For Reference

Not to be taken

from this room

Acronyms, Initialisms & Abbreviations Dictionary

Gale's publications in the acronyms and abbreviations field include:

Acronyms, Initialisms & Abbreviations Dictionary series:

Acronyms, Initialisms & Abbreviations Dictionary (Volume 1). A guide to acns, initialisms, abbreviations, and similar contractions, arranged alphabetically by abbren.

New Acronyms, Initialisms & Abbreviations (Volume 2). An interedition suppent in which terms are arranged both by abbreviation and by meaning.

Reverse Acronyms, Initialisms & Abbreviations Dictionary (Volume 3). A comon to Volume 1 in which terms are arranged alphabetically by meaning of the acm, initialism, or abbreviation.

Acronyms, Initialisms & Abbreviations Dictionary Subject Guide serie

Computer & Telecommunications Acronyms (Volume 1). A guide to acronymi-tialisms, abbreviations, and similar contractions used in the field of computerd telecommunications in which terms are arranged alphabetically both by abbrevn and by meaning.

Business Acronyms (Volume 2). A guide to business-oriented acronyms, initias, abbreviations, and similar contractions in which terms are arranged alphabeticallyh by abbreviation and by meaning.

International Acronyms, Initialisms & Abbreviations Dictionary series:

International Acronyms, Initialisms & Abbreviations Dictionary (Volume 1). A g to foreign and international acronyms, initialisms, abbreviations, and similar con-tions, arranged alphabetically by abbreviation.

New International Acronyms, Initialisms & Abbreviations (Volume 2). An intered supplement in which terms are arranged alphabetically both by abbreviation anc meaning.

Reverse International Acronyms, Initialisms & Abbreviations Dictionary (Volume A companion to Volume 1, in which terms are arranged alphabetically by meaning the acronym, initialism, or abbreviation.

Periodical Title Abbreviations series:

Periodical Title Abbreviations: By Abbreviation (Volume 1). A guide to abbreviatic commonly used for periodical titles, arranged alphabetically by abbreviation.

Periodical Title Abbreviations: By Title (Volume 2). A guide to abbreviations co monly used for periodical titles, arranged alphabetically by title.

New Periodical Title Abbreviations (Volume 3). An interedition supplement in whic terms are arranged alphabetically both by abbreviation and by title.

ISSN 0270-4404

Acronyms, Initialisms & Abbreviations Dictionary

A Guide to More Than 520,000 Acronyms, Initialisms, Abbreviations, Contractions, Alphabetic Symbols, and Similar Condensed Appellations

Covering: Aerospace, Associations, Banking, Biochemistry, Business, Data Processing, Domestic and International Affairs, Economics, Education, Electronics, Genetics, Government, Information Technology, Investment, Labor, Law, Medicine, Military Affairs, Periodicals, Pharmacy, Physiology, Politics, Religion, Science, Societies, Sports, Technical Drawings and Specifications, Telecommunications, Trade, Transportation, and Other Fields

Sixteenth Edition
1992

Volume 1

Part 1
A-F

Jennifer Mossman,
Editor

Pamela Dear
Prindle LaBarge
Ellen Paré,
Associate Editors

 Gale Research Inc. · DETROIT · LONDON

Senior Editor:	Donna Wood
Editor:	Jennifer Mossman
Associate Editors:	Pamela Dear, Prindle LaBarge, Ellen Paré
Assistant Editors:	Yvonne Y. Lee, Alice M. Walsh
Contributing Editors:	Leland G. Alkire, Jr., Mildred Hunt, Edwin B. Steen, Miriam M. Steinert
Data Entry Supervisor:	Benita L. Spight
Data Entry Associate:	Merrie Ann Carpenter
Production Manager:	Mary Beth Trimper
Production Assistant:	Mary Winterhalter
Art Director:	Arthur Chartow
Keyliners:	C.J. Jonik, Yolanda Y. Latham
Supervisor of Systems and Programming:	Theresa A. Rocklin
Programmers:	Charles Beaumont, David Trotter

The paper used in this publication meets the minimum requirements of American National Standard for Information Sciences—Permanence Paper for Printed Library Materials, ANSI Z39.48-1984.™

Copyright © 1991
Gale Research Inc.
835 Penobscot Building
Detroit, MI 48226-4094

Library of Congress Catalog Card Number 84-643188
ISBN 0-8103-5077-7 (Volume 1 Complete)
ISBN 0-8103-5099-8 (Part 1: A-F only)
ISBN 0-8103-5352-0 (Part 2: G-O only)
ISBN 0-8103-5353-9 (Part 3: P-Z only)
ISSN 0270-4404

Printed in the United States of America

Published simultaneously in the United Kingdom
by Gale Research International Limited
(An affiliated company of Gale Research Inc.)

Contents

Volume 1
Part 1 A-F

Highlights vii

User's Guide ix

Preface xi

Acknowledgments xiii

List of Selected Sources xv

Acronyms, Initialisms, and Abbreviations
    A-F 1

Volume 1
Part 2 G-O

User's Guide vii

List of Selected Sources ix

Acronyms, Initialisms, and Abbreviations
    G-O 1397

Volume 1
Part 3 P-Z

User's Guide vii

List of Selected Sources ix

Acronyms, Initialisms, and Abbreviations
    P-Z 2631

Highlights

520,000 Total Entries
20,000 New Terms
Comprehensive Coverage
Subject Categories
Source Citations

The sixteenth edition of *Acronyms, Initialisms, and Abbreviations Dictionary (AIAD)* offers increased coverage in all fields of human endeavor. Many of the 20,000 new terms are from the subject areas of:

- Aviation
- Business
- Computer Science
- Military Affairs
- Oceanography

Of major value to librarians and researchers is the inclusion of:

- information systems
- library symbols
- organizations
- periodical title abbreviations
- radio/television station call letters
- research centers
- stock exchange symbols
- tradeshows

Subject Categories Provided

Where possible, and if not already implied in the entry itself, a category or identifier follows many terms. Its purpose is to provide a subject context for entries that require clarification.

Major Sources Cited

Codes are provided to indicate the source from which the information was obtained. This feature allows you to verify the entries and may, in some instances, lead to additional information. Complete bibliographic data about the publications cited can be found in the List of Selected Sources following the acknowledgments. Terms that are obtained from miscellaneous newspapers and newsmagazines, are provided by outside contributors, or are discovered through independent research by the editorial staff remain uncoded.

User's Guide

The following examples illustrate the possible elements of entries in *AIAD*:

---

[1]   **[2]**   **[3]**   **[4]**   **[5]**

FATAC....Force Aerienne Tactique [*Tactical Air Force*] [*French*] (NATG)

                      [6]   **[7]**

MMT...*Multiple-Mirror Telescope [Mount Hopkins, AZ] [Jointly operated by Smithsonian Institution and the University of Arizona] [Astronomy]*
                                             [8]

---

[1] Acronym, Initialism, or Abbreviation

[2] Meaning or Phrase

[3] English translation

[4] Language (for non-English entries)

[5] Source code (Allows you to verify entries or find additional information. Decoded in the List of Selected Sources)

[6] Location or Country of origin (Provides geographic identifiers for airports, colleges and universities, libraries, military bases, political parties, radio and television stations, and others)

[7] Sponsoring organization

[8] Subject category (Clarifies entries by providing appropriate context)

The completeness of a listing is dependent upon both the nature of the term and the amount of information provided by the source. If additional information becomes available during future research, an entry is revised.

Arrangement of Entries

Acronyms, initialisms, and abbreviations are arranged alphabetically in letter-by-letter sequence. Spacing, punctuation, and capitalization are not considered. If the same term has more than one meaning, the various meanings are subarranged in word-by-word sequence.

Should you wish to eliminate the guesswork from acronym formation and usage, a companion volume could help. *Reverse Acronyms, Initialisms and Abbreviations Dictionary* contains essentially the same entries as *AIAD*, but arranges them alphabetically by meaning, rather than by acronym or initialism.

Preface

The use of acronyms and similar abbreviated terms is convenient, speedy, and particularly well suited to the needs of our highly technical society. Rapid growth of this "language" and the need to eliminate guesswork in translating terms led to the publication of *Acronyms, Initialisms, and Abbreviations Dictionary (AIAD)*. For over a quarter century, *AIAD* has served the needs of businesspeople, students, government officials, researchers, and other interested citizens whose work requires a high degree of accuracy.

What Is Included?

Most entries in *AIAD* are specifically identified with the United States. Thousands of British and Canadian terms can also be found. Other non-U.S. acronyms most likely to be encountered in magazines and daily newspapers are included as well. For users whose principal interest is foreign and international terms, a companion volume to the *AIAD* series is available. *International Acronyms, Initialisms, and Abbreviations Dictionary* includes terms that are local to specific foreign countries (and, as such, not eligible for inclusion in *AIAD*).

No attempt is made to list acronyms of local businesses or associations, local units of government, or other terms in limited use. Obsolete terms are retained for their historical interest. Only those found to be incorrect are deleted.

Slight Distinctions among Terms

Distinctions are not always made among the three terms used in the current title, nor are distinctions always necessary, since in many ways the definitions overlap. But the most commonly accepted, if somewhat simplified, explanations are as follows:

> An *acronym* is composed of the initial letters or parts of a compound term. It is usually read or spoken as a *single word*, rather than letter by letter. Examples include RADAR (Radio Detection and Ranging) and LASER (Light Amplification by Stimulated Emission of Radiation).

> An *initialism* is also composed of the initial letters or parts of a compound term, but is generally verbalized *letter by letter*, rather than as a single "word." Examples include PO (Post Office) and RPM (Revolutions per Minute).

> An *abbreviation* is a shortened form of a word or words that does not follow the formation of either of the above. Examples include APR (April), Ph D (Doctor of Philosophy), BCSTG (Broadcasting), and DR (Doctor).

Also included in *AIAD* are many alphabetic symbols, in which the letters used do not necessarily correspond to the words that they represent. Included in this category are R, a missile launch environment symbol for Ship, and T, representing Meridian Angle.

Need for a Guide Evident

There have been rumblings of discontent through the years because of the overuse or misuse of acronyms, initialisms, and abbreviations. In a lecture presented before the International Congress of Pharmaceutical Sciences,

Dr. Anatole Sliosberg, of the International Federation of Translators, expressed his dismay over the abuses of "abbreviomania"

> Whenever you open a scientific, technical, or economic publication, or even a daily newspaper, you are immediately struck by the number of apparently meaningless letter or syllable combinations which the most knowledgeable reader cannot decipher without the aid of a dictionary or a keen sense of divination.

The frustration of wrestling with inadequately identified designations or with the overuse of these terms is understandable. Yet, what H.L. Mencken called "the characteristic American habit of reducing complete concepts to starkest abbreviations" seems likely to continue unabated for some time. Accordingly, *AIAD* will continue to guide users through this expanding maze of linguistic shorthand.

Trends in the Field

Acronym formation often follows what might be termed the "chicken or egg" syndrome. Recent years have shown that in choosing a name or slogan, new organizations, ad hoc groups, or activist movements frequently will select a colorful acronym first—one that they hope will spotlight their philosophy and be associated easily in the public mind with their ideas or purposes. The catchy acronym will then be fleshed out with more-or-less appropriate words. This back-formation is common with political groups, fund-raising organizations, consumer-protection interests, and countless other topical coalitions.

A few editions ago, it was reported that there was a noticeable movement among corporations to abbreviate names, often because merger or expansion had rendered the original names meaningless or misleading. American District Telegraph Company changing its name to ADT, Incorporated and US Steel Corporation becoming USX Corporation are examples of this trend.

Another ongoing trend involves the creation of alternative translations to existing acronyms. These are usually facetious and sometimes quite clever. DT & I (Detroit, Toledo & Ironton Railroad) has also been translated as "Damned Tough and Independent;" IBM (International Business Machines Corp.) has been translated as "I Built a Macintosh;" PBS (Public Broadcasting Service) as "Petroleum Broadcasting Service;" and Ph D (Philosophiae Doctor) as "Piled Higher and Deeper." Proper names can be turned into acronyms in a similar process. Ford (in reference to Ford Motor Company products) has been translated as "Fix or Repair Daily;" and Lee Iacocca's surname has been interpreted as "I Am Chairman of the Chrysler Corporation of America." A related type of acronym formation occurs when an existing acronym is used as inspiration for other acronyms. The association MADD (Mothers Against Drunk Driving) has led to the formation of a related group, SADD (Students Against Drunk Driving), and also to the creation of the satirical DAMM (Drinkers Against Mad Mothers). Similarly, the famous MGM (Metro-Goldwyn-Mayer) logo was the basis for MTM (Mary Tyler Moore) Productions, Inc.; and BC (Before Christ) has been updated to BV (Before Video).

Currently the most rapid proliferation of this type of spinoff formation is of the terms based on Yuppie (Young Urban Professional). Examples include Buppie (Black Urban Professional); Fuppie (Female Urban Professional); and Guppie (Gay Urban Professional). The collection of this type of acronym currently exceeds eighty terms.

"Outstanding Reference Source"

New editions are prepared by adding thousands of previously unlisted terms and updating many entries from earlier editions. Substantial editorial research is required to ensure that the most complete and current information is provided. The editors were rewarded for their diligent efforts in 1985 when the Reference and Adult Services Division of the American Library Association selected *AIAD* as one of the twenty-five most distinguished reference titles published during the past quarter century. We take great pride in this achievement.

Suggestions Are Welcome

Many suggestions concerning individual terms to be included or subjects to be covered have been received from individual users and have been most helpful. The editors invite all such comments and will make every effort to incorporate them in future editions.

Acknowledgments

For suggestions, contributions of terms, permission to take material from personal or published sources, and for other courtesies extended during the preparation of previous editions and the present one, the editors are indebted to the following:

James Aguirre, former staff writer and editor, Quality Evaluation Laboratory, United States Naval Weapons Station, Concord, California

O.T. Albertini, Plans and Policy Directorate, Joint Chiefs of Staff, Department of Defense (retired)

Leland G. Alkire, Jr., humanities reference librarian, Eastern Washington University, editor of *Periodical Title Abbreviations*

Irving Allen, Professor of Sociology, University of Connecticut Associated Spring Corp., B-G-R Division (publisher of *Civilian's Dictionary*, a dictionary of wartime abbreviations)

Association of American Railroads

Paul Axel-Lute

Burroughs Corp. (publisher of *Computer Acronyms and Abbreviations Handbook*)

Butterworth & Co. (Publishers) Ltd. (publisher of *Index to Legal Citations and Abbreviations*)

Ethel M. Fair

David Glagovsky

Jack Gordon

Hoyt Hammer, Jr.

William S. Hein Co. (publisher of *Bieber's Dictionary of Legal Abbreviations*)

Charles C. Hinckley, executive vice president, Union Central Life Insurance Co.

Roy Hubbard

Mildred Hunt, editorial consultant International Business Machines Corp., Data Processing Division (publisher of *IBM Glossary for Information Processing*)

David J. Jones, compiler of *Australian Dictionary of Acronyms and Abbreviations* and *Australian Periodical Title Abbreviations*)

Kogan Page Ltd. (publisher of *Dictionary of British Qualifications*)

Steven C. Krems, computer specialist, Internal Revenue Service)

Ktav Publishing House, Inc. (publisher of *Biblical and Judaic Acronyms*)

Robert E. Lacey, journalist

Lawrence Marwick, late editor of *Biblical and Judaic Acronyms*

Divid Mattison

Mamie Meredith, late Professor of English, University of Nebraska

National Association of Securities Dealers (publisher of the *NASDAQ Company Directory*)

National Library of Canada

National Library of Medicine

Morgan Oates, late librarian, *Detroit Free Press*

Charles Parsons, formerly of Translation Research Institute

Eric Partridge, late author of *A Dictionary of Slang and Unconventional English*; *A Dictionary of Abbreviations, with Especial Attention to War-Time Abbreviations*; and other books

Rynd Communications (publisher of *Dictionary of Health Services Management*)

Harry Schechter, late chairman, Government Printing Office Style Board

Edward A. Schmerler

Brian Scott, editor of *Dictionary of Military Abbreviations*

Peter Sikli

Standard & Poor's Corporation (publisher of *Security Owner's Stock Guide*)

Edwin B. Steen, professor emeritus of biology, Western Michigan University, author of *Abbreviations in Medicine* and *Dictionary of Biology*

Miriam M. Steinert, editorial consultant

A. Marjorie Taylor, editor, *Language of World War II*

Edith Thompson

Toronto Stock Exchange

The University Press of Virginia (publisher of *Dictionary of Sigla and Abbreviations to and in Law Books before 1607*)

U.S. Air Force, Translation Section HQ

Donald Weeks

Witherby & Co. Ltd. (publisher of *Aviation Insurance Abbreviations, Organisations, and Institutions*; *Dictionary of Commercial Terms and Abbreviations*; *Dictionary of Shipping International Trade Terms and Abbreviations*)

Harvey J. Wolf

List of Selected Sources

Each of the print sources included in the following list contributed at least 50 terms. It would be impossible to cite a source for every entry in *Acronyms, Initialisms, and Abbreviations Dictionary (AIAD)* becuase the majority of terms are sent by outside contributors, are uncovered through independent research by the editorial staff, or surface as miscellaneous broadcast or print media references.

For sources used on an ongoing basis, only the latest edition is listed. For most of the remaining sources, the edition that was used is cited. The editors will provide further information about these sources upon request.

Unless further described in an annotation, the publications listed here contain no additional information about the acronym, initialism, or abbreviation cited in *AIAD*.

(AABC)   *Catalog of Abbreviations and Brevity Codes.* Washington, DC: U.S. Department of the Army, 1981. [Use of source began in 1969]

(AAG)   *Aerospace Abbreviations Glossary.* Report Number AG60-0014. Prepared by General Dynamics/Astronautics. San Diego: 1962.

(ADA)   *The Australian Dictionary of Acronyms and Abbreviations.* 2nd ed. Compiled by David J. Jones. Leura, NSW, Australia: Second Back Row Press Pty. Ltd., 1981.

(AFIT)   *Compendium of Authenticated Systems and Logistics.* Washington, DC: Air Force Institute of Technology. [Use of source began in 1984]

(AFM)   *Air Force Manual of Abbreviations.* Washington, DC: U.S. Department of the Air Force, 1975. [Use of source began in 1969]

(AIA)   *Aviation Insurance Abbreviations, Organisations and Institutions.* By M.J. Spurway. London: Witherby & Co. Ltd., 1983.

(APTA)   *Australian Periodical Title Abbreviations.* Compiled by David J. Jones. Leura, NSW, Australia: Second Back Row Press Pty. Ltd., 1985.

(ARC)   *Agricultural Research Centres: A World Directory of Organizations and Programmes.* 2 vols. Edited by Nigel Harvey. Harlow, Essex, England: Longman Group, 1983; distributed in the U.S. by Gale Research Inc., Detroit.
> A world guide to official, educational, industrial, and independent research centers which support research in the fields of agriculture, veterinary medicine, horticulture, aquaculture, food science, forestry, zoology, and botany.

(ASF)   *Guide to Names and Acronyms of Organizations, Activities, and Projects.* Food and Agriculture Organization of the United Nations. Fishery Information, Data, and Statistics Service and U.S. National Oceanic and Atmospheric Administration. Aquatic Sciences and Fisheries Information System Reference Series, Number 10, 1982. n.p.

(BIB)   *Bibliotech.* Ottawa, Canada: National Library of Canada, 1988-89.

(BJA)   *Biblical and Judaic Acronyms.* By Lawrence Marwick. New York: Ktav Publishing House, Inc., 1979.

(BUR) *Computer Acronyms and Abbreviations Handbook.* Tokyo: Burroughs Co. Ltd., 1978.

(BYTE) *Byte: The Small Systems Journal.* Peterborough, NH: McGraw- Hill Information Systems, Inc., 1987-89.

(CAAL) *CAAL COMOPTEVFOR Acronym and Abbreviation List.* Norfolk, VA: (CAAL-U) Operational Test and Evaluation Force, 1981.

(CB) *Centres & Bureaux: A Directory of Concentrations of Effort, Information and Expertise.* Edited by Lindsay Sellar. Beckenham, Kent, England: CBD Research Ltd., 1987.
> A guide to British organizations which include the words "centre" or "bureau" in their names. Entries include name and address; telephone and telex numbers; chief official; and a description of the purposes, activities, and services of the organization.

(CED) *Current European Directories.* 2nd ed. Edited by G.P. Henderson, Beckenham, Kent, England: CBD Research, 1981; distributed in U.S. by Gale Research Inc., Detroit.

(CET) *Communications-Electronics Terminology.* AFM 11-1. Vol. 3 U.S. Department of the Air Force, 1973.

(CINC) *A CINCPAC Glossary of Commonly Used Abbreviations and Short Titles.* By Ltc. J.R. Johnson. Washington, DC: 1968.

(CMD) *Complete Multilingual Dictionary of Computer Terminology.* Compiled by Georges Nania. Chicago: National Textbook Co., 1984.
> Computer-related terms in Spanish, French, Italian, Portuguese, and English. Indexes in French, Italian, Spanish, and Portuguese are also provided.

(CNC) *American National Standard Codes for the Representation of Names of Countries, Dependencies, and Areas of Special Sovereignty for Information Interchange.* U.S. National Bureau of Standards. Washington, DC: Government Printing Office, 1986. [Use of source began in 1977]
> These standard codes, approved by the International Organization for Standardization and the American National Standards Institute, are used in the international interchange of data in many fields.

(CRD) *Computer-Readable Databases: A Directory and Data Sourcebook.* 6th ed. Edited by Kathleen Young Marcaccio. Detroit: Gale Research Inc., 1990.
> A guide to online databases, offline files available in various magnetic formats, and CD-ROM files. Entries include producer name, address, telephone number, description of coverage, vendors, and contact person.

(CSR) *Computer Science Resources: A Guide to Professional Literature.* Edited by Darlene Myers. White Plains, NY: Knowledge Industry Publications, Inc., 1981.
> Covers several types of computer-related literature including journals, technical reports, directories, dictionaries, handbooks, and university computer center newsletters. Five appendices cover career and salary trends in the computer industry, user group acronyms, university computer libraries, and trade fairs and shows.

(CTT) *Corporate TrendTrac.* Edited by A. Dale Timpe. Detroit: Gale Research Inc., 1988-89.
> Covers mergers and acquisitions, stock exchange listings and suspensions, company name changes, bankruptcies, liquidations, and reorganizations.

(DAS) *Dictionary of Abbreviations and Symbols.* By Edward Frank Allen. London: Cassell and Co. Ltd.

(DBQ) *A Dictionary of British Qualifications.* London: Kogan Page Ltd., 1985.

(DCTA)   *Dictionary of Commercial Terms and Abbreviations.* By Alan E. Branch. London: Witherby & Co. Ltd., 1984.

(DEN)   *Dictionary of Electronics and Nucleonics.* By L.E.C. Hughes, R.W.B. Stephens, and L.D. Brown. New York: Barnes & Noble, 1969.

(DHSM)   *Dictionary of Health Services Management.* 2nd ed. By Thomas C. Timmreck. Owings Mills, MD: Rynd Communications, 1987.

(DIT)   *Dictionary of Informatics Terms in Russian and English.* By G.S. Zhdanov, E.S. Kolobrodov, V.A. Polushkin, and A.I. Cherny. Moscow: Nauka, 1971.

(DLA)   *Bieber's Dictionary of Legal Abbreviations.* 3rd ed. By Mary Miles Prince. Buffalo, NY: William S. Hein & Co., 1988.

(DMA)   *Dictionary of Military Abbreviations: British, Empire, Commonwealth.* By. B.K.C. Scott. Hastings, East Sussex, England: Tamarisk Books, 1982.

(DS)   *Dictionary of Shipping International Trade Terms and Abbreviations.* 3rd ed. By Alan E. Branch. London: Witherby & Co. Ltd., 1986.

(DSA)   *Dictionary of Sigla and Abbreviations to and in Law Books before 1607.* By William Hamilton Bryson. Charlottesville, VA: University Press of Virginia, 1975.

(DSUE)   *A Dictionary of Slang and Unconventional English.* 8th ed. By Eric Partridge. New York: Macmillan Publishing Co., 1984.

(EA)   *Encyclopedia of Associations.* 25th ed. Vol. 1, National Organizations of the U.S. Edited by Deborah M. Burek. Detroit: Gale Research Inc., 1990. (and supplement, 1991) [Use of source began in 1960]
            A guide to trade, professional, and other nonprofit associations that are national and international in scope and membership and that are headquartered in the United States. Entries include name and address; telephone and telex number; chief official; and a description of the purpose, activities, and structure of the organization.

(EAAP)   *Encyclopedia of Associations: Association Periodicals.* 3 vols. Edited by Denise M. Allard and Robert C. Thomas. Detroit: Gale Research Inc., 1987.
            A directory of publications issued by all types of national nonprofit organizations in the United States. Entries include title and organization name, address, telephone number; description of periodical, frequency of publication, and price.

(EAIO)   *Encyclopedia of Associations: International Organizations.* 24th ed. Edited by Kenneth Estell. Detroit: Gale Research Inc., 1990. [Use of source began in 1985]
            A guide to trade, professional, and other nonprofit associations that are national or international in scope and membership and that are headquartered outside the United States. Entries include name and address; principal foreign language name; telephone and telex number; chief official; and a description of the purpose, activities, and structure of the organization.

(ECON)   *The Economist.* London: The Economist Newspaper Ltd., 1991. [Use of source began in 1988]

(EGAO)   *Encyclopedia of Government Advisory Organizations.* 6th ed. Edited by Denise M. Allard and Donna Batten. Detroit: Gale Research Inc., 1988 [Use of source began in 1975]
>   A reference guide to permanent, continuing, and ad hoc U.S. presidential advisory committees, interagency committees, and other government-related boards, panels, task forces, commissions, conferences, and other similar bodies serving in a consultative, coordinating, advisory, research, or investigative capacity. Entries include name and address, telephone number, designated federal employee, history, recommendation and findings of the committee, staff size, publications, and subsidiaries. Also includes indexes to personnel, reports, federal agencies, presidential administration, and an alphabetical and keyword index.

(EY)   *The Europa Year Book 1987: A World Survey.* London: Europa Publications Ltd., 1987. distributed in U.S. by Gale Research Inc., Detroit.
>   An annual survey containing detailed information about the political, economic, statistical, and commercial situation of the regions and countries covered.

(FAAC)   *Contractions Handbook.* Changes. U.S. Department of Transportation. Federal Aviation Administration, 1985. [Use of source began in 1969]

(FAAL)   *Location Identifiers.* U.S. Department of Transportation. Federal Aviation Administration. Air Traffic Service, 1982.

(FEA)   *The Far East and Australasia 1987.* 18th ed. London: Europa Publications Ltd., 1986; distributed in U.S. by Gale Research Inc., Detroit.
>   Annual survey containing detailed information about the political, economic, statistical, and commercial situation of the regions and countries covered.

(GEA)   *Government Economic Agencies of the World: An International Directory of Governmental Organisations Concerned with Economic Development and Planning.* A Keesing's Reference Publication. Edited by Alan J. Day. Harlow, Essex, England: Longman Group Ltd., 1985; distributed in U.S. by Gale Research Inc., Detroit.
>   Covers over 170 countries and territories. Two introductory sections for each area cover economic data and prevailing economic and political conditions. Individual entries provide title, address, and names of chief officials of each agency. Current activities and financial structure of each agency are also detailed. An index of agency officials is provided.

(GPO)   *Style Manual.* Washington, DC: Government Printing Office, 1984. Terms are included in Chapter 24, Foreign Languages.

(GRD)   *Government Research Directory.* 5th ed. Edited by Kay Gill and Susan E. Tufts. Detroit: Gale Research Inc., 1989. (and supplement, 1989)
>   A descriptive guide to U.S. government research and development centers, institutes, laboratories, bureaus, test facilities, experiment stations, data collection and analysis centers, and grants management and research coordinating offices in agriculture, business, education, energy, engineering, environment, the humanities, medicine, military science, and basic applied sciences.

(IBMDP)   *IBM Data Processing Glossary.* 6th ed. White Plains, NY: IBM Corp., 1977.

(ICAO)   *Aircraft Type Designators.* 13th ed. International Civil Aviation Organization, August, 1981.

(ICDA)   *Designators for Aircraft Operating Agencies, Aeronautical Authorities and Services.* 49th ed. International Civil Aviation Organization, June 1982.
>   Document also includes telephony designators and postal and telegraphic addresses of government civil aviation authorities.

(ICLI)   *Location Indicators.* 51st ed. International Civil Aviation Organization, February 1987.
>   Document also contains addresses of flight information centers.

(IEEE)   *IEEE Standard Dictionary of Electrical and Electronics Terms.* Edited by Frank Jay. New York: The Institute of Electrical and Electronics Engineers, Inc., 1977, 1984.
Includes definitions for thousands of electrical and electronics terms. Each entry includes a numeric source code.

(IID)   *Information Industry Directory.* 11th ed. Edited by Bradley J. Morgan. Detroit: Gale Research Inc., 1991 (and supplement, 1991).
An international guide to computer-readable databases, database producers, and publishers, online vendors and time-sharing companies, telecommunications networks, and many other information systems and services. Entries include name and address, telephone number, chief official, and a detailed description of the purpose and function of the system or service.

(ILCA)   *Index to Legal Citations and Abbreviations.* By Donald Raistrick. Abingdon, Oxfordshire, England: Professional Books Ltd., 1981.

(IMH)   *International Marketing Handbook.* 2nd ed. Edited by Frank Bair. Detroit: Gale Research Inc., 1985.
An in-depth guide to commercial and trade data on 142 countries of the world. Features include a list of European trade fairs and a report on growth markets in Western Europe.

(INF)   *Infantry.* Fort Benning, GA: U.S. Army Infantry Training School, 1989. [Use of source began in 1983]

(IRC)   *International Research Centers Directory 1988-89.* 4th ed. Edited by Darren L. Smith. Detroit: Gale Research Inc., 1988.
A world guide to government, university, independent, nonprofit, and commercial research and development centers, institutes, laboratories, bureaus, test facilities, experiment stations, and data collection and analysis centers, as well as foundations, councils, and other organizations which support research.

(IRUK)   *Industrial Research in the United Kingdom.* 12th ed. Harlow, Essex, England: Longman Group UK Ltd., 1987.
A guide to all groups conducting or funding research relevant to British industrial development. Entries include name, address, telephone and telex numbers; chief officials; and scope of activities.

(IT)   *Information Today: The Newspaper for Users and Producers of Electronic Information Services.* Medford, NJ: Learned Information Inc., 1988-89.

(ITD)   *International Tradeshow Directory.* 5th ed. Frankfurt am Main: M + A Publishers for Fairs, Exhibitions and Conventions Ltd., 1989.
A guide to trade fairs and exhibitions throughout the world. Entries include event name, dates, frequency, location,description of purpose, profile of exhibitors and attendees.

(IYR)   *The 1989-92 International Yacht Racing Rules.* London: International Yacht Racing Union, 1989.

(KSC)   *A Selective List of Acronyms and Abbreviations.* Compiled by the Documents Department, Kennedy Space Center Library, 1971, 1973.

(LCCP)   *MARC Formats for Bibliographic Data.* Appendix II. Washington, DC: Library of Congress, 1982.

(LCLS)   *Symbols of American Libraries.* 13th ed. Washington, DC: Catalog Management and Publication Division, Library of Congress, 1985. [Use of source began in 1980]

(MCD)   *Acronyms, Abbreviations, and Initialisms.* Compiled by Carl Lauer. St. Louis: McDonnell Douglas Corp., 1989 [Use of source began in 1969]

(MDG)   *Microcomputer Dictionary and Guide.* By Charles J. Sippl. Champaign, IL: Matrix Publishers, Inc., 1975.
          A listing of definitions for over 5,000 microelectronics terms. Seven
          appendices.

(MENA) *The Middle East and North Africa 1987.* 33rd ed. London: Europa Publications Ltd., 1986; distributed in U.S. by Gale Research Inc., Detroit.
          An annual survey containing detailed information about the political, economic, statistical, and commercial situation of the regions and countries
          covered.

(MSA)   *Military Standard Abbreviations for Use on Drawings, and in Specifications, Standards, and Technical Documents.* MIL-STD-12D. U.S. Department of Defense, 1981. [Use of source began in 1975]

(MSC)   *Annotated Acronyms and Abbreviations of Marine Science Related Activities.* 3rd ed. Revised by Charlotte M. Ashby and Alan R. Flesh. Washington, DC: U.S. Department of Commerce. National Oceanographic and Atmospheric Administration. Environmental Data Service. National Oceanographic Data Center, 1976, 1981.

(MUGU) *The Mugu Book of Acronyms and Abbreviations.* Management Engineering Office, Pacific Missile Range, California, 1963, 1964.

(NASA) *Space Transportation System and Associated Payloads: Glossary, Acronyms, and Abbreviations.* Washington, DC: U.S. National Aeronautics and Space Administration, 1985.

(NATG) *Glossary of Abbreviations Used in NATO Documents.* AAP 15, n.p., 1979. [Use of source began in 1976]

(NG)   *NAVAIR Glossary of Unclassified Common-Use Abbreviated Titles and Phrases.* NAVAIRNOTE 5216 AIR-6031, n.p., July 1969.

(NLC)   *Symbols of Canadian Libraries.* 12th ed. National Library of Canada. Minister of Supply and Services Canada, 1987.

(NOAA) *NOAA Directives Manual.* 66-13 Acronyms. 1977.

(NQ)   *NASDAQ Company Directory.* New York: National Association of Securities Dealers Inc., 1990. [Use of source began in 1983]
          Entries include company name, SIC code, contact person's name, title,
          address, and telephone number.

(NRCH) *A Handbook of Acronyms and Initialisms.* Washington, DC: U.S. Nuclear Regulatory Commission. Division of Technical Information and Document Control, 1985.

(NVT)   *Naval Terminology.* NWP3. Rev. B. U.S. Department of the Navy. Office of the Chief of Naval Operations, 1980 [Use of source began in 1974]
          Includes a section on definitions of naval terminology.

(OAG)   *Official Airline Guide Worldwide Edition.* Oak Brook, IL: Official Airlines Guide, Inc., 1984. [Use of source began in 1975]

(OCD)   *Oxford Classical Dictionary.* 2nd ed. Edited by N.G. Hammond and H.H. Scullard. London: Oxford University Press, 1970.

(OCLC) *OCLC Participating Institutions Arranged by OCLC Symbol.* Dublin, OH: OCLC, 1981.

(OICC) *Abbreviations and Acronyms.* Des Moines, IA: Iowa State Occupational Information Coordinating Committee, 1986.

(OLDSS) *Online Database Search Services Directory.* 2nd ed. Edited by Doris Morris Maxfield. Detroit: Gale Research Inc., 1988.
> Provides detailed descriptions of the online information retrieval services offered by libraries, private information firms, and other organizations in the United States and Canada. Entries include name and address, telephone number, and key contact, as well as online systems accessed, frequently searched databases, and access hardware.

(PCM) *PC Magazine.* New York: Ziff-Davis Publishing Co., 1989. [Use of source began in 1987]

(PD) *Political Dissent: An International Guide to Dissident, Extra-Parliamentary, Guerrilla and Illegal Political Movements.* A Keesing's Reference Publication. Compiled by Henry W. Degenhardt. Edited by Alan J. Day. Harlow, Essex, England: Longman Group, 1983; distributed in U.S. by Gale Research Inc., Detroit.
> Includes the history and aims of approximately 1,000 organizations, with details of their leaderships.

(PPE) *Political Parties of Europe.* 2 vols. Edited by Vincent E. McHale. The Greenwood Historical Encyclopedia of the World's Political Parties. Westport, CT: Greenwood Press, 1983.
> One of a series of reference guides to the world's significant political parties. Each guide provides concise histories of the political parties of a region and attempts to detail the evolution of ideology, changes in organization, membership, leadership, and each party's impact upon society.

(PPW) *Political Parties of the World.* 2nd ed. A Keesing's Reference Publication. Compiled and edited by Alan J. Day and Henry W. Degenhardt. Harlow, Essex, England: Longman Group, 1980, 1984; distributed in U.S. by Gale Research Inc., Detroit.
> Covers historical development, structure, leadership, membership, policy, publications, and international affiliations. For each country, an overview of the current political situation and constitutional structure is provided.

(RCD) *Research Centers Directory.* 14th ed. Edited by Peter D. Dresser and Karen Hill. Detroit: Gale Research Inc., 1989 (and supplement, 1990). [Use of source began in 1986]
> A guide to university-related and other nonprofit research organizations carrying on research in agriculture, astronomy and space sciences, behavioral and social sciences, computers and mathematics, engineering and technology, physical and earth sciences and regional and area studies.

(RDA) *Army RD and A Magazine.* Alexandria, VA: Development, Engineering, and Acquisition Directorate, Army Materiel Command, 1989. [Use of source began in 1979]

(ROG) *Dictionary of Abbreviations.* By Walter T. Rogers. London: George Allen & Co. Ltd., 1913; reprinted by Gale Research Inc., 1969.

(SDI) *Report to the Congress on the Strategic Defense Initiative.* U.S. Department of Defense. Strategic Defense Initiative Organization, April 1987.

(SEIS) *Seismograph Station Codes and Characteristics.* Geological Survey. Circular 791. By Barbara B. Poppe, Debbi A. Naab, and John S. Derr. Washington, DC: U.S. Department of the Interior, 1978.

(SPSG) *Security Owner's Stock Guide.* New York: Standard & Poor's Corp., 1991. [Use of source began in 1988]

(TEL) *Telephony's Dictionary.* 2nd ed. By Graham Langley. Chicago: Telephony Publishing Corp., 1986.
> Includes definitions for U.S. and international telecommunications terms. Ten appendices.

(TSPED)   *Trade Shows and Professional Exhibits Directory.* 2nd ed. Edited by Robert J. Elster. Detroit: Gale Research Inc., 1987. [Use of source began in 1986]
> A guide to scheduled events providing commercial display facilities including conferences, conventions, meetings, fairs and festivals, etc. Entries include name of trade show; sponsor name, address, and telephone number; attendance figures; principal exhibits; special features; publications; and date and location of shows.

(TSSD)   *Telecommunications Systems and Services Directory.* 4th ed. (and supplement) Edited by John Krol. Detroit: Gale Research Inc., 1989. [Use of source began in 1985]
> An international descriptive guide to telecommunications organizations, systems, and services. Entries include name and address, telephone number, chief official, and a description of the purposes, technical structure, and background of the service or system.

Acronyms, Initialisms & Abbreviations Dictionary

A-F

A

A................ A/B Astra [*Sweden*] [*Research code symbol*]
A................ Abbey
A................ Abbott Laboratories [*Research code symbol*]
A................ Abitibi-Price, Inc. [*Toronto Stock Exchange symbol*] [*Vancouver Stock Exchange symbol*]
A................ Ablative [*Grammar*]   (ROG)
A................ Able [*Phonetic alphabet*] [*World War II*]   (DSUE)
A................ About
A................ Absent
A................ Absolute [*Temperature in Fahrenheit degrees*]
A................ Absolvo [*I Acquit*] [*Used by Romans in criminal trials*] [*Latin*]
A................ Absorbance [*Internal transmission density*] [*Symbol*] [*IUPAC*]
a................ Absorption Coefficient, Linear [*Symbol*] [*IUPAC*]
A................ Absorptivity
A................ Abstracts
A................ Abundant [*With respect to occurrence of species*]
A................ Academician [*or Academy*]
A................ Accelerating Contactor or Relay   (IEEE)
A................ Acceleration [*or Accelerator*]
a................ Accepte [*Accepted*] [*French*] [*Banking*]   (GPO)
A................ Accepted
A................ Acceptor [*Physiology*]
A................ Access [*Credit card*] [*British*]
A................ Accessed BIT [*Binary Digit*] [*Data processing*]
A................ Accessory [*Protein synthesis*]
A................ Accommodation
A................ Account
A................ Accumulator [*Data processing*]   (MDG)
A................ Accursius [*Deceased, 1263*] [*Authority cited in pre-1607 legal work*]   (DSA)
A................ Accusative [*Grammar*]   (ROG)
A................ Ace
A................ Aceite [*Acceptance*] [*Portuguese*] [*Business term*]
A................ Acheteur [*or Acheter*] [*Buyer*] [*French*] [*Business term*]
A................ Acid
A................ Ack [*Phonetic alphabet*] [*Pre-World War II*]   (DSUE)
A................ Acquiescence   (DLA)
A................ Acre
A................ Act
A................ Actin [*Muscle physiology*]
A................ Acting
A................ Actinomycin [*Also, act*] [*Antibiotic compound*]
a................ Action [*Share*] [*French*] [*Business term*]
A................ Action
A................ Active
A................ Activity
A................ Actual   (ADA)
A................ Acute
A................ Ad [*To or At*] [*Latin*]   (ROG)
A................ Adam's Justiciary Reports [*1893-1906*] [*Scotland*] [*A publication*]   (ILCA)
A................ Adaptable
A................ Adder [*Computer device*]
A................ Address [*Computer character*] [*Data processing*]
A................ Adenine [*Also, Ade*] [*Biochemistry*]
A................ Adenosine [*One-letter symbol; see Ado*] [*A nucleoside*]
A................ Adequate
A................ Adhibendus [*To Be Used*] [*Pharmacy*]   (ROG)
A................ Adjective
A................ Adjunct [*Linguistics*]
A................ Adjutant
A................ Admap [*A publication*]
A................ Administration
A................ Admiral
A................ Adolfo [*Couturier*]
A................ Adopted From [*or Adoption Of*] [*Etymology*]
A................ Adriamycin [*Also, ADM, ADR, D, H*] [*Antineoplastic drug*]
A................ Adult [*Film certificate*] [*British*]
A................ Adult
A................ Adulteress [*Letter embroidered on Hester Prynne's dress in Nathaniel Hawthorne's "The Scarlet Letter"*]

A................ Advance   (ADA)
A................ Advanced Level [*School graduating grade*] [*British*]
A................ Aerospace   (MCD)
A................ Affect
A................ Affirmation [*Linguistics*]
A................ Affirmed   (DLA)
A................ Affix [*Linguistics*]
A................ Africa Committee [*British*] [*World War II*]
A................ Aft
A................ After
A................ Aftercooled [*Automotive engineering*]
A................ Afternoon
A................ Age
A................ Agency
A................ Agglomerate [*Geology*]
A................ Agriculture Department [*US government*]
A................ Agusta [*Construzioni Aeronautiche Giovanni Agusta SpA*] [*Italy*] [*ICAO aircraft manufacturer identifier*]   (ICAO)
A................ Aided School [*British*]
A................ Air
A................ Air Force Training Category [*48 inactive duty training periods and 15 days active duty training per year*]
A................ Air-Launched [*Missile launch environment symbol*]
A................ Aircraft [*or Airplane*]
A................ Airman
A................ Akinetic
A................ Alabama Public Library Service, Montgomery, AL [*Library symbol*] [*Library of Congress*]   (LCLS)
A................ Alanine [*One-letter symbol; see Ala*]
A................ Alanine Nitrogen Mustard [*L-PAM*] [*Antineoplastic drug*]
A................ Alanus Anglicus [*Flourished, 1208-10*] [*Authority cited in pre-1607 legal work*]   (DSA)
A................ Alaskan Standard Time [*Aviation*]   (FAAC)
A................ Albedo [*Psychology*]
A................ Albericus de Porta Ravennate [*Flourished, 1165-94*] [*Authority cited in pre-1607 legal work*]   (DSA)
A................ [*Magister*] Albertus [*Authority cited in pre-1607 legal work*]   (DSA)
A................ Albertus Beneventanus [*Deceased, 1187*] [*Authority cited in pre-1607 legal work*]   (DSA)
a................ Albertus Longobardista [*Flourished, 12th century*] [*Authority cited in pre-1607 legal work*]   (DSA)
A................ Alcohol   (ADA)
A................ Alert Area [*Military*]
A................ Alfa [*Phonetic alphabet*] [*International*]   (DSUE)
A................ Alive
A................ Allele [*Genetics*]
A................ Allergy
A................ Allocator
A................ Alloy Container [*Shipping*]   (DCTA)
A................ Alpha
A................ Alphabetic
A................ Alternate [*Approach and landing charts*] [*Aviation*]
A................ Alternate Captain [*Sports*]
A................ Alternating Current
A................ Altezza [*Highness*] [*Italian*]
A................ Altimeter   (FAAC)
A................ Altitude Difference [*Navigation*]
A................ Alto
A................ Alveolar [*Gas*] [*Medicine*]
A................ Amateur
A................ Amber   (AAG)
A................ Ambient [*Electronics*]
A................ Ambiguity [*Used in correcting manuscripts, etc.*]
A................ Ambitendency [*Psychology*]
A................ Amended   (DLA)
A................ America [*A publication*]
A................ American
A................ American League [*Baseball*]
A................ American Medical Buildings, Inc. [*AMEX symbol*]   (SPSG)
A................ American Stock Exchange [*New York, NY*]

1

A................ Amethopterin [Methotrexate] [Antineoplastic drug]
A................ Ammeter (MDG)
A................ Amora (BJA)
A................ Amount (ROG)
A................ Ampere [Unit of electric current] [SI symbol]
A................ Amphetamine [Also, AMT, amphet] [CNS stimulant]
A................ Amphibian [or Amphibious]
A................ Ampicillin [Also, AM, AMP] [Antibacterial compound]
A................ Amplifier
A................ Amplitude [Physics]
A................ Ana [Of Each] [Pharmacy]
A................ Anaesthetics [Medical Officer designation] [British]
A................ Analog
A................ Anaphylaxis [Medicine]
A................ Anchorite
A................ And (ROG)
A................ Androecium [Botany]
A................ Anesthetic [Medicine]
A................ Angel (ROG)
A................ Anglican
A................ Angling
A................ Angstrom [Also, AU]
A................ Animal [Psychology]
A................ Anion
A................ Anisean [Geology]
A................ Anna [Monetary unit] [India]
A................ Anno [or Annus] [Year] [Latin]
A................ Annual
A................ Annular
A................ Anode [Technical drawings]
A................ Anonymous
A................ Answer [In transcripts]
A................ Antarctic
A................ Ante [Before] [Latin]
A................ Anterior
A................ Anther [Botany]
A................ Antiaircraft [Officer's rating] [British Royal Navy]
A................ Anticlockwise
A................ Antigen [Also, a, Ag] [Immunology]
A................ Antiquo [I Oppose] [Latin] [Used by Romans to signify a negative vote]
a................ Antisymmetric [Chemistry]
A................ Anus
A................ Apatite Subgroup [Apatite, fluorite, calcite, pyrite, iron] [CIPW classification] [Geology]
A................ Apostle [Church calendars]
A................ Apples [Phonetic alphabet] [Royal Navy] [World War I] (DSUE)
A................ Applique
A................ Approved
A................ Approximate [Rate] [Value of the English pound]
A................ April
A................ Aqua [Water] [Latin]
A................ Arab [or Arabic] (BJA)
a................ Arabinose [One-letter symbol; see Ara] [A sugar]
A................ Aramaic [Language, etc.]
A................ Architect
A................ Archiv fuer das Studium der Neueren Sprachen [A publication]
A................ Arctic [Air mass] [Meteorological symbol]
A................ Are [Also, a] [A unit of area in the metric system]
A................ Area
A................ Area Chart
A................ Argent [Heraldry]
A................ Argent [Money] [French]
A................ Argentina [IYRU nationality code] (IYR)
A................ Argon [Chemical symbol is Ar] [Chemical element]
A................ Armament
A................ Armored (ADA)
A................ Army
A................ Arousal
A................ Arrive (ADA)
A................ Art (ADA)
A................ Artery
A................ Arthuriana [A publication]
A................ Article
A................ Articulated (DCTA)
A................ Artillery
A................ Asbestos (MSA)
a------.......... Asia [MARC geographic area code] [Library of Congress] (LCCP)
A................ Asked
A................ Asparagine [One-letter symbol; see Asn]
A................ Assault [FBI standardized term]
A................ Assented [Investment term]
A................ Assessment [Medicine]
a................ Assinado [Signed] [Portuguese] [Business term]
A................ Assist [Sports]
A................ Assist [Health care]
A................ Assistant [Military]

A................ Assistant Captain [Worn on assistant captains' uniforms] [Hockey]
A................ Associate [In an academic degree]
A................ Association
A................ Asta Werke AG [Germany] [Research code symbol]
A................ Astragal (MSA)
A................ Asymmetric
A................ Asynchronous
A................ At
A................ Athletic (ADA)
A................ Atlantic Reporter [A publication] (DLA)
A................ Atom [or Atomic]
A................ Atomic Weight
A................ Attack [Designation for all US military aircraft]
A................ Attack [Men's lacrosse position]
A................ Attendance [Sports]
a................ Atto [A prefix meaning divided by 10 to the 18th power] [SI symbol]
A................ Atto [Act] [Italian]
A................ Attribute
A................ Audit [or Audited]
A................ Aufbau [A publication]
A................ Augmentation [Music]
A................ Auricular [or Auricle] [Also, AUR] [Medicine]
A................ Auris [Ear] [Latin]
A................ Ausgabestelle [Distribution Point] [German military - World War II]
A................ Australian
A................ [The] Australian [A publication] (APTA)
A................ Austria
A................ Authentic
A................ Authenticum [A publication] (DSA)
A................ Author
A................ Automation (DS)
A................ Automobile
A................ Autosome [Genetics]
A................ Autumn-Burned [Ecology]
A................ Available [or Availability] (MCD)
A................ Avancer [Fast, as clocks] [French]
A................ Axial
a................ [Jacobus] d'Azo [Flourished, 1191-1220] [Authority cited in pre-1607 legal work] (DSA)
A................ Buchanan's Reports of the Court of Appeal, Cape [1880-1910] [South Africa] [A publication] (ILCA)
A................ Burning Surface Area of Propellant [Symbol] [Aerospace]
A................ Class "A" Preferred or Common Stock [Investment term]
A................ Cleared to Airport [Point of intended landing] [Aviation] (FAAC)
A................ Codex Alexandrinus (BJA)
A................ Completely Reliable Source for Intelligence Information
A................ Eli Lilly & Co. [Research code symbol]
A................ General [Military aircraft identification prefix] [Air Force] (FAAC)
A................ Goals Against [Hockey]
A................ Hail [Meteorological symbol]
A................ Helmholtz Energy [Symbol] [IUPAC]
A................ High Medium [Moody's bond rating] [Investment term]
A................ Indian Reports, Allahabad Series [A publication] (DLA)
A................ L-Asparaginase [Also, L, L-ase, L-asnase, L-Asp] [An enzyme, an antineoplastic]
A................ Louisiana Annuals [A publication] (DLA)
A................ Magnetic Vector Potential [Symbol] (DEN)
A................ Mass Number [Symbol]
A................ Matthew Arnold [English poet, 1822-1888] [Initial used as pseudonym]
a................ Mean Sound Absorption [Symbol] [Aerospace]
A................ Narrow [Women's shoe width] [More than one "A" indicates increasing narrowness, up to AAAAA]
A................ Ordinary Combustibles [Fire classification]
A................ Recto (ROG)
A................ Semi-Major Axis [of a comet] [In astronomical units]
A................ Series "A" Bonds or Debentures [Investment term]
A................ Shape Descriptor [A-frame, for example. The shape resembles the letter for which it is named]
a................ Thermal Diffusivity [Symbol] [Thermodynamics]
A................ Total Average Dollar Inventory
A................ United Nations General Assembly Document (ILCA)
A................ United Nations Secretariat Member [License plate code assigned to foreign diplomats in the US]
A................ Upper Medium [Standard & Poor's bond rating] [Investment term]
A................ Warner-Lambert Pharmaceutical Co. [Research code symbol]
A_1............ Aortic First Heart Sound [Cardiology]
A1............ First Class [or First Quality]
A1............ Highest Hull [Symbol] [American Bureau of Shipping] (DS)
A-1 .... Personnel Section [of an air staff; also, officer in charge of this section] [Air Force]
1-A .... Selective Service Class [for Registrant Available for Military Service]
A^2............ Ann Arbor [Michigan]
A_2............ Aortic Second Heart Sound [Cardiology]

A-2	Intelligence Section [*of an air staff; also, officer in charge of this section*] [*Air Force*]
2-A	Selective Service Class [*for Registrant Deferred Because of Civilian Occupation, Other than Agriculture, or Non-Degree Study*]
A³	Accelerated Acquisition Approach [*Pronounced "a-cubed"*] [*Air Force*]
A3	Afterburner (AFIT)
3A	Monaco [*Aircraft nationality and registration mark*] (FAAC)
A-3	Operations and Training Section [*of an air staff; also, officer in charge of this section*] [*Air Force*]
3-A	Selective Service Class [*for Registrant Deferred by Reason of Extreme Hardship to Dependents; or Registrant with Child or Children*]
A-4	Materiel and Supply Section [*of an air staff; also, officer in charge of this section*] [*Air Force*]
4-A	Selective Service Class [*for Registrant with Sufficient Prior Active Service to Satisfy Requirements of Law (Veteran)*]
5A	Libya [*Aircraft nationality and registration mark*] (LCLS)
A10	Crater [*Costa Rica*] [*Seismograph station code, US Geological Survey*] (SEIS)
A-66	Alpha-66 (EA)
A-440	Designated international pitch to which pianos are tuned
4A's	American Association of Advertising Agencies [*New York, NY*]
A (Bomb)	Atom Bomb
A-(Day)	Act Day [*Financial Services*] [*British*]
A (Dolly)	Articulating Dolly [*Trailer engineering*]
AA	A & A Foods Ltd. [*Vancouver Stock Exchange symbol*]
aA	Abampere [*Also, Bi*] [*Unit of electric current*]
AA	Abbreviated Analysis [*Military*]
AA	Able and Available [*Unemployment insurance*] (OICC)
AA	Absolute Address (AAG)
AA	Absolute Altitude [*Navigation*]
AA	Abstracts in Anthropology [*A publication*]
AA	Academic Alliances (EA)
AA	Academy of Aphasia (EA)
AA	Academy Award [*Academy of Motion Picture Arts and Sciences film award*]
AA	Accelerated Assemblies (NASA)
AA	Accelerometer Assembly [*NASA*]
AA	Access America [*Commercial firm*] (EA)
AA	Access Authorization [*Nuclear energy*]
AA	Accompanied by Adult [*British Board of Film Censors*]
AA	Accuracy in Academia (EA)
AA	Acetylacrolein [*Organic chemistry*]
AA	Achieved Availability (MCD)
AA	Achievement Age [*Psychology*]
AA	Acoustics Associates (AAG)
AA	Acrylic Acid [*Organic chemistry*]
AA	Acting Appointment
AA	ActionAid [*London, England*] (EAIO)
AA	Activation Analysis [*Chemistry*]
AA	Active Air Defence [*British*] [*World War II*]
AA	Active Alkali [*Chemistry*]
AA	Active Army
AA	Active Assets
AA	Activity Account
AA	Acts of the Apostles [*New Testament book*] (BJA)
AA	Actual Availability (MCD)
AA	Actual Completion Date of Activity [*Business term*]
AA	Acute Appendicitis [*Medicine*]
AA	Addicts Anonymous (EA)
A & A	Additions and Amendments (ADA)
AA	Adenylic Acid [*Biochemistry*]
AA	Adjustment Assistance
AA	Adjuvant Arthritis
AA	Administration on Aging [*Defunct*] [*HEW*]
AA	Administrative Assistant
AA	Adoption Act [*British*]
AA	Adrenal [*or Adrenocortical*] Autoantibody
AA	Adult Accompaniment [*Restricted to age 14 and up unless accompanied by an adult*] [*Movie rating*] [*Canadian*]
AA	Adult Authority (OICC)
AA	Advance Airlines [*Australia*]
A & A	Advertise and Award (KSC)
AA	Advertising Age [*A publication*]
AA	Advertising Association (EAIO)
A/A	Advice of Allotment (AFM)
AA	Aegyptologische Abhandlungen [*A publication*]
A/A	Aerodrome to Aerodrome
AA	Aerosol Analyzer (KSC)
AA	Affected Areas
AA	Affiliate Artists (EA)
AA	Affiliate Assembly [*American Association of School Librarians*]
AA	Affirmative Action [*Employment policies for minorities*]
AA	Africa
AA	African Abstracts [*A publication*]
AA	African Affairs [*A publication*]
A & A	Afrique et l'Asie [*Later, Afrique et l'Asie Modernes*] [*A publication*]
AA	After All [*Message handling*]

AA	After Arrival
AA	Ah-Ah [*Lava-Flow*] [*Hawaiian*]
A to A	Air-to-Air (ADA)
AA	Air-to-Air [*NASA*]
AA	Air America, Inc. (CINC)
AA	Air Armament (NATG)
AA	Air Attache [*British*]
AA	Airborne Alert (AFM)
AA	Aircraft Artificer [*British*]
AA	Airlift Association (EA)
AA	Airman Apprentice [*Navy rating*]
AA	Airplane Avionics (NASA)
A/A	Airport and Airways (OICC)
AA	Airship Association [*London, England*] (EAIO)
AA	Airship Association - US (EA)
AA	Al Ahram [*Cairo*] [*A publication*]
aa	Albania [*MARC country of publication code*] [*Library of Congress*] (LCCP)
AA	Alcoa of Australia [*Commercial firm*]
AA	Alcoholics Anonymous World Services (EA)
AA	Alert Availability (MCD)
AA	Alkalyzing Agent
AA	All Ability School [*British*]
AA	All Abnormal [*Clinical hematology*]
AA	All [*Text*] After [*Specified Point*] [*Message handling*]
AA	All Along (ADA)
AA	Alopecia Areata [*Medicine*]
AA	Altesses [*Highnesses*] [*French*]
AA	Alttestamentliche Abhandlungen [*A publication*]
AA	Aluminum Association (EA)
AA	Aluminum Co. of America [*NYSE symbol*] [*Wall Street slang names: "Ack Ack" and "All American"*] (SPSG)
AA	Always Afloat [*Ship's charter*]
AA	Amazing Stories. Annual [*A publication*]
A & A	Amendments and Additions (DLA)
AA	American Airlines, Inc. [*ICAO designator*]
AA	American Annals of the Deaf [*A publication*]
AA	American Anthology [*A publication*]
AA	American Anthropologist [*A publication*]
AA	American Antiquity [*A publication*]
AA	American Archivist [*A publication*]
AA	American Army (DAS)
AA	American Assembly (EA)
AA	American Association [*Baseball league*]
A & A	American and Australian Line [*Shipping*] (ROG)
AA	Amino Acid [*Biochemistry*]
aa	Amino Acid [*As substituent on nucleoside*] [*Biochemistry*]
AA	Amino Acid Residue [*Biochemistry*]
AA	Aminoacetone [*Organic chemistry*]
AA	Amities Acadiennes [*Paris, France*] (EAIO)
AA	Amplitude of Accommodation [*Ophthalmology*]
aa----	Amur River and Basin [*MARC geographic area code*] [*Library of Congress*] (LCCP)
AA	AMVETS Auxiliary (EA)
AA	Amyloid-A [*Protein*] [*Medicine*]
AA	Ana [*Of Each*] [*Pharmacy*]
A/A	Analysis of Accounts
AA	Analytical Abstracts Online [*Royal Society of Chemistry*] [*Information service or system*] (CRD)
A and A	Ancient and Accepted [*Freemasonry*]
AA	Andrew Public Library, Alberta [*Library symbol*] [*National Library of Canada*] (NLC)
A/A	Angle of Attack [*Military*] (NG)
AA	Anglo-American
AA	Anglo-American Magazine [*A publication*]
AA	Angular Accelerometer [*NASA*] (MCD)
AA	Angular Aperture (MCD)
AA	Aniline Association (EA)
AA	Ann Arbor Railroad Co. [*AAR code*]
AA	Annales Africaines [*A publication*] (ILCA)
AA	Annals Australia: Journal of Catholic Culture [*A publication*] (APTA)
AA	Ant Guard Activity [*Ecology*]
AA	Anterior Aorta
AA	Anterograde Amnesia [*Medicine*]
AA	Anthranilic Acid [*Organic chemistry*]
AA	Antiaircraft [*Army*]
AA	Antibody Activity [*Immunology*]
AA	Anticipatory Avoidance [*Medicine*]
A & A	Antike und Abendland [*A publication*]
AA	Antioxidant Activity [*Food technology*]
AA	Antiproton Accumulator [*Particle physics*]
AA	Antonius Augustinus [*Deceased, 1586*] [*Authority cited in pre-1607 legal work*] (DSA)
AA	Antwerpsch Archievenblad [*A publication*]
A/A	Any Acceptable
AA	AOUON [*All of Us or None*] Archive [*An association*] (EA)
AA	Apicultural Abstracts [*Information service or system*] [*A publication*]
AA	Apollo Applications [*NASA*]

AA.............. Apostolicam Actuositatem [*Decree on the Apostolate of the Laity*] [*Vatican II document*]
AA.............. Appropriate Authority [*Office of Censorship*] [*World War II*]
AA.............. Appropriations and Allocations (OICC)
AA.............. Approving Authority
AA.............. Approximate Absolute [*Temperature*]
AA.............. Aptitude Test for Adults [*Psychoeducational test*]
AA.............. Arachidonic Acid [*Biochemistry*]
A & A......... Arbeitsschutz und Arbeitsmedizin [*Industrial Safety and Medicine*] [*German*]
AA.............. Arboricultural Association (EA)
AA.............. Archaeologischer Anzeiger [*A publication*]
AA.............. Archaeology Abroad (EAIO)
AA.............. Architectural Association [*London, England*] (EA)
AA.............. Archiv fuer Anthropologie [*A publication*]
A. A............ Argenteum Astrum [*Silver Star*] [*Secret occult society*]
AA.............. Arithmetic Average
AA.............. Arlington Annex [*Navy*]
AA.............. Armament Artificer [*British and Canadian*] [*World War II*]
AA.............. Armature Accelerator
AA.............. Armored Ambulance
AA.............. ARMS [*Action Research into Multiple Sclerosis*] of America (EA)
AA.............. Army Act (ILCA)
AA.............. Army Air Operations (MCD)
AA.............. Arrival Angle [*Army*]
AA.............. Arrival Approved [*Aviation*] (FAAC)
A-A .... Arrocillo Amarillo [*Race of maize*] [*Mexico*]
AA.............. Ars Aequi; Juridisch Studentenblad [*A publication*]
A & A .... Art and Archaeology [*A publication*]
AA.............. Art and Architecture [*A publication*]
A & A .... Arta si Arheologia [*A publication*]
AA.............. Arthrogryposis Association (EA)
AA.............. Artibus Asiae [*A publication*]
AA.............. Artificial Aerial (DEN)
AA.............. Arts Anonymous (EA)
A & A .... Arts and Architecture [*A publication*]
AA.............. Asanteman Association (EA)
AA.............. Asatru Alliance (EA)
AA.............. Ascending Aorta [*Anatomy*]
AA.............. Ascorbic Acid [*Vitamin C*] [*Biochemistry*]
AA.............. Asian Affairs [*A publication*]
AA.............. Aspergillus Asthma
AA.............. Assembly Area
AA.............. Assets Accounting [*Business term*]
AA.............. Assistant Adjutant
AA.............. Associate in Accounting
AA.............. Associate Administrator [*NASA*]
AA.............. Associate in Arts
AA.............. Association of Acrobats [*Australia*] (EA)
AA.............. Assumptionists [*Australia*]
AA.............. Aster Growth with Aster [*Ecology*]
AA.............. Astrological Association (EAIO)
A & A .... Astronautics and Aeronautics [*A publication*]
AA.............. Atheist Association (EA)
AA.............. Athletic Association
AA.............. Athro Arfon [*A publication*]
AA.............. Atlantic Area [*Services to the Armed Forces*] [*Red Cross*]
AA.............. Atlas Agena [*NASA*]
AA.............. Atmospheric Applications (MCD)
AA.............. Atomic Absorption [*Environmental Protection Agency*]
AA.............. Attack Assessment [*Military*]
AA.............. Auctores Antiquissimi [*Classical studies*] (OCD)
AA.............. Audit Agency
AA.............. Audubon Artists (EA)
AA.............. Augustiniani Assumptionis [*Assumptionists*] [*Roman Catholic men's religious order*]
AA.............. Ausfuehrungsanweisung [*Regulatory Instructions*] [*German*] (DLA)
AA.............. Australia Antigen [*Immunology*]
AA.............. Australian Archives
AA.............. Australian Army
AA.............. Auswaertiges Amt [*Foreign Ministry*] [*German*]
AA.............. Aut Aut [*A publication*]
AA.............. Authorized Allowance
AA.............. Author's Alteration [*Publishing*]
AA.............. Auto Acquisition [*RADAR*]
AA.............. Autoanalyzer
AA.............. Automatic Answer [*Telecommunications*] (TEL)
AA.............. Automatic Approval System [*Importation*] [*Japan*] (IMH)
AA.............. Automobile Association [*British*]
AA.............. Autonomous Area
AA.............. Auxiliary Assembly [*JETDS nomenclature*]
AA.............. Auxiliary Vessels [*Navy symbol*] (MUGU)
AA.............. Avenue of Approach [*Army*] (AABC)
AA.............. Average Adjuster [*Insurance*] (DS)
AA.............. Average Audience [*Television ratings*]
AA.............. Aviation Annex [*Air Force*]
Aa.............. Biblioteca Nacional, Buenos Aires, Argentina [*Library symbol*] [*Library of Congress*] (LCLS)
AA.............. Dry-Type Self-Cooled [*Transformer*] (IEEE)

AA.............. Grumman American Aviation [*ICAO aircraft manufacturer identifier*] (ICAO)
AA.............. High [*Standard & Poor's bond rating*] [*Investment term*]
Aa.............. High [*Moody's bond rating*] [*Investment term*]
AA.............. Sisters Auxiliaries of the Apostolate [*Roman Catholic religious order*]
AAA............ Abdominal Aortic Aneurysm [*or Aneurismectomy*] [*Medicine*]
AAA............ Aboriginal Arts Australia Ltd.
AAA............ Acta Academiae Aboensis [*A publication*]
AAA............ Acta Apostolorum Apocrypha [*A publication*]
AAA............ Action Against Allergy [*British*] (EAIO)
AAA............ Action on Alcohol Abuse [*British*]
AAA............ Active Antenna Array (MCD)
AAA............ Acute Anxiety Attack [*Medicine*]
AAA............ Advance Australia Award
AAA............ Advanced Attack Aircraft (CAAL)
AAA............ Aerosol Age [*A publication*]
AAA............ Aerosol Association of Australia
AAA............ Agency Activity Analysis [*LIMRA*]
AAA............ Agnew Association of America (EA)
AAA............ Agricultural Adjustment Act [*1933, 1938, 1980*] [*Department of Agriculture*]
AAA............ Agricultural Adjustment Administration [*or Agency*] [*Production and Marketing Administration*] [*Department of Agriculture*]
AAA............ Agricultural Aircraft Association [*Later, CAAA*] (EA)
AAA............ Alaska
AAA............ Alianza Anticomunista Argentina [*Argentine Anti-Communist Alliance*] (PD)
AAA............ Alianza Apostolica Anticomunista [*Anti-Communist Apostolic Alliance*] [*Spain*] (PD)
AAA............ Allegheny Airlines [*Air carrier designation symbol*]
AAA............ Allergy Association Australia
AAA............ Allied Airborne Association (EA)
AAA............ Allied Artists of America (EA)
AAA............ Allocation Assessment and Analysis [*Report*]
AAA............ Alma-Ata [*USSR*] [*Geomagnetic observatory code*]
AAA............ Alma-Ata [*USSR*] [*Seismograph station code, US Geological Survey*] (SEIS)
AAA............ Alternative Antenna Array (MCD)
AAA............ Amalgama [*Amalgamation*] [*Pharmacy*] (ROG)
AAA............ Amateur Astronomers Association [*Later, AAANY*]
AAA............ Amateur Athletic Association [*British*]
AA of A ...... Ambulance Association of America [*Later, AAA*]
AAA............ American Abstract Artists (EA)
AAA............ American Academy of Achievement (EA)
AAA............ American Academy of Actuaries [*Washington, DC*] (EA)
AAA............ American Academy of Advertising [*Charleston, SC*] (EA)
AAA............ American Academy of Allergy [*Later, AAAI*] (EA)
AAA............ American Academy of Art [*Chicago, IL*]
AAA............ American Accordionists' Association (EA)
AAA............ American Accounting Association [*Sarasota, FL*] (EA)
AAA............ American Acupuncture Association (EA)
AAA............ American Aerobics Association (EA)
AAA............ American Affenpinscher Association (EA)
AAA............ American Afghan Action [*Later, FAAA*] (EA)
AAA............ American Agents Association [*Indianapolis, IN*] (EA)
AAA............ American Airship Association [*Later, Airship Association*] (EA)
AAA............ American Albino Association [*Later, WWWCRW*]
AAA............ American Allergy Association (EA)
AAA............ American Ambulance Association (EA)
AAA............ American Angus Association (EA)
AAA............ American Antarctic Association (EA)
AAA............ American Anthropological Association (EA)
AAA............ American Aquatech International [*Vancouver Stock Exchange symbol*]
AAA............ American Arab Affairs [*A publication*]
AAA............ American Arbitration Association (EA)
AAA............ American Armwrestling Association (EA)
AAA............ American Art Association [*Predecessor of Parke-Bernet, New York*]
AAA............ American Arts Alliance (EA)
AAA............ American Association of Anatomists (EA)
AAA............ American Astronomers Association (EA)
AAA............ American Australian Association (EA)
AAA............ American Automobile Association (EA)
AAA............ Americans Against Abortion (EA)
AAA............ Aminoadipic Acid [*Organic chemistry*]
AAA............ Anarchist Association of the Americas (EA)
AAA............ Anglo-American Associates (EA)
AAA............ Annals. American Academy of Political and Social Science [*A publication*]
AAA............ Annals of Archaeology and Anthropology [*Liverpool*] [*A publication*]
AAA............ Ansett Airlines of Australia (ADA)
AAA............ Antiaircraft Armament
AAA............ Antiaircraft Artillery (GPO)
AAA............ Antique Airplane Association (EA)
AAA............ Apollo Access Arm [*NASA*] (KSC)
AAA.......... Apostolic Anti-Communist Alliance [*Spain*]

AAA	Appraisers Association of America (EA)
AAA	Approved as Amended
AAA	Archives of American Art (EA)
AAA	Archivio. Alto Adige [*A publication*]
AAA	Area Agency on Aging (DHSM)
AA & A	Armor, Armament, and Ammunition
AAA	Army Audit Agency
AAA	Aromatic Amino Acids [*Biochemistry*]
AAA	Assistant Air Attache [*British*]
AAA	Associate in Applied Arts
AAA	Associated Actors and Artistes of America
AAA	Associated Agents of America (EA)
AAA	Association of Accounting Administrators [*Commercial firm*] [*Washington, DC*] (EA)
AAA	Association of Attenders and Alumni of The Hague Academy of International Law
AAA	Association des Auditeurs et Anciens Auditeurs de l'Academie [*Association of Attenders and Alumni of the Hague Academy of International Law*] (EAIO)
AAA	Association of Authors' Agents (EAIO)
AAA	Association of Average Adjusters of the United States [*New York, NY*] (EA)
AAA	Astronaut-Actuated Abort [*NASA*] (MCD)
AAA	Athens Annals of Archaeology [*A publication*]
AAA	Auburn University, Auburn, AL [*OCLC symbol*] (OCLC)
AAA	Australian American Association (ADA)
AAA	Australian American Assurance Co. Ltd.
AAA	Australian Anglers' Association
AAA	Australian Anglo American Ltd. (ADA)
AAA	Australian Antarctic Adventures
AAA	Authorized Accounting Activity [*DoD*]
AAA	Authors at Auction [*A publication*]
AAA	Automated Agency Accounting
AAA	Automated Amino Acid Analysis [*Food technology*]
AAA	Awaiting Aircraft Availability
Aaa	Best [*Moody's bond rating*] [*Investment term*]
AAA	Highest [*Standard & Poor's bond rating*]
AAA	Lincoln, IL [*Location identifier*] [*FAA*] (FAAL)
AAA	Office of Accounting and Audit [*FAA*] (FAAC)
AAAA	Activities, Adaptation, and Aging [*A publication*]
AAAA	Aerial Agricultural Association of Australia
AAAA	Akro Agate Art Association (EA)
AAAA	Amateur Artists Association of America (EA)
AAAA	American-African Affairs Association (EA)
AAAA	American Association of Aardvark Aficionados (EA)
AAAA	American Association for the Advancement of Atheism [*Later, AA*] (EA)
AAAA	American Association of Advertising Agencies [*New York, NY*] (EA)
AAAA	American Association for Affirmative Action (EA)
AAAA	American Association Against Addiction [*Defunct*] (EA)
AAAA	American Association of Audio Analgesia [*Defunct*]
AAAA	Antique Aeroplane Association of Australia
AAAA	Antique Appraisal Association of America (EA)
AAAA	Army Aviation Association of America (EA)
AAAA	Artists and Athletes Against Apartheid (EA)
AAAA	Associated Actors and Artistes of America (EA)
AAAA	Australian Association for Applied Anthropology
AAA/AA	American Anthropologist. American Anthropological Association [*A publication*]
AAAAAA	Association for the Alleviation of Asinine Abbreviations and Absurd Acronyms [*Satirical nonassociation*]
AAAAPSF	American Association for Accreditation of Ambulatory Plastic Surgery Facilities (EA)
AAAB	American Association of Architectural Bibliographers
AAAB	Annales. Academie Royale d'Archeologie de Belgique [*A publication*]
AAABA	All-American Amateur Baseball Association (EA)
AAABC	Astronomy and Astrophysics. Abstracts [*A publication*]
AAABG	Australian Association of Animal Breeding and Genetics
AAAC	About Arts and Crafts. Department of Indian and Northern Affairs [*A publication*]
AAAC	All Aluminum Alloy Conductor (MCD)
AAAC	American-Arab Affairs Council (EA)
AAAC	American Association of Accompanists and Coaches (EA)
AAAC	Antiaircraft Artillery Command
AAAC	Archival Association of Atlantic Canada
AAAC	Association of Australian Acoustical Consultants
AAAC	Australian Aboriginal Affairs Council
AAAC	Australian Association of Agricultural Consultants
AAACC	Association of Asian-American Chambers of Commerce [*Washington, DC*] (EA)
AAACCA	Advances in Antimicrobial and Antineoplastic Chemotherapy [*A publication*]
AAACE	American Association for Adult and Continuing Education (EA)
AAACE	American Association of Agricultural College Editors [*Later, ACE*]
AAACI	American-Arab Association for Commerce and Industry [*New York, NY*] (EA)
AAACJ	All American Association of Contest Judges (EA)
AAA-CPA	American Association of Attorney-Certified Public Accountants [*Mission Viejo, CA*] (EA)
AAACU	Asian Association of Agricultural Colleges and Universities [*Philippines*]
AAAD	Airborne Antitank Armor Air Defense (MCD)
AAAD	American Athletic Association for the Deaf (EA)
AAAd	Antichita Altoadriatiche [*A publication*]
AAAd	Archivio. Alto Adige [*A publication*]
AAAD	Aromatic Amino Acid Decarboxylase [*Also, AADC*] [*An enzyme*]
AAAD	Association of Automotive Aftermarket Distributors (EA)
AAADC	Alvin Ailey American Dance Center
AAAE	Alliance of Associations for the Advancement of Education (EA)
AAAE	American Association of Academic Editors (EA)
AAAE	American Association for Agricultural Education (EA)
AAAE	American Association of Airport Executives (EA)
AAAE	Asian Automotive and Accessories Exhibition (TSPED)
AAAE	Association of Arts Administration Educators (EA)
AAAEE	American Afro-Asian Educational Exchange [*Later, AAEE*] (EA)
AAAF	Anglo-American Air Force (DAS)
AAAF	Arab Amateur Athletic Federation [*See also CAA*] (EAIO)
AAAG	Acting Assistant Adjutant-General [*Military*] [*British*] (ROG)
AAAG	Annals. Association of American Geographers [*A publication*]
AA Ag	Associate in Arts in Agriculture
AAAGA	Association of American Geographers. Annals [*A publication*]
AAAH	Acta Academiae Aboensis. Series A. Humaniora [*A publication*]
AAAH	Acta ad Archaeologiam et Artium Historiam Pertinentia [*A publication*]
AAAH	American Association for the Advancement of the Humanities
AAAHAIL	Association of Attenders and Alumni of The Hague Academy of International Law (EA)
AAAHAN	Australian Journal of Experimental Agriculture and Animal Husbandry [*A publication*]
AAAHC	Accreditation Association for Ambulatory Health Care (EA)
AAA Hum	Acta Academiae Aboensis. Series A. Humaniora [*A publication*]
AAAI	Affiliated Advertising Agencies International [*Aurora, CO*] (EA)
AAAI	Afro-American Art Institute (EA)
AAAI	American Academy of Allergy and Immunology (EA)
AAAI	American Association for Artificial Intelligence (EA)
AAAI	Associate of the Institute of Administrative Accounting and Data Processing [*British*] (DCTA)
AAAI	Association of Australian Aerospace Industries
AAAIBR	Aspects of Allergy and Applied Immunology [*A publication*]
AAAID	Arab Authority for Agricultural Investment and Development [*Khartoum, Sudan*] (EAIO)
AAAIMH	American Association for the Abolition of Involuntary Mental Hospitalization [*Defunct*]
AAAIS	Advanced Army Aircraft Instrument System (MCD)
AAAIS	Antiaircraft Artillery Information [*or Intelligence*] Service
AAAIWD	American Association of Aluminum Importers and Warehouse Distributors [*Later, AMIA*] (EA)
AA/AL	Airplane Avionics/AUTOLAND (NASA)
AAAL	American Academy of Arts and Letters [*Later, AAIAL*] (EA)
AAA & L	American Academy of Arts and Letters [*Later, AAIAL*] (EA)
AAAL	American Association for Applied Linguistics (EA)
AA/AL	Automatic Approach/AUTOLAND (NASA)
AAALAC	American Association for Accreditation of Laboratory Animal Care (EA)
AAAM	Advanced Air-to-Air Missile [*Military*]
AAAM	American Anthropological Association. Memoirs [*A publication*]
AAAM	Association for the Advancement of Automotive Medicine (EA)
AAAMA	Air-to-Air Armament Mission Analyses [*Air Force*] (MCD)
AAAMS	Advanced Antiarmor Missile Systems (MCD)
AAAN	Alaska Anthropological Association. Newsletter [*A publication*]
AAAN	American Academy of Applied Nutrition [*Later, ICAN*] (EA)
AAANA	American Academy of Ambulatory Nursing Administration (EA)
AAANA7	Arquivo de Anatomia e Antropologia [*A publication*]
AAA of NSW	Amateur Athletic Association of New South Wales [*Australia*]
AAANY	Amateur Astronomers Association of New York [*Formerly, AAA*] (EA)
AAANYC	Amateur Astronomers Association of New York City [*Later, AAA*] (EA)
AAAOB	Antiair Artillery Order of Battle (MCD)
AAAOC	Antiaircraft Artillery Operation Center
AAAOM	American Association for Acupuncture and Oriental Medicine (EA)
AAAP	Action Against Armageddon Project [*Defunct*] (EA)
AAAP	Airborne Associative Array Processor
AAAP	American Association of Applied Psychology [*Division of American Psychological Association*]
AAAP	American Association of Avian Pathologists (EA)
AAAPA	Afro-American Association of Performing Artists (EA)
AAAPSS	Annals. American Academy of Political and Social Science [*A publication*]

AAAR....... American Association for Aerosol Research   (EA)
AAAR....... Association for the Advancement of Aeronautical Research [*France*]
AAAR....... Association for the Advancement of Aging Research [*Defunct*]   (EA)
AAAr......... Atti. Accademia degli Arcadi [*A publication*]
AAAR....... Regional Office, Alberta Agriculture, Airdrie, Alberta [*Library symbol*] [*National Library of Canada*]   (NLC)
AAARBK... AGARD [*Advisory Group for Aerospace Research and Development*] Advisory Report [*A publication*]
AAARC..... Antiaircraft Artillery Reception Center
AAARG ..... American Atheist Addiction Recovery Groups [*Later, MOM*]   (EA)
AAAS........ American Academy of Arts and Sciences   (EA)
AAA & S.... American Academy of Arts and Sciences   (EA)
AAAS........ American Academy of Asian Studies   (EA)
AAAS........ American Association for the Advancement of Science   (EA)
AAAS........ Armored Antiaircraft System   (MCD)
AAA & S.... Associate in Arts in Arts and Science
AAAS........ Austrian Association for American Studies
AAAS........ Automated Attendance Accounting System [*Jet Propulsion Laboratory, NASA*]
AAASA...... Apparel Agents Association of South Australia
AAASA...... Association for the Advancement of Agricultural Sciences in Africa   (EAIO)
AAASAD... Armenian Assembly of America, Student Affairs Division   (EA)
AAASAH .. Acta Academiae Aboensis. Series A. Humaniora [*A publication*]
AAAS Bull ... American Association for the Advancement of Science. Bulletin [*A publication*]
AAASH ..... Acta Antiqua. Academiae Scientiarum Hungaricae [*A publication*]
AAAS Publication ... American Association for the Advancement of Science. Publication [*A publication*]
AAASS ...... American Association for the Advancement of Slavic Studies   (EA)
AAAS/S..... Science. American Association for the Advancement of Science [*A publication*]
AAAS Selected Symposia Series ... American Association for the Advancement of Science. Selected Symposia Series [*A publication*]
AAAS Sel Sympos Ser ... American Association for the Advancement of Science. Selected Symposia Series [*A publication*]
AAASUSS ... Association of Administrative Assistants and Secretaries to United States Senators   (EA)
AAATC...... American Association for the Advancement of Tension Control [*Later, ISTC*]
AAATC..... Association of American Air Travel Clubs   (EA)
AAATP...... Asian Alliance of Appropriate Technology Practitioners   (EA)
AAAUS ..... Association of Average Adjusters of the United States
AAAV .... American Alliance Against Violence   (EA)
AAAVYT... Asociacion Argentina de Agencias de Viajes y Turismo [*Argentine association of travel and tourism agencies*]   (EY)
AAAWC .... Alternate Antiair Warfare Commander   (NVT)
AAAZ .... Archaeologischer Anzeiger zur Archaeologischen Zeitung [*A publication*]
AAB........... AABCO Ventures, Inc. [*Vancouver Stock Exchange symbol*]
AAB........... Abhandlungen der Deutschen [*A publication*]
AAB........... Aboriginal Arts Board [*Australia*]
AAB........... Acquisition Advisory Board   (MCD)
AAB........... Action Against Burns [*Formerly, APBIC*]   (EA)
AAB........... Actualizing Assessment Battery [*Personality development test*] [*Psychology*]
AAB........... Adaptive Angle Bias
AAB........... Advertising Advisory Board of the Canadian Advertising Foundation
AAB........... Air Assault Brigade   (MCD)
AAB........... Air Force Air Base
AAB........... Aircraft Accident Board
AAB........... Aircraft Armament Bulletin [*Navy*] [*A publication*]   (MCD)
AAB........... Alianca Anticomunista Brasileira [*Brazilian Anti-Communist Alliance*]   (PD)
AAB........... Allied Arab Bank
AAB........... American Association of Bioanalysts   (EA)
AA/B .... Antiaircraft Balloon [*Obsolete*]
AAB........... Arab African Bank
AAB........... Army Air Base   (MCD)
AAB........... Army Artillery Board   (AAG)
AAB........... Army Aviation Board
AAB........... Artichoke Advisory Board   (EA)
AAB........... Associate in Arts in Business
AAB........... Association of Applied Biologists [*Midlothian, Scotland*]   (EA)
AAB........... Aviation Armament Bulletin   (MCD)
AAB........... Talgar [*Also, TLG*] [*Alma-Ata*] [*USSR*] [*Seismograph station code, US Geological Survey*]   (SEIS)
AABA .... American Anorexia/Bulimia Association   (EA)
AABAn ...... Annales. Academie Royale d'Archeologie de Belgique [*A publication*]
AABB........ American Association of Blood Banks   (EA)
AABB........ Association for the Advancement of British Biotechnology   (EAIO)

AABC .... Accrediting Association of Bible Colleges [*Later, American Association of Bible Colleges*]   (EA)
AABC .... All-American Bronze Club   (EA)
AABC .... American Amateur Baseball Congress   (EA)
AABC .... American Association of Backgammon Clubs   (EA)
AABC .... American Association of Bible Colleges   (EA)
AABC .... American Association of Biofeedback Clinicians   (EA)
AABC .... American Austin/Bantam Club   (EA)
AABC .... Associated Air Balance Council   (EA)
AABC .... Association for Advancement of Blind Children [*Later, AABR*]   (EA)
AABCAD... Anais. Academia Brasileira de Ciencias [*A publication*]
AABCC...... Australian Anti-Bases Campaign Coalition
AABCP...... Advanced Airborne Command Post
AABD........ Aid to the Aged, Blind, or Disabled [*Department of Health and Human Services*]
AABE........ American Association of Blacks in Energy   (EA)
AABEAJ ... Acta Anaesthesiologica Belgica [*A publication*]
AABEVM ... Association of American Boards of Examiners in Veterinary Medicine [*Later, AAVSB*]   (EA)
AABF........ American Australian Bicentennial Foundation [*Defunct*]   (EA)
AABFS ...... Amphibious Assault Bulk Fuel System [*Navy*]
AABFTFC ... Amalgamated Association of Brass Founders, Turners, Fitters, and Coppersmiths [*A union*] [*British*]
AABGA ..... American Association of Botanical Gardens and Arboreta   (EA)
AABGU ..... American Associates, Ben-Gurion University of the Negev   (EA)
AABH .... Broken Hill [*Australia*] [*ICAO location identifier*]   (ICLI)
AABHH..... American Association of Breeders of Holsteiner Horses   (EA)
AABI......... American Association of Bicycle Importers   (EA)
AABIAV ... Annals of Applied Biology [*A publication*]
AABL........ Advanced Atmospheric Burst Location   (MCD)
AABL........ Associated Australasian Banks in London
AABL........ Australian Amateur Boxing League
AABM ...... Airborne Antiballistic Missiles   (MCD)
AABM ...... Alberta Beach Municipal Library, Alberta [*Library symbol*] [*National Library of Canada*]   (NLC)
AABM ...... American Academy of Behavioral Medicine   (EA)
AABM ...... Association of American Battery Manufacturers [*Later, BCI*]   (EA)
AABM .... Australian Association of British Manufacturers
AABN .... Anti-Apartheids Beweging Nederland [*Anti-Apartheid Movement*] [*South Africa*] [*Political party*]   (EAIO)
AABNCP... Advanced Airborne National Command Post   (MCD)
AABNF...... African Association for Biological Nitrogen-Fixation   (EAIO)
AABO........ Assembly of Australian Business Organisations
AABP........ American Association of Bovine Practitioners   (EA)
AABP........ Aptitude Assessment Battery Programming [*Data processing*]   (IEEE)
AABP........ Association of Area Business Publications   (EA)
AABPA ..... American Association for Budget and Program Analysis   (EA)
AABR .... Association for Advancement of Blind and Retarded   (EA)
AABS........ All-Attitude Indicator Bombing System   (MCD)
AABS........ Association for the Advancement of Baltic Studies   (EA)
AABSHILL ... Aircraft Anticollision Beacon System High-Intensity Light [*Army*]   (MCD)
AABT........ American Association of Behavioral Therapists   (EA)
AABT........ Association for Advancement of Behavior Therapy   (EA)
AABTD...... Amalgamated Association of Beamers, Twisters, and Drawers [*A union*] [*British*]   (DCTA)
AABTM..... American Association of Baggage Traffic Managers [*Defunct*]   (EA)
AaBU .... Universidad de Buenos Aires, Buenos Aires, Argentina [*Library symbol*] [*Library of Congress*]   (LCLS)
AaBU-C..... Universidad de Buenos Aires, Facultad de Ciencias Exactas y Naturales, Buenos Aires, Argentina [*Library symbol*] [*Library of Congress*]   (LCLS)
AA Bus...... Associate in Arts in Business
AABW ...... American Association of Book Wholesalers   (EA)
AABW ...... Antarctic Bottom Water [*Oceanography*]
AABWA .... Association of Accountancy Bodies in West Africa [*Lagos, Nigeria*]   (EAIO)
AABWE..... American Association of Black Women Entrepreneurs [*Silver Spring, MD*]   (EA)
AABY .... As Amended By [*Army*]
AAC........... Aachen [*Federal Republic of Germany*] [*Seismograph station code, US Geological Survey*] [*Closed*]   (SEIS)
AAC........... Abort Advisory Channel [*NASA*]   (KSC)
AAC........... Acoustical Absorption Coefficient
AAC........... Acoustical Attenuation Constant
AAC........... Acquisition Advice Code [*NASA*]   (KSC)
AAC........... Acta Archaeologica (Copenhagen) [*A publication*]
AAC........... Activity Address Code [*DoD*]
AAC........... Adaptive Antenna Control   (MCD)
AAC........... Administration above the Company   (MCD)
AAC........... Aerated Autoclaved Concrete
AAC........... Aerial Ambulance Company [*Army*]   (AABC)
AAC........... Aeronautical Advisory Council
AAC........... Aeronautical Approach Chart [*Air Force*]
AAC........... Aeronca Aviators Club   (EA)
AAC........... African Association of Cartography   (EA)

AAC........... Afro-Asian Center (EA)
AAC........... Agreement and Account of Crew (ADA)
AAC........... Air Approach Control (MCD)
AAC........... Air Carbon Arc Cutting [*Welding*]
AAC........... Airborne Armament Control [*Air Force*] (MCD)
AAC........... Aircraft Armament Change
AAC........... Airworthiness Advisory Circular [*A publication*] (APTA)
AAC........... Al Arish [*Egypt*] [*Airport symbol*] (OAG)
AAC........... Alaskan Air Command [*Elmendorf Air Force Base*]
AAC........... Alkyl Amines Council
AAC........... All Aluminum Conductor
AAC........... Allied Longline Agency Annual Conference [*NATO*] (NATG)
AAC........... Alumnae Advisory Center [*Later, CCP*] (EA)
AAC........... Amateur Athletic Club
AAC........... American Academy of Criminalistics (EA)
AAC........... American Adoption Congress [*Later, NAAC*] (EA)
AAC........... American Alligator Council [*Defunct*] (EA)
AAC........... American Alpine Club (EA)
AAC........... American Alumni Council [*Later, Council for the Advancement and Support of Education*] (EA)
AAC........... American Archery Council (EA)
AAC........... American Association of Chiropractors (EA)
AAC........... Aminoacetylcatechol [*or Acetamidocatechol*] [*Biochemistry*]
AAC........... Amplitude Absorption Coefficient
AAC........... Anacomp, Inc. [*NYSE symbol*] (SPSG)
AAC........... Analytical Assessments Corporation (MCD)
AAC........... Anglo-American Code [*Cataloging*] (DIT)
AAC........... Anglo-American Committee [*World War II*]
AAC........... Anno ante Christum [*In the Year before Christ*] [*Latin*]
AAC........... Antarctic Circle (ROG)
AAC........... Anti-Aircraft Corps [*British military*] (DMA)
AAC........... Antiaircraft Cannon (KSC)
AAC........... Antiaircraft Command
AAC........... Antiaircraft Common [*Projectile*]
AAC........... Antibiotic-Associated Colitis [*Medicine*]
AAC........... Antimicrobial Agents and Chemotherapy
AAC........... Arabinosylazacytidine [*Biochemistry*]
AAC........... Architectural Anodizers Council (EA)
AAC........... Armor and Arms Club (EA)
AAC........... Army Air Corps
AAC........... Army Audiovisual Center
AAC........... Arsenic Atmosphere Czochralski [*System for growing crystals*]
AAC........... Assembly Area Command
AAC........... Assembly and Checkout [*Minuteman*] [*Military*] (AFIT)
AAC........... Assets Availability Code (MCD)
AAC........... Association Africaine de Cartographie [*African Association of Cartography*] (EAIO)
AAC........... Association of American Choruses [*Later, Drinker Library of Choral Music*] (EA)
AAC........... Association of American Colleges (EA)
AAC........... Association of Analytical Chemists, Inc.
AAC........... Athletes' Advisory Council [*See also CCA*] [*Canada*]
AAC........... Atomic Absorption Coefficient
AAC........... Attack Aircraft Carrier (MCD)
AA of C...... Auctioneers Association of Canada
AAC........... Augmentative and Alternative Communication [*A publication*]
AAC........... Australian Aero Club
AAC........... Australian Aircraft Consortium Proprietary Ltd.
AAC........... Automatic Amplitude Control (CET)
AAC........... Automatic Aperture Control
AAC........... Automatic Approach Control [*Aviation*] (AAG)
AAC........... Automatic Autocollimator
AAC........... Automotive Advertisers Council [*Chicago, IL*] (EA)
AAC........... Auxiliary Artillery Corps [*British military*] (DMA)
AAC........... Aviation Armament Change (MCD)
AAC........... Awami Action Committee [*India*] [*Political party*] (PPW)
AACA........ Allied Control Commission for Austria [*World War II*]
AACA........ American Apparel Contractors Association (EA)
AACA........ American Association of Certified Allergists (EA)
AACA........ American Association of Certified Appraisers [*Cincinnati, OH*] (EA)
AACA........ American Association of Creative Artists (EA)
AACA........ Amphibious Auto Club of America (EA)
AACA........ Antique Automobile Club of America (EA)
AACA........ Associate of the Association of Cost Accountants (ADA)
AACA........ Association of Americans and Canadians for Aliyah [*Later, North American Aliyah Movement*]
AACA........ Automotive Air Conditioning Association [*Later, IMACA*] (EA)
A Acad Sci Fenn ... Annales Academiae Scientiarum Fennicae [*A publication*]
AACAHPO ... American Association of Certified Allied Health Personnel in Ophthalmology (EA)
AACAP...... American Academy of Child and Adolescent Psychiatry (EA)
AACAR ..... Association for the Advancement of Central Asian Research (EA)
AACB .... Aeronautics and Astronautics Coordinating Board [*NASA*]
AACB .... Allied Control Commission for Bulgaria [*World War II*]
AACB .... American Association for Consumer Benefits (EA)
AACB .... Association of African Central Banks [*Dakar, Senegal*]
AACBC...... American Association of College Baseball Coaches (EA)
AACBP...... American Academy of Crown and Bridge Prosthodontics (EA)

AACC .... Administrative Area Control Centre [*Military*] [*British*]
AACC .... Affaires des Anciens Combattants du Canada [*Department of Canadian Veterans Affairs - DVA*]
AACC .... Affirmative Action Coordinating Center (EA)
AACC .... Airport Associations Coordinating Council [*Geneva Airport, Switzerland*] (EAIO)
AAcC .... Alexander City State Junior College, Alexander City, AL [*Library symbol*] [*Library of Congress*] (LCLS)
AACC .... All-Africa Conference of Churches [*Nairobi, Kenya*]
AACC .... All-Attitude Control Capability [*Aerospace*] (AAG)
AACC .... American Association of Cereal Chemists (EA)
AACC .... American Association of Clinical Chemistry (EA)
AACC .... American Association for Contamination Control [*Later, IES*] (EA)
AACC .... American Association for Continuity of Care (EA)
AACC .... American Association for Corporate Contributions [*Evanston, IL*] (EA)
AACC .... American Association of Credit Counselors [*Grayslake, IL*] (EA)
AACC .... American Automatic Control Council (EA)
AACC .... Army Air Corps Centre [*British military*] (DMA)
AACC .... Army Aviation Control Center
AACC .... Association of Agricultural Computer Companies (EA)
AACC .... Association for the Aid of Crippled Children [*Later, Foundation for Child Development*] (EA)
AACC .... Automatic Approach Control Coupler [*or Complex*] [*Aviation*] (MCD)
AACCA ..... Associate of Association of Certified and Corporate Accountants [*British*]
AACC (Am Assoc Cereal Chem) Monogr ... AACC (American Association of Cereal Chemists) Monograph [*A publication*]
AACCB...... All Africa Conference of Churches. Bulletin [*A publication*]
AACCC...... All-American Conference to Combat Communism (EA)
AACCLA ... Association of American Chambers of Commerce in Latin America (EA)
AACCN ..... American Association of Critical-Care Nurses (EA)
AACC News ... Affirmative Action Coordinating Center. Newsletter [*A publication*]
AACCP...... American Association of Colleges of Chiropody-Podiatry
AACD........ American Academy of Craniomandibular Disorders (EA)
AACD........ American Association for Counseling and Development (EA)
AACD........ Asian American Caucus for Disarmament (EA)
AACD........ Ceduna [*Australia*] [*ICAO location identifier*] (ICLI)
AACDP...... American Association of Chairmen of Departments of Psychiatry (EA)
AACE .... Airborne Alternate Command Echelon [*NATO*] (NATG)
AACE .... Aircraft Alerting Communications Electromagnetic Pulse (MCD)
AACE .... American Association for Cancer Education (EA)
AACE .... American Association for Career Education (EA)
AACE .... American Association of Cost Engineers (EA)
AACE .... Arrets et Avis du Conseil d'Etat [*Judgments and Opinions of the Council of State*] [*Belgium*] [*A publication*] (DLA)
AACE .... Association for Adult Continuing Education [*British*]
AACE .... Association des Assureurs Cooperatifs Europeens [*Association of European Cooperative Insurers - AECI*] [*Brussels, Belgium*] (EAIO)
AACE .... Association des Auteurs des Cantons de l'Est [*Association of Writers of Cantons of the East*] [*Canada*]
AACE (Am Assoc Cost Eng) Bull ... AACE (American Association of Cost Engineers) Bulletin [*A publication*]
AACE Bull ... American Association of Cost Engineers. Bulletin [*A publication*]
AACF........ Afro-American Cultural Foundation (EA)
AACF........ Army Area Calibration Facilities (MCD)
AACFAR ... Annales. ACFAS [*Association Canadienne Francaise pour l'Avancement des Sciences*] [*A publication*]
AACFO...... American Association of Correctional Facility Officers [*Later, IACO*] (EA)
AACFT ...... Army Aircraft (AABC)
AACG........ Acute Angle Closure Glaucoma [*Ophthalmology*]
AACG........ Allied Control Council for Germany [*World War II*]
AACG........ American Association for Crystal Growth (EA)
AACG........ Arrival Airfield Control Group [*Military*] (AABC)
AACGF...... All-American Collegiate Golf Foundation (EA)
AACH........ Allied Control Commission for Hungary [*World War II*]
AACHBY .. Acta Arachnologica [*A publication*]
Aachen Kuntsbl ... Aachener Kuntsblaetter [*A publication*]
AACHIR .... Augusta Area Committee for Health Information Resources [*Library network*]
Aach Kbl .... Aachener Kunstblaetter [*A publication*]
AACHP ..... American Association for Comprehensive Health Planning [*Later, AHPA*]
A A Chron ... Arthur Andersen Chronicle [*A publication*]
AACHS ..... Afro-American Cultural and Historical Society [*Later, AACHSM*]
AACHSA... Associate of the Australian College of Health Service Administrators
AACHSM ... Afro-American Cultural and Historical Society Museum (EA)
AACHT ..... American Association for Clinical Histocompatibility Testing [*Later, ASHI*] (EA)

AACI.........	Accredited Appraiser, Canadian Institute
AACI.........	Allied Control Commission for Italy [*World War II*]
AACI.........	American Academy of Crisis Interveners (EA)
AACI.........	American Association of Ceramic Industries (EA)
AACI.........	American Association for Conservation Information [*Later, ACI*] (EA)
AACI.........	American Association of Crop Insurers [*Washington, DC*] (EA)
AACI.........	Association of American Cancer Institutes (EA)
AACI.........	Association of Americans and Canadians in Israel (EA)
AACIA......	American Association for Clinical Immunology and Allergy (EA)
AACIA2.....	Advances in Analytical Chemistry and Instrumentation [*A publication*]
AACIGO ...	Association of American and Canadian Importers of Green Olives [*Later, Green Olive Trade Association*] (EA)
AACIL.......	All-Articles Configuration Inspection Log [*Aerospace*] (AAG)
AACIS	Association of American CIRP [*College Internationale pour l'Etude Scientifique des Techniques de Production Mechanique*] Industrial Sponsors (EA)
AACJ.........	Allied Control Council for Japan [*World War II*]
AACJC......	American Association of Community and Junior Colleges (EA)
AACL........	Affect Adjective Check List [*Psychology*]
AACL........	Anxiety Adjective Check List [*Psychology*]
AACL........	Association of American Correspondents in London [*England*] (EA)
AACLAME ...	Australian Advisory Council on Language and Multicultural Education
AACLS	Association of American Collegiate Literary Societies (EA)
AACM	Advanced Air Cycle Machine (MCD)
AACM	African Anti-Colonial Movement of Kenya
AACM	American Academy of Compensation Medicine [*Later, AALIM*] (EA)
AACM	ASEAN [*Association of Southeast Asian Nations*] - Australia Consultative Meeting
AACM	Associate of the Australian College of Music
AACM	Association for the Advancement of Creative Musicians (EA)
AACM	Automatic Armor Cluster Munition
AACM	Average Absolute Control Movement (MCD)
AACMP.....	Anales. Academia de Ciencias Morales y Politicas [*A publication*]
AACN........	American Association of Colleges of Nursing (EA)
AACN........	American Association of Critical-Care Nurses (EA)
AACN........	Anno ante Christum Natum [*In the Year before the Birth of Christ*] [*Latin*] (DLA)
AACN........	Arts and Culture of the North [*A publication*]
AACO........	Advanced and Applied Concepts Office [*MERDC*] [*Army*]
AACO........	American Association of Certified Orthoptists (EA)
AACO........	American Association of Correctional Officers [*Later, IACO*] (EA)
AACO........	Arab Air Carriers Organization (EAIO)
AACO........	Assault Airlift Control Officer
AACOB...	Applied Acoustics [*A publication*]
AACOBE...	Army Automation Command Operating Budget Estimate
AACOM	American Association of Colleges of Osteopathic Medicine (EA)
AACOMS ...	Army Area Communications System (MCD)
A & A Corp ...	Angell and Ames on Corporations [*A publication*] (DLA)
AACP.........	Advanced Airborne Command Post
AACP........	Air Carrier Contract Personnel
AACP........	American Academy for Cerebral Palsy [*Later, AACPDM*] (EA)
AACP........	American Academy of Child Psychiatry [*Later, AACAP*] (EA)
AACP........	American Academy of Clinical Psychiatrists (EA)
AACP........	American Association of Colleges of Pharmacy (EA)
AACP........	American Association of Colleges of Podiatry [*Later, AACPM*] (EA)
AACP.........	American Association of Commerce Publications [*Later, American Chamber of Commerce Executives Communications Council*] (EA)
AACP........	American Association of Community Psychiatrists (EA)
AACP........	American Association of Computer Professionals (EA)
AACP........	American Association of Convention Planners [*Defunct*] (EA)
AACP........	American Association for Correctional Psychology (EA)
AACP........	Associate of the Association of Computer Professionals [*British*] (DBQ)
AACP........	Association of American-Chinese Professionals (EA)
AACPA......	Asian American Certified Public Accountants
AACPDM ...	American Academy for Cerebral Palsy and Developmental Medicine (EA)
AACPDQ ..	Archives d'Anatomie et de Cytologie Pathologiques [*A publication*]
AACPM.....	American Association of Colleges of Podiatric Medicine (EA)
AACPP......	Association of Asbestos Cement Pipe Producers (EA)
AACPR......	American Association for Cleft Palate Rehabilitation [*Later, ACPA*]
AACPS	American Association of Clinic Physicians and Surgeons [*Defunct*] (EA)
AAC & R....	All American Cables & Radio, Inc.
AACR	Allied Control Commission for Rumania [*World War II*]
AACR	American Association for Cancer Research (EA)
AACR	American Association of Conservators and Restorers (EA)

AACR	Anglo-American Cataloguing Rules [*American Library Association*] [*A publication*]
AACR	Association for the Advancement of Civil Rights [*Gibraltar*] [*Political party*] (PPE)
AACR2	Anglo-American Cataloguing Rules, Second Edition [*American Library Association*] [*A publication*]
AACRA	Anesthesia and Analgesia (Cleveland) [*A publication*]
AACRAO ..	American Association of Collegiate Registrars and Admissions Officers (EA)
AACRC.....	American Association of Children's Residential Centers (EA)
AA-C & Ref Tech ...	Associate in Air-Conditioning and Refrigeration Technology
AACS........	Airborne Astrographic Camera System [*Air Force*] (MCD)
AACS........	Airspeed and Altitude Computer Set (CAAL)
AACS........	Airways and Air Communications Service [*Army*]
AACS........	American Academy of Cosmetic Surgery (EA)
AACS........	American Antiques and Crafts Society [*Defunct*] (EA)
AACS........	American Association for Chinese Studies (EA)
AACS........	American Association of Christian Schools (EA)
AACS........	Antiaircraft Control Station (MCD)
AACS........	Antiarmor Capabilities Study (MCD)
AACS........	Army Airways Communications System
AACS........	Army Alaska Communication System [*Air Force*]
AACS........	Association of Arts Centres in Scotland [*British*]
AACS........	Asynchronous Address Communications Systems
AACS........	Attitude and Antenna Control System [*NASA*] (MCD)
AACS........	Attitude and Articulation Control Subsystem [*NASA*]
AACS........	Auxiliary Attitude Control System [*Aviation*] (MCD)
AACSB......	American Assembly of Collegiate Schools of Business (EA)
AACSC......	Army Automation and Communication Steering Committee
AACSCEDR ...	Associates and Advisory Committee to the Special Committee on Electronic Data Retrieval (MCD)
AACSE......	American Association of Classified School Employees (EA)
AACSE2.....	Advances in Agronomy and Crop Science [*A publication*]
AACSL......	American Association for the Comparative Study of Law (EA)
AACSM.....	Airways and Air Communications Service Manual
AACSR.....	Aluminum Alloy Constructor Steel Reinforced (IEEE)
AACT	American Academy of Clinical Toxicology (EA)
AACT	American Association of Candy Technologists (EA)
AACT	American Association of Commodity Traders [*Inactive*] (EA)
AACT	American Association of Community Theatre (EA)
AACT	American Association of Crimean Turks (EA)
AACT	Armenian Assembly Charitable Trust (EA)
AACTE......	American Association of Colleges for Teacher Education (EA)
AACTO.....	American Association of Cable TV Owners [*Inactive*] (EA)
AACTP......	American Association of Correctional Training Personnel (EA)
AACTS......	Automatic Anechoic Chamber Test System [*Navy*] (MCD)
AACTVO...	American Association of Cable TV Owners
AACU	American Association of Clinical Urologists (EA)
AACU	Anti-Aircraft Co-Operation Unit [*British military*] (DMA)
AaCU.........	Universidad Nacional de Cordoba, Cordoba, Argentina [*Library symbol*] [*Library of Congress*] (LCLS)
AACUBO ..	American Association of College and University Business Officers [*Defunct*]
AACUO.....	Association for Affiliated College and University Offices [*Later, ACUO*] (EA)
AACVB.....	Asian Association of Convention and Visitor Bureaus (EA)
AACVPR...	American Association of Cardiovascular and Pulmonary Rehabilitation (EA)
AACX	Aries Air Cargo International [*Air carrier designation symbol*]
AAD..........	Acetoacetate Decarboxylase [*An enzyme*]
AAD..........	Active Acoustic Device
AAD..........	Admission and Disposition [*Military*] (AABC)
AAD..........	Advanced Academic Degree (AFM)
AAD..........	Advanced Airborne Demonstrator
AAD..........	Advanced Ammunition Depot
AAD..........	Air Assault Division [*Army*]
AAD..........	Airborne Assault Division (MCD)
AAD..........	Aircraft and Armament Development
AAD..........	Aircraft Assignment Directive
AAD..........	Alberta Alcoholism and Drug Abuse Commission Library, Edmonton, AB, Canada [*OCLC symbol*] (OCLC)
AAD..........	Alloxazine Adenine Dinucleotide [*Biochemistry*]
AAD..........	American Academy of Dentists [*Defunct*] (EA)
AAD..........	American Academy of Dermatology (EA)
AAD..........	American Academy of Diplomacy (EA)
AAD..........	American Daleco Technologies, Inc. [*Vancouver Stock Exchange symbol*]
Aad............	Aminoadipic Acid [*Biochemistry*]
AAD..........	Antiaircraft Defences [*British*]
AAD..........	Appropriation Account Data [*Business term*]
AAD..........	Arms and Ammunition Division [*Army*]
AAD..........	Army Air Defense
AAD..........	Army Automation Directorate [*Formerly, DMIS*] (MCD)
AAD..........	Army Aviation Digest [*A publication*]
AAD..........	Associate Administrator for Administration [*FAA*] (FAAC)
AAD..........	Association of American Dentists
AAD..........	At a Discount
AAD..........	Australian-Antarctic Discordance [*Geology*]
AAD..........	Average Absolute Deviation [*Statistics*]
AAD..........	Deputy Associate Administrator [*NASA*]

AADA........	Advanced Air Depot Area [Air Force]
AADA........	Airport and Airway Development Act of 1970 [FAA] (FAAC)
AADA........	Antiaircraft Defense Area [NATO]
AADA........	Army Adviser Discharge Affairs [British and Canadian] [World War II]
AADA........	Army Air Defense Area
AADA........	Associated Antique Dealers of America (EA)
AADA........	Association for Adult Development and Aging (EA)
AADA........	Australian Action for Development Alternatives
AADA........	Auxiliary to the American Dental Association (EA)
AADAOPA ...	American Association of Dealers in Ancient, Oriental, and Primitive Art (EA)
AADB........	American Association of the Deaf-Blind (EA)
AADB........	Army Air Defense Board (KSC)
AADC........	Advanced Avionics Digital Computer [Naval Air Systems Command]
AADC........	Air Aide-de-Camp [RAF] [British]
AADC........	Airborne Antiarmor Defense Concept (MCD)
AADC........	All Applications Digital Computer [Navy]
AADC........	American Association of Dental Consultants [Bloomington, MN] (EA)
AADC........	American Association of Disability Communicators (EA)
AADC........	Amino Acid Decarboxylase [An enzyme]
AADC........	Antiaircraft Defence Commander [British]
AADC........	Antiaircraft Director Center (MCD)
AADC........	Approach and Departure Control [Aviation] (FAAC)
AADC........	Army Air Defense Command [or Commander] [Later, AADCOM]
AADC........	Arnold Air Development Center [Air Force]
AADC........	Aromatic Amino Acid Decarboxylase [Also, AAAD] [An enzyme]
AADC........	Association of American Dance Companies [Defunct] (EA)
AADC........	Asthma and Allergic Disease Center [Department of Health and Human Services] (GRD)
AADC2......	Army Air Defense Command and Control (MCD)
AADCCS...	Army Air Defense Control and Coordination System (AABC)
AADCM......	Awaiting Action Deck Court-Martial
AADCOM ...	Army Air Defense Command [or Commander] [Formerly, AADC, ARADCOM] (AABC)
AADCP......	Army Air Defense Command Post
AADCS......	Automatic Air Data Calibration System [Aerospace]
AADE........	American Academy of Dental Electrosurgery (EA)
AADE........	American Association of Dental Editors (EA)
AADE........	American Association of Dental Examiners (EA)
AADE........	American Association of Diabetes Educators (EA)
AADE J	AADE [American Association of Dental Editors] Journal [A publication]
AADEP......	American Academy of Disability Evaluating Physicians (EA)
AADF........	Arab American Democratic Federation (EA)
AADF........	Association for the American Dance Festival (EA)
AADGE......	Allied Air Defense Ground Environment (MCD)
AADGP	American Academy of Dental Group Practice (EA)
AADHS	Advanced Avionics Data Handling System [Air Force] (MCD)
AA Dip.......	Diploma of the Architectural Association School of Architecture [British]
AADIS.......	Army Air Defense Information Service
AADLA	Art and Antique Dealers League of America (EA)
AADM.......	American Academy of Dental Medicine [Later, AAOM] (EA)
A Adm........	Associate in Administration
AADMC.....	Army Aviation Depot Maintenance Center (MCD)
AADMS	Advanced Academic Degree Management System (AFM)
AADN.......	American Association of Doctors' Nurses (EA)
AADO:.......	Accepted Alternative Designation Of
A-aDO₂......	Alveolar-Arterial Oxygen Difference [Physiology]
AADOO	Army Air Defense Operations Office [or Officer]
AADP........	Advanced Avionic Display Processor (MCD)
AADP........	Amyloid-A-Degrading Protease [An enzyme]
AADP........	Antiaircraft Defended Point (MUGU)
AADP........	Army Aviation Development Plan (MCD)
AADPA	American Academy of Dental Practice Administration (EA)
AA & DPD ...	Appropriation Accounts and Data Processing Division [Ministry of Agriculture, Fisheries, and Food] [British]
AADPRT ...	American Association of Directors of Psychiatric Residency Training (EA)
AADPSP ...	Activity Automatic Data Process Security Plan (MCD)
AADR.......	American Academy of Dental Radiology (EA)
AADR.......	American Association for Dental Research (EA)
AADS	Aboriginal Advisory and Development Services [Northern Territory, Australia]
AADS	Access Area Digital Switching System (MCD)
AADS	Advanced Air Defense System
AADS	Aero/Acoustic Detection System [Army] (MCD)
AADS	American Association of Dental Schools (EA)
AADS	Antiaircraft Defense System [Army] (AABC)
AADS	Area Air Defense System (MCD)
AADS	Army Air Defense School (KSC)
AADS	Army Air Defense Site
AADS	Army Air Defense Staff (MCD)
AADS	Army Air Defense System [Formerly, FABMDS]
AADS	Ascent Air Data System (NASA)
AADS	Automated Acoustic Detection System (MCD)
AADS	Automatic Aircraft Diagnostic System
AADSF	Advanced Automated Directional Solidification Furnace [Materials processing]
AADT	Annual Average Daily Traffic [on highways]
AADT	Association of Advanced Dental Technicians [Australia]
AADTS......	Association of Advisors in Design and Technical Studies [British]
AADV	Acquisition Aid Vehicle [Army] (AABC)
AADV	American Association of Dental Victims (EA)
AADW........	Advanced Air Defense Weapon
AAE	AACE [American Association of Cost Engineers] Transactions [A publication]
AAE	Abort Advisory Equipment [NASA] (KSC)
AAE	Accredited Airport Executive [Designation awarded by American Association of Airport Executives]
AAE	Active Assistive Exercise [Medicine]
AAE	Addis Ababa [Ethiopia] [Geomagnetic observatory code]
AAE	Addis Ababa [Ethiopia] [Seismograph station code, US Geological Survey] (SEIS)
AAE	Advertising Age Europe [A publication]
AAE	Aeronautical and Astronautical Engineering (MCD)
AAE	Aerospace Auxiliary Equipment [NASA]
AAE	Alliance for Arts Education (EA)
AAE	American Academic Environments, Inc.
AAE	American Association on Emeriti [Later, NCE] (EA)
AAE	American Association of Endodontists (EA)
AAE	American Association of Engineers [Later, NSPE] (EA)
AAE	American Association of Esthetics (EA)
AAe	Analecta Aegyptiaca [A publication]
AAE	Annaba [Algeria] [Airport symbol] (OAG)
AAE	Apparent Activation Energy
AAE	Appointment of Agents - Excise [Revenue Canada - Customs and Excise] [Information service or system] (CRD)
AAE	Appropriation and Expense (AFIT)
AAE	Architectural and Engineering (AFIT)
AAE	Armament and Electronics (AFIT)
AAE	Army Acquisition Executive
AAE	Army Aviation Element (AABC)
AAE	Army Aviation Engineers
AAe	Ars Aequi; Juridisch Studentenblad [Netherlands] (ILCA)
AAE	Asia Australia Express [Commercial firm] (DS)
AAE	Associate of Accountants' and Executives' Corporation of Canada
AAE	Associazione Archivistica Ecclesiastica [Rome, Italy] (EAIO)
AAE	Australasian Antarctic Expedition
AAE	Australian Antarctic Expedition [1911-14]
AAE	Automatic Adaptive Equalization [Telecommunications]
AAE	Average Absolute Error (MCD)
AAE	National Association of Aeronautical Examiners
AAEA	African Adult Education Association [Later, AALAE] (EAIO)
AAEA	Allied African Economic Affairs Committee [World War II]
AAEA	American Academy of Equine Art (EA)
AAEA	American Agricultural Economics Association (EA)
AAEA	American Agricultural Editors' Association (EA)
AAEC	Annuario. Accademia Etrusca di Cortona [A publication]
AAEC	Association of American Editorial Cartoonists (EA)
AAEC	Attitude Axis Emergency Control [Aerospace] (MCD)
AAEC Nucl News ...	AAEC [Australian Atomic Energy Commission] Nuclear News [A publication]
AAEC Nucl News (AU) ...	AAEC [Australian Atomic Energy Commission] Nuclear News (Australia) [A publication]
AAECo.......	Australian Aircraft and Engineering Co.
AAECS......	Auxiliary Area Environmental Control System [Nuclear energy] (NRCH)
AAED	Active Airborne Expendable Decoy
AAED	Alcoholism and Alcohol Education [A publication]
AAED	American Academy of Esthetic Dentistry (EA)
AAED	American Association of Entrepreneurial Dentists (EA)
AAED	Edinburgh [Australia] [ICAO location identifier] (ICLI)
AAEDC	American Agricultural Economics Documentation Center [Department of Agriculture] (IID)
AAEE.........	Aeroplane and Armament Experimental Establishment [British]
A & AEE....	Aircraft and Armament Experimental Establishment [British]
AAEE.........	American Academy of Environmental Engineers (EA)
AAEE.........	American-Asian Educational Exchange [Defunct] (EA)
AAEE.........	American Association of Electromyography and Electrodiagnosis [Later, AAEM] (EA)
A Ae E........	Associate in Aeronautical Engineering
AAEEH	American Association of Eye and Ear Hospitals (EA)
AAEF........	Academie Aeronautique de France [Aviation] (AIA)
AAEF........	American Afghan Education Fund (EA)
AAEF........	Australian Air Expeditionary Force (DMA)
AAEF.........	Automated Analytical Electrophoresis Facility [NASA] (MCD)
AAEFA......	Army Aviation Engineering Flight Activity
AAEGTS ...	Auxiliary Area Emergency Gas Treatment System [Nuclear energy] (NRCH)
AAEH........	Association to Advance Ethical Hypnosis (EA)
AAEI..........	American Association of Exporters and Importers [New York, NY] (EA)
AAEJ	American Association for Ethiopian Jews (EA)

AAEJN ...... American Association of English Jewish Newspapers [*Later, AJPA*] (BJA)
AAE/K/N/E ... American Association of Elementary/Kindergarten/Nursery Educators [*Defunct*]
AAEL .... American Association of Equipment Lessors (EA)
AAELSS .... Active Arm External Load Stabilization System [*Army*]
AAEM .... Acetoacetoxyethyl Methacrylate [*Organic chemistry*]
AAEM .... American Academy of Environmental Medicine (EA)
AAEM .... American Association of Electrodiagnostic Medicine (EA)
AAEO .... Astronomical, Atmospheric, Earth, and Ocean Sciences [*National Science Foundation*] (GRD)
AAEP .... American Association of Equine Practitioners (EA)
AAEPC ...... Anales. Asociacion Espanola para el Progreso de las Ciencias [*A publication*]
AAERA5 .... Alabama. Agricultural Experiment Station. Progress Report Series (Auburn University) [*A publication*]
AAES .... Advanced Aircraft Electrical System [*Navy*]
AAES .... American Archaeological Expedition to Syria. Publication [*A publication*]
AAES .... American Association of Engineering Societies (EA)
AAES .... American Association of Evangelical Students (EA)
AAES .... Anti-Aircraft Experimental Section [*British military*] (DMA)
AAES .... Association of Agricultural Education Staffs [*British*]
AAES .... Automated Aircrew Escape System (MCD)
AAESC ...... Association pour l'Avancement des Etudes Scandinaves au Canada [*Association for the Advancement of Scandinavian Studies in Canada - AASSC*]
AAESDA Bul ... AAESDA [*Association of Architects, Engineers, Surveyors, and Draughtsmen of Australia*] Bulletin [*A publication*] (APTA)
AAESWB .. Army Airborne Electronics and Special Warfare Board
AAETA ...... Asociacion Argentina Empresarios Transporte Automotor [*Transportation service*] [*Argentina*] (EY)
AA-EVP ..... American Association - Electronic Voice Phenomena (EA)
AAEW .... Atlantic Airborne Early Warning [*Military*]
AAEWR .... Advanced Aircraft Early Warning RADAR (MCD)
AAF .... Aboriginal-Australian Fellowship
AAF .... Accounting and Finance (AFIT)
AAF .... Acetic Acid, Alcohol, Formalin [*Biology*]
AAF .... Acetylaminofluorene [*Also, AcAF, AcNHFln, FAA*] [*Organic chemistry*]
AAF .... Advance Australia Foundation
a-af--- .... Afghanistan [*MARC geographic area code*] [*Library of Congress*] (LCCP)
AAF .... Agglutination Activating Factor [*Medicine*]
AAF .... Agricultural Aids Foundation
AAF .... Airway Facilities Service [*FAA*] (FAAC)
AAF .... Alder Flats Public Library, Alberta [*Library symbol*] [*National Library of Canada*] (NLC)
AAF .... Allied Air Forces
AAF .... American Advertising Federation [*Washington, DC*] (EA)
AAF .... American Aid for Afghans (EA)
AAF .... American Airforce [*World War II*]
AAF .... American Amputee Foundation (EA)
AAF .... American Architectural Foundation [*Later, AIAF*]
AAF .... American Astronautical Federation [*Defunct*] (EA)
AAF .... American Government Income Portfolio, Inc. [*NYSE symbol*] (CTT)
AAF .... Amino Acid Formula [*Biochemistry*]
AAF .... Anglo-American Forum [*A publication*]
AAF .... Anterior Auditory Field [*Physiology*]
AAF .... Antiarmor Fuze
AAF .... Apalachicola, FL [*Location identifier*] [*FAA*] (FAAL)
AAF .... Army Air Forces
AAF .... Army Airfield
AAF .... Ascorbic Acid Factor [*Biochemistry*]
AAF .... Association of Adventist Forums (EA)
AAF .... Atlantic Amphibious Force [*Navy*]
AAF .... Atti. Accademia Fiorentina [*A publication*]
AAF .... Australian Air Force
AAF .... Auxiliary Air Force [*Later, R Aux AF*] [*British*]
AAF .... Average Adjustment Factor (MCD)
AAFA .... American Aid for Afghans (EA)
AAFA .... American Alligator Farmers Association (EA)
AAFA .... Aplastic Anemia Foundation of America (EA)
A & AFA .... Army and Air Force Act [*British military*] (DMA)
AAFA .... Assistant Auditor Freight Accounts [*Business term*]
AAFA .... Associate in Arts in Fine Arts
A & AFA .... Asthma and Allergy Foundation of America (EA)
AAFAIS ..... Army and Air Force Air Intelligence School [*British*]
AAFAR ...... American Association of First Responders [*Later, National Association of First Aid Responders*] (EA)
AAFAS ...... Army Air Forces Aid Society [*World War II*]
AAFB .... Andrews Air Force Base [*Washington, DC*]
AAFB .... Army and Air Force Base
AAFB .... Army Air Force Board
AAFB .... Army Air Force Bulletin [*A publication*] (MCD)
AAFB .... Atypical Acid-Fast Bacilli [*Microbiology*]
AAFB .... Auxiliary Air Force Base
AAFBA ...... Annales Academiae Scientiarum Fennicae. Series A-IV (Biologica) [*A publication*]

AAFBAU ... Annales Academiae Scientiarum Fennicae. Series A-IV (Biologica) [*A publication*]
AAFBD ...... Army and Air Force Exchange and Motion Picture Service Board of Directors [*DoD*]
AAFBF ...... Anderson Air Force Base Flightline
AAFBI .... Ara Appaloosa and Foundation Breeders International (EA)
AAFBS ...... Army Air Forces Bombardier School
AAFBTC .... Army Air Forces Basic Training Center
AAFBU ...... Army Air Forces Base Unit
AAFC .... Air Accounting and Finance Center [*Air Force*]
AAFC .... Airborne Audio Frequency Coder
AAFC .... All-America Football Conference [*Major league 1946-49, merged with NFL 1950*]
AAFC .... Anglo-American Food Committee [*World War II*]
AAFC .... Antiaircraft Fire Control
AAFC .... Army Air Forces Center
AAFC .... Association of Advertising Film Companies
AAFCAX .. Annales Academiae Scientiarum Fennicae. Series A-II (Chemica) [*A publication*]
AAFCC ...... Army Air Force Classification Center
AAFCE ...... Allied Air Forces, Central Europe [*Later, AIRCENT*] [*NATO*]
AAFCFTC ... Army Air Force Central Flying Training Command
AAFCO ...... Association of American Feed Control Officials (EA)
AAFCO ...... Association of American Fertilizer Control Officials [*Later, AAPFCO*] (EA)
AAFCPB .... Army Air Force Clemency and Parole Board
AAFCS ...... Advanced Automatic Flight Control System (MCD)
AAFCTTC ... Army Air Force Central Technical Training Command
AAFCWF .. Army and Air Force Civilian Welfare Fund
AAFDBI ...... American Association of Fitness Directors in Business and Industry (EA)
AAFE .... Advanced Applications Flight Equipment (MCD)
AAFE .... Advanced Applications Flight Experiments [*NASA*] (MCD)
AAFE .... American Association of Feed Exporters [*Defunct*] (EA)
AAFE .... American Association of Forms Executives (EA)
AAFEB ...... Anaerobic Attached-Film Expanded-Bed [*For treating wastewater*]
AAFEC ...... Army Air Forces Engineer Command
AAFEESS ... Automated Armed Forces Examining and Entrance Station System (MCD)
AAFEFTC ... Army Air Force Eastern Flying Training Command
AAFEMPS ... Army and Air Force Exchange and Motion Picture Service
A & AFES ... Army and Air Force Exchange Service
AAFES ...... Army and Air Force Exchange Service
AAFETTC ... Army Air Force Eastern Technical Training Command
AAFFTD ... Army Air Force Flying Training Detachment
AAFG .... Amino Acid Formula with Glutamate [*Biochemistry*]
AAFGAB ... Annales Academiae Scientiarum Fennicae. Series A-III (Geologica-Geographica) [*A publication*]
AAFGH ..... Al-Anon Family Group Headquarters (EA)
AAFGL ...... Auxiliary Air Force General List [*British military*] (DMA)
AAFGS ...... Army Air Forces Gunnery School
AAFH .... Academy of American Franciscan History (EA)
AAFHA ...... African American Family History Association (EA)
AAFH/TAM ... [*The*] Americas. Academy of American Franciscan History [*A publication*]
AAFHTWF ... Amalgamated Association of Felt Hat Trimmers and Wool Formers [*A union*] [*British*] (DCTA)
AAFI .... Allied Air Forces in Italy [*World War II*]
AAFI .... Associated Accounting Firms International [*Washington, DC*] (EA)
AAFI .... Association des Anciens Fonctionnaires Internationaux [*Association of Former International Civil Servants - AFICS*] [*Geneva, Switzerland*] (EA)
AAFIF .... Automated Air Facilities Intelligence File [*Naval Oceanographic Office*]
AAFIF .... Automated Air Facility Information File [*Defense Mapping Agency*] (MCD)
AAFIR .... Army Air Force Intelligence Report (MCD)
AAFIS .... Advanced Avionic Fault Isolation System [*Navy*] (MCD)
AAFIS .... Army and Air Force Intelligence Staff [*British*]
AAFIS .... Army Air Forces Intelligence School
AAFLI .... Asian American Free Labor Institute (EA)
AAFM .... American Association of Feed Microscopists (EA)
AAFM .... Army Air Force Manual [*A publication*] (MCD)
AAFM .... Army/Air Force Motion Picture Service
AAFMAA ... Army and Air Force Mutual Aid Association (EA)
AAFMBU ... Annales Academiae Scientiarum Fennicae. Series A-V (Medica) [*A publication*]
AAFMC ..... American Association of Foundations for Medical Care [*Later, AMCRA*] (EA)
AAFMC ..... Army Air Forces Materiel Center
AAFMG ...... American Association of Foreign Medical Graduates [*Defunct*] (EA)
AAFMPS ... Army and Air Force Motion Picture Service
AAFMTO ... Army Air Force Headquarters, Mediterranean Theater of Operations
AAFNE ...... Allied Air Forces, Northern Europe [*Later, AIRNORTH*] [*NATO*]
AAFNS ...... Army Air Forces Navigation School
AAFNTIR ... Army Air Force Nontechnical Intelligence Report (MCD)

AAFO .... American Association for Functional Orthodontics (EA)
AAFO .... American Association of Functional Orthodontists [*Later, American Association for Functional Orthodontics*] (EA)
AAFOIC .... Army Air Force Officer-in-Charge
AAFP......... American Academy of Family Physicians [*Formerly, AAGP*] (EA)
AAFP......... American Academy of Forensic Psychology (EA)
AAFP......... American Association of Feline Practitioners (EA)
AAFP......... American Association of Financial Professionals (EA)
AAFPA...... Annales Academiae Scientiarum Fennicae. Series A-VI (Physica) [*A publication*]
AAFPC ...... Assistant Air Force Postal Clerk (AFM)
AAFPE ...... American Association for Paralegal Education (EA)
AAFPFS(P) ... Army Air Forces Pre-Flight School (Pilot)
AAFPOA .... Army Air Forces, Pacific Ocean Areas
AAFPOA (ADMIN) ... Army Air Forces, Pacific Ocean Areas (Administrative)
AAFPRS.... American Academy of Facial Plastic and Reconstructive Surgery (EA)
AAFPS ...... Army and Air Force Postal Service
AAFPS ...... Army Air Forces Pilot School
A Afr .... Annales Africaines [*A publication*]
AAFR......... Auxiliary Air Force Reserve [*British*]
AAFRA...... Arcispedale S. Anna di Ferrara [*A publication*]
AAFRC ...... American Association of Fund-Raising Counsel (EA)
AAFRCTP ... American Association of Fund-Raising Counsel Trust for Philanthropy (EA)
AAFS .... Academy of Ambulatory Foot Surgery (EA)
AAFS .... American Academy of Forensic Sciences (EA)
AAFS .... American Association of Foot Specialists (EA)
AAFS .... Amphibious Assault Fire System (CAAL)
AAFS .... Amphibious Assault Fuel System [*Navy*]
AAFS .... Association for the Advancement of Family Stability [*Later, AFCO*]
AAFS .... Atomic Absorption Flame Spectrometer
AAFSAT.... Army Air Forces School of Applied Tactics [*World War II*]
AAFSC ...... Additional Air Force Specialty Code (AFM)
AAFSC ...... Army Air Forces Service Command
AAFSD ...... American Association of Food Stamp Directors (EA)
AAFSE ...... Allied Air Forces, Southern Europe [*Later, AIRSOUTH*] [*NATO*]
AAFSETC ... Army Air Forces Southeast Training Command [*World War II*]
AAFSS ...... Advanced Aerial Fire Support System [*Army*]
AAFSSO ... Advanced Aerial Fire Support System Office [*Army*] (MCD)
AAFSW ..... Association of American Foreign Service Women (EA)
AAFSWPA ... Allied Air Forces, South West Pacific Area (ADA)
AAFT .... Alliance Against Fraud in Telemarketing (EA)
AAFT......... Army Air Force Translation (MCD)
AAFTAC ... Army Air Forces Tactical Center [*World War II*]
AAFTAD ... Army Air Forces Training Aids Division [*World War II*]
AAFTC ...... Army Air Forces Training Command [*World War II*]
AAFTIR .... Army Air Force Technical Intelligence Report (MCD)
AAFTO...... Army Air Force Technical Order (MCD)
AAFTS ...... Advanced Automatic Film Titles System (MCD)
AAFTS ...... Army Air Forces Technical School [*World War II*]
AAFTS ...... Automated Adaptive Flight Training System (MCD)
AAFTTC ... Army Air Forces Technical Training Command [*World War II*]
AAFU .... All-African Farmers' Union
AAFU .... Augmented Assault Fire Units [*Army*] (AABC)
AAFV......... Anuario. Asociacion Francisco de Vitoria [*A publication*]
AAFV......... Australian Armed Forces, Vietnam (CINC)
AAFWB..... Army and Air Force Wage Board
AAFWFTC ... Army Air Forces Western Flying Training Command [*World War II*]
AAFWSB .. Army Air Force Weather Service Bulletin (MCD)
AAFWSM ... Army Air Force Weather Service Manual [*A publication*] (MCD)
AAFWTTC ... Army Air Forces Western Technical Training Command [*World War II*]
AAG........... Abhandlungen. Akademie der Wissenschaften in Goettingen [*A publication*]
AAG........... Acquisition Advisory Group [*Business term*]
AAg........... Afrique Agriculture [*A publication*]
AAG........... Air Adjutant-General [*Military*]
AAG........... Alberta Agriculture Library [*UTLAS symbol*]
AAG........... Algemene Assurantie Groep [*Financial institution*] [*Netherlands*] (EY)
AAG........... American Association for the Gifted
AAG........... Annals of American Geographers [*A publication*]
AAg........... Archivo Agustiniano [*A publication*]
AAG........... Area Advisory Group [*British Overseas Trade Board*] (DS)
AAG........... Army Artillery Group (AABC)
AAG........... Assistant Adjutant-General [*Military*]
AAG........... Association of American Geographers (EA)
AAG........... Atlanta Gold Corp. [*Vancouver Stock Exchange symbol*] [*Toronto Stock Exchange symbol*]
AAGASE ... Australian Association of Graphic Art Sales Executives
AAGBA .... American Angora Goat Breeder's Association (EA)
AAGC .... All American Gourmet Company [*Stamford, CT*] [*NASDAQ symbol*] (NQ)
AAGC .... American Association for Gifted Children (EA)

AAGCA4 ... Atti. Accademia Gioenia di Scienze Naturali in Catania [*A publication*]
AAGCM .... Awaiting Action General Court-Martial
AAGE .... All Aspect Gunsight Evaluation (MCD)
AAGE .... Army Advisory Group on Energy
AAGEA ...... Arkhiv Anatomii, Gistologii, i Embriologii [*A publication*]
AAGEAA ... Arkhiv Anatomii, Gistologii, i Embriologii [*A publication*]
AAGFE...... American Association of Gravity Field Energy [*Inactive*] (EA)
AAGFO ...... American Academy of Gold Foil Operators (EA)
AAGI .... Anglo American Gold Investment Co. Ltd. [*NASDAQ symbol*] (NQ)
AAGIWA .. American Association of Grain Inspection and Weighing Agencies (EA)
AAGL .... American Association of Gynecological Laparoscopists (EA)
AAGL .... Antiaircraft Gun-Laying (DEN)
AAGM .... Antiaircraft Guided Missile (AAG)
AAGM .... Associate, Australian Guild of Music and Speech
AAGMC .... Antiaircraft Artillery and Guided Missile Center
AAGMS .... Antiaircraft Guided Missile System (NG)
AAGNA ...... Atti. Associazione Genetica Italiana [*A publication*]
AAGNA3... Atti. Associazione Genetica Italiana [*A publication*]
AAGNC .... Australian Association for Geriatric Nursing Care
AAGO........ American Academy of Gnathologic Orthopedics (EA)
AAGO........ Associate of American Guild of Organists
AAGp........ Aeromedical Airlift Group [*Air Force*] (AFM)
AAGP........ American Academy of General Practice [*Later, AAFP*] (EA)
AAGP........ American Association for Geriatric Psychiatry (EA)
AAGR .... Air-to-Air Gunnery Range [*Army*]
AAGRCH .. Australia. Commonwealth Scientific and Industrial Research Organisation. Division of Applied Geomechanics. Technical Report [*A publication*]
A Agri .... Associate in Agriculture
AAGS .... All-America Gladiolus Selections (EA)
AAGS .... American Antique Graphics Society (EA)
AAGS .... American Association for Geodetic Surveying (EA)
AAGS .... Army Air-Ground System
AAGS .... Association of African Geological Surveys [*See also ASGA*] (EAIO)
AAGSAI .... Annals of Agricultural Science [*Cairo*] [*A publication*]
AAGSSCS ... Antique and Art Glass Salt Shaker Collectors Society (EA)
AAGTCN .. Australia. Commonwealth Scientific and Industrial Research Organisation. Division of Applied Geomechanics. Technical Paper [*A publication*]
AAGTTS ... Advanced Aerial Gunnery TOW Target System
AAGUS ..... American Association of Genito-Urinary Surgeons (EA)
AAGW .... Air-to-Air Guided Weapons (NATG)
AAGWAU ... Acta Agrobotanica [*A publication*]
AAH .... Academy of Accounting Historians (EA)
AAH .... Acta Antiqua. Academiae Scientiarum Hungaricae [*A publication*]
AAH .... Advanced Attack Helicopter [*Army*]
AAH .... Air Arc Heater
AAH .... American Academy of Homiletics [*Later, AH*]
AAH .... Association of Ancient Historians (EA)
AAH .... Association for Applied Hypnosis (EAIO)
AAH .... Automated Attitude Hold [*Manned maneuvering unit*] [*Aerospace*] (NASA)
AAHA........ (Acetylalanyl)histidine Aluminum [*Biochemistry*]
AAHA........ American Academy of Health Administration (EA)
AAHA........ American Academy of Hospital Attorneys (EA)
AAHA........ American All-Hobbies Association (EA)
AAHA........ American Animal Hospital Association (EA)
AAHA........ American Association of Handwriting Analysts (EA)
AAHA........ American Association of Homes for the Aging (EA)
AAHA........ American Association of Hospital Accountants [*Later, HFMA*] (EA)
AAHA........ Awaiting Action [*of*] Higher Authority [*Army*]
AAHAA3... Australia. Commonwealth Scientific and Industrial Research Organisation. Division of Animal Health. Annual Report [*A publication*]
AAHBE .... Anglo-American-Hellenic Bureau of Education [*Defunct*]
AAHC........ American Albino Horse Club [*Later, WWWCRW*] (EA)
AAHC........ American Association of Healthcare Consultants (EA)
AAHC........ American Association of Hospital Consultants [*Later, American Association of Healthcare Consultants*] (EA)
AAHC........ Association of Academic Health Centers (EA)
AAHCC...... American Academy of Husband-Coached Childbirth (EA)
AAHCM .... Association for the Advancement of Health Care Managers (EA)
AAHCPA .. American Association of Hispanic CPA's [*Certified Public Accountants*] [*Houston, TX*] (EA)
AAHD .... American Academy of the History of Dentistry (EA)
AAHD .... American Association of Hospital Dentists [*Formerly, AAHDC*] (EA)
AAHDC...... American Association of Hospital Dental Chiefs [*Later, AAHD*]
AAHDS .... American Association of Health Data Systems [*Defunct*] (EA)
AAHE........ American Association for Higher Education (EA)
AAHE........ American Association of Housing Educators (EA)
AAHE........ Associate in Arts in Home Economics
AAHE........ Association for the Advancement of Health Education (EA)

AAHEAF... Archives d'Anatomie, d'Histologie, et d'Embryologie [*A publication*]

AAHED..... Association of Appliance and Home Entertainment Distributors [*Defunct*] (EA)

AAHFNPTO ... American Academy of Head, Facial, and Neck Pain and TMJ [*Temporomandibular Joint*] Orthopedics (EA)

AAHG........ Anzeiger fuer die Altertumswissenschaft. Herausgegeben von der Oesterreichischen Humanistischen Gesellschaft [*A publication*]

AAHGS..... Afro-American Historical and Genealogical Society (EA)

AAHH .... Air Arc Heater Housing

AAHI......... Association of American Historic Inns (EA)

AAHL........ Australian Animal Health Laboratory

AAHM....... American Academy of Homeopathic Medicine (EA)

AAHM...... American Association for the History of Medicine [*University of Rochester Medical Center*] (EA)

AAHM...... Association of Architectural Hardware Manufacturers (EA)

AAHN ...... American Association for the History of Nursing (EA)

AAHO ...... Afro-Asian Housing Organization [*Cairo, Egypt*] (EAIO)

AAHP........ American Association of Homeopathic Pharmacists (EA)

AAHP........ American Association for Hospital Planning [*Later, The Forum for Health Care Planning*] (EA)

AAHP........ American Association of Hospital Podiatrists (EA)

AAHP........ American Association for Humanistic Psychology [*Later, AHP*]

AAHPA..... American Association of Hospital Purchasing Agents (EA)

AAHPAE .. Australia. Commonwealth Scientific and Industrial Research Organisation. Division of Animal Health and Production. Technical Paper [*A publication*]

AAHPER... American Alliance for Health, Physical Education, and Recreation [*Later, AAHPERD*]

AAHPERD ... American Alliance for Health, Physical Education, Recreation, and Dance (EA)

AAHPhA ... American Animal Health Pharmaceutical Association [*Defunct*]

AAHQ ...... Advanced Allied Headquarters [*World War II*]

AAHQ .... Allied Air Headquarters [*Obsolete*]

AAHQS ..... Australian Agricultural Health and Quarantine Service

AAHRAK .. Arizona. Commission of Agriculture and Horticulture. Annual Report [*A publication*]

AAHS .... Abigail Adams Historical Society (EA)

AA(HS)...... Airman Apprentice (High School)

AAHS .... Alco Health Services Corp. [*Valley Forge, PA*] [*NASDAQ symbol*] (NQ)

AAHS .... American Association for Hand Surgery (EA)

AAHS .... American Aviation Historical Society (EA)

AAHSLD... Association of Academic Health Sciences Library Directors (EA)

AAHSLM ... American Association of Hides, Skins, and Leather Merchants [*Later, USHSLA*]

AAHSWAA ... Arpad Academy of Hungarian Scientists, Writers, and Artists Abroad (EA)

AAHT........ Antiarmor Helicopter Troop (MCD)

AAI .... Accordion for All International [*An association*] (EAIO)

AAI .... Adolescent Alienation Index [*Personality development test*] [*Psychology*]

AAI .... African-American Institute (EA)

AAI .... Agricultural Ammonia Institute [*Later, The Fertilizer Institute*] (EA)

AAI .... Air-to-Air Identification [*Air Force*]

AAI .... Air-to-Air Intercept (MCD)

AAI .... Air-to-Air Interrogation (MCD)

AAI .... Airborne Alert Indoctrination (AFM)

AAI .... Alfred Adler Institute (EA)

AAI .... All-Attitude Indicator

AAI .... Alliance of American Insurers [*Schaumburg, IL*] (EA)

AAI .... Allied Armies in Italy [*Obsolete*]

AAI .... Alternatives to Abortion International [*Later, AAI/WHEF*] (EA)

AAI .... Amateur Astronomers, Incorporated (EA)

AAI .... Ambon [*Indonesia*] [*Seismograph station code, US Geological Survey*] (SEIS)

AAI .... American Association of Immunologists (EA)

AAI .... American Association of Inventors (EA)

AAI .... American Audio Institute

AAI .... Angle-of-Approach Indicator [*Aviation*] (AFM)

AAI .... Angle-of-Attack Indicator [*Military*]

AAI .... Ankle Arm Index

AAI .... Arab American Institute (EA)

AAI .... Army Adaptation Inventory

AAI .... Army Analysis of Intelligence

AAI .... Associate of the Chartered Auctioneers' and Estate Agents' Institute [*British*]

AAI .... Association Actuarielle Internationale [*International Actuarial Association - IAA*] [*Brussels, Belgium*] (EAIO)

AAI .... Association Adjustment Inventory [*Psychology*]

AAI .... Association of Advertisers in Ireland (EAIO)

AAI .... Association of Art Institutions [*British*]

AAI .... Atlantic Art Institute

AAI .... Authorized Active Inventory (MCD)

AAI .... AUTODIN/AUTOVON Interface (CET)

AAI .... Azimuth Angle Increment

AAIA .... America-Australia Interaction Association (EA)

AAIA .... American Association for International Aging (EA)

AAIA .... Associate of the Association of International Accountants [*British*]

AAIA .... Association on American Indian Affairs (EA)

AAIA .... Association of Asian Indians in America (EA)

AAIAL....... American Academy and Institute of Arts and Letters (EA)

AAIAN...... Association for the Advancement of Instruction about Alcohol and Narcotics [*Defunct*]

AAIANSW ... Association of American Indian and Alaska Native Social Workers [*Later, NISWA*] (EA)

AAIB......... Aircraft Accident Investigation Board

AAIB......... American Association for the Improvement of Boxing (EA)

AAIB......... American Association of Instructors of the Blind [*Later, AEVH*] (EA)

AAIB......... Arab African International Bank

AAIC......... Air Accidents Investigation Committee [*Australia*]

AAIC......... Allied Air Intelligence Center

AAIC......... American Amateur Inventors Club (EA)

AAIC......... Asian Association of Insurance Commissioners (EAIO)

AAIC......... Australian Artificial Intelligence Conference

AAICD....... American Association of Imported Car Dealers [*Defunct*] (EA)

AAICJ .... American Association for the International Commission of Jurists (EA)

AAICP .... Air-to-Air Identification Control Panel [*Air Force*] (MCD)

AAICPC .... Association of Administrators of the Interstate Compact on the Placement of Children (EA)

AAICS .... Automatic Aircraft Intercept Control System

AAICV....... Amphibious, Armored Infantry Combat Vehicle (MCD)

AAID .... American Academy of Implant Dentistry (EA)

AAID .... American Association of Industrial Dentists [*Defunct*] (EA)

AAID .... Angular Accelerometer Input Device (MCD)

AAID .... Arithmetic Array Identification

AAID .... Asian Americans Information Directory [*A publication*]

AAIE......... American Association of Industrial Editors [*Later, IABC*] (EA)

AAIE......... American Association of Industrial Engineers

AAIE......... Association for the Advancement of International Education (EA)

AAIE......... Association of Applied Insect Ecologists (EA)

AAIEE....... Associate of the American Institute of Electrical Engineers

AAIEx....... Associate of the Australian Institute of Export

AAIFF .... Air-to-Air Identification Friend or Foe [*Air Force*] (MCD)

AAIH......... American Academy of Industrial Hygiene (EA)

AAII .... American Association of Individual Investors [*Chicago, IL*] (EA)

AAII .... Association for the Advancement of Invention and Innovation [*Patent lobby*] [*Defunct*]

AAIIS .... Australasian Association of Institutes of Inspectors of Schools

AAIL......... Airborne Argon Ion LASER

AAIM .... Airdrie Municipal Library, Alberta [*Library symbol*] [*National Library of Canada*] (NLC)

AAIM .... American Association of Industrial Management [*Springfield, MA*] (EA)

AAIMC...... All-American Indian Motorcycle Club (EA)

AAIMCo.... American Association of Insurance Management Consultants [*Houston, TX*] (EA)

AAIMME ... Associate of the American Institute of Mining and Metallurgical Engineers

AAIN .... American Association of Industrial Nurses [*Later, AAOHN*] (EA)

AAIND ...... American Association of Independent News Distributors (EA)

A A Intgnc ... Applied Artificial Intelligence Reporter [*A publication*]

AAIP......... Academic Administration Internship Program [*Later, AFP*] (EA)

AAIP........ Advanced Avionics Integration Program (MCD)

AAIP........ American Academy of Implant Prosthodontics (EA)

AAIP........ Associate of the American Institute of Physics

AAIP........ Association of American Indian Physicians (EA)

AAIPS .... Automated Air Information Production System (MCD)

AAIR .... Advanced Atmospheric Sounder and Imaging Radiometer [*NASA*] (NASA)

A AIR SC... Army Air Support Control [*British and Canadian*] [*World War II*]

AAIS......... Administrative Analysis, Information, and Statistics [*Red Cross*]

AAIS......... American Association of Insurance Services [*Bensenville, IL*] (EA)

AAIS......... Antiaircraft Artillery Information [*or Intelligence*] Service

AAIS......... Associate Administrator for Information Systems [*Social and Rehabilitation Service, HEW*]

AAISW...... American Association of Industrial Social Workers (EA)

AAISW...... Association of American Indian Social Workers [*Later, NISWA*] (EA)

AAIT......... American Association of Inhalation Therapists [*Later, AART*] (EA)

AAITC....... Australian Automobile Industry Training Committee

AAITO ...... Association of African Industrial Technology Organizations

AAIV .... American Association of Industrial Veterinarians (EA)

AAIVT....... American Association of IV Therapy (EA)

AAI/WHEF ... Alternatives to Abortion International/Women's Health and Education Foundation (EA)

AAIX .... Aeroamerica, Incorporated [*Air carrier designation symbol*]

AAJ............ American Association of Judges (EA)
AAJ............ Arab Airways (Jerusalem) Ltd.
AAJ............ Association of American Jurists (EA)
AAJ............ Augmented Air Jet
AAJ............ Australian Anthropological Journal [*A publication*] (APTA)
AAJ............ Binghamton, NY [*Location identifier*] [*FAA*] (FAAL)
AAJA......... Afro-Asian Journalists' Association (NATG)
AAJA......... Asian American Journalists Association (EA)
AAJAC...... Automatic Antijam Circuit (CET)
AAJBDJ.... Al-Khalij Al-Arabi [*A publication*]
AAJC......... American Association of Junior Colleges [*Later, AACJC*] (EA)
AAJCS....... Anglo-American Joint Chiefs of Staff
AAJDAI .... Archaeologischer Anzeiger. Beiblatt zum Jahrbuch des Kaiserlich Deutschen Archaeologischen Instituts [*A publication*]
AAJE.,....... American Academy of Judicial Education (DLA)
AAJE......... American Association for Jewish Education [*Later, JESNA*] (EA)
AAJE......... Anglo-American Judicial Exchange (ILCA)
AAJID....... AJRI. American Journal of Reproductive Immunology [*A publication*]
AAJID6..... AJRI. American Journal of Reproductive Immunology [*A publication*]
AAJNDL... AJNR. American Journal of Neuroradiology [*A publication*]
AAJR........ American Academy for Jewish Research (EA)
AAJRD...... AJR. American Journal of Roentgenology [*A publication*]
AAJS........ American Association of Jesuit Scientists [*Defunct*] (EA)
AAJS........ Associate in Arts in Judaic Studies (BJA)
AAJSA ...... American Association of Journalism School Administrators (EA)
AAJWA..... Asian Agricultural Journalists and Writers Association [*Jakarta, Indonesia*] (EAIO)
AAK.......... Aranuka [*Kiribati*] [*Airport symbol*] (OAG)
AAK.......... Asiaamerica Holdings [*Vancouver Stock Exchange symbol*]
AAKF........ American Amateur Karate Federation (EA)
AAKP .... American Association of Kidney Patients (EA)
AAL........... Aalborg [*Denmark*] [*Airport symbol*] (OAG)
Aal............ Aalenian [*Geology*]
AAL .... Aboriginal Advancement League [*Australia*]
AAL .... Above Aerodrome Level
AAL .... Absolute Assembly Language [*Programming language*] (BUR)
AAL .... Academy of Art and Literature [*British*]
AAL .... Account Access Layer [*Data processing*]
AAL .... Acoustical Absorption Loss
AAL .... Additional Authorization List [*Army*] (AABC)
AAL .... Adelaide Airways Limited [*Australia*]
AAL .... Aeronautica and Air Label Collectors Club (EA)
AAL .... Aid Association for Lutherans (EA)
AAL .... Aircraft Approach Light (MSA)
AAL .... Aircraft Approach Limitation
AAL .... Aircraft Armament Laboratory [*Naval Air Development Center*]
AAL .... Aircraft Assignment Letter
AAL .... Alaskan Region [*FAA*] (FAAC)
AAL .... Alexander & Alexander Services, Inc. [*NYSE symbol*] (SPSG)
AAL .... Alliance Public Library, Alberta [*Library symbol*] [*National Library of Canada*] (NLC)
AAL .... American Airlines, Inc. [*Air carrier designation symbol*] (MCD)
AAL .... Ames Aeronautical Laboratory [*Air Force*]
AAL .... Angle of Attack Limiter (MCD)
AAL .... Annals of Archaeology. University of Liverpool [*A publication*]
AAL .... Anterior Axillary Line
AAL .... Arctic Aeromedical Laboratory [*Later, AMRL*] [*Fort Wainwright, AK*] [*Air Force*] (KSC)
AAL .... Arctic Approach Limitation (AFM)
AAL .... Artic Aerospace Laboratory [*Air Force*]
AAL .... Asia America Line [*Commercial firm*] (DS)
AAL .... Asien, Afrika, Lateinamerika [*A publication*]
AAL .... Association of Advertising Lawyers (EA)
AAL .... Association of Architectural Librarians (EA)
AAL .... Association of Assistant Librarians
AAL .... Atti. Accademia dei Lincei [*A publication*]
AAL .... Australian Acoustical Laboratory
AAL .... Authorized Allowance List (MCD)
AAL .... Aviation Armament Laboratory [*Later, Naval Air Development Center*] [*Navy*]
AALA .... AmerAlia, Inc. [*NASDAQ symbol*] (NQ)
AALA .... American Agricultural Law Association (EA)
AALA .... American Association for Laboratory Accreditation (EA)
AALA .... American Auto Laundry Association [*Later, ICA*]
AALA .... American Automotive Leasing Association (EA)
AALA .... Asian American Librarians Association [*Defunct*] (EA)
AALAE ..... Associate in Arts in Liberal Arts
AALAE...... African Association for Literacy and Adult Education (EA)
AALAS...... American Association for Laboratory Animal Science (EA)
AALASO... Afro-Asian Latin-American Students' Organization (NATG)
AALB........ Australian Administrative Law Bulletin [*A publication*]
AALBAQ... Atti. Accademia Nazionale dei Lincei. Memorie. Classe di Scienze Fisiche, Matematiche, e Naturali. Sezione 3a [*A publication*]

AAL Bull ... Australian Administrative Law Bulletin [*A publication*]
AALC........ Advanced Airborne Launch Center (MCD)
AALC........ African-American Labor Center (EA)
AALC........ Afro-Asian Lawyers' Conference (NATG)
AALC........ Amphibious Assault Landing Craft [*Navy symbol*]
AALC........ Amplified Automatic Level Control [*Air Force*]
AALC........ Asian American Librarians Caucus
AALC........ Leigh Creek [*Australia*] [*ICAO location identifier*] (ICLI)
AALCC...... Aeronautica and Air Label Collectors Club (EA)
AALCI...... Ateitis Association of Lithuanian Catholic Intellectuals (EA)
A Alciat .... Andreas Alciatus [*Deceased, 1550*] [*Authority cited in pre-1607 legal work*] (DSA)
AALDEF ... Asian American Legal Defense and Education Fund (EA)
AALE........ Associate in Arts in Law Enforcement
AALF........ Anglican Accredited Layworkers' Federation [*British*]
AALGA7 ... Atti. Accademia Ligure di Scienze e Lettere [*A publication*]
AALI......... Alix Public Library, Alberta [*Library symbol*] [*National Library of Canada*] (NLC)
AALIAM... Arcadia, Accademia Letteraria Italiana. Atti e Memorie [*A publication*]
AALIM..... American Academy of Legal and Industrial Medicine (EA)
AALIPS..... Arthur Adaptation of the Leiter International Performance Scale [*Psychology*]
AALL........ American Association of Law Libraries (EA)
AALM .... Advanced Air-Launched Missile (MCD)
AALM ...... Advanced Air-Launched Motor (MCD)
AALM ...... Atti. Reale Accademia dei Lincei. Memorie. Classe di Scienze Morali, Storiche, e Filologiche [*Rome*] [*A publication*]
AALMA .... American Association of Laban Movement Analysts (EA)
AALMG ... Antiaircraft Light Machine Gun
AALN .... Atti. Reale Accademia dei Lincei. Notizie degli Scavi di Antichita. Classe di Scienze Morali, Storiche, e Filologiche [*Rome*] [*A publication*]
AALP........ American Association of Limited Partners (EA)
AALP........ Automated Airload Planning System
AALPA...... Associate of the Incorporated Society of Auctioneers and Landed Property Agents [*British*]
AALPP ..... American Association for Legal and Political Philosophy (EA)
AALPS ..... Automated Air Load Planning System [*Developed for the Army by SRI International*]
AALR........ American Association for Leisure and Recreation (EA)
AALR........ Anglo-American Law Review [*A publication*]
AALR........ Australian Argus Law Reports [*A publication*] (APTA)
AALS........ Active Army Locator System (AABC)
AALS........ Association of American Law Schools (EA)
AALS9..... Association for Arid Lands Studies (EA)
AALSA9.... Acta Allergologica. Supplementum [*A publication*]
AALS News ... Association of American Library Schools. Newsletter [*A publication*]
AALS Proc ... Association of American Law Schools. Proceedings [*A publication*]
AALT......... American Association of Library Trustees [*Later, ALTA*]
AALT......... Automatic Azimuth Laying Theodolite (KSC)
AALU .... Association for Advanced Life Underwriting [*Washington, DC*] (EA)
AaLU .... Universidad Nacional de La Plata, La Plata, Argentina [*Library symbol*] [*Library of Congress*] (LCLS)
AALUE...... Asymptotically Admissible Linear Unbiased Estimator [*Statistics*]
AALW .... Assembled Air-Launched Weapon
AAM......... Acme Municipal Library, Alberta [*Library symbol*] [*National Library of Canada*] (NLC)
AAM......... Acoustical Analysis Memo [*Navy*] (MCD)
AAM......... Acting Air-Marshal [*British*]
AAM......... Advisory Agricultural Meteorologist (NOAA)
AAM......... Afro-American Museum of Detroit (EA)
AAM......... Agricultural Advisory Meteorologist (NOAA)
AAM......... Air-to-Air Missile [*Army*]
AAM......... Airborne Activity Monitor [*Nuclear energy*] (NRCH)
AAM......... Aircraft Availability Model (MCD)
AAM......... American Abolitionist Movement (EA)
AAM......... American Academy of Mechanics (EA)
AAM......... American Academy of Microbiology (EA)
AAM......... American Agriculture Movement (EA)
AAM......... American Association of Museums (EA)
AAM......... Angeborener Ausolsender Mechanismus [*Innate Release Mechanism*] [*Psychology*]
AAM......... Anglican Association of Musicians (EA)
AAM......... Anglo American Resources [*Vancouver Stock Exchange symbol*]
AAM......... Ann Arbor [*Michigan*] [*Seismograph station code, US Geological Survey*] (SEIS)
AAM......... Anti-Antimissile Missile
AAM......... Anti-Apartheid Movement [*South Africa*] [*Political party*] (EA)
AAM......... Antiaircraft Missile (KSC)
AAM......... Army Achievement Medal [*Military decoration*]
AAM......... Army Aircraft Maintenance (AABC)
AAM......... Arte Antica e Moderna [*A publication*]
AAM......... Asian and African American Materials [*Association for Library Collections and Technical Services*]

AA/M........ Associate Administrator for Management [*Social and Rehabilitation Service, HEW*]
AAM.......... Association of Amateur Magicians   (EA)
AAM.......... Association des Amidonneries de Mais de la CEE [*Association of the Maize Starch Industries of the European Economic Community*]
AAM.......... Association of Anglican Musicians   (EA)
AAM.......... Atti e Memorie. Accademia di Scienze, Lettere, ed Arti di Modena [*A publication*]
AAM.......... Atti e Memorie. Reale Accademia Virgiliana di Scienze, Lettere, ed Arti di Montova [*A publication*]
AAM.......... Auburn University at Montgomery, Montgomery, AL [*OCLC symbol*]   (OCLC)
AAM.......... AWS Ammunition Magazine   (MCD)
AAM.......... Fargo, ND [*Location identifier*] [*FAA*]   (FAAL)
AAMA....... African American Museums Association   (EA)
AAMA....... American Academy of Medical Administrators   (EA)
AAMA....... American Agricultural Marketing Association   (EA)
AAMA....... American Amusement Machine Association   (EA)
AAMA....... American Apparel Manufacturers Association   (EA)
AAMA....... American Architectural Manufacturers Association   (EA)
AAMA....... American Association of Medical Assistants   (EA)
AAMA....... American Award Manufacturers Association [*Later, TDMA*]
AAMA....... Asian American Manufacturers Association   (EA)
AAMAA.... Army Aviation Mission Area Analysis
AAMAP.... Army Automation Master Plan
AAMAREF ... American Academy of Medical Administrators Research and Educational Foundation   (EA)
AAMB....... Army Automation Memorandum Budget
AAMBER ... Australian Antarctic Marine Biological Ecosystem Research
AAMBP..... Association of American Medical Book Publishers [*Later, AMPA*]   (EA)
AAMC....... American Association of Marriage Counselors [*Later, AAMFT*]   (EA)
AAMC....... American Association of Medical Clinics [*Later, AGPA*]   (EA)
AAMC....... American Association of Medico-Legal Consultants   (EA)
AAMC....... Army Artillery and Missile Center   (MCD)
AAMC....... Army Aviation Materiel Command
AAMC....... Association of American Medical Colleges   (EA)
AAMCH.... American Association for Maternal and Child Health   (EA)
AAMD....... American Academy of Medical Directors [*Absorbed by American College of Physician Executives*]   (EA)
AAMD....... American Association on Mental Deficiency [*Later, AAMR*]   (EA)
AAMD....... Association of Art Museum Directors   (EA)
AAME .... American Antarctic Mountaineering Expedition
AAME .... American Association of Microprocessor Engineers
AAME .... Association for the Advancement of Medical Education [*Defunct*]   (EA)
AAME .... Atlantic American Corp. [*NASDAQ symbol*]   (NQ)
AAME .... Australian Association for Marriage Education
AAMEA6 .. Australasian Annals of Medicine [*A publication*]
A Amer Acad Polit Soc Sci ... Annals. American Academy of Political and Social Science [*A publication*]
AAMES..... American Association for Middle East Studies [*Defunct*]   (EA)
AAMESBIC ... American Association of Minority Enterprise Small Business Investment Companies [*Washington, DC*]   (EA)
AAMF .... Afro-American Music Foundation   (EA)
AAMF .... American Association of Music Festivals [*Defunct*]
AAMFA..... Atti. Accademia dei Fisiocritici in Siena. Sezione Medico-Fisica [*A publication*]
AAMFA9... Atti. Accademia dei Fisiocritici in Siena. Sezione Medico-Fisica [*A publication*]
AAMFC..... American Association of Marriage and Family Counselors [*Later, AAMFT*]
AAMFT..... American Association for Marriage and Family Therapy   (EA)
AAMG....... Antiaircraft Machine Gun [*Army*]
AAMGA.... American Association of Managing General Agents [*Washington, DC*]   (EA)
AAMGBD ... Annales Academiae Medicae Gedanensis [*A publication*]
AAMGE.... Air-to-Air Missile Guidance Element
AAMH....... American Academy of Medical Hypnoanalysts   (EA)
AAMHC.... Atlantic Alliance for Maritime Heritage Conservation   (EA)
AAMHPC ... American Association of Mental Health Professionals in Corrections   (EA)
AAMI .... Age-Associated Memory Impairment [*Medicine*]
AAMI .... All-Aspect Maneuvering Index   (MCD)
AAMI .... American Association of Machinery Importers [*Defunct*]
AAMI .... American Association of Microcomputer Investors   (EA)
AAMI .... Amisk Public Library, Alberta [*Library symbol*] [*National Library of Canada*]   (NLC)
AAMI .... Associate of the Australian Marketing Institute
AAMI .... Association for the Advancement of Medical Instrumentation   (EA)
AAMI .... Association of Allergists for Mycological Investigations [*Defunct*]   (EA)
AAMI .... Association of Assistant Mistresses, Inc. [*British*]
AAM/ICOM ... International Council of Museums Committee of the American Association of Museums   (EA)

AAMID ..... Accomplishment of Assigned Mission Impeded by Deadline [*Army*]   (AABC)
AAMIH .... American Association for Maternal and Infant Health [*Later, AAMCH*]   (EA)
AAML .... American Academy of Matrimonial Lawyers   (EA)
AAML .... Arctic Aeromedical Laboratory [*Later, AMRL*] [*Air Force*]
AAML .... Army Aviation Materiel Laboratory
AAMLA .... American Academy of Medical-Legal Analysis   (EA)
AAMLAR ... Atti. Accademia Medica Lombarda [*A publication*]
AAMLS.... Association of Accredited Medical Laboratory Schools [*Later, NAHCS*]   (EA)
AAMM...... AN [*Army-Navy*] and MS [*Manufacturing Status*] Manual   (AAG)
AAMMAU ... Archives d'Anatomie Microscopique et de Morphologie Experimentale [*A publication*]
AAMMC ... American Association of Medical Milk Commissions   (EA)
AAMMP .. Active Army Military Manpower Program
AAMN...... American Assembly for Men in Nursing   (EA)
AAMO....... Asian Association of Management Organisations [*Kuala Lumpur, Malaysia*]
AAMO....... Association of Area Medical Officers [*British*]
AAMOA.... Afro-American Music Opportunities Association   (EA)
AAMod...... Atti e Memorie. Accademia di Scienze, Lettere, ed Arti di Modena [*A publication*]
AAMP .... Advanced Architecture Microprocessor   (MCD)
AAMP .... American Academy of Maxillofacial Prosthetics   (EA)
AAMP ...... American Academy of Medical Preventics [*Later, ACAM*]   (EA)
AAMP .... American Association of Meat Processors   (EA)
AAMP .... Army Aviation Modernization Plan   (MCD)
AAMR ...... American Academy on Mental Retardation   (EA)
AAMR ...... American Association on Mental Retardation   (EA)
AAMRDL ... Army Air Mobility Research and Development Laboratories [*Army*]
AAMREP ... Air-to-Air Missile Weapons System Flight Report   (NG)
AAMRH.... International Association of Agricultural Medicine and Rural Health   (EAIO)
AAMRL..... American Association of Medical Record Librarians [*Later, AMRA*]   (EA)
AAMRL..... [*Harry G.*] Armstrong Aerospace Medical Research Laboratory [*Wright-Patterson Air Force Base, OH*]   (GRD)
AAMRR ... Association of American Motorcycle Road Racers   (EA)
AAMS .... Advanced Antitank Missile System   (MCD)
AAMS .... Airborne Auxiliary Memory System
AAMS .... American Accordion Musicological Society   (EA)
AAMS .... American Air Mail Society   (EA)
AAMS .... American Association of Meta-Science   (EA)
AAMS .... Arab-American Media Society   (EA)
AAMS .... Army Aircraft Maintenance Shop   (AABC)
AAMS .... Army Armor School   (AAG)
AAMS .... Army Artillery and Missile School
AAMS .... Associate Member of the Association of Medical Secretaries, Practice Administrators, and Receptionists [*British*]   (DBQ)
AAMS .... Australian Army Medical Service   (DMA)
AAMS .... Automated Azimuth Measuring System   (MCD)
AAMSA..... Army Aviation Maintenance Support Activity
AAMSBN ... Antiaircraft Missile Battalion [*Marine Corps*]
AAMSC..... Annals. Academy of Medicine (Singapore) [*A publication*]
AAMSDH ... Annales Academiae Medicae Stetinensis. Suplement [*A publication*]
AAMSE..... American Association of Medical Society Executives   (EA)
AA/MSF ... Associate Administrator for Manned Space Flight [*NASA*]   (KSC)
AAMSI...... American Association for Medical Systems and Informatics [*Later, AMIA*]   (EA)
AAMSL..... American Association of Media Specialists and Librarians   (EA)
AAMSU ... Army Air Movement Support Unit   (MCD)
AAMT ...... American Association for Medical Transcription   (EA)
AAMT ...... American Association for Music Therapy   (EA)
AAMTAP ... Army Aircraft Mobile Technical Assistance Program
AAMU...... Army Advanced Marksmanship Unit
AAMUC.... Association of American Military Uniform Collectors   (EA)
AAMus ..... Associate in Arts in Music
AAMV...... American Association for Museum Volunteers   (EA)
AAMVA..... American Association of Motor Vehicle Administrators   (EA)
AAMW...... Amalgamated Association of Machine Workers [*A union*] [*British*]
AAMW...... Association of Advertising Men and Women [*Later, Advertising and Marketing Association*]   (EA)
AAMX....... Acetoacet-m-xylidide [*Organic chemistry*]
AAMX....... Air America, Inc. [*Air carrier designation symbol*]
AAMZ....... Abhandlungen. Akademie der Wissenschaften und der Literatur in Mainz [*Wiesbaden*] [*A publication*]
AAMZ....... Association des Amis de Maurice Zundel [*Paris, France*]   (EAIO)
AAMZAZ ... Acta Amazonica [*A publication*]
AAN.......... Aanwinsten van de Centrale Bibliotheek [*Brussels*] [*A publication*]
AAn........... Acta Antiqua [*Budapest*] [*A publication*]
AAN........... Advance Alteration Notice   (MSA)

AAN.......... Aeronautical Army and Navy (AAG)
AAN.......... Aliphatic Ammonium Nitrate (MCD)
AAN.......... American Academy of Neurology (EA)
AAN.......... American Academy of Nursing (EA)
AAN.......... American Academy of Nutrition (EA)
AAn.......... American Anthropologist [*A publication*]
AAN.......... American Association of Nurserymen (EA)
AAN.......... Amino Acid Nitrogen [*Analytical biochemistry*]
AAN.......... Aminoacetonitrile [*Organic chemistry*]
AAN.......... Analgesic-Associated Nephropathy [*Medicine*]
AAN.......... Annuaire de l'Afrique du Nord [*A publication*]
AAn.......... Archiv fuer Anthropologie [*A publication*]
AAN.......... Arnada Resources [*Vancouver Stock Exchange symbol*]
AAN.......... Assemblee de l'Atlantique Nord [*North Atlantic Assembly*] [*Brussels, Belgium*] (EAIO)
AAN.......... Assignment Action Number (AFM)
AAN.......... Associate in Arts in Nursing
AAN.......... Atti. Accademia di Scienze Morali e Politiche della Societa Nazionale di Scienze, Lettere, ed Arti di Napoli [*A publication*]
AAN.......... Atti. Reale Accademia di Archeologia, Lettere, e Belle Arti di Napoli [*A publication*]
AAN.......... Automotive Aftermarket News [*A publication*]
AANA....... American Anorexia Nervosa Association [*Later, AABA*] (EA)
AANA....... American Association of Nurse Anesthetists (EA)
AANA....... [*The*] American Association of Nurse Attorneys (EA)
AANA....... American Association of Nursing Assistants (EA)
AANA....... Arthroscopy Association of North America (EA)
AANA J..... AANA [*American Association of Nurse Anesthetists*] Journal [*A publication*]
AANC....... American Association of Nutritional Consultants (EA)
AANDD..... Aparatura Naukowa i Dydaktyczna [*A publication*]
AANEAB... Acta Anaesthesiologica Scandinavica [*A publication*]
AANEBC... Archivio per l'Antropologia e la Etnologia [*A publication*]
AANFA..... Annales de l'Anesthesiologie Francaise [*A publication*]
AANFP..... American Academy of Natural Family Planning (EA)
AANG....... Angle between Leaf Apex and Widest Point [*Botany*]
AANI........ Associate of the Australian Naval Institute
AANIBO ... Acta Anaesthesiologica Italica [*A publication*]
AANL....... Atti. Accademia Nazionale dei Lincei [*A publication*]
AANLAW ... Atti. Accademia Nazionale dei Lincei. Rendiconti. Classe di Scienze Fisiche, Matematiche, e Naturali [*A publication*]
AANLR ... Atti. Accademia Nazionale dei Lincei. Rendiconti. Classe di Scienze Morali, Storiche, e Filologiche [*A publication*]
AANM...... American Association of Nurse-Midwives [*Later, ACNM*]
AANN....... American Association of Neuroscience Nurses (EA)
AANN....... American Association of Neurosurgical Nurses [*Later, ABNN*] (EA)
AAnn....... Anniston Public Library, Anniston, AL [*Library symbol*] [*Library of Congress*] (LCLS)
AAnnM...... Anniston Museum of Natural History, Anniston, AL [*Library symbol*] [*Library of Congress*] (LCLS)
AANNT..... AANNT [*American Association of Nephrology Nurses and Technicians*] Journal [*A publication*]
AANNT..... American Association of Nephrology Nurses and Technicians [*Later, ANNA*] (EA)
AaNo.......... Aarboeger foer Nordisk Oldkyndighed og Historie [*A publication*]
AANO........ Albanian-American National Organization
AANP....... Aircraft Accident Notification Procedures [*Manual*] (FAAC)
AANP....... American Association of Naturopathic Physicians (EA)
AANP....... American Association of Neuropathologists (EA)
AANR....... American Association of Newspaper Representatives [*Later, NASA*] (EA)
AANS .... American Academy of Neurological Surgery (EA)
AANS .... American Association of Neurological Surgeons (EA)
AANSAJ ... Acta Anatomica. Supplementum [*A publication*]
AANSW ... Ansett Airlines of New South Wales [*Australia*] (ADA)
aant......... Aantekening [*Note*] [*Netherlands*] (ILCA)
AAnt .... Acta Antiqua. Academiae Scientiarum Hungaricae [*A publication*]
AANT........ Arctic Anthropology [*A publication*]
AANTA ..... American Antiquity [*A publication*]
A ANTH ... American Anthropologist [*A publication*]
AAnthr...... American Anthropologist [*A publication*]
AAntHung ... Acta Antiqua. Academiae Scientiarum Hungaricae [*A publication*]
A Antiqua Acad Sci Hung ... Acta Antiqua. Academiae Scientiarum Hungaricae [*A publication*]
A Antropol ... Anales de Antropologia [*A publication*]
AANZ........ Archaeologischer Anzeiger zur Archaeologischen Zeitung [*A publication*]
AAO.......... AAO Aquaculture [*Vancouver Stock Exchange symbol*]
AAO.......... Administrative Arrangements Order (ADA)
AAO.......... Advanced Assembly Outline (MCD)
AAO.......... Am Angefuehrten Örte [*At the Place Quoted*] [*German*]
AAO.......... American Academy of Ophthalmology (EA)
AAO.......... American Academy of Optometry (EA)
AAO.......... American Academy of Organ (EA)
AAO.......... American Academy of Osteopathy (EA)

AAO.......... American Association of Ophthalmology [*Absorbed by American Academy of Ophthalmology - AAO*]
AAO.......... American Association of Orthodontists (EA)
AAO.......... Amino Acid Oxidase [*An enzyme*]
AAO.......... Anaco [*Venezuela*] [*Airport symbol*] (OAG)
AAO.......... Anglo-Australian Observatory
AAO.......... Antiair Output
AAO.......... Army Acquisition Objective
AAO.......... Association for the Advancement of Ophthalmology (EA)
AAO.......... Astronaut Activities Office [*NASA*] (KSC)
AAO.......... Atlantis Airlines [*Myrtle Beach, SC*] [*FAA designator*] (FAAC)
AAO.......... Australian Academy of Osteopathy
AAO.......... Australian Archives Office
AAO.......... Australian Archives Organization
AAO.......... Authorized Acquisition Objective [*Army*] (AABC)
AAOA....... Ambulance Association of America [*Later, AAA*] (EA)
AAOA....... American Academy of Otolaryngologic Allergy (EA)
AAOA....... Auxiliary to the American Optometric Association [*Later, AFVA*] (EA)
AAOA....... Auxiliary to the American Osteopathic Association (EA)
AAOBPPH ... American Association of Owners and Breeders of Peruvian Paso Horses (EA)
AAOC....... American Association of Osteopathic Colleges [*Later, AACOM*] (EA)
AAOC....... Antiaircraft Operations Center [*Air Force*]
AAOD....... Army Aviation Operating Detachment
AAODC....... American Association of Oilwell Drilling Contractors [*Later, IADC*] (EA)
AAOE....... Airborne Antarctic Ozone Experiment
AAOE....... American Association of Osteopathic Examiners (EA)
AAOG....... American Association of Obstetricians and Gynecologists [*Later, AGOS*] (EA)
AAOGP ..... American Academy of Orthodontics for the General Practitioner (EA)
AAOH .... Asian Association of Occupational Health (EA)
AAOHN .... American Association of Occupational Health Nurses (EA)
AAOHN J ... American Association of Occupational Health Nurses. Journal [*A publication*]
AAO-HNS ... American Academy of Otolaryngology - Head and Neck Surgery (EA)
AAOI .... American Association of Inventors
AAOJ .... American Antiquarian and Oriental Journal [*A publication*]
AAOM...... American Academy of Occupational Medicine (EA)
AAOM...... American Academy of Oral Medicine (EA)
AAOM...... American Association of Orthomolecular Medicine (EA)
AAOM...... American Association of Orthopaedic Medicine (EA)
AAOME...... American Association of Osteopathic Medical Examiners (EA)
AAOMS ...... American Association of Oral and Maxillofacial Surgeons (EA)
AAONMS ... Imperial Council of the Ancient Arabic Order of the Nobles of the Mystic Shrine for North America [*Freemasonry*] (EA)
AAOO .... American Academy of Ophthalmology and Otolaryngology (EA)
AAOP....... American Academy of Oral Pathology (EA)
AAOP....... American Academy of Orthotists and Prosthetists (EA)
AAOP....... Antiaircraft Observation Post
AAOR....... American Academy of Oral Roentgenology [*Later, AADR*]
AAOR....... Antiaircraft Operations Room (MCD)
AAOrthMed ... American Association of Orthopedic Medicine (EA)
AAOS .... American Academy of Orthopaedic Surgeons (EA)
AAOS .... American Association of Osteopathic Specialists (EA)
AAOT........ American Association of Orthoptic Technicians [*Later, AACO*] (EA)
AAP.......... Academy of American Poets (EA)
AAP.......... Acquisition and Inoculation Access Period [*Immunology*]
AAP.......... Advanced Acquisition Plan (MCD)
AAP.......... Advise If Able to Proceed [*Aviation*] (FAAC)
AAP.......... Aerodynamics Advisory Panel [*AEC*] (MCD)
AAP.......... Affirmative Action Plan [*or Program*] [*Equal opportunity employment*]
AAP.......... Aggregation-Attachment Pheromone [*Entomology*]
AAP.......... Agribusiness Accountability Project [*Public interest research group*] [*Defunct*]
AAP.......... Aircraft Actually Possessed [*Air Force*] (AFIT)
AAP.......... Aircraft Assembly Plant
AAP.......... Airlock Adapter Plate (MCD)
AAP.......... Allied Administrative Publication [*NATO*] (AFM)
AAP.......... Allied Army Procedures (NATG)
AAP.......... Allied Army Publications (NATG)
AAP.......... Allied Authorized Publication
AAP.......... Allowance Appendix Page
AAP.......... Alpha Antiprotease [*Biochemistry*]
AAP.......... American Academy of Pediatrics (EA)
AAP.......... American Academy of Pedodontics [*Later, AAPD*] (EA)
AAP.......... American Academy of Periodontology (EA)
AAP.......... American Academy of Philately [*Later, APC*] (EA)
AAP.......... American Academy of Psychoanalysis (EA)
AAP.......... American Academy of Psychotherapists (EA)
AAP.......... American Association for Parapsychology (EA)
AAP.......... American Association of Pathologists (EA)
AAP.......... American Association of the Professions (EA)
AAP.......... American Association of Psychiatrists (EA)

AAP .... Amstar American Petroleum [*Vancouver Stock Exchange symbol*]
AAP .... Analog Antenna Positioner
AAP .... Analog Autopilot (KSC)
AAP .... Analysis and Production (MCD)
AAP .... Antenna Aspect Processor
AAP .... Apollo Applications Program [*NASA*]
A & AP ...... Arms & Armour Press [*Publisher*] [*British*]
AAP .... Army Ammunition Plant (AABC)
AAP .... Army Apprenticeship Program
AAP .... Army Avionics Program
AAP .... Associate Administrator for Airports [*FAA*] (FAAC)
AAP .... Association of Academic Physiatrists (EA)
AAP .... Association des Administrateurs du Personnel de la Fonction Publique [*Association of Personnel Administrators of Public Functions*] [*Canada*]
AAP .... Association for Advancement of Psychoanalysis (of the Karen Horney Psychoanalytic Institute and Center) (EA)
AAP .... Association for Advancement of Psychology (EA)
AAP .... Association for the Advancement of Psychotherapy (EA)
AAP .... Association of American Physicians (EA)
AAP .... Association of American Publishers (EA)
AAP .... Association for Applied Poetry (EA)
AAP .... Association for Applied Psychoanalysis (EA)
AAP .... Association for Astrological Psychology (EA)
AAP .... Association of Aviation Psychologists (EA)
AAP .... Association of Publishers
AAP .... Associative Array Processor (MCD)
AAP .... Athlete Assistance Program [*See also PAA*] [*Canada*]
AAP .... Atmospheric Analysis and Prediction [*National Center for Atmospheric Research*]
AAP .... Attached Applications Processor
AAP .... Atti. Accademia di Palermo [*A publication*]
AAP .... Atti. Accademia Pontaniana [*Naples*] [*A publication*]
AAP .... Atti e Memorie. Reale Accademia di Scienze, Lettere, ed Arti in Padova [*A publication*]
AAP .... Auburn University, Auburn, AL [*Library symbol*] [*Library of Congress*] (LCLS)
AAP .... Australia Air Publications [*A publication*]
AAP .... Australian Associated Press Party Ltd.
AAP .... Automotive Aftermarket Professional [*AWDA University*]
AAP .... Auxiliary Acceleration Pump [*Automotive engineering*]
AAP .... Houston, TX [*Location identifier*] [*FAA*] (FAAL)
AAP .... M. Able Aviation Co. [*Houston, TX*] [*FAA designator*] (FAAC)
AAPA .... Advocates Against Psychic Abuse (EA)
AAPA .... American Academy of Physician Assistants (EA)
AAPA .... American Academy of Podiatry Administration (EA)
AAPA .... American Alfalfa Processors Association (EA)
AAPA .... American Amateur Press Association (EA)
AAPA .... American Art Pottery Association (EA)
AAPA .... American Association of Pathologists' Assistants (EA)
AAPA .... American Association of Physical Anthropologists (EA)
AAPA .... American Association of Physicians' Assistants [*Defunct*] (EA)
AAPA .... American Association of Port Authorities (EA)
AAPA .... American Association of Psychiatric Administrators (EA)
AAPA .... Asian American Psychological Association (EA)
AAPA .... Association of Authorized Public Accountants (EAIO)
AAPA .... Australian Aborigines Progressive Association
AAPA .... Australian Air Pilots Association
AAPAA ...... American Academy of Psychiatrists in Alcoholism and Addictions (EA)
AAPAA ...... Association of Asian/Pacific American Artists (EA)
AAPad .... Atti e Memorie. Accademia di Padova [*A publication*]
AAPal .... Atti. Accademia di Scienze, Lettere, ed Arti di Palermo [*A publication*]
AAPA Newsl ... AAPA [*Australian Asphalt Pavement Association*] Newsletter [*A publication*] (APTA)
AAPAP ...... Anglo-American Press Association of Paris [*See also APAAP*] [*France*] (EA)
AAPat .... Atti e Memorie. Accademia Patavina [*A publication*]
AAPB .... American Association of Pathologists and Bacteriologists [*Later, AAP*] (EA)
AAPB .... Association for Applied Psychophysiology and Biofeedback (EA)
AAPB .... [*An*] Australian Prayer Book [*A publication*] (APTA)
AAPBA ...... Amino(aminophenyl)benzamide [*Organic chemistry*]
AAPBBD ... Advances in Aquatic Microbiology [*A publication*]
AAPBC ...... American Association of Professional Bridal Consultants (EA)
AAPBCE ... Archiv fuer Acker und Pflanzenbau und Bodenkunde [*A publication*]
AAPBG ...... Army Automation Program Budget Guidance
AAPC .... Adjusted Average Per Capita Cost
AAPC .... Advertising Agency Production Club of New York [*Later, APC*] (EA)
AAPC .... All African Peoples' Conference
AAPC .... American Association of Pastoral Counselors (EA)
AAPC .... American Association of Political Consultants (EA)
AAPC .... American Association of Professional Consultants [*Manchester, NH*] (EA)
AAPC .... American Association for Protecting Children (EA)

AAPC .... Application of Autonomous Passive Classification (MCD)
AAPC .... Association pour l'Anthropologie Physique au Canada [*Association for Physical Anthropology in Canada*]
AAPCC ...... Adjusted Average per Capita Cost
AAPCC ...... American Association of Poison Control Centers (EA)
AAPCC ...... American Association of Psychiatric Clinics for Children [*Later, AAPSC*] (EA)
AAPCK ..... Acetyl(alanyl)phenylalanylchloromethyl Ketone [*Biochemistry*]
AAPCM ..... Association of American Playing Card Manufacturers [*Defunct*] (EA)
AAPCO ..... Association of American Pesticide Control Officials (EA)
AAPD .... Absolute Average Percent Deviation [*Mathematics*]
AAPD .... American Academy of Pediatric Dentistry (EA)
AAPD .... American Academy of Physiologic Dentistry (EA)
AAPD .... Automated Astronomic Positioning Device [*Defense Mapping Agency*] (MCD)
AAPDA ..... Australasian Apple Programmers and Developers Association
AAPE .... American Academy of Physical Education (EA)
AAPE .... American Association for Paralegal Education (EA)
AAPE .... Average Absolute Percentage Error [*Statistics*]
AAPEP ...... Adolescent and Adult Psychoeducational Profile [*Educational testing*]
AAPERS.... Active Army Personnel Reporting System [*Europe*] (MCD)
AAPES ...... Army Automation Planning, Programming, and Evaluation System (MCD)
AAPF .... Arctos. Acta Philologica Fennica [*A publication*]
AAPFCO ... Association of American Plant Food Control Officials (EA)
AAPFP ...... American Association of Personal Financial Planners (EA)
AAPG .... Affirmative Action Planning Guide [*Executive Telecom System, Inc.*] [*Information service or system*] (CRD)
AAPG .... Allowance Appendix Package
AAPG .... American Association of Petroleum Geologists (EA)
AAPG .... American Association of Petroleum Geologists. Bulletin [*A publication*]
AAPG .... Arab-American Press Guild (EA)
AAPG .... Armament and Avionics Planning Guidance (MCD)
AAPG (Am Assoc Pet Geol) Bull ... AAPG (American Association of Petroleum Geologists) Bulletin [*A publication*]
AAPGB..... American Association of Petroleum Geologists. Bulletin [*A publication*]
AAPG Bull ... AAPG [*American Association of Petroleum Geologists*] Bulletin [*A publication*]
AAPG Continuing Education ... American Association of Petroleum Geologists. Continuing Education [*A publication*]
AAPG Explorer ... American Association of Petroleum Geologists. Explorer [*A publication*]
AAPG Mem ... AAPG [*American Association of Petroleum Geologists*] Memoir [*A publication*]
AAPG Memoir ... American Association of Petroleum Geologists. Memoir [*A publication*]
AAPG Stud Geol ... AAPG [*American Association of Petroleum Geologists*] Studies in Geology [*A publication*]
AAPH .... American Association for Partial Hospitalization (EA)
AAPH .... American Association of Professional Hypnologists (EA)
AAPH .... American Association of Professional Hypnotherapists (EA)
AAPH .... ASEAN [*Association of South East Asian Nations*] Association for Planning and Housing (EAIO)
AAPHD ..... American Association of Public Health Dentistry (EA)
AAPHP ..... American Association of Public Health Physicians (EA)
AAPHR ..... American Association of Physicians for Human Rights (EA)
AAPI .... Arizona Appetito's Stores, Incorporated [*Phoenix, AZ*] [*NASDAQ symbol*] (NQ)
AAPI .... Australian Architectural Periodicals Index (ADA)
AAPICU ... American Association of Presidents of Independent Colleges and Universities (EA)
AAPIS .... Australian Associated Press Information Services Proprietary Ltd.
AAPIU...... Allied Aerial Photographic Interpretation Unit [*Obsolete*]
AAPJ .... Acta Academiae Paedagogicae Jyvaskylaensis [*A publication*]
AAPJDE ... Australian Association for Peace, Justice, and Development Education
AAPL........ Afro-American Police League (EA)
AAPL........ American Academy of Psychiatry and the Law (EA)
AAPL........ American Artists Professional League (EA)
AAPL........ American Association of Petroleum Landmen (EA)
AAPL........ Apple Computer, Inc. [*NASDAQ symbol*] (NQ)
AAPL........ [*An*] Array Processing Language [*Programming language*]
AAPLA ..... Annales de l'Amelioration des Plantes [*A publication*]
AAPLA8 ... Annales de l'Amelioration des Plantes [*Paris*] [*A publication*]
AAPLC ..... Association of African American People's Legal Council (EA)
AAPLE ...... American Academy for Professional Law Enforcement (EA)
AAPLOG... American Association of Pro Life Obstetricians and Gynecologists (EA)
AAPLP ...... American Academy of Pro-Life Physicians (EA)
AAPLP ...... American Association of Pro-Life Pediatricians (EA)
AAPM .... American Association of Physicists in Medicine (EA)
AAPM .... Army Aviation Planning Manual (AABC)
AAPMC..... Antibiotic-Associated Pseudomembranous Colitis [*Medicine*]
AAPMR..... American Academy of Physical Medicine and Rehabilitation (EA)
AAPN .... Atti. Accademia Pontaniana (Naples) [*A publication*]

AAPNA ..... Association of African Physicians in North America (EA)
AAPO .... Advanced Aircraft Programs Office
AAPO .... American Academy of Podiatry Administration (EA)
AAPO .... Apollo Applications Program Office [*NASA*] (MCD)
AAPODK .. Acta Alimentaria Polonica [*A publication*]
AAPont ..... Atti. Accademia Pontaniana [*Naples*] [*A publication*]
AAPOR ..... American Association for Public Opinion Research (EA)
AAPO & S ... American Association for Pediatric Ophthalmology and Strabismus (EA)
AAPP .... Affirmative Action Program Plans [*DoD*]
AAPP .... American Association of Police Polygraphists (EA)
AAPP .... Auxiliary Airborne Power Plant
AAPP Abstr ... Amino Acids, Peptides, and Proteins. Abstracts [*A publication*]
AAPPCM .. Specialist Periodical Reports. Amino-Acids, Peptides, and Proteins [*A publication*]
AAPPDN ... Australasian Plant Pathology [*A publication*]
AAPPES .... Army Auto Plan and Progress Evaluation System
AAPPES .... Army Automation Planning, Programming, and Evaluation System
AAPPO ...... American Association of Preferred Provider Organizations [*Alexandria, VA*] (EA)
AAPPP ...... American Association of Planned Parenthood Physicians [*Later, APPP*] (EA)
AAPPS ...... American Association of Podiatric Physicians and Surgeons (EA)
AAPPTMP ... American Association of Physicians Practicing the Transcendental Meditation Program [*Later, WMAFPH*] (EA)
AAPR .... Army Aviation Program Review (MCD)
AAPRCO ... American Association of Private Railroad Car Owners (EA)
AAPRD ...... American Academy for Plastics Research in Dentistry [*Later, Academy of Dental Materials - ADM*]
AAPRDTW ... Association for the Advancement of Policy, Research, and Development in the Third World (EA)
AAPRM ...... American Association of Passenger Rate Men [*Defunct*] (EA)
A-APRP ..... All-African People's Revolutionary Party
AAPRSO ... Army Aviation Personnel Requirements of Sustained Operations Study (MCD)
AAPS .... Active Aircraft Plume Suppression (MCD)
AAPS .... Advanced Automotive Power Systems
AAPS .... Airborne Angular Position Sensor
AAPS .... Alternative Automotive Power Systems [*Environmental Protection Agency*]
AAPS .... American Association of Pharmaceutical Scientists (EA)
AAPS .... American Association of Phonetic Sciences (EA)
AAPS .... American Association of Plastic Surgeons (EA)
AAPS .... American Association for the Promotion of Science
AAPS .... Annals. American Academy of Political and Social Science [*A publication*]
AAPS .... Association of Alternate Postal Systems (EA)
AAPS .... Association for Ambulatory Pediatric Services [*Later, APA*] (EA)
AAPS .... Association of American Physicians and Surgeons (EA)
AAPS .... Automated Astronomic Positioning System [*Defense Mapping Agency*]
AAPSAT ... Archives d'Anatomie Pathologique [*Paris*] [*A publication*]
AAPSC ..... Afro-Asian Peoples Solidarity Council
AAPSC ...... American Association of Psychiatric Services for Children (EA)
AAPSE ...... American Association of Professors in Sanitary Engineering [*Later, AEEP*]
AAP/SHORAD ... Air-Augmented Propulsion for Short-Range Air Defense (MCD)
AAPSM ..... American Academy of Podiatric Sports Medicine (EA)
AAPS Newsletter ... Association of American Physicians and Surgeons. Newsletter [*A publication*]
AAPSO ...... Afro-Asian People's Solidarity Organization [*Cairo, Egypt*] (EAIO)
AAPSRO ... American Association of Professional Standards Review Organizations [*Later, AMPRA*] (EA)
AAPSS ...... American Academy of Political and Social Science (EA)
AAPSSA .... American Academy of Political and Social Science. Annals [*A publication*]
AAPSS Mg ... American Academy of Political and Social Science. Monographs [*A publication*]
AAPT .... American Association of Philosophy Teachers (EA)
AAPT .... American Association of Physics Teachers (EA)
AAPT .... Association of Asphalt Paving Technologists (EA)
AAPTCY ... Australia. Commonwealth Scientific and Industrial Research Organisation. Division of Atmospheric Physics. Technical Paper [*A publication*]
AAPTO ..... American Association of Passenger Traffic Officers [*Defunct*] (EA)
AAPU .... Airborne Auxiliary Power Unit
AAPVA4 .... Archives des Recherches Agronomiques et Pastorales au Vietnam [*A publication*]
AAPWA ..... American Association of Public Welfare Attorneys (EA)
AAPWISM ... American Association of Public Welfare Information Systems Management (EA)
AAPY .... American Association of Professors of Yiddish (EA)
AAPYAD ... Annual of Animal Psychology [*A publication*]

AAQ .... Architectural Association. Quarterly [*A publication*]
AAQ .... Armed Aircraft Qualification
AAQM .... Acting Assistant Quartermaster [*Marine Corps*]
AA & QMG ... Assistant Adjutant and Quartermaster-General [*British*]
AAQU-A ... Architectural Association. Quarterly [*A publication*]
AAR .... Aarhus [*Denmark*] [*Airport symbol*] (OAG)
AAR .... Accumulation Area Ratio
AAR .... Acupuncture Association and Register Ltd. [*British*]
AAR .... Administrative Appeals Reports [*Australia*] [*A publication*]
A/AR .... Aero/Acoustic Rotor (RDA)
AAR .... Affirmative Action Register [*A publication*]
AAR .... After Action Report [*Military*]
AAR .... After Action Review [*Military*] (MCD)
AAR .... Against All Risks [*Insurance*]
AAR .... Aid for Afghan Refugees [*An association*] (EA)
AAR .... Air-to-Air Refueling (MCD)
AAR .... Air Attack RADAR
AAR .... Air-Augmented Rocket
AAR .... Airborne Attack Recorder (MCD)
AAR .... Aircraft Accident Record [*Obsolete*] [*Military*]
AAR .... Aircraft Accident Report [*Military*]
A-Ar .... Alabama Department of Archives and History, Montgomery, AL [*Library symbol*] [*Library of Congress*] (LCLS)
AAR .... Alabama Department of Archives and History, Montgomery, AL [*OCLC symbol*] (OCLC)
AAR .... [*The*] Alaska Railroad [*Department of Transportation*] (FAAC)
AAR .... Alliance for Aging Research (EA)
AAR .... Alternate Acquisition RADAR (MCD)
AAR .... Americair [*Washington, DC*] [*FAA designator*] (FAAC)
AAR .... American Academy of Religion (EA)
AAR .... American Academy in Rome (EA)
AAR .... American Association of Rabbis (EA)
AAR .... Amino Acid Racemization [*Dating process*]
A and AR ... Ancient and Accepted Rite [*Freemasonry*]
AAR .... Ann Arbor Review [*A publication*]
AAR .... Annales. Academie des Sciences de Russie [*A publication*]
AAR .... Applied Agricultural Research, Inc. [*Research center*] (RCD)
AAR .... Approved Auto Repair [*American Automobile Association*]
AAR .... Arabesque Resources Ltd. [*Vancouver Stock Exchange symbol*]
AAR .... Army Area Representative
AAR .... Association of American Railroads (EA)
AAR .... Association of American Rhodes Scholars
AAR .... Association for Automated Reasoning (EA)
AAR .... Atti. Reale Accademia d'Italia (Roma). Memorie. Classe di Scienze Morali e Storiche [*A publication*]
AAR .... Automatic Alternative Routing [*Telecommunications*] (TEL)
AAR .... Automotive Affiliated Representatives (EA)
AARA .... Access and Amendment Refusal Authority [*Army*] (AABC)
AARA .... American Amateur Racquetball Association (EA)
AARA .... American Ambulance and Rescue Association [*Defunct*] (EA)
AARA .... American Arab Relief Agency [*Defunct*]
AARA .... Antique Auto Racing Association (EA)
AARA .... Atti. Accademia Roveretana degli Agiati [*A publication*]
AARAAJ ... Acta Albertina Ratisbonensia [*A publication*]
AARAB ..... Annales. Academie Royale d'Archeologie de Belgique [*A publication*]
AARAD ...... Aspect Angle Radiation Code (MCD)
AARB .... Advanced Air Refueling Boom [*Air Force*] (MCD)
AARB .... Annuaire. Academie Royale de Belgique [*A publication*]
Aarbok Univ Bergen Mat-Naturvitensk Ser ... Aarbok foer Universitetet i Bergen. Matematisk-Naturvitenskapelig Serie [*A publication*]
AARC .... Alliance for Acid Rain Control (EA)
AARC .... American Aircraft Corp. [*NASDAQ symbol*] (NQ)
AARC .... American-Arab Relations Committee (EA)
AARC .... American Association for Respiratory Care (EA)
AARC .... Army Attrition Rates Committee (NATG)
AARC .... Assassination Archives and Research Center (EA)
AARC .... Australian Applied Research Centre
AARCDS ... University of the Orange Free State. Publication. Series C [*A publication*]
AArch .... Acta Archaeologica [*A publication*]
A Arch .... American Archivist [*A publication*]
A Arch .... Associate in Architecture
A Arch Acad Sci Hung ... Acta Archaeologica. Academiae Scientiarum Hungaricae [*A publication*]
AArchAnthr ... Annals of Archaeology and Anthropology [*A publication*]
A Arch Carpathica ... Acta Archaeologica Carpathica [*Crakow*] [*A publication*]
AArchHung ... Acta Archaeologica. Academiae Scientiarum Hungaricae [*A publication*]
A Arch Lodziensia ... Acta Archaeologica Lodziensia [*A publication*]
AArchSlov ... Acta Archaeologica/Arheoloski Vestnik. Slovenska Akademija [*A publication*]
AArchSyr ... Annales Archeologiques de Syrie [*A publication*]
AARCKW ... Association of Airborne Ranger Companies of the Korean War (EA)
AARD .... American Academy of Restorative Dentistry (EA)
AARDAC .. Army Air Reconnaissance for Damage Assessment in the Continental United States (AABC)

AARDCO .. Association of American Railroad Dining Car Officers   (EA)
AARDL...... Artillery Ammunition and Rocket Development Laboratory
          [*Army*]   (MCD)
AARDS...... Australian Advertising Rate and Data Service [*A
          publication*]   (APTA)
AAREA...... Anesthesie, Analgesie, Reanimation [*Paris*] [*A publication*]
AAREC...... Adaptive Agile RADAR ECCM [*Electronic Counter-
          Countermeasures*]   (MCD)
AARF......... Arab American Republican Federation   (EA)
AARF........ Australian Accounting Research Foundation
AAR Facts ... Association of American Railroads. Yearbook of Railroad Facts
          [*A publication*]
AARG........ Association of Artist-Run Galleries   (EA)
AARG........ Atlantic Amphibious Ready Group   (MCD)
AARGCE... Association of American Rod and Gun Clubs, Europe   (EA)
Aarhus Univ Lab Fys Geogr Skr ... Aarhus Universitet. Laboratoriet foer
          Fysisk Geografi Skrifter [*A publication*]
AARL......... Advanced Automation Research Laboratory [*Purdue
          University*]
AARL........ Army Aeromedical Research Laboratory   (RDA)
AARL........ Army Aeronautical Research Center [*Ames Research Center*]
AARL........ Australian Academic and Research Libraries [*A
          publication*]   (APTA)
AARM....... Advanced Antiradiation Missile   (MCD)
A-ARM...... Army Armor Board   (MCD)
AARM....... Arrowwood Municipal Library, Alberta [*Library symbol*]
          [*National Library of Canada*]   (NLC)
AARMA...... Assistant [*US*] Army Military Attache   (CINC)
AArmL....... Annual of Armenian Linguistics [*A publication*]
AARMTO ... All Australian Register of Massage Therapists Organisation
AARN........ Aaron Brothers Art Marts, Inc. [*City Of Commerce, CA*]
          [*NASDAQ symbol*]   (NQ)
AARN Newsl ... AARN [*Alberta Association of Registered Nurses*] Newsletter
          [*A publication*]
AARN News Lett ... AARN [*Alberta Association of Registered Nurses*] News
          Letter [*A publication*]
AARO........ Association of Americans Resident Overseas   (EA)
AARP........ American Association of Retired Persons   (EA)
AARP........ Annual Advance Retainer Pay
AARP........ Art and Archaeology. Research Papers [*A publication*]
AARPLS.... Advanced Airborne Radio Position Location System
          [*Army*]   (MCD)
AARPS...... Air-Augmented Rocket Propulsion System
AARPUT... Average Aptitude Requirement per Unit Time
AARR........ Argonne Advanced Research Reactor
AARRC...... Army Aircraft Requirements Review Committee
AARRC...... Atlanta Aerospace Rescue and Recovery Center [*Air Force*]
AARRO..... Afro-Asian Rural Reconstruction Organization [*New Delhi,
          India*]
AARS........ Accrual Accounting and Reporting System
AARS........ Advanced Airborne RADAR System   (MCD)
AARS........ Air-to-Air Refueling Squadron
AARS........ Air Force Aerospace Rescue and Recovery Service   (MCD)
AARS........ All-America Rose Selections [*An association*]   (EA)
AARS........ American Association of Railroad Superintendents   (EA)
AARS........ American Association of Railway Surgeons   (EA)
AARS........ Annals of Regional Science [*A publication*]
AARS........ Anonymous Arts Recovery Society   (EA)
AARS........ Army Aerial Reconnaissance System
AARS........ Army Aircraft Repair Ship
AARS........ Army Amateur Radio System
AARS........ Association of American Rhodes Scholars   (EA)
AARS........ Automated Attendance Reporting System   (MCD)
AARS........ Automatic Address Recognition System [*or Subsystem*] [*Data
          processing*]
Aarsberet Inst Sterilitetsforsk K Vet Landbohoejsk ... Aarsberetning Institut
          foer Sterilitetsforskning Kongelige Veterinaer og
          Landbohoejskole [*A publication*]
AARSS ..... Austere Airborne Ranging and Sighting System   (MCD)
Aarsskr K Vet Landbohoejsk (DK) ... Aarsskrift den Kongelige Veterinaer og
          Landbohoejskole (Denmark) [*A publication*]
Aarsskr Yearb Annu Jahrb Copenh Vet Landbohojsk ... Aarsskrift/Yearbook/
          Annuaire/Jahrbuch. Copenhagen Veterinaer og
          Landbohoejskole [*A publication*]
AARST ...... American Association of Radon Scientists and
          Technologists   (EA)
AArt........... American Artist [*A publication*]
AART .... American Association for Rehabilitation Therapy   (EA)
AART .... American Association of Religious Therapists   (EA)
AART .... American Association for Respiratory Therapy [*Later,
          AARC*]   (EA)
A-ART ...... Army Artillery Board   (MCD)
AARTA...... American Association of Railroad Ticket Agents
          [*Defunct*]   (EA)
AARTI....... Australian Art Index [*Australian National Gallery Library*]
          [*Database*]   (ADA)
AARTimes ... American Association for Respiratory Therapy. Times [*A
          publication*]
AARTS...... Association of Advanced Rabbinical and Talmudic
          Schools   (EA)
AARU........ Agricultural Aviation Research Unit [*British*]   (ARC)

AARU........ Association of Arab Universities [*Amman, Jordan*]   (EAIO)
AARV .... Aerial Armored Reconnaissance Vehicle
AARV .... Armored Artillery Resupply Vehicle   (MCD)
AARV-A ... Architectural Review [*A publication*]
AARWBA ... American Auto Racing Writers and Broadcasters
          Association   (EA)
AAS .... Abort Advisory System [*NASA*]
AAS .... Academiae Americanae Socius [*Fellow of the American
          Academy (Academy of Arts and Sciences)*] [*Latin*]   (GPO)
AAS .... Academy of Applied Science
AAS .... Achievement Anxiety Scale [*Psychology*]
AAS .... Acta Apostolicae Sedis [*Cittal del Vaticano*] [*A publication*]
AAS .... Activity Accreditation Schedule   (MCD)
AAS .... Acts of the Apostolic See
AAS .... Adjusted Air Speed [*Navigation*]
AAS .... Advanced Accounting System
AAS .... Advanced Active Sonobuoy   (MCD)
AAS .... Advanced Administrative System [*IBM Corp.*]
AAS .... Advanced Aero-Wing Systems Corp. [*Vancouver Stock
          Exchange symbol*]
AAS .... Advanced Air Station   (DAS)
AAS .... Advanced Antenna System [*Air Force*]
AAS .... Advanced Automated System
AAS .... Advanced Automation System
AAS .... Advanced Avionic System   (MCD)
AAS .... Aeromedical Airlift Squadron [*Air Force*]
AAS .... Air Armament School [*British military*]   (DMA)
AAS .... Airborne Antenna System
AAS .... Aircraft Airworthiness Section
AAS .... Airport Advisory Service   (FAAC)
AAS .... Alabama Department of Archives and History, State
          Documents, Montgomery, AL [*OCLC symbol*]   (OCLC)
AAS .... Alert Area Supervisor [*Military*]   (AFM)
AAS .... All-America Selections   (EA)
AAS .... American Academy of Sanitarians   (EA)
AAS .... American Academy of Somnology   (EA)
AAS .... American Amaryllis Society   (EA)
AAS .... American Antiquarian Society   (EA)
AAS .... American Antiquarian Society. Proceedings [*A publication*]
AAS .... American Artists Series
AAS .... American Association of Shotgunning   (EA)
AAS .... American Association of Suicidology   (EA)
AAS .... American Astronautical Society   (EA)
AAS .... American Astronomical Society   (EA)
AAS .... American Auditory Society   (EA)
A-AS .... American-Austrian Society   (EA)
AAS .... Analog Alarm Section
AAS .... Ancient Astronaut Society   (EA)
AAS .... Angular Acceleration Susceptibility [*Orientation*]
AAS .... Annales Archeologiques de Syrie [*Damascus*] [*A publication*]
AAS .... Annual Abstracts of Statistics [*Baghdad*] [*A publication*]
AAS .... Annual Authorizations Service [*of the Copyright Clearance
          Center*]
AAS .... Annual Automated Controls Survey [*of a ship*]   (DS)
AAS .... Annual Average Score   (AABC)
AAS .... Anthrax Antiserum [*Medicine*]
AAS .... Aortic Arch Syndrome [*Medicine*]
AAS .... Architectural Acoustics Society   (EA)
AAS .... Arithmetic Assignment Statement
AAS .... Arms and Armour Society   (EA)
AAS .... Army Air Service
AAS .... Army Attache System
AAS .... Arnold Air Society   (EA)
AAS .... Ashmont Public Library, Alberta [*Library symbol*] [*National
          Library of Canada*]   (NLC)
AAS .... Asian and African Section [*Association of College and Research
          Libraries*]
AAS .... Asian and African Studies [*A publication*]
AAS .... Associate in Applied Science
AAS .... Association for Academic Surgery   (EA)
AAS .... Association of Academies of Science [*Later, NAAS*]
AAS .... Association for Archery in Schools   (EAIO)
AAS .... Association for Asian Studies   (EA)
AAS .... Atomic Absorption Spectrometer [*or Spectrophotometer or
          Spectroscopy*]
AAS .... Attack Assessment System   (MCD)
AAS .... Australian Aircraft Sales
AAS .... Automated Accounting System   (BUR)
AAS .... Automatic Addressing System [*Data processing*]
AAS .... Automatic Announcement Subsystem
          [*Telecommunications*]   (TEL)
AAS .... Auxiliary Ambulance Service   (DAS)
AAS .... Azimuth Alignment System [*Aerospace*]   (AAG)
AAS .... Campbellsville, KY [*Location identifier*] [*FAA*]   (FAAL)
AASA......... Academy of Arts and Sciences of the Americas   (EA)
AASA......... Administrative Assistant to the Secretary of the Army
AASA......... Advances in Alcohol and Substance Abuse [*A publication*]
AASA......... Afro-American Student Association   (EA)
AASA......... American Association of School Administrators   (EA)
AASA......... American Association of Surgeon's Assistants   (EA)
AASA......... Ansett Airlines of South Australia   (ADA)

AASAAO... Acta Agriculturae Suecana [*A publication*]

AASACM ... American Association of Swiss Alpine Club Members [*Defunct*] (EA)

AASADR... Advances in Alcohol and Substance Abuse [*A publication*]

AAS (Am Astronaut Soc) Sci Technol Ser ... AAS (American Astronautical Society) Science and Technology Series [*A publication*]

AASANA... Administracion de Aeropuertos y Servicios Auxiliares a la Navegacion Aerea [*Bolivian airline*]

AASB........ American Association of Small Business [*Later, NSBU*]

AASB........ Atti. Accademia delle Scienze. Istituto di Bologna [*A publication*]

AASBA...... American Astronomical Society. Bulletin [*A publication*]

AASBEVM ... Association of American State Boards of Examiners in Veterinary Medicine [*Later, AAVSB*] (EA)

AASC........ Acta Agriculturae Scandinavica [*A publication*]

AASC........ African-American Scholars Conference [*Defunct*] (EA)

AASC........ Alliance Against Sexual Coercion (EA)

AASC........ Allied Air Support Command [*Mediterranean*]

AASC....... American Association of Small Cities (EA)

AASC....... American Association of Specialized Colleges (EA)

AASC....... American Association of State Climatologists (EA)

AASC........ Anglo-American Sporting Club

AASC........ Army Area Signal Center (AABC)

AASC........ Army Automation Steering Committee

AASC........ Association for the Advancement of Science in Canada

AASC........ Association of African Sports Confederations [*See also UCSA*] [*Yaounde, Cameroon*] (EAIO)

AASCAU... Acta Agriculturae Scandinavica [*A publication*]

AASCIN.... American Association of Spinal Cord Injury Nurses (EA)

AASCM..... Awaiting Action Summary Court-Martial

AASCO...... Association of American Seed Control Officials (EA)

AASCU..... American Association of State Colleges and Universities (EA)

AASD........ American Academy of Stress Disorders (EA)

AASD .... Antiaircraft Self-Destroying

AASDJ ...... American Association of Schools and Departments of Journalism (EA)

AASDMCC ... American Association for Small Dredging and Marine Construction Companies (EA)

AASE........ American Academy of Safety Education (EA)

AASE........ American Association of Special Educators [*Inactive*] (EA)

AASE........ Army Aviation Support Element (AABC)

AASE........ Association for Applied Solar Energy [*Later, International Solar Energy Society*]

AASE........ Australian Associated Stock Exchanges (ADA)

AASEC ...... American Association of Sex Educators and Counselors [*Later, AASECT*] (EA)

AASECT ... American Association of Sex Educators, Counselors, and Therapists (EA)

AASF .... Advanced Air Striking Force [*British*]

AASF .... Annales Academiae Scientiarum Fennicae [*A publication*]

AASF .... Army Aviation Support Facility (MCD)

AASF .... Asian Amateur Swimming Federation [*Dhaka, Bangladesh*] (EAIO)

AASF .... Associate Administrator for Space Flight [*NASA*] (MCD)

AASFE ...... American Association of Sunday and Feature Editors (EA)

AASG .... American Association of Students of German (EA)

AASG .... Association of American State Geologists [*Defunct*] (EA)

AASGP...... American Association of Sheep and Goat Practitioners [*Later, AASRP*] (EA)

AAS & GP ... American Association of Soap and Glycerin Producers [*Later, SDA*]

AASH .... Adrenal Androgen Stimulating Hormone [*Medicine*]

AASH .... Alumni Association of Shriners Hospitals

AASH .... American Association for the Study of Headache (EA)

AASH .... Australian Association of Speech and Hearing

AASHAB.. Acta Agronomica. Academiae Scientiarum Hungaricae [*A publication*]

AASHCD .. Aliphatic, Alicyclic, and Saturated Heterocyclic Chemistry [*A publication*]

AASHO ...... American Association of State Highway Officials [*Later, AASHTO*] (EA)

AASHTO .. American Association of State Highway and Transportation Officials (EA)

AASI.......... Advertising Agency Service Interchange [*Defunct*] (EA)

AASI.......... Amherst Associates [*NASDAQ symbol*] (NQ)

AASI.......... Associate of the Ambulance Service Institute [*British*] (DBQ)

A'ASIA ...... Australasia (ADA)

A'ASIAN... Australasian (ADA)

A/asian Irrigator ... Australasian Irrigator and Pasture Improver [*A publication*] (APTA)

A/asian J Philos ... Australasian Journal of Philosophy [*A publication*] (APTA)

AASIP .... Appalachian Airport Safety Improvement Program (FAAC)

AASIR .... Advanced Atmospheric Sounder and Imaging Radiometer [*NASA*] (MCD)

AASIR .... Afro-American Society for International Relations (EA)

AASK......... Aid to Adoption of Special Kids [*An association*] (EA)

AASL......... American Association of School Librarians (EA)

AASL......... American Association of State Libraries [*Later, ASCLA*]

AASL......... Antiaircraft Searchlight

AASLA...... Atti. Accademia di Scienze, Lettere, ed Arti di Palermo [*A publication*]

AASLAN... Atti. Accademia di Scienze, Lettere, ed Arti di Palermo. Parte Prima. Scienze [*A publication*]

AASLD...... African Association for the Study of Liver Diseases (EAIO)

AASLD...... American Association for the Study of Liver Diseases (EA)

AASLH...... American Association for State and Local History (EA)

AASL NPSS ... AASL [*American Association of School Librarians*] Non-Public Schools Section

AASLS...... Afro-American Studies Librarians Section [*Association of College and Research Libraries*]

AASL SLMES ... AASL [*American Association of School Librarians*] School Library Media Educators Section

AASL SLMQ ... AASL [*American Association of School Librarians*] School Library Media Quarterly [*A publication*]

AASL SS ... AASL [*American Association of School Librarians*] Supervisors Section

AASLT ...... Air Assault [*Army*] (AABC)

AASM .... Advanced Air-to-Surface Missile (MCD)

AASM .... Association of American Steel Manufacturers

AASM .... Association of Aviation and Space Museums [*Defunct*] (EA)

AASMD .... Airborne Antiship Missile Defense (MCD)

AASME...... Associate of the American Society of Mechanical Engineers

AASMM ... Associated African States, Madagascar, and Mauritius (DS)

AASMMA ... Advanced Avionic System for Multi-Mission Application (MCD)

AASMS ..... Advanced Air-to-Surface Missile Seeker [*Navy*] (MCD)

AASN .... Atti. Accademia di Scienze Morali e Politiche di Napoli [*A publication*]

AASNAT... Acta Agriculturae Scandinavica. Supplementum [*A publication*]

AASND ...... American Association for Study of Neoplastic Diseases (EA)

AASNS ...... Asian-Australasian Society of Neurological Surgeons [*Kowloon, Hong Kong*] (EAIO)

AASO .... Administrative Aircraft Standardization Office [*NASA*]

AASO .... Afro-Asian Solidarity Organization (NATG)

AASO .... Assigned Activity Standardization Office [*Air Force*] (AFIT)

AASO .... Association of American Ship Owners

AASOR...... Annual. American Schools of Oriental Research [*A publication*]

AASP........ Advanced Automated Sample Processor

AASP........ American Academy of Sports Physicians (EA)

AASP........ American Aid Society of Paris [*France*] (EA)

AASP........ American Association of Senior Physicians (EA)

AASP........ American Association for Social Psychiatry (EA)

AASP........ American Association of Stratigraphic Palynologists (EA)

AASP........ American Association of Swine Practitioners (EA)

AASP........ Army Automation Security Program

AASP........ Association for the Advancement of Sports Potential (EA)

AASP........ Association of African Studies Programs (EA)

AASPA ...... American Association of School Personnel Administrators (EA)

AAS Photo-Bull ... AAS [*American Astronomical Society*] Photo-Bulletin [*A publication*]

AASPRC ... American Association of Sheriff Posses and Riding Clubs (EA)

AASq .... Aeromedical Airlift Squadron [*Air Force*] (AFM)

AASR........ Advanced Army System Requirements

AASR........ Airport and Airways Surveillance RADAR [*Air Force*]

AASR........ American Association of Securities Representatives

AASR........ Ancient and Accepted Scottish Rite [*Freemasonry*]

A & ASR .... Ancient and Accepted Scottish Rite [*Freemasonry*] (ROG)

AASRA7.... Atti. Accademia delle Scienze di Ferrara [*A publication*]

AASRC...... American Association of Small Research Companies (EA)

AASRC Newsl ... AASRC [*American Association of Small Research Companies*] Newsletter [*A publication*]

AASRE...... American Association of Schools of Religious Education [*Later, ATS*] (EA)

AASREC ... Asian Association of Social Science Research Councils

AASRI .... Arctic and Antarctic Scientific Research Institute

AASR-NMJ ... Supreme Council, Ancient Accepted Scottish Rite of Freemasonry - Northern Masonic Jurisdiction (EA)

AASRP ...... American Association of Small Ruminant Practitioners (EA)

AASR-SMJ ... Supreme Council, Ancient Accepted Scottish Rite of Freemasonry - Southern Masonic Jurisdiction (EA)

AASS .... Academiae Antiquarinae Societales Socius

AASS .... Advanced Acoustic Search Sensors (MCD)

AASS .... Advanced Airborne Surveillance Sensor (MCD)

AASS .... Afro-Asian Solidarity Secretariat (NATG)

AASS .... Aid Auto Stores, Inc. [*NASDAQ symbol*] (NQ)

AASS .... American Academy of Spinal Surgeons (EA)

AASS .... American Association for Social Security (EA)

AASS .... Americanae Antiquarianae Societatis Socius [*Fellow of the American Antiquarian Society*] [*Latin*]

AASS .... Armenian Assembly Student Services [*Later, AAASAD*] (EA)

AASS .... Automatic Abort-Sensing System [*NASA*]

AASSA ...... Association of American Schools in South America (EA)

AASSC ...... Association for the Advancement of Scandinavian Studies in Canada [*See also AAESC*]

AAS Sci Technol Ser ... AAS [*American Astronautical Society*] Science and Technology Series [*A publication*]

AASSCPA ... American Associations of Spanish Speaking CPA's (EA)

A Assoc Amer Geogr ... Annals. Association of American Geographers [*A publication*]

AASSREC ... Association of Asian Social Science Research Councils [*New Delhi, India*]
AASSWB .. American Association of State Social Work Boards (EA)
AAST .... Action Auto Stores, Inc. [*NASDAQ symbol*] (NQ)
AAST .... American Association for the Surgery of Trauma (EA)
AAST .... Atti. Reale Accademia delle Scienze di Torino. Classe di Scienze Morali, Storiche, e Filologiche [*A publication*]
AASTA ...... Antiaircraft Station
AASTA ...... Army Aviation Systems Test Activity [*Also, USAASTA*]
AASTD ...... ASSET. Abstracts of Selected Solar Energy Technology [*A publication*]
A-ASTP-P ... Association of Apollo-Soyuz Test Project Philatelists (EA)
AASU .... All Africa Students Union [*See also UPE*] (EAIO)
AASW .... Airborne Antisubmarine Warfare
AASW .... American Association of Scientific Workers [*Later, USFSS*] (EA)
AASW .... American Association of Social Workers
AASWI ...... American Aid Society for the West Indies (EA)
AASWS ..... Antimassed Armor Strike Weapon System (MCD)
AASXAP .... Acta Anaesthesiologica Scandinavica. Supplementum [*A publication*]
AASYA ...... Arkiv foer Astronomi [*A publication*]
AASZBW .. Acta Agraria et Silvestria. Series Zootechnia [*A publication*]
AAT .... Abaton Resources Ltd. [*Vancouver Stock Exchange symbol*]
AAT .... Academic Aptitude Test [*Vocational guidance test*]
AAT .... Accelerated Apprenticeship Training (ADA)
AAT .... Activation Acceptance Team [*NASA*] (NASA)
AAT .... Administrative Appeals Tribunal (ADA)
AAT .... Aerodynamic Accounting Technique (MCD)
AAT .... Air Traffic Service [*of FAA*] [*Also known as AT, ATS*] (FAAC)
AAT .... Airports Authority of Thailand (DS)
AAT .... Alanine Aminotransferase [*Also, ALAT, ALT, GPT*] [*An enzyme*]
AAT .... Alpha-Antitrypsin [*Biochemistry*]
AAT .... Altay [*China*] [*Airport symbol*] (OAG)
AAT .... American Academy of Thermology (EA)
AAT .... American Academy of Transportation
AAT .... Anglo-Australian Telescope
AAT .... Antiaircraft Technician (MCD)
AAT .... Aspartate Aminotransferase [*Also, ASAT, AST, GOT*] [*An enzyme*]
AAT .... Association of Accounting Technicians (EAIO)
AAT .... Atti. Accademia delle Scienze di Torino [*A publication*]
AAT .... Attitude Acquisition Technique
AAT .... Attitude Angle Transducer
AAT .... Auditory Apperception Test [*Psychology*]
AAT .... Australian Antarctic Territory
AAT .... Automated Assessment Tool (MCD)
AAT .... Automatic Antenna Timer
AAT .... Les Apocryphes de l'Ancien Testament [*A publication*] (BJA)
A₁AT .... Alpha-1-Antitrypsin [*Protease inhibitor*] [*Serology*]
AATA .... African Association of Tax Administrators (EAIO)
AATA .... American Art Therapy Association (EA)
AATA .... American Association of Teachers of Arabic (EA)
AATA .... American Automobile Touring Alliance (EA)
AATA .... Animal Air Transportation Association (EA)
AATA .... Art and Archaeology. Technical Abstracts [*Information service or system*] [*A publication*]
AATAAT ... Avances en Alimentacion y Mejora Animal [*A publication*]
AATACB ... American Athletic Trainers Association and Certification Board (EA)
AATB .... Advanced Amphibious Training Base [*Navy*]
AATB .... Afro-Asian Theatre Bulletin [*A publication*]
AATB .... American Association of Tissue Banks (EA)
AATB .... Army Aviation Test Board
AATBN ..... Aromatic Amine Terminated Butadiene/Acrylonitrile [*Organic chemistry*]
AATC .... Advanced Air Training Command [*Military*]
AATC .... American-ASEAN [*Association of South East Asian Nations*] Trade Council (EA)
AATC .... Antiaircraft Training Center [*Navy*]
AATC .... Army Aviation Test Command [*ATEC*]
AATC .... Atti e Memorie. Accademia Toscana la Colombaria [*A publication*]
AATC .... Automatic Air Traffic Control [*System*] (IEEE)
AATCAN .. Army Air Traffic Control and Navigation System (MCD)
AATCC ...... Airhead Air Traffic Coordination Center [*Army*] (AFIT)
AATCC ...... American Association of Textile Chemists and Colorists (EA)
AATCC Nat Tech Conf Book Pap ... AATCC [*American Association of Textile Chemists and Colorists*] National Technical Conference. Book of Papers [*A publication*]
AATCC Symp Flock Technol ... AATCC [*American Association of Textile Chemists and Colorists*] Symposium. Flock Technology [*A publication*]
AATCE ...... American Association of Temporary and Contract Employees (EA)
AATCLC ... American Association of Teachers of Chinese Language and Culture [*Later, AACS*] (EA)
AATCM .... Academy of Air Traffic Control Medicine
AATCO ..... Army Air Traffic Coordinating Office (AABC)
AATCS ...... [*An*] Automatic Test Control System (MCD)

AATD .... Aviation Applied Technology Directorate [*Fort Eustis, VA*] [*Army*] (RDA)
AATDC ..... Army Air Transport Training and Development Centre [*England*]
AATDEC ... Administrative Appeals Tribunal Decisions [*Database*] [*Australia*]
AATE .... American Association of Teachers of Esperanto (EA)
AATE .... Atlantic Association of Teacher Educators [*Canada*]
AATE .... Avionics Automatic Transmission Line
AATEA ...... American Association of Teacher Educators in Agriculture [*Later, AAAE*] (EA)
AA Tech ..... Associate in Automotive Technology
AA Ter Ed ... Associate in Arts in Terminal Education
AATESL .... American Association of Teachers of English as a Second Language
AATF .... Active Air Target Fuse (MCD)
AATF .... American Association of Teachers of French (EA)
AATF .... Anechoic Acoustic Test Facility (MCD)
AATFAA .... Atti. Accademia delle Scienze di Torino. I. Classe di Scienze Fisiche, Matematiche e Naturali [*A publication*]
AATFNB ... American Association of Teachers of French. National Bulletin [*A publication*]
AATG .... American Association of Teachers of German (EA)
AATH .... American Association for Therapeutic Humor (EA)
AATH .... Athabasca Public Library, Alberta [*Library symbol*] [*National Library of Canada*] (NLC)
AAthC .... Athens College, Athens, GA [*Library symbol*] [*Library of Congress*] (LCLS)
AATI .... American Anti-Terrorism Institute (EA)
AATI .... American Association of Teachers of Italian (EA)
AATI .... Analysis & Technology, Incorporated [*North Stonington, CT*] [*NASDAQ symbol*] (NQ)
AATM .... American Academy of Tropical Medicine (EA)
AATM .... At All Times (FAAC)
AATMA ...... Archiwum Automatyki i Telemechaniki [*A publication*]
AATMS ..... Advanced Air Traffic Management System [*Department of Transportation*]
AATNAY .. Archivos Argentinos de Tisiologia y Neumonologia [*A publication*]
AATNU ..... Administration de l'Assistance Technique des Nations Unies [*United Nations Technical Assistance Administration*]
AATO .... All Africa Teachers' Organization (EAIO)
AATO .... Army Air Transport Organization
AATP .... American Academy of Tuberculosis Physicians (EA)
AATP .... American Association of Testifying Physicians (EA)
AATPA ...... American Association of Traveling Passenger Agents [*Defunct*]
AATPO ..... Association of African Trade Promotion Organizations [*Tangier, Morocco*] (EAIO)
AATR .... Apollo Applications Test Requirements [*NASA*] (MCD)
AATR .... Association of Auto and Truck Recyclers [*Later, ADRA*] (EA)
AATRACEN ... Antiaircraft Training Center [*Navy*]
AATRI .... Army Air Traffic Regulation and Identification
AATRIS ..... Army Air Traffic Regulation and Identification System (AFM)
AA-tRNA .. Ribonucleic Acid, Transfer - Aminoacyl [*or Aminoacylated*] [*Biochemistry, genetics*]
AATS .... Alternate Aircraft Takeoff System (MCD)
AATS .... American Academy of Teachers of Singing (EA)
AATS .... American Association of Theological Schools [*Later, ATS*] (EA)
AATS .... American Association for Thoracic Surgery (EA)
AATS .... American Association of Trauma Specialists [*Defunct*] (EA)
AATS .... Armament Auxiliaries Test Set (MCD)
AATS .... Atikameg-Sovereign School, Alberta [*Library symbol*] [*National Library of Canada*] (BIB)
AATS .... Automatic Altitude Trim System [*for helicopters*] (NG)
AATS .... Automatic Antitheft System [*Electronic lock*]
AATSEEL ... American Association of Teachers of Slavic and East European Languages (EA)
AATSEEL Bull ... American Association of Teachers of Slavic and East European Languages. Bulletin [*A publication*]
AATSEEL Jour ... American Association of Teachers of Slavic and East European Languages. Journal [*A publication*]
AATSP ...... American Association of Teachers of Spanish and Portuguese (EA)
AATT .... American Association of Teachers of Turkish (EA)
AATT .... American Association for Textile Technology (EA)
AATT .... Australian Army Training Team
AATT .... Australian Association for Theatre Technology
AATTC ..... American Airlines Technical Training Corporation
AAT & TC ... Antiaircraft Training and Test Center [*Navy*]
AATTV ...... Australian Army Training Team, Vietnam (CINC)
AATU .... American Aid to Ulster (EA)
AATU .... Association of Air Transport Unions [*Defunct*] (EA)
AATVA ...... American All-Terrain Vehicle Association (EA)
AATW .... Advanced Antitank Weapon [*Army*] (MCD)
AATY .... American Association of Theatre for Youth (EA)
AAU .... Acoustic Add-On Unit (MCD)
AAU .... Activation Analysis Unit [*British*]
AAU .... Add-On Audio Unit (MCD)
AAU .... Address Arithmetic Unit [*Data processing*]
AAU .... Administrative Area Unit [*Army*]

AAU........... Alta [*Utah*] [*Seismograph station code, US Geological Survey*] [*Closed*] (SEIS)

AAU........... Amanda Resources Ltd. [*Vancouver Stock Exchange symbol*]

AAU........... Amateur Athletic Union of the United States (EA)

AAU........... American Aid to Ulster (EA)

AAU........... Americas [*A publication*]

AAU........... Angular Accelerometer Unit

AAU........... Ashland, OH [*Location identifier*] [*FAA*] (FAAL)

AAU........... Association of African Universities (EAIO)

AAU........... Association of American Universities (EA)

AAU........... Atti. Accademia di Scienze, Lettere, ed Arti di Udine [*A publication*]

AAU........... Automatic Answering Unit [*Telecommunications*] (TEL)

AAU........... Auxiliary Air Units [*Naval Reserve*]

AAU........... United States Air Force, Air University Library, Maxwell AFB, AL [*OCLC symbol*] (OCLC)

AaUA........ Altaramaeische Urkunden aus Assur [*A publication*] (BJA)

AAUA........ American Association of University Administrators (EA)

AAUAP ..... American Association of University Affiliated Programs for Persons with Developmental Disabilities (EA)

AAUAPDD ... American Association of University Affiliated Programs for Persons with Developmental Disabilities [*Later, AAUAP*]

AAU/BNA ... Association of Atlantic Universities/Blackwell North America [*Project*] [*Information service or system*] (IID)

AAUCG ...... Americans Against University Control of Government (EA)

AAug .... Analecta Augustiniana [*A publication*]

AAUG .... Association of Arab-American University Graduates (EA)

A August .... Antonius Augustinus [*Deceased, 1586*] [*Authority cited in pre-1607 legal work*] (DSA)

AAUN .... American Association for the United Nations [*Later, United Nations Association of the United States*] (EA)

AAUNZ ...... Aus Alter und Neuer Zeit [*Illustrated Addition to Israelitisches Familienblatt, Hamburg*] [*A publication*] (BJA)

AAUP .... American Association of University Affiliated Programs for the Developmentally Disabled [*Washington, DC*]

AAUP .... American Association of University Professors (EA)

AAUP .... Association of American University Presses (EA)

AAUPB...... American Association of University Professors. Bulletin [*A publication*]

AAUPB...... Proceedings. Astronomical Society of Australia [*A publication*]

AAUP Bul ... American Association of University Professors. Bulletin [*A publication*]

AAUP Bull ... American Association of University Professors. Bulletin [*A publication*]

AAUPF...... American Association of University Professors Foundation (EA)

AAUP-UAES ... American Association of University Professors of Urban Affairs and Environmental Sciences (EA)

AAUQ .... Associate in Accountancy, University of Queensland [*Australia*]

AAUS .... American Association of University Students (EA)

AAus .... Americana-Austriaca. Beitraege zur Amerikakunde [*A publication*]

AAUTC ..... Army Aviation Unit Training Command (MCD)

AAUTI....... American Association of University Teachers of Insurance [*Later, ARIA*]

AAU/USA JO ... AAU [*Amateur Athletic Union of the United States*]/USA Junior Olympics (EA)

AAUW .... American Association of University Women (EA)

AAUWEF ... American Association of University Women Educational Foundation (EA)

AAV .... Acta Academiae Velehradensis [*A publication*]

AAV .... Acupuncture Association of Victoria

AAV .... Adeno-Associated Viruses

AAV .... Advanced Aerospace Vehicle (MCD)

AAV .... Airborne [*or Amphibious or Armored*] Assault Vehicle

AAV .... Alah [*Philippines*] [*Airport symbol*] (OAG)

AAV .... Alternative Access Vendor [*Telecommunications*]

AAV .... Antiaircraft Volunteer

AAV .... Assault Amphibian Vehicle [*Military*]

AAV .... Assessed Annual Value [*Accounting*] (ADA)

AAV .... Association of American Vintners (EA)

AAV .... Association of Avian Veterinarians (EA)

AAV .... Atti. Accademia di Agricoltura, Scienze, e Lettere di Verona [*A publication*]

AAV .... Aus Aachens Vorzeit [*A publication*]

AAV .... Avatar Resources Corp. [*Vancouver Stock Exchange symbol*]

AAV .... Ayrshire Artillery Volunteers [*British military*] (DMA)

AAVA .... American Association of Veterinary Anatomists (EA)

AAVB .... American Association of Veterinary Bacteriologists [*Defunct*] (EA)

AAVC .... Anomalous Atrioventricular Conduction [*Cardiology*]

AAVC .... Asian American Voters Coalition (EA)

AAVC .... Association des Assureurs-Vie du Canada [*Association of Life Insurers of Canada*]

AAVCA .... Australian Affiliation of Voluntary Care Agencies

AAVCRS ... Airborne Automatic Voice Communications System (MCD)

AAVCS ..... Automatic Aircraft Vectoring Control System [*Air Force*]

AAVCT...... American Academy of Veterinary and Comparative Toxicology (EA)

AAVD .... American Academy of Veterinary Dermatology (EA)

AAVD .... Automatic Alternate Voice/Data [*Data processing*]

AAVIM ..... American Association for Vocational Instructional Materials (EA)

AAVLD ..... American Association of Veterinary Laboratory Diagnosticians (EA)

AAVM .... Acting Air Vice-Marshal [*British*] (DAS)

AAVMC .... Association of American Veterinary Medical Colleges (EA)

AAVN .... American Academy of Veterinary Nutrition (EA)

AAVN .... Army Aviation (AABC)

AAVN .... Australian Audio-Visual News [*A publication*] (APTA)

AAVNA .... American Affiliation of Visiting Nurses Associations and Services [*Later, VNAA*] (EA)

AAVP .... American Association of Veterinary Parasitologists (EA)

AAVP .... Association of American Volunteer Physicians (EA)

AAVPC...... Annuarium van de Apologetische Vereeniging (Petrus Canisius) [*A publication*]

AAVPT ...... American Academy of Veterinary Pharmacology and Therapeutics (EA)

AAVRB...... Australian Audio-Visual Reference Book [*A publication*] (APTA)

AAVRPHS ... American Association for Vital Records and Public Health Statistics [*Later, AVRHS*] (EA)

AAVRS ..... All-Attitude Vertical Reference System [*Aerospace*]

AAVS......... Aerospace Audiovisual Service [*Air Force*] (MCD)

AAVS......... American Anti-Vivisection Society (EA)

AAVS......... Association for Administration of Volunteer Services [*Later, AVA*] (EA)

AAVS......... Automatic Aircraft Vectoring System [*Air Force*] (MUGU)

AAVSB...... American Association of Veterinary State Boards (EA)

AAVSC...... American Association of Volunteer Services Coordinators [*Later, AVA*]

AAVSED ... Automatic Air-Valving Surface Effects Device [*Army*] (MCD)

AAVSO ..... American Association of Variable Star Observers (EA)

AAVSO Circ ... AAVSO [*American Association of Variable Star Observers*] Circular [*A publication*]

AAVT .... Association of Audio-Visual Technicians (EA)

A Av Tech.. Associate in Aviation Technology

AAW .... Aberdeen Airways Ltd.

AAW .... Advertising Association of the West [*Later, AAF*] (EA)

AAW .... Aeromedical Airlift Wing [*Air Force*] (MCD)

AAW .... Afro-Asian Writings [*A publication*]

AAW .... Air Acetylene Welding

AAW .... American Academy of Wine (EA)

AAW .... American Agri-Women (EA)

AAW .... American Association of Women (EA)

AAW .... American Association of Woodturners (EA)

AAW .... American Atheist Women (EA)

AAW .... Annales. Cercle Archeologique du Pays de Waes [*A publication*]

AAW .... Antiair Warfare

AAW .... Anzeiger. Akademie der Wissenschaften [*Vienna*] [*A publication*]

AAW .... Anzeiger fuer die Altertumswissenschaft [*Innsbruck*] [*A publication*]

AAW .... Austin Airways Ltd. [*Timmins, ON, Canada*] [*FAA designator*] (FAAC)

AAW .... Talkeetna Mountains, AK [*Location identifier*] [*FAA*] (FAAL)

AAWA ...... Afro-Asian and World Affairs [*A publication*]

AAWB ...... American Association of Workers for the Blind [*Later, AER*] (EA)

AAWBOT ... Aviation Antisubmarine Warfare Basic Operational Trainer

AAWC .... All-African Women's Conference [*or Congress*]

AAWC .... American Association of Workers for Children

AAWC .... Antiair Warfare Center

AAWC .... Antiair Warfare Commander [*or Coordinator*] (NVT)

AAWCJC .. American Association of Women in Community and Junior Colleges (EA)

AAWD ...... American Association of Women Dentists (EA)

AAWE ...... Association of American Wives of Europeans (EA)

AAWEX .... Antiair Warfare Exercise [*Navy*] (NG)

AAWEXINPT ... Antiair Warfare Exercise in Port [*Navy*] (NVT)

AAWF .... Auxiliary Aviation Weather Facility [*FAA*] (FAAC)

AAWG .... Abhandlungen. Akademie der Wissenschaften in Goettingen [*A publication*]

AAWg........ Aeromedical Airlift Wing [*Air Force*] (AFM)

AAWGPh .. Abhandlungen. Akademie der Wissenschaften in Goettingen. Philologisch-Historische Klasse [*A publication*]

AAWH...... American Association for World Health (EA)

AAWHA .... Australian Amateur Women's Hockey Association

AAWIPT ... Antiair Warfare Training in Port [*Navy*] (NVT)

AAWL .... Abhandlungen. Akademie der Wissenschaften und der Literatur in Mainz. Geistes- und Sozialwissenschaftliche Klasse [*A publication*]

AAWL .... Australia Asia Worker Links

AAWM ...... Abhandlungen. Akademie der Wissenschaften in Mainz. Geistes- und Sozialwissenschaftliche Klasse [*A publication*]

AAWM ...... American Association of Waterbed Manufacturers [*Later, WMA*]

AAWM ...... American Association of Women Ministers [*Later, IAWM*] (EA)

AAWO....... Afro-Asian Workers' Organization (NATG)

AAWO.......	Association of American Weather Observers (EA)
AAWORD ...	Association of African Women for Research and Development (EAIO)
AAWP	American Association for Women Podiatrists (EA)
AAWPB.....	Afro-Asian Writers' Permanent Bureau (NATG)
AAWPC.....	Asian-American Women's Political Caucus (EA)
AAWPI......	Association of American Wood Pulp Importers (EA)
AAWR	American Association of Women Radiologists (EA)
AAW(R).....	Antiair Warfare Reporting [*Navy*] (NVT)
AAWR	Woomera [*Australia*] [*ICAO location identifier*] (ICLI)
AAWRATS ...	Antiair Warfare Readiness Assessment Training System (MCD)
AAWRC	American Agri-Women Resource Center (EA)
AAWS	Airborne Alert Weapon System
AAWS	Alcoholics Anonymous World Services [*Canada*]
AAWS	Antiair Warfare Systems [*Navy*] (MCD)
AAWS	Automatic Attack Warning System (AFM)
AAWS	Automatic Aviation Weather Service (FAAC)
AAWSAU ...	Abhandlungen. Deutschen Akademie der Wissenschaften zu Berlin [*A publication*]
AAWS-H...	Advanced Antitank Weapon System - Heavy
AAWS-M ..	Advanced Antiarmor Weapon System, Medium [*Army*] (INF)
AAWS-M ..	Advanced Antitank Weapon System - Medium [*Pronounced "awesome"*] (RDA)
AAWSSC ..	Army Atomic Weapons Systems Safety Committee [*Later, DNA*] (AABC)
AAWSUP ...	Antiair Warfare Support (NVT)
AAWTD2 ..	Abhandlungen. Akademie der Wissenschaften der DDR. Abteilung Mathematik, Naturwissenschaften, Technik [*A publication*]
AAWTG	Agricultural and Allied Workers' National Trade Group [*British*]
AAWV	American Association of Wildlife Veterinarians (EA)
AAWW	Anzeiger. Oesterreichische Akademie der Wissenschaften (Wien). Philosophisch-Historische Klasse [*A publication*]
AAWWS...	Airborne Adverse Weather Weapons System (MCD)
AAWWW ..	Amalgamated Association of Wistful War Wives [*World War II*]
AAX	Araxa [*Brazil*] [*Airport symbol*] (OAG)
AAXICO....	American Air Export & Import Company
AAXRAW ...	ANARE [*Australian National Antarctic Research Expeditions*] Interim Reports. Series A [*A publication*]
AAY	Alloway Air [*Oak Harbor, WA*] [*FAA designator*] (FAAC)
AAYA	Authors and Artists for Young Adults [*A publication*]
AAYM	American Association of Youth Museums (EA)
AAYO........	All-American Youth Orchestra
AAYPA......	Annals. American Academy of Political and Social Science [*A publication*]
AAYPL......	Atlantic Association of Young Political Leaders (EA)
AAYPP......	American Association of Yellow Pages Publishers [*Defunct*] (EA)
AAYSO......	Afro-Asian Youth Solidarity Organization (NATG)
AAZ	Oakland, CA [*Location identifier*] [*FAA*] (FAAL)
AAZK	American Association of Zoo Keepers (EA)
AAZN	American Association for Zoological Nomenclature (EA)
AAZPA......	American Association of Zoological Parks and Aquariums (EA)
AAZPA (Am Assoc Zool Parks Aquariums) Annu Proc ...	AAZPA (American Association of Zoological Parks and Aquariums) Annual Proceedings [*A publication*]
AAZPA (Am Assoc Zool Parks Aquariums) Natl Conf ...	AAZPA (American Association of Zoological Parks and Aquariums) National Conference [*A publication*]
AAZV	American Association of Zoo Veterinarians (EA)
AB	AB Bookman's Weekly [*A publication*]
Ab..............	Abbas Antiquus [*Deceased, 1296*] [*Authority cited in pre-1607 legal work*] (DSA)
AB	Abbey [*or Abbot*]
AB	Abbreviation (ROG)
AB	Abdomen [*Medicine*]
AB	ABI American Businessphones [*AMEX symbol*] (SPSG)
AB	Able-Bodied Seaman
AB	Aboriginal [*Australian*] (DSUE)
AB	Abortion Patient [*Medicine*]
Ab..............	Aboth (BJA)
AB	About
Ab..............	Abridgment (DLA)
Ab..............	Abruzzo [*A publication*]
AB	Absent (ROG)
AB	Abstract [*Online database field identifier*]
AB	Abstracting Board [*International Council of Scientific Unions*] [*Information service or system*] (IID)
Ab..............	Abstracts of Treasury Decisions [*United States*] [*A publication*] (DLA)
AB	Abyssinia
AB	Accessories Bulletin (MCD)
AB	Accident Benefits [*Insurance*]
AB	Acquisition Beacon
AB	Acta Baltica [*A publication*]
AB	Actividades Aereas Aragonesas [*ICAO designator*] (FAAC)
AB	Acute Bisectrix [*Crystallography*]
AB	Adapter Booster
AB	Adapter, Bulkhead
AB	Adaptive Behavior [*Psychology*]
AB	Additional Benefits [*Unemployment insurance*]
AB	Address Buffer (MCD)
AB	Address Bus [*Data processing*]
AB	Adjustment Bond [*Investment term*]
AB	Administrative Battalion [*British military*] (DMA)
AB	Administrative Bulletin (MCD)
AB	Admiralty Board [*British*]
AB	Advance Purchase Required [*Also, AP*] [*Airline fare code*]
AB	Advisory Board
AB	Advocatenblad [*A publication*]
AB	Aerial Burst Bombs
AB	Aero Talleres Boero SRL [*Argentina*] [*ICAO aircraft manufacturer identifier*] (ICAO)
AB	Aeronautical Board [*Air Force*]
AB	African Business [*A publication*]
AB	Africana Bulletin [*Warsaw*] [*A publication*]
AB	After Body
AB	Afterburner [*on jet engines*]
AB	Aid to the Blind
AB	Air Bags
AB	Air Base
AB	Air Bearing (KSC)
AB	Air Berlin USA [*ICAO designator*] (ICDA)
AB	Air Blast (MSA)
AB	Air Board [*RAF*] [*British*]
AB	Air Bomber
A/B	Air Breather [*Aerospace*]
AB	Air Brick
AB	Air-Cushion Vehicle built by Air Bearings [*England*] [*Usually used in combination with numerals*]
A > B........	Air Greater Than Bone [*Conduction*]
AB	Airborne
A/B	Aircraft Bulletin
AB	Airman Basic
AB	Aktiebolag [*or Aktiebolaget*] [*Joint-Stock Company*] [*Sweden*]
Ab.............	Aktiebolag [*Joint-Stock Company*] [*Finland*]
Ab.............	Alabamine [*Superseded by astatine*] [*Chemical element*]
AB	Alberta [*Canadian province*] [*Postal code*]
ab..............	Albite [*CIPW classification*] [*Geology*]
AB	Alcian Blue [*A biological stain*]
AB	Alert Building (NATG)
AB	All [*Text*] Before [*Specified Point*] [*Message handling*]
A-B...........	Allen-Bradley Co.
AB	Alliance Balkanique [*Balkan Alliance*]
AB	Alternative Broadcasting [*An association*] (EA)
AB	Ambush
AB	American Association of Teachers of Slavic and East European Languages. Bulletin [*A publication*]
AB	American Banker [*A publication*]
AB	American Bookman [*A publication*]
AB	American Bureau of Shipping
AB	AminoAzobenzene [*Organic chemistry*]
AB	Aminobenzamide [*Organic chemistry*]
AB	Aminobenzophenone [*Organic chemistry*]
AB	Ammunition Bearer [*Military*] (INF)
AB	Analecta Biblica [*Rome*] [*A publication*]
AB	Analecta Bollandiana [*A publication*]
AB	Anchor Bolt [*Technical drawings*]
AB	Anheuser-Busch, Inc.
AB	Ankina Breeders [*Inactive*] (EA)
A/B	Ankle/Brachial Pressure Index
AB	Anonymous Reports at End of Benloe [*1661*] [*England*] [*A publication*] (DLA)
AB	Antenna Supports [*JETDS nomenclature*] [*Military*] (CET)
AB	Anterior Burster [*Neuron*]
Ab.............	Antibody [*Also, aby*] [*Immunology*]
AB	Antigen-Binding [*Immunology*]
AB	Antiquarian Bookman [*A publication*]
AB	Apex Beat [*Medicine*]
AB	Application Block (MSA)
AB	Applied Biosystems, Inc.
AB	Arc Brazing
AB	Archbishop (ROG)
A/B	Architectural Barriers
AB	Arctic Bibliography [*A publication*]
AB	Armor Board (MCD)
AB	Armour Pharmaceutical Co. [*Research code symbol*]
AB	Army Book [*British and Canadian*] [*World War II*]
AB	Art Bulletin [*A publication*]
Ab.............	Artbibliographies Modern [*A publication*]
AB	Artium Baccalaureus [*Bachelor of Arts*]
AB	As Before
AB	Asbestos Corp. Ltd. [*Toronto Stock Exchange symbol*]
A & B	Assault and Battery
AB	Assault Breaker (MCD)
AB	Assembly Bill [*in state legislatures*]
AB	Assistance for the Blind
AB	Assistant Barrister [*British*] (ROG)

AB.............. Associate in Business
AB.............. Associated with Brokers [London Stock Exchange]
AB.............. Association of Bankrupts (EAIO)
AB.............. Association of Brewers [Later, AOB] (EA)
AB.............. Aster Growth with Brown Sedge [Ecology]
AB.............. Asthmatic Bronchitis [Medicine] (ADA)
AB.............. At Bat [Baseball]
AB.............. Audio Bandwidth
AB.............. Auer Bodies [Medicine]
aB.............. Auf Bestellung [On Order] [German] (ILCA)
AB.............. Augustana Bulletin [A publication]
AB.............. Australian Ballet
AB.............. Australian Baptist [A publication] (APTA)
AB.............. Australian Boating [A publication]
AB.............. Australian Bridge [A publication]
AB.............. Australian Business [A publication] (APTA)
AB.............. Auto Beacon (KSC)
AB.............. Automated Banking
AB.............. Automated Bibliography
AB.............. Automatic Blow Down (IEEE)
AB.............. Aviation Battalion [Army]
AB.............. Aviation Boatswain [Navy rating]
AB.............. Avionics Bay (MCD)
AB.............. Banff Library, Alberta [Library symbol] [National Library of Canada] (NLC)
ab----- .... Bengal, Bay of [MARC geographic area code] [Library of Congress] (LCCP)
AB.............. Birmingham Public and Jefferson County Free Library, Birmingham, AL [Library symbol] [Library of Congress] (LCLS)
AB.............. Bond Adjustment [Finance]
AB.............. Crane Ship [Navy symbol] [Obsolete]
AB.............. Dainippon Pharmaceutical Co. [Japan] [Research code symbol]
AB.............. Faulty Abbreviation [Used in correcting manuscripts, etc.]
AB.............. Roswell Park Memorial Institute [Research code symbol]
AB1............ Aviation Boatswain's Mate, First Class [Navy rating]
AB2............ Aviation Boatswain's Mate, Second Class [Navy rating]
AB3............ Aviation Boatswain's Mate, Third Class [Navy rating]
A 1888 B .... Australia 1888 Bulletin [A publication] (APTA)
A 1938-1988 B ... Australia 1938-1988 Bicentennial History Project. Bulletin [A publication] (APTA)
A 1938 B .... Australia 1938 Bulletin [A publication]
AB's .... Abdominal Muscles
AB's .... Asbestos Bodies
ABA.......... Aaron Burr Association (EA)
Aba............ Abaco [A publication]
ABA.......... Abacus [Australia] [A publication]
ABA.......... Abhandlungen. Bayerische Akademie der Wissenschaften [Munich] [A publication]
ABA.......... Abscisic Acid [Biochemistry]
ABA.......... Achievable Benefit Achieved
ABA.......... Aerial Biosensing Association (EA)
ABA.......... African Bar Association (EAIO)
ABA.......... African Business Association
ABA.......... Air Brake Association (EA)
ABA.......... Air New York, Inc. [Albany, NY] [FAA designator] (FAAC)
ABA.......... Airborne Assault (CINC)
ABA.......... Aktiebolaget Aero Transport [Swedish airline]
ABA.......... Aktiebolaget Atomenergi [Swedish nuclear development company]
ABA.......... Alger-Bouzareah [Algeria] [Seismograph station code, US Geological Survey] (SEIS)
ABA.......... Alien Business Act [1979] [Thailand] (IMH)
ABA.......... Allergic Bronchopulmonary Aspergillosis [Medicine]
ABA.......... Amateur Boxing Association [British]
ABA.......... American Badminton Association [Later, USBA] (EA)
ABA.......... American Bakers Association (EA)
ABA.......... American Bandmasters Association (EA)
ABA.......... American Bankers Association [Washington, DC] (EA)
ABA.......... American Bantam Association (EA)
ABA.......... American Baptist Association
ABA.......... American Bar Association (EA)
ABAC........ American Bartenders' Association (EA)
ABA.......... American Basketball Association [Later, NBA] [League of professional basketball players] (EA)
ABA.......... American Bass Association (EA)
ABA.......... American Battleship Association (EA)
ABA.......... American Beauty Association (EA)
ABA.......... American Beefalo Association (EA)
ABA.......... American Behcet's Association (EA)
ABA.......... American Bell Association [Later, ABAI] (EA)
ABA.......... American Benedictine Academy (EA)
ABA.......... American Berkshire Association (EA)
ABA.......... American Bicycle Association (EA)
ABA.......... American Billiard Association (EA)
ABA.......... American Birding Association (EA)
ABA.......... American Board of Anesthesiology (EA)
ABA.......... American Boccaccio Association (EA)
ABA.......... American Book Awards [Formerly, TABA]
ABA.......... American Booksellers Association (EA)
ABA.......... American Bowhunters Association [Defunct] (EA)

ABA .... American Bralers Association (EA)
ABA .... American Brazilian Association [Later, Brazilian American Chamber of Commerce] (EA)
ABA .... American Breed Association (EA)
ABA .... American Breweriana Association (EA)
ABA .... American Bridge Association (EA)
ABA .... American, British, Australian [Military] (AABC)
ABA .... American Buddhist Academy (EA)
ABA .... American Buddhist Association (EA)
ABA .... American Buffalo Association (EA)
ABA .... American Bullmastiff Association (EA)
ABA .... American Burn Association (EA)
ABA .... American Bus Association (EA)
ABA .... American Business Association [New York, NY] (EA)
ABA .... Aminobutyric Acid [Also, Abu] [Organic chemistry]
ABA .... Amplifier Buffer Attenuator (MCD)
A de Ba...... Andreas Bonellus de Barulo [Flourished, 1260-71] [Authority cited in pre-1607 legal work] (DSA)
ABa............ Annee Balzacienne [A publication]
ABA .... Annual Budget Authorization (AFM)
ABA .... Antiquarian Booksellers Association [International]
ABA .... Antoniani Benedictini Armeni [Mechitarists]
ABA .... Applied Behavior Analysis [Psychology]
ABA .... Appropriation and Budget Activity [Army] (AABC)
ABA .... Arab Bankers' Association
ABA .... Archives of the Canadian Rockies, Banff, Alberta [Library symbol] [National Library of Canada] (NLC)
ABA .... Armadillo Breeders Association [Defunct] (EA)
ABA .... ASEAN [Association of South East Asian Nations] Bankers Association [Singapore, Singapore] (EAIO)
ABA .... Associate in Business Administration
ABA .... Association for Behavior Analysis (EA)
ABA .... Association Belgo-Americaine [Belgian-American Association] (EA)
ABA .... Association of Black Anthropologists (EA)
ABA .... Ateba Mines, Inc. [Toronto Stock Exchange symbol]
ABA .... Australian Bicentennial Authority
ABA .... Australian Biotechnology Association
ABA .... Australian Blue Asbestos
ABA .... Australian Braille Authority
ABA .... Authorized Bond Allotment (MCD)
ABA .... Ayrshire Breeders' Association (EA)
ABA .... Azobenzenearsonate [Also, ARS] [Organic chemistry]
a-ba--- .... Bahrain [MARC geographic area code] [Library of Congress] (LCCP)
ABA .... Whyte Museum of the Canadian Rockies (Archives), Banff, Alberta [Library symbol] [National Library of Canada] (NLC)
ABAA .... Airman Apprentice, Aviation Boatswain's Mate, Striker [Navy rating]
ABAA .... American Beverage Alcohol Association (EA)
ABAA .... American Blonde d'Aquitaine Association (EA)
ABAA .... Antiquarian Booksellers Association of America (EA)
ABA Antitrust L J ... American Bar Association. Antitrust Law Journal [A publication]
ABAAR...... Regional Office, Alberta Agriculture, Barrhead, Alberta [Library symbol] [National Library of Canada] (NLC)
ABABA..... Annales de Biologie Animale, Biochimie, et Biophysique [A publication]
ABA Banking J ... ABA [American Bankers Association] Banking Journal [A publication]
ABA Bank J ... ABA [American Bankers Association] Banking Journal [A publication]
ab Abr .... Ab Abraham [The chronological reckoning from the first year of Abraham; St. Jerome's translation and enlargement of Eusebius' Chronicle] [Classical studies] (OCD)
ABAC .... Abraham Baldwin Agricultural College [Tifton, GA]
ABAC .... Alpine Club, Banff, Alberta [Library symbol] [National Library of Canada] (NLC)
ABAC .... American Bosch Arma Corporation (AAG)
ABAC .... Antiquarian Booksellers Association of Canada
ABAC .... Association of Balloon and Airship Constructors (EA)
ABACC....... Alcoholic Beverages Advertising Code Council [Australia]
ABACCL..... ABA [American Bar Association] Center on Children and the Law (EA)
ABA Comp L Bull ... American Bar Association. Comparative Law Bureau. Annual Bulletin [A publication]
ABACPD... American Bar Association Center for Professional Discipline (DLA)
ABACPR ... American Bar Association Center for Professional Responsibility (EA)
ABACS...... Distance Education Research Centre Library, Alberta Correspondence School, Barrhead, Alberta [Library symbol] [National Library of Canada] (BIB)
ABACUS... Air Battle Analysis Center Utility System [Air Force]
ABACUS... Aktiebolaget Atomenergi Computer-Based User-Oriented Service
ABACUS... Association of Bibliographic Agencies of Britain, Australia, Canada, and the United States (ADA)
ABACUS... Autonetics Business & Control United Systems, Inc.
ABAD .... Air Base Air Defense [Air Force] (MCD)

ABAD .... Air Battle Analysis Division [*Air Force*]
ABADRL ... Arthropod-Borne Animal Diseases Research Laboratory [*Department of Agriculture*] (GRD)
ABAE .... Amateur Boxing Association of England (EAIO)
ABAE .... American Body Armor & Equipment, Inc. [*NASDAQ symbol*] (NQ)
ABaeG .... Amsterdamer Beitraege zur Aelteren Germanistik [*A publication*]
ABAF .... Brisbane/Archerfield [*Australia*] [*ICAO location identifier*] (ICLI)
ABAFAOILSS ... Association of Black Admissions and Financial Aid Officers of the Ivy League and Sister Schools (EA)
ABAFLSMAC ... American Bar Association, Family Law Section, Mediation and Arbitration Committee [*Defunct*] (EA)
ABAG .... Amsterdamer Beitraege zur Aelteren Germanistik [*A publication*]
ABAH .... Alberta Horticultural Research Centre, Brooks, Alberta [*Library symbol*] [*National Library of Canada*] (NLC)
ABAI .... American Bell Association International (EA)
ABAI .... American Board of Allergy and Immunology (EA)
ABA J .... American Bar Association. Journal [*A publication*]
ABA Jo ...... American Bar Association. Journal [*A publication*]
ABA Jour .... American Bar Association. Journal [*A publication*]
Abak Artikulaere Periartikulaere Entzuendungen ... Abakterielle, Artikulaere, und Periartikulaere Entzuendungen [*A publication*]
ABAKO ..... Alliance des Bakongo [*Alliance of the Bakongo People*]
ABAKWA ... Alliance de Baboma-Bateke du Kwamouth [*Alliance of Baboma-Bateke People of Kwamouth*]
ABAL .... Aminobutyraldehyde [*Organic chemistry*]
ABA/LSD ... Law Student Division - American Bar Association (EA)
ABalt-Slav .. Acta Baltico-Slavica [*A publication*]
A Balzac .... Annee Balzacienne [*A publication*]
ABAM .... Amberley [*Australia*] [*ICAO location identifier*] (ICLI)
ABAM .... Bawlf Municipal Library, Alberta [*Library symbol*] [*National Library of Canada*] (NLC)
ABAMP .... Absolute Ampere
AbAn .... Abstracts in Anthropology [*A publication*]
ABAN .... Airman, Aviation Boatswain's Mate, Striker [*Navy rating*]
ABAN .... Asian Bureau Australia Newsletter [*A publication*]
ABANA ...... Artist Blacksmith Association of North America (EA)
ABAND ..... Abandoned
ABAND LT HO ... Abandoned Lighthouse
ABANDT ... Abandonment
ABAP .... Alabama Power Co., Birmingham, AL [*Library symbol*] [*Library of Congress*] (LCLS)
ABAP .... Anais. Bibliotecas e Arquivos de Portugal [*A publication*]
ABAPSTAS ... Association of Blind and Partially-Sighted Teachers and Students [*British*]
ABAR .... Advanced [*or Alternate*] Battery Acquisition RADAR
ABAR .... Alberta RCMP Century Library, Beaverlodge, Alberta [*Library symbol*] [*National Library of Canada*] (NLC)
ABAR .... Auxiliary Battery Acquisition RADAR (MCD)
ABARE ...... Australian Bureau of Agricultural and Resource Economics
ABA Rep .... American Bar Association Reporter [*A publication*] (DLA)
ABA Rep .... American Bar Association Reports [*A publication*] (DLA)
ABA Rep Int'l & Comp L Sec ... American Bar Association. International and Comparative Law Section. Reports [*A publication*] (DLA)
ABARHP ... American Bar Association Representation of the Homeless Project (EA)
ABARM .... Barnwell Municipal Library, Alberta [*Library symbol*] [*National Library of Canada*] (NLC)
ABARR ...... Barrhead Public Library, Alberta [*Library symbol*] [*National Library of Canada*] (NLC)
ABAS .... Alice Springs [*Australia*] [*ICAO location identifier*] (ICLI)
ABAS .... American Board of Abdominal Surgery (EA)
ABAS .... Bassano Public Library, Alberta [*Library symbol*] [*National Library of Canada*] (NLC)
ABASCDR ... American Bar Association Special Committee on Dispute Resolution (EA)
ABA Sec Lab Rel L ... American Bar Association. Section of Labor Relations Law (DLA)
ABA Sect Antitrust L ... American Bar Association. Section of Antitrust Law [*A publication*]
ABA Sect Crim L ... American Bar Association. Section of Criminal Law [*A publication*]
ABA Sect Ins N & CL ... American Bar Association. Section of Insurance, Negligence, and Compensation Law [*A publication*]
ABA Sect Int & Comp L Bull ... American Bar Association. Section of International and Comparative Law. Bulletin [*A publication*]
ABA Sect Lab Rel L ... American Bar Association. Section of Labor Relations Law [*A publication*]
ABA Sect M & NRL ... American Bar Association. Section of Mineral and Natural Resources Law [*A publication*]
ABA Sect Real Prop L ... American Bar Association. Section of Real Property, Probate, and Trust Law. Proceedings [*A publication*]
ABASH ..... Bashaw Public Library, Alberta [*Library symbol*] [*National Library of Canada*] (NLC)
ABASILP .. American Bar Association Section of International Law and Practice (EA)
ABASS ...... Air Base Augmentation Support Set [*Air Force*] (AFM)

ABASS ...... Assembly for Behavioral and Social Sciences [*National Research Council*]
ABAT .... Abatement [*Legal term*] (DLA)
ABAT .... Air Base Advisory Team (CINC)
ABA/TCP ... Traffic Court Program of the American Bar Association (EA)
ABATE ...... Alliance des Bateke [*Alliance of Bateke*]
Ab Atomenergi (Stockholm) AE ... Aktiebolaget Atomenergi (Stockholm). Rapport AE [*A publication*]
Ab Atomenergi Stockholm Rapp ... Aktiebolaget Atomenergi Stockholm Rapport [*A publication*]
A Batt .... A Battuta [*Music*]
ABATU ...... Advanced Base Aviation Training Unit [*Navy*]
ABAU .... University of Alabama in Birmingham, Birmingham, AL [*Library symbol*] [*Library of Congress*] (LCLS)
ABAU-M... University of Alabama in Birmingham, Lister Hill Library of the Health Sciences, Birmingham, AL [*Library symbol*] [*Library of Congress*] (LCLS)
ABAUSA... Amateur Basketball Association of the United States of America [*Later, USA Basketball*] (EA)
ABAW .... Abhandlungen. Bayerische Akademie der Wissenschaften. Philosophisch-Historische Klasse [*A publication*]
ABAYLD... American Bar Association Young Lawyers Division (EA)
ABAZI .... Alliance des Bayanzi [*Alliance of Bayanzis*]
Abb .... Abbassamento [*Music*]
Abb .... Abbey [*Record label*]
ABB .... Abbey [*or Abbess or Abbot*]
ABB .... Abbey Exploration, Inc. [*Toronto Stock Exchange symbol*]
Abb .... Abbildungen [*Illustration, Figure*] [*German*] (BJA)
Abb .... Abbott Laboratories
Abb .... Abbott. United States Circuit and District Court Reports [*A publication*] (DLA)
ABB .... Abbreviation (ROG)
ABB .... Ablating Blunt Body
ABB .... Absatzwirtschaft; Zeitschrift fuer Marketing [*A publication*]
ABB .... Added Belly Band [*Military*] (CAAL)
ABB .... [*The*] Akron & Barberton Belt Railroad Co. [*AAR code*]
AbB .... Altbabylonische Briefe im Umschrift und Uebersetzung [*A publication*] (BJA)
ABB .... American Board of Bioanalysis (EA)
ABB .... Anterior Basal Body
ABB .... Applied Biochemistry and Biotechnology [*A publication*]
ABB .... Archives et Bibliotheques de Belgique [*A publication*]
ABB .... Arizona Business [*A publication*]
ABB .... Artificial Breeding Box
ABB .... ASEA [*Allmaenna Svenska Elektriska Aktiebolaget*]-Brown Boveri [*Commercial firm*] (ECON)
ABB .... Australian Bankruptcy Bulletin [*A publication*] (APTA)
ABB .... Automatic Back Bias [*RADAR*]
ABB .... Axisymmetric Blunt Body
ABB .... Nabb, IN [*Location identifier*] [*FAA*] (FAAL)
ABBA .... Agnetha Faltskog, Bjorn Ulvaeus, Benny Andersson, Anni-Frid Lyngstad [*Swedish singing group; acronym formed from first letters of their first names*]
ABBA .... American Bail Bondsman Association (EA)
ABBA .... American Bed and Breakfast Association (EA)
ABBA .... American Bee Breeders Association (EA)
ABBA .... American Blind Bowling Association (EA)
ABB-A .... American Board of Bio-Analysis [*Defunct*] [*No connection with ABB*] (EA)
ABBA .... American Brahman Breeders Association (EA)
ABBA .... Arbejdsloshedsstatistikkens Bruger-Bank [*Danmarks Statistik*] [*Denmark*] [*Information service or system*] (CRD)
ABBACG ... Analele. Universitatii Bucuresti. Biologie Animala [*A publication*]
Abb Ad ...... Abbott's Admiralty Reports [*United States*] [*A publication*] (DLA)
ABBADH .. Acta Botanica Barcinonensia [*A publication*]
Abb Adm.... Abbott's Admiralty Reports [*United States*] [*A publication*] (DLA)
Abb Ad R ... Abbott's Admiralty Reports [*United States*] [*A publication*] (DLA)
Abb Ap Dec ... Abbott's Court of Appeals Decisions [*New York*] [*A publication*] (DLA)
Abb App Dec ... Abbott's Court of Appeals Decisions [*New York*] [*A publication*] (DLA)
ABBB .... Association of Better Business Bureaus [*Later, CBBB*] (EA)
ABBB .... Brisbane [*Australia*] [*ICAO location identifier*] (ICLI)
Abb Beech Tr .. Abbott's Reports of the Beecher Trial [*A publication*] (DLA)
ABBBMR .. Another Boring Book Bi-Monthly Rag [*Subtitle for the periodical Slightly Soiled*] [*British*] [*A publication*]
ABBC .... American Baptist Black Caucus (EA)
ABBC .... Association of Bottled Beer Collectors (EAIO)
Abb CC ...... Abbott's Circuit Court Reports [*United States*] [*A publication*] (DLA)
Abb Cl Ass ... Abbott's Clerks and Conveyancers' Assistant [*A publication*] (DLA)
Abb Ct App ... Abbott's Court of Appeals Decisions [*New York*] [*A publication*] (DLA)
Abb Ct of App Dec ... Abbott's Court of Appeals Decisions [*New York*] [*A publication*] (DLA)
Abb Dec ..... Abbott's Decisions [*A publication*] (DLA)

Abb Dict..... Abbott's Dictionary [*A publication*] (DLA)
Abb Dig...... Abbott's New York Digest [*A publication*] (DLA)
Abb Dig Corp ... Abbott's Digest of the Law of Corporations [*A publication*] (DLA)
ABBE......... Advisory Board on the Built Environment [*Formerly, BRAB*] (EA)
Abb F .... Abbott's Forms of Pleading [*A publication*] (DLA)
ABBF .... Advanced Beef Breeds Federation (EA)
Abb F Sup ... Abbott's Forms of Pleading, Supplement [*A publication*] (DLA)
ABBGB...... Animal Blood Groups and Biochemical Genetics [*A publication*]
ABBIA4..... Archives of Biochemistry and Biophysics [*A publication*]
AB (Bible) ... Bachelor of Arts in Bible
ABBIM...... Association of Brass and Bronze Ingot Manufacturers (EA)
Abb Ind Dig ... Abbott's Indiana Digest [*A publication*] (DLA)
Abb Int........ Abbott's Introduction to Practice under the Codes [*A publication*] (DLA)
ABBK......... Abington Bancorp, Inc. [*NASDAQ symbol*] (NQ)
AB Bkman's W ... AB Bookman's Weekly [*A publication*]
Abb Law Dict ... Abbott's Law Dictionary [*1879*] [*A publication*] (DLA)
Abb L Dic... Abbott's Law Dictionary [*1879*] [*A publication*] (DLA)
Abb Leg Rem ... Abbott's Legal Remembrancer [*A publication*] (DLA)
ABBM....... Baptist Medical Center, School of Nursing, Birmingham, AL [*Library symbol*] [*Library of Congress*] (LCLS)
ABBM-M .. Baptist Medical Center (Montclair), Medical Library, Birmingham, AL [*Library symbol*] [*Library of Congress*] (LCLS)
Abb Mo Ind ... Abbott's Monthly Index [*A publication*] (DLA)
ABBM-P.... Baptist Medical Center (Princeton), Medical Library, Birmingham, AL [*Library symbol*] [*Library of Congress*] (LCLS)
ABBMS..... American Board of Bloodless Medicine and Surgery (EA)
ABBN .... Brisbane [*Australia*] [*ICAO location identifier*] (ICLI)
Abb Nat Dig ... Abbott's National Digest [*A publication*] (DLA)
Abb NC...... Abbott's New Cases [*New York*] [*A publication*] (DLA)
Abb N Cas ... Abbott's New Cases [*New York*] [*A publication*] (DLA)
Abb New Cas ... Abbott's New Cases [*New York*] [*A publication*] (DLA)
Abb NS ...... Abbott's Practice Reports, New Series [*New York*] [*A publication*] (DLA)
Abb NY App ... Abbott's Court of Appeals Decisions [*New York*] [*A publication*] (DLA)
Abb NY Dig ... Abbott's New York Digest [*A publication*] (DLA)
Abb NY Dig 2d ... Abbott's New York Digest, Second [*A publication*] (DLA)
ABBO .... Associate of the British Ballet Organisation
ABBOTSB ... Abbotsbury [*England*]
Abbott........ Abbott on Merchant Ships and Seaman [*1802-1901*] [*A publication*] (DLA)
Abbott .... Abbott's Dictionary [*A publication*] (DLA)
Abbott Civ Jur Tr ... Abbott on Civil Jury Trials [*A publication*] (ILCA)
Abbott Civ Jury Trials ... Abbott on Civil Jury Trials [*A publication*] (DLA)
Abbott Crim Tr Pr ... Abbott on Criminal Trial Practice [*A publication*] (DLA)
Abbott PR .. Abbott's Practice Reports [*New York*] [*A publication*] (DLA)
Abbott Pract Cas ... Abbott's Practice Reports [*New York*] [*A publication*] (DLA)
Abbott Pr Rep ... Abbott's Practice Reports [*New York*] [*A publication*] (DLA)
Abbott's Adm ... Abbott's Admiralty Reports [*United States*] [*A publication*] (DLA)
Abbott's Ad Rep ... Abbott's Admiralty Reports [*United States*] [*A publication*] (DLA)
Abbott's NC ... Abbott's New Cases [*New York*] [*A publication*] (DLA)
Abbott's Prac Rep ... Abbott's Practice Reports [*New York*] [*A publication*] (DLA)
Abbott's Pr Rep ... Abbott's Practice Reports [*New York*] [*A publication*] (DLA)
Abbott USR ... Abbott's United States Circuit and District Courts Reports [*A publication*] (DLA)
Abbott US Rep ... Abbott's United States Circuit and District Courts Reports [*A publication*] (DLA)
Abb Pl........ Abbott's Pleadings under the Code [*A publication*] (DLA)
Abb PR ...... Abbott's Practice Reports [*New York*] [*A publication*] (DLA)
Abb Prac.... Abbott's Practice Reports [*New York*] [*A publication*] (DLA)
Abb Prac NS ... Abbott's Practice Reports, New Series [*New York*] [*A publication*] (DLA)
Abb Pr NS ... Abbott's Practice Reports, New Series [*New York*] [*A publication*] (DLA)
Abb Pr Rep ... Abbott's Practice Reports [*New York*] [*A publication*] (DLA)
ABBR......... Abbreviation (AFM)
ABBR......... Brisbane [*Australia*] [*ICAO location identifier*] (ICLI)
ABBRA...... American Boat Builders and Repairers Association (EA)
ABBREV ... Abbreviation (EY)
Abbrev Plac ... Placitorum Abbreviatio, Record Commissioner [*England*] [*A publication*] (DLA)
ABBRON .. Abbreviation (ROG)
ABBRP...... American Board of Bionic Rehabilitative Psychology (EA)
ABBR PO... Abbreviated Purchase Order
Abb RPS ... Abbott's Real Property Statutes [*A publication*] (DLA)
ABBS......... American Brittle Bone Society (EA)
ABBS .... Apple Bulletin Board System [*Pronounced "abbies"*]
ABBS .... Australian Bird Banding Scheme

ABBS .... Beaverlodge High School, Alberta [*Library symbol*] [*National Library of Canada*] (BIB)
ABBSAY ... Archives Belges de Dermatologie et de Syphiligraphie [*A publication*]
Abb Sh ...... Abbott on Shipping [*A publication*] (DLA)
Abb Ship.... Abbott on Shipping [*A publication*] (DLA)
ABBT......... Animated Backlighted Burtek Trainer
Abb Tr Ev .. Abbott's Trial Evidence [*A publication*] (DLA)
ABBU .... Bundaberg [*Australia*] [*ICAO location identifier*] (ICLI)
Abb US ...... Abbott's Circuit Court Reports [*United States*] [*A publication*] (DLA)
Abb USCC ... Abbott's United States Circuit and District Courts Reports [*A publication*] (DLA)
Abb US Pr ... Abbott's Practice in the United States Courts [*A publication*] (DLA)
ABBWA..... American Black Book Writers Association (EA)
ABBX......... Brisbane [*Australia*] [*ICAO location identifier*] (ICLI)
Abb Y Bk ... Abbott's Year Book of Jurisprudence [*A publication*] (DLA)
ABBZAL ... Acta Botanica Instituti Botanici. Universitatis Zagrebensis [*A publication*]
ABC .... Abacus [*A publication*]
ABC .... Abeche [*Chad*] [*Seismograph station code, US Geological Survey*] [*Closed*] (SEIS)
ABC .... Aberford Resources Ltd. [*Toronto Stock Exchange symbol*]
ABC .... Aberrant Behavior Checklist [*Treatment effectiveness test*] [*Psychology*]
ABC .... [*To Be*] Able-Bodied, Bold, Courageous [*Promise made by members of the Junior Woodchucks, organization to which comic strip character Donald Duck's nephews belonged*]
ABC .... Abridged Building Classification for Architects, Builders, and Civil Engineers
ABC .... Abstracts in Biocommerce [*Biocommerce Data Ltd.*] [*England*] [*Information service or system*] [*A publication*]
ABC .... Academia Brasileira de Ciencias [*Brazil*] (MCD)
ABC .... Accent before Cooking [*Advertising slogan*]
ABC .... Acceptable Biological Catch [*Fishery management*] (MSC)
ABC .... Aconite, Belladonna, and Chloroform [*Liniment compound*]
ABC .... Act for Better Child Care Services
ABC .... Action Bell Canada
ABC .... Action for Brain-Handicapped Children [*Defunct*] (EA)
ABC .... Activating Event [*or Experience*], Belief System, Consequence [*Irrational behavior theory*] [*Psychotherapy*]
ABC .... Active Bioprosthetic Composition [*Artificial ligament*]
ABC .... Activity-Based Cost [*Management accounting system*]
ABC .... Adaptable Board Computer [*Signetics*]
ABC .... Administration by Competency [*Business term*]
ABC .... Adriamycin, BCNU [*Carmustine*], Cyclophosphamide [*Antineoplastic drug regimen*]
ABC .... Adriatic Base Command [*Military*]
ABC .... Advance Base Components [*Military*] (AFIT)
ABC .... Advance Baseline Configuration (MCD)
ABC .... Advance Booking Charter [*Airline fare*]
ABC .... Advanced Ballistics Concepts [*Air Force*] (MCD)
ABC .... Advanced Biomedical Capsule
ABC .... Advancing Blade Concept [*Helicopter*]
ABC .... Aerated Bread Company [*Chain of restaurants in London*]
ABC .... Afghan Border Crusade [*Later, NWFF*] (EA)
ABC .... African Bibliographic Center (EA)
ABC .... After Bottom Center [*Valve position*]
ABC .... Agricultural Biotechnology Center [*University of Maryland*] [*Research center*]
ABC .... Agricultural Business and Commerce
ABC .... Air Balance Consultants (EA)
ABC .... Air Bath Chamber
ABC .... Air Bubble Craft
ABC .... Airborne Control [*System*]
ABC .... Aircraft of Bomber Command [*British*]
ABC .... Aircraft Builders Council [*British*] (AIA)
ABC .... Airway Opened, Breathing Restored, and Circulation Restored [*Cardiopulmonary resuscitation*] [*Medicine*]
abc .... Alberta [*MARC country of publication code*] [*Library of Congress*] (LCCP)
ABC .... Alberta Ballet Company [*Canada*]
ABC .... Alcobaca [*Brazil*] [*Airport symbol*] (OAG)
ABC .... Alcoholic Beverage Control [*Board*]
ABC .... Ale, Bread, and Cheese
ABC .... Alexander Bonaparte Cust [*Antagonist of Agatha Christie's novel "The ABC Murders"*]
ABC .... Algemene Bedrijfsgroepen Centrale [*General Union of Workers in Miscellaneous Industries*] [*Netherlands*]
ABC .... All-in-One Business Contactbook [*A publication*]
ABC .... Alliance of British Clubs (EAIO)
ABC .... Allocations for Budgetary Control
ABC .... Allowable Biological Catch
ABC .... Almond Board of California (EA)
ABC .... Alpha Block Control Number [*Data processing*]
ABC .... Alum, Blood, and Charcoal [*A method of deodorizing by addition of a compound of these*] [*Medicine*]
ABC .... AmBase Corp. [*NYSE symbol*] (SPSG)
ABC .... American Ballet Competition (EA)
ABC .... American Baptist Churches

ABC	American Baptists Concerned (EA)
ABC	American Barefoot Club (EA)
ABC	American Beagle Club (EA)
ABC	American Beveren Club
ABC	American Bibliographical Center
ABC	American Blade Collectors (EA)
ABC	American Blood Commission (EA)
ABC	American Bloodhound Club (EA)
ABC	American Board for Certification in Orthotics and Prosthetics (EA)
ABC	American Book Collector [*A publication*]
ABC	American Book Council [*Defunct*] (EA)
ABC	American-Born Chinese
ABC	American Botanical Council (EA)
ABC	American Bowling Congress (EA)
ABC	American Boxer Club (EA)
ABC	American Brahma Club (EA)
ABC	American, British, and Canadian
ABC	American and British Commonwealth Association
ABC	American-British Conversation [*as ABC-1, a 1941 report that set forth Allied worldwide strategy*] [*World War II*]
ABC	American Brittany Club (EA)
ABC	American Broadcasting Companies, Inc. [*Subsidiary of Capital Cities/ABC, Inc.*]
ABC	American Bugatti Club (EA)
ABC	American Business Cancer [*in name "ABC Research Foundation"*]
ABC	American Business Conference [*Washington, DC*] (EA)
ABC	American Business Council, Malaysia (EA)
ABC	Americans for Better Care (EA)
ABC	Americans by Choice (EA)
ABC	AMIGOS [*Access Method for Indexed Data Generalized for Operating System*] Bibliographic Council (EA)
ABC	Amities Belgo-Congolaises [*Belgian-Congolese Friendship Association*]
ABC	Anchor Bible Commentary [*A publication*] (BJA)
ABC	Answer-Back Code [*Telecommunications*] (TEL)
ABC	Anterior Bulbar Cell [*Neurobiology*]
ABC	Antigen-Binding Capacity [*Immunology*]
ABC	Antiquarian Booksellers' Center (EA)
ABC	Any Boy Can [*Program*] [*Defunct*] (EA)
ABC	Anybody but Carter [*1976 presidential campaign*]
ABC	Apparel Business Control [*System*] [*Data processing*]
ABC	Applied Business Telecommunications [*San Ramon, CA*] [*Information service or system*] [*Telecommunications*] (TSSD)
ABC	Approach by Concept [*Information retrieval*]
ABC	Arab Banking Corporation
ABC	Architectural Barriers Committee (EA)
ABC	Argentina, Brazil, Chile
ABC	Arts and Business Council (EA)
ABC	Aruba, Bonaire, and Curacao [*Islands*]
ABC	Asian Basketball Confederation (EA)
ABC	Asian Benevolent Corps (EA)
ABC	Asphaltenic Bottom Cracking [*Hydrocarbon processing*]
ABC	Aspiration Biopsy Cytology [*Medicine*]
ABC	Assessment of Basic Competencies [*Child development test*]
ABC	Assessment Biological and Chemical [*Warfare*] (NATG)
ABC	Associated British Cinemas
ABC	Associated Builders and Contractors (EA)
ABC	Association des Banquiers Canadiens [*Canadian Bankers Association*]
ABC	Association of Baptist Chaplains (EA)
ABC	Association of Bendectin Children [*Later, ABDC*] (EA)
ABC	Association of Biotechnology Companies (EA)
ABC	Association of Bituminous Contractors (EA)
ABC	Association of Black Cardiologists (EA)
ABC	Association of Boards of Certification (EA)
ABC	Association of Bridal Consultants (EA)
ABC	Association of British Climatologists (EAIO)
ABC	Association for Business Communication [*Urbana, IL*] (EA)
ABC	Atanasoff-Berry Computer [*Early computer*]
AB & C	Atlanta, Birmingham & Coast Railroad Co.
ABC	Atomic, Biological, and Chemical [*as, ABC Officer, ABC Warfare*] [*Obsolete*]
ABC	Audit Bureau of Circulations (EA)
ABC	Augmented Bibliographic Citation (ADA)
ABC	Australia Bulk Carrier [*Shipping*]
ABC	Australian Bank of Commerce (ADA)
ABC	Australian Bankruptcy Cases [*A publication*] (APTA)
ABC	Australian Broadcasting Co.
ABC	Australian Business Computer [*A publication*] (APTA)
ABC	Auto Body Computer [*Software*] [*Automotive Computer Group*] [*Automotive engineering*]
ABC	Automatic Bandwidth Control
ABC	Automatic Bar Checker
ABC	Automatic Bass Compensation [*Radio*]
ABC	Automatic Bass Control
ABC	Automatic Bias Compensation
ABC	Automatic Bias Control
ABC	Automatic Bill Calling [*Later, MCCS*] [*Telecommunications*]
ABC	Automatic Binary Computer (ADA)
ABC	Automatic Blip Counter
ABC	Automatic Block Controller (MCD)
ABC	Automatic Boiling-Column Reactor
ABC	Automatic Bridge Control [*Navy*] (MCD)
ABC	Automatic Brightness Control [*Telecommunications*] (TEL)
ABC	Automation of Bibliography through Computerization [*ABC-Clio Press*]
ABC	Automotive Booster Clubs International (EA)
ABC	Aviation Boatswain's Mate, Chief [*Navy rating*]
ABC	Avidin-Biotin Complex [*Immunochemistry*]
ABC	Axiobuccocervical [*Dentistry*]
ABC	[*A*] Better Chance (EA)
ABC	[*A*] Brilliant Career
ABC	Brownvale Community Library, Alberta [*Library symbol*] [*National Library of Canada*] (NLC)
ABC	Jefferson County Court House, Birmingham, AL [*Library symbol*] [*Library of Congress*] (LCLS)
ABC	Refers to federal-aid program for improvement of (A) primary highway system, (B) secondary highway system, and (C) extensions of federal-aid primary and secondary highway systems in urban areas.
ABC	University of Alabama in Birmingham, Birmingham, AL [*OCLC symbol*] (OCLC)
ABCA	America, Britain, Canada, Australia (ADA)
ABCA	American Baseball Coaches Association (EA)
ABCA	American Black Chiropractors Association (EA)
ABCA	American Blade Collectors Association (EA)
ABCA	American Blue Cheese Association [*Defunct*] (EA)
ABCA	American Building Contractors Association (EA)
ABCA	American Business Communication Association [*Later, ABC*]
ABCA	Antique Bicycle Club of America (EA)
ABCA	Antique Bottle Collectors Association [*Defunct*]
ABCA	Army Bureau of Current Affairs [*To encourage British soldiers to think and talk about what they were fighting for*] [*World War II*]
ABCA	Association des Banques Centrales Africaines [*Association of African Central Banks*] (EAIO)
ABCA	Association of Biological Collections Appraisers (EA)
Ab Ca	Crawford and Dix's Irish Abridged Cases [*A publication*] (DLA)
ABCAA......	Arquivos Brasileiros de Cardiologia [*A publication*]
ABCAAJ ...	Arquivos Brasileiros de Cardiologia [*A publication*]
ABCA Bul ...	ABCA [*American Business Communication Association*] Bulletin [*A publication*]
ABCAIRSTD ...	American-British-Canadian Air Standardization Agreement (NG)
ABC-ASP ..	American-British-Canadian Army Standardization Program
ABCB........	Air Blast Circuit Breaker
ABCB........	American Board of Clinical Biofeedback (EA)
ABCB........	American Bottlers of Carbonated Beverages [*Later, NSDA*] (EA)
ABCBC......	Bear Point Community Library, Bear Canyon, Alberta [*Library symbol*] [*National Library of Canada*] (NLC)
ABCC.........	Airborne Battlefield Command and Control Center (MCD)
ABCC.........	Airborne Command Center
ABCC.........	Airborne Communications Center [*Military*]
ABCC.........	Alternative Birth Crisis Coalition (EA)
ABCC.........	American Board of Clinical Chemistry (EA)
ABCC.........	American Business Card Club (EA)
ABCC.........	American Business Computers Corp. [*NASDAQ symbol*] (NQ)
ABCC.........	Arab British Chamber of Commerce (DCTA)
ABCC.........	Association of British Chambers of Commerce
ABCC.........	Association of British Correspondence Colleges (EAIO)
ABCC.........	Atomic Bomb Casualty Commission [*Later, RERF*]
ABCC.........	Circuit Court Library, Birmingham, AL [*Library symbol*] [*Library of Congress*] (LCLS)
ABCCC......	Airborne Battlefield Command and Control Center [*Air Force*] (AFM)
ABCCTC ...	Advanced Base Combat Communication Training Center [*Pearl Harbor*]
ABCD	Able Seaman Clearance Diver
ABCD	Accelerated Business Collection and Delivery [*Postal Service*]
ABCD	Add BCD [*Binary Coded Decimal*] Number with Extend [*Data processing*]
ABCD	Adriamycin, Bleomycin, CCNU [*Lomustine*], Dacarbazine [*Antineoplastic drug regimen*]
ABCD	Advanced Base Construction Depot
ABCD	Agency for Business and Career Development (EA)
ABCD	Agrophysics Breeding Control Device [*Birth-control device for dogs*]
ABCD	Airway Opened, Breathing Restored, Circulation Restored, and Definitive Therapy [*Cardiopulmonary resuscitation*] [*Medicine*]
ABCD	America, Britain, China, and Dutch East Indies [*The ABCD Powers*] [*World War II*]
ABCD	Apache, Black Hawk, and Chinook Self-Deployments [*Military*]
ABCD	Archives, Bibliotheques, Collections, Documentation [*A publication*]
ABCD	Associacao Brasileiro dos Colecionadores de Discos [*Record label*] [*Brazil*]

ABCD .... Associated Baby Carriage Dealers (EA)
ABCD .... Association of Better Computer Dealers [*Later, ABCD: The Microcomputer Industry Association*] (EA)
ABCD .... Association of Biomedical Communication Directors (EA)
ABCD .... Association for Bridge Construction and Design (EA)
ABCD .... Asymmetry, Border, Color, and Diameter [*Rule*] [*Dermatology*]
ABCD .... [*USS*] Atlanta, [*USS*] Boston, [*USS*] Chicago, [*USS*] Dolphin [*The ABCD ships, so called because their construction began in the same year, 1883*]
ABCD .... Atomic, Biological, Chemical, and Damage Control
ABCD .... Automated Biological and Chemical Data [*System*]
ABCD .... Awaiting Bad Conduct Discharge [*Military*]
ABCDEF ... Allein bei Christo die Ewige Freude [*With Christ Alone Is Eternal Joy*] [*German*] [*Motto of Albrecht Gunther, Count Schwarzburg (1582-1634)*]
ABCDEF ... American Boys Club in Defense of Errol Flynn [*Facetious organization*]
ABCDEFGHIJ ... Automobile Builders' Combination Designed Especially for Getting Hitler including Japan [*Suggested name for Automotive Council for War Production*] [*World War II*]
ABCDE News ... Association of British Columbia Drama Educators. Newsletter [*A publication*]
ABCE .... Ann Baker College of English [*Australia*]
AB in CE .... Bachelor of Arts in Civil Engineering
ABCF .... As-Built Configuration File (MCD)
ABCFM ..... American Board of Commissioners for Foreign Missions [*Later, UCBWM*]
ABCG .... Coolangatta [*Australia*] [*ICAO location identifier*] (ICLI)
ABCH .... American Board of Clinical Hypnosis (EA)
AB in Ch E ... Bachelor of Arts in Chemical Engineering
ABCI .... Advanced Business Communications, Incorporated [*McLean, VA*] [*Telecommunications*] (TSSD)
ABCI .... Airport Business Center, Incorporated [*Minneapolis, MN*] [*Telecommunications*] (TSSD)
ABCI .... American Biomaterials Corporation [*Plainsboro, NJ*] [*NASDAQ symbol*] (NQ)
ABCI .... Automotive Booster Clubs International (EA)
ABCIA .... American Board of Clinical Immunology and Allergy (EA)
ABCIL .... Antibody Mediated Cell Dependent Immune Lympholysis [*Immunology*]
ABCK .... Alaska British Columbia Transportation Co. [*AAR code*]
ABCL .... American Board of Criminal Lawyers (EA)
ABCL .... As-Built Configuration Lists
ABCLA ...... Annales de Biologie Clinique [*A publication*]
ABCLDL .... Acta Bioquimica Clinica Latinoamericana [*A publication*]
ABCM .... Adriamycin, Bleomycin, Cyclophosphamide, Mitomycin C [*Antineoplastic drug regimen*]
ABCM .... Air Burst Contact Maker
ABCM .... Association of Building Component Manufacturers (EAIO)
ABCM .... Master Chief Aviation Boatswain's Mate [*Navy rating*]
ABCMC ..... Automotive Battery Charger Manufacturers Council (EA)
ABCMR ..... Army Board for Correction of Military Records
ABC Newsl ... International Association of Accident Boards and Commissions. Newsletter [*A publication*] (DLA)
ABCO .... Advanced Base Components [*Military*]
ABCP .... Airborne Command Post
ABCP .... American Board of Cardiovascular Perfusion (EA)
ABCP .... Asian Buddhists Conference for Peace (EAIO)
ABCP .... Association of Blind Chartered Physiotherapists
ABCP .... Automatic Bias Compensation (MSA)
ABCPAF .... Association of Black CPA [*Certified Public Accountant*] Firms [*Washington, DC*] (EA)
ABC Pol Sci ... Advance Bibliography of Contents: Political Science and Government [*A publication*]
ABCR .... American Bashkir Curly Registry (EA)
ABCR .... As-Built Configuration Record (NASA)
ABCR .... Association of Beverage Container Recyclers (EA)
ABCR .... Atomic, Biological, Chemical, and Radiological [*Warfare*] (NATG)
ABCRA ...... American-Byelorussian Cultural Relief Association (EA)
ABCRA2 .... Acta Botanica Croatica [*A publication*]
ABCRETT ... American Board of Certified and Registered Encephalographic Technicians and Technologists (EA)
ABCRF ...... American Business Cancer Research Foundation [*Later, ABFCR*] (EA)
ABCRS .... American Board of Colon and Rectal Surgery (EA)
ABCS .... Advanced Brake Control System (MCD)
ABCS .... Advisory Board for Cooperative Systems [*of ICIREPAT*]
ABCS .... American Bicentennial Commemorative Society [*Defunct*]
ABCS .... American Board of Cosmetic Surgery (EA)
ABCS .... American Board on Counseling Services [*Later, IACS*] (EA)
ABCS .... American British Cab Society (EA)
ABCS .... American Business Council of Singapore (EA)
ABCS .... Associated Body of Church Schoolmasters [*A union*] [*British*]
ABCS .... Automatic Blip Counter System
ABCS .... Automatic Broadcasting Control System [*Japan*]
ABCS .... Aviation Boatswain's Mate, Senior Chief [*Navy rating*]
ABCS .... Avionics Bay Cooling System
ABCS .... Bear Canyon School, Alberta [*Library symbol*] [*National Library of Canada*] (BIB)

ABCS .... Cairns [*Australia*] [*ICAO location identifier*] (ICLI)
ABCSC ...... American-British-Canadian Stores Catalogue (DEN)
ABCSP ...... American-British-Canadian Standardization Program
ABCST .... Automatic Broadcast (FAAC)
ABCT .... American Board of Chelation Therapy (EA)
ABCUDE .... Acta Botanica Cubana [*A publication*]
ABCV .... Affiliated Banc Corp. [*NASDAQ symbol*] (SPSG)
ABCV .... Charleville [*Australia*] [*ICAO location identifier*] (ICLI)
ABCW .... American Bakery and Confectionery Workers' International Union [*Later, BCTWIU*]
ABCW .... Atomic, Biological, Chemical Warfare
ABCWIU .... Aluminum, Brick, and Clay Workers International Union (EA)
ABCXA ..... Annales Biologiques [*A publication*]
ABD .... Abadan [*Iran*] [*Airport symbol*] (OAG)
ABD .... Abdicated (ROG)
ABD .... Abdomen
ABD .... Abduction [*FBI standardized term*]
ABD .... Aberdeen [*City and county in Scotland*] (ROG)
ABD .... Abiomed, Inc. [*AMEX symbol*] (SPSG)
ABD .... Aboard (FAAC)
ABD .... Access Block Diagram
ABD .... Adhesive Bonding [*Welding*]
ABD .... Adriamycin, Bleomycin, Dacarbazine [*Antineoplastic drug regimen*]
ABD .... Advanced Base Depot [*or Dock*] [*Obsolete*] [*Navy*]
ABD .... Aged, Blind, or Disabled [*HEW*]
ABD .... Airborne Ballistics Division [*NASA*] (KSC)
ABD .... Airborne Data Marketing Ltd. [*Vancouver Stock Exchange symbol*]
ABD .... Alien Business Decree [*Enacted in 1972*] [*Thailand*] (IMH)
ABD .... All But the Dissertation [*PhD candidates*]
ABD .... American Board of Dermatology (EA)
ABD .... Aminobenzamide [*Biochemistry*]
ABD .... Annular Base Drag
ABD .... Area Business Databank [*Information Access Co.*] [*Belmont, CA*] [*Information service or system*] (IID)
ABD .... Army Budget Directive
ABD .... Association of Blauvelt Descendants (EA)
ABD .... Australian Business Directory [*A publication*]
ABD .... Average Business Day [*Bell System*]
ABDA .... American, British, Dutch, Australian (ADA)
ABDA .... Bundesvereinigung Deutscher Apothekerverbande [*German Pharmaceutical Association Research Institute*] [*Information service or system*] (IID)
ABDACOM ... Advanced Base Depot Area Command
ABDACOM ... American-British-Dutch-Australian Supreme Command [*1942*]
ABDAFLOAT ... American-British-Dutch-Australian Naval Operational Command [*1942*]
ABDAIR .... American-British-Dutch-Australian Air Operational Command [*1942*]
ABDARM ... American-British-Dutch-Australian Army Operational Command [*1942*]
ABDC .... After Bottom Dead Center [*Valve position*]
ABDC .... Association of Birth Defect Children (EA)
ABDE .... Airport Bird Detection Equipment
ABDE .... Anfang Bedenk das Ende [*At the Beginning Consider the End*] [*German*] [*Motto of Bruno II, Count of Mansfeld (1545-1615)*]
ABDEB3 .... Anais Brasileiros de Dermatologia [*A publication*]
ABDER ...... Abduction, External Rotation [*Physiology*]
ABDFC ...... American Bouvier des Flandres Club (EA)
ABDI .... Administrative Board - Dress Industry (EA)
ABDIC .... Adriamycin, Bleomycin, Dacarbazine, CCNU [*Lomustine*] [*Antineoplastic drug regimen*]
ABDIR .... Abduction, Internal Rotation [*Physiology*]
ABDL .... Automatic Binary Data Link [*Data processing*] (CET)
ABDM .... Black Diamond Municipal Library, Alberta [*Library symbol*] [*National Library of Canada*] (NLC)
ABDMAQ ... Archives Belges de Dermatologie [*A publication*]
ABDMS ...... American Board of Dental Medicine and Surgery (EA)
ABDNSHP ... Abandon Ship (MSA)
Abdnt .... Abandonment [*Insurance*]
ABDOM ..... Abdomen
Abdom Surg ... Abdominal Surgery [*A publication*]
ABDP .... Association of British Directory Publishers (EAIO)
ABDPH ..... American Board of Dental Public Health (EA)
ABDR .... Aberdare [*Welsh depot code*]
ABDR .... Association of Blood Donor Recruiters (EA)
ABDS .... Accounting and Budget Distribution System [*Air Force*]
ABDS .... Associate of the British Display Society (DBQ)
ABDSA ...... Association of British Dental Surgery Assistants
ABDSAA ... Anais Brasileiros de Dermatologia e Sifiligrafia [*A publication*]
ABD/SCADS ... Air Base Defense/Sensor Communications and Display System [*Air Force*] (MCD)
ABDSRC ..... Sheep River Community Library, Black Diamond, Alberta [*Library symbol*] [*National Library of Canada*] (NLC)
ABDUC .... Abduction
ABDV .... Adriamycin, Bleomycin, Dacarbazine, Vinblastine [*Antineoplastic drug regimen*]
Abdy R Pr .. Abdy's Roman Civil Procedure [*A publication*] (DLA)

Abdy & W Gai ... Abdy and Walker's Gaius and Ulpian [*A publication*] (DLA)
Abdy & W Just ... Abdy and Walker's Justinian [*A publication*] (DLA)
ABE .... Aberdeen [*Scotland*] [*Seismograph station code, US Geological Survey*] (SEIS)
ABE .... Acetone, Butanol, and Ethanol [*Fermentation products*]
ABE .... Acute Bacterial Endocarditis [*Medicine*]
ABE .... Adult Basic Education
ABE .... Air-Based Electronics (MCD)
ABE .... Air-Breathing Engine (KSC)
ABE .... Air Burst Effect
A/BE .... Airborne Equipment (AAG)
ABE .... Akron Business and Economic Review [*A publication*]
ABE .... Allentown/Bethlehem/Easton [*Pennsylvania*] [*Airport symbol*]
ABE .... American Board of Endodontics (EA)
ABE .... Americans for Budget Equity (EA)
ABE .... Arithmetic Building Element [*Data processing*]
ABE .... Army Background Experiment
ABE .... Associated Borrowers Endorsement [*British*]
ABE .... Association of British Editors (EAIO)
ABE .... Aviation Boatswain's Mate, Launch and Recovery Equipment [*Navy rating*]
ABEA .... American Baptist Education Association [*Defunct*] (EA)
ABEA .... American Broncho-Esophagological Association (EA)
ABEAA ...... Aviation Boatswain's Mate, Launch and Recovery Equipment, Airman Apprentice [*Navy rating*]
ABEAG ...... Research Station, Agriculture Canada. Station de Recherches, Agriculture Canada, Beaverlodge, Alberta [*Library symbol*] [*National Library of Canada*] (NLC)
ABEAM ...... Beaumont Municipal Library, Alberta [*Library symbol*] [*National Library of Canada*] (NLC)
ABEAN ..... Aviation Boatswain's Mate, Launch and Recovery Equipment, Airman [*Navy rating*]
ABEAS ...... Association Belge des Entreprises d'Alimentation a Succursales [*Food chain stores*] [*Belgium*] (EY)
ABEBA ...... Annales Universitatis Scientiarum Budapestensis de Rolando Eoetvoes Nominatae. Sectio Biologica [*A publication*]
ABEC .... American Baptist Extension Corporation
ABEC .... Amphenol-Borg Electronics Corporation (MCD)
ABEC .... Annular Bearing Engineers Committee (EA)
ABEC .... Australian Business Education Council Ltd.
A'Beckett ... A'Beckett's Reserved Judgements [*Port Phillip*] [*A publication*] (APTA)
A'Beckett ... Judgments of the Supreme Court of New South Wales for the District of Port Philip [*1846-51*] [*A publication*] (DLA)
A'Beckett Res Judg ... A'Beckett's Reserved Judgements [*Victoria*] [*A publication*] (ILCA)
A'Beck Judg (Vic) ... A'Beckett's Reserved Judgements (Victoria) [*A publication*] (APTA)
A'Beck Judg (Vict) ... A'Beckett's Reserved Judgements (Victoria) [*A publication*]
A'Beck Res ... A'Beckett's Reserved Judgments [*Port Phillip*] [*Australia*] [*A publication*]
A'Beck Res Judg ... A'Beckett's Reserved Judgements [*A publication*] (ILCA)
A'Beck Res Judgm ... A'Beckett's Reserved Judgements [*A publication*] (APTA)
A'Beck RJ (NSW) ... A'Beckett's Reserved Judgements (New South Wales) [*A publication*] (APTA)
A'Beck RJ (PP) ... A'Beckett's Reserved Judgements (Port Phillip) [*A publication*] (APTA)
AB Ed .... Bachelor of Arts in Education
ABEDA ...... Arab Bank for Economic Development in Africa
ABEDIA ... Arab Bank for Economic Development in Africa
AB in EE ... Bachelor of Arts in Electrical Engineering
ABEEA ...... Annual Bulletin of the Electric Statistics for Europe [*A publication*]
ABEEG ...... Aberbeeg [*Welsh depot code*]
ABEF .... Brisbane [*Australia*] [*ICAO location identifier*] (ICLI)
ABEGB ...... Advances in Biomedical Engineering [*A publication*]
ABEGBE ... Advances in Biomedical Engineering [*A publication*]
ABEI .... (Aminobutyl)ethylisoluminol [*Biochemistry*]
Abeille Fr ... Abeille de France [*Later, Abeille de France et l'Apiculteur*] [*A publication*]
Abeille Fr Apic ... Abeille de France et l'Apiculteur [*A publication*]
Abeille Med (Paris) ... Abeille Medicale (Paris) [*A publication*]
Abeill Fr Apicul ... Abeille de France et l'Apiculteur [*A publication*]
ABEL .... Acid/Base Electrolyte [*Disorder diagnosed by an experimental medical system of the same name*]
ABEL .... Air-Breathing Electric LASER (MCD)
ABelges ...... Archives Belges [*A publication*]
ABELL ...... Annual Bibliography of English Language and Literature [*A publication*]
ABELM ..... Bellevue Municipal Library, Alberta [*Library symbol*] [*National Library of Canada*] (NLC)
ABEM .... American Board of Emergency Medicine (EA)
ABEM .... American Board of Environmental Medicine (EA)
ABEM .... Beiseker Municipal Library, Alberta [*Library symbol*] [*National Library of Canada*] (NLC)
ABEN .... Bentley Public Library, Alberta [*Library symbol*] [*National Library of Canada*] (NLC)

ABENA ..... Arquivos Brasileiros de Endocrinologia e Metabolia [*A publication*]
ABENAY ... Arquivos Brasileiros de Endocrinologia e Metabolia [*A publication*]
ABEND ..... Abnormal End [*Data processing*]
ABE News ... Action for Better Education Newsletter [*A publication*] (APTA)
A Ben R ..... American Benedictine Review [*A publication*]
AbEnSt ...... Abstracts of English Studies [*A publication*]
ABEP .... American Board of Examiners in Psychotherapy (EA)
ABEPC ...... American Board of Examiners in Pastoral Counseling (EA)
ABEPH ...... American Board of Examiners in Psychological Hypnosis [*Later, ABPH*] (EA)
ABEPP ...... American Board of Examiners in Professional Psychology [*Later, ABPP*]
ABEPSGP ... American Board of Examiners of Psychodrama, Sociometry, and Group Psychotherapy (EA)
ABER .... Aber Resources Ltd. [*NASDAQ symbol*] (NQ)
ABER .... Aberdeen [*City and county in Scotland*] (ROG)
ABERD ..... Aberdeen [*City and county in Scotland*]
Aberdeen Univ Rev ... Aberdeen University. Review [*A publication*]
Aberdeen Univ Stu ... Aberdeen University. Studies [*A publication*]
ABERT ...... Automatic BIT [*Binary Digit*] Error Rate Test [*Data processing*] (MCD)
ABERU ...... Airborne Emergency Reaction Unit
ABERY ...... Aberystwyth [*Borough in Wales*]
ABES .... Aerospace Business Environment Simulator [*Computer-programmed management game*]
ABES .... Air-Breathing Engine System
ABES .... Alliance for Balanced Environmental Solutions (EA)
ABES .... American Biblical Encyclopedia Society (EA)
ABES .... American Broncho-Esophagological Association (EA)
ABES .... Association for Broadcast Engineering Standards (EA)
ABES .... Beaverlodge Elementary School, Alberta [*Library symbol*] [*National Library of Canada*] (BIB)
ABESH ...... Antarjatik Beshamarik Sheba Sangstha [*An association*] (EAIO)
ABESPA ... American Boards of Examiners in Speech Pathology and Audiology [*Later, COPS*] (EA)
ABESS ...... St. Mary's School, Beaverlodge, Alberta [*Library symbol*] [*National Library of Canada*] (BIB)
ABET .... Accreditation Board for Engineering and Technology (EA)
ABETS ...... Airborne Beacon Electronic Test Set
ABEX .... Ab Extra [*From Without*] [*Latin*]
ABEXed .... Absorbance Expanded [*Spectroscopy*]
ABEZS ...... Bezanson School, Alberta [*Library symbol*] [*National Library of Canada*] (BIB)
ABF .... Abaiang [*Kiribati*] [*Airport symbol*] (OAG)
ABF .... Absolutely Bloody Final [*Especially with reference to a drink*]
ABF .... Adaptive Beam Forming (NVT)
ABF .... Advance Booking Fare [*Airlines*]
ABF .... Advanced Beamformer (MCD)
ABF .... Air Burst Fuze
ABF .... Airborne Freight Corp. [*NYSE symbol*] (SPSG)
ABF .... Aircraft Battle Force [*Obsolete*] [*Navy*]
ABF .... America the Beautiful Fund (EA)
ABF .... American Bach Foundation (EA)
ABF .... American Ballads and Folk Songs [*A publication*]
ABF .... American Banjo Fraternity (EA)
ABF .... American Bar Foundation (EA)
ABF .... American Beekeeping Federation (EA)
ABF .... American Behcet's Foundation (EA)
ABF .... American Bikeways Foundation [*Defunct*] (EA)
ABF .... American Blake Foundation (EA)
ABF .... American Buyers Federation (EA)
ABF .... Americas Boychoir Federation (EA)
ABF .... Anaerobic Bacterial Flora [*Microbiology*]
ABF .... Army Benevolent Fund [*British*]
ABF .... Asian Baptist Federation [*Quezon City, Metro Manila, Philippines*] (EAIO)
ABF .... Asset [*or Availability*] Balance File [*Military*] (AABC)
ABF .... Associated British Foods [*Commercial firm*]
ABF .... Association of British Factors
ABF .... Audio Bandpass Filter
ABF .... Australian Basketball Federation
ABF .... Availability Balance File [*Military*] (AABC)
ABF .... Aviation Boatswain's Mate, Fuel [*Navy rating*]
ABFA .... American Baseball Fans Association (EA)
ABFA .... American Board of Forensic Anthropology (EA)
ABFA .... Azobisformamide [*Organic chemistry*]
ABFAA ...... Aviation Boatswain's Mate, Fuel, Airman Apprentice [*Navy rating*]
ABFAB ...... Absolutely Fabulous (DSUE)
ABFAN ...... Aviation Boatswain's Mate, Fuel, Airman [*Navy rating*]
ABFCC ...... Advanced Base Functional Component [*Military*]
ABFCC ...... American Border Fancy Canary Club (EA)
ABFCR ...... American Business Foundation for Cancer Research (EA)
ABFCS ...... Advanced Base Functional Component System [*Military*]
A/B F & D ... Airborne Fill-and-Drain (AAG)
ABFDS ...... Aerial Bulk Fuel Delivery System [*Military*] (AFIT)
ABFE .... Acta Botanica Fennica [*A publication*]
ABFE .... Association of Black Foundation Executives (EA)

ABFEAC ... Acta Botanica Fennica [*A publication*]
ABFLO...... Association of Bedding and Furniture Law Officials (EA)
ABFM....... American Board of Foreign Missions
ABFM........ Association of Business Forms Manufacturers [*Defunct*] (EA)
ABFMS ..... American Baptist Foreign Mission Society [*Congo - Leopoldville*]
AbFolkSt ... Abstracts of Folklore Studies [*A publication*]
ABFOR...... American-British Forces [*World War II*]
ABFP .... American Board of Family Practice (EA)
ABFP .... American Board of Forensic Psychiatry (EA)
ABFP .... American Board of Forensic Psychology (EA)
ABF Research J ... American Bar Foundation. Research Journal [*A publication*]
ABF Research Reptr ... American Bar Foundation. Research Reporter [*A publication*] (DLA)
ABF Research Reptr J ... American Bar Foundation. Research Reporter Journal [*A publication*] (DLA)
ABF Res J ... American Bar Foundation. Research Journal [*A publication*]
ABF Res Newsl ... American Bar Foundation. Research Newsletter [*A publication*] (DLA)
AbFS......... Abstracts of Folklore Studies [*A publication*]
ABFS .... Auxiliary Building Filter System [*Nuclear energy*] (NRCH)
ABFSE....... American Board of Funeral Service Education (EA)
ABFSWS... Associated Blacksmiths, Forge, and Smithy Workers Society [*A union*] [*British*]
ABFZA ...... Analele. Universitatii Bucuresti. Fizica [*A publication*]
ABG .... Abingdon [*Australia*] [*Airport symbol*] (OAG)
ABG .... Abington Township Public Library, Abington, PA [*OCLC symbol*] (OCLC)
ABG .... Abnormal Blood Gas
ABG .... Air Base Group [*Obsolete*] [*Navy*]
ABG .... Alibag [*India*] [*Geomagnetic observatory code*]
ABG .... American Budgetel, Inc. [*Vancouver Stock Exchange symbol*]
ABG .... American Ship Building Co. [*NYSE symbol*] (SPSG)
ABG .... Antibacklash Gear
ABG .... Archiv fuer Begriffsgeschichte [*A publication*]
ABG .... Arterial Blood Gas [*Medicine*]
ABG .... Association of British Geodesists
ABG .... Aural Bearing Generator
ABG .... Axiobuccogingival [*Dentistry*]
a-bg--- ... Bangladesh [*MARC geographic area code*] [*Library of Congress*] (LCCP)
ABG .... Big Sandy, TX [*Location identifier*] [*FAA*] (FAAL)
ABGA .... Allied Bankshares, Inc. [*NASDAQ symbol*] (NQ)
ABGA .... American Brussels Griffon Association (EA)
ABGA .... Australian Blueberry Growers Association
ABGB .... Allgemeines Buergerliches Gesetzbuch [*Austrian Civil Code*] (DLA)
ABGCP...... Association of Boys and Girls Clubs Professionals (EA)
ABGE .... Albertan Geographer [*Canada*] [*A publication*]
ABGG .... (Amanitinylazobenzoyl)glycylglycine
ABGK........ Abgekuerzt [*Abbreviated*] [*German*]
ABGL......... Gladstone [*Australia*] [*ICAO location identifier*] (ICLI)
ABGLA ...... Analele. Universitatii Bucuresti. Geologie [*A publication*]
ABGMT .... Arizona Bureau of Geology and Mineral Technology [*University of Arizona*] [*Research center*] (RCD)
ABGP......... Air Base Group [*Air Force*]
Ab G R .... Above the Ground Review [*A publication*]
ABGR .... American Businessmen's Group of Riyadh (EA)
ABGR .... Australian Biographical and Genealogical Record [*A publication*] (ADA)
ABGTS...... Auxiliary Building Gas Treatment System [*Nuclear energy*] (NRCH)
ABGW ...... Aluminum, Brick, and Glass Workers International Union
ABGWIU .. Aluminum, Brick, and Glass Workers International Union (EA)
ABH........... Aberystwyth [*Welsh depot code*]
ABH........... Abhandlungen [*Transactions*] [*German*] [*Business term*]
ABH........... Advanced Base Hospital [*British*]
ABH........... Aims Biotech Corp. [*Vancouver Stock Exchange symbol*]
ABH........... Air-Britain Historians [*An association*] (EAIO)
ABH........... Alpha [*Australia*] [*Airport symbol*] (OAG)
ABH........... Alpha Benzene Hexachloride [*Organic chemistry*] (ADA)
ABH........... American Bureau of Shipping (Hellas) (DS)
ABH........... Association for the Bibliography of History (EA)
ABH........... Association of British Hairdressers and Hairdressing Schools
ABH........... Association of British Hispanists
ABH........... Average Busy Hour [*Telecommunications*] (TEL)
ABH........... Aviation Boatswain's Mate, Handler [*Navy rating*]
ABH........... Samford University, Birmingham, AL [*Library symbol*] [*Library of Congress*] (LCLS)
ABH........... University of Alabama in Birmingham, Health Sciences Library, Birmingham, AL [*OCLC symbol*] (OCLC)
ABHA....... Associate of the British Hypnotherapy Association (DBQ)
ABHAA..... Aviation Boatswain's Mate, Handler, Airman Apprentice [*Navy rating*]
Abh Abt Phytomorphogenese ... Abhandlungen. Abteilung fuer Phytomorphogenese der Timiriaseff. Instituts fuer Biologie [*A publication*]

Abh Akad Wiss DDR Abt Math Naturwiss Tech ... Abhandlungen. Akademie der Wissenschaften der DDR. Abteilung Mathematik, Naturwissenschaften, Technik [*A publication*]
Abh Akad Wiss DDR Abt Math Naturwiss Tech 1978 ... Abhandlungen. Akademie der Wissenschaften der DDR. Abteilung Mathematik, Naturwissenschaften, Technik. 1978 [*Berlin*] [*A publication*]
Abh Akad Wiss DDR Abt Math Naturwiss Tech 1979 ... Abhandlungen. Akademie der Wissenschaften der DDR. Abteilung Mathematik, Naturwissenschaften, Technik. 1979 [*Goettingen*] [*A publication*]
Abh Akad Wiss DDR Abt Math Naturwiss Tech 1981 ... Abhandlungen. Akademie der Wissenschaften der DDR. Abteilung Mathematik, Naturwissenschaften, Technik. 1981 [*A publication*]
Abh Akad Wiss Goettingen Math-Physik Kl ... Abhandlungen. Akademie der Wissenschaften in Goettingen. Mathematisch-Physikalische Klasse [*West Germany*] [*A publication*]
Abh Akad Wiss Goettingen Math-Phys Kl ... Abhandlungen. Akademie der Wissenschaften in Goettingen. Mathematisch-Physikalische Klasse [*A publication*]
AbhAkWiss Berlin ... Abhandlungen. Deutsche Akademie der Wissenschaften zu Berlin [*A publication*]
ABHAN..... Aviation Boatswain's Mate, Handler, Airman [*Navy rating*]
A Bhandarkar Or Res Inst ... Annals. Bhandarkar Oriental Research Institute [*A publication*]
Abhandl Akad Wiss Lit Geistes Sozialwiss Kl ... Akademie der Wissenschaften und der Literatur. Abhandlungen der Geistes- und Sozialwissenschaftlichen Klasse [*A publication*]
Abhandl Akad Wiss Lit Mainz Math Naturwiss Kl ... Abhandlungen. Akademie der Wissenschaften und der Literatur in Mainz. Mathematisch-Naturwissenschaftliche Klasse [*A publication*]
Abhandl Bayer Akad Wiss Math Naturwiss Abt ... Abhandlungen. Bayerische Akademie der Wissenschaften. Mathematisch-Naturwissenschaftliche Abteilung [*A publication*]
Abhandl Bayer Akad Wiss Math Phys Kl ... Abhandlungen. Bayerische Akademie der Wissenschaften. Mathematisch-Physikalische Klasse [*A publication*]
Abhandl Bayer Akad Wiss Phil Hist Abt ... Abhandlungen. Bayerische Akademie der Wissenschaften. Philosophisch-Historische Abteilung [*A publication*]
Abhandl Bayer Akad Wiss Phil Philol Hist Kl ... Abhandlungen. Bayerische Akademie der Wissenschaften. Philosophisch-Philologische und Historische Klasse [*A publication*]
Abhandl Ber Deut Mus ... Abhandlungen und Berichte. Deutsches Museum [*A publication*]
Abhandl Ber Ver Naturk ... Abhandlungen und Berichte des Vereins fuer Naturkunde zu Cassel [*A publication*]
Abhandl Braunschweig Wiss Ges ... Abhandlungen. Braunschweigische Wissenschaftliche Gesellschaft [*A publication*]
Abhandl Deut Akad Wiss Kl Math Phys Tech ... Abhandlungen. Deutsche Akademie der Wissenschaften zu Berlin. Klasse fuer Mathematik, Physik, und Technik [*A publication*]
Abhandl Deut Akad Wiss Math Naturwiss Kl ... Abhandlungen. Deutsche Akademie der Wissenschaften zu Berlin. Mathematisch-Naturwissenschaftliche Klasse [*A publication*]
Abhandl Deut Akad Wiss Phil Hist Kl ... Abhandlungen. Deutsche Akademie der Wissenschaften zu Berlin. Philosophisch-Historische Klasse [*A publication*]
Abhandl Geb Naturwiss ... Abhandlungen. Gebiet der Naturwissenschaften [*A publication*]
Abhandl Gesamtgeb Med ... Abhandlungen aus dem Gesamtgebiete der Medizin [*A publication*]
Abhandl Gesch Math Wiss ... Abhandlungen zur Geschichte der Mathematischen Wissenschaften mit Einschluss Ihrer Anwendungen [*A publication*]
Abhandl Gesch Naturwiss Med ... Abhandlungen zur Geschichte der Naturwissenschaften und der Medizin [*A publication*]
Abhandl Gesch Veterinaermed ... Abhandlungen aus der Geschichte der Veterinaermedizin [*A publication*]
Abhandl Ges Wiss Goettingen Math Phys Kl ... Abhandlungen. Koenigliche Gesellschaft der Wissenschaften zu Goettingen. Mathematisch-Physikalische Klasse [*A publication*]
Abhandl Ges Wiss Goettingen Philol Hist Kl ... Abhandlungen. Koenigliche Gesellschaft der Wissenschaften zu Goettingen. Philologisch-Historische Klasse [*A publication*]
Abhandl Herder-Ges Herder Inst ... Abhandlungen der Herder-Gesellschaft und des Herder Instituts zu Riga [*A publication*]
Abhandl Kunde Morgenlandes ... Abhandlungen fuer die Kunde des Morgenlandes [*Herausgegeben von der Deutschen Gesellschaft*] [*A publication*]
Abhandl Med Fak Sun Yatsen-Univ Canton ... Abhandlungen der Medizinischen Fakultaet der Sun Yatsen-Universitaet Canton [*A publication*]
Abhandl Naturforsch Ges Goerlitz ... Abhandlungen der Naturforschenden Gesellschaft zu Goerlitz [*A publication*]
Abhandl Naturhist Ges Nuernberg ... Abhandlungen der Naturhistorischen Gesellschaft zu Nuernberg [*A publication*]

Abhandl Naturwiss Ver Bremen ... Abhandlungen Herausgegeben vom Naturwissenschaftlichen Verein zu Bremen [*A publication*]

Abhandl Preuss Akad Wiss Math Naturwiss Kl ... Abhandlungen. Preussische Akademie der Wissenschaften. Mathematisch-Naturwissenschaftliche Klasse [*A publication*]

Abhandl Preuss Akad Wiss Phil Hist Kl ... Abhandlungen. Preussische Akademie der Wissenschaften. Philosophisch-Historische Klasse [*A publication*]

Abhandl Preuss Akad Wiss Phys Math Kl ... Abhandlungen. Preussische Akademie der Wissenschaften. Physikalisch-Mathematische Klasse [*A publication*]

Abhandl Saechs Akad Wiss Philol Hist Kl ... Abhandlungen. Saechsische Akademie der Wissenschaften. Philologisch-Historische Klasse [*A publication*]

Abhandl Saechs Ges Wiss Philol Hist Kl ... Abhandlungen. Saechsische Gesellschaft der Wissenschaften. Philologisch-Historische Klasse [*A publication*]

Abhandl Schlesischen Ges Vaterlaend Cult Geisteswiss Reihe ... Abhandlungen. Schlesische Gesellschaft fuer Vaterlaendische Cultur. Geisteswissenschaftliche Reihe [*A publication*]

Abhandl Theor Biol ... Abhandlungen zur Theoretischen Biologie [*A publication*]

Abh Arbgem Tier- u Pflageogr ... Abhandlungen. Arbeitsgemeinschaft fuer Tier- und Pflanzengeographische Heimatforschung im Saarland [*A publication*]

AbhBAW ... Abhandlungen. Bayerische Akademie der Wissenschaften [*A publication*]

Abh Bayer Akad Wiss Math-Naturwiss Kl ... Abhandlungen. Bayerische Akademie der Wissenschaften. Mathematisch-Naturwissenschaftliche Klasse [*A publication*]

Abh Ber Dtsch Mus ... Abhandlungen und Berichte. Deutsches Museum [*West Germany*] [*A publication*]

Abh (Berlin) ... Abhandlungen (Berlin) [*A publication*]

Abh Ber Naturkundemus Goerlitz ... Abhandlungen und Berichte. Naturkundemuseums Goerlitz [*East Germany*] [*A publication*]

Abh Ber Staat Mus Volk Dres ... Abhandlungen und Berichte. Staatlichen Museum fuer Voelkerkunde Dresden [*Forschungsstelle*] [*A publication*]

Abh Braunschweig Wiss Gesellsch ... Abhandlungen. Braunschweigische Wissenschaftliche Gesellschaft [*A publication*]

Abh Braunschw Wiss Ges ... Abhandlungen. Braunschweigische Wissenschaftliche Gesellschaft [*A publication*]

ABHC .... American Belgian Hare Club   (EA)

ABHC .... Association of Bank Holding Companies [*Washington, DC*]   (EA)

Abh Deut Akad Wiss Berlin Kl Math ... Abhandlungen. Deutsche Akademie der Wissenschaften zu Berlin. Klasse fuer Mathematik, Physik, und Technik [*A publication*]

Abh Deutsch Akad Wiss Berlin Kl Math Phys Tech ... Abhandlungen. Deutsche Akademie der Wissenschaften zu Berlin. Klasse fuer Mathematik, Physik, und Technik [*A publication*]

Abh Dtsch Akad Wiss Berl ... Abhandlungen. Deutsche Akademie der Wissenschaften zu Berlin [*A publication*]

Abh Dtsch Akad Wiss Berlin Kl Bergbau Huettenwes Montangeol ... Abhandlungen. Deutsche Akademie der Wissenschaften zu Berlin. Klasse fuer Bergbau, Huettenwesen, und Montangeologie [*A publication*]

Abh Dtsch Akad Wiss Berlin Kl Chem Geol Biol ... Abhandlungen. Deutsche Akademie der Wissenschaften zu Berlin. Klasse fuer Chemie, Geologie, und Biologie [*A publication*]

Abh Dtsch Akad Wiss Berlin Kl Math Allg Naturwiss ... Abhandlungen. Deutsche Akademie der Wissenschaften zu Berlin. Klasse fuer Mathematik und Allgemeine Naturwissenschaften [*A publication*]

Abh Dtsch Akad Wiss Berlin Kl Math Phys Tech ... Abhandlungen. Deutsche Akademie der Wissenschaften zu Berlin. Klasse fuer Mathematik, Physik, und Technik [*East Germany*] [*A publication*]

Abh Dtsch Akad Wiss Berlin Kl Med ... Abhandlungen. Deutsche Akademie der Wissenschaften zu Berlin. Klasse fuer Medizin [*A publication*]

Abh Dtsch Akad Wiss Berlin Math-Naturwiss Kl ... Abhandlungen. Deutsche Akademie der Wissenschaften zu Berlin. Mathematisch-Naturwissenschaftliche Klasse [*A publication*]

Abh Dtsch Akad Wiss Berl Kl Chem Geol Biol ... Abhandlungen. Deutsche Akademie der Wissenschaften zu Berlin. Klasse fuer Chemie, Geologie, und Biologie [*A publication*]

Abh Dtsch Akad Wiss Berl Kl Med ... Abhandlungen. Deutsche Akademie der Wissenschaften zu Berlin. Klasse fuer Medizin [*A publication*]

Abh Dtsch Kaelte Klimatech Ver ... Abhandlungen des Deutschen Kaelte und Klimatechnischen Vereins [*A publication*]

Abh Dtsch Kaeltetech Ver ... Abhandlungen. Deutscher Kaeltetechnische Verein [*A publication*]

AB in H Ec ... Bachelor of Arts in Home Economics

ABHES ...... Accrediting Bureau of Health Education Schools   (EA)

Abh Geb Hirnforsch Verhaltenphysiol ... Abhandlungen. Gebiet der Hirnforschung und Verhaltensphysiologie [*A publication*]

Abh Geol Dienstes (Berl) ... Abhandlungen. Geologischer Dienst (Berlin) [*A publication*]

Abh Geol Landesamtes Baden Wuerttemb ... Abhandlungen. Geologisches Landesamt in Baden Wuerttemberg [*A publication*]

Abh Gesamtgeb Hyg ... Abhandlungen aus dem Gesamtgebiete der Hygiene [*A publication*]

Abh zu Gesch d Math ... Abhandlungen zur Geschichte der Mathematischen Wissenschaften [*A publication*]   (OCD)

Abh zu Gesch d Med ... Abhandlungen zur Geschichte der Naturwissenschaften und der Medizin [*A publication*]   (OCD)

AbhGWG ... Abhandlungen. Gesellschaft der Wissenschaften zu Goettingen [*A publication*]

ABHH .... Association of Baptist Homes and Hospitals [*Later, ABHHA*]   (EA)

ABHHA ..... American Baptist Homes and Hospitals Association   (EA)

Abh Inst Hochspannungstech Elektr Anlagen ... Abhandlungen. Institut fuer Hochspannungstechnik und Elektrische Anlagen [*West Germany*] [*A publication*]

Abh Inst Hochspannungstechnik Elektr Anlagen ... Abhandlungen. Institut fuer Hochspannungstechnik und Elektrische Anlagen [*A publication*]

Abh Inst Metallhuettenwes Elektrometall Tech Hochsch Aachen ... Abhandlungen. Institut fuer Metallhuettenwesen und Elektrometallurgie der Technischen Hochschule (Aachen) [*A publication*]

ABHJ .... Angle Bulkhead Jack

Abh Kinderheilkd Ihren Grenzgeb ... Abhandlungen aus der Kinderheilkunde und Ihren Grenzgebieten [*A publication*]

AbhKM ...... Abhandlungen fuer die Kunde des Morgenlandes [*A publication*]

Abh Koenigl Akad Wiss Berlin ... Abhandlungen. Koeniglichen Akademie der Wissenschaften in Berlin [*A publication*]

Abh Kunde Morgenl ... Abhandlungen fuer die Kunde des Morgenlandes [*A publication*]

ABH-L .... Samford University, Cumberland School of Law, Cordell Hull Law Library, Birmingham, AL [*Library symbol*] [*Library of Congress*]   (LCLS)

Abh Landesmus Naturkd Muenster Westfalen ... Abhandlungen. Landesmuseum fuer Naturkunde zu Muenster in Westfalen [*A publication*]

Abh Landes Prov Westfalen Mus Naturkd ... Abhandlungen. Landesmuseum der Provinz Westfalen. Museum fuer Naturkunde [*A publication*]

ABHM .... American Board of Homeopathic Medicine   (EA)

ABHM .... Association of Builders' Hardware Manufacturers   (EAIO)

ABHM .... Hamilton Island [*Australia*] [*ICAO location identifier*]   (ICLI)

Abh Math-Phys Kl Saechs Akad Wiss ... Abhandlungen. Mathematisch-Physische Klasse der Saechsischen Akademie der Wissenschaften [*A publication*]

Abh Math Sem Univ (Hamburg) ... Abhandlungen aus dem Mathematischen Seminar der Universitaet (Hamburg) [*A publication*]

Abh Meteorol Dienstes DDR ... Abhandlungen. Meteorologischer Dienst der Deutschen Demokratischen Republik [*A publication*]

ABHMS .... American Baptist Home Mission Society [*Later, Board of National Ministries*]   (EA)

Abh Naturwiss Ver Bremen ... Abhandlungen. Naturwissenschaftlicher Verein zu Bremen [*A publication*]

Abh Naturwiss Ver Hamb ... Abhandlungen. Naturwissenschaftlicher Verein in Hamburg [*A publication*]

Abh Naturw Ver Bremen ... Abhandlungen. Naturwissenschaftlicher Verein zu Bremen [*A publication*]

ABHP .... American Board of Health Physics   (EA)

Abh Pathophysiol Regul ... Abhandlungen ueber die Pathophysiologie der Regulationen [*A publication*]

ABHPBS ... Blue Hills Community School, Buffalo Head Prairie, Alberta [*Library symbol*] [*National Library of Canada*]   (BIB)

Abh Philos Ges ... Abhandlungen zur Philosophie und Ihrer Geschichte [*A publication*]

Abh Preuss Akad Wiss Math Naturwiss Kl ... Abhandlungen. Preussische Akademie der Wissenschaften. Mathematisch-Naturwissenschaftliche Klasse [*A publication*]

Abh Preuss Akad Wiss Phys Math Kl ... Abhandlungen. Preussische Akademie der Wissenschaften. Physikalisch-Mathematische Klasse [*A publication*]

ABHPS ...... Buffalo Head Prairie School, Alberta [*Library symbol*] [*National Library of Canada*]   (BIB)

ABHR .... American Bay Horse Registry   (EA)

ABHRAR .. Anais Botanicos. Herbario "Barbosa Rodrigues" [*A publication*]

Abh Rheinisch-Westfael Akad Wiss ... Abhandlungen. Rheinisch-Westfaelische Akademie der Wissenschaften [*A publication*]

ABHS .... American Baptist Historical Society   (EA)

ABHS .... American Board of Hand Surgery   (EA)

ABHSA ..... American Behavioral Scientist [*A publication*]

Abh Sachs Ges Wiss ... Abhandlungen. Saechsische Gesellschaft der Wissenschaften [*A publication*]   (OCD)

Abh Saechs Akad Wiss Leipzig Math-Natur Kl ... Abhandlungen. Saechsische Akademie der Wissenschaften zu Leipzig. Mathematisch-Naturwissenschaftliche Klasse [*A publication*]

Abh Saechs Akad Wiss Leipzig Math Naturwiss Kl ... Abhandlungen. Saechsische Akademie der Wissenschaften zu Leipzig. Mathematisch-Naturwissenschaftliche Klasse [*A publication*]

Abh Senckenb Naturforsch Ges ... Abhandlungen. Senckenbergische Naturforschende Gesellschaft [*A publication*]

Abh Staatl Mus Mineral Geol Dresden ... Abhandlungen. Staatliches Museum fuer Mineralogie und Geologie zu Dresden [*A publication*]

AbhTANT ... Abhandlungen zur Theologie des Alten und Neuen Testaments [*A publication*]

Abh Verh Naturwiss Ver Hamb ... Abhandlungen und Verhandlungen. Naturwissenschaftlicher Verein in Hamburg [*A publication*] [*A publication*]

Abh Verh Naturwiss Ver Hamburg ... Abhandlungen und Verhandlungen. Naturwissenschaftlicher Verein in Hamburg [*A publication*]

ABHX .... Air Blast Heat Exchanger [*Nuclear energy*] (NRCH)

ABI .... Abilene [*Texas*] [*Airport symbol*] (OAG)

ABI .... About Books, Inc. [*An association*] (EA)

ABI .... Abstracted Business Information, Inc.

ABI .... Accademia e Biblioteche d'Italia [*A publication*]

ABI .... Advance Book Information [*Publishing*]

ABI .... Advanced Biotechnologies, Inc.

ABI .... Agile-Beam Illuminator (MCD)

ABI .... Allgemeines Bucher-Lexikon [*A publication*]

ABI .... AmBrit, Incorporated [*AMEX symbol*] (SPSG)

ABI .... American Bankruptcy Institute (EA)

ABI .... American Bell, Incorporated

ABI .... American-British Intelligence [*NATO*] (NATG)

ABI .... American Butter Institute (EA)

ABI .... Ankle/Brachial Pressure Index

ABI .... Application Binary Interface [*Data processing*] (BYTE)

ABI .... Associacao Brasileira de Imprensa [*Brazilian Press Association*]

ABI .... Association of British Insurers (EAIO)

ABI .... Association of British Investigators (EAIO)

ABI .... Australian Business Index [*A publication*] (APTA)

ABI .... Automated Behavioral Intelligence (MCD)

ABI .... Auxiliary Building Isolation [*Nuclear energy*] (NRCH)

ABI .... Bow Island Public Library, Alberta [*Library symbol*] [*National Library of Canada*] (NLC)

ABIA .... American Boardsailing Industries Association (EA)

ABIA .... Association of British Introduction Agencies (EAIO)

ABIA .... Australian Boating Industry Association

ABIA Assoc Bras Ind Aliment ... ABIA. Associacao Brasileira das Industrias da Alimentacao [*A publication*]

ABIAS .... Air Bag Impact Attenuation System (MCD)

ABIA SAPRO Bol Inf ... ABIA [*Associacao Brasileira das Industrias de Alimentacao*] SAPRO [*Setor de Alimentos Calorico-Proteicos*] Boletim Informativo [*A publication*]

ABIBD .... Applied Biochemistry and Biotechnology [*A publication*]

ABIBUZ .... Acta Botanica. Instituti Botanici. Universitatis Zagrebensis [*A publication*]

ABIC .... Adaptive Behavior Inventory for Children [*Psychology*]

ABIC .... Army Battlefield Interface/Interface Concept (MCD)

ABICC .... Associate of the British Institute of Certified Carpenters

ABID .... Associate of the British Institute of Interior Design (DBQ)

Abidjan Univ Ann Sci ... Abidjan Universite. Annales. Sciences [*A publication*]

ABIDM ..... Improvement District No. 9/Banff Municipal Library, Alberta [*Library symbol*] [*National Library of Canada*] (NLC)

ABIFT .... Arab Bank for Investment and Foreign Trade

ABIG .... American Bankers Insurance Group, Inc. [*NASDAQ symbol*] (NQ)

ABIH .... American Board of Industrial Hygiene (EA)

ABIL .... Airborne Beacon Interference Locator (MCD)

ABILAE .... Archives de Biologie [*Archives of Biology*] [*A publication*]

ABILS .... Automated Bulk Items List System (MCD)

ABIM .... Abridged Index Medicus [*A publication*]

ABIM .... American Board of Internal Medicine (EA)

ABIM .... American Board of International Missions (EA)

ABIMS ...... American Board of Industrial Medicine and Surgery (EA)

ABING ...... Abingdon [*England*]

AB INIT .... Ab Initio [*From the Beginning*] [*Latin*]

ABIO .... Applied Biosystems, Inc. [*NASDAQ symbol*] (NQ)

ABIOAN .. Acta Biotheoretica [*A publication*]

ABIOL .... Advanced Base Initial Outfitting List [*Military*]

A Biol Colloq Ore St Coll ... Annual Biology Colloquium. Oregon State College [*A publication*]

ABIP .... Australian Books in Print [*Information service or system*] [*A publication*] (APTA)

ABIPB .... Proceedings. Australian Biochemical Society [*A publication*]

ABIPC .... Abstract Bulletin. Institute of Paper Chemistry [*A publication*]

ABIPP .... Associate of the British Institute of Professional Photography (DBQ)

ABIR .... All-Band Intercept Receiver

ABIRA .... American Biographical Institute Research Association (EA)

ABIRBD .... Australia. Commonwealth Scientific and Industrial Research Organisation. Division of Irrigation Research. Report [*A publication*]

ABIRD .... Aircraft-Based Infrared Detector

ABIS .... Acta Botanica Islandica [*A publication*]

ABIS .... Anglo-Brazilian Information Service [*Information service or system*] (IID)

ABIS .... Audit Base Inventory System [*IRS*]

ABISL .... Advanced Base Initial Support Lists [*Navy*] (AFIT)

ABISS .... American Bough of the International Society of Shropshires (EA)

Abit .... Abitur [*School Exit Examination*] [*German*]

ABIT .... Aircraft Blast Interaction Tests (MCD)

ABITA .... American Biology Teacher [*A publication*]

ABIX .... Abatix Environmental Corp. [*NASDAQ symbol*] (NQ)

ABIX .... Australian Business Index [*Information service or system*] [*A publication*] (ADA)

ABJ .... Abashiri [*Japan*] [*Seismograph station code, US Geological Survey*] (SEIS)

ABJ .... Abidjan [*Ivory Coast*] [*Airport symbol*] (OAG)

ABJ .... Adhesively Bonded Joint [*or Junction*]

ABJ .... American Businessmen of Jeddah (EA)

ABJ .... Angle Bulkhead Jack

AB in J .... Bachelor of Arts in Journalism

ABJ .... Birmingham-Jefferson Library, Birmingham, AL [*OCLC symbol*] (OCLC)

ABJ .... Jefferson County Law Library, Birmingham, AL [*Library symbol*] [*Library of Congress*] (LCLS)

ABJCAQ ... Annales. Universite d'Abidjan. Serie C. Sciences [*A publication*]

ABJOA ...... American Bee Journal [*A publication*]

ABJS .... Association of Bone and Joint Surgeons (EA)

ABJS .... Jefferson State Junior College, Birmingham, AL [*Library symbol*] [*Library of Congress*] (LCLS)

ABK .... Aachener Beitraege zur Komparatistik [*A publication*]

ABK .... Abisko [*Sweden*] [*Geomagnetic observatory code*]

ABK .... Abisko [*Sweden*] [*Seismograph station code, US Geological Survey*] [*Closed*] (SEIS)

ABK .... Airborne Identification Kit (DEN)

ABK .... Ajia Bunka [*Asian Culture*] [*A publication*]

ABK .... Alliance Bancorporation [*AMEX symbol*] (SPSG)

ABK .... Angular Blocky Soil [*Agronomy*]

ABK .... Kabri Dar [*Ethiopia*] [*Airport symbol*] (OAG)

ABKA .... American Boarding Kennels Association (EA)

ABKC .... ABKCO Industries [*NASDAQ symbol*] (NQ)

ABKK .... Amtliche Berichte. Koenigliche Kunstsammlungen [*Berlin*] [*A publication*]

AbKM .... Abhandlungen fuer die Kunde des Morgenlandes [*A publication*]

ABKR .... Anchor Savings Bank FSB [*NASDAQ symbol*] (NQ)

AbKSGW ... Abhandlungen. Koenigliche Saechsische Gesellschaft der Wissenschaften [*A publication*]

ABKUFI .... Abkuerzungsfimmel [*Abbreviation Craze*]

AbL .... Abelson-Murine Leukemia [*Virus*]

ABL .... Ablative

ABL .... Above Baseline

ABL .... ABS Resources Ltd. [*Vancouver Stock Exchange symbol*]

ABL .... Accepted Batch Listing [*Accounting*]

ABL .... Action for Better Living [*Defunct*] (EA)

ABL .... Adaption Binary Load [*Program*] (CET)

ABL .... Air BC Ltd. [*British Columbia, Canada*] [*FAA designator*] (FAAC)

ABL .... Air Blast Loading

ABL .... Airborne LASER (MCD)

ABL .... Alameda Belt Line [*AAR code*]

ABL .... All Busy Low [*AT & T*]

ABL .... Allegheny Ballistics Laboratory [*Cumberland, MD*] (MCD)

ABL .... Allocated Baseline (MCD)

ABL .... Ambler [*Alaska*] [*Airport symbol*] (OAG)

ABL .... American Biltrite, Inc. [*AMEX symbol*] (SPSG)

ABL .... American Biotechnology Laboratory [*A publication*]

ABL .... American-British Laboratory [*Harvard University*]

ABL .... American Bulgarian League [*Defunct*] (EA)

ABL .... American Business Law Journal [*A publication*]

ABL .... Ammunition Base Load (MCD)

ABL .... Amtsblatt [*Official Gazette*] [*German*] (DLA)

ABL .... Architectural Block Diagram Language

ABL .... Archives of Business and Labour [*Australian National University*]

ABL .... Armament Boresight Line

ABL .... Armored Box Launcher [*Shipboard launching system*]

ABL .... Army Biological Laboratory

ABL .... Asian Business League [*Later, ABL-SF*] (EA)

ABL .... Assembly Breakdown List

ABL .... Assyrian and Babylonian Letters Belonging to the Kouyunjik Collection(s) of the British Museum [*A publication*] (BJA)

ABL .... Atlas Basic Language [*Data processing*]

ABL .... Atmospheric Burst Locator (MCD)

ABL .... Australian Bank Limited (ADA)

ABL .... Automated Biological Laboratory [*NASA*]

ABL .... Automatic Bootstrap Loader [*Data processing*]

ABL .... Axiobuccolingual [*Dentistry*]

ABL .... Blairmore Public Library, Alberta [*Library symbol*] [*National Library of Canada*] (NLC)

ABL .... Business Law Cases for Australia [*Commerce Clearing House*] [*A publication*]

ABL .... Law for the Australian Businessman [*A publication*]
ABLA .... Amateur Bicycle League of America [*Later, USCF*]
ABLA .... American Blind Lawyers Association (EA)
ABLA .... American Business Law Association (EA)
AB & LA .... Australian Builder and Land Advertiser [*A publication*]
ABLA .... Blackfalds Public Library, Alberta [*Library symbol*] [*National Library of Canada*] (NLC)
ABLAT ...... Ablative (KSC)
Ablauf-Planungsforsch ... Ablauf- und Planungsforschung [*A publication*]
ABLB .... Alternate Binaural Loudness Balancing [*Audiometry*]
ABLC .... Alcohol Beverage Legislative Council (EA)
ABLC .... American Brown Leghorn Club (EA)
ABLC .... Amphotericin B Lipid Complex [*Antifungal*]
ABLC .... Automatic Backlight Compensation [*Photography*]
ABLCHG ..... Airborne Launching (FAAC)
ABLCWS .. Altogether Builders, Labourers, and Constructional Workers Society [*A union*] [*British*]
ABLE .... [A] programming language [*1966*] (CSR)
ABLE .... Acquisition Based on Consideration of Logistic Effects [*Air Force*]
ABLE .... Activity Balance Line Evaluation [*PERT*]
ABLE .... Adult Basic Learning Examination (NVT)
ABLE .... Advanced Bio-Mechanical Linkage Enablement [*Rehabilitation technology*]
ABLE .... Advanced Blown Lift Enhancement (MCD)
ABLE .... Agricultural-Biological Literature Exploitation [*Systems study of National Agricultural Library*]
ABLE .... Amazon Boundary Layer Experiment (MCD)
ABLE .... Association for Biology Laboratory Education (EA)
ABLE .... Atmospheric Boundary Layer Experiment [*National Oceanic and Atmospheric Administration*]
ABLE .... Audit Basic Learning Examination (MCD)
ABLE .... Autonetics Base-Line Equipment
ABLE .... Viable Resources [*NASDAQ symbol*] (NQ)
ABLES ...... Airborne Battlefield Light Equipment System [*Army*]
ABLF .... Atmosphere Boundary Layer Facility (MCD)
ABLG .... Antibacklash Gear
ABLI .... Abraham Lincoln Birthplace National Monument
ABLISS ..... Association of British Library and Information Science Schools
ABLJ .... Adjustable Buoyancy Life Jacket
ABLK .... Laverack Barracks [*Australia*] [*ICAO location identifier*] (ICLI)
ABLO .... Australian Botanical Liaison Officer
ABLP .... Air Bearing Lift Pad (KSC)
ABLP .... Aniline Blue-Lactophenol Medium [*Botany*]
ABLR .... Australian Business Law Review [*A publication*]
ABLR .... Longreach [*Australia*] [*ICAO location identifier*] (ICLI)
ABLS .... Abelson Lymphosarcoma [*Oncology*]
ABLS .... American Board of Laser Surgery (EA)
ABLS .... American Bryological and Lichenological Society (EA)
ABLS .... Association of British Library Schools
ABLS .... Atlas Biomedical Literature System
ABLS .... Bachelor of Arts in Library Science
ABLSAG ... Archives of Biological Sciences [*English Translation of Arhiv Bioloskih Nauka*] [*A publication*]
ABL-SF ..... Asian Business League of San Francisco [*California*] (EA)
ABLSS....... Advanced Ballistic-Type Logistic Spacecraft System (MCD)
ABLUE...... Asymptotically Best Linear Unbiased Estimator [*Statistics*]
ABM .... Abducens Motoneuron [*Neuroanatomy*]
ABM .... Abeam
ABM .... Abermin Corp. [*Toronto Stock Exchange symbol*]
ABM .... Abingdon Mile [*Newmarket Racecourse*] [*Horseracing*] [*British*]
ABM .... Academie Royale de Belgique [*A publication*]
ABM .... Acquisition Bus Monitor [*Data processing*] (MCD)
ABM .... Acute Bacterial Meningitis [*Medicine*]
ABM .... Adjusted Balance Method
ABM .... Advanced Bill of Material [*Accounting*] (AAG)
ABM .... Allen, Brady & Marsh [*British advertising agency*]
ABM .... American Buddhist Movement (EA)
ABM .... American Building Maintenance Industries [*NYSE symbol*] (SPSG)
ABM .... Amino-Form Bind Medium [*Analytical biochemistry*]
ABM .... Anderson-Brinkman-Morel State [*Superconductivity*]
ABM .... Antiballistic Missile [*Air Force*]
ABM .... Anybody but McGovern [*1972 presidential campaign*]
ABM .... Apogee Boost Motor [*Aerospace*] (MCD)
ABM .... Art Bibliographies Modern [*A publication*]
ABM .... Artbibliographies Modern [*Database*] [*Clio Press Ltd.*] [*Information service or system*] (CRD)
ABM .... Assistant Beach Master [*British*]
ABM .... Associate in Business Management
ABM .... Associated Building Material Distributors of America (EA)
ABM .... Association of Breastfeeding Mothers (EAIO)
ABM .... Association for British Music (EAIO)
ABM .... Association of Button Merchants (EAIO)
ABM .... Asynchronous Balanced Mode
ABM .... Atomic Beam Method
ABM .... Automated [*or Automatic*] Batch Mixing [*Data processing*]
ABM .... Avian Basal Medium [*Culture media*]
ABM .... Aviation Boatswain's Mate [*Navy rating*]

ABM .... Bamaga [*Australia*] [*Airport symbol*] (OAG)
ABM .... Bonnyville Municipal Library, Alberta [*Library symbol*] [*National Library of Canada*] (NLC)
ABM .... Miles College, Birmingham, AL [*Library symbol*] [*Library of Congress*] (LCLS)
ABMA ...... American Boiler Manufacturers Association (EA)
ABMA ...... American Brush Manufacturers Association (EA)
ABMA ...... Army Ballistic Missile Agency [*Redstone Arsenal, AL*]
ABMA ...... Mount Isa [*Australia*] [*ICAO location identifier*] (ICLI)
ABMAA ... American Black Maine-Anjou Association (EA)
ABMAC ... American Bureau for Medical Advancement in China (EA)
ABMAE5... Acta Botanica Malacitana [*A publication*]
ABMAG .... Aviation Boatswain's Mate, Arresting Gear and Barriers [*Navy rating*]
ABMB ...... Archives, Bibliotheques, et Musees de Belgique [*Later, Archives et Bibliotheques de Belgique*] [*A publication*]
ABMC ...... ABM Computer Systems [*NASDAQ symbol*] (NQ)
ABMC ...... American Bandstand Memory Club [*Later, 1950's American Bandstand Fan Club*] (EA)
ABMC ...... American Battle Monuments Commission [*Independent government agency*]
ABMC ...... American Bike Month Committee [*Defunct*] (EA)
ABMC ...... American Business Media Council [*Defunct*] (EA)
ABMC ...... Maroochydore [*Australia*] [*ICAO location identifier*] (ICLI)
ABMCP.... Aviation Boatswain's Mate, Catapult [*Navy rating*]
ABMD ...... Advanced Ballistic Missile Defense [*Army*]
ABMD ...... Air Ballistics Missile Division [*Air Force*]
ABMDA .... Advanced Ballistic Missile Defense Agency [*Alexandria, VA*] [*Army*]
ABMDA .... Associated Building Material Distributors of America (EA)
ABME ...... American Board of Master Educators (EA)
AB in ME .. Bachelor of Arts in Mechanical Engineering
ABME ...... Bachelor of Arts in Mechanical Engineering
ABMEAD ... Arquivos Brasileiros de Medicina [*A publication*]
ABMEC.... Annals of Biomedical Engineering [*A publication*]
ABMEC.... Association of British Mining Equipment Companies (EAIO)
ABMEEH ... Annals of Behavioral Medicine [*A publication*]
ABMEWS ... Antiballistic Missile Early Warning System [*Air Force*]
ABMF........ John E. Meyer Eye Foundation, Eye Foundation Hospital, Birmingham, AL [*Library symbol*] [*Library of Congress*] (LCLS)
ABMG ...... American Board of Medical Genetics (EA)
ABMGA .... Acta Biologica et Medica Germanica [*A publication*]
ABMGA .... Aviation Boatswain's Mate, Gasoline System [*Navy rating*]
ABMHAM ... Archives Belges de Medecine Sociale, Hygiene, Medecine du Travail, et Medecine Legale [*A publication*]
ABMI ...... Author Biographies Master Index [*A publication*]
AbMilt ...... Abstracts of Military Bibliography [*A publication*]
ABMIS...... Airborne Ballistic Missile Intercept System
ABMIT ..... American Buyers of Meeting and Incentive Travel (EA)
ABMJ ...... American Board of Missions to the Jews [*Later, CPM*] (EA)
ABMK ...... Archiwa, Biblioteki, i Muzea Koscielne [*A publication*]
ABMK ...... Mackay [*Australia*] [*ICAO location identifier*] (ICLI)
ABMLAMS ... American Board of Medical-Legal Analysis in Medicine and Surgery (EA)
ABMLS ..... Accrediting Bureau of Medical Laboratory Schools [*Later, ABHES*]
ABMM ...... American Board of Medical Microbiology
ABMM ...... Antiballistic-Missile Missile [*Air Force*] (AFM)
ABMMC ... Analele. Universitatii Bucuresti. Matematica-Mecanica [*A publication*]
ABMOC .... [*Manual*] Air Battle Management Operations Center [*Army*] (RDA)
ABMP........ American Board of Medical Psychotherapists (EA)
ABMP........ Associated Bodywork and Massage Professionals (EA)
ABMPEG ... Medica Physica [*A publication*]
ABMPH .... Aviation Boatswain's Mate, Plane Handler [*Navy rating*]
ABMPTP .. Association of Black Motion Picture and Television Producers (EA)
ABMR ...... ABM [*Australian Board of Missions*] Review [*A publication*] (APTA)
ABMR ...... Academy of Behavioral Medicine Research (EA)
ABMR ...... Antiquarian Book Monthly Review [*A publication*]
ABMR ...... Atlantic Ballistic Missile Range
ABM Rev ... ABM [*Australian Board of Missions*] Review [*A publication*] (APTA)
ABMRF ..... American Business Men's Research Foundation [*Later, ARIS*]
ABMS ...... Advanced Ballistic Missile Systems (KSC)
ABMS........ American Board of Medical Specialties (EA)
ABMS........ American Bureau of Metal Statistics (EA)
ABMS........ Artillery Ballistic Meteorological System (MCD)
ABMT ...... American Board of Medical Toxicology (EA)
ABMU ...... American Baptist Missionary Union [*Later, Board of International Ministries*]
ABMXA .... Archivos de Biologia y Medicina Experimentales [*Chile*] [*A publication*]
ABMXA2 ... Archivos de Biologia y Medicina Experimentales [*A publication*]
ABMZDB ... Arquivo Brasileiro de Medicina Veterinaria e Zootecnia [*A publication*]

ABN.......... Abinger [*United Kingdom*] [*Later, HAD*] [*Geomagnetic observatory code*]
AbN........... Abr-Nahrain (BJA)
Ab N........... Abstracts of Treasury Decisions, New Series [*A publication*] (DLA)
ABN........... Aerodrome Beacon (FAAC)
ABN........... Airborne (AFM)
ABN........... Alban Exploration Ltd. [*Vancouver Stock Exchange symbol*]
ABN........... Algemene Bank Nederland [*General Bank of the Netherlands*]
ABN........... Allied Bank of Nigeria Ltd.
ABN........... American Bionetics, Inc.
ABN........... American Board of Nutrition (EA)
ABN........... Anais. Biblioteca Nacional [*Rio De Janeiro*] [*A publication*]
ABN........... Anti-Bolshevik Bloc of Nations [*Munich, Federal Republic of Germany*] (EAIO)
ABN........... Arhiv Bioloskih Nauka [*A publication*]
ABN........... Arnold Bennett Newsletter [*A publication*]
ABN........... Aseptic Bone Necrosis [*Medicine*]
ABN........... Asian Business [*Hong Kong*] [*A publication*]
ABN........... Associated Broadcast News [*Cable-television system*]
ABN........... Association of British Neurologists
ABN........... Auburn [*Nebraska*] [*Seismograph station code, US Geological Survey*] (SEIS)
ABN........... Australian Bibliographic Network [*National Library of Australia*] [*Information service or system*] (IID)
a-bn--- .... Borneo Island [*MARC geographic area code*] [*Library of Congress*] (LCCP)
ABNA...... Achievable Benefit Not Achieved
ABNCP..... Airborne Command Post [*Air Force*]
ABNCP..... Airborne National Command Force [*DoD*]
ABND........ Abandon (FAAC)
ABNDASC ... Airborne Direct Air Support Center
ABNDT ..... Abundant (FAAC)
ABNF .... Association of Black Nursing Faculty in Higher Education (EA)
ABNG........ Amsterdamer Beitraege zur Neueren Germanistik [*A publication*]
ABNGAO ... Abhandlungen und Berichte. Naturkundemuseums Goerlitz [*A publication*]
ABNH....... American Bank Note Holographics, Inc.
ABNI .... Available but Not Installed
ABNINF .... Airborne Infantry [*Military*]
ABNK .... Ameribanc, Inc. [*NASDAQ symbol*] (NQ)
ABNL .... Abnormal (MSA)
ABNM...... American Board of National Missions (EA)
ABNM...... American Board of Neurological Microsurgery (EA)
ABNM...... American Board of Nuclear Medicine (EA)
ABNML .... Abnormal (FAAC)
ABNN....... Alberta Native News [*A publication*]
ABNN....... American Board of Neuroscience Nursing (EA)
ABNO....... All but Not Only
ABNOC..... Airborne Operations Center [*NATO*] (NATG)
ABNOMS ... American Board of Neurological and Orthopaedic Medicine and Surgery (EA)
ABNOR..... Abnormal
ABNP .... Alan R. Barton Nuclear Plant (NRCH)
ABNRAN .. Acta Botanica Neerlandica [*A publication*]
ABN Review ... ABN [*Algemene Bank Nederland*] Economic Review [*A publication*]
Ab NS .... Abstracts of Treasury Decisions, New Series [*A publication*] (DLA)
ABNS....... American Board of Neurological Surgery (EA)
ABNS....... American British Numismatic Society (EA)
ABNT .... Associacao Brasileira de Normas Tecnicas [*Brazilian national standards organization*]
ABNUAW ... Arquivos Brasileiros de Nutricao [*A publication*]
ABO.......... Aboriginal [*Australian*] (DSUE)
ABO.......... Absatz- und Bezugsorganisation [*Marketing and Purchasing Organization*] [*German*]
ABO.......... Absent Bed Occupancy [*Medicine*]
ABO.......... Accessory Boring Organ [*of a gastropod*]
ABO.......... Administration by Objectives
ABO.......... Affiliated Boards of Officials (EA)
ABO.......... Agents of Biological Origin [*Military*]
ABO.......... American Board of Ophthalmology (EA)
ABO.......... American Board of Opticianry [*Later, NAO*] (EA)
ABO.......... American Board of Orthodontics (EA)
ABO.......... American Board of Otolaryngology (EA)
ABO.......... Arbor Capital, Inc. [*Toronto Stock Exchange symbol*]
ABO.......... Arecibo, PR [*Location identifier*] [*FAA*] (FAAL)
ABO.......... Army Budget Office
ABO.......... Association of British Orientalists
ABO.......... Association of Buying Offices [*Defunct*] (EA)
ABO.......... Astable Blocking Oscillator
ABO.......... Aviator's Breathing Oxygen [*Air Force*]
ABO.......... Boyle Public Library, Alberta [*Library symbol*] [*National Library of Canada*] (NLC)
ABOA .... Acta Borealia. B. Humaniora [*A publication*]
ABOA .... Aminobenzoic Acid [*Organic chemistry*]
ABOA .... Australian Bibliography of Agriculture [*Information service or system*] [*A publication*] (APTA)

ABOA .... Bon Accord Public Library, Alberta [*Library symbol*] [*National Library of Canada*] (NLC)
ABOAAB... Acta Borealia. A. Scientia [*A publication*]
ABOB........ Anhydrobis(beta-hydroxyethyl)biguanide [*Antiviral agent*]
ABOBAE... Anais. Congresso Nacional. Sociedade Botanica do Brasil [*A publication*]
ABOC .... Arnolt-Bristol Owners Club [*Later, ABR*] (EA)
Abo Child School ... Aboriginal Child at School [*A publication*]
ABOD........ Arbeiten zur Bayerisch-Oesterreichischen Dialektgeografie [*A publication*]
ABOF .... American Berlin Opera Foundation (EA)
ABOF .... Annales Botanici Fennici [*A publication*]
ABOFA...... Annales Botanici Fennici [*A publication*]
ABOG........ American Board of Obstetrics and Gynecology (EA)
Abogada Int'l ... Abogada Internacional [*A publication*] (DLA)
ABOHAW ... Acta Botanica. Academiae Scientiarum Hungaricae [*A publication*]
ABOHE2... Acta Botanica Hungarica [*A publication*]
ABOHN .... American Board for Occupational Health Nurses (EA)
A Bohuslaens Hembygds ... Aarsskrift. Bohuslaens Hembygdsfoerbund [*A publication*]
ABOI .... Association of British Oceanic Industries (DS)
ABOIB....... Acta Botanica Indica [*A publication*]
ABOIP...... Amended Basis of Issue Plan [*DoD*]
ABOIPFD ... Amended Basis of Issue Plan, Feeder Data [*DoD*]
Abo Island Forum ... Aboriginal and Islander Forum [*A publication*]
ABOJK..... [*A*] Bunch of Jewish Kids [*Slang*] (BJA)
ABOK .... Oakey [*Australia*] [*ICAO location identifier*] (ICLI)
ABOL .... Abolished
abol .... Abolitionist
ABOL .... Adviser Business Oriented Language [*Programming language*]
ABOM...... American Board of Orthopaedic Microneurosurgery (EA)
ABOM...... Assistant Base Operations Manager [*NASA*] (KSC)
ABOM....... Bowden Pioneer Museum, Alberta [*Library symbol*] [*National Library of Canada*] (BIB)
Abomac ... [*A*] Bit of Money and a Cat [*Lifestyle classification*]
ABOMS..... American Board of Oral and Maxillofacial Surgery (EA)
AB ONE ... Air Bases Command, 1st Naval District
ABOP .... American Board of Oral Pathology (EA)
ABOPAM ... Arquivos de Botanica do Estado de Sao Paulo [*A publication*]
ABOPS..... Association of Business Officers of Preparatory Schools (EA)
ABOR .... Aborigine
ABOR .... Abortion [*Medicine*]
ABORI...... Annals. Bhandarkar Oriental Research Institute [*A publication*]
Aborig Aff Info Paper ... Aboriginal Affairs Information Paper [*A publication*] (APTA)
Aborig Child Sch ... Aboriginal Child at School [*A publication*] (APTA)
Aboriginal Q ... Aboriginal Quarterly [*A publication*] (APTA)
ABORIGINE ... Aircooled Beryllium Oxide with Integrated Gas Turbine
Aborig LB .. Aboriginal Law Bulletin [*A publication*] (APTA)
Abor N....... Aboriginal News [*A publication*] (APTA)
Abortion Law Rep ... Abortion Law Reporter [*A publication*]
Abortion L Rep ... Abortion Law Reporter [*A publication*] (DLA)
ABOS .... Advanced Banking On-Line System (BUR)
ABOS .... American Board of Oral Surgery [*Later, ABOMS*] (EA)
ABOS .... American Board of Orthopedic Surgery (EA)
ABOS .... Bonaza School, Alberta [*Library symbol*] [*National Library of Canada*] (BIB)
ABOSS...... Advanced Bombardment System
ABoT .... Ankara Arkeoloji Muzesinde Bulunan Bogazkoy Tableteri [*Istanbul*] [*A publication*]
ABOTA ..... American Board of Trial Advocates (EA)
ABourg...... Annales de Bourgogne [*A publication*]
About Distance Educ ... About Distance Education [*A publication*]
ABOVA6 ... Acta Botanica Venezuelica [*A publication*]
ABOW .... Bowden Public Library, Alberta [*Library symbol*] [*National Library of Canada*] (NLC)
ABP .... Abra De Llog [*Philippines*] [*Seismograph station code, US Geological Survey*] [*Closed*] (SEIS)
ABP .... Absolute Boiling Point
ABP .... Acetyl Benzoyl Peroxide [*Organic chemistry*]
ABP .... Actin-Binding Protein [*Cytology*]
ABP .... Actual Block Processor [*IBM Corp.*] [*Data processing*] (BUR)
ABP .... Adapter, Binding Post
ABP .... Adriamycin, Bleomycin, Prednisone [*Antineoplastic drug regimen*]
ABP .... Advanced Business Processor [*Datapoint Corp.*]
ABP .... Air Bearing Platform
ABP .... Airborne Beacon Processor
ABP .... Aldosterone-Binding Protein [*Endocrinology*]
ABP .... American Board of Pathology (EA)
ABP .... American Board of Pediatrics (EA)
ABP .... American Board of Pedodontics [*Later, ABPD*] (EA)
ABP .... American Board of Periodontology (EA)
ABP .... American Board of Prosthodontics (EA)
ABP .... American Business Press [*Later, American Business Publishers*]
ABP .... American Business Products, Inc. [*NYSE symbol*] (SPSG)
ABP .... Androgen Binding Protein [*Endocrinology*]
ABP .... Arabinose Binding Protein [*Biochemistry*]
ABP .... Archbishop
ABP .... Arquivo de Bibliografia Portuguesa [*A publication*]

ABP .... Arterial Blood Pressure [*Medicine*]
ABP .... Associated Book Publishers [*Subsidiary of International Thomson Organisation*]
ABP .... Associated British Ports (DS)
ABP .... Association for Birth Psychology (EA)
ABP .... Association of Black Psychologists (EA)
ABP .... Association of Business Publishers (EA)
ABP .... Asteroid Belt Probe
AB & P ...... Australian Bookseller and Publisher [*A publication*] (APTA)
ABP .... Centraal Planbureau. Bibliotheek. Aanwinsten ['*S-Gravenhage*] [*A publication*]
ABPA........ Acoustical and Board Products Association
ABPA........ Advanced Base Personnel Administration
ABPA........ Aftermarket Body Parts Association (EA)
ABPA........ Allergic Bronchopulmonary Aspergillosis [*Medicine*]
ABPA........ American Backgammon Players Association (EA)
ABPA........ American Board Products Association [*Later, AHA*] (EA)
ABPA........ American Book Producers Association (EA)
ABPA........ Association des Bibliotheques des Provinces de l'Atlantique [*Atlantic Provinces Association of Libraries*] [*Canada*]
ABPAC...... Association des Bibliothecaires Parlementaires au Canada [*Association of Parliamentary Librarians of Canada*]
ABPANC.... American Board of PostAnesthesia Nursing Certification (EA)
AB-PAS-Pbh ... Alcian Blue-Periodic Acid Schiff-Lead Hematoxylin Procedure [*Biotechnology*]
ABPBBK ... Annual Review of Biophysics and Bioengineering [*A publication*]
ABPC........ Abaxial Leaflet Pubescence - Curly [*Botany*]
ABPC........ Abelson Plasmacytoma [*Oncology*]
ABPC........ Alaska Pacific Bancorp [*NASDAQ symbol*] (NQ)
ABPC........ American Book Prices Current [*A publication*]
ABPC........ American Book Publishers Council [*Later, AAP*]
ABPC........ Association of British Pewter Craftsmen
ABPCA...... Abstract Bulletin. Institute of Paper Chemistry [*A publication*]
ABPCA...... Aluminum Building Products Credit Association [*Defunct*]
ABPD .... American Board of Pediatric Dentistry (EA)
ABPD .... American Board of Podiatric Dermatology (EA)
ABPDA...... Aftermarket Body Parts Distributors Association [*Later, ABPA*] (EA)
ABPDC...... American Board of Professional Disability Consultants (EA)
ABPE........ Acute Bovine Pulmonary Emphysema [*Cattle disease*]
ABPF........ Audio Bandpass Filter
ABPG........ Advanced Base Proving Ground
ABPH .... American Board of Psychological Hypnosis (EA)
AbPhoto..... Abstracts of Photographic Science and Engineering Literature [*A publication*]
ABPI......... American Businessphones, Incorporated [*Irvine, CA*] [*NASDAQ symbol*] (NQ)
ABPI......... Ankle/Brachial Pressure Index
ABPI......... Association of the British Pharmaceutical Industry
ABPK........ Amtliche Berichte. Preussische Kunstsammlunge [*Berlin*] [*A publication*]
ABPL........ Abelson Plasmacytoid Lymphosarcoma [*Oncology*]
ABPLA ...... American Board of Professional Liability Attorneys [*Chicago, IL*] (EA)
ABPM....... American Board of Preventive Medicine (EA)
ABPM....... Association of Business Product Manufacturers (EA)
ABPM....... Authorized in Accordance with Bureau of Naval Personnel Manual
ABPMR..... American Board of Physical Medicine and Rehabilitation (EA)
ABPN .... American Board of Psychiatry and Neurology (EA)
ABPN .... Association of British Paediatric Nurses
ABPN .... Proserpine [*Australia*] [*ICAO location identifier*] (ICLI)
ABPO .... Advanced Base Personnel Officer
ABPO .... American Board of Podiatric Orthopedics (EA)
ABPP .... American Board of Professional Psychology (EA)
ABPP .... Amino(bromo)(phenyl)pyrimidinone [*Antiherpes compound*]
ABPP .... Amyloid Beta Protein Precursor [*Biochemistry*]
ABPPAC.... American Book Publishers Political Action Committee (EA)
ABPR....... African Book Publishing Record [*A publication*]
ABPR....... American Book Publishing Record [*A publication*]
ABPR....... Association of Baptist Professors of Religion
ABPR....... Association of British Picture Restorers
ABPRBC.... American Barred Plymouth Rock Bantam Club [*Defunct*] (EA)
ABPRC...... American Barred Plymouth Rock Club [*Later, Plymouth Rock Fanciers Club*] (EA)
ABPRC...... American Buff Plymouth Rock Club (EA)
ABPS .... Air-Breathing Propulsion System [*or Subsystem*] [*NASA*]
ABPS .... Airborne Beacon Processing System
A/BPS ...... Airborne Propellant System (AAG)
ABPS .... American Board of Plastic Surgery (EA)
ABPS .... American Board of Podiatric Surgery (EA)
ABPsi........ Association of Black Psychologists (EA)
AB Ps S .... Associate of the British Psychological Society
ABPSTS .... Association of Blind and Partially Sighted Teachers and Students [*British*]
ABPU .... Advanced Base Personnel Unit
ABPW....... Agency Broadcast Producers Workshop [*Defunct*] (EA)
ABPWC..... Association of Business and Professional Women in Construction (EA)

ABPWG..... Whyte Museum of the Canadian Rockies (Gallery), Banff, Alberta [*Library symbol*] [*National Library of Canada*] (NLC)
ABQ.......... Admiralty Berthing Officer [*British*]
ABQ.......... Albuquerque [*New Mexico*] [*Airport symbol*] (OAG)
ABQ.......... Albuquerque [*New Mexico*] [*Seismograph station code, US Geological Survey*] (SEIS)
ABQ.......... Erasmusuniversiteit Rotterdam. Universiteitsbibliotheek. Aanwinstenlijst [*A publication*]
ABQAUR .. American Board of Quality Assurance and Utilization Review (EA)
ABQAURP ... American Board of Quality Assurance and Utilization Review Physicians [*Later, ABQAUR*] (EA)
ABQC .... ABQ Corp. [*NASDAQ symbol*] (NQ)
ABQI .... Antipyrylbenzoquinoneimine [*Organic chemistry*]
ABR .... Abaterra Energy Ltd. [*Toronto Stock Exchange symbol*] [*Vancouver Stock Exchange symbol*]
ABR .... Aberdeen [*South Dakota*] [*Airport symbol*] (OAG)
ABR .... Aberrant Banding Region [*Genetics*]
ABR .... Abnormal Banding Region [*Genetics*]
ABR .... Abortus Bang Ringprobe [*Test*] [*Medicine*]
ABR .... Abridged
ABR .... Absolute Bed Rest [*Medicine*]
ABR .... Accounting and Business Research [*A publication*]
ABR .... Acrylate-Butadiene Rubber
ABR .... Active Business Records [*Bell & Howell Co.*]
ABR .... Additional Billet Requirements [*Military*]
ABR .... Adhesive Bonding Repair
ABR .... Airborne Resupply (CINC)
ABr .... Altbabylonische Briefe [*A publication*]
ABR .... American Bankruptcy Reports [*A publication*] (DLA)
ABR .... American Benedictine Review [*A publication*]
ABR .... American Board of Radiology (EA)
ABR .... American Book Review [*A publication*]
ABR .... Amphibian Boat Reconnaissance Aircraft
ABr .... Annales de Bretagne et des Pays de l'Ouest [*A publication*]
aBR .... Anti-Beevers-Ross [*Beta-alumina crystallography*]
ABR .... Arnolt-Bristol Registry (EA)
ABR .... Association for Biomedical Research (EA)
ABR .... Auditory Brainstem Response [*Neurophysiology*]
ABR .... Australian Biblical Review [*A publication*]
ABR .... Australian Book Review [*A publication*] (APTA)
ABR .... Automatic Band Rate (IEEE)
ABR .... Brooks Public Library, Alberta [*Library symbol*] [*National Library of Canada*] (NLC)
a-br---.......... Burma [*MARC geographic area code*] [*Library of Congress*] (LCCP)
Abr .... De Abrahamo [*Philo*] (BJA)
ABR .... Real-Aerovias Brasil [*Brazilian international airline*]
ABRA .... Abracadabra. Association of British Columbia Drama Educators [*A publication*]
ABRA .... American Blood Resources Association (EA)
ABRA .... American Buckskin Registry Association (EA)
ABRA .... Asociacion de Bancos de la Republica Argentina [*Bankers' association*] [*Argentina*] (EY)
ABRAC...... Abracadabra (DSUE)
ABRAC...... Agriculture Biotechnology Research Advisory Committee [*Department of Agriculture*] (EGAO)
ABRACADABRA ... Abbreviations and Related Acronyms Associated with Defense, Astronautics, Business, and Radio-Electronics [*Raytheon Co. publication*]
Abrasive Clean Methods ... Abrasive and Cleaning Methods [*A publication*]
Abrasive Eng ... Abrasive Engineering [*A publication*]
Abrasive Eng Soc Mag ... Abrasive Engineering Society. Magazine [*A publication*]
Abrasiv Eng ... Abrasive Engineering [*A publication*]
ABRB........ Advanced Base Receiving Barracks
ABRC........ [*The*] Advisory Board for the Research Councils [*British*]
ABRC........ Association des Bibliotheques de Recherche du Canada [*Canadian Association of Research Libraries*] (EAIO)
ABRC........ Auto Body Representatives Council (EA)
Abr Ca Eq.. Abridgment of Cases in Equity [*1667-1744*] [*A publication*] (DLA)
Abr Cas...... Crawford and Dix's Irish Abridged Cases [*A publication*] (DLA)
Abr Cas Eq ... Equity Cases Abridged [*2 vols.*] [*21, 22 English Reprint*] [*A publication*] (DLA)
ABRD .... Advanced Base Receiving Depot
ABRD .... Advanced Base Repair Depot
ABRD .... Advanced Base Reshipment Depot
ABRDA ..... American Bill of Rights Day Association [*Defunct*] (EA)
ABRE........ Air Battalion Royal Engineers [*Later, Royal Aircraft Establishment*] [*British*]
ABRE........ Army Board of Review for Eliminations
AB (Rel).... Bachelor of Arts with Religious Major
AB Rep...... American Bankruptcy Reports [*A publication*] (DLA)
Abr Eq Cas ... Equity Cases Abridged [*2 vols.*] [*21, 22 English Reprint*] [*A publication*] (DLA)
ABRES ..... Advanced Ballistic Reentry System
A'B Res Judgm ... A'Beckett's Reserved Judgements [*Port Phillip*] [*A publication*] (APTA)

ABRET ...... American Board of Registration of EEG [*Electroencephalographic*] Technologists (EA)

ABret .... Annales de Bretagne [*Later, Annales de Bretagne et des Pays de l'Ouest*] [*A publication*]

AB Rev ...... American Bankruptcy Review [*A publication*] (DLA)

ABRF .... Brisbane [*Australia*] [*ICAO location identifier*] (ICLI)

ABRI .... Abrams Industries, Inc. [*NASDAQ symbol*] (NQ)

AB & RI ..... Animal Breeding and Research Institute [*Western Australia*]

Abridg (Brit) Pat ... Abridgments of Specification Patents for Inventions (Great Britain) [*A publication*]

Abridg Wkly Weath Rep Canb ... Abridged Weekly Weather Report for Canberra [*A publication*] (APTA)

AbrIMed.... Abridged Index Medicus [*A publication*]

Abr Index Med ... Abridged Index Medicus [*A publication*]

A'B RJ (NSW) ... A'Beckett's Reserved and Equity Judgements (New South Wales) [*A publication*] (APTA)

A'B RJPP .. A'Beckett's Reserved Judgements (Port Phillip) [*A publication*]

ABRK .... Rockhampton [*Australia*] [*ICAO location identifier*] (ICLI)

ABRL......... Aviation Base Responsibility List (AFIT)

ABRM ...... Anterior Byssus Retractor Muscle [*Mollusk anatomy*]

ABRM .... Breton Municipal Library, Alberta [*Library symbol*] [*National Library of Canada*] (NLC)

ABRMS..... American Board of Ringside Medicine and Surgery (EA)

ABRNS...... American Bankruptcy Reports, New Series [*A publication*] (DLA)

ABRO .... Animal Breeding Research Organisation [*British*]

ABRO .... Army in Burma Reserve of Officers [*British military*] (DMA)

ABRO .... Brocket Public Library, Alberta [*Library symbol*] [*National Library of Canada*] (NLC)

Ab Rom Proc ... Abdy's Roman Civil Procedure [*A publication*] (DLA)

ABROW .... Brownfield Public Library, Alberta [*Library symbol*] [*National Library of Canada*] (NLC)

Abr Read Guide ... Abridged Readers' Guide to Periodical Literature [*A publication*]

Abr RG....... Abridged Reader's Guide to Periodical Literature [*A publication*]

ABRS......... Adolescent Behavior Rating Scale [*Devereaux*] [*Also, DAB*] [*Psychology*]

A Br Sch Archeol Athens ... Annual. British School of Archaeology at Athens [*A publication*]

Abr Sci Publ Kodak Res Lab ... Abridged Scientific Publications from the Kodak Research Laboratories [*A publication*]

Abr Sci Pubs ... Abridged Scientific Publications [*A publication*]

ABRSV....... Abrasive (MSA)

ABRT......... Abort (MCD)

ABRT......... Assyrian and Babylonian Religious Texts [*A publication*] (BJA)

ABRTDI .... Advances in Behaviour Research and Therapy [*A publication*]

ABRTREQ ... Abort Request (MCD)

ABRUM .... Bruderheim Municipal Library, Alberta [*Library symbol*] [*National Library of Canada*] (NLC)

ABRV .... Advanced Ballistic Reentry Vehicle (MCD)

ABS........... ABAC Resources [*Vancouver Stock Exchange symbol*]

ABS........... Abastumani [*USSR*] [*Seismograph station code, US Geological Survey*] [*Closed*] (SEIS)

ABS........... Abbess

ABS........... Abdominal Surgery [*Medical specialty*] (DHSM)

ABS........... [*Assays for Chromosome*] Aberrations [*Oncology*]

ABS........... Abitibi Asbestos Mining Co. Ltd. [*Vancouver Stock Exchange symbol*]

ABS........... Able-Bodied Seaman

Abs........... Absatz [*Paragraph*] [*German*] (ILCA)

ABS........... Absatzwirtschaft [*A publication*]

ABS........... Absent (AFM)

ABs........... Abside [*A publication*]

ABS........... Absolute [*Flowchart*]

ABS........... Absorb

Abs........... Abstain (ILCA)

ABS........... Abstract

Abs........... Abstracts of Treasury Decisions [*A publication*] (DLA)

ABS........... Abu Simbel [*Egypt*] [*Airport symbol*] (OAG)

ABS........... Acrylonitrile-Butadiene-Styrene [*Organic chemistry*]

ABS........... Acta Baltico-Slavica [*A publication*]

ABS........... Active Boom Suspension [*Engineering*]

ABS........... Acute Brain Syndrome [*Medicine*]

ABS........... Adaptive Behavior Scale [*American Association on Mental Deficiency*] [*Psychology*]

ABS........... Additional Budget Submissions [*DoD*]

ABS........... Affects Balance Scale [*Personality development test*] [*Psychology*]

ABS........... Air Base Simulator [*Air Force*]

ABSCS....... Air Base Squadron [*Air Force*]

ABS........... Air Base Survivability

ABS........... Air-Brake Switch

ABS........... Air-Breathing System

ABS........... Airborne Backing Store

ABS........... Albertson's, Inc. [*NYSE symbol*] (SPSG)

ABS........... Albumin-Buffered Saline [*Clinical chemistry*]

ABS........... Alkyl Benzenesulfonate [*Organic chemistry*]

ABS........... Amalgamated Book Services [*British*]

ABS........... American Backgammon Society

ABS........... American Ballads and Songs [*A publication*]

ABS........... American Bamboo Society (EA)

ABS........... American Beethoven Society (EA)

ABS........... American Begonia Society (EA)

ABS........... American Behavioral Scientist [*A publication*]

ABS........... American Bible Society (EA)

ABS........... American Biological Society (EA)

ABS........... American Bladesmith Society (EA)

ABS........... American Board of Surgery (EA)

ABS........... American Bonanza Society (EA)

ABS........... American Bonsai Society (EA)

ABS........... American Boxwood Society (EA)

ABS........... American Breeder Service

ABS........... American Bryological Society [*Later, ABLS*] (EA)

ABS........... American Budgerigar Society (EA)

ABS........... American Bureau of Shipping (EA)

ABS........... Anheuser-Busch, Inc., Corporation Library, St. Louis, MO [*OCLC symbol*] (OCLC)

ABS........... Animal Behavior Society (EA)

ABS........... Antenna Base Spring

ABS........... Antilock Braking System [*Automotive engineering*]

ABS........... Antique Boat Society (EA)

ABS........... Antiskid Braking System [*General Motors Corp.*]

ABS........... Approved to British Standard [*British Standards Institution*]

ABS........... Armoured Boarding Steamer [*British military*] (DMA)

ABS........... Asset-Backed Security [*Finance*]

ABSD........ Associate of the Building Services Institute [*Australia*]

ABS........... Associate in Business Science

ABS........... Associated Biomedic Systems, Inc.

ABS........... Associated Blacksmiths of Scotland [*A union*]

ABS........... Associated Broadcasting Services [*Australia*]

ABS........... Association of Black Sociologists (EA)

ABS........... Association of Black Storytellers (EA)

ABS........... Association of Broadcasting Staff [*A union*] [*British*] (DCTA)

ABS........... Association on Broadcasting Standards [*Later, Association for Broadcast Engineering Standards*]

ABS........... Atlantic Base Section

ABS........... ATLAS Block Structure (MCD)

ABS........... Australian Building Specification [*A publication*] (APTA)

ABS........... Australian Bureau of Statistics [*Information service or system*] (IID)

ABS........... Automated Bioassay System (MCD)

ABS........... Automatic Braking System (MCD)

ABS........... Aux Bons Soins De [*Care Of, c/o*] [*French*] [*Correspondence*]

ABS........... Auxiliary Building Sump [*Nuclear energy*] (IEEE)

ABS........... Average Busy Season [*Telecommunications*] (TEL)

ABS........... Birmingham Southern College, Birmingham, AL [*Library symbol*] [*Library of Congress*] (LCLS)

Abs........... Ohio Law Abstract [*A publication*] (DLA)

ABSA........ Annual. British School at Athens [*A publication*]

ABSA........ Association of British Secretaries in America

ABSA........ Association for Business Sponsorship of the Arts [*British*] (EAIO)

ABSA........ Australian Bird Study Association

ABSAME .. Association for Behavioral Sciences and Medical Education (EA)

ABSAP ...... Airborne Search and Attack Plotter

ABSB .... Air Burst/Surface Burst (MCD)

ABSB .... Alexander Brown, Inc. [*Baltimore, MD*] [*NASDAQ symbol*] (NQ)

ABSBH...... Average Busy Season Busy Hour [*Telecommunications*] (TEL)

Abs Bull Inst Paper Chem ... Abstract Bulletin. Institute of Paper Chemistry [*A publication*]

ABSC......... Applied Behavioural Studies Centre [*Australia*]

ABSC......... Associate of the British Society of Commerce

ABSC......... Association des Bibliotheques de la Sante du Canada [*Canadian Association of Health Libraries*]

ABSC......... Automatic Bass Compensation [*Radio*] (MSA)

ABSC......... Automatic Blip-Scan Counter

ABSCAM .. FBI "sting" operation, 1979, in which agents posing as Arabs tried to entice members of Congress and other public officials into taking bribes. Acronym is said to stand for either "Arab Scam," "Arab Businessmen Scam," or "Abdul Scam" (after Abdul Enterprises, phony FBI company used as a front for the operation).

ABSCD6.... Annales. Universite de Brazzaville. Serie C. Sciences [*A publication*]

Abschn....... Abschnitt [*Paragraph, Chapter*] [*German*] (ILCA)

ABS CLG... Absolute Ceiling [*Aviation*]

ABSCM..... Association of Boys and Students Clothing Manufacturers (EA)

Abs Crim Pen ... Abstracts on Criminology and Penology [*A publication*]

ABSCS....... Automatic Blip-Scan Counter System

ABSD........ Advance Base Section Dock [*Floating drydock, first used in World War II*]

ABSD........ Advanced Base Supply Depot

AB in Sec Ed ... Bachelor of Arts in Secondary Education

ABSEL ...... Association for Business Simulation and Experiential Learning [*Tulsa, OK*] (EA)

ABSE RE... Absente Reo [*The Defendant Being Absent*] [*Legal term*] [*Latin*] (ADA)

ABSF .... American Blind Skiing Foundation (EA)

ABSFA ...... Banff Centre Library, Alberta [*Library symbol*] [*National Library of Canada*] (NLC)

ABS FEB ... Absente Febre [*In the Absence of Fever*] [*Pharmacy*]

ABS FEBR ... Absente Febre [*In the Absence of Fever*] [*Pharmacy*] (ROG)

ABSHF ...... Annuaire-Bulletin. Societe de l'Histoire de France [*A publication*]

ABSHP ...... Archbishop

ABSI .... ABS Industries, Inc. [*Willoughby, OH*] [*NASDAQ symbol*] (NQ)

ABSI .... Adaptive Behavior Scale for Infants and Early Childhood [*Child development test*]

ABSIE .... American Broadcasting Station in Europe [*OWI*]

ABSIG .... Anti-Bureaucracy Special Interest Group [*Mensa*] (EA)

ABSJM ..... Amicable and Brotherly Society of Journeymen Millwrights [*A union*] [*British*]

ABSLA ...... Approved Basic Stock Level of Ammunition (MCD)

ABSLAU ... Danish Pest Infestation Laboratory. Annual Report [*A publication*]

ABSLDR ... Absolute Loader [*Data processing*]

ABSLY ...... Absolutely (ROG)

ABSM .... Associate of the Birmingham and Midland Institute School of Music [*British*]

ABSM .... Association of British Steriliser Manufacturers (EAIO)

ABSMA ..... American Bleached Shellac Manufacturers Association (EA)

ABSN .... Adoptee-Birthparent Support Network (EA)

Abs (NS) .... Abstracts of Treasury Decisions, New Series [*A publication*] (DLA)

AbSocWk ... Abstracts for Social Workers [*A publication*]

ABSOL ...... Absolute

ABSORB ... Absorption

Absorpt Distrib Transform Excretion Drugs ... Absorption, Distribution, Transformation, and Excretion of Drugs [*A publication*]

Absorpt Spectra Ultraviolet Visible Reg ... Absorption Spectra in the Ultraviolet and Visible Region [*A publication*]

ABSORS ... American Bureau of Shipping Information Retrieval System (MSC)

ABSP .... About Buttonhooks, Spoons, and Patents [*An association*] [*Defunct*] (EA)

Abs Pap ACS ... Abstracts of Papers. American Chemical Society [*A publication*]

ABSPDB ... Acta Botanica Slovaca. Academiae Scientiarum Slovacae. Series B. Physiologica, Pathophysiologica [*A publication*]

ABSq .... Air Base Squadron [*Air Force*]

ABSR .... Southern Research Institute, Birmingham, AL [*Library symbol*] [*Library of Congress*] (LCLS)

ABS RE ..... Absente Reo [*The Defendant Being Absent*] [*Legal term*] [*Latin*] (ADA)

ABSS .... Air Bag Skid System (MCD)

ABSS .... American Board of Spinal Surgery (EA)

ABS-SE ..... Adaptive Behavior Scale, School Edition [*Child development test*]

ABSSOP .... Committee for the Application of the Behavioral Sciences to the Strategies of Peace (EA)

ABST .... Abstract

ABST .... Adult Basic Skill Training (NVT)

ABST .... Auxiliary Building Sump Tank [*Nuclear energy*] (NRCH)

Abst .... De Abstinentia [*of Porphyry*] [*Classical studies*] (OCD)

Abst CSICMR ... Abstracts. Centre for the Study of Islam and Christian-Muslim Relations [*A publication*]

ABSTD ...... ABS [*Australian Bureau of Statistics*] Time-Series Database [*Information service or system*] (CRD)

ABSTEE .... Absentee

ABSTR ...... Abstract

Abstracts Amer Math Soc ... Abstracts of Papers Presented to the American Mathematical Society [*A publication*]

Abstracts Bulgar Sci Lit Math Phys Sci ... Abstracts of Bulgarian Scientific Literature. Mathematical and Physical Sciences [*A publication*]

Abstr Annu Meet Am Soc Microbiol ... Abstracts of the Annual Meeting. American Society for Microbiology [*A publication*]

Abstr Anthropol ... Abstracts in Anthropology [*A publication*]

Abstr Bacteriol ... Abstracts of Bacteriology [*A publication*]

Abstr Bot .... Abstracta Botanica [*A publication*]

Abstr Bulg Scient Lit ... Abstracts of Bulgarian Scientific Literature [*A publication*]

Abstr Bulg Sci Lit Agric For Vet Med ... Abstracts of Bulgarian Scientific Literature. Agriculture and Forestry, Veterinary Medicine [*A publication*]

Abstr Bulg Sci Lit Biol Biochem ... Abstracts of Bulgarian Scientific Literature. Biology and Biochemistry [*A publication*]

Abstr Bulg Sci Lit Biol Med ... Abstracts of Bulgarian Scientific Literature. Biology and Medicine [*A publication*]

Abstr Bulg Sci Lit Chem ... Abstracts of Bulgarian Scientific Literature. Chemistry [*A publication*]

Abstr Bulg Sci Lit Chem Chem Technol ... Abstracts of Bulgarian Scientific Literature. Chemistry and Chemical Technology [*A publication*]

Abstr Bulg Sci Lit Geol Geogr ... Abstracts of Bulgarian Scientific Literature. Geology and Geography [*A publication*]

Abstr Bulg Sci Lit Geosci ... Abstracts of Bulgarian Scientific Literature. Geosciences [*A publication*]

Abstr Bulg Sci Lit Math Phys Astron Geophys Geod ... Abstracts of Bulgarian Scientific Literature. Mathematics, Physics, Astronomy, Geophysics, Geodesy [*A publication*]

Abstr Bulg Sci Lit Ser A Plant Breed For Econ ... Abstracts of Bulgarian Scientific Literature. Series A. Plant Breeding and Forest Economy [*A publication*]

Abstr Bulg Sci Med Lit ... Abstracts of Bulgarian Scientific Medical Literature [*A publication*]

Abstr Bull .. Monthly Abstract Bulletin [*A publication*]

Abstr Bull Geol Surv S Aust ... Abstracts Bulletin. Geological Survey of South Australia [*A publication*] (APTA)

Abstr Bull Inst Pap Chem ... Abstract Bulletin. Institute of Paper Chemistry [*A publication*]

Abstr Bull Inst Paper Chem ... Abstract Bulletin. Institute of Paper Chemistry [*A publication*]

Abstr Collect Eur Neurosci Meet ... Abstract Collection. European Neurosciences Meeting [*A publication*]

Abstr Comput Lit ... Abstracts of Computer Literature [*A publication*]

Abstr Congr Eur Soc Exp Surg ... Abstracts. Congress of the European Society for Experimental Surgery [*A publication*]

Abstr Congr Pol Phthisiopneumonol Soc ... Abstracts. Congress of the Polish Phthisiopneumonological Society [*A publication*]

Abstr Crime Juv Del ... Abstracts on Crime and Juvenile Delinquency [*A publication*]

Abstr Criminol Penol ... Abstracts on Criminology and Penology [*A publication*]

Abstr Crim & Pen ... Abstracts on Criminology and Penology [*A publication*]

Abstr Curr Lit Aerosp Med Assoc ... Abstracts of Current Literature. Aerospace Medical Association [*A publication*]

Abstr Doct Diss Ohio St Univ ... Abstracts of Doctoral Dissertations. Ohio State University [*A publication*]

Abstr Engl Stud ... Abstracts of English Studies [*A publication*]

Abstr Entomol ... Abstracts of Entomology [*A publication*]

Abstr Eur Soc Surg Res Congr ... Abstracts. European Society for Surgical Research. Congress [*A publication*]

Abstr Folk Stud ... Abstracts of Folklore Studies [*A publication*]

Abstr Geochronology Isot Geol ... Abstracts of Geochronology and Isotope Geology [*A publication*]

Abstr Health Care Manage Stud ... Abstracts of Health Care Management Studies [*A publication*]

Abstr Health Eff Environ Pollut ... Abstracts on Health Effects of Environmental Pollutants [*A publication*]

Abstr Health Environ Pollutants ... Abstracts on Health Effects of Environmental Pollutants [*A publication*]

Abstr Hospit Manage Stud ... Abstracts of Hospital Management Studies [*A publication*]

Abstr Hosp Manage Stud ... Abstracts of Hospital Management Studies [*A publication*]

Abstr Hyg .. Abstracts on Hygiene [*A publication*]

Abstr Hyg Commun Dis ... Abstracts on Hygiene and Communicable Diseases [*A publication*]

Abstr Jap Lit Forest Genet ... Abstracts of Japanese Literature in Forest Genetics and Related Fields [*A publication*]

Abstr J Chem React Doc Serv ... Abstracts Journal. Chemical Reaction Documentation Service [*A publication*]

Abstr J Earthq Eng ... Abstract Journal in Earthquake Engineering [*A publication*]

Abstr J Inf (Moscow) ... Abstract Journal Informations (Moscow) [*A publication*]

Abstr Jpn Med ... Abstracts of Japanese Medicine [*A publication*]

Abstr Meet Weed Soc Am ... Abstracts. Meeting of the Weed Society of America [*A publication*]

Abstr Mil Bibl ... Abstracts of Military Bibliography [*A publication*]

Abstr Mil Bibliogr ... Abstracts of Military Bibliography [*A publication*]

Abstr Mtg ACS ... Abstracts of Papers. Meeting of the American Chemical Society [*A publication*]

Abstr Mtg Weed Soc Amer ... Abstracts. Meeting of the Weed Society of America [*A publication*]

Abstr Mycol ... Abstracts of Mycology [*A publication*]

Abstr N Amer Geol ... Abstracts of North American Geology [*A publication*]

Abstr Natl Congr Ital Soc Mar Biol ... Abstracts. National Congress of the Italian Society of Marine Biology [*A publication*]

Abstr New World Archaeol ... Abstracts of New World Archaeology [*A publication*]

Abstr North Am Geol ... Abstracts of North American Geology [*A publication*]

Abstr Pap Am Chem Soc ... Abstracts of Papers. American Chemical Society [*A publication*]

Abstr Pap Aust Workshop Coal Hydrogenation ... Australian Workshop on Coal Hydrogenation. Abstract and Papers [*A publication*] (APTA)

Abstr Pap Commun R Soc (London) ... Abstracts of the Papers Communicated to the Royal Society (London) [*A publication*]

Abstr Pap Int Conf At Sptrosc ... Abstracts of Papers Accepted for Presentation. International Conference on Atomic Spectroscopy [*A publication*]

Abstr Pap J Jpn Soc Intern Med ... Abstracts of Papers. Journal of the Japanese Society of Internal Medicine [*A publication*]

Abstr Pap Jt Conf Chem Inst Can Am Chem Soc ... Abstracts of Papers. Joint Conference. Chemical Institute of Canada and American Chemical Society [*A publication*]

Abstr Pap Pac Sci Congr ... Abstracts of the Papers. Pacific Science Congress [*A publication*]
Abstr Pap Presented Ann Meet Am Soc Range Mange ... Abstracts of Papers Presented at the Annual Meeting. American Society of Range Management [*A publication*]
Abstr Pap Presented Annu Meet Korean Surg Soc ... Abstracts of Papers Presented at the Annual Meeting. Korean Surgical Society [*A publication*]
Abstr Pap Printed Philos Trans R Soc (London) ... Abstracts of the Papers Printed in the Philosophical Transactions of the Royal Society (London) [*A publication*]
Abstr Pap Sci Poult Conf ... Abstracts of Papers Presented at the Scientific Poultry Conference [*A publication*]
Abstr Pap Soc Amer For ... Abstracts of Papers. Society of American Foresters Meeting [*A publication*]
Abstr Photogr Sci Eng Lit ... Abstracts of Photographic Science and Engineering Literature [*A publication*]
Abstr Police Sci ... Abstracts on Police Science [*A publication*]
Abstr Pop Cult ... Abstracts of Popular Culture [*A publication*]
Abstr Proc Linn Soc NSW ... Abstracts of the Proceedings. Linnean Society of New South Wales [*A publication*] (APTA)
Abstr Proc Soc NSW ... Abstracts of Proceedings. Royal Society of New South Wales [*A publication*] (APTA)
Abstr Programs Geol Soc Am ... Abstracts with Programs. Geological Society of America [*A publication*]
Abstr Publ Pap List Transl CSIRO (Aust) ... Abstracts of Published Papers and List of Translations. Commonwealth Scientific and Industrial Research Organisation (Australia) [*A publication*]
Abstr Refin Lit ... Abstracts of Refining Literature [*A publication*]
Abstr Rep Geol Surv West Austr ... Abstracts. Reports of the Geological Survey of Western Australia [*A publication*] (APTA)
Abstr Res Pastor Care Couns ... Abstracts of Research in Pastoral Care and Counseling [*A publication*]
Abstr Res Tob Salt Camphor ... Abstracts of Researches. Tobacco, Salt, Camphor [*A publication*]
Abstr Rom Sci Tech Lit ... Abstracts of Romanian Scientific and Technical Literature [*A publication*]
Abstr Rom Tech Lit ... Abstracts of Romanian Technical Literature [*A publication*]
Abstr Soc Work ... Abstracts for Social Workers [*A publication*]
Abstr Sov Med ... Abstracts of Soviet Medicine [*A publication*]
Abstr Sov Med Part A ... Abstracts of Soviet Medicine. Part A. Basic Medical Sciences [*A publication*]
Abstr Sov Med Part B ... Abstracts of Soviet Medicine. Part B. Clinical Medicine [*A publication*]
Abstr T ... Abstracts of Title [*A publication*] (DLA)
Abstr Tech Pap Water Pollut Control Fed ... Abstracts of Technical Papers. Water Pollution Control Federation [*A publication*]
Abstr Trop Agri ... Abstracts on Tropical Agriculture [*A publication*]
Abstr Trop Agric ... Abstracts on Tropical Agriculture [*A publication*]
Abstr Uppsala Diss Med ... Abstracts of Uppsala Dissertations in Medicine [*A publication*]
Abstr Uppsala Diss Sci ... Abstracts of Uppsala Dissertations in Science [*A publication*]
Abstr Wld Med ... Abstracts of World Medicine [*A publication*]
Abstr World Med ... Abstracts of World Medicine [*A publication*]
Absts Soc Workers ... Abstracts for Social Workers [*A publication*]
ABSTT ...... Abstract [*Legal*] [*British*] (ROG)
ABSTURN ... Absence and Turnover Rates [*Database*]
ABSU .... Aid to Believers in the Soviet Union [*See also ACU*] [*Paris, France*] (EAIO)
ABSUD ...... Amtsblatt. Bayerisches Staatsministerium fuer Landesentwicklung und Umweltfragen [*A publication*]
ABS U N .... Absque Ulla Nota [*Without Any Marking or Note*] [*Latin*] (ROG)
ABSV .... Absorptive Technology, Inc. [*NASDAQ symbol*] (NQ)
ABSVS ...... Auxiliary Building Special Ventilation System [*Nuclear energy*] (NRCH)
ABSW .... Air-Brake Switch
ABSW .... Association of British Science Writers
ABT .... Abbot Energy Corp. [*Vancouver Stock Exchange symbol*]
ABT .... Abbott Laboratories [*NYSE symbol*] (SPSG)
ABT .... Abort
ABT .... About (MUGU)
ABT .... Abstract Planning Tool
ABT .... Abteilung [*Department, Division, Section*] [*German*]
abT .... Abtesla [*Unit of magnetic induction*]
ABT .... Advanced Booster Technology (MCD)
ABT .... Air Blast Transformer (MSA)
ABT .... Airborne Tracking (MCD)
ABT .... All Body Type [*Army*] (AABC)
ABT .... Allied Board of Trade
ABT .... American Ballet Theater
ABT .... American Board of Toxicology (EA)
ABT .... American Board of Trade
ABT .... Animated Burtek Trainer
ABT .... Applied Business Technology Corp.
ABT .... Associate in Business Technology
ABT .... Association of Beauty Teachers [*British*]
ABT .... Association of Book Travelers (EA)

ABT .... Association of Building Technicians [*A union*] [*British*]
ABT .... Atlantic Booster Test (KSC)
ABT .... Automatic Battery Test
ABT .... Automatic Bus Terminal [*Data processing*] (MCD)
ABT .... Automatic Bus Transfer (NVT)
ABT .... Auxiliary Ballast Tank
a-bt--- ...... Bhutan [*MARC geographic area code*] [*Library of Congress*] (LCCP)
ABTA .... American Board of Trial Advocates
ABTA .... American Bridge Teachers' Association (EA)
ABTA .... Association of British Travel Agents
ABTA Bull ... Australian-British Trade Association. Bulletin [*A publication*]
ABTAPL ...... Association of British Theological and Philosophical Libraries
ABTB .... Association of Bank Travel Bureaus [*Defunct*] (EA)
ABTC .... American Belgian Tervuren Club (EA)
ABTC .... Australian Book Trade Committee
ABTCA ...... American Black and Tan Coonhound Association (EA)
ABTD .... American Book Trade Directory [*A publication*]
ABTD .... Australian Book Trade Directory [*A publication*] (APTA)
ABTD .... Automatic Bulk Tape Degausser
ABTD .... Thursday Island [*Australia*] [*ICAO location identifier*] (ICLI)
ABTF .... Aborigines Benefit Trust Fund [*Australia*]
ABTF .... Airborne Task Force
ABTF .... Assault Battalion Task Force (MCD)
AB in TH ... Bachelor of Arts in Theology
ABTIBR ...... Acta Botanica Islandica [*A publication*]
ABTICS ..... Abstract and Book Title Index Card Service [*United Kingdom*]
ABTL .... Townsville [*Australia*] [*ICAO location identifier*] (ICLI)
ABTM ...... American Board of Tropical Medicine [*Inactive*] (EA)
ABTM ...... Association of British Transport Museums
ABTNOMS ... American Board of Thoracic Neurological Orthopaedic Medicine and Surgery (EA)
ABTR .... Association for Brain Tumor Research (EA)
ABTS .... American Board of Thoracic Surgery (EA)
ABTSA ...... Association for the Behavioral Treatment of Sexual Abusers (EA)
ABTSS ...... Airborne Transponder Subsystem
ABTT .... Associate of British Theatre Technicians
ABTT .... Townsville [*Australia*] [*ICAO location identifier*] (ICLI)
ABTTA ...... American Bridge, Tunnel, and Turnpike Association [*Later, IBTTA*] (EA)
ABTTAP ... Arquivos de Biologia e Tecnologia [*Curitiba*] [*A publication*]
ABTU .... Advanced Base Torpedo Unit [*Navy*]
ABTU .... Advanced Base Training Unit [*Navy*]
ABTU .... Air Bombers Training Unit [*Navy*]
ABTU .... Army Basic Training Unit [*British military*] (DMA)
ABTV .... Townsville [*Australia*] [*ICAO location identifier*] (ICLI)
ABU .... ABO Resource Corp. [*Vancouver Stock Exchange symbol*]
ABU .... Abuyama [*Japan*] [*Seismograph station code, US Geological Survey*] (SEIS)
ABU .... Administrative Base Unit [*British military*] (DMA)
ABU .... Alliance Biblique Universelle
ABU .... American Board of Urology (EA)
Abu .... Aminobutyric Acid [*Also, ABA*] [*Biochemistry*]
ABU .... Asia Pacific Broadcasting Union (EAIO)
ABU .... Australian Business Law Review [*A publication*]
ABU .... Office of Budget [*FAA*] (FAAC)
ABU of A ... Amateur Boxing Union of Australia
ABUAHP .. American Board of Urologic Allied Health Professionals (EA)
ABUC .... Archivio Bibliographico. Bibliotheca da Universidade de Coimbra [*A publication*]
ABUG .... Rid-a-Bug Co. [*NASDAQ symbol*] (NQ)
ABUIC .... Association des Bureaux de l'Information des Universites [*Association of University Information Bureaus*] [*Canada*]
ABul .... Art Bulletin [*A publication*]
ABull .... Art Bulletin [*A publication*]
ABus .... Associate in Business Administration
A Bus L Rev ... Australian Business Law Review [*A publication*] (APTA)
ABU Tech Rev ... ABU [*Asian Broadcasting Union*] Technical Review [*A publication*]
ABV .... Above (MSA)
ABV .... Abschnittsbevollmaechtiger [*Section Deputy*] [*German*]
ABV .... Absolute Value (BUR)
ABV .... Absorptive Technology, Inc. [*Vancouver Stock Exchange symbol*]
ABV .... Abuja [*Nigeria*] [*Airport symbol*] (OAG)
ABV .... Actinomycin D, Bleomycin, Vincristine [*Antineoplastic drug regimen*]
ABV .... Adriamycin, Bleomycin, Vinblastine [*Antineoplastic drug regimen*]
ABV .... Air Blast Valve
ABV .... Air Bubble Vehicle
ABV .... Anegada [*Virgin Islands*] [*Seismograph station code, US Geological Survey*] (SEIS)
ABV .... Armed Boarding Vessel
ABV .... Attic Black-Figure Vase Painters [*A publication*]
ABV .... Auxiliary Building Ventilation [*Nuclear energy*] (NRCH)
ABV .... Repeat the Figures in Abbreviated Form [*Aviation code*]
ABVA .... United States Veterans Administration Hospital, Birmingham, AL [*Library symbol*] [*Library of Congress*] (LCLS)

ABVD .... Adriamycin, Bleomycin, Vinblastine [*Oncovin*], Dacarbazine [*Antineoplastic drug regimen*]
ABVE .... American Board of Vocational Experts (EA)
ABVEAO ... Acta Biologica Venezuelica [*A publication*]
AbVoc .... Abstracts of Research and Related Materials in Vocational and Technical Education [*A publication*]
ABVS .... Advisory Board on Veterinary Specialties (EA)
ABVSD ...... Annales. Association Belge de Radioprotection [*A publication*]
ABVT .... American Board of Veterinary Toxicology (EA)
ABW .... ABC Technology, Inc. [*Vancouver Stock Exchange symbol*]
ABW .... Air Base Wing [*Air Force*] (MCD)
ABW .... American Baptist Women (EA)
ABW .... Anybody but Wallace [*Political slogan referring to Alabama governor George Wallace*]
ABW .... Aruba [*ANSI three-letter standard code*] (CNC)
ABW .... Autobond Welder
ABW .... Automated Batch Weighing
ABW .... St. Louis, MO [*Location identifier*] [*FAA*] (FAAL)
ABWA ...... American Bottled Water Association [*Later, IBWA*] (EA)
ABWA ...... American Business Women's Association (EA)
ABWA ...... American Business Writing Association [*Later, ABCA*] (EA)
ABWA ...... Associated Business Writers of America (EA)
ABWADK ... Australian Birdwatcher [*A publication*]
abWb .... Abweber [*Also, Mx*] [*Unit of magnetic flux*]
ABWC ...... American Buff Wyandotte Club [*Defunct*] (EA)
ABWC ...... Automatic Bandwidth Control (MSA)
ABWE ...... Association of Baptists for World Evangelism (EA)
ABWG ...... Air Base Wing [*Air Force*]
ABWGA .... Abhandlungen. Braunschweigische Wissenschaftliche Gesellschaft [*A publication*]
ABWGAZ ... Abhandlungen. Braunschweigische Wissenschaftliche Gesellschaft [*A publication*]
ABWH ...... Association of Black Women Historians (EA)
ABWHE .... Association of Black Women in Higher Education (EA)
ABWIK ..... Assault and Battery with Intent to Kill
ABWM ...... Berwyn WI Municipal Library, Alberta [*Library symbol*] [*National Library of Canada*] (NLC)
ABWP .... Weipa [*Australia*] [*ICAO location identifier*] (ICLI)
ABWR .... Advanced Boiling Water Reactor
ABWR .... American Beefalo World Registry (EA)
ABWRC .... American Blue and White Rabbit Club (EA)
ABWRC ..... Army Biological Warfare Research Center
ABWS .... Berwyn School, Alberta [*Library symbol*] [*National Library of Canada*] (BIB)
ABX .... Airborne Express, Inc. [*Wilmington, OH*] [*FAA designator*] (FAAC)
ABX .... Albury [*Australia*] [*Airport symbol*] (OAG)
ABX .... American Barrick Resources Corp. [*NYSE symbol*] [*Toronto Stock Exchange symbol*] (SPSG)
a-bx--- .... Brunei [*MARC geographic area code*] [*Library of Congress*] (LCCP)
ABXL .... Abaxial (MSA)
ABY .... Abby Investment [*Vancouver Stock Exchange symbol*]
ABY .... Abitibi-Price, Inc. [*NYSE symbol*] (SPSG)
Aby .... Abyssinia
ABY .... Abyssinian [*Cat species*]
ABY .... Albany [*Georgia*] [*Airport symbol*] (OAG)
aby .... Antibody [*Also, Ab*] [*Immunology*]
ABYC .... American Boat and Yacht Council (EA)
ABYC .... Antique Boat and Yacht Club (EA)
ABYSS ...... Abyssinia
ABZ .... Aber Resources Ltd. [*Toronto Stock Exchange symbol*]
ABZ .... Aberdeen [*Scotland*] [*Airport symbol*] (OAG)
AbZ .... Aboda Zara (BJA)
ABZ .... Albendazole [*Anthelmintic*]
ABZ .... Arkansas Best Corp. [*NYSE symbol*] (SPSG)
AbZar .... Aboda Zara (BJA)
AbzG .... Abzahlungsgesetz [*Law on hire purchase agreements*] [*German*] (ILCA)
a/c .... A Cargo [*Debit Of*] [*Spanish*] [*Banking, investment*]
AC .... A. Christiaens [*Belgium*] [*Research code symbol*]
a/c .... A Conto [*On Account*] [*Italian*] [*Banking, investment*] (GPO)
a/c .... A Cuenta [*On Account*] [*Spanish*] [*Banking, investment*]
aC .... Abcoulomb [*Unit of electric charge*]
AC .... Abdominal Circumference
AC .... Able Chief (MCD)
AC .... Absolute Ceiling [*Aviation*]
AC .... AC [*Asbestos and Cement*]. The Fibrecement Review [*A publication*]
AC .... Acceded to Throne (ROG)
AC .... Accelerator (AAG)
Ac .... Accelerator [*Hematology*]
AC .... Accent on Worship, Music, and the Arts [*A publication*]
Ac .... Acceptance Number [*Business term*]
AC .... Accepted (ROG)
AC .... Access [*Telecommunications*] (TEL)
AC .... Accessory Cells [*Histology*]
AC .... Accommodation Convergence [*Ophthalmology*]
AC .... Account
AC .... Account Control (AFM)
A/C .... Account Current [*Business term*]

AC .... Accountants and Controllers
AC .... Accounting Program [*Association of Independent Colleges and Schools specialization code*]
AC .... Accumulator [*Data processing*]
Ac .... Accursius [*Deceased, 1263*] [*Authority cited in pre-1607 legal work*] (DSA)
AC .... Acetate [*Also, ACTT*] [*Organic chemistry*]
ac .... Acetyl [*As substituent on nucleoside*] [*Biochemistry*]
AC .... Achimoowin. James Smith Reserve [*Saskatchewan, Canada*] [*A publication*]
AC .... Acid Concentrator [*Nuclear energy*] (NRCH)
AC .... Acidus [*Acid*] [*Latin*] (ROG)
ac .... Acmite [*CIPW classification*] [*Geology*]
ac .... Acompte [*Payment on Account*] [*French*] [*Business term*]
AC .... Acoustic Coupler [*Computer MODEM*]
AC .... Acoustical [*Technical drawings*]
AC .... Acquisition Costs
AC .... Acre
AC .... Acromioclavicular [*Medicine*] (DHSM)
AC .... Acting (ROG)
Ac .... Actinium [*Chemical element*]
AC .... Action Civile [*Civil Action*] [*French*] (ILCA)
AC .... Activation Coefficient
AC .... Activator [*Genetics*]
AC .... Active Capital [*Investment term*]
AC .... Active Cirrhosis [*Medicine*]
AC .... Active Component
AC .... Activity Captain (MCD)
AC .... Activity Code [*DoD*]
Ac .... Acts of the Apostles [*New Testament book*] (BJA)
AC .... Actual Cost [*Accounting*]
AC .... Acupuncture Clinic [*British*]
AC .... Acute [*Medicine*]
Ac .... Acyl [*Organic chemistry*]
AC .... Adapter Cable
AC .... Adaptive Control [*Manufacturing term*]
A & C .... Addenda and Corrigenda (ADA)
AC .... Additional Claim [*Unemployment insurance*] (OICC)
AC .... Address Coding [*Business term*]
AC .... Adenylate Cyclase [*An enzyme*]
AC .... Adirondack Council (EA)
AC .... Adjustment-Calibration
A & C .... Administrative and Clerical (ADA)
AC .... Admiral Commanding
AC .... Admiral's Club [*American Airlines' club for frequent flyers*] [*Dallas/Ft. Worth Airport*] [*Texas*] (EA)
AC .... Adopted Child
AC .... Adrenal Cortex [*Medicine*]
AC .... Adrenocorticoid [*Medicine*]
AC .... Adriamycin, CCNU [*Lomustine*] [*Antineoplastic drug regimen*]
AC .... Adriamycin, Cyclophosphamide [*Antineoplastic drug regimen*]
AC .... Adult-Contemporary [*Music*]
AC .... Advance California Reports [*A publication*]
AC .... Advanced Certification [*Canadian Society of Radiological Technicians*]
AC .... Advertising Council (EA)
AC .... Advice of Charge [*Telecommunications*] (TEL)
AC .... Advisory Circular
AC .... Advisory Committee (NRCH)
AC .... Advisory Council on Scientific Research and Technical Development [*British*]
AC .... Aero Club [*Australia*]
AC .... Aerodynamics Center [*NASA*]
AC .... Aeronautical Approach Chart [*Air Force*]
AC .... Aeronautical Center [*FAA*]
AC .... Aeronca Club (EA)
AC .... Aerospace Center [*Defense Mapping Agency*]
AC .... Aerospace Corporation (AAG)
AC .... Aesculapian Club (EA)
AC .... After Christ
AC .... Aging, Federal Council (OICC)
AC .... Agribusiness Council (EA)
AC .... Air Canada [*ICAO designator*] (OAG)
AC .... Air Canada Corp. [*Vancouver Stock Exchange symbol*] [*Toronto Stock Exchange symbol*]
AC .... Air Command (ADA)
A/C .... Air Commodore [*RAF, RCAF*]
AC .... Air Compressor (AAG)
AC .... Air Conditioning (KSC)
AC .... Air Conduction
AC .... Air Controller (NVT)
AC .... Air Controlman [*Navy rating*]
AC .... Air Corps [*Obsolete*]
AC .... Air Council (ADA)
AC .... Aircraft
AC .... Aircraft [*Public-performance tariff class*] [*British*]
AC .... Aircraft Carrier Flag [*Navy*] [*British*]
AC .... Aircraft Commander
AC .... Aircraft Control (MUGU)
AC .... Aircraftman [*British*]
AC .... Aircrewman

AC.............. Airframe Change
AC.............. Airfreight Container [*Shipping*] (DCTA)
AC.............. Airworthiness Certificate (MCD)
AC.............. Airworthiness Committee
a/c.............. Al Cuidado [*Care Of*] [*Spanish*] [*Correspondence*]
AC.............. Alaska Coalition (EA)
AC.............. Alaskan Command [*Discontinued, 1975*] [*Military*]
AC.............. Albia Christiana [*A publication*]
AC.............. Alcuin Club (EAIO)
AC.............. Alfalfa Club (EA)
AC.............. Algoma Central Railway [*AAR code*]
ac.............. Alicyclic [*Chemistry*]
AC.............. Alien Cell
AC.............. Alkali Cellulose [*Chemistry*]
A/C.............. All the Conveniences
AC.............. Allens Creek [*Nuclear power plant*] (NRCH)
AC.............. Allergic Conjunctivitis [*Ophthalmology*]
AC.............. Alliance Capital Management LP [*NYSE symbol*] (SPSG)
AC.............. Allied Commission [*World War II*]
A-C.............. Allied Corporation [*Initialism is trademark*]
AC.............. Allis-Chalmers Corp.
AC.............. Allowable Cost (OICC)
AC.............. Allyl Chloride [*Organic chemistry*]
AC.............. Alpine Club [*British*]
A/C.............. Alter Course [*Navigation*]
AC.............. Alternate Call Listing [*Telecommunications*] (TEL)
AC.............. Alternating Current
AC.............. Altocumulus [*Cloud*] [*Meteorology*]
AC.............. Ambassador's Club [*TWA's club for frequent flyers*] (EA)
AC.............. Ambulance Corps (ADA)
AC.............. American Cause [*An association*] (EA)
AC.............. American City [*A publication*]
AC.............. American Conditions [*Insurance*]
AC.............. Amphibious Car [*British*]
AC.............. Amphibious Corps [*Marine Corps*]
AC.............. Analecta Cisterciensia [*A publication*]
AC.............. Anales Cervantinos [*A publication*]
AC.............. Analog Computer (AAG)
AC.............. Analysis Console (MCD)
AC.............. Analytic [*or Analytical*] Chemist
A/C.............. Anchored Catheter [*Medicine*]
AC.............. Ancilla College [*Formerly, Ancilla Domini College*] [*Donaldson, IN*]
AC.............. Andre and Coquelin [*Often used as a pattern on clothes designed by Courreges, the initials represent the first names of the couturier and his wife*]
AC.............. Anglican Communion
AC.............. Annales-Conferencia [*A publication*]
AC.............. Annee Courante [*Of the Current Year*] [*French*]
AC.............. Anni Currentis [*Of the Current Year*] [*Latin*] (ROG)
AC.............. Anno Christi [*In the Year of Christ*] [*Latin*]
AC.............. Anno Corrente [*In the Current Year*] [*Latin*] (ADA)
ac.............. Anno Corrente [*Of the Current Year*] [*Italian*] (GPO)
AC.............. Annual Conference (ADA)
AC.............. Annual Cycle of Readings from Torah and Prophets (BJA)
AC.............. Annulment of Certification
AC.............. Anodal Closure [*Physiology*]
AC.............. Anodal Contraction [*Physiology*]
AC.............. Anode Circuit
AC.............. Another Copy (ROG)
AC.............. Answer Complete [*Telecommunications*] (TEL)
AC.............. Answer Construct
AC.............. Ante Christum [*Before Christ*] [*Latin*]
AC.............. Ante Cibum [*Before Meals*] [*Pharmacy*]
AC.............. Ante-Communion
AC.............. Anterior Chamber [*Ophthalmology*]
AC.............. Anterior Commissure [*Neuroanatomy*]
AC.............. Anterior Connective [*Anatomy*]
AC.............. Anterior Cortical [*Anatomy*]
AC.............. Anthracenecarboxylic Acid [*Organic chemistry*]
A-C.............. Anti-Communist (ADA)
AC.............. Anti-Inflammatory Corticoid [*Endocrinology*]
AC.............. Anticenter
AC.............. Anticlutter (NATG)
AC.............. Anticoagulant [*or Anticoagulation*]
AC.............. Anticomplementary [*Immunology*]
AC.............. Anticorrosive
AC.............. Antiquite Classique [*A publication*]
A/C.............. Ao Cuidado [*Care Of*] [*Portuguese*] [*Business term*]
AC.............. Aortic Closure [*Cardiology*]
AC.............. Apical Cell [*Botany*]
AC.............. Apostolic Church
AC.............. Appalachian Consortium (EA)
AC.............. Appeal Cases [*Canada*] [*A publication*] (DLA)
AC.............. Appeal Cases [*Ceylon*] [*A publication*] (DLA)
AC.............. Appeal Court [*Legal*] [*British*] (ROG)
AC.............. Appeals Council [*Social Security Administration*] (OICC)
AC.............. Appellate Court
AC.............. Application Control [*or Controller*] [*Data processing*] (NASA)
AC.............. Applied Christianity [*A publication*]
AC.............. Apprenticeship Committee [*Department of Labor*]

AC.............. Approach Chart
A/C.............. Approach Control [*Aviation*]
AC.............. Approved Cult
AC.............. Arc Cutting [*Welding*]
AC.............. Arch-Chancellor
AC.............. Archaeologia Cambrensis [*A publication*]
AC.............. Archaeologia Classica [*A publication*]
AC.............. Archaeological Conservancy (EA)
AC.............. Architect of the Capitol [*US*]
AC.............. Archivos del Folklore Chileno [*A publication*]
AC.............. Archonist Club (EA)
AC.............. Archons of Colophon (EA)
AC.............. Arctic Circle
AC.............. Area Code
AC.............. Area Commander [*British military*] (DMA)
AC.............. Area Coverage
ac.............. Argent Comptant [*Ready Money*] [*French*] [*Business term*]
AC.............. Arithmetic Computation Test [*Military*]
AC.............. Arkansas College [*Batesville*]
AC.............. Arm Circumference
AC.............. Armament Control
AC.............. Armaments Command [*Formerly, Munitions Command*] [*Rock Island, IL*] [*Army*]
AC.............. Armored Cable
AC.............. Armoured Car [*Military*] [*British*]
AC.............. Army Circular [*British military*] (DMA)
AC.............. Army Co-Operation [*British military*] (DMA)
AC.............. Army Corps
AC.............. Army Council (ADA)
AC.............. Art Complete (MCD)
AC.............. Arthritis Care [*An association*] (EAIO)
AC.............. Artillery Controller (NATG)
AC.............. Arts of the Church [*A publication*]
AC.............. Arts Council (EAIO)
A & C......... Arts and Crafts Movement [*c. 1860-1920*]
AC.............. Asbestos Cement [*Technical drawings*]
ac.............. Ashmore and Cartier Islands [*at (Australia) used in records cataloged after January 1978*] [*MARC country of publication code*] [*Library of Congress*] (LCCP)
ac-----......... Asia, Central [*MARC geographic area code*] [*Library of Congress*] (LCCP)
AC.............. Asian CineVision [*Later, ACV*] [*An association*] (EA)
AC.............. Asparagus Club (EA)
AC.............. Asphalt Composition (KSC)
AC.............. Asphaltic Concrete
AC.............. Assegno Circolare [*Banker's Check*] [*Italian*] [*Business term*]
A/C.............. Assemble and Checkout (MCD)
AC.............. Assessment Center [*Business term*]
AC.............. Assistant Cashier [*Banking*]
AC.............. Assistant Chief (FAAC)
AC.............. Assistant Clerk [*Navy*] [*British*] (ROG)
AC.............. Assistant Commissioner
AC.............. Assistant Controller (DCTA)
AC.............. Associacao Comercial [*Commercial Association*] [*Portuguese*]
AC.............. Associate in Commerce
AC.............. Associate Contractor
AC.............. [*The*] Associated Clubs (EA)
AC.............. Association of Cosmetologists [*Later, ACH*] (EA)
AC.............. Astronomical Constant
AC.............. Athletic Club [*Usually in combination with proper noun, as, DAC, Detroit Athletic Club*]
AC.............. Atlantic Charter
AC.............. Atlantic Congress
AC.............. Atlantic Council [*Later, ACUS*] [*NATO*] (NATG)
A-C.............. Atlas-Centaur [*Missile*]
AC.............. Atriocarotid [*Medicine*]
AC.............. Attack Center
AC.............. Attack Characterization (MCD)
AC.............. Attack Console
AC.............. Attitude Control [*System*] [*Aerospace*]
AC.............. Audio Center [*Command and Service Module*] [*NASA*]
AC.............. Audit Compliance (MCD)
AC.............. Auditor Camerae [*Auditor of the Papal Treasury*]
AC.............. Auditory Cortex [*Neurology*]
AC.............. Augmentation Concentration [*Biochemistry*]
AC.............. Australian Christian [*A publication*] (APTA)
AC.............. Australian Cruiser (DMA)
AC.............. Author Catalogue (ROG)
AC.............. Authorization and Consent (OICC)
AC.............. Authorization under Consideration (DCTA)
AC.............. Author's Correction [*Publishing*]
AC.............. Auto/Axial Compression [*Chromatography*]
AC.............. Auto-Cite [*VERALEX, Inc.*] [*Information service or system*] (CRD)
AC.............. Autocollimator
AC.............. Autocontex [*Freight-forwarding company*] [*British*]
AC.............. Automatic Checkout (BUR)
AC.............. Automatic Computer
AC.............. Automatic Control

A & C .... Automation and Control
AC .... Automobile Club
AC .... Auxiliary Command
AC .... Availability Code
AC .... Average Consumer
AC .... Aviation Cadet [*Air Force*]
AC .... Awaiting Connection [*Telecommunications*]   (TEL)
AC .... Awareness Center [*Defunct*]   (EA)
AC .... Axial Centrifugal   (AAG)
AC .... Axiocervical [*Dentistry*]
AC .... Axiom of Choice [*Logic*]
AC .... Azacytidine [*or Azacitidine*] [*Also, AZA, Aza-C*]
                [*Antineoplastic drug*]
AC .... Azimuth Comparator
AC .... Blood Gas [*US Chemical Corps symbol*]
AC .... Buchanan. Cape Colony Court of Appeal Reports [*South Africa*]
                [*A publication*]   (DLA)
AC .... Calgary Public Library, Alberta [*Library symbol*] [*National
                Library of Canada*]   (NLC)
AC .... Canadian Reports, Appeal Cases [*1828-1913*] [*A
                publication*]   (DLA)
AC .... Case on Appeal   (DLA)
AC .... Collier [*Navy symbol*] [*Obsolete*]
AC .... Companion of the Order of Australia
AC .... Hercules, Inc. [*Research code symbol*]
AC .... Hydrogen Cyanide [*Also, HCN*] [*Poison gas*] [*Army symbol*]
AC .... Law Reports, Appeal Cases [*England*] [*A publication*]   (DLA)
AC .... Quebec dans le Monde [*An association*]
AC .... Rockwell International Corp. [*ICAO aircraft manufacturer
                identifier*]   (ICAO)
AC1 .... Air Controlman, First Class [*Navy rating*]
AC1 .... Aircraftman, First Class [*Canadian*]
A/1C .... Airman, First Class
AC2 .... Air Controlman, Second Class [*Navy rating*]
AC2 .... Aircraftman, Second Class [*Canadian*]
A/2C .... Airman, Second Class
AC3 .... Air Controlman, Third Class [*Navy rating*]
A/3C .... Airman, Third Class
ACA .... Acapulco [*Mexico*] [*Airport symbol*]
ACA .... Accession Compensatory Account   (DCTA)
AC/A .... Accomodative Convergence/Accomodation (Ratio)
                [*Ophthalmology*]
ACA .... Accounts Control Area   (AFM)
ACA .... Accreditation Council for Accountancy [*Later, ACAT*]   (EA)
ACA .... Acute Care Admission [*Medicine*]
ACA .... Adjacent Channel Attenuation
ACA .... Administrative Committee on Administration [*United
                Nations*]
ACA .... Advance California Appellate Reports [*A publication*]
ACA .... Advanced Cargo Aircraft
ACA .... Advanced Combat Aircraft   (MCD)
ACA .... Advanced Contract Administrator
ACA .... Advisory Committee on the Arts [*Terminated, 1973*]   (EGAO)
ACA .... Aero Club of America [*Later, National Aeronautic Association
                of the USA*]
ACA .... Affenpinscher Club of America [*Later, AAA*]
ACA .... Afghan Community in America   (EA)
ACA .... Afro-Caribbean Alliance [*London, England*]
ACA .... Agence Centrale des Approvisionnements [*Central Supplies
                Agency*]   (NATG)
ACA .... Agile Combat Aircraft [*Proposed*]
ACA .... Agricultural Computer Association   (EA)
ACA .... Agricultural Credit Administration [*Philippines*]   (DS)
ACA .... Agriculture Council of America   (EA)
ACA .... Air Canada   (MCD)
ACA .... Air Canada Library [*UTLAS symbol*]
ACA .... Air Combat Analysis
ACA .... Air Commando Association   (EA)
ACA .... Aircraft Change Analysis   (AAG)
ACA .... Aircrew Association   (EAIO)
ACA .... Airflow Club of America   (EA)
ACA .... Airlift Clearance Authority   (AFM)
ACA .... Airspace Coordination Area   (MCD)
ACA .... Akita Club of America   (EA)
ACA .... Alaska Carriers Association, Inc., Anchorage AK [*STAC*]
ACA .... Alaska Coastal Airlines
ACA .... All Composite Aircraft   (MCD)
ACA .... Alliance for Capital Access   (EA)
ACA .... Alliance for Communities in Action   (EA)
ACA .... Allied Command Atlantic   (EAIO)
ACA .... Allied Commission, Austria [*World War II*]
ACA .... Allied Control Authority [*Allied German Occupation Forces*]
ACA .... Allocated Configuration Audit   (MCD)
ACA .... Altitude Controller Assembly   (MCD)
ACA .... Amchitka Central A [*Alaska*] [*Seismograph station code, US
                Geological Survey*] [*Closed*]   (SEIS)
ACA .... American Cadet Alliance   (EA)
ACA .... American Camping Association   (EA)
ACA .... American Canoe Association   (EA)
ACA .... American Capital Management & Research, Inc. [*NYSE
                symbol*]   (SPSG)

ACA .... American Carnivals Association   (EA)
ACA .... American Cartographic Association   (EA)
ACA .... American Casting Association   (EA)
ACA .... American Cat Association   (EA)
ACA .... American Cement Alliance   (EA)
ACA .... American Cemetery Association   (EA)
ACA .... American Chain Association   (EA)
ACA .... American Chaplain's Association   (EA)
ACA .... American Cheerleader Association
ACA .... American Chess Academy [*Commercial firm*]   (EA)
ACA .... American Chianina Association   (EA)
ACA .... American Chiropractic Association   (EA)
ACA .... American Citizens Abroad   (EA)
ACA .... American Civic Association   (EA)
ACA .... American Collection Association [*Orem, UT*]   (EA)
ACA .... American Collectors Association [*Minneapolis, MN*]   (EA)
ACA .... American College of Allergists   (EA)
ACA .... American College of Anesthesiologists   (EA)
ACA .... American College of Angiology   (EA)
ACA .... American College of Apothecaries   (EA)
ACA .... American Color Association   (EA)
ACA .... American Communications Association
ACA .... American Commuters Association
ACA .... American Compensation Association   (EA)
ACA .... American Composers Alliance   (EA)
ACA .... American Composers Alliance. Bulletin [*A publication*]
ACA .... American Congregational Association   (EA)
ACA .... American Consumers Association [*Chicago, IL*]   (EA)
ACA .... American Coptic Association   (EA)
ACA .... American Correctional Association   (EA)
ACA .... American Corriedale Association   (EA)
ACA .... American Council on Alcoholism   (EA)
ACA .... American Council for the Arts   (EA)
ACA .... American Counseling Association [*Absorbed by NACFT*]   (EA)
ACA .... American Crossbow Association   (EA)
ACA .... American Cryptogram Association   (EA)
ACA .... American Crystallographic Association   (EA)
ACA .... American Culture Association   (EA)
ACA .... American Cyanamid Co., Princeton, NJ [*OCLC
                symbol*]   (OCLC)
ACA .... Americans for Constitutional Action   (EA)
ACA .... Amerifax Cattle Association   (EA)
ACA .... Aminocephalosporanic Acid [*Pharmacology*]
ACA .... Ammoniacal Copper Arsenate [*Wood preservative*]
ACA .... Analytica Chimica Acta [*A publication*]
ACA .... Annunciator Control Assembly   (MCD)
ACA .... Anticentromere Antibody [*Immunology*]
ACA .... Anticollagen Antibody [*Immunology*]
ACA .... Armaments Control Agency [*Western European
                Union*]   (NATG)
ACA .... Armistice Terms and Civil Administration [*British*] [*World
                War II*]
ACA .... Arms Control Association   (EA)
ACA .... Arthritis Care Association [*British*]
ACA .... Arts Councils of America [*Later, American Council for the
                Arts*]
ACA .... Asian Christian Association   (EAIO)
ACA .... Assembly Coordination Advice   (MCD)
ACA .... Assignment of Claims Act [*1940*]   (OICC)
ACA .... Assignment Control Authority [*Military*]   (NVT)
ACA .... Assistant Catering Accountant [*British military*]   (DMA)
ACA .... Assistant Clerks Association [*A union*] [*British*]
ACA .... Assistant County Architect [*British*]
ACA .... Associate in Commercial Arts
ACA .... Associate Contractor Agreement   (MCD)
ACA .... Associate of the Institute of Chartered Accountants
                [*British*]   (EY)
ACA .... Associated Chiropodists of America
ACA .... Associated Councils of the Arts [*Later, American Council for
                the Arts*]
ACA .... Association of Canadian Archivists
ACA .... Association Canadienne de l'Acoustique [*Canadian Acoustics
                Association*]
ACA .... Association Canadienne d'Archaeologie [*Canadian
                Archaeological Association - CAA*]
ACA .... Association Canadienne d'Athletisme [*Canadian Athletics
                Association*]
ACA .... Association Canado-Americaine   (EA)
ACA .... Association for the Care of Asthma   (EA)
ACA .... Association of Certified Accountants   (EAIO)
ACA .... Association of Child Advocates   (EA)
ACA .... Association for Communication Administration   (EA)
ACA .... Association of Commuter Airlines [*Later, NATA*]
ACA .... Association of Consultant Architects   (EAIO)
ACA .... Association of Consulting Actuaries   (EAIO)
ACA .... Association of Consulting Architects [*New South Wales,
                Australia*]
ACA .... Association of Correctional Administrators
ACA .... Attitude Controller Assembly [*NASA*]   (KSC)
ACA .... Australasian Corrosion Association   (EAIO)
ACA .... Australia Canada Association   (ADA)

ACA .... Australian Casting Association
ACA .... Australian Choral Association
ACA .... Australian Corporate Affairs Reporter [*A publication*]　(APTA)
ACA .... Australian Council for Aeronautics
ACA .... Australian Council of Archives
ACA .... Automatic Circuit Analyzer
ACA .... Automatic Conference Arranger　(CET)
ACA .... Awaiting Combat Assignment　(MUGU)
ACA .... Azimuth Control Amplifier
ACA .... Camrose Public Library, Alberta [*Library symbol*] [*National Library of Canada*]　(NLC)
A7CA .... Austin Seven Clubs Association　(EAIO)
ACAA .... Advisory Council on Australian Archives
ACAA .... Airman Apprentice, Air Controlman, Striker [*Navy rating*]
ACAA .... American Coal Ash Association　(EA)
ACAA .... Army Concepts Analysis Agency
ACAA .... Asthma Care Association of America [*Defunct*]　(EA)
ACAA .... Automatic Chemical Agent Alarm [*Military*]　(RDA)
ACAA .... Aviation Cadet Alumni Association
ACAAB ...... Annales de Cardiologie et d'Angeiologie [*A publication*]
ACAAC ...... American College Admissions Advisory Center [*Later, ACAACCC*]　(EA)
ACAACCC ... American College Admissions Advisory and Career Counseling Center (EA)
ACAAD ...... Authorized Commanders Atomic Air Defense　(CINC)
ACAAR ...... Action Committee on American-Arab Relations [*Later, AARC*]
ACAAS ...... Automatic Chemical Agent Alarm System　(MCD)
ACAB .... Air Cavalry Attack Brigade　(MCD)
ACAB .... Allied Central Air Bureau [*World War II*]
ACAB .... Army Contract Adjustment Board
ACAB .... Association Canadienne des Arbitres de Badminton [*Canadian Association of Badminton Referees*]
ACABQ ...... Advisory Committee on Administrative and Budgetary Questions [*United Nations*]
ACABRIT ... Allied Commission, Austria, British Element [*World War II*]
ACABUG .. American, Canadian, Australian, British Urban Game [*Computer-assisted simulation wargame*] [*Army*]　(INF)
ACAC .... Acacia [*Gum Arabic*] [*Chemistry*]　(ROG)
Acac .... Acetylacetonate [*Organic chemistry*]
ACAC .... Acetylacetone [*Organic chemistry*]
ACAC .... Admiral Commanding Aircraft-Carriers [*Navy*] [*British*]
ACAC .... Air Control Area Commander　(NVT)
ACAC .... Air Crew Association Canada
ACAC .... Allied Container Advisory Committee [*Obsolete*]
ACAC .... American Christian Action Council [*Later, NCBBC*]　(EA)
ACAC .... American College Admissions Center [*Later, ACAAC*]
ACAC .... American Croatian Academic Club [*Later, ACAS*]
ACAC .... AMOCO Canada Petroleum Co. Ltd., Calgary, Alberta [*Library symbol*] [*National Library of Canada*]　(NLC)
ACAC .... Anti-Communist Advisory Committee　(EA)
ACAC .... Association of College Admissions Counselors [*Later, NACAC*]　(EA)
ACAC .... Australian College of Aesthetics and Cosmetology
ACACA ...... Analytica Chimica Acta [*A publication*]
ACACA ...... Army Command and Administration Communication Agency　(NATG)
ACACB ...... Acta Crystallographica. Section A. Crystal Physics, Diffraction, Theoretical and General Crystallography [*A publication*]
ACACC ...... Advisory Council, Allied Control Commission [*Italy*] [*World War II*]
ACACC ...... Association des Cartotheques et des Archives Cartographiques du Canada [*Association of Canadian Map Libraries and Archives*]　(EAIO)
ACACE ...... Advisory Council for Adult and Continuing Education [*British*]
ACACH ..... Alberta Children's Hospital, Calgary, Alberta [*Library symbol*] [*National Library of Canada*]　(NLC)
ACACJC ... Genealogical Society Library, Church of Jesus Christ of Latter-Day Saints, Cardston, Alberta [*Library symbol*] [*National Library of Canada*]　(NLC)
ACACN ...... American Council of Applied Clinical Nutrition　(EA)
ACACP ...... Americans Concerned about Corporate Power　(EA)
ACACP ...... Canadian Park Service, Environment Canada [*Service Canadien des Parcs, Environnement Canada*], Canmore, Alberta [*Library symbol*] [*National Library of Canada*]　(BIB)
ACACS ...... Air Cycle Air-Conditioning System　(MCD)
ACACS ...... Annales. Cercle Archeologique du Canton de Soignies [*A publication*]
ACACW .... Athletic Conference of American College Women [*Later, ARFCW*]
Acad .... Academicae Quaestiones [*of Cicero*] [*Classical studies*]　(OCD)
ACAD .... Academician [*or Academy*]　(EY)
Acad .... Academy [*Record label*]
Acad .... [*The*] Academy [*A publication*]
ACAD .... Acadia National Park
ACAD .... Air Containment Atmosphere Dilution [*Nuclear energy*]　(NRCH)
ACAD .... Alarm Communications and Display System　(MCD)
ACAD .... Alcoholism and Drug Abuse Commission, Calgary, Alberta [*Library symbol*] [*National Library of Canada*]　(NLC)
ACAD .... American Conference of Academic Deans　(EA)

ACAD .... Autodesk, Inc. [*Sausalito, CA*] [*NASDAQ symbol*]　(NQ)
ACAD .... Automotive Committee for Air Defense [*World War II*]
ACADA ..... Advanced Chemical Agent Detector Alarm　(MCD)
ACADA ..... Automatic Chemical Agent Alarm [*Military*]　(RDA)
Acad Ag France Comptes Rendus ... Academie d'Agriculture de France. Comptes Rendus des Seances [*A publication*]
Acad Ag France Compt Rend ... Academie d'Agriculture de France. Comptes Rendus des Seances [*A publication*]
Acad Boliviana Ciencias Econs R ... Academia Boliviana de Ciencias Economicas. Revista [*A publication*]
Acad Bookman ... Academy Bookman [*A publication*]
Acad Brasileira Cienc Anais ... Academia Brasileira de Ciencias. Anais [*A publication*]
Acad Bul .... Academy of Motion Picture Arts and Sciences. Bulletin [*A publication*]
Acad Cienc Artes Barc ... Academia de Ciencias y Artes de Barcelona. Memorias [*A publication*]
Acad Cienc Cuba Inst Geol Actas ... Academia de Ciencias de Cuba. Instituto de Geologia. Actas [*A publication*]
Acad Cienc Cuba Inst Geol Paleontol Publ Espec ... Academia de Ciencias de Cuba. Instituto de Geologia y Paleontologia. Publicacion Especial [*A publication*]
Acad Cienc Cuba Inst Geol Ser Geol ... Academia de Ciencias de Cuba. Instituto de Geologia. Serie Geologica [*A publication*]
Acad Cienc Cuba Ser Biol ... Academia de Ciencias de Cuba. Serie Biologica [*A publication*]
Acad Cienc Exactas Fis Nat Madrid Mem Ser Cienc Fis Quim ... Academia de Ciencias Exactas, Fisicas, y Naturales de Madrid. Memorias. Serie de Ciencias Fisico-Quimicas [*A publication*]
Acad Cienc Med Cataluna Baleares ... Academia de Ciencias Medicas de Cataluna y Baleares [*A publication*]
Acad Cienc Med Fis y Naturales Habana Anales ... Academia de Ciencias Medicas, Fisicas, y Naturales de la Habana. Anales [*A publication*]
ACADE ..... Association for Computer Art and Design Education　(EA)
Academy of Mgmt Jrnl ... Academy of Management. Journal [*A publication*]
Academy of Mgmt Review ... Academy of Management. Review [*A publication*]
Acad Esp Bol ... Real Academia Espanola. Boletin [*A publication*]
Acad d Inscrip Memoires ... Academie des Inscriptions et Belles-Lettres. Memoires [*Paris*] [*A publication*]
Acad d Inscr Mon et Mem ... Academie des Inscriptions et Belles-Lettres. Monuments et Memoires [*Paris*] [*A publication*]
Acad d Inscr (Paris) Mem ... Academie des Inscriptions et Belles-Lettres. Memoires (Paris) [*A publication*]
Acad Inscr (Paris) Mem Div Savants ... Academie des Inscriptions et Belles-Lettres. Memoires Presentes par Divers Savants (Paris) [*A publication*]
Acad d Inscr (Paris) Mon et Mem ... Academie des Inscriptions et Belles-Lettres. Monuments et Memoires (Paris) [*A publication*]
Acad Inscr (Paris) Mon et Mem ... Institut de France (Paris). Academie des Inscriptions et Belles-Lettres. Monuments et Memoires [*A publication*]
Acad L Rev ... Academy Law Review [*Kerala, India*] [*A publication*]
Acad Manage J ... Academy of Management. Journal [*A publication*]
Acad Manage Rev ... Academy of Management. Review [*A publication*]
Acad Mangt J ... Academy of Management. Journal [*A publication*]
Acad Marketing Science J ... Academy of Marketing Science. Journal [*A publication*]
Acad Med NJ Bull ... Academy of Medicine of New Jersey. Bulletin [*A publication*]
Acad Mgt J ... Academy of Management. Journal [*A publication*]
Acad Mgt R ... Academy of Management. Review [*A publication*]
Acad Nac Cienc Mem Rev ... Academia Nacional de Ciencias. Memorias y Revista [*A publication*]
Acad Nac Cienc Misc (Cordoba) ... Academia Nacional de Ciencias. Miscelanea (Cordoba) [*A publication*]
Acad Nac Med Bol (Braz) ... Academia Nacional de Medicina. Boletim (Brazil) [*A publication*]
Acad of Nat Sci Jour ... Academy of Natural Sciences. Journal [*A publication*]
Acad Nat Sci Philadelphia Spec Pub ... Academy of Natural Sciences of Philadelphia. Special Publication [*A publication*]
Acad Natur Sci Phila Proc ... Academy of Natural Sciences of Philadelphia. Proceedings [*A publication*]
Acad Pap.... Academy Papers. American Academy of Physical Education [*A publication*]
Acad Pol Sci Bull Ser Sci Terre ... Academie Polonaise des Sciences. Bulletin. Serie des Sciences de la Terre [*A publication*]
Acad Pol Sci Proc ... Academy of Political Science. Proceedings [*A publication*]
Acad Post... Academica Posteriora [*of Cicero*] [*Classical studies*]　(OCD)
Acad Pr...... Academica Priora [*of Cicero*] [*Classical studies*]　(OCD)
Acad R Belg Annu ... Academie Royale de Belgique. Annuaire [*A publication*]
Acad R Belg Cl Sci Collect Octavo Mem ... Academie Royale de Belgique. Classe des Sciences. Collection in Octavo. Memoires [*A publication*]
Acad R Belg Cl Sci Collect Quarto Mem ... Academie Royale de Belgique. Classe des Sciences. Collection in Quarto. Memoires [*A publication*]

Acad R Belg Cl Sci Mem ... Academie Royale de Belgique. Classe des Sciences. Memoires [*A publication*]

Acad R Belg Mem Cl Sci Collect Octavo ... Academie Royale de Belgique. Memoires. Classe des Sciences. Collection in Octavo [*A publication*]

Acad R Belg Mem Cl Sci Collect Quarto ... Academie Royale de Belgique. Memoires. Classe des Sciences. Collection in Quarto [*A publication*]

Acad Rep Fac Eng Tokyo Inst Polytech ... Academic Reports. Faculty of Engineering. Tokyo Institute of Polytechnics [*A publication*]

Acad Repub Pop Rom Bul Stiint A ... Academia Republicii Populare Romine. Buletin Stiintific. Seria A [*Romania*] [*A publication*]

Acad Repub Pop Rom Bul Stiint Sect Biol Stiinte Agric ... Academia Republicii Populare Romine. Buletin Stiintific. Sectia de Biologie si Stiinte Agricole [*A publication*]

Acad Repub Pop Rom Bul Stiint Sect Geol Geogr ... Academia Republicii Populare Romine. Buletin Stiintific. Sectia de Geologie si Geografie [*A publication*]

Acad Repub Pop Rom Bul Stiint Sect Stiinte Mat Fiz ... Academia Republicii Populare Romine. Buletin Stiintific. Sectia de Stiinte Matematice si Fizice [*A publication*]

Acad Repub Pop Rom Bul Stiint Sect Stiinte Med ... Academia Republicii Populare Romine. Buletin Stiintific. Sectia de Stiinte Medicale [*A publication*]

Acad Repub Pop Rom Bul Stiint Sect Stiinte Teh Chim ... Academia Republicii Populare Romine. Buletin Stiintific. Sectiunea de Stiinte Tehnice si Chimice [*A publication*]

Acad Repub Pop Rom Bul Stiint Ser Mat Fiz Chim ... Academia Republicii Populare Romine. Buletin Stiintific. Seria Matematica, Fizica, Chimie [*A publication*]

Acad Repub Pop Rom Cen Cercet Metal Stud Cercet Metal ... Academia Republicii Populare Romine. Centrul de Cercetari Metalurgice. Studii si Cercetari de Metalurgie [*A publication*]

Acad Repub Pop Rom Fil (Cluj) Stud Cercet Agron ... Academia Republicii Populare Romine Filiala (Cluj). Studii si Cercetari de Agronomie [*A publication*]

Acad Repub Pop Rom Fil (Cluj) Stud Cercet Biol ... Academia Republicii Populare Romine Filiala (Cluj). Studii si Cercetari de Biologie [*A publication*]

Acad Repub Pop Rom Fil (Cluj) Stud Cercet Chim ... Academia Republicii Populare Romine Filiala (Cluj). Studii si Cercetari de Chimie [*A publication*]

Acad Repub Pop Rom Fil (Cluj) Stud Cercet Geol Geogr ... Academia Republicii Populare Romine Filiala (Cluj). Studii si Cercetari de Geologie, Geografie [*A publication*]

Acad Repub Pop Rom Fil (Cluj) Stud Cercet Mat Fiz ... Academia Republicii Populare Romine Filiala (Cluj). Studii si Cercetari de Matematica si Fizica [*A publication*]

Acad Repub Pop Rom Fil (Cluj) Stud Cercet Med ... Academia Republicii Populare Romine Filiala (Cluj). Studii si Cercetari de Medicina [*A publication*]

Acad Repub Pop Rom Fil (Cluj) Stud Cercet Stiint ... Academia Republicii Populare Romine Filiala (Cluj). Studii si Cercetari Stiintifice [*A publication*]

Acad Repub Pop Rom Fil (Cluj) Stud Cercet Stiint Ser 1 ... Academia Republicii Populare Romine Filiala (Cluj). Studii si Cercetari Stiintifice. Seria 1. Stiinte Matematice, Fizice, Chimice, si Tehnice [*A publication*]

Acad Repub Pop Rom Fil (Cluj) Stud Cercet Stiint Ser 2 ... Academia Republicii Populare Romine Filiala (Cluj). Studii si Cercetari Stiintifice. Seria 2. Stiinte Biologice, Agricole, si Medicale [*A publication*]

Acad Repub Pop Rom Fil (Iasi) Stud Cercet Stiint Chim ... Academia Republicii Populare Romine Filiala (Iasi). Studii si Cercetari Stiintifice. Chimie [*A publication*]

Acad Repub Pop Rom Fil (Iasi) Stud Cercet Stiint Med ... Academia Republicii Populare Romine Filiala (Iasi). Studii si Cercetari Stiintifice. Medicina [*A publication*]

Acad Repub Pop Rom Fil Iasi Stud Cercet Stiint Ser 1 ... Academia Republicii Populare Romine Filiala (Iasi). Studii si Cercetari Stiintifice. Seria 1. Stiinte Matematice, Fizice, Chimice, si Tehnice [*A publication*]

Acad Repub Pop Rom Fil (Iasi) Stud Cercet Stiint Ser 2 ... Academia Republicii Populare Romine Filiala (Iasi). Studii si Cercetari Stiintifice. Seria 2. Stiinte Biologice, Medicale, si Agricole [*A publication*]

Acad Repub Pop Rom Stud Cercet Biochim ... Academia Republicii Populare Romine. Institutul de Biochimie. Studii si Cercetari de Biochimie [*Romania*] [*A publication*]

Acad Repub Pop Rom Stud Cercet Biol Ser Biol Anim ... Academia Republicii Populare Romine. Studii si Cercetari de Biologie. Seria Biologie Animala [*A publication*]

Acad Repub Pop Rom Stud Cercet Biol Ser Biol Veg ... Academia Republicii Populare Romine. Studii si Cercetari de Biologie. Seria Biologie Vegetala [*A publication*]

Acad Repub Pop Rom Stud Cercet Chim ... Academia Republicii Populare Romine. Studii si Cercetari de Chimie [*A publication*]

Acad Repub Pop Rom Stud Cercet Fiz ... Academia Republicii Populare Romine. Institutul de Fizica Atomica si Institutul de Fizica. Studii si Cercetari de Fizica [*Romania*] [*A publication*]

Acad Repub Pop Rom Stud Cercet Fiziol ... Academia Republicii Populare Romine. Institutul de Fiziologie Normala si Patologica Dr. D. Danielolpolu. Studii si Cercetari de Fiziologie [*Romania*] [*A publication*]

Acad Repub Pop Rom Stud Cercet Geol ... Academia Republicii Populare Romine. Studii si Cercetari de Geologie [*A publication*]

Acad Repub Pop Rom Stud Cercet Stiint Ser Stiinte Med ... Academia Republicii Populare Romine. Studii si Cercetari Stiintifice. Seria Stiinte Medicina [*A publication*]

Acad Repub Pop Rom Stud Cercet Stiint Ser Stiint Med ... Academia Republicii Populare Romine. Studii si Cercetari Stiintifice. Seria Stiinte Medicina [*A publication*]

Acad Rev .... Academy Review [*A publication*]

Acad Rev Calif Acad Periodontol ... Academy Review. California Academy of Periodontology [*A publication*]

Acad R Med Belg Bull ... Academie Royale de Medecine de Belgique. Bulletin [*A publication*]

Acad R Med Belg Bull Mem ... Academie Royale de Medecine de Belgique. Bulletin et Memoires [*A publication*]

Acad R Med Belg Mem ... Academie Royale de Medecine de Belgique. Memoires [*A publication*]

Acad Roy Belg Bull Cl Sci ... Academie Royale de Belgique. Bulletin. Classe des Sciences [*A publication*]

Acad Roy Belg Cl Sci Mem Coll in-8 ... Academie Royale de Belgique. Classe des Sciences. Memoires. Collection in Octavo [*A publication*]

Acad Roy Belg Cl Sci Mem Collect 8o ... Academie Royale de Belgique. Classe des Sciences. Memoires. Collection in Octavo [*A publication*]

Acad Roy Sci O-Mer B ... Academie Royale des Sciences d'Outre-Mer. Bulletin des Seances [*A publication*]

Acad Roy Sci Outre-Mer Bul Seances ... Academie Royale des Sciences d'Outre-Mer. Bulletin des Seances [*A publication*]

Acad R Sci Colon (Brussels) Bull Seances ... Academie Royale des Sciences Coloniales (Brussels). Bulletin des Seances [*Belgium*] [*A publication*]

Acad R Sci Colon (Brussels) Cl Sci Nat Med Mem Collect ... Academie Royale des Sciences Coloniales (Brussels). Classe des Sciences Naturelles et Medicales. Memoires. Collection in Octavo [*A publication*]

Acad R Sci Lett B-Arts Belg Cl Sci Bull ... Academie Royale des Sciences, des Lettres, et des Beaux-Arts de Belgique. Classe des Sciences. Bulletin [*A publication*]

Acad R Sci Outre-Mer (Brussels) Bull Seances ... Academie Royale des Sciences d'Outre-Mer (Brussels). Bulletin des Seances [*A publication*]

Acad R Sci Outre-Mer Bull ... Academie Royale des Sciences d'Outre-Mer. Bulletin des Seances [*A publication*]

ACADS ...... Alarm Communications and Display Segment   (MCD)

Acad Sci Belg Bul Cl Beaux-Arts ... Academie Royale de Belgique. Bulletin. Classe des Beaux-Arts [*A publication*]

Acad Sci Belg Bul Cl Lett ... Academie Royale de Belgique. Bulletin. Classe des Lettres et des Sciences Morales et Politiques [*A publication*]

Acad Sci Belg Bul Cl Sci ... Academie Royale de Belgique. Bulletin. Classe des Sciences [*A publication*]

Acad d Sci d Belgique Mem 4 Cl d Lett ... Academie Royale des Sciences, des Lettres, et des Beaux-Arts de Belgique. Memoires 4. Classe des Lettres [*A publication*]

Acad d Sci d Belgique Mem 8 Cl d Lett ... Academie Royale des Sciences, des Lettres, et des Beaux-Arts de Belgique. Memoires 8. Classe des Lettres [*A publication*]

Acad d Sci d Belgique Mem 4 Cl d Sci ... Academie Royale des Sciences, des Lettres, et des Beaux-Arts de Belgique. Memoires 4. Classe des Sciences [*A publication*]

Acad d Sci d Belgique Mem 8 Cl d Sci ... Academie Royale des Sciences, des Lettres, et des Beaux-Arts de Belgique. Memoires 8. Classe des Sciences [*A publication*]

Acad Sci Belg Mem 8 Cl Lett ... Academie Royale de Belgique. Memoires. Classe des Lettres et des Sciences Morales et Politiques. Collection in Octavo [*A publication*]

Acad Sci Belg Mem 8 Cl Sci ... Academie Royale de Belgique. Memoires. Classe des Sciences. Collection in Octavo [*A publication*]

Acad Scient Hung Acta Hist ... Academia Scientiarum Hungarica. Acta Historica [*A publication*]

Acad Scient Hung Acta Microbiol ... Academia Scientiarum Hungarica. Acta Microbiologica [*A publication*]

Acad Scient Hung Act Bot ... Academia Scientiarum Hungarica. Acta Botanica [*A publication*]

Acad Sci Fenn Ann Ser A-III Geol-Geogr ... Academia Scientiarum Fennicae. Annales. Series A-III (Geologica-Geographica) [*A publication*]

Acad Sci Lith SSR Math Trans ... Academy of Sciences of the Lithuanian SSR. Mathematical Transactions [*A publication*]

Acad d Sci Mor et Pol (Paris) Mem ... Academie des Sciences Morales et Politiques (Paris). Memoires [*A publication*]

Acad Sci (Paris) CR Ser B ... Academie des Sciences (Paris). Comptes Rendus Hebdomadaires des Seances. Serie B. Sciences Physiques [*A publication*]
Acad Sci (Paris) CR Ser C ... Academie des Sciences (Paris). Comptes Rendus Hebdomadaires des Seances. Serie C. Sciences Chimiques [*A publication*]
Acad Sci (Paris) CR Ser D ... Academie des Sciences (Paris). Comptes Rendus Hebdomadaires des Seances. Serie D. Sciences Naturelles [*A publication*]
Acad Sci (Paris) Mem ... Academie des Sciences (Paris). Memoires [*A publication*]
Acad d Sci (Paris) Mem ... Academie des Sciences (Paris). Memoires [*A publication*]
Acad d Sci (Paris) Mem Div Savants ... Academie des Sciences (Paris). Memoires Presentes par Divers Savants [*A publication*]
Acad Sci St Louis Trans ... Academy of Science of St. Louis. Transactions [*A publication*]
Acad of Sci of St Louis Trans ... Academy of Science of St. Louis. Transactions [*A publication*]
Acad Sci Toulouse Mem ... Academie des Sciences, Inscriptions, et Belles-Lettres de Toulouse. Memoires [*A publication*]
Acad Sci USSR ... Academic Science USSR [*A publication*]
Acad Sci USSR Dokl Earth Sci Sec ... Doklady Academy of Sciences of the USSR. Earth Science Sections [*A publication*]
Acad Sci USSR Math Notes ... Academy of Sciences of the USSR. Mathematical Notes [*A publication*]
Acad Serbe Sci et Arts (Glas) Cl Sci Tech ... Academie Serbe des Sciences et des Arts (Glas). Classe des Sciences Techniques [*A publication*]
Acad Serb Sci Arts Classe Sci Math Nat (Glas) ... Academie Serbe des Sciences et des Arts. Classe des Sciences Mathematiques et Naturelles (Glas) [*A publication*]
Acad Sin Inst Bot Annu Rep ... Academia Sinica. Institute of Botany. Annual Report [*A publication*]
Acad Sin Inst Vertebr Palaeontol Palaeoanthropol Mem ... Academia Sinica. Institute of Vertebrate Palaeontology and Palaeoanthropology. Memoir [*A publication*]
Acad Sin Inst Zool Monogr Ser ... Academia Sinica. Institute of Zoology. Monograph Series [*A publication*]
Acad Sin Mem Inst Chem ... Academia Sinica. Memoirs. Institute of Chemistry [*A publication*]
Acad Sin Nanjing Inst Geol Palaeontol Mem ... Academia Sinica. Nanjing Institute of Geology and Palaeontology. Memoirs [*A publication*]
Acad Soc Lorraines Sci ... Academie et Societe Lorraines des Sciences [*A publication*]
Acad (Syr) ... Academy (Syracuse) [*A publication*]
Acad Tcheque Sci Bull Int Cl Sci Math Nat Med ... Academie Tcheque des Sciences. Bulletin International. Classe des Sciences Mathematiques et Naturelles, et de la Medecine [*A publication*]
Acad Ther .. Academic Therapy [*A publication*]
Acad Therapy ... Academic Therapy [*A publication*]
ACAE .... Actes. Congres International des Sciences Anthropologiques et Ethnologiques [*A publication*]
ACAE .... Alberta Energy Company, Calgary, Alberta [*Library symbol*] [*National Library of Canada*]   (NLC)
ACAE .... American Council for the Arts in Education [*Defunct*]   (EA)
ACAE .... Annales. Cercle Archeologique d'Enghien [*A publication*]
ACAE .... Association of Chinese and American Engineers
ACAE .... Association of Cuban Architects in Exile   (EA)
ACAE .... Canada Awards for Business Excellence
ACAEA ...... Acta Anaesthesiologica [*A publication*]
ACAEAS .. Acta Anaesthesiologica [*Padua*] [*A publication*]
ACAEL ...... Library & Records Centre, Alsands Energy Ltd., Calgary, Alberta [*Library symbol*] [*National Library of Canada*]   (NLC)
ACAEN ..... Association Canadienne pour l'Avancement des Etudes Neerlandaises [*Canadian Association for the Advancement of Netherlandic Studies - CAANS*]
A CAES ..... Anni Caesar [*Era of the Caesars*] [*Latin*]   (ROG)
AcAF .... Acetylaminofluorene [*Also, AAF, AcNHFln, FAA*] [*Organic chemistry*]
ACAF .... Amphibious Corps, Atlantic Fleet [*Marine Corps*]
ACAF .... Association Canadienne de l'Ataxie de Friedreich [*Canadian Association of Friedreich's Ataxia*]
ACAF .... Automatic Circuit Assurance Feature   (CET)
ACAFDCS ... Autograph Chapter of the American First Day Cover Society [*Defunct*]   (EA)
ACAG .... Afro-Caribbean Action Group [*London, England*]
ACAG .... Alberta Gas Ethylene Co., Calgary, Alberta [*Library symbol*] [*National Library of Canada*]   (NLC)
ACAGAY ... Acta Agronomica [*Palmira*] [*A publication*]
ACAGR ..... Allied Commission, Agriculture Subcommission [*World War II*]
ACAH .... Accreted Crystaline Anthropoid Homologue
ACAH .... Acylcholine Acyl-Hydrolase [*Same as PCE*] [*An enzyme*]
ACAH .... Autoimmune Chronic Active Hepatitis [*Medicine*]
ACAH .... Horse Industry Branch, Alberta Agriculture, Calgary, Alberta [*Library symbol*] [*National Library of Canada*]   (NLC)

ACAHA ..... Acta Chirurgica. Academiae Scientiarum Hungaricae [*A publication*]
ACAHA ..... Association of Chief Administrators of Health Authorities [*British*]
ACAHE7 ... Czechoslovak Academy of Sciences. Institute of Landscape Ecology. Section of Hydrobiology. Annual Report [*A publication*]
ACAHR ..... American Council for the Advancement of Human Rights   (EA)
ACAI .... Alkali and Clean Air Inspectorate [*British*]   (DCTA)
ACAI .... American Christian Association for Israel [*Later, American-Israel Cultural Foundation*]   (EA)
ACAI .... Associazione fra i Costruttori in Acciaio Italiani [*Steel constructors association*]   (EY)
ACAJ .... Aca Joe [*San Francisco, CA*] [*NASDAQ symbol*]   (NQ)
ACA J Chiropr ... American Chiropractic Association. Journal of Chiropractic [*A publication*]
ACAL .... Aircal, Inc. [*NASDAQ symbol*]   (NQ)
ACAL .... Aircraft Change Application List   (MCD)
ACAL .... Camrose Lutheran College, Alberta [*Library symbol*] [*National Library of Canada*]   (NLC)
ACALA ...... Administration for Civil Affairs in Liberated Areas [*World War II*]
ACALAF ... Acta Allergologica [*A publication*]
ACALD ...... Association for Children and Adults with Learning Disabilities [*Later, LDA*]   (EA)
ACALDI .... Acta Alimentaria [*A publication*]
ACALJ ...... Association Canadienne pour l'Avancement de la Litterature de Jeunesse [*Canadian Association for the Advancement of Children's Literature*]
ACALLS .... Calling Lake School, Alberta [*Library symbol*] [*National Library of Canada*]   (BIB)
ACALM ..... American College of Animal Laboratory Medicine   (RDA)
ACALM ..... Calmar Public Library, Alberta [*Library symbol*] [*National Library of Canada*]   (NLC)
ACALS ...... Cadotte Lake School, Alberta [*Library symbol*] [*National Library of Canada*]   (BIB)
ACAM .... American College of Advancement in Medicine   (EA)
ACAM .... Annales. Cercle Archeologique de Mons [*A publication*]
ACAM .... Apollo Computer Address Matrix [*NASA*]
ACAM .... Augmented Content-Addressed Memory
ACAM .... Canmore Municipal Library, Alberta [*Library symbol*] [*National Library of Canada*]   (NLC)
ACAMAR ... Asociacion Centroamericana de Armadores [*Central American Association of Shipowners*] [*Guatemala, Guatemala*]   (EAIO)
ACAmp ...... AC [*Alternating Current*] Amperometric [*Electromagnetics*]
ACAMP ..... Allied Camouflage and Concealment Publication [*NATO*]   (NATG)
ACAMPS .. Automated Communications and Message Processing System [*Army*]   (RDA)
ACAMR .... Associate Committee on Aviation Medical Research [*Canada*]
ACAMS ..... Automatic Continuous Air Monitoring System   (MCD)
AcAn .... Acta Antiqua. Academiae Scientiarum Hungaricae [*Budapest*] [*A publication*]
ACAN .... Action Committee Against Narcotics
ACAN .... Advisory Committee on Antarctic Feature Names [*Board on Geographic Names*]   (NOAA)
ACAN .... Agencia Centroamericana de Noticias SA [*Press agency*] [*Panama*]
ACAN .... Airman, Air Controlman, Striker [*Navy rating*]
ACAN .... Army Communications Administrative Network [*Domestic and overseas integrated system of fixed radio, wire, cable, and associated communications facilities*]
ACAN .... Australasian Child Abuse Network
ACAN .... Media Resource Centre, Access Network, Calgary, Alberta [*Library symbol*] [*National Library of Canada*]   (NLC)
ACANDO ... Acta Anthropogenetica [*A publication*]
ACAO .... Alaska Construction and Oil [*A publication*]
ACAO .... Allied Civil Affairs Office [*World War II*]
ACAO .... Official Committee on Armistice Terms and Civil Administration [*British*] [*World War II*]
ACAP .... Acap Corp. [*Houston, TX*] [*NASDAQ symbol*]   (NQ)
ACAP .... Advanced Combat Air Patrol   (MCD)
ACAP .... Advanced Composite Airframe Program [*Air Force*]
ACAP .... Advanced Computer for Array Processing
ACAP .... Agence Camerounaise de Presse [*Cameroon Press Agency*]
ACAP .... American Council on Alcohol Problems   (EA)
ACAP .... Analyst Capability
ACAP .... Army Child Advocacy Program   (MCD)
ACAP .... Army Combat Artist Program
ACAP .... Army Contract Appeals Panel
ACAP .... Army Cost Analysis Paper
ACap .... Australian Capitol [*Record label*]
ACAP .... Australian Cooperative Assessment Program
ACAP .... Automatic Circuit Analysis Program
ACAP .... Aviation Consumer Action Project   (EA)
ACAPA ...... American Concrete Agricultural Pipe Association [*Defunct*]
A CAPO .... A Capriccio [*At One's Fancy*] [*Music*]   (ROG)
A Capp ...... A Cappella [*Unaccompanied*] [*Music*]
ACAPS ...... Automated Chemical Analysis for Process Solutions System [*Hughes Aircraft Co.*]   (ECON)

ACAPW..... Annales. Cercle Archeologique du Pays de Waes [*A publication*]
ACAQE ..... Aquatic Environments Ltd., Calgary, Alberta [*Library symbol*] [*National Library of Canada*] (NLC)
Ac Ar.......... Acta Archaeologica [*A publication*]
ACAR .... Acta Arctica [*A publication*]
ACAR .... Aluminum Conductor Alloy Reinforced (MCD)
A Car........... Analecta Cartusiana [*A publication*]
ACAR .... Army Contract Adjustment Region (MCD)
ACAR .... Cardston Public Library, Alberta [*Library symbol*] [*National Library of Canada*] (NLC)
ACARC...... Arctec Canada Ltd., Calgary, Alberta [*Library symbol*] [*National Library of Canada*] (NLC)
Ac Arch (Ljub) ... Acta Archaeologica (Ljubljana) [*A publication*]
ACARCZ.... Acta Arctica [*A publication*]
A Card....... Acta Cardiologica [*A publication*]
ACARD ..... Advisory Council for Applied Research and Development [*British government*]
ACARM .... Association of Commonwealth Archivists and Records Managers (EAIO)
ACARM .... Carbon Municipal Library, Alberta [*Library symbol*] [*National Library of Canada*] (NLC)
ACARMA ... Carmanguay Public Library, Alberta [*Library symbol*] [*National Library of Canada*] (NLC)
ACARO ..... Caroline Public Library, Alberta [*Library symbol*] [*National Library of Canada*] (NLC)
Acarol .... Acarologia [*A publication*]
Acarol Newsl ... Acarology Newsletter [*A publication*]
ACARS....... ARINC Communication Addressing Reporting System (IEEE)
ACARS...... Carstairs Public Library, Alberta [*Library symbol*] [*National Library of Canada*] (NLC)
ACARTSD ... African Centre for Applied Research and Training in Social Development (EAIO)
ACARU ..... Association Canadienne d'Administrateurs de Recherche Universitaire [*Canadian Association of University Research Administrators - CAURA*]
Ac As.......... Acta Asiatica [*A publication*]
ACAS......... Advisory, Conciliation, and Arbitration Service [*London, England*]
ACAS........ African Commission on Agricultural Statistics (EA)
ACAS........ Air Cycle Air-Conditioning System (MCD)
ACAS........ Airborne Collision-Avoidance System [*Later, TCAS*]
ACAS........ American Croatian Academic Society [*Formerly, ACAC*] (EA)
ACAS........ Analytical Chemistry and Applied Spectroscopy (MUGU)
ACAS........ Anchored Cell Analysis and Sorting [*Cell culture*]
ACAS........ Army Crisis Action System
ACAS........ Assistant Chief of Air Staff [*Army*] [*British*]
AC of AS.... Assistant Chief of Air Staff [*Army*] [*British*]
ACAS......... Associate of the Casualty Actuarial Society [*Designation awarded by Casualty Actuarial Society*]
ACAS........ Association Canadienne des Administrateurs Scolaires [*Canadian Association of Academic Administrators*]
ACAS........ Association of Casualty Accountants and Statisticians [*Later, SIA*]
ACAS........ Association for Central Asian Studies (EA)
ACAS........ Association of College Auxiliary Services [*Later, NACAS*] (EA)
ACAS........ Association of Concerned African Scholars (EA)
ACAS........ Atlantic Coast Air Service
ACAS........ Automatic Collision Avoidance System [*Aviation*] (FAAC)
ACAS........ AUTOVON Centralized Alarm System
ACAS........ Caslan Public Library, Alberta [*Library symbol*] [*National Library of Canada*] (NLC)
ACAS......... Chinese Art Society of America. Archives [*A publication*]
ACASA...... Chinese Art Society of America. Archives [*A publication*]
ACASD..... Air Clutch Antislack Device (CAAL)
ACASG...... Alberta & Southern Gas Co. Ltd., Calgary, Alberta [*Library symbol*] [*National Library of Canada*] (BIB)
ACAS(I).... Assistant Chief of Air Staff (Intelligence) [*Army*] [*British*]
ACASLA ... Association of Chief Architects of Scottish Local Authorities (EAIO)
ACAS(O)... Assistant Chief of Air Staff (Operations) [*Army*] [*British*]
ACAS(P).... Assistant Chief of Air Staff (Policy) [*Army*] [*British*]
ACASPP.... American Committee to Advance the Study of Petroglyphs and Pictographs (EA)
ACAST...... Advisory Committee on the Application of Science and Technology to Development [*Also, ACASTD, ACST*] [*United Nations*]
ACAS(T) ... Assistant Chief of Air Staff (Technical) [*Army*] [*British*]
ACAST ...... Castor Public Library, Alberta [*Library symbol*] [*National Library of Canada*] (NLC)
ACASTD ... Advisory Committee on the Application of Science and Technology to Development [*Also, ACAST, ACST*] [*United Nations*]
ACAS(TR) ... Assistant Chief of Air Staff (Technical Requirements) [*Army*] [*British*]
ACAT .... Accreditation Council for Accountancy and Taxation (EA)
ACAT .... Acquisition Category (CAAL)
ACAT .... Advanced Computer Audit Techniques [*Arthur Andersen & Co.*]
ACAT .... Advanced Conformal Antenna Technique
ACAT .... Air Conditioner Air Transportable (MCD)
ACAT .... American Center for the Alexander Technique (EA)

ACAT .... Christian Action for the Abolition of Torture (EA)
ACATA...... American College of Addiction Treatment Administrators (EA)
ACATA5.... Acta Anatomica [*A publication*]
A Catedra F Suarez ... Anales. Catedra Francisco Suarez [*A publication*]
ACATEI .... American Committee for the Advancement of Torah Education in Israel [*Later, OTII*] (EA)
ACATT...... Aviation Combined Arms Team Trainer
ACAV .... Agence Centrafricaine de Voyages [*Airline*] (FAAC)
ACAV .... Armored Cavalry Assault Vehicle
ACAVS ..... Advanced Cab and Visual System [*Army*] (RDA)
ACAW ...... Aircraft Control and Warning (MCD)
ACAX .... Air California [*Air carrier designation symbol*]
ACB .... Acceptance and Certification Branch [*Social Security Administration*]
ACB .... Access Method Control Block [*Data processing*] (BUR)
ACB .... Accounting and Business Research [*A publication*]
ACB .... Adapter Control Block [*Data processing*] (IBMDP)
ACB .... Advertising Checking Bureau
ACB .... African Continental Bank Ltd.
ACB .... Air Circuit Breaker
ACB .... Air Corps Board [*Obsolete*] (MCD)
ACB .... Air Crew System Bulletin (MCD)
ACB .... Air-Cushion Barge (MCD)
ACB .... Airfield Construction Branch [*British military*] (DMA)
ACB .... Airmen Classification Battery [*Military tests*]
ACB .... Amchitka Central B [*Alaska*] [*Seismograph station code, US Geological Survey*] [*Closed*] (SEIS)
ACB .... American Biodynamics, Inc. [*Vancouver Stock Exchange symbol*]
ACB .... American Capital Bond Fund, Inc. [*NYSE symbol*] (SPSG)
ACB .... American City Bureau [*An association*] (EA)
ACB .... American Council of the Blind (EA)
ACB .... Aminochlorobenzophenone [*Organic chemistry*]
ACB .... Amphibious Construction Battalion [*Also, PHIBCB*]
ACB .... Annoyance Call Bureau [*Telephone-pest control*]
ACB .... Antibody-Coated Bacteria [*Immunology*]
ACB .... Antrum-Corpus Boundary [*Anatomy*]
ACB .... Aortocoronary Bypass [*Cardiology*]
ACB .... Army Classification Battery [*Military tests*]
ACB .... Army Communications Board
ACB .... Asbestos-Cement Board [*Technical drawings*]
ACB .... Associated Credit Bureaus [*Houston, TX*] (EA)
ACB .... Association Canadienne de Badminton [*Canadian Badminton Association*]
ACB .... Association Canadienne des Bibliotheques [*Canadian Library Association - CLA*]
ACB .... Association of Clinical Biochemists [*British*]
ACB .... Association of Concert Bands (EA)
ACB .... Association of Customers' Brokers [*Later, AIB*] (EA)
ACB .... Association of the Customs Bar [*Later, CITBA*] (EA)
ACB .... Australian Computer Bulletin [*A publication*] (APTA)
ACB .... Bellaire, MI [*Location identifier*] [*FAA*] (FAAL)
ACB .... Brascon Resources Ltd., Calgary, Alberta [*Library symbol*] [*National Library of Canada*] (NLC)
a-cb--------- Cambodia [*Democratic Kampuchea*] [*MARC geographic area code*] [*Library of Congress*] (LCCP)
ACB .... University of South Alabama, Biomedical Library, Mobile, AL [*OCLC symbol*] (OCLC)
ACBA .... Academy of Comic Book Artists
ACBA .... Aircrew Body Armor [*System*] [*Army*]
ACBA .... American Cavy Breeders Association (EA)
ACBA .... American Charbray Breeders Association [*Later, AICA*] (EA)
ACBA .... Appaloosa Color Breeders Association (EA)
ACBA .... Association of Concert Bands of America [*Later, ACB*] (EA)
ACBB....... American Council for Better Broadcasts (EA)
ACBB....... Foothills Christian College, Calgary, Alberta [*Library symbol*] [*Obsolete*] [*National Library of Canada*] (NLC)
ACBC...... Biotechnica Canada, Calgary, Alberta [*Library symbol*] [*National Library of Canada*] (BIB)
ACBCA ..... Acta Crystallographica. Section B. Structural Crystallography and Crystal Chemistry [*A publication*]
ACBCC...... Advisory Committee to the Board and to the Committee on Commodities [*UNCTAD*]
ACBCC...... Australia-China Business Co-Operation Committee
ACBCT...... Automatic Circuit Board Card Tester
AC/BD....... Acrylonitrile/Butadiene
ACBD .... Active Commission Base Date [*Military*]
ACBD .... Association Canadienne des Bibliotheques de Droit [*Canadian Association of Law Libraries - CALL*]
ACBDP...... Burnet, Duckworth & Palmer, Calgary, Alberta [*Library symbol*] [*National Library of Canada*] (BIB)
ACBE........ Association for Community Based Education (EA)
ACBE........ Australian Centre for Business Education
ACBEI .... Association for Community Based Educational Institutions [*Later, ACBE*] (EA)
Ac Belg B ... Academie Royale de Belgique. Bulletin [*A publication*]
ACBEP...... Calgary Board of Education Professional Library, Alberta [*Library symbol*] [*National Library of Canada*] (NLC)
ACBES ...... American Council of the Blind Enterprises and Services (EA)
ACBFC...... Academy of Comic-Book Fans and Collectors [*Defunct*]

ACBFC ...... American Church Building Fund Commission [*Later, Episcopal Church Building Fund*] (EA)
ACBFE ...... American Council of the Blind Federal Employees (EA)
ACBG .... Aortacoronary Bypass Graft [*Cardiology*]
ACBIS .... Academic Collective Bargaining Information Service (EA)
ACBL .... American Commercial Barge Lines, Inc. [*AAR code*]
ACBL .... American Contract Bridge League (EA)
ACBL .... American Council of Blind Lions (EA)
ACBLF ...... Association Canadienne des Bibliothecaires de Langue Francaise [*Later, ASTED*]
ACBLF Bul ... Association Canadienne des Bibliothecaires de Langue Francaise. Bulletin [*A publication*]
ACBLT .... Airlift Contingency Battalion Landing Team (NVT)
ACBM .... Advisory Committee for Biology and Medicine [*AEC*]
ACBM .... Associated Corset and Brassiere Manufacturers (EA)
ACBM .... Association Canadienne des Bibliotheques Musicales [*Canadian Association of Music Libraries*]
ACBM .... Atomic Cesium Beam MASER
ACBMAG ... Aviation Chief Boatswain's Mate, Arresting Gear and Barriers [*Navy rating*]
ACBMCP .. Aviation Chief Boatswain's Mate, Catapult [*Navy rating*]
ACBMGA ... Aviation Chief Boatswain's Mate, Gasoline System [*Navy rating*]
ACBMPH ... Aviation Chief Boatswain's Mate, Plane Handler [*Navy rating*]
ACBNM .... Acute Care Bed Need Methodology [*Hospital management*]
ACBO .... Acta Borealia [*A publication*]
ACBO .... Army Central Budget Office
ACBOA ..... American Citizens Band Operators Association (EA)
ACBOBU .. Annals of Clinical Biochemistry [*A publication*]
ACBP .... American Council of the Blind Parents [*Later, CFVI*] (EA)
ACBPAW .. Acta Biologica Paranaense [*A publication*]
ACBPE ...... BP Exploration Canada Ltd., Calgary, Alberta [*Library symbol*] [*National Library of Canada*] (NLC)
ACBR .... Association Canadienne des Boursiers Rhodes [*Canadian Association of Rhodes Scholars - CARS*]
ACBRA ...... ACB [*American Council of the Blind*] Radio Amateurs [*An association*] (EA)
ACBRA ...... American CB Radio Association (EA)
ACBS .... Accrediting Commission for Business Schools (EA)
ACBS .... Alert Crew Billet Security (AFM)
ACBS .... Antique and Classic Boat Society (EA)
ACBSI .... Associate of the Chartered Building Societies Institute [*British*] (DBQ)
ACBT .... Automatic Circuit Board Tester
ACBTDD ... Acta Biotechnologica [*A publication*]
ACBWG .... Apollo Reentry Communications Blackout Working Group [*NASA*]
ACBWS ..... Automatic Chemical Biological Warning System
ACC .... Aboriginal Coordinating Council [*Australia*]
ACC .... Academic Computation Center [*Georgetown University*] [*Research center*] (RCD)
ACC .... Academic Computer Center [*University of Washington*] [*Research center*] (RCD)
ACC .... Academic Computing Center [*University of Vermont*] [*Research center*] (RCD)
ACC .... Academic Computing Center [*University of California, Riverside*] [*Research center*] (RCD)
ACC .... Academy of Canadian Cinema [*Academie du Cinema Canadien*]
Acc .... Accademia [*Academy*] [*Italian*] (BJA)
ACC .... Accelerando [*Quickening the Pace*] [*Music*]
ACC .... Acceleration
ACC .... Accent [*A publication*]
ACC .... Acceptable Container Condition [*Shipping*] (DS)
ACC .... Acceptance [*Banking*]
ACC .... Access
ACC .... Accessory
ACC .... Accident
ACC .... Accommodation
ACC .... Accompagnamento [*Accompaniment*] [*Music*]
ACC .... Accompanied
Acc .... Accord (DLA)
ACC .... According (To)
ACC .... Account (EY)
ACC .... Accountancy [*A publication*]
ACC .... Accountant [*London*] [*A publication*]
ACC .... Accounting Careers Council [*Later, AICPA*]
ACC .... Accounting Classification Code (AFM)
ACC .... Accounting Controllers Committee
ACC .... Accra [*Ghana*] [*Airport symbol*] (OAG)
ACC .... Accumulator [*Flowchart*] (MSA)
Acc .... Accursius [*Deceased, 1263*] [*Authority cited in pre-1607 legal work*] (DSA)
ACC .... Accusative
ACC .... Acetyl-CoA Carboxylase [*An enzyme*]
ACC .... Acetylcysteine [*Biochemistry*]
ACC .... Acid Copper Chromate [*Wood preservative*]
ACC .... Acinic Cell Carcinoma [*Medicine*]
ACC .... Acora [*Ghana*] [*Airport symbol*]
ACC .... Action Change Card
ACC .... Active Citizenship Campaign

ACC .... Adaptive Control Constrained [*Manufacturing term*]
ACC .... Additives and Containments Committee [*British*]
ACC .... Adelaide City Council [*Australia*]
ACC .... Adenoid Cystic Carcinoma [*Medicine*]
ACC .... Administrative Committee on Coordination [*of the United Nations*] [*Aviation*]
ACC .... Admiralty Corrosion Committee [*British*] (KSC)
ACC .... Adrenocortical Carcinoma [*Medicine*]
ACC .... Advanced Carbon-Carbon (MCD)
ACC .... Advanced Concepts Center [*General Motors Corp.*] [*Automotive engineering*]
ACC .... Advisory Council on Camps (EA)
ACC .... Aeroplane Construction Committee [*Australia*]
ACC .... Aft Cargo Carrier (IEEE)
ACC .... Aft Cargo Compartment (MCD)
ACC .... Air Center Commander
ACC .... Air Chief Commandant [*British*]
ACC .... Air Component Command [*Military*] (MCD)
ACC .... Air Conditioning Clutch Compressor [*Automotive engineering*]
ACC .... Air Control Center [*Military*]
ACC .... Air Control Commission (AAG)
ACC .... Air Controlman, Chief [*Navy rating*]
ACC .... Air Coordinating Committee [*Governmental policy body for civil aviation in US; terminated, 1960*]
ACC .... Air Crew Change
ACC .... Airborne Control Computer
A/CC .... Aircraft Carrier
ACC .... Aircraft Controlling Custodian (MCD)
ACC .... Airport Consultants Council (EA)
ACC .... Airspace Control Center (MCD)
ACC .... Alarm Control Center (NVT)
ACC .... Alaskan Collectors Club (EA)
ACC .... Alcuin Club. Collections [*A publication*]
ACC .... Allahabad Criminal Cases [*India*] [*A publication*] (DLA)
ACC .... Allied Chemical Corporation [*Later, Allied Corp.*] (MCD)
ACC .... Allied Chief Commissioner [*World War II*]
ACC .... Allied Commander-in-Chief [*World War II*]
ACC .... Allied Control Center [*NATO*] (NATG)
ACC .... Allied Control Commission [*World War II*]
ACC .... Allied Control Council [*World War II*]
ACC .... Alpena Community College [*Michigan*]
ACC .... Alpine Club of Canada (EA)
ACC .... Alternate Command Center [*Navy*] (CINC)
ACC .... Alternating Current Circuit
ACC .... Altocumulus Castellanus [*Cloud*] [*Meteorology*]
ACC .... Aluminum Company of Canada Ltd. [*Toronto Stock Exchange symbol*] [*Vancouver Stock Exchange symbol*]
ACC .... Amarillo College, Amarillo, TX [*OCLC symbol*] (OCLC)
ACC .... Amazonian Cooperation Council (EAIO)
ACC .... Amchitka Central C [*Alaska*] [*Seismograph station code, US Geological Survey*] [*Closed*] (SEIS)
ACC .... American Capital Corporation [*AMEX symbol*] (SPSG)
ACC .... American Catholic Committee (EA)
ACC .... American Catholic Conference (EA)
ACC .... American Chamber of Commerce (DCTA)
ACC .... American Chesapeake Club (EA)
ACC .... American Cimflex Corporation [*Pittsburgh, PA*]
ACC .... American Citizenship Center (EA)
ACC .... American College of Cardiology (EA)
ACC .... American College of Chemosurgery (EA)
ACC .... American College of Counselors (EA)
ACC .... American College of Cryosurgery (EA)
ACC .... American Communications Consultants, Inc. [*Telecommunications service*] (TSSD)
ACC .... American Concert Choir [*Defunct*]
ACC .... American Conference of Cantors (EA)
ACC .... American Continental Corp.
ACC .... American Copper Council (EA)
ACC .... American Copyright Council (EA)
ACC .... American Corporation Cases, by Withrow [*1868-87*] [*A publication*] (DLA)
ACC .... American Craft Council (EA)
ACC .... American Crystallographic Community
ACC .... American Cyanamid Company (KSC)
ACC .... Aminocyclopropane-Carboxylic Acid [*Organic chemistry*]
ACC .... Amphibious Command Car (NATG)
ACC .... Analytical Calibration Curve
ACC .... Anglican Church of Canada
ACC .... Anglican Consultative Council [*London, England*] (EAIO)
ACC .... Annual Capital Charge
ACC .... Annual Contributions Contract [*Public housing development*]
ACC .... Anodal Closure Contraction [*Also, AnCC*] [*Physiology*]
ACC .... Antarctic Circumpolar Current [*Oceanography*]
ACC .... Antenna Control Console
ACC .... Anti-Communist Committee (EA)
ACC .... Antibody-Containing Cell [*Immunology*]
A-CC .... Antiphlogistic-Corticoid Conditioning Effect [*Medicine*]
ACC .... Aortic Cross Clamping [*Cardiology*]
ACC .... Appleton-Century-Crofts [*Publisher*]
ACC .... Approach Control Center (MCD)
ACC .... Approved Capital Costs [*Canada*]

ACC .... Arab Co-Operation Council   (ECON)
ACC .... Area Control Center [*Aviation*]   (FAAC)
ACC .... Area Coordination Center
ACC .... Argonne Code Center [*Department of Energy*]   (IID)
ACC .... Armament Control Computer   (MCD)
ACC .... Armored Column Cover   (MCD)
ACC .... Army Catering Corps [*British*]
ACC .... Army Chemical Center
ACC .... Army Commanders' Conference
ACC .... Army Communications Command [*Fort Huachuca, AZ*]
ACC .... Army Component Command   (CINC)
ACC .... Army Cooperation Command [*British*]
ACC .... Artillery Control Console [*British*]
ACC .... Asbestos Claims Council   (EA)
ACC .... Asbestos Compensation Coalition   (EA)
ACC .... Ashland Community College [*Ashland, KY*]
ACC .... Asian Coconut Community [*Later, APCC*]
ACC .... Asian Cultural Council   (EA)
ACC .... Assault Crisis Center
ACC .... Assistant Camp Commandant [*British*]
ACC .... Associated Communications Corp.
ACC .... Association Canadienne des Communications [*Canadian Communication Association - CCA*]
ACC .... Association Canadienne de la Construction [*Canadian Construction Association*]
ACC .... Association of Chiropractic Colleges   (EA)
ACC .... Association Chiropratique Canadienne [*Canadian Chiropractic Association*]
ACC .... Association of Choral Conductors   (EA)
ACC .... Association of Computer Consultants   (EA)
ACC .... Association des Consommateurs du Canada [*Consumers' Association of Canada - CAC*]
ACC .... Association of County Councils [*British*]
ACC .... Association for Creative Change within Religious and Other Social Systems   (EA)
ACC .... Astronaut Control Console [*NASA*]
ACC .... Astronomical Great Circle Course
ACC .... Asynchronous Communications Control
ACC .... Atlantic Christian College [*Wilson, NC*]
ACC .... Atlantic Coast Conference   (EA)
ACC .... Attack Control Concept
ACC .... Attack Control Console
ACC .... Auburn Community College [*New York*]
ACC .... Audio Control Center
ACC .... Australasian Corrosion Centre   (EAIO)
ACC .... Australia-China Council
ACC .... Australian Company Law Cases [*A publication*]   (APTA)
ACC .... Automatic Carrier Control [*Telecommunications*]   (TEL)
ACC .... Automatic Chrominance Control   (DEN)
ACC .... Automatic Color Control
ACC .... Automatic Combustion Control
ACC .... Automatic Contrast Control
ACC .... Automatic Control Certified   (DCTA)
ACC .... Automatic Control Console   (NASA)
ACC .... Automatic Course Control [*Air Force*]
ACC .... Auxiliary Crew Compartment   (MCD)
ACC .... Aviation Control Center
ACC .... Aviation Credit Corps
ACC .... Cessford Community Library, Alberta [*Library symbol*] [*National Library of Canada*]   (NLC)
a-cc--- .... China, Mainland [*MARC geographic area code*] [*Library of Congress*]   (LCCP)
ACC .... Classic Record Club [*Record label*]
ACCA .... Accelerated Capital Cost Allowance [*Accounting*]
ACCA .... Ad Hoc Crypto-Coordination Agency   (MUGU)
ACCA .... Aeronautical Chamber of Commerce of America [*Later, AIA*]
ACCA .... Agricultural Credit Corporation Act [*1932*]
ACCA .... Air Conditioning Contractors of America   (EA)
ACCA .... Air Courier Conference of America   (EA)
ACCA .... American Cave Conservation Association   (EA)
ACCA .... American Chamber of Commerce in Austria   (EA)
ACCA .... American Child Custody Alliance   (EA)
ACCA .... American Clinical and Climatological Association   (EA)
ACCA .... American College of Cardiovascular Administrators   (EA)
ACCA .... American College of Clinic Administrators [*Defunct*]   (EA)
ACCA .... American Commercial Collectors Association   (EA)
ACCA .... American Corporate Counsel Association   (EA)
ACCA .... American Correctional Chaplains Association   (EA)
ACCA .... American Cotton Cooperative Association   (EA)
ACCA .... American Council for Coordinated Action   (EA)
ACCA .... Angel Collectors Club of America   (EA)
ACCA .... Antenna Counterbalance Cylinder Assembly
ACCA .... Armed Career Criminal Act of 1984
ACCA .... Art Collectors Club of America   (EA)
ACCA .... Associated Colleges of the Chicago Area
ACCA .... Association of Certified and Corporate Accountants [*British*]
ACCA .... Asynchronous Communications Control Attachment
ACCA .... Australian Centre for Contemporary Art
ACCA .... Australian Current Case Annotator [*A publication*]
ACCA .... Auto Cycle Council of Australia
ACCAA ...... Acta Cardiologica [*Bruxelles*] [*A publication*]

ACC-ACO ... Army Communications Command Advanced Concepts Office [*Fort Huachuca, AZ*]
ACCAD ..... Accademia
Accad Bibliot d'Italia ... Accademia e Biblioteche d'Italia [*A publication*]
Accad Bibl Ital ... Accademia e Biblioteche d'Italia [*A publication*]
Accad e Bibl Italia ... Accademia e Biblioteche d'Italia [*A publication*]
Accad Ital Vite Vino (Siena) Atti ... Accademia Italiana della Vite e del Vino (Siena). Atti [*A publication*]
Accad Med ... Accademia Medica [*A publication*]
Accad Naz Lincei Atti Cl Sci Fis Mat Nat Rend ... Accademia Nazionale dei Lincei. Atti. Classe di Scienze Fisiche, Matematiche, e Naturali. Rendiconti [*A publication*]
Accad Naz Lincei Atti Cl Sci Fis Mat e Nat Rend ... Atti. Accademia Nazionale dei Lincei. Rendiconti. Classe di Scienze Fisiche, Matematiche, e Naturali [*A publication*]
Accad Naz Sci Lett Arti (Modena) Atti Mem ... Accademia Nazionale di Scienze, Lettere, ed Arti (Modena). Atti e Memorie [*A publication*]
Accad Pata Sci Lett Arti Collana Accad ... Accademia Patavina di Scienze, Lettere, ed Arti. Collana Accademica [*A publication*]
Accad Patavina Sci Lett Arti Atti Mem ... Accademia Patavina di Scienze, Lettere, ed Arti. Atti e Memorie [*Padua*] [*A publication*]
Accad Pugliese Sci Att Relaz Parte 2 ... Accademia Pugliese delle Scienze. Atti e Relazioni. Parte 2. Classe di Scienze Fisiche, Mediche, e Naturali [*A publication*]
Accad Sci Fis e Mat Rend ... Accademia delle Scienze Fisiche e Matematiche. Rendiconto [*A publication*]
a-cc-an........ Anhwei Province [*China, Mainland*] [*MARC geographic area code*] [*Library of Congress*]   (LCCP)
ACCAP...... Autocoder-to-COBOL Conversion Aid Program [*IBM Corp.*] [*Data processing*]
ACCAS...... Altocumulus Castellanus [*Cloud*] [*Meteorology*]   (FAAC)
ACCAS...... Association of Crossroads Care Attendant Schemes   (EAIO)
ACCASP ... Air Coordinating Committee [*Terminated*] Airspace Subcommittee
ACCAT...... Advanced Command and Control Architectural Testbed   (MCD)
ACCB........ Air Cavalry Combat Brigade [*Army*]
ACCB........ Aircraft Change Control Board [*DoD*]
ACCB........ Aircraft Configuration Change Board
ACCB........ Aircraft Configuration Control Board [*DoD*]
ACCB........ Airframe Change Control Board   (MCD)
ACCB........ American Chamber of Commerce of Bolivia   (EA)
ACCB........ Atlas Configuration Control Board [*Aerospace*]   (AAG)
ACCB........ Australian Copyright Council. Bulletin [*A publication*]   (APTA)
ACCB........ Library Services, Colonel Belcher Hospital, Calgary, Alberta [*Library symbol*] [*National Library of Canada*]   (BIB)
ACCB/TRICAP ... Air Cavalry Combat Brigade/Triple Capability Division [*Army*]   (MCD)
Acc Bus Res ... Accounting and Business Research [*A publication*]
ACCC........ ACC Corporation [*Rochester, NY*] [*NASDAQ symbol*]   (NQ)
ACCC........ Advisory Council on College Chemistry
ACCC........ Alternate Central Computer Complex   (MCD)
ACCC........ Alternate Command and Control Center [*Air Force*]   (MCD)
ACCC........ American Council of Christian Churches   (EA)
ACCC........ Antique Comb Collectors Club   (EA)
ACCC........ Association of Canadian Choral Conductors [*Association des Chefs des Choeurs Canadiens*]
ACCC........ Association of Canadian Community Colleges [*Association des Colleges Communautaires du Canada*]
ACCC........ Association of Child Care Centres [*Australia*]
ACCC........ Association of Community Cancer Centers   (EA)
ACCCA...... Acta Cientifica Compostelana [*A publication*]
ACCCA...... American Catholic Correctional Chaplains Association   (EA)
ACCCA...... American Community Cultural Center Association   (EA)
ACC-CCC ... Action Coordinating Council for Comprehensive Child Care
ACCCE...... Allied Commission, Commerce Subcommission, Exports [*World War II*]
ACC & CE ... Association of Consulting Chemists and Chemical Engineers   (EA)
ACCCF...... American Concert Choir and Choral Foundation [*Later, ACF*]
a-cc-ch........ Chekiang Province [*China, Mainland*] [*MARC geographic area code*] [*Library of Congress*]   (LCCP)
Acc Chem Re ... Accounts of Chemical Research [*A publication*]
Acc Chem Res ... Accounts of Chemical Research [*A publication*]
ACCCI...... American Coke and Coal Chemicals Institute   (EA)
ACCCI....... Australia-China Chamber of Commerce and Industry
Acc Cient Int ... Accion Cientifica International [*A publication*]
ACC/COM ... Air Coordinating Committee [*Terminated*] Communications Subcommittee
ACCCS...... Crooked Creek Colony School, Alberta [*Library symbol*] [*National Library of Canada*]   (BIB)
ACCD .... Accelerated Construction Completion Date   (NATG)
ACCD .... Accident
ACCD .... Advance Corporate Contract Directive   (MCD)
ACCD .... Aerospace Communication and Controls Division [*NASA*]   (KSC)
ACCD .... Aircraft Compatibility Control Drawing   (MCD)
ACCD .... American Coalition of Citizens with Disabilities   (EA)
ACCDCE .... Accordance   (ROG)
ACCE......... Acceptance [*Banking*]

ACCE......... American Chamber of Commerce Executives (EA)
ACCE......... American College for Continuing Education (EA)
ACCE......... American Council for Construction Education (EA)
ACCE......... American Council on Cosmetology Education [*Defunct*] (EA)
ACCE......... Association Canadienne des Chercheurs en Education [*Canadian Educational Researchers Association - CERA*]
ACCE......... Association of Christian Church Educators (EA)
ACCE......... Association of County Chief Executives [*British*] (EAIO)
ACCE......... Canterra Energy Ltd., Calgary, Alberta [*Library symbol*] [*National Library of Canada*] (NLC)
ACCEC...... Australian Chamber of Commerce Export Council
AC-CEF...... Allis-Chalmers Critical Experimental Facility
ACCEH ..... Access Committee Centre on Environment for the Handicapped [*British*]
ACCEL...... Accelerando [*Quickening the Pace*] [*Music*]
ACCEL...... · Accelerate (AABC)
ACCEL...... Accelerator [*Automotive engineering*]
ACCEL...... Accelerometer
ACCEL...... American College of Cardiology. Extended Learning [*A publication*]
ACCEL...... Automated Circuit Card Etching Layout [*Data processing*]
ACCEL...... Canuck Engineering Ltd., Calgary, Alberta [*Library symbol*] [*National Library of Canada*] (NLC)
ACCELO... Accelerando [*Quickening the Pace*] [*Music*] (ROG)
ACCEM..... Advanced Composite Cost Estimating Model (MCD)
ACCENT... Autogenetically-Controlled Cesium Electro-Nuclear Thrust System (MCD)
ACCEPN... Acceptation [*Acceptance*] [*French*] [*Banking*] (ROG)
ACCEPT... Access Electronic Payment Terminals [*for credit cards*] [*British*]
ACCEPT... Automated Cargo Clearance and Enforcement Processing Technique [*US Customs Service*]
ACCEPTCE ... Acceptance [*Banking*] (ROG)
ACCEPTN ... Acceptance
ACCES.... Accessory
ACCES...... American Chamber of Commerce of El Salvador (EA)
ACCES...... Cenlor Services Ltd., Calgary, Alberta [*Library symbol*] [*National Library of Canada*] (NLC)
ACCESD ... Australian Council of Chairmen of Earth Science Departments
ACCESS.... Accessory (KSC)
ACCESS.... Action Center for Educational Service and Scholarships
ACCESS.... Action Coordinating Committee to End Segregation in the Suburbs
ACCESS.... Afloat Consumption Cost and Effectiveness Surveillance System [*Navy*]
ACCESS.... Aircraft Communication Control and Electronic Signaling System [*Air Force*]
ACCESS.... American and Canadian Connection for Efficient Securities Settlement [*Canada*]
ACCESS.... American College of Cardiology Extended Study Services
ACCESS.... American Coordinating Committee for Equality in Sport and Society (EA)
ACCESS.... AMOCO Chemicals Customer Service System
ACCESS.... Army Commissary Computer Entry Store System (AABC)
ACCESS.... Assembly Concept for Construction of Erectable Space Structures [*Space shuttle experiment*] [*NASA*]
ACCESS.... Assessment for Community Care Services [*Health Care Financing Administration*]
ACCESS.... Association of Community Colleges for Excellence in Systems and Services [*Consortium*]
ACCESS.... Australian Contribution to the Cost of Education for Students Scheme
ACCESS.... Automated Computer Controlled Editing Sound System
ACCESS.... Automated CONARC Command Echelon Standard Systems (MCD)
ACCESS.... Automated Control and Checking of Electrical Systems Support (MCD)
ACCESS.... Automatic Card Control Entrance Security System [*Data processing*]
ACCESS.... Automatic Computer-Controlled Electronic Scanning System [*National Institute of Standards and Technology*]
ACCESS.... Automatic Crane Control Storage System
ACCESS.... [*A*] Complete Computerized Examination System [*Anatomy and physiology*]
Access Index Little Mag ... Access Index to Little Magazines [*A publication*]
Access V... Access Video [*Australia*] [*A publication*]
ACCF........ American Council for Capital Formation (EA)
ACCF........ Asia Christian Communications Fellowship [*Defunct*] (EAIO)
ACCFA...... Agricultural Credit Cooperative Farmers' Association [*Philippines*]
ACCFA...... Association des Citoyens de Culture Francaise d'Amerique [*American Association of Citizens of French Culture*] [*Canada*]
ACCFC...... Ag Chem and Commercial Fertilizer [*Later, Farm Chemicals*] [*A publication*]
a-cc-fn .... Fukien Province [*China, Mainland*] [*MARC geographic area code*] [*Library of Congress*] (LCCP)
ACCG .... Association Canadienne des Chirurgiens Generaux [*Canadian Association of General Surgeons - CAGS*]
ACCG .... Clarkson Gordon Library, Calgary, Alberta [*Library symbol*] [*National Library of Canada*] (BIB)

a-ccg-- .... Yangtze River and Basin [*China, Mainland*] [*MARC geographic area code*] [*Library of Congress*] (LCCP)
Acc Gar Equip ... Accessory and Garage Equipment [*A publication*]
ACCGET ... American Council on Capital Gains and Estate Taxation [*Later, ACCF*] [*Tax lobbying organization*]
ACCGS...... Air Cadet Central Gliding School [*British*]
ACCH....... American College of Clinical Hypnosis [*Defunct*] (EA)
ACCH....... Association for the Care of Children's Health (EA)
ACCH....... Calgary Herald, Alberta [*Library symbol*] [*National Library of Canada*] (NLC)
ACCHAN ... Allied Command Channel [*NATO*]
a-cc-he....... Heilungkiang Province [*China, Mainland*] [*MARC geographic area code*] [*Library of Congress*] (LCCP)
a-cc-hh .... Hupeh Province [*China, Mainland*] [*MARC geographic area code*] [*Library of Congress*] (LCCP)
ACCHO..... Association Canadienne des Communications entre l'Homme et l'Ordinateur [*Canadian Association of Communications between Man and Computers*]
a-cc-ho....... Honan Province [*China, Mainland*] [*MARC geographic area code*] [*Library of Congress*] (LCCP)
a-cc-hp....... Hopeh Province [*China, Mainland*] [*MARC geographic area code*] [*Library of Congress*] (LCCP)
AcChR .... Acetylcholine Receptor [*Also, AChR*] [*Biochemistry*]
a-cc-hu....... Hunan Province [*China, Mainland*] [*MARC geographic area code*] [*Library of Congress*] (LCCP)
ACCI......... Accident Injury
ACCI......... Adult Career Concerns Inventory [*Test*]
ACCI......... American Consulting Corporation, Inc. [*NASDAQ symbol*] (NQ)
ACCI......... American Corporate Counsel Institute [*Washington, DC*] (EA)
ACCI......... American Cottage Cheese Institute [*Later, ACDPI*] (EA)
ACCI......... American Council on Consumer Interests (EA)
ACCI......... Association of Crafts and Creative Industries (EA)
Acciaio Inossid ... Acciaio Inossidabile [*A publication*]
ACCID....... Initial Notification of an Aircraft Accident [*Aviation code*]
Accid Anal Prev ... Accident Analysis and Prevention [*A publication*]
Accid Anal Prev (Elmsford NY) ... Accident Analysis and Prevention (Elmsford, New York) [*A publication*]
Accident Anal Prev ... Accident Analysis and Prevention [*A publication*]
Accident Prevention Bul ... Accident Prevention Bulletin [*A publication*] (APTA)
ACCIDSUB ... Subsequent Notification of an Aircraft Accident [*Aviation code*]
Ac Cienc Med Habana An ... Academia de Ciencias Medicas, Fisicas, y Naturales de la Habana. Annales [*A publication*]
a-cc-im .... Inner Mongolia Autonomous Region [*China, Mainland*] [*MARC geographic area code*] [*Library of Congress*] (LCCP)
Accion Farm ... Accion Farmaceutica [*A publication*]
A & C Cir ... Accounts and Collection Unit Circulars [*A publication*] (DLA)
ACCIS .... Advisory Committee for the Co-Ordination of Information Systems [*Database producer*] [*United Nations*] [*Geneva, Switzerland*]
ACCIS .... Air Command and Control Improvement System [*NATO*]
ACCJ......... American Chamber of Commerce in Japan (EA)
ACCJC ...... Genealogical Society Library, Church of Jesus Christ of Latter-Day Saints, Calgary, Alberta [*Library symbol*] [*National Library of Canada*] (NLC)
a-cck-- .... Kunlun Mountain Region [*China, Mainland*] [*MARC geographic area code*] [*Library of Congress*] (LCCP)
ACCK .... Librarians Committee of the Associated Colleges of Central Kansas [*Library network*]
a-cc-ka....... Kansu Province [*China, Mainland*] [*MARC geographic area code*] [*Library of Congress*] (LCCP)
a-cc-kc....... Kwangsi Chuang Autonomous Region [*China, Mainland*] [*MARC geographic area code*] [*Library of Congress*] (LCCP)
a-cc-ki .... Kiangsi Province [*China, Mainland*] [*MARC geographic area code*] [*Library of Congress*] (LCCP)
a-cc-kn .... Kwangtung Province [*China, Mainland*] [*MARC geographic area code*] [*Library of Congress*] (LCCP)
a-cc-kr........ Kirin Province [*China, Mainland*] [*MARC geographic area code*] [*Library of Congress*] (LCCP)
a-cc-ku .... Kiangsu Province [*China, Mainland*] [*MARC geographic area code*] [*Library of Congress*] (LCCP)
a-cc-kw....... Kweichow Province [*China, Mainland*] [*MARC geographic area code*] [*Library of Congress*] (LCCP)
ACCL........ All Canadian Congress of Labour
ACCL........ American Citizens Concerned for Life Education Fund/ACCL Communications Center (EA)
ACCL........ American College of Computer Lawyers (EA)
ACCL........ American Council of Christian Laymen [*Later, LCACCC*] (EA)
ACCL........ American Council of Commercial Laboratories [*Later, ACIL*] (KSC)
ACCL........ Army Coating and Chemical Laboratory (MCD)
ACCL........ Calgary Library Service Centre, Alberta [*Library symbol*] [*National Library of Canada*] (NLC)
ACCLAIMS ... Army COMSEC [*Communications Security*] Commodity, Logistical, and Accounting Information Management System (AABC)

a-cc-lp .... Liaoning Province [*China, Mainland*] [*MARC geographic area code*] [*Library of Congress*] (LCCP)
ACCLRM .. Accelerometer
ACCM .... Acoustic Counter-Countermeasures [*Navy*] (NG)
ACCM .... Advanced Concept Cost Model (MCD)
ACCM .... Advisory Council for the Church's Ministry [*Church of England*]
ACCM .... Air Controlman, Master Chief [*Navy rating*]
ACCM .... American College of Clinic Managers [*Later, ACMGA*] (EA)
ACCM .... Associated Communications Corp. [*NASDAQ symbol*] (NQ)
ACCME ..... Accreditation Council for Continuing Medical Education (EA)
Acc Med (A) ... Accion Medica (Argentina) [*A publication*]
Acc Med (B) ... Accion Medica (Bolivia) [*A publication*]
Acc Med (M) ... Accion Medica (Mexico) [*A publication*]
ACC/MET ... Air Coordinating Committee [*Terminated*] Meteorological Subcommittee
ACCMIS .... Army Command and Control Management Information System
ACCML ..... Army Chemical Corps Medical Laboratories (KSC)
ACCMS ..... American Center for Chinese Medical Sciences (EA)
ACCN .... Accommodation
ACCN .... American Court and Commercial Newspapers (EA)
ACCN .... Arms Control Computer Network (EA)
ACCN .... Audit Central Control Network (MCD)
ACCN .... Australian Council of Community Nursing
ACCN .... Australian Customs Clearance Statistics [*Database*]
ACCNET ... Army Command and Control Network (AABC)
a-cc-nn .... Ningsia Hui Autonomous Region [*China, Mainland*] [*MARC geographic area code*] [*Library of Congress*] (LCCP)
ACCNR ..... Alaska Climate Center. News and Review [*A publication*]
ACCNR ..... Library and Records Center, Crows Nest Resources Ltd., Calgary, Alberta [*Library symbol*] [*National Library of Canada*] (NLC)
ACCO .... Adolph Coors Company [*NASDAQ symbol*] (NQ)
ACCO .... American College of Chiropractic Orthopedists (EA)
ACCO .... American Cyanamid Company
ACCO .... Associate of the Canadian College of Organists
ACCO .... [*The*] Associated Christian Colleges of Oregon [*Library network*]
AcCoA .... Acetyl Coenzyme A [*Biochemistry*]
ACCOM .... Accommodate (AFM)
ACCOM .... Accompaniment [*Music*]
ACCOM .... Accompany (AFM)
Accom ad Lib ... Accompaniment ad Libitum [*Music*]
ACCOMMODON ... Accommodation (ROG)
Accom Oblto ... Accompaniment Obligato [*Music*]
ACCOMP ... Academic Computing Group
ACCOMP ... Accompaniment [*Music*]
ACCOMP ... Accomplish (AFM)
ACCOMPL ... Accomplish (MUGU)
ACCON ..... Acoustic Control (NVT)
ACCOP ...... Canadian Occidental Petroleum Ltd., Calgary, Alberta [*Library symbol*] [*National Library of Canada*] (NLC)
ACCOR ..... Army COMSEC [*Communications Security*] Central Office of Record (AABC)
ACCORD .. According
Accord .... Accordion [*Music*]
ACCORD .. Association for Co-Ordinated Rural Development [*Government body*] [*British*]
ACCORDCE ... Accordance (ROG)
ACCORDG ... According (ROG)
ACCORDS ... Acoustic Correlation and Detection System
ACCOS ...... Automatic Computer Calculation of Optical Systems (MCD)
ACCOS ...... Canstar Oil Sands Ltd., Calgary, Alberta [*Library symbol*] [*National Library of Canada*] (NLC)
ACCOSCA ... African Confederation of Cooperative Savings and Credit Associations [*See also ACECA*] [*Nairobi, Kenya*] (EAIO)
Accountancy L Rep ... Accountancy Law Reporter [*A publication*] (DLA)
Accountancy L Rep CCH ... Accountancy Law Reports. Commerce Clearing House [*A publication*]
Accountants and Secretaries' Educ J ... Accountants and Secretaries' Educational Journal [*A publication*] (APTA)
Account Bus Res ... Accounting and Business Research [*A publication*]
Account Dig ... Accountants Digest [*A publication*]
Account Fin ... Accounting and Finance [*A publication*]
Account Index Suppl ... Accountants' Index. Supplement [*A publication*]
Accounting and Bus Research ... Accounting and Business Research [*A publication*]
Accounting R ... Accounting Review [*A publication*]
Account J ... Accountants' Journal [*A publication*]
Account Mag ... Accountant's Magazine [*A publication*]
Account R .. Accounting Review [*A publication*]
Account Res ... Accounting Research [*A publication*]
Account Rev ... Accounting Review [*A publication*]
ACCOVAM ... Association Canadienne des Courtiers en Valeurs Mobilieres [*Investment Dealers' Association of Canada - IDA*]
ACCOW .... Assistant Combat Cargo Officer, Well Deck (CAAL)
ACCOY ..... Accompany (ROG)
ACCP .... Advisory Committee on Civilian Policy [*World War II*]
ACCP .... American Chamber of Commerce of the Philippines (EA)
ACCP .... American College of Chest Physicians (EA)
ACCP .... American College of Clinical Pharmacology (EA)

ACCP .... American College of Clinical Pharmacy (EA)
ACCP .... American Council on Chiropractic Physiotherapy [*Later, CCPT*] (EA)
ACCP .... Army Correspondence Course Program
ACCP .... Arquivos. Centro Cultural Portugues [*A publication*]
ACCP .... Association Canadienne des Chefs de Pompiers [*Canadian Association of Fire Chiefs*]
ACCP .... Association of Casualty Care Personnel [*Canada*]
ACCP .... Canadian Petroleum Association, Calgary, Alberta [*Library symbol*] [*National Library of Canada*] (NLC)
a-ccp-- .... Pohai Sea and Area [*China, Mainland*] [*MARC geographic area code*] [*Library of Congress*] (LCCP)
ACCPA ..... Army Chemical Center Procurement Agency
a-cc-pe .... Peking Municipality [*China, Mainland*] [*MARC geographic area code*] [*Library of Congress*] (LCCP)
ACCPFF .... Anti-Communist Confederation of Polish Freedom Fighters in USA (EA)
ACCPL ...... Accomplice [*FBI standardized term*]
ACCPT ...... Accept [*or Acceptance*] [*Banking*] (KSC)
ACCR .... Accrued (AFM)
ACCR .... American Christian Committee for Refugees [*Post-World War II, Europe*]
ACCR .... American Council on Chiropractic Roentgenology [*Later, Council on Roentgenology of the American Chiropractic Association*] (EA)
ACCR .... Association Canadienne du Canotage Recreatif [*Canadian Association of Recreational Boating*]
ACCRA ..... American Chamber of Commerce Researchers Association (EA)
Accrd .... Accrued
ACCRED ... Accredited (EY)
Acc Res ...... Accounting Research [*A publication*]
ACCRES ... Accrescinto [*Increased*] [*Music*] (ROG)
Acc Review ... Accounting Review [*A publication*]
ACC-ROC ... American Chamber of Commerce in Republic of China (EA)
ACCRS ...... Ridgevalley School, Crooked Creek, Alberta [*Library symbol*] [*National Library of Canada*] (BIB)
ACCRU ..... American Constitutional and Civil Rights Union (EA)
ACCRY ...... Accessory (KSC)
ACCRY ...... Accuracy (AFM)
ACCS .... Advanced Communications Control System (CAAL)
ACCS .... Afloat Command and Control System (CAAL)
ACCS .... Air Command and Control System
ACCS .... Air Controlman, Senior Chief [*Navy rating*]
ACCS .... Airborne Command Control Squadron [*Air Force*] (CINC)
ACCS .... Airborne Command and Control System
ACCS .... Aircraft Communications System
ACCS .... American Child Care Services (EA)
ACCS .... American Christmas Crib Society [*Defunct*] (EA)
ACCS .... Amphibious Command and Control System (MCD)
ACCS .... Armored Crashworthy Crew Set (MCD)
ACCS .... Army Command and Control Study (MCD)
ACCS .... Army Command and Control System (RDA)
ACCS .... Association Catholique Canadienne de la Sante [*Canadian-Catholic Health Association*]
ACCS .... Attitude Coordinate Converter System (AAG)
ACCS .... Automated Circulation Control System [*Library management*]
ACCS .... Automated Command and Control System (MCD)
ACCS .... Automated Communications and Control System [*Navy*] (MCD)
ACCS .... Automatic Calling Card Service [*Telecommunications*] (TEL)
ACCS .... Automatic Case Control System
ACCS .... Automatic Checkout and Control System
a-ccs-- .... Sikiang River and Basin [*China, Mainland*] [*MARC geographic area code*] [*Library of Congress*] (LCCP)
ACC/SCN ... Administrative Committee on Coordination - Subcommittee on Nutrition [*United Nations*] (EAIO)
ACCSEATO ... Air Component Commander, Southeast Asia Treaty Organization (CINC)
a-cc-sh .... Shansi Province [*China, Mainland*] [*MARC geographic area code*] [*Library of Congress*] (LCCP)
ACCSIC ..... Atomic Collision Cross Sections Information Center [*ORNL*]
ACCSL ...... Accessorial (AABC)
a-cc-sm .... Shanghai Municipality [*China, Mainland*] [*MARC geographic area code*] [*Library of Congress*] (LCCP)
a-cc-sp .... Shantung Province [*China, Mainland*] [*MARC geographic area code*] [*Library of Congress*] (LCCP)
ACCSq ...... Airborne Command Control Squadron [*Air Force*] (AFM)
a-cc-ss .... Shensi Province [*China, Mainland*] [*MARC geographic area code*] [*Library of Congress*] (LCCP)
a-cc-su .... Sinkiang Uighur Autonomous Region [*China, Mainland*] [*MARC geographic area code*] [*Library of Congress*] (LCCP)
a-cc-sz .... Szechuan Province [*China, Mainland*] [*MARC geographic area code*] [*Library of Congress*] (LCCP)
ACCT .... Accent
ACCT .... Accompaniment [*Music*]
ACCT .... Account [*or Accountant*] (AFM)
Acct .... Accountants Journal [*A publication*]
ACCT .... Agence de Cooperation Culturelle et Technique [*Agency for Cultural and Technical Cooperation*] (EAIO)

ACCT........	Alliance for Coal and Competitive Transportation
ACCT........	American Chamber of Commerce in Thailand (EA)
ACCT........	American Council for Competitive Telecommunications [*Formerly, Ad Hoc Committee for Competitive Telecommunications*] (EA)
ACC-T.......	Association Canadienne de Cinema-Television [*Canada*]
ACCT........	Association of Community College Trustees (EA)
ACCT........	CARD TEL, Inc. [*NASDAQ symbol*] (NQ)
ACCTA......	Association Canadienne du Controle du Trafic Aerien [*Canadian Air Traffic Control Association - CATCA*]
ACCTANT ...	Accountant (DLA)
Acct & Bus Res ...	Accounting and Business Research [*A publication*]
Acct Chem Res ...	Accounts of Chemical Research [*A publication*]
ACCTCY	Accountancy
ACCTG......	Accounting
ACCTG & FINO ...	Accounting and Finance Officer [*Air Force*]
Acctg Rev ...	Accounting Review [*A publication*]
a-cc-ti........	Tibetan Autonomous Region [*China, Mainland*] [*MARC geographic area code*] [*Library of Congress*] (LCCP)
ACCTID....	Account Identifier [*Data processing*]
ACCTLC ...	Association of Canadian Commercial Testing Laboratories and Consultants
Acct L Rep ...	Accountant Law Reports [*England*] [*A publication*] (DLA)
ACCTNG....	Accounting
Acct R	Accounting Review [*A publication*]
ACCTS	Accounts [*Secondary school course*] [*British*]
a-cc-ts........	Tsinghai Province [*China, Mainland*] [*MARC geographic area code*] [*Library of Congress*] (LCCP)
Accts Sec Educ J ...	Accountants and Secretaries' Educational Journal [*A publication*] (APTA)
ACCTSTR ...	Accountable Strength (AABC)
ACCTVS ...	Association of CCTV [*Closed Circuit Television*] Surveyors (EAIO)
ACCU	Asian Confederation of Credit Unions [*of the World Council of Credit Unions*] [*Bangkok, Thailand*] (EAIO)
ACCU	Asian Cultural Centre for UNESCO
ACCU	Association of Catholic Colleges and Universities (EA)
ACCU	Audio Central Control Unit (NASA)
ACCU	Automatic Control Certified for Unattended Engine Room (DS)
ACCU	Award Central Control Unit [*NASA*] (NASA)
ACCUM	Accumulate (KSC)
ACCUM	Accumulations [*Finance*]
ACCUM	Accumulator [*Data processing*]
ACCUMULON ...	Accumulation (ROG)
Accumu Vet Index ...	Accumulative Veterinary Index [*A publication*]
ACCU-OS ...	Automatic Control Certified for Unattended Engine Room - Open Seas (DS)
ACCUR	Accurate (MSA)
Accur..........	Accursius [*Deceased, 1263*] [*Authority cited in pre-1607 legal work*] (DSA)
ACCUS......	Accusative
ACCUS......	Automobile Competition Committee for the United States FIA [*Federation Internationale de l'Automobile*] (EA)
ACC-USA ...	American Comet Club - United Spoilers of America [*Later, MERCPAC*] (EA)
ACCUTF ...	Association of Canadian College and University Teachers of French
ACCV	Anales. Centro de Cultura Valenciana [*A publication*]
ACCV	Armored Cavalry Cannon Vehicle (MCD)
ACCW	Alternating Current Continuous Wave
ACCW	American Council for Career Women [*New Orleans, LA*] (EA)
ACCWS.....	Assistant Chief, Chemical Warfare Service
ACCWS.....	Auxiliary Component Cooling Water System [*Nuclear energy*] (NRCH)
ACCY	Accessory (AFM)
ACCY	Accountancy (AFM)
a-ccy--	Yellow River and Basin [*China, Mainland*] [*MARC geographic area code*] [*Library of Congress*] (LCCP)
a-cc-yu........	Yunnan Province [*China, Mainland*] [*MARC geographic area code*] [*Library of Congress*] (LCCP)
ACD..........	Absolute Cardiac Dullness [*Medicine*]
ACD..........	Academy Airlines [*Griffin, GA*] [*FAA designator*] (FAAC)
ACD..........	Acandi [*Colombia*] [*Airport symbol*] (OAG)
ACD..........	Access Control Document [*NASA*] (NASA)
ACD..........	Accord (AABC)
ACD..........	Accuracy Control Document (NASA)
ACD..........	Acid-Citrate-Dextrose [*Hematology*]
ACD..........	Acta Classica. Universitatis Scientiarum Debreceniensis [*A publication*]
ACD..........	Action-Chart Diagramer [*Data processing*]
ACD..........	Adjournment in Contemplation of Dismissal [*Law*]
ACD..........	Administrative Commitment Document
ACD..........	Administrative Contract Document (MCD)
ACD..........	Advanced Copies Delivered
ACD..........	Aerodynamic Configuration Drivers (MCD)
ACD..........	Air Condensate Drain [*Aerospace*] (AAG)
ACD..........	Aircraft Damage (ADA)
ACD..........	Airlift Communications Division [*Military*]
ACD..........	Alarm Control and Display (TEL)
ACD..........	Allergic Contact Dermatitis [*Dermatology*]
ACD..........	Alliance for Cultural Democracy (EA)
ACD..........	Allied Civil Defense [*World War II*]
ACD..........	Allied-Signal, Inc. [*Toronto Stock Exchange symbol*]
ACD..........	Alternating Current Dump
ACD..........	Amchitka Central D [*Alaska*] [*Seismograph station code, US Geological Survey*] [*Closed*] (SEIS)
ACD..........	American Capital Income Trust [*NYSE symbol*] (SPSG)
ACD..........	American Center for Design (EA)
ACD..........	American College of Dentists (EA)
ACD..........	Anamilo Club of Detroit [*Michigan*] (EA)
ACD..........	Antenna Control Display
ACD..........	Anterior Chest Diameter
ACD..........	Anticoagulant Citrate Dextrose [*Hematology*]
ACD..........	Archaeologiae Christianae Doctor [*Doctor of Christian Archeology*]
ACD..........	Arms Control and Disarmament [*A publication*]
ACD..........	Army Chaplains Department [*British military*] (DMA)
ACD..........	Army Communications Division
ACD..........	Assistant Command Director [*Military*] (MCD)
ACD..........	Associated Construction Distributors International (EA)
ACD..........	Association Canadienne des Dietetistes [*Canadian Association of Dietitians*]
ACD..........	Associative Computer Device
ACD..........	Attack Center Display
ACD..........	Attitude toward Caring for the Dying Scale
ACD..........	Aulus Caius Decimus [*Coin inscription*] (ROG)
ACD..........	Automatic Call Distribution [*Switching system*] [*Telecommunications*]
ACD..........	Automatic Contour Digitizer
ACDA........	Afan Cooperative Development Agency [*British*]
ACDA........	American Choral Directors Association (EA)
ACDA........	American Component Dealers Association (EA)
ACDA........	Arms Control and Disarmament Act [*1961*]
ACDA........	Arms Control and Disarmament Agency [*Washington, DC*]
ACDA........	Association Canadienne pour le Droit a l'Avortement [*Canadian Abortion Rights Action League - CARAL*]
ACDA........	Association of Catholic Diocesan Archivists (EA)
ACDA........	Australian Club Development Association
ACDA........	Aviation Combat Development Agency [*CDC*]
ACDACX...	Australia. Commonwealth Scientific and Industrial Research Organisation. Division of Applied Chemistry. Annual Report [*A publication*]
ACDA/MEA ...	Arms Control and Disarmament Agency Military and Economic Affairs Bureau [*Washington, DC*]
ACDAR	Acoustic Detection and Ranging [*Geophysics*]
ACDA/WEC ...	Arms Control and Disarmament Agency Weapons Evaluation and Control Bureau [*Washington, DC*]
ACDA/WEC/FO ...	Arms Control and Disarmament Agency Weapons Evaluation and Control Bureau Field Operations Division [*Washington, DC*]
ACDB	Airport Characteristics Data Bank [*International Civil Aviation Organization*] [*Information service or system*] (IID)
ACDC	Administrative Communications Distribution Center [*Air Force*] (AFM)
ACDC	Advanced Coherent Deception Countermeasure (MCD)
A-C/D-C....	Alternating Current/Direct Current
ACDC	Army Combat Development Committee [*British*]
ACDC	Army Combat Developments Command
ACDC	Auburn-Cord-Duesenberg Club (EA)
ACDC	Australian Counter Disaster College
AC-DC.......	Bisexual Person [*Pun on electricity's 'AC or DC' - alternating current or direct current*]
ACDCA	Australian Cattle Dog Club of America (EA)
ACDCS......	Automated Classified Document Control System
ACDD........	Accreditation Council on Services for People with Developmental Disabilities (EA)
ACDDS......	Advanced Cartographic Data Digitizing System (MCD)
A CDE	Air Commodore [*RAF, RCAF*]
ACDE	American Council for Drug Education (EA)
ACDE	Association Canadienne du Droit de l'Environnement [*Canadian Association of Environmental Law*]
ACDE	Association of Commercial Diving Educators (EA)
ACDEC......	Army Combat Development Experimental Center (AAG)
ACD-ESS ..	Automatic Call Distributor - Electronic Switching System [*Telecommunications*] (TEL)
ACDFA......	American College Dance Festival Association (EA)
ACDFG......	American Committee for Democracy and Freedom in Greece (EA)
ACDG	American Community Development Group, Inc. [*St. Petersburg, FL*] [*NASDAQ symbol*] (NQ)
ACDG	Devonian Group of Charitable Foundations, Calgary, Alberta [*Library symbol*] [*National Library of Canada*] (NLC)
ACDH	Deloitte, Haskins & Sells, Calgary, Alberta [*Library symbol*] [*National Library of Canada*] (BIB)
ACDHA.....	American Cream Draft Horse Association (EA)
ACDI	Agence Canadienne de Developpement International [*Canadian International Development Agency - CIDA*]
ACDI	Agricultural Cooperative Development International (EA)
ACDI	Associated Construction Distributors, International
ACDIFOT ...	Active Duty in a Flying Status, Operational and Training Flights [*Navy*]

ACDIFOTCREW ... Active Duty in a Flying Status, Operational and Training Flights as Crewmember [*Navy*]
ACDIFOTINS ... Active Duty under Instruction in a Flying Status, Operational and Training Flights [*Navy*]
ACDIFOTINSCREW ... Active Duty under Instruction in a Flying Status, Operational and Training Flights as Crewmember [*Navy*]
ACDIFOTINSNONCREW ... Active Duty under Instruction in a Flying Status, Operational and Training Flights as Noncrewmember [*Navy*]
ACDIFOTNONCREW ... Active Duty in a Flying Status, Operational and Training Flights as Noncrewmember [*Navy*]
ACDL .... Association for Constitutional Democracy in Liberia   (EA)
ACDLAU .. Australia. Commonwealth Scientific and Industrial Research Organisation. Division of Land Use Research. Technical Paper [*A publication*]
ACDM .... Assessment of Career Decision Making [*Vocational guidance test*]
ACDM .... Association Canadienne pour les Deficients Mentaux [*Canadian Association for the Mentally Retarded*]
ACDM .... Association of Chairmen of Departments of Mechanics   (EA)
ACDMS ..... Automated Control of a Document Management System [*Data processing*]   (DIT)
Acdmy Mgt J ... Academy of Management. Journal [*A publication*]
Acdmy Mgt R ... Academy of Management. Review [*A publication*]
ACDN .... Alaska Census Data Network [*Alaska State Department of Labor*] [*Juneau*] [*Information service or system*]   (IID)
ACDNT ..... Accident   (AFM)
ACDO .... Air Carrier District Office
ACDO .... Assistant Command Duty Officer [*Military*]   (MCD)
ACDP .... Advisory Committee on Dangerous Pathogens [*British*]
ACDP .... Antenna Control and Display Panel   (MCD)
ACDP .... Association of Compact Disk Publishers   (EA)
ACDP .... Australian Committee of Directors and Principals in Advanced Education
ACDP .... Dome Petroleum Ltd., Calgary, Alberta [*Library symbol*] [*National Library of Canada*]   (NLC)
ACDPI .... American Cultured Dairy Products Institute   (EA)
ACDR .... Alpha-Cedrene
ACDRB ...... Active Contract Data Review Board [*Air Force*]   (AFIT)
A Cdre .... Air Commodore [*RAF, RCAF*]   (DMA)
ACDRU ..... Arms Control and Disarmament Research Unit [*British*]
ACDS .... Advanced Combat Direction System   (MCD)
ACDS .... Advanced Command Data System   (NG)
ACDS .... Advisory Committee on Dangerous Substances [*British*]
ACDS .... Anglo-Continental Dental Society [*British*]
ACDS .... Assistant Chief of Defence Staff [*British*] [*Australia*]   (NATG)
ACDS .... Associated Chain Drug Stores   (EA)
ACDS .... Association Canadienne Droit et Societe [*Canadian Law and Society Association - CLSA*]
ACDS .... Association for Children with Down Syndrome   (EA)
ACDS .... Attitude Control and Determination Subsystem   (MCD)
ACDS .... Automatic Comprehensive Display System [*Data processing*]
ACDSG ...... Australian Coastal Defences Study Group
ACDT .... Accident   (AABC)
A CDT .... Air Commandant [*British*]
ACDTR ...... Airborne Central Data Tape Recorder   (MCD)
ACDU .... Active Duty
ACDUINS ... Active Duty under Instruction [*Navy*]
ACDUOBLI ... Active Duty Obligation [*DoD*]
ACDUTRA ... Active Duty for Training [*Army*]   (MCD)
ACE .... Academic Courseware Exchange [*Combined Apple University Consortium and Kinko's project*] [*Software distributor*]
ACE .... Academie Canadienne d'Endodontie [*Canadian Academy of Endodontics*]   (EAIO)
ACE .... Accelerated Christian Education [*An association*]
ACE .... Accelerated Co-Pilot Enrichment [*Program*]
ACE .... Acceptance Checkout Equipment [*NASA*]
ACE .... Accountancy (England) [*A publication*]
ACE .... Accounting, Cost, Estimating
ACE .... Acme Electric Corp. [*NYSE symbol*]   (SPSG)
ACE .... Active Corps of Executives [*Maintained by the Service Corps of Retired Executives Association*]
ACE .... Adjusted Current Earnings
ACE .... Adrenal Cortical Extract [*Endocrinology*]
ACe .... Adriamycin, Cyclophosphamide [*Antineoplastic drug regimen*]
ACE .... Adult Continuing Education   (OICC)
ACE .... Advanced Clean Emission [*Automotive engineering*]
ACE .... Advanced Compilation Equipment   (MCD)
ACE .... Advanced Compound Engine
ACE .... Advanced Computational Element   (MCD)
ACE .... Advanced Control Experiments   (MCD)
ACE .... Advisory Centre for Education [*British*]
ACE .... Aerial Combat Evaluator   (MCD)
ACE .... Aerosol Climatic Effects [*NASA*]
ACE .... Aerospace Contract Engineers   (MCD)
ACE .... Aerospace Control Environment [*Air Force*]
ACE .... After the Christian Era   (BJA)
ACE .... Age Concern England [*An association*] [*British*]
ACE .... Agricultural Communicators in Education   (EA)

ACE .... Agricultural, Construction, and Earthmoving Equipment [*Acronym is the name of a metal coating painting product*] [*Imperial Chemical Industries Ltd.*] [*British*]
ACE .... Aid for Commonwealth English Scheme [*British*]
ACE .... Air Cargo Exhibition [*British*]   (ITD)
ACE .... Air Collection and Enrichment
ACE .... Air Combat Element   (MCD)
ACE .... Air Combat Emulator [*Computer game*]
ACE .... Air Combat Engagement   (MCD)
ACE .... Air-Conditioning Equipment   (AAG)
ACE .... Air Crew Error   (MCD)
ACE .... Airborne Communications and Electronics   (MCD)
ACE .... Airborne Cooperational Equipment
ACE .... Aircraft Catering Equipment [*British airlines*]
ACE .... Aircraft Condition Evaluation [*Navy*]   (MCD)
ACE .... Airspace Control [*or Coordination*] Element [*Army*]
ACE .... Alcohol, Chloroform, Ether [*An early anesthetic mixture*]
ACE .... Alliance for Clean Energy   (EA)
ACE .... Allied Command Europe [*NATO*]
ACE .... Allied Forces Central Europe [*NATO*]   (MCD)
ACE .... Alternate Command Elements [*Navy*]   (CINC)
ACE .... Altimeter Control Equipment [*Aviation*]
ACE .... Altitude Control Electronics
ACE .... Amateur Cartoonist Extraordinary [*National Cartoonists' Society award*]
ACE .... Ambush Communication Equipment [*Military*]
ACE .... Amchitka Central E [*Alaska*] [*Seismograph station code, US Geological Survey*] [*Closed*]   (SEIS)
ACE .... American Chemical Exchange
ACE .... American Cinema Editors   (EA)
ACE .... American Coaster Enthusiasts   (EA)
ACE .... American College of Ecology   (EA)
ACE .... American College of Epidemiology   (EA)
ACE .... American Council on Education   (EA)
ACE .... American Council on the Environment   (EA)
ACE .... AMEX [*American Stock Exchange*] Commodities Exchange
ACE .... An Chomhairle Ealaion [*Arts Council*]   (EAIO)
ACE .... Angiotensin Converting Enzyme [*Biochemistry*]
ACE .... Animated Computer Education
ACE .... Annals of Collective Economy [*Later, Annals of Public and Co-Operative Economy*] [*A publication*]
ACE .... Annals of Public and Cooperative Economy [*A publication*]
ACE .... Anno Christianis Aerae [*In the Year of the Christian Era*] [*Latin*]
ACE .... April Computing Executive [*Commercial firm*] [*British*]
ACE .... Armored Combat Earthmover [*Army*]
ACE .... Army/American Council on Education   (INF)
ACE .... Army Combat Engineers   (CINC)
ACE .... Army Corps of Engineers
ACE .... Arrecife [*Canary Islands*] [*Airport symbol*]   (OAG)
ACE .... Assessment of Combat Effectiveness [*Army*]   (AABC)
ACE .... Assistant Chief of Engineers [*Military*]
ACE .... Associate of the College of Engineering [*British*]   (ROG)
ACE .... Associate Credit Executive [*Designation awarded by Society of Certified Consumer Credit Executives*]
ACE .... Associated Corpuscular Emission
ACE .... Associates in Childbirth Education [*Australia*]
ACE .... Association Canadienne d'Economique [*Canadian Economics Association - CEA*]
ACE .... Association Canadienne d'Education [*Canadian Education Association - CEA*]
ACE .... Association Canadienne des Entraineurs [*Canadian Association of Coaches*]
ACE .... Association Canadienne d'Exportation [*Canadian Export Association*]
ACE .... Association for Childhood Education International
ACE .... Association for Christian Ethics [*Vatican*]   (EA)
ACE .... Association of Clandestine Radio Enthusiasts   (EA)
ACE .... Association of Collegiate Entrepreneurs   (EA)
ACE .... Association of Comics Enthusiasts   (EAIO)
ACE .... Association of Communication Engineers [*Charlotte, NC*]   (TSSD)
ACE .... Association for Comparative Economics [*Later, ACES*]
ACE .... Association for the Conservation of Energy [*British*]   (IRUK)
ACE .... Association of Conservation Engineers   (EA)
ACE .... Association of Consulting Engineers of Great Britain
ACE .... Association for Continuing Education   (EA)
ACE .... Association for Cooperation in Engineering [*Defunct*]
ACE .... Association of Cooperative Educators   (EA)
ACE .... Association of Country Entertainers   (EA)
ACE .... Association for Cultural Exchange
ACE .... Association of Cultural Executives [*Canada*]
ACE .... Association of Cycle Exhibitors [*Later, NABEA*]   (EA)
ACE .... Atmospheric Control Experimentation
ACE .... Attitude Control Electronics [*Aerospace*]
ACE .... Attorneys, Certified Public Accountants, and Enrolled Agents [*In "Operation ACE," IRS investigation of these occupations as sources of income tax evasion*]
ACE .... Aurally Coded English [*in The ACE Spelling Dictionary*] [*British*]
ACE .... Australian College of English

ACE .... Automated Cost Estimates
ACE .... Automated Credit Enquiry [*Great Britain*] [*Information service or system*] (IID)
ACE .... Automatic Calling Equipment [*Telecommunications*] (BUR)
ACE .... Automatic Checkout Equipment
ACE .... Automatic Circuit Exchange
ACE .... Automatic Clutter Eliminator [*FAA*]
ACE .... Automatic Computer Evaluation (BUR)
ACE .... Automatic Computing Engine [*Early computer*] [*National Physical Laboratory*]
ACE .... Automatic Continuity Equipment
ACE .... Automatic Continuous Evaporation
ACE .... Automatic Control Equipment
ACE .... Automatic Controlled Exposure
ACE .... Autumn Circulation Experiment [*Denmark, Great Britain, Norway, West Germany*] [*1987-88*] [*Oceanography*]
ACE .... Auxiliary Conversion Equipment
ACE .... Aviation and Computer Enthusiasts (EA)
ACE .... Aviation Construction Engineers [*Military*]
ACE .... Avion de Combat European [*France*]
ACE .... Awards for Cablecasting Excellence
ACE .... Central Region [*FAA*] (FAAC)
a-ce--- .... Ceylon [*Sri Lanka*] [*MARC geographic area code*] [*Library of Congress*] (LCCP)
ACE .... Engineering Library, City of Calgary, Alberta [*Library symbol*] [*National Library of Canada*] (BIB)
ACE .... Homer, AK [*Location identifier*] [*FAA*] (FAAL)
ACEA .... Air Line Communication Employees Association
ACEA .... American Cotton Exporters' Association (EA)
ACEA .... Assistant Civil Engineer Adviser [*Military*] [*British*]
ACEA .... Association Canadienne des Etudes Asiatiques [*Canadian Asian Studies Association - CASA*]
ACEA .... Association of Cost and Executive Accountants [*London, England*] (EAIO)
ACEA .... Australian Coal Exporters' Association (ADA)
ACEAA ...... Advisory Committee on Electrical Appliances and Accessories
ACEA Bull ... ACEA [*Australian Council for Educational Administration*] Bulletin [*A publication*] (APTA)
ACE-ACCIS ... Allied Command Europe Automated Command Control and Information System [*Proposed*] [*NATO*]
ACEARTS ... Airborne Countermeasures Environment and RADAR Target Simulation
ACEAS ...... Association Canadienne pour l'Etude de l'Administration Scolaire [*Canadian Association for the Study of Academic Administration*]
ACEB .... Army Clothing and Equipment Board (MCD)
ACEB .... Association Canadienne des Ecoles de Bibliothecaires [*Canadian Association of Library Schools*]
ACEB .... Association Canadienne d'Entraineurs de Badminton [*Canadian Association of Badminton Coaches*]
ACEBAC ... Association Catholique des Etudes Bibliques au Canada [*Catholic Association of Bible Studies in Canada*]
ACEBD ...... Airborne and Communications-Electronics Board [*Army*] (RDA)
Ac Ec .... Acta Ecclesiastica [*A publication*]
ACEC .... Actes. Congres de la Federation International des Associations d'Etudes Classiques [*A publication*]
ACEC .... Advisory Council on Energy Conservation [*British*]
ACEC .... American Consulting Engineers Council (EA)
ACEC .... Area of Critical Environmental Concern [*Bureau of Land Management designation*]
ACEC .... Army Communications and Electronic Command
AC & EC ..... Army Communications and Equipment Coordination
ACEC .... Association Canadienne des Entrepreneurs en Couverture [*Canadian Association of Bedding Entrepreneurs*]
ACEC .... Association Canadienne des Etudes Cinematographiques [*Canadian Association of Film Studies*]
ACEC .... Association Canadienne pour les Etudes en Cooperation [*Canadian Association for Studies in Cooperation - CASC*]
ACEC .... Association of Consulting Engineers of Canada
ACEC .... Australian Computer Education Conference
ACECA ...... Association des Cooperatives d'Epargne et de Credit d'Afrique [*African Confederation of Cooperative Savings and Credit Associations - ACCOSCA*] [*Nairobi, Kenya*] (EAIO)
ACECO ..... Allied Commission, Economic Section [*World War II*]
ACEC Rev ... ACEC [*Ateliers de Constructions Electriques de Charleroi*] Reviews [*A publication*]
ACEC/RMF ... ACEC [*American Consulting Engineers Council*] Research and Management Foundation (EA)
ACED .... Advanced Communications Equipment Depot (NATG)
ACED .... Aerospace Crew Equipment Development
ACED .... Agnostic Christians for Equality for Dignity (EA)
ACED .... Anticompromise Emergency Destruction (MCD)
AC Ed .... Associate in Commercial Education
ACED .... Association Canadienne de l'Enseignement a Distance [*Canadian Association for Distance Education - CADE*]
ACEE .... Adult Cost per Entered Employment [*Job Training and Partnership Act*] (OICC)
ACEE .... Air Combat Engagement Experiment
ACEE .... Aircraft Emission Estimator (MCD)
ACEE .... Aircraft Energy Efficiency (MCD)

ACEE .... Area Council for Economic Education (EA)
ACEE .... Association Canadienne des Etudes Ecossaises [*Canadian Association for Scottish Studies - CASS*]
ACEEA ...... Association Canadienne pour l'Etude de l'Education des Adultes [*Canadian Association for the Study of Adult Education - CASAE*]
ACEEE ...... American Council for an Energy Efficient Economy (EA)
ACEF .... Acta Entomologica Fennica [*A publication*]
ACEF .... Adult Children Educational Foundation (EA)
ACEF .... Adult Christian Education Foundation (EA)
ACEF .... Asian Cultural Exchange Foundation (EA)
ACEF .... Association Canadienne pour les Etudes sur les Femmes [*Canadian Women's Studies Association - CWSA*]
ACEF .... Association Canadienne pour les Etudes du Folklore [*Canadian Folklore Studies Association*]
ACEF .... Association of Commodity Exchange Firms [*Later, Futures Industry Association*] (EA)
ACEFO ...... Association Canadienne des Etudes Finno-Ougriennes [*Finno-Ugrian Studies Association - FUSAC*]
ACEGB ..... Association of Consulting Engineers of Great Britain
ACEH .... Acid Cholesteryl Ester Hydrolase [*An enzyme*]
ACEH .... Association Canadienne des Etudes Hongroises [*Canadian Association of Hungarian Studies - CAHS*]
ACEHI J/REV ACEDA ... Association of Canadian Educators of the Hearing Impaired. Journal/Association Canadienne des Educateurs des Deficients-Auditifs. Revue [*A publication*]
ACEHSA... Accrediting Commission on Education for Health Services Administration (EA)
ACEI .... Association for Childhood Education International (EA)
ACEI .... Association of Consulting Engineers of Ireland (EAIO)
ACEJ .... American Council on Education for Journalism [*Later, ACEJMC*] (EA)
ACEJMC .. Accrediting Council on Education in Journalism and Mass Communications (EA)
ACEL .... Aerospace Crew Equipment Laboratory [*Philadelphia, PA*] (MCD)
ACEL .... Air Crew Equipment Laboratory (MCD)
ACEL .... Alfacell Corp. [*NASDAQ symbol*] (NQ)
ACELA ...... Association Canadienne des Etudes Latino-Americaines [*Canadian Association of Latin American Studies - CALAS*]
ACELAC ... Association Canadienne des Etudes Latino-Americaines et Caraibes [*Canadian Association of Latin American and Caribbean Studies*]
ACELB ...... Actas. Coloquio Internacional de Estudos Luso-Brasileiros [*A publication*]
ACELLC.... Association Canadienne pour l'Etude de la Litterature et des Langues du Commonwealth [*Canadian Association for Commonwealth Literature and Language Studies - CACLALS*]
ACEM .... Association Canadienne des Editeurs de Musique [*Canadian Music Publishers Association - CMPA*]
ACEM .... Aviation Chief Electrician's Mate [*Navy*]
ACEM .... Southern Materials Resource Centre, Alberta Education, Calgary, Alberta [*Library symbol*] [*National Library of Canada*] (NLC)
A Cemb ...... A Cembalo [*Music*]
ACEMIS ... Automated Communications and Electronics Management Information System [*Army*]
ACEN .... Alberta Environment, Calgary, Alberta [*Library symbol*] [*National Library of Canada*] (NLC)
ACEN .... Assembly of Captive European Nations (EA)
ACEN .... Association Canadienne des Enseignants Noirs [*Canadian Association of Black Teachers*]
ACENEB... Advances in Clinical Enzymology [*A publication*]
Ac Energ .... Acero y Energia [*A publication*]
ACENET .... Allied Command Europe Communications Network [*NATO*] (NATG)
ACE News ... ACE [*Agricultural Communication in Education*] Newsletter [*A publication*]
ACEORP... Automotive and Construction Equipment Overhaul and Repair Plant [*Navy*]
ACEP .... Advisory Committee on Export Policy [*Department of Commerce*]
ACEP .... American College of Emergency Physicians (EA)
ACEP .... American Council for Emigres in the Professions [*Defunct*] (EA)
ACEP .... Arms Control Education Project (EA)
ACEP .... Association Canadienne des Etudes Patristiques [*Canadian Society of Patristic Studies - CSPS*]
ACEP .... Association Canadienne des Etudes Prospectives [*Canadian Association for Future Studies - CAFS*]
ACEPA ...... Australian Childbirth Education and Parenting Association
ACEPC ...... Preprints of Papers Presented at National Meeting. Division of Environmental Chemistry. American Chemical Society [*A publication*]
ACEPD...... Automotive and Construction Equipment Parts Depot [*Navy*]
ACEQ .... Association Canadienne des Editeurs de Quotidiens [*Canadian Association of Newspaper Editors*]
ACER......... Afro-Caribbean Educational Resource Centre [*British*]

ACER........ Alberta Energy Resources Conservation Board, Calgary, Alberta [*Library symbol*] [*National Library of Canada*] (NLC)
ACER........ American Council of Executives in Religion (EA)
ACer.......... Anales Cervantinos [*A publication*]
ACER........ Ancient Classics for English Readers [*A publication*]
ACER........ Annales. Centre d'Etude des Religions [*A publication*]
ACER........ Association Canadienne pour les Etudes Rurales [*Canadian Association of Rural Studies - CARS*]
ACER........ Australian Council for Educational Research [*Information service or system*] (ADA)
ACERA...... Air Carrier Economic Regulation Act
ACERB...... Allis-Chalmers Engineering Review [*A publication*]
ACER Bull ... Australian Council for Educational Research. Bulletin [*A publication*] (APTA)
ACERC...... Army Coastal Engineering Research Center
ACEREP ... Allied Command Europe Report (AFM)
ACERM..... Cereal Municipal Library, Alberta [*Library symbol*] [*National Library of Canada*] (NLC)
Acero Energ Numero Espec ... Acero y Energia. Numero Especial [*A publication*]
ACERP...... Advanced Communications-Electronics Requirements Plan [*Air Force*]
ACERR...... Energy Resources Research, Calgary, Alberta [*Library symbol*] [*National Library of Canada*] (NLC)
ACERS ..... Allied Command Europe Reporting System
ACerS .... American Ceramic Society (EA)
ACERT...... Advisory Committee for the Education of Romany and Other Travellers
ACertCM... Archbishop of Canterbury's Certificate in Church Music [*British*] (DBQ)
ACER Test News ... Australian Council for Educational Research. Test News [*A publication*] (APTA)
ACES........ Acceptance Checkout and Evaluation System [*NASA*] (NASA)
ACES........ Acceptance Control Equipment Section [*or System*] [*NASA*] (NASA)
ACES........ Access (FAAC)
ACES........ (Acetamidol)Aminoethanesulfonic Acid [*A buffer*]
ACES........ Acoustic Containerless Experiment System [*Materials processing*]
ACES........ Advanced Concept Ejection Seat [*Aviation*] (MCD)
ACES........ Advanced Concept Escape System (MCD)
ACES........ Aerolineas Centrales de Colombia [*Airline*] [*Colombian*]
ACES........ Air Carrier Engineering Service
ACES........ Air Collection Engine System
ACES........ Air Collection and Enrichment System
ACES........ Air Combat Expert Simulation [*Military*] (RDA)
ACES........ American Catholic Esperanto Society (EA)
ACES........ American Enterprises, Inc. [*Formerly, American Casino Enterprises, Inc.*] [*NASDAQ symbol*] (NQ)
ACES........ Americans for the Competitive Enterprise System [*Later, ACEE*] (EA)
ACES........ Annual Cycle Energy System [*Energy Research and Development Admininistration*]
ACES........ Antisubmarine Composite Engineering Squadron
ACES........ Area Cooperative Educational Services [*Information service or system*]
ACES........ ARMMS [*Automated Reliability and Maintenance Management System*] Control Executive System [*NASA*]
ACES........ Army Communications Electronics School (MCD)
ACES........ Army Communications Equipment Support (MCD)
ACES........ Army Continuing Education System
ACES........ Associated Collectors of El Salvador (EA)
ACES........ Association for Comparative Economic Studies [*Notre Dame, IN*] (EA)
ACES........ Association for Counselor Education and Supervision (EA)
ACES........ Assurance Control Economics System (MUGU)
ACES........ Automated Camera Effects System
ACES........ Automated Code Evaluation System
ACES........ Automatic Checkout Equipment Sequencer (NASA)
ACES........ Automatic Checkout and Evaluation System [*Air Force*]
ACES........ Automatic Control Evaluation Simulator [*Spaceflight training machine*]
ACES........ Automatically Controlled Electrical System [*NASA*] (MCD)
ACES........ Resource Centre, City of Calgary Electric System, Alberta [*Library symbol*] [*National Library of Canada*] (NLC)
ACES Bul .. ACES [*Association for Comparative Economic Studies*] Bulletin [*A publication*]
ACE-S/C ... Acceptance Checkout Equipment - Spacecraft [*NASA*] (KSC)
ACESEQ ... Annales de Chirurgie Plastique et Esthetique [*A publication*]
ACESG...... American Council on Educational Simulation and Gaming
ACESIA..... American Council for Elementary School Industrial Arts [*Later, TECC*] (EA)
ACESIS..... Army Corps of Engineers Socioeconomic Information System [*Information service or system*] (IID)
ACES Rev ... ACES [*Australian Council for Educational Standards*] Review [*A publication*] (APTA)
ACESS....... Association Canadienne des Ecoles du Service Social [*Canadian Association of Schools of Social Work - CASSW*]
ACET........ Aceto Corp. [*NASDAQ symbol*] (NQ)
Acet.......... Acetone [*Medicine*]
ACET........ Acetylene (MSA)

Acet.......... Acetylene [*A publication*]
ACET........ Advisory Committee on Electronics and Telecommunications [*International Electrotechnical Commission*] [*ISO*] (DS)
ACET........ Association Canadienne des Ecoles de Traduction
ACET........ Association Canadienne des Employes de Telephone [*Canadian Telephone Employees' Association - CTEA*]
ACET........ Association Canadienne des Entreprises de Telecommunications [*Canadian Association of Telecommunication Businesses*]
ACET........ Automatic Cancellation of Extended Targets (AABC)
ACETA...... Association Canadienne des Employes du Transport Aerien [*Canadian Air Line Employees' Association - CALEA*]
Acet J .... Acetylene Journal [*A publication*]
Acet Light Weld J ... Acetylene Lighting and Welding Journal [*A publication*]
ACETS ...... Air-Cushion Equipment Transportation System
Acet Weld .. Acetylene Welding [*A publication*]
Acetylene J ... Acetylene Journal [*A publication*]
ACEU........ Aerocontrol Electronics Unit [*NASA*] (NASA)
ACEUM .... Association Canadienne des Ecoles Universitaires de Musique [*Canadian Association of University Schools of Music - CAUSM*]
ACEUN .... Association Canadienne des Ecoles Universitaires de Nursing [*Canadian Association of University Schools of Nursing - CAUSN*]
ACEUR ..... Allied Command Europe [*NATO*]
ACEVAL.... Air Combat Evaluation (MCD)
ACEVF...... American Energy Corp. [*NASDAQ symbol*] (NQ)
ACEWA..... American Committee on East-West Accord [*Later, ACUSSR*] (EA)
ACF........... Abbreviated Cost Form (MCD)
ACF........... Academic Computer Facility [*Roosevelt University*] [*Research center*] (RCD)
ACF........... Access Control Facility
ACF........... Access Cost Factor [*Telecommunications*] (TEL)
ACF........... Accessory Clinical Findings [*Medicine*]
ACF........... Accounting and Finance [*Australia*] [*A publication*]
ACF........... Accounting Forum [*A publication*]
ACF........... ACI Holdings [*AMEX symbol*] (SPSG)
ACF........... Acid Concentrator Feed [*Nuclear energy*] (NRCH)
ACF........... Active Citizen Force [*British military*] (DMA)
ACF........... Active Contract File [*DoD*]
ACF........... Acute Care Facility [*Medicine*]
ACF........... Advanced Communications Function [*IBM Corp.*] [*Data processing*]
ACF........... African Colonial Forces [*British military*] (DMA)
ACF........... Air California (MCD)
ACF........... Air Combat Fighter (MCD)
ACF........... All for the Children Foundation (EA)
ACF........... All-Craft Foundation (EA)
ACF........... Alternate Command Facility [*Navy*] (NVT)
ACF........... Alternate Communications Facility [*Military*]
ACF........... Amchitka Central F [*Alaska*] [*Seismograph station code, US Geological Survey*] [*Closed*] (SEIS)
ACF........... American Car and Foundry
ACF........... American Checker Federation (EA)
ACF........... American Chess Foundation (EA)
ACF........... American Chestnut Foundation (EA)
ACF........... American Choral Foundation (EA)
ACF........... American Coal Foundation (EA)
ACF........... American Conservatives for Freedom (EA)
ACF........... American Crime Fighters (EA)
ACF........... American Crossword Federation (EA)
ACF........... American Culinary Federation (EA)
ACF........... Americans for Constitutional Freedom [*Later, MC/ACF*] (EA)
ACF........... Analog Computer Facility
ACF........... Annali. Facolta di Lingue e Litterature Straniere di Ca'Foscari [*A publication*]
ACF........... Annuaire. College de France [*A publication*]
ACF........... Appeal of Conscience Foundation (EA)
ACF........... Area Computing Facilities (CET)
ACF........... Area Confinement Facility [*Military*] (AABC)
ACF........... Area Coverage File (MCD)
ACF........... Army Cadet Force [*Military unit*] [*British*]
ACF........... Army Club Fund
ACF........... Asian Club Federation (EAIO)
ACF........... Association of Consulting Foresters (EA)
ACF........... Australian Chinese Forum of New South Wales
ACF........... Autocorrelation Function [*Statistics*]
ACF........... Automatic Control Features (NRCH)
ACF........... Axisymmetrical Conical Flow
ACF........... Foothills Pipe Lines (Yukon) Ltd., Calgary, Alberta [*Library symbol*] [*National Library of Canada*] (NLC)
ACFA........ Aero Club Federation of Australia
ACFA........ American Cat Fanciers Association (EA)
ACFA........ American Council for Free Asia (EA)
ACFA........ Army Cadet Force Association [*British military*] (DMA)
ACFA........ Association Canadienne de Football Amateur [*Canadian Association of Amateur Football*]
ACFA........ Association of Commercial Finance Attorneys (EA)
ACFA........ Australian Cystic Fibrosis Associations

ACFAS ...... Association Canadienne-Francaise pour l'Avancement des Sciences

ACFAS Assoc Can Fr Av Sci ... ACFAS. Association Canadienne Francaise pour l'Avancement des Sciences [*A publication*]

ACFB .... Association Canadienne Fournisseurs Bibliotheque [*Canadian Association of Library Suppliers*]

ACFBAA ... Anales. Academia Nacional de Ciencias Exactas, Fisicas, y Naturales de Buenos Aires [*A publication*]

ACFC .... Abbott and Costello Fan Club (EA)

ACFC .... American Center of Films for Children (EA)

ACFC .... Anne Christy Fan Club (EA)

ACFC .... Archie Campbell Fan Club (EA)

ACFC .... Association of Canadian Film Craftspeople

ACFC .... Association of Commercial Finance Companies of New York [*Later, NCFA*] (EA)

ACFC .... Aviation Chief Fire Controlman [*Navy*]

ACFC .... Fluor Canada Ltd., Calgary, Alberta [*Library symbol*] [*National Library of Canada*] (NLC)

ACFCBE.... Australia. Commonwealth Scientific and Industrial Research Organisation. Division of Fisheries and Oceanography. Circular [*A publication*]

ACFD .... Association of Canadian Faculties of Dentistry

ACFE .... American Car and Foundry, Electronics

ACFEA ...... Air Carrier Flight Engineers Association

ACFEL ...... Arctic Construction and Frost Effects Laboratory [*Boston, MA*] [*Army*]

ACFF .... Affinity Cross-Flow Filtration

ACFF .... Annales. Comite Flamand de France [*A publication*]

ACFFTU ... All Ceylon Federation of Free Trade Unions

ACFG........ Automatic Continuous Function Generation [*Data processing*]

ACFH .... Foothills Hospital, Calgary, Alberta [*Library symbol*] [*National Library of Canada*] (NLC)

ACFHE...... Association of Colleges for Further and Higher Education [*British*] (EAIO)

ACFI .... Advisory Committee on Flight Information [*FAA*]

ACFI .... American Car and Foundry Industries

ACFIA .... Associated Committee of Friends on Indian Affairs (EA)

ACFL .... Access Floor [*Technical drawings*]

ACFL .... Atlantic Coast Football League

ACFM .... Actual Cubic Feet per Minute (NRCH)

ACFM .... Association of Cereal Food Manufacturers (EAIO)

ACF-MR.... Accreditation Council for Facilities for the Mentally Retarded

ACFMR ..... Australian Cancer Fund for Medical Research

ACFN .... American Committee for Flags of Necessity [*Later, FACS*] (EA)

ACFNA...... Anarchist-Communist Federation of North America [*Canada*]

ACFNY...... Asthmatic Children's Foundation of New York (EA)

ACFO .... American College of Foot Orthopedists (EA)

ACFO .... Assistant Chief Fire Officer [*British*]

ACFOD-USA ... Asian Cultural Forum on Development - USA (EA)

ACFOR...... Association Canadienne des Cadres en Informatique [*Canadian Association of Information Officials*]

ACFPC ...... Arms Control and Foreign Policy Caucus (EA)

ACFR........ Advisory Council on Federal Reports

ACFR........ American College of Foot Roentgenologists [*Later, American College of Podiatric Radiologists*] (EA)

ACFRBP.... Australia. Commonwealth Scientific and Industrial Research Organisation. Division of Food Research. Report of Research [*A publication*]

ACFS .... American College of Foot Specialists [*Later, ACCE*] (EA)

ACFS .... American College of Foot Surgeons (EA)

ACFS .... Anales. Catedra Francisco Suarez [*A publication*]

ACFS .... Assistant Chief of Fleet Support [*Navy*] [*British*]

ACFS .... Australian Centre for Foreign Studies

ACFSA ...... American Correctional Food Service Association (EA)

ACFT........ Aircraft (AFM)

ACFT........ Aircraft Flying Training

AcftCrmnBad ... Aircraft Crewman Badge [*Military decoration*] (AABC)

ACFTTBI .. Aircraft to Be Identified [*Aviation*] (AIA)

ACFTU...... All-China Federation of Trade Unions [*Communist China*]

ACFUCY ... Actinomycin D, Fluorouracil, Cyclophosphamide [*Antineoplastic drug regimen*]

ACFW....... Australian Child and Family Welfare [*A publication*] (ADA)

ACFYAB .. Acta Fytotechnica [*A publication*]

ACG .... Aboriginal Consultative Group [*Australia*]

ACG .... Academie Canadienne du Genie [*Canadian Academy of Engineering*] (EAIO)

AcG .... Accelerator Globulin [*Medicine*]

ACG .... ACM Government Income Fund [*NYSE symbol*] (SPSG)

ACG .... Acycloguanosine [*Also, ACV, Acyclovir*] [*Antiviral compound*]

ACG .... Address Coding Guide

ACG .... Adjacent Charging Group [*Telecommunications*] (TEL)

ACG .... Advanced Concepts Group

ACG .... African Cavalry Guard [*British military*] (DMA)

ACG .... Air Cargo Express, Inc.

ACG .... Air Cargo Glider

ACG .... Air-Core Gauge (RDA)

ACG .... Airborne Coordinating Group

ACG .... Airline Carriers of Goods

ACG .... Alpha Control Guidance

ACG .... Alternating Current Generator

ACG .... American College of Gastroenterology (EA)

ACG .... American Council on Germany (EA)

ACG .... An Comunn Gaidhealach [*The Highland Association*] (EA)

ACG .... Angiocardiography [*Medicine*]

ACG .... Angle Closure Glaucoma [*Ophthalmology*]

ACG .... Apex Cardiogram [*Medicine*]

ACG .... Area Coordination Group [*Air Force*] (AABC)

ACG .... Arts Centre Group (EAIO)

ACG .... Assistant Chaplain-General [*British*]

ACG .... Assistant Commissary General

ACG .... Association Canadienne des Geographes [*Canadian Association of Geographers*]

ACG .... Association for Corporate Growth [*Deerfield, IL*] (EA)

ACG .... Atlantic Energy [*Vancouver Stock Exchange symbol*]

ACG .... Auto Car Guard

ACG .... Automatic Code Generator

ACG .... Automatic Correlation Guidance

ACG .... Automotive Component Group [*Automotive engineering*]

ACG .... Auxiliary Coastguard [*British*]

ACG .... Glenbow-Alberta Institute, Calgary, Alberta [*Library symbol*] [*National Library of Canada*] (NLC)

ACGA .... American Carnival Glass Association (EA)

ACGA .... American Community Gardening Association (EA)

ACGA .... American Cranberry Growers' Association [*Defunct*] (EA)

ACGA .... American Cricket Growers Association (EA)

ACGA .... American Cut Glass Association (EA)

ACGA .... Association Canadienne de Gestion des Achats [*Purchasing Management Association of Canada - PMAC*]

ACGB .... Arts Council of Great Britain

ACGBAF ... Acta Horti Gotoburgensis [*A publication*]

ACGBI...... Automobile Club of Great Britain and Ireland [*Later, Royal Automobile Club*]

ACGC .... American Checkered Giant Club [*Later, ACGRC*]

ACGC .... American Consolidated Gold Corp. [*NASDAQ symbol*] (NQ)

ACGC .... American Custard Glass Collectors (EA)

ACGCA ..... Advent Christian General Conference of America (EA)

ACGCBJ ... Acta Archaeologica. Academiae Scientiarum Hungaricae [*A publication*]

ACGD........ Association for Corporate Growth and Diversification [*Later, ACG*] (EA)

ACGE .... Association Canadienne du Genie Eolien [*Canada*]

ACGF....... American Child Guidance Foundation [*Defunct*] (EA)

ACGF....... Australian Citrus Growers' Federation

ACGF....... Autocovariance Generating Function [*Statistics*]

ACGG .... American Custom Gunmakers Guild (EA)

ACGG .... Associate Committee of Geodesy and Geophysics [*Canada*]

ACGH....... Calgary General Hospital, Alberta [*Library symbol*] [*National Library of Canada*] (NLC)

ACGHAX .. Acta Geologica Hispanica [*A publication*]

ACGI .... American Capacity Group, Incorporated [*Peoria, IL*] [*NASDAQ symbol*] (NQ)

ACGI .... Associate of the City and Guilds of London Institute [*British*]

ACGIH ...... American Conference of Governmental Industrial Hygienists (EA)

Ac Gioenia Sc Nat Catania B ... Accademia Gioenia de Scienze Naturali in Catania. Bollettino delle Sedute [*A publication*]

ACGKH ..... Aichi Daigaku Kenkyu Hokoku [*Bulletin of the Aichi Gakugei University: Cultural Sciences*] [*A publication*]

ACGLAB... Acta Ginecologica [*A publication*]

ACGM .... Advisory Committee on Genetic Manipulation [*Health and Safety Executive*] [*British*]

ACGM .... Aircraft Carrier General Memorandum

ACGME .... Accreditation Council for Graduate Medical Education [*American Medical Association*]

AC GN SCH ... Acidic Gneisses and Schists [*Agronomy*]

ACGO........ Gulf Canada Ltd., Calgary, Alberta [*Library symbol*] [*National Library of Canada*] (NLC)

ACGP .... American College of General Practice [*Later, ACM*] (EA)

ACGp........ Area Coordination Group [*Air Force*] (AFM)

ACGP .... Army Career Group

ACGPOMS ... American College of General Practitioners in Osteopathic Medicine and Surgery (EA)

ACGPSP.... Association Canadienne de la Gestion du Personnel des Services Publics [*Canadian Association of Public Service Personnel Management*]

ACGR .... Association Canadienne des Gerants de la Redaction [*Canadian Association of Editorial Directors*]

ACGRC...... American Checkered Giant Rabbit Club (EA)

ACGS........ Acting Commissary General of Subsistence [*Army*]

ACGS........ Aerospace Cartographic and Geodetic Service

ACGS........ American-Canadian Genealogical Society (EA)

ACGS........ American Council on German Studies

ACGS........ Australian Cashmere Goat Society

ACGSA ...... Annales Chirurgiae et Gynaecologiae Fenniae. Supplementum [*A publication*]

ACGSC...... Army Command and General Staff School

ACGS(OR) ... Assistant Chief of the General Staff (Operational Requirements) [*British*] (RDA)

ACGSq....... Aerial Cartographic and Geodetic Squadron [*Air Force*] (AFM)

ACGTL...... Alberta Gas Trunk Line Co. Ltd., Calgary, Alberta [*Library symbol*] [*National Library of Canada*] (NLC)

ACGYA ..... Annales Chirurgiae et Gynaecologiae Fenniae [*A publication*]
ACh............. Acetylcholine [*Biochemistry*]
Ach............. Acharnenses [*Acharnians*] [*of Aristophanes*] [*Classical studies*] (OCD)
Ach............. Achete [*Purchase*] [*French*] [*Business term*]
Ach............. Achiasaph (BJA)
ach............. Acholi [*MARC language code*] [*Library of Congress*] (LCCP)
ACH......... Acquisition Command Headquarters (AFIT)
ACH......... Adrenal Cortical Hormone [*Endocrinology*]
ACH......... Advanced Chain Home [*RADAR*]
ACH......... Aftercoming Head [*Obstetrics*]
ACH......... Air Change per Hour [*Ventilation and infiltration rates*]
ACH......... Aircraft Hangar (MCD)
ACH......... Aircrafthand [*British*]
ACH......... Aluminum Chlorohydrate [*Inorganic chemistry*]
ACH......... American Center for Homeopathy (EA)
ACH......... American College of Heraldry (EA)
ACH......... Anglican Church Handbooks [*A publication*]
A Ch......... Annales de Chimie [*A publication*]
A Ch......... Annales Chopin [*A publication*]
ACH......... Anton Chico, NM [*Location identifier*] [*FAA*] (FAAL)
ACH......... Area Combined Headquarters [*World War II*] (DMA)
ACH......... Arm Girth, Chest Depth, and Hip Width [*Anatomical index*]
ACh......... Associate of the Institute of Chiropodists [*British*] (DBQ)
ACH......... Association Canadienne des Hispanistes [*Canadian Association of Hispanists - CAH*]
ACH......... Association Canadienne des Humanites [*Humanities Association of Canada - HAC*]
ACH......... Association of Caribbean Historians [*Nassau, Bahamas*] (EAIO)
ACH......... Association for Computers and the Humanities (EA)
ACH......... Association of Contemporary Historians (EA)
ACH......... Association of Cosmetologists and Hairdressers (EA)
ACH......... Attempts per Circuit per Hour [*Telecommunications*] (TEL)
ACH......... Australian Commonwealth Horse (DMA)
ACH......... Automated Clearinghouse [*Banking*]
ACH......... Barcklay Flying Service [*Spokane, WA*] [*FAA designator*] (FAAC)
a-ch---......... China, Republic of [*Taiwan*] [*MARC geographic area code*] [*Library of Congress*] (LCCP)
a-ch---......... Formosa [*MARC geographic area code*] [*Library of Congress*] (LCCP)
ACH......... Home Oil Co. Ltd., Calgary, Alberta [*Library symbol*] [*National Library of Canada*] (NLC)
ACh......... L'Astrologie Chaldeenne [*A publication*] (BJA)
ACHA....... American Catholic Historical Association (EA)
ACHA....... American College Health Association (EA)
ACHA....... American College of Hospital Administrators [*Later, ACHE*] (EA)
ACHA....... American Coon Hunters Association (EA)
ACHA....... American Council of Highway Advertisers (EA)
ACHA....... Association Canadienne de Hockey Amateur [*Canadian Amateur Hockey Association - CAHA*]
ACHA....... Hardy Associates, Calgary, Alberta [*Library symbol*] [*National Library of Canada*] (NLC)
ACHAAH ... Acta Haematologica [*Basel*] [*A publication*]
ACHAM.... Champion Public Library, Alberta [*Library symbol*] [*National Library of Canada*] (NLC)
ACHAS ..... Haverlift Systems Ltd., Calgary, Alberta [*Library symbol*] [*National Library of Canada*] (NLC)
Achats et Entretien Mater Ind ... Achats et Entretien du Materiel Industriel [*A publication*]
Achats Entret Mater Ind ... Achats et Entretien du Materiel Industriel [*France*] [*A publication*]
ACHC....... American Capital Holdings, Inc. [*NASDAQ symbol*] (NQ)
ACHC....... Association to Combat Huntington's Chorea [*British*] (EAIO)
ACHC....... Holy Cross Hospital, Calgary, Alberta [*Library symbol*] [*National Library of Canada*] (NLC)
ACHCA ..... American College of Health Care Administrators (EA)
ACHCBO .. Acta Histochemica et Cytochemica [*A publication*]
ACHCL ..... Academy for Catholic Health Care Leadership (EA)
ACHCR ..... American Council for Health Care Reform (EA)
ACHCU ..... Canadian Union College, College Heights, Alberta [*Library symbol*] [*National Library of Canada*] (NLC)
Achdny....... Archdeanery
ACHDU..... Association Canadienne de l'Habitation et du Developpement Urbain [*Canadian Association of Housing and Urban Development*]
ACHDWU ... All-Ceylon Harbor and Dock Workers' Union
AchE......... Acetylcholineesterase [*An enzyme*]
ACHE......... Action Committee for Higher Education (EA)
ACHE......... American College of Healthcare Executives (EA)
ACHE......... American Council of Hypnotist Examiners (EA)
ACHE......... Association for Continuing Higher Education (EA)
ACHE......... Canadian Hunter Exploration Ltd., Calgary, Alberta [*Library symbol*] [*National Library of Canada*] (NLC)
A Chem ...... Associate in Chemistry
ACHEMA ... Air Cooled Heat Exchanger Manufacturers Association (EA)
ACHEMA ... Ausstellungs-Tegung fuer Chemisches Apparatewesen [*Triennial international chemical engineering exhibition*]

ACHEMA Jahr ... ACHEMA [*Ausstellungs- Tegung fuer Chemisches Apparatewesen*] Jahrbuch [*A publication*]
AChemS..... Association for Chemoreception Sciences (EA)
A Chem Scand ... Acta Chemica Scandinavica [*A publication*]
ACHFS...... Father R. Perin School, Chard, Alberta [*Library symbol*] [*National Library of Canada*] (BIB)
ACHG........ American Citizens for Honesty in Government [*Defunct*] (EA)
ACHI......... Application Channel Interface (TEL)
ACHI......... Association for Childbirth at Home, International (EA)
ACHIB....... African Chamber of Hawkers and Informal Business [*South Africa*] (ECON)
Achil........... Achilleis [*of Statius*] [*Classical studies*] (OCD)
A Chir Belg ... Acta Chirurgica Belgica [*A publication*]
A Chir It ... Acta Chirurgica Italica [*A publication*]
A Chir Jug ... Acta Chirurgica Jugoslavica [*A publication*]
A Chir Plast ... Acta Chirurgiae Plasticae [*A publication*]
A Chir Scand ... Acta Chirurgica Scandinavica [*A publication*]
A Ch J ... American Chemical Journal [*A publication*]
ACHL........ American Council for Healthful Living (EA)
ACHLAG .. Acta Historica Leopoldina [*A publication*]
ACHLIS .... Australian Clearing House for Library and Information Science [*South Australian College of Advanced Education Library*] [*Information service or system*] (IID)
ACHM...... Chauvin Municipal Library, Alberta [*Library symbol*] [*National Library of Canada*] (BIB)
ACHMDM ... Annales de Chirurgie de la Main [*A publication*]
ACHO........ American College of Home Obstetrics (EA)
ACHO........ Husky Oil Operations, Calgary, Alberta [*Library symbol*] [*National Library of Canada*] (NLC)
ACHOBS .. Assistant Chief Observer [*Navy*] (NVT)
ACHOD .... Acoustic Helicopter Overflight Detector (MCD)
ACHP .... Advisory Council on Historic Preservation (NRCH)
ACHP .... Association Canadienne d'Hygiene Publique [*Canadian Association of Public Health*]
ACHPIRST ... Australian Clearing House for Publications in Recreation, Sport, and Tourism [*Information service or system*] (IID)
ACHQ........ Area Combined Headquarters [*World War II*]
AChR .... Acetylcholine Receptor [*Also, AcChR*] [*Biochemistry*]
ACHR....... American Catholic Historical Researches [*A publication*]
ACHR....... American Committee for Human Rights (EA)
ACHR....... American Council of Human Rights [*Later, PHR*] (EA)
ACHR....... Argentine Commission for Human Rights (EA)
AChRAb ... Acetylcholine Receptor Antibody [*Immunology*]
ACHS........ American Camp and Hospital Service
ACHS........ American Catholic Historical Society (EA)
ACHS........ American Catholic Historical Society. Records [*A publication*]
AChS........ Associate of the Society of Chiropodists [*British*]
ACHS........ Association of College Honor Societies (EA)
ACHS........ Association of Community Home Schools [*British*]
ACHS........ Automatic Checkout System [*NASA*] (AAG)
ACHS .... Chevron Canada Resources Ltd., Calgary, Alberta [*Library symbol*] [*National Library of Canada*] (NLC)
ACHSA ..... American Correctional Health Services Association (EA)
ACHSB..... Annales. Cercle Hutois des Sciences et Beaux-Arts [*A publication*]
ACHSJ ...... Australian Catholic Historical Society. Journal [*A publication*] (ADA)
ACHSR...... American Catholic Historical Society. Records [*A publication*]
ACHSWW ... American Committee on the History of the Second World War (EA)
Acht Arb Fluess Krist Fluessigkrist Konf Soz Laender ... Acht Arbeiten ueber Fluessige Kristalle Fluessigkristall-Konferenz Sozialistischer Laender [*A publication*]
ACHU........ Aircrew Holding Unit [*British military*] (DMA)
ACHUD..... Advisory Committee to the Department of Housing and Urban Development
ACHV....... Archive Corp. [*NASDAQ symbol*] (NQ)
ACHVA..... Air Conditioning, Heating, and Ventilating [*A publication*]
ACHVIT..... Achievement
ACI .... Acid [*Pharmacy*] (ROG)
ACI .... Acoustic Comfort Index
ACI .... Actual Cost Incurred [*Accounting*] (MCD)
ACI .... Adenylate Cyclase Inhibitor [*Biochemistry*]
ACI .... Adjacent Channel Interference
ACI .... Adult-Child Interaction [*Test*]
ACI .... Advanced Chip Interconnect [*Data processing*]
ACI .... Age Controlled Item (NASA)
ACI .... Agence Congolaise d'Information [*Congolese Information Agency*]
ACI .... Air Combat Information
ACI .... Air Combat Intelligence [*Obsolete*] [*Navy*]
ACI .... Air Commuter, Incorporated (FAAC)
ACI .... Air Control Intercept
ACI .... Air Cortez [*Ontario, CA*] [*FAA designator*] (FAAC)
ACI .... Air Council Instruction [*World War II*]
ACI .... Air Couriers International, Inc. [*Defunct*] (TSSD)
ACI .... Air Curtain Incinerator (MCD)
ACI .... Airborne Controlled Intercept [*Air Force*]
ACI .... Aircraft Condition Inspection (MCD)
ACI .... Alderney [*Channel Islands*] [*Airport symbol*] (OAG)

ACI .... Alliance Co-Operative Internationale [*International Co-Operative Alliance*]   (EAIO)
ACI .... Allocated Configuration Identification [*NASA*]   (KSC)
ACI .... Allocated Configuration Item [*Navy*]
ACI .... Alloy Casting Institute [*Later, SFSA*]   (EA)
ACI .... Altered Commercial Item   (MCD)
ACI .... Altitude Command Indicator
ACI .... American Canvas Institute
ACI .... American Carpet Institute [*Later, CRI*]   (EA)
ACI .... American Concrete Institute   (EA)
ACI .... American Council on Consumer Interest. Proceedings [*A publication*]
ACI .... Amplifier-Control Intercommunications   (MCD)
ACI .... Analytical Condition Inspection [*Air Force*]   (MCD)
ACI .... Anti-Communism International   (EAIO)
ACI .... Anti-Communist International   (EA)
ACI .... Arcavacata [*Italy*] [*Seismograph station code, US Geological Survey*]   (SEIS)
ACI .... Arlen Communications, Incorporated [*Bethesda, MD*] [*Information service or system*] [*Telecommunications*]   (TSSD)
ACI .... Army Council Instruction [*World War II*]
ACI .... Ashland Coal [*NYSE symbol*]   (SPSG)
ACI .... Assist Card International   (EA)
ACI .... Associate of the Institute of Commerce [*British*]   (DCTA)
ACI .... Association of Canadian Interpreters
ACI .... Association Canadienne de l'Immeuble [*Canadian Real Estate Association - CREA*]
ACI .... Association Canadienne de l'Informatique [*Canadian Information Processing Society - CIPS*]
ACI .... Association of Chinese from Indochina [*Later, SEAC*]   (EA)
ACI .... Association of Commerce and Industry   (EA)
ACI .... Association for Conservation Information   (EA)
ACI .... Association for Cultural Interchange   (EA)
ACI .... Assure Contre l'Incendie [*Insured Against Fire*] [*French*]
ACI .... Austrian Cultural Institute   (EA)
ACI .... Automated Car Identification [*Railroads*]
ACI .... Automatic Card Identification
ACI .... Automatic Closure and Interlock [*Nuclear energy*]   (NRCH)
ACI .... Automatic Control Instrumentation
ACI .... Awana Clubs International   (EAIO)
ACI .... ESSO [*Standard Oil*] Resources Canada Ltd., Calgary, Alberta [*Library symbol*] [*National Library of Canada*]   (NLC)
ACIA .... Alternative Center for International Arts   (EA)
ACIA .... Associated Cooperage Industries of America   (EA)
ACIA .... Asynchronous Communications Interface Adapter [*Data processing*]   (MDG)
ACIA .... Aviation Career Incentive Act [*1974*]   (AABC)
ACIA .... Western Regional Office, Parks Canada [*Bureau Regional de l'Quest, Parcs Canada*] Calgary, Alberta [*Library symbol*] [*National Library of Canada*]   (NLC)
ACIAm ...... Actas. Congreso Internacional de Americanistas [*A publication*]
ACIArb ...... Associate of the Chartered Institute of Arbitrators [*British*]   (DBQ)
ACIAS .... American Council of Industrial Arts Supervisors   (EA)
ACIASAO ... American Council of Industrial Arts State Association Officers [*Later, CTEA*]   (EA)
ACIATE .... American Council on Industrial Arts Teacher Education [*of the International Technology Education Association*] [*Later, CTTE*]   (EA)
ACIB .... Associate of the Corporation of Insurance Brokers [*British*]
ACIBAP .... Australia. Commonwealth Scientific and Industrial Research Organisation. Bulletin [*A publication*]
ACIC .... Aeronautical Chart and Information Center [*St. Louis, MO*] [*Later, DMAAC*] [*Air Force*]
ACIC .... Air Corps Information Circular [*Obsolete*]
ACIC .... Albanian Catholic Information Center   (EA)
ACIC .... Allied Captured Intelligence Center [*US and Britain*]
ACIC .... American Capitol Insurance Company [*NASDAQ symbol*]   (NQ)
ACIC .... American Committee for International Conservation   (EA)
ACIC .... Apollo Contractor Information Center [*NASA*]   (KSC)
ACIC .... Associate of Canadian Institute of Chemistry
ACIC .... Association Canadienne pour l'Integration Communautarie [*Canadian Association for Community Living*]   (EAIO)
ACIC .... Automatic Combat Intelligence Center   (MCD)
ACIC .... Auxiliary Combat Information Center
ACICA ...... Australian Centre for International Commercial Arbitration
ACICAFE ... Association du Commerce et de l'Industrie du Cafe dans la CEE [*Association for the Coffee Trade and Industry in the EEC*]
ACICO ...... Assistant Combat Information Center Officer   (MUGU)
ACIC-TC .. Aeronautical Chart and Information Center Technical Translation Section [*Air Force*]
ACID .... Acidus [*Acid*] [*Latin*]   (ROG)
ACID .... Aircraft Identification   (KSC)
ACID .... Arithmetic, Coding, Information, and Digit Symbols [*Psychometrics*]
ACID .... Association of Canadian Industrial Designers
ACID .... Association of Colleges Implementing the Diploma of Higher Education [*British*]
ACID .... Attempted Corporate Integration of Dividends [*Economics*]

ACID .... Automatic Classification and Interpretation of Data   (BUR)
ACIDB .... Acta Ciencia Indica [*A publication*]
Acidic Proteins Nucl ... Acidic Proteins of the Nucleus [*A publication*]
Acid Open Hearth Res Assoc Bull ... Acid Open Hearth Research Association. Bulletin [*A publication*]
Acid Sulphate Soils Proc Int Symp ... Acid Sulphate Soils. Proceedings. International Symposium on Acid Sulphate Soils [*A publication*]
ACIDY .... Allied Commission, Industry Subcommission [*World War II*]
Aciers Spec ... Aciers Speciaux [*A publication*]
Aciers Spec Leurs Emplois ... Aciers Speciaux et Leurs Emplois [*A publication*]
Aciers Spec Met Alliages ... Aciers Speciaux, Metaux, et Alliages [*A publication*]
ACIF .... American Collectors of Infant Feeders   (EA)
ACIF .... Anticomplement Immunofluorescence Test [*Immunochemistry*]
ACIF .... Associacao Catolica Interamericana de Filosofia   (EAIO)
ACIFA ...... Analele Stiintifice ale Universitatii Al. I. Cuza din Iasi. Sectiunea 1. Matematica, Fizica, Chimie [*A publication*]
ACIFIC ...... Aspartame Committee of the International Food Information Council   (EA)
ACIG .... Academy Insurance Group, Inc. [*NASDAQ symbol*]   (NQ)
ACIG .... Advanced Computer Image Generator   (MCD)
ACIG .... Information Group West Corp., Calgary, Alberta [*Library symbol*] [*National Library of Canada*]   (BIB)
ACIGS ...... Assistant Chief of the Imperial General Staff [*British*]
ACIGY ...... Advisory Council of the International Geophysical Year
ACII .... Associate of the Chartered Insurance Institute [*British*]   (EY)
ACII .... Association Canadienne des Implantes Intraoculaires [*Canadian Implant Association*]   (EAIO)
ACII .... Astradyne Computer Industries, Incorporated [*NASDAQ symbol*]   (NQ)
ACIIB .... American Civilian Internee Information Bureau [*Army*]   (AABC)
ACIID .... [*A*] Critical Insight into Israel's Dilemmas [*Jewish student newspaper*]
ACIIW ...... American Council of the International Institute of Welding   (EA)
ACIL .... Aberration-Compensated Input Lens [*Optics*]
ACIL .... American Center for International Leadership   (EA)
ACIL .... American Council of Independent Laboratories   (EA)
ACIL .... Automatic Controlled Instrument Landing   (NASA)
ACILA ...... Associate of the Chartered Institute of Loss Adjustors [*Insurance*]
ACILL .... Australian Construction Industry Law Letter [*A publication*]
ACIM .... Accident Cost Indicator Model [*US Bureau of Mines*]
ACIM .... Advanced Common Intercept Missile   (MCD)
ACIM .... American Committee on Italian Migration   (EA)
ACIM .... Auxiliary Computer Input Multiplexer
ACIM .... Availability Centered Inventory Model   (MCD)
ACIM .... Axis Crossing Interval Meter [*SONAR*]
ACIMALL ... Associazione Costruttori Italiani Macchine e Accessori per la Lavorazione del Legno [*Italian Woodworking Machinery and Tool Manufacturers*]   (EY)
ACIMD ..... Advanced Common Intercept Missile Demonstration   (MCD)
ACIMGA... Associazione Costruttori Italiani Macchine Grafiche Cartotecniche e Affini [*Italian Printing, Converting, and Paper Machinery Manufacturers Association*]   (EY)
ACIMIT .... Associazione Costruttori Italiani di Macchinario per l'Industria Tessile [*Italian Textile Machinery Makers Association*]   (EY)
ACIMO ..... Association de Coureurs Internationaux en Multicoques Oceaniques [*Association of International Competitors on Oceanic Multihulls*]   (EAIO)
Ac Imp Lyon Cl Sc Mem ... Academie Imperiale des Sciences, Belles-Lettres, et Arts de Lyon. Classe des Sciences. Memoires [*A publication*]
ACIMS ...... Aerial Color Infrared Management System   (MCD)
ACIMS ...... Aircraft Component Intensive Management System [*Military*]   (AABC)
ACIN .... Australian Curriculum Information Network
ACINF ...... Advisory Committee on Irradiated and Novel Foods [*Government body*] [*British*]
ACINF ...... Airborne Acoustic Information System (Intelligence)
ACINT ...... Acoustic Intelligence [*Military*]   (NG)
ACINTEL ... Assistant Chief of Staff, Intelligence   (NATG)
ACIO .... Air Combat Intelligence Office [*or Officer*] [*Navy*]
ACIOA ...... Advisory Committee on International Oceanographic Affairs [*British*]
ACIOP...... Atlantic Command Intelligence Operating Procedures   (MCD)
ACIOPJF .. Association Catholique Internationale des Oeuvres de Protection de la Jeune Fille [*Later, ACISJF*]
ACIP......... Active Certificate Information Program [*for stock certificates*] [*Data processing*]
ACIP......... Advisory Committee on Immunization Practices [*Public Health Service*]
ACIP......... Aerodynamic Coefficient Identification Package   (NASA)
ACIP......... Aerodynamic Coefficient Instrumentation Package   (NASA)
ACIP......... American College of International Physicians   (EA)

ACIP.......... American Council on International Personnel [*New York, NY*] (EA)
ACIP.......... Analytical Condition Inspection Program [*Air Force*] (MCD)
ACIP.......... Attack Center Indicator Panel
ACIP.......... Australian Certified Investment Planners
ACIP.......... Aviation Career Incentive Pay [*Air Force*] (AFM)
ACIPRD.... Production Research Division, Esso Resources Canada Ltd., Calgary, Alberta [*Library symbol*] [*National Library of Canada*] (NLC)
ACIR.......... Advisory Commission on Intergovernmental Relations [*Washington, DC*]
ACIR.......... Association Culturelle Internationale: Reliance [*Leucate, France*] (EAIO)
ACIR.......... Automotive Crash Injury Research
ACIR.......... Aviation Crash Injury Research (MUGU)
ACIRC....... Air Circulating
ACIRC....... Asian Community Information Resource Centre [*Australia*]
AC/IREF... American Chapter, International Real Estate Federation (EA)
ACIS.......... Advanced Credit Information System
ACIS.......... Africa Church Information Service (EAIO)
ACIS.......... Air Cargo Integrated System (MCD)
ACIS.......... Aircraft Crew Interphone System (MCD)
ACIS.......... American Conference for Irish Studies (EA)
ACIS.......... American Council on International Sports (EA)
ACIS.......... American Council for International Studies (EA)
ACIS.......... Applied Communications [*NASDAQ symbol*] (NQ)
ACIS.......... Arms Control Impact Statement (MCD)
ACIS.......... Army Combat Identification Systems
ACIS.......... Associate of the Chartered Institute of Secretaries [*Later, Institute of Chartered Secretaries and Administrators*] [*British*] (EY)
ACIS.......... Avionics, Control, and Information Systems (MCD)
ACIS.......... Infocon Information Services Ltd., Calgary, Alberta [*Library symbol*] [*National Library of Canada*] (NLC)
ACIS.......... US Army Combat Identification System (RDA)
ACISE....... Atti. Convegno Internazionale di Studie Etiopici [*A publication*]
ACISJF...... Association Catholique Internationale des Services de la Jeunesse Feminine [*International Catholic Society for Girls*] [*Geneva, Switzerland*] (EAIO)
ACIS Newsletter ... American Committee for Irish Studies. Newsletter [*A publication*]
ACISQ........ Aeronautical Chart and Information Squadron [*Air Force*]
ACISR....... Atti. Congresso Internazionale di Studi Romanzi [*A publication*]
ACist.......... Analecta Cisterciensia [*A publication*]
AcIT.......... Academie Internationale du Tourisme [*International Academy of Tourism*] (EAIO)
ACIT News/Bu CATP ... Associate Committee on Instructional Technology. Newsletter/Bulletin. Comite Associe de Technologie Pedagogique [*A publication*]
ACIU........ Allied Central Interpretation Unit [*World War II*]
ACIU........ ASAP and Computer Interface Unit
ACIWLP... American Committee for International Wild Life Protection [*Later, ACIC*]
ACIX.......... American Carriers, Incorporated [*NASDAQ symbol*] (NQ)
ACJ............ Alternative Criminology Journal [*A publication*] (APTA)
ACJ............ Amcham Journal (Manila) [*A publication*]
ACJ............ American Citizens for Justice
ACJ............ American Committee on Japan (EA)
ACJ............ American Council for Judaism (EA)
ACJ............ Americus, GA [*Location identifier*] [*FAA*] (FAAL)
ACJ............ Ancillae Sacri Cordis Jesu [*Handmaids of the Sacred Heart of Jesus*] [*Roman Catholic religious order*]
ACJ............ Andean Commission of Jurists [*See also CAJ*] (EAIO)
ACJ............ Asociacion Cristiana de Jovenes [*Young Men's Christian Association*] (EAIO)
ACJ............ Associate in Criminal Justice
ACJ............ Attitude Control Jet [*Aerospace*]
ACJ............ Australian Commercial Journal [*A publication*] (APTA)
ACJ............ Sacred Heart College, Cullman, AL [*Library symbol*] [*Library of Congress*] (LCLS)
ACJA......... American Congregation of Jews from Austria (EA)
ACJA........ American Criminal Justice Association [*A publication*] (DLA)
ACJA-LAE ... American Criminal Justice Association - Lambda Alpha Epsilon (EA)
ACJC......... Association Catholique de la Jeunesse Canadienne-Francaise [*Catholic Association of Francophone Youth*] [*Canada*]
ACJI......... A Coeur Joie International (EAIO)
ACJ (Mad Pr) ... Accident Compensation Journal [*Madhya Pradesh, India*] [*A publication*] (DLA)
ACJS......... Academy of Criminal Justice Sciences (EA)
ACJS......... Alliance Carpenters and Joiners Society [*A union*] [*British*]
ACJSS....... Associated Carpenters and Joiners Society of Scotland [*A union*]
ACK.......... Acklands Ltd. [*Toronto Stock Exchange symbol*]
ACK.......... Acknowledge (AFM)
ACK.......... Acknowledgment Character [*Keyboard*] [*Data processing*]
ACK.......... Altitude Conversion Kit
ACK.......... American Committee for KEEP (EA)
ACK.......... Archiv fuer Christliche Kunst [*A publication*]

ACK.......... Armstrong World Industries, Inc. [*Formerly, Armstrong Cork Co.*] [*NYSE symbol*] (SPSG)
ACK.......... Assistant Cook [*British military*] (DMA)
ACK.......... Automatic Color Killer [*Video recording*]
ACK.......... Nantucket [*Massachusetts*] [*Airport symbol*] (OAG)
ACK0........ Even Positive Acknowledgment [*Data processing*] (IBMDP)
ACK1........ Odd Positive Acknowledgment [*Data processing*] (IBMDP)
ACK'D....... Acknowledged [*Business term*]
ACKGT...... Acknowledgment
ACKNE..... Acknowledge
ACKNOWL ... Acknowledgement (DLA)
ACKNT...... Acknowledgment (ROG)
ACKTX...... Automatic Circuit Exchange (MSA)
ACL.......... Accion Ciudadana Liberal [*Liberal Citizens' Action*] [*Spain*] [*Political party*] (PPE)
ACL.......... Achilles Resources [*Vancouver Stock Exchange symbol*]
ACL.......... Acme Precision Products, Inc. [*AMEX symbol*] (SPSG)
AcL........... Acta Linguistica [*A publication*]
ACL.......... Action-Centered Leadership [*Management term*]
ACL.......... Adjective Check List [*Psychology*]
ACL.......... Advanced CMOS Logic [*Texas Instruments, Inc.*]
ACL.......... Aerial Company Ltd. [*Australia*]
ACL.......... Aeronautical Computers Laboratory [*Johnsville, PA*] [*Navy*]
ACL.......... Air Cal [*Newport Beach, CA*] [*FAA designator*] (FAAC)
ACL.......... Air Cleaner Gasket [*Automotive engineering*]
ACL.......... Aircraft Circular Letter (MCD)
ACL.......... Aircraft Control Link
ACL.......... Aircraft Load
ACL.......... Alberta Case Locator [*University of Alberta*] [*Canada*] [*Information service or system*] (CRD)
ACL.......... Alberta Education Libraries [*Professional collection*] [*UTLAS symbol*]
ACL.......... Alicudi [*Lipari Islands*] [*Seismograph station code, US Geological Survey*] (SEIS)
ACL.......... Allen Cognitive Levels Test
ACL.......... Allowable Cabin Load [*in an aircraft*]
ACL.......... Allowable Cargo Load [*Air Force*] (AFIT)
ACL.......... Allowable Container Load [*in an aircraft*] (NASA)
ACL.......... Alternaria Citri (Lemon race) [*A toxin-producing fungus*]
ACL.......... Alternate Concentration Limit [*Nuclear energy*] (NRCH)
ACL.......... Altimeter Check Location [*Aviation*] (FAAC)
ACL.......... Ambassador College, Pasadena, CA [*OCLC symbol*] (OCLC)
ACL.......... American Classical League (EA)
ACL.......... American Coalition for Life (EA)
ACL.......... American Collegians for Life (EA)
ACL.......... American Commercial Lines, Inc.
ACL.......... American Committee for Liberation [*Later, RFE/RL*]
ACL.......... American Consultants League (EA)
ACL.......... Aminocaprolactam [*Organic chemistry*]
ACL.......... Analytical Chemistry Laboratory [*Department of Energy*]
ACL.......... Analytical and Computer Laboratory
ACL.......... Anterior Cruciate Ligament [*Anatomy*]
ACL.......... Anti-Catholic League (EA)
ACL.......... Antigen-Carrier Lipid [*Immunology*]
ACl........... Antiquite Classique [*A publication*]
ACL.......... Application Control Language [*Data processing*] (BUR)
ACL.......... Ascent Closed Loop (MCD)
ACL.......... Association Canadienne Linguistique [*Canadian Linguistic Association - CLA*]
ACL.......... Association of Christian Librarians (EA)
ACL.......... Association of Cinema Laboratories [*Later, ACVL*] (EA)
ACL.......... Association for Computational Linguistics (EA)
ACL.......... Atlantic Coast Line R. R. [*AAR code*]
ACL.......... Atlantic Container Line [*British*]
ACL.......... Atlas Commercial Language [*Data processing*] (BUR)
ACL.......... Attained Competency Level
ACL.......... Audit Command Language
ACL.......... Australian Centre for Languages
ACL.......... Australian Chess Lore [*A publication*] (APTA)
ACL.......... Australian College Libraries [*A publication*] (APTA)
ACL.......... Australian Companies Legislation [*A publication*]
ACL.......... Australian Current Law [*A publication*] (APTA)
ACL.......... Authorized Consumption List [*Military*] (AABC)
ACL.......... Automated Coagulation Laboratory
ACL.......... Automatic Carrier Landing System [*Military*]
ACL.......... Automator Control Language [*Data processing*]
ACL.......... Aviation Circular Letter
ACL.......... Avionics Cooling Loop (MCD)
ACL.......... Law Society of Alberta, Calgary, Alberta [*Library symbol*] [*National Library of Canada*] (NLC)
ACL.......... Monsanto Chemical Co. [*Research code symbol*]
ACLA........ American Citizens and Lawmen Association (EA)
ACLA........ American Clinical Laboratory Association (EA)
ACLA........ American Comparative Literature Association (EA)
ACLA........ American Cotton Linter Association [*Defunct*] (EA)
ACLA........ American Country Life Association (EA)
ACLA........ Anti-Communist League of America (EA)
ACLA........ Association Canadienne de Linguistique Appliquee [*Canadian Association of Applied Linguistics - CAAL*]
ACLA........ Lavalin Services, Inc., Calgary, Alberta [*Library symbol*] [*National Library of Canada*] (NLC)

ACLALS.... Association for Commonwealth Literature and Language Studies (EAIO)
ACLAM..... American College of Laboratory Animal Medicine (EA)
ACLAN ..... American Comparative Literature Association. Newsletter [*A publication*]
ACLANT... Allied Command Atlantic [*NATO*]
ACLANTREP ... Allied Command Atlantic Reporting System [*NATO*] (MCD)
ACLAR...... Claresholm Public Library, Alberta [*Library symbol*] [*National Library of Canada*] (NLC)
AClass........ Acta Classica. Verhandelinge van die Klassieke Vereniging van Suid-Afrika [*A publication*]
ACL AT .... Australian Current Law Articles [*A publication*]
ACLB........ Aircraft Launching Bulletin
ACLB........ Association of Christians in Local Broadcasting [*British*]
ACLB........ Australian Corporation Law Bulletin [*A publication*]
ACL Bull.... Australian Current Law Bulletin [*A publication*] (APTA)
ACLC........ Adaptive Communication Live Controller (MCD)
ACLC........ Air Cadet League of Canada [*World War II*]
AC/LC........ Anti-Axial Compression/Liquid Chromatography
ACLC........ Assessment of Children's Language Comprehension [*Education*]
ACLC........ Association Canadienne de Litterature Comparee [*Canadian Comparative Literature Association - CCLA*]
ACLC........ Australian Company Law Cases [*A publication*] (APTA)
AC/LC........ Auto/Axial Compression/Liquid Chromatography
ACLCA9..... Advances in Clinical Chemistry [*A publication*]
ACLCP...... Associated College Libraries of Central Pennsylvania [*Library network*]
ACLCS ...... Airborne Command-Launch Control Subsystem (CAAL)
ACLD .... Above Clouds [*Aviation*] (FAAC)
ACLD .... Aircooled (MSA)
ACLD .... Association for Children with Learning Disabilities [*Later, LDA*] (EA)
ACLD .... Australian Current Law Digest [*A publication*] (APTA)
ACLD-A .... Architectural Design [*A publication*]
ACLDB...... Army Central Logistics Data Bank (AABC)
ACLDB...... Australian Corporate Law Database
ACLE........ Accel International Corp. [*Formerly, Acceleration Corp.*] [*NASDAQ symbol*] (NQ)
ACLE........ Automatic Clutter Eliminator (MSA)
ACLEA...... Association of Continuing Legal Education Administrators (EA)
ACLG .... Air-Cushion Landing Gear
ACLGO ..... Australian Council of Local Government Officers
ACLI......... Adrian C. and Leon Israel [*in company name "ACLI International"*]
ACLI......... American Council of Life Insurance [*Washington, DC*] (EA)
ACLI......... Clive Public Library, Alberta [*National Library of Canada*] (NLC)
ACLICS..... Airborne Communications Location Identification and Collection System
ACLIS .... Australian Council of Libraries and Information Services
ACLJ .... American Civil Law Journal [*A publication*] (DLA)
AcLLB .... Academie Royale de Langue et de Litterature Francaise de Belgique. Bulletin [*A publication*]
ACLLS...... Little Buffalo School, Cadotte Lake, Alberta [*Library symbol*] [*National Library of Canada*] (BIB)
ACLM .... American College of Legal Medicine (EA)
ACLM .... Antigua Caribbean Liberation Movement [*Political party*] (EAIO)
ACLM .... Cold Lake Municipal Library, Alberta [*Library symbol*] [*National Library of Canada*] (NLC)
ACLMS...... Menno Simons Community School, Cleardale, Alberta [*Library symbol*] [*National Library of Canada*] (BIB)
ACLN .... Australian Construction Law Newsletter [*A publication*]
A/CLNR.... Air Cleaner [*Automotive engineering*]
ACLO .... Agena Class Lunar Orbiter [*NASA*]
ACLO .... Association of Cooperative Library Organizations [*Later, ASCLA*]
ACLOG ..... Assistant Chief of Staff, Logistics (NATG)
ACLOS...... Advisory Committee on the Law of the Sea [*Department of State*] [*Terminated, 1983*] (NOAA)
ACLOS...... Automatic Command to Line of Sight [*Military*] [*British*]
ACLP........ Above Core Load Pad [*Nuclear energy*] (NRCH)
ACLP........ Above Core Load Plane [*Nuclear energy*] (NRCH)
ACLP........ Air Cushion Launch Platform (MCD)
ACLPDH... Advances in Clinical Pharmacology [*A publication*]
ACLPS...... Academic Clinical Laboratory Physicians and Scientists
ACLR........ Australian Company Law Reports [*A publication*] (APTA)
ACLR........ Australian Construction Law Reporter [*A publication*] (APTA)
ACLR........ Australian Current Law Review [*A publication*] (APTA)
ACLRBL... Annals of Clinical Research [*A publication*]
ACL Rev .... Australian Current Law Review [*A publication*] (APTA)
ACLRR...... Atlantic Coast Line R. R.
ACLS........ Advanced Cardiac Life Support System
ACLS........ African Communications Liaison Service (EA)
ACLS........ Air-Cushion Landing System
ACLS........ All-Weather Carrier Landing System [*Navy*]
ACLS........ American Council of Learned Societies (EA)
ACLS......... Automated Carrier Landing System [*Military*]

ACLS .... Automated Control and Landing System [*Aerospace*]
ACLSC ...... Annals of Clinical and Laboratory Science [*A publication*]
ACLSN...... American Council of Learned Societies. Newsletter [*A publication*]
ACLS Newsl ... ACLS [*American Council of Learned Societies*] Newsletter [*A publication*]
ACLSP....... Automated Carrier Landing Systems Project [*Military*]
ACLSVF.... Armored Combat Logistics Support Vehicle Family
ACLT........ Accelerate (FAAC)
ACLT........ Association of Canadian Law Teachers
ACLTR...... Accelerator (MSA)
ACLU .... American Civil Liberties Union (EA)
ACLU .... American College of Life Underwriters [*Later, The American College*] (EA)
ACLUF...... American Civil Liberties Union Foundation (EA)
ACLU Leg Act Bull ... American Civil Liberties Union. Legislative Action Bulletin [*A publication*] (ILCA)
ACLU Leg Action Bull ... American Civil Liberties Union. Legislative Action Bulletin [*A publication*] (DLA)
ACLV........ Accrued Leave [*Military*]
ACLV........ Air-Cushion Logistic Vehicle [*Helicopter*]
ACLV......... Autoclave Engineers, Inc. [*NASDAQ symbol*] (NQ)
ACLZAA ... Anais. Congresso Latino-Americano de Zoologia [*A publication*]
ACM.......... Academy of Country Music (EA)
ACM.......... Accountant's Magazine [*A publication*]
ACM.......... Acoustic Countermeasures [*Navy*] (NG)
ACM.......... Acquisition and Control Module (MCD)
Ac M .... Acta Musicologica [*A publication*]
ACM.......... Active Countermeasures
ACM.......... Additional Crew Member [*Military*] (AFM)
ACM.......... Adriamycin, Cyclophosphamide, Methotrexate [*Antineoplastic drug regimen*]
ACM.......... Advanced Circuit Module
ACM.......... Advanced Concepts Missile (MCD)
ACM.......... Advanced Consumer Marketing
ACM.......... Advanced Conventional Munitions
ACM.......... Advanced Cruise Missile
ACM.......... Aerodynamic Configured Missile (MCD)
ACM.......... Aerospun Cluster Munitions (MCD)
ACM.......... Air Chief Marshal [*RAF*] [*British*]
ACM.......... Air Combat Maneuvering (AFM)
ACM.......... Air Commerce Manual
ACM.......... Air Court-Martial
ACM.......... Air Cycle Machine [*Aerospace*]
ACM.......... Aircraft Coloring and Marking (NATG)
AC/M.......... Aircraft Meteorological (NATG)
ACM.......... Alarm Control Module [*Telecommunications*] (TEL)
ACM.......... Alkaline Contaminant Material [*In used frying oils*]
ACM.......... Allocated Configuration Management [*NASA*] (NASA)
ACM.......... Alterable Control Memory
ACM.......... Alternative Communities Movement [*British*]
ACM.......... American Campaign Medal [*Military decoration*]
ACM.......... American College of Medicine (EA)
ACM.......... American College of Musicians (EA)
ACM.......... American Conservatory of Music [*Chicago, IL*]
ACM.......... American Council on Marijuana and Other Psychoactive Drugs [*Later, ACDE*] (EA)
ACM.......... Amsterdam Center for Mathematics and Computer Sciences
ACM.......... Annual Corrective Maintenance (CAAL)
ACM.......... Antiarmor Cluster Munition (MCD)
ACM.......... Anticruise Missile (MCD)
ACM.......... Anuarul Comisiunii Monumentelor Istorice. Sectia pentru Transilvania [*A publication*]
ACM.......... Arab Common Market [*United Arab Republic, Iraq, Jordan, Kuwait, and Syria*]
ACM.......... Archconfraternity of Christian Mothers (EA)
ACM.......... Area Club Management [*Military*]
ACM.......... Arnold-Chiari Malformation [*Medicine*]
ACM.......... Artificial Compression Method
ACM.......... Asbestos-Containing Material
ACM.......... Asbestos-Covered Metal [*Technical drawings*]
ACM.......... Assistant Chief of Mission [*Foreign Service*]
ACM.......... Assistant Cub Master [*Scouting*]
ACM.......... Associated Colleges of the Midwest (EA)
ACM.......... Association for Classical Music [*Later, MA*] (EA)
ACM.......... Association for Computing Machinery (EA)
ACM.......... Associative Communication Multiplexer
ACM.......... Astral Bellevue Pathe, Inc. [*Toronto Stock Exchange symbol*]
ACM.......... Astrocyte-Conditioned Medium [*Analytical biochemistry*]
ACM.......... Atlas Consolidated Mining & Development Corp. [*AMEX symbol*] (SPSG)
ACM.......... Australian Chamber of Manufactures
ACM.......... Authorized Controller Material
ACM.......... Automatic Clutter Mapping
ACM.......... Automatic Coating Machine
ACM.......... Automatic Control Module Switch (MCD)
ACM.......... Auxiliary Core Memory [*Data processing*] (MCD)
ACM.......... Auxiliary Minelayer [*Navy symbol*]
ACM.......... Aviation Chief Metalsmith [*Navy*]
ACM.......... Avion de Combat Marine [*France*]

ACM.......... Axon Cylinder Membrane
ACM.......... Court Martial Reports, Air Force Cases [*A publication*] (DLA)
ACM.......... Mobil Oil Canada Ltd., Calgary, Alberta [*Library symbol*] [*National Library of Canada*] (NLC)
ACM.......... Natchitoches, LA [*Location identifier*] [*FAA*] (FAAL)
ACM.......... University of South Alabama, Mobile, AL [*OCLC symbol*] (OCLC)
ACMA....... Acidproof Cement Manufacturers Association [*Defunct*] (EA)
ACMA....... Advanced Civil/Military Aircraft (MCD)
ACMA....... Air Carrier Mechanic Association
ACMA....... Alliance Cabinet Makers Association [*A union*] [*British*]
ACMA....... Alumina Ceramic Manufacturers Association [*Defunct*] (EA)
ACMA....... American Cast Metals Association (EA)
ACMA....... American Catfish Marketing Association (EA)
ACMA....... American Certified Morticians Association [*Defunct*] (EA)
ACMA....... American Circus Memorial Association (EA)
ACMA....... American Comedy Museum Association [*Defunct*] (EA)
ACMA....... American Cutlery Manufacturers Association (EA)
ACMA....... Army Class Manager Activity (AABC)
ACMA....... Associate of the Institute of Cost and Management Accountants [*British*]
ACMA....... Australian Crane Marketers Association
ACMA....... [*A*] Contractor Managed Account (AAG)
ACMAC .... ACM [*Association for Computing Machinery*] Accreditation Committee
ACMAF..... Association des Classes Moyennes Africaines [*African Middle Classes Association*]
ACM (Arq Catarinenses Med) Ed Cult ... ACM (Arquivos Catarinenses de Medicina) Edicao Cultural [*A publication*]
ACMAS...... Automated Classified Material Accountability System
ACMB .... Applications Configuration Management Board [*NASA*] (NASA)
ACMC .... Advanced Cruise Missile Combustor (MCD)
ACMC .... American Cemetery-Mortuary Council (EA)
ACMC .... American and Common Market Club (EAIO)
ACMC .... Area Combined Movements Center [*Army*] (AABC)
ACMC .... Association des Chantiers Maritimes Canadiens [*Association of Canadian Maritime Shipyards*]
ACMC .... Association of Church Missions Committees (EA)
ACMC .... Automotive Chemical Manufacturers Council (EA)
ACMC .... Information Centre, Manalta Coal Ltd., Calgary, Alberta [*Library symbol*] [*National Library of Canada*] (NLC)
ACMD....... Advanced Concepts and Missions Division [*NASA*]
ACMD....... African Cassanova Mosaic Disease [*Botany*]
ACMD....... Assistant Chief Medical Director
ACMD....... Macleod Dixon Library, Calgary, Alberta [*Library symbol*] [*National Library of Canada*] (NLC)
ACMDOSq ... Air Commando Squadron [*Air Force*]
ACME .... Academy of Country Music Entertainment [*Canada*]
ACME .... Acme Steel Co. [*Riverdale, IL*] [*NASDAQ symbol*] (NQ)
ACME .... Adult Community Movement for Equality [*Civil rights*]
ACME .... Advanced Computer for Medical Research [*Stanford University*]
ACME .... Advisory Council on Medical Education
ACME .... Advisory Council for Minority Enterprise [*Department of Commerce*]
ACME .... Aircraft Component Mating Evaluation (MCD)
ACME .... American Council on the Middle East [*Defunct*] (EA)
ACME .... Antenna Contour Measuring Equipment
ACME .... Application of Computers to Manufacturing Engineering
ACME .... Association of Consulting Management Engineers (EA)
ACME .... Association for Couples in Marriage Enrichment (EA)
ACME .... Attitude Control and Maneuvering Electronics [*Aerospace*] (MCD)
ACME .... Monenco Consultants Ltd., Calgary, Alberta [*Library symbol*] [*National Library of Canada*] (NLC)
ACMEE...... Australian Conference on Management Education for Engineers
ACMEL...... Associated Continental Middle East Lines (DS)
ACMES..... Army Countermine Mobility Equipment System (MCD)
ACMES..... Attitude Control and Maneuvering Electronics System [*Aerospace*]
Ac Mex Cienc An ... Academia Mexicana de Ciencias Exactas, Fisicas, y Naturales. Anuario [*A publication*]
ACMF........ Air Corps Medical Forces [*Obsolete*]
ACMF........ Allied Central Mediterranean Force [*Later, AAI*] [*World War II*]
ACMF........ American Corn Millers' Federation (EA)
ACMFP..... Association Canadienne des Manufacturiers de Fenetres et Portes [*Canadian Association of Window and Door Manufacturers*]
ACMFS..... Automated Combat Mission Folder System (MCD)
ACMG .... Allied Commission, Military Government Subcommission [*World War II*]
ACMGA .... American College of Medical Group Administrators (EA)
ACM-GAMM ... Association for Computing Machinery - German Association for Applied Mathematics and Mechanics [*Federal Republic of Germany*] (CSR)
ACM Guide Comput Lit ... ACM [*Association for Computing Machinery*] Guide to Computing Literature [*A publication*]
ACMH....... Advisory Committee on Major Hazards [*British*]
ACMHA.... American College of Mental Health Administration (EA)

ACMHN.... Australian Congress of Mental Health Nurses
ACMI .... Advisory Committee on Medical Uses of Isotopes [*Nuclear energy*] (NRCH)
ACMI .... Air Combat Maneuvering Instrumentation System [*Air Force*] (MCD)
ACMI .... American Cotton Manufacturers Institute [*Later, ATMI*]
ACMI .... Art and Craft Materials Institute (EA)
ACMI .... Australian Contemporary Music Institute
ACMIC...... Application of Computer Methods in the Mineral Industry. Proceedings of the International Symposium [*A publication*]
ACMIP...... Army Force/Materiel Cost Methodology Improvement Project
ACMIS...... Automated Career Management Information System
ACMLA..... Association of Canadian Map Libraries and Archives (EAIO)
ACMLC..... Army Chemical Center
ACMM ...... Association Canadienne de Maisons Mobiles [*Canadian Association of Mobile Homes*]
ACMM ...... Aviation Chief Machinist's Mate [*Navy*]
ACMM ...... I. N. McKinnon Memorial Library, Calgary, Alberta [*Library symbol*] [*National Library of Canada*] (NLC)
ACMMBB ... Annals. College of Medicine [*Mosul*] [*A publication*]
ACMMC ... Aviation Chief Machinist's Mate, Carburetor Mechanic [*Navy*]
ACMMF... Aviation Chief Machinist's Mate, Flight Engineer [*Navy*]
ACMMH... Aviation Chief Machinist's Mate, Hydraulic Mechanic [*Navy*]
ACMMI ... Aviation Chief Machinist's Mate, Instrument Mechanic [*Navy*]
ACMMP ... Aviation Chief Machinist's Mate, Propeller Mechanic [*Navy*]
ACMMT ... Aviation Chief Machinist's Mate, Gas Turbine Mechanic [*Navy*]
ACMN....... Aircrewman [*British military*] (DMA)
ACMNG.... Allied Commission, Mining Subcommission [*World War II*]
ACMNP .... [*A*] Christian Ministry in the National Parks (EA)
ACMO....... ACE [*Allied Command Europe*] Communication Management Organization [*NATO*] (NATG)
ACMO....... Afloat Communications Management Office [*Naval Ship Engineering Center*] (IEEE)
ACMO...... Alaska Coastal Management Office
ACMO...... Assistant Chief of Mission Operations [*NASA*]
ACMO...... Authorized Controlled Material Order [*Military*] (AFIT)
ACMODJ ... Acta Morphologica [*Sofia*] [*A publication*]
ACMP....... Accompany (AABC)
ACMP .... Advanced Cruise Missile Program [*Navy*]
ACMP .... Amateur Chamber Music Players (EA)
ACMP .... Anthropology Case Materials Project [*National Science Foundation*]
ACMP .... Assistant Commissioner of the Metropolitan Police [*British*] (DAS)
AC2MP ..... Army Command and Control Master Plan
ACMPA..... Association Canadienne des Maitres de Poste et Adjoints [*Canadian Postmasters and Assistants Association - CPAA*]
ACMPD..... Annual Conference on Materials for Coal Conversion and Utilization. Proceedings [*A publication*]
ACMPM ... Air Combat Maneuvering Performance Measurement (MCD)
ACM Proc ... ACM [*Association for Computing Machinery*] National Conference Proceedings [*A publication*]
ACMPS..... Automated Communications and Message Processing System [*Army*] (MCD)
ACMR .... Air Combat Maneuvering Range
ACMR .... Attitude Control and Maneuver Rate [*Aerospace*]
ACMR .... Mount Royal College, Calgary, Alberta [*Library symbol*] [*National Library of Canada*] (NLC)
ACMRA .... Association of Commercial Mail Receiving Agencies [*Defunct*] (EA)
AC/MRDD ... Accreditation Council for Services for Mentally Retarded and Other Developmentally Disabled Persons [*Later, ACDD*] (EA)
ACMRR .... Advisory Committee on Marine Resources Research
ACMRU.... Audio Commercial Message Repeating Unit [*Device delivering a recorded commercial from cigarette vending machines*]
ACMS....... Advanced Configuration Management System
ACMS....... African Centre for Monetary Studies (EAIO)
ACMS........ Air Call Medical Services [*British*]
ACMS........ Air Combat Maneuvering Simulator (MCD)
ACMS....... Air Conditioned Microclimate System [*Army*] (RDA)
ACMS....... American Chinese Medical Society [*Later, CAMS*] (EA)
ACMS........ American Coordinated Medical Society (EA)
ACMS........ Application Control Management System (MCD)
ACMS........ Army Command Management System
ACMS........ Automated Career Management System
ACMS........ Automated Configuration Management System [*NASA*] (NASA)
ACMS........ Special Court-Martial, Air Force [*United States*] (DLA)
ACMSC..... ACM [*Association for Computing Machinery*] Standards Committee
ACMT .... ACMAT Corp. [*NASDAQ symbol*] (NQ)
ACMT .... Advanced Cruise Missile Technology (MCD)
ACMT .... Aerial Combat Maneuvering Training (MCD)
ACMT .... American College of Medical Technologists (EA)
ACMT .... American Commission on Ministerial Training (EA)
ACMTBW ... Museo "Felipe Poey." Academia de Ciencias de Cuba. Trabajos de Divulgacion [*A publication*]

ACM Trans ... ACM [*Association for Computing Machinery*] Transactions [*A publication*]

ACM Trans Comp ... ACM [*Association for Computing Machinery*] Transactions on Computer Systems [*A publication*]

ACM Trans Comput Syst ... ACM [*Association for Computing Machinery*] Transactions on Computer Systems [*A publication*]

ACM Trans Database Syst ... ACM [*Association for Computing Machinery*] Transactions on Database Systems [*A publication*]

ACM Trans Database Systems ... ACM [*Association for Computing Machinery*] Transactions on Database Systems [*A publication*]

ACM Trans Graphics ... ACM [*Association for Computing Machinery*] Transactions on Graphics [*A publication*]

ACM Trans Math Softw ... ACM [*Association for Computing Machinery*] Transactions on Mathematical Software [*A publication*]

ACM Trans Math Software ... ACM [*Association for Computing Machinery*] Transactions on Mathematical Software [*A publication*]

ACM Trans Off Inf Syst ... ACM [*Association for Computing Machinery*] Transactions on Office Information Systems [*A publication*]

ACM Trans OIS ... ACM [*Association for Computing Machinery*] Transactions on Office Information Systems [*A publication*]

ACM Trans Program Lang Syst ... ACM [*Association for Computing Machinery*] Transactions on Programming Languages and Systems [*A publication*]

ACMU .... American Canoe Manufacturers Union   (EA)

ACMV .... Assist-Control Mechanical Ventilation [*Medicine*]

ACMVA3 .. Acta Medica Venezolana [*A publication*]

ACMVS ...... Air Combat Maneuvering Visual System   (MCD)

ACMYAC ... Acta Mycologica [*A publication*]

ACN .... Academia Cosmologica Nova [*International Free Academy of New Cosmology - IFANC*]   (EAIO)

ACN .... Access Network, Media Resource Center [*UTLAS symbol*]

ACN .... Accession Number [*Online database field identifier*]

ACN .... Acetone Cyanohydrin [*Organic chemistry*]

ACN .... Acetonitrile [*Organic chemistry*]

ACN .... Acrylonitrile [*Organic chemistry*]

ACN .... Action Control Number [*Army*]   (MCD)

ACN .... Activity Control Number [*Navy*]

ACN .... Acuson Corp. [*NYSE symbol*]   (CTT)

ACN .... Acute Conditioned Neurosis

ACN .... Advance Change Notice   (AAG)

ACN .... Agricultural Communications Network [*Purdue University*] [*Telecommunications service*]   (TSSD)

ACN .... Aid to the Church in Need   (EA)

ACN .... Air Central, Inc. [*Enid, OK*] [*FAA designator*]   (FAAC)

ACN .... Air Commander, Norway [*NATO*]   (NATG)

ACN .... Air Consignment Note   (ADA)

ACN .... All Concerned Notified

ACN .... American Cablesystems [*AMEX symbol*]   (SPSG)

ACN .... American College of Neuropsychiatrists   (EA)

ACN .... American College of Nutrition   (EA)

ACN .... American Council on NATO [*Later, Atlantic Council of the United States*]

ACN .... Ante Christum Natum [*Before the Birth of Christ*] [*Latin*]

ACN .... Anthocyanin [*Fruit pigment*]

ACN .... Artificial Cloud Nucleation [*Rainmaking*]

ACN .... Ascension Island Tracking Station [*NASA*]   (NASA)

ACN .... Assignment Control Number [*Army*]

AC of N ..... Assistant Controller of the Navy [*British*]

ACN .... Australian Customs Notice [*A publication*]

ACN .... Authorized Code Number   (AFM)

ACN .... Auto Chek Centres [*Vancouver Stock Exchange symbol*]

ACN .... Automatic Celestial Navigation [*Air Force*]

ACN .... TransCentral, Inc. [*Oklahoma City, OK*] [*FAA designator*]   (FAAC)

ACNA .... Advisory Council on Naval Affairs

ACNA .... Nova, An Alberta Corporation, Calgary, Alberta [*Library symbol*] [*National Library of Canada*]   (NLC)

ACNAAD .. Anales. Academia Chilena de Ciencias Naturales [*A publication*]

ACNAC ..... Anglican Council of North America and the Caribbean

ACNAM .... Associations Council of the National Association of Manufacturers   (EA)

ACNAS ...... Admiral Commanding North Atlantic Station [*Navy*] [*British*]   (DMA)

ACNAS ...... Advanced Cableship Navigation Aid System   (TEL)

ACNBC ..... Associate Committee on the National Building Code [*National Research Council Canada*]

ACNC .... Novacor Chemicals Ltd., Calgary, Alberta [*Library symbol*] [*National Library of Canada*]   (NLC)

ACNCT ..... Technical Library, Novacor Chemicals Ltd., Calgary, Alberta [*Library symbol*] [*National Library of Canada*]   (BIB)

ACND .... Advisory Committee on Northern Development [*Canada*]

ACNE .... Northern Engineering Services Co. Ltd., Calgary, Alberta [*Library symbol*] [*National Library of Canada*]   (NLC)

ACNEAP ... Acta Neurovegetativa [*A publication*]

ACNEE ...... Action Committee for Narcotics Education and Enforcement

ACNER ..... Norcen Energy Resources Ltd., Calgary, Alberta [*Library symbol*] [*National Library of Canada*]   (NLC)

ACNET ...... AC Network   (MCD)

ACNET ...... Alternating Current Network

AcNeu .... Acetylneuraminic Acid [*Also, NAN, NANA*] [*Biochemistry*]

ACNF .... American Central NOTAM [*Notice to Airmen*] Facility [*Military*]

ACNFP ...... Advisory Committee on Novel Foods and Processes [*British*]

ACNGS ..... Allens Creek Nuclear Generating Station   (NRCH)

ACNH .... Nova/Husky Research Corp. Ltd., Calgary, Alberta [*Library symbol*] [*National Library of Canada*]   (NLC)

ACNHA ..... American College of Nursing Home Administrators [*Later, ACHCA*]

AcNHFln .... Acetylaminofluorene [*Also, AAF, AcAF, FAA*] [*Organic chemistry*]

ACNI .... Acta Naturalia Islandica [*A publication*]

ACNI .... All Chiefs, No Indians [*Slang*]   (AAG)

ACNLAC... Acta Neurologica [*Naples*] [*A publication*]

ACNM .... American College of Nuclear Medicine   (EA)

ACNM .... American College of Nurse-Midwives   (EA)

ACNM .... American Cordage and Netting Manufacturers   (EA)

ACNMS .... Advisory Committee on Nuclear Materials Safeguards

ACNN .... Air Commander, North Norway [*NATO*]   (NATG)

ACNO .... Assistant Chief of Naval Operations

ACNO .... Association des Comites Nationaux Olympiques [*Association of National Olympic Committees - ANOC*] [*Paris, France*]   (EAIO)

ACNOA ..... Association de Comites Nationaux Olympiques d'Afrique [*Association of National Olympic Committees of Africa - ANOCA*]   (EA)

ACNOC ..... Technical Library, Novatel Communications Ltd., Calgary, Alberta [*Library symbol*] [*National Library of Canada*]   (NLC)

ACNOE ..... Association des Comites Nationaux Olympiques d'Europe [*Association of the European National Olympic Committees - ENOC*] [*Brussels, Belgium*]   (EAIO)

ACNOR ..... Association Canadienne de Normalisation [*Canadian Association of Standardization*]

ACNOT ..... Accident Notice [*Aviation*]   (FAAC)

ACNOT .... Assistant Chief of Naval Operations (Transportation)

ACNP .... American College of Neuropsychopharmacology   (EA)

ACNP .... American College of Nuclear Physicians   (EA)

ACNP .... Northern Pipeline Agency, Calgary, Alberta [*Library symbol*] [*National Library of Canada*]   (NLC)

AcNPV ...... Autographa Californica Nuclear Polyhedrosis Virus

ACNRA ..... Archivum Chirurgicum Neerlandicum [*A publication*]

ACNRCW ... Advances in Cyclic Nucleotide Research [*A publication*]

ACNREY ... Advances in Cyclic Nucleotide and Protein Phosphorylation Research [*A publication*]

ACNS .... Academic Computing and Network Services [*Northwestern University*] [*Information service or system*]   (IID)

ACNS .... Advisory Committee on Nuclear Safety [*Canada*]

ACNS .... American Council of Nanny Schools   (EA)

ACNS .... American Council for Nationalities Service   (EA)

ACNS .... Assistant Chief of the Naval Staff [*British*]

ACNS .... Associated Correspondents News Service

ACNSA ...... Activitas Nervosa Superior [*Praha*] [*A publication*]

ACNS(A)... Assistant Chief of the Naval Staff (Air) [*British*]

ACNSA ...... Association Canadienne de Nage Synchronisee Amateur [*Canadian Association of Amateur Synchronized Swimmers*]

Ac N Sc Phila J ... Academy of Natural Sciences of Philadelphia. Journal [*A publication*]

Ac N Sc Phila Min G Sec Pr ... Academy of Natural Sciences of Philadelphia. Mineralogical and Geological Section. Proceedings [*A publication*]

Ac N Sc Phila Pr ... Academy of Natural Sciences of Philadelphia. Proceedings [*A publication*]

ACNSFI .... American Committee for the National Sick Fund of Israel   (EA)

ACNUA5... Acta Neurochirurgica [*A publication*]

ACNWS ..... Nowsco Well Service Ltd., Calgary, Alberta [*Library symbol*] [*National Library of Canada*]   (NLC)

ACNX .... Automatic Cancellation   (CAAL)

ACNY .... Adventurers Club of New York [*Defunct*]   (EA)

ACNY .... Advertising Club of New York [*New York, NY*]   (EA)

ACO .... Abell-Corwin-Olowin Clusters [*Galaxy cluster*]

ACO .... Abort Once around Cutoff   (MCD)

ACO .... Acceptance Checkout [*NASA*]   (NASA)

ACO .... ACCO World Corp. [*NYSE symbol*]   (SPSG)

AcO .... Acetoxy [*Biochemistry*]

ACo .... Acta Comeniana [*A publication*]

ACO .... Acta Oeconomica [*Budapest*] [*A publication*]

ACO .... Actes. Congres International des Orientalistes [*A publication*]

ACO .... Action Cut-Out

ACO .... Adaptive Control Optimized [*Manufacturing term*]

ACO .... Administrative Contracting Office [*or Officer*]

ACO .... Admiralty Compass Observatory [*British*]   (DEN)

ACO .... Advance Contracting Officer   (AAG)

ACO .... Adviser on Combined Operations [*British*]

ACO .... Agricultural Climatological Office [*Department of Commerce*]

ACO .... Air [*or Airborne*] Control [*or Contract*] Officer [*Military*] [*British*]

ACO .... Aircraft Control Operator   (MUGU)

ACO.......... Akron, OH [*Location identifier*] [*FAA*]   (FAAL)
ACO.......... Alabaster Cavern State Park [*Oklahoma*] [*Seismograph station code, US Geological Survey*]   (SEIS)
ACO.......... Alpha Cutoff
ACO.......... American College of Orgonomy   (EA)
ACO.......... American College of Otorhinolaryngologists   (EA)
ACO.......... American Composers Orchestra
ACO.......... American Council of Otolaryngology [*Later, ACO-HNS*]   (EA)
ACO.......... Annual Cost of Ownership
ACO.......... Anodal Closing Odor [*Physiology*]
ACO.......... Area Clearance Officer   (MUGU)
ACO.......... Armament Concepts Office [*Army*]   (RDA)
A & CO ...... Assembly and Checkout [*Minuteman*] [*Military*]   (AFIT)
ACO.......... Association of Canadian Orchestras
ACO.......... Association Canadienne des Optometristes [*Canadian Association of Optometrists*]
ACO.......... Association of Charity Officers   (EAIO)
ACO.......... Association of Conservation Officers   (EAIO)
ACO.......... Atco Ltd. [*Toronto Stock Exchange symbol*]
ACO.......... Atomic Coordination Office [*British*]
ACO.......... Attack Cut Out [*Military*]   (NG)
ACO.......... Austin Community College, Austin, MN [*OCLC symbol*]   (OCLC)
ACO.......... Automatic Call Origination [*Telecommunications*]
ACO.......... Automatic Cutout [*Valve*] [*Aviation*]   (AIA)
ACO.......... Coaldale Public Library, Alberta [*Library symbol*] [*National Library of Canada*]   (NLC)
ACoA........ Adult Children of Alcoholics [*Bestseller by Janet Geringer Woititz*]
ACOA....... American Committee on Africa   (EA)
ACOA....... American Construction Owners Association [*Washington, DC*]   (EA)
ACOA....... Associate Committee on Aerodynamics [*National Research Council*] [*Canada*]
ACOA....... Atlantic Canada Opportunities Agency
ACOA(F & A) ... Assistant Comptroller of the Army for Finance and Accounting
ACOA JI.... ACOA [*Administrative and Clerical Officers Association*] Journal [*A publication*]
ACOB....... ASCII COBOL [*Data processing*]
ACOC....... A. C. Owners Club - American Centre   (EA)
ACOC....... Air Command Operations Center [*NATO*]   (NATG)
AC/OC...... Air Cooperation Command [*RAF*] [*British*]
ACOC....... Allied Command Operations Center
ACOC....... American Clipper Owners Club   (EA)
ACOC....... Area Communications Operations Center [*Telecommunications*]   (TEL)
ACOC....... Associated Contractor Originated Change   (AAG)
ACOCA ..... Army Communication Operations Center Agency
ACOCC ..... Atlantic [*Fleet*] Commander Operational Control Center [*Navy*]
ACOD....... Adjournment in Contemplation of Dismissal [*Law*]
ACODAC .. Acoustic Data Capsule [*Oceanography*]   (MSC)
ACODS ..... Army Container-Oriented Distribution Systems
ACOE....... Automatic Checkout Equipment
ACOED ..... Actualite, Combustibles, Energie [*A publication*]
ACOEP...... American College of Osteopathic Emergency Physicians   (EA)
ACOF .... Attendant Control of Facilities [*Western Electric Co.*]
ACOFAR... Agrupacion de Cooperativas Farmaceuticas [*A publication*]
ACOFS...... Assistant Chief of Staff   (MCD)
ACOG....... Agence Civile OTAN [*Organisation du Traite de l'Atlantique Nord*] du Temps de Guerre [*NATO Civil Wartime Agency*]   (NATG)
ACOG....... Aircraft on Ground [*Navy*]
ACOG....... American College of Obstetricians and Gynecologists   (EA)
ACOGFL... Australian Council of Government Film Libraries
ACOH .... Advisory Committee for Operational Hydrology [*WMO*]   (MSC)
ACOHA..... American College of Osteopathic Hospital Administrators [*Later, COHE*]   (EA)
ACO-HNS ... American Council of Otolaryngology - Head and Neck Surgery [*Later, AAO-HNS*]   (EA)
ACOHS ..... Occupational Health and Safety Library, Alberta Workers' Health, Safety and Compensation, Calgary, Alberta [*Library symbol*] [*National Library of Canada*]   (NLC)
ACOI .... American College of Osteopathic Internists   (EA)
ACOI .... American Credit Optical, Inc. [*NASDAQ symbol*]   (NQ)
ACOID ...... Alaska Construction and Oil [*A publication*]
ACOJ........ Association Canadienne des Orchestres de Jeunes [*Canadian Association of Youth Orchestras - CAYO*]
ACOL .... American Colloid Co. [*NASDAQ symbol*]   (NQ)
ACOL .... Analytical Chemistry by Open Learning [*A publication*]
ACOL .... Annualized Cost of Living Model
ACOL .... Antiproton Collector [*Particle physics*]
ACOL .... Crowsnest Public Library, Coleman, Alberta [*Library symbol*] [*National Library of Canada*]   (NLC)
ACOLI...... Advance Circuit Order and Layout Information [*Telecommunications*]   (TEL)
ACom........ Acta Comeniana [*A publication*]
ACOM....... Advisory Committee on Objective Measurement [*Australia*]

ACOM....... Asian Communist [*Later, B Group*] [*Division of National Security Agency*]
A Com ...... Associate in Commerce
ACOM....... Association for Computer Operations Management   (EA)
ACOM....... Association for Convention Operations Management   (EA)
ACOM....... Astrocom Corp. [*NASDAQ symbol*]   (NQ)
ACOM....... Australian College of Occupational Medicine
ACOM....... Automatic Coding Machine [*Data processing*]   (CET)
ACOM....... Aviation Chief Ordnanceman [*Navy*]
ACOM....... Cochrane Municipal Library, Alberta [*Library symbol*] [*National Library of Canada*]   (NLC)
ACOMARS ... Association of Centers of Medieval and Renaissance Studies [*Later, CARA*]   (EA)
A-Com-in-C ... Air-Commodore-in-Chief [*RAF, RCAF*]   (DAS)
ACOMD.... Ars Combinatoria [*A publication*]
ACOMDAILY ... Australian Commodities Database
ACOME .... Archivum Combustionis [*A publication*]
A Comm .... Air Commodore [*RAF, RCAF*]   (DAS)
A Comm A ... Associate of the Society of Commercial Accountants [*British*]
ACOMPLINE ... [*A*] Computerised London Information System Online [*Greater London Council Research Library*] [*Bibliographic database*] [*British*]
ACOMPLIS ... [*A*] Computerised London Information Service [*Greater London Council Research Library*] [*British*]
ACOMS .... American College of Oral and Maxillofacial Surgeons   (EA)
ACOMS .... Automated Collection Management System
ACOMT .... Aviation Chief Ordnanceman, Turret Mechanic [*Navy*]
ACONA .... Advisory Council on Naval Affairs of the Navy League
A/COND... Air Conditioning [*Automotive engineering*]
ACONDA ... Activities Committee on New Directions for ALA [*American Library Association*]
ACONM.... Consort Municipal Library, Alberta [*Library symbol*] [*National Library of Canada*]   (NLC)
ACONS .... Conklin Community School, Alberta [*Library symbol*] [*National Library of Canada*]   (BIB)
ACOOG..... American College of Osteopathic Obstetricians and Gynecologists   (EA)
ACOP .... Adriamycin, Cyclophosphamide, Oncovin [*Vincristine*], Prednisone [*Antineoplastic drug regimen*]
ACOP .... Airborne Corps Operation Plan [*Military*]   (AABC)
ACOP .... American College of Optometric Physicians   (EA)
ACOP .... American College of Osteopathic Pediatricians   (EA)
ACOP .... Approved Code of Practice   (DS)
ACOP .... Army Customer Order Program
ACOP .... Copeland [*Al*] Enterprises, Inc. [*NASDAQ symbol*]   (NQ)
ACOPAT... Acta Ophthalmologica [*A publication*]
ACOPD .... ASEE [*American Society for Engineering Education*] Annual Conference Proceedings [*A publication*]
A-COPE .... Adolescent-Coping Orientation for Problem Experiences [*Psychology*]
ACOPP...... Abbreviated COBOL Preprocessor [*Data processing*]   (IEEE)
ACOPP...... Adriamycin, Cyclophosphamide, Oncovin [*Vincristine*], Procarbazine, Prednisone [*Antineoplastic drug regimen*]
ACOPS..... Advisory Committee on Pollution of the Sea   (EAIO)
Acor.......... Acoreana [*A publication*]
AcOr .... Acta Orientalia [*A publication*]
ACOR....... Coronation Public Library, Alberta [*Library symbol*] [*National Library of Canada*]   (NLC)
AcOr(B)..... Acta Orientalia. Academiae Scientiarum Hungaricae [*Budapest*] [*A publication*]
ACORBAT ... Association for Cooperation in Banana Research in the Caribbean and Tropical America [*Guadeloupe, French West Indies*]   (EAIO)
ACORD..... Action through Creative Organization, Research, and Discussion [*An association*]   (EA)
ACORD..... Advanced Concepts for Ordnance
ACORD..... Advisory Committee on Energy Research and Development [*British government*]
ACORDD.. Action Council of Regional Dissemination Directors
ACORE ..... Advisory Council for Orthopaedic Resident Education   (EA)
AcOr(K)..... Acta Orientalia (Copenhagen) [*A publication*]
AcOr(L).... Acta Orientalia (Leiden) [*A publication*]
ACORN..... Acronym-Oriented Nut
ACORN..... Association of Community Organizations for Reform Now   (EA)
ACORN..... Associative Content Retrieval Network [*A. D. Little, Inc.*] [*Information service or system*]
ACORN..... Australian Confederation of Operating Room Nurses
ACORN..... Automated Coder of Report Narrative [*Data processing*]   (DIT)
ACORN..... Automatic Checkout and Recording Equipment
ACORN..... [*A*] Classification of Residential Neighborhoods [*Database*] [*CACI*] [*Information service or system*]   (CRD)
ACORP...... Aviation Committee of Review Proposal [*Australia*]
ACOS .... Advanced Computer Oriented System   (BUR)
ACOS .... Advisory Committee on Safety [*International Electrotechnical Commission*] [*ISO*]   (DS)
ACOS .... American College of Osteopathic Surgeons   (EA)
ACOS .... Arms Control Observation Satellite
ACOS .... Assistant Chief of Staff
ACOS .... Australian Chamber of Shipping
ACOS .... Automated Cloud Observation System   (MCD)

ACOS .... Automatic Checkout Set (AAG)
ACOS .... [A] Common Operational Software (MCD)
ACOS .... [A] Computer Series [*Nippon Electric Company*] [*Japan*]
ACOSCA... African Cooperative Savings and Credit Association [*See also ACECA*] [*Later, ACCOSCA*] (EAIO)
ACOSS..... Active Control of Space Structures
ACOSS Q .. ACOSS [*Australian Council of Social Service*] Quarterly [*A publication*] (APTA)
ACOST...... Advisory Committee on Science and Technology [*Great Britain*]
ACOT .... Apple Classroom of Tomorrow
ACOT .... Assistant Chief of Staff, Organization and Training Division (NATG)
ACOTANC ... Australasian Conference on Tree and Nut Crops
ACOU........ Coutts Public Library, Alberta [*Library symbol*] [*National Library of Canada*] (NLC)
ACOUS ..... Acoustic (KSC)
ACOUSID ... Acoustic-Seismic Intrusion Detector (MCD)
ACOUST... Acoustics (ROG)
Acoust Abstr ... Acoustics Abstracts [*A publication*]
Acoust Bull ... Acoustics Bulletin [*A publication*]
Acoust Hologr ... Acoustical Holography [*A publication*]
Acoustical Soc Am ... Acoustical Society of America. Journal [*A publication*]
Acoustics Abs ... Acoustics Abstracts [*A publication*]
Acoust Imaging ... Acoustical Imaging [*A publication*]
ACOUSTINT ... Acoustical Intelligence [*Military*] (AABC)
Acoust Lett ... Acoustics Letters [*A publication*]
Acoust and Noise Control Can ... Acoustics and Noise Control in Canada [*A publication*]
Acoust Noise Control Can ... Acoustics and Noise Control in Canada [*A publication*]
Acoust Soc Am J ... Acoustical Society of America. Journal [*A publication*]
Acoust Ultrason Abstr ... Acoustics and Ultrasonics Abstracts [*A publication*]
ACO(W) .... Atomic Coordinating Office (Washington, DC) [*British Defense Staff*]
ACP .... Abnormal Control Plasma [*Clinical chemistry*]
ACP .... Acceptance Checkout Procedure (KSC)
ACP .... Acceptance Message [*Aviation code*]
A & CP ...... Access and Control Point [*Telecommunications*] (TEL)
ACP .... Accion Democratica Popular [*Popular Democratic Action*] [*Costa Rica*] [*Political party*]
ACP .... Accomplishment/Cost Procedure
ACP .... Acetophenone [*Organic chemistry*]
ACP .... Acid Phosphatase [*Also, ACPH, AP*] [*An enzyme*]
ACP .... Acoustic Communication Program
ACP .... Action for Child Protection (EA)
ACP .... Action Congress Party [*Ghana*] [*Political party*] (PPW)
ACP .... Action Control Point [*Telecommunications*]
ACP .... Acyl Carrier Protein [*Biochemistry*]
ACP .... Adaptive Control Process
ACP .... Additional Conditional Purchase [*Business term*] (ADA)
ACP .... Additive Color Process
ACP .... Advance Command Post (NATG)
ACP .... Advanced Computational Processor
ACP .... Advanced Cooperative Project [*NASA*]
ACP .... Advisory Caution Panel (MCD)
ACP .... Advisory Committee on Pesticides [*British*]
ACP .... Aerospace Computer Program [*Air Force*]
ACP .... African, Caribbean, and Pacific Countries [*Associated with the EEC*]
ACP .... After Conning Position [*British military*] (DMA)
ACP .... Agence Congolaise de Presse [*Congolese Press Agency*]
ACP .... Agricultural Conservation Program [*Department of Agriculture*]
ACP .... Air-Conditioning Pack
ACP .... Air Control Point
ACP .... Airborne Command Post [*Air Force*]
ACP .... Aircraft Communication Procedures [*Navy*] (MCD)
ACP .... Airlift Command Post (AFM)
ACP .... Airline Carriers of Passengers
ACP .... Airlines Control Program [*IBM Corp.*]
ACP .... Airman Commissioning Program [*Air Force*] (AFM)
ACP .... Alarm Control Panel
ACP .... Alignment Control Panel
ACP .... Allied Collection Point [*World War II*]
ACP .... Allied Communications Publications [*Military*]
ACP .... Alternate Care Plan [*Health Care Financing Administration*]
ACP .... Alternate Command Post [*Military*] (CET)
ACP .... Alternative Coated Paper
ACP .... Alternative Complement Pathway [*Hematology*]
ACP .... Altimeter Checkpoint [*Aviation*] (FAAC)
ACP .... American Club of Paris (EA)
ACP .... American College of Pharmacists (EA)
ACP .... American College of Physicians (EA)
ACP .... American College of Podopediatrics (EA)
ACP .... American College of Prosthodontists (EA)
ACP .... American College of Psychiatrists (EA)
ACP .... American Collegiate Press
ACP .... American Real Estate Partnership [*NYSE symbol*] (SPSG)
Acp............ Aminocaproic Acid [*Biochemistry*]
ACP .... Amino(chloro)Pentenoic Acid [*Organic chemistry*]

ACP .... Ammunition Control Point (AFM)
ACP .... Amorphous Hydrous Calcium Phosphate [*Inorganic chemistry*]
ACP .... Analytical Computer Program
A & CP ..... Anchors and Chains Proved [*Shipping*]
ACP .... Ancillary Control Processor
ACP .... Animal Care Panel [*Later, AALAS*]
ACP .... Anodal Closing Picture [*Physiology*]
ACP .... Anthology of Catholic Poets [*A publication*]
ACP .... Anti-Comintern Pact
A-CP .... Anti-Concorde Project (EA)
ACP .... Apparent Candle Power
ACP .... Archiv fuer die Civilistische Praxis [*A publication*] (ILCA)
ACP .... Area Command Post (FAAC)
ACP .... Area Concept Papers [*Military*]
ACP .... Area Coordinating Paper
ACP .... Arithmetic and Control Processor
ACP .... Armament Control Panel
ACP .... Army Capabilities Plan
ACP .... Army Controllership Program
ACP .... Asphaltic Concrete Pavement
ACP .... Associate Client Program [*Business International Corp.*] [*Information service or system*] (IID)
ACP .... Associate of the College of Preceptors [*British*]
ACP .... Associate Collegiate Players
ACP .... Associated Church Press (EA)
ACP .... Associated Collegiate Press (EA)
ACP .... Associated Construction Publications (EA)
ACP .... Associates of Clinical Pharmacology (EA)
ACP .... Association of Canadian Publishers
ACP .... Association Canadienne de Philosophie [*Canadian Philosophical Association - CPA*]
ACP .... Association for Child Psychoanalysis (EA)
ACP .... Association of Child Psychotherapists (EAIO)
ACP .... Association of Clinical Pathologists
ACP .... Association of Computer Professionals (EA)
ACP .... Association of Correctional Psychologists
ACP .... Association of Coupon Processors (EA)
ACP .... Astronaut Control Panel [*NASA*] (NASA)
ACP .... Atlantic City Free Public Library, Atlantic City, NJ [*OCLC symbol*] (OCLC)
ACP .... Atmospheric Contamination Potential
ACP .... Attack Center Panel
ACP .... Atypical Chest Pain [*Medicine*]
ACP .... Audio Control Panel (NASA)
ACP .... Audit Control Point
ACP .... Australian Christian Party [*Political party*] (ADA)
ACP .... Australian City Properties
ACP .... Australian Company Law and Practice [*A publication*]
ACP .... Automated Chemistry Program [*Data processing*]
ACP .... Automated Communications Publications (AFIT)
ACP .... Automated Computer Program
ACP .... Auxiliary Checkpoint
ACP .... Auxiliary Control Panel [*Aerospace*] (AAG)
ACP .... Azimuth Change Pulse
ACP .... Groupe des Sept pour la Cooperation du Secteur Prive Europeen avec l'Afrique, les Caribes et le Pacific [*Group of Seven for European Private Sector Cooperation with Africa, the Caribbean, and the Pacific*] (EAIO)
ACP .... University Animal Care Program [*Arizona State University*] [*Research center*] (RCD)
ACP 80...... Air Cargo Processing in the 80's [*British Telecom*]
ACPA........ ACPA [*Affiliated Conference of Practicing Accountants*] International (EA)
ACPA........ Activated Carbons Producers' Association [*European Council of Chemical Manufacturers Federations*] [*Brussels, Belgium*] (EAIO)
ACPA........ Adaptive Controlled Phased Array (CAAL)
ACPA........ Adjusted Compensation Payment Act [*1936*]
ACPA........ Advisory Commission on Parliamentary Accommodation [*Canada*]
ACPA........ Affiliated Chiropodists-Podiatrists of America (EA)
ACPA........ Agriculture and Consumer Protection Act of 1973
ACPA........ American Capon Producers Association (EA)
ACPA........ American Catholic Philosophical Association (EA)
ACPA........ American Catholic Psychological Association [*Later, PIRI*] (EA)
ACPA........ American Chronic Pain Association (EA)
ACPA........ American Citizens for Political Action (EA)
ACPA........ American Cleft Palate Association [*Later, ACPCA*] (EA)
ACPA........ American College Personnel Association (EA)
ACPA........ American College of Physicians Assistants [*Defunct*] (EA)
ACPA........ American Concrete Pavement Association (EA)
ACPA........ American Concrete Pipe Association (EA)
ACPA........ American Concrete Pumping Association (EA)
ACPA........ Amino(chloro)pentenedioic Acid [*Organic chemistry*]
A-CPA .... Asbestos-Cement Products Association [*Defunct*] (EA)
ACPA........ Associate of the Institution of Certified Public Accountants [*British*]
ACPA........ Association Canadienne de Patinage Artistique [*Canada*]
ACPA........ Association of Computer Programmers and Analysts (EA)
ACPA........ Australian Commercial Parachute Association

ACPAC...... Annual Conference Program Advisory Committee [*American Occupational Therapy Association*]
ACPAE...... Association of Certified Public Accountant Examiners [*Later, NASBA*] (EA)
ACPAI....... Affiliated Conference of Practicing Accountants International [*Later, ACPA*] (EA)
ACPANDP ... Assistant Chief of Staff, Plans and Policy Division (NATG)
ACPAP...... American Catholic Philosophical Association. Proceedings [*A publication*]
ACPATT..... All Commands Process as Attached [*Army*] (AABC)
ACPAU ..... Association Canadienne du Personnel Administratif Universitaire [*Canadian Association of University Administration Personnel*]
ACPBAQ... Advances in Comparative Physiology and Biochemistry [*A publication*]
ACPC........ Aircraft Camera Parameter Control
ACPC........ All Canada Poetry Contests
ACPC........ American Christian Palestine Committee [*Defunct*]
ACPC........ American College Personnel Accreditation (OICC)
ACPC........ American College of Probate Counsel [*Later, ACTEC*] (EA)
ACPC........ American Council of Parent Cooperatives [*Later, PCPI*] (EA)
ACPC........ American Council for Polish Culture (EA)
ACPC........ Association Canadienne des Periodiques Catholiques [*Canadian Association of Catholic Periodicals*]
ACPC........ Association Canadienne des Professeurs de Comptabilite [*Canadian Association of Professors of Accounting*]
ACPC........ Petro-Canada, Calgary, Alberta [*Library symbol*] [*National Library of Canada*] (NLC)
ACPCA...... American Cleft Palate-Craniofacial Association (EA)
ACPCA...... Association Cinematographique Professionnelle de Conciliation et d'Arbitrage (EAIO)
ACPCC...... American Council of Polish Cultural Clubs [*Later, ACPC*] (EA)
ACPCD...... Annual Reports on the Progress of Chemistry. Section C. Physical Chemistry [*A publication*]
ACPCDW ... Annual Reports on the Progress of Chemistry. Section C. Physical Chemistry [*A publication*]
ACPCP...... Australian College of Private Consulting Psychologists
ACPCQJ ... Australian Crime Prevention Council. Quarterly Journal [*A publication*]
ACPD .... Amino(cyclopentyl)dicarboxylate [*Organic chemistry*]
ACPD .... Army Control Program Directive
ACPD .... Association Canadienne des Professeurs de Droit [*Canadian Association of Law Teachers - CALT*]
ACPDA...... Acta Paedopsychiatrica [*A publication*]
ACPDA...... Association Canadienne des Presidents de Departements d'Anglais [*Canadian Association of Chairmen of English Departments - CACE*]
ACPDS ...... Advisory Committee on Personal Dosimetry Services [*National Science Foundation*] (NRCH)
ACPE........ American College of Physician Executives (EA)
ACPE........ American Council on Pharmaceutical Education (EA)
ACPE........ Association Canadienne des Pigistes de l'Edition [*Canada*]
ACPE........ Association for Clinical Pastoral Education (EA)
ACPE........ Association for Continuing Professional Education [*Formerly, AFSTE*] (EA)
ACPE........ Australian Chemical Processing and Engineering [*A publication*] (APTA)
ACPEN...... Aircraft Penetration Model (MCD)
ACPERS.... Army Civilian Personnel System
ACPF........ Acoustic Containerless Processing Facility
ACPF........ Amphibious Corps, Pacific Fleet [*Marine Corps*]
ACPF........ Asia Crime Prevention Foundation (EAIO)
ACPF........ Asociacion del Congreso Panamericano de Ferrocarriles [*Pan American Railway Congress Association*] (EAIO)
ACPF........ Australian Cancer Patients' Federation
ACPF........ Plasti-Fab Ltd., Calgary, Alberta [*Library symbol*] [*National Library of Canada*] (NLC)
ACPFA ...... Association Canadienne des Producteurs de Films d'Animation [*Canada*]
ACPFM..... Amitie Charles Peguy. Feuillets Mensuels [*A publication*]
ACPH........ Acid Phosphatase [*Also, ACP, AP*] [*An enzyme*]
ACPH........ Air Change per Hour [*Ventilation and infiltration rates*]
ACPI......... Advisory Committee on Prices and Incomes [*Australia*]
ACPI......... American City Planning Institute
ACPI......... American Consumer Products, Inc. [*NASDAQ symbol*] (NQ)
ACPI......... Assistant Chief Patrol Inspector [*Immigration and Naturalization Service*]
ACPI......... Aviation Crime Prevention Institute (EA)
ACPIC....... American Council for Private International Communications, Inc. [*Proposed corporation to replace Radio Free Europe*]
ACPK........ Action Packets, Inc. [*Ocala, FL*] [*NASDAQ symbol*] (NQ)
ACPL........ Acoustical Plaster [*Technical drawings*]
ACPL........ Assistant Controller, Personnel and Logistics [*Navy*] [*British*]
ACPL........ ATLAS Crew Procedures Laboratory [*NASA*] (MCD)
ACPL........ Atmospheric Cloud Physics Laboratory [*Spacelab*] [*NASA*]
ACPL........ Planning Library & Resource Centre, Calgary, Alberta [*Library symbol*] [*National Library of Canada*] (NLC)
ACPLC ...... Peter Lougheed Centre, Calgary General Hospital, Alberta [*Library symbol*] [*National Library of Canada*] (BIB)
ACPM .... Acoustic Containerless Processing Module (MCD)

ACPM .... Activity Career Program Manager [*Military*]
ACPM .... American College of Preventive Medicine (EA)
ACPM .... Associate of the Confederation of Professional Management [*British*] (DBQ)
ACPM .... Associate Contractor Program Manager [*NASA*] (NASA)
ACPM .... Association of Canadian Pension Management
ACPM .... Attitude Control Propulsion Motor [*Aerospace*]
ACPMA..... Actualites Pharmacologiques [*A publication*]
ACPMC..... Alberta Petroleum Marketing Commission, Calgary, Alberta [*Library symbol*] [*National Library of Canada*] (NLC)
ACPMME ... Association of Concentrated and Powdered Milk Manufacturers of the EEC (EAIO)
ACPMR..... American Congress of Physical Medicine and Rehabilitation [*Later, ACRM*] (EA)
ACPn .... American College of Psychoanalysts (EA)
ACPO .... Associate Contractor Projects Office [*NASA*] (NASA)
ACPO .... Association of Chief Police Officers [*British*]
ACPO .... PanArctic Oils Ltd., Calgary, Alberta [*Library symbol*] [*National Library of Canada*] (NLC)
ACPOC...... Association of Children's Prosthetic-Orthotic Clinics (EA)
ACPP........ Adrenocorticopolypeptide [*Endocrinology*]
ACPP........ Advisory Committee on Polar Programs [*National Science Foundation*] (MSC)
ACPP........ Advisory Council on Personnel Policy [*Canada*]
ACPP........ Aircraft Crashworthiness Program Plan (MCD)
ACPP........ American Concrete Pressure Pipe Association (EA)
ACPP........ Association Canadienne des Patineurs Professionnels [*Canadian Association of Professional Skaters*]
ACPP........ Association for Child Psychology and Psychiatry [*British*]
ACPP........ Pan Canadian Petroleum Ltd., Calgary, Alberta [*Library symbol*] [*National Library of Canada*] (NLC)
ACPPA ...... American Concrete Pressure Pipe Association (EA)
ACPPD..... Average Cost per Patient Day [*Medicine*]
ACPR........ Advanced Core Performance Reactor (NRCH)
ACPR........ Advanced Core Pulsed Reactor (NRCH)
ACPR........ American Clinical Products Review [*A publication*]
ACPR........ American College of Podiatric Radiologists (EA)
ACPR........ American Crossbred Pony Registry (EA)
ACPR........ Annular Core Pulsed Reactor
ACPRA...... American College Public Relations Association [*Later, Council for the Advancement and Support of Education*]
ACPROG... Assistant Chief of Staff, Programs Division (NATG)
ACPRS ...... Ames Cubic Precision Ranging System [*NASA*]
ACPRTS.... Association Canadienne des Professeurs de Redaction Technique et Scientifique [*Canadian Association of Teachers of Technical Writing - CATTW*]
ACPS........ Air-Conditioning and Pneumatic System (MCD)
ACPS........ Alkaline Calcium Petroleum Sulfonate
ACPS........ American Coalition of Patriotic Societies (EA)
ACPS........ American Color Print Society (EA)
ACPS........ American Connemara Pony Society (EA)
ACPS........ Armament Control Processor Set (CAAL)
ACPS........ Association Canadienne de la Presse Syndicale [*Canadian Syndicated Press Association*]
ACPS........ Attitude Control Propulsion System [*or Subsystem*] [*NASA*]
ACPS........ Planning Section Library, Calgary Police Service, Alberta [*Library symbol*] [*National Library of Canada*] (NLC)
ACPSAHMWA ... American Commission for Protection and Salvage of Artistic and Historical Monuments in War Areas [*World War II*] [*Defunct*]
ACPS/B..... Boletin. Academia de Ciencias Politicas y Sociales [*A publication*]
ACPSM ..... Association of Chartered Physiotherapists in Sports Medicine (EAIO)
ACPT........ Accept (AABC)
ACPT........ Acceptance Insurance Holdings, Inc. [*Omaha, NE*] [*NASDAQ symbol*] (NQ)
ACPT........ Acid Phosphatase with Tartrate [*Clinical chemistry*]
ACPT........ Asian Confederation of Physical Therapy (EAIO)
ACPTC...... Association of College Professors of Textiles and Clothing (EA)
ACPTEC ... Action Committee of Public Transport of the European Communities [*See also CATPCE*] (EAIO)
ACPTR...... Acceptor (MSA)
ACPTT ...... Air Combat Part Task Trainer
ACPU .... Association Canadienne des Professeurs d'Universite [*Canadian Association of University Professors*]
ACPU .... Auxiliary Computer Power Unit
ACPY........ Accompany (FAAC)
ACQ........... Acquest Enterprises Ltd. [*Vancouver Stock Exchange symbol*]
ACQ........... Acquire (ROG)
ACQ........... Acquisition (AFM)
ACQ........... Acquittal (AFM)
ACQ........... Admiral Commanding Battlecruisers [*Obsolete*] [*Navy*] [*British*]
ACQ........... All Courses and Quadrants [*Aviation*] (FAAC)
ACQ........... American Catholic Quarterly [*A publication*]
ACQ........... Annual Contracted Quantity (ADA)
ACQ........... Areas of Change Questionnaire
ACQ........... Waseca, MN [*Location identifier*] [*FAA*] (FAAL)
Acq Divest ... Acquisition/Divestiture Weekly Report [*A publication*]

ACQE .... Acquisition and Control Query Executive [*Programming language*]
ACQL .... Association for Canadian and Quebec Literatures
Acq Month ... Acquisitions Monthly [*A publication*]
ACQR .... American Catholic Quarterly Review [*A publication*]
ACQSEL ... Acquisition Select Switch   (MCD)
AC & QT ... Acceptance, Conforming, and Qualification Test
Acqt .... Acquit [*Paid in Full*] [*French*] [*Accounting*]
ACQT .... Aviation Cadet Qualifying Test [*Military*]
Acqua Ind... Acqua Industriale [*Italy*] [*A publication*]
Acqua Ind Inquinamento ... Acqua Industriale. Inquinamento [*A publication*]
ACQUIS.... Acquisition
Acquis Med Recent ... Acquisitions Medicales Recentes [*A publication*]
ACQWL .... American Center for the Quality of Work Life   (EA)
ACR .... Abandon Call and Retry [*Telecommunications*]
ACR .... Abstracts of Classified Reports [*A publication*]
ACR .... Accelerated Cost Recovery [*Accounting*]   (ADA)
ACR .... Access Control Register
ACR .... Accounting Review [*A publication*]
ACR .... Accura Resources [*Vancouver Stock Exchange symbol*]
acr .... Acreedor [*Creditor*] [*Spanish*] [*Business term*]
Acr .... Acriflavine [*Anti-infective mixture*]
Acr .... Acropole. Revue du Monde Hellenique [*A publication*]
ACR .... Across   (MSA)
Acr .... Acrylic [*Organic chemistry*]
ACR .... Active Cavity Radiometer
ACR .... Actual Cost Report   (NASA)
ACR .... Address Correction Requested
ACR .... Adenomatosis of the Colon and Rectum [*Medicine*]
ACR .... Adjacent Channel Rejection
ACR .... Admiral Commanding Reserves [*Navy*] [*British*]
ACR .... Advanced Capabilities RADAR
ACR .... Advanced Cargo Rotorcraft [*Later, Advanced Cargo Aircraft - ACA*]
ACR .... Advanced Combat Rifle [*Military*]   (INF)
ACR .... Advanced Confidential Report   (MCD)
ACR .... Advanced Converter Reactor [*Atomic energy*]
ACR .... Advanced Cracking Reactor [*Fuel technology*]
ACR .... Aerial Combat Reconnaissance
ACR .... Aeroelastically Conformable Rotor   (RDA)
ACR .... Air Carrier   (FAAC)
ACR .... Air Cavalry Regiment
ACR .... Air Control RADAR
ACR .... Air Control and Reporting   (NATG)
ACR .... Air Control Room   (MUGU)
ACR .... Air Corps Reserve [*Obsolete*]
ACR .... Air Crew Rescue   (CINC)
ACR .... Aircraft Checker's Report   (AAG)
ACR .... Aircraft Control Room
ACR .... Airfield Control RADAR [*Air Force*]
ACR .... Alaskan Communications Region [*Air Force*]
ACR .... Alliance for Consumer Rights   (EA)
ACR .... Allied Commission on Reparations
ACR .... Allowance Change Request
ACR .... Alternate CPU [*Central Processing Unit*] Recovery [*IBM Corp.*] [*Data processing*]   (BUR)
AC & R ...... American Cable & Radio Corp.
ACR .... American Choral Review [*A publication*]
ACR .... American Classical Review [*A publication*]
ACR .... American College of Radiology   (EA)
ACR .... American College of Rheumatology   (EA)
ACR .... American Council for Romanians   (EA)
ACR .... American Criminal Reports, Edited by Hawley [*A publication*]   (DLA)
ACR .... Americans for Children's Relief [*Defunct*]   (EA)
ACR .... Ameriscribe Corp. [*NYSE symbol*]   (SPSG)
ACR .... Ammunition Condition Report
ACR .... Annual Confidential Report
ACR .... Antenna Coupler Receiver   (MCD)
ACR .... Antenna Coupling Regulator   (IEEE)
ACR .... Anti-Camout Ribbed Bit [*Screwdriving tool*]
ACR .... Anticircling Run [*Navy*]   (NG)
ACR .... Anticonstipation Regimen [*Medicine*]
ACR .... Appeal Court Reports [*Ceylon*] [*A publication*]   (DLA)
ACR .... Applied Communication Research, Inc. [*Information service or system*]   (IID)
ACR .... Applied Computer Research [*Information service or system*]   (IID)
ACR .... Approach Control RADAR [*Aviation*]
ACR .... Araracuara [*Colombia*] [*Airport symbol*]   (OAG)
ACR .... Area Coordination Review
ACR .... Armored Cavalry Regiment
ACR .... Armored Cruiser [*Navy symbol*] [*Obsolete*]
ACR .... Assistant Chief for Research
ACR .... Association of College Registrars [*British*]
ACR .... Association of Computer Retailers   (EA)
ACR .... Association for Conflict Resolution   (EA)
ACR .... Association for Consumer Research   (EA)
ACR .... Audio Cassette Recorder   (RDA)
ACR .... Australasian Catholic Record [*A publication*]   (ADA)
ACR .... Australian Coin Review [*A publication*]

ACR .... Australian Criminal Reports [*A publication*]   (APTA)
ACR .... Australian and New Zealand Conveyancing Report [*A publication*]
ACR .... Automatic Call Recording [*Telecommunications*]   (CMD)
ACR .... Automatic Card Reader
ACR .... Automatic Carriage Return
ACR .... Automatic Compression Regulator   (IEEE)
ACR .... Automatic Compression - Release
ACR .... Auxiliary Computer Room [*Apollo*] [*NASA*]
ACR .... AVCAL Change Request   (MCD)
ACR .... Calgary Research Centre, Alberta [*Library symbol*] [*National Library of Canada*]   (NLC)
ACR .... Office of Civil Rights [*FAA*]   (FAAC)
ACRA .... Accuray Corp. [*NASDAQ symbol*]   (NQ)
ACRA .... Airlift Concepts and Requirements Agency
ACRA .... American Car Rental Association   (EA)
ACRA .... American Collegiate Retailing Association   (EA)
ACRA .... American Commercial Rabbit Association   (EA)
ACRA .... American Constitutional Rights Association   (EA)
ACRA .... American Cotswold Record Association   (EA)
ACRA .... American Craft Retailers Association   (EA)
ACRA .... Anti-Char Rapide Autopropulse [*French antitank weapon system*]
ACRA .... Approved Conference Rate and Interconference Agreement [*of Steamship Lines in the Foreign Commerce of the United States*]
ACRA .... Association of College Registrars and Administrators [*British*]
ACRAAX... Acta Radiologica [*A publication*]
ACRAF.... Artists Civil Rights Assistance Fund [*Defunct*]
ACRB .... Acrobe Automation Technology, Inc. [*Denver, CO*] [*NASDAQ symbol*]   (NQ)
ACRB .... Army Council of Review Boards
ACRB .... Royal Bank of Canada, Calgary, Alberta [*Library symbol*] [*Obsolete*] [*National Library of Canada*]   (NLC)
ACRBA ...... American Chinchilla Rabbit Breeders Association   (EA)
ACRBT ...... Acrobatic   (FAAC)
AC & RC ... Active Components and Reserve Components
ACRC .... Air Compressor Research Council [*Defunct*]
A Cr C ...... Allahabad Criminal Cases [*India*] [*A publication*]   (DLA)
ACRC .... American Capital & Research Corp. [*NASDAQ symbol*]   (NQ)
ACRC .... Arkansas Cancer Research Center [*Little Rock*]
ACRC .... Association of Commercial Records Centers   (EA)
ACRC .... Audio Center - Receiver   (KSC)
ACRC .... Calgary Branch Library, Alberta Research Council, Alberta [*Library symbol*] [*National Library of Canada*]   (NLC)
ACRCP ...... Reid Crowther & Partners Ltd., Calgary, Alberta [*Library symbol*] [*National Library of Canada*]   (BIB)
AC(R & D) ... Assistant Controller, Research and Development [*Admiralty*] [*British*]
ACRD .... Automatic Compression - Release Device
ACRDA .... Acta Radiologica. Diagnosis [*A publication*]
ACRDL .... Army Chemical Research and Development Labs   (MCD)
ACRDM .... Centre for Research & Development in Masonry [*Centre de Recherche et de Developpement en Maconnerie*] Calgary, Alberta [*Library symbol*] [*National Library of Canada*]   (NLC)
ACRE .... Action Committee for Rural Electrification   (EA)
ACRE .... Advanced Chemical Rocket Engine [*Air Force*]
ACRE .... Associate Citizens for Responsible Education [*Group opposing sex education in schools*]
ACRE .... Atlantic City Remodelers Exposition [*Remodeling Contractors Association*]   (TSPED)
ACRE .... Automatic Call Recording Equipment [*Telecommunications*]
ACRE .... Automatic Checkout and Readiness Equipment
ACRE .... Cremona Public Library, Alberta [*Library symbol*] [*National Library of Canada*]   (NLC)
ACREC ...... American College of Real Estate Consultants [*Later, RECP*]   (EA)
ACREF ...... Association Canadienne pour la Recherche en Economie Familiale [*Canadian Association for Research in Home Economics - CARHE*]
ACRE-FT/D ... Acre-Feet per Day
ACREIT .... American Conference of Real Estate Investment Trusts   (EA)
ACREP ...... Association Canadienne de Recherche et d'Education pour la Paix [*Canadian Peace Research and Education Association - CPREA*]
ACREQ ..... Allied Commission, Requisitions Subcommittee [*World War II*]
ACRES ...... Airborne Communication Relay Station [*Air Force*]
ACRES ...... Association Canadienne pour la Recherche en Economie de Sante [*Canadian Health Economics Research Association - CHERA*]
ACRES ...... Australian Centre for Remote Sensing
ACRFAET ... Aircraft Crash Rescue Field Assistance and Evaluation Team [*Air Force*]   (AFM)
ACRFLT.... Across Flats
ACRFT...... Aircraft
ACRH .... Argonne Cancer Research Hospital [*Illinois*]
ACRHDN .... Acta Rhumatologica [*A publication*]
ACRHU .... Association Canadienne des Responsables de l'Habitation et de l'Urbanisme [*Canada*]

ACRI......... Air-Conditioning and Refrigeration Institute (MSA)
ACRI......... American Cocoa Research Institute (EA)
ACRI......... Association Canadienne des Relations Industrielles [*Canadian Industrial Relations Association - CIRA*]
ACRI......... Industrial Development Department, Alberta Research Council, Calgary, Alberta [*Library symbol*] [*National Library of Canada*] (BIB)
ACRIM...... Active Cavity Radiometer Irradiance Monitor
ACRIM...... Association for Correctional Research and Information Management (EA)
A Crim R.... Australian Criminal Reports [*A publication*] (APTA)
ACRIP...... Adrenocortical Renin Inhibitory Peptide [*Biochemistry*]
ACRIP....... Australian Computer Research in Progress [*Database*]
ACRIS ...... AID [*Agency for International Development*] Consultant Registry Information System (EISS)
ACRL......... Aero-Chem Research Laboratories, Inc. (KSC)
ACRL......... Altemaria citri Rough Lemon-specific Toxins
ACRL......... American Cruise Lines, Inc. [*Haddam, CT*] [*NASDAQ symbol*] (NQ)
ACRL......... Association of College and Research Libraries (EA)
ACRL AAS ... ACRL [*Association of College and Research Libraries*] Asian and African Section
ACRL ANSS ... ACRL [*Association of College and Research Libraries*] Anthropology and Sociology Section
ACRL ARTS ... ACRL [*Association of College and Research Libraries*] Art Section
ACRL BIS ... ACRL [*Association of College and Research Libraries*] Bibliographic Instruction Section
ACRL CJCLS ... ACRL [*Association of College and Research Libraries*] Community and Junior College and Research Libraries
ACRL CLS ... ACRL [*Association of College and Research Libraries*] College Libraries Section
ACRL C & RL ... ACRL [*Association of College and Research Libraries*] College and Research Libraries [*A publication*]
ACRL EBSS ... ACRL [*Association of College and Research Libraries*] Education and Behavioral Sciences Section
ACRL LPSS ... ACRL [*Association of College and Research Libraries*] Law and Political Science Section
ACRL Monogr ... Association of College and Research Libraries. Monographs [*A publication*]
ACRL RBMS ... ACRL [*Association of College and Research Libraries*] Rare Books and Manuscripts Section
ACRL SEES ... ACRL [*Association of College and Research Libraries*] Slavic and East European Section
ACRL STS ... ACRL [*Association of College and Research Libraries*] Science and Technology Section
ACRL ULS ... ACRL [*Association of College and Research Libraries*] University Libraries Section
ACRL WESS ... ACRL [*Association of College and Research Libraries*] Western European Specialists Section
AC/RM...... Air-Conditioning Room (AAG)
ACRM ...... American College of Radio Marketing (EA)
ACRM ...... American Congress of Rehabilitation Medicine (EA)
ACRM ...... Aviation Chief Radioman [*Navy*]
ACRM ...... Crossfield Municipal Library, Alberta [*Library symbol*] [*National Library of Canada*] (NLC)
ACRMA .... Air-Conditioning and Refrigerating Machinery Association [*Later, ARI*] (KSC)
A/CRMD... Association for Children with Retarded Mental Development (EA)
ACRMPIA ... Alliance of Canadian Regional Motion Picture Industry Associations
ACRN ...... Accounting Classification Reference Number (MCD)
ACRN ...... Accounting Code Reference Number
ACRO ...... Acro Energy Corp. [*NASDAQ symbol*] (NQ)
ACRO ...... Acrobat (DSUE)
ACRO ...... Aircraft Control Room Officer [*British military*] (DMA)
ACRO ...... Association Canadienne de la Recherche Operationnelle [*Canadian Association of Operational Research*]
ACRODABA ... Acronym Data Base
ACRONYM ... Anti-Cronyism Movement [*Philippines*]
ACRONYM ... [*A*] Contrived Reduction of Nomenclature Yielding Mnemonics [*Humorous interpretation of the term*]
Across the Bd ... Across the Board [*A publication*]
Across Board (NY) ... Across the Board. Conference Board (New York) [*A publication*]
ACROWE ... Association of Cooperative Retailers-Owned Wholesalers of Europe (EAIO)
ACRP......... Advisory Committee on Radiological Protection [*Canada*]
ACRP......... Airborne Communications Reconnaissance Platform
ACRP......... Airborne Communications Reconnaissance Program (AFM)
ACRP......... Armament Control Relay Panel (MCD)
ACRP......... Army Cost Reduction Program (AABC)
ACRP......... Asian Conference on Religion and Peace [*Singapore, Singapore*] (EAIO)
ACRP......... Association Canadienne des Restaurateurs Professionnels [*Canadian Association of Professional Conservators - CAPC*]
ACRPP...... Association pour la Conservation et la Reproduction Photographique de la Presse, Paris, France [*Library symbol*] [*Library of Congress*] (LCLS)

A Cr R....... Allahabad Criminal Reports [*India*] [*A publication*] (DLA)
ACRR .... American Council on Race Relations
ACRR .... Annular Core Research Reactor [*Nuclear energy*] (NRCH)
ACRRT..... American Chiropractic Registry of Radiologic Technologists (EA)
ACRS......... Accelerated Capital Recovery System [*Accounting*]
ACRS......... Accelerated Cost Recovery Schedule [*Accounting*]
ACRS......... Accelerated Cost Recovery System [*Accounting*]
ACRS......... Across (FAAC)
ACRS......... Active Contrast Reduction System (MCD)
ACRS......... Advisory Committee on Reactor Safeguards [*Nuclear Regulatory Commission*]
ACRS......... Air Cushion Recovery System (MCD)
ACRS......... Air-Cushion Restraint System [*General Motors*]
ACRS......... Association for Correctional Research and Statistics (OICC)
ACRS......... Australian Coral Reef Society
ACRS......... Automatic Chemical Reaction System
ACRS......... Southern Branch Library, Alberta Research Council, Calgary, Alberta [*Library symbol*] [*National Library of Canada*] (NLC)
ACRSA ..... Association Canadienne de Recherches Sociales Appliquees [*Canadian Association of Applied Social Research - CAASR*]
ACRSE...... American Council on Rural Special Education (EA)
ACRSS...... Association for Children with Russell-Silver Syndrome (EA)
ACRT........ Aviation Chief Radio Technician [*Navy*]
ACRTC...... Advanced CRT Controller [*Computer chip*]
ACRU....... Applied Climate Research Unit [*University of Queensland*] [*Australia*]
ACRV .... Armored Command and Reconnaissance Vehicle (AABC)
ACRV .... Association Canadienne des Regulateurs de Vols [*Canadian Air Line Dispatchers' Association - CALDA*]
ACRV .... Audio Center - Receiver (KSC)
ACRV .... Automated Command Response Verification (MCD)
ACRV .... Rocky View School Division, Calgary, Alberta [*Library symbol*] [*National Library of Canada*] (NLC)
ACRVH ..... Library Services, Rocky View General Hospital, Calgary, Alberta [*Library symbol*] [*National Library of Canada*] (BIB)
ACRW ...... Aircrew (AFM)
ACRW ...... American Council of Railroad Women (EA)
ACRY .... Acrylic
ACRYL...... Acrylic (MSA)
ACRYL-BIS ... Acrylamide Bis-Acrylamide
ACS........... Academic Computer Service [*Generic*] [*Research center*] (RCD)
ACS........... Access [*Telecommunications*] (MSA)
ACS........... Accounting Control System
ACS........... Accumulator Switch [*Data processing*]
ACS........... Acetylstrophanthidin [*Organic chemistry*]
ACS........... Acquisition and Command Support (MCD)
ACS........... Acting Commissary of Subsistence
ACS........... Activity Characteristics Sheet [*Agency for International Development*]
ACS........... Adaptive Control System
ACS........... Additional Curates' Society [*British*]
ACS........... Administrative Computing Service
ACS........... Administrative Control System [*Telecommunications*] (TEL)
ACS........... Advance Count Switch
ACS........... Advanced Cardiovascular Systems
ACS........... Advanced Ceramic System
ACS........... Advanced Civil Schooling [*Army*] (INF)
ACS........... Advanced Communications Service [*Later, AIS*] [*AT & T*]
ACS........... Advanced Computer Services [*Honeywell Information Systems*] (IEEE)
ACS........... Advanced Computer System [*IBM Corp.*] (IEEE)
ACS........... Advanced Cryptographic System [*Air Force*] (MCD)
ACS........... Advertisers Casting Service
AC(S)......... Advisory Committee, Statistics [*British*]
ACS........... Aerodrome Control Service
ACS........... Affiliated Computer Systems [*Telecommunications*] [*Later, MPEC Co.*] (TSSD)
ACS........... Affinely Connected Space
ACS........... Aft Crew Station [*NASA*] (MCD)
ACS........... Age Concern Scotland [*An association*] (EAIO)
ACS........... Agena Control System [*NASA*]
ACS........... Agricultural Cooperative Service [*Washington, DC*] [*Department of Agriculture*] (GRD)
ACS........... Air Capable Ship (MCD)
ACS........... Air Central, Inc. [*Harlinger, TX*] [*FAA designator*] (FAAC)
ACS........... Air Commando Squadron (CINC)
ACS........... Air Conditioning System
ACS........... Air Force Communications Service, Scott AFB, IL [*OCLC symbol*] (OCLC)
ACS........... Aircraft Carrier Squadron [*British military*] (DMA)
ACS........... Aircraft Communications System
ACS........... Aircraft Control and Surveillance [*Air Force*]
ACS........... Aircraft Control System (MUGU)
A/CS......... Aircraft Security Vessel
ACS........... Airfield Construction Squadron [*Australia*]
ACS........... Airline Charter Service

ACS........... Airways Communication Station (NATG)
ACS........... Alarm and Control System [*Telecommunications*] (TEL)
ACS........... Alaska Conservation Society (EA)
ACS........... Alaskan Communications System [*Air Force*]
A-CS......... Alignment Countdown Set [*Aerospace*] (AAG)
ACS........... Allied Chiefs of Staff [*World War II*]
ACS........... Alternate Core Spray [*Nuclear energy*] (NRCH)
ACS........... Alternating Current, Synchronous
ACS........... Alternating Current Synthesizer [*Exxon Corp.*]
ACS........... Altitude Control System
ACS........... American Camellia Society (EA)
ACS........... American Canal Society (EA)
ACS........... American Cancer Society (EA)
ACS........... American Capital Convertible Securities, Inc. [*NYSE symbol*] (SPSG)
ACS........... American Carbon Society (EA)
ACS........... American Carnation Society [*Defunct*] (EA)
ACS........... American Carousel Society (EA)
ACS........... American Celiac Society [*Later, ACS/DSC*] (EA)
ACS........... American Ceramic Society (EA)
ACS........... American Cetacean Society (EA)
ACS........... American Cheese Society (EA)
ACS........... American Chemical Society (EA)
ACS........... American Cockatiel Society (EA)
ACS........... American College of Surgeons (EA)
ACS........... American Colonization Society
ACS........... American Committee of Slavists (EA)
ACS........... American Communication Services [*Evanston, IL*] [*Telecommunications*] (TSSD)
ACS........... American Community Schools [*In foreign countries*]
ACS........... American Conifer Society (EA)
ACS........... American Contemplative Society (EA)
ACS........... American Copyright Society (EA)
ACS........... American Cryonics Society (EA)
ACS........... American Cultural Society [*Defunct*]
ACS........... Americans for Common Sense [*Defunct*] (EA)
ACS........... Analog Computer System
ACS........... Analysis Computer System
ACS........... Analysis of Coping Style [*Test*]
ACS........... Anglo-Chilean Society (EAIO)
ACS........... Anglo-Continental Society [*British*]
ACS........... Anisotropically Conductive Silicone [*Rubber*] [*Robotics*]
ACS........... Annealed Copper-Covered Steel
ACS........... Anodal Closing Sound [*Physiology*]
ACS........... Anterior Convex Side
ACS........... Anti-Communist Society [*Belize*] (PD)
ACS........... Antireticular Cytotoxic Serum
ACS........... Aperture Current Setting [*In Coulter counter*] [*Microbiology*]
ACS........... Apollo Command [*or Communications*] System [*NASA*]
ACS........... Applied Computer Solution
ACS........... Approximate Cubic Search [*Mathematics*]
A & CS...... Area and Culture Studies [*Tokyo*] [*A publication*]
ACS........... Armament Control System [*Air Force*]
ACS........... Armored Crew Seat
ACS........... Army Calibration System
ACS........... Army Commanding Service
ACS........... Army Communicative Systems [*Provisional*] (RDA)
ACS........... Army Community Service
ACS........... ARPA Calibration Satellite (MCD)
ACS........... Art Center School
ACS........... Artillery Computer System
ACS........... Asbestos Cement Sheet (ADA)
ACS........... Assembly Control System [*IBM Corp.*] (BUR)
ACS........... Asset Control System [*or Subsystem*] [*Army*] (AABC)
ACS........... Assistant Chief of Staff
AC of S...... Assistant Chief of Staff
ACS........... Assistant Chief Statistician
ACS........... Assistant Chief of Supplies [*British military*] (DMA)
ACS........... Associate in Commercial Science
ACS........... Association for Canadian Studies [*See also AEC*]
ACS........... Association Canadienne de Semiotique [*Canadian Semiotic Association - CSA*]
ACS........... Association Canadienne des Slavistes [*Canadian Association of Slavists - CAS*]
ACS........... Association of Caribbean Studies (EA)
ACS........... Association of Certified Servers (EA)
ACS........... Association for Christian Schools (EA)
ACS........... Association of Clinical Scientists (EA)
ACS........... Association of Contemplative Sisters (EA)
ACS........... Association of Council Secretaries [*Later, NAES*] (EA)
ACS........... Association of Cricket Statisticians (EAIO)
ACS........... Astro Communications System [*NASA*] (KSC)
ACS........... Asynchronous Communications Server [*Data processing*] (IT)
AC & S...... Atlantic City & Shore Railroad
ACS........... Atmosphere Climate Study [*National Science Foundation*] (MSC)
ACS........... Atmosphere Control System [*NASA*] (KSC)
ACS........... Attack Center Switchboard
ACS........... Attitude Command System (IEEE)
ACS........... Attitude Control and Stabilization [*NASA*] (KSC)
ACS........... Attitude Control System [*or Subsystem*] [*Aerospace*]

ACS........... Audio Communications System
ACS........... Australia Container Service (DS)
ACS........... Australian Card Service
ACS........... Australian Computer Society
ACS........... Australian Construction Services
ACS........... Australian Customs Service
ACS........... Autograph Card Signed [*Manuscript descriptions*]
ACS........... Automated Circulation System [*Data processing*]
ACS........... Automated Commercial System [*US Customs Service computerized system*]
ACS........... Automated Communications Set (BUR)
ACS........... Automatic Cartographic System
ACS........... Automatic Checkout System [*NASA*]
ACS........... Automatic Control System
ACS........... Automatic Counter System
ACS........... Automation Composition System (MCD)
ACS........... Auxiliary Cooling System [*Nuclear energy*] (NRCH)
ACS........... Auxiliary Core Storage [*Data processing*] (BUR)
ACS........... Azimuth Control System
ACS........... Civil Aviation Security Service [*FAA*] (FAAC)
ACS........... J. C. Sproule & Associates Ltd., Calgary, Alberta [*Library symbol*] [*National Library of Canada*] (NLC)
ACS2........ Las Acacias [*Argentina*] [*Geomagnetic observatory code*]
AC2S........ Army Command and Control System (MCD)
ACSA........ Acoustical Society of America
ACSA........ Aero Club of South Australia
ACSA........ Allied Communications Security Agency [*Brussels, Belgium*] [*NATO*] (AABC)
ACSA........ Allied Communications Support Area
ACSA........ American Center for Students and Artists (EA)
ACSA........ American Cormo Sheep Association (EA)
ACSA........ American Cotton Shippers Association (EA)
ACSA........ American Council of Spotted Asses (EA)
ACSA........ Americans Concerned about Southern Africa (EA)
ACSA........ Aqua-Cat Catamaran Sailing Association (EA)
ACSA........ Association of Cambodian Survivors of America (EA)
ACSA........ Association Canadienne de Sociologie et d'Anthropologie [*Canadian Sociology and Anthropology Association - CSAA*]
ACSA........ Association Canadienne de Softball Amateur [*Canadian Association of Amateur Softball*]
ACSA........ Association of Collegiate Schools of Architecture (EA)
ACSA........ Australian Collieries Staff Association
ACSA........ Southern Alberta Institute of Technology, Calgary, Alberta [*Library symbol*] [*National Library of Canada*] (NLC)
ACSAA...... Alberta College of Art, Calgary, Alberta [*Library symbol*] [*National Library of Canada*] (NLC)
ACSAA...... American Committee for South Asian Art [*Defunct*] (EA)
ACSAC...... Assistant Chief of Staff for Automation and Communications [*Military*] (AABC)
ACSAD...... Arab Center for the Study of Arid Zones and Dry Lands [*of the League of Arab States*] [*Damascus, Syria*] [*Research center*] (IRC)
AC/SAF..... Assistant Chief of Staff, Air Force
ACSALF.... Association Canadienne des Sociologues et Anthropologues de Langue Francaise [*Canadian Association of French-Language Sociologists and Anthropologists*]
ACSANZ... Association for Canadian Studies in Australia and New Zealand
ACSAP...... Automated Cross-Section Analysis Program [*Data processing*]
ACSAS...... Advanced Conformal Submarine Acoustic Sensor
ACSB........ Americans for a Common Sense Budget [*Inactive*] (EA)
ACSB........ Amplitude Companded Single Sideband [*Electronics*]
ACSB........ Apollo Crew Systems Branch [*NASA*] (KSC)
ACSB........ Appraisal. Children's Science Books [*A publication*]
ACSBA...... American Ceramic Society. Bulletin [*A publication*]
ACSC........ Accrediting Commission for Specialized Colleges (EA)
ACSC........ ACS Industries, Inc. [*NASDAQ symbol*] (NQ)
ACSC........ Air Carrier Service Corporation
ACSC........ Air Command and Staff College [*Maxwell AFB, AL*] [*Air Force*] (MCD)
AC & SC.... Air Command and Staff College [*Maxwell AFB, AL*] [*Air Force*]
ACSC........ American Council on Schools and Colleges (EA)
ACSC........ AMTRAK Commuter Services Corporation [*Later, CSC*]
ACSC........ Applied Communications Systems Center [*AT & T*]
ACSC........ Armaments Cooperation Steering Committee
ACSC........ Army Computer Systems Command [*Also, CSC*]
ACSC........ Association of Casualty and Surety Companies [*Later, AIA*] (EA)
ACSC........ Atlanta Cancer Surveillance Center [*Emory University*] [*Research center*] (RCD)
ACSC2...... Automated Contingency Support Capability (AFM)
ACSC........ Technical Library, Shell Canada Resources Ltd., Calgary, Alberta [*Library symbol*] [*National Library of Canada*] (NLC)
ACSCC...... Australian Consumer Sales and Credit Law Cases [*A publication*]
ACSCCIM ... Assistant Chief of Staff for Command and Control Information Management
ACSC-E..... Assistant Chief of Staff for Communications - Electronics [*Army*] (AABC)

ACSCI .... Association for Computer-Based Systems for Career Information (OICC)
Ac Sc Kansas City Tr ... Academy of Science of Kansas City. Transactions [*A publication*]
ACSCL ...... Calgary Research Centre Library, Shell Canada Ltd., Alberta [*Library symbol*] [*National Library of Canada*] (NLC)
ACSCOT ..... American College of Surgeons Committee on Trauma
Ac Sc (Paris) C R ... Academie des Sciences (Paris). Comptes Rendus [*A publication*]
Ac Sc Sioux City Pr ... Academy of Science and Letters of Sioux City, Iowa. Proceedings [*A publication*]
Ac Sc St L Tr ... Academy of Science of St. Louis. Transactions [*A publication*]
ACSD .... Academic Computer Services Division [*Milwaukee School of Engineering*] [*Research center*] (RCD)
ACSD .... Army Communications - Service Division
ACSD .... Australian Confederation of Sports for the Disabled
ACSD .... Automatic Color-Scanned Device (MCD)
ACSDI .... Sulphur Development Institute of Canada, Calgary, Alberta [*Library symbol*] [*National Library of Canada*] (NLC)
ACS Div Environ Chem Prepr ... American Chemical Society. Division of Environmental Chemistry. Preprints [*A publication*]
ACS Div Fuel Chem Prepr ... American Chemical Society. Division of Fuel Chemistry. Preprints [*A publication*]
ACS Div Pet Chem Prepr ... American Chemical Society. Division of Petroleum Chemistry. Preprints [*A publication*]
ACSDO ..... Air Carrier Safety District Office
ACS/DSC ... American Celiac Society/Dietary Support Coalition (EA)
ACSE .... ACS Enterprises, Inc. [*NASDAQ symbol*] (NQ)
ACSEA ...... Air Command, Southeast Asia
ACSEA ...... Allied Command Southeast Asia [*World War II*]
ACSEB ...... Aviation Clothing and Survival Equipment Bulletin (MCD)
ACSED ...... Automated Computer Science Education
ACSES .... Automated Computer Science Education System
ACSET ...... Advisory Committee on the Supply and Education of Teachers [*British*]
ACSF .... Artificial Cerebrospinal Fluid [*Medicine*]
ACSF .... Association of French Host Centers [*Paris*] [*Information service or system*] (IID)
ACSF .... Attack Carrier Striking Force
ACSFOR ... Assistant Chief of Staff for Force Development [*Army*]
AC-SG ...... Alternating Current Signal Generator
ACSG .... Area Coordination Subgroup [*Air Force*] (AFM)
ACSGp .... Area Coordination Subgroup [*Air Force*] (AFM)
ACSGRP ..... Area Coordination Subgroup [*Air Force*]
ACSH .... American Council on Science and Health (EA)
ACSHRD .... Atlantic Canada Society for Human Resource Development
ACSI .... American Communication Services, Incorporated [*Evanston, IL*] (TSSD)
ACSI .... American Community Services [*NASDAQ symbol*] (NQ)
ACSI .... Assistant Chief of Staff for Intelligence [*Washington, DC*] [*Army*]
ACSI .... Association Canadienne des Sciences de l'Information [*Canadian Association for Information Science*]
ACSI .... Association of Christian Schools International (EA)
ACSI .... Automotive Cooling Systems Institute (EA)
ACSICR ..... Association Canadienne des Societes d'Investissement en Capital de Risque
ACSIEC ..... [*The*] Suicide Information and Education Centre, Calgary, Alberta [*Library symbol*] [*National Library of Canada*] (NLC)
ACSIF .... Alaska Communication System Industrial Fund (AFM)
ACSIG .... Alignment Countdown Set Inertial Guidance [*Aerospace*] (AAG)
ACSIL ...... Admiralty Centre for Scientific Information and Liaison [*British*]
ACSIM ...... Assistant Chief of Staff for Information Management [*Army*]
Acsius .... Accursius [*Deceased, 1263*] [*Authority cited in pre-1607 legal work*] (DSA)
ACSJ .... Academic Committee on Soviet Jewry (EA)
AC & SJ .... Australian Conveyancer and Solicitors' Journal [*A publication*] (APTA)
ACSJC .... Australian Catholic Social Justice Council
ACSL .... Advanced Continuous Simulation Language [*Pronounced "axle"*] [*Data processing*] (CSR)
ACSL .... Advanced Continuous System Language (MCD)
ACSL .... American Computer Science League (EA)
ACSL .... Australian Company Secretary's Letter [*A publication*]
ACSL .... Standing Lenticular Altocumulus [*Meteorology*]
AcSM .... Academy Sergeant-Major [*British military*] (DMA)
ACSM .... Acoustic Warfare Support Measures (NVT)
ACSM .... Advanced Conventional Standoff Missile (MCD)
ACSM .... American College of Sports Medicine (EA)
ACSM .... American Congress on Surveying and Mapping (EA)
ACSM .... Assemblies, Components, Spare Parts, and Materials (NATG)
ACSM .... Associate of the Camborne School of Mines [*British*]
ACSM .... Stockmen's Memorial Foundation, Calgary, Alberta [*Library symbol*] [*National Library of Canada*] (NLC)
ACSMA ..... American Cloak and Suit Manufacturers Association (EA)
ACSMA6 ... Archivio Stomatologico [*A publication*]

ACSMH ...... Association of Clerks and Stewards in Mental Hospitals [*A union*] [*British*]
ACS Monogr ... ACS [*American Chemical Society*] Monograph [*A publication*]
ACSN .... Advanced Change Study Notice [*Aerospace*]
ACSN .... Appalachian Community Service Network [*Cable-television system*]
ACSN .... Association of Collegiate Schools of Nursing [*Later, NLN*]
ACS Natl Meet Abstr Pap ... American Chemical Society. National Meeting. Abstracts of Papers [*A publication*]
ACS-O ...... Access Opening (AAG)
ACSO .... Aircraft Capable of Satellite Operations
ACSO .... SUNCOR Inc., Calgary, Alberta [*Library symbol*] [*National Library of Canada*] (NLC)
ACSOC ...... Acoustical Society of America
ACSP .... Advanced Control Signal Processor [*For spacecraft*]
ACSP .... Advisory Council on Scientific Policy
ACSP .... Aircraft Cross-Servicing Program [*Military*]
ACSP .... Association Canadienne de Science Politique [*Canadian Political Science Association - CPSA*]
ACSP .... Association of Collegiate Schools of Planning (EA)
ACSP .... Institute of Sedimentary and Petroleum Geology, Calgary, Alberta [*Library symbol*] [*National Library of Canada*] (NLC)
ACSPCH ... Australia. Commonwealth Scientific and Industrial Research Organisation. Forest Products Laboratory. Division of Applied Chemistry. Technological Paper [*A publication*]
ACSPD ...... Aciers Speciaux [*A publication*]
ACSPFT .... Asian Committee for Standarization of Physical Fitness Tests [*Obu-Shi, Japan*] (EAIO)
ACSR .... Advanced Combat Surveillance RADAR
ACSR .... Aluminum Cable Steel Reinforced
ACSR .... Aluminum Conductor Steel Reinforced
ACSR .... American Catholic Sociological Review [*A publication*]
ACSR .... Arizona Cactus and Succulent Research (EA)
ACSR .... Association Canadienne des Sciences Regionales [*Canadian Regional Science Association - CRSA*]
ACSR .... Australian Corporations and Securities Reports [*A publication*]
ACSRC ...... Assistant Chief of Staff for Reserve Components [*Army*]
A/CS REC ... Accounts Receivable [*Accounting*]
ACSRNAS ... Armoured Car Section, Royal Naval Air Service [*British military*] (DMA)
ACSS .... Air Combat and Surveillance System (MCD)
ACSS .... Air Command and Staff School [*Air Force*]
AC & SS ..... Air Command and Staff School [*Air Force*]
ACSS .... American Catholic Sociological Society [*Later, ASR*] (EA)
ACSS .... American Cheviot Sheep Society (EA)
ACSS .... Analog Computer Subsystem
ACSS .... Analytical Chemistry Symposia Series [*Elsevier Book Series*] [*A publication*]
ACSS .... Army Chief of Support Services
ACSS .... Associated Carters Society of Scotland [*A union*]
ACSS .... Association Canadienne des Sciences Sportives [*Canadian Association of Sports Sciences*]
ACSS .... Association of Colleges and Secondary Schools [*Later, SACS*] (EA)
ACSS .... Augmented Contact Support Set [*TOW*]
ACSS .... Automated Contingency Support System
ACSS .... Automated Contract Specification System
ACS/S & A ... Assistant Chief of Staff, Studies and Analysis [*Air Force*] (MCD)
ACSSAVO ... Association of Chief State School Audio-Visual Officers [*Defunct*] (EA)
ACSSBP .... Annales de Chirurgie Thoracique et Cardio-Vasculaire [*A publication*]
ACSSCQ .... AIChE [*American Institute of Chemical Engineers*] Symposium Series [*A publication*]
ACSSDR .... Analytical Chemistry Symposia Series [*A publication*]
ACS-SIA ... Australian Computer Society - Software Industries Association
ACSSN ...... Association of Colleges and Secondary Schools for Negroes [*Later, ACSS*]
ACSSR ...... Ammunition Consolidated Stock Status Report
ACS Symp S ... ACS [*American Chemical Society*] Symposium Series [*A publication*]
ACS Symp Ser ... ACS [*American Chemical Society*] Symposium Series [*A publication*]
ACST .... Access Time
ACST .... Acoustic (MSA)
ACST .... Advisory Committee on the Application of Science and Technology to Development [*Also, ACAST, ACASTD*] [*United Nations*]
ACST .... Army Clerical Speed Test
ACSTA ...... American Center for Stanislavski Theatre Art (EA)
ACSTA ...... Society for Treatment of Autism, Calgary, Alberta [*Library symbol*] [*National Library of Canada*] (NLC)
ACSTBS .... Australia. Commonwealth Scientific and Industrial Research Organisation. Soil Mechanics Section. Technical Memorandum [*A publication*]
ACSTCW .. Association of Civil Service Temporary Clerks and Writers [*A union*] [*British*]
ACSTDU ... Advances in Cereal Science and Technology [*A publication*]

ACSTFA.... Advisory Committee on Science and Technology and Foreign Affairs [*Terminated, 1975*] [*Department of State*] (EGAO)
ACSTH...... Artistic Crafts Series of Technical Handbooks [*A publication*]
ACSTI ...... Advisory Committee for Scientific and Technical Information [*British*]
ACSTIS..... Advanced Circular Scan Thermal Imaging System (MCD)
ACSTN...... ACST [*Alaska Council on Science and Technology*] Notes [*A publication*]
ACSTT ...... Advisory Committee of the Supply and Training of Teachers [*British*]
ACSU .... Army Civil Services' Union [*Singapore*]
ACSU .... Atti. Colloquio Slavistico di Uppsala [*A publication*]
ACSUB..... Annals of Clinical Research. Supplement [*A publication*]
ACSUS ...... Association for Canadian Studies in the United States (EA)
ACSVAX ... Anales. Casa de Salud Valdecilla (Santander) [*A publication*]
ACSW........ Academy of Certified Social Workers
ACSW........ Advanced Conventional Standoff Weapon
ACSW........ Advanced Crew-Served Weapon [*Army*] (INF)
ACSW........ Advisory Council on the Status of Women [*Canada*]
ACSWC.... American Committee of the Slovak World Congress (EA)
ACSWC.... American Council of the Slovak World Congress (EA)
ACSWC.... Australian Catholic Social Welfare Commission
ACSYNT ... Aircraft Synthesis [*Data processing*]
ACSYS ...... Accounting Computer System [*Burroughs Corp.*]
ACSZJ ...... American Committee for Shaare Zedek in Jerusalem (EA)
ACT .... Accountant [*A publication*]
ACT .... Accounting Control Table (CMD)
ACT .... Accumulation Time
ACT .... Accumulator, Temporary
ACT .... Acetate Cloth Tape
ACT .... Achievement through Counselling and Treatment
ACT .... Acoustic Charge Transport [*Data processing*]
ACT .... Acoustical Tile [*Technical drawings*]
ACT .... Acquisition, Control of Test [*Units*] (NASA)
ACT .... Act in Crisis Today [*Fund sponsored by the Lutheran Church in America*]
ACT .... Acting
ACT .... Actinidin
act.............. Actinomycin [*Also, A*] [*Generic form*] [*Antibiotic compounds*]
ACT .... Action [*NATO*]
Act.............. Action [*Tunis*] [*A publication*]
ACT .... Action for Children in Trouble (EA)
ACT .... Action for Children's Television (EA)
ACT .... Action by Christians Against Torture (EAIO)
ACT .... Action Library, Washington, DC [*OCLC symbol*] (OCLC)
ACT .... Activated Clotting [*or Coagulation*] Time [*Medicine*]
ACT .... Activation (NVT)
ACT .... Active (AFM)
ACT .... Active Cleaning Technique [*Optical surface*]
ACT .... Active Control Technique [*or Technology*]
ACT .... Activity (MSA)
ACT .... Activity Completion Technique [*Personality development test*] [*Psychology*]
Act.............. Acton's Prize Cases, Privy Council [*A publication*] (DLA)
ACT .... Actor's Conservatory Theater
ACT .... Actual (KSC)
ACT .... Actuarial Data Base [*I. P. Sharp Associates*] [*Database*]
ACT .... Actuary [*Insurance*]
ACT .... Actuate (KSC)
ACT .... Adaptive Computer Technologies [*San Jose, CA*]
ACT .... Adaptive Control of Thought [*Psychology*]
ACT .... Adjuvant Chemotherapy [*Oncology*]
ACT .... Administrative Clerical and Technical Programs [*Department of Labor*]
ACT .... Advance Corporation Tax [*British*]
ACT .... Advanced Capability Tanker (MCD)
ACT .... Advanced Career Training
ACT .... Advanced Chassis Technology [*Automotive engineering*]
ACT .... Advanced Color Technology, Inc. [*Chelmsford, MA*] [*Printer manufacturer*]
ACT .... Advanced Communications Technology [*Tymshare, Inc.*]
ACT .... Advanced Computer Techniques (MCD)
ACT .... Advanced Concept Tire [*Firestone Tire & Rubber Co.*]
ACT .... Advanced Concept Train [*Aerospace*]
ACT .... Advanced Concepts Team [*Army*] (RDA)
ACT .... Advanced Concepts Test (MCD)
ACT .... Advanced Conversion Technology (MCD)
ACT .... Advanced Core Test [*Nuclear energy*]
ACT .... Advanced Coronary Treatment Foundation
ACT .... Advertised Computer Technologies [*Data Courier, Inc.*] [*Information service or system*] [*Defunct*] (IID)
ACT .... Advertising/Communications Times [*A publication*]
ACT .... Advisory Council on Technology [*British*]
ACT .... Agricultural Central Trading [*British*]
ACT .... Air-Charged Temperature [*Automotive engineering*]
ACT .... Air Combat Tactics (AFM)
ACT .... Air Combat Training (FAAC)
A Ct .... Air Commandant [*British*] (DMA)
ACT .... Air Control Team [*Air Force*]
ACT .... Air Council for Training [*British*] (DAS)
ACT .... Air-Cushion Trailer [*or Transporter*]

ACT .... Aircraft Commander Time
ACT .... Aircrew Classification Test (AFM)
ACT .... Airport Control Tower
ACT .... Algebraic Compiler and Translator [*Data processing*]
ACT .... Alliance for Cannabis Therapeutics (EA)
ACT .... Allied Chemical Technology [*Trademark*]
ACT .... Alpha Counter Tube
ACT .... Alternaria citri (Tangerine race) [*A toxin-producing fungus*]
ACT .... Alumina Ceramic Test
ACT .... American Association of Agricultural Communicators of Tomorrow (EA)
ACT .... American Century Corp. [*Formerly, American Century Trust SBI*] [*NYSE symbol*] (SPSG)
ACT .... American College Testing Program (EA)
ACT .... American College of Theriogenologists (EA)
ACT .... American College of Toxicology (EA)
ACT .... American Conference of Therapeutic Selfhelp/Selfhealth Social Action Clubs (EA)
ACT .... American Conservative Trust (EA)
ACT .... American Conservatory Theatre
ACT .... American Council of Taxpayers [*Formerly, COST*] (EA)
ACT .... American Council on Transplantation (EA)
ACT .... American Council for Turfgrass (EA)
ACT .... Americans Combatting Terrorism [*Commercial firm*] (EA)
ACT .... Americans for Constitutional Training (EA)
ACT .... Analog Control Technology [*Data processing*]
ACT .... Anglo-Canadian Telephone Co. [*Toronto Stock Exchange symbol*]
ACT .... Annual Change Traffic
ACT .... Antenna Cross Talk
ACT .... Anticar Theft [*Campaign or Committee*]
ACT .... Antichymotrypsin [*Biochemistry*]
ACT .... Anticoagulant Therapy [*Medicine*]
ACT .... Anticompromise Technique
ACT .... Apparatus Carrier Telephone [*British military*] (DMA)
ACT .... Applied Computer Techniques (TEL)
ACT .... Area Correlation Tracker [*Air Force*]
ACT .... Armored Cavalry Trainer [*Army*] (AABC)
ACT .... Army Chemical Typewriter [*Data processing*]
ACT .... Army Communicative Technology (RDA)
ACT .... Artists in Christian Testimony (EA)
ACT .... Asset Control Techniques [*TRW, Inc.*]
ACT .... Assignment Control Trainee (MCD)
AC of T ..... Assistant Chief of Transportation [*Army*]
ACT .... Associate of the College of Technology [*British*]
ACT .... Associated Container Transportation
ACT .... Association of Career Teachers [*British*]
ACT .... Association of Catholic Teachers [*Defunct*]
ACT .... Association of Charter Trustees [*British*]
ACT .... Association of Christian Teachers [*British*] (EAIO)
ACT .... Association of Civilian Technicians (EA)
ACT .... Association of Classroom Teachers [*Defunct*]
ACT .... Association of Communications Technicians (EA)
ACT .... Association for Commuter Transportation (EA)
ACT .... Association for Composite Tanks (EA)
ACT .... Association of Corporate Treasurers (EAIO)
ACT .... Association of Cycle Traders (EAIO)
ACT .... Association of Cytogenetic Technologists (EA)
ACT .... Assure Competitive Transportation [*Truckers' lobby*]
ACT .... At the Center of Things [*Slang*]
ACT .... Atlantic Canada Teacher [*A publication*]
ACT .... Attention Control Training
ACT .... Augmented Catalytic Thruster (MCD)
ACT .... Australian Capital Territory (PPW)
ACT .... Auto-Lock Channel Tuning [*Television technology*]
ACT .... Automated Contingency Translator [*Data processing*]
ACT .... Automated Control and Distribution of Trainees [*Army*] (MCD)
ACT .... Automatic Cable Tester
ACT .... Automatic Cannon Technology (MCD)
ACT .... Automatic Capacitor Tester
ACT .... Automatic Channel and Time [*Toshiba Corp.*] [*Programmable television set*]
ACT .... Automatic Checkout Technician [*or Technique*] (MCD)
ACT .... Automatic Circuit Tester
ACT .... Automatic Code Translation [*Data processing*]
ACT .... Automatic Component Tester
ACT .... Automatically Controlled Transportation [*Airport passenger shuttle*] [*Ford Motor Co.*]
ACT .... Aviation Classification Test
ACT .... Azimuth Control Torquer
ACT .... Treehouse Books, Calgary, Alberta [*Library symbol*] [*National Library of Canada*] (NLC)
ACT .... Waco [*Texas*] [*Airport symbol*] (OAG)
a cta.......... A Cuenta [*On Account*] [*Spanish*] [*Banking, investment*]
Acta.......... Acta Academiae Universalis Jurisprudentiae Comparativae [*Berlin, Germany*] [*A publication*] (DLA)
Acta.......... Acta Musicologica [*A publication*]
ACTA .... Activate Test Article [*Military*] (NASA)
ACTA .... Active Test Article (MCD)
ACTA .... Advanced Cargo/Tanker Aircraft

ACTA .... Advanced Combat Training Academy [*Army*]　(AABC)
ACTA .... Air Coach Transport Association
ACTA .... Alliance of Canadian Travel Associations
ACTA .... Alternative Carrier Telecommunications Association　(EA)
ACTA .... American Cardiology Technologists Association [*Later, NSCPT*]　(EA)
ACTA .... American Cement Trade Alliance [*Later, ACA*]　(EA)
ACTA .... American Community Theatre Association　(EA)
ACTA .... American Corrective Therapy Association [*Later, AKA*]　(EA)
ACTA .... Association Canadienne pour la Technologie des Animaux de Laboratoire [*Canadian Association for Laboratory Animals Technology*]
ACTA .... Association Canadienne de Technologie Avancee [*Canadian Association of Advanced Technology*]
ACTA .... Association Canadienne de Therapie Animale [*Canadian Animal Therapy Association*]
ACTA .... Association of Chart and Technical Analysts [*British*]
ACTA .... Australian Capital Territory Administration
ACTA .... Australian Council on Tertiary Awards
ACTA .... Automated Calibration Temperature Activated [*Electronic balance*]
ACTA .... Automatic Centrifugal Tinning Apparatus
ACTA .... Automatic Computerized Transverse Axial [*Computer X-ray system*]
Acta A .... Acta Archaeologica [*A publication*]
ActaA .... Acta Asiatica [*A publication*]
Acta Acad Aboensis ... Acta Academiae Aboensis [*A publication*]
Acta Acad Abo Ser B ... Acta Academiae Aboensis. Series B. Mathematica et Physica [*A publication*]
Acta Acad Abo Ser B Math Phys Mat Naturvetensk Tek ... Acta Academiae Aboensis. Series B. Mathematica et Physica. Matematik Naturvetenskaper Teknik [*A publication*]
Acta Acad Int Hist Med ... Acta Academiae Internationalis Historiae Medicinae [*A publication*]
Acta Acad Med Sichuan ... Acta Academiae Medicinae Sichuan [*A publication*]
Acta Acad Paedagog Civitate Pecs Ser 6 Math-Phys-Chem-Tech ... Acta Academiae Paedagogicae in Civitate Pecs. Seria 6. Mathematica-Physica-Chemica-Technica [*A publication*]
Acta Acad Polytech Pollack Mihaly Pecs ... Acta Academiae Polytechnicae Pollack Mihaly Pecs [*A publication*]
Acta Acad Reeks A ... Acta Academica. Reeks A [*A publication*]
Acta Acad Reeks B ... Acta Academica. Reeks B [*A publication*]
Acta Acad Regiae Sci Ups ... Acta Academiae Regiae Scientiarum Upsaliensis [*A publication*]
Acta Acad Sci Pol ... Acta Academiae Scientiarum Polonae [*A publication*]
Acta Acust ... Acta Acustica [*A publication*]
Acta Adriat ... Acta Adriatica [*A publication*]
Acta Agrar Silvestria ... Acta Agraria et Silvestria [*A publication*]
Acta Agrar Silvestria Ser Agrar ... Acta Agraria et Silvestria. Series Agraria [*A publication*]
Acta Agrar Silvestria Ser Silvestris ... Acta Agraria et Silvestria. Series Silvestris [*A publication*]
Acta Agrar Silvestria Ser Zootech ... Acta Agraria et Silvestria. Series Zootechnia [*A publication*]
Acta Agrar Silv Ser Agrar ... Acta Agraria et Silvestria. Series Agraria [*A publication*]
Acta Agrar Silv Ser Silv ... Acta Agraria et Silvestria. Series Silvestris [*A publication*]
Acta Agric Scand ... Acta Agriculturae Scandinavica [*A publication*]
Acta Agric Scand Suppl ... Acta Agriculturae Scandinavica. Supplementum [*A publication*]
Acta Agric Sin ... Acta Agriculturae Sinica [*A publication*]
Acta Agric Suec ... Acta Agriculturae Suecana [*A publication*]
Acta Agric Suecana ... Acta Agriculturae Suecana [*A publication*]
Acta Agric Univ Pekinensis ... Acta Agriculturae Universitatis Pekinensis [*A publication*]
Acta Agrobot ... Acta Agrobotanica [*A publication*]
Acta Agron ... Acta Agronomica [*A publication*]
Acta Agron Acad Sci Hung ... Acta Agronomica. Academiae Scientiarum Hungaricae [*Budapest*] [*A publication*]
Acta Agron (Budapest) ... Acta Agronomica. Academiae Scientiarum Hungaricae [*A publication*]
Acta Agron Hung ... Acta Agronomica. Academiae Scientiarum Hungaricae [*Budapest*] [*A publication*]
Acta Agron (Palmira) ... Acta Agronomica (Palmira) [*A publication*]
Acta Agr Scand ... Acta Agriculturae Scandinavica [*A publication*]
Acta Agr Silv Ser Roln ... Acta Agraria et Silvestria. Series Rolnictwo [*A publication*]
Acta Agr Sinica ... Acta Agriculturae Sinica [*A publication*]
Acta Albert ... Acta Albertina [*A publication*]
Acta Aliment Acad Sci Hung ... Acta Alimentaria. Academiae Scientiarum Hungaricae [*A publication*]
Acta Aliment Pol ... Acta Alimentaria Polonica [*A publication*]
Acta Allergol ... Acta Allergologica [*A publication*]
Acta Allergol Suppl ... Acta Allergologica. Supplementum [*A publication*]
Acta Am ... Acta Americana [*A publication*]
Acta Anaesth ... Acta Anaesthesiologica [*A publication*]
Acta Anaesthesiol ... Acta Anaesthesiologica [*A publication*]
Acta Anaesthesiol Belg ... Acta Anaesthesiologica Belgica [*A publication*]
Acta Anaesthesiol Ital ... Acta Anaesthesiologica Italica [*A publication*]

Acta Anaesthesiol (Padova) ... Acta Anaesthesiologica (Padova) [*A publication*]
Acta Anaesthesiol Scand ... Acta Anaesthesiologica Scandinavica [*A publication*]
Acta Anaesthesiol Scand Suppl ... Acta Anaesthesiologica Scandinavica. Supplementum [*A publication*]
Acta Anaesthes Scand ... Acta Anaesthesiologica Scandinavica [*A publication*]
Acta Anaesth Scandinav ... Acta Anaesthesiologica Scandinavica [*A publication*]
Acta Anat... Acta Anatomica [*A publication*]
Acta Anat (Basel) ... Acta Anatomica (Basel) [*A publication*]
Acta Anat Nippon ... Acta Anatomica Nipponica [*A publication*]
Acta Anat Sin ... Acta Anatomica Sinica [*A publication*]
Acta Anat Suppl ... Acta Anatomica. Supplementum [*A publication*]
Acta Ant H ... Acta Antiqua. Academiae Scientiarum Hungaricae [*A publication*]
Acta Anthr Biol ... Acta Anthropobiologica [*A publication*]
Acta Anthr (Mex) ... Acta Anthropologica (Mexico) [*A publication*]
Acta Anthropogen ... Acta Anthropogenetica [*A publication*]
Acta Anthropogenet ... Acta Anthropogenetica [*A publication*]
Acta Antiq Magyar Tud Akad ... Acta Antiqua. Magyar Tudomanyos Akademia [*A publication*]
Acta Arachnol ... Acta Arachnologica [*A publication*]
Acta Arch... Acta Archaeologica [*A publication*]
Acta Archaeol Acad Sci Hung ... Acta Archaeologica. Academiae Scientiarum Hungaricae [*A publication*]
Acta Archaeol (Budapest) ... Acta Archaeologica (Budapest) [*A publication*]
Acta Archaeol (Kobenhavn) ... Acta Archaeologica (Kobenhavn) [*A publication*]
Acta Arch Carp ... Acta Archaeologica Carpathica [*A publication*]
Acta Arch Lund ... Acta Archaeologica Lundensia [*A publication*]
Acta Arct... Acta Arctica [*A publication*]
Acta Argent Fisiol Fisiopatol ... Acta Argentina de Fisiologia y Fisiopatologia [*A publication*]
Acta Arith ... Acta Arithmetica [*A publication*]
Acta Asiat.. Acta Asiatica [*A publication*]
Acta Astron ... Acta Astronomica [*A publication*]
Acta Astronaut ... Acta Astronautica [*A publication*]
Acta Astronom Sinica ... Acta Astronomica Sinica [*A publication*]
Acta Astron Sin ... Acta Astronomica Sinica [*A publication*]
Acta Astron Sinica ... Acta Astronomica Sinica [*People's Republic of China*] [*A publication*]
Acta Astrophys Sinica ... Acta Astrophysica Sinica [*A publication*]
Acta Audiol Foniat Hispano-Amer ... Acta Audiologica y Foniatrica Hispano-Americana [*A publication*]
Acta Automat Sinica ... Acta Automatica Sinica [*People's Republic of China*] [*A publication*]
Acta Autom Sin ... Acta Automatica Sinica [*A publication*]
Acta Balt ... Acta Baltica [*A publication*]
Acta Belg Arte Med Pharm Mil ... Acta Belgica de Arte Medicinali et Pharmaceutica Militari [*A publication*]
Acta Biochim ... Acta Biochimica [*A publication*]
Acta Biochim Biophys ... Acta Biochimica et Biophysica [*A publication*]
Acta Biochim Biophys Acad Sci Hung ... Acta Biochimica et Biophysica. Academiae Scientiarum Hungaricae [*A publication*]
Acta Biochim Biophys Hung ... Acta Biochimica et Biophysica. Academiae Scientiarum Hungaricae [*A publication*]
Acta Biochim Biophys Sin ... Acta Biochimica et Biophysica Sinica [*A publication*]
Acta Biochim Biophys Sinica ... Acta Biochimica et Biophysica Sinica [*A publication*]
Acta Biochim Iran ... Acta Biochimica Iranica [*A publication*]
Acta Biochim Pol ... Acta Biochimica Polonica [*A publication*]
Acta Biochim Polon ... Acta Biochimica Polonica [*A publication*]
Acta Biochim Pol (Trans) ... Acta Biochimica Polonica (Translation) [*A publication*]
Acta Biochim Sin ... Acta Biochimica Sinica [*A publication*]
Acta Biol .... Acta Biologica [*A publication*]
Acta Biol Acad Sci Hung ... Acta Biologica. Academiae Scientiarum Hungaricae [*A publication*]
Acta Biol Acad Sci Hung Suppl ... Acta Biologica. Academiae Scientiarum Hungaricae. Supplementum [*A publication*]
Acta Biol (Budapest) ... Acta Biologica. Academiae Scientiarum Hungaricae (Budapest) [*A publication*]
Acta Biol Cracov Ser Bot ... Acta Biologica Cracoviensia. Series Botanica [*A publication*]
Acta Biol Cracov Ser Zool ... Acta Biologica Cracoviensia. Series Zoologia [*A publication*]
Acta Biol Debrecina ... Acta Biologica Debrecina [*A publication*]
Acta Biol Exp ... Acta Biologiae Experimentalis [*A publication*]
Acta Biol Exper Sinica ... Acta Biologiae Experimentalis Sinica [*A publication*]
Acta Biol Exp Pol Acad Sci ... Acta Biologiae Experimentalis. Polish Academy of Sciences [*A publication*]
Acta Biol Exp Sin ... Acta Biologiae Experimentalis Sinica [*A publication*]
Acta Biol Exp (Warsaw) ... Acta Biologiae Experimentalis (Warsaw) [*A publication*]
Acta Biol Hung ... Acta Biologica. Academiae Scientiarum Hungaricae [*A publication*]
Acta Biol Iugosl Ser B Mikrobiol ... Acta Biologica Iugoslavica. Serija B. Mikrobiologija [*A publication*]

Acta Biol Iugosl Ser C Iugosl Physiol Pharmacol Acta ... Acta Biologica Iugoslavica. Serija C. Iugoslavica Physiologica et Pharmacologica Acta [*A publication*]

Acta Biol Iugosl Ser D Eko ... Acta Biologica Iugoslavica. Serija D. Ekologija [*A publication*]

Acta Biol Iugosl Ser E Ichthyol ... Acta Biologica Iugoslavica. Serija E. Ichthyologia [*A publication*]

Acta Biol Iugosl Ser F ... Acta Biologica Iugoslavica. Serija F. Genetika [*A publication*]

Acta Biol Katowice ... Acta Biologica Katowice [*A publication*]

Acta Biol Latv ... Acta Biologica Latvica [*A publication*]

Acta Biol Med ... Acta Biologica et Medica [*A publication*]

Acta Biol Med (Gdansk) ... Acta Biologica et Medica (Gdansk) [*A publication*]

Acta Biol Med Ger ... Acta Biologica et Medica Germanica [*A publication*]

Acta Biol Parana ... Acta Biologica Paranaense [*A publication*]

Acta Biol (Szeged) ... Acta Biologica (Szeged) [*A publication*]

Acta Biol Venez ... Acta Biologica Venezuelica [*A publication*]

Acta Bio-Med Ateneo Parmense ... Acta Bio-Medica de l'Ateneo Parmense [*A publication*]

Acta Bioquim Clin Latinoam ... Acta Bioquimica Clinica Latinoamericana [*A publication*]

Acta Biotheor ... Acta Biotheoretica [*Leiden*] [*A publication*]

Acta Biotheor (Leiden) ... Acta Biotheoretica (Leiden) [*A publication*]

Acta Borealia A Sci ... Acta Borealia. A. Scientia [*A publication*]

Acta Bot ..... Acta Botanica [*A publication*]

Acta Bot Acad Sci Hung ... Acta Botanica. Academiae Scientiarum Hungaricae [*A publication*]

Acta Bot Barc ... Acta Botanica Barcinonensia [*A publication*]

Acta Bot (Budapest) ... Acta Botanica. Academiae Scientiarum Hungaricae (Budapest) [*A publication*]

Acta Bot Colomb ... Acta Botanica Colombiana [*A publication*]

Acta Bot Croat ... Acta Botanica Croatica [*A publication*]

Acta Bot Fenn ... Acta Botanica Fennica [*A publication*]

Acta Bot Horti Bucur ... Acta Botanica Horti Bucurestiensis [*A publication*]

Acta Bot Hung ... Acta Botanica. Academiae Scientiarum Hungaricae [*A publication*]

Acta Bot Hung ... Acta Botanica Hungarica [*A publication*]

Acta Bot Indica ... Acta Botanica Indica [*A publication*]

Acta Bot Indica (IN) ... Acta Botanica Indica (India) [*A publication*]

Acta Bot Inst Bot Univ Zagreb ... Acta Botanica Instituti Botanici. Universitatis Zagrebensis [*A publication*]

Acta Bot Isl ... Acta Botanica Islandica [*A publication*]

Acta Bot Malacitana ... Acta Botanica Malacitana [*A publication*]

Acta Bot Neerl ... Acta Botanica Neerlandica [*A publication*]

Acta Bot Neerland ... Acta Botanica Neerlandica [*A publication*]

Acta Bot Sin ... Acta Botanica Sinica [*A publication*]

Acta Bot Sinica ... Acta Botanica Sinica [*A publication*]

Acta Bot Taiwan ... Acta Botanica Taiwanica [*A publication*]

Acta Bot Venez ... Acta Botanica Venezuelica [*A publication*]

Acta Brevia Neerl Physiol Pharmacol Microbiol ... Acta Brevia Neerlandica de Physiologia, Pharmacologia, Microbiologia [*A publication*]

Acta Brev Neerl Physiol ... Acta Brevia Neerlandica de Physiologia, Pharmacologia, Microbiologia [*A publication*]

Acta Brev Sin ... Acta Brevia Sinensia [*A publication*]

ACTAC ...... Association of Community Technical Aid Centres (EAIO)

Acta Cancerol ... Acta Cancerologica [*A publication*]

Acta Cardiol (Brux) ... Acta Cardiologica (Bruxelles) [*A publication*]

Acta Cardiol Suppl ... Acta Cardiologica. Supplementum [*Bruxelles*] [*A publication*]

Acta Chem Fenn ... Acta Chemica Fennica [*Finland*] [*A publication*]

Acta Chem Mineralog Phys ... Acta Chemica, Mineralogica, et Physica [*A publication*]

Acta Chem Mineral Phys ... Acta Chemica, Mineralogica, et Physica [*A publication*]

Acta Chem Scand ... Acta Chemica Scandinavica [*A publication*]

Acta Chem Scand (B) ... Acta Chemica Scandinavica. Series B. Organic Chemistry and Biochemistry [*A publication*]

Acta Chem Scand (DK) ... Acta Chemica Scandinavica (Denmark) [*A publication*]

Acta Chem Scand Ser A ... Acta Chemica Scandinavica. Series A. Physical and Inorganic Chemistry [*A publication*]

Acta Chem Scand Ser A Phys Inorg Chem ... Acta Chemica Scandinavica. Series A. Physical and Inorganic Chemistry [*A publication*]

Acta Chem Scand Ser B ... Acta Chemica Scandinavica. Series B. Organic Chemistry and Biochemistry [*A publication*]

Acta Chem Scand Ser B Org Chem Biochem ... Acta Chemica Scandinavica. Series B. Organic Chemistry and Biochemistry [*A publication*]

Acta Chim Acad Sci Hung ... Acta Chimica. Academiae Scientiarum Hungaricae [*A publication*]

Acta Chim Hung ... Acta Chimica Hungarica [*A publication*]

Acta Chir Acad Sci Hung ... Acta Chirurgica. Academiae Scientiarum Hungaricae [*A publication*]

Acta Chir Austriaca ... Acta Chirurgica Austriaca [*A publication*]

Acta Chir Austriaca Suppl ... Acta Chirurgica Austriaca. Supplement [*A publication*]

Acta Chir Belg ... Acta Chirurgica Belgica [*A publication*]

Acta Chir Belg Suppl ... Acta Chirurgica Belgica. Supplement [*A publication*]

Acta Chir Hell ... Acta Chirurgica Hellenica [*A publication*]

Acta Chir Ital ... Acta Chirurgica Italica [*A publication*]

Acta Chir Iugosl ... Acta Chirurgica Iugoslavica [*A publication*]

Acta Chir Maxillo-Facialis ... Acta Chirurgiae Maxillo-Facialis [*A publication*]

Acta Chir Orthop Traumatol Cech ... Acta Chirurgiae, Orthopaedicae, et Traumatologiae Cechoslovaca [*A publication*]

Acta Chir Plast ... Acta Chirurgiae Plasticae [*Czechoslovakia*] [*A publication*]

Acta Chir Plast (Prague) ... Acta Chirurgiae Plasticae (Prague) [*A publication*]

Acta Chir Scand ... Acta Chirurgica Scandinavica [*A publication*]

Acta Chir Scandinav ... Acta Chirurgica Scandinavica [*A publication*]

Acta Chir Scand Suppl ... Acta Chirurgica Scandinavica. Supplementum [*A publication*]

Acta Ci Compostelana ... Acta Cientifica Compostelana [*A publication*]

Acta Cienc Indica ... Acta Ciencia Indica [*A publication*]

Acta Cienc Indica Chem ... Acta Ciencia Indica. Series Chemistry [*A publication*]

Acta Cienc Indica (IN) ... Acta Ciencia Indica (India) [*A publication*]

Acta Cienc Indica Math ... Acta Ciencia Indica. Mathematics [*A publication*]

Acta Cienc Indica Physica ... Acta Ciencia Indica. Physica [*A publication*]

Acta Cienc Indica Ser Chem ... Acta Ciencia Indica. Series Chemistry [*India*] [*A publication*]

Acta Cienc Indica Ser Math ... Acta Ciencia Indica. Series Mathematics [*India*] [*A publication*]

Acta Cient.. .. Acta Cientifica [*A publication*]

Acta Cient Compostelana ... Acta Cientifica Compostelana [*A publication*]

Acta Cient Potosina ... Acta Cientifica Potosina [*A publication*]

Acta Cient Venez ... Acta Cientifica Venezolana [*A publication*]

Acta Cient Venezolana ... Acta Cientifica Venezolana. Asociacion Venezolana para el Avance de la Ciencia [*A publication*]

Acta Cient Venez Supl ... Acta Cientifica Venezolana. Suplemento [*Venezuela*] [*A publication*]

Acta Ci Indica ... Acta Ciencia Indica [*A publication*]

Acta Ci Venezolana ... Acta Cientifica Venezolana. Asociacion Venezolana para el Avance de la Ciencia [*A publication*]

Acta Cl .... Acta Classica [*A publication*]

Acta Clin Belg ... Acta Clinica Belgica [*A publication*]

Acta Clin Belg Suppl ... Acta Clinica Belgica. Supplementum [*A publication*]

Acta Clin Odontol ... Acta Clinica Odontologica [*A publication*]

Acta Comment Univ Dorp ... Acta et Commentationes Universitatis Dorpatensis [*A publication*]

Acta Criminol Med Leg Jpn ... Acta Criminologiae Medicinae Legalis Japonica [*A publication*]

Acta Cryst ... Acta Crystallographica [*A publication*]

Acta Crystallogr ... Acta Crystallographica [*A publication*]

Acta Crystallogr A ... Acta Crystallographica. Section A [*A publication*]

Acta Crystallogr B ... Acta Crystallographica. Section B [*A publication*]

Acta Crystallogr Sect A ... Acta Crystallographica. Section A. Crystal Physics, Diffraction, Theoretical and General Crystallography [*Denmark*] [*A publication*]

Acta Crystallogr Sect B ... Acta Crystallographica. Section B. Structural Crystallography and Crystal Chemistry [*Denmark*] [*A publication*]

Acta Crystallogr Sect B Struct Crystallogr Cryst Chem ... Acta Crystallographica. Section B. Structural Crystallography and Crystal Chemistry [*A publication*]

Acta Crystallogr Sect C ... Acta Crystallographica. Section C. Crystal Structure Communications [*A publication*]

Acta Cryst Sect A ... Acta Crystallographica. Section A. Crystal Physics, Diffraction, Theoretical and General Crystallography [*A publication*]

Acta Cuyana Ing ... Acta Cuyana de Ingenieria [*A publication*]

Acta Cybernet ... Acta Cybernetica [*A publication*]

Acta Cytol ... Acta Cytologica [*A publication*]

Acta Cytol (Baltimore) ... Acta Cytologica (Baltimore) [*A publication*]

Act Adapt Aging ... Activities, Adaptation, and Aging [*A publication*]

Acta Davos ... Acta Davosiana [*A publication*]

Acta Dermatol ... Acta Dermatologica [*Japan*] [*A publication*]

Acta Dermatol (Kyoto) (Engl Ed) ... Acta Dermatologica (Kyoto) (English Edition) [*A publication*]

Acta Dermato-Venereol ... Acta Dermato-Venereologica [*A publication*]

Acta Dermat Vener ... Acta Dermato-Venereologica [*A publication*]

Acta Derm-Venereol ... Acta Dermato-Venereologica [*A publication*]

Acta Derm-Venereol (Stockh) ... Acta Dermato-Venereologica (Stockholm) [*A publication*]

Acta Derm-Venereol Suppl ... Acta Dermato-Venereologica. Supplementum [*Stockholm*] [*A publication*]

Acta Derm-Venereol Suppl (Stockh) ... Acta Dermato-Venereologica. Supplementum (Stockholm) [*A publication*]

Acta Diabetol Lat ... Acta Diabetologica Latina [*A publication*]

Acta Eccl .... Acta Ecclesiastica [*A publication*]

Acta Ecol ... Acta Ecologica [*A publication*]

Acta Electron ... Acta Electronica [*A publication*]

Acta Embryol Exp ... Acta Embryologiae Experimentalis [*Later, Acta Embryologiae et Morphologiae Experimentalis*] [*Palermo*] [*A publication*]

Acta Embryol Exp (Palermo) ... Acta Embryologiae Experimentalis [*Later, Acta Embryologiae et Morphologiae Experimentalis*] (Palermo) [*A publication*]

Acta Embryol Morphol Exp ... Acta Embryologiae et Morphologiae Experimentalis [*A publication*]

Acta Endocrinol ... Acta Endocrinologica [*A publication*]

Acta Endocrinol (Copenh) ... Acta Endocrinologica (Copenhagen) [*A publication*]

Acta Endocrinol Cubana ... Acta Endocrinologica Cubana [*A publication*]
Acta Endocrinol Panam ... Acta Endocrinologica Panamericana [*A publication*]
Acta Endocrinol Suppl ... Acta Endocrinologica. Supplementum [*Copenhagen*] [*A publication*]
Acta Endocrinol Suppl (Copenh) ... Acta Endocrinologica. Supplementum (Copenhagen) [*A publication*]
Acta Energ Solaris Sin ... Acta Energiae Solaris Sinica [*People's Republic of China*] [*A publication*]
Acta Ent..... Acta Entomologica [*A publication*]
Acta Ent Bohemoslov ... Acta Entomologica Bohemoslovaca [*A publication*]
Acta Ent Fenn ... Acta Entomologica Fennica [*A publication*]
Acta Ent Jugosl ... Acta Entomologica Jugoslavica [*A publication*]
Acta Ent Litu ... Acta Entomologica Lituanica [*A publication*]
Acta Ent Mus Natn (Prague) ... Acta Entomologica. Musei Nationalis (Prague) [*A publication*]
Acta Entomol Bohemoslov ... Acta Entomologica Bohemoslovaca [*A publication*]
Acta Entomol Fenn ... Acta Entomologica Fennica [*A publication*]
Acta Entomol Jugosl ... Acta Entomologica Jugoslavica [*A publication*]
Acta Entomol Litu ... Acta Entomologica Lituanica [*A publication*]
Acta Entomol Mus Natl Pragae ... Acta Entomologica. Musei Nationalis Pragae [*A publication*]
Acta Entomol Sin ... Acta Entomologica Sinica [*A publication*]
Acta Entomol Sinica ... Acta Entomologica Sinica [*A publication*]
Acta Ent (Prag) ... Acta Entomologica. Musei Nationalis (Prague) [*A publication*]
Acta Ent Sin ... Acta Entomologica Sinica [*A publication*]
Acta Erudit ... Acta Eruditorum [*A publication*]
Acta Ethn... Acta Ethnologica [*A publication*]
Acta Ethnog Hung ... Acta Ethnographica. Academiae Scientiarum Hungaricae [*A publication*]
Acta Ethnogr Acad Sci Hung ... Acta Ethnographica. Academiae Scientiarum Hungaricae [*A publication*]
Acta Ethnogr (Budapest) ... Acta Ethnographica (Budapest) [*A publication*]
Acta Ethnogr Hung ... Acta Ethnographica. Academiae Scientiarum Hungaricae [*A publication*]
Acta Eur Fertil ... Acta Europaea Fertilitatis [*A publication*]
Acta Fac Med Fluminensis ... Acta Facultatis Medicae Fluminensis [*A publication*]
Acta Fac Med Univ Brun ... Acta Facultatis Medicae Universitatis Brunensis [*A publication*]
Acta Fac Paedagog Ostra Ser E ... Acta Facultatis Paedagogicae Ostraviensis. Series E [*A publication*]
Acta Fac Pharm Bohemoslov ... Acta Facultatis Pharmaceuticae Bohemoslovenicae [*A publication*]
Acta Fac Pharm Brun Bratisl ... Acta Facultatis Pharmaceuticae Brunensis et Bratislavensis [*A publication*]
Acta Fac Pharm Univ Comenianae ... Acta Facultatis Pharmaceuticae Universitatis Comenianae [*A publication*]
Acta Fac Rerum Nat Univ Comenianae Anthropol ... Acta Facultatis Rerum Naturalium Universitatis Comenianae. Anthropologica [*A publication*]
Acta Fac Rerum Nat Univ Comenianae Bot ... Acta Facultatis Rerum Naturalium Universitatis Comenianae. Botanica [*A publication*]
Acta Fac Rerum Nat Univ Comenianae Chim ... Acta Facultatis Rerum Naturalium Universitatis Comenianae. Chimia [*A publication*]
Acta Fac Rerum Nat Univ Comenianae Form Prot Nat (CS) ... Acta Facultatis Rerum Naturalium Universitatis Comenianae. Formatio et Protectio Naturae (Czechoslovakia) [*A publication*]
Acta Fac Rerum Nat Univ Comenianae Genet ... Acta Facultatis Rerum Naturalium Universitatis Comenianae. Genetica [*A publication*]
Acta Fac Rerum Nat Univ Comenianae Microbiol ... Acta Facultatis Rerum Naturalium Universitatis Comenianae. Microbiologia [*A publication*]
Acta Fac Rerum Nat Univ Comenianae Phys ... Acta Facultatis Rerum Naturalium Universitatis Comenianae. Physica [*A publication*]
Acta Fac Rerum Nat Univ Comenianae Physiol Plant ... Acta Facultatis Rerum Naturalium Universitatis Comenianae. Physiologia Plantarum [*A publication*]
Acta Fac Rerum Nat Univ Comenianae Zool ... Acta Facultatis Rerum Naturalium Universitatis Comenianae. Zoologia [*A publication*]
Acta Fac Rerum Natur Univ Comenian Math ... Acta Facultatis Rerum Naturalium Universitatis Comenianae. Mathematica [*A publication*]
Acta Faun Entomol Mus Natl Pragae ... Acta Faunistica Entomologica. Musei Nationalis Pragae [*A publication*]
Acta For Fenn ... Acta Forestalia Fennica [*A publication*]
Acta Fytotech ... Acta Fytotechnica [*A publication*]
Acta Fytotech Univ Agric (Nitra) ... Acta Fytotechnica. Universitatis Agriculturae (Nitra) [*A publication*]
ActaG......... Acta Germanica [*Capetown*] [*A publication*]
Acta Gastro-Enterol Belg ... Acta Gastro-Enterologica Belgica [*A publication*]
Acta Gastroenterol Latinoam ... Acta Gastroenterologica Latinoamericana [*A publication*]

Acta Genet Med Gemellol ... Acta Geneticae, Medicae, et Gemellologiae [*A publication*]
Acta Genet Sin ... Acta Genetica Sinica [*A publication*]
Acta Genet Stat Med ... Acta Genetica et Statistica Medica [*A publication*]
Acta Geobot Barc ... Acta Geobotanica Barcinonensia [*A publication*]
Acta Geod Geophys Montan ... Acta Geodaetica, Geophysica, et Montanistica [*A publication*]
Acta Geod Geophys Montanistica ... Acta Geodaetica, Geophysica, et Montanistica [*Hungary*] [*A publication*]
Acta Geogr ... Acta Geographica [*A publication*]
Acta Geogr Lodz ... Acta Geographica Lodziensia [*A publication*]
Acta Geogr Sinica ... Acta Geographica Sinica [*A publication*]
Acta Geol Acad Sci Hung ... Acta Geologica. Academiae Scientiarum Hungaricae [*A publication*]
Acta Geol Geogr Univ Comenianae Geol ... Acta Geologica et Geographica. Universitatis Comenianae. Geologica [*A publication*]
Acta Geol Hisp ... Acta Geologica Hispanica [*A publication*]
Acta Geol Hung ... Acta Geologica. Academiae Scientiarum Hungaricae [*A publication*]
Acta Geol Lilloana ... Acta Geologica Lilloana [*A publication*]
Acta Geol Pol ... Acta Geologica Polonica [*A publication*]
Acta Geol Sin ... Acta Geologica Sinica [*A publication*]
Acta Geol Sin (Engl Transl) ... Acta Geologica Sinica (English Translation) [*A publication*]
Acta Geol Sinica ... Acta Geologica Sinica [*A publication*]
Acta Geol Taiwan ... Acta Geologica Taiwanica [*A publication*]
Acta Geol Taiwanica ... Acta Geologica Taiwanica [*A publication*]
Acta Geophys Pol ... Acta Geophysica Polonica [*A publication*]
Acta Geophys Polonica ... Acta Geophysica Polonica [*A publication*]
Acta Geophys Sin ... Acta Geophysica Sinica [*A publication*]
Acta Gerontol ... Acta Gerontologica [*A publication*]
Acta Gerontol Belg ... Acta Gerontologica Belgica [*A publication*]
Acta Gerontol Geriatr Belg ... Acta Gerontologica et Geriatrica Belgica [*A publication*]
Acta Gerontol Jpn ... Acta Gerontologica Japonica [*A publication*]
Acta Ginecol (Madr) ... Acta Ginecologica (Madrid) [*A publication*]
Act Agron H ... Acta Agronomica. Academiae Scientiarum Hungaricae [*Budapest*] [*A publication*]
Acta Gynaecol Obstet Hispano Lusitana ... Acta Gynaecologica et Obstetrica Hispano Lusitana [*Portugal*] [*A publication*]
Acta Haematol ... Acta Haematologica [*A publication*]
Acta Haematol (Basel) ... Acta Haematologica (Basel) [*A publication*]
Acta Haematol Jpn ... Acta Haematologica Japonica [*A publication*]
Acta Haematol Pol ... Acta Haematologica Polonica [*A publication*]
Acta Helvet ... Acta Helvetica Physico-Mathematico-Botanico-Medica [*A publication*]
Acta Hepato-Gastroenterol ... Acta Hepato-Gastroenterologica [*Stuttgart/New York*] [*A publication*]
Acta Hepato-Gastroenterol (Stuttg) ... Acta Hepato-Gastroenterologica (Stuttgart/New York) [*A publication*]
Acta Hepatol ... Acta Hepatologica [*A publication*]
Acta Hepatol Jpn ... Acta Hepatologica Japonica [*A publication*]
Acta Hepatosplen ... Acta Hepato-Splenologica [*A publication*]
Acta Hepato-Splenol ... Acta Hepato-Splenologica [*West Germany*] [*A publication*]
Acta Herpetol Jpn ... Acta Herpetologica Japonica [*A publication*]
Acta Hist Art ... Magyar Tudomanyos Akademia. Acta Historiae Artium [*A publication*]
Acta Hist Leopold ... Acta Historica Leopoldina [*A publication*]
Acta Hist Med Pharm Vet ... Acta Historica Medicinae Pharmaciae Veterinae [*A publication*]
Acta Histochem ... Acta Histochemica [*A publication*]
Acta Histochem Cytochem ... Acta Histochemica et Cytochemica [*A publication*]
Acta Histochem (Jena) ... Acta Histochemica (Jena) [*A publication*]
Acta Histochem Supplementb ... Acta Histochemica. Supplementband [*Jena*] [*A publication*]
Acta Histochem Suppl (Jena) ... Acta Histochemica. Supplementband (Jena) [*A publication*]
Acta Hist Rerum Natur Nec Non Tech ... Acta Historiae Rerum Naturalium Nec Non Technicarum [*A publication*]
Acta Hist Sci Nat Med ... Acta Historica Scientiarum, Naturalium, et Medicinalium [*Odense*] [*A publication*]
Acta Hist Sci Nat Med (Odense) ... Acta Historica Scientiarum, Naturalium, et Medicinalium (Odense) [*A publication*]
Acta Hort... Acta Horticulturae [*A publication*]
Acta Hort... Acta Horticulturalia [*Peking*] [*A publication*]
Acta Hortic (Peking) ... Acta Horticulturalia (Peking) [*A publication*]
Acta Hortic Sin ... Acta Horticulturae Sinica [*A publication*]
Acta Hortic (The Hague) ... Acta Horticulturae (The Hague) [*A publication*]
Acta Horti Gotob ... Acta Horti Gotoburgensis [*A publication*]
Acta Horti Gotoburg ... Acta Horti Gotoburgensis [*A publication*]
Acta Hosp ... Acta Hospitalia [*A publication*]
Acta Humanistica Sci Univ Sangio Kyotiensis ... Acta Humanistica et Scientifica. Universitatis Sangio Kyotiensis [*A publication*]
Acta Human Sci Univ Sangio Kyotien Natur Sci Ser ... Acta Humanistica et Scientifica. Universitatis Sangio Kyotiensis. Natural Science Series [*A publication*]
Acta Humboldtiana Ser Geog et Ethnograph ... Acta Humboldtiana. Series Geographica et Ethnographica [*A publication*]
Acta Hydrobiol ... Acta Hydrobiologica [*A publication*]

Acta Hydrobiol Sin ... Acta Hydrobiologica Sinica [*People's Republic of China*] [*A publication*]
Acta Hydrochim Hydrobiol ... Acta Hydrochimica et Hydrobiologica [*East Germany*] [*A publication*]
Acta Hydrophys ... Acta Hydrophysica [*East Germany*] [*A publication*]
Acta Hydrophys (Berl) ... Acta Hydrophysica (Deutsche Akademie der Wissenschaften zu Berlin. Zentralinstitut Physik der Erde. Selbstaendige Abteilung Physikalische Hydrographie) [*A publication*]
Acta Hymenopt (Tokyo) ... Acta Hymenopterologica (Tokyo) [*A publication*]
Acta Iber Radiol-Cancerol ... Acta Iberica Radiologia-Cancerologica [*A publication*]
Acta Ichthyol Piscatoria ... Acta Ichthyologica et Piscatoria [*A publication*]
Acta Inf ...... Acta Informatica [*A publication*]
Acta Inform ... Acta Informatica [*A publication*]
Acta Informat ... Acta Informatica [*A publication*]
Acta Inst Anesthesiol ... Acta. Institut d'Anesthesiologie [*A publication*]
Acta Inst For Zvolenensis ... Acta Instituti Forestalis Zvolenensis [*A publication*]
Acta Inst For Zvolenensis Vysk Ustav Lesn Hospod ... Acta Instituti Forestalis Zvolenensis. Vyskumny Ustav Lesneho Hospodarstva [*A publication*]
Acta Inst Psychol Univ Zagrabiensis ... Acta Instituti Psychologici Universitatis Zagrabiensis [*A publication*]
Acta Isot ..... Acta Isotopica [*A publication*]
Acta Jur Acad Sci Hung ... Acta Juridica. Academiae Scientiarum Hungaricae [*A publication*]
Acta Jur (Budapest) ... Acta Juridica (Budapest) [*A publication*]
Acta Jur (Cape Town) ... Acta Juridica (Cape Town) [*A publication*]
Acta Juridica ... Acta Juridica. Academiae Scientiarum Hungaricae [*A publication*]
Acta Juridica Acad Sci Hungaricae ... Acta Juridica. Academiae Scientiarum Hungaricae [*A publication*]
Acta Krausi Cuad Inst Nac Microbiol (B Aires) ... Acta Krausi. Cuaderno del Instituto Nacional de Microbiologia (Buenos Aires) [*A publication*]
Acta Krausi Cuad Inst Nac Microbiol (Buenos Aires) ... Acta Krausi. Cuaderno del Instituto Nacional de Microbiologia (Buenos Aires) [*A publication*]
ActaL .... Acta Latgalica [*A publication*]
Acta Leiden ... Acta Leidensia [*A publication*]
Acta Leiden Inst Trop Geneeskd ... Acta Leidensia. Instituut voor Tropische Geneeskunde [*A publication*]
Acta Leprol (Geneve) ... Acta Leprologica (Geneve) [*A publication*]
Acta Limnol Indica ... Acta Limnologica Indica [*A publication*]
Acta Linguist ... Acta Linguistica [*A publication*]
Acta Linguist Hung ... Acta Linguistica. Academiae Scientiarum Hungaricae [*A publication*]
Acta Lit Hung ... Acta Litteraria. Academiae Scientiarum Hungaricae [*A publication*]
Act Allerg ... Acta Allergologica [*A publication*]
Acta Lund .. Acta Universitatis Lundensis [*A publication*]
ACTA Mag ... ACTA [*Art Craft Teachers Association*] Magazine [*A publication*] (APTA)
Acta Manilana A ... Acta Manilana. Series A. Natural and Applied Sciences [*A publication*]
Acta Manilana Ser A ... Acta Manilana. Series A [*A publication*]
Acta Manilana Ser A Nat Appl Sci ... Acta Manilana. Series A. Natural and Applied Sciences [*A publication*]
Acta Marx-Lenin ... Acta Marxistica-Leninistica [*A publication*]
Acta Math ... Acta Mathematica [*A publication*]
Acta Math Acad Sci Hungar ... Acta Mathematica. Academiae Scientiarum Hungaricae [*A publication*]
Acta Math Appl Sin ... Acta Mathematicae Applicatae Sinica [*A publication*]
Acta Math Appl Sinica ... Acta Mathematicae Applicatae Sinica [*A publication*]
Acta Math Sci ... Acta Mathematica Scientia [*A publication*]
Acta Math Sin ... Acta Mathematica Sinica [*A publication*]
Acta Math Sinica ... Acta Mathematica Sinica [*A publication*]
Acta Math Univ Comenian ... Acta Mathematica. Universitatis Comenianae [*A publication*]
Acta Math Vietnam ... Acta Mathematica Vietnamica [*A publication*]
Acta Mech ... Acta Mechanica [*A publication*]
Acta Mech Sin ... Acta Mechanica Sinica [*People's Republic of China*] [*A publication*]
Acta Mech Sinica ... Acta Mechanica Sinica [*A publication*]
Acta Mech Solida Sin ... Acta Mechanica Solida Sinica [*A publication*]
Acta Med Acad Sci Hung ... Acta Medica. Academiae Scientiarum Hungaricae [*A publication*]
Acta Med Austriaca ... Acta Medica Austriaca [*A publication*]
Acta Med Austriaca Suppl ... Acta Medica Austriaca. Supplement [*A publication*]
Acta Med Biol ... Acta Medica et Biologica [*A publication*]
Acta Med Bulg ... Acta Medica Bulgarica [*A publication*]
Acta Med Costarric ... Acta Medica Costarricense [*A publication*]
Acta Med (Fukuoka) ... Acta Medica (Fukuoka) [*A publication*]
Acta Med Hidalg ... Acta Medica Hidalguense [*A publication*]
Acta Med Hist Patav ... Acta Medicae Historiae Patavina [*A publication*]
Acta Med Hondur ... Acta Medica Hondurena [*A publication*]
Acta Med Hung ... Acta Medica Hungarica [*A publication*]
Acta Medicotech ... Acta Medicotechnica [*A publication*]

Acta Med Iran ... Acta Medica Iranica [*A publication*]
Acta Med Ital Med Trop Subtrop ... Acta Medica Italica di Medicina Tropicale e Subtropicale e di Gastroenterologia [*A publication*]
Acta Med Iugosl ... Acta Medica Iugoslavica [*A publication*]
Acta Med Iugosl (Eng Transl) ... Acta Medica Iugoslavica (English Translation) [*A publication*]
Acta Med Keijo ... Acta Medicinalia in Keijo [*A publication*]
Acta Med Leg Soc ... Acta Medicinae Legalis et Socialis [*Liege*] [*A publication*]
Acta Med Leg Soc (Liege) ... Acta Medicinae Legalis et Socialis (Liege) [*A publication*]
Acta Med Medianae ... Acta Medica Medianae [*A publication*]
Acta Med (Mex) ... Acta Medica (Mexico) [*A publication*]
Acta Med Nagasaki ... Acta Medica Nagasakiensia [*A publication*]
Acta Med Okayama ... Acta Medica Okayama [*A publication*]
Acta Med Orient ... Acta Medica Orientalia [*A publication*]
Acta Med Pat ... Acta Medica Patavina [*A publication*]
Acta Med Pata ... Acta Medica Patavina [*A publication*]
Acta Med Peru ... Acta Medica Peruana [*A publication*]
Acta Med Philipp ... Acta Medica Philippina [*A publication*]
Acta Med Pol ... Acta Medica Polona [*A publication*]
Acta Med (Rio De Janeiro) ... Acta Medica (Rio De Janeiro) [*A publication*]
Acta Med Roman ... Acta Medica Romana [*A publication*]
Acta Med Romana ... Acta Medica Romana [*A publication*]
Acta Med Scand ... Acta Medica Scandinavica [*A publication*]
Acta Med Scandinav ... Acta Medica Scandinavica [*A publication*]
Acta Med Scand Suppl ... Acta Medica Scandinavica. Supplementum [*A publication*]
Acta Med Tenerife ... Acta Medica de Tenerife [*A publication*]
Acta Med Turc ... Acta Medica Turcica [*A publication*]
Acta Med Turc Suppl ... Acta Medica Turcica. Supplementum [*A publication*]
Acta Med Univ Kagoshima ... Acta Medica Universitatis Kagoshimaensis [*A publication*]
Acta Med Venez ... Acta Medica Venezolana [*A publication*]
Acta Med Vet ... Acta Medica Veterinaria [*A publication*]
Acta Med Vet (Madr) ... Acta Medica Veterinaria (Madrid) [*A publication*]
Acta Med Vietnam ... Acta Medica Vietnamica [*A publication*]
Acta Metall ... Acta Metallurgica [*A publication*]
Acta Metall Sin ... Acta Metallurgica Sinica [*A publication*]
Acta Meteorol Sin ... Acta Meteorologica Sinica [*A publication*]
Acta Met Sin ... Acta Metallurgica Sinica [*A publication*]
Acta Mex Cienc y Tecnol ... Acta Mexicana de Ciencia y Tecnologia [*A publication*]
Acta Mexicana Cienc Tecn ... Acta Mexicana de Ciencia y Tecnologia. Instituto Politecnico Nacional [*A publication*]
Acta Mexicana Ci Tecn ... Acta Mexicana de Ciencia y Tecnologia [*A publication*]
Acta Microbiol ... Acta Microbiologica [*A publication*]
Acta Microbiol Acad Sci Hung ... Acta Microbiologica. Academiae Scientiarum Hungaricae [*A publication*]
Acta Microbiol Bulg ... Acta Microbiologica Bulgarica [*A publication*]
Acta Microbiol Hell ... Acta Microbiologica Hellenica [*A publication*]
Acta Microbiol Hung ... Acta Microbiologica Hungarica [*A publication*]
Acta Microbiol Pol ... Acta Microbiologica Polonica [*A publication*]
Acta Microbiol Polon ... Acta Microbiologica Polonica [*A publication*]
Acta Microbiol Pol Ser A ... Acta Microbiologica Polonica. Series A. Microbiologia Generalis [*A publication*]
Acta Microbiol Pol Ser A Microbiol Gen ... Acta Microbiologica Polonica. Series A. Microbiologia Generalis [*A publication*]
Acta Microbiol Pol Ser B ... Acta Microbiologica Polonica. Series B. Microbiologia Applicata [*A publication*]
Acta Microbiol Pol Ser B Microbiol Appl ... Acta Microbiologica Polonica. Series B. Microbiologia Applicata [*A publication*]
Acta Microbiol Sin ... Acta Microbiologica Sinica [*A publication*]
Acta Microbiol Sinica ... Acta Microbiologica Sinica [*A publication*]
Acta Microbiol Virol Immunol ... Acta Microbiologica, Virologica, et Immunologica [*A publication*]
Acta Microbiol Virol Immunol (Sofiia) ... Acta Microbiologica, Virologica, et Immunologica (Sofiia) [*A publication*]
Acta Mineral-Petrogr ... Acta Mineralogica-Petrographica [*A publication*]
Acta Mineral-Petrogr (Szeged) ... Acta Mineralogica-Petrographica (Acta Universitatis Szegediensis) [*A publication*]
Acta Mont ... Acta Montana [*A publication*]
Acta Moravs Muz ... Acta Moravske Muzeum [*A publication*]
Acta Morphol Acad Sci Hung ... Acta Morphologica. Academiae Scientiarum Hungaricae [*A publication*]
Acta Morphol Acad Sci Hung Suppl ... Acta Morphologica. Academiae Scientiarum Hungaricae. Supplementum [*A publication*]
Acta Morphol Neerl-Scand ... Acta Morphologica Neerlando-Scandinavica [*A publication*]
Acta Morphol (Sofia) ... Acta Morphologica (Sofia) [*A publication*]
Acta Mus ... Acta Musicologica [*A publication*]
Acta Mus Hist Nat ... Acta Musei Historiae Naturalis [*A publication*]
Acta Mus Horti Bot Bohemiae Borealis Hist Nat ... Acta Musei et Horti Botanici Bohemiae Borealis. Historia Naturalis [*A publication*]
Acta Music ... Acta Musicologica [*A publication*]
Acta Mus Macedonici Sci Nat ... Acta Musei Macedonici. Scientiarum Naturalium [*A publication*]

Acta Mus Maced Sci Nat ... Acta Musei Macedonici. Scientiarum Naturalium [*A publication*]
Acta Mus Morav ... Acta Musei Moraviae [*A publication*]
Acta Mus Morav Sci Natur ... Acta Musei Moraviae. Scientiae Naturales [*A publication*]
Acta Mus Morav Sci Soc ... Acta Musei Moraviae. Scientiae Sociales [*A publication*]
Acta Mus Nap ... Acta Musei Napocensis [*A publication*]
Acta Mus Napocensis ... Acta Musei Napocensis [*A publication*]
Acta Mus Natl Pragae Ser B Hist Nat ... Acta Musei Nationalis Pragae. Series B. Historia Naturalis [*A publication*]
Acta Mus Silesiae Ser A Sci Nat ... Acta Musei Silesiae. Series A. Scientiae Naturales [*A publication*]
Acta Mycol ... Acta Mycologica [*A publication*]
Act Anae Sc ... Acta Anaesthesiologica Scandinavica [*A publication*]
Acta Nat Isl ... Acta Naturalia Islandica [*A publication*]
Act Anatom ... Acta Anatomica [*A publication*]
ActAndr ..... Acts of Andrew   (BJA)
Acta Neerl Morphol Norm Pathol ... Acta Neerlandica Morphologiae Normalis et Pathologicae [*A publication*]
Acta Neurobiol Exp ... Acta Neurobiologiae Experimentalis [*A publication*]
Acta Neurobiol Exp Suppl ... Acta Neurobiologiae Experimentalis. Supplementum [*A publication*]
Acta Neurobiol Exp (Warsaw) ... Acta Neurobiologiae Experimentalis (Warsaw) [*A publication*]
Acta Neurobiol Exp (Warsz) ... Acta Neurobiologiae Experimentalis (Warszawa) [*A publication*]
Acta Neurochir ... Acta Neurochirurgica [*A publication*]
Acta Neurochir Suppl ... Acta Neurochirurgica. Supplementum [*Wien*] [*A publication*]
Acta Neurochir Suppl (Wien) ... Acta Neurochirurgica. Supplementum (Wien) [*A publication*]
Acta Neurochir (Wien) ... Acta Neurochirurgica (Wien) [*A publication*]
Acta Neurol ... Acta Neurologica [*A publication*]
Acta Neurol Belg ... Acta Neurologica Belgica [*A publication*]
Acta Neurol Latinoam ... Acta Neurologica Latinoamericana [*A publication*]
Acta Neurol Latinoamer ... Acta Neurologica Latinoamericana [*A publication*]
Acta Neurol (Naples) ... Acta Neurologica (Naples) [*A publication*]
Acta Neurol (Napoli) ... Acta Neurologica (Napoli) [*A publication*]
Acta Neurol Psychiatr Belg ... Acta Neurologica et Psychiatrica Belgica [*A publication*]
Acta Neurol Quad ... Acta Neurologica. Quaderni [*A publication*]
Acta Neurol Scand ... Acta Neurologica Scandinavica [*A publication*]
Acta Neurol Scand Suppl ... Acta Neurologica Scandinavica. Supplementum [*A publication*]
Acta Neuropathol ... Acta Neuropathologica [*A publication*]
Acta Neuropathol (Berl) ... Acta Neuropathologica (Berlin) [*A publication*]
Acta Neuropathol Suppl ... Acta Neuropathologica. Supplementum [*Berlin*] [*A publication*]
Acta Neuropathol Suppl (Berl) ... Acta Neuropathologica. Supplementum (Berlin) [*A publication*]
Acta Neuropsiquiat Argent ... Acta Neuropsiquiatrica Argentina [*A publication*]
Acta Neuroveg ... Acta Neurovegetativa [*A publication*]
Acta Neuroveg Suppl ... Acta Neurovegetativa. Supplementum [*A publication*]
Acta Nipp Med Trop ... Acta Nipponica Medicinae Tropicalis [*A publication*]
Acta Nippon Med Trop ... Acta Nipponica Medicinae Tropicalis [*A publication*]
Act An-Path ... Actualites Anatomo-Pathologiques [*A publication*]
ActAntHung ... Acta Antiqua Hungarica [*A publication*]
Act Antiq H ... Acta Antiqua. Academiae Scientiarum Hungaricae [*A publication*]
Acta Num... Acta Numismatica [*A publication*]
Acta Nutr Sin ... Acta Nutrimenta Sinica [*A publication*]
Acta O........ Acta Orientalia [*A publication*]
Acta Obstet Ginecol Hisp-Lusit ... Acta Obstetrica y Ginecologica Hispano-Lusitana [*A publication*]
Acta Obstet Ginecol Hisp-Lusit Supl ... Acta Obstetrica y Ginecologica Hispano-Lusitana. Suplemento [*A publication*]
Acta Obstet Gynaecol Jpn ... Acta Obstetrica et Gynaecologica Japonica [*A publication*]
Acta Obstet Gynaecol Jpn (Engl Ed) ... Acta Obstetrica et Gynaecologica Japonica (English Edition) [*A publication*]
Acta Obstet Gynecol Scand ... Acta Obstetrica et Gynecologica Scandinavica [*A publication*]
Acta Obstet Gynecol Scand Suppl ... Acta Obstetrica et Gynecologica Scandinavica. Supplement [*A publication*]
Acta Obst Gynec Scandinav ... Acta Obstetrica et Gynecologica Scandinavica [*A publication*]
Acta Oceanogr Taiwan ... Acta Oceanographica Taiwanica [*A publication*]
Acta Odont ... Acta Odontologica [*A publication*]
Acta Odontol Latinoam ... Acta Odontologica Latinoamericana [*A publication*]
Acta Odontol Scand ... Acta Odontologica Scandinavica [*A publication*]
Acta Odontol Scand Suppl ... Acta Odontologica Scandinavica. Supplementum [*A publication*]
Acta Odontol Venez ... Acta Odontologica Venezolana [*A publication*]
Acta Oecol Oecol Appl ... Acta Oecologica. Oecologia Applicata [*A publication*]

Acta Oecol Oecol Plant ... Acta Oecologica. Oecologica Plantarum [*A publication*]
Acta Oecon ... Acta Oeconomica [*Budapest*] [*A publication*]
Acta Oeconomica ... Acta Oeconomica. Academiae Scientiarum Hungaricae [*A publication*]
Acta Oncol ... Acta Oncologica [*Madrid*] [*A publication*]
Acta Oncol Bras ... Acta Oncologica Brasileira [*A publication*]
Acta Oncol (Madr) ... Acta Oncologica (Madrid) [*A publication*]
Acta Oper-Oecon ... Acta Operativo-Oeconomica [*A publication*]
Acta Ophth ... Acta Ophthalmologica [*A publication*]
Acta Ophthalmol ... Acta Ophthalmologica [*A publication*]
Acta Ophthalmol (Copenh) ... Acta Ophthalmologica (Copenhagen) [*A publication*]
Acta Ophthalmol Iugosl ... Acta Ophthalmologica Iugoslavica [*A publication*]
Acta Ophthalmol Suppl ... Acta Ophthalmologica. Supplementum [*Kobenhavn*] [*A publication*]
Acta Ophthalmol Suppl (Copenh) ... Acta Ophthalmologica. Supplementum (Copenhagen) [*A publication*]
Acta Or ...... Acta Orientalia [*A publication*]
Acta Or (B) ... Acta Orientalia. Academiae Scientiarum Hungaricae (Budapest) [*A publication*]
Acta Orient ... Acta Orientalia [*A publication*]
Acta Orient Acad Sci Hungar ... Acta Orientalia. Academiae Scientiarum Hungaricae [*A publication*]
Acta ORL Belg ... Acta Oto-Rhino-Laryngologica Belgica [*A publication*]
Acta ORL Espan ... Acta Oto-Rino-Laringologica Espanola [*A publication*]
Acta Ornith ... Acta Ornithologica [*A publication*]
Acta Ornithol (Engl Transl) ... Acta Ornithologica (English Translation) [*A publication*]
Acta Ornithol (Warsaw) ... Acta Ornithologica (Warsaw) [*A publication*]
Acta Ornithol (Warsaw) (Engl Transl) ... Acta Ornithologica (Warsaw) (English Translation) [*A publication*]
Acta Orthop Belg ... Acta Orthopaedica Belgica [*A publication*]
Acta Orthop Scand ... Acta Orthopaedica Scandinavica [*A publication*]
Acta Orthop Scand Suppl ... Acta Orthopaedica Scandinavica. Supplementum [*A publication*]
Acta Oto-Laryng ... Acta Oto-Laryngologica [*A publication*]
Acta Oto-Laryngol ... Acta Oto-Laryngologica [*A publication*]
Acta Otolaryngol (Stockh) ... Acta Otolaryngologica (Stockholm) [*A publication*]
Acta Oto-Laryngol Suppl ... Acta Oto-Laryngologica. Supplementum [*A publication*]
Acta Otolaryngol Suppl (Stockh) ... Acta Otolaryngologica. Supplement (Stockholm) [*A publication*]
Acta Oto-Rhino-Lar Belg ... Acta Oto-Rhino-Laryngologica Belgica [*A publication*]
Acta Oto-Rhino-Laryngol Belg ... Acta Oto-Rhino-Laryngologica Belgica [*A publication*]
Acta Oto-Rino-Laringol Esp ... Acta Oto-Rino-Laringologica Espanola [*A publication*]
Acta Oto-Rino-Laringol Ibero-Am ... Acta Oto-Rino-Laringologica Ibero-Americana [*A publication*]
Acta Paed Hung ... Acta Paediatrica. Academiae Scientiarum Hungaricae [*A publication*]
Acta Paediat ... Acta Paediatrica [*A publication*]
Acta Paediatr ... Acta Paediatrica [*A publication*]
Acta Paediatr Acad Sci Hung ... Acta Paediatrica. Academiae Scientiarum Hungaricae [*A publication*]
Acta Paediatr Belg ... Acta Paediatrica Belgica [*A publication*]
Acta Paediatr Jpn (Overseas Ed) ... Acta Paediatrica Japonica (Overseas Edition) [*A publication*]
Acta Paediatr Lat ... Acta Paediatrica Latina [*A publication*]
Acta Paediatr Scand ... Acta Paediatrica Scandinavica [*A publication*]
Acta Paediatr Scand Suppl ... Acta Paediatrica Scandinavica. Supplementum [*A publication*]
Acta Paediatr Sin ... Acta Paediatrica Sinica [*A publication*]
Acta Paediatr (Stockholm) ... Acta Paediatrica (Stockholm) [*A publication*]
Acta Paediatr Suppl ... Acta Paediatrica. Supplement [*A publication*]
Acta Paediat Scandinav ... Acta Paediatrica Scandinavica [*A publication*]
Acta Paediat (Uppsala) ... Acta Paediatrica (Uppsala) [*A publication*]
Acta Paed Lat ... Acta Paediatrica Latina [*A publication*]
Acta Paedopsychiat ... Acta Paedopsychiatrica [*A publication*]
Acta Paedopsychiatr ... Acta Paedopsychiatrica [*A publication*]
Acta Paedopsychiatr (Basel) ... Acta Paedopsychiatrica (Basel) [*A publication*]
Acta Palaeobot ... Acta Palaeobotanica [*A publication*]
Acta Palaeontol Pol ... Acta Palaeontologica Polonica [*A publication*]
Acta Palaeontol Sin ... Acta Palaeontologica Sinica [*A publication*]
Acta Paracels ... Acta Paracelsica [*A publication*]
Acta Parasitol Iugosl ... Acta Parasitologica Iugoslavica [*A publication*]
Acta Parasitol Lith ... Acta Parasitologica Lithuanica [*A publication*]
Acta Parasitol Pol ... Acta Parasitologica Polonica [*A publication*]
Acta Pathol Jpn ... Acta Pathologica Japonica [*A publication*]
Acta Pathol Microbiol Immunol Scand Sect A ... Acta Pathologica, Microbiologica, et Immunologica Scandinavica. Section A [*A publication*]
Acta Pathol Microbiol Immunol Scand Sect A Suppl ... Acta Pathologica, Microbiologica, et Immunologica Scandinavica. Section A. Supplement [*A publication*]
Acta Pathol Microbiol Immunol Scand Sect B Microbiol ... Acta Pathologica, Microbiologica, et Immunologica Scandinavica. Section B. Microbiology [*A publication*]

Acta Pathol Microbiol Immunol Scand Sect C Immunol ... Acta Pathologica, Microbiologica, et Immunologica Scandinavica. Section C. Immunology [*A publication*]
Acta Pathol Microbiol Immunol Scand Suppl ... Acta Pathologica, Microbiologica, et Immunologica Scandinavica. Supplement [*A publication*]
Acta Pathol Microbiol Scand ... Acta Pathologica et Microbiologica Scandinavica [*A publication*]
Acta Pathol Microbiol Scand (A) ... Acta Pathologica et Microbiologica Scandinavica. Section A [*A publication*]
Acta Pathol Microbiol Scand (B) ... Acta Pathologica et Microbiologica Scandinavica. Section B [*A publication*]
Acta Pathol Microbiol Scand (C) ... Acta Pathologica et Microbiologica Scandinavica. Section C [*A publication*]
Acta Pathol Microbiol Scand Sect A ... Acta Pathologica et Microbiologica Scandinavica. Section A [*A publication*]
Acta Pathol Microbiol Scand Sect A Pathol ... Acta Pathologica et Microbiologica Scandinavica. Section A. Pathology [*A publication*]
Acta Pathol Microbiol Scand Sect A Suppl ... Acta Pathologica et Microbiologica Scandinavica. Section A. Supplement [*A publication*]
Acta Pathol Microbiol Scand Sect B ... Acta Pathologica et Microbiologica Scandinavica. Section B [*A publication*]
Acta Pathol Microbiol Scand Sect B Microbiol ... Acta Pathologica et Microbiologica Scandinavica. Section B. Microbiology [*A publication*]
Acta Pathol Microbiol Scand Sect B Microbiol Immunol ... Acta Pathologica et Microbiologica Scandinavica. Section B. Microbiology and Immunology [*A publication*]
Acta Pathol Microbiol Scand Sect B Suppl ... Acta Pathologica et Microbiologica Scandinavica. Section B. Supplement [*A publication*]
Acta Pathol Microbiol Scand Sect C ... Acta Pathologica et Microbiologica Scandinavica. Section C [*A publication*]
Acta Pathol Microbiol Scand Sect C Immunol ... Acta Pathologica et Microbiologica Scandinavica. Section C. Immunology [*A publication*]
Acta Pathol Microbiol Scand Suppl ... Acta Pathologica et Microbiologica Scandinavica. Supplementum [*A publication*]
Acta Pathol Microbiol Sect A ... Acta Pathologica et Microbiologica Scandinavica. Section A. Pathology [*A publication*]
Acta Ped Esp ... Acta Pediatrica Espanola [*A publication*]
Acta Pediatr Esp ... Acta Pediatrica Espanola [*A publication*]
Acta Pedol Sin ... Acta Pedologica Sinica [*A publication*]
Acta Pedol Sinica ... Acta Pedologica Sinica [*A publication*]
Acta Pet Sin ... Acta Petrolei Sinica [*A publication*]
Acta Phaenol ... Acta Phaenologica [*A publication*]
Acta Pharm ... Acta Pharmaceutica [*A publication*]
Acta Pharmaceut Jugoslav ... Acta Pharmaceutica Jugoslavica [*A publication*]
Acta Pharmacol ... Acta Pharmacologica et Toxicologica [*A publication*]
Acta Pharmacol Sin ... Acta Pharmacologica Sinica [*A publication*]
Acta Pharmacol Toxicol ... Acta Pharmacologica et Toxicologica [*A publication*]
Acta Pharmacol Toxicol (Copenh) ... Acta Pharmacologica et Toxicologica (Copenhagen) [*A publication*]
Acta Pharmacol Toxicol Suppl ... Acta Pharmacologica et Toxicologica. Supplementum [*A publication*]
Acta Pharmac Tox ... Acta Pharmacologica et Toxicologica [*A publication*]
Acta Pharm Fenn ... Acta Pharmaceutica Fennica [*A publication*]
Acta Pharm Hung ... Acta Pharmaceutica Hungarica [*A publication*]
Acta Pharm Int ... Acta Pharmaceutica Internationalia [*A publication*]
Acta Pharm Iugosl ... Acta Pharmaceutica Iugoslavica [*A publication*]
Acta Pharm Jugosl ... Acta Pharmaceutica Jugoslavica [*A publication*]
Acta Pharm Sin ... Acta Pharmaceutica Sinica [*A publication*]
Acta Pharm Sinica ... Acta Pharmaceutica Sinica [*People's Republic of China*] [*A publication*]
Acta Pharm Suec ... Acta Pharmaceutica Suecica [*A publication*]
Acta Pharm Tox ... Acta Pharmacologica et Toxicologica [*A publication*]
Acta Phil Fennica ... Acta Philosophica Fennica [*A publication*]
Acta Philol Scand ... Acta Philologica Scandinavica [*A publication*]
Acta Philos Fenn ... Acta Philosophica Fennica [*A publication*]
Acta Phys Acad Sci Hung ... Acta Physica. Academiae Scientiarum Hungaricae [*A publication*]
Acta Phys Acad Sci Hungar ... Acta Physica. Academiae Scientiarum Hungaricae [*A publication*]
Acta Phys Austriaca ... Acta Physica Austriaca [*A publication*]
Acta Phys Austriaca Suppl ... Acta Physica Austriaca. Supplementum [*A publication*]
Acta Phys Chem ... Acta Physica et Chemica [*A publication*]
Acta Phys Chem Univ Szeged ... Acta Physica et Chemica. Nova Series. Acta Universitatis Szegediensis [*A publication*]
Acta Phys Chim (Debrecina) ... Acta Physica et Chimica (Debrecina) [*Hungary*] [*A publication*]
Acta Phys Hung ... Acta Physica Hungarica [*A publication*]
Acta Phy Sin Abstr ... Acta Physica Sinica. Abstracts [*A publication*]
Acta Physiochim ... Acta Physiochimica [*A publication*]
Acta Physiol Acad Sci Hung ... Acta Physiologica. Academiae Scientiarum Hungaricae [*A publication*]
Acta Physiol Hung ... Acta Physiologica. Academiae Scientiarum Hungaricae [*A publication*]

Acta Physiol Hung ... Acta Physiologica Hungarica [*A publication*]
Acta Physiol Lat Am ... Acta Physiologica Latino Americana [*A publication*]
Acta Physiol Lat Am (Supl) ... Acta Physiologica Latino Americana. Suplemento [*A publication*]
Acta Physiol Latinoam ... Acta Physiologica Latinoamericana [*Argentina*] [*A publication*]
Acta Physiol Pharmac Neerl ... Acta Physiologica et Pharmacologica Neerlandica [*A publication*]
Acta Physiol Pharmacol Bulg ... Acta Physiologica et Pharmacologica Bulgarica [*A publication*]
Acta Physiol Pharmacol Latinoam ... Acta Physiologica et Pharmacologica Latinoamericana [*A publication*]
Acta Physiol Pharmacol Neerl ... Acta Physiologica et Pharmacologica Neerlandica [*A publication*]
Acta Physiol Pol ... Acta Physiologica Polonica [*A publication*]
Acta Physiol Pol (Engl Transl) ... Acta Physiologica Polonica (English Translation) [*A publication*]
Acta Physiol Pol Supl ... Acta Physiologica Polonica. Suplement [*Poland*] [*A publication*]
Acta Physiol Pol (Transl) ... Acta Physiologica Polonica (Translation) [*A publication*]
Acta Physiol Scand ... Acta Physiologica Scandinavica [*A publication*]
Acta Physiol Scand Suppl ... Acta Physiologica Scandinavica. Supplementum [*A publication*]
Acta Physiol Sin ... Acta Physiologica Sinica [*A publication*]
Acta Phys Pol ... Acta Physica Polonica [*A publication*]
Acta Phys Pol A ... Acta Physica Polonica. Series A [*A publication*]
Acta Phys Pol B ... Acta Physica Polonica. Series B [*A publication*]
Acta Phys Polon A ... Acta Physica Polonica. Series A [*Warsaw*] [*A publication*]
Acta Phys Polon B ... Acta Physica Polonica. Series B [*A publication*]
Acta Phys Pol Ser A ... Acta Physica Polonica. Series A [*A publication*]
Acta Phys Pol Ser B ... Acta Physica Polonica. Series B [*A publication*]
Acta Phys Sin ... Acta Physica Sinica [*A publication*]
Acta Phys Sinica ... Acta Physica Sinica [*A publication*]
Acta Phys Slov ... Acta Physica Slovaca [*A publication*]
Acta Phys Slovaca ... Acta Physica Slovaca [*A publication*]
Acta Phys Temp Humilis Sin ... Acta Physica Temperaturae Humilis Sinica [*A publication*]
Acta Phys Univ Comenianae ... Acta Physica Universitatis Comenianae [*A publication*]
Acta Phytochim ... Acta Phytochimica [*A publication*]
Acta Phytogeogr Suec ... Acta Phytogeographica Suecica [*A publication*]
Acta Phytomed ... Acta Phytomedica [*A publication*]
Acta Phytopathol ... Acta Phytopathologica [*A publication*]
Acta Phytopathol Acad Sci Hung ... Acta Phytopathologica. Academiae Scientiarum Hungaricae [*A publication*]
Acta Phytopathol (Budapest) ... Acta Phytopathologica (Budapest) [*A publication*]
Acta Phytopathol Sinica ... Acta Phytopathologica Sinica [*A publication*]
Acta Phytophylacica Sin ... Acta Phytophylacica Sinica [*A publication*]
Acta Phytophyl Sinica ... Acta Phytophylacica Sinica [*A publication*]
Acta Phytophysiol Sinica ... Acta Phytophysiologica Sinica [*A publication*]
Acta Phytotaxon Barc ... Acta Phytotaxonomica Barcinonensia [*A publication*]
Acta Phytotaxon Geobot ... Acta Phytotaxonomica et Geobotanica [*A publication*]
Acta Phytotaxon Sin ... Acta Phytotaxonomica Sinica [*A publication*]
Acta Phytother ... Acta Phytotherapeutica [*A publication*]
Acta Polit ... Acta Politica [*A publication*]
Acta Politec Mex ... Acta Politecnica Mexicana [*A publication*]
Acta Pol Mar ... Acta Poloniae Maritima [*A publication*]
Acta Pol Pharm ... Acta Poloniae Pharmaceutica [*A publication*]
Acta Pol Pharm (Engl Transl) ... Acta Poloniae Pharmaceutica (English Translation) [*A publication*]
Acta Pol Pharm (Transl) ... Acta Poloniae Pharmaceutica (English Translation) [*A publication*]
Acta Polym ... Acta Polymerica [*East Germany*] [*A publication*]
Acta Polytech Ceske Vys Uceni Tech v Pr III ... Acta Polytechnica. Ceske Vysoke Uceni Technicke v Prace III [*A publication*]
Acta Polytech Chem Incl Metall Ser ... Acta Polytechnica. Chemistry Including Metallurgy Series [*Sweden*] [*A publication*]
Acta Polytech III ... Acta Polytechnica. Series III [*A publication*]
Acta Polytech IV (Prague) ... Acta Polytechnica. Rada IV. Technicko-Teoreticka (Prague) [*A publication*]
Acta Polytech Prace CVUT ... Acta Polytechnica. Prace CVUT v Praze [*A publication*]
Acta Polytech Rada III Elektrotech ... Acta Polytechnica. Rada III. Elektrotechnicka [*A publication*]
Acta Polytech Rada IV Tech-Teor ... Acta Polytechnica. Rada IV. Technicko-Teoreticka [*A publication*]
Acta Polytech Rada 1 Stavebni ... Acta Polytechnica. Rada 1. Stavebni [*A publication*]
Acta Polytech Scand ... Acta Polytechnica Scandinavica [*A publication*]
Acta Polytech Scand Appl Phys Ser ... Acta Polytechnica Scandinavica. Applied Physics Series [*Finland*] [*A publication*]
Acta Polytech Scand Chem Incl Metall Ser ... Acta Polytechnica Scandinavica. Chemistry Including Metallurgy Series [*A publication*]

Acta Polytech Scand Chem Technol Metall Ser ... Acta Polytechnica Scandinavica. Chemical Technology and Metallurgy Series [*A publication*]

Acta Polytech Scand Civ Eng Build Constr Ser ... Acta Polytechnica Scandinavica. Civil Engineering and Building Construction Series [*Sweden*] [*A publication*]

Acta Polytech Scand Civ Eng Build Constru Ser ... Acta Polytechnica Scandinavica. Civil Engineering and Building Construction Series [*A publication*]

Acta Polytech Scand Elec Eng Ser ... Acta Polytechnica Scandinavica. Electrical Engineering Series [*A publication*]

Acta Polytech Scand Electr Ser ... Acta Polytechnica Scandinavica. Electrical Series [*A publication*]

Acta Polytech Scandinavica Chem Incl Met Series ... Acta Polytechnica Scandinavica. Chemistry Including Metallurgy Series [*A publication*]

Acta Polytech Scand Math Comput Mach Ser ... Acta Polytechnica Scandinavica. Mathematics and Computing Machinery Series [*Finland*] [*A publication*]

Acta Polytech Scand Math and Comput Mach Ser ... Acta Polytechnica Scandinavica. Mathematics and Computing Machinery Series [*A publication*]

Acta Polytech Scand Math Comput Sci Ser ... Acta Polytechnica Scandinavica. Mathematics and Computer Science Series [*A publication*]

Acta Polytech Scand Mech Eng Ser ... Acta Polytechnica Scandinavica. Mechanical Engineering Series [*A publication*]

Acta Polytech Scand Phys Incl Nucleon Ser ... Acta Polytechnica Scandinavica. Physics Including Nucleonics Series [*Finland*] [*A publication*]

Acta Polytech Scand Phys Incl Nucl Ser ... Acta Polytechnica Scandinavica. Physics Including Nucleonics Series [*A publication*]

Acta Polytech Scand Phys Nucl Ser ... Acta Polytechnica Scandinavica. Physics Including Nucleonics Series [*A publication*]

Acta Pontif Acad Sci ... Acta Pontificia. Academia Scientiarum [*A publication*]

Acta Pont Inst Bibl ... Acta Pontificii Instituti Biblici [*A publication*]

Acta Praehist ... Acta Praehistorica [*A publication*]

Acta Praehist et Archaeol ... Acta Praehistorica et Archaeologica [*A publication*]

Acta Protozool ... Acta Protozoologica [*A publication*]

Acta Psiquiatr Psicol Am Lat ... Acta Psiquiatrica y Psicologica de America Latina [*A publication*]

Acta Psiquiatr Psicol (Argent) ... Acta Psiquiatrica y Psicologica (Argentina) [*A publication*]

Acta Psychiat Belg ... Acta Psychiatrica Belgica [*A publication*]

Acta Psychiatr Belg ... Acta Psychiatrica Belgica [*A publication*]

Acta Psychiatr Neurol Scand ... Acta Psychiatrica et Neurologica Scandinavica [*A publication*]

Acta Psychiatr Neurol Scand Suppl ... Acta Psychiatrica et Neurologica Scandinavica. Supplementum [*A publication*]

Acta Psychiatr Scand ... Acta Psychiatrica Scandinavica [*A publication*]

Acta Psychiatr Scand Suppl ... Acta Psychiatrica Scandinavica. Supplementum [*A publication*]

Acta Psychiat Scand ... Acta Psychiatrica et Neurologica Scandinavica [*A publication*]

Acta Psychiat Scand ... Acta Psychiatrica Scandinavica [*Denmark*] [*A publication*]

Acta Psychiat Scandinav ... Acta Psychiatrica Scandinavica [*A publication*]

Acta Psychiat Scand Suppl ... Acta Psychiatrica Scandinavica. Supplementum [*Denmark*] [*A publication*]

Acta Psychol ... Acta Psychologica [*Amsterdam*] [*A publication*]

Acta Psychol (Amst) ... Acta Psychologica (Amsterdam) [*A publication*]

Acta Psychol Fenn ... Acta Psychologica Fennica [*A publication*]

Acta Psychol Taiwan ... Acta Psychologica Taiwanica [*A publication*]

Acta Psychotherap Psychosom Orthopaedagog ... Acta Psychotherapeutica, Psychosomatica, et Orthopaedagogica [*A publication*]

Acta Psychother Psychosom ... Acta Psychotherapeutica et Psychosomatica [*A publication*]

Acta Psychother Psychosom Orthopaedagog ... Acta Psychotherapeutica, Psychosomatica, et Orthopaedagogica [*A publication*]

Acta Psych Scand ... Acta Psychiatrica Scandinavica [*A publication*]

ACTAR ...... Acoustics of the Target

Acta Radiobot Genet ... Acta Radiobotanica et Genetica [*Japan*] [*A publication*]

Acta Radiol ... Acta Radiologica [*A publication*]

Acta Radiol Diagn ... Acta Radiologica. Series One. Diagnosis [*Stockholm*] [*A publication*]

Acta Radiol Diagn (Stockh) ... Acta Radiologica. Series One. Diagnosis (Stockholm) [*A publication*]

Acta Radiol Interam ... Acta Radiologica Interamericana [*A publication*]

Acta Radiol Oncol Radiat Phys Biol ... Acta Radiologica. Series Two. Oncology, Radiation, Physics, and Biology [*Stockholm*] [*A publication*]

Acta Radiol Oncol Radiat Therapy Phys and Biol ... Acta Radiologica. Oncology, Radiation Therapy, Physics, and Biology [*A publication*]

Acta Radiol Oncol Radiat Ther Phys Biol ... Acta Radiologica. Oncology, Radiation Therapy, Physics, and Biology [*Stockholm*] [*A publication*]

Acta Radiol (Stockh) ... Acta Radiologica (Stockholm) [*A publication*]

Acta Radiol Suppl ... Acta Radiologica. Supplementum [*Stockholm*] [*A publication*]

Acta Radiol Suppl (Stockh) ... Acta Radiologica. Supplementum (Stockholm) [*A publication*]

Acta Radiol Ther Phys Biol ... Acta Radiologica. Therapy, Physics, Biology [*Later, Acta Radiologica. Series Two. Oncology, Radiation, Physics, and Biology (Stockholm)*] [*A publication*]

Acta Radiol Ther (Stockh) ... Acta Radiologica. Therapy, Physics, Biology (Stockholm) [*Later, Acta Radiologica. Series Two. Oncology, Radiation, Physics, and Biology (Stockholm)*] [*A publication*]

Act Archaeo ... Acta Archaeologica [*A publication*]

Acta Regiae Soc Sci Litt Gothob Zool ... Acta Regiae Societatis Scientiarum et Litterarum Gothoburgensis. Zoologica [*A publication*]

Acta Reprod Turc ... Acta Reproductiva Turcica [*A publication*]

Acta Rerum Nat Mus Nat Slov Bratisl ... Acta Rerum Naturalium. Musei Nationalis Slovaci Bratislava [*A publication*]

Acta Rheumatol Scand ... Acta Rheumatologica Scandinavica [*A publication*]

Acta Rheumatol Scand Suppl ... Acta Rheumatologica Scandinavica. Supplementum [*A publication*]

Acta Rheumat Scand ... Acta Rheumatologica Scandinavica [*A publication*]

Acta Rhumatol ... Acta Rhumatologica [*A publication*]

Acta Rhumatol Belg ... Acta Rhumatologica Belgica [*A publication*]

Act Arith .... Acta Arithmetica [*A publication*]

ACTAS ...... Army Consideration of Tactical Air Support

Actas Acad Nac Cienc Exact Fis Natur Lima ... Actas. Academia Nacional de Ciencias Exactas, Fisicas, y Naturales de Lima [*A publication*]

Acta Sag ..... Acta Sagittariana [*A publication*]

Acta Salmant Cien ... Acta Salmanticensia. Serie de Ciencias [*A publication*]

Acta Salmanticensia Ser Cienc ... Acta Salmanticensia. Serie de Ciencias [*A publication*]

Acta Salmanticensia Ser Filos Letra ... Acta Salmanticensia. Serie Filosofia y Letras [*A publication*]

Acta Salmanticensia Ser Med ... Acta Salmanticensia. Serie de Medicina [*A publication*]

Acta Salmant Ser Cienc ... Acta Salmanticensia. Serie de Ciencias [*A publication*]

Actas Bioquim ... Actas Bioquimicas [*A publication*]

Acta Scaenograph ... Acta Scaenographica [*A publication*]

Acta Sch Med Gifu ... Acta Scholae Medicinalis Universitatis in Gifu [*Japan*] [*A publication*]

Acta Sch Med Univ Gifu ... Acta Scholae Medicinalis Universitatis in Gifu [*A publication*]

Acta Sch Med Univ Imp (Kioto) ... Acta Scholae Medicinalis Universitatis Imperialis (Kioto) [*A publication*]

Acta Sch Med Univ Kioto ... Acta Scholae Medicinalis Universitatis in Kioto [*A publication*]

Acta Sci Math (Szeged) ... Acta Scientiarum Mathematicarum (Szeged) [*A publication*]

Acta Sci Nat Acad Sci Bohemoslov (Brno) ... Acta Scientiarum Naturalium. Academiae Scientiarum Bohemoslovacae (Brno) [*A publication*]

Acta Sci Nat Univ Pekin ... Acta Scientiarum Naturalium. Universitatis Pekinensis [*People's Republic of China*] [*A publication*]

Acta Sci Nat Univ Sunyatseni (Zhongshandaxue Xuebao) ... Acta Scientiarum Naturalium. Universitatis Sunyatseni (Zhongshandaxue Xuebao) [*A publication*]

Acta Sci Nat Univ Szechuan ... Acta Scientiarum Naturalium. Universitatis Szechuanensis [*People's Republic of China*] [*A publication*]

Acta Sci Natur Univ Pekinensis ... Acta Scientiarum Naturalium. Universitatis Pekinensis [*A publication*]

Acta Sci Sin ... Acta Scientia Sinica [*A publication*]

Acta Sci Vietnam ... Acta Scientiarum Vietnamicarum [*A publication*]

Actas Clin Yodice ... Actas. Clinica Yodice [*A publication*]

Actas Cong Geol Argent ... Actas. Congreso Geologico Argentino [*A publication*]

Actas Congr Int Hist Descobrimentos ... Actas. Congreso Internacional de Historia dos Descobrimentos [*A publication*]

Actas Congr Mund Vet ... Actas. Congreso Mundial de Veterinaria [*A publication*]

Actas Congr Uniao Fitopatol Mediterr ... Actas. Congresso da Uniao Fitopatologica Mediterranea [*A publication*]

Actas Dermosifiliogr ... Actas Dermosifiliograficas [*A publication*]

Acta Seismol Sin ... Acta Seismologica Sinica [*People's Republic of China*] [*A publication*]

Acta Sericol ... Acta Sericologica [*A publication*]

Actas Int Congr Hist Med ... Actas. Congreso Internacional de Historia de la Medicina [*A publication*]

Actas Jornadas For ... Actas Jornadas Forestales [*A publication*]

Actas Jornadas Geol Argent ... Actas Jornadas Geologicas Argentinas [*A publication*]

Actas Luso-Esp Neurol Psiquiatr ... Actas Luso-Espanolas de Neurologia, Psiquiatria, y Ciencias Afines [*A publication*]

Actas-Luso Esp Neurol Psiquiatr Cienc Afines ... Actas Luso-Espanolas de Neurologia, Psiquiatria, y Ciencias Afines [*A publication*]

Actas Mem Congr Nat Esp ... Actas y Memorias. Congreso de Naturalistas Espanoles [*A publication*]

Acta Soc ..... Acta Sociologica [*A publication*]

Acta Soc Bot Pol ... Acta Societatis Botanicorum Poloniae [*A publication*]

Acta Soc Bot Polon ... Acta Societatis Botanicorum Poloniae [*A publication*]
Acta Soc Ent Jugosl ... Acta Societatis Entomologicae Jugoslavensis [*A publication*]
Acta Soc Entomol Cech ... Acta Societatis Entomologicae Cechosloveniae [*A publication*]
Acta Soc Ent Serbo Cro Slov ... Acta Societatis Entomologicae Serbo-Croato-Slovenae [*A publication*]
Acta Soc Fauna Flora Fenn ... Acta Societatis pro Fauna et Flora Fennica [*A publication*]
Acta Sociol ... Acta Sociologica [*A publication*]
Acta Soc Med Fenn Duodecim ... Acta Societatis Medicorum Fennicae Duodecim [*A publication*]
Acta Soc Med Fenn Duodecim Ser A ... Acta Societatis Medicorum Fennicae Duodecim. Serie A [*A publication*]
Acta Soc Med Fenn Duodecim Ser B ... Acta Societatis Medicorum Fennicae Duodecim. Serie B [*A publication*]
Acta Soc Med Ups ... Acta Societatis Medicorum Upsaliensis [*A publication*]
Acta Soc Med Upsal ... Acta Societatis Medicorum Upsaliensis [*A publication*]
Acta Soc Med Ups Suppl ... Acta Societatis Medicorum Upsaliensis. Supplementum [*A publication*]
Acta Soc Ophthalmol Jpn ... Acta Societatis Ophthalmologicae Japonicae [*A publication*]
Acta Soc Paed Hell ... Acta Societatis Paediatricae Hellenicae [*A publication*]
Acta Soc Path Jap ... Acta Societatis Pathologicae Japonicae [*A publication*]
Acta Soc Phil Lips ... Acta Societatis Philologae Lipsiensis [*A publication*]
Acta Soc Sci Fenn Ser B ... Acta Societatis Scientiarum Fennicae. Series B [*A publication*]
Acta Soc Sci Natur Moravicae ... Acta Societatis Scientiarum Naturalium Moravicae [*A publication*]
Acta Soc Zool Cechosl ... Acta Societatis Zoologicae Cechoslovenicae [*A publication*]
Actas Reun Argent Cienc Suelo ... Actas. Reunion Argentina de la Ciencia del Suelo [*A publication*]
Act Ass....... Acts of the General Assembly, Church of Scotland [*1638-1842*] [*A publication*] (DLA)
Acta Stereol ... Acta Stereologica [*A publication*]
Acta Stomatol Belg ... Acta Stomatologica Belgica [*A publication*]
Acta Stomatol Croat ... Acta Stomatologica Croatica [*A publication*]
Acta Stom Pat ... Acta Stomatologica Patavina [*A publication*]
Act Astron ... Acta Astronautica [*A publication*]
Actas Urol Esp ... Actas Urologicas Espanolas [*A publication*]
Acta Symp Evolut Insect ... Acta Symposii de Evolutione Insectorum [*A publication*]
Acta Tech Acad Sci Hung ... Acta Technica. Academiae Scientiarum Hungaricae [*A publication*]
Acta Tech Agric ... Acta Technologica Agriculturae [*Brno*]. A. Facultas Agronomica [*A publication*]
Acta Tech (Budap) ... Acta Technica (Budapest) [*A publication*]
Acta Tech CSAV ... Acta Technica. CSAV [*Ceskoslovenska Akademie Ved*] [*A publication*]
Acta Tech Hung ... Acta Technica Hungarica [*A publication*]
Acta Techn Gedan ... Acta Technica Gedanensia [*A publication*]
Acta Techn Hung ... Acta Technica Hungarica [*A publication*]
Acta Tech (Prague) ... Acta Technica (Prague) [*A publication*]
Acta Teilhard ... Acta Teilhardiana [*A publication*]
Acta Theriol ... Acta Theriologica [*A publication*]
Acta Trop... Acta Tropica [*A publication*]
Acta Trop (Basel) ... Acta Tropica (Basel) [*A publication*]
Acta Trop Suppl ... Acta Tropica. Supplementum [*A publication*]
Acta Tuberc Belg ... Acta Tuberculosea Belgica [*A publication*]
Acta Tuberc Jpn ... Acta Tuberculosea Japonica [*A publication*]
Acta Tuberc Pneumol Belg ... Acta Tuberculosea et Pneumologica Belgica [*A publication*]
Acta Tuberc Pneumol Scand ... Acta Tuberculosea et Pneumologica Scandinavica [*A publication*]
Acta Tuberc Pneumol Scand Suppl ... Acta Tuberculosea et Pneumologica Scandinavica. Supplementum [*A publication*]
Acta Tuberc Scand ... Acta Tuberculosea Scandinavica [*A publication*]
Acta Tuberc Scand Suppl ... Acta Tuberculosea Scandinavica. Supplementum [*A publication*]
Acta Unio Int Contra Cancrum ... Acta Unio Internationalis Contra Cancrum [*A publication*]
Acta Univ Agr (Brno) ... Acta Universitatis Agriculturae (Brno). Facultas Silviculturae. Series C [*A publication*]
Acta Univ Agric (Brno) Fac Agron ... Acta Universitatis Agriculturae (Brno). Facultas Agronomica [*A publication*]
Acta Univ Agric (Brno) Fac Silvic ... Acta Universitatis Agriculturae (Brno). Facultas Silviculturae [*A publication*]
Acta Univ Agric (Brno) Fac Vet ... Acta Universitatis Agriculturae (Brno). Facultas Veterinaria [*A publication*]
Acta Univ Agric Fac Agroecon Rada D Spisy Fak Provozne Ekon ... Acta Universitatis Agriculturae. Facultas Agroeconomica. Rada D. Spisy Fakulty Provozne Ekonomicke [*A publication*]
Acta Univ Agric Fac Agron ... Acta Universitatis Agriculturae. Facultas Agronomica [*A publication*]
Acta Univ Agric Fac Silvic ... Acta Universitatis Agriculturae. Facultas Silviculturae [*A publication*]
Acta Univ Agric Fac Vet ... Acta Universitatis Agriculturae. Facultas Veterinaria [*A publication*]

Acta Univ Agric Fac Vet Rada B ... Acta Universitatis Agriculturae. Facultas Veterinaria. Rada B [*A publication*]
Acta Univ Agric Ser C (Brno) ... Acta Universitatis Agriculturae (Brno). Facultas Silviculturae. Series C [*A publication*]
Acta Univ Bergen Ser Math Rerumque Nat ... Acta Universitatis Bergensis. Series Mathematica. Rerumque Naturalium [*A publication*]
Acta Univ Bergen Ser Med Nova Ser ... Acta Universitatis Bergensis. Series Medica. Nova Series [*A publication*]
Acta Univ Carol Biol ... Acta Universitatis Carolinae. Biologica [*A publication*]
Acta Univ Carol Geogr ... Acta Universitatis Carolinae. Geographica [*A publication*]
Acta Univ Carol Geol ... Acta Universitatis Carolinae. Geologica [*A publication*]
Acta Univ Carol Geol Monogr ... Acta Universitatis Carolinae. Geologica. Monographia [*A publication*]
Acta Univ Carol Geol Suppl ... Acta Universitatis Carolinae. Geologica. Supplementum [*A publication*]
Acta Univ Carol Hist ... Acta Universitatis Carolinae. Historia [*A publication*]
Acta Univ Carolinae Geol ... Acta Universitatis Carolinae. Geologica [*A publication*]
Acta Univ Carolinae Math et Phys ... Acta Universitatis Carolinae. Mathematica et Physica [*A publication*]
Acta Univ Carolin Math Phys ... Acta Universitatis Carolinae. Mathematica et Physica [*A publication*]
Acta Univ Carol Math Phys ... Acta Universitatis Carolinae. Mathematica et Physica [*A publication*]
Acta Univ Carol Med ... Acta Universitatis Carolinae. Medica [*A publication*]
Acta Univ Carol Med Monogr ... Acta Universitatis Carolinae. Medica. Monographia [*A publication*]
Acta Univ Carol Med Monogr (Praha) ... Acta Universitatis Carolinae. Medica. Monographia (Praha) [*A publication*]
Acta Univ Carol Med (Praha) ... Acta Universitatis Carolinae. Medica (Praha) [*A publication*]
Acta Univ Carol Med Suppl ... Acta Universitatis Carolinae. Medica. Supplementum [*Czechoslovakia*] [*A publication*]
Acta Univ Debrecen Ludovico Kossuth Nominatae ... Acta Universitatis Debreceniensis de Ludovico Kossuth Nominatae [*A publication*]
Acta Univ Debrecen Ludovico Kossuth Nominatae Ser Biol ... Acta Universitatis Debreceniensis de Ludovico Kossuth Nominatae. Series Biologica [*A publication*]
Acta Univ Debrecen Ludovico Kossuth Nominatae Ser Phys Chim ... Acta Universitatis Debreceniensis de Ludovico Kossuth Nominatae. Series Physica et Chimica [*A publication*]
Acta Univ Gothoburgensis ... Acta Universitatis Gothoburgensis [*A publication*]
Acta Univ Latviensis ... Acta Universitatis Latviensis [*A publication*]
Acta Univ Lodz ... Acta Universitatis Lodziensis [*A publication*]
Acta Univ Lodz Ser 2 ... Acta Universitatis Lodziensis. Seria 2. Nauki Matematyczno-Przyrodnicze [*A publication*]
Acta Univ Lodz Ser 2 Nauk Mat-Przyr ... Acta Universitatis Lodziensis. Seria 2. Nauki Matematyczno-Przyrodnicze [*A publication*]
Acta Univ Lund Sect II Med Math Sci Rerum Nat ... Acta Universitatis Lundensis. Sectio II. Scientiae Rerum Naturalium Medica, Mathematica [*A publication*]
Acta Univ Nicolai Copernici Biol ... Acta Universitatis Nicolai Copernici. Biologia [*A publication*]
Acta Univ Nicolai Copernici Geogr ... Acta Universitatis Nicolai Copernici. Geografia [*A publication*]
Acta Univ Nicolai Copernici Pr Limnol ... Acta Universitatis Nicolai Copernici. Prace Limnologiczne [*A publication*]
Acta Univ Ouluensis Ser A ... Acta Universitatis Ouluensis. Series A. Scientiae Rerum Naturalium. Geologica [*A publication*]
Acta Univ Ouluensis Ser A Sci Rerum Nat Biol ... Acta Universitatis Ouluensis. Series A. Scientiae Rerum Naturalium. Biologica [*A publication*]
Acta Univ Ouluensis Ser C ... Acta Universitatis Ouluensis. Series C. Technica [*A publication*]
Acta Univ Oulu Ser A Sci Rerum Natur Math ... Acta Universitatis Ouluensis. Series A. Scientiae Rerum Naturalium. Mathematica [*A publication*]
Acta Univ Palack Fac Med ... Acta Universitatis Palackianae. Facultatis Medicae [*A publication*]
Acta Univ Palacki Olomuc ... Acta Universitatis Palackianae Olomucensis [*A publication*]
Acta Univ Palacki Olomuc Fac Med ... Acta Universitatis Palackianae Olomucensis. Facultatis Medicae [*A publication*]
Acta Univ Palacki Olomuc Fac Med Suppl ... Acta Universitatis Palackianae Olomucensis. Facultatis Medicae. Supplementum [*A publication*]
Acta Univ Palacki Olomuc Fac Rerum Nat ... Acta Universitatis Palackianae Olomucensis. Facultas Rerum Naturalium [*A publication*]
Acta Univ Palacki Olomuc Fac Rerum Nat Biol ... Acta Universitatis Palackianae Olomucensis. Facultas Rerum Naturalium. Biologica [*A publication*]
Acta Univ Palacki Olomuc Fac Rerum Nat Chem ... Acta Universitatis Palackianae Olomucensis. Facultas Rerum Naturalium. Chemica [*A publication*]

Acta Univ Palacki Olomuc Fac Rerum Nat Math ... Acta Universitatis Palackianae Olomucensis. Facultas Rerum Naturalium. Mathematica [*A publication*]
Acta Univ Palacki Olomuc Fac Rerum Nat Phys ... Acta Universitatis Palackianae Olomucensis. Facultas Rerum Naturalium. Physica [*A publication*]
Acta Univ Szeged Acta Biol ... Acta Universitatis Szegediensis. Acta Biologica [*A publication*]
Acta Univ Szeged Acta Phys et Chem ... Acta Universitatis Szegediensis. Acta Physica et Chemica [*A publication*]
Acta Univ Tamper Ser A ... Acta Universitatis Tamperensis. Series A [*A publication*]
Acta Univ Tsinghuan ... Acta Universitatis Tsinghuanensis [*A publication*]
Acta Univ Ups ... Acta Universitatis Upsaliensis [*A publication*]
Acta Univ Ups Abstr Upps Diss Med ... Acta Universitatis Upsaliensis. Abstracts of Uppsala Dissertations in Medicine [*Sweden*] [*A publication*]
Acta Univ Ups Abstr Upps Diss Sci ... Acta Universitatis Upsaliensis. Abstracts of Uppsala Dissertations in Science [*A publication*]
Acta Univ Upsal Abstr Uppsala Diss Fac Sci ... Acta Universitatis Upsaliensis. Abstracts of Uppsala Dissertations. Faculty of Science [*A publication*]
Acta Univ Upsal Abstr Upps Diss Fac Sci ... Acta Universitatis Upsaliensis. Abstracts of Uppsala Dissertations. Faculty of Science [*A publication*]
Acta Univ Ups Nova Acta Regiae Soc Sci Up Ser VC ... Acta Universitatis Upsaliensis. Nova Acta Regiae Societatis Scientiarum Upsaliensis. Series VC [*A publication*]
Acta Univ Ups Nova Acta Regiae Soc Sci Ups Ser VC ... Acta Universitatis Upsaliensis. Nova Acta Regiae Societatis Scientiarum Upsaliensis. Series VC [*A publication*]
Acta Univ Ups Symb Bot Ups ... Acta Universitatis Upsaliensis. Symbolae Botanicae Upsalienses [*A publication*]
Acta Univ Wratislav ... Acta Universitatis Wratislaviensis [*A publication*]
Acta Univ Wratislaviensis ... Acta Universitatis Wratislaviensis [*Poland*] [*A publication*]
Acta Univ Wratislav Mat Fiz Astron ... Acta Universitatis Wratislaviensis. Matematyka, Fizyka, Astronomia [*A publication*]
Acta Univ Wratislav Pr Geol Mineral ... Acta Universitatis Wratislaviensis. Prace Geologiczno-Mineralogiczne [*A publication*]
Acta Univ Wratislav Pr Zool ... Acta Universitatis Wratislaviensis. Prace Zoologiczne [*Poland*] [*A publication*]
Acta Urol Belg ... Acta Urologica Belgica [*A publication*]
Acta Urol Jpn ... Acta Urologica Japonica [*A publication*]
Acta Vertebr ... Acta Vertebratica [*A publication*]
Acta Vet Acad Sci Hung ... Acta Veterinaria. Academiae Scientiarum Hungaricae [*A publication*]
Acta Vet (Belgr) ... Acta Veterinaria (Belgrade) [*A publication*]
Acta Vet (Beogr) ... Acta Veterinaria (Beograd) [*Yugoslavia*] [*A publication*]
Acta Vet (Brno) ... Acta Veterinaria (Brno) [*A publication*]
Acta Vet (Brno) Suppl ... Acta Veterinaria (Brno). Supplementum [*A publication*]
Acta Vet Hung ... Acta Veterinaria Hungarica [*A publication*]
Acta Vet Scand ... Acta Veterinaria Scandinavica [*A publication*]
Acta Vet Scand Suppl ... Acta Veterinaria Scandinavica. Supplementum [*A publication*]
Acta Vet Zootech Sin ... Acta Veterinaria et Zootechnica Sinica [*A publication*]
Acta Virol ... Acta Virologica [*A publication*]
Acta Virol (Engl Ed) ... Acta Virologica (English Edition) [*A publication*]
Acta Virol (Prague) ... Acta Virologica (Prague) [*A publication*]
Acta Virol (Prague) (Engl Ed) ... Acta Virologica (Prague) (English Edition) [*A publication*]
Acta Virol (Praha) ... Acta Virologica (Praha) [*A publication*]
Acta Vitaminol ... Acta Vitaminologica [*Later, Acta Vitaminologica et Enzymologica*] [*A publication*]
Acta Vitaminol Enzymol ... Acta Vitaminologica et Enzymologica [*Milano*] [*A publication*]
Acta Vitaminol Enzymol (Milano) ... Acta Vitaminologica et Enzymologica (Milano) [*A publication*]
Acta Zool ... Acta Zoologica [*A publication*]
Acta Zool Acad Sci Hung ... Acta Zoologica. Academiae Scientiarum Hungaricae [*A publication*]
Acta Zool Bulg ... Acta Zoologica Bulgarica [*A publication*]
Acta Zool Colomb ... Acta Zoologica Colombiana [*A publication*]
Acta Zool Cracov ... Acta Zoologica Cracoviensia [*A publication*]
Acta Zool Cracov (Engl Transl) ... Acta Zoologica Cracoviensia (English Translation) [*A publication*]
Acta Zool Fenn ... Acta Zoologica Fennica [*A publication*]
Acta Zool Hung ... Acta Zoologica. Academiae Scientiarum Hungaricae [*A publication*]
Acta Zool Lilloana ... Acta Zoologica Lilloana [*A publication*]
Acta Zool Mex ... Acta Zoologica Mexicana [*A publication*]
Acta Zool Mex Nueva Ser ... Acta Zoologica Mexicana. Nueva Serie [*A publication*]
Acta Zool Oecol Univ Lodz ... Acta Zoologica et Oecologica. Universitatis Lodziensis [*A publication*]
Acta Zool Pathol Antverp ... Acta Zoologica et Pathologica Antverpiensia [*A publication*]

Acta Zool Pathol Antverpiensia ... Acta Zoologica et Pathologica Antverpiensia [*A publication*]
Acta Zool Sin ... Acta Zoologica Sinica [*A publication*]
Acta Zool (Stockh) ... Acta Zoologica (Stockholm) [*A publication*]
Acta Zool Taiw ... Acta Zoologica Taiwanica [*A publication*]
Acta Zootech ... Acta Zootechnica [*A publication*]
Acta Zootech Univ Agric (Nitra) ... Acta Zootechnica. Universitatis Agriculturae (Nitra) [*A publication*]
ACTB .... Aircrew Classification Test Battery
ACTBC ...... Medical Library, Tom Baker Cancer Center, Calgary, Alberta [*Library symbol*] [*National Library of Canada*]   (NLC)
Act Bio C B ... Acta Biologica Cracoviensia. Series Botanica [*A publication*]
Act Bioch H ... Acta Biochimica et Biophysica. Academiae Scientiarum Hungaricae [*A publication*]
Act Biochim ... Actualites Biochimiques [*A publication*]
Act Bioch P ... Acta Biochimica Polonica [*A publication*]
Act Bio C Z ... Acta Biologica Cracoviensia. Series Zoologia [*A publication*]
Act Bio Ira ... Acta Biochimica Iranica [*A publication*]
Act Biol H ... Acta Biologica. Academiae Scientiarum Hungaricae [*A publication*]
Act Bio Med ... Acta Biologica et Medica Germanica [*A publication*]
Act Bot Nee ... Acta Botanica Neerlandica [*A publication*]
act-C .... Actinomycin-C [*Antineoplastic drug*]
ACTC .... Art Class Teacher's Certificate [*British*]
ACTC .... Association of Community Travel Clubs   (EA)
ACTC .... Association Culturelle et Touristique des Cantons [*Cultural and Tourist Association of Cantons*] [*Canada*]
ACTC .... Bureau of Air Commerce Type Certificate
ACTC .... CSIRO [*Commonwealth Scientific and Industrial Research Organisation*] Activities Archive [*Database*]   (ADA)
ACTC .... TCPL Resources Ltd., Calgary, Alberta [*Library symbol*] [*National Library of Canada*]   (NLC)
Act Can ...... Acta Cancellariae, by Monroe [*England*] [*A publication*]   (DLA)
Act Card ..... Actualites Cardiologiques et Angeiologiques Internationales [*A publication*]
Act Cart ..... Acta Cartographica [*A publication*]
Act Chem A ... Acta Chemica Scandinavica. Series A. Physical and Inorganic Chemistry [*A publication*]
Act Chem B ... Acta Chemica Scandinavica. Series B. Organic Chemistry and Biochemistry [*A publication*]
Act Chim H ... Acta Chimica. Academiae Scientiarum Hungaricae [*A publication*]
Act Chir B ... Acta Chirurgica Belgica [*A publication*]
Act Chir H ... Acta Chirurgica. Academiae Scientiarum Hungaricae [*A publication*]
Act Chir Sc ... Acta Chirurgica Scandinavica [*A publication*]
Act Ci .... Actas Ciba [*A publication*]
Act Cient V ... Acta Cientifica Venezolana [*A publication*]
Act Clin B .. Acta Clinica Belgica [*A publication*]
Act Clin Ther ... Actualites de Clinique Therapeutique [*A publication*]
Act Coll ...... Actes et Colloques [*A publication*]
Act Colloq Int Inst Etud Renaissance Hum ... Actes. Colloque International. Institut pour l'Etude de la Renaissance et de l'Humanisme. Universite Libre de Bruxelles [*A publication*]
ACTCOM ... Army Authority for Major Commands to Disseminate Information and Take Appropriate Action
Act Congr Benelux Hist Sci ... Actes. Congres Benelux d'Histoire des Sciences [*A publication*]
Act Congr Int Etud Byzantines ... Actes. Congres International des Etudes Byzantines [*A publication*]
Act Congr Int Hist Sci ... Actes. Congres International d'Histoire des Sciences [*A publication*]
Act Congr Int Phil Sci ... Actes. Congres International. Union Internationale de Philosophie des Sciences [*A publication*]
ACTCP ...... Trans-Canada Pipelines, Calgary, Alberta [*Library symbol*] [*National Library of Canada*]   (NLC)
ACTCR ...... Texaco Canada Resources Ltd., Calgary, Alberta [*Library symbol*] [*National Library of Canada*]   (NLC)
Act Cryst A ... Acta Crystallographica. Section A [*A publication*]
Act Cryst B ... Acta Crystallographica. Section B [*A publication*]
ACTCS ...... Active Thermal Control System [*NASA*]   (MCD)
ACTCS ...... Air Conditioning and Temperature Control System [*Aerospace*]
Act Cult Vet ... Actualites et Culture Veterinaires [*A publication*]
Act Cur Ad Sc ... Acta Curiae Admiralatus Scotiae (Wade) [*A publication*]   (DLA)
Act Cytol .... Acta Cytologica [*A publication*]
act-D .... Actinomycin-D [*Also, AMD, DACT*] [*Antineoplastic drug*]
ACTD .... Attitude Control Torquing Device [*Aerospace*]
ACTDEC .... Supreme Court of the Australian Capital Territory Decisions [*Database*]
Act Dent ... Actualite Dentaire [*A publication*]
Act Der-Ven ... Acta Dermato-Venereologica [*A publication*]
Act Develop ... Action for Development [*A publication*]
Act Diabet ... Acta Diabetologica Latina [*A publication*]
ACTDS ...... Automatically Cued Target Detecting System   (MCD)
ACTE .... Actuate
ACTE .... Agkistrodon Contortrix Thrombin-Like Enzyme
ACTe .... Anodal Closure Tetanus [*Physiology*]
ACTE .... Association of Corporate Travel Executives   (EA)
ACTE .... Automatic Checkout Test Equipment   (AAG)

ACTE......... Techman Engineering Ltd., Calgary, Alberta [*Library symbol*] [*National Library of Canada*] (NLC)
ACTEA...... Accrediting Council for Theological Education in Africa [*of the Association of Evangelicals of Africa and Madagascar*] [*See also COHETA*] (EAIO)
Act Ec........ Actualite Economique [*A publication*]
ACTEC...... American Coalition on Trade Expansion with Canada (EA)
ACTEC...... American College of Trust and Estate Counsel (EA)
ACTEDS ... Army Civilian Training, Education, and Development System
Act Endocr ... Acta Endocrinologica [*A publication*]
Act Ent Boh ... Acta Entomologica Bohemoslovaca [*A publication*]
ACTER...... Anticountermeasures Trainer
ACTERS.... ADD-H [*Attention Deficit Disorder with Hyperactivity*] Comprehensive Teachers Rating Scale
Actes Colloq Int ... Actes. Colloque International [*A publication*]
Actes Congr Int Hist Sci ... Actes. Congres International d'Histoire des Sciences [*A publication*]
Actes Congr Mond Soc Int Etude Corps Gras ... Actes. Congres Mondial. Societe Internationale pour l'Etude des Corps Gras [*A publication*]
Actes Rech Sci Soc ... Actes de la Recherche en Sciences Sociales [*A publication*]
Actes Semin Physiol Comp ... Actes. Seminaire de Physiologie Comparee [*A publication*]
Actes Soc Helv Sci Nat Parte Sci ... Actes. Societe Helvetique des Sciences Naturelles. Parte Scientifique [*A publication*]
Act Ethn H ... Acta Ethnographica. Academiae Scientiarum Hungaricae [*A publication*]
Act Ethnogr ... Acta Ethnographica [*A publication*]
ACTEW..... Australian Capital Territory Electricity and Water
ACTF........ Activities File [*CSIRO database*] (ADA)
ACTF........ Altitude Control Test Facility
ACTF........ American College Theater Festival
ACTF........ American Conservatory Theatre Foundation (EA)
ACTF........ CSIRO [*Commonwealth Scientific and Industrial Research Organisation*] Activities File [*Database*] (ADA)
ACTFL...... American Council on the Teaching of Foreign Languages (EA)
ACTG .... Acting (AFM)
ACTG .... Actuating (KSC)
ACTG .... Advance Carrier Training Group [*Navy*]
ACTG .... AIDS [*Acquired Immune Deficiency Syndrome*] Clinical Trials Group (EA)
ACTG .... [*A*] Chance to Grow (EA)
Act Gastr B ... Acta Gastro-Enterologica Belgica [*A publication*]
Act Genet M ... Acta Geneticae, Medicae, et Gemellologiae [*A publication*]
Act Geod Geophys et Montan ... Acta Geodaetica, Geophysica, et Montanistica [*A publication*]
Act Geogr ... Acta Geographica [*France*] [*A publication*]
Act Gyn...... Actualites Gynecologiques [*A publication*]
Act Gynaecol Obstet Hisp Lusit ... Acta Gynaecologica et Obstetrica Hispano Lusitana [*A publication*]
ACTH........ Adrenocorticotrophic Hormone [*Endocrinology*]
ACTH........ Arbitrary Correction to Hit [*Gunnery term*] [*Navy*]
ACTH........ Association for Canadian Theatre History
Act Haemat ... Acta Haematologica [*A publication*]
Act Hem..... Actualites Hematologiques [*A publication*]
ACTheol .... Australian College of Theology
Act Hep-Gas ... Acta Hepato-Gastroenterologica [*Stuttgart/New York*] [*A publication*]
Act Hist Ar ... Acta Historiae Artium. Academiae Scientiarum Hungaricae [*A publication*]
Act Hist Cy ... Acta Histochemica et Cytochemica [*A publication*]
Act Hist H ... Acta Historica. Academiae Scientiarum Hungaricae [*A publication*]
Act Histoch ... Acta Histochemica [*A publication*]
ACTH-LI... Adrenocorticotrophin-Like Immunoreactivity [*Immunochemistry*]
Act Hydrobiol Sin ... Acta Hydrobiologica Sinica [*A publication*]
ACTI......... Acacia Confusa Trypsin Inhibitor [*Biochemistry*]
ACTI......... Advisory Committee on Technology Innovation [*Board on Science and Technology for International Development*] [*Office of International Affairs*] [*National Research Council*] (EGAO)
ACTIAC .... Arms Control Technical Information and Analysis Center [*Department of State*]
ACT/IC ..... Active in Commission [*Vessel status*] [*Navy*]
ACTICE .... Authority Coordinating the Transport of Inland Continental Europe [*NATO*]
ACTIE3..... Anales. Catedra de Tisioneumologia [*A publication*]
ACTIFS..... Active Control for Total In-Flight Simulator (MCD)
ACTIIV ..... Advisory Centre on Technology for Industry in Victoria [*Australia*]
ACTIME... Agency for the Coordination of Transport in the Mediterranean [*NATO*] (MCD)
ACTIMED ... Agency for the Coordination of Transport in the Mediterranean [*NATO*] (NATG)
Actinides Electron Struct Relat Prop ... Actinides. Electronic Structure and Related Properties [*A publication*]
Actinides Lanthanides Rev ... Actinides and Lanthanides. Reviews [*A publication*]
Actinides Rev ... Actinides Reviews [*A publication*]

Actinomycetes Relat Org ... Actinomycetes and Related Organisms [*A publication*]
ACTION ... Action International Ministries (EAIO)
ACTION ... [*An*] independent government agency, created in 1971. Although always written in uppercase, the word is not an acronym
ACTION ... American Council to Improve Our Neighborhoods [*Later, NUC*]
ACTION ... [*A*] Commitment to Improve Our Nation [*Canada*]
Action........ United Evangelical Action [*A publication*]
Action Ageing Proc Symp ... Action on Ageing. Proceedings of a Symposium [*A publication*]
Action Med ... Action Medicale [*A publication*]
Action Univ ... Action Universitaire [*A publication*]
ACTIRF..... Association Canadienne de Traitement d'Images et Reconnaissance des Formes [*Canada*]
ACT/IS...... Active in Service [*Vessel status*] [*Navy*]
ACTIS .... Advanced Circular Scan Thermal Imaging System (MCD)
ACTIS .... AIDS [*Acquired Immune Deficiency Syndrome*] Clinical Trials Information Service (EISS)
ACTISUD ... Authority for the Coordination of Inland Transport in Southern Europe [*NATO*]
ACTIV....... Activation (NASA)
ACTIV....... Army Concept Team in Vietnam
Actividad Econ ... Actividad Economica [*A publication*]
Activity Bul ... Activity Bulletin for Teachers in Secondary Schools [*A publication*] (APTA)
Activ Nerv ... Activitas Nervosa Superior [*Praha*] [*A publication*]
Activ Nerv Super ... Activitas Nervosa Superior [*Czechoslovakia*] [*A publication*]
Activ Petrol ... Actividades Petroleras [*A publication*]
ActJn .... Acts of John (BJA)
Act Jpn Med Trop ... Acta Japonica Medicinae Tropicalis [*A publication*]
Act Jur .... Actualite Juridique [*A publication*]
ACTL........ Actual (MSA)
ACTL........ American College of Trial Lawyers (EA)
Act Lawt Ct ... Acts of Lawting Court [*Scotland*] [*A publication*] (DLA)
Act Ld Aud C ... Acts of Lords Auditors of Causes [*Scotland*] [*A publication*] (DLA)
Act Ld Co CC ... Acts of Lords of Council in Civil Causes [*1478-1501*] [*Scotland*] [*A publication*] (DLA)
Act Ld Co Pub Aff ... Acts of Lords of Council in Public Affairs [*Scotland*] [*A publication*] (DLA)
ActLingH... Acta Linguistica. Academiae Scientiarum Hungaricae [*A publication*]
ActLitH...... Acta Litteraria. Academiae Scientiarum Hungaricae [*A publication*]
Act Litt Sci Regiae Univ Hung Francisco-Josephinae Sect Med ... Acta Litterarum ac Scientiarum Regiae Universitatis Hungaricae Francisco-Josephinae. Sectio Medicorum [*A publication*]
ACTLTA ... Australian Capital Territory Lawn Tennis Association
ACTM .... Actmedia, Inc. [*NASDAQ symbol*] (NQ)
ACTM .... Ashridge Centre for Transport Management [*Ashridge Management College*] [*British*] (CB)
ACTM .... Association of Cotton Textile Merchants of New York [*Later, ATMI*] (EA)
ACTM .... Audio Center - Transmitter (KSC)
Act Macrophages Proc Workshop Conf Hoechst ... Activation of Macrophages Proceedings. Workshop Conference Hoechst [*A publication*]
Act Math.... Acta Mathematica [*A publication*]
Act Math H ... Acta Mathematica. Academiae Scientiarum Hungaricae [*A publication*]
ACTMC.... Army Clothing, Textile, and Materiel Center
Act Mechan ... Acta Mechanica [*A publication*]
Act Med ..... Actualidad Medica [*A publication*]
Act Med H ... Acta Medica. Academiae Scientiarum Hungaricae [*A publication*]
Act Med Oka ... Acta Medicinae Okayama [*A publication*]
Act Med Per ... Actualidad Medica Peruana [*A publication*]
Act Med Sc ... Acta Medica Scandinavica [*A publication*]
Act Metall ... Acta Metallurgica [*A publication*]
Act Mic P A ... Acta Microbiologica Polonica. Series A. Microbiologia Generalis [*A publication*]
Act Mic P B ... Acta Microbiologica Polonica. Series B. Microbiologia Applicata [*A publication*]
Act Micro H ... Acta Microbiologica. Academiae Scientiarum Hungaricae [*A publication*]
Act Morph H ... Acta Morphologica. Academiae Scientiarum Hungaricae [*A publication*]
Act Morph N ... Acta Morphologica Neerlando-Scandinavica [*A publication*]
Act Mozart ... Acta Mozartiana [*A publication*]
ACTMR..... Association Canadienne Contre la Tuberculose et les Maladies Respiratoires [*Canadian Association Against Tuberculosis and Respiratory Diseases*]
Act Mus Hist Natur Rouen ... Actes. Museum d'Histoire Naturelle de Rouen [*A publication*]
Act Music ... Acta Musicologica [*A publication*]
ACTN .... Action
ActN.......... Action Nationale [*A publication*]
Act Nat....... Action Nationale [*A publication*]

Act Nerv Super ... Activitas Nervosa Superior [*A publication*]
Act Nerv Super (Praha) ... Activitas Nervosa Superior (Praha) [*A publication*]
Act Neurob ... Acta Neurobiologiae Experimentalis [*A publication*]
Act Neuroch ... Acta Neurochirurgica [*A publication*]
Act Neurop ... Acta Neuropathologica [*A publication*]
Act Neuro-Phys ... Actualites Neurophysiologiques [*A publication*]
Act Neur Sc ... Acta Neurologica Scandinavica [*A publication*]
ACTNT...... Accountant   (MUGU)
ACTO........ Action Officer [*Army*]   (AABC)
ACTO........ Advanced Control Test Operation [*Oak Ridge National Laboratory*]
ACTO........ Army Communicative Technology Office
ACTO........ Association of Chief Technical Officers   (EAIO)
ACTO........ Automatic Computing Transfer Oscillator   (IEEE)
Act Obst Sc ... Acta Obstetrica et Gynecologica Scandinavica [*A publication*]
ACT/OC.... Active out of Commission [*Vessel status*] [*Navy*]
Act Odon Sc .. Acta Odontologica Scandinavica [*A publication*]
Act Oecon ... Acta Oeconomica [*Budapest*] [*A publication*]
Act O-Mer ... Actualites d'Outre-Mer [*A publication*]
Acton......... Acton's Prize Cases, Privy Council [*A publication*]   (DLA)
Act Ophth (K) ... Acta Ophthalmologica (Kobenhavn) [*A publication*]
ActOr......... Acta Orientalia [*Copenhagen*] [*A publication*]
ACTOR ..... Askania Cine-Theodolite Optical-Tracking Range
ACTORD .. Australian Capital Territory Ordinances [*Database*]
ActOrHung ... Acta Orientalia. Academiae Scientiarum Hungaricae [*Budapest*] [*A publication*]
Act Orth Sc ... Acta Orthopaedica Scandinavica [*A publication*]
ACT/OS.... Active out of Service [*Vessel status*] [*Navy*]
Act Oto-Lar ... Acta Oto-Laryngologica [*A publication*]
ACTOV ..... Accelerated Turn-Over to Vietnamese [*Military*]
ACTP......... Adrenocorticotrophic Polypeptide [*Endocrinology*]
ACTP......... Advanced-Composite Thermoplastic [*Materials engineering*]
ACTP......... Advanced Computer Techniques Corp. [*NASDAQ symbol*]   (NQ)
ACTP......... Advanced Computer Techniques Project   (KSC)
ACTP......... Advanced Control Technology Program [*Oak Ridge National Laboratory*]
ACTP......... Australian Capital Territory Police
ACTP......... Total Petroleum (North America) Ltd., Calgary, Alberta [*Library symbol*] [*National Library of Canada*]   (NLC)
Act Paed H ... Acta Paediatrica. Academiae Scientiarum Hungaricae [*A publication*]
Act Paedops ... Acta Paedopsychiatrica [*A publication*]
Act Paed Sc ... Acta Paediatrica Scandinavica [*A publication*]
ACT Pap Educ ... ACT [*Australian Capital Territory*] Papers on Education [*A publication*]   (APTA)
Act Pat Jap ... Acta Pathologica Japonica [*A publication*]
Act Pat S A ... Acta Pathologica et Microbiologica Scandinavica. Section A [*A publication*]
Act Pat S B ... Acta Pathologica et Microbiologica Scandinavica. Section B [*A publication*]
Act Pat S C ... Acta Pathologica et Microbiologica Scandinavica. Section C [*A publication*]
ActPaul...... Acts of Paul   (BJA)
ACTPC...... Acting Pay Clerk [*Navy*]
Act PC........ Acts of the Privy Council (Dasent) [*England*] [*A publication*]   (DLA)
ACTPCM .. Australia. Commonwealth Scientific and Industrial Research Organisation. Division of Food Research. Technical Paper [*A publication*]
Act PC NS ... Acts of the Privy Council, New Series (Dasent) [*England*] [*A publication*]   (DLA)
Act Ped....... Actualidad Pediatrica [*A publication*]
ActPet........ Acts of Peter   (BJA)
Act Pharm ... Action Pharmaceutique [*A publication*]
Act Pharm S ... Acta Pharmaceutica Suecica [*A publication*]
Act Pharm T ... Acta Pharmacologica et Toxicologica [*A publication*]
Act Phar Si ... Acta Pharmacologica Sinica [*A publication*]
Act Phy P A ... Acta Physica Polonica. Series A [*A publication*]
Act Phy P B ... Acta Physica Polonica. Series B [*A publication*]
Act Phys Au ... Acta Physica Austriaca [*A publication*]
Act Phys Ch ... Acta Physica et Chemica [*A publication*]
Act Phys H ... Acta Physica. Academiae Scientiarum Hungaricae [*A publication*]
Act Physl H ... Acta Physiologica. Academiae Scientiarum Hungaricae [*A publication*]
Act Physl L ... Acta Physiologica Latino Americana [*A publication*]
Act Physl P ... Acta Physiologica Polonica [*A publication*]
Act Physl S ... Acta Physiologica Scandinavica [*A publication*]
ACTPO...... Accountable Property Officer [*Military*]   (AABC)
Act Pol His ... Acta Poloniae Historica [*A publication*]
Act Pol Ph ... Acta Poloniae Pharmaceutica [*A publication*]
Act Poly Ch ... Acta Polytechnica Scandinavica. Chemistry Series [*A publication*]
Act Poly Ci ... Acta Polytechnica Scandinavica. Civil Engineering and Building Construction Series [*A publication*]
Act Poly El ... Acta Polytechnica Scandinavica. Electrical Engineering Series [*A publication*]
Act Poly Ma ... Acta Polytechnica Scandinavica. Mathematics and Computing Machinery Series [*A publication*]

Act Poly Me ... Acta Polytechnica Scandinavica. Mechanical Engineering Series [*A publication*]
Act Poly Ph ... Acta Polytechnica Scandinavica. Physics Including Nucleonics Series [*A publication*]
Act Pr C ..... Acton's Reports, Prize Cases [*England*] [*A publication*]   (DLA)
Act Pr C Col S ... Acts of the Privy Council, Colonial Series [*England*] [*A publication*]   (DLA)
Act Psiq Ps ... Acta Psiquiatrica y Psicologica de America Latina [*A publication*]
Act Psychol ... Acta Psychologica [*Amsterdam*] [*A publication*]
Act Psych T ... Acta Psychologica Taiwanica [*A publication*]
Act Psyc Sc ... Acta Psychiatrica Scandinavica [*A publication*]
ACTR......... Actuator   (KSC)
ACTR......... Air Corps Technical Report [*Obsolete*]
ACTR......... American Council of Teachers of Russian   (EA)
ACTR......... Australian Capital Territory. Reports [*A publication*]   (APTA)
ACTR......... Touche Ross & Co., Calgary, Alberta [*Library symbol*] [*National Library of Canada*]   (NLC)
ACTRA...... Association of Canadian Television and Radio Artists
ACTRA...... Australian Capital Territory Reading Association
ACTRAC... Accurate Tracking   (MUGU)
Act Rad Dgn ... Acta Radiologica. Series One. Diagnosis [*Stockholm*] [*A publication*]
Act Rad TPB ... Acta Radiologica. Therapy, Physics, Biology [*Later, Acta Radiologica. Series Two. Oncology, Radiation, Physics, and Biology (Stockholm)*] [*A publication*]
ACTRAM ... Advisory Committee on the Transport of Radioactive Materials [*British*]
ACTRAN... Analog Computer Translator
ACTRAN... Autocoder-to-COBOL Translating Service [*Data processing*]   (IEEE)
Act Reg ...... Acta Regia; An Abstract of Rymer's Foedera [*A publication*]
ACTREG.... Australian Capital Territory Regulations [*Database*]
ACTREP.... Activities Report [*Shipping*]
Act Rep Res Dev Assoc Mil Food Packag Syst ... Activities Report. Research and Development Associates for Military Food and Packaging Systems [*A publication*]
Act Rep Res Dev Assoc Mil Food Packag Syst Inc ... Activities Report. Research and Development Associates for Military Food and Packaging Systems, Incorporated [*A publication*]
ACT Res Rep ... American College Testing. Research Reports [*A publication*]
ACTRL...... Acoustic Trials   (NVT)
ACTRM..... Association Canadienne des Techniciens en Radiation Medicale [*Canadian Association of Medical Radiation Technologists*]   (EAIO)
ACTRS ...... Association of Catholic TV and Radio Syndicators   (EA)
ACTRUS ... Automatically Controlled Turbine Run-Up System [*Navigation*]
ACTS......... Accounts, Collection, and Taxpayer Service [*Internal Revenue Service*]
ACTS......... Acoustic Control and Telemetry System
ACTS......... Acquisitions, Cataloguing, Technical Systems [*Library service*]
ACTS......... Action for Child Transportation Safety [*Defunct*]   (EA)
ACTS......... Action Staffing, Inc. [*NASDAQ symbol*]   (NQ)
ACTS......... Activated Carbon Treatment System   (MCD)
ACTS......... Advanced Communication Technology Satellite Program [*Washington, DC*] [*Office of Space Science and Applications*] [*NASA*]   (GRD)
ACTS......... [*The*] Advanced Construction Technology Show [*British*]   (ITD)
ACTS......... Advisory Commission on Textbook Specifications
ACTS......... Aid for Commonwealth Teaching of Science Scheme [*British*]
ACTS......... Air Corps Tactical School [*Obsolete*]
ACTS......... Air Crew Training System
ACTS......... Air-Cushion Takeoff System   (MCD)
ACTS......... Airlines Computer Tracing System [*Luggage retrieving system*]
ACTS......... Alfred C. Toepfer Schiffahrt, MB [*Commercial firm*] [*Federal Republic of Germany*]   (DS)
ACTS......... American Catholic Truth Society [*Defunct*]   (EA)
ACTS......... American Christian Television Service [*Cable-television system*]
ACTS......... American Coalition for Traffic Safety   (EA)
ACTS......... Analog Conditioning and Test System
ACTS......... Arc Current Time Simulator
ACTS......... Area Communications Terminal Subsystem [*Ground Communications Facility, NASA*]
ACTS......... Army Criteria Tracking System
ACTS......... Association of Cable Television Suppliers   (EA)
ACTS......... Association Canadienne des Travailleurs Sociaux [*Canadian Association of Social Workers - CASW*]
ACTS......... Association of Career Training Schools [*Defunct*]   (EA)
ACTS......... Association for Christian Training and Service   (EA)
ACTS......... Association of Clerical, Technical, and Supervisory Staffs [*British*]   (DCTA)
ACTS......... Association of Community Tribal Schools   (EA)
ACTS......... Attitude Control and Translation System [*Aerospace*]   (MCD)
ACTS......... Automated Commitment Tracking System [*Nuclear energy*]   (NRCH)
ACTS......... Automated Component Trading System
ACTS......... Automated Computer Time Service
ACTS......... Automated Configuration Tracking System   (MCD)

ACTS......... Automated Custom Terminal System
ACTS......... Automatic Coin Telephone Service
ACTS......... Automatic Computer Telex Services
ACTS......... Commonwealth Acts [Database]
Acts Austl P ... Acts of the Australian Parliament [A publication] (DLA)
Acts Austl Parl ... Acts of the Australian Parliament [A publication] (ILCA)
Act Scand Juris Gent ... Nordisk Tidsskrift foer International Ret.; Acta Scandinavica, Juris Gentium [Copenhagen, Denmark] [A publication] (DLA)
Act Sci Mat ... Acta Scientiarum Mathematicarum [A publication]
ACTSECNAV ... Acting Secretary of the Navy
Act of Sed... Act of Sederunt (DLA)
Act Sed....... Act of Sederunt (DLA)
Act Sludge Process Control Ser ... Activated Sludge Process Control Series [A publication]
ACT-SO .... Afro-American Cultural Technological Scientific Olympics
Act Sociol... Acta Sociologica [A publication]
Act Soc Linn Bordeaux ... Actes. Societe Linneenne de Bordeaux [A publication]
Acts & Ords Interreg ... Acts and Ordinances of the Interregnum [1642-60] [United Kingdom] [A publication] (ILCA)
Acts & Ords Interregnum ... Acts and Ordinances of the Interregnum [1642-60] [United Kingdom] [A publication] (DLA)
ACTS/PROP ... Attitude Control and Translation System/Propulsion [Aerospace]
Acts S Austl ... Acts of South Australia [A publication] (DLA)
ACTS/SCE ... Attitude Control and Translation System/Stabilization and Control Electronics [Aerospace]
Acts Tasm ... Acts of Tasmania [A publication] (DLA)
ACTSU .... Association of Computer Time-Sharing Users
Acts Van Diem L ... Acts of Van Dieman's Land [Australia] [A publication] (DLA)
Acts Vict .... Acts of the Parliament of Victoria [Australia] [A publication] (DLA)
Act Symp Int Sci Phys Math 17 Siecle ... Actes. Symposium International des Sciences Physiques et Mathematiques dans la Premiere Moitie du 17e Siecle [A publication]
Act Syst (GB) ... Active Systems (Great Britain) [A publication]
ACTT........ Acetate [Also, AC] [Organic chemistry] (MSA)
ACTT........ Approved Course of Teacher Training [Australia]
ACTT........ Association of Cinematograph, Television, and Allied Technicians [Canada]
ACTT........ [A] Christmas Trains and Trucks Program [Marine Corps program in Vietnam]
ACTTAB ... Australian Capital Territory Totalizator Agency Board
ACT Teach ... ACT [Australian Capital Territory] Teachers Federation. Teacher [A publication] (APTA)
Act Techn H ... Acta Technica. Academiae Scientiarum Hungaricae [A publication]
ACTU .... Association of Catholic Trade Unionists (EA)
ACTU .... Transalta Utilities, Calgary, Alberta [Library symbol] [National Library of Canada] (NLC)
ACTUAL... American Council of Teachers of Uncommonly Taught Asian Languages [Defunct] (EA)
Actual Agron ... Actualites Agronomiques [A publication]
Actual Auto ... Actualite Automobile [A publication]
Actual Biochim ... Actualites Biochimiques [A publication]
Actual Biol ... Actualidades Biologicas [A publication]
Actual Biol (Paris) ... Actualites Biologiques (Paris) [A publication]
Actual Chim ... Actualite Chimique [A publication]
Actual Chim Can ... Actualite Chimique Canadienne [A publication]
Actual Chim Ind ... Actualite Chimique et Industrielle [A publication]
Actual Chine Popul ... Actualite en Chine Populaire [A publication]
Actual Combust Energ ... Actualite, Combustibles, Energie [France] [A publication]
Actual Econ Soc Can Sci Econ ... Actualite Economique. Societe Canadienne de Science Economique [A publication]
Actual Endocrinol (Paris) ... Actualites Endocrinologiques (Paris) [A publication]
Actual Formation Perm ... Actualite de la Formation Permanente [A publication]
Actual Hemat ... Actualites Hematologiques [A publication]
Actual Hematol ... Actualites Hematologiques [A publication]
Actual Hepato-Gastro-Enterol Hotel-Dieu ... Actualites Hepato-Gastro-Enterologiques de l'Hotel-Dieu [France] [A publication]
Actual Hotel-Dieu ... Actualites de l'Hotel-Dieu [A publication]
Actual Industr Lorraines ... Actualites Industrielles Lorraines [A publication]
Actualite Econ ... Actualite Economique [A publication]
Actualites Sci Indust ... Actualites Scientifiques et Industrielles [A publication]
Actual Jur .. Actualite Juridique [A publication]
Actual Mar ... Actualites Marines [A publication]
Actual Med ... Actualidad Medica [A publication]
Actual Med ... Actualidades Medicas [A publication]
Actual Med ... Actualite Medicale [A publication]
Actual Med-Chir (Mars) ... Actualites Medico-Chirurgicales (Marseille) [A publication]
Actual Nephrol Hop Necker ... Actualites Nephrologiques. Hopital Necker [A publication]
Actual Neurophysiol ... Actualites Neurophysiologiques [Paris] [A publication]

Actual Neurophysiol (Paris) ... Actualites Neurophysiologiques (Paris) [A publication]
Actual Odontostomatol ... Actualites Odontostomatologiques [Paris] [A publication]
Actual Pedagog ... Actualites Pedagogiques [A publication]
Actual Pharm ... Actualites Pharmacologiques [A publication]
Actual Pharmacol ... Actualites Pharmacologiques [A publication]
Actual Pharmacol (Paris) ... Actualites Pharmacologiques (Paris) [A publication]
Actual Protozool ... Actualites Protozoologiques [A publication]
Actual Psychiatr ... Actualites Psychiatriques [A publication]
Actual Rel Mo ... Actualite Religieuse dans le Monde [A publication]
Actual Sci Ind ... Actualites Scientifiques et Industrielles [A publication]
Actual Sci Techn ... Actualites Scientifiques et Techniques [A publication]
Actual Specif Eng ... Actual Specifying Engineer [A publication]
Actual Ther ... Actualite Therapeutique [A publication]
Actuar Note ... Actuarial Note [A publication]
ACTU Bul ... ACTU [Australian Council of Trade Unions] Bulletin [A publication] (APTA)
Actu Econ... Actualite Economique [A publication]
Actuel Dev ... Actuel Developpement [A publication]
Actuel Develop ... Actuel Developpement [A publication]
Actuel Dr Person ... Actuelles des Droits de la Personne [A publication]
Actuelle Gerontol ... Actuelle Gerontologie [A publication]
Act Univ La Plata ... Actos Universitarios. Universidad Nacional de La Plata [A publication]
ACT UP..... AIDS [Acquired Immune Deficiency Syndrome] Coalition to Unleash Power
ACTV........ Activate (AFM)
ACTV........ Activity (AABC)
ACTV........ Advanced Compatible Television [Wide-screen, high-resolution system utilizing standard broadcast channels] [RCA Corp.]
ACTV........ American Coalition for Traditional Values (EA)
Act Vet H ... Acta Veterinaria. Academiae Scientiarum Hungaricae [A publication]
Act Vet Sc .. Acta Veterinaria Scandinavica [A publication]
Act Virolog ... Acta Virologica [English Edition] [A publication]
Act Vit Enz ... Acta Vitaminologica et Enzymologica [Milano] [A publication]
ACTVNANAL ... Activation Analysis (MSA)
ACTVT...... Activate (MSA)
ACTVTR ... Activator (MSA)
ACTVTY ... Activity
ACTWU ...... Amalgamated Clothing and Textile Workers Union (EA)
AC & TWU ... Atlantic Communication and Technical Workers Union
ACTY........ Activity (AFM)
ACTY........ Actuary (ROG)
Act Zool H ... Acta Zoologica. Academiae Scientiarum Hungaricae [A publication]
ACU.......... AC [Alternating Current] Control Unit
ACU.......... Acceleration Compensation [or Control] Unit [Aviation]
ACU.......... Accugraph Corp. [Toronto Stock Exchange symbol]
Acu.......... Accursius [Deceased, 1263] [Authority cited in pre-1607 legal work] (DSA)
ACU.......... Achutupo [Panama] [Airport symbol] (OAG)
ACU.......... Acknowledgement Unit [Telecommunications] (TEL)
ACU.......... Acme United Corp. [AMEX symbol] (SPSG)
ACU.......... Actors' Church Union [Episcopalian]
ACU.......... Acute Care Unit [Medicine]
ACU.......... Address Control Unit [Data processing] (MDG)
ACU.......... Administration of the Customs Union [EEC] (DS)
ACU.......... Advanced Connector Unit [Telecommunications] (TSSD)
ACU.......... Aide aux Croyants de l'URSS [Aid to Believers in the Soviet Union - ABSU] [Paris, France] (EAIO)
ACU.......... Air Cleanup Unit [Nuclear energy] (NRCH)
ACU.......... Air-Conditioning Unit
ACU.......... Airborne Control Unit [Telecommunications] (TSSD)
ACU.......... Aircraft Control Unit (NVT)
ACU.......... Alarm Control Unit [Bell System] [Telecommunications]
ACU.......... Altocumulus [Cloud] [Meteorology] (MUGU)
ACU.......... American Catholic Union (EA)
ACU.......... American Church Union (EA)
ACU.......... American Congregational Union
ACU.......... American Conservative Union (EA)
ACU.......... American Cycling Union (EA)
ACU.......... Analysis Control Unit
ACU.......... Annunciator Control Unit [Military] (MCD)
ACU.......... Antenna Control Unit
ACU.......... Anticrime Unit
ACU.......... Arithmetic Computer
ACU.......... Arithmetic and Control Unit (BUR)
ACU.......... Asian Clearing Union
ACU.......... Asian Currency Unit
ACU.......... Assault Craft Unit (NVT)
ACU.......... Association Canadienne d'Urbanisme [Canadian City Planning Association]
ACU.......... Association of College Unions [Later, ACU-I] (EA)
ACU.......... Association of Commonwealth Universities [London, England] (EAIO)
ACU.......... Association of Computer Users (EA)
ACU.......... Association of Cricket Umpires (EAIO)

ACU.......... Autocycle Union [*British*]
ACU.......... Automatic Calling Unit [*Telecommunications*] (TEL)
ACU.......... Auxiliary Conditioning Unit
ACU.......... Avionics Cooling Unit [*Aerospace*] (NASA)
ACU.......... East Kurupa, AK [*Location identifier*] [*FAA*] (FAAL)
ACU.......... University of Calgary, Alberta [*Library symbol*] [*National Library of Canada*] (NLC)
ACUA....... Accugraph Corp. [*NASDAQ symbol*] (NQ)
ACUA....... Airline Credit Union Association (EA)
ACUA....... Association of College and University Auditors [*Madison, WI*] (EA)
ACUA....... University of Calgary Archives, Alberta [*Library symbol*] [*National Library of Canada*] (BIB)
ACUAI...... Arctic Institute of North America, University of Calgary, Alberta [*Library symbol*] [*National Library of Canada*] (NLC)
ACUC....... American Coalition of Unregistered Churches (EA)
ACUC....... Association of Canadian Underwater Councils
ACUCA .... Association of Christian Universities and Colleges in Asia (EA)
ACUCAA .. Association of College, University, and Community Arts Administrators [*Later, APAP*] (EA)
ACUCDN.. Acute Care [*A publication*]
ACUCES ... Research Centre for Canadian Ethnic Studies, University of Calgary, Alberta [*Library symbol*] [*National Library of Canada*] (NLC)
ACUCM .... Association of College and University Concert Managers [*Later, ACUCAA*]
ACUCTF ... Association of Canadian University and College Teachers of French
ACUE........ American Committee of United Europe
ACU-ERI... American Conservative Union Education and Research Institute (EA)
ACUF .... Advisory Committee on Undersea Feature Names [*Board on Geographic Names*] [*NOAA*]
ACUFE..... Faculty of Education, University of Calgary, Alberta [*Library symbol*] [*National Library of Canada*] (NLC)
ACUG........ Atex Commercial Users Group (EA)
ACUHO .... Association of College and University Housing Officers [*Later, ACUHO-I*] (EA)
ACUHO-I ... Association of College and University Housing Officers - International (EA)
ACU-I........ Association of College Unions - International (EA)
ACUI......... Automatic Calling Unit Interface [*Telecommunications*] (IEEE)
ACUIB....... Association of Canadian University Information Bureaus [*See also ABUIC*]
ACUIIS ..... Association of Colleges and Universities for International-Intercultural Studies [*Defunct*] (EA)
ACUJ........ American Committee for Ulster Justice (EA)
ACUL .... Law Library, University of Calgary, Alberta [*Library symbol*] [*National Library of Canada*] (BIB)
ACULE..... Association of Credit Union League Executives (EA)
ACUM....... Annales. Centre Universitaire Mediterraneen de Nice [*A publication*]
ACUM....... Medical Library, University of Calgary, Alberta [*Library symbol*] [*National Library of Canada*] (NLC)
ACUMA .... Map Library, University of Calgary, Alberta [*Library symbol*] [*National Library of Canada*] (NLC)
ACUMC .... Materials Centre Library, University of Calgary, Alberta [*Library symbol*] [*National Library of Canada*] (NLC)
ACUMG .... Association of College and University Museums and Galleries (EA)
ACUN........ Annales. Centre Universitaire de Nice [*A publication*]
ACUNO..... Union Oil Co. of Canada Ltd., Calgary, Alberta [*Library symbol*] [*National Library of Canada*] (NLC)
ACUNS ..... Association of Canadian Universities for Northern Studies
ACUNSOP ... Association of Canadian Universities for Northern Studies. Occasional Publications [*A publication*]
ACUNY ..... Associated Colleges of Upper New York
ACUO........ Association of College and University Offices (EA)
ACUO........ Avionics Cooling Unit Operator (MCD)
ACUP .... Association of Canadian University Presses
ACUP .... Association of College and University Printers (EA)
ACUPAE... American Council for University Planning and Academic Excellence (EA)
Acupunct Electro-Ther Res ... Acupuncture and Electro-Therapeutics Research [*A publication*]
ACUR-A.... Architectural Record [*A publication*]
ACURA .... Association for the Coordination of University Religious Affairs (EA)
ACURAD .. Acoustic Underwater Range Determination Systems
ACURIL.... Association of Caribbean University and Research Institute Libraries
ACURM .... Association of Concern for Ultimate Reality and Meaning (EA)
ACURP..... American College of Utilization Review Physicians (EA)
ACUS .... Administrative Conference of the United States [*Independent government agency*] [*Washington, DC*]
ACUS .... Amendment to the Constitution of the United States (DLA)
ACUS .... AT & T College and University System [*Bedminster, NJ*] [*Telecommunications service*] (TSSD)
ACUS .... Atlantic Council of the United States (EA)

ACUSA...... Acustica [*A publication*]
ACUSD ..... Acta Classica. Universitatis Scientiarum Debreceniensis [*A publication*]
ACUSSR ... American Committee on US-Soviet Relations (EA)
Acust.......... Acustica [*A publication*]
Acustica Akust Beih ... Acustica. Akustische Beihefte [*A publication*]
ACUSYST ... Automated Culture System
ACUTA ...... Association of College and University Telecommunications Administrators (EA)
ACUTE....... Accountants Computer Users Technical Exchange (EA)
ACUTE....... Association of Canadian University Teachers of English
Acute Care ... Acute Care Journal. International Society on Biotelemetry [*A publication*]
Acute Diarrhoea Child Symp ... Acute Diarrhoea in Childhood Symposium [*A publication*]
Acute Fluid Replacement Ther Shock Pro Conf ... Acute Fluid Replacement in the Therapy of Shock. Proceedings. Conference [*A publication*]
ACUTF..... Association of Canadian University Teachers of French
ACUU........ Acta Universitatis Upsaliensis. Abstracts of Uppsala Dissertations. Faculty of Science [*A publication*]
ACV .... ACTION Cooperative Volunteer Program
ACV .... Actual Cash Value [*Accounting*]
ACV .... Acyclovir [*Also, ACG, Acycloguanosine*] [*Antiviral compound*]
ACV .... Air Control Valve (MCD)
ACV .... Air-Cushion Vehicle
ACV .... Alarm Check Valve (MSA)
ACV .... Alberto-Culver Co. [*NYSE symbol*] (SPSG)
ACV .... Alternating Current Volts
ACV .... Amount of Critical View
ACV .... Anthology of Commonwealth Verse [*A publication*]
ACV .... Armored Cannon Vehicle (MCD)
ACV .... Armored Cavalry Vehicle
ACV .... Armored Combat Vehicle
ACV .... Armoured Command Vehicle [*British*]
ACV .... Asian CineVision (EA)
ACV .... Associate, College of Violinists
ACV .... Association Canadienne des Veterinaires [*Canadian Veterinary Medical Association*] (EAIO)
ACV .... Australian and New Zealand Conveyancing Report [*A publication*] (APTA)
ACV .... Auxiliary Aircraft Carrier [*Navy symbol*]
ACV .... Eureka/Arcata [*California*] [*Airport symbol*] (OAG)
ACVA .... Advisory Committee on Voluntary Foreign Aid [*Department of State*]
ACVAFS.... American Council of Voluntary Agencies for Foreign Service [*Later, I/ACVIA*] (EA)
ACVC .... Ada Compiler Validation Capacity [*Data processing*]
ACVC .... Alberta Vocational Centre, Calgary, Albert [*Library symbol*] [*National Library of Canada*] (NLC)
ACVC .... American Council of Venture Clubs (EA)
ACVC .... Armament and Combat Vehicle Center (MCD)
ACVC .... Arms Control Verification Committee [*Pronounced "acey-veecee"*]
ACVC .... Army Commercial Vehicle Code (AABC)
ACVCC..... Association of Canadian Venture Capital Companies
ACVD .... American College of Veterinary Dermatology (EA)
ACV-DP .... Acyclovir Diphosphate [*Antiviral compound*]
ACVE........ Accelerometer Calibration Vibration Exciter
ACVE........ Advisory Committee on Voter Education [*Defunct*] (EA)
ACVEN ..... Advisory Committee on Vehicle Emission and Noise [*Australia*]
ACVF......... Advanced Composite Vertical Fin (MCD)
ACVFA...... Advisory Committee on Voluntary Foreign Aid [*Department of State*]
ACVH........ Association Canadienne des Veterans du Hockey [*Canadian Association of Hockey Veterans*]
ACVIA9..... Acta Vitaminologica [*A publication*]
ACVIM..... American College of Veterinary Internal Medicine (EA)
ACVL........ Association of Cinema and Video Laboratories (EA)
ACVM .... American College of Veterinary Microbiologists (EA)
ACVMC .... Armored Combat Vehicle Material Center (MCD)
ACV-MP ... Acyclovir Monophosphate [*Antiviral compound*]
ACVNAO.... Atti. Museo Civico di Storia Naturale di Triesti [*A publication*]
ACVO........ American College of Veterinary Ophthalmologists (EA)
ACVP........ Additive Color Viewer Printer
ACVP........ American College of Veterinary Pathologists (EA)
ACVR .... American College of Veterinary Radiology (EA)
ACVS........ American College of Veterinary Surgeons (EA)
ACVSA...... Acta Cientifica Venezolana. Suplemento [*A publication*]
ACVT......... American College of Veterinary Toxicologists [*Later, AAVCT*] (EA)
ACVT........ Armored Combat Vehicle Technology (RDA)
ACVTA...... Acta Veterinaria [*A publication*]
ACVTB9.... Acta Veterinaria [*Brno*] [*A publication*]
ACVTP ...... Acyclovir Triphosphate [*Antiviral compound*]
ACVTP ...... Armored Combat Vehicle Technology Program
ACVV .... Afrikaanse Christelike Vrouevereniging
ACVV .... Association Canadienne de Vol a Voile [*Canada*]
ACVZS...... V. Zay, Smith Associates Ltd., Calgary, Alberta [*Library symbol*] [*National Library of Canada*] (NLC)

AC & W ..... Air Communications and Weather [*Group*] [*Navy*]
ACW .... Air [*or Aircraft*] Control and Warning [*Military*]
AC & W ..... Air [*or Aircraft*] Control and Warning [*Military*]
ACW .... Airborne Collision Warning
ACW .... Aircraftwoman [*British*]
ACW .... Alcoholism Center for Women   (EA)
ACW .... Alternating Continuous Wave [*Radio*]
ACW .... American Canadian Systems, Inc. [*Vancouver Stock Exchange symbol*]
ACW .... American Chain of Warehouses   (EA)
ACW .... Ancient Christian Writers [*Westminster, MD*] [*A publication*]
ACW .... Anticarrier Warfare   (MCD)
ACW .... Apostolate of Christ the Worker
ACW .... Association of Community Workers [*British*]
ACW .... Western Canada High School, Calgary, Alberta [*Library symbol*] [*National Library of Canada*]   (NLC)
ACWA .... Amalgamated Clothing Workers of America [*Later, ACTWU*]   (EA)
ACWA .... American Civil War Association   (EA)
ACWA .... American Clean Water Association   (EA)
ACWA .... Associate of the Institute of Cost and Works Accountants [*British*]
ACWA .... Automatic Car Wash Association International [*Later, ICA*]
ACWB .... Williams Brothers Canada Ltd., Calgary, Alberta [*Library symbol*] [*National Library of Canada*]   (NLC)
ACWBBS .. American Civil War Bulletin Board System [*Information service or system*]   (EISS)
ACWC .... Advisory Committee on Weather Control [*Terminated, 1957*]
ACWC .... American Council of Women Chiropractors [*Later, Council of Women Chiropractors*]   (EA)
ACWC .... Association of Canadian Women Composers
ACWCN .... Action Will Be Cancelled   (NOAA)
ACWE .... American Cotton Waste Exchange   (EA)
ACWF .... Actual Cost of Work Flow [*Accounting*]
ACWF .... American Council for World Freedom   (EA)
ACWF .... Army Central Welfare Fund
ACWIS ...... American Committee for the Weizmann Institute of Science   (EA)
ACWL .... Army Chemical Warfare Laboratory
ACWM ...... Americans for Customary Weight and Measure   (EA)
ACWO ...... Aircraft Control and Warning Officer [*Military*]
ACWP .... Actual Cost for Work Performed [*Accounting*]
ACWR ...... Alaska Cooperative Wildlife Research Unit [*A publication*]
ACWR ...... William Roper Hull Home, Calgary, Alberta [*Library symbol*] [*National Library of Canada*]   (NLC)
ACWRD .... Western Research & Development Ltd., Calgary, Alberta [*Library symbol*] [*National Library of Canada*]   (NLC)
ACWRON ... Aircraft Control and Warning Squadron [*Military*]
ACWRRE .. American Cargo War Risk Reinsurance Exchange   (EA)
ACWRT ..... American Civil War Round Table   (EAIO)
AC & WS .. Aircraft Control and Warning Stations [*Military*]
ACWS .... Aircraft Control and Warning System [*Military*]
ACWS .... All-Canada Weekly Summaries [*Canada Law Book Ltd.*] [*Database*]
ACWS .... Amalgamated Carriage and Wagon Society [*A union*] [*British*]
ACWS .... Assistant Casework Supervisor [*Red Cross*]
AC & WSq ... Aircraft Control and Warning Squadron [*Air Force*]
ACWW ...... Associated Country Women of the World [*London, England*]
ACX .... Action Industries, Inc. [*AMEX symbol*]   (SPSG)
ACX .... American Can Canada [*Toronto Stock Exchange symbol*]
ACXM ...... Acxiom Corp. [*NASDAQ symbol*]   (NQ)
AC/XRT .... Adriamycin, Cyclophosphamide/X-Ray Therapy [*Antineoplastic drug regimen*]
ACY .... Acoyapa [*Nicaragua*] [*Seismograph station code, US Geological Survey*]   (SEIS)
ACY .... [*The*] Akron, Canton & Youngstown Railroad Co. [*AAR code*]
ACY .... Amcan Cyphermaster Ltd. [*Vancouver Stock Exchange symbol*]
ACY .... American Cyanamid Co. [*NYSE symbol*]   (SPSG)
ACY .... Atlantic City [*New Jersey*] [*Airport symbol*]   (OAG)
a-cy--- .... Cyprus [*MARC geographic area code*] [*Library of Congress*]
ACYC .... Anticyclonic [*Meteorology*]   (FAAC)
ACYD .... Association of Cotton Yarn Distributors [*Later, AYD*]
A-CY-DIC ... Adriamycin, Cyclophosphamide, Dacarbazine [*Antineoplastic drug regimen*]
ACYF .... Administration for Children, Youth, and Families [*Office of Human Development Services*]
ACYOA ..... Armenian Church Youth Organization of America   (EA)
ACYPL ...... American Council of Young Political Leaders   (EA)
ACYT .... American Cytogenetics, Inc. [*NASDAQ symbol*]   (NQ)
ACYTA ..... Acta Cytologica [*A publication*]
ACZ .... Acheron Resources Ltd. [*Vancouver Stock Exchange symbol*]
ACZ .... Czar Public Library, Alberta [*Library symbol*] [*National Library of Canada*]   (NLC)
ACZ .... PROSI [*Public Relations Office of the Sugar Industry*] Bulletin Mensuel [*A publication*]
ACZ .... Wallace, NC [*Location identifier*] [*FAA*]   (FAAL)
ACZA .... Ammoniacal Copper Zinc Arsenate [*Wood preservative*]
ACZBA8.... Centro de Estudos Zoologicos. Universidade do Brasil. Avulso [*A publication*]
ACZCS ...... Advanced Coastal Zone Color Scanner   (MCD)

ACZMN .... Arctic Coastal Zone Management. Newsletter [*A publication*]
ACZOAD .. Acta Zootechnica [*A publication*]
AD.............. Abdominal Diameter [*Roentgenology*]
AD.............. Above Deck [*of a ship*]   (DS)
AD.............. Abwehrdienst [*Counterintelligence Service*] [*German military - World War II*]
AD.............. Access Door
AD.............. Accessions Document [*Air Force*]
AD.............. Accidental Discharge [*Firearms*]
AD.............. Accion Democratica [*Democratic Action*] [*Venezuela*] [*Political party*]   (PPW)
AD.............. Accion Democratica [*Democratic Action*] [*El Salvador*] [*Political party*]   (PD)
A & D........ Accounting and Disbursing   (MCD)
AD.............. Accounting and Disbursing   (MCD)
AD.............. Accrued Dividend
AD.............. Acknowledgment Due
AD.............. Acquisition Director
AD.............. Action for Development [*FAO*] [*United Nations*]
AD.............. Action Directe [*Direct Action*] [*Terrorist group*] [*French*]   (PD)
AD.............. Active Dosimeter
AD.............. Active Duty
AD.............. AD 2000: a Journal of Religious Opinion [*A publication*]   (APTA)
AD.............. Adamantane [*Organic chemistry*]
AD.............. Adapt
AD.............. Adaptation Of [*Etymology*]
Ad.............. Addams' Ecclesiastical Reports [*A publication*]   (DLA)
AD.............. Adde [*Add or Up To*] [*Pharmacy*]
AD.............. Addendum
AD.............. Addict [*Drug*] [*Slang*]
Ad.............. Adelphi [*A publication*]
Ad.............. Adelphoe [*of Terence*] [*Classical studies*]   (OCD)
AD.............. Aden Airways
AD.............. Adenoid Degenerative [*Viruses*]
AD.............. Adenovirus [*Also, ADV*]
AD.............. Adipose Fin [*Fish anatomy*]
AD.............. Adjective   (ROG)
Ad.............. Administration   (DLA)
Ad.............. Administrative   (DLA)
AD.............. Administrative Department   (ADA)
AD.............. Administrative Directive   (MCD)
AD.............. Administrative District   (ADA)
AD.............. Administrative Operation and Support Services [*Kennedy Space Center*] [*NASA*]   (NASA)
Ad.............. Administrator   (DLA)
AD.............. Admission Directive [*London Stock Exchange*]
A & D........ Admission and Discharge
AD.............. Adopted By
AD.............. Adoption Directory [*A publication*]
Ad.............. Adrenal [*Medicine*]
A/D.............. Advance/Decline   (MCD)
A-D.............. Advance-Decline Line [*Investment term*]
AD.............. Advanced Design   (IEEE)
AD.............. Advanced Development
AD.............. Advanced Ruling Expiration Date [*IRS*]
AD.............. Adverb   (ROG)
AD.............. Advertisement
AD.............. Advertisement Digest [*A publication*]
AD.............. Advice   (AABC)
AD.............. Advisory Direction   (NATG)
AD.............. Aerial Delivery   (MCD)
AD.............. Aerodrome
AD.............. Aerodynamic Decelerator   (AAG)
AD.............. Aeronautical Data
AD.............. Africa Diary [*A publication*]
AD.............. African Law Reports, Appellate Division [*A publication*]   (DLA)
AD.............. After Dark [*A publication*]
AD.............. After Date [*Business term*]
AD.............. After Digital [*Post-computer revolution*]
AD.............. Afterdischarge [*Electrophysiology*]
AD.............. Aggregate Demand
AD.............. Agnus Dei [*Lamb of God*] [*Latin*]
AD.............. Agricultural Decisions [*A publication*]
AD.............. Ahead Flag [*Navy*] [*British*]
AD.............. Aid to the Disabled
AD.............. Air Data   (MCD)
AD.............. Air Defense [*Air Force*]
AD.............. Air Density [*Explorer satellite*] [*NASA*]
AD.............. Air Department of the Admiralty [*British*]
AD.............. Air Depot
AD.............. Air Despatch [*British military*]   (DMA)
AD.............. Air Director   (DAS)
AD.............. Air Division [*Air Force*]
AD.............. Air-Dried [*Lumber*]
AD.............. Air Duct   (MSA)
AD.............. Airborne Designator   (MCD)
AD.............. Aircraft Depot [*British military*]   (DMA)
AD.............. Aircraft Division   (MCD)
AD.............. Airdrome

AD.............. Airframe Design Division [*Bureau of Aeronautics; later, NASC*] [*Navy*]
AD.............. Airworthiness Directive
AD.............. Akcijska Druzba [*Joint-Stock Company*]
AD.............. Akcionarsko Drustvo [*Joint-Stock Company*]
AD.............. Albrecht Durer [*German artist, 1471-1528*]
AD.............. Alcohol Dehydrogenase [*Also, ADH*] [*An enzyme*]
A & D........ Alcohol and Drug [*Type of addiction*]
AD.............. Aleutian Disease [*of mink*]
AD.............. Alexandra [*Newport and South Wales*] Docks & Railway [*Wales*]
AD.............. Algerian Dinar [*Monetary unit*]
AD.............. Alianca Democratica [*Democratic Alliance*] [*Portugal*] [*Political party*]   (PPE)
AD.............. Alianza Democratica [*Democratic Alliance*] [*Chile*] [*Political party*]   (PPW)
AD.............. Allergic Disease
AD.............. Allied Distribution [*An association*]   (EA)
AD.............. Allowable Deficiency   (MCD)
AD.............. Alpha Delta [*Society*]
AD.............. Alternate Days
A/D.......... Alternate Definition of Accident [*Insurance*]
AD.............. Alternate Drop [*Electroanalysis*]
AD.............. Altitude Deviation
AD.............. Alzheimer's Disease [*Medicine*]
AD.............. Amazing Detective Tales [*A publication*]
AD.............. Ambulance Driver
AD.............. American Decisions [*A publication*]   (DLA)
AD.............. American Defenders   (EA)
AD.............. American Documentation [*A publication*]
AD.............. Ampere Demand Meter   (MSA)
AD.............. Amplifier Detector
AD.............. Amplifier Discriminator [*Instrumentation*]
AD.............. Analgesic Dose
AD.............. Analog-to-Digital [*Converter*] [*Data processing*]   (AFM)
A-to-D...... Analog-to-Digital [*Converter*] [*Data processing*]
AD.............. Anderson - Darling Test [*Statistics*]
AD.............. Andorra [*ANSI two-letter standard code*]   (CNC)
AD.............. Androstenedione [*Endocrinology*]
AD.............. Anima Dulcis [*Sweet Soul*] [*Latin*]
Ad.............. Animal Detail [*Rorschach*] [*Psychology*]
AD.............. Anno Domini [*In the Year of Our Lord*] [*Latin*]   (GPO)
AD.............. Annual Digest and Reports of Public International Law Cases [*A publication*]   (DLA)
AD.............. Anodal Deviation [*Physiology*]
AD.............. Anode   (MSA)
ad.............. Ante Diem [*Before the Day*] [*Latin*]   (GPO)
AD.............. Anterior Deltoid [*Myology*]
AD.............. Anti-Disturbance   (MCD)
AD.............. Antidiarrhea [*Medicine*]
AD.............. Antigenic Determinant [*Medicine*]
AD.............. Apollo Development [*NASA*]   (KSC)
AD.............. Appellate Division [*Legal term*]
A D............ Appellate Division Reports [*New York*] [*A publication*]
AD.............. Approximate Digestibility
AD.............. Aptechnoe Delo [*A publication*]
AD.............. Archdeaconry
AD.............. Archduke
A & D........ Architects and Designers [*Building*] [*New York City*]
AD.............. Architectural Design [*A publication*]
AD.............. Architectural Digest [*A publication*]
AD.............. Archiv fuer Diplomatik [*A publication*]
AD.............. Area Dean [*Church of England in Australia*]
AD.............. Area Director
AD.............. Area Discriminator [*SAGE*]
AD.............. Area Drain [*Technical drawings*]
AD.............. Arista International Airlines [*ICAO designator*]   (FAAC)
AD.............. Arithmetic Device
A/D.......... Arm/Destruct   (KSC)
AD.............. Armament Depot [*Military*] [*British*]
AD.............. Armament Division [*Air Force Systems Command*] [*Eglin Air Force Base, FL*]
AD.............. Armored Division [*Military*]   (MCD)
AD.............. Army Dental Corps [*British*]
AD.............. Army Department [*British*]   (RDA)
AD.............. Army Depot   (AABC)
AD.............. Army Digest [*A publication*]
AD.............. Art Digest [*A publication*]
AD.............. Art Director [*Films, television, etc.*]
AD.............. Artificer Diver [*British military*]   (DMA)
AD.............. Artillery Division [*Military*]   (MCD)
AD.............. Artist Direct [*Record label*]
AD.............. As Drawn   (MSA)
A/D.......... Assembly/Disassembly Facility
AD.............. Assembly District
AD.............. Assembly Drawing
A/D.......... Assets and Depreciation [*Accounting*]
AD.............. Assignment Age [*Telecommunications*]   (TEL)
AD.............. Assistant Director
AD.............. Associate Degree
AD.............. Associate Director

AD.............. Associated with Dual Capacity Firms [*London Stock Exchange*]
AD.............. Assured Destruction [*Capability*] [*of missiles*]
AD.............. ASTIA [*Armed Services Technical Information Agency*] Document
AD.............. Athletic Director
AD.............. Atomic Drive   (AAG)
AD.............. Attack Director [*Military*]   (MCD)
AD.............. Attendant [*Telecommunications*]   (TEL)
AD.............. Attention Display [*Communications device*]
AD.............. Auris Dextra [*Right Ear*] [*Latin*]
AD.............. Australia Day
AD.............. Australian Digest [*A publication*]   (APTA)
AD.............. Auto-Diesel Technician Program [*Association of Independent Colleges and Schools specialization code*]
AD.............. Autograph Document [*Manuscript descriptions*]
AD.............. Automatic Depositor [*Banking*]   (BUR)
AD.............. Automatic Detection [*Air Force*]
AD.............. Automatic Display [*Data processing*]
AD.............. Autosomal Dominant [*Genetics*]
AD.............. Availability Date [*Banking*]
AD.............. Avalanche Diode   (KSC)
AD.............. Average Deviation [*Statistics*]
AD.............. Average Diameter
AD.............. Avia [*Francis Lombardi eC*] [*Italy*] [*ICAO aircraft manufacturer identifier*]   (ICAO)
AD.............. Aviation Daily
AD.............. Aviation Machinist's Mate [*Navy rating*]
AD.............. Aviatsionnaya Diviziya [*Air Division*] [*USSR*]
AD.............. Avoidable Delay
A/D.......... Awaiting Delivery   (MCD)
AD.............. Awaiting Disconnection [*Telecommunications*]   (TEL)
AD.............. Axiodistal [*Dentistry*]
Ad.............. C. H. Boehringer Sohn, Ingelheim [*Germany*] [*Research code symbol*]
AD.............. Deputy Administrator [*NASA*]
AD.............. Destroyer Tender [*Navy symbol*]
AD.............. Devon Public Library, Alberta [*Library symbol*] [*National Library of Canada*]   (NLC)
AD.............. Doctor of Arts
AD.............. [*A*] Drink
AD.............. Lab. Miquel [*Spain*] [*Research code symbol*]
AD.............. New York Supreme Court, Appellate Division Reports [*A publication*]   (DLA)
AD.............. Norfolk, Franklin & Danville Railway Co. [*The Atlantic & Danville Railway Co.*] [*AAR code*]
AD.............. Servantes de l'Agneu Divin [*Sisters of the Lamb of God*] [*Roman Catholic religious order*]
AD.............. South African Supreme Court Appellate Division Reports [*A publication*]   (DLA)
AD.............. Travel-Agent Discount [*For air travel*]
AD1............ Great Sitkin [*Alaska*] [*Seismograph station code, US Geological Survey*]   (SEIS)
A2d............ Atlantic Reporter, Second Series [*A publication*]   (DLA)
AD2............ Umak [*Alaska*] [*Seismograph station code, US Geological Survey*]   (SEIS)
AD3............ Kagalaska [*Alaska*] [*Seismograph station code, US Geological Survey*]   (SEIS)
AD4............ Hidden Bay [*Alaska*] [*Seismograph station code, US Geological Survey*]   (SEIS)
AD5............ Yakak [*Alaska*] [*Seismograph station code, US Geological Survey*]   (SEIS)
AD6............ South Kanaga [*Alaska*] [*Seismograph station code, US Geological Survey*]   (SEIS)
AD7............ North Kanaga [*Alaska*] [*Seismograph station code, US Geological Survey*]   (SEIS)
AD8............ Adagdak [*Alaska*] [*Seismograph station code, US Geological Survey*]   (SEIS)
AD 86........ Accion Democratica 86 [*Democratic Action 1986*] [*Aruba*] [*Political party*]   (EY)
AD 2000..... Areas of Development International Conference and Exhibition [*British*]   (ITD)
Ada.............. [*A*] programming language [*1979*] [*Named after Ada Augusta Byron, 1815-52, who coded the instructions for Charles Babbage's mechanical calculators and is considered the first computer programmer*]   (CSR)
ADA........... Academy of Dispensing Audiologists   (EA)
ADA........... (Acetamidol)Iminodiacetic Acid [*A buffer*]
ADA........... Action Data Automation [*British*]   (NATG)
ADA........... Action for Dysphasic Adults [*British*]
ADA........... Active Duty Agreement
ADA........... Adak [*Island*] [*Alaska*] [*Seismograph station code, US Geological Survey*] [*Closed*]   (SEIS)
ADA........... Adana [*Turkey*] [*Airport symbol*]   (OAG)
ADA........... Adenosine Deaminase [*An enzyme*]
ADA........... Adjusted Daily Average   (ADA)
ADA........... Adola Mining Corp. [*Vancouver Stock Exchange symbol*]
ADA........... Advanced Development Analysis
ADA........... Advertising Age [*A publication*]
ADA........... Advisory Area [*Aviation*]   (FAAC)
ADA........... Aerojet Differential Analyzer
ADA........... After Date of Award of Contract [*Telecommunications*]   (TEL)

ADA........... Agrupament Democratic d'Andorra [*Andorran Democratic Association*] [*Political party*]   (PPW)
ADA........... Aiken Dynamic Algebra   (MCD)
ADA........... Air Data Assembly   (NASA)
ADA........... Air Defense Area [*Army*]
ADA........... Air Defense Artillery [*Military*]
AD-A .... Air Density A [*Explorer satellite*] [*NASA*]
ADA........... Airborne Data Automation   (AFM)
ADA........... Aircraft Defense Analysis   (MCD)
ADA........... Airlines Deregulation Act [*1978*]
ADA........... Aluminum Dihydroxyaminoacetate [*Also, ALGLYN*] [*Pharmacology*]
ADA........... American Dairy Association   (EA)
ADA........... American Dance Asylum
ADA........... American Dart Association [*Inactive*]   (EA)
ADA........... American Dehydrators Association [*Later, AAPA*]   (EA)
ADA........... American Dental Association   (EA)
ADA........... American Dermatological Association   (EA)
ADA........... American Diabetes Association   (EA)
ADA........... American Dietetic Association   (EA)
ADA........... American Dove Association   (EA)
ADA........... American Down Association   (EA)
ADA........... Americans for Democratic Action   (EA)
ADA........... Ammonium Dihydrogen Arsenate [*Inorganic chemistry*]
ADA........... Amplifier Detector Assembly
ADA........... Analog Drive Assembly   (MCD)
ADA........... Andover Distributors Association   (EA)
ADA........... Angle Data Assembly
ADA........... Angular Differentiating-Integrating Accelerometer
ADALCON... Anthraquinone Disulfonic Acid [*Organic chemistry*]
ADA........... Antiques Dealers' Association of America   (EA)
ADA........... Anzeiger fuer Deutsches Altertum und Deutsche Literatur [*A publication*]
ADA........... Applied Decision Analysis
ADA........... Arming Device Assemblies [*Army*]   (MCD)
ADA........... Arquivo do Distrito de Aveiro [*A publication*]
ADA........... Art Directors Annual [*A publication*]
ADA........... Assistant Defence Advisor [*British military*]   (DMA)
ADA........... Assistant Director of Artillery [*British*]
ADA........... Assistant District Attorney
ADA........... Association of Dairymen's Assistants [*A union*] [*British*]
ADA........... Association of Drainage Authorities [*British*]   (DCTA)
ADA........... Atomic Development Authority [*Proposed by Bernard Baruch to exercise control over those aspects of atomic energy inimical to global security; never organized*]
ADA........... Audio Distribution Amplifier
ADA........... Australian Deer Association
ADA........... Authority Directing Arrest or Confinement [*Military*]
ADA........... Auto Directional Antenna
ADA........... Automatic Damper Arm   (KSC)
ADA........... Automatic Data Acquisition
ADA........... Automatic Data Aids   (MCD)
ADA........... Automatic Document Analysis   (DIT)
ADA........... Automobile Dealers Association
ADA........... Average Daily Allowance   (ADA)
ADA........... Average Daily Attendance
ADA........... Azimuth Drive Assembly   (MCD)
ADA........... Daysland Public Library, Alberta [*Library symbol*] [*National Library of Canada*]   (NLC)
ADA........... Office of Deputy Administrator [*FAA*]   (FAAC)
ADA........... Troy State University, Troy, AL [*OCLC symbol*]   (OCLC)
2ADA........ Second Air Division Association   (EA)
ADAA....... Air-Driven Air Amplifier
ADAA....... American Dental Assistants Association   (EA)
ADAA....... Anxiety Disorders Association of America   (EA)
ADAA........ Art Dealers Association of America   (EA)
ADAB....... Assistant Director of the Army Budget
ADABAS... Adaptable Database System [*Database management system*]
ADAB (FSM) ... Assistant Director of the Army Budget (Financial Systems Management)
ADAC....... Acoustic Data Analysis Center
ADAC....... ADAC Laboratories [*NASDAQ symbol*]   (NQ)
ADAC....... Air Defence Artillery Commander [*Military*] [*British*]
AD/AC .... Air Defense Aircraft   (MCD)
ADAC....... Air Defense Artillery Complex   (MCD)
ADAC....... Airfoil Design and Analysis Center [*Ohio State University*]   (MCD)
ADAC....... All-Digital Attack Center   (MCD)
ADAC....... Allgemeiner Deutscher Automobil Club [*Pre-World War II*] [*Germany*]
ADAC....... Association Danse au Canada [*Dance Association of Canada*]
AD/AC ...... Automatic Detection/Automatic Classification [*Antisubmarine warfare*]   (MCD)
ADAC....... Automatic Direct Analog Computer   (BUR)
ADAC....... Aviation Development Advisory Committee   (FAAC)
ADACAT... Advances in Acarology [*A publication*]
ADACC ..... Automatic Data Acquisition and Computer Complex [*Air Force*]
ADACIOM ... Associated Drug and Chemical Industries of Missouri
ADACS...... Attitude Determination and Control System   (MCD)
ADACS...... Automated Data Acquisition and Control System   (MCD)

A-DACT .... Adriamycin, Dactinomycin [*Antineoplastic drug regimen*]
ADACT ..... Advise Action Taken   (NOAA)
ADAD....... After Date of Award   (MCD)
ADAD....... Air Defense Alerting Device [*Military*]
ADAD....... Air Defense Artillery, Director [*Air Force*]
ADADA .... Advise Approximate Date   (NOAA)
ADADS ..... Army Depot Automatic Diagnostic System   (RDA)
ADAE .... Advanced Diploma in Art Education [*British*]
ADAE .... Association pour le Developpement de l'Administration de l'Education [*Association for the Development of Educational Administration*] [*Canada*]
ADAF .... Association pour la Diffusion des Accordeonistes Francophones [*Pleine Fougeres, France*]   (EAIO)
ADAG....... Adagio [*Slow*] [*Music*]
ADAGA7... Advances in Agronomy [*A publication*]
Ad Age ...... Advertising Age [*A publication*]
ADAGE ..... Air Defense Air-to-Ground Engagement [*Simulation*]
Ad Age Eur ... Advertising Age Europe [*A publication*]
ADAGO..... Adagio [*Slow*] [*Music*]   (ROG)
ADAH .... Assistant Director of Army Health [*British*]
ADAHF....... American Dental Association Health Foundation
ADAI .... Abhandlungen. Deutsches Archaeologisches Institut [*Cairo*] [*A publication*]
ADAI .... Apollo Documentation Administration Instruction [*NASA*]   (KSC)
Adair Lib.... Adair on Law Libels [*A publication*]   (DLA)
ADAIS....... Aerodynamic Data Analysis and Integration System [*Data processing*]
ADAJ........ Annual. Department of Antiquities of Jordan [*A publication*]
ADALCON ... Advise All Concerned
ADALINE ... Adaptive Linear   (KSC)
AD/ALT.... Advanced Destroyer/Aircraft Lightweight Torpedo   (MCD)
ADAM...... Adams National Historic Site
ADAM...... Adaptive Arithmetical Method
ADAM...... Adaptive Digital Avionics Module
ADAM...... Advanced Data Management
ADAM...... Advanced Direct-Landing Apollo Mission [*NASA*]   (IEEE)
ADAM...... Advanced Dynamic Anthropomorphic Manikin [*Air Force*]
ADAM...... Agriculture Department's Automated Manpower
ADAM...... Air Base Damage Assessment Model   (MCD)
ADAM...... Air Defense Antimissile
ADAM...... Air Defense Area Monthly Report [*Army*]
ADAM...... Air Deflection and Modification [*NASA*]   (KSC)
ADAM...... Air Deflection and Modulation [*Air Force*]   (MCD)
ADAM...... Air-Delivered Attack Marker [*Air Force*]   (MCD)
ADAM...... All-Digital Answering Machine [*PhoneMate, Inc.*]
ADAM...... American Defenders Against Animal Mistreatment [*Inactive*]   (EA)
ADAM...... American Divorce Association for Men
ADAM...... Analog Data Acquisition Module
ADAM...... Angular Distribution Auger Microscopy
ADAM...... Aperture Distribution and Maintenance [*System*]
ADAM...... Area Denial Artillery Munition   (AABC)
ADAM...... Artillery-Delivered Antipersonnel Mine   (RDA)
ADAM...... Artillery Delivered Antipersonnel Munitions   (MCD)
ADAM...... Association of Distributors of Advertising Material   (EAIO)
ADAM...... Associometrics Data Management System   (IEEE)
ADAM...... Automated Deposition of Advanced Materials [*Materials technology*]
ADAM...... Automatic Distance and Angle Measurement
ADAM...... Axisymmetric Duct Aeroacoustic Modeling   (MCD)
Adam.......... Justiciary Reports [*1893-1916*] [*Scotland*] [*A publication*]   (DLA)
ADAMAP ... Advances in Applied Microbiology [*A publication*]
ADA/MH ... Alcohol, Drug Abuse, and Mental Health [*Block grant*]
ADAMHA ... Alcohol, Drug Abuse, and Mental Health Administration [*Formerly, HSMHA*] [*Department of Health and Human Services*] [*Rockville, MD*]
ADAM II... Aerial Port Documentation and Management System
ADAM Int R ... ADAM [*Arts, Drama, Architecture, Music*] International Review [*A publication*]
Adam Jur Tr ... Adam on Trial by Jury [*A publication*]   (DLA)
ADAML .... Advise by Airmail [*Army*]
Adam Mickiewicz Univ Inst Chem Ser Chem ... Adam Mickiewicz University. Institute of Chemistry. Seria Chemia [*A publication*]
Adams........ Adams County Legal Journal [*Pennsylvania*] [*A publication*]   (DLA)
Adams........ Adams' Reports [*1 New Hampshire*] [*A publication*]   (DLA)
Adams........ Adams' Reports [*41, 42 Maine*] [*A publication*]   (DLA)
ADAMS .... Advanced Action Manipulator System
ADAMS .... Advanced Design Aluminum Metal Shelter [*A prefabricated building known as an ADAMS hut*]
ADAMS .... Airborne Data Acquisition Multifunction System   (MCD)
ADAMS .... Airborne Data Analysis and Monitoring System   (MCD)
ADAMS .... Automated Dynamic Analysis of Mechanical Systems [*Mechanical Dynamics, Inc.*] [*Automotive engineering*]
Adams Eq .. Adams' Equity [*A publication*]   (DLA)
Adam Sl ..... Adam on the Law of Slavery in British India [*A publication*]   (DLA)
Adams Leg J (PA) ... Adams' Legal Journal [*Pennsylvania*] [*A publication*]   (DLA)

Adams LJ .. Adams County Legal Journal [*Pennsylvania*] [*A publication*] (DLA)
Adams Rom Ant ... Adams' Roman Antiquities [*A publication*] (DLA)
AD AN.... Ad Annum [*Up to the Year*] [*Latin*]
ADaN........ Alabama State Normal School, Daphne, AL [*Library symbol*] [*Library of Congress*] [*Obsolete*] (LCLS)
ADANDAC ... Administrative and Accounting Purposes
Ad Ang Sax L ... Adams' Essay on Anglo-Saxon Law [*A publication*] (DLA)
ADAOD..... Air Defense Artillery Operations Detachment
ADAOO .... Air Defense Artillery Operations Office [*or Officer*]
ADAP........ Adaptive Intercommunication Requirement (MCD)
ADAP........ Adaptor (KSC)
ADAP....... Airport Development Aid Program [*FAA*]
ADAP........ Alzheimer's Disease Associated Protein [*Medicine*]
ADAP........ American Dental Assistant's Program
ADAP........ Assistant Director of Administrative Planning [*Military*] [*British*]
ADAP....... Assistant Director of Army Psychiatry [*British*]
ADAPCP... Alcohol and Drug Abuse Prevention and Control Program [*Military*] (AABC)
ADAPS..... Automatic Display and Plotting System (BUR)
ADAPSO... Association of Data Processing Service Organizations (EA)
ADAPSP .. Association of Data Processing Service Organizations Panels
ADAPT..... Accent on Developing Abstract Processes of Thought
ADAPT..... Active Duty Assistance Program Team
ADAPT..... Adaptation
ADAPT..... Adapter
ADAPT...... Adoption of Automatically Programmed Tools [*Data processing*] (IEEE)
ADAPT..... Advanced Development Aims Processor Transponder [*Military*] (MCD)
ADAPT..... Alcohol and Drug Abuse Prevention Treatment
ADAPT..... American Disabled for Accessible Public Transit (EA)
ADAPT..... Analog-Digital Automatic Program Tester [*Data processing*]
ADAPT..... Automated Data Analysis and Presentation Techniques (MCD)
ADAPT..... Automatic Data Acquisition and Processing Techniques [*Army*] (RDA)
ADAPT..... Avco Data Analysis and Prediction Technique [*for sunspot prediction*]
ADAPT...... [*A*] Diagnostic and Prescriptive Technique [*Teaching process*]
Adapt Environ Essays Physiol Mar Anim ... Adaptation to Environment. Essays on the Physiology of Marine Animals [*A publication*]
Adapt Osob Evol Ptits Plenarnye Dokl Vses Ornitol Konf ... Adaptivnye Osobennosti i Evolyutsiya Ptits Plenarnye Doklady Vsesoyuznoi Ornitologicheskoi Konferentsii [*A publication*]
Adapt Pingvinov ... Adaptatsii Pingvinov [*A publication*]
ADAPTS ... Air-Deliverable Antipollution Transfer System
Adapt Sistemy Avtomat Upravleniya ... Kievski Politekhnicheskii Institut Adaptivnye Sistemy Avtomaticheskogo Upravleniya [*A publication*]
ADAR .... Advanced Design Array RADAR
ADAR .... Air Defense Area [*Army*]
ADAR .... Analog Data Reduction System (CAAL)
ADAR .... Darwell Public Library, Alberta [*Library symbol*] [*National Library of Canada*] (NLC)
ADARA ..... American Dairy Review [*A publication*]
ADARA ..... American Deafness and Rehabilitation Association (EA)
ADARCO .. Advise Date of Reporting in Compliance with Orders [*Navy*]
ADARE ..... Advise Date of Receipt (NOAA)
ADARS..... Adaptive Antenna Receiver System
ADARS...... Airborne Data Acquisition and Recording System
ADARS...... Army Defense Acquisition Regulation Supplement (AABC)
ADAS .... Advanced Digital Avionics System (MCD)
ADAS .... Agricultural Development and Advisory Service [*British*] (ARC)
ADAS .... Airborne Data Acquisition System
ADAS .... Airborne Dynamic Alignment System (MCD)
ADAS .... Analog Data Aquisition System
ADAS .... Architecture Design and Assessment System [*Software package*]
ADAS .... Army Digital Avionics System (MCD)
ADAS .... Automated Data Acquisition System [*GCA Corp.*]
ADAS .... Auxiliary Data Annotation Set [*or System*]
ADASA9.... Advances in the Astronautical Sciences [*A publication*]
ADASH.... Advise Date of Shipment (NOAA)
ADASP..... Air Defense Annual Service Practice (AABC)
ADASP...... Automatic Data and Select Program (KSC)
ADAS Q Rev ... ADAS [*Agricultural Development and Advisory Service*] Quarterly Review [*A publication*]
ADAS Q Rev (GB) ... ADAS [*Agricultural Development and Advisory Service*] Quarterly Review (Great Britain) [*A publication*]
ADASSA ... Aerodynamic Design and Analysis System for Supersonic Aircraft (MCD)
ADAT .... Allied Directorate of Air Transport [*Australia*]
ADAT .... Automatic Data Accumulation and Transfer
ADATE...... Association pour le Developpement de l'Audiovisuel et de la Technologie en Education [*Canada*]
ADATE...... Automatic Digital Assembly Test Equipment (MCD)
ADATM ... Artillery-Delivered Antitank Mine (MCD)
ADatP........ Allied Data Processing Publications (NATG)

ADATS...... Air Defense Antitank System
ADATS...... Air Defense Artillery Threat Simulator (MCD)
ADATS...... Assistant Director, Auxiliary Territorial Service [*British military*] (DMA)
ADATT...... Advise Action to Be Taken by This Office (NOAA)
ADAUEJ.... Advances in Audiology [*A publication*]
ADAVAL... Advise Availability [*Army*]
ADAW...... Abhandlungen. Deutsche Akademie der Wissenschaften zu Berlin. Klasse fuer Sprachen, Literatur, und Kunst [*A publication*]
ADAWS .... Action Data Automation Weapons System (MCD)
ADAWS .... Assistant Director of Army Welfare Services [*British*]
ADAX....... American/Davey Corp. [*NASDAQ symbol*] (NQ)
ADAYAR .. Advances in Activation Analysis [*A publication*]
ADB.......... Accidental Death Benefit [*Insurance*]
ADB.......... Acoustic Distribution Box (CAAL)
ADB.......... Adjusted Debit Balance [*Accounting*]
ADB.......... Adobe Resources Corp. [*NYSE symbol*] (SPSG)
ADB.......... Aerodynamic Data Book (NASA)
ADB.......... African Development Bank [*Also, AfDB*]
ADB.......... Air Defense Board (AAG)
ADB.......... Algemeen Dagblad [*A publication*]
ADB.......... American Design Bicentennial [*An association*] [*Defunct*] (EA)
adb .... Another Debugger [*Data processing*] (BYTE)
ADB.......... Apollo Data Bank [*NASA*] (MCD)
ADB.......... Apple Desktop Bus [*Data processing*]
ADB.......... Arctic Drift Barge
ADB.......... Asian Development Bank
ADB.......... Association [*or Associate*] of Drama Boards [*British*]
ADB.......... Australian Dictionary of Biography [*A publication*] (APTA)
ADB.......... Australian Digest Bulletin [*A publication*] (APTA)
ADB.......... Average Daily Balance
ADB.......... Bachelor of Domestic Arts
ADB.......... United States Army Ballistic Research Laboratories, Aberdeen Proving Grounds, MD [*OCLC symbol*] (OCLC)
ADBA .... American Dog Breeders Association [*Defunct*] (EA)
ADBBBW .. Advances in Behavioral Biology [*A publication*]
ADBC .... Adriamycin, Dacarbazine, Bleomycin, CCNU [*Lomustine*] [*Antineoplastic drug regimen*]
ADBC .... American Defenders of Bataan and Corregidor (EA)
ADBD .... Active Duty Base Date [*Later, PSD*] [*Navy*]
ADBE .... Adobe Systems, Inc. [*Palo Alto, CA*] [*NASDAQ symbol*] (NQ)
ADBEA6.... Advances in Biochemical Engineering [*A publication*]
ADBED9.... Addictive Behaviors [*A publication*]
ADBEX...... Antarctic Division BIOMASS Experiment [*Australia*]
ADBF........ Australian Deer Breeders' Federation
ADBF........ Azurophil-Derived Bactericidal Factor
ADBM...... Apple Desktop Bus Microcontroller [*Computer processor*]
ADBMS..... Available Database Management System
ADBPE9.... Advances in Developmental and Behavioral Pediatrics [*A publication*]
ADBRDE... Australia. Commonwealth Scientific and Industrial Research Organisation. Division of Building Research. Annual Report [*A publication*]
ad Brut .... Epistulae ad Brutum [*of Cicero*] [*Classical studies*] (OCD)
ADBS........ Advanced Database System
ADC.......... Accretion Disk Corona [*Astrophysics*]
ADC.......... Acoustic Device, Countermeasure (CAAL)
ADC.......... Acta Dominorum Concilii [*3 vols.*] [*1839-1943*] [*Scotland*] [*A publication*] (DLA)
ADC.......... Action for Disabled Customers [*British Telecom*]
ADC.......... Active Diffusion Control (MCD)
ADC.......... Active Duty Commitment
ADC.......... Actuation Data Communication [*Naval Ordnance Laboratory*]
ADC.......... Adaptive Data Compression [*Data processing*]
ADC.......... Add with Carry
ADC.......... Address Complete, Charge [*Telecommunications*] (TEL)
AdC.......... Adrenal Cortex [*Medicine*]
ADC.......... Advance Delivery of Correspondence [*Military*]
ADC.......... Advanced Design [*or Drawing*] Change
ADC.......... Advanced Development Concept (CAAL)
ADC.......... Advancing Developing Countries [*Economics*]
AD and C ... Advise Duration and Charge [*British telephone term*]
ADC.......... Aerodrome Control [*British*]
ADC.......... Aerodrome Defence Corps [*British*]
ADC.......... Aerodynamic Data Correlation (MCD)
ADC.......... Aerophysics Development Corporation
ADC.......... Aerospace Defense Command [*Formerly, Air Defense Command*] [*Air Force*]
ADC.......... Agricultural Development Council [*Later, WIIAD*] (EA)
ADC.......... Aid to Dependent Children
ADC.......... Aide-de-Camp [*Military*] [*French*]
ADC.......... AIDS [*Acquired Immune Deficiency Syndrome*] Dementia Complex [*Medicine*]
ADC.......... Air Data Computer [*or Computing*] (MCD)
ADC.......... Air Data Converter
ADC.......... Air Defense Center (AAG)
ADC.......... Air Defense Command [*Peterson Air Force Base, CO*]
ADC.......... Air Defense Computer (AAG)
ADC.......... Air Development Center [*Air Force*]

ADC........... Air Diffusion Council (EA)
ADC........... Air Direction Center
ADC........... Airborne Digital Computer [*Air Force*]
ADC........... Aircraft Directives Configuration [*Navy*] (NG)
ADC........... Airdrome Defense Corps [*Air Force*]
ADC........... Alaska Defense Command [*Known to many of the soldiers who served in it as "All Damn Confusion"*] [*World War II*]
ADC........... Albumin, Dextrose, Catalase [*Media*]
ADC........... Alloy Data Center [*National Institute of Standards and Technology*]
ADC........... Allyl Diglycol Carbonate [*Organic chemistry*]
ADC........... Almost-Developed Country
ADC........... Amateur Dramatic Club [*British*]
ADC........... Ambulance Design Criteria [*National Highway Transportation Safety Administration*]
ADC........... American-Arab Anti-Discrimination Committee (EA)
ADC........... American Deserters Committee, France (EA)
AD & C ...... Ammunition Distribution and Control [*Military*] (NG)
ADC........... Ampere Direct Current (MCD)
ADC........... Amsterdam Depositary Company NV [*Netherlands*]
ADC........... Analog-to-Digital Computer [*Data processing*] (MCD)
ADC........... Analog-to-Digital Converter [*Data processing*] (MUGU)
ADC........... Analytic Decisions Corporation [*Information service or system*] (IID)
ADC........... Analytic Drag Control [*Aviation*] (NASA)
ADC........... Anchorage Dependent Cell [*Culture technology*]
ADC........... Anodal Duration Contraction [*Physiology*]
ADC........... Antenna Dish Control
ADC........... Anthracenedicarboxaldehyde [*Biochemistry*]
ADCL........ Anti-Drug Coalition [*Later, NADC*] (EA)
ADC........... Apollo Display Console [*NASA*]
ADC........... Apparent Depth of Compensation [*Geology*]
ADCM........ Appeal Cases, District of Columbia [*A publication*] (DLA)
ADC........... Ardeer Double Cartridge Test [*Sensitivity to propagation test of an explosive*]
ADC........... Area Damage Control (MCD)
ADC........... Area Data Center
ADC........... Area Defense Counsel [*Military*]
ADC........... Arginine Decarboxylase [*An enzyme*]
ADC........... Armament Development Center [*Army*]
ADC........... Army Dental Corps [*British*]
ADC........... Art Directors Club (EA)
ADC........... Asian Development Center
ADC........... Assistant Defense Counsel
ADC........... Assistant Director of Ceremonies [*Freemasonry*]
ADC........... Assistant Director of Contracts [*Military*] [*British*]
ADC........... Assistant Director, Curatorial
ADC........... Assistant District Commission (MCD)
ADC........... Assistant Division Commander [*Military*]
ADC........... Assistive Device Center [*Research center*] (RCD)
ADC........... [*The*] Associated Daimler Company [*British*] (DCTA)
ADC........... Association of Defense Counselors (EA)
ADC........... Association of District Councils [*British*]
ADC........... Association of Diving Contractors (EA)
ADC........... Asynchronous Data Channel (MCD)
ADC........... Asynchronous Digital Combiner (MCD)
ADC........... Auburn Dam [*California*] [*Seismograph station code, US Geological Survey*] (SEIS)
ADC........... Authorized Data Chain (AFM)
ADC........... Automatic Data Collector [*National Weather Service*]
ADC........... Automatic Depth Control (MCD)
ADC........... Automatic Deviation Control (MCD)
ADC........... Automatic Digital Calculator [*Data processing*] (ADA)
ADC........... Automatic Drift Control (AFM)
ADC........... Automatic Drip Coffee [*Brand name*]
ADC........... Average Daily Census
ADC........... Aviation Development Council (EA)
ADC........... Axiodistocervical [*Dentistry*]
ADC........... Chief Aviation Machinist's Mate (Reciprocating) [*Navy rating*]
ADC........... Debolt Community Library, Alberta [*Library symbol*] [*National Library of Canada*] (NLC)
ADCA........ Advanced Design Composite Aircraft (MCD)
ADCA........ Advisors Capital Technology Corp. [*NASDAQ symbol*] (NQ)
ADCA........ Advisory Dental Council of Australia
ADCA........ Aerospace Department Chairmen's Association (EA)
ADCA........ Allgemeine Deutsche Credit-Anstalt [*Bank*] [*Federal Republic of Germany*]
ADCA........ American Dexter Cattle Association (EA)
ADCA........ Aminodecephalosporanic Acid [*Biochemistry*]
ADCA........ Aminodeoxyclavulanic Acid [*Organic chemistry*]
ADCA........ Antique Doorknob Collectors of America (EA)
ADCAD...... Airways Data Collection and Distribution [*Data processing*]
ADCAP...... Advanced Capability
Ad Capt...... Ad Captandum [*For the Purpose of Captivating*] [*Latin*]
ADCAS....... Automatic Data Collection and Analysis System [*Fort Huachuca, AZ*] [*United States Army Electronic Proving Ground*] (GRD)
ADCASHAL ... Advance Cash Allowance Authorized
ADCAT ..... Air Defense Control and Targets Office [*Army*]
ADCB .... Abu Dhabi Commercial Bank (MENA)
ADCC .... Actual Development Cost Certification [*HUD*]

ADCC .... Air Defence Cadet Corps [*Military*] [*British*]
ADCC .... Air Defense Command Center
ADCC .... Air Defense Command and Control [*MICOM*] (RDA)
ADCC .... Air Defense Control Center [*Air Force*]
ADCC .... American Devon Cattle Club [*Later, Devon Cattle Association*] (EA)
ADCC .... Antibody-Dependent Cell-Mediated Cytotoxicity [*Immunology*]
ADCC .... Applied Data Communications, Inc. [*NASDAQ symbol*] (NQ)
ADCC .... Area Damage Control Center [*Army*]
ADCC .... Associated Day Care Centers
ADCC .... Asynchronous Data Communications Channel
ADCC .... Atlantic Development Council Canada
ADCCC ..... Air Defense Command Commendation Certificate
ADCCCS ... Air Defense Command, Control, and Coordination System (AABC)
ADCCM ..... Advanced Cooperative Countermeasure (MCD)
ADCCP...... Advanced Data Communications Control Procedure [*American National Standards Institute*]
ADCCS...... Air Defense Command and Control System (MCD)
ADCDA8 ... Advances in Child Development and Behavior [*A publication*]
ADCEO ..... Assistant Division Communications Electronics Officer [*Military*] (AABC)
ADCGEN .. Aide-de-Camp General [*Appointment to the Queen*] [*British*]
ADCI .... American Die Casting Institute (EA)
ADCII .... American Die Casting Institute, Incorporated
ADCIR....... Administrative Circular
ADCIS .... Association for Development of Computer-Based Instructional Systems (EA)
ADCL .... Accredited Dosimetry Calibration Laboratories
ADCLDZ... Advances in Cladistics [*A publication*]
ADCLS...... Advanced Data Collection and Location System
ADCM ...... Archbishop of Canterbury's Diploma in Church Music [*British*]
ADCMAZ ... Advances in Chemotherapy [*A publication*]
ADCMC .... Antibody-Dependent Cell-Mediated Cytotoxicity [*Immunology*]
ADCN........ Advanced Design [*or Drawing*] Change Notice
ADCND7... Advances in Cellular Neurobiology [*A publication*]
ADCNM .... Assistant Deputy Chief of Naval Material (MCD)
ADCO........ Advantage Companies, Inc. [*NASDAQ symbol*] (NQ)
ADCO........ Air Defense Communications Office (AABC)
ADCO........ Alcohol and Drug Control Office [*Military*] (AABC)
ADCO........ As Design Changes Occur (MCD)
ADC-OA.... Air Defense Command-Office of Operations Analysis [*Peterson Air Force Base, CO*]
ADCOC ..... Air Defense Command Operation Control (FAAC)
ADCOC ..... Area Damage Control Center [*Army*]
ADCOEB.... Advances in Contraception [*A publication*]
ADCOH .... Appalachian Ultradeep Core Hole [*Project of seismic profiling*]
ADCOINS ... Air Defense Command Interoperability System [*Army*]
ADCOM.... Administrative Command
ADCOM.... Advance Command
ADCOM.... Advanced Cooperative Countermeasure (MCD)
ADCOM.... Aerospace Defense Command [*Formerly, Air Defense Command*] [*Peterson Air Force Base, CO*] (FAAC)
ADCOMD ... Administrative Command [*Navy*] [*British*]
ADCOMINPAC ... Administrative Command, Minecraft, Pacific Fleet
ADCOMPHIBSPAC ... Administrative Command, Amphibious Forces, Pacific Fleet
Ad Compl... Advertising Compliance Service [*A publication*]
Ad Compli S ... Advertising Compliance Service. Special Report [*A publication*]
ADCOMSUBORDCOMPHIBSPAC ... Administrative Command, Amphibious Forces, Pacific Fleet, Subordinate Command
Ad Con .... Addison on Contracts [*A publication*] (DLA)
ADCON..... Address Constant [*Data processing*]
ADCON..... Administrative Control
ADCON..... Advance Concepts for Terrain Avoidance
ADCON..... Advise [*or Issue Instructions to*] All Concerned
ADCON..... Analog-to-Digital Converter [*Data processing*]
ADCON..... Archdeacon
ADCONSEN ... [*With the*] Advice and Consent of the Senate
Ad Cont...... Addison on Contract [*A publication*] (ILCA)
ADCOP ..... Acquisition and Distribution of Commercial Products [*Also, ADCP*] [*Department of Defense program*]
ADCOP ..... Air Defense Command Post
ADCOP ..... Area Damage Control Party [*Army*]
ADCOP ..... Associate Degree Completion Program [*Navy*] (NG)
ADCP .... Acoustic Doppler Current Profiler [*Oceanography*]
ADCP .... Acquisition and Distribution of Commercial Products [*Also, ADCOP*] [*Department of Defense program*] (MCD)
ADCP .... Advanced [*Flight*] Control Programmer
ADCP .... Advanced Data Communication Protocol [*Data processing*]
ADC(P)...... Aide-de-Camp Personal [*Appointment to the Queen*] [*British*]
ADCP .... Air Defense Command Post (AABC)
ADCPAA.... Advances in Chemical Physics [*A publication*]
ADC/PL.... Advanced Data Collection - Position Location (MCD)
ADCR........ Applicable Document Contractual Record [*Military*]
ADCR........ Devon Coal Research Centre, Alberta [*Library symbol*] [*National Library of Canada*] (NLC)
ADCS......... ADA Design and Coping Standards [*DoD*]

ADCS......... Advanced Defense Communications Satellite [*Air Force*] (AFM)
ADCS......... Air Data Computer Set
ADCS......... Air Data Computing System
ADCS......... AUTODIN Coordination Station (CET)
ADCS......... Automated Document Control System [*Data processing*]
ADCS......... Automatic Data Collection System (RDA)
ADCS......... Automatic Data Correlation System (MCD)
ADCS......... Senior Chief Aviation Machinist's Mate [*Navy rating*]
ADCSAJ... Advances in Chemistry Series [*A publication*]
ADCSC...... Australian Dairy Corporation Selection Committee
ADCSCD... Assistant Deputy Chief of Staff for Combat Developments [*Army*]
ADCSLOG ... Assistant Deputy Chief of Staff for Logistics [*Army*]
ADCSLOG-SA ... Assistant Deputy Chief of Staff for Logistics for Security Assistance [*Military*]
ADCSOPS ... Assistant Deputy Chief of Staff for Operations and Plans [*Military*]
ADCSOPS (JA) ... Assistant Deputy Chief of Staff for Operations and Plans (Joint Affairs) [*Military*]
ADCSP...... Advanced Defense Communications Satellite Program [*Air Force*]
ADCSPC ... Air Data Computer Static Pressure Compensator (MCD)
ADCSRDA ... Assistant Deputy Chief of Staff for Research, Development, and Acquisition [*Military*]
ADCSTE ... Assistant Deputy Chief of Staff, in Test and Evaluation [*Army*]
ADCT .... ADC Telecommunications, Inc. [*Bloomington, MN*] [*NASDAQ symbol*] (NQ)
ADCT .... Association of District Council Treasurers [*British*]
Ad Ct Dig... Administrative Court Digest [*A publication*] (DLA)
ADCU........ Air Vehicle Digital Computer Unit
ADCU........ Alarm Display and Control Unit [*Telecommunications*] (TEL)
ADCU........ Alternate Detection and Control Unit (MCD)
ADCU........ Association of Data Communications Users (EA)
ADCUS ..... Advise Customs [*Aviation*] (FAAC)
ADCWT .... Adipose Fin Clip with Coded Wire Tag [*Pisciculture*]
ADCYA3 ... Advances in Chromatography [*A publication*]
ADCYB4.... Advances in Cytopharmacology [*A publication*]
ADD.......... Abstracts of Declassified Documents [*A publication*]
AD and D... Accidental Death and Dismemberment [*Insurance*]
ADD.......... Acoustic Deception Device (CAAL)
ADD.......... Acoustic Detection Device (MCD)
ADD.......... Acoustic Discrimination of Decoys
Add............ Addams' Ecclesiastical Reports [*A publication*] (DLA)
add .... Addantur [*Let Them Be Added*] [*Latin*]
ADD.......... Adde [*Add or Up To*] [*Pharmacy*]
ADD.......... Addendum (KSC)
ADD.......... Addis Ababa [*Ethiopia*] [*Airport symbol*] (OAG)
Add........... Addison's Pennsylvania Supreme Court Reports [*A publication*] (DLA)
ADD.......... Addition (AABC)
ADD.......... Address
ADD.......... Adduction [*or Adductor*] [*Medicine*]
ADD.......... Administration on Developmental Disabilities [*Human Development Services*]
ADD.......... Advanced Development Design (CAAL)
AD & D..... Advanced Dungeons and Dragons
ADD.......... Aerospace Defense Division [*Air Force*]
ADD.......... Aerospace Digital Development
ADD.......... Air Defense Development
ADD.......... Air Defense District (NATG)
ADD.......... Alphanumeric Digital Display (CAAL)
ADD.......... American Dialect Dictionary [*A publication*]
ADD.......... American Doctoral Dissertations [*A publication*]
ADD.......... Ames Department Stores, Inc. [*NYSE symbol*] (SPSG)
ADD.......... Amino(dimethyl)dihydrobenzofuran [*Organic chemistry*]
ADD.......... Analog Data Digitizer
ADD.......... Analog-Digital-Designer [*Trademark*]
ADD.......... Armaments Design Department [*Ministry of Supply*] [*British*] [*World War II*]
ADD.......... Arming Decision Device (MUGU)
ADD.......... Attention Deficit Disorder [*Psychology*]
ADD.......... Auditory Discrimination in Depth [*Program*] [*Education*]
ADD.......... Automatic Data Descriptor
ADD.......... Automatic Distribution of Documents [*DoD*]
ADD.......... Automatic Document Distribution (MCD)
ADD.......... Automatic Drawing Office (DIT)
ADD.......... Aviatsiia Dalnego Deistviia [*Long-Range Aviation*] [*Strategic bombing force of USSR*]
ADD.......... United States Army ARRADCOM - STINFO Division, Dover, NJ [*OCLC symbol*] (OCLC)
A D 2d ...... Appellate Division Reports. Second Series [*New York*] [*A publication*]
AD 2d......... New York Supreme Court, Appellate Division Reports, Second Series [*A publication*] (DLA)
ADDA........ Air Defense Defended Area [*Army*]
ADDA........ American Design Drafting Association (EA)
AD/DA ...... Analog Digital/Digital Analog (RDA)
ADDA........ Attention-Deficit Disorder Association (EA)

ADDA........ Australian Database Development Association [*Database producer*] (IID)
ADDA........ Darwin [*Australia*] [*ICAO location identifier*] (ICLI)
Add Abr ..... Addington's Abridgment of Penal Statutes [*A publication*] (DLA)
ADDAC..... Analog Data Distributor and Control [*Data processing*] (KSC)
Add Agr Act ... Addison on the Agricultural Holdings Act [*A publication*] (DLA)
ADDAM.... Adaptive Dynamic Decision-Aiding Method
Addams...... Addams' Ecclesiastical Reports [*A publication*] (DLA)
Addams Ecc (Eng) ... Addams' Ecclesiastical Reports [*A publication*] (DLA)
ADDAR..... Automatic Digital Data Acquisition and Recording [*Data processing*]
ADDAS ..... Automatic Digital Data Assembly System [*Data processing*]
Add C........ Addison on Contracts [*A publication*] (DLA)
ADDC........ Addmaster Corporation [*NASDAQ symbol*] (NQ)
ADDC........ Air Defense Direction Center [*Air Force*]
ADDC........ Alignment and Diagnostic Display Console
ADDC........ Analog-to-Digital Data Converter [*Data processing*] (MCD)
ADDC........ Analog-Discrete Data Converter [*Data processing*] (MCD)
ADDC........ Association of Desk and Derrick Clubs (EA)
Add Ch ...... Addison Charges [*Addison's Pennsylvania Reports*] [*A publication*] (DLA)
Add Con ..... Addison on Contracts [*A publication*] (DLA)
Add Cont.... Addison on Contracts [*A publication*] (DLA)
ADDCS..... Aircraft Decontaminating, Deicing, Cleaning System (MCD)
ADDD....... Darwin [*Australia*] [*ICAO location identifier*] (ICLI)
ADDDS ..... Automatic Direct-Distance Dialing System [*Telecommunications*] (IEEE)
Add Ecc ..... Addams' Ecclesiastical Reports [*A publication*] (DLA)
Add Eccl..... Addams' Ecclesiastical Reports [*A publication*] (DLA)
Add Eccl Rep ... Addams' Ecclesiastical Reports [*A publication*] (DLA)
ADDED..... Additional Education
ADDEE ...... Addressee (NVT)
AD DEF AN ... Ad Defectionem Animi [*To the Point of Fainting*] [*Pharmacy*]
ADDEND ... Addendus [*To Be Added*] [*Pharmacy*]
Add ER ...... Addams' Ecclesiastical Reports [*A publication*] (DLA)
ADDER ..... Automatic Digital-Data-Error Recorder [*Data processing*]
AddEsther ... Additions to Esther [*Apocrypha*] (BJA)
ADDEV..... Advanced Development [*Army*] (AABC)
ADDF....... Automated Deferred Discrepancy File
ADD-H...... Attention Deficit Disorder with Hyperactivity [*Medicine*]
ADD-HA... Attention Deficit Disorder with Hyperactivity [*Medicine*]
ADDI........ Airborne Dual Detector Indicator (MCD)
ADDIC ...... Alcohol and Dependency Intervention Council [*Military*] (AABC)
Addict Behav ... Addictive Behaviors [*A publication*]
Addict Dis ... Addictive Diseases [*A publication*]
ADDIDV ... Addictive Diseases [*A publication*]
Addis.......... Addison's County Court Reports [*Pennsylvania*] [*A publication*] (DLA)
Addison (PA) ... Addison's County Court Reports [*Pennsylvania*] [*A publication*] (DLA)
Addison-Wesley Ser Comput Sci Inform Process ... Addison-Wesley Series in Computer Science and Information Processing [*A publication*]
addit .... Additional (DLA)
ADDIT ...... Association for Development of Design in Tasmania [*Australia*]
Additional Ser Roy Bot ... Additional Series. Royal Botanic Gardens [*A publication*]
Addit Rubber Plast Pap Meet ... Additives for Rubber and Plastics. Papers Presented at the Meeting of the Chemical Marketing Research Association [*A publication*]
ADDIV...... Air Defense of the Division (MCD)
ADDL....... Additional (KSC)
AD/DL...... Aircraft Division/Department List [*Air Force*]
ADDL....... Aircraft Dummy Deck Landing [*Navy*]
ADDL....... American Double Dutch League (EA)
ADDL....... Anti-Digit Dialing League (EA)
ADDLASS ... Air Deployable Drifting Linear Array SONAR System (MCD)
ADDM....... Addendum to Monthly Collection [*IRS*]
ADDM....... Automated Drafting and Digitizing Machine [*Data processing*] (RDA)
ADDMS .... Automatic Depth/Deployed Moored Sweep (MCD)
ADDN....... Addition
ADDN....... Darwin [*Australia*] [*ICAO location identifier*] (ICLI)
ADDNL...... Additional
ADDNR...... Assistant and Deputy Director of Naval Recruiting [*British*]
ADDP....... Air Defense Defended Point [*Army*]
Add PA ..... Addison's County Court Reports [*Pennsylvania*] [*A publication*] (DLA)
ADDPEP... Aerodynamic Deployable Decelerator Performance Evaluation Program
ADDPLA... Additional Places
ADDR....... Adder [*Computer device*]
ADDR....... Addington Resources, Inc. [*NASDAQ symbol*] (NQ)
ADDR....... Address [*Computer character*] [*Data processing*]
ADDR....... Address Register
Add Rep ..... Addison's County Court Reports [*Pennsylvania*] [*A publication*] (DLA)

ADDRESOR ... Analog-to-Digital Data Reduction System for Oceanographic Research
ADDRESS ... Automated Design of Damage Resistant Structures (MCD)
Address Proc Ontario Soil Crop Impr Ass ... Addresses and Proceedings. Ontario Soil and Crop Improvement Association [*A publication*]
Address Proc Saskatchewan Univ Farm Home Week ... Addresses and Proceedings. Saskatchewan University Farm and Home Week [*A publication*]
ADDRI ...... Apollo Document Distribution Requirements Index [*NASA*] (KSC)
ADDS .... Advanced Deep Diving Submersible
ADDS .... Air Defense Demonstration System (MCD)
ADDS .... Air Deployment Delivery System [*Military*] (NVT)
ADDS .... Airborne Detection Discrimination Sensor
ADDS .... American Digestive Disease Society (EA)
ADDS .... American Diopter and Decibel Society (EA)
ADDS .... American Diversified Dog Society (EA)
ADDS .... Apollo Data [*or Document*] Descriptions Standards [*NASA*] (MCD)
ADDS .... Applied Digital Data Systems, Inc. [*NASDAQ symbol*]
ADDS .... Army Data Distribution System
ADDS .... Army DEIS [*Defense Energy Information System*] Data Entry System
ADDS .... Assistant Director of Dental Services
ADDS .... Astrodigital Doppler Speedometer [*Electronics*]
ADDS .... ASW [*Antisubmarine Warfare*] Acoustic Deception Device (MCD)
ADDS .... Automated Digital Data System
ADDS .... Automated Digital Design System [*Raytheon Co.*]
ADDS .... Automatic Data Digitizing System [*Air Force*]
ADDS .... Automatic Data Distribution System [*Army*] (AABC)
ADDSC .... Association des Directeurs de Departements de Sante Communautaire [*Association of Public Health Department Directors*] [*Canada*]
Add T .... Addison on Torts [*A publication*] (DLA)
ADDT .... Additive (MSA)
ADDT .... All-Digital Data Tape (KSC)
ADDT .... Angular Distribution Data Tape
ADDTL ..... Additional
Add Tor ...... Addison on Torts [*A publication*] (DLA)
Add Torts ... Addison on Torts [*A publication*] (DLA)
Add Torts Abr ... Addison on Torts, Abridged [*A publication*] (DLA)
Add Torts D & B ... Addison on Torts, Dudley and Baylies' Edition [*A publication*] (DLA)
Add Torts Woods ... Addison on Torts, Woods Edition [*A publication*] (DLA)
ADD c TRIT ... Adde cum Tritu [*Add Trituration*] [*Pharmacy*]
ADDU .... Additional Duty
ADDU .... Alcohol and Drug Dependence Unit [*Northern Territory Health Commission*] [*Australia*]
ADDUNIFALW ... Additional Uniform Allowance [*Military*]
AD & Dur RP ... Adams and Durham on Real Property [*A publication*] (DLA)
ADDX .... Darwin [*Australia*] [*ICAO location identifier*] (ICLI)
ADE .... Accion Democratica Ecuatoriana [*Ecuadorean Democratic Action*] [*Political party*] (PPW)
ADE .... Acute Disseminated Encephalomyelitis [*Medicine*]
ADE .... Adelaide [*Mount Bonython*] [*Australia*] [*Seismograph station code, US Geological Survey*] (SEIS)
ADE .... Aden [*People's Democratic Republic of Yemen*] [*Airport symbol*] (OAG)
Ade .... Adenine [*Also, A*] [*Biochemistry*]
Ad & E .... Adolphus and Ellis' English King's Bench Reports [*A publication*] (DLA)
ADE .... Advanced Data Entry
ADE .... Aerial Delivery Equipment (MCD)
ADE .... After Delivery Economies
ADE .... Air Defense Element (AABC)
ADE .... Air Defense Emergency [*Military*] (AABC)
ADE .... Air Defense Evaluation
ADE .... Air Density [*Explorer satellite*] [*NASA*]
ADE .... Alpha Disintegration Energy
ADE .... Alphanumeric Display Equipment
ADE .... American Dance Ensemble
ADE .... American Demographics [*A publication*]
ADE .... Anglo Dominion Gold Exploration Ltd. [*Toronto Stock Exchange symbol*]
ADE .... Animal Disease Eradication Division [*of ARS, Department of Agriculture*]
ADE .... Antibody-Dependent Enhancement [*of viral infection*]
ADE .... Apparent Digestible Energy [*Nutrition*]
ADE .... Approved Data Element (AFM)
ADE .... Archivio di Diritto Ecclesiastico [*A publication*]
ADE .... Armament Design Establishment [*British*]
ADE .... Armored Division Equivalent [*Military*]
ADE .... Army Department Establishments [*British*]
ADE .... Arrhythmogenic Dose of Epinephrine [*Medicine*]
ADE .... Assessor's Data Exchange [*A publication*] (EAAP)
ADE .... Assistant Division Engineer [*Army*] (AABC)
ADE .... Association of Departments of English (EA)

ADE .... Association for Documentary Editing (EA)
ADE .... Association Europeenne pour l'Etude de l'Alimentation et Developpement de l'Enfant [*European Association of Nutrition and Child Development*] (EAIO)
ADE .... Atomic Defense Engineering (MUGU)
ADE .... Audible Doppler Enhancer [*Telecommunications*] (TEL)
ADE .... Authorized Data Element
ADE .... Automated Debugging Environment [*Applied Data Research, Inc.*]
ADE .... Automated Design Engineering [*Telecommunications*] (TEL)
ADE .... Automatic Data Entry [*Air Force*]
ADE .... Automatic Data Evaluation
ADE .... Automatic Drafting Equipment (IEEE)
ADE .... Chemical System Laboratory, Aberdeen Proving Grounds, MD [*OCLC symbol*] (OCLC)
ADE .... Delburne Public Library, Alberta [*Library symbol*] [*National Library of Canada*] (NLC)
ADEA .... Age Discrimination in Employment Act [*1967*] [*Department of Labor*]
ADEA .... American Driver Education Association [*Later, ADTSEA*] (EA)
ADEA .... Army Development and Employment Agency [*Fort Lewis, WA*] (INF)
ADEA .... Assistant Director of Expense Accounts [*Navy*] [*British*]
ADEA .... Australian Diabetes Educators Association
ADEB .... Association of Departments of English. Bulletin [*A publication*]
ADEB .... Association des Editeurs Belges [*Association of French-language book publishers*] [*Belgium*] (EY)
ADEC .... Aiken Dahlgren Electronic Calculator (MCD)
ADEC .... Association for Death Education and Counseling (EA)
ADEC .... Australian Drug Evaluation Centre
ADED .... Air Defense Effectiveness Demonstration [*Army*] (MCD)
ADED .... Air Delivery Equipment Division [*Natick Laboratories*] [*Army*]
ADED .... Association of Driver Educators for the Disabled (EA)
ADeD .... Decatur Daily, Decatur, AL [*Library symbol*] [*Library of Congress*] (LCLS)
ADEDA ..... Advise Effective Date (NOAA)
Ad Ed Act .. Adams on the Education Act [*A publication*] (DLA)
ADEDS .... Advanced Electronic Display System [*FAA*]
ADEDU ..... Assistant Director for Education [*Vietnam*]
ADEE .... Addressee (CINC)
ADEE .... Air Defence Experimental Establishment [*Later, ADRDE, RRE*] [*British*]
ADEE .... Association for Dental Education in Europe (EAIO)
AD EFFECT ... Ad Effectum [*Until Effectual*] [*Pharmacy*]
ADEFSq .... Air Defense Squadron [*Air Force*]
ADEFUCC ... Association des Directeurs de Departements d'Etudes Francaises des Universites et Colleges du Canada [*Association of Directors of Departments of French Studies of Canadian Universities and Colleges*]
ADEG .... Auxiliary Display Equipment Group (KSC)
ADEGB ..... Automotive Design Engineering [*A publication*]
Ad Ej .... Adams on Ejectment [*A publication*] (DLA)
ADEJB ...... Arizona Dental Journal [*A publication*]
ADEKS ...... Advanced Design Electronic Key System [*Telecommunications*]
Adel .... Adelphi [*A publication*]
ADEL .... Adelphia Communications Corp. [*Coudersport, PA*] [*NASDAQ symbol*] (NQ)
Ad & El ...... Adolphus and Ellis' English King's Bench Reports [*A publication*] (DLA)
Adel .... New Adelphi [*A publication*]
ADELA ...... Atlantic Community Development Group for Latin America [*Joint US-European private investment company*]
Adelaide Children's Hosp Records ... Adelaide Children's Hospital. Records [*A publication*] (APTA)
Adelaide Law Rev ... Adelaide Law Review [*A publication*] (APTA)
Adelaide LR ... Adelaide Law Review [*A publication*] (APTA)
Adelaide L Rev ... Adelaide Law Review [*A publication*]
Ad & El (Eng) ... Adolphus and Ellis' English King's Bench Reports [*A publication*] (DLA)
ADELF ...... Association des Distributeurs Exclusifs de Livres en Langue Francaise [*Association of Exclusive Distributors of French-Language Books*] [*Canada*]
ADELF ...... Association des Ecrivains de Langue Francaise [*Association of French-Language Writers*] (EAIO)
ADELF ...... Association des Epidemiologistes de Langue Francaise [*Association of French Language Epidemiologists - AFLE*] (EAIO)
ADELL ...... Adult Education and Lifelong Learning
Adel Law R ... Adelaide Law Review [*A publication*] (APTA)
Adel Law Rev ... Adelaide Law Review [*A publication*] (APTA)
Ad & Ell NS ... Adolphus and Ellis' English Queen's Bench Reports, New Series [*A publication*] (DLA)
Adel LR ...... Adelaide Law Review [*A publication*] (APTA)
Adel L Rev ... Adelaide Law Review [*A publication*] (APTA)
Ad & El NS ... Adolphus and Ellis' Reports, New Series [*A publication*] (ILCA)
Adelphi P .... Adelphi Papers [*A publication*]
Adel R .... Adelaide Review [*A publication*]

Adel Stock and Station J ... Adelaide Stock and Station Journal [*A publication*] (APTA)
A Delt......... Archaiologikon Deltion [*A publication*]
Adel Univ Grad Gaz ... Adelaide University Graduates Union. Gazette [*A publication*] (APTA)
Adel Univ Grad Union Gaz ... Adelaide University Graduates Union. Monthly Newsletter and Gazette [*A publication*] (APTA)
Adel Univ Mag ... Adelaide University. Magazine [*A publication*] (APTA)
ADEM....... Adaptively Data Equalized MODEM
ADEM....... Air Defences, Eastern Mediterranean [*British military*] (DMA)
ADEMAST ... Association Nationale pour le Developpment et la Maitrise des Sciences et des Techniques [*French*]
ADEMQA ... Office of Acid Deposition, Environmental Monitoring, and Quality Assurance [*Washington, DC*] [*Environmental Protection Agency*] (GRD)
ADEMRCM ... CANMET [*Canada Centre for Mineral and Energy Technology*] Library, Energy, Mines, and Resources Canada [*Bibliotheque CANMET, Energie, Mines, et Ressources Canada*], Devon, Alberta [*Library symbol*] [*National Library of Canada*] (NLC)
ADEMS..... Advanced Diagnostic Engine Monitoring System [*Air Force*]
ADEMS..... Airborne Display Electrical Management System (MCD)
ADEN........ Armament Development, Enfield
ADEN........ Augmented Deflector Exhaust Nozzle [*Aviation*]
ADEN/DEFA ... Armament Development, Enfield/Direction Etude Fabrication [*Military*] (MCD)
Adenine Arabinoside Antiviral Agent Symp ... Adenine Arabinoside; an Antiviral Agent. Symposium [*A publication*]
Aden LR..... Aden Law Reports [*A publication*] (ILCA)
adenoca...... Adenocarcinoma [*Medicine*]
Adeno-SCC ... Adenocarcinoma-Squamous Cell Carcinoma [*Oncology*]
ADEO........ Advance Development Engineering Order
ADEOS..... Advanced Earth Observing Satellite [*Japan*]
ADEOS..... Air Droppable, Expendable Ocean Sensor [*Oceanography*] (MSC)
ADEP........ Air Depot [*Army*]
A DEP........ Anno Depositionis [*In the Year of the Deposit*] [*Latin*] [*Freemasonry*]
ADEP........ [*Worldwide*] Asset Data Evaluation Program
ADEPO..... Automatic Dynamic Evaluation by Programmed Organizations
ADEPREP ... Army Deployment Reporting System (AABC)
ADEPS...... Antisubmarine Warfare Automated Detection Prediction System (MCD)
ADEPT...... Aerospace Draftsman's Education and Proficiency Training (MCD)
ADEPT...... Agricultural and Dairy Educational Political Trust
ADEPT...... Air Force Depot Equipment Performance Tester (AAG)
ADEPT...... Association d'Etudes Politiques Transeuropeennes [*Trans European Policy Studies Association - TEPSA*] (EA)
ADEPT...... Automated Direct Entry Packaging Technique
ADEPT...... Automatic Data Extractor and Plotting Table
ADEPT...... Automatic Dynamic Evaluation by Programmed Test
ADEPT...... [*A*] Distinctly Empirical Prover of Theorems
Ad Eq........ Adams' Equity [*A publication*] (DLA)
Adequacy Dial Pro Conf ... Adequacy of Dialysis. Proceedings of a Conference [*A publication*]
ADER........ Automatic Data Extraction Routine (CAAL)
ADER........ Derwent Public Library, Alberta [*Library symbol*] [*National Library of Canada*] (NLC)
ADERI....... American Disability Evaluation Research Institute [*Research center*] (RCD)
A Derm...... Acta Dermatologica [*A publication*]
A DES........ A Destra [*To the Right*] [*Italian*] (ADA)
ADES........ Air Defense Engagement System (MCD)
ADES........ Air Defense Engineering Service (MCD)
ADES........ Analysis, Design, and Evaluation System (MCD)
ADES........ Angle-Dispersed Electron Spectroscopy (MCD)
ADES........ Automatic Digital Encoding System [*Data processing*]
ADESAT..... Anales del Desarrollo [*Annals of Development*] [*A publication*]
ADESMS .. Mistassinity School, Desmarais, Alberta [*Library symbol*] [*National Library of Canada*] (BIB)
ADESPS..... Pelican Mountain School, Desmarais, Alberta [*Library symbol*] [*National Library of Canada*] (BIB)
ADETBX..... Australia. Commonwealth Scientific and Industrial Research Organisation. Division of Entomology. Annual Report [*A publication*]
ADEU........ Automatic Data Entry Unit
AD EUND ... Ad Eundem Gradum [*To the Same Degree*] [*Latin*] [*Of the admission of a graduate of one university to the same degree at another without examination*]
ADEVD..... Area Development [*A publication*]
ADEW....... Air Defense Early Warning (NATG)
ADeW....... Wheeler Basin Regional Library, Decatur, AL [*Library symbol*] [*Library of Congress*] (LCLS)
ADEWS..... Air Defense Electronic Warfare System (MCD)
AD EX........ Ad Extremum [*To the Extreme, To the End*] [*Latin*]
ADEX........ Advanced Antisubmarine Warfare Exercise (NVT)
ADEX........ Air Defense Exercise (MCD)
ADF.......... Acid-Detergent Fiber [*Food analysis*]
ADF.......... Acoustic Depth Finder
ADF.......... Acquisition Data Facility (MCD)

ADF.......... Ad Forum [*A publication*]
ADF.......... Adapter Definition File (BYTE)
ADF.......... Adera Financial Corp. Ltd. [*Vancouver Stock Exchange symbol*]
ADF.......... Aerial Direction Finding
ADF.......... Aeronutronics Division, Ford Motor Co. (AAG)
ADF.......... After Deducting Freight [*Billing*]
ADF.......... Air Defense Force
ADF.......... Air Development Force
ADF.......... Air Direction Finder
ADF.......... Airborne Direction Finder (MCD)
ADF.......... Aktion Demokratischer Fortschritt [*Action for Democratic Progress*] [*Federal Republic of Germany*] (PPE)
ADF.......... Alaska Defense Frontier [*Military*]
ADF.......... Alcohol and Drug Foundation [*Australia*]
ADF.......... Algorithm Development Facility [*for spacecraft data*] [*Jet Propulsion Laboratory*]
ADF.......... All Dielectric Filter
ADF.......... American Dance Festival [*Later, AADF*] (EA)
ADF.......... American Defense Foundation (EA)
ADF.......... American Ditchley Foundation (EA)
ADF.......... American Duty Free [*Freight*]
ADF.......... Anterior Dendritic Field [*Neurology*]
ADF.......... Application Development Facility [*IBM Corp.*] [*Data processing*]
ADF.......... Approved Deposit Fund (ADA)
ADF.......... Approximate Degrees of Freedom [*Statistics*]
ADF.......... Arab Deterrent Force [*Palestine*] (PD)
ADF.......... Archdiocesan Development Fund [*Catholic*]
ADF.......... Arkadelphia, AR [*Location identifier*] [*FAA*] (FAAL)
ADF.......... Army Distaff Foundation (EA)
ADF.......... Asian Development Fund [*Asian Development Bank*]
ADF.......... Assured Destruction Force [*Military*]
ADF.......... Australian Defence Force (ADA)
ADF.......... Automated Design Facility (MCD)
ADF.......... Automatic Direction Finder [*Military*]
ADF.......... Automatic Display Finder [*Data processing*] (NASA)
ADF.......... Automatic Document Feeder [*For copying machines*]
ADF.......... Auxiliary Detonation Fuze (NG)
ADF.......... Biomedical Laboratory, Aberdeen Proving Grounds, MD [*OCLC symbol*] (OCLC)
ADF.......... [*A*] Direction Finder
ADFAP...... Automatic Direction Finding Approach
ADFaS....... Australian Documentary Facsimile Society
ADFC........ Adiabatic Film Cooling
ADFC........ Admiral Financial Corporation [*NASDAQ symbol*] (NQ)
ADFC........ Air Defense Filter Center [*Military*]
ADFC........ Association des Femmes Collaboratrices [*Association of Feminine Collectives*] [*Canada*]
ADFCA...... Advances in Fluorine Chemistry [*A publication*]
ADFCAK.... Advances in Fluorine Chemistry [*A publication*]
ADFE........ Association Democratique des Francais de l'Etranger [*Democratic Association of French Citizens Abroad*] (PPW)
AD FEB .... Adstante Febre [*When Fever Is Present*] [*Pharmacy*]
ADFI......... American Dog Feed Institute [*Defunct*] (EA)
ADFIAP .... Association of Development Financing Institutions in Asia and the Pacific [*Manila, Philippines*] (EA)
ADFILS..... Australian Defence Families Information and Liaison Service
AD FIN ..... Ad Finem [*At or To the End*] [*Latin*]
ADFL........ Association of Departments of Foreign Languages (EA)
ADFLB...... Association of Departments of Foreign Languages. Bulletin [*A publication*]
ADFM....... Advertronics, Inc. [*NASDAQ symbol*] (NQ)
ADFO........ Assistant Director, Flight Operations [*NASA*] (KSC)
ADFOAM ... Australia. Commonwealth Scientific and Industrial Research Organisation. Division of Fisheries and Oceanography. Report [*A publication*]
ADFOR..... Adriatic Force [*Military*]
ADFORS.... Advertisement Format Selection [*Marketing*]
ADFP........ Atroxin-Defibrinated Plasma [*Clinical chemistry*]
ADFPBQ... Australia. Commonwealth Scientific and Industrial Research Organisation. Division of Food Preservation. Report of Research [*A publication*]
ADFR........ Automatic Direction Finder, Remote Control (AAG)
ADFRAV... Alaska. Department of Fisheries. Research Report [*A publication*]
ADFS........ American Dentists for Foreign Service (EA)
ADFS........ Automatic Direction Finding System
ADFSC..... Automatic Data Field Systems Command [*Fort Belvoir, VA*] [*Army*]
ADFT........ Artillery Direct Fire Trainer (AABC)
ADFU........ Air Defense Firing Unit (MCD)
ADFW....... Assistant Director of Fortifications and Works [*Military*] [*British*]
ADG.......... Accessory Drive Gear Box (MCD)
ADG.......... Adrian, MI [*Location identifier*] [*FAA*] (FAAL)
ADG.......... Advance Development Group [*Army*] (AABC)
ADG.......... Advantage Enterprises, Inc. [*Vancouver Stock Exchange symbol*]
ADG.......... Aeronautical Development Group [*Military*] (AFIT)

ADG.......... Air Defense Group [*Air Force*] (MCD)
ADG.......... Air Density Gauge [*Aviation*]
ADG.......... Air-Driven Generator (MCD)
ADG.......... American Dance Guild (EA)
ADG.......... Antenna Directive Gain
ADG.......... Archives Historiques du Departement de la Gironde [*A publication*]
ADG.......... Assistant Director-General [*British*]
ADG.......... Attack Display Group (MCD)
ADGp........ Automotive Development Group [*LTV Steel Corp.*]
ADG.......... Auxiliary Deception Generator (MCD)
ADG.......... Average Daily Gain [*of weight*] [*Cattle*]
ADG.......... Aviation Depot Group (AAG)
ADG.......... Axiodistogingival [*Dentistry*]
ADG.......... Degaussing Ship [*Navy symbol*]
ADGA....... American Dairy Goat Association (EA)
ADGB....... Accessory Drive Gear Box (MCD)
ADGB....... Air Defense of Great Britain
ADGB....... Archiv fuer Geschichte des Buchwesens [*A publication*]
ADGE....... Adage, Inc. [*NASDAQ symbol*] (NQ)
ADGE....... Air Defense Ground Environment [*NATO*] (MCD)
ADGEA...... Advances in Genetics [*A publication*]
Adgez Rasplavov Paika Mater ... Adgeziya Rasplavov i Paika Materialov [*A publication*]
ADGINT..... Advanced GPS/Inertial Integration (MCD)
ADGL ..... Adrenal Gland [*Anatomy*]
ADGMS .... Assistant Director-General of Medical Services [*Military*] [*British*]
ADGN....... American Diagnostics Corp. [*NASDAQ symbol*] (NQ)
ADGO........ Adagio [*Slow*] [*Music*]
ADGOA..... Advances in Geophysics [*A publication*]
ADGp........ Air Defense Group [*Air Force*]
AD GR ACID ... Ad Gratum Aciditatem [*To an Agreeable Sourness*] [*Pharmacy*]
Ad Grat Acid ... Ad Gratum Aciditatem [*To an Agreeable Sourness*] [*Pharmacy*]
AD GR GUST ... Ad Gratum Gustum [*To an Agreeable Taste*] [*Pharmacy*]
ADGRU..... Advisory Group [*Military*]
ADGT........ Assistant Director-General of Transportation [*British military*] (DMA)
ADGV........ Gove [*Australia*] [*ICAO location identifier*] (ICLI)
ADGZ........ Arbeiten der Deutschen Gesellschaft fuer Zuechtungskunde [*A publication*]
ADH .... Academy of Dentistry for the Handicapped (EA)
ADH .... Ada, OK [*Location identifier*] [*FAA*] (FAAL)
ADH .... Adhere (MSA)
ADH .... Adherent [*A publication*]
ADH .... Adhesive (KSC)
ADH .... Adhibendus [*To Be Used*] [*Pharmacy*] (ROG)
ADH .... Alcohol Dehydrogenase [*Also, AD*] [*An enzyme*]
ADH .... Angra Do Heroismo [*Azores*] [*Seismograph station code, US Geological Survey*] (SEIS)
ADH .... Antidiuretic Hormone [*Vasopressin*] [*Endocrinology*]
ADH .... Assistant Director of Hygiene [*Military*] [*British*]
ADH .... Automatic Data Handling [*Data processing*]
ADHA .... American Dental Hygienists' Association (EA)
Adhaes ...... Adhaesion [*A publication*]
ADHC....... Air Defense Hardware Committee [*NATO*] (NATG)
ADHCA ..... Advise This Headquarters of Complete Action [*Army*]
ADHCS ..... Amalgamated Drillers and Hole Cutters Society [*A union*] [*British*]
ADHD .... Attention Deficit Hyperactivity Disorder [*Medicine*]
ADHEL..... Air Defense High Energy LASER (MCD)
Adhes Adhes ... Adhesion and Adhesives [*Japan*] [*A publication*]
Adhes Age ... Adhesives Age [*A publication*]
Adhesive D ... Adhesives Age Directory [*A publication*]
Adhesives... Adhesives Age [*A publication*]
Adhes Res ... Adhesives and Resins [*A publication*]
Adhes Resins ... Adhesives and Resins [*A publication*]
Adhes Tech Ann ... Adhesives Technology Annual [*A publication*]
ADHEVE .. Adhesive (ROG)
ADHGA..... Advances in Human Genetics [*A publication*]
ADHGB..... Allgemeines Deutsches Handelsgesetzbuch von 1861 [*German commercial code*] (ILCA)
ADHI......... Area Defense Homing Interceptor
ADHIBEND ... Adhibendus [*To Be Used*] [*Pharmacy*]
A & D High ... Angell and Durfee on Highways [*A publication*] (DLA)
AD HL ..... Ad Hunc Locum [*To (or At) This Place*] [*Latin*]
AdHM .... Adler. Handbuch der Musikgeschichte [*A publication*]
ADHOS..... Alternative to Dedicated Hospital Ship (CAAL)
ADHP....... Association for the Development of Human Potential (EA)
ADHS........ Analog Data Handling System (AAG)
ADHS........ Armidale and District Historical Society. Journal [*A publication*] (APTA)
ADHYA..... Advances in Hydroscience [*A publication*]
ADI .... Academy of Dentistry International (EA)
ADI .... Acceptable Daily Intake [*Toxicology*]
ADI .... Accounting Department Instructions
ADI .... Acoustical Door Institute [*Defunct*] (EA)
ADI .... Ad-Dome International Ltd. [*Vancouver Stock Exchange symbol*]

ADI .... Address Incomplete [*Telecommunications*] (TEL)
ADI .... Air Defense Initiative [*DoD*]
ADI .... Air Defense Institute
ADI .... Air Defense Intercept [*Air Force*]
AD/I .... Air Density/Injun [*Explorer satellite*]
ADI .... Air Distribution Institute (EA)
ADI .... Alien Declared Intention
AdI .... Alliance des Independants [*Independent Party*] [*Switzerland*] [*Political party*] (PPE)
ADI .... Allied Distribution (EA)
ADI .... Allowable Daily Intake [*Toxicology*]
ADI .... Alternating Direction Implicit [*Algorithm*]
ADI .... Altitude Direction Indicator (AFM)
ADI .... Alzheimer's Disease International (EA)
ADI .... American Defense Institute (EA)
ADI .... American Directors Institute (EA)
ADI .... American Documentation Institute [*Later, American Society for Information Science*]
ADI .... American Dressage Institute
ADI .... Analog Devices, Incorporated [*NYSE symbol*] (SPSG)
ADI .... Analog Display Indicator (MCD)
AdI .... Annali. Istituto di Corrispondenza Archeologica [*A publication*]
ADI .... Antidetonation Injection
ADI .... Anuario. Departamento de Ingles [*Barcelona*] [*A publication*]
ADI .... Apollo Document Index [*NASA*] (KSC)
ADI .... Applied Dynamics International
ADI .... Approved Driving Instructor [*British*] (DBQ)
ADI .... Aquarian Digest International [*A publication*]
ADI .... Area of Dominant Influence [*Mapmaking*] [*Telecommunications*]
ADI .... Art Dreco Institute (EA)
ADGp........ Assembly Decay Indicator
ADI .... Assistance Dogs International (EA)
ADI .... Assistant Director of Intelligence [*British military*] (DMA)
ADI .... Association for Direct Instruction (EA)
ADI .... Attitude Direction Indicator [*Aerospace*]
ADI .... Attitude Display Indicator [*Aerospace*] (MCD)
ADI .... Australian Defence Industries Proprietary Ltd.
ADI .... Automatic Derivation of Invariants (MCD)
ADI .... Automatic Direction Indicator (AFM)
ADI .... Axiodistoincisal [*Dentistry*]
ADI .... Didsbury Public Library, Alberta [*Library symbol*] [*National Library of Canada*] (NLC)
ADI .... Doyon, AK [*Location identifier*] [*FAA*] (FAAL)
ADIA .... Adia Services, Inc. [*Menlo Park, CA*] [*NASDAQ symbol*] (NQ)
ADIA .... American Diamond Industry Association (EA)
ADIB .... Abu Dhabi International Bank, Inc.
A-DIC....... Adriamycin, Dacarbazine [*Antineoplastic drug regimen*]
ADIC .... Advanced Medical Imaging Corp. [*NASDAQ symbol*] (NQ)
ADIC .... American Dental Interfraternity Council (EA)
ADIC .... Analog-to-Digital Conversion System [*Data processing*]
ADIC .... Automated Digital Interior Communications (MCD)
A-DIC-DACT ... Adriamycin, Dacarbazine, Dactinomycin [*Antineoplastic drug regimen*]
ADICEP .... Association des Directeurs des Centres Europeens des Plastiques [*Association of Directors of European Centres for Plastics*] (EAIO)
ADIDAS.... Adi Dassler [*Founder of German sporting goods company; acronym used as brand name of shoes manufactured by the firm*]
ADIE .... Acquisition Data Input Equipment (AABC)
ADIE .... Autodie Corp. [*Grand Rapids, MI*] [*NASDAQ symbol*] (NQ)
A Dies Tech ... Associate in Diesel Technology
ADIF......... Autocrine Differentiation-Inhibiting Factor [*Biochemistry*]
ADIF......... Avionics Development and Integration Facility (MCD)
ADIG .... Tax Action Digest [*Australia*] [*A publication*]
ADIGE ...... Archivio Dati Italiani di Geologia [*Italian Geological Data Archive*] [*National Research Council*] [*Database*] (IID)
ADIHDJ.... Annual Research Reviews. Anti-Diuretic Hormone [*A publication*]
ADI(K)....... Assistant Director of Intelligence, Department K [*Air Ministry*] [*British*]
ADIL......... Air Defense Identification Line [*Air Force*]
ADIL......... Annual Digest of International Law [*A publication*]
ADILP....... Lone Pine Public Library, Didsbury, Alberta [*Library symbol*] [*National Library of Canada*] (NLC)
ADILR....... Annual Digest and Reports of Public International Law Cases [*A publication*] (DLA)
ADIMA ...... Advances in Immunology [*A publication*]
ADIMD .... Advise Immediately by Dispatch (NOAA)
ADINA ...... Automatic Dynamic Incremental Nonlinear Analysis (MCD)
AD INF..... Ad Infinitum [*To Infinity*] [*Latin*]
AD INIT .... Ad Initium [*At the Beginning*] [*Latin*]
ADINSP.... Administrative Inspection [*Military*] (NVT)
AD INT ..... Ad Interim [*In the Meantime*] [*Latin*]
ADINTELCEN ... Advanced Intelligence Center [*Navy*]
ADIOA ...... Journal. Audio Engineering Society [*A publication*]
ADIOS....... Analog-Digital Input/Output System [*Data processing*]
ADIOS....... Asian Dust Input to the Oceanic System [*Research project*]
ADIOS....... Automatic Diagnostic Input/Output System [*Data processing*]

ADIOS....... Automatic Digital Input/Output System [*Data processing*]
ADIP.......... Advanced Developing Institutions Program
ADIP.......... Air Defense, Interdiction, and Photographic
ADIP.......... Alloy Development for Irradiation Performance (MCD)
ADipA....... Associate Diploma in Arts (ADA)
ADIPA....... Association of Development Institutes for the Pacific and Asia
ADIPE....... Aircraft Design-Induced Pilot Error [*National Transportation Safety Board*]
Adipose Child Int Symp ... Adipose Child Medical and Psychological Aspects. International Symposium [*A publication*]
Adipose Tissue Regul Metab Funct ... Adipose Tissue. Regulation and Metabolic Functions [*A publication*]
Adipositas Kindesalter Symp ... Adipositas im Kindesalter Symposium [*A publication*]
ADIPU ...... Advise Whether Individual May Be Properly Utilized in Your Installation [*Army*] (AABC)
ADIRBD.... Australia. Commonwealth Scientific and Industrial Research Organisation. Division of Irrigation Research. Annual Report [*A publication*]
ADIRS....... ADIS [*Australasian Drug Information Services*] Drug Information Retrieval System [*ADIS Press Ltd.*] [*Auckland, New Zealand*]
ADIS.......... Air Defense Integrated System [*Military*]
ADIS.......... Airborne Digital Instrumentation System
ADIS.......... Association for Development of Instructional Systems [*Later, ADCIS*] [*Western Washington University*] [*Bellingham, WA*] (BUR)
ADIS.......... Australasian Drug Information Services
ADIS.......... Automatic Data Interchange System [*International Civil Aviation Organization*]
ADIS.......... Automatic Diffemic Identification of Speakers [*University of Bonn*]
ADISQ....... Association du Disque et de l'Industrie du Spectacle Quebecoise [*Quebec Association of the Record and Entertainment Industry*] [*Canada*]
ADISS ...... Advanced Defense Intelligence Support System (MCD)
ADIT .... Alien Documentation, Identification, and Telecommunications [*Immigration and Naturalization Service*]
ADIT .... Alliance Defense Industry and Technology (NATG)
ADIT .... Anadite, Inc. [*NASDAQ symbol*] (NQ)
ADIT .... Analog-Digital Integrating Translator [*Data processing*]
ADIT .... Automated Data on Instructional Technology
ADIT .... Automatic Detection and Integrated Tracking (MCD)
ADITC...... Australian Drilling Industry Training Committee
ADITS .... Aircraft Diagnostics and Integrated Test System (MCD)
ADIU .... Armament and Disarmament Information Unit [*British*]
A DIV .... Air Division [*Air Force*]
ADIZ .... Air Defense Identification Zone [*Air Force, FAA*]
ADJ .... Adjacent
ADJ .... Adjective
ADJ .... Adjoining
ADJ .... Adjornator [*British*]
ADJ .... Adjourned
ADJ .... Adjudged (ROG)
ADJ .... Adjunct
adj .... Adjunto [*Enclosure*] [*Spanish*] [*Business term*]
ADJ .... Adjustable
ADJ .... Adjuster [*Finance*]
ADJ .... Adjustment (AFM)
ADJ .... Adjutant (AFM)
ADJ .... American Adjustable Rate Term Trust 1995 [*NYSE symbol*] (SPSG)
ADJ .... Angle Deception Jamming
ADJ .... Aviation Machinist's Mate, Jet Engine Mechanic [*Navy rating*]
ADJ .... Improper Use of Adjective [*Used in correcting manuscripts, etc.*]
Adj A.......... Adjunct in Arts
ADJAA...... Airman Apprentice, Jet Striker [*Navy rating*]
ADJAC...... Adjacens [*Adjacent*] [*Pharmacy*] (ROG)
ADJAG...... Assistant Deputy Judge Advocate General [*Military*] [*British*]
ADJAN ..... Airman, Jet Striker [*Navy rating*]
ADJBLE.... Adjustable
ADJC........ Aviation Machinist Mate Jet, Chief [*Navy rating*]
ADJD .... Adjourned (ROG)
ADJD .... Adjudicated (ADA)
ADJF........ Adjustment File [*IRS*]
ADJFCUSA ... Adjusted on Basis of Photostat or Reviewed Copy of Temporary Pay Record from Finance Center, United States Army (AABC)
Adj-Gen ..... Adjutant-General (DAS)
ADJHDO .. Azabu Daigaku Juigakubu Kenkyu Hokoku [*A publication*]
ADJ L........ Adjoining Landowner (DLA)
ADJM .... Aviation Machinist Mate Jet, Master Chief [*Navy rating*]
ADJMOM ... Adjoint Gamma-Ray Moments [*Computer code*]
ADJN .... Adjourn (ROG)
ADJOING ... Adjoining (ROG)
ADJS........ Angle Deception Jamming System
ADJS........ Aviation Machinist Mate Jet, Senior Chief [*Navy rating*]
Adj Sess ..... Adjourned Session (DLA)
ADJT........ Adjustable [*Technical drawings*]
ADJT........ Adjutant

Adjt-Gen .... Adjutant-General [*British military*] (DMA)
ADJUN ...... Adjudication (ROG)
Ad Jus........ Adams' Justiciary Reports [*Scotland*] [*A publication*] (DLA)
Adjuvant Ther Cancer ... Adjuvant Therapy of Cancer. Proceedings of the International Conference [*A publication*]
Adjuvant Ther Cancer Proc Int Conf ... Adjuvant Therapy of Cancer. Proceedings of the International Conference on the Adjuvant Therapy of Cancer [*A publication*]
ADK.......... Adak Island [*Alaska*] [*Airport symbol*] (OAG)
ADK.......... Adak Island [*Alaska*] [*Seismograph station code, US Geological Survey*] (SEIS)
ADK.......... Adenylate Kinase [*An enzyme*]
ADK.......... Adirondack Mountain Club (EA)
ADK.......... Alliance for Democracy in Korea [*Defunct*] (EA)
ADK.......... Attach-Detach Kit
Adk.......... Awning Deck [*of a ship*] (DS)
Adk Town .. Adkinson on Township and Town Law in Indiana [*A publication*] (DLA)
AdL.......... A. de Lara Limited Edition Recordings [*Now Orfeo with same numbers*] [*Record label*] [*Great Britain*]
ADL.......... Acceptable Defect Level
ADL.......... Acid-Detergent Lignin [*Food analysis*]
ADL.......... Acoustic Delay Line
ADL.......... Active Duty List [*Army*] (INF)
ADL.......... Activities of Daily Living [*Medicine*]
AD L .... Ad Libitum [*At Pleasure, As Desired*] [*Music*] (ROG)
ADL.......... Adelaide [*Australia*] [*Airport symbol*] (OAG)
ADL.......... Adevarul Literar [*A publication*]
Ad L .... Administrative Law (DLA)
ADL.......... Adolescent Medicine [*Medical specialty*] (DHSM)
ADL.......... Adrian Resources [*Vancouver Stock Exchange symbol*]
ADL.......... Airborne Data Link
ADL.......... Aircraft Data Line (MCD)
AdL.......... Amor de Libro [*A publication*]
ADL.......... Andal Corp. [*AMEX symbol*] (SPSG)
ADL.......... Antenna Dummy Load
ADL.......... Anti-Defamation League of B'nai B'rith (EA)
AdL.......... Anuario de Letras [*A publication*]
ADL.......... Apollo Documentation List [*NASA*] (MCD)
ADL.......... Architecture Description Language [*Data processing*] (CSR)
ADL.......... Area Dental Laboratory [*Military*]
ADL.......... Armament Data Line [*Military*] (NVT)
ADL.......... Armament Datum Line (MCD)
ADL.......... Armament Development Laboratory [*Air Force*] (MCD)
ADL.......... Arthur D. Little, Inc. [*Cambridge, MA*] [*Research code symbol*]
ADL.......... Arthur D. Little, Inc., Cambridge, MA [*OCLC symbol*] (OCLC)
ADL.......... Associated Deliveries Limited [*British*]
ADL.......... Atmospheric Devices Laboratory [*Cambridge, MA*] (AAG)
ADL.......... Australian Deer Limited
ADL.......... Australian Development Ltd.
ADL.......... Authorized Data List [*DoD*]
ADL.......... Automatic Data Link [*Data processing*]
ADL.......... Average Decreasing Line
ADL.......... Avionics Development Laboratory [*Rockwell International-Space Division*] [*NASA*] (NASA)
ADLA .... Adventure Lands of America Corp. [*NASDAQ symbol*] (NQ)
ADLA .... Assistant Director for Legal and Legislative Affairs [*Obsolete*] [*National Security Agency*]
ADLAR..... Adaptive Lens Array (MCD)
ADLAT..... Advanced Low-Altitude Technique
ADLAT...... Advanced Low-Altitude Terrain System (MCD)
ADLATAD ... Advise Latest Address [*Military*] (AABC)
Ad Law Rev ... Administrative Law Review [*A publication*]
Ad LB .... Administrative Law Bulletin [*A publication*] (DLA)
AdLB .... Adyar Library Bulletin [*A publication*]
Ad L Bull ... Administrative Law Bulletin [*A publication*] (ILCA)
ADL Bull .... Australian Administrative Law Bulletin [*A publication*]
ADLC .... Advanced Data Link Control [*Data processing*]
ADLC .... Antibody-Dependent Lymphocyte-Mediated Cytotoxicity [*Clinical chemistry*]
Ad L 2d ..... Pike and Fischer's Administrative Law Reporter, Second Series [*A publication*] (DLA)
Ad L 2d(P & F) ... Pike and Fischer's Administrative Law Reporter, Second Series [*A publication*] (ILCA)
Adler Mus Bull ... Adler Museum Bulletin [*A publication*]
ADLI.......... Advanced Deck-Launched Interceptor (MCD)
AD LIB ...... Ad Libitum [*At Pleasure, As Desired*] [*Music*]
Ad Lib .... Adair on Libels [*A publication*] (DLA)
ADLIB....... Adaptive Library Management System [*Lipman Management Resources Ltd.*] [*Information service or system*] (IID)
ADLIB....... [*A*] Design Language for Indicating Behavior [*1967*] [*Data processing*] (CSR)
AD LIBIT ... Ad Libitum [*At Pleasure, As Desired*] [*Music*]
ADLIPS...... Automatic Data Link Plotting System
ADLM...... Aerial Delivered Land Mine (AFM)
ADLMS..... Air-Delivered Land Mine System [*Military*]
ADL-Nachr ... ADL-Nachrichten [*A publication*]
Ad L News ... Administrative Law News [*A publication*] (DLA)
Ad L Newsl ... Administrative Law Newsletter [*A publication*] (DLA)
ADLO........ Air Defense Liaison Officer
ADLO........ Association of Direct Labour Organisations [*British*]

AD LOC .... Ad Locum [*To (or At) the Place*] [*Latin*]
ADLOG ..... Advance Logistical Command [*Army*]
ADLP......... Adipose Fin and Left Pectoral Fin Clips [*Pisciculture*]
ADLP......... Australian Democratic Labor Party [*Political party*]   (PPW)
Ad L R........ Adelaide Law Reports [*A publication*]   (APTA)
Ad LR .... Administrative Law Review [*A publication*]
ADLR .... Assistant Director of Light Railways [*British military*]   (DMA)
ADLR .... Automated Direct Labor Reporting   (MCD)
Ad L Rep 2d (P & F) ... Administrative Law Reporter, Second (Pike and Fischer) [*A publication*]   (DLA)
Ad L Rev .... Administrative Law Review [*A publication*]
ADLS........ Air Dispatch Letter Service [*Navy*]
ADLS........ Airborne Data Link System
ADLS........ Anterior Dorsolateral Scale Count
ADLTDE..... Association of Dark Leaf Tobacco Dealers and Exporters   (EA)
ADLTY....... Adultery [*FBI standardized term*]
ADLV .... Adipose Fin and Left Ventral Fin Clips [*Pisciculture*]
ADM......... Academy of Dental Materials   (EA)
ADM......... Acoustic Digital Memory
ADM......... Acquisition Decision Memorandum   (MCD)
ADM......... Activity Data Method   (IEEE)
ADM......... Adams Exploration Ltd. [*Vancouver Stock Exchange symbol*]
ADM......... Adaptable Data Manager [*Hitachi Ltd.*] [*Japan*]
ADM......... Adaptive Delta Modulation [*Electronics*]
ADM......... Additional Dealer Markup [*Automobile retailing*]
ADM......... Administration   (EY)
ADM......... Admiral   (EY)
ADM......... Admiralty [*British*]
ADM......... Admissions
ADM......... Admove [*Apply*] [*Pharmacy*]
AdM......... Adrenal Medulla [*Anatomy*]
ADM......... Adriamycin [*Also, A, ADR, D, H*] [*Antineoplastic drug*]
ADM......... Advance Decoy Missile   (MCD)
ADM......... Advanced Data Management [*Information service or system*]   (IID)
ADM......... Advanced Deployment Model   (MCD)
ADM......... Advanced Development Memory   (MCD)
ADM......... Advanced Development Model
ADM......... Advanced Diploma in Midwifery [*British*]
ADM......... Aeronaves de Mexico SA [*Mexican airline*]   (MCD)
ADM......... Affiliated Dress Manufacturers   (EA)
ADM......... Agarose Diffusion Method [*Medical device safety test*]
ADM......... Air Decoy Missile   (AFM)
ADM......... Air Defense Missile
ADM......... American Dance Machine
ADM......... Ammonium Dimolybdate [*Inorganic chemistry*]
ADM......... Annals of Discrete Mathematics [*Elsevier Book Series*] [*A publication*]
ADM......... Annual Delegate Meeting [*British*]   (DCTA)
ADM......... Apollo Data Manager [*NASA*]   (KSC)
ADM......... Arbeitskreis Deutscher Marktforschungsinstitute eV [*Association of the German Market Research Institute*]
ADM......... Arc Data Monitor [*Welding*] [*Automotive engineering*]
ADM......... Archer-Daniels-Midland Co. [*NYSE symbol*]   (SPSG)
ADM......... Ardmore [*Oklahoma*] [*Airport symbol*] [*Obsolete*]   (OAG)
ADM......... Area Defense Missile
ADM......... Area Denial Munition   (MCD)
ADM......... Arrow Diagramming Method   (MCD)
ADM......... Assistant Deputy Minister [*Canada*]
ADM......... Assistant District Manager   (DCTA)
ADM......... Asynchronous Disconnected Mode
ADM......... Atomic Demolition Munition
ADM......... Authorized Data Item Description Manual [*A publication*]   (MCD)
ADM......... Automated Depot Maintenance
ADM......... Automated Drafting Machine
ADM......... Automatic Degreasing Machine
ADM......... Automatic Detection Mark   (NVT)
ADM......... Automatic Display Mode [*Data processing*]   (BUR)
ADM......... Automatic Distribution of Microfiche
ADM......... Average Daily Membership
ADM......... Delia Municipal Library, Alberta [*Library symbol*] [*National Library of Canada*]   (NLC)
Adm......... High Court of Admiralty [*England*]   (DLA)
ADM......... NRDS [*Nevada*] [*Seismograph station code, US Geological Survey*] [*Closed*]   (SEIS)
ADM......... Office Administration and Automation [*A publication*]
ADMA....... Agricultural Development and Marketing Authority [*Northern Territory, Australia*]
ADMA....... Alkyldimethylamine [*Acronym is a trademark of Ethyl Corp. for its brand of alkyldimethylamine products*]
ADMA....... American Drug Manufacturers' Association [*Later, PMA*]
ADMA....... Area-Dominant Military Aircraft
ADMA....... Association of Direct Marketing Agencies [*Defunct*]   (EA)
ADMA....... Automatic Damper Manufacturers Association   (EA)
ADMA....... Automatic Drafting Machine   (DIT)
ADMA....... Aviation Distributors and Manufacturers Association   (EA)
ADMAC....... Austrian Documentation Centre for Media and Communication Research [*Information service or system*]   (IID)
ADMAD.... Advise Method and Date of Shipment   (NOAA)

AD MAN MED ... Ad Manus Medici [*To Be Delivered into the Hands of the Physician*] [*Pharmacy*]
ADMAP .... Advise by Airmail as Soon as Practicable   (FAAC)
ADMAT .... Administrative-Material Inspection [*Military*]   (NVT)
Adm Bull.... Administrators' Bulletin [*A publication*]   (APTA)
ADMC....... Air Defense Missile Command   (AABC)
ADMC....... Antibody-Dependent Macrophage-Mediated Cytotoxicity [*Clinical chemistry*]
ADMCEN ... Administration Center
Adm Change ... Administrative Change [*A publication*]
ADMCS....... Allyl(dimethyl)chlorosilane [*Organic chemistry*]
ADMD....... Adjust Mode [*Data processing*]
ADMD....... Administration Management Domain [*Telecommunications*]   (TEL)
ADMD....... Administrative Division [*Municipality*] [*Board on Geographic Names*]
ADMDBP ... Advances in Metabolic Disorders. Supplement [*A publication*]
Adm y Desarr ... Administracion y Desarrollo [*A publication*]
ADME....... Assistant Director of Mechanical Engineering [*British military*]   (DMA)
Adm & Ecc ... English Law Reports, Admiralty and Ecclesiastical [*A publication*]   (DLA)
Adm & Eccl ... English Law Reports, Admiralty and Ecclesiastical [*A publication*]   (DLA)
ADMG....... Admitting   (MSA)
ADMG....... Advanced Magnetics, Inc. [*Cambridge, MA*] [*NASDAQ symbol*]   (NQ)
ADMG....... Air Defense Machine Gun   (MCD)
ADMG....... Assistant Deputy Military Governor [*US Military Government, Germany*]
ADMHA.... Alcohol, Drug Abuse, and Mental Health Administration [*Formerly, HSMHA*] [*Department of Health and Human Services*]   (OICC)
ADMI .... American Dry Milk Institute [*Later, ADPI*]   (EA)
ADMIA ..... Advances in Microwaves [*A publication*]
ADMIG Bulletin ... Australian Drug and Medical Information Group. Bulletin [*A publication*]   (APTA)
Admin .... Administration [*A publication*]
ADMIN..... Administration [*or Administrator*]   (EY)
Admin pub ... Administration Publique [*A publication*]   (ILCA)
ADMIN..... Administratrix [*Business term*]   (ADA)
Admin App Trib ... Administrative Appeals Tribunal [*Australia*]
Admin Bull ... Administrators' Bulletin [*A publication*]
Admin Cd... Administrative Code [*A publication*]   (DLA)
ADMINCEN ... Army Administration Center, Fort Benjamin Harrison   (AABC)
Admin Dec ... Administrative Decisions [*A publication*]   (DLA)
Admin Dig ... Administrative Digest [*A publication*]
ADMINI ... Administrative Instructions
ADMININSP ... Administrative Inspection [*Military*]   (NVT)
ADMININST ... Administrative Instructions
Administrn ... Administration   (DLA)
ADMIN L ... Administrative Law   (DLA)
Admin Law ... Administrative Law [*A publication*]
Admin L 2d P & F ... Administrative Law Second. Pike and Fischer [*A publication*]
Admin Man ... Administrator. Manitoba Association of Principals [*A publication*]
Admin Manage ... Administrative Management [*A publication*]
Admin Ment Hlth ... Administration in Mental Health [*A publication*]
Admin Mgmt ... Administrative Management [*A publication*]
ADMIN MOD ... Administration Module   (MCD)
ADMINO ... Administrative Office [*or Officer*]   (CINC)
ADMINO ... Administrative Order
ADMINORD ... Administrative Order   (NVT)
ADMINPLAN ... Administrative Plan   (NVT)
ADMINR .. Administrative
ADMINREP ... Administrative Report   (NVT)
Admin Rev ... Administrative Review [*A publication*]
Admin Science Q ... Administrative Science Quarterly [*A publication*]
Admin Sci Q ... Administrative Science Quarterly [*A publication*]
Admin Sci R ... Administrative Science Review [*A publication*]
Admin SO ... Administrative Staff Officer
Admin and Society ... Administration and Society [*A publication*]
Admin Staff Col India J Man ... Administrative Staff College of India. Journal of Management [*A publication*]
Adminstr.... Administrator   (DLA)
Adminstrv .. Administrative   (DLA)
ADMINSUP ... Administrative Support   (NVT)
Adm Interp ... Administrative Interpretations [*A publication*]   (DLA)
ADMINV .. Administrative
ADMIR .... Administrator   (FAAC)
Admir........ Admiralty Division   (DLA)
ADMIRAL ... Automatic and Dynamic Monitor with Immediate Relocation, Allocation, and Loading   (IEEE)
ADMIRE..... Automatic Diagnostic Maintenance Information Retrieval [*Data processing*]   (MCD)
ADMIS...... Admissions
ADMIS...... Aircraft Departing at [*number of minutes*] Intervals [*Aviation*]   (FAAC)
ADMIS...... Automated Data Management Information System

ADMIT ..... Aeronautical Depot Maintenance Industrial Technology [*Navy*] (AFIT)
ADMIT ..... Alcohol Drug Motorsensory Impairment Test [*Pharmometrics Corp.*]
ADMIV ..... Administrative (FAAC)
ADMIX ..... Administratrix [*Business term*] (ROG)
ADMK .... All-India Anna Dravida Munnetra Kazhagam [*Political party*] (PPW)
ADML .... Admiral (FAAC)
ADML .... Advanced Design Methods Laboratory [*Ohio State University*] [*Research center*] (RCD)
ADML .... Automatic Documentation and Mathematical Linguistics [*A publication*]
ADML .... Average Daily Member Load
Adm Law R ... Administrative Law Review [*A publication*]
ADMLBF .. Acta Dermatologica [*Kyoto*]. English Edition [*A publication*]
ADMLP ..... ASCII COBOL Data Manipulation Language-Preprocessor [*Data processing*]
Adm LR ..... Administrative Law Review [*A publication*]
Adm L Rev ... Administrative Law Review [*A publication*]
ADMM ...... Administrative Memo (NATG)
Adm Manage ... Administrative Management [*A publication*]
Adm Ment He ... Administration in Mental Health [*A publication*]
Adm Ment Health ... Administration in Mental Health [*A publication*]
Adm Mgmt ... Administrative Management [*A publication*]
Adm Mgt .... Administrative Management [*A publication*]
ADMN .... Administration
ADMN .... Administrative Appeals Tribunal Decisions [*Australia*] [*A publication*]
Adm Notebk ... Administrator's Notebook [*A publication*]
ADMO .... Air Defense Management Office (MCD)
ADMO .... Australian Directory of Music Organisations [*A publication*] (APTA)
ADMOA .... Advances in Morphogenesis [*A publication*]
ADMON ... Administration (ROG)
ADMON ... Admission (ROG)
ADMOR .... Administrator (ROG)
ADMOS .... Automatic Device for Mechanical Order Selection
ADMOV .... Admove [*Apply*] [*Pharmacy*]
ADMP .... Aerodynamic Damping Moment in Pitch [*Helicopter rotor*]
ADMP .... Association pour Defendre la Memoire de Petain
ADMPAQ ... Australia. Commonwealth Scientific and Industrial Research Organisation. Division of Mathematical Statistics. Technical Paper [*A publication*]
ADMR .... Absorbance-Detected Magnetic Resonance [*Physics*]
ADMR .... [*The*] Admar Group, Inc. [*Orange, CA*] [*NASDAQ symbol*] (NQ)
ADMR .... Administrator
ADMR .... Australian Directory of Music Research [*A publication*] (APTA)
AD-MRA ... American and Delaine-Merino Record Association (EA)
Adm Radiol ... Administrative Radiology [*A publication*]
ADMRB .... Advances in Materials Research [*A publication*]
ADM Rev .... ADM [*Asociacion Dental Mexicana*] Revista [*Mexico*] [*A publication*]
ADM Rev Asoc Dent Mex ... ADM. Revista de la Asociacion Dental Mexicana [*A publication*]
ADMRL .... Application Data Material Readiness List [*DoD*]
ADMRL .... Automatic Data Material Requirements List
ADMRX .... Administratrix [*Business term*] (ROG)
ADMS .... Advanced Marketing Services, Inc. [*NASDAQ symbol*] (NQ)
ADMS .... American Donkey and Mule Society (EA)
ADMS .... Analog and Digital Monitoring System [*Data processing*] (MCD)
ADMS .... Application Data Management Services (MCD)
ADMS .... Assistant Director of Medical Services
ADMS .... Asynchronous Data Multiplexer Synchronizer
ADMS .... Atmospheric Diffusion Measuring System
ADMS .... Automatic Digital Message Switching
ADMSB2 ... Advances in Microbiology of the Sea [*A publication*]
ADMSC ..... Automatic Digital Message Switching Center [*AUTODIN*]
Adm Sci ...... Administrative Science Quarterly [*A publication*]
Adm Sci Q ... Administrative Science Quarterly [*A publication*]
Adm Sci Qua ... Administrative Science Quarterly [*A publication*]
ADMSE ..... Automatic Digital Message Switch Equipment (MCD)
ADMSG .... Advise by [*Electronically Transmitted*] Message [*Army*] (AABC)
ADMSLBN ... Air Defense Missile Battalion [*Army*] (AABC)
ADMSN ..... Admission (AFM)
Adm and Soc ... Administration and Society [*A publication*]
Adm Socie ... Administration and Society [*A publication*]
Adm Soc Work ... Administration in Social Work [*A publication*]
ADMSPT .. Administrative Support (MCD)
ADMSTR .. Administrator
A/DM & T ... [*PTS*] Aerospace/Defense Markets & Technology [*Predicasts, Inc.*] [*Information service or system*] (IID)
ADMT .... Association for Dance Movement Therapy (EAIO)
ADMTR .... Administrator
ADMTRX ... Administratrix [*Business term*] (ROG)
Adm Tss ..... Administrativ Tidsskrift [*A publication*]
ADMTY .... Admiralty (NATG)

ADMU .... Air Data Measuring Unit (NATG)
ADMX .... Administratrix [*Business term*] (ROG)
ADMY .... Admiralty [*British*]
ADN .... Accession Designation Number [*Military*]
ADN .... Accion Democratica Nacionalista [*Nationalist Democratic Action*] [*Bolivia*] [*Political party*] (PPW)
ADN .... Adams [*New York*] [*Seismograph station code, US Geological Survey*] [*Closed*] (SEIS)
ADN .... Adanac Mining & Exploration Ltd. [*Toronto Stock Exchange symbol*] [*Vancouver Stock Exchange symbol*]
ADN .... Address Complete, No-Charge [*Telecommunications*] (TEL)
ADN .... Aden [*People's Democratic Republic of Yemen*]
ADN .... Adiponitrile [*Organic chemistry*]
ADN .... AgriData Network [*AgriData Resources, Inc.*] [*Milwaukee, WI*] [*Telecommunications service*] (TSSD)
ADN .... Alcohol and Drug News [*A publication*] (APTA)
ADN .... Allgemeiner Deutscher Nachrichtendienst [*German General News Service*] [*German Democratic Republic*]
ADN .... Archdeacon
ADN .... Ashley, Drew & Northern Railway Co. [*AAR code*]
ADN .... Associate Degree in Nursing
ADN .... Avionics Decision Notice (MCD)
ADNA .... Applied DNA Systems, Inc. [*NASDAQ symbol*] (NQ)
ADNA .... Assistant Director of Naval Accounts [*British*]
ADNAC ..... Air Defense of North American Continent [*Army*] (AABC)
Ad Nat ...... Ad Nationes [*of Tertullian*] [*Classical studies*] (OCD)
AD NAUS ... Ad Nauseum [*To the Extent of Producing Nausea*] [*Latin*]
ADNC .... Air Defense National Center (NATG)
ADNC .... Air Defense Notification Center (NATG)
ADNC .... Assistant Director of Naval Construction [*British*]
ADND .... ADM Industries, Inc. [*NASDAQ symbol*] (NQ)
ADNDA ..... Atomic Data and Nuclear Data Tables [*A publication*]
ADNE .... Alden Electronics, Inc. [*Westboro, MA*] [*NASDAQ symbol*] (NQ)
ADNEDZ .. Advances in Neurochemistry [*A publication*]
ADNET ..... Action Data Network (MCD)
AD NEUT ... Ad Neutralizandum [*To Neutralization*] [*Pharmacy*]
ADNI .... Assistant Director of Naval Intelligence [*British*]
ADNI .... Authorized Distribution Network, Inc. [*NASDAQ symbol*] (NQ)
ADNOK ..... Advise if Not Correct (FAAC)
ADNOMOVPEN ... Advised Not to Move Dependents until Suitable Quarters Located [*Military*]
ADNRA3 ... Advances in Neurology [*A publication*]
ADNSA6 ... Adansonia [*A publication*]
ADO .... Ad Com Marketing, Inc. [*Vancouver Stock Exchange symbol*]
ADO .... Adagio [*Slow*] [*Music*]
Ado .... Adenosine [*Also, A*] [*A nucleoside*]
ADO .... Administration Duty Officer (NATG)
ADO .... Advanced Development Objective [*Military*]
ADO .... Air Defence Officer [*Navy*] [*British*]
ADO .... Air Defense Operations (NATG)
ADO .... Air Drop Operator
ADO .... Airport District Office [*FAA*] (FAAC)
ADO .... Alleged Discrimination Official (MCD)
ADO .... American Darts Organization (EA)
A & DO ...... Analog and Discrete Output (MCD)
ADO .... Andamooka [*Australia*] [*Airport symbol*] (OAG)
ADO .... Animal Disease Occurrence [*Database*] [*Commonwealth Agricultural Bureaux*] [*Information service or system*] (CRD)
ADO .... Army Distribution Objective (MCD)
ADO .... Association of Dispensing Opticians [*British*] (DBQ)
ADO .... Audio Decode Oscillator
ADO .... Audiotronics Corp. [*AMEX symbol*] (SPSG)
ADO .... Auto Defense Ordinance (CINC)
ADO .... Automotive Diesel Oil (ADA)
ADO .... Automotive Distillate Oil (ADA)
ADO .... Avalanche Diode Oscillator
ADO .... Axiodisto-Occlusal [*Dentistry*]
ADO .... Data Automation Design Office [*Air Force*]
ADO .... Donalda Public Library, Alberta [*Library symbol*] [*National Library of Canada*] (BIB)
ADo .... George S. Houston Memorial Library, Dothan, AL [*Library symbol*] [*Library of Congress*] (LCLS)
ADO .... Louisville, KY [*Location identifier*] [*FAA*] (FAAL)
Ado .... Much Ado about Nothing [*Shakespearean work*]
ADOA .... American Dog Owners Association (EA)
ADOAP ..... Adriamycin, Oncovin, ara-C, Prednisone [*Antineoplastic drug regimen*]
ADOBE ..... Atmospheric Diffusion of Beryllium Program [*NASA*] (KSC)
A Dobr ...... Analele Dobrogei [*A publication*]
ADOC .... Agora/Documentaire [*Agence France-Presse*] [*French*] [*Information service or system*] (CRD)
ADOC .... Air Defense Operations Center [*Air Force*]
ADoC .... Houston County Court House, Dothan, AL [*Library symbol*] [*Library of Congress*] (LCLS)
ADOCA ..... Advances in Organic Chemistry [*A publication*]
ADOCBL ... Adenosylcobalamin [*Also, DBC*] [*A vitamin*]
ADOCS ..... Advanced Digital/Optical Control System

ADOD .... Assistant Director of Operations Division [*British military*]   (DMA)

ADOD .... Donalda and District Museum, Donalda, Alberta [*Library symbol*] [*National Library of Canada*]   (BIB)

ADOF .... Arbitrary Degree of Freedom   (MCD)

ADOF .... Assistant Director of Ordnance Factories [*Ministry of Supply*] [*British*] [*World War II*]

ADOG........ Abhandlungen. Deutsche Orient-Gesellschaft [*A publication*]

ADOGA...... American Dehydrated Onion and Garlic Association   (EA)

AdoHcy...... Adenosylhomocysteine [*Biochemistry*]

ADOIT ...... Automatically Directed Outgoing Intertoll Trunk [*Bell System*]

ADOL........ Adolescence [*A publication*]

ADOL........ Adolescent

ADOL........ American Directory of Organized Labor [*A publication*]

ADOLA ..... Adolescence [*A publication*]

Adol & El ... Adolphus and Ellis' English King's Bench Reports [*A publication*]   (DLA)

Adol & El NS ... Adolphus and Ellis' English Queen's Bench Reports, New Series [*A publication*]   (DLA)

Adoles .... Adolescence [*A publication*]

Adolesc Ment Health Abstr ... Adolescent Mental Health Abstracts [*A publication*]

Adolesc Psychiatry ... Adolescent Psychiatry [*A publication*]

Adol Med ... Adolescent Medicine [*A publication*]

Adolph & E ... Adolphus and Ellis' English King's Bench Reports [*A publication*]   (DLA)

ADOM....... Acid Deposition and Oxidant Model [*for acid rain*] [*Canada and Federal Republic of Germany*]

ADOM....... Administration

ADOM....... Army Depot Operations Management   (MCD)

ADOM....... Donnelly Municipal Library, Alberta [*Library symbol*] [*National Library of Canada*]   (NLC)

AdoMet...... Adenosylmethionine [*Also, SAM, SAMe*] [*Biochemistry*]

ADONIS ... Automatic Digital On-Line Instrumentation System

ADONIS ... Document delivery service based in Amsterdam

ADOP........ Additive Operational Project [*Army*]

ADOP........ Adriamycin, Oncovin [*Vincristine*], Prednisone [*Antineoplastic drug regimen*]

ADOP........ Advanced Distributed Onboard Processor   (SDI)

ADOPE ..... Automatic Decisions Optimizing Predicted Estimates

ADOPT ..... Adoption   (DLA)

ADOPT ..... Advanced Optics Technology   (MCD)

ADOPT ..... Automatic Design Optimization Techniques   (MCD)

ADORB .... Advances in Oto-Rhino-Laryngology [*A publication*]

ADOS .... Advanced Diskette Operating System

ADOS .... Area Distribution Officers [*Military*] [*British*] [*World War II*]

ADOS .... Assistant Director of Ordnance Services [*British*]

ADOS .... Astronautical Defensive-Offensive System

ADOS .... Authorization for Disposal of Overhead Supplies   (MCD)

ADOT .... Automatic Digital Optical Tracker [*Army*]   (AABC)

ADOT........ Automatically Directed Outgoing Trunk [*Bell System*]

ADOW....... Automatic Dial Order Wire [*Military*]   (NVT)

ADoW....... George C. Wallace Community College, Dothan, AL [*Library symbol*] [*Library of Congress*]   (LCLS)

ADP .... Academy of Denture Prosthetics   (EA)

ADP .... Acceptance Data Package   (KSC)

ADP .... Accountability Data Package   (MCD)

ADP .... Acid Dew Point

ADP .... Acoustic Data Processor   (MCD)

adp .... Adapter [*MARC relator code*] [*Library of Congress*]   (LCCP)

ADP .... Adenosine Diphosphate [*Biochemistry*]

ADP .... Administrative Data Processing   (KSC)

ADP .... Advanced Development Plan [*Air Force*]   (MCD)

ADP .... Advanced Passenger Train [*British*]

ADP .... African Democratic Party [*Political party*]

ADP .... Agence Dahomeene de Presse [*Dahomean Press Agency*]

ADP .... Agent Development Program [*LIMRA*]

ADP .... Agricultural Development Project [*London, England*]

ADP .... Air Data Package

ADP .... Air Data Probe [*Aerospace*]   (MCD)

ADP .... Air Defense Position [*Military*]

ADP .... Air Driven Pump

ADP .... Airborne Data Processor [*Air Force*]

ADP .... Airport Development Program

ADP .... Alclometasone Dipropionate [*Glucocorticoid*]

ADP .... Allied Defense Publications   (NATG)

ADP .... Allied Products Corp. [*NYSE symbol*]   (SPSG)

ADP .... Alpha Delta Phi [*Fraternity*]

ADP .... Alpha Delta Pi [*Sorority*]

ADP .... Americans for Due Process   (EA)

ADP .... Aminodiphenyl [*Organic chemistry*]

ADP .... Ammonium Dihydrogen Phosphate [*Inorganic chemistry*]

ADP .... Anatuberculina Diagnostica Petragnani [*Petragnani Diagnostic Anatuberculin*] [*Medicine*]

ADP .... Anguilla Democratic Party [*Political party*]   (EY)

ADP .... Animal Disease and Parasite Research Division [*of ARS, Department of Agriculture*]

ADP .... Apollo Dynamic Programs [*NASA*]   (KSC)

ADP .... Approach Deterioration Parameter   (MCD)

ADP .... Archiv fuer Deutsche Postgeschichte [*A publication*]

ADP .... Archivo de Derecho Publico [*A publication*]

ADP .... Area Distribution Panel

ADP .... Armor Development Corp. [*Vancouver Stock Exchange symbol*]

ADP .... Army Depot Police [*British military*]   (DMA)

ADP .... Artillery Destruction Program

ADP .... Assistant Director of Pathology [*Military*] [*British*]

ADP .... Assistant District Postmaster [*British*]   (DCTA)

ADP .... Association of Database Producers   (IID)

ADP .... Association for Denture Prosthesis   (EAIO)

ADP .... Association of Directors and Producers [*British*]

ADP .... Association of Disabled Professionals   (EAIO)

ADP .... Atmospheric Dynamics Program [*National Oceanic and Atmospheric Administration*]

ADP .... Australian Democratic Party [*Political party*]   (PPW)

ADP .... Automatic Data Plotter

ADP .... Automatic Data Processing

ADP .... Automatic Data Processing, Inc. [*Trademark for data processing services*]

ADP .... Automatic Destruct Program   (MUGU)

ADP .... Automatic Digital Processor   (MCD)

ADP .... Azerbaijan Democratic Party [*Iran*] [*Political party*]

ADP .... United States Army ARRADCOM - PLASTEC Division, Dover, NJ [*OCLC symbol*]   (OCLC)

ADPA .... Accounting and Data Processing Abstracts [*A publication*]

ADPA .... Air Data Probe Assemblies [*Aerospace*]   (NASA)

ADPA .... Alcohol and Drug Problems Association of North America   (EA)

ADPA .... American Defense Preparedness Association   (EA)

ADPA .... Automobile Dealers Parts Association

ADPAC...... American Democratic Political Action Committee   (EA)

AD-PAC .... American Druze Public Affairs Committee   (EA)

ADPADX... Advances in Pathobiology [*A publication*]

Ad Part Dol ... Ad Partes Dolentes [*To the Painful Parts*] [*Pharmacy*]

ad part dolent ... Ad Partes Dolentes [*To the Painful Parts*] [*Pharmacy*]

ADPase...... Adenosine Diphosphatase [*An enzyme*]

ADPASS.... Advanced Patrol Sensor System   (MCD)

ADPB .... Air Defense Planning Board   (MCD)

ADPBCT.... Automatic Data Processing Budget Control Totals

ADP/BISG ... ADP [*Automatic Data Processing, Inc.*] Brokerage Information Services Group [*Also, an information service or system*]   (IID)

ADPC .... Adaxial Leaflet Pubescence - Curly [*Botany*]

ADPC .... Agricultural Development Planning Center [*ASEAN*] [*Research center*] [*Thailand*]   (IRC)

ADPC .... Automatic Data Processing Center

ADPCA...... Advances in Photochemistry [*A publication*]

ADPCM .... Adaptive Differential Pulse Code Modulation [*Telecommunications*]   (MCD)

ADPCMT ... Adaptive Differential Pulse Code Modulated Transcoder [*Telecommunications*]

ADPE .... Automatic Data Processing Engineering

ADPE .... Automatic Data Processing Equipment

ADPE .... Auxiliary Data Processing Equipment

ADPEA...... Advances in Pediatrics [*A publication*]

ADP-EFS .. ADP [*Automatic Data Processing, Inc.*] Electronic Financial Services [*Telecommunications service*]   (TSSD)

ADPEP...... Automated Data Preparation by Electronic Photocomposition   (MCD)

ADPEP...... Automated Data Preparation Evaluation Program   (MCD)

ADPERSACT ... Advise by Message of Action the Following Individual Is Taking [*Military*]

ADPES...... Automatic Data Processing by Equipment Systems

ADPESO... Automatic Data Processing Equipment Selection Office [*Navy*]

ADPEV...... Aid to Displaced Persons and Its European Villages   (EAIO)

ADPFB...... Automatic Data Processing Field Branch [*BUPERS*]

ADP/FIS ... ADP [*Automatic Data Processing, Inc.*] Financial Information Services, Inc. [*Information service or system*] [*Later, ADP/BISG*]   (IID)

ADPG .... Air Defense Planning Group   (MCD)

ADPh.......... Arbeiten zur Deutschen Philologie [*A publication*]

ADPHDK.. Advances in Pharmacotherapy [*A publication*]

ADPI......... American Dairy Products Institute   (EA)

ADPI......... Association Internationale d'Etudes pour la Protection des Investissements

ADPKD ..... Autosomal Dominant Polycystic Kidney Disease [*Medicine*]

ADPL......... Assistant Director for Policy and Liaison [*Obsolete*] [*National Security Agency*]

ADPL......... Automated Drawing Parts List   (MCD)

ADPL......... Average Daily Patient Load [*Medicine*]

ADPLL...... All-Digital Phase-Locked Loop   (KSC)

ADPLO ..... Automatic Data Processing Liaison Officer [*Military*]   (MCD)

ADPLS ...... Automated Drawing Parts List System   (MCD)

ADPM .... Automatic Data Processing Machine

ADPMG ..... Assistant Deputy Postmaster-General [*Canada*]

ADPMIS ... Automatic Data Processing Management Information System   (AABC)

ADPMO .... Automatic Data Processing Modification Order

ADPO .... Advanced Development Program Office

AD POND OM ... Ad Pondus Omnium [*To the Weight of the Whole*] [*Pharmacy*]

ADPP......... ACTION Drug Prevention Program

ADPP........ Assembly Detail Purchased Parts   (AAG)
ADPP........ Automatic Data Processing Programs   (FAAC)
ADPPB...... Advances in Particle Physics [*A publication*]
ADPPB...... Automatic Data Processing Production Branch [*BUPERS*]
ADPP & DB ... Automatic Data Processing Planning and Development Branch [*BUPERS*]
ADPP & PB ... Automatic Data Processing Programming and Processing Branch [*BUPERS*]
ADPPRS ... Automatic Data Processing Program Reporting System [*Military*]   (MCD)
ADPR .... ADP [*Adenosine Diphosphate*] Ribosylated Enzyme
ADPR .... Assistant Director for Plans and Resources [*Obsolete*] [*National Security Agency*]
ADPR .... Assistant Director of Public Relations [*Military*] [*British*]
ADPRA...... Advances in Parasitology [*A publication*]
ADPREP.... Automatic Data Processing Resource Estimating Procedures
ADPRID.... Advanced Degree Program for ROTC Instructor Duty   (MCD)
ADPRO ..... Automatic Data Processing Requirements Office [*Jet Propulsion Laboratory, NASA*]
ADPRORED ... Advise by Message Why Individual Is Being Reduced [*Military*]
ADPRT...... Adenosine Diphosphate Ribosyltransferase [*An enzyme*]
ADP(S)...... Advanced Development Plan (System)
ADPS......... Advanced Digital Processing System
ADPS......... Apollo Document Preparation Standards [*Handbook*] [*NASA*]   (KSC)
ADPS...... Assistant Director, Army Postal Services [*British military*]   (DMA)
ADPS...... Automatic Data Processing Security [*Military*]   (MCD)
ADPS......... Automatic Data Processing Services
ADPS......... Automatic Data Processing System [*or Subsystem*]
ADPS........ Automatic Display Plotting System   (MCD)
ADPSC...... Automatic Data Processing Service Center [*Service of the US military*]   (AABC)
ADPSDJ.... Adolescent Psychiatry [*A publication*]
ADPSO...... Association of Data Processing Service Organizations [*Includes American and Canadian companies*] [*Later, ADAPSO - The Computer Software and Services Industry Association*]   (EA)
ADPSO...... Automatic Data Processing Selection Office [*Military*]   (MCD)
ADPSR...... Architects/Designers/Planners for Social Responsibility   (EA)
ADPSS ...... Archivio Dati e Programmi per le Scienze Sociali [*Data and Program Archive for the Social Sciences*] [*University of Milan*] [*Italy*] [*Information service or system*]   (IID)
ADPSSO ... Automatic Data Processing System Security Officer   (MCD)
ADPT .... Adaptec, Inc. [*Milpitas, CA*] [*NASDAQ symbol*]   (NQ)
ADPT .... Adapter   (KSC)
ADPT .... Adenosine Phosphoribosyltransferase [*An enzyme*]
ADP-T .... Automated Data Processing Telecommunications   (MCD)
ADPTC...... Automatic Data Processing Training Center [*Military*]   (MCD)
ADP/TCS ... ADP [*Automatic Data Processing, Inc.*] Telephone Computing Services, Inc. [*Telecommunications service*]   (TSSD)
ADPTR...... Adapter   (MSA)
ADPU .... Airborne Digital Processing Unit
ADPV .... Abhandlungen. Deutscher Palaestina-Verein [*A publication*]
ADQ........... Almost Differential Quasiternary Code [*Telecommunications*]   (TEL)
ADQ........... Australia Newsletter [*A publication*]
ADQ........... Kodiak [*Alaska*] [*Airport symbol*]   (OAG)
ADQEA ...... Advances in Quantum Electronics [*A publication*]
ADQT .... Adequate   (FAAC)
ADR............ Accepted Dental Remedies [*A publication*]
ADR........... Accident Data Recorder [*Aviation*]   (AIA)
ADR........... Accord Dangereuse Routier [*European agreement on the carriage of dangerous goods by road*]
ADR........... Achievable Data Rate   (MCD)
ADR........... Acid-Detergent Residue [*Food analysis*]
ADR........... Adder [*Computer device*]   (MDG)
ADR........... Address [*Computer character*] [*Data processing*]
ADR........... Address Register   (BUR)
Adr............. Adrenaline [*Endocrinology*]
adr............. Adres [*Address*] [*Poland*] [*Correspondence*]
adr............. Adress [*Address*] [*Sweden*] [*Correspondence*]   (GPO)
adr............. Adresse [*Address*] [*Denmark*] [*Correspondence*]   (GPO)
adr............. Adresse [*Address*] [*Norway*] [*Correspondence*]   (GPO)
Adr............. Adresse [*Address*] [*German*] [*Correspondence*]   (GPO)
ADR........... Adriamycin [*Also, A, ADM, D, H*] [*Antineoplastic drug*]
ADR........... Advance Deviations Report   (AAG)
ADR........... Advanced Dated Remittances [*IRS*]
ADR........... Advanced Development Report [*NASA*]   (KSC)
ADR........... Adverse Drug Reaction [*Medicine*]
ADR........... Advisory Route [*Aviation*]   (FAAC)
ADR........... Aeronautical Data Report [*Navy*]
ADR........... Air Defense Region   (NATG)
ADR........... Air Design Review   (MCD)
ADR........... Airborne Data Recorder   (MCD)
ADR........... Airborne Digital Recorder
ADR........... Aircraft Design Research Division [*Navy*]
ADR........... Aircraft Destination Record   (MCD)
ADR........... Aircraft Direction Room [*Navy*]
ADR........... Aircraft Discrepancy Report

ADR.......... Airfield Damage Repair [*Military*]
ADR.......... Alianza Democratica Revolucionaria [*Democratic Revolutionary Alliance*] [*Bolivia*]
ADR.......... Alternative Dispute Resolution
ADR.......... American Depositary Receipt
ADR.......... Ammunition Disposition Request [*or Report*]
ADR.......... Analog-Digital Recorder [*Data processing*]
ADR.......... Anderson Reservoir [*California*] [*Seismograph station code, US Geological Survey*]   (SEIS)
ADR.......... Angle Data Recorder
A Dr .... Annales de Droit [*A publication*]
ADR.......... Appellate Division Reports [*Massachusetts*] [*A publication*]   (DLA)
ADR.......... Applied Data Research, Inc. [*Princeton, NJ*]   (TSSD)
ADR.......... Army Density Report
ADR.......... Asset Depreciation Range [*IRS*]
ADR.......... Audit Discrepancy Report   (NRCH)
ADR.......... Australian De Facto Relationships Law [*A publication*]
ADR.......... Automatic Dialogue Replacement
ADR.......... Automatic Dividend Reinvestment [*Investment term*]
ADR.......... Average Daily Rate [*Hotels*]
ADR.......... Aviation Design Research [*Navy*]
ADR.......... Aviation Machinist's Mate, Reciprocating Engine Mechanic [*Navy rating*]
ADR.......... Award Resources [*Vancouver Stock Exchange symbol*]
ADR.......... Journal of Advertising Research [*A publication*]
ADR1......... Aviation Machinist's Mate, Reciprocating Engine Mechanic, First Class [*Navy rating*]
ADR2......... Aviation Machinist's Mate, Reciprocating Engine Mechanic, Second Class [*Navy rating*]
ADR3......... Aviation Machinist's Mate, Reciprocating Engine Mechanic, Third Class [*Navy rating*]
ADRA........ Adventist Development and Relief Agency, International   (EA)
ADRA........ American Drag Racing Association [*Commercial firm*]   (EA)
ADRA........ Animal Diseases Research Association [*Moredun Institute*] [*British*]   (ARC)
ADRA........ Army Dollar Resource Allocation
ADRA........ Automotive Dismantlers and Recyclers Association   (EA)
ADRAA ..... Airman Apprentice, Aviation Machinist's Mate, Reciprocating Engine Mechanic, Striker [*Navy rating*]
ADRAC ..... Automatic Digital Recording and Control
ADRAMS ... Air Droppable Measurement System [*Oceanography*]   (MSC)
ADRAN..... Advanced Digital Ranging System [*NASA*]   (KSC)
ADRAN..... Airman, Aviation Machinist's Mate, Reciprocating Engine Mechanic, Striker [*Navy rating*]
ADRAO..... Association pour le Developpement de la Riziculture en Afrique de l'Ouest [*West Africa Rice Development Association - WARDA*]   (EAIO)
ADRAT ..... Advanced Deep-Running Acoustic Torpedo   (MCD)
ADRB........ Army Disability Review Board
ADRB........ Army Discharge Review Board
ADRC........ Alzheimer's Disease and Related Conditions [*Medicine*]
ADRC........ Alzheimer's Disease Research Center [*Bronx, NY*] [*Department of Health and Human Services*]   (GRD)
ADRC........ American Dutch Rabbit Club   (EA)
ADRC........ Animal Drug Research Center [*Denver, CO*] [*Department of Health and Human Services*]   (GRD)
ADRC........ Automatic Data Rate Changer
ADRC........ Aviation Machinist's Mate, Reciprocating Engine Mechanic, Chief [*Navy rating*]
ADRCAC... Annali Italiani di Dermatologia Clinica e Sperimentale [*A publication*]
ADRCM .... Aviation Machinist's Mate, Reciprocating Engine Mechanic, Master Chief [*Navy rating*]
ADRCS ...... Aviation Machinist's Mate, Reciprocating Engine Mechanic, Senior Chief [*Navy rating*]
ADRDA ..... Alzheimer's Disease and Related Disorders Association   (EA)
ADRDE ..... Advise Reason for Delay [*Aviation*]   (FAAC)
ADRDE ..... Air Defence Research and Development Establishment [*Later, RRE*] [*British*]
A Dr & Dgn ... Associate in Drafting and Design
ADRE......... Audre Recognition Systems, Inc. [*NASDAQ symbol*]   (NQ)
ADREA ..... American Dyestuff Reporter [*A publication*]
ADRECS .... Advanced Recovery System   (MCD)
ADRED ...... Archives for Dermatological Research [*A publication*]
ADREDL.... Archives for Dermatological Research [*A publication*]
ADREDPRED ... Advise by Message Reduction Current Period of Active Duty [*Military*]
ADREP...... Aircraft Accident/Incident Reporting System [*International Civil Aviation Organization*] [*Information service or system*]   (IID)
ADREP...... Automatic Data Processing Resource Estimating Procedures
ADRES...... Army Data Retrieval Engineering System   (MCD)
ADRG........ Applied Demographic Research Group [*Database producer*]   (IID)
ADRG........ Assistant Deputy Registrar General [*Canada*]
ADRG........ Automatic Data Routing Group   (AAG)
Adria-L-PAM ... Adriamycin, L-Phenylalanine Mustard [*Antineoplastic drug regimen*]
Adriamycin-Symp ... Adriamycin-Symposium [*A publication*]
ADRIES .... Advanced Digital RADAR Imagery Exploitation System

ADRIS .... Association for the Development of Religious Information Systems (EA)
ADRIS .... Automatic Dead Reckoning Instrument Systems [*Navigation*] [*Canada*]
ADRJ .... Australian Dispute Resolution Journal [*A publication*]
ADRK .... Auxiliary Display Request Keyboard
ADRM ...... Aerodrome
ADRM .... Darwin [*Australia*] [*ICAO location identifier*] (ICLI)
ADRM .... Drumheller Municipal Library, Alberta [*Library symbol*] [*National Library of Canada*] (NLC)
A Dr Marit Aer ... Annuaire de Droit Maritime et Aerien [*A publication*]
ADRMP .... Automatic Dialer with Recorded Message Player [*Telecommunications*]
ADRMPS .. Auto-Dialed Remote Message Players [*Telecommunications*]
ADRN .... Advance Drawing Release Notice (KSC)
ADRN .... Advanced Document Revision Notice [*NASA*] (KSC)
ADRNDCK ... Adirondack [*National Weather Service*] (FAAC)
ADROBN .. Airdrome Battalion
Ad Rom ...... Expositio of Epistulae ad Romanos [*of Augustine*] [*Classical studies*] (OCD)
Ad Rom Ant ... Adams' Roman Antiquities [*A publication*] (DLA)
ADRP .... Acoustic Data Reduction Program (CAAL)
ADRP .... Adipose Fin and Right Pectoral Fin Clips [*Pisciculture*]
ADRP .... Airdrop [*Military*] (AABC)
ADRP .... Autosomal Dominant Retinitis Pigmentosa [*Ophthalmology*]
ADRPB ...... Advances in Reproductive Physiology [*A publication*]
ADRPBI ...... Advances in Reproductive Physiology [*A publication*]
ADRPM ...... Acoustic Detection Range Prediction Model (MCD)
ADRRAN .. Advances in Drug Research [*A publication*]
ADRRB .... Army Disability Rating Review Board (AABC)
ADRRCP ... Australia. Commonwealth Scientific and Industrial Research Organisation. Division of Dairy Research. Annual Report [*A publication*]
ADRS .... Address [*Computer character*] [*Data processing*] (AFM)
ADRS .... Airborne Digital Recording System
ADRS .... Analog-to-Digital Data Recording System [*Data processing*] (IEEE)
ADRS .... Archivio. Reale Deputazione Romana di Storia Patria [*A publication*]
ADRS .... Asset Depreciation Range System [*Accounting*]
ADRS .... Automated Data Retrieval System (NRCH)
ADRS .... Automatic Data Reporting System (NATG)
ADRS .... Automatic Document Request Service [*or System*]
ADRS .... [*A*] Departmental Reporting System [*IBM Corp.*]
ADRSA ...... Assistant Data Recording System Analyst (MUGU)
ADRSP ...... Archivio. Reale Deputazione Romana di Storia Patria [*A publication*]
ADRSS ...... Automated Data Reports Submission System
ADRT .... Analog Data Recorder Transcriber
ADRT .... Assistant Director of Railway Transport [*British military*] (DMA)
ADRUSAR ... Army Density Report, United States Army Reserve
ADRV .... Adipose Fin and Right Ventral Fin Clips [*Pisciculture*]
A-DRV .... Atomic Drive
ADS .... Academie des Sciences [*Academy of Science*] [*French*]
ADS .... Accelerated Declassification System (NVT)
ADS .... Accessory Drive System (NG)
ADS .... Accounting Data System
ADS .... Accurately Defined System [*Data processing*]
ADS .... Acoustic Doppler Sounder (MCD)
ADS .... Active Deferral Service (MCD)
ADS .... Activity Data Sheet (IEEE)
Ads .... Ad Sectam [*At the Suit Of*] [*Legal term*] [*Latin*]
ADS .... Address (FAAC)
ADS .... Address Data Strobe [*Electronics*]
ADS .... Address Display System [*or Subsystem*]
ADS .... Administration of Designed Services (TEL)
ADS .... Administration and Society [*A publication*]
ADS .... Administrative Data Systems
Ads .... Adsorption
ADS .... Advanced Data Scalar
ADS .... Advanced Data System [*DoD*]
ADS .... Advanced Debugging System
ADS .... Advanced Declassification Schedule (MCD)
ADS .... Advanced Deep-Dive System (NVT)
ADS .... Advanced Display System
ADS .... Advanced Diving System
ADS .... Advanced Dressing Station [*British*]
ADS .... Adversus [*Against*] [*Latin*] (ROG)
ADS .... Advertising Dimensions Standards [*American Newspaper Publishers Association*]
ADS .... Aerial Delivery System
ADS .... Aerial Demonstration Squadron (MCD)
ADS .... Aeronautical Design Standard [*Army*]
ADS .... Aerospace Data Systems (MCD)
ADS .... Affiliated Drug Stores (EA)
ADS .... Agent Distributor Service [*Departments of State and Commerce*]
ADS .... Air Data Sensor [*Aerospace*] (MCD)
ADS .... Air Data System [*or Subsystem*] (RDA)
ADS .... Air Defense Sector [*Air Force*]

ADS .... Air Defense Ship (NATG)
ADS .... Air Defense System
ADS .... Air Development Service (MCD)
ADS .... Air Development Station [*Navy*]
ADS .... Aircraft Development Service [*Air Force*]
ADS .... Airport Data System [*FAA*]
ADS .... All-Digital Simulator
ADS .... Alliance Democratique Senegalaise [*Allied Democratic Party of Senegal*] [*Political party*]
AD(S) .... Allied Demands, Supplies [*World War II*]
ADS .... Alternate Delivery System [*Medicine*] (DHSM)
ADS .... Alternate Device Support [*NASA*]
ADS .... Alzheimer's Disease Society [*British*]
ADS .... American Daffodil Society (EA)
ADS .... American Dahlia Society (EA)
ADS .... American Denture Society
ADS .... American Depositary Share (ECON)
ADS .... American Dialect Society (EA)
ADS .... American Driving Society (EA)
ADS .... American Druze Society (EA)
ADS .... Angle Data Subsystem
ADS .... Anomaly Dynamics Study [*NORPAX*]
ADS .... Anti-Ice/De-Ice System [*or Subsystem*] (MCD)
ADS .... Anticoincidence Detection System
ADS .... Antidiuretic Substance
ADS .... Applicant Data System [*Department of Labor*]
ADS .... Application Design Service [*IBM Corp.*]
ADS .... Application Development Systems [*Data processing*]
ADS .... Applied Decision Systems [*Information service or system*] (IID)
ADS .... Arctic Drift Station
ADS .... Arctic Drilling System
ADS .... Army Dental Service
ADS .... Association of Diesel Specialists (EA)
ADS .... Association of District Secretaries [*British*]
ADS .... Association for Dressings and Sauces (EA)
ADS .... Aston Dark Space [*Physics*]
ADS .... Atmospheric Diving Suit [*Deep sea diving*]
ADS .... Atmospheric Diving System
ADS .... Attitude Display System (MCD)
A/DS .... Audio/Digital Systems [*Telecommunications service*] (TSSD)
ADS .... Audio Distribution System (NASA)
ADS .... August Derleth Society (EA)
ADS .... Autograph Document Signed [*Manuscript descriptions*]
ADS .... Automated Declassification System (MCD)
ADS .... Automated Design System (MCD)
ADS .... Automated Dispatch System [*Telecommunications*]
ADS .... Automated Documentation Systems [*Data processing*]
ADS .... Automated Drafting System
ADS .... Automatic Data System [*Data processing*]
ADS .... Automatic Defense System (MCD)
ADS .... Automatic Dependence Surveillance System [*International Civil Aviation Organisation*]
ADS .... Automatic Depressurization System [*Nuclear energy*] (NRCH)
ADS .... Automatic Development System (MCD)
ADS .... Automatic Digital Switch
ADS .... Automatic Dispatch System [*Nuclear energy*] (NRCH)
ADS .... Automatic Door Seal [*Technical drawings*]
ADS .... Autopilot Disengage Switch (MCD)
ADS .... Aviation Data Service, Inc. [*Information service or system*] (IID)
ADS .... Aviation Depot Squadron [*Air Force*]
ADS .... Azione Dynamico-Specifico [*Dynamic-Specific Action*] [*Italian*] [*Medicine*]
ADS .... Dallas, TX [*Location identifier*] [*FAA*] (FAAL)
ADSA .... Air-Derived Separation Assurance [*Aviation*]
ADSA .... American Dairy Science Association (EA)
ADSA .... American Dental Society of Anesthesiology (EA)
ADSA .... Art Deco Societies of America (EA)
ADSA .... Atomic Defense Support Agency
ADSAAB ..... Annali della Sanita Pubblica [*A publication*]
AD SAEC .. Ad Saeculum [*To the Century*] [*Latin*] (ADA)
ADSAF ...... Automatic Data System within the Army in the Field
ADSAI .... American Dermatologic Society of Allergy and Immunology (EA)
AD/SAM ... Air Defense - Surface-to-Air Missile
ADSAP ...... Advise as Soon as Possible (NOAA)
ADSARM ... Advanced Defense Suppression Antiradiation Missile
ADSAS .... Air-Derived Separation Assurance System [*Aviation*]
AD SAT ..... Ad Saturandum [*To Saturation*] [*Pharmacy*]
ADSAT ...... Anomalous Dispersion Spherical Array Target [*for increasing radio reflectivity*]
AD SATUR ... Ad Saturandum [*To Saturation*] [*Pharmacy*]
ADSB .... Allgemeine Deutsche Spediteurbedingungen [*General German Regulations for Shipping Agents*]
ADSC .... Active Duty Service Commitment [*Military*] (AFM)
ADSC .... Advanced Section Communication Zone [*World War II*]
ADSC .... Air Defense Software Committee (NATG)
ADSC .... Air Defense Systems Command
ADSC .... Association of Drilled Shaft Contractors (EA)
ADSC .... Automatic Data Service Center

ADSC......... Automatic Digital Switching Center (IEEE)
ADSC......... Average Daily Service Charge [Hospitals]
ADSCAH .. Advancement of Science [A publication]
Ad Sci....... Advancement of Science [A publication]
ADSCOM ... Advanced Shipboard Communications (MCD)
ADSCS...... Aided Display Submarine Control System [Navy] (MCD)
ADSD........ Air Defense Systems Directorate (NATG)
ADSDA ..... Advise Earliest Date (NOAA)
ADSDP...... Automated Data System Development Plan [Military] (MCD)
ADSE........ Addressee
ADSE........ American Dental Society of Europe (EA)
AD SEC ..... Advance Section [Military]
ADSEC...... Air Defense System Engineering Committee
ADSEL...... Address-Selective [British] (MCD)
ADSEP...... Automatic Data Set Editing Program [NASA] (KSC)
Ad Serv Leafl Timb Res Developm Ass ... Advisory Service Leaflet. Timber
          Research and Development Association [A publication]
ADSF........ Automated Directional Solidification Furnace [Materials
          processing]
ADSG .... Atomic Defense and Space Group [Westinghouse Electric
          Corp.] (MCD)
Ad Sh .... Advance Sheet (DLA)
ADSHIPDA ... Advise Shipping Data (AABC)
ADSHIPDA ... Advise Shipping Date
ADSHPDAT ... Advise Shipping Date
ADSI.......... Adapted Delivered Source Instruction
ADSI.......... American Drug Screens, Incorporated [NASDAQ
          symbol] (NQ)
ADSIA .... Allied Data System Interoperability Agency [Brussels, Belgium]
          [NATO]
ADSID....... Air Defense Systems Integration Division [Air Force]
ADSID....... Air-Delivered Seismic Intrusion Detectors
ADSIM...... Advanced Simulation [Missions project]
A & DSL .... Administrative and Direct Support Logistics [Company]
          [Army]
ADSL......... Assembly Department Shortage List
ADSL......... Authorized Depot Stockage List [Army]
ADSL......... Auxiliary of the Decalogue Society of Lawyers (EA)
ADSM .... Air Defense Suppression Missile (AABC)
ADSMO .... Air Defense System Management Office [Air Force]
ADSN .... Accounting and Disbursing Station Number [Air Force] (AFM)
ADSN .... Addison-Wesley Publishing Co., Inc. [NASDAQ symbol] (NQ)
ADSO .... Aerospace Defense Systems Officer [Air Force] (AFM)
ADSO .... Assistant Division Supply Officer [Army]
ADSO .... Automatic Display Switching Oscilloscope
ADSOC ..... Administrative Support Operations Center [Army]
ADSORB... Adsorbent
Adsorbtsiya Poristost Tr Vses Konf Teor Vopr Adsorbtsii ... Adsorbtsiya i
          Poristost Trudy Vsesoyuznoi Konferentsii po
          Teoreticheskim Voprosam Adsorbtsii [A publication]
ADSOS...... Advance Services of Supply [Army]
ADSOT ..... Automatic Daily System Operability Test
ADSP........ Adaptive Digital Signal Processor (MCD)
ADSP........ Advanced Digital SAR Processor (MCD)
ADSP........ Advanced Digital Signal Processor
ADSP........ Automatic Dispatching Stick Repeater
ADSPA ...... Annales de Dermatologie et de Syphiligraphie [Later, Annales
          de Dermatologie et de Venereologie] [A publication]
ADSPEC ... Additional Specialty [Military] (INF)
ADSPM..... Atti e Memorie. Deputazione di Storia Patria per le Antiche
          Provincie Modenesi [A publication]
ADSPN..... Advise Disposition [Aviation] (FAAC)
ADSPR...... Atti e Memorie. Deputazione di Storia Patria per le Provincie di
          Romagna [A publication]
ADSq .... Air Defense Squadron [Air Force] [Vietnam] (AFM)
ADSR........ Attack/Decay/Sustain/Release [Audio programming
          parameters]
ADSS........ Advanced Digital Simulation System (MCD)
ADSS........ Air Defense Suppression System (MCD)
ADSS........ Aircraft Damage Sensing System
ADSS........ Analysis of Digitized Seismic Signals [Data processing]
ADSS........ Army Decision Support System
ADSS........ Association of Directors of Social Services (EAIO)
ADSS........ Automated Data Subsystem (AABC)
ADSS........ Automatic Data Switching System [Deep Space Network]
ADS & T .... Assistant Director of Supplies and Transport [Military]
          [British]
ADST........ Association for the Development of Social Therapy (EA)
ADST........ AUTODIN Digital Subscriber Terminal (AABC)
ADSTADIS ... Advise Status and/or Disposition [Army]
ADSTAP ... Advancement, Strength, and Training Plan System
ADSTAR... Automatic Document Storage and Retrieval [Data processing]
Adsteam..... Adelaide Steamship Co. [Australia]
ADST FEB ... Adstante Febre [When Fever Is Present] [Pharmacy]
ADSTKOH ... Advise Stock on Hand [Army]
ADS-TP...... Administrative Data Systems - Teleprocessing (IEEE)
ADSU .... Advanced Direct Support Unit (NATG)
ADSU .... Air Data Sensor Unit
ADSU .... Airstream Direction Sensing Unit (MCD)
ADSU .... Albrecht Durer Study Unit [American Topical
          Association] (EA)

ADSU .... Australian Disabled Students' Union
ADSUA ..... Advances in Surgery [A publication]
ADSUP...... Automatic Data System Uniform Practices
ADSVAL .... Air Defense Simulator Evaluation (MCD)
AD SW ...... Advanced Defense Suppression Weapon
AD SW ...... Archiv der Deutschen Seewarte [A publication]
ADSW .... Association of Directors of Social Work (EAIO)
ADSWSO ... Air Defense Special Weapons Support Organization
ADT.......... Abstract Data Type [Data processing]
ADT.......... Accelerated Development Test (MUGU)
ADT.......... Accepted Dental Therapeutics
ADT.......... Active Disk Table [Data processing] (IBMDP)
ADT.......... Active Duty for Training [Army] (AABC)
ADT.......... Actual Departure Time (CINC)
ADT.......... Adaptive Technologies (Canada) [Vancouver Stock Exchange
          symbol]
ADT.......... Adformatie. Weekblad voor Reclame en Marketing [A
          publication]
ADT.......... Admission/Discharge/Transfer [Hospital records] (DHSM)
ADT.......... ADT, Inc. [Formerly, American District Telegraph Co.] [NYSE
          symbol] (SPSG)
ADT.......... Advanced Design Team
ADT.......... Advanced Development Technology (KSC)
ADT.......... Advanced Dispenser Technology (MCD)
ADT.......... Advanced Driver Training [British military] (DMA)
ADT.......... Aerated Drain Tank [Nuclear energy] (NRCH)
ADT.......... Aerial Demonstration Team (MCD)
ADT.......... Aided Tracking
ADT.......... Air Data Transducer [Aerospace] (MCD)
AD/T......... Air Detector/Tracker (CAAL)
ADT.......... Air-Dried Ton
ADT.......... Airborne Data Terminal (MCD)
ADT.......... Airborne Digital Timer
ADT.......... Alaskan Daylight Time
ADT.......... Alternate-Day Treatment [Medicine]
ADT.......... Amazing Detective Tales [A publication]
ADT.......... Amphibious Training Demonstrator
ADT.......... Anti-Dumping Tribunal [Canada]
ADT.......... Any Desired Thing [Notation in a placebo prescription]
          [Medicine]
ADT.......... Approved Departure Time (MCD)
ADT.......... Arizona Dance Theatre
ADT.......... Articulated Dump Truck [Caterpillar Tractor Co.]
ADT.......... Assistant Director of Torpedoes [Navy] [British]
ADT.......... Assistant Director for Training [National Security Agency]
ADT.......... Assured Depot Task
ADT.......... Asynchronous Data Transceiver
ADT.......... Atlantic Daylight Time
ADT.......... Atomic Damage Template [Military drafting]
ADT.......... Atwood, KS [Location identifier] [FAA] (FAAL)
ADT.......... Auditory Discrimination Test ["Wepman"] [Education]
ADT.......... Automatic Data Translator [or Transmitter]
ADT.......... Automatic Debit Transfer [Banking]
ADT.......... Automatic Detection and Tracking (MCD)
ADT.......... Autonomous Data Transfer
ADT.......... Average Daily Traffic
AdT........... Die Agada der Tannaiten (BJA)
ADTA .... Air Data Transducer Assembly [Aerospace] (NASA)
ADTA .... Aircraft Development Test Activity [Army] (MCD)
ADTA .... American Dance Therapy Association (EA)
ADTA .... American Dental Trade Association (EA)
ADTA .... Association of Defense Trial Attorneys (EA)
ADTA .... Aviation Development Test Activity [Test and Evaluation
          Command] [Army] (RDA)
ADTAC..... Air Defense Tactical Air Commander [Air Force]
ADTAC ..... Automatic Digital Tracking Analyzer Computer [Data
          processing] (FAAC)
ADTAC ..... Tactical Air Command, Deputy Commander for Air
          Defense (MCD)
ADTAKE... Action Decision [or Determination] Taken
ADTAKE... Advice Decision [or Determination] Taken
ADTAKE... Advise What Action Has Been Taken [Military] (NVT)
ADTAM ... Air-Delivered Target-Activated Munitions (AFM)
AdTb........ Altdeutsche Textbibliothek [A publication]
ADTC .... Air Defense Technical Center (NATG)
ADTC .... Armament Development and Test Center [Eglin Air Force Base,
          FL] (MCD)
ADTC .... Tennant Creek [Australia] [ICAO location identifier] (ICLI)
ADTD....... Apollo Docking Test Device [NASA]
ADTD....... Association of Data Terminal Distributors
ADTD....... Association of Disciples for Theological Discussion (EA)
ADTDS...... Air Defense Tactical Data Systems [Missile minder] (RDA)
ADTEAS... Advances in Teratology [A publication]
ADTECH .. Advanced Decoy Technology (MCD)
Ad Techniq ... Advertising and Graphic Arts Techniques [A publication]
AD TERT VIC ... Ad Tertiam Vicem [Three Times] [Pharmacy]
ADTF........ Aviation Development Test Facility (MCD)
ADTG .... Application Development Task Group [Navy]
ADTI .... Advance Display Technologies, Incorporated [Golden, CO]
          [NASDAQ symbol] (NQ)
ADTI .... American Dinner Theatre Institute (EA)

ADTI .... Association pour le Developpement du Tourisme International [*Louveciennes, France*] (EAIO)

ADTIC...... Arctic-Desert-Tropic Information Center [*Air University*] [*Maxwell Air Force Base, AL*]

ADTL .... ADT Ltd. [*NASDAQ symbol*] (CTT)

ADTLP...... Army-Wide Doctrinal and Training Literature Program

ADTMP..... Tyrrell Museum of Palaeontology, Drumheller, Alberta [*Library symbol*] [*National Library of Canada*] (NLC)

ADTN........ Aminodihydroxytetrahydronaphthalene [*Organic chemistry*]

ADTn........ Assistant Director of Transportation [*British military*] (DMA)

ADTN........ Tindal [*Australia*] [*ICAO location identifier*] (ICLI)

Ad Torts..... Addison on Torts [*A publication*] (DLA)

ADTP........ Accelerated Development Test Program (AAG)

AD-TR....... Armament Development Technical Report

Ad Tr M..... Adams on Trade Marks [*A publication*] (DLA)

ADTS........ Air Data Test System

ADTS........ Airborne Data Transfer System (MCD)

ADTS........ Automated Data and Telecommunications Service [*Later, Office of Information and Resources Management*]

ADTS........ Automatic Data Test System [*Bell System*]

ADTS........ Automatic Data Transfer System (MCD)

ADTS........ Avionics Depot Test Station (MCD)

ADTSC...... Auto Dealers Traffic Safety Council [*Absorbed by HUF*] (EA)

ADTSEA ... American Driver and Traffic Safety Education Association (EA)

ADTU........ Automatic Digital Test Unit

ADTU........ Auxiliary Data Translator Unit

ADTX........ Advatex Associates, Inc. [*NASDAQ symbol*] (NQ)

ADU.......... Acceleration-Deceleration Unit

ADU.......... Accumulation Distribution Unit [*Data processing*]

ADU.......... Adapter Unit (NG)

ADU.......... Aircraft Delivery Unit [*Air Force*]

ADU.......... Amdura Corp. [*NYSE symbol*] (SPSG)

ADU.......... Ammonium Diuranate [*Inorganic chemistry*]

ADU.......... Analog Delay Unit

ADU.......... Analog Display Unit

ADU.......... Annunciator Display Unit (MCD)

ADU.......... Arc Detector Unit

ADU.......... Audubon, IA [*Location identifier*] [*FAA*] (FAAL)

ADU.......... Automatic Data Unit

ADU.......... Automatic Dialing Unit [*Telecommunications*]

ADU.......... Auxiliary Display Unit

ADU.......... Duchess Public Library, Alberta [*Library symbol*] [*National Library of Canada*] (NLC)

AdUA........ Annales. Universite d'Abidjan [*A publication*]

AdUB........ Annales. Universite de Brazzaville [*A publication*]

ADUF .... Duffield Public Library, Alberta [*Library symbol*] [*National Library of Canada*] (NLC)

ADUL .... Annales. Association des Anciens Etudiants. Faculte de Droit. Universite de Louvain [*A publication*]

ADULT ..... Adultery (DLA)

Adult Dis.... Adult Diseases [*Japan*] [*A publication*]

Adult Ed..... Adult Education [*A publication*]

Adult Ed Bul ... Adult Education Bulletin [*A publication*]

Adult Ed J ... Adult Education Journal [*A publication*]

Adult Ed and Lib ... Adult Education and the Library [*A publication*]

Adult Educ ... Adult Education [*A publication*]

Adult Ed-W ... Adult Education-Washington [*A publication*]

Adult Lead ... Adult Leadership [*A publication*]

ADUM....... Automated Data Unit Movement (AABC)

Ad Us....... Ad Usum [*According to Custom*] [*Pharmacy*]

AD US EXTER ... Ad Usum Externum [*For External Use*] [*Pharmacy*]

ADUT........ Advanced Development Unit Test [*Army*]

ADV.......... Acid Degree Value [*Food technology*]

ADV.......... Acreage Diversion [*Agriculture*]

ADV.......... Actinomycin-D, Dacarbazine, Vincristine [*Antineoplastic drug regimen*]

ADV.......... Adenovirus [*Also, AD*]

ADV.......... Advance [*Flowchart*] (AFM)

ADV.......... Advanced Development Vehicle

ADV.......... Advanced Micro Devices, Inc.

ADV.......... Advantage

ADV.......... Advent

ADV.......... Adverb [*or Adverbial*]

ADV.......... Adversus [*Against*] [*Latin*]

ADV.......... Advertisement

ADV.......... Advertising World [*A publication*]

ADV.......... [*The*] Advest Group, Inc. [*NYSE symbol*] (SPSG)

ADV.......... Advice (ROG)

ADV.......... Advise [*Legal term*]

ADV.......... Advisory

adv.......... Advocaat [*Barrister*] [*Netherlands*] (ILCA)

Adv.......... Advocate [*Minneapolis*] [*1889-90*] [*A publication*] (ILCA)

Adv.......... Advocate [*Ife, Nigeria*] [*1968*] [*A publication*] (ILCA)

Adv.......... Advocate [*London*] [*1875*] [*A publication*] (ILCA)

Adv.......... Advocate [*Canada*] [*1943*] [*A publication*] (ILCA)

Adv.......... Advocate [*Cleveland*] [*1929*] [*A publication*] (ILCA)

ADV.......... Advocate

Adv.......... Advocatenblad [*A publication*]

ADV.......... Air Defense Variant

ADV.......... Airborne Digital Voltmeter

ADV.......... Aleutian Disease Virus [*of mink*]

ADV.......... Arbeitsgemeinschaft Deutscher Verfolgten-Organisationen [*A publication*]

ADV.......... Arc Drop Voltage

ADV.......... Archer International Developments Ltd. [*Vancouver Stock Exchange symbol*]

A/DV .... Arterio/Deep Venous [*Medicine*]

ADV.......... Atmospheric Dump Valves [*Nuclear energy*] (NRCH)

ADV.......... Drayton Valley Public Library, Alberta [*Library symbol*] [*National Library of Canada*] (NLC)

ADV.......... Improper Use of Adverb [*Used in correcting manuscripts, etc.*]

ADVA....... Advanced Digital Systems, Inc. [*NASDAQ symbol*]

ADVA....... Advanced Medical Products, Inc. [*NASDAQ symbol*] (NQ)

ADVA....... Advanced Soviet [*Combined with GENS to form A Group*] [*Division of National Security Agency*]

ADVA....... Americal Division Veterans Association (EA)

ADVA....... American Deaf Volleyball Association (EA)

Adv Abstr Contrib Fish Aquat Sci India ... Advance Abstracts of Contributions on Fisheries and Aquatic Sciences in India [*A publication*]

ADVAC ..... Advise Acceptance (NOAA)

Adv Acarol ... Advances in Acarology [*A publication*]

Adv Act Anal ... Advances in Activation Analysis [*A publication*]

Adv (Adel) ... Advertiser (Adelaide) [*A publication*]

Adv Aerosol Phys ... Advances in Aerosol Physics [*A publication*]

Adv Age ..... Advertising Age [*A publication*]

Adv Agency Mag ... Advertising Agency Magazine [*A publication*]

Adv Agric Technol AAT W US Dep Agric Sci Educ Adm West Reg ... Advances in Agricultural Technology. AAT-W. United States Department of Agriculture. Science and Education Administration. Western Region [*A publication*]

Adv Agron ... Advances in Agronomy [*A publication*]

Adv Agron Crop Sci ... Advances in Agronomy and Crop Science [*A publication*]

ADVAILTRANSCONUS ... Advise Appropriate Command Having Cognizance of Transportation when Available for Transportation to Continental United States [*Military*]

ADVAILTRANSPOE ... Advise [*Command Designated*] Date Available for Transportation from Port of Embarkation [*Military*]

AD VAL..... Ad Valorem [*According to the Value*] [*Latin*] [*Business term*]

ADVAL ..... Advise Availability [*Army*]

ADVAL ..... Air Defense Evaluation Tests (MCD)

Adv Alcohol & Subst Abuse ... Advances in Alcohol and Substance Abuse [*A publication*]

Adv Alcohol Subst Abuse ... Advances in Alcohol and Substance Abuse [*A publication*]

Adv Alicyclic Chem ... Advances in Alicyclic Chemistry [*A publication*]

ADVALT... Advice of Allotment (FAAC)

Advan Agron ... Advances in Agronomy [*A publication*]

Adv Anal Chem Instrum ... Advances in Analytical Chemistry and Instrumentation [*A publication*]

Advan Appl Mech ... Advances in Applied Mechanics [*A publication*]

Advan Appl Probab ... Advances in Applied Probability [*A publication*]

Advan Astronaut Sci ... Advances in the Astronautical Sciences [*A publication*]

Adv Anat Embryol Cell Biol ... Advances in Anatomy, Embryology, and Cell Biology [*A publication*]

ADVANCE ... Airborne Doppler Velocity Altitude Navigation Compass Equipment (MCD)

Advance Aust ... Advance Australia [*A publication*]

Advance Data ... Advance Data from Vital and Health Statistics [*A publication*]

Advanced Mgmt Jrnl ... Advanced Management Journal [*A publication*]

Advanced Mgt ... Advanced Management Journal [*A publication*]

Advanced Mgt J ... Advanced Management Journal [*A publication*]

Advanced Mgt-Office Exec ... Advanced Management-Office Executive [*A publication*]

Advanced Textbooks in Econom ... Advanced Textbooks in Economics [*Amsterdam*] [*A publication*]

ADVANCEM ... Advancement (DLA)

Advancement Sci ... Advancement of Science [*A publication*]

Advances in Appl Mech ... Advances in Applied Mechanics [*A publication*]

Advances in Appl Probability ... Advances in Applied Probability [*A publication*]

Advances Cancer Res ... Advances in Cancer Research [*A publication*]

Advances Carbohyd Chem ... Advances in Carbohydrate Chemistry [*Later, Advances in Carbohydrate Chemistry and Biochemistry*] [*A publication*]

Advances Chemother ... Advances in Chemotherapy [*A publication*]

Advances in Chem Ser ... Advances in Chemistry Series [*A publication*]

Advance Sci ... Advancement of Science [*A publication*]

Advances Geophys ... Advances in Geophysics [*A publication*]

Advances Immun ... Advances in Immunology [*A publication*]

Advances Int Med ... Advances in Internal Medicine [*A publication*]

Advances in Math Suppl Studies ... Advances in Mathematics. Supplementary Studies [*A publication*]

Advances Pediat ... Advances in Pediatrics [*A publication*]

Advances Pharmacol ... Advances in Pharmacology [*A publication*]

Advances Phys Sci ... Advances in Physical Sciences [*A publication*]

Advances Surg ... Advances in Surgery [*A publication*]

Advan Chem Eng ... Advances in Chemical Engineering [*A publication*]

Advan Chem Ser ... Advances in Chemistry Series [*A publication*]
Advan Clin Chem ... Advances in Clinical Chemistry [*A publication*]
Advan Cryog Eng ... Advances in Cryogenic Engineering [*A publication*]
Adv Androl ... Advances in Andrology [*A publication*]
Advan Electron and Electron Phys ... Advances in Electronics and Electron Physics [*A publication*]
Advan Front Plant Sci ... Advancing Frontiers of Plant Sciences [*A publication*]
Advan Genet ... Advances in Genetics [*A publication*]
Advan Geophys ... Advances in Geophysics [*A publication*]
Adv Anim Breed ... Advanced Animal Breeder [*A publication*]
Adv Anim Physiol Anim Nutr ... Advances in Animal Physiology and Animal Nutrition [*A publication*]
Advan Manage J ... Advanced Management Journal [*A publication*]
Advan Mol Relaxation Processes ... Advances in Molecular Relaxation Processes [*Later, Advances in Molecular Relaxation and Interaction Processes*] [*A publication*]
Advan Phys ... Advances in Physics [*A publication*]
Advan Polymer Sci Fortschr Hochpolym-Forsch ... Advances in Polymer Science/Fortschritte der Hochpolymeren-Forschung [*A publication*]
Advan Thanatol ... Advances in Thanatology [*A publication*]
Adv Anthracite Technol Res Proc Conf ... Advanced Anthracite Technology and Research. Proceedings of the Conference [*A publication*]
Adv Antimicrob Antineoplast Chemother ... Advances in Antimicrobial and Antineoplastic Chemotherapy [*A publication*]
Advan Virus Res ... Advances in Virus Research [*A publication*]
Adv Appl Ma ... Advances in Applied Mathematics [*A publication*]
Adv Appl Math ... Advances in Applied Mathematics [*A publication*]
Adv Appl Mech ... Advances in Applied Mechanics [*A publication*]
Adv Appl Microb ... Advances in Applied Microbiology [*A publication*]
Adv Appl Microbiol ... Advances in Applied Microbiology [*A publication*]
Adv Appl P ... Advances in Applied Probability [*A publication*]
Adv Appl Prob ... Advances in Applied Probability [*England*] [*A publication*]
Adv Appl Probab ... Advances in Applied Probability [*A publication*]
Adv Ap Pr .. Advances in Applied Probability [*A publication*]
Adv Aquat Microbiol ... Advances in Aquatic Microbiology [*A publication*]
Adv Artif Hip Knee Jt Technol ... Advances in Artificial Hip and Knee Joint Technology [*A publication*]
Adv Astron Astrophys ... Advances in Astronomy and Astrophysics [*A publication*]
Adv Astronaut Sci ... Advances in the Astronautical Sciences [*A publication*]
Adv At Mol Phys ... Advances in Atomic and Molecular Physics [*A publication*]
Adv Audiol ... Advances in Audiology [*A publication*]
Adv Autom Anal Technicon Int Congr ... Advances in Automated Analysis. Technicon International Congress [*A publication*]
ADVB .... Adverbial
Adv Behav Biol ... Advances in Behavioral Biology [*A publication*]
Adv Behav Pharmacol ... Advances in Behavioral Pharmacology [*A publication*]
Adv Behav Res Ther ... Advances in Behaviour Research and Therapy [*A publication*]
Adv Beta-Adrenergic Blocking Ther Sotalol Proc Int Symp ... Advances in Beta-Adrenergic Blocking Therapy. Sotalol Proceedings. International Symposium [*A publication*]
Adv Biochem Biophys ... Advances in Biochemistry and Biophysics [*People's Republic of China*] [*A publication*]
Adv Biochem Eng ... Advances in Biochemical Engineering [*A publication*]
Adv Biochem Psychopharmacol ... Advances in Biochemical Psychopharmacology [*A publication*]
Adv Bioeng ... Advances in Bioengineering [*A publication*]
Adv Bioeng Instrum ... Advances in Bioengineering and Instrumentation [*A publication*]
Adv Biol Dis ... Advances in the Biology of Disease [*A publication*]
Adv Biol Med Phys ... Advances in Biological and Medical Physics [*A publication*]
Adv Biol Psychiatry ... Advances in Biological Psychiatry [*A publication*]
Adv Biol Skin ... Advances in Biology of the Skin [*A publication*]
Adv Biomed Eng ... Advances in Biomedical Engineering [*A publication*]
Adv Biomed Eng Med Phys ... Advances in Biomedical Engineering and Medical Physics [*A publication*]
Adv Biophys ... Advances in Biophysics [*Tokyo*] [*A publication*]
Adv Biosci ... Advances in the Biosciences [*A publication*]
Adv Biotechnol Processes ... Advances in Biotechnological Processes [*A publication*]
Adv Bl .... Advokatbladet [*Denmark*] [*1921-*] [*A publication*]   (ILCA)
Adv Blood Grouping ... Advances in Blood Grouping [*A publication*]
Adv Bot Res ... Advances in Botanical Research [*A publication*]
Adv Bryol ... Advances in Bryology [*A publication*]
ADVC .... Advance Circuits, Inc. [*NASDAQ symbol*]   (NQ)
ADVC .... Advice   (FAAC)
Adv Cancer Chemother ... Advances in Cancer Chemotherapy [*A publication*]
Adv Cancer Res ... Advances in Cancer Research [*A publication*]
ADVCAP ... Advance Capability   (MCD)
Adv Carbohyd Chem ... Advances in Carbohydrate Chemistry and Biochemistry [*A publication*]
Adv Carbohydr Chem ... Advances in Carbohydrate Chemistry [*Later, Advances in Carbohydrate Chemistry and Biochemistry*] [*A publication*]

Adv Carbohydr Chem Biochem ... Advances in Carbohydrate Chemistry and Biochemistry [*A publication*]
Adv Cardiol ... Advances in Cardiology [*A publication*]
Adv Cardiopulm Dis ... Advances in Cardiopulmonary Diseases [*A publication*]
Adv Cardiovasc Phys ... Advances in Cardiovascular Physics [*A publication*]
Adv Catal ... Advances in Catalysis and Related Subjects [*A publication*]
Adv Cell Biol ... Advances in Cell Biology [*A publication*]
Adv Cell Cult ... Advances in Cell Culture [*A publication*]
Adv Cell Mol Biol ... Advances in Cell and Molecular Biology [*A publication*]
Adv Cell Neurobiol ... Advances in Cellular Neurobiology [*A publication*]
Adv Cereal Sci Technol ... Advances in Cereal Science and Technology [*A publication*]
Adv Cert in Ed ... Advanced Certificate in Education
Adv Cert in Mus Ed ... Advanced Certificate in Music Education
Adv Chem .. Advances in Chemistry [*A publication*]
Adv Chem Eng ... Advances in Chemical Engineering [*A publication*]
Adv Chemoreception ... Advances in Chemoreception [*A publication*]
Adv Chemother ... Advances in Chemotherapy [*A publication*]
Adv Chem Phys ... Advances in Chemical Physics [*A publication*]
Adv Chem Se ... Advances in Chemistry Series [*A publication*]
Adv Chem Ser ... Advances in Chemistry Series [*A publication*]
Adv Child Dev Behav ... Advances in Child Development and Behavior [*A publication*]
Adv Chromatogr ... Advances in Chromatography [*A publication*]
Adv Chron ... Advocates' Chronicle [*India*] [*A publication*]   (DLA)
Adv Cladistics ... Advances in Cladistics [*A publication*]
Adv Clin Chem ... Advances in Clinical Chemistry [*A publication*]
Adv Clin Enzymol ... Advances in Clinical Enzymology [*A publication*]
Adv Clin Pharmacol ... Advances in Clinical Pharmacology [*A publication*]
Adv Coll In ... Advances in Colloid and Interface Science [*A publication*]
Adv Coll Inter Sci ... Advances in Colloid and Interface Science [*A publication*]
Adv Colloid Interface Sci ... Advances in Colloid and Interface Science [*A publication*]
Adv Colloid and Interface Sci ... Advances in Colloid and Interface Science [*A publication*]
Adv Colloid Sci ... Advances in Colloid Science [*A publication*]
Adv Comp .. Advances in Computers [*A publication*]
Adv Comp Physiol Biochem ... Advances in Comparative Physiology and Biochemistry [*A publication*]
Adv Contracept ... Advances in Contraception [*A publication*]
Adv Contracept Deliv Syst ... Advances in Contraceptive Delivery Systems [*Kiawah Island, South Carolina*] [*A publication*]
Adv Control Syst ... Advances in Control Systems [*A publication*]
Adv Corros Sci Technol ... Advances in Corrosion Science and Technology [*A publication*]
Adv Cryog ... Advanced Cryogenics [*A publication*]
Adv Cryog Eng ... Advances in Cryogenic Engineering [*A publication*]
ADVCTN .. Advection   (FAAC)
Adv Cyclic Nucleotide Protein Phosphorylation Res ... Advances in Cyclic Nucleotide and Protein Phosphorylation Research [*A publication*]
Adv Cyclic Nucleotide Res ... Advances in Cyclic Nucleotide Research [*A publication*]
Adv Cytopharmacol ... Advances in Cytopharmacology [*A publication*]
Adv Data .... Advance Data [*A publication*]
Adv Desalin Proc Nat Symp Desalin ... Advances in Desalination. Proceedings. National Symposium on Desalination [*A publication*]
Adv Desert Arid Land Technol Dev ... Advances in Desert and Arid Land Technology and Development [*A publication*]
AdvDipEd ... Advanced Diploma in Education   (ADA)
ADVDISC ... Advance Discontinuance of Allotment
ADVDLA-DEP ... Advance Payment of Dislocation Allowance to Dependents [*Air Force*]   (AFM)
Adv Drug Res ... Advances in Drug Research [*A publication*]
Adv Drug Ther Ment Illness Proc Symp ... Advances in the Drug Therapy of Mental Illness. Based on the Proceedings of a Symposium [*A publication*]
Adv Earth Oriented Appl Space Technol ... Advances in Earth-Oriented Applications of Space Technology [*Later, Earth-Oriented Applications of Space Technology*] [*A publication*]
Adv Earth and Planet Sci ... Advances in Earth and Planetary Sciences [*A publication*]
Adv Earth Planet Sci ... Advances in Earth and Planetary Sciences [*A publication*]
Adv Ecol Res ... Advances in Ecological Research [*A publication*]
Adv Econ Bot ... Advances in Economic Botany [*A publication*]
ADVED7 ... Annales de Dermatologie et de Venereologie [*A publication*]
Adv Electrochem Electrochem Eng ... Advances in Electrochemistry and Electrochemical Engineering [*A publication*]
Adv Electron ... Advances in Electronics [*A publication*]
Adv Electron Circuit Packag ... Advances in Electronic Circuit Packaging [*A publication*]
Adv Electron Electron Phys ... Advances in Electronics and Electron Physics [*A publication*]
Adv Electron Electron Phys Suppl ... Advances in Electronics and Electron Physics. Supplement [*A publication*]
Adv Electron Tube Tech ... Advances in Electron Tube Techniques [*A publication*]

Adv Electrophor ... Advances in Electrophoresis [*A publication*]

adven .... Adventurer

Adv Energy Convers ... Advanced Energy Conversion [*England*] [*A publication*]

Adv Energy Syst Technol ... Advances in Energy Systems and Technology [*A publication*]

Adv Engng Software ... Advances in Engineering Software [*A publication*]

Adv Eng Sci Annu Meet Soc Eng Sci ... Advances in Engineering Science. Annual Meeting. Society of Engineering Science [*A publication*]

Adv Eng Sof ... Advances in Engineering Software [*A publication*]

Adv Eng Software ... Advances in Engineering Software [*A publication*]

Adventures Exp Phys ... Adventures in Experimental Physics [*A publication*]

Adv Environ Sci ... Advances in Environmental Sciences [*A publication*]

Adv Environ Sci Technol ... Advances in Environmental Science and Technology [*A publication*]

Adv Envir Sci ... Advances in Environmental Sciences [*A publication*]

Adv Enzym ... Advances in Enzymology [*A publication*]

Adv Enzyme Regul ... Advances in Enzyme Regulation [*A publication*]

Adv Enzymol ... Advances in Enzymology [*A publication*]

Adv Enzymol Relat Areas Mol Biol ... Advances in Enzymology and Related Areas of Molecular Biology [*A publication*]

Adv Enzymol Relat Subj Biochem ... Advances in Enzymology and Related Subjects of Biochemistry [*Later, Advances in Enzymology and Related Areas of Molecular Biology*] [*A publication*]

Adv Epileptol ... Advances in Epileptology [*A publication*]

Adv Epitaxy Endotaxy Sel Chem Probl ... Advances in Epitaxy and Endotaxy. Selected Chemical Problems [*A publication*]

Adverse Drug React Acute Poisoning Rev ... Adverse Drug Reactions and Acute Poisoning Reviews [*A publication*]

Adverse Drug React Bull ... Adverse Drug Reaction Bulletin [*A publication*]

Adverse Eff Environ Chem Psychotropic Drugs ... Adverse Effects of Environmental Chemicals and Psychotropic Drugs [*A publication*]

ADVERT ... Advertisement

Advert Age ... Advertising Age [*A publication*]

Advert Bus ... Advertising Business [*A publication*]   (APTA)

ADVERTIS ... Advertising   (DLA)

Advert L Anth ... Advertising Law Anthology [*A publication*]   (ILCA)

Advert Q ... Advertising Quarterly [*A publication*]

Advert World ... Advertising World [*A publication*]

Adv Ethol ... Advances in Ethology [*A publication*]

Adv Exp Med Biol ... Advances in Experimental Medicine and Biology [*A publication*]

Adv Exp Soc Psychol ... Advances in Experimental Social Psychology [*A publication*]

Adv Extr Metall Int Symp ... Advances in Extractive Metallurgy. International Symposium [*A publication*]

Adv Fertil Control ... Advances in Fertility Control [*A publication*]

Adv Fibrous Reinf Compos ... Advanced Fibrous Reinforced Composites [*A publication*]

Adv Fire Retardants ... Advances in Fire Retardants [*A publication*]

Adv Fluorine Chem ... Advances in Fluorine Chemistry [*A publication*]

Adv Fluorine Res Dent Caries Prev ... Advances in Fluorine Research and Dental Caries Prevention [*A publication*]

Adv Food Res ... Advances in Food Research [*A publication*]

Adv Food Res Suppl ... Advances in Food Research. Supplement [*A publication*]

Adv Forensic Haemogenet ... Advances in Forensic Haemogenetics [*A publication*]

Adv Free Radical Chem ... Advances in Free Radical Chemistry [*A publication*]

Adv Frontiers Plant Sci ... Advancing Frontiers of Plant Sciences [*A publication*]

Adv Front Plant Sci ... Advancing Frontiers of Plant Sciences [*A publication*]

Adv Front Pl Sci ... Advancing Frontiers of Plant Sciences [*A publication*]

Adv Fusion Glass Pro Int Conf ... Advances in the Fusion of Glass. Proceedings. International Conference [*A publication*]

ADVG .... Advantage   (MSA)

advg .... Advertising

Adv Gd .... Advanced Guard [*British military*]   (DMA)

Adv Gen Cell Pharmacol ... Advances in General and Cellular Pharmacology [*A publication*]

Adv Genet .. Advances in Genetics [*A publication*]

Adv Genetic ... Advances in Genetics [*A publication*]

Adv Geophys ... Advances in Geophysics [*A publication*]

Adv Gerontol Res ... Advances in Gerontological Research [*A publication*]

Advg Front Pl Sci ... Advancing Frontiers of Plant Sciences [*A publication*]

ADVGP ..... Advisory Group

Adv Heat Transfer ... Advances in Heat Transfer [*A publication*]

ADVHED ... Advanced Headquarters   (MUGU)

Adv Hematol ... Advanced Hematology [*A publication*]

Adv Heterocycl Chem ... Advances in Heterocyclic Chemistry [*A publication*]

Adv High Pressure Res ... Advances in High Pressure Research [*England*] [*A publication*]

Adv High Temp Chem ... Advances in High Temperature Chemistry [*A publication*]

Adv Hologr ... Advances in Holography [*A publication*]

Adv Host Def Mech ... Advances in Host Defense Mechanisms [*A publication*]

Adv Hum Fertil Reprod Endocrinol ... Advances in Human Fertility and Reproductive Endocrinology [*A publication*]

Adv Hum Gen ... Advances in Human Genetics [*A publication*]

Adv Hum Genet ... Advances in Human Genetics [*A publication*]

Adv Hydrosci ... Advances in Hydroscience [*A publication*]

AD 2 VIC ... Ad Duas Vices [*For Two Doses*] [*Pharmacy*]

ADVID ...... Advertising Videotape

Adv Image Pickup Disp ... Advances in Image Pickup and Display [*A publication*]

Adv Immun Cancer Ther ... Advances in Immunity and Cancer Therapy [*A publication*]

Adv Immunol ... Advances in Immunology [*A publication*]

Adv Inflammation Res ... Advances in Inflammation Research [*A publication*]

Adv Infrared Raman Spectrosc ... Advances in Infrared and Raman Spectroscopy [*A publication*]

Adv Inf Syst Sci ... Advances in Information Systems Science [*A publication*]

Adv Inorg Biochem ... Advances in Inorganic Biochemistry [*A publication*]

Adv Inorg Chem Radiochem ... Advances in Inorganic Chemistry and Radiochemistry [*A publication*]

Adv Insect Physiol ... Advances in Insect Physiology [*A publication*]

Adv Instrum ... Advances in Instrumentation [*A publication*]

ADV INTEL CEN ... Advanced Intelligence Center [*Navy*]

Adv Intern Med ... Advances in Internal Medicine [*A publication*]

Adv Iovinian ... Adversus Iovinianum [*of St. Jerome*] [*Classical studies*]   (OCD)

ADVISE .... Area Denial Visual Indication Security Equipment   (MCD)

ADVISER ... Airborne Dual-Channel Variable Input Severe Environmental Recorder/Reproducer [*Air Force*]   (MCD)

Advis Group Meet Modif Radiosensitivity Biol Syst ... Advisory Group Meeting on Modification of Radiosensitivity of Biological Systems [*A publication*]

Advis Group Meet Tumour Localization Radioact Agents ... Advisory Group Meeting on Tumour Localization with Radioactive Agents [*A publication*]

Advis Leafl Br Beekprs Ass ... Advisory Leaflet. British Beekeepers Association [*A publication*]

Advis Leafl Dep For Queensl ... Advisory Leaflet. Queensland Department of Forestry [*A publication*]   (APTA)

Advis Leafl Qd Dep Agric ... Advisory Leaflet. Queensland Department of Agriculture [*A publication*]

Advis Leafl W Scotl Agric Coll ... Advisory Leaflet. West of Scotland Agricultural College [*A publication*]

ADVISOR ... Advanced Integrated Safety and Optimizing Computer

ADV/L .... Advance Leave [*Military*]

ADVL .... Advanced Logic Systems, Inc. [*Sunnyvale, CA*] [*NASDAQ symbol*]   (NQ)

Adv Leafl Dep For Qd ... Advisory Leaflet. Queensland Department of Forestry [*A publication*]   (APTA)

Adv Leafl Min Agr Fish Food (Gt Brit) ... Advisory Leaflet. Ministry of Agriculture, Fisheries, and Food (Great Britain) [*A publication*]

Adv Leafl Queensland Dept Agr Stock Div Plant Ind ... Advisory Leaflet. Queensland Department of Agriculture and Stock. Division of Plant Industry [*A publication*]

Adv Leafl W Scot Agr Coll ... Advisory Leaflet. West of Scotland Agricultural College [*A publication*]

Adv Lectin Res ... Advances in Lectin Research [*A publication*]

Adv Lipid Res ... Advances in Lipid Research [*A publication*]

Adv Liq Cryst ... Advances in Liquid Crystals [*A publication*]

ADVLOGSYSCEN ... Advanced Logistics Systems Center [*Air Force*]

ADVM .... Adaptive Delta Voice Modulation [*Air Force*]

Adv Macromol Chem ... Advances in Macromolecular Chemistry [*A publication*]

Adv Magn Reson ... Advances in Magnetic Resonance [*A publication*]

Adv Manag ... Advanced Management [*A publication*]

Adv Manage Cardiovas Dis ... Advances in the Management of Cardiovascular Disease [*A publication*]

Adv Manage J ... Advanced Management Journal [*A publication*]

Adv Manage Stud ... Advances in Management Studies [*A publication*]

Adv Mar Bio ... Advances in Marine Biology [*A publication*]

Adv Mar Biol ... Advances in Marine Biology [*A publication*]

Adv Mass Spectrom ... Advances in Mass Spectrometry [*A publication*]

Adv Mater Res ... Advances in Materials Research [*A publication*]

Adv in Math ... Advances in Mathematics [*A publication*]

Adv Math ... Advances in Mathematics [*A publication*]

ADVMBT ... Advances in Microcirculation [*A publication*]

Adv in Mech ... Advances in Mechanics [*A publication*]

Adv Med Proc Int Congr Intern Med ... Advances in Medicine. Proceedings. International Congress of Internal Medicine [*A publication*]

Adv Membr Fluid ... Advances in Membrane Fluidity [*A publication*]

Adv Metab Disord ... Advances in Metabolic Disorders [*A publication*]

Adv Metab Disord Suppl ... Advances in Metabolic Disorders. Supplement [*A publication*]

Adv Methods Protein Sequence Determination ... Advanced Methods in Protein Sequence Determination [*A publication*]

Adv Mgmt ... Advanced Management [*A publication*]

Adv Mgmt J ... Advanced Management Journal [*A publication*]

Adv Microb Ecol ... Advances in Microbial Ecology [*A publication*]

Adv Microbial Physiol ... Advances in Microbial Physiology [*England*] [*A publication*]

Adv Microbiol Sea ... Advances in Microbiology of the Sea [*A publication*]
Adv Microb Physiol ... Advances in Microbial Physiology [*A publication*]
Adv Microcirc ... Advances in Microcirculation [*A publication*]
Adv Microwaves ... Advances in Microwaves [*A publication*]
Adv Mod Biol ... Advances in Modern Biology [*A publication*]
Adv Mod Environ Toxicol ... Advances in Modern Environmental Toxicology [*A publication*]
Adv Mod Gen ... Advances in Modern Genetics [*A publication*]
Adv Mod Nutr ... Advances in Modern Nutrition [*A publication*]
Adv Mod Toxicol ... Advances in Modern Toxicology [*A publication*]
Adv Mol Rel ... Advances in Molecular Relaxation Processes [*Later, Advances in Molecular Relaxation and Interaction Processes*] [*A publication*]
Adv Mol Relaxation and Interaction Processes ... Advances in Molecular Relaxation and Interaction Processes [*A publication*]
Adv Mol Relaxation Interact Processes ... Advances in Molecular Relaxation and Interaction Processes [*Netherlands*] [*A publication*]
Adv Mol Relaxation Processes ... Advances in Molecular Relaxation Processes [*Later, Advances in Molecular Relaxation and Interaction Processes*] [*A publication*]
Adv Mol Relax Interact Processes ... Advances in Molecular Relaxation and Interaction Processes [*A publication*]
Adv Molten Salt Chem ... Advances in Molten Salt Chemistry [*A publication*]
Adv Morphog ... Advances in Morphogenesis [*A publication*]
ADVMOS ... Advanced Military Occupational Specialty [*Army*]   (AABC)
ADV MTR ... Advertising Matter [*Freight*]
Advmt Sci .. Advancement of Science [*A publication*]
Advmt Sci (Lond) ... Advancement of Science (London) [*A publication*]
Adv Myocardiol ... Advances in Myocardiology [*A publication*]
ADVN........ Advance [*or Advancement*]   (FAAC)
ADVN........ ADVANTA Corp. [*NASDAQ symbol*]   (NQ)
Adv N........ Advocacy Now [*A publication*]
Adv Nephrol ... Advances in Nephrology [*A publication*]
Adv Nephrol Necker Hosp ... Advances in Nephrology. Necker Hospital [*A publication*]
Adv Neurochem ... Advances in Neurochemistry [*A publication*]
Adv Neurochem Proc All-Union Conf Neurochem ... Advances in Neurochemistry. Proceedings. All-Union Conference on Neurochemistry [*A publication*]
Adv Neurol ... Advances in Neurology [*A publication*]
Adv Neurol Sci ... Advances in Neurological Sciences [*A publication*]
Adv Neurosurg ... Advances in Neurosurgery [*A publication*]
Adv Nucl Phys ... Advances in Nuclear Physics [*A publication*]
Adv Nucl Quadrupole Reson ... Advances in Nuclear Quadrupole Resonance [*England*] [*A publication*]
Adv Nucl Sci Technol ... Advances in Nuclear Science and Technology [*A publication*]
Adv Nurs Sci ... Advances in Nursing Science [*A publication*]
Adv Nutr Res ... Advances in Nutritional Research [*A publication*]
Adv O......... Advance Opinions in Lawyers' Edition of United States Reports [*A publication*]   (DLA)
ADVO........ ADVO-System, Inc. [*Hartford, CT*] [*NASDAQ symbol*]   (NQ)
Adv Obstet ... Advances in Obstetrics and Gynecology [*A publication*]
Adv Obstet Gynaecol (Basel) ... Advances in Obstetrics and Gynaecology (Basel) [*A publication*]
Adv Obstet Gynecol (Baltimore) ... Advances in Obstetrics and Gynecology (Baltimore) [*A publication*]
Adv Obstet Gynecol (Osaka) ... Advances in Obstetrics and Gynecology (Osaka) [*Japan*] [*A publication*]
ADVOC..... Advocate   (DLA)
Advocates Q ... Advocates Quarterly [*A publication*]
Advocates Soc J ... Advocates Society. Journal [*A publication*]
ADVOCNET ... Adult and Vocational Educational Electronic Mail Network [*National Center for Research in Vocational Education*] [*Columbus, OH*] [*Telecommunications*]   (TSSD)
ADVOF..... Advise This Office   (NOAA)
ADVON..... Advanced Echelon [*Marine Corps*]
ADVON..... Advanced Operations Unit [*Navy*]
Adv Ophthal ... Advances in Ophthalmology [*A publication*]
Adv Ophthalmol ... Advances in Ophthalmology [*Netherlands*] [*A publication*]
Adv Ops..... Advance Opinions [*A publication*]   (DLA)
Adv Opt Electron Microsc ... Advances in Optical and Electron Microscopy [*A publication*]
Adv Oral Biol ... Advances in Oral Biology [*A publication*]
Adv Organometal Chem ... Advances in Organometallic Chemistry [*A publication*]
Adv Organomet Chem ... Advances in Organometallic Chemistry [*A publication*]
Adv Org Chem ... Advances in Organic Chemistry. Methods and Results [*A publication*]
Adv Org Chem Methods Results ... Advances in Organic Chemistry. Methods and Results [*A publication*]
Adv Oto-Rhino-Laryngol ... Advances in Oto-Rhino-Laryngology [*A publication*]
ADV/P....... Advanced Pay
ADVPA3 ... Advances in Pharmacology [*Later, Advances in Pharmacology and Chemotherapy*] [*A publication*]
Adv Pain Res Ther ... Advances in Pain Research and Therapy [*A publication*]
Adv Parasitol ... Advances in Parasitology [*A publication*]

Adv Particle Phys ... Advances in Particle Physics [*A publication*]
Adv Part Phys ... Advances in Particle Physics [*A publication*]
Adv Pathobiol ... Advances in Pathobiology [*A publication*]
ADVPB4.... Advances in Planned Parenthood [*A publication*]
Adv Pediatr ... Advances in Pediatrics [*A publication*]
Adv Pest Control Res ... Advances in Pest Control Research [*A publication*]
Adv Pet Chem Refin ... Advances in Petroleum Chemistry and Refining [*A publication*]
Adv Pet Recovery Upgrading Technol Conf ... Advances in Petroleum Recovery and Upgrading Technology Conference [*A publication*]
Adv Petrol Chem Refin ... Advances in Petroleum Chemistry and Refining [*A publication*]
Adv Pharmacol ... Advances in Pharmacology [*Later, Advances in Pharmacology and Chemotherapy*] [*A publication*]
Adv Pharmacol Chemother ... Advances in Pharmacology and Chemotherapy [*A publication*]
Adv Pharmacother ... Advances in Pharmacotherapy [*A publication*]
Adv Pharm Sci ... Advances in Pharmaceutical Sciences [*A publication*]
Adv Photochem ... Advances in Photochemistry [*A publication*]
Adv Phycol Japan ... Advance of Phycology in Japan [*A publication*]
Adv in Phys ... Advances in Physics [*A publication*]
Adv Phys.... Advances in Physics [*A publication*]
Adv Phy Sci ... Advances in Physical Sciences [*A publication*]
Adv Physics ... Advances in Physics [*A publication*]
Adv Phys Org Chem ... Advances in Physical Organic Chemistry [*A publication*]
Adv Phys Sci (USSR) ... Advances in Physical Sciences (USSR) [*A publication*]
Adv Planned Parent ... Advances in Planned Parenthood [*A publication*]
Adv Plann Parent ... Advances in Planned Parenthood [*A publication*]
Adv Plasma Phys ... Advances in Plasma Physics [*A publication*]
Adv Plast Reconstr Surg ... Advances in Plastic and Reconstructive Surgery [*A publication*]
Adv Pl Morph ... Advances in Plant Morphology [*A publication*]
ADVPMT ... Advance Payment [*Finance*]
Adv Pollen-Spore Res ... Advances in Pollen-Spore Research [*A publication*]
Adv Polyamine Res ... Advances in Polyamine Research [*A publication*]
Adv Polymer Sci ... Advances in Polymer Science [*A publication*]
Adv Polym Sci ... Advances in Polymer Science [*A publication*]
Adv Polym Technol ... Advances in Polymer Technology [*A publication*]
ADV POSS ... Adverse Possession [*Legal term*]   (DLA)
Adv Preconc Dehydr Foods Symp ... Advances in Preconcentration and Dehydration of Foods. Symposium [*A publication*]
Adv Primatol ... Advances in Primatology [*A publication*]
Adv Printing Sci ... Advances in Printing Science and Technology [*A publication*]
Adv Print Sci Technol ... Advances in Printing Science and Technology [*A publication*]
Adv Probab Related Topics ... Advances in Probability and Related Topics [*A publication*]
Adv Process Util For Prod ... Advances in Processing and Utilization of Forest Products [*A publication*]
Adv Proc Fluid Power Test Symp ... Advance Proceedings. Fluid Power Testing Symposium [*A publication*]
Adv Prostaglandin Thromboxane Leukotriene Res ... Advances in Prostaglandin, Thromboxane, and Leukotriene Research [*A publication*]
Adv Prostaglandin Thromboxane Res ... Advances in Prostaglandin and Thromboxane Research [*A publication*]
Adv Protein Chem ... Advances in Protein Chemistry [*A publication*]
Adv Psychoanal Theory Res Pract ... Advances in Psychoanalysis Theory, Research, and Practice [*A publication*]
Adv Psychobiol ... Advances in Psychobiology [*A publication*]
Adv Psychosom Med ... Advances in Psychosomatic Medicine [*A publication*]
Adv Psy Med ... Advances in Psychosomatic Medicine [*A publication*]
Adv Q......... Advocates Quarterly [*A publication*]
Adv Quantum Chem ... Advances in Quantum Chemistry [*A publication*]
Adv Quantum Electron ... Advances in Quantum Electronics [*A publication*]
ADVR........ Advance Release [*Military*]
ADVR........ Advisor   (AABC)
Adv Radia Res Biol Med ... Advances in Radiation Research, Biology, and Medicine [*A publication*]
Adv Radiat Biol ... Advances in Radiation Biology [*A publication*]
Adv Radiat Chem ... Advances in Radiation Chemistry [*A publication*]
Adv Raman Spectrosc ... Advances in Raman Spectroscopy [*A publication*]
Adv React Phys Des Econ Proc Int Conf ... Advanced Reactors. Physics, Design, and Economics. Proceedings. International Conference [*A publication*]
Adv Rel St ... Advanced Religious Studies [*A publication*]
Adv Rep NJ ... New Jersey Advance Reports and Weekly Law Review [*A publication*]   (DLA)
Adv Reprod Physiol ... Advances in Reproductive Physiology [*A publication*]
Adv Res Proj Agency Workshop Needs Dep Def Catal ... Advanced Research Projects. Agency Workshop on Needs of the Department of Defense for Catalysis [*A publication*]
Adv R Physl ... Advances in Reproductive Physiology [*A publication*]
ADVRS...... Assistant Director of Veterinary and Remount Services [*British military*]   (DMA)
ADVRY ..... Advisory   (FAAC)
ADVS .... Advanced Systems, Inc. [*NASDAQ symbol*]   (NQ)

ADVS .... Advise (AFM)
ADVS .... Assistant Director of Veterinary Services [*Military*] [*British*]
ADVS .... Dixonville School, Alberta [*Library symbol*] [*National Library of Canada*] (BIB)
ADVSA...... Advances in Veterinary Science [*Later, Advances in Veterinary Science and Comparative Medicine*] [*A publication*]
Adv Sci...... Advancement of Science [*A publication*]
Adv of Science ... Advancement of Science [*A publication*]
ADVSCOL ... Advanced Schools (MUGU)
ADVSDF... Advance Data [*A publication*]
Adv & Sell ... Advertising and Selling [*A publication*]
Adv Ser Agric Sci ... Advanced Series in Agricultural Sciences [*A publication*]
Adv Sex Horm Res ... Advances in Sex Hormone Research [*A publication*]
Adv Sh .... Advance Sheet (DLA)
Adv Shock Res ... Advances in Shock Research [*A publication*]
Adv Sleep Res ... Advances in Sleep Research [*A publication*]
Adv Small Anim Pract ... Advances in Small Animal Practice [*A publication*]
Adv Sociodent Res ... Advances in Socio-Dental Research [*A publication*]
Adv Sol Energy ... Advances in Solar Energy [*A publication*]
Adv Sol En Tech Newsl ... Advanced Solar Energy Technology Newsletter [*A publication*]
Adv Space Res ... Advances in Space Research [*A publication*]
Adv Space Sci ... Advances in Space Science [*A publication*]
Adv Space Sci Technol ... Advances in Space Science and Technology [*A publication*]
Adv Spa Sci ... Advances in Space Science and Technology [*A publication*]
Adv Spectros ... Advances in Spectroscopy [*A publication*]
Adv Spectrosc ... Advances in Spectroscopy [*A publication*]
ADVSR...... Advisor (AFM)
ADVST ...... Advance Stoppage (MUGU)
Adv Stereoencephalotomy ... Advances in Stereoencephalotomy [*A publication*]
Adv Steroid Biochem ... Advances in Steroid Biochemistry and Pharmacology [*A publication*]
Adv Steroid Biochem Pharmacol ... Advances in Steroid Biochemistry and Pharmacology [*A publication*]
Adv Struct Compos ... Advances in Structural Composites [*A publication*]
Adv Struct Res Diffr Methods ... Advances in Structure Research by Diffraction Methods [*A publication*]
Adv Study Behav ... Advances in the Study of Behavior [*A publication*]
Adv Study Birth Defects ... Advances in the Study of Birth Defects [*A publication*]
Adv Surf Coat Technol ... Advances in Surface Coating Technology [*England*] [*A publication*]
Adv Surg .... Advances in Surgery [*A publication*]
ADVSY...... Advisory (AFM)
ADVT .... Advanced Development Verification Test (RDA)
ADVT .... Advantage Life Products [*NASDAQ symbol*] (NQ)
ADVT .... Advertisement (AABC)
ADVT-C .... Advanced Development Verification Test - Coordinator (MCD)
Adv Tech Biol Electron Microsc ... Advanced Techniques in Biological Electron Microscopy [*A publication*]
Adv Tech Lib ... Advanced Technology Libraries [*A publication*]
Adv Tech Mater Invest Fabr ... Advanced Techniques for Material Investigation and Fabrication [*A publication*]
Adv Technol ... Advancing Technologies [*A publication*]
Adv Technol Libr ... Advanced Technology Libraries [*A publication*]
Adv Tech Stand Neurosurg ... Advances and Technical Standards in Neurosurgery [*A publication*]
Adv Teratol ... Advances in Teratology [*A publication*]
Adv Test Meas ... Advances in Test Measurement [*A publication*]
Adv Textile Process ... Advances in Textile Processing [*A publication*]
ADVT-G.... Advanced Development Verification Test - Government (MCD)
ADVTG ..... Advantage
ADVTG ..... Advertising
ADVTGE... Advantage (ROG)
Adv Theor Phys ... Advances in Theoretical Physics [*A publication*]
Adv Ther.... Advanced Therapeutics [*A publication*]
Adv Ther.... Advances in Therapy [*A publication*]
Adv Therm Conduct Pap Int Conf Thermal Conduct ... Advances in Thermal Conductivity. Papers. International Conference. Thermal Conductivity [*A publication*]
Adv Therm Eng ... Advances in Thermal Engineering [*A publication*]
ADVTM .... Advisory Team
ADVTNG.. Advanced Training [*Military*] (NVT)
Adv Tracer Methodol ... Advances in Tracer Methodology [*A publication*]
Adv Tuberc Res ... Advances in Tuberculosis Research [*A publication*]
Adv Tumour Prev Detect Charact ... Advances in Tumour Prevention, Detection, and Characterization [*A publication*]
ADVUL..... Air Defense Vulnerability Simulation [*Simulation game*]
Adv Urethane Sci Technol ... Advances in Urethane Science and Technology [*A publication*]
ADVUSWS ... Naval Advanced Undersea Weapons School
ADVV .... Adverbs (ADA)
Adv Valent ... Adversus Valentinianos [*of Tertullian*] [*Classical studies*] (OCD)
Adv Veg Sci ... Advances in Vegetation Science [*A publication*]
Adv Vehicle News ... Advanced Vehicle News [*A publication*]

Adv Vet Med (Berl) ... Advances in Veterinary Medicine (Berlin) [*A publication*]
Adv Vet Sci ... Advances in Veterinary Science [*Later, Advances in Veterinary Science and Comparative Medicine*] [*A publication*]
Adv Vet Sci Comp Med ... Advances in Veterinary Science and Comparative Medicine [*A publication*]
Adv Viral Oncol ... Advances in Viral Oncology [*A publication*]
Adv Virus Res ... Advances in Virus Research [*A publication*]
Adv Wash State Univ Coll Agric Res Cent ... Advance. Washington State University. College of Agriculture Research Center [*A publication*]
Adv Waste Treat Res ... Advances in Waste Treatment Research [*A publication*]
Adv Waste Treat Res Publ ... Advanced Waste Treatment Research Publication [*A publication*]
Adv Water Resour ... Advances in Water Resources [*England*] [*A publication*]
Adv Weld Processes Int Conf ... Advances in Welding Processes. International Conference [*A publication*]
Adv X-Ray Anal ... Advances in X-Ray Analysis [*A publication*]
ADVY .... Advisory (FAAC)
ADW......... Aerial Distribution Wire [*Telecommunications*] (TEL)
ADW......... Air Defense Warning [*Air Force*]
ADW......... Air Defense Weapon
ADW......... Andres Wines Ltd. [*Toronto Stock Exchange symbol*] [*Vancouver Stock Exchange symbol*]
ADW......... Arbeitsgemeinschaft der Deutschen Wertpapierbosen [*Federation of German Stock Exchanges*] [*Federal Republic of Germany*]
ADW......... Assault with Deadly Weapon
ADW......... Automated Data Wiring
ADW......... Camp Springs, MD [*Location identifier*] [*FAA*] (FAAL)
A5D5W...... Alcohol 5%, Dextrose 5% in Water
ADWA....... Atlantic Deeper Waterways Association (EA)
ADWAR.... Advanced Directional Warhead (MCD)
ADWC....... Air Defense Weapons Center [*Tyndall Air Force Base, FL*] (MCD)
ADWCP .... Automated Digital Weather Communications Program [*Air Force*] (AFM)
ADWCR .... Air Defense Weapons Center Regulation (MCD)
Adweek E... Adweek/Eastern Edition [*A publication*]
Adweek MW ... Adweek/Midwest Edition [*A publication*]
Adweek MWD ... Adweek Directory of Advertising. Midwestern Edition [*A publication*]
Adweek NE ... Adweek/New England Advertising Week [*A publication*]
Adweek Ntl ... Adweek/National Marketing Edition [*A publication*]
Adweek SAN ... Adweek/Southwest Advertising News [*A publication*]
Adweek SE ... Adweek/Southeast Edition [*A publication*]
Adweek SED ... Adweek Directory of Advertising. Southeastern Edition [*A publication*]
Adweek Spl ... Adweek. Special Report [*A publication*]
Adweek S W ... Adweek/Southwest Edition [*A publication*]
Adweek SWD ... Adweek Directory of Advertising. Southwestern Edition [*A publication*]
Adweek W ... Adweek/Western Edition [*A publication*]
Adweek WD ... Adweek Directory of Advertising. Western Edition [*A publication*]
ADWE & M ... Assistant Director of Works, Electrical and Mechanical [*Military*] [*British*]
ADWEPS .. Air Defense Weapons Cost Effectiveness Study (AABC)
ADWKP .... Air Defense Warning Key Point [*Air Force*]
ADWMA... Abhandlungen. Deutsche Akademie der Wissenschaften zu Berlin. Klasse fuer Medizin [*A publication*]
Ad World ... Advertising World [*A publication*]
ADWS ...... Air Defense Weapon System (MCD)
ADWS ...... Automatic Digital Weather Switch [*Air Force*] (AFM)
ADWS ...... Deadwood School, Alberta [*Library symbol*] [*National Library of Canada*] (BIB)
ADWSS..... Air Defense Weapon Simulation System (MCD)
ADX.......... [*The*] Adams Express Co. [*NYSE symbol*] (SPSG)
ADX.......... Address Complete, Coin-Box [*Telecommunications*] (TEL)
ADX.......... Adrenalectomized [*Medicine*]
ADX.......... Advanced Development Experimental [*Army*] (AABC)
ADX.......... Air Defense Exercise (AABC)
ADX.......... Asymmetric Data Exchange
ADX.......... Automatic Data Exchange
ADXR........ Association of DX [*Distance*] Reporters (EA)
ADY.......... Additional Duty (AABC)
Ad/y.......... Adet/Yil [*Items per Year*] [*Turkish*] [*Business term*]
ADY.......... Audre Recognition Systems, Inc. [*Vancouver Stock Exchange symbol*]
Adye CM ... Adye on Courts-Martial [*A publication*] (DLA)
ADYN........ Amplidyne [*Electricity*] (KSC)
Ad'yuvanty Vaktsinno Syvorot Dele ... Ad'yuvanty v Vaktsinno Syvorotochnom Dele [*A publication*]
ADZ.......... Advise
ADZ.......... Air Defense Zone (NATG)
ADz........... Akademiska Dzive [*A publication*]
ADZ.......... San Andres Island [*Colombia*] [*Airport symbol*] (OAG)
ADZAR ..... Advise Arrival (FAAC)
ADZI .... Advise Intentions (FAAC)
ADZOF ..... Advise This Office (FAAC)

ADZY	Advisory (FAAC)
AE	Abort Electronics [*Apollo*] [*NASA*]
AE	Above Elbow [*Medicine*]
AE	Abrechnungseinheit [*Accounting Unit*] [*German*] [*Business term*]
AE	Absolute Error
A/E	Absorptivity-Emissivity [*Ratio*]
AE	Academia Europaea
A & E	Accident and Emergency [*Ward, Department, or Services*] [*Medicine*]
AE	Accion Espanola [*Spanish Action*] [*Political party*] (PPE)
AE	Accommodation Endorsement [*Banking*]
AE	Account Executive [*Advertising, securities*]
AE	Accrued Expenditure [*Accounting*] (AFM)
AE	ACE Developments [*Vancouver Stock Exchange symbol*]
AE	Acoustic Emission
AE	Acrodermatitis Enteropathica [*Medicine*]
AE	Acta Ethnographica [*A publication*]
AE	Active Enhancement (MCD)
A/E	Activity Elements (MCD)
AE	Adam and Eve (EA)
AE	Adams Resources & Energy, Inc. [*AMEX symbol*] (SPSG)
AE	Added Entry [*Online database field identifier*]
AE	Additional Expenses
AE	Administrative Entity [*Job Training and Partnership Act*] (OICC)
A & E	Admiralty and Ecclesiastical (DLA)
A & E	Adolphus and Ellis' English Queen's Bench Reports [*A publication*] (DLA)
AE	Adult Education [*A publication*]
AE	Adult Education
Ae	Aegyptus [*A publication*]
AE	Aeon [*10⁹ years*] [*Geology*]
AE	Aero Flugzeugbau [*Federal Republic of Germany*] [*ICAO aircraft manufacturer identifier*] (ICAO)
AE	Aeroelectronic (IEEE)
AE	Aeromedical Evacuation [*Later, AME*] (AFM)
AE	Aeronautical Engineer
AE	Aerospace Education
AE	Aerospace Environment (MCD)
AE	Aes [*Obverse*] [*Numismatics*]
AE	Aesthetics [*A publication*]
AE	Aetatis [*Age*] [*Latin*]
Ae	Aevum [*A publication*]
AE	Affect Elaboration [*Scale*] [*Psychology*]
A(E)	Africa (Ethiopia) Committee [*British*] [*World War II*]
AE	After End [*Naval engineering*] (DAS)
AE	Age Equivalent [*Development level*] [*Education*]
AE	Agence Europe [*A publication*]
AE	Aggregate Expenditure [*Economics*]
AE	Agricultural Engineer
AE	Agricultural Engineering Research Division [*of ARS, Department of Agriculture*]
AE	Air Ecosse Ltd. [*British*]
AE	Air Efficiency Award [*RAF*] [*British*] (DMA)
AE	Air Ejector
AE	Air Electrical [*NATO*] (NATG)
AE	Air Engineering [*British*]
AE	Air Escape [*Technical drawings*]
AE	Air Europe Ltd. [*Great Britain*] [*ICAO designator*] (FAAC)
AE	Air Mechanic (Engines) [*British military*] (DMA)
AE	Airborne Electronics (MCD)
AE	Airborne Equipment Division [*Bureau of Aeronautics; later, NASC*] [*Navy*]
A & E	Aircraft and Engineering (MCD)
A & E	Aircraft and Engines (AAG)
AE	Aircraft Equipment
A and E	Airframe and Engine
AE	Alaska Economic Report [*A publication*]
ae	Algeria [*MARC country of publication code*] [*Library of Congress*] (LCCP)
AE	All England
AE	Almost Everywhere
AE	Alpha Epsilon (EA)
AE	Alternative Energy
AE	American Embassy
AE	American Ensemble [*A publication*]
AE	Ammunition Examiner [*British and Canadian*] [*World War II*]
AE	Ammunition Ship [*Navy symbol*]
A & E	Analysis and Evaluation
AE	Ancient Egypt [*A publication*]
ae	And Elsewhere [*Mathematics*]
AE	Angle of Elevation
A und E	Anglistik und Englischunterricht [*A publication*]
AE	Angstromeinheit [*Angstrom Unit*] [*German*]
AE	Annales de l'Est [*A publication*]
AE	Annales d'Ethiopie [*A publication*]
AE	Annee Epigraphique [*A publication*]
AE	Annuaire Europeen [*A publication*]
A/E	Annular Expansion Column [*Chromatography*]
AE	Anonymos Etaireia [*Joint Stock Company, Corporation*] [*Greek*]
AE	Anoxic Encephalopathy [*Medicine*]
AE	Antarctic Expedition
AE	Apostle and Evangelist [*Church calendars*]
A & E	Appeal and Error [*Legal term*] (DLA)
AE	Appearance Energy [*Surface ionization*]
AE	Application Engineering
AE	Applications Explorer [*NASA*]
AE	Applied Entomology
AE	Apportioned Effort (MCD)
A & E	Appropriation and Expense (AFM)
AE	Arab Economist [*A publication*]
AE	Arbeitseinheit [*Work Unit*] [*German*]
AE	Archaiologike Ephemeris [*A publication*]
A-E	Architect-Engineer
A & E	Architectural and Engineering [*Also, A-E*] (AFM)
A/E	Architectural Engineering (OICC)
A-E	Architectural and Engineering [*Also, A & E*] (KSC)
AE	Arheologija un Etnografija [*A publication*]
AE	Arithmetic Element (BUR)
AE	Arithmetic Expression (IEEE)
AE	Arkheograficheskii Ezhegodnik [*A publication*]
A & E	Armament and Electronics [*Air Force*]
AE	Armed Experimental [*British military*] (DMA)
AE	Armor, Artillery, and Engineers Aptitude Area [*Army*]
AE	Army Education
AE	Army in Europe
AE	Artificial Erythrocyte [*Hematology*]
A & E	Arts & Entertainment Network [*Cable-television system*]
ae-----	Asia, East [*MARC geographic area code*] [*Library of Congress*] (LCCP)
AE	Assault Echelon (NVT)
AE	Assault Engineer [*British military*] (DMA)
AE	Assimilation Efficiency
AE	Assistant Editor [*Publishing*]
AE	Assistant Engineer
AE	Associate Editor [*Publishing*]
AE	Associate in Education
AE	Associate in Engineering
AE	Associate Engraver [*British*] (ROG)
AE	Association of Entertainers (EA)
AE	Association Europeenne des Officiers Professionnels de Sapeurs-Pompiers [*European Association of Professional Fire Brigade Officers - EAPFBO*] (EAIO)
AE	Astronomische Einheit [*Astronomical Unit*] [*German*]
AE	Asymmetric Epoxidation [*Organic chemistry*]
AE	Atmospheric Entry
AE	Atmospheric Explorer [*Satellite*] [*NASA*]
AE	Atomic Emission
AE	Atomic Energy (ADA)
AE	Audit Entry [*Accounting, finance*] (BUR)
AE	Auroral Electrojet [*Index*]
AE	Austral [*or Australian*] English
AE	Australian E Class [*Submarine*]
AE	Australian Encyclopaedia [*A publication*] (APTA)
AE	Australian Engineers
AE	Autoclave Engineers, Inc.
AE	Autoimmune Encephalomyelitis [*Hematology*]
AE	Automatic Electric (MCD)
AE	Automatic Exposure Camera
AE	Automotive Engineer [*A publication*]
AE	Autumnal Equinox
AE	Auxiliary Equipment (KSC)
AE	Average Error (MCD)
AE	Aviation Electrician's Mate [*Navy rating*]
A & E	Azimuth and Elevation
A-E	Dow Chemical Co. [*Research code symbol*]
AE	Dubai [*IYRU nationality code*] (IYR)
AE	Edmonton Public Library, Alberta [*Library symbol*] [*National Library of Canada*] (NLC)
AE	George William Russell [*Irish poet, 1867-1935*] [*Pseudonym*]
AE	Internationales Archiv fuer Ethnographie [*A publication*]
AE	L'Annee Epigraphique [*A publication*] (OCD)
AE	United Arab Emirates [*ANSI two-letter standard code*] (CNC)
AE1	Aviation Electrician's Mate, First Class [*Navy rating*]
AE2	Aviation Electrician's Mate, Second Class [*Navy rating*]
AE3	Aviation Electrician's Mate, Third Class [*Navy rating*]
AEA	Abemama [*Kiribati*] [*Airport symbol*] (OAG)
AEA	Aboriginal Employment Action [*Australia*]
AEA	Abort Electronics Assembly [*Apollo*] [*NASA*]
AEA	Accountable Entertainment Allowance [*British*]
AEA	Active Element Array
AEA	Actors' Equity Association (EA)
AEA	Actual Expenses Allowable [*Military*] (AFM)
AEA	Adult Education Association of the USA (EA)
AEA	Advanced Engine Aerospace
AeA	Aegyptologische Abhandlungen [*Wiesbaden*] [*A publication*]
AEA	Aerospace Education Association (EA)
AEA	African Economic Affairs Committee [*London*] [*World War II*]
AEA	Aft End Assembly

AEA .... Agence Europeenne d'Approvisionnement
AEA .... Aggregate Expense Analysis [Insurance]
AEA .... Agricultural Education Association [British]
AEA .... Agricultural Engineers Association [United Kingdom]   (DS)
AEA .... Agro-Ecological Atlas of Cereal Growing in Europe [Elsevier Book Series] [A publication]
AEA .... Air East Airlines [Westfield, MA] [FAA designator]   (FAAC)
AEA .... Air Efficiency Award [RAF] [British]
AEA .... Air Entraining Agent [Freight]
AEA .... Aircraft Electronics Association   (EA)
AEA .... Aircraft Engineers Association
AEA .... Alberta Historical Resources, Alberta Culture and Multiculturalism, Edmonton, Alberta [Library symbol] [National Library of Canada]   (NLC)
AEA .... Alcohol, Ether, Acetone [Solvent mixture]
AEA .... Ambulance Employees Association [Australia]
AEA .... America. Revista de la Asociacion de Escritores y Artistas Americanos [A publication]
AEA .... American Economic Association   (EA)
AEA .... American Education Association   (EA)
AEA .... American Electrology Association   (EA)
AEA .... American Electronics Association   (EA)
AEA .... American Engineering Association [Defunct]   (EA)
AEA .... American Enterprise Association [Later, AEI]
AEA .... American Entrepreneurs Association [Los Angeles, CA]   (EA)
AEA .... American Equine Association   (EA)
AEA .... American Eskimo Association   (EA)
AEA .... American Evaluation Association   (EA)
AEA .... American Export Airlines
AEA .... Americans of European Ancestry [Psychometrics]
AEA .... Annus Erat Augusti [It Was in the Year of Augustus] [Coin inscription] [Latin]   (ROG)
AEA .... Antenna Elevation Angle
AEA .... Anuario de Estudios Atlanticos [A publication]
AEA .... Applied Economic Associates [Australia]
AEA .... Archivo Espanol de Arqueologia [A publication]
AEA .... Archivo Espanol de Arte [A publication]
AEA .... Area Education Agency   (OICC)
AEA .... Argenta Systems [Vancouver Stock Exchange symbol]
AEA .... Artists Equity Association [Later, NAEA]   (EA)
AEA .... [The] Arts, Education, and Americans   (EA)
AEA .... Assignment Eligibility and Availability [Military]   (AABC)
AEA .... Associate in Engineering Administration
AEA .... Association of Enrolled Agents [Later, NAEA]   (EA)
AEA .... Association of European Airlines   (EAIO)
AEA .... Association Europeenne de l'Asphalte [European Mastic Asphalt Association - EMAA]   (EAIO)
AEA .... Association Europeenne d'Athletisme [European Athletic Association - EAA]   (EA)
AEA .... Association Europeenne des Audioprothesistes [European Association of Hearing Aid Dispensers]   (EAIO)
AEA .... Association of Seventh-Day Adventist Engineers and Architects   (EA)
AEA .... Atlantic Education Association [Canada]
AEA .... Atomic Energy Act [1954]
AEA .... Atomic Energy Authority [British]
AEA .... Auger Electron Analysis
AEA .... Augustinian Educational Association   (EA)
AEA .... Autoerotic Asphyxiation [Medicine]
AEA .... Automatic Error Analysis
AEA .... Automation Economic Analysis
AEA .... Automotive Electric Association [Absorbed by ASIA]   (EA)
AEA .... Eastern Region [FAA]   (FAAC)
AEA .... United States Army, Corps of Engineers, South Atlantic Division, Atlanta, GA [OCLC symbol]   (OCLC)
AEAA .... Airman Apprentice, Aviation Electrician, Striker [Navy rating]
AEAA .... Archivo Espanol de Arte y Arqueologia [A publication]
AEAA .... Ascent Engine Arming Assembly [NASA]   (KSC)
AEA/AER ... American Economic Review. American Economic Association [A publication]
AeAb .... Aegyptologische Abhandlungen [Wiesbaden] [A publication]
AEAC .... Alternate Emergency Action Center   (CINC)
A & EAC.... American and English Annotated Cases [A publication]   (DLA)
AEACA2.... Aeromedica Acta [A publication]
AEACC...... East Coulee Community Library, Alberta [Library symbol] [National Library of Canada]   (NLC)
AEACP...... Airborne Emergency Alternate Command Post   (CINC)
AEAD .... Alcoholism and Drug Abuse Commission, Edmonton, Alberta [Library symbol] [National Library of Canada]   (NLC)
AEAE........ Alberta Advanced Education, Edmonton, Alberta [Library symbol] [National Library of Canada]   (NLC)
AEAF........ Allied Expeditionary Air Force
AEAG .... Agnico-Eagle Mines Ltd. [NASDAQ symbol]   (NQ)
AEAG .... Alberta Agriculture, Edmonton, Alberta [Library symbol] [National Library of Canada]   (NLC)
AEAGL...... Laboratory, Alberta Agriculture, Edmonton, Alberta [Library symbol] [Obsolete] [National Library of Canada]   (NLC)
AEAGLS ... Eaglesham School, Alberta [Library symbol] [National Library of Canada]   (BIB)

AEAGS...... Operating and Maintenance Division, Alberta Government Services, Edmonton, Alberta [Library symbol] [National Library of Canada]   (NLC)
AEAH........ Alberta Hospital, Edmonton, Alberta [Library symbol] [National Library of Canada]   (BIB)
AEAHA..... Resource Library, Alberta Hospital Association, Edmonton, Alberta [Library symbol] [National Library of Canada]   (NLC)
AEAI.......... Association Europeenne des Assures de l'Industrie [European Association of Industrial Insurers] [Brussels, Belgium]   (EAIO)
AEA Inf Ser LA Agric Exp Stn ... AEA Information Series. Louisiana Agricultural Experiment Station [A publication]
AEAIs .... Archives de l'Eglise d'Alsace [A publication]
AEAM .... Association des Evangeliques d'Afrique et Madagascar [Association of Evangelicals of Africa and Madagascar]   (EAIO)
AEAM .... Eaglesham Municipal Library, Alberta [Library symbol] [National Library of Canada]   (NLC)
AEAME...... Allsopp, Morgan Engineering Ltd., Edmonton, Alberta [Library symbol] [National Library of Canada]   (NLC)
AEAN........ Airman, Aviation Electrician, Striker [Navy rating]
A & E Ann Cas ... American and English Annotated Cases [A publication]   (DLA)
A & E Anno ... American and English Annotated Cases [A publication]   (DLA)
AEAO........ Airborne Emergency Actions Officer [SAC]
AEAONMS ... Ancient Egyptian Arabic Order Nobles of the Mystic Shrine   (EA)
AEAOS...... Alberta Oil Sands Information Centre, Edmonton, Alberta [Library symbol] [National Library of Canada]   (NLC)
AEAP........ Alliance Europeenne des Agences de Presse
AEAPA...... Alberta Personnel Administration, Edmonton, Alberta [Library symbol] [National Library of Canada]   (NLC)
AEAPS ...... Auger Electron Appearance Potential Spectroscopy
AEAR .... American Ear Association for Research   (EA)
AEAR .... Committee on American East Asian Relations [Defunct]   (EA)
AEARC...... Army Equipment Authorizations Review Center   (AABC)
AEARN...... Alberta Association of Registered Nurses, Edmonton, Alberta [Library symbol] [National Library of Canada]   (NLC)
AEArq........ Archivo Espanol de Arqueologia [A publication]
AEAS........ Air Equipment and Support [Army]   (AFIT)
AEAS........ Automatic Equalization/Analyzation System
AEASC...... Alberta Securities Commission, Edmonton, Alberta [Library symbol] [National Library of Canada]   (NLC)
AEASH ..... Acta Ethnographica. Academiae Scientiarum Hungaricae [A publication]
AEATG...... Alberta Attorney General, Edmonton, Alberta [Library symbol] [National Library of Canada]   (NLC)
AEAU .... Athabasca University, Alberta [Library symbol] [National Library of Canada]   (NLC)
AEAUC ..... Alberta Government Libraries Union Catalogue, Edmonton, Alberta [Library symbol] [National Library of Canada]   (NLC)
AEAWA .... Agricultural Educators Association of Western Australia
AEB .... Acquired Epidermolysis Bullosa [Medicine]
AEB .... Advanced Engine Bell
AEB .... Aerial Exploitation Battalion   (MCD)
AEB .... Aft Equipment Bay [NASA]   (KSC)
AEB .... Airborne and Electronics Board [Army]   (MCD)
AEB .... Amchitka [Alaska] [Seismograph station code, US Geological Survey] [Closed]   (SEIS)
AEB .... American Egg Board   (EA)
AEB .... American Ethnology Bureau [British]   (DAS)
AEB .... Analytical and Enumerative Bibliography [A publication]
AEB .... Annual Egyptological Bibliography [A publication]
Aeb............ Archives et Bibliotheques [A publication]
AEB .... Arctic Environmental Buoy System   (NOAA)
AEB .... Art Exhibitions Bureau
AEB .... Associated Examining Board [British]
AEB .... Association of Editorial Businesses   (EA)
AEB .... Association Europeenne de la Boyauderie [European Natural Sausage Casings Association - ENSCA]   (EA)
AE-B .... Atmosphere Explorer B [Satellite] [NASA]
AEB .... Australian Business and Estate Planning Reporter [A publication]
AEB .... Auxiliary Equipment Building [Nuclear energy]   (NRCH)
AEB .... Average Extent of Burning
AEB .... United States Army, Corps of Engineers, Coastal Engineering Research Center, Fort Belvoir, VA [OCLC symbol]   (OCLC)
AEBA........ Agricultural Economics Bulletin for Africa [A publication]
AEBE......... Approach End Barrier Engagement   (MCD)
AEBOED... Advances in Economic Botany [A publication]
AEBR........ Airborne Electron Beam Recorder
AEBSTA.... Atomic Energy Bureau of Science and Technics Agency [Japan]
AEC .... Academy of Electrical Contracting   (EA)
AEC .... Adaptive Echo Cancellation [Navy]   (MCD)
AEC .... Additional Extended Coverage [Insurance]
AEC .... Adult Education Centre [British]
AEC .... Affaires Exterieures Canada [External Affairs Canada]

AEC .... Aft End Cone [*NASA*]   (NASA)

AEC .... Aft Events Controller [*NASA*]   (MCD)

AEC .... Agricultural Economics Division [*of AMS, Department of Agriculture*]

AEC .... Agricultural Engineering Centre [*Australia*]

AEC .... Agricultural Executive Council [*British*]

AEC .... Air Emplaced Classifier   (MCD)

AEC .... Airship Experimental Center [*Navy*]

AEC .... Alaska Engineering Commission [*Later, the Alaska Railroad*]

AEC .... Alberta Department of Culture Library [*UTLAS symbol*]

AEC .... Alberta Energy Company Ltd. [*Toronto Stock Exchange symbol*] [*Vancouver Stock Exchange symbol*]

AEC .... Altitude Engine Control   (AAG)

AEC .... Aluminum Extruders Council   (EA)

AEC .... Amelia Earhart Collectors Club   (EA)

AEC .... American Economic Council   (EA)

AEC .... American Economist [*A publication*]

AEC .... American Education Coalition   (EA)

AEC .... American Election Commission   (EA)

AEC .... American Electrical Cases [*A publication*]   (DLA)

AEC .... American Engineering Council

AEC .... American Express Card [*Credit card*]

AEC .... Americans for Educational Choice   (EA)

AEC .... Amino(ethyl)carbazole [*Organic chemistry*]

AEC .... Analog Electronic Computer

AEC .... Arab Economist [*A publication*]

AEC .... Arancel Externo Comun [*Common External Tariff*] [*Andean pact*]

AEC .... Architects' Emergency Committee

AEC .... Architectural and Engineering Construction   (BYTE)

AEC .... Area Equipment Compounds [*Military*]   (AABC)

AEC .... Army Education Center

AEC .... Army Educational Corps [*Later, RAEC*] [*British*]

AEC .... Army Electronics Command

AEC .... Assembled Electronic Component

AEC .... Association des Editeurs Canadiens [*Association of Canadian Editors*]

AEC .... Association of Education Committees [*British*]

AEC .... Association of Electronic Cottagers   (EA)

AEC .... Association of Episcopal Colleges   (EA)

AEC .... Association des Etudes Canadiennes [*Association for Canadian Studies - ACS*]

AEC .... Association Europeenne de Ceramique [*European Ceramic Association*] [*France*]

AEC .... Association Europeenne des Conservatoires [*European Association of Conservatories - EAC*]   (EAIO)

AEC .... Association Europeenne des Contribuables [*European Taxpayers Association - ETA*]   (EA)

AEC .... Association Europeenne pour la Cooperation [*European Association for Cooperation*]

AEC .... Atlantic & East Carolina Railway Co. [*AAR code*]

AEC .... Atlas Educational Center   (EA)

AEC .... Atomic Energy Commission [*Functions divided, 1975, between Nuclear Regulatory Commission and Energy Research and Development Administration*]

AEC .... Atomic Energy Commission. Reports [*A publication*]   (DLA)

AEC .... Australian Education Centre

AEC .... Automatic Exciter Control

AEC .... Automatic Exposure Control

AEC .... Average Electrode Current

AEC .... Aviation Electrician's Mate, Chief [*Navy rating*]

AEC .... Business [*Formerly, Atlanta Economic Review*] [*A publication*]

AEC .... Concordia College, Edmonton, Alberta [*Library symbol*] [*National Library of Canada*]   (NLC)

AEC .... United States Army, Corps of Engineers, Los Angeles District, Los Angeles, CA [*OCLC symbol*]   (OCLC)

AECA .... Alberta Consumer and Corporate Affairs, Edmonton, Alberta [*Library symbol*] [*National Library of Canada*]   (NLC)

AECA .... American Edge Collectors Association   (EA)

A & ECA .... Anglican and Eastern Churches Association   (EA)

AECA .... Arms Export Control Act

AECA .... Association Europeenne des Centres d'Audiophonologie [*European Association of Audiophonological Centres - EAAC*]   (EAIO)

AEC-AFSWP-TP ... Atomic Energy Commission - Armed Forces Special Weapons Project Technical Publication   (MCD)

AECAH ..... Association Europeenne des Conservatoires, Academies de Musique, et Musikhochschulen [*European Association of Music Conservatories, Academies, and High Schools*]   (EAIO)

A & E Cas .. American and English Annotated Cases [*A publication*]   (DLA)

AECAWA ... Association of Episcopal Conferences of Anglophone West Africa   (EAIO)

AECB .... Arms Export Control Board

AECB .... Atomic Energy Control Board [*Canada*]

AECC .... Aeromedical Evacuation Control Center [*Military*]   (MCD)

AECC .... Alberta Cancer Clinic, Edmonton, Alberta [*Library symbol*] [*National Library of Canada*]   (NLC)

AECC .... Amelia Earhart Collectors Club   (EA)

A & ECC .... American and English Corporation Cases [*United States*] [*A publication*]   (DLA)

AECC .... Australian Export Statistics [*Database*]

AECC .... Automobile Emissions Control by Catalyst [*of the European Council of Chemical Manufacturers' Federations*]   (EAIO)

AECCG ...... African Elephant Conservation Coordinating Group

AECCH ..... Peter Wilcock Library, Charles Camsell General Hospital, Edmonton, Alberta [*Library symbol*] [*National Library of Canada*]   (NLC)

AECCI ...... Cross Cancer Institute, Edmonton, Alberta [*Library symbol*] [*National Library of Canada*]   (NLC)

AEC-DASA-TP ... Atomic Energy Commission - Defense Atomic Support Agency Technical Publication   (MCD)

AEC-DNA-TP ... Atomic Energy Commission - Defense Nuclear Agency Technical Publication   (MCD)

AECE .... AEC, Inc. [*NASDAQ symbol*]   (NQ)

AECE .... Airborne Engineer Contraction Equipment   (MCD)

AECF .... American Egyptian Cooperation Foundation   (EA)

AECG .... Ambulatory Electrocardiogram

AECGIS .... Automated Electrocardiograph Interpretive System [*Veterans Administration*]

Ae Ch Salz ... Aevum Christianum. Salzburger Beitraege zur Religions- und Geistesgeschichte des Abendlandes [*A publication*]

AECI .... Associate Member of the Institute of Employment Consultants [*British*]   (DBQ)

AECI .... Association of European Conjuncture Institutes   (EA)

AECI .... Association of European Cooperative Insurers [*Brussels, Belgium*]   (EAIO)

AECJC ...... Genealogical Society Library, Church of Jesus Christ of Latter-Day Saints, Edmonton, Alberta [*Library symbol*] [*National Library of Canada*]   (NLC)

AECK .... Eckville Public Library, Alberta [*Library symbol*] [*National Library of Canada*]   (NLC)

AECL .... Aircraft and Equipment Configuration List   (MCD)

AECL .... Alberta Culture, Edmonton, Alberta [*Library symbol*] [*National Library of Canada*]   (NLC)

AECL .... Atomic Energy of Canada Limited

AECL .... Atomic Energy Centre - Lahore   (MCD)

AE Clemson Agr Exp Sta ... AE. Clemson Agricultural Experiment Station [*A publication*]

AECL Res & Dev Eng ... AECL [*Atomic Energy of Canada Limited*] Research and Development in Engineering [*A publication*]

AECLS ...... Alberta Culture Library Services, Edmonton, Alberta [*Library symbol*] [*National Library of Canada*]   (NLC)

AECM .... Association of European Candle Manufacturers   (EA)

AECM .... Atomic Energy Commission Manual

AECM .... Aviation Electrician's Mate, Master Chief [*Navy rating*]

AECMA .... Association Europeenne des Constructeurs de Materiel Aerospatial [*European Association of Aerospace Manufacturers*]   (EAIO)

AECNP...... Association Europeenne des Centres Nationaux de Productivite [*European Association for National Productivity Centers - EANPC*]   (EAIO)

AECO .... Aeromedical Evacuation Control Officer [*Military*]   (AABC)

AECO .... Agora-Economie [*Agence France-Presse*] [*French*] [*Information service or system*]   (CRD)

AECO .... American Electromedics Corporation [*NASDAQ symbol*]   (NQ)

AECO .... Archivum Europae Centro-Orientalis [*A publication*]

AECO .... Concordia Lutheran Seminary, Edmonton, Alberta [*Library symbol*] [*National Library of Canada*]   (BIB)

AECODH ... Agro-Ecosystems [*A publication*]

AECOM ..... Army Electronics Command   (MUGU)

A Econ .... Actualite Economique [*A publication*]

A Econ (Clermont) ... Annales Economiques (Clermont) [*A publication*]

A Econ Polit ... Annales d'Economie Politique [*A publication*]

A Econ Publ Soc Coop ... Annales de l'Economie Publique, Sociale, et Cooperative [*A publication*]

A Econ Soc Measurement ... Annals of Economic and Social Measurement [*A publication*]

A & E Cor Cases ... American and English Corporation Cases [*United States*] [*A publication*]   (DLA)

A & E Corp Cas ... American and English Corporation Cases [*A publication*]   (DLA)

A & E Corp Cas NS ... American and English Corporation Cases, New Series [*A publication*]   (DLA)

AECP .... Advance Engineering Change Proposal   (MSA)

AECP .... Airman Education and Commissioning Program

AECP .... Altitude Engine Control Panel   (AAG)

AECP .... Army Extension Course Program   (AABC)

AECPR...... Atomic Energy Commission Procurement Regulations [*Obsolete*]

AECPSUPC ... Association for the Encouragement of Correct Punctuation, Spelling, and Usage in Public Communications   (EA)

A Ec R .... American Ecclesiastical Review [*A publication*]

AECR......... Association des Employes du Conseil de Recherches [*Research Council Employees' Association - RCEA*] [*Canada*]

AECS .... Advanced Environmental Control System   (MCD)

AECS .... Alberta Union of Provincial Employees, Edmonton, Alberta [*Library symbol*] [*National Library of Canada*]   (NLC)

AECS .... Association of European Correspondence Schools   (EA)

AECS .... Automated Environmental Control System   (MCD)

AECS .... Aviation Electrician's Mate, Senior Chief [*Navy rating*]

AEC Symp Ser ... AEC [*US Atomic Energy Commission*] Symposium Series [*A publication*]

AECT........ Association for Educational Communications and Technology [*Washington, DC*]

AECT........ Automatic Exposure Control Technique

AECTC...... Archives of Environmental Contamination and Toxicology [*West Germany*] [*A publication*]

AEC/TIC... Atomic Energy Commission/Technical Information Center (MCD)

AECTR...... American Emergency Committee for Tibetan Refugees [*Defunct*] (EA)

AECTRC ... Advanced Environmental Control Technology Research Center [*University of Illinois*] [*Environmental Protection Agency*] [*Research center*] (RCD)

AECU .... Canadian Utilities Ltd., Edmonton, Alberta [*Library symbol*] [*National Library of Canada*] (NLC)

AED .... Academy for Educational Development (EA)

AED .... Active Electronic Decoy (CAAL)

AED .... Advanced Electronic Design

AED .... Advanced Gravis [*Vancouver Stock Exchange symbol*]

AED .... Aeromedical Education Division [*FAA*]

AED .... Aeronautical Engineering Department [*NASA*] (KSC)

AED .... Aeronautical Engineering Duty [*Navy*]

AED .... Africa Economic Digest [*A publication*]

AED .... Air Equipment Department [*British military*] (DMA)

AED .... Aircraft Explosive Device (MCD)

AED .... ALGOL Extended for Design [*1967*] [*Data processing*]

AED .... Alphanumeric Entry Device

A Ed .... American Education [*A publication*]

AED .... Ammunition Engineering Directorate [*Army*] (MCD)

AED .... Anaelectrodiabatic [*Nuclear wave*]

AED .... Analog Event Distributor [*Data processing*] (MCD)

AED .... Antiepileptic Drug

AED .... Armament Engineering Directorate [*Dover, NJ*] [*Army*] (GRD)

AED .... Artium Elegantium Doctor [*Doctor of Fine Arts*]

AED .... Associate Administrator for Engineering and Development [*FAA*] (FAAC)

A Ed .... Associate in Education

AED .... Associated Equipment Distributors (EA)

AED .... Association for Educational Development (EA)

AED .... Association of Electronic Distributors (EA)

AED .... Astro-Electronics Division [*RCA*]

AED .... Atomic Emission Detector [*Instrumentation*]

AED .... Automated Engineering Design [*Programming language*] [*1960*] [*Data processing*]

AED .... Avionics Electrical Distribution (MCD)

Aed .... De Aedificiis [*of Procopius*] [*Classical studies*] (OCD)

AED .... Edson Public Library, Alberta [*Library symbol*] [*National Library of Canada*] (NLC)

AED .... United States Army, Corps of Engineers, Office of the Chief of Engineers, Washington, DC [*OCLC symbol*] (OCLC)

AEDA .... Ammunition, Explosives, and Other Dangerous Articles

AEDAAB... Anales de Edafologia y Agrobiologia [*A publication*]

AEDB .... Apollo Engineering Documentation Board [*NASA*] (MCD)

AEDC .... American Economic Development Council (EA)

AEDC .... American Educational Computer, Inc. [*NASDAQ symbol*] (NQ)

AEDC .... Arnold Engineering Development Center [*Arnold Air Force Base, TN*]

AEDCM .... Advanced Electrochemical Depolarized Concentrator Module [*NASA*]

AEDD .... Air Engineering Development Division [*Air Force*]

AEDE .... Airplane Economic Design Evaluator [*Boeing Co.*]

AEDE .... Association Europeenne des Enseignants [*European Association of Teachers - EAT*] [*Switzerland*]

AEDEC ...... Association Europeenne d'Etudes Chinoises [*European Association of Chinese Studies - EACS*] (EAIO)

AE Del Agr Exp Stat Dept Agr Econ ... AE. Delaware Agricultural Experiment Station. Department of Agricultural Economics [*A publication*]

AEDG .... Edgerton Public Library, Alberta [*Library symbol*] [*National Library of Canada*] (NLC)

AEDH........ Association Europeenne des Directeurs d'Hopitaux [*European Association of Hospital Administrators - EAHA*] (EA)

AEDI .... Association pour l'Etude du Developpement International [*Association for the Study of International Development - ASID*] [*Canada*]

AEDM........ Edberg Municipal Library, Alberta [*Library symbol*] [*National Library of Canada*] (NLC)

AEDN........ Distribution Networks, Edmonton, Alberta [*Library symbol*] [*National Library of Canada*] (NLC)

AEDO........ Aircraft Engineering District Office

AEDP .... Aboriginal Employment Development Policy [*Australia*]

AEDP .... Advanced Electrical Development Package (MCD)

AEDP .... Association for Educational Data Processing

AEDP .... Automated External Defibrillator-Pacemaker [*Cardiology*]

AEDPS ...... Automated Engineering Document Preparation System (MCD)

AEDR .... Avionics Equipment Design Review

AED/R & S ... Associated Equipment Distributors' Research and Services Operation

AEDS........ Advanced Electric Distribution System

AEDS........ Airport Engineering Data Sheet [*FAA*] (MCD)

AEDS........ Analog Event Distribution System [*Data processing*] (MCD)

AEDS........ Association for Educational Data Systems (EA)

AEDS........ Atmospheric Electric Detection System (KSC)

AEDS........ Atomic Energy Detection System [*Nuclear energy*]

AEDS J...... AEDS [*Association for Educational Data Systems*] Journal [*A publication*]

AEDS Jrnl ... AEDS [*Association for Educational Data Systems*] Journal [*A publication*]

AEDS Mon ... AEDS [*Association for Educational Data Systems*] Monitor [*A publication*]

AEDS Monit ... AEDS [*Association for Educational Data Systems*] Monitor [*A publication*]

AEDST ...... Australian Eastern Daylight Saving Time (ADA)

AEDT .... Association Europeenne des Organisations Nationales des Commercants Detaillants en Textiles [*European Association of National Organizations of Textile Manufacturers*]

AEDT .... Australian Eastern Daylight Saving Time

AEDU .... Admiralty Experimental Diving Unit [*British*]

AEE .... Absolute Essential Equipment

AEE .... Additional Expediting Expense [*Insurance*]

AEE .... AEI [*American Enterprise Institute*] Economist [*A publication*]

AeE .... Aeronautical Engineer

AEE .... Aileen, Inc. [*NYSE symbol*] (SPSG)

AEE .... Airborne Evaluation Equipment (IEEE)

AEE .... Alberta Education, Edmonton, Alberta [*Library symbol*] [*National Library of Canada*] (NLC)

AEE .... Alliance for Environmental Education (EA)

AEE .... American-European Express [*Railway*]

AEE .... Ancient Egypt and the East [*A publication*]

AEE .... Anomalously Enriched Element [*Environmental chemistry*]

AEE .... Antlers, OK [*Location identifier*] [*FAA*] (FAAL)

AEE .... Assistant Executive Engineer [*British*] (DCTA)

AEE .... Associate in Engineering

AEE .... Association of Energy Engineers (EA)

AEE .... Association for Experiential Education (EA)

AE-E .... Atmosphere Explorer E [*Satellite*] [*NASA*]

AEE .... Atomic Energy Establishment [*British*]

AEE .... United States Army, Corps of Engineers, New England Division, Waltham, MA [*OCLC symbol*] (OCLC)

AEEA.......... Aminoethylethanolamine [*Organic chemistry*]

AEEA.......... Association Europeenne des Editeurs d'Annuaires [*European Association of Directory Publishers - EADP*] (EA)

AEEA........ City of Edmonton Archives, Alberta [*Library symbol*] [*National Library of Canada*] (NLC)

AEEAE...... Atmospheric Environment Service, Environment Canada [*Service de l'Environnement Atmospherique, Environnement Canada*] Edmonton, Alberta [*Library symbol*] [*National Library of Canada*] (NLC)

AEEC........ Airlines Electronic Engineering Committee

AEECA...... Environment Council of Alberta, Edmonton, Alberta [*Library symbol*] [*National Library of Canada*] (NLC)

AEECAM ... Anales. Estacion Experimental de Aula Dei [*Zaragoza*] [*A publication*]

AEECEEC ... Association des Etudes de l'Europe Centrale et de l'Europe de l'Est du Canada [*Central and East European Studies Association of Canada - CEESAC*]

AEECW..... Conservation and Protection-Western and Northern Region, Environment Canada [*Conservation et Protection-Region de l'Ouest et du Nord, Environnement Canada*], Edmonton, Alberta [*Library symbol*] [*National Library of Canada*] (NLC)

AEED .... Alberta Economic Development and Trade, Edmonton, Alberta [*Library symbol*] [*National Library of Canada*] (NLC)

AEED .... Association Europeenne pour l'Etude du Diabete [*European Association for the Study of Diabetes - EASD*] (EAIO)

AEEE........ Army Equipment Engineering Establishment

AEEEA...... Advances in Electrochemistry and Electrochemical Engineering [*A publication*]

AEEF........ Association Europeenne des Exploitations Frigorifiques [*European Association of Refrigeration Enterprises*] [*Common Market*] [*Belgium*]

AEEGS...... American Electroencephalographic Society (EA)

AEEI.......... Employment and Immigration Canada [*Emploi et Immigration Canada*] Edmonton, Alberta [*Library symbol*] [*National Library of Canada*] (NLC)

AEEL........ Aeronautical Engineering and Electronic Laboratory [*Johnsville, PA*] [*Navy*]

AEEL........ Arctic Environmental Engineering Laboratory [*University of Alaska*]

AEELS ...... Airborne ELINT Emitter Location System (MCD)

AEEM .... Airborne Electronic Equipment Modification

AEEM .... Northern Materials Resource Centre, Alberta Education, Edmonton, Alberta [*Library symbol*] [*National Library of Canada*] (NLC)

AEEN .... Alberta Environment, Edmonton, Alberta [*Library symbol*] [*National Library of Canada*] (NLC)

A & E Enc .. American and English Encyclopedia of Law and Practice [*A publication*] (DLA)

A & E Enc L ...   American and English Encyclopedia of Law [*A publication*]   (DLA)
A & E Enc L & Pr ...   American and English Encyclopedia of Law and Practice [*A publication*]   (DLA)
A & E Ency ...   American and English Encyclopedia of Law [*A publication*]   (DLA)
A & E Ency Law ...   American and English Encyclopedia of Law and Practice [*A publication*]   (DLA)
AEENDO ..   Agriculture, Ecosystems, and Environment [*A publication*]
AeEng ....   Aeronautical Engineer   (IEEE)
AEEP ....   Association of Environmental Engineering Professors   (EA)
AEEP ....   Association Europeenne pour l'Etude de la Population [*European Association for Population Studies - EAPS*]   (EAIO)
AEEP ....   Automotive Energy Efficiency Program [*Department of Transportation*]
AEEP ....   Edmonton Power Co., Alberta [*Library symbol*] [*National Library of Canada*]   (NLC)
AEEPCW ..   Epec Consulting Western Ltd., Edmonton, Alberta [*Library symbol*] [*National Library of Canada*]   (NLC)
AEEPM .....   Association pour l'Etude des Etats Proches de la Mort [*International Association for Near-Death Studies*]   (EAIO)
AEER ....   Adult Entered Employment Rate [*Job Training and Partnership Act*]   (OICC)
AEERB ......   Army Enlisted Education Review Board   (MCD)
AEERL ......   Air and Energy Engineering Research Laboratory [*Research Triangle Park, NC*] [*Environmental Protection Agency*]   (GRD)
AEEW ....   Atomic Energy Establishment, Winfrith [*England*]
AEF ....   Advanced Electronics Field
AEF ....   Advertising Educational Foundation   (EA)
AeF ....   Aegyptologische Forschungen [*Glueckstadt*] [*A publication*]
AEF ....   Aerospace Education Foundation   (EA)
AEF ....   Africa Evangelical Fellowship   (EA)
AEF ....   Afrique Equatoriale Francaise [*French Equatorial Africa*] [*French*]
AEF ....   After England Failed [*Soldier slang for American Expeditionary Force in World War I*]
AEF ....   Air Experience Flight [*British military*]   (DMA)
AEF ....   Airborne Equipment Failure [*Air Force*]
AEF ....   Aircraft Engineering Foundation
AEF ..   Airfields Environment Federation   (EAIO)
AEF ....   Alliance Global Environmental Fund, Inc. [*NYSE symbol*]   (SPSG)
AEF ....   Allied Expeditionary Force
AEF ....   Allogeneic Effect Factor [*Immunochemistry*]
AEF ....   Alternative Environmental Futures [*An association*]
AEF ....   American Economic Foundation   (EA)
AEF ....   American European Foundation [*Later, SFMJF*]   (EA)
AEF ....   American Euthanasia Foundation   (EA)
AEF ....   American Expeditionary Force [*World War I*]
AEF ....   Americans for Economic Freedom   (EA)
AEF ....   America's Ekiden Federation   (EA)
AEF ....   Anejos de Estudios Filologicos [*A publication*]
AEF ....   Armenian Educational Foundation   (EA)
AEF ....   Artists Equity Fund [*of the National Artists Equity Association*]   (EA)
AEF ....   Auditory-Evoked Magnetic Field [*Neurophysiology*]
AEF ....   Aviation Engineer Force
AEF ....   Centre d'Action Europeenne Federaliste [*European Center for Federalist Action*]
AEF ....   Northern Forest Research Centre, Environment Canada [*Centre de Recherches Forestieres du Nord, Environnement Canada*] Edmonton, Alberta [*Library symbol*] [*National Library of Canada*]   (NLC)
AEF ....   United States Army, Corps of Engineers, Buffalo District, Buffalo, NY [*OCLC symbol*]   (OCLC)
AEFA ....   American Education Finance Association   (EA)
AEFA ....   Army Experimental Flight Activity   (MCD)
AEFA ....   Aviation Engineering Flight Activity [*Formerly, ASTA*] [*Edwards Air Force Base, CA*] [*Army*]
AEFC ....   Alkaline Electrolyte Fuel Cell
AEFC ....   Atlantic Estuarine Fisheries Center [*National Oceanic and Atmospheric Administration*]   (MSC)
AEFDAU ...   Alabama. Agricultural Experiment Station. Auburn University. Forestry Departmental Series [*A publication*]
AEFDV ......   Acute Encephalography and Fatty Degeneration of the Viscera [*Reye's syndrome*] [*Medicine*]
AEFIA ....   Alberta Federal and Intergovernmental Affairs, Edmonton, Alberta [*Library symbol*] [*National Library of Canada*]   (NLC)
AEFLLC ....   Allied Expeditionary Force Long Lines Control [*British military*]   (DMA)
AEFM ....   Association Europeenne des Festivals de Musique [*European Association of Music Festivals - EAMF*]   (EAIO)
AEFR ....   Aurora, Elgin & Fox River Electric R. R. [*AAR code*]
AEFS ....   Antiexposure Flight Suit
AEFVAG ...   Anales de Edafologia y Fisiologia Vegetal [*A publication*]
AEG ....   Active Element Group [*QCR*]
AEG ....   Acute Erosion Gastritis [*Medicine*]

AEG ....   Ad Eundem Gradum [*To the Same Degree*] [*Latin*] [*Of the admission of a graduate of one university to the same degree at another without examination*]
AEG ....   Aegrus [*or Aegra*] [*The Patient*] [*Medicine*]
Aeg ....   Aegyptus: Rivista Italiana di Egittologia e di Papirologia [*A publication*]
AEG ....   Air Encephalogram [*Medicine*]
AEG ....   All Edges Gilt [*Bookbinding*]   (ADA)
AEG ....   Allegis Corp. [*NYSE symbol*]   (SPSG)
AEG ....   Analytic Ephemeris Generator
AEG ....   Applied Energy, Inc. [*Vancouver Stock Exchange symbol*]
AEG ....   Association of Engineering Geologists   (EA)
AEG ....   Association of Esperantist Greens   (EAIO)
AEG ....   Association of Exploration Geochemists [*ICSU*]   (EAIO)
AEG ....   Atlantic Environmental Group [*National Marine Fisheries Service*]
AEG ....   Atrialelectrogram [*Cardiology*]
AEG ....   Australian Estate and Gift Duty Reporter [*A publication*]   (APTA)
AEG ....   Aviation Evaluation Group   (FAAC)
AEG ....   [*The*] Egyptian Era [*Beginning 747BC*]   (ROG)
AEG ....   Staff Library, Glenrose Provincial General Hospital, Edmonton, Alberta [*Library symbol*] [*National Library of Canada*]   (NLC)
AEG ....   United States Army, Corps of Engineers, Detroit District, Detroit, MI [*OCLC symbol*]   (OCLC)
Aeg Christ ...   Aegyptica Christiana [*A publication*]
Aegean Earth Sci ...   Aegean Earth Sciences [*A publication*]
Aeg Forsch ...   Aegyptologische Forschungen [*A publication*]
AEGH ....   Edmonton General Hospital, Alberta [*Library symbol*] [*National Library of Canada*]   (NLC)
AEGIS ....   Active Electronic Gimballess Inertial System
AEGIS ....   Agricultural, Ecological, and Geographical Information System
AEGIS ......   Aid for the Elderly in Government Institutions [*British*]
AEGIS ....   Airborne Early Warning/Ground Integration Segment
AEGIS ....   [*An*] Existing Generalized Information System [*Data processing*]
AEG Kernreakt ...   AEG [*Allgemeine Elektrizitaets-Gesellschaft*] Kernreaktoren [*A publication*]
AEGM ....   Association of Electronic Guard Manufacturers [*British*]
AEGMCR ...   Grant MacEwan Cromdale Campus LRC, Edmonton, Alberta [*Library symbol*] [*National Library of Canada*]   (NLC)
AEGMJP ..   Grant MacEwan Jasper Place Campus LRC, Edmonton, Alberta [*Library symbol*] [*National Library of Canada*]   (NLC)
AEGMMW ...   Grant MacEwan Mill Woods Campus LRC, Edmonton, Alberta [*Library symbol*] [*National Library of Canada*]   (NLC)
AEGMSS ..   Grant MacEwan Seventh Street Plaza Campus, Edmonton, Alberta [*Library symbol*] [*National Library of Canada*]   (NLC)
AEGN ....   AEGON NV [*Mariahoeveplein, Netherlands*] [*NASDAQ symbol*]   (NQ)
AEGp ....   Aeromedical Evacuation Group [*Air Force*]   (AFM)
AEGPL ......   Association Europeenne des Gaz de Petrole Liquefies [*European Liquefied Petroleum Gas Association - ELPGA*]   (EAIO)
AEG Prog ..   AEG [*Allgemeine Elektrizitaets-Gesellschaft*] Progress [*West Germany*] [*A publication*]
AEGR ....   Australian Estate and Gift Duty Reporter [*A publication*]   (APTA)
AEGRAFLEX ...   Association Europeenne des Graveurs et des Flexographes [*European Association of Engravers and Flexographers*]   (EAIO)
AEG S ....   Aegean Sea
AEGS ....   Alberta Public Works, Supply and Services, Edmonton, Alberta [*Library symbol*] [*National Library of Canada*]   (NLC)
AEGSA ......   Good Samaritan Auxiliary Hospital, Edmonton, Alberta [*Library symbol*] [*National Library of Canada*]   (NLC)
AEGT ....   Alberta Government Telephones, Edmonton, Alberta [*Library symbol*] [*National Library of Canada*]   (NLC)
AEGTCC J ...   Association of Educators of Gifted, Talented, and Creative Children in British Columbia. Journal [*A publication*]
AEG Telefunken Prog ...   AEG [*Allgemeine Elektrizitaets-Gesellschaft*] - Telefunken Progress [*A publication*]
AEG-Telefunken Progr ...   AEG [*Allgemeine Elektrizitaets-Gesellschaft*] - Telefunken Progress [*A publication*]
AEGTS ......   Annulus Exhaust Gas Treatment System [*Nuclear energy*]   (NRCH)
AEH ....   Academie Europeenne d'Histoire [*European Academy of History - EAH*]   (EAIO)
AEH ....   Acta Ethnographica. Academiae Scientiarum Hungaricae [*A publication*]
AEH ....   Anhydroenneaheptol [*Organic chemistry*]
AEH ....   Antenna Effective Height
AEH ....   United States Army, Corps of Engineers, Huntington District, Huntington, WV [*OCLC symbol*]   (OCLC)
AEHA ....   Anuario Espanol e Hispano-Americano [*A publication*]
AEHA ....   Army Environmental Health Agency
AEHA ....   Army Environmental Hygiene Agency
AEHA ....   Hardy Associates Ltd., Edmonton, Alberta [*Library symbol*] [*National Library of Canada*]   (NLC)
AEHC ....   Assembly of Episcopal Hospitals and Chaplains   (EA)

AEHC........ Housing Library, Alberta Housing and Public Works, Edmonton, Alberta [*Library symbol*] [*National Library of Canada*] (NLC)

AEHCI ...... Health Care Insurance Commission, Edmonton, Alberta [*Library symbol*] [*National Library of Canada*] (NLC)

AEHE........ Library Services Branch, Alberta Department of Health, Edmonton, Alberta [*Library symbol*] [*National Library of Canada*] (BIB)

AEHEG ..... Annales. Ecole des Hautes-Etudes de Gand [*A publication*]

AEHF .... Association for Employee Health and Fitness (EA)

AEHH .... Handicapped Housing Society of Alberta, Edmonton, Alberta [*Library symbol*] [*National Library of Canada*] (NLC)

AEHHC..... Association of Educators of Homebound and Hospitalized Children [*Later, DPH*] (EA)

AEHL .... Army Environmental Health Laboratory

AEHLA ..... Archives of Environmental Health [*A publication*]

AEHO........ Alberta Hospital Library, Oliver, Alberta [*Library symbol*] [*National Library of Canada*] (NLC)

AEHP .... Atmospheric Electricity Hazards Protection

AEHR .... Australian Economic History Review [*A publication*]

AEHRC ..... Association Executives Human Rights Caucus (EA)

Aehrodin Razrezh Gazov ... Aehrodinamika Razrezhennykh Gazov [*A publication*]

AEHSC...... Alberta Hospitals & Medical Care, Edmonton, Alberta [*Library symbol*] [*National Library of Canada*] (NLC)

AEHSD ..... Alberta Social Services and Community Health, Edmonton, Alberta [*Library symbol*] [*National Library of Canada*] (NLC)

AEHT .... Alberta Transportation, Edmonton, Alberta [*Library symbol*] [*National Library of Canada*] (NLC)

AEI .... Acclimatization Experiences Institute [*Later, IEE*] (EA)

AEI .... Acrylic Eye Illustrator [*Medicine*]

AEI .... Aerial Exposure Index

AEI .... Aerospace Education Instructor (AFM)

AEI .... Air Express International Corp.

AEI .... Albert Einstein Institution (EA)

AEI .... Allow Enable Intercept [*Military*] (CAAL)

AEI .... Alternate Energy Institute (EA)

AEI .... American Enterprise Institute for Public Policy Research (EA)

AEI .... Annual Efficiency Index [*Army*]

AEI .... Armor Enhancement Initiative [*Army*]

AEI .... Associated Electrical Industries [*British*]

AEI .... Associated Enterprises, Inc. (TSSD)

AEI .... Association des Ecoles Internationales

AEI .... Association of Escort/Interpreters (EA)

AEI .... Audio End Instrument (MCD)

AEI .... Australian Education Index [*Australian Council for Educational Research*] [*Information service or system*] [*A publication*] (IID)

AEI .... Auto Enthusiasts International [*Defunct*] (EA)

AEI .... Average Efficiency Index

AEI .... Azimuth Error Indicator

AEI .... United States Army, Corps of Engineers, Mobile District, Mobile, AL [*OCLC symbol*] (OCLC)

AEIA........ American Excess Insurance Association [*East Hartford, CT*] (EA)

AEIAF ...... Albert Einstein International Academy Foundation (EA)

AEI (Am Enterprise Inst) For Policy and Defense R ... AEI (American Enterprise Institute) Foreign Policy and Defense Review [*A publication*]

AEIAR...... Association Europeenne des Institutions d'Amenagement Rural [*European Association of Country Planning Institutions*] (EAIO)

AEIB........ Activation Engineering Information Bulletin (AAG)

AEIB........ Association for Education in International Business [*Later, AIB*] (EA)

AEIC........ Advanced Earned Income Credit [*IRS*]

AEIC........ Alberta Tourism and Small Business, Edmonton, Alberta [*Library symbol*] [*National Library of Canada*] (NLC)

AEIC........ Association of Edison Illuminating Companies (EA)

AEICA8..... Contributions. American Entomological Institute [*Ann Arbor*] [*A publication*]

AEICP ...... Association of Entertainment Industry Computer Professionals (EA)

AEIDC...... Arctic Environmental Information and Data Center [*University of Alaska, Fairbanks*] [*Research center*] (IID)

AEIE......... Agence d'Examen de l'Investissement Etranger [*Foreign Investment Review Agency - FIRA*] [*Canada*]

AEI Econom ... AEI [*American Enterprise Institute*] Economist [*A publication*]

AEI Eng..... AEI [*Associated Electrical Industries*] Engineering [*England*] [*A publication*]

AEI Eng Rev ... AEI [*Associated Electrical Industries*] Engineering Review [*A publication*]

AEIH .... Association Europeenne des Industries de l'Habillement [*European Association of Clothing Industries*] (EA)

AEIL.......... American Export Isbrandtsen Lines [*Later, American Export Industries Co.*]

AEIM .... Association of Evangelicals for Italian Missions (EA)

AEIMS ...... Administrative Engineering Information Management System

AEINE....... Engineering and Architecture, Indian and Northern Affairs Canada [*Genie et Architecture, Affaires Indiennes et du Nord Canada*], Edmonton, Alberta [*Library symbol*] [*National Library of Canada*] (BIB)

AE Inform Ser Univ NC State Coll Agr Eng Dept Agr Econ ... AE Information Series. University of North Carolina. State College of Agriculture and Engineering. Department of Agricultural Economics [*A publication*]

AEIOU ...... Albertus Electus Imperator Optimus Vivat [*Inscription used by Albert II, 15th-century German king*]

AEIOU ...... Aller Ehren Ist Oesterreich Voll [*Austria Is Crowned with All Honor*] [*Variation of 15th-century inscription*]

AEIOU ...... Aller Erst Ist Oesterreich Verdorben [*Variation of 15th-century inscription*]

AEIOU ...... Alles Erdreich Ist Oesterreich Unterthan [*Variation of 15th-century inscription*]

AEIOU ...... Austria Erit In Orbe Ultima [*Austria Will Be The Last in the World*] [*Variation of 15th-century inscription*]

AEIOU .... Austriae Est Imperare Orbi Universo [*It Is Given to Austria to Rule the Whole World*] [*Variation of 15th-century inscription*]

AEIOU ...... Austria's Empire Is Obviously Upset [*Variation of 15th-century inscription*]

AEIOU ...... Austria's Empire Is Overall Universal [*Variation of 15th-century inscription*]

AEIPPR...... American Enterprise Institute for Public Policy Research (EA)

AEIROF .... Anodically Electrodeposited Iridium Oxide Film [*Electrochemistry*]

AEIS .... Associate of the Educational Institute of Scotland

AEISDP...... Aerofizicheskie Issledovaniya [*A publication*]

AEJ............ Adult Education Journal [*A publication*]

AEJ............ Aluminum Extension Jacket

AEJ............ Association for Education in Journalism [*Later, AEJMC*] (EA)

AEJ............ Atlantic Economic Journal [*A publication*]

AEJ............ Canada Department of Justice [*Ministere de la Justice*] Edmonton, Alberta [*Library symbol*] [*National Library of Canada*] (NLC)

AEJGAE ... John Graham Architect Engineer Ltd., Edmonton, Alberta [*Library symbol*] [*National Library of Canada*] (NLC)

AEJI .... Association of European Jute Industries

AEJ/JQ..... Journalism Quarterly. Association for Education in Journalism [*A publication*]

AEJMC ..... Association for Education in Journalism and Mass Communication (EA)

AEJR .... Adult Education Journal Review [*A publication*] (ADA)

AEJUAX ... Aerztliche Jugendkunde [*A publication*]

AEK .... Aircraft Ejection Kit

AEK .... Aseki [*Papua New Guinea*] [*Airport symbol*] [*Obsolete*] (OAG)

AEK .... United States Army, Corps of Engineers, Rock Island District, Rock Island, IL [*OCLC symbol*] (OCLC)

AEKC........ [*The*] King's College, Edmonton, Alberta [*Library symbol*] [*National Library of Canada*] (NLC)

AEKG .... Archiv fuer Elsaessische Kirchengeschichte [*A publication*]

AEL .... Acceptor Energy Level

AEL .... Acta Ethnologica et Linguistica [*A publication*]

AEL .... Actuarial Engine Life (AFIT)

AEL .... Acute Erythroleukemia [*Oncology*]

AEL .... Admiralty Engineering Laboratory [*British*] (MCD)

AEL .... Advanced Engineering Laboratory [*Australia*]

Ael............. Aelianus [*c. 170-235AD*] [*Classical studies*] (OCD)

AEL .... Aerobiology and Evaluation Laboratory [*Army*] (KSC)

AEL .... Aeronautical Engine Laboratory [*Later, NAPC*] [*Navy*]

AEL .... Aeronautical Engineering Laboratory [*NASA*] (KSC)

AEL .... Aerospace Electronics Laboratories (MCD)

AEL .... Aircraft Engine Laboratory

AEL .... Aircraft Equipment List (MCD)

AEL .... Albert Lea, MN [*Location identifier*] [*FAA*] (FAAL)

AEL .... Alberta Environment Library [*UTLAS symbol*]

AEL .... Allowance Equipage List

AEL .... Aluminum Electrical Lead

AEL .... American Emigrants' League (EA)

AEL .... Americanism Educational League [*Buena Park, CA*] (EA)

AEL .... Ameritel Management, Inc. [*Vancouver Stock Exchange symbol*]

AEL .... Animal Educational League [*Defunct*]

AEL .... Appalachia Educational Laboratory [*Department of Education*] [*Charleston, WV*]

AEL .... Appalachian Environmental Laboratory [*University of Maryland Center for Environmental and Estuarine Studies*] [*Research center*] (RCD)

AEL .... Armament and Electronics Laboratory

AEL .... Army Electronics Laboratories (KSC)

AEL .... Association of Equipment Lessors [*Later, AAEL*]

AEL .... Association Europeenne du Laser [*European Laser Association - ELA*] (EA)

AEL .... Atomic Energy Level

AEL .... Atomic Energy Levels and Grotrian Diagrams [*Elsevier Book Series*] [*A publication*]

AEL .... Audit Entry Language [*Burroughs Corp.*]

AEL .... Audit Error List

AEL .... Australian Employment Legislation [*A publication*]

AEL .... Authorized Equipment Listing (AABC)

AEL .... Automation Engineering Laboratory

AEL .... Luscar Ltd., Edmonton, Alberta [*Library symbol*] [*National Library of Canada*] (NLC)

AEL .... United States Army, Corps of Engineers, Louisville District, Louisville, KY [*OCLC symbol*] (OCLC)

AELA........ Australian Equipment Lessors Association

AELAAH .. Aerztliche Laboratorium [*A publication*]

AELC........ Aerospace Engine Life Committee [*Air Force*] (AFIT)

AELC........ Architect-Engineers Liaison Commission

AELC........ Association of Evangelical Lutheran Churches

AELD .... Ascent Engine Latching Device [*NASA*] (KSC)

AELDC..... Atomic Energy Levels Data Center

AELE .... Americans for Effective Law Enforcement (EA)

AELE........ Association Europeenne de Libre-Echange [*European Free Trade Association - EFTA*] [*Geneva, Switzerland*]

A Electr .... Acta Electronica [*A publication*]

A El Ed .... Associate in Elementary Education

Aelf C .... Canons of Aelfric [*A publication*] (DLA)

AELIA .... Association d'Etudes Linguistiques Interculturelles Africaines [*Canada*]

AELJ .... Atomic Energy Law Journal [*A publication*] (DLA)

AELK........ Allgemeine Evangelisch-Lutherische Kirchenzeitung [*Luthardt*] [*A publication*]

AELK........ Elk Point Public Library, Alberta [*Library symbol*] [*National Library of Canada*] (NLC)

AELKZ...... Allgemeine Evangelisch-Lutherische Kirchenzeitung [*Luthardt*] [*A publication*]

AELL........ Province of Alberta Law Library System, Edmonton, Alberta [*Library symbol*] [*National Library of Canada*] (NLC)

AELMRP .. Atomic Energy Labor Management Relations Panel

AELMS ..... Elmworth School, Alberta [*Library symbol*] [*National Library of Canada*] (BIB)

AELN .... AEL Industries, Inc. [*NASDAQ symbol*] (NQ)

AELN .... Australian Environmental Law News [*A publication*]

AELN .... Local Networks, Edmonton, Alberta [*Library symbol*] [*National Library of Canada*] (NLC)

AELNO ..... Elnora Public Library, Alberta [*Library symbol*] [*National Library of Canada*] (NLC)

AELO .... Aeromedical Evacuation Liaison Officer [*Air Force*] (AFM)

AElP .... Allied Electrical Publications (NATG)

AELR........ All England Law Reports [*A publication*]

AELRAY ... Advances in Ecological Research [*A publication*]

AELRO ...... Army Electronics Logistics Research Office (KSC)

AELS .... Airborne Electronic LASER System

AELT .... Association Europeenne de Laboratoires de Teledetection [*European Association of Remote Sensing Laboratories - EARSEL*] (EA)

AELTC ...... All England Lawn Tennis Club

AEM .... Accelerated Evaluation Method

AEM .... Acoustical Emission Monitoring (NASA)

AEM .... Advance Engineering Memorandum

Aem........... Aemilius Paulus [*of Plutarch*] [*Classical studies*] (OCD)

AEM .... Aeronautical Mobile

AEM .... Air Efficiency Medal [*RAF*] [*British*]

AEM .... Aircraft and Engine Mechanic

AEM .... American Energy Month (EA)

AEM .... Analytical Electron Microscopy

AEM .... Anuario de Estudios Medievales [*A publication*]

AE & M .... Apostle, Evangelist, and Martyr [*Church calendars*] (ROG)

AEM .... Application Explorer Mission [*NASA*]

AEM .... Arabian Exhibition Management WLL [*Manama, Bahrain*] (TSSD)

AEM .... Archaeologisch-Epigraphische Mitteilungen aus Oesterreich [*Ungarn*] [*A publication*]

AEM .... Archeion Euboikon Meleton [*A publication*]

AEM .... Architect-Engineer-Manager [*Plan*]

AEM .... Arsenal Exchange Model (MCD)

AEM .... Association of Electronic Manufacturers [*Later, EIA*] (EA)

AEM .... Association Europeenne du Moulinage [*European Throwsters Association - ETA*] (EA)

AEM .... Attack Evaluation Model (MCD)

AEM .... Augmented Energy Management (MCD)

AEM .... Australian Employment Law Guide [*A publication*]

AEM .... Automatic Environment Monitoring (BUR)

AEM .... Automobile Engineering and Manufacturing [*Commercial firm*] [*British*]

AEM .... Aviation Electrician's Mate [*Navy rating*]

AEM .... Empress Municipal Library, Alberta [*Library symbol*] [*National Library of Canada*] (NLC)

AEM .... Missile Support Ship (NATG)

AEM .... United States Army, Corps of Engineers, Lower Mississippi Valley Division, Vicksburg, MS [*OCLC symbol*] (OCLC)

AEMA .... Alberta Municipal Affairs, Edmonton, Alberta [*Library symbol*] [*National Library of Canada*] (NLC)

AEMA .... Asphalt Emulsion Manufacturers Association (EA)

AEMA .... Athletic Equipment Managers Association (EA)

AEMAN ... Alberta Manpower, Edmonton, Alberta [*Library symbol*] [*National Library of Canada*] (NLC)

AEMB .... Alliance for Engineering in Medicine and Biology (EA)

AEMB .... Association Europeenne des Marches aux Bestiaux [*European Association of Livestock Markets - EALM*] [*Brussels, Belgium*] (EAIO)

AEMB .... Multilingual Biblioservice, Edmonton, Alberta [*Library symbol*] [*National Library of Canada*] (NLC)

AEMBA..... Advances in Experimental Medicine and Biology [*A publication*]

AEMBB.... Bulletin. Association des Anciens Eleves de l'Ecole Francaise de Meunerie [*A publication*]

A Embr Morph Exp ... Acta Embryologiae et Morphologiae Experimentalis [*A publication*]

AEMC .... Acryloyloxyethyl N-Methylcarbamate [*Organic chemistry*]

AEMC .... Albert Einstein Medical Center

AEMC .... American Electro Metal Corporation

AEMC .... Auger and Elevator Manufacturers Council (EA)

AEMCC.... Air and Expedited Motor Carriers Conference (EA)

AEMCO .... Aircraft Engineering Maintenance Company

AEME .... Association pour l'Enseignement Medical en Europe [*Association for Medical Education in Europe - AMEE*] (EA)

AEME .... Association of International Marketing (EAIO)

AEME .... Australian Electrical and Mechanical Engineers

AEMEA..... Aerospace Medicine [*A publication*]

AEMEAY .. Aerospace Medicine [*A publication*]

AEM-ED ... Association of Electronic Manufacturers, Eastern Division (EA)

AEMED3 .. Annals of Emergency Medicine [*A publication*]

AEMERO ... African, Eastern Mediterranean, and European Regional Office [*UNICEF*] (DS)

AEMH....... Misericordia Hospital, Edmonton, Alberta [*Library symbol*] [*National Library of Canada*] (NLC)

AEMHSM ... Association Europeenne des Musees de l'Histoire des Sciences Medicales [*European Association of Museums of the History of Medical Sciences - EAMHMS*] (EAIO)

AE Mich State Univ Agr Appl Sci Ext Div Agr Econ Dept ... AE. Michigan State University of Agriculture and Applied Science. Extension Division. Agricultural Economics Department [*A publication*]

Aemil Ferret ... Aemilius Ferretus [*Deceased, 1552*] [*Authority cited in pre-1607 legal work*] (DSA)

Aemil Pap .. Aemilius Papinianus [*Deceased, 212*] [*Authority cited in pre-1607 legal work*] (DSA)

AEMIS ...... Aerospace and Environmental Medicine Information System (IID)

AEML....... Alberta Labour, Edmonton, Alberta [*Library symbol*] [*National Library of Canada*] (NLC)

AEMMBP ... Annales d'Embryologie et de Morphogenese [*A publication*]

AEMO .... Advance Engineering Material Order

AEMO....... African Elected Members Organization

AEMP........ Atmospheric Electromagnetic Pulse

AEMR .... Myrias Research Corp., Edmonton, Alberta [*Library symbol*] [*National Library of Canada*] (NLC)

AEMS........ Agro-Environmental Monitoring System [*Computerized Data Collection*]

AEMS........ Aircraft Engine Management System (MCD)

AEMS........ American Engineering Model Society (EA)

AEMS........ Aminoethyl(methyl)sulfone [*Biochemistry*]

AEMS........ Automated Edge Match System (MCD)

AEMS........ Automated Electrophoresis Microscope System (MCD)

AEMS........ Milner & Steer, Edmonton, Alberta [*Library symbol*] [*National Library of Canada*] (BIB)

AEMSA..... Army Electronics Material Support Agency

AEMSAT .. Association of European Manufacturers of Self-Adhesive Tapes (EA)

AEMSM.... Association of European Metal Sink Manufacturers (EAIO)

A & EMSq .. Armament and Electronic Maintenance Squadron [*Air Force*]

AEMT .... Association of Electrical Machinery Trades (EAIO)

AEMT .... Automated Electronic Maintenance Training (MCD)

AEMT .... Automatically Erectable Modular Torus

AEMT .... Regional Library, Transport Canada [*Bibliotheque Regionale de Transports Canada*] Edmonton, Alberta [*Library symbol*] [*National Library of Canada*] (NLC)

AEMTC..... Western Region, Engineering and Architecture Library, Transport Canada [*Region de l'Ouest, Bibliotheque d'Ingenierie et d'Architecture, Transports Canada*], Edmonton, Alberta [*Library symbol*] [*National Library of Canada*] (NLC)

AEMTCA ... Civil Aviation Branch, Canadian Air Transportation Administration, Transport Canada [*Direction Generale de l'Aviation Civile, Administration Canadienne des Transports Aeriens, Transports Canada*] Edmonton, Alberta [*Library symbol*] [*National Library of Canada*] (NLC)

AEMTM ... Association of European Machine Tool Merchants [*Berkhamsted, Hertfordshire, England*] (EAIO)

AEMXA .... Acta Embryologiae et Morphologiae Experimentalis [*A publication*]

AEN........... Adaption Error Note

AEN........... Address Enable [*Data processing*]

AEN........... Advance Evaluation Note

Aen:........... Aeneid [*of Vergil*] [*Classical studies*] (OCD)

AEN .... Agence de l'OCDE pour l'Energie Nucleaire [*OECD Nuclear Energy Agency - NEA*] (EAIO)
AEN .... Alberta Environmental Centre Library [*UTLAS symbol*]
AEN .... AMC Entertainment, Inc. [*AMEX symbol*] (SPSG)
AEN .... Annales de l'Est et du Nord [*A publication*]
A En .... Associate in English
AEN .... Association of Educational Negotiators [*Later, NAEN*] (EA)
AEN .... Enchant Public Library, Alberta [*Library symbol*] [*National Library of Canada*] (NLC)
AEN .... United States Army, Corps of Engineers, New Orleans District, New Orleans, LA [*OCLC symbol*] (OCLC)
AENA .... All England Netball Association (EAIO)
AENA .... American Ephemeris and Nautical Almanac [*A publication*]
AENA .... Northern Alberta Institute of Technology, Edmonton, Alberta [*Library symbol*] [*National Library of Canada*] (NLC)
AENABC... North American Baptist College and Divinity School, Edmonton, Alberta [*Library symbol*] [*National Library of Canada*] (NLC)
AENAC ..... Nova, an Alberta Corporation, Edmonton, Alberta [*Library symbol*] [*National Library of Canada*] (BIB)
AENBAU .. Anales. Escuela Nacional de Ciencias Biologicas [*Mexico*] [*A publication*]
AENC .... Avian Embryo Nutrient Cartridge
AENDA2... Annee Endocrinologique [*A publication*]
AEN Dep Agric Eng Univ KY ... AEN. Department of Agricultural Engineering. University of Kentucky [*A publication*]
A End Gyn ... Acta Endocrinologica et Gynaecologica Hispanolusitana [*A publication*]
A End Ib..... Acta Endocrinologica Iberica [*A publication*]
A Energy O ... Annual Energy Outlook [*A publication*]
A Energy R ... Annual Energy Review [*A publication*]
AENF .... Annales Entomologici Fennici [*A publication*]
AENF .... Network Facilities-Development, Edmonton, Alberta [*Library symbol*] [*National Library of Canada*] (NLC)
AENG .... Airways Engineer
A Eng .... Associate in Engineering
A Eng Elect ... Associate in Engineering Electronics
A Engr .... Associate in Engineering
AENI .... Technical Data Control Centre, Edmonton, Alberta [*Library symbol*] [*National Library of Canada*] (NLC)
AENORS... Anticipated Engine Not Operationally Ready Supply [*Military*] (AFIT)
AENR .... Alberta Energy and Natural Resources, Edmonton, Alberta [*Library symbol*] [*National Library of Canada*] (NLC)
A & E (NS) ... Adolphus and Ellis' English Queen's Bench Reports, New Series [*A publication*] (DLA)
AENT .... Entwistle Public Library, Alberta [*Library symbol*] [*National Library of Canada*] (NLC)
AEO .... Acoustoelectric Oscillator (IEEE)
AEO .... Advance Engineering Order
AEO .... Aioun El Atrouss [*Mauritania*] [*Airport symbol*] (OAG)
AEO .... Air Electronics Officer [*British*]
AEO .... Air Engineer Officer
AEO .... All Engines Operating [*Aviation*]
AEO .... American Eagle Petroleums Corp. [*Toronto Stock Exchange symbol*]
AEO .... Ammunition Executive Office [*Military*] [*British*]
AEO .... Appeals Examining Office [*CSC*]
AEO .... Area Education Officer [*Military*] [*British*]
AEO .... Area Engineering Officer [*Army Corps of Engineers*] (AAG)
AEO .... Army Energy Office
AEO .... Assistant Experimental Officer [*Ministry of Agriculture, Fisheries, and Food*] [*Also, AExO, AXO*] [*British*]
AEO .... Association of Education Officers [*British*]
AEO .... ATM [*Apollo Telescope Mount*] Experiments Officer [*NASA*]
AEO .... Author Earn-Out [*Publishing*]
AEO .... Oblate Archives of Alberta-Saskatchewan, Edmonton, Alberta [*Library symbol*] [*National Library of Canada*] (NLC)
AEO .... United States Army, Corps of Engineers, Ohio River District, Cincinnati, OH [*OCLC symbol*] (OCLC)
AEOA .... Annales de l'Extreme Orient et de l'Afrique [*A publication*]
AEOB .... Advanced Engine Overhaul Base
AEOC .... Aquatic Ecosystem Objectives Committee [*Great Lakes Science Advisory Board*] [*Canada*]
AEOD........ Office for Analysis and Evaluation of Operational Data [*Nuclear Regulatory Commission*]
AEODA7... Anales Espanoles de Odontoestomatologia [*A publication*]
AEODP ..... Allied Explosive Ordnance Disposal Publication (MCD)
AEOE .... Association for Environmental and Outdoor Education (EA)
AEOG .... Air Ejection Off Gas (IEEE)
AEOH........ Alberta Occupation Health and Safety, Edmonton, Alberta [*Library symbol*] [*National Library of Canada*] (NLC)
AEOK .... Alexander Energy Corp. [*NASDAQ symbol*] (NQ)
AEOM .... Alberta Office of the Ombudsman, Edmonton, Alberta [*Library symbol*] [*National Library of Canada*] (NLC)
AEOO........ Aeromedical Evacuation Operations Office [*or Officer*] [*Military*] (MCD)
AEoP.......... Allied Ordnance Disposal Publications (NATG)
AEOP .... Amend Existing Orders Pertaining To
AEOP .... Australian and New Zealand Equal Opportunity Law and Practice [*A publication*]

AEOS .... After Engineering Operating Station (CAAL)
AEOS .... Ancient Egyptian Order of Sciots (EA)
AEOSS ...... Advanced Electro-Optical Sensor Simulation
AEOTD ..... Advances in Earth-Oriented Applications of Space Technology [*Later, Earth-Oriented Applications of Space Technology*] [*A publication*]
AEOTR ..... Advanced Electro-Optical Tracker/Ranger (MCD)
AEOW....... Air Engineer Officer's Writer [*British military*] (DMA)
AEP .... A. E. Lepage Capital Prop. [*Limited Partnership Units*] [*Toronto Stock Exchange symbol*]
AEP .... Abstract Enterprise [*Vancouver Stock Exchange symbol*]
AEP .... Accrued Expenditure Paid [*Accounting*] (AFM)
AEP .... Acoustic Evoked Potential [*Physiology*]
AEP .... Adaptive Escalator Predictor (MCD)
AEP .... Adult Education Program
AEP .... Advanced Energy Projects [*Department of Energy*]
AEP .... Aggregate Exercise Price [*Investment term*]
AEP .... Air Evacuation Patients (AFIT)
AEP .... Aircraft Equipment Procedures (MCD)
AEP .... Akathariston Engkhorion Proion [*Gross National Product*] [*Greek*]
AEP .... Alberta Legislature Library, Edmonton, Alberta [*Library symbol*] [*National Library of Canada*] (NLC)
AEP .... Allied Engineering Publications (NATG)
AEP .... Allied Equipment Publications
AEP .... Alternative Education Project (EA)
AE & P....... Ambassador Extraordinary and Plenipotentiary [*Diplomacy*]
AEP .... American Electric Power Co., Inc. [*Group of investor-owned public utility companies*] [*NYSE symbol*]
AEP .... Aminoethylphosphonic Acid [*Organic chemistry*]
AEP .... Aminoethylpiperazine [*Organic chemistry*]
AeP .... Anima e Pensiero [*A publication*]
AEP .... Annual Engineering Plan (AFIT)
AEP .... Annual Execution Plan (RDA)
AEP .... Anterior Extreme Position [*Medicine*]
AEP .... Apollo Experiment Pallet [*NASA*]
AEP .... Apollo Extension Program [*NASA*]
AEP .... Aqueous Extraction Process
AEP .... Army Equipment Policy [*British military*] (DMA)
AEP .... Artificial Endocrine Pancreas [*Medicine*]
AEP .... Association d'Economie Politique [*Political Economic Association*] [*Canada*]
AEP .... Association of Educational Psychologists [*British*]
AEP .... Atomic Energy Project
AEP .... Auditory-Evoked Potential [*Neurophysiology*]
AEP .... Australian Economic Papers [*A publication*]
AEP .... AUTODIN Enhancement Program [*Data processing*] (MCD)
AEP .... Automated Environmental Prediction (CAAL)
AEP .... Automatic End Point
AEP .... Automatic Extracting Program
AEP .... Average Evoked Potential [*Neurophysiology*]
AEP .... Buenos Aires [*Argentina*] Jorge Newbery Airport [*Airport symbol*] (OAG)
AEP .... United States Army, Corps of Engineers, Memphis District, Memphis, TN [*OCLC symbol*] (OCLC)
AEPA......... Bibliography Section, Alberta Public Affairs Bureau, Edmonton, Alberta [*Library symbol*] [*National Library of Canada*] (NLC)
AEPAA...... Provincial Archives of Alberta, Edmonton, Alberta [*Library symbol*] [*National Library of Canada*] (NLC)
AE Pap Okla State Univ Coop Ext Serv ... AE Paper. Oklahoma State University. Cooperative Extension Service [*A publication*]
A & E Pat Cas ... American and English Patent Cases [*A publication*] (DLA)
AEPB......... Active Enlisted Plans Branch [*BUPERS*]
AEPC......... Alberta Provincial Courts, Edmonton, Alberta [*Library symbol*] [*National Library of Canada*] (NLC)
AEPC......... Army Equipment Policy Committee (AAG)
AEPCF ...... Premier's Commission on Future Health Care for Albertans, Edmonton, Alberta [*Library symbol*] [*National Library of Canada*] (BIB)
AEPD .... Amino(ethyl)propanediol [*Organic chemistry*]
AEPDS...... Automated EAM Processing and Dissemination System (MCD)
AEPE .... Association pour l'Etude des Problemes de l'Europe [*Association for the Study of European Problems*]
AEPEM..... Association of Electronic Parts and Equipment Manufacturers [*Later, EIA*]
AEPFC ..... Associates of Elvis Presley Fan Clubs (EA)
AEPG........ Army Electronic Proving Ground
AEPHAO .. Annales des Epiphyties et de Phytogenetique [*A publication*]
AEPI........ AEP Industries, Inc. [*Moonachie, NJ*] [*NASDAQ symbol*] (NQ)
AEPI......... Aerospace Engineering Process Institute
AEPI......... American Educational Publishers Institute [*Later, AAP*]
AEPI......... Atmospheric Emissions Photometric Imaging [*Plasma physics*]
AEPIAR ... Annales des Epiphyties [*Paris*] [*A publication*]
AEPIC .... Architecture and Engineering Performance Information Center [*University of Maryland*] [*College Park*] [*Information service or system*] (IID)
AEpigr .... Annee Epigraphique [*A publication*]

AEPJ .... Association of Educational Psychologists. Journal [*A publication*]
AEPL......... Approved Equivalent Parts List
AEPL......... Professional Library, Edmonton Catholic School District, Edmonton, Alberta [*Library symbol*] [*National Library of Canada*]   (NLC)
AEPM....... Association of Evangelical Professors of Missions   (EA)
A & EP & P ... American and English Pleading and Practice [*A publication*]   (DLA)
AEPP......... Association of Existential Psychology and Psychiatry   (EA)
AEPP......... Southeast/East Asian English Publications in Print [*Japan Publications Guide Service*] [*Japan*] [*Information service or system*]   (CRD)
AEPPF....... Albert Einstein Peace Prize Foundation   (EA)
A & EP & Pr ... American and English Pleading and Practice [*A publication*]   (DLA)
AEPR......... Resource Center, City of Edmonton Personnel Department, Alberta [*Library symbol*] [*National Library of Canada*]   (NLC)
AEPRD...... Planning, Research and Development Division, Alberta Attorney General, Edmonton, Alberta [*Library symbol*] [*National Library of Canada*]   (NLC)
AEPRT ...... All Equipment Production Reliability Tests   (MCD)
AEPS......... Advanced Extravehicular Protective System [*NASA*]
AEPS......... Aircraft Electrical Power System
AEPS......... Aircrew Escape Propulsion System [*Navy*]
AEPS......... Alfred E. Packer Society   (EA)
AEPS......... Asphalt Employees Protection Society [*A union*] [*British*]
AEPS......... ATM [*Apollo Telescope Mount*] Electrical Power System [*NASA*]
AEPS......... Automated Environmental Prediction System   (MCD)
AEPU .... Alberta Public Utilities Board, Edmonton, Alberta [*Library symbol*] [*National Library of Canada*]   (NLC)
AEPW....... Aircraft Emergency Procedures over Water
AEPW....... College Plaza Resource Centre, Alberta Public Works, Supply and Services, Edmonton, Alberta [*Library symbol*] [*National Library of Canada*]   (NLC)
AEPWW.... Western Region Library, Public Works Canada [*Bibliotheque de la Region de l'Ouest, Travaux Publics Canada*] Edmonton, Alberta [*Library symbol*] [*National Library of Canada*]   (NLC)
AEQ........... Aequales [*Equal*] [*Latin*]
Aeq............. Aequatoria [*A publication*]
AEQ........... Asiamerica Equities Ltd. [*Vancouver Stock Exchange symbol*]
AEQ........... Office of Environmental Quality [*FAA*]   (FAAC)
AEQBDE... Anales. Escuela de Quimica y Farmacia. Bioquimica. Universidad de Concepcion [*A publication*]
AEQI .... Agricultural Environmental Quality Institute [*Department of Agriculture*] [*Beltsville, MD*]
AEqP .... Allied Equipment Publications   (NATG)
AEQTS ...... American Equity Investment Trust [*NASDAQ symbol*]   (NQ)
AEQUA ..... Aequatoria [*A publication*]
Aequ Math ... Aequationes Mathematicae [*A publication*]
AER .... Abbreviated Effectiveness Report [*Air Force*]
AER .... Academic Evaluation Report [*Military*]   (INF)
AER .... Adler/Sochi [*USSR*] [*Airport symbol*]   (OAG)
AER .... Aerolift, Inc. [*Vancouver Stock Exchange symbol*]
AER .... Aeronautical Engineering Report
AER .... Aeronautics   (MCD)
AER .... Aeroplane   (ADA)
AER .... After Engine Room
AER .... Agri-Energy Roundtable   (EA)
AER .... Agricultural Economic Reports
AER .... Air Equivalence Ratio [*For hydrocarbon combustion*]
AER .... Airborne Extended Range
AER .... Airman Effectiveness Report [*Air Force*]
AER .... Alberta Research Council, Edmonton, Alberta [*Library symbol*] [*National Library of Canada*]   (NLC)
AER .... Albumin Excretion Rate [*Physiology*]
AER .... Aldosterone Excretion Rate [*Endocrinology*]
AER .... All England Law Reports [*A publication*]
AER .... Alliance to End Repression   (EA)
AER .... Alteration Equivalent to a Repair
AER .... Aluminum Efficient Radiator [*General Motors Corp.*] [*Automotive engineering*]
AER .... American Ecclesiastical Review [*A publication*]
AER .... American Economic Review [*A publication*]
AER .... Antenna Effective Resistance
AER .... Apical Ectodermal Ridge [*Embryology, genetics*]
AER .... Approach End Runway [*Aviation*]   (FAAC)
AER .... Army Emergency Relief   (EA)
AER .... Army Emergency Reserve [*British*]
AER .... Assemblee des Regions d'Europe [*Assembly of European Regions*]   (EAIO)
AER .... Association for Education and Rehabilitation of the Blind and Visually Impaired   (EA)
AER .... Association Europeenne pour l'Etude du Probleme des Refugies
AER .... Association Europeenne de Radiologie [*European Association of Radiology - EAR*]   (EA)
AeR .... Atene e Roma [*A publication*]
AER .... Atomic Energy Review [*A publication*]

AER .... Auditory-Evoked Response [*Neurophysiology*]
AER .... Australian Economic Review [*A publication*]
AER .... Average Evoked Response [*Neurophysiology*]
AER .... Azimuth Elevation Range   (KSC)
AER .... Thai-American Treaty of Amity and Economic Relations   (IMH)
AER .... United States Army, Corps of Engineers, Omaha District, Omaha, NE [*OCLC symbol*]   (OCLC)
AERA .... Airborne Electronics Research Activity [*Lakehurst, NJ*] [*United States Army Communications-Electronics Command*]   (GRD)
AERA .... American Educational Research Association   (EA)
AERA .... Associate Engraver, Royal Academy [*British*]
AERA .... Australian Endurance Riders Association
AERA .... Automated En-Route Air Traffic Control [*Proposed*] [*FAA*]
AERA .... Automotive Engine Rebuilders Association   (EA)
AERA .... Royal Alexandra Hospital, Edmonton, Alberta [*Library symbol*] [*National Library of Canada*]   (NLC)
AERAA...... Advances in Enzymology and Related Areas of Molecular Biology [*A publication*]
AERASN ... School of Nursing, Royal Alexandra Hospital, Edmonton, Alberta [*Library symbol*] [*National Library of Canada*]   (NLC)
AERB........ Army Education Review Board
AERB........ Army Educational Requirements Board
AERC........ Amelia Earhart Research Consortium   (EA)
AERC........ American Endurance Ride Conference   (EA)
A & ERC .... American and English Railroad Cases [*A publication*]   (DLA)
AERC........ Association of Ecosystem Research Centers   (EA)
AERC........ Association of Executive Recruiting Consultants [*Later, AESC*]   (EA)
AERC........ Atlantic Educational Research Council [*Canada*]
AERC........ Clover Bar Branch, Alberta Research Council, Edmonton, Alberta [*Library symbol*] [*National Library of Canada*]   (NLC)
AERCAB... Advanced [*or Aircrew*] Escape/Rescue Capability [*Navy - Air Force*]
A & ER Cas ... American and English Railroad Cases [*A publication*]   (DLA)
A & ER Cas NS ... American and English Railroad Cases, New Series [*A publication*]   (DLA)
AERCW..... Auxiliary Essential Raw Cooling Water [*Nuclear energy*]   (NRCH)
AERD .... Agricultural Engineering Research and Development [*Canada*]
AERD .... Atomic Energy Research Department [*NASA*]   (KSC)
AERDA ..... Army Electronics Research and Development Activity [*White Sands Missile Range, NM*]
AERDC...... Agricultural Extension and Rural Development Centre [*University of Reading*] [*British*]   (CB)
AERDDP... Australian Energy Research, Development, and Demonstration Projects
AERDL...... Army Electronics Research and Development Laboratory   (AABC)
AerE........... Aeronautical Engineer   (ADA)
AERE........ Association of Environmental and Resource Economists   (EA)
AERE........ Atomic Energy Research Establishment [*of United Kingdom Atomic Energy Authority*]
AERE/RPS ... Atomic Energy Research Establishment, Great Britain. Registered Publications Section [*A publication*]
AE Res Dep Agric Econ Cornell Univ Agric Exp Stn ... AE Research. Department of Agricultural Economics, Cornell University. Agricultural Experiment Station [*A publication*]
AE Res NY State Coll Agr Dept Agr Econ ... AE Research. New York State College of Agriculture. Department of Agricultural Economics [*A publication*]
AERF......... Atlas Economic Research Foundation   (EA)
Aerftliga Aemnesomsaettningsrubbningar Symp ... Aerftliga Aemnesomsaettningsrubbningar. Symposium [*A publication*]
AERG .... Advanced Environmental Research Group [*Commercial firm*]
AERG .... Alternative Education Resource Group [*Australia*]
AERG .... Army Engineer Reactors Group [*Fort Belvoir, VA*]
AERGB...... Applied Ergonomics [*A publication*]
AERI......... Agricultural Economics Research Institution [*British*]
AERI......... Automotive Exhaust Research Institute [*Defunct*]   (EA)
Aerial Archaeol ... Aerial Archaeology [*A publication*]
AERIC....... Applied Economic Research and Information Centre [*Conference Board of Canada*] [*Ottawa, ON*]
AERIS .... Airborne Electronic Ranging Instrumentation System
AERIS .... Airways Environmental RADAR Information System   (IEEE)
AERIS .... Automatic Electronic Range Instrumentation System   (MCD)
AERIS .... Industrial Information, Alberta Research Council, Edmonton, Alberta [*Library symbol*] [*National Library of Canada*]   (NLC)
AERJ......... American Educational Research Journal [*A publication*]
AERL......... Aerial   (AFM)
AERL......... Aero-Elastic Research Laboratory [*MIT*]   (MCD)
AERL......... Arctic Environmental Research Laboratory [*Environmental Protection Agency*]   (NOAA)
AERL......... Avco-Everett Research Laboratory   (MCD)
AERM .... Aerographer's Mate [*Navy rating*]

AERM .... R. M. Hardy & Associates Ltd., Edmonton, Alberta [*Library symbol*] [*National Library of Canada*] (NLC)
AERNA ..... American Economic Review [*A publication*]
AERNO ..... Aeronautical Equipment Reference Number [*Military*]
AERO .... Aero Services International, Inc. [*NASDAQ symbol*] (NQ)
Aero .... Aerobacter [*Microbiology*]
AERO .... Aerodynamic (NASA)
AERO .... Aerographer
AERO .... Aeronautics (AFM)
AERO .... Aerospace
AERO .... Aerosurfaces (NASA)
AERO .... Alternative Energy Resources Organization (EA)
AERO .... Automatic Earnings Recomputation Operation [*Social Security*]
AERO .... Aviation Routine Weather Report (FAAC)
Aero Amer ... Aerospace America [*A publication*]
AEROBEE ... Aerojet/Bumblebee [*Navy missile*]
AEROCOM ... Aeronautical Communications Equipment Corp.
AEROCONDOR ... Aerovias Condor de Colombia Ltda. [*Condor Airlines of Colombia Ltd.*]
Aero Def Mark Technol ... Aerospace/Defense Markets and Technology [*A publication*]
Aero Dig ..... Aero Digest [*A publication*]
Aerodin Razrezh Gazov ... Aerodinamika Razrezhennykh Gazov [*USSR*] [*A publication*]
AERODYN ... Aerodynamic (KSC)
Aerodyn Note ... Aerodynamics Note [*A publication*] (APTA)
Aerodyn Techn Mem ... Aerodynamics Technical Memorandum [*A publication*] (APTA)
Aero Eng .... Aerospace Engineering [*A publication*]
Aero Eng R ... Aeronautical Engineering Review [*A publication*]
AER OF ..... Aerological Officer
Aero F & F ... Aerospace Facts and Figures [*A publication*]
AEROFLOT ... Aero Flotilla [*Airline*] [*USSR*]
AEROG ...... Aerologist
AEROHEAT ... Aerodynamic Heating (NG)
Aero J .... Aeronautical Journal [*A publication*]
AEROL ...... Aerological
Aerol .... Aerologist [*A publication*]
AEROMED ... Aeromedical
Aeromed Acta ... Aeromedica Acta [*A publication*]
Aeromed Rev ... Aeromedical Reviews [*A publication*]
AEROMOD ... Aerodynamic Modeling [*Module*]
Aeromod .... Aeromodeller [*A publication*]
Aero Mund ... Aero Mundial [*A publication*]
Aeron .... Aeronautica [*A publication*]
AERON ..... Aeronautical
Aeron .... Aeronautique [*A publication*]
Aeronaut Astronaut ... Aeronautique et l'Astronautique [*A publication*]
Aeronaut Astronaut News Lett ... Aeronautical and Astronautical News Letter [*A publication*]
Aeronaut Eng Rev ... Aeronautical Engineering Review [*A publication*]
Aeronaut J ... Aeronautical Journal [*A publication*]
Aeronaut Q ... Aeronautical Quarterly [*A publication*]
Aeronaut Res Lab Dep Def Aust Rep ... Aeronautical Research Laboratories. Department of Defence. Australia. Reports [*A publication*]
Aeron J ...... Aeronautical Journal [*A publication*]
AERONL .. Aeronautical
Aeron Q ..... Aeronautical Quarterly [*A publication*]
Aeron Res Rep ... Aeronautical Research Report [*A publication*] (APTA)
Aeron Rev .. Aeronautic Review [*A publication*]
Aeron Wld ... Aeronautical World [*A publication*]
AEROPERU ... Linea Aerea Peruana [*Peruvian State Airlines*]
Aeropl Astron ... Aeroplane and Astronautics [*A publication*]
AEROPOST ... Aerodynamic Post-Processing [*Module*]
Aero Quart ... Aeronautical Quarterly [*London*] [*A publication*]
AERO R Bn ... Aeronautical Radiobeacon [*Nautical charts*]
Aero Res Aircr Bull ... Aero Research Aircraft Bulletin [*A publication*]
Aero Res Tech Notes ... Aero Research Technical Notes [*A publication*]
AERO R Rge ... Aeronautical Radio Range [*Nautical charts*]
AEROS ...... Advanced Earth Resources Observation System
AEROS ...... Aerometric and Emissions Reporting System [*Environmental Protection Agency*]
AEROS ...... Artificial Earth Research and Orbiting Satellite (NATG)
Aero Safe ... Aerospace Safety [*A publication*]
Aeros Age ... Aerosol Age [*A publication*]
AEROSAT ... Aeronautical Communications Satellite System
AEROSAT ... Aeronautical Satellite
Aeros Bull ... Aerosol Bulletin [*A publication*]
Aerosl Age ... Aerosol Age [*A publication*]
AEROS-NATE ... Aeronomy Satellite - Neutral Atmosphere Temperature Experiment
Aeros Ne .... Aerosol News [*A publication*]
AEROSOL ... Aerospace Spin-Off Laboratory
Aerosol 82 ... Aerosol Review 1982 [*A publication*]
Aerosol Rep ... Aerosol Report [*A publication*]
Aerosol Sci ... Aerosol Science [*England*] [*A publication*]
AEROSP ... Aerospace (MSA)
AEROSPACE ... Aeronautics and Space
AEROSPACECOM ... Aerospace Communications
Aero/Space Eng ... Aero/Space Engineering [*A publication*]
Aerospace Hist ... Aerospace Historian [*A publication*]

Aerospace Med ... Aerospace Medicine [*A publication*]
Aerospace Tech ... Aerospace Technology [*A publication*]
Aerosp and Def Rev ... Aerospace and Defence Review [*A publication*]
Aerosp Dly ... Aerospace Daily [*A publication*]
Aerosp Eng ... Aerospace Engineering [*A publication*]
Aerosp Med ... Aerospace Medicine [*A publication*]
Aerosp Med Biol ... Aerospace Medicine and Biology [*A publication*]
Aerosp Med Res Lab Tech Rep ... Aerospace Medical Research Laboratory. Technical Report [*A publication*]
AEROSPRSCHPLTSCH ... Aerospace Research USAF Test Pilot School [*Later, USAFTESTPLTSCH*]
Aerosp Technol ... Aerospace Technology [*A publication*]
AEROSSq ... Aerospace Support Squadron [*Air Force*]
AERO Sun-T ... AERO [*Alternative Energy Resources Organization*] Sun-Times [*A publication*]
Aerot .... Aerotecnica [*A publication*]
Aerotechn... Aerotechnique [*A publication*]
Aerotec Missili & Spazio ... Aerotechnica Missili e Spazio [*A publication*]
Aerotec Missili Spazio ... Aerotechnica Missili e Spazio [*A publication*]
AERPW..... Alberta Recreation and Parks, Edmonton, Alberta [*Library symbol*] [*National Library of Canada*] (NLC)
A & E RRC ... American and English Railroad Cases [*A publication*] (DLA)
A & ERR Cas ... American and English Railroad Cases [*A publication*] (DLA)
A & ERR Cas (NS) ... American and English Railroad Cases, New Series [*A publication*] (DLA)
AER Rep.... All England Law Reports (Reprint) [*1558-1935*] [*A publication*] (DLA)
AER Rep Ext ... All England Law Reports (Reprint) Australian Extension Volumes [*A publication*] (DLA)
AERS........ Aero Systems Engineering, Inc. [*St. Paul, MN*] [*NASDAQ symbol*] (NQ)
AERS........ Airborne Environmental Reporting System
AERS........ Airborne Equipment Repair Squadron (MCD)
AERS........ Airborne Expendable Rocket System (MCD)
AERS........ Aircraft Equipment Requirement Schedule
AERS........ Atlantic Estuarine Research Society (EA)
AERSG ..... African Elephant and Rhino Specialist Group [*of the International Union for Conservation of Nature and Natural Resources*] (EA)
AE RS PA State Univ Agr Sta Dept Agr Econ Rural Sociol ... AE and RS. Pennsylvania State University. Agricultural Experiment Station. Department of Agricultural Economics and Rural Sociology [*A publication*]
AERSWE .. Solar and Wind Energy Research Program Information Centre, Alberta Research Council, Edmonton, Alberta [*Library symbol*] [*Obsolete*] [*National Library of Canada*] (NLC)
AERT........ Acceptable Environmental Range Test
AERT........ Advanced Environmental Recycling Technology, Inc. [*NASDAQ symbol*] (NQ)
AERT........ Advanced Environmental Research and Technology (MCD)
AErt .... Archaeologiai Ertesito [*A publication*]
AERTC...... Association pour les Etudes sur la Radio-Television Canadienne [*Association for the Study of Canadian Radio and Television - ASCRT*]
AERTEL ... Association Europeenne Rubans, Tresses, Tissus Elastiques [*European Ribbon, Braid, and Elastic Material Association*]
AERTJ ...... Association of Education by Radio-Television. Journal [*A publication*]
AERTP...... Terrace Plaza Branch Library, Alberta Research Council, Edmonton, Alberta [*Library symbol*] [*National Library of Canada*] (NLC)
AERU .... University Branch, Alberta Research Council, Edmonton, Alberta [*Library symbol*] [*National Library of Canada*] (NLC)
AERX........ Aero Spacelines [*Air carrier designation symbol*]
Aerztebl Baden-Wuerttemb ... Aerzteblatt fuer Baden-Wuerttemberg [*A publication*]
Aerztebl Rheinl Pfalz ... Aerzteblatt Rheinland-Pfalz [*A publication*]
Aerztl Forsch ... Aerztliche Forschung [*A publication*]
Aerztl Fortbildungskurse Zuercher Kanton Liga Tuberk Arosa ... Aerztliche Fortbildungskurse der Zuercher Kantonalen Liga Gegen die Tuberkulose in Arosa [*A publication*]
Aerztl Jugendkd ... Aerztliche Jugendkunde [*A publication*]
Aerztl Kosmetol ... Aerztliche Kosmetologie [*A publication*]
Aerztl Lab ... Aerztliche Laboratorium [*A publication*]
Aerztl Monatsh Berufliche Fortbild ... Aerztliche Monatshefte fuer Berufliche Fortbildung [*A publication*]
Aerztl Praxis ... Aerztliche Praxis [*A publication*]
Aerztl Psychol ... Aerztliche Psychologie [*A publication*]
Aerztl Rundsch ... Aerztliche Rundschau [*A publication*]
Aerztl S Bl ... Aerztliche Sammebaetter [*A publication*]
Aerztl Wochenschr ... Aerztliche Wochenschrift [*A publication*]
AES........... Aalesund [*Norway*] [*Airport symbol*] (OAG)
AES........... Abrasive Engineering Society (EA)
AES........... Abstracts of English Studies [*A publication*]
AES........... Adult Emergency Service [*In TV series "A.E.S. Hudson Street"*]
AES........... Advanced Engineering Services [*General Motors Corp.*] [*Automotive engineering*]
AES........... Advanced Extravehicular Suit [*NASA*]

AeS............ Aegyptologische Studien [Berlin] [A publication]
AES............ Aerospace Electrical Society (EA)
AES............ Aerospace and Electronic Systems (MCD)
AES............ Agricultural Economics Society (EAIO)
AES............ Agricultural Estimates Division [of AMS, Department of Agriculture]
AES............ Agricultural Extension Service (OICC)
AES............ Air and Earth Shock (MCD)
AE & S....... Air Equipment and Support [Army] (AABC)
AES............ Aircraft Ejection Seat
AES............ Airways Engineering Society [Defunct] (EA)
AES............ Alkylethoxylated Sulfate [Surfactant] [Organic chemistry]
AES............ All-England Series
AES............ Alternative Economic Strategy
AES............ Amateur Entomologists' Society (EA)
AES............ American Ecology Services (EA)
AES............ American Educational Society (EA)
AES............ American Electrochemical Society [Later, ECS]
AES............ American Electroencephalographic Society (EA)
AES............ American Electromechanical Society
AES............ American Electronical Society
AES............ American Electroplaters' Society (EA)
AES............ American Endodontic Society (EA)
AES............ American Entomological Society (EA)
AES............ American Epidemiological Society (EA)
AES............ American Epilepsy Society (EA)
AES............ American Equilibration Society (EA)
AES............ American Ethnological Society (EA)
AES............ American Eugenics Society [Later, SSSB] (EA)
AES............ American Journal of Economics and Sociology [A publication]
AES............ Analog Event System [Data processing] (MCD)
AES............ Apollo Earth-Orbiting Station [NASA]
AES............ Apollo Experiment Support [NASA]
AES............ Apollo Extension System [NASA]
AES............ Applications Environment System
AES............ Archives Europeennes de Sociologie [A publication]
AESMC......... Area Electronic Supervisor
AES............ Army Excess Property (AABC)
AES............ Army Exchange Service [Centralized the control of PX's in US] [World War II]
AES............ Array Element Study
AES............ Artificial Earth Satellite [NASA]
AES............ Artillery Equipment School [British] (DAS)
AES............ Astronomical Explorer Satellite
AES............ Atlantic Economic Society (EA)
AES............ Atlantic Estuarine Society
AES............ Atmospheric Environment Service [Canada]
AES............ Atomic Emission Spectroscopy
AES............ Audio Engineering Society (EA)
AES............ Auger Electron Spectrometry [or Spectroscopy]
AES............ Australian Economic Statistics [Database] [I. P. Sharp Associates] [Information service or system] (CRD)
AES............ Automatic Emission Spectroscopy (MCD)
AES............ Automatic External Standard [or Standardization] [Radioactivity measurement]
AES............ Auxiliary Encoder System
AES............ Avionics Expert System (MCD)
AES............ Guam Agricultural Experiment Station [University of Guam] [Research center] (RCD)
AES............ Missouri Agricultural Experiment Station [University of Missouri - Columbia] [Research center] (RCD)
AES............ Northway, AK [Location identifier] [FAA] (FAAL)
AES............ Statistics Canada [Statistique Canada] Edmonton, Alberta [Library symbol] [National Library of Canada] (NLC)
AES............ United States Army, Corps of Engineers, Southwest Division, Dallas, TX [OCLC symbol] (OCLC)
AESA......... Aerolineas de El Salvador [Airline] [El Salvador]
AESA......... American Educational Studies Association (EA)
AESA......... Association pour l'Enseignement Social en Afrique [Association for Social Work Education in Africa - ASWEA] (EAIO)
AESA......... Association of Environmental Scientists and Administrators [Inactive] (EA)
AESAA...... Annals. Entomological Society of America [A publication]
AES/AE .... American Ethnologist. American Ethnological Society [A publication]
AESAE...... Stanley Associates Engineering Ltd., Edmonton, Alberta [Library symbol] [National Library of Canada] (NLC)
AESAL...... Academie Europeenne des Sciences, des Arts, et des Lettres [European Academy of Arts, Sciences, and Humanities] (EAIO)
AESAP...... Army Entertainment Scholarships and Awards Program (AABC)
AESB......... Architect-Engineers - Spanish Bases
AESBNW ... Association of Engineers and Scientists of the Bureau of Naval Weapons [Later, ASE]
AESC......... Aerojet Electrosystems Co. (MCD)
AESC......... AmerEco Environmental Services, Inc. [NASDAQ symbol] (NQ)
AESC......... American Engineering Standards Committee [Later, ANSI]
AESC......... Annales: Economies, Societes, Civilisations [A publication]
AESC......... Association of Executive Search Consultants (EA)

AESC......... Automatic Electronic Switching Center
AESC......... Syncrude Canada Ltd., Edmonton, Alberta [Library symbol] [National Library of Canada] (NLC)
AE SC Agric Exp Stn Clemson Univ ... AE. South Carolina Agricultural Experiment Station. Clemson University [A publication]
AESCH...... Aeschylus [Greek poet, 525-456BC] [Classical studies] (ROG)
Aeschin...... Aeschines [c. 397-322BC] [Classical studies] (OCD)
AESCO...... Association Europeenne des Ecoles et Colleges d'Optometre [European Association of Schools and Colleges of Optometry - EASCO] (EA)
AESD........ Acoustic Environmental Support Detachment [Office of Naval Research] [Arlington, VA]
AESD........ Alberta School for the Deaf, Edmonton, Alberta [Library symbol] [National Library of Canada] (NLC)
AESE........ Association of Earth Science Editors (EA)
AESES....... Association of Employees Supporting Education Services [Canada]
AESFS....... American Electroplaters' and Surface Finishers Society (EA)
AESG........ Alberta Solicitor General, Edmonton, Alberta [Library symbol] [National Library of Canada] (NLC)
AESGP...... Association Europeenne des Specialites Pharmaceutiques Grand Public [European Proprietary Association] (EA)
AES(I) .... Association of Engineers and Scientists (Independent)
AESIR ...... Aerospace Instrumentation Range Station
AESIS ...... Australian Earth Sciences Information System [Australian Mineral Foundation] [Information service or system] (IID)
AESIS....... Schick Information Systems, Edmonton, Alberta [Library symbol] [Obsolete] [National Library of Canada] (NLC)
AESIS Quarterly ... Australian Earth Sciences Information System. Quarterly [A publication]
AESL........ Aero Engine Service Ltd. [Australia]
AESL........ Associated Engineering Services [Canada]
AESM........ Aero Systems, Inc. [NASDAQ symbol] (NQ)
AESM........ American Ethnological Society. Monographs [A publication]
AESM........ Association for Equine Sports Medicine (EA)
AESMC...... Automotive Exhaust Systems Manufacturers Council (EA)
AESMD...... Aircraft Escape System Maintenance Data (MCD)
AESNL...... American Ethnological Society. Newsletter [A publication]
AESO .... Acupuncture Ethics and Standards Organisation [Australia]
AESO .... Airborne Electronic Sensor Operator [Canadian Navy]
AESO .... Aircraft Environmental Support Office [Naval Air Rework Facility] [North Island, CA]
AESOP...... Accounts Enquiry Sales and Order Processing (ADA)
AESOP...... Artificial Earth Satellite Observation Program [Navy]
AESOP...... Automated Educational Services On-Line Processing (MCD)
AESOP...... Automated Engineering and Scientific Optimization Program [NASA]
AESOP...... [An] Evolutionary System for On-Line Processing [Data processing]
AESOPS.... AMSAA [Army Materiel Systems Analysis Agency] Evade Sustained Operations Performance Simulation (MCD)
AESP........ American Ethnological Society. Publications [A publication]
AEsp......... Archivo Espanol de Arqueologia [A publication]
A Esp .... Arte Espanol [A publication]
AESP........ Auxiliary Engineering Signal Processor
A Esp Arqu ... Archivo Espanol de Arqueologia [A publication]
AES Pr....... American Ethnological Society. Proceedings [A publication]
AESQ........ Air Explorer Squadron
AESQAW ... Anais. Escola Superior de Agricultura "Luiz De Queiroz." Universidade de Sao Paulo [A publication]
AESR........ Aeronautical Equipment Service Record (MCD)
AESR........ Army Equipment Status Report
AESRC...... American English Spot Rabbit Club (EA)
AESRS...... Army Equipment Status Reporting System (AABC)
AESRS...... Automatic Electronic Switching System
AESS .... Aerospace and Electronics Systems (IEEE)
AESS .... Aircraft Ejection Seat System
AESS .... Association des Economistes, Sociologues, et Statisticiens [Economists', Sociologists', and Statisticians' Association - ESSA] [Canada]
AESS .... Automatic Electronic Switching System (MCD)
AESS .... IEEE Aerospace and Electronics Systems Society (EA)
AEST .... Aeromedical Evacuation Support Team
AESTC ...... Advances in Environmental Science and Technology [A publication]
AESTD...... Atomnye Elektricheskie Stantsii [A publication]
AESTH...... Aesthetics
Aesthetic Plast Surg ... Aesthetic Plastic Surgery [A publication]
Aesthet Med ... Aesthetische Medizin [West Germany] [A publication]
AESU......... Aerospace Environmental Support Unit [Air Weather Service] (IID)
AESUAB ... Agricultural Experiment Station. University of Alaska. Bulletin [A publication]
AESUATB ... Agricultural Experiment Station. University of Alaska. Technical Bulletin [A publication]
AESV........ Association Europeene de Saint Vladimir (EAIO)
AET .... Absorption Equivalent Thickness
AET .... Actual Elapsed Time
AET .... Actual Equipment Trainer (MCD)
AET .... Actual Evapotranspiration [Biology]

AET .... Actual Exposure Time (MUGU)
AET .... Advanced Energy Technology
AET .... Aerlinte Eireann Teoranta [*Irish Air Lines*]
AET .... Aeromedical Evacuation Technician
AET .... Aerosurface End-to-End Test (MCD)
aet. .... Aetas [*or Aetatis*] [*Age or Aged*] [*Latin*]
Aet. .... Aetia [*of Callimachus*] [*Classical studies*] (OCD)
AET .... Aetna Life & Casualty Co. [*NYSE symbol*] (SPSG)
AET .... Aircraft Equipment Trainer (MCD)
AET .... Aircrew Egress Trainer (MCD)
AET .... Airfields Environment Trust [*British*]
AET .... Alberta Treasury, Edmonton, Alberta [*Library symbol*]
            [*National Library of Canada*] (NLC)
AET .... Allakaket [*Alaska*] [*Airport symbol*] (OAG)
Aet. .... Aminoethyl [*Biochemistry*]
AET .... Aminoethylisothiuronium [*Radiology*]
AET .... Apparent Elastic Thickness [*Geoscience*]
AET .... Applied Electronics Technology Proprietary Ltd. [*Australia*]
AET .... Approximate Exposure Time
AET .... Associate in Electrical Technology
AET .... Associate in Engineering Technology
AET .... Association des Employes du Trafic [*Association of Traffic
            Employees*] [*Canada*]
AET .... Association Europeenne Thyroide [*European Thyroid
            Association - ETA*] (EAIO)
AET .... Atrial Ectopic Tachycardia [*Medicine*]
AET .... Auto Exhaust Testing
Aet. .... De Aeternitate Mundi [*Philo*] (BJA)
AET .... United States Army, Corps of Engineers, North Atlantic
            Division, New York, NY [*OCLC symbol*] (OCLC)
AETA .... Amatex Export Trade Association (EA)
AETA .... American Educational Theatre Association [*Later, ATA*] (EA)
AETA .... American Embryo Transfer Association (EA)
AETA .... Antique Engine and Thresher Association (EA)
AETA .... Australian Exhibition Touring Agency
AETAC ...... Aviation Electronic Technician's Mate, Combat Aircrewman
            [*Navy*]
AETAT ...... Aetatis [*Age*] [*Latin*]
AETATE ... Facility Engineering and Systems Development Library,
            Transport Canada [*Bibliotheque de l'Ingenierie des
            Installations et de la Mise au Point des Systemes,
            Transports Canada*], Edmonton, Alberta [*Library symbol*]
            [*National Library of Canada*] (NLC)
AETATE ... Telecommunications and Electronics, Canadian Air
            Transportation Administration, Transport Canada
            [*Telecommunications et Electronique, Administration
            Canadienne des Transports Aeriens, Transports Canada*]
            Edmonton, Alberta [*Library symbol*] [*National Library of
            Canada*] (NLC)
AETATES ... Facility Engineering and Systems Development Sub-Library,
            Edmonton International Airport, Transport Canada
            [*Succursale de la Bibliotheque de l'Ingenierie des
            Installations et de la Mise au Point des Systemes, Aeroport
            International d'Edmonton, Transports Canada*], Alberta
            [*Library symbol*] [*National Library of Canada*] (NLC)
AETBS ...... Bureau of Statistics, Alberta Treasury, Edmonton, Alberta
            [*Library symbol*] [*National Library of Canada*] (NLC)
AETC .... Accessory and Equipment Technical Committee (KSC)
AETCT ...... Corporate Tax Administration, Alberta Treasury, Edmonton,
            Alberta [*Library symbol*] [*National Library of
            Canada*] (NLC)
AETD .... Aero-Electronic Technology Department [*Navy*] (MCD)
AETDA ...... Aminoethyltricosadiynamide [*Organic chemistry*]
AETE .... Aerospace Engineering Test Establishment [*Canada*]
AETEB ...... Aerospace Technology [*A publication*]
AETF .... Azimuth Error Test Feature
AETF .... Azimuth Error Test Fixture (MCD)
AETFA4 .... Annales Entomologici Fennici [*A publication*]
AETh .... Abhandlungen zur Evangelischen Theologie [*Bonn*] [*A
            publication*]
AETH .... Aether [*Ether*] (ROG)
Aetherische Oele Riechst Parfuem Essenzen Aromen ... Aetherische Oele,
            Riechstoffe, Parfuemerien, Essenzen, und Aromen [*A
            publication*]
AETI .... Apollo Engineering and Technology Index [*NASA*] (KSC)
A Et Int ...... Annales d'Etudes Internationales [*A publication*]
AETIS .... Army Extension Training Information System
AETJA ...... Automatic Electric Technical Journal [*A publication*]
AETL .... Approved Engineering Test Laboratory [*Military*] (CAAL)
AETL .... Armament and Electronics Test Laboratory [*NATO*]
AETL .... Army Engineer Topographic Laboratories (RDA)
AETM .... Aviation Electronic Technician's Mate [*Navy*]
AETMS ..... Airborne Electronic Terrain Map System (MCD)
AETN .... Alberta Tree Nursery and Horticultural Centre, Edmonton,
            Alberta [*Library symbol*] [*National Library of
            Canada*] (BIB)
AETN .... American Educational Television Network [*Cable-television
            system*]
AETODY .. Advances in Modern Environmental Toxicology [*A
            publication*]
AEtP .... Allied Electronics Publications (NATG)

AETQA ..... Annales. Societe Entomologique du Quebec [*A publication*]
AETQA3 ... Annals. Entomological Society of Quebec [*A publication*]
AETR........ Advanced Engineering Test Reactor
AETR........ Advanced Epithermal Thorium Reactor
AETS........ Army Extension Training System
AETS........ Association for the Education of Teachers in Science (EA)
AETT........ Acetyl Ethyl Tetramethyl Tetralin [*Musk fragrance, neuro-toxic
            compound*]
AETT........ Association for Educational and Training Technology (EAIO)
AEU.......... Accrued Expenditure Unpaid [*Accounting*] (AFM)
AEU.......... Altitude Encoder Unit (MCD)
AEU.......... Amalgamated Engineering Union [*United Kingdom*]
AEU.......... American Ethical Union (EA)
AEU.......... Archiv fuer Elektronik und Uebertragungstechnik [*A
            publication*]
AEU.......... Army Exhibit Unit
AEU.......... Asia Electronics Union (EAIO)
AEU.......... Asia Electronics Union. Journal [*A publication*]
AEU.......... United States Army, Corps of Engineers, St. Louis District, St.
            Louis, MO [*OCLC symbol*] (OCLC)
AEU.......... University of Alberta, Edmonton, Alberta [*Library symbol*]
            [*National Library of Canada*] (NLC)
AEUA........ University of Alberta Archives, Edmonton, Alberta [*Library
            symbol*] [*National Library of Canada*] (NLC)
AEUAG ..... Department of Agricultural Engineering, University of Alberta,
            Edmonton, Alberta [*Library symbol*] [*National Library of
            Canada*] (NLC)
AEUAH..... Learning Resource Centre, Agnes Macleod Memorial Library,
            University of Alberta Hospitals, Edmonton, Alberta
            [*Library symbol*] [*National Library of Canada*] (BIB)
AEU-Arch El ... AEU-Archiv fuer Elektronik und Uebertragungstechnik [*A
            publication*]
AEU-Arch Elektron Uebertragungstech ... AEU-Archiv fuer Elektronik und
            Uebertragungstechnik [*A publication*]
AEUB .... Boreal Institute for Northern Studies, University of Alberta,
            Edmonton, Alberta [*Library symbol*] [*National Library of
            Canada*] (NLC)
AEUC .... Association des Employes d'Universites et de Colleges
            [*Association of University and College Employees -
            AUCE*] [*Canada*]
AEUCA ..... Ukrainian Canadian Archives and Museum, Edmonton, Alberta
            [*Library symbol*] [*National Library of Canada*] (BIB)
AEUIA....... Alleluia [*An old abbreviation, formed from the vowels of the
            word*]
AEUL .... Law Library, University of Alberta, Edmonton, Alberta [*Library
            symbol*] [*National Library of Canada*] (NLC)
AEULS ...... Faculty of Library Science, University of Alberta, Edmonton,
            Alberta [*Library symbol*] [*National Library of
            Canada*] (NLC)
AEUM .... University Map Collection, University of Alberta, Edmonton,
            Alberta [*Library symbol*] [*National Library of
            Canada*] (NLC)
AEUMJ ..... Amalgamated Engineering Union. Monthly Journal [*A
            publication*] (APTA)
AEU Mon J ... Amalgamated Engineering Union. Monthly Journal [*A
            publication*] (APTA)
AEUN........ Unifarm, Edmonton, Alberta [*Library symbol*] [*National
            Library of Canada*] (NLC)
AEUNA ..... AEU. Asia Electronics United [*A publication*]
AE Univ Ill Coll Agr Exp Sta Coop Ext Serv ... AE. University of Illinois.
            College of Agriculture. Experiment Station. Cooperative
            Extension Service [*A publication*]
AEUS........ Absolute Electrical Unit Scale
AEUS........ Bruce Peel Special Collections Library, University of Alberta,
            Edmonton, Alberta [*Library symbol*] [*National Library of
            Canada*] (NLC)
AEUSJ ...... Faculte Saint-Jean, University of Alberta, Edmonton, Alberta
            [*Library symbol*] [*National Library of Canada*] (NLC)
AEUT .... Alberta Utilities and Telephones, Edmonton, Alberta [*Library
            symbol*] [*National Library of Canada*] (NLC)
AEV .... Aerothermodynamic Elastic Vehicle
Aev .... Aevum [*A publication*]
AEV .... Anthology of English Verse [*A publication*]
AEV .... Armored Engineer Vehicle (MCD)
AEV .... Asian Economic Review [*A publication*]
AEV .... Avian Erythroblastosis Virus
AEV .... Evansburg Public Library, Alberta [*Library symbol*] [*National
            Library of Canada*] (NLC)
AEV .... United States Army, Corps of Engineers, Savannah District,
            Savannah, GA [*OCLC symbol*] (OCLC)
AEVAC...... Air Evacuation
AEVC........ Alberta Vocational Centre, Edmonton, Alberta [*Library
            symbol*] [*National Library of Canada*] (NLC)
AEVH........ Association for Education of the Visually Handicapped [*Later,
            AER*] (EA)
AEVS........ Automatic Electronic Voice Switch (RDA)
AEW .... Admiralty Experiment Works [*British*]
AEW .... Airborne [*or Aircraft*] Early Warning Station
AEW .... Airborne Electronic Warfare (NG)
AEW .... American Education Week
AEW .... American Energy Week [*Later, AEM*] [*An association*] (EA)

AEW .... Appalachian Power Co. [*NYSE symbol*]   (SPSG)
AEW .... Association of Electrical Wiremen [*A union*] [*British*]
AEW .... United States Army, Corps of Engineers, Fort Worth District, Fort Worth, TX [*OCLC symbol*]   (OCLC)
AEWA ...... Airborne Early Warning Aircraft
AEWB ...... Army Electronic Warfare Board   (MCD)
AEW & C... Airborne Early Warning and Control [*Army*]   (AFM)
AEWC ...... Airborne Early Warning and Control [*Army*]   (AABC)
AEWCAP.. Airborne Early Warning Combat Air Patrol   (NVT)
AEW & CSq ... Airborne Early Warning and Control Squadron [*Air Force*]
AEWES..... Army Engineer Waterways Experiment Station [*Vicksburg, MS*]
AEWF....... Airborne Early Warning Fighter
AEWHA.... All England Women's Hockey Association   (EAIO)
AEWIB..... Army Electronic Warfare and Intelligence Board
AEWICS.... Airborne Early Warning and Interceptor Control System
AEWIS...... Army Electronic Warfare Information System
AEWLA.... All England Women's Lacrosse Association   (EAIO)
AEWP....... Aerospace Education Workshop Project
AEWRON ... Airborne Early Warning Squadron
AEWS....... Advanced Earth Satellite Weapon System [*Air Force*]
AEWS....... Advanced Electronic Warfare System   (MCD)
AEWSP.... Aircraft Electronics Warfare Self-Protection System [*Army*]
AEWSPS... Aircraft Electronics Warfare Self-Protection System [*Army*]
AEWTF..... Aircrew Electronic Warfare Tactics Facility   (NATG)
AEWTS..... Advanced Electronic Warfare Test Set   (MCD)
AEWTU .... Airborne Early Warning Training Unit
AEWVH .... [*The*] Association for the Education and Welfare of the Visually Handicapped [*British*]
AEWW ...... Airborne Early Warning Wing   (MUGU)
AEX .... Agreement to Extend Enlistment [*Military*]
AEX .... Air Express International Corp. [*AMEX symbol*]   (SPSG)
AEX .... Airway Express, Inc. [*Mesa, AZ*] [*FAA designator*]   (FAAC)
AEX .... Alexandria, LA [*Location identifier*] [*FAA*]   (FAAL)
AEX .... American Import/Export Management [*A publication*]
AEX .... Export [*A publication*]
AEX .... United States Army, Corps of Engineers, North Central Division, Chicago, IL [*OCLC symbol*]   (OCLC)
AEXC........ Exshaw Community Library, Alberta [*Library symbol*] [*National Library of Canada*]   (NLC)
AExO........ Assistant Experimental Officer [*Ministry of Agriculture, Fisheries, and Food*] [*Also, AEO, AXO*] [*British*]
AEXP........ Applications Experience
AEY .... Aero Energy Ltd. [*Toronto Stock Exchange symbol*]
AEY .... Akureyri [*Iceland*] [*Airport symbol*]   (OAG)
AEY .... Alcohol Education for Youth   (EA)
AEY .... United States Army, Corps of Engineers, Jacksonville District, Jacksonville, FL [*OCLC symbol*]   (OCLC)
AEY .... Waverly, TN [*Location identifier*] [*FAA*]   (FAAL)
AEYC........ Alcohol Education for Youth and Community   (EA)
AeZ .... Aegyptische Zeitschrift [*A publication*]
AEZ .... United States Army Engineer District, Nashville, Nashville, TN [*OCLC symbol*]   (OCLC)
AEZRA...... Advances in Enzyme Regulation [*A publication*]
AF .... A Favor [*In Favor*] [*Spanish*]
A & F......... Abercrombie & Fitch [*Retail stores*]
aF .... Abfarad [*Unit of capacitance*]
AF .... Abnormal Frequency
AF .... Abortion Fund   (EA)
AF .... Accokeek Foundation   (EA)
A & F......... Accounting and Finance   (AFM)
AF .... Accumulation Factor   (DEN)
AF .... Accuracy Figure [*British and Canadian*] [*World War II*]
AF .... Acid-Fast [*Microbiology*]
AF .... Acre-Foot
AF .... Activating Factor [*Biochemistry*]
AF .... Ad Finem [*At or To the End*] [*Latin*]
AF .... Addison Foster [*Record label*]
AF .... Admiral of the Fleet [*British*]
AF .... Advance Freight [*Shipping*]
AF .... Aeronautically Fixed
AF .... Affiliation of Author [*Online database field identifier*]
AF .... Affirmative Flag [*Navy*] [*British*]
AF .... Affix [*Linguistics*]
AF .... Afghani [*Monetary unit*] [*Afghanistan*]
af .... Afghanistan [*MARC country of publication code*] [*Library of Congress*]   (LCCP)
AF .... Afghanistan [*ANSI two-letter standard code*]   (CNC)
AF .... Africa
AF .... [*The*] Africa Fund   (EA)
Af .... African [*Derogatory nickname for blacks in Zimbabwe and South Africa*]
AF .... Aft Fuselage   (NASA)
AF .... After Ford [*Calendar used in Aldous Huxley's novel, "Brave New World;" refers to Henry Ford*]
AF .... Agape Force
AF .... Aggregation Factor [*Biochemistry*]
AF .... Agricultural Forecaster   (NOAA)
A & F......... Agriculture and Forestry Committee [*US Senate*]
AF .... Agriservices Foundation   (EA)
AF .... Air Filter
AF .... Air Forager [*Ornithology*]

AF .... Air Force
AF .... Air Foundation
AF .... Air Frame   (MCD)
AF .... Air France [*ICAO designator*]
A/F .... Air/Fuel [*Mixture ratio*]
AF .... Air-to-Fuel Ratio   (MCD)
A & F......... Aircraft and Facilities [*Navy appropriation*]
A/F .... Airfield   (NATG)
A/F .... Airfile   (FAAC)
AF .... Airframe   (KSC)
AF .... Akumulacija Fondova [*Accumulation of Funds*] [*Yugoslavian*] [*Business term*]
AF .... Al Fine [*To the End*] [*Music*]
AF .... Albumin-Free [*Medicine*]
AF .... Aldehyde Fuchsin [*A dye*]
AF .... Ale Firkin [*Unit of measurement*]   (ROG)
AF .... Alternating Field
AF .... Alternating Flow
AF .... Alternative Fertility [*Demography*]
AF .... Aluminium Federation
AF .... Ambassadors for Friendship   (EA)
AF .... America First   (EA)
AF .... American Fabrics [*A publication*]
AF .... American Forests [*A publication*]
AF .... Americanism Foundation [*Norwalk, OH*]   (EA)
AF .... America's Foundation   (EA)
AF .... America's Future [*New Rochelle, NY*]   (EA)
AF .... Amerind Foundation   (EA)
AF .... Amerique Francaise [*A publication*]
AF .... Aminofluorene [*Also, FA*] [*Carcinogen*]
AF .... Amniotic Fluid [*Obstetrics*]
AF .... Amphiphilic Flavin [*Chemistry*]
AF .... Amplification Factor
A & F......... Analysis and Forecasting, Inc. [*Database producer*]   (IID)
AF .... Anarchist Federation [*British*]
AF .... Anchoring Fibril [*Anatomy*]
AF .... Ancien Franc [*Old Franc*] [*Monetary unit*] [*French*]
AF .... Angelini Francesco [*Italy*] [*Research code symbol*]
AF .... Angiogenesis Factor [*Biochemistry*]
AF .... Anglistische Forschungen [*A publication*]
AF .... Anglo-French [*Language, etc.*]
AF .... Anglo-Frisian [*Language, etc.*]
AF .... Anno Futuro [*In the Next Year*] [*Latin*]   (ADA)
AF .... Anterior [*Part of*] Foot
AF .... Aortic Flow [*Cardiology*]
AF .... Apply Force [*Industrial engineering*]
AF .... Appropriated Funds
AF .... Architectural Forum [*A publication*]
AF .... Archivio di Filosofia [*A publication*]
AF .... Area Weapon Forward   (MCD)
AF .... Aristos Foundation   (EA)
AF .... Armed Forces
A & F......... Arming and Fusing   (AFM)
AF .... Army Force
AF .... Army Form
AF .... Arpad Federation   (EA)
AF .... Arte Figurativa [*A publication*]
AF .... Arthritis Foundation   (EA)
AF .... Artificially Fed
AF .... Artilleriefuehrer [*Division artillery commander*] [*German military - World War II*]
AF .... Artists' Fellowship   (EA)
AF .... Asiatic Fleet [*Obsolete*] [*Navy*]
AF .... Asiatische Forschungen [*A publication*]
Af .... Aspergillus fumigatus [*A fungus*]
AF .... Assembly and Fabrication
AF .... Assembly Fixture   (MCD)
AF .... Associate Fellow   (ADA)
AF .... Associational Fluency [*Personality research*] [*Psychology*]
AF .... Asymmetry Factor [*Mathematics*]
AF .... Atmospheric Flight
AF .... Atomic Fluorescence
AF .... Atomic Forum   (IEEE)
AF .... Atrial Fibrillation [*Cardiology*]
Af .... Atrial Flutter [*Cardiology*]
AF .... Attiyeh Foundation   (EA)
AF .... Audio Frequency [*Data transmission*]
A & F......... August and February [*Denotes semiannual payments of interest or dividends in these months*] [*Business term*]
AF .... Auranofin [*An organogold*]
AF .... Auricular Fibrillation [*Medicine*]
AF .... Aurora Foundation   (EA)
AF .... Ausgrabungen und Funde. Nachrichtenblatt fuer Vor- und Fruehgeschichte [*A publication*]
AF .... Austrian Forum   (EA)
AF .... Auto-Fiche   (MCD)
AF .... Autofocus [*Cameras*]
AF .... Automatic Filter   (ADA)
AF .... Automatic Focusing [*Photography*]
AF .... Automatic Following [*RADAR*]

AF .... Automation Foundation
AF .... Auxiliary Feed [*Nuclear energy*] (NRCH)
AF .... Auxiliary Feedwater [*Nuclear energy*] (NRCH)
AF .... Auxiliary Field (MUGU)
AF .... Availability Factor [*Generating time ratio*] (IEEE)
AF .... Aviation Facilities (FAAC)
AF .... Aviation Forum [*British*]
AF .... Award Fee
AF .... Axial Flow (AAG)
AF .... Axle Flange Gasket [*Automotive engineering*]
AF .... Flug & Fahrzeugwerke AG Altenrhein [*Switzerland*] [*ICAO aircraft manufacturer identifier*] (ICAO)
AF .... Forestburg Public Library, Alberta [*Library symbol*] [*National Library of Canada*] (NLC)
Af .... Frontal Area [*Automotive engineering*]
AF .... Office of Alcohol Fuels [*Department of Energy*]
af----- .... Siam, Gulf of [*MARC geographic area code*] [*Library of Congress*] (LCCP)
AF .... Store Ship [*Navy symbol*]
AF2 .... Popular name for an identification card issued to Air Force military personnel and certain civilian personnel
2-A-F .... Selective Service Class [*for Man Physically Disqualified for Military Service but Engaged in Work in the National Health, Safety, or Interest*] [*Obsolete*]
A & F 15 ..... August 15 and February 15 [*Denotes interest payable on these dates*] [*Business term*]
AFA .... Actors' Fund of America (EA)
AFA .... Acute Focal Appendicitis [*Medicine*]
AFA .... Adams Family Association (EA)
AFA .... Advertising Federation of America [*Later, AAF*]
AFA .... Aerial Field Artillery (MCD)
AFA .... Aerophilatelic Federation of the Americas (EA)
Af A .... Afrique et l'Asie [*Later, Afrique et l'Asie Modernes*] [*A publication*]
afa .... Afro-Asiatic [*MARC language code*] [*Library of Congress*] (LCCP)
AFA .... Air Force Academy
AFA .... Air Force Act [*British military*] (DMA)
AFA .... Air Force Advisory
AFA .... Air Force Association (EA)
AFA .... Air Force Auxiliary [*British*]
AFA .... Air Frame Assembly (MCD)
AFA .... Air Freight Association of America (EA)
AFA .... Aircraft Finance Association [*Later, NAFA*] (EA)
AFA .... Alien Firearms Act
AFA .... Allergy Foundation of America [*Later, A & AFA*]
AFA .... Allied Financial Agency [*World War II*]
AFA .... Allied Fiscal Administration [*World War II*]
AFA .... Amateur Fencing Association (EAIO)
AFA .... American Family Association (EA)
AFA .... American Fan Association (EA)
AFA .... American Farriers Association (EA)
AFA .... American Fashion Association (EA)
AFA .... American Federation of Arts (EA)
AFA .... American Federation of Astrologers (EA)
AFA .... American Federation of Aviculture (EA)
AFA .... American Finance Association (EA)
AFA .... American Firearm Association (EA)
AFA .... American Firewalking Association (EA)
AFA .... American Fitness Association (EA)
AFA .... American Flag Association [*Defunct*] (EA)
AFA .... American Flock Association (EA)
AFA .... American Flyers Airline (MCD)
AFA .... American Forces in Action [*Military*]
AFA .... American Forensic Association (EA)
AFA .... American Forest Adventures (EA)
AFA .... American Forestry Association (EA)
AFA .... American Formalwear Association [*Later, IFA*] (EA)
AFA .... American Foundrymen's Association [*Later, AFS*]
AFA .... American Fracture Association (EA)
AFA .... American Franchise Association (EA)
AFA .... American Freedom Association
AFA .... American Freeman Association (EA)
AFA .... Amfonelic Acid [*Biochemistry*]
AFA .... Analog Filter Assembly (MCD)
AFA .... Anorexic Family Aid and National Information Centre [*British*] (CB)
AFA .... Anthology Film Archives (EA)
AFA .... Application for Federal Assistance (OICC)
AFA .... Application Fit Analysis
AFAS .... Archiv fuer Anthropologie [*A publication*]
AFA .... Archivo de Filologia Aragonesa [*A publication*]
AFA .... Armed Forces Act
AFA .... Army Finance Association [*Defunct*] (EA)
AFA .... Army Flight Activity
AFA .... Arthritis Foundation of Australia
AFA .... Asatru Free Assembly [*Later, AA*] (EA)
AFA .... Asociacion Folklorica Argentina. Anales [*A publication*]
AFA .... Aspirin Foundation of America
AFA .... Assemblee des Franco-Americains/Association of Franco-Americans (EA)

AFA .... Assembly Fixture Accessory (MCD)
AFA .... Assistant Freight Agent
AFA .... Associate of the Faculty of Actuaries [*British*]
AFA .... Associate in Fine Arts
AFA .... Associated Fraternities of America
AFA .... Association of Federal Appraisers [*Later, Association of Governmental Appraisers*]
AFA .... Association of Federal Architects
AFA .... Association of Flight Attendants (EA)
AFA .... Association of Fraternity Advisors (EA)
AFA .... Athletic Footwear Association (EA)
AFA .... Atlanta, GA [*Location identifier*] [*FAA*] (FAAL)
AFA .... Audio Frequency Amplifier
AFA .... Audio Frequency Apparatus
AFA .... Auditor Freight Accounts
AFA .... Australian Family Association
AFA .... Automatic Field Assistant (MCD)
AFA .... Azimuth Follow-Up Amplifier
AFA .... Fort Assiniboine Public Library, Alberta [*Library symbol*] [*National Library of Canada*] (NLC)
AFA .... San Rafael [*Argentina*] [*Airport symbol*] (OAG)
AFA .... United States Army, Corps of Engineers, Wilmington District, Wilmington, NC [*OCLC symbol*] (OCLC)
AFAA .... Adult Film Association of America (EA)
AFAA .... Aerobics and Fitness Association of America (EA)
AFAA .... Air Force Audit Agency
AFAA .... Airline Flight Attendants Association [*Commercial firm*] (EA)
AFAA .... American Fighter Aces Association (EA)
AFAA .... Application for Federal Assistance and Assurances (OICC)
AFAA .... Automatic Fire Alarm Association (EA)
AFAAC ..... Air Force Comptroller
AFAADS ... Advanced Forward Area Air Defense System
AFAADW ... Advanced Forward Area Air Defense Weapon
AFAAEC ... Air Force Academy and Aircrew Examining Center
AFAAR ..... American Fund for Alternatives to Animal Research (EA)
AFAAR ..... Regional Office, Alberta Agriculture, Fairview, Alberta [*Library symbol*] [*National Library of Canada*] (NLC)
AFAA Rept ... AFA [*Aborigines' Friends' Association*] Annual Report [*A publication*] (APTA)
AFA Art .... Associate in Fine Arts in Art
AFAAV ...... Veterinary Laboratory, Alberta Agriculture, Fairview, Alberta [*Library symbol*] [*National Library of Canada*] (NLC)
AFAB .... Air Force Academy Board
AFAB .... Air Force Audit Branch (AFM)
AFABA ...... Association des Federations Africaines de Basketball Amateur [*African Association of Basketball Federations*] (EAIO)
AFABBN ... American Friends of the Anti-Bolshevik Bloc of Nations (EA)
AF-ABN ... American Friends of the Anti-Bolshevik Bloc of Nations (EA)
AFABS ...... Air Force Arctic Broadcasting Squadron [*New York, NY*] (EY)
AFABT ...... Australian Federation of Aestheticians and Beauty Therapists
AFAC .... Air Force Acquisition Circular (MCD)
AFAC .... Air Force Armament Center [*Eglin Air Force Base, FL*]
AFAC .... Airborne Forward Air Controller
AFAC .... Allied Finance Adjusters Conference [*Greensboro, NC*] (EA)
AFAC .... Amateur Fishermen's Advisory Council [*New South Wales, Australia*]
AFAC .... American Fisheries Advisory Committee
AFAC .... Army Finance and Accounting Center (MCD)
AFAC .... Automatic Field Analog Computer
A Fac Agrar (Bari) ... Annali. Facolta di Agraria (Bari) [*A publication*]
A Fac Agrar (Milano) ... Annali. Facolta di Agraria (Milano) [*A publication*]
AFACAL ... Associate Fellow of American College of Allergists (DHSM)
A Fac Dr Liege ... Annales. Faculte de Droit de Liege [*A publication*]
A Fac Dr Lyon ... Annales. Faculte de Droit de Lyon [*A publication*]
A Fac Dr Sci Polit (Clermont) ... Annales. Faculte de Droit et de Science Politique (Clermont) [*A publication*]
AFACE ...... Army Field Artillery Combat Effectiveness Model (MCD)
A Fac Econ Com (Palermo) ... Annali. Facolta di Economia e Commercio (Palermo) [*A publication*]
AFACG ...... Army Air Forces Commanding General [*World War II*]
AFAC & IC ... Air Force Aeronautical Chart and Information Center (MUGU)
A Fac Sci Polit (Genova) ... Annali. Facolta di Scienze Politica (Genova) [*A publication*]
AFAD .... Air Force Acquisition Document (MCD)
AFAD .... Air Force Authorization Document (MCD)
AFAD .... Armed Forces Acquisition Document (NASA)
AFA Dance ... Associate in Fine Arts in Dance
AFADGRU ... Air Force Advisory Group (CINC)
AFA Drama ... Associate in Fine Arts in Drama
AFADS ...... Advanced Forward Air Defense System [*Missiles*] (IEEE)
AFADTC ... Air Force Armament Development and Test Center (MCD)
AFADVMC ... Air Force Advanced Management Class
AFAE .... Air Force Acquisition Executive (MCD)
AFAE .... American Foundation on Automation and Employment [*Later, CNB-TV*] (EA)
AFAEBG ... Acta Faunistica Entomologica. Musei Nationalis Pragae [*A publication*]
AFAEP ...... Association of Fashion Advertising and Editorial Photographers (EAIO)
AFAF .... Air Force Assistance Fund

AFAF......... Air Force Auxiliary Field
AFAF......... Air Force Director of Accounting and Financing (AAG)
AFAF......... Atlantic Fleet Amphibious Force [*Navy*]
AFAFC...... Air Force Accounting and Finance Center
AFAFC...... American Friends of Anne Frank Center (EA)
AFAFFO ... Air Force Aerospace Fuels Field Office (AFM)
AFAFPSO ... Air Force Aerospace Fuel Petroleum Supply Office
AFAG .... Air Force Advisory Group
AFAHC ..... American Foundation for Alternative Health Care [*Later, AFAHCRD*] (EA)
AFAHCRD ... American Foundation for Alternative Health Care, Research, and Development (EA)
AFAI.......... Air Force Agent Installation (AFM)
AFAIAA .... Associate Fellow of the American Institute of Aeronautics and Astronautics [*Formerly, AFIAS*]
AFAITC .... Armed Forces Air Intelligence Training Center
AFAIU....... American Friends of the Alliance Israelite Universelle (EA)
AFA/JFA .. Journal of Field Archaeology. Boston University Association for Field Archaeology [*A publication*]
AFAK........ Armed Forces Assistance to Korea [*Military*]
AFAL......... Air Force Astronautics Laboratory [*Edwards Air Force Base, CA*] (GRD)
AFAL......... Association Francophone d'Amitie et de Liaison (EA)
AFALC...... Air Force Acquisition Logistics Center (MCD)
AFALD...... Air Force Acquisition Logistics Division [*Wright Patterson Air Force Base*] (MCD)
AFALLS.... Air Force Alaskan Long Line System [*Communications*] (MCD)
AFALT ...... Air Force Alternate Headquarters
AFAM .... Air Field Attack Munition (MCD)
AFAM ...... Air Force Achievement Medal [*Military decoration*]
AFAM ...... Air Force Armament Museum
AFAM .... Ancient Free and Accepted Masons [*Freemasonry*]
AF & AM .. Ancient Free and Accepted Masons [*Freemasonry*]
AFAM ...... Australian Family Law Guide [*A publication*]
AFAM .... Automatic Frequency Assignment Model [*Telecommunications*]
AFAMA..... Air Force Air Materiel Area
AFAMA5... Anais. Faculdade de Medicina de Porto Alegre [*A publication*]
AFAMF ..... American Fighter Aces Museum Foundation (EA)
A Family Stud ... Annals of Family Studies [*A publication*]
AFAMM .... Aerial Field Artillery Multi-Mode (MCD)
AFAMRL .. Air Force Aerospace Medical Research Laboratory [*Wright-Patterson Air Force Base, OH*]
AFA Mus.. Associate in Fine Arts in Music
AFANPERA ... African National People's Empire Re-Established (EA)
AFAO .... Air Force Administrative Order [*Canada, 1946-1964*]
AFAO .... Approved Force Acquisition Objective [*Army*] (AABC)
AFAP......... AFA Protective Systems, Inc. [*NASDAQ symbol*] (NQ)
AFAP......... Air Forces, Arabian Peninsula [*British military*] (DMA)
AFAP......... Artillery-Fired Atomic Projectile
AFAPL ...... Air Force Aero-Propulsion Laboratory [*Wright-Patterson Air Force Base, OH*] (AFM)
AFAPO...... Air Force Accountable Property Officer (AAG)
AFAR........ Advanced Field Array RADAR
AFAR........ Aid for Afghan Refugees [*An association*] (EA)
AFAR........ Airborne Fixed Array RADAR (MSA)
AFAR........ American Federation for Aging Research (EA)
AFAR........ American Foundation for Aging Research (EA)
AFAR........ American Foundation for AIDS Research (EA)
AFAR........ American Friends of Afghan Refugees (EA)
AFAR........ Attorneys for Animal Rights (EA)
AFAR........ Australian Foreign Affairs Record [*A publication*] (APTA)
AFAR........ Automatic False Alarm Rate
AFAR........ Azores Fixed Acoustic Range [*NATO*]
Afar Cont Oceanic Rifting Proc Int Symp ... Afar between Continental and Oceanic Rifting. Proceedings of an International Symposium [*A publication*]
AFARD...... Association des Femmes Africaines pour la Recherche sur le Developpement [*Association of African Women for Research and Development - AAWORD*] (EAIO)
AFARS ...... Army Federal Acquisition Regulations Supplement [*Army*]
AFARV...... Armored Forward Area Rearm Vehicle (MCD)
AFARV...... Armored Forward Area Resupply Vehicle (MCD)
AFAS......... Advanced Field Artillery System
AFAS......... Afrique et l'Asie. Revue Politique, Sociale, et Economique et Bulletin des Anciens du CHEAM [*A publication*]
AFAS......... Afro-American Studies Librarians Section [*Association of College and Research Libraries*]
AFAS......... Air Flow Actuated Switch
AFAS......... Air Force Aid Society (EA)
AFAS......... American Fine Arts Society (EA)
AFAS......... Area Fire Armor System
AFAS......... Associate of the Faculty of Architects and Surveyors [*British*]
AFAS......... Associate of the Faculty of Astrological Studies [*British*]
AFAS......... Automated Frequency Assignment System [*Telecommunications*]
AFAS......... Auxiliary Feedwater Actuating System [*Nuclear energy*] (NRCH)
AFAS-C..... Advanced Field Artillery System - Cannon
AFASC .... Air Force Aeronautical Systems Command

AFASD...... Air Force Aeronautical Systems Division
AFASE ...... Association for Applied Solar Energy [*Later, International Solar Energy Society*]
AFASED ... African Association of Education for Development (EAIO)
AFA-SEF... Air Force Association - Space Education Foundation
AFASIC..... Association for All Speech Impaired Children (EAIO)
AFASPO ... Air Force Automated Systems Project Office
AF/ASPR .. Air Force/Armed Service Procurement Regulation
AFAST ...... Army Field Assistance and Technology
AFAT........ Air Force Acceptance Team (MCD)
AFAT........ Air Force Advisory Team
AFATDS.... Advanced Field Artillery Tactical Data System
AFATL ...... Air Force Armament Technology Laboratory [*Eglin Air Force Base, FL*] (AFM)
AFAUD ..... Air Force Auditor General
AF/AUR.... Air University. Review. US Air Force [*A publication*]
AFAUSSS ... Association of Former Agents of the US Secret Service (EA)
AFAUX .... Air Force Auxiliary Field
AFAW .... Fawcett Public Library, Alberta [*Library symbol*] [*National Library of Canada*] (NLC)
AFAX........ Amerifax, Inc. [*NASDAQ symbol*] (NQ)
AFaxA ...... American Facsimile Association [*Later, IFAXA*] (EA)
AFB........... Acid-Fast Bacillus [*Microbiology*]
AFB........... Aflatoxin B [*Mycotoxin*]
AfB............ Africana Bulletin [*Warsaw*] [*A publication*]
AFB........... Air Force Base
AFB........... Air Force Bulletin
AFB........... Air Freight Bill [*Shipping*]
AFB........... Aircooled Fluidized Bed [*Chemical engineering*]
AFB........... Airframe Bulletin (MCD)
AFB........... All Former Buyers
AFB........... American Farm Bureau
AFB........... American Festival Ballet
AFB........... American Fibre Corp. [*Vancouver Stock Exchange symbol*]
AFB........... American Foulbrood [*Honeybee disease*]
AFB........... American Foundation for the Blind (EA)
AFB........... Anal Fin Base [*Fish anatomy*]
AFB........... Anarchist Federation of Britain
AFB........... Antifriction Bearing
AFB........... Aorto-Femoral Bypass [*Medicine*]
AFB........... Atmospheric Fluidized Bed [*Chemical engineering*]
AFB........... Australian Fringe Benefits Tax Guide for Employers [*A publication*]
AFBA........ Armed Forces Broadcasters Association (EA)
AFBAA...... Armed Forces Benefit and Aid Association (EA)
AFBALTAP ... Allied Forces Baltic Approaches [*NATO*] (MCD)
AFBC......... Atmospheric Fluidized-Bed Combustion [*Fuel technology*]
AFBD........ Association of Futures Brokers and Dealers (EAIO)
AFBDA...... Anti-Friction Bearing Distributors Association [*Later, BSA*] (EA)
AFBF........ American Farm Bureau Federation (EA)
AFBFAR.... Air Force Bent Fin Artillery Rocket (MCD)
AFBG......... Arteriofemoral Bypass Graft [*Medicine*]
AFBH .... American Friends of Beit Halochem (EA)
AFBH .... American Friends of Beth Hatefutsoth (EA)
AFBITS..... Air Force Base Information Transfer System (MCD)
AFBK........ Affiliated Bankshares of Colorado, Inc. [*NASDAQ symbol*] (NQ)
AFBM........ Air Force Ballistic Missile (KSC)
AFBM........ Association of Fancy Box Makers [*A union*] [*British*]
AFBMA.... Air Force Ballistic Missile Arsenal
AFBMA.... Anti-Friction Bearing Manufacturers Association (EA)
AFBMAA ... Anales. Facultad de Farmacia y Bioquimica. Universidad Nacional Mayor de San Marcos de Lima [*A publication*]
AFBMC..... Air Force Ballistic Missile Center
AFBMC..... Air Force Ballistic Missile Committee
AFBMD..... Air Force Ballistic Missile Division [*Inglewood, CA*]
AFBMIR ... Air Force Ballistic Missile Installation Regulation
AFBMTC .. Air Force Ballistic Missile Training Center
AFBO .... Approved Force Budget Objective [*Army*] (AABC)
AFBODJ ... Acta Farmaceutica Bonaerense [*A publication*]
AFBP......... Air Force Bailment Property
AFBR........ Air Force Board of Review
AFBRB ...... American Foundation for the Blind. Research Bulletin [*A publication*]
AFB Res Bull ... American Foundation for the Blind. Research Bulletin [*A publication*]
AFBRF ...... American Farm Bureau Research Foundation (EA)
AFBRMC .. Air Force Business Research Management Center [*Wright-Patterson Air Force Base, OH*]
AFBS .... Air Force Board Structure (MCD)
AFBS .... American and Foreign Bible Society
AFBSD ...... Air Force Ballistic Systems Division [*Later, Space and Missile Systems Operations*]
AFBTAV ... Archivos de Farmacia y Bioquimica del Tucuman [*A publication*]
AFBTBW .. Australia. Commonwealth Scientific and Industrial Research Organisation. Forest Products Laboratory. Technological Paper [*A publication*]
AFBTR ...... Association for Brain Tumor Research (EA)

AFBU......... Agriculture and Forestry Bulletin. University of Alberta [*A publication*]
AFBU......... Air Force Base Unit
AFBUD3.... Agriculture and Forestry Bulletin [*A publication*]
AFBW........ Analog Fly by Wire [*Aviation*]
AFC............ Acadian Friendship Committee [*See also CAA*] (EAIO)
AFC............ Acupuncture Foundation of Canada
AFC............ Adjustable Focus Control   (MCD)
AFC............ Adult Foster Care
AFC............ Advanced Fighter Capability   (MCD)
AFC............ Advanced Fire Control   (MCD)
AFC............ Aerodynamic Flight Control   (MCD)
AFC0.......... Affiliation Code [*IRS*]
AFC............ African Farmers Committee [*See also CPA*]   (EAIO)
AFC............ African Football Confederation   (EAIO)
AFC............ African Forestry Commission [*UN Food and Agriculture Organization*]
AFC............ Air Flow Control [*Automotive engineering*]
AFC............ Air Force Circulars
AFC............ Air Force Component
AFC............ Air Force Comptroller   (AAG)
AFC............ Air Force Council [*Advisory board to Air Force*]
AFC............ Air Force Cross [*Military decoration*] [*US and British*]
AFC............ Airflex Clutch   (DS)
AFC............ Airframe Change   (MCD)
AFC............ Airworthiness and Flight Characteristics   (MCD)
AFC............ Alabama Fan Club   (EA)
AFC............ ALIBI Fan Club   (EA)
AFC............ Alkaline Fuel Cell
AFC............ Alliance for Fair Competition [*Falls Church, VA*]   (EA)
AFC............ Aluminum Field Coil
AFC............ American Filtrona Corp.
AFC............ American Finance Conference [*Later, NCFA*]   (EA)
AFC............ American Flag Committee   (EA)
AFC............ American Flight Center, Inc. [*Fort Worth, TX*] [*FAA designator*]   (FAAC)
AFC............ American Folklife Center [*Library of Congress*]
AFC............ American Football Conference [*of NFL*]
AFC............ American Forest Council   (EA)
AFC............ American Foxhound Club   (EA)
AFC............ American Freedom Center   (EA)
AFC............ American Fructose Corporation [*AMEX symbol*]   (SPSG)
AFC............ Anales de Filologia Clasica [*A publication*]
AFC............ Analog to Frequency Converter
AFC............ Antenna for Communications
AFC............ Antibody-Forming Cell [*Immunology*]
AFC............ Apollo Flight Control [*NASA*]   (MCD)
AFC............ Apostolate for Family Consecration   (EA)
AFC............ April Fan Club   (EA)
AFC............ Aquatic Federation of Canada
AFC............ Area Forecast Center   (FAAC)
AFC............ Area Frequency Coordinator   (MUGU)
A & FC...... Armament and Fire Control   (MCD)
AFC............ Armament and Fuel Coordinator   (MCD)
AFC............ Armed Forces Comptroller [*A publication*]
AFC............ Armed Forces Council
AFC............ Army Field Commands
AFC............ Army Finance Center
AFC............ Army Flying Corps [*British*]   (AIA)
AFC............ Asian Football Confederation   (EAIO)
AFC............ Assimilation and Fractional Crystallization [*Geology*]
AFC............ Association of Feminine Collectives [*Canada*]
AFC............ Association of Film Commissioners   (EA)
AFC............ Athletic Footwear Council [*Later, AFA*]   (EA)
AFC............ Atomic Fuel Corporation [*Japan*]
AFC............ Audio Frequency Change
AFC............ Audio Frequency Choke
AFC............ Audio Frequency Coder
AFC............ Auditor Freight Claims
AFC............ Australia Fan Club   (EA)
AFCK.......... Australian Fluorine Chemicals
AFC............ Automated Fare Collection
AFC............ Automatic Fidelity Control
AFC............ Automatic Fire Control
AFC............ Automatic Flight Control
AFC............ Automatic Flow Control
AFC............ Automatic Frequency Control [*Electronics*]
AFC............ Average Fixed Cost [*Economics*]
AFC............ Aviation Fire Controlman [*Navy*]
AFC............ Axial Flow Compressor
AFC............ Faust Community Library, Alberta [*Library symbol*] [*National Library of Canada*]   (NLC)
AFC............ Fayette County Court House, Fayette, AL [*Library symbol*] [*Library of Congress*]   (LCLS)
AFC............ United States Army, Concepts Analysis Agency, Bethesda, MD [*OCLC symbol*]   (OCLC)
AFCA......... American Fastener and Closure Association   (EA)
AFCA......... American Football Coaches Association   (EA)
AFCA......... Anadromous Fish Conservation Act [*1965*]
AFCA......... Armed Forces Chemical Association [*Later, ADPA*]   (EA)

AFCA......... Armed Forces Communications Association [*Later, AFCEA*]   (MCD)
AFCA......... Assistant Freight Claim Agent
AFCA......... Association Francaise pour la Communaute Atlantique [*French Association for the Atlantic Community*]   (NATG)
AFCAC...... African Civil Aviation Commission [*See also CAFAC*]   (EAIO)
AFCAC...... Air Force Computer Acquisition Center
AFCAI...... Associate Fellow of the Canadian Aeronautical Institute
AFCAL...... Association Francaise de Calcul [*French computing association*]   (MCD)
AFCAM..... Air Force Coated Aluminum Metal   (MCD)
AFCAN..... Analog Factor Calibration Network
AFCAO..... Air Force Computer Acquisition Office
AFCARA .. Air Force Civilian Appellate Review Agency
AFCAS ...... Advanced Flight Control Actuation System [*Navy*]   (MCD)
AFCAS ...... Army Air Forces Chief of the Air Staff [*World War II*]
AFCAS ...... Athabaska Delta Community School, Fort Chipewyan, Alberta [*Library symbol*] [*National Library of Canada*]   (BIB)
AFCAS-AE ... Advanced Flight Control Actuation System - All Electric   (MCD)
AFCASOLE ... Association des Fabricants de Cafe Soluble des Pays de la CEE [*Association of Soluble Coffee Manufacturers of the Countries of the European Economic Community*]
AFCAT ...... Alert Force Capability Test   (MCD)
AFC-AU .... American Friends of Chung-Ang University   (EA)
AFCB......... Armed Forces Combat Bulletin
AFCC......... Air Force Combat Command
AFCC......... Air Force Communication Center
AFCC......... Air Force Component Commander   (AFM)
AFCC......... Arsenal Family and Children's Center [*Research center*]   (RCD)
AFCC......... Assault Fire Command Console [*Army*]
AFCC......... Association of Family and Conciliation Courts   (EA)
AFCCB ...... Air Force Configuration Control Board   (AAG)
AFCCDC ... Air Force Command and Control Development Center
AFCCDD... Air Force Command and Control Development Division [*Bedford, MA*]   (AAG)
AFCCDM ... Anales. Facultad de Ciencias Quimicas y Farmacologicas. Universidad de Chile [*A publication*]
AFCCE ...... Association of Federal Communications Consulting Engineers   (EA)
AFCCG...... Atlantic Fleet Combat Camera Group [*Obsolete*]
AFCCP...... Air Force Command and Control Post
AFCCP...... Air Force Component Command Post   (AFM)
AFCCPC... Air Force Communications Computer Programming Center
AFCCS...... Air Force Command and Control System
AFCD........ Advanced Fighter Capability Demonstrator   (MCD)
AFCD........ Air Force Cryptologic Depot   (AFM)
AFCE........ Air Force Civil Engineer [*A publication*]
AFCE........ Air Force Civil Engineering Unit   (MCD)
AFCE........ Allied Forces Central Europe [*NATO*]   (MCD)
AFCE........ American Foundation for Continuing Education   (EA)
AFCE........ Automatic Flight Control Equipment
AFCEA ...... Armed Forces Communications and Electronics Association   (EA)
AFCEC...... Air Force Civil Engineering Center [*Tyndall Air Force Base, FL*]
AFCEL ...... Air Force Contractor Experience List   (AFM)
AFCENT ... Allied Forces Central Europe [*NATO*]
AFCET ...... Association Francaise Cybernetique, Economique, et Technique [*French Association for Economic and Technical Cybernetics*]
AFCF .... Anthropology Film Center Foundation   (EA)
AFCFP....... Arab Federation of Chemical Fertilizer Producers   (EA)
AFCG........ American Fine China Guild   (EA)
AFCGRB .. American Friends of Covent Garden and the Royal Ballet   (EA)
AFCH .... Air Force Component Headquarters
AFCI .... American Foot Care Institute [*Defunct*]   (EA)
AFCI .... Associate of the Faculty of Commerce and Industry [*British*]   (DBQ)
AFCIA .... Armed Forces Civilian Instructors Association   (EA)
AFCIS-L.... Armor Full Crew Research Simulator Center - Laboratory
AFCK........ Antenna Field Charge Kit
AFCM....... Air Force Commendation Medal [*Military decoration*]   (AFM)
AFCM....... Association for Classical Music [*Later, MA*]   (EA)
AFCM....... Association of First Class Mailers
AFCM....... Fox Creek Municipal Library, Alberta [*Library symbol*] [*National Library of Canada*]   (NLC)
AFCM....... Master Chief Aircraft Maintenanceman [*Navy rating*]
AFCMA..... Aluminum Foil Container Manufacturers Association   (EA)
AFCMC .... Air Force Contract Maintenance Center   (AFM)
AFCMCH ... Acta Facultatis Rerum Naturalium Universitatis Comenianae. Microbiologia [*A publication*]
AFCMD..... Air Force Contract Management Division [*Los Angeles, CA*]
AFCMO .... Air Force Contract Management Office
AFCN .... American Friends of the Captive Nations [*Defunct*]   (EA)
AFCNF ..... Air Force Central Notice to Airmen Facility
AFCO .... Admiralty Fleet Confidential Order [*British*]   (DMA)
AFCO .... Air Force Contracting Officer
AFCO .... Air Force Control Office   (AAG)
AFCO .... American Family Communiversity   (EA)
AFCO .... American First Corporation [*NASDAQ symbol*]   (NQ)
AFCO .... Automatic Fuel Cutoff [*NASA*]   (KSC)

AFCOA...... Air Force Chief of Operations Analysis (MUGU)
AFCOA...... Air Force Contracting Office Approval
AFCOLR... Air Force Coordinating Office for Logistics Research (MCD)
AFCOM.... AFTN [*Aeronautical Fixed Telecommunications Network*] Communications Center [*FAA*] (FAAC)
AFCOM.... Air Force Commendation Medal [*Military decoration*]
AFCOM.... Air Force Communications [*Satellite*]
AFCOMMSTA... Air Force Communications Station
AFCOMPMET... Air Force Comptroller Management Engineering Team
AFCOMS.. Air Force Commissary Service
AFCOMSEC... Air Force Communications Security
AFCOMSECCEN... Air Force Communications Security Center (AFM)
AFCOMSECM... Air Force Communications Security Manual
AFCON..... Air Force Controlled [*Units*]
AFCORS... Advanced Fire Control RADAR System (MCD)
AFCOS...... Air Force Combat Operations Staff
AFCOS...... Armed Forces Courier Service
AFCP........ Advanced Flight Control Programmer
AFCP........ Air Force Command Post
AFCP........ Automatic Flight Control Panel (MCD)
AFCPDR... Symposium on Fundamental Cancer Research [*A publication*]
AFCR....... American Federation for Clinical Research (EA)
AFCR....... American Foster Care Resources (EA)
AFCR....... American Fund for Czechoslovak Refugees (EA)
AFCRB..... Air Force Central Review Board (AAG)
AFCRC...... Air Force Cambridge Research Center [*Obsolete*]
AFCRL...... Air Force Cambridge Research Laboratories [*Later, AFGL*] [*Hanscom Air Force Base, MA*]
AFCRL...... Air Force Cambridge Research Library (MCD)
AFCRP...... Air Force Cost Reduction Program (AFM)
AFCRS...... Airborne Fire Control RADAR Set (MCD)
AFCS........ Active Federal Commissioned Service
AFCS........ Adaptive Flight Control System
AFCS........ Advanced Flight Control System (MCD)
AFCS........ Air Force Communications Service [*or System*] [*Scott Air Force Base, IL*]
AFCS........ Air Force Communications Squadron (MCD)
AFCS........ Army Facilities Components System (AABC)
AFCS........ Army Functional Component System
AFCS........ Automatic Fare Collection System
AFCS........ Automatic Fire Control System (AAG)
AFCS........ Automatic Flight Control System [*Aerospace*]
AFCS........ Avionic Flight Control System
AFCS........ Fox Creek School, Alberta [*Library symbol*] [*National Library of Canada*] (BIB)
AFCSC...... Air Force Command and Staff College
AFCSC...... Air Force Cryptologic Support Center
AFCSCP.... Automatic Flight Control System Control Panel (MCD)
AFCSDG... Air Force Container System Development Group
AFCS E & I... Air Force Communications Service, Engineering and Installation (CET)
AFCSL...... Air Force Communications Security Letter
AFCSM..... Air Force Communications Security Manual
AFCSM..... Air Force Communications Service Manual
AFCSP...... Air Force Communications Security Pamphlet (MCD)
AFCSS....... Air Force Communications Support System
AFCSS....... Army in the Field Containers System Study (MCD)
AFCT........ Affect
AFCT........ Alert Force Capability Test (MCD)
AFCTCP.... Air Force Combat Theater Communications Program (AFIT)
AFC & TO... Air Force Clothing and Textile Office (AFIT)
AFCTS...... Air Force Combined Tomography System (MCD)
AFCTV...... Action for Children's Television
AFCU........ American and Foreign Christian Union (EA)
AFCU........ American Friends of Cambridge University (EA)
AFCU........ Archivos del Folklore Chileno. Universidad de Chile [*A publication*]
AFCU........ Association of Federal Computer Users (EA)
AFCVC...... Vice Chief of Staff [*Air Force*]
AFCWB..... American Federation of Catholic Workers for the Blind [*Later, CAPVI*] (EA)
AFCWBVH... American Federation of Catholic Workers for the Blind and Visually Handicapped [*Later, CAPVI*] (EA)
AFCWF..... Air Force Civilian Welfare Fund (AFM)
AFCX........ Anchor Financial Corporation [*Myrtle Beach, SC*] [*NASDAQ symbol*] (NQ)
AFD.......... Accelerated Freeze-Drying [*Food processing*]
AFD.......... Acoustic Firing Device (CAAL)
AFD.......... Active Filter Design
AFD.......... Admiralty Floating Dock [*British*]
AFD.......... African Development [*A publication*]
AFD.......... Aft Flight Deck (NASA)
AFD.......... Air Force Depot
AFD.......... Air Force Directive (AAG)
AFD.......... Airborne Frequency Doubler
AFD.......... Airport/Facility Directory (FAAC)
AFD.......... Alternating Field Demagnetization
AFD.......... Americans for Decency (EA)
AFD.......... Ammunition Ship
AFD.......... Amplitude-Frequency Distortion
AFD.......... April Fools' Day

AfD.......... Archiv fuer Diplomatik [*A publication*]
AFD.......... Arithmetic Function Designator
AFD.......... Arm/Fire Device (MCD)
AFD.......... Armed Forces Day
AFD.......... Arming and Fusing Device
AFD.......... Assistant Field Director [*Red Cross*]
AFD.......... Assistant Flight Director [*NASA*] (KSC)
AFD.......... Association of Food Distributors [*Later, AFI*] (EA)
AFD.......... Association of Footwear Distributors (EA)
AFD.......... Australian Faculty Directory [*A publication*]
AFD.......... Australian Federation for Decency
AFD.......... Automated Flaw Detector
AFD.......... Automatic Fast Demagnetization
AFD.......... Auxiliary Floating Dry Dock [*Navy symbol*]
AFD.......... Axial Flux Density (IEEE)
AFD.......... Axial Flux Difference [*Nuclear energy*] (NRCH)
AFD.......... Bibliotheque Dentinger [*Dentinger Library*] Falher, Alberta [*Library symbol*] [*National Library of Canada*] (NLC)
AFD.......... Doctor of Fine Arts
AFD.......... Panorama Flight Service [*White Plains, NY*] [*FAA designator*] (FAAC)
AFD.......... Watford City, ND [*Location identifier*] [*FAA*] (FAAL)
AFDA........ Axial Flux Difference Alarm (IEEE)
AFDAA...... Air Force Data Automation Agency (AFM)
AFDAG..... Airborne Forward Delivery Airfield Group
AFDAMET... Air Force Data Automation Management Engineering Team
AFDAP...... Air Force Data Automation Planning Concepts [*Manual*]
AFDAP...... Air Force Designated Acquisition Program
AFDAP...... Assistant for Development Planning [*Air Force*]
AFDAR...... Air Force Defense Acquisition Regulations (MCD)
AFDAS...... Aircraft Fatigue Data Analysis System (ADA)
AFDAS...... Airframe Fatigue Data Analysis System (MCD)
AFDASTA... Air Force Data Station
AFDAT...... Air Force Directorate of Advanced Technology
AFDATACOM... Air Force Data Communications System
AFDATASTA... Air Force Data Station (CET)
AfDB......... African Development Bank [*Also, ADB*] (EY)
AFDB........ Air Force Decorations Board
AFDB........ Alternative Fuel Data Bank [*Bartlesville Energy Technology Center*] [*Database*]
AFDB........ Armed Forces Development Board
AFDB........ Auxiliary Floating Dry Dock (Big) [*Non-self-propelled*] [*Navy symbol*]
AFDC......... Agriculture and Fishery Development Corporation [*South Korea*]
AFDC........ Aid to Families with Dependent Children
AFDC........ Air Force Department Constabulary [*British military*] (DMA)
AFDC........ Association des Facultes Dentaires du Canada [*Association of Dentistry Faculties in Canada*]
AFDC........ Australian Film Development Corporation
AFDC........ Automatic Formation Drone Control (MCD)
AFDC........ Auxiliary Floating Dry Dock (Concrete) [*Non-self-propelled*] [*Navy symbol*]
AFDCAO... Advances in Fluorine Research and Dental Caries Prevention [*A publication*]
AFDCB...... Armed Forces Disciplinary Control Board
AFDCCO... Air Force Departmental Catalog Coordinating Office
AFDCF...... American First Day Cover Foundation (EA)
AFDCO...... Air Force Distribution Control Office
AFDCP...... Aft Flight Deck Control Panel (MCD)
AFDCP...... Air Force Decision Coordinating Paper (MCD)
AFDCS...... American First Day Cover Society (EA)
AFDCS...... Association of First Division Civil Servants [*British*]
AFDCS...... Automatic Film Data Collection System (MCD)
AFDCUF... Aid to Families with Dependent Children of Unemployed Fathers
AFDC-UP... Aid to Families with Dependent Children - Unemployed Parents
AFDDA...... Air Force Director of Data Automation (IEEE)
AFDDC...... Deputy Chief of Staff, Development, Air Force
AFDE........ American Fund for Dental Education [*Later, AFDH*] (EA)
AFDE........ Arctic Fuel Dispensing Equipment (MCD)
AFDE........ Association of Forensic Document Examiners (EA)
AFDEA...... American Funeral Directors and Embalmers Association (EA)
AFDEC...... Association of Franchised Distributors of Electronic Components [*British*]
AFDEN..... Adult Females, Density Of [*Ecology*]
AFDF........ African Development Fund
AFDFO...... Development Field Office [*Air Force*]
AFDFR...... Air Force Development Field Representative (AAG)
AFDFS...... Air Force Department Fire Service [*British military*] (DMA)
AFDH....... American Fund for Dental Health (EA)
AFDI......... Annuaire Francais de Droit International [*A publication*]
AFDI......... Australian Forest Development Institute
AFDIERSS... Air Force Departmental Industrial Equipment Reserve Storage Site
Afd Inform... Afdeling Informatica [*A publication*]
AFDIS....... Air Force Director of Inspection Services (MUGU)
AFDIT....... Associazione Italiana dei Fornitori e Distributori di Informazione Telematica [*Italian Association for the Production and Distribution of Online Information*] [*Rome*] [*Information service or system*] (IID)

AFDK .... After Dark (FAAC)
AFDL .... Annales. Faculte de Droit de Liege [*A publication*]
AFDL .... Auxiliary Floating Dry Dock (Little) [*Non-self-propelled*] [*Navy symbol*]
AFDL(C) ... Auxiliary Floating Dry Dock (Little, Concrete) [*Non-self-propelled*] [*Navy symbol*]
AFDM .... Air Force Driver Magazine [*A publication*]
AFDM .... Ash-Free Dry Mass [*Analytical chemistry*]
AFDM .... Auxiliary Floating Dry Dock (Medium) [*Non-self-propelled*] [*Navy symbol*]
Afd Math Beslisk ... Afdeling Mathematische Besliskunde [*Amsterdam*] [*A publication*]
Afd Math Statist ... Afdeling Mathematische Statistiek [*Amsterdam*] [*A publication*]
AFDMP ..... Air Force Directorate of Materials and Processes (KSC)
AFDMS ...... Airborne Flight Detection Measurement System (MCD)
Afd Numer Wisk ... Afdeling Numerieke Wiskunde [*A publication*]
AFDO .... Aft Flight Deck Operator (MCD)
AFDO .... Air Force Duty Officer
AFDO .... Assistant Fighter Director Office [*Navy*]
AFDO .... Assistant Flight Dynamics Officer [*NASA*]
AFDO .... Association of Food and Drug Officials (EA)
AFDOA ..... Armed Forces Dental Officers Association (EA)
AFDOUS .... Association of Food and Drug Officials of the United States [*Later, AFDO*] (EA)
AFDP .... Army Force Development Plan
AFDPDB .... Aft Flight Deck Power Distribution Box (MCD)
AFDR .... Air Force Directorate of Requirement (AAG)
AFDRB ...... Air Force Disability Review Board
AFDRB ...... Air Force Discharge Review Board
AFDRD ..... Air Force Director [*or Directorate*] of Research and Development
AFDRIF ..... Air Force Directory of Resident Inspection Facilities (AAG)
AFDRQ ..... Air Force Director of Requirements
AFDS .... Advanced Fighter Diagnostic System (MCD)
AFDS .... Amphibious Flagship Data System [*Military*] (NVT)
AFDS .... Associated Funeral Directors Service (EA)
AFDS .... Association for the Free Distribution of the Scriptures [*British*]
AFDS .... Automatic Flight Director System (MCD)
AFDS .... Auxiliary Fighter Director Ship [*Navy*]
AFDSC ...... Air Force Data Services Center
AFDSDC ... Air Force Data Systems Design Center [*Gunter Air Force Station, AL*] (AFM)
AFDSEC .... Air Force Data Systems Evaluation Center
AFDSI .... Associated Funeral Directors Service International (EA)
AFDT .... AEELS [*Airborne ELINT Emitter Location System*] Fixed Downlink Terminal (MCD)
AFDT .... Air Freight Decision Tool (MCD)
AFDTL ...... Air Force Drug Testing Laboratory [*Brooks Air Force Base, TX*] (GRD)
Afd Toegepaste Wisk ... Afdeling Toegepaste Wiskunde [*A publication*]
AFDU .... Air Fighting Development Unit [*British*]
AFDVT ...... Affidavit
Afd Zuiv Wisk ... Afdeling Zuivere Wiskunde [*A publication*]
AFE .... Accredited Financial Examiner [*Designation awarded by Society of Financial Examiners*]
AFE .... Aerospace Facilities Engineer
AFE .... African Trade Review [*A publication*]
AFE .... Agricultural Futures Exchange [*London, England*]
AFE .... Air Force in Europe
AFE .... Air Force Experiment
AFE .... Allowed Failure Effect
AFE .... Alternate Fighter Engine (MCD)
AFE .... Americans for the Environment (EA)
AFE .... Amniotic Fluid Embolism [*Obstetrics*]
AFE .... Apple File Exchange [*Data processing*]
AFE .... Authority for Expenditure
AFE .... Automatic Fire Extinguisher (MCD)
AFE .... Royal Air Force Establishments [*British*]
AFEA .... American Farm Economic Association [*Later, AAEA*] (EA)
AFEA .... American Film Export Association (EA)
AFEA .... Automobile Fuel Efficiency Act of 1980
AFEA .... Aviation Facilities Energy Association (EA)
AFEAS .... Association Feminine d'Education et d'Action Sociale [*Women's Association of Education and Social Action*] [*Canada*]
AFEB .... Armed Forces Epidemiological Board [*Washington, DC*]
AFEB .... Award Fee Evaluation Board [*NASA*] (NASA)
AFEBS .... Air Force European Broadcasting Squadron
AFEC .... Association Francaise des Etudes Canadiennes [*French Association of Canadian Studies*]
AFEC .... Association Francophone d'Education Comparee [*French-Speaking Comparative Education Association - FSCEA*] (EAIO)
AFEC .... Award Fee Evaluation Committee [*NASA*] (NASA)
AFECI .... Association des Fabricants Europeens de Chauffe-Bains et Chauffe-Eau Instantanes et de Chaudieres Murales au Gaz [*Association of European Manufacturers of Instantaneous Gas Water Heaters and Wall-Hung Boilers*] (EA)

AFECOGAZ ... Association des Fabricants Europeens d'Appareils de Controle [*European Control Manufacturers Association*] (EAIO)
AFED .... Atlanfed Bancorp, Inc. [*NASDAQ symbol*] (NQ)
AFEDEF ...... Association des Fabricants Europeens d'Equipements Ferroviaires [*Association of European Railway Equipment Manufacturers*] (EAIO)
AFEDPC .... Air Force Electronic Data Processing Center (AAG)
AFEE .... Association for Evolutionary Economics [*Lincoln, NE*] (EA)
AFEE .... Association Francaise pour l'Etude des Eaux [*French Water Study Association*] [*Paris*] [*Information service or system*] (IID)
AFEES .... Air Forces Escape and Evasion Society (EA)
AFEES .... Armed Forces Examining and Entrance Stations (AFM)
AFEES .... Automated Armed Forces Examining and Entrance Station
AFEFL ...... Andelin Foundation for Education in Family Living (EA)
AFEI .... Americans for Energy Independence (EA)
AFEI .... Association of Finnish Electric Industries
AFEIS .... Armed Forces Examining and Induction Stations
AFELIS ..... Air Force Engineering and Logistics Information System (IEEE)
AFEM .... Armed Forces Expeditionary Medal [*Military decoration*] (AFM)
AFEMMIS ... Air Force Equipment Maintenance Management Information System (MCD)
AFEMS ...... Air Force Equipment Management System (AFM)
AFEMST ... Air Force Equipment Management Survey Team
AFEMT ...... Air Force Equipment Management Team (AFIT)
AFEO .... ASEAN [*Association of South East Asian Nations*] Federation of Engineering Organizations (EAIO)
AFEOAR .... Air Force European Office of Aerospace Research (KSC)
AFEOC ...... Air Force Emergency Operations Center (CET)
AFEOS ...... Air Force Electro-Optical Site (CET)
AFEP .... Army Facilities Energy Program (MCD)
AFEPBA .... Armed Forces Enlisted Personnel Benefit Association [*Later, MBA*]
AFEPI .... Air Force Equipment Procurement Instruction
AFEQD ..... Air Force Engineering and Services Quarterly [*A publication*]
AFER .... African Ecclesial Review [*A publication*]
AFER .... Air Force Engineering Responsibility (CET)
AFERA ...... Association des Fabricants Europeens de Rubans Auto-Adhesifs [*Association of European Manufacturers of Self-Adhesive Tapes - AEMSAT*] (EAIO)
AFERB ...... Air Force Educational Requirements Board (AFM)
AFERC ...... Air Force Edwards Research Center
AFERSS .... Air Force Environmental Rocket-Sounding System [*Meteorology*]
AFES .... Admiralty Fuel Experimental Station [*British*]
AFES .... Aggregate Field Expense Study [*LIMRA*]
AFES .... Air Force Exchange Service (AFM)
AFES .... American Far Eastern Society (EA)
AFES .... Armed Forces Examining Station
AFES .... Automatic Feature Extraction System (MCD)
AFESC ...... Air Force Electronic Security Command
AFESC .... Air Force Engineering and Services Center [*Tyndall Air Force Base, FL*]
AFESC/ESL ... Air Force Engineering and Services Center/Engineering and Services Laboratory [*Tyndall Air Force Base, FL*]
AFESD ...... Air Force Electronic Systems Division
AFESD ...... Arab Fund for Economic and Social Development
AFESMET ... Air Force Engineering and Services Management Engineering Team
AFest .... Australian Festival [*Record label*]
AFETAC ... Air Force Environmental Technical Applications Center (MCD)
AFETO ...... Air Force Engineering Technology Office [*Tyndall Air Force Base, FL*]
AFETR ...... Air Force Eastern Test Range [*Later, ESMC*] [*Patrick Air Force Base, FL*]
AFETRM .. Air Force Eastern Test Range Manual [*A publication*] (MCD)
AFETS .... Air Force Engineering and Technical Service (AFM)
AFEU .... Association France-Etats-Unis [*France-United States Association*] (EA)
AFEWC ...... Air Force Electronic Warfare Center (CAAL)
AFEWES ... Air Force Electronic Warfare Evaluation Simulator
AFEX .... Air Forces Europe Exchange
AFEX .... American Frontier Explorations [*NASDAQ symbol*] (NQ)
AFEX .... Ammonia Freeze Explosion [*Chemical engineering*]
AFF .... Above Finished Floor [*Technical drawings*]
AFF .... Accelerator Free Fall [*Parachuting*]
AFF .... Acceptance and Ferry Flight [*NASA*] (NASA)
AFF .... Affairs (AFM)
AFF .... Affecting (ROG)
AFF .... Affectionately [*Correspondence*]
AFF .... Afferent [*Medicine*]
AFF .... Affiliated (ADA)
Aff .... Affinity Column [*Chromatography*]
AFF .... Affirmative
AFF .... Affirming (ROG)
AFF .... Agriculture, Forestry, Fishing [*Department of Employment*] [*British*]

AFF............ American Family Foundation (EA)
AFF............ American Farm Foundation (EA)
AFF............ An Foras Forbartha [*National Institute for Physical Planning and Construction Research*] [*Research center*] [*Ireland*] (IRC)
AFF............ Anali Filoloskog Fakulteta [*Belgrade*] [*A publication*]
AFF............ Anne Frank Foundation (EAIO)
AFF............ Anne Frank Fund [*Basel, Switzerland*] (EAIO)
AFF............ Armenian Film Foundation (EA)
AFF............ Army Field Forces
AFF............ Asociacion Filatelica de Filipinas [*Philatelic Association of the Philippines*] (EA)
AFF............ Associated Fresh Foods [*British*]
AFF............ Association of Family Farmers (EA)
AFF............ Automated Field Fire
AFF............ Automatic Frequency Follower
AFF............ Axisymmetrical Flow Field
AFF............ Colorado Springs, CO [*Location identifier*] [*FAA*] (FAAL)
AFFA........ Aerobics and Fitness Foundation of America (EA)
AFFA........ Air Freight Forwarders Association of America [*Later, AFA*] (EA)
AFFA........ Association for Field Archaeology (EA)
Aff Action Compl Man BNA ... Affirmative Action Compliance Manual for Federal Contractors. Bureau of National Affairs [*A publication*]
Affarsvarld ... Affarsvarlden [*A publication*]
AFFAS....... Armed Forces Financial Advisory Services [*British*]
AFFB........ Army Field Forces Board
AFFBC ...... Ahrens-Fox Fire Buffs Club (EA)
AFFC........ Advanced Fire/Flight Control System (MCD)
AFFC........ Air Force Finance Center
AFFC........ Air Forces Ferry Command
AFFC........ Alan Feinstein Fan Club (EA)
AFFC........ Aluminum Foil Field Coil
AFFC........ Annette Funicello Fan Club (EA)
AFFC........ Atlanta Flames Fan Club (EA)
AFFCO...... Alaska Forest Fire Council
AFFCS....... Advanced Fuze Function Control System (MCD)
AFFD........ Affirmed
AFFDL ...... Air Force Flight Dynamics Laboratory [*Wright-Patterson Air Force Base, OH*] (AFM)
AFFE........ Air Force Far East
AFFE......... Airborne Fire Fighting Equipment [*Air Force*] (MCD)
AFFE......... Army Forces Far East
AFFEC ...... Affectionate (ADA)
AFFECTLY ... Affectionately [*Correspondence*] (ROG)
Aff Est........ Affari Esteri [*A publication*]
AFFET........ Affettuoso [*With Expression*] [*Music*]
AFFETAIR ... Compagnie Gabonaise d'Affretement Aerien [*Airline*] (FAAC)
AFFETT .... Affettuoso [*With Expression*] [*Music*]
AFFETTO ... Affettuoso [*With Expression*] [*Music*]
AFFF .... America First Financial Fund 1987 (NQ)
AFFF .... American Family Farm Foundation (EA)
AFFF .... American Fish Farmers Federation (EA)
AFFF .... Aqueous Film-Forming Foam [*Firefighting chemical for ships*]
AFFFA...... American Forged Fitting and Flange Association [*Defunct*] (EA)
AFFFT...... Academy of Family Films and Family Television (EA)
AFFG........ Affirming
AFFHF ...... American Freedom from Hunger Foundation [*Later, MFM/FFH*]
AFFHO ..... Australasian Federation of Family History Organizations (EAIO)
AFFI .... Affidavit [*Legal term*] (DLA)
AFFI .... American Frozen Food Institute (EA)
AFFI .... Arab Federation for Food Industries (EA)
AFFIL........ Affiliate
Affil RSH... Affiliate of the Royal Society of Health [*British*]
AffilSLAET ... Affiliate of the Society of Licensed Aircraft Engineers and Technologists [*British*] (DBQ)
AFFILTN .. Affiliation
Affin........ Affinity [*Laboratory analysis*]
Affinity Tech Enzyme Purif Part B ... Affinity Techniques. Enzyme Purification. Part B [*A publication*]
AffIP.......... Affiliate of the Institute of Plumbing [*British*] (DBQ)
AFFIRM.... Association for Federal Information Resources Management (EA)
AffIWHTE ... Affiliate of the Institution of Works and Highways Technician Engineers [*British*] (DBQ)
A & F Fix ... Amos and Ferard on Fixtures [*A publication*] (DLA)
AFFJ.......... American Fund for Free Jurists (EA)
AFFL......... Affiliate (MUGU)
AFFL......... Affluent
AFFLC....... Air Force Film Library Center
Affli............ [*Matthaeus de*] Afflictis [*Deceased, 1528*] [*Authority cited in pre-1607 legal work*] (DSA)
Afflict......... [*Matthaeus de*] Afflictis [*Deceased, 1528*] [*Authority cited in pre-1607 legal work*] (DSA)
AFFLIZ...... Afflizione [*Afflictedly*] [*Music*] (ROG)
AFFLY....... Affectionately [*Correspondence*] (ROG)
AFFM........ Australian Financial Futures Market

AF(F)MMIU ... Amphibious Forces Ordnance Material Mobile Instruction Unit [*Obsolete*] [*Navy*]
AFFMO..... Affezionatissimo [*Very Tenderly, Pathetically*] [*Music*] (ROG)
AFFOM..... Air Force Field Office Manager (AAG)
AFFOR...... Air Force Forces [*Element of a joint task force*]
AFFORD... Analysis for Forces Objectives and Resources Determination (MCD)
AFFOR/DC ... Air Force Forces Deputy [*or Director*] Communications-Electronics (AFIT)
AFFPA5 .... Anais. Faculdade de Farmacia do Porto [*A publication*]
AFFPC ..... Air Force Financial Postal Clerk (AFM)
AFFR .... Affair
Affr............ Affranchi [*Paid*] [*French*] [*Business term*]
AFFR .... Affray [*FBI standardized term*]
AFFRA ...... American Family Farm and Ranch Association (EA)
Aff Reh...... Affirmed [*or Affirming*] on Rehearing [*Legal term*] (DLA)
AFFRET.... Affrettando [*Hurrying the Pace*] [*Music*]
AFFRETTO ... Affrettando [*Hurrying the Pace*] [*Music*]
AFFRI........ Armed Forces Radiobiology Institute
AFFRMN .. Affirmation (ROG)
AFFS .... American Federation of Film Societies (EA)
AFFSAE.... Anais. Faculdade de Farmacia e Odontologia. Universidade de Sao Paulo [*A publication*]
AFFSE....... Armed Forces Food Science Establishment [*Australia*]
AFFSIM.... Airborne Formation Flight Simulator (MCD)
Aff Soc Int ... Affari Sociali Internazionali [*A publication*]
AFFT .... Affidavit
AFFT .... Association of Federal Fiscal Technicians (EA)
AFFTC ...... Air Force Field Technical Center [*Edwards Air Force Base, CA*] (MCD)
AFFTC ...... Air Force Flight Test Center [*Edwards Air Force Base, CA*]
AFFTD ...... Air Force Foreign Technology Division (KSC)
AFFTE....... Affectionate [*Correspondence*] (ROG)
AFFTIS ..... Air Force Flight Test Instrumentation System
AFFTU ..... Augmentor Fuel Flow Test Unit (MCD)
AFFUS ...... Association of Free French in the US (EA)
AFFX .... Air Freight [*Air carrier designation symbol*]
AFFY .... Affectionately [*Correspondence*] (ROG)
AFG .... AFG Industries, Inc. [*NYSE symbol*] (SPSG)
AFG .... Afghani
AFG .... Afghanistan [*ANSI three-letter standard code*] (CNC)
AFG .... Afghanite [*A zeolite*]
AFG .... Aflatoxin G [*Mycotoxin*]
AFG .... ALANON Family Group Headquarters (EA)
AFG .... Allied Freighter Guard (NATG)
AFG .... Alternative Force Generator (MCD)
AFG .... American Federation of Guards (EA)
AFG .... American Friends of Greece (EA)
AFG .... Americans for God (EA)
AFG .... Amniotic Fluid Glucose [*Obstetrics*]
AFG .... Analog Function Generator
AFG .... Antenna Field Gain
AFG .... Arbitrary Function Generator (MUGU)
AFG .... Argyrophil, Fluorescent, Granulated [*Cells*] [*Anatomy*]
AFG .... Army Force Guidance
AFG .... Association des Fabricants de Glucose de la CEE [*Association of the Glucose Producers in the European Economic Community*]
AFG .... Audio Function Generator (MCD)
AFG .... Auslandsanfragen. Waren Vertretungen Kooperationen [*A publication*]
AFG .... Pro Air Service [*Opa Locka, FL*] [*FAA designator*] (FAAC)
AFGC........ American Forage and Grassland Council [*Lexington, KY*]
AFGCM.... Air Force Good Conduct Medal [*Military decoration*] (AFM)
AFGE........ American Federation of Government Employees (EA)
AFGE........ American Forum for Global Education (EISS)
AFGF .... Acidic Fibroblast Growth Factor [*Biochemistry*]
AFGH .... Afghanistan
Afghanistan J ... Afghanistan Journal [*A publication*]
AFGI.......... Ambassador Financial Group, Incorporated [*Tamarac, FL*] [*NASDAQ symbol*] (NQ)
AFGIL .... Alaska. Department of Fish and Game. Information Leaflet [*A publication*]
AFGIS .... Aerial Free Gunnery Instructions School [*Obsolete*]
AFGK .... Archiv fuer Frankfurts Geschichte und Kunst [*A publication*]
AFGL .... Air Force Geophysics Laboratory [*Formerly, AFCRL*] [*Hanscom Air Force Base, MA*]
AFGM .... American Federation of Grain Millers (EA)
AFGM .... American Friends of the Gutenberg Museum (EA)
AFGO .... Air Force General Order
AFGOM .... Air Force Command and Control System Graphic Operator Macros (MCD)
AFGP......... Air Force Advisory Group
AFGP......... Antifreeze Glycoprotein [*Biochemistry*]
AFGPAA ... Annali. Universita di Ferrara. Sezione IX. Scienze Geologiche e Paleontologiche [*A publication*]
AFGPRB ... Alaska. Department of Fish and Game. Project Progress Reports on Bears [*A publication*]
AFGPRC ... Alaska. Department of Fish and Game. Project Progress Reports on Caribou [*A publication*]

AFGPRD ... Alaska. Department of Fish and Game. Project Progress Reports on Deer [*A publication*]
AFGPRG ... Alaska. Department of Fish and Game. Project Progress Reports on Mountain Goats [*A publication*]
AFGPRM .. Alaska. Department of Fish and Game. Project Progress Reports on Moose [*A publication*]
AFGPRS .... Alaska. Department of Fish and Game. Project Progress Reports on Sheep [*A publication*]
AFGPRWQ ... Alaska. Department of Fish and Game. Project Progress Reports on Wildlife [*A publication*]
AFGR .... Approved Force Gross Requirement [*Army*]   (AABC)
AFGRR ...... Alaska. Department of Fish and Game. Research Reports [*A publication*]
AFGS .... Air Force Guide Specification   (MCD)
AFGS .... American-French Genealogical Society   (EA)
AFGSDTP ... Alaska. Department of Fish and Game. Subsistence Division. Technical Paper [*A publication*]
AFGT .... Alaska Fish Tales and Game Trails [*A publication*]
AFGU .... Aerial Free Gunnery Unit
AFGW .... American Flint Glass Workers' Union of North America [*Later, AFGWU*]
AFGWC ..... Air Force Global Weather Central [*or Control*] [*Offutt Air Force Base, NE*]
AFGWRP .. Air Force Global Weather Reconnaissance Program
AFGWTB .. Alaska. Department of Fish and Game. Wildlife Technical Bulletin [*A publication*]
AFGWU .... American Flint Glass Workers Union   (EA)
AFH .... Acceptance for Honor [*Business term*]
afh .... Afrihili [*MARC language code*] [*Library of Congress*]   (LCCP)
AFH .... Afrika Heute [*A publication*]
AFH .... Air Force Hospital
AFH .... American Foundation for Health   (EA)
AFH .... American Foundation for Homeopathy   (EA)
AFH .... Angiofollicular (Lymph Node) Hyperplasia [*Oncology*]
AFH .... Antenna Feed Horn
AFH .... Anterior Facial Height
AFH .... Archivum Franciscanum Historicum [*Firenze*] [*A publication*]
AFH .... Army Family Housing
AFH .... Australian Federation of Haemophilia
AFH .... United States Army, Cold Regions Research and Engineering Laboratory Library, Hanover, NH [*OCLC symbol*]   (OCLC)
AFHA .... Armed Forces Hostess Association   (EA)
AFHC .... Air Force Headquarters Command
AFHC .... Association of Fair Housing Committees [*Defunct*]
AFHF .... Air Force Historical Foundation   (EA)
AFHF .... American Foot Health Foundation   (EA)
Afh Fys Kemi Mineral ... Afhandlingar i Fysik, Kemi, och Mineralogi [*A publication*]
AFHG .... Additive-Free Hard Gold [*Metallurgy*]
AFHHA ..... American Federation of Home Health Agencies   (EA)
AFHL .... Annuaire. Federation Historique de Lorraine [*A publication*]
AFHMM ... American Friends of the Haifa Maritime Museum   (EA)
AFHOAC .. Anales de Farmacia Hospitalaria [*A publication*]
AFHP .... Anonymous Families History Project   (EA)
AFHPSP ..... Air Force Health Professions Scholarship Program
AFHPSP ..... Armed Forces Health Profession Scholarship Program
AFHQ .... African Force Headquarters [*World War II*]
AFHQ .... Air Force Headquarters
AFHQ .... Allied Forces Headquarters [*Might refer to any theater of war*] [*World War II*]
AFHQ (CIC) ... Allied Forces Headquarters (Counter Intelligence Corps) [*World War II*]
AFHQPS ..... Allied Forces Headquarters Petroleum Section [*World War II*]
AFHRL ...... Air Force Human Resources Laboratory [*Brooks Air Force Base, TX*]   (AFM)
AFHRL/FT ... Air Force Human Resources Laboratory/Flying Training Division [*Williams Air Force Base, AZ*]
AFHRL/MD ... Air Force Human Resources Laboratory/Manpower Development Division [*Alexandria, VA*]
AFHS .... American Family Heritage Society [*Defunct*]   (EA)
AFHS .... Average Flying Hours per Sortie [*Air Force*]   (AFIT)
AFHSC .... American Fashion Homesewing Council
AFHTWF ... Amalgamated Association of Felt Hat Trimmers and Wool Formers [*A union*] [*British*]   (DCTA)
AFHU .... American Friends of the Hebrew University   (EA)
AFHV .... America's Funniest Home Videos [*Television program*]
AFHW .... American Federation of Hosiery Workers [*Later, ACTWU*]
AFHZAB ... Allgemeine Forst- und Holzwirtschaftliche Zeitung [*A publication*]
AFI .... Afiamalu [*Samoa Islands*] [*Seismograph station code, US Geological Survey*]   (SEIS)
AFI .... African/Indian Ocean [*Aviation*]
AFI .... Agence Fonciere Industrielle [*Industrial Property Agency*] [*Tunisian*]   (GEA)
AFI .... Air Filter Institute [*Later, ARI*]   (EA)
AFI .... Air Flow Indicator
AFI .... Air Forces, Iceland   (MCD)
AFI .... Amaurotic Familial Idiocy
AFI .... American Fiber Institute
AFI .... American Film Institute   (EA)

AFI .... American Firearms Industry [*A publication*]   (EAAP)
AFI .... American Flag Institute   (EA)
AFI .... American Forest Institute [*Later, AFC*]
AFI .... American Friends of Israel   (EA)
AFI .... American Fur Industry   (EA)
AFI .... Amities France-Israel [*A publication*]
AFI .... Anthropology Film Institute [*Later, AFCF*]   (EA)
AFI .... Armed Forces Institute
AFI .... Association of Federal Investigators   (EA)
AFI .... Association of Food Industries   (EA)
AFI .... Automatic Fault Isolation
AFI .... Auxiliary Force, India [*British military*]   (DMA)
AFI .... United States Army, Corps of Engineers, Philadelphia District, Philadelphia, PA [*OCLC symbol*]   (OCLC)
AFIA .... American Feed Industry Association   (EA)
AFIA .... American Female Impersonators Association   (EA)
AFIA .... American Footwear Industries Association [*Later, FIA*]
AFIA .... American Foreign Insurance Association   (EA)
AFIA .... Associate of the Federal Institute of Accountants [*Australia*]
AFIAAWW ... American Film Institute Alumni Association Writers Workshop   (EA)
AFIAS ...... Army Air Forces Deputy Chiefs of Air Staff [*World War II*]
AFIAS ...... Associate Fellow of the Institute of Aeronautical Sciences [*Later, AFAIAA*]
AFIB .... Atrial Fibrillation [*Cardiology*]
AFIC .... Air Force Intelligence Center
AFIC .... Asian Finance/Investment Corp. [*Proposed*]   (ECON)
AFIC .... Association of Fashion and Image Consultants   (EA)
AFIC .... Australian Federation of Islamic Councils
AFICCS ..... Air Force Integrated Command and Control System   (AFM)
AFICD ...... Associate Fellow of the Institute of Civil Defence [*British*]
AFICE .... Air Forces, Iceland
AFICE .... Association for International Cotton Emblem [*Brussels, Belgium*]   (EAIO)
AFICS .... Association of Former International Civil Servants   (EA)
AFID .... Alkali Flame Ionization Detector [*Instrumentation*]
AFID .... Arithmetic Function Identifier
AFIDA ...... Agricultural Foreign Investment Disclosure Act [*1978*]
AFIDA ...... Asociacion de Ferias Internacionales de America [*Association of International Trade Fairs of America*]   (EAIO)
AFIDES ..... Association Francophone Internationale des Directeurs d'Etablissements Scolaires [*International Association of French-Speaking Directors of Educational Institutions*] [*Anjou, PQ*]
AFIDS .... Automatic Firearms Identification System [*Jet Propulsion Laboratory, NASA*]
AFIE .... Abnormal Fluctuation in the Economy   (MCD)
AFIE .... American Federation of Italian Evangelicals [*Later, AEIM*]   (EA)
AFIE .... Armed Forces Information and Education   (MCD)
AFIED ...... Armed Forces Information and Education Division
AFI Ed News ... AFI [*American Film Institute*] Education Newsletter [*A publication*]
AFIF .... Air Force Industrial Fund   (AFM)
AFIF .... Armed Forces Information Film   (AFM)
AFIF .... Associated Fraternity of Iron Forgers [*A union*] [*British*]
AFIF .... Association of Foremen Iron Founders [*A union*] [*British*]
AFig .... Arti Figurative. Rivista d'Arte Antica e Moderna [*A publication*]
AFIGAC .... Air Force Inspector General Activities Center
AFIGAP .... Association Francophone Internationale des Groupes d'Animation de la Paraplegie [*International French-Speaking Association of Paraplegic Therapy Groups*] [*Brie-Comte-Robert, France*]   (EAIO)
AFII .... American Federation of International Institutes [*Later, ACNS*]
AFIIM .... Associate Fellow of the Institute of Industrial Managers [*British*]
AFIL .... American Filtrona Corp. [*NASDAQ symbol*]   (NQ)
AFIL .... Flight Plan Filed in the Air [*Aviation code*]
A-FILE ...... Adolescent-Family Inventory of Life Events and Changes [*Psychology*]
AFilos .... Archivio di Filosofia [*A publication*]
AFILR .... Approved Force Investment Level Requirement   (AFIT)
AFIM .... Air Force Inventory Manager
AFIM .... American Friends of the Israel Museum   (EA)
AFIMA ...... Associate Fellow of the Institute of Mathematics and Its Applications [*British*]   (DBQ)
AFIMA ...... Australian Fellowship of the Israel Medical Association
AFIMS ...... Air Force Information Management Study
AFIN .... American Financial Corp. [*NASDAQ symbol*]   (NQ)
AFIN .... Assistant Chief of Staff, Intelligence [*Air Force*]   (MCD)
AFIN .... Association Francaise des Informaticiens [*France*]   (CSR)
AFIN .... Australian Finance Availability Guide [*A publication*]
AFINS .... Airways Flight Inspector
AF Inst Pet ... Associate Fellow of the Institute of Petroleum [*British*]
AFINTELMET ... Air Force Intelligence Management Engineering Team
AFIO .... Agreement for Fighter Interceptor Operations
AFIO .... Approved Force Inventory Objective [*Army*]   (AABC)
AFIO .... Association of Former Intelligence Officers   (EA)
AFIO .... Authorization for Interceptor Operations   (MCD)
AFIP .... American Federation of Information Processing

AFIP .... Anne Frank Institute of Philadelphia [*Formerly, NIH*]   (EA)
AFIP .... Armed Forces Information Program
AFIP .... Armed Forces Institute of Pathology [*DoD*]   (EA)
AFIPS .... American Federation of Information Processing Societies   (EA)
AFIPS Conf Proc ... AFIPS [*American Federation of Information Processing Societies*] Conference Proceedings [*A publication*]
AFIPS Conf Proc Fall Jt Comput Conf ... American Federation of Information Processing Societies. Conference Proceedings. Fall Joint Computer Conference [*A publication*]
AFIPS Conf Proc Fall Spring Jt Comput Conf ... American Federation of Information Processing Societies. Conference Proceedings. Fall and Spring Joint Computer Conferences [*A publication*]
AFIPS Conf Proc Spring Jt Comput Conf ... American Federation of Information Processing Societies. Conference Proceedings. Spring Joint Computer Conference [*A publication*]
AFIPS Nat Comput Conf Expo Conf Proc ... AFIPS [*American Federation of Information Processing Societies*] National Computer Conference and Exposition. Conference Proceedings [*A publication*]
AFIPS Natl Comp Conf Expo Conf Proc ... American Federation of Information Processing Societies. National Computer Conference and Exposition. Conference Proceedings [*A publication*]
AFIPS Washington Rep ... AFIPS [*American Federation of Information Processing Societies*] Washington Report [*A publication*]
AFIR .... Air Force Installation Representative
Afir .... Firkin of Ale [*Unit of measurement*]   (DAS)
AFIRB .... Armed Forces Identification Review Board [*US Total Army Personnel Agency*]   (EGAO)
AFIRE .... Association of Foreign Investors in US Real Estate   (EA)
AFIRE .... Association of Fundamental Institutions of Religious Education
AFIRM ...... Affirmative   (AABC)
AFIRO .... Air Force Installation Representative Officer
A-FIRST .... Advanced - Far Infrared Search/Track
AFIS .... Aerodrome Flight Information Service
AFIS .... Air Force Intelligence Service
AFIS .... American Forces Information Service [*DoD*]
AFIS .... Armed Forces Induction Station
AFIS .... Armed Forces Information School
AFIS .... Armed Forces Information Service [*DoD*]
AFIS .... Army Force Integration Study
AFIS .... Automated Field Interview System
AFIS .... Automated Fingerprint Identification System [*NEC Corp.*]
AFISAT ..... Atti. Accademia delle Scienze di Siena. Detta de Fisiocritici [*A publication*]
AFISC .... Air Force Inspection and Safety Center
AFISM ...... Aluminum-Free Inorganic Suspended Material
AFISOL ..... Aerodrome Flight Information Service Officer's Licence [*British*]   (DBQ)
AFISR .... Air Force Industrial Security Regulations
AFIT .... Air Force Institute of Technology [*Wright-Patterson Air Force Base, OH*]
AFIT .... Airblast Fuel Injection Tube [*Gas turbine engine*]
AFIT .... American Fabricating Institute of Technology [*Defunct*]   (EA)
AFIT .... Armed Forces Institute of Technology
AFIT .... Australian Families Income Transfer [*Project*]
AFIT .... Automatic Fault Isolation Test
AFIT .... University of North Alabama, Florence, AL [*Library symbol*] [*Library of Congress*]   (LCLS)
AFITC .... Armed Forces Intelligence Training Center
AFIT(RS) .. Air Force Institute of Technology, Residence School
AFIX .... Air Freighters [*Air carrier designation symbol*]
AFJ .... Air Force Jet
AFJ .... Armed Forces Journal [*A publication*]
AFJAG ...... Air Force Judge Advocate General
AF JAG L Rev ... Air Force JAG [*Judge Advocate General*] Law Review [*Later, Air Force Law Review*] [*A publication*]
AFJCC .... American Forum for Jewish-Christian Cooperation   (EA)
AFJCE .... American Federation of Jews from Central Europe   (EA)
AFJFCINV ... American Federation of Jewish Fighters, Camp Inmates and Nazi Victims   (EA)
AFJITR ..... American Friends of the Jerusalem Institute for Talmudic Research   (EA)
AFJKT .... Air Force Job Knowledge Test
AFJMG ..... American Friends of the Jewish Museum of Greece   (EA)
AFJMSNS .. Air Force Justification for Major System New Start   (MCD)
AFJN .... Africa Faith and Justice Network   (EA)
AFJROTC ... Air Force Junior Reserve Officers Training Corps   (AFM)
AFJSWF ... American Friends of the Jerusalem Society for World Fellowship   (EA)
AFJZA .... Allgemeine Forst- und Jagdzeitung [*A publication*]
AfK .... Archiv fuer Keilschriftforschung [*A publication*]
AfK .... Archiv fuer Kulturgeschichte [*Cologne/Graz*] [*A publication*]
AFK .... Armed Forces of the Republic of Korea   (CINC)
AFK .... Fort Kent Public Library, Alberta [*Library symbol*] [*National Library of Canada*]   (NLC)
AFK .... New African [*A publication*]
AFKAC ...... Air Force Cryptographic Code System   (CET)
AFKAG ...... Air Force Cryptographic Aid, General

AFKAI .... Air Force Cryptographic Aid, Recognition and Identification Systems   (CET)
AFKAM ..... Air Force Cryptographic Maintenance Manual   (CET)
AFKAP ...... Air Force Cryptographic One Time Pads   (CET)
AFKMAL .. Ankara Universitesi. Tip Fakultesi. Mecmuasi. Supplementum [*A publication*]
AFL .... Above Field Level [*Aerospace*]   (AAG)
AFL .... Abstract Family of Languages [*Data processing*]
AFL .... Active Fuel Length [*Nuclear energy*]   (NRCH)
AFL .... Actresses' Franchise League [*British*]
AFL .... Adolescent Family Life Program [*Department of Health and Human Services*]
AFL .... Advanced Flow LASER   (MCD)
AFL .... Aflatoxicol [*Metabolite of AFB*] [*Biochemistry*]
Af L .... Afroasiatic Linguistics [*A publication*]
AFL .... Air Force Letter
AFL .... Air Force Liaison
AFL .... Air Force List [*British military*]   (DMA)
AFL .... American Family Corp. [*NYSE symbol*]   (SPSG)
AF of L .... American Federation of Labor [*Later, AFL-CIO*]
AFL .... American Federation of Labor [*Later, AFL-CIO*]   (GPO)
AFL .... American Football League [*Reorganized as part of AFC and NFC*]   (EA)
AFL .... American Friends of Lafayette   (EA)
AFL .... Americans for Life   (EA)
AFL .... Animated Film Language   (BUR)
AFL .... Antifatty Liver [*Medicine*]
AFL .... Association for Family Living [*Defunct*]   (EA)
AFL .... Association for Library Information, Pittsburgh, PA [*OCLC symbol*]   (OCLC)
AFL .... Australian Family Law and Practice [*A publication*]   (APTA)
AFL .... Australian Family Lawyer [*A publication*]
AFL .... Australian Freedom League
AFL .... AUTOLAND [*Automatic Landing*] Flight Tests [*NASA*]   (MCD)
AFL .... Automatic Fault Location
AFL .... Flatbush Public Library, Alberta [*Library symbol*] [*National Library of Canada*]   (NLC)
AFL .... French Institute/Alliance Francaise Library [*UTLAS symbol*]
AFLA .... Adolescent Family Life Act [*of 1981*]
AFLA .... Amateur Fencers League of America [*Later, USFA*]   (EA)
AFLA .... American Foreign Law Association   (EA)
AFLA .... Annales. Faculte des Lettres d'Aix [*A publication*]
AFLA .... Armed Forces Leave Act of 1946
AFLA .... Asian Federation of Library Associations
AFLA .... Automotive Fleet and Leasing Association   (EA)
AFLANT .. Air Forces, Atlantic
AFLAS ...... Aviation Fuels Logistical Area Summary [*Air Force*]   (AFIT)
AFLAT ...... Air Force Language Aptitude Test
AF Law Rev ... Air Force Law Review [*A publication*]
AFLB .... Annali. Facolta di Lettere e Filosofia. Universita di Bari [*A publication*]
AFLB .... Australian Family Law Bulletin [*A publication*]
AFLC .... Air Force Logistics Center   (MCD)
AFLC .... Air Force Logistics Command [*Formerly, Air Materiel Command*] [*Wright-Patterson Air Force Base, OH*]
AFLC .... Annali. Facolta di Lettere, Filosofia, e Magistero. Universita di Cagliari [*A publication*]
AFLC .... Association of Free Lutheran Congregations
AFLC .... Australian Federal Libraries Committee
AFLCA ...... American Fur Liner Contractors Association   (EA)
AFL Cagl ... Annali. Facolta di Lettere. Universita di Cagliari [*A publication*]
AFLCF ...... Air Force Logistics Command Form
AFLCG ...... Air Force Logistics Control Group
AFL-CIO ... American Federation of Labor and Congress of Industrial Organizations
AFL-CIO Am Fed ... AFL-CIO [*American Federation of Labor and Congress of Industrial Organizations*] American Federationist [*A publication*]
AFLCL .... Air Force Logistics Command Letter   (MCD)
AFLCM ..... Air Force Logistics Command Manual   (MCD)
AFLCON ... Air Force Logistics Command Operations Network   (MCD)
AFLCON ... Air Force Logistics Communications Network   (AFM)
AFLCP ...... Air Force Logistics Command Pamphlets
AFLCR ...... Air Force Logistics Command Regulations
AFLD .... Airborne Fraunhofer Line Discriminator
AFLD .... Airfield   (AFM)
AFLD .... American Foundation for Learning Disabilities
AFLD .... Annales. Faculte des Lettres et Sciences Humaines de l'Universite de Dakar [*A publication*]
AFLE .... Association of French Language Epidemiologists   (EAIO)
AFLETS .... Air Force Law Enforcement Terminal System
AFLFB ...... Annali. Facolta di Lettere e Filosofia. Universita di Bari [*A publication*]
AFLFI .... About Face/Let's Face It   (EA)
AFLFP ...... Annali. Facolta di Lettere e Filosofia. Universita di Perugia [*A publication*]
AFLFUM .. Annali. Facolta di Lettere e Filosofia. Universita di Macerata [*A publication*]

AFLI .... African Library [*Belgium Ministry of Foreign Affairs*] [*Information service or system*] (CRD)

AFLI .... Air Force Legislative Item

AFLI .... Association for Library Information [*Duquesne University Library*] [*Information service or system*] (IID)

AFLIR ...... Advanced Forward-Looking Infrared

AFLL .... Annali. Facolta di Lettere di Lecce [*A publication*]

AFLL .... Army Fuels and Lubricants Laboratory

AFLL .... Association of French-Language Leprologists [*Paris, France*] (EAIO)

AFLM........ Annali. Facolta di Lettere e Filosofia. Universita di Macerata [*A publication*]

AFLMC ..... Air Force Logistics Management Center [*Gunter Air Force Station, AL*] (AFM)

AFLN........ Annali. Facolta di Lettere e Filosofia. Universita di Napoli [*A publication*]

AFLNice .... Annales. Faculte des Lettres et Sciences Humaines de Nice [*A publication*]

AFLNW..... Arbeitsgemeinschaft fuer Forschung des Landes Nordrhein-Westfalen. Geisteswissenschaften [*A publication*]

AFLNW/G ... Veroeffentlichungen. Arbeitsgemeinschaft fuer Forschung des Landes Nordrhein/Westfalen/Geisteswissenschaften [*Cologne/Opladen*] [*A publication*]

AFLP .... Acute Fatty Liver of Pregnancy [*Medicine*]

AFLP .... Armed Forces Language Program

AFLPer...... Annali. Facolta di Lettere e Filosofia (Perugia) [*A publication*]

AFLQ........ Archives de Folklore. Universite Laval (Quebec) [*A publication*]

AF L R .... Air Force Law Review [*A publication*]

AFLR........ Armed Forces Liaison Representative [*Red Cross*]

AFL Rev.... Air Force Law Review [*A publication*]

AFLRL ...... Army Fuels and Lubricants Research Laboratory

AFLRS...... Allied Forces Local Resources Section [*World War II*]

AFLS .... Active Flight Load System (MCD)

AFLS .... Armed Forces Librarians Section [*Public Library Association*]

AFLSA ...... Air Force Longevity Service Award [*Military decoration*] (AFM)

AFLSC....... Air Force Legal Services Center

AFLSHY ... Annales. Faculte des Lettres et Sciences Humaines de Yaounde [*A publication*]

Af L Studies ... African Law Studies [*A publication*] (DLA)

AFLT........ African Literature Today [*A publication*]

AFLT........ American Fletcher Corp. [*NASDAQ symbol*] (NQ)

AFLT........ Annales Publiees par la Faculte des Lettres de Toulouse [*A publication*]

AFLT Forum ... Arizona Foreign Language Teachers Forum [*A publication*]

AFLToul .... Annales Publiees par la Faculte des Lettres et Sciences Humaines de Toulouse [*Via Domitia*] [*A publication*]

AFLU........ Available for Local Use (MCD)

AFLUB...... Annales. Faculte des Lettres. Universite de Bordeaux [*A publication*]

AFLX........ Air Florida [*Air carrier designation symbol*]

AFM .... Academy of Family Mediators (EA)

AFM .... Accredited Farm Manager [*Designation given by American Society of Farm Managers and Rural Appraisers*]

AFM .... Acting Fort Major [*Military*] [*British*] (ROG)

AFM .... Adhesive Film Mechanism

AFM .... Aflatoxin M [*Mycotoxin*]

AFM .... After Full Moon [*Freemasonry*] (ROG)

AFM .... Air Force Manual [*A publication*]

AFM .... Air Force Medal [*British*]

AFM .... Air Force Museum

AFM .... Air Freight Motor Carriers Conference, Inc., Arlington VA [*STAC*]

AFM .... American Family Member

AFM .... American Federation of Musicians of the United States and Canada [*Later, THFC*] (EA)

AFM .... Analysis and Forecasting Mode

AFM .... Ancient Freemasons

AFM .... Annales Fonds Maeterlinck [*A publication*]

AFM .... Annular Fire Missile

AFM .... Antifriction Metal

AFM .... Application Functions Module [*Data processing*]

AFM .... Approved Flight Manual [*FAA*] [*A publication*] (MCD)

AfM .... Archiv fuer Musikwissenschaft [*A publication*]

A/FM........ Arm/Firing Mechanism (MCD)

AFM .... Armed Forces Management (AABC)

AFM .... Armed Forces Movement [*Portugal*]

AFM .... Aspects de la France et du Monde [*A publication*]

AFM .... Associated Foam Manufacturers (EA)

AFM .... Associated Fur Manufacturers (EA)

AFM .... Atomic Force Microscope

AFM .... Audio Frequency Modulation

AFM .... Australian Family Movement

AFM .... Automatic Flight Management

AFM .... Aviation Fleet Maintenance (NVT)

AFM .... Fort McMurray Public Library, Alberta [*Library symbol*] [*National Library of Canada*] (NLC)

AFM .... United States Army, Corps of Engineers, Waterways Experiment Station, Vicksburg, MS [*OCLC symbol*] (OCLC)

AFMA .... Access Floor Manufacturing Association (EA)

AFMA .... American Federation of Medical Accreditation (EA)

AFMA .... American Feed Manufacturers Association [*Later, AFIA*] (EA)

AFMA .... American Fiber Manufacturers Association (EA)

AFMA .... American Film Marketing Association (EA)

AFMA .... American Footwear Manufacturers' Association [*Later, FIA*]

AFMA .... American Fur Merchants' Association (EA)

AFMA .... American Furniture Manufacturers Association (EA)

AFMA .... Armed Forces Management Association [*Later, ADPA*] (EA)

AFMA .... Association of Food Marketing Agencies in Asia and the Pacific (EA)

AFMA .... Australian Folk Music Associates

AFMA .... Autobody Filler Manufacturers Association [*Absorbed by ASEMC*]

AFMA .... Fort Macleod Public Library, Alberta [*Library symbol*] [*National Library of Canada*] (NLC)

AFMAA..... Annales Academiae Scientiarum Fennicae. Series A-V (Medica) [*A publication*]

AFMAAT ... Annales Academiae Scientiarum Fennicae. Series A-V (Medica-Anthropologica) [*A publication*]

AFMAB..... Atmospheric Forcings for the Mid-Atlantic Bight [*Oceanography*] (MSC)

AFMADW ... Armed Forces Medical Journal [*Arab Republic of Egypt*] [*A publication*]

AFMAEX. Aquaculture and Fisheries Management [*A publication*]

AFMAG .... Air Force Management Analysis Group (MCD)

AFMag ...... Annali. Facolta di Magistero. Universita di Palermo [*A publication*]

AFMAG .... Army Air Forces Air Adjutant General [*World War II*]

AFMAG .... Audiofrequency Magnetic Fields [*Prospecting technique*]

AFMAS..... Anzac Community School, Fort McMurray, Alberta [*Library symbol*] [*National Library of Canada*] (BIB)

AFMB........ America First Federal Guaranteed Mortgage [*Omaha, NE*] [*NASDAQ symbol*] (NQ)

AFMBT ..... Artificial Flower Manufacturers Board of Trade (EA)

AFMC........ American Floral Marketing Council (EA)

AFMC........ Armed Forces Mail Call (EA)

AFMC........ Armed Forces Marketing Council (EA)

AFMC........ Asian Fluid Mechanics Committee (EAIO)

AFMC........ Association des Facultes de Medecine du Canada [*Association of Medical Faculties of Canada*]

AFMC........ Association of Former Members of Congress [*Formerly, FMC*] (EA)

AFMC........ Automotive Filter Manufacturers Council [*Later, FMC*] (EA)

AFMC........ Auxiliary Force Medical Corps [*British military*] (DMA)

AFMCC..... Air Freight Motor Carriers Conference [*Later, AEMCC*] (EA)

AFMCH ... American Foundation for Maternal and Child Health (EA)

AFMCO ... Army Force Modernization Coordination Office

AFMDA4 .. Anais. Faculdade de Medicina. Universidade de Sao Paulo [*A publication*]

AFMDBX ... Asian Journal of Medicine [*A publication*]

AFMDC ... Air Force Machinability Data Center (MCD)

AFMDC..... Air Force Missile Development Center [*AFSC*]

AFME........ Airframe

AFME........ American Friends of the Middle East [*Later, AMIDEAST*] (EA)

AFMEA..... Air Force Management Engineering Agency

AFMEA7... Anales. Facultad de Medicina. Universidad de la Republica [*Montevideo*] [*A publication*]

AFMEB8... Afrique Medicale [*A publication*]

AFMED..... Allied Forces Mediterranean [*NATO*]

AFMEDMET ... Air Force Medical Management Engineering Team

AFMEEB .. Agricultural and Forest Meteorology [*A publication*]

AFMEI...... Association of Free Methodist Educational Institutions (EA)

AFMENS.. Air Force Mission Element Need Statement

AFMF........ Air Fleet Marine Force

AfMf.......... Archiv fuer Musikforschung [*A publication*]

AFMFIC.... Associated Factory Mutual Fire Insurance Companies [*Later, FMS*] (EA)

AFMFP ..... Aircraft, Fleet Marine Force, Pacific [*Obsolete*]

AFMH...... American Foundation for Mental Hygiene

AFMH...... Association for Faculty in the Medical Humanities (EA)

AFMH...... Fort McMurray Regional Hospital, Alberta [*Library symbol*] [*National Library of Canada*] (NLC)

AFMI........ Association of French Mechanical Industries (EA)

AFMIBK .. Armed Forces Medical Journal [*India*] [*A publication*]

AFMIC...... Air Force Materials Information Center (DIT)

AFMIC...... Armed Forces Medical Intelligence Center [*Fort Detrick*] [*Frederick, MD*]

AFMIDPAC ... [*US*] Army Forces, Middle Pacific [*Official name for the theater of war more commonly called MIDPAC*] [*World War II*]

AF-MIPR.. Air Force - Military Interdepartmental Purchase Requests

AFMK .... Keyano College, Fort McMurray, Alberta [*Library symbol*] [*National Library of Canada*] (NLC)

AFMKS..... Fort McKay School, Alberta [*Library symbol*] [*National Library of Canada*] (BIB)

AFML........ Air Force Materials Laboratory [*Wright-Patterson Air Force Base, OH*]

AFML........ Annali. Facolta di Magistero. Universita di Lecce [*A publication*]

AFML........ Armed Forces Medical Library [*Later, National Library of Medicine, 1956*]
AFMM ...... American Festival of Microtonal Music   (EA)
AFMM ...... Heritage Park, Fort McMurray, Alberta [*Library symbol*] [*National Library of Canada*]   (BIB)
AFMMAV ... Anais. Faculdade de Medicina. Universidade Federal de Minas Gerais [*Belo Horizonte*] [*A publication*]
AFMMBW ... Archivos. Facultad de Medicina de Madrid [*A publication*]
AFMMFO ... Air Force Medical Materiel Field Office   (AFM)
AFMML.... Air Force Medical Materiel Letter
AFMMO ... Air Force MIPR [*Military Interdepartmental Purchase Request*] Management Office   (AFIT)
AFmMP..... United States Army, Military Police School, Fort McClellan, AL [*Library symbol*] [*Library of Congress*]   (LCLS)
Af Mo........ African Monthly [*Grahamstown*] [*A publication*]
AFMP........ Association of Free Magazines and Periodicals [*British*]   (EAIO)
AFMPA ...... Air Force Medical Publications Agency
AFMPA ...... Armed Forces Medical Procurement Agency
AFMPC ..... Air Force Manpower and Personnel Center   (MCD)
AFMPC ..... Air Force Military Personnel Center [*Randolph Air Force Base, TX*]
AFMPC ..... Assistant for Materiel Program Control [*Air Force*]
AFMPMET ... Air Force Manpower and Personnel Management Engineering Team
AFMR........ American Foundation for Management Research [*Later, AMA*]   (EA)
AFMR........ Antiferromagnetic Resonance
AFMR........ Armed Forces Master Records [*Solicited phonograph records, and money to buy records, for the armed forces*] [*See also RFOFM*] [*World War II*]
AFMR........ Armed Forces Military Report [*DoD*]
AFMR........ Assistant Firemaster [*British*]
AFMRB..... Air Force Material Review Board   (MCD)
AFMRS ..... ASW [*Antisubmarine Warfare*] Formatted Message Reporting System
AFMS........ Air Force Manpower Standards
AFMS........ Air Force Medical Service
AFMS........ Airborne Frequency Multiplexing System
AFMS........ Airlift Field Maintenance Section
AFMS........ American Federation of Mineralogical Societies   (EA)
AFMS........ Operations Library, Syncrude Canada Ltd., Fort McMurray, Alberta [*Library symbol*] [*National Library of Canada*]   (NLC)
AFMSBG .. African Journal of Medical Sciences [*Later, African Journal of Medicine and Medical Sciences*] [*A publication*]
AFMSC ..... Air Force Medical Service Center   (MCD)
AFMSC ..... Air Force Medical Specialist Corps
AFMSC ..... Armed Forces Menu Service Committee   (AABC)
AFMSI ...... Information Centre, SUNCOR Inc. Resources Group, Fort McMurray, Alberta [*Library symbol*] [*National Library of Canada*]   (NLC)
AFMSL ..... Air Force Measurement Standards Laboratories   (AFIT)
AFMSMET ... Air Force Maintenance and Supply Management Engineering Team [*Wright-Patterson Air Force Base, OH*]
AFMSO..... Air Force Mortuary Services Office
AFMSP ..... Air Force Meteorological Satellite Program   (NOAA)
AFMT........ Air Force Manufacturing Technology
AFMTC..... Air Force Military Training Center   (AFM)
AFMTC..... Air Force Missile Test Center [*Later, AFETR*] [*Patrick Air Force Base, FL*]
AFMU .... Acetylamino(formylamino)methyluracil [*Biochemistry*]
AFMUAL ... Anales. Facultad de Medicina. Universidad Nacional Mayor de San Marcos de Lima [*Peru*] [*A publication*]
AFMUB.... Annali. Facolta di Magistero. Universita di Bari [*A publication*]
Af Mus....... African Music [*A publication*]
AFMUSC .. American Federation of Musicians of the United States and Canada [*Later, THFC*]
AFMVB..... Annali. Facolta di Medicina Veterinaria. Universita di Pisa [*A publication*]
AFMW ...... Action for Former Military Wives [*An association*] [*Later, NAFMW*]   (EA)
AfMw......... Archiv fuer Musikwissenschaft [*A publication*]
AFN .... Active Filter Network
AFN .... Address Complete, Subscriber Free, No-Charge [*Telecommunications*]   (TEL)
AFN .... Air Force Finance Center
AF/N .... Air Force/Navy   (AAG)
AFN .... Alaska Federation of Natives   (EA)
AFN .... Alfin Fragrances, Inc. [*AMEX symbol*]   (SPSG)
AFN .... All Figure Number [*Telecommunications*]   (TEL)
AFN .... American Forces Network   (AABC)
AFN .... Armed Forces Network [*Military*]
AFN .... Asian Finance [*A publication*]
AFN .... Assembly of First Nations [*Canadian Indian organization*]
AFN .... Association of Free Newspapers [*British*]   (EAIO)
AFN .... Automatic Feature Negotiation [*Data processing*]
AFN .... Average Failure Number
AFN .... Jaffrey, NH [*Location identifier*] [*FAA*]   (FAAL)
AFN .... United States Army, Corps of Engineers, New York District, New York, NY [*OCLC symbol*]   (OCLC)
AFNA .... Accordion Federation of North America   (EA)

AFNA .... Air Force - Navy
AF/NA....... Air Force/Navy Aeronautical
AFNA .... American Foundation for Negro Affairs   (EA)
AFNAB...... Air Force - Navy Aeronautical Bulletin
AFNABZ ... Acta Facultatis Rerum Naturalium Universitatis Comenianae. Anthropologica [*A publication*]
AFNAG ...... Air Force NATO Agreement   (MCD)
AFNAS ...... Air Force - Navy Aeronautical Standard
AFNB .... Armed Forces News Bureau [*Later, AFPS*]
AFNBA3 ... Acta Facultatis Rerum Naturalium Universitatis Comenianae. Botanica [*A publication*]
AFNC .... Air Force Nurse Corps
AFNCOAR ... Air Force Noncommissioned Officer Academy [*Graduate*] Ribbon [*Military decoration*]   (AFM)
AFNE .... Allied Forces Northern Europe [*NATO*]
AFNE .... American Forces Network, Europe   (AABC)
AFNE .... Americans for Nuclear Energy   (EA)
AFNEA ...... Air Force NOTAM [*Notice to Airmen*] Exchange Area
AFNEO ..... Air Force NOTAM [*Notice to Airmen*] Exchange Office
AF NETF... Air Force Nuclear Engineering Test Facility [*Reactor*]
AFNETSTA ... Air Force Networks Station
AFNFICM ... Atlantic Fleet Naval Forces Intelligence Collection Manual   (MCD)
AFNG .... Arbeitsgemeinschaft fuer Forschung des Landes Nordrhein-Westfalen. Geisteswissenschaften [*A publication*]
AFNGAI.... Acta Facultatis Rerum Naturalium Universitatis Comenianae. Genetica [*A publication*]
AFNN .... AFN [*Alaska Federation of Natives*] Newsletter [*A publication*]
AFNON ..... Allied Forces North Norway [*NATO*]   (MCD)
AFNOR ..... Association Francaise de Normalisation [*French Association for Standardization*] [*Database producer*]   (IID)
AFNORTH ... Allied Forces Northern Europe [*NATO*]
AFNRC...... Armed Forces National Research Council [*National Academy of Sciences*]
AFNRD ..... Air Force National Range Division
AFNS......... Air Force News Service
AFNY .... Alliance Francaise de New York [*Later, FIAF*]
AFNZA7... Acta Facultatis Rerum Naturalium Universitatis Comenianae. Zoologia [*A publication*]
AFNZRB... American Federation of New Zealand Rabbit Breeders   (EA)
AFO .... Accounting and Finance Office [*or Officer*]
AFO .... Admiralty Fleet Order [*Obsolete*] [*British*]
AFO .... Advanced File Organization
AFO .... AEI [*American Enterprise Institute*] Economist [*A publication*]
AFO .... Afton, WY [*Location identifier*] [*FAA*]   (FAAL)
AFO .... Airports Field Office
A Fo .... Allgemeine Forstzeitung [*A publication*]
AFO .... Ankle-Foot Orthosis [*Orthopedics*]
AFO .... Announced [*or Announcement of*] Flight Opportunity [*NASA*]   (KSC)
AFO .... Anti-Fascist Organization [*Later, AFPFL*] [*Burma*] [*World War II*]
AFO .... Archiv fuer Orientforschung [*A publication*]
AFO .... Army Forwarding Officer [*British*]
AFO .... Artillery Forward Observer
AFO .... Assaulting Federal Officer [*FBI standardized term*]
AFO .... Association of Field Ornithologists   (EA)
AFO .... Atlantic Fleet Organization
AFO .... Axial Flux Offset   (IEEE)
AFOAA5 ... Agricultural Research Council. Food Research Institute [*Norwich*]. Annual Report [*A publication*]
AFOAB6.... Australia. Commonwealth Scientific and Industrial Research Organisation. Division of Fisheries and Oceanography. Annual Report [*A publication*]
AFOAO ..... Air Force Operations Analysis Office   (KSC)
AFOAR ..... Air Force Office of Aerospace Research [*AFSC*]
AFOAS...... Air Force Office of Aerospace Sciences [*AFOAR*]
AFOAT ..... Air Force Office of Atomic Energy
AFOB .... Air Force Operations Base
AFOB .... American Foundation for Overseas Blind [*Later, HKI*]   (EA)
AFOBIC .... Alliance of Female Owned Businesses Involved in Construction   (EA)
AFOC .... Air Force Comptroller
AFOC .... Air Force Operations Center
AFOC .... Alaska Field Operations Center [*Anchorage, AK*] [*Department of the Interior*]   (GRD)
AFOC .... Auditor Freight Overcharge Claim
AFOC .... Automatic Flight Operation Center [*Army*]   (RDA)
AFOCC..... Air Force Director of Command Control and Communications
AFOCEL... Association Foret-Cellulose [*A publication*]
AFOD .... Arab Federation for the Organs of the Deaf [*Damascus, Syria*]   (EAIO)
AFODC ..... Deputy Chief of Staff for Operations, Air Force
AFOE .... Amphibious Follow-on-Echelon [*Navy*]   (MCD)
AFOE .... Assault Follow-On Echelon [*Marine Corps*]   (MCD)
AFOEP...... Air Force Officer Education Program   (AFM)
AfOF......... Archiv fuer Orientforschung [*Berlin*] [*A publication*]
AFOIC ...... Air Force Officer in Charge
AFOJP ...... American Fans of Jon Pertwee   (EA)
AFOLDS ... Air Force On-Line Data System
A Folk .... Archives de Folklore [*A publication*]

AFOM	Foremost Municipal Library, Alberta [*Library symbol*] [*National Library of Canada*] (NLC)
AFOMO	Air Force Office of Manpower and Organization
AFONA	Arizona Forestry Notes [*A publication*]
AFONAA ..	Arizona Forestry Notes [*A publication*]
A Fond G Feltrinelli ...	Annali. Fondazione Giangiacomo Feltrinelli [*A publication*]
A Fond L Einaudi ...	Annali. Fondazione Luigi Einaudi [*A publication*]
AFOP	Association of Farmworker Opportunity Programs (EA)
AFOPA	Air Force Office of Public Affairs
AFOPAG ...	Australia. Commonwealth Scientific and Industrial Research Organisation. Division of Fisheries and Oceanography. Technical Paper [*A publication*]
AFOQT	Air Force Officer Qualifying Test
AFOR	Air Force Operations Room [*British military*] (DMA)
AFORA	Air Force Office of Research Analysis (AFM)
AFORD	Air Force Overseas Replacement Depot [*World War II*]
AFOREP ...	Air Force Operational Report (AFM)
AFORG	Air Force Overseas Replacement Group [*World War II*]
AFORMS ..	Air Force Operations Resource Management Systems
A FORT	A Fortiori [*With More Reason*] [*Latin*] (ROG)
AForum	African Forum: A Quarterly Journal of Contemporary Affairs [*A publication*]
AFOS	Advanced Field Operating System [*National Weather Service*]
AFOS	Air Force Objective Series [*Papers*]
AFOS	Armed Forces Optometric Society (EA)
AFOS	Automation of Field Observations and Services
AFOS	Automation of Field Operations and Services [*National Weather Service*] (MSC)
AFO(S)	Auxiliary Fuel Oil (System) [*Nuclear energy*] (NRCH)
AFOSAP ...	Annual Report. Institute for Fermentation (Osaka) [*A publication*]
AFOSCR	Air Force Organization Status Change Report
AFOSH	Air Force Occupational Safety and Health [*Standards*]
AFOSI	Air Force Office of Special Investigation
AFOSP	Air Force Office of Security Police
AFOSR	Air Force Office of Scientific Research [*Bolling Air Force Base*] [*Washington, DC*]
AFOT	American Friends of Turkey (EA)
AFOTC	Air Force Operational Test Center (MCD)
AFOTEC ...	Air Force Operational Test and Evaluation Center [*Kirtland Air Force Base, NM*]
AFOUA	Air Force Outstanding Unit Award [*Military decoration*] (AFM)
AFOUAR ..	Air Force Outstanding Unit Award Ribbon [*Military decoration*]
AFOUE	Air Force Outstanding Unit Emblem [*Military decoration*]
AFP	ACE [*American Council on Education*] Fellows Program (EA)
AFP	Advanced Fileable Processor
AFP	Advanced Flexible Processor (MCD)
AFP	Affiliated Publications, Inc. [*NYSE symbol*] (SPSG)
AFP	Aflatoxin P [*Mycotoxin*]
AFP	African Construction, Building, Civil Engineering, Land Development [*A publication*]
AFP	Agence France-Presse [*French Press Agency*] (IID)
AFP	Air Force Pamphlet
AFP	Air Force Plan (MCD)
AFP	Air Force Police (NATG)
AFP	Alpha-Fetoprotein [*Clinical chemistry*]
AFPJ	Alternate Flight Plan
AFP	Alternative Fertility Proportion [*Demography*]
AFP	American Federation of Police (EA)
AFP	American Federation of Priests
A & FP	American & Foreign Power Co., Inc.
AFP	Americans for Peace [*Defunct*] (EA)
AFP	Amniotic Alphafetoprotein [*Obstetrics*]
AFP	Anglican Fellowship of Prayer (EA)
AFP	Annual Financial Plan
AFP	Annual Funding Program [*Army*]
AFP	Antifreeze Polypeptide [*Biochemistry*]
AFP	Antifreeze Protein
AFP	Aperture File Protocol [*Data processing*]
AFP	AppleTalk Filing Protocol [*Apple Computer, Inc.*] (BYTE)
AfP	Archiv fuer Papyrusforschung [*Leipzig*] [*A publication*]
AFP	Archivum Fratrum Praedicatorum [*Roma*] [*A publication*]
AFP	Armed Forces Police
AFP	Army Force Program
AFP	Army Fuze Program (MCD)
AFP	Associated Fantasy Publishers
AFP	Association des Familles Paguin [*Association of the Paguin Family*] [*Canada*]
AFP	Association of Federal Photographers (EA)
AFP	Association for Finishing Processes of SME [*Society of Manufacturing Engineers*] (EA)
AFP	Association of Flock Processors [*Defunct*] (EA)
AFP	Attached FORTRAN Processor [*Burroughs Corp.*] [*Data processing*] (BUR)
AFP	Audio Flat Panel [*Speaker system*]
AFP	Authority for Purchase
AFP	United States Army, Corps of Engineers, Portland District, Portland, OR [*OCLC symbol*] (OCLC)

AFP	Wadesboro, NC [*Location identifier*] [*FAA*] (FAAL)
AFPA	Agricultural Fair Practices Act of 1967
AFPA	Airborne Flat Plate Array
AFPA	American Fisheries Protection Act
AFPA	American Folklife Preservation Act [*1976*]
AFPA	Automatic Flow Process Analysis (IEEE)
AFPAC	[*US*] Army Forces in the Pacific [*World War II*]
AFPAM	Air Force Pamphlet
AFPAM	Automatic Flight Planning and Monitoring
AFPAV	Airfield Pavement [*Air Force*]
AFPB	Air Force Personnel Board
AFPBS	Air Force Pacific Broadcasting Squadron
AFPC	AFP Imaging Corporation [*NASDAQ symbol*] (NQ)
AFPC	Air Force Personnel Council
AFPC	Air Force Policy Council (AAG)
AFPC	Air Force Postal Clerk (AFM)
AFPC	Air Force Procurement Circulars
AFPC	Alliance de la Fonction Publique du Canada [*Public Service Alliance of Canada - PSAC*]
AFPC	American Federation for the Pueri Cantores (EA)
AFPC	American Food for Peace Council [*Defunct*] (EA)
AFPC	Armed Forces Policy Council
AFPC	Association des Facultes de Pharmacie du Canada [*Association of Faculties of Pharmacy of Canada*]
AF/PC	Automatic Frequency/Phase-Controlled [*Loop*] (IEEE)
AFPCA	Air Force of the People Chinese Liberation Army
AFPCAG ...	Acta Facultatis Pharmaceuticae Universitatis Comenianae [*A publication*]
AFPCB	Armed Forces Pest Control Board [*Washington, DC*]
AFPCH	Army Force Planning Cost Handbook
AFPCP	Air Force Potential Contractor Program (MCD)
AFPCS	Association for Fair Play for Children in Scotland (EAIO)
AFPD	Armed Forces Police Department [*or Detachment*]
AFPD	Authorization for Program Development [*NASA*] (NASA)
AFPDA	Army Force Planning Data and Assumptions (AABC)
AFPDAB ..	Air Force Physical Disability Appeal Board
AFPDC	Deputy Chief of Staff, Personnel [*Air Force*]
AFPE	Air Force Planning Element
AFPE	Air Force Preliminary Evaluation (MCD)
AFPE	American Foundation for Pharmaceutical Education (EA)
AFPE	American Foundation for Political Education
AFPE	Association for Progressive Education (EA)
AFPEA	Air Force Packaging Evaluation Agency (MCD)
AFPEAM ..	Archives Francaises de Pediatrie [*A publication*]
AFPEB	Air Force Professional Entertainment Branch
AFPEC	Armed Forces Product Evaluation Committee (AABC)
AFPEO	Armed Forces Professional Entertainment Office
AFPF	America First Preferred Equity Mortgage LP [*NASDAQ symbol*] (NQ)
AFPFL	Anti-Fascist People's Freedom League [*Formerly, AFO*] [*Burma*] [*World War II*]
AFPG	Air Force Personnel Processing Group
AFPG	Air Force Planning Guide
AFPH	American Federation of the Physically Handicapped
AFPhys	Associate of the Faculty of Physiatrics [*British*]
AFPI	Air Force Procurement Instructions
AFPI	American Foreign Policy Institute [*Defunct*] (EA)
AFPI	American Forest Products Industries [*Later, AFC*]
AFPID	Air Force Purchase Item Description
AFPJ	American Federation of Polish Jews (EA)
AFPL	Air Force Packaging Laboratory
AFPLC	Air Force Policy Letter for Commanders
AFPM	Aircraft Force Projection Model [*Computer*] [*Navy*]
AFPMO	Air Force Polaris Material Office
AFPMP	Army Air Forces Military Personnel [*World War II*]
AFPMPMS ...	Air Force Professional Manpower and Personnel Management School
AFPO	Air Force Property Officer (MCD)
AFPO	Air Force Purchasing Office (MUGU)
AFPOAI	Anais. Faculdade de Ciencias. Universidade do Porto [*A publication*]
AFPOB	American Friends of the Paris Opera and Ballet (EA)
AFPOM	Air Force Program Objectives Memorandum (MCD)
AFPP	Acute Fibrinopurulent Pneumonia [*Medicine*]
AFPP	Air Force Procurement Procedures
AFPPA	American Federation of Poultry Producers Associations [*Defunct*] (EA)
AFPPAL	Australia. Commonwealth Scientific and Industrial Research Organisation. Division of Forest Products. Technological Paper [*A publication*]
AFPPCN	Acta Facultatis Rerum Naturalium Universitatis Comenianae. Physiologia Plantarum [*A publication*]
AFPPF	Automatic Fluorescent Penetrant Processing Facility (MCD)
AFPPG	American Foundation for Psychoanalysis and Psychoanalysis in Groups (EA)
AFPPS	American Forces Press and Publications Service
AFPR	Air Force Plant Representative
AFPR	Air Force Procurement Regulation
AFPR	Air Force Procurement Representative
AFPR	Air Force Project Representative
AFPR	Armed Forces Procurement Regulation

AFPRDS.... Air Force Petroleum Retail Distribution Station (AFM)
AFPRL ...... Air Force Personnel Research Lab (MCD)
AFPRO ...... Air Force Plant Representative Office
AFPRO ...... Air Force Program Representative Office (MCD)
AFPRP ...... Air Force Production Reserve Policy
AFPS .... American Forces Press Service [*Formerly, AFNB*]
AFPS .... Army Film and Photographic Section [*British military*] (DMA)
AFPS .... Aseptic Food Processing System
AFPSC....... Armed Forces Philippines Supply Center (CINC)
AFPT .... Aftenposten [*A publication*]
AFPT .... Air Force Personnel Test (AFM)
AFPT .... Auxiliary Feed Pump Turbine (IEEE)
AFPTC ...... Agricultural Farm Produce Trade Corporation [*Burma*] (DS)
AFPTRC.... Air Force Personnel and Training Research Center [*Later, Air
               Force Personnel Research Laboratory*] [*Lackland Air
               Force Base, TX*]
AFPU......... Air Force Postal Unit
AFPU......... Army Film and Photographic Unit [*British military*] (DMA)
AFPVD...... American Foundation for the Prevention of Venereal
               Disease (EA)
AFPYA ...... American Family Physician [*A publication*]
AFPYB ...... American Family Physician [*A publication*]
AFPZU ...... American Family Pizza Uts [*NASDAQ symbol*] (NQ)
AFQ .... Aflatoxin Q [*Mycotoxin*]
AFQ .... Air Afrique (MCD)
AFQ .... Airframe Flight Qualification
AFQ .... Alberta Folklore Quarterly [*A publication*]
AFQA .... Air Force Quality Assurance (KSC)
AFQAR...... Air Force Quality Assurance Representative
AFQC .... Air Force Quality Control
AFQCR...... Air Force Quality Control Representative
AFQFAU... Anales. Facultad de Quimica y Farmacia. Universidad de Chile
               [*A publication*]
AFQFBV ... Anales. Facultad de Quimica y Farmacia. Universidad de
               Concepcion [*A publication*]
AFQQPRI ... Amendment to the Final Qualitative and Quantitative
               Personnel Requirements Information (MCD)
AFQSAZ ... Anais de Farmacia e Quimica de Sao Paulo [*A publication*]
AFQSB2 .... Advance Abstracts of Contributions on Fisheries and Aquatic
               Sciences in India [*A publication*]
AFQT........ Armed Forces Qualification Test
AFQTVA ... Armed Forces Qualification Test, Verbal Arithmetic Subtest
AFR .... Absolute Filtration Rating
AFR .... Acceptable Failure Rate
AFR .... Access Function Register
AFR .... Acid Fractionator Recycle [*Nuclear energy*] (NRCH)
AFR .... Afareaitu [*Society Islands*] [*Seismograph station code, US
               Geological Survey*] (SEIS)
AFR .... Afore [*Papua New Guinea*] [*Airport symbol*] (OAG)
AFR .... Africa
AFR .... Africa Confidential [*A publication*]
AFR .... Africa. Revista Espanola de Colonizacion [*A publication*]
afr.............. Afrikaans [*MARC language code*] [*Library of
               Congress*] (LCCP)
AFR .... Air Force Regulation
AFR .... Air Force Reserve
AFR .... Air-Fuel Ratio (ADA)
AFR .... Aircraft Flight Report (AAG)
AFR .... Airframe
AFR .... Alaska. Department of Fish and Game. Sport Fish Division.
               Federal Aid in Fish Restoration Studies [*A publication*]
A Fr .... Alt-Franken [*A publication*]
AFR .... Alternating Frequency Rejection [*Automotive technology*]
AFR .... American Friends of Refugees [*Defunct*]
AFR .... America's Freedom Ride (EA)
AFR .... Anglo-French [*Language, etc.*]
AFR .... Anglo-French Review [*A publication*]
AFR .... Aqueous Flare Response [*Physiology*]
AFR .... Archiv fuer Reformationsgeschichte. Texte und
               Untersuchungen [*A publication*]
AfR............. Archiv foer Retsvidenskaben og dens Anvendelse [*Denmark*]
               [*A publication*] (ILCA)
AFR .... Armed Forces Radio (ADA)
AFR .... Armed Forces Radiobiology Research Institute, Bethesda, MD
               [*OCLC symbol*] (OCLC)
AFR .... Artillery Flash Ranging [*Army*] (AABC)
AFR .... Ascorbic Free Radical [*Biochemistry*]
AFR .... Auditor Freight Receipts
AFR .... Australian Financial Review [*A publication*] (APTA)
AFR .... Automatic Format Recognition [*Data processing*] (ADA)
AFR .... Available for Release (MCD)
AFR .... Avon Fantasy Reader [*A publication*]
AFR .... Awaiting Forward Release [*Telecommunications*] (TEL)
AFR .... Away from Reactor [*Storage facilities*]
AFR .... Axial Flow Reactor [*Chemical engineering*]
AfrA .... African Arts [*Los Angeles*] [*A publication*]
AFRA........ American Family Records Association (EA)
AFRA........ American Farm Research Association [*Superseded by
               AFBRF*] (EA)
AFRA......... American Federation of Radio Artists
AFRA......... Armed Forces Reserve Act of 1952, as Amended

AFRA........ Average Freight Rate Assessment [*Shipping*]
AFRAA...... African Airlines Association [*Kenya*]
AfrAb........ African Abstracts [*A publication*]
Afr Abstr.... African Abstracts [*A publication*]
AFRACA ... African Regional Agricultural Credit Association (EAIO)
AFRADBIORSCHINST ... Armed Forces Radiobiology Research Institute
AF/RADC ... Air Force Rome Air Development Center
AFR Ae S... Associate Fellow of the Royal Aeronautical Society [*British*]
AfrAf.......... African Affairs [*A publication*]
Afr Aff........ African Affairs [*A publication*]
Afr Affairs ... African Affairs [*A publication*]
Afr Agric.... Afrique Agriculture [*A publication*]
AFRAIDS ... Acute Fear Regarding AIDS
AfrAm S..... Afro-American Studies [*A publication*]
AFRAMS .. Air Force Recoverable Assembly Management System (AFM)
Afr-Am Stud ... Afro-American Studies [*A publication*]
AFRAP...... Air Force Recruiter Assistance Program (MCD)
AFRAP...... American Foundation of Religion and Psychiatry [*Later,
               Institutes of Religion and Health*] (EA)
AFRAPT ... Air Force Research in Aircraft Propulsion Technology Program
               [*West Lafayette, IN*] (GRD)
Afr Arch..... African Architect [*A publication*]
Afr Art .... African Arts [*A publication*]
Afr Arts...... African Arts [*Los Angeles*] [*A publication*]
Afr et As..... Afrique et l'Asie [*Later, Afrique et l'Asie Modernes*] [*A
               publication*]
AFRAS ...... Associate Fellow of the Royal Aeronautical Society [*British*]
AFrAS .... United States Army Aviation School, Fort Rucker, AL [*Library
               symbol*] [*Library of Congress*] (LCLS)
AFRASEC ... Afro-Asian Organization for Economic Cooperation
AFRASIA ... Africa and Asia
Afr Asie...... Afrique et l'Asie Modernes [*A publication*]
Afr et Asie Mod ... Afrique et l'Asie Modernes [*A publication*]
Afr Asie Mod ... Afrique et l'Asie Modernes [*A publication*]
Afr et Asie Modernes ... Afrique et l'Asie Modernes [*A publication*]
Afr B .... Africana Bulletin [*A publication*]
AFRB......... Air Force Retiring Board
AFRB......... Australian Family Research Bulletin [*A publication*] (ADA)
AFRB........ Award Fee Review Board
AFRBA ...... Armed Forces Relief and Benefit Association (EA)
Afr Beekeep ... African Beekeeping [*A publication*]
AFRBSGP ... Air Force Reserve Base Support Group
Afr Bull ...... Africana Bulletin [*A publication*]
Afr Bus Chamber Commer Rev ... African Business and Chamber of
               Commerce Review [*A publication*]
Afr Business ... African Business [*A publication*]
AFRC......... Adoption and Family Reunion Center (EA)
AFRC......... Agricultural and Food Research Council [*United Kingdom*]
               [*Research center*] (IRC)
AFRC........ Air Force Records Center
AFRC......... Armed Forces Recreation Center
AFRC......... Armed Forces Reserve Center (AABC)
AFRC......... Armed Forces Revolutionary Council [*Ghana*] (PPW)
AFRCA ...... Acta Facultatis Rerum Naturalium Universitatis Comenianae.
               Chimia [*A publication*]
AFRCC...... Air Force Rescue Coordination Center
AFRCC...... Air Force Reserve Coordination Center (AFM)
AFRCE ...... Air Force Regional Civil Engineers
Afr Ch .... Altfraenkische Chronik [*A publication*]
Afr Communist ... African Communist [*A publication*]
Afr Contemp ... Afrique Contemporaine [*A publication*]
Afr Contemporaine ... Afrique Contemporaine [*A publication*]
AFRCSTC ... Air Force Reserve Combat Support Training Center
AFRCTC ... Air Force Reserve Combat Training Center
AFRD .... Acute Febrile Respiratory Disease [*Medicine*]
AFRD .... Air Force Research Directorate (KSC)
AFRD .... Air Force Research Division
AFRD .... Air Force Reserve Division
AFRDB...... Air Force Research and Development Branch
Afr Develop ... African Development [*A publication*]
Afr Dig .... Africa Digest [*A publication*]
AFRDR...... Air Force Director of Reconnaissance and Electronic
               Warfare (IEEE)
AFRE......... African Environment [*A publication*]
AFRE......... Australian Family Reformation [*Project*]
AFRE......... Australian Financial Review [*Information service or system*] [*A
               publication*] (ADA)
AFREA ...... Advances in Food Research [*A publication*]
Afr Econ H ... African Economic History [*A publication*]
Afr Econ Hist ... African Economic History [*A publication*]
AFREDCOM ... Armed Forces Readiness Command (MCD)
Afr Eng ...... African Engineering [*A publication*]
AFREP...... Air Force Representative [*to the FAA*] (FAAC)
AF Rep....... Alaska Federal Reports [*A publication*] (DLA)
AFREQ...... Army Air Forces Requirements Division [*World War II*]
AFRES ...... Air Force Reserve
AFRESBSGP ... Air Force Reserve Regions Base Support Group
AFRESM..... Armed Forces Reserve Medal [*Military decoration*]
AFRESNAVSQ ... Air Force Reserve Navigation Squadron
AFRESR.... Air Force Reserve Regions
AFRESRGP ... Air Force Reserve Regions Group

AFRESS .... Air Force Reserve Sectors
AFRF .... American Freedom of Residence Fund [*Defunct*] (EA)
AFRF .... American Friends of Russian Freedom [*Later, AFR*] (EA)
AFRFAZ .... Acta Forestalia Fennica [*A publication*]
AFRFI .... American Friends of Religious Freedom in Israel [*Defunct*] (EAIO)
Afr Franc ... Afrique Francaise [*A publication*]
Afr Fr Chir ... Afrique Francaise Chirurgicale [*A publication*]
AFRFTC .... Air Force Reserve Flying Training Center
Afr Heute ... Afrika Heute [*A publication*]
Afr Hist Stud ... African Historical Studies [*A publication*]
AFRI .... Action from Ireland [*An association*] (EAIO)
AFRI .... Acute Febrile Respiratory Illness [*Medicine*]
AfrI .... African Imprint Library Services, Bedford, NY [*Library symbol*] [*Library of Congress*] (LCLS)
Afri .... [*Sextus Caecilius*] Africanus [*Flourished, 2nd century*] [*Authority cited in pre-1607 legal work*] (DSA)
AFRI .... American Foundation for Resistance International (EA)
AFRI .... American Fur Resources Institute (EA)
AFRI .... Applied Forest Research Institute [*Syracuse University*]
AFRIAA .... Africana [*A publication*]
Afric .... [*Sextus Caecilius*] Africanus [*Flourished, 2nd century*] [*Authority cited in pre-1607 legal work*] (DSA)
Africa .... Africa. Fouilles. Monuments et Collections Archeologiques en Tunisie [*A publication*]
Africa .... [*Sextus Caecilius*] Africanus [*Flourished, 2nd century*] [*Authority cited in pre-1607 legal work*] (DSA)
Afric Affairs ... African Affairs [*A publication*]
Africa IAI .. Africa. International African Institute [*A publication*]
AfricaL .... Africa (London) [*A publication*]
Africana ..... Africana Bulletin [*Warsaw*] [*A publication*]
African Admin Studies ... African Administrative Studies [*A publication*]
Africana J .. Africana Journal [*A publication*]
Africana Lib J ... Africana Library Journal [*A publication*]
Africana Marburg ... Africana Marburgensia [*A publication*]
Africana Res B ... Africana Research Bulletin [*A publication*]
African Bus ... African Business [*A publication*]
African Econ Hist ... African Economic History [*A publication*]
AFRICA NEWS ... Africa News Service (EA)
African J Ednl Research ... African Journal of Educational Research [*A publication*]
African LD ... African Law Digest [*A publication*] (ILCA)
African LR Comm ... African Law Reports, Commercial Series [*A publication*] (DLA)
African LR Mal ... African Law Reports, Malawi Series [*A publication*] (DLA)
African LRSL ... African Law Reports, Sierra Leone Series [*A publication*] (DLA)
African LS ... African Law Studies [*A publication*]
AfricanM ... African Music [*A publication*]
African R ... African Review [*A publication*]
African Stud ... African Studies [*A publication*]
African Stud Bul ... African Studies Bulletin [*A publication*]
African Studies R ... African Studies Review [*A publication*]
African Stud R ... African Studies Review [*A publication*]
Africa R ...... Africa Report [*A publication*]
Africa Rep ... Africa Report [*A publication*]
Africa Rept ... Africa Report [*A publication*]
Africa T ...... Africa Today [*A publication*]
Africa Th J ... Africa Theological Journal [*A publication*]
Afric Dev ... New African Development [*A publication*]
Afric Df Jl ... African Defence Journal [*A publication*]
Afric Lit Today ... African Literature Today [*A publication*]
AFRICOBRA ... African Commune of Bad Relevant Artists [*Chicago*]
Afric Stud ... African Studies [*A publication*]
Afric Stud R ... African Studies Review [*A publication*]
Afri Econ .... Review of African Political Economy [*A publication*]
AFRIK .... Afrikaans
Afrika Mat ... Afrika Matematika. The First Pan-African Mathematical Journal [*A publication*]
Afr Ind .... African Industries [*A publication*]
Afr Industr Infrastruct ... Afrique Industrie Infrastructures [*A publication*]
Afr Insight ... Africa Insight [*A publication*]
Afr Inst B ... Africa Institute. Bulletin [*A publication*]
Afr Inst Bull ... Africa Institute. Bulletin [*A publication*]
Afr Insur Rec ... African Insurance Record [*A publication*]
AfrIt .... Africa Italiana [*A publication*]
Afr J Clin Exp Immunol ... African Journal of Clinical and Experimental Immunology [*A publication*]
Afr J Ecol ... African Journal of Ecology [*A publication*]
Afr J Int Afr Inst ... Africa. Journal of the International African Institute [*A publication*]
Afr J Med Med Sci ... African Journal of Medicine and Medical Sciences [*A publication*]
Afr J Med Sci ... African Journal of Medical Sciences [*Later, African Journal of Medicine and Medical Sciences*] [*A publication*]
Afr J Psychiatr ... African Journal of Psychiatry [*A publication*]
Afr J Trop Hydrobiol Fish ... African Journal of Tropical Hydrobiology and Fisheries [*A publication*]
Afr J Trop Hydrobiol Fish Spec Issue ... African Journal of Tropical Hydrobiology and Fisheries. Special Issue [*A publication*]

AFRKB ...... American Federation of Retail Kosher Butchers (EA)
AfrL .... Africana Linguistica [*Tervuren*] [*A publication*]
Afr Lab N ... African Labour News [*A publication*]
Afr Lang Stud ... African Language Studies [*A publication*]
Afr Law Stud ... African Law Studies [*A publication*]
Afr L Digest ... African Law Digest [*A publication*]
Afr Ling ...... Africana Linguistica [*A publication*]
Afr Lit Assoc Bul ... African Literature Association. Bulletin [*A publication*]
Afr Lit Assoc Newsl ... African Literature Association. Newsletter [*A publication*]
Afr Litt Artist ... Afrique Litteraire et Artistique [*A publication*]
Afr Litter et Artist ... Afrique Litteraire et Artistique [*A publication*]
Afr Lit Tod ... African Literature Today [*A publication*]
AfrLJ .... Africana Library Journal [*A publication*]
Afr LR .... African Law Reports [*A publication*] (DLA)
AfrLRev ..... African Language Review [*A publication*]
Afr LR Mal Ser ... African Law Reports, Malawi Series [*A publication*] (DLA)
Afr LR Sierre L Ser ... African Law Reports, Sierra Leone Series [*A publication*] (DLA)
AfrLS .... African Language Studies [*A publication*]
Afr L Stud ... African Law Studies [*A publication*]
AfrM .... Africana Marburgensia [*A publication*]
AFRM .... Airframe (AABC)
AFRM .... Armed Forces Reserve Medal [*Military decoration*]
AFRMA ..... American Fancy Rat and Mouse Association (EA)
Afr Man Min ... African Manual on Mining [*A publication*]
Afr Med ...... Afrique Medicale [*A publication*]
Afr Mus ..... African Music [*A publication*]
Afr Music ... African Music [*A publication*]
AfrN .... African Notes [*Ibadan*] [*A publication*]
AFRNA ...... Acta Facultatis Rerum Naturalium Universitatis Comenianae. Physica [*A publication*]
Afr Natuurlewe ... Afrika Natuurlewe [*A publication*]
Afr Ne Lett ... African Newsletter [*A publication*]
Afr Notes News ... Africana Notes and News [*A publication*]
AFRO .... African Regional Organization
AFRO .... Air Force Research Objectives
AFRO .... Air Force Reserve Orders
AFRO .... Air Force Route Routine Order [*Canada, 1920-1945*]
AFROASI ... Authority for Removal of Accepted Spacecraft Installations (MCD)
Afroasiatic Ling ... Afroasiatic Linguistics [*A publication*]
AFROC ...... Air Force Retired Officer's Community
AFROC ...... Association of Freestanding Radiation Oncology Centers (EA)
AFROIC .... Air Force Resident Officer in Charge
AFROSAI ... African Organization of Supreme Audit Institutions [*Lome, Togo*] (EAIO)
AFROSAT ... African Satellite
AFROTC ... Air Force Reserve Officers Training Corps [*Washington, DC*]
AFRP .... Air Force Recurring Publication (AFM)
AFRP .... American Foundation of Religion and Psychiatry [*Later, Institutes of Religion and Health*]
AFrP .... Athlone French Poets [*A publication*]
AFRPC ...... Air Force Reserve Policy Committee
Afr Perspect ... Africa Perspective [*A publication*]
AFRPL ...... Air Force Rocket Propulsion Laboratory [*Later, AFAL*] [*Edwards Air Force Base, CA*]
Afr Post ...... Afrika Post [*A publication*]
Afr Q .... Africa Quarterly [*A publication*]
Afr R .... African Review [*A publication*]
AFRR .... Air Force Reserve Regions (AFM)
AFRR .... Air Force Resident Representative (AAG)
Afr Relig Res ... African Religious Research [*A publication*]
Afr Rep ...... Africa Report [*A publication*]
Afr Report ... Africa Report [*A publication*]
Afr Res Bull ... Africa Research Bulletin Series [*A publication*]
Afr Res Bul Ser A Pol ... Africa Research Bulletin. Series A. Political [*A publication*]
Afr Res Doc ... African Research and Documentation [*A publication*]
AFRRGp .... Air Force Reserve Recovery Group (AFM)
AFRRI ...... Armed Forces Radiobiology Research Institute [*Bethesda, MD*] [*DoD*]
AFRS .... Advanced Fighter RADAR System
AfrS .... African Studies [*Johannesburg*] [*A publication*]
AFRS .... Agricultural and Food Research Service [*Ministry of Agriculture, Fisheries, and Food*] [*British*] (IRUK)
AFRS .... Air Force Rescue Service
AFRS .... Air Force Reserve Sectors (AFM)
AFRS .... Approved Force Retention Stock [*Air Force*] (AFIT)
AFRS .... Armed Forces Radio Service [*Military*]
AFRS .... Armed Forces Recruiting Stations [*DoD*]
AFRS .... Auxiliary Flight Reference System
AFRSC ...... Armed Forces Recipe Service Committee (AABC)
AfrSch .... African Scholar [*A publication*]
AFRSF .... Air Force Range Support Facility
AFRSI .... Advanced Flexible Reusable Surface Insulation [*For space shuttles*]
Afr Soc Pretoria Yearb ... Africana Society of Pretoria. Yearbook [*A publication*]
Afr Soc Res ... African Social Research [*A publication*]

Afr Soc Secur Ser ... African Social Security Series [*A publication*]
Afr Soils..... African Soils [*A publication*]
Afr South ... Africa South [*A publication*]
Afr Spectrum ... Afrika Spectrum [*A publication*]
AfrSR........ African Studies Review [*A publication*]
Afr St .... African Studies [*A publication*]
AFRST ...... American Friends of the Royal Shakespeare Theatre   (EA)
AFRST ...... Automatic Focusing Random Scene Tracker   (MCD)
AFRSTC.... Air Force Reserve Specialist Training Center
Afr Stud ..... African Studies [*A publication*]
Afr Stud B ... African Studies Bulletin [*A publication*]
Afr Stud Newsl ... African Studies Newsletter [*A publication*]
Afr Stud R ... African Studies Review [*A publication*]
Afr-T.......... Africa-Tervuren [*A publication*]
AFRT........ Air Freight   (FAAC)
AFRT........ American [*formerly, Armed*] Forces Radio and Television [*DoD*]
AFrT .... Troy State University at Fort Rucker, Fort Rucker, AL [*Library symbol*] [*Library of Congress*]   (LCLS)
AFRTC...... Air Force Research Training Center
AFRTC...... Air Force Reserve Training Center
AFRTD...... Air Force Research and Technology Division
Afr Tervuren ... Africa-Tervuren [*A publication*]
Afr Th J ..... Africa Theological Journal [*A publication*]
Afr Today... Africa Today [*A publication*]
Afr T Rev ... African Trade Review [*A publication*]
AFRTS ...... American [*formerly, Armed*] Forces Radio and Television Service [*or System*]
AFRTS ...... Armed Forces Radio and Telegraph Service
AFRTS ...... Armed Forces Radio-Television [*Cable-television system*]
AFRU ...... Armed Forces Reporting Unit [*Red Cross*]
Afr Uebersee ... Afrika und Uebersee [*A publication*]
Afr Violet Mag ... African Violet Magazine [*A publication*]
Afr Wildl.... African Wildlife [*A publication*]
Afr Wild Life ... African Wild Life [*A publication*]
Afr-Wirtsch ... Afrika-Wirtschaft [*A publication*]
Afr WS...... African Writers Series [*A publication*]
AFS........... Active Fuzing System
AFS........... Adirondack Forty-Sixers   (EA)
AFS........... Administrative Fact Sheet [*Vocational education*]   (OICC)
AFS........... Advanced Fermentation System
AFS........... Advanced Figure Sensor   (KSC)
AFS........... Advanced Firing Systems   (MSA)
AFS........... Advanced Flying School [*British military*]   (DMA)
AFS........... Aerial Film Speed
AFS........... Aerial Fire Support
AFS........... Aerodrome Fire Service [*British*]   (AIA)
AFS........... Aeronautical Fixed Service
AFS........... African Studies [*Johannesburg*] [*A publication*]
AFS........... AFS [*American Field Service*] Intercultural Programs   (EA)
AFS........... Air Force Specialty
AFS........... Air Force Standard   (NASA)
AFS........... Air Force Station
AFS........... Air Force Stock   (AAG)
AFS........... Air Force Supply
AFS........... Airline Feed System
AFS........... Airways Facilities Sector   (FAAC)
AFS........... Alaska. Department of Fish and Game. Sport Fish Division. Anadromous Fish Studies [*A publication*]
AFS........... American Family Society   (EA)
AFS........... American Feline Society   (EA)
AFS........... American Fern Society   (EA)
AFS........... American Fertility Society   (EA)
AFS........... American Field Service [*Later, AFSIIP*]
AFS........... American Fisheries Society   (EA)
AFS........... American Folklore Society   (EA)
AFS........... American Foundrymen's Society   (EA)
AFS........... American Fuchsia Society   (EA)
AFS........... Anne Frank Stichting [*Anne Frank Foundation*]   (EAIO)
AFS........... Antenna Feed System
AFS........... Applicant File Search [*US Employment Service*] [*Department of Labor*]
AFS........... Armed Forces and Society [*A publication*]
AFS........... Arming and Fusing System   (MSA)
AFS........... Army Fire Service
AFS........... Asian Folklore Studies [*A publication*]
AFS........... Associate of the Faculty of Architects and Surveyors [*British*]   (DBQ)
AFS........... Association for Food Self-Sufficiency   (EAIO)
AFS........... Association for Stammerers   (EAIO)
AFS........... Atlantic Ferry Service [*World War II*]
AFS........... Atomic Fluorescence Spectroscopy
AFS........... Atomic Frequency Standard
AFS........... Audio Frequency Shift   (IEEE)
AFS........... Automatic Fault Simulator
AFS........... Automatic Firing Sequencer
AFS........... Automatic Flight System [*Aviation*]   (AIA)
AFS........... Automatic Frequency Stabilization
AFS........... Auxiliary Feedwater System [*Nuclear energy*]   (NRCH)
AFS........... Auxiliary Fire Service [*British*]
AFS........... Aviation Facilities Service [*of FAA*]

AFS........... Azimuth Follow-Up System
AFS........... Combat Store Ship [*Navy symbol*]
AFS........... United States Army, Corps of Engineers, Seattle District, Seattle, WA [*OCLC symbol*]   (OCLC)
AFSA........ Air Force Senior Advisory
AFSA........ Air Force Sergeants Association   (EA)
AFSA........ American Federation of School Administrators   (EA)
AFSA........ American Financial Services Association [*Washington, DC*]   (EA)
AFSA........ American Fire Sprinkler Association   (EA)
AFSA........ American Flagship Available
AFSA........ American Flight Strips Association   (EA)
AFSA........ American Foreign Service Association   (EA)
AFSA.......... Armed Forces Security Agency [*Obsolete*]
AFSA........ Association of Former Senate Aides   (EA)
AFSA........ Association for Spiritual Awareness   (EA)
AFSA.......... Automated Fire Support Artillery   (MCD)
AFSA........ Aviation Force Structure for the Army   (MCD)
AFSAB...... Air Force Scientific Advisory Board   (MCD)
AFSAC...... Air Force Special Activities Center
AFSAC...... Armed Forces Security Agency Council [*Abolished, 1952*]
AFSAC/IRC ... Armed Forces Security Agency Council Intelligence Requirements Committee [*Obsolete*]
AFSAG...... Armed Forces Security Agency [*Obsolete*]
AFSA-JB.... Air Force Senior Advisory - Jefferson Barracks
AFSAM..... Air Force School of Aviation Medicine
AFSAMSO ... Air Force Space and Missile Systems Organization   (KSC)
AFSARC.... Air Force System Acquisition Review Council
AFSARI.... Automation for Storage and Retrieval of Information
AFSAS...... Academy for Friends of Secretarial Arts and Sciences   (EA)
AFSAS....... Advanced Fire Support Avionics System
AFSAS....... American Federation of School Administrators and Supervisors [*AFL-CIO*]
AFSATCOM ... Air Force Satellite Communications System   (AFM)
AFSATLCF ... Air Force Satellite Control Facility
AFSAW..... Air Force Special Activities Wing
AFSAWC .. Air Force Special Air Warfare Center   (MCD)
AFSB........ Air Force Specification Bulletin
AFSB .... American Federation of Small Business [*Chicago, IL*]   (EA)
AFSB .... Association of Friends of Schloss Blutenburg [*See also VFSB*] [*Munich, Federal Republic of Germany*]   (EAIO)
AFSB .... Australian Flying Saucer Bureau [*Defunct*]
AFSBC...... Assembly of Free Spirit Baptist Churches   (EA)
AFSC........ Air Force Service Center [*or Command*]
AFSC........ Air Force Skill Code
AFSC........ Air Force Specialty Code
AFSC........ Air Force Supply Catalog
AFSC........ Air Force Supply Code
AFSC........ Air Force Systems Command [*Andrews Air Force Base, MD*]
AFSC........ American Federation of Soroptimist Clubs [*Later, Soroptimist International of the Americas*]
AFSC .... American Friends Service Committee   (EA)
AFSC .... Armed Forces Sports Committee   (EA)
AFSC .... Armed Forces Staff College
AFSC .... Assessment of Fluency in School-Age Children [*Speech evaluation test*]
AFSCA ...... Amalgamated Flying Saucer Clubs of America   (EA)
AFSCAG ... Air Force Service Contract Advisory Group   (MCD)
AFS Cast Met Res J ... AFS [*American Foundrymen's Society*] Cast Metals Research Journal [*A publication*]
AFSCC ...... Air Force Satellite Control Center   (CET)
AFSCC ...... Air Force Security Communications Center   (MCD)
AFSCC ...... Air Force Special Communications Center   (CET)
AFSCC ...... Armed Forces Supply Control Center [*DoD*]
AFSC-DH ... Air Force Systems Command Design Handbooks
AFSCE...... American Fertility Society Classification of Endometriosis
AFSCE....... Association of Former Students of the College of Europe   (EAIO)
AFSCF...... Air Force Satellite [*or Spacecraft*] Control Facility [*Sunnyvale Air Force Station, CA*]   (AFM)
AFSCF...... Air Force Systems Command Form
AFSCI....... American Foundation for the Science of Creative Intelligence   (EA)
AFSCL....... Air Force Systems Command Letter
AFSCM..... Air Force Systems Command Manual
AFSCME... American Federation of State, County, and Municipal Employees   (EA)
AFSCN..... Air Force Satellite Control Network   (MCD)
AFSCO...... Air Force Security Clearance Office
AFSCOORD ... Assistant Fire Support Coordinator [*Military*]   (AABC)
AFSCP....... Air Force Systems Command Pamphlet
AFSCP....... Air Force Systems Command Concept Paper   (MCD)
AFSCPP ... Air Force Systems Command Procurement Production   (MCD)
AFSCR ...... Air Force Systems Command Regulation
AFSCS....... Air Force Satellite Communications System   (MCD)
AFSCS....... Army Field Stock Control System   (AABC)
AFSC/SSD ... Air Force Systems Command Space Systems Division
AFSC/STLO ... Air Force Systems Command, Scientific Technical Liaison Office   (MUGU)
AFSD......... Aforesaid
AF/SD .... Air Force and Space Digest [*A publication*]

AFSD........ Air Force Space Division (MCD)
AFSD........ Air Force Supply Date
AFSD........ Air Force Supply Depot
AFSD........ Air Force Supply Directive (MCD)
AFSD........ Central Library, Dow Chemical of Canada Ltd., Fort Saskatchewan, Alberta [*Library symbol*] [*National Library of Canada*] (NLC)
AFSE........ Allied Forces Southern Europe [*NATO*] (NATG)
AFSec........ Air Force Section (AFM)
AFSEC...... Armed Forces Stamp Exchange Club (EA)
AFSEM..... Army Food Service Energy Management (AABC)
AFSERT.... Associate Fellow of the Society of Electronic and Radio Technicians [*British*] (DBQ)
AFSF........ Advanced Field Site Facility
AFSF........ Air Force Satellite Facility
AFSF........ Air Force Stock Fund
AFSF........ Air Force Supply Force
AFSFO...... Airways Facilities Sector Field Office (FAAC)
AFSFOU ... Airways Facilities Sector Field Office Plus Unit (FAAC)
AFSG........ Asian Folklore Studies Group [*Later, ISA*] (EA)
AFSHP...... Association of Federal Safety and Health Professionals (EA)
AFSHRC ... Albert F. Simpson Historical Research Center (AFM)
AFSI......... Americans for a Safe Israel (EA)
AFSI......... Architectural Fabric Structures Institute (EA)
AFSI......... Association of Suppliers to the Furniture Industries Show [*Wood Work Industrial Exhibition*] (TSPED)
AFSI......... Aviation Financial Services, Incorporated
AFSIG....... Ascent Flight Systems Integration Group [*NASA*] (NASA)
AFSINC .... Air Force Service Information and News Center
AFS Int Cast Met J ... AFS [*American Foundrymen's Society*] International Cast Metals Journal [*A publication*]
AFSIP........ Air Force Standard Intelligence Publication (AFM)
AFSIR....... Air Force Salary Impact Report
AFS/JAF... Journal of American Folklore. American Folklore Society [*A publication*]
AFSK........ Audio Frequency Shift Key
AFSL .... AmFed Financial Corp. [*Formerly, American Federal Savings & Loan Association of Colorado*] [*NASDAQ symbol*] (NQ)
AFSL .... Approved Fastener Substitution List (MCD)
AFSLAET ... Associate Fellow of the Society of Licensed Aircraft Engineers and Technologists [*British*] (DBQ)
AFSM........ Air Force Screen Magazine [*A publication*]
AFSM........ Artillery Forces Simulation Model (MCD)
AFSM........ Association of Field Service Managers [*Later, ASMI*] (EA)
AFSM........ Association for Food Service Management [*Later, SFM*] (EA)
AFSM........ Fort Saskatchewan Municipal Library, Alberta [*Library symbol*] [*National Library of Canada*] (NLC)
AFSMAAG ... Air Force Section, Military Assistance Advisory Group
AFSMAS... Association Francophone de Spectrometrie de Masse de Solides [*French-Speaking Association of Solids Mass Spectrometry*] (EAIO)
AFSMI ...... Association of Field Service Managers, International [*Later, ASMI*] (EA)
AFSN........ Air Force Serial Number
AFSN........ Air Force Service Number
AFSN........ Air Force Stock Number
AFSNCOA ... Air Force Senior Noncommissioned Officers' Academy (AFM)
AFSO........ Aerial Fire Support Officer [*Army*] (INF)
AFSO........ Air Force Service Office (AFM)
AFSO........ Airways Facilities Sector Office (FAAC)
AFSO........ American Friends of Scottish Opera (EA)
AFSOB...... Air Force Special Operation Base (MCD)
AFSONOR ... Allied Forces South Norway [*NATO*] (MCD)
AFSOON .. Air Force Solar Observing Optical Network (MCD)
AFSOUTH .. Allied Forces Southern Europe [*NATO*]
AFSP .... Acute Fibrinoserous Pneumonia [*Medicine*]
AFSP .... Air Force Space Plane (AAG)
AFSP .... Air Force Space Program
AFSP .... Air Force Standard Practice
AFSP .... Anglo-French Supply and Purchases [*World War II*]
AFSP .... Australian Foundation for the Peoples of the South Pacific
AFSPA ...... American Foreign Service Protective Association [*Washington, DC*] (EA)
AFSPBRSIO ... Armed Forces Surplus Property Bidders Registration and Sales Information Office [*Later, Defense Surplus Bidders Control Office*]
AFSPCOMMCEN ... Air Force Special Communications Center (AFM)
AFSPD ...... Air Force Systems Project Division (MCD)
AFSPEC.... Afrika Spectrum [*A publication*]
AFSPMET ... Air Force Security Policy Management Engineering Team
AFSR......... Advanced Foreign System Requirements
AFSR........ American Fund for Slovak Refugees (EA)
AFSR........ Argonne Fast Source Reactor
AFSR........ Armed Forces Screen Reports
AFSRAN .. Air Force Stock Record Account Number (AAG)
AFSS .... Africa South of the Sahara [*A publication*]
AFSS .... Air Force Security Service [*Later, AFESC*] (AFM)
AFSS .... Air Force Service Statement
AFSS .... Air Force Supply Services System
AFSS .... Automated Flight Service Station (FAAC)

AFSSC...... Armed Forces Supply Support Center [*Merged with Defense Logistics Services Center*]
AFSSD...... Air Force Space Systems Division
AFSSG...... Sherritt Gordon Mines Ltd., Fort Saskatchewan, Alberta [*Library symbol*] [*National Library of Canada*] (NLC)
AFSSMET ... Air Force Special Staff Management Engineering Team
AFSSO ...... Air Force Special Security Office [*or Officer*] (AFM)
AFSSOP.... Air Force Security Service Office of Production
AFST .... Assured Field Shop Task
AFST .... Auxiliary Feedwater Storage Tank [*Nuclear energy*] (IEEE)
AFSTC...... Air Force Satellite Test Center (MCD)
AFSTC...... Air Force Space Technology Center [*Kirtland Air Force Base, NM*] (MCD)
AFSTC...... Air Force Space Test Center [*Later, Western Test Range*]
AFSTC...... Army Foreign Science and Technology Center
AFSTDH... Animal Feed Science and Technology [*A publication*]
AFSTE....... Association for Field Services in Teacher Education [*Later, ACPE*]
AFSTRIKE ... Air Force Strike Command (MCD)
AFSU........ American Fraternal Snowshoe Union (EA)
AFSU........ Auxiliary Ferry Service Unit
AFSUB...... Army Air Forces Antisubmarine Command
AFSV......... American Franciscan Society for Vocations [*Later, FVC*] (EA)
AFSWA..... Armed Forces Special Weapons Agency
AFSWA..... Army Air Forces Assistant Secretary of War for Air [*World War II*]
AFSWB..... American Friends of Scottish War Blinded [*Inactive*] (EA)
AFSWC..... Air Force Special Weapons Center [*AFSC*] [*Kirtland Air Force Base, NM*]
AFSWP..... Armed Forces Special Weapons Project [*Later, DASA*]
AFSWP-TP ... Armed Forces Special Weapons Project [*later, DASA*]. Technical Publications [*A publication*]
AFT........... Acetate Film Tape
AFT........... Active File Table [*Data processing*] (IBMDP)
AFT........... Aerodynamic Flight Test (NASA)
AFT........... Aflatoxin [*Mycotoxin*] [*Generic form*]
AFT........... After (KSC)
AFT........... Afternoon
AFT........... Air Freight Terminal
AFT........... Algemeen Fiscaal Tijdschrift [*A publication*]
AFT........... American Farmland Trust (EA)
AFT........... American Federation of Teachers (EA)
AFT........... American Film Theater
AFT........... American Friends of Turkey (EA)
AFT........... An Foras Taluntais [*Agricultural Institute*] [*Research center*] [*Ireland*] (IRC)
AFT........... Analog Facility Terminal [*Data processing*] (TEL)
AFT........... Animal-Facilitated Therapy
AFT........... Annual Field Training [*Army*] (AABC)
AFT........... Annual Financial Target [*DoD*]
AFT........... Anterior Fold from Typhlosole
AFT........... Assembly Facility Tool (MCD)
AFT........... Asynchronous Framing Technique [*Data processing*]
AFT........... Atmospheric Flight Test (NASA)
AFT........... Audio Frequency Transformer
AFT........... Auditor Freight Traffic
AFT........... Australian Federal Tax Reporter [*A publication*] (APTA)
AFT........... Autogenic Feedback Training (MCD)
AFT........... Automatic Fine Tuning
AFT........... Automatic Flight Termination
AFT........... Automatic Frequency Tuner
AFT........... Automatic Funds Transfer
AFT........... Fort Smith, AR [*Location identifier*] [*FAA*] (FAAL)
AFT........... United States Army, Corps of Engineers, Tulsa District, Tulsa, OK [*OCLC symbol*] (OCLC)
AFTA......... Acoustic Fatigue Test Article (NASA)
AFTA......... Aft Frame Tilt Actuator [*Aviation*] (NASA)
AFTA......... American Family Therapy Association (EA)
AFTA......... Arab Fund for Technical Assistance to Arab and African Countries
AFTA......... Association of French Teachers in Africa [*See also AFPA*] [*Khartoum, Sudan*] (EAIO)
AFTA......... Atlantic Free Trade Area
AFTA......... Automated Fault Tree Analyzer (MCD)
AFTA......... Avionics Fault Tree Analyzer (MCD)
AFTAAS... Advanced Fast Time Acoustic Analysis System (MCD)
AFTAC...... Air Force Tactical Air Command (MCD)
AFTAC...... Air Force Technical Applications Center [*Patrick Air Force Base, FL*]
AFTAC...... American Fiber, Textile, Apparel Coalition (EA)
AFTAT...... Air Force Technical Approval Team (AAG)
AFTAU...... American Friends of the Tel Aviv University (EA)
AFTB......... Afterburner [*on jet engines*]
AFTB........ Air Force Test Base
AFTBC.... Air Flow Thermal Balance Calorimeter
AFTC......... Air Force Flight Training Command
AFTC......... American Fox Terrier Club (EA)
AFTC......... Apparent Free Testosterone Concentration [*Clinical chemistry*]
AFTCA...... Amateur Field Trial Clubs of America (EA)
AFTCC...... Air Force Troop Carrier Command [*British military*] (DMA)
AFTCLR.... After Cooler

AFTCM..... American Foundation of Traditional Chinese Medicine (EA)
AFTCom.... Associate of the Faculty of Teachers in Commerce [*British*] (DBQ)
AFTD......... Air Force Test Director (MCD)
AFTDS..... Automated Flight Test Data System (MCD)
AFTE......... American Federation of Technical Engineers [*Later, International Federation of Professional and Technical Engineers*] (EA)
AFTE......... Arab Federation for Technical Education [*Baghdad, Iraq*] (EAIO)
AFTE......... Association of Firearm and Tool Mark Examiners (EA)
AFTE......... Authority for Tooling Expenditures
AFTEC...... Air Force Flight Test Center [*Edwards Air Force Base, CA*] (MCD)
AFTEC...... Air Force Test and Evaluation Center [*Kirtland Air Force Base, NM*] (AFM)
AFTER...... Ask a Friend to Explain Reconstruction [*An association*] (EA)
AFTER...... Automatic Functional Test and Evaluation Routine [*Raytheon Co.*]
AFTERM.. Association Francaise de Terminologie [*French Association of Terminology*] [*Canada*]
AFTEX..... Australia France Technical Exchange Program
AFTF......... Air Force Task Force (AFM)
AFTFWC... Air Force Tactical Fighter Weapons Center (MCD)
AFTHBA... American Fox Trotting Horse Breed Association (EA)
AFTI......... Advanced Fighter Technology Integration [*Air Force*]
AFTI......... American Film Technologies, Incorporated [*NASDAQ symbol*] (NQ)
AFTIA...... Armed Forces Technical Information Agency (NATG)
AFTIC...... Air Force Technical Intelligence Center
AFTJ........ Airborne Fuze Test Jammer (CAAL)
AFTLI....... Association Feeling Truth and Living It
AFTM....... Additive Full-Time Manning (MCD)
AFTM....... American Foundation for Tropical Medicine (EA)
AFTM....... Assistant Freight Traffic Manager
AFTMA..... American Fishing Tackle Manufacturers Association (EA)
AFTN........ Aeronautical Fixed Telecommunication Network [*United Kingdom*]
AFTN........ Afternoon (FAAC)
AFTN........ Autonomously Functioning Thyroid Nodule [*Endocrinology*]
AFTO........ Air Force Technical Order
AFTOC..... Air Force Technical Order Management Center (MCD)
AFTOD..... Air Force Technical Objectives Documents
AFTOD7 ... Archivos de Farmacologia y Toxicologia [*A publication*]
AFTOSB ... Air Force Technical Order Standardization Board
A/FTP....... Acceptance Functional Test Procedure [*NASA*] (KSC)
AFTP........ Additional Flight Training Period (AABC)
AFTP........ Aircrew Flight Training Period (AABC)
AFTPS...... Air Force Test Pilot School (MCD)
AFTR........ Air Force Technical Report
AFTR........ American Federal Tax Reports [*Prentice-Hall, Inc.*] [*A publication*] (DLA)
AFTR........ Army Flying Time Report (MCD)
AFTR........ Association of Foreign Trade Representatives (EA)
AFTRA...... American Federation of Television and Radio Artists (EA)
AFTRANSMET ... Air Force Transportation Management Engineering Team
AFTRC...... Air Force Training Command
AFTRCC... Aerospace and Flight Test Radio Coordinating Council (MCD)
AFTR2d..... American Federal Tax Reports, Second Series [*Prentice-Hall, Inc.*] [*A publication*] (DLA)
AFTR 2d P-H ... American Federal Tax Reports. Second Series. Prentice-Hall [*A publication*]
AFTRRC ... Animal Feed and Tissue Residue Research Center [*Department of Health and Human Services*] (GRD)
AFTRS...... Australian Film, Television, and Radio School
AFTS........ Adaptive Flight Training System (MCD)
AFTS........ Aeronautical Fixed Telecommunications Service
AFTS........ Air Force Tactical Shelter (MCD)
AFTS........ Airborne Flight Test System (MCD)
AFTS........ Aseptic Fluid Transfer System [*NASA*]
AFTS........ Australian Flying Training School
AFTS........ Automatic Flexible Test Station
AFTSC...... Automatic Frequency Tone Shift (NVT)
AFTSC...... Air Force Technical Service Command
AFTTH...... Air Force Technical Training Headquarters
AFTU........ Air Force Test Unit (MCD)
AFTU........ Archiv fuer Reformationsgeschichte. Texte und Untersuchungen [*A publication*]
AFTU........ Association of Free Trade Unions [*USSR*]
AFTU-V .... Air Force Test Unit, Vietnam
AFTWDS .. Afterwards (ROG)
AFTX........ America First Tax Exempt Mortgage [*Omaha, NE*] [*NASDAQ symbol*] (NQ)
AFU.......... Advanced Flying Unit [*Air Force*]
AFU.......... Air Force Units
AFU.......... All Fouled-Up [*Bowdlerized version*] (AAG)
AFU.......... American Fraternal Union [*Ely, MN*] (EA)
AFU.......... Arkivet for UFO-Forskning [*Archives for UFO Research*] (EAIO)
AFU.......... Assault Fire Unit [*Army*]
AFU.......... Auxiliary Functional Unit [*Data link*] (NG)

AFU.......... University of Arkansas, Fayetteville, Fayetteville, AR [*OCLC symbol*] (OCLC)
AFUA........ ARMS/FIRMS Users Association (EA)
AFUD....... American Foundation for Urologic Disease (EA)
AFUDC ..... Allowance for Funds Used during Construction
AFUE........ Annual Fuel Utilization Efficiency [*Furnaces*]
AFUPBD... Anais. Faculdade de Medicina. Universidade Federal de Pernambuco [*A publication*]
AFUPO ..... Air Force Unit Post Office
AFUR .... American Furniture Co. [*NASDAQ symbol*] (NQ)
AFUR........ Amplified Failure or Unsatisfactory Report
AFUS........ Air Force of the United States
AFUS........ Armed Forces of the United States
AFUW Bul ... Australian Federation of University Women. Bulletin [*A publication*] (APTA)
AFV .... Aerospace Flight Vehicle
AFV .... Afluidal Variant [*Bacteriology*]
AFV .... Alliance for Volunteerism [*Defunct*] (EA)
AFV .... American Friends of Vietnam (EA)
AFV .... Anti-Flood Valve (MCD)
AFV .... Armored Family of Vehicles [*Military*] (RDA)
AFV .... Armored Fighting Vehicle [*Marine Corps*]
AFV .... Armored Force Vehicle
AFV .... Australian Force, Vietnam [*Military*]
AFV .... Fairview Public Library, Alberta [*Library symbol*] [*National Library of Canada*] (NLC)
AFVA........ Air Force Visual Aid
AFVA........ American Film and Video Association (EA)
AFVA........ American Foundation for Vision Awareness (EA)
AFVBM..... American Federation of Violin and Bow Makers (EA)
AFVC........ Auxiliary Force Veterinary Corps [*British military*] (DMA)
AFVC........ Fort Vermilion Community Library, Alberta [*Library symbol*] [*National Library of Canada*] (NLC)
AFVCS ...... Automatic Fingerprint Verification Computer System
AFVES ...... E. E. Oliver School, Fairview, Alberta [*Library symbol*] [*National Library of Canada*] (BIB)
AFVG........ Anglo-French Variable-Geometry [*Combat aircraft*]
AFVHS...... Hillcrest Community School, Fort Vermilion, Alberta [*Library symbol*] [*National Library of Canada*] (BIB)
AFVL........ American Friends of the Vatican Library (EA)
AFVLA5..... Anales. Facultad de Veterinaria de Leon [*A publication*]
AFVN........ American [*formerly, Armed*] Forces Vietnam Network
AFVPA ..... Advertising Film and Videotape Producers' Association [*British*]
AFVPS....... Fort Vermilion Public School, Alberta [*Library symbol*] [*National Library of Canada*] (BIB)
AFVRLS.... Rocky Lane School, Fort Vermilion, Alberta [*Library symbol*] [*National Library of Canada*] (BIB)
AFVS......... Fairview High School, Alberta [*Library symbol*] [*National Library of Canada*] (BIB)
AFVSMS... St. Mary's School, Fort Vermilion, Alberta [*Library symbol*] [*National Library of Canada*] (BIB)
AFVSTS.... St. Thomas More School, Fairview, Alberta [*Library symbol*] [*National Library of Canada*] (BIB)
AFVTG ...... Armed Forces Vocational Testing Group [*Randolph Air Force Base, TX*] (AFM)
AFVUBX... Anales. Facultad de Veterinaria del Uruguay [*A publication*]
AFW .... Advocates for Women (EA)
AFW .... Air Force Weapon
AFw........... Akkadische Fremdwoerter als Beweis fuer Babylonischen Kultureinfluss [*A publication*] (BJA)
AFW .... Army Field Workshop
AFW .... Auxiliary Feedwater [*Nuclear energy*] (NRCH)
AFW .... Axial Flow Wheel
AFW .... United States Army, Corps of Engineers, Walla Walla District, Walla Walla, WA [*OCLC symbol*] (OCLC)
AFWA .... Air Force with Army
AFWA .... Australian Federation for the Welfare of Animals
AFWAB..... Army Fixed Wing Aptitude Battery (AABC)
AFWAL..... Air Force Wright Aeronautical Laboratories [*Wright-Patterson Air Force Base, OH*]
AFWAR..... Air Force Personnel on Duty with Army
AFWAR.... Association of Federal Woman's Award Recipients (EA)
AFWAS..... Auxiliary Feedwater Actuating System [*Nuclear energy*] (NRCH)
AFWB........ Air Force Welfare Board (AFM)
AFWC....... Affiliated Woodcarvers Ltd. (EA)
AFWC....... American Federation of World Citizens [*Later, Fellowship of World Citizens*] (EA)
AFWC....... Auxiliary Feedwater Control [*Nuclear energy*] (NRCH)
AFWE....... Air Forces, Western Europe [*NATO*] (NATG)
AFWESPAC ... [*US*] Army Forces, Western Pacific
AFWET..... Air Force Weapons Effectiveness Testing (AFM)
AFWETS... Air Force Weapons Effectiveness Testing System
AFWFA..... Australian Fresh Water Fishermen's Assembly
AFWL....... Air Force Weapons Laboratory [*Kirtland Air Force Base, NM*]
AFWL........ Armed Forces Writers League [*Later, NAGC*] (EA)
AFWLA..... African Wildlife [*A publication*]
AFWL/LEAPS ... AFWL [*Air Force Weapons Laboratory*] LASER Engineering and Applications to Prototype Systems (MCD)

AFWMAA ... Air Force Wide Mission Area Analysis (MCD)
AFWN .... Air Force Personnel on Duty with Navy
AFWOFS .. Air Force Weather Observing and Forecasting System
AFWR .... Approved Force War Reserves (AFM)
AFWR .... Atlantic Fleet Weapons Range [*Later, AFRSF*] [*Navy*]
AFWS .... Advanced Filament Wound Structure
AFWS .... Auxiliary Feedwater System [*Nuclear energy*] (NRCH)
AFWST ..... Armed Forces Women's Selection Test
AFWTF ..... Atlantic Fleet Weapons Training Facility [*Navy*]
AFWTR ..... Air Force Western Test Range [*Later, Space and Missile Test Center*] [*Vandenberg Air Force Base, CA*]
AFWTRM ... Air Force Western Test Range Manual (MCD)
AFWWMCCS ... Air Force World Wide Military Command and Control System (MCD)
AFWY .... Arkansas Freightways Corp. [*NASDAQ symbol*] (NQ)
AFWYU .... American Foundation for World Youth Understanding (EA)
AFX .... Address Complete, Subscriber Free, Coin-Box [*Telecommunications*] (TEL)
AFXF .... Advanced Flash X-Ray Facility
AFYDP ...... Army's Five-Year Defense Program
AFYMOSAP ... Additional Fiscal Year Money Is Authorized by the Secretary of the Army (AABC)
AFZSA ..... Allgemeine Forstzeitschrift [*A publication*]
AFZTA ...... Allgemeine Forstzeitung [*A publication*]
AG .... Abbott Laboratories [*Research code symbol*]
AG .... Accessory Gland
AG .... Accountant General
AG .... Acting (ADA)
AG .... Acts of the Gods (BJA)
AG .... Ad Gentes [*Decree on the Church's Missionary Activity*] {*Vatican II document*]
AG .... Adjutant General
AG .... Advance Guard [*A publication*]
AG .... Advanced Guard
AG .... Advisory Group [*Military*]
AG .... Aerographer's Mate [*Navy rating*]
AG .... Aerojet-General Corp.
AG .... Aeronautical Standards Group [*Military*]
AG .... Aerospace Group
AG .... Aerospace Guidance and Metrology Center [*Air Force*] (AFIT)
AG .... Affretair [*Zimbabwe*] [*ICAO designator*] (FAAC)
AG .... Africa Guild (EA)
AG .... After Goetz [*A reference to "vigilante" Bernhard Goetz, who shot four youths on a New York subway in 1984 after allegedly being threatened by them*] [*See also BG*]
Ag .... Agada (BJA)
AG .... Again [*Telecommunications*] (TEL)
AG .... Against (ROG)
AG .... Against Grain
Ag .... Agamemnon [*of Aeschylus*] [*Classical studies*] (OCD)
AG .... Age of Primary Taxpayer [*IRS*]
AG .... Agefi [*A publication*]
AG .... Agency (EY)
AG .... Agent General
AG .... Aggressive Growth [*Investment term*]
AG .... Agitate (MSA)
Ag .... Agnus Dei [*Lamb of God*] [*Latin*]
AG .... Agorot [*Monetary unit*] [*Israel*]
Ag .... Agree (ILCA)
AG .... Agreement (ADA)
AG .... Agriculture
AG .... Air Gap
AG .... Air Gauge
AG .... Air-to-Ground [*Photos, missiles, etc.*]
AG .... Air Group
AG .... Air Gunner [*British*]
A/G .... Aircraft Arresting Gear (NG)
A/G .... Airgraph (ADA)
AG .... Airplane Group (MCD)
AG .... Aktiengesellschaft [*Corporation*] [*German*]
A/G .... Albumin/Globulin [*Medicine*]
AG .... Alignment Group
AG .... Allegheny International, Inc. [*NYSE symbol*] (SPSG)
AG .... Alternating Gradient
AG .... Americans for God (EA)
AG .... Aminoguanosine [*Biochemistry*]
AG .... Amtsgericht [*Inferior Court*] [*German*]
AG .... Anales Galdosianos [*A publication*]
AG .... Analytical Grade [*Organic chemistry*]
AG .... Anastomosis Group [*Plant pathology*]
AG .... Anatomische Gesellschaft [*Anatomical Society*] (EAIO)
AG .... And Gate [*Logic element*] [*Data processing*]
AG .... Anderson Galleries
AG .... Anglica Germanica [*A publication*]
AG .... Annales de Geographie [*A publication*]
AG .... Annales Geophysicae [*A publication*]
AG .... Annual Goal [*Education*]
AG .... Antigas [*Military*]
Ag .... Antigen [*Also, A, a*] [*Immunology*]
AG .... Antiglobulin [*Clinical chemistry*]
AG .... Antigravity

AG .... Antigua-Barbuda [*ANSI two-letter standard code*] (CNC)
AG .... Apparel Guild (EA)
AG .... Arbeitsgericht [*Labor Court*] [*German*]
AG .... Archivo Giuridico [*A publication*]
ag .... Argentina [*MARC country of publication code*] [*Library of Congress*] (LCCP)
Ag .... Argentum [*Silver*] [*Chemical element*]
AG .... Aristos Guild (EA)
AG .... Armed Guard
AG .... Armor Grating [*Technical drawings*]
AG .... Army Group (NATG)
AG .... Army Guidance
A-G .... Arresting Gear [*Aviation*]
AG .... Art Gallery
AG .... Artificial Gravity (NASA)
AG .... Artists Guild
AG .... Assault Gun (MCD)
AG .... Association for Gnotobiotics (EA)
AG .... Assumption Guild (EA)
AG .... Atlas Gemini [*NASA*] (KSC)
AG .... Atrial Gallop [*Cardiology*]
AG .... Attention Getting [*by the hearing-impaired*]
AG .... Attitude Gyro (MCD)
AG .... Attorney General
AG .... Attorney General's Opinions [*A publication*] (DLA)
AG .... Auditor General [*Military*]
aG .... Auf Gegenseitigkeit [*Mutual*] [*German*]
AG .... Aufklaerungsgruppe [*Air Forces Reconnaissance Unit*] [*German military - World War II*]
AG .... August
Ag .... August [*A publication*]
Ag .... Augustine [*Deceased, 430*] [*Authority cited in pre-1607 legal work*] (DSA)
AG .... Australian Geographer [*A publication*] (APTA)
AG .... Authors Guild (EA)
AG .... Autoleather Guild (EA)
AG .... Automatic Gauge
AG .... Availability Guarantee [*Military*]
AG .... Axiogingival [*Dentistry*]
AG .... Galahad Public Library, Alberta [*Library symbol*] [*National Library of Canada*] (NLC)
ag----- .... Mekong River and Basin [*MARC geographic area code*] [*Library of Congress*] (LCCP)
AG .... Miscellaneous Auxiliary Ship [*Navy ship symbol*]
AG .... Try Again [*Telecommunications*] (TEL)
AG1 .... Aerographer's Mate, First Class [*Navy rating*]
AG2 .... Aerographer's Mate, Second Class [*Navy rating*]
AG3 .... Aerographer's Mate, Third Class [*Navy rating*]
AGA .... Abrasive Grain Association (EA)
AGA .... Accelerated Growth Area [*Embryology*]
AGA .... Accredited Gemologists Association (EA)
AGA .... Aceglutamide Aluminum [*Biochemistry*]
AGA .... Adjutants General Association of the United States [*Later, AGAUS*] (EA)
AGA .... Aerodrome and Ground Aids [*A publication*] (APTA)
AGA .... Aerodromes, Air Routes, and Ground Aids [*Aviation*]
AGA .... Agadir [*Morocco*] [*Airport symbol*] (OAG)
AGA .... Agricultural Administration [*A publication*]
AGA .... Air-to-Ground-to-Air
AGA .... Alliance of Gay Artists (EA)
AGA .... Amalgamated Gas Accumulation [*Stove designed by Gustaf Dalen in 1922*]
AGA .... Amateur Golfers' Association of America (EA)
AGA .... American Galvanizers Association (EA)
AGA .... American Gas Association (EA)
AGA .... American Gas Association. Monthly [*A publication*]
AGA .... American Gastroenterological Association (EA)
AGA .... American Gay Atheists (EA)
AGA .... American Gelbvieh Association (EA)
AGA .... American Genetic Association (EA)
AGA .... American Girl Resources [*Vancouver Stock Exchange symbol*]
AGA .... American Glassware Association [*Defunct*]
AGA .... American Go Association (EA)
AGA .... American Goiter Association [*Later, American Thyroid Association*]
AGA .... American Gold Association [*Defunct*] (EA)
AGA .... American Grand Prix Association (EA)
AGA .... American Graniteware Association (EA)
AGA .... American Guernsey Association (EA)
AGA .... American Guides Association (EA)
AGA .... American Guppy Association [*Later, IFGA*] (EA)
AGA .... Animal Guild of America (EA)
AGA .... Antigliadin Antibodies [*Immunology*]
AGA .... Appropriate for Gestational Age [*Medicine*]
AGA .... As Good As
AGA .... Associated Geographers of America
AGA .... Association of Government Accountants [*Arlington, VA*] (EA)
AGA .... Association of Governmental Appraisers [*Absorbed by American Society of Appraisers*] (EA)
AGA .... Association of the Graphic Arts (EA)
AGA .... Astrologers' Guild of America (EA)

AGA.......... Attitude Gyro Assembly (MCD)
AGA.......... Automated Genetic Analyzer [*Instrumentation*]
AGA.......... Automatic Gas Analyzer [*Nuclear energy*] (NRCH)
AGA.......... Average Global Automobile [*Emissions to atmosphere*]
AGA.......... Azimuth Gimbal Assembly (MCD)
AGA.......... Office of General Aviation [*FAA*] (FAAC)
AGA.......... United States National Arboretum, Washington, DC [*OCLC symbol*] (OCLC)
AGA 2000 ... Gas Energy Supply Outlook, 1980-2000. American Gas Association [*A publication*]
AGAA....... Airman Apprentice, Aerographer's Mate, Striker [*Navy rating*]
AGAA....... Amateur Golfers' Association of America (EA)
AGAA....... American Guild of Animal Artists (EA)
AGAA....... Association des Groupes d'Astronomes Amateurs [*Association of Amateur Astronomy Groups*] [*Canada*]
AGAA....... Attitude Gyro Accelerometer Assembly (MCD)
AGAA....... Automatic Gain Adjusting Amplifier [*Telecommunications*]
Ag-AB....... Antigen-Antibody [*Immunology*]
Ag Abh....... Aegyptologische Abhandlungen [*A publication*]
AGAC...... Aero Geo Astro Corporation
AGAC...... American Guild of Authors and Composers (EA)
AGAC...... Association of Graphic Arts Consultants (EA)
AGACS..... Air-Ground-Air Communications System
AGACS..... Automatic Ground-to-Air Communications System
AGADS..... Advanced Graphics Avionics Display System (MCD)
AGA Facts ... Gas Facts. American Gas Association [*A publication*]
AGAFBO... Atlantic and Gulf American Flag Berth Operators
AGAG...... Acidic Glycoaminoglycan [*Biochemistry*]
AGAGAS... AGARD [*Advisory Group for Aerospace Research and Development*] Agardograph [*A publication*]
AGAH....... Association for Government Assisted Housing (EA)
AGAHAV ... Acta Geologica. Academiae Scientiarum Hungaricae [*A publication*]
AGAI........ Ally & Gargano, Incorporated [*NASDAQ symbol*] (NQ)
AGAJU...... Arbeiten zur Geschichte des Antiken Judentums und des Urchristentums [*A publication*]
AGAL....... American Gas Association Laboratories
AGALA ..... Authors Guild of the Authors League of America (EA)
AGA Lab Res Bull Res Rep ... American Gas Association. Laboratories. Research Bulletins, Research Reports [*A publication*]
AGald........ Anales Galdosianos [*A publication*]
AGALEV... Anders Gaan Leven [*Live Differently*] [*Belgium*] [*Political party*] (PPW)
Ag Am....... Agriculture in the Americas [*A publication*]
AGAMA .... American Gas Association. Monthly [*A publication*]
AGA Mon.. American Gas Association. Monthly [*A publication*]
AGAMP .... Automatic Gain Adjusting Amplifier [*Telecommunications*] (TEL)
AGAN....... Airman, Aerographer's Mate, Striker [*Navy rating*]
AGANI...... Apollo Guidance and Navigation Information [*NASA*]
AGA Oper Sec Proc ... American Gas Association. Operating Section. Proceedings [*A publication*]
AgAp.......... Against Apion [*Josephus*] (BJA)
AGAP .... Attitude Gyro Accelerometer Package (KSC)
AGAP .... Automated Graphics Application Program (MCD)
AGARD ..... Advisory Group for Aerospace Research and Development [*NATO*]
AGARD Advis Rep ... AGARD [*Advisory Group for Aerospace Research and Development*] Advisory Report [*A publication*]
AGARD Adv Rep ... AGARD [*Advisory Group for Aerospace Research and Development*] Advisory Report [*A publication*]
AGARD Agardogr ... AGARD [*Advisory Group for Aerospace Research and Development*] Agardograph [*A publication*]
AGARD Annu Meet ... AGARD [*Advisory Group for Aerospace Research and Development*] Annual Meeting [*A publication*]
AGARD Conf Proc ... AGARD [*Advisory Group for Aerospace Research and Development*] Conference Proceedings [*A publication*]
AGARD CP ... AGARD [*Advisory Group for Aerospace Research and Development*] Conference Proceedings [*A publication*]
AGARD Lect Ser ... AGARD [*Advisory Group for Aerospace Research and Development*] Lecture Series [*A publication*]
AGARD (NATO) ... AGARD [*Advisory Group for Aerospace Research and Development*] (North Atlantic Treaty Organization) [*A publication*]
AGARD Rep ... AGARD [*Advisory Group for Aerospace Research and Development*] Report [*A publication*]
AGARD Specif ... AGARD [*Advisory Group for Aerospace Research and Development*] Specification [*A publication*]
AGAS .... Aviation Gasoline [*Navy*]
AGASIA .... Asian Agriculture, Agrotechnology, and Agribusiness Exhibition and Conference (TSPED)
AGATE...... Air-to-Ground Acquisition and Tracking Equipment
AGAU....... Archief voor de Geschiedenis van het Aartsbisdom Utrecht [*A publication*]
AGAUS ..... Adjutants General Association of the United States (EA)
AGAVE ..... Automatic Gimbaled-Antenna Vectoring Equipment [*Air Force*]
AGAW....... AG Automotive Warehouses, Inc. [*NASDAQ symbol*] (NQ)
AGB.......... Accessory Gear Box
AGB.......... Advanced Geometry Blade [*Military*] (RDA)
AGB.......... Afton, OK [*Location identifier*] [*FAA*] (FAAL)

A/GB .... Agriculture (Great Britain). Ministry of Agriculture, Fisheries, and Food [*A publication*]
AGB.......... Allgemeine Geschäftsbedingungen [*General Conditions of Contracts, Transactions, Etc.*] [*German*] (DLA)
AGB.......... Angora Goat Breeders [*Australia*]
AGB.......... Anhaltische Geschichtsblaetter [*A publication*]
AGB.......... Any Good Brand
AGB.......... Archiv fuer Geschichte des Buchwesens [*A publication*]
AGB.......... Assault Gun Battalion (INF)
AGB.......... Association of German Broadcasters (EA)
AGB.......... Association of Governing Boards of Universities and Colleges (EA)
AGB.......... Association Guillaume Bude. Bulletin [*A publication*]
AGB.......... Asymptotic Giant Branch [*Astronomy*]
AGB.......... Audits of Great Britain
AGB.......... Canadian Angus Resources [*Vancouver Stock Exchange symbol*]
AGB.......... Icebreaker [*Navy ship symbol*]
AGB.......... United States Department of Agriculture, Food and Nutrition Information Center, Beltsville, MD [*OCLC symbol*] (OCLC)
AGBA....... Agriculture Bulletin. University of Alberta [*Later, Agriculture and Forestry Bulletin*] [*A publication*]
AGBA....... Alexander Graham Bell Association for the Deaf (EA)
AGBA....... American Galloway Breeders' Association (EA)
AGBAAF... Acta Geobotanica Barcinonensia [*A publication*]
AGBAD.... Alexander Graham Bell Association for the Deaf (EA)
AGBC....... Avocado Growers Bargaining Council (EA)
AGBESA ... Empresa de Aguas del Rio Besos, Sociedad Anonima [*Spanish*] [*Business term*]
AGBGB ..... Ausfuehrungsgesetz zur Burgerlichen Gesetzbuch [*Implementing law to the civil code*] [*German*] (ILCA)
AGBI .... Artists' General Benevolent Institution [*British*]
AGBIZ....... Agribusiness Information [*G. V. Olsen Associates*] [*Information service or system*] (CRD)
AGBM ...... Antiglomerular Basement Antibody Test
AGBO .... Agroborealis [*A publication*]
AGBOBO.. Agroborealis [*A publication*]
AGBS........ Artillery Ground Burst Simulator (MCD)
AGBU .... Armenian General Benevolent Union (EA)
AGBUA ..... Armenian General Benevolent Union of America [*Later, AGBU*] (EA)
AGBUS...... Analog Ground Bus
AGC .... Adjutant General's Corps
AGC .... Advanced Gas Centrifuge
AGC .... Advanced Graduate Certificate
AGC .... Aerographer's Mate, Chief [*Navy rating*]
AGC .... Aerojet-General Corporation
AGC .... African Business [*A publication*]
AGC .... African Groundnut Council [*See also CAA*] [*Nigeria*]
AGC .... Agricultural Genetics Co. Ltd. [*British*] (IRUK)
AGC .... Agriculture Canada
AGC .... Air-Ground Chart (AFM)
AGC .... Air-Ground Communications (CET)
AGC .... Alaska Game Commission [*Terminated, 1959*]
AGC .... American General Life Insurance Company [*NYSE symbol*] (SPSG)
AGC .... American Grassland Council [*Later, AFGC*] (EA)
AGC .... Amphibious Force Flagship [*Later, LCC*] [*Navy symbol*]
AGC .... Amphibious Group Command [*NATO*] (NATG)
AGC .... Amplitude Gain Control
AGC .... Ancient Gneiss Complex [*Geology*]
AGC .... Angel Island [*California*] [*Seismograph station code, US Geological Survey*] (SEIS)
AGC .... Apollo Guidance Computer [*NASA*]
AGC .... Armed Guard Center
AGC .... Army Advisory Group, China
AGC .... Artists Guild of Chicago (EA)
AGC .... Asahi Blass Company [*Japan*]
AGC .... Assessment Guidance Centre [*British*]
AGC .... Associated General Contractors of America (EA)
AGC .... Athena Gold Corp. [*Vancouver Stock Exchange symbol*]
AGC .... Atlantic-Gulf Coastwise Steamship Freight Bureau, Elizabeth NJ [*STAC*]
AGC .... Australian Girls Choir
AGC .... Automatech Graphics Corporation [*Information service or system*] (IID)
AGC .... Automatic Gain Control [*Electronics*]
AGC .... Automatic Gauge Control [*or Controller*]
AGC .... Avocado Growers Council [*Later, AGBC*] (EA)
AGC .... General Communications Vessel [*Navy ship symbol*] [*World War II*]
AGC .... Grande Cache Public Library, Alberta [*Library symbol*] [*National Library of Canada*] (NLC)
AGC .... Office of Chief Counsel [*FAA*] (FAAC)
AGC .... Pittsburgh, PA [*Location identifier*] [*FAA*] (FAAL)
AGC .... United States Department of Agriculture, Forest Service, North Central Forest Experiment Station, St. Paul, MN [*OCLC symbol*] (OCLC)
AGCA........ Altitude Gyroscope Control Assembly [*Military*] (CAAL)
AGCA........ American Game Collectors Association (EA)

AGCA .... Associated General Contractors of America

AGCA .... Automatic Ground-Controlled Approach [*RADAR*]

AGCACM ... Agrichemical Age [*A publication*]

AGCAP...... Automated Generic Case Analysis Program (MCD)

AGCB .... Association Geologique Carpatho-Balkanique [*Carpathian Balkan Geological Association - CBGA*] (EA)

AGCC .... Air-Ground Communications Channel

AGCC .... Airborne and Ground Communications Central (MCD)

AGCC .... American Guernsey Cattle Club [*Later, AGA*] (EA)

AGCC .... Association of Gifted-Creative Children (EA)

AGCCBR... Agrociencia [*A publication*]

AGCE .... Atmosphere General Circulation Experiment (MCD)

AGCF .... Air-Ground Correlation Factor (AABC)

AGCFAZ... Agriculteurs de France [*A publication*]

AGCG .... Associated Granite Craftsmen's Guild (EA)

AGCHA7... Agricultural Chemicals [*A publication*]

Ag Chem .... Agricultural Chemicals [*A publication*]

Ag Chem Commer Fert ... Ag Chem and Commercial Fertilizer [*Later, Farm Chemicals*] [*A publication*]

Ag Chemicals ... Agricultural Chemicals [*A publication*]

AGCI .... Associazione Generale delle Cooperative Italiane [*Cooperative union*] [*Italy*] (EY)

AGCI .... Australian Genealogical Computer Index

AGCI .... Automatic Ground-Controlled Intercept (MCD)

AGCIC....... Association of German Chambers of Industry and Commerce (EA)

AGCL .... Associate Member of the Guild of Cleaners and Launderers [*British*] (DBQ)

AGCL .... Automatic Ground-Controlled Landing

AGCM .... Aerographer's Mate, Master Chief [*Navy rating*]

AGCM .... Atmospheric General Circulation Model [*Meteorology*]

AGCM .... Grand Centre Municipal Library, Alberta [*Library symbol*] [*National Library of Canada*] (NLC)

AGCMDL ... Army Good Conduct Medal

AGCNCR .. Agrociencia. Serie A [*A publication*]

AGCO .... Air-Ground Cooperation Officer

AGCODV .. Agronomia Costarricense [*A publication*]

Ag Consult Fieldman ... Ag Consultant and Fieldman [*A publication*]

AGCP .... Automatic Gain Calibration Program

AGCPA...... AGARD [*Advisory Group for Aerospace Research and Development*] Conference Proceedings [*A publication*]

AGCPAV... AGARD [*Advisory Group for Aerospace Research and Development*] Conference Proceedings [*A publication*]

Ag & Cr Outlk ... Agricultural and Credit Outlook [*A publication*]

AGCRSP ... Army Gas-Cooled Reactor Systems Program

AGCS........ Advanced Guidance and Control System (MCD)

AGCS........ Aerographer's Mate, Senior Chief [*Navy rating*]

AGCS........ Association of Golf Club Secretaries (EAIO)

AGCS........ Automatic Ground Checkout System (KSC)

AGCS........ Automatic Ground Computer System (KSC)

AGCS........ Automatic Ground Control Station (KSC)

AGCSB...... Atlantic-Gulf Coastwise Steamship Freight Bureau

AGCSC...... Automatic Ground Control System Computer (KSC)

AGCT .... Army General Classification Test [*Measurement of intelligence*]

AGCTS...... Armed Guard Center Training School [*Obsolete*]

AGCU .... Air-Ground Cooling Unit (MCD)

AGCU .... Attitude Gyro Coupling Unit (KSC)

AGCU .... Autopilot Ground Control Unit (AAG)

AGCY .... Agency (AFM)

AGD........... Academy of General Dentistry (EA)

AGD........... Adjutant General's Department [*Army*]

AGD........... Agar-Gel Diffusion [*Clinical chemistry*]

AGD........... Agreed

AGD........... Aircraft Gunfire Detector

AGD........... American Gauge Design Committee

AGD........... Associated Gas Distributors

AGD........... Attorney General's Department (ADA)

AGD........... Auditor General's Department [*Air Force*]

AGD........... Australian Geodetic Datum

AGD........... Australian Government Digest [*A publication*] (APTA)

AGD........... Seagoing Dredge [*Navy symbol*]

AGD........... United States Department of Agriculture, Forest Service, Engineering-TIC, Washington, DC [*OCLC symbol*] (OCLC)

AGDA........ American Gasoline Dealers Association (EA)

AGDA........ American Gun Dealers Association (EA)

AGDATA .. Agricultural Commodities Data Base [*Alberta Department of Agriculture*] [*Information service or system*] (IID)

AGDBAS... Abhandlungen. Geologischer Dienst [*Berlin*] [*A publication*]

AGDC........ American Gauge Design Committee (MCD)

AGDC........ Assistant Grand Director of Ceremonies [*Freemasonry*]

AGDE........ Escort Research Ship [*Navy symbol*]

AG Dec ...... Attorney General's Decisions [*A publication*] (DLA)

AGDIC....... Astro Guidance Digital Computer (IEEE)

Ag Digest ... Agricultural Digest [*A publication*]

A-GDL....... Army Gas Dynamic LASER (MCD)

AGDL .... Attorney General of the Duchy of Lancaster (ILCA)

AG/DR ...... Assistant Gunner/Driver [*Military*] (INF)

AGDS .... American Gauge Design Standard

AGDS .... Auxiliary Deep Submergence Support Ship [*Navy symbol*] (NVT)

AGDSAB... Aichi-Gakuin Daigaku Shigakkai-Shi [*Aichi Gakuin Journal of Dental Science*] [*A publication*]

AGE........... Admiralty Gunnery Establishment [*British*]

AGE........... Adult Growth Examination [*Test*]

AGE........... Advanced Glycosylated End-Product [*Biochemistry*]

AGE........... Advisory Group on Energy [*Army*] (RDA)

AGE........... Aerospace Ground Equipment [*NASA*]

AGE........... Aerospace Guidance and Metrology Center [*Air Force*]

AGE........... Affiliated Government Employees' Distributing Co. [*California*]

AGE........... Agarose Gel Zone Electrophoresis

AGE........... Agenahambo [*Papua New Guinea*] [*Seismograph station code, US Geological Survey*] [*Closed*] (SEIS)

AGE........... Agency Sales Magazine [*A publication*]

AGE........... Agnico-Eagle Mines Ltd. [*Toronto Stock Exchange symbol*]

AgE........... Agricultural Engineer

AGE........... Air-Ground Equipment

AGe........... Akkadische Goetterepitheta [*A publication*] (BJA)

AGE........... Allyl Glycidyl Ether [*Organic chemistry*]

AGE........... Amarillo Grain Exchange (EA)

AGE........... Amazon Ground Emissions (MCD)

AGE........... Americans for Generational Equity (EA)

AGE........... Angle of Greatest Extension

AgE........... Antigen E

AGE........... Apollo Guidance Equipment [*NASA*] (KSC)

AGE........... Asian Geotechnical Engineering Information Center [*Information service or system*] (EISS)

AGE........... Asian Geotechnology Engineering Database [*Asian Institute of Technology*] [*Information service or system*] (CRD)

AGE........... Assembly of Governmental Employees (EA)

AGE........... Associate in General Education

AGE........... Associated Ground Equipment (CINC)

AGE........... Attorney General of England (ROG)

AGE........... Auditory Gross Error

AGE........... Australian Government Employment

AGE........... Automatic Ground Equipment

AGE........... Automatic Guidance Electronics

AGE........... Auxiliary Ground Equipment

AGE........... Edwards [*A. G.*] & Sons, Inc. [*NYSE symbol*] (SPSG)

AGE........... Gem Public Library, Alberta [*Library symbol*] [*National Library of Canada*] (NLC)

AGE........... United States Department of Agriculture, Eastern Regional Research Center, Philadelphia, PA [*OCLC symbol*] (OCLC)

AGE........... Wangerooge [*West Germany*] [*Airport symbol*] (OAG)

AGEAA ..... An Gluaiseacht Eireannach in Aghaidh Apartheid [*Irish Anti-Apartheid Movement*] (EAIO)

Age & Ageing ... Age and Ageing Science. Annuals [*A publication*]

Age Ageing Suppl ... Age and Ageing. Supplement [*A publication*]

AGEAS....... Automatic Ground Effect Augmentation System (MCD)

AGEBAX... Acta Gastro-Enterologica Belgica [*A publication*]

AGEC .... Arbeitsgemeinschaft Europaeischer Chorverbaende [*Federation of European Choirs*] [*Utrecht, Netherlands*] (EAIO)

AGEC .... Army General Equipment Command

AGECON .. Agricultural Economics [*Database*] [*Department of Agriculture*] [*Washington, DC*]

Ag Econ Res ... Agricultural Economics Research [*A publication*]

AGED........ Advisory Group on Electron Devices [*Army*] [*Washington, DC*]

AGED........ Aerospace Ground Equipment Department

Ag Ed........ Agricultural Education Magazine [*A publication*]

AGED........ Army Group Effects Department

AGEd........ Associate in General Education

A in G Ed ... Associate in General Education

AGED........ Association des Grandes Entreprises de Distribution de Belgique [*Trade organization*] [*Belgium*] (EY)

AGED........ Automated General Experimental Device [*Animal performance testing*]

Aged Care Serv Rev ... Aged Care and Services Review [*A publication*]

Aged High Risk Surg Patient Med Surg Anesth Manage ... Aged and High Risk Surgical Patient. Medical, Surgical, and Anesthetic Management [*A publication*]

AGEFAB ... Archiv fuer Gefluegelkunde [*Archives of Poultry Science*] [*A publication*]

AGEFI .... Agence Economique et Financiere [*A publication*]

AGEG .... Association Generale des Etudiants Guadeloupeens [*Guadeloupe*] (PD)

AGEH .... Hydrofoil Research Ship [*Navy symbol*]

AGEHR.... American Guild of English Handbell Ringers (EA)

AGEI .... Aerospace Ground Equipment Installation

AGEI .... Associates of the Graymoor Ecumenical Institute (EA)

Ageing Fish Proc Int Symp ... Ageing of Fish. Proceedings. International Symposium [*A publication*]

AGEL........ Angel Entertainment, Inc. [*NASDAQ symbol*] (NQ)

AGELAT ... Acta Geologica Lilloana [*A publication*]

Age Lit Supp ... Age Literary Supplement [*A publication*] (APTA)

Age MR ..... Age Monthly Review [*A publication*]

AGENAZ ... Agricultural Engineering [*A publication*]

Agence Spat Eur Rev Sci Tech ... Agence Spatiale Europeenne. Revue Scientifique et Technique [*A publication*]

AGEND4... Agriculture and Environment [*A publication*]

Ag Eng ...... Agricultural Engineering [*St. Joseph, MI*] [*A publication*]
AGENT ..... Advanced Graphite Experiments Testing [*Military*]
Agent Actio ... Agents and Actions [*A publication*]
Agents Actions Suppl ... Agents and Actions. Supplement [*A publication*]
Age Nucl .... Age Nucleaire [*A publication*]
AGEOCP... Aerospace Ground Equipment Out of Commission for Parts
                 [*Air Force*]
A Geogr...... Annales de Geographie [*A publication*]
AGEP......... Advisory Group on Electronic Parts [*Military*]
AGEP......... Agence Generale d'Editions Professionnelles [*Agency General of
                 Professional Publishing*] [*Canada*]
AGEPA..... Annales de Geophysique [*A publication*]
AGEPB...... Archiv fuer die Gesamte Psychologie [*A publication*]
AGEPC...... Acetyl-Glyceryl-Ether Phosphorylcholine
AGER .... Agricultural Economics Research [*A publication*]
AGER .... Environmental Research Ship [*Navy symbol*]
AGERAD .. Acta Gerontologica [*A publication*]
AGERD...... Aerospace Ground Equipment Requirements Data
AGERS...... Auxiliary General Electronics Research Ship [*Navy*]
Ages .... Agesilaus [*of Plutarch*] [*Classical studies*]   (OCD)
Ages .... Agesilaus [*of Xenophon*] [*Classical studies*]   (OCD)
AGES......... Air-Ground Engagement Simulation   (RDA)
AGES......... Air-to-Ground Engagement System   (MCD)
AGES......... Aircrew Gliding Escape System   (MCD)
AGES......... American Gas and Electric Services
AGES......... American Greek Exchange Society   (EA)
AGE/SE ..... Aerospace Ground Equipment/Support Equipment   (MCD)
AGET .... Advisory Group on Electron Tubes
AGETS ..... Automated Ground Engine Test System   (MCD)
Ag Europe ... Agra Europe [*A publication*]
AGF .... Adjutant-General to the Forces [*British*]
AGF .... Agen [*France*] [*Airport symbol*]   (OAG)
AGF .... AGF Management Ltd. [*Toronto Stock Exchange symbol*]
AGF .... Alternating Gradient Focusing
AGF .... American Government Income Fund [*NYSE symbol*]   (SPSG)
AGF .... Angle of Greatest Flexion
AGF .... Army Ground Forces
AGF .... Atlantic Gulf Airlines, Inc. [*Clearwater, FL*] [*FAA
                 designator*]   (FAAC)
AGF .... Automatic Guided Flight   (MUGU)
AGF .... Aviation Guided Flight   (MUGU)
AGF .... Forest Product Laboratory, Madison, WI [*OCLC
                 symbol*]   (OCLC)
AGF .... Miscellaneous Command Ship [*Navy symbol*]
AGFA .... Aktiengesellschaft fuer Anilinfabrikaten [*German photographic
                 manufacturer*]
AGFA .... Assistant General Freight Agent
AGFA .... Avant-Garde Francaise d'Amerique [*French Avant-Garde of
                 America*] [*Canada*]
Agfa Kinetech Mitt ... Agfa Kinetechnische Mitteilungen [*A publication*]
AGFB......... Association de Geographes Francais. Bulletin [*A publication*]
AGF/B....... Bulletin. Association des Geographes Francais [*A publication*]
AG FEB ..... Aggrediente Febre [*When the Fever Increases*] [*Pharmacy*]
AGFF......... Research Frigate [*Navy symbol*]   (NVT)
AGFIS .... Assemblee Generale des Federations Internationales Sportives
                 [*General Assembly of International Sports Federations*]
AGFIS .... Association Generale des Federations Internationales de Sports
                 [*General Association of International Sports Federations -
                 GAISF*]   (EA)
AGFL......... Airborne Ground Fire Locator
AGFLS ...... Airborne Ground Fire Locating System
AGF Mitt... AGF [*Arbeitsgemeinschaft der Grossforschungseinrichtungen*]
                 Mitteilungen [*A publication*]
AgFo .... Aegyptologische Forschungen [*Glueckstadt*] [*A publication*]
Ag Food Jl .. Agriculture and Food Chemistry. Journal [*A publication*]
AGFRTS.... Air and Ground Forces Resources and Technical Staff [*Army*]
AGFSA ...... American Ground Flat Stock Association   (EA)
AGFSR ...... Aircraft Ground Fire Suppression and Rescue [*Air
                 Force*]   (MCD)
AGFSRS.... Aircraft Ground Fire Suppression and Rescue Systems [*Air
                 Force*] [*Wright-Patterson Air Force Base, OH*]
AGFYA...... Arkiv foer Geofysik [*A publication*]
AGG.......... Abhandlungen. Gesellschaft der Wissenschaften zu Goettingen.
                 Philosophisch-Historische Klasse [*A publication*]
AGG.......... Agent to the Governor-General [*British*]
Agg.......... Aggadah   (BJA)
Agg.......... Aggadic   (BJA)
AGG.......... Agglutination [*Immunology*]
AGG.......... Aggregate
AGG.......... American Groomer's Guild   (EA)
AGG.......... Angoram [*Papua New Guinea*] [*Airport symbol*]   (OAG)
AGG.......... United States Department of Agriculture, Plum Island Animal
                 Disease Center, Greenport, NY [*OCLC symbol*]   (OCLC)
AGGAA6... Agricultura y Ganaderia [*A publication*]
AGGAFT... American Grape Growers Alliance for Fair Trade   (EA)
Ag Gaz of Canada ... Agricultural Gazette of Canada [*A publication*]
Ag Gaz of New South Wales ... Agricultural Gazette of New South Wales [*A
                 publication*]
Ag Gaz NSW ... Agricultural Gazette of New South Wales [*A
                 publication*]   (APTA)

AGGBA9 ... Bureau of Mineral Resources. Geology and Geophysics Bulletin
                 [*Canberra*] [*A publication*]
AGGBBA ... Acta Gerontologica et Geriatrica Belgica [*A publication*]
AGGCA ..... Acta Geologica et Geographica. Universitatis Comenianae.
                 Geologica [*A publication*]
AGGD....... Apollo Guidance Ground Display [*NASA*]   (MCD)
AGGD....... Automatic Gravity Gradient
AGGE .... Balalae, Shortland Islands [*Solomon Islands*] [*ICAO location
                 identifier*]   (ICLI)
AGGEDL... Archives of Gerontology and Geriatrics [*A publication*]
AGGG....... Honiara [*Solomon Islands*] [*ICAO location identifier*]   (ICLI)
AGGH .... Honiara/Henderson, Guadalcanal Island [*Solomon Islands*]
                 [*ICAO location identifier*]   (ICLI)
AGGHAR ... Archiv fuer Gewerbepathologie und Gewerbehygiene [*A
                 publication*]
Aggiorn Clinico Ter ... Aggiornamenti Clinico Terapeutici [*A publication*]
Aggiorn Mal Infez ... Aggiornamenti sulle Malattie da Infezione [*Italy*] [*A
                 publication*]
Aggiorn Pediatr ... Aggiornamento Pediatrico [*A publication*]
Aggiorn Soc ... Aggiornamenti Sociali [*A publication*]
AGGL .... Graciosa Bay/Luova, Santa Cruz Islands [*Solomon Islands*]
                 [*ICAO location identifier*]   (ICLI)
AGGLA5... Agronomski Glasnik [*A publication*]
Agglom...... Agglomeration [*A publication*]
agglut .... Agglutination [*Medicine*]
AGGM....... Munda, New Georgia Islands [*Solomon Islands*] [*ICAO
                 location identifier*]   (ICLI)
AGGN....... Gizo/Nusatupe, Gizo Island [*Solomon Islands*] [*ICAO location
                 identifier*]   (ICLI)
AGGR....... Aggregate   (AABC)
AGGR....... Air-to-Ground Gunnery Range
AGGRAN.. Bureau of Mineral Resources. Geology and Geophysics Report
                 [*Canberra*] [*A publication*]
AGGRBO .. Ahrokhimiia i Hruntoznavstvo Respublikanskii
                 Mizhvidomchyi Tematichnyi Zbirnyk [*A publication*]
Aggred Feb ... Aggrediente Febre [*When the Fever Increases*] [*Pharmacy*]
Aggregate Resour Inventory Pap Ontario Geol Surv ... Aggregate Resources
                 Inventory Paper. Ontario Geological Survey [*A
                 publication*]
Aggressive Behav ... Aggressive Behavior [*A publication*]
AGGRO ...... Aggravation   (DSUE)
AGGS .... American Gloxinia and Gesneriad Society   (EA)
AGGS .... American Good Government Society   (EA)
AGGS .... Antigas Gangrene Serum [*Medicine*]
AGGY .... Aggie Oil Co. [*NASDAQ symbol*]   (NQ)
Ag H.......... Agricultural History [*A publication*]
AGH .... American Guild of Hypnotherapists   (EA)
AGH .... Angelholm/Helsingbord [*Sweden*] [*Airport symbol*]   (OAG)
AGH .... Arc Gas Heater
AGH .... Army Group Headquarters
AGH .... Atlantis Group [*AMEX symbol*]   (SPSG)
AGH .... United States Department of Agriculture, APHIS [*Animal and
                 Plant Health Inspection Service*], Plant Protection and
                 Quarantine, Hyattsville, MD [*OCLC symbol*]   (OCLC)
AGHA....... Acadian Genealogical and Historical Association
                 [*Defunct*]   (EA)
AGHA....... American Gotland Horse Association   (EA)
AGHA....... Archiv fuer Geschichte des Hochstifts Augsburg [*A publication*]
AGHDAK ... International Journal of Aging and Human Development [*A
                 publication*]
AGHDEA ... Association of General Heating and Domestic Engineer
                 Assistants [*A union*] [*British*]
AGHE....... Association for Gerontology in Higher Education   (EA)
Ag Hist...... Agricultural History [*A publication*]
Ag Hist R... Agricultural History Review [*A publication*]
AGHJA4 ... Agrohemija [*A publication*]
AGHPB ...... Annales de Gastroenterologie et d'Hepatologie [*A publication*]
AGHS .... Patrol Combatant Support Ship [*Navy symbol*]
AGHTM.... Association Generale des Hygienistes et Techniciens
                 Municipaux [*General Association of Municipal Health and
                 Technical Experts*]   (EAIO)
AGHUE7... Acta Geologica Hungarica [*A publication*]
AGHVA6... Abhandlungen. Gebiet der Hirnforschung und
                 Verhaltensphysiologie [*A publication*]
AGHVA6... Brain and Behavior Research Monograph Series [*A publication*]
AGI .... Adjusted Gross Income [*Income taxes*]
AGI .... Agenzia Giornalistica Italia [*Press agency*] [*Italy*]
AGI .... Agio Resources Corp. [*Vancouver Stock Exchange symbol*]
AGI .... Agreement Item   (MCD)
AGI .... Air Gunnery Instructor [*British military*]   (DMA)
AGI .... Alan Guttmacher Institute   (EA)
AGI .... Alliance Graphique Internationale [*International League of
                 Graphic Artists*] [*Zurich, Switzerland*]   (EAIO)
AGI .... Alpine Group, Incorporated [*AMEX symbol*]   (SPSG)
AGI .... American Geographical Institute
AGI .... American Geological Institute   (EA)
AGI .... Annual General Inspection [*Army*]
A/GI .... Anti-Gas Instructor [*British military*]   (DMA)
agi............. Anyagi [*Financial, Economic*] [*Hungarian*]
AGI .... Archivio Glottologico Italiano [*Torino*] [*A publication*]
AGI .... Associate of the Institute of Certificated Grocers [*British*]

AGI .... Augustine Island [*Alaska*] [*Seismograph station code, US Geological Survey*]   (SEIS)
AGI .... Australian Grain Institute
AGI .... Autorisation Globale d'Importation [*Global Import Quotas*] [*Algerian*]
AGI .... Auxiliary Intelligence Collection Ship [*Navy*]   (CAAL)
AGI .... Gibbons Public Library, Alberta [*Library symbol*] [*National Library of Canada*]   (NLC)
AGI .... United States Department of Agriculture, Forest Service, Intermountain Forest and Range Experiment Station, Ogden, UT [*OCLC symbol*]   (OCLC)
AGIAA ...... Associazione Geofisica Italiana. Atti del Convegno Annuale [*A publication*]
AGIC .... Air-Ground Information Center
AGIC .... Andrus Gerontological Information Center [*University of Southern California*]   (IID)
AGIC .... Auto Glass Industry Council   (EA)
AGICHS.... Auto Glass Industry Committee for Highway Safety [*Later, AGIC*]   (EA)
AGICOA ... Association de Gestion Internationale Collective des Oeuvres Audiovisuelles [*Association for the International Collective Management of Audiovisual Works*] [*Geneva, Switzerland*]   (EAIO)
AGID .... Association of Geoscientists for International Development [*Bangkok, Thailand*]   (EAIO)
AGIF .... American GI Forum   (OICC)
AGIFORS ... Airline Group of International Federation of Operational Research Societies [*Denmark*]   (MCD)
AGII .... Argonaut Group, Incorporated [*Los Angeles, CA*] [*NASDAQ symbol*]   (NQ)
AGIL .... Airborne General Illumination Light
AGILE .... Auto-Graphics Interactive Library Exchange [*Auto-Graphics, Inc.*] [*Information service or system*]   (IID)
AGILE .... Autonetics General Information Learning Equipment
AGIMBJ ... Allergologia et Immunopathologia [*A publication*]
AG IMPS HND ... Agricultural Implements Hand [*Freight*]
AG IMPS O T HND ... Agricultural Implements Other Than Hand [*Freight*]
AGINEP... Agriculture International [*A publication*]
Aging Gametes Proc Int Symp ... Aging Gametes, Their Biology and Pathology. Proceedings. International Symposium on Aging Gametes [*A publication*]
Aging Hum Dev ... Aging and Human Development [*A publication*]
Aging Immunol Infect Dis ... Aging, Immunology, and Infectious Disease [*A publication*]
Aging Leis Living ... Aging and Leisure Living [*A publication*]
Ag Inst R ... Agriculture Institute Review [*A publication*]
AGIO .... Armed Guard Inspection Officer
AGIPA .... Adaptive Ground-Implemented Phased Array [*NASA*]
AGIPA....... Agricoltura Italiana (Pisa) [*A publication*]
AGIPAR.... Agricoltura Italiana (Pisa) [*A publication*]
AGIR .... Ateliers de Gestion Integree des Ressources Limitees [*Canada*]
AGIS .... Aegis Industries, Inc. [*NASDAQ symbol*]   (NQ)
AGIS .... Air-Ground Integration System
AGIS .... Armed Guard Inspection Service
AGIS .... Associazione Generale Italiana dello Spettacolo [*General Italian Entertainments Association*] [*Italy*]   (EY)
AGIS .... Attorney General's Information Service [*A publication*]   (APTA)
AGIT .... Agita [*Shake*] [*Pharmacy*]
Agit .... Agitato [*Agitatedly*] [*Music*]
Agitation Ind Chim Symp Int Genie Chim ... Agitation dans l'Industrie Chimique. Symposium International de Genie Chimique [*A publication*]
AGIT A US ... Agita ante Usum [*Shake before Using*] [*Pharmacy*]
AGIT BENE ... Agita Bene [*Shake Well*] [*Pharmacy*]
AGITO ...... Agitato [*Agitatedly*] [*Music*]
AGIT-PROP ... Agitation and Propaganda [*Military*]
Agit Vas ..... Agitato Vase [*The Vessel Being Shaken*] [*Pharmacy*]
AGJ .... Aguni [*Japan*] [*Airport symbol*]   (OAG)
AGJ .... Australian Guitar Journal [*A publication*]   (APTA)
Ag J of British Columbia ... Agricultural Journal of British Columbia [*A publication*]
Ag J of Egypt ... Agricultural Journal of Egypt [*A publication*]
AGJHS...... American Gathering of Jewish Holocaust Survivors   (EA)
Ag J of India ... Agricultural Journal of India [*A publication*]
AGJOAT... Agronomy Journal [*A publication*]
AGJU .... Arbeiten zur Geschichte des Antiken Judentums und des Urchristentums [*A publication*]
AGK .... Roman L. Hruska United States Meat Animal Research Center, Clay Center, NE [*OCLC symbol*]   (OCLC)
AGKBZH .. Archiwum Glownej Komisji Badania Zbrodni Hitlerowskich [*A publication*]
AGKKN ..... Archief voor de Geschiedenis van de Katholieke Kerk in Nederland [*A publication*]
AGKO........ Arginine, Glutamate, alpha-Ketoglutarate Oxalacetate
AGKYAU .. Agrokhimiya [*A publication*]
AGL .... Above Ground Level
AGL .... Absolute Ground Level   (MCD)
AGL .... Acute Granulocytic Leukemia [*Medicine*]
AGL .... Aglow [*A publication*]
AGL........... Agricultural   (ROG)

AGL .... Airborne Gun-Laying
AGL .... American Guild of Luthiers   (EA)
AGL .... Angelica Corp. [*NYSE symbol*]   (SPSG)
AGL .... Anglesey [*Welsh island and county*]   (ROG)
AGL .... Argon Gas LASER
AGL .... Argon Glow Lamp
AGL .... Argrel Resources Ltd. [*Formerly, Sundance Gold Ltd.*] [*Vancouver Stock Exchange symbol*]
AGL .... Automatic Gun-Laying   (DEN)
AGL .... Computation Center-Advanced Graphics Laboratory [*University of Texas at Austin*] [*Research center*]   (RCD)
AGL .... Glenwood Public Library, Alberta [*Library symbol*] [*National Library of Canada*]   (NLC)
AGL .... Great Lakes Region [*FAA*]   (FAAC)
AGL .... Lighthouse Tender [*Navy symbol*] [*Obsolete*]
AGL .... National Agricultural Library, Beltsville, MD [*OCLC symbol*]   (OCLC)
AGL .... Priority Air Freight D/B/A Skytrain Airlines [*Chicago, IL*] [*FAA designator*]   (FAAC)
AGL .... Wanigela [*Papua New Guinea*] [*Airport symbol*]   (OAG)
AGLA .... AGLA [*Australian Government Lawyers' Association*] Bulletin [*A publication*]
AGLA .... Alliance for Gay and Lesbian Artists in the Entertainment Industry   (EA)
AGLA .... Australian Government Lawyers' Association
AGLAA ..... Association of German Language Authors in America [*Defunct*]   (EA)
AGLAAV... Agricultura (Lisboa) [*A publication*]
AGLABW ... Agricultural Research Council. Meat Research Institute [*Bristol*]. Annual Report [*A publication*]
AGLBIC .... Association for Gay, Lesbian, and Bisexual Issues in Counseling   (EA)
AGLC .... Air-to-Ground Liaison Code [*Air Force*]
AGLF........ Association for Governmental Leasing and Finance [*Washington, DC*]   (EA)
AglGr .... Anglo-German Review [*A publication*]
AGLIBS..... Attorney General's Information Service Library Subject Headings [*Database*] [*Australia*]
AGLIC .... Association for Gay and Lesbian Issues in Counseling [*Later, AGLBIC*]   (EA)
AGLINET ... Agricultural Libraries Information Network [*Department of Agriculture*] [*Library network*]
AGLINET ... Agricultural Library Networks [*IAALD*] [*United Kingdom*]
Ag & Livestock India ... Agriculture and Livestock in India [*A publication*]
AGLME....... (Acetylglycyl)lysine Methyl Ester Acetate [*Biochemistry*]
AGLO .... Air-Ground Liaison Officer [*Marine Corps*]
AGLO .... Melcorp Securities Ltd. [*NASDAQ symbol*]   (NQ)
AGLOA ..... Angeiologie [*A publication*]
AGLP........ Association of Gay and Lesbian Psychiatrists   (EA)
AGLPA8.... Acta Geologica Polonica [*A publication*]
AGLR .... Airborne Gun-Laying RADAR   (AFM)
AGLRA ..... American Glass Review [*A publication*]
AGLS......... Anchor Glass Container Corp. [*Tampa, FL*] [*NASDAQ symbol*]   (NQ)
AGLS......... Association for General and Liberal Studies   (EA)
AGLS......... Gift Lake School, Alberta [*Library symbol*] [*National Library of Canada*]   (BIB)
AGLSP ...... Association of Graduate Liberal Studies Programs   (EA)
AGLT........ Acidified Glycerol Lysis Test [*Clinical chemistry*]
AGLT........ Airborne Gun-Laying for Turrets
AGLT........ Automatic Gun-Laying Turrets [*World War II*] [*British*]
AGLTBL .... Acta Gastroenterologica Latinoamericana [*A publication*]
AGL(T)TRG ... Automated Gun Laying (Turret) Training [*British military*]   (DMA)
AGLUAN .. Agronomia Lusitana [*A publication*]
AGM......... Acting Grand Master [*Freemasonry*]
AGM......... Admiralty General Message [*Obsolete*] [*British*]
AGM......... Air-to-Ground Missile
AGM......... Allagash [*Maine*] [*Seismograph station code, US Geological Survey*]   (SEIS)
AGM......... American Green Movement   (EA)
AGM......... American Guild of Music   (EA)
AGM......... Annual General Meeting
AGM......... Assistant General Manager [*AEC*]
AGM......... Attorney General's Ministry [*Canada*]
AGM......... Auxiliary General Missile
AGM......... Avalon Resources, Inc. [*Vancouver Stock Exchange symbol*]
AGM......... Gleichen Municipal Library, Alberta [*Library symbol*] [*National Library of Canada*]   (NLC)
AGM......... Missile Range Instrumentation Ship [*Navy symbol*]
AGM......... Sudhoffs Archiv fuer Geschichte der Medizin und der Naturwissenschaften [*A publication*]
AGM......... United States Department of Agriculture, Forest Service, Rocky Mountain Station, Fort Collins, CO [*OCLC symbol*]   (OCLC)
AGMA ...... American Gear Manufacturers Association   (EA)
AGMA ...... American Guild of Musical Artists   (EA)
AGMA ...... Amusement Game Manufacturers Association [*Later, AAMA*]   (EA)
AGMA ...... Assistant General Manager for Administration [*AEC*]

AGMA .... Athletic Goods Manufacturers Association [*Later, SGMA*]   (EA)
AGMA News Bul ... Art Galleries and Museums Association of Australia and New Zealand. News Bulletin [*A publication*]   (APTA)
AGMANZ News ... AGMANZ News. Art Galleries and Museums Association of New Zealand [*A publication*]
AGMAP ..... Agricultural and Food Products Market Development Assistance Program [*Canada*]
AGMAzine ... American Guild of Musical Artists Magazine [*A publication*]   (EAAP)
AG & MC .. Aerospace Guidance and Metrology Center [*Air Force*]
AGMC .... Aerospace Guidance and Metrology Center [*Newark Air Force Station, OH*]   (AFM)
AGMC .... American Gold Minerals [*NASDAQ symbol*]   (NQ)
AGMC .... Association of General Merchandise Chains [*Absorbed by NMRI*]   (EA)
AGMD ...... Angiomedics, Inc. [*Plymouth, MN*] [*NASDAQ symbol*]   (NQ)
AGMEF ..... Ana G. Mendez Educational Foundation
AGMEPS .. Advisory Group on Management of Electronic Parts Specifications
AGMF .... Agents Master File [*IRS*]
AGMGAK ... Acta Geneticae, Medicae, et Gemellologiae [*A publication*]
AGMIA ..... Assistant General Manager for International Activities [*AEC*]
AgMIL .... Agricultural Materials in Libraries [*Later, Agriculture Library*] [*Online Computer Library Center, Inc.*] [*Information service or system*]   (CRD)
AGMIS ...... Adjutant General Management Information System
AGMIV ..... African Green Monkey Immunodeficiency Virus
AGMK ...... African Green Monkey Kidney [*Type of cell line*]
AGMMA4 ... Annales Geologiques. Service des Mines [*Madagascar*] [*A publication*]
AGMO ...... Assistant General Manager for Operations [*AEC*]
AGMOAA ... Agronomia [*Monterrey, Mexico*] [*A publication*]
AGMPP ...... Assistant General Manager for Plans and Production [*AEC*]
AGMR ...... Major Communications Relay Ship [*Navy symbol*]
AGMRD .... Assistant General Manager for Research and Development [*AEC*]
AGMS .... Aircraft Ground Mobility System   (MCD)
AGMS .... American Gem Market System [*Information service or system*]   (IID)
AGMSA .... American Gem and Mineral Suppliers Association   (EA)
AGMT .... Agreement   (ROG)
AGMT .... Augment   (MSA)
AGMTI ...... Air-to-Ground Moving Target Indicator
AGMYA6 .. Agricultural Meteorology [*A publication*]
AGN .... Active Galactic Nucleus [*Astronomy*]
AGN .... Acute Glomerulonephritis [*Medicine*]
AGN .... Additive Gaussian Noise
AGN .... Aerojet-General Nucleonics [*of Aerojet-General Corp.*]
AGN .... Again
AgN .... Age Nouveau [*A publication*]
AGN .... Agincourt [*Canada*] [*Later, OTT*] [*Geomagnetic observatory code*]
AGN .... Agnosia [*Medicine*]
AGN .... Allergan, Inc. [*NYSE symbol*]   (SPSG)
AGN .... Angoon [*Alaska*] [*Airport symbol*]   (OAG)
AGN .... Anzeiger. Germanisches Nationalmuseum [*A publication*]
AGN .... Applied Genetics News [*A publication*]
AGN .... Argcen Holdings [*Vancouver Stock Exchange symbol*]
AGN .... Articles for the Government of the Navy [*Obsolete*]
AGN .... Augmentation
AGN .... United States Department of Agriculture, Northern Regional Research Center, Peoria, IL [*OCLC symbol*]   (OCLC)
AGNBC ..... Advisory Group on National Bibliographic Control
AGNC .... Agency Rent-A-Car, Inc. [*NASDAQ symbol*]   (NQ)
AGNCS ..... Nose Creek School, Grovedale, Alberta [*Library symbol*] [*National Library of Canada*]   (BIB)
AGNCY ..... Agency
Agn Fr .... Agnew on the Statute of Frauds [*A publication*]   (DLA)
Agni .... Agni Review [*A publication*]
AGNIB ...... Association des Groupements de Negoce Interieur du Bois et des Produits Derives dans les Pays de la CEE [*Association of National Trade Groups for Wood and Derived Products in Countries of the European Economic Community*]
AGNIS .... Apollo Guidance and Navigation Industrial Support [*NASA*]
AGNIS ...... Azimuth Guidance Nose in Stands   (MCD)
AGNKA3 ... Archiv fuer Genetik [*A publication*]
Ag NL .... Agricultural Newsletter [*A publication*]
AGNM ...... Anzeiger. Germanisches Nationalmuseum [*A publication*]
AGNMBA ... Agronomia [*Caracas*] [*A publication*]
AGNNAC ... Agricultural Research News Notes [*Lima*] [*A publication*]
AGNO .... Agriculture North [*Canada*] [*A publication*]
AGNOS ..... Agnostic
Agn Pat ...... Agnew on Patents [*A publication*]   (DLA)
AGNPP ...... Aboveground Net Primary Production [*Of biomass*]
AGNQ .... Apollo/GOSS [*Ground Operations Support System*] Navigation Qualifications [*NASA*]
AGNRAO ... Advances in Gerontological Research [*A publication*]
AGNS .... Allied-General Nuclear Services   (NRCH)
AGNS .... Grouard Northland School, Alberta [*Library symbol*] [*National Library of Canada*]   (BIB)

AGNSAR ... Agricultural Gazette of New South Wales [*A publication*]
AGNST ...... Against   (ROG)
AGNY .... Artists Guild of New York   (EA)
AGO .... Adjutant General's Office [*Washington, DC*] [*Army*]
AGO .... Administration Group Office
AGO .... Agitato [*Agitatedly*] [*Music*]   (ROG)
AGO .... Air Gunnery Officer
AGO .... Algo Resources Ltd. [*Vancouver Stock Exchange symbol*]
AGO .... American Guild of Organists   (EA)
AGO .... American Guild of Organists. Quarterly [*A publication*]
AGO .... Angola [*ANSI three-letter standard code*]   (CNC)
AGO .... Arresting Gear Officer [*Military*]   (MCD)
AGO .... Art Gallery of Ontario [*UTLAS symbol*]
AGO .... Atmospheric Gas Oil [*Petroleum technology*]
AGO .... Attorney General's Opinions
AGO .... Auditor General's Office
AGO .... Magnolia, AR [*Location identifier*] [*FAA*]   (FAAL)
AGO .... Santiago, Chile, Tracking Station [*NASA*]   (NASA)
AGODDS .. AGOR [*Auxiliary General Oceanographic Research*] Oceanographic Digital Data System   (MCD)
AGOES ...... Advanced Geosynchronous Observation Environment Satellite [*NASA*]   (NASA)
AGOP .... Australian Government Offsets Program
AGOR .... Auxiliary General Oceanographic Research [*Navy*]   (MSC)
AGor .... Gordo Public Library, Gordo, AL [*Library symbol*] [*Library of Congress*]   (LCLS)
AGORA ..... Archiwum Gornictwa [*A publication*]
Agora Inf Changing World ... Agora. Informatics in a Changing World [*A publication*]
Agora Math ... Agora Mathematica [*Paris*] [*A publication*]
AGOS .... Air-Ground Operations Section [*or School or System*]
AGOS .... American Gynecological and Obstetrical Society   (EA)
AGOS .... Aviation Gunnery Officers School
AGOS .... Ocean Surveillance Ship [*Navy*]   (CAAL)
AGOSP ...... Ad Hoc Advisory Group on Science Programs [*Terminated, 1976*] [*National Science Foundation*]   (EGAO)
AGOSS ...... Automated Ground Operations Scheduling System [*Also, AUTO-GOSS*]   (MCD)
AGOTUOC ... [*A*] Gentleman of the University of Cambridge [*Pseudonym used by Owen Manning*]
Ag Outlook ... Agricultural Outlook [*A publication*]
AGP .... Acid Glycoprotein [*Biochemistry*]
AGP .... Adjutant General Pool [*for Army officers*]
AGP .... Advanced Guided Projectile   (MCD)
AGP .... Agence Guineenne de Presse [*Guinean Press Agency*]
AGP .... Aircraft Grounded for Lack of Parts
AGP .... Aircraft Gun Pod   (NG)
AGP .... Anthology of German Poetry through the Nineteenth Century [*A publication*]
AGP .... Antisymmetrized Geminal Power [*Chemical physics*]
AGP .... Archiv fuer Geschichte der Philosophie [*A publication*]
AGP .... Arctic Gas Profile [*A publication*]
AGP .... Argonaut Resources Ltd. [*Vancouver Stock Exchange symbol*]
AGP .... Army Ground Pool [*for officers*]
AGP .... Army Group
AGP .... Asom Gana Parishad [*Assam People's Council*] [*India*] [*Political party*]   (FEA)
AGP .... Association of Gay Psychologists [*Later, ALGP*]   (EA)
AGP .... Australian Government Publications [*Information service or system*] [*A publication*]   (APTA)
AGP .... Automatic Guidance Programming   (NATG)
AGP .... Auxiliary Generating Plant [*Aviation*]   (AIA)
AGP .... Average Goals Against per Period [*Hockey*]
AGP .... Grande Prairie Public Library, Alberta [*Library symbol*] [*National Library of Canada*]   (NLC)
AGP .... Malaga [*Spain*] [*Airport symbol*]   (OAG)
AGP .... Motor Torpedo Boat Tender [*Navy symbol*] [*Obsolete*]
AGP .... Pacific Southwest Forest and Range Experiment Station, Berkeley, CA [*OCLC symbol*]   (OCLC)
AGP .... Patrol Craft Tender [*Navy symbol*]
AGPA .... American Group Practice Association   (EA)
AGPA .... American Group Psychotherapy Association   (EA)
AGPA .... Ammunition Group - Picatinny Arsenal   (MCD)
AGPA .... Australian Greek Presidential Awards
AGPAAH ... Agriculture (Paris) [*A publication*]
AGPAEA ... Association de Gestion Portuaire de l'Afrique de l'Est et de l'Afrique Australe [*Port Management Association of Eastern and Southern Africa - PMAESA*]   (EAIO)
AGPAM ...... American Guild of Patient Account Management   (EA)
AGPB .... Advanced General Purpose Bomb   (MCD)
AGPC .... Adjutant General Publications Center [*Army*]
AGPC .... Australasian Guild of Professional Cooks
AGPC .... Grande Prairie College, Alberta [*Library symbol*] [*National Library of Canada*]   (NLC)
AGP-CNO ... Assemblee Generale Permanente des Comites Nationaux Olympiques [*Permanent General Assembly of National Olympic Committees*]
AGPDC ..... Aeronutronic General Perturbations Differential Correction Program
AGPERSCEN ... [*US*] Army Enlisted Personnel Support Center   (AABC)

AGPES ...... Penson Elementary School, Grovedale, Alberta [*Library symbol*] [*National Library of Canada*] (BIB)
AGPGAZ ... Agricultural Progress [*A publication*]
AGPGS ...... Grandview Colony School, Grande Prairie, Alberta [*Library symbol*] [*National Library of Canada*] (BIB)
AGPH .... Agouron Pharmaceuticals, Inc. [*NASDAQ symbol*] (NQ)
AGPh .... Archiv fuer Geschichte der Philosophie [*A publication*]
AGPH .... Grande Prairie Regional Hospital, Alberta [*Library symbol*] [*National Library of Canada*] (NLC)
AGPHBS ... Harry Balfour School, Grande Prairie, Alberta [*Library symbol*] [*National Library of Canada*] (BIB)
AGPHS ..... Holy Cross School, Grande Prairie, Alberta [*Library symbol*] [*National Library of Canada*] (BIB)
AGPI .... Automatic Ground Position Indicator [*Military*]
AGPKS ...... Kateri Mission School, Grande Prairie, Alberta [*Library symbol*] [*National Library of Canada*] (BIB)
AGPLAG ... Agroplantae [*A publication*]
AGPM .... Associated Glass and Pottery Manufacturers (EA)
AGPMR .... Agricultural Property Management Regulations
AgPp .... Aggregates of P-Protein [*Botany*]
AGPP .... Association for Group Psychoanalysis and Process . (EA)
AGPPAS ... Archiv fuer die Gesamte Physiologie des Menschen und der Tiere [*Pfluegers*] [*A publication*]
AGPPI .... American Grain Products Processing Institute (EA)
AGPQAV .. Agriculture Pratique [*A publication*]
AGPR .... Agricultural Procurement Regulations
AGPS .... St. Patrick Community School, Grande Prairie, Alberta [*Library symbol*] [*National Library of Canada*] (BIB)
AGPSCS ... St. Clement School, Grande Prairie, Alberta [*Library symbol*] [*National Library of Canada*] (BIB)
AGPSGS ... St. Gerard School, Grande Prairie, Alberta [*Library symbol*] [*National Library of Canada*] (BIB)
AGPSJS .... St. Joseph School, Grande Prairie, Alberta [*Library symbol*] [*National Library of Canada*] (BIB)
AGPT .... Agar-Gel Precipitation Test [*Clinical chemistry*]
AGPTT ...... Aerial Gunnery Part Task Trainer [*MCD*]
AGPU .... Aviation Ground Power Unit (MCD)
AGPYAL ... Agrochemophysica [*A publication*]
AGQ .... Ambergate Exploration [*Vancouver Stock Exchange symbol*]
AGQ .... United States Department of Agriculture, Southern Forest Experiment Station, New Orleans, LA [*OCLC symbol*] (OCLC)
AG & QMG ... Adjutant-General and Quartermaster-General [*British*]
AGQT .... Attorney General of the Queen's Troop [*Military*] [*British*] (ROG)
AGR .... Active Guard Reserve [*DoD*]
AGR .... Advanced Gas-Cooled Reactor [*British*]
AGR .... Agra [*India*] [*Airport symbol*] (OAG)
AGR .... Agra [*India*] [*Seismograph station code, US Geological Survey*] [*Closed*] (SEIS)
AGR .... Agra Industries Ltd. [*Toronto Stock Exchange symbol*]
AGR .... Agrarwirtschaft [*A publication*]
AGR .... Agree (FAAC)
Agr .... Agricola [*of Tacitus*] [*Classical studies*] (OCD)
Agr .... Agricultura [*A publication*]
Ag R .... Agricultural Review [*A publication*]
AGR .... Agriculture
AGR .... Agriculture Division [*Census*] (OICC)
AGR .... Air-to-Ground Ranging
AGR .... Air-to-Ground Rocket (MCD)
AGR .... Alien Grange
AGR .... American-German Review [*A publication*]
AGR .... Annual Growth Rate
AGR .... Anticipatory Goal Response [*Medicine*]
AGR .... Auditor General's Report [*Canada*] [*Information service or system*] (IID)
AGR .... Autonetics Generalized Reset
AGR .... Avon Park, FL [*Location identifier*] [*FAA*] (FAAL)
Agr .... De Agricultura [*Philo*] · (BJA)
AGR .... Department of Agriculture [*Hyattsville, MD*] [*FAA designator*] (FAAC)
AGR .... Faulty Agreement [*Used in correcting manuscripts, etc.*]
AGR .... Granum Public Library, Alberta [*Library symbol*] [*National Library of Canada*] (NLC)
AGR .... Journal of Agricultural Taxation and Law [*A publication*]
AGR .... RADAR Picket Ship [*Navy symbol*]
AGR .... United States Department of Agriculture, Russell Agricultural Research Center, Athens, GA [*OCLC symbol*] (OCLC)
AGRA .... AGORA-GENERAL [*Agence France-Presse*] [*Information service or system*] (CRD)
Agra .... Agra High Court Reports [*India*] [*A publication*] (ILCA)
AGRA .... Army Group Royal Artillery [*British*]
AGRA .... Automatic Gain Ranging Amplifier (MCD)
Agr Abroad ... Agriculture Abroad [*A publication*]
A Graefe's A ... Albrecht Von Graefe's Archiv fuer Klinische und Experimentelle Ophthalmologie [*A publication*]
Agra FB ...... Agra Full Bench Rulings [*India*] [*A publication*] (ILCA)
Agra HC ..... Agra High Court Reports [*India*] [*A publication*] (DLA)
Agr Alger ... Agriculture Algerienne [*A publication*]
Agr Amer ... Agricultura de las Americas [*A publication*]
Agr Ammonia News ... Agricultural Ammonia News [*A publication*]

Agr Anim Husb ... Agriculture and Animal Husbandry [*A publication*]
Agrarpolit Rev ... Agrarpolitische Revue [*A publication*]
Agrar Rundsch ... Agrarische Rundschau [*A publication*]
Agrartoert Szle ... Agrartoerteneti Szemle [*A publication*]
Agrartort Szemle ... Agrartoerteneti Szemle [*A publication*]
Agrartud ..... Agrartudomany [*A publication*]
Agrartud Egy Agrarkozgazd Kar Kiad ... Agrartudomanyi Egyetem Agrarkozgazdasagi Karanak Kiadvanyai [*A publication*]
Agrartud Egy Agron Kar Kiad ... Agrartudomanyi Egyetem Agronomiai Karanak Kiadvanyai [*A publication*]
Agrartud Egy Allattenyesz Karanak Kozl (Godollo) ... Agrartudomanyi Egyetem Allattenyesztesi Karanak Koezlemenyei (Goedoelloe) [*A publication*]
Agrartud Egyetem Mezoegazdasagtud Kar Koezlem (Goedoelloe) ... Agrartudomanyi Egyetem Mezoegazdasagtudomanyi Karanak Koezlemenyei (Goedoelloe) [*A publication*]
Agrartud Egyetem Tud Tajekoz (Goedoelloe) ... Agrartudomanyi Egyetem Tudomanyos Tajekoztatoja (Goedoelloe) [*A publication*]
Agrartud Egyet Mezoegtud Kar Koezl (Goedoelloe) ... Agrartudomanyi Egyetem Mezoegazdasagtudomanyi Karanak Koezlemenyei (Goedoelloe) [*A publication*]
Agrartud Egy Kert Szologazdasagtud Karanak Evk ... Agrartudomanyi Egyetem Kert-es Szologazdasagtudomanyi Karanak Evkonyve [*A publication*]
Agrartud Egy Kert Szologazdasagtud Karanak Kozl ... Agrartudomanyi Egyetem Kert-es Szologazdasagtudomanyi Karanak Koezlemenyei [*A publication*]
Agrartud Egy Kozl ... Agrartudomanyi Egyetem Koezlemenyei [*A publication*]
Agrartud Egy Kozl (Godollo) ... Agrartudomanyi Egyetem Koezlemenyei (Goedoelloe) [*A publication*]
Agrartud Egy Mezogazdasagtud Karanak Kozl ... Agrartudomanyi Egyetem Mezoegazdasagtudomanyi Karanak Koezlemenyei [*Hungary*] [*A publication*]
Agrartud Egy Mezogazd Gepeszmern Karanak Kozl ... Agrartudomanyi Egyetem Mezoegazdasagi Gepeszmernoki Karanak Koezlemenyei [*A publication*]
Agrartud Egy Mezogazd Karanak Evk ... Agrartudomanyi Egyetem Mezoegazdasagi Karanak Evkonyve [*A publication*]
Agrartud Egy Tud Tajek ... Agrartudomanyi Egyetem Tudomanyos Tajekoztatoja [*Hungary*] [*A publication*]
Agrartud Foisk Tud Koezlem (Debrecen) ... Agrartudomanyi Foiskola Tudomanyos Koezlemenyei (Debrecen) [*A publication*]
Agrartud Foisk Tud Ulesszakanak Eloadasai Debreceni ... Agrartudomanyi Foiskola Tudomanyos Ulesszakanak Eloadasai Debreceni [*A publication*]
Agrartud Kozl ... Agrartudomanyi Koezlemenyek [*A publication*]
Agrartud Sz ... Agrartudomanyi Szemle [*A publication*]
Agrarwirt ... Agrarwirtschaft [*A publication*]
Agrarwirt und Agrarsoziol ... Agrarwirtschaft und Agrarsoziologie [*Economie et Sociologie Rurales*] [*A publication*]
Agrarwirts ... Agrarwirtschaft [*A publication*]
AGRAS ...... Grassland Public Library, Alberta [*Library symbol*] [*National Library of Canada*] (NLC)
Agr Asia ..... Agriculture Asia [*A publication*]
Agra Univ Bul ... Agra University. Bulletin [*A publication*]
Agra Univ J Res ... Agra University. Journal of Research [*India*] [*A publication*]
Agra Univ J Res Sci ... Agra University. Journal of Research Science [*A publication*]
Agr Aviation ... Agricultural Aviation [*A publication*]
Agrawirts ... Agrarwirtschaft [*A publication*]
Agr Banking Finan ... Agricultural Banking and Finance [*A publication*]
AGRBAU .. Agrobiologiya [*A publication*]
Agr Biol Ch ... Agricultural and Biological Chemistry [*Tokyo*] [*A publication*]
Agr Biol Chem ... Agricultural and Biological Chemistry [*Tokyo*] [*A publication*]
Agr Bresciano ... Agricoltore Bresciano [*A publication*]
Agr Bull Canterbury Chamber Commer ... Agricultural Bulletin. Canterbury Chamber of Commerce [*A publication*]
Agr Bull Oreg Dept Agr ... Agricultural Bulletin. Oregon Department of Agriculture [*A publication*]
Agr Bull Saga Univ ... Agricultural Bulletin. Saga University [*A publication*]
AGR C .... Agreed Case [*Legal term*] (DLA)
AGRC .... American Graves Registration Command [*Military*]
AGRCAX ... Agrochimica [*A publication*]
AGRCCZ ... Agrociencia. Serie C [*A publication*]
Agr Chem ... Agricultural Chemicals [*A publication*]
AGRCO ..... American Graves Registration Command [*Military*]
AGRE .... American Greetings Corp. [*NASDAQ symbol*] (NQ)
AGRE .... Army Group, Royal Engineers [*British and Canadian*] [*World War II*]
AGREA5 ... Agricultural Research [*Washington, DC*] [*A publication*]
AGRECE ... Agrupacion de Exportadores del Centro de Espana [*Trade association*] [*Spain*] (EY)
Agr Econ Inform Ser Univ MD Coop Ext Serv ... Agricultural Economics Information Series. University of Maryland. Cooperative Extension Service [*A publication*]
Agr Econ Mimeo Mich State Univ Agr Appl Sci Coop Ext Serv ... Agricultural Economics Mimeo. Michigan State University of Agriculture and Applied Science. Cooperative Extension Service [*A publication*]

Agr Econ Mimeo Rep Fla Agr Exp Sta ... Agricultural Economics Mimeo Report. Florida Agricultural Experiment Station [*A publication*]
Agr Econ Pam S Dak Agr Exp Sta ... Agricultural Economics Pamphlet. South Dakota Agricultural Experiment Station [*A publication*]
Agr Econ Re ... Agricultural Economics Research [*A publication*]
Agr Econ Rep Kans Agr Exp Sta ... Agricultural Economics Report. Kansas Agricultural Experiment Station [*A publication*]
Agr Econ Rep Mich State Univ Agr Appl Sci Coop Ext Serv ... Agricultural Economics Report. Michigan State University of Agriculture and Applied Science. Cooperative Extension Service [*A publication*]
Agr Econ Rep N Dak Agr Exp Sta ... Agricultural Economics Report. North Dakota Agricultural Experiment Station [*A publication*]
Agr Econ Res ... Agricultural Economics Research [*A publication*]
AGRED8 ... Agricultural Record [*South Australia*] [*A publication*]
Agr Educ Ma ... Agricultural Education Magazine [*A publication*]
AGREE...... Advisory Group on Reliability of Electronic Equipment [*Military*]
AGREET ... Agreement   (ROG)
AGREMC ... Assemblee des Gestionnaires de Reseaux Electriques Municipalises et Cooperatives [*Assembly of Managers of Municipal and Cooperative Electrical Systems*] [*Canada*]
Agr Eng...... Agricultural Engineering [*St. Joseph, MI*] [*A publication*]
Agr Eng Ext Bull NY State Coll Agr Dept Agr Eng ... Agricultural Engineering Extension Bulletin. New York State College of Agriculture. Department of Agricultural Engineering [*A publication*]
Ag Rep .... Agricultural Representative [*Canada*]
AGREP...... [*Permanent Inventory of*] Agricultural Research Projects [*Commission of the European Communities*] [*Information service or system*] [*A publication*]
Ag Res........ Agricultural Research [*A publication*]
Agressolog ... Agressologie [*A publication*]
AGRF........ American Geriatric Research Foundation [*Later, ARI*]
Agr Ferrarese ... Agricoltore Ferrarese [*A publication*]
Agr Ganad ... Agricultura y Ganaderia [*A publication*]
Agr Gaz NSW ... Agricultural Gazette of New South Wales [*A publication*]
Agr (Gt Brit) ... Agriculture (Great Britain). Ministry of Agriculture, Fisheries, and Food [*A publication*]
Agr Hist..... Agricultural History [*A publication*]
Agr Hist Rev ... Agricultural History Review [*A publication*]
Agr Hor Gen ... Agri Hortique Genetica [*A publication*]
Agr Hort .... Agriculture and Horticulture [*A publication*]
AGRI .... Agriculture   (DLA)
AGRI .... American Genealogical Research Institute
AGRIAH ... Agricultura (Heverlee) [*A publication*]
Agribus Decis ... Agribusiness Decision [*A publication*]
Agribus W ... Agribusiness Worldwide [*A publication*]
AGRIC...... Agriculture
Agric .... Agriculture [*A publication*]
AGRIC ...... Agriculture Canada
Agric 2000 ... Agriculture. Toward 2000 [*A publication*]
Agric Abroad ... Agriculture Abroad [*A publication*]
Agric Adm ... Agricultural Administration [*A publication*]
Agric Agroind J ... Agriculture and Agro-Industries Journal [*A publication*]
Agric Alger ... Agriculture Algerienne [*Algeria*] [*A publication*]
Agric Am.... Agricultura de las Americas [*A publication*]
Agric Anim Hub ... Agriculture and Animal Husbandry [*A publication*]
Agric Asia ... Agriculture Asia [*A publication*]
Agric Biol Chem ... Agricultural and Biological Chemistry [*Tokyo*] [*A publication*]
Agric & Biol Chem ... Agricultural and Biological Chemistry [*Tokyo*] [*A publication*]
Agric Biotechnol News ... Agricultural Biotechnology News [*A publication*]
Agric Bull... Agriculture Bulletin [*A publication*]
Agric Bull Fed Malay States ... Agricultural Bulletin. Federated Malay States [*A publication*]
Agric Bull Saga Univ ... Agricultural Bulletin. Saga University [*A publication*]
Agric Bur NSW State Congr ... Agricultural Bureau of New South Wales. State Congress [*A publication*]   (APTA)
Agric C....... Agricultural Code [*A publication*]   (DLA)
Agric Can Annu Rep ... Agriculture Canada. Annual Report [*A publication*]
Agric Can Monogr ... Agriculture Canada. Monograph [*A publication*]
Agric Can Rapp Annu ... Agriculture Canada. Rapport Annuel [*A publication*]
Agric Can Res Branch Rep ... Agriculture Canada. Research Branch Report [*A publication*]
Agric Can Weed Surv Ser ... Agriculture Canada. Weed Survey Series [*A publication*]
Agric Chem ... Agricultural Chemicals [*A publication*]
Agric Circ US Dep Agric ... Agriculture Circular. United States Department of Agriculture [*A publication*]
Agric Colon ... Agricoltura Coloniale [*A publication*]
Agric Conspectus Sci ... Agriculturae Conspectus Scientificus [*A publication*]
Agric Dec ... Agricultural Decisions [*A publication*]   (DLA)
Agric Econ ... Agricultural Economist [*A publication*]
Agric Econ B Afr ... Agricultural Economics Bulletin for Africa [*A publication*]
Agric Econ Ext Ser Univ KY Coop Ext Serv ... Agricultural Economics Extension Series. University of Kentucky. Cooperative Extension Service [*A publication*]

Agric Econ Fm Mgmt Occ Pap Dep Agric Qd Univ ... Agricultural Economics and Farm Management Occasional Paper. Department of Agriculture. University of Queensland [*A publication*]   (APTA)
Agric Econ Rep Dep Agric Econ Mich State Univ ... Agricultural Economics Report. Department of Agricultural Economics. Michigan State University [*A publication*]
Agric Econ Res ... Agricultural Economics Research [*A publication*]
Agric Econ Research ... Agricultural Economics Research [*A publication*]
Agric Econ Res Rep Miss Agric For Exp Sta ... Agricultural Economics Research Report. Mississippi Agricultural and Forestry Experiment Station [*A publication*]
Agric Econ Res US Dep Agric Econ Res Serv ... Agricultural Economics Research. United States Department of Agriculture. Economic Research Service [*A publication*]
Agric Ecosyst & Environ ... Agriculture, Ecosystems, and Environment [*A publication*]
Agric Educ ... Agricultural Education [*A publication*]
Agric Educ Mag ... Agricultural Education Magazine [*A publication*]
Agric Electr Inst Rep ... Agricultural Electricity Institute. Report [*A publication*]
Agric El Salv ... Agricultura en El Salvador [*A publication*]
Agric El Salvador ... Agricultura en El Salvador [*A publication*]
Agric-Energy Transp Dig ... Agricultural-Energy Transportation Digest [*A publication*]
Agric Eng ... Agricultural Engineering [*A publication*]
Agric Eng (Aust) ... Agricultural Engineering (Australia) [*A publication*]   (APTA)
Agric Engin ... Agricultural Engineering [*St. Joseph, MI*] [*A publication*]
Agric Eng J ... Agricultural Engineering Journal [*A publication*]
Agric Eng (Lond) ... Agricultural Engineer (London) [*A publication*]
Agric Engng (Aust) ... Agricultural Engineering (Australia) [*A publication*]   (APTA)
Agric Eng (S Afr) ... Agricultural Engineering (South Africa) [*A publication*]
Agric Eng (St Joseph Mich) ... Agricultural Engineering (St. Joseph, MI) [*A publication*]
Agric Environ ... Agriculture and Environment [*A publication*]
Agric Exp... Agricultura Experimental [*A publication*]
Agric Exp Stn Univ VT Bull ... Agricultural Experiment Station. University of Vermont. Bulletin [*A publication*]
Agric Fact Sh US Dep Agric ... Agriculture Fact Sheet. US Department of Agriculture [*A publication*]
Agric Fd Chemy ... Agricultural and Food Chemistry [*A publication*]
Agric Financ Rev US Dep Agric Econ Stat Coop Serv ... Agricultural Finance Review. United States Department of Agriculture. Economics, Statistics, and Cooperative Service [*A publication*]
Agric Fin R ... Agricultural Finance Review [*A publication*]
Agric Fin Rev ... Agricultural Finance Review [*A publication*]
Agric For Bull ... Agriculture and Forestry Bulletin [*A publication*]
Agric For Meteorol ... Agricultural and Forest Meteorology [*A publication*]
Agric Ganad ... Agricultura y Ganaderia [*A publication*]
Agric Gaz Can ... Agricultural Gazette of Canada [*A publication*]
Agric Gaz NSW ... Agricultural Gazette of New South Wales [*A publication*]
Agric Gaz Tasm ... Agricultural Gazette of Tasmania [*A publication*]   (APTA)
Agric Handb US Dep Agric ... Agriculture Handbook. United States Department of Agriculture [*A publication*]
Agric Handb US Dep Agric Agric Res Serv ... Agriculture Handbook. United States Department of Agriculture. Agricultural Research Service [*A publication*]
Agrichem Age ... Agrichemical Age [*A publication*]
Agrichem W ... Agrichemical West [*A publication*]
Agric Hist .. Agricultural History [*A publication*]
Agric Hist R ... Agricultural History Review [*A publication*]
Agric Hist Rev ... Agricultural History Review [*A publication*]
Agric Hoje ... Agricultura de Hoje [*A publication*]
Agric Hokkaido ... Agriculture in Hokkaido [*Japan*] [*A publication*]
Agric Hort ... Agriculture and Horticulture [*Japan*] [*A publication*]
Agric Hort Engng Abstr ... Agricultural and Horticultural Engineering Abstracts [*A publication*]
Agric Index ... Agricultural Index [*A publication*]
Agric Inf Bull US Dep Agric ... Agriculture Information Bulletin. United States Department of Agriculture [*A publication*]
Agric Inform Bull US Dep Agric ... Agriculture Information Bulletin. United States Department of Agriculture [*A publication*]
Agric Inst Rev ... Agricultural Institute Review [*A publication*]
Agric Int..... Agriculture International [*A publication*]
Agric Ital (Pisa) ... Agricoltura Italiana (Pisa) [*A publication*]
Agric Ital (Rome) ... Agricoltura Italiana (Rome) [*A publication*]
Agric J Br Guiana ... Agricultural Journal of British Guiana [*A publication*]
Agric J (Bridgetown Barbados) ... Agricultural Journal (Bridgetown, Barbados) [*A publication*]
Agric J Cape GH ... Agricultural Journal of the Cape Of Good Hope [*A publication*]
Agric J (Cape Town) ... Agricultural Journal (Cape Town) [*A publication*]
Agric J Dep Agric (Fiji) ... Agricultural Journal. Department of Agriculture (Suva, Fiji) [*A publication*]
Agric J Dep Agric Fiji Isl ... Agricultural Journal. Department of Agriculture. Fiji Islands [*A publication*]
Agric J Dept Agric (Victoria BC) ... Agricultural Journal. Department of Agriculture (Victoria, British Columbia) [*A publication*]

Agric J Egypt ... Agricultural Journal of Egypt [*A publication*]
Agric J India ... Agricultural Journal of India [*A publication*]
Agric J & Mining Rec Maritzburg ... Agricultural Journal and Mining Record. Maritzburg [*A publication*]
Agric J S Afr ... Agricultural Journal of South Africa [*A publication*]
Agric J (Suva Fiji) ... Agricultural Journal. Department of Agriculture (Suva, Fiji) [*A publication*]
Agric J Union S Afr ... Agricultural Journal of the Union of South Africa [*A publication*]
Agric Lit Czech ... Agricultural Literature of Czechoslovakia [*A publication*]
Agric Livestock India ... Agriculture and Livestock in India [*A publication*]
Agric Mach J ... Agricultural Machinery Journal [*A publication*]
Agric Mark (Washington) ... Agricultural Marketing (Washington, DC) [*A publication*]
Agric Mech Asia ... Agricultural Mechanization in Asia [*Japan*] [*A publication*]
Agric Met... Agricultural Meteorology [*A publication*]
Agric Meteorol ... Agricultural Meteorology [*A publication*]
Agric Mexicano ... Agricultor Mexicano y Hogar [*A publication*]
Agric & Mkts ... Agriculture and Markets [*A publication*] (DLA)
Agric News (Barbados) ... Agricultural News (Barbados) [*A publication*]
Agric News Lett E I Du Pont De Nemours Co ... Agricultural News Letter. E. I. Du Pont De Nemours and Company [*A publication*]
Agric Newsl (Manila) ... Agricultural Newsletter (Manila) [*A publication*]
Agric Nuova ... Agricoltura Nuova [*A publication*]
AGRICOLA ... Agricultural On-Line Access [*Formerly, CAIN*] [*National Agricultural Library, Information Systems Division*] [*Bibliographic database*] [*Information service or system*] (IID)
Agricoltura Ital (Pisa) ... Agricoltura Italiana (Pisa) [*A publication*]
Agric Outl ... Agricultural Outlook [*A publication*]
Agric Outlook ... Agricultural Outlook [*A publication*]
Agric Pak ... Agriculture Pakistan [*A publication*]
Agric Pakistan ... Agriculture Pakistan [*A publication*]
Agric Prat .. Agriculture Pratique [*France*] [*A publication*]
Agric Prog ... Agricultural Progress [*A publication*]
Agric Pugliese ... Agricoltura Pugliese [*A publication*]
Agric Rec ... Agricultural Record [*A publication*] (APTA)
Agric Rec (S Aust) ... Agricultural Record (South Australia) [*A publication*]
Agric Rec South Aust Dep Agric ... Agricultural Record. South Australia Department of Agriculture [*A publication*]
Agric Res ... Agricultural Research [*A publication*]
Agric Res Corp (Gezira) Tech Bull ... Agricultural Research Corporation (Gezira). Technical Bulletin [*A publication*]
Agric Res Counc Food Res Inst (Norwich) Annu Rep ... Agricultural Research Council. Food Research Institute (Norwich). Annual Report [*A publication*]
Agric Res Counc (GB) Letcombe Lab Annu Rep ... Agricultural Research Council (Great Britain). Letcombe Laboratory. Annual Report [*A publication*]
Agric Res Counc (GB) Radiobiol Lab ... Agricultural Research Council (Great Britain). Radiobiological Laboratory [*A publication*]
Agric Res Counc (GB) Radiobiol Lab ARCRL ... Agricultural Research Council (Great Britain). Radiobiological Laboratory. ARCRL [*A publication*]
Agric Res Counc Meat Res Inst Bien Rep (Bristol) ... Agricultural Research Council. Meat Research Institute. Biennial Report (Bristol) [*A publication*]
Agric Res Counc Meat Res Inst (Bristol) Annu Rep ... Agricultural Research Council. Meat Research Institute (Bristol). Annual Report [*A publication*]
Agric Res Counc Meat Res Inst (Bristol) Memo ... Agricultural Research Council. Meat Research Institute (Bristol). Memorandum [*A publication*]
Agric Res Counc Rep ... Agricultural Research Council. Report [*A publication*]
Agric Res Dev ... Agricultural Research for Development [*A publication*]
Agric Res Guyana ... Agricultural Research Guyana [*A publication*]
Agric Res Inst Ukiriguru Prog Rep ... Agricultural Research Institute Ukiriguru. Progress Report [*A publication*]
Agric Res J Kerala ... Agricultural Research Journal of Kerala [*A publication*]
Agric Res (Kurashiki) ... Agricultural Research (Kurashiki) [*A publication*]
Agric Res Man US Dep Agric Sci Educ Adm ... Agricultural Research Manual. US Department of Agriculture. Science and Education Administration [*A publication*]
Agric Res (New Delhi) ... Agricultural Research (New Delhi) [*A publication*]
Agric Res News Notes (Lima) ... Agricultural Research News Notes (Lima) [*A publication*]
Agric Res Organ Dep For Ilanot Leaf ... Agricultural Research Organization. Department of Forestry. Ilanot Leaflet [*A publication*]
Agric Res Organ Div For Ilanot Leafl ... Agricultural Research Organization. Division of Forestry. Ilanot Leaflet [*A publication*]
Agric Res Organ Pam (Bet-Dagan) ... Agricultural Research Organization. Pamphlet (Bet-Dagan) [*A publication*]
Agric Res Organ Prelim Rep (Bet-Dagan) ... Agricultural Research Organization. Preliminary Report (Bet-Dagan) [*A publication*]
Agric Res Organ Volcani Cent Spec Publ ... Agricultural Research Organization. Volcani Center. Special Publication [*A publication*]

Agric Res Rep (Wageningen) ... Agricultural Research Reports (Wageningen) [*A publication*]
Agric Res Rep (Wageningen) (Versl Landbouwk Onderz) ... Agricultural Research Reports (Wageningen) (Verslagen van Landbouwkundige Onderzoekingen) [*A publication*]
Agric Res Rev ... Agricultural Research Review [*A publication*]
Agric Res Rev (Cairo) ... Agricultural Research Review (Cairo) [*A publication*]
Agric Res Seoul Natl Univ ... Agricultural Research. Seoul National University [*A publication*]
Agric Res US Dep Agric Res Serv ... Agricultural Research. United States Department of Agriculture. Research Service [*A publication*]
Agric Res (Wash DC) ... Agricultural Research (Washington, DC) [*A publication*]
Agric Romande ... Agriculture Romande [*A publication*]
Agric Sao Paulo ... Agricultura em Sao Paulo [*A publication*]
Agric Sci Dig ... Agricultural Science Digest [*A publication*]
Agric Sci (Jogjakarta) ... Agricultural Science (Jogjakarta) [*A publication*]
Agric Sci R ... Agricultural Science Review [*A publication*]
Agric Sci Rev ... Agricultural Science Review [*A publication*]
Agric Sci Rev Coop State Res Serv US Dep Agric ... Agricultural Science Review. Cooperative State Research Service. US Department of Agriculture [*A publication*]
Agric Sci (Sofia) ... Agricultural Science (Sofia) [*A publication*]
Agric Serv Bull FAO ... Agricultural Services Bulletin. Food and Agriculture Organization of the United Nations [*A publication*]
Agric Situa ... Agricultural Situation [*Later, Farmline Magazine*] [*A publication*]
Agric Situation India ... Agricultural Situation in India [*A publication*]
Agric Syst .. Agricultural Systems [*A publication*]
Agric Tech ... Agricultural Technologist [*A publication*]
Agric Technol ... Agricultural Technologist [*A publication*]
Agric Tec Mex ... Agricultura Tecnica en Mexico [*A publication*]
Agric Tec (Santiago) ... Agricultura Tecnica (Santiago) [*A publication*]
Agric Trop ... Agricultura Tropical [*A publication*]
Agricultura Am ... Agricultura de las Americas [*A publication*]
Agricultura Tec ... Agricultura Tecnica [*A publication*]
Agricultura Tec Mex ... Agricultura Tecnica en Mexico [*A publication*]
Agricultura Trop ... Agricultura Tropical [*A publication*]
Agriculture in Ire ... Agriculture in Northern Ireland [*A publication*]
Agriculture Pakist .. Agriculture Pakistan [*A publication*]
Agric Univ (Wageningen) Pap ... Agricultural University (Wageningen). Papers [*A publication*]
Agric Venez ... Agricultura Venezolana [*A publication*]
Agric Venezie ... Agricoltura delle Venezie [*Italy*] [*A publication*]
Agric Vet Chem ... Agricultural and Veterinary Chemicals [*A publication*]
Agric Wastes ... Agricultural Wastes [*England*] [*A publication*]
Agric Water Manage ... Agricultural Water Management [*A publication*]
Agric Weather Res Ser ... Agricultural Weather Research Series [*A publication*]
Agri Dec..... Agriculture Decisions [*A publication*]
AGRIDOC ... Agricultural Documentation Network [*France*]
Agri Hort Genet ... Agri Hortique Genetica [*A publication*]
Agri Ind...... Agriculture Index [*A publication*]
AGRIMATION ... Agricultural Automation
AGRI/MECH Rep Econ Comm Eur ... AGRI/MECH Report. Economic Commission for Europe [*A publication*]
Agri Mktg ... Agri Marketing [*A publication*]
AGRINDEX ... Agricultural Research Information Index [*United Nations*]
Agr Inform Bull USDA ... Agriculture Information Bulletin. United States Department of Agriculture [*A publication*]
Agr Inst Rev ... Agricultural Institute Review [*A publication*]
Agri Res Seoul Nat Univ ... Agricultural Research. Seoul National University [*A publication*]
AGRIS....... International Information System for the Agricultural Sciences and Technology [*Food and Agriculture Organization*] [*United Nations*] [*Information service or system*] (IID)
Agriscene (Aust) ... Agriscene (Australia) [*A publication*] (APTA)
Agr Israel... Agriculture in Israel [*A publication*]
AgRISTARS ... Agriculture and Resources Inventory Survey through Aerospace Remote Sensing
AGRISTARS ... Agriculture and Resources Inventory Surveys through Aerospace (MCD)
Agr Ital ...... Agricoltura d'Italia [*Rome*] [*A publication*]
AGRJAK... Agronomia [*Rio De Janeiro*] [*A publication*]
AGRL .... Agricultural
AGRLAQ .. Agriculture (London) [*A publication*]
Agr Leaders Dig ... Agricultural Leaders Digest [*A publication*]
Agr (Lisboa) ... Agricultura (Lisboa) [*A publication*]
Agr Livestock India ... Agriculture and Livestock in India [*A publication*]
Agr LJ........ Agricultural Law Journal [*A publication*]
AGRM .... Adjutant-General of the Royal Marines [*British*]
AGRM .... Agreement (AABC)
Agr Market (Nagpur) ... Agricultural Marketing (Nagpur) [*A publication*]
Agr Market (Washington DC) ... Agricultural Marketing (Washington, DC) [*A publication*]
AGRMBU ... Agronomia [*Manizales*] [*A publication*]
Agr Mech... Agricultural Mechanization [*A publication*]
Agr Merchant ... Agricultural Merchant [*A publication*]
Agr Meteor ... Agricultural Meteorology [*A publication*]
Agr Meteorol ... Agricultural Meteorology [*A publication*]

Agr Milanese ... Agricoltura Milanese [*A publication*]
Agr (Montreal) ... Agriculture (Montreal) [*A publication*]
AGRMT .... Agreement (FAAC)
Agr Napoletana ... Agricoltura Napoletana [*A publication*]
AGRNAW ... Agronomico [*Campinas*] [*A publication*]
AGRNDZ .. Agronomie [*Paris*] [*A publication*]
Agr Newslett ... Agricultural Newsletter [*A publication*]
Agr N Ireland ... Agriculture in Northern Ireland [*A publication*]
AGROB2 ... Agrochemia (Bratislava) [*A publication*]
Agrobiol ..... Agrobiologiya [*A publication*]
Agroborealis Alaska Agric Exp Stn (Fairbanks) ... Agroborealis. Alaska
     Agricultural Experiment Station (Fairbanks) [*A
     publication*]
Agrobot ...... Agrobotanika [*A publication*]
Agrochem ... Agrochemia [*Bratislava*] [*A publication*]
Agrochem Cour ... Agrochem Courier [*A publication*]
Agrochim ... Agrochimica [*A publication*]
Agrocienc Ser A ... Agrociencia. Serie A [*A publication*]
Agrocienc Ser C ... Agrociencia. Serie C [*A publication*]
Agro-Ecosyst ... Agro-Ecosystems [*A publication*]
Agro Inds ... Agro Industries [*A publication*]
AGROINFORM ... Agricultural Information Services [*HUD*] [*Information
     service or system*] (IID)
AGROINFORM ... Information Center of the Ministry of Agriculture and
     Food [*Ministry of Agriculture and Food*] [*Information
     service or system*] (IID)
Agrokem Talajtan ... Agrokemia es Talajtan [*A publication*]
Agrokem Talajtan Suppl ... Agrokemia es Talajtan. Supplement [*A
     publication*]
Agrokhim ... Agrokhimiya [*A publication*]
Agrokhim Gruntoznst ... Agrokhimiya i Gruntoznaustvo [*A publication*]
Agrokhim Kharakt Pochv BSSR ... Agrokhimicheskaya Kharakteristika
     Pochv BSSR [*A publication*]
AGROMASH ... Mezhdunarodnoe Obshchestvo po Mashinam dlja
     Ovoshchevodstva, Sadovodstva, i Vinogradstva
     [*International Association for Vine, Fruit, and Vegetable-
     Growing Mechanization*] (EAIO)
AGROMEK ... International Exhibition for Agricultural Mechanization and
     Breeding Stock (TSPED)
AGRON ..... Agronomy
Agron .... Agronomy [*A publication*]
Agron Abstr ... Agronomy Abstracts [*A publication*]
Agron Angol ... Agronomia Angolana [*A publication*]
Agron Angolana ... Agronomia Angolana [*A publication*]
Agron Branch Rep (South Aust Dep Agric Fish) ... Agronomy Branch Report
     (South Australia Department of Agriculture and Fisheries)
     [*A publication*] (APTA)
Agron Costarric ... Agronomia Costarricense [*A publication*]
Agron Dept Ser Ohio Agr Exp Sta ... Agronomy Department Series. Ohio
     Agricultural Experiment Station [*A publication*]
Agron Food Contrib Challenges Pap Annu Meet Am Soc Agron ...
     Agronomists and Food. Contributions and Challenges.
     Papers Presented at the Annual Meeting. American Society
     of Agronomy [*A publication*]
Agron Glas ... Agronomski Glasnik [*A publication*]
Agron Glasn ... Agronomski Glasnik [*A publication*]
Agron J ...... Agronomy Journal [*A publication*]
Agron (Lima) ... Agronomia (Lima) [*A publication*]
Agron Lusit ... Agronomia Lusitana [*A publication*]
Agron Lusitana ... Agronomia Lusitana [*Portugal*] [*A publication*]
Agron (Manizales) ... Agronomia (Manizales) [*A publication*]
Agron (Mexico) ... Agronomia (Monterrey, Mexico) [*A publication*]
Agron Mimeogr Circ N Dak Agr Exp Sta ... Agronomy. Mimeograph Circular.
     North Dakota Agricultural Experiment Station [*A
     publication*]
Agron Mocambicana ... Agronomia Mocambicana [*A publication*]
Agronomia Angol ... Agronomia Angolana [*A publication*]
Agronomia Lusit ... Agronomia Lusitana [*A publication*]
Agronomia Trop ... Agronomia Tropical. Revista del Instituto Nacional de
     Agricultura [*A publication*]
Agron Pam S Dak Agr Exp Sta ... Agronomy Pamphlet. South Dakota
     Agricultural Experiment Station [*A publication*]
Agron Res Food Pap Annu Meet Am Soc Agron ... Agronomic Research for
     Food. Papers Presented at the Annual Meeting of the
     American Society of Agronomy [*A publication*]
Agron Res Rep LA State Univ Agric Mech Coll Dep Agron ... Agronomy
     Research Report. Louisiana State University and
     Agricultural and Mechanical College. Department of
     Agronomy [*A publication*]
Agron Soc NZ Spec Publ ... Agronomy Society of New Zealand. Special
     Publication [*A publication*]
Agron Soils Res Ser Clemson Agr Exp Sta ... Agronomy and Soils Research
     Series. Clemson Agricultural Experiment Station [*A
     publication*]
Agron Sulriogr ... Agronomia Sulriograndense [*A publication*]
Agron Sulriograndense ... Agronomia Sulriograndense [*A publication*]
Agron Trop ... Agronomia Tropical [*Maracay, Venezuela*] [*A publication*]
Agron Trop Agron Gen Etude Tech ... Agronomie Tropicale. Serie Agronomie
     Generale. Etudes Techniques [*Paris*] [*A publication*]
Agron Trop Agron Gen Etud Sci ... Agronomie Tropicale. Serie Agronomie
     Generale. Etudes Scientifiques [*Paris*] [*A publication*]

Agron Trop (Maracay) ... Agronomia Tropical (Maracay, Venezuela) [*A
     publication*]
Agron Trop (Paris) ... Agronomie Tropicale (Paris) [*A publication*]
Agron Trop Riz Rizic Cult Vivrieres Trop ... Agronomie Tropicale. Serie Riz et
     Riziculture et Cultures Vivrieres Tropicales [*A publication*]
Agron Trop Ser Agron Gen Etud Sci ... Agronomie Tropicale. Serie
     Agronomie Generale. Etudes Scientifiques [*A publication*]
Agron Trop Ser Agron Gen Etud Tech ... Agronomie Tropicale. Serie
     Agronomie Generale. Etudes Techniques [*A publication*]
Agron Trop Ser Riz Rizic Cult Vivrieres Trop ... Agronomie Tropicale. Serie
     Riz et Riziculture et Cultures Vivrieres Tropicales [*A
     publication*]
Agron Vet ... Agronomia y Veterinaria [*A publication*]
Agron Views Univ Nebr Coll Agr Home Econ Ext Serv ... Agronomy Views.
     University of Nebraska. College of Agriculture and Home
     Economics. Extension Service [*A publication*]
Agros (Lisb) ... Agros (Lisboa) [*A publication*]
AGROT ..... Agrotikon Komma [*Agrarian Party*] [*Greek*] [*Political
     party*] (PPE)
Agrotec (Madrid) ... Agrotecnia (Madrid) [*A publication*]
Agrotekh Provid Kul'tur ... Agrotekhnika Providnikh Kul'tur [*A publication*]
AGRP .... Andrews Group, Inc. [*NASDAQ symbol*] (NQ)
AGRPA4 .... Agriculture Pakistan [*A publication*]
Agr Pakistan ... Agriculture Pakistan [*A publication*]
Agr (Paris) ... Agriculture (Paris) [*A publication*]
Agr Policy Rev ... Agricultural Policy Review [*A publication*]
Agr Prat ...... Agriculture Pratique [*A publication*]
Agr Progr ... Agricultural Progress [*A publication*]
AGRR .... Angora Goat Record and Registry (EA)
AGRRA ...... Agricultural Research Review [*A publication*]
AGRRAA .. Agricultural Research Review [*Cairo*] [*A publication*]
Agr Res ...... Agricultural Research [*A publication*]
Agr Res (India) ... Agricultural Research (India) [*A publication*]
Agr Res J Kerala ... Agricultural Research Journal of Kerala [*A publication*]
Agr Res (Pretoria) ... Agricultural Research (Pretoria) [*A publication*]
Agr Res Rev ... Agricultural Research Review [*Cairo*] [*A publication*]
Agr Res (Washington DC) ... Agricultural Research (Washington, DC) [*A
     publication*]
Agr Romande ... Agriculture Romande [*A publication*]
Agr Rust Orig ... De Agricultura or De Re Rustica Origines [*of Cato*]
     [*Classical studies*] (OCD)
AGRS .... Acid Gas Removal System [*Chemical engineering*]
AGRS .... Agristar, Inc. [*NASDAQ symbol*] (NQ)
AGRS .... American Graves Registration Service [*Military*]
Agr (Santo Domingo) ... Agricultura (Santo Domingo) [*A publication*]
Agr Sao Paulo ... Agricultura em Sao Paulo [*A publication*]
Agr Sci Rev ... Agricultural Science Review [*A publication*]
Agr Sit Ind ... Agricultural Situation in India [*A publication*]
Agr Situation ... Agricultural Situation [*Later, Farmline Magazine*] [*A
     publication*]
Agr Situation India ... Agricultural Situation in India [*A publication*]
Agr Spezia ... Agricoltura della Spezia [*A publication*]
Agr Statist N Dak Crop Livestock Rep Serv ... Agricultural Statistics. North
     Dakota Crop and Livestock Reporting Service [*A
     publication*]
AGRT .... Agreement
AGRT .... Automatic Guard Receiver Terminals [*Navy*] (MCD)
Agr Tec .... Agricultura Tecnica [*A publication*]
Agr Tec Mex ... Agricultura Tecnica en Mexico [*A publication*]
Agr Trop ..... Agricultura Tropical [*A publication*]
AGR Univ KY Coop Ext Serv ... AGR. University of Kentucky. Cooperative
     Extension Service [*A publication*]
Agr Venezie ... Agricoltura delle Venezie [*A publication*]
Agr Vet Chem ... Agricultural and Veterinary Chemicals [*A publication*]
Agr Wastes ... Agricultural Wastes [*A publication*]
AGRYAV ... Agronomy [*A publication*]
AGS .... Abort Guidance Section [*NASA*] (KSC)
AGS .... Abort Guidance System [*or Subsystem*] [*Apollo*] [*NASA*]
AGS .... Adipic, Glutaric, and Succinic [*Acids for flue-gas cleaning*]
AGS .... Adrenogenital Syndrome [*Medicine*]
AGS .... Advanced Genetic Sciences, Inc.
AGS .... Advanced Guidance System
AGS .... Aero Gun Sights
AGS .... Agencies (EY)
AGS .... Agency Sales [*A publication*]
AGS .... AGS Computers, Inc. [*NYSE symbol*] (SPSG)
AGS .... Air-Ground System
AGS .... Airborne Gunsight
AGS .... Aircraft General Standards [*British*]
AGS .... Aircraft Generation Squadron (MCD)
AGS .... [*The*] Alabama Great Southern Railroad Co. [*AAR code*]
AGS .... Allied Geographic Section [*Southwest Pacific*] [*Obsolete*]
AGS .... Alpine Garden Society (EA)
AGS .... Alternating Gradient Synchrotron
AGS .... Alternating Guidance Section
AGS .... American Gem Society (EA)
AGS .... American Geographical Society (EA)
AGS .... American Geriatrics Society (EA)
AGS .... American Gesneria Society [*Later, GSI*] (EA)
AGS .... American Glovebox Society (EA)
AGS .... American Gloxinia Society [*Later, AGGS*] (EA)

AGS .... American Goat Society (EA)
AGS .... American Golf Sponsors (EA)
AGS .... American Gourd Society (EA)
AGS .... American Graphological Society (EA)
AGS .... American Gynecological Society [*Later, AGOS*] (EA)
AGS .... Anesthetic Gas Standards
AGS .... Angus [*County in Scotland*] (ROG)
AGS .... Angus Resources Ltd. [*Vancouver Stock Exchange symbol*]
AGS .... Annulus Gas System [*Nuclear energy*] (NRCH)
AGS .... Antigravity Suit [*NASA*] (MCD)
AGS .... Armed Guard School
AGS .... Armored Gun System [*Army*]
AGS .... Army General Staff
AGS .... Arnold's Geological Series
AGS .... Art Gallery Society [*New South Wales, Australia*]
AGS .... Artificial Gravity Structure
AGS .... Ascent Guidance and Control System [*NASA*] (KSC)
AGS .... Assistant General Secretary (DCTA)
AGS .... Assistant Grand Sojourner [*Freemasonry*]
AGS .... Associate in General Studies
AGS .... Association of Graduate Schools in Association of American Universities (EA)
AGS .... Association for Gravestone Studies (EA)
AGS .... Atlantic Generating Station [*Nuclear energy*] (NRCH)
AGS .... Atlantic Geoscience Association
AGS .... Augusta [*Georgia*] [*Airport symbol*]
AGS .... Australian Gallery of Sport
AGS .... Australian Geographical Studies [*A publication*]
AGS .... Australian Government Solicitor's Office
AGS .... Automatic Gain Stabilization
AGS .... Auxiliary General Survey [*Navy*] (MSC)
AGS .... Gadsden State Junior College, Gadsden, AL [*Library symbol*] [*Library of Congress*] (LCLS)
AGS .... Surveying Ship [*Navy symbol*]
AGS .... United States Department of Agriculture, Southern Regional Research Center, New Orleans, LA [*OCLC symbol*] (OCLC)
AGSA .... Art Glass Suppliers Association (EA)
AGSAF ...... Australian Government Student Assistance Fund
AGSAS ...... Andy Griffith Show Appreciation Society (EA)
AGSCC ...... Army General Supplies Commodity Center
Ag Sci J ...... Agricultural Science Journal [*A publication*]
Ag Sci R ...... Agricultural Science Review [*A publication*]
AGSCPO ... Army General Staff Civilian Personnel Office, Office of the Chief of Staff
AGSD .... Acta Germanica zur Sprache und Dichtung Deutschlands [*A publication*]
AGSD .... Association for Glycogen Storage Disease (EA)
AGSE .... Aerospace Ground Support Equipment
AGSE .... Aircraft Ground Support Equipment (MCD)
AGSES .... Association of Girl Scout Executive Staff (EA)
AGSG .... Alliance of Genetic Support Groups (EA)
AGS/GR .... Geographical Review. American Geographical Society [*A publication*]
AGSI .... Advanced Genetic Sciences, Incorporated [*NASDAQ symbol*] (NQ)
AGSI .... Automatic Government Source Inspection
AGSIDC .... Arab Gulf States Information Documentation Center [*Information service or system*] (EISS)
AGSIM ...... American Graduate School of International Management [*Formerly, Thunderbird Graduate School of International Management*] [*Glendale, AZ*]
Ag Situation ... Agricultural Situation [*Later, Farmline Magazine*] [*A publication*]
AGSL .... Satellite Launching Ship [*Navy symbol*] [*Obsolete*]
AGSLAV ... Agronomia Sulriograndense [*A publication*]
AGSM .... American Gold Star Mothers (EA)
AGSM .... Associate of the Guildhall School of Music [*British*]
AGSM .... Australian Graduate School of Management Corporate Data [*Information service or system*] (CRD)
AGSMAY ... Acta Genetica et Statistica Medica [*A publication*]
AGSOA ..... Agressologie [*A publication*]
AGSP .... Alignment Group Sensing Platform (AAG)
AGSP .... Atlas General Survey Program (IEEE)
Ag Sply Ind ... Agricultural Supply Industry [*A publication*]
AGSPW ..... Association of Girl Scout Professional Workers [*Later, AGSES*] (EA)
AGSq .... Aircraft Generation Squadron [*Air Force*]
AGSR .... Advanced Ground Surveillance RADAR (MCD)
AGSR .... All-Weather Ground Surveillance RADAR
AGSRO ..... Association of Government Supervisors and Radio Officers [*British*]
AGS-RTO ... Automatic Ground Spoiler - Rejected Takeoff (MCD)
AGSS .... American Geographical and Statistical Society
AGSS .... Attitude Ground Support System (MCD)
AGSS .... Auxiliary Submarine [*Navy symbol*]
AGSSAI ..... Acta Obstetrica et Gynecologica Scandinavica. Supplement [*A publication*]
AGST .... Against
Ag Stat .... Agricultural Statistics [*A publication*]

AGSU .... Arbeiten zur Geschichte des Spaetjudentums und Urchristentums [*A publication*]
AGSW .... Air-to-Ground Standoff Weapon (MCD)
AGSYD5 .... Agricultural Systems [*A publication*]
AGT .... Adage Graphics Terminal
AGT .... Additional Gunner Training (MCD)
AGT .... Advanced Gas Turbine
AGT .... Advanced Ground Transport
AGT .... Advanced Guidance Technology [*SAMSO*] [*Air Force*] (MCD)
AGT .... Against
AGT .... Agent (AABC)
AGT .... Agreement
AGT .... Aircraft Gas and Turbine
AGT .... Alberta Government Telephones [*Part of Telecom Canada*] [*Calgary, AB*] [*Telecommunications service*] (TSSD)
AGT .... Allison Gas Turbine [*Engine*]
AGT .... American Government Term Trust [*NYSE symbol*] (SPSG)
AGT .... Antiglobulin Test [*Hematology*]
AGT .... Army Gunner Training (MCD)
AGT .... Arresting Gear Tester
AGT .... Audiographic Teleconference
AGT .... Australian Grade Teacher [*A publication*] (APTA)
AGT .... Aviation Gas Turbine (KSC)
AGT .... United States Department of Agriculture, Food Safety and Quality Service Library - Agricultural South Building, Washington, DC [*OCLC symbol*] (OCLC)
AGTA .... Airline Ground Transportation Association [*Defunct*] (EA)
AGTA .... Airport Ground Transportation Association (EA)
AGTA .... American Gem Trade Association (EA)
AGTBA6.... Agricultura Tropical [*A publication*]
AGTC .... Airport Ground Traffic Control [*Department of Transportation*]
AGTCA9 ... Agricultura Tecnica [*Santiago*] [*A publication*]
AGTD .... Athletic Goods Team Distributors (EA)
AGTDC ..... Accord General sur les Tarifs Douaniers et le Commerce [*General Agreement on Tariffs and Trade*] (EAIO)
AGTE .... Association of Group Travel Executives (EA)
AGTELIS ... Army Ground Transportable Emitter Location Identification System
AGTELIS ... Automatic Ground Transportable Emitter Location and Identification System [*Army*]
AGTG .... Agenutemagen. Indians of New Brunswick [*Canada*] [*A publication*]
AGTI .... Allein Gott Traue Ich [*I Trust in God Alone*] [*German*] [*Motto of Dorothee, Duchess of Braunschweig-Lunebert (1546-1617)*]
agto .... Agosto [*August*] [*Spanish*] [*Correspondence*]
agto .... Agosto [*August*] [*Portuguese*] [*Correspondence*] (GPO)
AGTOA ..... American Greyhound Track Operators Association (EA)
AGTOAB .. Agronomie Tropicale. Serie Agronomie Generale. Etudes Techniques [*A publication*]
AGTP .... Automatically Generated Test Analysis and Programs (MCD)
AGTQA ..... Annales de Genetique [*A publication*]
AGTr......... Adrenoglomerulotrophin [*Also, ASH*] [*Endocrinology*]
AGTR .... Agitator [*FBI standardized term*]
AGTR .... Technical Research Ship [*Navy symbol*]
AGTS........ Advanced Gunnery Target Systems (MCD)
AGTS........ Aerial Gunnery Target System (MCD)
AGTS........ Association for Gifted and Talented Students (EA)
AGTS........ Automated Gyro Test Set
AGTSAN ... Agrokemia es Talajtan. Supplement [*A publication*]
AGTT .... Abnormal Glucose Tolerance Test [*Medicine*]
AGTT .... Aerial Gunnery TOW Target (MCD)
AGU.......... Aerospace Ground Unit
AGU.......... Aguascalientes [*Mexico*] [*Airport symbol*] (OAG)
AGU.......... All Got Up (ADA)
AGU.......... American Agricultural Economics Documentation Center, Washington, DC [*OCLC symbol*] (OCLC)
AGU.......... American Geophysical Union (EA)
AGU.......... Angle Resources Ltd. [*Vancouver Stock Exchange symbol*]
AGU.......... Anhydroglucose Unit [*Biochemistry*]
AGU.......... Automatic Ground Unit
AGU.......... Aviation Ground Unit [*Naval Reserve*]
Agua Energ ... Agua y Energia [*A publication*]
AGUEAK .. Annales Guebhard [*A publication*]
AGUSD ..... Gas + Architecture [*A publication*]
AGV.......... Acarigua [*Venezuela*] [*Airport symbol*] (OAG)
AGV.......... Alkali-Gravity-Viscosity [*Glass technology*]
AGV.......... Aniline Gentian Violet
AGV.......... Argyle Ventures [*Vancouver Stock Exchange symbol*]
AGV.......... Automatic Guided Vehicle [*Robotic manufacturing equipment*]
AGV.......... Avion a Grande Vitesse
AGV.......... United States Department of Agriculture, Cooperative Information System Agriculture Canada Library, Ontario, ON, Canada [*OCLC symbol*] (OCLC)
AGVA .... American Guild of Variety Artists (EA)
AGVC .... Alberta Vocational Centre, Grouard, Alberta [*Library symbol*] [*National Library of Canada*] (NLC)
AGVC .... Automatic Governing Valve Control [*Nuclear energy*] (NRCH)
AGVEAP... Agricultura Venezolana [*A publication*]
AGVGA ..... American Greenhouse Vegetable Growers Association (EA)

AGVIA3 .... Archiv fuer die Gesamte Virusforschung [*A publication*]
AGVM .... Giroux ville Public Library, Alberta [*Library symbol*] [*National Library of Canada*] (NLC)
AGVO .... Arbeitsgemeinschaft Vorderer Orient [*A publication*]
AGVS .... Air-to-Ground Voice System [*or Subsystem*] (MCD)
AGVS .... Automatic Guided Vehicle System [*Robotics*]
AGVS .... Automatic Guided Vehicle Systems (EA)
AGVT .... Advanced Ground Vehicle Technology Project [*Army*]
AGW .... Abhandlungen. Gesellschaft der Wissenschaften zu Goettingen [*A publication*]
AGW .... Acoustic-Gravity Wave
AGW .... Actual Gross Weight [*Railroads*]
AGW .... Adjusted Gross Weight (MCD)
AGW .... Aging and Work [*A publication*]
AGW .... Air Gap Width
AGW .... Allowable [*Takeoff*] Gross Weight [*for an aircraft*]
AGW .... Alternate Gross Weight (MCD)
AGW .... Association of Golf Writers (EAIO)
A & GW ..... Atlantic & Great Western Railroad
AGW .... United States Department of Agriculture, Western Regional Research Center, Berkeley, CA [*OCLC symbol*] (OCLC)
AGWAGS ... Albany Group, Western Australia Genealogical Society
AGWAR .... Adjutant General, War Department [*Obsolete*]
Agway Coop ... Agway Cooperator [*A publication*]
AGWD .... Australian Government Weekly Digest [*A publication*] (APTA)
AGWG .... Abhandlungen. Gesellschaft der Wissenschaften zu Goettingen [*A publication*]
AGWHS .... Holy Family School, Grimshaw, Alberta [*Library symbol*] [*National Library of Canada*] (BIB)
AGWI .... American Gulf West Indies Co.
AGWKS ..... Kennedy Elementary School, Grimshaw, Alberta [*Library symbol*] [*National Library of Canada*] (BIB)
AGWM ...... Grimshaw WI Municipal Library, Alberta [*Library symbol*] [*National Library of Canada*] (NLC)
AGWS .... Advanced Gun Weapon System (MCD)
AGWS .... Grimshaw Junior/Senior High School, Alberta [*Library symbol*] [*National Library of Canada*] (BIB)
AGWSE ..... Association of Ground Water Scientists and Engineers (EA)
AGWT .... American Ground Water Trust (EA)
AGX .... Agincourt Exploration, Inc. [*Vancouver Stock Exchange symbol*]
AGY .... Agency (ADA)
AGY .... Argosy Mining Corp. Ltd. [*Toronto Stock Exchange symbol*]
AGYRA .... Agricultural Research [*A publication*]
AGYRAB... Agricultural Research [*New Delhi*] [*A publication*]
AGZ .... Actual Ground Zero [*Nuclear explosions*]
AGZ .... Actual Ground Zone (MUGU)
AGZ .... Agassiz Resources Ltd. [*Toronto Stock Exchange symbol*]
AGZ .... Aggeneys [*South Africa*] [*Airport symbol*] (OAG)
AGZ .... Wagner, SD [*Location identifier*] [*FAA*] (FAAL)
AGZPAA... Agrikultura (Nitre) [*A publication*]
AH .... Abdominal Hysterectomy [*Medicine*]
aH .... Abhenry [*Unit of inductance*]
AH .... Aboriginal History [*A publication*] (APTA)
AH .... Academy of Homiletics (EA)
AH .... Accelerated Hypertension [*Medicine*]
AH .... Access for the Handicapped (EA)
A & H .... Accident and Health Insurance
AH .... Accidental Hypothermia [*Medicine*]
AH .... Accumulator High [*Data processing*]
AH .... Adenomatous Hyperplasia [*Medicine*]
AH .... Adult Heart
AH .... After Hatch [*Shipping*]
AH .... After Hours (ADA)
AH .... After-Hyperpolarization [*Also, AHP*] [*Neurophysiology*]
AH .... Agricultural History [*A publication*]
A & H .... Agricultural and Horticultural
AH .... Agriculture Handbook
AH .... Agudas Harabonim [*Union of Orthodox Rabbis of the United States and Canada*]
Ah .... Ahikar (BJA)
Ah .... Ahilot (BJA)
AH .... Air Algerie [*Algeria*] [*ICAO designator*] (FAAC)
AH .... Air-Cushion Vehicle built by Ajax Hovercraft [*England*] [*Usually used in combination with numerals*]
A/H .... Air Handling [*Nuclear energy*] (NRCH)
A/H .... Air Over Hydraulic (AAG)
AH .... Aircraft Handler [*British*]
AH .... Airfield Heliport
AH .... Alan Hutchison Publishing Ltd. [*British*]
AH .... Alcoholic Hepatitis [*Medicine*]
AH .... Algemeen Handelsblad [*A publication*]
AH .... Allen & Hanburys [*Great Britain*] [*Research code symbol*]
AH .... Allied Health Program [*Association of Independent Colleges and Schools specialization code*]
AH .... Allis-Chalmers Corp. [*NYSE symbol*] [*Wall Street slang name: "Alice"*] (SPSG)
A/H .... Already Had (FAAC)
AH .... Alter Heading [*Navigation*]
AH .... Alternate Headquarters [*Military*] (NVT)
A/H .... Amenorrhea/Hyperprolactinemia [*Endocrinology*]

AH .... American Hebrew (BJA)
AH .... American Heritage [*A publication*]
AH .... American Historical Review [*A publication*]
AH .... American Horizons (EA)
AH .... American Humanics (EA)
AH .... Anhydrous Hydrazine [*Rocket propellant*]
AH .... Animal Husbandry Research Division [*of ARS, Department of Agriculture*]
AH .... Anjou Historique [*A publication*]
AH .... Anno Hebraico [*In the Hebrew Year*] [*Since 3761 BC*] [*Latin*]
AH .... Anno Hegirae [*In the Year of the Hegira*] [*The flight of Mohammed from Mecca*] [*AD 622*] [*Latin*]
AH .... Anterior Hypothalamic Nucleus [*Brain anatomy*]
AH .... Antihalation
AH .... Antihunt [*Circuit*] [*Electronics*]
AH .... Antihyaluronidase [*Clinical chemistry*]
A/H .... Antwerp/Hamburg [*Range of ports between and including these two cities*] [*Shipping*] (DS)
AH .... Apache Helicopter [*Anti-armor attack helicopter*]
AH .... Archivium Hibernicum [*A publication*]
AH .... Archivo Hispalense [*A publication*]
A & H .... Arm and Hammer [*Brand of soda*]
AH .... Army Helicopter [*British military*] (DMA)
AH .... Army Hospital
A & H .... Arnold and Hodges' English Queen's Bench Reports [*1840-41*] [*A publication*] (DLA)
AH .... Art for Humanity [*A publication*]
AH .... Arterial Hypertension [*Medicine*]
AH .... Artificial Heart [*Medicine*]
AH .... Artificial Horizon (MCD)
AH .... Arts and Humanities
AH .... Ascites Hepatoma [*Medicine*]
AH .... Asia House [*An association*] (EA)
AH .... Association of Hispanists [*British*]
AH .... Astigmatism, Hypermetropic [*Also, AsH*] [*Ophthalmology*]
AH .... Atrial His-Bundle [*Cardiology*]
AH .... Attack Helicopter (CINC)
AH .... Attitude Hold (MCD)
AH .... Autonomic Hyperreflexia [*Medicine*]
AH .... Available Hours [*Electronics*] (IEEE)
ah----- .... Himalaya Mountain Region [*MARC geographic area code*] [*Library of Congress*] (LCCP)
AH .... Hinton Public Library, Alberta [*Library symbol*] [*National Library of Canada*] (NLC)
AH .... Hospital Ship [*Navy symbol*]
AH .... Huntsville Public Library, Huntsville, AL [*Library symbol*] [*Library of Congress*] (LCLS)
AHA .... Additive Histologic Assessment [*Medicine*]
AHA .... Adirondack Historical Association (EA)
AHA .... Agricultural and Horticultural Engineering Abstracts [*A publication*]
AHA .... AHA Automotive Technologies Corp. [*Toronto Stock Exchange symbol*]
AHA .... Ahua [*Hawaii*] [*Seismograph station code, US Geological Survey*] (SEIS)
AHA .... Alberta Hospital Association [*Edmonton*] (TSSD)
AHA .... Alpha Industries, Inc. [*AMEX symbol*] (SPSG)
AHA .... American Habonim Association [*Later, Labor Zionist Alliance*]
AHA .... American Hardboard Association (EA)
AHA .... American Healing Association (EA)
AHA .... American Health Association (EA)
AHA .... American Heart Association (EA)
AHA .... American Hellenic Alliance (EA)
AHA .... American Hepatitis Association (EA)
AHA .... American Herb Association (EA)
AHA .... American Hereford Association (EA)
AHA .... American Herens Association (EA)
AHA .... American Historical Association (EA)
AHA .... American Hitchhiker Association
AHA .... American Hobbit Association (EA)
AHA .... American Homebrewers Association (EA)
AHA .... American Homeowners Association [*Commercial firm*] (EA)
AHA .... American Hominological Association (EA)
AHA .... American Hospital Association (EA)
AHA .... American Hotel Association [*Later, AH & MA*]
AHA .... American Hound Association
AHA .... American Hovercraft Association [*Superseded by HA*] (EA)
AHA .... American Humane Association (EA)
AHA .... American Humanist Association (EA)
AHA .... American Hypnosis Association (EA)
AHA .... American Hypnotists' Association (EA)
AHA .... Anterior Hypothalamic Area
AHA .... Area Health Authority
AHA .... Associate of the Institute of Health Service Administrators [*British*] (DCTA)
AHA .... Association of Handicapped Artists (EA)
AHA .... Association of Hispanic Arts (EA)
AHA .... Autoimmune Hemolytic Anemia [*Hematology*]
AHA .... Hardisty Public Library, Alberta [*Library symbol*] [*National Library of Canada*] (NLC)
AHA .... Hitotsubashi Academy. Annals [*A publication*]

AHA .... Hitotsubashi Journal of Economics [*A publication*]
AHA .... United States Army Environmental Hygiene Agency, Aberdeen Proving Grounds, MD [*OCLC symbol*]   (OCLC)
AHAB .... Australian Historical Association. Bulletin [*A publication*]   (APTA)
AHACM .... Ancient and Honorable Artillery Company of Massachusetts   (EA)
AHAF .... American Handwriting Analysis Foundation   (EA)
AHAF .... American Health Assistance Foundation   (EA)
AHAG .... Annales. Societe d'Histoire et d'Archeologie de Gand [*A publication*]
AHAL .... Hay Lakes Public Library, Alberta [*Library symbol*] [*National Library of Canada*]   (NLC)
AHAM ...... Anales de Historea Antigua y Medieval [*A publication*]
AHAM ...... Association of Home Appliance Manufacturers   (EA)
AHAM ...... Association of Home Appliance Manufacturers. Trends and Forecasts [*A publication*]
AHAM Facts ... Major Appliance Industry Facts Book. Association of Home Appliance Manufacturers [*A publication*]
AHAMS .... Advanced Heavy Antitank Missile System [*Army*]   (MCD)
AHA Newsletter ... American Historical Association. Newsletter [*A publication*]
AHAP .... Apartment House Addressing Program [*US Postal Service*]
AHAPAS... Archivos Argentinos de Pediatria [*A publication*]
AHA Publ ... American Hospital Association. Publications [*A publication*]
AHARAY .. Archivos Argentinos de Reumatologia [*A publication*]
AHAS .... Acetohydroxyacidsynthase [*An enzyme*]
AHAS .... Association of Heritage Approved Specialists [*An association*]   (EAIO)
AHAS .... Automatic Helicopter Approach System [*Army*]
AHASC ..... Airport Handling Agreements Sub-Committee [*IATA*]   (DS)
AHA Stat... Hospital Statistics. American Hospital Association [*A publication*]
AHA(T) ..... Area Health Authority (Teaching) [*British*]
AHAT .... Arylhydroxamic(acyltransferase) [*An enzyme*]
AHAU .... University of Alabama in Huntsville, Huntsville, AL [*Library symbol*] [*Library of Congress*]   (LCLS)
AHAUS ..... Amateur Hockey Association of the United States   (EA)
AHAW .... Abhandlungen. Heidelberger Akademie der Wissenschaften [*A publication*]
AHAWPK ... Abhandlungen. Heidelberger Akademie der Wissenschaften. Philosophisch-Historische Klasse [*A publication*]
AHAWS .... Advanced Heavy Antitank Weapon System   (MCD)
AHB .... Abha [*Saudi Arabia*] [*Airport symbol*]   (OAG)
AHB.......... Air Heater Blower
AHB.......... Air Historical Branch [*Air Ministry*] [*British*]
AHB.......... American Highways and Byways [*British*]
AHB.......... Archaeologisch-Historische Bijdragen [*A publication*]
AHB.......... Assault Helicopter Battalion [*Military*]
AHB.......... Athabaska Gold [*Vancouver Stock Exchange symbol*]
AHB.......... Attack Helicopter Battalion
AHB.......... Australian Honey Board
AHB.......... [*The*] Australian Hymn Book [*A publication*]   (APTA)
AHBA .... American Home Business Association [*Greenwich, CT*]   (EA)
AHBAI ...... American Health and Beauty Aids Institute   (EA)
AH-Bank ... Aussenhandelsbank [*Foreign Trade Bank*] [*German*]
A & H Bank ... Avery and Hobbs' Bankrupt Law of United States [*A publication*]   (DLA)
AHBD........ Alpha-Hydroxybutyric Dehydrogenase [*An enzyme*]
AHBPAX... Acta Hydrobiologica [*A publication*]
AHBS .... Army Health Benefit Society [*Australia*]
AHC.......... Academy of Hospital Counselors [*Later, AHCC*]   (EA)
AHC.......... Accepting Houses Committee [*Banking*] [*British*]
AHC.......... Air Hawaii [*Honolulu, HI*] [*FAA designator*]   (FAAC)
AHC.......... Airport Handling Committee [*IATA*]   (DS)
AHC.......... Allan Hancock College [*Santa Maria, CA*]
AHC.......... Allied High Commission [*Germany*]   (NATG)
AHC.......... Amerada Hess Corp. [*NYSE symbol*] [*Toronto Stock Exchange symbol*]   (SPSG)
AHC.......... American Health Consultants [*Information service or system*]   (IID)
AHC.......... American Helicopter Company [*Air Force*]   (MCD)
AHC.......... American Hellenic Congress   (EA)
AHC.......... American Horse Council   (EA)
AHC.......... American Horticultural Council [*Later, AHS*]
AHC.......... American Hospital Corps
AHC.......... American Hostage Committee   (EA)
AHC.......... Ampere-Hour Capacity
AHC.......... Animal Health Committee [*Australia*]
AHC.......... Annuarium Historiae Conciliorum [*A publication*]
AHC.......... Anthropogenic Hydrocarbons
AHC.......... Appaloosa Horse Club
AHC.......... Army Hospital Corps
AHC.......... Assault Helicopter Company [*Army*]   (AABC)
AHC.......... Association of Hebrew Catholics   (EA)
AHC.......... Association Henri Capitant   (EA)
AHC.......... Association for the History of Chiropractic   (EA)
AHC.......... Association des Hopitaux du Canada [*Association of Hospitals of Canada*]
AHC.......... Atlas Historique du Canada [*Historical Atlas of Canada*] [*Project*]

AHC.......... Attack Helicopter Company [*Military*]
AHC.......... Australian Horticultural Corporation
AHC.......... Automatic Headway Control
AHC.......... Herlong, CA [*Location identifier*] [*FAA*]   (FAAL)
AHCA .... Afghan Hound Club of America   (EA)
AHCA .... American Health Care Association   (EA)
AHCA .... American Hockey Coaches Association   (EA)
AHCA .... Austin-Healey Club of America   (EA)
AHCAA ..... American Health Care Advisory Association   (EA)
AHCADM ... African Heritage Center for African Dance and Music   (EA)
AHCADU ... Aspects of Homogeneous Catalysis [*A publication*]
AHCAS ..... Ad Hoc Committee for American Silver   (EA)
AHCBAU ... Acta Hydrochimica et Hydrobiologica [*A publication*]
AHCBSU... Ad Hoc Committee on the Baltic States and the Ukraine   (EA)
AHCC....... Academy of Health Care Consultants [*Defunct*]   (EA)
AHCC....... American-Hellenic Chamber of Commerce   (EA)
AHCC....... Association des Hopitaux Catholiques du Canada [*Association of Catholic Hospitals of Canada*]
AHCCAX .. Aichi Cancer Center Research Institute. Annual Report [*A publication*]
AHCCBSU ... Ad Hoc Congressional Committee on the Baltic States and the Ukraine   (EA)
AHCCIA.... Ad Hoc Congressional Committee for Irish Affairs   (EA)
AHCCL .... Ad Hoc Committee on Copyright Law   (EA)
AHCE....... Asociacion para la Historia de la Ciencia Espanola [*A publication*]
AHCEI ...... Ad Hoc Committee on Equipment Interoperability [*NATO*]   (NATG)
AHCEI ...... American Histadrut Cultural Exchange Institute   (EA)
AHCF .... Alternate Headquarters Command Facility [*Military*]   (MCD)
AHCFSI .... Ad Hoc Committee on Freedom of Scholarly Inquiry   (EA)
AHCGS ..... Grace Shepherd School, Hines Creek, Alberta [*Library symbol*] [*National Library of Canada*]   (BIB)
AHCI........ Arts and Humanities Citation Index [*A publication*]
AHCIET.... Asociacion Hispanoamericana de Centros de Investigacion y Estudios de Telecomunicaciones   (EA)
AHCIMA .. Associate of the Hotel, Catering, and Institutional Management Association [*British*]   (DBQ)
AHCIS....... Ambulatory Health Care Information System
AHCLF...... Ad Hoc Committee for Lebanese Freedom [*Defunct*]   (EA)
AHCM....... Academy of Hazard Control Management   (EA)
AHCM....... Hines Creek Municipal Library, Alberta [*Library symbol*] [*National Library of Canada*]   (NLC)
AHCo......... Assault Helicopter Company [*Air Force*]   (AFM)
AHCP .... Arquivos de Historia de Cultura Portuguesa [*A publication*]
AHCRA ..... Arabian Horse Club Registry of America [*Later, AHR*]
AHCS .... Advanced Hybrid Computer System
AHCS .... Alternative Health Care Systems, Inc. [*Naugatuck, CT*] [*NASDAQ symbol*]   (NQ)
AHCS .... American Historic and Cultural Society   (EA)
AHCS .... American Hungarian Catholic Society [*Later, William Penn Association*]   (EA)
AHCS .... Hines Creek High School, Alberta [*Library symbol*] [*National Library of Canada*]   (BIB)
AHCTL ..... Acetylhomocysteinethiolactone [*Citiolone*] [*Organic chemistry*]
AHD .... Ahead   (FAAC)
AHD .... Airhead [*Army*]   (AABC)
AHD .... Airport Hotel Directory [*National Association of Business Travel Agents*] [*A publication*]
AHD .... American Health Decisions   (EA)
AHD .... American Heritage Dictionary [*A publication*]
AHD .... Anti-Helicopter Device
AHD .... Antihypertensive Drug [*Medicine*]
AHD .... Arc Heating Device
AHD .... Archives d'Histoire Dominicaine [*A publication*]
AHD .... Ardmore [*Oklahoma*] [*Airport symbol*] [*Obsolete*]   (OAG)
Ahd .... Arrowhead [*Military decoration*]   (AABC)
AHD .... Arteriosclerotic Heart Disease [*Cardiology*]
AHD .... Audio High Density
AHD .... Australian Height Datum
AHD .... Autoimmune Hemolytic Disease [*Medicine*]
AHDE....... Anuario de la Historia del Derecho Espanol [*A publication*]
AHDGA..... American Hot Dip Galvanizers Association [*Later, AGA*]   (EA)
AH Dienst ... Aussenhandels-Dienst [*A publication*]
AHDL........ Archives d'Histoire Doctrinale et Litteraire [*Paris*] [*A publication*]
AHDLMA ... Archives d'Histoire Doctrinale et Litteraire du Moyen-Age [*A publication*]
AHDME.... Association of Hospital Directors of Medical Education [*Later, AHME*]   (EA)
AHDO .... Archives d'Histoire du Droit Oriental [*A publication*]
AHDP........ Azacycloheptane Diphosphonate [*Organic chemistry*]
AHDPA..... Association of House Democratic Press Assistants   (EA)
AHDR....... Air Header
AHDRA....... Archiwum Hydrotechniki [*A publication*]
AHE......... Air to Heat Exchanger [*Aerospace*]   (AAG)
AHE.......... Alternatives in Higher Education [*Program*] [*National Science Foundation*]
AHE.......... American Health Properties [*NYSE symbol*]   (SPSG)
AHE.......... Ammunition Handling Equipment
AHE.......... Annales d'Histoire Economique [*A publication*]

AHE.......... Armament Handling Equipment (MCD)
AHE.......... Associate in Home Economics
AHE.......... Association for Higher Education [of the NEA] [Later, AAHE] (EA)
AHE...... Association for Human Emergence [Defunct] (EA)
AHE...... Association for Humanistic Education (EA)
AHE.......... Heinsburg Public Library, Alberta [Library symbol] [National Library of Canada] (NLC)
AHE.......... University of Arkansas for Medical Sciences, Area Health Education Center, Little Rock, AR [OCLC symbol] (OCLC)
AHEA....... American Home Economics Association (EA)
AHEA....... American Hungarian Educators' Association (EA)
AHEAD..... Army Help for Education and Development
AHEAD..... Association for Humanistic Education and Development (EA)
AHEAD..... Australian Health Education Advisory Digest [A publication] (APTA)
AHEB....... Analectes pour Servir a l'Histoire Ecclesiastique de la Belgique [A publication]
AHEC....... American Hardwood Export Council (EA)
AHEC....... Appropriate Home Energy Cooperative [Canada]
AHEC....... Area Health Education Center [Veterans Administration] (DHSM)
AHEC....... Arrowhead Energy Corporation [NASDAQ symbol] (NQ)
AH Ec...... Associate in Home Economics
AHEL....... Army Human Engineering Laboratory (MCD)
AHEM...... Association of Hydraulic Equipment Manufacturers
AHEMA..... Anatomia, Histologia, Embryologia [A publication]
AHEPA.... American Hellenic Educational Progressive Association
AHERA..... Asbestos Hazard Emergency Response Act of 1986
AHES....... American Humane Education Society (EA)
AHES....... Annales d'Histoire Economique et Sociale [A publication]
AHESC...... Airport Handling Equipment Sub-Committee [IATA] (DS)
AHEY....... Army Handicapped Employe of the Year (RDA)
AHF.......... Abba Hushi Files [Haifa] [A publication]
AHF.......... Active History File [Army]
AHF.......... Acute Heart Failure [Medicine]
AHF.......... American Health Foundation (EA)
AHF.......... American Hepatic Foundation (EA)
AHF.......... American Heritage Foundation (EA)
AHF.......... American Hobby Federation [Defunct] (EA)
AHF.......... American Homeowners Foundation (EA)
AHF.......... American Hospital Formulary [A publication]
AHF.......... American Host Foundation (EA)
AHF.......... American Humanics Foundation [Later, AH] (EA)
AHF.......... American Hungarian Federation (EA)
AHF.......... American Hungarian Foundation (EA)
AHF.......... Antihemophilic Factor [Factor VIII] [Also, AHG, PTF, TPC] [Hematology]
AHF.......... Architectural Heritage Foundation (EA)
AHF.......... Architectural History Foundation (EA)
AHF.......... Archivum Historii, Filozofii, i Mysli Spolecznej [A publication]
AHF.......... Area Health Authority Full Time [Chiropody] [British]
AHF.......... Army Historical Foundation (EA)
AHF.......... Asian Hospital Federation [Jakarta, Indonesia] (EAIO)
AHF.......... Associated Health Foundation (EA)
AHF.......... Australian High Court and Federal Court Practice [A publication] (APTA)
AHF.......... Auto Hold Fire (KSC)
AHF.......... Azad Hind Fauj [Indian National Army]
AHFA....... African Heritage Federation of the Americas (EA)
AHFC....... American Hungarian Folklore Centrum (EA)
AHFLCD... Association of Health Facility Licensure and Certification Directors (EA)
AHFMR.... Alberta Heritage Foundation for Medical Research [Canada]
AHFPAJ ... Allan Hancock Foundation. Publications. Occasional Paper [A publication]
AHFR....... Argonne High-Flux Reactor (NRCH)
AHFR....... Aussenhandels-Finanzierungs-Rundschreiben [Circular Letter on Financing of Foreign Trade] [German]
AHFRAC... Army Human Factors Research Advisory Committee
AHFRDC .. Army Human Factors Research and Development Committee (AABC)
AHFS........ American Hospital Formulary Service
AHG .... American High-Density Gradient
AHG .... Anchor Gold Corp. [Vancouver Stock Exchange symbol]
AHG .... Anhydroglucose [Biochemistry]
AHG .... Antihemophilic Globulin [Factor VIII] [Also, AHF, PTF, TPC] [Hematology]
AHG .... Antihuman Globulin [Consumption test] [Medicine]
AHG .... Archconfraternity of the Holy Ghost (EA)
AHG .... Archives Historique de la Gironde [A publication]
AHG .... Aussenhandelsgesellschaft [Foreign Trade Company] [German]
AHG .... Australian Historical Geography [A publication]
AHGAK.... Archiv fuer Hessische Geschichte und Altertumskunde [A publication]
AHGB....... Allgemeines Handelsgesetzbuch [German] [A publication] (DLA)
AHGBS ..... Association of Heads of Girls Boarding Schools [British]
AHGC........ Advanced Hardened Guidance Computer (MCD)

AHGC....... Australian Horticultural Growers' Council
AHGF....... Antique and Historical Glass Foundation (EA)
AHGMRF ... Ad Hoc Group for Medical Research Funding (EA)
AHGS....... Acute Herpetic Gingival Stomatitis [Dentistry]
AHGS....... Advanced Harpoon Guidance System (MCD)
AHGS..... Attitude Heading Gyroscope System
AHGS....... Church of Jesus Christ of Latter-Day Saints, Genealogical Society Library, Huntsville Branch, Huntsville, AL [Library symbol] [Library of Congress] (LCLS)
AHGSBY... Acta Hepato-Gastroenterologica [A publication]
AHGTC..... Ancient and Honourable Guild of Town Criers (EAIO)
AHGUSPTUN ... Ad Hoc Group on US Policy toward the UN (EA)
AHH.......... AmeriHealth, Inc. [AMEX symbol] (SPSG)
AHH.......... Amery, WI [Location identifier] [FAA] (FAAL)
AHH.......... Arc Heater Housing
AHH.......... Aromatic Hydrocarbon Hydroxylase [An enzyme]
AHH.......... Aryl Hydrocarbon Hydroxylase [An enzyme]
AHH.......... Association for Hispanic Handicapped of New Jersey (EA)
AHH.......... Association for Holistic Health [Inactive] (EA)
AHH.......... Hairy Hill Public Library, Alberta [Library symbol] [National Library of Canada] (NLC)
AHHA ...... American Holstein Horse Association (EA)
AHHAP..... Association of Halfway House Alcoholism Programs of North America (EA)
AHHI .... Alon Hahevra Hanumismatit le'Israel [A publication]
AHHS....... American Hackney Horse Society (EA)
AHHSA...... American Holistic Health Sciences Association (EA)
AHI.......... Active Hostility Index [Psychology]
AHI.......... Aerodynamic Heating Indicator (MCD)
AHI.......... Afro-Hispanic Institute (EA)
AHI.......... Amahai [Indonesia] [Airport symbol] (OAG)
AHI.......... American Healthcare Institute [Later, AMHS Institute] (EA)
AHI.......... American Hellenic Institute (EA)
AHI.......... American Honey Institute [Later, HICA] (EA)
AHI.......... Animal Health Institute (EA)
AHI.......... Artificial Horizon Indicator [Aerospace] (MCD)
AHI.......... Augmented Human Intellect (KSC)
AHI.......... Axel Heiberg Island [Canada]
AHIC......... American Home Industries Corporation [NASDAQ symbol] (NQ)
AHIC......... Art Hazards Information Center (EA)
AHIDGS ... Association of Heads of Independent and Direct Grant Girls Schools [British]
AHIHA...... American Hearing Impaired Hockey Association (EA)
AHII .... American Health Industries Institute (EA)
AHIL .... Association of Hospital and Institution Libraries [of ALA] [Later, ASCLA]
AHIL Q ..... Association of Hospital and Institution Libraries. Quarterly [A publication]
AHIP .... Advanced Helicopter Improvement Program [Army] (RDA)
AHIP .... Army Helicopter Improvement Program
AHIP .... Assisted Health Insurance Plan
AHIPAC.... American Hellenic Institute Public Affairs Committee (EA)
AHIS .... American Hull Insurance Syndicate [New York, NY] (EA)
AHIS .... Association of Heads of Independent Schools [British]
AHIS .... Automated Hospital Information System [Veterans Administration] (IID)
AHISA9..... Acta Histochemica [A publication]
A HistHung ... Acta Historica. Academiae Scientiarum Hungaricae [A publication]
AHIT .... Attack Helicopter Instrument Test (MCD)
AHJCP....... Association of Hillel/Jewish Campus Professionals (EA)
AHJOA ..... American Heart Journal [A publication]
AHJPB6..... Archivum Histologicum Japonicum [A publication]
AHK.......... Amhawk Resources Corp. [Vancouver Stock Exchange symbol]
a-hk---........ Hong Kong [MARC geographic area code] [Library of Congress] (LCCP)
AHL.......... Abstracts of Hungarian Economic Literature [A publication]
AHL.......... Acetate Halftone Litho [Du Pont]
AHL.......... Ad Hunc Locum [To (or At) This Place] [Latin]
AHL.......... Adam, Harding & Lueck [Commercial firm] [British]
AHL.......... AHL Group [Formerly, Automotive Hardware Limited] [Toronto Stock Exchange symbol]
AHL.......... Aishalton [Guyana] [Airport symbol] [Obsolete] (OAG)
AHL.......... America: History and Life [ABC-Clio Information Services] [Database] [A publication]
AHL.......... American Heritage Life Investment Corp. [NYSE symbol] (SPSG)
AHL.......... American Hockey League (EA)
AHL.......... Annuaire d'Histoire Liegeoise [A publication]
AHL.......... Association for Holistic Living (EA)
AHL.......... Auroral Hydrogen Line
AHL.......... Average Hearing Level
AHL.......... High Level Municipal Library, Alberta [Library symbol] [National Library of Canada] (NLC)
AHLE .... Auroral Hydrogen Line Emission
AHLFAJ ... Annales d'Hygiene de Langue Francaise. Medecine et Nutrition [A publication]
AHLFS...... Florence MacDougall Community School, High Level, Alberta [Library symbol] [National Library of Canada] (BIB)
A-HLH ...... Amphipathic Helix-Loop-Helix [Genetics]

AHLHS..... American Hungarian Library and Historical Society (EA)
AHLI .... American Home Lighting Institute (EA)
AHLMA .... American Home Laundry Manufacturers Association [Later, AHAM] (EA)
AHLPS...... High Level Public School, Alberta [Library symbol] [National Library of Canada] (BIB)
AHLZS...... Zama City School, High Level, Alberta [Library symbol] [National Library of Canada] (BIB)
AHM .... Aaronson, Huchra, and Moruld [Method of determining age of the universe]
AHM .... Acutely Hazardous Material
AHM .... Ahmanson [H. F.] & Co. [NYSE symbol] (SPSG)
AHM .... Airport Handling Manual [IATA] (DS)
AHM .... Ammonium Heptamolybdate [Inorganic chemistry]
AHM .... Ampere-Hour Meter
AHM .... Anterior Hyaloid Membrane [Ophthalmology]
AHM .... Auxiliary Handling Machine [Nuclear energy] (NRCH)
AHM .... Hanna Municipal Library, Alberta [Library symbol] [National Library of Canada] (NLC)
AHMA....... Advanced Hypersonic Manned Aircraft
AHMA....... Allied Hat Manufacturers Association (EA)
AHMA....... American Hardware Manufacturers Association (EA)
AHMA....... American Holistic Medical Association (EA)
AH & MA .... American Hotel & Motel Association (EA)
AHMA....... Archives d'Histoire Doctrinale et Litteraire du Moyen-Age [A publication]
AHMB....... American Hotel and Motel Brokers [Formerly, MBAA] (EA)
AHMC....... American Horticultural Marketing Council (EA)
AHMC....... Association of Hospital Management Committees
AHMC....... Australian Health Ministers Conference
AHMD ...... Airborne Helmet Mounted Display
AHME....... Association for Hospital Medical Education (EA)
AHME J.... Association for Hospital Medical Education. Journal [A publication]
AHMF....... American Holistic Medical Foundation (EA)
AHMGSA ... Ad Hoc Monitoring Group on Southern Africa (EA)
AHMH ...... Association of High Medicare Hospitals
AHMHAU ... Annales Historico-Naturales. Musei Nationalis Hungarici [A publication]
AHMI....... American Holistic Medical Institute [of the American Holistic Medical Association] [Formerly, BIA] [Later, AHMF] (EA)
AHMI....... Appalachian Hardwood Manufacturers, Incorporated (EA)
AHMI....... Association of Head Mistresses, Incorporated [British]
AHMJ .... Arc-Heated Materials Jet [Langley Research Center]
AHMOAH ... American Heart Association. Monograph [A publication]
AHMPS .... Association of Headmistresses of Preparatory Schools [British]
AHMS .... Abstracts of Hospital Management Studies [A publication]
AHMS .... American Home Mission Society
AHN .... Acta Historiae Neerlandica [A publication]
AHN .... Adventist Health Network of North America [Inactive] (EA)
AHN .... Army Health Nurse (AABC)
AHN .... Athens [Georgia] [Airport symbol] (OAG)
AHNA .... Accredited Home Newspapers of America [Later, SNA]
AHNA .... American Holistic Nurses Association (EA)
AHNO .... Association of Head and Neck Oncologists of Great Britain
AHNRH .... Annalen des Historischen Vereins fuer den Niederrhein [A publication]
A/H/O....... Abort/Hold/Orbit [NASA]
AHO .... Albright's Hereditary Osteodystrophy [Medicine]
AHO .... Alghero [Italy] [Airport symbol] (OAG)
AHO .... Applicant Holding Office [Employment]
AHO .... Association of Holocaust Organizations (EA)
AHO .... Attack Helicopter Operations (CAAL)
AHO .... Aussenhandelsorganisation [Foreign Trade Organization] [German]
AHO .... Oakwood College, Huntsville, AL [Library symbol] [Library of Congress] (LCLS)
AHO .... Technische Hogeschool Delft. Bibliotheek. Aanwinsten [A publication]
AHOAG .... Attack Helicopter Operations and Analysis Group
AHOBAM ... Acta Horti Bergiani [A publication]
AHOD .... Areal Hypolimnetic Oxygen Deficit [Hydrobiology]
AHOF....... Arabian Horse Owners Foundation (EA)
AHOF....... Automotive Hall of Fame
AHOM ...... American Home Patient Center [NASDAQ symbol] (NQ)
AHOM ...... Holden Municipal Library, Alberta [Library symbol] [National Library of Canada] (BIB)
AHOP....... Assisted Home-Ownership Program [Canada]
AHORA..... Acta Horticulturae [A publication]
AHOS........ Automatic Hydrologic Observing System [National Weather Service]
AHOSA5... Anales. Hospital de la Santa Cruz y San Pablo [A publication]
AHOTE..... Association of Health Occupations Teacher Educators (EA)
AHP.......... Absorption Heat Pumping [Engineering]
AHP.......... Afterhyperpolarization [Also, AH] [Neurophysiology]
AHP.......... Air Horsepower [Air Force]
AHP.......... Allied Health Professionals
AHP.......... Allied Hydrographic Publication [NATO]
AHP.......... Alternating Hamiltonian Path
AHP.......... American Health Professionals

AHP.......... American Home Products Corp. [NYSE symbol] (SPSG)
AHP.......... American Homeopathic Pharmacopoeia [Last published in 1920]
AHP.......... American Horse Publications (EA)
AHP.......... Americans for Historic Preservation (EA)
AHP.......... Analytic Hierarchy Process
AHP.......... Archivum Historiae Pontificiae [A publication]
AHP.......... Army Heliport (AABC)
AHP.......... Assistant Head Postmaster (DCTA)
AHP.......... Assistant House Physician
AHP.......... Association for Humanistic Psychology (EA)
AHP.......... Attitude Hold Pitch [Axis]
AHP.......... Awards, Honors, and Prizes [A publication]
AHP.......... Evacuation Hospital Ship [Navy symbol] [Obsolete]
AHPA....... Accumulator High-Pressure Air
AHPA....... (Adeninyl)hydroxypropanoic Acid [Antiviral]
AHPA....... American Half-Paso Association [Defunct] (EA)
AHPA....... American Health Planning Association (EA)
AHPA....... American Herbal Products Association (EA)
AHPA....... American Honey Producers Association (EA)
AHPA....... American Horse Protection Association (EA)
AHPA....... Arthritis Health Professions Association (EA)
AHPAA .... Annales. Institut Henri Poincare. Section A. Physique Theorique [A publication]
AHPAT .... Allied Health Professions Admissions Test [Admissions and selection test]
AHPB....... Association for Humanistic Psychology in Britain (EAIO)
AHPBA ..... Annales. Institut Henri Poincare. Section B. Calcul des Probabilites et Statistique [A publication]
AHPBS..... Bishop Routhier School, High Prairie, Alberta [Library symbol] [National Library of Canada] (BIB)
AHPC....... Aging Health Policy Center [Research center] (RCD)
AHPCS..... American Historical Print Collectors Society (EA)
AHPD....... High Prairie and District Centennial Museum, High Prairie, Alberta [Library symbol] [National Library of Canada] (BIB)
AHPFA5... Annales Homeopathiques Francaises [A publication]
AHPGSMBS ... Amalgamated Hackle Pin Grinders Sick and Mutual Benefit Society [British]
AHPL........ [A] Hardware Programming Language [1971] [Data processing] (CSR)
AHPLBO... Acta Haematologica Polonica [A publication]
AHPM....... High Prairie Municipal Library, Alberta [Library symbol] [National Library of Canada] (NLC)
AHPNAS... Advanced High-Performance Nuclear Attack Submarine
AHPOA..... Anterior Hypothalamus, Preoptic Area [Brain anatomy]
AHPP........ Association of Humanistic Psychology Practitioners (EAIO)
AHPR....... Academy of Hospital Public Relations [Later, Hospital Academy - HA]
AHPRB ..... Advances in High Pressure Research [England] [A publication]
AHPS .... American Helvetia Philatelic Society (EA)
AHPS .... American Historical Philatelic Society [Formerly, AHPS-CWPS] (EA)
AHPS .... Auxiliary Hydraulic Power Supply
AHPSAS ... St. Andrew's School, High Prairie, Alberta [Library symbol] [National Library of Canada] (BIB)
AHPSC...... Airport Handling Procedures Sub-Committee [IATA] (DS)
AHPS-CWPS ... American Historical Philatelic Society - Civil War Philatelic Society [Later, AHPS]
AHQ .... Air Headquarters
AHQ .... Allied Headquarters
AHQ .... Anthrahydroquinone [Organic chemistry]
AHQ .... Area Headquarters (NATG)
AHQ .... Arkansas Historical Quarterly [A publication]
AHQ .... Army Headquarters
AHQ .... Association for Healthcare Quality (EA)
AHQ .... Wahoo, NE [Location identifier] [FAA] (FAAL)
AHR.......... A. H. Robins Co. [Research code symbol]
AHR.......... Ablative Heat Rate (MCD)
AHR.......... Academy of Human Rights
AHR.......... Acceptable Hazard Rate (IEEE)
AHR.......... Active High Resolution (MCD)
AHR.......... Adsorptive Heat Recovery [Chemical engineering]
AHR.......... Afro-Hispanic Review [A publication]
AHR.......... [International] Air Conditioning, Heating, Refrigerating Exposition (ITD)
AHR.......... American Historical Review [A publication]
AHR.......... Americana Hotels & Realty Corp. [NYSE symbol] (SPSG)
A/HR......... Ampere/Hour (MCD)
AHR.......... Anchor (MSA)
AHR.......... Andalusian Horse Registry (EA)
AHR.......... Annual History Review (MCD)
AHR.......... Annual Hospital Report [Program of the Department of Health and Human Services]
AHR.......... Aqueous Homogeneous Reactor
AHR.......... Arabian Horse Registry of America (EA)
AHR.......... Arnhem Resources, Inc. [Vancouver Stock Exchange symbol]
AHR.......... Association for Health Records [Later, AHQ] (EA)
AHR.......... Association for Human Rights
AHR.......... Association of Humanistic Rabbis (EA)
AHR.......... Attitude Hold Roll [Axis] (NASA)

AHR............ Australasian Home Reader [*A publication*] (APTA)
AHR............ Provincial Archives of Alberta, Historical Resource Library [*UTLAS symbol*]
AHRA........ Advanced Helmet Sight Reticle Assembly [*Air Force*] (MCD)
AHRA........ African Human Rights Research Association [*Formerly, African Human Rights Study Group*] (EA)
AHRA........ American Hair Replacement Association [*Inactive*] (EA)
AHRA........ American Healthcare Radiology Administrators (EA)
AHRA........ American Himalayan Rabbit Association (EA)
AHRA........ American Hot Rod Association (EA)
AHRC........ Alister Hardy Research Centre [*Manchester College*] [*British*] (CB)
AHRC........ American Harlequin Rabbit Club (EA)
AHRF........ American Hearing Research Foundation (EA)
AHRF........ Annales Historiques de la Revolution Francaise [*A publication*]
AHRL........ Arctic Health Research Laboratory [*HEW*]
AHRM....... High River Municipal Library, Alberta [*Library symbol*] [*National Library of Canada*] (NLC)
AHRMA.... American Historic Racing Motorcycle Association (EA)
Ahrokhim Hruntozn Resp Mizhvid Temat Zb ... Ahrokhimiia i Hruntoznavstvo Respublikanskii Mizhvidomchyi Tematichnyi Zbirnyk [*A publication*]
Ahrokhimiia Hruntozn ... Ahrokhimiia i Hruntoznavstvo [*A publication*]
AHRP........ Academy on Human Rights and Peace (EA)
AHRRBI.... Australia. Commonwealth Scientific and Industrial Research Organisation. Division of Horticulture. Research Report [*A publication*]
AHRS........ Attitude Heading Reference System (NG)
AHRS........ Automatic Heading Reference System
AHRSJ...... Americans for Human Rights and Social Justice (EA)
AHRTA..... Arhiv za Higijenu Rada i Toksikologiju [*A publication*]
AHRTAG.. Appropriate Health Resources and Technologies Action Group [*London, England*]
AHRTAN.. Arhiv za Higijenu Rada i Toksikologiju [*A publication*]
AHRU........ Americans for Human Rights in Ukraine (EA)
AHRU........ Attitude Heading Reference Unit
AHRU........ Aviation Human Research Unit [*Army*]
AHRW....... Alcohol Health and Research World [*A publication*]
AHS........... Ablative Heat Shield
AHS........... Academy of Health Sciences [*Health Services Command*] [*Fort Sam Houston, TX*] [*Army*]
AHS........... Acute Hospital Syndrome [*Used facetiously to explain the popularity of a West German soap opera*]
AHS........... Agricultural History Society (EA)
AHS........... Aigner Holdings [*Vancouver Stock Exchange symbol*]
AHS........... Airborne Hardware Simulator (MCD)
AHS........... Alternate Health Services
AHS........... American Hanoverian Society (EA)
AHS........... American Harp Society (EA)
AHS........... American Hearing Society [*Later, NAHSA*] (EA)
AHS........... American Heartworm Society (EA)
AHS........... American Helicopter Society (EA)
AHS........... American Hemerocallis Society (EA)
AHS........... American Heritage Society (EA)
AHS........... American Hibiscus Society (EA)
AHS........... American Hiking Society (EA)
AHS........... American Horticultural Society (EA)
AHS........... American Hospital Society
AHS........... American Hosta Society (EA)
AHS........... American Humane Society
AHS........... American Hypnodontic Society (EA)
AHS........... Ammunition Handling System (MCD)
AHS........... Amtrak Historical Society (EA)
AHS........... Annales d'Histoire Sociale [*A publication*]
AHS........... Anno Humanae Salutis [*In the Year of Human Salvation*] [*Latin*]
AHS........... Annual Hull Survey (DS)
AHS........... Antenna Homing System
AHS........... Antiquarian Horological Society (EA)
AHS........... Arab Horse Society (EAIO)
AHS........... Archives Heraldiques Suisses [*A publication*]
AHS........... Arlington Hall Station [*Virginia*] [*Army*] (AABC)
AHS........... Assistant Head of Section (DCTA)
AHS........... Assistant House Surgeon
AHS........... Associated Heat Services [*Energy management contractor*] [*British*]
AHS........... Associated Humane Societies (EA)
AHS........... Association for Humanist Sociology (EA)
AHS........... Association of Hungarian Students in North America [*Defunct*] (EA)
AHS........... At Home Series [*Baseball*]
AHS........... Attack Helicopter Support (MCD)
AHS........... Augustana Historical Society (EA)
AHS........... Australian Hibiscus Society
AHS........... Australian Historical Statistics [*A publication*]
AHS........... Australian Historical Studies [*A publication*] (APTA)
AHS........... Aviation Historical Society (EA)
AHS........... Harding College, Searcy, AR [*OCLC symbol*] (OCLC)
AHS........... International Association of Hydrological Sciences [*See also AISH*] [*British*]
AHSA .... African Heritage Studies Association (EA)

AHSA .... American Hampshire Sheep Association (EA)
AHSA .... American Home Satellite Association (EA)
AHSA .... American Home Sewing Association [*Later, AHSCA*] (EA)
AHSA .... American Horse Shows Association (EA)
AHSA .... American Humor Studies Association (EA)
AHSA .... Association of Hospital Security Administrators
AHSC .... American Home Sewing Council [*Later, AHSCA*] (EA)
AHSC .... American Home Shield Corp. [*NASDAQ symbol*] (NQ)
AHSCA ...... American Home Sewing and Craft Association (EA)
AHSCo ...... Assault Helicopter Support Company [*Air Force*] (AFM)
AHSCP....... Army High School Completion Program (MCD)
AHSE .... Assembly, Handling, and Shipping Equipment
AHSF......... American Hungarian Studies Foundation [*Later, AHF*] (EA)
AHSGR ..... American Historical Society of Germans from Russia (EA)
AHSI .... Advanced Human Systems Institute [*San Jose State University*] [*Research center*] (RCD)
AHSI .... Archivum Historicum Societatis Iesu [*A publication*]
AHSM .... Academy for Health Services Marketing [*Chicago, IL*] (EA)
AHSM .... Alpha Hand and Shoe Monitor [*Radiation detection*]
AHSM .... Antiquarian Horological Society. Monograph [*A publication*]
AHSMA7.. Acta Historica Scientiarum, Naturalium, et Medicinalium [*A publication*]
AHSME .... Annual High School Mathematics Examination [*Educational test*]
AHSN....... Assembly of Hospital Schools of Nursing (EA)
AHSoc ...... Annales d'Histoire Sociale [*A publication*]
AHSPI....... Actions Having Significant Personnel Implications (MCD)
AHSR .... Air Height Surveillance RADAR
AHSR .... Association for Health Services Research (EA)
AHSRC...... Arctic Health Services Research Center [*HEW*]
AHSS........ Association of Home Study Schools [*Later, ACTS*] (EA)
AHSS........ Augusta Huiell Seaman Society (EA)
AHSSOP... Alberta. Historic Sites Service. Occasional Papers [*Canada*] [*A publication*]
AHSSPPE ... Association on Handicapped Student Service Programs in Postsecondary Education (EA)
AHST .... Anchor Handling Salvage Tug (DS)
AHST .... Associated Hosts, Inc. [*NASDAQ symbol*] (NQ)
AHST .... Association of Health Service Treasurers [*British*]
AHST .... Association of Highway Steel Transporters (EA)
AHST .... Attack Helicopter Self Test (MCD)
AHSTC...... Austin-Healey Sports and Touring Club (EA)
AHSUA ..... Acta Histochemica. Supplementband [*A publication*]
AHT........... Acoustic Homing Torpedo
AHT........... AIRCOA Hotel Partnership LP [*AMEX symbol*] (SPSG)
AHT........... Alaska Hydro-Train [*AAR code*]
AHT........... Amchitka, AK [*Location identifier*] [*FAA*] (FAAL)
AHT........... Anchor Handling Tug (DS)
AHT........... Arabian Horse Trust (EA)
AHT........... Assembly History Tag
AHT........... Attack Helicopter Team
AHT........... Average Holding Time [*Telecommunications*] (TEL)
AHTA....... Antigua Hotels and Tourist Association (EY)
AHTAE ..... American Hotel Trade Association Executives (EA)
AHTC....... Association d'Histoire du Theatre du Canada [*Association for Canadian Theatre History - ACTH*]
AHTCB .... Advances in High Temperature Chemistry [*A publication*]
AHTCBH .. Advances in High Temperature Chemistry [*A publication*]
AHTD....... Association of High Tech Distributors (EA)
AHTGG.... Antihuman Thymocyte Gamma Globulin [*Immunochemistry*]
AHTJA...... Archivum Histologicum Japonicum [*A publication*]
AHTN....... Association of Hospital Television Networks (EA)
AHTP .... Aerodynamic Heat Test Plans
AHTR....... Acute Hemolytic Transfusion Reaction [*Medicine*]
AHTRA ..... Advances in Heat Transfer [*A publication*]
AHTS .... American Health Services Corp. [*NASDAQ symbol*] (NQ)
AHTS .... American Health and Temperance Society (EA)
AHTS .... Anchor Handling Tug Supply Vessel (DS)
AHU .... Ahuachapan [*El Salvador*] [*Seismograph station code, US Geological Survey*] (SEIS)
AHU .... Al Hoceima [*Morocco*] [*Airport symbol*] (OAG)
AHU .... Hughenden Public Library, Alberta [*Library symbol*] [*National Library of Canada*] (NLC)
AHUBBJ... Annals of Human Biology [*A publication*]
AHUD .... Austere Heads-Up Display [*Aviation*] (MCD)
AHUM ...... Hussar Municipal Library, Alberta [*Library symbol*] [*National Library of Canada*] (NLC)
A Humor .... American Humor [*A publication*]
AHUNA ..... Archivos de Hospitales Universitarios [*A publication*]
AHUTA ..... Archiwum Hutnictwa [*A publication*]
AHV........... Ad Hanc Vocem [*At This Word*] [*Latin*]
AHV........... Aircraft Handling Vehicle (MCD)
AHV........... Alters- und Hinterlassenen-Versicherung [*Old Age and Dependents Insurance*] [*State insurance company*] [*Liechtenstein*] (EY)
AHVMA .... American Holistic Veterinary Medical Association (EA)
AHVMF .... Archiv des Historischen Vereins von Mainfranken [*A publication*]
AHVN .... American Hospital Video Network [*Satellite television system*]
AHVNR..... Annalen des Historischen Vereins fuer den Niederrhein [*A publication*]

AHVNRh...	Annalen des Historischen Vereins fuer den Niederrhein [*A publication*]
AHVsLund ...	Kungliga Humanistiska Vetenskapssamfundet i Lund. Arsberattelse [*A publication*]
AHVsUppsala ...	Kungliga Humanistiska Vetenskapssamfundet i Uppsala. Arsbok [*A publication*]
AHVUA.....	Archiv des Historischen Vereins von Unterfranken und Aschaffenburg [*A publication*]
AHW	[*The*] Ahnapee & Western Railway Co. [*Formerly, AW*] [*AAR code*]
AHw..........	Akkadisches Handwoerterbuch [*A publication*] (BJA)
AHW	Altona, Hamburg, Wandsbek [*A publication*]
AHW	Atomic Hydrogen Welding
AHWA......	American Hazardous Waste Association (EA)
AH-WC	Associate of Heriot-Watt College, Edinburgh
AHWG	Ad Hoc Working Group [*Army*]
Ahx	Aminohexanoic Acid [*Biochemistry*]
AHX..........	Athens, TX [*Location identifier*] [*FAA*] (FAAL)
AHX..........	Azahypoxanthine [*Biochemistry*]
AHYBB5 ...	Annales d'Hydrobiologie [*A publication*]
AHYD.......	Aromatics Hydrogenation [*Fuel technology*]
AHYM.......	Hythe Municipal Library, Alberta [*Library symbol*] [*National Library of Canada*] (NLC)
AHZ..........	Allgemeine Homoeopathische Zeitung [*A publication*]
AI	Aaland Islands
A & I	Abstracting and Indexing
AI	Accent on Information (EA)
AI	Access/Information [*Information service or system*] (EISS)
A/I	Accident/Incident
A & I	Accident and Indemnity [*Insurance*]
AI	Accident Intelligence [*British police term*]
AI	Accidental Injury
AI	Accidentally Incurred
AI	ACCION International (EA)
AI	Accrued Interest [*Investment term*]
AI	Accumulated Interest [*Banking*]
AI	Acquisition Institute [*Defunct*] (EA)
AI	Acta Iranica [*A publication*]
AI	Action Item (NASA)
AI	Active Ingredient
AI	Activity Index
AI	Actuator/Indicator
AI	Ad Interim [*In the Meantime*] [*Latin*] (EY)
AI	Adas [*or Adath*] Israel (BJA)
AI	Address Incomplete [*Telecommunications*] (TEL)
AI	Adjustment Inventory [*Psychology*]
AI	Administrative Instructions
AI	Admiralty Instruction [*A publication*] (DLA)
AI	Admiralty Islands
AI	Advocacy Institute (EA)
AI	Aeronautica Industrial SA [*Spain*] [*ICAO aircraft manufacturer identifier*] (ICAO)
AI	Aerospace Intelligence [*A publication*]
AI	Africa Italiana [*A publication*]
AI	Afrique Industrie [*A publication*]
AI	After Image [*Psychology*]
AI	Aged Individual [*Title XVI*] [*Social Security Administration*] (OICC)
AI	Aged Intact Animal [*Endocrinology*]
AI	Agenda Item (MCD)
AI	Agricultural Index
A & I	Agricultural and Industrial [*In a college name*]
AI	Agudath Israel [*Union of Israel*] [*World organization of Orthodox Jews*]
AI	Air India [*ICAO designator*] (FAAC)
AI	Air Injection [*Automotive engineering*]
AI	Air Inspector
AI	Air Installations
AI	Air Intelligence (NVT)
AI	Air Interdiction (MCD)
AI	Airborne Intercept [*RADAR*] [*Air Force*] (AFM)
AI	Aircraft Identification (AAG)
AI	Aircraft Industry (AAG)
AI	Aircraft Instruments and Aircrew Stations [*NATO*] (NATG)
AI	Aircraft Interceptor (MCD)
AI	Airfield Index
AI	Airship Industries Ltd. [*British*]
AI	Airspeed Indicator (MSA)
AI	Airways Inspector
AI	Alban Institute (EA)
AI	Alianza Interamericana (EA)
AI	All Iron
AI	Allergy and Immunology [*Medical specialty*] (DHSM)
AI	Alpines International (EA)
A & I	Alteration and Improvement Program [*Navy*]
A & I	Alteration and Inspection
AI	Altesse Imperiale [*Imperial Highness*] [*French*]
AI	Altimeter Indicator (MCD)
AI	Altitude Indicator (MCD)
AI	Altitude Indoctrination (MCD)
AI	Altrusa International (EA)

AI	Amcot, Incorporated (EA)
AI	America Indigena [*A publication*]
AI	American Imago [*A publication*]
AI	American Indian
AI	American Institute
AI	American Israelite (BJA)
AI	Amity International (EAIO)
AI	Amnesty International [*London, England*] (EAIO)
AI	Amorphous Inclusion [*Cytology*]
AI	Amplifier Input
AI	Ancient India [*A publication*]
AI	Angiogenesis Inhibitor [*Physiology*]
AI	Angle Iron [*Freight*]
AI	Anglo-Indian [*Language, etc.*]
AI	Anglo-Irish [*Language, etc.*]
AI	Anglo-Israelism [*or Anglo-Israelite*]
AI	Anguilla [*ANSI two-letter standard code*] (CNC)
AI	Annals of Iowa [*A publication*]
AI	Anno Inventionis [*In the Year of the Discovery*] [*Latin*]
AI	Antecedent Index (NOAA)
AI	Antenna Impedance
AI	Anthracite Institute [*Absorbed by PCMA*]
AI	Anti-Icing [*Technical drawings*]
AI	Anxiety Index [*Psychology*]
AI	Aortic Incompetence [*or Insufficiency*] [*Medicine*]
AI	Applications and Industry (MCD)
AI	Appraisal Institute (EA)
AI	Appreciation Index [*Television ratings*] [*British*]
AI	Aprovecho Institute (EA)
AI	Aptitude Index
AI	Archives Israelites de France [*Paris*] [*A publication*]
AI	Arctic Institute
AI	Area Inspector [*British railroad term*]
AI	Arica Institute (EA)
AI	Army Intelligence
AI	Arrival Approved Request for IFR [*Instrument Flight Rules*] Flight [*Aviation*] (FAAC)
AI	Arrow Automotive Industries, Inc. [*AMEX symbol*] (SPSG)
AI	Ars Islamica [*A publication*]
AI	Art International [*A publication*]
AI	Articulation Index
AI	Artificial Insemination [*Medicine*]
AI	Artificial Intelligence
AI	Artificial Intelligence [*Elsevier Book Series*] [*A publication*]
AI	Arts International (EA)
AI	Asbestos Institute (EA)
AI	Aslib Information [*A publication*]
AI	Asphalt Institute (EA)
AI	Assignment Instructions
AI	Assistance and Instructions (MCD)
AI	Assistant Inspector (DCTA)
AI	Assistant Instructor
AI	Association Institute (EA)
AI	Assurex International (EA)
AI	Astrologers International [*Defunct*] (EA)
AI	Atherogenic Index [*Medicine*]
AI	Athletic Institute (EA)
AI	Atomics International (NRCH)
AI	Attenuation Index
AI	Attitude Indicator [*NASA*] (KSC)
AI	Auditory Induction
AI	Australian Independent
AI	Australian Internationals (EA)
AI	Australian Investor [*A publication*] (ADA)
AI	Austrian Institute [*Later, ACI*] (EA)
AI	Authority for Issue Indicator (AFIT)
AI	Authorized Inspector
AI	Autographics International (EA)
AI	Automatic Input [*Data processing*] (BUR)
AI	Automation Institute (MCD)
AI	Automotive Industries [*A publication*]
AI	Avian Influenza
AI	Avionic Instrument (MCD)
AI	Axioincisal [*Dentistry*]
AI	Azimuth Indicator
ai-----	Indochina [*MARC geographic area code*] [*Library of Congress*] (LCCP)
AI	Inherent Availability
AI	Interpreter, Second Class [*British*]
AI	Irricana Municipal Library, Alberta [*Library symbol*] [*National Library of Canada*] (NLC)
AI	L'Avenir Illustre [*Casablanca*] [*A publication*]
3AI	Affiliated Advertising Agencies International (EA)
AIA	Academy of Irish Art
AIA	Accuracy in Academia
AIA	Acupuncture International Association (EA)
AIA	Advise If Able [*Aviation*] (FAAC)
AIA	Aerialift Industries Association (EA)
AIA	Aerospace Industries Association of America (EA)
AIA	Aestheticians International Association (EA)
AIA	Aging in America (EA)

AIA .... Agudath Israel of America (EA)
AIA .... Airborne Integration Area (MCD)
AIA .... Allergy Information Association [Canada]
AIA .... Alliance [Nebraska] [Airport symbol] (OAG)
AIA .... Allylisopropylacetamide [Biochemistry]
AIA .... American Imagery Association (EA)
AIA .... American Importers Association [Later, AAEI]
AIA .... American Institute of Architects (EA)
AIA .... American Insurance Association [New York, NY] (EA)
AIA .... American International Academy [Defunct] (EA)
AIA .... American International Association for Economic and Social
                 Development [Defunct] (EA)
AIA ...... American Inventors Association
AIA .... Americans for International Aid (EA)
AIA .... Amylase Inhibitor Activity [Food technology]
AIA .... Anglo-Irish Agreement [1985]
AIA .... Anguilla [ANSI three-letter standard code] (CNC)
AIa .... Annals of Iowa [A publication]
AIA .... Anthracite Industry Association (EA)
AIA .... Anti-Icing Additive (NATG)
AIA .... Anti-Inflation Act [Canada]
AIA .... Anti-Intrusion Alarm
AIA .... Anything Invented Anywhere [As opposed to NIH, Not
                 Invented Here, an acronym indicating refusal to accept
                 foreign technology]
AIA .... Apiary Inspectors of America (EA)
AIA .... Appliance Industry Association [Australia]
AIA .... Archaeological Institute of America (EA)
AIA .... Archivo Ibero-Americano [Madrid] [A publication]
AIA .... Argentine Interplanetary Association
AIA .... Argentine Island [Antarctica] [Seismograph station code, US
                 Geological Survey] (SEIS)
AIA .... Argentine Island [Antarctica] [Geomagnetic observatory code]
AIA .... Army Information Architecture
AIA .... Army Institute of Administration (MCD)
AIA .... Army Intelligence Agency
AIA .... Art in America [A publication]
AIA .... Artificially Induced Aurora
AIA .... Asbestos International Association [London, England] (EAIO)
AIA .... Assistant Inspector Armourer [British and Canadian] [World
                 War II]
AIA .... Associate in Arts (ROG)
AIA .... Associate of the Institute of Actuaries [British]
AIA .... Association of Immigration Attorneys (EA)
AIA .... Association of Indians in America (EA)
AIA .... Association of Industrial Advertisers [Later, B/PAA] (EA)
AIA .... Association of Industrial Archaeology (EAIO)
AIA .... Association of Insolvency Accountants [Chicago, IL] (EA)
AIA .... Association of Insurance Advertisers [Defunct] (EA)
AIA .... Association of Insurance Attorneys [Later, ADTA] (EA)
AIA .... Association of International Accountants [Bedford,
                 England] (EAIO)
AIA .... Association Internationale d'Allergologie [International
                 Association of Allergology]
AIA .... Association Internationale des Arbitres de Water Polo
                 [International Association of Water Polo Referees -
                 IAWPR] (EAIO)
AIA .... Athletes in Action (EA)
AIA .... Authors Institute of America (EA)
AIA .... Auto Internacional Association (EA)
AIA .... Automated Image Analysis [Instrumentation]
AIA .... Automated Imaging Association (EA)
AIA .... Automobile Importers of America [Later, AIAM] (EA)
AIA .... Automotive Industries Association of Canada
AIA .... Automotive Industry Authority [Australia]
AIA .... Office of International Aviation Affairs [FAA] (FAAC)
AIAA .... Aerospace [formerly, Aircraft] Industries Association of
                 America (MCD)
AIAA .... American Industrial Arts Association (EA)
AIAA .... American Institute of Aeronautics and Astronautics (EA)
AIA/A........ Archaeology. Archaeological Institute of America [A
                 publication]
AIAA .... Associate of the Institute of Affiliate Accountants [Australia]
AIAA .... Association of International Advertising Agencies (EA)
AIAA Bull ... AIAA [American Institute of Aeronautics and Astronautics]
                 Bulletin [A publication]
AIAADR.... Anales. Instituto Nacional de Investigaciones Agrarias. Serie
                 Agricola [A publication]
AIAA J ...... AIAA [American Institute of Aeronautics and Astronautics]
                 Journal [A publication]
AIAA Journal ... American Institute of Aeronautics and Astronautics. Journal
                 [A publication]
AIAAM ..... Advanced Interceptor Air-to-Air Missile (MCD)
AIAA Monogr ... AIAA [American Institute of Aeronautics and Astronautics]
                 Monographs [A publication]
AIAA Pap ... AIAA [American Institute of Aeronautics and Astronautics]
                 Paper [A publication]
AIAA Stud J ... AIAA [American Institute of Aeronautics and Astronautics]
                 Student Journal [A publication]
AIAA-TIS ... Technical Information Service - of American Institute of
                 Aeronautics and Astronautics (EA)

AIAB......... Associate of the International Association of Book-
                 Keepers (DCTA)
AIAC......... Associate of the Institute of Company Accountants [British]
AIAC......... Association Internationale des Aeroports Civils [International
                 Civil Airports Association - ICAA] (EAIO)
AIAC......... Associazione Internazionale di Archeologia Classica
                 [International Association for Classical Archaeology -
                 IACA] (EAIO)
AIAD .... Acronyms, Initialisms, and Abbreviations Dictionary
                 [Formerly, AID] [A publication]
AIADA ...... American International Automobile Dealers Association (EA)
AIADAX.... Annals. Indian Academy of Medical Sciences [A publication]
AIADMK .. All-India Anna Dravida Munnetra Kazhagam [Political party]
                 [Tamil Nadu]
AIAE......... Associate of the Institute of Automobile Engineers
                 [British] (MCD)
AIAE......... Australian Institute of Art Education
AIAEA2 .... Archivio Italiano di Anatomia e di Embriologia [A publication]
AIAEE....... Association for International Agricultural and Extension
                 Education (EA)
AIAF .... American Institute of Architects Foundation (EA)
AIAG .... Association Internationale des Assureurs Contre la Grele
                 [International Association of Hail Insurers]
AIAG .... Automotive Industry Action Group (EA)
AIAgrE ...... Associate of the Institution of Agricultural Engineers
                 [British] (DBQ)
AIAHAB ... Anales. Instituto Nacional de Antropologia e Historia [A
                 publication]
AIAI.......... AIA Industries, Inc. [NASDAQ symbol] (NQ)
AIAI.......... American Indian Archaeological Institute (EA)
AIAIAE ..... Archivio Italiano di Anatomia e Istologia Patologica [A
                 publication]
AIAIS .... American In-Vitro Allergy/Immunology Society (EA)
AIA J .... AIA [American Institute of Architects] Journal [A publication]
AIA Jnl ...... AIA [American Institute of Architects] Journal [A publication]
AIAK .... Akten des Internationalen Amerikanisten-Kongresses [A
                 publication]
AIAL......... American Indian Assistance League (OICC)
AIAL......... Annales. Institut Archeologique du Luxembourg [A
                 publication]
AIAL......... Associate Member of the International Institute of Arts and
                 Letters
AIAL......... Association of International Institute of Arts and Letters
AIA Lux..... Annales. Institut Archeologique du Luxembourg [A
                 publication]
AIAM .... Association of International Automobile Manufacturers (EA)
AIA/NA..... Asbestos Information Association/North America (EA)
AIANAT.... Arctic Institute of North America. Annual Report [A
                 publication]
AIANNA ... American Indian/Alaska Native Nurses Association (EA)
AIAOS....... Academic Instructor and Allied Officer School
                 [Military] (AFM)
AIAP......... Army's Incentive Awards Program (RDA)
AIAP......... Association Internationale des Arts Plastiques [International
                 Association of Art - IAA] (EAIO)
AIAPN...... Australian Institute of Air Pilots and Navigators
AIAQA4 .... Annales. Institut National Agronomique [A publication]
AIAR .... American Institute for Aerological Research (MCD)
AIAR .... American Institute for Archaeological Research (EA)
AIARA...... Archives of Interamerican Rheumatology [A publication]
AI Arb....... Associate of the Institute of Arbitrators [British]
AIARD ...... Association for International Agriculture and Rural
                 Development (EA)
AIAS......... American Institute of Architecture Students (EA)
AIAS......... Anti-Intrusion Alarm Set
AIAS......... Army Institute of Advanced Studies
AIAS......... Associate Surveyor Member of the Incorporated Association of
                 Architects and Surveyors [British]
AIASA...... American Industrial Arts Student Association [Later,
                 TSA] (EA)
AIASAA .... Arctic Institute of North America. Special Publication [A
                 publication]
AIA/SC ..... American Institute of Architects Service Corporation
                 [Information service or system] (IID)
AIAS News ... Australian Institute of Aboriginal Studies. Newsletter [A
                 publication] (APTA)
AIAS Newslett ... AIAS [Australian Institute of Aboriginal Studies]
                 Newsletter [A publication] (APTA)
AIASS .... American-Israel Anti-Smoking Society (EA)
AIAT......... Anti-Inflation Appeal Tribunal [Canada]
AIAT......... Association of the Institute of Asphalt Technology
                 [British] (DBQ)
AIAT......... Attitude-Interest Analysis Test [Psychology]
AIAT......... Auditory Integrative Abilities Test
AIATAD.... Arctic Institute of North America. Technical Paper [A
                 publication]
AIATSC..... All International Air Traffic Switching Centers [FAA] (FAAC)
AIAVA....... Amino(iodoacetamido)valeric Acid [Organic acid]
AIAW .... Association for Intercollegiate Athletics for Women (EA)
AIAX .... Alaska International Air, Inc. [Air carrier designation symbol]

AIB	Academie des Inscriptions et Belles-Lettres. Memoires Presentes par Divers Savants [*A publication*]
AIB	Academy of International Business [*Cleveland, OH*] (EA)
AIB	Accidents Investigation Branch [*Air Force*] [*British*]
AIB	Admiralty Interview Board [*British*]
AIB	Advances in Inorganic Biochemistry [*Elsevier Book Series*] [*A publication*]
AIB	Agency Investigation Board
AIB	Agricultural Information Bulletin
AIB	Aircraft Instrument Bulletin [*Navy*] (NG)
AIB	Allied Intelligence Bureau (ADA)
AIB	Allied Irish Banks ADS [*NYSE symbol*] (SPSG)
AIB	American Institute of Baking (EA)
AIB	American Institute of Banking (EA)
AIB	Aminoisobutyric Acid [*Biochemistry*]
AIB	Anthracite Information Bureau [*Defunct*]
AIB	Anti-Inflation Board
AIB	Aptitude Index Battery [*LIMRA*]
AIB	Arab Information Bank [*Information service or system*] (EISS)
AIB	Arkheologiia i Istoriia Bospora. Sbornik Statei [*A publication*]
AIB	Armored Infantry Battalion
AIB	Army Infantry Board (RDA)
AIB	Assassination Information Bureau [*An association*] (EA)
AIB	Associate of the Institute of Bankers [*British*] (EY)
AIB	Association of Independent Businesses (EAIO)
AIB	Association Internationale de Bibliophile [*International Association of Bibliophiles - IAB*] [*Paris, France*] (EAIO)
AIB	Association Internationale de Bryozoologie [*International Bryozoology Association - IBA*] [*Paris, France*] (EAIO)
AIB	Association of Investment Brokers [*New York, NY*] (EA)
AIB	Athlete Information Bureau [*Canada*]
AIB	Augustana Institute Bulletin [*A publication*]
AIB	Australian Insolvency Bulletin [*A publication*]
AIB	Australian Institute of Biology
AIB	Automatic Intercept Bureau [*Telecommunications*] (TEL)
AIB	Avionics Integration Bench (MCD)
AIB	Community College of Allegheny County, Boyce Campus, Monroeville, PA [*OCLC symbol*] [*Inactive*] (OCLC)
AIBA	Agricultural Information Bank for Asia [*Southeast Asian Regional Center for Graduate Study and Research in Agriculture*] [*Information service or system*] (IID)
AIBA	Air Intercept Battle Analysis
AIBA	Alpha-Aminoisobutyric Acid [*Organic chemistry*]
AIBA	American Industrial Bankers Association [*Later, NCFA*] (EA)
AIBA	Associate of the Institute of Business Administration [*Australia*]
AIBA	Associate of the Institution of Business Agents [*British*] (DBQ)
AIBA	Association of International Border Agencies (EA)
AIBA	Association Internationale de Boxe Amateur [*International Amateur Boxing Association*] (EA)
AIB Boll	Associazione Italiana Biblioteche. Bollettino d'Informazioni [*A publication*]
AIBC	American Irish Bicentennial Committee (EA)
AIBD	American Institute of Building Design (EA)
AIBD	Asia-Pacific Institute for Broadcasting Development (EAIO)
AIBD	Associate of the Institute of British Decorators
AIBD	Association of International Bond Dealers [*Zurich, Switzerland*] (EAIO)
AIBDA	Asociacion Interamericana de Bibliotecarios y Documentalistas Agricolas [*Inter-American Association of Agricultural Librarians and Documentalists*] (EAIO)
AIBDQ	Association of International Bond Dealers Quotation [*Stock exchange term*]
AIBEA	All-India Bank Employees' Association
AIBEF	All-India Bank Employees' Federation
AIBF	Advanced Internally Blown Jet Flag (MCD)
AIBGAD....	Annales. Instituti Biologici [*Tihany*]. Hungaricae Academiae Scientiarum [*A publication*]
AIBI	Association Internationale de la Boulangerie Industrielle [*International Association of the Bread Industry*] (EAIO)
AIBL	Academie des Inscriptions et Belles-Lettres. Comptes Rendus des Seances [*A publication*]
AIBLA	Archives Italiennes de Biologie [*A publication*]
AIBLAS.....	Archives Italiennes de Biologie [*A publication*]
AIBLCr......	Academie des Inscriptions et Belles-Lettres. Comptes Rendus des Seances [*A publication*]
AIBM	Association Internationale des Bibliotheques, Archives, et Centres de Documentation Musicaux [*International Association of Music Libraries, Archives, and Documentation Centres - IAML*] (EAIO)
AIBN	Azobisisobutyronitrile [*Organic chemistry*]
AIBNRM...	American Institute of Bolt, Nut, and Rivet Manufacturers [*Later, Industrial Fasteners Institute*]
AIBOA3	Arquivos. Instituto Biologico [*Sao Paulo*] [*A publication*]
AIBP.........	Anglo-Irish Beef Processors Ltd. [*Northern Ireland*]
AIBP.........	Associate of the Institute of British Photographers
AIBPD.......	Annales. Institut du Petrole (Belgium) [*A publication*]
AIBR.........	Australian Insurance and Banking Record [*A publication*] (APTA)
AIBS	Active Isolation/Balance System [*for aircraft*] (RDA)
AIBS	American Institute of Biological Sciences (EA)

AIBS Bull ..	AIBS [*American Institute of Biological Sciences*] Bulletin [*A publication*]
AIB(Scot)...	Associate of the Institute of Bankers in Scotland (DBQ)
AIBS Newsl ...	AIBS [*American Institute of Biological Sciences*] Newsletter [*A publication*]
AIBVAO....	Arquivos. Instituto de Biologia Vegetal [*Rio De Janeiro*] [*A publication*]
AIC	Academie Internationale de la Ceramique [*International Academy of Ceramics - IAC*] (EAIO)
AIC	Accelerator Information Center [*ORNL*]
AIC	Accretion-Induced Collapse [*Astrophysics*]
AIC	Acoustic Isolation Chamber
AIC	Activity Identification Code [*Navy*]
AIC	Adaptive Inferential Control [*Control technology*]
AIC	Address Information Center [*Memphis, TN*] [*US Postal Service*]
AIC	Adriatic Resources Corporation [*Vancouver Stock Exchange symbol*]
AIC	Advanced Image Compression (MCD)
AIC	Advanced Intelligence Center [*Navy*]
AIC	Advances in Consumer Research Proceedings [*A publication*]
AIC	Aerodynamic-Influence Coefficient
AIC	Aeronautical Information Circular [*A publication*] (APTA)
AIC	Afghanistan Information Center [*Later, ASAP*] (EA)
AIC	Agricultural Improvement Council [*British*]
AIC	Agricultural Institute of Canada
AIC	Air Information Center (NATG)
AIC	Air Information Codification (NATG)
AIC	Air Inlet Controller (MCD)
AIC	Air Intercept [*or Interception*] Control [*or Controller*]
AIC	Air Interception Committee [*Air Ministry*] [*British*]
AIC	Airborne Information Correlation (MCD)
AIC	Aircraft in Commission
AIC	Aircraft Industries Center (AAG)
AIC	Aircraft Industry Conference [*Navy*]
AIC	Aircraft Information Correlator (CAAL)
AIC	Allied Intelligence Committee [*London*]
AIC	Alternative Information Center [*Israeli news organization*]
AIC	American Institute of Chefs [*Later, ACF*]
AIC	American Institute of Chemists (EA)
AIC	American Institute for Conservation of Historic and Artistic Works (EA)
AIC	American Institute of Constructors (EA)
AIC	American Institute of Cooperation (EA)
AIC	American International College [*Springfield, MA*]
AIC	American International Communications Corp. [*Boulder, CO*]
AIC	American Italian Congress (EA)
AIC	Americans for Immigration Control (EA)
AIC	Aminoimidazolecarboxamide [*Also, AICA*] [*Organic chemistry*]
AIC	Ammunition Identification Code
AIC	Anacapa Island [*California*] [*Seismograph station code, US Geological Survey*] (SEIS)
AIC	Apollo Intermediate Chart [*NASA*] (MCD)
AIC	Appraisal Institute of Canada
AIC	Apprenticeship Information Center [*Department of Labor*]
AIC	Aquaculture Information Center [*Department of Agriculture*] [*Information service or system*] (IID)
AIC	Army Industrial College
AIC	Army Intelligence Center
AIC	Art Information Center (EA)
AIC	Art Institute of Chicago
AIC	Arthritis Information Clearinghouse [*Public Health Service*] (EA)
AIC	Asbestos Information Centre Ltd. [*British*] (CB)
AIC	Asociacion Interamericana de Contabilidad [*Interamerican Accounting Association - IAA*] [*Mexico City, Mexico*] (EAIO)
AIC	Asset Investors Corp. [*NYSE symbol*] (SPSG)
AIC	Associate of the Institute of Chemistry [*Later, ARIC*] [*British*]
AIC	Association of Image Consultants (EA)
AIC	Association of Independent Camps (EA)
AIC	Association of Independent Cinemas [*British*]
AIC	Association des Industries des Carrieres [*Federations of Quarrying Industries*] [*Belgium*] (EY)
AIC	Association des Infirmieres Canadiennes [*Canadian Nurses' Association - CNA*]
AIC	Association Internationale des Charites [*International Association of Charities - IAC*] (EAIO)
AIC	Association Internationale des Charites de St. Vincent De Paul [*International Association of Charities of St. Vincent De Paul*] (EAIO)
AIC	Association Internationale des Cordeliers [*International Songwriters' Association - ISA*] (EAIO)
AIC	Association Internationale de la Couleur [*International Color Association*] [*Soesterberg, Netherlands*] (EA)
AIC	Association Internationale de Cybernetique [*International Association for Cybernetics - IAC*] (EAIO)
AIC	Association of Interstate Motor Carriers, Newark NJ [*STAC*]
AIC	Asymmetric Illumination Contrast [*Microscopy*]
AIC	Atlantic Intelligence Center [*Navy*]

AIC .... Attack Information Center (AFM)
AIC .... Automatic Initiation Circuit (IEEE)
AIC .... Automatic Intercept Center [*Bell System*]
AIC .... Automotive Information Council (EA)
AIC .... Awaiting Incoming Continuity [*Telecommunications*] (TEL)
AIC .... Ayer Information Center [*Information service or system*] (IID)
AIC .... Community College of Allegheny County, Pittsburgh, PA [*OCLC symbol*] (OCLC)
AICA .... Alliance of Independent Colleges of Art (EA)
AICA .... American Institute of Commemorative Art (EA)
AICA .... American-International Charolais Association (EA)
AICA .... Aminoimidazolecarboxamide [*Also, AIC*] [*Organic chemistry*]
AICA .... Aminoimidazolecarboxylic Acid [*Organic chemistry*]
AICA .... Anterior Inferior Cerebellar Artery [*Anatomy*]
AICA .... Anterior Inferior Communicating Artery [*Anatomy*]
AICA .... Associate Member of the Commonwealth Institute of Accountants [*British*]
AICA .... Association Internationale pour le Calcul Analogique [*International Association for Analogue Computation*] [*Later, IMACS*]
AICA .... Association Internationale des Critiques d'Art [*International Association of Art Critics*] (EAIO)
AICA .... Associazione degli Industriali delle Conserve Animali [*Meat Products Manufacturers Association*] [*Italy*] (EY)
AICA .... Associazione Italiana per il Calcolo Automatico [*Italian Association for Automatic Data Processing*] (CSR)
AICA .... Automobile Importers Compliance Association (EA)
AICA Bull ... AICA [*Australasian Institute of Cost Accountants*] Bulletin [*A publication*] (APTA)
AICAE .... American Indian Council of Architects and Engineers (EA)
AICAP .... American Institute of Computerized Accounting Professionals (EA)
AICAR .... Aminoimidazolecarboxamide Ribonucleotide [*Also, AICR*] [*Biochemistry*]
AICB .... Association Internationale Contre le Bruit [*International Association Against Noise*] [*ICSU*] (EAIO)
AICBM ...... Anti-Intercontinental Ballistic Missile
AICC .... Action Item Control Card (MCD)
AICC .... All-India Congress Committee
AICC .... American Immigration and Citizenship Conference (EA)
AICC .... American Indian Crafts and Culture [*A publication*]
AICC .... American Indonesian Chamber of Commerce (EA)
AICC .... Asian Indian Chamber of Commerce (EA)
AICC .... Association of Independent Corrugated Converters (EA)
AICC .... Association des Ingenieurs-Conseils du Canada [*Association of Canadian Engineer-Councils*]
AICC .... Association Internationale de Chimie Cerealiere [*International Association for Cereal Chemistry*] [*Also, ICC*]
AICC .... Australian Import Statistics [*Database*]
AICC .... Automatic Interactive Computer Control (MCD)
AICCA .... Australian International Cabin Crew Association
AICCC .... Alarm Industry Committee for Combating Crime [*Defunct*] (EA)
AICCC .... American Institute of Child Care Centers [*Defunct*]
AICCER .... All India Congress Committee. Economic Review [*A publication*]
AICCF .... Association Internationale du Congres des Chemins de Fer [*International Railway Congress Association - IRCA*] (EAIO)
AICCM ...... Australian Institute for the Conservation of Cultural Materials
AICCP .... Association of the Institute for Certification of Computer Professionals (EA)
AICCP .... Association of Interstate Commerce Commission Practitioners (EA)
AICCT .... Association for the Improvement of Community College Teaching (EA)
AICD .... Activation-Induced Cell Death [*Immunology*]
AICD .... Automatic Implantable Cardioverter-Defibrillator [*Cardiology*]
AICE .... American Institute for Character Education [*Later, CEI*] (EA)
AICE .... American Institute of Chemical Engineers [*New York, NY*]
AICE .... American Institute of Consulting Engineers [*Later, ACEC*] (EA)
AICE .... American Institute of Crop Ecology (EA)
AICE .... Associate of the Institute of Civil Engineers [*British*]
AI-CE .... Atomic International - Combustion Engineering
AI Ceram ... Associate of the Institute of Ceramics [*British*]
AICES .... Association of International Courier and Express Services (EAIO)
AICF .... Action Internationale Contre la Faim [*International Action Against Hunger*] [*Paris, France*] (EAIO)
AICF .... America-Israel Cultural Foundation (EA)
AICF .... American Immigration Control Foundation (EA)
AICF .... American Inns of Court Foundation (EA)
AICF .... Autoimmune Complement Fixation [*Immunochemistry*]
AICGS .... American Institute for Contemporary German Studies (EA)
AICHAL..... Annali Italiani di Chirurgia [*A publication*]
AICHDO.. Annals. Institute of Child Health [*Calcutta*] [*A publication*]
AIChE......... American Institute of Chemical Engineers (EA)
AIChE Annu Meet Prepr ... AIChE [*American Institute of Chemical Engineers*] Annual Meeting. Preprints [*A publication*]

AIChE Annu Meet Program Abstr ... AIChE [*American Institute of Chemical Engineers*] Annual Meeting. Program Abstracts [*A publication*]
AIChEJ ..... AIChE [*American Institute of Chemical Engineers*] Journal [*A publication*]
AIChE Journal ... American Institute of Chemical Engineers. Journal [*A publication*]
AIChE Monograph Series ... American Institute of Chemical Engineers. Monograph Series [*A publication*]
AIChE Monogr Ser ... AIChE [*American Institute of Chemical Engineers*] Monograph Series [*A publication*]
AIChE Natl (or Annu) Meet Prepr ... AIChE [*American Institute of Chemical Engineers*] National (or Annual) Meeting. Preprints [*A publication*]
A I Ch E Natl Meet Program Abstr ... American Institute of Chemical Engineers. National Meeting. Program Abstracts [*A publication*]
AIChE Pap ... AIChE [*American Institute of Chemical Engineers*] Papers [*A publication*]
AIChE Symp Ser ... AIChE [*American Institute of Chemical Engineers*] Symposium Series [*A publication*]
AIChE Symp Series ... American Institute of Chemical Engineers. Symposium Series [*A publication*]
Aichi Cancer Cent Res Inst Annu Rep ... Aichi Cancer Center Research Institute. Annual Report [*A publication*]
Aichi Gakuin ... Aichi-Gakuin Daigaku Shigakkai-Shi [*Aichi-Gakuin Journal of Dental Science*] [*A publication*]
Aichi-Gakuin J Dent Sci ... Aichi-Gakuin Journal of Dental Science [*A publication*]
Aichi J Exp Med ... Aichi Journal of Experimental Medicine [*A publication*]
Aichi Univ Educ Res Rep Nat Sci ... Aichi University of Education. Research Report. Natural Sciences [*Japan*] [*A publication*]
AIChor....... Associate of the Benesh Institute of Choreology [*British*] (DBQ)
AICI.......... Apparel Industry Committee on Imports (EA)
AICIA .... Archivio Italiano di Chirurgia [*A publication*]
AICIAO...... Archivio Italiano di Chirurgia [*A publication*]
AICIPP..... America-Israel Council for Israeli-Palestinian Peace (EA)
AICL.......... Association Internationale des Critiques Litteraires [*International Association of Literary Critics*] (EAIO)
AICLC....... American Israeli Civil Liberties Coalition (EA)
AICM .... Association of Independent Colleges of Music (EA)
AICMA...... Association Internationale des Constructeurs de Materiel Aerospatial [*International Association of Aerospace Equipment Manufacturers*]
AICMDM ... Association of Independent Copy Machine Dealers and Manufacturers (EA)
AICMIP .... All-India Coordinated Millet Improvement Programme
AICMR...... Association Internationale des Constructeurs de Materiel Roulant [*International Association of Rolling Stock Builders - IARSB*] (EAIO)
AICO .... Action Information Control Officer [*Navy*]
AICO .... American Insulator Corporation
AICO .... American Investors Corporation [*Austin, TX*] [*NASDAQ symbol*] (NQ)
AICO .... Asociacion Iberoamericana de Camaras de Comercio [*Ibero-American Association of Chambers of Commerce - IAACC*] [*Bogota, Colombia*] (EAIO)
AICP.......... American Institute of Certified Planners (EA)
AICP.......... Anthropological Index to Current Periodicals in the Library of the Royal Anthropological Institute [*A publication*]
AICP......... Army Inventory Control Point
AICP.......... Association of Independent Commercial Producers [*New York, NY*] (EA)
AICP.......... Association of Independent Composers and Performers (EA)
AICP.......... Association Internationale des Circuits Permanents [*Circuits International*] [*Nuremburg, Federal Republic of Germany*] (EAIO)
AICP......... Atomic Incident Control Plan
AICPA .... American Institute of Certified Public Accountants [*New York, NY*] (EA)
AICPA-Prof Stand (CCH) ... American Institute for Certified Public Accountants - Professional Standards (Commerce Clearing House) [*A publication*] (DLA)
AIC/PMG ... Photographic Materials Specialty Group of the American Institute for Conservation of Historic and Artistic Works (EA)
AICPOA.... Advanced Intelligence Center, Pacific Ocean Areas [*Navy*]
AICR......... American Institute for Cancer Research [*Research center*] (RCD)
AICR......... Aminoimidazolecarboxamide Ribonucleotide [*Also, AICAR*] [*Biochemistry*]
AICR......... Association for International Cancer Research (EAIO)
AICRA....... Advances in Inorganic Chemistry and Radiochemistry [*A publication*]
AICRC....... American Indian Culture Research Center (EA)
AI Cr D ...... All India Criminal Decisions [*A publication*] (DLA)
AICRIP...... All-India Coordinated Rice Improvement Program
AICRO ...... Association of Independent Contract Research Organisations [*British*]
AICS.......... Action Item Closeout Sheet (MCD)

AICS......... Adaptive Interference Cancellation System (CAAL)
AICS......... Advanced Imaging Communications System (MCD)
AICS......... Advanced Interior Communication System
AICS......... Air Induction Control System [Air Force]
AICS......... Air Inlet Control System
AICS......... Air Intercept Control School
AICS......... Air Intercept Controller Supervisor (NVT)
AICS......... American Institute of Ceylonese Studies (EA)
AICS......... American International Checkers Society (EA)
AICS......... Amnesty International Canadian Section
AICS......... Anuarul. Institutul de Studii Clasice [A publication]
AICS......... Army Intelligence Center and School (MCD)
AICS......... Assistance for Isolated Children Scheme [Australia]
AICS......... Associate of the Institute of Chartered Shipbrokers [British]
AICS......... Association of Independent Colleges and Schools (EA)
AICS......... Association of Independent Computer Specialists (EAIO)
AICS......... Association of Industrial Colleges and Schools (OICC)
AICS......... Association Internationale du Cinema Scientifique
   [International Scientific Film Association]
AICS......... Automatic Inlet Control System (NG)
AICS......... Automatic Intersection Control System
AICSA....... Australian Intervarsity Choral Societies' Association
AICSC...... Aircraft Integrated Crew Station Concepts (MCD)
AICSTS..... Air Inlet Control System Test Set
AICT......... Association Internationale Contre la Torture [International
   Association Against Torture] [Milan, Italy] (EAIO)
AICT......... Association Internationale des Critiques de Theatre
   [International Association of Theatre Critics]
AICT......... Atlantic Information Centre for Teachers [Defunct] (EA)
AICT......... Automatic Integrated Circuit Tester
AICTA....... Associate of the Imperial College of Tropical Agriculture
   [British]
AICU........ Association of International Colleges and Universities (EA)
AICU........ AUTODIN Interface Control Unit (MCD)
AICUZ....... Air Installation Compatible Use Zoning [Air Force]
AICV........ Armored Infantry Combat Vehicle
AICVS....... Association Internationale Contre la Violence dans le Sport
   [International Association for Non-Violent Sport -
   IANVS] [Monte Carlo, Monaco] (EAIO)
AICW .... Advanced Individual Combat Weapon [Army] (INF)
AICY........ Association for International Children and Youth (EA)
AICYEE .... Association of the International Christian Youth Exchange in
   Europe (EAIO)
AID........... Abbreviated Item Description (NASA)
AID........... Abortion Information Data Bank [of Zero Population Growth,
   Inc.] [Defunct]
AID........... Acceptable Intake Daily [of foods and additives]
AID........... Accident, Incident, Deficiencies (AFM)
AID........... Accident/Injury/Damages (DLA)
AID........... Acquired Immunodeficiency [Also, AIDS, GRID] [Medicine]
AID........... Acquisition Integrated Data Base [Army] (RDA)
AID........... Acronyms and Initialisms Dictionary [Later, AIAD] [A
   publication]
AID........... Action Item Directive (AAG)
AID........... Active Integral Defense (AFM)
AID........... Acute Infectious Disease [Medicine]
AID........... Adriamycin, Ifosfamide, Dacarbazine [Antineoplastic drug
   regimen]
AID........... Adult Information on Drugs [Referral service]
AID........... Advance Information Document (MCD)
AID........... Advanced Integrated Diagnostics (BUR)
AID........... Advanced Ionization Detector
AID........... Advanced Ionization Development (MCD)
AID........... Advertising Investigation Department [British]
AID........... Aeronautical Inspection Directorate [British] (MCD)
AID........... Aerospace Information Digest [A publication]
AID........... Aerospace Information Division [Library of Congress]
AID........... Agency for International Development [State Department]
   [Also, USAID] [US International Development
   Cooperation Agency]
AID........... Agency for International Development, Washington, DC
   [OCLC symbol] (OCLC)
AID........... Aidu [Inawashiro] [Seismograph station code, US Geological
   Survey] [Closed] (SEIS)
AID........... Ailing-In Difficulty
AID........... Air Information Division [Library of Congress] (MCD)
AID........... Air Inlet Damper (NRCH)
AID........... Air Inspection Directorate [British]
AID........... Airborne Intelligent Display (MCD)
AID........... Airline Interline Development
AID........... Airport Information Desk
AID........... Algebraic Interpretive Dialogue [Data processing] (BUR)
AID........... Alliance Internationale de la Distribution par Cable
   [International Alliance for Distribution by Cable] (EAIO)
AID........... American Institute of Interior Designers [Later, ASID]
AID........... American Instructors of the Deaf [Also known as CAID] (EA)
AID........... Americans of Italian Descent (EA)
AID........... Analog Input Differential (MCD)
AID........... Analytical Instrument Development, Inc.
AID........... Anderson, IN [Location identifier] [FAA] (FAAL)
AID........... Apogee Intercept Defense (MCD)

AID........... Applied Information and Documentation [Database
   producer] (IID)
AID........... Area Imaging Device (MCD)
AID........... Argonne Interactive Display
AID........... Army Information Digest
AID........... Army Intelligence Department [British]
AID........... Artificial Insemination by Donor [Medicine]
AID........... Artikkel-Indeks Database [Norwegian Center for Informatics]
   [Information service or system]
AID........... Assistance and Independence for the Disabled [British]
AID........... Associated In-Group Donors
AID........... Associated Independent Distributors [Later, IDA] (EA)
AID........... Association of Institutional Distributors [Later, FOOD] (EA)
AID........... Association for International Development [Defunct] (EA)
AID........... Association Internationale des Debardeurs [International
   Longshoremen's Association - ILA] [Canada]
AID........... Association Internationale des Documentalistes et Techniciens
   de l'Information [International Association of
   Documentalists and Information Officers]
AID........... Association Internationale des Documentaristes [International
   Association of Documentary Filmmakers]
AID........... Associative Interactive Dictionary [for databases] [National
   Library of Medicine]
AID........... Attached Inflatable Decelerator [Aerodynamics]
AID........... Attached Inflatable Detector
AID........... Audit Item Disposition (MCD)
AID........... Auditory Information Display
AID........... Australian Industries Development Association. Bulletin [A
   publication]
AID........... Auto-Interactive Design [Combines operator-executed and
   automatic features] [Data processing]
AID........... Autoimmune Deficiency [or Disease] [Immunology]
AID........... Automatic Implantable Defibrillator [Cardiology]
AID........... Automatic Interaction Detection [or Detector] [Data
   processing]
AID........... Automotive Industry Data [British]
AID........... Avalanche Injection Diode
AIDA........ Air Base Damage Assessment Model (MCD)
AIDA........ American Independent Designers Association (EA)
AIDA........ American Indian Development Association (EA)
AIDA........ American Indicator Digest Average [American Stock Exchange]
AIDA........ American International Dragon Association (EA)
AIDA........ Asociacion Internacional de Derecho de Aguas [International
   Association for Water Law - IAWL] [Spanish] (EAIO)
AIDA........ Associated Independent Dairies of America (EA)
AIDA........ Association Internationale de Defense des Artistes
   [International Association for the Defence of
   Artists] (EAIO)
AIDA........ Association Internationale de la Distribution des Produits
   Alimentaires et des Produits de Grande Consommation
   [International Association for the Distribution of Food
   Products and General Consumer Goods] (EAIO)
AIDA........ Association Internationale de Droit des Assurances
   [International Association for Insurance Law]
   [Belgium] (EAIO)
AIDA........ Associazione Italiana per la Documentazione Avanzata [Italian
   Association for Advanced Documentation] [Information
   service or system] (IID)
AIDA........ Attention-Interest-Desire-Action [Formula] [Marketing]
AIDA........ Automated Inspection of Data
AIDA........ Automatic Instrumented Diving Assembly
AIDA........ Automatic Intruder Detector Alarm [Military] [British]
AIDA........ Automobile Information Disclosure Act [1958]
AIDAC....... Assistance Information and Data Acquisition Center [Navy]
AIDAC....... Association Internationale de Developpement et d'Action
   Communautaires [International Association for
   Community Development] [Marcinelle, Belgium] (EAIO)
Ai Daig Bung R ... Aichi Daigaku Bungaku Ronso [A publication]
AIDAP....... Automatic Inspection, Diagnostic, and Prognostic [System]
   [Army]
AIDAPS .... Automatic Inspection, Diagnostic, and Prognostic System
   [Army]
AIDAS....... Advanced Instrumentation and Data Analysis System
AIDAT....... Automatic Integrated Dynamic Avionics Tester
AIDATS .... Army In-Flight Data Transmission System (MCD)
AIDA-USA ... Association Internationale de Defense des Artistes
   [International Association for the Defense of Artists] -
   USA (EA)
AIDBA....... Association Internationale pour le Developpement des
   Bibliotheques en Afrique [International Association for the
   Development of Libraries in Africa]
AIDC .... AID Corporation [Des Moines, IA] [NASDAQ symbol] (NQ)
AIDC .... Alliance Internationale de la Distribution par Cable
   [International Alliance for Distribution by Cable -
   IADC] (EAIO)
AIDC .... American Industrial Development Council [Later,
   AEDC] (EA)
AIDC .... Association Internationale de Droit Constitutionnel
   [International Association of Constitutional Law -
   IACL] (EAIO)

AIDC (Am Ind Development Council) J ... AIDC (American Industrial Development Council) Journal [*A publication*]

AIDD .... American Institute for Design and Drafting [*Later, ADDA*] (EA)

AIDD .... Association of Insulin-Dependent Diabetics [*Defunct*] (EA)

AIDDDH ... Analysis and Intervention in Developmental Disabilities [*A publication*]

AIDDE ...... AMES Interactive Dynamic Display Editor (MCD)

AIDE .... Action Internationale pour les Droits de l'Enfant [*International Action for the Rights of the Child - IARC*] [*Paris, France*] (EAIO)

AIDE .... Adapted Identification Decision Equipment

AIDE .... Adaptive and Integrated Decision Expeditor (MCD)

AIDE .... Aerospace [*or Aircraft*] Installation Diagnostic Equipment (KSC)

AIDE .... Agence Internationale pour le Developpement [*Paris, France*] (EAIO)

AIDE .... Aide Informatisee pour le Developpement des Entreprises [*Automated Information for Management - AIM*]

AIDE .... Airborne Insertion Display Equipment

AIDE .... Aircraft Installation Diagnostic Equipment (MCD)

AIDE .... Association Internationale des Distributions d'Eau

AIDE .... Automated Image Device Evaluator [*Electronics*]

AIDE .... Automated Integrated Design Engineering (IEEE)

AIDE .... Automatic Integrated Director Equipment

AIDECS .... Automatic Inspection Device for Explosive Charge Shell (AABC)

AIDELF ..... Association Internationale des Demographes de Langue Francaise (EAIO)

AIDES ...... Airborne Infrared Decoy Evaluation System (MCD)

AIDES ...... American Independent Designers and Engineers Society

AIDES ...... Analyst Intelligence Display and Exploitation System

AIDES ...... Automated Image Data Extraction System (MCD)

AIDI .... Annuaire. Institut de Droit International [*A publication*]

AIDI .... Associazione Industrie Dolciarie Italiane [*Confectioners association*] [*Italy*] (EY)

AIDIS .... Asociacion Interamericana de Ingeniera Sanitaria [*Inter-American Assocation of Sanitary and Environmental Engineering*] (EA)

AIDJEX ..... Arctic Ice Dynamics Joint Experiment [*National Science Foundation - Canada*]

AIDL .... Asociacion Interamericana pro Democracia y Libertad [*Interamerican Association for Democracy and Freedom*]

AIDLCM ... Association Internationale pour la Defense des Langues et Cultures Menacees [*International Association for the Defence of Threatened Languages and Cultures*] (EAIO)

AIDLD .... Architects, Interior Designers, Landscape Designers [*British*]

AIDLUPA ... Association Internationale des Docteurs (Lettres et Sciences Humaines) de l'Universite de Paris et des Autres Universites de France [*International Association of Doctors (Letters and Liberal Studies) of the University of Paris and Other Universities of France*] [*Canada*]

AIDMS ...... Applied Information and Data Management Systems Section [*Battelle Memorial Institute*] [*Information service or system*] (IID)

AIDN .... Association Internationale du Droit Nucleaire [*International Nuclear Law Association - INLA*] (EA)

AIDO .... Arab Industrial Development Organization (EA)

AIDOAO ... Association Internationale des Diffuseurs d'Oeuvres d'Art Originales [*International Association of Original Art Diffusors - IAOAD*] (EAIO)

AIDP .... Advanced Institutional Development Program [*Under Title III of the Higher Education Act*]

AIDP .... Advances in Disease Prevention [*A publication*]

AIDP .... Association Internationale de Droit Penal [*International Association of Penal Law*]

AIDPA ...... American Institute of Industrial Engineers. Detroit Chapter. Proceedings of the Annual Conference [*A publication*]

AID/PEP ... Agency for International Development/Private Enterprise Promotion

AIDPM ...... Associate of the Institute of Data Processing Management [*British*] (DCTA)

AIDPR .... Agency for International Development, Procurement Regulations

AIDR .... Aerospace Internal Data Report [*Air Force*] (MCD)

AIDR .... Army Institute of Dental Research (RDA)

AIDRB ...... Army Investigational Drug Review Board (AABC)

AID Res Dev Abstr ... AID [*Agency for International Development*] Research and Development Abstracts [*A publication*]

AIDS .... Abort Inertial Digital System [*NASA*] (KSC)

AIDS .... Abstract Information Digest Service [*Forest Products Research Society*] [*Information service or system*] (IID)

AIDS .... Academy of International Dental Studies (EAIO)

AIDS .... Accident/Incident Data System [*Database*] [*FAA*]

AIDS .... Account Identification and Description Services [*Dun & Bradstreet*] (IID)

AIDS .... Accretive Industrial Development Syndrome [*Real estate phenomenon*]

AIDS .... Acoustic Intelligence Data System [*Navy*]

AIDS .... Acquired Immune Deficiency Syndrome [*Also, AID, GRID*] [*Medicine*]

AIDS .... Action Information Display System

AIDS .... Adaptive Intrusion Data System (MCD)

AIDS .... Administrative Information Data System (AFM)

AIDS .... Advanced Integrated Data System (AFM)

AIDS .... Advanced Integrated Display System [*Military*]

AIDS .... Advanced Interactive Debugging System

AIDS .... Aerospace Intelligence Data System [*IBM Corp.*] (DIT)

AIDS .... Agricultural Information Development Scheme (EAIO)

AIDS .... Agricultural Information and Documentation Section [*Royal Tropical Institute*] [*Netherlands*] [*Information service or system*] (IID)

AIDS .... Air Force Intelligence Data Handling System [*ESD*]

AIDS .... Airborne Integrated Data System

AIDS .... Aircraft Integrated Data System (MCD)

AIDS .... Aircraft Integrated Design System (MCD)

AIDS .... Aircraft Interface Data Summaries (MCD)

AIDS .... Aircraft Intrusion Detection System [*RADAR*]

AIDS .... All Individuals Deserve Support [*Alternative translation of AIDS, Acquired Immune Deficiency Syndrome, used as a slogan by AWARE*]

AIDS .... Almost Ideal Demand System [*Agriculture*]

AIDS .... Amdahl Internally Developed Software

AIDS .... American Institute for Decision Sciences [*Later, DSI*] (EA)

AIDS .... Analyst Intelligence Data System (MCD)

AIDS .... Architectural Interaction Design System

AIDS .... Area Intrusion Detection System (MCD)

AIDS .... Army Inventory Data Systems

AIDS .... Artwork-Interactive Design System (MCD)

AIDS .... Association for Independent Disabled Self-Sufficiency [*British*]

AIDS .... Association of Interior Decor Specialists [*Later, ASCR*]

AIDS .... Attitudinal Information Data System (NVT)

AIDS .... Augmented Ignition Delay Sensor (CAAL)

AIDS .... Automated Identification Division System [*FBI*]

AIDS .... Automated Information Data System

AIDS .... Automated Integrated Debugging System (MCD)

AIDS .... Automated Intelligence Data System [*Air Force*]

AIDS .... Automated Inventory Distribution System

AIDS .... Automatic Illustrated Documentation System [*Information International, Inc.*]

AIDS .... Automatic Integrated Debugging System [*Data processing*] (BUR)

AIDS .... Automation Instrument Data Service [*Computer-based industrial information system*] [*Indata Ltd.*] [*British*]

AIDS .... North Atlantic Institute for Defense Study [*NATO*] (NATG)

AIDSCOM ... Army Information and Data Systems Command

AIDSEARCH ... American International Data Search, Inc. [*Information service or system*] [*Defunct*] (IID)

AIDS Res ... AIDS [*Acquired Immune Deficiency Syndrome*] Research [*A publication*]

AIDS Res Ther ... AIDS [*Acquired Immune Deficiency Syndrome*] Research and Therapy [*A publication*]

AID/TA ..... Agency for International Development, Bureau for Technical Assistance [*Department of State*]

AIDTA .... Associate of the International Dance Teachers' Association [*British*] (DBQ)

AIDUIM ... Association Internationale pour le Developpement des Universites Internationales et Mondiales [*International Association for the Development of International and World Universities - IADIWU*] [*Aulnay-Sous-Bois, France*] (EAIO)

AIDUM ..... Association Internationale pour le Developpement des Universites Internationales et Mondiales [*International Association for the Development of International and World Universities - IADIWU*]

AIDUS .... Automated Input and Document Update Service [*International Data Corp.*]

AIE .... Acceptance Inspection Equipment [*Army*] (AABC)

AIE .... Aiome [*Papua New Guinea*] [*Airport symbol*] (OAG)

AIE .... Airborne Interceptor Equipment

AIE .... Aries Resources [*Vancouver Stock Exchange symbol*]

AIE .... Associate of the Institute of Education [*Australia*]

AIE .... Association Internationale des Entreprises d'Equipement Electrique [*International Association of Electrical Contractors - IAEC*] (EAIO)

AIE .... Association Internationale de l'Etancheite [*International Waterproofing Association - IWA*] (EAIO)

AIE .... Authorized "In Excess"

AIEA .... Agence Internationale de l'Energie Atomique

AIEA .... Archivos. Instituto de Estudios Africanos [*A publication*]

AIEA .... Association Internationale des Etudiants en Agriculture [*International Association of Agriculture Students - IAAS*] (EAIO)

AIEA .... Australian Institute of Engineering Associates

AIEAS ...... Association Internationale des Etudes de l'Asie du Sud-Est [*Paris, France*] (EAIO)

AIEB .... Association Internationale des Etudes Byzantines [*International Association for Byzantine Studies - IABS*] (EAIO)

AIEC .... Advanced Ion Exchange Cellulose [*Analytical biochemistry*]

AIEC .... All-Industry Electronics Conference

AIEC .... American Indian Environmental Council (EA)

AIEC......... American Indian Ethnohistorical Conference [*Later, American Society for Ethnohistory*]   (EA)
AIEC......... Anales. Instituto de Etnografia Americana. Universidad Nacional de Cuyo [*A publication*]
AIEC......... Anuario. Institut de'Estudios Catalans [*A publication*]
AIECA....... Associated Independent Electrical Contractors of America [*Later, IEC*]   (EA)
AIECE....... Association d'Instituts Europeens de Conjoncture Economique [*Association of European Conjuncture Institutes*]   (EAIO)
AIECF ...... American Indian and Eskimo Cultural Foundation [*Defunct*]
AIECM...... Association Internationale d'Etude des Civilisations Mediterraneennes [*International Association of Studies on Mediterranean Civilizations*]   (EAIO)
AIED .... American Institute for Economic Development   (EA)
AI Ed......... Associate in Industrial Education
AIEd .... Associate of the Institute of Education [*Australia*]
AIED .... Association Internationale des Etudiants Dentaires [*International Association of Dental Students - IADS*] [*London, England*]   (EA)
AIEDP...... Asian Institute for Economic Development and Planning
AIEE......... American Institute of Electrical Engineers [*Later, IEEE*]
AIEE......... Associate of the Institute of Electrical Engineers [*British*]
AIEE......... Association des Instituts d'Etudes Europeennes [*Association of Institutes for European Studies*]
AIEE......... Australia's International Engineering Exhibition   (TSPED)
AIEE Proc ... American Institute of Electrical Engineers. Proceedings [*A publication*]
AIEE Trans ... Transactions. American Institute of Electrical Engineers [*A publication*]
AIEF .... Association Internationale pour l'Etude du Foie [*International Association for the Study of the Liver*]   (EAIO)
AIEF .... Association Internationale des Etudes Francaises [*Paris, France*]   (EAIO)
AIEG .... Anales. Instituto de Estudios Gerundenses [*A publication*]
AIEGA...... Association Internationale d'Eutonie Gerda Alexander [*International Association for Gerda Alexander Eutony*] [*Switzerland*]   (EAIO)
AIEGL....... Association Internationale d'Epigraphie Grecque et Latine [*International Association for Greek and Latin Epigraphy*]   (EAIO)
AIEI.......... Association Internationale pour l'Education Integrative [*International Association for Integrative Education - IAIE*]   (EAIO)
AIEID........ Asociacion Internacional de Estudio Integral del Deporte [*International Association of Sport Research*]
AIEJI........ Association Internationale des Educateurs de Jeunes Inadaptes [*International Association of Workers for Troubled Children and Youth*]   (EAIO)
AIEKF ...... Adaptive Iterated Extended Kalman Filtering   (MCD)
AIEL......... Asociacion Internacional de Estructuras Laminares y Espaciales [*International Association for Shell and Spatial Structures*]
AIEL......... Association Internationale d'Epigraphie Latine [*International Association for Latin Epigraphy*]
AIEM .... Anales. Instituto de Estudios Madrilenos [*A publication*]
AIEM .... Associate of the Institute of Executives and Managers [*British*]   (DBQ)
AIEMA...... Association Internationale pour l'Etude de la Mosaique Antique [*International Association for the Study of Ancient Mosaics*]
AIEN .... Anales. Instituto Etnico Nacional, Argentina [*A publication*]
AIENDF .... Atomics International Evaluated Nuclear Data Files   (KSC)
AIEO .... Annales. Institut d'Etudes Occitanes [*A publication*]
AIEO .... Annales. Institut d'Etudes Orientales [*Alger*] [*A publication*]
AIEP......... Asociacion Internacional de Escritores Policiacos [*International Association of Crime Writers*]   (EAIO)
AIEP......... Association Internationale d'Etudes Patristiques [*International Association for Patristic Studies*]   (EAIO)
AIEP......... Association Internationale des Usagers d'Embranchements Particuliers [*International Association of Users of Private Sidings*]
AIEPE ...... Association Internationale des Ecoles Privees Europeennes
AIEQ .... Association Internationale pour l'Etude du Quaternaire [*International Association for the Study of the Quaternary*] [*Canada*]
AIER......... American Institute for Economic Research [*Great Barrington, MA*]   (EA)
AIERE....... Associate of the Institution of Electronic and Radio Engineers [*British*]
AIERI........ Association Internationale des Etudes et Recherches sur l'Information [*International Association of Mass Communications Research*]
AIERS .... Association Internationale pour l'Evaluation du Rendement Scolaire [*International Association for the Valuation of Educational Achievement*]   (EAIO)
AIES .... Accreditation and Institutional Eligibility Staff [*Office of Education*]
AIES .... Artificial Intelligence Expert System
AIES .... Australian Institute of Emergency Services

AIESEC..... Association Internationale des Etudiants en Sciences Economiques et Commerciales [*International Association of Students in Economics and Commerce*] [*Brussels, Belgium*]   (EAIO)
AIESEE..... Association Internationale d'Etudes du Sud-Est Europeen [*International Association of South-East European Studies - IASEES*]   (EAIO)
AIESEP..... Association Internationale des Ecoles Superieures d'Education Physique [*International Association for Physical Education in Higher Education*]   (EAIO)
AIESI......... Association Internationale des Ecoles des Sciences de l'Information [*International Association of Information Sciences Schools*] [*Montreal, PQ*]   (EAIO)
AIESS....... Association Internationale des Ecoles de Service Social [*International Association of Schools of Social Work - IASSW*]   (EA)
AIEST .... Association Internationale d'Experts Scientifiques du Tourisme [*International Association of Scientific Experts in Tourism*]   (EAIO)
AIET......... American International Exhibition for Travel   (ITD)
AIET......... Average Instruction Execution Time [*Computer parameter*]
AIETA...... Airborne Infrared Equipment for Target Analysis
AIETAX .... Annales. Institut Experimental du Tabac de Bergerac [*A publication*]
AIEWROC ... Army Intelligence/Electronic Warfare Reorganization Overwatch Committee   (MCD)
AIExpE...... Associate of the Institute of Explosives Engineers [*British*]   (DBQ)
AIF............ Aerospace Intelligence File   (CINC)
AIF............ Affiliated Inventors Foundation   (EA)
AIF............ Agenzia Internazionale Fides [*News agency*] [*Vatican City*]   (EY)
AIF............ AIFS, Inc. [*AMEX symbol*]   (SPSG)
AIF............ Air Intelligence Force
AIF............ Air Interceptor Fuze
AIF............ Alliance Internationale des Femmes [*International Alliance of Women - IAW*] [*Valetta, Malta*]   (EAIO)
AIF............ Allied Invasion Forces [*World War II*]
AIF............ American Institute of France [*Defunct*]   (EA)
AIF............ American Ireland Fund   (EA)
AIF............ American Issues Forum [*American bicentennial project*]
AIF............ Amphibian Imperial Forces
AIF............ Animal Industry Foundation   (EA)
AIF............ Annales. Institut Francais de Zagreb [*A publication*]
AIF............ Annual Improvement Factor   (MCD)
AIF............ Anti-Invasion Factor [*In bone resorption*]
AIF............ Anzeiger fuer Indogermanische Sprach- und Altertumskunde [*A publication*]
AIF............ Army Industrial Fund
AIF............ Asociacion Internacional de Fomento [*International Development Association*]
AIF............ Association Internationale Futuribles [*Futuribles International*]   (EAIO)
AIF............ Atomic Industrial Forum [*Later, USCEA*]   (EA)
AIF............ Audience Interest Factor
AIF............ Australian Imperial Forces
AIF............ Automated Installation File   (MCD)
AIF............ Automated Intelligence File [*Military*]   (AABC)
AIFA......... Association Internationale Francophone des Aines [*Quebec, PQ*]   (EAIO)
AIFAAF.... Anales. Instituto de Farmacologia Espanola [*A publication*]
AIFAN....... Association Internationale des Femmes d'Affaires Noires [*Black Business Women - International - BBWI*] [*French*]   (EAIO)
AIFB......... American Institute of Financial Brokers   (EA)
AIFC......... American Indemnity Financial Corporation [*NASDAQ symbol*]   (NQ)
AIFCBM ... Annali. Istituto Sperimentale per la Frutticoltura [*A publication*]
AIFCS....... Airborne Interception Fire Control System [*Air Force*]
AIFD......... Alaska Institute for Fisheries Development
AIFD......... American Institute of Floral Designers   (EA)
AIFD......... American Institute of Food Distribution   (EA)
AIFE .... American Institute for Exploration   (EA)
AIFEA ...... Archivos. Instituto de Farmacologia Experimental [*Madrid*] [*A publication*]
AIFEE ...... All-India Federation of Electricity Employees
AIFI.......... Automatic In-Flight Insertion   (NG)
AIFireE ...... Associate of the Institution of Fire Engineers [*British*]
AIFL......... America Israel Friendship League   (EA)
AIFLD....... American Institute for Free Labor Development   (EA)
AIFM........ Association Internationale des Femmes Medicins [*Medical Women's International Association - MWIA*] [*Cologne, Federal Republic of Germany*]   (EAIO)
AIFM........ Automatic Integrating Fluctuation Meter
AIF News... Agricultural, Insecticide, and Fungicide Association. News [*A publication*]
AIFOS ...... Academic Instructor and Foreign Officer School [*Military*]
AIFP .... Activate IFR [*Instrument Flight Rules*] Flight Plan [*Aviation*]   (FAAC)

AIFP .... Association Internationale de la Fonction Publique [*Avignon, France*] (EAIO)
AIFR .... American Institute of Family Relations
AIFRB .... American Institute of Fishery Research Biologists (EA)
AIFS .... Advanced Indirect Fire System
AIFS .... Advanced Instruction Flying School
AIFS .... Advanced Integrated Flight System (MCD)
AIFS .... American Institute for Foreign Study (EA)
AIFS .... Australian Institute of Family Studies
AIFS .... Australian Institute of Forensic Sciences
AIFSA .... American Institutions Food Service Association (EA)
AIFSIA ...... Australian International Simulator Instructors' Association
AIFSSF ...... American Institute for Foreign Study Scholarship Foundation (EA)
AIFST .... Associate of the Institute of Food Science and Technology [*British*] (DBQ)
AIFT .... Ackerman Institute for Family Therapy (EA)
AIFT .... American Institute for Foreign Trade
AIFT .... Audio Input Frequency Tolerance
AIFTA .... Anglo-Irish Free Trade Area [*British*]
AIFTA .... Associate of the Institute of Freight Trades Association (DS)
AIFTDS ..... Airborne Integrated Flight Test Data System [*NASA*]
AIFUA .... Annales. Institut Fourier. Universite de Grenoble [*A publication*]
AIFURC .... Assignment Instructions Were Furnished Your Command [*Military*]
AIFV .... Armored Infantry Fighting Vehicle (NATG)
AIFZAM ... Acta Instituti Forestalis Zvolenensis [*A publication*]
AIG .... Accident Investigation [*Aviation*]
AIG .... Address Indicating Group [*Data processing*]
AIG .... Adjutant Inspector General [*Military*]
AIG .... Air Inspector General (MCD)
AIG .... Air Intelligence Group [*Military*] (MCD)
AIG .... All Inertial Guidance [*Aerospace*] (AAG)
AIG .... Alltransport International Group
AIG .... American Insurance Group [*Commercial firm*]
AIG .... American International Group, Inc. [*NYSE symbol*]
AIG .... Angle of Inner Gimbal
AIG .... Antigo, WI [*Location identifier*] [*FAA*] (FAAL)
AIG .... Architectural Inventory Group [*Association of Canadian Archivists*]
AIG .... Army Inspector General (MCD)
AIG .... Artificial Intelligence Group [*MIT*]
AIG .... Assistant Inspector General [*Military*]
AIG .... Assistant Instructor in Gunnery [*British military*] (DMA)
AIG .... Association Internationale de Geodesie [*International Association of Geodesy*]
AIG .... Australian Institute of Geoscientists
AIGA .... American Institute of Graphic Arts (EA)
AIGA .... Association Internationale de Geomagnetisme et d'Aeronomie [*International Association of Geomagnetism and Aeronomy*]
AIGC .... American Indian Graduate Center (EA)
AIGC .... American Institute of Group Counseling [*Defunct*] (EA)
AIGC .... Annuario. Istituto Giapponese di Cultura in Roma [*A publication*]
AIGCM ..... Associate of the Incorporated Guild of Church Musicians [*British*]
AIGE .... Asociacion Interamericana de Gastroenterologia [*Interamerican Association of Gastroenterology*] [*Guatemala*]
AIGE .... Association for Individually Guided Education (EA)
AIGE .... Astroinertial Guidance Equipment
AIGI .... Association Internationale de Geologie de l'Ingenieur [*International Association of Engineering Geology*]
AIGM .... Association Internationale de Grands Magasins [*International Association of Department Stores - IADS*] (EAIO)
AIGMA ..... Anales. Instituto de Geofisica. Universidad Nacional Autonoma de Mexico [*A publication*]
AIGP .... Association Internationale de la Gestion du Personnel [*International Association of Personnel Administration*] [*Canada*]
AIGPAV .... Atti. Istituto Geologico. Universita di Pavia [*A publication*]
AIGR .... Anuarul. Institutului Geologic al Romaniei [*A publication*]
AIGRIC ..... Assistant Inspector-General, Royal Irish Constabulary (ROG)
AIGS .... Acoustic Intelligence Gathering System [*Military*] (CAAL)
AIGS .... All Inertial Guidance System [*Aerospace*]
AIGS .... Auxiliary Inerting Gas Subsystem [*Nuclear energy*] (NRCH)
AIGSS .... Annual Inert Gas System Survey (DS)
AIH .... Academie Internationale d'Heraldique [*Bridel, Luxembourg*] (EAIO)
AIH .... Agmatine Iminohydrolase [*An enzyme*]
AIH .... Air Over Hydraulic (MCD)
AIH .... All in Hand (ADA)
AIH .... American Institute of Homeopathy (EA)
AIH .... American Institute of Hydrology (EA)
AIH .... Artificial Insemination by Husband [*Medicine*]
AIH .... Asociacion Internacional de Hispanistas [*International Association of Hispanists*] [*Aalst, Belgium*] (EA)
AIH .... Association Internationale d'Hotellerie [*International Hotel Association - IHA*] (EAIO)

AIH .... Association Internationale des Hydrogeologues [*International Association of Hydrogeologists - IAH*]
AIH .... Association Internationale d'Hydrologie Scientifique
AIH .... Aussenhandels-Dienst der Industriekammern und Handelskammern und Wirtschaftsverbande [*Frankfurt Am Main*] [*A publication*]
AIH .... Australian Institute of Health
AIHA .... American Indian Historical Association (EA)
AIHA .... American Industrial Hygiene Association (EA)
AIHA .... American Italian Historical Association (EA)
AIHA .... Associate of the Institute of Hospital Almoners [*British*]
AIHA .... Autoimmune Hemolytic Anemia [*Hematology*]
AIHAA ...... American Industrial Hygiene Association. Journal [*A publication*]
AIHAAP .... American Industrial Hygiene Association. Journal [*A publication*]
AIHADS .... Anales. Instituto Nacional de Investigaciones Agrarias. Serie Higiene y Sanidad Animal [*A publication*]
AIHC .... American Industrial Health Council (EA)
AIHCA ...... American Indian Health Care Association (EA)
AIHCE ...... Association Internationale d'Histoire Contemporaine de l'Europe [*International Association for Contemporary History of Europe*] (EAIO)
AIHE .... Asociacion Interamericana de Hombres de Empresa [*Inter-American Businessmen's Association*]
AIHE .... Association for Innovation in Higher Education (EA)
AIHED ...... American Institute for Human Engineering and Development (EA)
AIHEX ...... Asian International Hardware Exposition (TSPED)
AIHF .... American Indian Heritage Foundation (EA)
AIHI .... Archives Internationales d'Histoire des Idees [*A publication*]
AIHJA .... Association Internationale des Hautes Juridictions Administratives [*International Association of Supreme Administrative Jurisdictions*] (EAIO)
AIHM .... Archivos Iberoamericanos de Historia de la Medicina [*A publication*]
AIHP .... Academie Internationale d'Histoire de la Pharmacie [*International Academy of the History of Pharmacy*] (EAIO)
AIHP .... American Institute of the History of Pharmacy (EA)
AIHR .... African Institute of Human Rights (EAIO)
AIHR .... American Indian Horse Registry (EA)
AIHR .... Association of International Health Researchers (EA)
AIHS .... American Indian Historical Society (EA)
AIHS .... American Irish Historical Society (EA)
AIHS .... Archives Internationales d'Histoire des Sciences [*A publication*]
AIHS .... Aspen Institute for Humanistic Studies (EA)
AIHSA ...... American Insurers Highway Safety Alliance (EA)
AIHSAB .... Archives Internationales d'Histoire des Sciences [*A publication*]
AIHSC ...... Auto Industries Highway Safety Committee [*Later, DSMC*] (EA)
AIHSS .... American Institute for Hollow Structural Sections (EA)
AIHTDH ... Anais. Instituto de Higiene e Medicina Tropical [*A publication*]
AIHV .... Association Internationale pour l'Histoire du Verre [*International Association for the History of Glass*] (EAIO)
AIHX .... Auxiliary Intermediate Heat Exchanger [*Nuclear energy*] (NRCH)
AII .... Acceptance Inspection Instruction
AII .... Acquired Intelligence, Incorporated [*Information service or system*] (IID)
AII .... Aerial Inspection Instrument
AII .... Altex Industries, Incorporated [*AMEX symbol*] (SPSG)
AII .... American Institute, Incorporated (EA)
AII .... American Interprofessional Institute (EA)
AII .... Angiotensin II [*Biochemistry*]
AII .... Anthes Industries, Inc. [*Toronto Stock Exchange symbol*]
AII .... Apollo Implementing Instructions [*NASA*] (KSC)
AII .... Army Intelligence Interpreter
AII .... Automatic Imagery Interpretation
a-ii--- .... India [*MARC geographic area code*] [*Library of Congress*] (LCCP)
AI/I .... Interciencia. Asociacion Interciencia [*Caracas*] [*A publication*]
AIIA .... American Institute for Islamic Affairs (EA)
AIIA .... Associate of the Insurance Institute of America
AIIA .... Association of International Insurance Agents [*Later, Intersure*] (EA)
AIIA .... Atlantic Institute for International Affairs [*Paris, France*] (EA)
AIIA .... Australian Information Industry Association
AIIA .... Australian Institute of International Affairs
AIIB .... Allied Irish Investment Bank
AIIBD2 ..... Anales. Instituto de Investigaciones Marinas de Punta de Betin [*A publication*]
AIIBP .... Association Internationale de l'Industrie des Bouillons et Potages [*International Association of the Manufacture of Soups and Broths*] (EAIO)
AIIC .... American Integrity Corporation [*Philadelphia, PA*] [*NASDAQ symbol*] (NQ)
AIIC .... Apparel Industries Inter-Association Committee [*Defunct*] (EA)
AIIC .... Army Imagery Intelligence Corps

AIIC.......... Associate of the Insurance Institute of Canada
AIIC.......... Association Internationale des Interpretes de Conference [*International Association of Conference Interpreters*] (EAIO)
AIIDAP..... Association Internationale d'Information et de Documentation en Administration Publique [*International Association for Information and Documentation in Public Administration*] (EAIO)
AIIDC....... Authorized Item Identification Data Collaborator Code
AIIDR....... Authorized Item Identification Data Receiver Code
AIIDS....... Authorized Item Identification Data Submitter Code
AIIE.......... American Institute of Industrial Engineers [*Later, IIE*] (EA)
AIIE.......... Anales. Instituto de Investigaciones Esteticas [*A publication*]
AIIEA....... All-India Insurance Employees' Association
AIIE Ind Engng ... American Institute of Industrial Engineers. Industrial Engineering [*A publication*]
AIIE Trans ... AIIE [*American Institute of Industrial Engineers*] Transactions [*A publication*]
AIIE Transactions ... American Institute of Industrial Engineers. Transactions [*A publication*]
AIII.......... Association Internationale d'Irradiation Industrielle [*Association of International Industrial Irradiation*] (EAIO)
AIIJD .... Journal. American Intraocular Implant Society [*A publication*]
AIIM.......... Associate of the Institution of Industrial Managers [*British*] (DCTA)
AIIM.......... Association of Independent Investment Managers (EAIO)
AIIM.......... Association for Information and Image Management (EA)
AIIN .... Annali. Istituto Italiano di Numismatica [*A publication*]
AIIN .... Atti e Memorie. Istituto Italiano di Numismatica [*A publication*]
AI Inf Sc .... Associate of the Institute of Information Scientists [*British*]
AIIP........... Asociacion Internacional de Investigacion para la Paz [*International Peace Research Association*] (EAIO)
AIIP........... Association of Independent Information Professionals (EA)
AIIPA .... Associazione Italiana Industriali Prodotti Alimentari [*Food manufacturers association*] [*Italy*] (EY)
AIIRM....... Association Internationale des Interets Radio-Maritimes
AIIS .... Advanced IR Imaging Seeker (MCD)
AIIS .... American Institute for Imported Steel (EA)
AIIS .... American Institute of Indian Studies (EA)
AIIS .... American Institute for International Steel (EA)
AIIS .... American Institute of Iranian Studies (EA)
AIIS .... American Institute of Islamic Studies (EA)
AIIS .... Annali. Istituto Italiano per gli Studi Storici [*A publication*]
AIISUP...... Association Internationale d'Information Scolaire, Universitaire, et Professionelle [*International Association for Educational and Vocational Information - IAEVI*] (EAIO)
AIJ............ AIL Absorbent Industry [*Vancouver Stock Exchange symbol*]
AIJ............. Ampullary-Isthmic Junction [*Anatomy*]
AIJA.......... Alliance Internationale Jeanne d'Arc [*Saint Joan's International Alliance - SJIA*] (EAIO)
AIJA.......... Association Internationale des Jeunes Avocats [*Young Lawyers' International Association*] (EAIO)
AIJA.......... Australian Institute of Judicial Administration
AIJD......... Association Internationale des Juristes Democrates [*International Association of Democratic Lawyers*]
AIJE .... Association des Industries du Jute Europeennes [*Association of European Jute Industries*]
AIJE .... Association Internationale des Juges des Enfants
AIJE .... Association Internationale des Magistrats de la Jeunesse [*International Association of Youth Magistrates*]
AIJP .... Association Internationale des Journalistes Philateliques [*International Association of Philatelic Journalists*] [*Federal Republic of Germany*]
AIJPA........ Artificial Intelligence Job Performance Aid [*Army*]
AIJPF........ Association Internationale des Journalistes de la Presse Feminine et Familiale [*International Association of Women and Home Page Journalists - IAWHPJ*] (EAIO)
AIJWF....... All-India Jute Textile Workers' Federation
AIK .... Aikawa [*Japan*] [*Seismograph station code, US Geological Survey*] (SEIS)
AIK .... Aiken, SC [*Location identifier*] [*FAA*] (FAAL)
Aik .... Aikens' Vermont Supreme Court Reports [*1825-28*] [*A publication*] (DLA)
AIK .... Assistance-in-Kind [*Funds*]
AIK .... Aviacija i Kosmonavtika [*A publication*]
AIKD .... American Institute of Kitchen Dealers
Aik Dig ...... Aiken's Digest of Alabama Statutes [*A publication*] (DLA)
Aikens' Rep ... Aikens' Vermont Reports [*A publication*] (DLA)
Aikens (VT) ... Aikens' Vermont Reports [*A publication*] (DLA)
AIKI.......... Arden International Kitchens, Incorporated [*Lakeville, MN*] [*NASDAQ symbol*] (NQ)
Aik Rep...... Aikens' Vermont Reports [*A publication*] (DLA)
Aik Stat...... Aiken's Digest of Alabama Statutes [*A publication*] (DLA)
Aik (VT) Rep ... Aikens' Vermont Reports [*A publication*] (DLA)
AIL............ Action Item List (MCD)
AIL............ Adams International Limited
AIL............ Advance Information Letter [*Military*] (AABC)
AIL............ Aeronautical Instruments Laboratory [*Military*]

AIL............ Aerospace Instrumentation Laboratory [*Air Force*] (MCD)
AIL............ Aileron [*Aviation*]
AIL............ Aileron [*Martinique*] [*Seismograph station code, US Geological Survey*] (SEIS)
AIL............ Air Intelligence Liaison [*British*]
AIL............ Airborne Instruments Laboratory [*Mineola, NY*]
AIL............ Aircraft Instrument Laboratory [*Navy*] (AAG)
AIL............ American Institute of Laundering [*Later, IFI*] (EA)
AIL............ American Institute of Leisuretime (EA)
AIL............ American Israeli Lighthouse (EA)
AIL............ Anales. Instituto de Linguistica. Universidad Nacional de Cuyo [*A publication*]
AIL............ Angioimmunoblastic Lymphadenopathy [*Medicine*]
AIL............ Argon Ion LASER
AIL............ Array Interconnection Logic [*Data processing*]
AIL............ Art Institute of Light
AIL............ Artificial Intelligence Laboratory [*Massachusetts Institute of Technology*] [*Research center*] (RCD)
AIL............ Associate of the Institute of Linguists [*British*]
AIL............ Association of International Libraries
AIL............ Association Internationale pour la Lecture (EAIO)
AIL............ Audio Input Level
AIL............ Australian Industrial Law Review [*A publication*] (APTA)
AIL............ Average Inventory Level
AIL............ Aviation Instrument Laboratory [*Navy*]
AIL............ Avionics Integration Laboratories [*NASA*] (NASA)
AILA .... Airborne Instruments Laboratory Approach
AILA .... American Immigration Lawyers Association (EA)
AILA .... American Indian Library Association (EA)
AILA .... American Indian Lore Association (EA)
AILA .... American Institute of Landscape Architects [*Later, ASLA*] (EA)
AILA .... Asociacion de Industriales Latinoamericanos [*Latin American Industrialists Association - LAIA*] [*Montevideo, Uruguay*]
AILA .... Associate of the Institute of Landscape Architects [*British*]
AILA .... Association Internationale de Linguistique Appliquee [*International Association of Applied Linguistics*] (EA)
AILA .... Australian Insurance Law Association
AILAAB .... Archivii Italiani di Laringologia [*A publication*]
AILACT..... Association for Informal Logic and Critical Thinking (EA)
AILAM...... Associate of the Institute of Leisure and Amenity Management [*British*] (DBQ)
AILAS ...... Airborne Integrated Light Avionics System
AILAS ...... Automatic Instrument Landing Approach System [*Aviation*]
AILC .... American Indian Law Center (EA)
AILC .... American Indian Liberation Crusade (EA)
AILC .... American International Law Cases [*1783-1968*] [*A publication*] (DLA)
AILC .... Anales. Instituto de Linguistica. Universidad Nacional de Cuyo [*A publication*]
AILC .... Anales. Instituto de Literaturas Clasicas [*A publication*]
AILC .... Association Internationale de Litterature Comparee [*International Comparative Literature Association*]
AILD .... Angioimmunoblastic Lymphadenopathy with Dysproteinemia [*Medicine*]
AILE .... Arterial Insufficiency of the Lower Extremities [*Medicine*]
AILE .... Association Internationale des Lotteries d'Etat [*International Association of State Lotteries*] [*Montreal, PQ*] (EAIO)
AILI .... American Investors Life [*NASDAQ symbol*] (NQ)
AILM .... Anales. Istituto di Linguistica di Mendoza [*A publication*]
AILN .... Australian International Law News [*A publication*]
AIL/NA .... Association of International Libraries/North America
AILO .... Air Intelligence Liaison Officer [*British*]
AI Loco E... Associate of the Institution of Locomotive Engineers [*British*]
AILP .... ALPNET, Inc. [*NASDAQ symbol*] (NQ)
AILR .... Australian Industrial Law Review [*A publication*] (APTA)
AILS .... Advanced Integrated Landing System
AILS .... Airborne Infrared Live Scanner
AILS .... Angular Intensity Light Scattering [*Physics*]
AILS .... Automatic Instrument Landing System [*Aviation*] (FAAC)
AILSA .... Aerospace Industrial Life Sciences Association [*of Aerospace Medical Association*] (MCD)
AILSA .... American Indian Law Students Association [*Later, NALSA*]
AILSS........ Advanced Integrated Life-Support System
AILX......... Air Illinois, Inc. [*Air carrier designation symbol*]
AIM .... Aboriginal-Islander-Message [*A publication*] (APTA)
AIM .... Abridged Index Medicus [*A publication*]
AIM .... Abstracts of Instructional Materials in Vocational and Technical Education [*ERIC*]
AIM .... Academy for Interscience Methodology (EA)
AIM .... Accelerated Investment Mortgage
AIM .... Access to Information for Medicine [*Allegheny General Hospital, Health Sciences Library*] [*Information service or system*] (IID)
AIM .... Accuracy in Media (EA)
AIM .... Achievement Identification Measure [*Educational test*]
AIM .... Acquisition Information Management Program [*Army*]
AIM .... Acronyms in Moderation [*Term coined by Ralph Slovenko*]
AIM .... Action for Independent Maturity [*Later, AARP*]
AIM .... Active Inert Missile

AIM .... Active Integrated Module
AIM .... ADA Integrated Methodology   (MCD)
AIM .... Adaptive Injection Molding [*Engineering*]
AIM .... ADCOM Intelligence Memorandum   (MCD)
AIM .... Add, Initial, Multiprecision
AIM .... Adhesive Insulation Material
AIM .... Advance Information Memo   (MCD)
AIM .... Advanced Information Management [*Information service or system*]   (IID)
AIM .... Advanced Information Manager [*Fujitsu Ltd.*] [*Japan*]
AIM .... Advanced Intercept Missile
AIM .... Adventures in Movement for the Handicapped   (EA)
AIM .... Aerial Intercept Missile
AIM .... Aerospace Industrial Modernization
AIM .... Aerothermodynamic Integration Model
AIM .... Aesculapius International Medicine   (EA)
AIM .... Africa Inland Mission International   (EAIO)
AIM .... Agency for Industrial Mission [*Canada*]
AIM .... Aid to Improved Marksmanship [*Army training aid*]   (INF)
AIM .... Aid to Incarcerated Mothers   (EA)
AIM .... Aid for International Medicine   (EA)
AIM .... Ailuk [*Marshall Islands*] [*Airport symbol*]   (OAG)
AIM .... AIM Telephones, Inc. [*AMEX symbol*]   (SPSG)
AIM .... Air Intercept Missile   (AFM)
AIM .... Air Isolated Monolithic [*Circuit*]
AIM .... Air-Launched Interceptor Missile   (MCD)
AIM .... Airborne Infrared Mapper
AIM .... Aircraft Inventory Management Group [*Military*]   (AFIT)
AIM .... Airman's Information Manual [*FAA*]
AIM .... Alarm Indicating Monitor
AIM .... Alliance Internationale pour le Merite   (EA)
AIM .... Ambassadors in Mission [*Religious organization*] [*Canada*]
AIM .... American Indian Movement   (EA)
AIM .... American Inkmaker [*A publication*]
AIM .... American Innerspring Manufacturers   (EA)
AIM .... American Institute of Maintenance   (EA)
AIM .... American Institute of Management [*Quincy, MA*]   (EA)
AIM .... American Institute of Musicology   (EA)
AIM .... American Interactive Media, Inc. [*Software manufacturer*]
AIM .... American International Media [*Joint venture of Philips International and PolyGram BV International*]
AIM .... Amputees in Motion   (EA)
AIM .... Amsterdam Interprofessional Market [*Amsterdam stock exchange*] [*Netherlands*]
AIM .... Analog Input Module [*Data processing*]
AIM .... Annali dell'Isturzione Media [*A publication*]
AIM .... Apogee Injection Module [*NASA*]
AIM .... Application Integration Module [*Telecommunications*]   (TSSD)
AIM .... Appraisal Institute. Magazine [*A publication*]
AIM .... Area Interdiction Mine [*Air Force*]   (MCD)
AIM .... Armored-Infantry-Mechanized   (AABC)
AIM .... Army Installation Management
AIM .... Army Integrated Meteorological Systems   (NOAA)
AIM .... Artificial Intelligence in Medicine
AIM .... Asian Institute of Management [*Philippines*]
AIM .... Assembly Instruction Mnemonics [*Data processing*]
AIM .... Assistance in Ministries   (EA)
AIM .... Assistant Industrial Manager [*of Naval District*]   (MUGU)
AIM .... Associate in Industrial Management
AIM .... Associate of the Institution of Metallurgists [*British*]
AIM .... Associated Industries of Massachusetts
AIM .... Associated Information Managers   (EA)
AIM .... Association Europeenne des Industries de Produits de Marque [*European Association of Industries of Branded Products*]   (EAIO)
AIM .... Association of Independent Microdealers [*Later, CMC*]   (EA)
AIM .... Association of Independent Museums [*British*]   (EAIO)
AIM .... Association of Indian Muslims   (EA)
AIM .... Association for Infant Massage   (EA)
AIM .... Association of Information Managers for Financial Institutions [*Chicago, IL*]   (EA)
AIM .... Association for Innovative Marketing   (EA)
AIM .... Association for the Integration of Management [*New York, NY*]   (EA)
AIM .... Association Internationale de la Meunerie [*International Milling Association - IMA*]   (EAIO)
AIM .... Association Internationale du Mohair [*International Mohair Association*]   (EAIO)
AIM .... Association Internationale de la Mutualite [*International Association for Mutual Assistance*] [*Geneva, Switzerland*]   (EAIO)
AIM .... Association Internationale de Mycologie [*International Mycological Association*]   (EAIO)
AIM .... Association of Interracial Marriages
AIM .... Association of Mary Immaculate   (EA)
AIM .... Associative Index Method
AIM .... Astrometric Interferometry Mission [*to determine locations of stars*]   (ECON)
AIM .... Atlantic International Marketing Committee [*Maryland, Virginia, North Carolina, and South Carolina*]

AIM .... Australian Inland Mission
AIM .... Automated Information Management   (NASA)
AIM .... Automated Integrated Manufacturing   (MCD)
AIM .... Automated Intelligent Microscope
AIM .... Automatic Identification Manufacturers   (EA)
AIM .... Automatic Inflation Module
AIM .... Automotive Industrial Motor
AIM .... Automotive Industry Matters [*A publication*]   (ADA)
AIM .... Autonomous Infantry Mortar [*Military*]   (INF)
AIM .... Avalanche-Induced Migration   (MCD)
AIM .... Awaiting Incoming Message [*Telecommunications*]   (TEL)
AIM .... Irvine Municipal Library, Alberta [*Library symbol*] [*National Library of Canada*]   (NLC)
AIMA .... Acoustical and Insulating Materials Association [*Later, ABPA*]   (EA)
AIMA .... American Incense Manufacturers Association   (EA)
AIMA .... American Industrial Music Association   (EA)
AIMA .... American Insured Mortgage Investors [*New York, NY*] [*NASDAQ symbol*]   (NQ)
AIMA .... As Interest May Appear [*Insurance*]
AIMA .... Associate of the Institute of Municipal Administration [*Australia*]
AIMA .... Association Internationale des Musees d'Agriculture [*International Association of Agricultural Museums*]   (EAIO)
AIMA .... Australian Information Management Association
AIMA .... Australian International Movers Association
AIMAA ..... Archivio Italiano delle Malattie dell'Apparato Digerente [*A publication*]
AIMACC... Air Material Command [*later, Air Force Logistics Command*] Compiling [*System*]
AIMACO .. Air Material Command [*Later, Air Force Logistics Command*] [*Air Force*]
AIMACO .. Air Material Computer   (MCD)
AI Mar E .. Associate of the Institute of Marine Engineers [*Great Britain*] [*Australia*]
AIM/ARM ... Abstracts of Instructional Materials/Abstracts of Research Materials
AIMAS...... Academie Internationale de Medecine Aeronautique et Spatiale [*International Academy of Aviation and Space Medicine - IAASM*] [*Montreal, PQ*]   (EA)
AIMAV ..... Association Internationale pour la Recherche et la Diffusion des Methodes Audio-Visuelles et Structuro-Globales [*International Association for Research and Diffusion of Audio-Visual and Structural-Global Methods*]   (EA)
AIMAV ..... International Association for Cross Cultural Communication   (EAIO)
AIMB .... American Institute of Mortgage Brokers [*Washington, DC*]   (EA)
AIMB .... Integrated Resources American Insurance Mortgage Investors [*New York, NY*] [*NASDAQ symbol*]   (NQ)
AIMBE...... Association Internationale de Medecine et de Biologie de l'Environnement [*International Association of Medicine and Biology of Environment - IAMBE*] [*Paris, France*]   (EAIO)
AIMBI....... Associate Member of the Institute of Medical and Biological Illustration [*British*]   (DBQ)
AIMBM..... Associate of the Institute of Municipal Building Management [*British*]   (DBQ)
AIMBW..... American Institute of Men's and Boys' Wear [*Later, MFA*]
AIMC .... American Institute of Medical Climatology   (EA)
AIMC .... Army Installation Management Course
AIMC .... Association of Internal Management Consultants [*East Bloomfield, NY*]   (EA)
AIMC .... Association Internationale pour la Mobilisation de la Creativite [*International Association for the Mobilization of Creativity*] [*Canada*]
AIMC .... Association of Interstate Motor Carriers [*Defunct*]
AIMC .... Associazione Internazionale Mosaicisti Contemporanei [*International Association of Contemporary Mosaicists*]   (EAIO)
AIMC .... Auto-Initiate Manual-Confirm   (CAAL)
AIMCA...... Associate of the Institute of Management Consultants in Australia
AIMCAL ... Association of Industrial Metallizers, Coaters, and Laminators   (EA)
AIMCC...... Audi International Motor Car Club   (EA)
AIMCS...... African International Movement of Catholic Students   (EA)
AIMD .... Aircraft Intermediate Maintenance Department [*Navy*]   (NVT)
AIMDAP... Archives of Internal Medicine [*A publication*]
AIME .... American Institute of Mining, Metallurgical, and Petroleum Engineers   (EA)
AIME .... American Invitational Mathematics Examination [*Educational test*]
AIME .... Associate of the Institute of Marine Engineers [*British*]
AIME .... Associate of the Institute of Mechanical Engineers
AIME .... Associate of the Institute of Mining Engineers
AIME .... Association for Informational Media and Equipment   (EA)
AIME .... Automatic In-Process Microcircuit Evaluation   (MCD)
AIME .... Average Indexed Monthly Earnings [*Social Security Administration*]

AIMEA...... Annals of Internal Medicine [*A publication*]
AIMEA...... Applied Immunoenzymometric Assay [*Clinical chemistry*]
AIMEA...... Association Internationale des Metiers et Enseignements d'Art [*International Association for Crafts and the Teaching of Art*]
AI Mech E ... Associate of the Institution of Mechanical Engineers [*British*]
AIMED .... Association of Independent Mailing Equipment Dealers (EA)
AIMEE...... Associate of the Institution of Mechanical Engineers [*British*]
AIME Proc Annu Miner Symp ... American Institute of Mining, Metallurgical, and Petroleum Engineers. Proceedings. Annual Minerals Symposium [*A publication*]
AIMES...... Association of Independent Medical Equipment Suppliers (EA)
AIMES...... Automated Information and Management Systems (MCD)
AIMES...... Automated Inventory Management Evaluation System (IEEE)
AIMES...... Avionics Integrated Maintenance Expert System (MCD)
AIME Trans ... American Institute of Mining, Metallurgical, and Petroleum Engineers. Transactions [*A publication*]
AIMEVAL ... Airborne Intercept Missile Evaluation (MCD)
AIMF........ American International Music Fund (EA)
AIMF........ Association Internationale des Maires et Responsables des Capitales et Metropoles Partiellement ou Entierement Francophones [*International Association of Mayors Responsible for Capital Cities or Metropolises Partially or Entirely French-Speaking*] (EA)
AIMF........ Audit Information Management-Systems File [*IRS*]
AIMG........ Alliance Imaging, Inc. [*NASDAQ symbol*] (NQ)
AIMH........ Academy of International Military History [*Later, IMA*] (EA)
AIMHA3... Annales Immunologiae Hungaricae [*A publication*]
AIMI........ Airborne Infrared Measurement Instrument
AIMI........ Aircraft Intensively Managed Items
AIMI........ Associacao Internacional de Missoes dos Israelitas [*International Board of Jewish Missions*] (EAIO)
AIMI........ Aviation Intensive Management Items (AABC)
AIMILO.... Army/Industry Materiel Information Liaison Office [*or Officer*]
AIMIS....... Advanced Integrated Modular Instrumentation System (MCD)
AIMIT....... Associate of the Institute of Musical Instrument Technology [*British*] (DBQ)
AIMJA9.... Ain Shams Medical Journal [*A publication*]
AIMK .... Akademija Istorii Material'noj Kul'tury [*A publication*]
AIMLBG ... Annals of Immunology [*A publication*]
AIMLC...... Association of Island Marine Laboratories of the Caribbean (EA)
AIMLS ...... Associate of the Institute of Medical Laboratory Sciences [*British*] (DBQ)
AIMM .... Associate of the Institution of Mining and Metallurgy [*British*]
AIMM .... Association of Importers-Manufacturers for Muzzleloading (EA)
AIMME..... See AIME, for which sometimes used erroneously
AIMMPE.. See AIME, for which sometimes used erroneously
AIMNA ..... Advances in Internal Medicine [*A publication*]
AIMO........ Associazione Italiana Manufatture Ombrelli [*Umbrella manufacturers association*] [*Italy*] (EY)
AIMO........ Audibly Instructed Manufacturing Operations [*Military*]
AIMOSACGP ... Assignment Instructions Will Include MOS [*Military Occupational Specialty*] within Army Career Group (AABC)
AIMP........ Air Intercept Missile Package
AIMP........ Anchored Interplanetary Monitoring Platform
AIMP........ Association of Independent Music Publishers (EA)
AIMP........ Association of International Meeting Planners (EA)
AIMPAP ... Asbestos Inspection and Management Plan Assistance Program [*Environmental Protection Agency*]
AIMPCT ... Annales. Institut Michel Pacha [*A publication*]
AIMPES.... Associazione Italiana Manufatturieri Pelli-Cuoio e Succedanei [*Leather and imitation skins association*] [*Italy*] (EY)
AIMPG...... American Importers Meat Products Group (EA)
AIMR........ Association for the Improvement of the Mississippi River (EA)
AIM/R....... Association of Industry Manufacturers Representatives (EA)
AIMR .... Association for Investment Management and Research (EA)
AIMRA...... Agricultural and Industrial Manufacturers' Representatives Association (EA)
AIMRAX... Anales. Instituto de Medicina Regional [*A publication*]
AIMRT...... American Institute for the Medical Research of Trauma (EA)
AIMS........ Abnormal Involuntary Movement Scale [*Medicine*]
AIMS........ Academic Instructional Measurement System [*Academic achievement and aptitude test*]
AIMS........ Advanced Image Management Software [*Data processing*]
AIMS........ Advanced Imagery Manipulation System
AIMS........ Advanced Impact Management System [*Padding for sportswear*]
AIMS........ Advanced Inertial Measurement System
AIMS........ Advanced Institutional Management Software, Inc. [*Syosset, NY*] [*NASDAQ symbol*] (NQ)
AIMS........ Advanced Integrated Magnetic Anomaly Detection System (MCD)
AIMS........ Advanced Intercontinental Missile System
AIMS........ Agricultural Information and Marketing Services [*Department of Agriculture*] [*Information service or system*] (IID)
AIMS........ Air Infiltration Measurement Service [*National Association of Home Builders National Research Center*]
AIMS........ Air-Launched Intercept Missile Record System

AIMS........ Air Traffic Control RADAR Beacon/Identification Friend or Foe/Mark XII/System
AIMS........ Airborne Identification, Mark XII System
AIMS........ Airborne Identification, Mobile System [*Military*] (NVT)
AIMS........ Airborne Integrated Maintenance System
AIMS........ Aircraft Inflight Monitoring System (MCD)
AIMS........ Aircraft Integrated Munition System (MCD)
AIMS........ Airways Integrating and Monitoring System (MCD)
AIMS........ Allied Indian Metis Society [*Canada*]
AIMS........ Altitude Identification Military System (MCD)
AIMS........ Amalgamated Instrument Makers Society [*A union*] [*British*]
AIMS........ American Institute for Maghrib Studies (EA)
AIMS........ American Institute of Maritime Services
AIMS........ American Institute for Marxist Studies (EA)
AIMS........ American Institute for Mental Studies [*Later, AITSV*] (EA)
AIMS........ American Institute of Merchant Shipping [*Washington, DC*] (EA)
AIMS........ American Institute of Musical Studies (EA)
AIMS........ American International Managers Society
AIMS........ American International Marchigiana Society (EA)
AIMS........ Analysis of Internal Management Systems
AIMS........ Applied Information Management System [*Data processing*] (DIT)
AIMS........ Army Information Management System
AIMS........ Army Insecticide Measuring System (RDA)
AIMS........ Army Integrated Decision Equipment
AIMS........ Army Integrated Meteorological System
AIMS........ Army Integrated Microfilm System
AIMS........ Arson Information Management System [*Developed by National Fire Administration*] [*Emmitsburg, MD*]
AIMS........ Arthritis Impact Measurement Scales [*Medicine*]
AIMS........ Asociacion Internacional de Mercadotecnia Social [*Social Marketing International Association - SMIA*] [*Queretaro, Mexico*] (EAIO)
AIMS........ Assessment, Improvement, and Monitoring System [*School milk programs*]
AIMS........ Assessments for Integration into Mainstream Settings
AIMS........ Associated Iron Moulders of Scotland [*A union*]
AIMS........ Association for Improvements in the Maternity Services (EAIO)
AIMS........ Association of International Marathons and Road Races (EAIO)
AIMS........ Association for International Medical Study (EA)
AIMS........ Association of Irish Musical Societies (EAIO)
AIMS........ Audit Information Management System [*Department of the Treasury*]
AIMS........ Australian Industries Management Services
AIMS........ Automated Industrial Management System
AIMS........ Automated Information and Management System (BUR)
AIMS........ Automated Instructional Management System [*Army*]
AIMS........ Automated Instructional Materials Services [*Developed by the System Development Corp.*] (IID)
AIMS........ Automatic Interference Measurement System (MCD)
AIMS........ Automotive Information Management System [*Computer software*] [*Automotive engineering*]
AIMS........ AVSCOM [*Aviation Systems Command*] Integrated Microfilm Systems [*Army*]
AIMT .... Association for Integrated Manufacturing Technology [*Later, NCS/AIMTECH*] (EA)
AIMT .... Association Internationale de Musees de Transports [*International Association of Transport Museums - IATM*] (EAIO)
AIMTA...... Associate of the Institute of Municipal Treasurers and Accountants [*British*]
AIMTA5.... Anais. Instituto de Medicina Tropical [*Lisbon*] [*A publication*]
AIMTC...... Association Internationale de Medecine Traditionnelle Chinoise [*International Association of Traditional Chinese Medicine*] [*Canada*]
AIM Tech .. Association for Integrated Manufacturing Technology [*Later, NCS/AIMTECH*] (EAAP)
AIM-TWX ... Abridged Index Medicus Accessed by Teletypewriter Exchange Service [*National Library of Medicine*]
AIMU .... American Institute of Marine Underwriters [*New York, NY*] (EA)
AIMVAL... Air Intercept Missile Evaluation (MCD)
AIMVTE ... Abstracts of Instructional Materials in Vocational and Technical Education (OICC)
AIMX .... Aimexico, Inc. [*NASDAQ symbol*] (NQ)
AIMXS...... Aircraft IFF [*Identification, Friend or Foe*] Mark XII System (AABC)
AIN............ Ainahou [*Hawaii*] [*Seismograph station code, US Geological Survey*] (SEIS)
AIN .... Airframe Integrated Nozzle (MCD)
AIN .... Albany International Corp. [*NYSE symbol*] (CTT)
AIN .... Alternative Information Network (EA)
AIN .... American Information Network (EA)
AIN .... American Information Network Ltd. [*Information service or system*] (IID)
AIN .... American Institute of Nutrition (EA)
AIN .... Approved Item Name
AIN .... Assembly Identification Number (NG)

AIN .... Association of Interpretive Naturalists [*Later, NAI*]   (EA)
AIN .... Atlantis Resources Ltd. [*Toronto Stock Exchange symbol*]
AIN .... Atti e Memorie. Istituto Italiano di Numismatica [*A publication*]
AIN .... Auditory Interneuron [*Neurology*]
AIN .... Australian and New Zealand Insurance Reporter [*A publication*]
AIN .... Community College of Allegheny County, Center North, Pittsburgh, PA [*OCLC symbol*]   (OCLC)
AIN .... Innisfail Public Library, Alberta [*Library symbol*] [*National Library of Canada*]   (NLC)
AIN .... Wainwright [*Alaska*] [*Airport symbol*]   (OAG)
AINA .... American Institute of Nautical Archaeology [*Later, INA*]   (EA)
AINA .... American-Israel Numismatic Association   (EA)
AINA .... Arctic Institute of North America   (EA)
AINA .... Associate of the Institute of Naval Architects
AINAH ...... Anales. Instituto Nacional de Antropologia e Historia [*A publication*]
AINARP.... Arctic Institute of North America. Research Paper [*A publication*]
AINBA ...... Asociacion Internacional de Beisbol Amateur [*International Association of Amateur Baseball*]   (EA)
AINBN ...... Association for the Introduction of New Biological Nomenclature [*Kalmthout, Belgium*]   (EAIO)
AINC .... American Income Life Insurance Company [*NASDAQ symbol*]   (NQ)
AINC .... Ministere des Affaires Indiennes et du Nord Canadien [*Department of Indian Affairs and Northern Development*] [*Canada*]
AINCAR.... India. Coffee Board. Research Department. Annual Report [*A publication*]
AINCBS .... Anaesthesia and Intensive Care [*A publication*]
AIND........ Arnold Industries, Inc. [*NASDAQ symbol*]   (NQ)
AInd.......... Art Index [*A publication*]
AINDTN ... Air Induction
A-INF .... Army Infantry Board   (MCD)
AINGA5 .... Anales. Instituto Nacional de Investigaciones Agrarias. Serie General [*A publication*]
A/INL .... Air Inlet [*Automotive engineering*]
AINL .... Association of Immigration and Nationality Lawyers [*Later, AILA*]   (EA)
AINLF .... Association Internationale des Navigants de Langue Francaise [*French*]   (EAIO)
AINM .... Assistant Inspector of Naval Materiel
AINO .... Assistant Inspector of Naval Ordnance
AINP .... Association Internationale des Numismates Professionnels [*International Association of Professional Numismatists - IAPN*] [*Zurich, Switzerland*]   (EAIO)
AINRP....... Approved Item Name Reclassification Program [*DoD*]   (AFIT)
AINS......... Advanced Inertial Navigation System   (MCD)
AINS......... AIN Leasing Corp. [*NASDAQ symbol*]   (NQ)
AINSE .... Argonne Institute of Nuclear Science and Engineering [*AEC*]
AINSE .... Australian Institute of Nuclear Science and Engineering
Ain Shams Med J ... Ain Shams Medical Journal [*A publication*]
Ain Shams Sci Bull ... Ain Shams Science Bulletin [*A publication*]
Ain Shams Univ Fac Agric Bull ... Ain Shams University. Faculty of Agriculture. Bulletin [*A publication*]
Ain Shams Univ Fac Agric Res Bull ... Ain Shams University. Faculty of Agriculture. Research Bulletin [*A publication*]
AINSMAT ... Assistant Inspector of Naval Materiel
A Ins R ... American Insolvency Reports [*A publication*]   (DLA)
AInst .... Annales Institutorum Quae in Urbe Erecta Sunt [*A publication*]
A Inst AM ... Associate of the Institute of Administrative Management [*British*]   (DCTA)
A Inst Anat Univ Hels ... Acta Instituti Anatomici Universitatis Helsinkiensis [*A publication*]
A Inst Anesth ... Acta. Institut d'Anesthesiologie [*A publication*]
AInstBB..... Associate of the Institute of British Bakers   (DBQ)
AInstBCA ... Associate of the Institute of Burial and Cremation Administration [*British*]   (DBQ)
A Inst Comp Stud Cult ... Annals. Institute of Comparative Studies of Culture [*A publication*]
A Inst Et Trav Secur Soc ... Annales. Institut d'Etudes du Travail et de la Securite Sociale [*A publication*]
AInstFF ..... Associate of the Institute of Freight Forwarders [*British*]   (DBQ)
A Inst M .... Associate of the Institute of Marketing [*British*]   (DCTA)
A Inst MSM ... Associate of the Institute of Marketing and Sales Management [*British*]
AInstP....... Associate of the Institute of Physics and the Physical Society [*British*]   (EY)
AInstPI...... Associate of the Institute of Patentees and Inventors [*British*]   (EY)
A Inst PS ... Associate of the Institute of Purchasing and Supply [*British*]   (DCTA)
AInstSMM ... Associate of the Institute of Sales and Marketing Management [*British*]   (DBQ)
AInstTA..... Associate of the Institute of Transport Administration [*British*]   (DBQ)
Ainsw .... Ainsworth's Lexicon [*A publication*]   (DLA)

Ainsworth Lex ... Ainsworth's Latin-English Dictionary [*1837*] [*A publication*]   (DLA)
A Int Criminol ... Annales Internationales de Criminologie [*A publication*]
AINTELG ... Air Intelligence Group [*Military*]   (MCD)
AINTELO ... Air Intelligence Officer [*Air Force*]
AINTM ..... American Institute of Nail and Tack Manufacturers   (EA)
AINTSEC ... Air Intelligence Section [*Army*]
AINV .... Ameribanc Investors Group [*Annandale, VA*] [*NASDAQ symbol*]   (NQ)
A INV .... Anno Inventionis [*In the Year of the Discovery*] [*Latin*] [*Freemasonry*]
AIO .... Academie Internationale Olympique [*International Olympic Academy*] [*Athens, Greece*]   (EAIO)
AIO .... Action Information Organization
AIO .... Activity, Interest, and Opinion [*Factor scores*] [*Marketing*]
AIO .... African Insurance Organization   (EAIO)
AIO .... Air Installation Office
AIO .... Air Intelligence Officer [*Navy*]   (NVT)
AIO .... Air Intelligence Organization   (NATG)
AIO .... Air Intercept Officer   (MCD)
AIO .... Airborne Infrared Observatory [*NASA*]
AIO .... Airborne Interceptor Officer   (MCD)
AIO .... Airborne Ionospheric Observatory   (MCD)
AIO .... Allied Interrogating Organization
AIO .... Allstate Municipal Income Opportunities Trust III [*NYSE symbol*]   (SPSG)
AIO .... American Institute of Organbuilders   (EA)
AIO .... Americans for Indian Opportunity   (EA)
AIO .... Amyloid of Immunoglobulin Origin [*Medicine*]
AI & O ...... Annual Inspection and Overhaul [*Nuclear energy*]   (NRCH)
AIO .... Arakan Independence Organization [*Political party*] [*Burma*]
AIO .... Arecibo Ionospheric Observatory [*Later, National Astronomy and Ionospheric Observatory*] [*Puerto Rico*]
AIO .... Arion Resources, Inc. [*Vancouver Stock Exchange symbol*]
AIO .... Army Inventory Objective   (AABC)
AIO .... Artillery Intelligence Officer [*Army*]
AIO .... Assistant Information Officer   (DCTA)
AIO .... Atlantic, IA [*Location identifier*] [*FAA*]   (FAAL)
a-io--- ...... Indonesia [*a-pt (Portuguese Timor) used in records cataloged before April 1980*] [*MARC geographic area code*] [*Library of Congress*]   (LCCP)
AIOA .... American Iron Ore Association   (EA)
AIOB .... American Institute of Oral Biology   (EA)
AIOB .... Associate of the Institute of Builders [*British*]
AIOB .... Association Internationale pour l'Oceanographie Biologique [*International Association of Biological Oceanography - IABO*]   (EAIO)
AIOC .... Assistant Instrumentation Operations Coordination   (KSC)
AIOC .... Associate of the Institute of Carpenters [*British*]   (DBQ)
AIOCC...... Associate Infantry Officer Career Course [*Army*]
AIOCC...... Association Internationale des Organisateurs de Courses Cyclistes [*International Association of Organizers of Cycle Competitions*] [*Issy-Les-Moulineaux, France*]   (EAIO)
AIOD........ Aorto-Iliac Occlusive Disease [*Medicine*]
AIOD........ Automatic Identified Outward Dialing [*Telecommunications*]
AIOEC....... Association of Iron Ore Exporting Countries
AIOF......... American Israel Opera Foundation   (EA)
AIOIS........ American Intra-Ocular Implant Society [*Later, ASCRS*]   (EA)
AIOK........ Akten des Internationalen Orientalisten-Kongresses [*A publication*]
AIOK of M ... Ancient and Illustrious Order Knights of Malta [*East Canton, OH*]   (EA)
AiolikaG .... Aiolika Grammata [*A publication*]
AION........ Alphabetical Index of Names
AION........ Annali. Istituto Universitario Orientale (Napoli) [*A publication*]
AION-G..... Annali. Istituto Universitario Orientale. Sezione Germanica (Napoli) [*A publication*]
AION-L..... Annali. Istituto Universitario Orientale. Sezione Linguistica (Napoli) [*A publication*]
AION Ling ... Annali. Istituto Universitario Orientale. Sezione Linguistica [*Napoli*] [*A publication*]
AION-O .... Annali. Istituto Universitario Orientale. Sezione Orientale (Napoli) [*A publication*]
AION-R..... Annali. Istituto Universitario Orientale. Sezione Romanza (Napoli) [*A publication*]
AION-S..... Annali. Istituto Universitario Orientale. Sezione Slava (Napoli) [*A publication*]
AION-SG .. Annali. Istituto Universitario Orientale. Sezione Germanica (Napoli) [*A publication*]
AION-SL... Annali. Istituto Universitario Orientale. Sezione Linguistica (Napoli) [*A publication*]
AION-SO .. Annali. Istituto Universitario Orientale. Sezione Orientale (Napoli) [*A publication*]
AION-SR .. Annali. Istituto Universitario Orientale. Sezione Romanza (Napoli) [*A publication*]
AION-SS... Annali. Istituto Universitario Orientale. Sezione Slava (Napoli) [*A publication*]
AIOOD3.... Anuario. Instituto de Orientacion y Asistencia Tecnica del Oeste [*A publication*]
AIOP .... Analog Input/Output Package [*Data processing*]

AIOP .... Association Internationale d'Orientation Professionnelle
AIOPI .... Association of Information Officers in the Pharmaceutical Industry [*British*]
AIORA ...... Archivio Italiano di Otologia, Rinologia, e Laringologia [*A publication*]
AIOSP .... Association Internationale d'Orientation Scolaire et Professionnelle [*International Association for Educational and Vocational Guidance - IAEVG*] (EAIO)
AIOTT .... Action Information Operations Tactical Trainer (ADA)
AIOUAlger ... Annales. Institut Oriental. Universite d'Alger [*A publication*]
AIOW .... Association of Independent Optical Wholesalers [*Later, OLA*]
AIP .... Ablative Insulative Plastic
AIP .... Acceptance Inspection Package (KSC)
AIP .... Acute Intermittent Porphyria [*Medicine*]
AIP .... Advanced Interceptor Propulsion (MCD)
AIP .... Advances in Psychology [*Elsevier Book Series*] [*A publication*]
AIP .... Aeronautical Information Publication [*FAA*] [*A publication*] (APTA)
AIP .... Air Intake Panel
AIP .... Airborne Instrumentation Platform
AIP .... Aldosterone-Induced Protein [*Biochemistry*]
AIP .... Allied Intelligence Publications [*NATO*] (NATG)
AIP .... Alphanumeric Impact Printer
AIP .... Alpine Aviation, Inc. [*Provo, UT*] [*FAA designator*] (FAAC)
AIP .... Alternate Inspection Policy
AIP .... Aluminum Isopropoxide [*or Isopropylate*] [*Organic chemistry*]
AIP .... American Independent Party
AIP .... American Institute of Parliamentarians (EA)
AIP .... American Institute of Physics (EA)
AIP .... American Institute of Planners [*Later, American Planning Association*] (EA)
AIP .... American International Pictures, Inc.
AIP .... American Israeli Paper Mills Ltd. [*AMEX symbol*] (SPSG)
AIP .... Annual Implementation Plan [*Health Planning and Resource Development Act of 1974*]
AIP .... Approval in Principle (NRCH)
AIP .... Army Information Program
AIP .... Arylene Isopropylidene Polymers [*Organic chemistry*]
AIP .... Ascot Investment Corp. [*Toronto Stock Exchange symbol*] [*Vancouver Stock Exchange symbol*]
AIP .... Assault on Illiteracy Program (EA)
AIP .... Associacao Industrial Portuguesa [*Industrial organization*] [*Portugal*] (EY)
AIP .... Associate of the Institute of Physicians [*British*]
AIP .... Associate of the Institute of Physics (ADA)
AIP .... Associate of the Institute of Plumbing [*British*] (DBQ)
AIP .... Association of Independent Producers [*British*]
AIP .... Association Internationale de Papyrologues [*International Association of Papyrologists*] (EAIO)
AIP .... Association Internationale de Pediatrie [*International Pediatric Association - IPA*] [*Paris, France*] (EAIO)
AIP .... Association Internationale de Photobiologie [*International Photobiology Association*] [*Epalinges, Switzerland*] (EA)
AIP .... Association Internationale des Ports [*International Association of Ports and Harbors - IAPH*] [*Tokyo, Japan*] (EAIO)
AIP .... Associazione Italiana Pellicceria [*Furriers association*] [*Italy*] (EY)
AIP .... Australia in Print [*Book distributor*]
AIP .... Automated Immunoprecipitin [*System*] [*Clinical chemistry*]
AIP .... Automated Implementation Plan
AIP .... Automated Information Processing [*Data processing*] (MCD)
AIP .... Automatic Input Processing [*Data processing*] (MCD)
AIP .... Average Instructions per Second [*Data processing*]
AIP .... Avionics Integration Plan [*NASA*] (NASA)
AIP .... Journal. American Planning Association [*A publication*]
AIPA .... American Indian Press Association [*Defunct*] (EA)
AIPA .... American Ionospheric Propagation Association
AIPA .... Association of Importers and Producers of Admixtures (EAIO)
AIPA .... Association Internationale de la Psychologie Adlerienne [*International Association of Adlerian Psychology*]
AIPA .... Association Internationale de Psychologie Appliquee [*International Association of Applied Psychology*]
AIPA .... Australian Institute of Park Administration
AIPA .... Australian Investment Planners Association
AIPAA .... Annales. Institut Pasteur [*Paris*] [*A publication*]
AIPAC .... American Israel Public Affairs Committee (EA)
AIPACX .... Anales. Instituto Nacional de Investigaciones Agrarias. Serie Produccion Animal [*A publication*]
AIPAD ...... Association of International Photography Art Dealers (EA)
AIPBAY .... Archives Internationales de Physiologie et de Biochimie [*A publication*]
AIPBS .... American Institute for Patristic and Byzantine Studies (EA)
AIPC .... All Indian Pueblo Council (EA)
AIPC .... American Institute of Polish Culture (EA)
AIPC .... American Institute for Political Communication
AIPC .... Army Installations Planning Committee (AABC)
AIPC .... Association Internationale des Palais des Congres [*International Association of Congress Centers*] [*Zagreb, Yugoslavia*] (EA)

AIPC .... Association Internationale des Ponts et Charpentes [*International Association for Bridge and Structural Engineering*]
AIPC .... Association Internationale de Prophylaxie de la Cecite [*International Association for the Prevention of Blindness*]
AIPC .... Australian Intellectual Property Cases [*A publication*]
AIPCEE ..... Associations des Industries du Poisson de la CEE [*Association of the Fish Industries of the European Economic Community*]
AIP Conference Proceedings ... American Institute of Physics. Conference Proceedings [*A publication*]
AIP Conf Proc ... AIP [*American Institute of Physics*] Conference Proceedings [*A publication*]
AIP Conf Proc Part Fields Subser ... AIP [*American Institute of Physics*] Conference Proceedings. Particles and Fields Subseries [*A publication*]
AIPCR .... Association Internationale Permanente des Congres de la Route [*Permanent International Association of Road Congresses - PIARC*] (EAIO)
AIPD .... Army Institute for Professional Development (MCD)
AIPD .... Associated Industrial Photographic Dealers [*Defunct*]
AIPDPS ..... Association Internationale de Philosophie du Droit et de Philosophie Sociale [*See also IAPLSP*]
AIPDWF ... All-India Port and Dock Workers' Federation
AIPE .... American Institute of Park Executives [*Later, APRS*] (EA)
AIPE .... American Institute of Plant Engineers (EA)
AIPE .... American Institute for Professional Education (EA)
AIPE .... Associate of the Institution of Production Engineers [*British*]
AIPE .... Association Internationale de la Presse Echiquenne [*International Association of Chess Press*] [*Kerteminde, Denmark*] (EAIO)
AIPEA .... Association Internationale pour l'Etude des Argiles [*International Association for the Study of Clays*] (EAIO)
AIPEDD .... American Institute for the Prevention and Eradication of Dental Disease
AIPELF ..... Association Internationale de Pedagogie Experimentale de Langue Francaise [*International Association of Experimental French Language Education*] [*Canada*]
AIPE Newsl ... AIPE [*American Institute of Plant Engineers*] Newsletter [*A publication*]
AIPEPO .... Association Internationale de Presse pour l'Etude des Problemes d'Outre-Mer [*International Press Association for Studying Overseas Problems*]
AIPet .... Australian Institute of Petroleum
AIPEU .... American Institute on Problems of European Unity [*Later, AFPI*] (EA)
AIPF .... American Indian Projects Foundation [*Defunct*] (EA)
AIPF .... Asociacion Internacional de Planificacion Familiar [*Social Marketing International Association - SMIA*] (EAIO)
AIPG .... American Institute of Professional Geologists (EA)
AIPH .... Agricultural and Industrial Process Heat (MCD)
AIPH .... Association Internationale de Paleontologie Humaine (EAIO)
AIPH .... Association Internationale des Producteurs de l'Horticulture [*International Association of Horticultural Producers*] [*Netherlands*]
AIPH .... International Association of Horticultural Producers [*The Hague, Netherlands*] (EA)
AIPhO .... Annuaire. Institut de Philologie et d'Histoire Orientales [*Bruxelles*] [*A publication*]
AIPhOS ..... Annuaire. Institut de Philologie et d'Histoire Orientales et Slaves [*Bruxelles*] [*A publication*]
AIPI .... Associazione Internazionale dei Professori d'Italiano [*International Association of Teachers of Italian*] (EAIO)
AIP Inf Progm Newsl ... American Institute of Physics. Information Program Newsletter [*A publication*]
AIPJA .... Journal. American Institute of Planners [*A publication*]
AIPL .... Animal Improvement Programs Laboratory [*Formerly, DHIA*] (EA)
AIPLA .... American Intellectual Property Law Association (EA)
AIPLA .... Annales. Institut Pasteur de Lille [*A publication*]
AIPLB .... Australian Intellectual Property Law Bulletin [*A publication*]
AIPLF .... Association Internationale des Parlementaires de Langue Francaise [*International Association of French-Speaking Parliamentarians*] (EAIO)
AIPLU .... American Institute for Property and Liability Underwriters [*Malvern, PA*] (EA)
AIPM .... Associate of the Institute of Personnel Management (ADA)
AIPMI .... Acute Infero-Posterior Myocardial Infarction [*Medicine*]
AIPN .... American International Petroleum Corp. [*New York, NY*] [*NASDAQ symbol*] (NQ)
AIPO .... ASEAN [*Association of South East Asian Nations*] Inter-Parliamentary Organisation
AIPP .... Arctic Islands Pipeline Program [*Canada*]
AIPP .... Army Industrial Preparedness Program
AIPP .... Australian Institute of Professional Photography
AIPP .... Australian Institute for Public Policy
AIPPh .... Association Internationale des Professeurs de Philosophie [*International Association of Teachers of Philosophy*] (EAIO)

AIPPI .... Association Internationale pour la Protection de la Propriete Industrielle [*International Association for the Protection of Industrial Property*] [*Zurich, Switzerland*] (EA)
AIPR........... American Institute of Pacific Relations [*Defunct*]
AIPR........... Applied Imagery Pattern Recognition
AIPR........... Australian Institute of Psychic Research
AIPR........... Automated Information Processing Request (MCD)
AIPS .... Advanced Integrated Propulsion System [*Aerospace*]
AIPS .... Advanced Interactive Presentation System
AIPS .... American Institute of Pathologic Science (EA)
AIPS .... American Institute for Public Service (EA)
AIPS .... Annuaire. Institut de Philologie et d'Histoire Orientales et Slaves [*Bruxelles*] [*A publication*]
AIPS .... Applications Information Processing System (MCD)
AIPS .... Army Information Processing Standards (MCD)
AIPS .... Association Internationale de la Presse Sportive [*International Sport Press Association*] (EAIO)
AIPS .... Association Internationale pour la Prevention du Suicide [*International Association for Suicide Prevention*]
AIPS .... Association Internationale pour le Progres Social
AIPS .... Astronomical Image Processing System
AIPS .... Automated Intelligence Processing System (MCD)
AIPS .... Automatic Indexing and Proofreading System
AIP(SA)..... Australian Institute of Petroleum (South Australian Branch)
AIPSCJ ...... Acta Ichthyologica et Piscatoria [*A publication*]
AIPSO ...... Auto Insurance Plans Services Office [*A rule and rate-making association*]
AIPT .... Assistant Inspector of Physical Training [*Military*] [*British*]
AIPT........... Association for International Practical Training (EA)
AIPTAK .... Archives Internationales de Pharmacodynamie et de Therapie [*A publication*]
AIPTS......... Active Imaging Pointer-Tracker System (MCD)
AIPU .... Arab Inter-Parliamentary Union (EAIO)
AIPUA....... Archivio Italiano di Patologia e Clinica dei Tumori [*A publication*]
AIPUAN.... Archivio Italiano di Patologia e Clinica del Tumori [*A publication*]
AIPULF..... Association Internationale des Presses Universitaires de Langue Francaise [*International Association of French Language University Presses*] [*Canada*]
AIPVAQ.... Arquivos. Instituto de Pesquisas Veterinarias "Desiderio Finamor" [*A publication*]
AIPVCS..... Anales. Instituto Nacional de Investigaciones Agrarias. Serie Produccion Vegetal [*A publication*]
AIQ .... American Indian Quarterly [*A publication*]
AIQ .... Animal Inspection and Quarantine Division [*of ARS, Department of Agriculture*]
a-iq--- .... Iraq [*MARC geographic area code*] [*Library of Congress*] (LCCP)
AIQS......... Associate of the Institute of Quantity Surveyors [*British*]
AIQSA....... Annals of the IQSY [*International Quiet Sun Year*] [*A publication*]
AIR .... AAR Corp. [*NYSE symbol*] (SPSG)
AIR .... Abitibi Resources Ltd. [*Vancouver Stock Exchange symbol*]
AIR .... Accelerated Item Reduction [*Military*]
AIR .... Accountable Indirect Representational Supplement [*British*]
AIR .... Acoustic Intercept Receiver [*Navy*]
AIR .... Action for Industrial Recycling [*An association*]
AIR .... Action of Instant Recording [*Video technology*]
AIR .... Action Item Report (NASA)
AIR .... Acute Insulin Response [*Endocrinology*]
AIR .... ADAM [*Arts, Drama, Architecture, Music*] International Review [*A publication*]
AIR .... Adaptive Intercommunication Requirement (NASA)
AIR .... Additional Information Request (MCD)
AIR .... Aeronautical [*or Aerospace*] Information Report (MCD)
AIR .... After Initial Release (MCD)
AIR .... Air et Cosmos. Hebdomadaire de l'Actualite Aerospatiale et des Techniques Avancees [*A publication*]
AIR .... Air Force Comptroller [*A publication*]
AIR .... Air Inflatable Retarder [*for bombs*] (MCD)
AIR .... Air Injection Reactor
AIR .... Air Intercept Rocket (IEEE)
AIR .... Airborne Interceptor RADAR
AIR .... Airborne Interceptor Rocket (AFM)
AIR .... Aircraft Incident Report [*Navy*] (NG)
AIR .... Aircraft Inspections and Repair
AIR .... Aircraft Inventory Record (NVT)
AIR .... Aircraft Recovery (CINC)
AIR .... Airline Industrial Relations Conference (EA)
AIR .... Airworthiness
AIR .... All India Law Reporter [*Usually followed by a province abbreviation, [as AIR All., for Allahabad, Bom. for Bombay, Dacca for Dacca, HP for Himachal Pradesh, Hyd. for Hyderabad, etc.]*] [*A publication*] (DLA)
AIR .... All-India Radio
AIR .... All India Reporter [*A publication*]
AIR .... Alliance of Independent Retailers (EAIO)
AIR .... American Indian Refugees (EA)
AIR .... American Industrial Real Estate Association (EA)
AIR .... American Institute of Reciprocators (EA)

AIR .... American Institute of Refrigeration [*Defunct*]
AIR .... American Institute of Research (OICC)
AIR .... American Institutes for Research [*Information service or system*] (IID)
AIR .... American Institutes for Research in the Behavioral Sciences (EA)
AIR .... Aminoimidazole Ribonucleotide [*Biochemistry*]
AIR .... Antenna Input Resistance
AIR .... Applied Information Resources [*Research center*] (RCD)
air .... Armenian Soviet Socialist Republic [*MARC country of publication code*] [*Library of Congress*] (LCCP)
AIR .... Army Intelligence Reserve
AIR .... Asociacion Interamericana de Radiodifusion [*Inter-American Association of Broadcasters - IAAB*] [*Montevideo, Uruguay*] (EA)
AIR .... Asociacion Internacional de Radiodifusion [*International Association of Broadcasting - IAB*] (EAIO)
AIR .... Association for Institutional Research (EA)
AIR .... Australian Institute of Radiography (EAIO)
AIR .... Aviation Item Reports
AIR .... Bellaire, OH [*Location identifier*] [*FAA*] (FAAL)
a-ir--- .... Iran [*MARC geographic area code*] [*Library of Congress*] (LCCP)
AIR .... Iron River Public Library, Alberta [*Library symbol*] [*National Library of Canada*] (NLC)
AIRA .... Air Attache [*Air Force*]
AIRA .... All India Reporter, Allahabad Series [*A publication*] (ILCA)
AIRA .... Allergies and Intolerant Reactions Association [*Australian Capital Territory*]
AIRA .... American Independent Refiners Association (EA)
AIRA .... American-International Reiki Association (EA)
AIRAC....... Aeronautical Information Regulation and Control
AIRAC....... All-Industry Research Advisory Council [*Later, IRC*] (EA)
AIRAC....... Atmospheric Infrared Attenuation Coefficient
AIRACCDT ... Air Accident
AIRACLIS ... Air Activities Logistic Information System (MCD)
AIRACS .... Aircraft Acquisition and Support (NG)
AIRAD ...... Air Administrative Net [*Army*] (AABC)
AIRAD ...... Airmen's Advisory [*A notice to airmen*] (FAAC)
AIRAF ...... Aircraft, Asiatic Fleet
AIRAH ...... Australian Institute of Refrigeration, Air Conditioning, and Heating
AIR Aj....... All India Reporter, Ajmer Series [*A publication*] (ILCA)
AIR All ...... All India Reporter, Allahabad Series [*A publication*] (ILCA)
AIR And..... All India Reporter, Andhra Series [*A publication*] (ILCA)
AIR Andh .. All India Reporter, Andhra Series [*A publication*] (ILCA)
AIR Andh Pra ... All India Reporter, Andhra Pradesh Series [*A publication*] (ILCA)
AIRANTISUBRON ... Air Antisubmarine Squadron [*Navy*]
AIR Arch Interam Rheumatol ... AIR. Archives of Interamerican Rheumatology [*A publication*]
AIRARMUNIT ... Aircraft Armament Unit
AIRASDEVLANT ... Aircraft Antisubmarine Development Detachment, Atlantic Fleet
AIR Asm.... All India Reporter, Assam Series [*A publication*] (ILCA)
AIR Assam ... All India Reporter, Assam Series [*A publication*] (ILCA)
Air Atmos Chem Air Pollut Semin ... Air, Atmospheric Chemistry, and Air Pollution. Seminar [*A publication*]
AIRB.......... All India Reporter, Bombay Series [*A publication*] (ILCA)
AIRB.......... Aviation Insurance Rating Bureau (EA)
AIRBALTAP ... Allied Air Forces, Baltic Approaches [*NATO*] (NATG)
AIRBAREX ... Air Barrier Exercise [*Military*] (NVT)
AIRBASECOM ... Air Base Commander
AIRBATFORPAC ... Aircraft Battle Force, Pacific Fleet [*Navy*]
AIR Bhop... All India Reporter, Bhopal Series [*A publication*] (ILCA)
AIR Bilas... All India Reporter, Bilaspur Series [*A publication*] (ILCA)
AIRBM...... Anti-Intermediate Range Ballistic Missile
AIRBO....... Association Internationale pour les Recherches au Bas Fourneau d'Ougree
AIR Bom .... All India Reporter, Bombay Series [*A publication*] (ILCA)
AIRBR....... Association Internationale du Registre des Bateaux du Rhin [*International Association of the Rhine Ships Register*]
AIRBS .... American Institute for Research in the Behavioral Sciences
AIRBUT .... Automatic Resupply and Buildup Time [*Air Force*] (AFIT)
AIRC.......... AIRCOA Hospitality Services, Inc. [*Formerly, Associated Inns & Restaurants of America*] [*Denver, CO*] [*NASDAQ symbol*] (NQ)
AIRC.......... All India Reporter, Calcutta Series [*A publication*] (ILCA)
AIRC.......... American Indian Research Center (OICC)
AIRC.......... Association of Independent Radio Contractors [*British*]
AIRC.......... Association of International Relations Clubs (EA)
AIRC.......... Irma Community Library, Alberta [*Library symbol*] [*National Library of Canada*] (NLC)
AIRCAD.... Annales. Institut National de la Recherche Agronomique. Serie C. Annales des Epiphyties [*A publication*]
AIR Cal..... All India Reporter, Calcutta Series [*A publication*] (ILCA)
Airc Engng ... Aircraft Engineering [*A publication*]
AIRCENT ... Allied Air Forces, Central Europe [*Formerly, AAFCE*] [*NATO*]
AIRCEY .... Air Ceylon Ltd.
Aircft.......... Aircraft
Air CHV .... Air Conditioning, Heating, and Ventilating [*A publication*]

Air Classif Solid Wastes ... Air Classification of Solid Wastes [*A publication*]
Air Clean.... Air Cleaning [*Japan*] [*A publication*]
AIRCLNR ... Air Cleaner
AIRCO ...... Air Coordinator [*Air Force*]
AIRCO ...... Air Reduction Company   (KSC)
AIRCOM... Aerospace Communications Complex [*Air Force*]
AIRCOM... Air Command   (MCD)
AIRCOM... Air Force Communications Program
AIRCOM... Airways Communications System
AIRCOMD ... Air Command Net [*Army*]   (AABC)
Air Commerce Bul ... Air Commerce Bulletin [*A publication*]
AIRCOMNET ... Air Communications Network
AIRCON ... Automated Information and Reservation Computer Operated Network
Air Cond Heat & Refrig N ... Air Conditioning, Heating, and Refrigeration News [*A publication*]
Air Cond Heat Refrig News ... Air Conditioning, Heating, and Refrigeration News [*A publication*]
Air Cond Heat & Ven ... Air Conditioning, Heating, and Ventilating [*A publication*]
Air Cond Heat Vent ... Air Conditioning, Heating, and Ventilating [*A publication*]
Air Cond N ... Air Conditioning, Heating, and Refrigeration News [*A publication*]
Air Cond Oil Heat ... Air Conditioning and Oil Heat [*A publication*]
Aircond Refrig Bus ... Airconditioning and Refrigeration Business [*A publication*]
Air Cond & Refrig N ... Air Conditioning and Refrigeration News [*A publication*]
Air Cos S.... Air et Cosmos. Special 1000 [*A publication*]
Aircraft ...... Aircraft Engineering [*A publication*]
Aircr Eng ... Aircraft Engineering [*A publication*]
Aircr Missiles ... Aircraft and Missiles [*A publication*]
Aircr Prod ... Aircraft Production [*A publication*]
AIRCSC..... Air Command and Staff College [*Air Force*]
AIRD .... American Indian Research and Development [*An association*]   (EA)
AIRD .... Australian Industrial Research Directory [*A publication*]   (APTA)
AIR Dacca ... All India Reporter, Dacca Series [*A publication*]   (ILCA)
Air D Arty ... Air Defense Artillery Magazine [*A publication*]
Aird Black ... Aird. Blackstone Economised [*1873*] [*A publication*]   (ILCA)
Aird Civ Law ... Aird's Civil Laws of France [*A publication*]   (DLA)
AIRDEF ...... Air Defense Division [*NATO*]   (NATG)
AIRDEFCOM ... Air Defense Commander
AIRDELOPS ... Air Delivery Operations [*Aerial resupply*] [*Military*]   (NVT)
AIRDELPLT ... Air Delivery Platoon
AIRDEP.... Air Deputy [*NATO*]   (NATG)
AIRDEVRON ... Air Development Squadron [*Navy*]
AIRDIV ...... Air Division [*Air Force*]
AIRDIVDEF ... Air Division Defense [*Air Force*]   (MUGU)
AIREA....... American Institute of Real Estate Appraisers [*Later, AI*]   (EA)
AIREASTLANT ... Naval Air Forces East Atlantic Area [*NATO*]   (NATG)
AIR East Punjab ... All India Reporter, East Punjab Series [*A publication*]   (ILCA)
AIREEN.... AIDS Research [*A publication*]
AIRELO..... Air Electrical Officer
AIREN....... American Institute for Research and Education in Naturopathy   (EA)
Air Eng...... Air Engineering [*A publication*]
AIRENGPROPACCOVERHAUL ... Airplane Engine, Propeller, and Accessory Overhaul [*Navy*]
AIREO....... Air Engineer Officer
AIREP....... Air Report [*Aviation*]   (FAAC)
AIREP....... Aircraft Report
AIREPDIV ... Aircraft Repair Division [*Military*]
AIREPDN ... Aircraft Repair Division [*Military*]
AIRES .... Advanced Imagery Requirements and Exploitation System   (MCD)
Air-Espace Tech ... Air-Espace Techniques [*A publication*]
AIREVAC ... Air Evacuation
AIREVACWING ... Air Evacuation Wing
AIREW...... Airborne Infrared Early Warning
AIRF......... Aircraft Instrument Repair Facility
AIRF......... All-India Railwaymen's Federation
AIRF......... Assignment Instructions Remain Firm [*Army*]
AIRFA....... American Indian Religious Freedom Act [*1978*]
AIRFAM ... Aircraft Familiarization
AIRFC....... All India Reporter, Federal Court Series [*A publication*]   (ILCA)
Air F Civ Eng ... Air Force Civil Engineer [*A publication*]
Air F Comp ... Air Force Comptroller [*A publication*]
AIRFERRON ... Air Ferry Squadron [*Navy*]
AIR FIL..... Air Filter [*Freight*]
Air F J Log ... Air Force Journal of Logistics [*A publication*]
AIRFL .... Air Refueling   (FAAC)
AIRFMF..... Air Fleet Marine Force   (AFIT)
AIRFMFLANT ... Aircraft, Fleet Marine Force, Atlantic [*Obsolete*]
AIRFMFPAC ... Aircraft, Fleet Marine Force, Pacific [*Obsolete*]
Air F Mgz ... Air Force Magazine [*A publication*]
Air Force Civ Eng ... Air Force Civil Engineer [*A publication*]

Air Force Civil Eng ... Air Force Civil Engineer [*A publication*]
Air Force Eng Serv Q ... Air Force Engineering and Services Quarterly [*United States*] [*A publication*]
Air Force Eng Serv Quart ... Air Force Engineering and Services Quarterly [*A publication*]
Air Force Law R ... Air Force Law Review [*A publication*]
AIRFORWARD ... Shore-Based Air Force, Forward Area, Central Pacific
AIRGI....... Airman's Guide [*A publication*]
AIRGLO.... Airborne Infrared Gunfire Locator
AIRGRP.... Air Group
AIRHC ...... Alaska International Rail and Highway Commission [*Terminated, 1961*]
AIR Him Pra ... All India Reporter, Himachal Pradesh Series [*A publication*]   (ILCA)
AIRHP....... All India Reporter, Himachal Pradesh Series [*A publication*]   (ILCA)
AIR Hy ...... All India Reporter, Hyderabad Series [*A publication*]   (ILCA)
AIR Hyd .... All India Reporter, Hyderabad Series [*A publication*]   (ILCA)
AIRI.......... Associate of the Institute of the Rubber Industry [*British*]
AIRI.......... Association of Independent Research Institutes   (EA)
AIRIF .... Aiguebelle Resources [*NASDAQ symbol*]   (NQ)
AIRIMP .... Air Reservations Interline Message Procedure
Air Ind .... Air Industriel [*A publication*]
AIR Ind Dig ... All India Reporter, Indian Digest [*A publication*]   (ILCA)
Air Int .... Air International [*A publication*]
AIRIS .... Advanced Infrared Imaging Seeker   (MCD)
AIRIS .... Air Store Issuing Ship
AIRJ & K... All India Reporter, Jammu and Kashmir Series [*A publication*]   (ILCA)
AIR Kerala ... All India Reporter, Kerala Series [*A publication*]   (ILCA)
AIR Kutch ... All India Reporter, Kutch Series [*A publication*]   (ILCA)
AIRL.......... Aeronautical Icing Research Laboratory
Air L.......... Air Law [*A publication*]
AIRL.......... Automation Industries Research Laboratory   (KSC)
AIR Lahore ... All India Reporter, Lahore Series [*A publication*]   (ILCA)
AIRLANT ... Air Forces, Atlantic Fleet [*Navy*]
AIRLC........ Air Florida Systems [*NASDAQ symbol*]   (NQ)
AIRLEX ..... Air Landing Exercise [*Military*]   (NVT)
AIRLIGHT ... Airborne Lighting System [*Air Force*]   (MCD)
Air Line Emp ... Air Line Employee [*A publication*]
AIRLO....... Air Liaison Officer
AIRLOC.... Air Lines of Communication
AIRLORDS ... Airlines Load Optimization Recording and Display System [*Airport passenger-moving sidewalk*]
Air LR........ Air Law Review [*A publication*]
Air L Rev ... Air Law Review [*A publication*]
AIRM .... Airborne Infrared Mapper
AIRM .... All India Reporter, Madras Series [*A publication*]   (ILCA)
AIR Mad.... All India Reporter, Madras Series [*A publication*]   (ILCA)
AIR Madh Pra ... All India Reporter, Madhya Pradesh Series [*A publication*]   (ILCA)
AIR Manip ... All India Reporter, Manipur Series [*A publication*]   (ILCA)
AIRMAP... Air Monitoring Analysis and Prediction [*System*]
AIRMB...... All India Reporter, Madhya Bharat Series [*A publication*]   (ILCA)
AIRME...... Apollo Initiator Resistance Measuring Equipment [*NASA*]   (NASA)
AIRMEC.... Association Internationale pour la Recherche Medicale et les Echanges Culturels [*International Association for Medical Research and Cultural Exchange*] [*Paris, France*]   (EAIO)
AIRMET ... Airmen's Meteorological Information   (FAAC)
AIRMG ..... Aircraft Machine Gunner
AIRMIC .... Association of Insurance and Risk Managers in Industry and Commerce   (EAIO)
AIRMICS ... Army Institute for Research in Management Information and Computer Science [*Atlanta, GA*]   (IEEE)
AIRMILMIS ... Aircraft Military Mission
AIR/MMH ... Acoustic Intercept Receiver/Multimode Hydrophone System [*Navy*]
AIRMOVE ... Air Movement [*Message*]   (NVT)
AIRMOVEX ... Air Movement Exercise [*Military*]   (NVT)
AIRMP...... All India Reporter, Madhya Pradesh Series [*A publication*]   (ILCA)
AIRMSN... Air Mission [*Air Force*]
AIR My..... All India Reporter, Mysore Series [*A publication*]   (ILCA)
AIRN .... All India Reporter, Nagpur Series [*A publication*]   (ILCA)
AIR Nag..... All India Reporter, Nagpur Series [*A publication*]   (ILCA)
AIRNAVAID ... Air Navigational Aid [*Navy*]   (NG)
AIRNAVO ... Air Navigation Office [*Navy*]
AIRNON... Allied Air Forces, North Norway [*NATO*]   (NATG)
AIRNORSOLS ... Aircraft, Northern Solomons [*Military*]
AIRNORTH ... Allied Air Forces, Northern Europe [*Formerly, AAFNE*] [*NATO*]
Air NZ .... Air New Zealand Ltd. [*Airline*]
AIROPNET ... Air Operational Network [*Air Force*]
AIROPNSO ... Air Operations Officer [*Air Force*]
AIROPS .... Air Operations [*Military*]
AIR Oris .... All India Reporter, Orissa Series [*A publication*]   (ILCA)
AIR Oudh .. All India Reporter, Oudh Series [*A publication*]   (ILCA)
AIRP.......... All India Reporter, Patna Series [*A publication*]   (ILCA)

AIRP.......... Association Internationale de Relations Professionnelles [*International Industrial Relations Association - IIRA*] (EAIO)
AIRPA....... American Indian Registry for the Performing Arts (EA)
AIRPAC .... Air Forces, Pacific Fleet
AIRPAC(ADV) ... Air Forces Pacific Advanced
AIRPAC(PEARL) ... Air Forces Pacific, Pearl Harbor
AIRPACSUBCOMFORD ... Air Forces Subordinate Command, Forward Area
AIRPAP .... Air Pressure Analysis Program [*Bell System*]
Air Pap Symp ... Air. Papers Based on Symposia [*A publication*]
AIRPASS .. Airborne Interception RADAR and Pilot's Attack Sight System
AIR Pat...... All India Reporter, Patna Series [*A publication*] (ILCA)
AIRPAX .... Aircraft Expendable Bathythermograph Program in the Pacific [*National Science Foundation*] (MSC)
AIRPC....... All India Reporter, Privy Council [*A publication*] (ILCA)
AIR PEP.... All India Reporter, Patiala and East Punjab States Union Series [*A publication*] (ILCA)
AIR PEPSU ... All India Reporter, Patiala and East Punjab States Union Series [*A publication*] (ILCA)
AIR Pesh ... All India Reporter, Peshawar Series [*A publication*] (ILCA)
AIRPL .... Airplane [*Freight*]
AirPolAb.... Air Pollution Abstracts [*A publication*]
Air Poll Cont Assn J ... Air Pollution Control Association. Journal [*A publication*]
Air Poll Control Assn J ... Air Pollution Control Association. Journal [*A publication*]
Air Pollut ... Air Pollution [*A publication*]
Air Pollut Assoc J ... Air Pollution Control Association. Journal [*A publication*]
Air Pollut Cancer Man Proc Hanover Int Carcinog Meet ... Air Pollution and Cancer in Man. Proceedings of the Hanover International Carcinogenesis Meeting [*A publication*]
Air Pollut Control ... Air Pollution Control [*A publication*]
Air Pollut Control Assoc Annu Meet Pap ... Air Pollution Control Association. Annual Meeting. Papers [*A publication*]
Air Pollut Control Conf ... Air Pollution Control Conference [*A publication*]
Air Pollut Control Des Handb ... Air Pollution Control and Design Handbook [*A publication*]
Air Pollut Control Dist Cty Los Angeles Annu Rep ... Air Pollution Control District. County of Los Angeles. Annual Report [*A publication*]
Air Pollut Control Ind Energy Prod ... Air Pollution Control and Industrial Energy Production [*A publication*]
Air Pollut Control Off US Publ AP Ser ... Air Pollution Control Office. Publication. AP Series [*United States*] [*A publication*]
Air Pollut Control Transp Engines Symp ... Air Pollution Control in Transport Engines. Symposium [*A publication*]
Air Pollut Eff Plant Growth Symp ... Air Pollution Effects on Plant Growth. Symposium [*A publication*]
Air Pollut Found Rep ... Air Pollution Foundation. Report [*A publication*]
Air Pollut News ... Air Pollution News [*Japan*] [*A publication*]
Air Pollut Symp Low Pollut Power Syst Dev ... Air Pollution Symposium on Low Pollution Power Systems Development [*A publication*]
Air Pollut Tech Rep ... Air Pollution Technical Report [*A publication*]
Air Pollut Titles ... Air Pollution Titles [*A publication*]
Airports Int ... Airports International [*A publication*]
AIR Pun..... All India Reporter, Punjab Series [*A publication*] (ILCA)
Air Qual Control Print Ind ... Air Quality Control in the Printing Industry [*A publication*]
Air Qual Environ Factors ... Air Quality and Environmental Factors [*A publication*]
Air Qual Instrum ... Air Quality Instrumentation [*A publication*]
Air Qual Monogr ... Air Quality Monographs [*A publication*]
Air Qual Smoke Urban For Fires Proc Int Symp ... Air Quality and Smoke from Urban and Forest Fires. Proceedings of the International Symposium [*A publication*]
AIRR.......... Air Reservist [*A publication*]
AIRR.......... All India Reporter, Rajasthan Series [*A publication*] (ILCA)
AIR Raj..... All India Reporter, Rajasthan Series [*A publication*] (ILCA)
AIRRES..... Air Rescue (CINC)
Air Reserv ... Air Reservist [*A publication*]
AIRS.......... Ablator Insulated Ramjet Study [*NASA*] (KSC)
AIRS.......... Accident/Incident Reporting System [*National Transportation Safety Board*] [*Information service or system*] (IID)
AIRS.......... Accident Information Retrieval System (RDA)
AIRS.......... Advanced Inertial Reference Sphere [*ICBM technology*]
AIRS.......... Advanced Instrumentation for Reflood Studies [*Nuclear energy*] (NRCH)
AIRS.......... Aerobics International Research Society (EA)
AIRS.......... Aerometric Information Retrieval System [*Environmental Protection Agency*] [*Information service or system*] (CRD)
AIRS.......... Airborne Infrared Radiometer System
AIRS.......... Airborne Integrated Reconnaissance System (MCD)
AIRS.......... Aircraft Inventory Reporting System (AABC)
AIRS.......... Airport Information Retrieval System [*FAA*]
AIRS.......... Airship Industries Ltd. [*NASDAQ symbol*] (NQ)
AIRS.......... Alliance of Information and Referral Systems (EA)
AIRS.......... Army Information Radio Service (MCD)

AIRS.......... Audit Integrated Reporting System [*IRS*]
AIRS.......... Australian Information Retrieval Services
AIRS.......... Automated Information Reference Systems, Inc. [*Information service or system*] (IID)
AIRS.......... Automatic Image Retrieval System (MCD)
AIRS.......... Automatic Information Retrieval System [*Information service or system*] (BUR)
AirSA........ Air South Australia
Air Saf J..... Air Safety Journal [*A publication*]
Air Sampling Instrum Eval Atmos Contam ... Air Sampling Instruments for Evaluation of Atmospheric Contaminants [*A publication*]
AIR Sau ..... All India Reporter, Saurashtra Series [*A publication*] (ILCA)
AIRSC .... All India Reporter, Supreme Court [*A publication*] (ILCA)
AIRSCOFORPAC ... Aircraft Scouting Force, Pacific Fleet
AIRSEV...... Association for International Cancer Research. Symposia [*A publication*]
AIRSHIPGR ... Airship Group
AIRSHIPRON ... Airship Squadron
AIRSHTR ... Air Shutter
AIR Simla ... All India Reporter, Simla Series [*A publication*] (ILCA)
AIR Sind... All India Reporter, Sind Series [*A publication*] (ILCA)
AIRSKEDELFLT ... Aircraft Schedule for Delivery to Fleet
AIRSOLS ... Air Solomons Command [*US*]
AIRSONOR ... Allied Air Forces, South Norway [*NATO*] (NATG)
AIRSOPAC ... Aircraft, South Pacific Force [*Navy*]
AIRSOUTH ... Allied Air Forces, Southern Europe [*Formerly, AAFSE*] [*NATO*]
AIRSOWESPAC ... Aircraft, Southwest Pacific Force [*Navy*]
Air & Space Law ... Air and Space Lawyer [*A publication*] (DLA)
AIRSS........ ABRES [*Advanced Ballistic Reentry System*] Instrumentation Range Safety Systems [*Air Force*] (MCD)
AIR-STD... Air Force International Standard
AIRSTORDEP ... Air Stores Depot [*Navy*]
AIRSVC ... Air Services [*Military*] (NVT)
AIRSYSCOM ... Air Systems Command [*Navy*]
AIRT.......... Air Transportation Holding Co., Inc. [*Denver, NC*] [*NASDAQ symbol*] (NQ)
AIRTAS .... Air-Deployed Towed-Array Surveillance System (MCD)
AIRTASS.. Airborne Towed Array SONAR System (MCD)
AIRTC....... All India Reporter, Travancore-Cochin Series [*A publication*] (ILCA)
AIRTE .... Associate of the Institute of Road Transport Engineers (DBQ)
airtps.......... Airborne Troops [*British and Canadian*] [*World War II*]
AIRTRAINRON ... Air Training Squadron (MUGU)
AIRTRANS ... Airport Transportation
AIRTRANSEX ... Air Transportation Exercise [*Military*] (NVT)
Air Transp World ... Air Transport World [*A publication*]
AIRTRANSRON ... Air Transport Squadron
AIRTRANSRONLANT ... Air Transport Squadron, Atlantic
AIRTRANSRONPAC ... Air Transport Squadron, Pacific
AIRTRANSRONWESTCOAST ... Air Transport Squadron, West Coast
Air Trans W ... Air Transport World [*A publication*]
AIRTRARON ... Air Training Squadron
AIR Trip .... All India Reporter, Tripura Series [*A publication*] (ILCA)
AIRU .... Air University (MCD)
Air Univ Libr Index Mil Period ... Air University. Library. Index to Military Periodicals [*A publication*]
Air Univ R ... Air University. Review [*A publication*]
Air Univ Rev ... Air University. Review [*A publication*]
AirUnLibI ... Air University. Library. Index to Military Periodicals [*A publication*]
Air Un Rev ... Air University. Review [*A publication*]
Air U Rev... Air University. Review [*A publication*] (DLA)
AIRVAN.... Air Mobile Van [*Trailer unit for use on ground or in air*] [*Military*]
AIRVP .... All India Reporter, Vindhya Pradesh Series [*A publication*] (ILCA)
Air/Water Poll Rept ... Air/Water Pollution Report [*A publication*]
Air Water Pollut ... Air and Water Pollution [*A publication*]
AIRWC...... Air War College [*Air Force*]
AIRXRS..... American Industrial Radium and X-Ray Society [*Later, ASNT*]
AIRYX...... Air Express Division of the Railway Express Agency
AIS............ Ablating Inner Surface
AIS............ Academic Instructors School [*Air Force*]
AIS............ Academy of Independent Scholars (EA)
AIS............ Accounting Information System (BUR)
AIS............ Accumulator Injection System [*Nuclear energy*] (NRCH)
AIS............ Action Item Sheet (MCD)
AIS............ Adoptees in Search [*An association*] (EA)
AIS............ Advance in Schedule (KSC)
AIS............ Advanced Indications Structure (MCD)
AIS............ Advanced Indications System (MCD)
AIS............ Advanced Information System/Net 1 Service [*Formerly, ACS*] [*American Bell, Inc.*]
AIS............ Advanced Instructional System (MCD)
AIS............ Advanced Ionospheric Sounder [*A ground-based instrument*]
AIS............ Advanced Isotope Separation [*Process*] [*Nuclear energy*]
AIS............ Advertising Information Services
AIS............ Aeronautical Information Service
AIS............ Aeronautical Information Specialist (FAAC)
AIS............ Air Intelligence Service

AIS............ Airborne Imaging Spectrometer
AIS............ Airborne Infrared Spectrometer
AIS............ Airborne Instrumentation Subsystem (MCD)
AIS............ Aircraft Inspection System
AIS............ Aircraft Instrument Subsystem [*Navy*] (MCD)
AIS............ Airlock Illumination Subassembly (MCD)
AIS............ AIS Resources Ltd. [*Vancouver Stock Exchange symbol*]
AIS............ Akademio Internacia de la Sciencoj [*International Academy of Sciences - IAS*] (EAIO)
AIS............ Alarm Indication Signal [*Telecommunications*] (TEL)
AIS............ Alarm Inhibit Signal [*Telecommunications*] (TEL)
AIS............ Alcohol Insoluble Solids [*Food analysis*]
AIS............ Alternate Interim Successor [*Military*] (NVT)
AIS............ Altitude Indication System
AIS............ Altman Information Systems, Inc. [*Information service or system*] (IID)
AIS............ America-Italy Society (EA)
AIS............ American Indian Scholarships [*Later, AIGC*] (EA)
AIS............ American Indian Sign Language (BYTE)
AIS............ American Indians for Sobriety (EA)
AIS............ American Information Services [*Information service or system*] (IID)
AIS............ American Institute of Stress (EA)
AIS............ American Iris Society (EA)
AIS............ American Ivy Society (EA)
AIS............ Ampal-American Israel Corp. [*AMEX symbol*] (SPSG)
AIS............ Amron Information Services (IID)
AIS............ Analog-In Single-Ended (MCD)
AIS............ Analog Input System
AIS............ Analog Instrumentation Subsystem
AIS............ Androgen Insensitivity Syndrome [*Endocrinology*]
AIS............ Annual Inspection Summary (MCD)
AIS............ Antenna Interface Subsystem (CAAL)
AIS............ Anti-Icing System [*Aircraft*]
AIS............ Apollo Instrumentation Ships [*NASA*] (MCD)
AIS............ Arabidopsis Information Service
AIS............ Army Infantry School (KSC)
AIS............ Army Information Systems (RDA)
AIS............ Army Intelligence School
AIS............ Army Intelligence and Security
AIS............ Army Intelligence Survey [*ITAC*] (MCD)
AIS............ Arorae [*Kiribati*] [*Airport symbol*] (OAG)
AIS............ Associate of the Institute of Statisticians [*Later, MIS*] [*British*]
AIS............ Association for Integrative Studies (EA)
AIS............ Association Internationale de la Savonnerie et de la Detergence [*International Association of the Soap and Detergent Industry*] (EAIO)
AIS............ Association Internationale de Semiotique [*International Association of Semiotic Studies*] (EAIO)
AIS............ Association Internationale de Sociologie [*International Sociological Association - ISA*] (EAIO)
AIS............ Association Internationale de la Soie [*International Silk Association - ISA*] (EAIO)
AIS............ Attitude Indicating System (MCD)
AIS............ Automated Cell-Injection System
AIS............ Automated Indicator System (MCD)
AIS............ Automated Information System
AIS............ Automated Instrumentation System
AIS............ Automated Insurance Service
AIS............ Automatic Idle Speed [*Automotive engineering*]
AIS............ Automatic Image Screening
AIS............ Automatic Intercept System [*Bell System*]
AIS............ Automatic Intermediate Station (MCD)
AIS............ Automatic Interplanetary Station [*USSR*]
AIS............ Avionics Intermediate Shop (MCD)
AIS............ Award Information System [*Australia*]
AIS............ Community College of Allegheny County, South Campus, West Mifflin, PA [*OCLC symbol*] (OCLC)
a-is---........ Israel [*MARC geographic area code*] [*Library of Congress*] (LCCP)
AISA.......... American Indoor Soccer Association (EA)
AISA.......... American Institute for Shippers' Associations (EA)
AISA.......... American Institute of Supply Associations [*Later, ASA*] (EA)
AISA.......... Analytical Isoelectrofocusing Scanning Apparatus [*Analytical chemistry*]
AISA.......... Associate of Incorporated Secretaries Association
AISA.......... Association of International Schools in Africa (EA)
AISA.......... Association Internationale pour la Securite Aerienne [*International Air Safety Association*]
AISA.......... Association Internationale pour le Sport des Aveugles [*International Blind Sports Association - IBSA*] [*Farsta, Sweden*] (EAIO)
AISAM...... Association Internationale des Societes d'Assurance Mutuelle [*International Association of Mutual Insurance Companies*] [*Paris, France*] (EAIO)
AISAR....... Accidental Incident Sabotage Assistance Request (MCD)
AISB.......... Association Internationale de Standardisation Biologique [*International Association of Biological Standardization - IABS*] (EAIO)
AISC.......... American Indian Studies Center [*Research center*] (RCD)
AISC.......... American Institute of Steel Construction (EA)

AISC.......... Amnistie Internationale Section Canadienne [*Amnesty International Canadian Section*]
AISC.......... Argentine Information Service Center (EA)
AISC.......... Army Information Systems Command
AISC.......... Assessment and Information Services Center [*National Oceanic and Atmospheric Administration*] [*Information service or system*] (IID)
AISC.......... Association of Independent Software Companies [*Later, ADAPSO*] (EA)
AISC.......... Association of Informed Senior Citizens (EA)
AISC.......... Association Internationale des Skal Clubs [*International Association of Skal Clubs*] (EAIO)
AISC.......... Associazione Italiana di Studi Canadesi [*Italian Association of Canadian Studies*]
AISD.......... Abstracting and Indexing Services Directory [*A publication*]
AISD.......... Annali. Istituto di Studi Danteschi [*A publication*]
AISD.......... Army Intelligence School, Fort Devens (MCD)
AISE.......... American Intercultural Student Exchange (EA)
AISE.......... Association Internationale des Sciences Economiques [*International Economic Association - IEA*] [*Paris, France*] (EAIO)
AISE.......... Association Internationale des Sciences de l'Education [*International Association for the Advancement of Educational Research*]
AISE.......... Association Internationale des Statisticiens d'Enquetes [*International Association of Survey Statisticians*] (EAIO)
AISE.......... Association of Iron and Steel Engineers (EA)
AISEIT...... Association of Institute and School of Education In-Service Tutors [*British*]
AISES........ American Indian Science and Engineering Society (EA)
AISF........ Avionic Integration Support Facility (MCD)
AISFAR.... Archivio Italiano di Scienze Farmacologiche [*A publication*]
AISG.......... Accountants International Study Group [*Later, International Federation of Accountants*]
AISG.......... American Insurance Services Group [*New York, NY*] (EA)
AISG.......... Artists in Stained Glass [*Canada*]
AISH .... Association Internationale des Sciences Hydrologiques [*International Association of Hydrological Sciences*] (EAIO)
AISHWC... Australian Industrial Safety, Health, and Welfare Cases [*A publication*]
AISI .... Advanced International Studies Institute (EA)
AISI .... Airborne Instrumentation Subsystem Internal (MCD)
AISI .... American Iron and Steel Institute (EA)
AISI .... American-Italy Society, Incorporated
AISI .... Associate of the Iron and Steel Institute
AISIN........ Alon. Internal Quarterly of the Israel Numismatic Society [*A publication*]
AISI Rpt .... American Iron and Steel Institute. Annual Statistical Report [*A publication*]
AISIS......... Advanced Icing Severity Indication System [*Military*] (RDA)
AISI Steel Prod Man ... American Iron and Steel Institute. Steel Products Manual [*A publication*]
AISJ.......... Association Internationale des Sciences Juridiques [*International Association of Legal Science - IALS*] (EAIO)
AISJB........ Journal. American Society for Information Science [*A publication*]
AISL .... Aviation Information Services Limited (IID)
AISLE........ [*An*] Intersociety Liaison Committee on the Environment
AISLF........ Association Internationale des Sociologues de Langue Francaise [*International Association of French Language Sociologists*] (EAIO)
AISLLI ...... Associazione Internazionale per gli Studi di Lingua e Letteratura Italiane [*International Association for the Study of the Italian Language and Literature - IASILL*] (EAIO)
AISLN .... Annali. Istituto Superiore di Scienze e Lettere di Santa Chiera (Napoli) [*A publication*]
AISMAE ... Archivio Italiano di Scienze Mediche Tropicali e di Parassitologia [*A publication*]
AIS-MEBA ... Association of Industrial Scientists [*affiliated with*] Marine Engineers Beneficial Association [*A union*]
AIS/MR .... Alternative Intermediate Services for the Mentally Retarded
AISNC....... ASIS [*American Society for Information Science*] Newsletter [*A publication*]
AISOB....... Associate of the Incorporated Society of Organ Builders [*British*] (DBQ)
AISOBL .... Anwendung von Isotopen in der Organischen Chemie und Biochemie [*A publication*]
AISP.......... Annales. Institut Superieur de Philosophie [*A publication*]
AISP.......... Association of Information Systems Professionals (EA)
AISP.......... Association Internationale de Science Politique [*International Political Science Association - IPSA*] [*Canada*]
AISP.......... Association Internationale des Secretaires Professionnelles [*International Association of Professional Secretaries*] [*Canada*]
AISP.......... Australian Insolvency Management Practice [*A publication*]
AISq.......... Aerospace Intelligence Squadron [*Air Force*]
AISR.......... Army Institute of Surgical Research (RDA)
AISRCM ... Australian Institute of Swimming and Recreation Centre Management

AISS .... Air Intelligence Services Squadron [*Defunct*] [*Air Force*]
AISS .... Airborne Infrared Surveillance Set
AISS .... Association Internationale de la Science du Sol [*International Society of Soil Science - ISSS*] (EAIO)
AISS .... Association Internationale de la Securite Sociale [*International Social Security Association*]
AISS .... Australian Innovation Sourcing Service [*Database*]
AISS .... Automatic Intercom Switching System
AISSAW.... Annali. Istituto Superiore di Sanita [*A publication*]
AIST .... Agency of Industrial Science and Technology [*Japan*] (NASA)
AIST .... Association for Intelligent Systems Technology (EA)
AIST .... Automatic Information Station [*or System*] (BUR)
AISTC ...... Associate of the International Institute of Sports Therapy [*British*] (DBQ)
AISTD ...... Associate of the Imperial Society of Teachers of Dancing [*British*] (DBQ)
AISTD4..... Annali. Istituto Sperimentale per il Tabacco [*A publication*]
AIS Technical Soc Bul ... AIS [*Australian Iron and Steel*] Technical Society. Bulletin [*A publication*] (APTA)
AISTM ...... Associate of the Institute of Sales Technology and Management [*British*] (DBQ)
AI Struct E ... Associate of the Institute of Structural Engineers [*British*]
AISV .... Amphibious Infantry Support Vehicle
AISWG...... Air Interface Sub-Working Group [*NATO*] (NATG)
AISZAJ .... Annali. Istituto Sperimentale per la Zootecnia [*A publication*]
AIT .... Academy for Implants and Transplants (EA)
AIT .... Adelaide Institute of Technology [*Australia*]
AIT .... Advanced Identification Techniques (MCD)
AIT .... Advanced Individual Training [*Army*]
AIT .... Advanced Infantry Training
AIT .... Advanced Interceptor Technology (MCD)
AIT .... Adventures in Travel [*Oakland, CA*] [*Information service or system*] (IID)
A(IT).......... Africa Inland Transport [*British*] [*World War II*]
AIT .... Agency for Instructional Technology (EA)
AIT .... Agglutination-Inhibition Test [*Clinical chemistry*]
AIT .... AIT. Architektur Innenarchitektur Technischer Ausbau [*A publication*]
AIT .... Aitkin, MN [*Location identifier*] [*FAA*] (FAAL)
AIT .... Aitutaki [*Cook Islands*] [*Airport symbol*] (OAG)
AIT .... All-in-Together Programme for Parent Education [*Australia*]
AIT .... Allanco Iolite Monitor Corp. [*Vancouver Stock Exchange symbol*]
AIT .... Alliance Internationale de Tourisme [*International Touring Alliance*] (EAIO)
AIT .... American Industrial Transport, Inc.
AIT .... American Institute in Taiwan
AIT .... American Institute of Technology (MCD)
AIT .... American Institution in Thailand
AIT .... Ameritech Corp. [*NYSE symbol*] (SPSG)
AIT .... Analytic Intelligence Test [*Psychology*]
AIT .... Army Ammunition in Thailand (MCD)
AIT .... Army Intelligence Translator
AIT .... Asian Institute of Technology [*Bangkok, Thailand*] (MCD)
AIT .... Association of Inspectors of Taxes [*British*]
AIT .... Association Internationale des Travailleurs [*International Association of Workers*] [*France*]
AIT .... Assured Intermediate Task (MCD)
AIT .... Autoignition Temperature
AIT .... Automatic Information Test [*Military*]
AIT .... Automotive Information Test (AABC)
AIT .... Inter-American Translators Association [*Inactive*] (EA)
AITA.......... Act Inside the Army [*European antiwar group*]
AITA.......... Advanced Individual Training Available [*Military*]
AITA.......... Air Industries and Transports Association (MCD)
AITA.......... Association Internationale du Theatre Amateur [*International Amateur Theatre Association - IATA*] (EAIO)
AITAA...... Advanced Individual Training Attrition Analysis (MCD)
AITAA...... Asian Institute of Technology Alumni Association (EAIO)
AITADK.... Anales. Instituto Nacional de Investigaciones Agrarias. Serie Tecnologia Agraria [*A publication*]
AITBA ...... Annales. Institut Technique du Batiment et des Travaux Publics [*A publication*]
AITC.......... Action Information Training Center
AITC.......... Advocates of International Trade and Comity [*Defunct*] (EA)
AITC.......... Air Intelligence Training Center (MCD)
AITC.......... Alabama International Trade Center [*University of Alabama*] [*Research center*] (RCD)
AITC.......... Allyl Isothiocyanate [*Organic chemistry*]
AITC.......... American Indian Travel Commission [*Defunct*] (EA)
AITC.......... American Institute of Timber Construction (EA)
AITC.......... Association de l'Industrie Touristique du Canada [*Travel (later, Tourism) Industry Association of Canada - TIAC*]
AITC.......... Association Internationale des Traducteurs de Conference [*International Association of Conference Translators*] (EAIO)
AITC.......... Association of Investment Trust Companies [*British*]
AITC.......... Australian Industry and Technology Council
AITC.......... Australian Information Technology Council
AITD ...... Autoimmune Thyroid Disease [*Endocrinology*]
AITE.......... Advanced Indication Technology Experiment (MCD)

AITE.......... Aircraft Integrated Test Equipment
AITE.......... Australian International Technology Exhibition
AITEA ...... Archivum Immunologiae et Therapiae Experimentalis [*A publication*]
AITEC ...... Associazione Italiana Tecnico Economica del Cemento [*Cement association*] [*Italy*] (EY)
AITEP ...... Association for International Technical Promotion
AITES-ITA ... Association Internationale des Travaux en Souterrain - International Tunneling Association [*Bron, France*] (EA)
AITF .... All in the Family [*TV program*]
AITF .... Ammunition Initiatives Task Force (MCD)
AITF .... Army in the Field (MCD)
AITG ...... Australian Income Tax Guide [*A publication*]
AITI .... Aero Industries Technical Institute
AITI.......... Artikkel-Indeks Tidsskrifter [*Norwegian Center for Informatics*] [*Database*]
AITIA...... American Institute of Technical Illustrators Association (EA)
AITIT .... Association Internationale de la Teinture et de l'Impression Textiles [*International Association of Textile Dyers and Printers*] (EAIO)
AITL & P... Australian Income Tax Law and Practice [*A publication*] (APTA)
AITME...... Association des Instituts de Theologie du Moyen-Orient [*Association of Theological Institutes in the Middle East - A TIME*] (EAIO)
AITP.......... Allergy, Immunology, and Transplantation Program [*NIH*]
AITP.......... American Institute of Tax Practice (EA)
AITR.......... Australian Income Tax Reports [*A publication*] (APTA)
AITR.......... Australian and New Zealand Income Tax Reports [*A publication*] (APTA)
AITRC ...... Applied Information Technologies Research Center [*Information service or system*] (IID)
AITS .... Action Item Tracking System [*Radiation measurement*] (NRCH)
AITS .... Automated Information Transfer System [*Department of Commerce*] [*Database*]
AITSA ...... Associate of the Institute of Trading Standards Administration [*British*] (DBQ)
AITSV ...... American Institute - the Training School at Vineland [*Later, TTS*] (EA)
AITU.......... Alliance of Independent Telephone Unions [*Later, TIU*] (EA)
AITUC...... All-India Trade Union Congress
AITX.......... Automatix, Inc. [*NASDAQ symbol*] (NQ)
AIU .... Abort Interface Unit [*NASA*]
AIU .... Absolute Iodine Uptake [*Medicine*]
AIU .... Action for Interracial Understanding [*Defunct*] (EA)
AIU .... Alarm Interface Unit [*Telecommunications*] (TEL)
AIU .... Alliance Israelite Universelle [*Universal Israelite Alliance*]
AIU .... Allied Independent Unions [*Lebanon*]
AIU .... American International Underwriters
AIU .... Array Interface Unit [*Data processing*] (CAAL)
AIU .... ASAP Interface Unit
AIU .... Association Internationale des Universites [*International Association of Universities - IAU*] (EAIO)
AIU .... Association Internationale des Urbanistes [*International Society of City and Regional Planners - ISOCARP*] (EAIO)
AIU .... Atiu [*Cook Islands*] [*Airport symbol*] (OAG)
AIU .... Atlantic Independent Union
AIU .... Attack Helicopter Interface Unit (MCD)
AIU .... Auxiliary Interface Unit [*NASA*]
AIU .... Avionics Interface Unit (MCD)
AIUC.......... American Irish Unity Committee (EA)
AIUFFAS ... Association Internationale des Utilisateurs de Files de Fibres Artificielles et Synthetiques [*International Association of Users of Yarn of Man-Made Fibers*]
AIUM........ American Institute of Ultrasound in Medicine (EA)
AIUNAR ... Archivio Italiano di Urologia e Nefrologia [*A publication*]
AIUO........ Annali. Istituto Universitario Orientale. Sezione Germanica [*Napoli*] [*A publication*]
AI(U)ON ... Annali. Istituto Universitario Orientale (Napoli) [*A publication*]
AIURA ...... American Institute of Urban and Regional Affairs
AIUS.......... Associazione Internazionale Uomo nello Spazis [*Italian*] (MCD)
AIUSA...... Amnesty International of the USA (EA)
AIUTA...... Association Internationale des Universites du Troisieme Age [*International Association of Universities of the Third Age*] (EAIO)
AIV .... Accelerated Inverse Voltage
AIV .... Advanced Interactive Video
AIV .... Alcina Development Corp. [*Vancouver Stock Exchange symbol*]
AIV .... Aliceville, AL [*Location identifier*] [*FAA*] (FAAL)
AIV .... Armored Infantry Vehicle (MSA)
AIV .... Association Internationale de Volcanologie [*International Association of Volcanology*]
AIV .... Atti. Reale Istituto Veneto di Scienze, Lettere, ed Arti. Classe di Scienze Morali e Lettere [*A publication*]
AIVA ...... Association Internationale des Villes d'Avenir [*International Association of Cities of the Future*] (EA)
AIVF.......... Association of Independent Video and Filmmakers (EA)

AIVFC .... Association Internationale des Villes Francophones des Congres [*International Association of French-Speaking Congress Towns - IAFCT*] (EAIO)

AIVLAQ.... Atti. Istituto Veneto di Scienze, Lettere, ed Arti. Classe di Scienze Matematiche e Naturali [*A publication*]

AIVM .... Association Internationale pour les Voiles Minces [*en Beton*] [*International Association for Shell Structures*]

AIVMAT... Anales. Instituto de Investigaciones Veterinarias [*A publication*]

AIVMB...... Archivos de Investigacion Medica [*A publication*]

AIVMBU... Archivos de Investigacion Medica [*A publication*]

AIVNDZ.... Atti. Istituto Veneto di Scienze, Lettere, ed Arti. Classe di Scienze Fisiche, Matematiche, e Naturali [*A publication*]

AIVP......... American Institute of Vocal Pedagogy (EA)

AIVPA....... Association Internationale Veterinaire de Production Animale [*International Veterinary Association for Animal Production - IVAAP*] [*Brussels, Belgium*] (EAIO)

AIVR......... Accelerated Idioventricular Rhythm [*Cardiology*]

AIVS......... American Institute for Verdi Studies (EA)

AIVSML ... Atti. Reale Istituto Veneto di Scienze, Lettere, ed Arti. Classe di Scienze Morali e Lettere [*A publication*]

AIW .... Ardmore, OK [*Location identifier*] [*FAA*] (FAAL)

AIW .... Asbestos Insulated Wire

AIW .... Auroral Infrasonic Wave [*Substorm*]

AIW .... International Union, Allied Industrial Workers of America (EA)

AIWA .... Asian-Indian Women in America (EA)

AiWb......... Altiranisches Woerterbuch [*A publication*] (BJA)

AIWEC ...... Intelligence Watch Condition [*NATO*] (NATG)

AIWEC ...... Advanced/Innovative Wind Energy Concept (MCD)

AIWF........ American Institute of Wine and Food (EA)

AIWHAJ... Animals [*London*] [*A publication*]

AIWHTE... Associate of the Institution of Works and Highways Technician Engineers [*British*] (DBQ)

AIWI......... American Industrial Writing Institute

AIWM .... American Institute of Weights and Measures (EA)

AIWO .... Agudas Israel World Organization [*Jerusalem, Israel*]

AIWPHSA ... American Institute of Wholesale Plumbing and Heating Supply Associations [*Later, AISA*]

AIWR .... Arctic International Wildlife Range Society. Newsletter [*A publication*]

AIWRS...... Arctic International Wildlife Range Society (EA)

AIWS .... Advanced Interdiction Weapon System [*Military*]

AIWSc .... Associate Member of the Institute of Wood Science [*British*] (DBQ)

AIWSF ...... Association of the International Winter Sports Federations [*Berne, Switzerland*] (EAIO)

AIWSP ...... Associate Member of the Institute of Work Study Practitioners [*British*]

AIX .... Advanced Interactive Executive [*IBM RT Personal Computer*] (BYTE)

AIX .... Astrotech International Corp. [*AMEX symbol*] (SPSG)

AIX .... Australian International Tax Agreements [*A publication*]

AIX .... Mekoryuk, AK [*Location identifier*] [*FAA*] (FAAL)

AIY .... Atlantic City [*New Jersey*] [*Airport symbol*] (OAG)

AIY .... Ayrshire Imperial Yeomanry [*British military*] (DMA)

Aiyar........ Aiyar's Company Cases [*India*] [*A publication*] (DLA)

Aiyar CC ... Aiyar's Company Cases [*India*] [*A publication*] (DLA)

Aiyar LPC ... Aiyar's Leading Privy Council Cases [*India*] [*A publication*] (DLA)

Aiyar Unrep D ... Aiyar's Unreported Decisions [*India*] [*A publication*] (DLA)

AIZ .... Amcast Industrial [*NYSE symbol*] (SPSG)

AIZ .... Lake Of The Ozarks [*Missouri*] [*Airport symbol*] (OAG)

AIZAAD.... Annali. Istituto Sperimentale per la Zoologia Agraria [*A publication*]

AIZLA .... Archiwum Inzynierii Ladowej [*A publication*]

AJ .... Acta Juridica [*South Africa*] [*A publication*] (ILCA)

AJ .... Acting Judge (ADA)

AJ .... Acting Justice (ADA)

AJ .... Actualite Juridique [*A publication*] (ILCA)

AJ .... Adas [*or Adath*] Jeshurun (BJA)

AJ .... Adjustment [*Accounting*]

AJ .... Aero Filipinas, Inc. [*Philippines*] [*ICAO designator*] (FAAC)

AJ .... After Japan [*Industry*]

AJ .... Air Jordan [*Airline*]

Aj............. Ajax [*of Sophocles*] [*Classical studies*] (OCD)

AJ .... Ajoutez [*Add*] [*Music*]

AJ .... Alaska Journal of Commerce and Pacific Rim Reporter [*A publication*]

Aj............. All India Reporter, Ajmer Series [*A publication*] (ILCA)

AJ .... Alliance Journal [*A publication*]

AJ .... Alliance for Justice (EA)

AJ .... Alloy Junction

AJ .... [*The*] Alma & Jonquieres Railway Co. [*AAR code*]

AJ .... American Jurist [*A publication*] (DLA)

AJ .... Analog Junction (TEL)

AJ .... Anderson Jacobson, Inc. [*Terminal manufacturer*] [*AMEX symbol*] (SPSG)

AJ .... Andrew Jackson [*US general and president, 1767-1845*]

AJ .... Ankle Jerk [*Neurology*]

AJ .... Antijamming [*RADAR*]

AJ .... Antilliaans Juristenblad [*A publication*]

AJ .... Antiquaries Journal [*London*] [*A publication*]

AJ .... Antiquitates Judaicae [*Jewish Antiquities*] [*of Josephus*] [*Classical studies*] (OCD)

AJ .... Applejack

AJ .... Applied Journalism

AJ .... Arc Jet

AJ .... Archaeological Journal [*A publication*]

AJ .... Architects' Journal [*A publication*]

AJ .... Armee Juive (BJA)

AJ .... Art Journal [*A publication*]

AJ .... Asiatisches Jahrbuch [*A publication*]

AJ .... Assembly Jig

AJ .... Associate Jewelers [*Defunct*] (EA)

AJ .... Associate in Journalism

AJ .... Associate Justice [*US Supreme Court*]

AJ .... Associated with Jobbers [*London Stock Exchange*]

AJ .... Attack Jet

AJ .... Australian Journal [*A publication*]

AJ .... Australian Journalist [*A publication*]

AJ .... British Guiana Supreme Court, Appellate Jurisdiction (DLA)

AJ .... Jasper Public Library, Alberta [*Library symbol*] [*National Library of Canada*] (NLC)

AJA .... Adjacent (AFM)

AJA .... Ajaccio [*Corsica*] [*Airport symbol*] (OAG)

AJA .... American Jail Association (EA)

AJA .... American Jazz Alliance [*Formerly, CJOA*] (EA)

AJA .... American Jewish Archives [*An association*] (EA)

AJA .... American Jewish Archives [*A publication*]

AJA .... American Journal of Agricultural Economics [*A publication*]

AJA .... American Journal of Archaeology [*A publication*]

AJA .... American Judges Association (EA)

AJA .... American Judo Association (EA)

AJA .... Americans of Japanese Ancestry [*Psychometrics*]

AJA .... Anglo-Jewish Archives [*A publication*]

AJA .... Anglo-Jewish Association [*British*]

AJA .... Australian Jewellers' Association

a-ja--- .... Japan [*MARC geographic area code*] [*Library of Congress*] (LCCP)

AJA .... Jarvie Public Library, Alberta [*Library symbol*] [*National Library of Canada*] (NLC)

AJAC .... Automatic Jamming Avoidance Circuitry (AABC)

AJacT .... Jacksonville State University, Jacksonville, AL [*Library symbol*] [*Library of Congress*] (LCLS)

AJADD...... Australian Journal of Alcoholism and Drug Dependence [*A publication*] (APTA)

AJAE........ American Journal of Agricultural Economics [*A publication*]

AJAEB ...... American Journal of Agricultural Economics [*A publication*]

AJAFAC.... Agricultural Journal. Department of Agriculture. Fiji Islands [*A publication*]

AJAG........ Assistant Judge Advocate General [*Army*]

AJAG/CIV ... Assistant Judge Advocate General for Civil Law [*Army*] (AABC)

AJAG/MIL ... Assistant Judge Advocate General for Military Law [*Army*] (AABC)

AJ/AI .... Antijamming/Anti-Interference (CET)

AJAN .... Australian Journal of Advanced Nursing [*A publication*] (APTA)

AJANA...... American Journal of Anatomy [*A publication*]

AJANA2.... American Journal of Anatomy [*A publication*]

AJAO .... American Juvenile Arthritis Organization (EA)

AJAPB9 .... American Journal of Acupuncture [*A publication*]

AJAPW ..... Association of Jewish Anti-Poverty Workers [*Superseded by ECJF*]

AJAQ........ Army Job Activities Questionnaire

AJAr......... American Journal of Archaeology [*A publication*]

AJAR........ Association des Juifs Anciens Resistants [*Association of Jews in the Resistance*] [*Acronym is pseudonym of writer Romain Gary*]

AJ Arch ..... American Journal of Archaeology [*A publication*] (OCD)

AJ Archaeol ... American Journal of Archaeology [*A publication*]

AJAS .... AJAS: Australasian Journal of American Studies [*A publication*] (APTA)

AJAS .... American Junior Academy of Sciences

AJAS .... Associated Japan-America Societies of the United States (EA)

AJAS .... Australian Journal of Applied Science [*A publication*] (APTA)

AJASS .... African Jazz Art Society Studios

AJATA ...... American Journal of Art Therapy [*A publication*]

AJAX......... Ajax Resources Ltd. [*Vancouver, BC*] [*NASDAQ symbol*] (NQ)

AJAY......... Ajay Sports, Inc. [*NASDAQ symbol*] (NQ)

AJAZ........ American Jewish Alternatives to Zionism (EA)

AJB .... Administration of Justice Branch [*US Military Government, Germany*]

AJB .... Associated Japanese Bank (International) Ltd.

AJB .... Audio Junction Box (MCD)

AJB .... Australian Journal of Botany [*A publication*] (APTA)

AJB .... Jacksonville State University, Jacksonville, AL [*OCLC symbol*] (OCLC)

AJBA .... American Junior Brahman Association (EA)

AJBA........	Australian Journal of Biblical Archaeology [*A publication*]
AJBC........	American Junior Bowling Congress　(EA)
AJBI.........	Annual. Japanese Biblical Institute [*A publication*]
AJBIC.......	Arlin J. Brown Information Center　(EA)
AJBJAT.....	Arquivos. Jardim Botanico do Rio De Janeiro [*A publication*]
AJBO........	Antijamming Blackout
AJBOA.......	American Journal of Botany [*A publication*]
AJBOAA.....	American Journal of Botany [*A publication*]
AJBP........	Association of Jewish Book Publishers　(EA)
AJBTA.......	Australian Journal of Botany [*A publication*]
AJC...........	Academy of Japanese Culture [*Australia*]
AJC...........	Alvin Junior College [*Texas*]
AJC...........	American Jewish Committee　(EA)
AJC...........	American Jewish Conference
AJC...........	American Jewish Congress　(EA)
AJC...........	American Joint Committee for Cancer Staging and End Results Reporting [*Later, AJCC*]　(EA)
AJC...........	Arizona Job Colleges [*An association*] [*Defunct*]　(EA)
AJC...........	Austin Junior College [*Later, Austin Community College*] [*Minnesota*]
AJCA........	American Junior Chianina Association　(EA)
AJCAF......	Association of Jewish Chaplains of the Armed Forces　(EA)
AJCARF....	Office of Animal Care and the A. J. Carlson Animal Research Facility [*University of Chicago*] [*Research center*]　(RCD)
AJCBDD....	American Journal of Clinical Biofeedback [*A publication*]
AJCC........	Alternate Joint Command Center　(MCD)
AJCC........	Alternate Joint Communications Center
AJCC........	American Jersey Cattle Club　(EA)
AJCC........	American Joint Committee on Cancer　(EA)
AJC/C........	Commentary. American Jewish Committee [*A publication*]
AJCCA......	American Jewish Correctional Chaplains Association　(EA)
AJCDA......	American Journal of Cardiology [*A publication*]
AJCDAG...	American Journal of Cardiology [*A publication*]
AJCH........	American Jewish Commission on the Holocaust　(EA)
AJCHAS....	Australian Journal of Chemistry [*A publication*]
AJCHDV...	Australian Journal of Clinical and Experimental Hypnosis [*A publication*]
AJCIDY	African Journal of Clinical and Experimental Immunology [*A publication*]
AJCL........	American Journal of Comparative Law [*A publication*]
AJCMBA ..	American Journal of Chinese Medicine [*A publication*]
AJCNA......	American Journal of Clinical Nutrition [*A publication*]
AJCNAC...	American Journal of Clinical Nutrition [*A publication*]
AJCOD......	American Journal of Clinical Oncology [*A publication*]
AJCODI...	American Journal of Clinical Oncology [*A publication*]
AJCP........	Australian Joint Copying Project [*A publication*]　(APTA)
AJCPA......	American Journal of Clinical Pathology [*A publication*]
AJCPAI......	American Journal of Clinical Pathology [*A publication*]
AJCPD......	American Journal of Physiology. Cell Physiology [*A publication*]
AJCRW	Association of Jewish Community Relations Workers　(EA)
AJCS........	Australian Journal of Cultural Studies [*A publication*]
AJCU........	Air Jet Control Unit
AJCU........	Association of Jesuit Colleges and Universities　(EA)
AJCW........	Association of Jewish Center Workers　(EA)
AJD	Antijam Display
AJDA........	Actualite Juridique. Droit Administratif. Revue Mensuelle [*A publication*]
AJDA........	American Journal of Alcohol and Drug Abuse [*A publication*]
AJDABD...	American Journal of Drug and Alcohol Abuse [*A publication*]
AJDC........	American Joint Distribution Committee
AJDC........	American Journal of Diseases of Children [*A publication*]
AJDCA......	American Journal of Diseases of Children [*A publication*]
AJDCAI...	American Journal of Diseases of Children [*A publication*]
AJDDA......	American Journal of Digestive Diseases [*Later, Digestive Diseases and Sciences*] [*A publication*]
AJDDAL...	American Journal of Digestive Diseases [*Later, Digestive Diseases and Sciences*] [*A publication*]
AJDE........	Alperin Jet-Diffuser Ejector　(MCD)
AJDEBP....	Australasian Journal of Dermatology [*A publication*]
AJDG	Air Jet Distortion Generator　(MCD)
AJDKA8....	Azabu Juika Daigaku Kenkyu Hokoku [*Bulletin. Azabu Veterinary College*] [*A publication*]
AJDTAZ ...	Australian Journal of Dairy Technology [*A publication*]
AJE...........	Adjusting Journal Entry [*Accounting*]
AJE...........	Adult Jewish Education
AJE...........	American Journal of Economics and Sociology [*New York*] [*A publication*]
AJE...........	American Journal of Education [*A publication*]
AJE...........	Antijam Equipment
AJE...........	Australian Journal of Education [*A publication*]　(ADA)
AJEAEL.....	Australian Journal of Experimental Agriculture [*A publication*]
AJEBAK....	Australian Journal of Experimental Biology and Medical Science [*A publication*]
AJECDQ ...	Australian Journal of Ecology [*A publication*]
AJ Ecol	Australian Journal of Ecology [*A publication*]
AJ Ed	Australian Journal of Education [*A publication*]
AJEED	Abstract Journal in Earthquake Engineering [*A publication*]
AJEPA......	American Journal of Epidemiology [*A publication*]
AJEPAS....	American Journal of Epidemiology [*A publication*]
AJER	Alberta Journal of Educational Research [*A publication*]

AJES	Aligarh Journal of English Studies [*A publication*]
AJES	American Journal of Economics and Sociology [*New York*] [*A publication*]
AJESA.......	American Journal of Economics and Sociology [*New York*] [*A publication*]
AJET	Australian Journal of Educational Technology [*A publication*]
AJETA6	American Journal of EEG Technology [*A publication*]
AJEUNAL ...	Alliance de Jeunesse Angolaise pour la Liberte [*Alliance of Angolan Youth for Freedom*]
AJEV	American Journal of Enology and Viticulture [*A publication*]　(EAAP)
AJEVAC ...	American Journal of Enology and Viticulture [*A publication*]
AJF	Antijam Frequency
AJF	Association Jeunesse Fransaskoise [*Canada*]
AJF	Jouf [*Saudi Arabia*] [*Airport symbol*]　(OAG)
AJFCA	Association of Jewish Family and Children's Agencies　(EA)
AJFE	Alternatives. Journal of the Friends of the Earth [*Canada*] [*A publication*]
AJFH........	Antijam Frequency Hopper
AJFL.........	Australian Journal of Family Law [*A publication*]
AJFLD.......	Association des Industries des Fruits et Legumes Deshydrates de la CEE [*European Organization of the Dehydrated Fruit and Vegetable Industries*]　(EAIO)
AJFS.........	Australian Journal of Forensic Sciences [*A publication*]　(APTA)
AJFS.........	Australian Journal of French Studies [*A publication*]
AJG	Gallagher [*Arthur J.*] & Co. [*NYSE symbol*]　(SPSG)
AJGA........	American Junior Golf Association
AJGA........	Arizona Jojoba Growers Association　(EA)
AJGAA......	American Journal of Gastroenterology [*A publication*]
AJGAAR ...	American Journal of Gastroenterology [*A publication*]
AJGS	Association of Jewish Genealogical Societies　(EA)
AJGV........	Akademischer Verein fuer Juedische Geschichte und Literatur [*A publication*]
AJH	American Jewish History [*A publication*]
AJH	Antijam Hopper
AJHA	American Junior Hereford Association　(EA)
AJHC	American Jewish Heritage Committee　(EA)
AJHC	American Jewish History Center of the Jewish Theological Seminary [*Defunct*]　(EA)
AJHE........	Australian Journal of Higher Education [*A publication*]　(ADA)
AJHEA......	American Journal of Public Health [*A publication*]
AJHEAA...	American Journal of Public Health [*A publication*]
AJHED......	American Journal of Hematology [*A publication*]
AJHEDD..	American Journal of Hematology [*A publication*]
AJHGA	American Journal of Human Genetics [*A publication*]
AJHGAG ..	American Journal of Human Genetics [*A publication*]
AJHNA3 ...	American Journal of Clinical Hypnosis [*A publication*]
AJHPA	American Journal of Hospital Pharmacy [*A publication*]
AJHPA9....	American Journal of Hospital Pharmacy [*A publication*]
AJHPER ...	Australian Journal for Health, Physical Education, and Recreation [*A publication*]
AJHQ	American Jewish Historical Quarterly [*A publication*]
AJHS........	American Jewish Historical Society
AJHS........	American Jewish Historical Society. Publications [*A publication*]
AJHS J......	Australian Jewish Historical Society. Journal [*A publication*]　(APTA)
AJHSNME ...	American Junior High School National Mathematics Exam
AJHYA2....	American Journal of Hygiene [*A publication*]
AJI............	Ajiro [*Japan*] [*Seismograph station code, US Geological Survey*]　(SEIS)
AJI............	American Jewish Institute [*Later, JIB*]　(EA)
AJI............	American Justice Institute　(EA)
AJI............	Antijamming Improvements　(AABC)
Ajia Keizai ...	Ajia Keizai. Journal of the Institute of Developing Economies [*A publication*]
AJICDC	American Journal of Infection Control [*A publication*]
AJIL	Aca Joe Intercon Limited [*New York, NY*] [*NASDAQ symbol*]　(NQ)
AJIL	American Journal of International Law [*A publication*]
A J I Law ...	American Journal of International Law [*A publication*]
AJIMD8....	American Journal of Industrial Medicine [*A publication*]
AJINB	American Journal of International Law [*A publication*]
AJIS..........	Automated Jail Information System
AJJ............	American Chamber of Commerce in Japan. Journal [*A publication*]
AJJ	Americans for Justice on the Job　(EA)
AJJ	Angel, Jerald J., Los Angeles CA [*STAC*]
AJJ	Arizona Jojoba, Inc. [*Vancouver Stock Exchange symbol*]
AJJDC......	American Jewish Joint Distribution Committee　(EA)
AJJR........	Annales. Societe Jean-Jacques Rousseau [*A publication*]
AJKDD.....	American Journal of Kidney Diseases [*A publication*]
AJKSAX....	Archiv der Julius Klaus-Stiftung fuer Vererbungsforschung, Sozialanthropologie, und Rassenhygiene [*A publication*]
AJL...........	Association of Jewish Libraries
AJL...........	Association of Junior Leagues　(EA)
AJL...........	Australian Journal of Liturgy [*A publication*]　(APTA)
AJLA	Association of the Junior Leagues of America [*Later, AJL*]　(EA)

AJLA .... Automated Juvenile Law Archive [*National Center for Juvenile Justice*] [*Information service or system*] (CRD)
AJLAC ...... American Jewish League Against Communism (EA)
AJLC .... American Jewish Leadership Conference (EA)
AJLI .... American Jewish League for Israel (EA)
AJLL .... Australian Journal of Labour Law [*A publication*]
AJLMDN ... American Journal of Law and Medicine [*A publication*]
AJLO......... Avalanching Junction Light Output
AJLS .... Australian Journal of Law and Society [*A publication*] (APTA)
ajm .... Aljamia [*MARC language code*] [*Library of Congress*] (LCCP)
AJM .... Analog Junction Module (TEL)
AJM .... Archivo Jose Marti [*Cuba*] [*A publication*]
AJM .... Arthur Johnson Memorial Library, Raton, NM [*OCLC symbol*] (OCLC)
AJM .... Australian Journal of Management [*A publication*]
AJM .... Australian Journal of Mining [*A publication*]
AJMA....... American Jesuit Missionary Association [*Later, JM*] (EA)
AJMA....... American Jewelry Marketing Association (EA)
AJMA....... Antijam Manpack Antenna (MCD)
AJMAA ..... American Journal of Mathematics [*A publication*]
AJMD .... American Journal of Mental Deficiency [*A publication*]
AJMDA...... American Journal of Mental Deficiency [*A publication*]
AJMDAW ... American Journal of Mental Deficiency [*A publication*]
AJME........ Americans for Justice in the Middle East (EA)
AJME........ Australian Journal of Music Education [*A publication*] (APTA)
AJMEA ..... American Journal of Medicine [*A publication*]
AJMEA ..... Australian Journal of Music Education [*A publication*]
AJMEAZ .. American Journal of Medicine [*A publication*]
Ajmer-Merwara LJ ... Ajmer-Merwara Law Journal [*India*] [*A publication*] (DLA)
AJMFA ..... Australian Journal of Marine and Freshwater Research [*A publication*]
AJMFA4 ... Australian Journal of Marine and Freshwater Research [*A publication*]
AJMGDA ... American Journal of Medical Genetics [*A publication*]
AJMMAP ... Asian Journal of Modern Medicine [*A publication*]
AJMNA..... Australian Journal of Mental Retardation [*A publication*]
AJ/MRDN ... AND-JEF/Mouvement Revolutionnaire pour la Democratie Nouvelle [*AND-JEF/New Democratic Revolutionary Movement*] [*Senegal*] [*Political party*]
AJMSA ..... American Journal of the Medical Sciences [*A publication*]
AJMSA9 ... American Journal of the Medical Sciences [*A publication*]
AJMSDC .. African Journal of Medicine and Medical Sciences [*A publication*]
AJMTA ..... American Journal of Medical Technology [*A publication*]
AJMTAC .. American Journal of Medical Technology [*A publication*]
AjN .... Adjective Noun [*Used in correcting manuscripts, etc.*]
AJN .... American Journal of Numismatics [*A publication*]
AJN .... Anjouan [*Comoro Islands*] [*Airport symbol*] (OAG)
AJN .... Australian Jewish News [*A publication*] (APTA)
AJNAD ..... Arab Journal of Nuclear Sciences and Applications [*A publication*]
AJNED9.... American Journal of Nephrology [*A publication*]
AJNOD5 ... Ajia Nogyo [*A publication*]
AJNR........ AJNR. American Journal of Neuroradiology [*A publication*]
AJNR........ American Journal of Neuroradiology [*A publication*]
AJNR Am J Neuroradiol ... AJNR. American Journal of Neuroradiology [*A publication*]
AJNT........ Ajurnarmat. Inuit Cultural Institute [*A publication*]
AJNUA ..... American Journal of Nursing [*A publication*]
AJNum ...... American Journal of Numismatics [*A publication*]
AJO .... American Jazz Orchestra
AJO .... Antijam Operator (CET)
AJO .... Association of Jensen Owners (EA)
a-jo--- .... Jordan [*MARC geographic area code*] [*Library of Congress*] (LCCP)
AJOAAX... American Journal of Optometry and Archives of American Academy of Optometry [*Later, American Journal of Optometry and Physiological Optics*] [*A publication*]
AJOE......... Aca Joe Eastern Ltd. [*New York, NY*] [*NASDAQ symbol*] (NQ)
AJOEDE.... African Journal of Ecology [*A publication*]
AJOGA ..... American Journal of Obstetrics and Gynecology [*A publication*]
AJOGAH .. American Journal of Obstetrics and Gynecology [*A publication*]
AJOHA ..... American Journal of Orthodontics [*A publication*]
AJOHAK .. American Journal of Orthodontics [*A publication*]
AJOHBL... Australian Journal of Ophthalmology [*A publication*]
AJOIA....... American Jews Opposed to Israeli Aggression (EA)
AJOJ .... April, July, October, and January [*Denotes quarterly payments of interest or dividends in these months*] [*Business term*]
AJOMA .... Alabama Journal of Medical Sciences [*A publication*]
AJOMAZ ... Alabama Journal of Medical Sciences [*A publication*]
AJOOA7 ... American Journal of Orthodontics and Oral Surgery [*Later, American Journal of Orthodontics*] [*A publication*]
AJOPA...... American Journal of Ophthalmology [*A publication*]
AJOPAA .... American Journal of Ophthalmology [*A publication*]
AJOPs........ American Journal of Orthopsychiatry [*A publication*]
AJORA...... American Journal of Orthopsychiatry [*A publication*]
AJORAG... American Journal of Orthopsychiatry [*A publication*]
AJOT........ American Journal of Occupational Therapy [*A publication*]
AJOTA ...... American Journal of Occupational Therapy [*A publication*]

AJOTAM ... American Journal of Occupational Therapy [*A publication*]
AJOTBN... American Journal of Otology [*A publication*]
Ajour Ind-Tek ... Ajour Industril-Teknikk [*Norway*] [*A publication*]
AJOYA....... American Journal of Optometry [*A publication*]
AJP............ Alarm and Jettison Panel
AJP............ American Journal of Pharmacy [*A publication*]
AJP............ American Journal of Philology [*A publication*]
AJP............ American Journal of Psychiatry [*A publication*]
AJP............ American Journal of Psychoanalysis [*A publication*]
AJP............ Annales des Justices de Paix [*France*] [*A publication*] (ILCA)
AJP............ Australasian Journal of Philosophy [*A publication*] (APTA)
AJP............ Australian Journal of Psychology [*A publication*] (ADA)
AJPA .... American Jewish Press Association (EA)
AJPA .... American Journal of Physical Anthropology [*A publication*]
AJPA .... Australian Journal of Public Administration [*A publication*] (APTA)
AJPAA ...... American Journal of Pathology [*A publication*]
AJPAA4 .... American Journal of Pathology [*A publication*]
AJPBA ...... American Journal of Physical Medicine [*A publication*]
AJPBA7 .... American Journal of Physical Medicine [*A publication*]
AJPC .... American Jewish Periodical Center (EA)
AJPC .... American Jewish Physicians' Committee [*Later, AFHU*] (EA)
AJPCA ...... American Journal of Psychology [*A publication*]
AJPCAA .... American Journal of Psychology [*A publication*]
AJPDA ..... American Journal of Pharmaceutical Education [*A publication*]
AJPDAD ... American Journal of Pharmaceutical Education [*A publication*]
AJPEA ...... American Journal of Public Health and the Nation's Health [*Later, American Journal of Public Health*] [*A publication*]
AJPED ...... American Journal of Physiology. Endocrinology, Metabolism, and Gastrointestinal Physiology [*A publication*]
AJPEEK.... American Journal of Perinatology [*A publication*]
AJPF......... American Jewish Philanthropic Fund (EA)
AJPh......... American Journal of Philology [*A publication*]
AJPH........ American Journal of Public Health [*A publication*]
AJPH........ Australian Journal of Politics and History [*A publication*] (APTA)
AJPHA ...... American Journal of Physiology [*A publication*]
AJPHA ...... American Junior Paint Horse Association (EA)
AJPHA ...... American Junior Polled Hereford Association [*Later, NJPHA*] (EA)
AJPHAP ... American Journal of Physiology [*A publication*]
AJPhil .... American Journal of Philology [*A publication*]
AJPIA .... American Journal of Physics [*A publication*]
AJPM........ Ad Jesum per Mariam [*To Jesus through Mary*] [*Latin*]
AJPMEA .. American Journal of Preventive Medicine [*A publication*]
AJPNA...... American Journal of Physical Anthropology [*A publication*]
AJPNA9.... American Journal of Physical Anthropology [*A publication*]
AJPO......... Ada Joint Program Office [*DoD*] [*Later, Ada Board*] (RDA)
AJPOA...... American Journal of Proctology [*Later, American Journal of Proctology, Gastroenterology, and Colon and Rectal Surgery*] [*A publication*]
AJPOAC ... American Journal of Proctology [*Later, American Journal of Proctology, Gastroenterology, and Colon and Rectal Surgery*] [*A publication*]
AJ Pol & Hist ... Australian Journal of Politics and History [*A publication*] (APTA)
AJPPCH ... Australian Journal of Plant Physiology [*A publication*]
AJPPD ...... American Journal of Physiology. Heart and Circulatory Physiology [*A publication*]
AJPRA ...... American Journal of Pharmacy and the Sciences Supporting Public Health [*Later, American Journal of Pharmacy*] [*A publication*]
AJPRAL.... American Journal of Pharmacy and the Sciences Supporting Public Health [*Later, American Journal of Pharmacy*] [*A publication*]
AJPRS....... American Jewish Public Relations Society (EA)
AJPs .... American Journal of Psychology [*A publication*]
AJPSA...... American Journal of Psychiatry [*A publication*]
AJPSAO.... American Journal of Psychiatry [*A publication*]
AJPSBP .... Australian Journal of Pharmaceutical Sciences [*A publication*]
AJPst .... American Journal of Psychotherapy [*A publication*]
AJPsy .... American Journal of Psychiatry [*A publication*]
A J Psy...... American Journal of Psychology [*A publication*]
AJPsych .... American Journal of Psychology [*A publication*]
AJ Psychol ... American Journal of Psychology [*A publication*]
AJPTAR.... American Journal of Psychotherapy [*A publication*]
AJPTDU ... American Journal of Primatology [*A publication*]
AJPXA .... Australasian Journal of Pharmacy. Science Supplement [*A publication*]
AJPXA5 .... Australasian Journal of Pharmacy. Science Supplement [*A publication*]
AJPYA8 .... American Journal of Psychoanalysis [*A publication*]
AJQ .... Army Job Questionnaire
AJQ .... Australian Jazz Quarterly [*A publication*] (APTA)
AJQHA .... American Junior Quarter Horse Association (EA)
AJR........... Agent Job Review [*LIMRA*]
AJR........... Ajax Resources Ltd. [*Vancouver Stock Exchange symbol*]
AJR........... AJR. American Journal of Roentgenology [*A publication*]
AJR........... Assembly Joint Resolution [*Congress*]
AJR........... Association of Jewish Refugees in Great Britain
AJR........... Australian Journal of Reading [*A publication*] (APTA)

AJR........... Australian Journalism Review [*A publication*]   (APTA)
AJR........... Australian Jurist Reports [*A publication*]   (APTA)
AJR........... Automatic "J" Relay   (MCD)
ajr........... Azerbaijan Soviet Socialist Republic [*MARC country of publication code*] [*Library of Congress*]   (LCCP)
A (Jr A)...... Arizoniana (Journal of Arizona History) [*A publication*]
AJR Am J Roentgenol ... AJR. American Journal of Roentgenology [*A publication*]
AJRC........ American Junior Red Cross
AJRFD...... American Journal of Physiology. Renal, Fluid, and Electrolyte Physiology [*A publication*]
AJRI......... American Journal of Reproductive Immunology [*A publication*]
AJRI Am J Reprod Immunol ... AJRI. American Journal of Reproductive Immunology [*A publication*]
AJRIM Am J Reprod Immunol Microbiol ... AJRIM. American Journal of Reproductive Immunology and Microbiology [*A publication*]
AJRL........ Ross [*A. J.*] Logistics, Inc. [*Keasbey, NJ*] [*NASDAQ symbol*]   (NQ)
AJRMEK .. AJRIM. American Journal of Reproductive Immunology and Microbiology [*A publication*]
AJR (NC) .. Australian Jurist Reports (Notes of Cases) [*A publication*]   (APTA)
AJROA...... American Journal of Roentgenology [*A publication*]
AJROAM ... AJR. American Journal of Roentgenology [*A publication*]
AJRRA...... American Journal of Roentgenology, Radium Therapy, and Nuclear Medicine [*Later, American Journal of Roentgenology*] [*A publication*]
AJRRAV ... American Journal of Roentgenology, Radium Therapy, and Nuclear Medicine [*Later, American Journal of Roentgenology*] [*A publication*]
AJRTA ...... American Journal of Roentgenology and Radium Therapy [*Later, American Journal of Roentgenology*] [*A publication*]
AJS........... Actes Juridiques Susiens [*A publication*]
AJS........... Alliance des Jeunes pour le Socialisme [*Alliance of Youth for Socialism*] [*France*] [*Political party*]   (PPE)
AJS........... American Journal of Science [*A publication*]
AJS........... American Journal of Semiotics [*A publication*]
AJS........... American Journal of Sociology [*A publication*]
AJS........... American Judicature Society   (EA)
AJS........... Angle Jamming System
AJS........... Antijam Synthesizer
AJS........... Association for Jewish Studies   (EA)
AJS........... Axisymmetric Jet Stretcher
AJSA........ American Junior Shorthorn Association   (EA)
AJSA........ American Junior Simmental Association [*Later, ASA*]   (EA)
AJSBD...... American Journal of Small Business [*A publication*]
AJSC........ Association of Jewish Sponsored Camps   (EA)
AJSCA...... American Journal of Science [*A publication*]
AJSCAP ... American Journal of Science [*A publication*]
AJSci........ American Journal of Science [*A publication*]
AJSemL..... American Journal of Semitic Languages and Literatures [*A publication*]
AJSH........ Journal of Occupational Health and Safety - Australia and New Zealand [*A publication*]
AJSI......... Australian Journal of Social Issues [*A publication*]   (ADA)
AJSIA9...... Australian Journal of Science [*A publication*]
AJSL......... American Journal of Semitic Languages and Literatures [*A publication*]
AJSLL....... American Journal of Semitic Languages and Literatures [*Chicago, IL*] [*A publication*]
AJSMD..... American Journal of Sports Medicine [*A publication*]
AJSMF...... Australian Journal of Sex, Marriage, and Family [*A publication*]   (APTA)
AJSMOC .. AJS [*Albert John Stevens*] and Matchless Owners Club [*Mount Sorrel, Leicestershire, England*]   (EAIO)
AJSN........ Association for Jewish Studies. Newsletter [*A publication*]
AJSOA...... American Journal of Sociology [*A publication*]
AJ Soc....... American Journal of Sociology [*A publication*]
AJ Soc Is.... Australian Journal of Social Issues [*A publication*]
AJ Soc Iss ... Australian Journal of Social Issues [*A publication*]   (APTA)
AJSPDX.... American Journal of Surgical Pathology [*A publication*]
AJSR .... Australian Journal of Scientific Research [*A publication*]   (APTA)
AJSS......... American Jewish Society for Service   (EA)
AJSS......... Australian Joint Staff Service   (AABC)
AJSUA...... American Journal of Surgery [*A publication*]
AJSUAB.... American Journal of Surgery [*A publication*]
AJSW........ Australian Journal of Social Work [*A publication*]   (ADA)
AJT........... Advanced Jet Trainer
AJT........... American Journal of Theology [*A publication*]
AJT........... Amerijet International [*Fort Lauderdale, FL*] [*FAA designator*]   (FAAC)
AJT........... Antijam Technique
AJTC........ American Japanese Trade Committee   (EA)
AJTh......... American Journal of Theology [*A publication*]
AJTHA...... American Journal of Tropical Medicine and Hygiene [*A publication*]

AJTHAB ... American Journal of Tropical Medicine and Hygiene [*A publication*]
AJTHBC ... African Journal of Tropical Hydrobiology and Fisheries [*A publication*]
AJTI......... Association on Japanese Textile Imports [*Defunct*]   (EA)
AJTR........ Allowance Prescribed in Joint Travel Regulations [*Military*]   (AABC)
AJTRDA ... American Journal of Therapeutics and Clinical Reports [*A publication*]
AJTSBB .... African Journal of Tropical Hydrobiology and Fisheries. Special Issue [*A publication*]
AJT(UK) ... Association of Jamaican Trusts (United Kingdom) [*London, England*]
AJU .... Aracaju [*Brazil*] [*Airport symbol*]   (OAG)
AJu .... Archives Juives [*A publication*]
AJU .... Washington, DC [*Location identifier*] [*FAA*]   (FAAL)
A Jur Rep... Australian Jurist Reports [*A publication*]   (APTA)
AJUS .... Antarctic Journal of the United States [*A publication*]
AJVD........ Abrupt Junction Varactor Doubler
AJVRA...... American Journal of Veterinary Research [*A publication*]
AJVRAH.... American Journal of Veterinary Research [*A publication*]
AJW.......... Alexandria, MN [*Location identifier*] [*FAA*]   (FAAL)
AJWDFP... Arab-Jewish Women's Dialogue for Peace   (EA)
AJWR....... Alternate Joint War Room [*Later, ANMCC*]   (CINC)
AJWS .... American Jewish World Service   (EA)
AJY .... Agades [*Niger*] [*Airport symbol*]   (OAG)
AJY.......... Ajay Resources, Inc. [*Vancouver Stock Exchange symbol*]
AJY.......... American Jewish Yearbook [*A publication*]
AJY........... Ashland, KY [*Location identifier*] [*FAA*]   (FAAL)
AJY.......... Association for Jewish Youth [*British*]
AJYB........ American Jewish Yearbook [*A publication*]
AJZOA...... Australian Journal of Zoology [*A publication*]
AJZOAS ... Australian Journal of Zoology [*A publication*]
AJZSA6..... Australian Journal of Zoology. Supplementary Series [*A publication*]
AK........... Above Knee [*Medicine*]
AK........... Ackerley Communications, Inc. [*AMEX symbol*]   (SPSG)
AK........... Adapter Kit   (MCD)
AK........... Adaption Kit
AK........... Adenosine Kinase [*An enzyme*]
AK........... Adenylate Kinase [*An enzyme*]
AK........... Afterpiece Kisser [*Slang*] [*Bowdlerized version*]
AK........... Agoranomikos Kodix [*Marketing Code*] [*Greek*]
AK........... Air-Bridge Carriers Ltd. [*ICAO designator*]   (FAAC)
Ak........... Akademie [*Academy*] [*German*]   (BJA)
AK........... Aktienkapital [*Share Capital*] [*German*] [*Business term*]
AK........... Alaska [*Postal code*]
AK........... Alaska Music Educator [*A publication*]
Ak........... Alaska State Library, Juneau, AK [*Library symbol*] [*Library of Congress*]   (LCLS)
AK........... Albright-Knox Art Gallery [*Buffalo, NY*]
AK........... Allied Kommandatura
AK........... Alte Kaempfer [*Old Fighters*] [*German*]
AK........... Alternaria kikuchiana [*A toxin-producing fungus*]
AK........... Amplitude Keyed
AK........... Anterior [*Wall of*] Kidney
AK........... Antike Kunst [*A publication*]
AK........... Apogee Kick [*NASA*]   (KSC)
AK........... Apple's Kin [*An association*] [*Inactive*]   (EA)
ak........... Arany Korona [*Gold Crown (Hungarian currency before World War I, still used to estimate real estate values)*]
AK........... Arbeitskraft
AK........... Archaeologiai Koezlemenyek [*A publication*]
AK........... Archiv fuer Kulturgeschichte [*A publication*]
Ak........... Arkansas Reports [*A publication*]   (DLA)
AK........... Arkheologiia [*A publication*]
AK........... Armee Korps [*Army Corps*] [*German*]
AK........... 'Arse over Kettle [*Head over heels*] [*Slang*] [*British*]   (DSUE)
A to K ...... Assault to Kill [*FBI standardized term*]
AK........... Ateneum Kaplanskie [*A publication*]
AK........... Aviation Storekeeper [*Navy rating*]
AK........... Avtomat Kalashnikov [*Submachine Gun*] [*USSR*]
AK........... Cargo Ship [*of any type*] [*Navy symbol*]
ak-----...... Caspian Sea and Area [*MARC geographic area code*] [*Library of Congress*]   (LCCP)
AK........... E. Merck AG [*Germany*] [*Research code symbol*]
AK........... Kitscoty Public Library, Alberta [*Library symbol*] [*National Library of Canada*]   (NLC)
AK1.......... Aviation Storekeeper, First Class [*Navy rating*]
AK1.......... West Kanaga [*Alaska*] [*Seismograph station code, US Geological Survey*]   (SEIS)
AK2.......... Aviation Storekeeper, Second Class [*Navy rating*]
AK2.......... South Tanaga [*Alaska*] [*Seismograph station code, US Geological Survey*]   (SEIS)
AK3.......... Aviation Storekeeper, Third Class [*Navy rating*]
AK3.......... North Tanaga [*Alaska*] [*Seismograph station code, US Geological Survey*]   (SEIS)
AK5.......... North Tanaga [*Alaska*] [*Seismograph station code, US Geological Survey*]   (SEIS)
AKA .... Above Knee Amputation [*Medicine*]
AKA .... Alaska   (ROG)

AKA .... Albert Kahn Associates [*Founded in 1895, one of the oldest architectural firms in the US*]
AKA .... Also Known As
AKA .... American Killifish Association (EA)
AKA .... American Kinesiotherapy Association (EA)
AKA .... American Kitefliers Association (EA)
AKA .... Ankang [*China*] [*Airport symbol*] (OAG)
AKA .... Annals of the Kings of Assyria [*A publication*] (BJA)
AKA .... Arkansas Arts Center, Little Rock, AR [*OCLC symbol*] (OCLC)
AKA .... Attack Cargo Ship [*Navy symbol*]
AkA .... Z. J. Loussac Public Library, Anchorage, AK [*Library symbol*] [*Library of Congress*] (LCLS)
AKAA .... Airman Apprentice, Aviation Storekeeper [*Navy rating*]
AkAAH ..... Alaska Health Sciences Library, Anchorage, AK [*Library symbol*] [*Library of Congress*] (LCLS)
AkAAP ...... United States Department of the Interior, Alaska Pipeline Office, Anchorage, AK [*Library symbol*] [*Library of Congress*] (LCLS)
AkAAR ...... United States Department of the Interior, Alaska Resources Library, Anchorage, AK [*Library symbol*] [*Library of Congress*] (LCLS)
AkAAVS .... UAITC/CIT/Audio Visual Services, Anchorage, AK [*Library symbol*] [*Library of Congress*] (LCLS)
AKABA7 .... Arkansas. Agricultural Experiment Station. Bulletin [*A publication*]
AkAbF .... United States National Marine Fisheries Service, Auke Bay Fisheries Laboratory, Auke Bay, AK [*Library symbol*] [*Library of Congress*] (LCLS)
AkAbU ...... University of Alaska, Juneau-Douglas Southeastern College, Auke Bay, AK [*Library symbol*] [*Library of Congress*] (LCLS)
AkAC .... Anchorage Community College, Anchorage, AK [*Library symbol*] [*Library of Congress*] (LCLS)
AkACon ..... Anchorage Higher Education Consortium Library, Anchorage, AK [*Library symbol*] [*Library of Congress*] (LCLS)
AKADCOMRGN ... Alaskan ADCOM Region [*Military*]
Akad Ekon Poznaniu Zesz Nauk ... Akademia Ekonomiczna w Poznaniu Zeszyty Naukowe [*A publication*]
Akad Ekon Poznaniu Zesz Nauk Ser 2 ... Akademia Ekonomiczna w Poznaniu Zeszyty Naukowe. Seria 2. Prace Habilitacyjne i Doktorskie [*A publication*]
Akad Nauk Armjan SSR Dokl ... Akademija Nauk Armjanskoi SSR. Doklady [*A publication*]
Akad Nauk Arm SSR Dokl ... Akademiya Nauk Armyanskoy SSR. Doklady [*A publication*]
Akad Nauk Armyan SSR Izv Ser Mek ... Akademiya Nauk Armyanskoi SSR. Izvestiya. Seriya Mekhanika [*A publication*]
Akad Nauka Umjet Bosne Hercegov Rad Odjelj Prirod Mat Nauka ... Akademija Nauka i Umjetnosti Bosne i Hercegovine. Radovi Odjeljenje Prirodnih i Matematickih Nauka [*A publication*]
Akad Nauka Umjet Bosne Hercegov Rad Odjel Tehn Nauka ... Akademija Nauka i Umjetnosti Bosne i Hercegovine. Radovi Odjeljenje Tehnickih Nauka [*A publication*]
Akad Nauka i Umjet Bosne Hercegov Rad Odjelj Tehn Nauka ... Akademija Nauka i Umjetnosti Bosne i Hercegovine. Radovi Odjeljenje Tehnickih Nauka [*A publication*]
Akad Nauk Azerbaidzan SSR Dokl ... Akademija Nauk Azerbaidzanskoi SSR. Doklady [*A publication*]
Akad Nauk Azerb SSR Dokl ... Akademiya Nauk Azerbaydzhanskoy SSR. Doklady [*A publication*]
Akad Nauk Azerb SSR Izv Ser Nauk Zemle ... Akademiya Nauk Azerbaydzhanskoy SSR. Izvestiya. Seriya Nauk o Zemle [*A publication*]
Akad Nauk BSSR Dokl ... Akademiya Nauk BSSR. Doklady [*A publication*]
Akad Nauk Gruzin SSR Trudy Tbiliss Mat Inst Razmadze ... Akademija Nauk Gruzinskoi SSR. Trudy Tbilisskogo Matematiceskogo Instituta Imeni A. M. Razmadze [*A publication*]
Akad Nauk Gruz SSR Geol Inst Tr ... Akademiya Nauk Gruzinskoy SSR. Geologicheskiy Institut. Trudy [*A publication*]
Akad Nauk Gruz SSR Inst Neorg Khim Elektrokhim Sb ... Akademiya Nauk Gruzinskoy SSR. Institut Neorganicheskoi Khimii i Elektrokhimii Sbornik [*A publication*]
Akad Nauk Gruz SSR Soobshch ... Akademiya Nauk Gruzinskoy SSR. Soobshcheniya [*A publication*]
Akad Nauk Kazah SSR Trudy Astrofiz Inst ... Akademija Nauk Kazahskoi SSR. Trudy Astrofiziceskogo Instituta [*A publication*]
Akad Nauk Kazah SSR Trudy Inst Mat i Meh ... Akademija Nauk Kazahskoi SSR. Trudy Instituta Matematiki i Mehaniki [*A publication*]
Akad Nauk Kazakh SSR Trudy Astrofiz Inst ... Akademiya Nauk Kazakhskoy SSR. Trudy Astrofizicheskogo Instituta [*A publication*]
Akad Nauk Kazak SSR Izv Ser Fiz Mat ... Akademiya Nauk Kazakhskoi SSR. Izvestiya. Seriya Fiziko-Matematicheskaya [*A publication*]
Akad Nauk Kaz SSR Inst Geol Nauk Tr ... Akademiya Nauk Kazakhskoy SSR. Institut Geologicheskikh Nauk. Trudy [*A publication*]
Akad Nauk Kaz SSR Izv Ser Geol ... Akademiya Nauk Kazakhskoy SSR. Izvestiya. Seriya Geologicheskaya [*A publication*]
Akad Nauk SSSR Dokl ... Akademiya Nauk SSSR. Doklady [*A publication*]

Akad Nauk SSSR Doklady Izvestiia Ser Geol ... Akademiia Nauk SSSR. Doklady. Izvestiia. Seriia Geologicheskaia [*A publication*]
Akad Nauk SSSR Geol Inst Tr ... Akademiya Nauk SSSR. Geologicheskiy Institut. Trudy [*A publication*]
Akad Nauk SSSR Geol Inst Trudy ... Akademiya Nauk SSSR. Geologicheskiy Institut. Trudy [*A publication*]
Akad Nauk SSSR Geomorfol Kom Plenum Mater ... Akademiya Nauk SSSR. Geomorfologicheskaya Komissiya. Plenum. Materialy [*A publication*]
Akad Nauk SSSR Inst Nefti Trud ... Akademia Nauk SSSR Institut Nefti Trudy [*A publication*]
Akad Nauk SSSR Inst Prikl Mat Preprint ... Akademiya Nauk SSSR. Institut Prikladnoi Matematiki. Preprint [*A publication*]
Akad Nauk SSSR Izv Ser Fiz ... Akademiya Nauk SSSR. Izvestiya. Seriya Fizicheskaya [*A publication*]
Akad Nauk SSSR Izv Ser Geogr ... Akademiya Nauk SSSR. Izvestiya. Seriya Geograficheskaya [*A publication*]
Akad Nauk SSSR Izv Ser Geol ... Akademiya Nauk SSSR. Izvestiya. Seriya Geologicheskaya [*A publication*]
Akad Nauk SSSR Komi Fil Inst Geol Tr ... Akademiya Nauk SSSR. Komi Filial. Institut Geologii. Trudy [*A publication*]
Akad Nauk SSSR Kom Izuch Chetvertich Perioda Byull ... Akademiya Nauk SSSR. Komissiya po Izucheniyu Chetvertichnogo Perioda. Byulleten [*A publication*]
Akad Nauk SSSR Kom Opred Absol Vozrasta Geol Form Tr ... Akademiya Nauk SSSR. Kommissiya po Opredeleniyu Absolyutnogo Vozrasta Geologicheskikh Formatsiy. Trudy [*A publication*]
Akad Nauk SSSR Metallofizka ... Akademiya Nauk SSSR. Metallofizika [*A publication*]
Akad Nauk SSSR Mezhduvedomstv Geofiz Kom Geofiz Byull ... Akademiya Nauk SSSR Mezhduvedomstvennoyy Geofizicheskiy Komitet pri Presidiume Geofizicheskiy Byulleten [*A publication*]
Akad Nauk SSSR Paleontol Inst Tr ... Akademiya Nauk SSSR. Paleontologicheskiy Institut Trudy [*A publication*]
Akad Nauk SSSR Sibirsk Otdel Vychisl Tsentr Preprint ... Akademiya Nauk SSSR. Sibirskoe Otdelenie Vychislitelnyi Tsentr. Preprint [*A publication*]
Akad Nauk SSSR Sibirsk Otdel Vycisl Centr Preprint ... Akademija Nauk SSSR. Sibirskoe Otdelenie. Vycislitelnyi Centr. Preprint [*Novosibirsk*] [*A publication*]
Akad Nauk SSSR Sib Otd Inst Geol Geofiz Tr ... Akademiya Nauk SSSR. Sibirskoe Otdelenie. Institut Geologii i Geofiziki. Trudy [*A publication*]
Akad Nauk SSSR Sib Otd Limnol Inst Tr ... Akademiya Nauk SSSR. Sibirskoe Otdelenie. Limnologicheskiy Institut. Trudy Novosibirsk [*A publication*]
Akad Nauk SSSR Trudy Jakutsk Filial Ser Fiz ... Akademija Nauk SSSR. Trudy Jakutskogo Filiala. Serija Fiziceskaja [*A publication*]
Akad Nauk SSSR Ural Fil Tr Inst Khim ... Akademiya Nauk SSSR. Ural'skii Filial. Trudy Instituta Khimii [*A publication*]
Akad Nauk SSSR Ural Nauchn Tsentr Inst Geol Geokhim Tr ... Akademiya Nauk SSSR. Ural'skiy Nauchnyi Tsentr. Institut Geologii i Geokhimii. Trudy [*A publication*]
Akad Nauk SSSR Vestn ... Akademiya Nauk SSSR. Vestnik [*A publication*]
Akad Nauk Tadzh SSR Dokl ... Akademiya Nauk Tadzhikskoy SSR. Doklady [*A publication*]
Akad Nauk Tadzh SSR Otd Fiz-Mat Geol-Khim Nauk Izv ... Akademiya Nauk Tadzhikskoy SSR. Otdeleniye Fiziko-Matematicheskikh i Geologo-Khimicheskikh Nauk. Izvestiya [*A publication*]
Akad Nauk Turkm SSR Izv Ser Fiz-Tekh Khim Geol Nauk ... Akademiya Nauk Turkmenskoy SSR. Izvestiya. Seriya Fiziko-Tekhnicheskikh. Khimicheskikh i Geologicheskikh Nauk [*A publication*]
Akad Nauk Ukrain SSR Inst Mat Preprint ... Akademiya Nauk Ukrainskoi SSR. Institut Matematiki. Preprint [*A publication*]
Akad Nauk Ukr RSR Dopov Ser B ... Akademiya Nauk Ukrainskoy RSR. Dopovidi. Seriya B. Geologiya, Geofizika, Khimiya, ta Biologiya [*A publication*]
Akad Nauk Ukr RSR Inst Teploenerg Zb Pr ... Akademia Nauk Ukrainskoi RSR. Institut Teploenergetiki. Zbirnik Prats [*Ukrainian SSR*] [*A publication*]
Akad Nauk Ukr SSR Metallofiz ... Akademiya Nauk Ukrainskoi SSR. Metallofizika [*A publication*]
Akad Nauk Ukr SSR Ser Metallofiz ... Akademiya Nauk Ukrainskoi SSR. Seriya Metallofizika [*Ukrainian SSR*] [*A publication*]
Akad Roln Warszawie Zesz Nauk Ogrod ... Akademia Rolnicza w Warszawie Zeszyty Naukowe Ogrodnictwo [*A publication*]
Akad Roln Warszawie Zesz Nauk Roln ... Akademia Rolnicza w Warszawie. Zeszyty Naukowe. Rolnictwo [*A publication*]
Akad Roln Wroclawiu Zesz Nauk Melior ... Akademia Rolnicza we Wroclawiu Zeszyty Naukowe Melioracja [*A publication*]
Akad Roln Wroclawiu Zesz Nauk Zootech ... Akademia Rolnicza we Wroclawiu Zeszyty Naukowe Zootechnika [*A publication*]
Akad Wiss DDR Abt Math Naturwiss Tech Abh ... Akademie der Wissenschaften der DDR. Abteilung Mathematik, Naturwissenschaften, Technik. Abhandlungen [*A publication*]

Akad Wiss DDR Zentralinst Phys Erde Veroeff ... Akademie der Wissenschaften der DDR. Zentralinstitut fuer Physik der Erde. Veroeffentlichungen [*A publication*]

Akad d Wiss Denksch Philos-Hist Kl ... Akademie der Wissenschaften in Wien. Philosophisch-Historische Klasse. Denkschriften [*A publication*]

Akad Wiss Goettingen Math Phys Kl Abh Folge 3 ... Akademie der Wissenschaften in Goettingen. Mathematisch-Physikalische Klasse. Abhandlungen. Folge 3 [*A publication*]

Akad Wiss Gottingen Nachr Math-Physikal Kl ... Akademie der Wissenschaften in Goettingen. Nachrichten. Mathematisch-Physikalische Klasse [*A publication*]

Akad Wiss Lit Abh Math-Naturwiss Kl (Mainz) ... Akademie der Wissenschaften und der Literatur in Mainz. Abhandlungen der Mathematisch-Naturwissenschaftlichen Klasse [*A publication*]

Akad Wiss Lit Mainz Abh Math-Natur Kl ... Akademie der Wissenschaften und der Literatur in Mainz. Abhandlungen der Mathematisch-Naturwissenschaftlichen Klasse [*A publication*]

Akad Wiss Lit Mainz Abh Math-Naturwiss Kl ... Akademie der Wissenschaften und der Literatur in Mainz. Abhandlungen der Mathematisch-Naturwissenschaftlichen Klasse [*A publication*]

Akad Wiss Lit Mainz Jahrb ... Akademie der Wissenschaften und der Literatur in Mainz. Jahrbuch (Wiesbaden) [*A publication*]

Akad Wiss Lit Mainz Math-Naturwiss Kl Abh ... Akademie der Wissenschaften und der Literatur in Mainz. Abhandlungen der Mathematisch-Naturwissenschaftlichen Klasse (Wiesbaden) [*A publication*]

Akad Wiss Lit Mainz Math Naturwiss Kl Res Mol Biol ... Akademie der Wissenschaften und der Literatur in Mainz. Mathematisch-Naturwissenschaftliche Klasse. Research in Molecular Biology [*A publication*]

Akad d Wiss Sitzungsb Philos-Hist Kl ... Akademie der Wissenschaften in Wien. Philosophisch-Historische Klasse. Sitzungsberichte [*A publication*]

Akad Wiss Wien ... Sitzungsberichte. Akademie der Wissenschaften in Wien [*A publication*]

AkAF .... United States National Marine Fisheries Service, Area Office, Anchorage, AK [*Library symbol*] [*Library of Congress*] (LCLS)

AkAGS ...... Church of Jesus Christ of Latter-Day Saints, Genealogical Society Library, Anchorage Branch, Anchorage, AK [*Library symbol*] [*Library of Congress*] (LCLS)

AkAH .... United States Public Health Service, Arctic Health Research Center, Anchorage, AK [*Library symbol*] [*Library of Congress*] (LCLS)

AKAJAV ... Journal. American Killifish Association [*A publication*]

Ak Alm ...... Magyar Tudomanyos Akademia Almanachja [*A publication*]

AkAM .... Alaska Methodist University, Anchorage, AK [*Library symbol*] [*Library of Congress*] (LCLS)

AKAMA6 .. Arkansas. Agricultural Experiment Station. Mimeograph Series [*A publication*]

AKAN .... Airman, Aviation Storekeeper [*Navy rating*]

AKARAL ... Arkansas. Agricultural Experiment Station. Report Series [*A publication*]

AkAS .... Anchorage School District, Library Resources, Anchorage, AK [*Library symbol*] [*Library of Congress*] (LCLS)

AKASAO ... Arkansas Academy of Science. Proceedings [*A publication*]

AkAU .... University of Alaska, Anchorage, AK [*Library symbol*] [*Library of Congress*] (LCLS)

AKAW .... Abhandlungen. Koenigliche Preussische Akademie der Wissenschaften zu Berlin [*A publication*]

AKAW .... Anzeiger. Kaiserliche Akademie der Wissenschaften [*Wien*] [*A publication*]

AKB .... Internationales Afrikaforum [*A publication*]

AkB .... Kuskokwin Consortium Library, Bethel, AK [*Library symbol*] [*Library of Congress*] (LCLS)

AKB .... University of Arkansas at Pine Bluff, Pine Bluff, AR [*OCLC symbol*] (OCLC)

AkBarNA .. United States Navy, Naval Arctic Research Laboratory, Barrow, AK [*Library symbol*] [*Library of Congress*] (LCLS)

AKBCC ...... Australia-Korea Business Cooperation Committee

AkBIA .... United States Bureau of Indian Affairs, Bethel Regional Library, Bethel, AK [*Library symbol*] [*Library of Congress*] (LCLS)

AKBS .... Advanced Kinematic Bombing System

AKBZAG ... Archiv fuer Kreislaufforschung [*A publication*]

AKC .... American Kennel Club (EA)

AKC .... Anchor Machine & Manufacturing Ltd. [*Toronto Stock Exchange symbol*]

AKC .... Army Kinematograph Corporation [*British military*] (DMA)

AKC .... Associate of King's College [*London*]

AKC .... Australia Kangaroo Club [*Defunct*] (EA)

AKC .... Aviation Storekeeper, Chief [*Navy rating*]

AkC .... Cordova Public Library, Cordova, AK [*Library symbol*] [*Library of Congress*] (LCLS)

AKC .... Keg River Community Library, Alberta [*Library symbol*] [*National Library of Canada*] (NLC)

AKC .... University of Central Arkansas, Conway, AR [*OCLC symbol*] (OCLC)

AKCA .... Associated Koi Clubs of America (EA)

AKCBA ...... Akita-Kenkritsu Chuo Byoin Igaku Zasshi [*Akita Central Hospital. Medical Journal*] [*A publication*]

AKCBAH .. Akita-Kenkritsu Chuo Byoin Igaku Zasshi [*Akita Central Hospital. Medical Journal*] [*A publication*]

AKCL .... Associate of King's College London

AKCM .... Aviation Storekeeper, Master Chief [*Navy rating*]

AKCS .... Aviation Storekeeper, Senior Chief [*Navy rating*]

AKCVA ...... Archiv fuer Klinische Chirurgie. Langenbecks [*A publication*]

AKD .... Alkylketene Dimer [*Organic chemistry*]

AKD .... Automatic Key Distribution

AKD .... Cargo Ship, Dock [*Navy symbol*]

AKD .... Central Arkansas Library System, Little Rock, AR [*OCLC symbol*] (OCLC)

AKDDA ..... Bulletin. Akron Dental Society [*Ohio*] [*A publication*]

AKDEDY .. Aktuelle Dermatologie [*A publication*]

AkDil .... Dillingham Public Library, Dillingham, AK [*Library symbol*] [*Library of Congress*] (LCLS)

AkDj .... Delta Community Library, Delta Junction, AK [*Library symbol*] [*Library of Congress*] (LCLS)

AKDJA ...... Arkansas Dental Journal [*A publication*]

AKDV .... Anzeiger fuer Kunde der Deutschen Vorzeit [*A publication*]

AKE .... Akers Medical Technology Ltd. [*Vancouver Stock Exchange symbol*]

AKE .... Akieni [*Gabon*] [*Airport symbol*] (OAG)

AKE .... Ammunition Transport

AKE .... Hendrix College, Conway, AR [*OCLC symbol*] (OCLC)

AKEC .... Keephills Community Library, Alberta [*Library symbol*] [*National Library of Canada*] (NLC)

AKEDAX ... Archiv fuer Klinische und Experimentelle Dermatologie [*A publication*]

AkEiel .... United States Air Force, Base Library, Eielson AFB, AK [*Library symbol*] [*Library of Congress*] (LCLS)

AKEL .... Anorthotiko Komma Ergazomenou Laou [*Progressive Party of the Working People*] [*Cyprus*] [*Political party*] (PPW)

AkElm .... United States Air Force, Base Library, Elmendorf AFB, AK [*Library symbol*] [*Library of Congress*] (LCLS)

AkElmM .... United States Air Force, Hospital Medical Library/SGAL, Elmendorf Air Force Base, AK [*Library symbol*] [*Library of Congress*] (LCLS)

AKF .... Aga Khan Foundation (EAIO)

AKF .... American Kidney Fund (EA)

AKF .... American-Korean Foundation [*Later, IHAP*] (EA)

AKF .... Arkansas Library Commission, Little Rock, AR [*OCLC symbol*] (OCLC)

AkF .... Fairbanks North Star Borough Library, Fairbanks, AK [*Library symbol*] [*Library of Congress*] (LCLS)

AKF .... Kufrah [*Libya*] [*Airport symbol*] (OAG)

AKF .... Refrigerated Cargo Ship [*World War II*]

AkFg .... United States Army, Recreational Services Post Library, Fort Greeley, AK [*Library symbol*] [*Library of Congress*] (LCLS)

AkFGS ...... Church of Jesus Christ of Latter-Day Saints, Genealogical Society Library, Fairbanks Alaska District Branch, Fairbanks, AK [*Library symbol*] [*Library of Congress*] (LCLS)

AkFL .... Fairbanks Law Library, Fairbanks, AK [*Library symbol*] [*Library of Congress*] (LCLS)

AKFM .... Antokon'ny Kongresin'ny Fahaleovantenan'i Madagasikara [*Congress Party for Malagasy Independence*] [*Political party*]

AKFM .... Association of Knitted Fabrics Manufacturers (EA)

AkFM .... Fairbanks Memorial Hospital, Fairbanks, AK [*Library symbol*] [*Library of Congress*] (LCLS)

AkFr .... United States Army, Recreational Services Post Library, Fort Richardson, AK [*Library symbol*] [*Library of Congress*] (LCLS)

AKFSR ...... American Karakul Fur Sheep Registry [*Later, AKSR*] (EA)

AkFw .... United States Army, Recreational Services Post Library, Fort Wainwright, AK [*Library symbol*] [*Library of Congress*] (LCLS)

AkFwP ...... Alaskan Projects Office, Fort Wainwright, AK [*Library symbol*] [*Library of Congress*] (LCLS)

AkFy .... Fort Yukon Community/School Library, Fort Yukon, AK [*Library symbol*] [*Library of Congress*] (LCLS)

AKG .... Alaskagold Mines Ltd. [*Vancouver Stock Exchange symbol*]

AKG .... Alkoxyglycerol [*Organic chemistry*]

AKG .... Anguganak [*Papua New Guinea*] [*Airport symbol*] (OAG)

AKG .... Arbeiten zur Kirchengeschichte [*A publication*]

AKG .... Archiv fuer Kulturgeschichte [*A publication*]

AKG .... Auxiliary Killing Ground [*British and Canadian*] [*World War II*]

AKG .... Kerngetallen van Nederlandse Effecten (Amsterdam) [*A publication*]

AKGA .... American Knit Glove Association (EA)

AKGA .... Association of Kew Gardeners in America [*Defunct*] (EA)

AKGD .... Acknowledged (ROG)

AKGIA .... Akusherstvo i Ginekologiya [*A publication*]

AKGIAO ... Akusherstvo i Ginekologiya [*Moscow*] [*A publication*]

AKGRAH .. Aktuelle Gerontologie [*A publication*]

AKH .... Akhalkalaki [*USSR*] [*Seismograph station code, US Geological Survey*] [*Closed*] (SEIS)

AKH .... Allgemeines Krankenhaus [*Austria*] [*Largest hospital in Europe*]

AkH .... Haines Borough Public Library, Haines, AK [*Library symbol*] [*Library of Congress*] (LCLS)

AKH .... Henderson State University, Arkadelphia, AR [*OCLC symbol*] (OCLC)

AkHi .... Alaska Historical Library and Museum, Juneau, AK [*Library symbol*] [*Library of Congress*] (LCLS)

AkHom ...... Homer Public Library, Homer, AK [*Library symbol*] [*Library of Congress*] (LCLS)

AKI .... Akiak [*Alaska*] [*Airport symbol*] (OAG)

AKI .... Akiko-Lori Gold [*Vancouver Stock Exchange symbol*]

AKI .... Akita [*Japan*] [*Seismograph station code, US Geological Survey*] (SEIS)

AKI .... Anti-Knock Index [*Automotive industry*]

AKI .... Automix Keyboards, Incorporated

AKI .... General Stores Issue Ship [*Navy symbol*]

AKI .... Killam Public Library, Alberta [*Library symbol*] [*National Library of Canada*] (NLC)

Akita Cent Hosp Med J ... Akita Central Hospital. Medical Journal [*A publication*]

AKJ .... Asahikawa [*Japan*] [*Airport symbol*] (OAG)

AkJ .... Juneau Memorial (Public) Library, Juneau, AK [*Library symbol*] [*Library of Congress*] (LCLS)

AkJBM ...... United States Bureau of Mines, Alaska Field Operation Center, Juneau, AK [*Library symbol*] [*Library of Congress*] (LCLS)

AkJFG ...... Alaska Department of Fish and Game, Juneau, AK [*Library symbol*] [*Library of Congress*] (LCLS)

AkJFS .... Forestry Science Laboratory, Juneau, AK [*Library symbol*] [*Library of Congress*] (LCLS)

AkJU .... University of Alaska, Juneau Library, Juneau, AK [*Library symbol*] [*Library of Congress*] (LCLS)

AKK .... Akhiok [*Alaska*] [*Airport symbol*] (OAG)

akk .... Akkadian [*MARC language code*] [*Library of Congress*] (LCCP)

AKK .... Alpha Kappa Kappa [*Fraternity*]

AKK .... Antifaschistischer Kampf Kaiserslautern [*Kaiserslautern Antifascist Struggle*] [*Federal Republic of Germany*] (PD)

AKK .... Archiv fuer Katholisches Kirchenrecht [*A publication*]

AKK .... John Brown University, Siloam Springs, AR [*OCLC symbol*] (OCLC)

AkK .... Ketchikan Public Library, Ketchikan, AK [*Library symbol*] [*Library of Congress*] (LCLS)

Akkad .... Akkadian (BJA)

AkKe .... Kenai Community Library, Inc., Kenai, AK [*Library symbol*] [*Library of Congress*] (LCLS)

AkKeH ...... Kenai Central High School, Kenai, AK [*Library symbol*] [*Library of Congress*] (LCLS)

AkKeHi ...... Kenai Historical, Inc., Fort Kenai Museum, Kenai, AK [*Library symbol*] [*Library of Congress*] (LCLS)

AkKeK ...... Kenai Peninsula Libraries, Kenai, AK [*Library symbol*] [*Library of Congress*] (LCLS)

AkKF .... United States Bureau of Commercial Fisheries, Technological Laboratory Library, Ketchikan, AK [*Library symbol*] [*Library of Congress*] [*Obsolete*] (LCLS)

AkKo .... Kodiak Public Library (A. Holmes Johnson Memorial Library), Kodiak, AK [*Library symbol*] [*Library of Congress*] (LCLS)

AKKO .... Turkish Communist Party - Marxist-Leninist [*Political party*] (PD)

AkKoH ...... Kodiak High School Library, Kodiak, AK [*Library symbol*] [*Library of Congress*] (LCLS)

AkKoHi ...... Kodiak Historical Society, Kodiak, AK [*Library symbol*] [*Library of Congress*] (LCLS)

AKKR .... Archiv fuer Katholisches Kirchenrecht [*A publication*]

AkKTHi ...... Tongass Historical Society Museum, Ketchikan, AK [*Library symbol*] [*Library of Congress*] (LCLS)

Ak-L .... Alaska State Court System, Law Library, Anchorage, AK [*Library symbol*] [*Library of Congress*] (LCLS)

AKL .... Ark-La-Tex Industries [*Vancouver Stock Exchange symbol*]

AKL .... Auckland [*New Zealand*] [*Airport symbol*] (OAG)

AKL .... Haskell, TX [*Location identifier*] [*FAA*] (FAAL)

AKL .... Light Cargo Ship [*Navy symbol*]

AKL .... University of Akron, Law Library, Akron, OH [*OCLC symbol*] (OCLC)

AkLA .... Alaska Library Association

AKLM .... Acclaim Entertainment, Inc. [*NASDAQ symbol*] (NQ)

AKM .... Abhandlungen fuer die Kunde des Morgenlandes [*A publication*]

AKM .... Apogee Kick Motor [*NASA*] (KSC)

AKM .... Kinuso Municipal Library, Alberta [*Library symbol*] [*National Library of Canada*] (NLC)

AKM .... University of Arkansas Medical Science Campus, Little Rock, AR [*OCLC symbol*] (OCLC)

A K Marsh ... [*A. K.*] Marshall's Kentucky Supreme Court Reports [*1817-21*] [*A publication*] (DLA)

AKMC .... Azad Kashmir Muslim Conference [*Political party*] [*Pakistan*] (FEA)

AKMDA .... Arkhimedes [*A publication*]

AKMEA8 .. Archiv fuer Klinische Medizin [*A publication*]

AK Metro... Auckland Metro [*New Zealand*] [*A publication*]

AKML .... Abhandlungen zur Kunst, Musik, und Literaturwissenschaft [*A publication*]

AKML .... Aladdin Knights of the Mystic Light (EA)

AKMTA .... Arkiv foer Matematik [*A publication*]

AKN .... Alaskon Resources [*Vancouver Stock Exchange symbol*]

AkN .... Kegoayah Kozga Public Library, Nome, AK [*Library symbol*] [*Library of Congress*] (LCLS)

AKN .... King Salmon [*Alaska*] [*Airport symbol*] (OAG)

a-kn--- .... Korea, North [*MARC geographic area code*] [*Library of Congress*] (LCCP)

AKN .... Net Cargo Ship [*Navy symbol*] [*Obsolete*]

AkNak .... Martin Monsen Regional Library, Naknek, AK [*Library symbol*] [*Library of Congress*] (LCLS)

AKNF .... Adair-Koshland-Nemethy-Filmer [*Enzyme model*]

AKNHAM ... Annals of Kentucky Natural History [*A publication*]

AKNKDY .. Akita-Kenkritsu Nogyo Tanki Daigaku Kenkyu Hokoku [*A publication*]

AKNUAR ... Aktuelle Neurologie [*A publication*]

AKO......... Akron, CO [*Location identifier*] [*FAA*] (FAAL)

a-ko--- .... Korea, South [*MARC geographic area code*] [*Library of Congress*] (LCCP)

AKO......... Ouachita Baptist University, Arkadelphia, AR [*OCLC symbol*] (OCLC)

AKOGAO ... Albrecht Von Graefe's Archive for Clinical and Experimental Ophthalmology [*A publication*]

AKOL .... Australian Kompass Online [*Database*]

AKONA..... Archiv fuer Klinische und Experimentelle Ohren-, Nasen-, und Kehlkopfheilkunde [*A publication*]

AKONAB .. Archiv fuer Klinische und Experimentelle Ohren-, Nasen-, und Kehlkopfheilkunde [*A publication*]

A KorrBl .... Archaeologisches Korrespondenzblatt [*A publication*]

AKP .... Agence Khmere de Presse [*Cambodian Press Agency*]

AKP .... Alpha Kappa Psi [*Fraternity*]

AKP .... Anaktuvuk Pass [*Alaska*] [*Airport symbol*] (OAG)

AKP .... Arbeidernes Kommunistiske Parti [*Workers' Communist Party*] [*Norway*] [*Political party*] (PPE)

AKP .... Arkansas Technical University, Russellville, AR [*OCLC symbol*] (OCLC)

AkP .... Petersburg Public Library, Petersburg, AK [*Library symbol*] [*Library of Congress*] (LCLS)

AkPal .... Palmer Public Library, Palmer, AK [*Library symbol*] [*Library of Congress*] (LCLS)

AkPalA ...... Alaska Agricultural Experiment Station, Palmer, AK [*Library symbol*] [*Library of Congress*] (LCLS)

AkPalU ...... University of Alaska, Matanuska-Susitna Community College, Palmer, AK [*Library symbol*] [*Library of Congress*] (LCLS)

AKPIRG .... Alaska Public Interest Research Group [*Research center*] (RCD)

AKPOD ..... Avtomatizatsiya i Kontrol'no-Izmeritel'nye Pribory v Neftepererabatyvayushchei i Neftekhimicheskoi Promyshlennosti [*A publication*]

AkPP .... Petersburg Press, Petersburg, AK [*Library symbol*] [*Library of Congress*] (LCLS)

AkPT .... Tongass National Forest, Petersburg, AK [*Library symbol*] [*Library of Congress*] (LCLS)

AKQ.......... Wakefield, VA [*Location identifier*] [*FAA*] (FAAL)

AKR .... Address Key Register

AKR .... Akron, OH [*Location identifier*] [*FAA*] (FAAL)

AKR .... Auroral Kilometric Radiation [*Planetary science*]

a-kr--- .... Korea [*MARC geographic area code*] [*Library of Congress*] (LCCP)

AKR .... University of Akron, Akron, OH [*OCLC symbol*] (OCLC)

AKR .... Vehicle Cargo Ship [*Navy symbol*]

AKRHDB .. Aktuelle Rheumatologie [*A publication*]

Akr LR ...... Akron Law Review [*United States*] [*A publication*]

AKRN .... Akorn, Inc. [*NASDAQ symbol*] (NQ)

AKRO .... Acknowledge Receipt Of [*Telecommunications*] (TEL)

Akron Beaco ... Akron Beacon Journal [*United States*] [*A publication*]

Akron Bus & Econ R ... Akron Business and Economic Review [*A publication*]

Akron Bus and Econ Rev ... Akron Business and Economic Review [*United States*] [*A publication*]

Akron L Rev ... Akron Law Review [*A publication*]

AKS .... Advanced Kick Stage [*Missile launching*] (MCD)

AKS .... Arakis Capital [*Vancouver Stock Exchange symbol*]

AKS .... Associated Knowledge Systems [*Imperial Chemical Industries PLC*] [*Information service or system*] (IID)

AKS .... Association for Korean Studies (EA)

AKS .... Auki [*Solomon Islands*] [*Airport symbol*] (OAG)

AKS .... Four Sons Flying Service [*Dodge City, KS*] [*FAA designator*] (FAAC)

AKS .... General Stores Issue Ship [*Navy symbol*]

AkS .... Kettleson Memorial Library, Sitka, AK [*Library symbol*] [*Library of Congress*] (LCLS)

AkSB .... Blatchley Junior High School, Sitka, AK [*Library symbol*] [*Library of Congress*] (LCLS)

AkSeld .... Seldovia Public Library, Seldovia, AK [*Library symbol*] [*Library of Congress*] (LCLS)

AkSew .... Seward Community Library, Seward, AK [*Library symbol*] [*Library of Congress*] (LCLS)

AkSJ .... Sheldon Jackson College, Sitka, AK [*Library symbol*] [*Library of Congress*] (LCLS)

AkSk .... Skagway Public Library, Skagway, AK [*Library symbol*] [*Library of Congress*] (LCLS)

AkSol .... Soldotna Public Library (Joyce Carver Memorial Library), Soldotna, AK [*Library symbol*] [*Library of Congress*] (LCLS)

AKSR .... American Karakul Sheep Registry (EA)

AK(SS) ...... Cargo Submarine [*Navy symbol*] [*Obsolete*]

Ak St .... Auckland Star [*A publication*]

akt .... Aktiv [*Active*] [*German*]

AKT .... Applied Knowledge Test [*Vocational guidance test*]

AKT .... Auditory, Kinesthetic, Tactile Approach [*Teaching method*]

Akt Anal Nar Khoz ... Aktivatsionnyi Analiz v Narodnom Khozyaistve [*A publication*]

AktG .... Aktiengesetz [*Law governing public companies*] [*German*] (ILCA)

Akt-Ges ...... Aktiengesellschaft [*Corporation, Incorporated*] [*German*]

AKTLAU ... Agrokemia es Talajtan [*A publication*]

Akt Probl Inf Dokum ... Aktualne Problemy Informacji i Dokumentacji [*A publication*]

AKTRAE ... Aktuelle Traumatologie [*A publication*]

AKTRSch .. Die Alphabetischen Keilschrifttexte von Ras Schamra [*A publication*] (BJA)

Aktual Probl Biol Sinezelenykh Vodoroslei ... Aktual'nye Problemy Biologii Sinezelenykh Vodoroslei [*A publication*]

Aktual Probl Inf Dok ... Aktualne Problemy Informacji i Dokumentacji [*A publication*]

Aktual Probl Inf & Dok ... Aktualne Problemy Informacji i Dokumentacji [*A publication*]

Aktual Probl Onkol Med Radiol ... Aktual'nye Problemy Onkologii i Meditsinskoi Radiologii [*Belorussian SSR*] [*A publication*]

Aktual Probl Prof Patol Resp Mezhved Sb ... Aktual'nye Problemy Professional'noi Patologii Respublikanskoi Mezhvedomstvennyi Sbornik [*A publication*]

Aktual Probl Razvit Ptitsevod ... Aktual'nye Problemy Razvitiya Ptitsevodstva [*A publication*]

Aktual Vopr Dermatol Venerol ... Aktual'nye Voprosy Dermatologii i Venerologii [*A publication*]

Aktual Vopr Eksp Klin Med ... Aktual'nye Voprosy Eksperimental'noi i Klinicheskoi Meditsiny [*A publication*]

Aktual Vopr Epidemiol ... Aktual'nye Voprosy Epidemiologii [*A publication*]

Aktual Vopr Farm ... Aktual'nye Voprosy Farmatsii [*A publication*]

Aktual Vopr Gastroenterol ... Aktual'nye Voprosy Gastroenterologii [*A publication*]

Aktual Vopr Ginekol ... Aktual'nye Voprosy Ginekologii [*A publication*]

Aktual Vopr Khimioter Zlokach Opukholei ... Aktual'nye Voprosy Khimioterapii Zlokachestvennykh Opukholei [*A publication*]

Aktual Vopr Oftal ... Aktual'nye Voprosy Oftal'mologii [*A publication*]

Aktual Vopr Oftal'mol ... Aktual'nye Voprosy Oftal'mologii [*A publication*]

Aktual Vopr Patol Pecheni ... Aktual'nye Voprosy Patologii Pecheni [*A publication*]

Aktual Vopr Sovrem Biokhim ... Aktual'nye Voprosy Sovremennoi Biokhimii [*A publication*]

Aktual Vopr Sovrem Onkol ... Aktual'nye Voprosy Sovremennoi Onkologii [*A publication*]

Aktual Vopr Sovrem Petrogr ... Aktual'nye Voprosy Sovremennoi Petrografii [*A publication*]

Aktuel Fragen Psychiat Neurol ... Aktuelle Fragen der Psychiatrie und Neurologie [*Switzerland*] [*A publication*]

Aktuel Fragen Psychiatr Neurol ... Aktuelle Fragen der Psychiatrie und Neurologie [*A publication*]

Aktuel Fragen Psychother ... Aktuelle Fragen der Psychotherapie [*A publication*]

Aktuel Gerontol ... Aktuelle Gerontologie [*A publication*]

Aktuellt Lantbrukshogs ... Aktuellt fran Lantbrukshogskolan [*A publication*]

Aktuel Neurol ... Aktuelle Neurologie [*A publication*]

Aktuel Otorhinolaryngol ... Aktuelle Otorhinolaryngologie [*A publication*]

Aktuel Probl Chir ... Aktuelle Probleme in der Chirurgie [*Later, Aktuelle Probleme in Chirurgie und Orthopaedie*] [*A publication*]

Aktuel Probl Chir Orthop ... Aktuelle Probleme in Chirurgie und Orthopaedie [*A publication*]

Aktuel Probl Intensivmed ... Aktuelle Probleme der Intensivmedizin [*A publication*]

Aktuel Probl Phoniatr Logop ... Aktuelle Probleme der Phoniatrie und Logopaedie [*A publication*]

Aktuel Probl Polym-Phys ... Aktuelle Probleme der Polymer-Physik [*A publication*]

Aktuel Rheumatol ... Aktuelle Rheumatologie [*West Germany*] [*A publication*]

Aktuelt Landbruksdep Opplysningstjeneste (Norw) ... Aktuelt Landbruksdepartementet. Opplysningstjeneste (Norway) [*A publication*]

Aktuel Traumatol ... Aktuelle Traumatologie [*A publication*]

Aktuel Urol ... Aktuelle Urologie [*A publication*]

AKU .... Aksu [*China*] [*Airport symbol*] (OAG)

AKU .... Akulik, AK [*Location identifier*] [*FAA*] (FAAL)

AKU .... Akureyri [*Iceland*] [*Seismograph station code, US Geological Survey*] (SEIS)

aku .... Alaska [*MARC country of publication code*] [*Library of Congress*] (LCCP)

AKU .... Algemene Kunstzijde Unie [*Later, AKZO*] [*Commercial firm*] [*Netherlands*]

a-ku--- .... Kuwait [*MARC geographic area code*] [*Library of Congress*] (LCCP)

AkU .... University of Alaska, Fairbanks, AK [*Library symbol*] [*Library of Congress*] (LCLS)

AKU .... University of Arkansas at Little Rock, Little Rock, AR [*OCLC symbol*] (OCLC)

AkU-AB .... University of Alaska, Institute of Arctic Biology, Fairbanks, AK [*Library symbol*] [*Library of Congress*] (LCLS)

AKultG ...... Archiv fuer Kulturgeschichte [*Weimar*] [*A publication*]

AkU-M ...... University of Alaska, Bio-Medical Library, Fairbanks, AK [*Library symbol*] [*Library of Congress*] (LCLS)

AKUP .... Association of Korean University Presses

AKURON ... Autonetics Kalman Utilization of Reference for Optimal Navigation (MCD)

Akush Ginekol (Kiev) ... Akusherstvo i Ginekologiya (Kiev) [*A publication*]

Akush Ginekol (Mosc) ... Akusherstvo i Ginekologiya (Moscow) [*A publication*]

Akush Ginekol (Moscow) ... Akusherstvo i Ginekologiya (Moscow) [*A publication*]

Akush Ginekol (Sofia) ... Akusherstvo i Ginekologiya (Sofia) [*Bulgaria*] [*A publication*]

Akust Beih ... Akustische Beihefte [*Switzerland*] [*A publication*]

Akust Ul'trazvuk Tekh ... Akustika i Ul'trazvukovaya Tekhnika [*A publication*]

Akust Z ...... Akademija Nauk SSSR. Akusticeskii Zurnal [*A publication*]

Akust Z ...... Akustische Zeitschrift [*A publication*]

Akust Zh .... Akusticheskii Zhurnal [*A publication*]

AKV .... Akulivik [*Canada*] [*Airport symbol*] (OAG)

AKV .... Cargo Ship and Aircraft Ferry [*Navy symbol*]

AkV .... Valdez Public Library, Valdez, AK [*Library symbol*] [*Library of Congress*] (LCLS)

AKVBAA ... Arkiv foer Botanik [*A publication*]

AKW .... Amberger Kaolinwerke GmbH [*Business term*] [*Federal Republic of Germany*]

AkW .... Wrangell Public Library, Wrangell, AK [*Library symbol*] [*Library of Congress*] (LCLS)

Ak Waik Hist J ... Auckland-Waikato Historical Journal [*A publication*]

AKWAS ...... Author and Keywords in Alphabetical Sequence (ADA)

AkWas .... Wasilla Public Library, Wasilla, AK [*Library symbol*] [*Library of Congress*] (LCLS)

AKWIC ...... Author and Keyword in Context

AkWill .... Willow Public Library, Willow, AK [*Library symbol*] [*Library of Congress*] (LCLS)

Akw Notes ... Akwesasne Notes [*A publication*]

AKWS .... Akwesasne Notes [*A publication*]

AKY .... Air Kentucky [*Owensboro, KY*] [*FAA designator*] (FAAC)

AKY .... Akaitcho Yellowknife Gold Mines Ltd. [*Toronto Stock Exchange symbol*]

AKY .... Akyab [*Burma*] [*Airport symbol*] (OAG)

AKY .... San Antonio, TX [*Location identifier*] [*FAA*] (FAAL)

AKYFW ...... Albanian Kosovar Youth in the Free World (EA)

Akz .... Akzente [*A publication*]

AKZ .... Antiarmor Kill Zone [*Military*] (INF)

AKZHA ...... Akusticheskii Zhurnal [*A publication*]

AKZMA .... ATOMKI [*Atommag Kutato Intezet*] Koezlemenyek. Supplement [*A publication*]

AKZO .... Akzo NV [*NASDAQ symbol*] (NQ)

a/l .... A Livraison [*On Delivery of Goods*] [*French*] [*Business term*]

AL .... Abnormal Lungs [*Medicine*]

AL .... Abraham Lincoln [*US president, 1809-1865*]

AL .... Absolute Limen [*Psychophysics*]

AL .... Accession List

AL .... Accidental Loss [*Nuclear energy*]

AL .... Accrued Liability [*Accounting*]

AL .... Accumulator Low [*Data processing*]

AL .... Acoustics Laboratory

AL .... Acquisition of Land Act [*Town planning*] [*British*]

AL .... Acquisition Logistician (NG)

AL .... Acquisition and Logistics (MCD)

AL .... Acta Linguistica [*A publication*]

A/L .... Acting Lieutenant [*Navy*] [*British*]

AL .... Action [*Indicator*] Level [*Radiation measurement*] (NRCH)

AL .... Action for Life (EA)

AL .... Action Linkage [*An association*] (EA)

AL .... Acute Leukemia [*Medicine*]

AL .... Adaptation Level

AL .... Additional Listing [*Telecommunications*] (TEL)

AL .... Adductor Longus [*Anatomy*]

AL .... Administratief Lexicon [*A publication*]

A & L .... Administration and Logistics [*Military*] (INF)

AL .... Admiralty Letter [*British military*] (DMA)

AL .... Advisory Leaflet

AL...............	Aerodynamics Laboratory [*Naval Ship Research and Development Center*]
AL...............	Aeromechanics Laboratory [*Army*] (GRD)
AL...............	Aeronautical Laboratory
AL...............	Aeronautical Radionavigation Land Station [*ITU designation*]
AL...............	Aeronomy Laboratory [*National Institute of Standards and Technology*]
AL...............	Aerophysics Laboratory (MCD)
AL...............	Afar Locality [*Paleoanthropology*]
AL...............	Aft Left (MCD)
AL...............	Agricultural Labourer
AL...............	Air Electrical [*Special duties officer*] [*Military*] [*British*]
A/L.............	Air-Landing [*British military*] (DMA)
AL...............	Air League [*An association*] (EAIO)
AL...............	Air Letter
AL...............	Air Liaison
AL...............	Air Lock [*Technical drawings*]
AL...............	Aircraft Logistics Division [*Bureau of Aeronautics*] [*Later, NASC*] [*Navy*]
AL...............	Airlift (AABC)
AL...............	Ala Breve [*A publication*]
AL...............	Alabama [*Postal code*]
Al................	Alanus Anglicus [*Flourished, 1208-10*] [*Authority cited in pre-1607 legal work*] (DSA)
AL...............	Alarm [*Telecommunications*] (TEL)
AL...............	Albania [*ANSI two-letter standard code*] (CNC)
Al................	Albericus de Porta Ravennate [*Flourished, 1165-94*] [*Authority cited in pre-1607 legal work*] (DSA)
Al................	[*Magister*] Albertus [*Authority cited in pre-1607 legal work*] (DSA)
Al................	Albertus Beneventanus [*Deceased, 1187*] [*Authority cited in pre-1607 legal work*] (DSA)
Al................	Albertus Longobardista [*Flourished, 12th century*] [*Authority cited in pre-1607 legal work*] (DSA)
Al................	Albertus Magnus [*Teutonicus*] [*Deceased, 1280*] [*Authority cited in pre-1607 legal work*] (DSA)
Al................	Albertus Ranconis [*Flourished, 1369-72*] [*Authority cited in pre-1607 legal work*] (DSA)
AL...............	Albumin [*Also, ALB*] [*Biochemistry*]
AL...............	ALCAN Aluminium Ltd. [*NYSE symbol*] [*Toronto Stock Exchange symbol*] [*Vancouver Stock Exchange symbol*] (SPSG)
Al................	Aleyn's English King's Bench Reports [*A publication*] (DLA)
Al................	Alfven Number [*IUPAC*]
AL...............	Algeria [*IYRU nationality code*] (IYR)
AL...............	Alia [*Others*] [*Latin*]
AL...............	Alias [*Otherwise*] [*Latin*]
AL...............	Alibi [*Elsewhere*] [*Latin*] (ROG)
AL...............	Alighieri [*A publication*]
AL...............	Alignment Lab
Al................	Alinea [*Paragraph*] [*Belgian*] (ILCA)
Al................	Alinea [*Paragraph*] [*French*] (ILCA)
Al................	Alinea [*Paragraph*] [*Italian*] (ILCA)
Al................	Alinea [*Paragraph*] [*Dutch*] (ILCA)
AL...............	Alkane [*Organic chemistry*]
AL...............	All [*When used as prefix*] [*FAA*] (FAAC)
AL...............	All Lengths [*Lumber*]
Al................	Allosteric [*Biochemistry*]
AL...............	Allowance List
AL...............	Almanor Railroad Co. [*AAR code*]
AL...............	Alpavia [*France*] [*ICAO aircraft manufacturer identifier*] (ICAO)
Al................	Alternaria alternata f lycopersici [*A toxin-producing fungus*]
Al................	Alternating Light [*Navigation signal*]
AL...............	Alternative List [*Sweden*] [*Political party*]
AL...............	Alternative Liste [*Alternative List*] [*German*] [*Political party*]
AL...............	Alternative Liste [*Alternative List*] [*Austria*] [*Political party*]
Al................	Aluminum [*Chemical element*]
AL...............	Amber Light (MSA)
AL...............	American League [*Baseball*]
AL...............	American Legend (EA)
AL...............	American Legion (EA)
AL...............	American Libraries [*A publication*]
AL...............	American Literature [*A publication*]
AL...............	Analog Link [*Telecommunications*] (TEL)
AL...............	Analog Loop-Back [*Telecommunications*] (TEL)
AL...............	Analytical Laboratory (NRCH)
AL...............	Analytical Letters [*A publication*]
AL...............	Analytical Limits (NRCH)
AL...............	Angle Lock
AL...............	Angler's Library [*A publication*]
AL...............	Anglo-Latin [*Language, etc.*]
AL...............	Animal Liberation (EA)
AL...............	Annali Lateranensi [*A publication*]
AL...............	Annee de Lumiere [*Light Year*] [*French*]
AL...............	Anno Lucis [*In the Year of Light*] [*Since 4000 BC*] [*Latin*]
AL...............	Annual Leave [*US Civil Service*]
AL...............	Antenna Laboratory (MCD)
AL...............	Antennule Length [*of Crustacea*]
AL...............	Anterior Pituitary Lobe [*Anatomy*]

A & L.........	Approach and Landing [*Aviation*] (NASA)
AL...............	Apres Livraison [*After Delivery of Goods*] [*French*]
AL...............	Arab League
AL...............	Architectural League of New York (EA)
AL...............	Area Weapon Left (MCD)
AL...............	Argininosuccinate Lyase [*Also, ASL*] [*An enzyme*]
AL...............	Argyrophil
AL...............	Arm Length
AL...............	Army List [*British military*] (DMA)
AL...............	Arrival Locator
AL...............	Art and Letters [*A publication*]
AL...............	Artificial Luminance [*Theory proposed by James Clerk Maxwell in 1864*]
AL...............	Artistic License (EA)
A/L.............	Assemble/Load [*Data processing*]
AL...............	Assembly Language [*Data processing*]
AL...............	Associated Laboratories (EA)
AL...............	Assumed Latitude [*Navigation*]
AL...............	Astronomical League (EA)
AL...............	Astronuclear Laboratory [*Westinghouse Electric Corp.*] (MCD)
AL...............	Astropower Laboratory [*Douglas Aircraft Corp.*] (MCD)
AL/.............	At Least [*Followed by altitude*] [*Aviation*] (FAAC)
AL...............	Auris Laeva [*Left Ear*] [*Latin*]
AL...............	Autograph Letter [*Manuscript descriptions*]
A/L.............	AUTOLAND [*Automatic Landing*] (NASA)
AL...............	Automobile Liability [*Insurance*]
AL...............	Aviation Electronicsman [*Military*]
AL...............	Avionics Laboratory [*Air Force*]
AL...............	Awami League [*Bangladesh*] [*Political party*] (FEA)
AL...............	Axiolingual [*Dentistry*]
AL...............	Intoxicated [*Airline notation*]
AL...............	Laureate of Arts
AL...............	Lethbridge Public Library, Alberta [*Library symbol*] [*National Library of Canada*] (NLC)
AL...............	Lightship [*Navy symbol*] [*Obsolete*]
AL & L........	USAIR, Inc. [*ICAO designator*] (FAAC)
ALA.............	Aboriginal Languages Association [*Australia*]
ALA.............	Abraham Lincoln Association (EA)
ALA.............	Academy of Lighting Arts
ALA.............	Actual Leaf Area [*Botany*]
ALA.............	Adult Learning Association (EA)
ALA.............	African Literature Association (EA)
ALA.............	Afrique Litteraire et Artistique [*A publication*]
ALA.............	Air-Land Assault (CINC)
ALA.............	Ala Moana Hawaii Properties [*NYSE symbol*] (SPSG)
ALA.............	Alabama
Ala..............	Alabama Reports [*A publication*] (DLA)
Ala..............	Alabama Supreme Court Reports [*A publication*] (DLA)
ALA.............	Alamethicin [*An antibiotic*]
ALA.............	Alamo [*Nevada*] [*Seismograph station code, US Geological Survey*] (SEIS)
Ala..............	Alanine [*Also, A*] [*An amino acid*]
Ala..............	Alanus Anglicus [*Flourished, 1208-10*] [*Authority cited in pre-1607 legal work*] (DSA)
ALA.............	Alighting Area [*Aviation*]
ALA.............	Alina International Industries [*Vancouver Stock Exchange symbol*]
ALA.............	Alliance for Labor Action [*1968-1971*]
ALA.............	Alma-Ata [*USSR*] [*Airport symbol*] (OAG)
AlA.............	Aluminum Association
ALA.............	Amalgamated Lithographers of America [*Later, GAIU*]
ALA.............	American Laminators Association (EA)
ALA.............	American Land Alliance (EA)
ALA.............	American Landrace Association (EA)
ALA.............	American Laryngological Association (EA)
ALA.............	American Latvian Association in the United States (EA)
ALA.............	American Lawyers Association [*Later, TAG*] (EA)
ALA.............	American Lawyers Auxiliary (EA)
ALA.............	American League of Anglers (EA)
ALA.............	American Legion Auxiliary (EA)
ALA.............	American Liberal Association (EA)
ALA.............	American Library Association (EA)
ALA.............	American Lighting Association (EA)
ALA.............	American Literary Anthology
ALA.............	American Logistics Association (EA)
ALA.............	American Longevity Association (EA)
ALA.............	American Lung Association (EA)
ALA.............	Aminolaevulinate [*or Aminolaevulinic*] Acid [*Biochemistry*]
ALA.............	Annales. Faculte des Lettres d'Aix-en-Provence [*A publication*]
ALA.............	Antenna Lightning Arrester
ALA.............	Arab Liberation Army
ALA.............	Arc Lamp Assembly
ALA.............	Army Launch Area
ALA.............	Army Light Aviation [*Australia*]
ALA.............	Army Logistics Assessment
ALA.............	Asociacion Latinoamericana de Archivos [*Latin American Association of Archives - LAAA*] (EAIO)
ALA.............	Assembly of Librarians of the Americas [*Defunct*] (EA)
ALA.............	Associate in Liberal Arts
ALA.............	Associate of the Library Association [*British*] (EY)
ALA.............	Associated Locksmiths of America

ALA .... Association of Legal Administrators (EA)
ALA .... Austral Lineas Aereas [*Airline*] [*Argentina*] (EY)
ALA .... Authorized Landing Area (ADA)
ALA .... Authors League of America
ALA .... Automobile Legal Association [*Commercial firm*] (EA)
ALA .... Avis Licensee Association (EA)
ALa .... Axiolabial [*Dentistry*]
A2LA .... American Association for Laboratory Accreditation (RCD)
ALAA .... African Law Association in America [*Later,
          INTWORLSA*] (EA)
Ala A .... Alabama Appellate Court (DLA)
ALAA .... American Labor Arbitration Awards [*Prentice-Hall, Inc.*] [*A
          publication*] (DLA)
ALAA .... Associate of the Library Association of Australia
ALAA .... Associate of the London Association of Certified and Corporate
          Accountants [*British*] (EY)
ALAA .... Association of Legal Aid Attorneys of the City of New
          York (EA)
ALAA .... Aviation Law Association of Australia
ALAAC ...... Lakedell and Area Community Library, Westerose, Alberta
          [*Library symbol*] [*National Library of Canada*] (NLC)
Ala Acad Sci Jour ... Alabama Academy of Science. Journal [*A publication*]
Ala Acts ..... Acts of Alabama [*A publication*] (DLA)
Ala Admin Code ... Alabama Administrative Code [*A publication*]
ALAAF ...... Field Crops Branch, Alberta Agriculture, Lacombe, Alberta
          [*Library symbol*] [*National Library of Canada*] (NLC)
ALAAG ..... Research Station, Agriculture Canada [*Station de Recherches,
          Agriculture Canada*] Lacombe, Alberta [*Library symbol*]
          [*National Library of Canada*] (NLC)
Ala Ag Exp ... Alabama. Agricultural Experiment Station. Publications [*A
          publication*]
Ala Agribus ... Alabama Agribusiness [*A publication*]
Ala Agric Exp Stn Annu Rep ... Alabama. Agricultural Experiment Station.
          Annual Report [*A publication*]
Ala Agric Exp Stn Auburn Univ Agron Soils Dep Ser ... Alabama. Agricultural
          Experiment Station. Auburn University. Agronomy and
          Soils Departmental Series [*A publication*]
Ala Agric Exp Stn Auburn Univ Bull ... Alabama. Agricultural Experiment
          Station. Auburn University. Bulletin [*A publication*]
Ala Agric Exp Stn Auburn Univ Dep Agron & Soils Dep Ser ... Alabama.
          Agricultural Experiment Station. Auburn University.
          Department of Agronomy and Soils. Departmental Series
          [*A publication*]
Ala Agric Exp Stn Auburn Univ For Dep Ser ... Alabama. Agricultural
          Experiment Station. Auburn University. Forestry
          Departmental Series [*A publication*]
Ala Agric Exp Stn Auburn Univ Leafl ... Alabama. Agricultural Experiment
          Station. Auburn University. Leaflet [*A publication*]
Ala Agric Exp Stn Auburn Univ Prog Rep ... Alabama. Agricultural
          Experiment Station. Auburn University. Progress Report
          [*A publication*]
Ala Agric Exp Stn Auburn Univ Prog Rep Ser ... Alabama. Agricultural
          Experiment Station. Auburn University. Progress Report
          Series [*A publication*]
Ala Agric Exp Stn Bull ... Alabama. Agricultural Experiment Station. Bulletin
          [*A publication*]
Ala Agric Exp Stn Bull (Auburn Univ) ... Alabama. Agricultural Experiment
          Station. Bulletin (Auburn University) [*A publication*]
Ala Agric Exp Stn Cir ... Alabama. Agricultural Experiment Station. Circular
          [*A publication*]
Ala Agric Exp Stn Leafl ... Alabama. Agricultural Experiment Station. Leaflet
          [*A publication*]
Ala Agric Exp Stn Leafl (Auburn Univ) ... Alabama. Agricultural Experiment
          Station. Leaflet (Auburn University) [*A publication*]
Ala Agric Exp Stn Prog Rep Ser ... Alabama. Agricultural Experiment Station.
          Progress Report Series [*A publication*]
Ala Agric Exp Stn Prog Rep Ser (Auburn Univ) ... Alabama. Agricultural
          Experiment Station. Progress Report Series (Auburn
          University) [*A publication*]
ALAAP ...... Alabama Army Ammunition Plant (AABC)
Ala App ...... Alabama Appellate Court Reports [*A publication*] (DLA)
Ala App ...... Alabama Court of Appeals (DLA)
ALAB .... American Lung Association. Bulletin [*A publication*]
Alabama Geol Soc Bull ... Alabama. Geological Society. Bulletin [*A
          publication*]
Alabama Geol Survey Inf Ser ... Alabama. Geological Survey. Information
          Series [*A publication*]
Alabama Geol Survey Map ... Alabama. Geological Survey. Map [*A
          publication*]
Alabama L Rev ... Alabama Law Review [*A publication*]
Alabama Rep ... Alabama Reports [*A publication*] (DLA)
Ala Bar Bull ... Alabama Bar Bulletin [*A publication*]
ALABM ..... Air-Launched Antiballistic Missile
Alab (NS)... Alabama Reports, New Series [*A publication*] (DLA)
ALABOL... Algorithmic and Business Oriented Language [*Data processing*]
Alab Rep ... Alabama Reports [*A publication*] (DLA)
ALA Bul..... American Library Association. Bulletin [*A publication*]
Ala Bus ...... Alabama Business [*A publication*]
Ala Bus and Econ Repts ... Alabama Business and Economic Reports [*A
          publication*]
ALAC........ Alaska Air Command [*Air Force*]

ALAC........ American Lhasa Apso Club (EA)
ALAC........ Artificial Limb and Appliance Centre [*British*]
ALAC........ Association de la Librairie Ancienne du Canada [*Association of
          Antique Bookstores of Canada*]
ALAC........ Lacombe Public Library, Alberta [*Library symbol*] [*National
          Library of Canada*] (NLC)
ALACAT ... Asociacion Latinoamericana de Agentes de Carga Aerea y
          Transporte [*Latin American Association of Freight and
          Transport Agents - LAFTA*] (EA)
ALACF ...... Asociacion Latinoamericana de Ciencias Fisiologicas [*Latin
          American Association of Physiological Sciences*]
          [*ICSU*] (EAIO)
ALACFO... All Air Carrier Field Offices [*FAA*] (FAAC)
Ala Civ App ... Alabama Civil Appeals [*A publication*] (DLA)
Ala Code .... Code of Alabama [*A publication*] (DLA)
Ala Conserv ... Alabama Conservation [*A publication*]
Ala Const .... Alabama Constitution [*A publication*] (DLA)
Ala Corn Variety Rep ... Alabama Corn Variety Report [*A publication*]
ALACP...... American League to Abolish Capital Punishment
          [*Defunct*] (EA)
Ala Cr App ... Alabama Criminal Appeals [*A publication*] (DLA)
ALAD .... Academic Librarians Assisting the Disabled Discussion Group
          [*Association of Specialized and Cooperative Library
          Agencies*]
ALAD .... Aminolaevulinate Dehydratase [*Also, ALD*] [*An enzyme*]
ALAD .... Arid Lands Agricultural Development [*Program*] [*Later,
          ICARDA*] [*Middle East*]
ALAD .... Automatic Liquid Agent Detector (AABC)
ALADA ..... Asociacion Latinoamericana de Derecho Aeronautico y Espacial
ALADA ..... Associacao Latino-Americana de Direito Agrario
ALADAA... Asociacion Latinoamericana de Estudios Afroasiaticos [*Latin
          American Association for Afro-Asian Studies -
          LAAAS*] (EAIO)
ALADDIN ... Atmospheric Layer and Density Distribution of Ions and
          Neutrals [*Rocket*] [*NASA*]
ALADI....... Asociacion Latinoamericana de Integracion [*Latin American
          Integration Association - LAIA*] (EAIO)
ALADIM... Asociacion Latinoamericana para el Desarrollo y la Integracion
          de la Mujer [*Latin American Association for the
          Development and Integration of Women - LAADIW*]
          [*Santiago, Chile*] (EAIO)
ALADIN.... Automated Laboratory Diagnostic Instrument
ALADLO... All Air Defense Liaison Officers in Region [*FAA*] (FAAC)
ALADR...... Animal Diseases Research Institute (West), Agriculture Canada
          [*Institut de Recherches Veterinaires (Ouest), Agriculture
          Canada*] Lethbridge, Alberta [*Library symbol*] [*National
          Library of Canada*] (NLC)
ALAE........ Association of Licensed Aircraft Engineers [*A union*] [*British*]
ALAF........ Asociacion Latinoamericana de Ferrocarriles [*Latin American
          Railways Association - LARA*] [*Argentina*]
ALAF......... Lafond Public Library, Alberta [*Library symbol*] [*National
          Library of Canada*] (NLC)
ALAFEM .. Asociacion Latinoamericana de Facultades y Escuelas de
          Medicina de America Latina [*Latin American Association
          of Medical Schools and Faculties - LAAMSF*] [*Quito,
          Ecuador*] (EAIO)
ALAFFO... All Airway Facilities Sector and Field Offices [*FAA*] (FAAC)
Ala For....... Alabama Forests [*A publication*]
ALAFO R .. ALAFO [*Asociacion Latino Americana de Facultades de
          Odontologia*] Revista [*A publication*]
ALAG .... Agriculture Canada, Lethbridge, Alberta [*Library symbol*]
          [*National Library of Canada*] (NLC)
ALAG .... Alpine Luft-Transport Aktiengesellschaft [*Airline*] (FAAC)
ALaG .... Axiolabiogingival [*Dentistry*]
Ala Geol Surv Atlas Ser ... Alabama. Geological Survey. Atlas Series [*A
          publication*]
Ala Geol Surv Bull ... Alabama. Geological Survey. Bulletin [*A publication*]
Ala Geol Surv Circ ... Alabama. Geological Survey. Circular [*A publication*]
Ala Geol Surv Cty Rep ... Alabama. Geological Survey. County Report [*A
          publication*]
Ala Geol Survey and State Oil and Gas Board Ann Repts ... Alabama.
          Geological Survey and State Oil and Gas Board. Annual
          Reports [*A publication*]
Ala Geol Surv Geo-Petro Notes ... Alabama. Geological Survey. Geo-Petro
          Notes [*A publication*]
Ala Geol Surv Inf Ser ... Alabama. Geological Survey. Information Series [*A
          publication*]
Ala Geol Surv Map ... Alabama. Geological Survey. Map [*A publication*]
Ala Geol Surv Spec Rep ... Alabama. Geological Survey. Special Report [*A
          publication*]
Ala G S ...... Alabama. Geological Survey [*A publication*]
Ala His S .... Alabama Historical Society. Transactions [*A publication*]
Ala Hist ..... Alabama Historian [*A publication*]
Ala Hist Q ... Alabama Historical Quarterly [*A publication*]
ALA Hosp Bk Guide ... American Library Association. Association of
          Hospital and Institution Libraries. Book Guide [*A
          publication*]
AlaHQ .... Alabama Historical Quarterly [*A publication*]
ALAI.......... Agencia Latinoamericana de Informacion [*Latin American
          Information Agency*] [*Canada*]

ALAI......... Association Litteraire et Artistique Internationale [*International Literary and Artistic Association*]
ALAI......... Irrigation Division, Alberta Agriculture, Lethbridge, Alberta [*Library symbol*] [*National Library of Canada*] (NLC)
Ala Ind Sc Soc Pr ... Alabama Industrial and Scientific Society. Proceedings [*A publication*]
ALA Intellectual Freedom Newsl ... American Library Association. Intellectual Freedom Committee. Newsletter [*A publication*]
ALAIRC .... Alaskan Air Command [*Elmendorf Air Force Base*] [*Air Force*]
ALAIRS..... Advanced Low-Altitude Infrared Reconnaissance Sensor
ALAJ......... Alaska Journal [*A publication*]
Ala J Med Sci ... Alabama Journal of Medical Sciences [*A publication*]
ALaL......... Axiolabiolingual [*Dentistry*]
Ala Law...... Alabama Lawyer [*A publication*]
Ala Law R.. Alabama Law Review [*A publication*]
ALALC...... Asociacion Latinoamericana de Libre Comercio [*Also, LAFTA*] [*Latin American Free Trade Association*]
Ala Libn..... Alabama Librarian [*A publication*]
ALA Lib Period Round Table Newsl ... American Library Association. Library Periodicals Round Table. Newsletter [*A publication*]
ALA Lib Serv to Labor News ... American Library Association. Adult Services Division. Joint Committee on Library Service to Labor Groups. Library Service to Labor Newsletter [*A publication*]
Ala LJ....... Alabama Law Journal [*A publication*]
Ala LR ...... Alabama Law Review [*A publication*]
Ala L Rev... Alabama Law Review [*A publication*]
ALALY...... Aluminum Alloy (MCD)
ALAM .... Lamont Public Library, Alberta [*Library symbol*] [*National Library of Canada*] (NLC)
ALAMAR ... Asociacion Latinoamericana de Armadores [*Latin American Shipowners' Association*] (EAIO)
Ala Mar Resour Bull ... Alabama Marine Resources. Bulletin [*A publication*]
Ala Med ..... Alabama Medicine [*A publication*]
ALAMOC ... Asociacion Latinoamericana de Analisis y Modificacion del Comportamiento [*Latin American Association of Behavior Analysis and Modification*] (EAIO)
Al-An .... Al-Andalus [*A publication*]
ALAN .... Alanco Ltd. [*NASDAQ symbol*] (NQ)
ALANAM ... Latin American Association of National Academies of Medicine (EA)
ALANBH .. Archivos Latinoamericanos de Nutricion [*A publication*]
ALANET ... American Library Association's Electronic Information Service
ALANF...... Army Land Forces
ALANO...... All Accident Notice Offices [*FAA*] (FAAC)
ALANON ... Alcoholics Anonymous Family Groups (ADA)
Ala NS .... Alabama Reports, New Series [*A publication*] (DLA)
Ala Nurse.. Alabama Nurse [*A publication*]
ALAO........ Association of Life Agency Officers [*Later, LIMRA*]
ALAOLPR ... American Library Association Office for Library Personnel Resources (EA)
ALAP........ AppleTalk Link Access Protocol [*Apple Computer, Inc.*] (BYTE)
ALAP......... As Low as Possible [*or Practical*] (NRCH)
ALAP........ Asociacion Latinoamericana de Administracion Publica
ALAP........ Associative Linear Array Processor [*Data processing*]
ALAP......... Parkland Regional Library, Lacombe, Alberta [*Library symbol*] [*National Library of Canada*] (NLC)
ALAPCO ... Association of Local Air Pollution Control Officials (EA)
ALAPDP ... Arizona Land and People [*A publication*]
Ala Polytech Inst Eng Exp Stn Eng Bull ... Alabama Polytechnic Institute. Engineering Experiment Station. Engineering Bulletin [*A publication*]
ALAR........ Acapulco y Los Arcos Restaurantes [*NASDAQ symbol*] (NQ)
Ala R......... Alabama Reports [*A publication*] (DLA)
Ala R......... Alabama Review [*A publication*]
ALAR........ Regional Office, Alberta Agriculture, Lethbridge, Alberta [*Library symbol*] [*National Library of Canada*] (NLC)
ALARA...... As Low as Reasonably Achievable [*Radiation exposure*] [*Nuclear Regulatory Commission*]
ALARACT ... All Army Activities (AABC)
ALA Ref Serv Div ... American Library Association. Reference Services Division. Reference Quarterly [*A publication*]
Ala Rep...... Alabama Reports [*A publication*] (DLA)
Ala Rep NS ... Alabama Reports, New Series [*A publication*] (DLA)
Ala Reps.... Alabama Reports [*A publication*] (DLA)
Ala Rev ..... Alabama Review [*A publication*]
ALARM..... Advanced Low-Altitude RADAR Model (MCD)
ALARM..... Air-Launched Advanced Ramjet Missile (KSC)
ALARM..... Air-Launched AntiRADAR Missile
ALARM..... Airborne LASER Receiver Module (MCD)
ALARM..... Alerting Long-Range Airborne RADAR for MTI [*Moving Target Indicator*]
ALARM..... Australian Library Annual Reports on Microfiche [*A publication*] (APTA)
ALARM..... Automatic Light Aircraft Readiness Monitor
Ala RNS..... Alabama Reports, New Series [*A publication*] (DLA)
ALARR...... Air-Launched, Air-Recoverable Rocket
ALART...... Army Low-Speed Air Research Tasks
ALARTC ... All Air Route Traffic Control Centers in Region [*FAA*] (FAAC)

ALAS........ Aboriginal Legal Aid Service [*Australia*]
ALAS........ Accident Legal Advise Service [*British*]
ALAS........ Alaska [*A publication*]
ALAS........ Alaska (AFM)
ALAS........ Alliance of Latin Artistes Society (EA)
ALAS........ Aminolaevulinate Synthase [*An enzyme*]
ALAS........ Approach Landing Autopilot System [*or Subsystem*] [*Aviation*] (MCD)
ALAS........ Army Library Automated Systems (IID)
ALAS........ Artillery Location Acoustic System (MCD)
ALAS........ Associate of the Chartered Land Agents' Society [*British*]
ALAS........ Associate in Letters, Arts, and Sciences
ALAS........ Association for Latin American Studies [*Defunct*]
ALAS........ Association of Latvian Academic Societies (EA)
ALAS........ Asynchronous Look-Ahead Simulator (IEEE)
ALAS........ Automated Library Acquisitions System [*Suggested name for the Library of Congress computer system*]
ALAS........ Automated Literature Alerting System [*Data processing*] (DIT)
ALAS........ Automatic Landing Autopilot Subsystem (NASA)
ALAS........ Automatic Load Alleviation System (MCD)
ALAS........ Auxiliary Loans to Assist Students
ALASA...... Allergie und Asthma [*A publication*]
ALASAM.. Advanced Low-Altitude SAM (MCD)
ALASAV .. Allergie und Asthma [*A publication*]
ALASC...... Aircraft Launching Accessory Service Change (MCD)
Ala Sel Cas ... Alabama Select Cases (Supreme Court), by Shepherd [*37, 38, 39*] [*A publication*] (DLA)
ALASH...... Acta Linguistica. Academiae Scientiarum Hungaricae [*A publication*]
Alaska........ Alaska Reporter [*A publication*] (DLA)
Alaska Admin Code ... Alaska Administrative Code [*A publication*] (DLA)
Alaska Admin Jnl ... Alaska Administrative Journal [*A publication*]
Alaska Ag Exp ... Alaska. Agricultural Experiment Station. Publications [*A publication*]
Alaska Agric Exp Stn Bull ... Alaska. Agricultural Experiment Station. Bulletin [*A publication*]
Alaska Agric Exp Stn Circ ... Alaska. Agricultural Experiment Station. Circular [*A publication*]
Alaska BB ... Alaska Bar Brief [*A publication*]
Alaska B Brief ... Alaska Bar Brief [*A publication*] (DLA)
Alaska BJ .. Alaska Bar Journal [*A publication*] (DLA)
Alaska Bus and Development ... Alaska Business and Development [*A publication*]
Alaska Co .. Alaska Codes (Carter) [*A publication*] (DLA)
Alaska Const ... Alaska Constitution [*A publication*] (DLA)
Alaska Constr Oil ... Alaska Construction and Oil [*A publication*]
Alaska Dep Fish Res Rep ... Alaska. Department of Fisheries. Research Report [*A publication*]
Alaska Dept Mines Rept Commissioner Mines Bienn ... Alaska. Department of Mines. Report of the Commissioner of Mines. Biennium [*A publication*]
Alaska Dept Nat Resour Div Mines Miner Rep ... Alaska. Department of Natural Resources. Division of Mines and Minerals. Report [*A publication*]
Alaska Div Geol Geophys Surv Geochem Rep ... Alaska. Division of Geological and Geophysical Surveys. Geochemical Report [*A publication*]
Alaska Div Geol Geophys Surv Geol Rep ... Alaska. Division of Geological and Geophysical Surveys. Geologic Report [*A publication*]
Alaska Div Geol Surv Geochem Rep ... Alaska. Division of Geological Survey. Geochemical Report [*A publication*]
Alaska Div Mines Geol Geochem Rep ... Alaska. Division of Mines and Geology. Geochemical Report [*A publication*]
Alaska Div Mines Geol Geol Rep ... Alaska. Division of Mines and Geology. Geologic Report [*A publication*]
Alaska Div Mines and Geology Geochem Rept ... Alaska. Department of Natural Resources. Division of Mines and Geology. Geochemical Report [*A publication*]
Alaska Div Mines and Geology Geol Rept ... Alaska. Department of Natural Resources. Division of Mines and Geology. Geologic Report [*A publication*]
Alaska Div Mines Geol Rep ... Alaska. Division of Mines and Geology. Report [*A publication*]
Alaska Div Mines and Minerals Inf Circ Rept ... Alaska. Division of Mines and Minerals. Information Circular. Report [*A publication*]
Alaska Div Mines Miner Rep ... Alaska. Division of Mines and Minerals. Report [*A publication*]
Alaska Econ Trends ... Alaska Economic Trends [*A publication*]
Alaska Fed ... Alaska Federal Reports [*A publication*] (DLA)
Alaska Fed Rep ... Alaska Federal Reports [*A publication*] (DLA)
Alaska Ind ... Alaska Industry [*A publication*]
Alaska J..... Alaska Journal [*A publication*]
Alaska LJ .. Alaska Law Journal [*A publication*]
Alaska Med ... Alaska Medicine [*A publication*]
Alaskan Arct Tundra Proc Anniv Celebration Nav Arct Res Lab ... Alaskan Arctic Tundra Proceedings. Anniversary Celebration. Naval Arctic Research Laboratory [*A publication*]
Alaska Nat N ... Alaska Native News [*A publication*]
Alaska Q Rev ... Alaska Quarterly Review [*A publication*]

Alaska Reg Rep US Dep Agric For Serv ... Alaska Region Report. United States Department of Agriculture. Forest Service [*A publication*]
Alaska Rev Bus Econ Cond ... Alaska Review of Business and Economic Conditions [*A publication*]
Alaska R Social and Econ Conditions ... Alaska Review of Social and Economic Conditions [*A publication*]
Alaska Sci Conf Proc ... Alaska Science Conference. Proceedings [*A publication*]
Alaska Sess Laws ... Alaska Session Laws [*A publication*] (DLA)
Alaska Stat ... Alaska Statutes [*A publication*] (DLA)
Alaska Univ Anthrop Pa ... Alaska University. Anthropological Papers [*A publication*]
Alaska Univ Geophys Inst Rep ... Alaska University. Geophysical Institute. Report [*A publication*]
Alaska Univ Mineral Industry Research Lab Rept ... University of Alaska. Mineral Industry Research Laboratory. Report [*A publication*]
Alaska Univ School Mines Pub Bull ... Alaska University. School of Mines Publication. Bulletin [*A publication*]
ALA/SRRT/GLTF ... American Library Association/Social Responsibilities Round Table/Gay and Lesbian Task Force (EA)
ALASRU ... Asociacion Latinoamericana de Sociologia Rural [*Latin American Rural Sociological Association - LARSA*] (EAIO)
ALAST ...... Advanced LASER Spot Tracker (MCD)
Ala St B Found Bull ... Alabama State Bar Foundation. Bulletin [*A publication*] (DLA)
Ala St Found Bull ... Alabama State Foundation Bulletin [*A publication*] (ILCA)
ALAT........ Aircraft Latitude (MCD)
ALAT........ Alanine Transaminase [*Also, AAT, ALT, GPT*] [*An enzyme*]
ALAT........ Alaska Today [*A publication*]
ALAT........ All Air Traffic Service Personnel in Region [*FAA*] (FAAC)
ALAT........ Army Language Aptitude Test [*Later, DLAT*]
ALATAS ... All Air Traffic [*Area*] Supervisors in Region [*FAA*] (FAAC)
ALATF ..... All Air Traffic Field Facilities [*FAA*] (FAAC)
ALATFO... All Air Traffic Field Offices [*FAA*] (FAAC)
Ala-tRNA .. Ribonucleic Acid, Transfer - Alanyl [*Biochemistry, genetics*]
ALAU .... Union of Latin American Universities (EA)
Alauda Rev Int Ornithol ... Alauda. Revue Internationale d'Ornithologie [*A publication*]
ALAW .... Advanced Light Antitank Weapon (RDA)
ALA Wash Newsl ... American Library Association. Washington Newsletter [*A publication*]
ALAZ........ ALA [*American Latvian Association*] Zurnals [*A publication*]
ALB .... Aboriginal Law Bulletin [*A publication*] (APTA)
ALB .... Academic Libraries of Brooklyn [*Library network*]
ALB .... Adyar Library Bulletin [*A publication*]
ALB .... Air-Land Battle (MCD)
ALB .... Air-Launched Booster (MCD)
ALB .... Aircraft Launching Bulletin (MCD)
Alb .... Albania [*A publication*]
ALB .... Albania [*ANSI three-letter standard code*] (CNC)
alb .... Albanian [*MARC language code*] [*Library of Congress*] (LCCP)
ALB .... Albany [*New York*]
ALB .... Albany [*New York*] [*Airport symbol*] (OAG)
Alb .... Albericus de Porta Ravennate [*Flourished, 1165-94*] [*Authority cited in pre-1607 legal work*] (DSA)
Alb .... Albericus de Rosate [*Deceased, 1360*] [*Authority cited in pre-1607 legal work*] (DSA)
ALB .... Alberni [*British Columbia*] [*Seismograph station code, US Geological Survey*] (SEIS)
ALB .... Alberta [*Canadian province*]
ALB .... Alberta Business [*A publication*]
Alb .... [*Magister*] Albertus [*Authority cited in pre-1607 legal work*] (DSA)
Alb .... Albertus Longobardista [*Flourished, 12th century*] [*Authority cited in pre-1607 legal work*] (DSA)
Alb .... Albertus de Saliceto [*Authority cited in pre-1607 legal work*] (DSA)
ALB .... Albumin [*Also, AL*] [*Biochemistry*]
ALB .... Albus [*White*] [*Pharmacy*]
ALB .... Allgemeines Literaturblatt [*A publication*]
ALB .... Almanacco Letterario Bompiani [*A publication*]
ALB .... American Legion Baseball (EA)
ALB .... Annales. Faculte des Lettres de Besancon [*A publication*]
ALB .... Anticipated Level of Business
ALB .... Automatic Loc-Bottom [*Packaging*]
ALB .... Automobile Labor Board
ALB .... University of Alberta Library [*UTLAS symbol*]
ALBA........ Alberta [*Canadian province*]
ALBA........ American Lawn Bowls Association (EA)
ALBA........ American Leather Belting Association [*Later, NIBA*]
AL-BAAB ... Al Bahrain Arab African Bank
Alban .... Albania
Alban .... [*Johannes Hieronymus*] Albanus [*Deceased, 1591*] [*Authority cited in pre-1607 legal work*] (DSA)
Albany Felt Guide ... Albany Felt Guidelines [*A publication*]
Albany Inst Pr ... Albany Institute. Proceedings [*A publication*]
Albany Inst Tr ... Albany Institute. Transactions [*A publication*]

Albany L R ... Albany Law Review [*A publication*]
Albany L Rev ... Albany Law Review [*A publication*]
Albany News Dig ... Albany International Weekly News Digest [*A publication*]
Alb Arb ...... Albert Arbitration [*Lord Cairns' Decisions*] [*A publication*] (DLA)
Alb Brun .... Albertus Brunus [*Deceased, 1541*] [*Authority cited in pre-1607 legal work*] (DSA)
ALBC........ Alameda Bancorporation, Inc. [*NASDAQ symbol*] (NQ)
ALBC........ AntiLASER Beam Coating
AlBD........ All the Best Dog Poems [*A publication*]
ALBE........ Air/Land Battlefield Environment [*Army*] (RDA)
Albe............ Albericus de Rosate [*Deceased, 1360*] [*Authority cited in pre-1607 legal work*] (DSA)
Albe............ [*Magister*] Albertus [*Authority cited in pre-1607 legal work*] (DSA)
ALBEN...... Aerodynamic Load Balanced Elliptical Nozzle (MCD)
Alber .... Albericus de Rosate [*Deceased, 1360*] [*Authority cited in pre-1607 legal work*] (DSA)
Alber Bru ... Albertus Brunus [*Deceased, 1541*] [*Authority cited in pre-1607 legal work*] (DSA)
Alberic de Rosat ... Albericus de Rosate [*Deceased, 1360*] [*Authority cited in pre-1607 legal work*] (DSA)
Alber J Edu ... Alberta Journal of Educational Research [*A publication*]
Alber de Malet ... Albericus de Maletis [*Flourished, 1431-33*] [*Authority cited in pre-1607 legal work*] (DSA)
Alberta Bs ... Alberta Business [*A publication*]
Alberta Bus J ... Alberta Business Journal. Chamber of Resources [*A publication*]
Alberta Dep Lands For Annu Rep ... Alberta. Department of Lands and Forests. Annual Report [*A publication*]
Alberta Dept Mines and Minerals Mines Div Ann Rept ... Alberta. Department of Mines and Minerals. Mines Division. Annual Report [*A publication*]
Alberta Gaz ... Alberta Gazette [*A publication*]
Alberta His ... Alberta History [*A publication*]
Alberta Hog J ... Alberta Hog Journal [*A publication*]
Alberta J Educ Res ... Alberta Journal of Educational Research [*A publication*]
Alberta Lands For Annu Rep ... Alberta Lands and Forests. Annual Report [*A publication*]
Alberta L (Can) ... Alberta Law Reports (Canada) [*A publication*]
Alberta LQ ... Alberta Law Quarterly [*A publication*]
Alberta L R ... Alberta Law Review [*A publication*]
Alberta L Rev ... Alberta Law Review [*A publication*]
Alberta LRR ... Alberta Institute of Law Research and Reform [*Canada*] (ILCA)
Alberta Med Bull ... Alberta Medical Bulletin [*A publication*]
Alberta M L J ... Alberta Modern Language Journal [*A publication*]
Alberta Mot ... Alberta Motorist [*A publication*]
Alberta Res Annu Rep ... Alberta Research. Annual Report [*A publication*]
Alberta Res Counc Bull ... Alberta Research Council. Bulletin [*A publication*]
Alberta Res Counc Inf Ser ... Alberta Research Council. Information Series [*A publication*]
Alberta Res Counc Rep ... Alberta Research Council. Report [*A publication*]
Alberta Research Council Bull ... Alberta Research Council. Bulletin [*A publication*]
Alberta Research Council Inf Ser ... Alberta Research Council. Information Series [*A publication*]
Alberta Research Council Mem ... Alberta Research Council. Memoir [*A publication*]
Alberta Research Council Mimeo Circ ... Alberta Research Council. Mimeographed Circular [*A publication*]
Alberta Research Council Prelim Rept ... Alberta Research Council. Preliminary Report [*A publication*]
Alberta Research Council Prelim Soil Survey Rept ... Alberta Research Council. Preliminary Soil Survey Report [*A publication*]
Alberta Research Council Rept ... Alberta Research Council. Report [*A publication*]
Alberta Res Econ Geol Rep ... Alberta Research. Economic Geology Report [*A publication*]
Alberta Res Inf Ser ... Alberta Research. Information Series [*A publication*]
Alberta Res Rep ... Alberta Research. Report [*A publication*]
Alberta Soc Pet Geol Annu Field Conf Guideb ... Alberta Society of Petroleum Geologists. Annual Field Conference. Guidebook [*A publication*]
Alberta Soc Pet Geol Bull ... Alberta Society of Petroleum Geologists. Bulletin [*A publication*]
Alberta Soc Petroleum Geologists Jour News Bull ... Alberta Society of Petroleum Geologists. Journal. News Bulletin [*A publication*]
Alberta Univ Dep Chem Div Theor Chem Tech Rep ... Alberta. University. Department of Chemistry. Division of Theoretical Chemistry. Technical Report [*A publication*]
Alberta Univ Dept Civil Eng Struct Eng Rep ... Alberta University. Department of Civil Engineering. Structural Engineering Reports [*A publication*]
Alberta Wild Assoc Nl ... Alberta Wilderness Association. Newsletter [*A publication*]
ALBI.......... Air-Launched Ballistic Intercept
ALBI.......... Air-Launched Boost Intercept (MSA)

ALBI......... Alaska Business and Industry [*Supersedes Alaska Industry*] [*A publication*]

ALBI......... Albion International Resources, Inc. [*Laguna Beach, CA*] [*NASDAQ symbol*]   (NQ)

ALBIS....... Air-Launched Ballistic Intercept System   (MCD)

Albiswerk-Ber ... Albiswerk-Berichte [*A publication*]

ALBJ .... Alberta Business Journal [*A publication*]

Alb Law J .. Albany Law Journal [*A publication*]

ALBLB ...... American Lung Association. Bulletin [*A publication*]

Alb LJ .... Albany Law Journal [*A publication*]   (DLA)

Alb LQ...... Alberta Law Quarterly [*A publication*]   (DLA)

Alb LR .... Alberta Law Reports [*A publication*]

Alb LR .... Alberta Law Review [*A publication*]

Alb L Rev... Albany Law Review [*A publication*]

Alb LS Jour ... Albany Law School Journal [*A publication*]   (DLA)

ALBM....... Air-Land Battle Management

ALBM....... Air-Launched Ballistic Missile

ALBM....... Alpha 1 Biomedicals, Inc. [*Washington, DC*] [*NASDAQ symbol*]   (NQ)

ALBN ...... Alberta Naturalist [*A publication*]

ALBN .... Allied Bancshares, Inc. [*NASDAQ symbol*]   (NQ)

ALBO .... Automatic Line Buildout [*Bell Laboratories*]

Alb de Odofre ... Albertus Denarii de Odofredo [*Deceased, 1300*] [*Authority cited in pre-1607 legal work*]   (DSA)

Alb Pp........ Albertus Papiensis [*Flourished, 1211-40*] [*Authority cited in pre-1607 legal work*]   (DSA)

ALBr.......... Anuario da Literatura Brasileira [*A publication*]

Albrecht Thaer Arch ... Albrecht-Thaer-Archiv [*A publication*]

Albrecht V Graefe's Arch Ophthal ... Albrecht Von Graefe's Archiv fuer Ophthalmologie [*A publication*]

Albrecht Von Graefe's Arch Clin Exp Ophthalmol ... Albrecht Von Graefe's Archive for Clinical and Experimental Ophthalmology [*A publication*]

Albrecht Von Graefe's Arch Klin Exp Ophthalmol ... Albrecht Von Graefe's Archiv fuer Klinische und Experimentelle Ophthalmologie [*West Germany*] [*A publication*]

Albrecht Von Graefe's Arch Ophthalmol ... Albrecht Von Graefe's Archiv fuer Ophthalmologie [*A publication*]

Albri.......... Albericus de Porta Ravennate [*Flourished, 1165-94*] [*Authority cited in pre-1607 legal work*]   (DSA)

Albright-Knox Gal Notes ... Albright-Knox Art Gallery. Notes [*A publication*]

Albri de Rosa ... Albericus de Rosate [*Deceased, 1360*] [*Authority cited in pre-1607 legal work*]   (DSA)

Alb de Ros ... Albericus de Rosate [*Deceased, 1360*] [*Authority cited in pre-1607 legal work*]   (DSA)

ALBS......... African Love Bird Society   (EA)

ALBS......... Air-Launched Balloon System   (MCD)

ALBS......... Alaskana Book Series [*A publication*]

Alb Stud..... Albertina Studien [*A publication*]

ALBSU...... Adult Literacy and Basic Skills Unit [*British*]

ALBU .... Alaska Business Newsletter [*A publication*]

Albuquer Jl ... Albuquerque Journal [*A publication*]

Albuquerque BJ ... Albuquerque Bar Journal [*A publication*]   (DLA)

ALBUS...... All Bureaus [*Navy*]

ALBVA...... Animal Learning and Behavior [*A publication*]

ALBYBL.... American Laboratory [*Fairfield, Connecticut*] [*A publication*]

Alby LR ..... Albany Law Review [*A publication*]

ALC .... A la Carte [*According to the Menu, each item ordered individually*] [*French*]   (ADA)

ALC .... Adaptive Linear Combiner [*Data processing*]

ALC .... Adaptive Logic Circuit

ALC .... Administrative/Logistics Center [*Military*]   (INF)

ALC .... Advanced Library Concepts, Inc. [*Later, ALI'I*] [*Information service or system*]   (IID)

ALC .... Aeronca Lovers Club   (EA)

ALC ....: Aft Load Controller   (MCD)

ALC .... Air Launchable Concept

ALC .... Air Logistics Center [*McClellan Air Force Base, CA*]   (MCD)

ALC .... Alabama Central R. R. [*AAR code*]

Alc............ Alcaeus [*Seventh century BC*] [*Classical studies*]   (OCD)

Alc............ Alcantara [*A publication*]

Alc............ Alcestis [*of Euripides*] [*Classical studies*]   (OCD)

Alc............ [*Andreas*] Alciatus [*Deceased, 1550*] [*Authority cited in pre-1607 legal work*]   (DSA)

Alc............ Alcibiades [*of Plutarch*] [*Classical studies*]   (OCD)

Alc............ Alcibiades [*of Plato*] [*Classical studies*]   (OCD)

Alc............ Alcock's Registry Cases [*1832-41*] [*Ireland*] [*A publication*]   (DLA)

ALC .... Alcohol   (KSC)

ALC .... Alcove [*Classified advertising*]   (ADA)

ALC .... Alexanders, Laing & Cruickshank [*Broker*] [*British*]

ALC .... Algoma Central Railway [*Toronto Stock Exchange symbol*]

ALC .... Alicante [*Spain*] [*Airport symbol*]   (OAG)

ALC .... Alkali-Extractable Light Chain [*Biochemistry*]

ALC .... Alternative Lifestyle Checklist

ALC .... American Labor Cases [*Prentice-Hall, Inc.*] [*A publication*]   (DLA)

ALC .... American LaMancha Club   (EA)

ALC .... American Lamb Council   (EA)

ALC .... American Lancia Club   (EA)

ALC .... American Langshan Club   (EA)

ALC .... American Leading Cases [*A publication*]   (DLA)

ALC .... American Life Convention [*Later, ACLI*]

ALC .... American Lutheran Church [*Later, ELCA*]

ALC .... Analytical Liquid Chromatograph

ALC .... Antenna Loading Coil

ALC .... Area Logistics Command

ALC .... Army Legal Corps [*British military*]   (DMA)

ALC .... Army Logistics Center

ALC .... Army-Wide Library Council   (RDA)

ALC .... Artificial Luminous Cloud

ALC .... Assembly Language Coding [*Data processing*]

ALC .... Associated Lutheran Charities [*Later, Lutheran Social Welfare Conference of America*]   (EA)

ALC .... Astro Launch Circuit [*NASA*]   (KSC)

ALC .... Audio Load Compensator   (MCD)

ALC .... Automatic Level Control [*Camera*] [*Aviation*]

ALC .... Automatic Light Control   (KSC)

ALC .... Automatic Load Control

ALC .... Axiolinguocervical [*Dentistry*]

ALC .... Lethbridge College, Alberta [*Library symbol*] [*National Library of Canada*]   (NLC)

ALCA......... Aft Load Control Assembly   (MCD)

ALCA......... Aluminum Chlorohydroxyallantoinate [*Organic chemistry*]

ALCA......... American Leather Chemists Association   (EA)

ALCA......... American Lock Collectors Association   (EA)

ALCA......... Arts Law Centre of Australia

ALCA......... Associated Landscape Contractors of America   (EA)

ALCA......... Automatic Level Control Assembly   (MCD)

ALCA......... Automotive Legislative Council of America   (EA)

ALCAC..... Airlines Communications Administrative Council

AL CAC ... Alla Cacia [*In the Hunting Style*] [*Music*]   (ROG)

ALCA/ILD ... Interior Landscape Division of ALCA [*Later, ALCA/IPD*]   (EA)

ALCA/IPD ... Interior Plantscape Division of ALCA   (EA)

ALCAL..... Alloy-Coated Aluminum   (KSC)

ALCAN ..... Alaska-Canada [*Highway*]

ALCAN ..... Aluminum Co. of Canada Ltd.

Alcan N ..... Alcan News [*A publication*]

ALCANUS ... Alaska, Canada, United States   (AABC)

AL CAP .... Alla Capella [*In Church Style*] [*Music*]   (ROG)

ALCAP...... Aluminocalcium Phosphorous Oxide [*Inorganic chemistry*]

ALCAPP.... Automatic List Classification and Profile Production

ALCARS ... Airborne Launch Control and Recovery System   (MCD)

ALCATS.... Automated Lines of Communications and Target System   (MCD)

ALCC......... Acetyl Levo-Carnitine Chloride [*Biochemistry*]

ALCC......... Airborne Launch Control Center

ALCC......... Airlift Control Center   (AFM)

ALCC......... ALC Communications Corp. [*Birmingham, MI*] [*NASDAQ symbol*]   (NQ)

ALCC .... La Crete Community Library, Alberta [*Library symbol*] [*National Library of Canada*]   (NLC)

ALCCAM ... Army Life Cycle Cost Analysis Model   (MCD)

ALCCM.... Army Life Cycle Cost Model   (MCD)

ALCD .... Alcide Corp. [*NASDAQ symbol*]   (NQ)

ALCD .... Alclad [*Metallurgy*]

ALCD .... Aluminum-Clad   (MSA)

ALCD .... Associate of the London College of Divinity [*British*]

ALCE......... Airlift Control Element   (AFM)

ALCEA...... Air Line Communication Employees Association

ALCENT.... Airlift Center [*Air Force*]   (MCD)

ALCES ...... Association of Lecturers in Colleges of Education in Scotland

ALCF .... Association of Lutheran College Faculties   (EA)

ALCF .... Australian Law Council Foundation   (ADA)

ALCFA ...... American Lithuanian Catholic Federation Ateitis [*Later, LCFA*]   (EA)

ALCGP...... Annali del Liceo Classico Garibaldi di Palermo [*A publication*]

ALCH .... Alchemy

ALCH .... Alcohol

ALCH .... Approach Light Contact Height

Alcheringa (Assoc Australas Palaeontol) ... Alcheringa (Association of Australasian Palaeontologists) [*A publication*]

ALCHRNI ... American Labor Committee for Human Rights in Northern Ireland   (EA)

Alci............ [*Andreas*] Alciatus [*Deceased, 1550*] [*Authority cited in pre-1607 legal work*]   (DSA)

ALCI .... Allcity Insurance Co. [*NASDAQ symbol*]   (NQ)

ALCJ .... Army Logistics Command Japan   (CINC)

ALCJC....... Genealogical Society Library, Church of Jesue Christ of Latter-Day Saints, Lethbridge, Alberta [*Library symbol*] [*National Library of Canada*]   (NLC)

ALCKT ...... All stations or offices having send-receive teletypewriter service on circuit [*FAA*]   (FAAC)

ALCL......... Assembly Line Communications Link [*General Motors computerized automotive production*]

ALCLAN ... Air Logistics Command Local Area Network

ALCM .... Air-Launched Cruise Missile

Alcm.......... Alcman [*Seventh century BC*] [*Classical studies*]   (OCD)

ALCM .... American Lutheran Church Men   (EA)

ALCM .... Associate of the London College of Music [*British*]

ALCMGS .. Air-Launched Cruise Missile Guidance Set   (MCD)

Alc & N ...... Alcock and Napier's Irish King's Bench Reports [*A publication*] (ILCA)

Alc & Nap .. Alcock and Napier's Irish King's Bench Reports [*A publication*] (DLA)

ALCNAQ .. Alabama Conservation [*A publication*]

ALCO .... Airlift Coordinating Office [*or Officer*] (AFIT)

ALCO .... Airlift Launch Control Officer [*Air Force*] (AFM)

ALCO .... Airlift Liaison Coordination Officer [*Air Force*]

ALCO .... Alberta Conservationist [*A publication*]

ALCO .... Alico, Inc. [*NASDAQ symbol*] (NQ)

ALCO .... American Locomotive Company

ALCO .... Asset-Liability Committee [*Banking*]

ALCOA ..... Aluminum Company of America

ALCOA Res Lab Tech Pap ... ALCOA [*Aluminum Company of America*] Research Laboratories. Technical Paper [*A publication*]

Alco Bev ..... Alcoholic Beverage (DLA)

Alco Bev Cont ... Alcoholic Beverage Control (DLA)

Alcock & N ... Alcock and Napier's Irish King's Bench Reports [*A publication*] (DLA)

ALCOGS .... Advanced Low-Cost G-Cueing System

ALCOH ..... Alcohol

Alcoh Health & Res W ... Alcohol Health and Research World [*A publication*]

Alcohol Abnorm Protein Biosynth ... Alcohol and Abnormal Protein Biosynthesis [*A publication*]

Alcohol Alcohol ... Alcohol and Alcoholism [*A publication*]

Alcohol Aldehyde Metab Syst Pap Int Symp ... Alcohol and Aldehyde Metabolizing Systems. Papers. International Symposium on Alcohol and Aldehyde Metabolizing Systems [*A publication*]

Alcohol Clin Exp Res ... Alcoholism Clinical and Experimental Research [*A publication*]

Alcohol Clin Update ... Alcohol Clinical Update [*A publication*]

Alcohol Dig ... Alcoholism Digest [*A publication*]

Alcohol Drug Res ... Alcohol and Drug Research [*A publication*]

Alcohol Health Res World ... Alcohol Health and Research World [*A publication*]

Alcohol Liver Pathol Proc Int Symp Alcohol Drug Res ... Alcoholic Liver Pathology. Proceedings. Liver Pathology Section. International Symposia. Alcohol and Drug Research [*A publication*]

ALCOL ...... Alcohol

ALCOLIC ... Alcoholic [*Freight*]

ALCOM .... Alaskan Command [*Discontinued, 1975*] [*Military*]

ALCOM .... Algebraic Compiler [*Data processing*]

ALCOM .... ALGOL Compiler [*Data processing*] (DIT)

ALCOM .... All Commands [*A dispatch to all commands in an area*] [*Navy*]

ALCOMLANT ... All Commands, [*US*] Atlantic Fleet [*Navy*] (NVT)

ALCOMPAC ... All Commands, [*US*] Pacific Fleet [*Navy*] (NVT)

ALCON ..... All Concerned [*Army*] (AABC)

ALCONH ... Alianza Campesina de Organizaciones Nacionales de Honduras [*Peasant Alliance of National Organizations of Honduras*] [*Political party*] (PD)

ALcons ...... Articulation Loss of Consonants [*Audiology*]

ALCOP ...... Alternate Command Post [*Military*] (AFM)

Alco Prod Rev ... Alco Products Review [*A publication*]

ALCOR ..... ARPA [*Advanced Research Projects Agency*]/Lincoln C-Band Observable RADAR [*Army*] (AABC)

ALCORCEN ... Air Logistic Coordination Center

ALCORSS ... Australian Liaison Committee on Remote Sensing by Satellite

ALCP .... Alternate Command Post

ALCP .... Area Local Control Panel (NRCH)

Alc Per Prop ... Alcock on Personal Property [*A publication*] (DLA)

ALCQ .... Association des Litteratures Canadiennes et Quebecoises [*Association for Canadian and Quebec Literatures - ACQL*]

ALCR .... Alaska Conservation Review [*A publication*]

AlcR .... Alcohol Rub [*Medicine*]

AL CR .... Aluminum Crown [*Dentistry*]

ALCR .... American Land Cruisers, Inc. [*Miami, FL*] [*NASDAQ symbol*] (NQ)

ALCRD7 .... Advances in Liquid Crystals [*A publication*]

Alc Reg .... Alcock's Registry Cases [*Ireland*] [*1832-41*] [*A publication*] (ILCA)

Alc Reg C ... Alcock's Registry Cases [*1832-41*] [*Ireland*] [*A publication*] (DLA)

Alc Reg Cas ... Alcock's Registry Cases [*1832-41*] [*Ireland*] [*A publication*] (DLA)

ALCS .... Airborne Launch Control System [*Air Force*] (MCD)

ALCS .... American League Championship Series [*Baseball*]

ALCS .... Authors' Lending and Copyright Society [*British*]

ALCS/C ..... All AT [*Air Traffic Service*] Combined Station/Centers in Region [*FAA*] (FAAC)

ALCS/T ..... All AT [*Air Traffic Service*] Combined Station/Towers in Region [*FAA*] (FAAC)

ALCT .... Attempt to Locate (FAAC)

ALCTS ...... Association for Library Collections and Technical Services

ALCTS CCS ... ALCTS [*Association for Library Collections and Technical Services*] Cataloging and Classification Section

ALCTS RS ... ALCTS [*Association for Library Collections and Technical Services*] Resources Section

ALCU .... Altocumulus [*Cloud*] [*Meteorology*]

ALCU .... Arithmetic Logic and Control Unit [*Data processing*]

ALCU .... Asynchronous Line Control Unit [*Telecommunications*]

Al Culukidzis Sahelob Khutnaisi Sahelmc Ped Inst Srom ... Al. Culukidzis Sahelobis Khutnaisis Sahelmcipho Pedagogiuri Institutis Sromebi [*A publication*]

ALCUS ...... Association of Ladies of Charity of the United States (EA)

ALCVO ...... Association of Licensed Charter Vessel Owners [*Australia*]

ALCW .... American Lutheran Church Women (EA)

ALCYAP ... Aliphatic Chemistry [*A publication*]

ALD .... Acceptable Limit for Dispersion

ALD .... Activity Level Dependent (KSC)

ALD .... Administrative Law Decisions. Australian [*A publication*] (APTA)

ALD .... Adrenoleukodystrophy [*Medicine*]

ALD .... Advanced LASER Designator

ALD .... Advanced Logistics Development

ALD .... African Law Digest [*A publication*]

ALD .... Airborne Line Discriminator

ALD .... Alcoholic Liver Disease [*Medicine*]

Ald .... Alden's Condensed Reports [*Pennsylvania*] [*A publication*] (DLA)

ALD .... Alderman

ALD .... Aldolase [*An enzyme*]

Ald .... Aldricus [*Flourished, 1154-72*] [*Authority cited in pre-1607 legal work*] (DSA)

Ald .... Aldridge. History and Jurisdiction of the Courts of Law [*1835*] [*A publication*] (ILCA)

ALD .... Allendale, SC [*Location identifier*] [*FAA*] (FAAL)

ALD .... Alliance for Leadership Development (EA)

ALD .... Allied-Lyons [*Toronto Stock Exchange symbol*]

Ald .... Allied Record Sales [*Record label*]

ALD .... Allied-Signal, Inc. [*NYSE symbol*] (SPSG)

ALD .... Altadena Library District, Altadena, CA [*OCLC symbol*] (OCLC)

ALD .... Alter Ridge [*Washington*] [*Seismograph station code, US Geological Survey*] (SEIS)

ALD .... Alternative Lifestyles for the Disabled [*Australia*]

ALD .... American Library Directory [*R. R. Bowker Co.*] [*Online database*]

ALD .... American Lobbyists Directory [*A publication*]

ALD .... Aminolaevulinate Dehydratase [*Also, ALAD*] [*An enzyme*]

ALD .... Analog Line Driver [*Data processing*] (BUR)

ALD .... Anterior Lateral Dendrites [*Neurology*]

ALD .... Anterior Latissimus Dorsi [*Anatomy*]

ALD .... Appraisal of Language Disturbance [*Test*]

ALD .... Approximate Lethal Dose

ALD .... Asbestos Lung Disease

ALD .... Asian Literature Division - of MLA [*Modern Language Association of America*] (EA)

ALD .... Assistant Laboratory Director

ALD .... Assistant Local Director (DCTA)

ALD .... Asynchronous Line Driver [*Prentice Corp.*]

ALD .... At a Later Date

ALD .... Automated Logic Diagram [*Data processing*] (IBMDP)

ALD .... Automatic Locking Differential

ALD .... Available-to-Load Date (AABC)

ALD .... Fortschrittliche Betriebsfuehrung und Industrial Engineering [*A publication*]

ALDA .... Air Line Dispatchers Association [*Defunct*]

ALDA .... Allied Linens and Domestics Association [*Defunct*] (EA)

ALDA .... Aluminum(dihydroxy)allantoinate [*Organic chemistry*]

ALDA .... American Land Development Association (EA)

ALDA .... American Luggage Dealers Association [*Later, ALDC*] (EA)

ALDA .... Analytic Learning Disability Assessment [*Child development test*]

ALDA .... Aqua Lung Dealers Association [*Defunct*] (EA)

ALDA .... Association of Late-Deafened Adults (EA)

ALDA .... Association of Learning Disabled Adults (EA)

Ald Abr ...... Alden's Abridgment of Law [*A publication*] (DLA)

Ald Ans Cont ... Aldrich's Edition of Ansen on Contracts [*A publication*] (DLA)

ALDB .... Aldebaran Drilling Co. [*NASDAQ symbol*] (NQ)

ALDC .... Aldus Corp. [*NASDAQ symbol*] (NQ)

ALDC .... American Luggage Dealers Cooperative (EA)

ALDC .... Army Logistic Development Committee [*British*] (RDA)

ALDC .... Army Logistics Data Center

ALDC .... Asociacion Latinoamericana de Derecho Constitucional [*Latin American Constitutional Law Association - LACLA*] (EAIO)

ALDCS ...... Active Lift Distribution Control System [*Aerospace*]

ALDD .... Alidade [*Engineering*]

ALDEP ...... Automated Layout Design Program [*IBM Corp.*]

ALDF .... Animal Legal Defense Fund (EA)

ALDGA ..... Alloy Digest [*A publication*]

ALDH .... Aldehyde Dehydrogenase [*An enzyme*]

Ald Hist ..... Aldridge. History and Jurisdiction of the Courts of Law [*A publication*] (DLA)

ALDHU ..... Latin American Human Rights Association (EA)

ALDI .... Associated Long-Distance Interstate Message [*Telecommunications*] (TEL)

Al Dieb .... Alterius Diebus [*Every Other Day*] [*Pharmacy*]

Ald Ind	Alden's Index of United States Reports [*A publication*] (DLA)
ALDIS	Australian LASER Disk Information Services Pty. Ltd.
ALDJA	Journal. Alabama Dental Association [*A publication*]
ALDMN	Alderman (ROG)
ALDO	Activity Level Dependent Operations (NASA)
ALDO	Aldosterone [*Endocrinology*]
ALDOC	League of Arab States Documentation and Information Center [*Information service or system*] (IID)
ALDP	Automatic Language Data Processing
ALDPS	Automated Logistics Data Processing System
Ald Ques	Aldred's Questions on the Law of Property [*A publication*] (DLA)
Aldra	Aldracus [*Flourished, 13th century*] [*Authority cited in pre-1607 legal work*] (DSA)
Aldri	Aldricus [*Flourished, 1154-72*] [*Authority cited in pre-1607 legal work*] (DSA)
ALDRI	Automatic Low Date Rate Input
Aldridge	History and Jurisdiction of the Courts of Law [*1835*] [*A publication*] (DLA)
ALDS	Apollo Launch Data System [*NASA*]
ALDS	Automatic Lightning Detection System [*To aid in the prevention of forest fires*]
ALDT	Administrative and Logistics Downtime (MCD)
ALDT	Argon LASER Discharge Tube
ALDU	Association of Lawyers for the Defence of the Unborn (EAIO)
Ald & VH	Alden and Van Hoesen's Digest of Mississippi Laws [*A publication*] (DLA)
ALE	Actuarial Life Expectancy (AFIT)
ALE	Adaptive Line Enhancer (CAAL)
ALE	Additional Living Expense [*Insurance*]
ALE	Address Latch Enable [*Data processing*]
ALE	Admixture-Lathe-Cut + Eutectic [*Dental alloy*]
ALE	Airborne LASER Experiment [*Strategic Defense Initiative*]
ALE	Airport Landing Equipment (MCD)
ALE	Airport Lighting Equipment (NASA)
ALE	Alert [*Northwest Territories*] [*Seismograph station code, US Geological Survey*] (SEIS)
ale	Aleut [*MARC language code*] [*Library of Congress*] (LCCP)
AL E	Alia Editione [*Another Edition*] [*Latin*] (ROG)
ALE	Alliance Libre Europeenne [*European Free Alliance - EFA*] [*Political party*] [*Brussels, Belgium*] (EAIO)
ALE	Alliance Resources Ltd. [*Vancouver Stock Exchange symbol*]
ALE	Alternate Low Energy (CAAL)
ALE	American Lives Endowment (EA)
ALE	Antitrust Law and Economics Review [*A publication*]
ALE	Arid Land Ecology [*AEC project*]
ALE	Army Liaison Element (MCD)
ALE	Association for Liberal Education [*British*]
ALE	Atmospheric Lifetime Experiment [*Environmental science*]
ALE	Atomic Layer Epitaxy [*Physical chemistry*]
ALE	Automated Large Experiment [*NASA*]
ALE	Automatic LASER Encoder
a-le---	Lebanon [*MARC geographic area code*] [*Library of Congress*] (LCCP)
ALE	Leduc Public Library, Alberta [*Library symbol*] [*National Library of Canada*] (NLC)
ALEA	Air Line Employees Association, International (EA)
ALEA	Airborne Law Enforcement Association (EA)
ALEA	AirLine Employees Association, International (EA)
ALEA	American Lutheran Education Association [*Later, ELEA*] (EA)
ALEAA	American Lithuanian Engineers' and Architects' Association (EA)
A Lead	Adult Leadership [*A publication*]
ALEAS	Asociacion Latinoamericana de Educacion Agricola Superior
ALEBCI	Asociacion Latinoamericana de Escuelas de Bibliotecologia y Ciencias de la Informacion
ALEC	Alleco, Inc. [*NASDAQ symbol*] (NQ)
ALEC	American Labor Education Center (EA)
ALEC	American Legislative Exchange Council (EA)
ALEC	Anales de la Literatura Espanola Contemporanea [*A publication*]
ALEC	Australian Industrial and Intellectual Property [*A publication*]
ALECS	Air Force - Los Alamos EMP [*Electromagnetic Pulse*] Calibration Simulator
ALECSO	Arab League Educational, Cultural, and Scientific Organization [*Tunisia*]
ALED	Alaska Education News [*A publication*]
AL ED	Alia Editione [*Another Edition*] [*Latin*] (ADA)
ALED	Australian Libraries: the Essential Directory [*A publication*]
ALEDC	Associate Logistics Executive Development Course
ALEF	Alcor Life Extension Foundation (EA)
ALEF	Food Processing Development Center, Leduc, Alberta [*Library symbol*] [*National Library of Canada*] (NLC)
ALEG	Legal Public Library, Alberta [*Library symbol*] [*National Library of Canada*] (NLC)
ALEGEO	Asociacion Latinoamericana de Editores en Geociencias
ALEHU	Advanced Legal Education, Hamline University School of Law (DLA)
ALELWLE	American Literature, English Literature, and World Literature in English [*A publication*]
ALEM	Apollo Lunar Exploration Mission [*NASA*]
ALEMS	Apollo Lunar Excursion Module Sensors [*NASA*]
AL/EMU	Airlock/Extravehicle Mobility Unit (MCD)
ALEN	Alaska Education News [*A publication*]
ALEN	Alberta Environment, Lethbridge, Alberta [*Library symbol*] [*National Library of Canada*] (NLC)
ALEOA	American Law Enforcement Officers Association (EA)
ALEP	Atypical Lymphoepitheloid Cell Proliferation [*Medicine*]
ALEP	Audio Lingual Education Press (KSC)
ALEPB9	Asociacion Latinoamericana de Entomologia. Publicacion [*A publication*]
ALEPH	Automated Library Expandable Program, Hebrew University of Jerusalem [*Israel*] [*Information service or system*] (IID)
ALERFA	Alert Phase [*Aviation code*]
ALERT	Acute Launch Emergency Reliability Tip [*NASA*] (KSC)
ALERT	Adaptive LASER Resonator Technique (MCD)
ALERT	Alcohol Level Evaluation Road Tester
ALERT	American Library for Education, Research, and Training
ALERT	American Life Education and Research Trust (EA)
ALERT	American Lifesaving Emergency Response Team (EA)
ALERT	Automated Linguistic Extraction and Retrieval Technique
ALERT	Automated Local Evaluations in Real Time [*National Oceanic and Atmospheric Administration*]
ALERT	Automatic Logging Electronic Reporting and Telemetering System [*Maintains surveillance over petroleum wells and pipelines*]
ALERT	Automatic Logical Equipment Readiness Tester
ALERTCONS	Alert Conditions (MCD)
ALERTS	Airborne LASER Equipment Real-Time Surveillance
ALES	Alaska Earthlines/Tidelines. Alaska Geographic Society [*A publication*]
ALES	American Labor Education Service [*Defunct*]
ALESA	American League for Exports and Security Assistance [*Washington, DC*] (EA)
ALESC	Amiral Commandant l'Escadre [*Admiral, French Fleet*] (NATG)
ALESCO	American Library and Educational Services Company
ALESEP	Airfoil Leading Edge Separation (MCD)
ALET	Alaska Economic Trends [*A publication*]
ALET	Aloette Cosmetics, Inc. [*Malvern, PA*] [*NASDAQ symbol*] (NQ)
ALet	Armas y Letras [*A publication*]
ALet	Aspetti Letterari [*A publication*]
ALEX	Alert Exercise (NATG)
Alex	Alexander [*of Plutarch*] [*Classical studies*] (OCD)
Alex	Alexander [*of Lucian*] [*Classical studies*] (OCD)
ALEX	Alexander & Baldwin, Inc. [*NASDAQ symbol*] (NQ)
Alex	Alexander Tartagna de Imola [*Deceased, 1477*] [*Authority cited in pre-1607 legal work*] (DSA)
Alex	Alexandra [*of Lycophron*] [*Classical studies*] (OCD)
Alex	Alexipharmaca [*of Nicander*] [*Classical studies*] (OCD)
Alexan	Alexander Tartagna de Imola [*Deceased, 1477*] [*Authority cited in pre-1607 legal work*] (DSA)
Alexand	Alexander Tartagna de Imola [*Deceased, 1477*] [*Authority cited in pre-1607 legal work*] (DSA)
Alexander	Alexander's Reports [*66-72 Mississippi*] [*A publication*] (DLA)
Alexander Blain Hosp Bull	Alexander Blain Hospital. Bulletin [*A publication*]
Alexanderreich	Das Alexanderreich aus Prosopographischer Grundlage [*A publication*] (OCD)
Alexander Turnbull Libr Bull	Alexander Turnbull Library. Bulletin [*A publication*]
Alexandria J Agric Res	Alexandria Journal of Agricultural Research [*A publication*]
Alexandria J Agr Res	Alexandria Journal of Agricultural Research [*A publication*]
Alexandria Med J	Alexandria Medical Journal [*A publication*]
Alexanor Rev Lepid Fr	Alexanor; Revue des Lepidopteristes Francais [*A publication*]
Alex Br Stat	Alexander's British Statutes in Force in Maryland [*A publication*] (DLA)
Alex Cas	Report of the "Alexandra" Case, by Dudley [*A publication*] (DLA)
Alex Ch Pr	Alexander's Chancery Practice in Maryland [*A publication*] (DLA)
Alex Com Pr	Alexander's Practice of the Commissary Courts, Scotland [*A publication*] (DLA)
Alex Dent J	Alexandria Dental Journal [*A publication*]
Alex Dig	Alexander's Texas Digest [*A publication*] (DLA)
Alex Ins	Alexander on Life Insurance in New York [*A publication*] (DLA)
Alex J Agric Res	Alexandria Journal of Agricultural Research [*A publication*]
Alex Sev	Alexander Severus [*of Scriptores Historiae Augustae*] [*Classical studies*] (OCD)
ALEXSHIP	Alexandria Shipping & Navigation Co. [*Egypt*] (IMH)
Aleyn	Aleyn's Select Cases, English King's Bench [*82 English Reprint*] [*A publication*] (DLA)
Aleyn (Eng)	Aleyn's Select Cases, English King's Bench [*82 English Reprint*] [*A publication*] (DLA)
ALF	Absorption Limiting Frequency (DEN)
ALF	Accelerated Loading Facility (ADA)

ALF........... Afar Liberation Front [*Ethiopia*]   (PD)
ALF........... Airlift [*International*]
ALF........... [*Vittorio*] Alfieri [*Italian dramatist and poet, 1749-1803*]   (ROG)
ALF........... Alfred [*New York*] [*Seismograph station code, US Geological Survey*]   (SEIS)
ALF........... Alien Life Force [*Acronym is name of title character in television series*]
ALF........... Allied Land Forces
ALF........... Aloft   (FAAC)
ALF........... Alpha-Omega Industries, Inc. [*Vancouver Stock Exchange symbol*]
ALF........... Alta [*Norway*] [*Airport symbol*]   (OAG)
ALF........... American Land Forum [*Later, ALRA*]   (EA)
ALF........... American Leadership Forum   (EA)
ALF........... American Legal Foundation [*Absorbed by WLF*]   (EA)
ALF........... American Life Foundation [*Press*]
ALF........... American Liver Foundation   (EA)
ALF........... American Loan Fund
ALF........... Animal Liberation Front   (EA)
ALF........... Application Library File [*Data processing*]
ALF........... Arab Liberation Front
ALF........... Assisted-Living Facility [*Health care*]
ALF........... Association of Libertarian Feminists   (EA)
ALF........... Automatic Lead Former
ALF........... Automatic Letter Facer
ALF........... Automatic Line Feed [*Telecommunications*]
ALF........... Auxiliary Landing Field
ALF........... Average Load Factor
ALF........... Azania Liberation Front [*South Africa*]
ALFA....... Advanced LASER Flow Analysis   (MCD)
ALFA....... Advanced Liaison Forward Area   (MCD)
ALFA....... Air-Land Forces Agency [*Air Force*] [*Army*]   (MCD)
ALFA....... Air-Land Forces Applications
ALFA....... Air Lubricated Free Attitude [*NASA*]   (KSC)
ALFA....... Alfa Corp. [*NASDAQ symbol*]   (NQ)
ALFA....... Anonima Lombarda Fabbrica Automobili
ALFAA...... Air-Land Forces Applications Agency [*TAC-TRADOC*]   (MCD)
ALFAA...... All FAA [*Federal Aviation Administration*] Field Offices and Personnel   (FAAC)
Alfaatih Univ Bull Fac Eng ... Alfaatih University. Bulletin of the Faculty of Engineering [*A publication*]
ALFAB...... All FAA [*Federal Aviation Administration*] Offices on Service B   (FAAC)
ALFAD...... Acoustic Low-Flying-Aircraft Detector   (MCD)
ALFAL...... Asociacion de Linguistica y Filologia de America Latina
ALFAR...... American Law Firms for African Relief   (EA)
ALFB........ Abraham Lincoln Federal Savings Bank [*NASDAQ symbol*]   (NQ)
ALFC........ Automatic Local Frequency Control
ALFCE...... Allied Land Forces Central Europe [*NATO*]   (NATG)
ALFD........ Alabama Federal Savings & Loan Association [*Birmingham, AL*] [*NASDAQ symbol*]   (NQ)
ALFE........ Acta Lapponica Fenniae [*A publication*]
ALFE........ Alfa International Corp. [*NASDAQ symbol*]   (NQ)
ALFGL...... Automatic Low-Frequency Gain-Limiting Circuit   (RDA)
ALFI......... Air-Land Forces Integration   (MCD)
ALFI......... Air-Land Forces Interface
ALFI......... American League of Financial Institutions [*Washington, DC*]   (EA)
ALFL........ Alliance Financial Corp. [*Dearborn, MI*] [*NASDAQ symbol*]   (NQ)
ALFM........ Alaska Farm Magazine [*Superseded by Alaska Farm and Garden*] [*A publication*]
ALFMED.. Apollo Light-Flash Moving-Emulsion Detector [*NASA*]
ALFOAA.. Alberta Lands and Forests. Annual Report [*A publication*]
ALFOF...... All FAA [*Federal Aviation Administration*] Field Offices   (FAAC)
Alfold .... Alfoeld: Irodalmi es Muvelodesi Folyoirat [*A publication*]
ALFOODACT ... All Food Activities [*DoD*]
ALFOR...... Allied Forces
ALFORD... Appalachian Laboratory for Occupational Respiratory Diseases
ALFRA...... Alta Frequenza [*A publication*]
ALFRED ... Associative Learning from Relative Environmental Data
Alfred Benson Symp ... Alfred Benson Symposium [*A publication*]
Alfred P Sloan Found Rep ... Alfred P. Sloan Foundation. Report [*A publication*]
Alfred Univ NY State Coll Ceram Mon Rep ... Alfred University. New York State. College of Ceramics. Monthly Report [*A publication*]
Alfr Hosp Clin Rep ... Alfred Hospital. Clinical Reports [*A publication*]   (APTA)
ALFS .... Airborne Low-Frequency SONAR [*Sound Navigation and Ranging*] [*Navy*]
ALFSE...... Allied Land Forces Southern Europe [*NATO*]
ALFSEA... Allied Land Forces Southeast Asia [*NATO*]
ALFSEE... Allied Land Forces Southeastern Europe [*NATO*]
ALFSFO... All Flight Standards Field Offices [*FAA*]   (FAAC)
ALFSH...... Allied Land Forces Schleswig-Holstein [*NATO*]   (NATG)
ALFSS...... All Flight Service Stations in Region [*FAA*]   (FAAC)
ALFT .... Airlift

ALFT .... Approach and Landing Flight Test [*Aviation*]   (MCD)
ALFTRAN ... ALGOL-to-FORTRAN Translator [*Data processing*]   (MCD)
ALFY .... [*A*] New Life for You, Inc.
ALFZA9 .... Allgemeine Fischerei-Zeitung [*A publication*]
ALG .... Advanced Landing Ground [*Air Force*]
ALG .... Africa. An International Business, Economic, and Political Monthly [*A publication*]
ALG .... Air Logistics [*Lafayette, LA*] [*FAA designator*]   (FAAC)
ALG .... Aircraft Landing Gear
ALG .... Algebra
ALG .... Algeria
ALG .... Algiers [*Algeria*] [*Airport symbol*]   (OAG)
ALG .... Algiers [*Algeria*] [*Seismograph station code, US Geological Survey*]   (SEIS)
ALG .... Algol [*A publication*]
ALG .... Algoma Steel Corp. Ltd. [*Toronto Stock Exchange symbol*] [*Vancouver Stock Exchange symbol*]
alg .... Algonquian [*MARC language code*] [*Library of Congress*]   (LCCP)
ALG .... Along   (FAAC)
ALG .... Antilymphocyte Globulin [*Immunology*]
ALG .... Arkla, Inc. [*Formerly, Arkansas Louisiana Gas Co.*] [*NYSE symbol*]   (SPSG)
ALG .... Asbestos Litigation Group   (EA)
ALG .... Axiolinguogingival [*Dentistry*]
ALG .... Logistics Service [*FAA*]   (FAAC)
ALG .... University of Alabama, Graduate School of Library Science, University, AL [*OCLC symbol*]   (OCLC)
ALGA .... Associate in Local Government Administration   (ADA)
ALGA .... Australian Local Government Association
AlGaAs .... Aluminum Gallium Arsenide   (IEEE)
ALGAB..... Alberta Gazette [*A publication*]
ALGAC..... Alpine Geophysical [*NASDAQ symbol*]   (NQ)
ALGASM ... Amiral Commandant le Groupe Anti-Sous-Marin [*Commander, Antisubmarine Force*] [*French*]   (NATG)
AlgAU....... Universite d'Alger, Algiers, Algeria [*Library symbol*] [*Library of Congress*]   (LCLS)
ALGC .... La Glace Community Library, Alberta [*Library symbol*] [*National Library of Canada*]   (NLC)
ALGCU .... Association of Land Grant Colleges and Universities [*Later, NASULGC*]
ALGDGADLU ... A la Gloire du Grand Architecte de l'Univers [*French*] [*Freemasonry*]   (ROG)
ALGE........ Alaska Geographic [*A publication*]
ALGEB..... Algebra
ALGEC..... Algorithmic Language for Economic Calculations [*Data processing*]
ALGED..... Alaska Geographic [*A publication*]
Alger Agric ... Algerie Agricole [*A publication*]
Algerie Med ... Algerie Medicale [*Algeria*] [*A publication*]
Alger Med ... Algerie Medicale [*A publication*]
Alger Serv Geol Bull ... Algeria. Service Geologique. Bulletin [*A publication*]
Alger's Law Promoters & Prom Corp ... Alger's Law in Relation to Promoters and Promotion of Corporations [*A publication*]   (DLA)
ALGGM .... Annuario. Liceo Ginnasio G. Mameli [*A publication*]
ALGH........ Allegheny & Western Energy Corp. [*NASDAQ symbol*]   (NQ)
ALGHJ...... Arbeiten zur Literatur und Geschichte des Hellenistischen Judentums [*A publication*]
ALGHNY.. Allegheny [*National Weather Service*]   (FAAC)
ALGI......... American Locker Group, Inc. [*NASDAQ symbol*]   (NQ)
ALGIBW... Allergie et Immunologie [*Paris*] [*A publication*]
Alg Log ... Algebra and Logic [*A publication*]
ALGLYN... Aluminum Glycinate [*Also, ADA*] [*Pharmacology*]
ALGM .... Air-Launched Guided Missile [*Military*]
Alg Med ... Algemene Mededelingen [*Netherlands*] [*A publication*]   (DLA)
ALGN........ Alignment   (KSC)
ALGO .... Algorex Corp. [*NASDAQ symbol*]   (NQ)
ALGO .... Algorithm   (MSA)
Algodon Bol Cam Algodonera Peru ... Algodon Boletin de la Camara Algodonera del Peru [*A publication*]
Algodonero Bol ... Algodonero Boletin [*A publication*]
ALGOL ..... Algorithmic Language [*1958*] [*Formerly, IAL*] [*Data processing*]
Algol Stud ... Algological Studies [*A publication*]
Algorithms Chem Comput Symp ... Algorithms for Chemical Computations. A Symposium [*A publication*]
Algoritmy i Algoritm Jazyki ... Algoritmy i Algoritmiceskie Jazyki [*A publication*]
Algot Holmbergs Arsb ... Algot Holmbergs Arsbok [*A publication*]
ALGP........ Annuario. Liceo Ginnasio Statale G. Palmieri [*A publication*]
ALGP........ Association of Lesbian and Gay Psychologists   (EA)
Alg Pap-Rund ... Allgemeine Papier-Rundschau [*A publication*]
Alg Proefstn Alg Ver Rubberplant Oostkust Sumatra Vlugschr ... Algemeen Proefstation der Algemeene Vereniging van Rubberplanters ter Oostkust van Sumatra. Vlugschrift [*A publication*]
ALGR .... Allied Group, Inc. [*NASDAQ symbol*]   (SPSG)
ALGTG...... Alighting [*Aviation*]   (FAAC)
Alg Zuivelbl ... Algemeen Zuivelblad [*A publication*]
Alg Zuivel Melkhyg Weekbl ... Algemeen-Zuivel-en Melkhygienisch Weekblad [*A publication*]

ALH.......... Acta Linguistica. Academiae Scientiarum Hungaricae [*A publication*]
ALH.......... Acta Linguistica Hafniensia [*A publication*]
ALH.......... Albany [*Australia*] [*Airport symbol*]   (OAG)
ALH.......... Aleta Resource Industries [*Vancouver Stock Exchange symbol*]
ALH.......... Alicahue [*Chile*] [*Seismograph station code, US Geological Survey*]   (SEIS)
ALH.......... Allan Hills [*Antarctic meteorology*]
AL of H...... American Legion of Honor
ALH.......... Atypical Lymphoid Hyperplasia [*Medicine*]
ALHa........ Acta Linguistica Hafniensia [*A publication*]
ALHA....... American Labor Health Association [*Later, GHAA*]
ALHARD .. Air-Launched High-Altitude Reconnaissance Drone   (MCD)
ALHFA...... Association of Local Housing Finance Agencies   (EA)
ALHFAM ... Association for Living Historical Farms and Agricultural Museums   (EA)
ALHHS..... Association of Librarians in the History of the Health Sciences   (EA)
ALHI........ Alaska History Series [*A publication*]
ALHN....... Alaska History News [*A publication*]
ALHRT .... American Library History Round Table
ALHT....... Apollo Lunar Hand Tool [*NASA*]
ALHTC .... Apollo Lunar Hand Tool Carrier [*NASA*]
ALHY....... Alaska History [*A publication*]
ALI.......... Activity Level Independent   (KSC)
ALI.......... Aetna Life Insurance Co. of Canada [*Toronto Stock Exchange symbol*]
ALI.......... Agricultural Limestone Institute
ALI.......... Airborne LASER Illuminator
ALI.......... Alberta Legislation Information [*Alberta Public Affairs Bureau*] [*Canada*] [*Information service or system*]   (CRD)
ALI.......... ALI-ABA [*American Law Institute - American Bar Association*] Course Materials Journal [*A publication*]
Ali .... Alibi [*Elsewhere*] [*Latin*]
ALI.......... Alicante [*Spain*] [*Seismograph station code, US Geological Survey*]   (SEIS)
ALI.......... Alice, TX [*Location identifier*] [*FAA*]   (FAAL)
ALI.......... ALITALIA [*Aerolinee Italiane Internazionali*] [*Italian airline*]   (MCD)
ALI.......... Allstate Municipal Premium Fund [*NYSE symbol*]   (SPSG)
ALI.......... American Ladder Institute   (EA)
ALI.......... American Law Institute   (EA)
ALi .... Amor de Libro [*A publication*]
ALI.......... Arc Lamp Igniter
ALI.......... Argyll Light Infantry [*Military unit*] [*British*]
ALI.......... Arm Length Index
ALI.......... Arthur D. Little, Incorporated
ALI.......... Associate of the Landscape Institute [*British*]   (DBQ)
ALI.......... Association Lyrique Internationale [*Toulouse, France*]   (EAIO)
ALI.......... Asynchronous Line Interface [*Telecommunications*]
ALI.......... Australian Laser Institute
ALI.......... Australian Leisure Index [*Information service or system*] [*A publication*]
ALI.......... Automated Logic Implementation [*Data processing*]   (IEEE)
ALI.......... Automatic Language Identification   (MCD)
ALI.......... Automatic Line Integration   (NVT)
ALI.......... Automatic Location Identification [*Street crime locator*]
ALI.......... Automotive Lift Institute   (EA)
ALI.......... Autonomous Learner Index
ALI.......... Awaiting Laboratory Input
ALI.......... Linaria Public Library, Alberta [*Library symbol*] [*National Library of Canada*]   (NLC)
ALIA........ American Life Insurance Association [*Later, ACLI*]   (EA)
ALIA........ Association of Lecturers in Accountancy [*British*]
ALIA........ Royal Jordanian Airlines   (IMH)
ALI-ABA ... ALI-ABA [*American Law Instutute - American Bar Association*] Committee on Continuing Professional Education   (EA)
ALI ABA ... ALI-ABA [*American Law Institute - American Bar Association*] Course Materials Journal [*A publication*]
ALI-ABA CLE Rev ... American Law Institute - American Bar Association Council of Legal Education Review [*A publication*]   (DLA)
ALI-ABA Course Mat J ... ALI-ABA [*American Law Institute - American Bar Association*] Course Materials Journal [*A publication*]
ALI-ABA Course MJ ... American Law Institute - American Bar Association. Course Materials Journal [*A publication*]   (DLA)
ALIADS .... Alaskan Integrated Air Defense System
ALIANSA ... Alimentos para Animales, SA [*Feed plant*] [*Guatemala*]
ALIAS ...... Algebraic Logic Investigation of Apollo Systems   (MCD)
ALIAS .... Australia's Library, Information and Archives Services: an Encyclopaedia of Practice and Practitioners [*A publication*]
ALIATCS.. All International Air Traffic Communications Stations [*FAA*]
ALIATSC.. All International Aeronautical Telecommunications Switching Centers [*FAA*]   (FAAC)
ALIAZO.... Alliance of Natives of Zombo [*Angola*]
A Lib......... American Libraries [*Chicago*] [*A publication*]
ALIB........ Army Library
ALIC......... Arid Lands Information Center [*University of Arizona*] [*Tucson*]
ALIC......... Association of Life Insurance Counsel   (EA)

ALICAT .... Advanced Long-Wave IR Circuit and Array Technology   (MCD)
ALICE ...... Ada/Lattice ICE [*Integrated Conceptual Environment*] [*Data processing*]
ALICE ...... Adaptive Line Canceller and Enhancer   (CAAL)
ALICE ...... Adiabatic Low-Energy Injection and Capture Experiment
ALICE ...... Alaskan Integrated Communications Exchange
ALICE ...... All-Purpose Lightweight Individual Carrying Equipment [*Army*]   (RDA)
ALICE ...... Applicative Language Idealized Computing Engine
ALICE ...... Archivio dei Libri Italiani, su Calcolatore Elettronica [*Editrice Bibliografica*] [*Italian*] [*Information service or system*]   (CRD)
ALICE ...... Automated Location of Isolation and Continuity Error [*Module*] [*Raytheon Co.*]
ALICS ...... Advanced Logistics Information and Control System [*Air Force*]
ALICW...... All-Purpose Lightweight Individual Carrying Equipment [*Army*]
Alicyclic Chem ... Alicyclic Chemistry [*A publication*]
ALID........ Automated Library Issue Document   (NVT)
ALIDA...... Alliance Industrielle [*A publication*]
ALIDE...... Asociacion Latinoamericana de Instituciones Financieras de Desarrollo [*Latin American Association of Development Financing Institutions*] [*Lima, Peru*]   (EAIO)
ALIE......... America Latina Informe Economico [*A publication*]
ALIFAR.... Asociacion Latinoamericana de Industrias Farmaceuticas [*Latin American Association of Pharmaceutical Industries - LAAPI*]   (EAIO)
ALI Fed Income Tax Project ... American Law Institute Federal Income Tax Project [*A publication*]   (DLA)
ALIFO....... All International Field Offices [*FAA*]   (FAAC)
ALIFSS ..... All International Flight Service Stations in Region [*FAA*]   (FAAC)
ALIG......... Alco International Group, Inc. [*NASDAQ symbol*]   (NQ)
Aligarh Bull Math ... Aligarh Bulletin of Mathematics [*A publication*]
Aligarh J Statist ... Aligarh Journal of Statistics [*A publication*]
Aligarh Muslim Univ Publ Zool Ser ... Aligarh Muslim University Publications. Zoological Series [*A publication*]
Aligh Ras Bib Dante ... Alighieri. Rassegna Bibliografica Dantesca [*A publication*]
ALIGN ...... Alignment
ALII.......... Advanced Libraries & Information, Incorporated [*Information service or system*]   (IID)
ALII.......... Allied Capital Corp. II [*NASDAQ symbol*]   (NQ)
ALIL......... Anuar de Lingvistica si Istorie Literara [*A publication*]
ALIM........ Air-Launched Intercept Missile
ALIM........ America Latina Informe de Mercados [*A publication*]
ALIMC...... Allergie und Immunologie [*A publication*]
ALIMCL ... Allergie und Immunologie [*Leipzig*] [*A publication*]
ALIMDA... Association of Life Insurance Medical Directors of America   (EA)
Aliment Anim ... Alimentazione Animale [*A publication*]
Aliment Ital ... Alimentazione Italiana [*A publication*]
Aliment Nutr Anim ... Alimentos y Nutricion Animal [*A publication*]
Aliment Nutr Metab ... Alimentazione Nutrizione Metabolismo [*A publication*]
Aliment Vie ... Alimentation et la Vie [*A publication*]
ALIMPREPS ... Alert Implementation Reports   (NATG)
ALIMREP ... Alert Implementation Report   (MCD)
ALIMS ...... Automatic LASER Instrumentation Measuring System   (MCD)
ALIN .... Agricultural Libraries Information Network [*Department of Agriculture*] [*Library network*]
ALIN .... Alaska Industry [*A publication*]
ALing....... Archivum Linguisticum [*A publication*]
ALingHung ... Acta Linguistica. Academiae Scientiarum Hungaricae [*A publication*]
ALIO........ Activity Level Independent Operations   (NASA)
ALIP........ Abnormal Localization of Immature Precursors [*Clinical hematology*]
ALIP........ Alaska in Perspective [*A publication*]
ALIP........ America Latina Informe Politico [*A publication*]
ALIP........ Annular Linear Induction Pump [*Nuclear energy*]   (NRCH)
Aliphatic Alicyclic Saturated Heterocycl Chem ... Aliphatic, Alicyclic, and Saturated Heterocyclic Chemistry [*A publication*]
Aliphatic Chem ... Aliphatic Chemistry [*A publication*]
Aliphatic Relat Nat Prod Chem ... Aliphatic and Related Natural Product Chemistry [*A publication*]
ALI Proc ... American Law Institute. Proceedings [*A publication*]
ALIR......... Advanced LASER Intercept Receiver   (MCD)
ALIR......... Australian Library and Information Research [*A publication*]   (APTA)
ALIRATS ... Airborne LASER Illuminator Ranging and Tracking System
ALIRT .... Adaptive Long-Range Infrared Tracker
ALIS........ Advanced Life Information System [*Data processing*]
ALIS........ Arid Lands Information System [*University of Arizona*] [*Tucson*]   (IID)
ALIS........ Automated Library Information System [*Dataphase Systems, Inc.*]   (IID)

ALIS .... Automated Library Information System [*National Technological Library of Denmark*] [*Lyngby*] [*Information service or system*] (IID)
ALISE .... Association for Library and Information Science Education (EA)
Alison Pr .... Alison's Practice [*Scotland*] [*A publication*] (DLA)
Alis Princ Scotch Law ... Alison's Principles of the Criminal Law of Scotland [*A publication*] (DLA)
Alis Princ Scot Law ... Alison's Principles of the Criminal Law of Scotland [*A publication*] (ILCA)
A Lit .... Associate in Literature
ALit .... Athenaion Literaturwissenschaft [*A publication*]
ALIT .... Automatic Line Insulation Test [*or Tester*] [*Bell System*]
ALITALIA ... Aerolinee Italiane Internazionali [*Italian International Airline*] [*Facetious translation: Always Late in Takeoffs, Always Late in Arrivals*]
ALitASH ... Acta Litteraria. Academiae Scientiarum Hungaricae [*A publication*]
ALitH .... Acta Litteraria. Academiae Scientiarum Hungaricae [*A publication*]
A Litt .... Associate in Letters
ALIVE .... Air-Launched Instrumented Vehicle Evaluation (MCD)
ALJ .... Administrative Law Judge [*Also, HE*] [*Federal trial examiner*]
ALJ .... Albany Law Journal [*A publication*] (DLA)
ALJ .... Alemannisches Jahrbuch [*A publication*]
ALJ .... Alexander Bay [*South Africa*] [*Airport symbol*] (OAG)
ALJ .... Allahabad Law Journal [*A publication*]
ALJ .... American Law Journal [*A publication*]
ALJ .... Association for Legal Justice [*Northern Ireland*]
ALJ .... Australian Law Journal [*A publication*] (APTA)
ALJ .... Australian Library Journal [*A publication*]
ALJA .... Anuario de Legislacion (Nacional y Provincial). Revista de Jurisprudencia Argentina [*A publication*] (DLA)
ALJD .... Administrative Law Judge of the Department [*Department of Labor*] (OICC)
ALJH .... Association of Libraries of Judaica and Hebraica in Europe
ALJMAO ... Antonie Van Leeuwenhoek Journal of Microbiology and Serology [*Later, Antonie Van Leeuwenhoek Journal of Microbiology*] [*A publication*]
ALJNS ...... American Law Journal. New Series [*A publication*]
ALJOD ...... Australian Law Journal [*A publication*]
ALJR .... Australian Law Journal. Reports [*A publication*] (APTA)
ALK .... Alaska Air Group, Inc. [*NYSE symbol*] (SPSG)
Alk .... Alaska Reports [*A publication*] (DLA)
ALK .... Alkaline (KSC)
Alk .... Alkyl [*Chemistry*]
ALK .... Almanac (ROG)
ALK .... Altero Technology [*Vancouver Stock Exchange symbol*]
Al Kada ...... Native Tribunals' Reports [*Egypt*] [*A publication*] (DLA)
Alkalis Blast Furn Proc Symp ... Alkalis in Blast Furnaces. Proceedings. Symposium on "Alkalis in Blast Furnaces. State of the Art" [*A publication*]
Alkalmaz Mat Lapok ... Alkalmazott Matematikai Lapok [*A publication*]
Alkaloidal Clin ... Alkaloidal Clinic [*A publication*]
Alkaloids Chem Physiol ... Alkaloids Chemistry and Physiology [*A publication*]
ALKM .... Archiv fuer Literatur und Kirchengeschichte des Mittelalters [*A publication*]
Alkohol Ind ... Alkohol Industrie [*A publication*]
Alkohol Ind Wiss Tech Brennereibeil ... Alkohol Industrie. Wissenschaftliche Technische Brennereibeilage [*A publication*]
ALKY .... Alkalinity (MSA)
ALL .... Accelerated Learning of Logic
ALL .... Acute Lymphatic [*or Lymphoblastic or Lymphocytic*] Leukemia [*Medicine*]
ALL .... Address Locator Logic [*Data processing*]
ALL .... Admiralty List of Lights [*British*]
ALL .... Affiliated Leadership League of and for the Blind of America (EA)
ALL .... Airborne LASER Laboratory [*Air Force*]
ALL .... Aircraft Landing Lamp
ALL .... AirLifeLine (EA)
ALL .... Alii Air Hawaii [*Honolulu, HI*] [*FAA designator*] (FAAC)
All .... Allative (BJA)
all .... Allegata [*Schedules, Enclosures*] [*Italian*] (ILCA)
ALL .... Allegheny Airlines (MCD)
ALL .... Allegro [*Quick*] [*Music*] (ROG)
ALL .... Alleluia
All .... Allen's Massachusetts Reports [*A publication*] (DLA)
All .... Allen's New Brunswick Reports [*Canada*] [*A publication*] (DLA)
ALL .... Allentown College of Saint Francis De Sales, Center Valley, PA [*OCLC symbol*] (OCLC)
ALL .... Alley
ALL .... Allowance Load List (AFIT)
ALL .... Allstate Municipal Income Trust III [*NYSE symbol*] (SPSG)
AlL .... Almanach des Lettres [*A publication*]
ALL .... American League of Lobbyists (EA)
ALL .... American Lebanese League (EA)
ALL .... American Liberation League
ALL .... American Life League (EA)

ALL .... American Life Lobby (EA)
ALL .... Application Language Liberator (MCD)
ALL .... Arc LASER Light
ALL .... Archiv fuer Lateinische Lexikographie und Grammatik [*Munich/Leipzig*] [*A publication*]
ALL .... Argon LASER Lining
ALL .... Ariel Resources Ltd. [*Vancouver Stock Exchange symbol*]
ALL .... Association for Latin Liturgy (EA)
ALL .... Augustana Luther League [*Later, ILLL*]
ALL .... Australian Labour Law Reporter [*A publication*] (APTA)
All .... Indian Law Reports, Allahabad Series [*A publication*] (DLA)
All .... Liberal Alliance [*Political party*] [*British*]
AL/LA .... African Languages/Langues Africaines [*A publication*]
ALLA .... Allied Longline Agency [*NATO*]
AllaB .... Alla Bottega [*A publication*]
ALLACM .. Air-Launched Low-Altitude Cruise Missile (MCD)
Allahabad Fmr ... Allahabad Farmer [*A publication*]
Allahabad LJ ... Allahabad Law Journal [*A publication*]
Allahabad Univ Studies ... Allahabad University Studies [*A publication*]
Alla LJ .... Allahabad Law Journal [*A publication*]
Allam- es Jogtud ... Allam- es Jogtudomany [*A publication*]
Allan Hancock Found Occas Pap (New Ser) ... Allan Hancock Foundation. Occasional Papers (New Series) [*A publication*]
Allan Hancock Found Publ Occas Pap ... Allan Hancock Foundation. Publications. Occasional Paper [*A publication*]
Allan Hancock Found Pubs Occasional Paper ... Allan Hancock Foundation. Publications. Occasional Paper [*A publication*]
Allan Hancock Found Tech Rep ... Allan Hancock Foundation. Technical Reports [*A publication*]
Allan Hancock Monogr Mar Biol ... Allan Hancock Monographs in Marine Biology [*A publication*]
Allatgyogy Oltoanyagellenorzo Intez Evk ... Allatgyogyaszati Oltoanyagellenorzo Intezet Evkonyve [*A publication*]
Allat Lapok ... Allatorvosi Lapok [*A publication*]
Allatorv Koezl ... Allatorvosi Koezloeny [*A publication*]
Allatorv Lapok ... Allatorvosi Lapok [*A publication*]
Allattani Kozl ... Allattani Kozlemenyek [*A publication*]
Allatteny ... Allattenyesztestani Tanszek [*A publication*]
Allattenyesz Anim Breed ... Allattenyesztes/Animal Breeding [*A publication*]
Allattenyesz Takarmanyozas ... Allattenyesztes es Takarmanyozas [*A publication*]
Allatteny Kutatointez Evk ... Allattenyesztesi Kutatointezet Evkoenyve [*A publication*]
ALLB .... Lac La Biche Public Library, Alberta [*Library symbol*] [*National Library of Canada*] (NLC)
ALLBVC ... Alberta Vocational Centre, Lac La Biche, Alberta [*Library symbol*] [*National Library of Canada*] (NLC)
ALLC .... Allied Capital Corp. [*NASDAQ symbol*] (NQ)
ALLC .... Association for Literary and Linguistic Computing [*University College of North Wales*] [*Gwynedd*] (EA)
ALLCB ...... ALLC [*Association for Literary and Linguistic Computing*] Bulletin [*A publication*]
ALLC Bull ... ALLC [*Association for Literary and Linguistic Computing*] Bulletin [*A publication*]
ALLCE ...... Allowance (ROG)
ALLC J .... ALLC [*Association for Literary and Linguistic Computing*] Journal [*A publication*]
All Cr Cas .. Allahabad Criminal Cases [*India*] [*A publication*] (DLA)
ALLD .... Airborne LASER Locator Designator (MCD)
ALLD .... Allied
Alld .... Allied Record Sales [*Record label*]
ALLD .... Allowed
ALLEG ...... Allegiance
ALLEG ...... Allegory (ADA)
ALLEG ...... Amiral Commandant l'Escadre Legere [*Admiral, Light Squadron*] [*French*] (NATG)
Allegheny Ludlum Horiz ... Allegheny Ludlum Horizons [*A publication*]
ALLEGTO ... Allegretto [*Moderately Quick*] [*Music*] (ROG)
Allem Aujourd ... Allemagnes d'Aujourd'hui [*A publication*]
Allen .... Aleyn's English King's Bench Reports [*A publication*] (DLA)
Allen .... Allen's Massachusetts Supreme Judicial Court Reports [*1861-67*] [*A publication*] (DLA)
Allen .... Allen's New Brunswick Reports [*Canada*] [*A publication*] (DLA)
Allen .... Allen's Washington Territory Reports [*1854-85*] [*A publication*] (DLA)
All Eng .... All England Law Reports [*A publication*]
Allen NB .... Allen's New Brunswick Reports [*Canada*] [*A publication*] (DLA)
Allen's Rep ... [*Charles*] Allen's Reports [*1-14 Massachusetts*] [*A publication*] (DLA)
Allen Tel Cas ... Allen's Telegraph Cases [*A publication*] (DLA)
All ER .... All England Law Reports [*A publication*]
Allerg Abstr ... Allergy Abstracts [*A publication*]
Allerg Asthma ... Allergie und Asthma [*A publication*]
Allerg Asthmaforsch ... Allergie und Asthmaforschung [*A publication*]
Allerg Immunol ... Allergie und Immunologie [*A publication*]
Allerg Immunol (Leipz) ... Allergie und Immunologie (Leipzig) [*A publication*]
Allergol Immunopathol ... Allergologia et Immunopathologia [*Madrid*] [*A publication*]

Allergol Immunopathol Suppl ... Allergologia et Immunopathologia. Supplementum [*A publication*]

Allergol Proc Congr Int Assoc Allergol ... Allergology. Proceedings. Congress. International Association of Allergology [*A publication*]

Allergy 74 Proc Eur Congr Allergol Clin Immunol ... Allergy '74. Proceedings of the European Congress of Allergology and Clinical Immunology [*A publication*]

All ER Rep ... All England Law Reports (Reprint) [*1558-1935*] [*A publication*]   (DLA)

All ER Rep Ext ... All England Law Reports (Reprint), Australian Extension Volumes [*A publication*]   (DLA)

All ER Repr ... All England Law Reports (Reprint) [*1558-1935*] [*A publication*]   (DLA)

Allevamenti Vet ... Allevamenti e Veterinaria [*A publication*]

Alley Mus .. Alley Music [*A publication*]

ALLG .... Archiv fuer Lateinische Lexikographie und Grammatik [*A publication*]

All Gazdasag ... Allami Gazdasag [*A publication*]

Allg Bot Z .. Allgemeine Botanische Zeitschrift [*A publication*]

Allg Brau Hopfenztg ... Allgemeine Brauer- und Hopfenzeitung [*A publication*]

Allg Deutsche Naturh Ztg ... Allgemeine Deutsche Naturhistorische Zeitung [*A publication*]

Allg Dt Imkerztg ... Allgemeine Deutsche Imkerzeitung [*A publication*]

Allg Dtsch Imkerztg ... Allgemeine Deutsche Imkerzeitung [*A publication*]

Allgem .... Allgemein [*General*] [*Music*]

Allgem Berg- u Huettenm Ztg ... Allgemeine Berg- und Huettenmaennische Zeitung [*A publication*]

Allgemein Statist Arch ... Allgemeines Statistisches Archiv [*A publication*]

Allgett .... Allegretto [*Moderately Quick*] [*Music*]

Allg Fischwirtschaftsztg ... Allgemeine Fischwirtschaftszeitung [*A publication*]

Allg Fisch-Ztg ... Allgemeine Fischerei-Zeitung [*A publication*]

Allg Forst Holzwirtsch Zeit ... Allgemeine Forst- und Holzwirtschaftliche Zeitung [*A publication*]

Allg Forst Holzwirtsch Ztg ... Allgemeine Forst- und Holzwirtschaftliche Zeitung [*A publication*]

Allg Forst- u Jagdztg ... Allgemeine Forst- und Jagdzeitung [*A publication*]

Allg Forst Jagdztg ... Allgemeine Forst- und Jagdzeitung [*A publication*]

Allg Forstz ... Allgemeine Forstzeitschrift [*A publication*]

Allg Forstzeitschr ... Allgemeine Forstzeitschrift [*A publication*]

Allg Forsztg ... Allgemeine Forstzeitung [*A publication*]

Allg Gerber Ztg ... Allgemeine Gerber Zeitung [*A publication*]

Allg Gesch Bed ... Allgemeine Geschaftsbedingungen [*General conditions of contracts, transactions, etc.*] [*German*]   (ILCA)

Allg Imkerkal ... Allgemeine Imkerkalender [*A publication*]

Allg J Chem ... Allgemeines Journal der Chemie [*A publication*]

Allg Lederind Ztg ... Allgemeine Lederindustrie Zeitung [*A publication*]

ALLG Newsletter ... Australian Law Librarians' Group. Newsletter [*A publication*]   (APTA)

Allg Nord Ann Chem Freunde Naturkd Arzneiwiss ... Allgemeine Nordische Annalen der Chemie fuer die Freunde der Naturkunde und Arzneiwissenschaft [*A publication*]

Allg Oel-Fett-Ztg ... Allgemeine Oel- und Fett-Zeitung [*West Germany*] [*A publication*]

Allg Oesterr Chem Tech-Ztg ... Allgemeine Oesterreichische Chemiker und Techniker-Zeitung [*Austria*] [*A publication*]

Allg Papier-Rundschau ... Allgemeine Papier-Rundschau [*A publication*]

Allg Pap Rundsch ... Allgemeine Papier-Rundschau [*A publication*]

Allg Photogr Ztg ... Allgemeine Photographische Zeitung [*A publication*]

Allg Prakt Chem ... Allgemeine und Praktische Chemie [*A publication*]

Allg Rundsch ... Allgemeine Rundschau [*A publication*]

Allg Stat Arch ... Allgemeines Statistisches Archiv [*A publication*]

Allg Statis Arch ... Allgemeines Statistisches Archiv [*A publication*]

Allg Text Z ... Allgemeine Textil-Zeitschrift [*A publication*]

Allg Text Z Text Ring ... Allgemeine Textil-Zeitschrift und Textil-Ring [*A publication*]

Allg Tonind Ztg ... Allgemeine Tonindustrie Zeitung [*A publication*]

ALLGTTO ... Allegretto [*Moderately Quick*] [*Music*]   (ROG)

Allg VersBed ... Allgemeine Versicherungsbedingungen [*General conditions of insurance*] [*German*]   (ILCA)

Allg Waermetech ... Allgemeine Waermetechnik [*West Germany*] [*A publication*]

Allg Wien Med Ztg ... Allgemeine Wiener Medizinische Zeitung [*A publication*]

Allg Z Bierbrau Malzfabr ... Allgemeine Zeitschrift fuer Bierbrauerei und Malzfabrikation [*A publication*]

Allg Zellforsch Mikrosk Anat ... Allgemeine Zellforschung und Mikroskopische Anatomie [*A publication*]

Allg Z Ent ... Allgemeine Zeitschrift fuer Entomologie [*A publication*]

Allg Z Psychiat ... Allgemeine Zeitschrift fuer Psychiatrie [*A publication*]

Allg Z Psychiatr Ihre Grenzgeb ... Allgemeine Zeitschrift fuer Psychiatrie und Ihre Grenzgebiete [*A publication*]

Allg Ztschr Psychiat ... Allgemeine Zeitschrift fuer Psychiatrie und Psychisch-Gerichtliche Medizin [*A publication*]

All Hawaii ... All about Business in Hawaii [*A publication*]

ALLI .... Alliance/l'Alliance. Voice of Metis and Non-Status Indians of Quebec [*Canada*] [*A publication*]

ALLI .... Australian Legal Literature Index

ALLIAM ... Allionia [*Turin*] [*A publication*]

Alliance Ind ... Alliance Industrielle [*A publication*]

Alliance Recd ... Alliance Record [*A publication*]

Allianz Ber Betriebstech Schadenverhuetung ... Allianz Berichte fuer Betriebstechnik und Schadenverhuetung [*A publication*]

All ICR ...... All Indian Criminal Reports [*A publication*]   (DLA)

Allied Health & Behav Sci ... Allied Health and Behavioral Sciences [*A publication*]

Allied Ind Wkr ... Allied Industrial Worker [*A publication*]

Allied Irish Bank R ... Allied Irish Bank Review [*A publication*]

Allied Vet ... Allied Veterinarian [*A publication*]

Allin .... Allinson's Pennsylvania Superior and District Court Reports [*A publication*]   (DLA)

All Ind Crim Dec ... All India Criminal Decisions [*A publication*]   (ILCA)

All Ind Cr R ... All Indian Criminal Reports [*A publication*]   (DLA)

All Ind Cr T ... All India Criminal Times [*A publication*]   (DLA)

All India Crim Dec ... All India Criminal Decisions [*A publication*]   (DLA)

All-India Inst Ment Health Trans ... All-India Institute of Mental Health. Transactions [*A publication*]

All India Rep ... All India Reporter, Nagpur [*A publication*]   (DLA)

All India Rptr ... All India Reporter [*A publication*]

All Ind Rep ... All India Reporter [*A publication*]

All Ind Rep NS ... All India Reporter, New Series [*A publication*]   (DLA)

Allinson ...... Allinson's Pennsylvania Superior and District Court Reports [*A publication*]   (DLA)

All IR .... All India Reports [*A publication*]   (DLA)

Allis-Chalmers Electr Rev ... Allis-Chalmers Electrical Review [*A publication*]

Allis-Chalmers Eng Rev ... Allis-Chalmers Engineering Review [*A publication*]

Allison Res Eng ... Allison Research and Engineering [*A publication*]

Allison's Am Dict ... Allison's American Dictionary [*A publication*]   (DLA)

ALLKAS .... Allattani Kozlemenyek [*A publication*]

All LD of Mar ... Alleyne. Legal Decrees of Marriage [*1810*] [*A publication*]   (DLA)

All LJ .... Allahabad Law Journal [*India*] [*A publication*]   (DLA)

All LR .... Allahabad Law Review [*India*] [*A publication*]   (DLA)

All LT .... Allahabad Law Times [*India*] [*A publication*]   (DLA)

Allmaenna Svenska Utsaedesaktiebol Svaloef ... Allmaenna Svenska Utsaedesaktiebolaget Svaloef [*A publication*]

ALLMIS .... Army Lessons Learned Management Information System   (INF)

All & Mor Tr ... Allen and Morris' Trial [*A publication*]   (DLA)

Allm Sven Laekartidn ... Allmaenna Svenska Laekartidningen [*A publication*]

ALLN .... Anterior Lateral Line Nerve [*Fish anatomy*]

ALLNAVSTAS ... All Naval Stations [*A dispatch to all Naval stations in an area*]

All NB .... Allen's New Brunswick Reports [*Canada*] [*A publication*]   (DLA)

All Nig LR ... All Nigeria Law Reports [*A publication*]   (DLA)

All NLR ..... All Nigeria Law Reports [*A publication*]   (DLA)

Alln Part .... Allnat. Law of Partition [*1820*] [*A publication*]   (DLA)

Alln Wills .. Allnat on Wills [*A publication*]   (DLA)

ALLO .... All Others [*Later, G Group*] [*Division of National Security Agency*]

ALLO .... Allegro [*Quick*] [*Music*]

Allo .... Allegro-Elite [*Formerly, Allegro*] [*Record label*]

ALLO .... Atypical Legionella-Like Organism

ALLOC .... Allocate [*or Allocation*]   (AFM)

ALL'OTT .. All'Ottava [*At the Octave*] [*Music*]

All'Ova ...... All'Ottava [*At the Octave*] [*Music*]

ALLOW .... Allowance

Alloy Cast Bull ... Alloy Casting Bulletin [*A publication*]

Alloy Dig ..... Alloy Digest [*A publication*]

Alloy Met Rev ... Alloy Metals Review [*A publication*]

ALLP .... Alliance Pharmaceutical Corp. [*NASDAQ symbol*]   (NQ)

ALLP .... Arc LASER Light Pump

ALLP .... Audiolingual Language Programming [*Data processing*]

All Pak Legal Dec ... All Pakistan Legal Decisions [*A publication*]

All Pak Leg Dec ... All Pakistan Legal Decisions [*A publication*]

All Pak Sci Conf Proc ... All Pakistan Science Conference. Proceedings [*A publication*]

ALLR .... Alaska Law Review [*A publication*]

ALLR .... Australian Labour Law Reporter [*A publication*]   (APTA)

ALLRDI .... Allergologie [*A publication*]

ALLS .... Adult Life Long Learning Section [*Public Library Association*]

ALLS .... Allison's Place, Inc. [*Los Angeles, CA*] [*NASDAQ symbol*]   (NQ)

ALLS .... Apollo Lunar Logistic Support [*NASA*]

All Ser .... Allahabad Series, Indian Law Reports [*A publication*]   (DLA)

All Sher ...... Allen on Sheriffs [*A publication*]   (DLA)

All St Sales Tax Rep CCH ... All-State Sales Tax Reporter. Commerce Clearing House [*A publication*]

ALLT .... All American Television, Inc. [*New York, NY*] [*NASDAQ symbol*]   (NQ)

All T .... Allwedd y Tannau [*A publication*]

All Tel Cas ... Allen's Telegraph Cases [*A publication*]   (DLA)

ALLTO ...... Allegretto [*Moderately Quick*] [*Music*]   (ROG)

ALLTV ...... Active Low-Light-Level Television [*Night vision device*] [*Air Force*]   (MCD)

Allum Nuova Met ... Alluminio e Nuova Metallurgia [*A publication*]

Allum Nuova Metall ... Alluminio e Nuova Metallurgia [*Italy*] [*A publication*]

ALLUS ...... Allusion

ALLVRJ .... Air-Launched Low-Volume Ramjet (MCD)
All WN ...... Allahabad Weekly Notes (and Supplement) [*India*] [*A publication*] (DLA)
Allwood ...... Allwood's Appeal Cases under the Weights and Measures Act [*England*] [*A publication*] (DLA)
All WR .... Allahabad Weekly Reporter [*India*] [*A publication*] (DLA)
All the Year ... All the Year Round [*A publication*]
ALM .... Acral Lentiginous Melanoma [*Medicine*]
ALM .... Advanced List of Materials
ALM .... Aerophysics Laboratory Memorandum [*NASA*] (KSC)
ALM .... Air-Launched Missile
ALM .... Aircraft Limited Model
ALM .... Airlift Loading Model
ALM .... Al Markazi. Central Bank of Oman [*A publication*]
ALM .... Alamogordo [*New Mexico*] [*Airport symbol*] (OAG)
ALM .... Alarm (MSA)
ALM .... Alice Lake Mines [*Vancouver Stock Exchange symbol*]
ALM .... Allstate Municipal Income Trust [*NYSE symbol*] (SPSG)
ALM .... Almaden Air Charter [*San Jose, CA*] [*FAA designator*] (FAAC)
Alm .... Almagest [*of Ptolemy*] [*Classical studies*] (OCD)
ALM .... Almeria [*Spain*] [*Seismograph station code, US Geological Survey*] (SEIS)
ALM .... Almeria [*Spain*] [*Geomagnetic observatory code*]
alm .... Almost [*Philately*]
ALM .... American Law Magazine [*A publication*]
ALM .... American Leprosy Missions (EA)
ALM .... Antillaanse Luchtvaart Maatschappij [*Airline*] [*Netherlands Antilles*]
ALM .... Apollo Lunar Module [*NASA*]
ALM .... Archives des Lettres Modernes [*A publication*]
ALM .... Arkansas & Louisiana Missouri Railway Co. [*AAR code*]
ALM .... Arm Lock Magnet
ALM .... Artium Liberalium Magister [*Master of the Liberal Arts*]
ALM .... Assembler Language for MULTICS
ALM .... Asset/Liability Management [*Banking*]
ALM .... Associated Liquor Merchants Ltd. [*Australia*]
ALM .... Association of Lutheran Men (EA)
ALM .... Asynchronous Line Module
ALM .... Asynchronous Line Multiplexer [*Telecommunications*]
ALM .... Audio Level Meter
ALM .... Augmented Lunar Module (MCD)
ALM .... Linden Municipal Library, Alberta [*Library symbol*] [*National Library of Canada*] (NLC)
ALM .... University of Alabama, University, AL [*OCLC symbol*] (OCLC)
ALMA .... Adoptees Liberty Movement Association (EA)
ALMA .... Aircraft Locknut Manufacturers Association (EA)
ALMA .... Alphanumeric Language for Music Analysis
ALMA .... Alternative Living Manager's Association [*Defunct*] (EA)
ALMA .... American Lace Manufacturers Association
ALMA .... American Lithuanian Musicians Alliance (EA)
ALMA .... American Loudspeaker Manufacturers Association (EA)
ALMA .... Analytical Laboratory Managers Association (EA)
ALMA .... Archivum Latinitatis Medii Aevi [*A publication*]
ALMA .... Association of Labor Mediation Agencies [*Later, ALRA*] (EA)
ALMA .... Association of Literary Magazines of America [*Later, CCLM*]
Alma-Atin Gos Ped Inst Ucen Zap ... Alma-Atinskii Gosudarstvennyi Pedagogiceskii Institut Imeni Abaja. Ucenye Zapiski [*A publication*]
ALMACA ... Association of Labor-Management Administrators and Consultants on Alcoholism (EA)
ALMAJCOM ... All Major Commands
Alma Mater Philipp ... Alma Mater Philippina [*A publication*]
Almanak Agric Brasil ... Almanak Agricola Brasileiro [*A publication*]
ALMAR ..... All Marine Corps Activities (NVT)
ALMArv ...... Annales Latini Montium Arvernorum. Bulletin du Groupe d'Etudes Latines. Universite de Clermont [*A publication*]
ALMB .... Air-Launched Missile Ballistics (MCD)
ALMC .... Almanac (ROG)
ALMC .... Army Logistics Management College [*Fort Lee, VA*]
Alm Chas Pec ... Almanach Chasse et Peche [*A publication*]
ALMD .... Alaska Medicine [*A publication*]
ALMD ...... Australian Legal Monthly Digest [*A publication*] (APTA)
ALMDA ...... Airlock Multiple Docking Adapter [*NASA*] (MCD)
ALMDB ...... Alaska Medicine [*A publication*]
ALME .... Acetyllysine Methyl Ester [*Biochemistry*]
ALMG .... Alaska Mines and Geology [*A publication*]
ALMI .... Alpha Microsystems [*NASDAQ symbol*] (NQ)
ALMI .... Anterior Lateral Myocardial Infarct [*Cardiology*]
ALMICS .... Automated Logistics Management and Inventory Control System (MCD)
ALMIDO .. Amplitude and Latency Measuring Instrument with Digital Output (MCD)
ALMIDS ... Army Logistics Management Integrated Data Systems (AABC)
AL MIL ..... Alla Militaire [*In Military Style*] [*Music*] (ROG)
ALMILACT ... All Military Activities (AFM)
ALMIMSIP ... Air-Launched Missile Intermediate Maintenance System Program [*Navy*] (MCD)
ALMIOS .... Air-Launched Missile Inventory Objectives Study (MCD)

ALMIRBM ... Air-Launched Medium-Intermediate Range Ballistic Missile (MCD)
ALMM ...... Alaska Mining and Minerals [*A publication*]
ALMMB6 ... Allan Hancock Monographs in Marine Biology [*A publication*]
ALMNEC ... Alimentaria [*A publication*]
ALMO .... Alamo Savings Association of Texas [*NASDAQ symbol*] (NQ)
ALMO .... Army Logistics Manpower Office [*Merged with Operations Personnel Office*]
AlmOAW .. Almanach. Oesterreichische Akademie der Wissenschaften [*A publication*]
AL MOD ... Alla Moderna [*In Modern Style*] [*Music*] (ROG)
ALMOND ... Almondsbury [*England*]
ALMPB ..... Annals. Medical Section. Polish Academy of Sciences [*A publication*]
ALMPBF ... Annals. Medical Section. Polish Academy of Sciences [*A publication*]
ALMPT ...... Air-Launched Missile Propulsion Technology (MCD)
ALMRB .... Memorias. Academia das Ciencias de Lisboa. Classe de Ciencias [*A publication*]
ALMS .... Air-Launched Missile System
ALMS .... Aircraft Landing Measurement System (MCD)
ALMS .... Analytic Language Manipulation System
ALMS .... Atomic Line Molecular Spectroscopy
ALMS .... Auxiliary Liquid Metal System [*Nuclear energy*] (NRCH)
ALMSA ..... Army Logistics Management Systems Activity
ALMSA ..... Automated Logistics Management Systems Agency [*DoD*]
ALMTB ...... Alimenta [*A publication*]
ALMV .... Air-Launched Miniature Vehicle
Alm Ved ..... Almanach des Vedettes [*A publication*]
ALN .... Accounting Line Number (CINC)
ALN .... Adaptive Learning Network [*Data processing*]
ALN .... Administrative Law Decisions. Notes [*A publication*] (APTA)
ALN .... Administrative Law Notes [*Australia*] [*A publication*]
ALN .... Advanced Land Navigation (MCD)
ALN .... Albany & Northern Railway Co. [*AAR code*]
Al & N .... Alcock and Napier's Irish King's Bench Reports [*A publication*] (DLA)
ALN .... Alianca Libertadora Nacional [*National Liberation Alliance*] [*Brazil*] [*Political party*] (PD)
ALN .... Align
ALN .... [*The*] Allen Group, Inc. [*NYSE symbol*] (SPSG)
ALN .... Alton, IL [*Location identifier*] [*FAA*] (FAAL)
ALN .... American Law Network [*Telecommunications service*] (TSSD)
ALN .... Ameroil Energy Corp. [*Vancouver Stock Exchange symbol*]
ALN .... Ammunition Lot Number
ALN .... Anterior Lateral Nerve
ALN .... Armee de Liberation Nationale [*National Liberation Army*] [*Guadeloupe*] [*Political party*] (PD)
ALN .... Australian Law News [*A publication*] (APTA)
ALN .... Australian Library News [*A publication*] (APTA)
ALNA .... Armee de Liberation Nationale de l'Angola [*Angolan Army of National Liberation*]
Al & Nap .... Alcock and Napier's Irish King's Bench Reports [*A publication*] (DLA)
ALNAV ..... All Navy Activities [*A dispatch to all activities in an area*]
ALNAVSTA ... All Naval Stations [*A dispatch to all Naval stations in an area*]
ALND .... Australian Lawyers for Nuclear Disarmament
ALNICO .... Aluminum, Nickel, Cobalt [*Alloy*]
ALNK .... Armee de Liberation Nationale Kamerounaise [*Cameroonese National Liberation Army*]
ALNMT .... Alignment (AAG)
ALNN .... Alaska Native Magazine [*Formerly, Alaska Native News*] [*A publication*]
ALNN .... Alaska Native News [*A publication*]
ALNNO ..... Air-Launched Nonnuclear Ordnance
ALNO .... Alberta North [*A publication*]
ALNOT ..... Alert Notice
ALNT .... Alliant Computer Systems Corp. [*Littleton, MA*] [*NASDAQ symbol*] (NQ)
ALNTS ...... Automatic Liquid Nitrogen Transfer System
ALNU .... Alaska Nurse [*A publication*]
ALNY .... Architectural League of New York [*Later, AL*] (EA)
Al'O .... A l'Orient [*At the East*] [*French*] [*Freemasonry*] (ROG)
ALO .... Administrative Liaison Officer
ALO .... Admiralty Liaison Officer [*British*]
ALO .... Advanced Lunar Operation
ALO .... Air Liaison Officer
ALO .... Alamo Developments [*Vancouver Stock Exchange symbol*]
ALO .... Albuquerque Operations Office [*Department of Energy*]
ALO .... Allied Liaison Office [*Military*]
ALO .... Alternate Launch Officer [*Air Force*]
ALO .... Alternate Liaison Officer
ALO .... Alternative Liste Oesterreich [*Austrian Alternative List*] [*Political party*] (PPW)
ALO .... Amalgamated Lace Operatives of America
ALO .... American Liaison Office
ALO .... Apollo Lunar Orbit [*NASA*]
ALO .... Appropriate Labor Organization (OICC)
ALO .... Arm Length Order
ALO .... Army Liaison Officer

ALO	Authorized Level of Organization (AABC)
ALO	Automatic Lock-On (MCD)
ALO	Axiolinguo-Occlusal [*Dentistry*]
ALO	Lougheed Public Library, Alberta [*Library symbol*] [*National Library of Canada*] (NLC)
ALO	Waterloo [*Iowa*] [*Airport symbol*] (OAG)
ALOA	Amalgamated Lace Operatives of America (EA)
ALOA	Assembly of Librarians of the Americas [*Defunct*]
ALOA	Associated Locksmiths of America (EA)
ALOAL	Autonomous Lock-On After Launch (MCD)
ALoaLHi ...	Lee County Historical Society, Museum Library, Loachapoka, AL [*Library symbol*] [*Library of Congress*] (LCLS)
ALOC	Administrative and Logistics Operations Center [*Military*] (INF)
ALOC	Air Line of Communication [*Air Force*]
ALOC	Air Logistics Chain (MCD)
ALOC	Allocate [*or Allocation*] (AABC)
ALOC	Alternate Launch Officer Console [*Air Force*]
ALOC	Apollo Launch Operations Committee [*NASA*] (KSC)
ALOE	[*A*] Lady of England [*Pseudonym used by Charlotte Maria Tucker, 19th-century author of children's books*]
ALOF	Alaska Offshore [*A publication*]
ALOFT	Airborne Light Optical Fiber Technology
ALOFT	[*A*] Language Oriented to Flight Engineering and Testing [*NASA*] (KSC)
ALOG	Administration-Logistics [*Military*] (INF)
ALOG	Analogic Corp. [*NASDAQ symbol*] (NQ)
ALOG	Army Logistician [*A publication*]
ALOHA	Aboriginal Lands of Hawaiian Ancestry [*Hawaiian group seeking compensation for land*]
ALOM	Air-Land Operations Manual (MCD)
ALOM	Longview Municipal Library, Alberta [*Library symbol*] [*National Library of Canada*] (NLC)
ALOMA	American Lithuanian Organist - Musicians Alliance [*Formerly, ALRCOA*] (EA)
ALOMAD ...	Adriamycin, Leukeran [*Chlorambucil*], Oncovin [*Vincristine*], Methotrexate, Actinomycin D, Dacarbazine [*Antineoplastic drug regimen*]
ALOMO	Lomond Public Library, Alberta [*Library symbol*] [*National Library of Canada*] (NLC)
ALON	Air Liaison Officer Net (NATG)
ALON	Aircraft Longitude (MCD)
ALOO	Albuquerque Operations Office [*Department of Energy*] (GRD)
ALOP	Apollo Launch Operation Panel [*NASA*] (KSC)
ALOP	Army Logistics Objectives Program
ALOPE	Airborne LIDAR [*Light Detection and Ranging*] Oceanographic Probing Experiment [*NASA*]
A l'OR	A l'Orient [*At the East*] [*French*] [*Freemasonry*]
ALOR	Advanced Lunar Orbital Rendezvous (IEEE)
ALOR	Alter Orient [*A publication*]
ALOREP ...	Airlift Operational Report
ALOS	Annual. Leeds University Oriental Society [*A publication*]
ALOS	Apollo Lunar Orbital Science [*NASA*] (KSC)
ALOS	Average Length of Stay [*of patients in a health care institution*]
ALOSYN ...	Alouette Topside Sounder Synoptic [*NASA*]
ALOT	Adaptive LASER Optics Techniques (MCD)
ALOT	Adsorption Layer Open Tubular Column [*Chromatography*]
ALOT	Airborne Lightweight Optical Tracking [*Air Force*]
ALOT	Allotment (AABC)
ALOT	Astro-Med, Inc. [*NASDAQ symbol*] (NQ)
ALOTM	Allotment (AFM)
ALOTS	Airborne Lightweight Optical Tracking System [*Air Force*]
ALOW	Air Electrical Officer's Writer [*British military*] (DMA)
ALOXCON ...	Aluminum-Oxide Electrolytic Capacitor (MUGU)
ALOY	Alloy Computer Products, Inc. [*Framingham, MA*] [*NASDAQ symbol*] (NQ)
ALP	Administration Laboratory Project File [*University of Alberta*] [*Canada*] [*Information service or system*] (CRD)
ALP	Advanced Language Program [*Institute for Defense Analysis*]
ALP	Advanced Lunar Projects
ALP	Advisory Light Panel (MCD)
ALP	Agence Lao Presse [*Laos Press Agency*]
ALP	Air-Launched Platform (NVT)
ALP	Air Liaison Party
ALP	Air Logistics Pipeline Study (MCD)
ALP	Airborne Line Printer
ALP	Airport Layout Plan (FAAC)
ALP	Airport Location Point (FAAC)
ALP	Alabama Power Co. [*NYSE symbol*] (SPSG)
ALP	Aleppo [*Syria*] [*Airport symbol*] (OAG)
ALP	Alkaline Phosphatase [*Also, AP*] [*An enzyme*]
ALP	Allied Liaison and Protocol [*Military*]
ALP	Allied Logistics Publication [*Military*]
ALP	Alphalytic Protease [*An enzyme*]
AIP	Altro Polo [*A publication*]
ALP	Alprazolam [*Tranquilizer*]
ALP	Ambulance Loading Post [*Military*]
ALP	American Labor Party
ALP	Anterior Lobe of Pituitary [*Gland*]
ALP	Antigua Labour Party [*Political party*] (PPW)

ALP	Approved for Limited Production (MCD)
ALP	Arakan Liberation Party [*Political party*] [*Burma*]
ALP	Arithmetic Logic Processor
ALP	Articulated Leg Platform [*Drilling technology*]
ALP	Assembly Language Preprocessor [*Data processing*] (IEEE)
ALP	Assembly Language Program [*Data processing*]
ALP	Australian Labour Party [*Political party*] (PPW)
ALP	Automated Learning Process
ALP	Automated Library Program [*Data processing*] (DIT)
ALP	Elmira, NY [*Location identifier*] [*FAA*] (FAAL)
ALPA	Air Line Pilots Association, International (EA)
ALPA	Alaskan Long-Period Array
Al Pa	Albertus Papiensis [*Flourished, 1211-40*] [*Authority cited in pre-1607 legal work*] (DSA)
ALPA	American Legion Press Association [*Later, NALPA*] (EA)
ALPA	Amiral Commandant les Porte-Avions [*Admiral, Aircraft Carriers*] [*French*] (NATG)
ALPA	Asociacion Latinoamericana de Produccion Animal
ALPA	Australian Library Publishers Association
ALPAC	Automatic Language Processing Advisory Committee [*National Research Council*]
ALPAI	Air Line Pilots Association, International (EA)
ALPAK	Algebra Package [*Data processing*]
ALPAL	Algeria - Palma, Spain [*Submarine cable*] [*Telecommunications*] (TEL)
ALPB	Aircraft Logistics Planning Board (MCD)
ALPB	American Lutheran Publicity Bureau (EA)
ALPBC	American League of Professional Baseball Clubs (EA)
ALPC	Adaptive Linear Predictive Coding (TEL)
ALPC	Army Logistics Policy Council (AABC)
ALPCA	Automobile License Plate Collectors Association (EA)
ALPD	Australian Legal Profession Digest [*A publication*] (APTA)
ALPDA	Advances in Lipid Research [*A publication*]
ALPE	Airborne LASER Propagation Experiment (MCD)
ALPEC	Ammunition Loading Production Engineering Center [*Army*]
Alpenlaend Bienenztg ...	Alpenlaendische Bienenzeitung [*A publication*]
ALPERSCOM ...	All Personnel Communication [*Military*] (AFM)
Alpes Orient ...	Alpes Orientales [*A publication*]
ALPETH ...	Aluminum and Polyethylene [*Components of a type of telecommunications cable*]
ALPH	Alaskan Philatelist [*A publication*]
ALPH	Alphabetic Phonogram [*Egyptology*] (ROG)
ALPHA	Action League of Physically Handicapped Adults [*Canada*]
ALPHA	Alkali Plasma Hall Accelerator (MCD)
ALPHA	Alphabetical [*Flowchart*]
ALPHA	AMC [*Army Materiel Command*] Logistics Program - Hardcore Automated
ALPHA	Automatic Literature Processing, Handling, and Analysis
Alpha-Fetoprotein Hepatoma Jpn Cancer Assn Symp ...	Alpha-Fetoprotein and Hepatoma. Japanese Cancer Association. Symposium on Alpha-Fetoprotein and Hepatoma [*A publication*]
ALPHANUM ...	Alphanumeric
ALPHGR ...	Average Linear Planar Heat Generation Rate [*Nuclear energy*] (NRCH)
ALPI	Alarm Products International [*NASDAQ symbol*] (NQ)
ALPID	Analysis of Large Plastic Incremental Deformation (MCD)
Alpine J	Alpine Journal [*A publication*]
ALPL	Advanced Lunar Projects Laboratory
ALPLASMA ...	Aluminum Plasma Model (MCD)
ALPM	Assembly-Line Preventive Maintenance [*Automotive engineering*]
ALPM	Augmented Lunar Payload Module
ALPMBL ..	Asociacion Latinoamericana de Produccion Animal. Memoria [*A publication*]
ALPNA	American Licensed Practical Nurses Association (EA)
ALPO	Air-Land Programs Office
ALPO	Allegheny Portage Railroad National Historic Site
ALPO	Aluminophosphate [*Inorganic chemistry*]
ALPO	Anterolateral Pre-Olivary Nucleus [*Neuroanatomy*]
ALPO	Apollo Lunar Polar Orbiter [*NASA*]
ALPO	Association of Land and Property Owners
ALPO	Association of Lunar and Planetary Observers (EA)
ALPOS	Avionics Laboratory Predictive Operations and Support (MCD)
Al Pp	Albertus Papiensis [*Flourished, 1211-40*] [*Authority cited in pre-1607 legal work*] (DSA)
ALPPA	Agriculture and Livestock Professional Photographers Association (EA)
Al Pr	Alison's Principles of the Criminal Law of Scotland [*A publication*] (DLA)
ALPR	Argonne Low-Power Reactor [*Obsolete*]
ALPRA	American Lithuanian Press and Radio Association
ALPRA-V ...	American Lithuanian Press and Radio Association - Viltis (EA)
ALPRO	Alianza para el Progreso [*Alliance for Progress*] [*Washington, DC*]
ALPS	Accidental Launch Protection System [*Military*]
ALPS	Advanced Linear Programming System [*Operational research technique*]
ALPS	Advanced Liquid Propulsion System [*NASA*]
ALPS	Air-Launched Probe System (MCD)
ALPS	Air-Launched Projected Sonobuoy (MCD)

ALPS .... Alabama Linguistic and Philological Series [*A publication*]
ALPS .... Alternative Launch-Point System
ALPS .... Applied LASER Projects Staff
ALPS .... Approach and Landing Procedures Simulator
                  [*Aviation*]   (MCD)
ALPS .... Army Linguist Personnel Study
ALPS .... Arts, Letters, Printers and Publishers, and Systems [*A
                  publication*]
ALPS .... Asociacion Latinoamericana de Psicologia Social [*Latin
                  American Association for Social Psychology -
                  LAASP*]   (EAIO)
ALPS .... Associated Logic Parallel System   (BUR)
ALPS .... Association for Loss Prevention and Security   (EA)
ALPS .... Australian Library Publishers Society
ALPS .... Automated Library Processing Services [*System Development
                  Corp.*]   (IID)
ALPS .... Automated Logistics Planning System   (MCD)
ALPS .... Automatic Landing Positioning System
ALPS .... Automatic License Plate Scanning
ALPS .... Automatic Linear Positioning System
ALPSP .... Association of Learned and Professional Society Publishers
                  [*British*]
ALPSS .... Army Life-Support Power Source System   (MCD)
ALPTA .... American Low Power Television Association   (EA)
ALPURCOMS ... All-Purpose Communications System
ALPVB ...... Analyse et Prevision [*A publication*]
ALQ .... Abraham Lincoln Quarterly [*A publication*]
ALQ .... Albuquerque [*New Mexico*] [*Seismograph station code, US
                  Geological Survey*]   (SEIS)
ALQ .... Alegrete [*Brazil*] [*Airport symbol*] [*Obsolete*]   (OAG)
ALQ .... [*The*] Ancient Library of Qumran   (BJA)
ALQ .... Annales du Marche Commun; Revue Bimestrielle pour
                  l'Information et l'Harmonisation du Commerce et de
                  l'Industrie [*A publication*]
ALQDS ...... All Quadrants [*Aviation*]   (FAAC)
ALQS .... Aliquippa & Southern Railroad Co. [*AAR code*]
ALR .... Active Line Rotation [*Telecommunications*]   (TEL)
ALR .... Actual Loss Ratio [*Insurance*]
ALR .... Adelaide Law Review [*A publication*]   (APTA)
ALR .... Administrative Law Review [*A publication*]
ALR .... Advanced Logic Research Access 386 [*Microcomputer*]
ALR .... African Language Review [*A publication*]
ALR .... Afrika Spectrum [*A publication*]
ALR .... Air-Land Resupply   (CINC)
ALR .... Airborne LASER Range-Finder
ALR .... Alaska Aeronautical Industries [*Anchorage, AK*] [*FAA
                  designator*]   (FAAC)
ALR .... Alberta Law Reports [*A publication*]
ALR .... Alden's Law Reports [*A publication*]   (DLA)
ALR .... Alerting Message [*Aviation code*]
ALR .... Alexandra [*New Zealand*] [*Airport symbol*]   (OAG)
ALR .... Aliter [*Otherwise*] [*Latin*]   (ADA)
ALR .... Amagat-Leduc Rule [*Physics*]
ALR .... American Labor Cases [*Prentice-Hall, Inc.*] [*A
                  publication*]   (DLA)
ALR .... American Law Register [*A publication*]   (DLA)
ALR .... American Law Reports
ALR .... American Literary Realism, 1870-1910 [*A publication*]
ALR .... Arachidonic Linoleic Acid Ratio [*Clinical chemistry*]
ALR .... Arbeitsgruppe fuer Luft-und Raufahrt [*German*]
ALR .... Argus Law Reports [*A publication*]   (APTA)
ALR .... Artillery-Locating RADAR
ALR .... Australian Argus Law Reports [*A publication*]
ALR .... Australian Law Reports [*A publication*]   (APTA)
ALR .... Australian Left Review [*A publication*]   (APTA)
ALR .... Authors' Lending Royalty
ALR .... Automatic Level Recorder
ALR .... Automatic Load Regulator
ALR .... Office of Labor Relations [*FAA*]   (FAAC)
ALR .... University of Arkansas at Little Rock, Law Library, Little Rock,
                  AR [*OCLC symbol*]   (OCLC)
ALRA .... Abortion Law Reform Association   (EAIO)
ALRA .... Academy of Live and Recorded Arts [*British*]
ALRA .... Advanced LASER Requirements Assessment   (MCD)
ALRA .... American Land Resource Association   (EA)
ALRA .... Army Long-Range Appraisal
ALRA .... Associated Legislative Rabbinate of America   (EA)
ALRA .... Association of Labor Relations Agencies   (EA)
ALRAAM ... Air-Launched Long-Range Air-to-Air Missile   (MCD)
ALRAC ...... Australian Law Reform Agencies Conference [*A
                  publication*]   (APTA)
ALRAFAC ... All RADAR Air Traffic Control Facilities in Region [*FAA*]
ALRANL ... Abortion Law Reform Association. News Letter [*A
                  publication*]   (DLA)
ALRAWI ... Advanced Long-Range All-Weather Interceptor   (MCD)
ALRC .... Adoption Legislation Review Committee [*Victoria, Australia*]
ALRC .... Aerojet Liquid Rocket Company   (KSC)
ALRC .... Anti-Locust Research Centre [*Later, Centre for Overseas Pest
                  Research*] [*British*]   (MCD)
ALRC .... Area Learning Resource Center
ALRC .... Australian Law Reform Commission   (DLA)

ALRC DP .. Australian Law Reform Commission. Discussion Paper [*A
                  publication*]   (APTA)
ALR (CN) .. Argus Law Reports (Current Notes) [*A publication*]   (APTA)
ALRCOA... American Lithuanian Roman Catholic Organist Alliance [*Later,
                  ALOMA*]   (EA)
ALRCP ...... Army Long-Range Capabilities Plan
ALRCWA ... American Lithuanian Roman Catholic Women's Alliance
                  [*Later, LCW*]   (EA)
ALRD .... Army Logistics Research and Development
ALR 2d ...... American Law Reports, Annotated, Second Series [*A
                  publication*]   (DLA)
ALR 3d ...... American Law Reports, Annotated, Third Series [*A
                  publication*]   (DLA)
ALRE......... Aircraft Launch and Recovery Equipment [*Navy*]   (MCD)
AL Rec ...... American Law Record [*Cincinnati*] [*A publication*]   (DLA)
ALRED ...... Arizona Law Review [*A publication*]
AL Reg ...... American Law Register [*Philadelphia*] [*A publication*]   (DLA)
AL Reg (NS) ... American Law Register, New Series [*A publication*]   (DLA)
AL Reg (OS) ... American Law Register, Old Series [*A publication*]   (DLA)
ALREMP .. Aircraft Launch and Recovery Equipment Maintenance
                  Program [*Navy*]   (NG)
ALREP ...... Air-Launched Report [*Navy*]   (NG)
AL Rep...... Alabama Reports [*A publication*]   (DLA)
AL Rep...... American Law Reporter [*Davenport, IA*] [*A
                  publication*]   (DLA)
ALRES ...... Army Logistics Readiness Evaluation System
AL Rev ...... American Law Review [*A publication*]
ALR Fed .... American Law Reports, Annotated, Federal [*A
                  publication*]   (DLA)
ALRGN ..... All Regional Offices [*FAA*]   (FAAC)
ALRH .... Apollo Lunar Radioisotopic Heater [*NASA*]   (MCD)
ALRI.......... Advanced Long-Range Interceptor
ALRI.......... Airborne Long-Range Input   (KSC)
ALRI.......... Airborne Long-Range Intercept
ALRI.......... Anterolateral Rotatory Instability [*Orthopedics*]
ALRIAI .... Arid Lands Resource Information Paper [*A publication*]
ALRLCS... American Law Reports Later Case Service [*A
                  publication*]   (DLA)
ALR Mal ... African Law Reports, Malawi Series [*A publication*]   (DLA)
ALR (Malawi Ser) ... African Law Reports, Malawi Series [*A
                  publication*]   (DLA)
ALRN .... Altron, Inc. [*Wilmington, MA*] [*NASDAQ symbol*]   (NQ)
ALRNS...... American Law Register, New Series [*A publication*]   (ILCA)
ALROS...... American Laryngological, Rhinological, and Otological
                  Society   (EA)
ALRPG...... Army Long-Range Planning Guidance
ALRR........ Ames Laboratory Research Reactor
ALRRI .... Airborne Long-Range RADAR Input   (MUGU)
ALRS......... Admiralty List of Radio Signals [*British*]
ALR (Sierra L Ser) ... African Law Reports, Sierra Leone Series [*A
                  publication*]   (DLA)
ALRSL ...... African Law Reports, Sierra Leone Series [*A
                  publication*]   (DLA)
ALRT........ Advanced Light Rapid Transit
ALRTF....... Army Long-Range Technological Forecast   (AABC)
ALR 4th ..... American Law Reports, Annotated, Fourth Series [*A
                  publication*]   (DLA)
ALRU .... Automated Line Record Update [*Telecommunications*]   (TEL)
ALS........... Aboriginal Legal Service [*Australia*]
ALS........... Acetolactate Synthase [*An enzyme*]
ALS........... Active LASER Seeker   (MCD)
ALS........... ADA Language System   (MCD)
ALS........... Advanced Landing System
ALS........... Advanced Launch System [*Rocketry*]
ALS........... Advanced Library Systems, Inc. [*Information service or
                  system*]   (IID)
ALS........... Advanced Life Support [*System*]
ALS........... Advanced Light Source [*For Synchrotron radiation*] [*High-
                  energy physics*]
ALS........... Advanced Limb Scanner   (MCD)
ALS........... Advanced Logistic System   (AFM)
ALS........... Advanced Logistics Spacecraft
ALS........... Advanced Low-Power Schottky   (MCD)
ALS........... Advanced Lunar Studies
ALS........... African Language Studies [*A publication*]
ALS........... Agricultural Land Service [*Later, ADAS*] [*British*]
ALS........... Air Lock System   (MCD)
ALS........... Air Logistics Service [*or System*] [*Military*]
ALS........... Airborne LASER System
ALS........... Airborne Live Scanner
ALS........... Aircraft Landing System
ALS........... Airfield Lighting System
ALS........... Alabama Supreme Court and State Law Library, Montgomery,
                  AL [*OCLC symbol*]   (OCLC)
ALS........... Alamosa [*Colorado*] [*Airport symbol*]   (OAG)
ALS........... Alclare Resources [*Vancouver Stock Exchange symbol*]
ALS........... Aldolase [*An enzyme*]
ALS........... Alias [*Otherwise*] [*Latin*]
ALS........... Alishan [*Republic of China*] [*Seismograph station code, US
                  Geological Survey*]   (SEIS)
ALS........... All-Language Services, Inc.

ALS............	All-Weather Landing System [*Also, AWLS*]
ALS............	Allegheny Ludlum Corp. [*NYSE symbol*] (SPSG)
ALS............	Almond Leaf Scorch [*Plant pathology*]
ALS............	Alternate Landing Site [*NASA*] (NASA)
ALS............	Alternate Life Style
ALS............	[*The*] Alton & Southern Railway Co. [*AAR code*]
ALS............	American Lessing Society [*Later, LS*] (EA)
ALS............	American Library Society [*Defunct*]
ALS............	American Liszt Society (EA)
ALS............	American Literary Society [*Defunct*] (EA)
ALS............	American Littoral Society (EA)
ALS............	American Lumber Standards
ALS............	American Lunar Society (EA)
ALS............	American Luxembourg Society (EA)
ALS............	Ammunition Loading System (MCD)
ALS............	Amphibious Logistics Systems [*Navy*]
ALS............	Amyotrophic Lateral Sclerosis [*Medicine*]
ALS............	Anti-Collision Light System [*or Subsystem*] (MCD)
ALS............	Anticipated Life Span
ALS............	Antilymphocyte [*or Antilympholytic*] Serum [*Immunology*]
ALS............	Approach and Landing Simulator [*Aviation*]
ALS............	Approach Landing System [*Aviation*] (MCD)
ALSP..........	Approach Light System [*Aviation*]
ALS............	Arithmetic Logic Section [*Data processing*]
ALS............	Armenian Literary Society (EA)
ALS............	Arrowhead Library System [*Library network*]
AIS............	Asia Library Services, Auburn, NY [*Library symbol*] [*Library of Congress*] (LCLS)
ALS............	Associate of the Linnaean Society [*British*]
ALS............	Associative List Selection
ALS............	Augmented Logistics Support (MCD)
ALS............	Australian LANDSAT [*Land Satellite*] Station
ALS............	Australian Libraries Summit
ALS............	Australian Literary Studies [*A publication*]
ALS............	Australian Longitudinal Survey
ALS............	Autograph Letter Signed [*Manuscript descriptions*]
ALS............	Automated Library System [*Foundation for Library Research, Inc.*] [*Information service or system*] (IID)
ALS............	Automated Liquid Sampler [*Instrumentation*]
ALS............	Automatic Landing System
ALS............	Automatic Level Setting
ALS............	Autonomic Lability Score [*In ion detection*]
ALS............	Autonomous Listening Stations [*Instrumentation*]
ALS............	Azimuth Laying Set (AABC)
ALS............	Chartair, Inc. [*Los Angeles, CA*] [*FAA designator*] (FAAC)
a-ls---........	Laos [*MARC geographic area code*] [*Library of Congress*] (LCCP)
ALSA........	American Law Student Association [*Later, Law Student Division - American Bar Association*] (EA)
ALSA........	American Legal Studies Association (EA)
ALSA........	Amphibious Logistics Support Ashore [*Marine Corps*] (MCD)
ALSA........	Amyotrophic Lateral Sclerosis Association (EA)
ALSA........	Area Library Services Authority [*Indiana*]
ALSA........	Astronaut Life Support Assembly [*NASA*]
ALSA........	Australasian Law Students Association
ALSA........	Four Rivers Area Library Services Authority [*Library network*]
ALSA 2......	Area II Library Services Authority [*Library network*]
ALSA 6......	Area VI Library Services Authority [*Library network*]
ALSAA......	Allgemeines Statistisches Archiv [*A publication*]
ALSAA......	Americans (of Lebanese-Syrian Ancestry) for America (EA)
ALSAC......	Aiding Leukemia Stricken American Children [*Later, ALSAC - St. Jude Children's Research Hospital*] [*Fund-raising organization*]
ALSAC......	American Lebanese Syrian Association Charities (EA)
Alsace-Lorraine Serv Carte Geol Mem ...	Alsace-Lorraine. Service de la Carte Geologique. Memoires [*Strasbourg*] [*A publication*]
ALSA F......	ALSA [*American Legal Studies Association*] Forum [*A publication*]
ALSAFECOM ...	All Safety Commands [*Air Force*] (AFM)
Alsager......	Alsager's Dictionary of Business Terms (DLA)
ALSAM......	Air-Launched Ship-Attack Missile
ALSAM......	Air-Launched Surface Attack Missile
ALSAML ..	Ahvenanmaan Kokoomus; Alaendsk Samling [*Aland Coalition*] [*Finland*] (PPE)
ALSB........	Almond Leaf Scorch Bacterium [*Plant pathology*]
ALSC.........	Alaska Seas and Coast [*A publication*]
ALSC.........	American Lumber Standards Committee (EA)
ALSC.........	Army Logistics Specialty Committee (MCD)
ALSC.........	Association for Library Service to Children (EA)
ALSC.......	Auxiliary Library Service Collections
ALSCC......	Apollo Lunar Surface Closeup Camera [*Apollo 11*] [*NASA*]
Al Sc CrL...	Alison's Principles of the Criminal Law of Scotland [*A publication*] (DLA)
ALSCP.......	Appalachian Land Stabilization and Conservation Program
ALSCS......	Admixture-Lathe-Cut + Single Composition Spherical [*Dental alloy*]
ALSD.........	Apollo Lunar Surface Drill [*NASA*]
ALSE........	All Seasons Resorts, Inc. [*Costa Mesa, CA*] [*NASDAQ symbol*] (NQ)
ALSE	Apollo Lunar Sounder Experiment [*NASA*]
ALSE	Astronaut Life Support Equipment [*NASA*] (MCD)

ALSE........	Availability of Logistics Support Elements (MCD)
ALSE.........	Aviation Life Support Equipment (AABC)
AL SEA FRON ...	Alaskan Sea Frontier [*Navy*]
AL SEC	Alaskan Sector
ALSEC	All Sectors [*FAA*] (FAAC)
AL SEG	Al Segno [*At the Sign*] [*Music*]
ALSEP......	Apollo Lunar Surface Experiments Package [*NASA*]
Al Ser........	Indian Law Reports, Allahabad Series [*A publication*] (DLA)
ALSF	Abundant Life Seed Foundation (EA)
ALSF	Approach Lighting System with Sequenced Flashers [*Aviation*]
ALSFA......	Asa Lafitte Stark Family Association (EA)
ALSI	Aluminum Silicon [*An alloy*]
ALSIB.......	Alaska Industry [*A publication*]
ALSK........	Alaskana [*A publication*]
ALSL	Assembly List Shortage Log (AAG)
ALSM........	Air-Launched Strategic Missile
ALSNRF	ALS [*Amyotrophic Lateral Sclerosis*] and Neuromuscular Research Foundation (EA)
ALS-NSDI ...	Actual Loss Sustained - No Specified Daily Indemnity [*Insurance*]
ALSO........	Auxiliary Library Service Organization
ALSOR.....	Air Launch Sounding Rocket
ALSP	Army Logistics Study Program
ALSPAA.....	American Littoral Society. Special Publication [*A publication*]
ALSPAC....	Advanced Logistics System Project Advisory Committee [*Terminated, 1977*] [*DoD*] (EGAO)
ALS/P-D ...	Amyotrophic Lateral Sclerosis/Parkinsonism-Dementia [*Medicine*]
ALSPES	Automated LASER Seeker Performance Evaluation System (MCD)
ALSPT......	Associateship of the London School of Polymer Technology [*British*] (DBQ)
ALSR	Automated Logistics Systems Review (MCD)
ALSRC......	Apollo Lunar Sample Return Container [*NASA*]
ALSS	Acoustic Lens SONAR System (MCD)
ALSS	Adult Learning Satellite Service [*Public Broadcasting Service*] [*Telecommunications service*] (TSSD)
ALSS	Advanced LASER System Study
ALSS	Advanced Life Support System (MCD)
ALSS	Advanced Location Strike System [*Formerly, Airborne Location and Strike System*] [*Air Force*]
ALSS	Airborne Location and Strike System (MCD)
ALSS	Aircrew Life Support System (CAAL)
ALSS	Airline System Simulator
ALSS	Airlock Support System [*or Subsystem*] [*NASA*] (MCD)
ALSS	Apollo Logistic Support System [*NASA*]
ALSS	Association of Lutheran Secondary Schools (EA)
ALSS	Aviation Life Support Systems (MCD)
ALSSA.......	Air Line Stewards and Stewardesses Association (EA)
ALSSDM ...	Annual Reviews of Plant Sciences [*A publication*]
ALSSOA....	Amyotrophic Lateral Sclerosis Society of America (EA)
ALSSOC....	Amyotrophic Lateral Sclerosis Society of Canada
ALST	Adolescent Language Screening Test [*Speech development test*]
ALST	Alaska Standard Time
ALST	Altostratus [*Also, AS*] [*Meteorology*]
ALSTA	All Stations (KSC)
ALSTACON ...	All Stations, Continental United States (MUGU)
ALSTAR	Altitude Layer Surveillance Terminal Area RADAR
ALSTG	Altimeter Setting [*Aviation*] (FAAC)
ALSU.........	Autonomous Line Scanning Unit (MCD)
ALSV	Air-Launched Sortie Vehicle [*Aviation*] (AIA)
ALT	Above Local Terrain (MCD)
ALT	Accelerated Life Testing
ALT	Acquisition Lead Time
ALT	Administrative Lead Time
ALT	Aer Lingus Teoranta [*Ireland*]
ALT	African Literature Today [*A publication*]
ALT	Agricultural Laboratory Technology
ALT	Airborne LASER Tracker [*System*]
ALT	Alabama Trucking Association, Montgomery AL [*STAC*]
ALT	Alanine Aminotransferase [*Also, AAT, ALAT, GPT*] [*An enzyme*]
ALT	Allstate Municipal Income II [*NYSE symbol*] (SPSG)
ALT	Altamont Aviation, Inc. [*Livermore, CA*] [*FAA designator*] (FAAC)
ALT	Altar Gold & Resources [*Vancouver Stock Exchange symbol*]
ALT	Alteration
ALT	Altered (DCTA)
ALT	Altering [*FBI standardized term*]
Alt	Alternaria [*A fungus*]
ALT	Alternate
alt	Alternating [*Polymer*] [*Organic chemistry*]
Alt	Alternating Light [*Navigation signal*]
ALT	Alternative (ROG)
ALT	Alternator (KSC)
ALT	Altesse [*Highness*] [*French*]
ALT	Altimeter (NG)
ALT	Altintas [*Turkey*] [*Seismograph station code. US Geological Survey*] (SEIS)
ALT	Altitude (AFM)
ALT	Alto

ALT .... Altoona [*Pennsylvania*]
ALT .... Altus, OK [*Location identifier*] [*FAA*]   (FAAL)
ALT .... American Law Times [*A publication*]   (DLA)
ALT .... Annales. Faculte des Lettres de Toulouse [*A publication*]
ALT .... Approach and Landing Test [*Aviation*]   (MCD)
ALT .... [*The*] Association of Law Teachers [*British*]
ALT .... Australian Law Times [*A publication*]   (APTA)
ALT .... Automatic Line Testing [*Telecommunications*]   (TEL)
ALT I .... Automotive Layshaft Transmission
ALT .... Livingston University, Livingston, AL [*Library symbol*]
    [*Library of Congress*]   (LCLS)
ALT .... RADAR Altimeter   (TEL)
ALT .... Rohstoff-Rundschau; Fachblatt des Gesamten Handels mit
    Altstoffen und Abfallstoffen, mit Ausfuehrlichen Berichten
    ueber die Internationalen Rohstoffmarkte und
    Altstoffmarkte [*A publication*]
ALTA .... Adventist Language Teachers Association   (EA)
ALTA .... Airline Traffic Association
ALTA .... Alberta [*Canadian province*]
Alta .... Alberta Law Reports [*A publication*]
ALTA .... Alta Gold Co. [*NASDAQ symbol*]   (NQ)
ALTA .... American Land Title Association   (EA)
ALTA .... American Library Trustee Association   (EA)
ALTA .... American Literary Translators Association   (EA)
ALTA .... Association of Local Transport Airlines [*Defunct*]   (EA)
ALTAC ...... Algebraic Translator and Compiler [*Data processing*]   (MCD)
Alta Couns ... Alberta Counsellor [*A publication*]
Alta Counslttr ... Alberta Counselletter [*A publication*]
Alta Dir ...... Alta Direccion [*A publication*]
Alta Engl .... Alberta English [*A publication*]
Alta Freq .... Alta Frequenza [*A publication*]
Alta Freq Suppl ... Alta Frequenza. Supplemento [*A publication*]
Alta Gaz ..... Alberta Gazette [*A publication*]   (DLA)
Alta Hist .... Alberta History [*A publication*]
Alta Hist R ... Alberta Historical Review [*A publication*]
ALTAIR .... ARPA [*Advanced Research Projects Agency*] Long-Range
    Tracking and Instrument RADAR
ALTAIR .... Automatic Logical Translation and Information Retrieval [*Data
    processing*]   (DIT)
Alta L .... Alberta Law [*A publication*]   (DLA)
Alta Learn Res J ... Alberta Learning Resources Journal [*A publication*]
Alta Libr Ass Bull ... Alberta Library Association. Bulletin [*A publication*]
Alta LQ ...... Alberta Law Quarterly [*A publication*]   (DLA)
Alta LR .... Alberta Law Reports [*A publication*]
Alta LR (2d) ... Alberta Law Reports, Second Series [*A publication*]
Alta L Rev ... Alberta Law Review [*A publication*]
Alta Mod Lang J ... Alberta Modern Language Journal [*A publication*]
ALTAN ...... Alternate Alerting Network [*Air Force*]
ALTAPE .... Automatic Line Tracer and Programming Equipment
Alta Pers .... Alberta Perspective [*A publication*]
ALTARE .... Automatic Logic Testing and Recording Equipment
Alta Report ... Alberta Reports [*Information service or system*] [*A
    publication*]
Alta Rev Stat ... Alberta Revised Statutes [*Canada*] [*A publication*]   (DLA)
Alta Rev Stat ... Revised Statutes of Alberta [*A publication*]
Alta Sci Ed J ... Alberta Science Education Journal [*A publication*]
Alta Sci Teach ... Alberta Science Teacher [*A publication*]
Alta Stat..... Alberta Statutes [*Canada*] [*A publication*]   (DLA)
Alta Stat..... Statutes of Alberta [*A publication*]
ALTB .... Acute Laryngotracheobronchitis [*Virus*]
ALT Bankr ... American Law Times, Bankruptcy Reports [*A
    publication*]   (DLA)
ALTBR ...... Law Times Bankruptcy Reports [*United States*] [*A
    publication*]   (DLA)
ALTCGC ... Arizona Long Term Care Gerontology Center [*University of
    Arizona*] [*Research center*]   (RCD)
Alt C I .... Alternative Culture and Institutions [*A publication*]
ALTCOM ... Alternate Command [*or Commander*] [*Navy*]   (NVT)
ALTCOM ... Alternate Command, Atlantic Fleet   (MCD)
ALTCOMCEN ... Alternate Command Center [*Navy*]   (NVT)
ALTCOMLANT ... Alternate Commander, Atlantic [*Navy*]   (NVT)
ALTCOMLANTFLT ... Alternate Command, Atlantic Fleet
ALTCOMPAC ... Alternate Commander, Pacific [*Navy*]   (NVT)
Alt County Gov't ... Alternative County Government [*A publication*]   (DLA)
Alt Criminol J ... Alternative Criminology Journal [*A publication*]
ALT DIEB ... Alternis Diebus [*Every Other Day*] [*Pharmacy*]
ALTDS ...... Apollo Launch Trajectory Data System [*NASA*]   (KSC)
ALTDS ...... Army LASER Target Designator System
ALTE......... Alta Energy Corp. [*NASDAQ symbol*]   (NQ)
ALTE......... Altitude Error
ALTE......... Altitude Transmitting Equipment [*FAA*]   (MSA)
ALTE......... Apparent Life-Threatening Episode [*Medicine*]
Alt Eg........ Alter Ego [*My Other Self*] [*Latin*]
ALTEL ...... Association of Long Distance Telephone Companies   (EA)
Al Tel Ca.... Allen's Telegraph Cases [*A publication*]   (DLA)
Alte Mod Kunst ... Alte und Moderne Kunst. Oesterreichische Fachzeitschrift
    des Marktes fuer Antiquitaeten, Bilder, Kunstgegenstaende
    Alter und Moderner Kunst [*A publication*]
Alt En........ Alternative Energy [*A publication*]
Alt Energy ... Alternative Energy Trends and Forecasts [*A publication*]
Alt Energy ... Alternative Sources of Energy [*A publication*]

Alte Orient Beih ... Alte Orient Beihefte [*A publication*]
ALTER...... Alteration   (ROG)
ALTER...... Alternate
Alter Med .. Alternative Medicine [*A publication*]
Altern......... Alternate Futures [*A publication*]
Alternate Energy Mag ... Alternate Energy Magazine [*A publication*]
Alternative Technol Power Prod ... Alternative Technologies for Power
    Production [*A publication*]
Alternat Non-Violentes ... Alternatives Non-Violentes [*A publication*]
Alternatv ... Alternatives [*A publication*]
Altern Energy Sources ... Alternative Energy Sources [*A publication*]
ALTERN HOR ... Alternis Horis [*Every Other Hour*] [*Pharmacy*]
Altern Methods Toxicol ... Alternative Methods in Toxicology [*A publication*]
Altern Press Index ... Alternative Press Index [*A publication*]
Alternstheorien Memb Giessener Symp Exp Gerontol ... Alternstheorien
    Zellkern Membranen Giessener Symposion ueber
    Experimentelle Gerontologie [*A publication*]
ALTERON ... Alteration
Altes Haus-Mod ... Altes Haus - Modern [*West Germany*] [*A publication*]
ALTF .... Airlift Task Force [*Air Force*]   (AFM)
ALTFFL ...... Alternating Fixed and Flashing [*Lights*]
ALTFGPGL ... Alternating Fixed and Group Flashing [*Lights*]
ALTFL....... Alternating Flashing [*Lights*]
Alt Ftr .... Alternative Features [*A publication*]
ALTGA ...... Ark-La-Tex Genealogical Association   (EA)
ALTGPOCC ... Alternating Group Occulting [*Lights*]
ALTH .... Althaea [*Rose of Sharon*] [*Pharmacology*]   (ROG)
ALTH .... Alumina Trihydrate [*Inorganic chemistry*]
Althaus Mod ... Althaus Modernisierung [*West Germany*] [*A publication*]
ALT HOR ... Alternis Horis [*Every Other Hour*] [*Pharmacy*]
ALTHQ ...... Alternate Headquarters [*Military*]   (AABC)
ALTI .... Altai, Inc. [*NASDAQ symbol*]   (NQ)
Alt Id......... Alter Idem [*Another Self*] [*Latin*]
ALTID....... Alteration Identification
ALTIHP ..... Avionics Laboratory Technical Information Handling Profile
ALT INST ... Alteration of Instruments [*Legal term*]   (DLA)
ALTL........ Alaska Tidelines [*A publication*]
AL/TL........ Antennule Length to Total Body Length Ratio [*of Crustacea*]
ALTLIB...... Alternate Library [*Computer program*] [*NASA*]
ALTM....... Altimeter   (KSC)
ALTMEA ... Alternative Medicine [*A publication*]
Alt Media... Alternative Media [*A publication*]
ALTN .... Alternacare Corp. [*Los Angeles, CA*] [*NASDAQ symbol*]   (NQ)
ALTN .... Alternate   (AFM)
ALTN .... Alternative   (IEEE)
Alt-Neuindische Stud ... Alt- und Neuindische Studien [*Wiesbaden*] [*A
    publication*]
ALT NOCT ... Alternis Nocte [*Every Other Night*] [*Pharmacy*]
ALTNR...... Alternator
ALTNTR.... Alternator   (MSA)
ALTNV...... Alternative   (MSA)
ALTO .... Altos Computer Systems [*NASDAQ symbol*]   (NQ)
Alt O .... Der Alte Orient [*A publication*]
ALTOCC .... Alternating Occulting [*Lights*]
ALTOGR.... Altogether   (ROG)
AltOrAT .... Alter Orient und Altes Testament [*Kevelaer/Neukirchen*] [*A
    publication*]   (BJA)
ALTP........ Airline Transport Pilot's Licence [*British*]   (AIA)
ALTP........ American Legion Transportation Post
ALTP........ Automatic Linear Temperature Programmer
Alt Press Ind ... Alternative Press Index [*A publication*]
Alt Pr J ...... Alternative Press, Libraries, Journalism [*A publication*]
ALTPT ...... Alternate Airport   (FAAC)
ALTR........ Altera Corp. [*NASDAQ symbol*]   (NQ)
ALTR........ Alteration   (AABC)
ALTR........ Alternate   (KSC)
ALTR........ Alternator [*Automotive engineering*]
ALTR........ American Law Times Reports [*A publication*]   (DLA)
ALTR........ Approach and Landing Test Requirement [*NASA*]   (NASA)
ALTRAN.. Algebraic Translator [*Programming language*] [*1969*]
ALTRAN.. Assembly Language Translator [*Xerox Corp.*]
ALTRD...... Altered   (MSA)
ALTRD...... Alternatives [*A publication*]
ALTREC .... Automatic Life Testing and Recording of Electronic
    Components [*Canada*]
ALTREU... Allgemeine Treuhandstelle fuer die Juedische Auswanderung [*A
    publication*]
ALTRN...... Alteration   (MSA)
ALTRNS ... American Law Times Reports, New Series [*United States*] [*A
    publication*]   (DLA)
ALTRON .. Alteration   (ROG)
Alt Routes .. Alternate Routes [*A publication*]
ALTRV...... Altitude Reservation [*Air Force*]   (AFM)
ALTS .... Advanced Lunar Transportation Systems
ALTS .... Aided LASER Tracking System   (RDA)
ALTS .... Alterations   (ROG)
ALT & S... [*The*] Alton & Southern Railway Co.
ALTS .... Altus Bank, A Federal Savings Bank [*NASDAQ symbol*]   (NQ)
ALTS .... Amerikos Lietuviu Tautine Sajunga [*National Lithuanian
    Society of America*]   (EA)

ALTS......... Analog Line Termination Subsystem [*Telecommunications*] (TEL)
ALTS......... Automated Land Titles System (ADA)
ALTS......... Automated Library Technical Services [*Program*] [*Los Angeles Public Library*]
ALTS......... Automatic LASER Test Set [*Hughes Aircraft Co.*]
ALTS......... Automatic Line Test Set [*Telecommunications*] (TEL)
ALTU........ Adder, Logical, and Transfer Unit [*Computer*]
ALTWR..... All Air Traffic Control Towers in Region [*FAA*] (FAAC)
ALTX......... Altex Industustries, Inc. [*NASDAQ symbol*] (NQ)
ALTZAB ... Allattenyesztes [*Animal Breeding*] [*A publication*]
ALU.......... Adult Literacy Unit [*British*]
ALU.......... Advanced Levitation Unit [*Materials processing*]
alu.............. Alabama [*MARC country of publication code*] [*Library of Congress*] (LCCP)
ALU.......... Allou Health & Beauty Care, Inc. Class A [*AMEX symbol*] (SPSG)
ALU.......... Alula [*Somalia*] [*Airport symbol*] (OAG)
ALU.......... Aluminium [*British*] (ADA)
ALU.......... Alushta [*USSR*] [*Seismograph station code, US Geological Survey*] [*Closed*] (SEIS)
ALU.......... Amble Resources Ltd. [*Vancouver Stock Exchange symbol*]
ALU.......... Annual Life Unit (MCD)
ALU.......... Arab Lawyers Union [*See also UAA*] [*Cairo, Egypt*] (EAIO)
A & LU ..... Arithmetic and Logic Unit [*Data processing*]
ALU.......... Arithmetic Logic Unit [*Data processing*]
ALU.......... Association for the Liberation of Ukraine (EA)
ALU.......... Asynchronous Line Unit [*Telecommunications*]
ALU.......... University of Lethbridge, Alberta [*Library symbol*] [*National Library of Canada*] (NLC)
ALU.......... University of Lethbridge Library [*UTLAS symbol*] (NLC)
ALUB........ Alubec Industries, Inc. [*NASDAQ symbol*] (NQ)
ALUCARD ... Aircraft Loss, Utilization, Combat, and Repair Damage (MCD)
ALUE....... Admissible Linear Unbiased Estimator [*Statistics*]
ALUG........ Department of Geography, University of Lethbridge, Alberta [*Library symbol*] [*National Library of Canada*] (NLC)
ALUIA....... Automated Living User Intervention Anarchy [*Data processing*]
Alum........ Aluminium [*A publication*] (APTA)
ALUM....... Aluminum [*Chemical symbol is Al*]
ALUM....... Alumnus (ROG)
ALUM....... Underwood McLellan Ltd., Lethbridge, Alberta [*Library symbol*] [*National Library of Canada*] (NLC)
ALUMA .... Aluminium [*A publication*]
Alum Abstr ... Aluminum Abstracts [*A publication*]
Alum Arch ... Aluminum Archiv [*A publication*]
Alum Co Am Res Lab Tech Pap ... Aluminum Company of America. Research Laboratories. Technical Paper [*A publication*]
Alum Finish Soc Kinki J ... Aluminum Finishing Society of Kinki. Journal [*A publication*]
ALUMINAUT ... Aluminium Submarine for Deep-Ocean Research [*Navy symbol*] [*British*]
Alumin Cour ... Aluminium Courier [*A publication*]
Alumin Wld ... Aluminium World [*A publication*] (APTA)
Alum Magnesium ... Aluminum and Magnesium [*A publication*]
ALUMN ..... Aluminum [*Chemical symbol is Al*]
Alumnae Mag ... Alumnae Magazine [*A publication*]
Alumnae Mag (Baltimore) ... Alumnae Magazine. Johns Hopkins Hospital. School of Nursing. Alumnae Association (Baltimore) [*A publication*]
Alum News Lett ... Aluminum News Letter [*A publication*]
Alumni Bull Sch Dent Indiana Univ ... Alumni Bulletin. School of Dentistry. Indiana University [*A publication*]
Alumni Bull Univ Mich Sch Dent ... Alumni Bulletin. University of Michigan. School of Dentistry [*A publication*]
Alumni Bull Univ Virginia ... Alumni Bulletin. University of Virginia [*A publication*]
Alumni Gaz Coll William ... Alumni Gazette. College of William and Mary [*A publication*]
Alumni Mag ... Alumni Magazine [*A publication*]
Alumni Mag Columbia Univ Presbyt Hosp Sch Nurs ... Alumni Magazine. Columbia University - Presbyterian Hospital. School of Nursing. Alumni Association [*A publication*]
Alumni Mag (NY) ... Alumni Magazine. Columbia University. Presbyterian Hospital School of Nursing Alumni Association (New York) [*A publication*]
Alum Non Ferrous Rev ... Aluminum and The Non-Ferrous Review [*A publication*]
Alum Ranshofen Mitt ... Aluminum Ranshofen Mitteilungen [*A publication*]
Alum Res Lab Tech Pap ... Aluminum Research Laboratories. Technical Paper [*A publication*]
Alum Rev ... Aluminum Review [*A publication*]
Alum Stat... Aluminum Statistical Review [*A publication*]
Alum Suisse ... Aluminum Suisse [*A publication*]
Alum Wld .. Aluminium World [*A publication*] (APTA)
Alum World Brass Copper Ind ... Aluminum World and Brass and Copper Industries [*A publication*]
Alum Yalen ... Alumni Yalensia [*Alumni of Yale College*] [*Latin*]
ALUOS...... Leeds University Oriental Society. Annual [*A publication*]
ALUR .... Allure Cosmetics Ltd. [*NASDAQ symbol*] (NQ)

ALURE...... Alternative Land Uses and the Rural Economy [*Ministry of Agriculture*] [*British*]
ALUR Rep ... Arctic Land Use Research Report [*A publication*]
ALUSLO... American Legation, United States Naval Liaison Officer
ALUSNA... American Legation, United States Naval Attache (MUGU)
ALUSNLO ... American Legation, United States Naval Liaison Officer (MCD)
ALUSNOB ... American Legation, United States Naval Observer
ALUT........ Aluta [*Leather*] [*Pharmacy*] (ROG)
ALUT .... Associateship of Loughborough University of Technology [*British*] (DBQ)
ALUTN ..... Aleutian [*FAA*] (FAAC)
ALUTS...... Aleutian Islands
ALV .... Abelson Leukemia Virus
ALV .... Acadia Mineral Ventures Ltd. [*Toronto Stock Exchange symbol*]
ALV............ Air-Launched Vehicle (AFM)
alv............... Alveolar [*Anatomy*]
ALV .... Alvus [*Stomach*] [*Medicine*] (ROG)
ALV .... Anthology of Light Verse [*A publication*]
ALV .... Archiv fuer Literatur und Volksdichtung [*A publication*]
ALV .... Autonomous Land Vehicle [*Military*] (RDA)
ALV .... Avian Leukosis Virus
ALV .... Gaylord, MI [*Location identifier*] [*FAA*] (FAAL)
ALV ADST ... Alvo Adstricta [*When the Bowels Are Constipated*] [*Pharmacy*]
Alv Adstrict ... Alvo Adstricta [*When the Bowels Are Constipated*] [*Pharmacy*]
Alvar .... [*Jacobus*] Alvarottus [*Deceased, 1453*] [*Authority cited in pre-1607 legal work*] (DSA)
Alvarot .... [*Jacobus*] Alvarottus [*Deceased, 1453*] [*Authority cited in pre-1607 legal work*] (DSA)
ALV DEJECT ... Alvi Dejectiones [*Discharge from the Bowels*] [*Pharmacy*]
ALVE......... Australian Leave and Holidays Practice Manual [*A publication*]
Alves .... Dampier and Maxwell's British Guiana Reports [*A publication*] (DLA)
ALVIN....... Alex [*Aarons*] and Vinton [*Freedley*] [*Theatrical producers of the 1920's and 1930's, after whom the Alvin Theatre in New York City was named*]
ALVIN....... Antenna Lobe for Variable Ionospheric Nimbus (IEEE)
ALVINN... Autonomous Land Vehicle in a Neural Network [*Military*]
ALVRJ ...... Advanced Low-Volume Ramjet
ALVRJ ...... Air-Launched Low-Volume Ramjet
ALW .... Air-Launched Weapon
ALW .... Alawas Gold Corp. [*Vancouver Stock Exchange symbol*]
ALW .... Allowance (AFM)
ALW .... Allowance Race [*Horse racing*]
ALW .... Arch-Loop-Whorl [*Basis of Galton's System of Fingerprint Classifications*]
ALW .... Archiv fuer Liturgiewissenschaft [*A publication*]
ALW .... Association of Lithuanian Workers (EA)
ALW .... Walla Walla [*Washington*] [*Airport symbol*] (OAG)
ALWC .... Williams [*A. L.*] Corp. [*NYSE symbol*] (CTT)
ALWC .... Williams [*A. L.*] Corporation [*NASDAQ symbol*] (NQ)
ALWF........ Actual Wind Factor [*Meteorology*] (FAAC)
ALWG .... Australian Legal Workers Group (ADA)
ALWG Newsletter ... Australian Legal Workers Group. Newsletter [*A publication*] (APTA)
ALWL........ Army Limited War Laboratory
ALWLA..... American Lithuanian Workers Literary Association (EA)
ALWMI..... Anterolateral Wall Myocardial Infarction [*Cardiology*]
ALWNAO ... Abhandlungen. Landesmuseum der Provinz Westfalen. Museum fuer Naturkunde [*A publication*]
ALWOS...... Automated Low-Cost Weather Observation System (MCD)
ALWS........ Advanced Lightweight SONAR [*Military*]
ALWS........ Allwaste, Inc. [*Stafford, TX*] [*NASDAQ symbol*] (NQ)
ALWT........ Advanced Lightweight Torpedo [*Navy*]
ALX .... Albany Resources [*Vancouver Stock Exchange symbol*]
ALX .... Alexander Bay [*New York*] [*Seismograph station code, US Geological Survey*] (SEIS)
ALX .... Alexander City, AL [*Location identifier*] [*FAA*] (FAAL)
ALX .... Alexander's, Inc. [*NYSE symbol*] (SPSG)
ALY .... Alexandria [*Egypt*] [*Airport symbol*] (OAG)
ALY .... Alley (MCD)
ALY .... Allied Cellular [*Vancouver Stock Exchange symbol*]
ALY .... Alloy
ALY .... Alyeska Air Service [*Anchorage, AK*] [*FAA designator*] (FAAC)
ALYA........ Army Laboratory of the Year Award (RDA)
Alyum Splavy Sb Statei ... Alyuminievye Splavy. Sbornik Statei [*USSR*] [*A publication*]
ALYX......... Analytix, Inc. [*Cambridge, MA*] [*NASDAQ symbol*] (NQ)
ALZ .... Alitak [*Alaska*] [*Airport symbol*] (OAG)
Alz.............. Alzamento [*Raising, Lifting*] [*Music*]
ALZ............. Assault Landing Zone (AFM)
ALZ .... Lazy Bay, AK [*Location identifier*] [*FAA*] (FAAL)
ALZAAY... ALZA Conference Series [*A publication*]
ALZA Conf Ser ... ALZA Conference Series [*A publication*]
AM............. Above Mentioned
AM............. Academy of Management [*Mississippi State, MS*] (EA)
AM............. Access Method [*Data processing*]

AM............ Accounts Maintenance [*IRS*]
AM............ Acetoxymethyl Ester
AM............ Acoustic-Magnetic   (NVT)
AM............ Acquisition Manager
AM............ Acta Musicologica [*A publication*]
AM............ Action Monegasque [*Monegasque Action*] [*Political party*]   (PPE)
AM............ Active Market [*Investment term*]
AM............ Active Monitor [*Telecommunications*]
AM............ Actomyosin [*Biochemistry*]
AM............ Actuator Mechanism   (NASA)
AM............ Adaptive Multiplexer   (CAAL)
AM............ Address Mark [*Microprocessors*]
AM............ Address Mode [*Data processing*]
AM............ Address Modifier
AM............ Administration and Management Operations [*Kennedy Space Center*] [*NASA*]   (NASA)
A/M.......... Administrative Management [*A publication*]
AM............ Administrative Manual
AM............ Adrenal Medulla [*Anatomy*]
AM............ Aeromexico [*Airline*]   (DS)
AM............ Aeronautical Radionavigation Mobile Station [*ITU designation*]
AM............ Aeronaves de Mexico SA [*Mexico*] [*ICAO designator*]   (ICDA)
AM............ Aerospace Medicine   (MCD)
AM............ After Market [*Investment term*]
AM............ Agricultural Marketing
A & M........ Agricultural and Mechanical [*In a college name*]
AM............ Agricultural Missions   (EA)
AM............ Air Marshal [*British*]
AM............ Air Mass [*Solar energy research*]
AM............ Air Mattress [*Medicine*]
AM............ Air Mechanician
AM............ Air Medal [*Military decoration*]
AM............ Air Ministry [*British*]
AM............ Air Mobile
AM............ Aircooled Motor
AM............ Airlock Module [*NASA*]
AM............ Airmail
AM............ Albert Medal [*British*]
AM............ Alert Message   (CINC)
AM............ Algonquin Mercantile Corp. [*Toronto Stock Exchange symbol*]
AM............ Alice Meynell [*British poet, 1847-1922*]
AM............ Alma Mater [*A publication*]
A & M........ [*Herb*] Alpert and [*Jerry*] Moss [*Initialism, from surnames of founders, is used as name of record company*]
AM............ Alpes Maritimes [*French*]
AM............ Alpha Meter   (MCD)
AM............ Alternaria mali [*A toxin-producing fungus*]
AM............ Alternate Mode   (CAAL)
AM............ Aluminum Matting [*Military*]
AM............ Alveolar Macrophage [*Hematology*]
AM............ AM International, Inc. [*Formerly, Addressograph-Multigraph Corp.*] [*NYSE symbol*]   (SPSG)
AM............ Amacrine Cell [*of the retina*] [*Optics*]
AM............ Amalgam [*Dentistry*]
AM............ Amatol [*Materials*]
AM............ Ambassadors of Mary   (EA)
AM............ Amber
AM............ Ambient   (KSC)
AM............ Amendment
AM............ America [*A publication*]
AM............ America   (ROG)
AM............ American
AM............ American Machinist [*A publication*]
AM............ American Mercury [*A publication*]
AM............ American Motorcyclist [*A publication*]
Am............ Americana [*A publication*]
AM............ [*The*] Americas: A Quarterly Review of Inter-American Cultural History [*A publication*]
Am............ Americium [*Chemical element*]
AM............ Ametropia [*Ophthalmology*]
AM............ Aminophylline [*A drug*]
AM............ Ammeter
AM............ Ammunition   (ADA)
Am............ Amores [*of Ovid*] [*Classical studies*]   (OCD)
Am............ Amorphous Material [*Agronomy*]
am .... Amortissement [*Redemption of stock*] [*French*]
Am............ Amos [*Old Testament book*]
A/M.......... Ampere per Meter [*Unit of magnetic field strength*]
AM............ Ampicillin [*Also, A, AMP*] [*Antibacterial compound*]
AM............ Amplifier [*JETDS nomenclature*] [*Military*]   (CET)
AM............ Amplitude Modulation [*Electronics*]
AM............ Ampoule
Am............ Amyl [*Organic chemistry*]
AM............ Analog Module [*Telecommunications*]   (TEL)
AM............ Ananda Marga   (EA)
A and M..... Ancient and Modern [*Hymns*]
AM............ Ancient Monuments Act [*Town planning*] [*British*]
AM............ Anderson Model [*Physics*]
A & M .... Andrews & McMeel [*Publisher*]

AM............ Angular Momentum
AM............ Annales du Midi; Revue de la France Meridionale [*Toulouse*] [*A publication*]
A d M........ Annales du Midi; Revue de la France Meridionale [*A publication*]
AM............ Annali Manzoniani [*A publication*]
AM............ Anno Mundi [*In the Year of the World*] [*Since 4004 BC*] [*Latin*]   (GPO)
AM............ Annus Mirabilis [*The Wonderful Year (1666)*] [*Latin*]   (GPO)
AM............ Anovular Menstruation
AM............ Ante Meridiem [*Before Noon*] [*Latin*]   (GPO)
AM............ Antenna Management   (NASA)
AM............ Anterior Mitochondrion [*Cytology*]
AM............ Anterior Mitral Leaflet [*Cardiology*]
AM............ Antimateriel [*Munitions*]
A & M........ Antitrust and Monopoly Subcommittee [*US Senate*]
A & M :...... Apostle and Martyr [*Church calendars*]   (ROG)
AM............ Apostolatus Maris [*Apostleship of the Sea - AOS*]   (EA)
AM............ Appalachian Mountains
AM............ Archipelago Mundi [*An international association*]   (EA)
A & M........ Archives and Manuscripts [*A publication*]
AM............ Archives des Murasu [*A publication*]   (BJA)
AM............ Archivio Muratoriano [*A publication*]
AM............ Arctic Missions [*Later, IM*]   (EA)
AM............ Area Multiplexer   (CAAL)
AM............ Arithmetic Mean [*Statistics*]   (DCTA)
AM............ Armillaria mellea [*A fungus*]
AM............ Arms Material   (AABC)
AM............ Arms Memorandum
AM............ Army Manual
AM............ Arousal Mechanism [*Medicine*]
AM............ Artium Magister [*Master of Arts*]
A et M........ Arts et Metiers [*Arts and Crafts*] [*French*]
AM............ Asamblea Majorera [*Spain*] [*Political party*]   (EY)
AM............ Aseptic Meningitis [*Medicine*]
AM............ Asia Major [*A publication*]
A & M .... Assembly and Maintenance   (KSC)
AM............ Assignment Memorandum [*Army*]   (AABC)
AM............ Assistant Manager
AM............ Assistant Minister [*Church of England in Australia*]
AM............ Associate Member
AM............ Association of Management   (EA)
AM............ Associative Memory [*Data processing*]
AM............ Assumed Mean
AM............ Astigmatism, Myopic [*Also, AsM*] [*Ophthalmology*]
AM............ Asynchronous MODEM
AM............ Athenische Mitteilungen [*A publication*]
AM............ Atlantic Monthly [*A publication*]
AM............ Atomic Migration
A-M .... Austin-Moore [*Prosthesis*] [*Medicine*]
AM............ Australian Magazine [*A publication*]   (APTA)
AM............ Australian Ministry [*A publication*]   (APTA)
AM............ Australian Monthly [*A publication*]   (APTA)
A/M.......... Automatic/Manual   (MDG)
AM............ Automatic Monitoring   (CET)
AM............ Automedica Corp. [*An association*] [*Defunct*]   (EA)
AM............ Auxiliary Marker [*Telecommunications*]   (TEL)
AM............ Auxiliary Memory
AM............ Auxiliary Minesweeper [*NATO*]
AM............ Ave Maria
AM............ Aviamilano [*Construzioni Aeronautiche SpA*] [*Italy*] [*ICAO aircraft manufacturer identifier*]   (ICAO)
A/M.......... Aviation Medicine [*Medical officer designation*] [*British*]
AM............ Aviation Medicine
AM............ Aviation Metalsmith
AM............ Aviation Structural Mechanic [*Navy rating*]
AM............ Awaiting Maintenance
AM............ Award of Merit [*Royal Horticultural Society*] [*British*]
AM............ Axiomesial [*Dentistry*]
AM............ Magrath Public Library, Alberta [*Library symbol*] [*National Library of Canada*]   (NLC)
am---- .... Malaya [*MARC geographic area code*] [*Library of Congress*]   (LCCP)
AM............ Member of the Order of Australia
AM............ Mine Countermeasure Tender [*Navy symbol*]
AM............ Mistress of Arts
AM............ Montgomery Public Library, Montgomery, AL [*Library symbol*] [*Library of Congress*]   (LCLS)
AM1.......... Aviation Structural Mechanic, First Class [*Navy rating*]
AM2.......... Air Mail Route Number 2
A/M²......... Amperes per Square Meter
A²M.......... Automated Auger Microprobe
AM2.......... Aviation Structural Mechanic, Second Class [*Navy rating*]
AM3.......... Aviation Structural Mechanic, Third Class [*Navy rating*]
AMA.......... Abstaining Motorists' Association   (EA)
AMA.......... Academy of Management. Journal [*A publication*]
AMA.......... Academy of Model Aeronautics   (EA)
AMA.......... Accessory Meningeal Artery [*Anatomy*]
AMA.......... Acoustical Materials Association [*Later, ABPA*]   (EA)
AMA.......... Adaptive Multifunction Antenna   (MCD)
AMA.......... Adhesives Manufacturers Association   (EA)

AMA......... Advanced Medical, Inc. [*AMEX symbol*] (SPSG)
AMA......... Advanced Minuteman Accelerometer
A & MA ..... Advertising and Marketing Association
AMA......... Aerospace Medical Association (MCD)
AMA......... Against Medical Advice
AMA......... Agricultural Marketing Administration [*World War II*]
AMA......... Agricultural Mechanization in Asia [*Japan*] [*A publication*]
AMA......... Ahmadiyya Muslim Association (EAIO)
AMA......... Air Materiel Area [*Later, Air Logistics Centers*] [*Air Force*]
AMA......... Aircraft Manufacturers Association [*Superseded by MAA*] (EA)
AMA......... Airhead Maintenance Area [*Military*] [*British*]
AMA......... Alternative Medical Association (EA)
Ama......... Amadeo [*Record label*] [*Austria, etc.*]
AMA......... Amalgamated Mining [*Vancouver Stock Exchange symbol*]
AMA......... Amarillo [*Texas*] [*Airport symbol*] (OAG)
AMA......... Amatignak Island [*Alaska*] [*Seismograph station code, US Geological Survey*] [*Closed*] (SEIS)
AMA......... Amazing Stories. Annual [*A publication*]
AMA......... Ambulance Manufacturers Association [*Later, TBEA*] (EA)
AmA......... American Annual [*A publication*]
AmA......... American Anthropologist [*A publication*]
AMA......... American Machinery Association
AMA......... American Maltese Association (EA)
AMA......... American Management Association [*New York, NY*] (EA)
AMA......... American Maritain Association (EA)
AMA......... American Maritime Association (EA)
AMA......... American Marketing Association [*Chicago, IL*] (EA)
AMA......... American Marketing Association. Proceedings [*A publication*]
AMA......... American Matthay Association (EA)
AMA......... American McAll Association (EA)
AMA......... American Mead Association [*Inactive*] (EA)
AMA......... American Medical Association (EA)
AMA......... American Medical Association, Division of Library and Archival Services, Chicago, IL [*OCLC symbol*] (OCLC)
AMA......... American Metaphysical Association (EA)
AMA......... American Ministerial Association (EA)
AMA......... American Missionary Association
AMA......... American Mobilehome Association (EA)
AMA......... American Monument Association (EA)
AMA......... American Motel Association (EA)
AMA......... American Motivational Association (EA)
AMA......... American Motorcyclist Association (EA)
AMA......... American Mule Association (EA)
AMA......... American Municipal Association [*Later, NLC*] (EA)
AMA......... American Mustang Association (EA)
AMA......... American Mutual Alliance [*Insurance association*] [*Later, Alliance of American Insurers*]
AMA......... Amfac, Inc. [*NYSE symbol*] (SPSG)
AMA......... Aminomalonic Acid [*Organic chemistry*]
AMA......... Aminomethyl Anthracene [*Organic chemistry*]
AMA......... Amyl Acetate [*Organic chemistry*]
AMA......... Analog Major Alarm (MCD)
AMA......... Angular Measurement Accuracy
AMA......... Antimalarial Agent
AMA......... Antimitochondral Antibodies [*Immunology*]
AMA......... Apparel Manufacturers Association (EA)
AMA......... Apple Management Association (EA)
AMA......... Archery Manufacturers Association [*Later, AMO*]
AMA......... Arena Managers Association [*Defunct*] (EA)
AMA......... Army Mounteering Association [*British military*] (DMA)
AMA......... ASROC [*Antisubmarine Rocket*] Missile Assembly
AMA......... Asset Management Account
AMA......... Assistant Masters' Association [*British*]
AMA......... Associate of the Museums Association [*British*] (EY)
AMA......... Association of Metropolitan Authorities [*British*]
AMA......... Association of Municipal Authorities [*British*] (DCTA)
AMA......... Associative Memory Address [*Data processing*]
AMA......... Associative Memory Array [*Data processing*]
AMA......... Atti e Memorie dell'Arcadia [*A publication*]
AMA......... Australian Medical Association
AMA......... Automated Modification Analyzer [*Data processing*]
AMA......... Automatic Malfunction Analysis (KSC)
AMA......... Automatic Memory Allocation [*Data processing*] (BUR)
AMA......... Automatic Message Accounting [*Bell Laboratories*] [*Telecommunications*]
AMA......... Automobile Manufacturers' Association [*Later, MVMA*] (EA)
AMA......... Mayerthorpe Public Library, Alberta [*Library symbol*] [*National Library of Canada*] (NLC)
AMA......... Metropolitan Washington Airport Service [*FAA*] (FAAC)
AMAA....... Adhesives Manufacturers Association of America [*Later, AMA*] (EA)
AMAA....... Airman Apprentice, Aviation Structural Mechanic, Striker [*Navy rating*]
AMAA....... American Maine-Anjou Association (EA)
AMAA....... American Medical Association Auxiliary (EA)
AMAA....... American Medical Athletic Association (EA)
AMAA....... Armenian Missionary Association of America (EA)
AMAA....... Army Mutual Aid Association [*Later, AAFMAA*] (EA)
AMAA....... Art Museum Association of America (EA)
AMAA....... Art Museums Association of Australia

AMAA....... Association of Medical Advertising Agencies (EA)
AMAAA.... Atti e Memorie. Accademia di Storia dell'Arte Sanitaria [*A publication*]
AMAABJ.. INTA [*Instituto Nacional de Tecnologia Agropecuaria*]. Manual Agropecuario [*A publication*]
AMA Arch Dermatol ... AMA [*American Medical Association*] Archives of Dermatology [*A publication*]
AMA Arch Dermatol Syphilol ... AMA [*American Medical Association*] Archives of Dermatology and Syphilology [*A publication*]
AMA Arch Gen Psychiatry ... AMA [*American Medical Association*] Archives of General Psychiatry [*A publication*]
AMA Arch Ind Health ... AMA [*American Medical Association*] Archives of Industrial Health [*A publication*]
AMA Arch Ind Hyg Occup Med ... AMA [*American Medical Association*] Archives of Industrial Hygiene and Occupational Medicine [*A publication*]
AMA Archs Internal Med ... AMA [*American Medical Association*] Archives of Internal Medicine [*A publication*]
AMAB....... Air Ministry's Accident Branch [*British*]
AMAB....... Air Mobile Assault Brigade (MCD)
AMAB....... Alaska Mutual Bancorporation [*NASDAQ symbol*] (NQ)
AMABE..... Associate Member of the Association of Business Executives [*British*] (DCTA)
AMAC....... Aircraft Monitor and Control (NG)
AMAC....... American Medical Alert Corporation [*NASDAQ symbol*] (NQ)
AMAC....... Arlington Memorial Amphitheater Commission [*Abolished 1960, functions transferred to Department of Defense*]
AMAC....... Armament Monitor and Control (CAAL)
AMAC....... Automated Multiparameter Analyzer for Cells
AMACAB ... Allied Military Administration Civil Affairs Branch [*World War II*]
Am Acad Arts & Sci Mem ... American Academy of Arts and Sciences. Memoirs [*A publication*]
Am Acad Arts & Sci Proc ... American Academy of Arts and Sciences. Proceedings [*A publication*]
Am Acad Child Psychiat J ... American Academy of Child Psychiatry. Journal [*A publication*]
Am Acad Matri Law J ... American Academy of Matrimonial Lawyers. Journal [*A publication*] (DLA)
Am Acad Ophthalmol Otolaryngol Trans Sect Ophthalmol ... American Academy of Ophthalmology and Otolaryngology. Transactions. Section on Ophthalmology [*A publication*]
Am Acad Ophthalmol Otolaryngol Trans Sect Otolaryngol ... American Academy of Ophthalmology and Otolaryngology. Transactions. Section on Otolaryngology [*A publication*]
Am Acad Opthalmol Otolaryngol Trans ... American Academy of Ophthalmology and Otolaryngology. Transactions [*A publication*]
Am Acad Optom Ser ... American Academy of Optometry Series [*A publication*]
Am Acad Orthop Surg Lectures ... American Academy of Orthopedic Surgery. Instructional Course Lectures [*A publication*]
Am Acad Pol & Soc Sci ... American Academy of Political and Social Science (DLA)
Am Acad Pol & Soc Sci Ann ... American Academy of Political and Social Science. Annals [*A publication*]
Am Acad Psychoanal J ... American Academy of Psychoanalysis. Journal [*A publication*]
Am Acad Relig J ... American Academy of Religion. Journal [*A publication*]
Am Acad Rome Mem ... American Academy in Rome. Memoirs [*A publication*]
AMACC .... Antimicrobial Agents and Chemotherapy [*A publication*]
AMACCQ ... Antimicrobial Agents and Chemotherapy [*A publication*]
AMA-CIPP ... American Medical Association Committee on Insurance and Prepayment Plans (EA)
AMACS..... Automatic Message Accounting Collecting System [*Telecommunications*] (TEL)
AMACU.... Adults Molested as Children United (EA)
AMACUS ... Automated Microfilm Aperture Card Updating System [*Army*]
AMAD....... Activity Median Aerodynamic Diameter
AMAD....... Airframe-Mounted Accessory Drive (MCD)
AMAD....... Association Mondiale des Arts Divinatoires [*Divinatory Arts World Association - DAWA*] [*Rillieux-La-Pape, France*] (EAIO)
AMAD....... Auxilium Meum a Deo [*My Help Cometh from the Lord*] [(*Ps., CXXI. 2) Motto of Christian, Margrave of Brandenburg-Baireuth (1581-1655)*]
AMADA.... Alle Macht aan de Arbeiders [*All Power to the Workers*] [*Belgium*] [*Political party*] (PPW)
AMADA.... Archery Manufacturers and Dealers Association [*Later, AMO*] (EA)
AMADAC ... Aminomethylalizarindiacetic [*Organic chemistry*]
AMADBS ... Archives Francaises des Maladies de l'Appareil Digestif [*A publication*]
AMA-DE... American Medical Association Drug Evaluation
AMADE .... Association Mondiale des Amis de l'Enfance [*World Association of Children's Friends*] [*Monaco*] (EAIO)
AMADS .... Airframe-Mounted Accessory Drive System
AMAE....... Air Member for Aeronautical Engineering [*British and Canadian*] [*World War II*]

AMAE .... Association of Mexican-American Educators (OICC)
AMAEF ..... Amark Explorations Ltd. [*NASDAQ symbol*] (NQ)
AMA-ERF ... American Medical Association Education and Research Foundation (EA)
AMAF .... Air Member for Accounts and Finance [*British and Canadian*] [*World War II*]
AMAFA ..... Air Mass and Frontal Analysis [*Meteorology*]
AMAG .... American Aggregates Corp. [*NASDAQ symbol*] (NQ)
AMAG .... American Mission for Aid to Greece
AMAG .... Army Materiel Acquisition Guidance
AMA Gazette ... Australian Medical Association. Gazette [*A publication*]
Am Ag Br ... American Agent and Broker [*A publication*]
AMAHA5 ... Acta Microbiologica. Academiae Scientiarum Hungaricae [*A publication*]
AMA/I .... AMA [*American Management Association*]/International [*New York, NY*] (EA)
AMAI .... Arena Managers Association, Incorporated [*Defunct*]
AMAJ .... American Alpine Journal [*A publication*]
AMaJ .... Judson College, Marion, AL [*Library symbol*] [*Library of Congress*] (LCLS)
AMA J Dis Child ... AMA [*American Medical Association*] Journal of Diseases of Children [*A publication*]
AMAL .... Aeronautical Medical Acceleration Laboratory [*Air Force*]
AMAL .... Amalgamated (ADA)
Amal .... Amalvius de Claris Aquis [*Flourished, 14th century*] [*Authority cited in pre-1607 legal work*] (DSA)
AMAL .... Authorized Medical Allowance List (CAAL)
AMAL .... Aviation Medical Acceleration Laboratory (MCD)
AMAL .... Mallaig Public Library, Alberta [*Library symbol*] [*National Library of Canada*] (NLC)
Amal Engng Union Mon J ... Amalgamated Engineering Union. Monthly Journal [*A publication*]
Amal Engr Union MJ ... Amalgamated Engineering Union. Monthly Journal [*A publication*] (APTA)
AMALG .... Amalgamated (EY)
Am Alma.... American Almanac [*A publication*]
Am Alpine Jour ... American Alpine Journal [*A publication*]
Am Alpine N ... American Alpine News [*A publication*]
AM-ALRI ... Anteromedial-Anterolateral Rotatory Instability [*Medicine*]
Amalvis ...... Amalvius de Claris Aquis [*Flourished, 14th century*] [*Authority cited in pre-1607 legal work*] (DSA)
AMAM ...... Army Materiel Command Mission Area Manager
AMAM ...... Atti e Memorie. Accademia di Scienze, Lettere, ed Arti di Modena [*A publication*]
AMAM ...... Manning Municipal Library, Alberta [*Library symbol*] [*National Library of Canada*] (NLC)
AMAMP ... Army Multibus Avionics Multi-Process (MCD)
AMAMS ... Advanced Medium Antitank Missile (MCD)
AM Am Soc CE ... Associate Member of the American Society of Civil Engineers
AMan......... Accademia di Mantova. Atti e Memorie [*A publication*]
AMAN....... Airman, Aviation Structural Mechanic, Striker [*Navy rating*]
AMAN....... Mannville Public Library, Alberta [*Library symbol*] [*National Library of Canada*] (NLC)
AMANDA ... Automized Medical Anamnesis Dialog Assistant [*Computer*]
AMANET ... Atlantic Antisubmarine Warfare Communication Net (NVT)
Am An Hosp Assoc Bul ... American Animal Hospital Association. Bulletin [*A publication*]
Am Ann...... Americana Annual [*A publication*]
Am Annals Deaf ... American Annals of the Deaf [*A publication*]
Am Ann Cas ... American Annotated Cases [*A publication*] (DLA)
Am Ann Deaf ... American Annals of the Deaf [*A publication*]
Am Ant....... American Anthropologist [*A publication*]
Am Ant....... American Antiquity [*A publication*]
Am Anth .... American Anthropologist [*A publication*]
Am Anthro ... American Anthropologist [*A publication*]
Am Anthro Assoc Newsl ... American Anthropological Association. Newsletter [*A publication*]
Am Anthrop ... American Anthropologist [*A publication*]
Am Anthropol ... American Anthropologist [*A publication*]
Am Antiq ... American Antiquarian [*A publication*]
Am Antiq ... American Antiquity [*A publication*]
Am Antiq Soc Proc ... American Antiquarian Society. Proceedings [*A publication*]
Am Antiques ... American Antiques [*A publication*]
Am Antiquit ... American Antiquity [*A publication*]
AMAP .... Adaptive Mobile Access Protocol (MCD)
AMAP .... Aerojet Mass Analyzer Program (MCD)
AMAP .... As Much As Possible [*Medicine*]
AMAP .... Atelier de Modelisation de l'Architecture des Plantes [*Software manufacturer*] [*Paris, France*]
AMAP .... Atti e Memorie. Accademia Patavina di Scienze, Lettere, ed Arti [*A publication*]
AMAPAC ... American Medical Association Political Action Committee
AMAPe...... Atti e Memorie. Accademia Petrarca [*A publication*]
AMAPS..... Advanced Manufacturing, Accounting, and Production System (MCD)
AMAPS..... Apogee Motor Assembly with Paired Satellites [*NASA*]
AMAPS/G ... Advanced Manufacturing, Accounting, and Production System for Government Contractors (MCD)

Am A Psych L Bull ... American Academy of Psychiatry and the Law. Bulletin [*A publication*] (DLA)
AMAR ...... Alvin, Mid-Atlantic Ridge [*Oceanography*]
AMAR ...... Amarco Resources Corp. [*NASDAQ symbol*] (NQ)
AMAR ...... Antimissile Array RADAR
AMAR ...... Marwayne Public Library, Alberta [*Library symbol*] [*National Library of Canada*] (NLC)
Am Arab Affairs ... American Arab Affairs [*A publication*]
AMARC .... Army Material Acquisition Reorganization Committee (MCD)
AMARC .... Army Materiel Acquisition Review Committee [*Terminated, 1974*]
AMARC .... Automatic Message Accounting Recording Center [*Telecommunications*] (TEL)
Am Arch .... American Architect [*A publication*]
Am Arch .... American Architect and Building News [*A publication*]
Am Archiv ... American Archivist [*A publication*]
Am Archivis ... American Archivist [*A publication*]
Am Archivist ... American Archivist [*A publication*]
Am Arch Rehabil Ther ... American Archives of Rehabilitation Therapy [*A publication*]
AMARS..... Air Mobile Aircraft Refueling System
AMARS..... Automatic Message Accounting Recording System [*Bell System*]
AMARS..... Automatic Message Address Routing System (AABC)
AMARS..... Autonetics Modular Airborne RADAR System
Am Artist ... American Artist [*A publication*]
Am Art J ... American Art Journal [*A publication*]
Am Art Rev ... American Art Review [*A publication*]
AMARTS.. American Arts Documentation Centre (EA)
AMARV ... Advanced Maneuvering Reentry Vehicle (MCD)
AMAS ...... Advanced Midcourse Active System (MCD)
AMAS ...... Air Member for Air Staff [*British and Canadian*] [*World War II*]
AMAS ...... American Military Assistance Staff
AMAS ...... Automatic Maneuvering Attack System [*Air Force*]
AMAS ...... Automatic Message Accounting System (MCD)
AMASCP ... Air Material Area Stock Control Point (NG)
AMASEE .. Associate Member of the Association of Supervisory and Executive Engineers [*British*] (DBQ)
AMASLG ... Association of Management Analysts in State and Local Government (EA)
AMASM ... Air Materiel Area System Management [*Air Force*]
AMASME ... Associate Member of the American Society of Mechanical Engineers
Am As Museums Pr ... American Association of Museums. Proceedings [*A publication*]
Am As Petroleum G B ... American Association of Petroleum Geologists. Bulletin [*A publication*]
Am As Pr Mem ... American Association for the Advancement of Science. Proceedings. Memoirs [*A publication*]
AMASS..... Amplitude Miss Distance Acoustical Scoring System (MCD)
AMASS..... Automatic Multiaddress Segregation System (MCD)
Am Assn Coll Reg J ... American Association of Collegiate Registrars. Journal [*A publication*]
Am Assn Col Teach Educ Yrbk ... American Association of Colleges for Teacher Education. Yearbook [*A publication*]
Am Assn Pet Geol Bul ... American Association of Petroleum Geologists. Bulletin [*A publication*]
Am Assn Pet Geologists Bull ... American Association of Petroleum Geologists. Bulletin [*A publication*]
Am Assn Sch Adm Off Rep ... American Association of School Administrators. Official Report [*A publication*]
Am Assn Univ Prof B ... American Association of University Professors. Bulletin [*A publication*]
Am Assn Univ Women J ... American Association of University Women. Journal [*A publication*]
Am Assoc Adv Sci Abstr Pap Natl Meet ... American Association for the Advancement of Science. Abstracts of Papers. National Meeting [*A publication*]
Am Assoc Adv Sci Comm Desert Arid Zones Res Contrib ... American Association for the Advancement of Science. Committee on Desert and Arid Zones Research. Contribution [*A publication*]
Am Assoc Adv Sci Publ ... American Association for the Advancement of Science. Publication [*A publication*]
Am Assoc Adv Sci Symp ... American Association for the Advancement of Science. Symposium [*A publication*]
Am Assoc Cereal Chem Monogr Ser ... American Association of Cereal Chemists. Monograph Series [*A publication*]
Am Assoc Ind Nurses J ... American Association of Industrial Nurses. Journal [*A publication*]
Am Assoc Pet Geol Bull ... American Association of Petroleum Geologists. Bulletin [*A publication*]
Am Assoc Pet Geol Mem ... American Association of Petroleum Geologists. Memoir [*A publication*]
Am Assoc Pet Geol Repr Ser ... American Association of Petroleum Geologists. Reprint Series [*A publication*]
Am Assoc Pet Geol Study Geol ... American Association of Petroleum Geologists. Studies in Geology [*A publication*]
Am Assoc Petroleum Geologists Mem ... American Association of Petroleum Geologists. Memoir [*A publication*]

Am Assoc Petroleum Geologists Pacific Sec Correlation Sec ... American Association of Petroleum Geologists. Pacific Section. Correlation Section [*A publication*]

Am Assoc Ret Per News Bul ... American Association of Retired Persons. News Bulletin [*A publication*]

Am Assoc Sm Res Comp N ... American Association of Small Research Companies. News [*A publication*]

Am Assoc State Local Hist Bull ... American Association for State and Local History. Bulletin [*A publication*]

Am Assoc Stratigr Palynol Contrib Ser ... American Association of Stratigraphic Palynologists. Contribution Series [*A publication*]

Am Assoc Text Chem Color Natl Tech Conf Book Pap ... American Association of Textile Chemists and Colorists. National Technical Conference. Book of Papers [*A publication*]

Am Assoc Univ Prof Bull ... American Association of University Professors. Bulletin [*A publication*]

Am Assoc Vet Lab Diagn Proc Annu Meet ... American Association of Veterinary Laboratory Diagnosticians. Proceedings of Annual Meeting [*A publication*]

Am Assoc Zoo Vet Annu Proc ... American Association of Zoo Veterinarians. Annual Proceedings [*A publication*]

Am Astronaut Soc Publ Sci Technol ... American Astronautical Society. Publications. Science and Technology [*A publication*]

Am Astronaut Soc Sci Technol Ser ... American Astronautical Society. Science and Technology Series [*A publication*]

Am Astron Soc Bull ... American Astronomical Society. Bulletin [*A publication*]

Am Astron Soc Photo Bull ... American Astronomical Society. Photo Bulletin [*A publication*]

Amat .... Amatorius [*of Plutarch*] [*Classical studies*] (OCD)

AMAT .... American Mission for Aid to Turkey

A-MAT ...... Amorphous Material [*Clinical medicine*]

AMAT .... Applied Materials, Inc. [*NASDAQ symbol*] (NQ)

AMAT .... Atti e Memorie. Accademia Toscana la Colombaria [*A publication*]

Amat Build Man ... Amateur Builder's Manual [*A publication*]

AMATC .... Air Material Armament Test Center

Amat Cine World ... Amateur Cine World [*A publication*]

Amat Ent.... Amateur Entomologist [*A publication*]

Amat Geol ... Amateur Geologist [*A publication*]

AMATIS ... Automated Meteorological and Terminal Information Service

Amat Narr ... Narrationum Amatoriarum Libellus [*of Parthenius*] [*Classical studies*] (OCD)

Amat Photogr ... Amateur Photographer [*A publication*]

AMATYC ... American Mathematical Association of Two Year Colleges (EA)

AMAU .... United States Air University, Maxwell Air Force Base, Montgomery, AL [*Library symbol*] [*Library of Congress*] (LCLS)

AMAUBB ... Acta Medica Austriaca [*A publication*]

AM Aus IMM ... Associate Member of the Australian Institute of Mining and Metallurgy

AMAV .... Avalon [*Australia*] [*ICAO location identifier*] (ICLI)

Am Aviation ... American Aviation [*A publication*]

AMAVS ..... Advanced Metallic Air Vehicle Structure (MCD)

AMAW .... Advanced Medium Antitank Weapon (MCD)

AMAX .... American Metal Climax, Inc. [*Later, AMAX, Inc.*]

AMAY .... Albury [*Australia*] [*ICAO location identifier*] (ICLI)

AMAZAP ... Amazoniana [*A publication*]

AMB .... Abstracts of Military Bibliography [*A publication*]

AMB .... Acta Medica Bulgarica [*A publication*]

AMB .... Active Magnetic Bearing [*Mechanical engineering*]

AMB .... Adjusted Monetary Base [*Economics*]

AMB .... Administrative Machine Branch [*Army*] (AABC)

AMB .... Admiralty Medical Board [*British military*] (DMA)

AMB .... Aerospace Medicine and Biology

AMB .... Air-Launched Missile Bulletin (MCD)

AMB .... Air Ministry Bulletin [*British military*] (DMA)

AMB .... Aircraft Maintenance Base

AMB .... Airways Modernization Board [*Functions transferred to FAA*]

AMB .... AMB. Revista da Associacao Medica Brasileira [*A publication*]

AMB .... Ambassador

AMB .... Amber (MSA)

AMB .... Amberquest Resources Ltd. [*Vancouver Stock Exchange symbol*]

AMB .... Ambient (MSA)

AMB .... Ambiguous [*Used in correcting manuscripts, etc.*]

AMB .... Ambilobe [*Madagascar*] [*Airport symbol*] (OAG)

Amb............ Ambler's Reports, Chancery [*27 English Reprint*] [*A publication*] (DLA)

Amb............ [*Saint*] Ambrose of Milan [*Deceased, 397*] [*Authority cited in pre-1607 legal work*] (DSA)

AMB .... Ambulance (AFM)

AMB .... Ambulatory [*Also, AMBUL*] [*Medicine*]

AMB .... Ambulong [*Philippines*] [*Seismograph station code, US Geological Survey*] [*Closed*] (SEIS)

AMB .... Ambush

AMB .... American Brands, Inc. [*NYSE symbol*] (SPSG)

AmB .... American Brunswick [*Record label*]

AMB .... Amphotericin B [*Antifungal agent*]

AMB .... Antarctic Meteorite Bibliography [*Lunar and Planetary Institute*] [*Database*]

AMB .... Antimotorboat

AMB .... Armament Material Bulletin (NG)

AMB .... Armoured Motor Battery [*British military*] (DMA)

AMB .... Army Maintenance Board

AMB .... Asbestos Mill Board [*Technical drawings*]

AMB .... Astronomy Missions Board [*NASA*]

AMB .... Auto-Manual Bridge Control [*Telecommunications*] (TEL)

AMB .... Bachelor of Mechanic Arts

AMB .... Blount, Inc., Montgomery, AL [*Library symbol*] [*Library of Congress*] (LCLS)

AMB .... Minesweeper, Harbor [*Navy symbol*] [*Obsolete*]

AMBA .... Ambassador Group, Inc. [*NASDAQ symbol*] (NQ)

Am BA .... American Bar Association (DLA)

AMBA .... American Malting Barley Association (EA)

AMBA .... American-Mideast Business Association (EA)

AMBA .... American Mold Builders Association (EA)

AMBA .... American Mustang and Burro Association (EA)

AMBA .... Angora Mohair Breeders of Australia

AMBA .... Associate Member of the British Arts Association (DBQ)

AMBA .... Association of Military Banks of America [*Bethesda, MD*] (EA)

Am Baby .... American Baby for Expectant and New Parents [*A publication*]

Am Baby Expectant New Parents ... American Baby for Expectant and New Parents [*A publication*]

AMBAC .... American Bosch Arma Corporation (MCD)

AMBAC .... American Municipal Bond Assurance Corporation

AMBAE..... Association of Master of Business Administration Executives [*New York, NY*] (EA)

AMBAER ... Arquivos. Museu Bocage. Serie A [*A publication*]

Am Bank .... American Banker [*A publication*]

Am Bank Assoc Bank Comp ... American Bankers Association. Bank Compliance [*A publication*]

Am Bank Assoc Bank Jnl ... American Bankers Association. Banking Journal [*A publication*]

Am Bankr ... American Bankruptcy [*A publication*] (DLA)

Am Bank R ... American Bankruptcy Reports [*A publication*] (DLA)

Am Bank Rev ... American Bankruptcy Review [*A publication*] (DLA)

Am Bankr L J ... American Bankruptcy Law Journal [*A publication*]

Am Bankr NS ... American Bankruptcy, New Series [*A publication*] (DLA)

Am Bankr R ... American Bankruptcy Reports [*A publication*] (DLA)

Am Bankr Reg ... American Bankruptcy Register [*A publication*] (DLA)

AMBANKRREP ... American Bankruptcy Reports

Am Bankr Rep NS ... American Bankruptcy Reports, New Series [*A publication*] (DLA)

Am Bankr Rev ... American Bankruptcy Review [*A publication*] (DLA)

Am Bankr R (NS) ... American Bankruptcy Reports, New Series [*A publication*] (DLA)

Am Bankrupt ... American Bankruptcy Law Journal [*A publication*]

Am Bankruptcy Reps ... American Bankruptcy Reports [*A publication*] (DLA)

Am Ban LJ ... American Bankruptcy Law Journal [*A publication*]

Am Bapt Q ... American Baptist Quarterly [*A publication*]

Am Bar A J ... American Bar Association. Journal [*A publication*]

Am Bar Ass J ... American Bar Association. Journal [*A publication*]

Am Bar Assn J ... American Bar Association. Journal [*A publication*]

Am Bar Assoc J ... American Bar Association. Journal [*A publication*]

Am Bar Asso Jour ... American Bar Association. Journal [*A publication*]

Am Bar Asso Rep ... American Bar Association Reports [*A publication*] (DLA)

Am Bar Found Res J ... American Bar Foundation. Research Journal [*A publication*]

Am Bar N... American Bar News [*A publication*]

Ambass ...... Ambassador

AMBBA .... Associated Master Barbers and Beauticians of America [*Later, HI/AMBBA*] (EA)

AMBBB..... Acta Microbiologica Polonica. Series B. Microbiologia Applicata [*A publication*]

AMBC .... American Bancorporation [*NASDAQ symbol*] (NQ)

AMBC .... American Minor Breeds Conservancy (EA)

AMBCS ..... Associate Member of the British Computer Society (DBQ)

AMBD .... Aminomethyl(methyl)benzothiadiazinedioxide [*Biochemistry*]

Am Bee J.... American Bee Journal [*A publication*]

Am Beekeep Fed Newsl ... American Beekeeping Federation. Newsletter [*A publication*]

Am Behavioral Sci ... American Behavioral Scientist [*A publication*]

Am Behavioral Scientist ... American Behavioral Scientist [*A publication*]

Am Behav Sci ... American Behavioral Scientist [*A publication*]

AMBEI .... Associate Member of the Institution of Body Engineers [*British*] (DBQ)

AMBEL..... Ambiguity Eliminator [*Electronics*]

Am Benedictine Rev ... American Benedictine Review [*A publication*]

AmBenR .... American Benedictine Review [*St. Paul, MN*] [*A publication*]

AMBERS .... A. M. Best Electronic Retrieval Services [*A. M. Best Co.*] [*Database*]

AMBF....... Ambassador Food Services Corp. [*NASDAQ symbol*] (NQ)

AMBF....... Asset Master Balance File [*Military*] (AABC)

Am B Found Res J ... American Bar Foundation. Research Journal [*A publication*]

AMBGA7 .. Annals. Missouri Botanical Garden [*A publication*]

AMBHAA ... Acta Microbiologica Hellenica [*A publication*]
AMBI .... Ambitious (DSUE)
AMBI .... American Bionetics, Inc. [*NASDAQ symbol*] (NQ)
AMBIB...... Abhandlungen. Akademie der Wissenschaften in Goettingen. Mathematisch-Physikalische Klasse. Beitraege zum Internationalen Geophysikalischen Jahr [*A publication*]
Am Bibliop ... American Bibliopolist [*A publication*]
Am Bib Repos ... American Biblical Repository [*A publication*]
AMBIEH... Antibiotics and Medical Biotechnology [*A publication*]
AMBIEH... Antibiotiki i Meditsinskaya Biotekhnologiya [*A publication*]
AMBIG...... Ambiguity (MCD)
AMBIM..... Associate Member of the British Institute of Management
Am Biol Tea ... American Biology Teacher [*A publication*]
Am Biol Teach ... American Biology Teacher [*A publication*]
Ambio Spec Rep ... Ambio. Special Report [*A publication*]
Am Biotechnol Lab ... American Biotechnology Laboratory [*A publication*]
Am Birds.... American Birds [*A publication*]
AMBIT...... Algebraic Manipulation by Identity Translation
AMBIT...... Augmented Built-In Test
AMBIT/L ... Acronym May Be Ignored Totally [*Data processing*] (CSR)
AMBJ....... American City Business Journals, Inc. [*Kansas City, MO*] [*NASDAQ symbol*] (NQ)
Am Bk Collec ... American Book Collector [*A publication*]
Am Bk Collector ... American Book Collector [*A publication*]
Am B'kc'y Rep ... American Bankruptcy Reports [*A publication*] (DLA)
AMBL........ Airmobile (AABC)
Ambl .... Ambler's Reports, Chancery [*27 English Reprint*] [*A publication*] (DLA)
AMBLADS ... Advise Method, Bill of Lading, and Date Shipped
Am Bld....... American Builder [*A publication*]
AMBM...... Association of Men's Belt Manufacturers [*Absorbed by BA*] (EA)
AMBNA.... Acta Medica et Biologica (Niigata) [*A publication*]
AMBNDV ... Arquivos. Museu Bocage. Serie B. Notas [*A publication*]
Am B News ... American Bar News [*A publication*] (DLA)
Am B (NS) ... American Bankruptcy, New Series [*A publication*] (DLA)
Am Book Publ Recd ... American Book Publishing Record [*A publication*]
Am Book Rev ... American Book Review [*A publication*]
AMBOP ..... American Board of Oral Pathology [*Later, ABOP*] (EA)
Am Bottler ... American Bottler [*A publication*]
AMBPBZ .. Acta Pathologica et Microbiologica Scandinavica. Section A. Pathology [*A publication*]
Am B Q ...... American Baptist Quarterly [*A publication*]
AMBR .... Amber Resources Co. [*NASDAQ symbol*] (NQ)
Ambr .... [*Saint*] Ambrose of Milan [*Deceased, 397*] [*Authority cited in pre-1607 legal work*] (DSA)
Am BR .... American Bankruptcy Reports [*A publication*] (DLA)
Ambra .... Alhambra [*Record label*] [*Spain*]
AMBRDL ... Army Medical Bioengineering Research and Development Laboratory (RDA)
Am Brew .... American Brewer [*A publication*]
Am Brew Rev ... American Brewer's Review [*A publication*]
AM Brit IRE ... Associate Member of the British Institution of Radio Engineers [*Later, AMIERE*]
AMBRL..... Army Medical Biomechanical Research Laboratory
Am BR (NS) ... American Bankruptcy Reports, New Series [*A publication*] (DLA)
Ambr Opizo ... Ambrosius Opizonus [*Flourished, 15th century*] [*Authority cited in pre-1607 legal work*] (DSA)
AMBSDC ... Arquivos. Museu Bocage. Serie C. Suplementos [*A publication*]
Am Bsns..... American Business [*A publication*]
Am Bsns Ed ... American Business Education [*A publication*]
Am Bsns Ed Yrbk ... American Business Education Yearbook [*A publication*]
AMBT .... Ambulatory (AABC)
AMBT .... American Biology Teacher [*A publication*]
AMBUCS ... National Association of American Business Clubs (EA)
AMBUDI .. Acta Microbiologica Bulgarica [*A publication*]
AMBUEJ... American Malacological Bulletin [*A publication*]
AMBUL ..... Ambulatory [*Also, AMB*] [*Medicine*]
Ambulance J ... Ambulance Journal [*A publication*]
Am Bur Geog B ... American Bureau of Geography. Bulletin [*A publication*]
AMBUSH ... Advanced Model Builder Shell [*Programming language*] [*1970*] (CSR)
Am Business ... American Business [*A publication*]
Am Bus Law ... American Business Law Journal [*A publication*]
Am Bus Law J ... American Business Law Journal [*A publication*]
Am Bus L J ... American Business Law Journal [*A publication*]
Am Butter R ... American Butter and Cheese Review [*A publication*]
AMBV .... Auxiliary Mexican Border Veterans (EA)
Amb de Vig ... Ambrosius de Vignate [*Flourished, 15th century*] [*Authority cited in pre-1607 legal work*] (DSA)
AMBYAR ... Advances in Marine Biology [*A publication*]
AMC......... Absent-Minded Club (EA)
AMC......... Account Manager Code (TEL)
AMC......... Acquisition Method Coding (MCD)
AMC......... Adenoma Malignum of the Cervix [*Oncology*]
AMC......... Advanced Memory Concepts (MCD)
AMC......... Advanced Minuteman Computer
AMC......... Advanced Motor Case (MCD)
AMC......... Aerodrome Surface Movement Control
AMC......... Aeromedical Monitor Console

AMC.......... Aerospace Manufacturers Council [*Defunct*] (EA)
AMC.......... Aerospace Medical Command [*Air Force*]
AMC.......... Agency Management Conference [*LIMRA*]
AMC.......... Agricultural Mortgage Corp. [*Finance*] [*British*]
AMC.......... Air-Launched Missile Change (MCD)
AMC.......... Air Mail Center
AMC.......... Air Materiel Command [*Later, Air Force Logistics Command*]
AMC.......... Air Ministry Constabulary [*British military*] (DMA)
AMC.......... Air Mission Commander [*Military*] (INF)
AMC.......... Air Monitoring Center [*Rockwell International Corp.*]
AMC.......... Air Mounting Centre [*British military*] (DMA)
AMC.......... Airborne Mode Control
AMC.......... Aircraft Manufacturer's Council
AMC.......... Aircraft Manufacturing Company (MCD)
AMC.......... Aircraft Model Change
AMC.......... Aircraft Motion Compensation
AMC.......... AiResearch Manufacturing Company
AMC.......... Airspace Management Center (MCD)
AMC.......... Airspace Management and Control (MCD)
AMC.......... Alarm Monitor Computer
AMC.......... Alberta Microelectronic Centre [*University of Alberta*] [*Research center*] (RCD)
AMC.......... Albertus Magnus College [*New Haven, CT*]
AMC.......... All Major Commands (MCD)
AMC.......... Allied Mediterranean Commission [*World War II*]
AMC.......... Almaden [*California*] [*Seismograph station code, US Geological Survey*] (SEIS)
AMC.......... Alternate Media Center [*New York University*] [*New York, NY*] [*Telecommunications*]
AMC.......... Amador Central Railroad Co. [*AAR code*]
AMC.......... AMCA Resources Ltd. [*Vancouver Stock Exchange symbol*]
AmC.......... American Catalogue [*A bibliographic publication*]
AMC.......... American College, Bryn Mawr, PA [*OCLC symbol*] (OCLC)
AmC.......... American Columbia [*Record label*]
AMC.......... American Maritime Cases
AMC.......... American Mining Congress (EA)
AMC.......... American Mission to the Chinese [*Later, American Mission to the Chinese and Asian*] (EA)
AMC.......... American Monitor Corporation (MCD)
AMC.......... American Mothers Committee (EA)
AMC.......... American Motors Corporation
AMC.......... American Movers Conference (EA)
AMC.......... American Movie Classics [*Cable-television network*]
AMC.......... American Multi Cinema [*Third largest theatre chain in America*]
AMC.......... American Music Center (EA)
AMC.......... American Music Center. Newsletter [*A publication*]
AMC.......... American Music Conference (EA)
AMC.......... Amino-Methyl-Coumarin
AMC.......... Angular Motion Compensator
AMC.......... Animal Medical Center (EA)
AMC.......... Antimalaria Campaign
AMC.......... Appalachian Mountain Club (EA)
AmC.......... Arcata Microfilm Corporation, Winston-Salem, NC [*Library symbol*] [*Library of Congress*] (LCLS)
AMC.......... Archival and Manuscripts Control [*USMARC format*] [*Data processing*]
AMC.......... Arm Muscle Circumference
AMC.......... Armament Material Change (NG)
AMC.......... Armed Merchant Cruiser [*Obsolete*] [*Navy*] [*British*]
AMC.......... Army Materiel Command [*Formerly, DARCOM*] [*Alexandria, VA*]
AMC.......... Army Medical Center
AMC.......... Army Medical Corps
AMC.......... Army Missile Command
AMC.......... Army Mobility Command
AMC.......... Army Munitions Command [*Later merged with Army Weapons Command*]
AMC.......... Art Master's Certificate
AMC.......... Art Material Club [*Later, AMMA*] (EA)
AMC.......... Arthrogryposis Multiplex Congenita [*Medicine*]
AMC.......... Asian Media Coalition [*Inactive*] (EA)
AMC.......... Associated Merchandising Corporation
AMC.......... Associated Minority Contractors of America (EA)
AMC.......... Associated Motor Carriers Tariff Bureau, Saint Paul MN [*STAC*]
AMC.......... Association of Management Consultants (EA)
AMC.......... Association Medicale Canadienne [*Canadian Medical Association - CMA*]
AMC.......... Association of Mercy Colleges (EA)
AMC.......... Association of Municipal Corporations [*British*]
AMC.......... Associative Memory Computer [*Data processing*]
AMC.......... Atlantic Marine Center [*National Oceanic and Atmospheric Administration*]
AMC.......... Australian Media Contacts [*A publication*] (ADA)
AMC.......... Australian Medical Council
AMC.......... Auto-Manual Center [*Telecommunications*] (TEL)
AMC.......... Automatic Message Counting
AMC.......... Automatic Mission Control
AMC.......... Automatic Mixture Control
AMC.......... Automatic Modulation Control (DEN)

AMC......... Autonomous Multiplexer Channel
AMC......... Auxiliary Coastal Minesweepers [*Navy symbol*]
AMC......... Average Monthly Consumption   (MCD)
AMC......... Aviation Maintenance Costs
AMC......... Aviation Structural Mechanic, Chief [*Navy rating*]
AMC......... Avionics Materiel Conference   (EA)
AMC......... Axial Magma Chamber [*Geology*]
AMC......... Axiomesiocervical [*Dentistry*]
AMC......... Millarville Community Library, Alberta [*Library symbol*] [*National Library of Canada*]   (NLC)
AMCA....... Advanced Materiel Concepts Agency [*Alexandria, VA*] [*Army*]
AMCA....... Aft Motor Control Assembly   (NASA)
AM & CA... Air Movement and Control Association   (EA)
AMCA....... Air Movement and Control Association   (EA)
AMCA....... Alaskan Malamute Club of America   (EA)
AMCA....... American Appraisal Association [*Arlington Heights, IL*] [*NASDAQ symbol*]   (NQ)
AMCA....... American Medical Curling Association   (EA)
AMCA....... American Mission to the Chinese and Asian   (EA)
AMCA....... American Mosquito Control Association   (EA)
AMCA....... Amino(methyl)coumarinacetate [*Organic chemistry*]
AMcA........ Antimicrosomal Antibody [*Clinical chemistry*]
AMCA....... Antique Motorcycle Club of America   (EA)
AMC of A.. Associated Male Choruses of America   (EA)
AMCADC... Army Materiel Command Administrative Data Center
AMCADS... Army Materiel Command Announcement Distribution System   (RDA)
AMC-AF... Air Materiel Command [*later, Air Force Logistics Command*] - Air Force
AMCAL..... Allied Master Chemists of Australia Ltd.
AMCALMSA ... Army Materiel Command Automated Logistics Management Systems Agency   (AABC)
Am Camellia Yearb ... American Camellia Yearbook [*American Camellia Society*] [*A publication*]
AMCAPS.. Automatic Multiple-Parameter Collection Processing System [*Air Force*]   (MCD)
AMCARS.. Automated Maintenance Control and Records System   (MCD)
AMCAS..... American Medical College Application Service
AmCAS...... Centre for American and Commonwealth Arts and Studies [*British*]   (CB)
Am Cath His Rec ... American Catholic Historical Society. Records [*A publication*]
Am Cath His S ... American Catholic Historical Society. Records [*Philadelphia*] [*A publication*]
AmCathHS ... American Catholic Historical Society. Records [*A publication*]
Am Cath Q ... American Catholic Quarterly Review [*A publication*]
Am Cattle Prod ... American Cattle Producer [*A publication*]
AMCAWS ... Advanced Medium-Caliber Aircraft Weapon System   (MCD)
AMCB....... Aluminum Manufacturers Credit Bureau [*Defunct*]   (EA)
AMCB....... American Medical Center for Burma [*Defunct*]   (EA)
AMCB....... Army Materiel Command Board [*Aberdeen Proving Ground, MD*]   (MCD)
AMCBMC ... Air Materiel Command [*later, Air Force Logistics Command*] Ballistic Missile Center   (IEEE)
AMCBO.... Association of Major City Building Officials   (EA)
AMCBW ... Amalgamated Meat Cutters and Butcher Workmen of North America [*Later, UFCWIU*]   (EA)
AMCC....... American Continental Corporation [*NASDAQ symbol*]   (NQ)
AMCC....... American Mexican Claims Commission [*Terminated, 1947*]
AMCC....... Army Material Command Circular   (MCD)
AMCC....... Army Metrology and Calibration Center
AMCC....... Association of Manufacturers of Confectionery and Chocolate   (EA)
AMCCC..... Australian Maritime College Courses Committee
AMCCDO ... Army Materiel Command Catalog Data Office   (AABC)
AMCC-MM ... Army Metrology and Calibration Center Metrology Development and Engineering Division
AMCCOM ... US Army Armament, Munitions, and Chemical Command [*Pronounced "a-m-c-com"*] [*Rock Island, IL*]   (RDA)
AMCCOMR ... Armament, Munitions, and Chemical Command Regulation [*Military*]
AMCD....... Addressograph-Multigraph Copier Duplicator
AMCD....... Annular Momentum Control Device [*NASA*]
AMCD....... Association for Multicultural Counseling and Development   (EA)
AMCDC .... Army Materiel Command Data Center
AMCDDC ... Army Materiel Command Depot Data Center
AMCE .... American Claims Evaluation, Inc. [*NASDAQ symbol*]   (NQ)
AMCEA .... Advertising Media Credit Executives Association [*Toledo, OH*]   (EA)
AMCEC..... Allied Military Communications-Electronics Committee   (AABC)
AMCEE..... Association for Media-Based Continuing Education for Engineers   (EA)
Am Cent Dig ... American Digest (Century Edition) [*A publication*]   (DLA)
Am Ceramic Soc Jour ... American Ceramic Society. Journal [*A publication*]
Am Ceram S ... American Ceramic Society. Bulletin [*A publication*]
Am Ceram Soc Bull ... American Ceramic Society. Bulletin [*A publication*]
Am Ceram Soc Fall Meet Mater Equip Whitewares Div Proc ... American Ceramic Society. Fall Meeting. Materials and Equipment. Whitewares Division. Proceedings [*A publication*]

Am Cer Soc Bul ... American Ceramic Society. Bulletin [*A publication*]
Am Cer Soc J ... American Ceramic Society. Journal [*A publication*]
AMCF........ Air Materiel Command [*later, Air Force Logistics Command*] Forms
AMCF........ Alkali Metal Cleaning Facility [*Nuclear energy*]   (NRCH)
AMCFASC ... Army Materiel Command Facilities and Services Center   (AABC)
AMCFO .... Army Materiel Command Field Office   (RDA)
AMCFSA .. Army Materiel Command Field Safety Agency   (AABC)
AMCGO.... Army Materiel Command General Order
AMCH....... Crescent Heights High School, Medicine Hat, Alberta [*Library symbol*] [*National Library of Canada*]   (NLC)
AMCHA.... Aminomethylcyclohexanecarboxylic Acid [*Pharmacology*]
Am Chamber Commer Japan J ... American Chamber of Commerce in Japan. Journal [*A publication*]
AmCham HK ... American Chamber of Commerce in Hong Kong   (EA)
AMCHCCP ... Association for Maternal and Child Health and Crippled Children's Programs   (EA)
Am Ch Dig ... American Chancery Digest [*A publication*]   (DLA)
Am Chem... American Chemist [*A publication*]
Am Chem J ... American Chemical Journal [*A publication*]
Am Chem Soc Div Environ Chem Prepr ... American Chemical Society. Division of Environmental Chemistry. Preprints [*A publication*]
Am Chem Soc Div Fuel Chem Prepr ... American Chemical Society. Division of Fuel Chemistry. Preprints [*A publication*]
Am Chem Soc Div Fuel Chem Prepr Pap ... American Chemical Society. Division of Fuel Chemistry. Preprints of Papers [*A publication*]
Am Chem Soc Div Fuel Prepr ... American Chemical Society. Division of Fuel Chemistry. Preprints [*A publication*]
Am Chem Soc Div Gas Fuel Chem Prepr ... American Chemical Society. Division of Gas and Fuel Chemistry. Preprints [*A publication*]
Am Chem Soc Div Org Coat Plast Chem Pap ... American Chemical Society. Division of Organic Coatings and Plastics Chemistry. Papers [*A publication*]
Am Chem Soc Div Org Coat Plast Chem Pap Meet ... American Chemical Society. Division of Organic Coatings and Plastics Chemistry. Papers Presented at the Meeting [*A publication*]
Am Chem Soc Div Pet Chem Gen Pap Prepr ... American Chemical Society. Division of Petroleum Chemistry. General Papers. Preprints [*A publication*]
Am Chem Soc Div Pet Chem Prepr ... American Chemical Society. Division of Petroleum Chemistry. Preprints [*A publication*]
Am Chem Soc Div Pet Chem Symp ... American Chemical Society. Division of Petroleum Chemistry. Symposia [*A publication*]
Am Chem Soc Div Petr Chem Prepr ... American Chemical Society. Division of Petroleum Chemistry. Preprints [*A publication*]
Am Chem Soc Div Polym Chem Prepr ... American Chemical Society. Division of Polymer Chemistry. Preprints [*A publication*]
Am Chem Soc Div Water Air Waste Chem Gen Pap ... American Chemical Society. Division of Water, Air, and Waste Chemistry. General Papers [*A publication*]
Am Chem Soc J ... American Chemical Society. Journal [*A publication*]
Am Chem Soc Jt Conf Chem Inst Can Abstr Pap ... American Chemical Society. Joint Conference with the Chemical Institute of Canada. Abstracts of Papers [*A publication*]
Am Chem Soc Mon ... American Chemical Society. Monograph [*A publication*]
Am Chem Soc Rep Annu Meet Corp Assoc ... American Chemical Society. Report. Annual Meeting. Corporation Associates [*A publication*]
Am Chem Soc Rubber Div Symp ... American Chemical Society. Rubber Division. Symposia [*A publication*]
Am Chem Soc Symp Ser ... American Chemical Society. Symposium Series [*A publication*]
Am Child.... American Child [*A publication*]
Am Childh ... American Childhood [*A publication*]
Am Chiro ... American Chiropractor [*A publication*]
Am Choral R ... American Choral Review [*A publication*]
AMCHQ.... Air Materiel Command [*later, Air Force Logistics Command*] Headquarters
AmChQ...... American Church Quarterly [*New York*] [*A publication*]
Am Christmas Tree Grow J ... American Christmas Tree Growers' Journal [*A publication*]
Am Christmas Tree J ... American Christmas Tree Journal [*A publication*]
Am Church Mo ... American Church Monthly [*A publication*]
Am Church R ... American Church Review [*A publication*]
AMCI........ AM Communications, Inc. [*NASDAQ symbol*]   (NQ)
AMCI .... Ameritech Mobile Communications, Incorporated [*Schaumburg, IL*] [*Telecommunications*]   (TSSD)
AMCIA...... American City [*A publication*]
AMCIC...... Army Materiel Command Information Center
AMCID ..... Accumulation Mode Charge Injection Device   (MCD)
AMCID ..... Army Materiel Command Installation Division
AMCIGW ... Army Materiel Command Inspector General, Western Inspection Activity
AMCIL...... Army Materiel Command International Logistics Directorate   (MCD)

AMCILR ...   Actas y Memorias. Congreso Internacional de Linguistica Romanica [*A publication*]

AMCIM ....   Actes et Memoires. Congres International de Langue et Litterature du Midi de la France [*A publication*]

Am Cin.......   American Cinematographer [*A publication*]

Am Cinem ...   American Cinematographer [*A publication*]

Am Cinematgr ...   American Cinematographer [*A publication*]

Am Cinematog ...   American Cinematographer [*A publication*]

AMCI & SA ...   Army Materiel Command Installations and Service Agency   (AABC)

AMCISO...   Actes et Memoires. Congres International des Sciences Onomastiques [*A publication*]

AMCIT......   Actes et Memoires. Congres International de Toponymie [*A publication*]

Am City......   American City [*A publication*]

Am City (C ed) ...   American City (City Edition) [*A publication*]

Am City Cty ...   American City and County [*A publication*]

Am City (T & C ed) ...   American City (Town and Country Edition) [*A publication*]

Am Civ LJ ...   American Civil Law Journal [*A publication*]

AMCL ....   Air Materiel Command [*later, Air Force Logistics Command*] Letter

AMCL ....   Amended Clearance [*Aviation*]   (FAAC)

A-MCL......   Anterior Portion - Medial Collateral Ligament [*Anatomy*]

AMCL ....   Association of Metropolitan Chief Librarians [*London*]

AMCLDC ...   Army Materiel Command Logistic Data Center   (AABC)

Am Clin......   America Clinica [*A publication*]

Am Clin Climatol Assoc Trans ...   American Clinical and Climatological Association. Transactions [*A publication*]

Am CLJ .....   American Civil Law Journal [*A publication*]   (DLA)

AMCLO ....   Air Materiel Command [*later, Air Force Logistics Command*] Liaison Office [*or Officer*]

AMCLO ....   Air Materiel Command [*later, Air Force Logistics Command*] Logistics Office [*or Officer*]

AMCLSSA ...   Army Materiel Command Logistics Systems Support Agency   (AABC)

AMCM ......   Advanced Mine Countermeasures   (MCD)

AMCM ......   Air Materiel Command [*later, Air Force Logistics Command*] Manual

AMCM ......   Airborne Mine Countermeasure Equipment

AMCM ......   Anti-Mine Countermeasure   (MCD)

AMCM ......   Army Materiel Command Memorandum

AMCM ......   Aviation Structural Mechanic, Master Chief [*Navy rating*]

AMCMAU ...   Annales. Musee Colonial de Marseille [*A publication*]

AMCMFO ...   Air Materiel Command [*later, Air Force Logistics Command*] Missile Field Office

AMCMR ...   Army Materiel Command Materiel Requirements Directorate   (MCD)

AMCMS....   Airborne Mine Countermeasure System   (NG)

AMCN.......   Amacan Resources Corp. [*NASDAQ symbol*]   (NQ)

AMCN(NSW) ...   Associate Member of the College of Nursing (New South Wales) [*Australia*]

AMCO.......   Afro-Mauritian Common Organization

AmCo.........   American Micro Company, Kansas City, MO [*Library symbol*] [*Library of Congress*]   (LCLS)

AMCO.......   American Midland Corporation [*NASDAQ symbol*]   (NQ)

AMCODE ...   AMEX [*American Stock Exchange*] Computerized Order Display and Execution System

Am Coll......   American Collector [*A publication*]

Am Coll Physicians Bull ...   American College of Physicians. Bulletin [*A publication*]

Am Coll Physicians Obs ...   American College of Physicians. Observer [*A publication*]

Am Col Toxicol J ...   American College of Toxicology. Journal [*A publication*]

AMCOM...   AMEX [*American Stock Exchange*] Communications [*Network*]

AMCON....   American Consul

Am Concrete Inst J ...   American Concrete Institute. Journal [*A publication*]

Am Concr Inst J ...   American Concrete Institute. Journal [*A publication*]

Am Concr Inst Monogr ...   American Concrete Institute. Monograph [*A publication*]

Am Concr Inst Publ SP ...   American Concrete Institute. Publication SP [*A publication*]

Am Concr Inst SP ...   American Concrete Institute. Special Publication [*A publication*]

AMCONGEN ...   American Consulate General   (CINC)

AMCONREPO ...   American Consular Reporting Officer

Am Consul Bul ...   American Consular Bulletin [*A publication*]

Am Contract ...   American Contractor [*A publication*]

Am Co-Op J ...   American Co-Operative Journal [*A publication*]

AMCOR ....   Atlantic Margin Coring Project

Am Corp Cas ...   American Corporation Cases, by Withrow [*A publication*]   (DLA)

AMCORR ...   American Committee for Rescue and Resettlement of Iraqi Jews   (EA)

Am Correct Ther J ...   American Corrective Therapy Journal [*A publication*]

AMCOS ....   Aldermaston Mechanised Cataloging and Ordering System [*British*]   (DIT)

AMCOS ....   Army Manpower Cost   (RDA)

Am Cosmet Perfum ...   American Cosmetics and Perfumery [*A publication*]

Am Counc Cons Int Proc ...   American Council on Consumer Interest. Proceedings [*A publication*]

Am Counc Jud Issues ...   American Council for Judaism. Issues [*A publication*]

AMCP ....   ADL [*Avionics Development Laboratory*] Master Control Program [*NASA*]   (NASA)

AMCP ....   Allied Military Communications Panel

AMCP ....   Anhydrous Monocalcium Phosphate [*Inorganic chemistry*]

AMCP ....   Army Materiel Command Pamphlet   (MCD)

AMCPA......   American Managed Care Pharmacy Association   (EA)

AMCPI......   Army Materiel Command Procurement Instructions

AMCPP....   Army Materiel Command Procurement and Production Directorate

AMCR ....   Air Materiel Command [*later, Air Force Logistics Command*] Regulations

AMCR ....   Amcor Capital Corp. [*NASDAQ symbol*]   (NQ)

Am Cr ....   American Criminal Reports [*A publication*]   (DLA)

AMCR ....   Army Materiel Command Regulations

AMCRA ....   American Managed Care and Review Association   (EA)

Am Craft .....   American Craft [*A publication*]

AMCRC....   AMC [*American Motors Corporation*] Rambler Club   (EA)

AMCRD....   Army Materiel Command Research and Development

Am Creamery ...   American Creamery and Poultry Produce Review [*A publication*]

AMCRIC...   Aviation Material Combat Ready In-Country   (MCD)

Am Crim Law ...   American Criminal Law Review [*A publication*]

Am Crim L Q ...   American Criminal Law Quarterly [*A publication*]

Am Crim LR ...   American Criminal Law Review [*A publication*]

Am Crim L Rev ...   American Criminal Law Review [*A publication*]

AMCROSS ...   American Red Cross

Am Cr R ...   American Criminal Reports [*A publication*]   (DLA)

Am Cr Rep ...   American Criminal Reports, Edited by Hawley [*A publication*]   (DLA)

Am Cr R (Hawley) ...   American Criminal Reports, Edited by Hawley [*A publication*]   (DLA)

Am Cr Tr ...   American Criminal Trials (Chandler) [*A publication*]   (DLA)

Am Cryst Assoc Trans ...   American Crystallographic Association. Polycrystal Book Service. Transactions [*A publication*]

AMCS........   Advanced Mail Coding System   (MCD)

AMCS.......   Airborne Missile Control System

AMCS.......   Aircraft Mounted Control System

AMCS.......   Army Mobilization Capabilities Study

AMCS.......   Association for Mexican Cave Studies   (EA)

AMCS.......   Association of Military Colleges and Schools of the US   (EA)

AMCS.......   Automatic Motion Control System   (MCD)

AMCS.......   Aviation Structural Mechanic, Senior Chief [*Navy rating*]

AMCSA.....   Army Materiel Command Support Activity

AMCSI......   Associate Member of the Construction Surveyor's Institute [*British*]   (DBQ)

AMCSS .....   Advanced Materials Cargo Sling System   (MCD)

AMCSS .....   Airborne Missile Control Subsystem

AMCT ....   Associate of Manchester College of Technology [*British*]

AMCTAH ...   Antibiotic Medicine and Clinical Therapy [*A publication*]

AMCTB.....   Associated Motor Carriers Tariff Bureau   (EA)

AMCTC.....   Army Materiel Command Technical Committee

AMCTSO ...   Air Materiel Command [*later, Air Force Logistics Command*] Test Site Office

AMCU.......   Adults Molested as Children United   (EA)

AMC(U)....   Minesweeper, Coastal (Underwater Locator) [*Navy symbol*]

AM CUR ...   Amicus Curiae [*Friend of the Court*] [*Latin*] [*Legal term*]   (ADA)

AMCV ....   Australia's Military Commitment to Vietnam

Am Cyanamid Co Miner Dressing Notes ...   American Cyanamid Company. Mineral Dressing Notes [*A publication*]

Am Cyanamid Co Tech Bull ...   American Cyanamid Company. Technical Bulletin [*A publication*]

AMD........   Acacia Mineral [*Vancouver Stock Exchange symbol*]

AMD.........   Accident Model Document [*NASA*]   (KSC)

AMD.........   Actinomycin-D [*Also, act-D, DACT*] [*Antineoplastic drug*]

AMD.........   Administrative Machine Division [*Army*]   (AABC)

AMD.........   Administrative and Miscellaneous Duties [*RAF*] [*British*]

AMD.........   Advance Manufacturing Directive

AMD.........   Advanced Micro Devices, Inc. [*Computer manufacturer*] [*NYSE symbol*]   (SPSG)

AMD.........   Aero-Mechanics Department [*Navy*]   (MCD)

AMD.........   Aeromedical Data

AMD.........   Aerospace Materials Document   (MCD)

AMD.........   Aerospace Medical Division [*Brooks Air Force Base, TX*] [*Air Force*]

AMD.........   Age-Related Macular Degeneration [*Ophthalmology*]

AMD.........   Ahmedabad [*India*] [*Airport symbol*]   (OAG)

AMD.........   Air Movement Data [*Air Force*]

AMD.........   Air Movement Designator [*Army*]

AMD.........   Aircraft Maintenance Department [*Military*]   (AFIT)

AMD.........   Alliance pour Une Mauritanie Democratique [*Alliance for One Democratic Mauritania*]   (PD)

AMD.........   Alpha Activity Median Diameter [*Nuclear energy*]   (NRCH)

AMD.........   Alpha-Methyldopa [*Also, MD*] [*Antihypertensive compound*]

AMD.........   Alternating Monocular Deprivation [*Optics*]

AMD.........   Ambulance Manufacturers Division [*An association*]   (EA)

AMD......... Amderma [*USSR*] [*Seismograph station code, US Geological Survey*] [*Closed*] (SEIS)
AMD......... Amend
AmD.......... American Decca [*Record label*]
Am D......... American Decisions [*A publication*] (DLA)
AMD.......... American Demographics [*A publication*]
AmD.......... American Diagnostics Corp.
AmD........... American Dialog [*A publication*]
AMD......... America's Manifest Destiny [*An association*] (EA)
AMD......... Applied Mechanics Division [*American Society of Mechanical Engineers*]
AMD......... Approved Marine Devices Co. (MCD)
AMD......... Army Medical Department
AMD......... Association for Macular Diseases (EA)
AMD......... Associative Memory Device [*Data processing*] (DIT)
AMD......... Asteroid Meteoroid Detector
AMD......... Atomic and Molecular Physical Data Program [*American Society for Testing and Materials*] (IID)
AMD...:..... Automated Maintenance Depot
AMD......... Automated Mooney Decay [*Chemical engineering*]
AMD......... Automated Multiple Development [*Chromatography*]
AMD......... Automatic Map Display (MCD)
AMD......... Auxiliary Memory Drum
AMD......... Axiomesiodistal [*Dentistry*]
AMD......... Bozeman, MT [*Location identifier*] [*FAA*] (FAAL)
AMD......... Scheppend Ambacht. Tweemaandelijks Tijdschrift voor Toegepaste Kunst [*A publication*]
AMDA...... Advanced Maneuvering Demonstrator Aircraft (MCD)
AMDA...... Advances for Mutual Defense Assistance
AMDA...... Airline Medical Directors Association (EA)
AMDA...... American Medical Directors Association (EA)
AMDA...... American Microcomputer Dealers Association (EA)
AMDA...... American Milking Devon Association (EA)
AMDA...... Anglo-Malaysian Defence Agreement
AMDA...... Armada Corp. [*NASDAQ symbol*] (NQ)
AMDA...... Associated Minicomputer Dealers of America (EA)
AMDAC.... Amdahl Diagnostics Assistance Center
Am Daffodil Yearb ... American Daffodil Yearbook [*A publication*]
AMDAG.... American Decartelization Agency [*Post-World War II*]
Am Dairy Prod R ... American Dairy Products Review [*A publication*]
Am Dairy R ... American Dairy Review [*A publication*]
Am Dairy Rev ... American Dairy Review [*A publication*]
AMDAPS ... Automatic Meteorological Data Acquisition and Processing System (MCD)
AMDAR .... Automated Manpower Data Department of the Navy Reports (MCD)
AMDAS .... Automatic Magnetic Data Acquisition System (MCD)
AMD/BA... Avions Moral Dassault/Bregnet Aviation [*Later, GAMD*] [*French*]
AMDC....... American Dynamics Corporation [*Santa Ana, CA*] [*NASDAQ symbol*] (NQ)
AMDC....... American Modern Dance Caucus (EA)
AMDC....... Army Missile Defense Command (AABC)
AMDC....... Army Missile Development Center (MCD)
AMDC....... Assistant Marshal of the Diplomatic Corps [*British*]
AMDC....... Australian Mycotoxin Data Centre
AMDCL...... Association of Metropolitan District Chief Librarians [*British*]
AMDE....... Association of Medical Deans in Europe (EAIO)
Am Dec ...... American Decisions, Select Cases [*San Francisco, CA*] [*A publication*] (DLA)
Am Dec's.... American Decisions [*A publication*] (DLA)
AMDEL Bul ... AMDEL [*Australian Mineral Development Laboratories*] Bulletin [*A publication*]
AMDEL Bull ... AMDEL [*Australian Mineral Development Laboratories*] Bulletin [*A publication*]
Am Demogr ... American Demographics [*A publication*]
Am Demographics ... American Demographics [*A publication*]
AMDEN .... Adult Males, Density Of [*Ecology*]
Am Dent Surg ... American Dental Surgeon [*A publication*]
AMDEX .... Automated Maintenance Data Exchange (MCD)
AMDF....... Army Master Data File (AABC)
AMDFRMS ... Army Master Data File Reader Microfilm System [*Later, ARMS*] (AABC)
AMDGF .... Alveolar-Macrophage-Derived Growth Factor [*Biochemistry*]
AMDI .... Admiralty Merchant Ship Defense Instructions [*British*]
AMDI .... Applied Medical Devices [*NASDAQ symbol*] (NQ)
AMDI .... Automatic Miss Distance Indicator
AMDIB ...... Annales de Medecine Interne [*A publication*]
AMDIBO .. Annales de Medecine Interne [*A publication*]
Am Dietet Assn J ... American Dietetic Association. Journal [*A publication*]
Am Dig....... American Digest [*A publication*] (DLA)
Am Dig Cent Ed ... American Digest (Century Edition) [*A publication*] (DLA)
Am Dig Dec Ed ... American Digest (Decennial Edition) (West) [*A publication*] (DLA)
Am Dig Decen Ed ... American Digest (Decennial Edition) (West) [*A publication*] (DLA)
Am Dig Eighth Dec Ed ... American Digest (Eighth Decennial Edition) (West) [*A publication*] (DLA)
Am Dig Fifth Dec Ed ... American Digest (Fifth Decennial Edition) (West) [*A publication*] (DLA)

Am Dig Fourth Dec Ed ... American Digest (Fourth Decennial Edition) (West) [*A publication*] (DLA)
Am Dig Key No Ser ... American Digest (Key Number Series) (West) [*A publication*] (DLA)
Am Dig Secd Dec Ed ... American Digest (Second Decennial Edition) (West) [*A publication*] (DLA)
Am Dig Seventh Dec Ed ... American Digest (Seventh Decennial Edition) (West) [*A publication*] (DLA)
Am Dig Sixth Dec Ed ... American Digest (Sixth Decennial Edition) (West) [*A publication*] (DLA)
Am Dig Third Dec Ed ... American Digest (Third Decennial Edition) (West) [*A publication*] (DLA)
AMDL....... Abstract Machine Description Language [*1977*] [*Data processing*] (CSR)
AMDL....... Air Munitions Development Laboratory (MUGU)
AMDLEVAC ... Aeromedical Evacuation [*Later, AME*]
AMDLS...... Agricultural Meteorological Data Logging System (NOAA)
AMDM...... Association of Microbiological Diagnostic Manufacturers (EA)
AMDM...... Atti e Memorie. Deputazione di Storia Patria per le Antiche Provincie Modenesi [*A publication*]
AMDMA... American Metal Detector Manufacturers Association (EA)
AMDNA4 ... Annali di Medicina Navale [*A publication*]
AMDO...... Aeronautical Maintenance Duty Officer
AMDO....... American Merchandise Display Osaka [*Department of Commerce*] [*Japan*] (IMH)
AMDOC.... American Doctors [*Later, PCOS*] (EA)
Am Doc ...... American Documentation [*A publication*]
AMDP....... Air Member for Development and Production [*Air Ministry*] [*British*]
AMDP....... Aircraft Maintenance Delayed for Parts [*Military*]
AMDPAA ... Acta Medica Polona [*A publication*]
AMDR...... Advance Missile Deviation Report
AMDRA .... American Motorcycle Drag Racing Association [*of the National Hot Rod Association*] [*Later, NMRA*] (EA)
Am Drop Forger ... American Drop Forger [*A publication*]
Am Drug .... American Druggist [*A publication*]
Am Druggist ... American Druggist [*A publication*]
Am Druggist Merch ... American Druggist Merchandising [*A publication*]
Am Drug Pharm Rec ... American Druggist and Pharmaceutical Record [*A publication*]
Am Drycleaner ... American Drycleaner [*A publication*]
AMDS .... Advanced Missions Docking System [*or Subsystem*] [*NASA*] (NASA)
AMDS .... Agri-Markets Data Service [*Capitol Publications, Inc.*] [*Database*] [*Defunct*]
AMDS .... Airborne Mine Detection System (MCD)
AMDS .... Association of Military Dental Surgeons
AMDS .... Automatic Message Distribution System (CET)
AMDSB..... Amplitude Modulation, Double Sideband [*Electronics*]
AMDSB/SC ... Amplitude Modulation, Double Sideband, Suppressed Carrier [*Electronics*] (CET)
AMDSPAM ... Atti e Memorie. Deputazione di Storia Patria per le Antiche Provincie Modenesi [*A publication*]
AMDSPPM ... Atti e Memorie. Deputazione di Storia Patria per le Provincie delle Marche [*A publication*]
AMD Symp Ser (Am Soc Mech Eng) ... AMD Symposia Series (American Society of Mechanical Engineers) [*A publication*]
AMDT .... Active Maintenance Downtime
AMDT .... Amendment (AABC)
AMDU....... Aerospace Maintenance and Development Unit (MCD)
AMDV....... Devonport [*Australia*] [*ICAO location identifier*] (ICLI)
Am Dye Rep ... American Dyestuff Reporter [*A publication*]
Am Dyest Rep ... American Dyestuff Reporter [*A publication*]
Am Dyestuf ... American Dyestuff Reporter [*A publication*]
Am Dyestuff Reptr ... American Dyestuff Reporter [*A publication*]
AME......... Accord Monetaire Europeen
AME......... Admiralty Mining Establishment [*British*] (MCD)
AME......... Adult Migrant Education [*Department of Labor*]
AME......... Advanced Master of Education
AME......... Aeromedical Evacuation [*Formerly, AE, AMDLEVAC*] (AABC)
AME......... African Methodist Episcopal [*Church*]
AME......... Aircraft Mission Equipment (MCD)
AME......... Aircraft Movement Element (MCD)
AME......... Airspace Management Element (MCD)
AME......... Alliance Missionnaire Evangelique [*Missionary Evangelical Alliance - MEA*] [*Renens, Switzerland*] (EAIO)
AME......... Alliance for Monetary Education (EA)
AME......... Alternariol Methyl Ether [*Biochemistry*]
AME......... Alternate Mission Equipment (MCD)
AME......... Alveolar Mixing Efficiency [*Physiology*]
AME......... Amchitka East [*Alaska*] [*Seismograph station code, US Geological Survey*] [*Closed*] (SEIS)
AME......... American Economist [*A publication*]
AME......... Ametek, Inc. [*NYSE symbol*] (SPSG)
AME......... Amphotericin B Methyl Ester [*A drug*]
AME......... Amplitude Modulation Equivalent [*Telecommunications*] (TEL)
AME......... Angle Measuring Equipment
AME......... Antimultipath Equipment
A-ME........ Arcuate-Median Eminence [*Anatomy*]

AME......... Associated Memory Equipment
AME......... Association for Management Excellence [*Later, AAIM*]   (EA)
AME......... Association for Manufacturing Excellence   (EA)
AME......... Association of Membership Executives   (EA)
AME......... Astronaut Maneuvering Equipment [*NASA*]   (MCD)
AME......... Automatenmarkt [*A publication*]
AME......... Automatic Microfiche Editor
AME......... Automatic Monitoring Equipment
AME......... Automotive Mechanical and Electrical [*Test*]
AME......... Average Monthly Earnings
AME......... Aviation Medical Examiner
AME......... Aviation Structural Mechanic, Safety Equipment [*Navy rating*]
AME......... Medley Public Library, Alberta [*Library symbol*] [*National Library of Canada*]   (NLC)
AME......... MERADCOM [*Mobility Equipment Research and Development Command*] Technical Library, Fort Belvoir, VA [*OCLC symbol*]   (OCLC)
AMEA...... AME, Inc. [*NASDAQ symbol*]   (NQ)
AMEA...... Apparel Manufacturing Executives Association   (EA)
AMEA...... Association of Machinery and Equipment Appraisers   (EA)
AMEAA... Aviation Structural Mechanic, Safety Equipment, Airman Apprentice [*Navy rating*]
AMEAB5... Australia. Commonwealth Scientific and Industrial Research Organisation. Division of Mechanical Engineering. Annual Report [*A publication*]
AMEAMS ... Adaptive Multibeam Experiment for Aeronautical and Maritime Services   (MCD)
AMEAN.... Aviation Structural Mechanic, Safety Equipment, Airman [*Navy rating*]
AMEBA..... Annales Medicinae Experimentalis et Biologiae Fenniae [*A publication*]
AMEC ...... Acoustic Model Evaluation Committee [*Woods Hole Oceanographic Institution*]   (MSC)
AMEC ...... Advanced Manufacturing Engineering Council
AMEC ...... Aft Master Events Controller [*NASA*]   (NASA)
AMEC ...... Airframe Manufacturing Equipment Committee
AMEC ...... Association of Management Education Centres [*British*]
AMEC ...... Australian Manufacturers' Export Council
AMEC ...... Australian Marine Engineering Corp. Ltd.
Am Eccles Rev ... American Ecclesiastical Review [*A publication*]
AMECD .... Association for Measurement and Evaluation in Counseling and Development   (EA)
AMECEA ... Association of Member Episcopal Conferences in Eastern Africa [*Nairobi, Kenya*]   (EAIO)
AMECFA .. Aerospace Engineering Test Establishment, Canadian Forces Base Coal Lake, Medley, Alberta [*Library symbol*] [*National Library of Canada*]   (NLC)
AMECH .... Account Mechanical   (FAAC)
Am Ecl ...... American Eclectic [*A publication*]
Am Econ .... American Economist [*A publication*]
AMECON ... Australian Marine Engineering Consolidated Ltd.
Am Econ Assn Bul ... American Economic Association. Bulletin [*A publication*]
Am Econ Assoc ... American Economic Association. Publications [*A publication*]
Am Econ Assoc Publ ... American Economic Association. Publications [*A publication*]
Am Economist ... American Economist [*A publication*]
Am Econ R ... American Economic Review [*A publication*]
Am Econ Rev ... American Economic Review [*A publication*]
Am Econ R Pa & Proc ... American Economic Review. Papers and Proceedings [*A publication*]
Am & E Corp Cas ... American and English Corporation Cases [*A publication*]   (DLA)
Am & E Corp Cas NS ... American and English Corporation Cases, New Series [*A publication*]   (DLA)
AMECOS ... Automatic Measuring, Computing, and Sorting
AME/COTAR ... Angle Measuring Equipment, Correlation Tracking and Ranging
Am Ec R..... American Economic Review [*A publication*]
Am Ec Rev ... American Economic Review [*A publication*]
AMECZ..... Antimechanized [*Army*]   (AABC)
Am Ed ...... American Edition   (DLA)
AMED....... American Education [*A publication*]
AMED....... Automedix Sciences, Inc. [*NASDAQ symbol*]   (NQ)
A Med Biol ... Acta Medica et Biologica [*A publication*]
A Med Cost ... Acta Medica Costarricense [*A publication*]
AMEDD.... Army Medical Department   (AABC)
AMED/DC ... Army Medical Corps/Dental Corps
AMEDDPAS ... Army Medical Department Property Accounting System   (AABC)
A Med Hist Pat ... Acta Medicae Historiae Patavina [*A publication*]
A Med Ir .... Acta Medica Iranica [*A publication*]
A Med Nag ... Acta Medica Nagasakiensia [*A publication*]
A Med Ok ... Acta Medicinae Okayama [*A publication*]
A Med Or ... Acta Medica Orientalia [*A publication*]
AMed P...... Allied Medical Publications   (NATG)
A Med Pat ... Acta Medica Patavina [*A publication*]
AMEDPC ... Automotive Manufacturers EDP [*Electronic Data Processing*] Council   (EA)
A Med Phil ... Acta Medica Philippina [*A publication*]

Am Ed Res J ... American Educational Research Journal [*A publication*]
AMEDS..... Army Medical Science
AMEDS..... Army Medical Service
A Med Scand ... Acta Medica Scandinavica [*A publication*]
A Med Sci Hung ... Acta Medica. Academiae Scientiarum Hungaricae [*A publication*]
Am Educ .... American Education [*A publication*]
Am Educ Res ... American Educational Research Journal [*A publication*]
A Med Univ Kag ... Acta Medica Universitatis Kagoshimaensis [*A publication*]
A Med Ven ... Acta Medica Venezolana [*A publication*]
A Med Vietn ... Acta Medica Vietnamica [*A publication*]
AMEE .... Admiralty Marine Engineering Establishment [*British*]
AMEE .... Association for Medical Education in Europe [*Scotland*]
AMEEGA ... American Medical Electroencephalographic Association   (EA)
Am & E Eq D ... American and English Decisions in Equity [*A publication*]   (DLA)
A Meet Ent Soc Am ... Annual Meeting. Entomological Society of America [*A publication*]
A Meet Kans St Hort Soc ... Annual Meeting. Kansas State Horticultural Society [*A publication*]
AMEG .... Ambient Multimedia Environmental Goals [*Environmental Protection Agency*]
AMEG .... Association for Measurement and Evaluation in Guidance [*Later, AMECD*]   (EA)
Am Egg & Poultry R ... American Egg and Poultry Review [*A publication*]
AMEGS.... AMSAA [*Army Materiel Systems Analysis Agency*] Missile End Game Simulation   (MCD)
AMEI .... American Medical Electronics, Incorporated [*Dallas, TX*] [*NASDAQ symbol*]   (NQ)
AMEIC...... Associate Member of Engineering Institute of Canada
AMEL....... Aero-Mechanical Engineering Laboratory [*Army*]   (RDA)
AMEL....... Aeromedical Equipment Laboratory
AMEL....... Aircraft Multiengine Land [*Pilot rating*]   (IEEE)
AMELA3... American Journal of Medical Electronics [*A publication*]
Am El Ca ... American Electrical Cases [*A publication*]   (ILCA)
Am Elec Ca ... American Electrical Cases [*A publication*]   (ILCA)
Am Elect Cas ... American Electrical Cases [*A publication*]   (DLA)
Am Electl Cas ... American Electrical Cases [*A publication*]   (ILCA)
Am Electr Cas ... American Electrical Cases [*A publication*]   (DLA)
Am Electrochem Soc Trans ... American Electrochemical Society. Transactions [*A publication*]
Am Electroplat Soc Ann Tech Conf ... American Electroplaters' Society. Annual Technical Conference [*A publication*]
AMEM ...... African Methodist Episcopal Mission
AMEM ...... Association of Marine Engine Manufacturers   (EA)
AMEMA ... Anales de Mecanica y Electricidad [*A publication*]
AMEMB ... American Embassy   (AFM)
AMEMIC ... Association of Mill and Elevator Mutual Insurance Companies   (EA)
AMEN....... [*The*] Amnews Holding Corp. [*NASDAQ symbol*]   (NQ)
AMEN....... Association Mondiale pour l'Energie Non-Polluante [*Planetary Association for Clean Energy - PACE*]
AMEN....... Melbourne/Essendon [*Australia*] [*ICAO location identifier*]   (ICLI)
Amenage Territ Droit Foncier ... Amenagement du Territoire et Droit Foncier [*A publication*]
Amenag et Nature ... Amenagement et Nature [*A publication*]
Amenag Territ Develop Region ... Amenagement du Territoire et Developpement Regional [*A publication*]
Am Enameler ... American Enameler [*A publication*]
Am Enc Dict ... American Encyclopedic Dictionary [*A publication*]   (DLA)
AMEND.... Abusive Men Exploring New Directions [*In association name AMEND Network*]
AMEND.... Amendment
AMENDT ... Amendment
Am Eng ...... American Engineer [*A publication*]
Am & Eng Ann Cas ... American and English Annotated Cases [*A publication*]   (DLA)
Am-Eng Ann Cases ... American and English Annotated Cases [*A publication*]   (DLA)
Am & Eng Corp Cas ... American and English Corporation Cases [*A publication*]   (DLA)
Am Eng Corp Cas NS ... American and English Corporation Cases, New Series [*United States*] [*A publication*]   (DLA)
Am & Eng Corp Cas NS ... American and English Corporation Cases, New Series [*A publication*]   (DLA)
Am & Eng Dec in Eq ... American and English Decisions in Equity [*A publication*]   (DLA)
Am & Eng Dec Eq ... American and English Decisions in Equity [*A publication*]   (DLA)
Am & Eng Enc Law ... American and English Encyclopedia of Law [*A publication*]   (DLA)
Am & Eng Enc Law & Pr ... American and English Encyclopedia of Law and Practice [*A publication*]   (DLA)
Am & Eng Enc Law Sup ... American and English Encyclopedia of Law. Supplement [*A publication*]   (DLA)
Am & Eng Ency Law ... American and English Encyclopedia of Law [*A publication*]   (DLA)
Am & Eng Eq D ... American and English Decisions in Equity [*A publication*]   (DLA)

Am & Engl RC ... American and English Railway Cases [*A publication*] (DLA)
Am & Eng Pat Cas ... American and English Patent Cases [*A publication*] (DLA)
Am & Eng R Cas ... American and English Railroad Cases [*A publication*] (DLA)
Am & Eng R Cas NS ... American and English Railroad Cases, New Series [*A publication*] (DLA)
Am & Eng RR Ca ... American and English Railroad Cases [*A publication*] (DLA)
Am & Eng RR Cas ... American and English Railroad Cases [*A publication*] (DLA)
Am & Eng RR Cases ... American and English Railroad Cases [*A publication*] (DLA)
Am & Eng Ry Cas ... American and English Railway Cases [*A publication*] (DLA)
Am & Eng Ry Cas NS ... American and English Railroad Cases, New Series [*A publication*] (DLA)
Am Ens ...... American Ensemble [*A publication*]
Am Enterp Inst Public Policy Res Natl Energy Study ... American Enterprise Institute for Public Policy Research. National Energy Study [*A publication*]
Am Entomol Soc Trans ... American Entomological Society. Transactions [*A publication*]
AMEP .... Australian Mathematics Education Program
Am Ephem ... American Ephemeris and Nautical Almanac [*A publication*]
AMER ...... America [*or American*]
Amer .... American [*A publication*]
Am ER .... American Ecclesiastical Review [*A publication*]
Am ER .... American Economic Review [*A publication*]
AMER .... American Middle East Rehabilitation (EA)
Amer .... Amerman's Reports [*111-115 Pennsylvania*] [*A publication*] (DLA)
AMER .... Amersham [*England*]
AMERA .... American Arabic Association (EA)
Amer Acad of Arts and Sciences Proc ... American Academy of Arts and Sciences. Proceedings [*A publication*]
Amer Acad Arts & Sci Mem ... American Academy of Arts and Sciences. Memoirs [*A publication*]
Amer Acad Rome ... Memoirs. American Academy at Rome [*A publication*] (OCD)
AMERADC ... Army Mobility Equipment Research and Development Center (MCD)
Amer Ann Phot ... American Annual of Photography [*A publication*]
Amer Annual Phot ... American Annual of Photography [*A publication*]
Amer Anthropol ... American Anthropologist [*A publication*]
Amer Antiq ... American Antiquity [*A publication*]
Amer Antiq Soc Proc ... American Antiquarian Society. Proceedings [*A publication*]
Amer Archivist ... American Archivist [*A publication*]
Amer Arch Rehab Ther ... American Archives of Rehabilitation Therapy [*A publication*]
Amerasia J ... Amerasia Journal [*A publication*]
Amer Assoc Pet Geol Bull ... American Association of Petroleum Geologists. Bulletin [*A publication*]
Amer Avia Hist Soc Jnl ... American Aviation Historical Society. Journal [*A publication*]
Amer Baker ... American Baker [*A publication*]
Amer Bee J ... American Bee Journal [*A publication*]
Amer Behav Scientist ... American Behavioral Scientist [*A publication*]
Amer Bk Pub Rec ... American Book Publishing Record [*A publication*]
Amer Bookman ... Bookman [*Published in US*] [*A publication*]
Amer Brewer ... American Brewer [*A publication*]
Am & ER Cas ... American and English Railroad Cases [*A publication*] (DLA)
Am & ER Cas NS ... American and English Railroad Cases, New Series [*A publication*] (DLA)
Amer Cattle Prod ... American Cattle Producer [*A publication*]
Amer Ceram Soc Bull ... American Ceramic Society. Bulletin [*A publication*]
Amer Chem Soc Div Fuel Chem Prepr ... American Chemical Society. Division of Fuel Chemistry. Preprints [*A publication*]
Amer Chem Soc Div Org Coatings Plast Chem Prepr ... American Chemical Society. Division of Organic Coatings and Plastics Chemistry. Preprints [*A publication*]
Amer Chem Soc Div Petrol Chem Prepr ... American Chemical Society. Division of Petroleum Chemistry. Preprints [*A publication*]
Amer Chem Soc Div Water Air Waste Chem Gen Pap ... American Chemical Society. Division of Water, Air, and Waste Chemistry. General Papers [*A publication*]
Amer Chem Soc Petrol Chem Div Preprints ... American Chemical Society. Petroleum Chemistry Division. Preprints [*A publication*]
Amer Choral R ... American Choral Review [*A publication*]
Amer Cinematogr ... American Cinematographer [*A publication*]
Amer City .. American City [*A publication*]
Amer Classic Screen ... American Classic Screen [*A publication*]
Amer Concr Inst Monogr ... American Concrete Institute. Monograph [*A publication*]
Amer Concr Inst Stand ... American Concrete Institute. Standards [*A publication*]
Amer Corp ... American Corporation [*A publication*]

Amer Corp Cas ... American Corporation Cases [*A publication*] (DLA)
Amer Correct Ther J ... American Corrective Therapy Journal [*A publication*]
Amer Dairy Rev ... American Dairy Review [*A publication*]
Amer Dec ... American Decisions [*A publication*] (DLA)
Amer Demogr ... American Demographics [*A publication*]
Amer Doc ... American Documentation [*A publication*]
Amer Drug ... American Druggist [*A publication*]
Amer Dyestuff Rep ... American Dyestuff Reporter [*A publication*]
Amer Dyestuff Reporter ... American Dyestuff Reporter [*A publication*]
Amer Economist ... American Economist [*A publication*]
Amer Econ R ... American Economic Review [*A publication*]
Amer Econ Rev ... American Economic Review [*A publication*]
Amer Elec Ca ... American Electrical Cases [*A publication*] (DLA)
Amer Eng ... American Engineer [*A publication*]
Amer & Eng Enc Law ... American and English Encyclopedia of Law [*A publication*] (DLA)
Amer Ethnol ... American Ethnologist [*A publication*]
Amer F .... American Film [*A publication*]
Amer Feder ... American Federationist [*A publication*]
Amer Fed Tax Rep ... American Federal Tax Reports [*Prentice-Hall, Inc.*] [*A publication*] (DLA)
Amer Fern J ... American Fern Journal [*A publication*]
Amer Forests Forest Life ... American Forests and Forest Life [*A publication*]
Amer Gas Ass Mon ... American Gas Association. Monthly [*A publication*]
Amer Gas Ass Oper Sect Proc ... American Gas Association. Operating Section. Proceedings [*A publication*]
Amer Gas J ... American Gas Journal [*A publication*]
Amer Gear Mfr Ass Stand ... American Gear Manufacturers Association. Standards [*A publication*]
AmerH .... America: History and Life [*A publication*]
Amer Highways ... American Highways [*A publication*]
Amer Hist Rev ... American Historical Review [*A publication*]
AMERICAL ... Americans in New Caledonia [*Army's 23rd infantry; acronym used as name of division. Active in World War II, disbanded 1945; reactivated 1967-71*]
American Assoc Arch Bib ... American Association of Architectural Bibliographers. Papers [*A publication*]
American Business Law Jrnl ... American Business Law Journal [*A publication*]
American Church R ... American Church Review [*A publication*]
American F ... American Film [*A publication*]
American Inst Planners Jnl ... American Institute of Planners. Journal [*A publication*]
American Jrnl of Economics and Sociology ... American Journal of Economics and Sociology [*A publication*]
American Jrnl of Small Business ... American Journal of Small Business [*A publication*]
American Planning Assocn Jnl ... American Planning Association. Journal [*A publication*]
American Repts ... American Reports [*A publication*] (DLA)
American State Rep ... American State Reports [*A publication*] (DLA)
AMERIEZ ... Antarctic Marine Ecosystem Research at the Ice Edge Zone
amerik .... Amerikanisch [*American*] [*German*]
Amerikastud ... Amerikastudien [*American Studies*] [*A publication*]
Amer Imago ... American Imago [*A publication*]
AMERIMIC ... American Military Industrial Complex
AMERIND ... American Indian
Amer Indig ... America Indigena [*A publication*]
Amer Ind J ... American Indian Journal [*A publication*]
Amer Industr Hyg Assoc J ... American Industrial Hygiene Association. Journal [*A publication*]
Amer Iron Steel Inst Contrib Met Steel ... American Iron and Steel Institute. Contributions to the Metallurgy of Steel [*A publication*]
Amer Iron Steel Inst Reg Tech Meetings Addresses ... American Iron and Steel Institute. Regional Technical Meetings. Addresses [*A publication*]
Amer Iron Steel Steel Res Constr Bull ... American Iron and Steel Institute. Steel Research for Construction. Bulletin [*A publication*]
AMERITECH ... American Information Technologies Corp. [*Telecommunications*] [*Chicago, IL*]
Amer J Agr Econ ... American Journal of Agricultural Economics [*A publication*]
Amer J Agric Econ ... American Journal of Agricultural Economics [*A publication*]
Amer J Archaeol ... American Journal of Archaeology [*A publication*]
Amer J Art Ther ... American Journal of Art Therapy [*A publication*]
Amer J Bot ... American Journal of Botany [*A publication*]
Amer J Cardiol ... American Journal of Cardiology [*A publication*]
Amer J Chinese Medicine ... American Journal of Chinese Medicine [*A publication*]
Amer J Clin Hypnosis ... American Journal of Clinical Hypnosis [*A publication*]
Amer J Clin Nutr ... American Journal of Clinical Nutrition [*A publication*]
Amer J Clin Pathol ... American Journal of Clinical Pathology [*A publication*]
Amer J Comp L ... American Journal of Comparative Law [*A publication*]
Amer J Comp Law ... American Journal of Comparative Law [*A publication*]
Amer J Digest Dis ... American Journal of Digestive Diseases [*Later, Digestive Diseases and Sciences*] [*A publication*]
Amer J Dis Child ... American Journal of Diseases of Children [*A publication*]
Amer J Econ & Soc ... American Journal of Economics and Sociology [*New York*] [*A publication*]

Amer J Econ Sociol ... American Journal of Economics and Sociology [*New York*] [*A publication*]

Amer Jew Yearb ... American Jewish Yearbook [*A publication*]

Amer J Hosp Pharm ... American Journal of Hospital Pharmacy [*A publication*]

Amer J Hum Genetics ... American Journal of Human Genetics [*A publication*]

Amer J Hyg ... American Journal of Hygiene [*A publication*]

Amer J Int Law ... American Journal of International Law [*A publication*]

Amer J Int'l L ... American Journal of International Law [*A publication*]

Amer J Juris ... American Journal of Jurisprudence [*A publication*]

Amer J Math ... American Journal of Mathematics [*A publication*]

Amer J Math Management Sci ... American Journal of Mathematical and Management Sciences [*A publication*]

Amer J Med Sci ... American Journal of the Medical Sciences [*A publication*]

Amer J Ment Defic ... American Journal of Mental Deficiency [*A publication*]

Amer J Mining ... American Journal of Mining [*A publication*]

Amer Jnl Reprod Immun ... American Journal of Reproductive Immunology [*A publication*]

Amer Jnl Rural Health ... American Journal of Rural Health [*A publication*]

Amer J Nursing ... American Journal of Nursing [*A publication*]

Amer J Ophthalmol ... American Journal of Ophthalmology [*A publication*]

Amer J Optom and Arch Amer Acad Optom ... American Journal of Optometry and Archives of American Academy of Optometry [*Later, American Journal of Optometry and Physiological Optics*] [*A publication*]

Amer J Orthopsychiat ... American Journal of Orthopsychiatry [*A publication*]

Amer Jour Psych ... American Journal of Psychology [*A publication*]

Amer J Pathol ... American Journal of Pathology [*A publication*]

Amer J Philo ... American Journal of Philology [*A publication*]

Amer J Phys ... American Journal of Physics [*A publication*]

Amer J of Phys ... American Journal of Physics [*A publication*]

Amer J Phys Anthropol ... American Journal of Physical Anthropology [*A publication*]

Amer J Physiol ... American Journal of Physiology [*A publication*]

Amer J Phys Med ... American Journal of Physical Medicine [*A publication*]

Amer J Polit Sci ... American Journal of Political Science [*A publication*]

Amer J Psychiatry ... American Journal of Psychiatry [*A publication*]

Amer J Psychoanal ... American Journal of Psychoanalysis [*A publication*]

Amer J Psychol ... American Journal of Psychology [*A publication*]

Amer J Psychother ... American Journal of Psychotherapy [*A publication*]

Amer J Psychotherap ... American Journal of Psychotherapy [*A publication*]

Amer J Roentg ... American Journal of Roentgenology [*A publication*]

Amer J Roentgenol ... American Journal of Roentgenology [*A publication*]

Amer J Sci ... American Journal of Science [*A publication*]

Amer J Sci Radiocarbon Suppl ... American Journal of Science. Radiocarbon Supplement [*A publication*]

Amer J Semitic Lang ... American Journal of Semitic Languages [*A publication*]

Amer J Sociol ... American Journal of Sociology [*A publication*]

Amer J Surg ... American Journal of Surgery and Gynecology [*A publication*]

Amer J Theol Phil ... American Journal of Theology and Philosophy [*A publication*]

Amer Jur.... American Jurist [*A publication*]   (DLA)

Amer J Vet Res ... American Journal of Veterinary Research [*A publication*]

Amer Kenkyu ... America Kenkyu [*A publication*]

Amer Lat... America Latina [*A publication*]

Amer Law .. American Lawyer [*A publication*]

Amer Law Reg (NS) ... American Law Register, New Series [*A publication*]   (DLA)

Amer Law Reg (OS) ... American Law Register, Old Series [*A publication*]   (DLA)

Amer Law Rev ... American Law Review [*A publication*]

Amer Lawy ... American Lawyer [*A publication*]

Amer Lea Cas ... American Leading Cases [*A publication*]   (DLA)

Amer Liszt Soc J ... American Liszt Society. Journal [*A publication*]

Amer Lit... American Literature [*A publication*]

AmerLitAb ... American Literature Abstracts [*A publication*]

Amer Livestock J ... American Livestock Journal [*A publication*]

Amer Mach ... American Machinist [*A publication*]

Amer Manage Ass Res Stud ... American Management Associations. Research Study [*A publication*]

Amer Math Mon ... American Mathematical Monthly [*A publication*]

Amer Math Monthly ... American Mathematical Monthly [*A publication*]

Amer Math Soc Colloq Publ ... American Mathematical Society. Colloquium Publications [*A publication*]

Amer Math Soc Transl ... American Mathematical Society. Translations [*A publication*]

Amer Midl Nat ... American Midland Naturalist [*A publication*]

Amer Miller Process ... American Miller and Processor [*A publication*]

Amer Mineral ... American Mineralogist [*A publication*]

Amer M Instrument Soc J ... American Musical Instrument Society. Journal [*A publication*]

Amer Nat ... American Naturalist [*A publication*]

Amer Natur ... American Naturalist [*A publication*]

Amer Neptune ... American Neptune [*A publication*]

Amer Nurserym ... American Nurseryman [*A publication*]

Amer O ...... American Opinion [*A publication*]

Amer Oil Gas Reporter ... American Oil and Gas Reporter [*A publication*]

Amer Oriental Soc Jour ... American Oriental Society. Journal [*A publication*]

Amer Orient Ser ... American Oriental Series [*A publication*]

AMEROSE ... American Committee of OSE [*Defunct*]

Amer Pap Ind ... American Paper Industry [*A publication*]

Amer Petrol Inst Div Prod Drilling Prod Pract Pap ... American Petroleum Institute. Division of Production, Drilling, and Production Practice. Papers [*A publication*]

Amer Petrol Inst Stand ... American Petroleum Institute. Standards [*A publication*]

Amer Philos Quart Monograph Ser ... American Philosophical Quarterly. Monograph Series [*A publication*]

Amer Philos Soc Proc ... American Philosophical Society. Proceedings [*A publication*]

Amer Philos Soc Trans ... American Philosophical Society. Transactions [*A publication*]

Amer Phil Quart ... American Philosophical Quarterly [*A publication*]

Amer Phot ... American Photography [*A publication*]

Amer Photogr ... American Photographer [*A publication*]

Amer Phys Teacher ... American Physics Teacher [*A publication*]

Amer Polit Quart ... American Politics Quarterly [*A publication*]

Amer Polit Sci R ... American Political Science Review [*A publication*]

Amer Po R ... American Poetry Review [*A publication*]

Amer Prem ... American Premiere [*A publication*]

Amer Psychol ... American Psychologist [*A publication*]

Amer Quart ... American Quarterly [*A publication*]

Amer Recorder ... American Recorder [*A publication*]

Amer Rehab ... American Rehabilitation [*A publication*]

Amer Rep... American Reports [*A publication*]   (DLA)

Amer Reports ... American Reports [*A publication*]   (DLA)

Amer Reps ... American Reports [*A publication*]   (DLA)

Amer Rev E-W Tr ... American Review of East-West Trade [*A publication*]   (DLA)

Amer Rev Tuberc ... American Review of Tuberculosis [*A publication*]

Amer R'y Rep ... American Railway Reports [*A publication*]   (DLA)

AmerS... American Studies [*A publication*]

AMERSA .. Association of Medical Education and Research in Substance Abuse   (EA)

Amer Scholar ... American Scholar [*A publication*]

Amer Sci .... American Scientist [*A publication*]

Amer Sci Press Ser Math Management Sci ... American Sciences Press Series in Mathematical and Management Sciences [*A publication*]

Amer Slavic East Europe Rev ... American Slavic and East European Review [*A publication*]

Amer Soc Abrasive Method Nat Tech Conf Proc ... American Society for Abrasive Methods. National Technical Conference. Proceedings [*A publication*]

Amer Sociologist ... American Sociologist [*A publication*]

Amer Sociol R ... American Sociological Review [*A publication*]

Amer Soc Quality Contr Tech Conf Trans ... American Society for Quality Control. Annual Technical Conference. Transactions [*A publication*]

Amer Sp..... American Speech [*A publication*]

Amer Stat... American Statistician [*A publication*]

Amer State Reps ... American State Reports [*A publication*]   (DLA)

Amer Stat Ind ... American Statistics Index [*A publication*]

Amer Statist ... American Statistician [*A publication*]

Amer St Rep ... American State Reports [*A publication*]   (DLA)

Amer Univ L Rev ... American University Law Review [*A publication*]

Amer Veg Grower ... American Vegetable Grower [*A publication*]

AMERWAX ... American Wax Importers and Refiners Association   (EA)

Amer Welding Soc Stand ... American Welding Society. Standards [*A publication*]

Amer Woods US For Serv ... American Woods. United States Forest Service [*A publication*]

Amer Zool ... American Zoologist [*A publication*]

AMES........ Aeromedical Evacuation System [*Air Force*]   (AFM)

AMES........ Air Member for Engineering and Supply [*British and Canadian*] [*World War II*]

AMES...... Air Ministry Experimental Station [*British*]

AMES........ Aircraft Maintenance Effectiveness Simulation   (MCD)

AMES........ Aircraft Multiengine Sea [*Pilot rating*]   (AIA)

Ames .... Ames' Reports [*4-7 Rhode Island*] [*A publication*]   (DLA)

Ames .... Ames' Reports [*1 Minnesota*] [*A publication*]   (DLA)

AMES........ Association of Marine Engineering Schools [*Liverpool, Merseyside, England*]   (EAIO)

AMES........ Automatic Message Entry System [*Data processing*]   (MCD)

AMES........ East Sale [*Australia*] [*ICAO location identifier*]   (ICLI)

AMESA..... Archiwum Mechaniki Stosowanej [*Archives of Mechanics*] [*A publication*]

Ames Cas B & N ... Ames' Cases on Bills and Notes [*A publication*]   (DLA)

Ames Cas Par ... Ames' Cases on Partnership [*A publication*]   (DLA)

Ames Cas Pl ... Ames' Cases on Pleading [*A publication*]   (DLA)

Ames Cas Sur ... Ames' Cases on Suretyship [*A publication*]   (DLA)

Ames Cas Trusts ... Ames' Cases on Trusts [*A publication*]   (DLA)

Ames K & B ... Ames', Knowles', and Bradley's Reports [*8 Rhode Island*] [*A publication*]   (DLA)

Ames Lab Bull Ser ... Ames Laboratory. Bulletin Series [*A publication*]

AMESLAN ... American Sign Language [*for the deaf*]

AMESP..... Administration des Mesures d'Encouragement du Secteur Petrolier [*Petroleum Incentives Administration*] [*Canada*]

AmEsq....... American Esquire [*Record label*]

AMET .... Accelerated Mission Endurance Test   (MCD)

AMET ...... Africa - Middle East Theater [*World War II*]
A Met........ Annalen der Meteorologie [*A publication*]
A Met........ Associate in Metallurgy [*British*]
AMETA..... Army Management Engineering Training Agency   (RDA)
Am Ethnol ... American Ethnologist [*A publication*]
A Meth Th ... Advances in Archaeological Method and Theory [*A publication*]
AMETS..... Artillery Meteorological System   (NATG)
A Met Sin .. Acta Meteorologica Sinica [*A publication*]
AMEU .... Americans for Middle East Understanding   (EA)
AMEX .... Agencia Mexicana de Noticias SA [*Press agency*] [*Mexico*]
AMEX ...... Airletter Mail Express [*American Express Co.*]
Am Ex ...... American Examiner [*A publication*]
AMEX ...... American Exiles
AMEX ...... American Express Co.
AMEX ...... American Stock Exchange [*New York, NY*]   (EA)
AMEX ...... AMEX-Canada [*A publication*]
AMEXCO ... American Express Company
Am Exp Mark ... American Export Marketer [*A publication*]
Am Exporter ... American Exporter [*A publication*]
AMEZ .... African Methodist Episcopal Zion [*Church*]
AMEZAB ... Annali di Microbiologia. Edizione. Enzimologia [*A publication*]
AME Zion QR ... AME [*African Methodist Episcopal*] Zion Quarterly Review [*A publication*]
A Mezzogiorno ... Annali del Mezzogiorno [*A publication*]
AMF .... A. Merritt's Fantasy Magazine [*A publication*]
AMF .... Abort Motor Facility [*NASA*]   (NASA)
AMF .... ACE [*Allied Command Europe*] Mobile Force [*NATO*]
AMF .... ACM Managed Income Fund, Inc. [*NYSE symbol*]   (CTT)
AMF .... Acoustic Match Filter
AMF .... Actuarial Mail File [*IRS*]
AMF .... Advanced Maneuvering FLAP [*Flight Application Software*]   (MCD)
AMF .... Air Mail Facility [*Post Office*]
AMF .... Air Mail Field
AMF .... Air Materiel Force
AMF .... Airman Memorial Foundation   (EA)
AMF .... Airport Mail Facility   (AFM)
AMF .... Algonquin Minerals [*Vancouver Stock Exchange symbol*]
AMF .... Allied Mobile Force [*NATO*]
AMF .... Ama [*Papua New Guinea*] [*Airport symbol*]   (OAG)
AMF .... Ambler, AK [*Location identifier*] [*FAA*]   (FAAL)
AMF .... American Messianic Fellowship   (EA)
AMF .... American Missionary Fellowship   (EA)
AMF .... Americans for Medical Freedom [*Inactive*]   (EA)
AmF .... [*The*] Americas: A Quarterly Review of Inter-American Cultural History [*A publication*]
Amf .... Amfion [*Record label*] [*Mexico*]
AMF .... Analog Matched Filter
AMF .... Annual Material Forecast [*Military*]   (AFM)
AMF .... Antimuscle Factor [*Immunology*]
AMF .... Apogee Motor Fire [*Aerospace*]
AMF .... Applicant Master File [*State Employee Security Agency*]   (OICC)
AMF .... Arab Monetary Fund
AMF .... Arc Melting Furnace
A Mf.......... Archiv fuer Musikforschung [*A publication*]
AMF .... Area Maintenance Facility
AMF .... Army Management Fund
AMF .... Assembly Machine Fixture   (MCD)
AMF .... Australian Military Forces
AMF .... Autocrine Mobility Factor [*Oncology*]
AMFA .... Aircraft Mechanics Fraternal Association   (EA)
AMFA .... Allied Military Financial Agency [*World War II*]
AMF(A)..... Allied Mobile Force (Air) [*NATO*]
AMFA .... American Music Festival Association   (EA)
AMFA .... Association Medicale Franco-Americaine   (EA)
Am Fabrics ... American Fabrics [*A publication*]
Am Fam Phys ... American Family Physician [*A publication*]
Am Fam Physician ... American Family Physician [*A publication*]
Am Fam Physician GP ... American Family Physician - GP [*A publication*]
AmFAR...... American Foundation for AIDS Research [*New York, NY*]   (EA)
Am Farm Bur N L ... American Farm Bureau Federation. Weekly News Letter [*A publication*]
AMFAX..... Aviation Meteorological Facsimile [*National Weather Service*]
AMFB........ American Federal Bank [*NASDAQ symbol*]   (CTT)
AMFC........ Andrea McArdle Fan Club   (EA)
AMFC........ Anne Murray Fan Club   (EA)
AMFC........ Automotive Franchise Corporation [*Nashville, TN*] [*NASDAQ symbol*]   (NQ)
AMFD .... A & M Food Service, Inc. [*NASDAQ symbol*]   (NQ)
AMFDP..... Army Master Force Development Plan   (MCD)
AMFEA..... Air Materiel Force, European Area
Am Fed....... American Federationist [*A publication*]
Am Federationist ... American Federationist [*A publication*]
Am Fed Tax R ... American Federal Tax Reports [*Prentice-Hall, Inc.*] [*A publication*]   (DLA)
Am Fed Tax R 2d ... American Federal Tax Reports, Second Series [*Prentice-Hall, Inc.*] [*A publication*]   (DLA)

Am Feed Manuf Assoc Proc Meet Nutr Counc ... American Feed Manufacturers Association. Proceedings. Meeting of the Nutrition Council [*A publication*]
Am Fencing ... American Fencing [*A publication*]
AMFEP..... Association of Microbial Food Enzyme Producers   (EA)
Am & Fer ... Amos and Ferard on Fixtures [*A publication*]   (DLA)
Am Fern J ... American Fern Journal [*A publication*]
Am Fert...... American Fertilizer and Allied Chemicals [*A publication*]
Am Fert Allied Chem ... American Fertilizer and Allied Chemicals [*A publication*]
AMFF........ Advanced Materials Fabrication Facility [*Manufacturing*]   (MCD)
AMFFA..... American Medical Fly Fishing Association   (EA)
AMFGAR ... American Fruit Grower [*A publication*]
AMFGC..... Association of Midwest Fish and Game Commissioners [*Later, AMFWA*]
AMFHSTFU ... Association of Members and Friends of the Historic Southern Tenant Farmers Union   (EA)
AMFI........ Amcore Financial, Inc. [*Rockford, IL*] [*NASDAQ symbol*]   (NQ)
AMFI........ Aviation Maintenance Foundation, Incorporated   (EA)
AMFIE...... Association of Mutual Fire Insurance Engineers [*Later, ILCA*]
Am Film..... American Film [*A publication*]
AMFINFOS ... American Forces Information Service [*DoD*]   (AABC)
AMFIS...... Automatic Microfilm Information System
Am Fisheries Soc Trans ... American Fisheries Society. Transactions [*A publication*]
Am Fish Soc Monogr ... American Fisheries Society. Monograph [*A publication*]
Am Fish Soc Spec Publ ... American Fisheries Society. Special Publication [*A publication*]
Am Fish Soc Trans ... American Fisheries Society. Transactions [*A publication*]
AMF(L)..... Allied Mobile Force (Land) [*NATO*]
AMFL........ American Savings and Loan Association of Florida [*NASDAQ symbol*]   (NQ)
Am Flint ... American Flint [*A publication*]
Am Flor...... American Florist [*A publication*]
AMFM ...... Advisory Panel of Alternative Means of Financing and Managing Radioactive Waste Facilities [*Terminated, 1984*] [*Department of Energy*]   (EGAO)
AM-FM ..... Algorithm Mass-Factoring Method   (MCD)
AMFM ...... Association Mondiale des Federalistes Mondiaux [*World Association of World Federalists - WAWF*]   (EA)
AMFN .... AFN, Inc. [*NASDAQ symbol*]   (NQ)
AMFNAE ... Annales Medicinae Internae Fenniae [*A publication*]
AMFO....... American Forests [*A publication*]
AMFO....... Association of Manpower Franchise Owners   (EA)
AMFOA.... American Forests [*A publication*]
Am Folk Newsl ... American Folklore Newsletter [*A publication*]
Am Folk Soc Newsl ... American Folklore Society. Newsletter [*A publication*]
Am For...... American Forests [*A publication*]
Am Forests ... American Forests [*A publication*]
Am For L Ass'n Newsl ... American Foreign Law Association. Newsletter [*A publication*]   (DLA)
Am For Serv Jour ... American Foreign Service Journal [*A publication*]
Am Found Blind Res Bull ... American Foundation for the Blind. Research Bulletin [*A publication*]
Am Found Blind Res Ser ... American Foundation for the Blind. Research Series [*A publication*]
Am Foundryman ... American Foundryman [*A publication*]
Am Fox and Fur Farmer ... American Fox and Fur Farmer [*A publication*]
AMFPA..... Air Materiel Force, Pacific Area
AMFPS..... Association of Mutual Fund Plan Sponsors [*Later, ICI*]   (EA)
AMFR........ Aerospace Mechanical Fastening Requirements   (MCD)
Am Fruit Grow ... American Fruit Grower [*A publication*]
Am Fruit Grower ... American Fruit Grower [*A publication*]
Am Fruit Grow Mag ... American Fruit Grower Magazine [*A publication*]
AMFS........ Airframe Mechanical and Fluid Subsystems   (MCD)
AMFSO..... Assistant Missile Flight Safety Officer   (MUGU)
AMFUR..... Amplified Failure or Unsatisfactory Report [*Obsolete*]
AMFV....... [*A*] Mind Forever Voyaging [*Infocom*] [*Computer gaming*]
AMFWA ... Association of Midwest Fish and Wildlife Agencies   (EA)
AMFWC.... Association of Midwest Fish and Wildlife Commissioners [*Later, AMFWA*]
AMFWSCA ... AMF Windflite Sailboard Class Association   (EA)
AMG.......... Acquisition Management Guide [*Military*]   (AFIT)
AMG.......... Acreage Marketing Guide
AMG.......... Activation Management Group [*NASA*]   (NASA)
AMG.......... Aircraft Machine Gunner
AMG.......... Albertus Magnus Guild   (EA)
AMG.......... Algebraic Multigrid [*Computation method*]
AMG.......... Alles mit Gott [*Everything with God*] [*German*] [*Motto of Georg Albrecht, Margrave of Brandenburg-Baireuth (1619-66)*]
AMG.......... Allied Medical Group [*British*]
AMG.......... Allied Military Government [*of occupied territory*] [*Formerly, AMGOT*] [*Post-World War II*]
AMG.......... Alma, GA [*Location identifier*] [*FAA*]   (FAAL)
AMG.......... Alpha-Macroglobulin [*Biochemistry*]
AMG.......... Amboin [*Papua New Guinea*] [*Airport symbol*]   (OAG)

Am G.......... American Geologist [*A publication*]
AMG.......... American Military Government
AMG.......... American Mission to Greeks [*Later, AMG International*] (EA)
AMG.......... Americus [*Georgia*] [*Seismograph station code, US Geological Survey*] (SEIS)
AMG.......... Among
AMG.......... Amplitude Modulation Generator
AMG.......... Amyloglucosidase [*An enzyme*]
AMG.......... Angle of Middle Gimbal (KSC)
AMG.......... Annales. Musee Guimet [*A publication*]
AMG.......... Antenna Mast Group [*PATRIOT*] [*Army*] (RDA)
AMG.......... Applied Mathematics Group [*Brown University*] (MCD)
AMG.......... Applied Microbiology Group [*Natick Laboratories*] [*Army*] (RDA)
AMG.......... Armor Machine Gun (MCD)
AM-G .... Assistant Major-General [*Military*] [*British*] (ROG)
AMG.......... Association Management [*A publication*]
AMG.......... Automatic Magnetic Guidance
AMG.......... Axiomesiogingival [*Dentistry*]
AMG.......... Medicine Hat General Hospital, Alberta [*Library symbol*] [*National Library of Canada*] (NLC)
AMGA...... American Medical Golf Association (EA)
AMGA...... American Modified Golf Association (EA)
AMGA...... American Murray Grey Association (EA)
AMGA...... Australian Mushroom Growers Association
Am Game Bull Am Game Protect Ass ... American Game Bulletin. American Game Protective Association [*A publication*]
Am Gas As M ... American Gas Association. Monthly [*A publication*]
Am Gas Ass Mon ... American Gas Association. Monthly [*A publication*]
Am Gas Assoc Annu Rep ... American Gas Association. Annual Report [*A publication*]
Am Gas Assoc Bull Abstr ... American Gas Association. Bulletin of Abstracts [*A publication*]
Am Gas Assoc Mon ... American Gas Association. Monthly [*A publication*]
Am Gas Assoc Oper Sect Proc ... American Gas Association. Operating Section. Proceedings [*A publication*]
Am Gas Assoc Prepr ... American Gas Association. Preprints [*A publication*]
Am Gas Assoc Proc ... American Gas Association. Proceedings [*A publication*]
Am G As B ... American Geological Association. Bulletin [*A publication*]
Am Gas Eng J ... American Gas Engineering Journal [*A publication*]
Am Gas Inst Abstr ... American Gas Institute. Abstracts [*A publication*]
Am Gas J ... American Gas Journal [*A publication*]
Am Gas Jrl ... American Gas Journal [*A publication*]
Am Gas Light J ... American Gas Light Journal [*A publication*]
AMGBA .... American MGB Association (EA)
AMGBA .... Archiv fuer Meteorologie, Geophysik, und Bioklimatologie. Serie B [*A publication*]
AMGBCJ .. Argentina. Servicio Nacional Minero Geologico. Boletin [*A publication*]
AMGCR .... American MGC Register (EA)
AMGD...... American Vanguard Corp. [*NASDAQ symbol*] (NQ)
AMGDAN ... Annali. Museo Civico di Storia Naturale "Giacomo Doria" [*A publication*]
AMGE....... Association of Marine and General Engineers [*A union*] [*British*]
AMGE....... Association Mondiale des Guides et des Eclaireuses [*World Association of Girl Guides and Girl Scouts - WAGGGS*] [*London, England*] (EAIO)
Am Geneal ... American Genealogist [*A publication*]
Am Geog Soc B J ... American Geographical Society. Bulletin. Journal [*A publication*]
Am Geog Soc Bul ... American Geographical Society. Bulletin [*A publication*]
Am Geog Soc Jour ... American Geographical Society. Journal [*A publication*]
Am Geog Soc Special Pub ... American Geographical Society. Special Publication [*A publication*]
Am Geog Stat Soc J ... American Geographical and Statistical Society. Journal [*A publication*]
Am Geol..... American Geologist [*A publication*]
Am Geol Inst Repr Ser ... American Geological Institute. Reprint Series [*A publication*]
Am Geol Inst Rept ... American Geological Institute. Report [*A publication*]
Am Geophys Union Trans ... American Geophysical Union. Transactions [*A publication*]
AMGGA .... Archiv fuer Meteorologie, Geophysik, und Bioklimatologie. Serie A [*A publication*]
AMGHB2 ... Ameghiniana [*A publication*]
AMGI....... American Genetics International [*NASDAQ symbol*] (NQ)
Am Glass Rev ... American Glass Review [*A publication*]
AMGLU .... Amalgamated Machine and General Labourers Union [*British*]
AMGM....... Airmailgram
AMGN....... Amgen, Inc. [*NASDAQ symbol*] (NQ)
AMGO....... Assistant Master-General of Ordnance [*British*]
AMGOT.... Allied Military Government of Occupied Territory [*Later, AMG*] [*Post-World War II*]
AMGP .... Association of Medical Group Psychoanalysts (EA)
AMGR....... Airport Manager (FAAC)
AMGR....... American Guaranty Financial Corp. [*NASDAQ symbol*] (NQ)
AMGRA .... American Milk Goat Record Association [*Later, ADGA*] (EA)
Am Group Psychother Assoc Monogr Ser ... American Group Psychotherapy Association. Monograph Series [*A publication*]

AMGS .... Acceleration Monitoring Guidance System (MCD)
AMGST..... Amongst (ROG)
AMGYAI... Anales. Sociedad Medico-Quirurgica del Guayas [*A publication*]
Am Gynecol Soc Trans ... American Gynecological Society. Transactions [*A publication*]
AMH .... Aero Mech, Inc. [*Clarksburg, WV*] [*FAA designator*] (FAAC)
AMH .... Alaska Military Highway
AMH .... Almaden Resources Corp. [*Vancouver Stock Exchange symbol*]
AMH .... Amdahl Corp. [*AMEX symbol*] (SPSG)
amh .... Amharic [*MARC language code*] [*Library of Congress*] (LCCP)
AMH .... Amherst College, Amherst, MA [*OCLC symbol*] (OCLC)
AMH .... Association of Marian Helpers (EA)
AMH .... Association Mondiale de Hockey [*World Hockey Association - WHA*] [*Canada*]
AMH .... Automated Medical History
AMH .... Aviation Structural Mechanic, Hydraulic Mechanic [*Navy rating*]
AMH .... Harbor Minesweepers [*Navy symbol*]
AMH .... Huntingdon College, Montgomery, AL [*Library symbol*] [*Library of Congress*] (LCLS)
a-mh--- .... Macao [*MARC geographic area code*] [*Library of Congress*] (LCCP)
AMH .... Mixed Astigmatism with Exceeding Myopia [*Ophthalmology*]
AMHA...... American Miniature Horse Association (EA)
AMHA...... American Morab Horse Association (EA)
AMHA...... American Morgan Horse Association (EA)
AMHA...... American Motor Hotel Association (EA)
AMHA...... Army Management Headquarters Activity (MCD)
AMHA...... Association of Mental Health Administrators (EA)
AMHAA.... Aviation Structural Mechanic, Hydraulics, Airman Apprentice [*Navy rating*]
AMHAI..... Association for Mental Health Affiliation with Israel (EA)
AMHAN ... Aviation Structural Mechanic, Hydraulics, Airman [*Navy rating*]
Am Harp J ... American Harp Journal [*A publication*]
AMHA-TP ... Automated Microhemagglutination Assay for Antibodies to Treponema pallidum [*Serology*]
AMHAZ.... Ammunition and Hazardous Materials Handling Review Board (MCD)
AMHB...... Hobart [*Australia*] [*ICAO location identifier*] (ICLI)
AMHC...... Association of Mental Health Clergy (EA)
AMHCA.... American Mental Health Counselors Association (EA)
AMHCB.... Applied Mathematics and Computation [*A publication*]
AMHC Forum ... Association of Mental Health Chaplains. Forum [*A publication*]
AMHD ...... [*The*] American Museum of Historical Documents [*Las Vegas, NV*] [*NASDAQ symbol*] (NQ)
AMHE...... American Health [*A publication*]
AMHE....... Association des Medecins Haitiens a l'Etranger [*Association of Haitian Physicains Abroad*] (EA)
Am Health ... American Health [*A publication*]
Am Health Care Assoc J ... American Health Care Association. Journal [*A publication*]
Am Heart Assoc Monogr ... American Heart Association. Monograph [*A publication*]
Am Heart J ... American Heart Journal [*A publication*]
Am Her ... American Heritage [*A publication*]
Am Herit.... American Heritage [*A publication*]
Am Heritage ... American Heritage [*A publication*]
AMHF....... American Mental Health Foundation (EA)
AMHF....... American Mental Health Fund (EA)
AMHF....... American Motorcycle Heritage Foundation (EA)
AMHF....... Hobart [*Australia*] [*ICAO location identifier*] (ICLI)
AMHGD6 ... Arquivos. Museu de Historia Natural. Universidade Federal de Minas Gerais [*A publication*]
AMHI........ American Morgan Horse Institute (EA)
Am Highw ... American Highways [*A publication*]
Am His R... American Historical Review [*A publication*]
Am Hist Assn Ann Rep ... American Historical Association. Annual Report [*A publication*]
Am Hist Assn Rept ... American Historical Association. Reports [*A publication*]
Am Hist Ill ... American History Illustrated [*A publication*]
Am Hist Illus ... American History Illustrated [*A publication*]
Am Hist Life ... America. History and Life [*A publication*]
Am Hist Life Part A ... America. History and Life. Part A. Article Abstracts and Citations [*A publication*]
Am Hist Life Part B ... America. History and Life. Part B. Index to Book Reviews [*A publication*]
Am Hist Life Part C ... America. History and Life. Part C. American History Bibliography, Books, Articles, and Dissertations [*A publication*]
Am Hist Life Part D ... America. History and Life. Part D. Annual Index [*A publication*]
Am Hist Life Suppl ... America. History and Life. Supplement [*A publication*]
Am Hist M ... American Historical Magazine [*New York*] [*A publication*]
Am Hist R ... American Historical Review [*A publication*]
Am Hist Rec ... American Historical Record [*A publication*]
Am Hist Reg ... American Historical Register [*A publication*]
Am Hist Rev ... American Historical Review [*A publication*]

AMHL...... Association of Mental Health Librarians (EA)
AMHNAO ... Anales. Museo Nacional de Historia Natural de Montevideo [*A publication*]
Am Home... American Home [*A publication*]
Am Homes ... American Homes and Gardens [*A publication*]
Am Horol Jeweler ... American Horologist and Jeweler [*A publication*]
Am Hort ... American Horticulturist [*A publication*]
Am Hortic ... American Horticulturist [*A publication*]
Am Hort Mag ... American Horticultural Magazine [*A publication*]
AMHPD.... Association of Mental Health Practitioners with Disabilities [*Defunct*] (EA)
AMHPS .... Association of Minority Health Professions Schools (EA)
AMHR....... American Miniature Horse Registry (EA)
AMHR....... Annuaire. Musee d'Histoire de la Religion et de l'Atheisme [*A publication*]
AMHS....... American Material Handling Society [*Later, IMMS*] (EA)
AMHS....... Association of Mental Health Specialties (EA)
AMHS....... Association of Methodist Historical Societies [*Later, General Commission on Archives and History of the United Methodist Church*] (EA)
AMHS...... Automated Materials Handling System [*Data processing*]
AMHS...... Automated Message Handling System
AMHS...... Medicine Hat High School, Alberta [*Library symbol*] [*National Library of Canada*] (NLC)
AMHS...... Melbourne [*Australia*] [*ICAO location identifier*] (ICLI)
AMHSJ..... AMHS [*American Material Handling Society*] Journal [*A publication*]
AMHSJ..... Australasian Methodist Historical Society. Journal and Proceedings [*A publication*] (ADA)
AMHT...... Automated Multiphasic Health Testing
AMHTS .... Automated Multiphasic Health Testing and Services (KSC)
AMHTTA ... Associate Member of the Highway and Traffic Technicians' Association [*British*] (DBQ)
AMHUDE ... Acta Morphologica Hungarica [*A publication*]
AMHUEF ... Acta Microbiologica Hungarica [*A publication*]
Am Humanit Index ... American Humanities Index [*A publication*]
AMI.......... Absolute Memory Image (MCD)
AMI.......... Active Microwave Instrument
AMI.......... Acute Mesenteric Ischemia [*Medicine*]
AMI.......... Acute Myocardial Infarction [*Medicine*]
AMI.......... Advanced Manned Interceptor [*US Air Force Artillery Spotting Division interceptor*]
AMI.......... Advertising and Marketing Intelligence [*The New York Times Co.*] [*Information service or system*] (CRD)
AMI.......... Aerospace Materials Information
AMI.......... Africa Music International [*Lorient, France*] (EAIO)
AMI.......... Agence Maritime Internationale [*International Maritime Agency*]
AMI.......... Air Mileage Indicator [*Navigation*]
AMI.......... Air Movement Institute
AMI.......... Aircraft Multiplex Intercommunications
AMI.......... Airline Mutual Insurance [*International Air Transport Association*]
AMI.......... Airspeed Mach Indicator (MCD)
AMI.......... Alliance for the Mentally Ill [*Australia*]
AMI.......... Alliance of Metalworking Industries (EA)
AMI.......... Alpha/Mach Indicator (NASA)
AMI.......... Alternate Mark Inversion [*Telecommunications*] (IEEE)
AMI.......... Alternative Mortgage Instrument
AMI.......... American Meat Institute (EA)
AMI.......... American Medical Holdings [*AMEX symbol*] (SPSG)
AMI.......... American Microsystems, Incorporated (MCD)
AMI.......... American Military Institute (EA)
AMI.......... American Mothers, Incorporated (EA)
AMI.......... American Motorsport International (EA)
AMI.......... American Museum of Immigration (EA)
AMI.......... American Mushroom Institute (EA)
AMI.......... American Reserve Mining Corp. [*Vancouver Stock Exchange symbol*]
Ami.......... Amicus [*A publication*]
Ami.......... Amiga [*Record label*] [*East Germany*]
AMI.......... Amitriptyline [*Also, AT*] [*Antidepressant compound*]
AMI.......... Annual Military Inspection
AMI.......... Antimateriel Incendiary
AMI.......... Apogee Motor Igniter [*NASA*]
AMI.......... Applied Mathematics Institute [*University of Delaware*] [*Research center*] (RCD)
AMI.......... Archaeologische Mitteilungen aus Iran [*A publication*]
AMI.......... Arginine Maturity Index [*For prediction of peanut harvest date*]
AMI.......... Assistance Medicale Internationale [*International Medical Assistance*] [*Canada*]
AMI.......... Association of Meat Inspectors [*British*]
AMI.......... Association of Medical Illustrators (EA)
AMI.......... Association Montessori Internationale [*International Montessori Association*] [*Amsterdam, Netherlands*] (EAIO)
AMI.......... Association for Multi-Image (EA)
AMI.......... Australasian Medical Index
AMI.......... Automatic Motion Inhibit [*Nuclear energy*] (NRCH)
AMI.......... Auxiliary Inshore Minesweeper [*NATO*]
AMI.......... Axiomesioincisal [*Dentistry*]

AMI.......... Handmaids of Mary Immaculate [*Roman Catholic religious order*]
AMI.......... Journal of American Insurance [*A publication*]
AMI.......... Mataram [*Indonesia*] [*Airport symbol*] (OAG)
AMI.......... Millet Public Library, Alberta [*Library symbol*] [*National Library of Canada*] (NLC)
AMIA .... American Medical Informatics Association (EA)
AMIA .... American Metal Importers Association [*Defunct*] (EA)
AMIA .... American Mutual Insurance Alliance [*Later, Alliance of American Insurers*] (EA)
AMIA .... Angular Magnetic-Hydrodynamic Integrating Accelerometer
AMIA .... Australian Meat Industries Association
AMIAA ..... American Imago [*A publication*]
AMIADB ... Army Member, Inter-American Defense Board (AABC)
AMIAE...... Associate Member of the Institute of Automobile Engineers [*British*] (ROG)
AMI Ae E .. Associate Member of Institution of Aeronautical Engineers [*British*]
AMIAgrE .. Associate Member of the Institution of Agricultural Engineers [*British*]
AMIAP...... Associate of the Institution of Analysts and Programmers [*British*] (DBQ)
AMIAT...... Associate Member of the Institute of Asphalt Technology [*British*] (DBQ)
AMIB .... American Indian Basketry Magazine [*A publication*]
AMIB .... Army Military Intelligence Battalion (MCD)
AMIC .... Aerospace Materials Information Center [*Air Force*] (MCD)
AMIC .... Air Movement Information Center [*NATO*] (NATG)
AMIC .... American Marine Insurance Clearinghouse [*New York, NY*] (EA)
AMIC .... Analytical Methodology Information Center [*Environmental Protection Agency*]
AMIC .... Army Methods of Instruction Centre [*British military*] (DMA)
AMIC .... Asian Mass Communication Research and Information Centre [*Singapore*] (EAIO)
Amic.......... De Amicitia [*of Cicero*] [*Classical studies*] (OCD)
AMICA...... Automatic Module for Industrial Control Analysis
AMICA...... Automatic Musical Instrument Collectors Association (EA)
AMICA...... Automobile Mutual Insurance Company of America
AMICD ..... Annual Meeting. International Water Conference [*A publication*]
AMICE...... Associate Member of the Institution of Civil Engineers [*Later, MICE*] [*British*]
AMI Chem E ... Associate Member of the Institution of Chemical Engineers [*British*]
AMICO ..... Arab Multinational Investment Company (MENA)
AMICOM ... Army Missile Command
AMICorrST ... Associate Member of the Institution of Corrosion Science and Technology [*British*] (DBQ)
A Micr Acad Sci Hung ... Acta Microbiologica. Academiae Scientiarum Hungaricae [*A publication*]
AMid.......... Annales du Midi; Revue de la France Meridionale [*Toulouse*] [*A publication*]
AMIDA ..... Accommodation for Mildly Intellectually Disadvantaged Adults [*Australia*]
AMIDEAST ... America-Mideast Educational and Training Services [*Acronym is now organization's official name*] (EA)
AMIDS...... Advanced Multispectral Image Descriptor System [*Photography*]
AMIDS...... Airborne Minefield Detector System (MCD)
AMIDS...... Area Manpower Instructional Development Systems
AMIE .... Association of Mutual Insurance Engineers [*Later, ILCA*] (EA)
AMIE Aust ... Associate Member of the Institution of Engineers of Australia
AMIED ..... Associate Member of the Institution of Engineering Designers [*British*]
AMIED5 ... Advances in Microbial Ecology [*A publication*]
AMIEE...... Associate Member of the Institution of Electrical Engineers [*Later, MIEE*] [*British*] (EY)
AMIElecIE ... Associate Member of the Institution of Electrical and Electronics Incorporated Engineers [*British*] (DBQ)
AMIERE ... Associate Member of the Institution of Electronic and Radio Engineers [*Formerly, AM Brit IRE*] [*British*]
AMIEV...... Association Medicale Internationale pour l'Etudes des Conditions de Vie et de Sante [*International Medical Association for the Study of Living Conditions and Health*] [*Sofia, Bulgaria*] (EAIO)
AMIEx ...... Associate Member of the Institute of Export [*British*]
AMIF........ American Marine Insurance Forum [*New York, NY*] (EA)
AMIF........ American Meat Institute Foundation (EA)
AMIF........ Associate Member of the Institute of Fuel [*British*]
AMIFireE ... Associate Member of the Institution of Fire Engineers [*British*]
AMIGasE ... Associate Member of the Institution of Gas Engineers [*British*]
AMIGB...... Acta Microbiologica Polonica. Series A. Microbiologia Generalis [*A publication*]
AMIGeol ... Associate of the Geological Society [*British*] (DBQ)
AMIGO ..... Ants, Mice, and Gophers [*Electromagnetic antipest device*]
AMIGOS... Access Method for Indexed Data Generalized for Operating System [*Data processing*]
AMIGOS... Americans Mutually Interested in Giving Others a Start [*Defunct*] (EA)
AMIH........ Association for Middle-Income Housing [*Later, MMHA*] (EA)

AMIHA ..... AMA [*American Medical Association*] Archives of Industrial Health [*A publication*]

AMIHT ..... Associate Member of the Institution of Highway Engineers [*British*] (DBQ)

AMIIA .... Army Medical Intelligence and Information Agency (MCD)

AMIIISE..... Associate Member of the International Institute of Social Economics [*British*] (DBQ)

AMIJAH... JAAMI. Journal of the Association for the Advancement of Medical Instrumentation [*A publication*]

AMIK .... American Mission in Korea

AMIK .... (Amino)(Iodo)ketanserin [*Biochemistry*]

AMIKA ..... American Inkmaker [*A publication*]

AMILAN... Annales de Medecine Legale [*A publication*]

Am Ill......... Americana Illustrated [*A publication*]

AMILM.... Milo Municipal Library, Alberta [*Library symbol*] [*National Library of Canada*] (NLC)

AMILocoE ... Associate Member of the Institution of Locomotive Engineers [*British*]

Am Im .... American Imago [*A publication*]

AMIM .... Army Modernization Information Memorandum (RDA)

AMIM .... Associate Member of the Institute of Metallurgists [*British*] (DBQ)

AMIM .... Associated Mortgage Investors [*NASDAQ symbol*] (NQ)

Am Imago .. American Imago [*A publication*]

AMIManf ... Associate Member of the Institute of Manufacturing [*British*] (DBQ)

AMI Mar E ... Associate Member of the Institute of Marine Engineers [*British*]

AMIME..... Associate Member of the Institute of Marine Engineers [*British*] (DS)

AMIME..... Associate Member of the Institution of Mining Engineers [*British*]

AMIME(Aust) ... Associate Member of the Institution of Mining Engineers (Australia)

AMIMechE ... Associate Member of the Institution of Mechanical Engineers [*Later, MIMechE*] [*British*] (EY)

Am I M Eng Tr B ... American Institute of Mining Engineers. Transactions. Bulletin [*A publication*]

AMIMGTechE ... Associate Member of the Institution of Mechanical and General Technician Engineers [*British*] (DBQ)

AMIMH.... Associate Member of the Institute of Materials Handling [*British*] (DBQ)

AMIMI...... Associate Member of the Institute of the Motor Industry [*British*]

AMIMinE ... Associate Member of the Institution of Mining Engineers [*British*] (EY)

AMIMM ... Associate Member of the Institution of Mining and Metallurgy [*British*]

Am Import Export Bul ... American Import/Export Bulletin [*A publication*]

Am Import/Export Bull ... American Import/Export Bulletin [*A publication*]

Am Import/Export Manage ... American Import/Export Management [*A publication*]

Am Import/Export Mgt ... American Import/Export Management [*A publication*]

AMIMS..... Associate Member of the Institute of Management Specialists [*British*] (DBQ)

AMI Mun E ... Associate Member of the Institution of Municipal Engineers [*British*]

AMIN .... Advertising and Marketing International Network [*Stamford, CT*] (EA)

AMIN .... Amerindian [*A publication*]

AMINA ..... Associate Member of the Institution of Naval Architects [*British*]

AMINA ..... Association Mondiale des Inventeurs [*World Association of Inventors and Researchers*] (EAIO)

AMINCO.. American Instrument Company

AMINCO Lab News ... AMINCO [*American Instrument Company*] Laboratory News [*A publication*]

Am Ind .... America Indigena [*A publication*]

AMIND..... American Indian

Am Ind .... American Industries [*A publication*]

Am Ind Bas Mag ... American Indian Basketry Magazine [*A publication*]

Am Ind Hyg ... American Industrial Hygiene Association. Journal [*A publication*]

Am Ind Hyg Ass J ... American Industrial Hygiene Association. Journal [*A publication*]

Am Ind Hyg Assn J ... American Industrial Hygiene Association. Journal [*A publication*]

Am Ind Hyg Assoc J ... American Industrial Hygiene Association. Journal [*A publication*]

Am Ind Hyg Assoc Q ... American Industrial Hygiene Association. Quarterly [*A publication*]

Am Ind Hygiene Assn J ... American Industrial Hygiene Association. Journal [*A publication*]

Am Indian Art Mag ... American Indian Art Magazine [*A publication*]

Am Indian Index ... American Indian Index [*A publication*]

Am Indian J ... American Indian Journal [*A publication*]

Am Indian L Rev ... American Indian Law Review [*A publication*]

Am Indigena ... America Indigena [*A publication*]

Am Ind J.... American Indian Journal [*A publication*] (DLA)

Am Ind L Newsl ... American Indian Law Newsletter [*A publication*] (DLA)

Am Ind LR ... American Indian Law Review [*A publication*]

Am Ind L Rev ... American Indian Law Review [*A publication*] (DLA)

Am Indust Hyg A J ... American Industrial Hygiene Association. Journal [*A publication*]

Am Indust Hyg A Quart ... American Industrial Hygiene Association. Quarterly [*A publication*]

Amine Fluores Histochem Scand Jpn Seminar ... Amine Fluorescence Histochemistry. Scandinavia-Japan Seminar [*A publication*]

A Mines Belg ... Annales des Mines de Belgique [*A publication*]

Am Ink....... American Inkmaker [*A publication*]

Am Inkmaker ... American Inkmaker [*A publication*]

Amino Acids Anim Husb Int Symp Rep ... Amino Acids in Animal Husbandry. International Symposium. Reports [*A publication*]

Amino Acids Pept Prot Abstr ... Amino Acids, Peptide, and Protein Abstracts [*A publication*]

Amino Acids Pept Proteins ... Amino Acids, Peptides, and Proteins [*A publication*]

Amino Acid Transp Uric Acid Transp Symp ... Amino Acid Transport and Uric Acid Transport Symposium [*A publication*]

AMINOIL ... American Independent Oil Co.

Aminosaeuren Tierz Int Symp Vortr ... Aminosaeuren in Tierzucht. Internationales Symposium. Vortraege [*A publication*]

Am Insolv Rep ... American Insolvency Reports [*A publication*] (DLA)

Am Ins Rep ... American Insolvency Reports [*A publication*] (DLA)

AMInstAEA ... Associate Member of the Institute of Automotive Engineer Assessors [*British*] (DBQ)

Am Inst Aeronaut Astronaut Monogr ... American Institute of Aeronautics and Astronautics. Monographs [*A publication*]

Am Inst Aeronaut Astronaut Pap ... American Institute of Aeronautics and Astronautics. Paper [*A publication*]

Am Inst Archit J ... American Institute of Architects. Journal [*A publication*]

Am Inst Archit Q Bull ... American Institute of Architects. Quarterly Bulletin [*A publication*]

Am Inst Arch J ... American Institute of Architects. Journal [*A publication*]

Am Inst Bank Bul ... American Institute of Banking. Bulletin [*A publication*]

AMInstBE ... Associate Member of the Institution of British Engineers

Am Inst Biol Sci Publ ... American Institute of Biological Sciences. Publications [*A publication*]

Am Inst Biol Sci Symp ... American Institute of Biological Sciences. Symposia [*A publication*]

AMInstBTM ... Associate Member of the Institute of Business and Technical Management [*British*] (DBQ)

AMInstCE ... Associate Member of the Institution of Civil Engineers [*British*] (EY)

Am Inst Chem Eng Natl Heat Transfer Conf Prepr AIChE Pap ... American Institute of Chemical Engineers. National Heat Transfer Conference. Preprints. AIChE Paper [*A publication*]

AM Inst CM ... Associate Member of the Institute of Commercial Management [*British*] (DCTA)

Am Inst Dent Med Annu Meet ... American Institute of Dental Medicine. Annual Meeting [*A publication*]

AM Inst E ... Associate Member of the Institute of Electronics [*British*]

AmInstEE ... American Institute of Electrical Engineers [*Later, IEEE*]

AM Inst F ... Associate Member of the Institute of Fuel [*British*]

AM INST GE ... Associate Member of the Institute of Gas Engineers [*British*] (ROG)

AMInstHE ... Associate Member of the Institution of Highway Engineers [*British*]

Am Inst Ind Eng Detroit Chapter Proc Annu Conf ... American Institute of Industrial Engineers. Detroit Chapter. Proceedings of the Annual Conference [*A publication*]

Am Inst of Instruc ... American Institute of Instruction [*A publication*]

Am Instit Crim Law and Criminol Jour ... American Institute of Criminal Law and Criminology. Journal [*A publication*]

Am Inst Min Metall Eng Tech Publ ... American Institute of Mining and Metallurgical Engineers. Technical Publications [*A publication*]

Am Inst Min Metall Pet Eng Annu Meet Proc Sess ... American Institute of Mining, Metallurgical, and Petroleum Engineers. Annual Meeting. Proceedings of Sessions [*A publication*]

Am Inst Min Metall Pet Eng Minn Sect Annu Meet ... American Institute of Mining, Metallurgical, and Petroleum Engineers. Minnesota Section. Annual Meeting [*A publication*]

Am Inst Min Metall Petr Eng Inst Met Div Spec Rep Ser ... American Institute of Mining, Metallurgical, and Petroleum Engineers. Institute of Metals Division. Special Report Series [*A publication*]

Am Inst Min Metal Pet Eng Pet Trans ... Petroleum Transactions. AIME (American Institute of Mining, Metallurgy, and Petroleum Engineering) [*A publication*]

Am Inst Oral Biol Annu Meet ... American Institute of Oral Biology. Annual Meeting [*A publication*]

Am Inst Phys Conf Proc ... American Institute of Physics. Conference Proceedings [*A publication*]

Am Inst Plan ... American Institute of Planners. Journal [*A publication*]

Am Inst Plan J ... American Institute of Planners. Journal [*A publication*]

Am Inst Planners J ... American Institute of Planners. Journal [*A publication*]

Am Inst Plann J ... American Institute of Planners. Journal [*A publication*]

Am Inst Plann Pap ... American Institute of Planners. Papers [*A publication*]

Am Inst Plant Eng J ... American Institute of Plant Engineers. Journal [*A publication*]
Am Inst Prof Geol Calif Sect Annu Meet Proc ... American Institute of Professional Geologists. California Section. Annual Meeting. Proceedings [*A publication*]
AMInstR ... Associate Member of the Institute of Refrigeration [*British*]
Am Inst Refrig Proc ... American Institute of Refrigeration. Proceedings [*A publication*]
AMInstT ... Associate Member of the Institute of Transport [*British*]   (EY)
AM Inst TA ... Associate Member of the Institute of Transport Administration [*British*]   (DCTA)
AM Inst W ... Associate Member of the Institute of Welding [*British*]
AMINTAPHIL ... International Association for Philosophy of Law and Social Philosophy, American Section   (EA)
Am Int J ..... American Intelligence Journal [*A publication*]
AMIO .... Amiodarone [*Coronary vasodilator*] [*Cardiology*]
AMIOSH .. Associate Member of the Institution of Occupational Safety and Health [*British*]   (DCTA)
AMIP .... Allied Minimum Imports Program [*World War II*]
AMIP .... American Market for International Program [*Telecommunications*]
AMIP .... Army Management Information Program   (AABC)
AMIP .... Army Management Intern Program   (RDA)
AMIP .... Army Model Improvement Program   (RDA)
AMIPAC ... Americans in Israel Political Action Committee   (EA)
AMIPAZ ... Anais. Faculdade de Medicina. Universidade do Parana [*Curitiba*] [*A publication*]
AMIPC ...... Associate Member of the Institute of Production Control [*British*]   (DBQ)
AMIPE ...... Associate Member of the Institution of Production Engineers [*British*]
AMI Plant E ... Associate Member of the Institute of Plant Engineers [*British*]
AMIQ .... Associate Member of the Institute of Quarrying [*British*]   (DBQ)
AMIQ .... Association pour l'Avancement de la Micro-Informatique [*Association for the Advancement of Micro-Information*] [*Canada*]
AMIR .... Amicor, Inc. [*NASDAQ symbol*]   (NQ)
AMIR .... Mirror Public Library, Alberta [*Library symbol*] [*National Library of Canada*]   (NLC)
AMIRA ...... Amplified Immunoradiometric Assay
AMIRA ...... Australian Mineral Industries Research Association
AMIran ...... Archaeologische Mitteilungen aus Iran [*A publication*]
AMIREE (Aust) ... Associate Member of the Institute of Radio and Electronic Engineers (Australia)
Am Irish His S J ... American Irish Historical Society. Journal [*A publication*]
AMIRTE ... Associate Member of the Institute of Road Transport Engineers [*British*]   (DBQ)
AMIS .... Acquisition Management Information System [*Air Force*]
AMIS .... Advanced Management Information Service [*or System*] [*Air Force*]
AMIS .... Agricultural Management Information System   (ADA)
AMIS .... Air Movements Information Section
AMIS .... Airborne Modular Integrated System   (MCD)
AMIS .... Aircraft Movement Information Service [*Air Force*]
AMIS .... Aircraft Multiplex Intercommunications System
AMIS .... Airport Management Information System
AMIS .... American Musical Instrument Society   (EA)
AMIS .... AMI Systems, Inc. [*NASDAQ symbol*]   (NQ)
AMIS .... Amis du Film et de la Television [*A publication*]
AMIS .... Amistad Recreation Area [*National Park Service designation*]
AMIS .... Army Management Information System
AMIS .... Aspirin Myocardial Infarction Study [*Medicine*]
AMIS .... Australian Municipal Information System [*Computer Sciences of Australia Pty. Ltd.*] [*Information service or system*]   (CRD)
AMIS .... Automated Incendiary Submunition   (MCD)
AMIS .... Automated Maintenance Information System   (MCD)
AMIS .... Automated Management Information System   (DIT)
AMIS .... Automated Minerals Information System [*Bureau of Mines*] [*Database*]
AMISC ...... Army Management Information Systems Course
AMISEE ... Israel. Geological Society. Annual Meeting [*A publication*]
AMISIBR ... American Marine Insurance Syndicate for Insurance of Builder's Risks [*Defunct*]   (EA)
AMIS J ...... American Musical Instrument Society. Journal [*A publication*]
AMISM ..... Associate Member of the Institute of Supervisory Management [*British*]   (DBQ)
AMIS N ..... American Musical Instrument Society. Newsletter [*A publication*]
AMIStruct E ... Associate Member of the Institute of Structural Engineers [*British*]
AMITA ...... American-Italian Women of Achievement
AMITD ..... Associate Member of the Institute of Training and Development [*British*]   (DBQ)
AMIUA ..... Acta Medica Iugoslavica [*A publication*]
AMI-USA ... Association Montessori International - USA   (EA)
AMIW .... Associate Member of the Institute of Welding [*British*]
AMI Water E ... Associate Member of the Institute of Water Engineers [*British*]

AMIWHTE ... Associate Member of the Institution of Works and Highways Technician Engineers [*British*]   (DBQ)
AMIWM ... Associate Member of the Institution of Works Managers [*British*]
AMIWPC ... Associate Member of the Institute of Water Pollution Control [*British*]   (DBQ)
AMJ .... Academy of Management. Journal [*A publication*]
AMJ .... Advanced Management Journal [*A publication*]
AMJ .... Almenara [*Brazil*] [*Airport symbol*] [*Obsolete*]   (OAG)
AMJ .... Assemblee Mondiale de la Jeunesse [*World Assembly of Youth*]
AMJ .... Augustines de la Misericorde de Jesus [*Religious order*] [*Canada*]
AMJA .... American Medical Joggers Association [*Later, AMAA*]
Am J Acupunct ... American Journal of Acupuncture [*A publication*]
Am J Ag Econ ... American Journal of Agricultural Economics [*A publication*]
Am J Agr ... American Journal of Agriculture and Science [*A publication*]
Am J Agr Ec ... American Journal of Agricultural Economics [*A publication*]
Am J Agr Econ ... American Journal of Agricultural Economics [*A publication*]
Am J Agric Econ ... American Journal of Agricultural Economics [*A publication*]
AMJAMS ... Automated Military Justice Analysis and Management System
Am J Anat ... American Journal of Anatomy [*A publication*]
Am J Anc Hist ... American Journal of Ancient History [*A publication*]
Am J Arab St ... American Journal of Arabic Studies [*A publication*]
Am J Archae ... American Journal of Archaeology [*A publication*]
Am J Archaeol ... American Journal of Archaeology [*A publication*]
Am J Art Th ... American Journal of Art Therapy [*A publication*]
Am J Art Ther ... American Journal of Art Therapy [*A publication*]
Am J Bot .... American Journal of Botany [*A publication*]
Am J Canc ... American Journal of Cancer [*A publication*]
Am J Cancer ... American Journal of Cancer [*A publication*]
Am J Card ... American Journal of Cardiology [*A publication*]
Am J Cardiol ... American Journal of Cardiology [*A publication*]
Am J Chinese Med ... American Journal of Chinese Medicine [*A publication*]
Am J Chin Med ... American Journal of Chinese Medicine [*A publication*]
Am J Clin Biofeedback ... American Journal of Clinical Biofeedback [*A publication*]
Am J Clin Hypn ... American Journal of Clinical Hypnosis [*A publication*]
Am J Clin Hypnosis ... American Journal of Clinical Hypnosis [*A publication*]
Am J Clin Med ... American Journal of Clinical Medicine [*A publication*]
Am J Clin N ... American Journal of Clinical Nutrition [*A publication*]
Am J Clin Nutr ... American Journal of Clinical Nutrition [*A publication*]
Am J Clin Nutrition ... American Journal of Clinical Nutrition [*A publication*]
Am J Clin Oncol ... American Journal of Clinical Oncology [*A publication*]
Am J Clin P ... American Journal of Clinical Pathology [*A publication*]
Am J Clin Path ... American Journal of Clinical Pathology [*A publication*]
Am J Clin Pathol ... American Journal of Clinical Pathology [*A publication*]
Am J Community Psychol ... American Journal of Community Psychology [*A publication*]
Am J Comparative Law ... American Journal of Comparative Law [*A publication*]
Am J Compar Law ... American Journal of Comparative Law [*A publication*]
Am J Comp L ... American Journal of Comparative Law [*A publication*]
Am J Comp Law ... American Journal of Comparative Law [*A publication*]
Am J Comput Ling ... American Journal of Computational Linguistics [*A publication*]
Am J Conch ... American Journal of Conchology [*A publication*]
Am J Corr ... American Journal of Correction [*A publication*]
Am J Correction ... American Journal of Correction [*A publication*]
Am J Crim L ... American Journal of Criminal Law [*A publication*]
Am J 2d ... American Jurisprudence, Second Series [*A publication*]   (DLA)
Am J Dent Sci ... American Journal of Dental Science [*A publication*]
Am J Dermatopathol ... American Journal of Dermatopathology [*A publication*]
Am J Dig Di ... American Journal of Digestive Diseases [*Later, Digestive Diseases and Sciences*] [*A publication*]
Am J Dig Dis ... American Journal of Digestive Diseases [*Later, Digestive Diseases and Sciences*] [*A publication*]
Am J Dig Dis Nutr ... American Journal of Digestive Diseases and Nutrition [*A publication*]
Am J Digest Dis ... American Journal of Digestive Diseases [*A publication*]
Am J Dis Ch ... American Journal of Diseases of Children [*A publication*]
Am J Dis Child ... American Journal of Diseases of Children [*A publication*]
Am J Drug Alcohol Abuse ... American Journal of Drug and Alcohol Abuse [*A publication*]
Am J Econ ... American Journal of Economics and Sociology [*New York*] [*A publication*]
Am J Econ S ... American Journal of Economics and Sociology [*New York*] [*A publication*]
Am J Econ Soc ... American Journal of Economics and Sociology [*A publication*]
Am J Econ & Soc ... American Journal of Economics and Sociology [*New York*] [*A publication*]
Am J Econ & Sociol ... American Journal of Economics and Sociology [*New York*] [*A publication*]
Am J Econ Sociol ... American Journal of Economics and Sociology [*New York*] [*A publication*]
Am J Econ Sociol (New York) ... American Journal of Economics and Sociology (New York) [*A publication*]
Am J Educ ... American Journal of Education [*A publication*]

Am J EEG Technol ... American Journal of EEG Technology [A publication]
Am J Enol ... American Journal of Enology [A publication]
Am J Enol V ... American Journal of Enology and Viticulture [A publication]
Am J Enol Viti ... American Journal of Enology and Viticulture [A publication]
Am J Enol Vitic ... American Journal of Enology and Viticulture [A publication]
Am J Epidem ... American Journal of Epidemiology [A publication]
Am J Epidemiol ... American Journal of Epidemiology [A publication]
Am Jew Arch ... American Jewish Archives [A publication]
Am Jew H ... American Jewish History [A publication]
Am Jew His ... American Jewish Historical Society. Publications [A publication]
Am Jew Hist ... American Jewish History [A publication]
Am Jew Hist Q ... American Jewish Historical Quarterly [A publication]
Am Jew Hist Soc Publ ... American Jewish Historical Society. Publications [A publication]
Am Jewish A ... American Jewish Archives [A publication]
Am Jewish H ... American Jewish Historical Quarterly [A publication]
Am Jew Yb ... American Jewish Yearbook [A publication]
Am Jew Yr Bk ... American Jewish Yearbook [A publication]
Am J Forensic Med Pathol ... American Journal of Forensic Medicine and Pathology [A publication]
Am J For Psych ... American Journal of Forensic Psychiatry [A publication]   (DLA)
Am J Gastro ... American Journal of Gastroenterology [A publication]
Am J Gastroenterol ... American Journal of Gastroenterology [A publication]
Am J Health Plann ... American Journal of Health Planning [A publication]
Am J Hematol ... American Journal of Hematology [A publication]
Am J Hosp Care ... American Journal of Hospice Care [A publication]
Am J Hosp P ... American Journal of Hospital Pharmacy [A publication]
Am J Hosp Pharm ... American Journal of Hospital Pharmacy [A publication]
Am J Hu Gen ... American Journal of Human Genetics [A publication]
Am J Human Genet ... American Journal of Human Genetics [A publication]
Am J Hum Biol ... American Journal of Human Biology [A publication]
Am J Hum Genet ... American Journal of Human Genetics [A publication]
Am J Hyg .. American Journal of Hygiene [A publication]
Am J Hyg Monogr Ser ... American Journal of Hygiene. Monographic Series [A publication]
Am J Ind Med ... American Journal of Industrial Medicine [A publication]
Am J Ind Psych ... American Journal of Individual Psychology [A publication]
Am J Inf Con ... American Journal of Infection Control [A publication]
Am J Infect Control ... American Journal of Infection Control [A publication]
Am J Internat Law ... American Journal of International Law [A publication]
Am J Int L ... American Journal of International Law [A publication]
Am J Int Law ... American Journal of International Law [A publication]
Am J Int Law Proc ... American Journal of International Law. Proceedings [A publication]
Am J Int'l L ... American Journal of International Law [A publication]
Am J Int L Supp ... American Journal of International Law. Supplement [A publication]
Am J IV Clin Nutr ... American Journal of Intravenous Therapy and Clinical Nutrition [A publication]
Am J IV Ther ... American Journal of Intravenous Therapy [Later, American Journal of Intravenous Therapy and Clinical Nutrition] [A publication]
Am J IV Therapy ... American Journal of Intravenous Therapy [Later, American Journal of Intravenous Therapy and Clinical Nutrition] [A publication]
Am J IV Ther Clin Nutr ... American Journal of Intravenous Therapy and Clinical Nutrition [A publication]
Am J Jur.... American Journal of Jurisprudence [A publication]
Am J Juris ... American Journal of Jurisprudence [A publication]
Am J Jurispr ... American Journal of Jurisprudence [A publication]
Am J Jurisprud ... American Journal of Jurisprudence [A publication]
Am J Kidney ... American Journal of Kidney Diseases [A publication]
Am J Kidney Dis ... American Journal of Kidney Diseases [A publication]
Am J Law Med ... American Journal of Law and Medicine [A publication]
Am J Law & Med ... American Journal of Law and Medicine [A publication]
Am J Legal Hist ... American Journal of Legal History [A publication]
Am J Leg Forms Anno ... American Jurisprudence Legal Forms, Annotated [A publication]   (DLA)
Am J Leg Hist ... American Journal of Legal History [A publication]
Am JLH..... American Journal of Legal History [A publication]
Am JL and M ... American Journal of Law and Medicine [A publication]
Am JL & Med ... American Journal of Law and Medicine [A publication]
Am Jl Ph... American Journal of Pharmacy [A publication]
Am J L Rev ... American Journal Law Review [A publication]   (DLA)
Am J Math ... American Journal of Mathematics [A publication]
Am J Math Manage Sci ... American Journal of Mathematical and Management Sciences [A publication]
Am J Med ... American Journal of Medicine [A publication]
Am J Med Electron ... American Journal of Medical Electronics [A publication]
Am J Med Genet ... American Journal of Medical Genetics [A publication]
Am J Med Jurispr ... American Journal of Medical Jurisprudence [A publication]
Am J Med Sc ... American Journal of the Medical Sciences [A publication]
Am J Med Sci ... American Journal of the Medical Sciences [A publication]
Am J Med Te ... American Journal of Medical Technology [A publication]

Am J Med Technol ... American Journal of Medical Technology [A publication]
Am J Men Deficiency ... American Journal of Mental Deficiency [A publication]
Am J Mental Deficiency ... American Journal of Mental Deficiency [A publication]
Am J Ment D ... American Journal of Mental Deficiency [A publication]
Am J Ment Defic ... American Journal of Mental Deficiency [A publication]
Am J Ment Deficiency ... American Journal of Mental Deficiency [A publication]
Am J Ment Dis ... American Journal of Mental Diseases [A publication]
Am J Micr (NY) ... American Journal of Microscopy and Popular Science (New York) [A publication]
Am JM Sc ... American Journal of the Medical Sciences [A publication]
AMJN .... American Journal of Nursing [A publication]
Am J Nephr ... American Journal of Nephrology [A publication]
Am J Nephrol ... American Journal of Nephrology [A publication]
Am J Neurop ... American Journal of Neuropathy [A publication]
Am Jnl Archae ... American Journal of Archaeology [A publication]
Am Jnl Econ & Soc ... American Journal of Economics and Sociology [New York] [A publication]
Am Jnl Philol ... American Journal of Philology [A publication]
Am Jnl Soc ... American Journal of Sociology [A publication]
Am J Nurs ... American Journal of Nursing [A publication]
Am J Nursing ... American Journal of Nursing [A publication]
Am J Obstet Gynecol ... American Journal of Obstetrics and Gynecology [A publication]
Am J Obst G ... American Journal of Obstetrics and Gynecology [A publication]
Am J Obst Gynec ... American Journal of Obstetrics and Gynecology [A publication]
Am J Occup Ther ... American Journal of Occupational Therapy [A publication]
Am J Occup Therapy ... American Journal of Occupational Therapy [A publication]
Am J Occu T ... American Journal of Occupational Therapy [A publication]
Am J Ophth ... American Journal of Ophthalmology [A publication]
Am J Ophthalmol ... American Journal of Ophthalmology [A publication]
Am J Optom ... American Journal of Optometry and Physiological Optics [A publication]
Am J Optom Arch Am Acad Optom ... American Journal of Optometry and Archives of American Academy of Optometry [Later, American Journal of Optometry and Physiological Optics] [A publication]
Am J Optom and Arch Am Acad Optom ... American Journal of Optometry and Archives of American Academy of Optometry [Later, American Journal of Optometry and Physiological Optics] [A publication]
Am J Optom & Physiol Opt ... American Journal of Optometry and Physiological Optics [A publication]
Am J Optom Physiol Opt ... American Journal of Optometry and Physiological Optics [A publication]
Am J Orth ... American Journal of Orthopedics [A publication]
Am J Orthod ... American Journal of Orthodontics [A publication]
Am J Orthod Dentofacial Orthop ... American Journal of Orthodontics and Dentofacial Orthopedics [A publication]
Am J Orthod Oral Surg ... American Journal of Orthodontics and Oral Surgery [Later, American Journal of Orthodontics] [A publication]
Am J Orthod Oral Surg Oral Surg ... American Journal of Orthodontics and Oral Surgery [later, American Journal of Orthodontics]. Oral Surgery [A publication]
Am J Orthop ... American Journal of Orthopsychiatry [A publication]
Am J Orthopsych ... American Journal of Orthopsychiatry [A publication]
Am J Orthopsychiat ... American Journal of Orthopsychiatry [A publication]
Am J Orthopsychiatr ... American Journal of Orthopsychiatry [A publication]
Am J Orthopsychiatry ... American Journal of Orthopsychiatry [A publication]
Am J Orth Surg ... American Journal of Orthopedic Surgery [A publication]
Am J Otol .. American Journal of Otology [A publication]
Am J Otolaryngol ... American Journal of Otolaryngology [A publication]
Am J Otolaryngol ... American Journal of Otolaryngology [A publication]
Am Jour Econ Sociol ... American Journal of Economics and Sociology [New York] [A publication]
Am Jour Internatl Law ... American Journal of International Law [A publication]
Am Jour Legal Hist ... American Journal of Legal History [A publication]
Am Journ Phil ... American Journal of Philology [A publication]
Am Jour Phys Anthropol ... American Journal of Physical Anthropology [A publication]
Am Jour Pol ... American Journal of Politics [A publication]
Am Jour Psychiatry ... American Journal of Psychiatry [A publication]
Am Jour Soc ... American Journal of Sociology [A publication]   (DLA)
Am Jour Sociol ... American Journal of Sociology [A publication]
AMJP........ [A] Messianic Jewish Perspective   (EA)
Am JPA ... American Journal of Physical Anthropology [A publication]
Am J P Anth ... American Journal of Physical Anthropology [A publication]
Am J Path ... American Journal of Pathology [A publication]
Am J Pathol ... American Journal of Pathology [A publication]
Am J Pediatr Hematol Oncol ... American Journal of Pediatric Hematology/ Oncology [A publication]
Am J Perinatol ... American Journal of Perinatology [A publication]

AmJPh....... American Journal of Philology [*Baltimore*] [*A publication*]

Am J Phar E ... American Journal of Pharmaceutical Education [*A publication*]

Am J Pharm ... American Journal of Pharmacy [*A publication*]

Am J Pharm ... American Journal of Pharmacy and the Sciences Supporting Public Health [*Later, American Journal of Pharmacy*] [*A publication*]

Am J Pharm Educ ... American Journal of Pharmaceutical Education [*A publication*]

Am J Pharm Sci Supporting Public Health ... American Journal of Pharmacy and the Sciences Supporting Public Health [*Later, American Journal of Pharmacy*] [*A publication*]

Am J Phil... American Journal of Philology [*A publication*]

Am J Philol ... American Journal of Philology [*A publication*]

Am J Photogr ... American Journal of Photography [*A publication*]

Am J Phys ... American Journal of Physics [*A publication*]

Am J Phys Anthro ... American Journal of Physical Anthropology [*A publication*]

Am J Phys Anthrop ... American Journal of Physical Anthropology [*A publication*]

Am J Phys Anthrop ns ... American Journal of Physical Anthropology. New Series [*A publication*]

Am J Phys Anthropol ... American Journal of Physical Anthropology [*A publication*]

Am J Physics ... American Journal of Physics [*A publication*]

Am J Physiol ... American Journal of Physiology [*A publication*]

Am J Physiol Cell Physiol ... American Journal of Physiology. Cell Physiology [*A publication*]

Am J Physiol Endocrinol Metab Gastrointest Physiol ... American Journal of Physiology. Endocrinology, Metabolism, and Gastrointestinal Physiology [*A publication*]

Am J Physiol Heart Circ Physiol ... American Journal of Physiology. Heart and Circulatory Physiology [*A publication*]

Am J Physiol Regul Integr Comp Physiol ... American Journal of Physiology. Regulatory, Integrative, and Comparative Physiology [*A publication*]

Am J Physiol Renal Fluid Electrolyte Physiol ... American Journal of Physiology. Renal, Fluid, and Electrolyte Physiology [*A publication*]

Am J Physl ... American Journal of Physiology [*A publication*]

Am J Phys M ... American Journal of Physical Medicine [*A publication*]

Am J Phys Med ... American Journal of Physical Medicine [*A publication*]

Am J Phys Med Rehabil ... American Journal of Physical Medicine and Rehabilitation [*A publication*]

Am J Pl & Pr Forms Anno ... American Jurisprudence Pleading and Practice Forms, Annotated [*A publication*]   (DLA)

Am J Pol.... American Journal of Politics [*A publication*]

Am J Police Sci ... American Journal of Police Science [*A publication*]   (DLA)

Am J Pol Sc ... American Journal of Political Science [*A publication*]

Am J Pol Sci ... American Journal of Political Science [*A publication*]

Am J Pract Nurs ... American Journal of Practical Nursing [*A publication*]

Am J Prev Med ... American Journal of Preventive Medicine [*A publication*]

Am J Primatol ... American Journal of Primatology [*A publication*]

Am J Proct ... American Journal of Proctology [*A publication*]

Am J Proctol ... American Journal of Proctology [*Later, American Journal of Proctology, Gastroenterology, and Colon and Rectal Surgery*] [*A publication*]

Am J Proctol Gastroenterol Colon Rectal Surg ... American Journal of Proctology, Gastroenterology, and Colon and Rectal Surgery [*A publication*]

Am J Proctol Gastroenterol Colon Rectal Surg (Georgetown) ... American Journal of Proctology, Gastroenterology, and Colon and Rectal Surgery (Georgetown) [*A publication*]

Am J Progr Ther ... American Journal of Progressive Therapeutics [*A publication*]

Am J Proof of Facts ... American Jurisprudence Proof of Facts [*A publication*]   (DLA)

Am J Psych ... American Journal of Psychiatry [*A publication*]

Am J Psycha ... American Journal of Psychoanalysis [*A publication*]

Am J Psychi ... American Journal of Psychiatry [*A publication*]

Am J Psychiat ... American Journal of Psychiatry [*A publication*]

Am J Psychiatr ... American Journal of Psychiatry [*A publication*]

Am J Psychiatry ... American Journal of Psychiatry [*A publication*]

Am J Psycho ... American Journal of Psychology [*A publication*]

Am J Psychoanal ... American Journal of Psychoanalysis [*A publication*]

Am J Psychol ... American Journal of Psychology [*A publication*]

Am J Psychoth ... American Journal of Psychotherapy [*A publication*]

Am J Psychother ... American Journal of Psychotherapy [*A publication*]

Am J Psycht ... American Journal of Psychotherapy [*A publication*]

Am J Pub He ... American Journal of Public Health [*A publication*]

Am J Pub Health ... American Journal of Public Health [*A publication*]

Am J Pub Health ... American Journal of Public Health and the Nation's Health [*A publication*]

Am J Public Health ... American Journal of Public Health [*A publication*]

Am J Public Health Nation's Health ... American Journal of Public Health and the Nation's Health [*Later, American Journal of Public Health*] [*A publication*]

Am J Public Health Suppl ... American Journal of Public Health. Supplement [*A publication*]

Am Jr........ American Jurisprudence [*A publication*]   (DLA)

Am Jr......... American Jurist [*A publication*]   (DLA)

Am J Reprod Immunol ... American Journal of Reproductive Immunology [*A publication*]

Am J Reprod Immunol Microbiol ... American Journal of Reproductive Immunology and Microbiology [*A publication*]

Am J Respir Cell Mol Biol ... American Journal of Respiratory Cell and Molecular Biology [*A publication*]

Am J Roentg ... American Journal of Roentgenology [*A publication*]

Am J Roentgenol ... American Journal of Roentgenology [*A publication*]

Am J Roentgenol ... American Journal of Roentgenology, Radium Therapy, and Nuclear Medicine [*A publication*]

Am J Roentgenol Radium Ther ... American Journal of Roentgenology and Radium Therapy [*Later, American Journal of Roentgenology*] [*A publication*]

Am J Roentgenol Radium Ther Nucl Med ... American Journal of Roentgenology, Radium Therapy, and Nuclear Medicine [*Later, American Journal of Roentgenology*] [*A publication*]

Am JS........ American Journal of Sociology [*A publication*]

Am J Sc and Arts ... American Journal of Science and Arts [*A publication*]

Am J School Hygiene ... American Journal of School Hygiene [*A publication*]

Am J Sci ... American Journal of Science [*A publication*]

Am J Sci Arts ... American Journal of Science and Arts [*A publication*]

Am J Sem Lang ... American Journal of Semitic Languages and Literatures [*A publication*]

Am J Small Bus ... American Journal of Small Business [*A publication*]

Am J Soc.... American Journal of Sociology [*A publication*]

Am J Socio ... American Journal of Sociology [*A publication*]

Am J Sociol ... American Journal of Sociology [*A publication*]

Am J Soc Sci ... American Journal of Social Science [*A publication*]

Am J Sports Med ... American Journal of Sports Medicine [*A publication*]

Am J Stomat ... American Journal of Stomatology [*A publication*]

Am J Surg ... American Journal of Surgery [*A publication*]

Am J Surg Pathol ... American Journal of Surgical Pathology [*A publication*]

Am J Syph Gonorrhea Vener Dis ... American Journal of Syphilis, Gonorrhea, and Venereal Diseases [*A publication*]

Am J Tax Pol'y ... American Journal of Tax Policy [*A publication*]   (DLA)

AmJTh....... American Journal of Theology [*A publication*]

Am J Theol ... American Journal of Theology [*A publication*]

Am J Ther Clin Rep ... American Journal of Therapeutics and Clinical Reports [*A publication*]

Am J Th Ph ... American Journal of Theology and Philosophy [*A publication*]

Am J Trial Ad ... American Journal of Trial Advocacy [*A publication*]

Am J Trial Advoc ... American Journal of Trial Advocacy [*A publication*]   (DLA)

Am J Trial Advocacy ... American Journal of Trial Advocacy [*A publication*]

Am J Trials ... American Jurisprudence Trials [*A publication*]   (DLA)

Am J Trop Dis (New Orleans) ... American Journal of Tropical Diseases and Preventive Medicine (New Orleans) [*A publication*]

Am J Trop M ... American Journal of Tropical Medicine and Hygiene [*A publication*]

Am J Trop Med ... American Journal of Tropical Medicine [*Later, American Journal of Tropical Medicine and Hygiene*] [*A publication*]

Am J Trop Med Hyg ... American Journal of Tropical Medicine and Hygiene [*A publication*]

Am Jud Soc ... American Judicature Society. Journal [*A publication*]

Am Jud Soc'y ... Journal. American Judicature Society [*A publication*]

Am Jur...... American Jurisprudence [*A publication*]   (DLA)

Am Jur...... American Jurist [*A publication*]   (DLA)

Am Jur 2d .. American Jurisprudence, Second Series [*A publication*]   (DLA)

Am Jurist... American Jurist [*A publication*]   (DLA)

Am Jur Legal Forms ... American Jurisprudence Legal Forms [*A publication*]   (DLA)

Am Jur Legal Forms 2d ... American Jurisprudence Legal Forms, Second Series [*A publication*]   (DLA)

Am Jur Leg Forms Anno ... American Jurisprudence Legal Forms, Annotated [*A publication*]   (DLA)

Am Jur Pl & Pr Forms ... American Jurisprudence Pleading and Practice Forms, Annotated [*A publication*]   (DLA)

Am Jur Pl & Pr Forms (Rev Ed) ... American Jurisprudence Pleading and Practice Forms, Revised Editions [*A publication*]   (DLA)

Am Jur Proof of Facts ... American Jurisprudence Proof of Facts [*A publication*]   (DLA)

Am Jur Proof of Facts Anno ... American Jurisprudence Proof of Facts, Annotated [*A publication*]   (DLA)

Am Jur Trials ... American Jurisprudence Trials [*A publication*]   (DLA)

AMJV........ Alexander Marx Jubilee Volume [*A publication*]   (BJA)

Am J Vet Med ... American Journal of Veterinary Medicine [*A publication*]

Am J Vet Re ... American Journal of Veterinary Research [*A publication*]

Am J Vet Res ... American Journal of Veterinary Research [*A publication*]

AMJX........ American Federal Savings Bank of Duval County [*NASDAQ symbol*]   (NQ)

AMK.......... Academy of Marketing Science. Journal [*A publication*]

AMK.......... Amark Explorations Ltd. [*Vancouver Stock Exchange symbol*]

AMK.......... American Technical Ceramics [*AMEX symbol*]   (SPSG)

AMK.......... Antimisting Kerosene [*Aviation*]

a-mk--- .... Muscat and Oman [*Oman*] [*MARC geographic area code*] [*Library of Congress*]   (LCCP)

AMK.......... University of Arkansas at Monticello, Monticello, AR [*OCLC symbol*]   (OCLC)

AMKG....... Amoskeag Bank Shares, Inc. [*NASDAQ symbol*]   (NQ)

AMKI .... King Island [*Australia*] [*ICAO location identifier*]   (ICLI)

AMKITU... Amalgamated Moulders and Kindred Industries Trade Union [*British*]
AMKO....... American Mothers of Korean Orphans (EA)
AMKTU .... Army Marksmanship Training Unit [*CONARC*] (AABC)
AML.......... Abandoned Mine Land [*Department of the Interior*]
AML.......... Aberdeen Marine Laboratory
AML.......... Absolute Maximum Loss
AML.......... Acquisition Material List (MCD)
AML.......... Actual Measured Loss [*Telecommunications*] (TEL)
AML.......... Acute Myelogenous Leukemia [*Medicine*]
AML.......... Acute Myeloid [*or Myeloblastic or Myelocytic*] Leukemia [*Medicine*]
AML.......... Adaptive Maneuvering Logic (MCD)
AML.......... Admiralty Materials Laboratory [*British*]
AML.......... Aeromedical Laboratory
AML.......... Aeronautical Materials Laboratory
AML.......... Airfield Marking and Lighting (NATG)
AML.......... Allied Military Liaison [*Balkans*] [*World War II*]
AML.......... Amberley [*New Zealand*] [*Later, EYR*] [*Geomagnetic observatory code*]
AML.......... American Mail Line
AML.......... American Men of Letters [*A publication*]
AML.......... American Meteorite Laboratory
AmL.......... Amor de Libro [*A publication*]
AML.......... Amplitude-Modulated Link [*Electronics*]
AML.......... Animated Movie Language (BUR)
AML.......... Anterior Mitral Leaflet [*Cardiology*]
AML.......... Application Module Library [*IBM Corp.*]
AML.......... Applied Mathematics Laboratory
AML.......... Approved Materials List [*NASA*]
AML.......... Arctic Marine Locomotive [*An icebreaker used in oil exploration in the Arctic*]
AML.......... Area Medical Laboratory [*Military*] (AABC)
AML.......... Armee-Munitionslager [*Army ammunition depot*] [*German military - World War II*]
AML.......... Armel, Inc. [*AMEX symbol*] (SPSG)
AML.......... Army Medical Library [*Became Armed Forces Medical Library, 1952; later, NLM*]
AML.......... Army Missile Laboratory (RDA)
AML.......... Array Machine Language [*Data processing*]
AML.......... Automated Multitest Laboratory
AML.......... Automatic Machine Loading
AML.......... Automatic Magazine Loading
AML.......... Auxiliary Minelayer
AML.......... Aviation Materiel Laboratories [*Army*]
AML.......... [*A*] Manufacturing Language [*Data processing*]
AML.......... Washington, DC [*Location identifier*] [*FAA*] (FAAL)
AMLA .... Airplane Model List of America
AMLA .... American Mutual Life Association (EA)
Am Lab ..... American Laboratory [*A publication*]
Am Lab Arb Awards (P-H) ... American Labor Arbitration Awards (Prentice-Hall, Inc.) [*A publication*] (DLA)
Am Lab Arb Cas ... American Labor Arbitration Cases [*Prentice-Hall, Inc.*] [*A publication*] (DLA)
Am Lab Arb Serv ... American Labor Arbitration Services [*A publication*] (DLA)
Am Lab (Boston) ... American Laboratory (Boston) [*A publication*]
Am Lab Cas ... American Labor Cases [*Prentice-Hall, Inc.*] [*A publication*] (DLA)
Am Lab (Fairfield Conn) ... American Laboratory (Fairfield, Connecticut) [*A publication*]
Am Lab Leg Rev ... American Labor Legislation Review [*A publication*]
Am Labor Legis Rev ... American Labor Legislation Review [*A publication*]
Am Labor Leg R ... American Labor Legislation Review [*A publication*]
Am Landrace ... American Landrace [*A publication*]
Am Laund Dig ... American Laundry Digest [*A publication*]
Am Laundry Dig ... American Laundry Digest [*A publication*]
Am Law...... American Lawyer [*A publication*]
Am Law Inst ... American Law Institute. Restatement of the Law [*A publication*] (DLA)
Am Law J... American Law Journal [*A publication*]
Am Law J NS ... American Law Journal. New Series [*A publication*]
Am Law Mag ... American Law Magazine [*A publication*]
Am Law R.. American Law Review [*A publication*]
Am Law Rec ... American Law Record [*Cincinnati*] [*A publication*] (DLA)
Am Law Rec ... American Law Record [*Ohio*] [*A publication*] (DLA)
Am Law Record ... American Law Record (Reprint) [*Ohio*] [*A publication*] (DLA)
Am Law Reg ... American Law Register [*Philadelphia*] [*A publication*] (DLA)
Am Law Reg NS ... American Law Register, New Series [*A publication*] (DLA)
Am Law Reg (Old Ser) ... American Law Register (Reprint) [*Ohio*] [*A publication*] (DLA)
Am Law Reg OS ... American Law Register, Old Series [*A publication*] (DLA)
Am Law Rev ... American Law Review [*A publication*]
Am Law S Rev ... American Law School Review [*A publication*] (DLA)
Am Law T Rep ... American Law Times Reports [*A publication*] (DLA)
Am Lawy.... American Lawyer [*A publication*]

AMLB........ Advertising and Marketing Law Bulletin [*Australia*] [*A publication*]
AMLC .... Aerospace Medical Laboratory (Clinical) [*Lackland Air Force Base, TX*] (MCD)
Am LC ...... American Leading Cases [*A publication*] (DLA)
AMLC ...... Association of Marine Laboratories of the Caribbean (EAIO)
AMLC ...... Asynchronous Multiline Controller [*Telecommunications*]
Am L Cas ... American Leading Cases [*A publication*] (DLA)
AMLCD .... Active Matrix Liquid Crystal Display
Am LCRP .. Sharswood and Budd's Leading Cases on Real Property [*A publication*] (DLA)
AMLE........ Amcole Energy Corp. [*Fort Worth, TX*] [*NASDAQ symbol*] (NQ)
AMLE........ Aviation Maintenance and Logistics Evaluation (MCD)
Am Lead Ca (Ed of 1871) ... American Leading Cases (Edition of 1871) [*A publication*] (DLA)
Am Lead Cas ... American Leading Cases, Edited by Hare and Wallace [*A publication*] (DLA)
Am Lead Cases ... American Leading Cases [*A publication*] (DLA)
Am Lead Cas (H & W) ... American Leading Cases, Edited by Hare and Wallace [*A publication*] (DLA)
Am Leading Cas ... American Leading Cases [*A publication*] (DLA)
Am Lect Ser ... American Lecture Series [*A publication*]
Am Leg...... American Legislator [*A publication*] (DLA)
Am Legion M ... American Legion Magazine [*A publication*]
Am Leg N... American Legal News [*A publication*] (DLA)
Am L Elec.. American Law of Elections [*A publication*] (DLA)
AmLev........ Aminolaevulinic Acid [*Biochemistry*]
AMLG .... Allied Military Liaison, Greece [*World War II*]
AMLG .... Amalgam [*Metallurgy*]
AMLI......... Americans for a Music Library in Israel [*Defunct*] (EA)
Am Li .... Amor de Libro [*A publication*]
Am Lib ...... American Libraries [*Chicago*] [*A publication*]
Am Lib Assn Bul ... American Library Association. Bulletin [*A publication*]
Am Libr..... American Libraries [*Chicago*] [*A publication*]
Am Libr (Chicago) ... American Libraries (Chicago) [*A publication*]
Am Libs ..... American Libraries [*Chicago*] [*A publication*]
AMLICP ... [*A*] Monthly Lesson in Criminal Politics [*Center for Financial Freedom and Accuracy in Financial Reporting*] [*A publication*]
Am L Ins.... American Law Institute. Restatement of the Law [*A publication*] (DLA)
Am L Inst... American Law Institute. Restatement of the Law [*A publication*] (DLA)
AMLIPC ... Australian Meat and Livestock Industry Policy Council
AmLit........ American Literature [*A publication*]
Am Lit M... American Literary Magazine [*A publication*]
Am Lit Real ... American Literary Realism, 1870-1910 [*A publication*]
Am Lit Realism ... American Literary Realism, 1870-1910 [*A publication*]
Am Littoral Soc Spec Publ ... American Littoral Society. Special Publication [*A publication*]
Am Livestock J ... American Livestock Journal [*A publication*]
AMLJ........ Ajmer-Merwara Law Journal [*India*] [*A publication*] (DLA)
Am LJ....... American Law Journal [*A publication*]
Am LJNS... American Law Journal. New Series [*A publication*]
Am LJ (O) ... American Law Journal (Ohio) [*or Okey*] [*A publication*]
Am LJ OS ... American Law Journal. Old Series [*A publication*]
AMLL........ American Cellular Network Corp. [*NASDAQ symbol*] (NQ)
AMLLV .... Advanced Multipurpose Large Launch Vehicle (MCD)
Am LM ...... American Law Magazine [*A publication*]
AMLM ...... McLennan Municipal Library, Alberta [*Library symbol*] [*National Library of Canada*] (NLC)
Am L Mag ... American Law Magazine [*A publication*] (DLA)
AMLO .... Aeromedical Liaison Office [*or Officer*] [*Air Force*] (AFM)
AMLO .... Assistant Military Landing Officer [*British and Canadian*] [*World War II*]
Am Logger Lumberman ... American Logger and Lumberman [*A publication*]
AmLP........ American Lyric Poems: from Colonial Times to the Present [*A publication*]
AMLP........ Amplitude Modulation Link Program
AMLPAG ... Arquivos Mineiros de Leprologia [*A publication*]
AMLR .... Abandoned Mine Land Reclamation [*Department of the Interior*]
AMLR .... Autologous Mixed Lymphocyte Reaction [*Immunochemistry*]
Am L Rec ... American Law Record [*Ohio*] [*A publication*] (DLA)
Am L Rec (Ohio) ... American Law Record (Reprint) (Ohio) [*A publication*] (DLA)
Am L Reg... American Law Register [*Philadelphia*] [*A publication*] (DLA)
Am L Reg (NS) ... American Law Register, New Series [*A publication*] (DLA)
Am L Reg (OS) ... American Law Register, Old Series [*A publication*] (DLA)
Am L Reg & Rev ... American Law Register and Review [*A publication*] (DLA)
Am L Rep... American Law Reporter [*Davenport, IA*] [*A publication*] (DLA)
Am L Rev... American Law Review [*A publication*]
AMLS........ Adaptive Maneuvering Logic Score (MCD)
AMLS........ Advanced Manned Launch System [*NASA*]
AMLS........ Airspace Management Liaison Section (MCD)
Am L S...... American Library Scholarship [*A publication*]
AMLS........ Master of Arts in Library Science
AMLSBQ.. American Lecture Series [*A publication*]

Am L School Rev ... American Law School Review [*A publication*]   (DLA)
Am L Sch Rev ... American Law School Review [*A publication*]   (DLA)
Am LS Rev ... American Law School Review [*A publication*]   (DLA)
AMLSU..... Air Ministry Local Staff Union [*Singapore*]
Am LT....... American Law Times [*A publication*]   (DLA)
AMLT........ Armel, Inc. [*NASDAQ symbol*]   (NQ)
AMLT........ Launceston [*Australia*] [*ICAO location identifier*]   (ICLI)
AM LT Bankr ... American Law Times, Bankruptcy Reports [*A publication*]   (DLA)
Am LT Bankr Rep ... American Law Times, Bankruptcy Reports [*A publication*]   (DLA)
Am LTR..... American Law Times Reports [*A publication*]   (DLA)
Am LT Rep ... American Law Times Reports [*A publication*]   (DLA)
Am LTRNS ... American Law Times Reports, New Series [*A publication*]   (DLA)
AmLum...... American Lumen [*Record label*]
Am Lumberman ... American Lumberman [*A publication*]
Am Lung Assoc Bull ... American Lung Association. Bulletin [*A publication*]
Am Luth...... American Lutheran [*A publication*]
AMLV....... Laverton [*Australia*] [*ICAO location identifier*]   (ICLI)
AMM........ Adaptive Mathematical Model
AMM........ Additional Memory Module
AMM........ Advanced Multipurpose Missile   (MCD)
AMM........ Agnogenic Myeloid Metaplasia [*Medicine*]
AMM........ Air-Mining Mission [*Military*]
AMM........ Aircraft Maintenance Manual
AMM........ Allied Military Mission [*World War II*]
AMM........ Alpha-Methylmannoside [*Biochemistry*]
AMM........ Alternative Music Market
Am M........ American Magazine [*A publication*]
AmM........ American Mercury [*A publication*]
AMM........ American Money Management Association [*Barrington, IL*]   (EA)
AMM........ Amir Mines Ltd. [*Toronto Stock Exchange symbol*]
AMM........ Amman [*Jordan*] [*Airport symbol*]   (OAG)
AMM........ Ammeter
AMM........ Ammunition   (KSC)
AMM........ AMRE, Inc. [*NYSE symbol*]   (SPSG)
AMM........ Analog Monitor Module [*Data processing*]
AMM........ Annuaire du Monde Musulman [*A publication*]
AMM........ Anomalous Magnetic Moment
AMM........ Antimissile Missile [*Air Force*]
AMM........ Army Maintenance Management   (MCD)
AMM........ Army Mobility Model   (RDA)
AMM........ Asia Merchant Marine [*Commercial firm*]   (DS)
AMM........ Asian Marketing Monitor [*A publication*]
AMM........ Associated Maintenance Module [*Telecommunications*]   (TEL)
AMM........ Associated Millinery Men   (EA)
AMM........ Association Medicale Mondiale [*World Medical Association - WMA*] [*Ferney-Voltaire, France*]
AMM........ Australian Medal of Merit
AMM........ Automatic Maintenance Monitor
AMM........ Master of Mechanic Arts
AMM........ Medicine Hat College, Alberta [*Library symbol*] [*National Library of Canada*]   (NLC)
AMM........ United States Army Material and Mechanics Research Center, Watertown, MA [*OCLC symbol*]   (OCLC)
AMMA...... Advanced Memory Management Architecture [*Data processing*]   (BYTE)
AMMA...... American Mail-Order Merchants Association   (EA)
AMMA...... American Military Music Association   (EA)
AMMA...... American Millinery Manufacturers Association [*Defunct*]
AMMA...... American Museum of Marine Archaeology
AMMA...... Army Medical Material Agency   (MCD)
AMMA...... Art Material Manufacturers Association   (EA)
AMMAC..... Assistant Masters and Mistresses Association   (EAIO)
AMMAC..... Aviation Machinist's Mate, Combat Aircrewman [*Navy rating*]
Am Mach ... American Machinist [*A publication*]
Am Machin ... American Machinist [*A publication*]
Am Mach/Metalwork Manuf ... American Machinist/Metalworking Manufacturing [*A publication*]
Am Mag..... American Magazine [*A publication*]
Am Mag Art ... American Magazine of Art [*A publication*]
Am Malacol Bull ... American Malacological Bulletin [*A publication*]
Am Malacolog Union Ann Rept ... American Malacological Union. Annual Report [*A publication*]
Am Malacol Union Bull ... American Malacological Union. Bulletin [*Later, American Malacological Bulletin*] [*A publication*]
Am Malacol Union Inc Annu Rep ... American Malacological Union, Incorporated. Annual Report [*A publication*]
Am Malacol Union Inc Bull ... American Malacological Union, Incorporated. Bulletin [*Later, American Malacological Bulletin*] [*A publication*]
AMMAN... Ammanford [*District in Wales*]
Am Management R ... American Management Review [*A publication*]
Am Manuf ... American Manufacturer [*A publication*]
Am Mar Cas ... American Maritime Cases [*A publication*]
Am Marine Engineer ... American Marine Engineer [*A publication*]
Am M Art ... American Magazine of Art [*A publication*]
Am Math M ... American Mathematical Monthly [*A publication*]
Am Math Mo ... American Mathematical Monthly [*A publication*]

Am Math Mon ... American Mathematical Monthly [*A publication*]
Am Math Soc Bul ... American Mathematical Society. Bulletin [*A publication*]
Am Math Soc Mem ... American Mathematical Society. Memoirs [*A publication*]
Am Math Soc Memoirs ... American Mathematical Society. Memoirs [*A publication*]
AMMB...... Melbourne/Moorabbin [*Australia*] [*ICAO location identifier*]   (ICLI)
AMMBAD ... Argentina. Direccion Nacional de Geologia y Mineria. Boletin [*A publication*]
AMMC..... American Medcare Corp. [*NASDAQ symbol*]   (NQ)
AMMC..... Army Maintenance Management Center
AMMC..... Association of Map Memorabilia Collectors   (EA)
AMMC..... Aviation Machinist's Mate, Carburetor Mechanic [*Navy rating*]
AMMC..... Aviation Materiel Management Center   (AABC)
AMMC..... Melbourne [*Australia*] [*ICAO location identifier*]   (ICLI)
Am M Civics ... American Magazine of Civics [*A publication*]
Am M Cong ... American Mining Congress. Journal [*A publication*]
AMMDEL ... American Military Mission, Delhi [*World War II*]
AMME...... Automated Multimedia Exchange [*Communications*] [*Army*]   (MCD)
Am Meat Inst Found Bull ... American Meat Institute. Foundation Bulletin [*A publication*]
Am Meat Inst Found Circ ... American Meat Institute. Foundation Circular [*A publication*]
Am Med..... American Medicine [*A publication*]
Am Med Assn J ... American Medical Association. Journal [*A publication*]
Am Med Assoc Congr Environ Health ... American Medical Association. Congress on Environmental Health [*A publication*]
Am Med News ... American Medical News [*A publication*]
Am Med News Impact ... American Medical News Impact [*A publication*]
AmMerc..... American Mercury [*A publication*]
Am Mercury ... American Mercury [*A publication*]
Am Meteorological J ... American Meteorological Journal [*A publication*]
Am Meteorol Soc Bull ... American Meteorological Society. Bulletin [*A publication*]
Am Meth M ... American Methodist Magazine [*A publication*]
Am Met Mark ... American Metal Market [*A publication*]
Am Met Mark Metalwork News Ed ... American Metal Market. Metalworking News Edition [*A publication*]
Am Met Soc Bull ... American Meteorological Society. Bulletin [*A publication*]
AMMF...... Association Mondiale des Medecins Francophones [*Ottawa, ON*]   (EAIO)
AMMF...... Aviation Machinist's Mate, Flight Engineer [*Navy rating*]
AMMG...... Mount Gambier [*Australia*] [*ICAO location identifier*]   (ICLI)
AMMH...... Annual Maintenance Manhours [*Military*]   (AABC)
AMMH...... Aviation Machinist's Mate, Hydraulic Mechanic [*Navy rating*]
AMMI....... American Merchant Marine Institute [*Later, AIMS*]   (EA)
AMMI....... American Museum of the Moving Image [*New York City*]   (ECON)
AMMI....... Atlantis Mining & Manufacturing Company, Incorporated [*Las Vegas, NV*] [*NASDAQ symbol*]   (NQ)
AMMI....... Aviation Machinist's Mate, Instrument Mechanic [*Navy rating*]
AMMI....... Mildura [*Australia*] [*ICAO location identifier*]   (ICLI)
AMMIA..... American Mineralogist [*A publication*]
AMMIC.... Armament Maintenance Management Information Center [*Navy*]   (NG)
Am Micro Soc Pr ... American Microscopical Society. Proceedings [*A publication*]
Am Micros Soc Trans ... American Microscopical Society. Transactions [*A publication*]
Am Midland Natural ... American Midland Naturalist [*A publication*]
Am Midl Nat ... American Midland Naturalist [*A publication*]
Am Midl Natur ... American Midland Naturalist [*A publication*]
Am Milk R ... American Milk Review [*A publication*]
Am Milk Rev ... American Milk Review [*A publication*]
Am Milk Rev Milk Plant Mon ... American Milk Review and Milk Plant Monthly [*A publication*]
Am Miller Process ... American Miller and Processor [*A publication*]
Am Min...... American Mineralogist [*A publication*]
Am Min Congr J ... American Mining Congress. Journal [*A publication*]
Am Min Congr Proc ... American Mining Congress. Proceedings [*A publication*]
Am Miner .. American Mineralogist [*A publication*]
Am Mineral ... American Mineralogist [*A publication*]
Am Mineralogist ... American Mineralogist [*A publication*]
Am Miner J ... American Mineralogical Journal [*A publication*]
AMMIP..... Aviation Materiel Management Improvement Program [*Military*]   (NG)
AMMIS..... Aircraft Maintenance Management Information System
AMMIS..... Aircraft Maintenance Manpower Information System [*Air Force*]
AMMIS..... Automated Manpower Management Information System
AMMISCA ... American Military Mission to China [*World War II*]
AMMISSq ... Ammunition Supply Squadron [*Air Force*]
AMMKA... American Metal Market [*A publication*]
AMML....... Acute Myelomonocytic Leukemia [*Medicine*]
AMML....... Automated Microbial Metabolism Laboratory [*NASA*]
AMML...... Melbourne [*Australia*] [*ICAO location identifier*]   (ICLI)
AMMLA ... American Merchant Marine Library Association   (EA)

AMMM..... Melbourne [*Australia*] [*ICAO location identifier*]   (ICLI)
Amm Marc ... Ammianus Marcellinus [*c. 330-395AD*] [*Classical studies*]   (OCD)
AMMO...... Ammunition   (AFM)
AMMO...... Army Mobile Missile Operation
AMMO...... Army Model Improvement Program Management Office   (RDA)
AMMO...... Australian Mining, Minerals, and Oil [*A publication*]   (APTA)
AMMOBR ... Ammunition Bearer [*Military*]   (AABC)
AMMOHOUSE Bull ... AMMOHOUSE [*Ammunition House*] Bulletin [*A publication*]
AMMOL... Acute Myelomonoblastic Leukemia [*Medicine*]
AMMOLOG ... Ammunition Logistics [*Army*]   (RDA)
Am Mo M ... American Monthly Magazine [*A publication*]
ammon.... Ammonia
Ammonia Plant Saf ... Ammonia Plant Safety and Related Facilities [*A publication*]
Am Mo R ... American Monthly Review [*A publication*]
AMMORK ... Ammunition Rack
Am Mosq Control Assoc ... American Mosquito Control Association. Journal [*A publication*]
Am Mosq Control Assoc Bull ... American Mosquito Control Association. Bulletin [*A publication*]
AMMP...... Advanced Manned Missions Program [*NASA*]   (MCD)
AMMP...... Apollo Master Measurements Program [*NASA*]   (KSC)
AMMP...... Approved Modernization Maintenance Program   (AFM)
AMMP...... Aviation Machinist's Mate, Propeller Mechanic [*Navy rating*]
AMMQ...... Macquarie Island [*Australia*] [*ICAO location identifier*]   (ICLI)
AMMR...... Advanced Multimission RADAR
AMMR...... Aircraft Maintenance Manpower Requirement [*Air Force*]   (AFM)
AMMR...... Melbourne [*Australia*] [*ICAO location identifier*]   (ICLI)
AMMRC ... Army Materials and Mechanics Research Center [*Watertown, MA*]
AMMRES ... Advanced Missile Materials Research Technical Advisory Group [*Terminated, 1975*] [*DoD*]   (EGAO)
AMMRL ... Aircraft Maintenance Material Readiness List [*Navy*]   (NG)
AMMRS... Advanced Multimission Reconnaissance System [*Military*]   (MCD)
AMMS ...... Acquisition Management Milestone System [*DoD*]
AMMS ...... Advanced Magnetic Minesweeping   (MCD)
AMMS ...... Advanced Microwave Moisture Sensor   (MCD)
AMMS ...... Army Maintenance Management System   (MCD)
AMMS ...... Army Management Milestone System
AMMS ...... Automated Message Management System   (MCD)
AMMS ...... Automatic Multimode Mass Spectrometry
AMMSBV ... Acta Musei Macedonici. Scientiarum Naturalium [*A publication*]
AMMSDO ... Antimissile Missile and Space Defense Office
Am Ms Mag ... American Ms Magazine [*A publication*]
AMMSN ... Acta Musei Macedonici. Scientiarum Naturalium [*A publication*]
AMMSq .... Airborne Missile Maintenance Squadron [*Air Force*]
AMM SYS ... Ammonia System   (DS)
AMMT ...... Advanced Multimission Torpedo   (MCD)
AMMT ...... Aviation Machinist's Mate, Turret Mechanic [*Navy rating*]
Am Mtl Mkt ... American Metal Market [*A publication*]
AMMTR ... Antimissile Missile Test Range [*Military*]
Am Mus Dgt ... American Musical Digest [*A publication*]
Am Musicol Soc J ... American Musicological Society. Journal [*A publication*]
Am Mus J ... American Museum Journal [*A publication*]
Am Mus Nat History Bull ... American Museum of Natural History. Bulletin [*A publication*]
Am Mus Nat History Bull Sci Guide Special Pub ... American Museum of Natural History. Bulletin. Science Guide. Special Publication [*A publication*]
Am Mus N H B Mem ... American Museum of Natural History. Bulletin. Memoirs [*A publication*]
Am Mus Novit ... American Museum Novitates [*A publication*]
Am Mus Novitates ... American Museum Novitates [*A publication*]
Am Mus Tcr ... American Music Teacher [*A publication*]
Am Mus Teach ... American Music Teacher [*A publication*]
AMMV...... American Merchant Marine Veterans   (EA)
AMMX...... Melbourne [*Australia*] [*ICAO location identifier*]   (ICLI)
AMMYA ... American Mathematical Monthly [*A publication*]
AMMYAE ... American Mathematical Monthly [*A publication*]
AMN......... Adrenomyeloneuropathy [*Neurology*]
AMN......... Aircraft Mechanician [*British military*]   (DMA)
AMN......... Airman   (AFM)
AMN......... All Malignant Neoplasm [*Medicine*]
AMN......... Alloxazine Mononucleotide [*Pharmacology*]
AMN......... Alma, MI [*Location identifier*] [*FAA*]   (FAAL)
AMN......... Amanu [*Tuamotu Archipelago*] [*Seismograph station code, US Geological Survey*]   (SEIS)
AMN......... Amazing Stories. Science Fiction Novels [*A publication*]
AMN......... American Salesman [*A publication*]
AMN......... Ameron, Inc. [*NYSE symbol*]   (SPSG)
AMN......... Aminomethyl Naphthalene [*Organic chemistry*]
AMN......... Ammunition
AMN......... Analecta Mediaevalia Namurcensia [*A publication*]
AMN......... Arizona Music News [*A publication*]

AMN......... Atomic Mass Number
AMN......... SAM [*Society for Advancement of Management*] Advanced Management Journal [*A publication*]
AMNA...... Ammonia   (MSA)
AMNAA.... American Midland Naturalist [*A publication*]
AMNAAF ... American Midland Naturalist [*A publication*]
AMNADI .. Annales Medicales de Nancy et de l'Est [*A publication*]
Am Nat ...... American Naturalist [*A publication*]
Am Natl Red Cross Annu Sci Symp ... American National Red Cross. Annual Scientific Symposium [*A publication*]
Am Natl Stand Inst Stand ... American National Standards Institute. Standards [*A publication*]
Am Natural ... American Naturalist [*A publication*]
AMNCS ..... Advanced Multiplatform Navy Computer System   (MCD)
AMND...... Amend [*or Amendment*]   (AFM)
AMNDS .... Annales de la Mission de N.-D. de Sion en Terre Sainte (1877-1912) [*A publication*]
Am Neg Ca ... American Negligence Cases [*A publication*]   (DLA)
Am Neg Cas ... American Negligence Cases [*A publication*]   (DLA)
Am Neg Cases ... American Negligence Cases [*A publication*]   (DLA)
Am Neg Dig ... American Negligence Digest [*A publication*]   (DLA)
Am Negl Cas ... American Negligence Cases [*A publication*]   (DLA)
Am Negl R ... American Negligence Reports [*A publication*]   (DLA)
Am Negl Rep ... American Negligence Reports [*A publication*]   (DLA)
Am Neg Rep ... American Negligence Reports [*A publication*]   (DLA)
Am Nep...... American Neptune [*A publication*]
Am Neptune ... American Neptune [*A publication*]
AMNET...... American Network, Inc. [*Portland, OR*]   (TSSD)
AMNGA.... Arkiv foer Mineralogi och Geologi [*A publication*]
AMNGAX ... Arkiv foer Mineralogi och Geologi [*A publication*]
AMNH ...... American Museum of Natural History   (EA)
AMNHA2 ... Annals and Magazine of Natural History [*A publication*]
AMNH/NH ... Natural History. American Museum of Natural History [*A publication*]
AMNI........ Associate Member of the Nautical Institute [*British*]
AMNIB ..... Acta Manilana. Series A. Natural and Applied Sciences [*A publication*]
AMNIP ..... Adaptive Man-Machine Nonarithmetic Information Processing [*Documentation*]
AMNJA8... Arquivos. Museu Nacional do Rio De Janeiro [*A publication*]
AMNL ...... Army Medical Nutrition Laboratory   (MCD)
AmnM....... Airman's Medal [*Military decoration*]   (AFM)
A M Nordwest D ... Archaeologische Mitteilungen aus Nordwestdeutschland [*A publication*]
Am Notary ... American Notary [*A publication*]   (DLA)
Am Note Que ... American Notes and Queries [*A publication*]
Am Notes & Queries ... American Notes and Queries [*A publication*]
AmNP........ American Negro Poetry [*A publication*]
AMNP........ Annuaire. Musee National Archeologique (Plovdiv) [*A publication*]
Am N & Q ... American Notes and Queries [*A publication*]
A-MNR...... Alianza del Movimiento Nacionalista Revolucionario [*Bolivia*]   (PPW)
AMNSAZ ... Acta Morphologica Neerlando-Scandinavica [*A publication*]
AMNSWP ... Acoustic Minesweeping
AMNT....... [*The*] American Network Group, Inc. [*NASDAQ symbol*]   (NQ)
AMNTA .... American Naturalist [*A publication*]
AMNTA4 .. American Naturalist [*A publication*]
AMNU ...... American Nucleonics Corp. [*NASDAQ symbol*]   (NQ)
Am Nucl Soc Proc Pac Basin Conf Nucl Power Dev Fuel Cycle ... American Nuclear Society. Proceedings. Pacific Basin Conference on Nuclear Power Development and the Fuel Cycle [*A publication*]
Am Nucl Soc Top Meet Gas-Cooled React HTGR GCFBR ... American Nuclear Society Topical Meeting. Gas-Cooled Reactors. HTGR and GCFBR [*A publication*]
Am Nucl Soc Trans ... American Nuclear Society. Transactions [*A publication*]
AMNUDA ... Advances in Modern Nutrition [*A publication*]
Am Num Soc Mus Notes ... American Numismatic Society. Museum Notes [*A publication*]
Am Nurse... American Nurse [*A publication*]
Am Nurserman ... American Nurseryman [*A publication*]
Am Nurseryman ... American Nurseryman [*A publication*]
Am Nut J ... American Nut Journal [*A publication*]
AMNYAJ ... Annales Medicales de Nancy [*A publication*]
AM/O........ A Mon Ordre [*To My Order*] [*French*] [*Business term*]   (ROG)
AMO.......... Accredited Management Organization [*Designation awarded by Institute of Real Estate Management*]
AMO.......... Acta Medica Orientalia [*A publication*]
AMO.......... Administrative Medical Officer [*British*]
AMO.......... Admiralty Monthly Order [*British military*]   (DMA)
AMO.......... Advance Material Order [*Manufacturing*]
AMO.......... Air Mass Zero
AMO.......... Air Member for Organization [*British and Canadian*] [*World War II*]
AMO.......... Air Ministry Order [*British*]
AMO.......... Aircraft Material Officer
AMO.......... Alamogordo Public Library, Alamogordo, NM [*OCLC symbol*]   (OCLC)

AMO......... Allied Meteorological Office (NATG)
AMO......... Allstate Municipal Income Opportunities Trust [*NYSE symbol*] (CTT)
AMO......... Alternant Molecular Orbital [*Physical chemistry*]
AMO......... Amboina [*Indonesia*] [*Seismograph station code, US Geological Survey*] (SEIS)
AMO......... Amco Industrial Holdings Ltd. [*Toronto Stock Exchange symbol*]
AMO......... American Medical Technology, Inc. [*Vancouver Stock Exchange symbol*]
AMO......... American Motors Owners Association (EA)
AMO......... Answering Machine Owner
AMO......... Applied Methods in Oncology [*Elsevier Book Series*] [*A publication*]
AMO......... Archery Manufacturers Organization (EA)
AM & O..... Armstrong, Macartney, and Ogle's Irish Nisi Prius Reports [*A publication*] (DLA)
AMO......... Assistant Medical Officer
AMo.......... Atlantic Monthly [*A publication*]
AMO......... Atomic, Molecular, and Optical Physics
AMO......... Automation Management Office [*Military*] (AABC)
AMO......... Aviation Maintenance Officer [*Military*] (NVT)
AMO......... Aviation Marine-Outillage
AMO......... Aviation Material Office [*Military*] (AFIT)
AMO......... Aviation Medical Officer [*Military*] (AABC)
AMO......... Axiomesio-Occlusal [*Dentistry*]
AMO......... Morinville Public Library, Alberta [*Library symbol*] [*National Library of Canada*] (NLC)
AMOA....... American Mailorder Association (EA)
AMOA....... Amusement and Music Operators Association (EA)
AMOA....... Atmospheric Monitor Oxygen Analyzer (IEEE)
AMOAC.... Automatic Multiloop Optimal Approach Controller [*Navy*]
AMOAP.... Associated Marine Officers Association of the Philippines
AMOB....... Ancient Mystic Order of Bagmen of Bagdad Imperial Guild [*Roanoke, VA*] (EA)
AMOB....... Automatic Meteorological Oceanographic Buoy [*Marine science*] (MSC)
AMob........ Mobile Public Library, Mobile, AL [*Library symbol*] [*Library of Congress*] (LCLS)
AMOBAN ... AMMOHOUSE [*Ammunition House*] Bulletin [*A publication*]
AMobB...... Bishop State Junior College, Mobile, AL [*Library symbol*] [*Library of Congress*] (LCLS)
AMobHi .... Historic Mobile Preservation Society Headquarters, Mobile, AL [*Library symbol*] [*Library of Congress*] (LCLS)
AMobM.... Museum of the City of Mobile, Mobile, AL [*Library symbol*] [*Library of Congress*] (LCLS)
AMobS ...... Spring Hill College, Mobile, AL [*Library symbol*] [*Library of Congress*] (LCLS)
AMobU...... University of South Alabama, Mobile, AL [*Library symbol*] [*Library of Congress*] (LCLS)
AMobU-M ... University of South Alabama, Biomedical Library, Mobile, AL [*Library symbol*] [*Library of Congress*] (LCLS)
AMOC....... American Mission for Opening Churches (EA)
AMOC....... Aston Martin Owners Club (EA)
AMOC....... [*A*] Matter of Crime [*Novel by Matthew Bruccoli*]
AMOCBR ... Agronomia Mocambicana [*A publication*]
AMOCC .... American Mission for Opening Closed Churches [*Later, AMOC*] (EA)
AMOCO.... American Oil Company [*Later, Amoco Oil Co.*]
AMOCOM ... Army Mobility Command
AMOD....... Army's Mobility Opportunity Development Program
AMOF ...... [*A*] Matter of Fact [*Pierian Press, Inc.*] [*Information service or system*] (IID)
AMOHST ... Ammunition Hoist
AMOHSTDR ... Ammunition Hoist Drive
Am Oil Chemists Soc J ... American Oil Chemists' Society. Journal [*A publication*]
Am Oil Chem Soc J ... American Oil Chemists' Society. Journal [*A publication*]
AMOK....... Aerochemical Metal-Oxide Kinetics [*Program*] (MCD)
AMoL........ Acute Monocytic Leukemia [*Also, AMonoL*] [*Medicine*]
A Mold ...... Arheologia Moldovei [*A publication*]
AMOL-FD ... Acousto-Optic Mode Locker and Frequency Doubler (MCD)
AMOM...... Morrin Municipal Library, Alberta [*Library symbol*] [*National Library of Canada*] (NLC)
AMOMB.... Applied Mathematics and Optimization [*A publication*]
AMON ...... American Monitor Corp. [*NASDAQ symbol*] (NQ)
AMon........ Analecta Monastica [*A publication*]
AMon........ Atlantic Monthly [*A publication*]
AMonA...... University of Montevallo, Montevallo, AL [*Library symbol*] [*Library of Congress*] (LCLS)
AMonoL.... Acute Monoblastic Leukemia [*Also, AMoL*] [*Medicine*]
AMontserr ... Analecta Montserratensia [*A publication*]
AMON ZINGIB ... Amonium Zingiber [*Ginger*] [*Pharmacology*] (ROG)
AMOO ...... Aerospace Medical Operations Office [*NASA*] (KSC)
A Moo .... Moore's Reports [*Bosanquet and Puller*] [*England*] [*A publication*] (DLA)
A Moor....... [*A.*] Moore's Reports [*Bosanquet and Puller*] [*England*] [*A publication*] (DLA)
AMOOS .... Advanced Maneuvering Orbit-to-Orbit Shuttle [*NASA*] (NASA)

Am Opinion ... American Opinion [*A publication*]
AMOPS..... Army Mobilization and Operations Planning System
Am Optomet Assoc J ... American Optometric Association. Journal [*A publication*]
AMOR...... Army Mortar Requirements Study
AMORC.... Ancient Mystical Order Rosae Crucis [*Rosicrucian Order*] (EA)
Am Orchid Soc Bull ... American Orchid Society. Bulletin [*A publication*]
Am Orch Soc B ... American Orchid Society. Bulletin [*A publication*]
Am Orch Soc Yb ... American Orchid Society. Yearbook [*A publication*]
AMORE...... Analysis of Military Organizational Effectiveness (MCD)
AMORF..... Amore Resources, Inc. [*NASDAQ symbol*] (NQ)
Am Org...... American Organist [*A publication*]
Am Orient Soc J ... American Oriental Society. Journal [*A publication*]
Am Orn ...... American Ornithology [*A publication*]
amorph....... Amorphous
Amorphous Liq Semicond ... Amorphous and Liquid Semiconductors [*A publication*]
Amorphous Liq Semicond Proc Int Conf ... Amorphous and Liquid Semiconductors. Proceedings. International Conference [*A publication*]
AMORS .... Atomic Magneto-Optic Resonance Spectrometry
AMO(R)S ... Automatic Meteorological, Oceanographic, (and Radiation) Station
amort.......... Amortissable [*Redeemable*] [*French*] [*Business term*]
Am Orth J ... American Orthoptic Journal [*A publication*]
Am Orthopt J ... American Orthoptic Journal [*A publication*]
AMOS....... Acoustic, Meteorological, and Oceanographic Survey
AMOS....... Additionally Awarded Military Occupational Specialty
AMOS....... Aerospace Maintenance and Operational Status (AFM)
AMOS....... Air Force Maui Optical Station
AMOS....... Alpha Microsystems Operating System
AMOS....... Alternate Military Occupational Specialty (MUGU)
AMOS....... American Maritime Officers Service (EA)
AMOS....... AMEX [*American Stock Exchange*] Options Switching System
AMOS....... Amoskeag Co. [*NASDAQ symbol*] (NQ)
AMOS....... Ancient Mystic Order of Samaritans (EA)
AMOS....... Antireflection Coated Metal-Oxide Semiconductor (MCD)
AMOS....... ARPA [*Advanced Research Projects Agency*] Maui Optical Station (MUGU)
AMOS....... Assembly Management Operating System (MCD)
AMOS....... Associated Migrant Opportunity Services
AMOS....... Associative Memory Organizing System
AMOS....... Automated Military Outpatient System (RDA)
AMOS....... Automatic Computer, Ministry of Supply [*British*] (DEN)
AMOS....... Automatic Meteorological Observation [*or Observing*] Station [*or System*]
AMOS....... Avalanche Injection Metal-Oxide Semiconductor
AMOSA.... Association of Aviation Maintenance Organizations (EAIO)
AMOSC .... Authorized Military Occupational Specialty Code (AABC)
Amos Eng Code ... Amos on an English Code [*A publication*] (DLA)
Amos Engl Const ... Amos' Primer of the English Constitution [*A publication*] (DLA)
Amos & F... Amos and Ferard on Fixtures [*A publication*] (DLA)
Amos & F Fixt ... Amos and Ferard on Fixtures [*A publication*] (DLA)
Amos Fifty Years ... Amos' Fifty Years of the English Constitution [*A publication*] (DLA)
Amos Int Law ... Amos on International Law [*A publication*] (DLA)
AMOSIST ... Automated Military Outpatient System Specialist (MCD)
Amos Jur ... Amos' Science of Jurisprudence [*A publication*] (DLA)
Amos Reg Vice ... Amos on Laws for Regulation of Vice [*A publication*] (DLA)
AMOSS..... Adaptive Mission-Oriented Software System (MCD)
AMOSS..... Additional Mobile SAM [*Surface-to-Air Missile*] Site (NATG)
Am Osteopath Assoc J ... American Osteopathic Association. Journal [*A publication*]
AMOT....... Air Member for Organization and Training [*British and Canadian*] [*World War II*]
AMOT....... American Medical Technologies, Inc. [*NASDAQ symbol*] (NQ)
AMOTA9 .. Anales. Sociedad Mexicana de Otorrinolaringologia [*A publication*]
AmOx .... American Oxonian [*A publication*]
Amoxycillin (BRL 2333) Pap Int Symp ... Amoxycillin (BRL 2333) Papers. International Symposium [*A publication*]
AMP.......... Accelerometer Monitoring Program [*NASA*] (KSC)
AMP.......... Acid Mucopolysaccharide [*Biochemistry*]
AMP.......... Acquisition Management Plan [*Navy*]
AMP.......... Acta Medica Polona [*A publication*]
AMP.......... Active Medium Propagation [*Amplifier*]
AMP.......... Adaptation Mathematical Processor
AMP.......... Adaptive Microwave Proximity [*Military*] (MCD)
AMP.......... Add, Multiprecision
AMP.......... Additional Military Production
AMP.......... Adenosine Monophosphate [*Biochemistry*]
AMP.......... Advance Market Protection (MCD)
AMP.......... Advanced Management Program
AMP.......... Advanced Manned Penetrator
AMP.......... Advanced Microstructure Profiler [*Instrumentation, oceanography*]
AMP.......... Advanced Minuteman Platform

AMP......... Agence Madagascar - Presse [*Press agency*] [*Malagasy Republic*]
AMP......... Agricultural Marketing Project (EA)
AMP......... Air Mail Pioneers (EA)
AMP......... Air Member for Personnel [*Air Ministry*] [*British*]
AMP......... Aircraft/Missile Project (AFM)
AMP......... Airport Master Plan (FAAC)
AMP......... Allied Mining and Mine Countermeasures Publications
　　　　　　[*NATO*] (NATG)
AMP......... Altitude Manned Penetrator (MCD)
AMP......... Ambar [*Pakistan*] [*Seismograph station code, US Geological
　　　　　　Survey*] (SEIS)
AMP......... American Majority Party (EA)
AMP......... American Mathematics Project (EA)
AMP......... American Melting Point
AmP......... American Poetry [*A publication*]
Am P......... American Psychologist [*A publication*]
AMP......... Amino(methyl)propanol [*Organic chemistry*]
AMP......... Ammonium Molybdophosphate [*Inorganic chemistry*]
AMP......... AMP, Inc. [*NYSE symbol*] (SPSG)
AMP...... Ampac Petroleum Resources, Inc. [*Vancouver Stock Exchange
　　　　　　symbol*]
AMP......... Ampanihy [*Madagascar*] [*Airport symbol*] (OAG)
AMP......... Ampere [*Unit of electric current*] (AFM)
Amp......... Amperometric [*Electromagnetics*]
AMP......... Ampicillin [*Also, A, AM*] [*Antibacterial compound*]
AMP......... Amplifier (KSC)
AMP......... Amplitude
AMP......... Amplus [*Large*] [*Pharmacy*] (ROG)
AMP......... Ampule [*Pharmacy*]
Amp .... Ampurias [*A publication*]
AMP......... Amputation [*Medicine*]
AMP......... Analytical Maintenance Program [*Navy*] (NVT)
AMP......... Ancient and Modern Palestine [*A publication*] (BJA)
AM & P... Andrews, McMeel & Parker [*Later, A & M*] [*Publisher*]
AMP......... Another Mother for Peace (EA)
AMP......... Anteromedial Puncture [*Medicine*]
AMP......... Apollo Mission Programs [*NASA*] (KSC)
AMP......... Applied Mathematics Panel [*DoD*]
AMP......... Area Mail Processing [*US Postal Service*]
AMP......... Argonne Microprocessor
AMP......... Army Materiel Plan (AABC)
AMP......... Army Mine Planter
AMP......... Aseptic Maintenance by Pressurization [*NASA*]
AMP......... Assisted Maintenance Period [*British military*] (DMA)
AMP......... Association of Media Producers [*Absorbed by ICIA*] (EA)
AMP...... Association for Media Psychology (EA)
AMP......... Association for Men in Psychology
AMP......... Association of Multiracial Playgroups
AMP...... Associative Memory Processor [*Data processing*] (BUR)
AMP...... Atlantic Monthly Press
AMP......... Audiovisual Market Place [*A publication*]
A-MP....... Austin-Moore Prosthesis [*Medicine*]
AMP......... Australian Mutual Provident Society [*Insurance*]
AMP......... Automated Molding Plant [*Manufacturing*]
AMP...... Automatic Message Processor (MCD)
AMP...... Automatic Multipattern Metering [*Photography*]
AMP...... Avalanche Mode Photodiode
AMP......... Average Mean Pressure
AMP......... Average Month Program [*Air Force*] (AFIT)
AMP......... Axially Magnetized Plasma
AMP......... Medicine Hat Public Library, Alberta [*Library symbol*]
　　　　　　[*National Library of Canada*] (NLC)
AMP......... Mobile Public Library, Mobile, AL [*OCLC symbol*] (OCLC)
a-mp--- .... Mongolia [*MARC geographic area code*] [*Library of
　　　　　　Congress*] (LCCP)
AMP......... Tampa, FL [*Location identifier*] [*FAA*] (FAAL)
AMPA...... Adaptive Multibeam Phased Array [*RADAR*] (MCD)
AMPA...... American Manganese Producers Association [*Defunct*] (EA)
AMPA...... American Medical Publishers' Association
AMPA....... Associate Member of the Master Photographers Association
　　　　　　[*British*] (DBQ)
AMPA...... Associated Motion Picture Advertisers (EA)
AMPA....... Automotive Machine & Parts Association
AMPA....... Azimuth Mark Pulse Amplifier
AMPAC.... American Medical Political Action Committee (EA)
AMPAC..... American Motorcyclist Political Action Committee
Am P Advocate ... American Poultry Advocate [*A publication*]
Am Paint.... American Paint and Coatings Journal [*A publication*]
Am Paint Coat J ... American Paint and Coatings Journal [*A publication*]
Am Paint Contract ... American Painting Contractor [*A publication*]
Am Painter Decor ... American Painter and Decorator [*A publication*]
Am Paint J ... American Paint Journal [*Later, American Paint and Coatings
　　　　　　Journal*] [*A publication*]
Am Paper Ind ... American Paper Industry [*A publication*]
Am Paper Merch ... American Paper Merchant [*A publication*]
Am Pap Ind ... American Paper Industry [*A publication*]
AMPAS..... Academy of Motion Picture Arts and Sciences (EA)
Am Pat LA Bull ... American Patent Law Association. Bulletin [*A
　　　　　　publication*] (DLA)
Am Pat L Assoc Bull ... American Patent Law Association. Bulletin [*A
　　　　　　publication*] (DLA)

Am Pat LQJ ... APLA (American Patent Law Association). Quarterly Journal
　　　　　　[*A publication*]
AMPBAS .. Anais. Sociedade de Medicina de Pernambuco [*A publication*]
AmPC .... American Poems; a Contemporary Collection [*A publication*]
AMPC .... Area Mail Processing Center [*US Postal Service*]
AMPC .... Associated Mail and Parcel Centers (EA)
AMPC .... Automatic Message Processing Center
AMPC .... Auxiliary Military Pioneer Corps [*British*]
AMPC .... Point Cook [*Australia*] [*ICAO location identifier*] (ICLI)
AMPCA.... Archivio "E. Maragliano" di Patologia e Clinica [*A publication*]
AMPCAV ... Archivio e Maragliano di Patologia e Clinica [*A publication*]
AMPCB..... American Psychological Association. Proceedings of the Annual
　　　　　　Convention [*A publication*]
AMPCO .... Associated Missile Products Corporation
AMPD....... Amino(methyl)propanediol [*Organic chemistry*]
AMPD....... Ampad Corp. [*NASDAQ symbol*] (NQ)
AMPD....... Army Mobilization Program Directive
AMPD....... Aza(methyl)pregnanedione [*Biochemistry*]
AMPDA .... Adenosine Monophosphate Deaminase [*An enzyme*]
AMPDA .... Australian Machinery and Production Engineering [*A
　　　　　　publication*]
AMPDS..... Advanced Missile Propulsion Definition Study [*NASA*] (KSC)
AMPDS..... Automated Message Processing Dissemination System (MCD)
AMPEA3... American Miller and Processor [*A publication*]
AMPEC..... American Motion Picture Export Company (EA)
AMPECA ... American Motion Picture Export Company/Africa [*Later,
　　　　　　AMPEC*] [*An association*] (EA)
Am Pept Symp ... American Peptide Symposium [*A publication*]
AMPERE .. APL [*Applied Physics Laboratory*] Management Planning and
　　　　　　Engineering Resource Evaluation [*Navy*]
AMPEREDOC ... Association Multinationale des Producteurs et Revendeurs
　　　　　　d'Electricite-Documentation [*Multinational Association of
　　　　　　Producers and Retailers of Electricity-Documentation*]
　　　　　　[*Electricity Supply Board*] [*Information service or
　　　　　　system*] (IID)
Ampere Int Summer Sch Magn Reson Chem Biol ... Ampere International
　　　　　　Summer School on Magnetic Resonance in Chemistry and
　　　　　　Biology [*A publication*]
Am Perfum ... American Perfumer [*A publication*]
Am Perfum Aromat ... American Perfumer and Aromatics [*A publication*]
Am Perfum Cosmet ... American Perfumer and Cosmetics [*A publication*]
Am Perfum Cosmet Toilet Prep ... American Perfumer, Cosmetics, Toilet
　　　　　　Preparations [*A publication*]
Am Perfume ... American Cosmetics and Perfumery [*A publication*]
Am Perfumer ... American Perfumer and Cosmetics [*A publication*]
Am Perfumer Arom ... American Perfumer and Aromatics [*A publication*]
Am Perfumer & Aromatics ... American Perfumer and Aromatics [*A
　　　　　　publication*]
Am Perfumer Ess Oil Rev ... American Perfumer and Essential Oil Review [*A
　　　　　　publication*]
Am Perfum Esst Oil Rev ... American Perfumer and Essential Oil Review [*A
　　　　　　publication*]
Am Pet Inst Bul ... American Petroleum Institute. Bulletin [*A publication*]
Am Pet Inst Proc ... American Petroleum Institute. Proceedings [*A
　　　　　　publication*]
Am Pet Inst Publ ... American Petroleum Institute. Publication [*A
　　　　　　publication*]
Am Pet Inst Q ... American Petroleum Institute. Quarterly [*A publication*]
Am Pet Inst Refin Dep Proc ... American Petroleum Institute. Refining
　　　　　　Department. Proceedings [*A publication*]
Am Petr Inst Quart ... American Petroleum Institute. Quarterly [*A
　　　　　　publication*]
Am Petr Inst Wkly Stat Bull ... American Petroleum Institute. Weekly
　　　　　　Statistical Bulletin [*A publication*]
Am Petroleum Inst Drilling and Production Practice ... American Petroleum
　　　　　　Institute. Drilling and Production Practice [*A publication*]
AMPEX..... Alexander M. Poniatoff, Excellence [*Acronym is name of
　　　　　　electronics company and brand name of its products;
　　　　　　formed from name of firm's founder, plus "excellence"*]
AMPFION ... Auto-Magnetic Plasma-Filled Ion Diode (MCD)
AMPFTA .. American Military Precision Flying Teams Association (EA)
AMPFUR ... Amplifying Failure, Unsatisfactory, or Removal Report (MCD)
AMPG .... Air Material Proving Ground
AMPGATP ... Advanced Multipurpose Gas Turbine Program
AMPH....... American Pharmacy [*A publication*]
AMPH....... American Physicians Service Group, Inc. [*NASDAQ
　　　　　　symbol*] (NQ)
AMPH....... Amphibious (AFM)
Amph .... Amphibole [*A mineral*]
Amph .... Amphion [*Record label*] [*France*]
Amph .... Amphitruo [*of Plautus*] [*Classical studies*] (OCD)
AMPH....... Association of Management in Public Health [*Later,
　　　　　　AAHA*] (EA)
Am Pharm ... American Pharmacy [*A publication*]
AMPHDF ... American Pharmacy [*A publication*]
AMPHENOL ... American Phenolic Corp. (KSC)
amphet....... Amphetamine [*Also, A, AMT*] [*CNS stimulant*]
AMPHETAMINE ... Alpha-Methylphenethylamine [*CNS stimulant*]
AMPHFORLANT ... Amphibious Forces, Atlantic
AMPHFORMED ... Amphibious Forces, Mediterranean
AMPHFORPAC ... Amphibious Forces, Pacific

AMPHI ..... Aerial Mission Photographic Indoctrination (MCD)
AMPHI ..... Amphitheatre (ROG)
AMPHIB... Amphibious
AMPHIBEX ... Amphibious Exercise [*Navy, Marine Corps*]
AMPHIBFOR ... Amphibious Forces
AMPHIBFORCENPAC ... Amphibious Forces, Central Pacific
AMPHIBFORLANT ... Amphibious Forces, Atlantic (MUGU)
AMPHIBFORMED ... Amphibious Forces, Mediterranean (MUGU)
AMPHIBFORPAC ... Amphibious Forces, Pacific (MUGU)
Am Philos Q ... American Philosophical Quarterly [*A publication*]
Am Philos Soc Lib Bull ... American Philosophical Society. Library Bulletin
            [*A publication*]
Am Philos Soc Proc ... American Philosophical Society. Proceedings [*A*
            publication]
Am Philos Soc Trans ... American Philosophical Society. Transactions [*A*
            publication]
Am Philos Soc YB ... American Philosophical Society. Yearbook [*A*
            publication]
Am Philos Soc Yearbook ... American Philosophical Society. Yearbook [*A*
            publication]
Am Phot..... American Photography [*A publication*]
AMPHOTO ... American Photographic Book Publishing Co.
Am Photo Engraver ... American Photo Engraver [*A publication*]
Am Photog ... American Photography [*A publication*]
Am Photogr ... American Photography [*A publication*]
AMP-HR... Ampere-Hour (MDG)
Am Phys Ed Assn Res Q ... American Physical Education Association.
            Research Quarterly [*A publication*]
Am Phys Educ R ... American Physical Education Review [*A publication*]
Am Phys Teach ... American Physics Teacher [*A publication*]
Am Phytopathol Soc Monogr ... American Phytopathological Society.
            Monograph [*A publication*]
Am Phytopathol Soc Proc ... American Phytopathological Society. Proceedings
            [*A publication*]
AMPI........ Adolescent Multiphasic Personality Inventory [*Personality*
            development test] [*Psychology*]
AMPI........ Amplicon, Inc. [*NASDAQ symbol*] (NQ)
AMPI........ Annual Military Personnel Inspection
AMPI........ Associated Milk Producers, Incorporated
AMPIAF .... Acta Medica Philippina [*A publication*]
AMPI (Assoc Med Phys India) Med Phys Bull ... AMPI (Association of
            Medical Physicists of India) Medical Physics Bulletin [*A*
            publication]
AMPIB...... Advances in Microbial Physiology [*A publication*]
AMPIC...... Atomic and Molecular Processes Information Center [*ORNL*]
AMPIE...... [*The*] American Psycho/Info Exchange [*Information service or*
            system] (IID)
AMPIM..... Animal Models of Protecting Ischemic Myocardium
            [*Cardiology project*]
Am P J .... American Poultry Journal [*A publication*]
AMPL........ Advanced Microprocessor Programming Language [*Texas*
            Instruments, Inc.]
AMPL........ Advanced Microprocessor Prototyping Laboratory [*Texas*
            Instruments, Inc.]
AMPL........ Alaskan Malamute Protection League (EA)
AMPL........ Ampal-American Israel Corp. [*NASDAQ symbol*] (NQ)
AMPL........ Amplifier (AAG)
AMPL........ Amplitude
AMPL........ Amplus [*Large*] [*Pharmacy*]
AMPL........ [*A*] Macro Programming Language [*Data processing*]
AMPLA...... Australian Mining and Petroleum Law Association
Am Plan Assn J ... American Planning Association. Journal [*A publication*]
Am Plann Assoc J ... American Planning Association. Journal [*A publication*]
Am Planning ... American Planning and Civic Planning [*A publication*]
AMPLAS.... Apparatus Mounted in Plastic
Am Pl Ass ... American Pleader's Assistant [*A publication*] (DLA)
AMPLDN ... Amplidyne [*Electricity*]
AMPLFD.... Amplified
AMPLG..... Amplidyne Generator [*Electricity*]
AMPLJ ..... Australian Mining and Petroleum Law Journal [*A*
            publication] (APTA)
AMPLMG ... Amplidyne Motor Generator [*Electricity*]
AMPLTD.. Amplitude (FAAC)
AMPM ...... Institut de France. Academie des Sciences Morales et Politiques.
            Memoires [*A publication*]
AMPMA .... Archives des Maladies Professionnelles de Medecine du Travail
            et de Securite Sociale [*A publication*]
AMPME.... Assemblee Mondiale des Petites et Moyennes Entreprises
            [*World Assembly of Small and Medium Enterprises -*
            WASME] [*New Delhi, India*] (EAIO)
AMPMOD ... Army Materiel Plan Modernization
AMP News ... AMP [*Australian Mutual Provident Society*] News and Views
            [*A publication*] (APTA)
AmPo......... American Poetry [*A publication*]
AMPOAX ... Acta Microbiologica Polonica [*A publication*]
Am Poet Rev ... American Poetry Review [*A publication*]
Am Poetry ... American Poetry Review [*A publication*]
AMPOL .... [*The*] Almanac of American Politics [*National Journal Inc.*]
            [*Database*] [*A publication*]
Am Poli Sci ... American Political Science Review [*A publication*]
Am Politics Q ... American Politics Quarterly [*A publication*]

Am Polit Q ... American Politics Quarterly [*A publication*]
Am Polit Sci R ... American Political Science Review [*A publication*]
Am Pol Q ... American Politics Quarterly [*A publication*]
Am Pol Sci ... American Political Science Review [*Baltimore*] [*A publication*]
Am Pol Science R ... American Political Science Review [*A publication*]
Am Pol Science Rev ... American Political Science Review [*A publication*]
Am Pol Sci R ... American Political Science Review [*A publication*]
Am Pol Sci Rev ... American Political Science Review [*A publication*]
Am Pol Sc Rev ... American Political Science Review [*A publication*]
Am Pom Soc Pro ... American Pomological Society. Proceedings [*A*
            publication]
Am Postal Wkr ... American Postal Worker [*A publication*]
Am Potato J ... American Potato Journal [*A publication*]
Am Pot J .... American Potato Journal [*A publication*]
Am Poultry J ... American Poultry Journal [*A publication*]
AMPP........ Advanced Microprogrammable Processors (MCD)
AmPP........ American Poetry and Prose [*A publication*]
AMPP........ Arctic Meteorology Photographic Probe
AMPP........ Association of Motion Picture Producers [*Later,*
            AMPTP] (EA)
AMPPD..... Army Mobilization Planning and Programming
            Directive (AABC)
AMPPE..... Acute Multifocal Placoid Pigment Epitheliopathy
            [*Ophthalmology*]
AMPPGD ... Army Mobilization Planning and Programming Guidance
            Document (AABC)
AMPPS..... Automated Modular Preplanner Programming System (MCD)
AMPR ...... Aeronautical Manufacturers' Planning Report [*NASA*]
AMPR ...... Aeronautical Manufacturers Progress Report [*NASA*]
Am Pr........ American Practice [*A publication*] (DLA)
AMPR ...... Automatic Manifold Pressure Regulator [*Aviation*]
AMPRA..... American Medical Peer Review Association (EA)
Am Pract.... American Practitioner [*A publication*]
Am Pract Digest Treat ... American Practitioner and Digest of Treatment [*A*
            publication]
Am Pract Dig Treat ... American Practitioner and Digest of Treatment [*A*
            publication]
Am Practitioner ... American Practitioner [*A publication*]
AMPRB9... Annales de Medecine et de Pharmacie de Reims [*A publication*]
Am Prefs.... American Prefaces [*A publication*]
Am Presb R ... American Presbyterian Review [*A publication*]
Am Pressman ... American Pressman [*A publication*]
Am Pressman Rept ... American Pressman Reports [*A publication*]
AMPRI...... Association Member of the Plastics and Rubber Institute
            [*British*] (DBQ)
Am Print .... American Printer [*A publication*]
Am Prnt Lith ... American Printer and Lithographer [*Later, American Printer*]
            [*A publication*]
Am Prob..... American Probate Reports [*A publication*] (DLA)
Am Prob NS ... American Probate, New Series [*A publication*] (DLA)
Am Prob Rep ... American Probate Reports [*A publication*] (DLA)
Am Prod R ... American Produce Review [*A publication*]
Am Prof Pharm ... American Professional Pharmacist [*A publication*]
Am Property ... American Law of Property [*A publication*] (DLA)
Am Pro Rep ... American Probate Reports [*A publication*] (DLA)
Am Pr Rep ... American Practice Reports [*Washington, DC*] [*A*
            publication] (DLA)
Am Pr Rep NS ... American Practice Reports, New Series [*A*
            publication] (DLA)
AMPRS..... Automated Material Parts Request System (MCD)
AMPRT..... Asymptotically Most Powerful Rank Test [*Statistics*]
AMPS........ Accrued Military Pay System (AFM)
AMPS........ Acid Mucopolysaccharide [*Biochemistry*]
AMPS........ (Acrylamido)methylpropanesulfonic Acid [*Trademark of*
            Lubrizol] [*Organic chemistry*]
AMPS........ Adaptive Mode Planning System [*Computer program*]
AMPS........ Adenosine Monophosphate Succinate [*Biochemistry*]
AMPS........ Advanced Maneuvering Propulsion System
AMPS........ Advanced Manned Penetrator System
AMPS........ Advanced Mobile Phone Service [*Bell System*]
AMPS........ Aircraft Multispectral Photographic System [*NASA*]
AMPS........ Amazing Magic Pivot Swing [*Training device for baseball*
            batter's rear foot]
AMPS........ American Metered Postage Society [*Defunct*] (EA)
AMPS........ Americans for More Power Sources (EA)
AMPS........ Amperes (KSC)
AM-Ps....... Annales Medico-Psychologiques [*A publication*]
AMPS........ Arctic Marine Pipelaying System
AMPS........ Army Mine Planter Service
AMPS........ Army Motion Picture Service
AMPS........ Assembly of Mathematical and Physical Sciences [*National*
            Research Council]
AMPS........ Assessment of Motor and Process Skills [*Occupational therapy*]
AMPS........ Associated Music Publishers [*Musical slang*]
AMPS........ Association Mondiale de Prospective Sociale [*World Social*
            Prospects Study Association] [*Geneva,*
            Switzerland] (EAIO)
AMPS........ Atmosphere, Magnetosphere, and Plasmas in Space [*Space*
            shuttle payload] [*NASA*]
AMPS........ Atmospheric Magnetospheric Plasma System (NASA)
AMPS........ Auction-Market Preferred Stock

AMPS........ Automated Material Processing System [*Data processing*]
AMPS........ Automated Merchandise Processing System [*US Customs Service*]
AMPS........ Automated Program Search [*Tape recorder feature*]
AMPS....... Automatic Message Processing System [*USAERDL*]
AMPS........ Automatic Multi-Program Selection [*Photography*] [*Minolta Corp.*]
AMPS........ [*A*] Marriage Prediction Schedule [*Premarital relations test*]
AMPSA..... American Psychologist [*A publication*]
AMPSAB.. American Psychologist [*A publication*]
AMPSIN.... Adaptive Mode Planning System Input [*Computer program*]
AMPSS ..... Advanced Manned Precision Strike System [*Proposed Air Force plane*]
AMPSS ..... Airlift Mission Planning and Scheduling System [*Air Force*] (MCD)
Am Psychiatr Assoc Ment Hosp Serv Monogr Ser ... American Psychiatric Association. Mental Hospital Service. Monograph Series [*A publication*]
Am Psychoana Assn J ... American Psychoanalytic Association. Journal [*A publication*]
Am Psychoanal Assn J ... American Psychoanalytic Association. Journal [*A publication*]
Am Psychoanal Assoc J Monogr Ser ... American Psychoanalytic Association. Journal. Monograph Series [*A publication*]
Am Psychol ... American Psychologist [*A publication*]
Am Psychologist ... American Psychologist [*A publication*]
AMPT........ Advanced Maneuvering Propulsion Technology [*NASA*] (KSC)
AMPT........ Alpha-Methyl-p-tyrosine [*Also, MPT*] [*Pharmacology*]
AMPT....... Ampthill [*England*]
AMPT........ Association for Medical Physics Technology [*British*]
AMPTD..... Amplitude (MSA)
AMPTE..... Active Magnetospheric Particle Tracer Explorer [*Project*] [*NASA/West Germany*]
AMPTE..... Active Mesospheric Particle Tracer Explorer (MCD)
AMPTF ..... Apollo Mission Planning Task Force [*NASA*] (KSC)
AMPTP..... Alliance of Motion Picture and Television Producers (EA)
Am Ptr & Lith ... American Printer and Lithographer [*Later, American Printer*] [*A publication*]
Am Pub Health Ass Rep ... American Public Health Association. Reports [*A publication*]
Am Public Health Assoc Yearb ... American Public Health Association. Yearbook [*A publication*]
Am Public Works Assoc Yearb ... American Public Works Association. Yearbook [*A publication*]
AMPUL..... Ampulla [*Ampule*] [*Pharmacy*]
AMPYA..... Annales Medico-Psychologiques [*A publication*]
AMPYAT ... Annales Medico-Psychologiques [*A publication*]
AMPYF ..... American Pyramid Resources, Inc. [*NASDAQ symbol*] (NQ)
AMQ......... Amazing Stories. Quarterly [*A publication*]
AMQ......... Ambon [*Indonesia*] [*Airport symbol*] (OAG)
AMQ......... American Medical Qualification [*British*]
Am Q .... American Quarterly [*A publication*]
Am Q .... American Quarterly [*1827-1837*] [*A publication*]
AMQ......... Analog Multiplexer Quantitizer [*Data processing*] (KSC)
AMQ......... Apparent Molar Quantity
Am Q J Agr ... American Quarterly Journal of Agriculture and Science [*A publication*]
Am Q Micro J ... American Quarterly Microscopical Journal [*A publication*]
Am Q Obs ... American Quarterly Observer [*A publication*]
Am Q Reg .. American Quarterly Register [*A publication*]
AMQUA..... American Quaternary Association (EA)
Am Quar .... American Quarterly [*A publication*]
Am Quart ... American Quarterly [*A publication*]
AMR......... Abnormal Mission Routine
AMR......... Academy of Management. Review [*A publication*]
AMR......... Activity Metabolic Rate
AMR......... Ada, OK [*Location identifier*] [*FAA*] (FAAL)
AMR......... Advance Material Request
AMR......... Advanced Management Research [*A publication*] (DLA)
AMR......... Advanced Medium Rocket (MCD)
AMR......... Advanced Missile Receiver (MCD)
AMR......... Advanced Modular RADAR (MCD)
AMR......... Aerospace Medical Research
AMR......... Affiliated Medical Research, Inc. [*Research code symbol*]
AMR......... Air Movement Recorder
AMR......... Airborne Magnetic Recorder
AMR......... Airborne Microwave Refractometer (CAAL)
AMR......... Airman Military Record [*Air Force*]
AMR......... Alberta Education Materials Resource Centre [*UTLAS symbol*]
AMR......... Alternating Motion Rate
AMR......... Altitude Marking Range (KSC)
AMR......... Amazing Stories. Quarterly Reissue [*A publication*]
AMR......... Ambtenaar [*A publication*]
AMR......... American Book Review [*A publication*]
Am R .... American Reports [*A publication*] (DLA)
Am R .... American Review [*Formerly, New American Review*] [*A publication*]
AMR......... AMR Corp. [*NYSE symbol*] (SPSG)
AMR......... Amrinone [*Cardiotonic*]
AMR......... Analytic Mission Reliability (MCD)

AMR......... Annee Mondiale du Refugie
AMR......... Applied Mechanics Reviews [*A publication*]
AMR......... [*The*] Arcata & Mad River Rail Road Co. [*AAR code*]
AMR......... Area Manpower Review [*Department of Labor*]
AMR......... Assign Missile RADAR (CAAL)
AMR......... Associate of the Association of Health Care Information and Medical Record Officers [*British*] (DBQ)
AMR......... Association Marketing Roundtable (EA)
AMR......... Astro Musical Research (EA)
AMR......... Atlantic Missile Range [*Later, Eastern Test Range*]
AMR......... Auckland Mounted Rifles [*New Zealand*] (DMA)
AMR......... Australian Marketing Researcher [*A publication*] (APTA)
AMR......... Automated Management Reports (BUR)
AMR......... Automatic Message Recording
AMR......... Automatic Message Registering
AMR......... Automatic Message Routing (BUR)
AMR......... Automatic Meter Reading
AMR......... Auxiliary Machinery Room (CAAL)
AMR......... Aviation Medical Reports
AM(R) ...... Master of Arts in Research
AMR......... Milk River Public Library, Alberta [*Library symbol*] [*National Library of Canada*] (NLC)
AMR......... Reffton Corp., Montgomery, AL [*Library symbol*] [*Library of Congress*] (LCLS)
AMRA....... Abandoned Military Reservations Act [*1884*]
AMRA....... American Mechanical Rights Agency
AMRA....... American Medical Record Association (EA)
AMRA....... American Metal Repair Association [*Defunct*]
AMRA....... American Military Retirees Association (EA)
AMRA....... Ancient Mediterranean Research Association (EA)
AMRA....... Army Materials Research Agency [*Later, AMMRC*] [*Watertown, MA*]
AMRA....... Association of Medical Rehabilitation Administrators (EA)
AMRA....... Automatic Meter Reading Association (EA)
AMRAAM... Advanced Medium-Range Air-to-Air Missile (MCD)
Am Rabbit J ... American Rabbit Journal [*A publication*]
AMRAC..... Annales Musee Royal de l'Afrique Centrale [*A publication*]
AMRAC..... Anti-Missile Research Advisory Council
AMRAD.... Air Munitions Requirements and Development Committee [*DoD*] (MCD)
AMRAD.... Amateur Radio Research and Development Corp. (IID)
AMRAD.... Armament/Munitions Requirements, Acquisition and Development Committee [*Military*] [*Washington, DC*]
AMRAD.... ARPA [*Advanced Research Projects Agency*] Measurements RADAR [*Raytheon*]
AMRAD.... Australian Medical Research and Development Corporation
Am Rail Cas ... American Railway Cases [*A publication*] (DLA)
Am Rail R ... American Railway Reports [*A publication*] (DLA)
Am Railw Cas ... American Railway Cases [*A publication*] (DLA)
Am Railw Eng Assoc Bull ... American Railway Engineering Association. Bulletin [*A publication*]
Am Railw Eng Assoc Proc ... American Railway Engineering Association. Proceedings [*A publication*]
AMRAP..... Alaska Mineral Resource Assessment Program [*Department of the Interior*]
AMRBB5... Alabama Marine Resources. Bulletin [*A publication*]
AMRC....... Advanced Metals Research Corporation
AMRC....... American Recreation Centers, Inc. [*NASDAQ symbol*] (NQ)
AMRC....... Army Mathematics Research Center [*Madison, Wisconsin*]
AMRC....... Army Mobility Research Center
AMRC....... Association of Medical Record Consultants [*Defunct*] (EA)
AMRC....... Association of Medical Research Charities [*British*]
AMRC....... Automotive Market Research Council (EA)
AMRCA..... American Miniature Racing Car Association
Am R Ca ... American Railway Cases [*A publication*] (DLA)
AMRCFO ... Additional Material Required to Complete Fabrication Order
Am R & Corp ... American Railroad and Corporation Reports [*A publication*] (DLA)
Am R & C Rep ... American Railroad and Corporation Reports [*A publication*] (DLA)
AMRC Rev ... AMRC [*Australian Meat Research Committee*] Review [*A publication*] (APTA)
AMRCUS ... Alternative Marriage and Relationship Council of the United States
AMRD....... Air Member for Research and Development [*Later, TRE*] [*Air Ministry*] [*British*]
AMRD....... Air Mobility Research and Development Laboratory [*Also, AMR & DL, USAMR & DL*] [*Army*] (MCD)
AMRD....... Aircraft Maintenance and Repair Department [*British military*] (DMA)
AMRD....... Army Missile and Rockets Directorate
AMRD....... Automatic Message Routing Device
AMRDC .... Army Medical Research and Development Command
AMRDC .... Army Missile Research and Development Command (MCD)
AMRDC .... Army Mobility Research and Development Center
AMRDC .... Association of Medical Rehabilitation Directors and Coordinators [*Later, AMRA*] (EA)
AMR & DL ... Air Mobility Research and Development Laboratory [*Also, USAMR & DL*] [*Army*]
AMRD-NASC ... Army Missile and Rockets Division - NATO Supply Center
AMRE .... Air Ministry Reconnaissance Department [*British*] (DAS)

AMRE .... Air Ministry Research Establishment [*British military*] (DMA)
Am Real Estate & Urb Econ Assn J ... American Real Estate and Urban Economics Association. Journal [*A publication*]
Am Rec G ... American Record Guide [*A publication*]
Am Rec Guide ... American Record Guide [*A publication*]
AMRECOM ... Armament Material Readiness Command
Am Recorder ... American Recorder [*A publication*]
Am Record Gd ... American Record Guide [*A publication*]
Am Red Angus ... American Red Angus [*A publication*]
AMREE .... American Medical Research Expedition to Mount Everest
AMREEH ... Amphibia-Reptilia [*A publication*]
AMREF ..... African Medical and Research Foundation, USA (EA)
Am Ref Bk Ann ... American Reference Books Annual [*A publication*]
Am Refract Inst Inf Circ ... American Refractories Institute. Information Circular [*A publication*]
Am Refract Inst Tech Bull ... American Refractories Institute. Technical Bulletin [*A publication*]
Am Rehabil ... American Rehabilitation [*A publication*]
AMREP ..... Aircraft/Missile Maintenance - Production Compression Report
Am Rep ...... American Reports [*A publication*] (DLA)
Am Reports ... American Reports [*A publication*] (DLA)
Am Rev ...... American Review [*Formerly, New American Review*] [*A publication*]
Am Rev Resp Dis ... American Review of Respiratory Disease [*A publication*]
Am Rev Respir Dis ... American Review of Respiratory Disease [*A publication*]
Am Rev Sov Med ... American Review of Soviet Medicine [*A publication*]
Am Rev Sov Union ... American Review on the Soviet Union [*A publication*]
Am Rev Tub ... American Review of Tuberculosis and Pulmonary Diseases [*A publication*]
Am Rev Tuberc ... American Review of Tuberculosis [*A publication*]
Am Rev Tuberc Pulm Dis ... American Review of Tuberculosis and Pulmonary Diseases [*A publication*]
AMREX ..... American Real Estate Exchange
AMRF .... African Medical and Research Foundation (EA)
AMRF .... Amended Route of Flight [*Aviation*]
AMRF .... Amerford International Corp. [*NASDAQ symbol*] (NQ)
AMRF .... Automated Manufacturing Research Facility [*Gaithersburg, MD*] [*Department of Commerce*] (GRD)
AMRF .... Melbourne [*Australia*] [*ICAO location identifier*] (ICLI)
AMrhKG ... Archiv fuer Mittelrheinische Kirchengeschichte [*A publication*]
AMRI .... Amerifirst Bank FSB [*Miami, FL*] [*NASDAQ symbol*] (NQ)
AMRI .... Anteromedial Rotatory Instability [*Medicine*]
AMRI .... Association of Missile and Rocket Industries
AMRIA .... Americas [*A publication*]
AMRIB ..... America [*A publication*]
AMRICD ... Army Medical Research Institute of Chemical Defense (RDA)
AMRIID .... Army Medical Research Institute of Infectious Diseases (RDA)
AMRINA .. Associate Member of the Royal Institution of Naval Architects [*British*]
AMRIP ...... Avionics Module Repair Improvement Program [*Navy*]
AMRIR ...... Advanced Medium-Resolution Imaging Radiometer
AMRL .... Above Modern River Level [*Geology*]
AMRL .... Aerospace Medical Research Laboratory [*Later, MRL*] [*Wright-Patterson Air Force Base, OH*]
AMRL .... Air Medical Research Laboratory [*Later, MRL*] (MCD)
AMRL .... Applied Marine Research Laboratory [*Old Dominion University*] [*Research center*] (RCD)
AMRL .... Army Medical Research Laboratory
AMRLA ..... Army Medical Research Laboratory, Alaska (RDA)
AMRM ...... Australasian Model Railroad Magazine [*A publication*] (APTA)
AMRMC5 ... Agricultural Research Council. Meat Research Institute [*Bristol*]. Memorandum [*A publication*]
AMRNL .... Army Medical Research and Nutrition Laboratory
AMRO ...... Amsterdam-Rotterdam Bank
AMRO .... Association of Health Care Information and Medical Records Officers (EAIO)
AMRO .... Atlantic Missile Range [*later, Eastern Test Range*] Operations
AMROBA ... Acta Medica Romana [*A publication*]
Am Rocket Soc Pap ... American Rocket Society. Paper [*A publication*]
AMROO ...... Atlantic Missile Range [*later, Eastern Test Range*] Operations Office
Am Rose Annu ... American Rose Annual [*A publication*]
AMRPD .... Applied Manufacturing Research and Process Development
AMRPDF .. Advances in Molecular Relaxation and Interaction Processes [*A publication*]
Am R Public Admin ... American Review of Public Administration [*A publication*]
AMRPV ..... Advanced Multimission Remotely Piloted Vehicle (MCD)
AMRQC ..... Amarex, Inc. [*NASDAQ symbol*] (NQ)
AMRR .... Arctic Medical Research Report. Nordic Council [*A publication*]
AMRR .... Army Materials Research Reactor
Am RR Ca ... American Railway Cases [*A publication*] (DLA)
Am RR Cas ... American Railway Cases [*A publication*] (DLA)
Am RR & C Rep ... American Railroad and Corporation Reports [*A publication*] (DLA)
Am R Rep ... American Railway Reports [*A publication*] (DLA)
Am R Resp D ... American Review of Respiratory Disease [*A publication*]
Am RR Rep ... American Railway Reports [*A publication*] (DLA)

AMRS .... American Restaurants Corp. [*Ventura, CA*] [*NASDAQ symbol*] (NQ)
AMRSH .... Associate Member of the Royal Society of Health [*Formerly, ARSH*] [*British*]
AMRSHF ... Adrenal Metabolic Research Society of the Hypoglycemia Foundation (EA)
AMRV .... Astronaut Maneuvering Research Vehicle [*NASA*]
AMRV .... Atmospheric Maneuvering Reentry Vehicle (IEEE)
AMRWA ... Anglo-German Medical Review [*A publication*]
Am Ry Ca ... American Railway Cases [*A publication*] (DLA)
Am Ry Cases ... American Railway Cases [*A publication*] (DLA)
Am Ry Rep ... American Railway Reports [*A publication*] (DLA)
AMS .... Abortus, Militensis, Suis [*Microbiology*]
AMS .... Academy of Marketing Science [*Coral Gables, FL*] (EA)
AMS .... Academy of Marketing Science. Journal [*A publication*]
AMS .... Accelerator Mass Spectrometry
AMS .... Access Method Service [*Data processing*] (BUR)
AMS .... Accident Mitigation System [*Industrial engineering*]
AMS .... Accommodation and Messenger Service, Admiralty [*Obsolete*] [*British*]
AMS .... Acoustic Material Signature (MCD)
AMS .... Acoustic Measurement System (KSC)
AMS .... Acta Martyrum et Sanctorum [*A publication*]
AMS .... Actuation Mechanism Subsystem (MCD)
AMS .... Actuation Mine Simulator (MCD)
AMS .... Acute Mountain Sickness
AMS .... Adjustable Muzzle Stabilizer [*Rifles*] [*Army*] (INF)
AMS .... Administrative and Management Services (OICC)
AMS .... Administrative Management Society [*Willow Grove, PA*] (EA)
AMS .... Advanced Manned Spacecraft
AMS .... Advanced Manufacturing System (MCD)
AMS .... Advanced Manufacturing Systems Exposition and Conference (ITD)
AMS .... Advanced Mapping System [*Geography*]
AMS .... Advanced Marketing Services [*Book supplier*]
AMS .... Advanced Masking Systems [*Automotive engineering*] [*3M Co.*]
AMS .... Advanced Memory Specification [*Data processing*]
AMS .... Advanced Memory Systems, Inc. (IEEE)
AMS .... Advanced Metallic Structures [*Program*] [*Air Force*]
AMS .... Advanced Meteorological System (MCD)
AMS .... Advanced Minuteman System
AMS .... Advanced Missile System
AMS .... Advanced Mission Studies [*NASA*] (KSC)
AMS .... Advanced Monopulse Seeker
AMS .... Advances in Management Studies [*A publication*]
AMS .... Aerial Monitoring System [*Nuclear energy*] (NRCH)
AMS .... Aeronautical [*or Aerospace*] Material Specification
AMS .... Aeronautical Military Standards
AMS .... Aeronautical Mobile Service (FAAC)
AMS .... Aerospace Material Specification (MCD)
AMS .... Agency Manager Survey [*LIMRA*]
AMS .... Aggregate Measure of Support [*International trade*] (ECON)
AMS .... Agricultural Manpower Society [*British*] (EAIO)
AMS .... Agricultural Marketing Service [*Formerly, CMS*] [*Washington, DC*] [*Department of Agriculture*]
AMS .... Air Mail Service
AMS .... Air Management Station
AMS .... Air Mass (FAAC)
AMS .... Air Member for Supply [*British and Canadian*] [*World War II*]
AMS .... Air Missile System (NG)
AMS .... Airborne Maintenance System
AMS .... Aircraft Material Specifications [*Society of Automotive Engineers*]
AMS .... Airlock Module Station [*NASA*] (MCD)
AMS .... Alabama State University, Montgomery, AL [*Library symbol*] [*Library of Congress*] (LCLS)
AMS .... Alarm Monitoring System
AMS .... Alma Mater Society [*Canada*]
AMS .... Alpha-Methylstyrene [*Organic chemistry*]
AMS .... Alteration Management System (NVT)
AMS .... Altitude Measurement System
AMS .... Ambassador Industries Ltd. [*Vancouver Stock Exchange symbol*]
AMS .... American Magnolia Society [*Later, TMS*] (EA)
AMS .... American Management Systems, Inc. [*Information service or system*] (IID)
AMS .... American Market Selection [*Cigars*]
AMS .... American Mathematical Society (EA)
AMS .... American Meteor Society (EA)
AMS .... American Meteorological Society [*Boston, MA*]
AMS .... American Microchemical Society (EA)
AMS .... American Microscopical Society (EA)
AMS .... American Mohammedan Society [*Later, MM*] (EA)
AMS .... American Montessori Society (EA)
AMS .... American Motility Society (EA)
AMS .... American Museum of Safety (EA)
AMS .... American Musicological Society (EA)
AMS .... American Musicological Society. Journal [*A publication*]
AMS .... American Salesman [*A publication*]
AMS .... American Shared Hospital Services [*AMEX symbol*] (SPSG)

AmS .... American Speech [*A publication*]
AmS .... American Studies [*A publication*]
AMS .... [*The*] Americas: A Quarterly Review of Inter-American
        Cultural History [*A publication*]
AMS .... Ammonium Sulfamate [*Inorganic chemistry*]
AMS .... Amos [*California*] [*Seismograph station code, US Geological
        Survey*] (SEIS)
AMS .... Amplifier Subsystem (NASA)
AmS .... AMS Press, Inc., New York, NY [*Library symbol*] [*Library of
        Congress*] (LCLS)
AMS .... Amsterdam [*Netherlands*] [*Airport symbol*] (OAG)
AMS .... Ancient Monuments Society (EAIO)
AMS .... Anglo-Mongolian Society (EAIO)
AMS .... Angular Motion Simulator (MCD)
AMS .... Anisotropy of Magnetic Susceptibility [*Geophysics*]
AMS .... Annual Machinery Survey [*American Bureau of
        Shipping*] (DS)
AMS .... Antenna Mast Set (MCD)
AMS .... Apogee and Maneuvering Stage [*Space flight*]
AMS .... Apollo Mission Simulator [*NASA*]
AMS .... Applied Mathematics Series
AMS .... Arab-American Media Society (EA)
AMS .... Arbetsmarknadsstyrelsen [*National Labor Market Board*]
        [*Sweden*]
AMS .... Army Management School (KSC)
AMS .... Army Management Structure
AMS .... Army Management System
AMS .... Army Map Service [*Later, Defense Mapping Agency
        Topographic Center*] [*Washington, DC*]
AMS .... Army Medical Service [*British*]
AMS .... Army Medical Staff
AMS .... Arthritis and Musculoskeletal and Skin Diseases Database
        [*National Arthritis and Musculoskeletal and Skin Diseases
        Information Clearinghouse*] [*Information service or
        system*] (CRD)
AMS .... Arthur Machen Society [*Defunct*] (EA)
AMS .... Articulated Mirror System [*Astronomy*]
AMS .... Artillery and Missile School [*Army*] (MCD)
AMS .... Assets Management System
AMS .... Assistant Military Secretary [*British*]
AMS .... Associate of the Institute of Management Services
        [*British*] (DBQ)
AMS .... Associated Mariners' Society [*A union*] [*British*]
AMS .... Association of Marshall Scholars (EA)
AMS .... Association of Messenger Services
AMS .... Association of Military Surgeons of the United States (RDA)
AMS .... Association of Museum Stores (EA)
AMS .... Associative Memory System [*Data processing*] (DIT)
AMS .... Assurance Medical Society [*British*]
AMS .... Asymmetric Multiprocessing System [*IBM Corp.*]
AMS .... Atmospheric Monitor System (IEEE)
AMS .... Atypical Measles Syndrome [*Medicine*]
AMS .... Auditory Memory Span [*Psychometrics*]
AMS .... Australian MARC [*Machine-Readable Cataloguing*]
        Specification
AMS .... Australian Merino Society
AmS .... Australian Minesweeper [*A publication*]
AMS .... Australian Museum, Sydney
AmS .... Authority for Material Substitution (MCD)
AmS .... Automated Microbial Systems (MCD)
AMS .... Automated Minefield System (MCD)
AMS .... Automatic Meteorological System (RDA)
AMS .... Automatic Mode Status (CAAL)
AMS .... Automatic Monitoring System [*Aviation*]
AMS .... Automicrobic System
AMS .... Autopilot Mode Selector
AMS .... Auxiliary Memory Set (MCD)
AMS .... Auxiliary Minesweeper [*NATO*]
AMS .... Average Monthly Sales (MCD)
AMS .... Aviation Structural Mechanic, Structures [*Navy rating*]
AMS .... Avionics Maintenance Shop
AMS .... Avionics Maintenance Squadron [*Air Force/Navy*] (MCD)
AMS .... Avonics Management System
AMS .... Chandler, AZ [*Location identifier*] [*FAA*] (FAAL)
AMS .... Joseph Quincy Adams Memorial Studies [*A publication*]
AMS .... [*A*] Minehunting SONAR (MCD)
AMS .... Motor Minesweeper [*Navy symbol*] [*Obsolete*]
AMS .... National Arthritis and Musculoskeletal and Skin Diseases
        Information Clearinghouse [*US Public Health Service*]
        [*Information service or system*] (IID)
AMSA .... (Acridinylamino)methanesulfon-m-anisidide
AMSA .... Advanced Manned Strategic Aircraft [*Facetious translation:
        "America's Most Studied Aircraft"*] [*Air Force*]
AMSA .... Advanced Mutual Security Act
AMSA .... Aerospace Multiple Station Analysis (MCD)
AMSA .... American Meat Science Association (EA)
AMSA .... American Medallic Sculpture Association (EA)
AMSA .... American Medical Society on Alcoholism
AMSA .... American Medical Student Association (EA)
AMSA .... American Metal Stamping Association [*Later, PMA*] (EA)
AMSA .... American Music Scholarship Association (EA)

AMSA .... Anterior Middle Suprasylvian Association [*Area of cat cortex*]
AMSA .... Area Maintenance Support Activity (AABC)
AMSA .... Association of Metropolitan Sewerage Agencies (EA)
AMSA .... Australian Marine Sciences Association
AMSA .... Australian Museum Shops Association
AMS-A ...... Automatic Meteorological System - Artillery (MCD)
AMSAA ..... Ambulance and Medical Service Association of America [*Later,
        AAA*] (EA)
AMSAA ..... Army Materiel Systems Analysis Activity [*or Agency*]
        [*Aberdeen Proving Ground, MD*] (MCD)
AMSAA ..... Aviation Structural Mechanic, Structures, Airman Apprentice
        [*Navy rating*]
AMSAC .... American Society of African Culture [*Defunct*] (EA)
AMSAC ..... AMSAC [*American Society of African Culture*] Newsletter [*A
        publication*]
AMSAC ..... ATWS [*Anticipated Transient without Scram*] Mitigating
        System Actuation Circuitry [*Nuclear energy*] (NRCH)
AMS(Aff) .. Affiliate, Association of Medical Secretaries, Practice
        Administrators, and Receptionists [*British*] (DBQ)
AM SAM ... American Samoa
AMSAM ... Antimissile Surface-to-Air Missile
Am Samoa ... American Samoa Code [*A publication*] (DLA)
Am Samoa Code Ann ... American Samoa Code. Annotated [*A
        publication*] (DLA)
AMSAN .... Aviation Structural Mechanic, Structures, Airman [*Navy
        rating*]
AMSAODD ... American Medical Society on Alcoholism and Other Drug
        Dependencies [*Later, ASAM*] (EA)
AMSAPM ... Atti e Memorie. Deputazione di Storia Patria per le Antiche
        Provincie Modenesi [*A publication*]
AMSAT ..... American Satellite (MCD)
AMSAT ..... Radio Amateur Satellite Corp. (EA)
AMSB .... American Savings Financial Corp. [*Tacoma, WA*] [*NASDAQ
        symbol*] (NQ)
AMSC .... Advanced Military Spaceflight Capability
AMSC .... Advances in Molten Salt Chemistry [*Elsevier Book Series*] [*A
        publication*]
AMSC .... Alliance des Moniteurs de Ski du Canada [*Canadian Ski
        Instructors' Alliance*]
AMSC .... Allied Military Staff Conference [*Quebec, Yalta, etc.*] [*World
        War II*]
AMSC .... American Miniature Schnauzer Club (EA)
AMSC .... Archives, Manuscripts, and Special Collections [*Research
        Libraries Group project*] (IT)
AMSC .... Army Material Supply Command (KSC)
AMSC .... Army Mathematics Steering Committee
AMSC .... Army Medical Specialist Corps
AMSC .... Army Mobility Support Center
AMSC .... Automatic Message Switching Center (NOAA)
AMSC .... Averaged Magnitude Squared Coherence (MCD)
AMSCA ...... American Scientist [*A publication*]
AMSCAC .... American Scientist [*A publication*]
Am Scand R ... American-Scandinavian Review [*A publication*]
AMSCAT .. Airborne Microwave Scatterometer [*For measuring wind speed
        and direction*]
AMSCC ..... Advances in Molten Salt Chemistry [*A publication*]
Am Scenic and Historic Preservation Soc An Rp ... American Scenic and
        Historic Preservation Society. Annual Report [*A
        publication*]
Am Sch ...... American Scholar [*A publication*]
Am Sch Bd J ... American School Board Journal [*A publication*]
Am Sch Board J ... American School Board Journal [*A publication*]
Am Sch Brd J ... American School Board Journal [*A publication*]
Am Schol ... American Scholar [*A publication*]
Am Scholar ... American Scholar [*A publication*]
Am School Bd J ... American School Board Journal [*A publication*]
Am Sch Orient Res Bul ... American Schools of Oriental Research. Bulletin [*A
        publication*]
Am Sch & Univ ... American School and University [*A publication*]
Am Sci .... American Scientist [*A publication*]
Am Scient .. American Scientist [*A publication*]
Am Scientist ... American Scientist [*A publication*]
AMSCO ...... Acquisition Management System Control Officer (MCD)
AMSCO .... Aircraft Manufacturing and Supply Company of Australia
AMSCO .... American Mineral Spirits Company
AMSCO .... American Sterilizer Company
AMSCO .... Army Management Structure Code
AMSCO .... Army Medical Supply Control Officer
AMSCP .... Associate Member of the Society of Certified Professionals
        [*British*] (DBQ)
AMSDCL .... Acquisition Management Systems and Data Control List
AMSDEP .. Asian Manpower Skill Development Program [*United Nations*]
AMSDL .. Acquisition Management Systems and Data Control List
AMSDRP .. Acquisition Management Systems and Data Requirements
        Control Program [*Navy*]
AMSDSP .... Atti e Memorie. Societa Dalmata di Storia [*A publication*]
AMSE .... Aircraft Maintenance Support Equipment (MCD)
AMSE .... American Mobile Systems, Inc. [*NASDAQ symbol*] (NQ)
AMSE .... Associate Member of the Society of Engineers, Inc.
        [*British*] (DBQ)

AMSE........ Association for Advancement of Modelling and Simulation
Techniques in Enterprises (EAIO)
AMSE........ Association Mondiale des Sciences de l'Education [*World
Association for Educational Research - WAER*] (EAIO)
AMSE........ Association of Muslim Scientists and Engineers (EA)
AMSEC..... Analytic Methodology for System Evaluation and Control
[*Army*]
Am Sec Educ ... American Secondary Education [*A publication*]
AmSECT ... American Society of Extra-Corporeal Technology (EA)
AMSEF ..... Antiminesweeping Explosive Float
AMSEL ..... Aeronautical Maintenance Support Equipment List
[*Military*] (AFIT)
Am Seph .... American Sephardi [*A publication*]
AMSER..... Atti e Memorie. Reale Deputazione di Storia Patria per l'Emilia
et la Romagna [*A publication*]
AMSERT .. Associate Member of the Society of Electronic and Radio
Technicians [*British*] (DBQ)
AMSF........ Area Maintenance Supply Facility [*Army*] (AABC)
AMSF........ Army Morale Support Fund (AABC)
AMSFT ..... American Medical Support Flight Team [*Later, Operation
Angel Plane*] (EA)
AMSGS..... Army Medical Service Graduate School
AMS-H..... Advanced Missile System - Heavy (MCD)
AMSHAH ... Assessment Models in Support of Hazard Assessment
Handbook (MCD)
AMSHAR ... Acta Morphologica. Academiae Scientiarum Hungaricae [*A
publication*]
Am Sheep B & W ... American Sheep Breeder and Wool Grower [*A
publication*]
Am Shipp... American Shipper [*A publication*]
AMSI........ Admiralty Merchant Shipping Instructions [*British*]
AMSI........ Advanced Monitoring Systems, Inc. [*NASDAQ symbol*] (NQ)
AMSI........ Atlantic Merchant Shipping Instructions
AMSI........ Atti e Memorie. Societa Istriana di Archeologia e Storia Patria
[*A publication*]
AMSIF ...... International Fertilizer Development Center, Muscle Shoals,
Alberta [*Library symbol*] [*National Library of
Canada*] (NLC)
Am Silk J... American Silk Journal [*A publication*]
Am Silk Rayon J ... American Silk Rayon Journal [*A publication*]
AMSIS ..... Air Ministry Secret Intelligence Summary [*British
military*] (DMA)
AMSIstriana ... Atti e Memorie. Societa Istriana di Archeologia e Storia Patria
[*A publication*]
AMSJ .... American Musicological Society. Journal [*A publication*]
AMSJAX... Journal. Aero Medical Society of India [*A publication*]
AMS JI...... American Musicological Society. Journal [*A publication*]
AMSK....... American Solar King Corp. [*NASDAQ symbol*] (NQ)
AMSL........ Above Mean Sea Level [*Navigation*]
AMSL........ Acquisition Management System List (MCD)
Am Sl .... American Slavic and East European Review [*A publication*]
AMSL........ Applied Mathematics and Statistics Laboratory [*Stanford
University*] (MCD)
AMSL........ Approved Material Substitution List
AMSLAET ... Associate Member of the Society of Licensed Aircraft Engineers
and Technologists [*British*] (DBQ)
Am Slavic R ... American Slavic and East European Review [*A publication*]
AMSM ...... Atti e Memorie. Reale Deputazione di Storia Patria per le
Marche [*A publication*]
AMSMH ... Association of Medical Superintendents of Mental Hospitals
[*Later, AAPA*] (EA)
AMSMS.... Airborne Mechanical Special Mission System (MCD)
AMSO .... Air Member for Supply and Organisation [*Air Ministry*]
[*British*]
AMSO .... Ammunition Shipment Order [*Army*]
AMSO .... Association of Major Symphony Orchestra Volunteers (EA)
AMSO .... Association of Market Survey Organisations [*British*]
AMSOC .... American Miscellaneous Society (EA)
Am Soc...... American Sociologist [*A publication*]
Am Soc Abrasive Methods Natl Tech Conf Proc ... American Society for
Abrasive Methods. National Technical Conference.
Proceedings [*A publication*]
Am Soc Ag Eng ... American Society of Agricultural Engineers. Transactions
[*A publication*]
Am Soc Agron J ... American Society of Agronomy. Journal [*A publication*]
Am Soc Agron Spec Publ ... American Society of Agronomy. Special
Publication [*A publication*]
Am Soc Anim Prod Rec Proc Annu Meet ... American Society of Animal
Production. Record of Proceedings. Annual Meeting [*A
publication*]
Am Soc Brew Chem Proc ... American Society of Brewing Chemists.
Proceedings [*A publication*]
Am Soc C E Proc ... American Society of Civil Engineers. Proceedings [*A
publication*]
Am Soc Church Hist Papers ... American Society of Church History. Papers
[*A publication*]
Am Soc Civ E J Struct Div ... American Society of Civil Engineers. Journal.
Structural Division [*A publication*]
Am Soc Civ E J Waterway Port Div ... American Society of Civil Engineers.
Waterway, Port, Coastal, and Ocean Division [*A
publication*]

Am Soc Civ Eng Hydraul Div Annu Spec Conf Proc ... American Society of
Civil Engineers. Hydraulics Division. Annual Specialty
Conference. Proceedings [*A publication*]
Am Soc Civ Eng Proc Eng Issues J Prof Act ... American Society of Civil
Engineers. Proceedings. Engineering Issues. Journal of
Professional Activities [*A publication*]
Am Soc Civ Eng Proc J Hydraul Div ... American Society of Civil Engineers.
Proceedings. Journal. Hydraulics Division [*A publication*]
Am Soc Civ Eng Proc J Irrig Drain Div ... American Society of Civil
Engineers. Proceedings. Journal. Irrigation and Drainage
Division [*A publication*]
Am Soc Civ Eng Proc Transp Eng J ... American Society of Civil Engineers.
Proceedings. Transportation Engineering Journal [*A
publication*]
Am Soc Civ Eng Trans ... American Society of Civil Engineers. Transactions
[*A publication*]
Am Soc Civ E Transp Eng J ... American Society of Civil Engineers.
Transportation Engineering Journal [*A publication*]
Am Soc Civil Engineers Proc Jour Hydraulics Div ... American Society of
Civil Engineers. Proceedings. Journal. Hydraulics Division
[*A publication*]
Am Soc Civil Engineers Proc Jour Sanitary Eng Div ... American Society of
Civil Engineers. Proceedings. Journal. Sanitary Engineering
Division [*A publication*]
Am Soc Civil Engineers Proc Jour Structural Div ... American Society of Civil
Engineers. Proceedings. Journal. Structural Division [*A
publication*]
Am Soc Civil Engineers Proc Jour Surveying and Mapping Div ... American
Society of Civil Engineers. Proceedings. Journal. Surveying
and Mapping Division [*A publication*]
Am Soc Civil Engineers Trans ... American Society of Civil Engineers.
Transactions [*A publication*]
Am Soc Civil Eng Proc ... American Society of Civil Engineers. Proceedings [*A
publication*]
Am Soc Civil Eng Proc J Geotech Eng Div ... American Society of Civil
Engineers. Proceedings. Journal. Geotechnical Engineering
Division [*A publication*]
Am Soc Civil Engrs Constr ... American Society of Civil Engineers.
Proceedings. Journal. Construction Division [*A
publication*]
Am Soc Civil Engrs Geotech ... American Society of Civil Engineers.
Proceedings. Journal. Geotechnical Division [*A
publication*]
Am Soc Civil Engrs Struct ... American Society of Civil Engineers.
Proceedings. Journal. Structural Division [*A publication*]
Am Soc Civil Engrs Transpn ... American Society of Civil Engineers.
Proceedings. Journal of Transportation Engineering [*A
publication*]
Am Soc Civil Engrs Urb Plann ... American Society of Civil Engineers.
Journal of Urban Planning [*A publication*]
Am Soc Eng Educ COED Trans ... American Society for Engineering
Education. Computers in Education Division. Transactions
[*A publication*]
Am Soc Eng Educ Comput Educ Div Trans ... American Society for
Engineering Education. Computers in Education Division.
Transactions [*A publication*]
Am Soc Heat Vent Eng Guide ... American Society of Heating and Ventilating
Engineers. Guide [*A publication*]
Am Soc Hort Sci J ... American Society for Horticultural Science. Journal [*A
publication*]
Am Soc Info Science Bul ... Bulletin. American Society for Information
Science [*A publication*]
Am Soc Info Science J ... Journal. American Society for Information Science
[*A publication*]
Am Soc Inf Sci J ... American Society for Information Science. Journal [*A
publication*]
Am Soc Inf Sci Proc ... American Society for Information Science. Proceedings
[*A publication*]
Am Soc Inf Sci Proc Annu Meet ... American Society for Information Science.
Proceedings. Annual Meeting [*A publication*]
Am Soc Inf Sci Proc ASIS Annu Meet ... American Society for Information
Science. Proceedings of the ASIS Annual Meeting [*A
publication*]
Am Soc Int L ... American Society of International Law (DLA)
Am Soc Int Law Proc ... American Society of International Law. Proceedings
[*A publication*]
Am Soc Int'l L Proc ... American Society of International Law. Proceedings [*A
publication*]
Am Soc Int L Proc ... American Society of International Law. Proceedings [*A
publication*]
Am Sociol... American Sociologist [*A publication*]
Am Sociological R ... American Sociological Review [*A publication*]
Am Sociol R ... American Sociological Review [*A publication*]
Am Sociol Rev ... American Sociological Review [*A publication*]
Am Sociol S ... American Sociological Society. Publications [*A publication*]
Am Socio Rev ... American Sociological Review [*A publication*]
Am Soc Limnol Oceangr Spec Symp ... American Society of Limnology and
Oceanography. Special Symposium [*A publication*]
Am Soc Limnol Oceanogr Spec Symp ... American Society of Limnology and
Oceanography. Special Symposium [*A publication*]

Am Soc Lubr Eng Tech Prepr ... American Society of Lubrication Engineers. Technical Preprints [*A publication*]
Am Soc Mechanical Engineers Trans ... American Society of Mechanical Engineers. Transactions [*A publication*]
Am Soc Mech Eng Appl Mech Div (AMD) ... American Society of Mechanical Engineers. Applied Mechanics Division (AMD) [*A publication*]
Am Soc Mech Eng Appl Mech Div Appl Mech Symp Ser ... American Society of Mechanical Engineers. Applied Mechanics Division. Applied Mechanics Symposia Series [*A publication*]
Am Soc Mech Eng Heat Transfer Div Publ HTD ... American Society of Mechanical Engineers. Heat Transfer Division. Publication HTD [*A publication*]
Am Soc Mech Eng Met Prop Counc Publ MPC ... American Society of Mechanical Engineers and Metal Properties Council. Publication MPC [*A publication*]
Am Soc Mech Eng Pap ... American Society of Mechanical Engineers. Papers [*A publication*]
Am Soc Mech Eng Pressure Vessels Piping Div PVP ... American Society of Mechanical Engineers. Pressure Vessels and Piping Division. PVP [*A publication*]
Am Soc Met Mater Metalwork Technol Ser ... American Society for Metals Materials/Metalworking. Technology Series [*A publication*]
Am Soc Munic Eng Off Proc ... American Society of Municipal Engineers. Official Proceedings [*A publication*]
Am Soc Munic Imp ... American Society for Municipal Improvements. Proceedings [*A publication*]
Am Soc Naval Eng J ... American Society of Naval Engineers. Journal [*A publication*]
Am Soc Photogramm Annu Meet Proc ... American Society of Photogrammetry. Annual Meeting. Proceedings [*A publication*]
Am Soc Photogramm Fall Conv Proc ... American Society of Photogrammetry. Fall Convention. Proceedings [*A publication*]
Am Soc Plast Reconstr Surg Educ Found Proc Symp ... American Society of Plastic and Reconstructive Surgeons. Educational Foundation. Proceedings of the Symposium [*A publication*]
Am Soc Psychical Res J ... American Society for Psychical Research. Journal [*A publication*]
Am Soc Psych Res J ... American Society for Psychical Research. Journal [*A publication*]
Am Soc R ... American Sociological Review [*A publication*]
Am Soc Rev ... American Sociological Review [*A publication*]
Am Soc Safety Eng J ... American Society of Safety Engineers. Journal [*A publication*]
Am Soc Sci J ... American Journal of Social Science [*A publication*]
Am Soc Testing Materials Special Tech Pub ... American Society for Testing and Materials. Special Technical Publication [*A publication*]
Am Soc Testing and Materials Spec Tech Pub ... American Society for Testing and Materials. Special Technical Publication [*A publication*]
Am Soc Test Mater Annu Book ASTM Stand ... American Society for Testing and Materials. Annual Book of ASTM Standards [*A publication*]
Am Soc Test Mater ASTM Stand ... American Society for Testing and Materials. Book of ASTM Standards [*A publication*]
Am Soc Test Mater Spec Tech Publ ... American Society for Testing and Materials. Special Technical Publication [*A publication*]
Am Soc Trop Med Papers ... American Society of Tropical Medicine. Papers [*A publication*]
Am Soc Vet Clin Pathol Bull ... American Society of Veterinary Clinical Pathologists. Bulletin [*A publication*]
Am Soc'y Int'l Proc ... American Society of International Law. Proceedings [*A publication*] (DLA)
AMSOG .... Army Molecular Sieve Oxygen Generator (RDA)
AMSOL ... American Soldier
AMSORB ... Analysis of Multiple Source Obscurants on Realistic Battlefield (MCD)
AMSP .... Advanced Military Studies Program [*DoD*]
AMSP .... Allied Military Security Publication
Am Sp .... American Speech [*A publication*]
AMSP .... Army Maintenance and Supply Procedures [*or Publications*] (NATG)
AMSP .... Army Master Study Program (AABC)
AMSPA ..... Advances in Mass Spectrometry [*A publication*]
AMSPDC .. Association of Medical School Pediatric Department Chairmen (EA)
Am Spect .... American Spectator [*A publication*]
Am Spectator ... American Spectator [*A publication*]
Am Speech ... American Speech [*A publication*]
AMSPR ..... Atti e Memorie. Deputazione di Storia Patria per le Provincie di Romagna [*A publication*]
AMS P & S ... Agricultural Marketing Service, P and S Docket [*United States*] [*A publication*] (DLA)
AMSq .... Avionics Maintenance Squadron [*Air Force*] (AFM)
AMSR .... Advanced Microwave Scanning Radiometer (MCD)
AMSR .... Air Member for Supply and Research [*Air Ministry*] [*British*]
AMSR .... Alternate Management Summary Report (MCD)
AMSR .... Amer-Scandinavian Review [*A publication*]

Am SR .... American State Reports [*A publication*] (DLA)
AMSR .... Amserv, Inc. [*NASDAQ symbol*] (NQ)
AMSR .... Annotated Manual of Statutes and Regulations [*of the Federal Home Loan Bank Board*]
AMSR .... Automated Microfilm Storage and Retrieval [*Army*] (IID)
AMSR .... Autonomous Missile Site RADAR (AABC)
AMSRDC ... Army Medical Service Research and Development Command
AMSS .... Advanced Manned Space Simulator
AMSS .... Advanced Meteorological Sounding System
AMSS .... Advanced Mine-Hunting SONAR System (MCD)
AMSS .... Advanced Multimission Sensor System
AMSS .... Advanced Multipurpose Surfacing System (MCD)
AMSS .... American Milking Shorthorn Society (EA)
AmSS .... American Sea Songs and Chanteys [*A publication*]
AMSS .... Army Medical Service School [*Later, Medical Field Service School*]
AMSS .... Association of Muslim Social Scientists (EA)
AMSS .... Autograph Manuscript Signed [*Manuscript descriptions*]
AMSS .... Automated Multistage Substructuring (MCD)
AMSS .... Automatic Master Sequence Selector
AMSSA ..... Army Medical Supply Support Activity
AMSSAQ .. Acta Medica Scandinavica. Supplementum [*A publication*]
AMSSB ..... Amplitude Modulation, Single Sideband [*Electronics*]
AMSSB/SC ... Amplitude Modulation, Single Sideband, Suppressed Carrier [*Electronics*] (CET)
AMSSS ...... Actron Microprocessor Softwear Support System (MCD)
AMSST ..... Associate of the Society of Surveying Technicians [*British*] (DBQ)
AMST .... Advanced Medium STOL [*Short Takeoff and Landing*] Transport
AMST .... Advanced Military Spaceflight Technology (MCD)
AMST .... American States Leasing [*NASDAQ symbol*] (NQ)
Amst .... Amerikastudien [*American Studies*] [*A publication*]
AMST .... Association of Maximum Service Telecasters
AMSTAN ... American Radiator & Standard Sanitary Corp. [*Later, American Standard, Inc.*]
Am Sta Rep ... American State Reports [*A publication*] (DLA)
Am Stat ...... American Statistician [*A publication*]
Am Stat Assn J ... American Statistical Association. Journal [*A publication*]
Am Stat Assoc Quar Publ ... American Statistical Association. Quarterly Publications [*A publication*]
Am State Papers ... American State Papers [*A publication*] (DLA)
Am State Rep ... American State Reports [*A publication*] (DLA)
Am Stat Index ... American Statistics Index [*A publication*]
Am Statis Assn ... American Statistical Association. Quarterly Publications [*A publication*]
Am Statistician ... American Statistician [*A publication*]
Am Statistn ... American Statistician [*A publication*]
Amstel .... Amstelodamum [*A publication*]
Amsterdams Sociol Tijds ... Amsterdams Sociologisch Tijdschrift [*A publication*]
Am Stock Exch Rules ... Rules of the American Stock Exchange [*A publication*] (DLA)
Am Stock Ex Guide ... American Stock Exchange Guide [*Commerce Clearing House*] [*A publication*] (DLA)
Am Stock Ex Guide CCH ... American Stock Exchange Guide. Commerce Clearing House [*A publication*]
Am Stockman ... American Stockman [*A publication*]
Am Stomat ... American Stomatologist [*A publication*]
Am St P ...... American State Papers [*A publication*] (DLA)
Am St P ...... American Studies in Papyrology [*A publication*]
Am St Papers ... American State Papers [*A publication*] (DLA)
AMStPapyr ... American Studies in Papyrology [*New Haven, CT*] [*A publication*]
Am St R ..... American State Reports [*1886-1911*] [*A publication*] (DLA)
Am St RD .. American Street Railway Decisions [*A publication*] (DLA)
Am St Rep ... American State Reports [*A publication*] (DLA)
Am St Reports ... American State Reports [*A publication*] (DLA)
Am St Ry Dec ... American Street Railway Decisions [*A publication*] (DLA)
Am St Ry Rep ... American Street Railway Reports [*A publication*] (DLA)
AMSTS ...... Automatic Multiparameter Semiconductor Test Set
Amst St IV ... Amsterdam Studies in the Theory and History of Linguistic Science. Series IV. Current Issues in Linguistic Theory [*A publication*]
Am Stud ..... American Studies [*A publication*]
Am Stud Int ... American Studies International [*A publication*]
Am Stud Sc ... American Studies in Scandinavia [*A publication*]
AMSU .... Advanced Microwave Sounding Unit [*Satellite instrument for meteorology*]
AMSU .... Aeronautical Material Screening Unit (AFIT)
AMSU .... Air Motor Servo Unit (MCD)
AMSU .... Attitude Monitor Switching Unit (MCD)
AMSU .... Auto-Manual Switching Unit [*Telecommunications*] (DCTA)
AMSUA .... American Surgeon [*A publication*]
AMSUAW ... American Surgeon [*A publication*]
AMSUBX ... Acta Medica Turcica. Supplementum [*A publication*]
Am Sugar Ind ... American Sugar Industry [*A publication*]
Am Surg ..... American Surgeon [*A publication*]
Am Surgeon ... American Surgeon [*A publication*]
AMSUS ..... Association of Military Surgeons of the United States (EA)
AMSVAZ .. Acta Medica Scandinavica [*A publication*]

AMSW ...... American Software, Inc. [*NASDAQ symbol*] (NQ)
AMSWAG ... AMSAA [*Army Materiel Systems Analysis Agency*] Simulation
     Wargame (MCD)
AMSY........ American Management Systems, Inc. [*NASDAQ
     symbol*] (NQ)
AMT......... Accelerated Mission Testing (IEEE)
AMT......... Acme-Cleveland Corp. [*NYSE symbol*] (SPSG)
AMT......... Active Maintenance Time
AMT......... Active Memory Technology (ECON)
AMT......... Advanced Manufacturing Technology [*Technical Insights, Inc.*]
     [*Information service or system*] (CRD)
AMT......... Advanced Materials Technology [*Information service or
     system*] (IID)
AMT......... Aerial Mail Terminal (AFM)
AMT......... Air Mail Transfer (ADA)
AMT......... Air Mail Transmission
AMT......... Air Member for Training [*British and Canadian*] [*World War
     II*]
AMT......... Alkali-Metal Turbine
AMT......... Alternative Mating Technique [*Zoology*]
AMT......... Alternative Minimum Tax
AMT......... Amatsia [*Israel*] [*Geomagnetic observatory code*]
AMT......... American Medical Technologists (EA)
AMT......... American Medical Television
AMT......... American Mime Theatre (EA)
AMT......... American Music Teacher Magazine [*A publication*]
AMT......... American Telecommunications Corp. [*Vancouver Stock
     Exchange symbol*]
AMT......... American Trans Air, Inc. [*Indianapolis, IN*] [*FAA
     designator*] (FAAC)
AMT......... Aminomethyltrimethylpsoralen [*Cytology*]
AMT......... Aminomethyltrioxsalen [*Organic chemistry*]
AMT......... Aminopterin [*Antiviral compound*]
AMT......... Ammonium Metatungstate [*Inorganic chemistry*]
AMT......... Amount (AFM)
AMT......... Amphetamine [*Also, A, amphet*] [*CNS stimulant*]
AMT......... Amplitude-Modulated Transmitter [*Electronics*]
AMt .... Analecta Montserratensia [*A publication*]
AMT......... Angular Mapping Transformation [*Data processing*]
AMT......... Apogee Motor Timer [*NASA*]
AMT......... Army Modernization Training
AMT......... Associate in Mechanical Technology
AMT......... Associate in Medical Technology
AMT......... Association for Manufacturing Technology (EA)
AMT......... Assyrian Medical Texts [*A publication*] (BJA)
AMT......... Astrograph Mean Time [*Navigation*]
AMT......... Audio Frequency Magnetotelluric
AMT......... AUTODIN Multimedia Terminal (NVT)
AMT......... Automatic Moon Tracking
AMT......... Automatic Motor Tester
AMT......... Available Machine Time
AMT......... Master of Arts in Teaching
AM in T... Master of Arts in Teaching
AMT......... Troy State University at Montgomery, Montgomery, AL
     [*Library symbol*] [*Library of Congress*] (LCLS)
AMT......... West Union, OH [*Location identifier*] [*FAA*] (FAAL)
AMTA....... Airborne Moving Target Attack
AMTA....... American Massage Therapy Association (EA)
AMTA....... American Medical Tennis Association (EA)
AMTA....... Amistar Corp. [*NASDAQ symbol*] (NQ)
AMTA....... Antenna Measurement Techniques Association (EA)
AMTANK ... Amphibious Tank [*Military*]
AMTAS..... Army Modernization Training Automation System
AMTAS..... Automatic Modal Tuning and Analysis System (NASA)
Am Taxp Q ... American Taxpayers' Quarterly [*A publication*]
Am Tax Q .. American Taxpayers' Quarterly [*A publication*] (DLA)
AMTB....... Antimotor Torpedo Boat [*Navy*]
AMTC....... Air Material Armament Test Center [*Air Force*] (MCD)
AMTC....... American Fair Trade Council [*Sausalito, CA*] (EA)
AMTC....... American Manchester Terrier Club (EA)
AMTC....... Amtech Corp. [*NASDAQ symbol*] (NQ)
AMTC....... Apparel Manufacturing Technology Center [*Research
     center*] (RCD)
AMTC....... Army Missile Test Center [*White Sands Missile Range, NM*]
AMTC....... Art Master's Teaching Certificate [*British*]
AMTCL...... Association for Machine Translation and Computational
     Linguistics [*Later, Association for Computational
     Linguistics*] (EA)
Am Tcr...... American Teacher [*A publication*]
AMTD....... Adaptive Mobile Torpedo Decoy [*Navy*] (MCD)
AMTD....... Automatic Magnetic Tape Dissemination [*Defense
     Documentation Center*]
AMTD....... Automatic Magnetic Tape Distribution [*Program*]
AMTDA..... Advances in Metabolic Disorders [*A publication*]
AMTDA..... American Machine Tool Distributors Association (EA)
AMTE ...... Adjusted Megaton Equivalent (MCD)
AMTE ...... Admiralty Marine Technology Establishment [*Research center*]
     [*British*] (IRC)
AMTE ...... Association des Media et de la Technologie en Education au
     Canada [*Association for Media and Technology in
     Education in Canada - AMTEC*]

AMTEA..... American Machine Tool Export Associates (EA)
Am Teach... American Teacher [*A publication*]
AMTeC...... Advanced Manufacturing Technology Centre [*Research center*]
     [*British*] (CB)
AMTEC..... Alkali Metal Thermoelectric Converter [*Power source*]
AMTEC..... Association for Media and Technology in Education in Canada
     [*See also AMTE*]
Am Teleph J ... American Telephone Journal [*A publication*]
AMTE(PL) ... Admiralty Marine Training Establishment (Physiological
     Laboratory) [*Research center*] [*British*]
AMTESS... Army Maintenance Training and Evaluation Simulation
     System (MCD)
AMTESS... Army Training Effectiveness and Simulation System (MCD)
AMTEX.... Air-Mass Transformation Experiment [*National Science
     Foundation/Japan*]
AMTEX.... Australian Machine Tool Exhibition
Am Textil... America's Textiles [*A publication*]
AMTF....... Acoustic Model Test Facility [*NASA*] (NASA)
AMTF....... Air Mobile Task Force
AMTF....... Air Movements Training Flight
AMTF....... American Music Theater Festival
AMTFAQ ... Acta Medica de Tenerife [*A publication*]
Am Them... American Themis [*A publication*] (DLA)
Am Theol Lib Assn Newsl ... American Theological Library Association.
     Newsletter [*A publication*]
Am Thresherman ... American Thresherman [*A publication*]
AMTI .... Airborne Moving Target Indicator (CAAL)
AMTI .... American Trustee, Incorporated [*NASDAQ symbol*] (NQ)
AMTI .... Area Moving Target Indicator [*NASA*] (KSC)
AMTI .... Automatic Moving Target Indicator (MSA)
AMTIC...... Archivio Monaldi per la Tisiologia e le Malattie dell'Apparato
     Respiratorio [*A publication*]
AMTIDE... Aircraft Multipurpose Test Inspection and Diagnostic
     Equipment
AMTIR..... Advanced Moving Target Indicator, RADAR
AMTIS..... Australian Manufacturing Technology Information
     System (ADA)
AMTK ...... Amphibious Tank [*Military*]
AMTL....... Army Materials Technology Laboratory [*Watertown, MA*]
Amtl Ber .... Amtliche Berichte. Koenigliche Kunstsammlungen [*A
     publication*]
Amtl Ztg Deutsch Fleischer-Verbandes ... Amtliche Zeitung. Deutscher
     Fleischer-Verband [*A publication*]
AMTMA ... American Measuring Tool Manufacturers Association
     [*Defunct*] (EA)
Am T-M Cas ... American Trade-Mark Cases (Cox) [*A publication*] (DLA)
AMTODM ... Advances in Modern Toxicology [*A publication*]
AMTOEN ... Alternative Methods in Toxicology [*A publication*]
Am Tom Yb ... American Tomato Yearbook [*A publication*]
AMTP........ ARTEP [*Army Training and Evaluation Program*] Mission
     Training Plan (INF)
AMTPBN ... Annales. Belgische Verenigingen voor Tropische Geneeskunde
     voor Parasitologie en voor Menselijke en Dierlijke
     Mycologie [*A publication*]
AMTPI...... Associate Member of the Town Planning Institute
     [*British*] (EY)
AmTQ....... American Transcendental Quarterly [*A publication*]
AMTR .... Ameritrust Corp. [*NASDAQ symbol*] (NQ)
AMTR .... Ammeter
AMTR ...... Atlantic Missile Test Range (KSC)
AMTRAC... Amphibian [*or Amphibious*] Tractor [*or Truck*]
AMTRACBN ... Amphibian [*or Amphibious*] Tractor [*or Truck*] Battalion
Am Trade Mark Cas ... American Trade-Mark Cases (Cox) [*A
     publication*] (DLA)
AMTRAK ... American Track [*National Railroad Passenger Corp.; formerly,
     Railpax*]
AMTRALEASE ... American Truck Leasing Network, Inc.
AMTRAN ... Automatic Mathematical Translator [*Programming language*]
     [*1970*]
AMTRANS ... Army Missile Transport Systems (KSC)
AmTrans.... [*The*] Complete Bible, An American Translation [*A
     publication*] (BJA)
Am Transcen ... American Transcendental Quarterly [*A publication*]
Am Trav..... American Traveler [*A publication*]
AMTREX ... Amphibious Training Exercise [*Navy*] (NVT)
AMTRI..... Advanced Manufacturing Technology Research Institute
     [*United Kingdom*] [*Research center*] (IRC)
Am Trial Law J ... American Trial Lawyers Journal [*A publication*]
Am Tr M Cas ... Cox's American Trade-Mark Cases [*A publication*] (DLA)
Am Trop Med ... American Journal of Tropical Medicine and Hygiene [*A
     publication*]
Am Trust Rev Pacific ... American Trust Review of the Pacific [*A publication*]
AMTS........ Advanced Meteorological Temperature Sounder (MCD)
AMTS........ Advanced Mobile Telephone System (MCD)
AMTS........ AGE [*Air-Ground Equipment*] Module Test Set (MCD)
AMTS........ American Metals Service, Inc. [*NASDAQ symbol*] (NQ)
AMTS........ Association Mondiale des Travailleurs Scientifiques [*Scientific
     Workers World Association*] (NATG)
Amtsbl Bayer Staatsminist Landesentwickl Umweltfragen ... Amtsblatt.
     Bayerisches Staatsministerium fuer Landesentwicklung und
     Umweltfragen [*A publication*]

Amtsbl Eur Gem ... Amtsblatt. Europaeische Gemeinschaften [*A publication*]
Amts- Mitteilungsbl Bundesanst Materialpruef ... Amts- und Mitteilungsblatt. Bundesanstalt fuer Materialpruefung [*A publication*]
AMTT .... American Telecommunications Corp. [*NASDAQ symbol*] (NQ)
AMTU .... Army Marksmanship Training Unit [*CONARC*] (INF)
AMTU .... Melbourne [*Australia*] [*ICAO location identifier*] (ICLI)
AMTUA3 .. Acta Medica Turcica [*A publication*]
Am Tung News ... American Tung News [*A publication*]
Am Tung Oil Top ... American Tung Oil Topics [*A publication*]
AMTV .... AM Cable TV Industries, Inc. [*NASDAQ symbol*] (NQ)
AMTV .... Australian Medical Television
AMTY .... Amity Bancorp, Inc. [*NASDAQ symbol*] (NQ)
AMU .... African Mathematical Union (EA)
AMU .... Air Mileage Unit [*Navigation*]
AMU .... Air Mission Unit [*Air Force*]
AMU .... Alabama State University, Montgomery, AL [*OCLC symbol*] (OCLC)
AMU .... Alarm Monitor Unit [*Telecommunications*] (TEL)
AMU .... Alaska Methodist University
AMU .... Alternate Master Unit (MCD)
AMU .... Amanab [*Papua New Guinea*] [*Airport symbol*] (OAG)
AMU .... American Malacological Union (EA)
AMU .... American Musicians Union (EA)
AMU .... Anchorage [*Alaska Methodist University*] [*Alaska*] [*Seismograph station code, US Geological Survey*] [*Closed*] (SEIS)
AMu .... Annales Musicologiques [*A publication*]
AMU .... Antenna Matching Unit
AMU .... Aqueous Makeup [*Room*] [*Nuclear energy*] (NRCH)
AMU .... Arab Maghreb Union [*Morocco, Algeria, Mauritania, Tunisia, and Libya*]
AMU .... Army Marksmanship Unit
AMU .... Army Medical Unit
AMU .... Asian Monetary Unit
AMU .... Associated Metalworkers' Union [*British*] (DCTA)
AMU .... Associated Midwestern Universities, Inc.
AMU .... Association of Minicomputer Users (EA)
AMU .... Astronaut Maneuvering Unit [*Gemini*] [*NASA*]
AMU .... Atomic Mass Unit
AMU .... Auburn University at Montgomery, Montgomery, AL [*Library symbol*] [*Library of Congress*] (LCLS)
AMU .... Auxiliary Memory Unit
AMU .... Average Monthly Usage (KSC)
AMUBBK ... American Malacological Union, Incorporated. Bulletin [*Later, American Malacological Bulletin*] [*A publication*]
AMUCOM ... Army Munitions Command [*Later merged with Army Weapons Command*]
AMUDB ..... African and Mauritian Union of Development Banks (EAIO)
AMUE .... Association for the Monetary Union of Europe
AMUFOC ... Association des Etablissements Multiplicateurs de Semences Fourrageres des Communautes Europeennes [*Association of Forage Seed Breeders of the European Community*] [*Brussels, Belgium*]
AMUGAY ... Annales Musei Goulandris [*A publication*]
AMUGS .... Antike Muenzen und Geschnittene Steine [*A publication*]
AMuI .... International Fertilizer Development Center, Muscle Shoals, AL [*Library symbol*] [*Library of Congress*] (LCLS)
Am U Int L Rev ... American University Intramural Law Review [*A publication*] (DLA)
Am U Intra L Rev ... American University Intramural Law Review [*A publication*] (DLA)
AMUKAC ... Acta Medica Universitatis Kagoshimaensis [*A publication*]
Am U L ...... American University Law Review [*A publication*] (DLA)
Am ULR ... American University Law Review [*A publication*]
Am U L Rev ... American University Law Review [*A publication*]
A-MuLV ..... Abelson-Murine Leukemia Virus
AMUN .... Air Munitions
AMUNAL ... American Museum Novitates [*A publication*]
AMUNC .... Army Munitions Command [*Later merged with Army Weapons Command*]
Am Univ Beirut Fac Agric Sci Publ ... American University of Beirut. Faculty of Agricultural Sciences. Publication [*A publication*]
Am Univ Field Staff Rep Asia ... American Universities Field Staff. Reports. Asia [*A publication*]
Am Univ Field Staff Rep North Am ... American Universities Field Staff. Reports. North America [*A publication*]
Am Univ Field Staff Rep South Am ... American Universities Field Staff. Reports. South America [*A publication*]
Am Univ L Rev ... American University Law Review [*A publication*]
AMur .... Archivio Muratoriano [*A publication*]
AMURAX ... Anais. Faculdade de Medicina. Universidade do Recife [*A publication*]
AMURT .... Ananda Marga Universal Relief Team [*India*]
A Mus .... Acta Musicologica [*A publication*]
AMUS .... Alpha Micro Users Society (EA)
AMus .... Asian Music [*A publication*]
AMus .... Associate in Music
AMusAGM ... Associate in Music, Australian Guild of Music and Speech
A MUS LCM ... Associate in Music of the London College of Music (ROG)
A Mus Napocensis ... Acta Musei Napocensis [*A publication*]

A Mus Porol ... Acta Musei Porolissensis [*A publication*]
AMusTCL ... Associate in Music of Trinity College of Music, London [*British*] (DBQ)
AMUTA .... American Music Teacher [*A publication*]
AMUUS ... Association of Marine Underwriters of the United States (EA)
AMUX .... Avionics Multiplex
AMV .... Abbott Mead Vickers [*Commercial firm*] [*British*]
AMV .... Alfalfa Mosaic Virus
AMV .... AMEV Securities, Inc. [*NYSE symbol*] (SPSG)
AMV .... Ammonium Metavanadate [*Inorganic chemistry*]
AMV .... Amstar Venture Corp. [*Vancouver Stock Exchange symbol*]
AMV .... Archiv fuer Mathematische Versicherungswissenschaft [*A publication*]
AMV .... Armored Maintenance Vehicle
AMV .... Association Mondiale Veterinaire [*World Veterinary Association - WVA*] [*Madrid, Spain*] (EAIO)
AMV .... Astable Multivibrator
AMV .... Australian Merchant Vessel [*Shipping*] (ADA)
AMV .... Australian Mineral Ventures
AMV .... Avian Myeloblastosis Virus
AMVA .... Asociacion Mundial de Veterinaria de Avicola [*World Veterinary Poultry Association - WVPA*] [*Huntingdon, Cambridgeshire, England*] (EAIO)
AMVA .... United States Veterans Administration Hospital, Montgomery, AL [*Library symbol*] [*Library of Congress*] (LCLS)
AMvB .... Algemene Maatregel van Bestuur [*Order in Council*] [*Netherlands*] (ILCA)
AMVB .... Association of Music Video Broadcasters (EA)
AMVC .... American Vision Centers, Inc. [*NASDAQ symbol*] (NQ)
AMVEAX ... Acta Medica Veterinaria [*Naples*] [*A publication*]
Am Veg Grower ... American Vegetable Grower [*A publication*]
Am Veg Grower ... American Vegetable Grower [*A publication*]
Am Veg Grow Greenhouse Grow ... American Vegetable Grower and Greenhouse Grower [*A publication*]
AMVER ..... Automated [*formerly, Atlantic*] Merchant Vessel Report [*Coast Guard*]
AMVER ..... Automated Mutual-Assistance Vessel Rescue System (DS)
AMVERS .. Automated [*formerly, Atlantic*] Merchant Vessel Report System [*Coast Guard*]
Am Vet Med Assn J ... American Veterinary Medical Association. Journal [*A publication*]
Am Vet Med Assn Proc ... American Veterinary Medical Association. Proceedings [*A publication*]
Am Vet Med Assoc Sci Proc Annu Meet ... American Veterinary Medical Association. Scientific Proceedings of the Annual Meeting [*A publication*]
Am Vet Rev ... American Veterinary Review [*A publication*]
Am Vets ...... American Law of Veterans [*A publication*] (DLA)
AMVETS .. American Veterans of World War II, Korea, and Vietnam (GPO)
AMVHA .... Asociacion Mundial de Veterinarios Higienistas de los Alimentos [*World Association of Veterinary Food-Hygienists - WAVFH*] [*Berlin, Federal Republic of Germany*] (EAIO)
AMVIAB ... Acta Medica Vietnamica [*A publication*]
AMVIDE ... Acta Microbiologica, Virologica, et Immunologica [*A publication*]
AmVien ...... American Viennola [*Record label*]
AMVM ...... Administrative Motor Vehicle Management
AMVMI .... Association Mondiale des Veterinaires Microbiologistes, Immunologistes, et Specialistes des Maladies Infectieuses [*World Association of Veterinary Microbiologists, Immunologists, and Specialists in Infectious Diseases - WAVMI*] [*Maisons-Alfort, France*] (EAIO)
Am Voc J ... American Vocational Journal [*A publication*]
AmVox .... American Vox [*Record label*]
AMVPA ..... Asociacion Mundial Veterinaria de Pequenos Animales [*World Small Animal Veterinary Association - WSAVA*] [*Hatfield, Hertfordshire, England*] (EAIO)
AMVRA .... Annales de Medecine Veterinaire [*A publication*]
AMVRA4 .. Annales de Medecine Veterinaire [*A publication*]
AMVRT .... Avian Myeloblastosis Virus Reverse Transcription [*Genetics*]
AMVT .... Acute Mesenteric Venous Thrombosis [*Medicine*]
AMVTA .... Annali. Facolta di Medicina Veterinaria di Torino [*A publication*]
AMVX .... American Vaccine Corp. [*NASDAQ symbol*] (NQ)
AMW .... Active Microwave Workshop
AMW .... Actual Measurement Weight [*Railroads*]
AMW .... Air Midwest, Inc. [*Wichita, KS*] [*FAA designator*] (FAAC)
AMW .... Air Ministry Warden [*British military*] (DMA)
AMW .... American Mizrachi Women [*Formerly, MWOA*] (EA)
AMW .... America's Most Wanted [*Television program*]
AMW .... Ames, IA [*Location identifier*] [*FAA*] (FAAL)
AMW .... Amphibious Warfare [*Navy*] (NVT)
AMW .... Amwest Insurance Group, Inc. [*AMEX symbol*] (SPSG)
AMW .... Angular Momentum Wheel (KSC)
AMW .... Antimateriel Warhead
AMW .... Antimissile Warfare
AMW .... Archiv fuer Musikwissenschaft [*A publication*]
AMW .... Association of Married Women (EA)
AMW .... Average Monthly Wage

AMWA...... American Medical Women's Association (EA)
AMWA...... American Medical Writers' Association (EA)
AMWA...... Area Microwave Assembly [*Ground Communications Facility, NASA*]
AMWA...... Association of Metropolitan Water Agencies (EA)
AMWAC ... America/West Africa Conference [*Shipping*]
AMWAR ... Application of the 1973 Middle East War to CAA [*Concepts Analysis Agency*] War Games, Models, and Simulations
Am Water Resour Assoc Symp Proc ... American Water Resources Association. Symposium. Proceedings [*A publication*]
Am Water Works Assn J ... American Water Works Association. Journal [*A publication*]
Am Water Works Assoc J ... American Water Works Association. Journal [*A publication*]
Am Water Works Assoc Jour Southeastern Sec ... American Water Works Association. Journal. Southeastern Section [*A publication*]
AMWBPD ... Alliance of Minority Women for Business and Political Development (EA)
AMWD...... Advanced Millimeter Wave Device
AMWD...... American Woodmark Corp. [*Winchester, VA*] [*NASDAQ symbol*] (NQ)
Am Weld Soc J ... American Welding Society. Journal [*A publication*]
Am Weld Soc Publ ... American Welding Society. Publication [*A publication*]
AMWES..... Associate Member of the Women's Engineering Society [*British*] (DBQ)
Am West .... American West [*A publication*]
AMWG...... Academy of Master Wine Growers (EA)
AMWG...... American Movement for World Government (EA)
AMWH ..... Antimateriel Warhead
Am Whig R ... American Whig Review [*A publication*]
AMWI........ Air Midwest, Incorporated [*NASDAQ symbol*] (NQ)
Am Wine Liquor J ... American Wine and Liquor Journal [*A publication*]
Am Wine Soc J ... American Wine Society. Journal [*A publication*]
AMWL...... Amphibious Warfare Lift Capability [*Navy*] (MCD)
Am Wool Cotton Rep ... American Wool and Cotton Reporter [*A publication*]
AMWR...... Air Ministry War Room [*British*] [*World War II*]
AMWS ...... Advanced Manportable Weapons System (Provisional) [*Army*] (RDA)
AMWS ...... American Men and Women of Science [*R. R. Bowker Co.*] [*Information service or system*] [*A publication*] (IID)
AMWS ...... Associated Metal Workers Society [*A union*] [*British*]
AMWU...... Associated Metal Workers Union [*British*]
AMWY...... Wynyard [*Australia*] [*ICAO location identifier*] (ICLI)
AMX.......... AMAX, Inc. [*Formerly, Alumax, Inc., American Metal Climax, Inc.*] [*NYSE symbol*] [*Toronto Stock Exchange symbol*] (SPSG)
AMX.......... Automatic Message Exchange
AMXCB..... Acta Mexicana de Ciencia y Tecnologia [*A publication*]
AMY.......... Academy Resources Ltd. [*Vancouver Stock Exchange symbol*]
AMY.......... Ambatomainty [*Madagascar*] [*Airport symbol*] (OAG)
AMY.......... Amylase [*An enzyme*]
a-my--- .... Malaysia [*MARC geographic area code*] [*Library of Congress*] (LCCP)
AMY.......... Mynarski Public Library, Alberta [*Library symbol*] [*National Library of Canada*] (NLC)
AMYA .... American Model Yachting Association (EA)
AMYGD..... Amygdalus [*Almond*] [*Pharmacology*] (ROG)
Amyloidosis Proc Sigrid Juselius Found Symp ... Amyloidosis. Proceedings of the Sigrid Juselius Foundation Symposium [*A publication*]
Amyotrophic Lateral Scler Conf ... Amyotrophic Lateral Sclerosis Recent Research Trends. Conference on Research Trends in Amyotrophic Lateral Sclerosis [*A publication*]
AMYR .... Myrnam Public Library, Alberta [*Library symbol*] [*National Library of Canada*] (NLC)
AMZ.......... Allgemeine Musikalische Zeitung [*A publication*]
AMz.......... Allgemeine Musikzeitung [*A publication*]
AMZ.......... Amazing Stories [*A publication*]
AMZ.......... Amazon Petroleum Corp. [*Vancouver Stock Exchange symbol*]
AMZ.......... American List Corp. [*AMEX symbol*] (SPSG)
AMZ.......... Ardmore [*New Zealand*] [*Airport symbol*] (OAG)
AMZ.......... Association Mondiale de Zootechnie [*World Association for Animal Production*]
Am Zinc Inst J ... American Zinc Institute. Journal [*A publication*]
AMZOA..... American Zoologist [*A publication*]
AMZOAF ... American Zoologist [*A publication*]
Am Zool ..... American Zoologist [*A publication*]
Am Zoolog ... American Zoologist [*A publication*]
Am Zoologist ... American Zoologist [*A publication*]
AN.............. Abbott's New Cases [*New York*] [*A publication*] (DLA)
AN.............. Above-Named
AN.............. Abr-Nahrain (BJA)
AN.............. Acanthosis Nigricans [*Medicine*]
AN.............. Accession Number [*Online database field identifier*]
AN.............. Accion Nacional [*National Action*] [*Spain*] [*Political party*] (PPE)
AN.............. Account Number
AN.............. Acid Number [*Chemistry*]
AN.............. Acide Nucleique [*French*] [*Medicine*]
A/N............ Acidic and Neutral [*Chemical analysis*]
AN.............. Acrylonitrile [*Organic chemistry*]
AN.............. Acta Neophilologica [*A publication*]

AN.............. Action Nationale [*National Action for People and Homeland*] [*Switzerland*] [*Political party*] (PPE)
AN.............. Administrative Note
AN.............. Advanced Navigator [*Air Force*]
AN.............. Advertising News [*A publication*] (APTA)
AN.............. Advice Note (ADA)
AN.............. Aerodynamics Note
AN.............. Africa Network [*An association*] (EA)
AN.............. African Notes [*Ibadan*] [*A publication*]
AN.............. Afrique Nouvelle [*A publication*]
AN.............. Age Nouveau [*A publication*]
AN.............. Agencia Nacional [*National Agency*] [*Press agency*] [*Brazil*]
AN.............. Aids to Navigation
A to N......... Aids to Navigation
AN.............. Air Force - Navy
AN.............. Air Navigation
AN.............. Airman [*Nonrated enlisted man*] [*Navy*]
A & N........ Alcock and Napier's Irish King's Bench Reports [*A publication*] (DLA)
AN.............. Alianza Nacional [*National Alliance*] [*Spain*] [*Political party*] (PPE)
AN.............. All Normal [*Hematology*]
A/N............ Allied/Neutral [*Military*]
AN.............. Alphanumeric
AN.............. Ambient Noise [*Composite of sounds present at a given spot in the ocean*] (NVT)
AN.............. Ambulances for Nicaragua (EA)
AN.............. American Newspapers, 1821-1936 [*A bibliographic publication*]
AN.............. Americana Norvegica [*A publication*]
AN.............. Ammonium Nitrate [*Inorganic chemistry*]
AN.............. AMOCO Corp. [*NYSE symbol*] [*Toronto Stock Exchange symbol*] (SPSG)
An.............. Anabasis [*of Xenophon*] [*Classical studies*] (OCD)
an .... Andorra [*MARC country of publication code*] [*Library of Congress*] (LCCP)
An.............. [*Johannes*] Andreae [*Deceased, 1348*] [*Authority cited in pre-1607 legal work*] (DSA)
An.............. Andreas Bonellus de Barulo [*Flourished, 1260-71*] [*Authority cited in pre-1607 legal work*] (DSA)
An.............. Andreas de Capua [*Flourished, 1242-57*] [*Authority cited in pre-1607 legal work*] (DSA)
An.............. Andria [*of Terence*] [*Classical studies*] (OCD)
AN.............. Anemone [*Botany*]
AN.............. Anesthesiology [*Medical specialty*] (DHSM)
AN.............. Aneurysm
An.............. Angelus de Ubaldis [*Deceased, 1407*] [*Authority cited in pre-1607 legal work*] (DSA)
AN.............. Anglo-Norman [*Language, etc.*]
AN.............. Anhydrous
AN.............. Animal
AN.............. Anisometropia [*Ophthalmology*]
an .... Anisoyl [*As substituent on nucleoside*] [*Biochemistry*]
An.............. Annales. Revue Mensuelle de Lettres Francaises [*A publication*]
AN.............. Annex
AN.............. Anno [*or Annus*] [*Year*] [*Latin*]
AN.............. Anode
An.............. Anonymous Reports at End of Benloe [*1661*] [*England*] [*A publication*] (DLA)
AN.............. Anorexia Nervosa [*Medicine*]
an .... Anorthite [*CIPW classification*] [*Geology*]
AN.............. Ansett Airlines of Australia [*ICAO designator*] (FAAC)
AN.............. Answer
AN.............. Answering Flag [*Navy*] [*British*]
an .... Ante [*Before*] [*Latin*]
AN.............. Antenatal [*Medicine*]
AN.............. Anther [*Botany*]
An.............. Anthropos [*A publication*]
AN.............. Antilliaanse Nieuwsbrief [*A publication*]
An.............. Antonianum [*A publication*]
An.............. Antonius de Butrio [*Deceased, 1408*] [*Authority cited in pre-1607 legal work*] (DSA)
AN.............. Antonov [*USSR*] [*ICAO aircraft manufacturer identifier*] (ICAO)
AN.............. Apalachicola Northern Railroad Co. [*AAR code*]
AN.............. Appeals Notes [*A publication*] (DLA)
AN.............. Aquileia Nostra [*A publication*]
AN.............. Archdeacon Nares [*Pseudonym used by Robert Nares*]
AN.............. Arcuate Nucleus [*In the medulla oblongata*]
AN.............. Argentaffin [*Cytology*]
A & N........ Army and Navy
AN.............. Army and Navy
AN.............. Army-Navy Joint Type Ordnance
A/N............ Army/Navy Number
AN.............. Arrival Notice [*Shipping*]
AN.............. Art News [*A publication*]
A/N............ As Needed (NRCH)
AN.............. Ascending Neuron [*Neurology*]
AN.............. Aseptic Necrosis [*Medicine*]
AN.............. Aspergillus niger [*Factor*]
AN.............. Associate in Nursing
AN.............. Astronautics Notice (AAG)

AN............ Astronavigation (NATG)
AN............ Atomic Number
AN............ Autonetics (KSC)
AN............ Die Akkadische Namengebung [A publication] (BJA)
an----- .... East China Sea and Area [MARC geographic area code] [Library of Congress] (LCCP)
AN............ National Agreement [Paraguay] (PD)
AN............ Neerlandia Public Library, Alberta [Library symbol] [National Library of Canada] (NLC)
AN............ Net Laying Ship [Later, ANL] [Navy symbol]
AN............ Netherlands Antilles [ANSI two-letter standard code] (CNC)
AN............ Nicaragua [Aircraft nationality and registration mark] (FAAC)
AN............ Rhone-Poulenc [France] [Research code symbol]
AN1............ Anna [Ohio] [Seismograph station code, US Geological Survey] (SEIS)
AN3............ Anna [Ohio] [Seismograph station code, US Geological Survey] (SEIS)
ANA............ Acoustic Neuroma Association (EA)
A/NA........ Activated/Non-Activated [Cytology]
ANA............ Adaptive Null Antenna
ANA............ Aden News Agency [People's Democratic Republic of Yemen] (MENA)
ANA............ Administration for Native Americans [Office of Human Development Services]
ANA............ Aerojet Network Analyzer
ANA............ Air Force - Navy Aeronautical
ANA............ Air Force - Navy Aeronautical Bulletin (NASA)
ANA............ Air Navigation Act [British]
ANA............ Alabama Agricultural and Mechanical University, Normal, AL [Library symbol] [Library of Congress] (LCLS)
ANA............ Alanine Nitroanilide [Biochemistry]
ANA............ All-Nippon Airways Co. Ltd. [Japan]
ANA............ Alpha-Naphthyl Acetate [Organic chemistry]
ANA............ Amchitka [Alaska] [Seismograph station code, US Geological Survey] [Closed] (SEIS)
ANA............ American Naprapathic Association (EA)
ANA............ American Narcolepsy Association (EA)
ANA............ American National Archives (DIT)
ANA............ American Nature Association
ANA............ American Neurological Association (EA)
ANA............ American Newspaper Association
ANA............ American Normande Association (EA)
ANA............ American Numismatic Association (EA)
ANA............ American Nurses' Association (EA)
ANA............ American Nutritionists Association (EA)
ANA............ Anaheim, CA [Location identifier] [FAA] (FAAL)
ANA............ Analcime [A zeolite]
An A............ Anatomischer Anzeiger [A publication]
ANA............ Anguilla National Alliance (PPW)
ANA............ Antibodies to Nuclear Antigen [Immunology]
ANA............ Antinuclear Antibody [Immunology]
ANA............ Appropriate National Authorities [NATO] (NATG)
ANA............ Arlington Naval Annex (MCD)
ANA............ Army-Navy Aeronautical (KSC)
ANA............ Army-Navy-Air Force (MCD)
ANA............ Article Number Association (EAIO)
ANA............ Assigned Night Answer [Telecommunications] (TEL)
ANA............ Assistant Naval Attache [British]
ANA............ Associate, National Academician
ANA............ Associate of the National Academy of Design
ANA............ Association of National Advertisers (EA)
ANA............ Association of Naval Aviation (EA)
ANA............ Association of Nordic Aeroclubs (EA)
ANA............ Athenagence [News agency] [Greece] (EY)
ANA............ Athens News Agency [Greece]
ANA............ Atlantic Nutritional Association (EA)
ANA............ Australian National Airways
ANA............ Autoantibodies to Nuclear Antigens (MCD)
ANA............ Automatic Network Analyzer
ANA............ Automatic Number Announcer [Telecommunications] (TEL)
ANA............ Nanton Public Library, Alberta [Library symbol] [National Library of Canada] (NLC)
ANA............ Northern Arkansas Regional Library, Harrison, AR [OCLC symbol] (OCLC)
ANAA........ American Nursing Assistants' Association (EA)
Anab............ Anabasis [of Arrian] [Classical studies] (OCD)
AnAB........ Annales. Societe d'Archeologie de Bruxelles [A publication]
ANABA ..... Asociacion Nacional de Bibliotecarios, Arquiveros, y Arqueologos [Madrid] [A publication]
ANAC........ Alaska Native Arts and Crafts Cooperative Association
ANAC........ American Nobel Anniversary Committee (EA)
ANAC........ Anachronism
Anac............ Anacreon [Greek poet, 527-488BC] [Classical studies] (OCD)
AN AC .... Anno ante Christum [In the Year before Christ] (ROG)
ANAC........ Association of Nurses in AIDS [Acquired Immune Deficiency Syndrome] Care (EA)
ANAC........ Associazione Nazionale Autoservizi in Concessione [Bus service operators association] [Italy] (EY)
ANAC........ Australian National Airlines Commission
ANACAD4 ... Analytical Calorimetry [A publication]

An Acad Biol Univ Catol Chile ... Anales. Academia de Biologia. Universidad Catolica de Chile [A publication]
An Acad Bras Cienc ... Anais. Academia Brasileira de Ciencias [A publication]
An Acad Bras Cienc Supl ... Anais. Academia Brasileira de Ciencias. Suplemento [A publication]
An Acad Brasil Ci ... Anais. Academia Brasileira de Ciencias [A publication]
An Acad Brasil Cienc ... Anais. Academia Brasileira de Ciencias [A publication]
An Acad Chil Cienc Nat ... Anales. Academia Chilena de Ciencias Naturales [A publication]
An Acad Cienc Med Fis Nat Habana ... Anales. Academia de Ciencias Medicas, Fisicas, y Naturales de La Habana [A publication]
An Acad Farm (Madrid) ... Anales. Real Academia de Farmacia (Madrid) [A publication]
An Acad Nac Cienc Exactas Fis Nat B Aires ... Anales. Academia Nacional de Ciencias Exactas, Fisicas, y Naturales de Buenos Aires [A publication]
An Acad Nac Cienc Exactas Fis Nat Buenos Aires ... Anales. Academia Nacional de Ciencias Exactas, Fisicas, y Naturales de Buenos Aires [A publication]
An Acad Nac Farm ... Anales. Academia Nacional de Farmacia [A publication]
An Acad Port Hist ... Anais. Academia Portuguesa da Historia [A publication]
An Acad Repub Soc Rom ... Analele. Academiei Republicii Socialiste Romania [A publication]
An Acad Rom ... Analele. Academiei Romane [A publication]
An Ac Brasi ... Anais. Academia Brasileira de Ciencias [A publication]
ANACDUTRA ... Annual Active Duty for Training [Army]
ANACE ..... Army Net Assessment, Central Europe
Anach........ Anacharsis [of Lucian] [Classical studies] (OCD)
ANACH..... Asociacion Nacional de Campesinos Hondurenos [National Association of Honduran Peasants] (PD)
ANACHEM ... Association of Analytical Chemists, Inc. (EA)
A Nachr Bad ... Archaeologische Nachrichten aus Baden [A publication]
ANACITEC ... Asociacion Argentino-Norteamericana para el Avance de la Ciencia, Technologia, y Cultura [Argentine-North American Association for the Advancement of Science, Technology, and Culture] (EA)
ANA Clin Conf ... ANA [American Nurses' Association] Clinical Conferences [A publication]
ANA Clin Sess ... ANA [American Nurses' Association] Clinical Session [A publication]
ANACOM ... Analog Computer
ANACR ..... Anacreon [Greek poet, 572-488BC] [Classical studies] (ROG)
An Ac R...... Analele. Academiei Romane [A publication]
ANACS...... American Numismatic Association Certification Service
ANAD........ Anniston Army Depot [Alabama] (AABC)
An Ad......... Annuaire Administratif et Judiciaire de Belgique [A publication]
ANAD........ Anorexia Nervosa and Associated Disorders [Later, ANAD-National Association of Anorexia Nervosa and Associated Disorders] (EA)
An Adm Nac Bosques Minist Agric Ganad (Repub Argent) ... Anales. Administracion Nacional de Bosques. Ministerio de Agricultura y Ganaderia (Republica Argentina) [A publication]
Anadolu Aras ... Anadolu Arastirmalari [A publication]
ANADP...... Association of North American Directory Publishers (EA)
ANADS ..... Ambient Noise and Data System [Pacific Missile Range] (MCD)
ANAEA ..... Associate of the National Association of Estate Agents [British] (DBQ)
ANAEA3 ... Annals of Allergy [A publication]
ANAEC ..... All Naval Activities Employing Civilians (MCD)
AnAeg........ Analecta Aegyptiaca [Copenhagen] [A publication]
Anaerobic Bact Role Dis Int Conf ... Anaerobic Bacteria. Role in Disease. International Conference on Anaerobic Bacteria [A publication]
ANAES...... Anaesthesia [or Anaesthetic] (ADA)
ANAES...... Anaesthetist (ADA)
ANAESTH ... Anaesthesia [or Anaesthetic] (ADA)
Anaesth...... Anaesthesia [A publication]
Anaesth...... Anaesthesist [A publication]
ANAESTH ... Anaesthetist (ADA)
Anaesth Alter Ber Symp ... Anaesthesie im Alter. Bericht. Symposium. Anaesthesie und Intensivtherapie [A publication]
Anaesthesiol Intensive Care Med ... Anaesthesiology and Intensive Care Medicine [A publication]
Anaesthesiol Intensivmed ... Anaesthesiologie und Intensivmedizin [A publication]
Anaesthesiol Intensivmed Prax ... Anaesthesiologische und Intensivmedizinische Praxis [A publication]
Anaesthesiol Proc World Congr ... Anaesthesiology. Proceedings of the World Congress of Anaesthesiology [A publication]
Anaesthesiol Resusc ... Anaesthesiology and Resuscitation [A publication]
Anaesthesiol Resuscitation ... Anaesthesiology and Resuscitation [A publication]
Anaesthesiol Wiederbeleb ... Anaesthesiologie und Wiederbelebung [A publication]

Anaesthesiol Wiederbelebung ... Anaesthesiologie und Wiederbelebung [*A publication*]
Anaesth Intensive Care ... Anaesthesia and Intensive Care [*A publication*]
Anaesth Intensivther Notfallmed ... Anaesthesie, Intensivtherapie, Notfallmedizin [*A publication*]
Anaesth Pharmacol Spec Sect Prof Hazards ... Anaesthesia and Pharmacology, with a Special Section on Professional Hazards [*A publication*]
Anaesth Resusc Intensive Ther ... Anaesthesia, Resuscitation, and Intensive Therapy [*A publication*]
ANAF .... Army-Navy-Air Force
ANAFA6 ... Annales Agriculturae Fenniae [*A publication*]
ANAFJ ...... Army-Navy-Air Force Journal [*A publication*]
ANAG .... Abstracts of North American Geology [*A publication*]
ANAG .... Anagram   (ADA)
ANAG .... Australian National Action Group
ANAGA ..... Annales Agronomiques [*A publication*]
An Agron ... Anales Agronomicos [*A publication*]
ANAH .... Association Nationale d'Aide aux Handicapes [*National Association of Aids to Handicapped Persons*] [*Canada*]
ANAI .... African Network of Administrative Information [*Information service or system*]   (IID)
AnAI .... Annuaire des Archives Israelites [*A publication*]
ANAI .... Article Numbering Association of Ireland   (EAIO)
ANAIA ...... Annales de la Nutrition et de l'Alimentation [*A publication*]
ANAIDI ..... Annals. National Academy of Medical Sciences [*India*] [*A publication*]
Anais Acad Bras Cienc ... Anais. Academia Brasileira de Ciencias [*A publication*]
Anais Esc Sup Agric "Luiz Queiroz" ... Anais. Escola Superior de Agricultura "Luiz De Queiroz" [*A publication*]
Anais Fac Cienc Porto ... Anais. Faculdade de Ciencias. Universidade do Porto [*A publication*]
Anais II Congr Latin-Amer Zool ... Anais. II Congresso Latino-Americano de Zoologia [*A publication*]
Anais Inst Sup Agron Lisboa ... Anais. Instituto Superior de Agronomia. Universidade Tecnica de Lisboa [*A publication*]
Anais Inst Sup Agron Univ Tec Lisb ... Anais. Instituto Superior de Agronomia. Universidade Tecnica de Lisboa [*A publication*]
Anais Soc Ent Brasil ... Anais. Sociedade Entomologica do Brasil [*A publication*]
ANAL .... Analgesic [*Medicine*]
ANAL .... Analogy
ANAL .... Analysis   (AABC)
Anal .... Analyst [*A publication*]
ANALA ...... Analyst (London) [*A publication*]
Analabs Res Notes ... Analabs, Incorporated. Research Notes [*A publication*]
Anal Abstr ... Analytical Abstracts [*A publication*]
Anal Acad Nac Cienc Exactas Fis Nat ... Anales. Academia Nacional de Ciencias Exactas, Fisicas, y Naturales [*A publication*]
Anal Acad Rom ... Analele. Academiei Romane [*A publication*]
Anal Adv ... Analytical Advances [*A publication*]
Anal Appl Rare Earth Mater NATO Adv Study Inst ... Analysis and Application of Rare Earth Materials. NATO [*North Atlantic Treaty Organization*] Advanced Study Institute [*A publication*]
Anal Aug .... Analecta Augustiniana [*A publication*]
ANALB ...... Analytical Letters [*A publication*]
Anal Ber Gesellschaftswiss ... Analysen und Berichte aus Gesellschaftswissenschaften [*West Germany*] [*A publication*]
An Albg ...... Antonius Albergati [*Deceased, 1634*] [*Authority cited in pre-1607 legal work*]   (DSA)
Anal Biochem ... Analytical Biochemistry [*A publication*]
Anal Biochem Insects ... Analytical Biochemistry of Insects [*A publication*]
Anal Boll ... Analecta Bollandiana [*A publication*]
Anal Bolland ... Analecta Bollandiana [*A publication*]
Anal Calorim ... Analytical Calorimetry [*A publication*]
Anal Calorimetry ... Analytical Calorimetry [*A publication*]
Anal Charact Oils Fats Fat Prod ... Analysis and Characterization of Oils, Fats, and Fat Products [*A publication*]
Anal Chem ... Analytical Chemistry [*A publication*]
Anal Chem Nitrogen Its Compd ... Analytical Chemistry of Nitrogen and Its Compounds [*A publication*]
Anal Chem Nucl Fuels Proc Panel ... Analytical Chemistry of Nuclear Fuels. Proceedings of the Panel [*A publication*]
Anal Chem Phosphorus Compd ... Analytical Chemistry of Phosphorus Compounds [*A publication*]
Anal Chem Sulfur Its Compd ... Analytical Chemistry of Sulfur and Its Compounds [*A publication*]
Anal Chem Symp Ser ... Analytical Chemistry Symposia Series [*A publication*]
Anal Chem Synth Dyes ... Analytical Chemistry of Synthetic Dyes [*A publication*]
Anal Chim Ac ... Analytica Chimica Acta [*A publication*]
Anal Chim Acta ... Analytica Chimica Acta [*A publication*]
Anal Chimica Acta ... Analytica Chimica Acta [*A publication*]
Anal Cist .... Analecta Cisterciensia [*A publication*]

Anal Drugs Metab Gas Chromatogr Mass Spectrom ... Analysis of Drugs and Metabolites by Gas Chromatography. Mass Spectrometry [*A publication*]
Analecta Farm Gerund ... Analecta Farmacia Gerundense [*A publication*]
Analecta Geol ... Analecta Geologica [*A publication*]
Analecta Vet ... Analecta Veterinaria [*A publication*]
Anales Inst Biol UNAM Ser Bot ... Anales. Instituto de Biologia. Universidad Nacional Autonoma de Mexico. Serie Botanica [*A publication*]
Anales Jur ... Anales de Jurisprudencia [*Mexico*] [*A publication*]
Anale Stat Cent Apic Seri ... Anale. Statiunea Centrala de Apicultura si Sericultura [*A publication*]
Anal Financ ... Analyse Financiere [*A publication*]
Anal Fran ... Analecta Franciscana [*A publication*]
Anal Gas Chromatogr Biochem ... Analysis by Gas Chromatography of Biochemicals [*A publication*]
Anal Greg .. Analecta Gregoriana [*A publication*]
Anal Hus Yb ... Analecta Husserliana. Yearbook of Phenomenological Research [*A publication*]
Anali Accad Agric (Torino) ... Annali. Accademia di Agricoltura (Torino) [*A publication*]
AnaliFF ...... Anali Filoloskog Fakulteta Beogradskog Univerziteta [*A publication*]
Anal Inst Cent Cerc Agric Sect Pedol ... Anale. Institutul Central de Cercetari Agricole. Sectiei de Pedologie [*A publication*]
Anal Inst Cerc Agron ... Analele. Institutului de Cercetari Agronomice. Academia Republicii Populare Romine [*A publication*]
Anal Inst Cerc pentru Cereale Pl Tehn-Fundulea ... Analele. Institutului de Cercetari pentru Cereale si Plante Tehnice-Fundulea [*A publication*]
Anal Inst Cerc Prot Plantelor ... Analele. Institutului de Cercetari pentru Protectia Plantelor [*A publication*]
Anal Inst Cerc Zooteh ... Analele. Institutului de Cercetari. Zootehnice [*A publication*]
Anal Instrum ... Analysis Instrumentation [*A publication*]
Anal Intervention Dev Disabil ... Analysis and Intervention in Developmental Disabilities [*A publication*]
Analise Conjuntural Econ Nordestina ... Analise Conjuntural da Economia Nordestina [*A publication*]
ANALIT .... Analysis of Automatic Line Insulation Test [*Bell System*]
ANALIT .... Analysis of Intelligence   (MCD)
Anal Khim Neorg Soedin ... Analiticheskaya Khimiya Neorganicheskikh Soedinenij [*A publication*]
Anal Kontrol Proizvod Azotn Promsti ... Analiticheskii Kontrol Proizvodstva v Azotnoi Promyshlennosti [*A publication*]
Anal Lett .... Analytical Letters [*A publication*]
Anal Letter .... Analytical Letters [*A publication*]
Anal Letters ... Analytical Letters [*A publication*]
Anal Ling ... Analecta Linguistica [*A publication*]
Anal M .... Analectic Magazine [*A publication*]
Anal Math ... Analysis Mathematica [*A publication*]
Anal Methods Appl Air Pollut Meas ... Analytical Methods Applied to Air Pollution Measurements [*A publication*]
Anal Methods Pestic Plant Growth Regul ... Analytical Methods for Pesticides and Plant Growth Regulators [*A publication*]
Anal Methods Pestic Plant Growth Regul Food Addit ... Analytical Methods for Pesticides, Plant Growth Regulators, and Food Additives [*A publication*]
Anal Mon ... Analecta Monastica [*A publication*]
Anal Mont ... Analecta Montserratensia [*A publication*]
Anal Numer Theor Approx ... L'Analyse Numerique et la Theorie de l'Approximation [*A publication*]
Anal O .... Analecta Orientalia [*A publication*]
Anal Or ...... Analecta Orientalia [*A publication*]
Anal Pet Trace Met Symp ... Analysis of Petroleum for Trace Metals. A Symposium [*A publication*]
Anal Praem ... Analecta Praemonstratensia [*A publication*]
Anal Previs ... Analyse et Prevision [*A publication*]
Anal et Previs ... Analyse et Prevision [*A publication*]
Anal Prichin Avarii Povrezhdenii Stroit Konstr ... Analiz Prichin Avarii i Povrezhdenii Stroitel'nykh Konstruktsii [*A publication*]
Anal Proc ... Analytical Proceedings [*A publication*]
Anal Proc R Soc Chem ... Analytical Proceedings. Royal Society of Chemistry [*United Kingdom*] [*A publication*]
Anal Profiles Drug Subst ... Analytical Profiles of Drug Substances [*A publication*]
Anal Progn ... Analysen und Prognosen ueber die Welt von Morgen [*A publication*]
Anal Progn Welt Morgen ... Analysen und Prognosen ueber die Welt von Morgen [*West Germany*] [*A publication*]
Anal Psychol ... Analytische Psychologie [*A publication*]
Anal Pyrolysis ... Analytical Pyrolysis [*A publication*]
Anal Pyrolysis Proc Int Symp ... Analytical Pyrolysis. Proceedings of the International Symposium on Analytical Pyrolysis [*A publication*]
Anal Quant Cytol ... Analytical and Quantitative Cytology [*A publication*]
Anal Quant Cytol Histol ... Analytical and Quantitative Cytology and Histology [*A publication*]
Anal Quant Methods Microsc ... Analytical and Quantitative Methods in Microscopy [*A publication*]

Anal Rev Tech Merlin Gerin ... Analyses. Revue Technique Merlin Gerin [*A publication*]
Anal Rom ... Analecta Romana Instituti Danici [*A publication*]
Anal Sacra Tarraconensia ... Analecta Sacra Tarraconensia. Annuari de la Biblioteca Balmes [*A publication*]
Anal Sci Monogr ... Analytical Sciences Monographs [*A publication*]
Anal Simul Biochem Syst ... Analysis and Simulation of Biochemical Systems [*A publication*]
Anal Soc ..... Analise Social [*A publication*]
Anal Spectrosc Ser ... Analytical Spectroscopy Series [*A publication*]
Anal Stiint Univ Cuza Iasi Chim ... Analele Stiintifice ale Universitatii Al. I. Cuza din Iasi. Sectiunea 1c. Chimie [*A publication*]
Anal Struct Amplitudes Collision Les Houches June Inst ... Analyse Structurale des Amplitudes de Collision Les Houches. June Institute [*A publication*]
Anal Struct Compos Mater ... Analysis of Structural Composite Materials [*A publication*]
Anal Univ Buc Biol Anim ... Analele. Universitatii Bucuresti. Biologie Animala [*A publication*]
Anal Univ Buc Ser Stiint Nat Biol ... Analele. Universitatii Bucuresti. Seria Stiintele Naturii. Biologie [*A publication*]
Anal Univ Bucuresti ... Analele. Universitatii Bucuresti. Stiinte Sociale. Seria Istorie [*A publication*]
Anal Univ C I Parhon ... Analele. Universitatii C. I. Parhon [*A publication*]
ANALY ..... Analyze (MSA)
ANALYS ... Analysis
Analysts J ... Analysts Journal [*A publication*]
Analyt Abs ... Analytical Abstracts [*A publication*]
Analyt Abstr ... Analytical Abstracts [*A publication*]
Analyt Bioc ... Analytical Biochemistry [*A publication*]
Analyt Biochem ... Analytical Biochemistry [*A publication*]
Analyt Chem ... Analytical Chemistry [*A publication*]
Analyt Chim ... Analytica Chimica Acta [*A publication*]
Analytical Chem ... Analytical Chemistry in Memory of Professor Anders Ringbom [*A publication*]
Analyt Lett ... Analytical Letters [*A publication*]
Analyt Proc ... Analytical Proceedings [*A publication*]
Analyt Tables For Trade Sect D ... Analytical Tables of Foreign Trade. Section D [*A publication*]
ANAM .... Association of North American Missions (EA)
An Am Acad Pol Soc Sci ... Annals. American Academy of Political and Social Science [*A publication*]
ANAMD .... Archiwum Nauki o Materialach [*A publication*]
An-Am LR ... Anglo-American Law Review [*A publication*]
ANANA ..... Anatomischer Anzeiger; Zentralblatt fuer die Gesamte Wissenschaftliche Anatomie [*A publication*]
An Anat ...... Anales de Anatomia [*A publication*]
Anani .... [*Johannes de*] Anania [*Deceased, 1457*] [*Authority cited in pre-1607 legal work*] (DSA)
ANA Nurs Res Conf ... American Nurses' Association. Nursing Research Conferences [*A publication*]
ANAPA ..... Annales d'Anatomie Pathologique [*A publication*]
ANAPC4 ... Analytische Psychologie [*A publication*]
ANAPO ..... Alianza Nacional Popular [*National Popular Alliance*] [*Colombia*] (PD)
ANAPROP ... Anomalous Propagation [*Telecommunications*] [*Electronics*] (NVT)
ANA Publ .. American Nurses' Association. Publications [*A publication*]
ANAR .... An-Nahar Arab Report [*A publication*]
AnAr .... Anadolu Arastirmalari [*A publication*]
ANAR .... Approach, Naval Aviation Safety Review [*A publication*]
ANARA ..... Alcoholic and Narcotic Addict Rehabilitation Amendments
ANARC ..... Association of North American Radio Clubs (EA)
Anarch .... Anarchism [*A publication*]
AnArchSyr ... Annales Archeologiques de Syrie [*Damascus*] [*A publication*]
ANARE ..... Australian National Antarctic Research Expeditions [*1947-*]
ANARE (Aust Natl Antarct Res Exped) Res Notes ... ANARE (Australian National Antarctic Research Expeditions) Research Notes [*A publication*]
ANARE Data Rep ... ANARE [*Australian National Antarctic Research Expeditions*] Data Reports [*A publication*] (APTA)
ANARE Data Rep Ser B ... ANARE [*Australian National Antarctic Research Expeditions*] Data Reports. Series B [*A publication*] (APTA)
ANARE Data Rep Ser C ... ANARE [*Australian National Antarctic Research Expeditions*] Data Reports. Series C [*A publication*] (APTA)
ANARE Interim Rep ... ANARE [*Australian National Antarctic Research Expeditions*] Interim Reports [*A publication*] (APTA)
ANARE Interim Rep Ser A ... ANARE [*Australian National Antarctic Research Expeditions*] Interim Reports. Series A [*A publication*]
ANAREN .. ANARE [*Australian National Antarctic Research Expeditions*] News [*A publication*]
ANARE Rep ... ANARE [*Australian National Antarctic Research Expeditions*] Report [*A publication*] (APTA)
ANARE Rep Ser B ... ANARE [*Australian National Antarctic Research Expeditions*] Report. Series B [*A publication*] (APTA)
ANARE Rep Ser C ... ANARE [*Australian National Antarctic Research Expeditions*] Report. Series C [*A publication*] (APTA)

ANARE Sci Rep ... ANARE [*Australian National Antarctic Research Expeditions*] Scientific Reports [*A publication*] (APTA)
ANARE Sci Rep Ser A IV Publ ... ANARE [*Australian National Antarctic Research Expeditions*] Scientific Reports. Series A-IV. Publications [*A publication*] (APTA)
ANARE Sci Rep Ser B IV Med Sci ... ANARE [*Australian National Antarctic Research Expeditions*] Scientific Reports. Series B-IV. Medical Science [*A publication*]
ANARE Sci Rep Ser B I Zool ... ANARE [*Australian National Antarctic Research Expeditions*] Scientific Reports. Series B-I. Zoology [*A publication*]
An Arqueol Etnol ... Anales de Arqueologia y Etnologia [*A publication*]
ANAS .... Auditory Nerve Activating Substance [*Physiology*]
ANASA ...... Anaesthesia [*A publication*]
An Asoc Quim (Argent) ... Anales. Asociacion Quimica (Argentina) [*A publication*]
An Asoc Quim Farm Urug ... Anales. Asociacion de Quimica y Farmacia del Uruguay [*A publication*]
ANASP ...... Advanced Nuclear Attack Submarine Program (MCD)
An As Quim ... Anales. Asociacion Quimica [*Argentina*] [*A publication*]
An As Quim Farm Urug ... Anales. Asociacion de Quimica y Farmacia del Uruguay [*A publication*]
An Assoc Bras Quim ... Anais. Associacao Brasileira de Quimica [*A publication*]
An Assoc Quim Bras ... Anais. Associacao Quimica do Brasil [*A publication*]
Anasthesiol Intensivmed Prax ... Anaesthesiologische und Intensivmedizinische Praxis [*A publication*]
Anasth Intensivther Notfallmed ... Anaesthesie, Intensivtherapie, Notfallmedizin [*A publication*]
ANAT .... American National Insurance Co. [*NASDAQ symbol*] (NQ)
Anat .... Anatomie [*Anatomy*] [*German*]
ANAT .... Anatomy [*or Anatomical*]
ANATA ..... Der Anaesthesist [*A publication*]
ANATAE ..... Anaesthesist [*A publication*]
Anat Anz .... Anatomischer Anzeiger; Zentralblatt fuer die Gesamte Wissenschaftliche Anatomie [*A publication*]
ANATC ..... Air Navigation and Traffic Control
Anat Chir ... Anatomia e Chirurgia [*A publication*]
Anat Embryo ... Anatomy and Embryology [*A publication*]
Anat Embryol ... Anatomy and Embryology [*West Germany*] [*A publication*]
An Ateneo Clin Quir ... Anales. Ateneo de Clinica Quirurgica [*A publication*]
Anat Entw Gesch Monogr ... Anatomische und Entwicklungsgeschichtliche Monographien [*A publication*]
Anat His Em ... Anatomia, Histologia, Embryologia. Zentralblatt fuer Veterinaermedizin, Reihe C[*A publication*]
Anat Histol Embryol ... Anatomia, Histologia, Embryologia [*A publication*]
ANATRAN ... Analog Translator [*Data processing*]
Anat Rec .... Anatomical Record [*A publication*]
Anat Rec Suppl ... Anatomical Record. Supplement [*A publication*]
AnatS .... Anatolian Studies [*A publication*]
Anat Skr .... Anatomiske Skrifter [*A publication*]
AnatSt .... Anatolian Studies [*London*] [*A publication*]
Anat Stud ... Anatolian Studies [*A publication*]
A Natur Wiss ... Archaeologie und Naturwissenschaften [*A publication*]
ANAU .... Nauru Island [*ICAO location identifier*] (ICLI)
ANAUC ..... Anno Ab Urbe Condita [*In the Year from the Building of the City (Rome)*] [*Latin*] (ROG)
ANAV .... Area Navigation
ANAZAW ... Anais Azevedos [*A publication*]
ANAZBX ... Annals of Arid Zone [*A publication*]
An Azevedos ... Anais Azevedos [*A publication*]
ANB .... Aids to Navigation Boat
ANB .... Air Navigation Bureau [*British*] (AIA)
ANB .... Air Nebraska [*Kearny, NE*] [*FAA designator*] (FAAC)
ANB .... Alpha-Naphthyl Butyrate [*Organic chemistry*]
ANB .... Ambient Noise Background
ANB .... Amchitka [*Alaska*] [*Seismograph station code, US Geological Survey*] [*Closed*] (SEIS)
ANB .... Andover Newton Bulletin [*A publication*]
ANB .... Anglo-Bomarc Mines [*Vancouver Stock Exchange symbol*]
AnB .... Animal Behaviour [*A publication*]
AnB .... Annales de Bourgogne [*A publication*]
ANB .... Anniston [*Alabama*] [*Airport symbol*] (OAG)
An B .... Anonymous Reports at End of Benloe [*1661*] [*England*] [*A publication*] (DLA)
ANB .... Antitrust Bulletin [*A publication*]
ANB .... Arab National Bank
ANB .... Army-Navy-British
A & NB .... Army and Navy Munitions Board [*British*] (DAS)
ANB .... Australian National Bibliography [*Information service or system*] [*A publication*]
ANB .... Austrian National Bank (IMH)
Anbar Abs (Account Data) ... Anbar Abstracts (Accounting and Data) [*A publication*]
Anbar Abs (Mktng Distr) ... Anbar Abstracts (Marketing and Distribution) [*A publication*]
Anbar Abs (Personn Trng) ... Anbar Abstracts (Personnel and Training) [*A publication*]
Anbar Abs (Top Mgmt) ... Anbar Abstracts (Top Management) [*A publication*]
Anbar Abs (Wk Study) ... Anbar Abstracts (Work Study) [*A publication*]

Anbar Mgmt Serv ... Anbar Management Services Joint Index [*A publication*]
ANBCA ..... Analytical Biochemistry [*A publication*]
ANBE .... Alpha-Naphthyl Butyrate Esterase [*An enzyme*]
ANBEA ..... Animal Behaviour [*A publication*]
ANBF .... Australian National Boxing Federation
ANBFM ..... Adaptive Narrowband FM [*Frequency Modulation*] MODEM [*Telecommunications*] (TEL)
ANBG .... Australian Botanic Gardens
An Bhand Or Res Inst ... Annals. Bhandarkar Oriental Research Institute [*A publication*]
An Bi .... Analecta Biblica [*A publication*]
ANBI .... Annales Biologiques [*A publication*]
An Bibl ...... Analecta Biblica [*A publication*]
ANBKAQ .. Antibiotiki Respublikanskii Mezhvedomstvennyi Sbornik [*A publication*]
ANBLAT ... Annee Biologique [*A publication*]
ANBMAW ... Animal Behavior Monographs [*A publication*]
ANBN .... Alaska National Bank of the North [*Fairbanks, AK*] [*NASDAQ symbol*] (NQ)
ANBOA ..... Annals of Botany [*A publication*]
AnBol .... Analecta Bollandiana [*A publication*]
AnBoll .... Analecta Bollandiana [*Brussels*] [*A publication*]
An Bot Herb "Barbosa Rodrigues" ... Anais Botanicos. Herbario "Barbosa Rodrigues" [*A publication*]
ANBPA7 .... Anais. Sociedade de Biologia de Pernambuco [*A publication*]
AnBr .... Annales de Bretagne [*Later, Annales de Bretagne et des Pays de l'Ouest*] [*A publication*]
ANBRAD .. Anales de Bromatologia [*A publication*]
An Bras Dermatol ... Anais Brasileiros de Dermatologia [*A publication*]
An Bras Dermatol Sifilogr ... Anais Brasileiros de Dermatologia e Sifilografia [*A publication*]
An Bras Gin ... Anais Brasileiros de Ginecologia [*A publication*]
An Bras Ginecol ... Anais Brasileiros de Ginecologia [*Brazil*] [*A publication*]
AnBret .... Annales de Bretagne [*Later, Annales de Bretagne et des Pays de l'Ouest*] [*A publication*]
An Brom ..... Annales de Bromatologia [*A publication*]
An Bromat ... Anales de Bromatologia [*A publication*]
An Bromatol ... Anales de Bromatologia [*A publication*]
ANBS .... Air Navigation and Bombing School
ANBS .... Armed Nuclear Bombardment Satellite
An de Bu ... Antonius de Butrio [*Deceased, 1408*] [*Authority cited in pre-1607 legal work*] (DSA)
ANC .... Abbott's New Cases [*New York*] [*A publication*] (DLA)
ANC .... Absolute Neutrophil Count [*Hematology*]
ANC .... Academy of the New Church
ANC .... Acid-Neutralizing Capacity [*Chemistry*]
ANC .... Acoustic Noise Canceling [*Headsets*] [*Bose Corp.*]
ANC .... Active Nutation Control
ANC .... Adaptive Noise Cancelling (MCD)
ANC .... Advanced Nozzle Concepts (MCD)
ANC .... African National Congress [*South Africa*] (PD)
ANC .... African National Council [*Later, UANC*] [*Zimbabwe*] [*Political party*] (PPW)
ANC .... Air Force-Navy-Civil Committee on Aircraft Requirements
ANC .... Air Navigation Charge (ADA)
ANC .... Air Navigation Committee [*NATO*] (NATG)
ANC .... Air Navigation Conference [*ICAO*]
ANC .... Airborne Navigation Computer
ANC .... All Numbers Calling [*Telephone*]
ANC .... American National Cowbelles [*Later, ANCW*] (EA)
ANC .... American Nationalities Council (EA)
ANC .... American Negligence Cases [*A publication*] (DLA)
ANC .... Ancestor
ANC .... Anchor Glass Container Corp. [*NYSE symbol*] (SPSG)
ANC .... Anchorage [*Alaska*] [*Airport symbol*] (OAG)
ANC .... Ancient
ANC .... Ancillary (MCD)
AN C .... Anno Christi [*In the Year of Christ*] [*Latin*] (ROG)
ANC .... Antarctic [*Marguerite Bay*] [*Antarctica*] [*Seismograph station code, US Geological Survey*] [*Closed*] (SEIS)
ANC .... Ante Nativitatem Christi [*Before the Birth of Christ*] [*Latin*] (ROG)
ANC .... Antenatal Care
ANC .... Antenatal Clinic
ANC .... Anti-Nuclear Campaign [*British*]
ANC .... Antioch College, Yellow Springs, OH [*OCLC symbol*] (OCLC)
ANC .... Area Naval Commander [*NATO*] (NATG)
ANC .... Arlington National Cemetery
ANC .... Armee Nationale Congolaise [*Congolese National Army*]
ANC .... Armenian National Committee (EA)
ANC .... Army-Navy Anticorrosion Compound
ANC .... Army-Navy-Civil (MSA)
ANC .... Army-Navy-Commerce
ANC .... Army Nurse Corps
ANC .... Asia Research Bulletin [*A publication*]
ANC .... Asian Canadian Resources Ltd. [*Vancouver Stock Exchange symbol*]
ANC .... Assistant Network Controller [*NASA*] (KSC)
ANC .... Association of Neighbourhood Councils [*British*]
ANC .... Association of Noise Consultants [*British*]

ANC .... Association Nucleaire Canadienne [*Canadian Nuclear Association - CNA*]
ANC .... Average Net Cost [*Insurance*]
ANC .... New South Wales Conveyancing Law and Practice [*Australia*] [*A publication*]
ANCA .... Allied Naval Communications Agency [*London, England*] [*NATO*] (AABC)
ANCA .... American National Cattlemen's Association [*Later, NCA*] (EA)
ANCA .... American Nickel Collectors' Association (EA)
Anca .... [*Petrus de*] Ancharano [*Deceased, 1416*] [*Authority cited in pre-1607 legal work*] (DSA)
ANCA .... Armenian National Council of America (EA)
ANCA .... Australian National Council on AIDS
ANCAAA .. Association for Northern and Central Australia Aboriginal Artists
ANCAB ..... Alaska Native Claims Appeals Board (in United States Interior Decisions) [*A publication*] (DLA)
ANCACU .. American National Commission for the Accreditation of Colleges and Universities (EA)
ANCAM ..... Association of Newspaper Classified Advertising Managers (EA)
ANCAP ..... Ammonium Nitrate, Copper, Aluminum, and Plywood [*Proposed currency*]
An Casa Salud Valdecilla ... Anales. Casa de Salud Valdecilla [*A publication*]
An Casa Salud Valdecilla (Santander) ... Anales. Casa de Salud Valdecilla (Santander) [*A publication*]
ANCAT ..... Abatement of Nuisances Caused by Air Transport
An Catedra de Patol Clin Tuberc Univ B Aires ... Anales. Catedra de Patologia y Clinica de la Tuberculosis. Universidad de Buenos Aires [*A publication*]
An Cated Suarez ... Anales. Catedra Francisco Suarez [*A publication*]
ANCB .... American National Cowbelles [*Later, ANCW*] (EA)
ANCC .... Affiliated National Coaches Council (EA)
ANCC .... All Nations Christian College [*British*]
ANC-in-C .. Allied Naval Commander-in-Chief [*World War II*]
AnCC .... Anodal Closure Contraction [*Also, ACC*] [*Physiology*]
ANCC .... Army-Navy Country Club
Anc Charters ... Ancient Charters [*1692*] [*A publication*] (DLA)
ANCCSA ... American North Country Cheviot Sheep Association (EA)
Anc Dial Exch ... Ancient Dialogue upon the Exchequer [*A publication*] (DLA)
ANCE .... Assemblee des Nations Captives d'Europe [*Assembly of Captive European Nations*]
ANCE .... Associazione Nazionale Costruttori Edili [*Builders association*] [*Italy*] (EY)
ANCE .... Attitude Nutation Control Electronics (NASA)
AncEg .... Ancient Egypt [*A publication*]
An Cent Invest Tisiol ... Anales. Centro de Investigaciones Tisiologicas [*A publication*]
AnCEtRel .. Annales. Centre d'Etude des Religions [*Brussels*] [*A publication*]
ANCF .... Account Number Change File [*IRS*]
ANCFIL .... Anchored Filament
ANCG .... Announcing (MSA)
Anch .... [*Petrus de*] Ancharano [*Deceased, 1416*] [*Authority cited in pre-1607 legal work*] (DSA)
ANCH .... Anches [*Reeds*] [*Music*]
ANCH .... Anchorage [*Maps and charts*]
ANCH .... Anchored
ANCH .... Anechoic (MSA)
ANCHA ..... American National Committee to Aid Homeless Armenians (EA)
ANCHA ..... Analytical Chemistry [*A publication*]
Anchar .... [*Petrus de*] Ancharano [*Deceased, 1416*] [*Authority cited in pre-1607 legal work*] (DSA)
ANCHB ..... Annales de Chirurgie [*A publication*]
An Chem .... Analytical Chemistry [*A publication*]
ANCHEP .. American National Council for Health Education of the Public (EA)
An Chilenos Hist Med ... Anales Chilenos de Historia de la Medicina [*A publication*]
An Chopin ... Annales Chopin [*A publication*]
Anchorag DN ... Anchorage Daily News [*United States*] [*A publication*]
Anchor Rev ... Anchor Review [*A publication*]
ANCI .... Associazione Nazionale Calzaturifici Italiani [*Footwear manufacturers association*] [*Italy*] (EY)
ANCIAP ..... Anales de Cirugia [*Rosario*] [*A publication*]
ANCIB .... Army-Navy Communications Intelligence Board [*Later, STANCIB*]
ANCIC .... Australian National Copyright Information Center
ANCICC .... Army-Navy Communications Intelligence Coordinating Committee [*Later, ANCIB*]
An Cienc Natur ... Anales de Ciencias Naturales [*A publication*]
An Cient ..... Anales Cientificos [*A publication*]
An Cient (La Molina) ... Anales Cientificos (La Molina) [*A publication*]
An Cient (Lima) ... Anales Cientificos (Lima) [*A publication*]
Ancient Monuments Soc Trans ... Ancient Monuments Society. Transactions [*A publication*]

An Cient UNA (Univ Nac Agrar) ... Anales Cientificos. UNA (Universidad Nacional Agraria) [*A publication*]
ANCIF....... Automated Nautical Chart Index File [*System*] [*DoD*]
ANCIL....... Ancillary (MCD)
Anc Ind...... Ancient India [*A publication*]
An Circ Med Argent ... Anales. Circa Medico Argentino [*A publication*]
An Cir (Rosario) ... Anales de Cirugia (Rosario) [*A publication*]
AncIsr........ Ancient Israel: Its Life and Institutions [*A publication*] (BJA)
An Cist........ Analecta Cisterciensia [*A publication*]
AnCL......... Anthology of Contemporary Latin-American Poetry [*A publication*]
An Cl......... Antiquite Classique [*A publication*]
ANCLAV... Automatic Navigation Computer for Land and Amphibious Vehicles
ANCLAY... Australian National Clay [*A publication*]
AnClemOchr ... Annuaire. Academie Theologique (S. Clement D'Ochride) [*A publication*] (BJA)
An Clim...... Anales Climatologicos. Servicio Meteorologico Nacional [*Argentina*] [*A publication*]
An Clim Port ... Anuario Climatologico de Portugal [*A publication*]
ANCMA.... Associazione Nazionale Ciclo, Motociclo Accessori [*National Cycle, Motorcycle, and Accessories Association*] [*Italy*] (EY)
ANCN........ An-Con Genetics, Inc. [*NASDAQ symbol*] (NQ)
ANCO........ Alternate Net Control Officer [*Navy*] (NVT)
ANCO........ Annual Customer Order [*Air Force*] (AFIT)
ANCOA..... Aerial Nurse Corps of America
ANCOC..... Advanced Noncommissioned Officer Course [*Army*] (INF)
ANCOES... Advanced Noncommissioned Officer Education System (MCD)
ANCOLD Bull ... ANCOLD [*Australian National Committee on Large Dams*] Bulletin [*A publication*] (APTA)
ANCOM.... Andean Common Market (EAIO)
An Com...... Annales des Sciences Commerciales et Economiques [*A publication*]
An Com Ext Mex Banco Nac Com Ext ... Anuario de Comercio Exterior de Mexico. Banco Nacional de Comercio Exterior [*A publication*]
An Com Invest Cient Prov Buenos Aires ... Anales. Comision de Investigaciones Cientificas. Provincia de Buenos Aires [*A publication*]
An Cong Lat-Am Zool ... Anais. Congresso Latino-Americano de Zoologia [*A publication*]
An Cong Nac Soc Bot Bras ... Anais. Congresso Nacional. Sociedade Botanica do Brasil [*A publication*]
An Congr Nac Med Vet Zootec ... Anales. Congreso Nacional de Medicina Veterinaria y Zootecnia [*A publication*]
ANCOR...... American-Netherlands Club of Rotterdam
ANCOSE.... Associacao Nacional dos Corretores de Seguros [*Insurance representative body*] [*Portugal*] (EY)
ANCOVA.. Analysis of Covariance
ANCOVS.. Active Night Covert Viewing [*or Vision*] System
ANCPA..... Amino-(nitro)cyclopentanecarboxylic Acid [*Organic chemistry*]
ANCPA..... Annales de Chimie (Paris) [*A publication*]
ANCPCJ... Alliance of NGOs [*Nongovernmental Organizations*] on Crime Prevention and Criminal Justice (EA)
ANCPDF... AAZPA [*American Association of Zoological Parks and Aquariums*] National Conference [*A publication*]
ANCPEA... Army-Navy Communications Production Expediting Agency
ANCPT...... Anticipate (FAAC)
ANCR........ Aircraft Not Combat Ready (MCD)
AnCracov... Analecta Cracoviana [*Cracow*] [*A publication*]
ANCS........ Airborne Night Classification System (MCD)
ANCS........ Alternate Net Control Station (CET)
ANCS........ ANCSA News. Alaska Native Claims Settlement Act. Bureau of Land Management [*A publication*]
ANCSA...... African National Congress of South Africa
ANCSA...... Alaska Native Claims Settlement Act [*1971*]
ANCSBM ... Acta Neurochirurgica. Supplementum [*A publication*]
Anc Soc...... Ancient Society [*A publication*]
ANCT........ Ancient
ANCU........ Air Navigation Computer Unit (MCD)
ANCW....... American National Cattle Women (EA)
ANCWA.... American Naturalized Citizen Welfare Association [*Later, US Naturalized Citizen Association*] (EA)
Anc World ... Ancient World [*A publication*]
ANCXF...... Allied Naval Commander Expeditionary Forces
ANCYL...... African National Congress Youth League [*South Africa*] (PD)
AND.......... Active Nutation Damper
AND.......... Admiralty Net Defence [*Antitorpedo nets*] [*British*] [*World War II*]
AND.......... Air Force-Navy Design
ANDL........ Air Navigation Device
AND.......... Air Navigation Directions
AND.......... Airplane Nose Down
And............ All India Reporter, Andhra Series [*A publication*] (DLA)
AND.......... Alphanumeric Display
AND.......... Amchitka [*Alaska*] [*Seismograph station code, US Geological Survey*] [*Closed*] (SEIS)
AND.......... Andalusite [*Mineralogy*]
AND.......... Andaman Islands

AND.......... Andante [*Slow*] [*Music*]
and............ Andere [*Other*] [*German*]
And........... Anderseniana [*A publication*]
AND.......... Anderson [*South Carolina*] [*Airport symbol*] (OAG)
And........... Anderson's Agriculture Cases [*England*] [*A publication*] (DLA)
And........... Anderson's English Common Pleas Reports [*1534-1605*] [*A publication*] (DLA)
AND.......... Andorra [*ANSI three-letter standard code*] (CNC)
AND.......... Andrea Radio Corp. [*AMEX symbol*] (SPSG)
And........... [*Johannes*] Andreae [*Deceased, 1348*] [*Authority cited in pre-1607 legal work*] (DSA)
And........... Andreas Bonellus de Barulo [*Flourished, 1260-71*] [*Authority cited in pre-1607 legal work*] (DSA)
And........... Andrews' English King's Bench Reports [*95 English Reprint*] [*A publication*] (DLA)
And........... Andrews' Reports [*63-73 Connecticut*] [*A publication*] (DLA)
And........... Andromeda [*Constellation*]
AND.......... Androne Resources Ltd. [*Vancouver Stock Exchange symbol*]
AND.......... Army-Navy Design Standards
AND.......... Artists for Nuclear Disarmament (EA)
AND.......... Australian National Dictionary [*A publication*]
AND.......... Australian News Digest [*A publication*] (APTA)
AND.......... Automatic Network Dialing [*Telecommunications*] (TEL)
AND.......... National Jet Service, Inc. [*Indianapolis, IN*] [*FAA designator*] (FAAC)
ANDA........ Abbreviated New Drug Application [*FDA*]
ANDA........ Auxiliary to the National Dental Association (EA)
And Agr Dec ... Anderson's Agricultural Decisions [*Scotland*] [*A publication*] (DLA)
ANDAS..... Automatic Navigation and Data Acquisition System
ANDB........ Air Navigation Development Board [*Functions absorbed by the FAA*]
ANDB........ Andover Bancorp, Inc. [*NASDAQ symbol*] (NQ)
And de Baro ... Andreas Bonellus de Barulo [*Flourished, 1260-71*] [*Authority cited in pre-1607 legal work*] (DSA)
And de Ca .. Andreas de Capua [*Flourished, 1242-57*] [*Authority cited in pre-1607 legal work*] (DSA)
And Ch W ... Anderson on Church Wardens [*A publication*] (DLA)
And Com.... Anderson's History of Commerce [*A publication*] (DLA)
And Cr Law ... Andrews on Criminal Law [*A publication*] (DLA)
And Dig...... Andrews' Digest of the Opinions of the Attorneys-General [*A publication*] (DLA)
ANDE........ Active Nutation Damper Electronics
ANDE........ Alphanumeric Display Equipment
Andean Rpt ... Andean Report [*A publication*]
ANDEC...... Australian National Disease Eradication Campaign
ANDEF..... Action for Nuclear Disarmament Education Fund (EA)
Ander (Eng) ... Anderson's Reports, English Court of Common Pleas [*A publication*] (DLA)
Anders........ Anderson's Reports, English Court of Common Pleas [*A publication*] (DLA)
Anderson.... Anderson's Reports, English Court of Common Pleas [*A publication*] (DLA)
Anderson UCC ... Anderson's Uniform Commercial Code [*A publication*] (DLA)
ANDES...... Asociacion Nacional de Educadores Salvadorenos [*National Association of Salvadoran Teachers*] (PD)
An Desarrollo ... Anales del Desarrollo [*A publication*]
ANDFA..... American Annals of the Deaf [*A publication*]
ANDGAO ... Anales. Museo Nacional David J. Guzman [*A publication*]
Andh.......... All India Reporter, Andhra Series [*A publication*] (DLA)
Andh Pra.... All India Reporter, Andhra Pradesh Series [*A publication*] (DLA)
Andhra Agric J ... Andhra Agricultural Journal [*A publication*]
Andhra Agr J ... Andhra Agricultural Journal [*A publication*]
Andhra Pradesh Ground Water Dep Dist Ser ... Andhra Pradesh Ground Water Department. District Series [*A publication*]
Andhra Pradesh Ground Water Dep Res Ser ... Andhra Pradesh Ground Water Department. Research Series [*A publication*]
Andhra WR ... Andhra Weekly Reporter [*India*] [*A publication*]
Andh WR... Andhra Weekly Reporter [*India*] [*A publication*]
ANDIL...... Associazione Nazionale degli Industriali del Laterizi [*Brick industry association*] [*Italy*] (EY)
ANDIPS.... American National Dictionary for Information Processing Systems [*A publication*]
An Dir Gen Of Quim Nac (Argentina) ... Anales. Direccion General de Oficinas Quimica Nacionales (Argentina) [*A publication*]
An Dir Nac Quim (Argentina) ... Anales. Direccion Nacional de Quimica (Argentina) [*A publication*]
An Dispensario Publico Nac Enferm Apar Dig (Argentina) ... Anales. Dispensario Publico Nacional para Enfermedades del Aparato Digestivo (Argentina) [*A publication*]
ANDL........ Army Nuclear Defense Laboratory (MCD)
ANDLA..... Andrologie [*A publication*]
And Law Dict ... Anderson's Law Dictionary [*A publication*] (DLA)
And L & Cts ... Andrews on United States Laws and Courts [*A publication*] (DLA)
And Man Const ... Andrews' Manual of the United States Constitution [*A publication*] (DLA)
ANDN .... Andersen 2000, Inc. [*NASDAQ symbol*] (NQ)
AndNewQ.. Andover Newton Quarterly [*A publication*]

AndNewtQ ... Andover Newton Quarterly [*Newton, MA*] [*A publication*]

ANDNO .... Andantino [*Slow*] [*Music*]

ANDO .... Andantino [*Slow*] [*Music*]

ANDO .... Andover Controls Corp. [*NASDAQ symbol*] (NQ)

AN DO ...... Anno Domini [*In the Year of Our Lord*] [*Latin*]

Andoc .... Andocides [*Fifth century BC*] [*Classical studies*] (OCD)

And Pr Lea ... Andrews' Precedents of Leases [*A publication*] (DLA)

And Pr Mort ... Andrews' Precedents of Mortgages [*A publication*] (DLA)

ANDPVA .. Association for Native Development in the Performing and Visual Arts [*Canada*]

And Q & A ... Anderson's Examination Questions and Answers [*A publication*] (DLA)

ANDR .... Andersen Group, Inc. [*NASDAQ symbol*] (NQ)

And R .... Andover Review [*A publication*]

Andr .... Andreas Bonellus de Barulo [*Flourished, 1260-71*] [*Authority cited in pre-1607 legal work*] (DSA)

Andr .... Andreas de Isernia [*Deceased circa 1316*] [*Authority cited in pre-1607 legal work*] (DSA)

Andr .... Andrews' English King's Bench Reports [*95 English Reprint*] [*A publication*] (DLA)

Andr .... Andromache [*of Euripides*] [*Classical studies*] (OCD)

Andr .... Andromeda [*Constellation*]

Andr Acza .. Andreas Acconzaioco de Ravello [*Flourished, 1294-1300*] [*Authority cited in pre-1607 legal work*] (DSA)

Andr Alciat ... Andreas Alciatus [*Deceased, 1550*] [*Authority cited in pre-1607 legal work*] (DSA)

Andr Azaio ... Andreas Acconzaioco de Ravello [*Flourished, 1294-1300*] [*Authority cited in pre-1607 legal work*] (DSA)

ANDRB ..... Active Duty Nondisability Retirement Branch [*BUPERS*] [*Navy*]

Andr de Bar ... Andreas Bonellus de Barulo [*Flourished, 1260-71*] [*Authority cited in pre-1607 legal work*] (DSA)

Andr de Ca ... Andreas de Capua [*Flourished, 1242-57*] [*Authority cited in pre-1607 legal work*] (DSA)

Andr de Cap ... Andreas de Capua [*Flourished, 1242-57*] [*Authority cited in pre-1607 legal work*] (DSA)

Andre .... Andreas Bonellus de Barulo [*Flourished, 1260-71*] [*Authority cited in pre-1607 legal work*] (DSA)

Andre .... Andreas de Isernia [*Deceased circa 1316*] [*Authority cited in pre-1607 legal work*] (DSA)

ANDREE ... Association for Nuclear Development and Research in Electrical Engineering (MCD)

And Rev Law ... Andrews on the Revenue Law [*A publication*] (DLA)

Andrews (Eng) ... Andrews' English King's Bench Reports [*95 English Reprint*] [*A publication*] (DLA)

Andr Fachin ... Andreas Fachineus [*Deceased, 1622*] [*Authority cited in pre-1607 legal work*] (DSA)

Andr de Isern ... Andreas de Isernia [*Deceased circa 1316*] [*Authority cited in pre-1607 legal work*] (DSA)

Androgens Antiandrogens Pap Int Symp ... Androgens and Antiandrogens. Papers Presented at the International Symposium on Androgens and Antiandrogens [*A publication*]

Androgens Norm Pathol Cond Proc Symp Steroid Horm ... Androgens in Normal and Pathological Conditions. Proceedings. Symposium on Steroid Hormones [*A publication*]

Andr Pomat ... Andreas Pomates [*Authority cited in pre-1607 legal work*] (DSA)

Andr de Ra ... Andreas Acconzaioco de Ravello [*Flourished, 1294-1300*] [*Authority cited in pre-1607 legal work*] (DSA)

Andr Tiraq ... Andreas Tiraquellus [*Deceased, 1558*] [*Authority cited in pre-1607 legal work*] (DSA)

AndrUnSS ... Andrews University. Seminary Studies [*A publication*]

ANDS .... Advanced Navy Display System

ANDS .... Anderson Industries, Inc. [*NASDAQ symbol*] (NQ)

An D S P ... Annales de Droit et de Sciences Politiques [*A publication*]

And & Ston JA ... Andrews and Stoney's Supreme Court of Judicature Acts [*A publication*] (DLA)

ANDTE ..... Andante [*Slow*] [*Music*]

AnDTe .... Anodal Duration Tetanus [*Physiology*]

And Tiraq .. Andreas Tiraquellus [*Deceased, 1558*] [*Authority cited in pre-1607 legal work*] (DSA)

ANDTS ...... Associate of the Non-Destructive Testing Society [*British*]

An Dubrovnik ... Anali Historijskog Instituta u Dubrovniku [*A publication*]

ANDUS ...... Anglo-Dutch United States

ANDVT ...... Advanced Narrowband Digital Voice Terminal (MCD)

ANDW .... Andrew Corp. [*NASDAQ symbol*] (NQ)

And WR ..... Andhra Weekly Reporter [*India*] [*A publication*]

ANDY .... Andros, Inc. [*NASDAQ symbol*] (NQ)

ANDZ .... Anodize (MSA)

ANE .... Acoustic Noise Environment

ANE .... Aeronautical and Navigational Electronics (MCD)

ANE .... Aerospace and Navigational Electronics (MCD)

ANE .... Air National [*Monterey, CA*] [*FAA designator*] (FAAC)

ANE .... Alliance New Europe Fund [*NYSE symbol*] (SPSG)

ANE .... Alto Exploration [*Vancouver Stock Exchange symbol*]

ANE .... Americans for Nuclear Energy (EA)

ANE .... Ancient Near East (BJA)

AnE .... Annales de l'Est et du Nord [*A publication*]

ANE .... Annales du Notariat et de l'Enregistrement [*A publication*]

AnE .... Expression of Anger [*Psychology*]

ANE .... Minneapolis, MN [*Location identifier*] [*FAA*] (FAAL)

ANE .... New England Region [*FAA*] (FAAC)

ANE .... Newbrook Public Library, Alberta [*Library symbol*] [*National Library of Canada*] (NLC)

ANEA .... Associate of New Era Academy of Dance [*British*]

ANEC .... Air Navigation and Engineering Co. [*Australia*]

ANEC .... American Nuclear Energy Council (EA)

AnEC .... Ancient English Christmas Carols [*A publication*]

ANEC .... Association Nordique des Etudes Canadiennes [*Nordic Association for Canadian Studies*]

ANECInst ... Associate of the Northeast Coast Institution of Engineers and Shipbuilders [*British*]

ANED .... Associazione Nazionale Ex-Deportati Politici nei Campi Nazisti [*National Association of Political Ex-Deportees of the Nazi Camps*] [*Italy*] [*Political party*] (EAIO)

An Edafol Agrobiol ... Anales de Edafologia y Agrobiologia [*A publication*]

An Edafol Fisiol Veg ... Anales de Edafologia y Fisiologia Vegetal [*A publication*]

ANEEG ..... Army, Navy Electronics Evaluation Group

ANEF .... American-Nepal Education Foundation (EA)

AnEgB .... Annual Egyptological Bibliography [*Leiden*] [*A publication*]

Anekd .... Anekdote [*Anecdote*] [*German*]

ANEMD .... Anatomy and Embryology [*A publication*]

ANEMDG ... Anatomy and Embryology [*A publication*]

ANEN .... African NGOs [*Nongovernmental Organizations*] Environment Network (EAIO)

ANEN .... Anaren Microwave, Inc. [*NASDAQ symbol*] (NQ)

AnEN .... Annales de l'Est et du Nord [*A publication*]

ANENAG ... Annales d'Endocrinologie [*A publication*]

ANENDJ ... Annals of Nuclear Energy [*A publication*]

AnEnPo ..... Anthology for the Enjoyment of Poetry [*A publication*]

ANEP .... [*The*] Ancient Near East in Pictures [*A publication*] (BJA)

ANEPA ...... Army-Navy Electronics Production Agency

ANEPLA ... Associazione Nazionale Estrattori Produttori Lapidei Affini [*Polished stone slab manufacturers association*] [*Italy*] (EY)

ANER .... Aneroid (MSA)

ANERA ..... American Near East Refugee Aid (EA)

ANERAC ... Annual Northeast Regional Antipollution Conference

ANES .... Anesthesiology (AABC)

ANESA ...... Anesthesiology [*A publication*]

An Esc Farm Fac Cienc Med Univ Nac Mayor San Marcos ... Anales. Escuela de Farmacia. Facultad de Ciencias Medicas. Universidad Nacional Mayor de San Marcos [*A publication*]

An Esc Nac Cienc Biol (Mex) ... Anales. Escuela Nacional de Ciencias Biologicas (Mexico) [*A publication*]

An Esc Nac Saude Publica Med Trop ... Anais. Escola Nacional de Saude Publica e de Medicina Tropical [*A publication*]

An Esc Quim Farm Bioquim Univ Concepcion ... Anales. Escuela de Quimica y Farmacia y Bioquimica. Universidad de Concepcion [*A publication*]

An Esc Super Agric "Luiz De Queiroz" Univ Sao Paulo ... Anais. Escola Superior de Agricultura "Luiz De Queiroz." Universidade de Sao Paulo [*A publication*]

An Esc Super Agr "Luiz De Queiroz" ... Anais. Escola Superior de Agricultura "Luiz De Queiroz" [*A publication*]

An Esc Super Med Vet (Lisb) ... Anais. Escola Superior de Medicina Veterinaria (Lisbon) [*A publication*]

An Escuela Nac Cienc Biol ... Anales. Escuela Nacional de Ciencias Biologicas [*A publication*]

ANESG ...... Atomic/Nuclear Energy Study Group (EA)

An Esp Odontoestomatol ... Anales Espanoles de Odontoestomatologia [*A publication*]

An Esp Pediatr ... Anales Espanoles de Pediatria [*A publication*]

An Estac Exp Aula Dei ... Anales. Estacion Experimental de Aula Dei [*A publication*]

An Estac Exp Aula Dei Cons Super Invest Cient ... Anales. Estacion Experimental de Aula Dei. Consejo Superior de Investigaciones Cientificas [*A publication*]

An Estac Exp Aula Dei (Zaragoza) ... Anales. Estacion Experimental de Aula Dei (Zaragoza) [*A publication*]

Anesteziol Reanimatol ... Anesteziologiya i Reanimatologiya [*A publication*]

ANESTH ... Anesthesia [*or Anesthetic*] [*Medicine*]

Anesth Abstr ... Anesthesia Abstracts [*A publication*]

Anesth Anal ... Anesthesia and Analgesia [*Cleveland*] [*A publication*]

Anesth Analg ... Current Researches in Anesthesia and Analgesia [*A publication*]

Anesth Analg (Cleve) ... Anesthesia and Analgesia (Cleveland) [*A publication*]

Anesth Analg (Paris) ... Anesthesie, Analgesie, Reanimation (Paris) [*A publication*]

Anesth Analg Reanim ... Anesthesie, Analgesie, Reanimation [*Paris*] [*A publication*]

Anesth An R ... Anesthesie, Analgesie, Reanimation [*Paris*] [*A publication*]

Anesthesiol ... Anesthesiology [*A publication*]

Anesthesiol Clin ... International Anesthesiology Clinics [*A publication*]

Anesthesiol Reanim ... Anesthesiologie et Reanimation [*A publication*]

Anesth Intensive Care ... Anaesthesia and Intensive Care [*A publication*]

ANESTHLGY ... Anesthesiology

Anesth Prog ... Anesthesia Progress [*A publication*]

Anesth Prog Dent ... Anesthesia Progress in Dentistry [*A publication*]

Anest Reanim ... Anestezja i Reanimacja [*A publication*]

Anest Reanim Intensywna Ter ... Anestezja i Reanimacja. Intensywna Terapia [*A publication*]
ANET .... Ancient Near Eastern Texts Relating to the Old Testament [*A publication*] (BJA)
ANET .... Association of Nurses Endorsing Transplantation (EA)
ANETH ..... Anethum [*Dill Seed*] [*Pharmacology*] (ROG)
AnEth .... Annales d'Ethiopie [*Paris/Addis-Ababa*] [*A publication*]
A News .... Archaeological News [*A publication*]
ANEX .... Analyst-to-Analyst Exchange Message Format (MCD)
ANEXA ...... Acta Neurobiologiae Experimentalis [*A publication*]
ANEXAC .... Acta Neurobiologiae Experimentalis [*Warsaw*] [*A publication*]
ANEXBD ... Acta Neurobiologiae Experimentalis. Supplementum [*A publication*]
ANEXGOVT ... At No Expense to the Government
ANF .... Account Number File [*Integrated Data Retrieval System*] [*IRS*]
ANF .... Actinide Nitride-Fueled Reactor (NRCH)
ANF .... Agriculture, Nutrition, and Forestry (DLA)
ANF .... Air Navigation Facility
ANF .... Allied Naval Forces [*NATO*]
ANF .... Alpha-Naphthoflavone [*Biochemistry*]
ANF .... American Nurses' Foundation (EA)
ANF .... Anchored Filament
Anf .... Anfang [*Beginning*] [*German*]
AnF .... Angel Flight (EA)
ANF .... Angeles Finance Trust Class A [*AMEX symbol*] (SPSG)
ANF .... Antinuclear Factor [*Immunology*]
ANF .... Antofagasta [*Chile*] [*Airport symbol*] (OAG)
ANF .... Arkiv foer Nordisk Filologi [*A publication*]
ANEth ...... Army News Features
ANF .... Arrived Notification Form [*British*] (DCTA)
ANF .... Associazione la Nostra Famiglia [*Ponte Lambro, Italy*] (EAIO)
ANF .... Atlantic Nuclear Force [*NATO*]
ANF .... Atrial Natriuretic Factor [*Biochemistry*]
ANF .... Automatic Number Identification Failure [*Telecommunications*] (TEL)
ANF .... Aviation News Features
ANFA .... Australian National Flag Association
An Fac Cienc Fis Mat Univ Concepcion ... Anales. Facultad de Ciencias Fisicas y Matematicas. Universidad de Concepcion [*A publication*]
An Fac Cienc Univ Porto ... Anais. Faculdade de Ciencias. Universidade do Porto [*A publication*]
An Fac Ci Univ Porto ... Anais. Faculdade de Ciencias. Universidade do Porto [*A publication*]
An Fac Farm Bioquim Univ Nac Mayor San Marcos ... Anales. Facultad de Farmacia y Bioquimica. Universidad Nacional Mayor de San Marcos [*A publication*]
An Fac Farm Bioquim Univ Nac Mayor San Marcos Lima ... Anales. Facultad de Farmacia y Bioquimica. Universidad Nacional Mayor de San Marcos de Lima [*A publication*]
An Fac Farm Odontol Univ Sao Paulo ... Anais. Faculdade de Farmacia e Odontologia. Universidade de Sao Paulo [*A publication*]
An Fac Farm Porto ... Anais. Faculdade de Farmacia do Porto [*A publication*]
An Fac Ing Univ Concepcion ... Anales. Facultad de Ingenieria. Universidad de Concepcion [*A publication*]
An Fac Med Lima ... Anales. Facultad de Medicina. Universidad Nacional Mayor de San Marcos de Lima [*A publication*]
An Fac Med (Montevideo) ... Anales. Facultad de Medicina. Universidad de la Republica (Montevideo) [*A publication*]
An Fac Med Porto Alegre ... Anais. Faculdade de Medicina de Porto Alegre [*A publication*]
An Fac Med Univ Fed Minas Gerais (Belo Horizonte) ... Anais. Faculdade de Medicina. Universidade Federal de Minas Gerais (Belo Horizonte) [*A publication*]
An Fac Med Univ Fed Pernambuco ... Anais. Faculdade de Medicina. Universidade Federal de Pernambuco [*A publication*]
An Fac Med Univ Nac Mayor San Marcos Lima ... Anales. Facultad de Medicina. Universidad Nacional de San Marcos de Lima [*A publication*]
An Fac Med Univ Nac Mayor San Marcos Lima (Peru) ... Anales. Facultad de Medicina. Universidad Nacional Mayor de San Marcos de Lima (Peru) [*A publication*]
An Fac Med Univ Parana (Curitiba) ... Anais. Faculdade de Medicina. Universidade do Parana (Curitiba) [*A publication*]
An Fac Med Univ Recife ... Anais. Faculdade de Medicina. Universidade do Recife [*A publication*]
An Fac Med Univ Repub (Montev) ... Anales. Facultad de Medicina. Universidad de la Republica (Montevideo) [*A publication*]
An Fac Med Univ Sao Paulo ... Anais. Faculdade de Medicina. Universidade de Sao Paulo [*A publication*]
An Fac Odontol Univ Fed Rio De J ... Anais. Faculdade de Odontologia. Universidade Federal do Rio De Janeiro [*A publication*]
An Fac Odontol Univ Repub Urug ... Anales. Facultad de Odontologia. Universidad de la Republica [*Uruguay*] [*A publication*]
An Fac Quim Farm (Santiago) ... Anales. Facultad de Quimica y Farmacia. Universidad de Chile (Santiago) [*A publication*]
An Fac Quim Farm Univ Chile ... Anales. Facultad de Quimica y Farmacia. Universidad de Chile [*Santiago*] [*A publication*]
An Fac Quim Farm Univ Concepcion ... Anales. Facultad de Quimica y Farmacia. Universidad de Concepcion [*A publication*]

An Fac Quim Univ Repub Orient Urug ... Anales. Facultad de Quimica. Universidad de la Republica Oriental del Uruguay [*A publication*]
An Fac Vet Leon ... Anales. Facultad de Veterinaria de Leon [*A publication*]
An Fac Vet Univ Madrid Inst Invest Vet ... Anales. Facultad de Veterinaria. Universidad de Madrid. Instituto de Investigaciones Veterinarias [*A publication*]
An Fac Vet Urug ... Anales. Facultad de Veterinaria del Uruguay [*A publication*]
An Farm Bioquim (Buenos Aires) ... Anales de Farmacia y Bioquimica (Buenos Aires) [*A publication*]
An Farm Hosp ... Anales de Farmacia Hospitalaria [*A publication*]
An Farm Quim Sao Paulo ... Anais da Farmacia e Quimica de Sao Paulo [*A publication*]
ANFC .... Australian National Football Council
AN/FCC .... Army Navy/Fixed Communications Cabinet (MCD)
ANFCE ...... Allied Naval Forces Central Europe [*NATO*]
ANFE .... Aircraft Nonflying-Electronics (CINC)
ANFE .... Aircraft Not Fully Equipped
AnFE .... Anthology for Famous English and American Poetry [*A publication*]
ANFEBT ... Annali. Universita di Ferrara. Sezione I. Ecologia [*A publication*]
ANFES ..... Australian Nursing Federation Employee's Section
ANFI .... Automatic Noise Figure Indicator (MCD)
ANFIA .... Associazione Nazionale fra Industrie Automobilistiche [*Motor vehicle industries association*] [*Italy*] (EY)
ANFICM ... Atlantic Fleet Naval Forces Intelligence Collection Manual
ANFIDA .... Associazione Nazionale fra gli Industriali degli Acquedotti [*Waterworks constructors association*] [*Italy*] (EY)
ANFIMA ... Associazione Nazionale fra i Fabbricanti di Imballaggi Metallici ed Affini [*Manufacturers of metal containers and allied articles association*] [*Italy*] (EY)
An Fis .... Anales de Fisica [*A publication*]
An Fisica .... Anales de Fisica [*A publication*]
An Fis Quim ... Anales de Fisica y Quimica [*A publication*]
An Fis Ser A ... Anales de Fisica. Serie A [*A publication*]
An Fis Ser B ... Anales de Fisica. Serie B [*A publication*]
ANFLOW ... Anaerobic Upflow Fixed-Film Process [*For treating wastewater*]
ANFM .... August, November, February, and May [*Denotes quarterly payments of interest or dividends in these months*] [*Business term*]
ANFO .... Ammonium Nitrate and Fuel Oil [*Explosive*]
AnFP .... Analecta Sacri Ordinis Fratrum Praedicatorum [*A publication*]
AnFP .... Anthology of French Poetry [*A publication*]
ANFRIDI .. Annuaire Francais de Droit International [*A publication*]
ANFS .... Airport Network Flow Simulator (MCD)
AN/FSC .... Army Navy/Fixed Satellite Communication (MCD)
ANFTES ... Archives Nationales du Film, de la Television, et de l'Enregistrement Sonore [*National Film, Television, and Sound Archives*] [*NFTSA*] [*Canada*]
ANG .... Acoustic Noise Generator
ANG .... Acta Nuntiaturae Gallicae [*A publication*]
ANG .... Air National Guard
ANG .... Alarm Network Group
ANG .... Alberta Natural Gas Co. Ltd. [*Toronto Stock Exchange symbol*] [*Vancouver Stock Exchange symbol*]
ANG .... Alliance for Neighborhood Government [*Later, NAN*] (EA)
ANG .... American Needlepoint Guild (EA)
ANG .... American Newspaper Guild [*Later, TNG*] (EA)
ANG .... American Nominalist Group (EA)
ANG .... Angeles Corp. [*AMEX symbol*] (SPSG)
Ang .... Angelicum [*Rome*] [*A publication*]
Ang .... Angell and Durfee's Reports [*1 Rhode Island*] [*A publication*] (DLA)
Ang .... Angell's Rhode Island Reports [*A publication*] (DLA)
Ang .... Angelus de Gambilionibus de Aretio [*Flourished, 1422-51*] [*Authority cited in pre-1607 legal work*] (DSA)
Ang .... Angelus de Ubaldis [*Deceased, 1407*] [*Authority cited in pre-1607 legal work*] (DSA)
Ang .... Angestellte [*Employee*] [*German*]
ANG .... Angiogram [*Cardiology*]
ANG .... Angiotensin [*Biochemistry*]
ANG .... Angle (MSA)
ANG .... Anglesey [*Welsh island and county*]
Ang .... Anglia [*A publication*]
ANG .... Anglican
ang .... Anglo-Saxon [*MARC language code*] [*Library of Congress*] (LCCP)
ANG .... Angola
ANG .... Antigua [*Antigua*] [*Seismograph station code, US Geological Survey*] (SEIS)
ANG .... Applied Naturalist Guild [*Defunct*]
ANG .... Army National Guard
ANG .... Association of National Grasslands (EA)
ANG .... Australian National Gallery [*Information service or system*] (IID)
ANg .... Die Akkadische Namengebung [*A publication*] (BJA)
Ang & A Corp ... Angell and Ames on Corporations [*A publication*] (DLA)
Ang Adv Enj ... Angell on Adverse Enjoyment [*A publication*] (DLA)
ANGAM .... Australian National Guide to Archival Material

Ang Are...... Angelus de Gambilionibus de Aretio [*Flourished, 1422-51*] [*Authority cited in pre-1607 legal work*] (DSA)

Ang Ass...... Angell on Assignment [*A publication*] (DLA)

ANGAU..... Australia-New Guinea Administrative Unit [*World War II*]

ANGB........ Air National Guard Base

Ang Bbl ...... Anglia Beiblatt [*A publication*]

ANGBF........ Anglo-Bomarc Mines [*NASDAQ symbol*] (NQ)

Ang Bot ...... Angewandte Botanik [*A publication*]

Ang BT ...... Angell on Bank Tax [*A publication*] (DLA)

Ang Car...... Angell on Carriers [*A publication*] (DLA)

Ang Corp.... Angell and Ames on Corporations [*A publication*] (DLA)

Ang & D High ... Angell and Durfee on Highways [*A publication*] (DLA)

Ang & Dur ... Angell and Durfee's Reports [*1 Rhode Island*] [*A publication*] (DLA)

Ange.......... Angelus de Gambilionibus de Aretio [*Flourished, 1422-51*] [*Authority cited in pre-1607 legal work*] (DSA)

Ange........... Angelus de Ubaldis [*Deceased, 1407*] [*Authority cited in pre-1607 legal work*] (DSA)

ANGE........ Los Angeles Times [*A publication*]

Ange Aret... Angelus de Gambilionibus de Aretio [*Flourished, 1422-51*] [*Authority cited in pre-1607 legal work*] (DSA)

ANGED..... Annales Geophysicae [*A publication*]

Angel......... Angelus de Gambilionibus de Aretio [*Flourished, 1422-51*] [*Authority cited in pre-1607 legal work*] (DSA)

Angel de Clavas ... Angelus Carletus de Clavasio [*Deceased, 1492*] [*Authority cited in pre-1607 legal work*] (DSA)

Angelegenh ... Angelegenheit [*Affair*] [*German*]

ANGELL... Associated Nursery Guides Emphatically Lacking in Leisure

An Geog ..... Annales de Geographie [*A publication*]

Angest........ Angestellter [*Clerk, Employee*] [*German*]

Angew Bot ... Angewandte Botanik [*A publication*]

Angew Chem ... Angewandte Chemie [*A publication*]

Angew Chem Beil ... Angewandte Chemie. Beilage [*A publication*]

Angew Chem Int Ed Engl ... Angewandte Chemie. International Edition in English [*A publication*]

Angew Chem Int Ed Engl Suppl ... Angewandte Chemie. International Edition in English. Supplement [*A publication*]

Angew Chem Intern Ed ... Angewandte Chemie. International Edition in English [*A publication*]

Angew Elektron ... Angewandte Elektronik [*A publication*]

Angew Elektron Mess & Regeltech ... Angewandte Elektronik. Mess und Regeltechnik [*A publication*]

Angew Inf... Angewandte Informatik/Applied Informatics [*A publication*]

Angew Inf Appl Inf ... Angewandte Informatik/Applied Informatics [*A publication*]

Angew Infor ... Angewandte Informatik/Applied Informatics [*A publication*]

Angew Kosmet ... Angewandte Kosmetik [*A publication*]

Angew Makro ... Angewandte Makromolekulare Chemie [*A publication*]

Angew Makromol Chem ... Angewandte Makromolekulare Chemie [*A publication*]

Angew Met ... Angewandte Meteorologie [*A publication*]

Angew Meteorol ... Angewandte Meteorologie [*A publication*]

Angew Ornithol ... Angewandte Ornithologie [*A publication*]

Angew Parasit ... Angewandte Parasitologie [*A publication*]

Angew Parasitol ... Angewandte Parasitologie [*A publication*]

Angew Pflanzensoziol ... Angewandte Pflanzensoziologie [*A publication*]

Angew Statist Okonometrie ... Angewandte Statistik und Okonometrie [*A publication*]

Angew Systemanal ... Angewandte Systemanalyse [*West Germany*] [*A publication*]

Angew Systemanal ... Angewandte Systemanalyse. Theorie und Praxis [*A publication*]

Ang High ... Angell and Durfee on Highways [*A publication*] (DLA)

Ang Highw ... Angell and Durfee on Highways [*A publication*] (DLA)

ANGIA ... Angiology [*A publication*]

Angim .... Epic Angim Dimma (BJA)

Ang Ins ...... Angell on Insurance [*A publication*] (DLA)

angio........ Angiogram [*Cardiology*]

Angiol .... Angiologia [*A publication*]

Angiol Symp ... Angiologisches Symposion [*A publication*]

Angiol Symp (Kitzbuehel) ... Angiologisches Symposion (Kitzbuehel) [*A publication*]

ANGL........ Anglican

ANGL........ Anglice [*In English*] [*Latin*]

Angl .... Anglistik [*Study of English language and literature*] [*German*]

ANGL........ Anglo American Corp. of South Africa Ltd. [*NASDAQ symbol*] (NQ)

ANGL........ Annals of Glaciology [*A publication*]

ANGLA ..... Angiologica [*A publication*]

AnglB........ Anglia Beiblatt [*A publication*]

Angl Bei ..... Anglia Beiblatt [*A publication*]

Angle Orthod ... Angle Orthodontist [*A publication*]

Angl F .... Anglistische Forschungen [*A publication*]

Anglican R ... Anglican Review [*A publication*] (APTA)

ANGLICO ... Air and Naval Gunfire Liaison Company [*Military*]

Ang Lim ...... Angell on Limitation of Actions [*A publication*] (DLA)

Anglo-Am Law Rev ... Anglo-American Law Review [*A publication*]

Anglo-Am LR ... Anglo-American Law Review [*A publication*]

Anglo-Am L Rev ... Anglo-American Law Review [*A publication*]

Anglo Bat Soc Proc ... Anglo Batarian Society. Proceedings [*A publication*]

Anglo-Ger Med Rev ... Anglo-German Medical Review [*A publication*]

Angl Orthod ... Angle Orthodontist [*A publication*]

Anglosax En ... Anglosaxon England [*A publication*]

Anglo-Saxon Engl ... Anglo-Saxon England [*A publication*]

Anglo-Sp Q Rev ... Anglo-Spanish Quarterly Review [*A publication*]

Anglo-Welsh ... Anglo-Welsh Review [*A publication*]

Angl Th R .. Anglican Theological Review [*A publication*]

AnglTR .... Anglican Theological Review [*Evanston, IL/Sewanee, TN*] [*A publication*]

ANGM...... Anglican Messenger [*A publication*]

ANGN ...... Angeion Corp. [*NASDAQ symbol*] (NQ)

ANGNDT ... Abhandlung. Naturhistorische Gesellschaft Nuernberg [*A publication*]

An Go........ Antonius Gomez [*Flourished, 16th century*] [*Authority cited in pre-1607 legal work*] (DSA)

ANGO .... Association du Negoce des Grains Oleagineuses, Huiles, et Graisses Animales et Vegetales et Leurs Derives de la CEE [*Trade Association for Oilseeds, Oil, Vegetable and Animal Fats, and Their Derivatives of the European Economic Community*]

ANGOA..... Angiologia [*A publication*]

ANGOC..... Asian Nongovernmental Organizations Coalition for Agrarian Reform and Rural Development (EAIO)

Angola Serv Geol Minas Bol ... Angola. Servicos de Geologia e Minas. Boletim [*A publication*]

ANGOP..... Angolan News Agency

Angora Goat Mohair J ... Angora Goat and Mohair Journal [*A publication*]

ANGOS ..... Air National Guard Optometric Society (EA)

AnGP......... Anthology of German Poetry [*A publication*]

An G Paleont ... Annales de Geologie et de Paleontologie [*A publication*]

Ang Paras ... Angewandte Parasitologie [*A publication*]

ANGPC..... Air National Guard Policy Council

Ang de Perigl ... Angelus de Periglis [*Deceased, 1446*] [*Authority cited in pre-1607 legal work*] (DSA)

ANGRY ..... Anti-Nuclear Group Representing York (NRCH)

Ang-Sax..... Anglo-Saxon

ANGSC .... Air National Guard Support Center

ANGSOC... Anglican Society [*Australia*] (ADA)

ANGTA .... Alaska Natural Gas Transportation Act of 1976

Ang Theol Rev ... Anglican Theological Review [*A publication*]

Ang Tide Waters ... Angell on Tide Waters [*A publication*] (DLA)

ANGTS..... Alaska Natural Gas Transportation System

Ang TW ..... Angell on Tide Waters [*A publication*] (DLA)

ANGUS ..... Acoustically Navigated Geological Underwater Survey [*Unmanned vehicle*]

ANGUS ..... Air National Guard of the United States

Angus Wildl Rev ... Angus Wildlife Review [*A publication*]

ANGW....... Alles nach Gottes Willen [*Everything According to the Will of God*] [*Motto of Heinrich Julius, Duke of Braunschweig-Wolfenbuttel (1564-1613); Marie, Margravine of Brandenburg (1579-1649); Sophie, Duchess of Schleswig-Holstein (1579-1618); Elisabeth, Duchess of Schleswig-Holstein (1580-1653); Christian, Margrave of Brandenburg-Baireuth (1581-1655); Erdmann August, Margrave of Brandenburg-Baireuth (1615-51)*]

Ang Wat..... Angell on Water Courses [*A publication*] (DLA)

Ang Water Courses ... Angell on Water Courses [*A publication*] (DLA)

ANGWS .... Advanced Naval Gun Weapon System (MCD)

ANGYBQ .. Advances in Nephrology [*A publication*]

ANH .... All-North Resources Ltd. [*Vancouver Stock Exchange symbol*]

An H .... Anatomische Hefte [*A publication*]

ANH .... Anhang [*Appendix*] [*German*]

ANH .... Anhydrous

ANH .... Associated Newspaper Holdings [*British*]

ANHA ...... American National Heritage Association (EA)

ANHA ...... American Nursing Home Association [*Later, AHCA*] (EA)

Anharmonic Lattices Struct Transitions Melting ... Anharmonic Lattices, Structural Transitions, and Melting [*A publication*]

ANH/B...... Boletin. Academia Nacional de la Historia [*A publication*]

ANHC....... American National Holding Company [*NASDAQ symbol*] (NQ)

ANHC....... Army Native Hospital Corps [*British military*] (DMA)

ANHEA4... Animal Health [*A publication*]

ANHGAA ... Annals of Human Genetics [*A publication*]

ANHIAG ... Annales d'Histochimie [*A publication*]

ANHIDJ .... Archives of Natural History [*A publication*]

An Hisp .... Anales. Universidad Hispalense [*A publication*]

An Hist ...... Anais de Historia [*A publication*]

An Hist Der ... Anuario de la Historia del Derecho Espanol [*A publication*]

An Hist Inst Dubrovniku ... Anali Historijski Institut u Dubrovniku [*A publication*]

ANHNAV ... Annuaire. Museum National d'Histoire Naturelle [*A publication*]

An Hosp Mil Cent (Lima Peru) ... Anales. Hospital Militar Central (Lima, Peru) [*A publication*]

An Hosp St Cruz San Pablo ... Anales. Hospital de la Santa Cruz y San Pablo [*A publication*]

ANHS........ American Natural Hygiene Society (EA)

ANHSA ..... Aeronias Nacionales de Honduras Sociedad Anonima [*Airline*] [*Honduras*]

ANHSCSR ... Association of National Health Service Corps Scholarship Recipients (EA)

ANHSO..... Association of National Health Service Officers [*British*]
ANHY .... Anhydrous
ANHYD .... Anhydride (MSA)
ANHYD .... Anhydrous
ANI........... Adizes Network International [*Santa Monica, CA*] (EA)
ANI........... Advanced Network Integration (TEL)
ANI........... Agencia Nacionale de Informacoes [*National Information Agency*] [*Portugal*]
ANI........... Ambient Noise Index (CAAL)
ANI........... American National Insurance Co.
ANI........... American Nuclear Insurers [*Farmington, CT*] (EA)
ANI........... Americans for the National Interest (EA)
ANI........... Aniak [*Alaska*] [*Airport symbol*] (OAG)
ANI........... Animal
ANI........... Anina Resources, Incorporated [*Vancouver Stock Exchange symbol*]
ANI........... Apprentices National Insurance [*British*]
ANI........... Army-Navy-Industry (MCD)
ANI........... Association Nationale pour l'Infographie [*National Computer Graphics Association of Canada*]
ANI........... Associazione Nazionalista Italiana [*Italian Nationalist Association*] [*Political party*] (PPE)
ANI........... Atmosphere Normale Internationale [*International Normal Atmosphere*]
ANI........... Authorized Nuclear Inspector (NRCH)
ANI........... Automatic Number Identification [*Telecommunications*]
ANIA .... Association Nationale des Industries Agro-Alimentaires [*Industrial organization*] [*France*] (EY)
ANIA .... Associazione Nazionale fra le Imprese [*Insurance association*] [*Italy*] (EY)
ANICA ...... Associazione Nazionale Industrie Cinematografiche e Audiovisive [*Cinematograph and allied industries association*] [*Italy*] (EY)
ANICA ...... Associazione Nazionale fra gli Istituti de Credito Agrario [*Bankers' organization*] [*Italy*] (EY)
ANICAM .. Associazione Nazionale dell'Industria dei Componenti Accessori e Materiali per Calzature e Pelletterie [*Footwear Components and Accessories Association*] [*Italy*] (EY)
ANICAV.... Associazione Nazionale Industriali Conserve Alimentari Vegetali [*Manufacturers of canned vegetable foods association*] [*Italy*] (EY)
ANICD6 .... Annals. ICRP [*International Commission on Radiological Protection*] [*A publication*]
ANICO ...... American National Insurance Company
ANIFA .... Annales de Chirurgie Infantile [*A publication*]
ANIGDI .... Anales. Instituto Nacional de Investigaciones Agrarias. Serie Ganadera [*A publication*]
ANIH......... Associate of the National Institute of Hardware [*British*] (DBQ)
anil .... Aniline [*Philately*]
AnIL .... Anthology of Irish Literature [*A publication*]
ANILCA .... Alaska National Interest Land Conservation Act [*1980*]
Anilinokras Promst ... Anilinokrasochnaya Promyshlennost [*A publication*]
An Ilus Col Of Med Prov Lerida ... Anales Ilustrados. Colegio Oficial de Medicina. Provincia de Lerida [*A publication*]
ANIM .... Acute Necrosis of Intestinal Mucosa [*Gastroenterology*]
ANIM .... Agence Internationale d'Information du Mali [*Press agency*] [*Mali*]
ANIM .... Animal
ANIM .... Animation [*Films, television, etc.*]
ANIM .... Association of Nuclear Instrument Manufacturers [*Later, SAMA*]
Animal Behav ... Animal Behaviour [*A publication*]
Animal Prod ... Animal Production [*A publication*]
Animal Rights L Rep ... Animal Rights Law Reporter [*A publication*] (DLA)
Anim Behav ... Animal Behaviour [*A publication*]
Anim Behav Abstr ... Animal Behavior Abstracts [*A publication*]
Anim Behav Monogr ... Animal Behaviour. Monographs [*A publication*]
Anim Blood Groups Biochem Genet ... Animal Blood Groups and Biochemical Genetics [*A publication*]
Anim Blood Groups Biochem Genet (Suppl) ... Animal Blood Groups and Biochemical Genetics (Supplement) [*A publication*]
Anim Breed ... Animal Breeding [*A publication*]
Anim Breed Abstr ... Animal Breeding Abstracts [*A publication*]
Anim Breed Feed ... Animal Breeding and Feeding [*A publication*]
ANIMC ...... Annales d'Immunologie [*A publication*]
Anim Compagnie ... Animal de Compagnie [*A publication*]
ANIMD2... Anaesthesiologie und Intensivmedizin [*A publication*]
ANIMD2... Anaesthesiology and Intensive Care Medicine [*A publication*]
Anim Def Anti-Viv ... Animals Defender and Anti-Vivisectionist [*A publication*]
Anim Feed S ... Animal Feed Science and Technology [*A publication*]
Anim Feed Sci Technol ... Animal Feed Science and Technology [*Netherlands*] [*A publication*]
Anim Genet ... Animal Genetics [*A publication*]
Anim Health ... Animal Health [*A publication*]
Anim Hlth ... Animal Health [*A publication*]
Anim Hlth Yb ... Animal Health Yearbook [*A publication*]
Anim Husb ... Animal Husbandry [*A publication*]
Anim Husb Agric J ... Animal Husbandry and Agricultural Journal [*A publication*]

Anim Husb Mimeogr Ser Fla Agr Exp Sta ... Animal Husbandry Mimeograph Series. Florida Agricultural Experiment Station [*A publication*]
Anim Husb (Tokyo) ... Animal Husbandry (Tokyo) [*A publication*]
Anim Ind Today ... Animal Industry Today [*A publication*]
Anim Kingdom ... Animal Kingdom [*A publication*]
Anim Lear B ... Animal Learning and Behavior [*A publication*]
Anim Learn Behav ... Animal Learning and Behavior [*A publication*]
Anim Models Thromb Hemorrhagic Dis ... Animal Models of Thrombosis and Hemorrhagic Diseases [*A publication*]
Anim Nutr Health ... Animal Nutrition and Health [*A publication*]
Anim Nutr Res Counc Proc Annu Meet ... Animal Nutrition Research Council. Proceedings of the Annual Meeting [*A publication*]
ANIMO..... Animato [*Lively, Animated*] [*Music*]
Anim Plant Microb Toxins Proc Int Symp M ... Animal, Plant, and Microbial Toxins. Proceedings of the International Symposium on Animal, Plant, and Microbial Toxins [*A publication*]
Anim Prod ... Animal Production [*A publication*]
Anim Produc ... Animal Production [*A publication*]
Anim Quar ... Animal Quarantine [*A publication*] (APTA)
Anim Regul Stud ... Animal Regulation Studies [*A publication*]
Anim Res Lab Tech Pap Aust CSIRO ... Animal Research Laboratories Technical Paper. Australia Commonwealth Scientific and Industrial Research Organisation [*A publication*]
Anim Rights L Rep ... Animal Rights Law Reporter [*A publication*]
Anim Sci J Pak ... Animal Science Journal of Pakistan [*A publication*]
Anim Sci Mimeogr Rep Fla Agr Exp Sta ... Animal Science Mimeograph Report. Florida Agricultural Experiment Station [*A publication*]
Anim Sci Mimeogr Ser Ohio State Agr Exp Sta ... Animal Science Mimeograph Series. Ohio State Agricultural Experiment Station [*A publication*]
Anim Sci (Sofia) ... Animal Science (Sofia) [*A publication*]
Anim Technol ... Animal Technology [*A publication*]
Anim Virol ... Animal Virology [*A publication*]
AnINA .... Anales. Instituto Nacional de Antropologia e Historia [*A publication*]
ANINE6 .... Analytical Instrumentation [*A publication*]
An Ing .... Anales de Ingenieria [*A publication*]
An Inst Agron (Lisboa) ... Anais. Instituto Superior de Agronomia (Lisboa) [*A publication*]
An Inst Antrop Hist ... Anales. Instituto Nacional de Antropologia e Historia [*A publication*]
An Inst Biol (Mexico) ... Anales. Instituto de Biologia. Universidad Nacional Autonoma de Mexico [*A publication*]
An Inst Biol Univ Mex ... Anales. Instituto de Biologia. Universidad Nacional Autonoma de Mexico [*A publication*]
An Inst Biol Univ Nac Auton Mex ... Anales. Instituto de Biologia. Universidad Nacional Autonoma de Mexico [*A publication*]
An Inst Biol Univ Nac Auton Mex Ser Biol Exp ... Anales. Instituto de Biologia. Universidad Nacional Autonoma de Mexico. Serie Biologia Experimental [*A publication*]
An Inst Biol Univ Nac Auton Mex Ser Bot ... Anales. Instituto de Biologia. Universidad Nacional Autonoma de Mexico. Serie Botanica [*A publication*]
An Inst Biol Univ Nac Auton Mex Ser Cienc Mar Limnol ... Anales. Instituto de Biologia. Universidad Nacional Autonoma de Mexico. Serie Ciencias del Mar y Limnologia [*A publication*]
An Inst Biol Univ Nac Auton Mex Ser Zool ... Anales. Instituto de Biologia. Universidad Nacional Autonoma de Mexico. Serie Zoologia [*A publication*]
An Inst Bot A J Cavanilles ... Anales. Instituto Botanico A. J. Cavanilles [*A publication*]
An Inst Bot A J Cavanilles (Madrid) ... Anales. Instituto Botanico A. J. Cavanilles (Madrid) [*A publication*]
An Inst Cent Cercet Agric Sect Pedol ... Analele. Institutul Central de Cercetari Agricole. Sectiei de Pedologie [*A publication*]
An Inst Cent Cercet Agr Sect Econ Agr (Bucharest) ... Anale. Institutul Central de Cercetari Agricole. Sectiei de Economice Agricole (Bucharest) [*A publication*]
An Inst Cent Cercet Agr Sect Prot Plant ... Anale. Institutul Central de Cercetari Agricole. Sectiei de Protectia Plantelor [*A publication*]
An Inst Cent Cercet Agr Ser A (Bucharest) ... Anale. Institutul Central de Cercetari Agricole. Series A (Bucharest) [*A publication*]
An Inst Cent Cercet Agr Ser B (Bucharest) ... Anale. Institutul Central de Cercetari Agricole. Series B (Bucharest) [*A publication*]
An Inst Cent Cercet Agr Ser C (Bucharest) ... Anale. Institutul Central de Cercetari Agricole. Series C (Bucharest) [*A publication*]
An Inst Cercet pentru Cereale Plante Teh-Fundulea ... Analele. Institutului de Cercetari pentru Cereale si Plante Tehnice-Fundulea [*Romania*] [*A publication*]
An Inst Cercet Cereale Plante Teh-Fundulea ... Analele. Institutului de Cercetari pentru Cereale si Plante Tehnice-Fundulea [*A publication*]
An Inst Cercet pentru Cereale Plante Teh-Fundulea Ser A ... Analele. Institutului de Cercetari pentru Cereale si Plante Tehnice-Fundulea. Seria A [*A publication*]

An Inst Cercet pentru Cereale Plante Teh-Fundulea Ser B ... Analele. Institutului de Cercetari pentru Cereale si Plante Tehnice-Fundulea. Seria B [*A publication*]

An Inst Cercet pentru Cereale Plante Teh-Fundulea Ser C ... Analele. Institutului de Cercetari pentru Cereale si Plante Tehnice-Fundulea. Seria C [*A publication*]

An Inst Cercet Cul Cartofului Sfeclei Zahar (Brasov) Cartofu ... Anale. Institutul de Cercetari pentru Cultura Cartofului si Sfeclei de Zahar (Brasov). Cartoful [*A publication*]

An Inst Cercet Imbunatatiri Funciare Pedol Ser Hidroteh ... Analele. Institutului de Cercetari pentru Imbunatatiri Funciare si Pedologie. Seria Hidrotehnica [*A publication*]

An Inst Cercet Imbunatatiri Funciare Pedol Ser Pedol ... Analele. Institutului de Cercetari pentru Imbunatatiri Funciare si Pedologie. Seria Pedologie [*A publication*]

An Inst Cercet Pedol Agrochim ... Analele. Institutului de Cercetari pentru Pedologie si Agrochimie [*A publication*]

An Inst Cercet Prot Plant ... Analele. Institutului de Cercetari pentru Protectia Plantelor [*A publication*]

An Inst Cercet Prot Plant Acad Stiinte Agric Silvice ... Analele. Institutului de Cercetari pentru Protectia Plantelor. Academia de Stiinte. Agricole si Silvice [*A publication*]

An Inst Cercet Prot Plant Inst Cent Cercet Agric (Bucharest) ... Analele. Institutului de Cercetari pentru Protectia Plantelor. Institutul Central de Cercetari Agricole (Bucharest) [*A publication*]

An Inst Cercet Zooteh (Bucharest) ... Analele. Institutului de Cercetari. Zootehnice (Bucharest) [*A publication*]

An Inst (Cluj) ... Anuarul. Institutului de Istorie si Arheologie (Cluj-Napoca) [*A publication*]

An Inst Corachan ... Anales. Instituto Corachan [*Spain*] [*A publication*]

An Inst Esp Edafol Ecol Fisiol Veg ... Anales. Instituto Espanol de Edafologia, Ecologia, y Fisiologia Vegetal [*A publication*]

An Inst Estud Madrilenos ... Anales. Instituto de Estudios Madrilenos [*A publication*]

An Inst Farmac Esp ... Anales. Instituto de Farmacologia Espanola [*A publication*]

An Inst Farmacol Esp ... Anales. Instituto de Farmacologia Espanola [*A publication*]

An Inst For Invest Exper (Madr) ... Anales. Instituto Forestal de Investigaciones y Experiencias (Madrid) [*A publication*]

An Inst Geofis UNAM ... Anales. Instituto de Geofisica. Universidad Nacional Autonoma de Mexico [*A publication*]

An Inst Geofis Univ Nac Auton Mex ... Anales. Instituto de Geofisica. Universidad Nacional Autonoma de Mexico [*A publication*]

An Inst Geol Mex ... Anales. Instituto Geologico de Mexico [*A publication*]

An Inst Geol Univ Nac Auton Mex ... Anales. Instituto de Geologia. Universidad Nacional Autonoma de Mexico [*A publication*]

An Inst Hig Med Trop ... Anais. Instituto de Higiene e Medicina Tropical [*Lisbon*] [*A publication*]

An Inst Hig Med Trop (Lisb) ... Anais. Instituto de Higiene e Medicina Tropical (Lisbon) [*A publication*]

An Insti Nac Invest Agrar (Spain) Ser Prot Veg ... Anales. Instituto Nacional de Investigaciones Agrarias (Spain). Serie Proteccion Vegetal [*A publication*]

An Inst Invest Cient Tecnol Univ Nac Litoral ... Anales. Instituto de Investigaciones Cientificas y Tecnologicas. Universidad Nacional del Litoral [*A publication*]

An Inst Invest Cient Univ Nuevo Leon ... Anales. Instituto de Investigaciones Cientificas. Universidad de Nuevo Leon [*A publication*]

An Inst Invest Odontol (Maracaibo) ... Anales. Instituto de Investigaciones Odontologicas. Universidad del Zulia (Maracaibo) [*A publication*]

An Inst Invest Vet ... Anales. Instituto de Investigaciones Veterinarias [*A publication*]

An Inst Invest Vet (Madrid) ... Anales. Instituto de Investigaciones Veterinarias (Madrid) [*A publication*]

An Inst Ist Arh (Cluj) ... Anuarul. Institutului de Istorie si Arheologie (Cluj-Napoca) [*A publication*]

An In St Ma ... Annals. Institute of Statistical Mathematics [*A publication*]

An Inst Mat Univ Nac Autonoma Mexico ... Anales. Instituto de Matematicas. Universidad Nacional Autonoma de Mexico [*A publication*]

An Inst Med Nac (Mexico) ... Anales. Instituto Medico Nacional (Mexico) [*A publication*]

An Inst Med Reg ... Anales. Instituto de Medicina Regional [*A publication*]

An Inst Med Trop ... Anais. Instituto de Medicina Tropical [*Lisbon*] [*A publication*]

An Inst Med Trop (Lisb) ... Anais. Instituto de Medicina Tropical (Lisbon) [*A publication*]

An Inst Mun Hig Zaragoza ... Anales. Instituto Municipal de Higiene de Zaragoza [*A publication*]

An Inst Munic Hig Z ... Anales. Instituto Municipal de Higiene de Zaragoza [*A publication*]

An Inst Nac Antropol Hist ... Anales. Instituto Nacional de Antropologia e Historia [*A publication*]

An Inst Nac Invest Agrar Ser Ganad ... Anales. Instituto Nacional de Investigaciones Agrarias. Serie Ganadera [*A publication*]

An Inst Nac Invest Agrar Ser Gen ... Anales. Instituto Nacional de Investigaciones Agrarias. Serie General [*A publication*]

An Inst Nac Invest Agrar Ser Hig Sanid Anim ... Anales. Instituto Nacional de Investigaciones Agrarias. Serie Higiene y Sanidad Animal [*A publication*]

An Inst Nac Invest Agrar Ser Prod Anim ... Anales. Instituto Nacional de Investigaciones Agrarias. Serie Produccion Animal [*A publication*]

An Inst Nac Invest Agrar Ser Prod Veg ... Anales. Instituto Nacional de Investigaciones Agrarias. Serie Produccion Vegetal [*A publication*]

An Inst Nac Invest Agrar Ser Prot Veg ... Anales. Instituto Nacional de Investigaciones Agrarias. Serie Proteccion Vegetal [*A publication*]

An Inst Nac Invest Agrar Ser Recur Nat ... Anales. Instituto Nacional de Investigaciones Agrarias. Serie Recursos Naturales [*A publication*]

An Inst Nac Invest Agrar Ser Tecnol Agrar ... Anales. Instituto Nacional de Investigaciones Agrarias. Serie Tecnologia Agraria [*A publication*]

An Inst Nac Invest Agrar (Spain) Ser Prod Anim ... Anales. Instituto Nacional de Investigaciones Agrarias (Spain). Serie Produccion Animal [*A publication*]

An Inst Nac Invest Agrar (Spain) Ser Prod Veg ... Anales. Instituto Nacional de Investigaciones Agrarias (Spain). Serie Produccion Vegetal [*A publication*]

An Inst Nac Invest Agron (Madr) ... Anales. Instituto Nacional de Investigaciones Agronomicas (Madrid) [*A publication*]

An Inst Nac Microbiol (B Aires) ... Anales. Instituto Nacional de Microbiologia (Buenos Aires) [*A publication*]

An Inst Oncol Angel H Roffo ... Anales. Instituto de Oncologia "Angel H. Roffo" [*A publication*]

An Inst Oncol Angel H Roffo (B Aires) ... Anales. Instituto de Oncologia "Angel H. Roffo" (Buenos Aires) [*A publication*]

An Inst Patagonia ... Anales. Instituto de la Patagonia [*A publication*]

An Inst Pinheiros ... Anais. Instituto Pinheiros [*A publication*]

An Inst Psicol ... Anales. Instituto de Psicologia [*Buenos Aires*] [*A publication*]

An Inst Radio Quir Guipuzcoa ... Anales. Instituto Radio Quirurgico de Guipuzcoa [*A publication*]

An Inst Stud Cercet Pedol ... Analele. Institutului de Studii si Cercetari Pedologice [*A publication*]

An Inst Super Agron (Lisboa) ... Anais. Instituto Superior de Agronomia (Lisboa) [*A publication*]

An Inst Super Agron Univ Tec Lisb ... Anais. Instituto Superior de Agronomia. Universidade Tecnica de Lisboa [*A publication*]

An Inst Vinho Porto ... Anais. Instituto do Vinho do Porto [*A publication*]

An Invest Agron ... Anales de Investigaciones Agronomicas [*A publication*]

An Invest Text ... Anales de Investigacion Textil [*A publication*]

Anionic Surfactants Chem Anal ... Anionic Surfactants Chemical Analysis [*A publication*]

AnIowa .... Annals of Iowa [*A publication*]

ANIP .... Army-Navy Instrumentation Program

ANIP .... Army Navy Integrated Presentation

ANIPA .... Animal Production [*A publication*]

ANIRAE ...... Acta Naturalia Islandica [*A publication*]

ANIRC .... Annual National Information Retrieval Colloquium

ANIS .... Anisum [*Anise Seed*] [*Pharmacology*]   (ROG)

Ani Sci .... Animal Science [*A publication*]

An de Iser ... Andreas de Isernia [*Deceased circa 1316*] [*Authority cited in pre-1607 legal work*]   (DSA)

aniso .... Anisocytosis [*Hematology*]

Anisometr .. Anisometropia [*Ophthalmology*]

Anisotropy Eff Supercond Proc Int Discuss Meet ... Anisotropy Effects in Superconductors. Proceedings of an International Discussion Meeting. Atominstitut der Oesterreichischen Universitaeten [*A publication*]

ANIT .... Alpha-Naphthylisothiocyanate [*Organic chemistry*]

ANITA ...... Associazione Nazionale Imprese Trasporti Automobilistici [*Motor transport concerns association*] [*Italy*]   (EY)

ANITA ...... [*A*] New Inspiration to Arithmetic

AnIV .... Anthology of Irish Verse [*A publication*]

ANIVK ...... Akademiia Nauk SSSR. Institut Vostokovedeniia. Kratkie Soobshcheniia [*A publication*]

ANix .... Australian Nixa [*Record label*]

ANJ .... Aintree Resources [*Vancouver Stock Exchange symbol*]

ANJ .... Atlantic Community College, Mays Landing, NJ [*OCLC symbol*]   (OCLC)

ANJ .... Australian Numismatic Journal [*A publication*]

ANJ .... Australian Nurses' Journal [*A publication*]   (APTA)

ANJ .... Zanaga [*Congo*] [*Airport symbol*]   (OAG)

An Jard Bot Madrid ... Anales. Jardin Botanico de Madrid [*A publication*]

ANJGG ..... Green Grove Community Library, Nilton Junction, Alberta [*Library symbol*] [*National Library of Canada*]   (NLC)

ANJSB ...... Army-Navy Joint Specifications Board

An Junta Invest Ultramar ... Anais. Junta de Investigacoes do Ultramar [*A publication*]

ANK .... Alphanumeric Keyboard

ANK .... American Neturei Karta [*Friends of Jerusalem*]   (EA)

ANK .... Ankara [*Turkey*] [*Airport symbol*]   (OAG)

ANK.......... Ankara [*Turkey*] [*Seismograph station code, US Geological Survey*] (SEIS)
ANK.......... Automatic Navigation Kit (MCD)
ANK.......... Consommation [*A publication*]
Ankara Nucl Res Cent Tech J ... Ankara Nuclear Research Center. Technical Journal [*A publication*]
Ankara Nucl Res Train Cent Tech J ... Ankara Nuclear Research and Training Center. Technical Journal [*A publication*]
Ankara Univ Tip Fak Mecm ... Ankara Universitesi. Tip Fakultesi. Mecmuasi [*A publication*]
Ankara Univ Tip Fak Mecm Suppl ... Ankara Universitesi. Tip Fakultesi. Mecmuasi. Supplementum [*A publication*]
Ankara Univ Vet Fak Derg ... Ankara Universitesi. Veteriner Fakultesi. Dergisi [*A publication*]
Ankara Univ Ziraat Fak Yayin ... Ankara Universitesi. Ziraat Fakultesi. Yayinlari [*A publication*]
ANKB........ Alphanumeric Keyboard
ANKIAV.... Animal Kingdom [*A publication*]
ANKIDY ... Annales de Kinesitherapie [*A publication*]
An Klin Boln Dr M Stojanovic ... Anali Klinicke Bolnice Dr. M. Stojanovic [*A publication*]
An Klin Boln Dr M Stojanovic Supl ... Anali Klinicke Bolnice Dr. M. Stojanovic. Suplement [*A publication*]
AnkUDerg ... Ankara Universitesi Dil ve Tarih-Cografya Fakultesi. Dergisi [*A publication*]
ANL.......... Above Normal Loss [*Insurance*]
ANL.......... Accademia Nazionale dei Lincei [*Rome*] [*A publication*]
ANL.......... Acute Nonlymphoblastic Leukemia [*Medicine*]
ANL.......... Air New Orleans [*New Orleans, LA*] [*FAA designator*] (FAAC)
ANL.......... Altnuernberger Landschaft. Mitteilungen [*A publication*]
ANL.......... American National Standard Labels (BUR)
ANL.......... Amplitude Noise Limiting
ANL.......... Analog (NASA)
ANL.......... Andalgala [*Argentina*] [*Seismograph station code, US Geological Survey*] [*Closed*] (SEIS)
Anl .... Anlage [*Enclosure*] [*German*] (ILCA)
ANL.......... Anneal (KSC)
ANL.......... Annoyance Level [*Aircraft noise*]
ANL.......... Annual (AABC)
AnL.......... Anthropological Linguistics [*A publication*]
ANL.......... Archaeological News Letter [*A publication*]
ANL.......... Argonne National Laboratory [*Argonne, IL*] [*Department of Energy*] (GRD)
ANL.......... Argonne National Laboratory, Argonne, IL [*OCLC symbol*] (OCLC)
ANL.......... Army Natick Laboratory
A & NL ..... Army and Navy Life [*New York*] [*A publication*] (ROG)
ANL.......... Atti. Reale Accademia Nazionale dei Lincei. Classe di Scienze Morali, Storiche, e Filologiche [*Rome*] [*A publication*]
ANL.......... Australian National Line (DS)
ANL.......... Automatic Noise Limiter [*Electronics*]
ANL.......... Net Laying Ship [*Formerly, AN*] [*Navy symbol*]
ANLA .... Atti. Reale Accademia Nazionale dei Lincei. Classe di Scienze Morali, Storiche, e Filologiche [*Rome*] [*A publication*]
ANLAAC... Acta Neurologica Latinoamericana [*A publication*]
An Lactol Quim Agric (Zaragoza) ... Anales de Lactologia y Quimica Agricola (Zaragoza) [*A publication*]
ANLADF... Auris Nasus Larynx [*A publication*]
ANLBA..... Bulletin. Australian Mathematical Society [*A publication*]
ANLC .... Alaska Native Language Center [*Research center*] (RCD)
ANLC .... Army-Navy Liquidation Commission [*World War II*]
ANLEDR... Antonie Van Leeuwenhoek Journal of Microbiology [*A publication*]
AnLeeds..... Annual. Leeds University Oriental Society [*Leiden*] [*A publication*]
An Leeds UOS ... Annual. Leeds University Oriental Society [*Leiden*] [*A publication*]
Anleit Bienenzuechter ... Anleitungen Bienenzuechter [*A publication*]
ANL/ETD ... Argonne National Laboratory Engineering and Technology Division [*Illinois*]
ANLF....... Afghanistan National Liberation Front
ANLG .... Analog (MSA)
ANLG .... Antilogarithmic Function
ANLGS...... Analogous (MSA)
ANLI .... Antibody-Negative Mice with Latent Infection [*Immunology*]
ANLIA2..... Annali. Accademia Italiana di Scienze Forestali [*A publication*]
ANLIB...... Annales de Limnologie [*A publication*]
ANL ID...... Argonne National Laboratory, Idaho Division
ANLKB..... Archiv fuer die Naturkunde Liv-, Est-, und Kurlands [*A publication*]
ANLL....... Acute Nonlymphocytic Leukemia [*Medicine*]
ANLLF ...... Association des Neurologues Liberaux de Langue Francaise [*Versailles, France*] (EAIO)
ANLM...... Accademia Nazionale dei Lincei. Memorie [*A publication*]
ANLMSF .. Accademia Nazionale dei Lincei. Rendiconti. Classe di Scienze Morali, Storiche, e Filologiche [*A publication*]
ANLOR..... Angle Order (IEEE)
AnLov...... Analecta Lovanensia [*A publication*]
ANL/PHY Rep ... Argonne National Laboratory. Physics Division. Report [*A publication*]
ANLR .... Angular

ANLR .... Annular
ANLRAT... Annales de Radiologie [*A publication*]
ANLS .... Analyst
ANLSBX ... Acta Neuropathologica. Supplementum [*A publication*]
ANLSC...... Additive Noise Linear Sequential Circuit
ANLSCY ... Analusis [*A publication*]
ANLSD..... Argonne National Laboratory. Energy and Environmental Systems Division. Report ANL/CNSV [*A publication*]
Anls Prob ... Annals of Probability [*A publication*]
Anls Stat ... Annals of Statistics [*A publication*]
ANLT .... Analytical Surveys, Inc. [*Colorado Springs, CO*] [*NASDAQ symbol*] (NQ)
ANLX .... New South Wales Land Tax [*Australia*] [*A publication*]
ANLY .... Analysis
ANLY .... Analysts International Corp. [*NASDAQ symbol*] (NQ)
ANLYS...... Analysis (FAAC)
ANLYZ...... Analyzer
ANM........ Acoustic Noise Making (CAAL)
ANM........ Acute Necrotic Myelopathy [*Medicine*]
ANM........ After New Moon [*Freemasonry*] (ROG)
ANM........ Airways of New Mexico [*Alamogordo, NM*] [*FAA designator*] (FAAC)
ANM........ Alliance of Nonprofit Mailers (EA)
ANM........ Ambient Noise Measurement (CAAL)
ANM........ Angeles Mortgage Investors Trust [*AMEX symbol*] (SPSG)
ANM........ (Anilinonaphthyl)maleimide [*Organic chemistry*]
ANM........ Anmerkung [*Note*] [*German*]
AnM........ Annales du Midi; Revue de la France Meridionale [*Toulouse*] [*A publication*]
AnM........ Annuale Mediaevale [*A publication*]
ANM........ Antalaha [*Madagascar*] [*Airport symbol*] (OAG)
An M........ Anuario Musical [*A publication*]
ANM........ Artesia Public Library, Artesia, NM [*OCLC symbol*] (OCLC)
ANM........ Nampa Municipal Library, Alberta [*Library symbol*] [*National Library of Canada*] (NLC)
ANM........ New Mexico Air [*Roswell, NM*] [*FAA designator*] (FAAC)
ANM........ New Music (Australia) [*Record label*]
ANMA...... American Naturopathic Medical Association (EA)
ANMA...... Auxiliary to the National Medical Association (EA)
An Mag N H ... Annals and Magazine of Natural History [*A publication*]
An Mat Fiz Chim Electroteh Univ Craiova ... Anale. Universitatea din Craiova. Seria Matematica, Fizica, Chimie, Electrotehnica [*A publication*]
ANMB...... Army-Navy Munitions Board [*Later, Munitions Board*]
ANMBC .... Annales de Microbiologie [*A publication*]
ANMBCM ... Annales de Microbiologie [*Paris*] [*A publication*]
An M Belgique ... Annales des Mines de Belgique [*A publication*]
ANMC...... American National Metric Council (EA)
ANMC...... Assistant Navy Mail Clerk
ANMCAN ... Annali di Microbiologia [*A publication*]
ANMCB .... Angewandte Makromolekulare Chemie [*A publication*]
ANMCC .... Alternate National Military Command Center [*Formerly, AJWR*] (AFM)
ANMCS .... Anticipated Not Mission Capable, Supply [*Military*] (NVT)
ANMDAQ ... Antioquia Medica [*A publication*]
ANME...... Angio-Medical Corp. [*NASDAQ symbol*] (NQ)
anme.......... Anonyme [*Anonymous*] [*Used to indicate limited liability*] [*French*]
An Mec Elect ... Anales de Mecanica y Electricidad [*A publication*]
An Mec Electr ... Anales de Mecanica y Electricidad [*Spain*] [*A publication*]
An Mec & Electr ... Anales de Mecanica y Electricidad [*A publication*]
An Med ... Anales de Medicina [*A publication*]
An Med Acad Cienc Med Cataluna Baleares ... Anales de Medicina. Academia de Ciencias Medicas de Cataluna y Baleares [*A publication*]
An Med Assoc Med Hosp Am Br Cowdray ... Anales Medicos. Asociacion Medica. Hospital Americano-Britanico Cowdray [*A publication*]
An Med Cir ... Anales de Medicina. Cirugia [*A publication*]
An Med Espec ... Anales de Medicina. Especialidades [*A publication*]
An Med (Lima) ... Anales de Medicina (Lima) [*A publication*]
An Med Med ... Anales de Medicina. Medicina [*A publication*]
An Med Publ ... Anales de Medicina Publica [*Argentina*] [*A publication*]
An Med Quir ... Anales Medicoquirurgicos [*A publication*]
An Med Sec Med ... Anales de Medicina. Seccion de Medicina [*Spain*] [*A publication*]
An Med (Sevilla) ... Anales de Medicina (Sevilla) [*A publication*]
ANMEDW ... Annals. Medicina Academia de Ciencies Mediques de Catalunya i de Balears [*A publication*]
AN & MEF ... Australian Naval and Military Expeditionary Force
An Mex Cienc ... Anales Mexicanos de Ciencias [*A publication*]
ANMI .... Airborne Navigational Multiple Indicators (MCD)
ANMI .... Allied Naval Maneuvering Instructions [*NATO*] (NATG)
ANMIC .... Alternate National Military Intelligence Center (MCD)
An Micr ... Anais de Microbiologia [*A publication*]
An Microbiol (Rio De J) ... Anais de Microbiologia (Rio De Janeiro) [*A publication*]
An Minelor Rom ... Analele Minelor din Romania [*A publication*]
An Mines ... Annales des Mines [*Paris*] [*A publication*]
AnML........ Anthology of Medieval Lyrics [*A publication*]
ANMM...... Australian National Maritime Museum

ANMO ...... Albuquerque [*New Mexico*] [*Seismograph station code, US Geological Survey*] (SEIS)

AnMoPo .... Anthology of Modern Poetry [*A publication*]

AN Morph ... Acta Neerlandica Morphologiae Normalis et Pathologicae [*A publication*]

AnMP .... Anthology of Mexican Poetry [*A publication*]

ANMR .... Advanced NMR Systems, Inc. [*NASDAQ symbol*] (NQ)

ANMR .... Alaska Native Management Report [*A publication*]

ANMRC2 .. Annales de Medecine de Reims [*A publication*]

ANMS .... Automated Notices to Mariners System

ANMS .... Automatic Network Management System (FAAC)

ANMUA9 ... Annale. Natalse Museum [*A publication*]

An Mun Faro ... Anais. Municipio de Faro [*A publication*]

An Mus Argent Cienc Nat Bernardino Rivadavia ... Anales. Museo Argentino de Ciencias Naturales Bernardino Rivadavia [*A publication*]

An Mus Hist Nat Valparaiso ... Anales. Museo de Historia Natural de Valparaiso [*A publication*]

An Mus Nac David J Guzman ... Anales. Museo Nacional David J. Guzman [*A publication*]

An Mus Nac Hist Nat Montev ... Anales. Museo Nacional de Historia Natural de Montevideo [*A publication*]

ANMWAF ... Annalen des Naturhistorischen Museums in Wien [*A publication*]

Ann .... Annales [*of Tacitus*] [*Classical studies*] (OCD)

AnN .... Annales de Normandie [*A publication*]

ANN .... Annals

Ann .... Annaly's Lee Tempore Hardwicke [*7-10 George II, King's Bench*] [*1733-38*] [*A publication*] (DLA)

ANN .... Annamalainagar [*India*] [*Geomagnetic observatory code*]

ANN .... Annealed

ANN .... Annette Island [*Alaska*] [*Airport symbol*] [*Obsolete*] (OAG)

ANN .... Annex

ANN .... Anno [*or Annus*] [*Year*] [*Latin*]

Ann .... Annotated (DLA)

ann .... Annotator [*MARC relator code*] [*Library of Congress*] (LCCP)

ANN .... Announce (AABC)

Ann .... Annuaire (BJA)

ANN .... Annual

ANN .... Annuity (ROG)

ANN .... Annunciator [*Electronically controlled signal board*] (KSC)

ANN .... Annus [*Year*] [*Latin*]

ANN .... Answer, No-Charge [*Telecommunications*] (TEL)

ANN .... Arts for a New Nicaragua (EA)

ANN .... Asia-Pacific News Network

Ann .... Cases in King's Bench [*7-10 George II Tempore*] [*A publication*] (DLA)

Ann .... Cunningham's English King's Bench Reports [*A publication*] (DLA)

Ann .... Queen Anne (DLA)

ANNA .... American Nephrology Nurses' Association (EA)

ANNA .... Annandale Corp. [*NASDAQ symbol*] (NQ)

ANNA .... Army, Navy, NASA, Air Force Geodetic Satellite

ANNAAM ... Annales de l'Abeille [*Paris*] [*A publication*]

AnnAB ...... Annuaire. Academie Royale de Belgique [*A publication*]

Ann Abeille ... Annales de l'Abeille [*A publication*]

Ann Acad Med Gedanensis ... Annales Academiae Medicae Gedanensis [*A publication*]

Ann Acad Med Lodz ... Annales Academiae Medicae Lodzensis [*A publication*]

Ann Acad Med Lodz Supl ... Annales Academiae Medicae Lodzensis. Suplement [*A publication*]

Ann Acad Med (Singapore) ... Annals. Academy of Medicine (Singapore) [*A publication*]

Ann Acad Med Stetin ... Annales Academiae Medicae Stetinensis [*A publication*]

Ann Acad Med Stetin Supl ... Annales Academiae Medicae Stetinensis. Suplement [*A publication*]

Ann Acad Regiae Sci Ups ... Annales Academiae Regiae Scientiarum Upsaliensis [*A publication*]

Ann Acad Sci Colon ... Annales. Academie des Sciences Coloniales [*A publication*]

Ann Acad Sci Fenn A I ... Annales Academiae Scientiarum Fennicae. Series A-I (Mathematica) [*A publication*]

Ann Acad Sci Fenn A II ... Annales Academiae Scientiarum Fennicae. Series A-II (Chemica) [*A publication*]

Ann Acad Sci Fenn A VI ... Annales Academiae Scientiarum Fennicae. Series A-VI (Physica) [*A publication*]

Ann Acad Sci Fenn (Biol) ... Annales Academiae Scientiarum Fennicae. Series A-IV (Biologica) [*A publication*]

Ann Acad Sci Fenn (Med) ... Annales Academiae Scientiarum Fennicae. Series A-V (Medica) [*A publication*]

Ann Acad Sci Fenn Ser A I ... Annales Academiae Scientiarum Fennicae. Series A-I (Mathematica) [*A publication*]

Ann Acad Sci Fenn Ser A II ... Annales Academiae Scientiarum Fennicae. Series A-II (Chemica) [*A publication*]

Ann Acad Sci Fenn Ser A II (Chem) ... Annales Academiae Scientiarum Fennicae. Series A-II (Chemica) [*A publication*]

Ann Acad Sci Fenn Ser A III ... Annales Academiae Scientiarum Fennicae. Series A-III (Geologica-Geographica) [*A publication*]

Ann Acad Sci Fenn Ser A I (Math) ... Annales Academiae Scientiarum Fennicae. Series A-I (Mathematica) [*A publication*]

Ann Acad Sci Fenn Ser AI (Math) Dissertationes ... Annales Academiae Scientiarum Fennicae. Series A-I (Mathematica). Dissertationes [*A publication*]

Ann Acad Sci Fenn Ser AI (Math Phy) ... Annales Academiae Scientiarum Fennicae. Series A-I (Mathematica-Physica) [*A publication*]

Ann Acad Sci Fenn Ser A IV ... Annales Academiae Scientiarum Fennicae. Series A-IV (Biologica) [*A publication*]

Ann Acad Sci Fenn Ser A IV (Biol) ... Annales Academiae Scientiarum Fennicae. Series A-IV (Biologica) [*A publication*]

Ann Acad Sci Fenn Ser A V ... Annales Academiae Scientiarum Fennicae. Series A-V (Medica) [*A publication*]

Ann Acad Sci Fenn Ser A VI ... Annales Academiae Scientiarum Fennicae. Series A-VI (Physica) [*A publication*]

Ann Acad Sci Fenn Ser A VI (Phys) ... Annales Academiae Scientiarum Fennicae. Series A-VI (Physica) [*A publication*]

Ann Acad Sci Fenn Ser A V (Med) ... Annales Academiae Scientiarum Fennicae. Series A-V (Medica) [*A publication*]

Ann Acad Sci Fenn Ser A V (Med-Anthropol) ... Annales Academiae Scientiarum Fennicae. Series A-V (Medica-Anthropologica) [*A publication*]

Ann Accad Agric (Torino) ... Annali. Accademia di Agricoltura (Torino) [*A publication*]

Ann Accad Ital Sci For ... Annali. Accademia Italiana di Scienze Forestali [*A publication*]

Ann ACFAS ... Annales. ACFAS [*Association Canadienne Francaise pour l'Avancement des Sciences*] [*A publication*]

Ann Ac Fenn ... Annales Academiae Scientiarum Fennicae [*A publication*]

Ann Ac Torino ... Annuario. Accademia delle Scienze di Torino [*A publication*]

Ann Agr Fenn ... Annales Agriculturae Fenniae [*A publication*]

Ann Agric Exp Stn Gov Gen Chosen ... Annals. Agricultural Experiment Station. Government General of Chosen [*A publication*]

Ann Agric Fenn ... Annales Agriculturae Fenniae [*A publication*]

Ann Agric Fenn Ser Agrogeol -Chim -Phys ... Annales Agriculturae Fenniae. Seria Agrogeologia, -Chimica, et -Physica [*Finland*] [*A publication*]

Ann Agric Fenn Suppl ... Annales Agriculturae Fenniae. Supplementum [*A publication*]

Ann Agric Sci (Cairo) ... Annals of Agricultural Science (Cairo) [*A publication*]

Ann Agric Sci (Moshtohor) ... Annals of Agricultural Science (Moshtohor) [*A publication*]

Ann Agric Sci Univ A'in Shams ... Annals of Agricultural Science. University of A'in Shams [*A publication*]

Ann Agri Sci ... Annals of Agriculture Science [*A publication*]

Ann Agron ... Annales Agronomiques [*A publication*]

Ann Agron Hors-Ser ... Annales Agronomiques. Hors-Serie [*France*] [*A publication*]

Ann Agron (Paris) ... Annales Agronomiques (Paris) [*A publication*]

An-Nahar Arab Rept and Memo ... An-Nahar Arab Report and Memo [*A publication*]

AnnAIF ...... Annuaire des Archives Israelites (de France) [*A publication*]

ANNA J ..... ANNA [*American Nephrology Nurses Association*] Journal [*A publication*]

Annales-ESC ... Annales: Economies, Societes, Civilisations [*A publication*]

Annales Int'l de Crimin ... Annales Internationales de Criminologie [*A publication*]

Ann Alger Chir ... Annales Algeriennes de Chirurgie [*A publication*]

Annali Accad Naz Agric (Bologna) ... Annali. Accademia Nazionale di Agricoltura (Bologna) [*A publication*]

Annali Chim Appl ... Annali di Chimica Applicata [*A publication*]

Annali Fac Agr Portici ... Annali. Facolta di Agraria di Portici della Reale Universita di Napoli [*A publication*]

Annali Fac Agr Univ Bari ... Annali. Facolta di Agraria. Universita di Bari [*A publication*]

Annali Fac Agr Univ Milano ... Annali. Facolta di Agraria. Universita di Milano [*A publication*]

Annali Fac Agr Univ Perugia ... Annali. Facolta di Agraria. Universita degli Studi di Perugia [*A publication*]

Annali Fac Sci Agr Univ Napoli ... Annali. Facolta di Scienze Agrarie. Universita degli Studi di Napoli [*A publication*]

Annali Fac Sci Agr Univ Torino ... Annali. Facolta di Scienze Agrarie. Universita degli Studi di Torino [*A publication*]

Annali Geofisica ... Annali di Geofisica [*A publication*]

Annali Idrol ... Annali Idrologici [*A publication*]

Annali Ig Sper ... Annali d'Igiene. Sperimentali [*A publication*]

Annali Ist Carlo Forlanini ... Annali. Istituto Carlo Forlanini [*A publication*]

Annali Ist Sper Zool Agr ... Annali. Istituto Sperimentale per la Zoologia Agraria [*A publication*]

Annali Microbiol ... Annali di Microbiologia. Edizione. Enzimologia [*A publication*]

Annali Mus Civ Stor Nat Giacomo Doria ... Annali. Museo Civico di Storia Naturale "Giacomo Doria" [*A publication*]

Annali Sper Agr ... Annali della Sperimentazione Agraria [*A publication*]

Annali Staz Chim-Agr Sper Roma ... Annali. Reale Stazione Chimico-Agraria Sperimentale di Roma [*A publication*]

Annali Staz Sper Risicolt Vercelli ... Annali. Stazione Sperimentale di Risicoltura e delle Colture Irrigue. Vercelli [*A publication*]

Ann Allergy ... Annals of Allergy [*A publication*]
Annals........ Annals. American Academy of Political and Social Science [*A publication*]
Annals Air and Space ... Annals of Air and Space Law [*A publication*]
Annals Air and Space L ... Annals of Air and Space Law [*A publication*]
Annals Am Acad ... Annals. American Academy of Political and Social Science [*A publication*]
Annals General Prac ... Annals of General Practice [*A publication*]   (APTA)
Annals of Gen Prac ... Annals of General Practice [*A publication*]   (APTA)
Annals Gen Pract ... Annals of General Practice [*A publication*]   (APTA)
Annals Internat Studies ... Annals of International Studies [*A publication*]
Annals KY Nat History ... Annals of Kentucky Natural History [*A publication*]
Annals Lib Sci ... Annals of Library Science [*A publication*]
Annals and Mag Nat History ... Annals and Magazine of Natural History [*A publication*]
Annals Math Log ... Annals of Mathematical Logic [*A publication*]
Annals Occup Hyg ... Annals of Occupational Hygiene [*A publication*]
Annals Public and Coop Economy ... Annals of Public and Cooperative Economy [*A publication*]
Annaly .... Lee's English King's Bench Reports Tempore Hardwicke, Annaly Edition [*1733-38*] [*A publication*]   (DLA)
Ann Am Acad ... Annals. American Academy of Political and Social Science [*A publication*]
Ann Am Acad Poli Soc Sci ... Annals. American Academy of Political and Social Science [*A publication*]
Ann Am Acad Pol Sci ... Annals. American Academy of Political and Social Science [*A publication*]
Ann Am Acad Pol Soc Sci (Philadelphia) ... Annals. American Academy of Political and Social Science (Philadelphia) [*A publication*]
Annamalai Univ Agric Res Annu ... Annamalai University. Agricultural Research Annual [*A publication*]
Ann Am Conf Gov Ind Hyg ... American Conference of Governmental Industrial Hygienists [*A publication*]
Ann Amelior Plantes ... Annales de l'Amelioration des Plantes [*Paris*] [*A publication*]
Ann Amelior Plantes Inst Nat Rech Agron Ser B ... Annales de l'Amelioration des Plantes. Institut National de la Recherche Agronomique. Serie B [*A publication*]
Ann Amelior Plant (Paris) ... Annales de l'Amelioration des Plantes (Paris) [*A publication*]
Ann Amer Acad Polit Soc Sci ... Annals. American Academy of Political and Social Science [*A publication*]
Ann Am Poli ... Annals. American Academy of Political and Social Science [*A publication*]
Ann Anat Pathol ... Annales d'Anatomie Pathologique [*Paris*] [*A publication*]
Ann Anat Pathol Anat Norm Med Chir ... Annales d'Anatomie Pathologique et d'Anatomie Normale. Medico Chirurgicale [*A publication*]
Ann Anat Pathol (Paris) ... Annales d'Anatomie Pathologique (Paris) [*A publication*]
Ann Anesthesiol Fr ... Annales de l'Anesthesiologie Francaise [*A publication*]
Ann Anim Ps ... Annual of Animal Psychology [*A publication*]
Ann Ap Biol ... Annals of Applied Biology [*A publication*]
Ann A Plant ... Annales de l'Amelioration des Plantes [*Paris*] [*A publication*]
Ann App Biol ... Annals of Applied Biology [*A publication*]
Ann Appl Biol ... Annals of Applied Biology [*A publication*]
Ann Appl Biol Suppl ... Annals of Applied Biology. Supplement [*A publication*]
Ann Arbor Obs ... Ann Arbor Observer [*A publication*]
Ann Arch ... Annales Archeologiques [*A publication*]
Ann Archeol Syrie ... Annales Archeologiques de Syrie [*A publication*]
Ann Arid Zone ... Annals of Arid Zone [*A publication*]
Ann As Am G ... Annals. Association of American Geographers [*A publication*]
Ann Ass Amer Geogr ... Annals. Association of American Geographers [*A publication*]
Ann Ass Int Calcul Analogique ... Annales. Association Internationale pour le Calcul Analogique [*A publication*]
Ann Assn Am Geog ... Annals. Association of American Geographers [*A publication*]
Ann Assoc Belge Radioprot ... Annales. Association Belge de Radioprotection [*Belgium*] [*A publication*]
Ann Assoc Int Calcul Analogique ... Annales. Association Internationale pour le Calcul Analogique [*A publication*]
Ann Assur Sci Proc Reliab Maint Conf ... Annals of Assurance Sciences. Proceedings of Reliability and Maintainability Conference [*A publication*]
Ann A Stor Ant ... Annali. Seminario di Studi del Mondo Classico. Sezione di Archeologia e Storia Antica [*Napoli*] [*A publication*]
Ann Astrophys ... Annales d'Astrophysique [*France*] [*A publication*]
Ann Astrophys Suppl ... Annales d'Astrophysique. Supplement [*A publication*]
Ann Aust Coll Dent Surg ... Annals. Australian College of Dental Surgeons [*A publication*]
Ann Bari .... Annali. Facolta di Lettere e Filosofia. Universita di Bari [*A publication*]
Ann Bar-Il ... Annual. Bar-Ilan University Studies in Judaica and Humanities [*A publication*]
Ann Behav Med ... Annals of Behavioral Medicine [*A publication*]
Ann Belg Med Mil ... Annales Belges de Medecine Militaire [*A publication*]

Ann Belg Ver Hosp ... Annalen Belg Vereniging voor Hospitaalgeschiedenis [*A publication*]
Ann Belg Ver Trop Geneeskd ... Annales. Belgische Vereniging voor Tropische Geneeskunde [*A publication*]
Ann Belg Ver Trop Geneeskd Parasitol Mensel Dierl Mycol ... Annales. Belgische Verenigingen voor Tropische Geneeskunde voor Parasitologie en voor Menselijke en Dierlijke Mycologie [*A publication*]
Ann Benac ... Annali Benacensi [*A publication*]
AnnBhI ...... Annals. Bhandarkar Oriental Research Institute [*A publication*]
Ann Biochem Exp Med ... Annals of Biochemistry and Experimental Medicine [*Calcutta and New Delhi*] [*A publication*]
Ann Biochem Exp Med (Calcutta) ... Annals of Biochemistry and Experimental Medicine (Calcutta and New Delhi) [*A publication*]
Ann Biol..... Annales Biologiques [*A publication*]
Ann Biol An ... Annales de Biologie Animale, Biochimie, et Biophysique [*A publication*]
Ann Biol Anim Biochim Biophys ... Annales de Biologie Animale, Biochimie, et Biophysique [*A publication*]
Ann Biol Cl ... Annales de Biologie Clinique [*Paris*] [*A publication*]
Ann Biol Clin (Paris) ... Annales de Biologie Clinique (Paris) [*A publication*]
Ann Biol (Ludhiana) ... Annals of Biology (Ludhiana) [*A publication*]
Ann Biol Norm Pathol ... Annali Biologia Normale e Pathologica [*A publication*]
Ann Biomed ... Annals of Biomedical Engineering [*A publication*]
Ann Biomed Eng ... Annals of Biomedical Engineering [*A publication*]
Ann Bogor ... Annales Bogoriensis [*A publication*]
Ann Bot...... Annals of Botany [*A publication*]
Ann Bot Fenn ... Annales Botanici Fennici [*A publication*]
Ann Bot (London) ... Annals of Botany (London) [*A publication*]
Ann Bot (Rome) ... Annali di Botanica (Rome) [*A publication*]
Ann Bot Soc Zool Bot Fenn "Vanamo" ... Annales Botanici Societatis Zoologicae Botanicae Fennicae "Vanamo" [*A publication*]
AnnBourg... Annales de Bourgogne [*A publication*]
Ann Bourgogne ... Annales de Bourgogne [*A publication*]
Ann Brass Distill ... Annales de la Brasserie et de la Distillerie [*A publication*]
Ann Bret .... Annales de Bretagne [*Later, Annales de Bretagne et des Pays de l'Ouest*] [*A publication*]
Ann de Bret ... Annales de Bretagne [*Later, Annales de Bretagne et des Pays de l'Ouest*] [*A publication*]
Ann Bretagne ... Annales de Bretagne et des Pays de l'Ouest [*A publication*]
Ann Brux I ... Annales. Societe Scientifique de Bruxelles. Serie I [*A publication*]
Ann B S Arch Ath ... Annual. British School of Archaeology at Athens [*A publication*]
Ann Bull Soc R Med Gand ... Annales et Bulletin. Societe Royale de Medecine de Gand [*A publication*]
Ann Bull Soc R Sci Med Nat Bruxelles ... Annales et Bulletin. Societe Royale des Sciences Medicales et Naturelles de Bruxelles [*A publication*]
Ann Byz Conf ... Annual Byzantine Studies Conference. Abstracts of Papers [*A publication*]
Ann C .... Annals of Congress [*A publication*]   (DLA)
ANNC........ Announce   (FAAC)
Ann Cagliari ... Annali. Facolta di Lettere, Filosofia, e Magistero. Universita di Cagliari [*A publication*]
Ann Cal Codes ... West's Annotated California Codes [*A publication*]   (DLA)
Ann Cape Prov Mus ... Annals. Cape Provincial Museums [*A publication*]
Ann Cape Prov Mus Hum Sci ... Annals. Cape Provincial Museums. Human Sciences [*A publication*]
Ann Cape Prov Mus Nat Hist ... Annals. Cape Provincial Museums. Natural History [*A publication*]
Ann Card An ... Annales de Cardiologie et d'Angeiologie [*A publication*]
Ann Cardiol Angeiol ... Annales de Cardiologie et d'Angeiologie [*A publication*]
Ann Carnegie Mus ... Annals. Carnegie Museum [*A publication*]
Ann Cas ..... American Annotated Cases [*A publication*]   (DLA)
Ann Cas ..... American and English Annotated Cases [*A publication*]   (DLA)
Ann Cas ..... New York Annotated Cases [*A publication*]   (DLA)
Ann Cattedra Petrarchesca ... Annali. Cattedra Petrarchesca. Reale Accademia Petrarca di Lettere, Arti, e Scienze. Arezzo [*A publication*]
Ann Cent Enseign Super Brazzaville ... Annales. Centre d'Enseignement Superieur de Brazzaville [*A publication*]
Ann Cerc Archeol Canton Soignies ... Annales. Cercle Archeologique du Canton de Soignies [*A publication*]
Ann Cerc Archeol Enghien ... Annales. Cercle Archeologique d'Enghien [*A publication*]
Ann Cerc Archeol Mons ... Annales. Cercle Archeologique de Mons [*A publication*]
Ann Chem ... Annalen der Chemie [*Justus Liebigs*] [*A publication*]
Ann Chem (Justus Liebigs) ... Annalen der Chemie (Justus Liebigs) [*A publication*]
Ann Chim ... Annali di Chimica [*A publication*]
Ann Chim Anal ... Annales de Chimie Analytique [*A publication*]
Ann Chim Anal Chim Appl ... Annales de Chimie Analytique et de Chimie Applique et Revue de Chimie Analytique Reunies [*A publication*]
Ann Chim Anal Rev Chim Anal Reunies ... Annales de Chimie Analytique et Revue de Chimie Analytique Reunies [*A publication*]
Ann Chim Appl ... Annali di Chimica Applicata [*Italy*] [*A publication*]

Ann Chim Farm ... Annali di Chimica Farmaceutica [*A publication*]
Ann Chim (Fr) ... Annales de Chimie (Paris, France) [*A publication*]
Ann Chim (Paris) ... Annales de Chimie (Paris, France) [*A publication*]
Ann Chim Phys ... Annales de Chimie et de Physique [*A publication*]
Ann Chim (Rome) ... Annali di Chimica (Rome) [*A publication*]
Ann Chir .... Annales de Chirurgie [*A publication*]
Ann Chir Gy ... Annales Chirurgiae et Gynaecologiae Fenniae [*Helsinki*] [*A publication*]
Ann Chir Gynaecol ... Annales Chirurgiae et Gynaecologiae Fenniae [*Helsinki*] [*A publication*]
Ann Chir Gynaecol Fenn ... Annales Chirurgiae et Gynaecologiae Fenniae [*Helsinki*] [*A publication*]
Ann Chir Gynaecol Fenn Suppl ... Annales Chirurgiae et Gynaecologiae Fenniae. Supplementum [*Helsinki*] [*A publication*]
Ann Chir Gynaecol Suppl ... Annales Chirurgiae et Gynaecologiae Fenniae. Supplementum [*Helsinki*] [*A publication*]
Ann Chir In ... Annales de Chirurgie Infantile [*A publication*]
Ann Chir Infant ... Annales de Chirurgie Infantile [*A publication*]
Ann Chir Main ... Annales de Chirurgie de la Main [*A publication*]
Ann Chir (Paris) ... Annales de Chirurgie (Paris) [*A publication*]
Ann Chir Pl ... Annales de Chirurgie Plastique [*A publication*]
Ann Chir Plast ... Annales de Chirurgie Plastique [*A publication*]
Ann Chir Plast Esthetique ... Annales de Chirurgie Plastique et Esthetique [*A publication*]
Ann Chir Sem Hop ... Annales de Chirurgie. Semaine des Hopitaux [*France*] [*A publication*]
Ann Chir Thorac Cardio-Vasc ... Annales de Chirurgie Thoracique et Cardio-Vasculaire [*A publication*]
Ann CIRP .. Annals of the CIRP [*A publication*]
Ann Cisalp Hist Soc ... Annales Cisalpines d'Histoire Sociale [*A publication*]
Ann Clin Biochem ... Annals of Clinical Biochemistry [*A publication*]
Ann Clin Lab Sci ... Annals of Clinical and Laboratory Science [*A publication*]
Ann Clin Med ... Annals of Clinical Medicine [*A publication*]
Ann Clin Med Med Sper ... Annali di Clinica Medica e di Medicina Sperimentale [*A publication*]
Ann Clin R ... Annals of Clinical Research [*A publication*]
Ann Clin Res ... Annals of Clinical Research [*A publication*]
Ann Clin Res Suppl ... Annals of Clinical Research. Supplement [*A publication*]
Ann Code ... Annotated Code [*A publication*] (DLA)
Ann Codes & St ... Bellinger and Cotton's Annotated Codes and Statutes [*Oregon*] [*A publication*] (DLA)
Ann Coll Med Antwerp ... Annales Collegii Medici Antwerpiensis [*A publication*]
Ann Coll Med (Mosul) ... Annals. College of Medicine (Mosul) [*A publication*]
Ann Coll R Med Chir Can ... Annales. College Royal des Medecins et Chirurgiens du Canada [*A publication*]
Ann Compos ... Annales des Composites [*A publication*]
Ann Conf Health Inspectors NSW ... Annual Conference of Health Inspectors of New South Wales [*A publication*] (APTA)
Ann Conf Res Med Ed ... Annual Conference on Research in Medical Education [*A publication*]
Ann Cong ... Annals of Congress [*A publication*] (DLA)
Ann Congr Federation Archeol Hist Belg ... Annales. Congres de la Federation Archeologique et Historique de Belgique [*A publication*]
Ann Corp Prof Comp Gen Lic Quebec ... Annuaire. Corporation Professionnelle des Comptables Generaux Licencies du Quebec [*A publication*]
ANNCR ..... Announcer
Ann Cryptogam Exot ... Annales de Cryptogamie Exotique [*A publication*]
Ann Cryptogam Phytopathol ... Annales Cryptogamici et Phytopathologici [*A publication*]
Ann D A (J) ... Annual. Department of Antiquities (Jordan) [*A publication*]
Ann Dakar Univ Fac Sci ... Annales. Dakar Universite. Faculte des Sciences [*A publication*]
Ann Dem Hist ... Annales de Demographie Historique [*A publication*]
Ann Demogr Hist ... Annales de Demographie Historique [*A publication*]
Ann Dent ... Annals of Dentistry [*A publication*]
Ann Dermatol Syphiligr ... Annales de Dermatologie et de Syphiligraphie [*Later, Annales de Dermatologie et de Venereologie*] [*A publication*]
Ann Dermatol Venereol ... Annales de Dermatologie et de Venereologie [*A publication*]
Ann Der Syp ... Annales de Dermatologie et de Syphiligraphie [*Later, Annales de Dermatologie et de Venereologie*] [*A publication*]
Ann Dev ..... Annals of Development [*A publication*]
Ann Dig ...... Annual Digest and Reports of Public International Law Cases [*A publication*] (DLA)
Ann Dig ILC ... Annual Digest and Reports of Public International Law Cases [*A publication*] (DLA)
Ann Dir Comp ... Annuario di Diritto Comparato e di Studi Legislativi [*A publication*]
Ann Dir Etud Equip Ser Exploit Ind Tab Allumettes Sec 1 ... Annales. Direction des Etudes et de l'Equipement. Service d'Exploitation Industrielle des Tabacs et des Allumettes. Section 1 [*A publication*]
Ann Dir Etud Equip Serv Exploit Ind Tab Allumettes Sec 2 ... Annales. Direction des Etudes et de l'Equipement. Service d'Exploitation Industrielle des Tabacs et des Allumettes. Section 2 [*A publication*]

Ann Dir Int ... Annali di Diritto Internazionale [*Milan*] [*A publication*] (DLA)
Ann Discrete Math ... Annals of Discrete Mathematics [*A publication*]
Ann Dog Watch ... Annual Dog Watch [*A publication*] (APTA)
Ann Dr .... Annales de Droit [*A publication*]
Ann Dr Com Fr Etr Int ... Annales de Droit Commercial Francais, Etranger, et International [*A publication*] (DLA)
Ann Dr Com Ind Fr Etr ... Annales de Droit Commercial et Industriel Francais, Etranger, et International [*A publication*] (DLA)
Ann de Droit ... Annales de Droit. Revue Trimestrielle de Droit Belge [*A publication*]
Ann de Droit Internat Med ... Annales de Droit International Medical [*A publication*]
Ann Droit Int Med ... Annales de Droit International Medical [*A publication*]
Ann Dr Sc Pol ... Annales de Droit et de Sciences Politiques. Revue Trimestrielle [*Brussels*] [*A publication*]
Ann Dr Sc Polit ... Annales de Droit et de Sciences Politiques [*A publication*]
AnNE .... Anthology of New England Poets [*A publication*]
Anne .... Queen Anne (DLA)
Ann Ec Fr Dr Beyrouth ... Annales. Faculte de Droit. Ecole Francaise de Droit de Beyrouth [*A publication*]
Ann Ec Natl Eaux For Stn Rech Exper For ... Annales. Ecole Nationale des Eaux et Forets et de la Station de Recherches et Experiences Forestieres [*A publication*]
Ann Ec Natl Super Agron (Montpellier) ... Annales. Ecole Nationale Superieure Agronomique (Montpellier) [*A publication*]
Ann Ecole Nat Agr Alger ... Annales. Ecole Nationale d'Agriculture d'Alger [*A publication*]
Ann Ecole Nat Super Agron ... Annales. Ecole Nationale Superieure Agronomique [*A publication*]
Ann Ecole Nat Sup Mec (Nantes) ... Annales. Ecole Nationale Superieure de Mecanique (Nantes) [*A publication*]
Ann Econ ... Annales de Droit Economique [*A publication*] (DLA)
Ann Econ ... Annales Economiques [*A publication*] (DLA)
Ann Econ Sm ... Annals of Economic and Social Measurement [*A publication*]
Ann Econ So ... Annales d'Economie et de Sociologie Rurales [*A publication*]
Ann Econ Soc Civ ... Annales: Economies, Societes, Civilisations [*A publication*]
Ann Econ Soc Civilis ... Annales: Economies, Societes, Civilisations [*A publication*]
Ann Ec Prat HEt ... Annuaire. Ecole Pratique des Hautes Etudes, IVeme Section [*A publication*]
Ann Ec Super Sci Inst Hautes Etud (Dakar) ... Annales. Ecole Superieure des Sciences. Institut des Hautes Etudes (Dakar) [*A publication*]
Ann Ed Read Educ ... Annual Editions. Readings in Education [*A publication*]
Ann Ed Read Soc ... Annual Editions. Readings in Sociology [*A publication*]
Annee Afr ... Annee Africaine [*A publication*]
Annee Agr ... Annee Agricole [*A publication*]
Annee Biol ... Annee Biologique [*A publication*]
Annee Biol (Paris) ... Annee Biologique (Paris) [*A publication*]
Annee Endocrinol ... Annee Endocrinologique [*A publication*]
Annee Med ... Annee Medicale [*A publication*]
Annee Pedagog ... Annee Pedagogique [*A publication*]
Annee Phil ... Annee Philosophique [*A publication*]
Annee Polit Econ ... Annee Politique et Economique [*A publication*]
Annee Psychol ... Annee Psychologique [*A publication*]
Annee Sociol ... Annee Sociologique [*A publication*]
Annee Ther Clin Ophtalmol ... Annee Therapeutique et Clinique en Ophtalmologie [*A publication*]
Ann Eg Bibl ... Annual Egyptological Bibliography [*A publication*]
Ann Egypt Bib ... Annual Egyptological Bibliography [*A publication*]
Ann Embryol Morphog ... Annales d'Embryologie et de Morphogenese [*A publication*]
Ann Emerg Med ... Annals of Emergency Medicine [*A publication*]
Ann Endocr ... Annales d'Endocrinologie [*Paris*] [*A publication*]
Ann Endocrinol ... Annales d'Endocrinologie [*Paris*] [*A publication*]
Ann Endocrinol (Paris) ... Annales d'Endocrinologie (Paris) [*A publication*]
Ann Ent Fenn ... Annales Entomologici Fennici [*A publication*]
Ann Entomol Fenn ... Annales Entomologici Fennici [*A publication*]
Ann Entomol Soc Am ... Annals. Entomological Society of America [*A publication*]
Ann Entomol Soc Que ... Annals. Entomological Society of Quebec [*A publication*]
Ann Entom Soc Am ... Annals. Entomological Society of America [*A publication*]
Ann Ent S A ... Annals. Entomological Society of America [*A publication*]
Ann Ent Soc Am ... Annals. Entomological Society of America [*A publication*]
Ann Ent Soc Queb ... Annals. Entomological Society of Quebec [*A publication*]
AnnEp .... L'Annee Epigraphique [*A publication*]
Ann Epigr ... Annee Epigraphique [*A publication*]
Ann Epiphyt ... Annales des Epiphyties [*Paris*] [*A publication*]
Ann Epiphyt (Paris) ... Annales des Epiphyties (Paris) [*A publication*]
Ann Epiphyt Phytogenet ... Annales des Epiphyties et de Phytogenetique [*Paris*] [*A publication*]
Ann ESC .... Annales. Economies, Societes, Civilisations [*A publication*]
Ann Est ...... Annales de l'Est [*A publication*]
Ann Esth ...... Annales d'Esthetique [*A publication*]
AnnEth ...... Annales d'Ethiopie [*A publication*]
Ann Eugen ... Annals of Eugenics [*A publication*]

Ann Eur ..... Annuaire Europeen [*A publication*]
Ann Exp For ... Annales pro Experimentis Foresticis [*A publication*]
Ann Fac Agrar Portici Regia Univ Napoli ... Annali. Facolta di Agraria de Portici. Regia Universita di Napoli [*A publication*]
Ann Fac Agrar Univ Bari ... Annali. Facolta di Agraria. Universita di Bari [*A publication*]
Ann Fac Agrar Univ Catt Sacro Cuore ... Annali. Facolta di Agraria. Universita Cattolica del Sacro Cuore [*A publication*]
Ann Fac Agrar Univ Pisa ... Annali. Facolta di Agraria. Universita di Pisa [*A publication*]
Ann Fac Agrar Univ Studi Milano ... Annali. Facolta di Agraria. Universita degli Studi di Milano [*A publication*]
Ann Fac Agrar Univ Stud Perugia ... Annali. Facolta di Agraria. Universita degli Studi di Perugia [*A publication*]
Ann Fac Agr (Perugia) ... Annali. Facolta di Agraria (Perugia) [*A publication*]
Ann Fac Agr Univ Cattol Sacro Cuore (Milan) ... Annali. Facolta di Agraria. Universita Cattolica del Sacro Cuore (Milan) [*A publication*]
Ann Fac Agr Univ Pisa ... Annali. Facolta di Agraria. Universita di Pisa [*A publication*]
Ann Fac Agr Univ Studii Perugia ... Annali. Facolta di Agraria. Universita degli Studi di Perugia [*A publication*]
Ann Fac Bari ... Annali. Facolta di Giurisprudenza. Universita di Bari [*A publication*] (DLA)
Ann Fac Beyrouth ... Annales. Faculte de Droit et des Sciences Economiques de Beyrouth. Faculte de Droit [*A publication*] (DLA)
Ann Fac Dr L ... Annales. Faculte de Droit de Liege [*A publication*] (DLA)
Ann de la Fac de Droit d'Istanbul ... Annales. Faculte de Droit d'Istanbul [*Istanbul, Turkey*] [*A publication*]
Ann de la Fac de Droit de Liege ... Annales. Faculte de Droit de Liege [*Liege, Belgium*] [*A publication*]
Ann de la Fac de Droit et des Sci Econ (Beyrouth) ... Annales. Faculte de Droit et des Sciences Economiques [*Beyrouth, Lebanon*] [*A publication*] (DLA)
Ann de la Fac de Droit et des Sci Econ de Lille ... Annales. Faculte de Droit et des Sciences Economiques de Lille, France [*A publication*] (DLA)
Ann Fac Econ Commer Univ Bari ... Annali. Facolta di Economia e Commercio. Universita di Bari [*A publication*]
Ann Fac Econ Commer Univ Studi Mesina ... Annali. Facolta di Economia e Commercio. Universita degli Studi di Messina [*A publication*]
Ann Fac Istanbul ... Annales. Faculte de Droit d'Istanbul [*A publication*]
Ann Fac Lett Filosof ... Annali. Facolta di Lettere e Filosofia [*A publication*]
Ann Fac Lett Filos Univ Padova ... Annali. Facolta di Lettere e Filosofia. Universita di Padova [*A publication*]
Ann Fac Liege ... Annales. Faculte de Droit de Liege [*A publication*]
Ann Fac Lyon ... Annales. Faculte de Droit et des Sciences Economiques de Lyon [*A publication*] (DLA)
Ann Fac Med Chir Univ Studi Perugia Atti Accad Anat Chir ... Annali. Facolta di Medicina e Chirurgia. Universita degli Studi di Perugia che Pubblicano gli Atti della Accademia Anatomico-Chirurgica [*A publication*]
Ann Fac Med Chirurg ... Annali. Facolta di Medicina e Chirurgia [*A publication*]
Ann Fac Med S Paulo ... Annales. Faculdade de Medicina de Sao Paulo [*A publication*]
Ann Fac Med Vet Torino ... Annali. Facolta di Medicina Veterinaria die Torino [*A publication*]
Ann Fac Med Vet Univ Pisa ... Annali. Facolta di Medicina Veterinaria. Universita di Pisa [*Italy*] [*A publication*]
Ann Fac Med Vet Univ Studi Pisa ... Annali. Facolta di Medicina Veterinaria. Universita degli Studi di Pisa [*A publication*]
Ann Fac Med Vet Univ Torino ... Annali. Facolta di Medicina Veterinaria. Universita di Torino [*A publication*]
Ann Fac Sci Agrar Napoli Portici ... Annali. Facolta di Scienze Agrarie. Universita degli Studi di Napoli Portici [*A publication*]
Ann Fac Sci Agrar Univ Palermo ... Annali. Facolta di Scienze Agrarie. Universita di Palermo [*A publication*]
Ann Fac Sci Agrar Univ Studi Napoli Portici ... Annali. Facolta di Scienze Agrarie. Universita degli Studi di Napoli Portici [*A publication*]
Ann Fac Sci Agrar Univ Studi Torino ... Annali. Facolta di Scienze Agrarie. Universita degli Studi di Torino [*A publication*]
Ann Fac Sci Agr Univ Napoli Ser 3 ... Annali. Facolta di Scienze Agrarie. Universita di Napoli. Serie 3 [*A publication*]
Ann Fac Sci Agr Univ Stud Napoli Portici ... Annali. Facolta di Scienze Agrarie. Universita degli Studi di Napoli Portici [*A publication*]
Ann Fac Sci Agr Univ Torino ... Annali. Facolta di Scienze Agrarie. Universita di Torino [*A publication*]
Ann Fac Sci Cameroun ... Annales. Faculte des Sciences du Cameroun [*A publication*]
Ann Fac Sci Mars ... Annales. Faculte des Sciences de Marseille [*A publication*]
Ann Fac Sci Marseille ... Annales. Faculte des Sciences de Marseille [*A publication*]
Ann Fac Sci Sect Biol Chim Sci Terre (Univ Natl Zaire) ... Annales. Faculte des Sciences. Section Biologie, Chimie, et Sciences de la Terre (Universite Nationale du Zaire) [*A publication*]

Ann Fac Sci Toulouse Math ... Annales. Faculte des Sciences de Toulouse. Mathematiques [*A publication*]
Ann Fac Sci Toulouse Math Ser 5 ... Toulouse. Faculte des Sciences. Annales Mathematiques. Serie 5 [*A publication*]
Ann Fac Sci Univ Clermont ... Annales. Faculte des Sciences. Universite de Clermont [*A publication*]
Ann Fac Sci Univ Clermont Ser Biol Anim ... Annales. Faculte des Sciences. Universite de Clermont. Serie Biologie Animale [*A publication*]
Ann Fac Sci Univ Dakar ... Annales. Faculte des Sciences. Universite de Dakar [*A publication*]
Ann Fac Sci Univ Nat Zaire (Kinshasa) Sect Math-Phys ... Annales. Faculte des Sciences. Universite Nationale du Zaire (Kinshasa). Sect ion Mathematique-Physique [*A publication*]
Ann Fac Sci Univ Toulouse ... Annales. Faculte des Sciences. Universite de Toulouse [*A publication*]
Ann Fac Sci Univ Yaounde Ser 3 ... Annales. Faculte des Sciences. Universite de Yaounde. Serie 3. Biologie-Biochimie [*A publication*]
Ann Fac Sci Yaounde ... Annales. Faculte des Sciences. Universite de Yaounde [*A publication*]
Ann Fals Expert Chim ... Annales des Falsifications et de l'Expertise Chimique [*Later, Annales des Falsifications et de l'Expertise Chimique et Toxicologique*] [*France*] [*A publication*]
Ann Falsif Expert Chim ... Annales des Falsifications et de l'Expertise Chimique [*Later, Annales des Falsifications et dde l'Expertise Chimique et Toxicologique*] [*A publication*]
Ann Falsif Expert Chim Toxicol ... Annales des Falsifications et de l'Expertise Chimique et Toxicologique [*A publication*]
Ann Falsif Expertise Chim ... Annales des Falsifications et de l'Expertise Chimique [*Later, Annales des Falsifications et de l'Expertise Chimique et Toxicologique*] [*A publication*]
Ann Falsif Fraudes ... Annales des Falsifications et des Fraudes [*Later, Annales des Falsifications et de l'Expertise Chimique*] [*A publication*]
Ann Ferment ... Annales des Fermentations [*A publication*]
Ann Fis ...... Annali di Fisica [*A publication*]
Ann Fitopatol ... Annali di Fitopatologia [*A publication*]
Ann Fogg ... Annual Report. Fogg Art Museum [*A publication*]
Ann Fond Louis Broglie ... Annales. Fondation Louis de Broglie [*France*] [*A publication*]
Ann Fond Louis de Broglie ... Annales. Fondation Louis de Broglie [*A publication*]
Ann Food Technol Chem ... Annals. Food Technology and Chemistry [*A publication*]
Ann For (Zagreb) ... Annales Forestales (Zagreb) [*A publication*]
Ann Fr Anesth Reanim ... Annales Francaises d'Anesthesie et de Reanimation [*A publication*]
Ann Fr Chronom ... Annales Francaises de Chronometrie [*A publication*]
Ann Fr Chronom Micromec ... Annales Francaises de Chronometrie et de Micromecanique [*Later, Annales Francaises des Microtechniques et de Chronolmetrie*] [*A publication*]
Ann Fr Microtech et Chronom ... Annales Francaises des Microtechniques et de Chronometrie [*A publication*]
Ann Gastro ... Annales de Gastroenterologie et d'Hepatologie [*A publication*]
Ann Gastroenterol Hepatol ... Annales de Gastroenterologie et d'Hepatologie [*A publication*]
Ann Gembloux ... Annales de Gembloux [*A publication*]
Ann Genet ... Annales de Genetique [*A publication*]
Ann Genet Sel Anim ... Annales de Genetique et de Selection Animale [*A publication*]
Ann Genie Chimie ... Annales du Genie Chimique [*A publication*]
Ann Gen Pract ... Annals of General Practice [*A publication*]
Ann Geofis ... Annali di Geofisica [*A publication*]
Ann Geog ... Annales de Geographie [*A publication*]
Ann Geogr ... Annales de Geographie [*A publication*]
Ann Geol Madagascar ... Annales Geologiques de Madagascar [*A publication*]
Ann Geol Opname Repub S Afr ... Annale van Geologiese Opname. Republiek van Suid-Afrika [*A publication*]
Ann Geol Pays Hell ... Annales Geologiques des Pays Helleniques [*A publication*]
Ann Geol Peninsule Balk ... Annales Geologiques de la Peninsule Balkanique [*A publication*]
Ann Geol Serv Mines (Madagascar) ... Annales Geologiques. Service des Mines (Madagascar) [*A publication*]
Ann Geol Surv ... Annals. Geological Survey [*A publication*]
Ann Geol Surv Egypt ... Annals. Geological Survey of Egypt [*A publication*]
Ann Geol Surv S Afr ... Annals. Geological Survey of South Africa [*A publication*]
Ann Geophy ... Annales de Geophysique [*A publication*]
Ann Geophys ... Annales de Geophysique [*A publication*]
Ann Geophys Ser A ... Annales Geophysicae. Series A. Upper Atmosphere and Space Sciences [*A publication*]
Ann Gifu College Ed ... Gifu College of Education. Annals [*A publication*]
ANNGS ..... Ad Novas. Norwegian Geographical Studies [*A publication*]
Ann Guebhard ... Annales Guebhard [*A publication*]
Ann Guebhard Severine ... Annales Guebhard Severine [*A publication*]
Ann Gynaec Pediat ... Annals of Gynaecology and Pediatry [*A publication*]
Ann Hebert Haug ... Annales. Hebert et Haug [*A publication*]
Ann Heb Union Coll ... Annals. Hebrew Union College [*A publication*]

Ann Hist A Lor ... Annuaire. Societe d'Histoire et d'Archeologie de la Lorraine [*A publication*]

Ann Hist Comput ... Annals of the History of Computing [*A publication*]

Ann Hist-Nat Mus Natl Hung ... Annales Historico-Naturales. Musei Nationalis Hungarici [*A publication*]

Ann Hist Natur Mus Nat Hung Pars Zool ... Annales Historico-Naturales. Musei Nationalis Hungarici. Pars Zoologica [*A publication*]

Ann Histoch ... Annales d'Histochimie [*A publication*]

Ann Histochim ... Annales d'Histochimie [*A publication*]

Ann Hist R ... Annales Historiques de la Revolution Francaise [*A publication*]

Ann Hitotsubashi Acad ... Annals. Hitotsubashi Academy [*A publication*] (DLA)

AnnHL....... Annuaire d'Histoire Liegeoise [*A publication*]

Ann Homeopath Fr ... Annales Homeopathiques Francaises [*A publication*]

Ann Human Genetics ... Annals of Human Genetics [*A publication*]

Ann Hum Bio ... Annals of Human Biology [*A publication*]

Ann Hum Gen ... Annals of Human Genetics [*A publication*]

Ann Hum Genet ... Annals of Human Genetics [*A publication*]

Ann Hydrob ... Annales d'Hydrobiologie [*A publication*]

Ann Hydrobiol ... Annales d'Hydrobiologie [*A publication*]

Ann Hydrogr ... Annales Hydrographiques [*A publication*]

Ann Hydrogr Marit Meteorol ... Annales. Hydrographie und Maritimen Meteorologie [*A publication*]

Ann Hyg Lang Fr Med Nutr ... Annales d'Hygiene de Langue Francaise. Medecine et Nutrition [*A publication*]

Ann Hyg et Med Colon ... Annales d'Hygiene et de Medecine Coloniales [*A publication*]

Ann Hyg Publique Ind Soc ... Annales d'Hygiene Publique. Industrielle et Sociale [*A publication*]

Ann Hyg Pub et Med Legale ... Annales d'Hygiene Publique et de Medecine Legale [*A publication*]

Ann IA .... Annals of Iowa [*A publication*]

Ann ICRP .. Annals. ICRP [*International Commission on Radiological Protection*] [*A publication*]

Ann Idrol ... Annali Idrologici [*A publication*]

AnnIEO ..... Annales. Institut d'Etudes Orientales. Faculte des Lettres d'Alger [*A publication*]

AnnIEOc ... Annales. Institut d'Etudes Occidentes [*A publication*]

Ann I Four ... Annales. Institut Fourier [*A publication*]

Ann Ig .... Annali d'Igiene [*A publication*]

Ann Ig Sper ... Annali d'Igiene. Sperimentali [*A publication*]

Ann I Hen A ... Annales. Institut Henri Poincare. Section A. Physique Theorique [*A publication*]

Ann I Hen B ... Annales. Institut Henri Poincare. Section B. Calcul des Probabilites et Statistique [*A publication*]

Ann Immunol ... Annales d'Immunologie [*A publication*]

Ann Immunol Hung ... Annales Immunologiae Hungaricae [*A publication*]

Ann Immunol (Paris) ... Annales d'Immunologie (Paris) [*A publication*]

Ann Indian Acad Med Sci ... Annals. Indian Academy of Medical Sciences [*A publication*]

Ann Ind Prop L ... Annual of Industrial Property Law [*A publication*]

Ann Indus Prop L ... Annual of Industrial Property Law [*A publication*]

Ann Ins ...... Annesley on Insurance [*A publication*] (DLA)

Ann INSEE ... Annales. INSEE [*Institut National de la Statistique et des Etudes Economiques*] [*A publication*]

Ann Inst ..... Annales Institutorum [*A publication*]

Ann Inst Agric Serv Rech Exp Agric Alger ... Annales. Institut Agricole et Services de Recherche et d'Experimentation Agricoles de l'Algerie [*A publication*]

Ann Inst Archeol Luxemb ... Annales. Institut Archeologique du Luxembourg [*A publication*]

Ann Inst Belge Petrol ... Annales. Institut Belge du Petrole [*A publication*]

Ann Inst Biol (Tihany) Hung ... Annales. Instituti Biologici (Tihany). Hungaricae Academiae Scientiarum [*A publication*]

Ann Inst Biol (Tihany) Hung Acad Sci ... Annales. Instituti Biologici (Tihany). Hungaricae Academiae Scientiarum [*A publication*]

Ann Inst Cent Ampelol R Hong ... Annales. Institut Central Ampelologique Royal Hongrois [*A publication*]

Ann Inst Child Health (Calcutta) ... Annals. Institute of Child Health (Calcutta) [*A publication*]

Ann Inst Dr Int ... Annuaire. Institut de Droit International [*A publication*]

Ann Inst Etud Orient Univ Alger ... Annales. Institut d'Etudes Orientales. Universite d'Alger [*A publication*]

Ann Inst Exp Tabac Bergerac ... Annales. Institut Experimental du Tabac de Bergerac [*A publication*]

Ann Inst Fourier ... Annales. Institut Fourier [*A publication*]

Ann Inst Fourier (Grenoble) ... Annales. Institut Fourier (Grenoble) [*A publication*]

Ann Inst Fourier Univ Grenoble ... Annales. Institut Fourier. Universite de Grenoble [*France*] [*A publication*]

Ann Inst Geol Publ Hung ... Annales. Instituti Geologici Publici Hungarici [*A publication*]

Ann Inst Henri Poincare ... Annales. Institut Henri Poincare [*A publication*]

Ann Inst Henri Poincare A ... Annales. Institut Henri Poincare. Section A. Physique Theorique [*A publication*]

Ann Inst Henri Poincare B ... Annales. Institut Henri Poincare. Section B. Calcul des Probabilites et Statistique [*A publication*]

Ann Inst Henri Poincare Sect A ... Annales. Institut Henri Poincare. Section A. Physique Theorique [*A publication*]

Ann Inst Henri Poincare Sect B ... Annales. Institut Henri Poincare. Section B. Calcul des Probabilites et Statistique [*France*] [*A publication*]

Ann Inst H Poincare Sect A ... Annales. Institut Henri Poincare. Section A [*A publication*]

Ann Inst H Poincare Sect A NS ... Annales. Institut Henri Poincare. Section A. Physique Theorique. Nouvelle Serie [*A publication*]

Ann Inst H Poincare Sect B ... Annales. Institut Henri Poincare. Section B [*A publication*]

Ann Inst H Poincare Sect B NS ... Annales. Institut Henri Poincare. Section B. Nouvelle Serie [*A publication*]

Ann Inst Hydrol Climatol ... Annales. Institut d'Hydrologie et de Climatologie [*A publication*]

Ann Inst Michel Pacha ... Annales. Institut Michel Pacha [*A publication*]

Ann Inst Nat Agron ... Annales. Institut National Agronomique [*Paris*] [*A publication*]

Ann Inst Natl Agron ... Annales. Institut National Agronomique [*Paris*] [*A publication*]

Ann Inst Natl Rech A ... Annales. Institut National de la Recherche Agronomique de Tunisie [*A publication*]

Ann Inst Natl Rech Agron Ser A ... Annales. Institut National de la Recherche Agronomique. Serie A. Annales Agronomiques [*A publication*]

Ann Inst Natl Rech Agron Ser B ... Annales. Institut National de la Recherche Agronomique. Serie B. Annales de l'Amelioration des Plantes [*A publication*]

Ann Inst Natl Rech Agron Ser C ... Annales. Institut National de la Recherche Agronomique. Serie C. Annales des Epiphyties [*A publication*]

Ann Inst Natl Rech Agron Ser C Ann Epiphyt ... Annales. Institut National de la Recherche Agronomique. Serie C. Annales des Epiphyties [*A publication*]

Ann Inst Natl Rech Agron Ser D ... Annales. Institut National de la Recherche Agronomique. Serie D. Annales de Zootechnie [*A publication*]

Ann Inst Natl Rech Agron Ser D Ann Zootech ... Annales. Institut National de la Recherche Agronomique. Serie D. Annales de Zootechnie [*A publication*]

Ann Inst Natl Rech Agron Ser E ... Annales. Institut National de la Recherche Agronomique. Serie E. Annales de Technologie Agricole [*A publication*]

Ann Inst Natl Rech Agron Ser E Ann Technol Agric ... Annales. Institut National de la Recherche Agronomique. Serie E. Annales de Technologie Agricole [*A publication*]

Ann Inst Natl Rech Agron Tunis ... Annales. Institut National de la Recherche Agronomique de Tunisie [*A publication*]

Ann Inst Nat Rech For Tunis ... Annales. Institut National de Recherches Forestieres de Tunisie [*A publication*]

Ann Inst Oceanogr ... Annales. Institut Oceanographique [*A publication*]

Ann Inst Pasteur ... Annales. Institut Pasteur [*A publication*]

Ann Inst Pasteur Immunol ... Annales. Institut Pasteur. Immunologie [*A publication*]

Ann Inst Pasteur Lille ... Annales. Institut Pasteur de Lille [*A publication*]

Ann Inst Pasteur Microbiol ... Annales. Institut Pasteur. Microbiologie [*A publication*]

Ann Inst Pasteur (Paris) ... Annales. Institut Pasteur (Paris) [*A publication*]

Ann Inst Phys Globe Univ Paris Bur Cent Magn Terr ... Annales. Institut de Physique du Globe. Universite de Paris et Bureau Central de Magnetisme Terrestre [*A publication*]

Ann Inst Phytopathol Benaki ... Annales. Institut Phytopathologique Benaki [*A publication*]

Ann Inst Poincare Sect A ... Annales. Institut Henri Poincare. Section A. Physique Theorique [*A publication*]

Ann Inst Poincare Sect B ... Annales. Institut Henri Poincare. Section B. Calcul des Probabilites et Statistique [*A publication*]

Ann Inst Statist Math ... Annals. Institute of Statistical Mathematics [*A publication*]

Ann Inst Super Phil Univ Cath Louvain ... Annales. Institut Superieur de Philosophie. Universite Catholique de Louvain [*A publication*]

Ann Inst Tech Batim Trav Publics ... Annales. Institut Technique du Batiment et des Travaux Publics [*A publication*]

Ann Inter Comm Radiol Prot ... Annals. International Commission of Radiological Protection [*A publication*]

Ann Internat Criminologie ... Annales Internationales de Criminologie [*A publication*]

Ann Intern Med ... Annals of Internal Medicine [*A publication*]

Ann Int Geophys Year ... Annals of the International Geophysical Year [*A publication*]

Ann Int Med ... Annals of Internal Medicine [*A publication*]

Ann I Ocean ... Annales. Institut Oceanographique [*A publication*]

AnnION ..... Annali. Istituto Universitario Orientale (Napoli) [*A publication*]

Ann Iowa .... Annals of Iowa [*A publication*]

AnnIPhO ... Annuaire. Institut de Philologie et d'Histoire Orientales et Slaves [*Bruxelles*] [*A publication*]

Ann IQSY ... Annals of the IQSY [*International Quiet Sun Year*] [*A publication*]

Ann Isnardi Auxol Norm Patol ... Annali Isnardi di Auxologia Normale e Patologica [*A publication*]

Ann Israel Phys Soc ... Annals. Israel Physical Society [*A publication*]

Ann Isr Phys Soc ... Annals. Israel Physical Society [*A publication*]
Ann Ist .... Annali. Istituto di Corrispondenza Archeologica [*A publication*] (OCD)
Ann I Stat .. Annals. Institute of Statistical Mathematics [*A publication*]
Ann Ist Carlo Forlanini ... Annali. Istituto Carlo Forlanini [*A publication*]
Ann Ist It Num ... Annali. Istituto Italiano di Numismatica [*A publication*]
Ann Ist Mus Stor ... Annali. Istituto e Museo di Storia della Scienza di Firenze [*A publication*]
Ann Ist Orient Napoli ... Annali. Istituto Orientale di Napoli [*A publication*]
Ann Ist Sper Agron ... Annali. Istituto Sperimentale Agronomico [*A publication*]
Ann Ist Sper Asses For Alpic ... Annali. Istituto Sperimentale per l'Assestamento Forestale e per l'Alpicoltura [*A publication*]
Ann Ist Sper Assestamento For Apic ... Annali. Istituto Sperimentale per l'Assestamento Forestale e per l'Apicoltura [*A publication*]
Ann Ist Sper Cereal ... Annali. Istituto Sperimentale per la Cerealicoltura [*A publication*]
Ann Ist Sper Cerealic ... Annali. Istituto Sperimentale per la Cerealicoltura [*A publication*]
Ann Ist Sper Colt Foraggere ... Annali. Istituto Sperimentale per le Colture Foraggere [*A publication*]
Ann Ist Sper Colt Ind ... Annali. Istituto Sperimentale per le Colture Industriali [*A publication*]
Ann Ist Sper Enol (Asti) ... Annali. Istituto Sperimentale per l'Enologia (Asti) [*A publication*]
Ann Ist Sper Flori ... Annali. Istituto Sperimentale per la Floricoltura [*A publication*]
Ann Ist Sper Floricolt ... Annali. Istituto Sperimentale per la Floricoltura [*A publication*]
Ann Ist Sper Fruttic ... Annali. Istituto Sperimentale per la Frutticoltura [*A publication*]
Ann Ist Sper Frutticolt ... Annali. Istituto Sperimentale per la Frutticoltura [*A publication*]
Ann Ist Sper Nutr Piante ... Annali. Istituto Sperimentale per la Nutrizione delle Piante [*A publication*]
Ann Ist Sper Selvi ... Annali. Istituto Sperimentale per la Selvicoltura [*A publication*]
Ann Ist Sper Selvic ... Annali. Istituto Sperimentale per la Selvicoltura [*A publication*]
Ann Ist Sper Stud Dif Suolo ... Annali. Istituto Sperimentale per lo Studio e la Difesa del Suolo [*A publication*]
Ann Ist Sper Tab .. Annali. Istituto Sperimentale per il Tabacco [*A publication*]
Ann Ist Sper Vitic (Conegliano Italy) ... Annali. Istituto Sperimentale per la Viticoltura (Conegliano, Italy) [*A publication*]
Ann Ist Sper Zool Agrar ... Annali. Istituto Sperimentale per la Zoologia Agraria [*A publication*]
Ann Ist Sper Zootec ... Annali. Istituto Sperimentale per la Zootecnia [*A publication*]
Ann Ist Sper Zootec Roma ... Annali. Istituto Sperimentale Zootecnico di Roma [*A publication*]
Ann Ist Super Sanita ... Annali. Istituto Superiore di Sanita [*A publication*]
Ann Ital Chir ... Annali Italiani di Chirurgia [*A publication*]
Ann Ital Dermatol Clin Sper ... Annali Italiani di Dermatologia Clinica e Sperimentale [*A publication*]
Ann Ital Dermatol Sifilol ... Annali Italiani di Dermatologia e Sifilologia [*A publication*]
Ann Ital Pediatr ... Annali Italiani di Pediatria [*A publication*]
ANNIV ...... Anniversary
Anniv Bull Chuo Univ ... Anniversary Bulletin. Chuo University [*A publication*]
Ann Japan Assoc Philos Sci ... Annals. Japan Association for Philosophy of Science [*A publication*]
Ann J Kerou ... Annals. Jack Kerouac School of Disembodied Poetics [*A publication*]
Ann JP .... Annales des Justices de Paix [*France*] [*A publication*] (DLA)
Ann Jpn Assoc Philos Sci ... Annals. Japan Association for Philosophy of Science [*A publication*]
Ann Jud ..... Annuaire Judiciaire. [*A publication*] (DLA)
Ann Kinesither ... Annales de Kinesitherapie [*A publication*]
Ann Kurashiki Cent Hosp ... Annals. Kurashiki Central Hospital [*A publication*]
Ann KY Nat Hist ... Annals of Kentucky Natural History [*A publication*]
ANNL .... Annual ·(ROG)
Ann Laringol ... Annali di Laringologia, Otologia, Rinologia, Laringologia [*A publication*]
Ann Laringol Otol Rinol Laringol ... Annali di Laringologia, Otologia, Rinologia, Laringologia [*A publication*]
AnnLat .... Annali Lateranensi [*A publication*]
Ann Lav Pubblici ... Annali dei Lavori Pubblici [*A publication*]
Ann Law Dig ... Annual Law Digest [*A publication*]
Ann Law Reg ... Annual Law Register of the United States [*A publication*]
Ann Law Review ... Annual Law Review [*Australia*] [*A publication*]
Ann Lecce .. Annali. Universita di Lecce. Facolta di Lettere e Filosofia e di Magistero [*A publication*]
Ann Leeds Un Or Soc ... Annual. Leeds University Oriental Society [*A publication*]
Ann de Leg ... Annuaire de Legislation Francaise et Etrangere [*A publication*] (DLA)
Ann Leg Bibliog ... Annual Legal Bibliography [*Harvard Law School Library*] [*A publication*] (DLA)

Ann Leg Forms Mag ... Annotated Legal Forms Magazine [*A publication*]
Ann Leg Fr ... Annuaire de Legislation Francaise [*A publication*] (DLA)
Ann Leg Fr Etr ... Annuaire de Legislation Francaise et Etrangere [*A publication*]
Ann Libr Sci ... Annals of Library Science and Documentation [*A publication*]
Ann Libr Sci Docum ... Annals of Library Science and Documentation [*A publication*]
Ann Life Ins Med ... Annals of Life Insurance Medicine [*A publication*]
Ann Limnol ... Annales de Limnologie [*A publication*]
Ann Liv ...... Annals of Archaeology and Anthropology (Liverpool) [*A publication*]
Annln Naturh Mus Wien ... Annalen des Naturhistorischen Museums in Wien [*A publication*]
Ann L Reg US ... Annual Law Register of the United States [*A publication*] (DLA)
Ann L Rep ... Annotated Law Reporter [*1932-35*] [*India*] [*A publication*] (DLA)
Annls Abeille ... Annales de l'Abeille [*A publication*]
Annls Agric Fenn ... Annales Agriculturae Fenniae [*A publication*]
Annls Agric Fenniae ... Annales Agriculturae Fenniae [*A publication*]
Annls Agron ... Annales Agronomiques [*A publication*]
Annls Amel Pl ... Annales de l'Amelioration des Plantes [*A publication*]
Annls Biol .. Annales de Biologie [*A publication*]
Annls Biol Anim Biochim Biophys ... Annales de Biologie Animale, Biochimie, et Biophysique [*A publication*]
Annls Cent Rech Agron Bambey ... Annales. Centre de Recherches Agronomiques de Bambey au Senegal [*A publication*]
Annls Endocr ... Annales d'Endocrinologie [*A publication*]
Annls Epiphyt ... Annales des Epiphyties et de Phytogenetique [*Paris*] [*A publication*]
Annls Fac Sci Marseille ... Annales. Faculte des Sciences de Marseille [*A publication*]
Annls Falsif Expert Chim ... Annales des Falsifications et de l'Expertise Chimique [*Later, Annales des Falsifications et de l'Expertise Chimique et Toxicologique*] [*A publication*]
Annls Gembloux ... Annales de Gembloux [*A publication*]
Annls Hist-Nat Mus Natn Hung ... Annalis. Historico-Naturales Musei Nationalis Hungarici [*A publication*]
Annls Histochim ... Annales d'Histochimie [*A publication*]
Annls Inst Agric Alger ... Annales. Institut Agricole et Services de Recherche et d'Experimentation Agricoles de l'Algerie [*A publication*]
Annls Inst Natn Agron (Paris) ... Annales. Institut National Agronomique (Paris) [*A publication*]
Annls Inst Natn Rech Agron Tunisie ... Annales. Institut National de la Recherche Agronomique de Tunisie [*A publication*]
Annls Inst Pasteur (Paris) ... Annales. Institut Pasteur (Paris) [*A publication*]
Annls Inst Phytopath Benaki ... Annales. Institut Phytopathologique Benaki [*A publication*]
Annls Med Vet ... Annales de Medecine Veterinaire [*A publication*]
Annls Mines Belg ... Annales des Mines de Belgique [*A publication*]
Annls Mines (Paris) ... Annales des Mines (Paris) [*A publication*]
Annls Mus R Afr Cent Ser 8vo ... Annales. Musee Royal de l'Afrique Centrale. Serie in Octavo [*A publication*]
Annls Nutr Aliment ... Annales de la Nutrition et de l'Alimentation [*A publication*]
Annls Pharm Fr ... Annales Pharmaceutiques Francaises [*A publication*]
Annls Physiol Veg (Brux) ... Annales de Physiologie Vegetale (Bruxelles) [*A publication*]
Annls Physiol Veg (Paris) ... Annales de Physiologie Vegetale (Paris) [*A publication*]
Annls Scient Univ Jassy ... Annales Scientifiques. Universite de Jassy [*A publication*]
Annls Sci Nat A Bot ... Annales des Sciences Naturelles. A. Botanique [*A publication*]
Annls SEITA ... Annales de la Direction des Etudes et de l'Equipement. Service d'Exploitation Industrielle des Tabacs et des Allumettes [*A publication*]
Annls Soc Belge Med Trop ... Annales. Societe Belge de Medecine Tropicale [*A publication*]
Annls Soc Ent Fr ... Annales. Societe Entomologique de France [*A publication*]
Annls Soc Lit Eston Am ... Annales Societatis Litterarum Estonicae in America [*A publication*]
Annls Soc R Zool Belg ... Annales. Societe Royale Zoologique de Belgique [*A publication*]
Annls Soc Tartu ... Annales Societatis Tartu [*A publication*]
Annls Univ Mariae Curie-Sklodowska ... Annales Universitatis Mariae Curie-Sklodowska [*A publication*]
Annls Zool Ecol Anim ... Annales de Zoologie - Ecologie Animale [*A publication*]
Annls Zool Fennici ... Annales Zoologici Fennici [*A publication*]
Annls Zootech ... Annales de Zootechnie [*A publication*]
Ann Lux ..... Annales. Institut Archeologique du Luxembourg [*A publication*]
ANNLY ..... Annually (ROG)
Ann Lyceum Nat Hist (NY) ... Annals. Lyceum of Natural History (New York) [*A publication*]
Ann M .... Annales Musicologiques [*A publication*]
AnnMAfrC ... Annales. Musee Royal de l'Afrique Centrale [*A publication*]
Ann Mag Nat Hist ... Annals and Magazine of Natural History [*A publication*]

Ann and Mag Nat Hist ... Annals and Magazine of Natural History [*A publication*]
Ann Mag Natur Hist ... Annals and Magazine of Natural History [*A publication*]
Ann Malg... Annales Malgaches [*A publication*] (DLA)
Ann Malg... Annales. Universite de Madagascar [*A publication*] (DLA)
Ann Math .. Annals of Mathematics [*A publication*]
Ann of Math (2) ... Annals of Mathematics. Second Series [*A publication*]
Ann Math Logic ... Annals of Mathematical Logic [*A publication*]
Ann Math Stat ... Annals of Mathematical Statistics [*A publication*]
Ann of Math Stud ... Annals of Mathematics. Studies [*A publication*]
Ann of Math Studies ... Annals of Mathematics. Studies [*A publication*]
Ann Mat Pura Appl ... Annali di Matematica Pura ed Applicata [*A publication*]
AnnMCB-L ... Annales. Musee Royal du Congo Belge. Linguistique [*A publication*]
Ann Med.... Annals of Medicine [*A publication*]
Ann Med.... Annuale Mediaevale [*A publication*]
Ann Med Acad Cienc Med Catalunya Balears ... Annals. Medicina Academia de Ciencias Mediques de Catalunya i de Balears [*A publication*]
Ann de Med Belge ... Annales de Medecine Belge et Etrangere [*A publication*]
Ann Med Belges ... Annales Medicales Belges [*A publication*]
Ann Med Chir Hainaut ... Annales Medico-Chirurgicales du Hainaut [*A publication*]
Ann Med et Chir Inf ... Annales de Medecine et Chirurgie Infantiles [*A publication*]
Ann Med Exp Biol Fenn ... Annales Medicinae Experimentalis et Biologiae Fenniae [*A publication*]
Ann Med Exp Biol Fenn Suppl ... Annales Medicinae Experimentalis et Biologiae Fenniae. Supplementum [*A publication*]
Ann Med (Hagerstown Maryland) ... Annals of Medicine (Hagerstown, Maryland) [*A publication*]
Ann Med Hist ... Annals of Medical History [*A publication*]
Ann Mediaev ... Annuale Mediaevale [*A publication*]
Ann Med In ... Annales de Medecine Interne [*A publication*]
Ann Med Intern ... Annales de Medecine Interne [*A publication*]
Ann Med Intern Fenn ... Annales Medicinae Internae Fenniae [*A publication*]
Ann Med Intern Fenn Suppl ... Annales Medicinae Internae Fenniae. Supplementum [*A publication*]
Ann Med Leg ... Annales de Medecine Legale [*A publication*]
Ann Med Leg Criminol ... Annales de Medecine Legale et de Criminologie [*A publication*]
Ann Med Leg Criminol Police Toxicol ... Annales de Medecine Legale, Criminologie, Police Scientifique, et Toxicologie [*A publication*]
Ann Med (Milan) ... Annali Medici (Milan) [*A publication*]
Ann Med Mil Fenn ... Annales Medicinae Militaris Fenniae [*A publication*]
Ann Med Nancy ... Annales Medicales de Nancy [*A publication*]
Ann Med Nancy Est ... Annales Medicales de Nancy et de l'Est [*A publication*]
Ann Med Nav ... Annali di Medicina Navale [*A publication*]
Ann Med Nav e Colon ... Annali di Medicina Navale e Coloniale [*A publication*]
Ann Med Nav Trop ... Annali di Medicina Navale e Tropicale [*A publication*]
Ann Med (Paris) ... Annales de Medecine (Paris) [*A publication*]
Ann Med et Pharm Colon ... Annales de Medecine et de Pharmacie Coloniales [*A publication*]
Ann Med Pharm Reims ... Annales de Medecine et de Pharmacie de Reims [*A publication*]
Ann Med-Psy ... Annales Medico-Psychologiques [*A publication*]
Ann Med-Psychol ... Annales Medico-Psychologiques [*A publication*]
Ann Med Reims ... Annales de Medecine de Reims [*A publication*]
Ann Med Sect Pol Acad Sci ... Annals. Medical Section. Polish Academy of Sciences [*A publication*]
Ann Med Sondalo ... Annali Medici di Sondalo [*A publication*]
Ann Med Vet ... Annales de Medecine Veterinaire [*A publication*]
Ann Mem Assoc Int Pedagog Univ ... Annuaire des Membres. Association Internationale de Pedagogie Universitaire [*A publication*]
Ann Merceol Sicil ... Annali di Merceol Siciliana [*A publication*]
Ann Meteorol ... Annales der Meteorologie [*A publication*]
Ann Microb ... Annales de Microbiologie [*Institut Pasteur*] [*Paris*] [*A publication*]
Ann Microbiol ... Annali di Microbiologia [*A publication*]
Ann Microbiol Enzimol ... Annali di Microbiologia. Edizione. Enzimologia [*A publication*]
Ann Microbiol (Milan) ... Annali di Microbiologia (Milan) [*A publication*]
Ann Microbiol (Paris) ... Annales de Microbiologie (Paris) [*A publication*]
Ann Midi ... Annales du Midi; Revue de la France Meridionale [*Toulouse*] [*A publication*]
Ann Mines ... Annales des Mines [*Paris*] [*A publication*]
Ann Mines Belg ... Annales des Mines de Belgique [*A publication*]
Ann Mines Doc ... Annales des Mines. Documentation [*A publication*]
Ann Mines Geol (Tunisia) ... Annales des Mines et de la Geologie (Tunisia) [*A publication*]
Ann Mines Mem ... Annales des Mines. Memoires [*A publication*]
Ann MO Bot ... Annals. Missouri Botanical Garden [*A publication*]
Ann MO Bot Gard ... Annals. Missouri Botanical Garden [*A publication*]
Ann MO Bot Gdn ... Annals. Missouri Botanical Garden [*A publication*]
Ann Mus Civ Stor Nat "Giacomo Doria" ... Annali. Museo Civico di Storia Naturale "Giacomo Doria" [*A publication*]

Ann Mus Colon Mars ... Annales. Musee Colonial de Marseille [*A publication*]
Ann Mus Goulandris ... Annales Musei Goulandris [*A publication*]
Ann Mus Guimet ... Annales. Musee Guimet [*A publication*]
Ann Mus Guimet Bibl Etud ... Annales. Musee Guimet. Bibliotheque d'Etudes [*A publication*]
Ann Mus Hist Nat Nice ... Annales. Museum d'Histoire Naturelle de Nice [*A publication*]
Ann Mus Nat Arch (Plovdiv) ... Annuaire. Musee National Archeologique (Plovdiv) [*A publication*]
Ann Mus R Afr Cent Ser Quarto Zool ... Annales. Musee Royal de l'Afrique Centrale. Serie in Quarto. Zoologie [*A publication*]
Ann Mus R Afr Cent Ser 8 Sci Geol ... Annales. Musee Royal de l'Afrique Centrale. Serie in Octavo. Sciences Geologiques [*Tervuren*] [*A publication*]
Ann Mus R Congo Belge Ser 8o Sci Geol ... Annales. Musee Royal du Congo Belge. Serie in Octavo. Sciences Geologiques [*A publication*]
Ann Nap..... Annali. Facolta di Lettere e Magistero. Universita di Napoli [*A publication*]
Ann Natal Mus ... Annale. Natalse Museum [*A publication*]
Ann Natl Acad Med Sci ... Annals. National Academy of Medical Sciences [*A publication*]
Ann Naturhist Mus Wien ... Annalen des Naturhistorischen Museums in Wien [*A publication*]
Ann Naturhist Mus Wien Ser B Bot Zool ... Annalen des Naturhistorischen Museums in Wien. Serie B. Botanik und Zoologie [*A publication*]
Ann Natur Kulturphil ... Annalen der Natur- und Kulturphilosophie [*A publication*]
Ann Naturphil ... Annalen der Naturphilosophie [*A publication*]
Ann Neur ... Annali di Neurologia [*A publication*]
Ann Neurol ... Annals of Neurology [*A publication*]
Ann Neuropsichiatr Psicoanal ... Annali di Neuropsichiatria e Psicoanalisi [*A publication*]
Ann Neur Psich Psic ... Annali di Neuropsichiatria e Psicoanalisi [*A publication*]
Ann New York Acad Sc ... Annals. New York Academy of Sciences [*A publication*]
Ann New York Acad Sci ... Annals. New York Academy of Sciences [*A publication*]
ANNNI...... Axial Next-Nearest-Neighbor Interactions [*Crystallography*]
AnnNorm... Annales de Normandie [*A publication*]
Ann Normandie ... Annales de Normandie [*A publication*]
Ann Not Enr ... Annales du Notariat et de l'Enregistrement [*A publication*]
Ann Notre Dame Est Plan Inst ... Annual. Notre Dame Estate Planning Institute [*A publication*]
Ann N Ph... Annalen der Naturphilosophie [*A publication*]
Ann Nuc Eng ... Annals of Nuclear Energy [*A publication*]
Ann Nucl Energy ... Annals of Nuclear Energy [*A publication*]
Ann Nucl Sci and Eng ... Annals of Nuclear Science and Engineering [*A publication*]
Ann Nucl Sci Eng ... Annals of Nuclear Science and Engineering [*A publication*]
Ann Nucl Sci Engng ... Annals of Nuclear Science and Engineering [*A publication*]
Ann Nutr Al ... Annales de la Nutrition et de l'Alimentation [*A publication*]
Ann Nutr Aliment ... Annales de la Nutrition et de l'Alimentation [*A publication*]
Ann Nutr Aliment Ann Nutr Food ... Annales de la Nutrition et de l'Alimentation/Annals of Nutrition and Food [*A publication*]
Ann Nutr Metab ... Annals of Nutrition and Metabolism [*A publication*]
Ann NY Acad ... Annals. New York Academy of Sciences [*A publication*]
Ann NY Acad Sci ... Annals. New York Academy of Sciences [*A publication*]
Ann NY Ac Sci ... Annals. New York Academy of Sciences [*A publication*]
Ann O .... Annals of Otology, Rhinology, and Laryngology [*A publication*]
Anno........ Annotated (DLA)
Ann Obs Besancon ... Annales. Observatoire de Besancon [*A publication*]
Ann Obs Nat ... Annales. Observatoire National d'Athenes [*A publication*]
Ann Obstet ... Annee Obstetricale [*A publication*]
Anno Cases ... American Annotated Cases [*A publication*] (DLA)
Ann Occup Hyg ... Annals of Occupational Hygiene [*A publication*]
Ann Ocul ... Annales d'Oculistique [*Paris*] [*A publication*]
Ann Oculist ... Annales d'Oculistique [*Paris*] [*A publication*]
Ann Ocul (Paris) ... Annales d'Oculistique (Paris) [*A publication*]
Ann Odonto-Stomatol ... Annales Odonto-Stomatologiques [*A publication*]
Ann Off Natl Combust Liq (France) ... Annales. Office National des Combustibles Liquides (France) [*A publication*]
Ann Oftalmol Clin Ocul ... Annali di Oftalmologia e Clinica Oculistica [*A publication*]
Ann Okla Acad Sci ... Annals. Oklahoma Academy of Science [*A publication*]
AnNoLy..... Anthology of Norwegian Lyrics [*A publication*]
Ann Ophth ... Annals of Ophthalmology [*A publication*]
Ann Ophthal ... Annals of Ophthalmology [*A publication*]
Ann Ophthalmol ... Annals of Ophthalmology [*A publication*]
Ann Ophth Otol ... Annals of Ophthalmology and Otology [*A publication*]
Ann OR...... Annals of Oriental Research. University of Madras [*A publication*]
Ann Or (Napoli) ... Annali. Istituto Universitario Orientale (Napoli) [*A publication*]

Ann Osp Maria Vittoria Torino ... Annali. Ospedale Maria Vittoria di Torino [*A publication*]
Ann Osserv Astron Torino ... Annali. Osservatorio Astronomico. Universita di Torino [*A publication*]
Ann Oss Vesuviano ... Annali. Osservatorio Vesuviano [*A publication*]
Ann Ostet Ginecol ... Annali di Ostetricia e Ginecologia [*Italy*] [*A publication*]
Ann Ostet Ginecol Med Perinat ... Annali di Ostetricia, Ginecologia, Medicina Perinatale [*A publication*]
Ann Ot .... Annals of Otology, Rhinology, and Laryngology [*A publication*]
ANNOT ..... Annotated
Annot Bibliogr Anim/Hum Ser Commonw Bur Anim Health ... Annotated Bibliography. Animal/Human Series. Commonwealth Bureau of Animal Health [*A publication*]
Annot Bibliography of Econ Geology ... Annotated Bibliography of Economic Geology [*A publication*]
Annot Bibliogr Commonw Bur Nutr ... Annotated Bibliography. Commonwealth Bureau of Nutrition [*A publication*]
Annot Bibliogr Commonw Bur Pastures Field Crops ... Annotated Bibliography. Commonwealth Bureau of Pastures and Field Crops [*A publication*]
Annot Bibliogr Commonw Bur Soils ... Annotated Bibliography. Commonwealth Bureau of Soils [*A publication*]
Annot Bibliogr Econ Geol ... Annotated Bibliography of Economic Geology [*A publication*]
Annot Bibliogr Med Myc ... Annotated Bibliography of Medical Mycology [*A publication*]
Annot Dokl Semin Inst Prikl Mat Tbilis Univ ... Annotatsii Dokladov. Seminar Instituta Prikladnoj Matematiki. Tbilisskij Universitet [*A publication*]
Annotness Zool Bot (Bratislava) ... Annotationes Zoologicae et Botanicae (Bratislava) [*A publication*]
Annotness Zool Jap ... Annotationes Zoologicae Japonenses [*A publication*]
Ann Oto-Lar ... Annales d'Oto-Laryngologie et de Chirurgie Cervico-Faciale [*A publication*]
Ann Oto-Laryngol ... Annales d'Oto-Laryngologie [*Later, Annales d'Oto-Laryngologie et de Chirurgie Cervico-Faciale*] [*A publication*]
Ann Oto-Laryngol Chir Cervico-Fac ... Annales d'Oto-Laryngologie et de Chirurgie Cervico-Faciale [*A publication*]
Ann Otol Rh ... Annals of Otology, Rhinology, and Laryngology [*A publication*]
Ann Otol Rhin Laryng ... Annals of Otology, Rhinology, and Laryngology [*A publication*]
Ann Otol Rhinol Laryngol ... Annals of Otology, Rhinology, and Laryngology [*A publication*]
Ann Otol Rhinol Laryngol Suppl ... Annals of Otology, Rhinology, and Laryngology. Supplement [*A publication*]
Ann Oto Rhinol Laryngol ... Annals of Otology, Rhinology, and Laryngology [*A publication*]
Ann Ottalmol Clin Ocul ... Annali di Ottalmologia e Clinica Oculistica [*A publication*]
Ann Ottalmol Clin Oculist ... Annali di Ottalmologia e Clinica Oculistica [*A publication*]
Annot Zool Bot ... Annotationes Zoologicae et Botanicae [*A publication*]
Annot Zool Jap ... Annotationes Zoologicae Japonenses [*A publication*]
Annot Zool Japon ... Annotationes Zoologicae Japonenses [*A publication*]
Annot Zool Jpn ... Annotationes Zoologicae Japonenses [*A publication*]
Ann Oudheidk Kring Land Waas ... Annalen van de Oudheidkundige Kring van het Land van Waas [*A publication*]
ANNPAC .. Association of National Non-Profit Artists' Centres [*Canada*]
Ann Paediatr ... Annales Paediatrici [*A publication*]
Ann Paediatr Fenn ... Annales Paediatriae Fenniae [*Finland*] [*A publication*]
Ann Paediatr Fenn Suppl ... Annales Paediatriae Fenniae. Supplementum [*A publication*]
Ann Paediatr Int Rev Pediatr ... Annales Paediatrici. International Review of Pediatrics [*A publication*]
Ann Paed Jap ... Annales Paediatrici Japonici [*A publication*]
Ann Paleontol ... Annales de Paleontologie [*A publication*]
Ann Paleontol Invertebr ... Annales de Paleontologie Invertebre [*A publication*]
Ann Paleontol Invertebr ... Annales de Paleontologie Invertebre [*A publication*]
Ann Paleontol Vertebr ... Annales de Paleontologie Vertebre [*A publication*]
Ann Parasit ... Annales de Parasitologie Humaine et Comparee [*A publication*]
Ann Parasitol ... Annales de Parasitologie Humaine et Comparee [*A publication*]
Ann Parasitol Hum Comp ... Annales de Parasitologie Humaine et Comparee [*A publication*]
Ann Paris ... Annales. Universite de Paris [*A publication*]
Ann Parl ... Annales Parlementaires [*Belgium*] [*A publication*]   (DLA)
Ann Pathol ... Annales de Pathologie [*A publication*]
Ann Paulist Med e Cirurg ... Annales Paulistas de Medicina e Cirurgia [*A publication*]
Ann Ped ..... Annee Pediatrique [*A publication*]
Ann Pediatr ... Annales de Pediatrie [*Paris*] [*A publication*]
Ann Pediatr Jpn Kioto Univ ... Annales Paediatrici Japonici. Kioto Universitatis [*A publication*]
Ann Pediatr (Paris) ... Annales de Pediatrie (Paris) [*A publication*]
Ann Perugia ... Annali. Facolta di Lettere e Filosofia. Universita degli Studi di Perugia [*A publication*]

Ann Pharm Belg ... Annales Pharmaceutiques Belges [*A publication*]
Ann Pharm F ... Annales Pharmaceutiques Francaises [*A publication*]
Ann Pharm Fr ... Annales Pharmaceutiques Francaises [*A publication*]
Ann Pharm (Lemgo Germany) ... Annalen der Pharmacie (Lemgo, Germany) [*A publication*]
Ann Pharm (Poznan) ... Annales Pharmaceutici (Poznan) [*A publication*]
Ann Phil ... Annals of Philosophy [*A publication*]
Ann Phil Hist ... Brussels. Universite Libre. Institut de Philologie et d'Histoire. Annuaire [*A publication*]
Ann Philos ... Annals of Philosophy [*A publication*]
Ann Phys ... Annales de Physique [*A publication*]
Ann Phys ... Annals of Physics [*New York*] [*A publication*]
Ann Phys Bi ... Annales de Physique Biologique et Medicale [*A publication*]
Ann Phys Biol Med ... Annales de Physique Biologique et Medicale [*A publication*]
Ann Phys (Germ) ... Annalen der Physik (Germany) [*A publication*]
Ann Physics ... Annals of Physics [*New York*] [*A publication*]
Ann Physik ... Annalen der Physik [*A publication*]
Ann Physik (7) ... Annales der Physik. 7 Folge [*A publication*]
Ann Physiol Anthropol ... Annals of Physiological Anthropology [*A publication*]
Ann Physiol Physicochim Biol ... Annales de Physiologie et de Physicochimie Biologique [*A publication*]
Ann Physiol Veg ... Annales de Physiologie Vegetale [*Bruxelles*] [*A publication*]
Ann Physiol Veg (Paris) ... Annales de Physiologie Vegetale (Paris) [*A publication*]
Ann Physiol Veg Univ Brux ... Annales de Physiologie Vegetale. Universite de Bruxelles [*A publication*]
Ann Physiq ... Annales de Physique [*Paris*] [*A publication*]
Ann Phys (Leipzig) ... Annalen der Physik (Leipzig) [*A publication*]
Ann Phys Med ... Annals of Physical Medicine [*A publication*]
Ann Phys (New York) ... Annals of Physics (New York) [*A publication*]
Ann Phys (Paris) ... Annales de Physique (Paris) [*A publication*]
Ann Phys Phys Chim ... Annales de Physiologie et de Physicochimie Biologique [*A publication*]
Ann Phytopath ... Annales de Phytopathologie [*A publication*]
Ann Phytopathol ... Annales de Phytopathologie [*A publication*]
Ann Phytopathol Soc Jap ... Annals. Phytopathological Society of Japan [*A publication*]
Ann Phytopathol Soc Jpn ... Annals. Phytopathological Society of Japan [*A publication*]
Ann Pisa .... Annali. Scuola Normale Superiore di Pisa [*A publication*]
Ann Pisa Univ Fac Agrar ... Annali. Pisa Universita. Facolta di Agraria [*A publication*]
Ann Plan Rep DC ... Annual Planning Report. District of Columbia [*A publication*]
Ann Plast Surg ... Annals of Plastic Surgery [*A publication*]
Ann Pol et Econ ... Annee Politique et Economique [*A publication*]
Ann Polit Litt ... Annales Politiques et Litteraires [*A publication*]
Ann Pol et Litt ... Annales Politiques et Litteraires [*A publication*]
Ann Pol Math ... Annales Polonici Mathematici [*A publication*]
Ann Polon Math ... Annales Polonici Mathematici [*A publication*]
Ann Pontif Mus Miss Etnol (Vatican) ... Annali. Pontificio Museo Missionario Etnologico (Vatican) [*A publication*]
Ann Ponts Chaussees ... Annales des Ponts et Chaussees [*A publication*]
Ann Pr .... Annual Practice [*A publication*]   (DLA)
Ann de la Pro ... Annales de la Propriete Industrielle, Artistique, et Litteraire [*A publication*]   (DLA)
Ann Probab ... Annals of Probability [*A publication*]
Ann Probability ... Annals of Probability [*A publication*]
Ann Proc Nat Asso R Coms ... Annual Proceedings. National Association of Railway Commissions [*A publication*]   (DLA)
Ann Prog Rep Geol Surv West Austr ... Annual Progress Report. Geological Survey. Western Australia [*A publication*]   (APTA)
Ann Prog Rep Nat Found Cancer Res ... Annual Progress Report. National Foundation for Cancer Research [*US*] [*A publication*]
Ann Prop Ind ... Annales de la Propriete Industrielle, Artistique, et Litteraire [*A publication*]
Ann Protist ... Annales de Protistologie [*A publication*]
Ann P S ...... Annales Parlementaires. Senat [*A publication*]
AnnPsych... Annee Psychologique [*A publication*]
Ann Psychol ... Annee Psychologique [*A publication*]
Ann Public and Coop Econ ... Annals of Public and Cooperative Economy [*Formerly, Annals of Collective Economy*] [*A publication*]
Ann Pur App ... Annals of Pure and Applied Logic [*A publication*]
Ann Purdue Air Qual Conf Proc ... Annual Purdue Air Quality Conference. Proceedings [*A publication*]
Ann Rad Diagn ... Annali di Radiologia Diagnostica [*A publication*]
Ann Radioelectr ... Annales de Radioelectricite [*France*] [*A publication*]
Ann Radiol ... Annales de Radiologie [*A publication*]
Ann Radiol Diagn ... Annali di Radiologia Diagnostica [*A publication*]
Ann Radiol Med Nucl ... Annales de Radiologie. Medecine Nucleaire [*France*] [*A publication*]
Ann Rainf Aust ... Annual Rainfall, Australia [*Australia Commonwealth Bureau of Meteorology*] [*A publication*]   (APTA)
Ann R Anthr ... Annual Review of Anthropology [*A publication*]
Ann R Astro ... Annual Review of Astronomy and Astrophysics [*A publication*]

Ann R Australas Coll Dent Surg ... Annals. Royal Australasian College of Dental Surgeons [*A publication*]
Ann R Bioch ... Annual Review of Biochemistry [*A publication*]
Ann R Bioph ... Annual Review of Biophysics and Bioengineering [*A publication*]
Ann R Coll Physicians Surg Can ... Annals. Royal College of Physicians and Surgeons of Canada [*A publication*]
Ann R Coll Surg Eng ... Annals. Royal College of Surgeons of England [*A publication*]
Ann R Coll Surg Engl ... Annals. Royal College of Surgeons of England [*A publication*]
Ann RC Surg ... Annals. Royal College of Surgeons of England [*A publication*]
Ann Readaptation Med Phys ... Annales de Readaptation et de Medecine Physique [*A publication*]
Ann R Earth ... Annual Review of Earth and Planetary Sciences [*A publication*]
Ann Rech For Maroc ... Annales de la Recherche Forestiere au Maroc [*A publication*]
Ann Rech Vet ... Annales de Recherches Veterinaires [*A publication*]
Ann Rech Vet Ann Vet Res ... Annales de Recherches Veterinaires/Annals of Veterinary Research [*A publication*]
Ann R Ecol ... Annual Review of Ecology and Systematics [*A publication*]
Ann Reg ..... American Annual Register [*A publication*]
Ann Reg ..... Annual Register [*London*] [*A publication*]   (DLA)
Ann Regia Super Agric (Portici) ... Annali. Regia Scuola Superiore di Agricoltura (Portici) [*A publication*]
Ann Regio Ist Super Agrar Portici ... Annali. Regio Istituto Superiore Agrario di Portici [*A publication*]
Ann Reg NS ... Annual Register, New Series [*A publication*]   (DLA)
Ann R Entom ... Annual Review of Entomology [*A publication*]
Ann Rep ..... Annual Report [*A publication*]   (DLA)
Ann Rep Acc India Man Assoc ... Annual Report and Accounts. All India Management Association [*A publication*]
Ann Rep Am Jud Soc ... Annual Report. American Judicature Society [*A publication*]
Ann Rep Argonne Nat Lab Div Bio Med Res ... Annual Report. Argonne National Laboratory. Division of Biological and Medical Research [*A publication*]
Ann Rep Bank Ceylon ... Annual Report. Bank of Ceylon [*A publication*]
Ann Rep Brooklyn ... Annual Report. Brooklyn Museum [*A publication*]
Ann Rep Calif Adm Law ... Annual Report. California. Office of Administrative Law [*A publication*]
Ann Rep Calif Pub Broadc Com ... Annual Report. California Public Broadcasting Commission [*A publication*]
Ann Rep Can Dept Fish Oceans Newfoundland Reg ... Annual Report. Canada Department of Fisheries and Oceans. Newfoundland Region [*A publication*]
Ann Rep Cent Adult Dis (Osaka) ... Annual Report. Center for Adult Diseases (Osaka) [*A publication*]
Ann Rep Cocoa Res Inst (Tafo Ghana) ... Annual Report. Cocoa Research Institute (Tafo, Ghana) [*A publication*]
Ann Rep Com Corp ... Annual Report. Committee on Corporations [*A publication*]
Ann Rep Dep Hlth NZ ... Annual Report. Department of Health [*New Zealand*] [*A publication*]
Ann Rep Dept Env (India) ... Annual Report. Department of Environment (India) [*A publication*]
Ann Rep Dept Lab Ind (West Aust) ... Annual Report. Department of Labour and Industry (Western Australia) [*A publication*]
Ann Rep Dir Civ Cons Corp (US) ... Annual Report. Director of the Civilian Conservation Corps (US) [*A publication*]
Ann Rep Dir Sea Fish (S Africa) ... Annual Report. Director of Sea Fisheries (South Africa) [*A publication*]
Ann Rep DS ... Annual Report. Dante Society [*A publication*]
Ann Rep Fla Att'y Gen ... Annual Report of the Attorney General of Florida [*A publication*]   (DLA)
Ann Rep Fogg Art Mus ... Annual Report. Fogg Art Museum [*Harvard University*] [*A publication*]
Ann Rep Hlth Med Serv ... Annual Report. Health and Medical Services of the State of Queensland [*A publication*]   (APTA)
Ann Rep Inst Med Vet Sci ... Annual Report. Institute of Medical and Veterinary Science [*A publication*]   (APTA)
Ann Rep Inst Vir Res ... Annual Report. Institute for Virus Research [*Kyoto*] [*A publication*]
Ann Rep Int Telecom Sat Org ... Annual Report. International Telecommunications Satellite Organization [*A publication*]
Ann Rep Maine Adv Counc Voc Ed ... Annual Report. Maine Advisory Council on Vocational Education [*A publication*]
Ann Rep Manag Adel Hosp ... Annual Report. Board of Management. Royal Adelaide Hospital [*A publication*]   (APTA)
Ann Rep Med Chem ... Annual Reports in Medicinal Chemistry [*A publication*]
Ann Rep Med Res Counc Nigeria ... Annual Report. Medical Research Council of Nigeria [*A publication*]
Ann Rep Min Res Div (Fiji) ... Annual Report. Mineral Resources Division (Fiji) [*A publication*]
Ann Rep NACA ... Annual Report. United States National Advisory Committee for Aeronautics [*A publication*]
Ann Rep Nat Res Counc Can ... Annual Report. National Research Council of Canada [*A publication*]

Ann Rep New Jersey Dept Transp ... Annual Report. New Jersey Department of Transportation [*A publication*]
Ann Rep & Op Ind Att'y Gen ... Annual Report and Official Opinions of the Attorney General of Indiana [*A publication*]   (DLA)
Ann Rep & Op MD Att'y Gen ... Annual Report and Official Opinions of the Attorney General of Maryland [*A publication*]   (DLA)
Ann Rep Past Ins SI ... Annual Report. Pasteur Institute of Southern India [*A publication*]
Ann Rep Prog Chem Sect C Phys Chem ... Annual Reports on the Progress of Chemistry. Section C. Physical Chemistry [*A publication*]
Ann Rep Rev Op (Port Melbourne) ... Annual Report and Review of Operations (Port of Melbourne) [*A publication*]
Ann Rep S Afr Inst Med Res ... Annual Report. South African Institute for Medical Research [*A publication*]
Ann Rep SC Att'y Gen ... Annual Report of the Attorney General of South Carolina to the General Assembly [*A publication*]   (DLA)
Ann Rep Smith Inst ... Annual Report. Smithsonian Institution [*A publication*]
Ann Rep Soc Libyan Stud ... Annual Report. Society for Libyan Studies [*A publication*]
Ann Rept Progr Chem ... Annual Reports on the Progress of Chemistry [*A publication*]
Ann Rept Tokyo Univ Agr Technol ... Annual Report. Tokyo University of Agriculture and Technology [*A publication*]
Ann Rep United Fruit Co Med Dept ... Annual Report. United Fruit Company. Medical Department [*A publication*]
Ann Rep Yearb Adv Res Found ... Annual Report and Yearbook. Advertising Research Foundation [*A publication*]
Ann Rep Yorkshire Phil Soc ... Annual Report. Yorkshire Philosophical Society [*A publication*]
Ann Res Inst Epidemiol Microbiol ... Annals. Research Institute of Epidemiology and Microbiology [*A publication*]
Ann Res Inst Micr Dis ... Annals. Research Institute for Microbial Diseases [*A publication*]
Ann Res Rep Red River Valley Agric Exp Stn ... Annual Research Report. Red River Valley Agricultural Experiment Station [*A publication*]
Ann Rev Acad Nat Sci Philad ... Annual Review. Academy of Natural Sciences of Philadelphia [*A publication*]
Ann Rev Analyt Chem ... Annual Review of Analytical Chemistry [*A publication*]
Ann Rev Austr Min Ind ... Annual Review. Australian Mineral Industry [*A publication*]
Ann Rev Biochem ... Annual Review of Biochemistry [*A publication*]
Ann Rev Ecol ... Annual Review of Ecology and Systematics [*A publication*]
Ann Rev Ent ... Annual Review of Entomology [*A publication*]
Ann Rev Entomol ... Annual Review of Entomology [*A publication*]
Ann Rev Gen ... Annual Review of Genetics [*A publication*]
Ann Rev Int'l Aff ... Annual Review of International Affairs [*A publication*]   (DLA)
Ann Rev Med ... Annual Review of Medicine [*A publication*]
Ann Rev Microbiol ... Annual Review of Microbiology [*A publication*]
Ann Rev Nuclear Sci ... Annual Review of Nuclear Science [*Later, Annual Review of Nuclear and Particle Science*] [*A publication*]
Ann Rev Nucl Sci ... Annual Review of Nuclear Science [*Later, Annual Review of Nuclear and Particle Science*] [*A publication*]
Ann Rev Pharm ... Annual Review of Pharmacology [*Later, Annual Review of Pharmacology and Toxicology*] [*A publication*]
Ann Rev Pharmacol ... Annual Review of Pharmacology [*A publication*]
Ann Rev Phys Chem ... Annual Review of Physical Chemistry [*A publication*]
Ann Rev Physiol ... Annual Review of Physiology [*A publication*]
Ann Rev Phytopath ... Annual Review of Phytopathology [*A publication*]
Ann Rev Plant Physiol ... Annual Review of Plant Physiology [*A publication*]
Ann R Fluid ... Annual Review of Fluid Mechanics [*A publication*]
Ann R Genet ... Annual Review of Genetics [*A publication*]
Ann Rheumat Dis ... Annals of the Rheumatic Diseases [*A publication*]
Ann Rheum D ... Annals of the Rheumatic Diseases [*A publication*]
Ann Rheum Dis ... Annals of the Rheumatic Diseases [*A publication*]
Ann R Infor ... Annual Review of Information Science and Technology [*A publication*]
Ann R Mater ... Annual Review of Materials Science [*A publication*]
Ann R Med ... Annual Review of Medicine [*A publication*]
Ann R Micro ... Annual Review of Microbiology [*A publication*]
Ann R Nucl ... Annual Review of Nuclear Science [*Later, Annual Review of Nuclear and Particle Science*] [*A publication*]
Ann Roentg ... Annals of Roentgenology [*A publication*]
Ann Roy Coll Surg ... Annals. Royal College of Surgeons of England [*A publication*]
Ann Rp Ch A ... Annual Reports on the Progress of Chemistry. Section A. General, Physical, and Inorganic Chemistry [*A publication*]
Ann Rp Ch B ... Annual Reports on the Progress of Chemistry. Section B. Organic Chemistry [*A publication*]
Ann R Pharm ... Annual Review of Pharmacology [*Later, Annual Review of Pharmacology and Toxicology*] [*A publication*]
Ann R Ph Ch ... Annual Review of Physical Chemistry [*A publication*]
Ann R Physl ... Annual Review of Physiology [*A publication*]
Ann R Phyto ... Annual Review of Phytopathology [*A publication*]
Ann R Plant ... Annual Review of Plant Physiology [*A publication*]
Ann R Psych ... Annual Review of Psychology [*A publication*]
Ann R Sociol ... Annual Review of Sociology [*A publication*]
AnnS .... Annales Silesiae [*A publication*]

ANNSA8 ... Annals of Science [*A publication*]
Ann S Afr Mus ... Annals. South Africa Museum [*A publication*]
Ann Sanita Pubblica ... Annali della Sanita Pubblica [*A publication*]
Ann Sanit Int ... Annuaire Sanitaire International [*A publication*]
Ann San Rep Prov Assam ... Annual Sanitary Report of the Province of Assam [*A publication*]
Ann Saudi Med ... Annals of Saudi Medicine [*A publication*]
Ann Sc Econ Appliq ... Annales des Sciences Economiques Appliquees [*A publication*]
Ann Schiapparelli ... Annali Schiapparelli [*A publication*]
Ann of Sci .. Annals of Science [*A publication*]
Ann Sci ...... Annals of Science [*London*] [*A publication*]
Ann Sci Agron ... Annales de la Science Agronomique [*A publication*]
Ann Sci Agron Fr ... Annales de la Science Agronomique Francaise et Etrangere [*A publication*]
Ann Sci Agron Fr Etrang ... Annales de la Science Agronomique Francaise et Etrangere [*A publication*]
Ann Sci Ec ... Annales Scientifiques. Ecole Normale Superieure [*A publication*]
Ann Sci Ecole Norm Sup ... Annales Scientifiques. Ecole Normale Superieure [*A publication*]
Ann Sci Econ Appl ... Annales des Sciences Economiques Appliquees [*A publication*]
Ann Sciences Econs Appliquees ... Annales des Sciences Economiques Appliquees [*A publication*]
Ann Sci For (Paris) ... Annales des Sciences Forestieres (Paris) [*A publication*]
Ann Sci Franche Comte ... Annales Scientifiques de Franche Comte [*A publication*]
Ann Sci Hom ... Annuaire Sciences de l'Homme [*A publication*]
Ann Sci Kanazawa Univ ... Annals of Science. Kanazawa University [*A publication*]
Ann Sci Kanazawa Univ Part 2 Biol-Geol ... Annals of Science. Kanazawa University. Part 2. Biology-Geology [*A publication*]
Ann Sci (Lond) ... Annals of Science (London) [*A publication*]
Ann Sci Math Quebec ... Annales des Sciences Mathematiques du Quebec [*A publication*]
Ann Sci Nat ... Annaes de Sciencias Naturaes [*A publication*]
Ann Sci Nat Bot ... Annales des Sciences Naturelles. A. Botanique [*A publication*]
Ann Sci Nat Bot Biol Veg ... Annales des Sciences Naturelles. Botanique et Biologie Vegetale [*A publication*]
Ann Sci Natur Bot Biol Veg ... Annales des Sciences Naturelles. Botanique et Biologie Vegetale [*A publication*]
Ann Sci Nat Zool ... Annales des Sciences Naturelles. B. Zoologie [*A publication*]
Ann Sci Nat Zool Biol Anim ... Annales des Sciences Naturelles. Zoologie et Biologie Animale [*A publication*]
Ann Sci Text Belg ... Annales Scientifiques Textiles Belges [*A publication*]
Ann Sci Univ Bes ... Annales Scientifiques. Universite de Besancon [*A publication*]
Ann Sci Univ Besancon Biol Veg ... Annales Scientifiques. Universite de Besancon. Biologie Vegetale [*A publication*]
Ann Sci Univ Besancon Bot ... Annales Scientifiques. Universite de Besancon. Botanique [*A publication*]
Ann Sci Univ Besancon Chim ... Annales Scientifiques. Universite de Besancon. Chimie [*A publication*]
Ann Sci Univ Besancon Climatol ... Annales Scientifiques. Universite de Besancon. Climatologie [*A publication*]
Ann Sci Univ Besancon Geol ... Annales Scientifiques. Universite de Besancon. Geologie [*A publication*]
Ann Sci Univ Besancon Hydrogr ... Annales Scientifiques. Universite de Besancon. Hydrographie [*A publication*]
Ann Sci Univ Besancon Math ... Annales Scientifiques. Universite de Besancon. Mathematiques [*A publication*]
Ann Sci Univ Besancon Math 3 ... Annales Scientifiques. Universite de Besancon. Mathematiques. 3e Serie [*A publication*]
Ann Sci Univ Besancon Mec Phys Theor ... Annales Scientifiques. Universite de Besancon. Mecanique et Physique Theorique [*A publication*]
Ann Sci Univ Besancon Med ... Annales Scientifiques. Universite de Besancon. Medecine [*A publication*]
Ann Sci Univ Besancon Meteorol ... Annales Scientifiques. Universite de Besancon. Meteorologie [*A publication*]
Ann Sci Univ Besancon Phys ... Annales Scientifiques. Universite de Besancon. Physique [*A publication*]
Ann Sci Univ Besancon Physiol Biol Anim ... Annales Scientifiques. Universite de Besancon. Physiologie et Biologie Animale [*A publication*]
Ann Sci Univ Besancon Zool ... Annales Scientifiques. Universite de Besancon. Zoologie [*A publication*]
Ann Sci Univ Besancon Zool Physiol ... Annales Scientifiques. Universite de Besancon. Zoologie et Physiologie [*A publication*]
Ann Sci Univ Besancon Zool Physiol Biol Anim ... Annales Scientifiques. Universite de Besancon. Zoologie, Physiologie, et Biologie Animale [*A publication*]
Ann Sci Univ Clermont ... Annales Scientifiques. Universite de Clermont [*A publication*]
Ann Sci Univ Clermont-Ferrand II Math ... Annales Scientifiques. Universite de Clermont-Ferrand. II. Mathematiques [*A publication*]
Ann Sci Univ Clermont Math ... Annales Scientifiques. Universite de Clermont. Serie Mathematique [*A publication*]

Ann Sci Univ Jass Sect 1 ... Annales Scientifiques. Universite de Jassy. Section 1. Mathematiques. Physique, Chimie [*A publication*]
Ann Sci Univ Jassy ... Annales Scientifiques. Universite de Jassy [*A publication*]
Ann Sci Univ Jassy Sect 2 ... Annales Scientifiques. Universite de Jassy. Section 2. Sciences Naturelles [*A publication*]
Ann Sci Univ Reims ARERS ... Annales Scientifiques. Universite de Reims et ARERS [*Association Regionale pour l'Etude et la Recherche Scientifiques*] [*A publication*]
Ann Sci Univ Reims ARERS (Assoc Reg Etude Rech Sci) ... Annales Scientifiques. Universite de Reims et ARERS (Association Regionale pour l'Etude et la Recherche Scientifiques) [*A publication*]
Ann Sclavo ... Annali Sclavo [*A publication*]
Ann Sc Nat ... Annales des Sciences Naturelles [*A publication*]
Ann Sc Nat Zool ... Annales des Sciences Naturelles. Zoologie [*A publication*]
Ann Sc Norm Super Pisa ... Annali. Scuola Normale Superiore di Pisa [*A publication*]
Ann Sc Norm Super Pisa Sci Fis Mat ... Annali. Scuola Normale Superiore di Pisa. Scienze, Fisiche, e Matematiche [*A publication*]
Ann Sc Pisa ... Annali. Scuola Normale Superiore di Pisa. Classe di Lettere e Filosofia [*A publication*]
Ann Scu Archeol Atene ... Annuario. Scuola Archeologica di Atene e Missioni Italiane in Oriente [*A publication*]
Ann Scu Norm Sup ... Annali. Scuola Normale Superiore [*A publication*]
Ann Scuola Norm Sup Pisa Cl Sci ... Annali. Scuola Normale Superiore di Pisa. Classe di Scienze [*A publication*]
Ann Scuola Norm Sup Pisa Cl Sci 4 ... Annali. Scuola Normale Superiore di Pisa. Classe di Scienze. Serie IV [*A publication*]
Ann Scuola Norm Sup Pisa Sci Fis Mat ... Annali. Scuola Normale Superiore di Pisa. Scienze, Fisiche, e Matematiche [*A publication*]
Ann Sect Dendrol Soc Bot Pol ... Annales. Section Dendrologique. Societe Botanique de Pologne [*A publication*]
Ann Seism ... Annuaire Seismique [*A publication*]
Ann Sem Giur ... Annali. Seminario Giuridico. Universita di Palermo [*A publication*]   (ILCA)
Ann Sem Giur Catania ... Annali. Seminario Giuridico. Universita Catania [*A publication*]   (ILCA)
Ann Seminar Metaf ... Annales. Seminario de Metafisica [*A publication*]
Ann Serv .... Annales. Service des Antiquites de l'Egypte [*A publication*]
Ann Serv Ant ... Annales. Service des Antiquites de l'Egypte [*A publication*]
Ann Serv Bot Agron Tunis ... Annales. Service Botanique et Agronomique de Tunisie [*A publication*]
Ann Service des Ant ... Annales. Service des Antiquites de l'Egypte [*A publication*]
Ann Sez Ling ... Annali. Sezione Linguistica. Istituto Universitario Orientale [*A publication*]
Ann Soc Arch Namur ... Annales. Societe Archeologique de Namur [*A publication*]
Ann Soc Belge Astr ... Annuaire. Societe Belge d'Astronomie [*A publication*]
Ann Soc Belge Med Trop ... Annales. Societe Belge de Medecine Tropicale [*A publication*]
Ann Soc Belge Neurol ... Annales. Societe Belge de Neurologie [*A publication*]
Ann Soc Belg Hist Hop ... Annales. Societe Belge d'Histoire des Hopitaux [*A publication*]
Ann Soc Belg Med Trop Parasitol Mycol ... Annales. Societes Belges de Medecine Tropicale, de Parasitologie, et de Mycologie [*A publication*]
Ann Soc Brass Enseign Prof ... Annales. Societe des Brasseurs pour l'Enseignement Professionel [*A publication*]
Ann Soc Chim Fr ... Annuaire. Societe Chimique de France [*A publication*]
Ann Soc Doctrinae Stud Acad Med Silesiensis ... Annales Societatis Doctrinae Studentium Academiae Medicae Silesiensis [*A publication*]
Ann Soc Emulation Bruges ... Annales. Societe d'Emulation de Bruges [*Handelingen van het Genootschap voor Geschiedenis te Bruges*] [*A publication*]
Ann Soc Ent ... Annales. Societe Entomologique de France [*A publication*]
Ann Soc Entomol Fr ... Annales. Societe Entomologique de France [*A publication*]
Ann Soc Entomol Que ... Annales. Societe Entomologique du Quebec [*A publication*]
Ann Soc Fr Econ Alp ... Annuaire. Societe Francaise d'Economie Alpestre [*A publication*]
Ann Soc Geol Belg ... Annales. Societe Geologique de Belgique [*A publication*]
Ann Soc Geol Belg Bull ... Annales. Societe Geologique de Belgique. Bulletin [*A publication*]
Ann Soc Geol Belg Mem ... Annales. Societe Geologique de Belgique. Memoires [*A publication*]
Ann Soc Geol Nord ... Annales. Societe Geologique du Nord [*A publication*]
Ann Soc Hist Archeol Arrondissement Saint Malo ... Annales. Societe Historique et Archeologique de l'Arrondissement de Saint-Malo [*A publication*]
Ann Soc Hydr Med ... Annales. Societe d'Hydrologie Medicale de Paris [*A publication*]
Ann Soc Ingeg ... Annali. Societa degli Ingegneri e degli Architetti Italiani [*A publication*]
Ann Soc Linn Lyon ... Annales. Societe Linneenne de Lyon [*A publication*]
Ann Soc Math Pol Ser IV Fundam Inf ... Annales Societatis Mathematicae Polonae. Series IV. Fundamenta Informaticae [*A publication*]

Ann Soc Med-Chir Bruges ... Annales. Societe Medico-Chirurgicale de Bruges [*A publication*]
Ann Soc Med Leg Belg ... Annales. Societe de Medecine Legale de Belgique [*A publication*]
Ann Soc Nat Hort Fr ... Annales. Societe Nationale de l'Horticulture de France [*A publication*]
Ann Soc Pol Math ... Annales. Societe Polonaise de Mathematique [*A publication*]
Ann Soc Roy Sci Med ... Annales. Societe Royale des Sciences Medicales et Naturelles de Bruxelles [*A publication*]
Ann Soc R Zool Belg ... Annales. Societe Royale Zoologique de Belgique [*A publication*]
Ann Soc Sci Bruxelles ... Annales. Societe Scientifique de Bruxelles [*A publication*]
Ann Soc Sci Bruxelles Ser 1 ... Annales. Societe Scientifique de Bruxelles. Serie 1 [*A publication*]
Ann Soc Sci Bruxelles Ser 2 ... Annales. Societe Scientifique de Bruxelles. Serie 2. Sciences Naturelles et Medicales [*A publication*]
Ann Soc Sci Bruxelles Ser 3 ... Annales. Societe Scientifique de Bruxelles. Serie 3. Sciences Economiques [*A publication*]
Ann Soc Sci Bruxelles Ser A ... Annales. Societe Scientifique de Bruxelles. Serie A. Sciences Mathematiques [*A publication*]
Ann Soc Sci Brux Ser 1 ... Annales. Societe Scientifique de Bruxelles. Serie 1 [*A publication*]
Ann Soc Scient Bruxelles S B Sc Phys Nat ... Annales. Societe Scientifique de Bruxelles. Serie B. Sciences Physiques et Naturelles [*A publication*]
Ann Soc Scient Bruxelles S C Sci Med ... Annales. Societe Scientifique de Bruxelles. Serie C. Sciences Medicales [*A publication*]
Ann Soc Sci Faeroe ... Annales Societatis Scientiarum Faeroensis [*A publication*]
Ann Soc Sci Litt Cannes ... Annales. Societe de Science et Litterature de Cannes [*A publication*]
Ann Soc Sci Nat Charente-Marit ... Annales. Societe des Sciences Naturelles de la Charente-Maritime [*A publication*]
Ann Soc Zool Belg ... Annales. Societe Royale Zoologique de Belgique [*A publication*]
Ann Speleol ... Annales de Speleologie [*A publication*]
Ann Sper Agr ... Annali della Sperimentazione Agraria [*A publication*]
Ann Sper Agrar ... Annali della Sperimentazione Agraria [*A publication*]
Ann Sports Med ... Annals of Sports Medicine [*A publication*]
AnnSR .... Annales. Societa Retorumantscha [*A publication*]
Ann St .... Annotated Statutes [*A publication*] (DLA)
Ann Sta Chim-Agr Sper Roma Ser 3 ... Annali. Stazione Chimico-Agraria Sperimentale di Roma. Serie 3 [*A publication*]
Ann Staedt Allg Krankenhaeuser Muenchen ... Annalen. Staedtische Allgemeine Krankenhaeuser zu Muenchen [*A publication*]
Ann Sta Sperim Agrumicoltura ... Annali. Reale Stazione Sperimentale di Agrumicoltura e Frutticoltura in Acireale [*A publication*]
Ann Stat Belg ... Annuaire Statistique de la Belgique [*A publication*]
Ann Stat Guid ... Annuario di Statistiche Guidiziarie [*A publication*] (ILCA)
Ann Statist ... Annals of Statistics [*A publication*]
Ann Statist Tun ... Annuaire Statistique de la Tunisie [*A publication*]
Ann St Dir ... Annali di Storia del Diritto [*A publication*] (ILCA)
Ann St Ind T ... Annotated Statutes of Indian Territory [*A publication*] (DLA)
Ann Stn Biol Besse-En-Chandesse ... Annales. Station Biologique de Besse-En-Chandesse [*A publication*]
Ann Stn Cent Hydrobiol Appl ... Annales. Station Centrale d'Hydrobiologie Appliquee [*A publication*]
Ann Stn Chim Agrar Sper Roma ... Annali. Stazione Chimico-Agraria Sperimentale di Roma [*A publication*]
Ann Stn Chim-Agrar Sper Roma Ser 3 Pubbl ... Annali. Stazione Chimico-Agraria Sperimentale di Roma. Serie 3. Pubblicazione [*A publication*]
Ann Stom ... Annali di Stomatologia [*A publication*]
Ann Stomatol ... Annali di Stomatologia [*Roma*] [*A publication*]
Ann Stomatol Ist Super Odontoiatr G Eastman ... Annali di Stomatologia. Istituto Superiore di Odontoiatria G. Eastman [*A publication*]
Ann Stomatol (Roma) ... Annali di Stomatologia (Roma) [*A publication*]
Ann Storia Nat ... Annali di Storia Naturale [*A publication*]
Ann Surg .... Annals of Surgery [*A publication*]
Ann Surv Afr L ... Annual Survey of African Law [*A publication*] (DLA)
Ann Surv Am ... Annual Survey of American Law [*A publication*] (DLA)
Ann Surv Am L ... Annual Survey of American Law [*A publication*]
Ann Surv of Aust Law ... Annual Survey of Australian Law [*A publication*]
Ann Surv Banking L ... Annual Survey of Banking Law [*A publication*] (DLA)
Ann Surv Colo L ... Annual Survey of Colorado Law [*A publication*] (DLA)
Ann Surv Comm L ... Annual Survey of Commonwealth Law [*A publication*]
Ann Surv Commonw L ... Annual Survey of Commonwealth Law [*A publication*]
Ann Survey ... Annual Survey of Massachusetts Law [*A publication*] (DLA)
Ann Survey Am L ... Annual Survey of American Law [*A publication*]
Ann Surv Ind L ... Annual Survey of Indian Law [*A publication*] (DLA)
Ann Surv Law ... Annual Survey of Law [*A publication*] (APTA)
Ann Surv of Law ... Annual Survey of Law [*A publication*] (APTA)
Ann Surv Mass L ... Annual Survey of Massachusetts Law [*A publication*]
Ann Surv S Afr L ... Annual Survey of South African Law [*A publication*] (DLA)

Ann Surv SAL ... Annual Survey of South African Law [*A publication*]
Ann Systems Res ... Annals of Systems Research [*A publication*]
Ann Syst Res ... Annals of Systems Research [*A publication*]
Ann Tab Sect 2 ... Annales du Tabac. Section 2 [*A publication*]
Ann Tax Cas ... Annotated Tax Cases [*England*] [*A publication*] (DLA)
Ann Tec Agr ... Annales de Technologie Agricole [*Paris*] [*A publication*]
Ann Tech Agric ... Annales de Technologie Agricole [*A publication*]
Ann Technol Agr ... Annales de Technologie Agricole [*Paris*] [*A publication*]
Ann Technol Agric (Paris) ... Annales de Technologie Agricole (Paris) [*A publication*]
Ann Telecom ... Annales des Telecommunications [*A publication*]
Ann Telecomm ... Annales des Telecommunications [*A publication*]
Ann Telecommun ... Annales des Telecommunications [*A publication*]
Ann Ther .... Annee Therapeutique [*A publication*]
AnnThijm .. Annalen van het Thijmgenootschap [*A publication*]
Ann Thijmgenoot ... Annales Thijmgenootschap [*A publication*]
Ann Thorac ... Annals of Thoracic Surgery [*A publication*]
Ann Thoracic Surg ... Annals of Thoracic Surgery [*A publication*]
Ann Thorac Surg ... Annals of Thoracic Surgery [*A publication*]
Ann Thor Surg ... Annals of Thoracic Surgery [*A publication*]
Ann Tokyo Astron Obs ... Annals. Tokyo Astronomical Observatory [*A publication*]
Ann Transvaal Mus ... Annals. Transvaal Museum [*A publication*]
Ann Transv Mus ... Annals. Transvaal Museum [*A publication*]
Ann Trav Agr Sci ... Annales des Travaux Agricoles Scientifiques [*A publication*]
Ann Trav Publics Belg ... Annales des Travaux Publics de Belgique [*A publication*]
AnnTriest ... Annali Triestini [*A publication*]
Ann Triest Cura Univ Trieste Sez II ... Annali Triestini a Cura. Universita di Trieste. Sezione II. Scienze ed Ingegneria [*A publication*]
Ann Trop M ... Annals of Tropical Medicine and Parasitology [*A publication*]
Ann Trop Med ... Annals of Tropical Medicine and Parasitology [*A publication*]
Ann Trop Med Paras ... Annals of Tropical Medicine and Parasitology [*A publication*]
Ann Trop Med Parasitol ... Annals of Tropical Medicine and Parasitology [*A publication*]
Ann Trop Paediatr ... Annals of Tropical Paediatrics [*A publication*]
Ann Trop Res ... Annals of Tropical Research [*A publication*]
Ann Tuberc ... Annals of Tuberculosis [*A publication*]
Ann Tvl Mus ... Annals. Transvaal Museum [*A publication*]
AnnUA .... Annals. Ukrainian Academy of Arts and Sciences in the US [*A publication*]
Annu A A A ... Annuaire des Auditeurs et Anciens Auditeurs. Academie de Droit International de la Haye [*A publication*]
Annu Acad Roy Belg ... Annuaire. Academie Royale de Belgique [*A publication*]
Annu Acad R Sci Outre Mer ... Annuaire. Academie Royale des Sciences d'Outre Mer [*A publication*]
Annu Accad Ital ... Annuario. Reale Accademia d'Italia [*A publication*]
Annu Accad Univ Stud ... Annuario Accademico. Regia Universita degli Studi de Siena [*A publication*]
Annu Afr Nord ... Annuaire de l'Afrique du Nord [*A publication*]
Annu Agric Suisse ... Annuaire Agricole de la Suisse [*A publication*]
Annuaire Francais Droit Int ... Annuaire Francais de Droit International [*A publication*]
Annuaire Univ Sofia Fac ... Annuaire. Universite de Sofia. Faculte de Mathematiques [*A publication*]
Annuaire Univ Sofia Fac Math Mec ... Annuaire. Universite de Sofia. Faculte de Mathematiques et Mecanique [*A publication*]
Annuaire Univ Sofia Fac Phys ... Annuaire. Universite de Sofia. Faculte de Physique [*A publication*]
Annu Air Pollut Control Conf ... Annual Air Pollution Control Conference [*A publication*]
Annual Br Sc Athens ... Annual. British School at Athens [*A publication*]
Annual Dep Jordan ... Annual. Department of Antiquities of Jordan [*A publication*]
Annual Law R ... Annual Law Review [*A publication*] (APTA)
Annual L Rev ... Western Australian Annual Law Review [*Nedlands, Australia*] [*A publication*] (DLA)
Annual R .... Louisiana Annual Reports [*A publication*] (DLA)
Annual Rep Fac Ed Univ Iwate ... Annual Report. Faculty of Education. University of Iwate [*A publication*]
Annual R Residential Care Assoc ... Annual Review. Residential Care Association [*A publication*]
Annu Amer Inst Coop ... Annual. American Institute of Cooperation [*A publication*]
Annu Anim Psychol ... Annual of Animal Psychology [*A publication*]
Annuario Acc Etr Cortona ... Annuario. Accademia Etrusca di Cortona [*A publication*]
Annuario Ac Etr ... Annuario. Accademia Etrusca di Cortona [*A publication*]
Annuario At ... Annuario. Scuola Archeologica di Atene e Missioni Italiani in Oriente [*A publication*]
Annu Ass Ott Ital ... Annuario. Associazione Ottica Italiana [*A publication*]
Annu Astron Osserv ... Annuario Astronomico. Osservatorio Astronomico. Universita di Torino [*A publication*]
Annu Bibliogr Engl Lang Lit ... Annual Bibliography of English Language and Literature [*A publication*]
Annu Bibliogr Mod Humanit Res Assoc ... Annual Bibliography. Modern Humanities Research Association [*A publication*]

Annu Biol Colloq ... Annual Biology Colloquium [*A publication*]
Annu Biol Fac Sci Nat Univ Kiril Metodij (Skopje) ... Annuaire. Biologie. Faculte des Sciences Naturelles. Universite Kiril. Metodij (Skopje) [*A publication*]
Annu Book ASTM Stand ... Annual Book of ASTM [*American Society for Testing and Materials*] Standards [*A publication*]
Annu Brit Sch Athens ... Annual. British School at Athens [*A publication*]
Annu Brit School Athens ... Annual. British School at Athens [*A publication*]
Annu Bull Int Dairy Fed ... Annual Bulletin. International Dairy Federation [*A publication*]
Annu Bull Soc Jersiaise ... Annual Bulletin. Societe Jersiaise [*A publication*]
Annu Bur Longitudes (Paris) ... Annuaire. Bureau de Longitudes (Paris) [*A publication*]
Annu Chim ... Annuaire de Chimie [*A publication*]
Annu Conf Aust Inst Met ... Annual Conference. Australian Institute of Metals [*Later, Annual Conference. Australasian Institute of Metals*] [*A publication*]
Annu Conf Australas Inst Met ... Annual Conference. Australasian Institute of Metals [*A publication*]
Annu Conf B C Water Waste Assoc Proc ... Annual Conference. British Columbia Water and Waste Association. Proceedings [*A publication*]
Annu Conf Calif Mosq Vector Control Assoc Proc Pap ... Annual Conference. California Mosquito and Vector Control Association. Proceedings and Papers [*A publication*]
Annu Conf Environ Toxicol ... Annual Conference on Environmental Toxicology [*A publication*]
Annu Conf Glass Prob ... Annual Conference on Glass Problems [*A publication*]
Annu Conf Glass Prob Collect Pap ... Annual Conference on Glass Problems. Collected Papers [*A publication*]
Annu Conf Hung Physiol Soc ... Annual Conference. Hungarian Physiological Society [*A publication*]
Annu Conf Manit Agron ... Annual Conference. Manitoba Agronomists [*A publication*]
Annu Conf Metall Proc ... Annual Conference of Metallurgists. Proceedings [*A publication*]
Annu Conf Microbeam Anal Soc Proc ... Annual Conference. Microbeam Analysis Society. Proceedings [*A publication*]
Annu Conf Natl Water Supply Improv Assoc Tech Proc ... Annual Conference. National Water Supply Improvement Association. Technical Proceedings [*A publication*]
Annu Conf Res Med Educ ... Annual Conference on Research in Medical Education [*A publication*]
Annu Conf Soil Mech Found Eng ... Annual Conference. Soil Mechanics and Foundation Engineering [*A publication*]
Annu Connector Symp Proc ... Annual Connector Symposium. Proceedings [*A publication*]
Annu Conv Proc Wash Ass Wheat Growers ... Annual Convention Proceedings. Washington Association of Wheat Growers [*A publication*]
Annu Dr Marit Aer ... Annuaire de Droit Maritime et Aerien [*A publication*]
Annu Ec Tech Super Phys ... Annuaire. Ecoles Techniques Superieures. Physique [*A publication*]
Annu Eng Conf Inst Eng Aust Pap ... Annual Engineering Conference. Institution of Engineers of Australia. Papers [*A publication*]
Annu Europ ... Annuaire Europeen [*A publication*]
Annu Fac Agric Sylvi Univ Skopje Pomol ... Annuaire. Faculte d'Agriculture et de Sylviculture. Universite de Skopje. Pomologie [*A publication*]
Annu Fac Agric Sylvi Univ Skopje Zootech ... Annuaire. Faculte d'Agriculture et de Sylviculture. Universite de Skopje. Zootechnie [*A publication*]
Annu Fac Agric Univ Skopje ... Annuaire. Faculte d'Agriculture et de Sylviculture. Universite de Skopje [*A publication*]
Annu de la Fac de Droit de Skopje ... Annuaire. Faculte de Droit de Skopje [*A publication*] (DLA)
Annu Fac Educ Gunma Univ Art Technol Ser ... Annual Report. Faculty of Education. Gunma University. Art and Technology Series [*A publication*]
Annu Fac Sci Nat Univ Kiril Metodij (Skopje) Biol ... Annuaire. Faculte des Sciences Naturelles. Universite Kiril et Metodij (Skopje). Biologie [*A publication*]
Annu Fac Sci Nat Univ Kiril Metodij (Skopje) Math Phys Chim ... Annuaire. Faculte des Sciences Naturelles. Universite Kiril et Metodij (Skopje). Mathematique, Physique, et Chimie [*A publication*]
Annu Franc Dr Homme ... Annuaire Francais des Droits de l'Homme [*A publication*]
Annu Franc Dr Int ... Annuaire Francais de Droit International [*A publication*]
Annu Franc de Droit Internat ... Annuaire Francais de Droit International [*A publication*]
Annu Freq Control Symp ... Annual Frequency Control Symposium [*A publication*]
Annu Freq Control Symp Proc ... Annual Frequency Control Symposium. Proceedings [*A publication*]
Annu Gas Compressor Inst ... Annual. Gas Compressor Institute [*A publication*]
Annu Gas Meas Inst ... Annual. Gas Measurement Institute [*A publication*]
Annu Hebrew Union Coll ... Annual. Hebrew Union College [*A publication*]

Annu Highway Geol Symp Proc ... Annual Highway Geology Symposium. Proceedings [*A publication*]
ANNUI ...... Annuity (DLA)
Annu Index Pop Music Rec Rev ... Annual Index to Popular Music Record Reviews [*A publication*]
Annu Inf Meet Heavy Sect Steel Technol Program ... Annual Information Meeting. Heavy Section Steel Technology Program [*A publication*]
Annu de l'Inst de Droit Internat ... Annuaire. Institut de Droit International [*A publication*]
Annu Inst Europ Secur Soc ... Annuaire. Institut Europeen de Securite Sociale [*A publication*]
Annu Inst Philol Hist Orient ... Annuaire. Institut de Philologie et d'Histoire Orientales et Slaves. Universite Libre de Bruxelles [*A publication*]
Annu Int Fonction Publ ... Annuaire International de la Fonction Publique [*A publication*]
ANNUIT ... Annuitant (ROG)
Annu J Inst Eng ... Annual Journal. Institution of Engineers [*A publication*]
Ann Ukr Acad Arts Sci US ... Annals. Ukrainian Academy of Arts and Sciences in the US [*A publication*]
ANNUL ..... Annulment (DLA)
Annu Leg Bibliogr ... Annual Legal Bibliography [*A publication*]
Annu Lightwood Res Conf Proc ... Annual Lightwood Research Conference. Proceedings [*A publication*]
Ann UMCS ... Annales Universitatis Mariae Curie-Sklodowska [*A publication*]
Annu Meat Sci Inst Proc ... Annual Meat Science Institute. Proceedings [*A publication*]
Annu Meet Am Coll Nutr ... Annual Meeting. American College of Nutrition [*A publication*]
Annu Meet Am Inst Oral Biol ... Annual Meeting. American Institute of Oral Biology [*A publication*]
Annu Meet Corp Assoc Am Chem Soc ... Annual Meeting. Corporation Associates. American Chemical Society [*A publication*]
Annu Meet Inf Counc Fabr Flammability Proc ... Annual Meeting. Information Council on Fabric Flammability. Proceedings [*A publication*]
Annu Meet Inter Soc Cytol Counc Trans ... Annual Meeting. Inter-Society Cytology Council. Transactions [*A publication*]
Annu Meet Int Soc Exp Hematol ... Annual Meeting. International Society for Experimental Hematology [*A publication*]
Annu Meet Int Water Conf ... Annual Meeting. International Water Conference [*A publication*]
Annu Meet Natl Mastitis Counc ... Annual Meeting. National Mastitis Council [*A publication*]
Annu Meet Proc Am Soc Photogramm ... Annual Meeting-Proceedings. American Society of Photogrammetry [*A publication*]
Annu Meet Proc Int Inst Synth Rubber Prod ... Annual Meeting Proceedings. International Institute of Synthetic Rubber Producers [*A publication*]
Annu Meet Soc Eng Sci Proc ... Annual Meeting. Society of Engineering Science. Proceedings [*A publication*]
Annu Miner Symp Proc ... Annual Minerals Symposium Proceedings [*American Institute of Mining, Metallurgical, and Petroleum Engineers*] [*A publication*]
Annu Min Symp ... Annual Mining Symposium [*A publication*]
Annu Min Symp Proc ... Annual Mining Symposium. Proceedings [*A publication*]
Annu Mus Natl Hist Nat ... Annuaire. Museum National d'Histoire Naturelle [*A publication*]
ANNUN .... Annunciation
Annu Natl Conf Plast Rubber Inst ... Annual National Conference. Plastics and Rubber Institute [*A publication*]
Annu Natl Inf Retr Colloq ... Annual National Information Retrieval Colloquium [*A publication*]
Ann Un Bud ... Annales Universitatis Scientiarum Budapestensis de Rolando Eoetvoes Nominatae. Sectio Classica [*A publication*]
ANNUNC ... Annunciation [*or Annunciator*] (ROG)
Ann Unidroit ... L'Unification du Droit - Annuaire [*A publication*] (DLA)
Ann Univ Abidjan Med ... Annales. Universite d'Abidjan. Medecine [*A publication*]
Ann Univ Abidjan Ser B Med ... Annales. Universite d'Abidjan. Serie B. Medecine [*A publication*]
Ann Univ Abidjan Ser C Sci ... Annales. Universite d'Abidjan. Serie C. Sciences [*A publication*]
Ann Univ Abidjan Ser E Ecol ... Annales. Universite d'Abidjan. Serie E. Ecologie [*A publication*]
Ann Univ Ankara ... Annales. Universite d'Ankara [*A publication*]
Ann Univ ARERS ... Annales. Universite et de l'ARERS [*Association Regionale pour l'Etude et la Recherche Scientifiques*] [*A publication*]
Ann Univ Besancon ... Annales Litteraires. Universite de Besancon [*A publication*]
Ann Univ Bp ... Annales Universitatis Scientiarum Budapestensis [*A publication*]
Ann Univ Brazzaville ... Annales. Universite de Brazzaville [*A publication*]
Ann Univ Brazzaville Ser C Sci ... Annales. Universite de Brazzaville. Serie C. Sciences [*A publication*]
Ann Univ Fenn Abo ... Annales Universitatis Fennicae Aboensis [*A publication*]

Ann Univ Ferrara ... Annali. Universita di Ferrara [*A publication*]
Ann Univ Ferrara Nuova Ser Sez XX Biol ... Annali. Universita di Ferrara. Nuova Serie. Sezione XX. Biologia [*A publication*]
Ann Univ Ferrara Sez I Ecol ... Annali. Universita di Ferrara. Sezione I. Ecologia [*A publication*]
Ann Univ Ferrara Sez III Biol Anim ... Annali. Universita di Ferrara. Sezione III. Biologia Animale [*A publication*]
Ann Univ Ferrara Sez IV ... Annali. Universita di Ferrara. Sezione IV. Fisiologia e Chimica Biologica [*A publication*]
Ann Univ Ferrara Sez IV Bot ... Annali. Universita di Ferrara. Sezione IV. Botanica [*A publication*]
Ann Univ Ferrara Sez IX ... Annali. Universita di Ferrara. Nuovo Serie. Sezione IX. Scienze Geologiche e Paleontologiche [*A publication*]
Ann Univ Ferrara Sez IX Sci Geol Mineral ... Annali. Universita di Ferrara. Sezione IX. Scienze Geologiche e Mineralogiche [*A publication*]
Ann Univ Ferrara Sez IX Sci Geol Paleontol ... Annali. Universita di Ferrara. Sezione IX. Scienze Geologiche e Paleontologiche [*A publication*]
Ann Univ Ferrara Sez V ... Annali. Universita di Ferrara. Sezione V. Chimica Pura ed Applicata [*A publication*]
Ann Univ Ferrara Sez VI Fisiol Chim Biol ... Annali. Universita di Ferrara. Sezione VI. Fisiologia e Chimica Biologica [*A publication*]
Ann Univ Ferrara Sez VII ... Annali. Universita di Ferrara. Nuovo Serie. Sezione VII. Scienze Matematiche [*A publication*]
Ann Univ Ferrara Sez VII NS ... Annali. Universita di Ferrara. Nuovo Serie. Sezione VII [*A publication*]
Ann Univ Ferrara Sez V Suppl ... Annali. Universita di Ferrara. Sezione V. Chimica Pura ed Applicata. Supplemento [*A publication*]
Ann Univ Ferrara Sez XI Farmacol Ter ... Annali. Universita di Ferrara. Sezione XI. Farmacologia e Terapia [*A publication*]
Ann Univ Ferrara Sez XIII Anat Comp ... Annali. Universita di Ferrara. Sezione XIII. Anatomia Comparata [*A publication*]
Ann Univ Genova ... Annali. Reale Universita di Genova [*A publication*]
Ann Univ Lyon 3e Ser Lett ... Annales. Universite de Lyon. 3e Serie. Lettres [*A publication*]
Ann Univ Lyon Fasc Spec ... Annales. Universite de Lyon. Fascicule Special [*A publication*]
Ann Univ Lyon Nouv Ser 2 ... Annales. Universite de Lyon. Nouvelle Serie 2. Droit. Lettres [*A publication*]
Ann Univ Lyon Sci Med ... Annales. Universite de Lyon. Sciences. Medecine [*A publication*]
Ann Univ Lyon Sci Sect A ... Annales. Universite de Lyon. Sciences. Section A. Sciences Mathematiques et Astronomie [*A publication*]
Ann Univ Lyon Sci Sect B ... Annales. Universite de Lyon. Sciences. Section B. Sciences Physiques et Chimiques [*A publication*]
Ann Univ Lyon Sci Sect C ... Annales. Universite de Lyon. Sciences. Section C. Sciences Naturelles [*A publication*]
Ann Univ Madagascar Ser Sci Nat Math ... Annales. Universite de Madagascar. Serie Sciences de la Nature et Mathematiques [*A publication*]
Ann Univ Madagascar Ser Sci Nature Math ... Annales. Universite de Madagascar. Serie Sciences de la Nature et Mathematiques [*A publication*]
Ann Univ Mariae Curie-Sklodowska Med ... Annales Universitatis Mariae Curie-Sklodowska. Sectio D. Medicina [*A publication*]
Ann Univ Mariae Curie-Sklodowska Sect A ... Annales Universitatis Mariae Curie-Sklodowska. Sectio A. Mathematica [*A publication*]
Ann Univ Mariae Curie-Sklodowska Sect AA ... Annales Universitatis Mariae Curie-Sklodowska. Sectio AA. Physica et Chemia [*A publication*]
Ann Univ Mariae Curie-Sklodowska Sect AAA ... Annales Universitatis Mariae Curie-Sklodowska. Sectio AAA (Physica) [*Poland*] [*A publication*]
Ann Univ Mariae Curie-Sklodowska Sect B ... Annales Universitatis Mariae Curie-Sklodowska. Sectio B. Geographia, Geologia, Mineralogia, et Petrographia [*A publication*]
Ann Univ Mariae Curie-Sklodowska Sect C ... Annales Universitatis Mariae Curie-Sklodowska. Sectio C. Biologia [*A publication*]
Ann Univ Mariae Curie-Sklodowska Sect C Biol ... Annales Universitatis Mariae Curie-Sklodowska. Sectio C. Biologia [*A publication*]
Ann Univ Mariae Curie-Sklodowska Sect C Suppl ... Annales Universitatis Mariae Curie-Sklodowska. Sectio C. Biologia. Supplementum [*A publication*]
Ann Univ Mariae Curie-Sklodowska Sect D ... Annales Universitatis Mariae Curie-Sklodowska. Sectio D. Medicina [*A publication*]
Ann Univ Mariae Curie-Sklodowska Sect DD ... Annales Universitatis Mariae Curie-Sklodowska. Sectio DD. Medicina Veterinaria [*A publication*]
Ann Univ Mariae Curie-Sklodowska Sect DD Med Vet ... Annales Universitatis Mariae Curie-Sklodowska. Sectio DD. Medicina Veterinaria [*A publication*]
Ann Univ Mariae Curie-Sklodowska Sect D Med ... Annales Universitatis Mariae Curie-Sklodowska. Sectio D. Medicina [*A publication*]
Ann Univ Mariae Curie-Sklodowska Sect E ... Annales Universitatis Mariae Curie-Sklodowska. Sectio E. Agricultura [*A publication*]

Ann Univ Mariae Curie-Sklodowska Sect E Agric ... Annales Universitatis Mariae Curie-Sklodowska. Sectio E. Agricultura [*A publication*]
Ann Univ Mariae Curie-Sklodowska Sect EE ... Annales Universitatis Mariae Curie-Sklodowska. Sectio EE. Agraria [*A publication*]
Ann Univ Mariae Curie-Sklodowska Sect E Suppl ... Annales Universitatis Mariae Curie-Sklodowska. Sectio E. Agricultura. Supplementum [*A publication*]
Ann Univ M Curie-Sklodowska Sect AA ... Annales Universitatis Mariae Curie-Sklodowska. Sectio AA. Physica et Chemia [*A publication*]
Ann Univ M Curie-Sklodowska Sect AAA (Phys) ... Annales Universitatis Mariae Curie-Sklodowska. Sectio AAA (Physica) [*A publication*]
Ann Univ M Curie-Sklodowska Sect C ... Annales Universitatis Mariae Curie-Sklodowska. Sectio C. Biologia [*A publication*]
Ann Univ M Curie-Sklodowska Sect D ... Annales Universitatis Mariae Curie-Sklodowska. Sectio D. Medicina [*A publication*]
Ann Univ Montp Suppl Sci Ser Bot ... Annales. Universite de Montpellier. Supplement Scientifique. Serie Botanique [*A publication*]
Ann Univ Padova ... Annale. Universita di Padova. Facolta di Economia e Commercio in Verona [*A publication*]
Ann Univ Paris ... Annales. Universite de Paris [*A publication*]
Ann Univ Provence Geol Mediterr ... Annales. Universite de Provence. Geologie Mediterraneenne [*A publication*]
Ann Univ Sara Math Naturwiss Fak ... Annales Universitatis Saraviensis (Reihe). Mathematisch-Naturwissenschaftliche Fakultaet [*A publication*]
Ann Univ Sara Naturwiss ... Annales Universitatis Saraviensis. Naturwissenschaften [*A publication*]
Ann Univ Sara Sci ... Annales Universitatis Saraviensis. Scientia [*A publication*]
Ann Univ Saraviensis Med ... Annales Universitatis Saraviensis. Medizin [*A publication*]
Ann Univ Saraviensis Naturwiss ... Annales Universitatis Saraviensis. Naturwissenschaften [*A publication*]
Ann Univ Saraviensis Phil ... Annales Universitatis Saraviensis. Philosophie [*A publication*]
Ann Univ Saraviensis Sci ... Annales Universitatis Saraviensis. Scientia [*A publication*]
Ann Univ Saraviensis Wiss ... Annales Universitatis Saraviensis. Wissenschaften [*A publication*]
Ann Univ Sarav Math-Natur Fak ... Annales Universitatis Saraviensis. Mathematisch-Naturwissenschaftliche Fakultaet [*A publication*]
Ann Univ Sarav Med ... Annales Universitatis Saraviensis. Medizin [*A publication*]
Ann Univ Sarav (Reihe) Math-Naturwiss Fak ... Annales Universitatis Saraviensis (Reihe). Mathematisch-Naturwissenschaftliche Fakultaet [*A publication*]
Ann Univ Sci Budapest Eotvos Sect Math ... Annales Universitatis Scientiarum Budapestensis de Rolando Eoetvoes Nominatae. Sectio Mathematica [*A publication*]
Ann Univ Sci Budapest Rolando Eotvos Nominatae Sect Chim ... Annales Universitatis Scientiarum Budapestensis de Rolando Eoetvoes Nominatae. Sectio Chimica [*A publication*]
Ann Univ Sci Budapest Sect Comput ... Annales Universitatis Scientiarum Budapestensis de Rolando Eoetvoes Nominatae. Sectio Computatorica [*A publication*]
Ann Univ Sci Budap Rolando Eotvos Nominatae Sect Biol ... Annales Universitatis Scientiarum Budapestensis de Rolando Eoetvoes Nominatae. Sectio Biologica [*A publication*]
Ann Univ Sci Budap Rolando Eotvos Nominatae Sect Chim ... Annales Universitatis Scientiarum Budapestensis de Rolando Eoetvoes Nominatae. Sectio Chimica [*A publication*]
Ann Univ Sci Budap Rolando Eotvos Nominatae Sect Geol ... Annales Universitatis Scientiarum Budapestensis de Rolando Eoetvoes Nominatae. Sectio Geologica [*A publication*]
Ann Univ Stellenbosch Ser A ... Annale. Universiteit van Stellenbosch. Serie A [*A publication*]
Ann Univ Stellenbosch Ser A II Sool ... Annale. Universiteit van Stellenbosch. Serie A-II. Soologie [*A publication*]
Ann Univ Stellenbosch Ser B ... Annale. Universiteit van Stellenbosch. Serie B [*A publication*]
Ann Univ Toscane ... Annali. Universita Toscane [*A publication*]
Ann Univ Turk Ser A II Biol-Geogr ... Annales Universitatis Turkuensis. Series A-II. Biologica-Geographica [*A publication*]
Ann Univ Turk Ser A II Biol-Geogr-Geol ... Annales Universitatis Turkuensis. Series A-II. Biologica-Geographica-Geologica [*A publication*]
Ann Univ Turku Ser A ... Annales Universitatis Turkuensis. Series A [*A publication*]
Ann Univ Turku Ser A I ... Annales Universitatis Turkuensis. Series A-I. Astronomica-Chemica-Physica-Mathematica [*A publication*]
Ann Univ Turku Ser A II ... Annales Universitatis Turkuensis. Series A-II. Biologica-Geographica [*A publication*]
Ann Uniw Marii Curie-Sklodowskiej Sect C Biol ... Annales. Uniwersytet Marii Curie-Sklodowskiej. Sectio C. Biologia [*A publication*]

Ann Uniw Marii Curie Sklodowskiej Sect E Agric ... Annales. Uniwersytet Marii Curie-Sklodowskiej. Sectio E. Agricultura [*A publication*]

Annu Northeast Reg Antipollu Conf ... Annual Northeastern Regional Antipollution Conference [*A publication*]

Annu Observ Belg Annu Meteorol ... Annuaire. Observatoire Royale de Belgique. Deuxieme Serie. Annuaire Meteorologique [*A publication*]

Annu Ordre Souverain Mil Malte ... Annuaire. Ordre Souverain Militaire de Malte [*A publication*]

AnnUP .... Annales. Universite de Paris [*A publication*]

Annu Polit Int ... Annuario di Politica Internazionale [*A publication*]

Annu Pontif Accad Sci ... Annuario. Pontificia Accademia delle Scienze [*A publication*]

Annu Priestley Lect ... Annual Priestley Lectures [*A publication*]

Annu Proc Am Assoc Zoo Vet ... Annual Proceedings. American Association of Zoo Veterinarians [*A publication*]

Annu Proc Assoc Sci & Tech Soc S Afr ... Annual Proceedings. Associated Scientific and Technical Societies of South Africa [*A publication*]

Annu Proc Gifu Coll Pharm ... Annual Proceedings. Gifu College of Pharmacy [*A publication*]

Annu Proc Gifu Pharm Univ ... Annual Proceedings. Gifu Pharmaceutical University [*A publication*]

Annu Proc Phytochem Soc ... Annual Proceedings. Phytochemical Society [*A publication*]

Annu Proc Phytochem Soc Eur ... Annual Proceedings. Phytochemical Society of Europe [*A publication*]

Annu Proc Reliab Phys (Symp) ... Annual Proceedings. Reliability Physics (Symposium) [*A publication*]

Annu Prog Child Psychiatry Chil Dev ... Annual Progress in Child Psychiatry and Child Development [*A publication*]

Annu Prog Rep SEATO Med Res Lab ... Annual Progress Report. SEATO [*Southeast Asia Treaty Organization*] Medical Research Laboratories [*A publication*]

Annu Psychoanal ... Annual of Psychoanalysis [*A publication*]

Annu R Accad Ital ... Annuario. Reale Accademia d'Italia [*A publication*]

Annu Rep Acc Cornish Chamber Mines ... Annual Report and Accounts. Cornish Chamber of Mines [*A publication*]

Annu Rep Agric Exp Stn (Nebr) ... Annual Report. Agricultural Experiment Station (Nebraska) [*A publication*]

Annu Rep Agric Exp Stn Univ MD ... Annual Report. Agricultural Experiment Station. University of Maryland [*A publication*]

Annu Rep Agric Res Inst North Irel ... Annual Report. Agricultural Research Institute of Northern Ireland [*A publication*]

Annu Rep Air Resour Atmos Turbul Diffus Lab ... Annual Report. Air Resources Atmospheric Turbulence and Diffusion Laboratory [*A publication*]

Annu Rep Akita Prefect Inst Public Health ... Annual Report. Akita Prefectural Institute of Public Health [*A publication*]

Annu Rep Ala Agr Exp Sta ... Annual Report. Alabama Agricultural Experiment Station [*A publication*]

Annu Rep AMDEL ... Annual Report AMDEL [*Australian Mineral Development Laboratories*] [*Frewville*] [*A publication*]

Annu Rep Amer Hist Ass ... Annual Report. American Historical Association [*A publication*]

Annu Rep Am Inst Phys ... Annual Report. American Institute of Physics [*A publication*]

Annu Rep Anal At Spectrosc ... Annual Reports on Analytical Atomic Spectroscopy [*A publication*]

Annu Rep Anim Nutr Allied Sci Rowett Res Inst ... Annual Report on Animal Nutrition and Allied Sciences. Rowett Research Institute [*A publication*]

Annu Rep Archaeol Surv India ... Annual Report. Archaeological Survey of India [*A publication*]

Annu Rep Aust At Energy Comm ... Annual Report. Australian Atomic Energy Commission [*A publication*]

Annu Rep Bean Improv Coop ... Annual Report. Bean Improvement Cooperative [*A publication*]

Annu Rep Biol Works Fac Sci Osaka Univ ... Annual Report of Biological Works. Faculty of Science. Osaka University [*A publication*]

Annu Rep Board Greenkeeping Res ... Annual Report. Board of Greenkeeping Research [*A publication*]

Annu Rep Br Non Ferrous Met Res Assoc ... Annual Report. British Non Ferrous Metals Research Association [*A publication*]

Annu Rep Bur Mines (Philipp) ... Annual Report. Bureau of Mines and Geo-Sciences (Philippines) [*A publication*]

Annu Rep Bur Rec Geol Min ... Annual Report. Bureau de Recherches Geologiques et Minieres [*Paris*] [*A publication*]

Annu Rep Cacao Res Univ West Indies ... Annual Report on Cacao Research. University of the West Indies [*A publication*]

Annu Rep Cancer Res Inst Kanazawa Univ ... Annual Report. Cancer Research Institute. Kanazawa University [*A publication*]

Annu Rep Can Seed Growers Ass ... Annual Report. Canadian Seed Growers Association [*A publication*]

Annu Rep Carnegie Inst Wash Dep Plant Biol ... Annual Report. Carnegie Institution of Washington. Department of Plant Biology [*A publication*]

Annu Rep Cent Adult Dis (Osaka) ... Annual Report. Center for Adult Diseases (Osaka) [*A publication*]

Annu Rep Cent Reg Arecanut Res Stn ... Annual Report. Central and Regional Arecanut Research Stations [*A publication*]

Annu Rep Centre Resour Stud ... Annual Report. Centre for Resource Studies [*Kingston, Ontario*] [*A publication*]

Annu Rep Chamber Mines Precambrian Res Unit ... Annual Report. Chamber of Mines Precambrian Research Unit. University of Cape Town [*A publication*]

Annu Rep Chem Soc Sect A Phys Inorg Chem ... Annual Reports. Chemical Society. Section A. Physical and Inorganic Chemistry [*A publication*]

Annu Rep Clemson Agr Exp Sta ... Annual Report. Clemson Agricultural Experiment Station [*A publication*]

Annu Rep Conf Electr Insul Dielectr Phenom ... Annual Report. Conference on Electrical Insulation and Dielectric Phenomena [*A publication*]

Annu Rep Cornish Min Dev Ass ... Annual Report. Cornish Mining Development Association [*A publication*]

Annu Rep Counc Miner Technol ... Annual Report. Council for Mineral Technology [*Randburg*] [*A publication*]

Annu Rep CSIR ... Annual Report. CSIR [*Council for Scientific and Industrial Research*] [*A publication*]

Annu Rep CSIRO Mar Biochem Unit ... Annual Report. Commonwealth Scientific and Industrial Research Organisation. Marine Biochemistry Unit [*A publication*]　(APTA)

Annu Rep CSIRO Plant Ind ... Annual Report. Commonwealth Scientific and Industrial Research Organisation. Plant Industry [*A publication*]

Annu Rep Dante Soc ... Annual Report. Dante Society [*A publication*]

Annu Rep Dep Agric Stock Queensl ... Annual Report. Department of Agriculture and Stock. Queensland [*A publication*]　(APTA)

Annu Rep Dep Agr NSW ... Annual Report. Department of Agriculture. New South Wales [*A publication*]　(APTA)

Annu Rep Dep At Energy Gov India ... Annual Report. Department of Atomic Energy. Government of India [*A publication*]

Annu Rep Dep Miner Energy (Victoria) ... Annual Report. Department of Minerals and Energy (Victoria) [*Melbourne*] [*A publication*]

Annu Rep Dep Miner Resour (NSW) ... Annual Report. Department of Mineral Resources (New South Wales) [*A publication*]

Annu Rep Dep Mines Energy (South Aust) ... Annual Report. Department of Mines and Energy (South Australia) [*A publication*]

Annu Rep Dep Mines (West Aust) ... Annual Report. Department of Mines (Western Australia) [*A publication*]

Annu Rep Dir Dep Terr Magn Carnegie Inst ... Annual Report of the Director. Department of Terrestrial Magnetism. Carnegie Institution [*A publication*]

Annu Rep Dir Res Philipp Sugar Assoc ... Annual Report. Director of Research. Philippine Sugar Association [*A publication*]

Annu Rep E Afr Agr Forest Res Organ ... Annual Report. East African Agriculture and Forestry Research Organization [*A publication*]

Annu Rep East Malling Res Stn (Kent) ... Annual Report. East Malling Research Station (Kent) [*A publication*]

Annu Rep Energy Mines Resour (Can) ... Annual Report. Energy, Mines, and Resources (Canada) [*A publication*]

Annu Rep Eng Res Inst Fac Eng Univ Tokyo ... Annual Report. Engineering Research Institute. Faculty of Engineering. University of Tokyo [*A publication*]

Annu Rep Eng Res Inst Tokyo Univ ... Annual Report. Engineering Research Institute. Tokyo University [*A publication*]

Annu Rep Eng Res Inst Univ Tokyo ... Annual Report. Engineering Research Institute. University of Tokyo [*A publication*]

Annu Rep Entomol Soc Ont ... Annual Report. Entomological Society of Ontario [*A publication*]

Annu Rep Environ Pollut Res Cent Fukui Prefect ... Annual Report. Environmental Pollution Research Center. Fukui Prefecture [*A publication*]

Annu Rep Environ Pollut Res Cent Ibaraki-Ken ... Annual Report. Environmental Pollution Research Center of Ibaraki-Ken [*A publication*]

Annu Rep Fac Educ Gunma Univ ... Annual Report. Faculty of Education. Gunma University [*A publication*]

Annu Rep Fac Educ Gunma Univ Art Technol Ser ... Annual Report. Faculty of Education. Gunma University. Art and Technology Series [*A publication*]

Annu Rep Fac Educ Iwate Univ ... Annual Report. Faculty of Education. Iwate University [*A publication*]

Annu Rep Fac Educ Univ Iwate ... Annual Report. Faculty of Education. University of Iwate [*A publication*]

Annu Rep Fac Pharm Sci Nagoya City Univ ... Annual Report. Faculty of Pharmaceutical Sciences. Nagoya City University [*A publication*]

Annu Rep Fac Pharm Sci Tokushima Univ ... Annual Reports. Faculty of Pharmaceutical Sciences. Tokushima University [*A publication*]

Annu Rep Farmers Union Grain Terminal Ass ... Annual Report. Farmers Union Grain Terminal Association [*A publication*]

Annu Rep Ferment Process ... Annual Reports on Fermentation Processes [*A publication*]

Annu Rep Finan Statements Inst Corn Agr Merchants ... Annual Report and Financial Statements. Institute of Corn and Agricultural Merchants [*A publication*]

Annu Rep Fla Univ Agr Exp Sta ... Annual Report. Florida University. Agricultural Experiment Station [*A publication*]

Annu Rep Food Res Inst Aichi Prefect ... Annual Report. Food Research Institute. Aichi Prefecture [*A publication*]

Annu Rep Geol Surv Dep (Cyprus) ... Annual Report. Geological Survey Department (Cyprus) [*A publication*]

Annu Rep Geol Surv Dep (Malawi) ... Annual Report. Geological Survey Department (Malawi) [*A publication*]

Annu Rep Geol Surv Div (Niger) ... Annual Report. Geological Survey Division (Nigeria) [*A publication*]

Annu Rep Geol Surv Fed Niger ... Annual Report. Geological Survey. Federation of Nigeria [*A publication*]

Annu Rep Geol Surv Malays ... Annual Report. Geological Survey of Malaysia [*A publication*]

Annu Rep Geol Surv Malaysia ... Annual Report. Geological Survey of Malaysia [*A publication*]

Annu Rep Geol Surv Mines Dep (Swaziland) ... Annual Report. Geological Survey and Mines Department (Swaziland) [*A publication*]

Annu Rep Geol Surv West Aust ... Annual Report. Geological Survey. Western Australia [*A publication*]   (APTA)

Annu Rep Geophys Comm (Norw) ... Annual Report. Geophysical Commission (Norway) [*A publication*]

Annu Rep Geophys Res Norw ... Annual Report on Geophysical Research in Norway [*A publication*]

Annu Rep Governor Kans Wheat Comm ... Annual Report to the Governor. Kansas Wheat Commission [*A publication*]

Annu Rep Hokkaido Branch For For Prod Res Inst ... Annual Report. Hokkaido Branch. Forestry and Forest Products Research Institute [*A publication*]

Annu Rep Hokkaido Branch Gov For Exp Stn ... Annual Report. Hokkaido Branch. Government Forest Experiment Station [*A publication*]

Annu Rep Hokusei Gakuin Jr Coll ... Annual Report. Hokusei Gakuin Junior College [*A publication*]

Annu Rep Ind Agric Exp Stn ... Annual Report. Indiana Agricultural Experiment Station [*A publication*]

Annu Rep Inorg Gen Synth ... Annual Reports in Inorganic and General Syntheses [*A publication*]

Annu Rep Inst Ferment (Osaka) ... Annual Report. Institute for Fermentation (Osaka) [*A publication*]

Annu Rep Inst Food Microbiol Chiba Univ ... Annual Report. Institute of Food Microbiology. Chiba University [*A publication*]

Annu Rep Inst Mar Eng ... Annual Report. Institute of Marine Engineers [*A publication*]

Annu Rep Inst Nucl Stud Univ Tokyo ... Annual Report. Institute for Nuclear Study. University of Tokyo [*A publication*]

Annu Rep Inst Phys Acad Sin ... Annual Report. Institute of Physics. Academia Sinica [*A publication*]

Annu Rep Inst Popul Probl ... Annual Reports. Institute of Population Problems [*A publication*]

Annu Rep Inst Sci Technol Meiji Univ ... Annual Report. Institute of Sciences and Technology. Meiji University [*A publication*]

Annu Rep Inst Sociol ... Annual Report. Institute of Sociology [*A publication*]

Annu Rep Inst Virus Res Kyoto Univ ... Annual Report. Institute for Virus Research. Kyoto University [*A publication*]

Annu Rep Int Assoc Milk Sanit ... Annual Report. International Association of Milk Sanitarians [*A publication*]

Annu Rep Int Crop Impr Ass ... Annual Report. International Crop Improvement Association [*A publication*]

Annu Rep Int Tin Res Counc ... Annual Report. International Tin Research Council [*A publication*]

Annu Rep Itsuu Lab ... Annual Report. Itsuu Laboratory [*A publication*]

Annu Rep John Innes Hortic Inst ... Annual Report. John Innes Horticultural Institution [*A publication*]

Annu Rep Jpn Assoc Tuberc ... Annual Report. Japanese Association for Tuberculosis [*A publication*]

Annu Rep Jpn Soc Tuber ... Annual Report. Japanese Society for Tuberculosis [*A publication*]

Annu Rep Kinki Univ At Energy Res Inst ... Annual Reports. Kinki University Atomic Energy Research Institute [*A publication*]

Annu Rep Kumamoto Livest Exp Stn ... Annual Report. Kumamoto Livestock Experiment Station [*A publication*]

Annu Rep Kyoritsu Coll Pharm ... Annual Report. Kyoritsu College of Pharmacy [*A publication*]

Annu Rep Lab Algol (Trebon) ... Annual Report. Laboratory of Algology (Trebon) [*A publication*]

Annu Rep Lab Exp Algol Dep Appl Algol (Trebon) ... Annual Report. Laboratory of Experimental Algology and Department of Applied Algology (Trebon) [*A publication*]

Annu Rep Lab Public Health Hiroshima Prefect ... Annual Report. Laboratory of Public Health. Hiroshima Prefecture [*A publication*]

Annu Rep Libr Counc Phila ... Annual Report. Library Council of Philadelphia [*A publication*]

Annu Rep MAFES Miss Agric For Exp St ... Annual Report. MAFES. Mississippi Agricultural and Forestry Experiment Station [*A publication*]

Annu Rep Med Chem ... Annual Reports in Medicinal Chemistry [*A publication*]

Annu Rep Miner Resour Dep (Fiji) ... Annual Report. Mineral Resources Department (Fiji) [*A publication*]

Annu Rep Miner Resour Div (Manitoba) ... Annual Report. Mineral Resources Division (Manitoba) [*A publication*]

Annu Rep Mines NS Dep Mines ... Annual Report on Mines. Nova Scotia Department of Mines [*A publication*]

Annu Rep Mines Serv (Cyprus) ... Annual Report. Mines Service (Cyprus) [*A publication*]

Annu Rep Miss State Univ Agr Exp Sta ... Annual Report. Mississippi State University. Agricultural Experiment Station [*A publication*]

Annu Rep Nat Inst Genet (Jap) ... Annual Report. National Institute of Genetics (Japan) [*A publication*]

Annu Rep Natl Inst Genet ... Annual Report. National Institute of Genetics [*A publication*]

Annu Rep Natl Inst Nutr ... Annual Report. National Institute of Nutrition [*A publication*]

Annu Rep Natl Inst Nutr (Tokyo) ... Annual Report. National Institute of Nutrition (Tokyo) [*A publication*]

Annu Rep Natl Vet Assay Lab ... Annual Report. National Veterinary Assay Laboratory [*A publication*]

Annu Rep Nat Prod Res Inst Seoul Natl Univ ... Annual Reports. Natural Products Research Institute. Seoul National University [*A publication*]

Annu Rep Natur Sci Home Econ Kinjo Gakuin Coll ... Annual Report of Natural Science and Home Economics. Kinjo Gakuin College [*A publication*]

Annu Rep Nat Veg Res Stn (Wellesbourne Eng) ... Annual Report. National Vegetable Research Station (Wellesbourne, England) [*A publication*]

Annu Rep Nebr Grain Impr Ass ... Annual Report. Nebraska Grain Improvement Association [*A publication*]

Annu Rep Nebr Wheat Comm ... Annual Report. Nebraska Wheat Commission [*A publication*]

Annu Rep Neth Inst Sea Res ... Annual Report. Netherlands Institute for Sea Research [*A publication*]

Annu Rep Nigeria Cocoa Res Inst ... Annual Report. Nigeria Cocoa Research Institute [*A publication*]

Annu Rep Nigerian Inst Oceanogr Mar Res (Lagos) ... Annual Report. Nigerian Institute for Oceanography and Marine Research (Lagos) [*A publication*]

Annu Rep N Mex Agr Exp Sta ... Annual Report. New Mexico Agricultural Experiment Station [*A publication*]

Annu Rep Noto Mar Lab ... Annual Report. Noto Marine Laboratory [*A publication*]

Annu Rep NS Fruit Grow Assoc ... Annual Report. Nova Scotia Fruit Growers' Association [*A publication*]

Annu Rep NY State Assoc Dairy Milk Insp ... Annual Report. New York State Association of Dairy and Milk Inspectors [*A publication*]

Annu Rep NY State Assoc Milk Food Sanit ... Annual Report. New York State Association of Milk and Food Sanitarians [*A publication*]

Annu Rep Ohio State Hortic ... Annual Report. Ohio State Horticultural Society [*A publication*]

Annu Rep Okla Agric Exp Stn ... Annual Report. Oklahoma Agricultural Experiment Station [*A publication*]

Annu Rep Ont Dep Mines ... Annual Report. Ontario Department of Mines [*A publication*]

Annu Rep Oreg Hortic Soc ... Annual Report. Oregon Horticultural Society [*A publication*]

Annu Rep Oreg State Hort Soc ... Annual Report. Oregon State Horticultural Society [*A publication*]

Annu Rep Orient Hosp ... Annual Report. Orient Hospital [*A publication*]

Annu Rep Orient Hosp (Beirut) ... Annual Report. Orient Hospital (Beirut) [*A publication*]

Annu Rep Osaka Prefect Radiat Res Inst ... Annual Report. Osaka Prefectural Radiation Research Institute [*A publication*]

Annu Rep Pak Cent Jute Comm ... Annual Report. Pakistan Central Jute Committee [*A publication*]

Annu Rep Peterborough Natur Hist Sci Archaeol Soc ... Annual Report. Peterborough Natural History, Scientific, and Archaeological Society [*A publication*]

Annu Rep PETROBRAS ... Annual Report PETROBRAS [*Petroleo Brasileiro SA*] [*Rio De Janeiro*] [*A publication*]

Annu Rep Philipp Sugar Assoc ... Annual Report. Philippine Sugar Association [*A publication*]

Annu Rep Prod Ammonia Using Coal Source Hydrogen ... Annual Report. Production of Ammonia Using Coal as a Source of Hydrogen [*A publication*]

Annu Rep Prog Chem ... Annual Reports on the Progress of Chemistry [*England*] [*A publication*]

Annu Rep Prog Chem Sect A ... Annual Reports on the Progress of Chemistry. Section A. General, Physical, and Inorganic Chemistry [*A publication*]

Annu Rep Prog Chem Sect A Gen Phys Inorg Chem ... Annual Reports on the Progress of Chemistry. Section A. General, Physical, and Inorganic Chemistry [*England*] [*A publication*]

Annu Rep Prog Chem Sect A Inorg Chem ... Annual Reports on the Progress of Chemistry. Section A. Inorganic Chemistry [*A publication*]

Annu Rep Prog Chem Sect B ... Annual Reports on the Progress of Chemistry. Section B. Organic Chemistry [*A publication*]

Annu Rep Prog Chem Sect B Org Chem ... Annual Reports on the Progress of Chemistry. Section B. Organic Chemistry [*A publication*]

Annu Rep Prog Chem Sect C ... Annual Reports on the Progress of Chemistry. Section C. Physical Chemistry [*England*] [*A publication*]

Annu Rep Prog Chem Sect C Phys Chem ... Annual Reports on the Progress of Chemistry. Section C. Physical Chemistry [*A publication*]

Annu Rep Prog Rubber Technol ... Annual Report on the Progress of Rubber Technology [*A publication*]

Annu Rep Queensland Dep Mines ... Annual Report. Queensland Department of Mines [*A publication*]

Annu Rep Radiat Cent Osaka Prefect ... Annual Report. Radiation Center of Osaka Prefecture [*A publication*]

Annu Rep Res Inst Chemobiodyn Chiba Univ ... Annual Report. Research Institute for Chemobiodynamics. Chiba University [*A publication*]

Annu Rep Res Inst Environ Med Nagoya Univ ... Annual Report. Research Institute of Environmental Medicine. Nagoya University [*A publication*]

Annu Rep Res Inst Environ Med Nagoya Univ (Engl Ed) ... Annual Report. Research Institute of Environmental Medicine. Nagoya University (English Edition) [*A publication*]

Annu Rep Res Inst Tuberc Kanazawa Univ ... Annual Report. Research Institute of Tuberculosis. Kanazawa University [*Japan*] [*A publication*]

Annu Rep Res Inst Wakan-Yaku Toyama Med Pharm Univ ... Annual Report. Research Institute for Wakan-Yaku Toyama Medical and Pharmaceutical University [*A publication*]

Annu Rep Res Mishima Coll Human Sci Nihon Univ ... Annual Report of the Researches. Mishima College of Humanities and Sciences. Nihon University [*A publication*]

Annu Rep Res Mishima Coll Human Sci Nihon Univ Nat Sci ... Annual Report of the Researches. Mishima College of Humanities and Sciences. Nihon University. Natural Sciences [*A publication*]

Annu Rep Res React Inst Kyoto Univ ... Annual Reports. Research Reactor Institute. Kyoto University [*A publication*]

Annu Rep Res Reactor Inst Kyoto Univ ... Annual Reports. Research Reactor Institute. Kyoto University [*A publication*]

Annu Rep Res Tech Work Dep Agric North Irel ... Annual Report on Research and Technical Work. Department of Agriculture for Northern Ireland [*A publication*]

Annu Rep Sado Mar Biol Stn Niigata Univ ... Annual Report. Sado Marine Biological Station. Niigata University [*A publication*]

Annu Rep Sankyo Res Lab ... Annual Report. Sankyo Research Laboratories [*A publication*]

Annu Rep Saranac Lab Stud Tuberc ... Annual Report. Saranac Laboratory for the Study of Tuberculosis [*A publication*]

Annu Rep Saskatchewan Energy Mines ... Annual Report. Saskatchewan Energy and Mines [*A publication*]

Annu Rep Sci Living Osaka City Univ ... Annual Report of the Science of Living. Osaka City University [*A publication*]

Annu Rep Sci Res Counc Jamaica ... Annual Report. Scientific Research Council of Jamaica [*A publication*]

Annu Rep Sci Works Fac Sci Osaka Univ ... Annual Report of Scientific Works. Faculty of Science. Osaka University [*Japan*] [*A publication*]

Annu Rep Secr State Hortic Soc Mich ... Annual Report. Secretary of the State Horticultural Society of Michigan [*A publication*]

Annu Rep Shionogi Res Lab ... Annual Report. Shionogi Research Laboratory [*A publication*]

Annu Rep Shizuoka Public Health Lab ... Annual Report. Shizuoka Public Health Laboratory [*Japan*] [*A publication*]

Annu Rep Smiths Inst ... Annual Report. Smithsonian Institution [*A publication*]

Annu Rep Soc Libyan Stud ... Annual Report. Society for Libyan Studies [*A publication*]

Annu Rep Soc Plant Prot N Jap ... Annual Report. Society of Plant Protection of North Japan [*A publication*]

Annu Rep Stud Anim Nutr Allied Sci Rowett Res Inst ... Annual Report of Studies in Animal Nutrition and Allied Sciences. Rowett Research Institute [*A publication*]

Annu Rep Stud Doshisha Women's Coll Lib Arts ... Annual Report of Studies. Doshisha Women's College of Liberal Arts [*A publication*]

Annu Rep Takeda Res Lab ... Annual Report. Takeda Research Laboratories [*A publication*]

Annu Rep Tanabe Seiyaku Co Ltd ... Annual Report. Tanabe Seiyaku Company Limited [*Japan*] [*A publication*]

Annu Rep Tob Inst PR ... Annual Report. Tobacco Institute of Puerto Rico [*A publication*]

Annu Rep Tob Res Inst ... Annual Report. Tobacco Research Institute [*A publication*]

Annu Rep Tob Res Inst Taiwan Tob & Wine Monop Bur ... Annual Report. Tobacco Research Institute. Taiwan Tobacco and Wine Monopoly Bureau [*A publication*]

Annu Rep Tohoku Coll Pharm ... Annual Report. Tohoku College of Pharmacy [*A publication*]

Annu Rep Tokushima Prefect Inst Public Health Environ Sci ... Annual Report. Tokushima Prefectural Institute of Public Health and Environmental Sciences [*A publication*]

Annu Rep Tokyo Coll Pharm ... Annual Report. Tokyo College of Pharmacy [*A publication*]

Annu Rep Tokyo Metrop Labs Med Sci ... Annual Report. Tokyo Metropolitan Laboratories for Medical Sciences [*A publication*]

Annu Rep Tokyo Metrop Res Inst Environ Prot ... Annual Report. Tokyo Metropolitan Research Institute for Environmental Protection [*A publication*]

Annu Rep Tokyo Metrop Res Inst Environ Prot Engl Transl ... Annual Report. Tokyo Metropolitan Research Institute for Environmental Protection. English Translation [*A publication*]

Annu Rep Tokyo Metrop Res Inst Environ Prot Jpn Ed ... Annual Report. Tokyo Metropolitan Research Institute for Environmental Protection. Japanese Edition [*A publication*]

Annu Rep Tokyo Univ Agric Technol ... Annual Report. Tokyo University of Agriculture and Technology [*A publication*]

Annu Rep Torry Res Stn (Aberdeen UK) ... Annual Report. Torry Research Station (Aberdeen, UK) [*A publication*]

Annu Rep United Dent Hosp Sydney Inst Dent Res ... Annual Report. United Dental Hospital of Sydney. Institute of Dental Research [*A publication*]

Annu Rep Univ GA Coll Agr Exp Sta ... Annual Report. University of Georgia. College of Agriculture. Experiment Stations [*A publication*]

Annu Rep US Crude Oil Nat Gas Reserves ... Annual Report. US Crude Oil and Natural Gas Reserves [*A publication*]

Annu Rep Veg Growers Ass Amer ... Annual Report. Vegetable Growers Association of America [*A publication*]

Annu Rep Veg Growers Assoc Am ... Annual Report. Vegetable Growers Association of America [*A publication*]

Annu Rep Welsh Plant Breed Stn Univ Coll Wales (Aberystwyth) ... Annual Report. Welsh Plant Breeding Station. University College of Wales (Aberystwyth) [*A publication*]

Annu Rep Yokohama City Inst Health ... Annual Report. Yokohama City Institute of Health [*A publication*]

Annu Res Rev Angina Pectoris ... Annual Research Reviews. Angina Pectoris [*A publication*]

Annu Res Rev Anti-Diuretic Horm ... Annual Research Reviews. Anti-Diuretic Hormone [*A publication*]

Annu Res Rev Biofeedback ... Annual Research Reviews. Biofeedback [*A publication*]

Annu Res Rev Duodenal Ulcer ... Annual Research Reviews. Duodenal Ulcer [*A publication*]

Annu Res Rev Eff Psychother ... Annual Research Reviews. Effects of Psychotherapy [*A publication*]

Annu Res Rev Hodgkin's Dis Lymphomas ... Annual Research Reviews. Hodgkin's Disease and the Lymphomas [*A publication*]

Annu Res Rev Horm & Aggression ... Annual Research Reviews. Hormones and Aggression [*A publication*]

Annu Res Rev Hypothal Releasing Factors ... Annual Research Reviews. Hypothalamic Releasing Factors [*A publication*]

Annu Res Rev Intrauterine Contracept ... Annual Research Reviews. Intrauterine Contraception [*A publication*]

Annu Res Rev Oral Contracept ... Annual Research Reviews. Oral Contraceptives [*A publication*]

Annu Res Rev Peripher Metab Action Thyroid Horm ... Annual Research Reviews. Peripheral Metabolism and Action of Thyroid Hormones [*A publication*]

Annu Res Rev Physiol Pathol Aspects Prolactin Secretion ... Annual Research Reviews. Physiological and Pathological Aspects of Prolactin Secretion [*A publication*]

Annu Res Rev Pineal ... Annual Research Reviews. Pineal [*A publication*]

Annu Res Rev Prolactin ... Annual Research Reviews. Prolactin [*A publication*]

Annu Res Rev Prostaglandins Gut ... Annual Research Reviews. Prostaglandins and the Gut [*A publication*]

Annu Res Rev Proteins Anim Cell Plasma Membr ... Annual Research Reviews. Proteins of Animal Cell Plasma Membranes [*A publication*]

Annu Res Rev Regul Growth Horm Secretion ... Annual Research Reviews. Regulation of Growth Hormone Secretion [*A publication*]

Annu Res Rev Renal Prostaglandins ... Annual Research Reviews. Renal Prostaglandins [*A publication*]

Annu Res Rev Renin ... Annual Research Reviews. Renin [*A publication*]

Annu Res Rev Rheum Arthritis Relat Cond ... Annual Research Reviews. Rheumatoid Arthritis and Related Conditions [*A publication*]

Annu Res Rev Somatostatin ... Annual Research Reviews. Somatostatin [*A publication*]

Annu Res Rev Sphingolipidoses Allied Disord ... Annual Research Reviews. Sphingolipidoses and Allied Disorders [*A publication*]

Annu Res Rev Subst P ... Annual Research Reviews. Substance P [*A publication*]

Annu Res Rev Ultrastruct Pathol Hum Tumors ... Annual Research Reviews. Ultrastructural Pathology of Human Tumors [*A publication*]

Annu Res Rev Vitam Trace Miner Protein Interact ... Annual Research Reviews. Vitamin-Trace Mineral-Protein Interactions [*A publication*]

Annu Rev Anthropol ... Annual Review of Anthropology [*A publication*]

Annu Rev Astron Astrophys ... Annual Review of Astronomy and Astrophysics [*A publication*]

Annu Rev Autom Program ... Annual Review in Automatic Programming [*A publication*]

Annu Rev Behav Ther Theory Pract ... Annual Review of Behavior Therapy Theory and Practice [*A publication*]

Annu Rev Biochem ... Annual Review of Biochemistry [*A publication*]

Annu Rev Biochem Allied Res India ... Annual Review of Biochemical and Allied Research in India [*A publication*]

Annu Rev Biophys Bioeng ... Annual Review of Biophysics and Bioengineering [*A publication*]

Annu Rev Biophys Biophys Chem ... Annual Review of Biophysics and Biophysical Chemistry [*A publication*]

Annu Rev Cell Biol ... Annual Review of Cell Biology [*A publication*]

Annu Rev Chronopharmacol ... Annual Review of Chronopharmacology [*A publication*]

Annu Rev Earth Planet Sci ... Annual Review of Earth and Planetary Sciences [*A publication*]

Annu Rev Ecol Syst ... Annual Review of Ecology and Systematics [*A publication*]

Annu Rev Energy ... Annual Review of Energy [*A publication*]

Annu Rev Entomol ... Annual Review of Entomology [*A publication*]

Annu Rev Fluid Mech ... Annual Review of Fluid Mechanics [*A publication*]

Annu Rev Food Technol ... Annual Review of Food Technology [*A publication*]

Annu Rev Food Technol (Mysore) ... Annual Review of Food Technology (Mysore) [*A publication*]

Annu Rev Genet ... Annual Review of Genetics [*A publication*]

Annu Rev Immunol ... Annual Review of Immunology [*A publication*]

Annu Rev Ind Eng Chem ... Annual Reviews of Industrial and Engineering Chemistry [*A publication*]

Annu Rev Inf Sci Technol ... Annual Review of Information Science and Technology [*Encyclopedia Britannica*] [*A publication*]

Annu Rev Inst Plasma Phys Nagoya Univ ... Annual Review. Institute of Plasma Physics. Nagoya University [*A publication*]

Annu Rev Mater Sci ... Annual Review of Materials Science [*A publication*]

Annu Rev Med ... Annual Review of Medicine [*A publication*]

Annu Rev Microbiol ... Annual Review of Microbiology [*A publication*]

Annu Rev Neurosci ... Annual Review of Neuroscience [*A publication*]

Annu Rev Nucl Part Sci ... Annual Review of Nuclear and Particle Science [*A publication*]

Annu Rev Nucl Sci ... Annual Review of Nuclear Science [*Later, Annual Review of Nuclear and Particle Science*] [*A publication*]

Annu Rev Nurs Res ... Annual Review of Nursing Research [*A publication*]

Annu Rev Nutr ... Annual Review of Nutrition [*A publication*]

Annu Rev Pharmacol ... Annual Review of Pharmacology [*Later, Annual Review of Pharmacology and Toxicology*] [*A publication*]

Annu Rev Pharmacol Toxicol ... Annual Review of Pharmacology and Toxicology [*A publication*]

Annu Rev Photochem ... Annual Review of Photochemistry [*A publication*]

Annu Rev Phys Chem ... Annual Review of Physical Chemistry [*A publication*]

Annu Rev Physiol ... Annual Review of Physiology [*A publication*]

Annu Rev Phytopathol ... Annual Review of Phytopathology [*A publication*]

Annu Rev Plant Physiol ... Annual Review of Plant Physiology [*A publication*]

Annu Rev Plant Sci ... Annual Reviews of Plant Sciences [*A publication*]

Annu Rev Psychol ... Annual Review of Psychology [*A publication*]

Annu Rev Public Health ... Annual Review of Public Health [*A publication*]

Annu Rev Rehabil ... Annual Review of Rehabilitation [*A publication*]

Annu Rev Rubber Res Inst Sri Lanka ... Annual Review. Rubber Research Institute of Sri Lanka [*A publication*]

Annu Rev Schizophr Syndr ... Annual Review of the Schizophrenic Syndrome [*A publication*]

Annu Rev Sociol ... Annual Review of Sociology [*A publication*]

Ann Urol .... Annales d'Urologie [*A publication*]

Annu Romant Bibliogr ... Annual Romantic Bibliography [*A publication*]

Annu Roum Anthropol ... Annuaire Roumain d'Anthropologie [*A publication*]

AnnUS .... Annales Universitatis Saraviensis. Philosophie- Lettres [*A publication*]

Annu Simul Symp (Rec Proc) ... Annual Simulation Symposium (Record of Proceedings) [*A publication*]

Annu Soc Arch Bruxelles ... Annuaire. Societe Royal d'Archeologie de Bruxelles [*A publication*]

Annu Soc Hist Sundgovienne ... Annuaire. Societe de l'Histoire de Sundgovienne [*A publication*]

Annu Sta Chim-Agr Sper Torino ... Annuario. Stazione Chimico-Agraria Sperimentale di Torino [*A publication*]

Annu Suisse Sci Polit ... Annuaire Suisse de Science Politique [*A publication*]

Annu Surv of Afr L ... Annual Survey of African Law [*A publication*]

Annu Surv Am Chem Nat Res Counc ... Annual Survey of American Chemistry. National Research Council [*A publication*]

Annu Surv of Amer L ... Annual Survey of American Law [*A publication*]

Annu Surv of Indian L ... Annual Survey of Indian Law [*A publication*]

Annu Surv of South Afr L ... Annual Survey of South African Law [*A publication*]

Annu Symp Biomath Comput Sci Life Sci Abstr ... Annual Symposium on Biomathematics and Computer Science in the Life Sciences. Abstracts [*A publication*]

Annu Symp East PA Branch Am Soc Microbiol Proc ... Annual Symposium. Eastern Pennsylvania Branch, American Society for Microbiology. Proceedings [*A publication*]

Annu Symp Found Comput Sci (Proc) ... Annual Symposium on Foundations of Computer Science (Proceedings) [*A publication*]

Annu Symp Nurs Fac Pract ... Annual Symposium on Nursing Faculty Practice [*A publication*]

Annu Tech Conf Am Electroplat Soc ... Annual Technical Conference. American Electroplaters' Society [*A publication*]

Annu Tech Conf Proc Soc Vac Coaters ... Annual Technical Conference Proceedings. Society of Vacuum Coaters [*A publication*]

Annu Tech Conf Trans Am Soc Qual Control ... Annual Technical Conference Transactions. American Society for Quality Control [*A publication*]

Annu Tiers-Monde ... Annuaire du Tiers-Monde [*A publication*]

Annu UMR-DNR Conf Energy Proc ... Annual UMR-DNR [*University of Missouri, Rolla - Department of Natural Resources*] Conference on Energy. Proceedings [*A publication*]

Annu Univ Modena ... Annuario. Reale Universita di Modena [*A publication*]

Annu Univ Sofia Fac Biol ... Annuaire. Universite de Sofia. Faculte de Biologie [*A publication*]

Annu Univ Sofia Fac Phys ... Annuaire. Universite de Sofia. Faculte de Physique [*A publication*]

Annu URSS ... Annuaire de l'URSS et des Pays Socialistes Europeens [*A publication*]

Annu Visit Lect Ser Coll Pharm Univ Tex ... Annual Visiting Lecture Series. College of Pharmacy. University of Texas [*A publication*]

Annu Vol Inst Mar Eng ... Annual Volume. Institute of Marine Engineers [*A publication*]

Ann Vet Res ... Annals of Veterinary Research [*A publication*]

Ann Villaggio Sanat Sondalo ... Annali. Villaggio Sanatoriale di Sondalo [*A publication*]

Ann Virol ... Annales de Virologie [*A publication*]

Ann Warsaw Agric Univ SGGW-AR Anim Sci ... Annals. Warsaw Agricultural University. SGGW-AR [*Szkola Glowna Gospodarstwa Wiejskiego - Akademia Rolnicza*]. Animal Science [*A publication*]

Ann Western Med Surg ... Annals of Western Medicine and Surgery. Los Angeles County Medical Association [*A publication*]

Ann Worc Art Mus ... Annual Report. Worcester Art Museum [*A publication*]

Ann Wyo .... Annals of Wyoming [*A publication*]

annx .... Annexure [*British and Canadian*] [*World War II*]

ANNX .... [*The*] Learning Annex, Inc. [*New York, NY*] [*NASDAQ symbol*] (NQ)

Anny .... Advertising News of New York [*Later, Adweek*] [*A publication*]

ANNY .... Annuity

AnNZ .... Anthology of New Zealand Verse [*A publication*]

Ann Zimbabwe Geol Surv ... Annals. Zimbabwe Geological Survey [*A publication*]

Ann Zool .... Annals of Zoology [*A publication*]

Ann Zool (Agra) ... Annals of Zoology (Agra) [*A publication*]

Ann Zool Ecol Anim ... Annales de Zoologie - Ecologie Animale [*A publication*]

Ann Zool Fenn ... Annales Zoologici Fennici [*A publication*]

Ann Zool Soc Zool-Bot Fenn "Vanamo" ... Annales Zoologici. Societatis Zoologicae-Botanicae Fennicae "Vanamo" [*A publication*]

Ann Zool (Warsaw) ... Annales Zoologici (Warsaw) [*A publication*]

Ann Zootech ... Annales de Zootechnie [*A publication*]

Ann Zootech Inst Nat Rech Agron ... Annales de Zootechnie. Institut National de la Recherche Agronomique [*A publication*]

Ann Zootech (Paris) ... Annales de Zootechnie (Paris) [*A publication*]

Ann Zymol ... Annales de Zymologie [*A publication*]

ANO .... Above-Named Officer [*Army orders*]

ANO .... Air Navigation Office [*Navy*]

ANO .... Air Navigation Order [*A publication*] (APTA)

ANO .... Air Navigation Order

ANO .... Alphanumeric Output

ANO .... Annus [*Year*] [*Latin*]

ANO .... Anodyne [*Medicine*] (ROG)

AnO .... Anordnung [*Direction, Instruction*] [*German*] (ILCA)

ANO .... Another

ANO .... Antipolo [*Philippines*] [*Later, MUT*] [*Geomagnetic observatory code*]

ANO .... Aricana Resources [*Vancouver Stock Exchange symbol*]

ANO .... Arkansas Nuclear One (NRCH)

ANO .... Nordegg Public Library, Alberta [*Library symbol*] [*National Library of Canada*] (NLC)

ANO .... University of North Alabama, Florence, AL [*OCLC symbol*] (OCLC)

ANOAAR ... Antropologicky Archiv [*A publication*]

An Obs Astr Met ... Analele Observatorului Astronomic si Meteorologic [*A publication*]

An Obs Buc ... Anuarul. Observatorului din Bucuresti [*A publication*]

ANOC .... Advanced Noncommissioned Officer Course [*Army*]

AnOC .... Anodal Opening Contraction [*Also, AOC*] [*Physiology*]

ANOC .... Association of National Olympic Committees [*See also ACNO*] [*Paris, France*] (EAIO)

ANOC .... Authorized Notice of Change

ANOCA ..... Association of National Olympic Committees of Africa (EA)

An OCD .... Analecta Ordinis Carmelitarum Discalceatorum [*A publication*]

An O Cist .... Analecta Sacri Ordinis Cisterciensis [*A publication*]

ANOD .... Airborne Night Observation Device (MCD)

ANOD .... Anodize (MSA)

ANODE ..... Ambient Noise Directionality Estimator (MCD)

ANODE..... Analytic Orbit Determination Program (MCD)
Anodic Behav Met Semicond Ser ... Anodic Behavior of Metals and Semiconductors Series [*A publication*]
ANODYN ... Anodynum [*A Soothing Medicament*] [*Pharmacy*] (ROG)
AnOE........ Anthology of Old English Poetry [*A publication*]
ANOG .... Australian National Observer Group
ANOH .... Aarboeger foer Nordisk Oldkyndighed og Historie [*A publication*]
ANOM ...... Assistant Network Operations Manager [*NASA*] (KSC)
ANOMA.... Alluminio e Nuova Metallurgia [*A publication*]
ANON .... Anonymous
ANOPO...... Aircraft Noise Prediction Office [*NASA*]
ANOPP ..... Aircraft Noise Prediction Program [*NASA*]
ANOPS ..... Aircraft Not Operationally Ready Supply (AFIT)
AnOr.......... Analecta Orientalia. Commentationes Scientificae de Rebus Orientis Antiqui. Pontificium Institutum Biblicum [*Rome*] [*A publication*]
ANOR........ Another (ROG)
ANORA..... Angle Orthodontist [*A publication*]
ANORBB .. Applied Ornithology [*A publication*]
Anorexia Nerv Multidisciplinary Conf ... Anorexia Nervosa. Multidisciplinary Conference of Anorexia Nervosa [*A publication*]
An ORL Ibero-Amer ... Anales Otorrinolaringologicos Ibero-Americanos [*A publication*]
A Norm ...... Annales de Normandie [*A publication*]
ANORM.... Anticipated Not Operationally Ready, Maintenance (NVT)
A d Normandie ... Annales de Normandie [*A publication*]
A Normandie ... Annales de Normandie; Revue Trimestrielle d'Etudes Regionales [*A publication*]
An Or Res ... Annals of Oriental Research [*A publication*]
ANORS ...... Anticipated Not Operationally Ready, Supply (AFM)
ANOT........ Annotate
An Otorrinolaringol Iber-Am ... Anales Otorrinolaringologicos Ibero-Americanos [*A publication*]
Anot Pediatr ... Anotaciones Pediatricas [*Colombia*] [*A publication*]
ANOV........ Analysis of Variance
ANOVA..... Analysis of Variance
An Oviedo Univ Fac Vet (Leon) ... Anales. Oviedo Universidad. Facultad de Veterinaria (Leon) [*A publication*]
ANP.......... Accao Nacional Popular [*National Popular Action*] [*Portugal*] [*Political party*] (PPE)
ANP.......... Acta Neurologica et Psychiatrica Belgica [*A publication*]
ANP.......... Aircraft Nuclear Power [*or Propulsion*]
ANP.......... Albert Rolland [*France*] [*Research code symbol*]
ANP.......... Algemeen Nederlandisch Persbureau [*Press agency*] [*Netherlands*]
ANP.......... Allied Navigation Publications [*NATO*] (NATG)
ANP.......... American NAZI Party [*Later, NSWWP*]
ANP.......... Anales de la Narrativa Espanola Contemporanea [*A publication*]
ANP.......... Anglo Canadian Mining Corp. [*Toronto Stock Exchange symbol*] [*Vancouver Stock Exchange symbol*]
ANP.......... Annapolis, MD [*Location identifier*] [*FAA*] (FAAL)
AnP.......... Annee Propedeutique [*A publication*]
ANP.......... Anpu [*Republic of China*] [*Seismograph station code, US Geological Survey*] (SEIS)
ANP.......... Atrial Natriuretic Peptide [*Biochemistry*]
ANP.......... Australian National Party [*Political party*] (ADA)
ANP.......... Awami National Party [*Pakistan*] [*Political party*] (FEA)
ANP.......... Lab. Anphar [*France*] [*Research code symbol*]
a-np--- .... Nepal [*MARC geographic area code*] [*Library of Congress*] (LCCP)
ANPA........ American Newspaper Publishers Association (EA)
ANPAC ..... Animal Political Action Committee (EA)
ANPAF...... American Newspaper Publishers Association Foundation (EA)
An Paleont ... Annales de Paleontologie [*A publication*]
ANPAM .... Associazione Nazionale Produttori Armi e Munizioni [*Arms and munitions producers association*] [*Italy*] (EY)
ANPA/RI Bull ... ANPA/RI [*American Newspaper Publishers Association. Research Institute*] Bulletin [*A publication*]
An Parques Nac (B Aires) ... Anales de Parques Nacionales (Buenos Aires) [*A publication*]
ANPASC... [*A*] National Plan for Arts in Small Communities (EA)
ANPA Stat ... American Newspaper Publishers Association. Newsprint Statistics [*A publication*]
ANPAT...... American Newspaper Publishers Abstracting Technique
ANPA/TEC ... American Newspaper Publishers' Association Technical Exposition and Conference (ITD)
An Paul Med Cir ... Anais Paulistas de Medicina e Cirurgia [*A publication*]
ANPB .... Army-Navy Petroleum Board
ANPBA...... Acta Neurologica et Psychiatrica Belgica [*A publication*]
ANPBAZ... Acta Neurologica et Psychiatrica Belgica [*A publication*]
ANPC .... Air-Nitrogen Pressurization Control
ANPC .... American Nail Producers Council
ANPC .... American National Petroleum Company [*NASDAQ symbol*] (NQ)
AnPC .... Annales de la Philosophie Chretienne [*A publication*]
ANPCD7 ... Specialist Periodical Reports. Aliphatic and Related Natural Product Chemistry [*A publication*]
ANPD .... Aircraft Nuclear Propulsion Department [*Navy*]
ANPEDD .. Annual Research Reviews. Angina Pectoris [*A publication*]

An Pediat ... Anales de Pediatria [*A publication*]
ANPERA... American National Postal Employees Retirees Association (EA)
An de Peru ... Angelus de Ubaldis de Perusio [*Deceased, 1407*] [*Authority cited in pre-1607 legal work*] (DSA)
AnPh.......... L'Annee Philologique [*Paris*] [*A publication*]
ANPHA ...... Annales de Physique [*A publication*]
ANPHCL .. Applied Neurophysiology [*A publication*]
An Phil Chin Hist Asso ... Annals. Philippine Chinese Historical Association [*A publication*]
ANPHI Pap ... ANPHI [*Academy of Nursing of the Philippines*] Papers [*A publication*]
An Physik .. Annalen der Physik und Chemie [*A publication*]
ANPI .... Alaska Northwest Properties, Incorporated [*NASDAQ symbol*] (NQ)
ANPIA....... Arquivos de Neuro-Psiquiatria [*A publication*]
ANPL .... Adoptee/Natural Parent Locators [*Later, ANPLI*] (EA)
ANPLI....... Adoptee/Natural Parent Locators - International [*Formerly, ANPL*] [*Later, MPI*] (EA)
ANPM .... African Nationalist Pioneer Movement [*Defunct*]
ANPMD3.. Acta Naturalia de l'Ateneo Parmense [*A publication*]
ANPO........ Aircraft Nuclear Propulsion Office [*of AEC*] [*Defunct*]
ANPO........ Association of National Park Officers [*British*]
ANPOD..... Antenna Positioning Device
An Post .... Analytica Posteriora [*of Aristotle*] [*Classical studies*] (OCD)
ANPP .... Above Ground Net Primary Production [*Ecology*]
A-NPP .... Adsorbed Normal Pool Plasma [*Clinical chemistry*]
ANPP .... Aircraft Nuclear Propulsion Program
ANPP .... Army Nuclear Power Program
ANPPF ...... Association of Negro Press Photographers
ANPPF ...... Aircraft Nuclear Power Plant Facility
ANPPM..... Asociacion Nacional pro Personas Mayores [*National Association for Hispanic Elderly*] (EA)
ANPPPC ... Army-Navy Petroleum Pool, Pacific Coast
ANPQA .... Annee Psychologique [*A publication*]
ANPR .... Advance Notice of Proposed Rulemaking [*Also, ANPRM*] [*US Government agencies*]
An Pr.......... Analytica Priora [*of Aristotle*] [*Classical studies*] (OCD)
ANPRA ..... American Native Press Research Association (EA)
AnPraem.... Analecta Praemonstratensia [*A publication*]
ANPRDI.... Analytical Proceedings [*A publication*]
ANPRM .... Advance Notice of Proposed Rulemaking [*Also, ANPR*] [*US Government agencies*]
An Programa Acad Med Univ Nac Mayor San Marcos (Lima) ... Anales. Programa Academico de Medicina. Universidad Nacional Mayor de San Marcos (Lima) [*A publication*]
ANPSAI .... Archives of Neurology and Psychiatry [*A publication*]
ANPSI .... Animal Psi [*Parapsychology*]
ANPT .... Aeronautical National Taper Pipe Threads
ANPTAL... Acta Neuropathologica [*A publication*]
ANPTBM .. Annales de Phytopathologie [*A publication*]
ANPV .... Adjusted Net Present Value (MCD)
ANPYA ..... Annalen der Physik [*A publication*]
ANQ .... American Notes and Queries [*A publication*]
AN & Q...... American Notes and Queries [*A publication*]
ANQ .... Andover Newton Quarterly [*A publication*]
ANQ .... Angola, IN [*Location identifier*] [*FAA*] (FAAL)
ANQU-A ... Anthropological Quarterly [*A publication*]
ANQUBU .. Anales de Quimica [*A publication*]
An Quim .... Anales de Quimica [*A publication*]
An Quim A-Fis Tec ... Anales de Quimica. Serie A. Quimica Fisica y Quimica Tecnica [*A publication*]
An Quim B Inorg Anal ... Anales de Quimica. Serie B. Quimica Inorganica y Quimica Analitica [*A publication*]
An Quim C Org Bioquim ... Anales de Quimica. Serie C. Quimica Organica y Bioquimica [*A publication*]
An Quim Farm ... Anales de Quimica y Farmacia [*A publication*]
An Quimica ... Anales de Quimica [*A publication*]
ANR.......... Active Noise Reduction (MCD)
ANR.......... Advanced Non-Rigid Airship [*British*]
ANR.......... Agricultural and Natural Resources
ANR.......... Air Navigation Regulations (ADA)
ANR.......... Alaskan NORAD Region
ANR.......... Alberta Energy and Natural Resources Library [*UTLAS symbol*]
ANR.......... American Negligence Reports, Current Series [*A publication*] (DLA)
ANR.......... Americans for Nonsmokers' Rights (EA)
ANR.......... Andizhan [*USSR*] [*Seismograph station code, US Geological Survey*] (SEIS)
ANR.......... Andrews, TX [*Location identifier*] [*FAA*] (FAAL)
ANR.......... Angelina & Neches River Railroad Co. [*AAR code*]
ANR.......... Another (ROG)
AnR.......... Antigonish Review [*A publication*]
ANR.......... Antwerp [*Belgium*] [*Airport symbol*] (OAG)
ANR.......... Awaiting Number Received [*Telecommunications*] (TEL)
ANR.......... National Economic and Legislative Report [*Commerce Clearing House*] [*A publication*] (DLA)
ANRA........ Affiliated Nutritional Retailers Association [*Commercial firm*] (EA)
ANRA........ Air Navigation Radio Aids

ANRAC ..... Aids to Navigation Radio Control [*Military*]
An R Acad Farm ... Anales. Real Academia de Farmacia [*A publication*]
An R Acad Med Cir Valladolid ... Anales. Real Academia de Medicina y Cirugia de Valladolid [*A publication*]
An R Acad Nacl Med (Madr) ... Anales. Real Academia Nacional de Medicina (Madrid) [*A publication*]
An R Acad Nac Med (Madr) ... Anales. Real Academia Nacional de Medicina (Madrid) [*A publication*]
ANRC .... Affiliated National Riding Commission   (EA)
ANRC .... American National Red Cross [*Later, ARC*]
ANRC .... Animal Nutrition Research Council   (EA)
ANRC .... Automatic Noise Reduction Circuit [*Electronics*]
ANRCEI ..... Annual Review of Chronopharmacology [*A publication*]
ANRCP ..... Additional Nonresidential Conditional Purchase   (ADA)
ANREA ..... Anatomical Record [*A publication*]
An Real Acad Farm ... Anales. Real Academia de Farmacia. Instituto de Espana [*A publication*]
ANRED ..... Anorexia Nervosa and Related Eating Disorders   (EA)
ANREP....... Annual Report
ANREP...... Appraisal of the Navy RDT & E [*Research, Development, Test, and Evaluation*] Program
An Rep Econ Keio Gijuku Univ ... Keio Gijuku University [*Tokyo*]. Annual Report. Economics [*A publication*]
An Reun Fitossanit Bras ... Anais. Reuniao de Fitossanitarisatas do Brasil [*A publication*]
An Reuniao Fitossanit Brasil ... Anais. Reuniao de Fitossanitarisatas do Brasil [*A publication*]
ANRGGSIC ... Alaska. Department of Natural Resources. Division of Geological and Geophysical Surveys. Information Circular [*A publication*]
ANRGGSSR ... Alaska. Department of Natural Resources. Division of Geological and Geophysical Surveys. Special Report [*A publication*]
Anritsu Tech Bull ... Anritsu Technical Bulletin [*A publication*]
ANRL .... Antihypertensive Neural Renomedullary Liquid
ANRM .... Alaska. Department of Natural Resources. Division of Mines and Geology [*A publication*]
An Rom Sov ... Analele Romino-Sovietice [*A publication*]
ANRORC .. Addition Nucleophile Ring Opening Ring Closure [*Organic chemistry*]
ANRP .... Association for a National Recycling Policy   (EA)
ANRPC...... Association of Natural Rubber Producing Countries [*Kuala Lumpur, Malaysia*]   (EAIO)
ANRPEN... ANARE [*Australian National Antarctic Research Expeditions*] Report [*A publication*]
ANRR .... Australian National Register of Records
AnRS .... Annual Reports of Studies [*Kyoto*] [*A publication*]
ANRSAS ... Acta Neurologica Scandinavica [*A publication*]
An R Soc Esp Fis Quim ... Anales. Real Sociedad Espanola de Fisica y Quimica [*A publication*]
An R Soc Esp Fis y Quim A ... Anales. Real Sociedad Espanola de Fisica y Quimica. Serie A [*A publication*]
An R Soc Esp Fis Quim Ser A ... Anales. Real Sociedad Espanola de Fisica y Quimica. Serie A. Fisica [*Spain*] [*A publication*]
An R Soc Esp Fis Quim Ser B Quim ... Anales. Real Sociedad Espanola de Fisica y Quimica. Serie B. Quimica [*A publication*]
ANRT .... Association Nationale de la Recherche Technique [*National Association of Technical Research - NATR*] [*France*] [*Information service or system*]   (IID)
ANRTB...... ANSI [*American National Standards Institute*] Reporter [*A publication*]
AnRts......... Writers for Animal Rights   (EA)
ANRU........ New South Wales Revenue Rulings [*Australia*] [*A publication*]
ANRVA ..... Argonne National Laboratory. Reviews [*United States*] [*A publication*]
ANS .... Academy of Natural Sciences of Philadelphia, Philadelphia, PA [*OCLC symbol*]   (OCLC)
ANS .... Active Network Synthesis
ANS .... Admiralty Naval Staff [*British*]
ANS .... Advanced Navigation School [*British military*]   (DMA)
ANS .... Advanced Network & Services, Inc. [*Nonprofit company formed to manage the National Science Foundation Network*]   (IID)
ANS .... Advanced Network System [*Data processing*]   (ECON)
ANS .... Advanced Neutron Source [*Proposed nuclear reactor*]
ANS .... Advances in Nursing Science [*A publication*]
ANS .... Agencia Noticiosa Saporiti [*Press agency*] [*Argentina*]
ANS .... Air Navigation School [*British*]
ANS .... Airborne Navigation Sensor
ANS .... Alternate [*or Alternative*] News Service   (ADA)
ANS .... American Name Society   (EA)
ANS .... American National Standard [*ANSI*]   (MCD)
ANS .... American Navion Society   (EA)
ANS .... American Neurotology Society   (EA)
ANS .... American Newcomen Society
ANS .... American Norwich Society   (EA)
ANS .... American Nuclear Society   (EA)
ANS .... American Numismatic Society   (EA)
ANS .... American Nutrition Society   (EA)
ANS .... Andahuaylas [*Peru*] [*Airport symbol*] [*Obsolete*]   (OAG)

ANS .... Anilinonaphthalenesulfonic Acid [*Also, ANSA*] [*Organic chemistry*]
ANS .... Ansco Resources (BC) [*Vancouver Stock Exchange symbol*]
Ans .... Anselmus de Baggio de Lucca [*Deceased, 1086*] [*Authority cited in pre-1607 legal work*]   (DSA)
ANS .... Answer   (AFM)
Ans .... Ansyl [*Organic radical*]
ANS .... Apollo Network Simulations [*NASA*]   (KSC)
ANS .... Archiv fuer das Studium der Neueren Sprachen [*A publication*]
ANS .... Armenian Numismatic Society   (EA)
ANS .... Army News Service
ANS .... Army Newspaper Service
ANS .... Army Nursing Service [*British*]
ANS .... Arteriolonephrosclerosis [*Urology*]
ANS .... Associated Nuclear Services [*British*]   (IRUK)
ANS .... Astronomical Netherlands Satellite
ANS .... Autograph Note Signed [*Manuscript descriptions*]
ANS .... Automatic Navigation System
ANS .... Autonomic Nervous System [*Medicine*]
ANS .... Autonomous Navigation System
ANS .... New Sarepta Public Library, Alberta [*Library symbol*] [*National Library of Canada*]   (NLC)
ANSA .... Advanced Network System Architecture   (BUR)
ANSA .... Agenzia Nazionale Stampa Associata [*Associated National Press Agency*] [*Italy*]
ANSA .... Aminohydroxynaphthalenesulfonic Acid [*Organic chemistry*]
ANSA .... Aminonaphtholsulfonic Acid [*Organic chemistry*]
ANSA .... (Anilino)naphthalenesulfonic Acid [*Also, ANS*] [*Organic chemistry*]
ANSA .... Australian National Shipping Agencies
ANSA .... Australian National Sportfishing Association   (EAIO)
ANSA .... Automatic New Structure Alert [*A publication*]
ANSABLE ... Answerable   (ROG)
ANSAC ... American Natural Soda Ash Corporation   (EA)
ANS Adv Nurs Sci ... ANS. Advances in Nursing Science [*A publication*]
ANSAS...... Automatic Null Steering/Surveillance Array System   (MCD)
AnSATarrac ... Analecta Sacra Tarraconensia [*Barcelona*] [*A publication*]
ANSC .... American National Standards (Institute) Committee [*Later, NISO*]
ANSC .... American Nuclear Science Corporation   (MCD)
ANSC .... Andover Service Center [*IRS*]
ANSC .... Antarctic Science [*A publication*]
ANSC .... Army and Navy Staff College [*Redesignated National War College, 1946*]
ANSC .... Autonomous Navigation System Concept   (MCD)
An Sc (Cleveland) ... Annals of Science (Cleveland) [*A publication*]
ANS Cent... American Numismatic Society. Centennial Publication [*A publication*]
An Sc Geol ... Annales des Sciences Geologiques [*A publication*]
anschl......... Anschliessend [*Following, Subsequent*] [*German*]
ANSCII .... American National Standard Code for Information Interchange   (MCD)
An Sc Nat Zool ... Annales des Sciences Naturelles. Zoologie [*A publication*]
ANSCOL... Army and Navy Staff College [*See ANSC*]
Ans Con ..... Anson on Contracts [*A publication*]   (DLA)
ANSCR...... Alphanumeric System for Classification of Recordings
ANSCS OCR ... American National Standard Character Set for Optical Character Recognition   (MCD)
ANSD........ Answered   (ROG)
ANSDB...... ANSI [*American National Standards Institute*] Standards Action [*A publication*]
ANSDL...... Australisch-Neuseelaendische Studien zur Deutschen Sprache und Literatur [*A publication*]   (APTA)
ANSDSL ... Australisch-Neuseelaendische Studien zur Deutschen Sprache und Literatur [*A publication*]
An Secc Cienc Col Univ Gerona Univ Auton Barcelona ... Anales. Seccion de Ciencias. Colegio Universitario de Gerona. Universidad Autonoma de Barcelona [*A publication*]
An Sect Pedol Inst Cent Cercet Agric ... Analele. Sectiei de Pedologie. Institutul Central de Cercetari Agricole [*A publication*]
An Sect Prot Plant Inst Cent Cercet Agric (Bucharest) ... Analele. Sectiei de Protectia Plantelor. Institutul Central de Cercetari Agricole (Bucharest) [*A publication*]
An Seminar Brasil Herbic Ervas Danin ... Anais. Seminario Brasileiro de Herbicidas e Ervas Daninhas [*A publication*]
An Seni ...... An Seni Respublica Gerenda Sit [*of Plutarch*] [*Classical studies*]   (OCD)
ANSER...... Agricultural Network Serving Extension and Research [*University of Kentucky*] [*Lexington*] [*Information service or system*] [*Research center*]   (IID)
ANSER...... Analytic Services, Inc.
An Ser Prod Anim Inst Nac Invest Agrar ... Anales. Serie Produccion Animal. Instituto Nacional de Investigaciones Agrarias [*A publication*]
An Serv Geol Nac Salvador Bol ... Anales. Servico Geologico Nacional de El Salvador. Boletin [*A publication*]
ANSETT ... Ansett Airlines of Australia
ANSFAS... Annales des Sciences Forestieres [*Paris*] [*A publication*]
ANSG .... Answering   (ROG)
ANSI.......... American National Standards Institute   (EA)
ANSIA....... Army-Navy Shipping Information Agency

ANSIC....... Aerospace Nuclear Safety Information Center (MCD)

ANSI Reptr ... ANSI [*American National Standards Institute*] Reporter [*A publication*]

ANSI Stand ... ANSI [*American National Standards Institute*] Standards [*A publication*]

ANSI Std Action ... ANSI [*American National Standards Institute*] Standards Action [*A publication*]

ANSL......... Action Savings Bank SLA [*NASDAQ symbol*] (NQ)

AnSL.......... Anthology of Swedish Lyrics [*A publication*]

ANSLA...... Acta Neurologica Scandinavica. Supplementum [*A publication*]

ANSMN .... American Numismatic Society. Museum Notes [*A publication*]

ANSMusN ... American Numismatic Society. Museum Notes [*A publication*]

ANSN........ American Numismatic Society. Museum Notes [*A publication*]

ANSNNM ... American Numismatic Society. Numismatic Notes and Monographs [*A publication*]

ANSNS...... American Numismatic Society. Numismatic Studies [*A publication*]

ANSO........ Anderson-Stokes, Inc. [*Rehoboth Beach, DE*] [*NASDAQ symbol*] (NQ)

AnSO........ Annual Service Order

ANSO........ Assistant Naval Stores Officer

AnSoc......... Ancient Society [*Leuven*] [*A publication*]

An Soc Biol Bogota ... Anales. Sociedad de Biologia de Bogota [*A publication*]

An Soc Biol Pernambuco ... Anais. Sociedade de Biologia de Pernambuco [*A publication*]

An Soc Bot Bras ... Anais. Sociedade Botanica do Brasil [*A publication*]

An Soc Cient Argent ... Anales. Sociedad Cientifica Argentina [*A publication*]

An Soc Cient Argent Sec S Fe ... Anales. Sociedad Cientifica Argentina. Seccion Santa Fe [*A publication*]

An Soc Cient S Fe ... Anales. Sociedad Cientifica de Santa Fe [*A publication*]

An Soc Entomol Bras ... Anais. Sociedade Entomologica do Brasil [*A publication*]

An Soc Espan Fis Quim ... Anales. Sociedad Espanola de Fisica y Quimica [*A publication*]

An Soc Esp Fis Quim ... Anales. Sociedad Espanola de Fisica y Quimica [*Spain*] [*A publication*]

An Soc Esp Hidrol Med ... Anales. Sociedad Espanola de Hidrologia Medica [*A publication*]

An Soc Geogr Hist ... Anales. Sociedad de Geografia e Historia [*A publication*]

An Soc Geogr Hist Guatem ... Anales. Sociedad de Geografia e Historia de Guatemala [*A publication*]

An Soc Med Pern ... Anais. Sociedade de Medicina de Pernambuco [*A publication*]

An Soc Med Pernambuco ... Anais. Sociedade de Medicina de Pernambuco [*A publication*]

An Soc Med-Quir Guayas ... Anales. Sociedad Medico-Quirurgica del Guayas [*A publication*]

An Soc Mex Hist Cienc Tecnol ... Anales. Sociedad Mexicana de Historia de la Ciencia de la Tecnologia [*A publication*]

An Soc Mex Oftalmol ... Anales. Sociedad Mexicana de Oftalmologia [*A publication*]

An Soc Mex Otorinolaringol ... Anales. Sociedad Mexicana de Otorrinolaringologia [*A publication*]

An Soc Mex Otorrinolaringol Broncoesofagol ... Anales. Sociedad Mexicana de Otorrinolaringologia y Broncoesofagologia [*A publication*]

An Soc Peruana Hist Med ... Anales. Sociedad Peruana de Historia de la Medicina [*A publication*]

An Soc Quim Argent ... Anales. Sociedad Quimica Argentina [*A publication*]

An Soc R Sci Med Nat Bruxelles ... Annales. Societe Royale des Sciences Medicales et Naturelles de Bruxelles [*A publication*]

An Soc Rural Argent ... Anales. Sociedad Rural Argentina [*A publication*]

An Soc Rur Argent ... Anales. Sociedad Rural Argentina [*A publication*]

An Soc Vet Zootec ... Anales. Sociedad Veterinaria de Zootecnia [*A publication*]

Anson Cont ... Anson on Contracts [*A publication*] (DLA)

ANSP........ Academy of Natural Sciences [*Acronym is based on former name, Academy of Natural Sciences of Philadelphia*] (EA)

ANSP........ Agency for National Security Planning [*Republic of Korea*] (ECON)

AnSP.......... Anthology of Spanish Poetry from Garsilaso to Garcia [*A publication*]

ANSP......... Association of Navy Safety Professionals (EA)

ANSPAO... Australia. Commonwealth Scientific and Industrial Research Organisation. National Standards Laboratory. Technical Paper [*A publication*]

Anspr......... Anspruch [*Claim, Title, Right*] [*German*] (ILCA)

ANSR .... Advanced Naval System Requirements

ANSR .... Answer (ROG)

ANSS......... American Nature Study Society (EA)

ANSS......... Anthropology and Sociology Section [*Association of College and Research Libraries*]

ANSS......... Associate of the Normal School of Science

ANSSIR .... [*A*] Network of Social Security Information Resources [*Health and Welfare Canada*] [*Defunct*] (IID)

ANSSR...... Aerodynamically Neutral Spin-Stabilized Rocket (MCD)

ANSSRAS ... Aerodynamically Neutral Spin-Stabilized Rocket Artillery System [*Army*] (MCD)

ANSSSR.... Akademija Nauk SSSR [*A publication*]

AnST.......... Analecta Sacra Tarraconensia [*A publication*]

AnSt.......... Anatolian Studies. Journal of the British Institute of Archaeology at Ankara [*London*] [*A publication*]

Anst........... Anstruther's English Exchequer Reports [*145 English Reprint*] [*A publication*] (DLA)

ANST........ New South Wales Strata Title Law and Practice [*Australia*] [*A publication*]

AnSTar...... Analecta Sacra Tarraconensia [*Barcelona*] [*A publication*]

An Staz Sper Agr M ... Annali. Stazione Sperimentale Agrario di Modena [*A publication*]

An St Casa Santos ... Anais. Santa Casa de Santos [*A publication*]

AnStEbr..... Annuario di Studi Ebraici. Collegio Rabbinico Italiano [*Rome*] [*A publication*]

Anst Eng Law ... Anstey's Guide to the English Law and Constitution [*A publication*] (DLA)

ANSTI....... African Network of Scientific and Technological Institutions (EAIO)

An Stiint Univ Al I Cuza Iasi Sect 1 ... Analele Stiintifice ale Universitatii Al. I. Cuza din Iasi. Sectiunea 1. Matematica, Fizica, Chimie [*Romania*] [*A publication*]

An Stiint Univ Al I Cuza Iasi Sect 2 ... Analele Stiintifice ale Universitatii Al. I. Cuza din Iasi. Sectiunea 2. Stiinte Naturale [*A publication*]

An Stiint Univ Al I Cuza Iasi Sect 1a ... Analele Stiintifice ale Universitatii Al. I. Cuza din Iasi. Sectiunea 1a. Matematica [*Romania*] [*A publication*]

An Stiint Univ Al I Cuza Iasi Sect 2a ... Analele Stiintifice ale Universitatii Al. I. Cuza din Iasi. Sectiunea 2a. Biologie [*Romania*] [*A publication*]

An Stiint Univ Al I Cuza Iasi Sect 2a Biol ... Analele Stiintifice ale Universitatii Al. I. Cuza din Iasi. Sectiunea 2a. Biologie [*A publication*]

An Stiint Univ Al I Cuza Iasi Sect 1a Mat ... Analele Stiintifice ale Universitatii Al. I. Cuza din Iasi. Seria Noua. Sectiunea 1a. Matematica [*A publication*]

An Stiint Univ Al I Cuza Iasi Sect 1a Mat NS ... Analele Stiintifice ale Universitatii Al. I. Cuza din Iasi. Seria Noua. Sectiunea 1a. Matematica [*A publication*]

An Stiint Univ Al I Cuza Iasi Sect 1b ... Analele Stiintifice ale Universitatii Al. I. Cuza din Iasi. Sectiunea 1b. Fizica [*Romania*] [*A publication*]

An Stiint Univ Al I Cuza Iasi Sect 2b ... Analele Stiintifice ale Universitatii Al. I. Cuza din Iasi. Sectiunea 2b. Geologie [*A publication*]

An Stiint Univ Al I Cuza Iasi Sect 1b Fiz N S ... Analele Stiintifice ale Universitatii Al. I. Cuza din Iasi. Sectiunea 1b. Fizica. Seria Noua [*A publication*]

An Stiint Univ Al I Cuza Iasi Sect 2 Biol Geol Geogr ... Analele Stiintifice ale Universitatii Al. I. Cuza din Iasi. Sectiunea 2. Biologie, Geologie, Geografie [*A publication*]

An Stiint Univ Al I Cuza Iasi Sect 1c ... Analele Stiintifice ale Universitatii Al. I. Cuza din Iasi. Sectiunea 1c. Chimie [*Romania*] [*A publication*]

An Stiint Univ Al I Cuza Iasi Sect 2c ... Analele Stiintifice ale Universitatii Al. I. Cuza din Iasi. Sectiunea 2c. Geografie [*A publication*]

An Stiint Univ Al I Cuza Iasi Stiinte Nat Biol ... Analele Stiintifice ale Universitatii Al. I. Cuza din Iasi. Stiinte Naturale. Biologia [*Romania*] [*A publication*]

An Sti Univ Al I Cuza Iasi Sect 1b Fiz ... Analele Stiintifice ale Universitatii Al. I. Cuza din Iasi. Sectiunea 1b. Fizica. Seria Noua [*A publication*]

An Sti Univ Al I Cuza Iasi Sect 1 Mat ... Analele Stiintifice ale Universitatii Al. I. Cuza din Iasi. Seria Noua. Sectiunea 1. Matematica [*A publication*]

ANSTO ..... Australian Nuclear Science and Technology Organisation [*Also, an information service or system*] (IID)

Anst Pl Gui ... Anstey's Pleader's Guide [*A publication*] (DLA)

Anstr.......... Anstruther's English Exchequer Reports [*145 English Reprint*] [*A publication*] (DLA)

Anstr (Eng) ... Anstruther's English Exchequer Reports [*145 English Reprint*] [*A publication*] (DLA)

AnStud....... Anatolian Studies. Journal of the British Institute of Archaeology at Ankara [*London*] [*A publication*]

ANSUA5 ... Annals of Surgery [*A publication*]

An Sumar (Zagreb) ... Anali za Sumarstvo (Zagreb) [*A publication*]

AnSur........ Antiquity and Survival [*The Hague*] [*A publication*]

An Sur Am L ... Annual Survey of American Law [*A publication*]

ANSVIP .... American National Standard Vocabulary for Information Processing

ANSW .... Air New South Wales [*Australia*]

ANSW .... Antinuclear Submarine Warfare [*Navy*]

ANSWER ... Automated Network Schedule with Evaluation of Resources (MCD)

ANSWERS ... Antisurface Weapons Exchange and Reaction Simulation (MCD)

ANSY .... American Nursery Products, Inc. [*NASDAQ symbol*] (NQ)

ANSYS ...... Analysis System for Static and Dynamic Problems (MCD)

ANT .... A. N. Tupolev [*Initialism used as designation for Russian aircraft designed by Tupolev*]

ANT .... Acoustic Noise Test

ANT .... Advanced Nosetip Test [*AEC*] (MCD)

ANT .... Altalanos Nyelveszeti Tanulmanyok [*A publication*]

ANT.......... American National Theater [*Kennedy Center for the Performing Arts*]
ANT.......... Anglo-Norman Texts [*A publication*]
Ant............ Antaios [*A publication*]
ANT.......... Antarctic
ANT.......... Antenna (AFM)
ANT.......... Antenna Noise Temperature
ANT.......... Anterior
ANT.......... Anthony Industries, Inc. [*NYSE symbol*] (SPSG)
Ant............ Antichthon. Journal of the Australian Society for Classical Studies [*A publication*]
ANT.......... Antient [*Archaic variation of "ancient"*] (ROG)
Ant............ Antigone [*of Sophocles*] [*Classical studies*] (OCD)
ANT.......... Antigua (ROG)
Ant............ Antike [*A publication*]
ANT.......... Antilliaanse Nieuwsbrief. Tweewekelijkse Uitgave van het Kabinet van de Gevolmachtigde Minister van de Nederlandse Antillen [*A publication*]
ANT.......... Antimonium [*Antimony*] [*Chemical element*] [*Symbol is Sb*] (ROG)
ANT.......... Antiphon
Ant............ Antiquary [*A publication*]
Ant............ Antiquitates Judaicae [*Jewish Antiquities*] [*of Josephus*] [*Classical studies*] (BJA)
ANT.......... Antiquities
Ant............ Antiquity [*Gloucester*] [*A publication*]
Ant............ Antlia [*Constellation*]
ANT.......... Antofagasta [*Chile*] [*Seismograph station code, US Geological Survey*] (SEIS)
Ant............ Antonius [*of Plutarch*] [*Classical studies*] (OCD)
Ant............ Antony and Cleopatra [*Shakespearean work*]
ANT.......... Antonym
ANT.......... Antrim [*County in Ireland*] (ROG)
ANT.......... [*The*] Apocryphal New Testament [*A publication*] (BJA)
ANT.......... Association Nationale des Telespectateurs [*National Association of Telespectators*] [*Canada*]
ANT.......... Australian Nouveau Theatre
ANT.......... Autonomous Navigation Technology (MCD)
ANT.......... Netherlands Antilles [*ANSI three-letter standard code*] (CNC)
ANT.......... San Antonio, TX [*Location identifier*] [*FAA*] (FAAL)
ANTA....... American National Theatre and Academy [*Defunct*] (EA)
ANTA....... Antarctic [*A publication*]
ANTA....... Australian Natural Therapists Association
ANTAC..... Air Navigation and Tactical Control
ANTACCS ... Advanced Navy Tactical Command and Control System (NG)
Ant Afr....... Antiquites Africaines [*A publication*]
ANTAR..... Antarctic Record [*Japan*] [*A publication*]
Antarc........ Antarctic
Antarct Geol Map Ser ... Antarctic Geological Map Series [*Tokyo*] [*A publication*]
Antarctic J ... Antarctic Journal of the United States [*A publication*]
ANTARCTICSUPPORT ... Antarctic Support Activities
Antarct J US ... Antarctic Journal of the United States [*A publication*]
Antarct Rec ... Antarctic Record [*A publication*]
Antarct Rec (Tokyo) ... Antarctic Record (Tokyo) [*A publication*]
Antarct Res Ser ... Antarctic Research Series [*A publication*]
Antar Jour US ... Antarctic Journal of the United States [*A publication*]
Antarktika Doklady Kom ... Antarktika Doklady Komissii [*A publication*]
AntAS........ Antike, Alte Sprachen und Deutsche Bildung [*A publication*]
Ant Ath ...... Antiquities of Athens [*A publication*]
Ant Aug...... Antonius Augustinus [*Deceased, 1586*] [*Authority cited in pre-1607 legal work*] (DSA)
Ant August ... Antonius Augustinus [*Deceased, 1586*] [*Authority cited in pre-1607 legal work*] (DSA)
ANTBAL... Antibiotiki [*Moscow*] [*A publication*]
ANTBDO... Antibiotics [*Berlin*] [*A publication*]
Ant Bk....... Antiquarian Bookman [*A publication*]
Ant Boid..... Antonius Boidus [*Flourished, 16th century*] [*Authority cited in pre-1607 legal work*] (DSA)
Ant de But ... Antonius de Butrio [*Deceased, 1408*] [*Authority cited in pre-1607 legal work*] (DSA)
ANTC........ Air Navigation Traffic Control
ANT-C....... Antennapedia Complex [*Gene cluster in fruit fly*]
ANTC........ Antichaff Circuit (IEEE)
AntC.......... Antiquite Classique [*A publication*]
ANTC........ Association of Nursery Training Colleges [*British*]
ANTC........ International Paper Corp./Anitec Image Technology Corp. [*NASDAQ symbol*] (NQ)
Ant Cl........ Antiquite Classique [*A publication*]
Ant Class ... Antiquite Classique [*A publication*] (OCD)
Ant Coll...... Australasian Antique Collector [*A publication*] (APTA)
ANTCOMDUSARCARIB ... Antilles Command, United States Army Caribbean
Ant Corse ... Antonius Corsettus [*Flourished, 15th century*] [*Authority cited in pre-1607 legal work*] (DSA)
ANTCP...... Anticipate (AABC)
ANTDEFCOM ... Antilles Defense Command (MCD)
Ant Denk .... Antike Denkmaeler [*A publication*]
ANTEC...... Annual Technical Conference [*Society of Plastics Engineers*]
ANTEDX... Animal Technology [*A publication*]

Antennas Propag Soc Int Symp ... Antennas and Propagation Society. International Symposium [*A publication*]
Ant F.......... Anthropological Forum [*A publication*]
ANTF........ Arbeiten zur NT Textforschung [*A publication*]
Ant Fab...... Antonius Faber [*Deceased, 1624*] [*Authority cited in pre-1607 legal work*] (DSA)
Ant Gab Rom ... Antonius Gabrielius (Romanus) [*Deceased, 1555*] [*Authority cited in pre-1607 legal work*] (DSA)
ANTGWDPEC ... Association of National Trade Groups of Wood and Derived Products in the EEC Countries (EAIO)
ANTH....... Anthelmintic [*Expelling Worms*] [*Medicine*] (ROG)
ANTH....... Anthology
Anth......... Anthon's New York Nisi Prius Reports [*A publication*] (DLA)
ANTH....... Anthropologica [*A publication*]
Ant H .... Antiquitas Hungarica [*A publication*]
Anth Black ... Anthon's Abridgment of Blackstone [*A publication*] (DLA)
AnThijm .... Annalen van het Thijmgenootschap [*Utrecht*] [*A publication*]
AnthL........ Anthropological Linguistics [*A publication*]
Anth Lat ..... Anthologia Latina [*A publication*] (OCD)
Anth LS ..... Anthon's Law Student [*A publication*] (DLA)
Anth Lyr Graec ... Anthologia Lyrica Graeca [*A publication*] (OCD)
Anth NP..... Anthon's New York Nisi Prius Reports [*A publication*] (DLA)
Anth NPR.... Anthon's New York Nisi Prius Reports [*A publication*] (DLA)
Anthol........ Anthologie [*Anthology*] [*German*]
ANTHOL ... Anthology
Anthol Med Santoriana ... Anthologica Medica Santoriana [*A publication*]
Anthon NP (NY) ... Anthon's New York Nisi Prius Reports [*A publication*] (DLA)
Anthon Rep ... Anthon's New York Nisi Prius Reports [*A publication*] (DLA)
Anthon's NP ... Anthon's New York Nisi Prius Reports [*A publication*] (DLA)
Anthon's NP (2d Ed) ... Anthon's Nisi Prius Reports [*2nd ed.*] [*A publication*] (DLA)
Anthon's Rep ... Anthon's New York Nisi Prius Reports [*A publication*] (DLA)
Anth Pal..... Anthologia Palatina [*Classical studies*] (OCD)
Anth Plan... Anthologia Planudea [*Classical studies*] (OCD)
Anth Prec... Anthon's New Precedents of Declarations [*A publication*] (DLA)
AnthQ........ Anthropological Quarterly [*A publication*]
Anth Quart ... Anthropological Quarterly [*A publication*]
Anthr......... Anthropos [*A publication*]
Anthr H ..... Anthropologia Hungarica [*A publication*]
Anthr J Can ... Anthropological Journal of Canada [*A publication*]
Anthr Kozl ... Anthropologiai Koezlemenyek [*A publication*]
Anthr Ling ... Anthropological Linguistics [*A publication*]
ANTHRO ... Anthropology
Anthro Anz ... Anthropologischer Anzeiger [*A publication*]
Anthro Forum ... Anthropological Forum [*A publication*]
Anthro I ..... Anthropologica Index [*A publication*]
Anthro Ling ... Anthropological Linguistics [*A publication*]
ANTHROP ... Anthropology
Anthrop Gesell Wien Mitt ... Anthropologische Gesellschaft in Wien. Mitteilungen [*A publication*]
Anthrop J... Anthropological Institute. Journal [*A publication*]
ANTHROPOL ... Anthropological
Anthropol... Anthropologie [*Anthropology*] [*German*]
Anthropol Anz ... Anthropologischer Anzeiger [*A publication*]
Anthropol Forum ... Anthropological Forum [*A publication*]
Anthropol (H) ... Anthropologie (Hamburg) [*A publication*]
Anthropol Index ... Anthropological Index [*A publication*]
Anthropol Koezlem ... Anthropologiai Koezlemenyek [*A publication*]
Anthropol Kozl ... Anthropologiai Koezlemenyek [*A publication*]
Anthropol Ling ... Anthropological Linguistics [*A publication*]
Anthropol Lit ... Anthropological Literature [*A publication*]
Anthropol (P) ... Anthropologie (Paris) [*A publication*]
Anthropol Pap Am Mus Nat Hist ... Anthropological Papers. American Museum of Natural History [*A publication*]
Anthropol Pap Mus Anthropol Univ Mich ... Anthropological Papers. Museum of Anthropology. University of Michigan [*A publication*]
Anthropol Quart ... Anthropological Quarterly [*A publication*]
Anthropol Rec Univ Calif ... Anthropological Records. University of California [*A publication*]
Anthrop Q ... Anthropological Quarterly [*A publication*]
Anthrop R .. Anthropological Review [*A publication*]
Anthr Pap .. Anthropological Papers. American Museum of Natural History [*A publication*]
Anthrplgica ... Anthropologica [*A publication*]
Anthr P Mic ... Anthropological Papers. Museum of Anthropology. University of Michigan [*A publication*]
Anthr Q...... Anthropological Quarterly [*A publication*]
Anth RR Cons ... Anthony on Consolidation of Railroad Companies [*A publication*] (DLA)
Anthr Rep Pap ... Anthropological Report of Papua [*A publication*] (APTA)
Anthr-UCLA ... Anthropology-UCLA [*A publication*]
Anth Shep ... Anthony's Edition of Shephard's Touchstone [*A publication*] (DLA)
Anth St....... Anthon's Study of Law [*A publication*] (DLA)
AntHung.... Antiquitas Hungarica [*A publication*]
ANTI .... Acetoxy-N-trimethylanilinium Iodide [*Organic chemistry*]

ANTI .... Antietam National Battlefield Site
ANTI .... Automated Near-Term Improvement　(MCD)
Antib .... [*Petrus*] Antibolus [*Authority cited in pre-1607 legal work*]　(DSA)
ANTIB .... Antincendio [*A publication*]
Antibakt Chemother Urol Norddtsch Therapiegespraeche ... Antibakterielle Chemotherapie in der Urologie. Norddeutsche Therapiegespraeche [*A publication*]
Antibio Med Clin Ther ... Antibiotic Medicine and Clinical Therapy [*A publication*]
Antibiot ...... Antibiotiki [*A publication*]
Antibiot Annu ... Antibiotics Annual [*A publication*]
Antibiot Chemother ... Antibiotica et Chemotherapia [*A publication*]
Antibiot and Chemother ... Antibiotics and Chemotherapy [*A publication*]
Antibiot Chemother (Basel) ... Antibiotics and Chemotherapy (Basel) [*A publication*]
Antibiot Chemother (Wash DC) ... Antibiotics and Chemotherapy (Washington, DC) [*A publication*]
Antibiotic Med Clin Therapy ... Antibiotic Medicine and Clinical Therapy [*A publication*]
Antibiotics Chemother ... Antibiotics and Chemotherapy [*A publication*]
Antibiot Khimioter ... Antibiotiki i Khimioterapiya [*A publication*]
Antibiot Med ... Antibiotic Medicine [*A publication*]
Antibiot Med Biotechnol ... Antibiotics and Medical Biotechnology [*A publication*]
Antibiot Med Clin Ther (London) ... Antibiotic Medicine and Clinical Therapy (London) [*A publication*]
Antibiot Med Clin Ther (NY) ... Antibiotic Medicine and Clinical Therapy (New York) [*A publication*]
Antibiot Monogr ... Antibiotics Monographs [*A publication*]
Antibiot Resp Mezhved Sb ... Antibiotiki Respublikanskii Mezhvedomstvennyi Sbornik [*A publication*]
Antibiot Vitam Horm ... Antibiotics, Vitamins, and Hormones [*A publication*]
Antibodies Hum Diagn Ther ... Antibodies in Human Diagnosis and Therapy [*A publication*]
Antibol .... [*Petrus*] Antibolus [*Authority cited in pre-1607 legal work*]　(DSA)
Anti-Cancer Drug Des ... Anti-Cancer Drug Design [*A publication*]
Anticancer Res ... Anticancer Research [*A publication*]
Anti-Corr Meth Mat ... Anti-Corrosion Methods and Materials [*A publication*]
Anti-Corros ... Anti-Corrosion Methods and Materials [*A publication*]
Anti-Corrosion ... Anti-Corrosion Methods and Materials [*A publication*]
Anti-Corrosion Meth & Mat ... Anti-Corrosion Methods and Materials [*A publication*]
Anti-Corrosion Methods Mats ... Anti-Corrosion Methods and Materials [*A publication*]
Anti-Corros Methods Mater ... Anti-Corrosion Methods and Materials [*A publication*]
Antifungal Compd ... Antifungal Compounds [*A publication*]
ANTIG ...... Antigua　(ROG)
Antigon Rev ... Antigonish Review [*A publication*]
AntigR .... Antigonish Review [*A publication*]
Antiinflammatory Agents Chem Pharmacol ... Antiinflammatory Agents. Chemistry and Pharmacology [*A publication*]
Antike Aben ... Antike und Abendland [*A publication*]
Anti-Locust Bull ... Anti-Locust Bulletin [*A publication*]
Anti-Locust Mem ... Anti-Locust Memoir [*A publication*]
Anti-Locust Res Cent Rep ... Anti-Locust Research Centre [*Later, Centre for Overseas Pest Research*] Report [*A publication*]
ANTILOG ... Antilogarithm
ANTIM ..... Antimonium [*Antimony*] [*Chemical element*] [*Symbol is Sb*]　(ROG)
Antim Ag Ch ... Antimicrobial Agents and Chemotherapy [*A publication*]
Antimicrob Agents Annu ... Antimicrobial Agents Annual [*A publication*]
Antimicrob Agents Chemother ... Antimicrobial Agents and Chemotherapy [*A publication*]
Antimicrob Newsl ... Antimicrobic Newsletter [*A publication*]
Antineoplast Immunosuppr Agents ... Antineoplastic and Immunosuppressive Agents [*A publication*]
Anti Nk ...... Anti Nuclear [*A publication*]
Antioch R ... Antioch Review [*A publication*]
Antioch Rev ... Antioch Review [*A publication*]
ANTIOPE ... L'Acquisition Numerique et Televisualisation d'Images Organisees en Pages d'Ecriture [*French videotex system*]
Antioquia Med ... Antioquia Medica [*A publication*]
ANTIQ ...... Antiquarian [*or Antiquities*]
ANTIQ ...... Antique [*Bookbinding*]　(ROG)
Antiq .... Antiques [*A publication*]
Antiq .... Antiquity [*A publication*]
Antiq Afr ... Antiquites Africaines [*A publication*]
Antiq Bkman ... Antiquarian Bookman [*A publication*]
Antiq Class ... Antiquite Classique [*A publication*]
Antiq Gesell in Zuerich Mitt ... Antiquarische Gesellschaft in Zuerich. Mitteilungen [*A publication*]
Antiq Horol ... Antiquarian Horology [*A publication*]
Antiq Horology ... Antiquarian Horology and the Proceedings of the Antiquarian Horological Society [*A publication*]
Antiq J .... Antiquaries Journal [*A publication*]
Antiq Jnl .... Antiquaries Journal [*A publication*]
Antiq Journ ... Antiquaries Journal [*A publication*]

Antiq (n s) .. Antiquary (New Series) [*A publication*]
Antiq S Afr ... Antiques in South Africa [*A publication*]
Antiq Sunderland ... Antiquities of Sunderland [*A publication*]
Antiqu Africaines ... Antiquites Africaines [*A publication*]
Antiquaries J ... Antiquaries Journal [*A publication*]
Antiquaries Jnl ... Antiquaries Journal [*A publication*]
Antiquar J ... Antiquaries Journal [*A publication*]
Antiquary ... Antiquary, Jewitt's [*A publication*]
Antique Eng ... Antique Engines [*A publication*]　(APTA)
Antiques J ... Antiques Journal [*A publication*]
Antiquite Cl ... Antiquite Classique [*A publication*]
Antiquit Rundsch ... Antiquitaten Rundschau [*A publication*]
Antiqu Journal ... Antiquaries Journal [*A publication*]
ANTI-SOC ... Anti-Socialist Party　(ADA)
ANTISUBFITRON ... Antisubmarine Fighter Squadron [*Navy*]
Antitr Law Symp ... Antitrust Law Symposium [*A publication*]
Antitr L and Ec R ... Antitrust Law and Economics Review [*A publication*]
Antitr LJ .... Antitrust Law Journal [*A publication*]
Antitrust B ... Antitrust Bulletin [*A publication*]
Antitrust Bull ... Antitrust Bulletin [*A publication*]
Antitrust Law and Econ R ... Antitrust Law and Economics Review [*A publication*]
Antitrust Law Econ Rev ... Antitrust Law and Economics Review [*A publication*]
Antitrust L & Econ Rev ... Antitrust Law and Economics Review [*A publication*]
Antitrust LJ ... Antitrust Law Journal [*A publication*]
Antitrust L Sym ... Antitrust Law Symposium [*A publication*]
Antitrust L & Trade Reg Rep ... Antitrust Law and Trade Regulations Report [*Bureau of National Affairs*] [*A publication*]　(ILCA)
Antitrust Newsl ... Antitrust Newsletter [*A publication*]
Antitrust & Trade Reg Rep ... Antitrust and Trade Regulation Report [*Bureau of National Affairs*] [*A publication*]
Antitrust & Trade Reg Rep BNA ... Antitrust and Trade Regulation Report. Bureau of National Affairs [*A publication*]
Antitumor Stud Nitrocaphane (AT-1258) ... Antitumor Studies on Nitrocaphane (AT-1258) [*A publication*]
Antiviral Res ... Antiviral Research [*A publication*]
ANTIVOX ... Antivoice-Operated Transmission　(CET)
AntJ .... Antiquaries Journal [*A publication*]
ANT JENTAC ... Ante Jentaculum [*Before Breakfast*] [*Pharmacy*]
Ant Journ ... Antiquaries Journal [*A publication*]　(OCD)
AntK .... Antike Kunst [*A publication*]
Ant Kunst ... Antike Kunst [*A publication*]
Ant Kunstpr ... Die Antike Kunstprosa [*A publication*]　(OCD)
Antl .... Antlia [*Constellation*]
ANTLAT ... Antique Latin　(ADA)
ANTLD ..... Antique Laid [*Paper*]　(ADA)
Ant Luc ...... Ante Lucem [*Before Daylight*] [*Latin*]
Ant Nat ...... Antiquites Nationales [*St.-Germain-En-Laye*] [*A publication*]
Anto .... Antonius de Butrio [*Deceased, 1408*] [*Authority cited in pre-1607 legal work*]　(DSA)
ANTO .... Austrian National Tourist Office　(EA)
Anto de But ... Antonius de Butrio [*Deceased, 1408*] [*Authority cited in pre-1607 legal work*]　(DSA)
Anto Fab .... Antonius Faber [*Deceased, 1624*] [*Authority cited in pre-1607 legal work*]　(DSA)
Anton .... Antonianum [*A publication*]
ANTON ..... Antonym　(ADA)
Anton Burg ... Antonius Burgos [*Deceased, 1525*] [*Authority cited in pre-1607 legal work*]　(DSA)
Anton Costan ... Antonius Guibertus Costanus [*Flourished, 16th century*] [*Authority cited in pre-1607 legal work*]　(DSA)
Anton Fab .. Antonius Faber [*Deceased, 1624*] [*Authority cited in pre-1607 legal work*]　(DSA)
Anton Gabr ... Antonius Gabrielius (Romanus) [*Deceased, 1555*] [*Authority cited in pre-1607 legal work*]　(DSA)
Anton Gabr Roman ... Antonius Gabrielius (Romanus) [*Deceased, 1555*] [*Authority cited in pre-1607 legal work*]　(DSA)
Anto Nice ... Antonius Nicellus [*Flourished, 15th century*] [*Authority cited in pre-1607 legal work*]　(DSA)
Anto Nice ... Antonius Nicenus [*Authority cited in pre-1607 legal work*]　(DSA)
Antonie Leeuwenhoek J Microbiol ... Antonie van Leeuwenhoek Journal of Microbiology [*A publication*]
Antonie Van Leewenhoek J Microbiol Serol ... Antonie Van Leeuwenhoek Journal of Microbiology and Serology [*A publication*]
ANTOPS ... Antarctic Operations [*Military*]　(NVT)
ANTOR ..... Assembly of National Tourist Office Representatives in New York　(EA)
Anto Rub .... [*Johannes*] Antonius Rubeus [*Deceased, 1544*] [*Authority cited in pre-1607 legal work*]　(DSA)
Anto Rube .. [*Johannes*] Antonius Rubeus [*Deceased, 1544*] [*Authority cited in pre-1607 legal work*]　(DSA)
ANTOS ..... Antique Old Style [*Paper*]　(ADA)
Anto de Trem ... Antonius de Tremolis [*Flourished, 16th century*] [*Authority cited in pre-1607 legal work*]　(DSA)
ANTOX ..... Antitoxin　(MSA)
AntP .... Antike Plastik [*A publication*]
ANTP .... Army Nozzle Technology Program　(MCD)
ANT PIT ... Anterior Pituitary [*Endocrinology*]

ANT PRAND ... Ante Prandium [*Before Dinner*] [*Pharmacy*]
ANTQ .... AA Importing Co., Inc. [*NASDAQ symbol*]   (NQ)
ANTR .... Antarctic Record [*New Zealand*] [*A publication*]
Ant R .... Antioch Review [*A publication*]
ANTRAC ... Andrulis Tracker [*Military*]   (CAAL)
An Trav Pub Belgique ... Annales des Travaux Publics de Belgique [*A publication*]
ANTRD ..... Anticancer Research [*A publication*]
ANTRD4 ... Anticancer Research [*A publication*]
Antrol .... Anthropological Index [*A publication*]
Ant Rom ... Antiquitates Romanae [*of Dionysius Halicarnassensis*] [*Classical studies*]   (OCD)
Antropol Arch ... Antropologicky Archiv [*A publication*]
Antropologi ... Antropologica [*A publication*]
Ant Rosel ... Antonius de Rosellis [*Deceased, 1466*] [*Authority cited in pre-1607 legal work*]   (DSA)
Ant de Rosell ... Antonius de Rosellis [*Deceased, 1466*] [*Authority cited in pre-1607 legal work*]   (DSA)
ANTRS ..... Antarctic Research Series [*A publication*]
ANTS .... Advanced Naval Training School
ANTS .... Airborne Night Television System [*Obsolete*] [*Army*]   (MCD)
ANTS .... Andover Newton Theological School [*Newton Center, MA*]
ANTS .... Anglo-Norman Text Society [*British*]
ANTS .... Antares Oil Corp. [*NASDAQ symbol*]   (NQ)
ANTS .... Any Tape Search [*Computer program*]   (KSC)
ANTS .... ARPA [*Advanced Research Projects Agency*] Network Terminal System
ANTS .... ATM [*Apollo Telescope Mount*] Navigation and Timing Summary [*NASA*]
ANTS .... Automatic Nitrogen Transfer System
ANTSPT ... Antiseptic   (MSA)
Ant St .... Anatolian Studies [*A publication*]
AntSurv ... Antiquity and Survival [*The Hague*] [*A publication*]
ANTsW ..... Algemeen Nederlands Tijdschrift voor Wijsbegeerte en Psychologie [*A publication*]
ANTU .... Air Navigation Training Unit
ANTU .... Alpha-Naphthylthiourea [*Organic chemistry*]
ANTUF ..... All-Nigeria Trade Union Federation
ANTW .... Algemeen Nederlands Tijdschrift voor Wijsbegeerte [*A publication*]
Antw .... Antwerpiensia [*A publication*]
antw bet ...... Antwoord Betaal [*Reply Paid*] [*Afrikaans*] [*Business term*]
AntWelt ..... Antike Welt [*Kuesnacht-Zuerich*] [*A publication*]
Antwerpen Tijdschr ... Antwerpen; Tijdschrift der Stad Antwerpen [*A publication*]
ANTWO .... Antique Wove [*Paper*]   (ADA)
Antybiot Badaniu Procesow Biochem ... Antybiotyki w Badaniu Procesow Biochemicznych [*A publication*]
ANU .... Airplane Nose Up   (NG)
AnU .... Anales de la Universidad [*A publication*]
ANU .... Antelope Island [*Utah*] [*Seismograph station code, US Geological Survey*]   (SEIS)
ANU .... Antigua [*Antigua*] [*Airport symbol*] [*IYRU nationality code*]
ANU .... Army and Navy Union, USA   (EA)
Anuario Estud Centroam ... Anuario de Estudios Centroamericanos [*A publication*]
AnuarioF .... Anuario de Filologia [*A publication*]
Anu Bago Invest Cient ... Anuario Bago de Investigaciones Cientificas [*A publication*]
ANUBBR .. Acta Neurologica Belgica [*A publication*]
AnUBLG ... Analele. Universitatii Bucuresti. Limbi Germanice [*A publication*]
AnUBLUC ... Analele. Universitatii Bucuresti. Literatura Universala Comparata [*A publication*]
Anu Bras Econ Florestal ... Anuario Brasileiro de Economia Florestal [*A publication*]
Anu Bras Econ Flor Inst Nac Pinho ... Anuario Brasileiro de Economia Florestal. Instituto Nacional de Pinho [*A publication*]
Anu Bras Odontol ... Anuario Brasileiro de Odontologia [*A publication*]
ANUC .... American Nuclear Corp. [*NASDAQ symbol*]   (NQ)
Anu Com Stat Geol Repub Soc Rom ... Anuarul. Comitetului de Stat al Geologiei. Republica Socialista Romania [*A publication*]
Anude .... Asamblea Nicaraguense de Unidad Democratica [*Nicaraguan Assembly Democratic Unity*]   (PD)
Anu Der Univ Panama ... Anuario de Derecho. Universidad de Panama [*A publication*]
ANUDS ..... Army Nuclear Data System [*Study*]   (AABC)
Anu Ecuator Der Int ... Anuario Ecuatoriano de Derecho Internacional [*A publication*]
Anu Estad Min Mex ... Anuario Estadistico de la Mineria Mexicana [*A publication*]
Anu Estud Atl ... Anuario de Estudios Atlanticos [*A publication*]
ANUF .... Account Number Update File [*IRS*]
Anu Fac Der ... Anuario. Facultad de Derecho [*A publication*]
Anu de Filos del Derecho ... Anuario de Filosofia del Derecho [*A publication*]
Anu Filosof ... Anuario Filosofico [*A publication*]
ANUG .... Acute Necrotizing Ulcerative Gingivitis [*Dentistry*]
AnUG .... Annales. Universite de Grenoble [*A publication*]
ANUG .... Atex Newspaper Users Group   (EA)
ANUGA ..... Allgemeine Nahrungs und Genussmittel Ausstellung [*General Food and Delicacies Fair*] [*West Germany*]

ANUHAA ... Animal Nutrition and Health [*A publication*]
Anu Hist J ... Annual History Journal [*A publication*]
ANU Hist J ... ANU [*Australian National University*] Historical Journal [*A publication*]   (APTA)
ANUHJ ..... Australian National University. Historical Journal [*A publication*]   (APTA)
AnUILingv ... Analele Stiintifice ale Universitatii Al. I. Cuza din Iasi. Seria Noua. Sectiunea 3e (Stiinte Sociale). Lingvistica [*A publication*]
AnUILit ..... Analele Stiintifice ale Universitatii Al. I. Cuza din Iasi. Serie Noua. Sectiunea 3f. Literatura [*A publication*]
Anu Indig ... Anuario Indigenista [*A publication*]
Anu Inst Cienc Pen Criminol ... Anuario. Instituto de Ciencias Penales y Criminologicas [*A publication*]
Anu Inst Geol (Rom) ... Anuarul. Institutului Geologic (Romania) [*A publication*]
Anu Inst Istor Arheologie ... Anuarul. Institutului de Istorie si Arheologie [*A publication*]
Anu Inst Patol Ig Anim ... Anuarul. Institutului de Patologie si Igiena Animala [*A publication*]
Anu Inst Patol Ig Anim (Bucur) ... Anuarul. Institutului de Patologie si Igiena Animala (Bucuresti) [*A publication*]
Anu Inst Stud Cl ... Anuarul. Institutul de Studii Clasice. Universitate din Cluj [*A publication*]
AnUL .... Annales. Universite de Lyon [*A publication*]
ANULAE .. Amalgamated National Union of Local Authorities Employees' Federation of Malaya
ANum .... Acta Numismatica [*A publication*]
Anu Miner Bras ... Anuario Mineral Brasileiro [*Brazil*] [*A publication*]
Anu Miner Brasil ... Anuario Mineral Brasileiro [*A publication*]
Anu Mus ... Anuario Musical [*A publication*]
ANU News ... Australian National University. News [*A publication*]   (APTA)
An Univ Barcelona ... Anales. Universidad de Barcelona [*A publication*]
An Univ Bucur Biol Anim ... Analele. Universitatii Bucuresti. Biologie Animala [*A publication*]
An Univ Bucur Biol Veg ... Analele. Universitatii Bucuresti. Biologie Vegetala [*A publication*]
An Univ Bucur Chim ... Analele. Universitatii Bucuresti. Chimie [*A publication*]
An Univ Bucuresti Fiz ... Analele. Universitatii Bucuresti. Fizica [*A publication*]
An Univ Bucuresti Geogr ... Analele. Universitatii Bucuresti. Geografie [*A publication*]
An Univ Bucuresti Geol ... Analele. Universitatii Bucuresti. Geologie [*A publication*]
An Univ Bucuresti Mat ... Analele. Universitatii Bucuresti. Matematica [*A publication*]
An Univ Bucuresti Mat Mec ... Analele. Universitatii Bucuresti. Matematica-Mecanica [*A publication*]
An Univ Bucuresti Seria Stiint Nat Mat Mec ... Analele. Universitatii Bucuresti. Seria Stiintele Naturii. Matematica-Mecanica [*A publication*]
An Univ Bucuresti Ser Mat ... Analele. Universitatii Bucuresti. Seria Matematica [*A publication*]
An Univ Bucuresti Ser Stiint Nat ... Analele. Universitatii Bucuresti. Seria Stiintele Naturii [*A publication*]
An Univ Bucuresti Ser Stiint Nat Biol ... Analele. Universitatii Bucuresti. Seria Stiintele Naturii. Biologie [*A publication*]
An Univ Bucuresti Ser Stiint Nat Chim ... Analele. Universitatii Bucuresti. Seria Stiintele Naturii. Chimie [*A publication*]
An Univ Bucuresti Ser Stiint Nat Fiz ... Analele. Universitatii Bucuresti. Seria Stiintele Naturii. Fizica [*Romania*] [*A publication*]
An Univ Bucuresti Ser Stiint Nat Geol Geogr ... Analele. Universitatii Bucuresti. Seria Stiintele Naturii. Geologie, Geografie [*A publication*]
An Univ Bucuresti Stiint Nat ... Analele. Universitatii Bucuresti. Stiintele Naturii [*A publication*]
An Univ Bucuresti Sti Natur ... Analele. Universitatii Bucuresti. Stiintele Naturii [*A publication*]
An Univ Bucur Fiz ... Analele. Universitatii Bucuresti. Fizica [*A publication*]
An Univ Bucur Geol ... Analele. Universitatii Bucuresti. Geologie [*A publication*]
An Univ Bucur Mat Mec ... Analele. Universitatii Bucuresti. Matematica-Mecanica [*A publication*]
An Univ Bucur Ser Stiint Nat Chim ... Analele. Universitatii Bucuresti. Seria Stiintele Naturii. Chimie [*A publication*]
An Univ Bucur Stiint Nat ... Analele. Universitatii Bucuresti. Stiintele Naturii [*A publication*]
An Univ Catol Valparaiso ... Anales. Universidad Catolica de Valparaiso [*A publication*]
An Univ Cent Ecuador ... Anales. Universidad Central del Ecuador [*A publication*]
An Univ Chile ... Anales. Universidad de Chile [*A publication*]
An Univ C I Parhon Ser Stiint Nat ... Analele. Universitatii C. I. Parhon. Seria Stiintele Naturii [*A publication*]
An Univ Craiova Biol Stiinte Agric Ser A 3a ... Analele. Universitatii din Craiova. Biologie Stiinte. Agricole. Seria A 3a [*A publication*]
An Univ Craiova Mat Fiz-Chim ... Analele. Universitatii din Craiova. Matematica. Fizica-Chimie [*A publication*]

An Univ Craiova Ser 3 ... Analele. Universitatii din Craiova. Seria 3a. Stiinte Agricole [*A publication*]
An Univ Craiova Ser Biol Med Stiinte Agr ... Analele. Universitatii din Craiova. Seria Biologie Medicina Stiinte Agricole [*A publication*]
An Univ Craiova Ser Mat Fiz Chim Electroteh ... Anale. Universitatea din Craiova. Seria Matematica, Fizica, Chimie, Electrotehnica [*A publication*]
An Univ Cuenca ... Anales. Universidad de Cuenca [*A publication*]
An Univ Galati Fasc 6 ... Analele. Universitatii din Galati. Fascicula 6. Tehnologia si Chimia Produselor Alimentare [*A publication*]
An Univ Hispalense ... Anales. Universidad Hispalense [*A publication*]
An Univ Hispalense Ser Cienc ... Anales. Universidad Hispalense. Serie de Ciencias [*A publication*]
An Univ Hisp Ser Cienc ... Anales. Universidad Hispalense. Serie de Ciencias [*A publication*]
An Univ Hisp Ser Med ... Anales. Universidad Hispalense. Serie Medicina [*A publication*]
An Univ Hisp Ser Vet ... Anales. Universidad Hispalense. Serie Veterinaria [*A publication*]
An Univ Madrid ... Anales. Universidad de Madrid [*A publication*]
An Univ Murcia ... Anales. Universidad de Murcia [*A publication*]
An Univ Murcia Cienc ... Anales. Universidad de Murcia. Ciencias [*A publication*]
An Univ Norte (Chile) ... Anales. Universidad del Norte (Chile) [*A publication*]
An Univ Patagonia San Juan Bosco Cienc Geol ... Anales. Universidad de la Patagonia San Juan Bosco. Ciencias Geologicas [*A publication*]
An Univ St Domingo ... Anales. Universidad de Santo Domingo [*A publication*]
An Univ Timisoara Ser Sti Fiz-Chim ... Analele. Universitatii din Timisoara. Seria Stiinte Fizice-Chimice [*A publication*]
An Univ Timisoara Ser Stiinte Fiz Chim ... Analele. Universitatii din Timisoara. Seria Stiinte Fizice-Chimice [*A publication*]
An Univ Timisoara Ser Stiinte Mat-Fiz ... Analele. Universitatii din Timisoara. Seria Stiinte Matematice-Fizice [*Romania*] [*A publication*]
An Univ Timisoara Ser Stiint Fiz-Chim ... Analele. Universitatii din Timisoara. Seria Stiinte Fizice-Chimice [*A publication*]
An Univ Timisoara Ser Stiint Mat ... Analele. Universitatii din Timisoara. Seria Stiinte Matematice [*A publication*]
An Univ Timisoara Ser Sti Mat ... Analele. Universitatii din Timisoara. Seria Stiinte Matematice [*A publication*]
An Univ Timisoara Stiinte Fiz Chim ... Analele. Universitatii din Timisoara. Seria Stiinte Fizice-Chimice [*A publication*]
ANUOA .... Actualites Neurophysiologiques [*A publication*]
ANUP .... Antineoplastic Urinary Protein
ANUPB ...... Advances in Nuclear Physics [*A publication*]
ANURD9 ... Advances in Nutritional Research [*A publication*]
AnUS .... Annual of Urdu Studies [*A publication*]
ANUSDC .. Annual Review of Nuclear and Particle Science [*A publication*]
Anu Soc Broteriana ... Anuario. Sociedade Broteriana [*A publication*]
An U S S ... Andrews University. Seminary Studies [*A publication*]
ANUSSM ... Australian National University. Social Science Monograph [*A publication*] (APTA)
ANUTA ..... Advances in Nuclear Science and Technology [*A publication*]
Anu Tec Inst Pesqui Zootec "Francisco Osorio" ... Anuario Tecnico. Instituto de Pesquisas Zootecnicas "Francisco Osorio" [*A publication*]
AnUTFil .... Analele. Universitatii din Timisoara. Seria Stiinte Filologice [*A publication*]
ANV .... Accion Nacional Vasca [*Basque National Action*] [*Spain*] [*Political party*] (PPE)
ANV .... Advanced Naval Vehicle (CAAL)
ANV .... Air Nevada Airlines, Inc. [*Las Vegas, NV*] [*FAA designator*] (FAAC)
ANV .... Anticipatory Nausea and Vomiting [*Medicine*]
ANV .... Anvik [*Alaska*] [*Airport symbol*] (OAG)
ANV .... Anvil Mountain [*Alaska*] [*Seismograph station code, US Geological Survey*] (SEIS)
ANV .... Army of Northern Virginia [*Civil War*]
ANV .... Australian and New Zealand Environmental Report [*A publication*]
ANVA .... Avhandlinger Utgitt av Norsk Videnskaps-Akademi I Oslo [*A publication*]
ANVAO ..... Avhandlinger Utgitt av Norsk Videnskaps-Akademi I Oslo. II [*A publication*]
ANVAR ..... Agence Nationale de Valorisation de la Recherche [*National Agency for the Promotion of Research*] [*Information service or system*] (IID)
ANVBAV .. Abhandlungen. Naturwissenschaftlicher Verein zu Bremen [*A publication*]
ANVCE ...... Advanced Naval Vehicle Concepts Evaluation (MCD)
ANVHEJ... Abhandlungen. Naturwissenschaftlicher Verein in Hamburg [*A publication*]
ANVIA ...... Americans for the National Voter Initiative Amendment (EA)
ANVIDL.... Annales de Virologie [*Paris*] [*A publication*]
ANVIS....... Aviator's Night Vision Imaging System (RDA)
ANVM....... Association of United States Night Vision Manufacturers (EA)

ANVO........ Accept No Verbal Orders
ANVS .... Advanced Night Viewer Subsystem (MCD)
ANVTAH ... Analecta Veterinaria [*A publication*]
ANW.......... Ainsworth, NE [*Location identifier*] [*FAA*] (FAAL)
ANW.......... American West Capital [*Vancouver Stock Exchange symbol*]
A/N/W ...... Andrews/Nelson/Whitehead [*Commercial firm*]
ANW.......... Apollo Network [*NASA*] (KSC)
a-nw---........ New Guinea Island [*MARC geographic area code*] [*Library of Congress*] (LCCP)
ANW.......... Northwest Region [*FAA*] (FAAC)
ANWA........ Abstracts of New World Archaeology [*A publication*]
ANWC...... American News Women's Club (EA)
ANWC...... Association for Non-White Concerns in Personnel and Guidance (EA)
ANWCG.... Army Nuclear Weapon Coordination Group
ANWD...... Alphanumeric Warning Display (MCD)
ANWES..... Association of Naval Weapons, Engineers, and Scientists [*Later, ASE*]
ANWG...... Apollo Navigation Working Group [*NASA*] (MCD)
ANWI........ American Network, Incorporated [*Portland, OR*] [*NASDAQ symbol*] (NQ)
ANWIAN .. Anaesthesiologie und Wiederbelebung [*Anaesthesiology and Resuscitation*] [*A publication*]
ANWL....... All Nations Women's League (EA)
ANWPP..... Accidental Nuclear War Prevention Project [*Nuclear Age Peace Foundation*] (EA)
An WR ...... Andhra Weekly Reporter [*India*] [*A publication*]
ANWR....... Arctic National Wildlife Refuge [*Alaska*]
ANWS ...... Association of Northwest Steelheaders (EA)
AN-WSC-3 ... Whiskey-3 [*Shipboard radio*]
ANWSRP ... Army Nuclear Weapons Stockpile Reliability Program
ANX.......... Andenes [*Norway*] [*Airport symbol*] (OAG)
ANX.......... Annalen der Gemeinwirtschaft [*A publication*]
ANX.......... Annex (AABC)
ANX.......... Napoleon, MO [*Location identifier*] [*FAA*] (FAAL)
ANXF .... Allied Naval Expeditionary Force [*British military*] (DMA)
ANY .... Ancom ATM International, Inc. [*Toronto Stock Exchange symbol*]
ANY.......... Anthony, KS [*Location identifier*] [*FAA*] (FAAL)
ANYAA .... Annals. New York Academy of Sciences [*A publication*]
ANYA9 .... Annals. New York Academy of Sciences [*A publication*]
ANYAS..... Annals. New York Academy of Sciences [*A publication*]
ANYTC ..... Alternative to the New York Times Committee (EA)
ANZ.......... Air New Zealand (MCD)
ANZ.......... Anzar Road [*California*] [*Seismograph station code, US Geological Survey*] (SEIS)
Anz............ Anzeiger [*or Anzeigen*] [*German*] (OCD)
ANZAAB... Australian and New Zealand Association of Antiquarian Booksellers
ANZAAS... Australian and New Zealand Association for the Advancement of Science
ANZAAS Congress ... Australian and New Zealand Association for the Advancement of Science. Congress [*A publication*] (APTA)
ANZAAS Papers ... Australian and New Zealand Association for the Advancement of Science. Papers [*A publication*] (APTA)
ANZAB..... Australian and New Zealand Association of Bellringers
ANZAC..... Australia-New Zealand Army Corps
ANZACS... Australian and New Zealand Association for Canadian Studies
ANZAEVH ... Australian and New Zealand Association of Educators of the Visually Handicapped
Anz Akad (Wien) ... Anzeiger der Oesterreichischen Akademie der Wissenschaften. Philosophisch-Historische Klasse (Wien) [*A publication*]
Anz Akad Wiss Wien Math Naturwiss Kl ... Anzeiger. Akademie der Wissenschaften in Wien. Mathematisch-Naturwissenschaftliche Klasse [*A publication*]
ANZALDATA ... Australian and New Zealand Academic Library Statistics [*Database*] (ADA)
ANZALS... Australian and New Zealand Association of Law Schools
Anz Alt....... Anzeiger fuer die Altertumswissenschaft [*A publication*]
Anz Altertumsw ... Anzeiger fuer die Altertumswissenschaft [*A publication*]
Anz Altertumswiss ... Anzeiger fuer die Altertumswissenschaft [*A publication*]
AnzAltW.... Anzeiger fuer die Altertumswissenschaft [*Innsbruck*] [*A publication*]
ANZAM .... Australia, New Zealand, and Malaysia (CINC)
ANZAOMS ... Australian and New Zealand Association of Oral and Maxillofacial Surgeons
ANZAPPL ... Australian and New Zealand Association of Psychiatry, Psychology, and the Law
ANZATS... Australian and New Zealand Association of Theological Schools
ANZATVH Newsl ... ANZATVH [*Australian and New Zealand Association of Teachers of the Visually Handicapped*] Newsletter [*A publication*] (APTA)
AnzAW ...... Anzeiger fuer die Altertumswissenschaft [*Innsbruck*] [*A publication*]
ANZBA ..... Australian and New Zealand Burn Association
ANZ Bank ... Australia and New Zealand Bank. Quarterly Survey [*A publication*] (APTA)
ANZ Bank Q ... ANZ [*Australia and New Zealand*] Bank. Quarterly [*A publication*] (APTA)

A & NZ Bank Quarterly Surv ... Australia and New Zealand Bank. Quarterly Survey [*A publication*] (APTA)

ANZCAN .. Australian-New Zealand-Canada [*Cable*] (ADA)

ANZCER ... Australia New Zealand Closer Economic Relationship

ANZC Hals ... Australian and New Zealand Commentary on Halsbury's Laws of England [*A publication*]

ANZCIES ... Australian and New Zealand Comparative and International Education Society

ANZ Conv R ... Australian and New Zealand Conveyancing Report [*A publication*] (APTA)

Anz f D Altert ... Anzeiger fuer Deutsches Altertum [*A publication*]

ANZDDQ ... Australian and New Zealand Journal of Developmental Disabilities [*A publication*]

Anz Germ Nat Mus ... Anzeiger. Germanisches Nationalmuseum [*A publication*]

Anz Ger Nazionalmus ... Anzeiger. Germanisches Nationalmuseum [*A publication*]

ANZHESJ ... ANZHES [*Australian and New Zealand History of Education Society*] Journal [*A publication*] (APTA)

ANZHES Jl ... ANZHES [*Australian and New Zealand History of Education Society*] Journal [*A publication*]

ANZIC ...... Associate of the New Zealand Institute of Chemistry

ANZ Ind .... Australia and New Zealand Bank. Business Indicators [*A publication*] (APTA)

ANZ Insp Sch J ... Australian and New Zealand Association of Inspectors of Schools. Journal [*A publication*] (APTA)

ANZ Insurance Cases ... Australian and New Zealand Insurance Cases [*A publication*] (APTA)

ANZITR .... Australian and New Zealand Income Tax Reports [*A publication*] (DLA)

ANZJC ...... Australian and New Zealand Journal of Criminology [*A publication*] (APTA)

ANZJ Crim ... Australian and New Zealand Journal of Criminology [*A publication*] (APTA)

ANZJ of Crim ... Australian and New Zealand Journal of Criminology [*A publication*] (APTA)

ANZJOS ... Australian and New Zealand Journal of Sociology [*A publication*] (APTA)

ANZJS ...... Australian and New Zealand Journal of Sociology [*A publication*] (ADA)

Anz Maschinenwes ... Anzeiger fuer Maschinenwesen [*A publication*]

ANZMSA ... Australian and New Zealand Merchants' and Shippers' Association (DS)

ANZOAM ... Archives Neerlandaises de Zoologie [*A publication*]

ANZOEQ .. Australian and New Zealand Journal of Ophthalmology [*A publication*]

Anz Oesterr Akad Wiss Math Naturwiss Kl ... Anzeiger. Oesterreichische Akademie der Wissenschaften [*Wien*]. Mathematisch-Naturwissenschaftliche Klasse [*A publication*]

Anz Orn Ges Bayern ... Anzeiger. Ornithologische Gesellschaft in Bayern [*A publication*]

Anz Ornithol Ges Bayern ... Anzeiger. Ornithologische Gesellschaft in Bayern [*A publication*]

Anz Osterr Akad Wiss Math-Naturwiss Kl ... Anzeiger. Oesterreichische Akademie der Wissenschaften. Mathematisch-Naturwissenschaftliche Klasse [*A publication*]

ANZQ .... ANZ [*Australia and New Zealand*] Bank. Quarterly Survey [*A publication*] (APTA)

ANZQ Survey ... ANZ [*Australia and New Zealand*] Bank. Quarterly Survey [*A publication*] (APTA)

ANZ Quart Surv ... ANZ [*Australia and New Zealand*] Bank. Quarterly Survey [*A publication*] (APTA)

Anz Schaedlingskd ... Anzeiger fuer Schaedlingskunde [*A publication*]

Anz Schaedlingskd Pflanz ... Anzeiger fuer Schaedlingskunde, Pflanzenschutz, Umweltschutz [*A publication*]

Anz Schaedlingskd Pflanzenschutz ... Anzeiger fuer Schaedlingskunde und Pflanzenschutz [*Later, Anzeiger fuer Schaedlingskunde, Pflanzenschutz, Umweltschutz*] [*A publication*]

Anz Schaedlingskd Pflanzenschutz Umweltschutz ... Anzeiger fuer Schaedlingskunde, Pflanzenschutz, Umweltschutz [*A publication*]

Anz Schaedlingskd Pflanzen- und Umweltschutz ... Anzeiger fuer Schaedlingskunde, Pflanzen- und Umweltschutz [*A publication*]

Anz Schaedlingskd Pflanz- Umweltschutz ... Anzeiger fuer Schaedlingskunde, Pflanzen- und Umweltschutz [*West Germany*] [*A publication*]

Anz Schw Alt ... Anzeiger fuer Schweizerische Altertumskunde [*A publication*]

Anz Schweiz ... Anzeiger fuer Schweizerische Altertumskunde [*A publication*]

Anz Schweiz Alt ... Anzeiger fuer Schweizerische Altertumskunde [*A publication*]

ANZSES ... Australian and New Zealand Schools Exploring Society

A-NZSNY ... Australian-New Zealand Society of New York (EA)

ANZSRL ... Australian and New Zealand Scientific Research Liaison

ANZSTS ... Australian and New Zealand Society for Theological Studies

ANZ Sur .... ANZ [*Australia and New Zealand*] Bank. Quarterly Survey [*A publication*] (APTA)

ANZTAC ... Australia and New Zealand Trade Advisory Committee [*British Overseas Trade Board*] (DS)

ANZTLA ... Australian and New Zealand Theological Library Association

ANZUK ..... Australia, New Zealand, and United Kingdom

ANZUS ..... Australia, New Zealand, and the United States [*Signatories to the Tripartite Security Treaty of 1951*]

Anz (Wien) ... Anzeiger. Akademie der Wissenschaften (Wien) [*A publication*]

Anz (Wien) ... Anzeiger. Oesterreichische Akademie der Wissenschaften (Wien) [*A publication*]

AO .... Abnormal Occurrence (NRCH)

A/O .... About or On (MCD)

AO .... Absolute Output [*Data processing*]

AO .... Abwehroffizier [*Counterintelligence Officer*] [*German military - World War II*]

AO .... Access Opening [*Technical drawings*]

AO .... Account Of [*Business term*]

AO .... Accountant [*or Accounting*] Officer

AO .... Accounts Office [*Army*] (AABC)

AO .... Acid Output [*Physiology*]

A-O .... Acousto-Optic (MCD)

AO .... Acridine Orange [*Dye*]

AO .... Acta Orientalia [*A publication*]

AO .... Action Officer [*Air Force*] (AFM)

A & O .... Actors and Others for Animals (EA)

AO .... Adjusted Output [*Data processing*]

AO .... Administration Office

AO .... Administrative Operations

AO .... Administrative Order (DLA)

AO .... Administrative and Overhead [*Costs*] (KSC)

AO .... Admiralty Office [*Navy*] [*British*] (ROG)

AO .... Adult Operculum

AO .... Adults Only (ADA)

AO .... Aerial Observer [*Military*] (NVT)

AO .... Aeromere SpA [*Italy*] [*ICAO aircraft manufacturer identifier*] (ICAO)

AO .... Aeronautical Order (AFM)

AO .... Aerosol Obscurant (MCD)

AO .... Affiliation Officer [*British*]

AO .... After Orders (MCD)

AO .... Air Observer [*Military*] [*British*]

AO .... Air Officer [*RAF*] [*British*]

AO .... Air Operator (NRCH)

AO .... Air Ordnance [*Special duties officer*] [*British*]

AO .... Air Over (MSA)

AO .... Airdrome Officer

AO .... Alandsk Odling: Arsbok [*A publication*]

AO .... Aldehyde Oxidase [*An enzyme*]

AO .... Algo Group, Inc. [*Toronto Stock Exchange symbol*]

AO .... Alliance for Opportunity (EA)

AO .... Alte Orient [*A publication*]

AO .... American Optical Corp.

AO .... American Oxonian [*A publication*]

AO .... Among Others

AO .... Amplifier Output [*Data processing*]

AO .... Analog Output [*Data processing*] (NASA)

AO .... And Others

AO .... Angola [*ANSI two-letter standard code*] (CNC)

ao .... Angola [*MARC country of publication code*] [*Library of Congress*] (LCCP)

AO .... Anno Ordinis [*In the Year of the Order*] [*Used by the Knights Templar*] [*Freemasonry*] (ROG)

AO .... Announcement of Opportunity [*NASA*] (MCD)

AO .... Anodal Opening [*Physiology*]

AO .... Anonim Ortaklari [*Partnership*] [*See also TAO*]

AO .... Anonim Ortakligi [*Joint-Stock Partnership*] [*Turkey*] (CED)

AO .... Anordnung [*Direction, Instruction*] [*German*] (ILCA)

AO .... Answer Only (TEL)

AO .... Aortic Valve Opening [*Cardiology*]

AO .... Appointing Order

A & O .... April and October [*Denotes semiannual payments of interest or dividends in these months*] [*Business term*]

A/O .... Aqueous to Organic [*Ratio*]

AO .... Arcane Order (EA)

AO .... Archiv Orientalni [*A publication*]

AO .... Archives Office (ADA)

AO .... Area Office

AO .... Area of Operations [*Military*] (AABC)

AO .... Arkansas & Ozarks Railway [*AAR code*]

AO .... Army Order [*British*]

AO .... Artillery/Ordnance (MCD)

AO .... Assembly Order

AO .... Assembly Outline

AO .... Assist Order

AO .... Astronomical Observatory

AO .... At Occupation [*An underwriting designation for an occupational accident*] [*Insurance*]

AO .... Atomic Orbital

AO .... Audio-Only

AO .... Audio Oscillator

AO .... Auramine-O [*A biological stain*]

AO .... Australian Outlook [*A publication*] (APTA)

AO .... Authenticator Organization (MCD)

AO .... Authority to Officiate [*Church of England in Australia*]

AO .... Authorized Order

AO	Autoimmune Oophoritis [*Medicine*]
AO	Automatic Observer
AO	Autonomous Oblast [*USSR*]
AO	Auxiliary Oiler (MCD)
AO	Auxiliary Oscillator
AO	Avanguardia Operaia [*Worker's Vanguard*] [*Italy*] [*Political party*] (PPE)
AO	Average Out [*Business term*]
AO	Aviacion y Comercio SA [*AVIACO*] [*Spanish airline*] [*ICAO designator*] (FAAC)
AO	Aviation Ordnanceman [*Navy rating*]
AO	Axio-Occlusal [*Dentistry*]
AO	Der Alte Orient. Gemeinverstaendliche Darstellungen [*Leipzig*] [*A publication*]
AO	Officer of the Order of Australia
AO	Oiler [*Navy ship symbol*]
AO	Onoway Public Library, Alberta [*Library symbol*] [*National Library of Canada*] (NLC)
ao-----	South China Sea and Area [*MARC geographic area code*] [*Library of Congress*] (LCCP)
AO1	Aviation Ordnanceman, First Class [*Navy rating*]
1-A-O	Selective Service Class [*for a Conscientious Objector Available for Noncombatant Military Service Only*]
AO2	Aviation Ordnanceman, Second Class [*Navy rating*]
AO3	Aviation Ordnanceman, Third Class [*Navy rating*]
AOA	Abort Once Around [*NASA*]
AOA	Action Outdoor Association [*Australia*]
AOA	Administration on Aging [*Defunct*] [*Department of Health and Human Services*]
AOA	Aerostar Owners Association (EA)
AOA	Air Officer in Charge of Administration [*RAF*] [*British*]
AOA	Airborne Optical Adjunct [*Army*] (RDA)
AOA	Airlines of Australia
AOA	Alabaster, AL [*Location identifier*] [*FAA*] (FAAL)
AOA	American Ontoanalytic Association (EA)
AOA	American Optometric Association (EA)
AOA	American [*or Army*] Ordnance Association [*Later, ADPA*] (EA)
AOA	American Orthopedic Association (EA)
AOA	American Orthopsychiatric Association (EA)
AOA	American Osteopathic Association (EA)
AOA	American Ostrich Association (EA)
AOA	American Overseas Airlines
AOA	American Overseas Association [*Later, ARCOA*] (EA)
AOA	Amphibious Objective Area [*Navy*]
AOA	Amphibious Operating Area
AOA	Angle of Arrival
AOA	Angle of Attack [*Military*] (MCD)
AOA	Any One Accident [*Insurance*] (AIA)
AOA	Any One Aircraft [*Insurance*] (AIA)
AOA	Aspira of America (EA)
AOA	Association of Official Architects [*British*]
AOA	Association of Otolaryngology Administrators (EA)
AOA	At or Above [*Aviation*]
AOA	Atlantic Ocean Area
AOA	Authorized Ordering Agency (MCD)
AOA	Office of Administrator [*FAA*] (FAAC)
AOAA	Aminooxyacetic Acid [*Biochemistry*]
AOAA	Aviation Ordnanceman, Airman Apprentice, Striker [*Navy rating*]
AOAC	Army Ordnance Ammunition Command [*Merged with Munitions Command*]
AOAC	Association of Official Analytical Chemists (EA)
AOAC	Automobile Owners Action Council [*Defunct*] (EA)
AOAC	Calibrated Angle of Attack (MCD)
AOAC	Olds College, Alberta [*Library symbol*] [*National Library of Canada*] (NLC)
AOACB	Aviation Ordnanceman, Combat Aircrewman, Air Bomber [*Navy rating*] [*Obsolete*]
AOAcc	Any One Accident [*Insurance*] (AIA)
AOAC Europe ...	Association of Official Analytical Chemists - Europe [*Bennekom, Netherlands*] (EAIO)
AOAD	Arab Organization for Agricultural Development (EAIO)
AOAD	Army Operating Availability Data
AOAF	Farm Business Management Branch, Alberta Agriculture, Olds, Alberta [*Library symbol*] [*National Library of Canada*] (NLC)
AOAI	Amateur Organist Association International (EA)
AOAI	Angle-of-Attack Indicator [*Military*]
AOAI	Avanti Owners Association International (EA)
AOAK	Oak Tree Construction Computers, Inc. [*NASDAQ symbol*] (NQ)
AOAL	Local Angle of Attack (MCD)
AOAN	Aviation Ordnanceman, Airman, Striker [*Navy rating*]
AOAO	Advanced Orbiting Astronautical Observatory
AOAO	American Osteopathic Academy of Orthopedics (EA)
AOAP	Army Oil Analysis Program (MCD)
AOAPA9 ...	Australia. Commonwealth Scientific and Industrial Research Organisation. Animal Research Laboratories. Technical Paper [*A publication*]
AOARRF...	Archbishop Oscar Arnulfo Romero Relief Fund (EA)

AOAS	American Osteopathic Academy of Sclerotherapy (EA)
AOAS	Angle-of-Attack Sensor [*Military*] (MCD)
AOAS	Arab Organization of Administrative Sciences (EAIO)
AOAS	Selected Angle of Attack (MCD)
AOASH	Acta Orientalia. Academiae Scientiarum Hungaricae [*A publication*]
AOASM	American Osteopathic Academy of Sports Medicine (EA)
AOAT	Allowed-Off Aircraft Time
AOAT	Alter Orient und Altes Testament [*A publication*]
AOAT	Alter Orient und Altes Testament. Veroeffentlichungen zur Kultur und Geschichte des Alten Orients und des Alten Testaments [*Kevelaer/Neukirchen/Vluyn*] [*A publication*] (BJA)
AOAT	Angle of Attack Transmitter [*Military*]
AOAT	True Angle of Attack (MCD)
AOATC	Atlantic Ocean Air Traffic Control [*NATO*] (NATG)
AOATS.....	Alter Orient und Altes Testament. Sonderreihe [*A publication*]
AOAW.......	Anzeiger. Oesterreichische Akademie der Wissenschaften [*Wien*]. Philosophisch-Historische Klasse [*A publication*]
AOB..........	Acta Orientalia [*Budapest*] [*A publication*]
AOB..........	Administrative Operations Branch [*NTIS*]
AOB..........	Advanced Operational Base [*Navy*]
AOB..........	Air Order of Battle (AFM)
AOB..........	Airborne Optical Beacon
AOB..........	Alcohol on Breath [*Police term*]
AOB..........	Altorientalische Bibliothek [*A publication*]
AOB..........	Altorientalische Texte und Bilder zum Alten Testament [*A publication*]
AOB..........	Angle of Bank
AOB..........	Angle of Beam
AOB..........	Angle on the Bow [*Navy*] (NVT)
AOB..........	Annual Operating Budget [*Army*]
AOB..........	Antediluvian Order of Buffaloes [*British*]
AOB..........	Any One Bottom [*Marine insurance*] (DS)
AOB..........	Any Other Business (ADA)
AOB..........	Approved Operating Budget [*Army*] (AABC)
AOB..........	Association of Brewers (EA)
AOB..........	At or Below [*Aviation*]
AOB..........	Automated Office Battery [*Selection and career development test*]
AOB..........	Automatic Optical Bench [*Hughes Aircraft Co.*]
AOB..........	[*An*] Old Bachelor [*Pseudonym used by William Lloyd Garrison*] [*Acronym also facetiously translated as "Ass, Oaf, and Blockhead"*]
AOBAA3 ...	Archivos de Oftalmologia de Buenos Aires [*A publication*]
AOBAT	Altorientalische Bilder zum Alten Testament [*A publication*] (BJA)
AOBC	American Overseas Book Company
AOBEAF ...	Acta Orthopaedica Belgica [*A publication*]
AOBEM	American Osteopathic Board of Emergency Medicine (EA)
AOBGP	American Osteopathic Board of General Practice (EA)
AOBIAR....	Archives of Oral Biology [*A publication*]
AOBMO....	Army Ordnance Ballistic Missile Office
AOBP	American Osteopathic Board of Pediatrics (EA)
AOBRDN...	Acta Oncologica Brasileira [*A publication*]
AOBS	Army Outward Bound School [*British military*] (DMA)
AOBS	Association of Oldetime Barbell and Strongmen (EA)
AOBSR	Air Observer [*Military*] (AFM)
AOBTS......	Air Order of Battle Textual Summary (MCD)
AOC..........	Adult Opportunity Center [*State employment service*]
AOC..........	Advanced Office Concepts Corp. [*Defunct*] [*Information service or system*] (IID)
AOC..........	Aerodrome Obstruction Chart
AOC..........	Air Officer Commanding [*RAF*] [*British*]
AOC..........	Air Oil Cooler
AOC..........	Air Operations Center [*Air Force*]
AOC..........	Air Operators Certificate [*British*] (AIA)
AOC..........	Airport Operating Certificate (FAAC)
AOC..........	Airport Operators Council [*Later, AOCI*] (EA)
AOC..........	Alianca Operaria Camponesa [*Peasants and Workers Alliance*] [*Portugal*] [*Political party*] (PPE)
AOC..........	Allard Owners Club [*British*] (EAIO)
AOC..........	Alvis Owners Club [*North Droitwich, Worcestershire, England*] (EAIO)
AOC..........	American Ophthalmological Color [*Chart*]
AOC..........	American Orthoptic Council (EA)
AOC..........	Amphicar Owners Club (EA)
AOC..........	Anno Orbis Conditi [*In the Year of the Creation*] [*Latin*]
AOC..........	Anodal Opening Contraction [*Also, AnOC*] [*Physiology*]
AOC..........	Aon Corporation [*NYSE symbol*] (SPSG)
AOC..........	Appellation d'Origine Controlle [*Official place name for wine*]
AOC..........	Architect of the Capitol [*US*]
AOC..........	Archives de l'Orient Chretien [*A publication*]
AOC..........	Area of Concentration (RDA)
AOC..........	Area of Concern (MCD)
AOC..........	[*The*] Army Operations Center
AOC..........	Army Ordnance Corps [*Later, RAOC*] [*British*]
AOC..........	Assimilable Organic Carbon [*Environmental chemistry*]
AOC..........	Association of Old Crows (EAIO)
AOC..........	Association Olympique Canadienne [*Canadian Olympic Association - COA*]

AOC............	Association of Orthopaedic Chairmen (EA)	
AOC............	Assumption of Control Message [*Aviation*]	
A to OC.....	Attached to Other Correspondence [*Business term*]	
AOC............	Attached to Other Correspondence [*Business term*]	
AOC............	Attention Operating Characteristic [*Psychometrics*]	
AOC............	Attock Oil Company [*Pakistan*]	
AOC............	Auditor Overcharge Claims	
AOC............	Automatic Operation Control	
AOC............	Automatic Output Control	
AOC............	Automatic Overload Circuit	
AOC............	Automatic Overload Control (IEEE)	
AOC............	Average Operating Cost (KSC)	
AOC............	Aviation Officer Candidate [*Navy*]	
AOC............	Aviation Ordnanceman, Chief [*Navy rating*]	
AOC............	Awaiting Outgoing Continuity [*Telecommunications*] (TEL)	
AOC............	Award of Contract	
AOCA........	American Osteopathic College of Anesthesiologists (EA)	
AOCAI	American Osteopathic College of Allergy and Immunology (EA)	
AOCBAF ...	Air Officer Commanding Base Air Forces [*RAF*] [*British*]	
AOCC........	Advanced Office Concepts Corporation [*Defunct*] (TSSD)	
AOC-in-C..	Air Officer Commanding-in-Chief [*RAF*] [*British*]	
AOCC.......	ARIA [*Apollo Range Instrumentation Aircraft*] Operations Control Center [*NASA*]	
AOCC.......	Australian Onion Coordinating Committee	
AOCCA	Annales d'Oto-Laryngologie et de Chirurgie Cervico-Faciale [*A publication*]	
AOC in CBAFO ...	Air Officer Commanding-in-Chief British Air Force Occupation [*RAF*]	
AOCD........	American Osteopathic College of Dermatology (EA)	
AOCE........	Attitude and Orbit Control Electronics [*Aerospace*] (NASA)	
AOCEDN..	Archaeology in Oceania [*A publication*]	
AOCEO......	Army Ordnance Combat Equipment Office	
AOCEUR ..	Alternative Operational Concepts in Europe [*Military*]	
AOCF	Association of Outplacement Consulting Firms (EA)	
AOCI	Accredited Off-Campus Instruction	
AOCI	Airport Operators Council International (EA)	
AOCIC.......	Air Officer Commanding-in-Chief [*RAF*] [*British*]	
AOCINC....	Air Officer Commanding-in-Chief [*RAF*] [*British*] (NATG)	
AOCJ.........	Association of Obedience Clubs and Judges (EA)	
AOCL	Anodal Opening Clonus [*Physiology*]	
AOCM.......	Advanced Optical Countermeasures (MCD)	
AOCM.......	Aircraft Out of Commission for Maintenance [*Military*]	
AOCM.......	Aviation Ordnanceman, Master Chief [*Navy rating*]	
AOC Newsl ...	Administrative Office of the Courts. Newsletter [*A publication*] (DLA)	
AOCNM....	American Osteopathic College of Nuclear Medicine (EA)	
AOCO........	Atomic Ordnance Cataloging Office	
AOCP	Airborne Operational Computer Program (MCD)	
AOCP	Aircraft Out of Commission for [*Lack of*] Parts [*Obsolete*] [*Military*]	
AOCP	American Osteopathic College of Pathologists (EA)	
AOCP	American Osteopathic College of Proctology (EA)	
AOCP	Aviation Officer Continuation Pay [*Navy*]	
AOCPA	American Osteopathic College of Pathologists	
AOCPM	American Osteopathic College of Preventive Medicine (EA)	
AOCPMR ...	American Osteopathic College of Physical Medicine and Rehabilitation [*Later, AOCRM*] (EA)	
AOCPR.......	American Osteopathic College of Proctology	
AOCR........	Advanced Optical Character Reader	
AOCR........	Aircraft Operating Cost Report (NG)	
AOCR........	American Osteopathic College of Radiology (EA)	
AOCR........	American Osteopathic College of Rheumatology (EA)	
AOCRD.....	Acceptance and Operational Checkout Requirements Document [*NASA*] (NASA)	
AOCRM	American Osteopathic College of Rehabilitation Medicine (EA)	
AOCS	Airline Operational Control Society (EA)	
AOCS	Alpha Omega Computer System (IEEE)	
AOCS	American Oil Chemists' Society (EA)	
AOCS	Atlantic Outer Continental Shelf	
AOCS	Attitude and Orbit Control System [*or Subsystem*] (MCD)	
AOCS	Automated Orbit Control System (MCD)	
AOCS	Aviation Officer Candidate School [*Navy*]	
AOCS	Aviation Ordnanceman, Senior Chief [*Navy rating*]	
AOCSSSR ...	Alaska Outer Continental Shelf Socioeconomic Studies Program. Special Reports [*A publication*]	
AOCSSTR ...	Alaska Outer Continental Shelf Socioeconomic Studies Program. Technical Reports [*A publication*]	
AOCT	Associated Overseas Countries and Territories (DS)	
AOCU........	Arithmetic Output Control Unit	
AOCU........	Associative Output Control Unit [*Data processing*]	
AOC-USA ...	Allard Owners Club USA (EA)	
AOD	Academy of Operative Dentistry (EA)	
AOD	Academy of Oral Dynamics (EA)	
AOD	Acousto-Optics Device	
AOD	Administrative Officer on Duty	
AOD	Advanced Ordnance Department [*British*]	
AOD	Advanced Ordnance Depot	
AOD	Air Officer of the Day [*Air Force*] (AFM)	
AOD	Aircraft Operations Division [*Johnson Space Center*] [*NASA*] (NASA)	

AOD	Airfield Operations Designator [*Air Force/Army*]	
AOD	Airlift Operations Directive (AFM)	
AOD	Alleged Onset Date [*of disability*] [*Social Security Administration*] (OICC)	
AOD	Allocate on Demand [*Data processing*] (BYTE)	
AOD	Analog Output Differential [*Data processing*] (MCD)	
AOD	Ancient Order of Druids	
AOD	Angle of Descent	
AOD	Area-Oriented Depots [*Military*] (RDA)	
AOD	Area-Oriented Distribution [*DoD*]	
AOD	Argon-Oxygen Decarburization [*Steelmaking*]	
AOD	Arithmetic Output Data [*Data processing*]	
AOD	Army Ordnance Department [*British*]	
AOD	Arsenal Operations Directorate [*Rock Island Arsenal*] [*Army*]	
AOD	Arterial Occlusive Disease [*Medicine*]	
AOD	As-Of Date (AFM)	
AOD	Assistant Operations Director [*Air Force/Army*] (MCD)	
AOD	Auriculo-Osteodysplasia [*Medicine*]	
AOD	Automatic Overdrive	
AOD	Aviation Operating Detachment (CINC)	
AOD	Ontario, CA [*Location identifier*] [*FAA*] (FAAL)	
AODAP	Office of Alcohol and Other Drug Abuse Programming [*University of Minnesota*] [*Research center*] (RCD)	
AODC........	Automobile Objets d'Art Club (EA)	
AODM.......	Adult-Onset Diabetes Mellitus [*Endocrinology*]	
AODME.....	Academy of Osteopathic Directors of Medical Education (EA)	
AODNS.....	Acta Orientalia [*A publication*]	
AODP........	Acquisition Orbit Determination Program Assembly [*Space Flight Operations Facility, NASA*]	
AODP........	Advanced Ocean Drilling Program [*National Science Foundation*]	
AODRA	American Oxford Down Record Association [*Later, AOSA*] (EA)	
AODRM....	Academy of Oral Diagnosis, Radiology, and Medicine (EA)	
AODS	All-Ordnance Destruct System	
AODS	Atlas [*Missile*] Operational Data Summary	
AOE	Abbreviated Operational Evaluation (MCD)	
AOE	Aerodrome [*or Airport*] of Entry	
AOE	Airborne Operational Equipment	
AOE	Alcoholic Onion Extract	
AOE	Army of Excellence [*Military program*] (INF)	
AOE	Association of Optometric Educators (EA)	
AOE	Association of Overseas Educators (EA)	
AOE	Auditing Order Error	
AOE	Fast Combat Support Ship [*Navy symbol*]	
AOE	Multipurpose Stores Ship	
AOEA	Awards for Outstanding Export Achievement [*Australia*]	
AOEC	Airways Operations Evaluation Center	
AOEHI	American Organization for the Education of the Hearing Impaired [*Later, IOEHI*] (EA)	
AOEL	Advanced Ocean Engineering Laboratory [*Scripps Institution of Oceanography*]	
AOEM.......	Automotive Original Equipment Manufacturers	
AOEMAK ...	Advances in Optical and Electron Microscopy [*A publication*]	
AOER	Arab Oil and Economic Review [*A publication*]	
AOER	Army Officers' Emergency Reserve [*British*]	
AOERP.......	Automated Overseas Employment Referral Program	
AOES	Advanced Orbit/Ephemeris Subsystem	
AOES	Arctic Ocean Environment Simulator	
AOET	Allowed Off-Engine Time (AFIT)	
AOF	ACM Government Opportunity Fund, Inc. [*NYSE symbol*] (CTT)	
AOF	Active Optical Fuze	
AOF	Advanced Operating Facility [*Computer Technology, Inc.*]	
AOF	Afrique Occidentale Francaise [*French West Africa*] [*French*]	
AOF	Aircraft Operating Fee (ADA)	
AOF	Altorientalische Forschungen [*A publication*]	
AOF	American Opportunity Foundation [*Washington, DC*] (EA)	
AOF	American Optometric Foundation (EA)	
AOF	[*The*] Ancient Order of Foresters	
AOF	Archiv fuer Orientforschung [*A publication*]	
AOF	Australian Orchid Foundation	
AOFA	Atlantic Offshore Fishermen's Association (EA)	
AOFAS	American Orthopedic Foot and Ankle Society (EA)	
AOFB	Ancient Order of Frothblowers [*British*]	
AOFC	Ancient Order of Foresters of California [*Later, AOFPCJ*] (EA)	
AOFC	Apple Octopus Fan Club (EA)	
AOFCG	American Order of the French Croix de Guerre (EA)	
AOFFA4....	Analysis and Characterization of Oils, Fats, and Fat Products [*A publication*]	
AOFPAY ...	Australia. Commonwealth Scientific and Industrial Research Organisation. Division of Food Preservation. Technical Paper [*A publication*]	
AOFPCJ....	Ancient Order of Foresters of the Pacific Coast Jurisdiction [*Hilo, HI*] (EA)	
AOFS	Active Optical Fuzing System	
AOFS	American Orthopedic Foot Society [*Later, AOFAS*] (EA)	
AOFSA9....	Australia. Commonwealth Scientific and Industrial Research Organisation. Division of Fisheries and Oceanography. Fisheries Synopsis [*A publication*]	
AOG..........	Acid Fractionator Off-Gas [*Nuclear energy*] (NRCH)	

AOG........... Aircraft on Ground [*Navy*]
AOG........... American Oil & Gas Corporation [*AMEX symbol*] (SPSG)
AOG........... Amino(octyl)guanidine [*Organic chemistry*]
AOG........... Archiv fuer Oesterreichische Geschichte [*A publication*]
AOG........... Assemblies of God (ADA)
AOG........... Association of Graduates of the United States Air Force
                    Academy (EA)
AOG........... Augmented Off-Gas System [*Nuclear energy*] (NRCH)
AOG........... Automated Onboard Gravimeter
AOG........... Gasoline Tanker [*Navy symbol*]
AOGA....... Aircraft Operations Group Association
AOGBAV .. Anzeiger. Ornithologische Gesellschaft in Bayern [*A
                    publication*]
AOGC....... Ambra Oil & Gas Company [*NASDAQ symbol*] (NQ)
AOGI......... Appalachian Oil & Gas Company, Incorporated [*Chattanooga,
                    TN*] [*NASDAQ symbol*] (NQ)
AOGJAL.... Australasian Oil and Gas Journal [*A publication*]
AOGLAR .. Acta Obstetrica et Gynaecologica Japonica [*English Edition*] [*A
                    publication*]
AOGM....... Army of Occupation of Germany Medal [*Military decoration*]
AOGMA.... Annali di Ostetricia, Ginecologia, Medicina Perinatale [*A
                    publication*]
AOGMS .... Army Ordnance Guided Missile School (MCD)
AOGN ...... Alaska Oil and Gas News [*A publication*]
AOGNAX ... Archivio di Ostetricia e Ginecologia [*A publication*]
AOGO .... Advanced Orbiting Geophysical Observatory
AOGRDE .. Australasian Oil and Gas Review [*A publication*]
AOGSAE... Acta Obstetrica et Gynecologica Scandinavica [*A publication*]
AOGYA .... Advances in Obstetrics and Gynecology [*A publication*]
AOH .... Accepted on Hire
AOH .... Acta Orientalia. Academiae Scientiarum Hungaricae [*A
                    publication*]
AOH .... Aircraft Requiring Overhaul (AFIT)
AOH .... Alternariol [*Biochemistry*]
AOH .... Ancient Order of Hibernians in America (EA)
AOH .... Annual Operating Hours (MCD)
AOH .... Apollo Operations Handbook [*NASA*]
AOH .... Aviator's Oxygen Helmet (NG)
AOH .... Awaiting Office Hours
AOH .... Awaiting Overhaul (NG)
AOH .... Lima, OH [*Location identifier*] [*FAA*] (FAAL)
AOHA ...... American Osteopathic Hospital Association (EA)
AOHI....... After Overhaul Inspection
AOHREF .. American Osteopathic Hospital Research and Education
                    Foundation (EA)
AOHS....... American Osteopathic Historical Society [*Defunct*] (EA)
AOHSA ..... Annals of Occupational Hygiene. Supplement [*A publication*]
AOHYA..... Annals of Occupational Hygiene [*A publication*]
AOI.......... Academia Ophthalmologica Internationalis (EAIO)
AOI........... Accent on Information [*Databank for the handicapped and
                    rehabilitation professionals*] [*Accent on Living*] (IID)
AOI........... Acousto-Optical Imaging
AOI........... Advance Ordering Information
AOI........... Airways Operations Instructions [*A publication*] (APTA)
AOI........... Ancona [*Italy*] [*Airport symbol*] (OAG)
AOI........... And-Or Invert (IEEE)
AOI........... AOI Coal Co. [*AMEX symbol*] (SPSG)
AOI........... Area of Interest (AABC)
AOI........... Avionics Operating Instruction (MCD)
AOIAA ...... Annals of Oto-Rino-Laryngologica Ibero-Americana [*A
                    publication*]
AOIAA4 .... Anales Otorrinolaringologicos Ibero-Americanos [*A
                    publication*]
AOIC .... Assistant Officer in Charge [*DoD*]
A OIL........ Aviation Oil [*Military*]
AOINST.... Administrative Office Instruction
AOIP .... Assault on Illiteracy Program (EA)
AOIPS .... Atmospheric and Oceanographic Information Processing
                    System [*Satellite image enhancing system*] (MCD)
AOIR .... Assembly Operation and Inspection Report
AOIRAL.... Australia. Commonwealth Scientific and Industrial Research
                    Organisation. Division of Plant Industry. Field Station
                    Record [*A publication*]
AOIV .... Automatically Operated Inlet Valve
AOJ .... Acquire on Jam
AOJ .... Angle on Jam (MCD)
AOJ .... Aomori [*Japan*] [*Airport symbol*] (OAG)
AOJC........ Association des Orchestres de Jeunes du Canada [*Canadian
                    Association of Youth Orchestras*]
AOJC........ Association of Orthodox Jews in Communications (EA)
AOJP........ Australian Official Journal of Patents, Trade Marks, and
                    Designs [*A publication*] (APTA)
AOJPTMD ... Australian Official Journal of Patents, Trade Marks, and
                    Designs [*A publication*] (APTA)
AOJS........ Association of Orthodox Jewish Scientists (EA)
AOJT........ Association of Orthodox Jewish Teachers (EA)
AOJTAW ... American Orthoptic Journal [*A publication*]
A-OK .... All Equipment OK [*Expression meaning "in perfect working
                    order." Popularized during early development of NASA's
                    space program*]
AOK........... All Out-of-Kilter [*Slang*]

AOK........... Karpathos [*Greece*] [*Airport symbol*] (OAG)
AOKAI ..... Amateur Organists and Keyboard Association
                    International (EA)
AOKAT ..... Altorientalischer Kommentar zum Alten Testament [*A
                    publication*]
AOKW....... Annalen van de Oudheidkundige Kring van het Land van Waas
                    [*A publication*]
AOL........... Absent over Leave [*Navy*]
AOL........... Acro-Osteolysis [*Medicine*]
AOL........... Admiralty Office, London (ROG)
AOL........... Admiralty Oil Laboratory [*British*]
AOL........... All Operator Letter (MCD)
AOL........... Any One Loss [*Insurance*] (AIA)
AOL........... Application Oriented Language [*Data processing*] (BUR)
AOL........... Archives de l'Orient Latin [*A publication*]
AOL........... Atlantic Oceanographic Laboratories [*of Environmental Science
                    Services Administration*]
AOL........... Olds Public Library, Alberta [*Library symbol*] [*National Library
                    of Canada*] (NLC)
AOL........... Paso De Los Libres [*Argentina*] [*Airport symbol*] (OAG)
AOLAA ..... Acta Oto-Laryngologica [*A publication*]
AOLAEN ... Acta Odontologica Latinoamericana [*A publication*]
AOLC .... Auxiliaries of Our Lady of the Cenacle (EA)
AOLIN ...... Australian Open Learning Information Network
AOLM .... Apollo Orbiting Laboratory Module [*NASA*]
AOLO .... Advanced Orbital Launch Operations
AOLOC ..... Any One Location [*Marine insurance*] (DS)
AOLPAU... Australia. Commonwealth Scientific and Industrial Research
                    Organisation. Division of Land Research and Regional
                    Survey. Technical Paper [*A publication*]
AOLR .... Amplifier Open Loop Response
AOLS........ Association of Our Lady of Salvation [*Defunct*]
AOLSA5.... Acta Oto-Laryngologica. Supplementum [*A publication*]
AOLVA ..... Archivio di Oceanografia e Limnologia [*A publication*]
AOLVAE... Archivio di Oceanografia e Limnologia [*A publication*]
AOM........... Aaron Mining Ltd. [*Vancouver Stock Exchange symbol*]
AOM........... Academy of Orthomolecular Medicine (EA)
AOM........... Acousto-Optic Modulator
AOM........... Active Oxygen Method [*Food fat stability test*]
AOM........... Acute Otitis Media [*Medicine*]
AOM........... Add One to Memory [*Data processing*]
AOM........... Altos Office Manager [*Altos Computer Systems*]
AOM........... Ancient Order of Maccabeans (BJA)
AOM........... Aomori [*Japan*] [*Seismograph station code, US Geological
                    Survey*] (SEIS)
AOM........... Army of Occupation Medal [*Military decoration*]
AOM........... Association of Operative Millers (EA)
AOM........... Aviation Ordnanceman [*Navy rating*] [*Obsolete*]
AOM........... Okotoks Municipal Library, Alberta [*Library symbol*] [*National
                    Library of Canada*] (NLC)
AOMA....... American Occupational Medical Association (EA)
AOMA....... Apartment Owners and Managers Association of America (EA)
AOMAC.... Aviation Ordnanceman, Combat Aircrewman [*Navy rating*]
                    [*Obsolete*]
AOMB....... Aviation Ordnanceman, Bombsight Mechanic [*Navy rating*]
                    [*Obsolete*]
AOMC....... Ariel Owners' Motorcycle Club (EA)
AOMC....... Army Ordnance Missile Center (MCD)
AOMC....... Army Ordnance Missile Command [*Later, Missile Command*]
                    [*Redstone Arsenal, AL*]
AOMCA.... Advances in Organometallic Chemistry [*A publication*]
AOMD...... Amended Operator and Maintenance Decision [*Army*]
AOME....... Assistant Ordnance Mechanical Engineer [*British
                    military*] (DMA)
AOMJ .... Aomori Outpost [*Japan*] [*Seismograph station code, US
                    Geological Survey*] (SEIS)
AOML .... Atlantic Oceanographic and Meteorological Laboratory [*Miami,
                    FL*] [*National Oceanic and Atmospheric Administration*]
AOMOD ... AOCS Monograph [*A publication*]
Aomori J Med ... Aomori Journal of Medicine [*A publication*]
AOMP....... Artisans Order of Mutual Protection [*Philadelphia, PA*] (EA)
AOMPAZ ... Australia. Commonwealth Scientific and Industrial Research
                    Organisation. Division of Meteorological Physics.
                    Technical Paper [*A publication*]
AOMPS..... Automatic Outgoing Message Processor System (NVT)
AOMS ...... Association of Organisers of Music, Scotland
AOMSA .... Army Ordnance Missile Support Agency
AOMSC .... Army Ordnance Missile Support Center (NATG)
AOMT...... Aviation Ordnanceman, Turret Mechanic [*Navy rating*]
AON .... Accessory Optic Nucleus [*Neuroanatomy*]
AON .... Acta Orientalia Neerlandica [*A publication*]
AO-N .... Administrative Office - Navy
AON .... Air One, Inc. [*St. Louis, MO*] [*FAA designator*] (FAAC)
AON .... All or None [*Investment, securities*]
AON .... Anterior Octaval Nucleus [*Neuroanatomy*]
AON .... Automated Optical Navigation (MCD)
AON .... Average of Normals
AONALS... Type "A" Off-Network Access Lines
                    [*Telecommunications*] (TEL)
AONB....... Area of Outstanding Natural Beauty [*Great Britain*]
AONCAZ .. Acta Oncologica [*A publication*]

AOND .... Administrative Office, Navy Department
AONE........ Air One [*NASDAQ symbol*]   (NQ)
AONE........ American Organization of Nurse Executives   (EA)
AONET ..... American Osteopathic Network [*American Osteopathic Association*] [*Information service or system*]   (IID)
AONGAD ... Archives. Office du Niger [*A publication*]
AONSEJ ... Archives of Otolaryngology and Head and Neck Surgery [*A publication*]
AONTAS... Aos-Oideachas Naisiunta Tri Aontu Saorlach [*National Association of Adult Education*]   (EAIO)
AOO .... Altoona [*Pennsylvania*] [*Airport symbol*]   (OAG)
AOO .... American Oceanic Organization   (EA)
AOO .... Amphibious Operations Officer [*British military*]   (DMA)
AOO .... Anodal Opening Odor [*Physiology*]
AOO .... Anticipated Operational Occurrence [*Nuclear energy*]   (NRCH)
AOO .... Area Operations Office [*Employment and Training Administration*]   (OICC)
AOO .... Aviation Ordnance Officer
AOOC........ Albertville Olympic Organizing Committee [*Albertville, France*]   (EAIO)
AOOcc .... Any One Occurrence [*Insurance*]   (AIA)
AOP .... Abnormal Operating Procedure   (NRCH)
AOP .... Academy of Orthomolecular Psychiatry [*Later, AOM*]   (EA)
AOP .... Accuracy of Position   (MCD)
AOP .... Acetoxypregnenolone [*Pharmacology*]
AOP .... Acidity Oxidation Potential [*Chemistry*]
A-OP.......... Acylated Octapeptide [*Biochemistry*]
AOP .... Additive Operational Project [*Army*]   (MCD)
AOP .... Administrative and Operational Procedure   (MCD)
AOP .... Advanced On-Board Processor [*Computer*]
AOP .... Aerospace Observation Platform
AOP .... Air Observation Post
AOP .... Airborne Optical Platform
AOP .... Aircraft Out for Parts   (MCD)
AOP .... All Other Perils [*Insurance*]
AOP .... All Over Pattern [*Quilting*]
AOP .... Allied Ordnance Publications   (NATG)
AOP .... Altoona Area Public Library, Altoona, PA [*OCLC symbol*]   (OCLC)
AOP.......... Amino-Oligopeptidase [*An enzyme*]
AOP .... Ammonia Oxidation Plant   (MCD)
AOP .... Analectes. Ordre de Premontre [*A publication*]
AOP .... Analyser og Problemer [*A publication*]
AOP .... Annals of Probability [*A publication*]   (EAAP)
AOP........... Annual Operating Program [*Army*]
AOP........... Anodal Opening Picture [*Physiology*]
AOP .... Anomalistic Observational Phenomena [*In study of UFO's*]
AOP .... Any One Person [*Insurance*]   (AIA)
AoP .... Aortic Pressure [*Medicine*]
AOP .... Applicant Outreach Program [*Department of Labor*]
AOP .... Apprenticeship Outreach Program [*Bureau of Apprenticeship and Training*]   (OICC)
AOP .... Archivum Orientale Pragense [*A publication*]
AOP .... Area of Probability   (NVT)
AOP .... Armoured Observation Post [*British and Canadian*] [*World War II*]
AOP .... Army Observation Post [*British military*]   (DMA)
AOP .... Artillery Observation Post [*British military*]   (DMA)
AOP .... Assembly and Operations Plan
AOP .... Association of Osteopathic Publications [*Defunct*]
AOP .... Atomic Ordnance Platoon   (NG)
AOP .... Automatic Operations Panel
AOP........... Rock Springs, WY [*Location identifier*] [*FAA*]   (FAAL)
AOPA .... Aircraft Owners and Pilots Association   (EA)
AOPA .... American Orthotic and Prosthetic Association   (EA)
AOPA .... Automotive Occupant Protection Association   (EA)
AOPA Mo Mag ... AOPA [*Aircraft Owners' and Pilots' Association*] Monthly Magazine [*A publication*]   (APTA)
AOPB .... Active Officer Promotion Branch [*BUPERS*]
AOPCD ..... Annual Report. Organization of the Petroleum Exporting Countries [*A publication*]
AOPE .... Associated Organizations for Professionals in Education   (EA)
AOPEC...... Arab Organization of Petroleum Exporting Countries
AOPES ...... Association of Organisers of Physical Education, Scotland
AOPF......... Air Observation Post Flight [*British military*]   (DMA)
aopf--- .... Paracel Islands [*MARC geographic area code*] [*Library of Congress*]   (LCCP)
AOPIBU.... Acta Ophthalmologica Iugoslavica [*A publication*]
AOPL .... Association of Oil Pipe Lines   (EA)
AOPM....... Airline Operations Planning Model   (NASA)
AOPOCF... American Journal of Optometry and Physiological Optics [*A publication*]
AOPRAM ... Australia. Commonwealth Scientific and Industrial Research Organisation. Division of Plant Industry. Annual Report [*A publication*]
AOPS........ Air Operations [*Military*]   (NVT)
AOPSA...... Advanced Optical Power Spectrum Analyzer   (MCD)
AOPSAP.... Acta Ophthalmologica. Supplementum [*A publication*]
AOPT........ Acrylic Optics Corp. [*NASDAQ symbol*]   (NQ)
AOPU........ Asian Oceanic Postal Union [*Later, APPU*] [*China, Korea, Philippines, Thailand*]

AOPV .... Air-Operated Plastic Valve
AOQ .... Alliance, NE [*Location identifier*] [*FAA*]   (FAAL)
AOQ .... Average Outgoing Quality [*Quality control*]
AOQ .... Aviation Officers' Quarters
AOQC........ Australian Organization for Quality Control
AOQL .... Average Outgoing Quality Laboratory
AOQL........ Average Outgoing Quality Level [*or Limit*] [*Quality control*]
AOR .... Accumulated Operating Results
AOR .... Advance List of Oversea-Returnees for Reassignment [*Army*]
AOR .... Air Operations Room
AOR .... Airborne Overland RADAR
AOR........... Aircraft Operating Report   (MCD)
AOR .... Album Oriented Rock [*Facetious translation: Another Old Record*] [*Broadcasting*]
AOR .... Allowance Override Requirement   (CAAL)
AOR .... Alor Setar [*Malaysia*] [*Airport symbol*]   (OAG)
AOR .... Analecta Orientalia [*A publication*]
AOR .... Anchor Order   (MSA)
A/OR .... And/Or
AOR .... Angle of Reflection
AOR .... Annals of Oriental Research [*A publication*]
AOR .... Antenna Ohmic Resistance
AOR .... Anuari. Oficina Romanica [*A publication*]
AOR........... Aorist [*Grammar*]   (ROG)
AOR .... Apollo Owners Register   (EA)
AOR .... Arbor Resources, Inc. [*Vancouver Stock Exchange symbol*]
AOR .... Area of Responsibility   (MCD)
AOR .... Army Operational Research
AOR .... Assembly Operations Record
AOR .... Atlantic Ocean Region [*INTELSAT*]
AOR .... Auxiliary Oil Replenisher [*or Replenishment*] [*Navy*] [*British*]
AOR .... Operational Replenishment Ship [*Canadian Navy*]
AOR .... Replenishment Oiler [*Navy ship symbol*]
AORA .... Atlantic Ocean Recovery Area [*NASA*]
AORBA ...... Advances in Oral Biology [*A publication*]
AORBAI.... Advances in Oral Biology [*A publication*]
AORC........ Association of Official Racing Chemists   (EA)
AORC .... Automotive Occupant Restraints Council   (EA)
AORD........ Astronaut Operations Requirement Document [*NASA*]   (KSC)
AORE .... Army Operational Research Establishment [*British*]
AOREDU.. Archivio di Ortopedia e Reumatologia [*A publication*]
AORF .... Amplifier Oscillator, Radiofrequency
AORG........ Allen Organ Co. [*NASDAQ symbol*]   (NQ)
AORG........ Army Operational Research Group [*British*]
AORHA...... Annals of Otology, Rhinology, and Laryngology [*A publication*]
AORIA ...... Acta Oto-Rino-Laringologica Ibero-Americana [*A publication*]
AOrientHung ... Acta Orientalia. Academiae Scientiarum Hungaricae [*A publication*]
AORL .... Apollo Orbital Research Laboratory [*NASA*]
AORLA ...... Acta Oto-Rhino-Laryngologica Belgica [*A publication*]
AORLCG... Archives of Oto-Rhino-Laryngology [*A publication*]
AORN....... Association of Operating Room Nurses   (EA)
AORNAK.. Acta Ornithologica [*Warsaw*] [*A publication*]
AORNBD.. Acta Ornithologica [*Warsaw*] [*English translation*] [*A publication*]
AORN J..... Association of Operating Room Nurses. Journal [*A publication*]
AORS .... Army Operations Research Symposia   (RDA)
AORT .... Association of Operating Room Technicians [*Later, AST*]   (EA)
AORTA ..... Australian Organisation of Retired Teachers Associations
AOS .... Accessory Optic System [*Neuroanatomy*]
AOS .... Accounting, Organizations, and Society [*A publication*]
AOS .... Acousto-Optical Spectrograph   (ADA)
AOS .... Acquisition of Signal
AOS .... Active Optical Sensor   (MCD)
AOS .... Active Oxygen Species [*Biochemistry*]
AOS .... Activity Operating Schedule
AOS .... Add-On Stabilization   (MCD)
AOS .... Add or Subtract
AOS .... Advanced Operating System [*Data General Corp.*]
AOS .... Aero Services, Inc. [*Wichita, KS*] [*FAA designator*]   (FAAC)
AOS .... Agency Officers School [*Formerly, FOS*] [*LIMRA*]
AOS .... Air Observer School [*British*]
AOS .... Air Oil Separator
AOS .... Air Operations Specialist
AOS .... Airborne Optical Sensor [*Military*]   (SDI)
AOS .... Airborne Optical Surveillance   (MCD)
AOS .... Airlift Operations School Library, Scott AFB, IL [*OCLC symbol*]   (OCLC)
AOS .... Algebraic Operating System [*Texas Instruments, Inc.*] [*Data processing*]
AOS .... All Over Set [*Quilting*]
AOS .... Alotta Resources Ltd. [*Vancouver Stock Exchange symbol*]
AOS .... Alpha-Olefin Sulfonate [*Surfactant*] [*Organic chemistry*]
AOS .... Alternative Operator Services [*Telecommunications*]
AOS .... American Ophthalmological Society   (EA)
AOS .... American Orchid Society   (EA)
AOS .... American Oriental Series [*A publication*]
AOS .... American Oriental Society   (EA)
AOS .... American Orthodontic Society   (EA)
AOS .... American Osler Society   (EA)
AOS .... American Otological Society   (EA)

AOS .... Amook [Alaska] [Airport symbol]   (OAG)
AOS .... Amphibious Objective Study [Navy]
AOS .... Amplifier Output Stage
AOS .... Ancient Order of Shepherds
AOS .... Angle of Site
AOS .... Annals of Statistics [A publication]   (EAAP)
AOS .... Anodal Opening Sound [Physiology]
AOS .... Any One Steamer [Marine insurance]   (DS)
AOS .... Apostleship of the Sea [See also AM] [Vatican City, Vatican City State]   (EAIO)
AOS .... Army Optical Station
AOS .... Army Ordnance Stores [British]
AOS .... Astronomical Observatory Satellite   (KSC)
AOS .... Atlantic Ocean Ship [INTELSAT]
AOS .... Australian Optical Society
AOS .... Azimuth Orientation System [Military]
AOS .... Special Liquids Tanker   (MCD)
AOSA .... Alden Ocean Shell Association   (EA)
AOSA .... American Optometric Student Association   (EA)
AOSA .... American Orff-Schulwerk Association   (EA)
AOSA .... American Oxford Sheep Association   (EA)
AOSA .... Association of Official Seed Analysts   (EA)
AOSAAK... Acta Orthopaedica Scandinavica [A publication]
AOSADN .. Acta Oecologica. Oecologia Applicata [A publication]
AOSAP....... Airway Operations Specialist [Airport]
AOSBAN... American Orchid Society. Bulletin [A publication]
AOSC .... Association of Oilwell Servicing Contractors   (EA)
AOSC .... Association of Student Councils [Canada]
AOSCA...... Acta Odontologica Scandinavica [A publication]
AOSCA...... Association of Official Seed Certifying Agencies   (EA)
AOSD .... Aeronautical Operating Systems Division [NASA]
AOSE .... American Order of Stationary Engineers
AOSEA...... American Office Supply Exporters Association [Defunct]   (EA)
AOSED ..... Association of Osteopathic State Executive Directors   (EA)
AOSERP .. Alberta Oil Sands Environmental Research Program [A publication]
AOSG .... Airways Operations Specialist (General)
AOSG .... Arbeiten aus dem Orientalischen Seminar der Universitaet Giessen [A publication]
AOSGA4 ... Attualita di Ostetricia e Ginecologia [A publication]
AOSGD7 ... Acta Oecologica. Oecologia Generalis [A publication]
AOSI.......... Alberta Oil Sands Index [Alberta Oil Sands Technology and Research Authority] [Information service or system]
AOSL......... Authorized Organizational Storage List [Army]
AOSLAJ.... Australia. Commonwealth Scientific and Industrial Research Organisation. Soils and Land Use Series [A publication]
AOSM .... Airline Operations Simulation Model   (MCD)
AOSM .... Annual Ordinary Shareholders' Meeting [Investment term]
AOSMAM ... Archivio. Ospedale al Mare [A publication]
AOSML..... Army Ordnance Submarine Mine Laboratory   (KSC)
AOSO .... Advanced Orbiting Solar Observatory [NASA]
AOSP .... Active Optics Simulation Program [NASA]   (KSC)
AOSP......... Army Occupational Survey Program [Formerly, MODB]
AOSP......... Automatic Operating and Scheduling Program [Data processing]
AOSPDY ... Acta Oecologica. Oecologia Plantarum [A publication]
AOSPS ...... American Otorhinologic Society for Plastic Surgery [Later, AAFPRS]   (EA)
AOSPV ...... Airways Operations Supervisor
AOSQ .... Activity Order and Shipping Quantity   (AFIT)
AO-SR .... Assembly Over-Ships Records
AOSRB4 ... Ambio. Special Report [A publication]
AOSRD6 ... Archiwum Ochrony Srodowiska [A publication]
AOSS .... Active Optics Simulation System [NASA]
AOSS .... Airborne Oil Surveillance System
AOSS .... Airways Operations Specialist
AOSS .... Americanae Orientalis Societatis Socius [Fellow of the American Oriental Society]
AO(SS) ...... Submarine Oiler [Navy ship symbol] [Obsolete]
AOSSM..... American Orthopaedic Society for Sports Medicine   (EA)
AOSTRA ... Alberta Oil Sands Technology and Research Authority   (IID)
AOSUAC .. Acta Orthopaedica Scandinavica. Supplementum [A publication]
AOSUS...... Apostleship of the Sea in the United States   (EA)
AOS/VS .... Advanced Operating System/Virtual Storage [Data General Corp.]
AOT .... Acquisition on Target
AOT .... Active on Target
AOT .... Actual Operating Time   (MCD)
AOT .... Alignment-Off-Time [Instrumentation]
AOT .... Alignment Optical Telescope
AOT .... Allstate Municipal Income Opportunities Trust II [NYSE symbol]   (SPSG)
AOT .... Altorientalische Texte zum Alten Testament [A publication]
AOT .... Angle on Target
AOT .... Antarctic Observation Team
AOT .... Anti-Ovotransferrin [Biochemistry]
AOT .... [The] Aramaic of the Old Testament [A publication]   (BJA)
AOT .... Army Orientation Training   (MCD)
AOT .... 'Arse over Top [Head over Heels] [Bowdlerized version]   (ADA)

AOT .... Ascot Resources Ltd. [Vancouver Stock Exchange symbol]
AOT .... Askania Optical Tracker
AOT .... Assembly Outline Tooling
AOT .... Assignment Oriented Training
AOT .... Association of Tutors [British]
AOT .... Automotive Organization Team   (EA)
AOT .... Auxiliary Output Tester
AOT .... Average Operation Time
AOT .... Avionics Operating Time   (MCD)
AOT .... Avionics Overall Test   (NASA)
AOT .... Transport Oiler   (MCD)
AOTA .... Absorber Open Test Assembly [Nuclear energy]   (NRCH)
AOTA .... American Occupational Therapy Association   (EA)
AOTADS... Acta Oceanographica Taiwanica [A publication]
AOTC .... Aviation Officers Training Corps
AOTCB...... American Occupational Therapy Certification Board [AOTA]
AOTD .... Active Optical Target Detector   (NVT)
AOTD .... Air Organisation and Training Division [British military]   (DMA)
AOTE .... Amphibious Operational Training Element
AOTE .... Associated Organizations for Teacher Education [Later, AOPE]
AOTFA...... American Old Time Fiddlers Association   (EA)
AOTH........ Active Optical Target Housing   (MCD)
AOTN........ ACE Operational Telegraph Network   (MCD)
AOTOI ...... American Organization of Tour Operators to Israel [Defunct]   (EA)
AOTOS ..... Admiral of the Ocean Sea [Annual award of US Merchant Marine; title originally bestowed on Christopher Columbus by the Spanish government]
AOTPAC... American Occupational Therapy Political Action Committee [AOTA]
AOTS .... Advanced On-the-Job Training System   (MCD)
AOTS .... Advanced Orbital Test Satellite [European Space Agency]
AOTSDE ... Archives of Orthopaedic and Traumatic Surgery [A publication]
AOTT .... All-Ordnance Thrust Termination   (KSC)
AOTT .... Automatic Outgoing Trunk Test [Bell System]
AOTU........ Altorientalische Texte und Untersuchungen [A publication]
AOTV .... Aeroassisted Orbital Transfer Vehicle
AOU .... Air-Operated Unit
AOU .... American Open University [Data processing]
AOU .... American Ornithologists' Union   (EA)
AOU .... Apparent Oxygen Utilization
AOU .... Area of Uncertainty   (CAAL)
AOU .... Arithmetic Output Unit
AOU .... Associative Output Unit [Data processing]
AOU .... Automated Offset Unit [Air Force]
AOU .... Azimuth Orientation Unit [Military]   (AABC)
AOUF .... Area of Uncertainty Factor
AOUNAZ ... Archiv fuer Orthopaedische und Unfall-Chirurgie [A publication]
AOUSC...... Administrative Office of United States Courts
A/OUT ...... Air Outlet [Automotive engineering]
AOUW ...... Ancient Order United Workmen [Seattle, WA]   (EA)
AOV .... Air-Operated Valve   (NRCH)
AOV .... Any One Vessel [Marine insurance]   (DS)
AOV .... Ava, MO [Location identifier] [FAA]   (FAAL)
AOVC .... Automatic Overload Circuit   (MSA)
AOVEBE... Acta Odontologica Venezolana [A publication]
AOVI .... Agent Orange Victims International [Later, VVAOVI]   (EA)
AOW......... Army Ordnance Workshop [British military]   (DMA)
AOW......... Articles of War
AOWC .... Army Ordnance Weapons Command
AOWG....... Agent Orange Working Group [Cabinet Council on Human Resources]
AOWP .... Automated Order Writing Process   (MCD)
AOWS .... Aircraft Overhaul Work Stoppage   (NG)
AOWS .... Automated Order Writing System   (MCD)
AOWSFM ... Association of Optical Workers and Spectacle Frame Makers [A union] [British]
A Ox........... Anecdota Oxonensia [A publication]
aoxp---........ Spratley Island [MARC geographic area code] [Library of Congress]   (LCCP)
Aoyama J Gen Educ ... Aoyama Journal of General Education [A publication]
AOYM....... Oyen Municipal Library, Alberta [Library symbol] [National Library of Canada]   (NLC)
AP .... A Protester [To Be Protested] [French] [Business term]
AP .... Abingdon Press [Publisher]
AP .... Above Proof
AP .... Absolute Pardon   (ADA)
AP .... Absolute Pitch [Physiology]
AP .... Academic Press, Inc. [Publishers]
AP .... Accelerometer Package   (KSC)
AP .... Access Panel [Technical drawings]
AP .... Access Permit [or Permittee] [Nuclear energy]
AP .... Access Point [Telecommunications]   (TEL)
AP .... Accion Popular [Popular Action] [Spain] [Political party]   (PPE)
AP .... Accion Popular [Popular Action] [Peru] [Political party]   (PPW)
AP .... Account Paid
A/P .... Account-Purchase   (ADA)

AP	Accounts Payable
AP	Acid Phosphatase [*Also, ACP, ACPH*] [*An enzyme*]
AP	Acidproof
AP	Acoustic-Pressure (NVT)
AP	Acquisition Plan
AP	Acquisition Point (MUGU)
AP	Action Potential [*of auditory nerve*]
AP	Activator Protein
AP	Adapter Panel
AP	Add Packed [*Data processing*]
AP	Additional Premium [*Insurance*]
AP	Adenosis Pattern [*Medicine*]
AP	Adjective Phrase [*Linguistics*]
AP	Adjustment and Preventative (MCD)
AP	Administrative Procedure (NRCH)
AP	Administrative Processor (TEL)
AP	Administrative Publication [*Navy*]
AP	Admiralty Pattern [*The right procedure, the correct thing to do*] [*British*]
AP	Adoratrici Perpetuae del Santissimo Sacramento [*Nuns of the Perpetual Adoration of the Blessed Sacrament*] [*Roman Catholic religious order*]
AP	Advance Pay (MCD)
AP	Advance Purchase Required [*Also, AB*] [*Airline fare code*]
AP	Advanced Placement [*Education*]
AP	Advanced Post [*Military*]
AP	Advanced Pressurized [*In name of nuclear reactor, AP 600, developed by Westinghouse Electric Corp.*]
AP	Advanced Procurement (NG)
AP	Advanced Purification [*Chromatography*]
AP	Advice of Payment
AP	Aerial Port
AP	Aero Spacelines [*ICAO aircraft manufacturer identifier*] (ICAO)
AP	Aeropelican
AP	Aeroplane Flag [*Navy*] [*British*]
AP	Aft Perpendicular [*Naval engineering*]
AP	After Peak (MSA)
AP	Agency Procedure
A & P	Agricultural and Pastoral (ADA)
AP	Aiming Point
AP	Air Passage (MSA)
AP	Air Pilot
AP	Air Police [*By extension, a person who is a member of the Air Police*]
AP	Air Pollution (KSC)
AP	Air Position
AP	Air Pressure (MCD)
AP	Air Processing Subsystem (MCD)
AP	Air Publication [*Navy*]
A & P	Airframe and Powerplant [*Aviation*]
AP	Airplane
AP	Airplane Pilot
AP	Airport
AP	Airway Pressure [*Pulmonary ventilation*]
AP	Algemeen Politieblad van het Koninkrijk der Nederlanden [*A publication*]
AP	Alianza Popular [*Popular Alliance*] [*Madrid, Spain*] (PPW)
AP	Alianza para el Progreso [*Alliance for Progress*] [*Washington, DC*]
AP	Alignment Periscope
AP	Alignment Procedures
AP	Alkaline Phosphatase [*Also, ALP*] [*An enzyme*]
AP	All-Purpose
AP	Alliance for Progress [*OAS*]
A/P	Allied Papers
AP	Allied Publication (RDA)
AP	Allophycocyanin [*Also, APC*] [*Biochemistry*]
A d P	Almanach der Psychoanalyse [*A publication*]
AP	Alpha Particle Spectrometer (KSC)
AP	Alphaprodine [*Anesthesiology*]
AP	Alternative Poland [*Defunct*] (EA)
AP	Alum Precipitated [*Medicine*]
AP	Aluminum Perchlorate (MCD)
AP	Ambush Patrol
AP	American Paper Co.
AP	American Pharmacopeia
AP	American Plan [*Hotel room rate*]
AP	American Platinum, Inc. [*Vancouver Stock Exchange symbol*]
AP	American Poetry [*A publication*]
AP	American Psychologist [*A publication*]
AP	Aminopurine [*Biochemistry*]
AP	Aminopyrine [*An antipyretic and anesthetic*]
AP	Ammonium Perchlorate [*Inorganic chemistry*]
AP	Ammunition Point
AP	Ampco-Pittsburgh Corp. [*NYSE symbol*] (SPSG)
AP	Amphibian Papilla [*An auditory organ*]
AP	Amusement Parks and Arcades [*Public-performance tariff class*] [*British*]
AP	Amyloid Protein [*Biochemistry*]
AP	Anal Pore
AP	Analecta Praemonstratensia [*A publication*]
AP	Analytical Psychology
AP	Anaphylactoid Purpura [*Medicine*]
AP	Anavatan Partisi [*Motherland Parties*] (EAIO)
AP	Ancient Parish
AP	Ancient Petition
AP	Andhra Pradesh [*State in southeast India*]
AP	[*The*] Angel Planes [*An association*] (EA)
AP	Angina Pectoris [*Medicine*]
AP	Angkutan Pertambangan [*Commercial firm*] (DS)
AP	Angle Point
AP	Aniline Point [*Measure of solvency*]
AP	Annalen der Philosophie und Philosophischen Kritik [*A publication*]
AP	Annealing Point (MCD)
AP	Annie People (EA)
AP	Annual Plan
AP	Annual Practice [*A publication*] (DLA)
AP	Anomalous Propagation [*Telecommunications*] [*Electronics*] (TEL)
AP	Antarctica Project (EA)
AP	Ante Partum [*Obstetrics*]
AP	Ante Prandium [*Before Dinner*] [*Pharmacy*]
A/P	Antennas and Propagation (MCD)
AP	Anterior Pituitary [*Endocrinology*]
AP	Anteroposterior
AP	Anther Primordium [*Botany*]
AP	Anthropological Papers [*Smithsonian Institution*] [*A publication*]
ap	Antiperiplanar [*Chemistry*]
AP	Antipersonnel [*Projectile*]
AP	Antiplasmin [*Hematology*]
AP	Aortic Plexus [*Anatomy*]
AP	Aortic Pressure [*Medicine*]
AP	Aortopulmonary [*Cardiology*]
ap	Apatite [*CIPW classification*] [*Geology*]
AP	Aperture
AP	Apical Meristem [*Botany*]
AP	Apical Pulse [*Medicine*]
Ap	Apocalypse (BJA)
AP	Apollo Program [*NASA*]
Ap	Apologia [*of Plato*] [*Classical studies*] (OCD)
Ap	Apologia Socratis [*of Xenophon*] [*Classical studies*] (OCD)
AP	Apostle
AP	Apostleship of Prayer (EA)
Ap	Apostolic (BJA)
AP	Apparent (ADA)
AP	Appearance Potential [*Physics*]
AP	Appendectomy [*Medicine*]
ap	Apple [*Philately*]
AP	Application Program [*Data processing*] (BUR)
AP	Applications Processor (IEEE)
AP	Applied Physics (IEEE)
AP	Apply Pressure [*Industrial engineering*]
AP	Approach Lights [*Aviation*] (AIA)
AP	Approaches (NATG)
Ap	April [*A publication*]
AP	April
AP	Apud [*At, In the Works Of, According To*] [*Latin*]
AP	Aquagenic Pruritus [*Medicine*]
AP	Aquatic Plant
AP	Aramaic Papyri Discovered at Assuan [*A publication*] (BJA)
AP	[*The*] Archaeology of Palestine [*A publication*] (BJA)
AP	Archaeus Project (EA)
AP	Archeion Pontou [*A publication*]
AP	Architectural Psychology Newsletter [*British*]
AP	Archiv Patologii [*A publication*]
AP	Archives de Philosophie [*A publication*]
AP	Area Planning
AP	Argument Programming (MSA)
AP	Argyre Planitia [*A filamentary mark on Mars*]
AP	Arithmetic Processor
AP	Arithmetic Progression
AP	Arithmetic Project [*National Science Foundation*]
AP	Armageddon Project [*Later, AAAP*] (EA)
AP	Armor-Piercing [*Ammunition*]
AP	Army Pensions
AP	Arqueologo Portugues [*A publication*]
AP	Array Processor [*Data processing*] (BUR)
AP	Ars Poetica [*A publication*]
AP	Arterial Presssure [*Medicine*] (DHSM)
AP	Artificial Personality
AP	Artificial Pneumothorax [*Medicine*]
AP	Artist's Proof
AP	Aryan Path [*A publication*]
AP	As Prescribed (AFM)
AP	As Purchased
AP	Ascent Phase
AP	Ashpit [*British*] (ROG)
AP	Asian Perspectives [*A publication*]
AP	Asking Price

AP .... Assembly of Parties [*INTELSAT*]
AP .... Assessment Paid [*Billing*]
AP .... Assistance Payments [*Social Security Administration*]
AP .... Assistant Paymaster
AP .... Associated Parishes   (EA)
AP .... Associated Person [*Stock exchange term*]
AP .... Associated Presbyterian [*British*]   (ROG)
AP .... Associated Press   (EA)
AP .... Associated Publishers   (EA)
AP .... Association for Psychotheatrics [*Defunct*]   (EA)
AP .... Associative Processor [*Data processing*]   (BUR)
AP .... Assumed Position [*Navigation*]
AP .... Assurance Problem
AP .... Atmospheric Pressure
AP .... Atomic Powered
AP .... Atriopeptin [*Biochemistry*]
AP .... Atrium Pace [*Cardiology*]
AP .... Attached Processor [*Data processing*]   (BUR)
AP .... Attachment Plaque
AP .... Attack Plan   (MCD)
AP .... Attack Plotter   (NVT)
AP .... Attitude and Pointing   (MCD)
AP .... Attitude Processor   (NASA)
A & P .... Attraktiv und Preiswert [*Attractive and Priced Right*] [*West German grocery products brand*]
A and P ...... Attrition and Pregnancy [*Reasons for high turnover rate among women employees*]
AP .... Aurea Parma [*A publication*]
A & P .... Auscultation and Percussion [*Medicine*]
A/P .... Authority to Pay [*or Purchase*]
A to P .... Authority to Prospect   (ADA)
AP .... Author's Proof [*Publishing*]
AP .... Auto Part   (NRCH)
A/P .... Automatic Pilot   (MCD)
A/P .... Automatic Programming [*Data processing*]
AP .... Automotive Products [*Commercial firm*] [*British*]
AP .... Auxiliary Patrol [*British military*]   (DMA)
AP ....: Auxiliary Power   (CAAL)
AP .... Average Price
AP .... Average Product [*Economics*]
AP .... Aviapolk [*Russian term for an air regiment*]
AP .... Aviation Pilot [*Navy*]
AP .... Awaiting Parts
AP .... Award Processing [*Social Security Administration*]   (OICC)
AP .... Axiopulpal [*Dentistry*]
AP .... Belgian International Air Services Cy. [*ICAO designator*]   (FAAC)
AP .... Ciba-Geigy [*France*] [*Research code symbol*]
Ap .... Contra Apionem [*Against Apion*] [*Josephus*]   (BJA)
A & P. .... Great Atlantic & Pacific Tea Co., Inc.
Ap .... Hymnus in Apollinem [*of Callimachus*] [*Classical studies*]   (OCD)
AP .... Nachschlagewerk des Bundesarbeitsgerichts. Arbeitsrechtliche Praxis [*German*] [*A publication*]   (DLA)
Ap .... New York Supreme Court, Appellate Division Reports [*A publication*]   (DLA)
AP .... Pakistan [*Aircraft nationality and registration mark*]   (FAAC)
AP .... Penhold Public Library, Alberta [*Library symbol*] [*National Library of Canada*]   (NLC)
ap----- .... Persian Gulf [*MARC geographic area code*] [*Library of Congress*]   (LCCP)
AP .... Small Hail [*Meteorology*]   (FAAC)
AP .... Transport [*Navy ship symbol*]
APA .... Abhandlungen. Akademie der Wissenschaften in Prag [*A publication*]
APA .... Abort Programmer Assembly [*NASA*]   (KSC)
APA .... Acetone Producers Association   (EAIO)
APA .... Acrylamide Producers Association   (EA)
APA .... Acta Praehistorica et Archaeologica [*A publication*]
APA .... Action Potential Amplitude [*Physiology*]
APA .... Additional Personal Allowance   (DLA)
APA .... Advance of Pay and Allowances   (AABC)
APA .... Advanced Programs Authorization
APA .... Advertising Photographers of America   (EA)
APA .... Aerovias Panama Airways
APA .... Agricultural Pilots Association [*Defunct*]   (EA)
APA .... Agricultural Publishers Association   (EA)
APA .... Air Pacific Airlines [*Eureka, CA*] [*FAA designator*]   (FAAC)
APA .... Air Pathway Analyses [*Environmental chemistry*]
APA .... Air Patrol Area   (NVT)
APA .... Air Products & Chemicals, Inc., Allentown, PA [*OCLC symbol*]   (OCLC)
APA .... Airborne Power Adapter
APA .... Aircraft Plume Analysis
APA .... Aircraft Procurement, Army   (AABC)
APA .... Alan Pascoe Associates [*British*]
APA .... Alaska Power Administration [*Department of Energy*]
APA .... Albanian People's Army
APA .... Aldosterone-Producing Adenoma [*Clinical chemistry*]
APA .... All Party Alliance [*British*]

APA .... All Points Addressable [*Data processing*]
APA .... Alliance of Poles of America   (EA)
APA .... Allied Pilots Association   (EA)
APA .... Allowance for Project Adjustment
APA .... Amalgamated Printers' Association   (EA)
APA .... Amateur Press Alliance [*Defunct*]   (EA)
APA .... Amateur Press Association [*Generic term*]
APA .... Amateur Publishers' Association
APA .... Ambulatory Pediatric Association   (EA)
APA .... American Pancreatic Association   (EA)
APA .... American Paralysis Association   (EA)
APA .... American Parquet Association   (EA)
APA .... American Patients Association   (EA)
APA .... American Pawnbrokers Association   (EA)
APA .... American Pax Association [*Later, PC-USA*]   (EA)
APA .... American Payroll Association   (EA)
APA .... American Pedestrian Association   (EA)
APA .... American Petanque Association USA   (EA)
APA .... American Pharmaceutical Association
APA .... American Philological Association   (EA)
APA .... American Philosophical Association   (EA)
APA .... American Photoplatemakers Association [*Later, IAP*]
APA .... American Physiotherapy Association [*Later, APTA*]
APA .... American Piedmontese Association   (EA)
APA .... American Pilots' Association   (EA)
APA .... American Pinzgauer Association   (EA)
APA .... American Planning Association   (EAIO)
APA .... American Plywood Association   (EA)
APA .... American Podiatry Association [*Later, APMA*]
APA .... American Poetry [*A publication*]
APA .... American Poetry Association   (EA)
APA .... American Police Academy   (EA)
APA .... American Polygraph Association   (EA)
APA .... American Poolplayers Association   (EA)
APA .... American Poultry Association   (EA)
APA .... American Produce Association   (EA)
APA .... American Protective Association [*Late-19th-century organization opposed to so-called encroachments of the Catholic Church in the US; initialism was also used by Catholics as an epithet for Protestants*]
APA .... American Protestant Association
APA .... American Psychiatric Association   (EA)
APA .... American Psychoanalytic Association   (EA)
APA .... American Psychological Association   (EA)
APA .... American Psychopathological Association
APA .... American Psychotherapy Association [*Inactive*]   (EA)
APA .... American Puffer Alliance [*An association*]   (EA)
APA .... American Pulpwood Association   (EA)
APA .... American Pyrotechnics Association   (EA)
APA .... Americans for Peace in the Americas   (EA)
APA .... Aminopenicillanic Acid [*Biochemistry*]
APA .... Aminophenylacetylene [*Organic chemistry*]
APA .... Animal Transport [*Navy ship symbol*] [*Obsolete*]
APA .... Animation Producers' Association [*Defunct*]   (EA)
APA .... Annual Procurement Agreement   (MCD)
APA .... Antenna Pattern Analyzer
APA .... Antiparietal Antibody
apa .... Apache [*MARC language code*] [*Library of Congress*]   (LCCP)
∴PA .... Apache Corp. [*NYSE symbol*]   (SPSG)
APA .... [*The*] Apache Railway Co. [*AAR code*]
APA .... Apachito [*Race of maize*]
APA .... Apatity [*USSR*] [*Seismograph station code, US Geological Survey*]   (SEIS)
APA .... Apple Processors Association   (EA)
APA .... Appropriation Purchases Account
APA .... Archconfraternity of Perpetual Adoration [*Defunct*]   (EA)
APA .... Architectural Photographers Association   (EA)
APA .... Architectural Precast Association   (EA)
APA .... Army Parachute Association [*British military*]   (DMA)
APA .... Army Procurement Appropriation
APA .... Asian/Pacific American
APA .... Assistance Payments Administration [*Later, Office of Family Assistance*] [*Social Security Administration*]
APA .... Associate Member of Institute of Accredited Public Accountants
APA .... Associate in Practical Arts
APA .... Associate in Public Administration
APA .... Association of Paediatric Anaesthetists of Great Britain and Ireland [*Birmingham, England*]   (EAIO)
APA .... Association of Paroling Authorities International   (EA)
APA .... Association for People with Arthritis   (EA)
APA .... Association of Port Authorities
APA .... Association of Producing Artists
APA .... Association for the Protection of the Adirondacks   (EA)
APA .... Association pour la Protection des Automobilistes [*Canada*]
APA .... Association of Public Analysts [*British*]
APA .... Associative Principle for Addition [*Mathematics*]
APA .... Atlantic Pilotage Authority
APA .... Attack Transport [*Later, LPA*] [*Navy symbol*]
APA .... Audio Publishers Association   (EA)
APA .... Augmented Predictive Analyzer [*Data processing*]   (DIT)
APA .... Australian Peace Alliance

APA .... Australian Planning Appeal Decisions [*A publication*]
APA .... Australian Press Association
APA .... Austria Presse Agentur [*Press agency*] [*Austria*]
APA .... Automatic Photographic Analysis
APA .... Automobile Protection Association [*Canada*]
APA .... Auxiliary Personnel, Attack [*Navy designation for combat landing craft*] [*World War II*]
APA .... Available Phosphoric Acid
APA .... Axial Pressure Angle [*Gears*]
APA .... Denver, CO [*Location identifier*] [*FAA*]   (FAAL)
APA .... International Airline Passengers Association
APAA .... Adelaide [*Australia*] [*ICAO location identifier*]   (ICLI)
APAA .... American Physicians Art Association   (EA)
APAA .... American Podiatry Association Auxiliary [*Later, APMAA*]   (EA)
APAA .... Art Patrons Association of America   (EA)
APAA .... ASEAN [*Association of South East Asian Nations*] Port Authorities Association   (DS)
APAA .... Asian Patent Attorneys Association   (EA)
APAA .... Atti. Pontificia Accademia Romana di Archeologia [*A publication*]
APAA .... Automotive Parts and Accessories Association   (EA)
APAAP ...... Alkaline Phosphatase:Antialkaline Phosphatase [*Immunochemistry*]
APAAP ...... Association de la Presse Anglo-Americaine de Paris [*Anglo-American Press Association of Paris*]   (EAIO)
APAC .... Administrator's Pesticide Advisory Committee [*Environmental Protection Agency*] [*Terminated, 1985*]
APAC .... Aerial Photographic Analysis Center
APAC .... Airborne Parabolic Arc Computer
APAC .... American Puppet Arts Council [*Defunct*]
APAC .... Antenna Pointing Angle Change
APAC .... Appointment and Promotion Advisory Committee [*UN Food and Agriculture Organization*]
APAC .... Area Planning-Action Councils
APAC .... Association of Patternmakers and Allied Craftsmen [*A union*] [*British*]   (DCTA)
APACAB ... Acta Physiologica. Academiae Scientiarum Hungaricae [*A publication*]
APACB ...... American Painting Contractor [*A publication*]
APACHE... Accelerated Project to Automate Critical Hardware Hardcore Systems
APACHE... Accelerator for Physics and Chemistry of Heavy Metals
APACHE... Active Thermal Protection for Avionics Crew and Heat-Sensitive Equipment [*Air Force*]   (MCD)
APACHE... Acute Physiology and Chronic Health Evaluation
APACHE... Analog Programming and Checking [*Data processing*]
APACHE... Analysis of Pacific Area Communications for Hardening to Electromagnetic Pulse
APACHE... Application Package for Chemical Engineers
APACHES ... Automated Personnel Accounting, Cost, Historical Estimating System [*Army*]
APACI .... Association for the Promotion of African Community Initiatives [*See also APACI*]   (EAIO)
APACL ...... Asian Peoples' Anti-Communist League
APACM..... American Physicians Association of Computer Medicine   (EA)
APACM..... Atmospheric Physical and Chemical Monitor
APACS ..... Adaptive Planning and Control Sequence [*Marketing*]
APACVS ... Association of Physician's Assistants in Cardio-Vascular Surgery   (EA)
APAD .... Acetylpyridineadenine Dinucleotide [*Biochemistry*]
APAD .... Adelaide [*Australia*] [*ICAO location identifier*]   (ICLI)
APAD .... Australian Planning Appeal Decisions [*A publication*]   (APTA)
APADAS ... Automatic Phase and Amplitude Data System   (MCD)
APADS ..... Automatic Programmer and Data System [*Air Force*]
A Paed........ Acta Paediatrica [*A publication*]
A f Paed...... Archiv fuer Paedagogik [*A publication*]
A Paed Belg ... Acta Paediatrica Belgica [*A publication*]
A Paed Lat ... Acta Paediatrica Latina [*A publication*]
APAETP .. (Aminopropylamino)ethylthiophosphate [*Biochemistry*]
APAF........ Antipernicious Anemia Factor [*Also, APA, EF, LLD*] [*Hematology*]
APAG .... American Photographic Artisans Guild   (EA)
APAG .... A: CO Argentina, Inc. [*NASDAQ symbol*]   (NQ)
APAG .... Association Europeenne des Producteurs d'Acides Gras [*European Association of Fatty Acid Producing Companies*]   (EAIO)
APAG .... Atlantic Political Advisory Group [*NATO*]
APAGA ..... Atlantic Provinces Art Gallery Association [*Canada*]
APAH........ Amino Polycyclic Aromatic Hydrocarbon [*Environmental chemistry*]
APAHC ..... Asian Pacific American Heritage Council   (EA)
APAIF .... Association de Prevention des Accidents dans l'Industrie Forestiere [*Forest Products Accident Prevention Association*] [*Canada*]
APAIS .... Australian Public Affairs Information Service [*Information service or system*] [*A publication*]
APAIS Aust Public Affairs Inf Serv ... APAIS. Australian Public Affairs Information Service [*A publication*]
A-PAL .... Activists for Protective Animal Legislation   (EA)
APAL......... Albany [*Australia*] [*ICAO location identifier*]   (ICLI)

APAL........ American Puerto-Rican Action League
APAL........ Array Processor Assembly Language [*Data processing*]
APALA...... Asian/Pacific American Librarians Association   (EA)
APALA4.... Arquivo de Patologia [*A publication*]
APA Legisl Bull ... American Pulpwood Association. Legislative Bulletin [*A publication*]
APALMER ... Atlantic Provinces Association of Learning Materials and Education Representatives [*Canada*]
APAM .... Anthropological Papers. American Museum of Natural History [*A publication*]
APAM .... Antipersonnel Antimaterial [*Weaponry*]   (MCD)
APAM .... Array Processor Access Method [*Data processing*]   (BUR)
APAM .... Association for the Preservation of the Auction Market [*New York, NY*]   (EA)
APAMNH ... Anthropological Papers. American Museum of Natural History [*A publication*]
APAMS.... Automated Pilot Aptitude Measurement System   (MCD)
APANA ..... Asian and Pacific Americans for Nuclear Awareness   (EA)
APANDD.. Avances en Produccion Animal [*A publication*]
APANEE.... Annals of Physiological Anthropology [*A publication*]
APANY ..... Association of Personnel Agencies of New York
APAO .... Amorphous Polyalphaolefin [*Plastics technology*]
APAO .... Asia-Pacific Academy of Ophthalmology [*Tokyo, Japan*]   (EAIO)
APAOBE... Archaeology and Physical Anthropology in Oceania [*Later, Archaeology in Oceania*] [*A publication*]
APAP........ Acetyl-para-aminophenol [*Pharmacology*]
APAP........ American People for American Prisoners   (EA)
APAP........ Apollo Propulsion Analysis Program [*NASA*]
APAP........ Army Pollution Abatement Program   (MCD)
APAP........ Association of Performing Arts Presenters   (EA)
APAP........ Association of Physician Assistant Programs   (EA)
APAPA...... Association for the Preservation of Anti-Psychiatric Artifacts   (EA)
APAPI .... Association Professionnelle des Aides Pedagogiques Individuels [*Professional Association of Individual Educational Assistants*] [*Canada*]
APA-PSIEP Rep ... APA-PSIEP [*American Psychological Association-Project on Scientific Information Exchange in Psychology*] Report [*A publication*]
APA Pulpwood Highl ... American Pulpwood Association. Pulpwood Highlights [*A publication*]
APA Pulpwood Statist ... American Pulpwood Association. Pulpwood Statistics [*A publication*]
APA Pulpwood Sum ... American Pulpwood Association. Monthly Pulpwood Summary [*A publication*]
APAR........ Adaptive Phase Array RADAR
APAR........ Adelaide [*Australia*] [*ICAO location identifier*]   (ICLI)
APAR........ Apparatus   (MUGU)
APar.......... Aurea Parma [*A publication*]
APAR........ Authorized Program Analysis Report [*Data processing*]   (IBMDP)
APAR........ Automatic Program Analysis Report [*Data processing*]   (BUR)
APAR........ Automatic Programming and Recording [*Data processing*]
APARA ..... Atti. Pontificia Accademia Romana di Archeologia [*A publication*]
APARAR... Atti. Pontificia Accademia Romana di Archeologia. Rendiconti [*A publication*]
Apar Nauk Dydakt ... Aparatura Naukowa i Dydaktyczna [*A publication*]
A Par Pol ... Acta Parasitologica Polonica [*A publication*]
Apar Respir Tuberc ... Aparato Respiratorio y Tuberculosis [*A publication*]
APARS...... Army Procurement Appropriation Reporting System
APART...... Adelphi Parent Administered Readiness Test [*Educational development test*]
APART...... Alliance of Pan American Round Tables
A-PART..... Alpha Particle   (ADA)
APART...... Apartment [*Classified advertising*]   (ADA)
APAS........ Academy of Psychic Arts and Sciences   (EA)
APAS........ Advanced Passive Array Sonobuoy [*Navy*]   (CAAL)
APAS........ American Passage Marketing Corp. [*Seattle, WA*] [*NASDAQ symbol*]   (NQ)
APAS........ Association of Personal Assistants and Secretaries [*Leamington Spa, Warwickshire, England*]   (EAIO)
APAS........ Automated Program for Aerospace-Vehicle Synthesis
APAS........ Automated Programmable Assembly System [*Data processing*]
APAS........ Automatic Performance Analysis System
APA Safety Alert ... American Pulpwood Association. Safety Alert [*A publication*]
APAT........ APA Optics, Inc. [*Blaine, MN*] [*NASDAQ symbol*]   (NQ)
APAT........ Atmospheric Pressure and Ambient Temperature
APATB...... Applied Atomics [*A publication*]
APA Tech Papers ... American Pulpwood Association. Technical Papers [*A publication*]
APA Tech Release ... American Pulpwood Association. Technical Release [*A publication*]
A Path Jap ... Acta Pathologica Japonica [*A publication*]
Apatitovye Proyavleniya Sev Kavk ... Apatitovye Proyavleniya Severnogo Kavkaza [*A publication*]
APATS...... Antenna Pattern Test System [*Army*]   (AABC)
APATS...... ARIA [*Advanced Range Instrumentation Aircraft*] Phased Array Telemetry System [*Air Force*]

APATS ...... Automatic Programmer and Test System [*Army*]

APAUC ..... Association des Professeurs d'Allemand des Universites Canadiennes [*Canadian Association of University Teachers of German - CAUTG*]

APAUC ..... Association des Professeurs d'Anglais des Universites Canadiennes [*Association of Canadian University Teachers of English - ACUTE*]

APAVE ...... APAVE. Revue Technique du Groupement des Associations de Proprietaires d'Appareils a Vapeur et Electriques [*A publication*]

APA VIC News ... Australian Pre-School Association. Victorian Branch. Newsletter [*A publication*] (APTA)

APAW .... Abhandlungen. Preussische Akademie der Wissenschaften [*A publication*]

APAW .... Association of Philippine-American Women (EA)

APAX......... Adelaide [*Australia*] [*ICAO location identifier*] (ICLI)

APAZINE ... Amateur Publishers' Association Magazine [*Generic term for one-person science-fiction fan magazine*]

APB .... Accounting Principles Board [*Later, Financial Accounting Standards Board*] [*American Institute of Certified Public Accountants*]

APB .... Advanced Planning Briefing [*Program*] [*DoD*] (RDA)

APB .... Algemeen Politieblad van het Koninkrijk der Nederlanden [*A publication*]

APB .... All Points Bulletin [*Police call*]

APB .... Allied Publications Board [*World War II*]

APB .... Amalgamate Paper Books [*British*]

APB .... American Pacific Bank [*Vancouver Stock Exchange symbol*]

APB .... American Part-Blooded Horse Registry (EA)

APB .... American Program Bureau [*Lectures*]

APB .... Aminophosphonobutyric Acid [*Organic chemistry*]

APB .... Antipersonnel Bomb

APB .... Antiphase Boundaries [*Mineralogy*]

APB .... Apollo Problem Bulletin [*NASA*]

APB .... Appalachian Business Review [*A publication*]

APB .... Applied Physics Branch [*Air Proving Ground Center*]

APB .... [*The*] Archaeology of Palestine and the Bible [*A publication*] (BJA)

APB .... Army Packaging Board (AABC)

APB .... Arterial Premature Beat [*Cardiology*]

APB .... Artillery Barge [*Navy symbol*] [*Obsolete*]

APB .... Ashurst's Paper Books, Lincoln's Inn Library [*A publication*] (DLA)

APB .... Asia Pacific Fund [*NYSE symbol*] (SPSG)

APB .... Associated Press Broadcasters (EA)

APB .... Association for Public Broadcasting (EA)

APB .... Atrial Premature Beats [*Cardiology*]

APB .... Picture Butte Public Library, Alberta [*Library symbol*] [*National Library of Canada*] (NLC)

APB .... Religiosae Adoratrices Pretiosissimo Sanguinis [*Sisters Adorers of the Precious Blood*] [*Roman Catholic religious order*]

APB .... Self-Propelled Barracks Ship [*Navy symbol*]

APB .... United States Army FORSCOM, Fort Bragg Command Reference Center and Main Post, Fort Bragg, NC [*OCLC symbol*] (OCLC)

APBA........ American Pet Boarding Association (EA)

APBA........ American Power Boat Association (EA)

APBA........ American Professional Basketball Association [*Game*] [*Pronounced "ap-bah"*]

APBA........ Amino(phenyl)butanoic Acid [*Organic chemistry*]

APBA........ Associated Press Broadcasters Association [*Later, APB*] (EA)

APBA........ Atlantic Professional Boatman's Association (EA)

APBA........ Australasian Power Boat Association

APBDAJ ... Archiv der Pharmazie und Berichte der Deutschen Pharmazeutischen Gesellschaft [*A publication*]

APBE........ Association for Professional Broadcasting Education [*Later, Broadcast Education Association*] (EA)

APBH .... After Peak Bulkhead [*Shipping*] (DS)

APBH .... Broken Hill [*Australia*] [*ICAO location identifier*] (ICLI)

APBI........ Advanced Planning Briefs for Industry (MCD)

APBI......... Applied Bioscience International, Inc. [*NASDAQ symbol*] (NQ)

APBIC ...... Action for Prevention of Burn Injuries to Children [*Later, AAB*] (EA)

Ap Bl .... Apologetische Blaetter [*A publication*]

APBMBD ... Annales de Physique Biologique et Medicale [*A publication*]

APBMDF .. Acta Pathologica et Microbiologica Scandinavica. Section B. Microbiology [*A publication*]

Ap Bon ...... Apud Bonifacium [*Latin*] (DSA)

APB Op ..... Accounting Principles Board Opinions [*A publication*] (DLA)

APBP........ Association of Professional Baseball Physicians (EA)

APBP........ Association of Professional Bridge Players (EA)

APBPA ...... Association of Professional Ball Players of America (EA)

APBR........ Broome [*Australia*] [*ICAO location identifier*] (ICLI)

Ap Bre ...... Appendix to Breese's Reports [*Illinois*] [*A publication*] (DLA)

APBS .... Advanced Post Boost System [*Military*]

APBS .... Automated PEMA [*Procurement of Equipment and Munition Appropriations*] Budget System [*Military*] (AABC)

APBT........ Aminopyrine Breath Test [*Clinical chemistry*]

APBV........ Advanced Post Boost Vehicle (MCD)

APC .... Abbreviated Performance Characteristics [*Army*]

APC .... Abingdon Pottery Club (EA)

APC .... Absolute Pressure Control

APC .... Academy of Parish Clergy (EA)

APC .... Accelerated Pacification Campaign [*South Vietnam*]

APC .... Accelerometer Pulse Converter

APC .... Accounting Processing Code (AABC)

APC .... Acetylsalicylic Acid [*Aspirin*], Phenacetin, and Caffeine Compound [*Slang translation is, "All Purpose Capsules"*] [*Pharmacy*]

APC .... Acoustical Phase Constant

APC .... Acoustical Plaster Ceiling [*Technical drawings*]

APC .... Acoustical Propagation Constant

APC .... Activated Protein C

APC .... Activity Processing Code

APC .... Adaptive Predictive Coding [*Telecommunications*] (TEL)

APC .... Address Plate Cabinet

APC .... Adenoidal-Pharyngeal-Conjunctival [*Virus*] [*Obsolete usage*]

APC .... Adjustable Pressure Conveyor

APC .... Advanced Performance Computer

APC .... Advanced Piston Coring [*Drilling technology*]

APC .... Advanced Procurement Change [*or Check*] (MCD)

APC .... Advanced Programming Course [*Data processing*]

APC .... Advanced Propulsion Comparison Study [*NASA*] (NASA)

APC .... Advanced Propulsion Cooling

APC .... Advertising Production Club of New York (EA)

APC .... Aerobic Plate Count [*Microbiology*]

APC .... Aeronautical Planning Chart [*Military*]

APC .... Aerospace Primus Club

APC .... African Peanut (Groundnut) Council

APC .... Aft Power Controller (MCD)

APC .... Aimpoint Correlator [*Weaponry*] (MCD)

APC .... Air Pollution Control

APC .... Airpac [*Seattle, WA*] [*FAA designator*] (FAAC)

APC .... Airport Forum News Services [*A publication*]

APC .... Alcohol Policy Council (EA)

APC .... Alien Property Custodian [*World War II*]

APC .... All-People's Congress [*Sierra Leone*] [*Political party*] (PPW)

APC .... All-Peoples Congress [*An association*] (EA)

APC .... Alliance for Philippine Concerns (EA)

APC .... Alliance Property and Construction [*Commercial firm*] [*British*]

APC .... Allied Purchasing Company (EA)

APC .... Allophycocyanin [*Also, AP*] [*Biochemistry*]

APC .... Alternative Press Center (EA)

APC .... AMARC [*Automatic Message Accounting Recording Center*] Protocol Converter (TEL)

APC .... AMCEL Propulsion Co. [*Later, Northrup Caroline Co.*] (KSC)

APC .... American Palestine Committee [*Defunct*] (EA)

APC .... American Parents Committee (EA)

APC .... American Philatelic Congress (EA)

APC .... American Pointer Club (EA)

APC .... American Pomeranian Club (EA)

APC .... American Power Committee (EA)

APC .... American President Companies Ltd.

APC .... American Productivity Center [*Houston, TX*] (EA)

APC .... Ammonium Perchlorate [*Inorganic chemistry*]

APC .... AMSA, Prednisone, and Chlorambucil [*Antineoplastic drug regimen*]

APC .... Amyloid Pack Core [*Pathology*]

APC .... Anadarko Petroleum [*NYSE symbol*] (SPSG)

APC .... Analog to Pressure Converter

APC .... Analytic Plotter Coordinagraph [*Geoscience*]

ApC............ Andronicus Publishing Company, Inc., New York, NY [*Library symbol*] [*Library of Congress*] (LCLS)

APC .... Annales de la Philosophie Chretienne [*A publication*]

APC .... Anno post Christum Natum [*In the Year after Christ Was Born*] [*Latin*] (ROG)

APC .... Annotated Predicate Calculus (MCD)

APC .... Annular Primary Combustor

APC .... Antenna Pattern Correction [*for spacecraft data*]

APC .... Antigen-Presenting Cell [*Immunology*]

APC .... Apneustic Center [*Brain anatomy*]

APC .... Appalachian Power Company

APC .... Applied to Previous Charge [*Business term*]

APC .... Applied Psychology Corporation (KSC)

APC .... Approach Control [*Aviation*]

APC .... Approach Power Compensator [*NASA*]

APC .... Apricot Producers of California (EA)

APC .... Archives Publiques du Canada [*Public Archives of Canada - PAC*]

APC .... Area Planning Council [*Department of Education*] (OICC)

APC .... Area of Positive Control [*FAA*]

APC .... Argon Purge Cart [*Nuclear energy*] (NRCH)

APC .... Arkansas Polytechnic College [*Later, Arkansas Technical University*]

APC .... Armament Practice Camp [*British military*] (DMA)

APC .... Armor-Piercing Capped [*Ammunition*]

APC .... Armored Personnel Carrier [*Military*]

APC .... Army Pay Corps [*Later, RAPC*] [*British*]

APC .... Army Petroleum Center

APC .... Army Pictorial Center

APC .... Army Policy Council
APC .... Army Postal Clerk　(AABC)
APC .... Arunachal People's Conference [*India*] [*Political party*]　(PPW)
APC .... Aspirin, Phenacetin, Caffeine [*Medicine*]　(DHSM)
APC .... Assistant Principal Chaplain [*British*]　(ADA)
APC .... Assisted Places Committee [*Education*] [*British*]
APC .... Associated Pimiento Canners [*Defunct*]　(EA)
APC .... Associated Porcupine Mines Ltd. [*Toronto Stock Exchange symbol*]
APC .... Association des Parlementaires du Commonwealth [*Commonwealth Parliamentary Association*] [*Canada*]
APC .... Association of Pathology Chairmen　(EA)
APC .... Association of Principals of Colleges [*British*]
APC .... Association of Private Camps [*Later, AIC*]　(EA)
APC .... Association of Profiles Consultants　(EA)
APC .... Association des Psychiatres du Canada [*Canadian Psychiatric Association*]　(EAIO)
APC .... Association of Public Corporations [*Miami, FL*]　(EA)
APC .... Association of Pulp Consumers, Inc. [*Later, American Paper Institute*]　(EA)
APC .... Associative Processor Control [*Data processing*]
APC .... Associu di Patrioti Corsi [*Association of Corsican Patriots*] [*France*] [*Political party*]　(PPE)
APC .... Atomic Power Construction Ltd.
APC .... Atrial Premature Contractions [*Cardiology*]
APC .... Auditing Practices Committee [*British*]
APC .... Australasian Petroleum Co.
APC .... Australian Peace Committee
APC .... Australian People's Congress
APC .... Australian Personal Computer [*A publication*]　(APTA)
APC .... Australian Production Committee
APC .... Australian Productivity Council
APC .... Autographed Presentation Copy
APC .... Automated Packaging Code [*Army*]　(MCD)
APC .... Automated Production and Control [*Industrial engineering*]
APC .... Automatic Performance Control
APC .... Automatic Phase Control [*Telecommunications*]　(TEL)
APC .... Automatic Pitch Control
APC .... Automatic Pressure Conveyor
APC .... Automotive Presidents Council　(EA)
A/PC .... Autopilot Capsule
APC .... Autoplot Controller　(IEEE)
APC .... Average Power Control [*Telecommunications*]　(TEL)
APC .... Average Propensity to Consume [*Economics*]
APC .... Cavalry Transport [*Navy ship symbol*] [*Obsolete*]
APc .... Compound Action Potential [*Biology*]
APC .... Napa, CA [*Location identifier*] [*FAA*]　(FAAL)
APC .... Pacific Region [*FAA*]　(FAAC)
APC .... Pincher Creek Public Library, Alberta [*Library symbol*] [*National Library of Canada*]　(NLC)
APC .... Small Coastal Transport [*Navy symbol*] [*Obsolete*]
APCA .... Abandoned Property Collection Act [*1863*]
APCA .... Aft Power Controller Assembly [*NASA*]　(MCD)
APCA .... Air Pollution Control Association　(EA)
APCA .... American Petroleum Credit Association [*Minneapolis, MN*]　(EA)
APCA .... American Planning Civic Association [*Later, NUC*]　(EA)
APCA .... Assemblee Permanente des Chambres d'Agriculture [*Industrial organization*] [*France*]　(EY)
APCA .... Audio Peak Clipping Amplifier
APCA .... Australian Pest Controllers Association
APCA .... Australian Port Charge Additional
APCA .... National Association of Aeronautical Production Controllers
APCA Abstr ... APCA [*Air Pollution Control Association*] Abstracts [*A publication*]
APCAC ...... Asia-Pacific Council of American Chambers of Commerce　(EA)
APCAD ...... Applied Catalysis [*A publication*]
APCAE ...... Association of Principals of Colleges for Adult Education [*British*]
APCA J ...... APCA [*Air Pollution Control Association*] Journal [*A publication*]
APCAPS .... Automated Payroll, Cost, and Personnel System [*Defense Supply Agency*]
APCAS ...... Asia and the Pacific Commission on Agricultural Statistics [*Formerly, Asia and the Far East Commission on Agricultural Statistics*]　(EA)
APCBC ...... Armor-Piercing-Capped, Ballistic-Capped [*Ammunition*]　(MSA)
APCBC ...... Armor-Piercing, Carbide, Ballistic Cap [*Ammunition*]　(NATG)
APCC .... American Power Conversion Corp. [*NASDAQ symbol*]　(NQ)
APCC .... American Public Communications Council　(EA)
APCC .... Animal and Plant Control Commission [*Australia*]
APCC .... Antique Phonograph Collectors Club　(EA)
APCC .... Apollo Program Control Center [*NASA*]　(KSC)
APCC .... Asian and Pacific Coconut Community [*Jakarta, Indonesia*]　(EAIO)
APCC .... Atmospheric Pressure and Composition Control　(NASA)
APCC .... Cocos Islands [*Australia*] [*ICAO location identifier*]　(ICLI)
APCCA ...... American Protestant Correctional Chaplains Association　(EA)

APCCBM .. Annual Progress in Child Psychiatry and Child Development [*A publication*]
APCCDO... Annual Reports on the Progress of Chemistry. Section A. Inorganic Chemistry [*A publication*]
APCChE ... Asian Pacific Confederation of Chemical Engineering　(EAIO)
APCCLA ... Aviation Petroleum Coordinating Committee, Latin American
APCD .... Air Pollution Control District
APCD .... Association of Philippine Coconut Desiccators
APCD .... Ceduna [*Australia*] [*ICAO location identifier*]　(ICLI)
APCE........ Annals of Public and Cooperative Economy [*Formerly, Annals of Collective Economy*] [*A publication*]
APCE........ Association Petroliere pour la Conservation de l'Environnement Canadien [*Petroleum Association for Conservation of the Canadian Environment*]
APCEAR ... Archiv foer Pharmaci og Chemi [*A publication*]
APCEC ...... Army Precommission Extension Course　(AABC)
APCEF ...... Advanced Power Conversion Experimental Facility
APCF .... Acute Pharyngo-Conjunctival Fever [*Medicine*]
APCG .... Aperture Plate Character Generator
APCG .... Apex Cardiogram [*Medicine*]
APCH .... Apache Energy & Mining Co. [*NASDAQ symbol*]　(NQ)
APCH .... Approach
APCHA ..... Advances in Protein Chemistry [*A publication*]
APCHE ..... Automatic Programmed Checkout Equipment
APCHG ..... Approaching
APCI........ Amusement Park Club International [*Defunct*]　(EA)
APCI........ Apollo Computer, Incorporated [*NASDAQ symbol*]　(NQ)
APCI........ Armor-Piercing-Capped Incendiary [*Ammunition*]
APCI........ Association of Pulp Consumers, Incorporated
APCI........ Atmospheric Pressure Chemical Ionization
APCISS .... Alumni Presidents' Council of Independent Secondary Schools　(EA)
APCIT ...... Armor-Piercing-Capped Incendiary with Tracer [*Ammunition*]
APCK........ Association for Promoting Christian Knowledge [*Church of Ireland*]
APCKD..... Adult-Onset Polycystic Kidney Disease [*Medicine*]
APCL .... American Postal Chess League [*Defunct*]　(EA)
APCL .... Association of Professional Color Laboratories　(EA)
APCL .... Atomic Power Construction Limited
APCLA ..... Australian Professional Colour Laboratories Association
APCM .... Adaptive Pulse Code Modulation [*Telecommunications*]　(TEL)
APCM .... American Presbyterian Congo Mission
APCM .... Asiatic-Pacific Campaign Medal [*Military decoration*]
APCM .... Associated Portland Cement Manufacturers of Great Britain
APCM .... Association of Professional Conservatories of Music　(EA)
APCMA..... Archivio di Patologia e Clinica Medica [*A publication*]
APCMAH ... Archivio di Patologia e Clinica Medica [*A publication*]
APCN .... Active Pulse Compression Network
APCN .... Anno post Christum Natum [*In the Year after Christ Was Born*] [*Latin*]
APCNY...... Analytical Psychology Club of New York　(EA)
APCO .... Air Pollution Control Office [*Obsolete*] [*Environmental Protection Agency*]
APCO .... Appomattox Court House National Historic Park
APCO .... Arab Political and Cultural Organization [*Iran*]　(PD)
APCO .... Asian Parasite Control Organization　(EAIO)
APCO .... Associated Public-Safety Communications Officers　(EA)
APCO .... Automobile Protection Corp. [*NASDAQ symbol*]　(NQ)
APCOB...... Archivio Putti di Chirurgia degli Organi di Movimento [*A publication*]
APCOD .... Applicability Code
APCOD .... Applied Physics Communications [*A publication*]
APCOL...... All-Pakistan Confederation of Labor
APCOM .... Application of Computers and Mathematics in the Mineral Industry [*A publication*]
APCOM .... International Symposium on the Application of Computers and Operations Research in the Mineral Industries
APCOM 77 Pap Int Symp Appl Comput Oper Res Miner Ind ... APCOM 77. Papers Presented at the International Symposium on the Application of Computers and Operations Research in the Mineral Industries [*A publication*]
APCON ..... Approach Control [*FAA*]
APCOPPLSRF ... Analysis and Program for Calculation of Optimum Propellant Performance for Liquid and Solid Rocket Fuels
APCOR...... Atomic Physics Consortium at Oak Ridge
APCP........ Activation Project Control Plan
APCP........ Association of Paid Circulation Publications　(EA)
APCPCS.... American Institute of Physics. Conference Proceedings [*A publication*]
APC/QC.... Armored Personnel Carrier/Qualification Course [*Army*]
APCR....... Air Pollution Control Regulation　(MCD)
A-PCR ...... Anchored Polymerase Chain Reaction [*Genetics*]
Apcr .... Apocrypha　(BJA)
APCR....... Apollo Program Control Room [*NASA*]　(KSC)
APCR....... Armor-Piercing Reduced (Caliber) [*Ammunition*]
APCR....... Armour-Piercing Composite Rigid [*British military*]　(DMA)
APCR........ Carnarvon [*Australia*] [*ICAO location identifier*]　(ICLI)
APCRAW ... Advances in Pest Control Research [*A publication*]
APC Review ... APC Review. Australian Parents Council [*A publication*]

APCRP......	Aquatic Plant Control Research Program [*Army Corps of Engineers Waterways Experiment Station*] (MSC)
APCS.........	Aeronautical Production Control System
APCS.........	Air Photographic and Charting Service
APCS.........	American Pencil Collectors Society (EA)
APCS.........	American Podiatric Circulatory Society (EA)
APCS.........	American Portuguese Cultural Society [*Later, APS*] (EA)
APCS.........	Applied Control Systems, Inc. [*Morrisville, NC*] [*NASDAQ symbol*] (NQ)
APCS.........	Approach Path Control System [*NASA*] (MCD)
APCS.........	Approach Power Compensator System [*NASA*]
APCS.........	Approach Power Control Set (NG)
APCS.........	Associative Processor Computer System
APCS.........	Attitude and Pointing Control System [*NASA*] (KSC)
APCSD4....	Annals of Plastic Surgery [*A publication*]
APCT.........	American Postal Chess Tournaments (EA)
APCT.........	Armor-Piercing-Capped with Tracer [*Ammunition*]
APCT.........	Association of Painting Craft Teachers [*British*]
A/P CTL...	Autopilot Control (AAG)
APCTT......	Asian and Pacific Centre for Transfer of Technology (EAIO)
APCU.........	Association of Presbyterian Colleges and Universities (EA)
APCV.........	Air-Piloted Control Valve
APCV.........	Association Professionnelle Catholique des Voyageurs de Commerce du Canada [*Catholic Professional Association of Commercial Representatives of Canada*]
APCVD......	Atmospheric Pressure Chemical Vapor Deposition [*Photovoltaic energy systems*]
APCYA......	[*A*] Presidential Classroom for Young Americans (EA)
APD...........	Action Potential Duration [*Electrophysiology*]
APD...........	Adjustable Pitch Device
APD...........	Admiralty Press Division [*British military*] (DMA)
APD...........	Adult Polycystic Disease [*Medicine*]
AP & D......	Advanced Planning and Design [*NASA*] (KSC)
APD...........	Advanced Planning Document [*DoD*] (AABC)
APD...........	Advanced Program Development
APD...........	Aerial Port Detachment
APD...........	Aeronautical Propulsion Division [*NASA*]
APD...........	Aerospace Power Division [*Air Force*]
APD...........	Agricultural Pipe Drain
APD...........	Aiming Point Determination
APD...........	Air Particulate Detector (IEEE)
APD...........	Air to Pneumatic Distribution [*Aerospace*]
APD...........	Air Procurement Directive (MCD)
APD...........	Air Procurement District [*Air Force*]
APD...........	Air Products & Chemicals, Inc. [*NYSE symbol*] (SPSG)
APD...........	Airport Directory [*FAA*]
APD...........	Albany Port District [*AAR code*]
APD...........	Alien Property Division [*Department of Justice*] (DLA)
APD...........	All-Purpose Decontaminant (MCD)
APD...........	Amino(hydroxy)propylidine [*Organic chemistry*]
APD...........	Amplitude Probability Distribution [*Telecommunications*]
APD...........	Analog-to-Pulse Duration
APD...........	Angiotensin Pressor Dose [*Medicine*]
APD...........	Angular Position Digitizer
A-PD........	Anteroposterior Diameter
APD...........	Antiphase Domains [*Mineralogy*]
APD...........	Antipsychotic Drug
APD...........	Apollo Program Directive [*NASA*] (KSC)
APD...........	Archives de Philosophie du Droit [*A publication*] (ILCA)
APD...........	Area Passive Dosimeter (MCD)
APD...........	Area Postal Directory [*Army*] (AFIT)
APD...........	Army Pay Department [*British*]
APD...........	Army Pictorial Division
APD...........	Army Procurement District
APD...........	Aslib Proceedings [*A publication*]
Apd............	Assessment Paid
APD...........	Associate Administrator for Policy Development and Review [*FAA*] (FAAC)
APD...........	Association for Prevention of Disabilities (EAIO)
APD...........	Atrial Premature Depolarization [*Cardiology*]
APD...........	Automated Payment and Deposit [*Banking*]
APD...........	Automated Peritoneal Dialysis [*Medicine*]
APD...........	Automated Powder Diffractometer
APD...........	Automated Program Debugging System (MCD)
APD...........	Automobile Physical Damage [*Insurance*]
APD...........	Auxiliary Personnel, Destroyer [*British military*] (DMA)
APD...........	Auxiliary Power Distribution (KSC)
APD...........	Avalanche Photodiode [*Solid state physics*]
APDU.........	Avalanche Photodiode Detector
APD...........	Average Particle Diameter
APD...........	Average Percentage Damage [*Meteorology*]
APD...........	Average Pore Diameter [*Filtration*]
APD...........	Average Power Dissipation
APD...........	High-Speed Transport [*Navy symbol*] [*Obsolete*]
APD...........	Pennsylvania State's Agricultural Progress Days (TSPED)
Ap 2d.......	New York Appellate Division Reports, Second Series [*A publication*] (DLA)
APDA	Acidified Potato-Dextrose Agar [*Microbiology*]
APDA	American Parkinson Disease Association (EA)
APDA	American Power Drinkers Association
APDA	Appliance Parts Distributors Association (EA)

APDA	Army Physical Disability Activity (MCD)
APDA	Atomic Power Development Associates, Inc.
APDA	Auxiliary Pump-Drive Assembly
APDAB.....	Army Physical Disability Appeal Board
APDB	Derby [*Australia*] [*ICAO location identifier*] (ICLI)
APDBA.....	Acta Physica et Chimica (Debrecina) [*A publication*]
APDC	Air Procurement District Commander [*Air Force*]
APDC	Ammonium Pyrrolidinedithiocarbamate [*Also, APDTC*] [*Organic chemistry*]
APDC	Asian and Pacific Development Centre (EAIO)
APDEA.....	Aminopropyldiethanolamine [*Organic chemistry*]
APDEAW ...	Aptechnoe Delo [*A publication*]
APDEB.....	Current Problems in Dermatology [*A publication*]
APDF........	Africa Project Development Facility [*United Nations*] (EY)
APDF........	Aircraft Program Data File
APDF.........	Association of Professional Design Firms (EA)
APDF/APRO ...	Asian Pacific Dental Federation/Asian Pacific Regional Organisation (EAIO)
APDIAO....	Annals of the Rheumatic Diseases [*A publication*]
APDIM......	Association of Program Directors in Internal Medicine (EA)
APDKA.....	Aktualne Problemy Informacji i Dokumentacji [*A publication*]
APDL........	American Protestant Defense League (EA)
APDM.......	Amended Program Decision Memorandum [*Navy*] (NVT)
APDME.....	Americans for Peace and Democracy in the Middle East (EA)
APDMS.....	Advanced Point Defense Missile System [*Navy*]
APDMS.....	Axial Power Distribution Monitoring Systems [*Nuclear energy*] (NRCH)
APDO.......	Airport District Office (FAAC)
APDP.......	Aminohydroxypropane Diphosphonate
APDP........	Apollo Program Definition Phase [*NASA*] (KSC)
APDPD.....	Annual Power Distribution Conference. Proceedings [*United States*] [*A publication*]
APDS.......	Advanced Personnel Data System (MCD)
APDS.......	Advanced Planning Data Sheet
APDS.........	Aminophenyl Disulfide [*Biochemistry*]
APDS.........	Armor-Piercing Discarding Sabot [*Ammunition*] (NATG)
APDSA......	Asian Pacific Dental Students' Association [*Singapore, Singapore*] (EAIO)
APDSFS.....	Armor-Piercing Discarding Sabot, Fin-Stabilized [*Ammunition*] (MCD)
APDSMS ..	Advanced Point Defense Surface Missile System [*Navy*]
APDS-T.....	Armor-Piercing Discarding Sabot with Tracer [*Ammunition*] (AABC)
APDTA9....	American Practitioner and Digest of Treatment [*A publication*]
APDTC......	Ammonium Pyrrolidinedithiocarbamate [*Also, APDC*] [*Organic chemistry*]
APDU........	Association of Public Data Users (EA)
Apdusa......	African People's Democratic Union of South Africa (PD)
APDVE......	Aide aux Personnes Deplacees et Ses Villages Europeens [*Aid to Displaced Persons and Its European Villages*] (EAIO)
APDW......	Advance Procurement Data Worksheets [*Air Force*] (AFIT)
APDW......	Advanced Personal Defense Weapon [*Army*] (INF)
APDW......	Apple and Pear Disease Workers (EA)
APDY	Appropriate Duty [*Air Force*] (AFM)
APE	Advanced Procurement Engineering (MCD)
APE	Advanced Production Engineering
APE	Aerial Port of Embarkation [*Military*]
APE	Agency to Prevent Evil [*Organization in TV series "Lancelot Link"*]
APE	Alfven Propulsion Engine [*Aerospace*]
APE	American Puritan Ethic
APE	American Pyramid Resources, Inc. [*Vancouver Stock Exchange symbol*]
APE	Aminopentanoic Acid [*An amino acid*]
APE	Ammunition Peculiar Equipment (AABC)
APE	Amphibious Pionier Erkundungsfahrzeug [*Amphibious Engineer Reconnaissance Vehicle*] [*German*] (MCD)
APE	Anchor Placement Equipment
APE	Annual Planning Estimate [*Navy*] (NVT)
APE	Anomalous Photovoltaic Effect (MCD)
APE	Anterior Pituitary Extract [*Endocrinology*]
APE	Apeiranthos Of Naxos [*Greece*] [*Seismograph station code, US Geological Survey*] (SEIS)
APE	Aperient [*Pharmacy*] (ROG)
APE	Appleton, OH [*Location identifier*] [*FAA*] (FAAL)
APE	Applied Economics [*United Kingdom*] [*A publication*]
APE	Aramaeische Papyri aus Elephantine [*A publication*] (BJA)
APE	Arecaidine Propargyl Ester [*Biochemistry*]
APE	Army Preliminary Evaluation
APE	Assemblee Parlementaire Europeenne
APE	Assistant Project Engineer
APE	Association for the Protection of Evolution [*British*]
APE	Associative Processing Element (MCD)
APE	Athinaikon Praktoreion Eidiseon [*Athens News Agency*] [*Greece*]
APE	Atomic Photoelectric Effect
APE	Automatic Positioning Equipment
APE	Available Potential Energy [*Geophysics*]
APE	Available Power Efficiency
APEA........	Agri-Products Exporters Association (EA)
APEA........	Antenna Pattern Error Analysis

APEA......... Association Parlementaire Europe-Afrique [*Eur-African Parliamentary Association*]

APEA......... Association for Petroleum and Explosives Administration [*British*]

APEA......... Association des Producteurs Europeens d'Azote [*European Association of Nitrogen Manufacturers*] (EAIO)

APEA J...... APEA [*Australian Petroleum Exploration Association*] Journal [*A publication*]

APEA Jl .... APEA [*Australian Petroleum Exploration Association*] Journal [*A publication*]

APEB......... Army Physical Evaluation Board

APEC......... All-Purpose Electronic Computer (IEEE)

APEC........ Alliance for the Preservation of English in Canada

APEC........ American Paper Exchange Club [*Later, PIR*] (EA)

APEC........ Atlantic Provinces Economic Council

APEC........ Automated Procedures for Engineering Consultants, Inc.

APEC........ Automotive Products Emissions Committee (EA)

APEC........ Automotive Products Export Council (EA)

APECA...... American Package Express Carriers Association (EA)

APECM..... Adaptive Polarization Electronic Countermeasure (MCD)

APECO...... American Photograph Equipment Company

AP Ed........ Associate in Physical Education

APED .... Edinburgh [*Australia*] [*ICAO location identifier*] (ICLI)

APEE........ Association of Private Enterprise Education (EA)

APE Eng.... APE [*Amalgamated Power Engineering Ltd.*] Engineering [*A publication*]

APE Engng ... APE [*Amalgamated Power Engineering Ltd.*] Engineering [*A publication*]

APEF........ Advance-Purchase Excursion Fare [*Airline fare code*] (ADA)

APEF........ Annual. Palestine Exploration Fund [*A publication*]

APEF........ Association des Pays Exportateurs de Mineral de Fer [*Association of Iron Ore Exporting Countries*] (EAIO)

APEI......... Associated Poultry and Egg Industries [*Defunct*] (EA)

APEID....... Asian Program for Education Innovation for Development

APEL........ Aeronautical Photographic Experimental Laboratory [*Johnsville, PA*] [*Navy*]

APELS....... Airborne Precision Emitter Location System (MCD)

APELSCOR ... Architects, Professional Engineers, Land Surveyors Council on Registration

APEM........ Association for Professional Education for Ministry [*Later, APT*] (EA)

APEM........ Association of Professional Energy Managers (EA)

APEMAR ... Archives Roumaines de Pathologie Experimentale et de Microbiologie [*A publication*]

APen .... Anima e Pensiero [*A publication*]

APENAC... Association du Personnel Navigant des Lignes Aeriennes Canadiennes [*Canadian Air Line Flight Attendants' Association - CALFA*]

APEND ..... Applied Energy [*A publication*]

APENPLAN ... Asian and Pacific Energy Planning Network [*of the Asian and Pacific Development Centre*] (EAIO)

APEO .... Advance Process Engineering Order [*Manufacturing*] (MCD)

APEO .... Alkylphenol Polyethoxylate [*Organic chemistry*]

APEQS...... Airborne Photography of the Eclipse of the Quiet Sun

APER......... Air Pollutant Emissions Report [*Environmental Protection Agency*]

APER........ Antipersonnel [*Projectile*]

APER........ Aperient [*Pharmacy*] (ROG)

APER......... Aperture

APER......... Association of Publishers' Educational Representatives [*British*]

APER......... Atlantic Permanent Savings Bank FSB [*NASDAQ symbol*] (NQ)

Apercus Econ Tchecosl ... Apercus sur l'Economie Tchecoslovaque [*A publication*]

APERS ...... Antipersonnel [*Projectile*] (AABC)

A PERS...... [*The*] Era of Persia [*Beginning 632AD*] (ROG)

APERT ...... Aperture (MSA)

APET......... Alpha Petrol Explorations [*NASDAQ symbol*] (NQ)

APEX........ Acid Precipitation Experiment

APEX........ Advance-Purchase Excursion [*Airline fare code*]

APEX........ Air Pollution Exercise

APEX........ Apparatus for Pore Examination [*Geophysics*]

APEX........ ARCAS [*Atlantic Research Corporation Atmospheric Sounding Missile*] Piggyback Emulsion Experiment (MUGU)

APEX........ Association of Professional and Executive Staff [*British*]

APEX........ Atlantische Passatwind Experiment [*Atlantic Tradewind Experiment*] [*US, England, Germany*] (MSC)

APEX........ Automated Procurement Planning, Execution, and Control

APEX........ Institute for Astrophysics and Planetary Exploration [*University of Florida*] [*Research center*] (RCD)

APExC....... All Purpose Electronic x Computer [*Early computer*] [*Birkbeck College*] [*British*]

APEXER ... Approach Indexer

APF........... Accurate Position Finder

APF........... Acidproof Floor [*Technical drawings*]

APF........... Acidulated Phosphofluoride

APF........... Acta Philosophica Fennica [*Elsevier Book Series*] [*A publication*]

APF........... Adjustable Pawl Fastener

APF........... Administrative Flagship [*Navy symbol*] [*Obsolete*]

APF........... Advanced Procurement Funding (MCD)

APF........... American Pathology Foundation (EA)

APF........... American Physicians Fellowship for Medicine in Israel (EA)

APF........... American Porphyria Foundation (EA)

APF........... American Progress Foundation

APF........... American Psychological Foundation

APF........... Anglican Pacifist Fellowship [*Oxford, England*] (EAIO)

APF........... Animal Protein Factor

APF........... Apple Preferred Format [*Data processing*]

APF........... Approach Control Function [*Aviation*] (AIA)

APF........... Appropriated Funds (AABC)

APF........... Archiv fuer Papyrusforschung und Verwandte Gebiete [*A publication*]

A-P-F .... Ashbrooke-Pembleton-Ffrench [*Mythical British family appearing in "Announcements" column of Times of London*]

APF........... Association of Pacific Fisheries [*Later, PSPA*] (EA)

APF........... Association of Professional Foresters (EAIO)

APF........... Atomic Packing Factor (IEEE)

APF........... Atrial Pore Field [*Botany*]

APF........... Australian Permanent Forces

APF........... Authorized Program Facility [*Data processing*] (BUR)

APF........... Automatic Press Feed

APF........... Automatic Program Finding [*Electronics*]

APF........... Naples [*Florida*] [*Airport symbol*] (OAG)

APFA........ Accelerator Pulsed Fast Assembly

APFA........ American Pipe Fittings Association (EA)

APFA........ American Professional Faceters Association [*Defunct*] (EA)

APFA........ Appalachian Finance Association [*Later, Eastern Finance Association*] (EA)

APFA......... Association des Professeurs de Francais en Afrique [*Association of French Teachers in Africa - AFTA*] [*Khartoum, Sudan*] (EAIO)

APFA........ Association des Professeurs Franco-Americains [*Defunct*] (EA)

APFA........ Association for Protection of Fur-Bearing Animals [*Canada*]

AP Faith .... Annals of the Propagation of the Faith [*A publication*]

APFBA...... Association for the Protection of Fur-Bearing Animals (EAIO)

APFC........ American Pacific Corporation [*NASDAQ symbol*] (NQ)

APFC........ American Printed Fabrics Council (EA)

APFC........ Asia-Pacific Forestry Commission [*UN Food and Agriculture Organization*]

APFC........ Association of Physical Fitness Centers (EA)

APFCS...... Automatic Power-Factor-Control Systems (IEEE)

APFD........ Autopilot Flight Director

APFHA...... American Paso Fino Horse Association (EA)

APFL........ Aero-Propulsion Fuels Laboratory [*Air Force*]

APFNC3.... Department of Primary Industries. Brisbane Fisheries Branch. Fisheries Notes [*New Series*] [*A publication*]

APFO........ Association on Programs for Female Offenders (EA)

APFO........ Automated Planning Fabrication Outline (MCD)

APFP........ Army Physical Fitness Program

APFRAD ... Annales Pharmaceutiques Francaises [*A publication*]

APFRI....... American Physical Fitness Research Institute (EA)

APFS .... Association of Podiatrists in Federal Service [*Later, FSPMA*] (EA)

APFS .... Australian Pacific Friendly Society

APFSDS .... Armor-Piercing Fin Stabilized Discarding Sabot [*Ammunition*] (MCD)

APFT........ Advanced [*or Army*] Physical Fitness Test (INF)

APFT........ Army Physical Fitness Test (INF)

APFT........ Forrest [*Australia*] [*ICAO location identifier*] (ICLI)

APFTU...... Amalgamated Picture Frame Trade Union [*British*]

APFUC...... Association des Professeurs de Francais des Universites Canadiennes [*Association of Canadian University Teachers of French*]

APFUCC ... Association des Professeurs de Francais des Universites et Colleges Canadiens [*Association of Canadian University and College Teachers of French - ACUCTF*]

APFX........ Apply Fixture (AAG)

APG .... Aberdeen, MD [*Location identifier*] [*FAA*] (FAAL)

APG .... Aberdeen Proving Ground [*Maryland*] [*Army*]

APG .... Accessory Pedal Ganglia

APG .... Acid-Precipitable Globulin [*Clinical chemistry*]

APG .... ACLANT [*Allied Command, Atlantic*] Planning Guidance [*NATO*]

APG .... Aerial Port Group [*Air Force*] (AFM)

APG .... Air Proving Ground

APG .... Airplane General (MCD)

APG .... American Pewter Guild (EA)

APG .... American Programmers Guild

APG .... American Publicists Guild (EA)

APG .... Antenna Power Gain

APG .... Apex Energy Corp. [*Vancouver Stock Exchange symbol*]

APG .... Apogee

APG .... Application Program Generator [*Data processing*]

APG .... Archiv fuer Politik und Geschichte [*A publication*]

APG .... Argus Press Group [*British*]

APG .... Army Planning Group

APG .... Army Proving Grounds

APG .... Association for Precision Graphics [*Defunct*] (EA)

APG .... Association of Professional Genealogists (EA)

APG .... Astronomiae Professor Greshamii [*Professor of Astronomy at Gresham College, London*]
APG .... Australian Property Group
APG .... Automatic Precipitation Gauge (NOAA)
APG .... Automatic Priority Group [*Fujitsu Ltd.*] [*Japan*] (MCD)
APG .... Azimuth Pulse Generator
APG .... Supporting Gunnery Ship [*Navy symbol*] [*Obsolete*]
APGA .... American Personnel and Guidance Association [*Later, AACD*] (EA)
APGA .... American Public Gas Association (EA)
APGA .... Aminopteroylglutamic Acid [*Organic chemistry*]
APGAAZ... Arquivos de Patologia Geral e Anatomia Patologica. Universidade de Coimbra [*A publication*]
APGAR...... Adaptability, Partnership, Growth, Affection, and Resolve [*Family Therapy Questionnaire*]
APGAR...... American Pediatric Gross Assessment Record
A Pg B........ Archiv fuer Postgeschichte in Bayern [*A publication*]
APGBRL ... Aberdeen Proving Ground/Ballistics Research Laboratory [*Army*]
APGC .... Air Proving Ground Center [*or Command*] [*Eglin Air Force Base, FL*]
APGCE....... Air Proving Ground Center - Eglin Air Force Base
APGCU ..... Autopilot Ground Control Unit
APGE......... Apogee Robotics, Inc. [*Fort Collins, CO*] [*NASDAQ symbol*] (NQ)
APGF......... Perth [*Australia*] [*ICAO location identifier*] (ICLI)
APGG .... Apogee Technology, Inc. [*NASDAQ symbol*] (NQ)
APG/HEL ... Aberdeen Proving Ground/Human Engineering Laboratory [*Army*]
APGI.......... Green [*A. P.*] Industries, Inc. [*NASDAQ symbol*] (NQ)
APG/MT... Aberdeen Ground/Materiel Testing Directorate [*Maryland*] [*Army*]
APGN .... Geraldton [*Australia*] [*ICAO location identifier*] (ICLI)
APGO .... Association of Professors of Gynecology and Obstetrics (EA)
APG/OBDC ... Aberdeen Proving Ground/Ordnance Bomb Disposal Center [*Army*] (KSC)
APG/OTC ... Aberdeen Proving Ground/Ordnance Training Command [*Army*] (KSC)
APGp .... Aerial Port Group [*Air Force*]
APGRA...... American Pediatric Gastroesophageal Reflux Association (EA)
Ap Greg...... Apud Gregorium [*Latin*] (DSA)
APGS......... Apollo Propellant Gauging System [*NASA*] (KSC)
APGS......... Association of Professional Geological Scientists [*Later, AIPG*] (EA)
APGTC...... Administration du Petrole et du Gaz des Terres du Canada [*Canada Oil and Gas Lands Administration*]
APH.......... Access Permit Holder
APh.......... Acta Philologica. Societas Academica Dacoromana [*A publication*]
APH.......... Acta Poloniae Historica [*A publication*]
APH.......... Actual Production History Program
APH.......... Airport Hangar [*New York*] [*Seismograph station code, US Geological Survey*] (SEIS)
APH.......... Alberta Hospital, Ponoka, Alberta [*Library symbol*] [*National Library of Canada*] (NLC)
APH.......... [*Sir*] Allan Patrick Herbert [*British humorist*]
APH.......... Alpha Aviation, Inc. [*Dallas, TX*] [*FAA designator*] (FAAC)
APH.......... American Printing House for the Blind (EA)
APH.......... Amino(phosphono)heptanoic Acid [*Organic chemistry*]
APH.......... Animal Pharm World Animal Health News [*A publication*]
APh.......... Annee Philologique [*A publication*]
APH.......... Antepartum Hemorrhage [*Medicine*]
APH.......... Anterior Pituitary Hormone [*Endocrinology*]
APH.......... Aphorism
APH.......... Approach Resources, Inc. [*Vancouver Stock Exchange symbol*]
A Ph .... Archiv fuer Philosophie [*A publication*]
A f Ph......... Archiv fuer Philosophie [*A publication*]
A Ph .... Associate in Philosophy
APH.......... Association of Private Hospitals (EA)
APH.......... Automatic Parts Handler
APH.......... Automotive Planner's Handbook
APH.......... Aviator's Protective Helmet (NG)
APH.......... Bowling Green, VA [*Location identifier*] [*FAA*] (FAAL)
APH.......... Fort Hood Post Library, Library Service Center, Fort Hood, TX [*OCLC symbol*] (OCLC)
a-ph--- .... Philippines [*MARC geographic area code*] [*Library of Congress*] (LCCP)
APH.......... Transport [*Fitted to evacuate wounded*] [*Navy ship symbol*] [*Obsolete*]
APHA .... American Paint Horse Association (EA)
APHA .... American Performance Horse Association (EA)
APhA .... American Pharmaceutical Association (EA)
APHA .... American Pinto Horse Association (EA)
APHA .... American Polled Hereford Association (EA)
APHA .... American Printing History Association (EA)
APHA .... American Protestant Health Association (EA)
APHA .... American Public Health Association (EA)
APHA .... American Public Health Association. Public Health Education. Section Newsletter [*A publication*]
APHA .... Associate of Public Health Association

APhA-ASP ... [*American Pharmaceutical Association*]-Academy of Students of Pharmacy (EA)
APhAP....... Archives de Philologie. Academie Polonaise des Sciences et des Lettres [*A publication*]
A Pharm..... Archiv der Pharmazie [*A publication*]
A Pharm Hung ... Acta Pharmaceutica Hungarica [*A publication*]
A Pharm Int ... Acta Pharmaceutica Internationalia [*A publication*]
APHB .... American Printing House for the Blind
APHB .... Army Pearl Harbor Board [*World War II*]
ApHC......... Appaloosa Horse Club (EA)
APhC........ Association Pharmaceutique Canadienne [*Canadian Pharmaceutical Association*] (EAIO)
APHC .... Halls Creek [*Australia*] [*ICAO location identifier*] (ICLI)
APHC .... Partech Holdings Corp. [*NASDAQ symbol*] (NQ)
APHCA ...... Annales de Parasitologie Humaine et Comparee [*A publication*]
APH-CARL ... American Printing House for the Blind Central Automated Resource List [*Information service or system*] (CRD)
APhD........ Acta Philologica. Societas Academica Dacoromana [*A publication*]
APHE .... Armor-Piercing High Explosive [*Ammunition*]
Aphe......... Audiophile [*Record label*]
APHEX ...... Aural Perception Heterodyne Exciter [*Inter-Technology Exchange Ltd.*] [*Psychoacoustics*]
APHF .... American Poultry and Hatchery Federation [*Later, PEIA*] (EA)
APHFFF.... Ames Prototype Hypersonic Free Flight Facility (KSC)
APHGAO ... Acta Pharmaceutica Hungarica [*A publication*]
APHH........ Port Hedland [*Australia*] [*ICAO location identifier*] (ICLI)
APHHDU ... Acta Physiologica Hungarica [*A publication*]
APHI .... Association of Public Health Inspectors
APHIA ...... Association for the Promotion of Humor in International Affairs (EA)
APhilos ..... Archives de Philosophie [*A publication*]
APHIS....... Animal and Plant Health Inspection Service [*Department of Agriculture*] [*Also, an information service or system*] (IID)
APHLC...... All-Party Hill Leaders' Conference [*India*] [*Political party*] (PPW)
APHMA8 .. Advances in Pharmaceutical Sciences [*A publication*]
A Ph Ph K ... Annalen der Philosophie und Philosophischen Kritik [*A publication*]
APHRA...... Ars Pharmaceutica [*A publication*]
APHRDQ.. Archives of Pharmacal Research [*Seoul*] [*A publication*]
APHRO...... Aphrodisiac [*Medicine*] (ROG)
APhS.......... Acta Philologica Scandinavica. Tidsskrift foer Nordisk Sprogforskning [*A publication*]
APHS .... American Photographic Historical Society (EA)
APHS .... American Poultry Historical Society (EA)
APHS .... Antique Powercraft Historical Society [*Defunct*] (EA)
A Ph S .... Asian Philosophical Studies [*A publication*]
APHS .... Australian Printing Historical Society
A Ph Sc ...... Acta Philologica Scandinavica [*A publication*]
APHYC ...... Applied Physics [*A publication*]
A Phys Pol ... Acta Physica Polonica [*A publication*]
A Phys Pol ... Acta Physiologica Polonica [*A publication*]
A Phys Scand ... Acta Physiologica Scandinavica [*A publication*]
A Phytother ... Acta Phytotherapeutica [*A publication*]
API............. Absolute Position Indication [*Nuclear energy*] (NRCH)
API............. Academic Press, Incorporated [*Publishers*] (MCD)
API............. Accel International Corp. Productivity Interface [*Data processing*] (BYTE)
API............. Accelerator Pedal with Idler [*Automotive engineering*]
API............. Acceptable Periodic Inspection
API............. Accountants for the Public Interest [*Washington, DC*]
API............. Accurate Position Indicator
API............. Advanced Performance Interceptor
API............. Advanced Procurement Information (MCD)
API............. Affective Perception Inventory [*Student personality test*]
API............. Air Position Indicator [*Air Force*]
API............. Alabama Polytechnic Institute (MCD)
API............. Alignment Progress Indicator (KSC)
API............. Allied Pacific Investments Ltd.
API............. Alternative Press Index [*A publication*]
API............. Amalgamated Publishers, Incorporated
API............. American Paper Institute (EA)
API............. American Paramedical Institute [*Hawaii*]
API............. American Petroleum Institute (EA)
API............. American Photonics, Incorporated [*Brookfield Center, CT*] (TSSD)
API............. American Pistol Institute (EA)
API............. American Potash Institute [*Later, PPI*] (EA)
API............. American Poultry International (EA)
API............. American Prepaid Legal Services Institute (EA)
API............. American Press Institute
API............. American Psychical Institute
API............. Americans for Progressive Israel (EA)
API............. AMP Exploration & Mining Co. Ltd. [*Vancouver Stock Exchange symbol*]
API............. Amyloplast Pressure Index [*Botany*]
API............. Analytical Profile Index [*Microbiology*]
API............. Angle Position Indicator
API............. Animal Protection Institute of America (EA)

API............ Annali della Pubblica Istruzione [*A publication*]
API............ Antecedent Precipitation Index
API............ Antenna Position Indicator
API............ Anthocyanin Pigmented Juices [*Food technology*]
API............ Apia [*Samoa Islands*] [*Seismograph station code, US Geological Survey*] (SEIS)
API............ Apia [*Samoa Islands*] [*Geomagnetic observatory code*]
API............ Application Program Interface [*Data processing*] (BUR)
API............ Appreciation of Capital, Protection, Income [*Finance*]
API............ Archconfraternity of Prayer for Israel (EA)
API............ Architectural Periodicals Index [*Royal Institute of British Architects*] [*Information service or system*] (IID)
API............ Armor-Piercing Incendiary [*Ammunition*]
API............ Associate of the Plastics Institute [*British*]
API............ Associated Paper Industries [*British*]
API............ Associated Photographers International (EA)
API............ Association Phonetique Internationale [*International Phonetic Association*]
API............ Association des Producteurs d'Isoglucose de la CE [*Association of the Producers of Isoglucose of the European Community*] [*Common Market*]
API............ Astro-Psychology Institute (EA)
API............ Atmospheric Pressure Ionization [*Physics*]
API............ Automated Pronunciation Instructor
API............ Automatic Priority Interrupt [*Data processing*]
API............ Automatic Programming Instruction [*Data processing*]
API............ Aviation Professionals International [*New Orleans*]
API............ Import Identification Number [*Indonesia*] (IMH)
APIA......... Antitrust Procedural Improvements Act of 1980
APIA......... Association pour la Promotion Industrie - Agriculture [*Association for the Promotion of Industry - Agriculture*] (EAIO)
APIA......... Australian Pipeline Industry Association
APIA......... Australian Poultry Industry Association
Apiary Circ BC Dep Agric ... Apiary Circular. British Columbia Department of Agriculture [*A publication*]
Apiary Circ (Victoria) ... Apiary Circular (Victoria) [*A publication*]
APIB......... Applications Program Integration Board [*NASA*]
APIC......... Alliance des Patriotes Independants du Congo [*Alliance of Independent Patriots of the Congo*]
APIC......... Alliance des Proletaires Independants du Congo [*Alliance of Independent Proletarians of the Congo*]
APIC......... Allied Press Information Center [*NATO*] (NATG)
APIC......... American Pacific International [*NASDAQ symbol*] (NQ)
APIC......... American Political Items Collectors (EA)
APIC......... Analytical Processing for Improved Composite (MCD)
APIC......... Apiculture
APIC......... Apollo Parts Information Center [*NASA*] (MCD)
APIC......... Army Photo Interpretation Center
APIC......... Association for Practitioners in Infection Control (EA)
APIC......... Association pour la Protection des Interets des Consommateurs [*Association for the Protection of Consumer Interests*] [*Canada*]
APIC......... Association of Psychology Internship Centers (EA)
APIC......... Automatic Power Input Controller
APIC......... Automatic Programming Information Centre [*British*]
APICA....... Association pour la Promotion des Initiatives Communautaires Africaines [*Association for the Promotion of African Community Initiatives - APACI*] (EAIO)
Apic Abstr ... Apicultural Abstracts [*Information service or system*] [*A publication*]
Apic Am ..... Apicultor Americano [*A publication*]
Apic Argent ... Apicultura Argentina [*A publication*]
APICE .... Asociacion Panamericana de Instituciones de Credito Educativo [*Pan American Association of Educational Credit Institutions - PAAECI*] (EAIO)
Apic Fr ...... Apiculture Francaise [*A publication*]
Apic Ital ..... Apicoltore d'Italia [*A publication*]
Apic Mod ... Apicoltore Moderno [*A publication*]
Apic Newsl Pl Ind Div Alberta Dep Agric ... Apiculture Newsletter. Plant Industry Division. Alberta Department of Agriculture [*A publication*]
Apic Nouv .. Apiculture Nouvelle [*A publication*]
Apicolt Ital ... Apicoltore d'Italia [*A publication*]
Apicolt Mod ... Apicoltore Moderno [*A publication*]
APICON.... Aircraft Position Information Converter [*Air Force*]
APICORP ... Arab Petroleum Investments Corporation [*of the Organization of Arab Petroleum Exporting Countries*]
APICP .... Association for the Promotion of the International Circulation of the Press [*Distipress*]
Apic Rom ... Apicultura in Romania [*A publication*]
APICS .... Air Pollution Information and Computation System
APICS .... American Production and Inventory Control Society (EA) ⏴
Apicult Abstr ... Apicultural Abstracts [*A publication*]
Apicult Alger ... Apiculteur Algerien [*A publication*]
Apicult Als-Lorr ... Apiculteur d'Alsace et de Lorraine [*A publication*]
Apicult Am ... Apicultor Americano [*A publication*]
Apicult Nord-Afr ... Apiculteur Nord-Africain [*A publication*]
Apic Venezol ... Apicultura Venezolana [*A publication*]
Apic W Aust ... Apiculture in Western Australia [*A publication*]
APID......... Army Photo Interpretation Detachment

APID......... Association of Photographic Importers and Distributors (EA)
APIE......... Antioch Program for Interracial Education [*Antioch College*] (EA)
APIE......... API Enterprises, Inc. [*Toronto, ON*] [*NASDAQ symbol*] (NQ)
APIE......... Atmospheric Pressure Ion Evaporation
APIF......... Aerodynamic Propulsive Interactive Force [*Air Force*]
APIF......... Automated Process Information File [*Library of Congress*]
API Food Add Ref ... American Paper Institute. Food Additives Reference Manual [*A publication*]
APIGAT .... Anuarul. Institutului de Patologie si Igiena Animala [*Bucuresti*] [*A publication*]
API-HH..... Americans for Progressive Israel - Hashomer Hatzair (EA)
APII .... Action Products International, Inc. [*NASDAQ symbol*] (NQ)
APIJ .... APIJ. Australian Planning Institute. Journal [*A publication*] (APTA)
API Journal ... Australian Planning Institute. Journal [*A publication*] (APTA)
APIL .... Axial Power Imbalance Limit (IEEE)
APILAS..... Armor-Piercing Infantry Light-Arm System [*Ammunition*]
APILIT...... API [*American Petroleum Institute*] Literature [*New York, NY*] [*Bibliographic database*]
APIM........ Association Professionnelle Internationale des Medicins [*International Professional Association of Physicians*]
API Med Res Publ ... American Petroleum Institute. Medical Research Publications [*A publication*]
APIN .... Alianza Popular de Integracion Nacional [*Bolivia*] [*Political party*] (PPW)
APIN .... Alpine International Corp. [*NASDAQ symbol*] (NQ)
APIN .... System of Computerized Processing of Scientific Information [*Technical University of Wroclaw*] [*Information service or system*] (IID)
API Newsprint Bull ... American Paper Institute. Newsprint Division. Bulletin [*A publication*]
AP Inf B ... Agerpres Information Bulletin [*A publication*]
APIO .... American Pioneer, Inc. [*NASDAQ symbol*] (NQ)
APIP .... Additional Personal Injury Protection [*Insurance*]
APIP .... AMDF [*Army Master Data File*] Positive Improvement Program (MCD)
APIP .... Apollo Personnel Identification [*or Investigation*] Program [*NASA*] (KSC)
APIP .... Associations' Publications in Print [*Database*] [*R. R. Bowker Co.*] [*Information service or system*] (CRD)
APIP .... Australian Periodicals in Print [*A publication*] (APTA)
APIPAM ... Australia. Commonwealth Scientific and Industrial Research Organisation. Division of Plant Industry. Technical Paper [*A publication*]
APIPOCC ... Appropriating Property in Possession of Common Carrier [*FBI standardized term*]
API Publ .... American Petroleum Institute. Publication [*A publication*]
APIR........ American Petroleum Institute Research (MCD)
APIRD...... Authorized Procurement Information Requirements Description [*NASA*] (NASA)
API Refining Dep Midyear Meet Prepr ... American Petroleum Institute. Refining Department. Midyear Meeting. Preprints [*A publication*]
APIRL....... Authorized Procurement Information Requirements List [*NASA*] (NASA)
APIRP .... American Petroleum Institute Research Project
APIS .... Approved Production Inspection System [*Manufacturing*] (MCD)
APIS .... Army Photographic Interpretation Section [*British*]
APIS .... Array Processing Instruction Set [*Data processing*] (MSA)
APIS .... Austrian Press and Information Service (EA)
API Statist Sum ... American Paper Institute. Monthly Statistical Summary [*A publication*]
APIT......... Armor-Piercing Incendiary Tracer [*Ammunition*]
APITCA .... American Producers of Italian Type Cheese Association (EA)
APIU .... Army Photo Interpretation Unit (NATG)
APIW........ Association of Professional Insurance Women [*Acronym is now organization's official name*] (EA)
API Wood Pulp Statist ... American Paper Institute. Wood Pulp Statistics [*A publication*]
APJ........... Aberdeen Press and Journal [*A publication*]
APJ........... American Paint and Coatings Journal [*A publication*]
APJ........... American Power Jet Co.
APJ........... Angle Panel Jack
Ap J........... Appenzellische Jahrbuecher [*A publication*]
APJ........... Appraisal Journal [*A publication*]
APJ........... Association for Public Justice (EA)
APJ........... Auspex Gold Ltd. [*Vancouver Stock Exchange symbol*]
APJ........... Public Library of Pine Bluff and Jefferson County, Pine Bluff, AR [*OCLC symbol*] (OCLC)
APJA........ Appliance Parts Jobbers Association [*Later, APDA*]
AP JC .... Apres Jesus-Christ [*After Christ*] [*French*]
APJE........ Association of Philosophy Journal Editors (EA)
APJEF....... Association for Public Justice Education Fund [*Later, CPJ*] (EA)
APJI .... Assistant Parachute Jump Instructor [*British military*] (DMA)
APJL......... Alpine Journal [*A publication*]
APJSA....... Astrophysical Journal. Supplement Series [*A publication*]
APJT .... Perth/Jandakot [*Australia*] [*ICAO location identifier*] (ICLI)
APJUA8.... Acta Pharmaceutica Jugoslavica [*A publication*]

Ap Just...... Apud Justinianum [*Latin*] (DLA)
Ap Justin ... Apud Justinianum [*Latin*] (DLA)
APK .... Accelerometer Package (KSC)
APK .... Amplitude Phase Shift Keying (MCD)
APK .... Angel's Peak [*Nevada*] [*Seismograph station code, US Geological Survey*] (SEIS)
APK .... Apataki [*French Polynesia*] [*Airport symbol*] (OAG)
APK .... Apple Bancorp., Inc. [*NYSE symbol*] (SPSG)
APK .... Arbetarpartiet Kommunisterna [*Communist Workers' Party*] [*Sweden*] (PPE)
APK .... Astronaut Preference Kit [*NASA*]
APK .... Aufsaetze zur Portugiesischen Kulturgeschichte [*A publication*]
APK .... Fort Campbell Post Library, Fort Campbell, KY [*OCLC symbol*] (OCLC)
a-pk--- ...... Pakistan [*MARC geographic area code*] [*Library of Congress*] (LCCP)
APKA .... Karratha [*Australia*] [*ICAO location identifier*] (ICLI)
APKCA ...... Allgemeine und Praktische Chemie [*A publication*]
APKCA ...... Associated Pot and Kettle Clubs of America [*Later, IPKC*] (EA)
APKD .... Adult-Onset Polycystic Kidney Disease [*Medicine*]
APKG .... Kalgoorlie [*Australia*] [*ICAO location identifier*] (ICLI)
APKK .... An Party Kenethlegek Kernow (EA)
APKTAA... Archeia tes Pharmakeutikes (Athens) [*A publication*]
APKU .... Kununurra [*Australia*] [*ICAO location identifier*] (ICLI)
APL .... Acceptable Process Level
APL .... Acceptable Productivity Level [*Quality control*]
APL .... Acute Progranulocytic [*or Promyelocytic*] Leukemia [*Hematology*]
APL .... Aden Protectorate Levies [*British military*] (DMA)
APL .... Adjustment Payment Level [*Social Security Administration*]
APL .... Adult Performance Level Project (EA)
APL .... Advance Procurement List (MCD)
APL .... Advanced Programming Language [*Data processing*]
APL .... Aero-Propulsion Laboratory [*Air Force*]
APL .... Airplane (KSC)
APL .... Airport Lights (FAAC)
APL .... Akron-Summit County Public Library, Akron, OH [*OCLC symbol*] (OCLC)
APL .... Allowance Parts List
APL .... American Poetry League
APL .... American President Lines
APL .... Amygdala Pars Lateralis [*Neuroanatomy*]
APL .... Ancien Pays de Looz [*A publication*]
APL .... Angleplied Laminate
APL .... Annales Politiques et Litteraires [*A publication*]
APL .... Annales. Prince de Ligne [*A publication*]
APL .... Anterior Pituitary-Like [*Endocrinology*]
APL .... Antigen-Presenting Liposome [*Immunochemistry*]
APL .... Aperture Lip
APL .... Appalachian Flying Service, Inc. [*Blountville, TN*] [*FAA designator*] (FAAC)
APL .... Applied Physics Laboratory [*Johns Hopkins University*]
ApLR .... Approdo Letterario [*A publication*]
APL .... Approved Parts List
APL .... April
APL .... Archivo de Prehistoria Levantina [*A publication*]
A/PL .... Armor Plate (MUGU)
APL .... Army Personnel Letter (AABC)
APL .... Army Promotion List (AABC)
APL .... As per List
APL .... Assembly Part List
APL .... Assembly Programming Language [*Data processing*]
APL .... Association of Private Libraries (EA)
APL .... Association of Programmed Learning [*London, England*] (MCD)
APL .... Associative Programming Language [*Data processing*] (BUR)
APL .... Authorized Possession Limits [*Nuclear energy*] (NRCH)
APL .... Authorized Price List
APL .... Automatic Phase Lock
APL .... Automatic Premium Loan [*Insurance*]
APL .... Automatic Production Line
APL .... Automatic Programming Language [*Data processing*] (CMD)
APL .... Automotive Pigeon Loft
APL .... Average Picture Level
APL .... Aviation Psychology Laboratory [*Ohio State University*] [*Research center*] (RCD)
APL .... Barracks Craft [*Non-self-propelled*] [*Navy symbol*]
APL .... Minneapolis, MN [*Location identifier*] [*FAA*] (FAAL)
APL .... Nampula [*Mozambique*] [*Airport symbol*] (OAG)
APL .... Plamondon Public Library, Alberta [*Library symbol*] [*National Library of Canada*] (NLC)
APL .... [*A*] Programming Language [*1960*] [*Data processing*] (CSR)
APLA .... American Patent Law Association [*Later, AIPLA*] (EA)
APLA .... Armenian Progressive League of America (EA)
APLA .... Arrowhead Professional Libraries Association [*Library network*]
APLA .... Asia-Pacific Lawyers Association
APLA .... Association of Parliamentary Librarians of Australasia
APLA .... Atlantic Provinces Linguistic Association [*Canada*]
APLA .... Authors' and Publishers' Lending Right Association Committee

APLA .... Aviation Pilot, Airship [*Navy*]
APLA .... Azanian People's Liberation Army [*South Africa*] (ECON)
APLA Bull ... Atlantic Provinces Library Association. Bulletin [*A publication*]
APLA Bull ... Bulletin. American Patent Law Association [*A publication*] (DLA)
APLAC ...... Analysis Program Linear Active Circuits (NASA)
Ap Laic ..... Apostolado Laico [*A publication*]
APLA QJ... APLA [*American Patent Law Association*] Quarterly Journal [*A publication*]
APLB .... Australian Property Law Bulletin [*A publication*]
APLC .... American Pro Life Council (EA)
APLC .... Army Propulsion Laboratory and Center (KSC)
APLC .... Assistant Poor Law Commissioner [*British*] (ROG)
APLC .... Automated Parking Lot Control (MCD)
APLC .... Leigh Creek [*Australia*] [*ICAO location identifier*] (ICLI)
APL Cas .... Archbold's Poor Law Cases [*1842-58*] [*A publication*] (DLA)
APL/CAT ... [*A*] Public Library/Community Access Tool [*Acronym used by Community Information Database*] [*Dallas Public Library*] [*Texas*] [*Information service or system*] (IID)
APL/CID... Allowance Parts List/Component Identification Number
APLCN...... Appalachian [*FAA*] (FAAC)
APLD........ Applied (MSA)
APLET ...... Association for Programmed Learning and Educational Technology
AP Lev ...... Archivo de Prehistoria Levantina [*A publication*]
APLF .... Alliance of Progressive and Left-Wing Forces [*Greek*] (PPE)
APLHGR... Average Planar Heat Generation Rate [*Nuclear energy*] (NRCH)
APLI .... AUI Peace Language International (EA)
APLIC ...... Association of Parliamentary Librarians in Canada
APLIC ...... Association for Population/Family Planning Libraries and Information Centers - International [*Also, an information service or system*] (IID)
APLIC-Intl ... Association for Population/Family Planning Libraries and Information Centers, International (EA)
APLIS........ Australasian Public Libraries and Information Services [*A publication*]
ApLit.......... Apocalyptic Literature [*A publication*]
APL/JHU ... Applied Physics Laboratory/Johns Hopkins University
APL JHU SR ... Applied Physics Laboratory. Johns Hopkins University. Special Report [*A publication*]
APLM........ Learmonth [*Australia*] [*ICAO location identifier*] (ICLI)
APLMAS .. Archives of Pathology and Laboratory Medicine [*A publication*]
Apl Mat ..... Aplikace Matematiky [*A publication*]
APLMI ...... Allowance Parts List Master Index (MCD)
APLN .... Apollo Program Logic Network [*NASA*] (KSC)
APLO .... Aerial Port Liaison Office [*or Officer*] [*Air Force*] (AFM)
APLO .... Aerial Port Logistics Office [*Air Force*]
APLO .... Alaska Apollo Gold Mines Ltd. [*NASDAQ symbol*] (NQ)
APLPB ..... Advances in Plasma Physics [*A publication*]
APLQ......... Agence de Presse Libre du Quebec [*Free Press Agency of Quebec*] [*Canada*]
APLQ......... Applique (MSA)
APLR......... Australian Product Liability Reporter [*A publication*]
APLRDC.... Advances in Polyamine Research [*A publication*]
APLS .... Administrator Professional Leadership Scale
APLS .... American Plant Life Society (EA)
APLS .... American Private Line Services, Inc. [*Newton, MA*] [*Telecommunications*] (TSSD)
AP-LS........ American Psychology-Law Society (EA)
APLS .... Apparel Performance Level Standards [*Pronounced "apples"*]
APLS .... Association for Politics and the Life Sciences (EA)
APL/S........ [*A*] Programming Language/Structured [*Data processing*] (CSR)
APLSA ..... Annales de Chirurgie Plastique [*A publication*]
APLSDF.... Aspects of Plant Sciences [*A publication*]
APLSTATPACK ... Advanced Programming Language Statistical Package (MCD)
APLSV ...... [*A*] Programming Language Shared Variables [*Data processing*]
APLTAF.... Acta Physiologica Latinoamericana [*A publication*]
APL Tech Dig ... APL [*Applied Physics Laboratory*] Technical Digest [*A publication*]
APLU......... Automatic Program Loading Unit [*Data processing*]
APLUM..... [*A*] Programming Language/University of Massachusetts [*Data processing*] (CSR)
APL/UW... Applied Physics Laboratory/University of Washington
APLY......... Applied Microbiology, Inc. [*Brooklyn, NY*] [*NASDAQ symbol*] (NQ)
APM .... Academy of Parapsychology and Medicine (EA)
APM .... Academy of Psychosomatic Medicine (EA)
APM .... Acid-Precipitable Material [*Antiviral agent*]
APM .... Acoustic Performance Monitor
APM .... Acquisition Project Manager
APM .... Advanced Penetration Model (MCD)
APM .... Advanced Progressive Matrices [*Intelligence test*]
APM .... African People's Movement [*London, England*]
APM .... Agricultural Production and Management
APM .... Aim-Point-Miss
APM .... Air Particulate Matter [*Environmental science*]
APM .... Air Particulate Monitor [*Nuclear energy*] (NRCH)
APM .... Air Permeability Meter

APM .... Air Pollution Meteorologist (NOAA)
APM .... Air Provost Marshal
APM .... Airpac, Inc. [Anchorage, AK] [FAA designator] (FAAC)
APM .... Alarm Panel Monitor (AFM)
APM .... Alfalfa Pest Management
APM .... Aluminum Powder Metallurgy
APM .... American People's Mobilization [Formerly, American Peace Mobilization] [World War II]
APM .... American Prison Ministry [An association] (EA)
APM .... Aminopimelic Acid [An amino acid]
APM .... Aminopropylmorpholine [Organic chemistry]
APM .... Amiprophos Methyl [Organic chemistry]
APM .... Amygdala Pars Medialis [Neuroanatomy]
APM .... Analog Panel Meter (IEEE)
APM .... Antenna Positioning Mechanism
APM .... Antipersonnel Missile
APM .... Anuario de Prehistoria Madrilena [A publication]
APM .... Applied Magnetics Corp. [NYSE symbol] (SPSG)
APM .... Army Program Memorandum (AABC)
APM .... Aspartame [Sweetening agent]
APM .... Assistant Paymaster [Marine Corps]
APM .... Assistant Project Manager [NASA] (NASA)
APM .... Assistant Provost Marshal [Facetious translation: "A Permanent Malingerer"]
APM .... Association of Professors of Medicine (EA)
APM .... Association of Professors of Mission (EA)
APM .... Association for Psychoanalytic Medicine (EA)
APM .... Associative Principle for Multiplication [Mathematics]
APM .... Australian Pacific Minerals
APM .... Australian Personnel Management [A publication] (APTA)
APM .... Australian Police Medal
APM .... Automated Performance Measurement (MCD)
APM .... Automated Plate Measuring [for Spectrography]
APM .... Automatic Programming Machine [Data processing]
APM .... Auxiliary Pastoral Ministry [Church of England]
APM .... Mechanized Artillery Transport [Navy symbol] [Obsolete]
APM .... Pro Musica [Record label]
APMA ...... Absorbent Paper Manufacturers Association [Defunct]
APMA ...... Advance Payment of Mileage Authorized [Army]
APMA ...... American Paper Machinery Association (EA)
APMA ...... American Podiatric Medical Association (EA)
APMA ...... American Podiatric Medical Students Association (EA)
APMA ...... American Productivity Management Association [Skokie, IL] (EA)
APMA ...... Aminophenylmercuric Acid [Organic chemistry]
APMA ...... Asia/Pacific Market Analysis [MMS International] [Information service or system] (CRD)
APMA ...... Australian Pharmaceutical Manufacturers Association
APMA ...... Automatic Phonograph Manufacturers Association
APMAA .... American Podiatric Medical Association Auxiliary (EA)
APMALTA ... Advance Payment of Monetary Allowance in Lieu of Transportation Is Authorized [Army]
APMAST .. Analysis of Packing Methods for Ammunition Storage and Transportation (MCD)
APMBA..... Assistant Project Manager for Business Administration
APMBAY ... Applied Microbiology [A publication]
APMC .... Academy of Psychologists in Marital Counseling [Later, APMSFT]
APMC .... Allied Political and Military Commission [World War II]
APMCA..... American Phonemeter Cl A [NASDAQ symbol] (NQ)
APMCA3... Anais Paulistas de Medicina e Cirurgia [A publication]
APMCB4... Annales Pharmaceutici [Poznan] [A publication]
APMCC5... Applied Mathematics and Computation [A publication]
A/P MCU ... Autopilot Monitor and Control Unit
APMDA6 .. Annals of Physical Medicine [A publication]
APME....... Area Precipitation Measurement Equipment
APME....... Associated Press Managing Editors (EA)
APME....... Association of Plastics Manufacturers in Europe (EA)
APME....... Association Professionnelle de Mesure en Education [Professional Association of Educational Measures] [Canada]
APME....... Associative Processor Microelectronic Element
ApMec ...... Applied Mechanics Reviews [A publication]
APMEDC ... Applied Psychological Measurement [A publication]
APMG .... Assistant Postmaster-General [British]
APMH....... Association of Professions for the Mentally Handicapped [British]
APMHAI .. Archives of Physical Medicine and Rehabilitation [A publication]
APMHC .... Association of Professional Material Handling Consultants (EA)
APMI........ American Powder Metallurgy Institute (EA)
APMI........ Area Precipitation Measurement Indicator (IEEE)
APMI........ Associate Member of the Pensions Management Institute [British] (DBQ)
APMIAL ... Acta Pathologica et Microbiologica Scandinavica [A publication]
APMIBM .. Acta Pathologica et Microbiologica Scandinavica. Section B. Microbiology and Immunology [A publication]
ApMicrobiol ... Applied Microbiology [Later, Applied and Environmental Microbiology] [A publication]

APMIS ...... Acta Pathologica, Microbiologica, et Immunologica Scandinavica [A publication]
APMIS ...... Automated Project Management Information System [Data processing]
APML........ Assistant Project Manager for Logistics
APMMRI ... Automatic Point Marking, Measuring, and Recording Instrument
APMNHOP ... Alberta Provincial Museum. Natural History. Occasional Paper [Canada] [A publication]
A/P MON ... Autopilot Monitor (AAG)
APMP........ Aluminum Powder Metallurgy Product
APMPPE .. Acute Posterior Multifocal Placoid Pigment Epitheliopathy [Ophthalmology]
APMR .... Ancient Philosophies for Modern Readers [A publication]
APMR .... Association for Physical and Mental Rehabilitation [Later, ACTA] (EA)
APMR .... Meekatharra [Australia] [ICAO location identifier] (ICLI)
APMS........ Advanced Power Management System [Jammer] (MCD)
APMS........ Airborne Particle Monitoring System (MCD)
APMS........ Altpreussische Monatschrift [A publication]
APMS........ Aquatic Plant Management Society (EA)
APMS........ Assistant Professor of Military Science (INF)
APMSDK .. Archives of Podiatric Medicine and Foot Surgery [A publication]
APMSFT... Academy of Psychologists in Marital Sex and Family Therapy (EA)
APMT........ Advanced Planetary Mission Technology [NASA]
APMT........ Antenna Pattern Measurement Test [Army] (AABC)
APMT........ Associated Professional Massage Therapists and Bodyworkers [Later, ABMP] (EA)
APMUAN ... Acta Pathologica et Microbiologica Scandinavica. Supplementum [A publication]
ApMV........ Apple Mosaic Virus
APMWA ... American Podiatric Medical Writers Association (EA)
APN .... Agentstvo Pechati Novosti [News agency] [USSR]
APN .... Aircraft Procurement, Navy (NVT)
APN .... Aircraft Pulse Navigation
APN .... All Pass Network
APN .... Alpena [Michigan] [Airport symbol] (OAG)
APN .... Apron [Aviation]
APN .... Armenian Express Canada [Vancouver Stock Exchange symbol]
APN .... Army Part Number (MCD)
APN .... Artificial Pneumothorax [Medicine]
APN .... Aspen Airways [Air carrier designation symbol]
APN .... Assyrian Personal Names [A publication] (BJA)
APN .... Australian Property News [A publication] (ADA)
APN .... Authorized Part Number
APN .... Aviation Procurement, Navy (MCD)
APn .... Die Aegyptischen Personnennamen [A publication] (BJA)
APN .... Nonmechanized Artillery Transport [Navy symbol] [Obsolete]
APNA .... American Power Net Association [Later, EFMCNTA] (EA)
APNA .... Atlantic Provinces Numismatic Association [Canada]
APNAA ..... Arhiv za Poljoprivredne Nauke [A publication]
APNAA2 ... Arhiv za Poljoprivredne Nauke [A publication]
APNC .... Administration du Pipeline du Nord Canada [Northern Pipeline Agency Canada - NPAC]
APNDAB... Anales de Parques Nacionales [Buenos Aires] [A publication]
APNEU ..... Auxiliary Pneumatic (AAG)
APNG .... Australia - Papua New Guinea [Submarine cable] [Telecommunications] (TEL)
APNGBCC ... Australia-Papua New Guinea Business Cooperation Committee
APNI .... Alliance Party of Northern Ireland [Political party] (EAIO)
APNIC....... Automatic Programming National Information Center
APNL .... Army Personnel Newsletter
APNM .... Amorite Personal Names in the Mari Texts [A publication] (BJA)
APNPA...... Archivio di Psicologia, Neurologia, e Psichiatria [A publication]
APNPAD... Archivio di Psicologia, Neurologia, e Psichiatria [A publication]
ApNPM ..... Apel. Notation of Polyphonic Music [A publication]
APNPS...... Acetyl(p-nitrophenyl)sulfanilamide [Pharmacology]
APNR .... American Professional Needlework Retailers (EA)
APNR .... Association for the Protection of Native Races [Australia]
APNRP...... American-Polish National Relief for Poland (EA)
APNSS...... American Plate Number Single Society (EA)
APNT .... Appoint (FAAC)
APNTAP... Arhiv za Poljoprivredne Nauke i Tehniku [A publication]
APNVAV... Archiv fuer Psychiatrie und Nervenkrankheiten [A publication]
APO.......... Accountable Property Officer [Military]
APO.......... Accounting Property Officer
APO.......... Acting Pilot Officer [British]
APO.......... Adriamycin, Prednisone, Oncovin [Vincristine] [Antineoplastic drug regimen]
APO.......... Advanced Post Office [Military]
APO.......... Advisory Panel for Oceanography [National Science Foundation] (MSC)
APO.......... Air Force Post Office
APO.......... Air Post Office (MCD)
APO.......... Air Procurement Office
APO.......... Air Programs Office [Environmental Protection Agency]
APO.......... Amorphous Polyolefin [Organic chemistry]

APO........... Andean Pact Organization [*Chile, Peru, Bolivia, Ecuador. Colombia*]
APO........... Animal Procurement Office [*Military*]
APO........... Annual Program Objectives [*Navy*]   (NG)
APO........... Apartado [*Colombia*] [*Airport symbol*]   (OAG)
APO........... Aphoxide [*Also, TEPA*] [*Mutagen*]
APO........... APO. The Australian Post Office Magazine [*A publication*]   (APTA)
APO.......... Apogee
Apo............. Apolipoprotein [*Biochemistry*]
Apo............. Apollo [*A publication*]
APO........... Apollo Program Office [*NASA*]   (KSC)
APO........... Apomorphine [*Neurochemistry, pharmacology*]
Apot........... Apoprotein [*Biochemistry*]
APO........... Area Petroleum Office [*or Officer*]
APO.......... Army Post Office
APO........... Asian Productivity Organization   (EAIO)
APO........... Asociacion Panamericana de Oftalmologia [*Panamerican Association of Ophthalmology*] [*Washington, DC*]
APO........... Assembly Production Order [*Manufacturing*]   (AAG)
APO........... Assistant Project Officer
APO........... Astrophysical Observatory [*Smithsonian Museum*]
APO........... Attach Points Only   (MCD)
APO........... Australian Patents Office
APO........... Ponoka Public Library, Alberta [*Library symbol*] [*National Library of Canada*]   (NLC)
APO........... Tris(aziridinyl)phosphine Oxide [*Organic chemistry*]
APOA........ APOA [*Arctic Petroleum Operators Association*] Review [*A publication*]
ApoA.......... Apolipoprotein A [*Biochemistry*]
APOA........ Arctic Petroleum Operators' Association [*Canada*]
APOAF...... All Present or Accounted For
APOAM..... Acting Petty Officer Air Mechanic [*British military*]   (DMA)
APOAR...... APOA [*Arctic Petroleum Operators Association*] Reports [*A publication*]
APOBA...... Associated Pipe Organ Builders of America   (EA)
APOC........ Aerial Port Operations Center
Apoc........... Apocalypse
Apoc........... Apocalyptic   (BJA)
Apoc........... Apocrypha   (BJA)
ApoC.......... Apolipoprotein C [*Biochemistry*]
APOC........ Army Point of Contact   (AABC)
APOC........ Army Post Office Corps [*British military*]   (DMA)
APOC........ Association of Postal Officials of Canada
APOCA...... Acta Polytechnica. Chemistry Including Metallurgy Series [*A publication*]
ApocAbr..... Apocalypse of Abraham   (BJA)
APOC BAR ... Apocalypse of Baruch [*Apocalyptic book*]
ApocElij.... Apocalypse of Elijah   (BJA)
ApocGen .... [*The*] Genesis Apocryphon from Qumran. Cave One   (BJA)
APOCH...... Apocrypha   (ROG)
ApocMos .. Apocalypse of Moses   (BJA)
Apocol........ Apocolocyntosis [*of Seneca the Younger*] [*Classical studies*]   (OCD)
ApocPet ..... Apocalypse of Peter   (BJA)
APOCR...... Apocrypha
Apocr .... [*The*] Genesis Apocryphon from Qumran. Cave One   (BJA)
APOD........ Aerial Port of Debarkation [*Military*]
APOD........ Australian Pocket Oxford Dictionary [*A publication*]   (APTA)
APOE........ Aerial Port of Embarkation [*Military*]
ApoE.......... Apolipoprotein E [*Biochemistry*]
APOFDF ... Application of Filters to Demand Forecasting   (MCD)
APOG........ Aerial Port Group [*Air Force*]   (AFM)
APOG........ Apogee
APOG........ Apogee Enterprises, Inc. [*NASDAQ symbol*]   (NQ)
APOGI...... Advanced Polaris Guidance Information
APOJA...... American Potato Journal [*A publication*]
APOJAY.... American Potato Journal [*A publication*]
APOJI .... Automatic Processing of Jezebel [*Sonobuoy System*] Information
APOL .... Apollo Savings & Loan Co. [*NASDAQ symbol*]   (NQ)
Apol............ Apologeticus [*of Tertullian*] [*Classical studies*]   (OCD)
Apol............ Apologia [*of Apuleius*] [*Classical studies*]   (OCD)
APOL .... Australian Political Register [*Australian Consolidated Press*] [*Database*]
A Pol Econ ... Annee Politique et Economique [*A publication*]
A Pol J .... Australian Police Journal [*A publication*]
APOLLO... Article Procurement with Online Local Ordering [*Document delivery system*] [*Telecommunications*]
Apollod ...... Apollodorus [*Second century BC*] [*Classical studies*]   (OCD)
A Polona .... Archaeologia Polona [*A publication*]
A Polski .... Archeologia Polski [*A publication*]
A Polytechn ... Acta Polytechnica [*A publication*]
APOMA .... American Precision Optics Manufacturers Association   (EA)
APOMS.... Automated Propeller Optical Measurement System
APON .... Association of Pediatric Oncology Nurses   (EA)
APOP .... Apollo Preflight Operations Procedures [*NASA*]   (KSC)
APOP .... Applied Optics, Inc. [*Kensington, MD*] [*NASDAQ symbol*]   (NQ)
APOPA...... Association of Private Office Personnel Agencies

APOPEC ... Agence de Presse de l'OPEC [*OPEC News Agency - OPECNA*] [*Vienna, Austria*]   (EAIO)
Apophth ..... Apophthegmata [*of Julian*] [*Classical studies*]   (OCD)
Ap Optics... Applied Optics [*A publication*]
APOR........ Advisory Panel for Operations Research
APORA ..... Advances in Physical Organic Chemistry [*A publication*]
APORS...... Army Performance-Oriented Review and Standards Program
APORS...... Army Performance-Oriented Reviews and Standards
A Port......... O Arqueologo Portugues [*A publication*]
APOS........ Advanced Polar Orbiting Satellite
APOS........ Advanced Polymer Systems, Inc. [*NASDAQ symbol*]   (NQ)
APOS........ Apostrophe
APOS........ Cocos Islands [*Australia*] [*ICAO location identifier*]   (ICLI)
apost........... Apostolic   (BJA)
APOSW..... Association of Pediatric Oncology Social Workers   (EA)
APOT .... [*The*] Apocrypha and Pseudepigrapha of the Old Testament [*A publication*]   (BJA)
APOTA ..... Automatic Positioning Telemetering Antenna
APOTH..... Apothecary
Apothekerprakt Pharm Tech Assist ... Apothekerpraktikant und Pharmazeutisch-Technischer Assistent [*A publication*]
Apoth Ztg... Apotheker-Zeitung [*A publication*]
Apoth Ztg (Hanslian Ed) ... Apotheker-Zeitung (Hanslian Edition) [*A publication*]
APOTV..... All Propulsive Orbited Transfer Vehicle [*NASA*]
APOW....... Ampower Instrument [*NASDAQ symbol*]   (NQ)
APP........... A Posteriori Probability   (MCD)
APP........... Abandoned Private Property
APP........... Academy of Pharmacy Practice   (EA)
APP........... Access Point Pace   (KSC)
APP........... Accion Politica Progresista [*Progressive Political Action*] [*Ecuador*] [*Political party*]   (PPW)
APP........... Acid-Precipitated Protein [*Food analysis*]
APP........... Acoustic Performance Prediction [*Navy*]   (MSC)
APP........... Acquisition Plan (Procurement)
APP........... Advance Port Purchase [*Investment term*]   (ECON)
APP........... Advance Procurement Plan [*Navy*]
APP........... Advanced Parts Procurement   (MCD)
APP........... Advanced Placement Program
APP........... Advanced Planetary Probe
APP........... Advanced Procurement Package   (MCD)
APP........... Advanced Procurement Plan [*Navy*] [*British*]
APP........... Advanced Project Planning
APP........... Air Parcel Post [*Shipping*]   (AABC)
APP........... Air Pollution Potential
APP........... All Purpose Paper [*Euphemism for toilet paper*]
APP........... Allied Procedures Publications   (NATG)
APP........... Allopurinol Phosphate [*Biochemistry*]
APP........... Alternative Pink Pages. Australasian Plant Pathology [*A publication*]   (APTA)
APP........... Aminopyrazolopyrimidine [*Biochemistry*]
APP........... Ammonium Polyphosphate [*Fertilizer*]
APP........... Ammunition Post Processor [*Data processing*] [*Military*]
APP........... Amorphous Polypropylene [*Organic chemistry*]
APP........... Amortization and Partial Prepayment [*Business term*]
APP........... Amyloid Protein Precursor [*Biochemistry*]
APP........... Analysis Production Persistency [*LIMRA*]
APP........... Ancient Peoples and Places [*A publication*]
APP........... Anguilla People's Party [*Later, ADP*] [*Political party*]   (PPW)
APP........... Antenna Position Programmer [*Manned Space Flight Network*]
APP........... Antipersonnel Projectile
APP........... Antipodal Propagation Phenomena
APP........... Apache Petroleum [*NYSE symbol*]   (SPSG)
APP........... Apostles
APP........... Apparatus   (KSC)
APP........... Apparently
APP........... Appeal   (ADA)
App .... Appeal Cases [*A publication*]   (DLA)
APP........... Appearance   (MSA)
APP........... Appelbo [*Sweden*] [*Seismograph station code, US Geological Survey*]   (SEIS)
APP........... Appellate [*Legal term*]   (DLA)
APP........... Append [*or Appendix*]   (AFM)
App .... Appian [*Second century AD*] [*Classical studies*]   (OCD)
App .... Appleton's Reports [*19, 20 Maine*]
APP........... Application
APP........... Application Date [*Bell System*]   (TEL)
APP........... Applied
APP........... Applied Psychology Panel [*of NDRC*] [*World War II*]
APP........... Appointed
APP........... Apprehend   (AABC)
APP........... Apprentice
APP........... Approach [*A publication*]
APP........... Approach
APP........... Approach Astrophysics Payload [*NASA*]   (MCD)
APP........... Approach Control Office [*Aviation code*]
APP........... Appropriated   (ROG)
APP........... Approval   (ADA)
APP........... Approximate
APP........... Army Procurement Procedure
APP........... Ashford Press Publishing [*British*]

APP............ Asia Pacific Capital Corp. [*Vancouver Stock Exchange symbol*]
APP............ Associated Press of Pakistan
APP............ Associated Purchasing Publications
APP............ Association of Pakistani Physicians (EA)
APP............ Association of Professional Photogrammetrists (EA)
APP............ Associative Parallel Processor [*Data processing*]
APP............ Astrophysics Payload [*NASA*] (MCD)
APP............ Atactic Polypropylene [*Organic chemistry*]
APP............ Automatic Plate Processor
APP............ Automatic Position Planning
APP............ Auxiliary Pneumatics Panel
APP............ Auxiliary Power Package (MCD)
APP............ Auxiliary Power Plant
APP............ Avian Pancreatic Polypeptide
APP............ Axactic Polypropylene
APP............ Fort McPherson Library System, Fort McPherson, GA [*OCLC symbol*] (OCLC)
App .... Illinois Appellate Court Reports [*A publication*] (DLA)
App .... Ohio Appellate Reports [*A publication*] (DLA)
a-pp--- .... Papua New Guinea [*MARC geographic area code*] [*Library of Congress*] (LCCP)
App .... Texas Court of Appeals Reports [*A publication*] (DLA)
APP............ Troop Barge, Class A [*Navy symbol*] [*Obsolete*]
APPA........ Advise Present Position and Altitude [*Aviation*] (FAAC)
APPA........ American Paper and Pulp Association [*Later, API*]
APPA........ American Physicians Poetry Association (EA)
APPA........ American Probation and Parole Association (EA)
APPA........ American Professional Practice Association (EA)
APPA........ American Psychological Practitioners Association (EA)
APPA........ American Psychopathological Association (EA)
APPA........ American Public Power Association (EA)
APPA........ Association of Philippine Physicians in America (EA)
APPA........ Association of Physical Plant Administrators of Universities and Colleges (EA)
APPA........ Association for the Preservation of Political Americana (EA)
APPA........ Association for the Preservation and Presentation of the Arts
APPA........ Port Hedland [*Australia*] [*ICAO location identifier*] (ICLI)
APPAC...... Aviation Petroleum Products Allocation Committee
APPAC-L.. Aviation Petroleum Products Allocation Committee, London
Appalachia Mag ... Appalachia Magazine [*A publication*]
Appalachian Geol Soc Bull ... Appalachian Geological Society. Bulletin [*A publication*]
Appalach J ... Appalachian Journal [*A publication*]
Appal J ...... Appalachian Journal [*A publication*]
APPALLING ... Acronym Production Particularly at Lavish Level Is No Good [*Term coined by Theodore M. Bernstein*]
APPAM..... Association for Public Policy Analysis and Management (EA)
App Anal.... Applicable Analysis [*A publication*]
APPAR...... Apparatus (AFM)
APPAR...... Apparent
APPARAT ... Archive Preservation Programme and Retrieval by Automated Techniques [*Data processing*]
Apparecch Idraul Pneum ... Apparecchiature Idrauliche e Pneumatiche [*A publication*]
Apparel Int ... Apparel International [*A publication*]
Appar Mash Kislorodn Kriog Ustanovok ... Apparaty i Mashiny Kislorodnykh i Kriogennykh Ustanovok [*A publication*]
Appar Metody Rentgenovskogo Anal ... Apparatura i Metody Rentgenovskogo Analiza [*A publication*]
APPATS.... Automated Program to Project AIT [*Advanced Individual Training*] Training Spaces [*DoD*]
APPAUC... Association of Physical Plant Administrators of Universities and Colleges (EA)
APPB........ Airborne Provisioning Parts Breakdown
APPB........ Applebee's International, Inc. [*NASDAQ symbol*] (NQ)
APPBD...... Acta Physiologica et Pharmacologica [*A publication*]
APPBDI ...... Acta Physiologica et Pharmacologica Bulgarica [*A publication*]
App Bd OCS ... Office of Contract Settlement, Appeal Board Decisions [*A publication*] (DLA)
APPC......... Advanced Program-to-Program Communication [*Data processing*]
APPC......... Automatic Power Plant Checker
App Ca .... Buchanan. Cape Colony Court of Appeal Reports [*South Africa*] [*A publication*] (DLA)
App Cas ..... Appeal Cases of the Different States [*A publication*] (DLA)
App Cas ..... Appeal Cases, District of Columbia [*1-74*] [*A publication*] (DLA)
App Cas ..... Appeal Cases, English Law Reports [*1875-90*] [*A publication*] (DLA)
App Cas ..... Appeal Cases in the United States [*A publication*] (DLA)
App Cas ..... Law Reports, Appeal Cases [*England*] [*A publication*] (DLA)
App Cas Beng ... Sevestre and Marshall's Bengal Reports [*A publication*] (DLA)
App Cas 2d ... Appeal Cases, English Law Reports, Second Series [*A publication*] (DLA)
App Cas (DC) ... Appeal Cases, District of Columbia [*1-74*] [*A publication*] (DLA)
App CC ...... Texas Civil Cases [*A publication*] (DLA)
App CC (White & W) ... Texas Civil Cases [*A publication*] (DLA)
App CC (Willson) ... Texas Civil Cases [*A publication*] (DLA)

APPCD...... Applied Physics. Part B. Photophysics and Laser Chemistry [*A publication*]
APPCE...... Appearance (ROG)
App Civ Cases ... Texas Civil Cases [*A publication*] (DLA)
APPCON... Approach Control [*Aviation*] (AFM)
App Court Ad Rev ... Appellate Court Administration Review [*A publication*]
APPC/PC.. Advanced Program-to-Program Communication/Personal Computer [*IBM Corp.*] (BYTE)
App Ct Rep ... Appeal Court Reports, New Zealand [*A publication*] (DLA)
App Ct Rep ... Bradwell's Illinois Appellate Reports [*A publication*] (DLA)
AP Pd .... Abhandlungen zur Philosophie und Paedagogik [*A publication*]
APPD........ Appeared (ROG)
APPD........ Approved (KSC)
APPD........ Aviation Personnel Planning Data [*Navy*] (NG)
APPD........ Port Hedland [*Australia*] [*ICAO location identifier*] (ICLI)
App D......... South Africa Law Reports, Appellate Division [*A publication*] (DLA)
APPDA...... Atlantic Provinces Power Development Act [*Canada*]
App DC...... Appeal Cases, District of Columbia [*A publication*] (DLA)
app den...... Appeal Denied (DLA)
App Dep't.. Appellate Department (DLA)
App Dept Super Ct ... Appellate Department of the Superior Court, California (ILCA)
APPDI .... American Professional Pet Distributors, Inc. [*An association*] (EA)
app dism..... Appeal Dismissed (DLA)
App Div ...... Appellate Division (DLA)
App Div ...... New York Supreme Court, Appellate Division Reports [*A publication*] (DLA)
App Div 2d ... New York Supreme Court, Appellate Division Reports, Second Series [*A publication*] (DLA)
App Div (NY) ... New York Supreme Court, Appellate Division Reports [*A publication*] (DLA)
App Div NY Sup Ct ... New York Supreme Court, Appellate Division Reports [*A publication*] (DLA)
App Div R .. New York Supreme Court, Appellate Division Reports [*A publication*] (DLA)
App Div Rep ... Massachusetts Appellate Division Reports [*A publication*] (DLA)
APPE......... Association of Petrochemicals Producers in Europe [*Brussels, Belgium*]
APPE......... Pearce [*Australia*] [*ICAO location identifier*] (ICLI)
APPEC...... Asia-Pacific Petroleum Conference
App Econ ... Applied Economics [*A publication*]
APPECS..... Adaptive Pattern-Perceiving Electronic Computer System
APPEM..... Anovulatory Persistent Proliferative Endometrium [*Medicine*]
APPEN...... Appendage
APPEN...... Asia-Pacific People's Environment Network [*Penang, Malaysia*] (EAIO)
Append....... Appendix (DLA)
Append Provis Nomencl Symb Terminol Conv IUPAC ... Appendices on Provisional Nomenclature Symbols, Terminology, and Conventions. International Union of Pure and Applied Chemistry [*A publication*]
App Environ Microbiol ... Applied and Environmental Microbiology [*A publication*]
App Ev .... Appleton's Rules of Evidence [*A publication*] (DLA)
App Exam ... Appeal [*or Appeals*] Examiner (DLA)
APPF .... Adelaide/Parafield [*Australia*] [*ICAO location identifier*] (ICLI)
APPF .... Australian Pork Producers' Federation
APPF .... Automated Payload Processing Facility [*NASA*] (NASA)
App Fish Com ... Appeals from Fisheries Commission [*1861-93*] [*Ireland*] [*A publication*] (DLA)
APPG........ Aqueous Procaine Penicillin G [*Antibiotic*]
APPG........ Australian Pensioner Pressure Group
App Geomech ... Applied Geomechanics [*A publication*]
APPGM..... Army Planning and Programming Guidance Memorandum (MCD)
APPH .... Perth/International [*Australia*] [*ICAO location identifier*] (ICLI)
APPHCZ... Annual Proceedings. Phytochemical Society [*A publication*]
APPHR...... American Peruvian Paso Horse Registry (EA)
APPI .... Advance Planning Procurement Information [*Army*] (MCD)
APPI .... International Association for the Promotion and Protection of Private Foreign Investments
APPIB .... American Paper Industry [*A publication*]
APPITA..... APPITA. Journal of the Australian and New Zealand Pulp and Paper Industry Technical Association [*A publication*] (APTA)
APPITA Proc ... Australian Pulp and Paper Industry Technical Association. Proceedings [*A publication*] (APTA)
App Jur Act 1876 ... Appellate Jurisdiction Act of 1876 [*39, 40 Victoria, c. 59*] (DLA)
APPL......... Appeal
APPL......... Appliance
APPL......... Applicable (AFM)
APPL......... Applied
APPL......... As Planned Parts List (MCD)
APPL........ Court of Appeal Judgements [*Database*] [*Australia*]
Appl Acoust ... Applied Acoustics [*A publication*]

Appl Agric Res ... Applied Agricultural Research [*A publication*]

APPLAN ... Applanation [*Ophthalmology*]

Appl Anal .. Applicable Analysis [*A publication*]

Appl Anim Behav Sci ... Applied Animal Behaviour Science [*A publication*]

Appl Anim Ethol ... Applied Animal Ethology [*A publication*]

Appl Anim Ethology ... Applied Animal Ethology [*A publication*]

Appl Anthrop ... Applied Anthropology [*A publication*]

Appl At ...... Applied Atomics [*England*] [*A publication*]

APPLAUSE ... Appeal, Plain Facts, Personalities, Local Angle, Action, Uniqueness [*or Universality*], Significance, Energy

Appl Biochem Bioeng ... Applied Biochemistry and Bioengineering [*A publication*]

Appl Biochem Biotechnol ... Applied Biochemistry and Biotechnology [*A publication*]

Appl Biochem Micr ... Applied Biochemistry and Microbiology [*A publication*]

Appl Biochem Microbiol ... Applied Biochemistry and Microbiology [*A publication*]

Appl Biochem Microbiol (Engl Transl Prikl Biokhim Mikrobiol) ... Applied Biochemistry and Microbiology (English Translation of Prikladnaya Biokhimiya i Mikrobiologiya) [*A publication*]

Appl Cardiol ... Applied Cardiology [*A publication*]

Appl Catal ... Applied Catalysis [*A publication*]

Appl Chem Eng Treat Sewage Ind Liq Effluents Symp ... Application of Chemical Engineering to the Treatment of Sewage and Industrial Liquid Effluents. Symposium [*A publication*]

Appl Chem Protein Interfaces Symp ... Applied Chemistry at Protein Interfaces. Symposium [*A publication*]

Appl Commer Oxygen Water Wastewater Syst ... Applications of Commercial Oxygen to Water and Wastewater Systems [*A publication*]

Appl Cryog Technol ... Applications of Cryogenic Technology [*A publication*]

APPLD ...... Applied

Appld Sci Res ... Applied Scientific Research [*A publication*]

APPLE ...... Advanced Propulsion Payload Effects [*NASA*]   (NASA)

APPLE ...... Aerotherm Prediction Procedure for LASER Effects   (MCD)

APPLE ...... AIDS [*Acquired Immune Deficiency Syndrome*] Prevention League   (EA)

APPLE ...... Apollo Payload Exploration [*NASA*]

APPLE ...... Applied Parallel Programming Language Experiment [*Data processing*]   (MCD)

APPLE ...... Association of Public and Private Labor Employees

APPLE ...... Associative Processor Programming Language Evaluation

Appl Econ .. Applied Economics [*A publication*]

APPLEF .... Acta Physiologica et Pharmacologica Latinoamericana [*A publication*]

Appl El Ann ... Applied Electronics Annual [*A publication*]

Appl Electron Struct Theory ... Applications of Electronic Structure Theory [*A publication*]

Appl Electr Phenom ... Applied Electrical Phenomena [*A publication*]

APPLE-MD ... Age; Prior Service; Physical, Legal, Educational, and Marital Status; and Dependents [*Army recruiting questionnaire*]

Appl Energy ... Applied Energy [*A publication*]

Appl Entomol Zool ... Applied Entomology and Zoology [*A publication*]

Appl Ent Zool ... Applied Entomology and Zoology [*A publication*]

Appl Envir Microbiol ... Applied and Environmental Microbiology [*A publication*]

Appl Environ Microbiol ... Applied and Environmental Microbiology [*A publication*]

Appl Ergon ... Applied Ergonomics [*A publication*]

Appl Ergonomics ... Applied Ergonomics [*A publication*]

APPLES .... Asian and Pacific Professional Language and Education Services   (EA)

Applesauc .. Applesauce [*A publication*]

Appleton .. Appleton's Journal [*A publication*]

Appleton .... Appleton's Reports [*19, 20 Maine*] [*A publication*]   (DLA)

Appleton M ... Appleton's Magazine [*A publication*]

Appl Fundam Aspects Plant Cell Tissue Organ Cult ... Applied and Fundamental Aspects of Plant Cell Tissue and Organ Culture [*A publication*]

Appl Herbic Oil Crops Plant ... Application of Herbicides in Oil Crops Plantings [*A publication*]

Appl High Mag Fields Semicond Phys Lect Int Conf ... Application of High Magnetic Fields in Semiconductor Physics. Lectures Presented at the International Conference [*A publication*]

Appl Hydraul ... Applied Hydraulics [*A publication*]

Appliance Manuf ... Appliance Manufacturer [*A publication*]

APPLIC ..... Applicatur [*Let It Be Applied*] [*Pharmacy*]   (ROG)

Applicable Anal ... Applicable Analysis [*A publication*]

Applic Anal ... Applicable Analysis [*A publication*]

APPLICAND ... Applicandus [*To Be Applied*] [*Pharmacy*]

APPLICAT ... Applicatur [*Let It Be Applied*] [*Pharmacy*]

Applications Math ... Applications of Mathematics [*A publication*]

Applied Econ ... Applied Economics [*A publication*]

Applied Phil ... Applied Philosophy [*A publication*]

Applied Radiol ... Applied Radiology [*A publication*]

Applied Sc ... Applied Science [*A publication*]

Appl Isot Tech Hydrol Hydraul ... Application of Isotope Techniques in Hydrology and Hydraulics [*A publication*]

Appl Mater Res ... Applied Materials Research [*England*] [*A publication*]

Appl Math ... Applications of Mathematics [*A publication*]

Appl Math and Comput ... Applied Mathematics and Computation [*A publication*]

Appl Math Comput ... Applied Mathematics and Computation [*A publication*]

Appl Math Comput (New York) ... Applied Mathematics and Computation (New York) [*A publication*]

Appl Math Mech ... Applied Mathematics and Mechanics [*A publication*]

Appl Math and Mech ... Applied Mathematics and Mechanics [*A publication*]

Appl Math Mech (English Ed) ... Applied Mathematics and Mechanics (English Edition) [*A publication*]

Appl Math Model ... Applied Mathematical Modelling [*A publication*]

Appl Math Modelling ... Applied Mathematical Modelling [*A publication*]

Appl Math Notes ... Applied Mathematics Notes [*A publication*]

Appl Math O ... Applied Mathematics and Optimization [*A publication*]

Appl Math Optim ... Applied Mathematics and Optimization [*A publication*]

Appl Math and Optimiz ... Applied Mathematics and Optimization [*A publication*]

Appl Math Sci ... Applied Mathematical Sciences [*A publication*]

Appl Mech Div Symp Ser (Am Soc Mech Eng) ... Applied Mechanics Division. Symposia Series (American Society of Mechanical Engineers) [*A publication*]

Appl Mech Rev ... Applied Mechanics Reviews [*A publication*]

Appl Mech Symp Ser ... Applied Mechanics Symposia Series [*A publication*]

Appl Mfr .... Appliance Manufacturer [*A publication*]

Appl Microb ... Applied Microbiology [*Later, Applied and Environmental Microbiology*] [*A publication*]

Appl Microbiol ... Applied Microbiology [*Later, Applied and Environmental Microbiology*] [*A publication*]

Appl Microbiol Biotechnol ... Applied Microbiology and Biotechnology [*A publication*]

Appl Mineral ... Applied Mineralogy. Technische Mineralogie [*A publication*]

Appl Moessbauer Spectrosc ... Applications of Moessbauer Spectroscopy [*A publication*]

APPLN ...... Application

Appl Neurop ... Applied Neurophysiology [*A publication*]

Appl Neurophysiol ... Applied Neurophysiology [*A publication*]

Appl Newer Tech Anal ... Applications of the Newer Techniques of Analysis [*A publication*]

Appl News ... Appalachian News Service [*A publication*]

Appl Nucl Radiochem ... Applied Nuclear Radiochemistry [*A publication*]

Appl Num M ... Applied Numerical Mathematics [*A publication*]

Appl Nutr ... Applied Nutrition [*A publication*]

Appl Ocean Res ... Applied Ocean Research [*A publication*]

APPLON ... Application

Appl Opt .... Applied Optics [*A publication*]

Appl Optics ... Applied Optics [*A publication*]

Appl Opt Suppl ... Applied Optics. Supplement [*A publication*]

Appl Ornithol ... Applied Ornithology [*A publication*]

Appl Pathol ... Applied Pathology [*A publication*]

Appl Phys .. Applied Physics [*A publication*]

Appl Phys A ... Applied Physics. Part A. Solids and Surfaces [*A publication*]

Appl Phys B ... Applied Physics. Part B. Photophysics and Laser Chemistry [*A publication*]

Appl Phys Comm ... Applied Physics Communications [*A publication*]

Appl Phys Commun ... Applied Physics Communications [*A publication*]

Appl Phys Eng ... Applied Physics and Engineering [*A publication*]

Appl Phys L ... Applied Physics Letters [*A publication*]

Appl Phys Lett ... Applied Physics Letters [*A publication*]

Appl Phys Part A ... Applied Physics. Part A. Solids and Surfaces [*West Germany*] [*A publication*]

Appl Phys Part B ... Applied Physics. Part B. Photophysics and Laser Chemistry [*West Germany*] [*A publication*]

Appl Phys Q ... Applied Physics Quarterly [*A publication*]

Appl Plast ... Applied Plastics [*A publication*]

Appl Plast Reinf Plast Rev ... Applied Plastics and Reinforced Plastics Review [*A publication*]

Appl Polym Symp ... Applied Polymer Symposia [*A publication*]

Appl Psych Monogr ... Applied Psychology Monographs [*A publication*]

Appl Psycholinguist ... Applied Psycholinguistics [*A publication*]

Appl Psychol Meas ... Applied Psychological Measurement [*A publication*]

Appl Radiol ... Applied Radiology [*A publication*]

Appl Radiol Nucl Med ... Applied Radiology and Nuclear Medicine [*Later, Applied Radiology*] [*A publication*]

Appl Res Ment Retard ... Applied Research in Mental Retardation [*A publication*]

Appl Sci Dev ... Applied Sciences and Development [*A publication*]

Appl Sci Re ... Applied Scientific Research [*A publication*]

Appl Sci Res ... Applied Scientific Research [*A publication*]

Appl Sci Res Corp Thail Annu Rep ... Applied Scientific Research Corporation of Thailand. Annual Report [*A publication*]

Appl Sci Res Sect A ... Applied Scientific Research. Section A. Mechanics, Heat, Chemical Engineering, Mathematical Methods [*Netherlands*] [*A publication*]

Appl Sci Res Sect B ... Applied Scientific Research. Section B. Electrophysics, Acoustics, Optics, Mathematical Methods [*Netherlands*] [*A publication*]

Appl Sci Res (The Hague) ... Applied Scientific Research (The Hague) [*A publication*]

Appl Sci Technol Index ... Applied Science and Technology Index [*A publication*]

Appl Solar Energy (Engl Transl) ... Applied Solar Energy (English Translation) [*A publication*]
Appl Sol Energ Proc Southeast Conf 1st ... Application of Solar Energy. Proceedings of the Southeastern Conference on Application of Solar Energy. 1st [*A publication*]
Appl Sol Energy ... Applied Solar Energy [*A publication*]
Appl Solid State Sci ... Applied Solid State Science [*A publication*]
Appl Spect ... Applied Spectroscopy [*A publication*]
Appl Spectr ... Applied Spectroscopy [*A publication*]
Appl Spectrosc ... Applied Spectroscopy [*A publication*]
Appl Spectrosc Rev ... Applied Spectroscopy Reviews [*A publication*]
Appl Spectry ... Applied Spectroscopy [*A publication*]
Appl Sp Rev ... Applied Spectroscopy Reviews [*A publication*]
Appl Stat ... Applied Statistics [*A publication*]
Appl Stats ... Applied Statistics [*A publication*]
Appl Surf Sci ... Applications of Surface Science [*A publication*]
Appl Theor Electrophor ... Applied and Theoretical Electrophoresis [*A publication*]
Appl Ther .. Applied Therapeutics [*A publication*]
APPM........ Association of Publication Production Managers (EA)
APPM........ Atom Parts per Million (MCD)
APPMA..... American Pet Products Manufacturers Association (EA)
App Math & Mech ... Applied Mathematics and Mechanics [*A publication*]
App Math Ser ... Applied Mathematics Series [*A publication*]
APPME..... American Professors for Peace in the Middle East (EA)
App ME..... Applied Mechanics Engineer [*Academic degree*]
App Metody Rentgenovskogo Anal ... Apparatura i Metody Rentgenovskogo Analiza [*USSR*] [*A publication*]
APPMI...... American Peanut Product Manufacturers, Incorporated (EA)
App Microbiol ... Applied Microbiology [*Later, Applied and Environmental Microbiology*] [*A publication*]
APPMT..... Appointment
APPN........ Appian Technology, Inc. [*NASDAQ symbol*] (SPSG)
APPN........ Appropriation
APPNET... MicroBilt Applications Network [*MicroBuilt Corp.*] [*Telecommunications service*] (TSSD)
App NZ...... Appeal Reports, New Zealand [*A publication*] (DLA)
App NZ 2d ... Appeal Reports, New Zealand, Second Series [*A publication*] (DLA)
AP & PO... Advance Programming and Proposal Operations (MCD)
APPO........ Advanced Product Planning Operation (MUGU)
A/P POI..... Autopilot Positioning Indicator
App Op ...... Applied Optics [*A publication*]
App Opt..... Applied Optics [*A publication*]
App Optics ... Applied Optics [*A publication*]
APPOR...... Army Power Procurement Officer Representative (MCD)
APPP........ Abhandlungen zur Philosophie, Psychologie, und Paedagogik [*A publication*]
APPP........ Advanced Procurement Planning Program
APPP........ Association of Planned Parenthood Professionals [*Later, ARHP*] (EA)
APPP........ Perth [*Australia*] [*ICAO location identifier*] (ICLI)
APPPA...... Association of Philippine Practicing Physicians in America [*Later, APPA*] (EA)
APPPC...... Asia and Pacific Plant Protection Commission [*Formerly, Plant Protection Committee for the Southeast Asia and Pacific Region*] (EA)
App Phys ... Applied Physics [*A publication*]
APPR........ Allopurinol Phosphate Ribonucleotide [*Biochemistry*]
APPR........ Aminopyrazolopyrimidine Ribonucleoside [*Biochemistry*]
APPR........ Appear (FAAC)
APPR........ Apprehend (AFM)
APPR........ Apprenticeship (AABC)
APPR........ Approval (AFM)
APPR........ Approximate (ADA)
APPR........ Army Package Power Reactor
APPR........ Perth [*Australia*] [*ICAO location identifier*] (ICLI)
Appraisal J ... Appraisal Journal [*A publication*]
Appraisal Jrnl ... Appraisal Journal [*A publication*]
APPRAIST ... Appraisement (ROG)
APPRC.... American Partridge Plymouth Rock Club (EA)
APPRCE.... Apprentice (ROG)
App Ref...... Appeal Referee (DLA)
APPRENT ... Apprentice
Apprent News ... Apprenticeship News [*A publication*]
Apprent Social ... Apprentissage et Socialisation [*A publication*]
App Rep..... Ontario Appeal Reports [*A publication*] (DLA)
App Rep Ont ... Ontario Appeal Reports [*A publication*] (DLA)
APPRES.... Applied Research
Appretur Ztg ... Appretur Zeitung [*A publication*]
App RNZ... Appeal Reports, New Zealand [*A publication*] (DLA)
APPRO...... Approbation
APPRO...... Approval
Approaches Cell Biol Neurons ... Approaches to the Cell Biology of Neurons [*A publication*]
APPROP ... Appropriation
Appropriate Technol ... Appropriate Technology [*England*] [*A publication*]
Approp Technol ... Appropriate Technology [*A publication*]
APPROX.... Approximate (EY)
Apprs........ Approaches [*Maps and charts*]
APPRV ...... Approve

apprvd........ Approved (ILCA)
APPRX...... Approximate
APPS......... Adenosine Phosphate Phosphosulfate [*Also, PAPS*] [*Biochemistry*]
APPS......... Advanced Planning Program Scheduling
APPS......... Advanced Protein Purification System
APPS......... Aerosol Physical Properties of the Stratosphere [*NASA*] (MCD)
APPS........ Analytical Photogrammetric Positioning System (MCD)
APPS........ Analytical Photogrammetric Processing System (MCD)
apps........... Appendixes (DLA)
APPS........ Association of Private Postal Systems [*Later, AAPS*] (EA)
APPS......... Atmospheric Pressure Plasma Sprayed [*Thermal barrier coating*]
APPS....... Automated Packaging Planning System (MCD)
APPS......... Automated Publication Preparation System [*Army*] (MCD)
APPS......... Automatic Point Positioning System (MCD)
APPS......... Auxiliary Payload Power System (MCD)
APPSDZ.... Applied Psycholinguistics [*A publication*]
APPS II..... Analytical Photogrammetric Positioning System - II
APPSMS... Automated Procurement and Production Scheduling and Management System [*Army*]
App et Soc ... Apprentissage et Socialisation [*A publication*]
APPSSA.... Advanced Procurement Planning System for Security Assistance
APPT........ Appointment (AFM)
App T......... Supreme Court Appellate Term (DLA)
App Tax Serv ... Appeals Relating to Tax on Servants [*1781*] [*England*] [*A publication*] (DLA)
APPTD...... Appointed
APPTNT ... Appointment (ROG)
App Trib ... Appeal Tribunal (DLA)
APPTS...... Appellants (ROG)
APPTT ...... Appointment (ROG)
APPTU...... All-Pakistan Post and Telegraph Union
APPU......... Air Photo Production Unit [*Canada*]
APPU........ Asian and Pacific Parliamentary Union
APPU........ Asian-Pacific Postal Union [*Manila, Philippines*] (EAIO)
APPURTS ... Appurtenances (ROG)
APPV......... Approve (MSA)
APPVAL ... Approval (ROG)
APPVL...... Approval (MSA)
App World ... Apparel World [*A publication*]
APPWP.... Association of Private Pension and Welfare Plans (EA)
APPX........ Appendix (KSC)
Appx Bre... Appendix to Breese's Reports [*Illinois*] [*A publication*] (DLA)
APPYA..... Annual Review of Phytopathology [*A publication*]
APPYAG ... Annual Review of Phytopathology [*A publication*]
APQ.......... American Philosophical Quarterly [*A publication*]
APQ.......... Asia-Pacific Resources [*Vancouver Stock Exchange symbol*]
APQAAH .. Arquivos. Instituto de Pesquisas Agronomicas [*A publication*]
APQPA...... Acta Psiquiatrica y Psicologica de America Latina [*A publication*]
APR .... Abdomino - Perineal Resection [*Medicine*]
APR .... Academy for Peace Research (EA)
APR .... Acoustic Paramagnetic Resonance [*Physics*]
APR .... Acute Phase Reactant [*Medicine*]
APR .... Acute Phase Response [*Medicine*]
APR .... Advance Production Release (NRCH)
APR .... Advanced Parts Release (NASA)
APR .... Aerial Photographic Reconnaissance
APR .... Agency Procurement Request
APR .... Agency Progress Report
APR .... Air Priority Rating
APR .... Airborne Profile Recorder
APR .... Airman Performance Report
APR .... Airports Program Report (FAAC)
APR .... Algemene Practische Rechtverzameling [*A publication*]
APR .... Alien Priory
APR .... All-Purpose Room
APR .... Alternate Path Reentry [*Fujitsu Ltd.*] [*Data processing*] (MCD)
APR .... American Poetry Review [*A publication*]
APR .... American Precision Industries, Inc. [*AMEX symbol*] (SPSG)
APR .... American Public Radio
APR .... Ammunition Performance Report [*Military*] (NVT)
APr........... Analecta Praemonstratensia [*A publication*]
APR .... Annual Percentage Rate
APR .... Annual Planning Report
APR .... Annual Progress Report
APR .... Anonymous Peer Refereeing
APR .... Antenna Position Recorder
APR .... Antiplugging Relay
APR .... Apollo Program Requirements [*NASA*] (KSC)
APR .... Applied Property Research [*British*]
APR .... Apprentice (AFM)
APR .... April (AFM)
APR .... Area Planning Report
APR .... Arecibo [*Puerto Rico*] [*Seismograph station code, US Geological Survey*] (SEIS)
APR .... Army Procurement Regulation [*or Requirement*]
APR .... Asian Profiles [*Database*] [*SRG International Ltd.*] [*Information service or system*] (CRD)
APR .... Assigned Procurement Responsibility (AAG)

APR .... Associated Press Radio
APR .... Association of Petroleum Re-Refiners (EA)
APR .... Association of Publishers Representatives [*Later, NAPR*] (EA)
APR .... Atlantic Province Reports [*Information service or system*] [*A publication*]
APR .... Atlantic Provinces Reports [*Canada*] [*A publication*]
APR .... Auburn-Placer County Library, Auburn, CA [*OCLC symbol*] (OCLC)
APR .... Auropalpebral Reflex [*Response to sound*]
APR .... Australasian Photo Review [*A publication*] (APTA)
APR .... Automatic Paralleling Relay (MCD)
APR .... Automatic Passbook Reader (BUR)
APR .... Automatic Pattern Recognition
APR .... Automatic Performance Reserve
APR .... Automatic Performance Review [*Aerospace*]
APR .... Automatic Power Reserve [*Aeronautics*]
APR .... Automatic Pressure Relief [*Nuclear energy*] (NRCH)
APR .... Automatic Production Recording
APR .... Automatic Programming and Recording [*Data processing*] (MCD)
APR .... Available Power Response
APR .... Provost Public Library, Alberta [*Library symbol*] [*National Library of Canada*] (NLC)
APR .... Rescue Transport [*Navy symbol*]
APRA .... Aircraft Production Resources Agency
APRA .... Alianza Popular Revolucionaria Americana [*American Revolutionary Popular Alliance*] [*Peru*] [*Political party*] (PPW)
APRA .... American Park Rangers Association (EA)
APRA .... American Petroleum Refiners Association [*Later, AIRA*] (EA)
APRA .... American Pigeon Racing Association (EA)
APRA .... American Pistol and Revolver Association [*Defunct*] (EA)
APRA .... American Popular Revolutionary Alliance [*Political party*] [*Peru*]
APRA .... American Prospect Research Association (EA)
APRA .... American Public Relations Association [*Later, PRSA*]
APRA .... Armed Forces Production Resources Agency (MUGU)
APRA .... Army Pulsed Experimental Research Assembly
APRA .... Association of Political Risk Analysts [*Later, CIBRM*] (EA)
APRA .... Australasian Performing Right Association (EAIO)
APRA .... Automotive Parts Rebuilders Association (EA)
APRAA ...... Auto Parts Recyclers Association of Australia
APRAC ..... Air Pollution Research Advisory Committee
APRACA ... Asian and Pacific Regional Agricultural Credit Association (EA)
APraem ...... Analecta Praemonstratensia [*A publication*]
APRAJ ...... Australasian Performing Right Association. Journal [*A publication*] (APTA)
APRAPS .... Active/Passive Reliable Acoustic Path SONAR (MCD)
APRB .... Acquisition Plan Review Board [*Army*]
APRC .... Anno post Roman Conditam [*In the Year after the Building of Rome*] [*753 BC*] [*Latin*]
APRC .... Army Personnel Research Committee (MCD)
APRC .... Army Physical Review Council
APRC .... Association for Promoting the Reform of Convocation [*British*]
APRC .... Automotive Public Relations Council (EA)
APRCH ..... Approach (MSA)
APRD .... Atmosphere Particulate Radioactivity Detector (IEEE)
APRE .... Aerospace Photographic Reconnaissance Equipment
APRE .... Air Procurement Region, Europe
APRE .... Alianza Popular Revolucionaria Ecuatoriana [*Ecuadorean Popular Revolutionary Alliance*] [*Political party*] (PPW)
APRE .... Army Personnel Research Establishment [*British*]
APREA ...... American Peanut Research and Education Association [*Later, APRES*] (EA)
APREF ...... A. Philip Randolph Educational Fund (EA)
A Pregl .... Arheoloski Pregled Arheolosko Drustvo Jugoslavije [*A publication*]
APREN ...... Alberta Environment, Peace River, Alberta [*Library symbol*] [*National Library of Canada*] (NLC)
APREQS ... Approval Requests [*Military*] (AABC)
APRES ...... American Peanut Research and Education Society (EA)
APRF .... Aberdeen Pulsed Reactor Facility
APRF .... Active Purchase Request File [*DoD*]
APRF .... Advanced Photon Research Facility [*Proposed, 1986, for high-energy physics*]
APRF .... All-Pakistan Railwaymen's Federation
APrF .... Altpreussische Forschungen [*A publication*]
APRF .... American Parapsychological Research Foundation [*Later, AAP*] (EA)
APRF .... Army Pulse Radiation Facility [*Aberdeen Proving Ground, MD*]
APRF .... Perth [*Australia*] [*ICAO location identifier*] (ICLI)
APRFE ...... Air Procurement Region, Far East (AFM)
APRFP ..... Americans for President Reagan's Foreign Policy (EA)
APRHC ..... Association for Puerto Rican-Hispanic Culture (EA)
Ap Rhod .... Apollonius Rhodius [*Third century BC*] [*Classical studies*] (OCD)
APRI .... A. Philip Randolph Institute (EA)
APRI .... Air Priority
APRI .... American Prosecutors Research Institute (EA)

APRIL .... Aquaplaning Risk Indicator for Landings
APRIL .... Automatically Programmed Remote Indication Logged
APRINT ..... Army's Program for Individual Training (MCD)
APRK .... Air Park
APRKAI .... Archiv fuer Protistenkunde [*A publication*]
APRL .... American Philatelic Research Library (EA)
APRL .... Architecture and Planning Research Laboratory [*University of Michigan*] [*Research center*] (RCD)
APRL .... Army Prosthetics Research Laboratory
APRM .... Adelaide [*Australia*] [*ICAO location identifier*] (ICLI)
APRM .... Automatic Position Reference Monitor (IEEE)
APRM .... Average Power Range Monitor [*Nuclear energy*] (NRCH)
APRM .... Peace River Municipal Library, Alberta [*Library symbol*] [*National Library of Canada*] (NLC)
APRMD .... Appointment Recommended (NOAA)
APRMD .... Association of Plastic Raw Material Distributors [*Defunct*] (EA)
APRN .... Alaska Public Radio Network
APRNT ...... Apparent (MSA)
APRO .... Aerial Phenomena Research Organization (EA)
APRO .... American Professional Racquetball Organization (EA)
APRO .... Army Personnel Research Office [*Washington, DC*]
APRO .... Army Plant Representative's Offices
APRO .... Army Procurement Research Office
APRO .... Association of Progressive Rental Organizations (EA)
A Proc Electron Microsc Soc Am ... Annual Proceedings. Electron Microscopy Society of America [*A publication*]
A Proc Gifu Coll Pharm ... Annual Proceedings. Gifu College of Pharmacy [*A publication*]
APROP .... Appropriate (AABC)
APROSE ... Associacao Portuguesa dos Produtores de Seguros [*Insurance representative body*] [*Portugal*] (EY)
APRPLS ..... Peace Library System, Peace River, Alberta [*Library symbol*] [*National Library of Canada*] (NLC)
APRRB ...... Airman Performance Report Review Board (AFM)
APRRE ...... Active Participation Rental Real Estate [*IRS*]
APRRE ...... Association of Professors and Researchers in Religious Education (EA)
APRRN ...... Advance Personnel Requirements Research Note
APRS .... Alliance for Perinatal Research and Services (EA)
APRS .... American Park and Recreation Society (EA)
APRS .... American Performing-Rights Society
APRS .... Applied Physics Research Section
APRS .... Army Personnel Research Service
APRS .... Ascension Poetry Reading Series (EA)
APRS .... Association for the Protection of Rural Scotland [*British*]
APRS .... Association of Public Radio Stations [*Later, NPR*] (EA)
APRS .... Automatic Position Reference System
APRS .... Automatic Pressure Relief System [*Military*] (CAAL)
APRS .... Automatic Production Record System
APRSCA ... Annual Progress Report. SEATO [*Southeast Asia Treaty Organization*] Medical Research Laboratories [*A publication*]
APRSEC .... Advances in Plastic and Reconstructive Surgery [*A publication*]
APRSS ...... Australian Photogrammetric and Remote Sensing Society
APRT .... Adenine Phosphoribosyltransferase [*An enzyme*]
APRT .... Advanced Productivity Research and Technology (MCD)
APRT .... Airport (AFM)
APRT .... Army Physical Readiness Test (INF)
APRT .... Association for Past-Life Research and Therapy (EA)
APRTA ...... Associated Press Radio-Television Association [*Later, APB*]
APRV .... Approve (KSC)
APRVL ...... Approval (KSC)
APRX .... Approximate (AFM)
APRXLY ... Approximately (DEN)
APS .... Aborigines Protection Society [*Later, Anti-Slavery Society for the Protection of Human Rights*]
APS .... Academy of Pharmaceutical Sciences (EA)
APS .... Academy of Political Science (EA)
APS .... Accelerated Photosynthetic System [*Sewage purification*]
APS .... Accelerated Propagation System [*Gardening*]
APS .... Accelerometer Parameter Shift
APS .... Accessory Power Supply (AABC)
APS .... Accion Politica Socialista [*Socialist Political Action*] [*Peru*] [*Political party*] (PPW)
APS .... Acta Philologica Scandinavica [*A publication*]
APS .... Acta Psychologica Sinica [*Hsin-Li Hsueh-Pao*] [*A publication*]
APS .... Acts of the Parliaments of Scotland
APS .... Acute Physiology Score [*In evaluating impact of intensive care*]
APS .... Adaptive Processor, SONAR (CAAL)
APS .... Adenosine Phosphosulfate [*Biochemistry*]
APS .... Administration and Program Support (MCD)
A & PS .... Administration and Program Support [*George C. Marshall Space Flight Center Directorate*] [*NASA*] (NASA)
APS .... Administration for Public Services [*Office of Human Development Services*]
APS .... Advanced Personnel System
APS .... Advanced Photon Source [*Particle accelerator*] [*Argonne National Laboratory*]
APS .... Advanced Photosynthetic System
APS .... Advanced Power System

APS............ Advanced Propellant System
APS............ Advanced Proton Source [*Physics*]
APS............ Aerial Port Squadron [*Air Force*]
APS............ Aft Propulsion System [*or Subsystem*] [*NASA*] (NASA)
APS............ Agathon Publication Services, Inc. [*Later, APS Publications*]
APS............ Agence de Presse Senegalaise [*Senegalese Press Agency*]
APS............ Air-Breathing Propulsion System [*or Subsystem*] [*NASA*] (NASA)
APS............ Air Pictorial Service
APS............ Air Pollution Syndrome
APS............ Air Pressure Switch
APS............ Airborne Power Supply   (KSC)
APS............ Airborne Pulse Search RADAR   (FAAC)
APS............ Aircraft Prepared for Service
APS............ Algerie Presse Service [*Press agency*] [*Algeria*]
APS............ All Africa Press Service   (EAIO)
APS............ Allegheny Power System, Inc.
APS............ Allied Provincial Securities [*British*]   (ECON)
APS............ Alphanumeric Photocomposer System   (IEEE)
APS............ Alternative Press Syndicate   (EA)
APS............ Altitude Proximity Sensor   (MCD)
APS............ American Pain Society   (EA)
APS............ American Paraplegia Society   (EA)
APS............ American Peace Society   (EA)
APS............ American Pediatric Society   (EA)
APS............ American Penstemon Society   (EA)
APS............ American Peony Society   (EA)
APS............ American Pheasant Society [*Later, AP & WS*]   (EA)
APS............ American Philatelic Society   (EA)
APS............ American Philosophical Society   (EA)
APS............ American Philosophical Society. Proceedings [*A publication*]
APS............ American Physical Society   (EA)
APS............ American Physiological Society   (EA)
APS............ American Phytopathological Society   (EA)
APS............ American Plant Selections [*An association*] [*Defunct*]   (EA)
APS............ American Poinsettia Society   (EA)
APS............ American Polar Society   (EA)
APS............ American Pomological Society   (EA)
APsA........ American Psychoanalytic Association   (EA)
APS............ American Portrait Society   (EA)
APS............ American Portuguese Society   (EA)
APS............ American President Companies Ltd. [*NYSE symbol*]   (SPSG)
APS............ American Primrose Society   (EA)
APS............ American Proctologic Society [*Later, ASCRS*]   (EA)
APS............ American Prosthodontic Society   (EA)
APS............ American Protestant Society
APs .... American Psychologist [*A publication*]
APS............ American Psychosomatic Society   (EA)
APS............ American Purchasing Society   (EA)
APS............ Ammonium Persulfate [*Inorganic chemistry*]
APS............ Ammonium Polysulfide [*Fertilizer*]
APS............ Amplifier Power Supply
APS............ Analytical Procedures Subsystem   (MCD)
APS............ Angstrom Pyrheliometric Scale
APS............ Angular Position Sensor
APS............ Animal Parasitic Systems
APS............ Annals. American Academy of Political and Social Science [*A publication*]
ApS .... Anpartsselskab [*Private Limited Company*] [*Sweden*]
APS............ Antenna Pointing Subsystem
APS............ Antiprostaglandin Antiserum [*Immunology*]
APS............ Apollo Program Specifications [*NASA*]   (KSC)
APS............ Appearance Potential Spectroscopy [*Physics*]
AP(S)........ Application Process [*or Program*] (Structure) [*Telecommunications*]   (TEL)
APS............ Application Process Subsystem [*Telecommunications*]   (TEL)
APS............ Applied Psychological Services   (KSC)
APS............ Approved Prescription Services Ltd. [*British*]
Aps............ Apus [*Constellation*]
APS............ Aqueous Powder Suspension [*For coating plastics*]
APS............ Arc-Plasma Spraying [*Magnetic film*]
APS............ Armament Practice Station [*British military*]   (DMA)
APS............ Army Pictorial Service
APS............ Army Pilot School
APS............ Army Postal Service
APS............ Array Processor Software [*Data processing*]   (IEEE)
APS............ Ascending Pharyngeal System [*Anatomy*]
APS............ Ascent Propulsion System [*NASA*]
APS............ Assembly Programming System [*Data processing*]   (IEEE)
APS............ Assimilations per Second
APS............ Associacao Portuguesa de Seguros [*Insurance representative body*] [*Portugal*]   (EY)
APS............ Associate of the Pharmaceutical Society [*British*]
APS............ Associated Patternmakers of Scotland [*A union*]
APS............ Associated Press Service
APS............ Association of Photo Sensitizers   (EA)
APS............ Association of Productivity Specialists   (EA)
APS............ Atmospheric Pollution Sensor
APS............ Atomic Power Station   (NRCH)
APS............ Attached Processor System [*Telecommunications*]   (TEL)
APS............ Attended Pay Station [*Attended Public Telephone*]   (TEL)
APS............ Attending Physician's Statement

APS............ Attitude and Pointing Control System [*NASA*]
APS............ Attitude Propulsion Subsystem
APS............ Austin Public Schools Media, Austin, MN [*OCLC symbol*]   (OCLC)
APS............ Australian Perinatal Society
APS............ Autocorrelator Photon Spectroscopy
APS............ Autograph Poem Signed [*Manuscript descriptions*]   (ADA)
APS............ Autograph Postcard Signed [*Manuscript descriptions*]
APS............ Automated Patent Searching [*Data processing*]
APS............ Automated Productivity Services   (MCD)
APS............ Automatic Patching System   (IEEE)
APS............ Automatic Phase Shifter
APS............ Automatic Phase Synchronization
APS............ Automatic Pilot System
APS............ Automatic Planetary Station [*Astronomy*]
APS............ Automatic Processing System   (MCD)
APS............ Automatic Program System [*Data processing*]
APS............ Automatic Provisioning System [*Military*]   (CAAL)
APS............ Auxiliary Power Subsystem   (MCD)
APS............ Auxiliary Power Supply
APS............ Auxiliary Power System   (NRCH)
APS............ Auxiliary Program Storage [*Data processing*]   (BUR)
APS............ Auxiliary Propulsion System [*or Subsystem*] [*Apollo*] [*NASA*]
APS............ Average Propensity to Save [*Economics*]
APS............ Avionics Processing System
APS............ IEEE Antennas and Propagation Society   (EA)
APS............ Minelaying Submarine [*Navy symbol*]
APS............ Transport, Submarine [*Later, SSP*] [*Navy symbol*]
APSA........ American Pediatric Surgical Association   (EA)
APSA........ American Political Science Association   (EA)
APSA........ American Polypay Sheep Association   (EA)
APSA........ American Professional Surfing Association   (EA)
APSA........ American Psychologists for Social Action [*Later, PSA*]
APSA........ Ammunition Procurement and Supply Agency [*Army*]
APSA........ Association of Point-of-Sale-Advertising [*British*]
APSA........ Association for the Psychiatric Study of Adolescents [*British*]
APSA........ Axisymmetrical and Planar Structural Analysis   (MCD)
APsaA....... American Psychoanalytic Association   (EA)
APSAC...... Acylated Plasminogen-Streptokinase Activator Complex [*Anticlotting agent*]
APSAC...... Anisoylated-Plasminogen-Streptokinase Activator Complex [*Thrombolytic*]
APSACT.... Annual of Psychoanalysis [*A publication*]
APSAP...... Auxiliary Propulsion System Aft POP   (MCD)
APSA/R .... American Political Science Review. American Political Science Association [*A publication*]
APSARA ... Australian Peace Studies and Research Association
APSBAU ... Archives Portugaises des Sciences Biologiques [*A publication*]
APSC......... Advanced Processing Science Center [*Oak Ridge National Laboratory*]
APSC......... Alabama Public Service Commission Decisions [*A publication*]   (DLA)
APSC......... Andorran Philately Study Circle   (EA)
APSC......... Arab Petroleum Services Company [*of the Organization of Arab Petroleum Exporting Countries*]
APSC......... Army Personnel System Committee
AP & SC .... Army Port and Service Command
APSC......... Asian-Pacific Society of Cardiology   (EA)
APSC......... Austin Peay State College [*Later, Austin Peay State University*] [*Tennessee*]
APSC......... Australian Police Staff College
APSCA ...... Acta Physiologica Scandinavica [*A publication*]
APSCD2 .... Acta Pathologica et Microbiologica Scandinavica. Section C. Immunology [*A publication*]
APSD......... American Professional Society of the Deaf   (EA)
APSDEP.... Asian and Pacific Skill Development Programme [*Database producer*]   (IID)
APSDIN .... APSDEP Information Network [*Islamabad, Pakistan*] [*Information service or system*]   (IID)
APSE......... Abstracts of Photographic Science and Engineering Literature [*A publication*]
APSE......... Ada Programming Support Environments [*Data processing*]   (RDA)
APSE......... Alternatives. Perspectives on Society and Environment [*Canada*] [*A publication*]
APSE......... Armour-Piercing Secondary Effects [*British military*]   (DMA)
APSE......... Associated Press Sports Editors [*Defunct*]   (EA)
APSET ...... Aviation Personnel and Survival Equipment Team [*Navy*]   (NG)
APSF......... Armed Public Security Force   (CINC)
APSFSL .... Assistant Private Secretary to the First Sea Lord [*Navy*] [*British*]
APSG......... After Passage [*or Passing*] [*Aviation*]   (FAAC)
APSGB...... Association of Police Surgeons of Great Britain
APSGD...... Army Procurement - Sharpe General Depot
APSGUSA ... Asian Political Scientists Group in USA   (EA)
APSHA...... Annales de Pediatrie [*A publication*]
ApSHA ...... Appaloosa Sport Horse Association   (EA)
APSHDH .. American Journal of Pharmacy and the Sciences Supporting Public Health [*Later, American Journal of Pharmacy*] [*A publication*]

APSI .... Academy for the Psychology of Sports International [*Later, ASPI*] (EA)
APSI .... Advanced Professional Sales, Incorporated [*NASDAQ symbol*] (NQ)
APSI .... Advanced Propulsion Subsystem Integration [*Air Force*]
APSI .... Aircraft Propulsion Subsystem Integration
APSI .... Allstates-Programming & Systems, Incorporated
APSI .... Amperes per Square Inch
APSIA .... Association of Professional Schools of International Affairs (EA)
APSID .... Advances in Polymer Science [*A publication*]
APSL .... Acting Paymaster Sub-Lieutenant [*Navy*] [*British*]
APSL .... Amsterdamer Publikationen zur Sprache und Literatur [*A publication*]
APSLF .... Association de Psychologie Scientifique de Langue Francaise [*French-Language Association of Scientific Psychology*] (EAIO)
APSM .... Academy of Product Safety Management (EA)
APSM .... Association for Physical and System Mathematics (EA)
APSN .... Architects and Planners in Support of Nicaragua (EA)
APSN .... Association Package Sequence Number (MCD)
APSNY ...... Austria Philatelic Society of New York (EA)
APSO .... Allied Petroleum Service Organization
APSO .... Asia-Pacific Socialist Organization [*Political party*] [*Tokyo, Japan*] (EAIO)
APSO .... Assistant Polaris Systems Officer [*British military*] (DMA)
APSO .... Association of Poultry Slaughterhouse Operators (EA)
APSOA ...... Acta Psychologica (Amsterdam) [*A publication*]
APSP .... Array Processor Subroutine Package [*Data processing*] (BUR)
APS/P .... Proceedings. American Philosophical Society [*A publication*]
APSPA4 ... Applied Spectroscopy [*A publication*]
APSQ .... Advance Payment of Subsistence and Quarters
APSq .... Aerial Port Squadron [*Air Force*] (AFM)
APSR .... Airport Surveillance RADAR (MSA)
APSR .... American Political Science Review [*A publication*]
APSR .... Axial Power Shaping Rods [*Nuclear energy*] (NRCH)
APSRA ...... Axial Power Shaping Rods Assembly [*Nuclear energy*] (NRCH)
APSRDD ... Advances in Pollen-Spore Research [*A publication*]
APSS .... Advanced Planetary Spacecraft System
APSS .... American Academy of Political and Social Science. Annals [*A publication*]
APSS .... American Polled Shorthorn Society (EA)
APSS .... Area/Point Search System (CAAL)
APSS .... Army Printing and Stationery Services [*British*]
APSS .... Associated Public School Systems
APSS .... Association of Professional Sleep Societies (EA)
APSS .... Association for the Psychophysiological Study of Sleep [*Later, Sleep Research Society - SRS*]
APSS .... Atmospheric Pressure Supply System [*or Subsystem*] [*NASA*] (NASA)
APSS .... Automated Program Support System [*Data processing*]
APSS .... Transport, Submarine [*Later, LPSS*] [*Navy symbol*] [*Obsolete*]
APSSEAR ... Association of Pediatric Societies of the Southeast Asian Region (EA)
APsSI .... Associate of the Psychological Society of Ireland
APSSNM .. Advisory Panel on Safeguarding Special Nuclear Material
APST .... Associate in Public Service Technology
APSTA ..... Applied Statistics [*A publication*]
APSTCI ..... Acta Psychologica Taiwanica [*A publication*]
APSU .... Austin Peay State University [*Tennessee*]
APSU .... Auxiliary Power Supply Unit (MCD)
APSVC ...... Acta Physica Slovaca [*A publication*]
APSWU .... American Philatelic Society Writers Unit (EA)
APSXAS .... Acta Pharmaceutica Suecica [*A publication*]
A Psy .... American Psychologist [*A publication*]
APsyc .... Archiv fuer die Gesamte Psychologie [*A publication*]
APsych ...... Acta Psychologica [*Amsterdam*] [*A publication*]
APsyOI ...... Association des Psychologues de l'Ocean Indien (EAIO)
APT .... Acta Psychologica Taiwanica [*A publication*]
APT .... Adaptive Programming Technology
APT .... Advanced Passenger Train [*British*]
APT .... Advanced Patent Technique
APT .... Advanced Pointing Tracking (MCD)
APT .... Aerial Profiling of Terrain [*System*] [*Department of the Interior*]
APT .... Aft Peak Tank [*Shipping*]
APT .... Airborne Pointer and Tracker
APT .... Airmen Proficiency Test
APT .... Airport (AFIT)
APT .... Airportable [*British military*] (DMA)
APT .... All-Purpose Terminal [*Computer technology*]
APT .... All-Purpose Tween [*Microorganism growth medium*]
APT .... Allarcom Pay Television Ltd. [*Canada*]
APT .... Alum Precipitated Toxoid [*Medicine*]
APT .... Amberhill Petroleum Ltd. [*Vancouver Stock Exchange symbol*]
APT .... American Peace Test (EA)
APT .... American Place Theatre (EA)
APT .... American Playwrights Theatre [*Defunct*]
APT .... Ammonium Paratungstate [*Metallurgy*]
APT .... Analog Pressure Transducer
APT .... Analog Program Tape [*Data processing*]

APT .... Angeles Participating Mortgage Class A SBI [*AMEX symbol*] (SPSG)
APT .... Animation Photo Transfer [*Animation technique developed by Disney Studio*]
APT .... Antiphosphotyrosine [*Biochemistry*]
APT .... Apartment
APT .... Apollo Pad Test [*NASA*] (KSC)
APT .... Applied Potential Tomography [*Medicine*]
APT .... Appoint (AABC)
APT .... Aptitude (AABC)
APT .... Arbitrage Pricing Theory [*Finance*]
APT .... Arizona Photopolarimeter Telescope
APT .... Armed Propaganda Team [*Military*]
APT .... Armor-Piercing with Tracer [*Ammunition*]
APT .... Army Parachute Team
APT .... Asia-Pacific Telecommunity [*Thailand*] [*Telecommunications*] (TSSD)
APT .... Asset Protection Trust
APT .... Association for Poetry Therapy [*Later, NAPT*] (EA)
APT .... Association of Polysomnographic Technologists (EA)
APT .... Association of Polytechnic Teachers [*British*]
APT .... Association for Practical Theology (EA)
APT .... Association for Preservation Technology [*Later, APTI*] (EA)
APT .... Association for Psychological Type (EA)
APT .... Astronaut Preference Test [*NASA*] (NASA)
APT .... AT & T Philips Telecommunications
APT .... Augmented Programming Training [*Data processing*] (IEEE)
APT .... Australia Prophetical Truth Centre
APT .... Automated Pit Trading [*Developed by London International Financial Futures Exchange*] [*Stock exchange term*]
APT .... Automatic Picture Taking (IEEE)
APT .... Automatic Picture Transmission [*NASA*]
APT .... Automatic Position Telemetering
APT .... Automatic Progression Testing (TEL)
APT .... Automatically Programmed Tool [*Computer software*] [*Data processing*]
APT .... Automation Planning and Technology
APT .... Avery Point [*Connecticut*] [*Seismograph station code, US Geological Survey*] [*Closed*] (SEIS)
APT .... Fort Stewart/Hunter AAF Library System, Fort Stewart, GA [*OCLC symbol*] (OCLC)
APT .... Jasper, TN [*Location identifier*] [*FAA*] (FAAL)
APT .... North Carolina State Agency for Public Telecommunications [*Raleigh*] (TSSD)
APT .... Office of Personnel and Training [*FAA*] (FAAC)
a-pt--- .... Portuguese Timor [*a-io (Indonesia) used in records cataloged after April 1980*] [*MARC geographic area code*] [*Library of Congress*] (LCCP)
APT .... Troop Barge, Class B [*Navy symbol*] [*Obsolete*]
APTA........ American Physical Therapy Association (EA)
APTA........ American Pioneer Trails Association (EA)
APTA........ American Platform Tennis Association (EA)
APTA........ American Public Transit Association (EA)
APTA........ Antigua Paddle Tennis Association (EAIO)
APTA........ Aptitude Area
APTA........ Atlantic Provinces Trucking Association [*Canada*]
APTA........ Automotive Products Trade Act of 1965
APT-AC...... Automatically Programmed Tool - Advanced Contouring [*IBM Corp.*]
APTC........ Aperture Card (MSA)
APTC........ Army Physical Training Corps [*British*]
APTC........ Association of Publicly Traded Companies (EA)
APTD ...... Aid to the Permanently and Totally Disabled [*HEW*]
APTD .... Air Pollution Technical Data [*Series*] [*A publication*]
APTE........ Abrams Power Train Evolution
APTE........ Avalanche Punch-Through Erase (MCD)
APTEC...... Appropriate Technology Ltd. [*British*] (IRUK)
Aptechn Delo ... Aptechnoe Delo [*A publication*]
APTEDD..... Acta Pharmaceutica Technologica [*A publication*]
APTEM..... Association of Passenger Transport Executives and Managers [*British*] (DCTA)
APTES ..... (Aminopropyl)triethoxysilane [*Organic chemistry*]
APTGAG... Anales. Catedra de Patologia y Clinica de la Tuberculosis. Universidad de Buenos Aires [*A publication*]
APTGS ...... Automatic Picture Transmission Ground System (NOAA)
APTHDM ... Applied Pathology [*A publication*]
APTI.......... Actions per Time Interval
APTI.......... Advanced Products & Technologies, Incorporated [*Redmond, WA*] [*NASDAQ symbol*] (NQ)
APTI.......... Arab Petroleum Training Institute [*Defunct*] (EA)
APTI.......... Association of Principals of Technical Institutions [*British*]
APTI.......... Automatic Point Transfer Instrument (MCD)
APTI.......... Automatic Programmed Test Input (NASA)
APTIC .... Air Pollution Technical Information Center [*Also, NAPTIC*] [*Environmental Protection Agency*] [*Bibliographic database*]
APT-IC ...... Automatically Programmed Tool - Intermediate Contouring [*IBM Corp.*]
APTIF....... Association of Publicly Traded Investment Funds (EA)
APTIRC .... Asian-Pacific Tax and Investment Research Centre [*Singapore*] (EA)

APTKAS ... Archiv fuer Physikalische Therapie [*A publication*]
APTLF...... Association de Psychologie du Travail de Langue Francaise [*French-Language Association of Work Psychology*] (EAIO)
APTO .... Association for the Professional Treatment of Offenders (EA)
APTOA6 ... Acta Pharmacologica et Toxicologica [*A publication*]
APTP......... Arithmetic Proficiency Training Program [*Computer-assisted training program*]
AP-TP....... Association of Part-Time Professionals (EA)
APTPDA ... Advance Payment of Travel per Diem Authorized [*Army*]
APTPED .... Advances in Psychoanalysis Theory, Research, and Practice [*A publication*]
APTR........ Advanced Pressure Tube Reactor [*Nuclear energy*]
APTRA...... Air Operational Training
APTRDI .... Advances in Prostaglandin and Thromboxane Research [*A publication*]
APTS......... Air Traffic Control Proficiency Training System [*Navy*]
APTS .... Apartments
APTS......... Apertus Technologies, Inc. [*NASDAQ symbol*] (SPSG)
APTS .... Army Physical Training Staff [*British military*] (DMA)
APTS .... Association for the Prevention of Thefts in Shops [*British*]
APTS .... Automatic Picture Transmission System [*or Subsystem*] [*NASA*]
APTS .... Automatic Programmer and Test System [*Army*] (MCD)
APTSAI..... Acta Pharmacologica et Toxicologica. Supplementum [*A publication*]
A/P TSTMN ... Autopilot Test Monitor (AAG)
A/P TSTPG ... Autopilot Test Programmer (AAG)
APTT......... Activated Partial Thromboplastin Time [*Hematology*]
APTT......... Aircrew Part Task Trainer (MCD)
APTT......... Apollo Part Task Trainer [*NASA*] (KSC)
APTU .... Aerodynamic and Propulsion Test Unit
APTU .... African Postal and Telecommunications Union
APTUA...... Archives. Institut Pasteur de Tunis [*A publication*]
APTUS...... Apparatus
APTVAR ... Anales. Instituto Nacional de Investigaciones Agrarias. Serie Proteccion Vegetal [*A publication*]
APTW........ Asiatic-Pacific Theater of War
APU .... Accessory Power Unit (MUGU)
APU .... Acoustics Propellant Utilization
APU .... Airborne Processing Unit
APU .... Aircraft Propulsion Unit
APU .... Alianca Popular Unida/Alianca Povo Unido [*United People's Alliance*] [*Portugal*] [*Political party*] (PPW)
APU .... Analytic Processing Unit
APU .... Applied Psychology Unit
APU .... Arab Postal Union
APU .... Arithmetic Processing Unit [*Data processing*]
APU .... Army Postal Unit
APU .... Asian Parliamentarians' Union
APU .... Assessment of Performance Unit [*Education*] [*British*]
APU .... Association for Philosophy of the Unconscious (EA)
APU .... Audio Playback Unit
APU .... Authorized Pick-Up [*Trucking terminology*]
APU .... Auxiliary Power [*or Propulsion*] Unit [*Military*]
APU .... Auxiliary Processing Unit
APU .... Avian Philately Unit (EA)
APUA .... Alliance for the Prudent Use of Antibiotics (EA)
APUA .... Anthropological Papers. University of Alaska [*A publication*]
A Pubbl Istr ... Annali della Pubblica Istruzione [*A publication*]
APUC .... Area Production Urgency Committee
APUC .... Association de Placement Universitaire et Collegial [*University and College Placement Association*] [*Canada*]
APUC .... Association des Presses Universitaires Canadiennes [*Association of Canadian University Presses - ACUP*]
APUC .... Association for Promoting Unity of Christendom
APUD........ Amine Precursor Uptake and Decarboxylation [*Cytology*]
APUG .... AutoPrep 5000 Users Group (EA)
APUHS ..... Automatic Program Unit, High-Speed [*Component of ADIS*]
Apul .... Apuleius [*Second century AD*] [*Classical studies*] (OCD)
APULS...... Automatic Program Unit, Low-Speed [*Component of ADIS*]
Apulum..... Apulum. Acta Musei Apulensis [*A publication*]
APUPA...... Alien, Penumbral, Umbral, Penumbral, Alien
APUR .... Atelier Parisien d'Urbanisme [*Paris Office of Urbanization*] [*France*] [*Information service or system*] (IID)
APURAK... Archivos de Pediatria del Uruguay [*A publication*]
APUS........ Auxiliary Power Unit Subsystem (MCD)
AP/USA .... Airline Passengers of America (EA)
APUSM...... Auxiliary Power Unit System Module (MCD)
A-Put....... Associate Pulmonary Technologist [*Academic degree*]
APUT .... Auxiliary Power Unit Test (MCD)
APV .... Air-Piloted Valve
APV .... All-Purpose Vehicle [*Automotive engineering*]
APV .... Amino(phosphono)valerate [*Organic chemistry*]
APV .... Amino(phosphono)valeric Acid [*An amino acid*]
APV .... Anomalous Photovoltaic Effect (MCD)
APV .... Apple Valley [*California*] [*Airport symbol*] [*Obsolete*] (OAG)
APV .... Approve
APV .... Autopiloted Vehicle
APV .... Paradise Valley Public Library, Alberta [*Library symbol*] [*National Library of Canada*] (NLC)

APV .... Transport and Aircraft Ferry [*Navy symbol*] [*Obsolete*]
APV .... Van Deusen Post Library, Fort Monmouth, Fort Monmouth, NJ [*OCLC symbol*] (OCLC)
APVA .... Association for the Preservation of Virginia Antiquities (EA)
APVAST ... Airborne Platform Versus Airbreathing Strategic Threats (MCD)
APVBAB ... Annales de Physiologie Vegetale. Universite de Bruxelles [*A publication*]
APVD .... Approved (MSA)
APVDC...... Association of Parents of Vaccine Damaged Children [*British*]
APVE......... Association of Professional Vocal Ensembles [*Later, Chorus America*] (EA)
APVGAQ .. Annales de Physiologie Vegetale [*Paris*] [*A publication*]
APVL........ Approval
APVO........ Soviet Air Defense Aviation (MCD)
APVOI....... Advanced PVO [*Protivo-Vozdushnaia Oborona*] Intercepter [*Military*] (MCD)
APW .... Accelerated Public Works [*Program*] [*Department of the Interior*]
APW .... Action Program for Women
APW .... American Prisoner of War (AABC)
A/PW........ Analog-to-Pulse Width Converter
APW .... Apia [*Samoa Islands*] [*Airport symbol*] (OAG)
APW .... Apparent Polar Wander [*Paleomagnetism*]
APW .... Architectural Projected Window [*Technical drawings*]
APW .... Armistice and Post-War Committee [*British*] [*World War II*]
APW .... Association of Petroleum Writers (EA)
APW .... Augmented Phase Wave [*Thermodynamics*]
APW .... Augmented Plane Wave
APWA ...... American Public Welfare Association (EA)
APWA ...... American Public Works Association (EA)
APWC .... Association of Professional Writing Consultants (EA)
APWD ...... Aircraft Proximity Warning Device
APWI........ Air Prisoner of War Interrogation
APWIB ..... American Prisoner of War Information Bureau (AABC)
APWL........ Automatically Processed WIR [*Weapons Inspection Report*] List (CET)
APWO .... Assistant Public Works Officer
APWP........ Accelerated Public Works Program [*Department of the Interior*]
APWP........ Apparent Polar Wander Path [*Paleomagnetism*]
APWR .... Advanced Pressurized-Water Reactor [*Nuclear energy*]
APWR ...... American Polish War Relief [*Post-World War II*]
APWR ...... Applied Power, Inc. [*NASDAQ symbol*] (NQ)
APWR ...... Woomera [*Australia*] [*ICAO location identifier*] (ICLI)
APWRC..... Association of Private Weather Related Companies (EA)
APWS........ Aircraft Proximity Warning System
AP & WS ... American Pheasant and Waterfowl Society (EA)
APWSS ..... Asian Pacific Weed Science Society (EA)
APWT........ Arterial Pulse Wave Transducer
APWU ...... American Postal Workers Union (EA)
APWUS...... Association of Polish Women in the United States (EA)
APX .... Advance Payment Plan [*Airlines*]
APX .... Apex Municipal Fund, Inc. [*NYSE symbol*] (SPSG)
APX .... Australian Tax Planning Report [*Commerce Clearing House*] [*A publication*] (DLA)
APX .... Fort Sam Houston Morale Support Library, Fort Sam Houston, TX [*OCLC symbol*] (OCLC)
APXM .... Christmas Island [*Australia*] [*ICAO location identifier*] (ICLI)
APY .... Apoyeque [*Nicaragua*] [*Seismograph station code, US Geological Survey*] (SEIS)
APY .... Australian Pay-Roll Tax Manual [*A publication*]
APY .... Giant "Y" Boat [*Navy symbol*] [*Obsolete*]
APYF......... Asian Pacific Youth Forum (EA)
APYFL ...... Asian Pacific Youth Freedom League [*Tokyo, Japan*] (EAIO)
APYMAP .. American Phytopathological Society. Monograph [*A publication*]
APYSA9 .... Acta Psychiatrica Scandinavica [*A publication*]
APYTA...... Acta Psychotherapeutica et Psychosomatica [*A publication*]
APZ .... Air Patrol Zone (NVT)
APZ .... Zapala [*Argentina*] [*Airport symbol*] (OAG)
APZA........ Asociacion pro Zarzuela en America (EA)
AQ.............. Accomplishment Quotient
AQ.............. Achievement Quotient
AQ.............. Acquisicorp Capital [*Vancouver Stock Exchange symbol*]
AQ.............. Acquisition Message
AQ.............. Africa Quarterly [*A publication*]
AQ.............. Air Queensland [*Australia*]
AQ.............. Aircraft Quality (AAG)
AQ.............. Alcohol Quotient
AQ.............. Aloha Airlines, Inc. [*ICAO designator*] (FAAC)
AQ.............. Amazing Stories. Quarterly [*A publication*]
AQ.............. American Quarterly [*A publication*]
AQ.............. Antarctica [*ANSI two-letter standard code*] (CNC)
AQ.............. Anthraquinone [*Organic chemistry*]
aq.............. Antigua [*MARC country of publication code*] [*Library of Congress*] (LCCP)
AQ.............. Any Quantity
AQ.............. Apollo Qualification [*NASA*] (KSC)
AQ.............. Aqua [*Water*] [*Pharmacy*]
AQ.............. Aqueous
Aq............... Aquila's Greek Translation of the Bible [*A publication*] (BJA)

AQ.............	Arizona Quarterly [*A publication*]
AQ.............	Art Quarterly [*A publication*]
AQ.............	Asiatic Quarterly [*A publication*]
AQ.............	Assimulatory Quotient
AQ.............	Atlantic Quarterly [*A publication*]
AQ.............	Attainment Quotient
AQ.............	Australian Quarterly [*A publication*]
AQ.............	Autoquote [*Data processing*] (TEL)
AQ.............	Aviation Fire Control Technician [*Navy rating*]
Aq.............	De Aquae Ductu Urbis Romae [*of Frontinus*] [*Classical studies*] (OCD)
AQ.............	Syria [*License plate code assigned to foreign diplomats in the US*]
AQ.............	Westminster Aquarium [*British music hall popular in the 1870s-80s*] (DSUE)
AQ1...........	Aviation Fire Control Technician, First Class [*Navy rating*]
AQ2...........	Aviation Fire Control Technician, Second Class [*Navy rating*]
AQ3...........	Aviation Fire Control Technician, Third Class [*Navy rating*]
AQA..........	Air Quality Act
AQA..........	Application Quality Assurance [*Automotive engineering*] [*3M Co.*]
AQA..........	Araraquara [*Brazil*] [*Airport symbol*] [*Obsolete*] (OAG)
a-qa---	Qatar [*MARC geographic area code*] [*Library of Congress*] (LCCP)
AQAA.......	Airman Apprentice, Aviation Fire Control Technician, Striker [*Navy rating*]
AQAB.......	Air Quality Advisory Board
AQA EMS ...	AST/Quadram/Ashton-Tate Enhanced Memory Specification [*Quadram*] [*Norcross, GA*] [*Data processing*]
AQAFO.....	Aeronautical Quality Assurance Field Office [*FAA*] (FAAC)
AQAM......	Air Quality Assessment Model [*Air Force*]
AQ AMMON ...	Aqua Ammoniae [*Ammoniated Water*] [*Pharmacy*] (ROG)
AQAN.......	Airman, Aviation Fire Control Technician, Striker [*Navy rating*]
AQ ANETH ...	Aqua Anethi [*Dill Water*] [*Pharmacy*] (ROG)
AQ ANIS...	Aqua Anisi [*Anise Water*] [*Pharmacy*] (ROG)
AQAP	Allied Quality Assurance Provision [*NATO*] (MCD)
AQAP	Allied Quality Assurance Publication [*NATO*] (NATG)
Aqar	Aquarius [*Constellation*]
AQARD.....	Acqua Aria [*A publication*]
AQAS.......	American Quasar Petroleum Co. [*NASDAQ symbol*] (NQ)
AQ ASTR ..	Aqua Astricta [*Frozen Water*] [*Pharmacy*] (ROG)
AQB..........	Alberta Attorney General, Queen's Bench Libraries [*UTLAS symbol*]
AQB..........	Aqua 1 Beverage [*Vancouver Stock Exchange symbol*]
AQB..........	Army Qualification Battery [*of tests*]
AQB..........	Aviation Fire Control Technician, Bomb Direction [*Navy rating*]
AQBOAP ..	Arquivos Brasileiros de Oftalmologia [*A publication*]
AQBODS ..	Aquatic Botany [*A publication*]
AQBPA......	Arquivos Brasileiros de Psicotecnica [*A publication*]
AQ BULL ...	Aqua Bulliens [*Boiling Water*] [*Pharmacy*]
AQ BULLIENS ...	Aqua Bulliens [*Boiling Water*] [*Pharmacy*] (ROG)
AQC..........	Alaska Quaternary Center [*University of Alaska, Fairbanks*] [*Research center*] (RCD)
A Q C	Analytical and Quantitative Cytology [*A publication*]
AQC.........	Associate of Queen's College [*London*]
AQC..........	Automatic Quench Calibration [*or Correction*]
AQC..........	Automatic Quench Compensation [*Beckman Instruments, Inc.*] [*Instrumentation*]
AQC.........	Aviation Fire Control Technician, Chief [*Navy rating*]
AQC.........	Queensland Conveyancing Law and Practice [*A publication*]
AQ CAL.....	Aqua Calida [*Hot Water*] [*Pharmacy*]
AQ CALID ...	Aqua Calida [*Hot Water*] [*Pharmacy*] (ROG)
AQCESS ...	Automated Quality of Care Evaluation Support System [*Military*]
AQCHED ...	Analytical and Quantitative Cytology and Histology [*A publication*]
AQ CINNAM ...	Aqua Cinnamoni [*Cinnamon Water*] [*Pharmacy*] (ROG)
AQCL	Analytical Quality Control Laboratory (IID)
AQCLAL...	Aquaculture [*A publication*]
AQCM......	Aviation Fire Control Technician, Master Chief [*Navy rating*]
AQ COM...	Aqua Communis [*Tap Water*] [*Pharmacy*]
AQCR.......	Air Quality Control Region [*Environmental Protection Agency*]
AQCS	Aviation Fire Control Technician, Senior Chief [*Navy rating*]
AQCYDT ..	Analytical and Quantitative Cytology [*A publication*]
AQD..........	Additional Qualification Designator (NVT)
AQD..........	Aeronautical Quality Assurance Directorate [*British*]
AQD..........	Alleged Quarter [*of the year*] Disability Began [*Social Security Administration*] (OICC)
AQD..........	Average Quarterly Demand
AQD..........	Hartford, CT [*Location identifier*] [*FAA*] (FAAL)
AQ DEST ...	Aqua Destillata [*Distilled Water*] [*Pharmacy*]
AQDHS.....	Air Quality Data Handling System [*or Subsystem*] [*Environmental Protection Agency*]
AQDM......	Air Quality Display Model
AQE..........	Airman Qualifying Examination
AQE..........	Greenville, NC [*Location identifier*] [*FAA*] (FAAL)
AQF..........	Air Quality Forecast
AQF..........	Aviation Fire Control Technician, Fire Control [*Navy rating*]
AQFEDI....	Aqua Fennica [*A publication*]

AQ FERV ..	Aqua Fervens [*Warm Water*] [*Pharmacy*]
AQ FLUV ...	Aqua Fluviatilis [*River Water*] [*Pharmacy*] (ROG)
AQ FONT ...	Aqua Fontis [*Spring Water*] [*Pharmacy*] (ROG)
AQ FORT ...	Aqua Fortis [*Sulphuric Acid*] [*Pharmacy*] (ROG)
AQ FRIG ...	Aqua Frigida [*Cold Water*] [*Pharmacy*]
AQ FRIGID ...	Aqua Frigida [*Cold Water*] [*Pharmacy*] (ROG)
AQ GEL	Aqua Gelida [*Cold Water*] [*Pharmacy*]
AQGV........	Azimuth Quantized Gated Video [*Air Force*]
AQHA	American Quarter Horse Association (EA)
AQI...........	Air Quality Index
AQI...........	American Quicksilver Institute [*Defunct*] (EA)
AQI...........	Qaisumah [*Saudi Arabia*] [*Airport symbol*] (OAG)
AQIC	Anima Quiescat in Christo [*May His, or Her, Soul Repose in Christ*] [*Latin*]
Aqil	Aquila [*Constellation*]
AQIND......	Aquatic Insects [*A publication*]
AQINDQ....	Aquatic Insects [*A publication*]
AQIS..........	Australian Quarantine and Inspection Service
AQJ...........	Aqaba [*Jordan*] [*Airport symbol*] (OAG)
AQJOAV...	Aquarium Journal [*A publication*]
AQL..........	Acceptable Quality Level [*Quality control*]
AQL..........	Airworthiness Qualification Program
Aql	Aquila [*Constellation*]
AQL..........	Average Quality Limit
AQM..........	Air Quality Management
AQM..........	American Antiquarian Society, Worcester, MA [*OCLC symbol*] (OCLC)
AQM..........	Assistant Quartermaster
AQM..........	Atmospheric Quality and Modification [*National Center for Atmospheric Research*]
AQM.........	Drone Target [*Navy symbol*] [*British*]
AQM.........	QMS, Inc. [*NYSE symbol*] (SPSG)
AQMAA4 ...	Aquarien Magazin [*A publication*]
AQMAD7 ...	Aquatic Mammals [*A publication*]
AQ MAR ...	Aqua Marina [*Sea Water*] [*Pharmacy*] (ROG)
AQMC.......	Army Quartermaster Corps [*Merged with Supply and Maintenance Command*]
AQ MENTH ...	Aqua Mentha [*Mint Water*] [*Pharmacy*] (ROG)
AQ MENTH PIP ...	Aqua Mentha Piperitae [*Peppermint Water*] [*Pharmacy*] (ROG)
AQMG.......	Assistant Quartermaster-General [*Military*]
AQMPAF ...	Arquivos. Museu Paranaense [*A publication*]
AQMS	Armourer Quartermaster Sergeant [*British*]
AQMS	Artificer Quartermaster Sergeant [*British*]
AQMS	Artisan Quartermaster Sergeant [*British*]
AQN	Acton, TX [*Location identifier*] [*FAA*] (FAAL)
AQN	Azimuthal Quantum Number
AQ NIV	Aqua Nivalis [*Snow Water*] [*Pharmacy*] (ROG)
AQNT........	Aquanautics Corp. [*NASDAQ symbol*] (NQ)
AQP..........	Airworthiness Qualification Plan
AQP..........	Airworthiness Qualification Program (MCD)
AQP..........	Arequipa [*Peru*] [*Airport symbol*] (OAG)
AQP..........	Association for Quality and Participation (EA)
AQPA	American Quarter Pony Association (EA)
AQPA	American Quick Printing Association (EA)
AQ PIMENT ...	Aqua Pimentae [*Allspice Water*] [*Pharmacy*] (ROG)
AQ PLUV ...	Aqua Pluvialis [*or Pluviatilis*] [*Rain Water*] [*Pharmacy*] (ROG)
AQPTA......	Arquivos de Patologia [*Lisbon*] [*A publication*]
AQ PUR	Aqua Pura [*Pure Water*] [*Pharmacy*] (ROG)
AQQ	Annual Qualifications Questionnaire [*Navy*] (NVT)
AQQ	Apalachicola, FL [*Location identifier*] [*FAA*] (FAAL)
AQQPRI....	Advanced Qualitative and Quantitative Personnel Requirements Information [*Army*]
AQR..........	Acceptable Quality Rate [*Quality control*]
AQR..........	Afterloaded Quick Release [*Physiology*]
AQR	Air Quality Region
Aqr	Aquarius [*Constellation*]
AQR..........	Aquarius Resources Ltd. [*Vancouver Stock Exchange symbol*]
AQR..........	Asiatic Quarterly Review [*A publication*]
AQR..........	Assembly Quality Record
AQR..........	Assessment Quality Report (MCD)
A Qr D	After Quarter Day [*Freemasonry*] (ROG)
AQREC	Army Quartermaster Research and Engineering Command (MCD)
AQRLF......	Aquarius Resources Ltd. [*NASDAQ symbol*] (NQ)
AQRMAV ...	Aquarium [*Wuppertal*] [*A publication*]
AQ ROS ...	Aqua Rosa [*Rose Water*] [*Pharmacy*] (ROG)
AQ RUT	Aqua Ruta [*Rue Water*] [*Pharmacy*] (ROG)
AQRV	Air Quality Related Values/Visibility Test [*Environmental Protection Agency*]
AQS	Air Quality Standard
AQS	Airworthiness Qualification Specification
AQS	American Quilter's Society (EA)
AQS	Approximate Quadratic Search [*Mathematics*]
AQS	Aquarius Seafarms [*Vancouver Stock Exchange symbol*]
AQS	Saqani [*Fiji*] [*Airport symbol*] (OAG)
AQSBD6....	Anales de Quimica. Serie C. Quimica Organica y Bioquimica [*A publication*]
AQSG	American Quilt Study Group (EA)

AQSI......... AquaSciences International, Inc. [*Lincoln Park, NJ*] [*NASDAQ symbol*] (NQ)
AQSLU...... Aqua-Sol, Inc. Uts [*NASDAQ symbol*] (NQ)
AQSM .... Air Quality Simulation Model [*Environmental Protection Agency*]
AQ SOD .... Aqua Soda [*Soda Water*] [*Pharmacy*] (ROG)
AQSZ........ Aquilo Serie Zoologica [*A publication*]
AQT.......... Acceptable Quality Test [*Quality control*] (MSA)
AQT.......... Acquisitor Mines Ltd. [*Vancouver Stock Exchange symbol*]
AQT.......... Applicant Qualification Test [*Navy*]
AQT.......... Aviation Qualification Test
AQTE .... Association Quebecoise des Techniques de l'Eau [*Canada*] (ASF)
AQTEAH .. Aqua Terra [*A publication*]
AQTEBI .... Aquarien Terrarien [*A publication*]
AQ TEP .... Aqua Tepida [*Lukewarm Water*] [*Pharmacy*]
AQ TEPID ... Aqua Tepida [*Lukewarm Water*] [*Pharmacy*] (ROG)
AQTN........ Aequitron Medical, Inc. [*Minneapolis, MN*] [*NASDAQ symbol*] (NQ)
AQTOD..... Aquatic Toxicology [*A publication*]
AQTSA...... Arquivos de Tisiologia [*A publication*]
AQU .... Acqualin Resources Ltd. [*Vancouver Stock Exchange symbol*]
AQU .... Aquila [*Italy*] [*Geomagnetic observatory code*]
AQU .... Aquila [*Italy*] [*Seismograph station code, US Geological Survey*] (SEIS)
AQU .... Aquila Airways Ltd.
AQUA....... Aquaculture Products Technology [*NASDAQ symbol*] (NQ)
Aqua.......... Aquamarine [*Philately*]
AQUA........ Aquatic
Aqua Biol Ab ... Aquatic Biology Abstracts [*A publication*]
Aquacult Fish Manage ... Aquaculture and Fisheries Management [*A publication*]
Aquaculture Mag ... Aquaculture Magazine [*A publication*]
Aqua Fenn ... Aqua Fennica [*A publication*]
AQUAID... Acquisition Aid
Aqualine Abstr ... Aqualine Abstracts [*A publication*]
Aquarien Mag ... Aquarien Magazin [*A publication*]
Aquarium J ... Aquarium Journal [*A publication*]
AQUARIUS ... [*A*] Query and Retrieval Interactive Utility System [*Data processing*] (ADA)
A Quart...... Australian Quarterly [*A publication*] (APTA)
Aqua Sci & Fish Abstr ... Aquatic Sciences and Fisheries Abstracts [*A publication*]
Aquat Bot... Aquatic Botany [*A publication*]
Aquat Insec ... Aquatic Insects [*A publication*]
Aquat Insects ... Aquatic Insects [*A publication*]
Aquat Mamm ... Aquatic Mammals [*A publication*]
Aquat Microbiol Ecol Proc ... Aquatic Microbial Ecology. Proceedings of the Conference [*A publication*]
Aquat Sci ... Aquatic Sciences [*A publication*]
Aquat Sci Fish Abst Part I ... Aquatic Sciences and Fisheries Abstracts. Part I. Biological Sciences and Living Resources [*A publication*]
Aquat Sci Fish Abst Part II ... Aquatic Sciences and Fisheries Abstracts. Part II. Ocean Technology, Policy, and Non-Living Resources [*A publication*]
Aquat Toxicol (Amst) ... Aquatic Toxicology (Amsterdam) [*A publication*]
Aquat Toxicol (NY) ... Aquatic Toxicology (New York) [*A publication*]
Aquat Weed Control Soc Proc ... Aquatic Weed Control Society. Proceedings [*A publication*]
Aquat Weeds South East Asia Proc Reg Semin Noxious Aquat Veg ... Aquatic Weeds in South East Asia. Proceedings of a Regional Seminar on Noxious Aquatic Vegetation [*A publication*]
Aquil Nost ... Aquileia Nostra [*A publication*]
Aquilo Ser Bot ... Aquilo Serie Botanica [*A publication*]
Aquilo Ser Zool ... Aquilo Serie Zoologica [*A publication*]
AQUIRE.... Aquatic Information Retrieval Database [*Chemical Information Systems, Inc.*] [*Information service or system*]
AQUIS....... Acquisition (KSC)
AQY.......... Girdwood, AK [*Location identifier*] [*FAA*] (FAAL)
AR............. Aberdeen & Rockfish Railroad Co. [*AAR code*]
AR............. Accept-Reject Rule [*Statistics*]
AR............. Acceptance Readiness (NASA)
AR............. Acceptance Requirement
AR............. Acceptance Review (NASA)
AR............. Accomplishment Ratio (ADA)
A & R .... Account and Risk [*Investment term*]
AR............. Accounting Review [*A publication*]
AR............. Accounts Receivable [*Accounting*]
AR............. Accounts Register [*Data processing*]
AR............. Accumulator Register [*Data processing*]
A/R .... Accumulator/Reservoir (MCD)
AR............. Achievement Ratio
AR............. Acid Resisting [*Technical drawings*]
AR............. Acknowledgment of Receipt [*Message handling*] [*Telecommunications*]
AR............. Acoustic Reflex
AR............. Acquisition RADAR
AR............. Acting Rector [*Church of England in Australia*]
AR............. Action Register
A/R .... Action and/or Reply [*Control system*]
AR............. Active Range (MCD)

AR............. Active Resistance [*Occupational therapy*]
AR............. Activity Report (MCD)
AR............. Additional Requirements (DLA)
AR............. Address Register (CMD)
AR............. Adelaide Rifles [*Australia*] (DMA)
AR............. Administrative Ruling [*US*]
AR............. Adrenergic Receptor [*Physiology*]
AR............. Advanced Reactor (KSC)
AR............. Advanced Readiness (MCD)
AR............. Advice of Receipt
AR............. Aerial [*In-Flight*] Refueling
AR............. Aero Repair (MCD)
AR............. Aerodynamic Report
AR............. Aerolineas Argentinas [*Argentine airline*] [*ICAO designator*] (FAAC)
AR............. Aeronautical [*or Aircraft*] Requirement [*Military*] (MCD)
AR............. Aeronca Manufacturing [*ICAO aircraft manufacturer identifier*] (ICAO)
AR............. Africa Report [*A publication*]
AR............. Aft Right (MCD)
AR............. Age Replacement
AR............. Agencja Robotricza [*Press agency*] [*Poland*]
AR............. Agent Report (MCD)
AR............. Agricultural Research
AR............. Air Conditioning and Refrigeration Program [*Association of Independent Colleges and Schools specialization code*]
AR............. Air Radio [*Special duties officer*] [*British*]
A & R .... Air and Rail [*Shipping*]
AR............. Air Receive
AR............. Air Refueling
AR............. Air Register [*Combustion emission control*]
AR............. Air Regulator
AR............. Air Rescue
AR............. Air Reserve
AR............. Air Resistance
AR............. Aircraft Ready (AFIT)
AR............. Aircraft Rocket (NVT)
AR............. Airman Records [*Air Force*] (AFM)
AR............. Airman Recruit
AR............. Airship Rigger
AR............. Alabama Review [*A publication*]
AR............. Alarm Reaction [*Physiology*]
AR............. Alberta Reports [*Information service or system*] [*A publication*]
AR............. All Rail [*Railroad*]
AR............. All Risks [*Insurance*]
A/R .... All Round [*Price*] (ROG)
AR............. Allard Register (EA)
AR............. Allegheny Region
AR............. Allergic Reaction [*Immunology*]
AR............. Allergic Rhinitis [*Medicine*]
AR............. Alliance Review [*New York*] [*A publication*]
AR............. Allocated Reserve
A/R .... Alternate Route [*Telecommunications*] (TEL)
AR............. Altesse Royale [*Royal Highness*] [*French*]
AR............. Amateur (Radio) Station [*ITU designation*] (CET)
AR............. Amendment Request [*Navy*]
AR............. America Remembers (EA)
AR............. American Record Guide [*A publication*]
AR............. American Recorder [*A publication*]
AR............. American Reports [*A publication*] (DLA)
AR............. American Review [*Formerly, New American Review*] [*A publication*]
AR............. American Rivers (EA)
AR............. Amilcar Register (EA)
AR............. Amphibian Reconnaissance [*Military*]
AR............. Amphiregulin [*Biochemistry*]
AR............. Amplification Ratio (MCD)
AR............. Amrinone [*Cardiotonic*]
AR............. Analytical Reagent [*Chemistry*]
AR............. Anaphylactoid Reaction [*Immunology*]
AR............. Androgen Receptors [*Endocrinology*]
AR............. Angle Resolved [*Physics*]
A & R .... Angus & Robertson [*Publisher*] [*Australia*]
AR............. Anna Regina [*Queen Anne*]
AR............. Anno Regni [*In the Year of the Reign*] [*Latin*]
AR............. Annual Register [*A publication*]
AR............. Annual Report
AR............. Annual Return
AR............. Annual Review (NATG)
AR............. Annual Reviews (EA)
AR............. Anode Reaction
AR............. Anomaly Report (MCD)
AR............. Anterior Resection [*Medicine*]
AR............. Antioch Review [*A publication*]
AR............. Antiphonale Sacrosanctae Romanae Ecclesiae
AR............. Antiquitaeten-Rundschau [*A publication*]
AR............. Antiracketeering
AR............. AntiRADAR (NATG)
AR............. Antireflection
AR............. Antireversionary [*Method of exhaust control*] [*Automotive engineering*]

AR	Antiviral Research [*A publication*]
AR	Aortic Regurgitation [*Medicine*]
AR	Aortic Root [*Cardiology*]
A/R	Apical/Radial [*Pulse*] [*Medicine*]
AR	Apical Rate [*Medicine*]
AR	Appeal Reports, Upper Canada [*1846-66*] [*A publication*] (DLA)
AR	Applied Research
AR	Applied Research [*of ASRA*] [*National Science Foundation*]
AR	Appointments Register
AR	Approved for Release
A & R	Approved and Removed
ar-----	Arabian Peninsula [*MARC geographic area code*] [*Library of Congress*] (LCCP)
AR	Arabic
Ar	Arabinoside
Ar	Arakhin [*or Arakin*] (BJA)
AR	Aramaic [*Language, etc.*] (ROG)
AR	Archaeological Reports [*A publication*]
Ar	Arche [*A publication*]
Ar	Archidiaconus [*Authority cited in pre-1607 legal work*] (DSA)
AR	Architectural Review [*A publication*]
AR	Architecture
AR	Archiv fuer Reformationsgeschichte [*A publication*]
Ar	Archive [*Quezon City*] [*A publication*]
Ar	Archivio [*A publication*]
AR	Archivum Romanicum [*A publication*]
AR	Arcuate [*Brain anatomy*]
Ar	[*Jacobus de*] Arditionibus [*Flourished, 1213-50*] [*Authority cited in pre-1607 legal work*] (DSA)
AR	Area
AR	Area of Resolution
AR	Area Weapon Right (MCD)
AR	Areito [*A publication*]
Ar	Arena [*A publication*]
AR	Argentina [*ANSI two-letter standard code*] (CNC)
AR	Argentum [*Silver*] [*Numismatics*]
Ar	Argon [*Preferred form, but also see A*] [*Chemical element*]
AR	Argus Corp. Ltd. [*Toronto Stock Exchange symbol*]
Ar	Ariprandus [*Flourished, 12th century*] [*Authority cited in pre-1607 legal work*] (DSA)
Ar	Aristophanes [*Greek playwright, c. 445-380BC*] [*Classical studies*] (OCD)
AR	Arithmetic Register
AR	Arizona Review [*A publication*]
AR	Arkansas [*Postal code*]
Ar	Arkansas Library Commission, Little Rock, AR [*Library symbol*] [*Library of Congress*] (LCLS)
AR	Armagh [*County in Ireland*] (ROG)
A/R	Armed Reconnaissance (MUGU)
AR	Armored Reconnaissance
AR	Army
AR	Army Regulation
AR	Army Reserve [*Formerly, ERC, ORC*]
ar	Aromatic [*Chemistry*]
AR	Arrested Relaxation [*Molecular dynamics*]
AR	Arrete [*Decision, Ordinance, By-law*] [*French*] (DLA)
AR	Arrete Royal [*Royal Decree*] [*Belgian*] (ILCA)
AR	Arrival
AR	Arrival and Return [*Shipping*]
Ar	Arsendinus de Forlivio [*Authority cited in pre-1607 legal work*] (DSA)
AR	Articulare [*Craniometric point*]
AR	Artificial Respiration [*Medicine*]
A & R	Artists and Repertory
Ar	Aryl [*Chemistry*]
AR	As Required (AFM)
AR	ASARCO, Inc. [*Formerly, American Smelting & Refining Company*] [*NYSE symbol*] (SPSG)
AR	Asian Review [*A publication*]
AR	Aspect Ratio
A & R	Assembly and Repair
AR	Assigned Rating [*Sailing*]
AR	Assistant Registrar (ROG)
AR	Associate in Retailing
AR	Associated Rediffusion [*Television*]
AR	Associative Register [*Data processing*]
AR	Asthma Rhinitis [*Immunology*]
A/R	At the Rate Of (MUGU)
A & R	Atene e Roma [*A publication*]
AR	Atlantic Reporter [*A publication*] (DLA)
AR	Atmospheric Revitalization (MCD)
AR	Atrial Rate [*Cardiology*]
AR	Attenuation Reaction
AR	Attrition Reserve
AR	Audio Response
AR	Auditor of Receipts
AR	Auditor of Revenue
AR	Aufsichtsrat [*Supervisory Board*] [*German*]
AR	Augmentation Reliability (MCD)
AR	Augmented Roman (ADA)

AR	Austin Rover [*British-built automobile*]
AR	Australian Republican
A/R	AUTOLAND [*Automatic Landing*] Rollout [*NASA*] (MCD)
AR	Automated Radioimmunoassay
AR	Automated Reagin [*Serology*]
AR	Automatic Radio Manufacturing Co., Inc.
AR	Automatic Resupply (NVT)
AR	Automatic Rifle [*or Rifleman*] [*DoD*]
AR	Autonomous Republic
AR	Autoradiographic
AR	Autoregressive [*Mathematical bioscience*]
AR	Autosomal Recessive [*Genetics*]
AR	Average Rating
AR	Average Revenue
AR	Aviation Radionavigation, Land [*FCC*] (IEEE)
AR	Avionics Requirements (MCD)
AR	Avis de Reception [*Return Receipt*] [*French*]
AR	Awaiting Reply [*Telecommunications*] (TEL)
A/R	Azimuth/Range (RDA)
AR	Bomber [*Russian aircraft symbol*]
AR	Egypt [*IYRU nationality code*] (IYR)
AR	Industrial Arbitration Reports [*New South Wales*] [*A publication*] (APTA)
AR	Ontario Appeal Reports [*A publication*] (DLA)
AR	Ralston Public Library, Alberta [*Library symbol*] [*National Library of Canada*] (NLC)
AR	Repair Ship [*Navy symbol*]
AR	Stanlabs, Inc. [*Research code symbol*]
AR1	Volcano Arenal [*Costa Rica*] [*Seismograph station code, US Geological Survey*] (SEIS)
AR2	Lago De Cote [*Costa Rica*] [*Seismograph station code, US Geological Survey*] (SEIS)
AR3	Tierras Morenas [*Costa Rica*] [*Seismograph station code, US Geological Survey*] (SEIS)
AR4	Solania [*Costa Rica*] [*Seismograph station code, US Geological Survey*] (SEIS)
AR5	Santa Elena [*Costa Rica*] [*Seismograph station code, US Geological Survey*] (SEIS)
AR6	Chripa [*Costa Rica*] [*Seismograph station code. US Geological Survey*] (SEIS)
AR7	Cabo Frio [*Costa Rica*] [*Seismograph station code, US Geological Survey*] (SEIS)
AR8	Nicoya [*Costa Rica*] [*Seismograph station code, US Geological Survey*] (SEIS)
AR9	Volcan Norte [*Costa Rica*] [*Seismograph station code, US Geological Survey*] (SEIS)
A²R²	Argonne Advanced Research Reactor (NRCH)
ARA	Abbreviated Registered Address
ARA	Academy of Rehabilitative Audiology (EA)
ARA	Accelerated Readiness Analysis (NG)
ARA	Accredited Rural Appraiser [*Designation awarded by American Society of Farm Managers and Rural Appraisers*]
ARA	Acetylene Reduction Assay [*Botany*]
ARA	Active Retrodirective Array (MCD)
ARA	Adapter, Right Angle
ARA	Aerial Refueling Area
ARA	Aerial Rocket Artillery
ARA	Aerospace Research Association (MCD)
ARA	Agricultural Research Administration [*Superseded by ARS, 1953*] [*Department of Agriculture*]
ARA	Air Reserve Association [*Later, Air Force Association*]
ARA	Airborne RADAR Approach (AFM)
ARA	Airborne Receiving Antenna
ARA	Aircraft Replaceable Assemblies
ARA	Aircraft Research Association (EAIO)
ARA	Allied Research Associates, Inc. (MCD)
ARA	Aluminum Recycling Association (EA)
ARA	Amateur Rocketeers of America
ARA	Amateur Rowing Association [*British*]
ARA	American Archives Association (EA)
ARA	American Radio Association (EA)
ARA	American Rafting Association (EA)
ARA	American Railway Association [*Later, AAR*]
ARA	American Recovery Association (EA)
ARA	American Recreational Activities
ARA	American Relief Administration Association
ARA	American Reloaders Association (EA)
ARA	American Remount Association
ARA	American Rental Association (EA)
ARA	American Republics Area [*Department of State*]
ARA	American Restitution Association (EA)
ARA	American Retreaders Association (EA)
ARA	American Revenue Association (EA)
ARA	American Rheumatism Association [*Later, ACR*] (EA)
ARA	American Romagnola Association (EA)
ARA	American Romanian Academy of Arts and Sciences (EA)
ARA	American Rowing Association (EA)
ARA	American Royal Association (EA)
ARA	Amsterdam, Rotterdam, Antwerp
ARA3	Analog RADAR Absorber
ARA	Ancient Records of Assyria [*A publication*] (BJA)

ARA .... [*PTS*] Annual Reports Abstracts [*Predicasts, Inc.*] [*Information service or system*] (IID)
ARA .... Antireceptor Antibody [*Immunology*]
ARA .... Arab Relief Agency
ARA .... Arab Roads Association [*Cairo, Egypt*] (EAIO)
ARA .... Arabesque [*Embossed*] [*Bookbinding*] (ROG)
ARA .... Arabic [*Language, etc.*]
ara .... Arabic [*MARC language code*] [*Library of Congress*] (LCCP)
Ara .... Arabinose [*Also, a*] [*A sugar*]
ARA .... ARAMCO [*Arabian American Oil Company*] World Magazine [*A publication*]
ARA .... Arapuni [*New Zealand*] [*Seismograph station code, US Geological Survey*] [*Closed*] (SEIS)
ARA .... Arcade & Attica Railroad Corp. [*AAR code*]
ARA .... Area Redevelopment Act
ARA .... Area Redevelopment Administration [*Terminated, 1965; functions transferred to Economic Development Administration*] [*Department of Commerce*]
ARA .... Army Rifle Association [*British military*] (DMA)
ARA .... Artists' Representatives Association [*Defunct*] (EA)
ARA .... Artists Rights Association [*Defunct*]
ARA .... Asian Recycling Association (EAIO)
ARA .... Assigned Responsible Agency [*DoD*]
ARA .... Associate Regional Administrator
ARA .... Associate in Religious Arts
ARA .... Associate of the Royal Academy [*British*]
ARA .... Associates for Radio Astronomy
ARA .... Association of Retired Americans (EA)
ARA .... Attitude Reference Assembly (MCD)
ARA .... Aurora Air Service, Inc. [*Fairbanks, AK*] [*FAA designator*] (FAAC)
ARA .... Australian Reading Association
ARA .... Australian Robot Association
ARA .... Auto Recovery Association of New South Wales [*Australia*]
ARA .... Auto-Resonant Accelerator [*For atomic particles*]
ARA .... Automatic Retailers of America (MCD)
ARA .... Automatic Route Advancement (MCD)
ARA .... Automotive Retailers Association [*Canada*]
ARA .... Auxiliary Recovery Antenna [*NASA*] (KSC)
ARA .... Average Response Amplitude
ARA .... Avionics Repairable Assemblies (AFIT)
ARA .... Avionics Research Aircraft (MCD)
ARA .... New Iberia, LA [*Location identifier*] [*FAA*] (FAAL)
ARA .... Society of American Registered Architects (EA)
ARAA .... Aerodrome RADAR/Radio Approach Aid
ARAA .... American Registry of Architectural Antiquities (EA)
ARAA .... American Russian Aid Association (EA)
ARAA .... Annual Review of Astronomy and Astrophysics [*A publication*]
ara-A .... Arabinofuranosyladenine [*or Adenine Arabinoside*] [*Also, Vira-A*] [*Antiviral compound*]
Ar A A .... Arbeiten aus Anglistik und Amerikanistik [*A publication*]
ARAAA ..... Annual Review of Astronomy and Astrophysics [*A publication*]
ara-AMP ... Adenine Arabinoside Monophosphate [*Biochemistry*]
ARAAS ..... Annual Reports on Analytical Atomic Spectroscopy [*Later, JAAS*] [*A publication*]
ara-ATP .... Adenine Arabinoside Triphosphate [*Biochemistry*]
ARAAV .... Armored Reconnaissance Airborne Assault Vehicle (AABC)
ARAB .... American Riding Association of Berlin [*Post-World War II*]
ARAB .... Ancient Records of Assyria and Babylonia [*A publication*] (BJA)
ARAB .... Arabic [*Language, etc.*] (ROG)
ARABAn ... Academie Royale d'Archeologie de Belgique. Annales [*A publication*]
ARABBull ... Academie Royale d'Archeologie de Belgique. Bulletin [*A publication*]
Arab Enrgy ... Arab Energy. Prospects to 2000 [*A publication*]
Arab F & TV ... Arab Film and Television Center News [*A publication*]
Arab Gulf J ... Arab Gulf Journal [*A publication*]
Arab Gulf J Sci Res ... Arab Gulf Journal of Scientific Research [*A publication*]
ARABHA .. Arab Historians Association (EAIO)
Arabian J Sci Eng ... Arabian Journal for Science and Engineering [*A publication*]
Arabian J Sci and Eng ... Arabian Journal for Science and Engineering [*A publication*]
Arabian J Sci Engrg ... Arabian Journal for Science and Engineering [*A publication*]
Arabin .... Decision of Sergeant Arabin [*A publication*] (DLA)
Arab J Math ... [*The*] Arab Journal of Mathematics [*A publication*]
Arab J Nucl Sci Appl ... Arab Journal of Nuclear Sciences and Applications [*A publication*]
Arab Metall News ... Arab Metallurgical News [*Algeria*] [*A publication*]
Arab Min J ... Arab Mining Journal [*A publication*]
ARABS ...... Active RADAR Augmentor Beacon System (MCD)
ARABS ...... Association of Religion and Applied Behavioral Science [*Later, ACC*] (EA)
ARABSAT ... Arab Satellite Communications Organization [*Saudi Arabia*] [*Telecommunications*] (TSSD)
Arab Studies Q ... Arab Studies Quarterly [*A publication*]
ArabW .... Arab World [*A publication*]

ARAC .... Academie Royale des Arts du Canada [*Royal Canadian Academy of Arts - RCA*]
ARAC .... Accredited Review Appraisers Council (EA)
ARAC .... Aerospace Research Applications Center [*Indiana University*] [*NASA*]
ARAC .... Alcoma Community Library, Rainier, Alberta [*Library symbol*] [*National Library of Canada*] (NLC)
ARAC .... Aracca Petroleum Corp. [*NASDAQ symbol*] (NQ)
ara-C .... Aracytidine [*Cytarabine*] [*Also, CA, CAR*] [*Antineoplastic drug*]
ARAC .... Area Airports Checked (FAAC)
ARAC .... Army RADAR Approach Control Facility (FAAC)
ARAC .... Art and Architecture [*A publication*]
ARAC .... Association of Rain Apparel Contractors (EA)
ARAC .... Atmospheric Release Advisory Capability [*Energy Research and Development Administration*]
ARAC .... Australian Refugee Advisory Council
ARACC ..... Archives of Acoustics [*A publication*]
ARACH ..... Arachnology
Arachno Entomol Lek ... Arachno Entomologia Lekarska [*A publication*]
ara-C-HU .. Aracytidine, Hydroxyurea [*Antineoplastic drug regimen*]
ARACI ...... Associate of the Royal Australian Chemical Institute
ara-CMP ... Cytosine Arabinoside Monophosphate [*Biochemistry*]
ara-CTP ..... Cytosine Arabinoside Triphosphate [*Biochemistry*]
ARAD .... Airborne RADAR and Doppler
ARAD .... Alpha Research and Development (KSC)
ARAD .... Altitude Radial [*Aviation*] (FAAC)
ARAD .... Associate of the Royal Academy of Dancing [*British*]
ARAD .... Automated Requirements Allocation Data (MCD)
ARAD .... Average Response Amplitude Data
ARAD .... Radway Public Library, Alberta [*Library symbol*] [*National Library of Canada*] (NLC)
ARADAS... Annual Report. Center for Adult Diseases [*Osaka*] [*A publication*]
ARADCOM ... Army Air Defense Command [*or Commander*] [*Later, AADCOM*]
ARADMAC ... Army Aeronautical Depot Maintenance Center [*AMC-ASMC*]
A Rad Raspr ... Arheoloski Radovi i Rasprave [*A publication*]
ARADS ...... Artillery Registration/Adjustment System [*ARRADCOM*] (MCD)
ARADSCH ... Army Air Defense School
ARAE .... American Retail Association Executives [*Defunct*] (EA)
ARAeS .... Associate of the Royal Aeronautical Society [*British*]
ARAF .... Associated Regional Accounting Firms [*Atlanta, GA*] (EA)
ARAFAY... Anales. Real Academia de Farmacia [*A publication*]
ara-FC....... Arabinofuranosylfluorocytosine [*Also, FCA*] [*Antineoplastic drug*]
ara-H......... Arabinosylhypoxanthine [*Biochemistry*]
ARAI .... Allied Research Corp. [*NASDAQ symbol*] (NQ)
ARAI .... Annuario. Reale Accademia d'Italia [*A publication*]
ARAL........ Annual Review of Applied Linguistics [*A publication*]
ARAL........ Association to Repeal Abortion Laws (EA)
ARAL........ Automatic Record Analysis Language [*Data processing*]
ARALL...... Aramid Reinforced Aluminum Laminate (MCD)
ARALNS... Atti. Reale Accademia dei Lincei. Notizie degli Scavi [*Rome*] [*A publication*]
ARAM ...... Aramaic [*Language, etc.*]
ARAM ...... Army Achievement Medal [*Military decoration*]
ARAM ...... Associate of the Royal Academy of Music [*British*]
ARAM ...... Association of Railroad Advertising and Marketing (EA)
ARAMCO ... Arabian-American Oil Company
ARAMCO W ... ARAMCO [*Arabian American Oil Company*] World Magazine [*A publication*]
ARAMCO World M ... ARAMCO [*Arabian American Oil Company*] World Magazine [*A publication*]
ARAMIS ... American Rheumatism Association Medical Information System [*Information service or system*] (IID)
ara-MP ...... Arabinosylmercaptopurine [*Antineoplastic drug*]
ARAN........ Association for the Reduction of Aircraft Noise (EA)
ARANA ..... Anales. Real Academia Nacional de Medicina [*Spain*] [*A publication*]
ARANAO ... Anales. Real Academia Nacional de Medicina [*Madrid*] [*A publication*]
ARANBP... Arctic Anthropology [*A publication*]
ARAND ..... Analysis of Random Data [*System documentation*] [*Oregon State University*]
ARANDR .. Archives of Andrology [*A publication*]
Araneta J Agric ... Araneta Journal of Agriculture [*A publication*]
Araneta Res J ... Araneta Research Journal [*A publication*]
ArAO .... Ouachita Baptist University, Arkadelphia, AR [*Library symbol*] [*Library of Congress*] (LCLS)
ARAOAR .. Agronomia Angolana [*A publication*]
ARAOLA... Association of Romanian-American Orthodox Ladies Auxiliaries (EA)
ARAP........ Administration du Retablissement Agricole des Prairies [*Prairie Farm Rehabilitation Administration - PFRA*]
ARAP........ Aeronautical Research Associates of Princeton (MCD)
ARAP........ Alternative Resource Allocation Priorities [*Military*]
ARAP........ Astronaut Rescue Air Pack [*NASA*] (KSC)
ARAP........ Automated Reliability Assessment Program [*FAA*]
ARAP........ Average Revenue/Average Physical Product [*Economics*]

ARAPCS ... Association for Research, Administration, Professional Councils, and Societies (EA)
ARAPCW ... Annual Review of Anthropology [*A publication*]
ARAPH ..... Automated Reading Aid for the Physically Handicapped
ARAPI .... Affiliate of the Royal Australian Planning Institute
ARAPT ...... Advanced Research Agency Project Tempo (MCD)
ARAR .... Arctic and Alpine Research [*A publication*]
ARARA ..... American Rock Art Research Association (EA)
ARAS .... Artillery Registration/Adjustment System [*ARRADCOM*] (MCD)
Ar As .... Arts Asiatiques [*A publication*]
ARAS .... Ascending Reticular Activating [*or Activation*] System
ARAS .... Associate of the Royal Astronomical Society [*British*]
ARAS .... Association of Regular Army Sergeants (EA)
ARAS .... Atomic Resonance Absorption Spectroscopy [*Physics*]
ARaS .... Redstone Scientific Information Center, United States Army Missile Command, Redstone Arsenal, AL [*Library symbol*] [*Library of Congress*] (LCLS)
ARASA5 ... Acta Radiologica. Supplementum [*A publication*]
ARASC7 ... Annual Reports on Analytical Atomic Spectroscopy [*A publication*]
ARAST ...... Atti. Reale Accademia delle Scienze di Torino [*A publication*]
ARASUSA ... Association of Russian-American Scholars in the United States of America (EA)
ARAT .... Advise [*names of*] Representatives, Accommodations, and Transportation [*desired*] [*Army*] (AABC)
ARAT .... Aerial Rocket Antitank Program (MCD)
ara-T .... Arabinofuranosylthymine [*Biochemistry*]
Arat .... Aratea [*of Germanicus*] [*Classical studies*] (OCD)
Arat .... Aratus [*of Plutarch*] [*Classical studies*] (OCD)
ARAT .... Automatic Random Access Transport
ArAT .... Henderson State University, Arkadelphia, AR [*Library symbol*] [*Library of Congress*] (LCLS)
ARATDL ... Air Resources Atmospheric Turbulence and Diffusion Laboratory [*National Oceanic and Atmospheric Administration*] (NOAA)
ARATE ...... Australian Financial Markets Database
A/RATLR ... Antirattler [*Automotive engineering*]
ara-U .... Uracil Arabinoside [*Biochemistry*]
Araucariana Ser Bot ... Araucariana. Serie Botanica [*A publication*]
Araucariana Ser Geocienc ... Araucariana. Serie Geociencias [*A publication*]
Araucariana Ser Zool ... Araucariana. Serie Zoologia [*A publication*]
AR Austrl ... Industrial Arbitration Reports, New South Wales (Australia) [*A publication*] (ILCA)
ARAV .... Army Aviator (AABC)
AR Av Bad ... Army Aviator Badge [*Military decoration*]
AR Av MO Bad ... Army Aviation Medical Officer's Badge [*Military decoration*]
ARAVS ...... Auxiliary and RADWASTE Area Ventilation System [*Nuclear energy*] (NRCH)
ARAWDK ... Abhandlungen. Rheinisch-Westfaelische Akademie der Wissenschaften [*A publication*]
ARAY .... Arrays, Inc. [*Van Nuys, CA*] [*NASDAQ symbol*] (NQ)
ARAY .... Raymond Public Library, Alberta [*Library symbol*] [*National Library of Canada*] (NLC)
ARB .... Academie Royale de Belgique. Bulletin. Classe des Lettres et des Sciences Morales et Politiques [*A publication*]
ARB .... Accounting Research Board Opinion [*A publication*] (DLA)
ARB .... Accounting Research Bulletin [*A publication*]
ARB .... Acquisition Review Board [*Military*] (CAAL)
ARB .... Administrative Research Bulletin
ARB .... Africa Research Bulletin [*A publication*]
ARB .... Africana Research Bulletin [*A publication*]
ARB .... Air Refueling Boom (MCD)
ARB .... Air Registration Board [*British*]
ARB .... Air Research Bureau
ARB .... Air Reserve Base
ARB .... Air Resources Board [*California*]
ARB .... Aircraft Reactors Branch
ARB .... Aircraft Recovery Bulletin (MCD)
ARB .... Airworthiness Requirements Board [*British*] (AIA)
ARB .... Alianza Revolucionaria Barrientista [*Bolivia*] [*Political party*] (PPW)
ARB .... All Routes Busy [*Telecommunications*] (TEL)
ARB .... Alternate Reproductive Behavior [*Zoology*]
ARB .... American Realty Trust SBI [*NYSE symbol*] (SPSG)
ARB .... American Research Bureau
ARB .... Amnesty Review Board [*Terminated, 1976*]
ARB .... Ann Arbor, MI [*Location identifier*] [*FAA*] (FAAL)
ARB .... Any Reliable Brand [*Pharmacology*]
ARB .... APCHE [*Automatic Program Checkout Equipment*] Relay Box
ARB .... Appeals Review Board [*Formerly, BAR*] [*Civil Service Commission*]
Arb .... Arbeidsblad [*A publication*]
ARB .... Arbiter (ADA)
Arb .... Arbitrageur [*Stock exchange term*]
ARB .... Arbitrary (MSA)
Arb .... Arbitration (DLA)
ARB .... Arbitration Journal [*A publication*]
Arb .... Arbitrator (DLA)

ARB .... Arbitron Radio Summary Data [*Arbitron Ratings Co.*] [*Information service or system*]
Arb .... Arbor [*A publication*]
ARB .... Armored Rifle Battalion
ARB .... Army Rearming Base
ARB .... Army Retiring Board
ARB .... ASTIA [*Armed Services Technical Information Agency*] Report Bibliography (MCD)
ARB .... Australian Ranger Bulletin [*A publication*] (APTA)
ARB .... Automatic RADAR Beacon
ARB .... Auxiliary Repair Battle Damage [*British military*] (DMA)
ARB .... Battle Damage Repair Ship [*Navy symbol*]
ARB .... Concise Australian Reference Book [*A publication*] (ADA)
ARB .... Labor Arbitration Awards [*Commerce Clearing House*] [*A publication*] (DLA)
ARBA .... American Rabbit Breeders Association (EA)
ARBA .... American Red Brangus Association (EA)
ARBA .... American Reference Books Annual [*A publication*]
ARBA .... American Revolution Bicentennial Administration [*Formerly, ARBC*] [*Disbanded, 1977*]
ARBA .... American Road Builders' Association [*Later, ARTBA*]
ARBA .... American Romney Breeders' Association (EA)
ARB & A ... Arbitration and Award [*Legal term*] (DLA)
ARBA .... Associate of the Royal Society of British Artists
ARBA .... Associated Retail Bakers of America [*Later, Retail Bakers of America*] (EA)
ArBaA .... Arkansas College, Batesville, AR [*Library symbol*] [*Library of Congress*] (LCLS)
ARBAC ...... American Revolution Bicentennial Advisory Council [*American Revolution Bicentennial Administration*]
Arb Anat Inst ... Arbeiten. Anatomisches Institut [*A publication*]
Arb Anat Inst Kais Jpn Univ Sendai ... Arbeiten. Anatomisches Institut. Kaiserlich Japanischen Universitaet zu Sendai [*A publication*]
ARBAT ...... Application of RADAR to Ballistic Acceptance Testing [*of ammunition*] (MCD)
Arb Ausgl G ... Gesetz u. d. Ausgleichs und Schiedsverfahren Arbeitsstreitigkeiten [*Law on Labor Arbitration*] [*German*] (ILCA)
ARBB .... American Revolution Bicentennial Board [*American Revolution Bicentennial Administration*]
ARBBA ...... American Railway Bridge and Building Association (EA)
ARBBCL ... Academie Royale de Belgique. Bulletin. Classe des Lettres et des Sciences Morales et Politiques [*A publication*]
Arb Ber Sueddtsch Ver Forschungsanst Milchwirtsch ... Arbeiten und Berichte. Sueddeutsche Versuchs und Forschungsanstalt fuer Milchwirtschaft [*A publication*]
Arb Biol Reichanst Land Forstw (Berlin) ... Arbeiten. Biologischen Reichsanstalt fuer Land- und Forstwirtschaft (Berlin) [*A publication*]
Arb Bl Rest ... Arbeitsblaetter fuer Restauratoren [*A publication*]
Arb Bot Inst Wurz ... Arbeiten. Botanischen Instituts in Wurzburg [*A publication*]
ARBBull .... Academie Royale de Belgique. Bulletin. Classe des Lettres et des Sciences Morales et Politiques et Classe des Beaux-Arts [*A publication*]
ARBC .... American Republic Bancorp [*NASDAQ symbol*] (NQ)
ARBC .... American Revolution Bicentennial Commission [*Later, ARBA*]
ARBC .... Associate of the Royal British Colonial Society of Artists
ARBC .... Attitude Reference Bombing Computer (MCD)
ARBCEY ... Annual Review of Biophysics and Biophysical Chemistry [*A publication*]
ARBCS ...... Attitude Reference Bombing Computer Set [*or System*] (MCD)
ARBDD ..... Arbeidervern [*A publication*]
Arb Deut Landwirt Ges ... Arbeiten. Deutsche Landwirtschafts-Gesellschaft [*A publication*]
Arb Dritten Abt Anat Inst Kais Univ Kyoto Ser A ... Arbeiten. Dritte Abteilung des Anatomischen Institutes der Kaiserlichen Universitaet Kyoto. Serie A. Untersuchungen ueber das Periphere Nervensystem [*A publication*]
Arb Dritten Abt Anat Inst Kais Univ Kyoto Ser C ... Arbeiten. Dritte Abteilung des Anatomischen Institutes der Kaiserlichen Universitaet Kyoto. Serie C. Experimentelle Tuberkuloseforschung [*A publication*]
Arb Dritten Abt Anat Inst Kais Univ Kyoto Ser D ... Arbeiten. Dritte Abteilung des Anatomischen Institutes der Kaiserlichen Universitaet Kyoto. Serie D. Lymphatologie [*A publication*]
ARBED ...... Acieries Reunies de Burbach-Eich-Dudelange [*Business term*] [*Luxembourg*]
ArBegriffsg ... Archiv fuer Begriffsgeschichte [*Bonn*] [*A publication*]
Arbeiten Angew Statist ... Arbeiten zur Angewandten Statistik [*A publication*]
Arbeiten Niedersaechs Staats- u Universitaetsbibl ... Arbeiten aus der Niedersaechsischen Staats- und Universitaetsbibliothek (Goettingen) [*A publication*]
Arbeitg .... Arbeitgeber [*Employer*] [*German*]
Arbeitneh Aus ... Arbeitnehmerverdienste im Ausland [*A publication*]
Arbeitsber Inst Math Masch Datenverarb Band 14 ... Arbeitsberichte. Instituts fuer Mathematische Maschinen und Datenverarbeitung. Band 14 [*A publication*]

Arbeitsber Inst Math Masch Datenverarb Band 15 ... Arbeitsberichte. Instituts fuer Mathematische Maschinen und Datenverarbeitung. Band 15 [*A publication*]

Arbeitsber Rechenzentrum ... Arbeitsberichte des Rechenzentrums [*Bochum*] [*A publication*]

Arbeitsgem ... Arbeitsgemeinschaft [*Study Group*] [*German*]

Arbeitsgem-Forsch Landes Nordrh-Westfalen ... Arbeitsgemeinschaft fuer Forschung des Landes Nordrhein-Westfalen [*West Germany*] [*A publication*]

Arbeitsmed Kolloq Ber Jahrestag Dtsh Ges Arbeitsmed ... Arbeitsmedizinisches Kolloquium Bericht ueber die Jahrestagung der Deutschen Gesellschaft fuer Arbeitsmedizin [*A publication*]

Arbeitsmed Sozialmed Arbeitshyg ... Arbeitsmedizin, Sozialmedizin, Arbeitshygiene [*Later, Arbeitsmedizin, Sozialmedizin, Praeventivmedizin*] [*A publication*]

Arbeitsmed Sozialmed Praeventivmed ... Arbeitsmedizin, Sozialmedizin, Praeventivmedizin [*A publication*]

Arbeit und Sozialpol ... Arbeit und Sozialpolitik [*A publication*]

Arbeitspapiere Pol Soziol ... Arbeitspapiere zur Politischen Soziologie [*A publication*]

Arbeitstag Physiol Pathophysiol Prostata ... Arbeitstagung ueber Physiologie und Pathophysiologie der Prostata [*A publication*]

Arbeit und Wirt ... Arbeit und Wirtschaft [*A publication*]

Arbejdsmark (Kob) ... Nationalmuseets Arbejdsmark (Kobenhavn) [*A publication*]

ArBerC....... Carroll County Heritage Center, Berryville, AR [*Library symbol*] [*Library of Congress*]   (LCLS)

Arb F Ber Saechs ... Arbeits- und Forschungsberichte zur Saechsischen Bodendenkmalpflege [*A publication*]

Arb Futterbau ... Arbeiten aus dem Gebiete des Futterbaues [*A publication*]

Arb G .... Arbeitsgericht [*Labor Court*] [*German*]   (DLA)

ARBGB9.... Acta Radiobotanica et Genetica [*A publication*]

Arb Gebiete Futterbaues ... Arbeiten aus dem Gebiete des Futterbaues [*A publication*]

Arb Geol Palaeontol Inst Univ Stuttgart ... Arbeiten aus dem Geologisch Palaeontologischen Institut der Universitaet Stuttgart [*A publication*]

ArbGeschAntJudUrchr ... Arbeiten zur Geschichte des Antiken Judentums und des Urchristentums [*Leiden*] [*A publication*]

Arb Gesund ... Arbeit und Gesundheit [*A publication*]

Arb GG ...... Arbeitsgerichtsgesetz [*Law on labor courts*] [*German*]   (ILCA)

ARBHC ..... Association of Registered Bank Holding Companies [*Later, ABHC*]   (EA)

ARBIDH ... Basel Institute for Immunology. Annual Report [*A publication*]

Arb Inst Gesch Med Univ Leipzig ... Arbeiten des Instituts fuer Geschichte der Medizin an der Universitaet Leipzig [*A publication*]

ARBITER ... Access Refusal and Barrier Interface Terminal [*Hardware-based security device from Computer Security Systems*]

Arbit J........ Arbitration Journal [*A publication*]

Arbitr .... Arbitration   (DLA)

Arbitration J ... Arbitration Journal [*A publication*]

Arbitration Jrnl ... Arbitration Journal [*A publication*]

Arbitrat J ... Arbitration Journal [*A publication*]

Arbitr J ...... Arbitration Journal [*A publication*]

ARBITRN ... Arbitration   (ADA)

ARBITS..... Army Base Information Transfer System   (MCD)

Arb J .... Arbitration Journal [*A publication*]

ARBJAH... American Rabbit Journal [*A publication*]

Arb J of the Inst of Arbitrators ... Arbitration Journal. Institute of Arbitrators [*A publication*]

Arb J (NS) ... Arbitration Journal (New Series) [*A publication*]

Arb J (OS) ... Arbitration Journal (Old Series) [*A publication*]

Arb Kais Biol Anst Land Forstwirtsch ... Arbeiten der Kaiserlichen Biologischen Anstalt fuer Land und Forstwirtschaft [*A publication*]

ARBKAK... Archiv fuer Bienenkunde [*A publication*]

ARBLAN... Arquivos de Biologia [*Sao Paulo*] [*A publication*]

Arb L Dig... Arbitration Law: A Digest of Court Decisions [*A publication*]   (DLA)

Arb Leist.... Arbeit und Leistung [*West Germany*] [*A publication*]

ArBlM .... Mississippi County Library System, Blytheville, AR [*Library symbol*] [*Library of Congress*]   (LCLS)

ARBMA .... Arbok fuer Universitetet i Bergen. Matematisk-Naturvitenskapelig Serie [*A publication*]

Arb Med Fak Okayama ... Arbeiten aus der Medizinischen Fakultaet Okayama [*A publication*]

Arb Med Univ Okayama ... Arbeiten aus der Medizinischen Universitaet Okayama [*A publication*]

ARBNE...... Associated Rare Breeds of New England [*Defunct*]   (EA)

ARBO........ Arthropod-Borne [*Also, ARBOR*] [*Virology*]

ARBOA ..... Annual Review of Biochemistry [*A publication*]

ARBOAW ... Annual Review of Biochemistry [*A publication*]

Arbog Dan Geol Unders ... Arbog-Danmarks Geologiske Undersoegelse [*Denmark*] [*A publication*]

Arbok Univ Bergen Mat-Natur Ser ... Arbok fuer Universitetet i Bergen. Matematisk-Naturvitenskapelig Serie [*A publication*]

Arbok Univ Bergen Mat-Naturvitensk Ser ... Arbok fuer Universitetet i Bergen. Matematisk-Naturvitenskapelig Serie [*A publication*]

Arbok Univ Bergen Med Ser ... Arbok fuer Universitetet i Bergen. Medisinsk Serie [*A publication*]

ARBOR ..... Arboriculture

ARBOR ..... Argonne Boiling Water Reactor   (NRCH)

ARBOR ..... Arthropod-Borne [*Also, ARBO*] [*Virology*]

Arbor Ass J ... Arboricultural Association. Journal [*A publication*]

Arbor Bull Arbor Found (Seattle) Univ Wash ... Arboretum Bulletin. Arboretum Foundation (Seattle). University of Washington [*A publication*]

Arbor Bull Assoc Morris Arbor ... Arboretum Bulletin. Associates of the Morris Arboretum [*A publication*]

Arboric Fruit ... Arboriculture Fruitiere [*A publication*]

Arboric J.... Arboricultural Journal [*A publication*]

Arboricult Fruit ... Arboriculture Fruitiere [*A publication*]

Arbor Kornickie ... Arboretum Kornickie [*A publication*]

Arbor Leaves ... Arboretum Leaves [*A publication*]

Arbor Scientiarum Beitraege Wissenschaftsgeschichte Reihe C ... Arbor Scientiarum. Beitraege Wissenschaftsgeschichte. Reihe C. Bibliographien [*A publication*]

Arbor Sun .. Ann Arbor Sun [*A publication*]

ARBP........ Associated Reinforcing Bar Producers   (EA)

Arb Paul-Ehrlich-Inst ... Arbeiten. Paul-Ehrlich-Institut [*A publication*]

Arb Paul Ehrlich Inst Georg Speyer Haus Ferdinand Blum Inst ... Arbeiten. Paul-Ehrlich-Institut, Georg-Speyer-Haus, und Ferdinand-Blum-Institut [*A publication*]

ARBPD4.... Annual Review of Behavior Therapy Theory and Practice [*A publication*]

Arb Physiol Angew Entomol Berlin Dahlem ... Arbeiten ueber Physiologische und Angewandte Entomologie aus Berlin Dahlem [*A publication*]

ARBQA4.... Koninklijk Academie van Belgie. Jaarboek [*A publication*]

ARBR........ Arbitrator   (ROG)

ARBR........ Arbor Drugs, Inc. [*Troy, MI*] [*NASDAQ symbol*]   (NQ)

ARBRA7.... Annual Review of Biochemical and Allied Research in India [*A publication*]

Arb Reinischen Landeskunde ... Arbeiten zur Reinischen Landeskunde [*West Germany*] [*A publication*]

ARBRL...... Army Armament Research Ballistic Research Laboratory [*Aberdeen Proving Ground, MD*]   (MCD)

ARBRON .. Arbitration   (ROG)

ARBROR... Arbitrator   (ROG)

Arb R Samml ... Entscheidungen des Reichsarbeitsgericht und der Landesarbeitsgerichte [*Labor court reports*] [*A publication*]   (ILCA)

ARBRSI..... Annual Report. Board of Regents of the Smithsonian Institution [*A publication*]

Arb R Slg ... Entscheidungen des Reichsarbeitsgericht und der Landesarbeitsgerichte [*Labor court reports*] [*A publication*]   (ILCA)

Arb Rspr .... Rechtsprechung in Arbeitssachen [*Labor Court Reports*] [*A publication*]   (ILCA)

ARBRY...... Arbitrary

ARBS........ Angle Rate Bombing System

ARBS........ Angular Rate Bombing System   (MCD)

ARBS........ Associate of the Royal Society of British Sculptors

ARBS........ Automatic RADAR Beacon Sequencer

ArbT .... Arbeiten zur Theologie [*Stuttgart/Berlin-Ost*] [*A publication*]

ARBTM..... Arab Times [*A publication*]

ARBU .... Arctic Bulletin [*A publication*]

Arb U B Mat ... Arbok fuer Universitetet i Bergen. Matematisk-Naturvitenskapelig Serie [*A publication*]

ARBUD...... Arctic Bulletin [*A publication*]

ARBUDJ ... Arctic Bulletin [*A publication*]

Arb Univ Hohenheim (Landwirtsch Hochsch) ... Arbeiten. Universitaet Hohenheim (Landwirtschaftliche Hochschule) [*A publication*]

Arbuth........ Arbuthnot's Select Criminal Cases [*Madras*] [*A publication*]   (DLA)

ARBWAM ... Annual Report of Biological Works. Faculty of Science. Osaka University [*A publication*]

ARC .... Abnormal [*or Anomalous*] Retinal Correspondence [*Ophthalmology*]

ARC .... Aboriginal Research Club   (EA)

ARC .... Academy of Roofing Contractors [*Defunct*]   (EA)

ARC .... Accelerating Rate Calorimeter [*Instrumentation*]

ARC .... Accounting Requirements Code [*Military*]   (AABC)

ARC .... Accounting Research and Education Centre [*McMaster University*] [*Canada*] [*Research center*]   (RCD)

ARC .... Acoustic Research Center   (MCD)

ARC .... Acquisition Review Committee [*Navy*]   (CAAL)

ARC .... Action Resource Centre [*British*]   (CB)

ARC .... Action Revolutionnaire Corse [*Corsican Revolutionary Action*]   (PD)

ARC .... Active Reduction of Contrast   (MCD)

ARC .... Ad Hoc Requirements Committee [*Later, COMOR*]

ARC .... Adaptive Residual Coding   (MCD)

ARC .... Addict Rehabilitation Counselor

ARC .... Addiction Research Center [*Department of Health and Human Services*] [*Baltimore, MD*]

ARC .... Adelaide Racing Club [*Australia*]

ARC .... Administrative Radio Conference [*International Telecommunications Union*]
ARC .... Adult Rehabilitation Centre [*Canada*]
ARC .... Advanced Reentry Concepts [*Aerospace*]
ARC .... Advanced Research Center [*Aerospace*]
ARC .... Aeronautical Research Council [*British*]
ARC .... Aerospace Remote Calculator　(MCD)
ARC .... Aerospace Research Chamber
ARC .... Afghanistan Relief Committee　(EA)
ARC .... Aggregation of Red Blood Cells [*Hematology*]
ARC .... Agreements for Recreation and Conservation [*Canada*]
ARC .... Agricultural Relations Council　(EA)
ARC .... Agricultural Research Center [*of ARS, Department of Agriculture*]
ARC .... Agricultural Research Council [*Research center*] [*British*]　(IRC)
ARC .... Agronomy Research Center [*Southern Illinois University at Carbondale*] [*Research center*]　(RCD)
ARC .... AIDS [*Acquired Immune Deficiency Syndrome*]-Related Complex [*Medicine*]
ARC .... Aiken Relay Calculator
ARC .... Air Reduction Center [*NASA*]　(KSC)
ARC .... Air Release Capacity [*Aviation*]
ARC .... Air Reporting Control　(NVT)
ARC .... Air Reserve Center
ARC .... Air Reserve Components [*Military*]
ARC .... Airborne Radio Communicating
ARC .... Airborne Radio Control
ARC .... Airborne Research Capsule
ARC .... Aircrew Reception Centre [*British military*]　(DMA)
ARC .... Airworthiness Requirements Committee
ARC .... Ajstra Resources Corp. [*Vancouver Stock Exchange symbol*]
ARC .... Alcohol Rehabilitation Center　(NVT)
ARC .... Alexander Railroad Company [*AAR code*]
ARC .... All-Breeds Rescue Conservancy　(EA)
ARC .... Alliance for Rail Commuter Progress [*Later, ARCP*]　(EA)
ARC .... Alliance Research Center [*Nuclear energy*]　(NRCH)
ARC .... Alternate Route Cancel [*Telecommunications*]　(TEL)
ARC .... Alternative Resource Center　(EA)
ARC .... Altitude Rate Command
ARC .... American Radio Company of the Air [*Radio program*]
ARC .... American Radio Council [*Later, PRO-IF*]　(EA)
ARC .... American Railway Cases [*Legal*]
ARC .... American Reading Council　(EA)
ARC .... American Recreation Coalition　(EA)
ARC .... American Red Cross　(EA)
ARC .... American Refugee Committee　(EA)
ARC .... American Rehabilitation Committee [*Absorbed by FEGS*]　(EA)
ARC .... American Rose Council　(EA)
ARC .... American Rottweiler Club　(EA)
ARC .... Ames Research Center [*Moffett Field, CA*] [*NASA*]
ARC .... Ammunition Readiness Concept　(MCD)
ARC .... Amphibious Research Craft
ARC .... Amplitude and Rise Time Compensation　(IEEE)
ARC .... Analog Response Conditioner　(MCD)
ARC .... Analyzer-Recorder-Controller
ARC .... Anarchist Red Cross
ARC .... Ancestry Research Club　(EA)
ARC .... Animal Research Centre [*Canada*]　(ARC)
ARC .... Animal Research Committee
ARC .... Animal Resources Center [*University of Texas at Austin*] [*Research center*]　(RCD)
ARC .... Annual Report Council　(EA)
ARC .... Annual Review Committee [*NATO*]　(NATG)
ARC .... Anomalous Retinal Correspondence [*Ophthalmology*]
ARC .... Anthropological Research Center [*Memphis State University*] [*Research center*]　(RCD)
ARC .... Anthropological Research Council [*British*]
ARC .... Anthropology Resource Center　(EA)
ARC .... Antigen-Reactive Cell [*Immunology*]
ARC .... Appalachian Regional Commission [*Washington, DC*]
A & RC .... Application and Resource Control　(NASA)
ARC .... Applied Research Corporation
ARC .... Aquaculture Research Center [*Texas A & M University*] [*Research center*]　(RCD)
ARC .... Arab Research Centre [*British*]　(CB)
arc .... Aramaic [*MARC language code*] [*Library of Congress*]　(LCCP)
ARC .... Arcade　(MCD)
Arc .... Arcadia [*Berlin*] [*A publication*]
ARC .... Arcata [*California*] [*Seismograph station code, US Geological Survey*]　(SEIS)
ARC .... Arcato [*With the Bow*] [*Music*]
ARC .... Architects' Registration Council [*British*]
ARC .... Arctic Ocean
ARC .... Arctic Village [*Alaska*] [*Airport symbol*]　(OAG)
Arc .... Arctos. Acta Philologica Fennica [*A publication*]
ARC .... Arcuate Nucleus [*Neuroanatomy*]
ARC .... Area Resource Center [*Library network*]
ARC .... Area of Responsibility Centre [*Aviation*]
ARC .... Argonne Reactor Computation　(IEEE)

ARC .... Armored Reconnaissance Carrier　(MCD)
ARC .... Army Radio Code
ARC .... Army Reserve Components　(MCD)
ARC .... Art and Requirements of Command　(MCD)
ARC .... Art Resources in Collaboration　(EA)
ARC .... Arthritis Rehabilitation Center　(EA)
ARC .... Arthritis and Rheumatism Council for Research [*British*]　(IRUK)
ARC .... Asbestosis Research Council [*British*]
ARC .... Asia Resource Center　(EA)
ARC .... Asian Racing Conference
ARC .... Assistant Regional Commissioner [*IRS*]
ARC .... Associated Retail Confectioners of North America [*Later, RCI*]　(EA)
ARC .... Association of Railway Communicators　(EA)
ARC .... Association of Rehabilitation Centers [*Later, NARF*]　(EA)
ARC .... Association for Research in Cosmecology　(EA)
ARC .... Association des Restauratrices-Cuisinieres　(EA)
ARC .... Association for Retarded Citizens　(EA)
ARC .... Association of Rover Clubs　(EAIO)
ARC .... Asthma Research Council [*British*]
ARC .... Astro Research Corporation　(KSC)
ARC .... Atlantic Research Center　(KSC)
ARC .... Atlantic Research Corporation　(MCD)
ARC .... Atlantic Richfield Company [*NYSE symbol*]　(SPSG)
ARC .... Atlantis Research Centre　(EA)
ARC .... Atomedic Research Center　(EA)
ARC .... Audio Response Control　(BUR)
ARC .... Augmentation Research Center [*Stanford Research Institute*]
ARC .... Austra Resources Corporation [*Vancouver Stock Exchange symbol*]
ARC .... Australian Research Council
ARC .... Australian Resuscitation Council
ARC .... Australian Rostrum Council
ARC .... Automated Rent Collections
ARC .... Automatic Radio Control
ARC .... Automatic Ram Control　(CAAL)
ARC .... Automatic Range Compensating [*Firearms*]
ARC .... Automatic Range Control
ARC .... Automatic Rate Changer
ARC .... Automatic Rate Control
ARC .... Automatic Relay Calculator [*Early computer*] [*Birkbeck College*] [*British*]　(MCD)
ARC .... Automatic Remote Control　(DEN)
ARC .... Automatic Reset Counter
ARC .... Automatic Responsivity Control　(MCD)
ARC .... Autopilot Rate Control
ARC .... Auxiliary Roll Control
ARC .... Average Response Computer
ARC .... Cable Repairing Ship [*Navy symbol*]
ARC .... Society for the Arts, Religion, and Contemporary Culture　(EA)
ARCA .... Acquired Red Cell Aplasia [*Hematology*]
ARCA .... American Arts and Crafts Alliance　(EA)
ARCA .... American Rehabilitation Counseling Association　(EA)
ARCA .... American Retail Coal Association　(EA)
ARCA .... Antique Radio Club of America　(EA)
ARCA .... Asbestos Removal Contractors Association　(EAIO)
ARCA .... Asbestos Removalists Contractors Association [*Australia*]
ARCA .... Associate of the Royal Cambrian Academy [*British*]
ARCA .... Associate of the Royal Canadian Academy
ARCA .... Associate of the Royal College of Art [*British*]　(EY)
ARCA .... Association of Romanian Catholics of America　(EA)
ARCA .... Automobile Racing Club of America
ARCAD ..... Association for Recreation and Cultural Activities with People in Detention [*Canada*]
ARCADE... Argonne Computer-Aided Diffraction Equipment
ARCADE... Automatic RADAR Control and Data Equipment
ARCADS... Armament Control and Delivery System　(MCD)
ARCAEX... Archives of Research on Industrial Carcinogenesis [*A publication*]
ARCAIDS ... Army Cost Analysis Information and Data System　(MCD)
ARCAM .... Army Reserve Components Achievement Medal [*Military decoration*]　(AABC)
ARCamA ... Associate of the Royal Cambrian Academy [*British*]
ARCAN ..... Aeronautical Radio of Canada
ARCAN ..... Atlantic Richfield Canada Ltd.
ARCAR...... American Romanian Committee for Assistance to Refugees　(EA)
ARCAS...... All-Purpose Rocket for Collecting Atmospheric Soundings [*Navy*]
ARCAS...... Atlantic Research Corporation Atmospheric Sounding [*Missile*]　(MUGU)
ARCAS..... Automatic RADAR Chain Acquisition System [*Air Force*]
ARCASP ... Army Reserve Civilian Acquired Skills Program　(MCD)
ARCAVEX ... Army Cavalry Scout Experiment　(MCD)
ARCB......... Association of Reserve City Bankers　(EA)
ARCBE2... Annual Review of Cell Biology [*A publication*]
ARCC .... American Restaurant China Council　(EA)
ARCC .... American Rivers Conservation Council [*Later, AR*]　(EA)
ARCC .... ARTADS Requirements Coordinating Committee

ARCC .... ARTINS [*Army Terrain Information System*] Requirements Coordination Committee (RDA)
ARCC .... Association for the Rights of Catholics in the Church (EA)
ArCCA .... University of Central Arkansas, Conway, AR [*Library symbol*] [*Library of Congress*] (LCLS)
ARCCD4 ... Australia. Commonwealth Scientific and Industrial Research Organisation. Division of Protein Chemistry. Annual Report [*A publication*]
ARCCF ...... American Red Cross Children's Fund
ARCCLMA ... Aromatic Red Cedar Closet Lining Manufacturers Association (EA)
ARCcMD... Abnormal Record Compatible with Myocardial Disease [*Lowercase c in acronym means "with"*] [*Cardiology*]
ARCcMDE ... Abnormal Record Compatible with Myocardial Drug Effect [*Lowercase c in acronym means "with"*] [*Cardiology*]
ARCCNET ... Army Command and Control Communications Network (MCD)
ARCCO ..... Associate of the Royal Canadian College of Organists
ARCCOS... Inverse Cosine [*Mathematics*]
ARCCOT... Inverse Cotangent [*Mathematics*]
ArCCP .... Arquivos. Centro Cultural Portugues [*Paris*] [*A publication*]
ARCCSE ... Inverse Cosecant [*Mathematics*]
ARCD .... Associate of the Royal College of Dancing [*British*]
ARCDI....... Assistant Regional Commissioner Disability Insurance [*Social Security Administration*] (OICC)
ARCE........ Academical Rank of Civil Engineers
ARCE........ Air Cargo Equipment Corp. [*NASDAQ symbol*] (NQ)
ARCE........ Amphibious River Crossing Equipment [*Military*]
ARCEA...... American Railway Car Export Association (EA)
ARCEDEM ... African Regional Centre for Engineering Design and Manufacturing (EA)
ARCFCP.... Alliance for Responsible CFC [*Chlorofluorocarbon*] Policy (EA)
ARCFOD... Asian Religio-Cultural Forum on Development
ARCGDG .. Archives of Gynecology [*A publication*]
ARCGSC ... Army Command and General Staff College
ARCH........ Advocacy Resource Centre for the Handicapped [*Canada*]
ARCH........ Arch Petroleum, Inc. [*Fort Worth, TX*] [*NASDAQ symbol*] (NQ)
ARCH........ Archaeologia [*A publication*]
Arch .... Archaeology [*Cambridge, MA*] [*A publication*]
ARCH........ Archaic
ARCH........ Archaism
Arch .... Archbishop (ADA)
ARCH........ Archdeacon (ROG)
Arch .... Archeology (BJA)
ARCH........ Archery
ARCH........ Arches National Monument
Arch .... Archidiaconus [*Authority cited in pre-1607 legal work*] (DSA)
ARCH........ Archipelago [*Maps and charts*]
ARCH........ Architect [*or Architecture*]
ARCH........ Architects Renewal Committee in Harlem [*Defunct*]
Arch .... Architecture in Australia [*Later, Architecture Australia*] [*A publication*] (APTA)
ARCH........ Archive (MSA)
Arch .... Archivio [*A publication*]
ARCH........ Archivist. Public Archives of Canada [*A publication*]
Arch .... Archivum [*Oviedo*] [*A publication*]
ARCH........ Articulated Computing Hierarchy [*British*]
ARCH........ Australian Architectural Database [*Stanton Library*] [*Information service or system*] (IID)
ARCH........ Automated Reports Control Handling (MCD)
ARCH........ Autoregressive Conditional Heteroscedastic [*Electronics*] (PCM)
Arch .... Court of Arches [*England*] (DLA)
ArCH .... Hendrix College, Conway, AR [*Library symbol*] [*Library of Congress*] (LCLS)
Arch .... Pro Archia [*of Cicero*] [*Classical studies*] (OCD)
Archa .... [*Bartholomaeus*] Archamonus [*Authority cited in pre-1607 legal work*] (DSA)
Arch Acad Ecuat Med ... Archivos. Academia Ecuatoriana de Medicina [*A publication*]
Arch Acker-Pflanzenbau Bodenkd ... Archiv fuer Acker-Pflanzenbau und Bodenkunde [*A publication*]
Arch Acoust ... Archives of Acoustics [*A publication*]
ARCHAE .. Archaeology [*or Archaeologist*]
Arch Ael..... Archaeologia Aeliana [*A publication*] (OCD)
Arch Aeliana ... Archaeologica Aeliana [*A publication*]
Archaeographie ... Archaeographie. Archaeologie und Elektronische Datenverarbeitung [*A publication*]
Archaeol..... Archaeologia [*A publication*]
ARCHAEOL ... Archaeology
Archaeol Aeliana 5 Ser ... Archaeologia Aeliana. Series 5 [*A publication*]
Archaeol Austr ... Archaeologia Austriaca [*A publication*]
Archaeol Austriaca ... Archaeologia Austriaca [*A publication*]
Archaeol Biblio ... Archaeologische Bibliographie [*A publication*]
Archaeol Brit ... Archaeology in Britain [*A publication*]
Archaeol Cambrensis ... Archaeologia Cambrensis [*A publication*]
Archaeol Cantiana ... Archaeologia Cantiana [*A publication*]
Archaeol J ... Archaeological Journal [*A publication*]
Archaeol J (London) ... Archaeological Journal (London) [*A publication*]

Archaeol Korrespbl ... Archaeologisches Korrespondenzblatt [*A publication*]
Archaeol Oceania ... Archaeology in Oceania [*A publication*]
Archaeological Jnl ... Archaeological Journal [*A publication*]
Archaeol Phy Anthrop Oceania ... Archaeology and Physical Anthropology in Oceania [*Later, Archaeology in Oceania*] [*A publication*]
Archaeol & Phys Anthropol Oceania ... Archaeology and Physical Anthropology in Oceania [*Later, Archaeology in Oceania*] [*A publication*]
Archaeol Phys Anthropol Oceania ... Archaeology and Physical Anthropology in Oceania [*Later, Archaeology in Oceania*] [*A publication*]
Archaeol Polona ... Archaeologia Polona [*A publication*]
Archaeol Rep ... Archaeological Reports [*A publication*]
Archaeol Rev ... Archaeological Review [*A publication*]
Archaeol Surv Alberta Occas Pap ... Archaeological Survey of Alberta. Occasional Paper [*A publication*]
Archaeometr ... Archaeometry [*A publication*]
Arch Akust ... Archiwum Akustyki [*A publication*]
Arch Alum ... Architectural Aluminum Industry. Annual Statistical Review [*A publication*]
Arch Am Art ... Archives of American Art. Journal [*A publication*]
Arch Anat Cytol Pathol ... Archives d'Anatomie et de Cytologie Pathologiques [*A publication*]
Arch An Ath ... Archaiologika Analekta ex Athenon [*A publication*]
Arch Anat Histol Embryol ... Archives d'Anatomie, d'Histologie, et d'Embryologie [*A publication*]
Arch Anat Histol Embryol Norm Exp ... Archives d'Anatomie, d'Histologie, et d'Embryologie; Normales et Experimentales [*A publication*]
Arch Anat Histol Embryol (Strasb) ... Archives d'Anatomie, d'Histologie, et d'Embryologie (Strasbourg) [*A publication*]
Arch Anat M ... Archives d'Anatomie Microscopique et de Morphologie Experimentale [*A publication*]
Arch Anat Microsc Morphol Exp ... Archives d'Anatomie Microscopique et de Morphologie Experimentale [*A publication*]
Arch Anat Pathol (Paris) ... Archives d'Anatomie Pathologique (Paris) [*A publication*]
Arch Anat Pathol Sem Hop ... Archives d'Anatomie Pathologique. Semaine des Hopitaux [*France*] [*A publication*]
Arch Anat Physiol Physiol Abt ... Archiv fuer Anatomie und Physiologie. Physiologische Abteilung [*A publication*]
Arch Anat Phys Wiss Med ... Archiv fuer Anatomie, Physiologie, und Wissenschaftliche Medizin [*A publication*]
Arch Androl (New York) ... Archives of Andrology (New York) [*A publication*]
Arch Anim Nutr ... Archives of Animal Nutrition [*A publication*]
Arch Anthrop ... Archiv fuer Anthropologie [*A publication*]
Arch Anthropol Criminelle ... Archives d'Anthropologie Criminelle, de Medecine Legale, et de Psychologie Normale et Pathologique [*A publication*]
Arch Antropol Crim Psichiatr Med Leg ... Archivio di Antropologia Criminale, Psichiatria, e Medicina Legale [*A publication*]
Arch Antropol Etnol ... Archivio per l'Antropologia e la Etnologia [*A publication*]
ArchAnz..... Archaeologischer Anzeiger [*Berlin*] [*A publication*]
Arch Anz.... Archaeologischer Anzeiger in Jahrbuch des [*Kaiserlichen*] Deutschen Archaeologischen Instituts [*A publication*] (OCD)
Archaol ...... Archaeologie [*Archeology*] [*German*]
Arch Apoth Ver Noerd Deutschl ... Archiv des Apotheker Vereins im Noerdlichen Deutschland [*A publication*]
Arch Arb.... Archbold's Law of Arbitration and Award [*A publication*] (DLA)
Arch Argent Dermatol ... Archivos Argentinos de Dermatologia [*A publication*]
Arch Argent Neurol ... Archivos Argentinos de Neurologia [*A publication*]
Arch Argent Pediatr ... Archivos Argentinos de Pediatria [*A publication*]
Arch Argent Reumatol ... Archivos Argentinos de Reumatologia [*A publication*]
Arch Argent Tisiol Neumonol ... Archivos Argentinos de Tisiologia y Neumonologia [*A publication*]
ArchArm..... Archeologie Armoricaine [*A publication*]
Arch & Arts ... Architecture and Arts [*A publication*] (APTA)
Arch Arzneither ... Archiv fuer Arzneitherapie [*A publication*]
Arch Atlas Norm Pathol Anat Roentgenbild ... Archiv und Atlas der Normalen und Pathologischen Anatomie in Typischen Roentgenbildern [*A publication*]
Arch ed Atti Soc Ital Chir ... Archivio ed Atti. Societa Italiana di Chirurgia [*A publication*]
Arch Augenheilkd ... Archiv fuer Augenheilkunde [*A publication*]
Arch d'Aujourd'hui ... Architecture d'Aujourd'hui [*A publication*]
Arch Aujourd'hui ... Architecture d'Aujourd'hui [*A publication*]
Arch in Aust ... Architecture in Australia [*Later, Architecture Australia*] [*A publication*] (APTA)
Arch Austr ... Archaeologia Austriaca [*A publication*]
Arch Automat Telemech ... Archiwum Automatyki i Telemechaniki [*A publication*]
Arch Automat i Telemech ... Archiwum Automatyki i Telemechaniki [*A publication*]
Arch Autom Telemech ... Archiwum Automatyki i Telemechaniki [*A publication*]
Arch & B.... Architecture and Building [*A publication*]

Arch Badewes ... Archiv des Badewesens [*A publication*]
Arch Baines' Act ... Archbold on Baines' Acts on Criminal Justice [*A publication*] (DLA)
Arch Balatonicum ... Archivum Balatonicum [*A publication*]
Arch Balkaniques Med Chir Spec ... Archives Balkaniques de Medecine. Chirurgie et Leurs Specialites [*A publication*]
Arch Bank ... Archbold on Bankruptcy [*1825-56*] [*A publication*] (DLA)
Arch-Bat-Constr ... Architecture-Batiment-Construction [*A publication*]
Archb Civil Pl ... Archbold's Civil Pleading [*A publication*] (DLA)
Archb Civ Pl ... Archbold's Civil Pleading and Evidence [*A publication*] (ILCA)
Archb Crim Pl ... Archbold's Criminal Pleading [*A publication*] (DLA)
Archb Cr Prac & Pl ... Archbold's Pleading and Evidence in Criminal Cases [*A publication*] (DLA)
Arch Begriff ... Archiv fuer Begriffsgeschichte [*A publication*]
Arch Begriffs Gesch ... Archiv fuer Begriffs-Geschichte [*A publication*]
Arch Belg Dermatol ... Archives Belges de Dermatologie [*A publication*]
Arch Belg Dermatol Syphiligr ... Archives Belges de Dermatologie et de Syphiligraphie [*A publication*]
Arch Belges Med Soc Hyg Med Trav Med Leg (Belgium) ... Archives Belges de Medecine Sociale, Hygiene, Medecine du Travail, et Medecine Legale (Belgium) [*A publication*]
Arch Belg Med Soc ... Archives Belges de Medecine Sociale, Hygiene, Medecine du Travail, et Medecine Legale [*A publication*]
Arch Belg Med Soc Hyg Med Trav Med Leg ... Archives Belges de Medecine Sociale, Hygiene, Medecine du Travail, et Medecine Legale [*A publication*]
Arch Bergbau ... Archiv fuer Bergbau und Huettenwesen [*A publication*]
ArchBg .... Archaeologische Bibliographie [*A publication*]
Arch Bibl ... Archives et Bibliotheques de Belgique [*A publication*]
Arch Bibl et Mus ... Archives, Bibliotheques, et Musees de Belgique [*Later, Archives et Bibliotheques de Belgique*] [*A publication*]
Arch Bienenk ... Archiv fuer Bienenkunde [*A publication*]
Arch Bienenkd ... Archiv fuer Bienenkunde [*A publication*]
Arch Bioch ... Archives of Biochemistry and Biophysics [*A publication*]
Arch Biochem ... Archives of Biochemistry [*A publication*]
Arch Biochem ... Archives of Biochemistry and Biophysics [*A publication*]
Arch Biochem Biophys ... Archives of Biochemistry and Biophysics [*A publication*]
Arch Biochem Biophys Suppl ... Archives of Biochemistry and Biophysics. Supplement [*A publication*]
Arch Biochim Cosmetol ... Archives de Biochimie et Cosmetologie [*A publication*]
Arch Biol .... Archives de Biologie [*Liege*] [*A publication*]
Arch Biol .... Archives of Biology [*A publication*]
Arch Biol Andina ... Archivos de Biologia Andina [*A publication*]
Arch Biol Hung ... Archiva Biologia Hungarica [*A publication*]
Arch Biol M ... Archivos de Biologia y Medicina Experimentales [*A publication*]
Arch Biol Med Exp ... Archivos de Biologia y Medicina Experimentales [*A publication*]
Arch Biol Med Exp Supl ... Archivos de Biologia y Medicina Experimentales. Suplemento [*A publication*]
Arch Biol Sci ... Archives of Biological Sciences [*A publication*]
Arch Biol Sci (Engl Transl) ... Archives of Biological Sciences (English Translation of Arhiv Bioloskih Nauka) [*A publication*]
Arch Biol Sci (Engl Transl Arh Biol Nauka) ... Archives of Biological Sciences (English Translation of Arhiv Bioloskih Nauka) [*A publication*]
Arch Bioquim Quim Farm ... Archivos de Bioquimica, Quimica, y Farmacia [*A publication*]
Arch Bioquim Quim Farm (Tucuman) ... Archivos de Bioquimica, Quimica, y Farmacia (Tucuman) [*A publication*]
Arch BL ..... Archbold's Bankrupt Law [*A publication*] (DLA)
Arch Black ... Archbold's Edition of Blackstone's Commentaries [*A publication*] (DLA)
Archb Landl & Ten ... Archbold's Landlord and Tenant [*A publication*] (DLA)
Arch & Bldg ... Architecture and Building [*A publication*]
Arch & BM ... Architects' and Builders' Magazine [*New York*] [*A publication*]
Archb New Pr ... Archbold's New Practice [*A publication*] (DLA)
Archb NP ... Archbold's Law of Nisi Prius [*A publication*] (DLA)
Archb N Prac ... Archbold's New Practice [*A publication*] (DLA)
Arch Bodenfruchtbarkeit Pflanzenprod ... Archiv fuer Bodenfruchtbarkeit und Pflanzenproduktion [*A publication*]
Arch Bot ..... Archivio Botanico [*A publication*]
Arch Bot Biogeogr Ital ... Archivio Botanico e Biogeografico Italiano [*A publication*]
ARCHBP ... Archbishop
Archb Pr .... Archbold's Practice [*A publication*] (DLA)
Archb Pr KB ... Archbold's Practice in the King's Bench [*A publication*] (DLA)
Arch Brasil Med ... Archivos Brasileiros de Medicina [*A publication*]
Arch Budowy Masz ... Archiwum Budowy Maszyn [*A publication*]
Arch Budowy Maszyn ... Archiwum Budowy Maszyn [*A publication*]
Arch Build Eng ... Architecture, Building, Engineering [*A publication*] (APTA)
Arch Build Eng ... Architecture, Building, Structural Engineering [*A publication*] (APTA)
Arch Byz Mnem ... Archeion ton Byzantinon Mnemeion tes Hellados [*A publication*]

Arch Cal Chiro ... Archives. California Chiropractic Association [*A publication*]
Arch Camb ... Archaeologia Cambrensis [*A publication*]
Arch Cambrensis ... Archaeologia Cambrensis [*A publication*]
Arch Can .... Architecture Canada [*A publication*]
Arch Cant .. Archaeologia Cantiana [*A publication*]
Arch Cantiana ... Archaeologia Cantiana. Transactions of the Kent Archaeological Society [*A publication*]
Arch Cardio y Hematol ... Archivos de Cardiologia y Hematologia [*A publication*]
Arch Cas .... Archivni Casopis [*A publication*]
Arch Chem Mikrosk ... Archiv fuer Chemie und Mikroskopie [*A publication*]
Arch Child Health ... Archives of Child Health [*A publication*]
Arch Chir Neerl ... Archivum Chirurgicum Neerlandicum [*A publication*]
Arch Chir Ortop Med ... Archivio di Chirurgia Ortopedica e di Medicina [*A publication*]
Arch Chir Torac Cardiovasc ... Archivio di Chirurgia Toracica e Cardiovascolare [*A publication*]
Arch Chir Torace ... Archivio di Chirurgia del Torace [*A publication*]
Arch Civ Pl ... Archbold's Civil Pleading and Evidence [*A publication*] (DLA)
Arch Cl ...... Archeologia Classica [*A publication*]
ArchClass .. Archeologia Classica [*A publication*]
Arch Clin Inst Endocrinol (Montevideo) ... Archivos. Clinica e Instituto de Endocrinologia (Montevideo) [*A publication*]
Arch CL Pr ... Archbold's New Common Law Practice [*A publication*] (DLA)
Arch Col Med El Salv ... Archivos. Colegio Medico de El Salvador [*A publication*]
Arch Col Med El Salvador ... Archivos. Colegio Medico de El Salvador [*A publication*]
Arch Concept ... Architecture Concept [*A publication*]
Arch CP ..... Archbold's Practice in the Common Pleas [*A publication*] (DLA)
Arch Cr ...... Archbold's Pleading and Evidence in Criminal Cases [*A publication*] (DLA)
Arch Criminol Neuro Psiquiatr Discip Conexas ... Archivos de Criminologia Neuro-Psiquiatria y Disciplinas Conexas [*A publication*]
Arch Cr L ... Archbold's Criminal Law [*A publication*] (DLA)
Arch Cr Law ... Archbold's Pleading and Evidence in Criminal Cases [*A publication*] (DLA)
Arch Cr Pl ... Archbold's Criminal Pleading [*A publication*] (DLA)
Arch Cr Prac ... Archbold's Criminal Practice [*A publication*] (DLA)
Arch Cr Proc ... Archbold's Criminal Procedure [*A publication*] (DLA)
Arch CS Pr ... Archibald. Country Solicitor's Practice in the Queen's Bench [*1881*] [*A publication*] (DLA)
Arch Cubanos Cancerol ... Archivos Cubanos de Cancerologia [*A publication*]
ARCHD ..... Archdeacon [*or Archdeaconry*]
ARCHD ..... Archduke
Arch Deputazione Romana Stor Patria ... Archivio. Reale Deputazione Romana di Storia Patria [*A publication*]
Arch Dermat ... Archives of Dermatology [*A publication*]
Arch Dermatol ... Archives of Dermatology [*A publication*]
Arch Dermatol Exp Funct ... Archivum de Dermatologia Experimentale et Functionale [*A publication*]
Arch Dermatol Forsch ... Archiv fuer Dermatologische Forschung [*A publication*]
Arch Dermatol Res ... Archives for Dermatological Research [*A publication*]
Arch Dermatol Syphilol ... Archives of Dermatology and Syphilology [*Chicago*] [*A publication*]
Arch Dermat u Syph ... Archiv fuer Dermatologie und Syphilis [*A publication*]
Arch Dermat and Syph (Chicago) ... Archives of Dermatology and Syphilology (Chicago) [*A publication*]
Arch Derm F ... Archiv fuer Dermatologische Forschung [*A publication*]
Arch Derm R ... Archives for Dermatological Research [*A publication*]
Arch Des ... Architectural Design [*A publication*]
Arch De Vecchi Anat Patol Med Clin ... Archivio "De Vecchi" per l'Anatomia Patologica e la Medicina Clinica [*Italy*] [*A publication*]
Arch Diagn ... Archives of Diagnosis [*A publication*]
ARCHDIOC ... Archdiocese (ADA)
Arch Dis Ch ... Archives of Disease in Childhood [*A publication*]
Arch Dis Child ... Archives of Disease in Childhood [*A publication*]
Arch Dis Childhood ... Archives of Disease in Childhood [*A publication*]
Arch Druck Pap ... Archiv fuer Druck und Papier [*A publication*]
Arch E .... Architectural Engineer
Arch Ed ...... Architectural Education [*A publication*]
ARCHEDDA ... Architectures for Heterogeneous European Distributed Databases (TEL)
Arch Eisenbahntech ... Archiv fuer Eisenbahntechnik [*A publication*]
Arch Eisenh ... Archiv fuer das Eisenhuettenwesen [*A publication*]
Arch Eisenhuettenwes ... Archiv fuer das Eisenhuettenwesen [*A publication*]
Arch Eisenhuttenwesen ... Archiv fuer das Eisenhuettenwesen [*West Germany*] [*A publication*]
Arch Elektr ... Archiv fuer Elektrotechnik [*Berlin*] [*A publication*]
Arch Elektron und Uebertragungstech ... Archiv fuer Elektronik und Uebertragungstechnik [*A publication*]
Arch Elektron Uebertragungstech ... Archiv fuer Elektronik und Uebertragungstechnik [*A publication*]
Arch Elektrotech ... Archiwum Elektrotechniki [*Warsaw*] [*A publication*]
Arch Elektrotech (Berlin) ... Archiv fuer Elektrotechnik (Berlin) [*A publication*]

Arch Elektr Uebertrag ... Archiv der Elektrischen Uebertragung [*A publication*]
Arch Elek Ubertr ... Archiv fuer Elektronik und Uebertragungstechnik [*A publication*]
Arch Elek Uebertragung ... Archiv der Elektrischen Uebertragung [*A publication*]
Arch "E Maragliano" Patol Clin ... Archivio "E. Maragliano" di Patologia e Clinica [*A publication*]
Arch Energ ... Archiwum Energetyki [*A publication*]
Arch Energiewirtsch ... Archiv fuer Energiewirtschaft [*A publication*]
Arch & Eng ... Architect and Engineer [*A publication*]
Arch Entwicklungsmech Org ... Archiv fuer Entwicklungsmechanik der Organismen [*A publication*]
Arch Entwicklungsmech Org (Wilhelm Roux) ... Archiv fuer Entwicklungsmechanik der Organismen (Wilhelm Roux) [*A publication*]
Arch Entwmech Org ... Archiv fuer Entwicklungsmechanik der Organismen [*A publication*]
Arch Env He ... Archives of Environmental Health [*A publication*]
Arch Envir Health ... Archives of Environmental Health [*A publication*]
Arch Environ Contam Toxicol ... Archives of Environmental Contamination and Toxicology [*A publication*]
Arch Environ Health ... Archives of Environmental Health [*A publication*]
Arch Environ Hlth ... Archives of Environmental Health [*A publication*]
Arch Environ Prot ... Archives of Environmental Protection [*A publication*]
Archeogr Triest ... Archeolgrafo Triestino [*A publication*]
ARCHEOL ... Archeological
Archeologia (Paris) ... Archeologia. Tresors des Ages (Paris) [*A publication*]
Archeologia (Warzawa) ... Archeologia. Rocznik Instytutu Historii Kultury Materialnej Polskiej Akademii Nauk (Warszawa) [*A publication*]
Archeologija (Kiev) ... Archeologija. Akademija Nauk Ukrains'koi RSR. Institut Archeologii (Kiev) [*A publication*]
Archeologija (Sof) ... Archeologija. Organ na Archeologiceskija Institut i Muzej pri B'lgarskata Akademija na Naukite (Sofia) [*A publication*]
Archeol Pol ... Archeologia Polski [*A publication*]
Archeol Rozhl ... Archeologicke Rozhledy [*A publication*]
Arch Eph.... Archaiologike Ephemeris [*A publication*]
Arch Ephemeris ... Archaiologike Ephemeris [*A publication*]
Archer........ Archer's Reports [*2 Florida*] [*A publication*]   (DLA)
Arch Erbergbau Erzaufbereit Metallhuettenwes ... Archiv fuer Erzbergbau, Erzaufbereitung, Metallhuettenwesen [*A publication*]
Archer & H ... Archer and Hogue. Reports [*2 Florida*] [*A publication*]   (DLA)
Arch Ert ... Archaeologiai Ertesito [*A publication*]
Archery Wld ... Archery World [*A publication*]
Arch Esp.... Archivo Espanol de Arte y Arqueologia [*A publication*]
Arch Esp Ar ... Archivo Espanol de Arte [*A publication*]
Arch Esp Arq ... Archivo Espanol de Arqueologia [*A publication*]
Arch Esp Art ... Archivo Espanol de Arte [*A publication*]
Arch Esp Morfol ... Archivo Espanol de Morfologia [*A publication*]
Arch Esp Urol ... Archivos Espanoles de Urologia [*A publication*]
Arch Estud Med Aragon ... Archivos de Estudios Medicos Aragoneses [*A publication*]
ArchEurCO ... Archivum Europae Centro-Orientalis [*A publication*]
Arch Eur So ... Archives Europeennes de Sociologie [*A publication*]
Arch Eur Sociol ... Archives Europeennes de Sociologie [*A publication*]
Arch Exp Pathol Pharmakol ... Archiv fuer Experimentelle Pathologie und Pharmakologie [*A publication*]
Arch Exp Path Pharmak ... Archiv fuer Experimentelle Pathologie und Pharmakologie [*A publication*]
Arch Exp Ve ... Archiv fuer Experimentelle Veterinaermedizin [*A publication*]
Arch Exp Veterinaermed ... Archiv fuer Experimentelle Veterinaermedizin [*A publication*]
Arch Exp Vetmed ... Archiv fuer Experimentelle Veterinaermedizin [*A publication*]
Arch Fac Med Madrid ... Archivos. Facultad de Medicina de Madrid [*A publication*]
Arch Fac Med Zaragoza ... Archivos. Facultad de Medicina de Zaragoza [*A publication*]
ArchFAr .... Archivo de Filologia Aragonesa [*A publication*]
Arch Farmacol Sper Sci Affini ... Archivio di Farmacologia Sperimentale e Scienze Affini [*A publication*]
Arch Farmacol Toxicol ... Archivos de Farmacologia y Toxicologia [*A publication*]
Arch Farm (Bago) ... Archivos Farmaceuticos (Bago) [*A publication*]
Arch Farm Bioquim Tucuman ... Archivos de Farmacia y Bioquimica del Tucuman [*A publication*]
Arch Filosof ... Archivio di Filosofia [*A publication*]
Arch Fisch ... Archiv fuer Fischereiwissenschaft [*A publication*]
Arch Fischereiwiss ... Archiv fuer Fischereiwissenschaft [*A publication*]
Arch Fischereiwiss Beih ... Archiv fuer Fischereiwissenschaft. Beiheft [*A publication*]
Arch Fisiol ... Archivio di Fisiologia [*A publication*]
Arch Folk... Archives de Folklore [*A publication*]
Arch Forms ... Archbold. Indictments, with Forms [*1916*] [*A publication*]   (DLA)
Arch Forms Ind ... Archbold's Forms of Indictment [*A publication*]   (DLA)
Arch Forstw ... Archiv fuer Forstwesen [*A publication*]
Arch Forstwes ... Archiv fuer Forstwesen [*A publication*]

Arch Forum ... Architectural Forum [*A publication*]
Arch Franciscanum Hist ... Archivum Franciscanum Historicum [*A publication*]
Arch Fratrum Praedicatorum ... Archivum Fratrum Praedicatorum [*A publication*]
Arch Freunde Naturgesch Mecklenburg ... Archiv. Freunde der Naturgeschichte in Mecklenburg [*A publication*]
Arch Fr Mal ... Archives Francaises des Maladies de l'Appareil Digestif [*A publication*]
Arch Fr Mal App Dig ... Archives Francaises des Maladies de l'Appareil Digestif [*A publication*]
Arch Fr Ped ... Archives Francaises de Pediatrie [*A publication*]
Arch Fr Pediatr ... Archives Francaises de Pediatrie [*A publication*]
Arch Fund Roux-Ocefa ... Archivos. Fundacion Roux-Ocefa [*A publication*]
Arch Gartenb ... Archiv fuer Gartenbau [*A publication*]
Arch Gartenbau ... Archiv fuer Gartenbau [*A publication*]
Arch Gastroenterol ... Archives of Gastroenterology [*A publication*]
Arch Gefluegelk ... Archiv fuer Gefluegelkunde [*A publication*]
Arch Gefluegelkd ... Archiv fuer Gefluegelkunde [*A publication*]
Arch Gefluegelz Kleintierk ... Archiv fuer Gefluegelzucht und Kleintierkunde [*A publication*]
Arch Gefluegelzucht Kleintierk ... Archiv fuer Gefluegelzucht und Kleintierkunde [*A publication*]
Arch Geflugelkd Eur Poult Sci Rev Sci Avicole Eur ... Archiv fuer Gefluegelkunde/European Poultry Science/Revue de Science Avicole Europeenne [*A publication*]
Arch Genet ... Archiv fuer Genetik [*Zurich*] [*A publication*]
Arch Gen Med ... Archives Generales de Medecine [*A publication*]
Arch Gen Psychiat ... Archives of General Psychiatry [*A publication*]
Arch Gen Psychiatr ... Archives of General Psychiatry [*A publication*]
Arch Gen Psychiatry ... Archives of General Psychiatry [*A publication*]
Arch Geogr ... Archaeologia Geographica [*A publication*]
Arch Geol Vietnam ... Archives Geologiques du Vietnam [*A publication*]
Arch Gerontol Geriatr ... Archives of Gerontology and Geriatrics [*A publication*]
Arch Gesamte Naturl ... Archiv fuer die Gesamte Naturlehre [*A publication*]
Arch Gesamte Physiol Mens Tiere (Pfluegers) ... Archiv fuer die Gesamte Physiologie des Menschen und der Tiere (Pfluegers) [*A publication*]
Arch Gesamte Virusforsch ... Archiv fuer die Gesamte Virusforschung [*A publication*]
Arch Gesamte Waermetech ... Archiv fuer die Gesamte Waermetechnik [*A publication*]
Arch Gesch ... Archiv fuer Geschichte der Philosophie [*A publication*]
Arch Gesch Math Naturwiss Techn ... Archiv fuer Geschichte der Mathematik, der Naturwissenschaften, und der Technik [*A publication*]
Arch Gesch Med ... Archiv fuer Geschichte der Medizin [*A publication*]
Arch Gesch Naturwiss Tech ... Archiv fuer die Geschichte der Naturwissenschaften und der Technik. Berliner Gesellschaft fuer Geschichte der Naturwissenschaften und Medizin [*A publication*]
Arch Gesch Phil ... Archiv fuer Geschichte der Philosophie [*A publication*]
Arch Geschw ... Archiv fuer Geschwulstforschung [*A publication*]
Arch Geschwulstforsch ... Archiv fuer Geschwulstforschung [*A publication*]
Arch Gewerbepathol Gewerbehyg ... Archiv fuer Gewerbepathologie und Gewerbehygiene [*A publication*]
Arch Giur... Archivio Giuridico [*A publication*]   (ILCA)
Arch Gl It... Archivio Glottologico Italiano [*A publication*]
Arch Gorn ... Archiwum Gornictwa [*A publication*]
Arch Gorn Hutn ... Archiwum Gornictwa i Hutnictwa [*A publication*]
Arch G Psyc ... Archives of General Psychiatry [*A publication*]
Arch G Utrecht ... Archief voor de Geschiedenis van het Aartsbisdom Utrecht [*A publication*]
Arch Gynaekol ... Archiv fuer Gynaekologie [*A publication*]
Arch Gynecol ... Archives of Gynecology [*A publication*]
Arch Helv .. Archaeologia Helvetica [*A publication*]
Arch Herald Suisses ... Archives Heraldiques Suisses. Annuaire [*A publication*]
Arch Hib.... Archivium Hibernicum [*A publication*]
Arch Hisp .. Archivo Hispalense [*A publication*]
Arch Hist Carm ... Archivum Historicum Carmelitanum [*A publication*]
Arch Hist Doctrinale Litt Moyen Age ... Archives d'Histoire Doctrinale et Litteraire du Moyen-Age [*A publication*]
Arch Hist Dom ... Archives d'Histoire Dominicaine [*A publication*]
Arch Hist E ... Archive for History of Exact Sciences [*A publication*]
Arch Hist Exact Sci ... Archive for History of Exact Sciences [*A publication*]
Arch Hist J ... Archivum Histologicum Japonicum [*A publication*]
Arch Hist Jap ... Archivum Histologicum Japonicum [*A publication*]
Arch Hist Lev ... Archivo de Prehistoria Levantina [*A publication*]
Arch Hist Med ... Archiwum Historii Medycyny [*A publication*]
Arch Hist Med Argent ... Archivos de Historia de la Medicina Argentina [*A publication*]
Arch Hist Med Venezuela ... Archivos de Historia Medica de Venezuela [*A publication*]
Arch Hist Med (Warsz) ... Archiwum Historii Medycyny (Warszawa) [*A publication*]
Arch Hist Nat ... Archives d'Histoire Naturelle [*A publication*]
Arch Histol Jpn ... Archivum Histologicum Japonicum [*A publication*]
Arch Histol Norm Patol ... Archivos de Histologia Normal y Patologica [*A publication*]

Arch History Exact Sci ... Archive for History of Exact Sciences [*A publication*]
Arch Hist Sci ... Archives de l'Histoire des Sciences [*A publication*]
Arch Hist Soc Iesu ... Archivum Historicum Societatis Iesu [*A publication*]
Arch Hist Ver Unterfranken ... Archiv des Historischen Vereins von Unterfranken und Aschaffenburg [*A publication*]
Arch Hom .. Archaeologia Homerica [*A publication*]
Arch Hosp ... Archives Hospitalieres [*A publication*]
Arch Hosp Cruz Roja ... Archivos. Hospital de la Cruz Roja de Barcelona [*A publication*]
Arch Hosp Univ (Havana) ... Archivos de Hospitales Universitarios (Havana) [*A publication*]
Arch Hosp Vargas ... Archivos. Hospital Vargas [*A publication*]
Arch Hosp Vargas (Caracas) ... Archivos. Hospital Vargas (Caracas) [*A publication*]
Arch Hung ... Archaeologia Hungarica [*A publication*]
Arch Hutn ... Archiwum Hutnictwa [*A publication*]
Arch Hydrob ... Archiv fuer Hydrobiologie [*A publication*]
Arch Hydrobiol ... Archiv fuer Hydrobiologie [*A publication*]
Arch Hydrobiol u Planktonkunde ... Archiv fuer Hydrobiologie und Planktonkunde [*A publication*]
Arch Hydrobiol Rybactwa ... Archivum Hydrobiologii i Rybactwa [*A publication*]
Arch Hydrobiol Suppl ... Archiv fuer Hydrobiologie. Supplementband [*A publication*]
Arch Hydrobiol Supplementb ... Archiv fuer Hydrobiologie. Supplementband [*A publication*]
Arch Hydrotech ... Archiwum Hydrotechniki [*A publication*]
Arch Hyg ... Archiv fuer Hygiene [*A publication*]
Arch Hyg (Athens) ... Archives of Hygiene (Athens) [*A publication*]
Arch Hyg Bakt ... Archiv fuer Hygiene und Bakteriologie [*A publication*]
Arch Hyg Bakteriol ... Archiv fuer Hygiene und Bakteriologie [*A publication*]
Archi .... Archidiaconus [*Authority cited in pre-1607 legal work*] (DSA)
ArchIA .... Archivo Ibero-Americano [*Madrid*] [*A publication*]
Arch Ib Am Hist Med ... Archivo Iberoamericano de Historia de la Medicina y de Antropologia Medica [*A publication*]
Arch Iberoamer Hist Med ... Archivos Iberoamericanos de Historia de la Medicina y Antropologia Medica [*A publication*]
Arch I Card ... Archivos. Instituto de Cardiologia de Mexico [*A publication*]
Archid .... Archidiaconus [*Authority cited in pre-1607 legal work*] (DSA)
Archidi .... Archidiaconus [*Authority cited in pre-1607 legal work*] (DSA)
ARCHIDIAC ... Archidiaconal [*Ecclesiastical*] (ROG)
Arch IE Afr ... Archivos. Instituto de Estudios Africanos [*A publication*]
Archig .... Archiginnasio [*A publication*]
Archi Hosp Rev Sci Sante Reunies ... Archives Hospitalieres et Revue de Science et Sante Reunies [*A publication*]
Archil .... Archilochus [*Seventh century BC*] [*Classical studies*] (OCD)
Archi & Manu ... Archives and Manuscripts [*A publication*] (APTA)
Arch Immunol Ter Dosw ... Archiwum Immunologii i Terapii Doswiadczalnej [*A publication*]
Arch Immunol Ther Exp ... Archivum Immunologiae et Therapiae Experimentalis [*A publication*]
Arch Immunol Ther Exp (Warsz) ... Archivum Immunologiae et Therapiae Experimentalis (Warszawa) [*A publication*]
Arch Ind Hlth ... Archives of Industrial Health [*A publication*]
Arch Ind Hyg Occup Med ... Archives of Industrial Hygiene and Occupational Medicine [*A publication*]
Arch Indust Health ... Archives of Industrial Health [*A publication*]
Arch Industr Hlth ... Archives of Industrial Health [*A publication*]
Arch In Med ... Archives of Internal Medicine [*A publication*]
Arch Inn Med ... Archiv fuer Innere Medizin [*A publication*]
Arch Insect Biochem Physiol ... Archives of Insect Biochemistry and Physiology [*A publication*]
Arch Inst Aclim (Almeria Esp) ... Archivos. Instituto de Aclimatacion (Almeria, Espana) [*A publication*]
Arch Inst Biol ... Archivos. Instituto Biologico [*A publication*]
Arch Inst Biol Andina (Lima) ... Archivos. Instituto de Biologia Andina (Lima) [*A publication*]
Arch Inst Bot Univ Liege ... Archives. Institut de Botanique. Universite de Liege [*A publication*]
Arch Inst Cardiol Mex ... Archivos. Instituto de Cardiologia de Mexico [*A publication*]
Arch Inst Farmacol Exp (Madrid) ... Archivos. Instituto de Farmacologia Experimental (Madrid) [*A publication*]
Arch Inst Farmacol Exp (Med) ... Archivos. Instituto de Farmacologia Experimental (Medicina) [*A publication*]
Arch Inst Farm Exp ... Archivos. Instituto de Farmacologia Experimental [*A publication*]
Arch Inst Grand-Ducal Luxemb Sect Sci ... Archives. Institut Grand-Ducal de Luxembourg. Section des Sciences Naturelles, Physiques, et Mathematiques [*A publication*]
Arch Inst Hessarek (Inst Razi) ... Archives. Institut d'Hessarek (Institut Razi) [*A publication*]
Arch Inst Past Alg ... Archives. Institut Pasteur d'Algerie [*A publication*]
Arch Inst Pasteur Afrique Nord ... Archives. Instituts Pasteur de l'Afrique du Nord [*A publication*]
Arch Inst Pasteur Alger ... Archives. Institut Pasteur d'Algerie [*A publication*]
Arch Inst Pasteur Algerie ... Archives. Institut Pasteur d'Algerie [*A publication*]
Arch Inst Pasteur Hell ... Archives. Institut Pasteur Hellenique [*A publication*]

Arch Inst Pasteur Indochine ... Archives. Instituts Pasteur d'Indochine [*A publication*]
Arch Inst Pasteur Madagascar ... Archives. Institut Pasteur de Madagascar [*A publication*]
Arch Inst Pasteur Tunis ... Archives. Institut Pasteur de Tunis [*A publication*]
Arch Inst Past Tunis ... Archives. Institut Pasteur de Tunis [*A publication*]
Arch Inst Prophyl ... Archives. Institut Prophylactique [*A publication*]
Arch Inst Razi ... Archives. Institut Razi [*A publication*]
Arch Int Chir ... Archives Internationales de Chirurgie [*A publication*]
Arch Int Claude Bernard ... Archives Internationales Claude Bernard [*A publication*]
Arch Interamerican Rheumatol ... AIR. Archives of Interamerican Rheumatology [*A publication*]
Arch Interam Rheumatol ... Archives of Interamerican Rheumatology [*Brazil*] [*A publication*]
Arch Internat Histoire Sci ... Archives Internationales d'Histoire des Sciences [*Paris*] [*A publication*]
Arch Internat Hist Sci ... Archives Internationales d'Histoire des Sciences [*A publication*]
Arch Intern Med ... Archives of Internal Medicine [*A publication*]
Arch Int Etnogr Preist ... Archivio Internazionale di Etnografia e Preistoria [*A publication*]
Arch Int Hidatidosis ... Archivos Internacionales de la Hidatidosis [*A publication*]
Arch Int Hist Sci ... Archives Internationales d'Histoire des Sciences [*A publication*]
Arch Int Med ... Archives of Internal Medicine [*A publication*]
Arch Int Med Exp ... Archives Internationales de Medecine Experimentale [*A publication*]
Arch Int Neur ... Archives Internationales de Neurologie [*A publication*]
Arch Int Neurol ... Archives Internationales de Neurologie [*A publication*]
Arch Int Pharmacodyn Ther ... Archives Internationales de Pharmacodynamie et de Therapie [*A publication*]
Arch Int Physiol ... Archives Internationales de Physiologie [*A publication*]
Arch Int Physiol Biochim ... Archives Internationales de Physiologie et de Biochimie [*A publication*]
Arch Invest Med ... Archivos de Investigacion Medica [*A publication*]
Arch Inv M ... Archivos de Investigacion Medica [*A publication*]
Arch Inz Ladowej ... Archiwum Inzynierii Ladowej [*A publication*]
Arch I Phar ... Archives Internationales de Pharmacodynamie et de Therapie [*A publication*]
Arch I Phys ... Archives Internationales de Physiologie et de Biochimie [*A publication*]
Arch Ist Biochim Ital ... Archivio. Istituto Biochimico Italiano [*A publication*]
Arch Ist Osp St Corona ... Archivio. Istituti Ospedalieri Santa Corona [*A publication*]
ARCHIT .... Architecture
Archit .... Architecture in Australia [*Later, Architecture Australia*] [*A publication*] (APTA)
Arch Ital Anat Embriol ... Archivio Italiano di Anatomia e di Embriologia [*A publication*]
Arch Ital Anat Istol Patol ... Archivio Italiano di Istologia Patologica [*A publication*]
Arch Ital Biol ... Archives Italiennes de Biologie [*A publication*]
Arch Ital Chir ... Archivio Italiano di Chirurgia [*A publication*]
Arch Ital Clin Med ... Archivio Italiano di Clinica Medica [*A publication*]
Arch Ital Dermatol Sifilogr Venereol ... Archivio Italiano di Dermatologia, Sifilografia, e Venereologia [*A publication*]
Arch Ital Dermatol Venereol Sessuol ... Archivio Italiano di Dermatologia, Venereologia, e Sessuologia [*A publication*]
Arch Ital Laringol ... Archivii Italiani di Laringologia [*A publication*]
Arch Ital Mal Appar Dig ... Archivio Italiano delle Malattie dell'Apparato Digerente [*Italy*] [*A publication*]
Arch Ital Mal Nerv Ment ... Archivio Italiano per le Malattie Nervose e Mentali [*A publication*]
Arch Ital Med Sper ... Archivio Italiano di Medicina Sperimentale [*A publication*]
Arch Ital Otol Rinol Laringol ... Archivio Italiano di Otologia, Rinologia, e Laringologia [*A publication*]
Arch Ital Otol Rinol-Laringol Patol Cervico-Facciale ... Archivio Italiano di Otologia, Rinologia-Laringologia, e Patologia Cervico-Facciale [*A publication*]
Arch Ital Patol Clin Tumori ... Archivio Italiano di Patologia e Clinica dei Tumori [*A publication*]
Arch Ital Pediatr Pueri ... Archivio Italiano di Pediatria e Puericoltura [*A publication*]
Arch Ital Sci Farmacol ... Archivio Italiano di Scienze Farmacologiche [*A publication*]
Arch Ital Sci Med Trop Parassitol ... Archivio Italiano di Scienze Mediche Tropicali e di Parassitologia [*A publication*]
Arch Ital Sc Med Colon ... Archivio Italiano di Scienze Mediche Coloniali [*A publication*]
Arch Ital Urol ... Archivio Italiano di Urologia [*A publication*]
Arch Ital Urol Nefrol ... Archivio Italiano di Urologia e Nefrologia [*A publication*]
Archit Archaeol Soc Durham Northumberl Trans ... Architectural and Archaeological Society of Durham and Northumberland. Transactions [*A publication*]
Archit Assoc Q ... Architectural Association. Quarterly [*A publication*]
Archit Auj .. Architecture d'Aujourd'hui [*A publication*]
Archit Aujourd ... Architecture d'Aujourd'hui [*A publication*]

Archit d'Aujourd'hui ... Architecture d'Aujourd'hui [*A publication*]
Archit Aust ... Architecture Australia [*A publication*] (APTA)
Archit in Aust ... Architecture in Australia [*Later, Architecture Australia*] [*A publication*] (APTA)
Arch It Bio ... Archives Italiennes de Biologie [*A publication*]
Archit Build ... Architect and Builder [*A publication*]
Archit Concept ... Architecture Concept [*Canada*] [*A publication*]
Archit Cronache Storia ... Architettura Cronache e Storia [*A publication*]
Archit Des ... Architectural Design [*A publication*]
Archit Dig ... Architectural Digest [*A publication*]
Architect Hist ... Architectural History [*A publication*]
Architects J ... Architects' Journal [*A publication*]
Architects' LR ... Architects' Law Reports [*British*] [*A publication*] (DLA)
Architecture & Comportement/Archre & Behavior ... Architecture et Comportement/Architecture and Behavior [*A publication*]
Archit Eng ... Architect and Engineer [*A publication*]
Archit Forum ... Architectural Forum [*A publication*]
Archit Hist ... Architectural History [*A publication*]
Archit J ...... Architects' Journal [*A publication*]
Archit Met ... Architectural Metals [*A publication*]
Archit Mono ... Architectural Monographs [*A publication*]
Archit Per Ind ... Architectural Periodicals Index [*A publication*]
Archit Period Index ... Architectural Periodicals Index [*A publication*]
Archit Plus ... Architecture Plus [*A publication*]
Archit R ..... Architectural Review [*A publication*]
Archit Rec ... Architectural Record [*A publication*]
Archit Rev ... Architectural Review [*A publication*]
Archit Sci Rev ... Architectural Science Review [*A publication*]
Archits News ... Architects News [*A publication*]
Archit Surv ... Architect and Surveyor [*A publication*]
Archit Wohnwelt ... Architektur und Wohnwelt [*West Germany*] [*A publication*]
ArchIug ...... Archaeologia Iugoslavica [*A publication*]
Archiv .... Archiv fuer Reformationsgeschichte [*A publication*]
Archiv .... Archiv fuer das Studium der Neueren Sprachen und Literaturen [*A publication*]
Archiv Anthrop ... Archiv fuer Anthropologie und Voelkerforschung [*A publication*]
Archiv Antropol Etnol ... Archivio per l'Antropologia e la Etnologia [*A publication*]
Archiv As Art ... Archives of Asian Art [*A publication*]
Archiv Diplom Consul ... Archives Diplomatiques et Consulaires [*A publication*]
·ArchiveP .... [*The*] Archive (Philippines) [*A publication*]
Archives & Bibl ... Archives et Bibliotheques de Belgique [*A publication*]
Archives Environ Health ... Archives of Environmental Health [*A publication*]
Archives Environ Hlth ... Archives of Environmental Health [*A publication*]
Archives Eur Sociol ... Archives Europeennes de Sociologie [*A publication*]
Archives Gen Psychiat ... Archives of General Psychiatry [*A publication*]
Archives Ind Hyg & Occup Med ... Archives of Industrial Hygiene and Occupational Medicine [*A publication*]
Archives and Mss ... Archives and Manuscripts [*A publication*] (APTA)
Archives Neurol ... Archives of Neurology [*A publication*]
Archives Philos ... Archives de Philosophie [*A publication*]
Archives Sci ... Archives des Sciences [*A publication*]
Archives of Science Orleans Co Soc N Sc Tr ... Archives of Science. Orleans County Society of Natural Sciences. Transactions [*A publication*]
Archives Sci Sociales Relig ... Archives de Sciences Sociales des Religions [*A publication*]
Archives Sociol Relig ... Archives de Sociologie des Religions [*A publication*]
Archives Suisses Anthrop Gen ... Archives Suisses d'Anthropologie Generale [*A publication*]
Archiv Europ Sociol ... Archives Europeennes de Sociologie [*A publication*]
Archiv Eur Sociol ... Archives Europeennes de Sociologie [*A publication*]
Archiv Exp Zellforsch Besonders Gewebezuecht ... Archiv fuer Experimentelle Zellforschung Besonders Gewebezuechtung [*A publication*]
Archiv Gesch Buchw ... Archiv fuer Geschichte des Buchwesens [*A publication*]
Archiv Gesch Buchwes ... Archiv fuer Geschichte des Buchwesens [*A publication*]
Archiv Ibero ... Archivo Ibero-Americano [*A publication*]
Archiv Int Sociol Coop Develop ... Archives Internationales de Sociologie de la Cooperation et du Developpement [*A publication*]
Archiv Kommunalwiss ... Archiv fuer Kommunalwissenschaften [*A publication*]
Archiv Ling ... Archivum Linguisticum [*A publication*]
Archiv Meteorologie Geophysik u Bioklimatolgie Ser A ... Archiv fuer Meteorologie, Geophysik, und Bioklimatologie. Serie A. Meteorologie und Geophysik [*A publication*]
Archiv Mis ... Archives des Missions Scientifiques et Litteraires [*A publication*]
Archiv fuer Mus ... Archiv fuer Musikwissenschaft [*A publication*]
Archivo Espanol Arqu ... Archivo Espanol de Arqueologia [*A publication*]
Archivo Esp Arq ... Archivo Espanol de Arqueologia [*A publication*]
Archivo Esp Arte ... Archivo Espanol de Arte [*A publication*]
Archiv Oesterr Gesch ... Archiv fuer Oesterreichische Geschichte [*A publication*]
Archiv f Oesterr Geschichte ... Archiv fuer Oesterreichische Geschichte [*A publication*]

Archiv Off Rechts ... Archiv des Oeffentlichen Rechts [*A publication*]
Archiv Or ... Archiv Orientalni [*A publication*]
Archiv Orientforsch ... Archiv fuer Orientforschung [*A publication*]
Archiv Pap ... Archiv fuer Papyrusforschung und Verwandte Gebiete [*A publication*]
ArchivPhilos ... Archiv fuer Philosophie [*A publication*]
Archiv Philos Dr ... Archives de Philosophie du Droit [*A publication*]
Archiv Rechts u Soz-Philos ... Archiv fuer Rechts- und Sozialphilosophie [*A publication*]
Archiv Rom ... Archivum Romanicum [*A publication*]
Archiv Sci Soc Rel ... Archives de Sciences Sociales des Religions [*A publication*]
Archiv Sci Soc Relig ... Archives de Sciences Sociales des Religions [*A publication*]
Archiv Sex Behav ... Archives of Sexual Behavior [*A publication*]
Archiv Soc Rel ... Archives de Sociologie des Religions [*A publication*]
Archiv Stor ... Archivio Storico [*A publication*]
Archiv f Stud ... Archiv fuer das Studium der Neueren Sprachen und Literaturen [*A publication*]
Archiv Suisses Anthropol Gen ... Archives Suisses d'Anthropologie Generale [*A publication*]
Archivum Hist Soc Iesu ... Archivum Historicum Societatis Iesu [*A publication*]
Archiv Urk ... Archiv fuer Urkundenforschung [*A publication*]
Archiv Voelkerk ... Archiv fuer Voelkerkunde [*A publication*]
Archiv Volkerrechts ... Archiv des Voelkerrechts [*A publication*]
Arch J .... Archaeological Journal [*A publication*]
Arch J .... Architects' Journal [*A publication*]
Arch JC Pr ... Archibald on Practice of Judges' Chambers [*A publication*] (DLA)
Arch Journ ... Archaeological Journal [*A publication*] (OCD)
Arch JP ...... Archbold. Justice of the Peace [*7th ed.*] [*1859*] [*A publication*] (DLA)
Arch Jpn Chir ... Archiv fuer Japanische Chirurgie [*A publication*]
Arch Jug .... Archaeologia Jugoslavica [*A publication*]
Arch Juives ... Archives Juives. Cahiers de la Commission des Archives Juives [*A publication*]
Arch Julius Klaus-Stift Vererbforsch ... Archiv der Julius Klaus-Stiftung fuer Vererbungsforschung, Sozialanthropologie, und Rassenhygiene [*A publication*]
ArchK .... Archiv fuer Kulturgeschichte [*A publication*]
Arch KB Forms ... Archbold's Forms in King's Bench and Common Pleas [*A publication*] (DLA)
Arch KB Pr ... Archbold's King's Bench Practice [*A publication*] (DLA)
Arch Kinderh ... Archiv fuer Kinderheilkunde [*A publication*]
Arch Kinderheilkd ... Archiv fuer Kinderheilkunde [*A publication*]
Arch Kinderheilkd Beih ... Archiv fuer Kinderheilkunde. Beihefte [*A publication*]
Arch Klaerung Wuenschelrutenfrage ... Archiv zur Klaerung der Wuenschelrutenfrage [*A publication*]
Arch Klin Chir ... Archiv fuer Klinische Chirurgie [*A publication*]
Arch Klin Chir Langenbecks ... Archiv fuer Klinische Chirurgie. Langenbecks [*West Germany*] [*A publication*]
Arch Klin Exp Dermatol ... Archiv fuer Klinische und Experimentelle Dermatologie [*A publication*]
Arch Klin Exp Ohren- Nasen- Kehlkopfheilkd ... Archiv fuer Klinische und Experimentelle Ohren-, Nasen-, und Kehlkopfheilkunde [*A publication*]
Arch Klin Exp Ophtalmol ... Archiv fuer Klinische und Experimentelle Ophtalmologie [*A publication*]
Arch Klin Med ... Archiv fuer Klinische Medizin [*A publication*]
Arch Kohno Clin Med Res Inst ... Archives. Kohno Clinical Medicine Research Institute [*A publication*]
Arch Kommunalwiss ... Archiv fuer Kommunalwissenschaften [*A publication*]
Arch Kreislaufforsch ... Archiv fuer Kreislaufforschung [*A publication*]
Arch Kriminol ... Archiv fuer Kriminologie [*A publication*]
Arch Kulturgesch ... Archiv fuer Kulturgeschichte [*A publication*]
ArchL .... Archivum Linguisticum [*A publication*]
Arch Lagerstaettenforsch ... Archiv fuer Lagerstaettenforschung [*A publication*]
Arch Lagerstaettenforsch Ostalpen ... Archiv fuer Lagerstaettenforschung in den Ostalpen [*A publication*]
Arch Lagerstattenforsch Geol Bundesanst ... Archiv fuer Lagerstaettenforschung der Geologischen Bundesanstalt [*A publication*]
Arch Landtech ... Archiv fuer Landtechnik [*A publication*]
Archl Assocn Annual Review ... Architectural Association. Annual Review [*A publication*]
Arch Latinoamer Nutr ... Archivos Latinoamericanos de Nutricion [*A publication*]
Arch Latinoam Nutr ... Archivos Latinoamericanos de Nutricion [*A publication*]
Arch Latr Epistem ... Archeion Iatrikon Epistemon [*A publication*]
Arch Lebensm Hyg ... Archiv fuer Lebensmittel-Hygiene [*A publication*]
Arch Lebensmittelhyg ... Archiv fuer Lebensmittelhygiene [*A publication*]
Arch Ling ... Archivum Linguisticum [*A publication*]
Arch Linguist ... Archivum Linguisticum [*A publication*]
ArchLit ...... Archiv fuer Literatur und Volksdichtung [*A publication*]
ArchLitg .... Archiv fuer Liturgiewissenschaft [*Regensburg*] [*A publication*]
ARCHLR ... Architects' Law Reports [*British*]

Arch L & T ... Archbold. Law of Landlord and Tenant [*3rd ed.*] [*1864*] [*A publication*] (DLA)

Arch Lun.... Archbold. Lunacy Laws [*5th ed.*] [*1915*] [*A publication*] (DLA)

Arch Mal Appar Dig Mal Nutr ... Archives des Maladies de l'Appareil Digestif et des Maladies de la Nutrition [*A publication*]

Arch Mal C ... Archives des Maladies du Coeur et des Vaisseaux [*A publication*]

Arch Mal Coeur ... Archives des Maladies du Coeur et des Vaisseaux [*A publication*]

Arch Mal Coeur Vaiss ... Archives des Maladies du Coeur et des Vaisseaux [*A publication*]

Arch Mal Pr ... Archives des Maladies Professionnelles de Medecine du Travail et de Securite Sociale [*A publication*]

Arch Mal Prof ... Archives des Maladies Professionnelles de Medecine du Travail et de Securite Sociale [*A publication*]

Arch Mal Prof Hyg Toxicol Ind ... Archives des Maladies Professionnelles, Hygiene, et Toxicologie Industrielles [*A publication*]

Arch Mal Prof Med Trav Secur Soc ... Archives des Maladies Professionnelles de Medecine du Travail et de Securite Sociale [*A publication*]

Arch & Manus ... Archives and Manuscripts [*A publication*] (APTA)

Arch Manuscr ... Archives and Manuscripts [*A publication*]

Arch and Manuscripts ... Archives and Manuscripts [*A publication*] (APTA)

Arch Maragliano Patol Clin ... Archivio e Maragliano di Patologia e Clinica [*A publication*]

Arch Mass Spectral Data ... Archives of Mass Spectral Data [*A publication*]

Arch Math ... Archiv der Mathematik [*A publication*]

Arch Math (Basel) ... Archiv der Mathematik (Basel) [*A publication*]

Arch Math (Brno) ... Archivum Mathematicum (Brno) [*A publication*]

Arch Math Log ... Archiv fuer Mathematische Logik und Grundlagenforschung [*A publication*]

Arch Math Logik Grundlag ... Archiv fuer Mathematische Logik und Grundlagenforschung [*Stuttgart*] [*A publication*]

Arch Math Logik Grundlagenforsch ... Archiv fuer Mathematische Logik und Grundlagenforschung [*A publication*]

Arch Math Logik und Grundlagenforsch ... Archiv fuer Mathematische Logik und Grundlagenforschung [*A publication*]

Arch Mat Naturvidensk ... Archiv foer Matematik og Naturvidenskab [*Norway*] [*A publication*]

Arch Meat Fish Dairy Sci ... Archives of Meat, Fish, and Dairy Science [*A publication*]

Arch Mech ... Archives of Mechanics [*Archiwum Mechaniki Stosowanej*] [*A publication*]

Arch Mech (Arch Mech Stosow) ... Archives of Mechanics (Archiwum Mechaniki Stosowanej) [*A publication*]

Arch Mech Stosow ... Archiwum Mechaniki Stosowanej [*Archives of Mechanics*] [*A publication*]

Arch Mech Stosowanej ... Archiwum Mechaniki Stosowanej [*Archives of Mechanics*] [*A publication*]

Arch Med... Archives Medicales [*A publication*]

Arch Med Angers ... Archives Medicales d'Angers [*A publication*]

Arch Med Belg ... Archiva Medica Belgica [*A publication*]

Arch Med Chir Appar Respir ... Archives Medico-Chirurgicales de l'Appareil Respiratoire [*A publication*]

Arch Med Cuba ... Archivos Medicos de Cuba [*A publication*]

Arch Med Enf ... Archives de Medecine des Enfants [*A publication*]

Arch Med Enfants ... Archives de Medecine des Enfants [*A publication*]

Arch Med Exp ... Archivos de Medicina Experimental [*A publication*]

Arch Med Exper et Anat Path ... Archives de Medecine Experimentale et d'Anatomie Pathologique [*A publication*]

Arch Med Gen Trop ... Archives de Medecine Generale et Tropicale [*A publication*]

Arch Med Hydrol ... Archives of Medical Hydrology [*A publication*]

Arch Med Leg ... Archivo de Medicina Legal [*A publication*]

Arch Med (Lisbon) ... Archivos de Medicina (Lisbon) [*A publication*]

Arch Med Mex ... Archivos Medicos Mexicanos [*Mexico*] [*A publication*]

Arch Med (Mexico City) ... Archivos Medicos (Mexico City) [*A publication*]

Arch Med Nav ... Archives de Medecine Navale [*A publication*]

Arch Med Normandie ... Archives Medicales de Normandie [*A publication*]

Arch Med Panameno ... Archivos Medicos Panamenos [*A publication*]

Arch Med Pharm Nav ... Archives de Medecine et Pharmacie Navales [*A publication*]

Arch Med Sadowej Kryminol ... Archiwum Medycyny Sadowej i Kryminologii [*A publication*]

Arch Med Soc Hyg Rev Pathol Physiol Trav ... Archives de Medecine Sociale et d'Hygiene et Revue de Pathologie et de Physiologie du Travail [*A publication*]

Arch Med Vet (Valdivia) ... Archivos de Medicina Veterinaria (Valdivia) [*A publication*]

Arch Metallkd ... Archiv fuer Metallkunde [*West Germany*] [*A publication*]

Arch Meteorol Geophys Bioclimatol Ser B Theor Appl Climatol ... Archives for Meteorology, Geophysics, and Bioclimatology. Series B. Theoretical and Applied Climatology [*A publication*]

Arch Meteorol Geophys Bioklimatol Ser A ... Archiv fuer Meteorologie, Geophysik, und Bioklimatologie. Serie A [*A publication*]

Arch Meteorol Geophys Bioklimatol Ser B ... Archiv fuer Meteorologie, Geophysik, und Bioklimatologie. Serie B [*A publication*]

Arch Met Geophys Bioklim Ser A Meteorologie und Geophysik ... Archiv fuer Meteorologie, Geophysik, und Bioklimatologie. Serie A. Meteorologie und Geophysik [*A publication*]

Arch Mex Anat ... Archivos Mexicanos de Anatomia [*A publication*]

Arch Mex Neurol Psiquiatr ... Archivos Mexicanos de Neurologia y Psiquiatria [*A publication*]

Arch Mex Venereol Dermatol ... Archivos Mexicanos de Venereologia y Dermatologia [*A publication*]

Arch MGB A ... Archiv fuer Meteorologie, Geophysik, und Bioklimatologie. Serie A [*A publication*]

Arch MGB B ... Archiv fuer Meteorologie, Geophysik, und Bioklimatologie. Serie B [*A publication*]

Arch Microb ... Archives of Microbiology [*A publication*]

Arch Microbiol ... Archives of Microbiology [*A publication*]

Arch Mikr Anat ... Archiv fuer Mikroskopische Anatomie [*A publication*]

Arch Mikrobiol ... Archiv fuer Mikrobiologie [*A publication*]

Arch Mikrosk Anat Entwicklungsmech ... Archiv fuer Mikroskopische Anatomie und Entwicklungsmechanik [*A publication*]

Arch Mikrosk Anat Entwmech ... Archiv fuer Mikroskopische Anatomie und Entwicklungsmechanik [*A publication*]

Arch Miner ... Archiv fuer Mineralogie, Geognosie, Bergbau, und Huettenkunde [*A publication*]

Arch Mineral ... Archiwum Mineralogiczne [*A publication*]

ArchMIran ... Archaeologische Mitteilungen aus Iran. Neue Folge [*Berlin*] [*A publication*]

Arch Miss ... Archives des Missions Scientifiques et Litteraires [*A publication*]

Arch Molluskenkd ... Archiv fuer Molluskenkunde [*A publication*]

Arch Monaldi ... Archivio Monaldi [*A publication*]

Arch Monaldi Tisiol Mal Appar Respir ... Archivio Monaldi per la Tisiologia e le Malattie dell'Apparato Respiratorio [*A publication*]

Arch Ms..... Archives and Manuscripts [*A publication*]

Arch Mun Corp ... Archbold. Municipal Corporations Act [*1836*] [*A publication*] (DLA)

Arch Mus ... Archiv fuer Musikwissenschaft [*A publication*]

Arch Mus Hist Nat Lyon ... Archives. Museum d'Histoire Naturelle de Lyon [*A publication*]

Arch Musik ... Archiv fuer Musikwissenschaft [*A publication*]

Arch Mus Natl Hist Nat (Paris) ... Archives. Museum National d'Histoire Naturelle (Paris) [*A publication*]

Arch Mus Teyler ... Archives. Musee Teyler [*A publication*]

Arch N ... Archaeological News [*A publication*]

Arch Nachr Baden ... Archaeologische Nachrichten aus Baden [*A publication*]

Arch Nat Hist ... Archives of Natural History [*A publication*]

Arch Naturg ... Archiv fuer Naturgeschichte [*A publication*]

Arch Naturg (Berlin) ... Archiv fuer Naturgeschichte (Berlin) [*A publication*]

Arch Naturgesch ... Archiv fuer Naturgeschichte [*A publication*]

Arch Naturkd Liv- Est- Kurlands ... Archiv fuer die Naturkunde Liv-, Est-, und Kurlands [*Estonian SSR*] [*A publication*]

Arch Naturschutz Landschaftsforsch ... Archiv fuer Naturschutz und Landschaftsforschung [*A publication*]

Arch Naturw ... Archaeologie und Naturwissenschaften [*A publication*]

Arch Nauki Mater ... Archiwum Nauki o Materialach [*Poland*] [*A publication*]

Arch Neerl Phon Exp ... Archives Neerlandaises de Phonetique Experimentale [*A publication*]

Arch Neerl Physiol ... Archives Neerlandaises de Physiologie [*A publication*]

Arch Neerl Sci Exactes Nat ... Archives Neerlandaises des Sciences Exactes et Naturelles [*Netherlands*] [*A publication*]

Arch Neerl Sci Exactes Nat Ser 3A ... Archives Neerlandaises des Sciences Exactes et Naturelles. Serie 3A. Sciences Exactes [*A publication*]

Arch Neerl Sci Exactes Nat Ser 3B ... Archives Neerlandaises des Sciences Exactes et Naturelles. Serie 3B. Sciences Naturelles [*A publication*]

Arch Neerl Zool ... Archives Neerlandaises de Zoologie [*A publication*]

Arch Neurobiol ... Archivos de Neurobiologia [*Madrid*] [*A publication*]

Arch Neurol ... Archives of Neurology [*A publication*]

Arch Neurol (Chicago) ... Archives of Neurology (Chicago) [*A publication*]

Arch Neurol Psychiatry ... Archives of Neurology and Psychiatry [*A publication*]

Arch News ... Archaeological News [*A publication*]

Arch NP... Archbold's Law of Nisi Prius [*A publication*] (DLA)

ArchNPhonExp ... Archives Neerlandaises de Phonetique Experimentale [*A publication*]

Arch Oceanogr Limnol ... Archivio di Oceanografia e Limnologia [*A publication*]

Arch Odontoestomatol ... Archivos de Odontoestomatologia [*A publication*]

Arch Oeff Recht ... Archiv des Oeffentlichen Rechts [*A publication*]

ArchOF...... Archiv fuer Orientforschung [*Graz, Austria*] [*A publication*]

Arch Off Niger ... Archives. Office du Niger [*A publication*]

Arch Off R ... Archiv des Oeffentlichen Rechts [*A publication*] (ILCA)

Arch Oftal Hispano-Am ... Archivos de Oftalmologia Hispano-Americanos [*A publication*]

Arch Oftalmol B Aires ... Archivos de Oftalmologia de Buenos Aires [*A publication*]

Arch Oftalmol Hisp-Am ... Archivos de Oftalmologia Hispano-Americanos [*A publication*]

Arch Ohrenh ... Archiv fuer Ohrenheilkunde [*A publication*]

Arch Ohren- Nasen- Kehlkopfheilkd ... Archiv fuer Ohren-, Nasen-, und Kehlkopfheilkunde [*West Germany*] [*A publication*]

Arch Ohr-Nas Kehlkopfheilk ... Archiv fuer Ohren-, Nasen-, und Kehlkopfheilkunde [*A publication*]

ARCHOLOGY ... Archeology and Ecology [*Coined by Paolo Soleri, Italian-born architect*]

Archo Patol Clin Med ... Archivio di Patologia e Clinica Medica [*A publication*]
Arch Ophtal ... Archives d'Ophtalmologie [*A publication*]
Arch Ophtalmol ... Archives d'Ophtalmologie [*A publication*]
Arch Ophtalmol (Paris) ... Archives d'Ophtalmologie et Revue Generale d'Ophtalmologie (Paris) [*A publication*]
Arch Ophtalmol Rev Gen Ophtalmol ... Archives d'Ophtalmologie et Revue Generale d'Ophtalmologie [*A publication*]
Arch Ophth ... Archives of Ophthalmology [*Chicago*] [*A publication*]
Arch Ophthalmol ... Archives of Ophthalmology [*Chicago*] [*A publication*]
Arch Opht (Paris) ... Archives d'Ophtalmologie (Paris)
Arch Opt .... Archiv fuer Optik [*A publication*]
ArchOr .... Archiv Orientalni [*Prague*] [*A publication*]
Arch Oral B ... Archives of Oral Biology [*A publication*]
Arch Oral Biol ... Archives of Oral Biology [*A publication*]
ArchOrient ... Archiv Orientalni [*A publication*]
Arch Orthop ... Archiv fuer Orthopaedische und Unfall-Chirurgie [*A publication*]
Arch Orthop Trauma Surg ... Archives of Orthopaedic and Traumatic Surgery [*A publication*]
Arch Orthop Unfall-Chir ... Archiv fuer Orthopaedische und Unfall-Chirurgie [*A publication*]
Arch Ortop ... Archivio di Ortopedia [*Later, Archivio di Ortopedia e Reumatologia*] [*Italy*] [*A publication*]
Arch Ortop Reumatol ... Archivio di Ortopedia e Reumatologia [*A publication*]
Archos Bioquim Quim Farmac (Tucuman) ... Archivos de Bioquimica, Quimica, y Farmacia (Tucuman) [*A publication*]
Archos Bromat ... Archivos de Bromatologia [*A publication*]
Archos Inst Aclim (Almeria) ... Archivos. Instituto de Aclimatacion (Almeria, Espana) [*A publication*]
Archos Inst Antrop (Natal) ... Archivos. Instituto Antropologia (Natal) [*A publication*]
Archos Inst Biol (S Paulo) ... Archivos. Instituto Biologico (Sao Paulo) [*A publication*]
Archos Mus Paranaie ... Archivos. Museu Paranaie [*A publication*]
Arch Osp Mare ... Archivio. Ospedale al Mare [*A publication*]
Archos Soc Biol Montev ... Archivos. Sociedad de Biologia de Montevideo [*A publication*]
Arch Ostet Ginecol ... Archivio di Ostetricia e Ginecologia [*A publication*]
Archos Venez Nutr ... Archivos Venezolanos de Nutricion [*A publication*]
Archos Zootecnia ... Archivos de Zootecnia [*A publication*]
Arch Otol ... Archives of Otology [*A publication*]
Arch Otolar ... Archives of Otolaryngology [*A publication*]
Arch Otolaryng ... Archives of Otolaryngology [*A publication*]
Arch Otolaryngol ... Archives of Otolaryngology [*A publication*]
Arch Otolaryngol Head and Neck Surg ... Archives of Otolaryngology and Head and Neck Surgery [*A publication*]
Arch Otolaryngol Head Neck Surg ... Archives of Otolaryngology and Head and Neck Surgery [*A publication*]
Arch Oto-R ... Archives of Oto-Rhino-Laryngology [*A publication*]
Arch Oto-Rhino-Laryngol ... Archives of Oto-Rhino-Laryngology [*A publication*]
Arch Otorhinolaryngol Suppl ... Archives of Oto-Rhino-Laryngology. Supplement [*A publication*]
Arch Ottalmol ... Archivio di Ottalmologia [*A publication*]
Archo Vet Ital ... Archivio Veterinario Italiano [*A publication*]
Archo Zool Ital ... Archivio Zoologico Italiano [*A publication*]
Arch P .... Archiv fuer Papyrusforschung [*A publication*]
Arch Pap ...... Archiv fuer Papyrusforschung [*A publication*] (OCD)
Arch Parasitol (Paris) ... Archives de Parasitologie (Paris) [*A publication*]
Arch Part ... Archbold's Law of Partnership [*A publication*] (DLA)
Arch Path ... Archives of Pathology [*Later, Archives of Pathology and Laboratory Medicine*] [*A publication*]
Arch Path Anat ... Archiv fuer Pathologische Anatomie und Physiologie und fuer Klinische Medizin [*A publication*]
Arch Path and Lab Med ... Archives of Pathology and Laboratory Medicine [*A publication*]
Arch Pathol ... Archives of Pathology [*Later, Archives of Pathology and Laboratory Medicine*] [*A publication*]
Arch Pathol Lab Med ... Archives of Pathology and Laboratory Medicine [*A publication*]
Arch Patol Clin Med ... Archivio di Patologia e Clinica Medica [*A publication*]
Arch Patol e Clin Med ... Archivio di Patologia e Clinica Medica [*A publication*]
Arch PC ..... Archbold's Pleas of the Crown [*A publication*] (DLA)
Arch P Ch ... Archbold's Practice, by Chitty [*A publication*] (DLA)
Arch PCP ... Archbold. Practice of the Court of Common Pleas [*1829*] [*A publication*] (DLA)
Arch Pediat ... Archives of Pediatrics [*A publication*]
Arch Pediatr ... Archives of Pediatrics [*A publication*]
Arch Pediatr Urug ... Archivos de Pediatria del Uruguay [*A publication*]
Arch Peru Patol Clin ... Archivos Peruanos de Patologia y Clinica [*A publication*]
Arch Peru Patol Clin (Lima) ... Archivos Peruanos de Patologia y Clinica (Lima) [*A publication*]
Arch PF ..... Archiv fuer Papyrusforschung und Verwandte Gebiete [*A publication*]
Arch Pflanzenschutz ... Archiv fuer Pflanzenschutz [*A publication*]
Arch Pflsch ... Archiv fuer Pflanzenschutz [*A publication*]

Arch Pflschutz ... Archiv fuer Pflanzenschutz [*A publication*]
Arch Pharm ... Archiv der Pharmazie [*A publication*]
Arch Pharmacal Res (Seoul) ... Archives of Pharmacal Research (Seoul) [*A publication*]
Arch Pharmacol ... Archives of Pharmacology [*A publication*]
Arch Pharmakol Exp Pathol ... Archiv fuer Pharmakologie und Experimentelle Pathologie. Naunyn-Schmiedebergs [*Later, Archiv fuer Pharmakologie. Naunyn-Schmiedebergs*] [*West Germany*] [*A publication*]
Arch Pharmakol Naunyn-Schmiedebergs ... Archiv fuer Pharmakologie. Naunyn-Schmiedebergs [*Formerly, Archiv fuer Pharmakologie und Experimentelle Pathologie. Naunyn-Schmiedebergs*] [*West Germany*] [*A publication*]
Arch Pharm (Athens) ... Archeia tes Pharmakeutikes (Athens) [*A publication*]
Arch Pharm Ber Dtsch Pharm Ges ... Archiv der Pharmazie und Berichte der Deutschen Pharmazeutischen Gesellschaft [*A publication*]
Arch Pharm (Berl) ... Archiv der Pharmazie und Berichte der Deutschen Pharmazeutischen Gesellschaft (Berlin) [*A publication*]
Arch Pharm Chem ... Archiv foer Pharmaci og Chemi [*A publication*]
Arch Pharm Chem Sci Ed ... Archiv foer Pharmaci og Chemi. Scientific Edition [*A publication*]
Arch Pharm (Weinheim Ger) ... Archiv der Pharmazie (Weinheim, Germany) [*A publication*]
Arch Phil ... Archives de Philosophie [*A publication*]
Arch Phil Dr ... Archives de Philosophie du Droit [*A publication*]
Arch Philos ... Archives de Philosophie [*A publication*]
Arch Phys Biol ... Archives de Physique Biologique [*A publication*]
Arch Phys Biol Chim Phys Corps Organ ... Archives de Physique Biologique et de Chimie Physique des Corps Organises [*A publication*]
Arch Phys M ... Archives of Physical Medicine and Rehabilitation [*A publication*]
Arch Phys Med ... Archives of Physical Medicine [*A publication*]
Arch Phys Med ... Archives of Physical Medicine and Rehabilitation [*A publication*]
Arch Phys Med Rehab ... Archives of Physical Medicine and Rehabilitation [*A publication*]
Arch Phys Med Rehabil ... Archives of Physical Medicine and Rehabilitation [*A publication*]
Arch Phys Ther ... Archiv fuer Physikalische Therapie [*A publication*]
Arch Phytopathol Pflanzenschutz ... Archiv fuer Phytopathologie und Pflanzenschutz [*A publication*]
Arch Phytopath Pflschutz ... Archiv fuer Phytopathologie und Pflanzenschutz [*A publication*]
Arch PKB .. Archbold's Practice in the King's Bench [*A publication*] (DLA)
Arch PL ..... Archbold's Poor Law [*1840-1930*] [*A publication*] (DLA)
Arch PLC ... Archbold's Poor Law Cases [*1842-58*] [*A publication*] (DLA)
Arch PL Cas ... Archbold's Abridgment of Poor Law Cases [*1842-58*] [*A publication*] (DLA)
Arch PL Pr ... Archbold's New Practice in Poor Law Removals and Appeals [*A publication*] (DLA)
Arch Podiatr Med Foot Surg ... Archives of Podiatric Medicine and Foot Surgery [*A publication*]
Arch Pol ..... Archeologia Polski [*A publication*]
Arch Pol Criminelle ... Archives de Politique Criminelle [*A publication*]
Arch Polon ... Archaeologia Polona [*A publication*]
Arch Polona ... Archaeologia Polona [*A publication*]
Arch Port Sci Biol ... Archives Portugaises des Sciences Biologiques [*A publication*]
Arch Post und Fernmeldewes ... Archiv fuer das Post- und Fernmeldewesen [*A publication*]
Arch Poult Sci ... Archives of Poultry Science [*A publication*]
Arch Pract Pharm ... Archives of Practical Pharmacy [*Japan*] [*A publication*]
Arch Pr Ch ... Archbold's Practice, by Cholty [*A publication*] (DLA)
Arch Pr CP ... Archbold's Practice in the Common Pleas [*A publication*] (DLA)
Arch Pr Hist Lev ... Archivo de Prehistoria Levantina [*A publication*]
Arch Pr JC ... Archbold's Practice in Judges Chambers [*A publication*] (DLA)
Arch Procesow Spalania ... Archiwum Procesow Spalania [*Poland*] [*A publication*]
Arch Protistenkd ... Archiv fuer Protistenkunde. Protozoen-Algen-Pilze [*A publication*]
Arch Pr QS ... Archbold's Practice in Quarter Sessions [*A publication*] (DLA)
Arch Psicol Neurol Psichiatr ... Archivio di Psicologia, Neurologia, e Psichiatria [*A publication*]
Arch Psych ... Archiv fuer Psychologie [*A publication*]
Arch Psychi ... Archiv fuer Psychiatrie und Nervenkrankheiten [*A publication*]
Arch Psychiat Nervenkr ... Archiv fuer Psychiatrie und Nervenkrankheiten [*A publication*]
Arch Psychiatr Nervenkr ... Archiv fuer Psychiatrie und Nervenkrankheiten [*A publication*]
Arch Psychiatr Nervenkrankh ... Archiv fuer Psychiatrie und Nervenkrankheiten [*A publication*]
Arch Psychiatry Neurol Sci ... Archives of Psychiatry and Neurological Sciences [*A publication*]
Arch Psychol (Frankf) ... Archiv fuer Psychologie (Frankfurt Am Main) [*A publication*]
Arch Putti Chir Organi Mov ... Archivio Putti di Chirurgia degli Organi di Movimento [*A publication*]

Arch QB..... Archbold's Practice in the Queen's Bench [*A publication*] (DLA)
Arch R........ Architectural Review [*A publication*]
Arch Radiol ... Archivio di Radiologia [*A publication*]
Arch Radiol (Napoli) ... Archivio di Radiologia (Napoli) [*A publication*]
Arch Rass- u Ges Biol ... Archiv fuer Rassen- und Gesellschafts-Biologie Einschliessend Rassen- und Gesellschaftshygiene [*A publication*]
Arch Rass Ital Ottalmol ... Archivio e Rassegna Italiana di Ottalmologia [*A publication*]
Arch Rational Mech Anal ... Archive for Rational Mechanics and Analysis [*A publication*]
Arch Ration Mech and Anal ... Archive for Rational Mechanics and Analysis [*A publication*]
Arch Ration Mech Anal ... Archive for Rational Mechanics and Analysis [*A publication*]
Archre Australia ... Architecture Australia [*A publication*]
Archre in Australia ... Architecture in Australia [*Later, Architecture Australia*] [*A publication*]
Arch Rec .... Architectural Record [*A publication*]
Arch Rech Agron Pastorales Vietnam ... Archives des Recherches Agronomiques et Pastorales au Vietnam [*A publication*]
Arch Rechts Soz ... Archiv fuer Rechts- und Sozialphilosophie [*A publication*]
Archre East Midlands ... Architecture East Midlands [*A publication*]
Arch Reformation Hist ... Archive for Reformation History [*A publication*]
Archre in Greece ... Architecture in Greece [*A publication*]
Archre in Ireland ... Architecture in Ireland [*A publication*]
Archre in Israel ... Architecture in Israel [*A publication*]
Archre Nebr ... Architecture Nebraska [*A publication*]
Arch Rep .... Archaeological Reports [*A publication*] (OCD)
Archre SA ... Architecture South Africa [*A publication*]
Archre from Scandinavia ... Architecture from Scandinavia [*A publication*]
Arch Res Ind Carcinog ... Archives of Research on Industrial Carcinogenesis [*A publication*]
Arch Rev .... Architectural Review [*A publication*]
Archre West Midlands ... Architecture West Midlands [*A publication*]
Arch Ricam ... Archivio del Ricambio [*A publication*]
Arch R Inst Bacteriol Camara Pestana ... Archivos. Real Instituto Bacteriologico Camara Pestana [*A publication*]
Arch R Mech ... Archive for Rational Mechanics and Analysis [*A publication*]
Arch Rom... Archivum Romanicum [*A publication*]
Arch Roum Pathol Exp Microbiol ... Archives Roumaines de Pathologie Experimentale et de Microbiologie [*A publication*]
Arch Rozhledy ... Archeologicke Rozhledy [*A publication*]
Arch R Soz Phil ... Archiv fuer Rechts und Sozialphilosophie [*A publication*] (ILCA)
Arch Rubber Cultiv (Bogor) ... Archives of Rubber Cultivation (Bogor) [*A publication*]
ArchRW..... Archiv fuer Religionswissenschaft [*A publication*]
ARCHS...... Army Reactor Systems Health and Safety Review Committee (AABC)
Archs Anat Microsc ... Archives d'Anatomie Microscopique [*A publication*]
Archs Anat Microsc Morph Exp ... Archives d'Anatomie Microscopique et de Morphologie Experimentale [*A publication*]
Arch S A Of ... Archivos. Sociedad Americana de Oftalmologia y Optometria [*A publication*]
Archs Biochem ... Archives of Biochemistry [*A publication*]
Archs Biochem Biophys ... Archives of Biochemistry and Biophysics [*A publication*]
Archs Biol (Liege) ... Archives de Biologie (Liege) [*Belgium*] [*A publication*]
Arch Schiffs-u Tropen-Hyg ... Archiv fuer Schiffs-und Tropen-Hygiene [*A publication*]
Arch Schlesische Kirchengesch ... Archiv fuer Schlesische Kirchengeschichte [*A publication*]
Arch Sci ..... Archives des Sciences [*A publication*]
Arch Sci Avicole ... Archives de Science Avicole [*A publication*]
Arch Sci Biol ... Archivio di Scienze Biologiche [*Bologna*] [*A publication*]
Arch Sci Biol (Belgrade) ... Archives des Sciences Biologiques (Belgrade) [*A publication*]
Arch Science R ... Architectural Science Review [*A publication*] (APTA)
Arch Sci (Geneva) ... Archives des Sciences (Geneva) [*A publication*]
Arch Sci Med ... Archivio per le Scienze Mediche [*Torino*] [*A publication*]
Arch Sci Ph ... Archives des Sciences Physiologiques [*A publication*]
Arch Sci Physiol ... Archives des Sciences Physiologiques [*A publication*]
Arch Sci Phys Nat ... Archives des Sciences Physiques et Naturelles. Supplement a la Bibliotheque Universelle [*A publication*]
Arch Sci Rev ... Architectural Science Review [*A publication*] (APTA)
Arch Sci Soc Coop Dev ... Archives de Sciences Sociales de la Cooperation et du Developpement [*A publication*]
Arch Sci Soc Phys Hist Nat Geneve ... Archives des Sciences. Societe de Physique et d'Histoire Naturelle de Geneve [*A publication*]
Arch Sc Med (Torino) ... Archivio per le Scienze Mediche (Torino) [*A publication*]
Arch Sc Phys Nat ... Archives des Sciences Physiques et Naturelles [*A publication*]
Archs Derm ... Archives of Dermatology [*A publication*]
Archs Envir Contam Toxic ... Archives of Environmental Contamination and Toxicology [*A publication*]
Archs Envir Hlth ... Archives of Environmental Health [*A publication*]
Arch Serv Sante Armee Belge ... Archives. Service de Sante de l'Armee Belge [*A publication*]

Arch Sex Be ... Archives of Sexual Behavior [*A publication*]
Arch Sex Behav ... Archives of Sexual Behavior [*A publication*]
Archs Inst Gr-Duc Luxemb ... Archives. Institut Grand-Ducal de Luxembourg [*A publication*]
Archs Insts Pasteur Afr N ... Archives. Instituts Pasteur de l'Afrique du Nord [*A publication*]
Archs Intern Med ... Archives of Internal Medicine [*A publication*]
Archs Int Pharmacodyn Ther ... Archives Internationales de Pharmacodynamie et de Therapie [*A publication*]
Archs Int Physiol ... Archives Internationales de Physiologie [*A publication*]
Archs Int Physiol Biochim ... Archives Internationales de Physiologie et de Biochimie [*A publication*]
Archs Man ... Archives and Manuscripts [*A publication*]
Archs Med-Chir Normandie ... Archives Medico-Chirurgicales de Normandie [*A publication*]
Archs Neerl Zool ... Archives Neerlandaises de Zoologie [*A publication*]
Arch Soc Am Oftalmol Optom ... Archivos. Sociedad Americana de Oftalmologia y Optometria [*A publication*]
Arch Soc Biol Montev ... Archivos. Sociedad de Biologia de Montevideo [*A publication*]
Arch Soc Esp Oftalmol ... Archivos. Sociedad Espanola de Oftalmologia [*A publication*]
Arch Soc Estud Clin Habana ... Archivos. Sociedad de Estudios Clinicos de la Habana [*A publication*]
Arch Soc Oftalmol Hisp-Am ... Archivos. Sociedad Oftalmologica Hispano-Americana [*A publication*]
Arch Soc Zool-Bot Fenn "Vanamo" ... Archivum Societatis Zoologicae-Botanicae Fennicae "Vanamo" [*A publication*]
Arch (Sofia) ... Archeologie (Sofia) [*A publication*]
ArchSS....... Archivio Storico Siciliano [*A publication*]
Archs Sci Physiol ... Archives des Sciences Physiologiques [*A publication*]
Arch SS Rel ... Archives de Sciences Sociales des Religions [*A publication*]
Arch Stomatol ... Archivio Stomatologico [*A publication*]
Arch Stor ... Archivio Storico Italiano [*A publication*]
Arch Stor Calabria ... Archivio Storico per la Calabria e la Lucania [*A publication*]
Arch Stor I ... Archivio Storico Italiano [*A publication*]
Arch Stor Lodigiano ... Archivo Storico Lodigiano [*A publication*]
Arch Stor Patria ... Archivio. Societa Romana di Storia Patria [*A publication*]
Arch Stor Pugl ... Archivio Storico Pugliese [*A publication*]
Arch Stor Sicilia ... Archivio Storico per la Sicilia Orientale [*A publication*]
Arch Stor Sicilia Orient ... Archivio Storico per la Sicilia Orientale [*A publication*]
Arch Stud Fisiopatol Clin Ricamb ... Archivio per lo Studio della Fisiopatologia e Clinica del Ricambio [*A publication*]
Arch Suisses Anthrop ... Archives Suisses d'Anthropologie Generale [*A publication*]
Arch Suisses Anthropol Gen ... Archives Suisses d'Anthropologie Generale [*A publication*]
Arch Suisses Neurol Neurochir Psychiatr ... Archives Suisses de Neurologie, Neurochirurgie, et de Psychiatrie [*A publication*]
Arch Sum ... Archbold's Summary of Laws of England [*A publication*] (DLA)
Archs Un Med Balkan ... Archives. Union Medicale Balkanique [*A publication*]
Arch Surg... Archives of Surgery [*A publication*]
Archs Virol ... Archives of Virology [*A publication*]
Archs Zool Exp Gen ... Archives de Zoologie Experimentale et Generale [*A publication*]
ArchT........ Archeion Thrakes [*A publication*]
ARCHT ... Architect
Archt & Bldr ... Architect and Builder [*South Africa*] [*A publication*]
Arch Tea Cultiv ... Archives of Tea Cultivation [*A publication*]
Arch Tech .. Architectural Technology [*A publication*]
Arch Tech Mess Ind Messtech ... Archiv fuer Technisches Messen und Industrielle Messtechnik [*A publication*]
Arch Tech Mess und Ind Messtech ... Archiv fuer Technisches Messen und Industrielle Messtechnik [*A publication*]
Arch Tech Mess und Messtech Prax ... Archiv fuer Technisches Messen und Messtechnische Praxis [*A publication*]
Arch Tech Mess Messtech Prax ... Archiv fuer Technisches Messen und Messtechnische Praxis [*A publication*]
Arch Termodyn ... Archiwum Termodynamiki [*A publication*]
Arch Termodyn Spal ... Archiwum Termodynamiki i Spalania [*A publication*]
Arch Tierernaehr ... Archiv fuer Tierernaehrung [*A publication*]
Arch Tierernahr Arch Anim Nutr ... Archiv fuer Tierernaehrung/Archives of Animal Nutrition [*A publication*]
Arch Tierz ... Archiv fuer Tierzucht [*East Germany*] [*A publication*]
Arch Tisiol Mal Appar Respir ... Archivio di Tisiologia e delle Malattie dell'Apparato Respiratorio [*A publication*]
Arch Tisiol Mal App Resp ... Archivio di Tisiologia e delle Malattie dell'Apparato Respiratorio [*Italy*] [*A publication*]
Archtl Bull ... Architectural Bulletin [*A publication*]
Archtl Design ... Architectural Design [*A publication*]
Archtl Forum (Dublin) ... Architectural Forum (Dublin) [*A publication*]
Archtl History ... Architectural History [*A publication*]
Archtl Jnl... Architectural Journal [*A publication*]
Archtl Magazine Egyptian Assocn of Archts ... Architectural Magazine. Egyptian Association of Architects [*A publication*]
Archtl Monographs ... Architectural Monographs [*A publication*]
Archtl Preservation ... Architectural Preservation [*A publication*]

Archtl Psychology Newsletter ... Architectural Psychology Newsletter [*A publication*]
Archtl Record ... Architectural Record [*A publication*]
Archtl Review ... Architectural Review [*A publication*]
Archtl Science Review ... Architectural Science Review [*A publication*]
Arch Today ... Architecture Today [*A publication*]   (APTA)
Arch Toxic ... Archives of Toxicology [*Berlin*] [*A publication*]
Arch Toxicol ... Archives of Toxicology [*Berlin*] [*A publication*]
Arch Toxicol (Berl) ... Archives of Toxicology (Berlin) [*A publication*]
Arch Toxicol (Suppl) ... Archives of Toxicology. Supplement (Berlin) [*A publication*]
Arch Toxikol ... Archiv fuer Toxikologie [*Later, Archives of Toxicology*] [*A publication*]
Arch Triest ... Archeolgrafo Triestino [*A publication*]
Archt Sci Rev ... Architectural Science Review [*A publication*]   (APTA)
Archts Forum ... Architects Forum [*A publication*]
Archts Jnl ... Architects' Journal [*A publication*]
Archts News ... Architects News [*A publication*]
Archts Trade Jnl ... Architects' Trade Journal [*A publication*]
Archt & Surveyor ... Architect and Surveyor [*A publication*]
Arch Union Med Balk ... Archives. Union Medicale Balkanique [*A publication*]
Arch Urug Med Cir Espec ... Archivos Uruguayos de Medicina, Cirujia, y Especialidades [*A publication*]
ArchV ... Archiv fuer Voelkerkunde [*A publication*]
Arch De Vecchi Anat Patol ... Archivio "De Vecchi" per l'Anatomia Patologica e la Medicina Clinica [*A publication*]
Arch Venez Med Trop Parasitol Med ... Archivos Venezolanos de Medicina Tropical y Parasitologia Medica [*A publication*]
Arch Venez Nutr ... Archivos Venezolanos de Nutricion [*A publication*]
Arch Venez Patol Trop Parasitol Med ... Archivos Venezolanos de Patologia Tropical y Parasitologia Medica [*A publication*]
Arch Venez Pueric Pediatr ... Archivos Venezolanos de Puericultura y Pediatria [*A publication*]
Arch Verdau Kr ... Archiv fuer Verdauungs-Krankheiten [*A publication*]
Arch Verdau Kr Stoffwechselpathol Diaet ... Archiv fuer Verdauungs-Krankheiten mit Einschluss der Stoffwechselpathologie und der Diaetetik [*A publication*]
Arch Verdauungskr ... Archiv fuer Verdauungs-Krankheiten mit Einschluss der Stoffwechselpathologie und der Diaetetik [*A publication*]
Arch Vet ... Archiva Veterinaria [*A publication*]
Arch Vet (Buchar) ... Archiva Veterinaria (Bucharest) [*A publication*]
Arch Vet Ital ... Archivio Veterinario Italiano [*A publication*]
Arch Vet Pol ... Archivum Veterinarium Polonicum [*A publication*]
Arch Virol ... Archives of Virology [*A publication*]
Arch Voelkerrechts ... Archiv des Voelkerrechts [*A publication*]
Arch Volkswohlfahrt ... Archiv fuer Volkswohlfahrt [*A publication*]
Arch Waermewirtsch ... Archiv fuer Waermewirtschaft [*A publication*]
Arch Waermewirtsch Dampfkesselwes ... Archiv fuer Waermewirtschaft und Dampfkesselwesen [*West Germany*] [*A publication*]
Arch Wissensch u Prakt Tierh ... Archiv fuer Wissenschaftliche und Praktische Tierheilkunde [*A publication*]
Arch Wiss Phot ... Archiv fuer Wissenschaftliche Photographie [*A publication*]
Arch Wiss Prakt Tierheilkd ... Archiv fuer Wissenschaftliche und Praktische Tierheilkunde [*A publication*]
Archwm Gorn ... Archiwum Gornictwa [*A publication*]
Archwm Hutn ... Archiwum Hutnictwa [*A publication*]
Arch Yearb S Afr Hist ... Archives Yearbook for South African History [*A publication*]
Arch Yr ... Architect's Yearbook [*A publication*]
Arch Yrbk ... Architect's Yearbook [*A publication*]
Arch Zellforsch ... Archiv fuer Zellforschung [*A publication*]
Arch Z Ges ... Architectura. Zeitschrift fuer Geschichte der Baukunst [*A publication*]
Arch Ziv Pr ... Archiv fuer die Zivilistische Praxis [*A publication*]   (ILCA)
Arch Zool Exper et Gen ... Archives de Zoologie Experimentale et Generale [*A publication*]
Arch Zool Exp Gen ... Archives de Zoologie Experimentale et Generale [*A publication*]
Arch Zool Exp Gen Notes Rev ... Archives de Zoologie Experimentale et Generale. Notes et Revue [*A publication*]
Arch Zool Ital ... Archivio Zoologico Italiano [*A publication*]
Arch Zootec ... Archivos de Zootecnia [*A publication*]
ArchZtg ... Archaeologische Zeitung [*A publication*]
Arch Zuechtungsforsch ... Archiv fuer Zuechtungsforschung [*A publication*]
ARCI ... Addiction Research Center Inventory [*Psychology*]
ARCI ... Aid Refugee Chinese Intellectuals [*Defunct*]   (EA)
ARCI ... American Railway Car Institute   (EA)
ARCI ... Arctic Circular [*A publication*]
ARCI ... Associate of the Royal Colonial Institute [*British*]
ARCI ... Association of Racing Commissioners International   (EA)
ARCI ... Association Regionale Caraibeenne des Infirmieres   (EAIO)
ARCIC-II ... Anglican-Roman Catholic International Commission
Arcisp S Anna di Ferrara ... Arcispedale S. Anna di Ferrara [*Italy*] [*A publication*]
ARCIXS ... Area Command Information Exchange System   (MCD)
ARCK ... Advanced Research Craft Hydrokeel   (MCD)
ArClC ... College of the Ozarks, Clarksville, AR [*Library symbol*] [*Library of Congress*]   (LCLS)

ARCLEW ... Czechoslovak Academy of Sciences. Institute of Landscape Ecology. Hydrobiological Laboratory. Annual Report [*A publication*]
ARCLUB ... Archonist Club   (EA)
ArcM ... Archival Micrographics, Midland Park, NJ [*Library symbol*] [*Library of Congress*]   (LCLS)
ARCM ... Army Commendation Medal [*Military decoration*]
ARCM ... Associate of the Royal College of Music [*British*]   (EY)
ARCMR ... Atlantic Research Centre for Mental Retardation [*Dalhousie University*] [*Canada*] [*Research center*]   (RCD)
ARCNET ... Army Command and Control Network   (MCD)
ARCO ... Aerolineas Colonia SA [*Airline*] [*Uruguay*]
ARCO ... Agricultural Research Center Operations [*of ARS, Department of Agriculture*]
ARCO ... Aircraft Resources Control Office
ARCO ... Airspace Reservation Coordination Office [*Canada*]   (FAAC)
ARCO ... Arcato [*With the Bow*] [*Music*]   (ROG)
ARCO ... Army Requirements Control Office   (AABC)
ARCO ... Associate of the Royal College of Organists [*British*]   (EY)
ARCO ... Atlantic Richfield Company
ARCO ... Auxiliary Resources Control Office
ARCOA ... American Red Cross Overseas Association   (EA)
ARCO(CHM) ... Associate of the Royal College of Organists (Choir-Training Diploma) [*British*]
ARCOM ... Army Commendation Medal [*Military decoration*]
ARCOM ... Army Reserve Command
ARCOMET ... Area Commanders' Meeting [*NATO*]   (NATG)
ARCOMS ... Armor Combat Operations Model Support [*TCATA*]   (RDA)
ARCOMSAT ... Arabian Communication Satellite
ARCON ... Advanced Research Consultants   (MCD)
ARCON ... Automatic Rudder Control   (MUGU)
ARCONA ... Austin Rover Cars of North America, Inc.
ARCONET ... Army Command and Control Communications Network   (MCD)
ARCOPS ... Arctic Operations [*Military*]   (NVT)
ARCOST ... Army Cohesion and Stability Program
ARCOST ... Army Cohesion Study   (MCD)
ARCOV ... Army Combat Operations Vietnam   (AABC)
ARCP ... Air Refueling Control Point   (AFM)
ARCP ... Alliance of Rail Citizens for Progress   (EA)
ArcP ... Archeion Pontou [*A publication*]
ARCP ... Army [*Forces*] Command Post
ARC-PA ... Accreditation Review Committee on Education for Physicians Assistants   (EA)
ARCPACS ... American Registry of Certified Professionals in Agronomy, Crops, and Soils   (EA)
ARCPEA ... Australia Commonwealth Scientific and Industrial Research Organisation. Tropical Crops and Pastures. Annual Report [*A publication*]
ARCRBD ... Annual Report on Cacao Research. University of the West Indies [*A publication*]
ARCRDF ... Australia. Commonwealth Scientific and Industrial Research Organisation. Division of Forest Research. Annual Report [*A publication*]
ARCRL ... Agricultural Research Council Radiological Laboratory [*British*]
ARCRL Rep ... Agricultural Research Council. Radiobiology Laboratory Report [*United Kingdom*] [*A publication*]
ARCRT ... American Registry of Clinical Radiography Technologists   (EA)
ARCS ... Accrediting and Recording Centralized System   (MCD)
ARCS ... Achievement Rewards for College Scientists [*Foundation*]
ARCS ... Acoustic Optical RADAR Classification System   (CAAL)
ARCS ... Acquisition RADAR and Control System
ARCS ... Advanced Reconfigurable Computer System
ARCS ... Aerial Rocket Control System [*or Subsystem*]   (MCD)
ARCS ... Aft Reaction Control System [*or Subsystem*] [*NASA*]   (NASA)
ARCS ... Air Resupply and Communication Service
ARCS ... Aircraft Requirements Computer System
ARCS ... Alternative Remedial Contracting Systems [*Environmental Protection Agency*]
ARCS ... Altitude Rate Command System   (MCD)
ARCS ... AMSAA [*Army Materiel Systems Analysis Agency*]/RARDE [*Royal Armament Research and Development Establishment*] Combat Simulation   (MCD)
ARCS ... Army Ration Credit System   (AABC)
ARCS ... Associate of the Royal College of Science [*British*]   (EY)
ARCS ... Associate of the Royal College of Surgeons [*British*]   (ROG)
ARCS ... Association of Retail Candy Shops
ARCS ... Automated Records Control System
ARCS ... Automated Reproduction and Collating System   (MCD)
ARCS ... Automated Ring Code Search   (DIT)
ARCS ... Automatic Route Control System [*Truck-delivery computer system*]
ARCS ... Autonomous Remotely Controlled Submersible [*Autonomous underwater vehicle*]
ARCSA ... Annals. Royal College of Surgeons of England [*A publication*]
ARCSA ... Aviation Requirements for the Combat Structure of the Army   (AABC)
ARCSB ... Archivio Stomatologico [*A publication*]
ARCSc ... Associate of the Royal College of Science [*British*]
ARCSEC ... Arcseconds

ARCSEC ...   Inverse Secant [*Mathematics*]
ARCSF ......   Active Requisition Control and Status File [*DoD*]
ARCSIN ....   Inverse Sine [*Mathematics*]
ARCSIP .....   Automated Requirement Computation System Initial Provisioning [*Army*]
ARCSL ......   Army Armament Research and Development Command Chemical Systems Laboratory
ARCSS ......   Center for Social Science Research and Documentation for the Arab Region [*UNESCO*] [*Information service or system*]   (IID)
ARCST ......   Associate of the Royal College of Science and Technology, Glasgow [*Later, ARTC*] [*Scotland*]
ARCSTAR ...   Area Recruiting Concept Special Test Army Reserve
ARCT ....   African Regional Centre for Technology [*See also CRAT*]   (EA)
ARCT ....   Air Refueling Control Time   (AFM)
Arct ....   Arctic
ARCT ....   Arctic [*A publication*]
ARCT ....   Army Radio Code Aptitude Test
ARCT ....   Associate of the Royal Conservatory of Music of Toronto
ArCT ....   State College of Arkansas, Conway, AR [*Library symbol*] [*Library of Congress*]   (LCLS)
Arct Aeromed Lab (US) Tech Doc Rep ...   Arctic Aeromedical Laboratory (United States). Technical Documentary Report [*A publication*]
Arct Aeromed Lab (US) Tech Note ...   Arctic Aeromedical Laboratory (United States). Technical Note [*A publication*]
Arct Aeromed Lab (US) Tech Rep ...   Arctic Aeromedical Laboratory (United States). Technical Report [*A publication*]
Arct Alp Res ...   Arctic and Alpine Research [*A publication*]
Arct Alp Res (Boulder Colo) ...   Arctic and Alpine Research (Boulder, Colorado) [*A publication*]
ARCTAN...   Inverse Tangent [*Mathematics*]
Arct Anthropol ...   Arctic Anthropology [*A publication*]
Arct Bibl ....   Arctic Bibliography [*A publication*]
Arct Bibliogr ...   Arctic Bibliography [*A publication*]
Arct Bull ....   Arctic Bulletin [*A publication*]
Arctic Anthropol ...   Arctic Anthropology [*A publication*]
Arctic Bul...   Arctic Bulletin [*A publication*]
Arctic Inst North America Research Paper ...   Arctic Institute of North America. Research Paper [*A publication*]
Arctic Inst North America Special Pub ...   Arctic Institute of North America. Special Publication [*A publication*]
Arctic Inst North America Tech Paper ...   Arctic Institute of North America. Technical Paper [*A publication*]
Arctic Med Res ...   Arctic Medical Research [*A publication*]
Arct Inst N Am Annu Rep ...   Arctic Institute of North America. Annual Report [*A publication*]
Arct Inst N Am Spec Publ ...   Arctic Institute of North America. Special Publication [*A publication*]
Arct Inst N Am Tech Pap ...   Arctic Institute of North America. Technical Paper [*A publication*]
Arct Inst North Am Annu Rep ...   Arctic Institute of North America. Annual Report [*A publication*]
Arct Inst North America Tech Pap ...   Arctic Institute of North America. Technical Paper [*A publication*]
Arct Land Use Res Program Rep ALUR (Can) ...   Arctic Land Use Research Program Report. ALUR (Canada) [*A publication*]
ARCU ....   Architektura a Urbanizmus [*A publication*]
ARCU ....   Arcturus. Department of Education. Northwest Territories [*Canada*] [*A publication*]
ARCUS ......   Agricultural Research Council Unit of Statistics [*British*]   (ARC)
ARCUS ......   Associated Retail Confectioners of the United States [*Later, RCI*]
ARCVBP ...   Annales de Recherches Veterinaires [*Annals of Veterinary Research*] [*A publication*]
ARCVS ......   Associate of the Royal College of Veterinary Surgeons [*British*]
ARC/W ......   Arc Weld   (KSC)
ARCWD ....   Architektur und Wohnwelt [*A publication*]
ARCWRO ...   Agricultural Research Council Weed Research Organization [*British*]
ARCYANA ...   Collective name for seven scientists based on the names of the submersibles Archimede and Cyana
ARD ....   Absolute Reaction of Degeneration
ARD ....   Accelerated Rural Development
ARD ....   Active Range of the Day   (MCD)
ARD ....   Acute Respiratory Disease [*Medicine*]
ARD ....   Advanced Reactors Division [*of the Nuclear Regulatory Commission*]   (NRCH)
AR & D ......   Advanced Research and Development
ARD ....   Advanced Research Division
ARD ....   Aeronautical Research Division [*NASA*]
ARD ....   Air-Raid Defence [*British*] [*World War II*]
AR & D ......   Air Research and Development
ARD ....   Air Reserve District
ARD ....   Alor [*Indonesia*] [*Airport symbol*]   (OAG)
ARD ....   Ammunition Reliability Division [*Military*]
ARD ....   Answering, Recording, and Dialing
ARD ....   Antimicrobial Removal Device
ARD ....   Application for Review Decisions [*A publication*]   (DLA)

ARD ....   Arbeits Gemeinschaft der Offentlichrechtlichen Rundfunk Anstalten der Bundesrepublik Deutschland [*Broadcasting organization*]
Ard ....   Archidiaconus [*Authority cited in pre-1607 legal work*]   (DSA)
ARD ....   Architectural Record [*A publication*]
ARD ....   Ardent   (DSUE)
Ard ....   [*Jacobus de*] Arditionibus [*Flourished, 1213-50*] [*Authority cited in pre-1607 legal work*]   (DSA)
ARD ....   Ardito [*Ardently*] [*Music*]   (ROG)
ARD ....   Arida [*Japan*] [*Seismograph station code, US Geological Survey*]   (SEIS)
ARD ....   Armament Research Development [*British*]   (MCD)
ARD ....   Armaments Research Department [*Ministry of Supply*] [*British*]
ARD ....   Armored Training Devices [*Army*]   (RDA)
ARD ....   Army Renegotiation Division [*of ASRB*]
ARD ....   Arthritis and Rheumatic Diseases Abstracts [*A publication*]
ARD ....   Association of Research Directors   (EA)
ARD ....   Association for Responsible Dissent   (EA)
ARD ....   Automatic Release Date [*Military*]   (AABC)
ARD ....   Auxiliary Repair Dry Dock [*Non-self-propelled*] [*Navy ship symbol*]
ARD ....   Average Response Data
ARD ....   Red Deer Public Library, Alberta [*Library symbol*] [*National Library of Canada*]   (NLC)
ARD ....   Yardley, PA [*Location identifier*] [*FAA*]   (FAAL)
ARDA ....   Advanced Reactor Development Associates
ARDA ....   Agricultural and Rural Development Act [*Canada*]
ARDA ....   American Railway Development Association   (EA)
ARDA ....   American Rescue Dog Association   (EA)
ARDA ....   Analog Recording Dynamic Analyzer [*Data processing*]
ARDA ....   Appalachian Regional Development Act of 1965
ARDAA .....   Army Research, Development, and Acquisition
ARDAAY ..   Annali di Radiologia Diagnostica [*A publication*]
ARDAC .....   Army Research, Development, and Acquisition
ARDAD .....   Army R D and A [*Research, Development, and Acquisition*] [*Later, R, D & A*] [*United States*] [*A publication*]
ArDar ....   Arkansas River Valley Regional Library, Dardanelle, AR [*Library symbol*] [*Library of Congress*]   (LCLS)
ARDAR .....   Regional Office, Alberta Agriculture, Red Deer, Alberta [*Library symbol*] [*National Library of Canada*]   (NLC)
ARDB ....   Analytical Results Database
ARDBA .....   Advances in Radiation Biology [*A publication*]
ARDBC......   American Rubberband Duckpin Bowling Congress   (EA)
ARDC ....   Aberdeen Research and Development Center   (MCD)
ARDC ....   Air Research and Development Center [*Later, Air Force Systems Command*]
ARDC ....   Air Research and Development Command [*Washington, DC*] [*Air Force*]
ARDC ....   Air Research and Development Council [*NATO*]   (NATG)
ARDC ....   American Racing Driver's Club   (EA)
ARDC ....   Applied Research and Design Center [*Research center*]   (RCD)
ARDC ....   Arctic Research Directors Committee [*Canada*]
ARDC ....   Armament Research and Development Center [*Army*]   (RDA)
ARDC ....   Association des Redacteurs de Devis du Canada [*Specification Writers Association of Canada*]
ARDC ....   Australian Racing Drivers Club
ARDC ....   Auxiliary Repair Dry Dock, Concrete [*Later, AFDL*] [*Navy symbol*] [*Obsolete*]
ARDC ....   Red Deer College, Alberta [*Library symbol*] [*National Library of Canada*]   (NLC)
ARDCA .....   Air Research and Development Command - Andrews Air Force Base
ARDCB .....   Advances in Radiation Chemistry [*A publication*]
ARDCF .....   Air Research and Development Command Forms
ARDCM ....   Air Research and Development Command Manual
ARDCOM ...   Armament Research and Development Command   (MCD)
ARDCR .....   Air Research and Development Command Regulations
ARDE ....   Aircraft and Rocket Design Engineers
ARDE ....   Alianza Revolucionaria Democratica [*Democratic Revolutionary Alliance*] [*Nicaragua*] [*Political party*]   (PD)
ARDE ....   Armament Research and Development Establishment [*British*]   (MCD)
ARDEC......   Armament Research, Development, and Engineering Center [*Picatinny Arsenal*] [*Dover, NJ*] [*Army*]   (RDA)
ARDEMS ...   Airborne Delivered Multi-Purpose Submunition   (MCD)
ARDEMS ...   Artillery-Delivered Multipurpose Submunition   (AABC)
Arden's Sydney Mag ...   Arden's Sydney Magazine [*A publication*]   (APTA)
ARDF ....   Air Reconnaissance Detection Force   (CINC)
ARDF ....   Airborne Radiation Detection and Fixing [*Military*]
ARDF ....   Airborne Radio Direction Finding   (AFM)
ARDF ....   Association Reunion Departement Francais [*Association for Reunion as a French Department*] [*Political party*]   (PPW)
ARDG ....   Army Research and Development Group   (MCD)
ARDG(E)...   Army Research and Development Group (Europe)
ARDG(FE) ...   Army Research and Development Group (Far East)
ARDH-A ...   Architecture d'Aujourd'hui [*A publication*]

ARDIC....... Association pour la Recherche et le Developpement en Informatique Chimique [*Association for Research and Development of Chemical Informatics*] [*Information service or system*]   (IID)
ARDIS....... Advanced Radio Data Information Service [*IBM Corp., Motorola, Inc.*]
ARDIS....... Army Research and Development Test and Evaluation Information Systems
ARDISC .... Argonne Dispersion Code   (MCD)
ARDISO.... Army Research and Development Information Systems Office   (RDA)
ARDL .... Ardleigh [*England*]
ARDM....... Association of Refrigerant and Desuperheating Manufacturing   (EA)
ARDM....... Medium Auxiliary Repair Dry Dock [*Navy symbol*]
ARDMA .... Asset Requirements Depot Maintenance Data   (MCD)
ARDMC .... Michener Centre Library, Red Deer, Alberta [*Library symbol*] [*National Library of Canada*]   (NLC)
ARDMD.... Autosomal Recessive Distal Muscular Dystrophy [*Medicine*]
ARDME .... Automatic RADAR Data Measuring Equipment
ARDME .... Automatic RADAR Distance Measuring Equipment   (MSA)
ARDME .... Automatic Range Detection and Measuring Equipment
ARDMS..... American Registry of Diagnostic Medical Sonographers   (EA)
ARDN........ Arden Group, Inc. [*NASDAQ symbol*]   (NQ)
Ardn........ Arnoldian [*A publication*]
Ardo.......... Ardito [*Ardently*] [*Music*]
ARDP .... Army Requirements Development Plan   (AABC)
ARDRA ..... Australian Road Research [*A publication*]
ARDRH..... Red Deer Regional Hospital Center, Red Deer, Alberta [*Library symbol*] [*National Library of Canada*]   (NLC)
ARDRSP ... Archivio. Reale Deputazione Romana di Storia Patria [*A publication*]
ARDS........ Acute Respiratory Distress Syndrome [*Medicine*]
ARDS........ Annual Report. Dante Society [*A publication*]
ARDS........ Associate of the Royal Drawing Society [*British*]
ARDS........ Atmospheric Resid Desulfurization [*Petroleum technology*]
ARDS........ Automated Requirements Development System   (MCD)
ARDS........ Aviation Research and Development Service [*FAA*]
ARDSA...... Agriculture and Rural Development Subsidiary Agreement [*Canada*]
ARDSB ...... American Review of Respiratory Disease [*A publication*]
ARDSBL .... American Review of Respiratory Disease [*A publication*]
ARDSDN .. Zimbabwe. Division of Livestock and Pastures. Annual Report [*A publication*]
ARDU........ Analytical Research and Development Unit [*British*]
ARDVA ..... Army Research and Development [*Later, R, D & A*] [*United States*] [*A publication*]
ARDYA4 ... Applied Radiology [*A publication*]
ARE .... Acoustic Radiation Element
ARE .... Activated Reactive Evaporation [*Coating technology*]
ARE .... Active Resistive Exercise
ARE .... Admiralty Research Establishment [*British*]   (IRUK)
ARE .... Advanced Real-Time Executive   (BUR)
ARE .... Advanced Research Engine   (MCD)
ARE .... Aerothermal Re-Entry Experiment   (MCD)
ARE .... Air Reactor Experiment
ARE .... Aircraft Reactor Equipment
ARE .... Aircraft Recovery Equipment
ARE .... Ancient Records of Egypt [*A publication*]   (BJA)
ARE .... Anion-Responsive Electrode
ARE .... Antenna Range Equipment
ARE .... Apollo Reliability Engineering [*NASA*]   (KSC)
ARE .... Arab Republic of Egypt
Ar E.......... Architectural Engineer
A Re .... Archiv fuer Religionswissenschaft [*A publication*]
Are .... [*Jacobus de*] Arena [*Deceased, 1297*] [*Authority cited in pre-1607 legal work*]   (DSA)
ARE .... Arequipa [*Peru*] [*Seismograph station code, US Geological Survey*]   (SEIS)
ARE .... Armbro Enterprises, Inc. [*Toronto Stock Exchange symbol*]
ARE .... Aspect Ratio Enhancement   (MCD)
ARE .... Assembly of European Regions   (EAIO)
ARE .... Associate in Religious Education
ARE .... Associate of the Royal Society of Painter-Etchers and Engravers [*British*]
ARE .... Association of Railroad Editors [*Formerly, ARMEA*]   (EA)
ARE .... Association for Recurrent Education [*British*]
ARE .... Association for Religious Education
ARE .... Association for Research and Enlightenment   (EA)
ARE .... Asymptotic Relative Efficiency [*Statistics*]
ARE .... Atmospheric Research Equipment
ARE .... Attack Response Evaluation   (MCD)
ARE .... Attack Response Exercise   (MCD)
ARE .... Automated Responsive Environment   (BUR)
ARE .... Automatic Record Evaluation
ARE .... Auxiliary Rocket Engine
ARE .... Aviation Readiness Evaluation   (NVT)
ARE .... Axiomatic Requirements Engineering   (MCD)
ARE .... Characato [*Formerly, Arequipa*] [*Peru*] [*Later, FRD*] [*Geomagnetic observatory code*]

ARE .... Redcliff Public Library, Alberta [*Library symbol*] [*National Library of Canada*]   (NLC)
ARE .... United Arab Emirates [*ANSI three-letter standard code*]   (CNC)
AREA .... Academic Research Enhancement Award [*NIH*]
AREA .... Aerovias Ecuatoriana SA
AREA .... American Railway Engineering Association   (EA)
AREA .... American Recreational Equipment Association   (EA)
AREA .... Arctic Research in Environmental Acoustics [*Navy*]   (MSC)
AREA .... Army Reactor Experimental Area
AREA .... Association for Rational Environmental Alternatives   (EA)
AREA .... Association of Records Executives and Administrators [*Later, ARMA*]   (EA)
AREA .... Association for Religious Education Aspects of Education. Bulletin [*A publication*]
AREA .... Association for Research, Exploration, and Aid [*Australia*]
AREACORD ... Area Coordination to Command Designated in Appropriate Instructions   (MCD)
Area Dev ... Area Development [*A publication*]
AREAER ... Annual Report on Exchange Arrangements and Exchange Restrictions [*A publication*]
AREAOPREP ... Area Commanders Operations Report
AREBA .... Accelerated Reeducation of Emotions, Behavior, and Attitudes [*Rehabilitation program*]
AREBA8.... Bulletin. ARERS [*Association Regionale des Amis de l'Universite et de l'Enseignement Superieur pour la Promotion de l'Etude et la Recherche Scientifiques*] [*A publication*]
AREC........ Agricultural Research and Education Center, Belle Glade [*University of Florida*] [*Research center*]   (RCD)
AREC........ Agricultural Research and Education Center, Fort Lauderdale [*University of Florida*] [*Research center*]   (RCD)
AREC........ Agricultural Research and Educational Center [*American University of Beirut*]
AREC........ Air Element Coordinator [*Military*]   (CAAL)
AREC........ Amateur Radio Emergency Corps [*of ARPSC*]
ARECB...... Annual Review of Ecology and Systematics [*A publication*]
ARECBC ... Annual Review of Ecology and Systematics [*A publication*]
ARECS ..... Australian Real Estate Computer Systems
ARED ...... Acoustic Reflex Ear Defender
ARED .... Aperture Relay Experiment Definition   (MCD)
ARED .... Redwater Public Library, Alberta [*Library symbol*] [*National Library of Canada*]   (NLC)
AREDD ..... Annual Report on Energy Research, Development, and Demonstration. International Energy Agency [*A publication*]
AREDS...... Acoustic Reflex Ear Defender System   (RDA)
AREE........ Apollo Reliability Engineering Electronics [*NASA*]   (KSC)
AREE........ Association of Radio and Electrical Engineers [*A union*] [*British*]
AREFS ...... Air Refueling Squadron
AREFSQ ... Air Refueling Squadron
AREG .... Apparatus Repair - Strategy Evaluation Guidelines [*Telecommunications*]   (TEL)
AREGB...... Archiwum Energetyki [*A publication*]
AREHDT .. Annual Review of Public Health [*A publication*]
AREIS .... Army Education Information System   (MCD)
AREL........ Air Resources Environmental Research Laboratory [*National Oceanic and Atmospheric Administration*]   (NOAA)
AREL........ Alpharel, Inc. [*NASDAQ symbol*]   (NQ)
A Rel .... Associate in Religion
ARELA...... Archiwum Elektrotechniki [*A publication*]
ARELEM .. Arithmetic Element Program
ARELS ...... Association of Recognised English Language Schools [*British*]
AREMA .... Antoky ny Revolosiona Malagasy [*Vanguard of the Malagasy Revolution*]   (PPW)
AREMA .... Avantgarde de la Revolution Malgache [*Vanguard of the Malagasy Revolution*] [*Political party*]   (PPW)
AREN .... American Rehabilitation Educational Network [*Pittsburgh, PA*] [*Telecommunications service*]   (TSSD)
AREN .... Argosy Energy, Inc. [*NASDAQ symbol*]   (NQ)
ARENA ..... Adoption Resource Exchange of North America [*Later, NAIES*]   (EA)
ARENA ..... Alianca Renovadora Nacional [*Alliance for National Renewal*] [*Brazil*] [*Political party*]   (PPW)
ARENA ..... Alianza Republicana Nacionalista [*Nationalist Republican Alliance*] [*El Salvador*] [*Political party*]   (PPW)
ARENA ..... Annual Review of Entomology [*A publication*]
ARENA ..... Applied Research Ethics National Association   (EA)
ARENAA ... Annual Review of Entomology [*A publication*]
Arena Rev .. Arena Review [*A publication*]
AREND ..... Annual Review of Energy [*A publication*]
ARENTS ... ARPA [*Advanced Research Projects Agency*] Environmental Test Satellite
ARENUM ... Analysis, Refinement, and Extension of Nuclear Methodology [*Military*]
AREO .... Area Real Estate Office
AREP........ Air Refueling Egress Point [*FAA*]   (FAAC)
A Rep .... American Reports [*A publication*]   (DLA)
A Rep .... Atlantic Reporter [*A publication*]   (DLA)
AREP........ Office of Applied Research, Evaluation, and Planning [*West Virginia University*] [*Research center*]   (RCD)

A Rep (London) ... Archaeological Report (London) [*A publication*]
A Rep Natn Inst Anim Ind (Japan) ... Annual Report. National Institute for Animal Industry. Ministry of Agriculture and Forestry (Japan) [*A publication*]
A Rep Rec Res ... Annual Report. Record Research. East African Agriculture and Forestry Research Organisation [*A publication*]
A Rep Res Tech Wk Minist Agric Nth Ire ... Annual Report on Research and Technical Work. Ministry of Agriculture for Northern Ireland [*A publication*]
AREPT ...... Agent Report [*Army*] (AABC)
A Rep Tokyo Metropol Res Lab Publ Hlth ... Annual Report. Tokyo Metropolitan Research Laboratory of Public Health [*A publication*]
ARERAM ... Arerugi [*A publication*]
ARERI ...... Australian Renewable Energy Resources Index [*A publication*] (APTA)
ARES .... Advanced Radiation Effects Simulation
ARES .... Advanced Railroad Electronics System [*A space guidance system made by Collins Air Transport*]
ARES .... Advanced Research EMP [*Electromagnetic Pulse*] Simulator
ARES .... Advanced Rocket Engine Storable (MCD)
ARES .... Aeroelastic Rotor Experimental System (MCD)
ARES .... Agile Responsive Effective Support Aircraft [*Military*]
ARES .... Agricultural Research [*A publication*]
ARES .... Airplane Responsive Engine Selection (MCD)
ARES .... Amateur Radio Emergency Service
ARES .... American Real Estate Society (EA)
ARES .... Army Readiness Evaluation System (MCD)
ARES .... Artillery Engagement Simulation System (MCD)
ARES .... Association of Real Estate Syndicators (EA)
ARES .... Automatic Record Evaluation System
ARES .... Automatic Requirements Engineering Systems (MCD)
ARESDS .... Animal Regulation Studies [*A publication*]
A Res Nerv Ment Dis Proc ... Association for Research in Nervous and Mental Disease. Proceedings [*A publication*]
ArEspArq .. Archivo Espanol de Arqueologia [*Madrid*] [*A publication*]
AREST ...... Advanced RADAR Experimental Systems Technology [*Army*]
ARESTEM ... [*A*] Recording Stray Energy Monitor
Aret .... [*Angelus de Gambilionibus de*] Aretio [*Flourished, 1422-51*] [*Authority cited in pre-1607 legal work*] (DSA)
Areth .... Arethusa [*A publication*]
ARETL ...... Associate for Religious Education for Teachers and Lecturers [*British*]
ARETS ...... Arizona Regional Ecological Test Site [*Department of the Interior*]
ARETS ...... Armor Remoted Target System (RDA)
AREUEA ... American Real Estate and Urban Economics Association (EA)
AREUEA Jrnl Amer Real Estate and Urban Economics Assn ... AREUEA Journal. American Real Estate and Urban Economics Association [*A publication*]
A Rev Biochem ... Annual Review of Biochemistry [*A publication*]
A Rev Ecol Syst ... Annual Review of Ecology and Systematics [*A publication*]
A Rev Ent ... Annual Review of Entomology [*A publication*]
A Rev Genet ... Annual Review of Genetics [*A publication*]
A Rev Microbiol ... Annual Review of Microbiology [*A publication*]
A Rev Pharmac Toxic ... Annual Review of Pharmacology and Toxicology [*A publication*]
A Rev Phytopath ... Annual Review of Phytopathology [*A publication*]
A Rev Pl Physiol ... Annual Review of Plant Physiology [*A publication*]
A Rev Psychol ... Annual Review of Psychology [*A publication*]
AREX .... Air Refueling Exit [*Aviation*] (FAAC)
AREX .... Arctic Explorer. Travel Arctic. Northwest Territories [*Canada*] [*A publication*]
ARF .... Acoustic Range-Finder (MCD)
ARF .... Acute Renal Failure [*Medicine*]
ARF .... Acute Respiratory Failure [*Medicine*]
ARF .... Acute Rheumatic Fever [*Medicine*]
ARF .... Addiction Research Foundation of Ontario Library [*UTLAS symbol*]
ARF .... ADP [*Adenosine Diphosphate*]-Ribosylation Factor [*Biochemistry*]
ARF .... Adventitious Root Formation [*Botany*]
ARF .... Advertising Research Foundation (EA)
ARF .... Aeronautical Research Foundation
ARF .... Aerospace Recovery Facility (MCD)
ARF .... Aesthetic Realism Foundation (EA)
ARF .... Afghan Refugee Fund (EA)
ARF .... African Research Foundation (EA)
ARF .... Agricultural Research Foundation [*Oregon State University*] [*Research center*] (RCD)
ARF .... Air Reserve Forces
ARF .... Airborne Relay Facility (MCD)
ARF .... Albertville, AL [*Location identifier*] [*FAA*] (FAAL)
ARF .... Almost Ready to Fly [*Remote-control plane*]
ARF .... American Railroad Foundation [*Defunct*] (EA)
ARF .... American Rationalist Federation (EA)
ARF .... American Rehabilitation Foundation [*Later, SKI*] (EA)
ARF .... American Retail Federation [*Later, NRF*] (EA)
ARF .... American Rose Foundation (EA)
ARF .... Animal Research Facilities
ARF .... Apparel Research Foundation [*Defunct*]

ARF .... Application Replacement Factor
ARF .... Aquarian Research Foundation (EA)
ArF .... Archivio di Filosofia [*A publication*]
ARF .... Area Resource File [*Public Health Service*] [*Information service or system*] (IID)
ARF .... Arfendazam [*Biochemistry*]
arf .... Arfolyam [*Current Price, Rate of Exchange, Quotation*]
ARF .... Armenian Revolutionary Federation (EA)
ARF .... Armour Research Foundation [*Later, IITRI*]
ARF .... Arthritis and Rheumatism Foundation [*Later, Arthritis Foundation*]
ARF .... Auburn Research Foundation (KSC)
ARF .... Automatic Reporting Feature (MCD)
ARF .... Automatic Return Fire [*ARPA*]
ARF .... Aviation Route Forecast (MCD)
ARF .... Awareness Research Foundation (EA)
ARF .... Axial Rotating Filtration
ARFA .... Allied Radio Frequency Agency [*Formerly, ERFA*] [*Brussels, Belgium*] [*NATO*]
AR & FA .... American Running and Fitness Association (EA)
ARFA .... Antirecession Fiscal Assistance
ARFA .... Armenian Revolutionary Federation of America [*Later, ARF*] (EA)
ARFAA ...... Academia Republicii Populare Romine. Institutul de Fizica Atomica si Institutul de Fizica. Studii si Cercetari de Fizica [*A publication*]
ARFC .... Air Reserve Flying Center [*Air Force*]
ARFC .... Aldo Ray Fan Club (EA)
ARFC .... Autologous Rosette-Forming Cell[*s*] [*Immunology*]
ARFCOS ... Armed Forces Courier Service
ARFCOSTA ... Armed Forces Courier Station (AFM)
ARFCW ...... Athletic and Recreation Federation of College Women (EA)
ARFDS ...... Automatic Reentry Flight Dynamics Simulator [*NASA*] (NASA)
ARFF .... Air Reserve Forces Facility [*Military*]
ARFF .... Angry Revengeful Frequent Fliers [*Aeronautics*]
ARFHA ...... Australian Refrigeration, Air Conditioning, and Heating [*A publication*]
Ar Fi .... Archivio di Filosofia [*A publication*]
ARFIA ...... Archivio di Fisiologia [*A publication*]
ARFIAY .... Archivio di Fisiologia [*A publication*]
Ar Fil .... Archivio di Filosofia [*A publication*]
ARFLBA .... Agricultural Research Organization. Division of Forestry. Ilanot Leaflet [*A publication*]
ARFMA ..... Arhiv za Farmaciju [*A publication*]
ARFMAC ... Arhiv za Farmaciju [*Belgrade*] [*A publication*]
ARFMSA .. Air Reserve Forces Meritorious Service Award [*Military decoration*]
ARFMSR .. Air Reserve Forces Meritorious Service Ribbon [*Military decoration*] (AFM)
ArFO .... Ozarks Regional Library, Fayetteville, AR [*Library symbol*] [*Library of Congress*] (LCLS)
ARFOR ...... Area Forecast [*Aviation*]
ARFOR ...... Army Forces [*Element of a joint task force*]
Ar de For .... Arsendinus de Forlivio [*Authority cited in pre-1607 legal work*] (DSA)
ARFORA ... Asociatiunea Reuniunilor Femeilor Ortodoxe Romane-Americane [*Association of Romanian-American Orthodox Ladies Auxiliaries*]
ARFORM ... Atomic Resonance Filter Optical Receiver Module (MCD)
ARFORSTAT ... Army Force Status Reporting System (AABC)
ARFPC .... Air Reserve Forces Policy Committee
ARFPC .... Army Reserve Forces Policy Council (MCD)
ARFPDS .... Air Reserve Forces Personnel Data System (AFM)
ArFs .... Fort Smith Carnegie City Library, Fort Smith, AR [*Library symbol*] [*Library of Congress*] (LCLS)
ArFsD .... Donrey Media Group, Fort Smith, AR [*Library symbol*] [*Library of Congress*] (LCLS)
ARFSU ...... Australian Rugby Football Schools Union
ARFTAX ... Annual Review of Food Technology [*Mysore*] [*A publication*]
ARG .... Abridged Reader's Guide to Periodical Literature [*A publication*]
ARG .... Aerolineas Argentinas [*Argentine airline*]
ARG .... African Rhino Group (EA)
ARG .... Airgas, Inc. [*NYSE symbol*] (SPSG)
ARG .... Alcohol Research Group [*Research center*] (RCD)
ARG .... American Record Guide [*A publication*]
ARG .... American Resources Group (EA)
ARG .... Americans for Responsible Government (EA)
ARG .... Amphibious Ready Group
ARG .... Archangelos [*Greece*] [*Seismograph station code, US Geological Survey*] (SEIS)
ARG .... Archiv fuer Reformationsgeschichte [*A publication*]
Arg .... Argensola [*A publication*]
ARG .... Argent [*Heraldry*]
ARG .... Argentina [*ANSI three-letter standard code*] (CNC)
ARG .... Argentum [*Silver*]
Arg .... Arginine [*Also, R*] [*An amino acid*]
ARG .... Argo [*Constellation*]
ARG .... Argo Development Corp. [*Vancouver Stock Exchange symbol*]
ARG .... Argosy [*A publication*] (ROG)

ARG........... Argosy Air Lines, Inc. [*Ft. Lauderdale, FL*] [*FAA designator*] (FAAC)
ARG........... Argument (OCD)
ARG........... Argumento [*By an argument drawn from such a law*] [*Latin*]
ARG........... Argyll [*County in Scotland*]
ARG........... Armoured Replacement Group [*British and Canadian*] [*World War II*]
ARG........... Arresting
ARG........... Atlantic Fleet Amphibious Ready Group (MCD)
ARG........... Atlantis Research Group (EA)
ARG........... Atlas Reliability Group
ARG........... Austin Rover Group Ltd.
ARG........... Automation Resource Group [*Wellesley, MA*]
ARG........... Autoradiography
ARG........... Internal Combustion Engine Repair Ship [*Navy symbol*]
ARG........... Walnut Ridge, AR [*Location identifier*] [*FAA*] (FAAL)
ARGA........ Antique Radio Guild of America
ARGA........ Appliance, Range, Adjust [*Data processing*]
ArgA......... Argentine Angel [*Record label*]
ARGADS... Army Gun Air Defense Systems (RDA)
ARGAP...... [*A*] Research Guide to Australian Politics [*A publication*] (APTA)
Arg Bills Ex ... Argles' French Law of Bills of Exchange [*A publication*] (DLA)
ArgC......... Argentine Columbia [*Record label*]
ARGC........ Graham Community Library, Ralston, Alberta [*Library symbol*] [*National Library of Canada*] (NLC)
ARGCA ..... American Rice Growers Cooperative Association [*Defunct*] (EA)
ArgD......... Argentine Decca [*Record label*]
ARGE........ Arbeitsgemeinschaft der Verbande der Europaischen Schloss- und Beschlagindustrie [*European Federation of Associations of Lock and Builders' Hardware Manufacturers*] (EAIO)
ARGE ALP ... Arbeitsgemeinschaft Alpenlaender [*Working Group of Alpine Regions*] (EAIO)
ARGEAR... Archiv fuer Geschwulstforschung [*A publication*]
Argent .... Argentinien [*Argentina*] [*German*]
Argent Com Nac Energ At CNEA NT ... Argentina. Comision Nacional de Energia Atomica. CNEA NT [*A publication*]
Argent Com Nac Energ At Inf ... Argentina. Comision Nacional de Energia Atomica. Informe [*A publication*]
Argent Dir Gen Ind Minera Bol ... Argentina. Direccion General de Industria Minera. Boletin [*A publication*]
Argent Dir Minas Geol Bol ... Argentina. Direccion de Minas y Geologia. Boletin [*A publication*]
Argent Dir Nac Geol Min An ... Argentina. Direccion Nacional de Geologia y Mineria. Anales [*A publication*]
Argent Dir Nac Geol Min Bol ... Argentina. Direccion Nacional de Geologia y Mineria. Boletin [*A publication*]
Argent Dir Nac Geol Min Inf Tec ... Argentina. Direccion Nacional de Geologia y Mineria. Informe Tecnico [*A publication*]
Argent Dir Nac Geol Min Publ ... Argentina. Direccion Nacional de Geologia y Mineria. Publicacion [*A publication*]
Argent Eco ... Economic Report. Summary (Argentina) [*A publication*]
Argent Electroenerg ... Argentina Electroenergetica [*A publication*]
Argent Inst Nac Geol Min An ... Argentina. Instituto Nacional de Geologia y Mineria. Anales [*A publication*]
Argent Inst Nac Geol Min Bol ... Argentina. Instituto Nacional de Geologia y Mineria. Boletin [*A publication*]
Argent Inst Nac Tecnol Agropecu Man Agropecu ... Argentina. Instituto Nacional de Tecnologia Agropecuaria. Manual Agropecuario [*A publication*]
Argent Inst Nac Tecnol Ind Bol Tec ... Argentina. Instituto Nacional de Tecnologia Industrial. Boletin Tecnico [*A publication*]
Argent Repub Minist Agric Ganad Publ ... Republica de Argentina. Ministerio de Agricultura y Ganaderia. Publicacion Miscelanea [*A publication*]
Argent Repub Minist Agric Ganad Publ Tec ... Republica de Argentina. Ministerio de Agricultura y Ganaderia. Publicacion Tecnia [*A publication*]
Argent Repub Subsecr Min Ser Argent ... Republica de Argentina. Subsecretaria de Mineria. Serie Argentina [*A publication*]
Argent Serv Nac Min Geol Rev ... Argentina. Servicio Nacional Minero Geologica. Revista [*A publication*]
Argent Text ... Argentina Textil [*A publication*]
ArGeO .... Ozark Academy, Gentry, AR [*Library symbol*] [*Library of Congress*] (LCLS)
Arg Fr Merc Law ... [*Napoleon*] Argles' Treatise upon French Mercantile Law, Etc. [*A publication*]
ARGG........ Annual Review of Gerontology and Geriatrics [*A publication*]
ARGH........ Adult Rat Growth Hormone [*Endocrinology*]
ARGI......... ARGOSystems, Incorporated [*NASDAQ symbol*] (NQ)
Arg Inform ... Informe Economico (Argentina) [*A publication*]
Arg Inst...... Institution au Droit Francais, par M. Argon [*A publication*] (DLA)
ArgLon....... Argentine London [*Record label*]
ArGlottIt.... Archivio Glottologico Italiano [*Florence*] [*A publication*]
Arg LR .... Argus Law Reports [*A publication*] (APTA)
ARGMA .... Army Rocket and Guided Missile Agency [*Redstone Arsenal, AL*]

Arg Mo ...... Moore's English King's Bench Reports (Arguments of Moore) [*A publication*] (DLA)
ARGN........ Argonaut Energy Corp. [*NASDAQ symbol*] (NQ)
ARGOA..... Argosy [*A publication*]
ArgOd........ Argentine Odeon [*Record label*]
Argomenti Farmacoter ... Argomenti de Farmacoterapia [*A publication*]
Argon .... Argonautica [*of Apollonius Rhodius*] [*Classical studies*] (OCD)
ARGONAUT ... Argonne Nuclear Assembly for University Training
Argonne Natl Lab News Bull ... Argonne National Laboratory. News Bulletin [*A publication*]
Argonne Natl Lab Phys Div Rep ... Argonne National Laboratory. Physics Division. Report [*A publication*]
Argonne Natl Lab Rep ANL ... Argonne National Laboratory. Report ANL [*A publication*]
Argonne Natl Lab Rev ... Argonne National Laboratory. Reviews [*A publication*]
Argonne Natl Lab Water Resour Res Program (Rep) ANL/WR ... Argonne National Laboratory. Water Resources Research Program (Report) ANL/WR [*A publication*]
Argonne Rev ... Argonne Reviews [*A publication*]
ArgP.......... Argentine Parlophone [*Record label*]
ARGPA...... Archives of General Psychiatry [*A publication*]
ARGPAQ .. Archives of General Psychiatry [*A publication*]
ArgPat .... Argentine Pathe [*Record label*]
ARGR .... Association for Research in Growth Relationships (EA)
Arg Rep ...... Argus Law Reports [*A publication*] (APTA)
Arg Rep...... Reports Printed in Melbourne Argus [*Australia*] [*A publication*] (DLA)
ARGS........ American Rock Garden Society (EA)
ARGS........ Antiradiation Guidance Sensor
ARGTU ..... Archiv fuer Reformationsgeschichte. Texte und Untersuchungen [*A publication*]
ARGUC9... Agricultural Research Guyana [*A publication*]
ARGUS ..... Analytical Reports Gathering and Updating System [*Navy*] (NG)
ARGUS ..... Associative Registers for Generalized User Switching [*Computer typesetting system*]
ARGUS ..... Automatic Routine Generating and Updating System [*Compiler*] [*Data processing*]
Argus LR ... Argus Law Reports [*A publication*] (APTA)
Argus LR (CN) ... Argus Law Reports (Current Notes) [*A publication*] (APTA)
Argus L Rep ... Argus Law Reports [*A publication*]
Argus (Newspr) (VIC) ... Argus Reports (Newspaper) (Victoria) [*A publication*] (APTA)
ArgV .... Argentine Victor [*Record label*]
ARGYAJ ... Archiv fuer Gynaekologie [*A publication*]
ARGYL...... Argyllshire [*County in Scotland*]
ARGYLLS ... Argyllshire [*County in Scotland*] (ROG)
ARH.......... Advanced Reconnaissance Helicopter
ARH.......... Ammunition Railhead
ARH.......... Anchor Hocking Corp. [*NYSE symbol*] (SPSG)
ARH.......... Antenna RADOME [*RADAR Dome*] Heater
ARH.......... Antiradiation Homer
ARH.......... Archignac [*France*] [*Seismograph station code, US Geological Survey*] (SEIS)
ArH.......... Archivo Hispalense [*A publication*]
ARH.......... Atlantic Richfield Hanford Co. (MCD)
ARH.......... Audit Reports Handbook [*IRS*]
ARH.......... Heavy-Hull Repair Ship [*Navy symbol*] [*Obsolete*]
ARH.......... Rolling Hills Public Library, Alberta [*Library symbol*] [*National Library of Canada*] (NLC)
ARHA........ American Rural Health Association (EA)
ARHA........ Associate of the Royal Hibernian Academy [*British*]
ARHAG..... African Refugee Housing Action Group [*British*]
Arh Biol Nauka ... Arhiv Bioloskih Nauka [*A publication*]
ARHCO..... Atlantic Richfield Hanford Company
ARHEA ..... Arthritis and Rheumatism [*A publication*]
Arh Farm (Belgr) ... Arhiv za Farmaciju (Belgrade) [*A publication*]
Arh Hig Rada ... Arhiv za Higijenu Rada [*A publication*]
Arh Hig Rada Toksikol ... Arhiv za Higijenu Rada i Toksikologiju [*A publication*]
Arh Hig Rad Toksikol ... Arhiv za Higijenu Rada i Toksikologiju [*A publication*]
Ar-Hi .... Arkansas History Commission, Department of Archives and History, Little Rock, AR [*Library symbol*] [*Library of Congress*] (LCLS)
Arhitekt SSSR ... Arhitektura SSSR [*A publication*]
Arh Kem ..... Arhiv za Kemiju [*A publication*]
ARHMB.... Archiwum Historii Medycyny [*A publication*]
ARHMBN ... Archiwum Historii Medycyny [*A publication*]
Arh Minist Poljopr (Yugoslavia) ... Arhiv Ministarstva Poljoprivrede (Yugoslavia) [*A publication*]
Arh Moldovei ... Arheologia Moldovei [*A publication*]
ArHN........ North Arkansas Regional Library, Harrison, AR [*Library symbol*] [*Library of Congress*] (LCLS)
ARHO .... Arapaho Petroleum, Inc. [*NASDAQ symbol*] (NQ)
ARHOC.... Army Housing Committee (AABC)
ARHP........ Association of Reproductive Health Professionals (EA)
Arh Poljopriv Nauke ... Arhiv za Poljoprivredne Nauke [*A publication*]
Arh Poljopr Nauke ... Arhiv za Poljoprivredne Nauke [*A publication*]

Arh Poljopr Nauke Teh ... Arhiv za Poljoprivredne Nauke i Tehniku [*A publication*]
ArHPont .... Archivum Historiae Pontificiae [*Rome*] [*A publication*]
ArHQ .... Arkansas Historical Quarterly [*A publication*]
Arh Rud Tehnol ... Arhiv za Rudarstvo i Tehnologiju [*A publication*]
ARHS .... Anthracite Railroads Historical Society (EA)
ARHS .... Australian Railway Historical Society
ARHS Bull ... Australian Railway Historical Society. Bulletin [*A publication*] (APTA)
Arh Tehnol ... Arhiv za Tehnologiju [*A publication*]
ArhV .... Arheoloski Vestnik [*A publication*]
ARI .... Acne Research Institute (EA)
ARI .... Activity Routing Indicator (MCD)
ARI .... Actuarial Removal Interval (AFIT)
ARI .... Acupuncture Research Institute (EA)
ARI .... Aerial RADIAC Instrument
ARI .... Aeronautical Radio, Incorporated (KSC)
ARI .... Aging Research Institute [*Defunct*] (EA)
ARI .... Agricultural Research Institute (EA)
ARI .... Aileron Rudder Interconnect (MCD)
ARI .... Air-Conditioning and Refrigeration Institute (EA)
ARI .... Airborne Radio Installation [*RADAR*]
ARI .... Airborne Radio Instrument
ARI .... Airpower Research Institute [*Air University*] [*Research center*] (RCD)
ARI .... Airway Reactivity Index [*Physiology*]
ARI .... Allied Research Institute [*Later, Aluminum Recycling Association*] (EA)
ARI .... Alternate Rod Insertion [*Nuclear energy*] (NRCH)
ARI .... Aluminum Research Institute
ARI .... Amaryllis Research Institute (EA)
ARI .... American Rayon Institute [*Defunct*]
ARI .... American Reliance Group, Inc. [*AMEX symbol*] (SPSG)
ARI .... Animal Rights International (EA)
ARI .... Aquatic Research Institute (EA)
ARI .... Archaeology and the Religion of Israel [*A publication*] (BJA)
ArI .... Archivo Ibero-Americano [*Madrid*] [*A publication*]
ARI .... Ariadne [*A publication*]
ARI .... Arica [*Chile*] [*Airport symbol*] (OAG)
ARI .... Arica [*Chile*] [*Seismograph station code, US Geological Survey*] (SEIS)
Ari .... Aries [*Constellation*]
Ari .... Ariprandus [*Flourished, 12th century*] [*Authority cited in pre-1607 legal work*] (DSA)
ARI .... Arizona
ARI .... Army Research Institute for the Behavioral and Social Sciences [*Alexandria, VA*]
ARI .... Artist-Run Initiative [*Australia*]
ARI .... Association Resource Institute [*Commercial firm*] (EA)
ARI .... Attribute Requirement Inventory
ARI .... ATWS [*Anticipated Transient without Scram*] Rod Injection System [*Nuclear energy*] (NRCH)
ARI .... Australasian Religion Index [*A publication*] (APTA)
ARI .... Authority Is Requested to Inter [*the remains of*] [*Army*] (AABC)
ARI .... Automated Readability Index (MCD)
ARI .... Automatic Radio Information [*System which relays traffic information through car radios*]
ARI .... Automatic Return Items (AABC)
ARI .... Average Relationship Index
ARI .... Ayn Rand Institute (EA)
ARI .... Rimbey Public Library, Alberta [*Library symbol*] [*National Library of Canada*] (NLC)
ARIA .... Accounting Researchers International Association [*Defunct*] (EA)
ARIA .... Acetylcholine Receptor-Inducing Activity [*Biochemistry*]
ARIA .... Administration, Ryukyu Islands, Army (AABC)
ARIA .... Adult Reading Improvement Association
ARIA .... Advanced Range Instrumentation Aircraft
ARIA .... American Radio Importers Association (EA)
ARIA .... American Risk and Insurance Association [*Orlando, FL*] (EA)
ARIA .... Apollo Range Instrumentation Aircraft [*NASA*]
ARIA .... Autoradiographic Immunoassay (MCD)
ARIADS .... Industrial Environmental Research Laboratory [*Research Triangle Park*]. Annual Report [*A publication*]
ARIAS ...... Associate of the Royal Incorporation of Architects in Scotland
ARIB .... Aspen Imaging International [*NASDAQ symbol*] (NQ)
ARIB .... Asphalt Roofing Industry Bureau [*Later, ARMA*] (EA)
ARIBA ...... Associate of the Royal Institute of British Architects
ARIC .... Admission Referral and Information Center [*Commission on Independent Colleges and Universities*]
ARIC .... Agricultural Research Information Centre [*Indian Council of Agricultural Research*] (IID)
ARIC .... Air Resources Information Clearinghouse [*Also, an information service or system*] (EA)
ARIC .... Arctic in Colour [*A publication*]
ARIC .... Arizona Research Information Center [*Information service or system*] (IID)
ARIC .... Associate of the Royal Institute of Chemistry [*Formerly, AIC*] [*British*]

ARICD ...... American Research Institute for Community Development (EA)
ARICS ...... Associate of the Royal Institution of Chartered Surveyors [*Formerly, PASI*] [*British*]
ARID .... Analecta Romana Instituti Danici [*A publication*]
ARID .... Aridtech, Inc. [*Manhattan Beach, CA*] [*NASDAQ symbol*] (NQ)
Ari D .... Arion's Dolphin [*A publication*]
ARID .... Australian Resources Industry Database
Arid Lands Resour Inf Pap ... Arid Lands Resource Information Paper [*A publication*]
Aridnye Pochvy Ikh Genezis Geokhim Ispol ... Aridnye Pochvy Ikh Genezis Geokhimiya Ispol'zovanie [*A publication*]
Arid Soils Their Genesis Geochem Util ... Arid Soils. Their Genesis, Geochemistry, Utilization [*A publication*]
Arid Zone Newsl Div Land Res CSIRO ... Arid Zone Newsletter. Division of Land Research. Commonwealth Scientific and Industrial Research Organisation [*A publication*] (APTA)
Arid Zone Res ... Arid Zone Research [*A publication*]
Arid Zone Res UNESCO ... Arid Zone Research. United Nations Educational, Scientific, and Cultural Organization [*A publication*]
Arie .... Aries [*Constellation*]
ARIEL ...... Automated Real-Time Investments Exchange [*NASDAQ trading computer*]
Ariel E .... Ariel: a Review of International English Literature [*A publication*]
ARIEM ...... Army Research Institute for Environmental Medicine
ARIES ...... Advanced RADAR Information Evaluation System
ARIES ...... Airborne Reconnaissance Integrated Electronic System (MCD)
ARIES ...... Airborne Research Integration Engineering Support (MCD)
ARIES ...... Aircraft Reply and Interference Environment Simulator (MCD)
ARIES ...... Ammunition Reliability Information Evolution System (MCD)
ARIES ...... Animal Rights Information and Education Service (EA)
ARIES ...... Astronomical Radio Interferometric Earth Survey [*or Surveying*] [*NASA*]
ARIES ...... Authentic Reproduction of an Independent Earth Satellite
ARIES ...... Automated Registration, Indexing, and Enquiries System [*Data processing*]
ARIES ...... Automated Reliability Estimation Program [*Data processing*]
ARIF .... Association pour le Retablissement des Institutions et Oeuvres Israelites en France (EA)
ARIFD9 ..... International Commission for the Northwest Atlantic Fisheries. Annual Report [*A publication*]
ARIHSL .... Association of Rhode Island Health Sciences Librarians [*Library network*]
AR II .... American Revolution II Committee (EA)
ARIL .... [*The*] ARIL Group [*NASDAQ symbol*] (NQ)
ARIL .... Associates for Religion and Intellectual Life (EA)
ARIL .... Automatic Return Item List (MCD)
ARIM .... Accelerator and Reactor Improvement and Modification
ARIMA ...... Autoregressive-Integrated-Moving-Average [*Statistics*]
ARIMDU .. Annual Review of Immunology [*A publication*]
ARIMO ..... Association of Russian Imperial Medical Officers [*Defunct*] (EA)
ARIMS ...... Airborne RADAR Inflight Monitoring System
ARIN .... Arista Investors Corp. [*NASDAQ symbol*] (NQ)
ARIN .... National Aeronautics and Space Administration Library Network [*Information service or system*] (IID)
ARINAU ... Annual Report. Research Institute of Environmental Medicine. Nagoya University [*English Edition*] [*A publication*]
ARINC ...... Aeronautical Radio, Incorporated
ARINC ...... Aeronautical Research, Incorporated (MCD)
ARINC ...... Aircraft Radio, Incorporated (MCD)
ARINCO ... Aeronautical Radio, Incorporated
ARINOA ... Association of Russian Imperial Naval Officers in America (EA)
ARIP .... Air Refueling Ingress Point [*FAA*] (FAAC)
ARIP .... Air Refueling Initial Point [*Air Force*] (AFM)
Arip .... Ariprandus [*Flourished, 12th century*] [*Authority cited in pre-1607 legal work*] (DSA)
ARIP .... Automatic Rocket Impact Predictor
ARIPHH ... Associate of the Royal Institute of Public Health and Hygiene [*British*]
Aripnd .... Ariprandus [*Flourished, 12th century*] [*Authority cited in pre-1607 legal work*] (DSA)
ARIPUC .... Annual Report. Institute of Phonetics. University of Copenhagen [*A publication*]
ARIQD8 .... Annual Report. Nigerian Institute for Oceanography and Marine Research [*A publication*]
ARIS .... Advanced Range Instrumentation Ship [*Navy symbol*]
ARIS .... Advanced Range Instrumentation Systems (MCD)
ARIS .... Advanced Research Instrument System, Inc.
ARIS .... Aerial RADIAC Instrument System
ARIS .... Aeronautical Research Institute of Sweden (MCD)
ARIS .... Airborne Range Instrumentation Station
ARIS .... Aircraft Recording Instrumentation System [*British*]
ARIS .... Aircraft Research Instrumentation System
ARIS .... Alabama Resources Information System [*Auburn University*] [*Information service or system*] (IID)
ARIS .... Alcohol Research Information Service (EA)

ARIS .... Apoenzyme Reactivation Immunoassay System [*Clinical chemistry*]
ARIS .... Aristek Communities [*NASDAQ symbol*]   (NQ)
ARIS .... Association Referral Information Service
ARIS .... Atlantic Range Instrumentation Ship
ARIS .... Atomic Reactor in Space   (MUGU)
ARIS .... Attitude and Rate Indicating System
ARIS .... Automated Reactor Inspection System [*Nuclear energy*]   (NRCH)
ARIS .... Automated Real-Time Imaging System
ARIS .... Automatic Recording Infrared Spectrometer
ARISBC ..... Annual Review of Information Science and Technology [*A publication*]
ARISDE .... Institute of Oceanographic Sciences. Annual Report [*A publication*]
ARISF .... Association of the IOC Recognized International Sports Federations [*Seoul, Republic of Korea*]   (EAIO)
Aris Phil C ... Aris and Phillips Central Asian Studies [*A publication*]
Aris Soc ...... Aristotelian Society. Supplementary Volume [*A publication*]
ARIST .... Annual Review of Information Science and Technology [*A publication*]
ARIST .... Aristophanes [*Greek playwright, c. 445-380BC*] [*Classical studies*]   (ROG)
ARIST .... Aristotle [*Greek philosopher, 384-322BC*] [*Classical studies*]   (ROG)
Arist .... Letter of Aristeas (Pseudepigrapha)   (BJA)
ARISTO .... Aristocrat   (DSUE)
ARISTOTLE ... Annual Review and Information Symposium on the Technology of Training, Learning, and Education [*DoD*]
Aristot Panepist Thessalonikis Epet Geopon Dasolog Skol ... Aristoteleion Panepistemion Thessalonikis Epetiris tis Geoponikis kai Dasologikis Skolis [*A publication*]
Aristox .... Aristoxenus [*Fourth century BC*] [*Classical studies*]   (OCD)
ARIT .... American Registered Inhalation Therapist [*Academic degree*]
ARIT .... American Registry of Inhalation Therapists [*Later, NBRT*]   (EA)
ARIT .... American Research Institute of Turkey [*University of Pennsylvania*] [*Research center*]   (RCD)
ARIT .... Aritech Corp. [*Framingham, MA*] [*NASDAQ symbol*]   (NQ)
ARITH ...... Arithmetic [*Flowchart*]
ARITHMETIC ... A Rat in the House May Eat the Ice Cream [*Mnemonic guide for spelling "arithmetic"*]
Arith Teach ... Arithmetic Teacher [*A publication*]
ARITHU ... Arithmetic Unit [*Data processing*]
ARIVAK .... Annual Report. Institute for Virus Research. Kyoto University [*A publication*]
ARIX .... ARIX Corp. [*NASDAQ symbol*]   (CTT)
ARIZ .... Arizona   (AFM)
Ariz .... Arizona Reports [*A publication*]
Ariz .... Arizona Supreme Court Reports [*A publication*]
Ariz Admin Comp ... Arizona Official Compilation of Administrative Rules and Regulations [*A publication*]   (DLA)
Ariz Admin Comp R ... Arizona Official Compilation of Administrative Rules and Regulations [*A publication*]   (DLA)
Ariz Admin Dig ... Arizona Administrative Digest [*A publication*]   (DLA)
Ariz Ag Exp ... Arizona. Agricultural Experiment Station. Publications [*A publication*]
Ariz Agric Exp Stn Bull ... Arizona. Agricultural Experiment Station. Bulletin [*A publication*]
Ariz Agric Exp Stn Rep ... Arizona. Agricultural Experiment Station. Report [*A publication*]
Ariz Agric Exp Stn Res Rep ... Arizona. Agricultural Experiment Station. Research Report [*A publication*]
Ariz Agric Exp Stn Tech Bull ... Arizona. Agricultural Experiment Station. Technical Bulletin [*A publication*]
Ariz App .... Arizona Appeals Reports [*A publication*]   (DLA)
Ariz BJ .... Arizona Bar Journal [*A publication*]
Ariz Bsn G ... Arizona Business Gazette [*A publication*]
Ariz Bur Mines Bull ... Arizona. Bureau of Mines. Bulletin [*A publication*]
Ariz Bur Mines Bull Geol Ser ... Arizona. Bureau of Mines. Bulletin. Geological Series [*A publication*]
Ariz Bur Mines Bull Mineral Technology Ser ... Arizona. Bureau of Mines. Bulletin. Mineral Technology Series [*A publication*]
Ariz Bur Mines Circ ... Arizona. Bureau of Mines. Circular [*A publication*]
Ariz Bur Mines Field Notes ... Arizona. Bureau of Mines. Field Notes [*A publication*]
Ariz Bus ..... Arizona Business [*A publication*]
Ariz Comm Agric Hortic Annu Rep ... Arizona. Commission of Agriculture and Horticulture. Annual Report [*A publication*]
Ariz Comp Admin R & Regs ... Arizona Official Compilation of Administrative Rules and Regulations [*A publication*]
Ariz Const ... Arizona Constitution [*A publication*]   (DLA)
Ariz Dent J ... Arizona Dental Journal [*A publication*]
Ariz Dept Mineral Res Ann Rept ... Arizona. Department of Mineral Resources. Annual Report [*A publication*]
Ariz For Notes ... Arizona Forestry Notes [*A publication*]
Ariz For Note Sch For Nth Ariz Univ ... Arizona Forestry Notes. School of Forestry. Northern Arizona University [*A publication*]
Ariz Game Fish Dep Wildl Bull ... Arizona. Game and Fish Department. Wildlife Bulletin [*A publication*]

Ariz Geol Soc Digest Ann ... Arizona Geological Society. Digest. Annual [*A publication*]
Ariz H .... Arizona Highways [*A publication*]
Ariz His R ... Arizona Historical Review [*A publication*]
Ariz Hist Rev ... Arizona Historical Review [*A publication*]
Ariz Land & People ... Arizona Land and People [*A publication*]
Ariz Law R ... Arizona Law Review [*A publication*]
Ariz Legis Serv ... Arizona Legislative Service [*A publication*]
Ariz Legis Serv (West) ... Arizona Legislative Service (West) [*A publication*]
Ariz Libn .... Arizona Librarian [*A publication*]
Ariz Librn .. Arizona Librarian [*A publication*]
Ariz LR ...... Arizona Law Review [*A publication*]
Ariz L Rev ... Arizona Law Review [*A publication*]
Ariz Med ..... Arizona Medicine [*A publication*]
Ariz Nurse ... Arizona Nurse [*A publication*]
Arizona Acad Sci Jour ... Arizona Academy of Science. Journal [*A publication*]
Arizona Bur Mines Bull ... Arizona. Bureau of Mines. Bulletin [*A publication*]
Arizona Med ... Arizona Medicine [*A publication*]
Arizona R ... Arizona Review [*A publication*]
Arizona State LJ ... Arizona State Law Journal [*A publication*]
Ariz Q .... Arizona Quarterly [*A publication*]
Ariz R .... Arizona Review [*A publication*]
Ariz Repub ... Arizona Republic [*A publication*]
Ariz Rev Stat ... Arizona Revised Statutes [*A publication*]   (DLA)
Ariz Rev Stat Ann ... Arizona Revised Statutes, Annotated [*A publication*]   (DLA)
Ariz Rev State ... Arizona Revised Statutes [*A publication*]   (DLA)
Ariz Sess Laws ... Arizona Session Laws [*A publication*]   (DLA)
Ariz State Land Dept Water Res Rept ... Arizona State Land Department. Water Resources Report [*A publication*]
Ariz State Land Dep Water Resour Rep ... Arizona State Land Department. Water Resources Report [*A publication*]
Ariz State Law J ... Arizona State Law Journal [*A publication*]
Ariz State LJ ... Arizona State Law Journal [*A publication*]   (DLA)
Ariz St Bur Mines B ... Arizona State Bureau of Mines. Bulletin [*A publication*]
Ariz St LF .. Arizona State Law Forum [*A publication*]
Ariz St L J ... Arizona State Law Journal [*A publication*]
Ariz SU Ant ... Arizona State University. Anthropological Research Papers [*A publication*]
Ariz Teach ... Arizona Teacher [*A publication*]
Ariz Univ Agr Expt Bull ... Arizona University. Agricultural Experiment Station. Bulletin [*A publication*]
Ariz Univ Agr Expt Bull Phys Sci Bull ... Arizona University. Agricultural Experiment Station. Bulletin. Physical Science Bulletin [*A publication*]
Ariz Univ Lab Tree-Ring Res Pap ... Arizona University. Laboratory of Tree-Ring Research. Papers [*A publication*]
Ariz Univ Lunar Planet Lab Commun ... Arizona University. Lunar and Planetary Laboratory. Communications [*A publication*]
ArizW .... Arizona and the West [*A publication*]
Ariz Water Comm Bull ... Arizona. Water Commission. Bulletin [*A publication*]
Ariz and West ... Arizona and the West [*A publication*]
Ariz West ... Arizona and the West [*A publication*]
ARJ .... Acquisition RADAR Jamming
ARJ .... Anciens de la Resistance Juive   (BJA)
Ar J .... Arbitration Journal [*A publication*]
arj .... Arjegyzek [*Price List, Catalog*] [*Hungarian*]
arj .... Arjegyzes [*Price Quotation*] [*Hungarian*]
ARJ .... Austin Rover Japan
ARJ .... Providence, RI [*Location identifier*] [*FAA*]   (FAAL)
ARJCC ...... Andrew R. Jennings Computing Center [*Case Western Reserve University*] [*Research center*]   (RCD)
ARJID .... Japan. Atomic Energy Research Institute. Annual Report and Account [*A publication*]
ARJKAQ ... Agricultural Research Journal of Kerala [*A publication*]
A and R (JP) ... A and R. Analysis and Research (Japan) [*A publication*]
ARJS .... Airborne RADAR Jamming System   (MCD)
ARJSAG .... Japanese Society for Tuberculosis. Annual Report [*A publication*]
ARJU .... Arjungnagimmat. Inuit Cultural Institute [*A publication*]
ARK .... Air Center, Inc. [*El Dorado, AR*] [*FAA designator*]   (FAAC)
ARK .... Ark Energy Ltd. [*Vancouver Stock Exchange symbol*]
ARK .... Arkansas   (AFM)
ARK .... Arkansas Business and Economic Review [*A publication*]
Ark .... Arkansas Reports [*A publication*]
Ark .... Arkansas Supreme Court Reports [*A publication*]   (DLA)
ARK .... Arkhangelsk [*USSR*] [*Geomagnetic observatory code*]
ARK .... Arkla Exploration Co. [*NYSE symbol*]   (SPSG)
Ark .... Arkley's Justiciary Reports [*Scotland*] [*A publication*]   (DLA)
ARK .... Arrick, Douglas B., Denver CO [*STAC*]
ARK .... Reconnaissance Seaplane [*Russian symbol*]
Ark Acad Sci Proc ... Arkansas Academy of Science. Proceedings [*A publication*]
Ark Acts ..... General Acts of Arkansas [*A publication*]   (DLA)
Ark Admin Reg ... Arkansas Register [*A publication*]   (DLA)
Ark Ag Exp ... Arkansas. Agricultural Experiment Station. Publications [*A publication*]

Arkansas Acad Sci Proc ... Arkansas Academy of Science. Proceedings [*A publication*]

Arkansas Agric Exp Stn Bull ... Arkansas. Agricultural Experiment Station. Bulletin [*A publication*]

Arkansas Agric Exp Stn Mimeogr Ser ... Arkansas. Agricultural Experiment Station. Mimeograph Series [*A publication*]

Arkansas Agric Exp Stn Rep Ser ... Arkansas. Agricultural Experiment Station. Report Series [*A publication*]

Arkansas Agric Exp Stn Res Ser ... Arkansas. Agricultural Experiment Station. Research Series [*A publication*]

Arkansas Agric Exp Stn Spec Rep ... Arkansas. Agricultural Experiment Station. Special Report [*A publication*]

Arkansas Anim Morb Rep ... Arkansas Animal Morbidity Report [*A publication*]

Arkansas B ... Arkansas Business [*A publication*]

Arkansas Cattle Bus ... Arkansas Cattle Business [*A publication*]

Arkansas Dent J ... Arkansas Dental Journal [*A publication*]

Arkansas Eng Exp Stn Bull ... Arkansas. Engineering Experiment Station. Bulletin [*A publication*]

Arkansas Farm Res ... Arkansas Farm Research [*A publication*]

Arkansas Farm Res Arkansas Agric Exp Stn ... Arkansas Farm Research. Arkansas Agricultural Experiment Station [*A publication*]

Arkansas Geol Comm Bull ... Arkansas. Geological Commission. Bulletin [*A publication*]

Arkansas Geol Comm Inform Circ ... Arkansas. Geological and Conservation Commission. Information Circular [*A publication*]

Arkansas Geol Comm Water Resour Circ ... Arkansas. Geological Commission. Water Resources Circular [*A publication*]

Arkansas Geol Comm Water Resour Summ ... Arkansas. Geological Commission. Water Resources Summary [*A publication*]

Arkansas Geol Conserv Comm Inf Circ ... Arkansas. Geological and Conservation Commission. Information Circular [*A publication*]

Arkansas Hist Q ... Arkansas Historical Quarterly [*A publication*]

Arkansas Lib ... Arkansas Libraries [*A publication*]

Arkansas L Rev ... Arkansas Law Review [*A publication*]

Arkansas Univ Eng Exp Sta Res Rep ... Arkansas University. Engineering Experiment Station. Research Report [*A publication*]

Arkansas Univ Eng Exp Stn Res Rep Ser ... Arkansas University. Engineering Experiment Station. Research Report Series [*A publication*]

Arkansas Univ Seismol Bull ... Arkansas University. Seismological Bulletin [*A publication*]

Arkansas Water Sewage Conf Short Course Proc ... Arkansas Water and Sewage Conference and Short Course. Proceedings [*A publication*]

Arkans Fm Res ... Arkansas Farm Research [*A publication*]

Ark App ..... Arkansas Appellate Reports [*A publication*]   (DLA)

Ark App Rep ... Arkansas Appellate Reports [*A publication*]   (DLA)

Ark Astron ... Arkiv foer Astronomi [*A publication*]

Ark BA .... Arkansas Bar Association. Proceedings [*A publication*]   (DLA)

Ark Bot ...... Arkiv foer Botanik [*A publication*]

Ark Bus and Econ R ... Arkansas Business and Economic Review [*A publication*]

Ark CC .... Arkansas Corporation Commission Report [*A publication*]   (DLA)

ARKCDA ... Kenya Tuberculosis Investigation Centre. Annual Report [*A publication*]

ARKCEB ... Kenya Tuberculosis and Respiratory Diseases Research Centre. Annual Report [*A publication*]

Ark Const .. Arkansas Constitution [*A publication*]   (DLA)

ARKEAD ... Arkiv foer Kemi [*A publication*]

ArKF .... Archiv fuer Keilschriftforschung [*A publication*]

Ark Farm Res ... Arkansas Farm Research [*A publication*]

Ark Fys ...... Arkiv foer Fysik [*A publication*]

Ark Fys Semin Trondheim ... Arkiv foer det Fysiske Seminar i Trondheim [*A publication*]

Ark Gazet... Arkansas Gazette [*A publication*]

Ark Geofys ... Arkiv foer Geofysik [*A publication*]

Ark G S ...... Arkansas. Geological Survey [*A publication*]

Arkh Anat Gistol Embriol ... Arkhiv Anatomii, Gistologii, i Embriologii [*A publication*]

Arkh Biol Nauk ... Arkhiv Biologicheskikh Nauk [*A publication*]

Arkheologiia ... Arkheologiia Organ na Arkheologicheskiia Institut i Muzei pri B'lgarskata Akademiia na Naukite [*A publication*]

Ark His As ... Arkansas Historical Association. Publications [*A publication*]

Ark Hist Assoc Publ ... Arkansas Historical Association. Publications [*A publication*]

Ark Hist Q ... Arkansas Historical Quarterly [*A publication*]

Ark Hist Quar ... Arkansas Historical Quarterly [*A publication*]

Arkhit Stroit Leningrada ... Arkhitektura i Stroitelstvo Leningrada [*A publication*]

Arkhivi Ukr ... Arkhivi Ukraini. Naukovo Informatsiinii Biuleten` Arkhivnogo Upravliniia pri Radi Ministriv URSR [*A publication*]

Arkh Klin i Eksper Med (Moskva) ... Arkhiv Klinicheskoi i Eksperimental'noi Meditsiny (Moskva) [*A publication*]

Arkh Med Nauk ... Arkhiv Meditsinskikh Nauk [*A publication*]

Arkh Patol ... Arkhiv Patologii [*A publication*]

ArkHQ .... Arkansas Historical Quarterly [*A publication*]

Arkh Russk Protist Obsh ... Arkhiv Russkogo Protistologicheskogo Obshchestva [*A publication*]

ARKIAP .... Archiv fuer Kinderheilkunde [*A publication*]

Arkiv .... Arkiv foer Nordisk Filologi [*A publication*]

Arkiv f Nord Filologi ... Arkiv foer Nordisk Filologi [*A publication*]

Ark Just ..... Arkley's Justiciary Reports [*Scotland*] [*A publication*]   (DLA)

ARKK-A .... Arkkitehti [*A publication*]

Ark Kemi ... Arkiv foer Kemi [*A publication*]

Ark Kemi Mineral Geol ... Arkiv foer Kemi, Mineralogi, och Geologi [*Sweden*] [*A publication*]

Ark Kemi Miner Geol ... Arkiv foer Kemi, Mineralogi, och Geologi [*A publication*]

Ark (Kiev) .. Arkheologiia (Kiev) [*A publication*]

Arkl .... Arkley's Justiciary Reports [*Scotland*] [*A publication*]   (DLA)

ARKLA ..... Arkansas Louisiana Gas Co.

Ark Law ..... Arkansas Lawyer [*A publication*]

Ark Law R ... Arkansas Law Review [*A publication*]

ARKLAY ... Arkheologiya (Kiev) [*A publication*]

Arkley .... Arkley's Justiciary Reports [*Scotland*] [*A publication*]   (DLA)

Ark Lib ...... Arkansas Libraries [*A publication*]

Ark Light Newsl ... Ark-Light Newsletter [*A publication*]

Ark LJ .... Arkansas Law Journal [*A publication*]   (DLA)

Ark LR .... Arkansas Law Review [*A publication*]

Ark L Rev ... Arkansas Law Review [*A publication*]

Ark Mat ...... Arkiv foer Matematik [*A publication*]

Ark Mat Astron Fys ... Arkiv foer Matematik, Astronomi, och Fysik [*Sweden*] [*A publication*]

Ark Matemat ... Arkiv foer Matematik [*A publication*]

Ark Mineral Geol ... Arkiv foer Mineralogi och Geologi [*A publication*]

Ark Nurse .. Arkansas Nurse [*A publication*]

ar kor .... Arany Korona (Hungarian currency before World War I, still used to estimate real estate values)]

Ark Otkr .... Arkheologicheskie Otkrytiia [*A publication*]

Ark Pam URSR ... Arkheologichi Pamiatniki URSR [*A publication*]

Ark PU ...... Arkansas Department of Public Utilities Report [*A publication*]   (DLA)

Ark R .... Arkansas Reports [*A publication*]   (DLA)

ARKRAI .... Archiv fuer Kriminologie [*A publication*]

Ark Reg ...... Arkansas Register [*A publication*]

Ark Rep ...... Arkansas Reports [*A publication*]   (DLA)

Ark Res Devel Comm Div Geology Bull Inf Circ ... Arkansas. Resources and Development Commission. Division of Geology Bulletin. Information Circular [*A publication*]

Ark Riv ...... Ark River Review [*A publication*]

Ark's .... Arkansas Reports [*A publication*]   (DLA)

ARKSN ...... Annuarium des Roomsch-Katholieke Studenten in Nederland [*A publication*]

Ark Stat Ann ... Arkansas Statutes, Annotated [*A publication*]   (DLA)

Ark State Nurses Assoc Newsl ... Arkansas State Nurses' Association. Newsletter [*A publication*]

Ark Stats .... Arkansas Statutes [*A publication*]   (DLA)

ARKT-B ..... Architektura [*A publication*]

ArkUkr ...... Arkheologija. Publies par l'Academie des Sciences d'Ukraine [*A publication*]

ArKulturg .. Archiv fuer Kulturgeschichte [*A publication*]

Ark Univ Inst Sci and Technology Research Ser ... Arkansas University. Institute of Science and Technology. Research Series [*A publication*]

Ark Zool .... Arkiv foer Zoologi [*A publication*]

Ark Zool (Stockholm) ... Arkiv foer Zoologi (Stockholm) [*A publication*]

ARL .... Acceptable Reliability Level [*Quality control*]

ARL .... Admiralty Research Laboratory [*British*]

ARL .... Aerial   (FAAC)

ARL .... Aerial Reconnaissance Laboratory

ARL .... Aeromedical Research Laboratory [*Army*]   (KSC)

ARL .... Aeronautical Research Laboratory [*OAR*] [*Australia*]

ARL .... Aerospace Research Laboratory [*Wright-Patterson Air Force Base, OH*]   (AFM)

ARL .... Age Run Length

ARL .... Air Resources Laboratory [*Silver Spring, MD*] [*National Oceanic and Atmospheric Administration*]

ARL .... Aircraft Radio Laboratory

ARL .... American Leduc Petroleums Ltd. [*Toronto Stock Exchange symbol*]

ARL .... American Roque League   (EA)

ARL .... Americans for Religious Liberty   (EA)

ARL .... Antiriot Laws

ARL .... Applied Research Laboratories [*Commercial firm*]

ARL .... Applied Research Laboratory [*Johns Hopkins University, University of Texas at Austin, Pennsylvania State University*] [*Research center*]

ARL .... Archeological Research Laboratory [*Texas A & M University*] [*Research center*]

ArL .... Archivum Linguisticum [*A publication*]

ARL .... Arctic Research Laboratory [*Point Barrow, AK*] [*Army*]

ARL .... Army Radiation Laboratory

ARL .... Arundel Corp. [*AMEX symbol*]   (SPSG)

ARL .... Associate in Recreation Leadership

ARL .... Association of Research Libraries   (EA)

ARL .... Atlantic Research Laboratories [*National Research Council of Canada*]   (MCD)

ARL .... Authorized Retention Level [*Military*]   (AABC)
ARL .... Average Run Length [*Statistics*]
ARL .... Aviation Research Laboratory [*University of Illinois*]   (MCD)
ARL .... Aviator Readiness Level   (MCD)
ARL .... Landing Craft, Repair Ship [*Navy symbol*]
ArL .... Little Rock Public Library, Little Rock, AR [*Library symbol*]
                [*Library of Congress*]   (LCLS)
ARL .... United States Army Library, Washington, DC [*OCLC symbol*]   (OCLC)
ArLA .... Arkansas Arts Center, Little Rock, AR [*Library symbol*]
                [*Library of Congress*]   (LCLS)
ARLAB ...... Archiv fuer Landtechnik [*A publication*]
ARLABANK ... Arab Latin American Bank
ArLAD .... Arkansas Democrat, Little Rock, AR [*Library symbol*] [*Library of Congress*]   (LCLS)
ARLANT ... Army Forces Atlantic   (MCD)
ARLCAP ... Association of Research Libraries Collection Analysis Project
ARLE .... Admiralty Research Laboratory Extension [*British*]
ARLEA ...... Army Logistics Evaluation Agency   (MCD)
ARL-FRO ... Air Resources Laboratory - Field Research Office [*National Oceanic and Atmospheric Administration*]   (NOAA)
ARLFT ...... Airlift
ARLIS .... Arctic Research Laboratory Island [*A floating ice island in the Arctic Ocean*] [*Navy*]
ARLIS/NA ... Art Libraries Society/North America   (EA)
ARLIS Newsl ... ARLIS [*Art Libraries Society/North America*] Newsletter [*A publication*]
ARLL .... Advanced Run Length Limited [*Data processing*]
ARLL .... Audible Rumble Loudness Level [*Stereo*]
ARLLUC ... Alpha Roster Locator List (United States Army Reserve) Colonels
ARLM .... Rainbow Lake Municipal Library, Alberta [*Library symbol*] [*National Library of Canada*]   (NLC)
ARL Mech Eng Rep Aust Aeronaut Res Lab ... ARL Mechanical Engineering Report. Australia Aeronautical Research Laboratories [*A publication*]
ARL Mins ... Association of Research Libraries. Minutes [*A publication*]
ARLO .... Air Reconnaissance Liaison Officer
ARLO .... Army Liaison Officer   (FAAC)
ARLO .... Art Research Libraries of Ohio [*Library network*]
ARLP .... Alliance Republicaine pour les Libertes et le Progres [*Republican Alliance for Liberties and Progress*] [*France*] [*Political party*]   (PPE)
ARLP .... Association of Rugby League Players [*Australia*]
ArlQ .... Arlington Quarterly [*A publication*]
ARLS .... Association for Recognizing the Life of Stillborns   (EA)
ARLS .... Automated Runbook/Library System
ARLS .... Automatic Resupply Logistics System   (AFM)
ARLSEA .... Active-Retired Lighthouse Service Employees' Association   (EA)
ArLSJ .... Saint John's Seminary, Little Rock, AR [*Library symbol*] [*Library of Congress*]   (LCLS)
ARLT......... Associate for Reform of Latin Teaching [*British*]
ARL/TR .... Australian Radiation Laboratory. Technical Report [*A publication*]   (APTA)
ArLUA .... University of Arkansas at Little Rock, Little Rock, AR [*Library symbol*] [*Library of Congress*]   (LCLS)
ArLUA-L... University of Arkansas at Little Rock, Law Library, Little Rock, AR [*Library symbol*] [*Library of Congress*]   (LCLS)
ArLVA .... United States Veterans Administration Hospital, Little Rock, AR [*Library symbol*] [*Library of Congress*]   (LCLS)
Ar Lw .... Archiv fuer Liturgiewissenschaft [*A publication*]
ARM.......... Abstracts of Research and Related Materials in Vocational and Technical Education [*A publication*]
ARM.......... Accredited Resident Manager [*Designation awarded by Institute of Real Estate Management of the National Association of Realtors*]
ARM.......... Action Research Model [*Program of Keep America Beautiful, Inc.*]
ARM.......... Adjustable Rate Mortgage
ARM.......... Advanced Rifle Marksmanship [*Military*]   (INF)
ARM.......... African Resistance Movement [*South Africa*]   (PD)
ARM.......... Agent Reference Material [*Used by airline agents*]
ARM.......... Aircraft Regression Model   (MCD)
ARM.......... Algorithmic Remote Manipulation [*Programming language*]
ARM.......... All Risk Management [*Insurance*]
ARM.......... Allergy Recognition and Management, Inc. [*Australia*]
ARM.......... Allergy Relief Medicine [*Trademark*]
ARM.......... Alliance Reformee Mondiale [*World Alliance of Reformed Churches - WARC*] [*Geneva, Switzerland*]   (EAIO)
ARM.......... Amateur Radio Monitor
ARM.......... Anhysteretic Remanent Magnetization
ARM.......... Animal Rights Mobilization   (EA)
ARM.......... AntiRADAR Missile
ARM.......... Antiradiation Missile
ARM.......... Apollo Requirements Manual [*NASA*]   (KSC)
ARM.......... Applied Research Management
ARM.......... Archives Royales de Mari [*A publication*]
ARM.......... Area Radiation Monitor   (NRCH)
ARM.......... Armada Gold & Mining [*Vancouver Stock Exchange symbol*]

ARM.......... Armadillo Airways Helicopters [*Houston, TX*] [*FAA designator*]   (FAAC)
ARM.......... Armament
ARM.......... Armature   (KSC)
ARM.......... Armed Resistance Movement   (EA)
ARM.......... Armed Revolutionary Movement [*Puerto Rico*]
ARM.......... Armenia
arm.......... Armenian [*MARC language code*] [*Library of Congress*]   (LCCP)
ARM.......... Armidale [*Australia*] [*Airport symbol*]   (OAG)
ARM.......... Arming   (MSA)
ARM.......... Armored   (CINC)
ARM.......... Armorican
ARM.......... Armtek Corp. [*NYSE symbol*]   (SPSG)
ARM.......... Army Ready Materiel
ArM .... Arte (Milan) [*A publication*]
ARM.......... Artificial Rupture of Membranes [*Medicine*]
ARM.......... Assistant Regional Manager
ARM.......... Association of Railway Museums   (EA)
ARM.......... Association of Recovering Motorcyclists   (EA)
ARM.......... Association of Rotational Molders   (EA)
ARM.......... Asynchronous Response Mode [*Data processing*]
ARM.......... Atmosphere Radiation Monitor   (IEEE)
ARM.......... Atomic Resolution Microscope
ARM.......... Attenuated RADAR Monitor
ARM.......... Automated RADAR Monitor System
ARM.......... Automated Route Management   (DEN)
ARM.......... Automatic Reel Mounting
ARM.......... Availability, Reliability, and Maintainability [*Computer performance*]
ARM.......... Aviation Radioman [*Navy*]
ARM.......... Heavy Machinery Repair Ship [*Navy symbol*]
ARM.......... Internal Revenue Bureau Committee on Appeals and Review, Memorandum [*United States*] [*A publication*]   (DLA)
ARM.......... Rocky Mountain Region [*FAA*]   (FAAC)
ARM.......... Rockyford Municipal Library, Alberta [*Library symbol*] [*National Library of Canada*]   (NLC)
ARM.......... Wharton, TX [*Location identifier*] [*FAA*]   (FAAL)
ARMA ...... Accumulator Reservoir Manifold Assembly
ARMA ...... American Bosch Arma Corp.   (AAG)
ARMA ...... American Registry of Medical Assistants   (EA)
ARMA ...... Armature
ARMA ...... Army Attache
ARMA ...... Asphalt Roofing Manufacturers Association   (EA)
ARMA ...... Association of Records Managers and Administrators   (EA)
ARMA ...... Autoregressive Moving Average [*Statistics*]
ARMAAP ... Army Resource Management Advisory and Assessment Program
ARMAC .... Aviation Radioman, Combat Aircrewman [*Navy*]
ARMACS.. Aviation Resources Management and Control System
ARMAD.... Armored and Mechanized Unit Air Defense [*Army*]
ARMADA ... American Record Merchandisers and Distributors Association [*Defunct*]   (EA)
ArMagS..... Southern State College, Magnolia, AR [*Library symbol*] [*Library of Congress*]   (LCLS)
Arma Int .... Armada International [*A publication*]
ARMAN ... Artificial Methods Analyst   (MCD)
ARMATSC ... Army Materiel Status Committees   (AABC)
ARMB ...... Army Requirements and Management Board
ARMC .... American Resources Management [*NASDAQ symbol*]   (NQ)
ARMC .... Architecture, Mouvement, Continuite [*A publication*]
ArmC .... Arms Control and Disarmament [*A publication*]
ARMCA .... Annual Review of Medicine [*A publication*]
ARMCAH ... Annual Review of Medicine [*A publication*]
ARMCBI ... Annual Reports in Medicinal Chemistry [*A publication*]
Armchair Det ... [*The*] Armchair Detective [*A publication*]
ARMCM ... Associate, Royal Manchester College of Music [*British*]   (ROG)
ARMCOM ... Armament Command [*Army*]   (AABC)
ARMD ...... American Red Magen David for Israel [*An association*]
Arm D .... [*The*] Armchair Detective [*A publication*]
ARMD....... Armed   (CINC)
ARMD....... Armored   (AFM)
ARMD....... Armored Division [*Army*]
Armdale & Dist Hist Soc J & Proc ... Armidale and District Historical Society. Journal and Proceedings [*A publication*]   (APTA)
ARMDAS ... Army Damage Assessment System   (AABC)
ARMDEV ... Arming Device
ARMDI .... American Red Magen David for Israel   (EA)
ARME .... Automatic Reseau Measuring Equipment   (MCD)
ARMEA .... American Railway Magazine Editors Association [*Later, Association of Railroad Editors*]   (EA)
ARMEA .... Arizona Medicine [*A publication*]
ARMEAN ... Arizona Medicine [*A publication*]
ARMED .... Armement [*A publication*]
ARMED .... Army Medical Department
ARMEDASH ... Armed Advanced Scout Helicopter   (AABC)
Armed Forces Chem J ... Armed Forces Chemical Journal [*A publication*]
Armed Forces Med J (Arab Repub Egypt) ... Armed Forces Medical Journal (Arab Republic of Egypt) [*A publication*]
Armed Forces Med J (India) ... Armed Forces Medical Journal (India) [*A publication*]

Armed Forces Soc ... Armed Forces and Society [*A publication*]
Armed Forces & Soc ... Armed Forces and Society [*A publication*]
Armees Aujourd ... Armees d'Aujourd'hui [*A publication*]
Armement Bull Inf Liaison ... Armement. Bulletin d'Information et de Liaison [*A publication*]
Armen .... Armenian (BJA)
Armenian N J ... Armenian Numismatic Journal [*A publication*]
ARMET ..... Area Forecast of Upper Winds and Temperatures [*Aviation code*] (FAAC)
ARMF .... Advanced Reactivity Measurement Facility [*Department of Energy*] [*Idaho Falls, ID*]
ARMF .... All-Russian Monarchist Front (EA)
Arm FJ Int ... Armed Forces Journal International [*A publication*]
Arm Frc ..... Armed Forces [*A publication*]
ARMGRD .... Armed Guard (MUGU)
ARMH .... Academy of Religion and Mental Health [*Later, Institutes of Religion and Health*]
ARMH .... Association for Rural Mental Health [*Later, NARMH*] (EA)
ARMH .... Rocky Mountain House Public Library, Alberta [*Library symbol*] [*National Library of Canada*] (NLC)
Arm Hist Soc J ... Armidale Historical Society. Journal [*A publication*]
ARMHS .... American Rat, Mouse, and Hamster Society (EA)
ARMI .... American Research Merchandising Institute [*Later, NASM*] (EA)
ARMI .... Associated Risk Managers International [*Austin, TX*] (EA)
ARMIA ...... Annual Review of Microbiology [*A publication*]
ARMIAZ ... Annual Review of Microbiology [*A publication*]
Armidale Dist Hist Soc J ... Armidale and District Historical Society. Journal [*A publication*] (APTA)
Armidale Hist Soc J ... Armidale and District Historical Society. Journal [*A publication*] (APTA)
Armidale New Engl Univ Explor Soc Rep ... Armidale. University of New England. Exploration Society. Report [*A publication*] (APTA)
Armidale Teach Coll Bull ... Armidale Teachers' College. Bulletin [*A publication*] (APTA)
Armid Teach Coll Bul ... Armidale Teachers' College. Bulletin [*A publication*] (APTA)
ARMINGF ... Armingford [*England*]
ARMIP ...... Accounting and Reporting Management Improvement Program [*Army*] (AABC)
ARMIS ...... Arsenal Management Information System
ARMISH ... United States Military Mission with the Iranian Army
ARMIS-LOG ... Armor Management Information System - Logistics
Armjan Gos Ped Inst Sb Naucn Trud Ser Fiz-Mat ... Armjanskii Gosudarstvennyi Pedagogiceskii Institut Imeni H. Abovjana. Sbornik Naucnyh Trudov. Serija Fiziko-Matematiceskaja [*A publication*]
Arm Khim Zh ... Armyanskii Khimicheskii Zhurnal [*A publication*]
ARML .... Airmail (FAAC)
ARMLA ...... Ayn Rand Memorial Library Association [*Defunct*] (EA)
ARMLO ...... Army Liaison Officer (MCD)
ARMM ...... Accelerated Refuge Maintenance Management [*Department of the Interior*]
ARMM ...... Analysis and Research of Methods for Management
ARMM ...... Association of Reproduction Materials Manufacturers (EA)
ARMMA ... American Railway Master Mechanics' Association
Arm Mac & Og ... Armstrong, Macartney, and Ogle's Irish Nisi Prius Reports [*A publication*] (DLA)
Arm M & O ... Armstrong, Macartney, and Ogle's Irish Nisi Prius Reports [*A publication*] (DLA)
ARMMS .... Automated Reliability and Maintenance Management [*or Measurement*] System [*Navy*] (NG)
ARMMS .... Automatically Reconfigurable Modular Multiprocessor [*or Multiprocessing*] System [*Data processing*]
ARMM/TTC ... Auxiliary Removable Memory Media/Tape-Transport Cartridge (MCD)
ARMN .... Airman [*British military*] (DMA)
Arm Nauchno-Issled Inst Stroit Mater Sooruzh Nauchn Soobshch ... Armyanskii Nauchno-Issledovatel'skii Institut Stroitel'nykh Materialov i Sooruzhenii Nauchnye Soobshcheniya [*A publication*]
ARMND .... Annales de Radiologie. Medecine Nucleaire [*A publication*]
Arm & O .... Armstrong, Macartney, and Ogle's Irish Nisi Prius Reports [*A publication*] (DLA)
ArMonD .... Southeast Arkansas Regional Library, Monticello, AR [*Library symbol*] [*Library of Congress*] (LCLS)
ARMOP .... Army Mortar Program (RDA)
Armored Cavalry J ... Armored Cavalry Journal [*A publication*]
Armotsem Konstr ... Armotsementnye Konstruktsii [*A publication*]
Armour .... Manitoba Queen's Bench Tempore Wood, by Armour [*A publication*] (DLA)
Armour Res Found Rep ... Armour Research Foundation. Report [*A publication*]
ARMP ...... Allied Reliability and Maintainability Publication (MCD)
ARMP ...... Average Revenue/Marginal Physical Product [*Economics*]
ARMPEQ ... Annales de Readaptation et de Medecine Physique [*A publication*]
ARM-PL .... Armor Plate (KSC)
ARMR .... Armor All Products Corp. [*Irvine, CA*] [*NASDAQ symbol*] (NQ)

ARMR .... Armorer (AABC)
ARMR .... Army Readiness and Mobilization Regions (MCD)
Arm Rev ..... Armenian Review [*A publication*]
ARMREW ... Applied Research in Mental Retardation [*A publication*]
ARMS .... Acid Rain Mitigation Strategies
ARMS .... Action Research into Multiple Sclerosis [*See also Arms of America - AA*] [*British*]
ARMS .... ADPE [*Automatic Data Processing Equipment*] Resources Management System (AFM)
ARMS .... Advanced Receiver Model System
ARMS .... Aerial Radiological Measurement and Survey [*Program*]
ARMS .... Aerial Radiological Measurements System [*Nuclear energy*] (NRCH)
ARMS .... Aircraft Readiness Maintainability Simulator (MCD)
ARMS .... Aircraft Reliability and Maintainability Simulation
ARMS .... Aircraft Resources Management System [*Military*]
ARMS .... AMDF [*Army Master Data File*] Reader Microfilm System [*Formerly, AMDFRMS*] (AABC)
ARMS .... Ammunition Reporting Management System [*Air Force*] (AFM)
ARMS .... Application of Remote Manipulators in Space [*Robot*] [*NASA*]
ARMS .... Archaeological Resources Management Service [*Ball State Univesity*] [*Research center*] (RCD)
ARMS .... Area Radiological Monitoring System (NRCH)
ARMS .... Army Readiness Management [*or Measurement*] System (MCD)
ARMS .... Associate of the Royal Society of Miniature Painters [*British*]
ARMS .... Association of Racquetsports Manufacturers and Suppliers [*Inactive*] (EA)
ARMS .... Association of Researchers in Medical Sciences [*British*]
ARMS .... Atmospheric or Remote Manipulator System [*Deep-sea diving*]
ARMS .... Automated RADAR Measurement System
ARMS .... Automated Range Management System (MCD)
ARMS .... Automated Resource Management System (MCD)
ARMS .... Automatic Radiation Monitoring System (MCD)
ARMS .... Automatic Receiving and Measuring System (MCD)
ARMS .... Automatic Remote Manned System (MCD)
ARMS .... Automatic Reporting Maintenance System (MCD)
ARMS .... Automotive Repair Management Systems [*3M Co.*]
ARMS .... [*Special*] Aviation Resources Management Survey Team (MCD)
Arms Br P Cas ... Armstrong's Breach of Privilege Cases, New York [*A publication*] (DLA)
Arms Con El ... Armstrong. Contested Election Cases [*New York*] [*A publication*] (DLA)
Arms Con Elec ... Armstrong's New York Contested Elections [*A publication*] (DLA)
Arms Con T ... Arms Control Today [*A publication*]
ARMSEF ... Atmospheric Reentry Materials and Structural Evaluation Facility (MCD)
Arms Elect Cas ... Armstrong's Cases of Contested Elections, New York [*A publication*] (DLA)
Arms Explos ... Arms and Explosives [*A publication*]
ARMSHT ... Armature Shunt [*Electromagnetism*]
ARMSLC ... Army Missile Command (MUGU)
Arms Mac & Og ... Armstrong, Macartney, and Ogle's Irish Nisi Prius Reports [*A publication*] (DLA)
Arms M & O ... Armstrong, Macartney, and Ogle's Irish Nisi Prius Reports [*A publication*] (DLA)
ARMSPAC ... Aircraft Resources Management System, Pacific [*Military*] (NVT)
ArmSSR ..... Armenian Soviet Socialist Republic
Arms Tr ..... Armstrong's Limerick Trials [*Ireland*] [*A publication*] (DLA)
Armstrong M & O (Ir) ... Armstrong, Macartney, and Ogle's Irish Nisi Prius Reports [*A publication*] (DLA)
ARMT .... Archives Royales de Mari. Textes Administratives [*A publication*]
ARMT .... Archives Royales de Mari. Transcriptions et Traductions [*Paris*] [*A publication*]
ARMT .... Armament (AFM)
ARMT .... Australian Register of Massage Therapists
ARMTE ..... Army Materiel Test and Evaluation Directorate [*White Sands Missile Range, NM*]
ARMTE ..... Army Missile Test and Evaluation
armtr .... Armature
ARMU .... Addressable Remote Multiplexer Unit (MCD)
ARMU .... Associated Rocky Mountain Universities [*AEC*]
ARMUA3 .. American Malacological Union, Incorporated. Annual Report [*A publication*]
ARMUB .... Arts et Manufactures [*A publication*]
ARMVAL ... Advanced Antiarmor Vehicle Evaluation Test (RDA)
ARMY .... Armistice Resources Ltd. [*NASDAQ symbol*] (NQ)
Army .... Australian Army [*A publication*] (APTA)
Army Adm ... Army Administrator [*A publication*]
Armyanskii Khim Zh ... Armyanskii Khimicheskii Zhurnal [*A publication*]
Army Av D ... US Army. Aviation Digest [*A publication*]
Army Comm ... Army Communicator [*United States*] [*A publication*]
Army Law .. Army Lawyer [*A publication*]
Army Lawy ... Army Lawyer [*A publication*]
Army Log ... Army Logistician [*United States*] [*A publication*]
Army Logis ... Army Logistician [*A publication*]

Army Med Bull ... Army Medical Bulletin [*A publication*]
Army Med Dept Rep (London) ... Army Medical Department. Reports (London) [*A publication*]
Army Q Def J ... Army Quarterly and Defence Journal [*A publication*]
Army Res & Devel ... Army Research and Development [*Later, R, D & A*] [*A publication*]
Army Reserv ... Army Reserve Magazine [*A publication*]
ARN .... Aboth [*or Avot*] d'Rabbi Nathan (BJA)
ARN .... Acorn Resources Ltd. [*Vancouver Stock Exchange symbol*]
ARN .... Additional Reference Number [*NASA*] (NASA)
ARN .... Air Reporting Net (NATG)
ARN .... Airborne RADAR Navigational Aid (MCD)
ARN .... Airborne Radio Navigation
ARN .... Alteration Request Number
ARN .... Animal Rights Network (EA)
arn .... Araucanian [*MARC language code*] [*Library of Congress*] (LCCP)
ARN .... Arnold Ranch [*California*] [*Seismograph station code, US Geological Survey*] (SEIS)
Arn .... Arnold's English Common Pleas Reports [*1838-39*] [*A publication*] (DLA)
Arn .... Arnot's Criminal Trials [*1536-1784*] [*Scotland*] [*A publication*] (DLA)
Arn .... Arnould on Marine Insurance [*A publication*] (DLA)
ARN .... Association of Rehabilitation Nurses (EA)
ARN .... Atmospheric Radio Noise
ARN .... Australian Radio Network
ARN .... Stockholm [*Sweden*] Arlanda Airport [*Airport symbol*] (OAG)
ARNA .... Alfa Romeo Nissan Autoveicoli [*Italian-Japanese alliance for the joint manufacture of automobiles with Alfa engines and Nissan bodies*]
ARNA .... Arab Revolution News Agency
ARNA .... Army with Navy [*Personnel*]
ARNA .... Association of Radio News Analysts [*Later, ARTNA*]
ARNAAG .. Annuaire Roumain d'Anthropologie [*A publication*]
ARNBBK ... Archivos de Neurobiologia [*A publication*]
ARNCAM ... Agronomia [*La Molina*] [*A publication*]
ARND .... Arctic and Northern Development Digest [*A publication*]
ARND .... Around (FAAC)
ARNE .... Accion Revolucionaria Nacional Ecuatoriana [*National Revolutionary Action*] [*Ecuador*] [*Political party*]
ARNE .... Accountant's Resource Network [*Information service or system*] (EISS)
ARNE .... Arctic News [*A publication*]
ARNEA ..... Archives of Neurology [*A publication*]
ARNEAS ... Archives of Neurology [*A publication*]
ArNeJM .... James Logan Morgan, Jr., Newport, AR [*Library symbol*] [*Library of Congress*] (LCLS)
Arn El Cas ... Arnold's Election Cases [*England*] [*A publication*] (DLA)
ARNG .... Arcing (MSA)
ARNG .... Army National Guard
ARNG .... Arrange (AABC)
ARNG-TSP ... Army National Guard Troop Structure Program
ARNGUS .. Army National Guard of the United States
Arn & H ..... Arnold and Hodges' English Queen's Bench Reports [*1840-41*] [*A publication*] (DLA)
Arn & HBC ... Arnold and Hodges' English Bail Court Reports [*A publication*] (DLA)
Arn & Hod ... Arnold and Hodges' English Queen's Bench Reports [*1840-41*] [*A publication*] (DLA)
Arn & Hod BC ... Arnold and Hodges' English Bail Court Reports [*A publication*] (DLA)
Arn & Hod PC ... Arnold and Hodges' English Practice Cases [*A publication*] (DLA)
Arn & Hod Pr Cas ... Arnold and Hodges' English Practice Cases [*A publication*] (DLA)
ARNI .... Association of Rhodesian and Nyasaland Industries
Arn Ins .... Arnould on Marine Insurance [*A publication*] (DLA)
ARN J .... American Rehabilitation Nursing Journal [*A publication*]
ARN J .... ARN [*Association of Rehabilitation Nurses*] Journal [*A publication*]
ARNLBG ... Archiv fuer Naturschutz und Landschaftsforschung [*A publication*]
ARNMD .... Association for Research in Nervous and Mental Disease (EA)
ARNMDL ... Applied Radiology and Nuclear Medicine [*Later, Applied Radiology*] [*A publication*]
Arn Mun Cor ... Arnold's Municipal Corporations [*A publication*] (DLA)
ARNNA ..... Annual Report. National Institute of Nutrition [*A publication*]
ARNO .... Air Indicator Not Operating [*Aviation*] (FAAC)
ARNO .... Association of Retired Naval Officers [*British military*] (DMA)
ARNOAO ... Arnoldia [*Boston*] [*A publication*]
Arnold .... Arnold's English Common Pleas Reports [*1838-39*] [*A publication*] (DLA)
Arnold Arboretum J ... Arnold Arboretum. Journal [*A publication*]
Arnold Arbor J ... Harvard University. Arnold Arboretum Journal [*A publication*]
Arnold & H ... Arnold and Hodges' English Queen's Bench Reports [*1840-41*] [*A publication*] (DLA)
Arnold (Zim) ... Arnoldia (Zimbabwe) [*A publication*]
ARNOON ... Afternoon (ROG)
ARNOT ..... Area Office Notice [*FAA*] (FAAC)

Arnot Cr C ... Arnot's Criminal Cases [*1536-1784*] [*Scotland*] [*A publication*] (DLA)
ARNOVA .. Association for Research on Nonprofit Organizations and Voluntary Action (EA)
ARNP .... Advanced Registered Nurse Practitioner
ARNPBS ... Arnoldia Rhodesia [*A publication*]
Arn Pub M ... Arnold. Public Meetings and Political Societies [*1833*] [*A publication*] (DLA)
Arn Pub Meet ... Arnold. Public Meetings and Political Societies [*1833*] [*A publication*] (DLA)
ARNS .... Airborne Reference Noise Source (MCD)
ARNSD5 ... Annual Review of Neuroscience [*A publication*]
AR(NSW) ... Industrial Arbitration Reports (New South Wales) [*A publication*]
ARNTD8 ... Annual Review of Nutrition [*A publication*]
ARNUA ..... Annual Review of Nuclear Science [*Later, Annual Review of Nuclear and Particle Science*] [*A publication*]
ARNUA8 ... Annual Review of Nuclear Science [*Later, Annual Review of Nuclear and Particle Science*] [*A publication*]
ArNVA ...... Arbok det Norske Videnskapsakademi [*A publication*]
ARNX .... ARNOX Corp. [*Greenwich, CT*] [*NASDAQ symbol*] (NQ)
ARNYA ..... Annual Report. Natural Science Research Institute. Yonsei University [*A publication*]
ARO .... Advanced Research Objective (MCD)
ARO .... Aerial Refueling Operator (MCD)
ARO .... After Receipt of Order
ARO .... Air Radio Officer
ARO .... Air Traffic Services Reporting Office [*Aviation*]
ARO .... Airborne Range Only [*RADAR ranging set for use with various gun computers*]
ARO .... Airport Reservation Office (FAAC)
ARO .... Algonquin Radio Observatory [*Research center*] (RCD)
ARO .... Alignment Requirements Outline (MCD)
ARO .... All Rods Out [*Nuclear energy*] (NRCH)
ARO .... Anciennes Religions Orientales [*A publication*]
ARO .... Applied Research Objective
ARO .... Arboletas [*Colombia*] [*Airport symbol*] (OAG)
ArO .... Archiv Orientalni [*A publication*]
ARO .... Area Records Officer (MCD)
ARO .... Armeno Resources, Inc. [*Vancouver Stock Exchange symbol*]
ARO .... Army Research Office [*Research Triangle Park, NC*]
ARO .... Army Routine Order
ARO .... Arrow Aviation Ltd. [*Abbotsford, BC*] [*FAA designator*] (FAAC)
ARO .... Arta Observatory [*Djibouti*] (SEIS)
ARO .... Asian Regional Organization
ARO .... Assembly and Rework Operation
ARO .... Assistant Research Officer [*Ministry of Agriculture, Fisheries, and Food*] [*British*]
ARO .... Association for Research in Ophthalmology [*Later, ARVO*] (EA)
ARO .... Automatic Range Only
ARO .... Auxiliary Readout (CAAL)
ARO .... Rosemary Public Library, Alberta [*Library symbol*] [*National Library of Canada*] (NLC)
AROABM ... Agroanimalia [*A publication*]
AROBDR .. Acta Radiologica. Oncology [*A publication*]
AROC .... Air Rescue Operations Center [*Air Force*]
AROC .... Alfa Romeo Owners Club (EA)
AROC .... Rochester Public Library, Alberta [*Library symbol*] [*National Library of Canada*] (NLC)
AROCC ..... Association for Research of Childhood Cancer (EA)
AROD .... Airborne Ranging and Orbit Determination System
AROD .... Airborne Remotely Operated Device [*Marine Corps*]
ARO-D ...... Army Research Office - Durham
ARODS ..... Airborne RADAR Orbital Determination System
ARODYN ... Aerodynamics
ARO-E ...... Army Research Office - Europe
AROF .... Arctic Offshore. Publication of the Alaska Oil and Gas Association [*A publication*]
AROF .... Atomic Resonance Optical Filter (MCD)
ARO-FE .... Army Research Office - Far East (AABC)
AROHA8 ... Archives d'Ophtalmologie et Revue Generale d'Ophtalmologie [*A publication*]
AROI .... Annual Return of Investment [*Business term*]
ARO-ICFTU ... Asian Regional Organization - International Confederation of Free Trade Unions
ARO-J .... Army Research Office - Japan
AROM .... Active Range of Motion [*Medicine*]
AROM .... Alterable Read-Only Memory [*Data processing*]
ARom .... Archivum Romanicum [*A publication*]
AROM .... Aromatic (MSA)
Aroma Res Proc Int Symp A ... Aroma Research. Proceedings of the International Symposium on Aroma Research. Central Institute for Nutrition and Food Research [*A publication*]
AROMAT ... Aromatica [*Essence*] [*Chemistry*] (ROG)
Aromat Amino Acids Brain Symp ... Aromatic Amino Acids in the Brain. Symposium [*A publication*]
Aromat Heteroaromat Chem ... Aromatic and Heteroaromatic Chemistry [*A publication*]
ARON .... Aaron Rents, Inc. [*NASDAQ symbol*] (NQ)

ARONDT .. Acta Radiologica. Oncology, Radiation Therapy, Physics, and Biology [*A publication*]
AR (Ont).... Ontario Appeal Reports [*A publication*] (DLA)
AROP .... Activity Reorder Point [*Military*] (AFIT)
AROPAW ... Archives of Ophthalmology [*A publication*]
AROPDZ... Archives d'Ophtalmologie [*A publication*]
AROPS...... Association of Representatives of Old Pupils' Societies [*British*]
Ar Or......... Archiv Orientalni [*A publication*]
ARORA ..... Archivio di Ortopedia [*Later, Archivio di Ortopedia e Reumatologia*] [*A publication*]
AROS .... Advance Ross Corp. [*NASDAQ symbol*] (NQ)
AROS .... Alterable Read-Only Operating System [*Data processing*]
AROTA ...... Archives of Otolaryngology [*A publication*]
AROTAA ... Archives of Otolaryngology [*A publication*]
AROTC ..... Air Reserve Officers' Training Corps [*Air Force*]
AROU........ Aviation Repair and Overhaul Unit
AROUSPHS ... Association of Reserve Officers of the US Public Health Service (EA)
AROW....... Apprenticeship, Referral, and Outreach for Women [*An association*] [*Defunct*] (EA)
AROW....... Arrow Bank Corp. [*NASDAQ symbol*] (NQ)
AROWA .... Applied Research: Operation Weather Analysis [*Navy*]
AROWF .... Association of Retailer-Owned Wholesalers in Foodstuffs [*Later, ACROWE*] (EAIO)
AROY .... American Romanian Orthodox Youth (EA)
AROY .... Armeno Resources, Inc. [*NASDAQ symbol*] (NQ)
A Rozhl ..... Archeologicke Rozhledy [*A publication*]
ARP .... Abrasion-Resistant Print Coating [*for plastic laminates*] [*Nevamar*]
ARP .... Absolute Refractory Period
ARP .... Account Reconciliation Plan
ARP .... Acres, Roods, Perches [*Land measurement*] [*British*] (ROG)
ARP .... Address Resolution Protocol (BYTE)
ARP .... Adult Retraining Program
ARP .... Advanced Reentry Program [*Aerospace*]
ARP .... Advanced Research Projects
ARP .... Aerodrome Reference Point (FAAC)
ARP .... Aeronautical [*or Aerospace*] Recommended Practice
ARP .... Aerospace Recommended Practice (MCD)
ARP .... Aerospace Reference Project [*Formerly, ATP*] [*Library of Congress*]
ARP .... After Receipt of Proposal
ARP .... Air Raid Precautions [*British*] [*World War II*]
ARP .... Air Raid Protection (NATG)
ARP .... Air Refueling Probe
ARP .... Air Report [*Aviation*]
ARP .... Airborne RADAR Platform [*Air Force*]
ARP .... Aircraft Reference Point
ARP .... Aircrew Respiratory Protection
ARP .... Airport Reference Point
ARP .... Airport Reservation Position (FAAC)
ARP .... Airports [*Public-performance tariff class*] [*British*]
ARP .... Alternative Release Procedures (MCD)
ARP .... Alternator Research Package
ARP .... Altitude Reconnaissance Probe (MUGU)
ARP .... American Registry of Pathologists
ARP .... American Registry of Pathology (EA)
ARP .... American Relief for Poland [*Defunct*] (EA)
ARP .... Ammunition Refilling Point
ARP .... Analytical Rework Program [*Navy*] (NG)
ARP .... Angle-Resolved Photoemission (MCD)
ARP .... Animal Resources Program [*Bethesda, MD*] [*Department of Health and Human Services*] (GRD)
ARP .... Annunciator Response Procedure [*Nuclear energy*] (NRCH)
ARP .... Antenna Radiation Pattern
ARP .... Anti-Revolutionaire Partij - Evangelische Volkspartij [*Antirevolutionary Party*] [*Netherlands*] [*Political party*] (PPW)
ARP .... Antilles Research Program [*Yale University*]
ARP .... Antiradiation Projectile
ARP .... Aragip [*Papua New Guinea*] [*Airport symbol*] (OAG)
ar p .... Arany Pengo [*Gold Pengo (Hungarian currency in 1925-45, still used to estimate real estate values)*]
arp.............. Arapaho [*MARC language code*] [*Library of Congress*] (LCCP)
ARP .... Arbeiten zur Romanischen Philologie [*A publication*]
ARp............ Archaeological Report Comprising the Recent Work of the Egypt Exploration Fund and the Progress of Egyptology [*London*] [*A publication*]
ARP .... Archaeology Research Program [*Southern Methodist University*] [*Research center*] (RCD)
Ar (P) .... Archeologia (Paris) [*A publication*]
ARP .... Arctic Red Resources [*Vancouver Stock Exchange symbol*]
ARP .... Area Redevelopment Program
Arp............ Ariprandus [*Flourished, 12th century*] [*Authority cited in pre-1607 legal work*] (DSA)
ARP .... Armament Recording Program [*Military*]
ARP .... Army Research Plan
Arp............ Arpeggio [*Record label*] [*Italy*]
ARP .... Arpeggio [*Music*]
ArP............ Aryan Path [*A publication*]
ARP .... As-Run Procedure [*Military*] (MCD)

ARP .... Assisted Rental Program [*Canada*]
ARP .... Associated Reformed Presbyterian
ARP .... Association for Realistic Philosophy [*Defunct*] (EA)
ARP .... Association of Retired Persons International [*Later, IARP*]
ARP .... Attack Reference Point
ARP .... Autofocus RADAR Projector
ARP .... Automatic Recovery Process (MCD)
ARP .... Automatic Reporting Post [*Air defense*] [*NATO*] (NATG)
ARP .... Aviation Regulatory Proposal [*Australia*]
ARP .... Azimuth Reference Pulse [*Aviation*] (FAAC)
ARP .... Azimuth Reset Pulse
ARPA........ Advanced Research Projects Agency [*Later, DARPA*] [*DoD*]
ARPA........ American Rape Prevention Association (EA)
ARPA........ American Red Poll Association (EA)
ARPA........ Archeological Resources Protection Act [*1979*]
ARPA........ Arctic Research and Policy Act of 1984
ARPA........ Association pour les Recherches sur les Parodontopathies [*International Association for Research in Paradentosis*]
ARPA........ Association of Representatives of Professional Athletes (EA)
ARPA........ Australian Reinforced Plastics Association
ARPA........ Automatic RADAR Plotting Aids
ARPAAQ... Archives of Pathology [*Later, Archives of Pathology and Laboratory Medicine*] [*A publication*]
ARPAC...... Agricultural Research Policy Advisory Committee [*Terminated, 1977*] [*Department of Agriculture*]
ARPAC...... Army Pacific (CINC)
ARPAD...... Army Armament Research and Development Command Product Assurance Directorate
ARPANET ... Advanced Research Projects Agency Network [*DoD*]
ArPapF ..... Archiv fuer Papyrusforschung [*Leipzig*] [*A publication*]
ARPAS...... Air Reserve Pay and Allowance System
ARPAS...... Automated Resource Planning and Analysis System (MCD)
ARPAT...... Advanced Research Projects Agency Terminal [*DoD*]
ArPb.......... Pine Bluff and Jefferson County Public Library, Pine Bluff, AR [*Library symbol*] [*Library of Congress*] (LCLS)
ArPbUA..... University of Arkansas at Pine Bluff, Pine Bluff, AR [*Library symbol*] [*Library of Congress*] (LCLS)
ARPC........ Air Raid Precautions Controller [*British*] [*World War II*]
ARPC........ Air Reserve Personnel Center [*Air Force*]
ARPC........ Annual Report Producers Council
ARPCS...... Atmospheric Revitalization Pressure Control System (MCD)
ARPD .... Advanced Research Planning Document
ARPD .... Advanced Research Program Directive (MCD)
ARPDP...... Association of Rehabilitation Programs in Data Processing (EA)
ARPE........ American Registry of Professional Entomologists (EA)
ARPE........ Army Physiological Research Establishment [*British*]
ARPEA4.... Archives of Pediatrics [*A publication*]
ARPEFS.... Angle-Resolved Photoemission Extended Fine Structure [*Analytical technique*]
ARPEL ...... Asistencia Reciproca Petrolera Estatal Latinoamericana [*Mutual Assistance of the Latin American Government Oil Companies*] (EAIO)
ARPERCEN ... Army Reserve Personnel Center [*St. Louis, MO*] (INF)
ARPES ...... Angle-Resolved Photoelectron Spectroscopy
ARPESH ... Accurate and Reliable Prototype Earth Sensor Head [*NASA*]
Ar Pf .... Archiv fuer Papyrusforschung [*A publication*]
ARPG .... Asphalt Rubber Producers Group (EA)
ARPH .... Annual Review of Public Health [*A publication*]
ARPh .... Archiv fuer Rechts- und Wirtschaftsphilosophie [*A publication*]
Ar Ph......... Archives de Philosophie [*A publication*]
ARPHA ...... Annual Review of Physiology [*A publication*]
ARPHAD .. Annual Review of Physiology [*A publication*]
ARPI.......... Absolute Rod Position Indication [*Nuclear energy*] (NRCH)
ARPI.......... Automotive Refrigeration Products Institute (EA)
ARPIC .... Aerospace Radioisotope Power Information Center (KSC)
ARPLA ...... Annual Review of Physical Chemistry [*A publication*]
ARPM .... Average Revenue per Message
ARPMA..... Advanced Remotely Piloted Modular Aircraft (MCD)
ARPMAS .. Archiv der Pharmazie [*Weinheim, Germany*] [*A publication*]
ARPN .... Aircraft and Related Procurement, Navy
Arpn.......... Ariprandus [*Flourished, 12th century*] [*Authority cited in pre-1607 legal work*] (DSA)
ARPO .... Air Raid Precautions Officer [*British*] [*World War II*]
ARPO .... Applied Research Program
ARPO .... Arkansas Post National Monument
ARPO .... Arpeggio [*Music*]
ARPP......... Africa Research and Publications Project (EA)
ARPPA ...... Annual Review of Plant Physiology [*A publication*]
ARPPA3 .... Annual Review of Plant Physiology [*A publication*]
ARPPRN ... Adenine-D-ribose-phosphate-phosphate-D-ribose-nicotinamide [*Also, NAD, DPN*] [*Biochemistry*]
ARPR......... Academy of Religion and Psychical Research (EA)
ARPR........ Advanced RADAR Pattern Recognition
ARPR........ Arctic Policy Review [*A publication*]
ARPR........ Automatic RADAR Pattern Recognition (MCD)
ARPRD...... Arbitrazni Praxe [*A publication*]
ArPreC....... Nevada County Library, Prescott, AR [*Library symbol*] [*Library of Congress*] (LCLS)
Ar Preg....... Arheoloski Pregled [*A publication*]
ARPRINT ... Army Program for Individual Training

ARPROIMREP ... Arrival Further Proceed Immediately and Report [*Navy*]
ARPROPORICH ... Arrival Furthèr Proceed Port in which Activity Designated May Be [*Navy*]
ARPRT ...... Airport
ARPS .... Adjustable Rate Preferred Stock
ARPS .... Advanced RADAR Processing System
ARPS .... Aerospace Research Pilot School [*Air Force*]
ARPS .... Air Reserve Pay System   (AFM)
ARPs .... Archiv fuer Religionspsychologie [*A publication*]
ARPS .... Associate of the Royal Photographic Society [*British*]
ARPS .... Association of Railway Preservation Societies Ltd. [*British*]
ARPS .... Automatic RADAR Plotting System [*Collision avoidance aid*]
ARPSA ...... Annual Review of Psychology [*A publication*]
ARPSA ...... Army Postal Service Agency   (AFM)
ARPSAC ... Annual Review of Psychology [*A publication*]
ARPSC ...... Amateur Radio Public Service Corps
ARPSD ...... Annual Review of Nuclear and Particle Science [*A publication*]
ARPSE ...... Aerospace Research Pilot School - Edwards Air Force Base [*Air Force*]
ARPSIM ... Antiradiation Projectile Simulation   (MCD)
ARPT .... Airport
ARPT .... American Registry of Physical Therapists [*Defunct*]   (EA)
ARPT .... Army Registry of Physical Therapists
ARPTA ...... Arkhiv Patologii [*A publication*]
ARPTAF ... Arkhiv Patologii [*A publication*]
ARPTD ...... Annual Review of Pharmacology and Toxicology [*A publication*]
ARPTDI .... Annual Review of Pharmacology and Toxicology [*A publication*]
ARPTT ...... Air Refueling Part Task Trainer
ARPU .... American Racing Pigeon Union   (EA)
ARPV .... Advanced Remotely Piloted Vehicle [*Aviation*]   (AIA)
ARQ .... Andoraq Resources Corp. [*Vancouver Stock Exchange symbol*]
ARQ .... Annual Review Questionnaire [*Military*]   (AABC)
ARQ .... Answer-Return Query
ArQ .... Arizona Quarterly [*A publication*]
ARQ .... Asterriquinone [*Antineoplastic drug*]
ARQ .... Automated Response to Query
ARQ .... Automatic Error Correction [*Aviation*]   (FAAC)
ARQ .... Automatic Error Correction Equipment [*Aviation*]   (FAAC)
ARQ .... Automatic Error Request Equipment [*Aviation*]
ARQ .... Automatic Repeat Request [*Data processing*]   (MCD)
Arq Anat Antrop ... Arquivo de Anatomia e Antropologia [*A publication*]
Arq Anat Antropol ... Arquivo de Anatomia e Antropologia [*A publication*]
Arq Beja ..... Arquivo de Beja [*A publication*]
Arq Biol (Sao Paulo) ... Arquivos de Biologia (Sao Paulo) [*A publication*]
Arq Biol Tecnol ... Arquivos de Biologia e Tecnologia [*A publication*]
Arq Biol Tecnol (Curitiba) ... Arquivos de Biologia e Tecnologia (Curitiba) [*A publication*]
Arq Bot Estado Sao Paulo ... Arquivos de Botanica do Estado de Sao Paulo [*A publication*]
Arq Bras Cardiol ... Arquivos Brasileiros de Cardiologia [*A publication*]
Arq Bras Endocrinol Metabol ... Arquivos Brasileiros de Endocrinologia e Metabologia [*A publication*]
Arq Brasil Cardiol ... Arquivos Brasileiros de Cardiologia [*A publication*]
Arq Bras Med ... Arquivos Brasileiros de Medicina [*A publication*]
Arq Bras Med Nav ... Arquivos Brasileiros de Medicina Naval [*A publication*]
Arq Bras Nutr ... Arquivos Brasileiros de Nutricao [*A publication*]
Arq Bras Oftal ... Arquivos Brasileiros de Oftalmologia [*A publication*]
Arq Bras Oftalmol ... Arquivos Brasileiros de Oftalmologia [*A publication*]
Arq Bras Ps ... Arquivos Brasileiros de Psicologia Aplicada [*A publication*]
Arq Bras Tuberc Doencas Torax ... Arquivos Brasileiros de Tuberculose e Doencas do Torax [*A publication*]
Arq Bromatol ... Arquivos de Bromatologia [*A publication*]
ARQC .... Australian Rope Quoit Council
Arq Catarinenses Med ... Arquivos Catarinenses de Medicina [*A publication*]
Arq Cent Estud Curso Odontol Univ Fed Minas Gerais ... Arquivos. Centro de Estudos do Curso de Odontologia. Universidade Federal de Minas Gerais [*A publication*]
Arq Cent Estud Fac Odontol Univ Fed Minas Gerais ... Arquivos. Centro de Estudos da Faculdade de Odontologia. Universidade Federal de Minas Gerais [*A publication*]
Arq Cent Estud Fac Odontol Univ Minas Gerais (Belo Horiz) ... Arquivos. Centro de Estudos da Faculdade de Odontologia. Universidade de Minas Gerais (Belo Horizonte) [*A publication*]
Arq Centro Cult Port ... Arquivos. Centro Cultural Portugues [*A publication*]
Arq Cienc Mar ... Arquivos de Ciencias do Mar [*A publication*]
Arq Cir Clin Exp (Sao Paulo) ... Arquivos de Cirurgia Clinica e Experimental (Sao Paulo) [*A publication*]
Arq Dep Assist Psicop S Paulo ... Arquivos. Departamento de Assistencia a Psicopates. Estado de Sao Paulo [*A publication*]
Arq Dermatol Sifiligr Sao Paulo ... Arquivos de Dermatologia e Sifiligrafia de Sao Paulo [*A publication*]
Arq Entomol Ser A ... Arquivos de Entomologia. Serie A [*A publication*]
Arq Entomol Ser B ... Arquivos de Entomologia. Serie B [*A publication*]
Arq Esc Super Vet Univ Rur Estado Minas Gerais ... Arquivos. Escola Superior de Veterinaria. Universidade Rural. Estado de Minas Gerais [*A publication*]
Arq Esc Vet Univ Fed Minas Gerais ... Arquivos. Escola de Veterinaria. Universidade Federal de Minas Gerais [*A publication*]

Arq Esc Vet Univ Minas Gerais ... Arquivos. Escola de Veterinaria. Universidade Federal de Minas Gerais [*A publication*]
Arq Estac Biol Mar Univ Ceara ... Arquivos. Estacao de Biologia Marinha da Universidade Federal do Ceara [*A publication*]
Arq Estac Biol Mar Univ Fed Ceara ... Arquivos. Estacao de Biologia Marinha da Universidade Federal do Ceara [*A publication*]
Arq Fac Hig Saude Publica Univ Sao Paulo ... Arquivos. Faculdade de Higiene e Saude Publica. Universidade de Sao Paulo [*A publication*]
Arq Fac Hig S Paul ... Arquivos. Faculdade de Higiene e Saude Publica. Universidade de Sao Paulo [*A publication*]
Arq Fac Nac Med ... Arquivos. Faculdade Nacional de Medicina [*A publication*]
Arq Fac Nac Med (Rio De Janeiro) ... Arquivos. Faculdade Nacional de Medicina (Rio De Janeiro) [*A publication*]
ARQGAF ... Archives of Gastroenterology [*A publication*]
Arq Gastroenterol ... Arquivos de Gastroenterologia [*A publication*]
Arq Geol ...... Arquivos de Geologia [*A publication*]
Arq Hig (Rio De J) ... Arquivos de Higiene (Rio De Janeiro) [*A publication*]
Arq Hig Saude Publica (Sao Paulo) ... Arquivos de Higiene e Saude Publica (Sao Paulo) [*A publication*]
Arq Hyg Saude Publica ... Arquivos de Higiene e Saude Publica [*A publication*]
Arq Inst Anat Univ Rio Grande Do Sul ... Arquivos. Instituto de Anatomia. Universidade do Rio Grande Do Sul [*A publication*]
Arq Inst Bacteriol Camara Pestana ... Arquivos. Instituto Bacteriologico. Camara Pestana [*A publication*]
Arq Inst Bacteriol Cam Pestana ... Arquivos. Instituto Bacteriologico. Camara Pestana [*A publication*]
Arq Inst Biol ... Arquivos. Instituto Biologico [*A publication*]
Arq Inst Biol Anim (Rio De J) ... Arquivos. Instituto de Biologia Animal (Rio De Janeiro) [*A publication*]
Arq Inst Biol Exerc ... Arquivos. Instituto de Biologia do Exercito [*A publication*]
Arq Inst Biol (Sao Paulo) ... Arquivos. Instituto Biologico (Sao Paulo) [*A publication*]
Arq Inst Biol (Sao Paulo) Supl ... Arquivos. Instituto Biologico (Sao Paulo). Suplemento [*A publication*]
Arq Inst Biol Veg (Rio De J) ... Arquivos. Instituto de Biologia Vegetal (Rio De Janeiro) [*A publication*]
Arq Inst Mil Biol (Rio De Janeiro) ... Arquivos. Instituto Militar de Biologia (Rio De Janeiro) [*A publication*]
Arq Inst Pesqui Agron ... Arquivos. Instituto de Pesquisas Agronomicas [*A publication*]
Arq Inst Pesqui Vet Desiderio Finamor ... Arquivos. Instituto de Pesquisas Veterinarias "Desiderio Finamor" [*A publication*]
Arq Interam Reumatol ... Arquivos Interamericanos de Reumatologia [*A publication*]
Arq Jard Bot Rio De J ... Arquivos. Jardim Botanico do Rio De Janeiro [*A publication*]
Arq Min Leprol ... Arquivos Mineiros de Leprologia [*A publication*]
Arq Mus Bocage ... Arquivos. Museu Bocage [*A publication*]
Arq Mus Bocage Ser A ... Arquivos. Museu Bocage. Serie A [*A publication*]
Arq Mus Bocage Ser C Supl ... Arquivos. Museu Bocage. Serie C. Suplementos [*A publication*]
Arq Mus Hist Nat Univ Fed Minas Gerais ... Arquivos. Museu de Historia Natural. Universidade Federal de Minas Gerais [*A publication*]
Arq Mus Nac Rio De J ... Arquivos. Museu Nacional do Rio De Janeiro [*A publication*]
Arq Mus Parana ... Arquivos. Museu Paranaense [*A publication*]
Arq Neuro-Psiquiatr ... Arquivos de Neuro-Psiquiatria [*A publication*]
ARQOA5 ... Arquivos de Oncologia [*A publication*]
Arq Oncol .. Arquivos de Oncologia [*A publication*]
Arq Patol ... Arquivo de Patologia [*A publication*]
Arq Patol Geral Anat Patol Univ Coimbra ... Arquivos de Patologia Geral e Anatomia Patologica. Universidade de Coimbra [*A publication*]
Arq Patol (Lisbon) ... Arquivos de Patologia (Lisbon) [*A publication*]
Arq Pediat ... Arquivos de Pediatria [*A publication*]
Arq Port ..... Arqueologo Portugues [*A publication*]
Arq Port Bioquim ... Arquivos Portugueses de Bioquimica [*A publication*]
Arq Serv Florestal (Rio De J) ... Arquivos. Servico Florestal (Rio De Janeiro) [*A publication*]
ARQT .... Arquitectura [*A publication*]
Arq Tisiol ... Arquivos de Tisiologia [*A publication*]
Arqu Bol ..... Arqueologia Boliviana [*A publication*]
Arquivo Inst Gulbenkian Ci A Estud Mat Fis-Mat ... Arquivo. Instituto Gulbenkian de Ciencia. A. Estudos Matematicos e Fisico-Matematicos [*A publication*]
Arquivos Brasil Psicol Ap ... Arquivos Brasileiros de Psicologia Aplicada [*A publication*]
Arqu Mus Nac ... Arquivos. Museu Nacional do Rio De Janeiro [*A publication*]
Arq Univ Bahia Fac Med ... Arquivos. Universidade de Bahia. Faculdade de Medicina [*A publication*]
Arq Univ Fed Rural Rio De Janeiro ... Arquivos. Universidade Federal Rural do Rio De Janeiro [*A publication*]
ARQZA4 ... Arquivos de Zoologia [*Sao Paulo*] [*A publication*]
Arq Zool Estado Sao Paulo ... Arquivos de Zoologia do Estado de Sao Paulo [*A publication*]

Arq Zool (Sao Paulo) ... Arquivos de Zoologia (Sao Paulo) [*A publication*]
ARR .... Accounting Rate of Return   (ADA)
ARR .... Advance Release Record   (AAG)
ARR .... Advanced Restricted Report
ARR .... Advanced Rocket Ramjet   (MCD)
ARR .... Aerial Refueling Receptacle   (MCD)
ARR .... Aeronautical Radionavigation RADAR
ARR .... Aerospace Rescue and Recovery
ARR .... AFOS [*Automation of Field Operations and Services*] Regional Representative [*National Weather Service*]   (NOAA)
ARR .... Air Regional Representative
ARR .... Airborne Radio Receiver
ARR .... Aircraft Radio Regulations
ARR .... [*The*] Alaska Railroad [*AAR code*]
ARR .... Allowance Requirement Register   (MCD)
ARR .... Altitude Referenced Radiometer
ARR .... Alto Rio Senguerr [*Argentina*] [*Airport symbol*]   (OAG)
ARR .... American Railway Reports [*A publication*]   (DLA)
ARR .... American Review of Reviews [*A publication*]
ARR .... American Right to Read [*Defunct*]   (EA)
ARR .... Andean Group Regional Report [*A publication*]
ARR .... Anno Regni Regis [*or Reginae*] [*In the Year of the King's, or Queen's, Reign*] [*Latin*]
ARR .... Antenna Radiation Resistance
ARR .... Antenna Rotation Rate   (NVT)
ARR .... Antirepeat Relay
ARR .... Arab Report & Record [*A publication*]
ArR .... Archivi (Rome) [*A publication*]
ARR .... Arges [*Romania*] [*Seismograph station code, US Geological Survey*]   (SEIS)
ARR .... Armour Research Foundation Reactor
ARR .... Army Readiness Region   (AABC)
ARR .... Army Retail Requirements
ARR .... Arranged
ARR .... Arrangement [*Music*]
arr .... Arranger [*MARC relator code*] [*Library of Congress*]   (LCCP)
ARR .... Array   (NASA)
ARR .... Arrester [*Electricity*]   (KSC)
Arr .... Arrete [*Decision, Order*] [*French*]   (ILCA)
Arr .... Arrian [*Second century AD*] [*Classical studies*]   (OCD)
ARR .... Arrington [*England*]
ARR .... Arrival [*or Arrive*]
ARR .... Arrival Message [*Aviation code*]
ARR .... Associate for Radiation Research [*British*]
ARR .... Association for Radiation Research [*British*]   (NRCH)
ARR .... Association for Regulatory Reform   (EA)
ARR .... Aurora, IL [*Location identifier*] [*FAA*]   (FAAL)
ARR .... Australian Rifle Regiment   (DMA)
ARR .... Automatic Rerouting [*Telecommunications*]   (TEL)
ARR .... Internal Revenue Bureau Committee on Appeals and Review, Recommendation [*United States*] [*A publication*]   (DLA)
ARRA .... American Road Racing Association   (EA)
ARRA .... Asphalt Recycling and Reclaiming Association   (EA)
ARRA .... Association of Road Racing Athletes   (EA)
ARRADCOM ... Army Armament Research and Development Command [*Dover, NJ*]   (MCD)
Arrang .... Arrangement   (DLA)
ARRANGT ... Arrangement
Arran Nat .. Arran Naturalist [*A publication*]
Arr et Av Cons Etat ... Arrets et Avis du Conseil d'Etat [*A publication*]
ARRB .... Australian Road Research Board [*Information service or system*]   (IID)
ARRC .... Aeronautical RADAR Research Complex
ARRC .... Aerospace Rescue and Recovery Center [*Air Force*]   (AFM)
ARRC .... Air Reserve Records Center
ARRC .... American Road Race of Champions
ARRC .... Area Reference Resource Center [*Library network*]
ARRC .... Associate of the Royal Red Cross [*British*]
ARRC .... Association of Regional Religious Communicators   (EA)
ARRC .... Audio Recording Rights Coalition [*Defunct*]   (EA)
ARRCOM ... Army Armament Materiel Readiness Command
ARRCOM ... Army Reserve Command   (MCD)
ARRCS ...... Air Raid Reporting Control Ship [*Navy*]   (NVT)
ARRD .... Arranged
ARRD .... Arrived
ARRD .... Australian Road Research Documentation [*Australian Road Research Board*] [*Information service or system*]   (IID)
ARRDA ..... American Resort and Residential Development Association   (EA)
ARRDA ..... American Review of Respiratory Disease [*A publication*]
ARRE .... Alarm Receiving and Reporting Equipment [*Telecommunications*]   (TEL)
ARRE .... Antigen Receptor Response Element [*Immunology*]
ARRE .... Arrange   (ROG)
ARRE .... Assault Regiment Royal Engineers [*British military*]   (DMA)
ARRED ...... Army Forces Readiness Command   (MCD)
ARRED ...... Army Readiness Region
ARREEI ...... Annual Review of Rehabilitation [*A publication*]
ArRefg .... Archiv fuer Reformationsgeschichte [*Guetersloh*] [*A publication*]
Ar Rep .... Argus Reports [*A publication*]

ARREP ...... Arrival Report [*Navy*]
ARREPCOVES ... Arrival Report Commanding Officer that Vessel Duty [*Navy*]
ARREPISIC ... Arrival Report Immediate Superior in Command [*Navy*]
ARRES ...... Automatic RADAR Reconnaissance Exploitation System
ARREST .... Acoustic Response of Reusable Shuttle Tiles   (MCD)
AR-RET-ST ... Arm Retracting Strut [*Nuclear energy*]   (AAG)
ARRF .... Automatic Recording and Reduction Facility
ARRG .... Association for Research into Restricted Growth [*British*]
ARRGp .... Aerospace Rescue and Recovery Group [*Air Force*]   (AFM)
ARRGT ...... Arrangement   (ROG)
ARRHA ..... American RSROA [*Roller Skating Rink Operators Association of America*] Roller Hockey Association   (EA)
ARRI .... Arriflex [*Camera*] [*Named for manufacturers Arnold and Richter*]
ARRI .... Automation and Robotics Research Institute [*University of Texas at Arlington*] [*Research center*]   (RCD)
ARRIP .... Australian Road Research in Progress [*A publication*]   (APTA)
ARRIVEDREP ... Arrival Report [*Navy*]   (NVT)
ARRJ .... Advanced Rocket Ramjet
ARRL .... Aeronautical Radio and RADAR Laboratory [*Navy*]
ARRL .... Air Resources Solar Radiation Laboratory [*National Oceanic and Atmospheric Administration*]   (NOAA)
ARRL .... American Radio Relay League   (EA)
ARRLF ..... ARRL [*American Radio Relay League*] Foundation   (EA)
ARRO .... Afro-Asian Rural Reconstruction Organization   (EAIO)
ARRO .... Archery Range and Retailers Organization   (EA)
ARROAA ..... Annual Report. Radiation Center of Osaka Prefecture [*A publication*]
ARROND ... Arrondissement [*District*] [*French*]
ARROTCA ... Army Reserve and Reserve Officers Training Corps Affairs
ARROW .... Army's Requirement to Own and Operate Watercraft   (MCD)
ARRP .... Australian Recommended Retail Price
ARRR .... American Railway Reports [*A publication*]   (DLA)
ARRS .... Advanced Rescue and Recovery System [*Proposed VTOL aircraft*] [*Also, ARS*]   (MCD)
ARRS .... Aerospace Rescue and Recovery Service [*Scott Air Force Base, IL*]   (MCD)
ARRS .... Air Recovery and Rescue Service   (NASA)
ARRS .... Air Rescue and Recovery Squadron
ARRS .... Airborne Radioactivity Removal System   (NRCH)
ARRS .... Aircraft Refuel/Rearm Study   (MCD)
ARRS .... American Roentgen Ray Society   (EA)
ARRS .... Association of Radio Reading Services   (EA)
ARRS .... Attitude-Referenced Radiometer Study [*NASA*]
AR & RSq .. Aerospace Rescue and Recovery Squadron [*Air Force*]
ARRSq .... Aerospace Rescue and Recovery Squadron [*Air Force*]   (AFM)
ARRT .... Absolute Reaction Rate Theory [*Physical chemistry*]
ARRT .... American Registered Respiratory Therapist
ARRT .... American Registry of Radiologic Technologists   (EA)
ARRT .... American Revolution Round Table   (EA)
ARRT .... Anti-Repression Resource Team   (EA)
ARRTC ...... Aerospace Rescue and Recovery Training Center [*Air Force*]   (AFM)
ARRTC ...... Army Reserve Readiness Training Center [*Fort McCoy, WI*]   (INF)
ARRTL .... Arranged Total Loss [*Insurance*]
ARRTVC ... Association for Restriction of Radio and Television Commercials   (EA)
ArRuA .... Arkansas Polytechnic College [*Later, Arkansas Technical University*], Russellville, AR [*Library symbol*] [*Library of Congress*]   (LCLS)
ARRUS ...... Arrived Within Continental Limits of US [*Navy*]
ARRW .... Aerospace Rescue and Recovery Wing [*Air Force*]   (MCD)
ArRW .... Archiv fuer Religionswissenschaft [*Leipzig/Berlin*] [*A publication*]
ARRWB ...... Argonne Reviews [*A publication*]
ARRWg ..... Aerospace Rescue and Recovery Wing [*Air Force*]   (AFM)
ARS .... Accelerated Random Search   (MCD)
ARS .... Accidents and Road Safety [*British*]
ARS .... Accion Revolucionaria Socialista [*Socialist Revolutionary Action*] [*Peru*] [*Political party*]   (PPW)
ARS .... Accounting Research Study
ARS .... Acid-Rinsing Solution [*Clinical chemistry*]
ARS .... Action Republicaine et Sociale [*Republican and Social Action*] [*France*] [*Political party*]   (PPE)
ARS .... Active RADAR Seeker
ARS .... Active Repeater Satellite [*Air Force*]
ARS .... Admiralty Recruiting Service [*British*]
ARS .... Advanced Reconnaissance Satellite
ARS .... Advanced Reconnaissance System   (MUGU)
ARS .... Advanced Record System [*Air Force*]
ARS .... Advanced Reentry System [*Aerospace*]
ARS .... Advanced Regulating Station [*British military*]   (DMA)
ARS .... Advanced Religious Studies [*A publication*]
ARS .... Advanced Rescue System [*Proposed VTOL aircraft*] [*Also, ARRS*]
ARS .... Aerial Reconnaissance and Security
ARS .... Aerial Reconnaissance Surveillance   (MCD)
ARS .... Aeronautical Research Scientist
ARS .... Aerospace Research Satellite

ARS............	Agricultural Research Service [*Washington, DC*] [*Department of Agriculture*] [*Also, an information service or system*]
ARS............	Agricultural Research Station (ADA)
ARS............	Air Regulating Squadron
ARS............	Air Rescue Science (NASA)
ARS............	Air Rescue Service [*Air Force*]
ARS............	Air Rescue Ship
ARS............	Air Revitalization System (MCD)
ARS............	Air Security Transport Corp. [*Titusville, FL*] [*FAA designator*] (FAAC)
ARS............	Airborne Ranging System
ARS............	Airborne Rapid-Scan Spectrometer
ARS............	Airborne Refrigeration System
ARS............	Airborne Relay Stations (MCD)
ARS............	Aircraft Repair Ship [*Navy*]
ARS............	Aircraft Report, Special (ADA)
ARS............	Aircraft Rocket Subsystem [*Army/Air Force*]
ARS............	Alizarin Red S [*An indicator*] [*Chemistry*]
ARS............	All Red Series [*A publication*]
ARS............	Alpha Ray Spectrometer
ARS............	American Racing Series
ARS............	American Radium Society (EA)
ARS............	American Recorder Society (EA)
ARS............	American Recreation Society [*Later, APRS*] (EA)
ARS............	American Repair Service
ARS............	American Rhinologic Society (EA)
ARS............	American Rhododendron Society (EA)
ARS............	American Robot Society (EA)
ARS............	American Rocket Society [*Later, AIAA*]
ARS............	American Rose Society (EA)
ARS............	Amplified Response Spectrum [*Nuclear energy*] (NRCH)
ARS............	Anaesthetic Research Society (EAIO)
ARS............	Analog Recording System
ARS............	Anchored Radiosight
ARS............	Anglo-Rhodesian Society (EA)
ARS............	Angular Rate Sensor
ARS............	Anno Reparatae Salutis [*In the Year of Our Redemption*] [*Latin*]
ARS............	Annual Refrigerated Machinery Survey [*of a vessel*] (DS)
ARS............	Annual Report to Shareholders [*Securities and Exchange Commission*] (IID)
ARS............	Antigen Recognition Site [*Genetics*]
ARS............	Antirabies Serum [*Medicine*]
ARS............	Apollo Reentry Ship [*NASA*]
ARS............	Aragarcas [*Brazil*] [*Airport symbol*] (OAG)
ARS............	Area Resupply
ARS............	Aristech Chemical [*NYSE symbol*] (SPSG)
ARS............	Arizona Revised Statutes [*A publication*] (DLA)
ARS............	Armenian Relief Society [*Later, ARSNA*] (EA)
ARS............	Armenian Rugs Society (EA)
ARS............	Army Radio School [*British military*] (DMA)
ARS............	Army Records Society (EAIO)
ARS............	Army Relief Society [*Absorbed by AER*] (EA)
ARS............	Arsanilic Acid [*Organic chemistry*]
ARS............	Arsenal (AABC)
ARS............	Arshan [*USSR*] [*Seismograph station code, US Geological Survey*] (SEIS)
ARS............	Arsine [*Inorganic chemistry*]
ARS............	Arsphenamine [*Antisyphilitic compound*]
ARS............	Artina Resources Ltd. [*Vancouver Stock Exchange symbol*]
ARSF............	Asbestos Roof Shingles [*Technical drawings*]
ARS............	Atmosphere Revitalization Section [*or System*] [*NASA*]
ARS............	Attitude Reference System (KSC)
ARS............	Audio Response System
ARS............	Augustan Reprint Society (EA)
ARS............	Automated Reference Service [*Ohio State University Libraries*] (OLDSS)
ARS............	Automatic Recording Spectrometer
ARS............	Automatic Recovery System
ARS............	Automatic Reference System (MCD)
ARS............	Automatic Route Selection [*Also, MERS*] [*Bell System*] [*Telecommunications*]
ARS............	Autonomously Replicating Sequence [*Genetics*]
ARS............	Azimuth Reference System (MCD)
ARS............	Azobenzenearsonate [*Also, ABA*] [*Organic chemistry*]
ARS............	Defence Research Establishment Suffield, Canada Department of National Defence [*Centre de Recherches pour la Defense Suffield, Ministere de la Defense Nationale*] Ralston, Alberta [*Library symbol*] [*National Library of Canada*] (NLC)
ARS............	Salvage Ship [*Navy symbol*]
Ar S............	Sister of Arts
ARS............	Special Air-Report [*Aviation code*]
ARS............	Sverdlovsk (Arti) [*USSR*] [*Geomagnetic observatory code*]
ARSA.........	Aeronautical Repair Station Association (EA)
ARSA.........	Airport RADAR Service Area [*Aeronautics*]
ARSA.........	Allied Railway Supply Association [*Later, RSA*]
ARSA.........	American Reye's Syndrome Association (EA)
ARSA.........	Annual Reevaluation of Safe Areas (MCD)
ARSA.........	Associate of the Royal Scottish Academy
ARSA.........	Associate of the Royal Society of Antiquaries [*British*]
ARSA.........	Associate of the Royal Society of Arts [*British*] (EY)
ARSA.........	Austrian RADAR Site Analysis
ARSAG.........	Aerial Refueling Systems Advisory Group [*Military*] (CAAL)
Ars Am.........	Ars Amatoria [*of Ovid*] [*Classical studies*] (OCD)
ARSANI....	Associate of the Royal Sanitary Institute [*British*] (ROG)
ARSAP.....	Army Small Arms Program
ARSASA	Associate of the Royal South Australian Society of Artists
ARSB.........	Air Reconnaissance Support Battalion
ARSB.........	Aircraft Repair and Supply Base (AFIT)
ARSB.........	Anchored Radio Sonobuoy
ARSB.........	Arctic Seas Bulletin. Canadian Arctic Resources Committee [*A publication*]
ARSB.........	Automated Repair Service Bureau (TEL)
ARSBA.........	American Rambouillet Sheep Breeders Association (EA)
Arsber Danm Fisk Havund ...	Arsberetning fra Danmarks Fiskeri og Havundersogelser [*A publication*]
Arsberet Nor Fisk ...	Arsberetning Norges Fiskerier [*A publication*]
Arsberet Statens Forsoegsmejeri ...	Arsberetning. Statens Forsoegsmejeri [*A publication*]
Arsberet Vedkomm Nor Fisk ...	Arsberetning Vedkommende Norges Fiskerier [*A publication*]
Arsber Sver Geol Unders ...	Arsberaettelse. Sverings Geologiska Undersoekning [*A publication*]
Arsb Finska Vetensk Soc ...	Arsbok. Finska Vetenskaps Societeten [*A publication*]
Arsb Foren Skogstradsfor ...	Arsbok. Foreningen Skogstradsforadling [*A publication*]
Arsb Sodermanlands Lans Hushallningssallsk ...	Arsbok. Sodermanlands Lans Hushallningssallskaps [*A publication*]
Arsb Sver Met Hydrol Inst ...	Arsbok. Sveriges Meteorologisk och Hydrologiska Institut [*A publication*]
Arsb Vet Soc Lund ...	Arsbok. Vetenskaps-Societetn i Lund [*A publication*]
ARSC.........	Aircraft Repair and Supply Center
ARSC.........	Analog Rotation Speed Control
ARSC.........	Annals of Regional Science [*A publication*]
Ar-SC.........	Arkansas Supreme Court Library, Little Rock, AR [*Library symbol*] [*Library of Congress*] (LCLS)
ARSC.........	ARUS Corporation [*Utica, NY*] [*NASDAQ symbol*] (NQ)
ARSC.........	Association for Recorded Sound Collections (EA)
ARSC.........	Association for Recorded Sound Collections. Journal [*A publication*]
ARSCAD....	Acta Rheumatologica Scandinavica [*A publication*]
ARSCBS.....	Academie Royale des Sciences Coloniales (Brussels). Bulletin des Seances [*A publication*]
ARSCJ.......	Association for Recorded Sound Collections. Journal [*A publication*]
ARSCM.....	Associate Member of the Royal School of Church Music [*British*]
Ars Comb...	Ars Combinatoria [*Canada*] [*A publication*]
Ars Combin ...	Ars Combinatoria [*A publication*]
Ars Curandi Odontol ...	Ars Curandi em Odontologia [*A publication*]
ARSD.........	Arabian Shield Development Co. [*NASDAQ symbol*] (NQ)
ARSD.........	Aviation Repair Supply Depot
ARSD.........	Salvage Lifting Ship [*Navy symbol*]
ARSDA.....	Advanced Radiation Space Defense Application (MCD)
ARSE.........	Alpha Ray Spectrometric Equipment
ArSeH........	Harding College, Searcy, AR [*Library symbol*] [*Library of Congress*] (LCLS)
ARSEM.....	Army Registry of Special Educational Materials (AABC)
Arsenical Pestic Symp ...	Arsenical Pesticides. Symposium [*A publication*]
ARSF.........	Artistic Roller Skating Federation (EA)
ARSFA......	Anales. Real Sociedad Espanola de Fisica y Quimica. Serie A. Fisica [*A publication*]
ARSH	Associate of the Royal Society of Health [*Later, AMRSH*] [*British*]
ARSI.........	Associate of the Royal Sanitary Institute [*British*]
ARSIA	Annuario. Regia Scuola Archeologica Italiana di Atene [*A publication*]
ARSIP	Arrears in Pay [*Military*]
Ars Islam ...	Ars Islamica [*A publication*]
ARSJ	American Rocket Society. Journal [*A publication*]
Ars J	Ars Journal [*A publication*]
ArSK..........	Archiv fuer Schriftkunde [*A publication*]
ARSL.........	Arsenal (MCD)
ARSL.........	Associate of the Royal Society of Literature [*British*]
ARSL.........	Atmospheric Rendezvous Space Logistics [*NASA*] (MCD)
AR/SLA	Automatic Reference System/Sequential Launch (MCD)
ARSLOE	Atlantic Remote Sensing Land Ocean Experiment (MCD)
ARSM........	Acute Respiratory System Malfunction [*Medicine*]
ARSM........	Associate of the Royal School of Mines [*British*] (EY)
ARSM.......	Associate of the Royal Society of Musicians [*British*]
ARSMBA ..	Ars Medici [*Edition Francaise*] [*A publication*]
Ars Med (Ed Fr) ...	Ars Medici (Edition Francaise) [*A publication*]
Arsmelding St Smabrlaerarsk ...	Arsmelding Statens Smabrukslaerarskole [*A publication*]
ARSN	AirSensors, Inc. [*Seattle, WA*] [*NASDAQ symbol*] (NQ)
ARSNA......	Armenian Relief Society of North America (EA)
ARS NE US Agric Res Serv Northeast Reg ...	ARS NE. United States Agricultural Research Service. Northeastern Region [*A publication*]
ARSNSP....	Atti. Reale Scuola Normale Superiore di Pisa [*A publication*]

ARSO .... African Regional Organization for Standardization [*Kenya*]

ARSO .... Armament Supply Officer [*British Navy slang*] [*World War II*]   (DSUE)

ARSOB ...... Arts in Society [*A publication*]

ArSocRel .... Archives de Sociologie des Religions [*Paris*] [*A publication*]

A R Soc Sci Rel ... Annual Review of the Social Sciences of Religion [*A publication*]

Arson Anal Newsl ... Arson Analysis Newsletter [*A publication*]

ARSOP ...... Airborne Remote Sensing Oceanography Project

ArsOr .... Ars Orientalis [*A publication*]

Ars Orient ... Ars Orientalis [*A publication*]

ARSP .... Action Reconciliation/Services for Peace [*An association*]   (EAIO)

ARSP .... Aerospace Research Support Program [*Air Force*]

ARSP .... Analog RADAR Signal Processor   (MCD)

ARSP .... Applied Remote Sensing Program   (MCD)

ARSP .... Archiv fuer Rechts- und Sozialphilosophie [*A publication*]

Ars P .... Ars Poetica [*of Horace*] [*Classical studies*]   (OCD)

ARSPA ...... Aerial Reconnaissance and Surveillance Penetration Analysis [*Army*]

Ars Pharm ... Ars Pharmaceutica [*A publication*]

ARSPT ...... Air Reconnaissance Support   (AABC)

ARSQA ...... Anales. Real Sociedad Espanola de Fisica y Quimica. Serie B. Quimica [*A publication*]

ARSQAL ... Anales. Real Sociedad Espanola de Fisica y Quimica. Serie B. Quimica [*A publication*]

ARSR .... Air Route Surveillance RADAR

Ar SR .... Archives de Sociologie des Religions [*A publication*]

ARSR .... Arrester [*Electricity*]

ARSR .... Australian Religion Studies Review [*A publication*]   (APTA)

ARSRDR ... Antiviral Research [*A publication*]

ARSR Mem Sect Stiint Ist ... Academia Republicii Socialiste Romania. Memoriile. Sectei de Stiinte Istorice [*A publication*]

ARSS .... Active Relaxed Static Stability   (MCD)

ARSS .... Airborne Remote Sensing System [*Coast Guard*]   (MCD)

ARSS .... American Radiator & Standard Sanitary Corp. [*Later, American Standard, Inc.*]

ARSS .... Antiquariorum Regiae Societatis Socius [*Fellow of the Royal Society of Antiquaries*] [*Latin*]

Ars S .... Ars Semiotica [*A publication*]

ARSS .... Atmosphere Reactants Supply Subsystem

ARSSA ...... Aerial Reconnaissance and Surveillance Survivability Analysis [*Army*]

ARSSAR .... Acta Rheumatologica Scandinavica. Supplementum [*A publication*]

ARSSC ...... Associate of the Royal Society of Sciences [*British*]   (ROG)

Ars Semiot ... Ars Semiotica [*A publication*]

ARSSG ...... Atmosphere Reactants Supply Subsystem Group   (MCD)

ArSsJ .... John Brown University, Siloam Springs, AR [*Library symbol*] [*Library of Congress*]   (LCLS)

Arsskr K Vet Landbohoejsk ... Ariskrift den Kongelige Veterinaer og Landbohoejskole [*A publication*]

Arsskr f Modersmalslararnas Foren ... Arsskrift foer Modersmalslararnas Forening [*A publication*]

Arsskr Nor Skogplanteskoler ... Arsskrift foer Norske Skogplanteskoler [*A publication*]

ARS S US Agric Res Serv South Reg ... ARS S. United States Agricultural Research Service. Southern Region [*A publication*]

ARST .... Aerial Reconnaissance and Security Troop

ARST .... Army Requirements for Space Technologies   (MCD)

ARST .... Salvage Craft Tender [*Navy ship symbol*]

ARSTADS ... Army Staff Automated Administrative Support System   (MCD)

ARSTAF .... [*The*] Army Staff   (AABC)

ArStC .... Arkansas State University, State University, AR [*Library symbol*] [*Library of Congress*]   (LCLS)

ARSTRIKE ... [*US*] Army Strike [*STRICOM*]

ARSTS ...... Air Reserve Specialist Training Squadron

ARSUAX ... Archives of Surgery [*A publication*]

ArSuL .... Public Library, Sulphur Springs, AR [*Library symbol*] [*Library of Congress*]   (LCLS)

ArSuN .... New Subiaco Abbey, Subiaco, AR [*Library symbol*] [*Library of Congress*]   (LCLS)

ARSUP ...... Area Supervisor [*FAA*]   (FAAC)

ARSV .... Armored Reconnaissance Scout Vehicle [*Army*]   (AABC)

ARSV-TF ... Armored Reconnaissance Scout Vehicle - Task Force   (MCD)

ARSZAE ... Acta Regiae Societatis Scientiarum et Litterarum Gothoburgensis. Zoologica [*A publication*]

ART .... Absolute Rate Theory [*Statistics*]

ART .... Academic Remedial Training [*Navy*]

ART .... Accredited Record Technician [*American Medical Record Association*]

ART .... Acoustic Reflex Test [*Audiology*]

A & RT .... Adams & Rountree Technology, Inc. [*Information service or system*]   (IID)

ART .... Additional Reference Carrier Transmission [*Telecommunications*]   (TEL)

ART ....: Adjustable Ranging Telescope [*Army*]   (MCD)

ART .... Admissible Rank Test [*Statistics*]

ART .... Advanced Reactor Technology   (IEEE)

ART .... Advanced Research and Technology

AR & T .... Advanced Research and Technology   (MUGU)

ART .... Aerosol Release and Transport [*Nuclear energy*]   (NRCH)

ART .... Air Reserve Technician [*Air Force*]

ART .... Airborne Radiation Thermometer

ART .... Airwolf Recovery Team [*An association*]   (EA)

ART .... Alarm Reporting Telephone [*Telecommunications*]   (TEL)

ART .... Alarm Response Team [*Military*]

ART .... Alert Reaction Time

ART .... Algebraic Reconstruction Technique

ART .... Almine Resources [*Vancouver Stock Exchange symbol*]

ART .... Ambiguity Reference Tone   (MCD)

ART .... American Radiography Technologists   (EA)

ART .... American Refrigeration Transit Co. [*AAR code*]

ART .... American Repertory Theatre

ART .... Angst, Revolution, Titillation [*Art films*]

ART .... Animated Reconstruction of Telemetry

ART .... Annual Renewable Term [*Insurance*]

ART .... Anticipatory Reactor Trips   (NRCH)

ART .... Approximate Ray Tracing [*Of seismic waves*]

ART .... Arc Resistance Tester

ART .... Arithmetic Reading Test [*Military*]

ART .... Arithmetic Reasoning Test

ART .... Armatron International, Inc. [*AMEX symbol*]   (SPSG)

ART .... Army Reserve Technician

ART .... Army Resident Training   (MCD)

Art .... Art/Film/Criticism [*A publication*]

ART .... Arta [*Djibouti*] [*Seismograph station code, US Geological Survey*] [*Closed*]   (SEIS)

ART .... Artery

ART .... Article   (AFM)

ART .... Articulated   (ADA)

ART .... Artificer

ART .... Artificial   (TEL)

ART .... Artificial Resynthesis Technology [*Mechanical mouth used in dental research*]

ART .... Artillery

ART .... Artillery Repair Truck [*British*]

ART .... Artist

art .... Artist [*MARC relator code*] [*Library of Congress*]   (LCCP)

ART .... Arts in Society [*A publication*]

ART .... Asphalt Residual Treatment [*Petroleum refining*]

ART .... Association pour la Recherche en Tourisme [*Travel Research Association*] [*Canada*]

ART .... Audio Renaissance Tapes [*Los Angeles, CA*]

ART .... Automated Reagin Test [*Serology*]

ART .... Automated Reasoning Tool   (MCD)

ART .... Automatic Radiating Tester

ART .... Automatic Radiotheodolite [*Meteorology*]

ART .... Automatic Range Tracker [*or Tracking*]

ART .... Automatic Ranging Telescope [*Weaponry*]   (INF)

ART .... Automatic Reasoning Tool   (MCD)

ART .... Automatic Reporting Telephone [*Telecommunications*]   (TEL)

ART .... Aviation Radio Technician

ART .... Watertown [*New York*] [*Airport symbol*]   (OAG)

ARTA ...... American Reuseable Textile Association   (EA)

ARTA ...... American River Touring Association

ARTA .... Association of Retail Travel Agents   (EA)

ARTA .... Aviation Research and Technology Activity [*Moffett Field, CA*] [*Army*]   (RDA)

ARTAC ...... Advanced Reconnaissance and Target Acquisition Capabilities

ARTACOM ... Army Requirements for Tactical Communications   (AABC)

ARTADS ... Army Tactical Data Systems   (AABC)

Art Am ...... Art in America [*A publication*]

Art in Am ... Art in America [*A publication*]

Art in Amer ... Art in America [*A publication*]

Art & Arch ... Art and Archaeology [*A publication*]

ArtArch ...... Art and Archaeology. Technical Abstracts [*A publication*]

Art Archaeol Res Papers ... Art and Archaeology. Research Papers [*A publication*]

Art Archaeol Tech Abstr ... Art and Archaeology. Technical Abstracts [*A publication*]

Art & Archre ... Art et Architecture [*A publication*]

Art As ...... Artibus Asiae [*A publication*]

Art Asia ..... Arts of Asia [*A publication*]

Art and Aust ... Art and Australia [*A publication*]   (APTA)

Art Aust ..... Art and Australia [*A publication*]

ArtB .... Art Bulletin [*A publication*]

ARTBA ...... American Road and Transportation Builders Association   (EA)

ARTBASS ... Army Training Battle Simulation System   (MCD)

ARTBCH ... Agricultural Research Corporation [*Gezira*]. Technical Bulletin [*A publication*]

ARTbibliogr Curr Titles ... ARTbibliographies. Current Titles [*A publication*]

ARTbibliogr Mod ... ARTbibliographies Modern [*A publication*]

ARTBSS ...... Army Training Battle Simulation System

Art Bul .... Art Bulletin [*A publication*]

Art Bull .... Art Bulletin [*A publication*]

ARTC .... Addiction Research and Treatment Corporation   (EA)

ARTC .... Air Research and Testing Committee   (MUGU)

ARTC .... Air Route Traffic Control [*Aviation*]

ARTC .... Aircraft Research and Testing Committee   (MCD)

ARTC .... Articulation Control Subsystem [*NASA*]

ARTC......... Associate of the Royal Technical College. Glasgow [Formerly, ARCST]

ARTC......... Association des Routes et Transports du Canada [Roads and Transportation Association of Canada]

ARTC......... Auxiliary Rescue Team Chief [Air Force]

ARTCA...... Association of Round Tables in Central Africa

ARTCC...... Air Route Traffic Control Center [Aviation]

ARTCLD... Articulated

Art Crit ...... Art Criticism [A publication]

ARTCS...... Advanced RADAR Traffic Control System [Air Force]   (AFM)

ARTC(S).... Associate of the Royal Technical College (Salford) [British]

AR & TD..... Advanced Research and Technology Development Program [Department of Energy]

Art D.......... Doctor of Arts

ARTDA ..... Art Direction [A publication]

Art & Dec... Art and Decoration [A publication]

Art Des Photo ... Art, Design, Photo [A publication]

Art Dir .... Art Direction [A publication]

Art Direct... Art Direction [A publication]

ARTDO...... Asian Regional Training and Development Organization

ARTE....... Admiralty Reactor Test Establishment   (MCD)

ARTEC...... Association of Radio and Television Employees of Canada

Art Educ.... Art Education [A publication]

ARTEF...... Arbeiter Teater Farband [A publication]

Arte Lomb ... Arte Lombarda [A publication]

ARTEMIS ... Automatic Retrieval of Text from Europe's Multinational Information Service

Arte Mus.... Arte Musical [A publication]

ARTEP...... Army Training and Evaluation Program   (AABC)

ArteP....... Arte e Poesia [A publication]

Arte y Var .. Arte y Variedades [A publication]

Artf............. Artforum [A publication]

ARTF........ Artificial   (MSA)

ARTG .... Artistic Greetings, Inc. [Elmira, NY] [NASDAQ symbol]   (NQ)

ARTG .... Azimuth Range and Timing Group   (KSC)

Art Gall NSW Q ... Art Gallery of New South Wales. Quarterly [A publication]   (APTA)

ArTGran.... Archivo Teologico Granadino [Granada] [A publication]

Arth............ Arthaniti [A publication]

Artha Vij.... Artha Vijnana [A publication]

Artha Vijnana J Gokhale Inst Polit Econ ... Artha Vijnana. Journal of the Gokhale Institute of Politics and Economics [A publication]

Artha Vik... Artha Vikas [A publication]

Art Hist...... Art History [A publication]

Arth Rheum ... Arthritis and Rheumatism [A publication]

Arthritis Rheum ... Arthritis and Rheumatism [A publication]

Arthropods Fla Neighboring Land Areas ... Arthropods of Florida and Neighboring Land Areas [A publication]

ARTI.......... Acute Respiratory Tract Illness

ARTI.......... Advanced Rotorcraft Technology Integration   (MCD)

ArtI .... Art Index [A publication]

ARTIA2..... Archiv fuer Tierernaehrung [Archives of Animal Nutrition] [A publication]

Artibus A ... Artibus Asiae [A publication]

Artibus As ... Artibus Asiae [A publication]

ARTIC....... Articulation

ARTIC....... Associometrics Remote Terminal Inquiry Control System   (IEEE)

Artic Anth ... Arctic Anthropology [A publication]

Artic Cl ...... Articled Clerk [1867-68] [A publication]   (DLA)

Artic Cl Deb ... Articled Clerk and Debater [1866] [A publication]   (DLA)

Artic Cleri ... Articuli Cleri [Articles of the Clergy] [Latin]   (DLA)

Artic Cl J Exam ... Articled Clerks' Journal and Examiner [1879-81] [A publication]   (DLA)

Artic Sup Chart ... Articuli Super Chartas [Articles upon the Charters] [Latin]   (DLA)

ARTID5..... Annual Report on Research and Technical Work. Department of Agriculture for Northern Ireland [A publication]

ARTIF .... Artificer   (ADA)

ARTIF .... Artificial

ARTIFCL.. Artificial

Artif Earth Satell (USSR) ... Artificial Earth Satellites (USSR) [A publication]

Artif Intel... Artificial Intelligence [A publication]

Artif Intell ... Artificial Intelligence [A publication]

Artif Lungs Acute Respir Failure Pap Int Conf ... Artificial Lungs for Acute Respiratory Failure. Theory and Practice. Papers Presented at the International Conference on Membrane Lung Technology and Prolonged Extracorporeal Perfusion [A publication]

Artif Organs ... Artificial Organs [A publication]

Artif Satell ... Artificial Satellites [Poland] [A publication]

Artif Silk World ... Artificial Silk World [A publication]

ARTIL .... Artillery

ARTILL ...... Artillery

Arti M .... Arti Musices [A publication]

Arti Mus .... Arti Musices [A publication]

Art Ind .... Art Index [A publication]

Art & Ind ... Art and Industry [A publication]

ARTINS .... Army Terrain Information System   (MCD)

ARTINS .... Automated Terrain Information System

Art Inst of Chicago Bull ... Art Institute of Chicago. Bulletin [A publication]

Art Int .... Art International [A publication]

ARTIS .... Airborne Real-Time Instrumentation System   (MCD)

ARTIS .... ALPHA [AMC Logistics Program - Hardcore Automated] Remote Terminal Interactive System

ARTISS..... Advanced Requirements Tasking Information and Support System   (MCD)

Art J........... Art Journal [A publication]

Art Jnl....... Art Journal [A publication]

Art Jour ..... Art Journal [A publication]

Art J P E.... Art Journal. Paris Edition [A publication]

ARTK .... Artech Recovery Systems, Inc. [NASDAQ symbol]   (NQ)

Art & L....... Art and the Law [A publication]

Artl............. Artillerie [Artillery] [German]

ARTL......... Awaiting Results of Trial [Military]

Art & Law .. Art and the Law [A publication]   (DLA)

ARTLF ...... Association of Railway Trainmen and Locomotive Firemen   (EA)

Art Lib J .... Art Libraries Journal [A publication]

Art Libraries Jnl ... Art Libraries Journal [A publication]

ARTLY ...... Artillery

Art Mag ..... Arts Magazine [A publication]

Art Mthly... Art Monthly [A publication]

Art N.......... Art News [A publication]

ARTNA ..... Association of Radio-Television News Analysts   (EA)

ARTNB...... Art News [A publication]

ART/NY..... Alliance of Resident Theatres/New York   (EA)

Art NZ....... Art New Zealand [A publication]

ARTO .... Advanced Radiation Technology Office [Military]

ARTO .... Area Railway Transport Officer [British military]   (DMA)

ARTOC ...... Army Tactical Operations Central

ARTODN .. Archives of Toxicology/Archiv fuer Toxikologie [A publication]

ARTP......... Advanced Resident Training Plan [Military]   (AABC)

ARTP......... Air Reserve Technician Program [Air Force]

ARTP......... Army Rocket Transportation System   (MCD)

ARTPA...... American Review of Tuberculosis and Pulmonary Diseases [A publication]

ARTPAN... American Review of Tuberculosis and Pulmonary Diseases [A publication]

ART PF ...... Artist's Proof   (ADA)

Art Psychot ... Art Psychotherapy [A publication]

ArtQ........... Art Quarterly [A publication]

ART/R........ Airframe Repair Technician-Repairman   (AAG)

ARTRAC... Advanced Range Testing, Reporting, and Control

ARTRAC... Advanced Real-Time Range Control   (IEEE)

ARTRD...... Arteriosclerosis (Dallas) [A publication]

ARTRON .. Artificial Neuron

ARTS......... Acquisition Requirements Tracking System   (MCD)

ARTS......... Active RADAR Test System   (MCD)

ARTS......... Advanced RADAR Terminal System   (IEEE)

ARTS......... Advanced RADAR Traffic Control System [Air Force]

ARTS......... Advanced Real-Time Simulation   (MCD)

ARTS......... Advanced Real-Time System   (MCD)

ARTS......... Advanced Remote Tracking Station   (MCD)

ARTS......... Adventist Radio Television Services [Canada]

ARTS......... Aerial Relay Transportation System   (MCD)

ARTS......... Airborne RADAR Target Simulator

ARTS......... All-Altitude Air-Bearing Research and Training Simulator

ARTS......... Alpha Repertory Television Service [Cable-television system]

ARTS......... American Radio Telephone System   (TEL)

ARTS......... Annual Report on Transport Statistics

ARTS......... Annual Research Task Summary

ARTS......... Arkansas Research Test Station

ARTS......... Army Research Task Summary

ARTS......... Army Training Study

ARTS......... Arts Documentation Service [Australian Council Library] [Information service or system]

Arts........... Arts Magazine [A publication]

ARTS......... Arts Recognition and Talent Search [National Foundation for Advancement in the Arts]

ARTS......... Automated RADAR Terminal System   (FAAC)

ARTS......... Automated RADAR Tracking System   (MCD)

ARTS......... Automated Remote Tracking Station   (MCD)

ARTS......... Automatic Resistance Test Set

Arts Afr Noire ... Arts d'Afrique Noire [A publication]

Arts & Arch ... Arts and Architecture [A publication]

Arts & Archre ... Arts and Architecture [A publication]

Arts As....... Arts of Asia [A publication]

Arts Asiat... Arts Asiatiques [A publication]

Artscan....... Artscanada [A publication]

ARTSD...... Army Armament Research and Development Center [or Command] Technical Support Directorate [Dover, NJ]

Arts & D..... Arts and Decoration [A publication]

Arts D .... Doctor of Arts

Arts and Dec ... Arts and Decoration [A publication]

ARTSDOC ... Arts Documentation Service [Australian Council Library] [Information service or system]   (IID)

Arts Doc Mthly ... Arts Documentation Monthly [A publication]

ARTSEM .. Artificial Insemination [From George Orwell's novel, "1984"]

Arts Humanit Citation Index ... Arts and Humanities Citation Index [A publication]

Arts & Hum Cit Ind ... Arts and Humanities Citation Index [*A publication*]
Arts Mag.... Arts Magazine [*A publication*]
Arts Manuf ... Arts et Manufactures [*A publication*]
Arts Metiers ... Arts et Metiers [*A publication*]
Arts Psychother ... Arts in Psychotherapy [*A publication*]
ARTSq....... Aerospace Reconnaissance Technical Squadron [*Air Force*]
Arts Reptg Ser ... Arts Reporting Service [*A publication*]
Arts Rev ..... Arts Review [*A publication*]
ArtsS.......... Arts in Society [*A publication*]
Arts in Soc ... Arts in Society [*A publication*]
Art St .... Art Stamps [*A publication*]
ArtSt .... Arte Stampa [*A publication*]
ARTT........ Annual Review Traveling Team [*NATO*] (NATG)
Art & T....... Art and Text [*A publication*]
artt.............. Artikelen [*Articles*] [*Dutch*] (ILCA)
Art Teach... Art Teacher [*A publication*]
Art Technol Health Phys Educ Sci Hum Living Ser ... Art, Technology, Health, and Physical Education and Science of Human Living Series [*A publication*]
ARTU .... Archiv fuer Reformationsgeschichte. Texte und Untersuchungen [*A publication*]
ARTU .... Arcturus, Inc. [*Acton, MA*] [*NASDAQ symbol*] (NQ)
ARTU .... Automatic Range Tracking Unit [*Military*]
ARTUD7 ... Acta Reproductiva Turcica [*A publication*]
ARTVC...... Association for Restriction of TV Commercials [*Later, ARRTVC*] (EA)
Art Vict ..... Arts Victoria [*A publication*]
ARTW ...... Aerospace Reconnaissance Technical Wing (MCD)
ARTW .... Art's Way Manufacturing Co., Inc. [*NASDAQ symbol*] (NQ)
art wks coy ... Artisan Works Company [*British and Canadian*] [*World War II*]
ARTX........ Art Explosion, Inc. [*NASDAQ symbol*] (NQ)
ARTY........ Artillery (AFM)
arty R .... Artillery Reconnaissance [*British and Canadian*] [*World War II*]
ARU.......... Acoustic Resistance Unit
ARU.......... Address Recognition Unit
ARU.......... Aeromedical Research Unit [*Army*] (MCD)
ARU.......... Air Reserve Unit
ARU.......... Allure Industries Corp. [*Vancouver Stock Exchange symbol*]
ARU.......... Alturas, CA [*Location identifier*] [*FAA*] (FAAL)
ARU.......... Alure Resource Corp. [*Vancouver Stock Exchange symbol*]
ARU.......... American Railway Union
ARU.......... Analog Remote Unit (MCD)
ARU.......... Analog Response Unit
ARU.......... Aracatuba [*Brazil*] [*Airport symbol*] (OAG)
aru .... Arkansas [*MARC country of publication code*] [*Library of Congress*] (LCCP)
ARU.......... Armed Resistance Unit (EA)
ARU.......... Arti [*USSR*] [*Seismograph station code, US Geological Survey*] (SEIS)
ARu.......... Assyrische Rechtsurkunden [*A publication*] (BJA)
ARU.......... Attitude Reference Unit
ARU.......... Audio Response Unit
ARU.......... Automatic Range Unit
ArU............ University of Arkansas, Fayetteville, AR [*Library symbol*] [*Library of Congress*] (LCLS)
ARUB....... Authorized Repair Unaccomplished at Base [*Military*] (AFIT)
ARUCAN.. Archives of Rubber Cultivation [*Bogor*] [*A publication*]
ARUCC ..... Association des Registraires d'Universites et de Colleges du Canada [*Association of Registrars of the Universities and Colleges of Canada*]
ARUCC ..... Association of Registrars of the Universities and Colleges of Canada
ARUG........ Air Reserve Unit (General Training)
ARUM....... Rumsey Municipal Library, Alberta [*Library symbol*] [*National Library of Canada*] (NLC)
ArU-M....... University of Arkansas Medical Center, Little Rock, AR [*Library symbol*] [*Library of Congress*] (LCLS)
ARUMD.... Argumente [*A publication*]
ArU-Mon.. University of Arkansas at Monticello, Monticello, AR [*Library symbol*] [*Library of Congress*] (LCLS)
ARUNK..... Arrival Unknown [*Aviation*]
Arun Mines ... Arundell on the Law of Mines [*A publication*] (DLA)
ARUPAS... Annales Academiae Regiae Scientiarum Upsaliensis [*A publication*]
Arup J........ Arup Journal [*A publication*]
Arup Jnl...... Arup Journal [*A publication*]
ARUPS....... Angle-Resolved Ultraviolet Photoelectron Spectroscopy
ARUS .... Arctic Research in the United States [*A publication*]
ARUSA....... Abarth Register, USA (EA)
ARUSE7.... University of Maine at Orono. Maine Agricultural Experiment Station. Annual Report [*A publication*]
ARUSNP... Air Reserve Unit (General Training, Nonpay)
ARUSP...... Air Reserve Unit (General Training, Pay)
ARV .... Aeroballistic Reentry Vehicle
ARV .... Aerospace Research Vehicle
ARV .... AIDS [*Acquired Immune Deficiency Syndrome*]-Associated Retrovirus
ARV .... Air Recreational Vehicle
ARV .... Air Research Vehicle (MCD)

ARV .... Airborne Relay Vehicle
ARV .... Aircraft Repair Ship [*Navy symbol*]
ARV .... Aircraft Rescue Vessel [*Navy*] (MCD)
ARV .... Allgemeiner Rabbiner-Verband [*A publication*]
ARV .... Alternate Record-Voice
ARV .... Alternative Reproduction Vehicle [*Medicine*]
ARV .... American Revised Version [*of the Bible*]
ARV .... Arch Development Corp. [*Vancouver Stock Exchange symbol*]
ARV .... Armored Reconnaissance Vehicle (MCD)
ARV .... Armored Recovery Vehicle
ARV .... Army Vietnam
ARV .... Arvin Industries, Inc. [*NYSE symbol*] (SPSG)
ARV .... Attic Red-Figure Vase Painters [*A publication*]
ARV .... Avian Retrovirus
ARV .... Minocqua/Woodruff, WI [*Location identifier*] [*FAA*] (FAAL)
ARV .... Rich Valley Public Library, Alberta [*Library symbol*] [*National Library of Canada*] (NLC)
ARVA .... Aircraft Repair Ship (Aircraft) [*Navy symbol*]
ARVA .... Associate of the Rating and Valuation Association [*British*] (DBQ)
ARVAC..... Association of Researchers in Voluntary Action and Community Involvement [*British*]
ARVD .... Arteriosclerotic Renal Vascular Disease [*Medicine*]
ARVE .... Aircraft Repair Ship (Engine) [*Navy symbol*]
ARVEBZ .... Archiva Veterinaria [*Bucharest*] [*A publication*]
ARVEE...... Recreational Vehicle [*Formed by phonetic spelling of initials R and V*]
ARVFA...... Annual Review of Fluid Mechanics [*A publication*]
ARVFA3.... Annual Review of Fluid Mechanics [*A publication*]
ARVGB....... Annual Review of Genetics [*A publication*]
ARVGB7.... Annual Review of Genetics [*A publication*]
ARVH........ Aircraft Repair Ship (Helicopter) [*Navy symbol*]
ARVIA....... Associate of the Royal Victoria Institute of Architects [*British*]
ARVIC........ Association for Religious and Value Issues in Counseling (EA)
ARVID....... Archives of Virology [*A publication*]
ARVIDA.... Arthur Vining Davis Corp.
ARVIDF..... Archives of Virology [*A publication*]
ARVIN ...... Army of the Republic of Vietnam [*Also, ARVN*] [*South Vietnam*]
Ar Vk .... Archiv fuer Voelkerkunde [*A publication*]
ARVLA...... American Recreational Vehicle Living Association [*Defunct*] (EA)
ARVm........ American Revised Version [*of the Bible*], Margin
ARVN .... Army of the Republic of Vietnam [*Also, ARVIN*] [*Defunct*] [*South Vietnam*]
ARVO........ Association for Research in Vision and Ophthalmology (EA)
ARVPA...... Annual Review of Pharmacology [*Later, Annual Review of Pharmacology and Toxicology*] [*A publication*]
ARVPAX... Annual Review of Pharmacology [*Later, Annual Review of Pharmacology and Toxicology*] [*A publication*]
ARVR 22.... Anno Regni Victoriae Regina Vicesimo Secundo (DLA)
ARVSDB.. Annual Review of Sociology [*A publication*]
ARVSG...... Air Reserve Volunteer Support Group
ARVT .... North Atlantic Airlines [*NASDAQ symbol*] (NQ)
ARW .... Advanced Recoilless Weapon (MCD)
ARW .... Advanced Research Workshop
ARW .... Aerial Refueling Wing [*Aeronautics*]
ARW .... Aeroelastic Research Wing (MCD)
ARW .... Air-Conditioning and Refrigeration Wholesalers (EA)
ARW .... Air Raid Warden
ARW .... Air Raid Warning [*Air Force*]
ARW .... American Rescue Workers (EA)
ARW .... Ammunition Repair Workshop (NATG)
ARW .... Arad [*Romania*] [*Airport symbol*] (OAG)
arw .... Arawak [*MARC language code*] [*Library of Congress*] (LCCP)
ARW .... Archiv fuer Religionswissenschaft [*A publication*]
ARW .... [*The*] Arkansas Western Railway Co. [*AAR code*]
ARW .... Arrow Electronics, Inc. [*NYSE symbol*] (SPSG)
ARW .... Arrowfield Resources [*Vancouver Stock Exchange symbol*]
ARW .... Atmospheric Radio Wave
ARW .... Attitude Reaction Wheel
ARWA .... American Right of Way Association [*Later, IRWA*] (EA)
ARWA ...... Associate of the Royal West of England Academy
ARWAB ... Army Rotary Wing Aptitude Battery (AABC)
ARWAF.... Army Personnel Attached to the Air Force for Duty
ARWARCOL ... Army War College (MCD)
ARWBA ...... American Railway Engineering Association. Bulletin [*A publication*]
ARWC .... Army War College
ARWDS..... Afterwards (ROG)
ARWI .... Association of Russian War Invalids of World War II (EA)
ARWMA .... Archiwum Mineralogiczne [*A publication*]
ARWP .... Archiv fuer Rechts- und Wirtschaftsphilosophie [*A publication*]
ARWR .... Advanced RADAR Warning Receiver (MCD)
ARWS........ Advanced RADAR Warning System (MCD)
ARWS....... Air Wisconsin Services, Inc. [*NASDAQ symbol*] (NQ)
ARWS....... Aircraft Response to Wind Spectrum (MCD)
ARWS....... Antiradiation Weapon System (NVT)
ARWS........ Associate of the Royal Society of Painters in Water Colours [*British*]
ARWS........ Associate of the Royal Water-Colour Society [*British*] (ROG)

ARWSDG ... US Department of Agriculture. Science and Education Administration. Agricultural Research Results. ARR-W [*A publication*]
ARX .... Air Regenerative Exhaust
ARX .... Air Xpress, Inc. [*Greensboro, NC*] [*FAA designator*]   (FAA)
ARX .... ARX, Inc. [*NYSE symbol*]   (SPSG)
ARX .... Asbury Park/Monmouth County [*New Jersey*] [*Airport symbol*]   (OAG)
ARX .... Aurex Resources, Inc. [*Vancouver Stock Exchange symbol*]
ARX .... Automatic Retransmission Exchange [*ITT World Communications, Inc.*] [*Secaucus, NJ*]   (TSSD)
ARX .... Soviet and Eastern European Foreign Trade. A Journal of Translations [*A publication*]
ARY .... Antilles Resources Ltd. [*Vancouver Stock Exchange symbol*]
ARY .... Ararat [*Australia*] [*Airport symbol*] [*Obsolete*]   (OAG)
ARY .... Artillery Resources Ltd. [*Vancouver Stock Exchange symbol*]
ArY .... Marion County Library, Yellville, AR [*Library symbol*] [*Library of Congress*]   (LCLS)
ARY .... Ryley Public Library, Alberta [*Library symbol*] [*National Library of Canada*]   (NLC)
ARYM .... Rycroft Municipal Library, Alberta [*Library symbol*] [*National Library of Canada*]   (NLC)
ARYT .... Aryt Optronics Industries Ltd. [*Tel Aviv, Israel*] [*NASDAQ symbol*]   (NQ)
ARZ .... Active Reconnaissance Zone
ARZ .... Arizona Business [*A publication*]
ARZ .... Arizona Silver Corp. [*Vancouver Stock Exchange symbol*]
ARZ .... Aurizon Mines Ltd. [*Toronto Stock Exchange symbol*] [*Vancouver Stock Exchange symbol*]
ARZ .... N'Zeto [*Angola*] [*Airport symbol*]   (OAG)
ARZA .... Association of Reform Zionists of America   (EA)
Arzi .... Hed-Arzi [*Israel*] [*Record label*]
ARZMAA ... Aerztliche Monatshefte fuer Berufliche Fortbildung [*A publication*]
ARZNA ..... Arzneimittel-Forschung [*Drug Research*] [*A publication*]
ARZNAD .. Drug Research [*A publication*]
Arznei-For ... Arzneimittel-Forschung [*Drug Research*] [*A publication*]
Arzneim-Forsch ... Arzneimittel-Forschung [*Drug Research*] [*A publication*]
Arzneim Forsch Beih ... Arzneimittel-Forschung. Beiheft [*A publication*]
Arzneim Forsch Drug Res ... Arzneimittel-Forschung/Drug Research [*A publication*]
Arzneimittelallerg Kongr Dtsch Ges Allerg Immunitaetsforsch ... Arzneimittelallergie. Kongress der Deutschen Gesellschaft fuer Allergie- und Immunitaetsforschung [*A publication*]
Arzneimittel-Forsch ... Arzneimittel-Forschung [*Drug Research*] [*A publication*]
ARZNF ...... Arizona Silver Corp. [*NASDAQ symbol*]   (NQ)
ARZOA ..... Arkiv foer Zoologi [*A publication*]
ARZOAG .. Arkiv foer Zoologi [*A publication*]
Arzt Apoth Krankenhaus ... Arzt, Apotheker, Krankenhaus [*A publication*]
Arzt Krankenh ... Arzt im Krankenhaus [*A publication*]
ARZWA6 .. Aerztliche Wochenschrift [*A publication*]
AS .... Abilene & Southern Railway Co. [*AAR code*]
A & S .... Abraham & Straus [*Retail store*]
aS .... Absiemens [*Unit of conductance*]
AS .... Academy of Sciences
A & S .... Accident and Sickness Insurance
AS .... Account Sales
AS .... Accumulated Surplus [*Profit margin*]
AS .... Acetosyringone [*Organic chemistry*]
AS .... Acquisition Strategy [*Army*]   (RDA)
AS .... Acquisitions Section [*Resources and Technical Services Division of ALA*]
AS .... Acrylic Styrene [*Plastics technology*]
AS .... Act of Sederunt   (DLA)
AS .... Action Socialiste [*Socialist Action*] [*Congo*]
AS .... Active Security [*Investment term*]
AS .... Active Sleep [*Physiology*]
AS .... Actors Studio   (EA)
A-S .... Adams-Stokes [*Cardiology*]
AS .... Adapter Section [*NASA*]   (KSC)
AS .... Adapter, Straight
AS .... Add-Subtract
AS .... Additional Sources
AS .... Address Strobe [*Signal*] [*Data processing*]
AS .... Adhesion Society   (EA)
AS .... Administrative Support
AS .... Admiral Superintendent [*Obsolete*] [*British*]
AS .... Advanced Supplementary [*Education level*] [*British*]
AS .... Advanced System [*NAS*]
AS .... Aerial Surveillance   (MCD)
AS .... Aeronaut Society   (EA)
AS .... Aeronautical Specifications
AS .... Aeronautical Standards
AS .... Aerospace   (IEEE)
AS .... Aerospace Standards
AS .... Aerospace Studies [*AFROTC*]   (AFM)
AS .... Aerospray [*Ionization*] [*Physics*]
AS .... Aetherius Society   (EA)
As .... Aethestan [*King of England, 895-940*]   (ILCA)
AS .... Affective System

AS .... Affirmist Society   (EA)
AS .... African Star [*Decoration*] [*British*]
AS .... Afrika Spectrum [*A publication*]
AS .... Afrolit Society   (EAIO)
AS .... Aftersight [*Billing*]
AS .... Aged Spouse [*Social Security Administration*]   (OICC)
AS .... Aggregate Supply
AS .... Aileron Station   (MCD)
AS .... Ain Shems   (BJA)
AS .... Air Sacculitis [*Avian pathology*]
AS .... Air Screw
AS .... Air Section
AS .... Air Service
AS .... Air Specification   (NG)
AS .... Air Staff [*Air Force*]
AS .... Air Station
AS .... Air Steward [*British military*]   (DMA)
A/S .... Air Strike
AS .... Air Superiority   (MCD)
AS .... Air Supply   (NRCH)
AS .... Air Support
AS .... Air-to-Surface [*Missiles*]   (NATG)
AS .... Air Surveillance [*Air Force*]
AS .... Aircraft Standards
AS .... Airports Service [*of FAA*]
AS .... Airscoop
AS .... Airspeed
as .... Akciova Spolecnost [*Joint-Stock Company*]
A/S .... Aksjeselskap [*Joint-Stock Company*] [*Norway*]   (GPO)
A/S .... Aktieselskab [*Joint-Stock Company*] [*Sweden*]
AS .... Al Segno [*At the Sign*] [*Music*]   (ROG)
AS .... Alaska Airlines, Inc. [*ICAO designator*]   (OAG)
AS .... Albanian Society   (EAIO)
AS .... Alcuin Society   (EA)
AS .... Alimentary System [*Medicine*]
AS .... Alkan Society [*Surrey, England*]   (EAIO)
AS .... Alkyl Sulfate [*Surfactant*] [*Organic chemistry*]
AS .... Alongside
AS .... Alten Sprachen [*A publication*]
AS .... Alternative Society [*British*]
A & S .... Alton & Southern Railroad
AS .... Altostratus [*Also, ALST*] [*Meteorology*]
AS .... Aluminium Suisse, SA [*Commercial firm*]
AS .... Aluminum and Steel [*Freight*]
AS .... American Samoa [*ANSI two-letter standard code*] [*Postal code*]   (CNC)
as .... American Samoa [*MARC country of publication code*] [*Library of Congress*]   (LCCP)
AS .... American Scholar [*A publication*]
AS .... American Songbag [*A publication*]
AS .... American Speech [*A publication*]
AS .... American Standard
AS .... American Statesmen [*A publication*]
AS .... American String Teacher [*A publication*]
AS .... Americas Society   (EA)
AS .... Amertool Services
AS .... Ammeter Switch   (MSA)
As .... Ampere Second
AS .... Amyloid Substance [*Medicine*]
AS .... Anatolian Studies [*A publication*]
AS .... Anatomical Society   (EAIO)
AS .... Anglican Society   (EA)
AS .... Anglistisches Seminar [*A publication*]
A-S .... Anglo-Saxon [*Language, etc.*]
AS .... Ankylosing Spondylitis [*Medicine*]
AS .... Anno Salvatoris [*or Salutis*] [*In the Year of Salvation*] [*Latin*]
AS .... Anomalous Scattering [*Crystallography*]
AS .... Anonim Sirketi [*Corporation, Joint-Stock Company*]
AS .... Antarctican Society   (EA)
AS .... Antennas, Complex [*JETDS nomenclature*] [*Military*]   (CET)
AS .... Anthologie Sonore [*Record label*] [*France*]
AS .... (Anthroyloxy)stearic Acid [*Organic chemistry*]
AS .... Antiquity and Survival [*The Hague and Jerusalem*] [*A publication*]
AS .... Antisense Orientation
AS .... Antiserum [*Immunology*]
AS .... Antisubmarine
A/S .... Antisurface [*Military*]   (NVT)
AS .... Anxiety Score [*Psychology*]
AS .... Anxiety State [*Psychology*]
AS .... Aortic Stenosis [*Medicine*]
AS .... Apollo-Saturn [*NASA*]   (MCD)
AS .... Apostolado Sacerdotal [*A publication*]
AS .... Application System   (ADA)
AS .... Applied Science
AS .... Applied Statistics [*A publication*]
AS .... Apprentice Seaman
AS .... Aqueous Solution
AS .... Aqueous Suspension
AS .... Arator Society   (EA)
AS .... Arba Sicula [*Sicilian Dawn*]   (EA)

AS	Arbeit und Sitte in Palaestina [*A publication*] (BJA)
AS	Archeology Section (EA)
AS	Area Specialized Division (MCD)
AS	Area Supervisor [*Bureau of Apprenticeship and Training*] [*Department of Labor*]
AS	Area Surveillance
AS	Arginase [*An enzyme*]
AS	Argininosuccinate Synthetase [*An enzyme*]
AS	Armco, Inc. [*Formerly, Armco Steel Corp.*] [*NYSE symbol*] (SPSG)
AS	Armed Services
AS	Armor School [*Army*] (MCD)
AS	Army Security
AS	Army Service [*British*] (ROG)
AS	Army Staff
As	Arsenic [*Chemical element*]
AS	Art Scholar [*A publication*]
AS	Arteriosclerosis [*Medicine*]
AS	Articulation Score [*Percentage of words correctly understood over a radio channel perturbed by interference*] [*Telecommunications*]
AS	Artificial Satellite
AS	Artificial Sweetener
AS	Artists Space (EA)
A & S	Arts and Sciences
A & S	Arts and Sciences [*A publication*]
AS	Arts in Society [*A publication*]
AS	As Stated
AS	Asbury Seminarian [*A publication*]
AS	Ascendance-Submission [*Psychology*]
AS	Ascent Stage [*NASA*] (MCD)
AS	Ashoka Society [*Later, Ashoka: Innovators for the Public*] (EA)
AS	Asia
AS	Asia Society (EA)
as-----	Asia, Southeastern [*MARC geographic area code*] [*Library of Congress*] (LCCP)
AS	Asian Survey [*A publication*]
AS	Asiatische Studien [*A publication*]
AS	Asmonean (BJA)
As	Asomante [*A publication*]
AS	Assault Squadron [*British military*] (DMA)
AS	Assembly System
AS	Assented Security [*Investment term*]
AS	Assessable Stock [*Investment term*]
A & S	Assignment and Status Chart
AS	Assistant Secretary
AS	Assistant Surgeon (DAS)
AS	Associate in Science
AS	Association for Singles (EA)
AS	Assyriological Studies. Oriental Institute. University of Chicago [*A publication*]
As	Astigmatism [*Also, Ast*] [*Ophthalmology*]
AS	Astronomy (ROG)
as	Asymmetric [*Chemistry*]
AS	At Sight
AS	Atmosphere and Space
AS	Attitude Set [*Aerospace*] (MCD)
AS	Audio Sensitivity
AS	Audiogenic Seizure [*Neurophysiology*]
AS	Augmentation System
AS	Augmented Surveyor [*NASA*] (MCD)
AS	Augustan Society (EA)
AS	Auris Sinistra [*Left Ear*] [*Latin*]
AS	Auslieferungsschein [*Delivery Permit, Certificate of Delivery, Delivery Order*] [*German*]
AS	Australasian Sketcher [*A publication*]
AS	Australia (AABC)
AS	Australian Society [*A publication*] (ADA)
AS	Austrian Schilling [*Monetary unit*]
AS	Authorizations Subsystem [*Military*]
AS	Auto Sequential (NRCH)
AS	Automatic Skin [*NASA*] (KSC)
AS	Automatic Sprinkler [*Technical drawings*]
AS	Automatic Synchronizer
AS	Automation Society (EA)
AS	Autosampler
A/S	Aux Soins De [*Care Of, c/o*] [*French*]
A/S	Auxiliary Stage [*NASA*] (NASA)
AS	Auxiliary Steam [*Nuclear energy*] (NRCH)
AS	Auxiliary Storage [*Data processing*]
AS	Aviaeskadra [*Russian term for an air squadron*]
AS	Aviation Support Equipment Technician [*Navy rating*]
AS	[*The*] Avicultural Society [*British*]
AS	Das Akkadische Syllabar [*A publication*] (BJA)
AS	Dr. Madaus & Co. [*Germany*] [*Research code symbol*]
AS	Hawker Siddeley Aviation Ltd. [*Great Britain*] [*ICAO aircraft manufacturer identifier*] (ICAO)
As	Oesterreichische Nationalbibliothek, Vienna, Austria [*Library symbol*] [*Library of Congress*] (LCLS)
AS	Sister of Arts
AS	Standard Atmosphere
AS	Start of Answer [*Telecommunications*] (TEL)
AS	Submarine Tender [*Navy symbol*]
AS	Wait [*Morse telephony*] (FAAC)
AS1	Aviation Support Equipment Technician, First Class [*Navy rating*]
AS2	Angel, Second Class [*Classification of angel Clarence Oddbody in 1947 film, "It's a Wonderful Life"*]
AS2	Aviation Support Equipment Technician, Second Class [*Navy rating*]
A3S	Army Aircraft Avionics Study (MCD)
AS3	Aviation Support Equipment Technician, Third Class [*Navy rating*]
A²S²	Accelerated Active Search System (CAAL)
ASA	Abort Sensor Assembly [*Apollo*] [*NASA*]
ASA	Accommodation Sales Authorization (MCD)
ASA	Acetylsalicylic Acid [*Aspirin*]
ASA	Acoustical Society of America (EA)
ASA	Acrylic-Styrene-Acrylonitrile [*Organic chemistry*]
ASA	Active Surface Area (MCD)
ASA	Actuarial Society of America [*Later, SA*]
ASA	Adapter Service Area
ASA	Adastral Resources Ltd. [*Vancouver Stock Exchange symbol*]
ASA	Adjustable Shock Absorber
ASA	Administrative Support Airlift (MCD)
ASA	Advanced Surveillance Aircraft (MCD)
ASA	Advanced System Avionics [*Air Force*]
ASA	Advertising Standards Authority [*British*]
ASA	Aerospace Amplifier (MCD)
ASA	Aerosurface Amplifier (NASA)
ASA	Aerosurface Servo Amplifier [*NASA*] (NASA)
ASA	Afghanistan Studies Association (EA)
ASA	African Studies Association (EA)
ASA	Air Security Agency (MCD)
ASA	Air Stagnation Advisories [*National Weather Service*]
ASA	Airline Services Association [*Absorbed by ARSA*] (EA)
ASA	Airlines of South Australia
ASA	Alaska Airlines, Inc. [*Air carrier designation symbol*]
ASA	Alkylsuccinic Anhydride [*Organic chemistry*]
ASA	Aluminium Stockholders' Association [*British*]
ASA	Aluminum Siding Association [*Later, AAMA*] (EA)
ASA	Amateur Softball Association of America (EA)
ASA	Amateur Swimming Association
ASA	Amegroid Society of America (EA)
ASA	American Sailing Association (EA)
ASA	American Salers Association (EA)
ASA	American Saluki Association (EA)
ASA	American Schizophrenia Association (EA)
ASA	American Schools Association (EA)
ASA	American Schooner Association (EA)
ASA	American Scientific Affiliation (EA)
ASA	American Sentic Association
ASA	American Shark Association (EA)
ASA	American Shellfisheries Association
ASA	American Shiatsu Association (EA)
ASA	American Shorthorn Association (EA)
ASA	American Shrimpboat Association (EA)
ASA	American Sightseeing Association [*Later, ASI*]
ASA	American Simmental Association (EA)
ASA	American Ski Association (EA)
ASA	American Snowmobile Association [*Defunct*]
ASA	American Snowplowing Association (EA)
ASA	American Society for Abrasives [*Superseded by AES*] (EA)
ASA	American Society for Aesthetics (EA)
ASA	American Society on Aging (EA)
ASA	American Society of Agronomy (EA)
ASA	American Society of Anesthesiologists (EA)
ASA	American Society of Appraisers [*Acronym also used as designation awarded to group's senior members*] [*Washington, DC*] (EA)
ASA	American Society of Artists (EA)
ASA	American Society of Auctioneers [*Defunct*] (EA)
ASA	American Sociological Association (EA)
ASA	American Sociometric Association [*Defunct*] (EA)
ASA	American Soybean Association (EA)
ASA	American Sportscasters Association (EA)
ASA	American Standards Association [*Later, USASI, ANSI*]
ASA	American Statistical Association (EA)
ASA	American Sternwheel Association (EA)
ASA	American Student Association (EA)
ASA	American Studies Association (EA)
ASA	American Subcontractors Association (EA)
ASA	American Sugar Alliance (EA)
ASA	American Sunbathing Association (EA)
ASA	American Supply Association (EA)
ASA	American Surety Association (EA)
ASA	American Surfing Association (EA)
ASA	American Surgical Association (EA)
ASA	American Survival Association [*Defunct*] (EA)
ASA	American-Swiss Association (EA)
ASA	Aminosalicylic Acid [*Biochemistry*]
ASA	Amplifier and Switch Assembly (MCD)

ASA	Amputee Sports Association (EA)
ASA	Anterior Septal Artery [*Anatomy*]
ASA	Anterior Sorting Area
AS & A	Anthony, Smallhorn & Associates [*British*]
ASA	Anthroposophical Society in America (EA)
ASA	Antistatic Additive
ASA	Anzeiger fuer Schweizerische Altertumskunde [*A publication*]
ASA	Appropriate Superior Authority [*British military*] (DMA)
ASA	Architectural Secretaries Association [*Later, SAA*] (EA)
ASA	Area Scanning Alarm
ASA	Armenian Students Association of America (EA)
ASA	Army Seal of Approval
ASA	Army Security Agency [*Later, INSCOM*] [*Arlington, VA*]
ASA	Army Ski Association [*British military*] (DMA)
ASA	Army Strategic Appraisal
ASA	Articulation Screening Assessment [*Speech development test*]
ASA	ASA Ltd. [*Formerly, American-South African Investment Co. Ltd.*] [*NYSE symbol*] (SPSG)
ASA	Asahikawa [*Japan*] [*Seismograph station code, US Geological Survey*] (SEIS)
ASA	Asian Students' Association [*Kowloon, Hong Kong*] (EAIO)
ASA	Asian Surgical Association (EAIO)
As A	Asie et l'Afrique [*A publication*]
ASA	Assab [*Ethiopia*] [*Airport symbol*] (OAG)
AS of A	Assistant Secretary of the Army
ASA	Assistant Secretary of the Army
ASA	Assistant Stores Accountant [*British military*] (DMA)
ASA	Associate Administrator for Aviation Safety [*FAA*] (FAAC)
ASA	Associate in Secretarial Administration
ASA	Associate of the Society of Actuaries [*Designation awarded by Society of Actuaries*]
ASA	Associated Stenotypists of America [*Later, NSRA*] (EA)
ASA	Association of Social Anthropologists of the Commonwealth [*London, England*] (EAIO)
ASA	Association of South East Asia [*Later, ASEAN*]
ASA	Association des Statisticiens de l'Athletisme [*Association of Track and Field Statisticians*] (EAIO)
ASA	Association for the Study of Abortion [*Later, NAF*]
ASA	Atlantic Salmon Association (EA)
ASA	Atlantic Southeast Airlines, Inc.
ASA	Atomic Scientists' Association [*Great Britain*]
ASA	Atomic Security Agency [*Army*]
ASA	Auditory Sensation Area
ASA (FM)	Australian Science Action
ASA	Autism Society of America (EA)
ASA	Automatic Steering Antenna
ASA	Automatic Systems Analysis (KSC)
ASA	Automotive Service Association (EA)
ASA	Aviation Supply Annex
ASA	Avicultural Society of America (EA)
ASA	Azalea Society of America (EA)
ASA	Azimuth Servo Assembly
ASA	Die Aramaeische Sprache unter den Achaimeniden [*A publication*] (BJA)
ASA	St. Albert Public Library, Alberta [*Library symbol*] [*National Library of Canada*] (NLC)
ASA	Southern Arkansas University, Magnolia, AR [*OCLC symbol*] (OCLC)
ASA	(Specification) Standards Association of Australia [*A publication*] (APTA)
ASAA........	Airman Apprentice, Aviation Support Equipment Technician, Striker [*Navy rating*]
ASAA........	Annuario. Reale Scuola Archeologica di Atene [*A publication*]
ASAA........	Armenian Students Association of America (EA)
ASAA........	Army Special Award for Accomplishment (RDA)
ASAA........	ASA International Ltd. [*NASDAQ symbol*] (NQ)
ASAA........	Associate of the Society of Incorporated Accountants and Auditors [*British*]
ASAAD......	American Society for Advancement of Anesthesia in Dentistry (EA)
ASAA-I......	Aviation Security Association of America - International [*Defunct*] (EA)
ASAAN	Annales. Societe Archeologique de l'Arrondissement de Nivelles [*A publication*]
ASAA Rev ...	Asian Studies Association of Australia. Review [*A publication*]
ASAAS	Asymmetric Stress Analysis of Axisymmetric Solids [*Computer program*]
ASA/ASR ...	American Sociological Review. American Sociological Association [*A publication*]
ASAAWE..	Association of South Asian Archaeologists in Western Europe (EAIO)
ASAB........	Annales. Societe d'Archeologie de Bruxelles [*A publication*]
ASAB........	Association for the Study of Animal Behavior
ASAB........	Atlanta & Saint Andrews Bay Railway Co. [*AAR code*]
ASA Bull....	ASA [*Australian Society of Accountants*] Bulletin [*A publication*] (APTA)
ASAC........	Active Satellite Attitude Control
ASAC........	Administrative Sciences Association of Canada [*Association des Sciences Administratives du Canada*]
ASAC........	Aerodynamic Surface Assembly and Checkout [*NASA*] (NASA)

ASAC........	Air Service Area Command
ASAC........	Air Surveillance and Airspace Control (MCD)
ASAC........	All Source Analysis Center (MCD)
ASAC........	Altostratus and Altocumulus [*Meteorology*]
ASAC........	American Samoa Administrative Code [*A publication*] (DLA)
ASAC........	American Society of Agricultural Consultants (EA)
AS of AC...	American Society of Arms Collectors
ASAC........	American Society of Arms Collectors (EA)
ASAC........	American-Southern Africa Council [*Defunct*]
ASAC........	Antisubmarine Air Control [*Navy*] (MCD)
ASAC........	Army Study Advisory Committee
ASAC........	Asian Securities Analysts Council [*See also CAAF*] [*Japan*] (EAIO)
ASAC........	Association of Surf Angling Clubs (EA)
ASAC........	Automated Systems Army Commissaries (AABC)
ASACG......	Army Security Assistance Coordinating Group
ASACOT...	American-Southern Africa Chamber of Trade and Industry (EA)
ASACS	Airborne Surveillance and Control System [*ASD*]
ASACT......	Advanced Strategic Aerodynamic Configuration Technology (MCD)
ASA(CW)..	Assistant Secretary of the Army (Civil Works)
ASAD	Assembly Aid [*Tool*] (AAG)
ASAD	Authorized Shortages and Discrepancies (KSC)
ASADA......	Atomic Space and Development Authority [*Nuclear energy*] (NRCH)
ASAE........	American Society of Aeronautical Engineers [*Later, SAE*] (KSC)
ASAE........	American Society for Aerospace Education (EA)
ASAE........	American Society of Agricultural Engineers (EA)
ASAE........	American Society of Association Executives (EA)
ASAE........	Annales. Service des Antiquites de l'Egypte [*A publication*]
ASAE Tech Pap ...	ASAE [*American Society of Agricultural Engineers*] Technical Paper [*A publication*]
ASAE Trans ...	American Society of Agricultural Engineers. Transactions [*A publication*]
ASAF	Assistant Secretary of the Air Force (MCD)
AS of AF	Assistant Secretary of the Air Force
ASAFED ...	Association Africaine d'Education pour le Developpement [*African Association of Education for Development - AFASED*] (EAIO)
As Aff (L)...	Asian Affairs (London) [*A publication*]
As Aff (NY) ...	Asian Affairs (New York) [*A publication*]
ASA (FM) ...	Assistant Secretary of the Army (Financial Management)
ASAFMA ..	Assistant Secretary of the Air Force (Materiel)
ASAF(RD & A) ...	Assistant Secretary of the Air Force (Research, Development, and Acquisition) (MCD)
ASAF(RDL) ...	Assistant Secretary of the Air Force (Research, Development, and Logistics) (MCD)
As Afr Stud (B) ...	Asian and African Studies (Bratislava) [*A publication*]
ASAGAD...	American Society for Advancement of General Anesthesia in Dentistry [*Later, ASAAD*] (EA)
ASAH	American Squadron of Aviation Historians (EA)
ASAHC	American Society of Architectural Hardware Consultants [*Later, DHI*] (EA)
ASAHP......	American Society of Allied Health Professions (EA)
ASAI.........	American Society of Ancient Instruments (EA)
ASAI.........	Annales. Service Archeologique de l'Iran [*A publication*]
ASAI.........	Atlantic Southeast Airlines, Incorporated [*NASDAQ symbol*] (NQ)
ASAIA	Associate of the South Australian Institute of Architects
ASAIC	Assistant Special Agent in Charge
ASAIHL....	Association of Southeast Asian Institutions of Higher Learning [*Bangkok, Thailand*]
ASA (I & L) ...	Assistant Secretary of the Army (Installations and Logistics)
ASA(IL & FM) ...	Assistant Secretary of the Army (Installations, Logistics, and Financial Management) (AABC)
ASAI Mech E ...	Associate of the South African Institute of Mechanical Engineers
ASAIO.......	American Society for Artificial Internal Organs (EA)
ASAIO Trans ...	Transactions. American Society for Artificial Internal Organs [*A publication*]
ASAK........	Anzeiger fuer Schweizerische Altertumskunde [*A publication*]
ASal	Acta Salmanticensia [*A publication*]
ASAL........	Annuaire. Societe d'Histoire et d'Archeologie de la Lorraine [*A publication*]
ASAL........	Annual Survey of African Law [*A publication*]
ASAL........	Annual Survey of American Law [*A publication*]
ASAL........	Annual Survey of Australian Law [*A publication*]
ASAL........	Bank Atlantic, A Federal Savings Bank [*NASDAQ symbol*] (NQ)
ASALA	Armenian Secret Army for the Liberation of Armenia [*Turkey*] (PD)
ASALAP....	Acta Salmanticensia. Serie de Ciencias [*A publication*]
ASALH......	Association for the Study of Afro-American Life and History (EA)
ASALM.....	Advanced Strategic Air-Launched Missile (MCD)
ASALT......	Assessment of Survivability Against LASER Threat (MCD)
ASAM	American Society for Abrasive Methods [*Later, AES*] (EA)
ASAM	American Society of Addiction Medicine (EA)
ASAM	American Society of Asset Managers (EA)

ASAM .... Annals. South Africa Museum [*A publication*]
ASAM .... Assistant Secretary for Administration and Management [*Department of Labor*]
ASAM .... Associate of the Society of Art Masters [*British*]
ASAM .... Association of Sales Administration Managers   (EA)
ASAMAS .. Annals. South African Museum [*A publication*]
As Am Geog ... Association of American Geographers. Annals [*A publication*]
As Am G Rp ... Association of American Geologists and Naturalists. Reports [*A publication*]
ASAMLM ... MLM Groundwater Engineering, St. Albert, Alberta [*Library symbol*] [*National Library of Canada*]   (NLC)
ASAMN .... American Society of Anthropometric Medicine and Nutrition [*Defunct*]   (EA)
ASAMP..... Airplane Sizing and Mission Performance [*Computer program*]
ASAMPE .. Allied States Association of Motion Picture Exhibitors [*Later, NATO*]
ASA (M & RA) ... Assistant Secretary of the Army (Manpower and Reserve Affairs)   (AABC)
ASAMS..... Austere Surface-to-Air Missile System
ASAMS..... Automatic Structure Analysis of Mass Spectra
ASAN .... Airman, Aviation Support Equipment Technician, Striker [*Navy rating*]
ASAN .... Annales. Societe Archeologique de Namur [*A publication*]
ASA Newsl ... ASA [*American Society of Agronomy*] Newsletter [*A publication*]
ASA Newsl ... Association for the Study of Abortion. Newsletter [*A publication*]   (DLA)
ASA Newsletter ... American Society of Anesthesiologists. Newsletter [*A publication*]
ASANS...... Sangudo Public and School Library, Alberta [*Library symbol*] [*National Library of Canada*]   (NLC)
ASAO .... Association of Show and Agricultural Organisations [*British*]
ASAO .... Association for Social Anthropology in Oceania   (EA)
ASAOP...... Archaeological Survey of Alberta. Occasional Papers [*A publication*]
ASAOTT ... Australian Society of Anaesthetic and Operating Theatre Technicians
ASAP........ Academic and Social Anxiety Program [*Cornell University*]
ASAP........ Accelerated Solicitation to Award Process [*National Institutes of Health*]
ASAP........ Advanced Space Applications Program [*Military*]
ASAP........ Advanced Supersonic All-Purpose Dispenser   (MCD)
ASAP........ Advanced Survival Avionics Program   (MCD)
ASAP........ Advanced Symbolic Artwork Preparation   (MCD)
ASAP........ [*The*] Aerospace Safety Advisory Panel [*NASA/Air Force*]   (NASA)
ASAP........ After Sale Assurance Program
ASAP........ AIDS Services and Prevention Coalition   (EA)
ASAP........ Aircraft Synthesis Analysis Program
ASAP........ Aircraft Systems Activation Program [*Military*]
ASAP........ Aircrew Systems Advisory Panel [*NASA, Air Force*]   (MCD)
ASAP........ Alcohol Safety Action Project [*Department of Transportation*]
ASAP........ American Society of Access Professionals   (EA)
ASAP........ American Society for Adolescent Psychiatry   (EA)
ASAP........ American Society of Aerospace Pilots [*Defunct*]   (EA)
ASAP........ American Society of Animal Production [*Later, ASAS*]
ASAP........ American Society for Association Publishing   (EA)
ASAP........ Americans for a Sound AIDS [*Acquired Immune Deficiency Syndrome*] Policy   (EA)
AS/AP .... Amplified Substrate/Alkaline Phosphatase
ASAP........ Analog System Assembly Pack
ASAP........ Annular Suspension and Pointing System   (MCD)
ASAP........ Antisubmarine Attack Plotter [*Navy*]
ASAP........ Applied Systems and Personnel   (BUR)
ASAP........ Army Scientific Advisory Panel [*Later, ASB*]
ASAP........ Army Scientific Assistance Program   (RDA)
ASAP........ Army Streamlined Acquisition Process [*or Program*]   (RDA)
ASAP........ As Soon as Possible
ASAP........ Australian Science Archives Project
ASAP........ Australian Seniors Action Plan
ASAP........ Auto-Trace Steam Analysis Program [*Computer software*]
ASAP........ Automated Statistical Analysis Program
ASAP........ Auxiliary Storage and Playback [*Assembly*] [*Apollo Telescope Mount*] [*NASA*]
ASAP........ North American Society of Adlerian Psychology [*Later, NASAP*]   (EA)
ASAPA3.... Archives Suisses d'Anthropologie Generale [*A publication*]
ASAPAC .... Army Security Agency, Pacific   (CINC)
ASAPHA... Association of Sea and Air Ports Health Authority [*British*]
ASAPR...... Accelerated Strike Aircraft Program Requirement [*DoD*]   (MCD)
ASA Pro Bu Ec ... American Statistical Association. Proceedings of Business and Economic Statistics Section [*A publication*]
ASA Pro So St ... American Statistical Association. Proceedings of Social Statistics Section [*A publication*]
ASA Pro St Cp ... American Statistical Association. Proceedings of Statistical Computing Section [*A publication*]
ASAPS....... American Society for Aesthetic Plastic Surgery   (EA)
ASAPSS.... American Society for Amusement Park Security and Safety   (EA)

ASAPT ...... Americans for Substance Abuse Prevention and Treatment   (EA)
ASA Publ... ASA [*American Society of Agronomy*] Publication [*A publication*]
ASAR......... Advanced Surface-to-Air Ramjet [*Navy*]
ASAR........ Air Search Acquisition RADAR   (CAAL)
ASAR........ All South Africa Law Reports [*A publication*]   (DLA)
ASAR........ Army Selective Aerial Rocket   (MCD)
ASARB...... Association of Statisticians of American Religious Bodies   (EA)
ASARC...... Army Systems Acquisition Review Council
ASARC IET ... Army Systems Acquisition Review Council Independent Evaluation Team   (MCD)
ASA (R & D) ... Assistant Secretary of the Army (Research and Development)
ASA(RDA) ... Assistant Secretary of the Army (Research, Development, and Acquisition)
ASAR-ER .. Advanced Surface-to-Air Ramjet, Extended Range   (MCD)
Asarh .... Asarhaddon [*BJA*]
ASAR-MR ... Advanced Surface-to-Air Ramjet, Medium Range   (MCD)
ASARR...... Advanced Surface-to-Air Rocket Ramjet   (MCD)
ASARS ..... Advance Synthetic Aperture RADAR System   (MCD)
ASARS ...... Advanced Sensor Analog Relay System [*Army*]   (MCD)
ASARS ...... Advanced Strategic Airborne RADAR System
ASARS ...... Army Small Arms Requirements Simulation [*Battle model*]   (MCD)
ASARS ...... Army Small Arms Requirements Studies   (MCD)
ASAS......... Active Scattering Aerosol Spectrometer [*Aerosol measurement device*]
ASAS......... Aerodynamic Stability Augmentation System [*or Subsystem*] [*NASA*]   (NASA)
ASAS......... Agostiniani Secolari Agustinos Seculares [*Order Secular of St. Augustine - OSSA*] [*Rome, Italy*]   (EAIO)
ASAS......... All Source Analysis System [*DoD*]
ASAS........ American Society of Abdominal Surgery   (EA)
ASAS........ American Society of Animal Science   (EA)
ASAS........ Amorphous Sodium Aluminosilicate [*Inorganic chemistry*]
ASAS........ Amsterdam Security Account System [*Amsterdam stock exchange*] [*Netherlands*]
ASAS........ Army Security Agency School [*Merged with Defense Security Agency School*]
ASAS........ Association of South-East Asian States
ASAS........ Atkins Structural Analysis System   (MCD)
ASAS........ Australian Science and Application Spacecraft
ASASDF.... Advanced Series in Agricultural Sciences [*A publication*]
ASASP....... Active Scattering Aerosol Spectrometer Probe   (MCD)
ASA Spec Publ ... ASA [*Archaeological Survey Association*] Special Publication [*A publication*]
ASA Spec Publ ... ASA [*American Society of Agronomy*] Special Publication [*A publication*]
ASASTSM ... Amalgamated Society of Anchorsmiths, Ship Tackle, and Shackle Makers [*A union*] [*British*]
ASAT......... Acoustic Surface Analysis Technology
ASAT........ Air Search Attack Team [*Military*]
ASA/T .... Airframe and System Assembly/Test   (MCD)
ASAT........ Antisatellite
ASAT........ Antisatellite Satellite
ASAT........ Antisubmarine Attack Teacher
ASAT........ Aspartate Aminotransferase [*Also, AAT, AST, GOT*] [*An enzyme*]
ASAT........ Automatic Spares Analysis Technique
ASA Tech Bul ... ASA [*Australian Society of Accountants*] Technical Bulletin [*A publication*]   (APTA)
A S Atene... Annuario. Scuola Archeologica di Atene e delle Missioni Italiane in Oriente [*A publication*]
ASATT ...... Advanced Small Axial Turbine Technology   (RDA)
ASATTU ... Antisubmarine Attack Teacher Training Unit
ASAU .... Air Search Attack Unit [*Military*]
ASAUK...... African Studies Association United Kingdom
ASAW .... Abhandlungen. Saechsische Akademie der Wissenschaften zu Leipzig. Philosophisch-Historische Klasse [*A publication*]
ASAW .... American Society of Aviation Writers [*Later, IATJ*]   (EA)
ASAW .... Association of Southern Agricultural Workers [*Later, SAAS*]
ASAWL..... Abhandlungen. Saechsische Akademie der Wissenschaften zu Leipzig [*A publication*]
ASAWL PHK ... Abhandlungen. Saechsische Akademie der Wissenschaften zu Leipzig. Philosophisch-Historische Klasse [*A publication*]
ASAWS ..... Advance Surface-to-Air Weapons System
ASAXP...... Average Sorties per Aircraft Actually Possessed [*Air Force*]   (AFIT)
ASB............ Accademia delle Scienze di Bologna. Memorie [*A publication*]
ASB............ Acoustical Standards Board   (MUGU)
ASB............ Administration and Storage Building
ASB............ Advanced Systems Buying
ASB............ Aerated Stabilization Basin [*For water purification*]
ASB............ African Studies Bulletin [*A publication*]
ASB............ Agricultural Statistics Board [*Department of Agriculture*] [*Information service or system*]   (IID)
ASB............ Air Safety Board
ASB............ Air Staff Board   (AFM)
ASB............ Air Supply Board [*Ministry of Aircraft Production*] [*British*]
ASB............ Air Surveillance Broadcast   (MCD)

ASB............	Airborne Special Bombing
ASB............	Aircraft Safety Beacon
ASB............	Aircraft Services Base
ASB............	Airlock Stowage Bag [*NASA*] (MCD)
ASB............	Allied Staff, Berlin [*Post-World War II*]
AS & B.......	Aloin, Strychnine, and Belladonna [*Pharmacy*]
ASB............	Altitude Sensor Bypass
ASB............	Amchitka [*Alaska*] [*Seismograph station code, US Geological Survey*] [*Closed*] (SEIS)
ASB............	American Journal of Small Business [*A publication*]
ASB............	American Savings Bank [*NYSE symbol*] (SPSG)
ASB............	American Society of Bariatrics [*Later, ASBP*]
ASB............	Amphibious Support Battalion [*Military*]
ASB............	Anesthesia Standby [*Medicine*]
ASB............	Annales. Societe Scientifique de Bruxelles. Section Sciences Economiques [*A publication*]
ASB............	Antishock Body
ASB.........	Antisurface Boat
ASB........	Anxiety Scale for the Blind [*Psychology*]
Asb........	Apostilb [*Unit of luminance*]
ASB...........	Aptitude Test for School Beginners [*Child development test*]
ASB......	Armed Services Bulletin
ASB......	Armor Support Battalion (MCD)
ASB........	Army Science Board [*Formerly, ASAP*] (RDA)
ASB........	Asbestos (KSC)
ASB........	Ashburton Oil Ltd. [*Vancouver Stock Exchange symbol*]
ASB........	Ashkhabad [*USSR*] [*Airport symbol*] (OAG)
ASB...........	Asia Letter. An Authoritative Analysis of Asian Affairs [*A publication*]
ASB...........	Associate in Science in Business
ASB...........	Associate in Specialized Business
ASB........	Associated Services for the Blind (EA)
ASB........	Association of Software Brokers (EA)
ASB........	Asymmetrical Sideband
ASB........	Australian Space Board
ASB.......	Australian Stud Book [*A publication*] (APTA)
ASB.......	Automated Status Board
ASB...........	Seba Beach Public Library, Alberta [*Library symbol*] [*National Library of Canada*] (NLC)
ASBA........	American Shore and Beach Preservation Association (NOAA)
ASBA........	American Shorthorn Breeders Association [*Later, ASA*]
ASBA........	American Skibob Association [*Later, USSBF*] (EA)
ASBA........	American Small Businesses Association (EA)
ASBA........	American Southdown Breeders' Association (EA)
ASBA........	American Standardbred Breeders Association (EA)
ASBA........	Association of Ship Brokers and Agents - USA (EA)
ASBA........	Association for Small Business Advancement [*Rockville, MD*] (EA)
ASBA........	Atas. Simposio Sobre a Biota Amazonica [*A publication*]
ASBAH.....	Association for Spina Bifida and Hydrocephalus [*Australia*] [*British*] (IRUK)
ASBAL......	[*A*] Stack Based Abstraction Language [*1978*] [*Data processing*] (CSR)
ASB Bull....	ASB [*Association of Southeastern Biologists*] Bulletin [*A publication*]
ASBC........	American Seat Belt Council [*Later, AORC*] (EA)
ASBC........	American Silkie Bantam Club (EA)
ASBC........	American Society of Biological Chemists [*Later, ASBMB*] (EA)
ASBC........	American Society of Brewing Chemists (EA)
ASBC........	American Standard Building Code (IEEE)
ASBC........	Associated Banc-Corp [*NASDAQ symbol*] (NQ)
ASBC........	Australian Second Board Consultants
ASBCA......	Armed Services Board of Contract Appeals
ASBC & D ...	American Society of Bookplate Collectors and Designers (EA)
ASBCM......	Association of Southern Baptist Campus Ministers (EA)
ASBCS......	Association of Southern Baptist Colleges and Schools (EA)
ASBD........	Advanced Sea-Based Deterrent [*Navy*]
ASBD........	American Society of Bank Directors [*Arlington, VA*] (EA)
ASBDA......	American School Band Directors' Association (EA)
ASBDC......	Association of Small Business Development Centers [*Washington, DC*] (EA)
ASBE........	American Society of Bakery Engineers (EA)
ASBE........	American Society of Body Engineers (EA)
ASBE........	Associate in Science in Basic Engineering
ASBEA9......	Annales Scientifiques. Universite de Besancon. Medecine [*A publication*]
ASBEB......	Acta Stomatologica Belgica [*A publication*]
ASBFC......	Archivio Storico per Belluno, Feltre, e Cadore [*A publication*]
ASBGAF ...	Annales Scientifiques. Universite de Besancon. Geologie [*A publication*]
ASBHCA...	Average Season Busy Hour Call Attempts [*Telecommunications*] (TEL)
ASBHCC...	Average Season Busy Hour Call Completions [*Telecommunications*] (TEL)
ASB & I	Aloin, Strychnine, Belladonna, and Ipecac [*Pharmacy*]
ASBI........	Ameriana Savings Bank FSB [*NASDAQ symbol*] (NQ)
ASBIA	Archivio di Scienze Biologiche [*Bologna*] [*A publication*]
ASBIAL.....	Archivio di Scienze Biologiche [*A publication*]
ASBIPC.....	American Sugar Beet Industry Policy Committee [*Defunct*] (EA)

ASBK.........	Sydney/Bankstown [*Australia*] [*ICAO location identifier*] (ICLI)
ASBL.........	Assemble (AABC)
ASBLAU ..	Archivos. Sociedad de Biologia de Montevideo [*A publication*]
ASBLY	Assembly (AFM)
ASBM........	Air-to-Surface Ballistic Missile
ASBM........	Associate in Business Management
ASBMAX ..	Annales. Belgische Vereniging voor Tropische Geneeskunde [*A publication*]
ASBMB	American Society for Biochemistry and Molecular Biology (EA)
ASBMR	American Society for Bone and Mineral Research (EA)
ASBO	Asbestos and Small Business Ombudsman [*Environmental Protection Agency*]
ASBO	Association of School Business Officials International (EA)
ASBOA5....	Annales Scientifiques. Universite de Besancon. Botanique [*A publication*]
A Sbor	Archeologiceskij Sbornik Gosudarstvennyj Ordena Lenina Ermitaz [*A publication*]
ASBP........	American Society of Bariatric Physicians (EA)
ASBPA	American Shore and Beach Preservation Association (EA)
ASBPAC....	America's Small Business Political Action Committee (EA)
ASBPE	American Society of Business Press Editors (EA)
ASBRAE ...	Anuario. Sociedade Broteriana [*A publication*]
ASBS	American Striped Bass Society (EA)
ASBS	Asbestec Industries, Inc. [*Pennsauken, NJ*] [*NASDAQ symbol*] (NQ)
ASBS	Association of Social and Behavioral Scientists (EA)
ASBSBSW ...	Amalgamated Society of Boilermakers, Shipwrights, Blacksmiths, and Structural Workers [*A union*] [*British*] (DCTA)
AsbSem......	Asbury Seminarian [*Wilmore, KY*] [*A publication*]
ASBSTS	Asbestos
ASBTh.......	Associate of the Society of Health and Beauty Therapists [*British*] (DBQ)
ASBU.........	Arab States Broadcasting Union
ASBV.........	Avocado-Sunblotch Viroid
ASBW.........	Amalgamated Society of Brass Workers [*A union*] [*British*]
ASBWMMA ...	Amalgamated Scale, Beam, and Weighing Machine Makers Association [*A union*] [*British*]
ASBYP........	Appraisal. Science Books for Young People [*A publication*]
ASBZA4	Annales Scientifiques. Universite de Besancon. Zoologie et Physiologie [*A publication*]
ASC............	Abbe Sine Condition
ASC............	Above Suspended Ceiling [*Technical drawings*]
ASC............	Accelerometer Signal Conditioner (KSC)
ASC............	Accounting Standards Committee [*British*]
ASC............	Acetylsulfanilyl Chloride [*Organic chemistry*]
ASC............	Acid-Soluble Collagen [*Biochemistry*]
ASC............	Action Socialiste Congolaise [*Congolese Socialist Action*]
ASC............	Active Signal Correction [*Video technology*]
ASC............	Activity Sections Council [*Association of College and Research Libraries*]
ASC............	Adams State College [*Alamosa, CO*]
ASC............	Adhesive and Sealant Council (EA)
ASC............	Administrative Service Centers (AABC)
ASC............	Adorers of the Blood of Christ [*Roman Catholic women's religious order*]
ASC............	Advanced Scientific Computer [*Texas Instruments, Inc.*]
ASC............	Advanced Ship Concepts
ASC............	Advanced Simulation Center [*Army*] (MCD)
ASC............	Advanced Sonobuoy Communications Link [*Navy*] (MCD)
ASC............	Advanced Surgical Centre [*British and Canadian*] [*World War II*]
ASC............	Advanced System Concept (MCD)
ASC............	Advertising Standards Council [*Canada*] [*Australia*]
ASC............	Aerodynamics Surface Control (MCD)
ASC............	Aeronautical Systems Center [*Air Force*]
ASC............	Aeronca Sedan Club (EA)
ASC............	Aerospace Control [*Air Force*] (MCD)
ASC............	Aerospace Planning Charts
ASC............	Aerospace Static Converter
AS & C	Aerospace Surveillance and Control [*Air Force*] (AFM)
ASC............	Aerospace Systems Center [*Dayton, OH*] [*Air Force*] (MCD)
ASC............	Aerosurface Control [*NASA*] (NASA)
ASC............	African Studies Center [*Michigan State University*] [*Research center*] (RCD)
ASC............	Agnes Scott College [*Decatur, GA*]
ASC............	Agricultural Stabilization and Conservation
ASC............	Air Service Command
ASC............	Air Support Command
ASC............	Air Support Control
ASC............	Air Support Coordinator (MCD)
ASC............	Air Systems Command [*Navy*]
ASC............	Airborne Software Change (MCD)
ASC............	Aircraft Service Change [*Navy*]
ASC............	Aircraft Supply Council [*Ministry of Aircraft Production*] [*British*]
ASC............	Aircrew Systems Change (MCD)
ASC............	Airport Security Council (EA)

A-SC .... Alabama State Supreme Court Library, Montgomery, AL [*Library symbol*] [*Library of Congress*] (LCLS)
ASC............ Albany State College [*Georgia*]
ASC............ Alcohol Studies Centre [*British*] (CB)
ASC............ All Savers Certificate [*Banking*]
ASC............ All-Sky Camera
ASC............ Allied Staff Chiefs [*World War II*]
ASC............ Allied Supreme Council [*World War II*]
ASC............ Allowance Source Code [*Military*] (AFM)
ASC............ Allowance Summary Code
ASC............ Altered State of Consciousness [*Parapsychology*]
ASC............ Alternate Source Council (MCD)
ASC............ Alternate Squadron Commander [*Air Force*]
ASC............ Amalgamated Society of Casters [*A union*] [*British*]
ASC............ Amchitka [*Alaska*] [*Seismograph station code, US Geological Survey*] [*Closed*] (SEIS)
ASC............ American Safety Council (EA)
ASC............ American Sailing Council [*of the National Marine Manufacturers Association*] [*Chicago, IL*]
ASC............ American Satellite Company [*Rockville, MD*] [*Telecommunications*] (TSSD)
ASc............ American Scholar [*A publication*]
ASC............ American Security Council (EA)
ASC............ American Shuffleboard Company (EA)
ASC............ American Silk Council [*Defunct*] (EA)
ASC............ American Singers Club (EA)
ASC............ American Society of Cartographers (EA)
ASC............ American Society of Cinematographers (EA)
ASC............ American Society of Criminology (EA)
ASC............ American Society for Cybernetics (EA)
ASC............ American Society of Cytology (EA)
ASC............ American Spaniel Club (EA)
ASC............ American Spanish Committee (EA)
ASC............ American Spoon Collectors (EA)
ASC............ American Sportsman's Club [*Commercial firm*] (EA)
ASC............ American Stores Company [*NYSE symbol*] (SPSG)
ASC............ American Sunroof Corporation, Inc.
ASC............ Amicable Society of Coachmakers [*A union*] [*British*]
ASC............ Analog Signal Converter
ASC............ Analog Signal Correlator
ASC............ Analog Strip Chart
ASC............ Anglo-Saxon Chronicle
ASc............ Annals of Science [*London*] [*A publication*]
ASC............ Annapolis Science Center
ASC............ Annual Support Cost (MCD)
ASC............ Annual Survey of Colleges [*The College Board*] [*Information service or system*] (CRD)
ASC............ Antique Studebaker Club (EA)
ASC............ Antistatic Compound
ASC............ Apple Sound Chip [*Apple Computer, Inc.*] (BYTE)
ASC............ Applied Science Corp. (MCD)
ASC............ Applied Superconductivity Conference, Inc. (MCD)
ASC............ Applied Superconductivity Research Center [*University of Wisconsin - Madison*] [*Research center*] (RCD)
ASC............ Approvisionnements et Services Canada [*Supply and Services Canada - SSC*]
ASC............ Arab Sports Confederation [*Saudi Arabia*] (EAIO)
ASC............ Archivio Storico di Corsica [*A publication*]
A-SC .... Area Signal Conditioner (MCD)
ASC............ Arizona Silver Corp. [*Vancouver Stock Exchange symbol*]
ASC............ Arizona State College
ASC............ Arkansas State College [*Later, ASU*]
ASC............ Arlington State College [*Texas*]
ASC............ Armed Services Committee [*US Senate*] (AAG)
ASC............ Army Selection Centre [*British*]
ASC............ Army Service Corps [*Initialism also facetiously translated during World War I as "Ally Sloper's Cavalry," Ally Sloper being a comic-paper buffoon*] [*Later, RASC*] [*British*]
ASC............ Army Signal Corps [*Later, CEC*]
ASC............ Army Specialist Corps [*Functions transferred to Officer Procurement Service*]
ASC............ Army Staff Council
ASC............ Army Subsistence Center
ASC............ Arteriosclerosis [*Medicine*]
ASC............ Ascend To [*or Ascending To*] [*Aviation*] (FAAC)
ASC............ Ascending
ASC............ Ascension [*Bolivia*] [*Airport symbol*] [*Obsolete*] (OAG)
ASC............ Ascent (MCD)
ASC............ ASCI [*Administrative Staff College of India*] Journal of Management [*A publication*]
ASC............ Ashland College, Ashland, OH [*OCLC symbol*] (OCLC)
ASC............ Asian Socialist Conference
ASC............ Asian Studies Centre [*St. Antony's College*] [*British*] (CB)
ASC............ Assembly Shortage Control (MCD)
ASC............ Assessment of Skills in Computation [*Mathematics test*]
ASC............ Asset Status Cards
ASC............ Assigned Service Contractor
AS(C)......... Assistant Secretary, Controller [*Admiralty*] [*British*]
ASc............ Associate in Science
ASC............ Associate in Science in Commerce
ASC............ Associated Sandblasting Contractors (EA)

ASC............ Associated Schools of Construction (EA)
ASC............ Associated Specialty Contractors (EA)
ASC............ Association of Systematics Collections (EA)
ASC............ Associative Structure Computer (BUR)
ASC............ Astronautical Society of Canada
ASC............ Astronautics Support Center
ASC............ Asynchronous Communication Procedure (BUR)
ASC............ Atlantic Seaboard Circuit [*Horse racing*]
ASC............ Atlantic Systems Conference [*Navy/NATO*] (MCD)
ASC............ Aughey Spark Chamber
ASC............ Australian Consumer Sales and Credit Law Cases [*Commerce Clearing House*] [*A publication*] (DLA)
ASC............ Australian Consumer Sales and Credit Law Reporter [*A publication*] (APTA)
ASC............ Australian Securities Commission
ASC............ Australian Seeds Committee
ASC............ Australian Shipping Commission
ASC............ Australian Signal Corps
ASC............ Australian Sports Commission
ASC............ Australian Studies Centre [*University of Queensland*]
ASC............ Austrian Shippers Council (DS)
ASC............ Authorized Signature Card (MCD)
ASC............ Autism Services Center (EA)
ASC............ Autism Society Canada
ASC............ AUTODIN Switching Center
ASC............ Automatic Scan Counter
ASC............ Automatic Selectivity Control (DEN)
ASC............ Automatic Sensitivity Control [*Aviation*]
ASC............ Automatic Stability Control System [*Bavarian Motor Works*] [*Automotive engineering*]
ASC............ Automatic Submarine Control [*Navy*] (MCD)
ASC............ Automatic Switching Center
ASC............ Automatic Synchronized Control (DEN)
ASC............ Automatic System Control
ASC............ Automotive Sales Council (EA)
ASC............ Automotive Service Councils [*Later, ASA*] (EA)
ASC............ Auxiliary Switch [*Breaker*] Normally Closed [*Electricity*]
ASC............ Average Standing Crop
ASC............ Aviation Service Code (AFM)
ASC............ Aviation Support Equipment Technician, Chief [*Navy rating*]
ASC............ Aviation Systems Command [*Army*] (RDA)
ASC............ Movimiento de Accion Social Cristiana [*Christian Social Action Movement*] [*Dominican Republic*] [*Political party*] (PPW)
ASCA........ Airlines Sports and Cultural Association (EA)
ASCA........ American School Counselor Association (EA)
ASCA........ American Senior Citizens Association (EA)
ASCA........ American-Serbian Cultural Association (EA)
ASCA........ American Shrimp Canners Association [*Later, ASPA*]
ASCA........ American Society for Church Architecture [*Later, IFRAA*] (EA)
ASCA........ American Society for Conservation Archaeology (EA)
ASCA........ American Society of Consulting Arborists (EA)
ASCA........ American Society of Contemporary Artists (EA)
ASCA........ American Standard Chinchilla Association [*Later, ASCRA*]
ASCA........ American Swimming Coaches Association (EA)
ASCA........ AMF Apollo Sailing Class Association (EA)
ASCA........ Architectural Spray Coaters Association (EA)
ASCA........ Associate of the Society of Company and Commercial Accountants [*British*] (DCTA)
ASCA........ Association for Sickle Cell Anemia [*Defunct*]
ASCA........ Association of State Correctional Administrators (EA)
ASCA........ Atlantic Salmon Convention Act of 1982
ASCA........ Automatic Science Citation Alerting (IEEE)
ASCA........ Automatic Subject Citation Alert [*A publication*]
ASCA........ Canberra [*Australia*] [*ICAO location identifier*] (ICLI)
ASCAA...... Anales. Sociedad Cientifica Argentina [*A publication*]
ASCAA...... Automobile Seat Cover Association of America (EA)
ASC/ABT ... Ascent/Abort (MCD)
ASCAC...... Acoustical Signal Classification and Analysis Center [*Navy*] (CAAL)
ASCAC...... Antisubmarine Classification and Analysis Center [*Navy*]
ASC/AIA... Association of Student Chapters, American Institute of Architects
ASCAM..... Aerospace Catalog Automated Microfilm, Inc. (MCD)
ASCAM..... Anti-Shipping Campaign Model (MCD)
ASCAP ..... American Society of Composers, Authors, and Publishers (EA)
ASCAP ..... ASCAP [*American Society of Composers, Authors, and Publishers*] in Action [*A publication*]
ASCAP ..... ASCAP [*American Society of Composers, Authors, and Publishers*] Today [*A publication*]
ASCAP ..... At-Sea Calibration Procedure
ASCAP Cop L Symp ... Copyright Law Symposium. American Society of Composers, Authors, and Publishers [*A publication*]
ASCAP Copyright L Sym ... ASCAP [*American Society of Composers, Authors, and Publishers*] Copyright Law Symposium [*A publication*]
ASCAP Copyright L Symp ... Copyright Law Symposium. American Society of Composers, Authors, and Publishers [*A publication*]
ASCAP Sympos ... Copyright Law Symposium. American Society of Composers, Authors, and Publishers (DLA)

ASCAS ...... All-Service Close Air Support [*Military*]
ASCAS ...... Automated System for the Control of Atmospheric Sampling [*Marine science*] (MSC)
ASCAT ...... Air Service Command Advisory Team
ASCAT ...... Analog Self-Checking Automatic Tester
ASCAT ...... Antisubmarine Classification Analysis Test
ASCAT ...... Association Internationale des Editeurs de Catalogues de Timbres-Poste [*International Association of Publishers of Postage Stamp Catalogues*] (EA)
ASCATS .... Apollo Simulation Checkout and Training System [*NASA*]
ASCB .... American Society for Cell Biology (EA)
ASCB .... Army Sports Control Board [*British*]
ASCB .... Canberra [*Australia*] [*ICAO location identifier*] (ICLI)
ASCBull..... Academie des Sciences de Cracovie. Bulletin International [*A publication*]
ASCC .... Aeronautical Services Communication Center [*Great Britain*]
ASCC .... Air Standardization Coordinating Committee
ASCC .... Air Support Coordination and Control (MCD)
ASCC .... American Social Communications Conference (EA)
ASCC .... American Society of Camera Collectors (EA)
ASCC .... American Society of Check Collectors (EA)
ASCC .... American Society for Concrete Construction (EA)
ASCC .... Area Security Coordination Center
ASCC .... Army Strategic Communications Command
ASCC .... Asian Studies Co-Ordinating Committee [*Australia*]
ASCC .... Association des Syndicats de Cheminots Canadiens [*Canadian Railway Labour Association - CRLA*]
ASCC .... Automatic Sequence Controlled Calculator [*First all-automatic calculating machine*]
ASCC .... Aviation Supply Control Center (NVT)
ASCCI .... American Society for Crippled Children in Israel (EA)
ASC Commun ... ASC [*American Society for Cybernetics*] Communications [*A publication*]
ASCCP ...... American Society for Colposcopy and Cervical Pathology (EA)
ASCCSS .... Army Signal Corps, Communications Security Service (MUGU)
ASCD .... Academy of Stress and Chronic Disease (EA)
ASCD .... Advanced Ship Concept Development
ASCD .... Aircraft Sensor Correlation Device (MCD)
ASCD .... American Society of Computer Dealers (EA)
ASCD .... Association for Supervision and Curriculum Development (EA)
ASCE .... Abrupt Space Charge Edge [*Algorithm*]
ASCE .... Airlock Signal Conditioning Electronics (MCD)
ASCE .... American Society of Childbirth Educators [*Inactive*] (EA)
ASCE .... American Society of Christian Ethics [*Later, SCE*]
ASCE .... American Society of Civil Engineers (EA)
ASCE .... Association of Safety Council Executives (EA)
ASCE Annu Comb Index ... ASCE [*American Society of Civil Engineers*] Annual Combined Index [*A publication*]
ASCE Combined Sewer Separation Proj Tech Memo ... ASCE [*American Society of Civil Engineers*] Combined Sewer Separation Project. Technical Memorandum [*A publication*]
ASCE Eng Issues ... ASCE [*American Society of Civil Engineers*] Engineering Issues [*A publication*]
ASCE Eng Issues J Prof Activ ... ASCE [*American Society of Civil Engineers*] Engineering Issues. Journal of Professional Activities [*A publication*]
ASCE J Constr Div ... ASCE [*American Society of Civil Engineers*] Journal of the Construction Division [*A publication*]
ASCE J Eng Mech Div ... ASCE [*American Society of Civil Engineers*] Journal of the Engineering Mechanics Division [*A publication*]
ASCE J Geotech Eng Div ... ASCE [*American Society of Civil Engineers*] Journal of the Geotechnical Engineering Division [*A publication*]
ASCE J Hydraul Div ... ASCE [*American Society of Civil Engineers*] Journal of the Hydraulics Division [*A publication*]
ASCE J Irrig Drain Div ... ASCE [*American Society of Civil Engineers*] Journal of the Irrigation and Drainage Division [*A publication*]
ASCE J Power Div ... ASCE [*American Society of Civil Engineers*] Journal of the Power Division [*A publication*]
ASCE J Prof Activ ... ASCE [*American Society of Civil Engineers*] Journal of Professional Activities [*A publication*]
ASCE J Sanit Eng Div ... ASCE [*American Society of Civil Engineers*] Journal of the Sanitary Engineering Division [*A publication*]
ASCE J Soil Mech Found Div ... ASCE [*American Society of Civil Engineers*] Journal of the Soil Mechanics and Foundations Division [*A publication*]
ASCE J Struct Div ... ASCE [*American Society of Civil Engineers*] Journal of the Structural Division [*A publication*]
ASCE J Surv Mapp Div ... ASCE [*American Society of Civil Engineers*] Journal of the Surveying and Mapping Division [*A publication*]
ASCE J Urban Plann Dev Div ... ASCE [*American Society of Civil Engineers*] Journal of the Urban Planning and Development Division [*A publication*]
ASCE J Waterw Harbors Coastal Eng Div ... ASCE [*American Society of Civil Engineers*] Journal of the Waterways, Harbors, and Coastal Engineering Division [*A publication*]

ASCE Man Rep Eng Pract ... ASCE [*American Society of Civil Engineers*] Manuals and Reports on Engineering Practice [*A publication*]
ASCEND... Advanced System for Communications and Education in National Development (MCD)
ASCENT ... Assembly System for Central Processor [*Data processing*]
ASCEP ...... American Society for Clinical Evoked Potentials (EA)
ASCE Proc Transp Eng J ... American Society of Civil Engineers. Proceedings. Transportation Engineering Journal [*A publication*]
ASCE Publ Abstr ... ASCE [*American Society of Civil Engineers*] Publications Abstracts [*A publication*]
ASCE Publ Inf ... ASCE [*American Society of Civil Engineers*] Publications Information [*A publication*]
ASCES...... Antisubmarine Contact Evaluation System [*Navy*] (MCD)
ASCET ...... American Society of Certified Engineering Technicians (EA)
ASCE Transp Eng J ... ASCE [*American Society of Civil Engineers*] Transportation Engineering Journal [*A publication*]
ASCE Urban Water Resour Res Program Tech Mem ... ASCE [*American Society of Civil Engineers*] Urban Water Resources Research Program. Technical Memorandum [*A publication*]
ASCE Urban Water Resour Res Program Tech Memo IHP ... ASCE [*American Society of Civil Engineers*] Urban Water Resources Research Program. Technical Memorandum IHP [*International Hydrological Programme*] [*A publication*]
ASCF .... American Security Council Foundation (EA)
ASCG........ Automatic Solution Crystal Growth [*Materials processing*]
ASCGB ...... American Stamp Club of Great Britain (EA)
ASCGBI .... Amalgamated Society of Coremakers of Great Britain and Ireland [*A union*]
ASCGD...... American Society of Clinical Genetics and Dysmorphology [*Later, BDCGS*] (EA)
ASCGD...... Anales. Seccion de Ciencias. Colegio Universitario de Gerona. Universidad Autonoma de Barcelona [*A publication*]
ASCGW...... Action-Study Center for a Governed World [*Defunct*] (EA)
ASch .... American Scholar [*A publication*]
ASCH .... American Society of Church History (EA)
ASCH .... American Society of Clinical Hypnosis (EA)
ASCH .... Coffs Harbour [*Australia*] [*ICAO location identifier*] (ICLI)
ASCHB...... Association for Studies in the Conservation of Historic Buildings [*British*]
ASCH/CH ... Church History. American Society of Church History. University of Chicago [*A publication*]
ASCHDQ .. Assignment Children [*A publication*]
Aschener Bl Aufbereit Verkoken Briket ... Aschener Blaetter fuer Aufbereiten Verkoken Brikettieren [*A publication*]
ASCH-ERF ... American Society of Clinical Hypnosis - Education and Research Foundation (EA)
A Schw .... Archaeologie der Schweiz. Mitteilungsblatt der Schweizerischen Gesellschaft fuer Ur- und Fruehgeschichte [*A publication*]
ASci .... American Scientist [*A publication*]
ASCI .... American Society for Clinical Investigation (EA)
ASCI .... American Society of Construction Inspectors (EA)
ASCI .... Associated Companies, Incorporated [*NASDAQ symbol*] (NQ)
ASCI (Admin Staff Col India) J Mgt ... ASCI (Administrative Staff College of India) Journal of Management [*A publication*]
ASCID .... Altered State of Consciousness Induction Device [*Parapsychology*]
A Sci Econ Appl ... Annales des Sciences Economiques Appliquees [*A publication*]
ASCII .... American Standard Code for Information Interchange [*Pronounced "ask-ee"*] [*American National Standards Institute*] [*Data processing*]
ASCIS........ Australian Schools Cooperative Information Service
ASCJ .... Apostles of the Sacred Heart of Jesus [*Roman Catholic women's religious order*]
ASCL .... Advanced Sonobuoy Communications Link [*Navy*] (MCD)
ASCL .... Advanced System Concepts Laboratory [*Army*]
ASCL .... Airborne Sonobuoy Communications Link
ASCL .... American Safety Closure Corp. [*Farmingdale, NY*] [*NASDAQ symbol*] (NQ)
ASCL .... American Sugar Cane League of the USA (EA)
ASCL .... Annual Survey of Commonwealth Law [*A publication*]
ASCL .... Archivio Storico per la Calabria e la Lucania [*A publication*]
ASCLA ...... Association of Specialized and Cooperative Library Agencies (EA)
ASCLA LSSPS ... ASCLA [*Association of Specialized and Cooperative Library Agencies*] Libraries Serving Special Populations Section
ASCLA LSSPS ALAD ... ASCLA LSSPS [*Association of Specialized and Cooperative Library Agencies - Libraries Serving Special Populations Section*] Academic Librarians Assisting the Disabled Discussion Group
ASCLA LSSPS BF ... ASCLA LSSPS [*Association of Specialized and Cooperative Library Agencies - Libraries Serving Special Populations Section*] Bibliotherapy Forum
ASCLA LSSPS HCLF ... ASCLA LSSPS [*Association of Specialized and Cooperative Library Agencies - Libraries Serving Special Populations Section*] Health Care Libraries Forum

ASCLA LSSPS LSBPHF ... ASCLA LSSPS [*Association of Specialized and Cooperative Library Agencies - Libraries Serving Special Populations Section*] Library Service to the Blind and Physically Handicapped Forum
ASCLA LSSPS LSDDP MAG ... ASCLA LSSPS [*Association of Specialized and Cooperative Library Agencies - Libraries Serving Special Populations Section*] Library Service to Developmentally Disabled Persons Membership Activity Group
ASCLA LSSPS LSDF ... ASCLA LSSPS [*Association of Specialized and Cooperative Library Agencies - Libraries Serving Special Populations Section*] Library Service to the Deaf Forum
ASCLA LSSPS LSIEF ... ASCLA LSSPS [*Association of Specialized and Cooperative Library Agencies - Libraries Serving Special Populations Section*] Library Service to the Impaired Elderly Forum
ASCLA LSSPS LSPF ... ASCLA LSSPS [*Association of Specialized and Cooperative Library Agencies - Libraries Serving Special Populations Section*] Library Service to Prisoners Forum
ASCLA Multi-LINCS ... ASCLA [*Association of Specialized and Cooperative Library Agencies*] Multitype Library Networks and Cooperatives Section
ASCLA SLAS ... ASCLA [*Association of Specialized and Cooperative Library Agencies*] State Library Agency Section
ASCLD ...... American Society of Crime Laboratory Directors (EA)
Asclep .... Asclepius [*of Apuleius*] [*Classical studies*] (OCD)
Ascls .... Ascension of Isaiah (BJA)
ASCLT ...... American Society of Clinical Laboratory Technicians [*Later, ASMT*]
ASCLU ...... American Society of Chartered Life Underwriters [*Later, ASCLU, ChFC*] (EA)
ASCLU & ChFC ... American Society of CLU [*Chartered Life Underwriters*] and ChFC [*Chartered Financial Consultants*] [*Bryn Mawr, PA*] (EA)
ASCM........ Acquisition Strategy Comparison Model (MCD)
ASCM........ Aluminum, Silicon, Calcium, Magnesium [*Geology*]
ASCM........ American Society of Chinese Medicine [*Inactive*]
ASCM........ American Society of Country Music (EA)
ASCM........ Antiship Capable Missile (NVT)
ASCM........ Antiship Cruise Missile
ASCM........ Association of Sprocket Chain Manufacturers [*Defunct*]
ASCM........ Aviation Support Equipment Technician, Master Chief [*Navy rating*]
ASCM........ Cooma [*Australia*] [*ICAO location identifier*] (ICLI)
ASCMA..... American Sprocket Chain Manufacturers Association [*Later, American Chain Association*]
ASCMP..... Association of Second Class Mail Publishers (EA)
ASCMS.... American Society of Contemporary Medicine and Surgery (EA)
ASCN .... American Society for Clinical Nutrition (EA)
ASCN .... Camden [*Australia*] [*ICAO location identifier*] (ICLI)
ASCO .... Abort Sensing Control Unit
ASCO .... Advanced Systems Concepts Office [*Army*] (RDA)
ASCO .... Alpha Solarco, Inc. [*NASDAQ symbol*] (NQ)
ASCO .... American Society of Clinical Oncology (EA)
ASCO .... American Society of Contemporary Ophthalmology (EA)
ASCO .... Arab Satellite Communications Organization [*League of Arab States*] [*Riyadh, Saudi Arabia*] (EAIO)
ASCO .... Associated Spring Corporation
ASCO .... Association of Schools and Colleges of Optometry (EA)
ASCO .... ATMDC [*Apollo Telescope Mount Digital Computer*] Software Control Officer [*NASA*]
ASCO .... Automatic Sustainer Cutoff (MUGU)
ASCO .... Canberra [*Australia*] [*ICAO location identifier*] (ICLI)
ASCOA..... American Scholar [*A publication*]
ASCOA..... Antique Snowmobile Club of America (EA)
ASCOD..... Army Systems Coordinating Documents
AS Code..... American Samoa Code [*A publication*] (DLA)
ASCOFAM ... Association Mondiale de Lutte Contre la Faim [*World Association for the Struggle Against Hunger*]
ASCOM .... Army Service Command
ASCOMACE ... Association des Constructeurs de Machines a Coudre de la CEE [*Association of Sewing Machine Manufacturers of the EEC*]
ASCON ..... Automated Switched Communications Network (MCD)
ASCOP..... Advanced Submarine Control Program (MCD)
ASCOP..... Applied Science Corporation of Princeton (MCD)
ASCOP...... [*A*] Statistical Computing Procedure
ASCOPE ... ASEAN [*Association of South East Asian Nations*] Council on Petroleum [*Indonesia*]
ASCORE... Automatic Shipboard Checkout and Readiness Equipment (MCD)
ASCOT..... Adaptive Signal Control Optimization Techniques
ASCOT...... Analogue Simulation of Competitive Operational Tactics [*Game*]
ASCOT...... Asphalt Coking Technology
ASCOT...... Association of Soil Conservation Officer Trainees
ASCOTA... American Student Committee of the Occupational Therapy Association [*American Occupational Therapy Association*]
ASCP .... African Safari Club of Philadelphia (EA)
ASCP .... Air Standardization Coordination Program [*NATO*]
ASCP .... American Society of Clinical Pathologists (EA)

ASCP........ American Society of Consultant Pharmacists (EA)
ASCP........ American Society of Consulting Planners (EA)
ASCP........ Anglo-Saxon Christian Patriot (EA)
ASCP........ Army Strategic Capabilities Plan
ASCP........ Attitude Set Control Panel [*Aerospace*] (NASA)
ASCP........ Automatic System Checkout Program
ASCPA ...... American Shrimp Canners and Processors Association [*Later, ASPA*] (EA)
ASCR........ Advanced Sodium-Cooled Reactor
ASCR........ American Screen Co. [*NASDAQ symbol*] (NQ)
ASCR........ American Society of Chiropodical Roentgenology
ASCR........ American Society of Clinic Radiologists (EA)
ASCR........ Analog Strip Chart Recorder
ASCR........ Association of Specialists in Cleaning and Restoration (EA)
ASCR........ Asymmetric Silicon Controlled Rectifier [*Electronics*] (TEL)
ASCRA...... American Standard Chinchilla Rabbit Association (EA)
ASCRE ...... Assistant Secretary for Conservation and Renewable Energy
ASCRO..... Active Service Career for Reserve Officers
ASCRS ...... American Society of Cataract and Refractive Surgery (EA)
ASCRS ...... American Society of Colon and Rectal Surgeons (EA)
ASCRT ...... Association for the Study of Canadian Radio and Television [*Pronounced "Askrat"*] [*See also AERTC*]
ASCS........ Admission Scheduling and Control System [*Hospital management*]
ASCS........ Advanced Stirling Conversion System [*Mechanical engineering*]
ASCS........ Aerospace Surveillance and Control Squadron [*Air Force*]
ASCS........ Agricultural Stabilization and Conservation Service [*Department of Agriculture*]
ASCS........ American Society of Corporate Secretaries [*New York, NY*] (EA)
ASCS........ American Society of Cosmetic Surgeons [*Later, AACS*] (EA)
ASCS........ Area Surveillance Control System (IEEE)
ASCS........ Association des Conseils Sub-Aquatiques Canadiens [*Association of Canadian Underwater Councils*]
ASCS........ Atmospheric Storage and Control Section [*Spacelab*] [*NASA*]
ASCS........ Attitude and Spin Control Subsystem [*NASA*]
ASCS........ Attitude Stabilization and Control System (MCD)
ASCS........ Automated Ship Classification System (MCD)
ASCS........ Automated Storage Control System (MCD)
ASCS........ Automatic Scan Counter System
ASCS........ Automatic Stabilization and Control System
ASCS........ Aviation Support Equipment Technician, Senior Chief [*Navy rating*]
ASCSA ...... American School and Community Safety Association [*Later, The Safety Society*]
ASCT........ American Society for Cytotechnology (EA)
ASCT........ Americans for Safe and Competitive Trucking (EA)
ASCT........ Associate Member of the Society of Cardiological Technicians [*British*] (DBQ)
ASCT........ Associate Member of the Society of Commercial Teachers [*British*] (DBQ)
ASCTRLA ... Alliance of State Car and Truck Renting and Leasing Associations (EA)
ASCU .... Air Support Control Units
ASCU .... Alarm System Control Unit
ASCU .... Armament Station Control Unit
ASCU .... Armament Systems Control Unit (MCD)
ASCU .... Association of Small Computer Users [*Later, ACU*] (EA)
ASCU .... Association of State Colleges and Universities [*Later, AASCU*]
ASCU .... Automatic Scanning Control Unit
ASCUE...... Association of Small Computer Users [*Later, ACU*] (CSR)
ASCUFRO ... Association of State Colleges and Universities Forestry Research Organizations
As Cult Q ... Asian Culture Quarterly [*A publication*]
A Scuol Pisa ... Annali. Scuola Normale Superiore di Pisa. Classe di Lettere e Filosofia [*A publication*]
ASCUS...... Association for School, College, and University Staffing (EA)
ASCVD...... Arteriosclerotic Cardiovascular Disease [*Cardiology*]
ASCVIS...... Armed Services - Civilian Interest Survey [*Test*]
AScW........ Association of Scientific Workers [*British*]
ASCY........ Allied Security, Inc. [*NASDAQ symbol*] (NQ)
ASD .... Academy for Sports Dentistry (EA)
ASD .... Accao Social Democratica [*Social Democratic Action*] [*Portugal*] [*Political party*] (PPE)
ASD .... Adaptive Seating Device [*Occupational therapy*]
ASD .... Adjustable Speed Drive
ASD .... Administrative Services Division [*Census*] (OICC)
ASD .... Admiralty Salvage Department [*British military*] (DMA)
ASD .... Adult Services Division [*American Library Association*] [*Later, RASD*] (EA)
ASD .... Advanced Ship Development
ASD .... Advanced Submarine Detection (MCD)
ASD .... Advanced Surveillance Drone (MCD)
ASD .... Advanced Systems and Design
ASD .... Advanced Systems Division [*IBM Corp.*]
ASD .... Aeronautical System Development (NG)
ASD .... Aeronautical Systems Division [*Wright-Patterson Air Force Base, OH*] [*Air Force*]
ASD .... Aerospace Services Division [*NASA*] (KSC)
ASD .... Air Support Director [*Military*] (NVT)
ASD .... Aircraft Statistical Data

ASD .... Airspace Docket (FAAC)
ASD .... All Saints' Day
ASD .... Alternate Source Development
ASD .... Amchitka [*Alaska*] [*Seismograph station code, US Geological Survey*] [*Closed*] (SEIS)
ASD .... American Society of Dermatopathology (EA)
ASD .... American Society of Dowsers (EA)
ASD .... (Amino)selenadiazole [*Antiviral compound*]
ASD .... Amistad Airlines [*Del Rio, TX*] [*FAA designator*] (FAAC)
ASD .... Ammunition Subdepot [*United Kingdom*] (NATG)
ASD .... Ammunition Supply Depot
ASD .... Ammunition Supply Dump [*British*] [*World War II*]
ASD .... Amplitude Spectral Density [*Physics*]
ASD .... Andros Town [*Bahamas*] [*Airport symbol*] (OAG)
ASD .... Annali di Storia del Diritto [*A publication*]
ASD .... Anthracene Scintillation Dosimeter
ASD .... Anti-Submarine Division [*British military*] (DMA)
ASD .... Antislack Device
ASD .... Apollo Standard Detonator [*NASA*]
ASD .... Apollo Support Department [*NASA*] (KSC)
ASD .... Application Systems Developer [*Army*]
ASD .... Archivio Storico per la Dalmazia [*A publication*]
ASD .... Armament Supply Department [*Navy*] [*British*]
ASD .... Army Schools Department [*British military*] (DMA)
ASD .... Army Shipping Document
ASD .... Artillery Spotting Division [*Air Force*]
ASD .... Assented [*Investment term*]
ASD .... Assignment Selection Date [*Military*] (AFM)
ASD .... Assistant Secretary of Defense
ASD .... Assistant State Director
ASD .... Associated Surplus Dealers (EA)
ASD .... Association for Social Design [*Later, BRI*] (EA)
ASD .... Association of Steel Distributors (EA)
ASD .... Association for the Study of Dreams (EA)
ASD .... Assumed
ASD .... Atomic Solution Diffusion
ASD .... Atrial Septal Defect [*Cardiology*]
ASD .... Australian Sentencing Digest [*A publication*]
ASD .... Automated Structural Design [*NASA*]
ASD .... Automatic Shutdown [*Automotive engineering*]
ASD .... Automatic Synchronized Discriminator (DEN)
ASD .... Average Sorties per Day [*Air Force*] (AFIT)
ASD .... Aviation Safety Digest [*A publication*] (APTA)
ASD .... Aviation Service Date (AFM)
ASD .... Aviation Supply Depot
ASDA .... Accelerate/Stop Distance Available [*Aviation*] (FAAC)
ASDA .... Accountable Supply Distribution Activity (MCD)
ASDA .... All Star Dairy Association (EA)
ASDA .... American Seafood Distributors Association (EA)
ASDA .... American Society for Dental Aesthetics (EA)
ASDA .... American Stamp Dealers Association (EA)
ASDA .... American Student Dental Association (EA)
ASDA .... Asbestos & Danville [*AAR code*]
ASD (A) ..... Assistant Secretary of Defense (Administration) (AABC)
ASDA .... Associated Dairies [*Commercial firm*] [*British*]
ASDA .... Association of Structural Draftsmen of America (EA)
ASDA .... Association for the Support and Diffusion of Art (EA)
ASDA .... Atomic Space and Development Authority [*Nuclear energy*]
ASDACS .... Acoustic Signal Data Analysis and Conversion System [*Navy*]
ASDAE ...... Association of Seventh-Day Adventist Educators (EA)
ASD(A & L) ... Assistant Secretary of Defense for Acquisition and Logistics
ASDAL ...... Association of Seventh-Day Adventist Librarians (EA)
ASD/AMD ... Associated Surplus Dealers and Associated Merchandise Dealers Trade Show (ITD)
ASDA News ... American Student Dental Association. News [*A publication*]
ASDAP ...... Army Systems Development and Acquisition Priorities (MCD)
ASDAR ...... Aircraft-to-Satellite Data Relay [*Meteorology*]
AsDB .... Asian Development Bank (EY)
ASDC .... Aeronomy and Space Data Center [*Later, NGSDC*] [*National Oceanic and Atmospheric Administration*]
ASDC .... Alaska State Data Center [*Alaska State Department of Labor*] [*Information service or system*] (IID)
ASDC .... Alternative System Design Concept
ASDC .... American Society for Deaf Children (EA)
ASDC .... American Society of Dentistry for Children (EA)
ASD (C) ..... Assistant Secretary of Defense (Comptroller)
ASDC .... Associate of the Society of Dyers and Colourists [*British*] (DBQ)
ASDC .... Association of Sleep Disorders Centers (EA)
ASDC .... Association of State Democratic Chairs (EA)
ASD (CD) .. Assistant Secretary of Defense (Civil Defense)
ASD(C3I) .. Assistant Secretary of Defense (Communications, Command-Control, and Intelligence) (AABC)
ASDD .... Antisubmarine Development Detachment [*Atlantic Fleet*] [*Norfolk, VA*]
ASDD .... Apollo Signal Definition Document [*NASA*] (KSC)
ASDE .... Airport Surface Detection Equipment [*RADAR*]
ASDE .... American Society of Danish Engineers (EA)
ASDE .... American Society of Design Engineers (EA)
A/S DE ...... Aux Soins De [*Care Of, c/o*] [*French*]
ASDEC ...... Applied Systems Development and Evaluation Center

ASDEC ...... Automatic Selection of Digital Electronic Computers
As Def J ..... Asian Defence Journal [*A publication*]
ASDEFORLANT ... Antisubmarine Defense Forces, Atlantic [*Obsolete*] [*Navy*]
ASDEFORPAC ... Antisubmarine Defense Forces, Pacific [*Obsolete*] [*Navy*]
ASDEVLANT ... Antisubmarine Development Detachment, Atlantic Fleet [*Navy*]
ASDF .... Aeronautical Systems Division Form
ASDF .... Air Self-Defense Force [*Japan*] (CINC)
ASDF .... Air Staff Defense Force (CINC)
ASDG .... Aircraft Storage and Disposition Group [*Air Force*]
ASDG .... Antisubmarine Defense Group
ASDH .... Acute Subdural Hematoma [*Medicine*]
ASD(HA) ... Assistant Secretary of Defense (Health Affairs) (AABC)
ASD (H & E) ... Assistant Secretary of Defense (Health and Environment)
ASD/H & M ... Assistant Secretary of Defense (Health and Medical)
ASD (I) ...... Assistant Secretary of Defense (Intelligence)
ASDI .... Associacao Social Democrata Independente [*Independent Social Democrat Association*] [*Portugal*] [*Political party*] (PPE)
ASDI .... Automatic Selective Dissemination of Information
ASDIC .... Antisubmarine Detection Investigation Committee [*A group in World War I that gave rise to the device that bore its name in World War II*]
ASDIC .... Armed Services Documents Intelligence Center [*DoD*]
ASDIDY .... Agricultural Science Digest [*A publication*]
ASD (I & L) ... Assistant Secretary of Defense (Installations and Logistics)
ASDIRS ..... Army Study Documentation and Information Retrieval System [*Later, ALAS*]
ASD/ISA ... Assistant Secretary of Defense (International Security Affairs)
ASDJ .... American Society of Disk Jockeys [*Defunct*] (EA)
ASDL .... Advanced STANO [*Surveillance, Target Acquisition, and Night Observation*] Data Link [*Military*] (MCD)
ASDL .... Automated Ship Data Library (IEEE)
ASDM .... Aeronautical Systems Division Manual
ASDM .... Aerosurface Driver/Monitor [*NASA*] (MCD)
ASDM .... America's Society of Separated and Divorced Men (EA)
ASDM .... Apollo-Soyuz Docking Module [*NASA*]
ASD (M) .... Assistant Secretary of Defense (Manpower)
ASDMA ..... Advances in Structure Research by Diffraction Methods [*United States-Germany*] [*A publication*]
ASD/MP & R ... Assistant Secretary of Defense (Manpower, Personnel, and Reserves)
ASD (M & RA) ... Assistant Secretary of Defense (Manpower and Reserve Affairs) [*Later, ASD (MRA & L)*] (AABC)
ASD (MRA & L) ... Assistant Secretary of Defense (Manpower, Reserve Affairs, and Logistics) [*Formerly, ASD (M & RA)*]
ASD-NSC ... Aviation Supply Depot - Naval Supply Center (MCD)
ASDO .... Assistant Staff Duty Officer (CINC)
ASDO .... Aviation Safety District Office
ASDP .... Advance Sensor Development Program [*Military*] (MCD)
ASDP .... Assistant Secretary for Defense Programs
ASDP .... Automatic Shot Dispensing Pump
ASD (PA) .. Assistant Secretary of Defense (Public Affairs)
ASDPA ...... Association of Seventh Day Pentecostal Assemblies (EA)
ASD (PA & E) ... Assistant Secretary of Defense (Program Analysis and Evaluation) (AABC)
ASD/P & I ... Assistant Secretary of Defense (Properties and Installations)
ASDPSIM ... Advanced System Data Processing Simulation (AABC)
ASDR .... Aeronautical Systems Division Regulation
ASDR .... Airport Surface Detection RADAR
ASDR .... American Society of Dental Radiographers
ASDR .... ASDAR Group [*NASDAQ symbol*] (NQ)
ASD/R & D ... Assistant Secretary of Defense (Research and Development)
ASD/R & E ... Assistant Secretary of Defense (Research and Engineering)
ASDS .... Aircraft Sound Description Scheme [*FAA*]
ASDS .... American Society for Dermatologic Surgery (EA)
ASDS .... Association for the Study of Dada and Surrealism (EA)
ASD (SA) ... Assistant Secretary of Defense (Systems Analysis) (AABC)
ASDSAR ... Annali. Istituto Sperimentale per lo Studio e la Difesa del Suolo [*A publication*]
ASD/S & L ... Assistant Secretary of Defense (Supply and Logistics)
ASDSO ...... Association of State Dam Safety Officials (EA)
ASDSRS .... Automatic Spectrum Display and Signal Recognition System (IEEE)
ASDSVN .... Army Switched Data and Secure Voice Network
ASD (T) ..... Assistant Secretary of Defense (Telecommunications)
ASDT .... Timorese Social Democratic Association [*Indonesia*] (PD)
ASDTIC .... Analog Signal to Discrete Time Interval Converter [*NASA*]
ASDTP ...... Apollo Spacecraft Development Test Plan [*NASA*] (KSC)
ASDU .... Dubbo [*Australia*] [*ICAO location identifier*] (ICLI)
ASDVS ...... American Society of Directors of Volunteer Services (EA)
ASDWA ..... Association of State Drinking Water Administrators (EA)
ASE .... Active Seismic Experiment [*NASA*] (MCD)
ASE .... Administration Support Equipment (MCD)
ASE .... Admiralty Signal Establishment [*British*]
ASE .... Advanced Space Engine (NASA)
ASE .... Advanced Systems Engineering
ASE .... Aerospace Support Equipment
ASE .... Agence Spatiale Europeenne [*European Space Agency*] (EAIO)
ASE .... Air Standard Efficiency

ASE............ Airborne Search Equipment
ASE............ Airborne Support Equipment   (MCD)
ASE............ Aircraft Stores Establishment [*Navy*]
ASE............ Aircraft Survivability Equipment
ASE............ All-Steel Equipment, Inc.
ASE............ Alliance to Save Energy   (EA)
ASE............ Allied Supply Executive [*World War II*]
ASE............ Allowable Steering Error
ASE............ Alternative Sources of Energy   (EA)
ASE............ Alternative System Exploration   (MCD)
ASE............ Amalgamated Society of Engineers [*A union*] [*British*]
AS & E...... American Science & Engineering, Inc.
ASE............ American Science & Engineering, Inc. [*AMEX symbol*]   (SPSG)
ASE............ American Scientific Engineering   (KSC)
ASe............ American Sephardi   (BJA)
ASE............ American Society of Echocardiography   (EA)
ASE............ American Society of Educators [*Later, AAMSL*]   (EA)
ASE............ American Society of Engineers
ASE............ American Society of Enologists   (EA)
ASE............ American Society for Ethnohistory   (EA)
ASE............ American Stock Exchange   (EA)
ASE............ Amplified Spontaneous Emission   (MCD)
ASE............ Anglo-Saxon England [*A publication*]
ASE............ Annales des Sciences Economiques Appliquees [*A publication*]
ASE............ Annuario di Studi Ebraici [*A publication*]
ASE............ Antisubmarine Establishment [*Navy*] [*British*]
ASE............ Archaeological Survey of Egypt [*A publication*]
ASE............ Arizona State University, College of Educational Technology
     and Library Science, Tempe, AZ [*OCLC symbol*]   (OCLC)
ASE............ Armed Services Edition [*Publishing*] [*World War II*]
ASE............ Army School of Education [*British*]
ASE............ Aserradero [*Nicaragua*] [*Seismograph station code, US
     Geological Survey*]   (SEIS)
ASE............ Aspen [*Colorado*] [*Airport symbol*]   (OAG)
ASE............ Associate in Engineering
ASE............ Associate in Science in Engineering
ASE............ Association for Science Education [*British*]   (DEN)
ASE............ Association of Scientists and Engineers of the Naval Sea
     Systems Command   (EA)
ASE............ Association of Senior Engineers [*NAVSHIPS*]
ASE............ Association for Social Economics   (EA)
ASE............ Association of Space Explorers [*Later, ASE-USA*]   (EA)
ASE............ Association for Stamp Exhibitions [*Defunct*]
ASE............ Association Suisse des Electriciens   (MCD)
ASE............ Association for Surgical Education   (EA)
ASE............ Asymptotic Standard Error [*Statistics*]
ASE............ Audio Support Equipment
ASE............ Australasian Society of Engineers
ASE............ Australian Stock Exchange Indices [*Database*] [*Sydney Stock
     Exchange*] [*Information service or system*]   (CRD)
ASE............ Automatic Stabilization Equipment
ASE............ Automatic Support Equipment [*Military*]
ASE............ Automotive Service Excellence
ASE............ Aviation Support, Electrical [*Navy rating*]
ASE............ Aviation Support Equipment   (CAAL)
ASE............ Axilla, Shoulder, Elbow [*Bandage*]
ASE............ Memoirs. Archaeological Survey of Egypt [*A publication*]
ASE............ National Institute for Automotive Service Excellence   (EA)
ASE............ Office of Investigation and Security [*FAA*]   (FAAC)
ASE............ Sedgewick Public Library, Alberta [*Library symbol*] [*National
     Library of Canada*]   (NLC)
ASEA........ American Society for Eastern Arts
ASEA........ American Society of Engineers and Architects
ASEA........ American Solar Energy Association   (EA)
ASEA........ ASEA AB [*NASDAQ symbol*]   (NQ)
ASEA........ Asiatische Studien/Etudes Asiatiques [*A publication*]
ASEA........ Augustinian Secondary Educational Association   (EA)
ASEA........ Australian Shorthorn Export Association
ASEA Bul .. Australian Society for Education through the Arts. Bulletin [*A
     publication*]   (APTA)
ASEA Bull ... Australian Society for Education through the Arts. Bulletin [*A
     publication*]
ASEA J...... ASEA [*Allmaenna Svenska Elektriska Aktiebolaget*] Journal [*A
     publication*]
ASEAN...... Association of Southeast Asian Nations   (ECON)
ASEANAM ... ASEAN [*Association of South East Asian Nations*]
     Association of Museums   (EAIO)
ASEAN (Assn South East Asian Nations) Bus Q ... ASEAN (Association of
     South East Asian Nations) Business Quarterly [*A
     publication*]
ASEAN Bus ... ASEAN [*Association of South East Asian Nations*] Business
     Quarterly [*A publication*]
ASEANIS ... Association of South East Asian Nations: Indonesia-Singapore
     [*Submarine cable*] [*Telecommunications*]   (TEL)
ASEANPS ... Association of South East Asian Nations: Philippines-Singapore
     [*Submarine cable*] [*Telecommunications*]   (TEL)
ASEA Res ... ASEA [*Allmaenna Svenska Elektriska Aktiebolaget*] Research
     [*A publication*]
ASEAS(UK) ... Association of Southeast Asian Studies in the (United
     Kingdom)

ASEA Tidn ... ASEA [*Allmaenna Svenska Elektriska Aktiebolaget*] Tidning [*A
     publication*]
ASEAUS ... Association of Southeast Asian University Students
ASEA Z ..... ASEA [*Allmaenna Svenska Elektriska Aktiebolaget*] Zeitschrift
     [*A publication*]
ASEB........ Aeronautics and Space Engineering Board [*National Academy
     of Engineering*]
ASEB........ Annales. Societe d'Emulation de Bruges [*A publication*]
ASEBS....... Association of Senior Engineers of the Bureau of Ships [*Later,
     ASE*]   (EA)
ASEC........ Action Sports Entertainment Cable [*Cable TV programming
     service*]
ASEC........ Airworthiness Standards Evaluation Committee [*FAA*]
ASEC........ Albert Schweitzer Ecological Centre   (EAIO)
ASEC........ Alice Springs Education Centre [*Australia*]
ASEC........ Allied Secretariat [*Allied German Occupation Forces*]
ASE(C)...... Allied Supply Executive, China [*World War II*]
ASEC........ American Security Corp. [*NASDAQ symbol*]   (NQ)
ASEC........ American Standard Elevator Code
ASECA...... Association for Education and Cultural Advancement [*South
     Africa*]
ASECC...... American Stock Exchange Clearing Corporation
ASECNA... Agency for the Security of Air Navigation   (AFM)
As Econ..... Asian Economies [*A publication*]
ASECS....... American Society for Eighteenth-Century Studies   (EA)
ASECUC ... Association des Services aux Etudiants des Colleges et
     Universites du Canada [*Canadian Association of College
     and University Student Services*]
ASED........ Ammoniaque Synthetique et Derives [*Belgium*]
ASED........ Assessment Statute Expiration Date [*IRS*]
ASEd.......... Associate in Science Education
ASED........ Automated Speed Enforcement Device
ASED........ Aviation Service Entry Data   (AABC)
ASED........ Aviation and Surface Effects Department [*David W. Taylor
     Naval Ship Research and Development Center*]
ASED........ Avionics Systems Engineering Division [*Johnson Space Center*]
     [*NASA*]   (NASA)
ASEE........ Advanced Semiconductor Equipment Exposition   (TSPED)
ASEE........ American Society for Engineering Education   (EA)
ASEE........ American Society for Environmental Education   (EA)
A/SEE .... Antisubmarine Experimental Establishment
ASEE........ Association of Supervisory and Executive Engineers [*A union*]
     [*British*]
ASE/E .... Ethnohistory. Journal of the American Society for Ethnohistory
     [*A publication*]
ASEER ...... American Slavic and East European Review [*A publication*]
ASEET ...... Associate in Science in Electronic Engineering Technology
ASEF .... Annales. Societe d'Emulation pour l'Etude de l'Histoire et des
     Antiquites de Flandre [*A publication*]
ASEF .... Association of Stock Exchange Firms [*Later, SIA*]   (EA)
ASEG........ All-Services Evaluation Group [*Military*]
ASEG........ Arquivos. Seminario de Estudos Galegos [*A publication*]
ASEGB...... Australian Society of Exploration Geophysicists. Bulletin [*A
     publication*]
ASEH .... American Society for Environmental History   (EA)
ASEI .... American Sports Education Institute   (EA)
ASEIB ...... American Sanitary Engineering Intersociety Board [*Later,
     AAEE*]   (EA)
ASEJ .... Annuaire. Societe des Etudes Juives [*A publication*]
ASEL .... Airplane Single-Engine Land [*Aviation rating*]
ASEL......... Annual Survey of English Law [*A publication*]
ASeLC .... Alabama Lutheran College, Selma, AL [*Library symbol*]
     [*Library of Congress*]   (LCLS)
ASELT ...... Association Europeenne pour l'Echange de la Litterature
     Technique dans le Domaine de la Siderurgie [*European
     Association for the Exchange of Technical Literature in the
     Field of Ferrous Metallurgy - EAETLFFM*]   (EAIO)
ASEM........ American Society for Engineering Management   (EA)
ASEM........ Analytical Scanning Electron Microscope
ASEMC..... Autobody Supply and Equipment Manufacturers Council   (EA)
ASEMC..... Aviation, Space, and Environmental Medicine [*A publication*]
ASEMCG .. Aviation, Space, and Environmental Medicine [*A publication*]
ASE(ME)... Allied Supply Executive, Middle East [*World War II*]
ASEMSMP ... Amalgamated Society of Engineers, Machinists, Smiths,
     Millwrights, and Pattern Makers [*A union*] [*British*]
ASENBI .... Anais. Sociedade Entomologica do Brasil [*A publication*]
As Eng Soc J ... Association of Engineering Societies. Journal [*A publication*]
ASE(OA)... Allied Supply Executive, Other Allies [*World War II*]
ASEOAK... Archivos. Sociedad Espanola de Oftalmologia [*A publication*]
ASE(OC)... Allied Supply Executive, Chinese Oil Supplies [*World War II*]
ASEODCG ... Armed Services Explosive Ordnance Disposal Coordinating
     Group
ASEP .... Accident Sequence Evaluation Program [*Nuclear
     energy*]   (NRCH)
ASEP .... Advanced Science Education Program [*National Science
     Foundation*]
ASEP .... Advanced Skills Education Program [*Army*]
ASEP .... American Society of Electroplated Plastics   (EA)
ASEP......... American Society for Experimental Pathology [*Later,
     AAP*]   (EA)
ASEP .... Automated Signal Excess Prediction   (MCD)

ASEP .... Automatic Sequence Execution and Processor   (MCD)
ASEPAN ... Australia. Commonwealth Scientific and Industrial Research Organisation. Division of Entomology. Technical Paper [*A publication*]
ASEPELT ... Association Scientifique Europeenne pour la Prevision Economique a Moyen et Long Terme [*European Scientific Association for Medium and Long-Term Economic Forecasts*]
ASE(PG).... Allied Supply Executive, Persian Gulf [*World War II*]
ASE-PM.... Aircraft Survivability Equipment - Product Manager
ASEPS .... Automatic Signal Excess Prediction System [*Military*]   (CAAL)
ASE(R) ...... Allied Supply Executive, Russia and Persian Gulf [*World War II*]
ASER .... Amplification by Stimulated Emission of Radiation
ASER .... Armed Services Exchange Regulation [*DoD*]
ASERL ...... Association of Southeastern Research Libraries [*Library network*]
ASERTT .... Alliance for Simple, Equitable, and Rational Truck Taxation   (EA)
ASES .... Aircraft Single Engine Sea [*Pilot rating*]   (AIA)
ASES .... American Shoulder and Elbow Surgeons   (EA)
ASES .... American Solar Energy Society   (EA)
ASES .... Assistant Secretary for Employment Standards [*Department of Labor*]
A Se S .... Associate in Secretarial Science
ASESA .... Automated Software Evaluation System
ASESA .... Armed Services Electro-Standards Agency [*Later, DESC*]
ASESB ...... Armed Services Explosives Safety Board [*Army*]
ASESBD.... Armed Services Explosives Safety Board [*Army*]   (AABC)
A Se Sc ...... Associate in Secretarial Science
ASESH ...... Assistant Secretary for Environment, Safety, and Health
ASESS .... Aerospace Environment Simulation System
ASET .... Academy of Security Educators and Trainees   (EA)
ASET .... Adaptive Subbands Excited Transform [*Data processing*]
ASET .... Advanced Sensor Evaluation and Test [*NASA*]
ASET .... Advanced Surface Engineering Technologies
ASET .... Aircrew Standardization and Evaluation Team [*Military*]
ASE(T) ...... Allied Supply Executive, Transportation [*World War II*]
ASET .... American Society of Electro-Neurodiagnostic Technologists   (EA)
ASET .... American Society of Electroencephalographic Technologists   (EA)
ASET .... Assistant Secretary for Employment and Training [*Department of Labor*]
ASET .... Association for Special Education Technology
ASETA ...... Asociacion de Empresas Estatales de Telecomunicaciones del Acuerdo Subregional Andino [*Association of State Telecommunication Undertakings of the Andean Subregional Agreement*] [*Quito, Ecuador*]   (EAIO)
ASETC ...... Armed Services Electron Tube Committee
ASETDS.... Aeronautical Support Equipment Type Designation System
ASETS .... Advanced System Environment and Threat Simulation
ASETS .... Airborne Seeker Evaluation Test System [*Air Force*]
ASET Yearb ... Australian Society of Educational Technology. Yearbook [*A publication*]   (APTA)
ASEU .... Archivo per la Storia Ecclesiastica dell'Umbria [*A publication*]
ASE-USA .. Association of Space Explorers - USA   (EAIO)
ASEV .... American Society for Enology and Viticulture   (EA)
ASEV .... Arctic Surface Effects Vehicle [*Navy*]
ASEW .... Airborne and Surface Early Warning
AS & EWD ... Air, Surface, and Electronic Warfare Division [*Navy*]   (MCD)
ASEX .... Atlantic Southeast Airlines, Inc. [*Air carrier designation symbol*]
ASF .... Additional Selection Factor
ASF .... Advanced Simulation Facility [*Army*]   (MCD)
ASF .... Advisory Support Force [*Military*]
ASF .... Aeromedical Staging Facility
ASF .... Aerospace Security Force   (AFM)
ASF .... African Swine Fever [*Veterinary medicine*]
ASF .... Aim Safety Co. [*Vancouver Stock Exchange symbol*]
ASF .... Air Superiority Fighter
ASF .... Aircraft Services Facility
ASF .... Aktion Suehnezeichen/Friedensdienste [*Action Reconciliation/ Services for Peace*]   (EAIO)
ASF .... Alaska Synthetic Aperture RADAR Facility [*NASA*]   (GRD)
ASF .... Alaskan Sea Frontier [*Navy*]
ASF .... Albert Schweitzer Fellowship   (EA)
ASF .... American Sailing Foundation   (EA)
ASF .... American-Scandinavian Foundation   (EA)
ASF .... American Scottish Foundation   (EA)
ASF .... American Sephardi Federation   (EA)
ASF .... American Ski Federation   (EA)
ASF .... American Space Foundation   (EA)
ASF .... Ammunition Storage Facility [*Military*]
ASF .... Amperes per Square Foot
ASF .... Analog Science Fiction [*A publication*]
ASF .... Arab Sugar Federation [*Khartoum, Sudan*]   (EAIO)
ASF .... Archivio di Storia della Filosofia [*A publication*]
ASF .... Area Sampling Frames
ASF .... Area Spatial Filtering   (MCD)
ASF .... Arithmetic Statement Function

ASF .... Army Service Forces [*Formerly, SOS*]
ASF .... Army Stock Fund
ASF .... Assignable Square Feet
ASF .... Assist Ship's Force Funds [*Navy*]   (NVT)
ASF .... Association of State Foresters [*Later, NASF*]
ASF .... Astounding Science Fiction [*A publication*]
ASF .... Atlantic Salmon Federation   (EA)
ASF .... Atmospheric Science Facility [*NASA*]   (NASA)
ASF .... Atmospheric Simulation Facility   (MCD)
ASF .... Atomic Scattering Factor
ASF .... Australian Ski Federation
ASF .... Automatic Sheet Feeder
ASF .... Automatic Store and Forward
ASF .... Automotive Safety Foundation   (EA)
ASF .... Auxiliary Stabilizing Support - "A" Frame
ASF .... Auxiliary Supporting Feature   (IEEE)
ASF .... Aviation sans Frontieres [*Humanitarian organization*] [*France*]   (EY)
ASFA .... Agricultural Subterminal Facilities Act of 1980
ASFA .... American Science Fiction Association   (EA)
ASFA .... American Science Film Association   (EA)
ASFA .... American Sighthound Field Association   (EA)
ASFA .... American Society for Apheresis   (EA)
ASFA .... American Steel Foundrymen's Association
ASFA .... Aquatic Sciences and Fisheries Abstracts [*United Nations*] [*Information service or system*] [*A publication*]
ASFA .... Association de Solidarite Franco-Arabe   (EAIO)
ASFALEC ... Association des Fabricants de Laits de Conserve des Pays de la CEE [*Association of Powdered Milk Manufacturers of the EEC*]
ASFAR ...... Active SONAR Frequency Analysis and Recording
AS(FBM)... Submarine Tender (Fleet Ballistic Missile) [*Navy symbol*]
ASFC .... Air Supply Fan Club   (EA)
ASFC .... Aircraft Specification Forum Committee
ASFC .... Allison Smith Fan Club   (EA)
ASFC .... American Space Frontier Committee   (EA)
ASFC .... Andrews Sisters Fan Club   (EA)
ASFC .... Association of Sea Fisheries Committees of England and Wales   (DCTA)
ASFD .... American Society of Furniture Designers   (EA)
A/SFDO ... Antisubmarine Fixed Defenses Officer [*Navy*]
ASFE .... Accelerometer Scale Factor Error
ASFE .... Assistant Secretary for Fossil Energy
ASFE .... Association of Soil and Foundation Engineers [*Later, ASFE/The Association of Engineering Firms Practicing in the Geosciences*]   (EA)
ASFE .... Association of Specialized Film Exhibitors [*Defunct*]   (EA)
ASFEAEFPG ... ASFE [*Association of Soil and Foundation Engineers*]/ Association of Engineering Firms Practicing in the Geosciences   (EA)
ASFF .... Acta Societatis pro Fauna et Flora [*A publication*]
ASFFHF ..... Academy of Science Fiction, Fantasy, and Horror Films   (EA)
ASFG .... Atmospheric Sound-Focusing Gain
ASFIP .... Accelerometer Scale Factor Input Panel
ASFIR .... Active Swept-Frequency Interferometer RADAR [*RADC*]
ASFIS .... Aquatic Sciences and Fisheries Information System [*Food and Agriculture Organization*] [*United Nations*]   (IID)
ASFISS ...... Advance Simulation Facility Interconnection and Setup System [*or Subsystem*] [*Air Force*]
ASFJAA .... Arquivos. Servico Florestal [*Rio De Janeiro*] [*A publication*]
ASFL .... Australian State Family Law Legislation [*A publication*]
ASFLH ...... American Society of the French Legion of Honor   (EA)
AS-FLUGZEUG ... Luftuberlegenheits Flugzeug (Air Superiority) [*German*]   (MCD)
ASFM .... Anuario. Sociedad Folklorico de Mexico [*A publication*]
ASFMRA .. American Society of Farm Managers and Rural Appraisers   (EA)
ASFN .... Allstate Financial Corp. [*NASDAQ symbol*]   (NQ)
ASF/NSF ... Army Stock Fund/Non-Stock Fund
ASFO .... American Society of Forensic Odontology   (EA)
As Folk Stud ... Asian Folklore Studies [*A publication*]
As For .... Asiatische Forschungen [*A publication*]
ASFP .... Association of Smoked Fish Processors   (EA)
ASFPAS .... Australia. Commonwealth Scientific and Industrial Research Organisation. Division of Food Preservation and Transport. Technical Paper [*A publication*]
ASFPM ..... Association of State Floodplain Managers   (EA)
ASFR .... Australian Science Fiction Review [*A publication*]   (APTA)
ASFR .... Avon Science Fiction Reader [*A publication*]
As Franc C R ... Association Francaise pour l'Avancement des Sciences. Comptes-Rendus [*A publication*]
ASFS .... American Seamen's Friend Society [*Defunct*]   (EA)
ASFS .... American Society for Friendship with Switzerland [*Later, ASA*]   (EA)
ASFS .... Automated Shipboard Forecasting System
ASFSA ...... American School Food Service Association   (EA)
ASFSE .... American Swiss Foundation for Scientific Exchange   (EA)
ASFTC .... Army Service Forces Training Center
ASFTCU .... Army Service Forces Training Center Unit
ASFTRNTRARONPAC ... Auxiliary Service Force, Transition Training Squadron, Pacific

ASFTS...... Auxiliary Systems Function Test Stand [*NASA*] (KSC)
ASFX........ Assembly Fixture [*Tool*] (AAG)
ASFZA ...... Analele. Universitatii Bucuresti. Seria Stiintele Naturii. Fizica [*A publication*]
ASG .... Abhandlungen. Koenigliche Saechsische Gesellschaft der Wissenschaften [*A publication*]
ASG .... Abhandlungen. Philosophisch-Historische Klasse der Saechsischen Gesellschaft [*A publication*]
ASG .... Administrative Support Group [*Army*]
ASG .... Advance Strike Gully [*Mining engineering*]
ASG .... Advanced Studies Group [*Air Force*]
ASG .... Advocates for Self-Government (EA)
ASG .... Aeronautical Standards Group [*Military*]
ASG ...... African Seabird Group (EAIO)
ASG .... Air Safety Group [*British*]
ASG .... Air Service Group [*Air Force*]
ASG .... Aircraft Supply Group
ASG .... Aktion Soziale Gemeinschaft, die Partei der Sozialversicherten Arbeitnehmer und Rentner [*Social Community Action (Party of Socially Insured Employees and Pensioners)*] [*Federal Republic of Germany*] [*Political party*] (PPW)
ASG .... American Sewing Guild (EA)
ASG .... American Society of Genealogists (EA)
ASG .... American Society of Geolinguistics (EA)
ASG .... Antenna Steering Group
ASG .... Area Support Group [*Military*] (AABC)
ASG .... Army Surgeon General
ASG .... Art Services Grants [*British*]
ASG .... ASG Industries, Inc. [*Formerly, American St. Gobain*]
ASG .... Asialoglycoprotein [*Biochemistry*]
ASG .... Assessment Subgroup [*NATO*] (NATG)
ASG .... Assign (AABC)
asg .... Assignee [*MARC relator code*] [*Library of Congress*] (LCCP)
ASG .... Assistant Secretary General (NATG)
ASG .... Assistant Solicitor-General (DAS)
ASG .... Assistant Surgeon General (DAS)
ASG .... Association of Student Governments
ASG .... Australasian Seabird Group (EA)
ASG .... Automatic Spray Gun
ASG .... Auxiliary Steam Generator [*Nuclear energy*] (NRCH)
ASG .... Avionics Subsystem Group [*NASA*] (NASA)
ASG .... Spruce Grove Public Library, Alberta [*Library symbol*] [*National Library of Canada*] (NLC)
ASGA .... Advertising Specialty Guild of America
ASGA .... American Sugarbeet Growers Association (EA)
ASGA .... Association des Services Geologiques Africains [*Association of African Geological Surveys - AAGS*] [*ICSU*] (EAIO)
ASGA .... Neues Archiv fuer Saechsische Geschichte und Altertumskunde [*A publication*]
ASGAN ..... Assistant Secretary General for Air Navigation [*ICAO*]
ASGB........ Anthroposophical Society in Great Britain (EAIO)
ASGBI .... Anatomical Society of Great Britain and Ireland
ASGC .... Australian Standard Geographic Classification
ASGCA...... American Society of Golf Course Architects (EA)
ASGD .... American Society for Geriatric Dentistry (EA)
ASGD .... Assigned (AABC)
ASGE......... Acoustic Signal Generator System
ASGE......... American Society of Gas Engineers (EA)
ASGE......... American Society for Gastrointestinal Endoscopy (EA)
ASGE......... Amputee Shoe and Glove Exchange (EA)
ASGE......... Association for the Study of the Grants Economy (EA)
ASGED...... Assigned
ASGEN...... As Generated (MCD)
ASGF........ Association of Scottish Games and Festivals (EA)
ASGH .... Anales. Sociedad de Geografia e Historia [*A publication*]
ASGHA9 ... Anales. Sociedad de Geografia e Historia [*A publication*]
ASGIDF .... Woods Hole Oceanographic Institution. Annual Sea Grant Report [*A publication*]
ASGJA ...... American Society for Geriatric Dentistry. Journal [*A publication*]
ASGLM..... Atti. Sodalizio Glottologico Milanese [*A publication*]
ASGLS ...... Advanced Space Ground Link Subsystem (MCD)
ASGLSSC ... American Society for German Literature of the 16th and 17th Centuries (EA)
ASGM .... American Scripture Gift Mission [*Later, SGM/USA*] (EA)
ASGM .... Atti. Sodalizio Glottologico Milanese [*A publication*]
ASGMT..... Assignment
ASGN .... Assign (AFM)
ASGOBS... Army Standard Group Order of Battle System (MCD)
ASGOSDZ ... American Society of the Greek Order of Saint Dennis of Zante (EA)
ASGP........ Aeronautical Standards Group [*Military*] (AFIT)
ASGP........ Annali. Seminario Giuridico di Palermo [*A publication*]
ASGP........ Association of Secretaries General of Parliaments (EA)
AS/GPD .... Attitude Set and Gimbal Position Display [*NASA*] (KSC)
AS/GPI..... Attitude Set and Gimbal Position Indicator [*NASA*]
ASGPP ...... American Society of Group Psychotherapy and Psychodrama (EA)
ASGRO ..... Armed Services Graves Registration Office [*Later, AFIRB*]
ASGS......... American Scientific Glassblowers Society (EA)
ASGS......... Assistant Secretary of the General Staff

ASGTMEM ... Amalgamated Society of General Tool Makers, Engineers, and Machinists [*A union*] [*British*]
AsGTU ...... Technische Universitat Graz, Graz, Austria [*Library symbol*] [*Library of Congress*] (LCLS)
ASGVAH .. Archives des Sciences (Geneva) [*A publication*]
ASGW .... Abhandlungen. Philologisch-Historische Klasse. Koenigliche Saechsische Gesellschaft der Wissenschaften [*A publication*]
ASGW .... Association for Specialists in Group Work (EA)
ASGY......... Yellowhead Regional Library, Spruce Grove, Alberta [*Library symbol*] [*National Library of Canada*] (NLC)
ASH .... Academy of Scientific Hypno Therapy (EA)
ASH .... Action on Smoking and Health (EA)
ASH .... Advanced Scout Helicopter [*Military*]
ASH .... Aerial Scout Helicopter (MCD)
ASH .... Aldosterone-Stimulating Hormone [*Also, AGTr*] [*Endocrinology*]
ASH .... American Society of Hematology (EA)
ASH .... American-Soviet Homestays (EA)
ASH .... Antiself Homing [*System*] [*Torpedo safety device*] [*Navy*]
A & SH ...... Argyll and Sutherland Highlanders [*Military unit*] [*British*]
ASH .... Armature Shunt [*Electromagnetism*]
ASH .... Ashendon [*England*]
ASH .... Ashkhabad [*USSR*] [*Seismograph station code, US Geological Survey*] (SEIS)
ASH .... Ashkhabad [*USSR*] [*Geomagnetic observatory code*]
ASH .... Ashland Oil, Inc. [*NYSE symbol*] (SPSG)
Ash............ Ashmead's Pennsylvania Reports [*1808-41*] [*A publication*] (DLA)
ASH .... Assault Support Helicopter [*Military*]
ASH .... Assistant Secretary for Health [*HEW*]
ASH .... Association for the Sexually Harassed (EA)
AsH............ Astigmatism, Hypermetropic [*Also, AH*] [*Ophthalmology*]
Ash............ Astonishing Stories [*A publication*]
ASH .... Asymmetric Septal Hypertrophy [*Medicine*]
ASH .... Australian Industrial Safety, Health, and Welfare [*A publication*]
ASH .... Author of "Southern Harmony" [*Initials singer Billy Walker put after his name*]
ASH .... Aviation Support, Hydraulic [*Navy rating*]
ASH .... Nashua, NH [*Location identifier*] [*FAA*] (FAAL)
ASH .... Spring Hill College, Mobile, AL [*OCLC symbol*] (OCLC)
ASH .... Submarine-Exhaust Detector [*Navy*] [*British*]
ASH .... Swan Hills Public Library, Alberta [*Library symbol*] [*National Library of Canada*] (NLC)
ASHA .... Amalgamated Shipyard Helpers Association [*A union*] [*British*]
ASHA .... American Saddlebred Horse Association (EA)
ASHA .... American School Health Association (EA)
ASHA .... American Schools and Hospitals Abroad [*Program*] [*Agency for International Development*]
ASHA .... American Shire Horse Association (EA)
ASHA .... American Social Health [*formerly, Hygiene*] Association (EA)
ASHA .... American Society of Hospital Attorneys (EA)
ASHA .... American Speech-Language-Hearing Association (EA)
ASHA .... American Spelean Historical Association (EA)
ASHA .... American Suffolk Horse Association (EA)
ASHA .... Arabian Sport Horse Association (EA)
ASHA .... Asha Corp. [*NASDAQ symbol*] (NQ)
ASHA .... ASHA. Journal of the American Speech and Hearing Association [*A publication*]
ASHA .... Australian Society for Historical Archaeology
ASHA .... Australian Software Houses Association
ASHA .... Aviation Safety and Health Association (EA)
ASHACE... American Society of Heating and Air-Conditioning Engineers [*Later, ASHRAE*]
ASHAE ..... American Society of Heating and Air-Conditioning Engineers [*Later, ASHRAE*]
ASHAG ..... Annales. Societe d'Histoire et d'Archeologie de Gand [*A publication*]
ASHA J Am Speech Hear Assoc ... ASHA. Journal of the American Speech and Hearing Association [*A publication*]
ASHAL...... Annuaire. Societe d'Histoire et d'Archeologie de la Lorraine [*A publication*]
ASHA Monogr ... ASHA [*American Speech and Hearing Association*] Monographs [*A publication*]
ASHA Rep ... ASHA [*American Speech and Hearing Association*] Reports [*A publication*]
ASHAT ..... Annales. Societe Historique et Archeologique de Tournai [*A publication*]
Ashb.......... Ashburner. Principles of Equity [*2nd ed.*] [*1933*] [*A publication*] (DLA)
ASHBA ..... American Saddle Horse Breeders Association [*Later, ASHA*] (EA)
ASHBA ..... American Scotch Highland Breeders' Association (EA)
ASHBEAMS ... American Society of Hospital-Based Emergency Air Medical Services (EA)
ASHC .... Aeronautics and Space Historical Center (EA)
ASHC .... All States Hobby Club [*Later, NASHC*]
ASHC .... American Society of Hospice Care (EA)
AShC .... Spring Hill College, Spring Hill, AL [*Library symbol*] [*Library of Congress*] (LCLS)

ASHCMPR ... American Society for Health Care Marketing and Public Relations (EA)

ASHCSP ... American Society for Healthcare Central Service Personnel [*American Hospital Association*] (EA)

ASHD .... Arteriosclerotic Heart Disease [*Cardiology*]

ASHE .... American Society for Hospital Engineering - of the American Hospital Association (EA)

Ashe .... Ashe's Tables to the Year Books, Coke's Reports, or Dyer's Reports [*A publication*] (DLA)

ASHE .... Association for the Study of Higher Education (EA)

ASheR .... Reynolds Metals, Reduction Research Division, Sheffield, AL [*Library symbol*] [*Library of Congress*] (LCLS)

Ashers Guide Bot Period ... Asher's Guide to Botanical Periodicals [*A publication*]

ASHES ...... American Society for Healthcare Environmental Services of the American Hospital Association (EA)

ASHET ...... American Society for Healthcare Education and Training - of the American Hospital Association (EA)

ASHF .... American Swedish Historical Foundation and Museum (EA)

ASHFSA ... American Society for Hospital Food Service Administrators (EA)

ASHFY ...... American Swedish Historical Foundation. Yearbook [*A publication*]

ASHG .... American Society of Human Genetics (EA)

Ash G Bot Per ... Asher's Guide to Botanical Periodicals [*A publication*]

ASHHRA .. American Society for Healthcare Human Resources Administration (EA)

ASHI .... American Society for Histocompatibility and Immunogenetics (EA)

ASHI .... American Society of Home Inspectors (EA)

Ashken ...... Ashkenazic [*Jews from Central or Eastern Europe*] (BJA)

ASHL .... ASCIS [*Australian Schools Cooperative Information Service*] Subject Headings List

Ashm .... Ashmead's Pennsylvania Reports [*1808-41*] [*A publication*] (DLA)

Ash M .... Ashmolean Museum [*A publication*]

Ashmead .... Ashmead's Pennsylvania Reports [*1808-41*] [*A publication*] (DLA)

Ashmead (PA) ... Ashmead's Pennsylvania Reports [*1808-41*] [*A publication*] (DLA)

Ashmead's Penn Rep ... Ashmead's Pennsylvania Reports [*1808-41*] [*A publication*] (DLA)

ASHMM ... American Society for Hospital Materials Management (EA)

Ashm (PA) ... Ashmead's Pennsylvania Reports [*1808-41*] [*A publication*] (DLA)

ASHMPR ... American Society for Hospital Marketing and Public Relations [*Later, ASHCMPR*] (EA)

ASH-NI ..... Action on Smoking and Health - Northern Ireland (EAIO)

ASHNS ..... American Society for Head and Neck Surgery (EA)

ASHOF ...... Air Shutoff

ASHORAD ... Advanced Short-Range Air Defense System (MCD)

ASHP .... Airship

ASHP .... American Society of Handicapped Physicians (EA)

ASHP .... American Society of Hospital Pharmacists (EA)

ASHP .... American Society for Hospital Planning (EA)

ASHPA ...... American Society for Hospital Personnel Administration [*Later, ASHHRA*] (EA)

ASHPMM ... American Society for Hospital Purchasing and Materials Management [*Later, ASHMM*] (EA)

ASHPREF ... American Society of Hospital Pharmacists Research and Education Foundation (EA)

ASHPS ...... American Scenic and Historic Preservation Society (EA)

ASHR .... African Society for Human Rights [*Defunct*] (EA)

ASHR .... American Sport Horse Registry (EA)

ASHRA ...... American Spa and Health Resort Association (EA)

ASHRAE ... American Society of Heating, Refrigerating, and Air-Conditioning Engineers (EA)

ASHRAE B ... American Society of Heating, Refrigerating, and Air-Conditioning Engineers. Bulletin [*A publication*]

ASHRAE Handb Fundam ... American Society of Heating, Refrigerating, and Air-Conditioning Engineers. Handbook of Fundamentals [*A publication*]

ASHRAE Handb Prod Dir ... ASHRAE [*American Society of Heating, Refrigerating, and Air-Conditioning Engineers*] Handbook and Product Directory [*A publication*]

ASHRAE J ... American Society of Heating, Refrigerating, and Air-Conditioning Engineers. Journal [*A publication*]

ASHRAE Jol ... American Society of Heating, Refrigerating, and Air-Conditioning Engineers. Journal [*A publication*]

ASHRAE Trans ... American Society of Heating, Refrigerating, and Air-Conditioning Engineers. Transactions [*A publication*]

ASHRF ...... African Starvation and Hunger Relief Fund (EA)

ASHRM .... American Society for Healthcare Risk Management (EA)

ASHS .... American Society for Horticultural Science (EA)

ASHT .... American Society of Hand Therapists (EA)

ASH-TF ..... Advanced Scout Helicopter Task Force [*Army*] (RDA)

Ashton .... Ashton's Reports [*9-12 Opinions of the United States Attorneys General*] [*A publication*] (DLA)

ASHUR ..... Apollo Spacecraft Hardware Utilization Request [*NASA*]

Ashurst ...... Ashurst's Manuscript Reports, Printed in Volume 2, Chitty [*A publication*] (DLA)

Ashurst ...... Ashurst's Paper Books, Lincoln's Inn Library [*A publication*] (DLA)

Ashurst MS ... Ashurst's Manuscript Reports, Printed in Volume 2, Chitty [*A publication*] (DLA)

Ashurst MS ... Ashurst's Paper Books, Lincoln's Inn Library [*A publication*] (DLA)

ASHVE ...... American Society of Heating and Ventilating Engineers

ASHW ...... Action on Smoking and Health in Wales (EAIO)

ASHW ...... Holsworthy [*Australia*] [*ICAO location identifier*] (ICLI)

ASHY .... Agudath Shofte ha-Hakhra'ah ha-Yehudit (BJA)

ASHY .... American Swedish Historical Foundation. Yearbook [*A publication*]

ASHYC ..... American Saddle Horse Youth Club (EA)

ASI .... Action Surveys, Incorporated [*Information service or system*] (IID)

ASI .... Adam Smith Institute (EA)

ASI .... Additional Skill Identifier [*Military*]

ASI .... Admiralty Supply Item

ASI .... Adoption Search Institute [*Inactive*] (EA)

ASI .... Advanced Sales Index [*LIMRA*]

ASI .... Advanced Scientific Instruments [*AMR, Inc.*]

ASI .... Advanced Study Institutes (NATG)

ASI .... Aerospace Static Inverter

ASI .... Aerospace Studies Institute [*Air Force*] (MCD)

ASI .... Africa Service Institute of New York [*Defunct*]

ASI .... African Scientific Institute (EA)

ASI .... Agri-Silviculture Institute (EA)

ASI .... Air Sea International [*British*]

ASI .... Air Society, International (EA)

ASI .... Aircraft Sampling Inspection (MCD)

ASI .... Airspeed Indicator

ASI .... Allied Stone Industries (EA)

ASI .... Alphabetic Subject Index [*A publication*]

ASI .... Althydusamband Islands [*Icelandic Federation of Labor*]

ASI .... Altimeter Setting Indicator [*Aviation*] (FAAC)

ASI .... Amended Shipping Instruction [*Military*]

ASI .... Amended Shipping Instrument (MCD)

ASI .... American Sightseeing International (EA)

ASI .... American Society of Indexers (EA)

ASI .... American Society of Interpreters (EA)

ASI .... American Society of Inventors (EA)

ASI .... American Soybean Institute [*Defunct*] (EA)

ASI .... American Specification Institute [*Defunct*]

ASI .... American Statistics Index [*Congressional Information Service, Inc.*] [*Bibliographic database*] [*A publication*]

ASI .... American Supplier Institute (EA)

ASI .... American Swedish Institute (EA)

ASI .... Ammunition Supply Installation [*Army*] (INF)

ASI .... Andrei Sakharov Institute [*Later, FUWPH*] (EA)

ASI .... Annual Supply Inspection [*Military*] (NVT)

ASI .... Answer Search Interface (MCD)

ASI .... Antisaturation Inverter

ASI .... Apollo Standard Initiator [*NASA*]

ASI .... Architects and Surveyors Institute (EAIO)

ASI .... Archivio Storico Italiano [*A publication*]

ASI .... Arctic Survival Instructor [*British military*] (DMA)

ASI .... ARGO Systems, Inc., Sunnyvale, CA [*OCLC symbol*] (OCLC)

ASI .... Aril Society International (EA)

ASI .... Armaments Standardization and Interoperability [*NATO*] (NATG)

ASI .... Arnold Schoenberg Institute [*University of Southern California*] [*Research center*] (RCD)

ASI .... Asian Statistical Institute

ASI .... Association of Privately Owned Seventh-Day Adventist Services and Industries (EA)

ASI .... Association of Seafood Importers (EA)

ASI .... Association Stomatologique Internationale [*International Stomatological Association*]

ASI .... Associative Surface Ionization [*Organic chemistry*]

ASI .... Astrex, Incorporated [*AMEX symbol*] (SPSG)

ASI .... Audience Studies, Incorporated [*Television program testing system*]

ASI .... Augmented Spark Igniter [*NASA*]

ASI .... Augmented System Ignition [*NASA*] (KSC)

ASI .... Augustana Swedish Institute [*Later, AHS*]

ASI .... Australian Science Index [*Information service or system*] [*A publication*] (APTA)

ASI .... Australian Shipbuilding Industries Ltd.

ASI .... Australian Society of Indexers

ASI .... Australian Swimming, Inc.

ASI .... Automatic Sampling Injector

ASI .... Aviation Safety Institute (EA)

ASI .... Aviation Services, Incorporated

ASI .... Axial Shape Index (NRCH)

ASI .... Azimuth Speed Indicator

a-si--- .... Singapore [*MARC geographic area code*] [*Library of Congress*] (LCCP)

ASIA .... Airlines Staff International Association (EAIO)

ASIA .... American Sheep Industry Association (EA)

ASIA .... American Society of Industrial Auctioneers (EA)

ASIA .... American Spinal Injury Association (EA)

ASIA .... American Stone Importers Association (EA)
ASIA .... Army Signal Intelligence Agency
Asia .... Asia and the Americas [*A publication*]
ASIA .... Asia Pacific Business [*A publication*]
ASIA .... Asiamerica Equities Ltd. [*NASDAQ symbol*] (NQ)
ASIA .... Associate of the Society of Investment Analysts [*British*] (DBQ)
ASIA .... Association of Sri-Lankans in America (EA)
ASIA .... Australian Scientific Industry Association
ASIA .... Automotive Service Industry Association (EA)
ASIA .... Avionics System Integration and Acquisition (MCD)
Asia Afr R ... Asia and Africa Review [*A publication*]
ASIAC .... Aerospace Structures Information and Analysis Center [*Air Force*] [*Wright-Patterson Air Force Base, OH*] (MCD)
ASIAC .... Australian Surveying Industry Advisory Committee
ASIA(Ed)... Associate of the Society of Industrial Artists (Education) [*British*]
ASIAEE..... Assistant Secretary for International Affairs and Energy Emergencies
Asia Folkl Stud ... Asian Folklore Studies [*A publication*]
Asia Found News ... Asia Foundation News [*A publication*]
Asia J Econ ... Asian Journal of Economics [*A publication*]
ASIAM...... [*The*] Asian American Magazine [*A publication*]
Asia Min.... Asia Mining [*Manila*] [*A publication*]
Asia Mon ... Asia Monitor [*A publication*]
Asian Aff.... Asian Affairs [*A publication*]
Asian Aff (London) ... Asian Affairs. Journal of the Royal Central Asian Society (London) [*A publication*]
Asian Aff (New York) ... Asian Affairs (New York) [*A publication*]
Asian & African Stud (Bratislava) ... Asian and African Studies (Bratislava) [*A publication*]
Asian Arch Anaesthesiol Resusc ... Asian Archives of Anaesthesiology and Resuscitation [*A publication*]
Asian Australas J Anim Sci ... Asian-Australasian Journal of Animal Science • [*A publication*]
A'sian Baker ... Australasian Baker and Millers' Journal [*A publication*] (APTA)
Asian Bldg & Construction ... Asian Building and Construction [*A publication*]
A'sian Boating ... Australasian Boating [*A publication*] (APTA)
Asian Bus... Asian Business and Industry [*Later, Asian Business*] [*A publication*]
A'sian Bus Cond Bul ... Australasian Business Conditions Bulletin [*A publication*] (APTA)
Asian Bus and Industry ... Asian Business and Industry [*Later, Asian Business*] [*A publication*]
A'sian Catholic R ... Australasian Catholic Record [*A publication*] (APTA)
A'sian Catholic Rec ... Australasian Catholic Record [*A publication*] (APTA)
Asian Comp L Rev ... Asian Comparative Law Review [*A publication*] (DLA)
A'sian Confectioner ... Australasian Confectioner and Restaurant Journal [*A publication*] (APTA)
Asian Dev .. Asian Development. Quarterly Newsletter [*A publication*]
Asian Econ ... Asian Economics [*A publication*]
Asian Econ R ... Asian Economic Review [*A publication*]
A'sian Eng ... Australasian Engineering [*A publication*] (APTA)
A'sian Engineer ... Australasian Engineer [*A publication*] (APTA)
A'sian Exhibitor ... Australasian Exhibitor [*A publication*] (APTA)
Asian Fin ... Asian Finance [*A publication*]
Asian Folk ... Asian Folklore Studies [*A publication*]
Asian Folkl Stud ... Asian Folklore Studies [*A publication*]
A'sian Grocer ... Australasian Grocer [*A publication*] (APTA)
A'sian Inst Min & Metallurgy Proc ... Australasian Institute of Mining and Metallurgy. Proceedings [*A publication*] (APTA)
Asian Inst Tech Newsl ... Asian Institute of Technology. Newsletter [*A publication*]
Asian Inst Tech Rev ... Asian Institute of Technology. Review [*A publication*]
A'sian Insurance & Banking Rec ... Australasian Insurance and Banking Record [*A publication*] (APTA)
A'sian Insurance J ... Australasian Insurance Journal [*A publication*] (APTA)
A'sian Irrigator ... Australasian Irrigator [*A publication*] (APTA)
Asian J Chem ... Asian Journal of Chemistry [*A publication*]
Asian J Dairy Res ... Asian Journal of Dairy Research [*A publication*]
Asian J Infect Dis ... Asian Journal of Infectious Diseases [*A publication*]
Asian J Med ... Asian Journal of Medicine [*A publication*]
Asian J Mod Med ... Asian Journal of Modern Medicine [*A publication*]
Asian J Pharm ... Asian Journal of Pharmacy [*A publication*]
A'sian J Pharmacy ... Australasian Journal of Pharmacy [*A publication*] (APTA)
Asian J Pharm Sci ... Asian Journal of Pharmaceutical Sciences [*A publication*]
A'sian J Phil ... Australasian Journal of Philosophy [*A publication*] (APTA)
A'sian Leather and Footwear R ... Australasian Leather and Footwear Review [*A publication*] (APTA)
A'sian Leather Trades R ... Australasian Leather Trades Review [*A publication*] (APTA)
Asian M ..... Asian Music [*A publication*]
A'sian Manuf ... Australasian Manufacturer [*A publication*] (APTA)
A'sian Manufacturer ... Australasian Manufacturer [*A publication*] (APTA)
A'sian Manuf Ind Ann ... Australasian Manufacturer. Industrial Annual [*A publication*] (APTA)
Asian Med J ... Asian Medical Journal [*Tokyo*] [*A publication*]

A'sian Meth Hist Soc J & Proc ... Australasian Methodist Historical Society. Journal and Proceedings [*A publication*] (APTA)
Asian Mus ... Asian Music [*A publication*]
A'sian Oil & Gas J ... Australasian Oil and Gas Journal [*A publication*] (APTA)
Asian Pac Cens Forum ... Asian and Pacific Census Forum [*A publication*]
Asian Pacif Quart Cult Soc Aff ... Asian Pacific Quarterly of Cultural and Social Affairs [*A publication*]
Asian Pac J Allergy Immunol ... Asian Pacific Journal of Allergy and Immunology [*A publication*]
Asian Pac Popul Programme News ... Asian and Pacific Population Programme News [*A publication*]
Asian Persp ... Asian Perspectives [*A publication*]
Asian Perspect ... Asian Perspectives [*A publication*]
A'sian Post ... Australasian Post [*A publication*] (APTA)
A'sian Pr.... Australasian Printer [*A publication*] (APTA)
A'sian Printer ... Australasian Printer [*A publication*] (APTA)
Asian R .... Asian Review [*A publication*]
A'sian R'way & Locomotive Hist Soc Bul ... Australasian Railway and Locomotive Historical Society. Bulletin [*A publication*] (APTA)
Asian S....... Asian Survey [*A publication*]
Asian Sch... Bulletin of Concerned Asian Scholars [*A publication*]
Asian Soc Sci Bibliogr Annot Abstr ... Asian Social Science Bibliography with Annotations and Abstracts [*A publication*]
Asian Stud ... Asian Studies [*A publication*]
Asian Stud Prof R ... Asian Studies. Professional Review [*A publication*]
Asian Surv ... Asian Survey [*A publication*]
A'sian Univ Mod Lang Assoc Congress Proc ... Australasian Universities Modern Language Association. Proceedings of Congress [*A publication*] (APTA)
Asian WSJ ... Asian Wall Street Journal [*A publication*]
Asia & Oceania Cong Endocrinol ... Asia and Oceania Congress of Endocrinology [*A publication*]
Asia Oceania J Obstet Gynaecol ... Asia Oceania Journal of Obstetrics and Gynaecology [*A publication*]
Asia Pac Com ... Asia Pacific Community [*A publication*]
ASIAPACK ... South East Asia International Exhibition of Packaging Machinery and Materials and Food Processing Machinery (TSPED)
Asia Pac Q ... Quarterly Bulletin of Statistics for Asia and the Pacific [*A publication*]
Asia Q........ Asia Quarterly [*A publication*]
Asia Quart ... Asia Quarterly [*A publication*]
Asia R .... Asiatic Review [*A publication*]
Asia Res Bul ... Asia Research Bulletin [*A publication*]
ASIAS ...... Airline Schedules and Interline Availability Study [*IATA*] (DS)
Asia Ship ... Asia Pacific Shipping [*A publication*]
ASIATEX ... South East Asia's International Exhibition of Textile and Garment Machinery and Fabrics Trade (TSPED)
Asiatic R .... Asiatic Review [*A publication*]
Asiatic R ns ... Asiatic Review. New Series [*A publication*]
Asiatic Soc Japan Trans ... Asiatic Society of Japan. Transactions [*A publication*]
Asiatische Stud ... Asiatische Studien [*A publication*]
Asiat Stud .. Asiatische Studien [*A publication*]
ASIB .... American Society of Independent Business (EA)
ASIC .... Air Service Information Circular
ASIC .... All Source Intelligence Center (MCD)
ASIC .... American Society of Irrigation Consultants (EA)
ASIC .... Antique Stove Information Clearinghouse (EA)
ASIC .... Application-Specific Integrated Circuit [*Electronics*]
ASIC .... Area Security Information Center
ASIC .... Associated States of Indochina (NATG)
ASIC .... Association Scientifique Internationale du Cafe [*International Scientific Association of Coffee*] (EAIO)
ASIC .... Association de la Securite Industrielle du Canada [*Industrial Security Association of Canada*]
ASIC .... Avionics Subsystems Interface Contractor [*Air Force*]
ASIC .... St. Isidore Community Library [*Bibliotheque de St-Isidore*] Alberta [*Library symbol*] [*National Library of Canada*] (NLC)
ASICA .... Association Internationale pour le Calcul Analogique [*International Association for Analogue Computation*] [*Later, IMACS*]
ASID .... Address Space Identifier (BUR)
ASID .... Advanced System Integration Demonstration [*Military*]
ASID .... American Society of Industrial Designers [*Later, IDSA*] (EA)
ASID .... American Society of Interior Designers (EA)
ASID .... Association of Sports Information Directors (EA)
ASID .... Association for the Study of International Development [*See also AEDI*] [*Canada*]
ASID .... Automatic Station Identification Device
ASIDIC ..... Association of Information and Dissemination Centers (EA)
ASIDIC News ... ASIDIC [*Association of Information and Dissemination Centers*] Newsletter [*A publication*]
ASIDS .... Airborne Surveillance and Intercept Defense System
ASIDS .... Aircraft Stores Interface Data Systems
ASIDSI...... American Sudden Infant Death Syndrome Institute (EA)
ASIE .... American Society of International Executives [*Blue Bell, PA*] (EA)

Asien Afr Lateinam ... Asien, Afrika, Lateinamerika [*A publication*]
Asie Nouv .. Asie Nouvelle [*A publication*]
ASIEP....... Autism Screening Instrument for Educational Planning
Asie Sud-Est Monde Insulind ... Asie du Sud-Est et Monde Insulindien [*A publication*]
ASIF .... Airlift Service Industrial Fund [*Military*]
ASIF .... Aldosterone Secretion Inhibitory Factor [*Endocrinology*]
ASIFA .... Association Internationale du Film d'Animation [*International Animated Film Association*] (EAIO)
ASIG......... Alarm System Improvement Guide (MCD)
ASIGCEN ... Area Signal Center [*Army*] (AABC)
ASIGSCH ... Army Signal School (MCD)
ASIH .... American Society of Ichthyologists and Herpetologists (EA)
ASII .... American Science Information Institute
ASII........... Automated Systems, Incorporated [*Brookfield, WI*] [*NASDAQ symbol*] (NQ)
ASIL.......... American Society of International Law (EA)
ASIL.......... Annual Survey of Indian Law [*A publication*]
ASILO....... Adalbert Stifter Institut des Landes Oberoesterreich. Vierteljahresschrift [*A publication*]
ASIL Proc ... Proceedings. American Society of International Law [*A publication*]
ASILS....... Association of Student International Law Societies (EA)
ASILS Intl LJ ... ASILS [*Association of Student International Law Societies*] International Law Journal [*A publication*]
ASIM........ Aircraft Stores Interface Manual (MCD)
ASIM........ American Society of Insurance Management [*Later, RIMS*] (EA)
ASIM........ American Society of Internal Medicine (EA)
ASIM........ Associate in Industrial Management
ASIM........ Australian Scientific Instrument Manufacturers
ASIMAY ... Atti. Societa Italiana di Scienze Naturali. Museo Civico di Storia Naturale di Milano [*A publication*]
ASIMIS..... Aircraft Structural Integrity Management Information System [*Air Force*] (AFIT)
ASIMS ...... Army Standard Information Management System
ASIN......... Agricultural Sciences Information Network [*National Agricultural Library*] [*Beltsville, MD*]
ASIN......... Arts in Alaska. Newsletter. Alaska State Council on the Arts [*A publication*]
Asin........... Asinaria [*of Plautus*] [*Classical studies*] (OCD)
ASInt .... American Studies International [*A publication*]
ASIO......... Australian Security Intelligence Organisation (PD)
ASIOE....... Associated Support Items of Equipment (MCD)
ASIP......... Aircraft Structural Integrity Program
ASIP .... Airspace Flight Inspection Pilot (FAAC)
ASIP .... All-Sky Imaging Photometer
ASIP .... Army Stationing and Installation Plan (AABC)
ASIP .... Australian Serials in Print [*A publication*]
ASIP .... Avionic System Integration Plan (MCD)
ASIP .... Joint Air-Sea Interaction Panel [*Federal Council for Science and Technology*] (NOAA)
ASIPI........ Asociacion Interamericana de la Propiedad Industrial [*Inter-American Association of Industrial Property - IAAIP*] (EAIO)
ASIPRE..... Army Snow, Ice, and Permafrost Research Establishment
ASIR......... Aeronautical Shipboard Installation Representative (NVT)
ASIR .... Airspeed Indicator Reading
ASIRAF..... Australia. Commonwealth Scientific and Industrial Research Organisation. Annual Report [*A publication*]
ASIRC....... Aquatic Sciences Information Retrieval Center [*University of Rhode Island*]
ASIRC ...... Armed Services Industrial Readiness Council
ASIS .... Abort Sensing and Implementation System
ASIS .... Alcohol Safety Interlock System
ASIS .... American Society for Industrial Security (EA)
ASIS .... American Society for Information Science [*Formerly, ADI*] (EA)
ASIS .... American Student Information Service
ASIS .... Ammunition Stores Issue Ship
ASIS .... Amphibious Support Information System (NVT)
ASIS .... Anterior Superior Iliac Spine [*Anatomy*]
ASIS .... Arbeitsschutzinformationssystem [*Information System for Occupational Safety and Health*] [*West Germany*] (IID)
ASIS .... Army Space Initiatives Study
ASIS .... Aromatic Solvent-Induced Shift [*Physical chemistry*]
ASIS .... Assateague Island National Seashore [*National Park Service designation*]
ASIS .... Atti. Societa Italiana di Statistica [*A publication*]
ASIS .... Automated Schedule Information System
ASIS .... Automotive Sensor Instrumentation System Van [*Automotive engineering*]
ASIS .... Auxiliary Ship Information System [*Navy*] (CAAL)
ASISAI...... Atti. Societa Italiana delle Scienze Veterinarie [*A publication*]
AS of ISES ... American Section of the International Solar Energy Society (EA)
ASIS Newsl ... ASIS [*American Society for Information Science*] Newsletter [*A publication*]
ASISS........ Alpine Science Information Service [*Information service or system*] (IID)

ASIST....... Accelerated Specialized Inspection Sites [*Customs inspection at airports*]
ASIST....... Advanced Scientific Instruments Symbolic Translator [*Assembly program*] (DEN)
ASIST....... Alberta Statistical Information System [*Alberta Treasury, Bureau of Statistics*] [*Database*]
Asi St/Et As ... Asiatische Studien/Etudes Asiatiques [*A publication*]
ASIT .... Adaptable Surface Interface Terminal (MCD)
ASIT .... Army School on Instructional Technology [*British*]
ASITC .... Association des Scientifiques, Ingenieurs, et Techniciens du Canada [*Association of the Scientific, Engineering, and Technological Community of Canada*]
AsIU .... Leopold-Franzens Universitat Insbruck, Insbruck, Austria [*Library symbol*] [*Library of Congress*] (LCLS)
ASIWPCA ... Association of State and Interstate Water Pollution Control Administrators (EA)
ASIX .... Assix International, Inc. [*NASDAQ symbol*] (NQ)
ASJ .... AAA Stamp & Coin [*Vancouver Stock Exchange symbol*]
ASJ .... Action for Soviet Jewry (EA)
ASJ .... Ahoskie, NC [*Location identifier*] [*FAA*] (FAAL)
ASJ .... Alianca Socialista de Juventude [*Socialist Youth Alliance*] [*Portugal*] [*Political party*] (PPE)
ASJ .... Amami O Shima [*Japan*] [*Airport symbol*] (OAG)
ASJ .... American Suzuki Journal [*A publication*]
ASJ .... Asosan [*Japan*] [*Seismograph station code, US Geological Survey*] (SEIS)
ASJ .... Association for Scientific Journals (EA)
ASJA .... American Salers Junior Association (EA)
ASJA .... American Society of Journalists and Authors (EA)
ASJA .... Assistant Staff Judge Advocate [*Air Force*]
ASJB .... Australian Sentencing Judgements Bulletin [*A publication*]
ASJFHAW ... Amalgamated Society of Journeymen Felt Hatters and Allied Workers [*A union*] [*British*] (DCTA)
ASJG .... Albanian Society Jusuf Gervalla (EA)
ASJJA .... Association of State Juvenile Justice Administrators [*Absorbed by NAJCA*] (EA)
ASJL......... Association for the Study of Jewish Languages [*Haifa, Israel*] (EAIO)
ASJM .... American Society for Jewish Music (EA)
ASJMC ..... Association of Schools of Journalism and Mass Communication (EA)
ASJPA....... Australian Journal of Psychology [*A publication*]
ASJPAE.... Australian Journal of Psychology [*A publication*]
ASJR .... Army Summary Jurisdiction Regulations [*British military*] (DMA)
ASJSA....... American Society of Journalism School Administrators (EA)
ASK .... Actively Shared Knowledge [*Data processing system*]
ASK .... Adjustable Stroke Kit
ASK .... Aeolian-Skinner Organ Co. [*Record label*]
ASK .... Agent Selection Kit [*LIMRA*]
ASK .... Aircraft Station Keeper (MCD)
ASK .... Alaska Apollo Gold Mines Ltd. [*Vancouver Stock Exchange symbol*]
ASK .... Alerting Search Service from Kinokuniya [*Kinokuniya Co. Ltd.*] [*Japan*] [*Information service or system*] (IID)
ASK .... American Simplified Keyboard [*Typewriter*]
ASK .... Amplitude Shift Keying
ASK .... Analog Select Keyboard [*Data processing*] (KSC)
ASK .... Antistreptokinase [*Immunology*]
ASK .... Askania Theodolite Camera (MUGU)
ASK .... Association for Study of Karma (EA)
ASK .... Astronaut Survival Kit [*NASA*]
a-sk---....... Sikkim [*MARC geographic area code*] [*Library of Congress*] (LCCP)
ASK .... Yamoussoukro [*Ivory Coast*] [*Airport symbol*] (OAG)
ASKA......... Alaska Bancorporation [*NASDAQ symbol*] (NQ)
ASKA......... Automatic Systems for Kinematic Analysis [*NASA*] (NASA)
ASKARS.... Automated Storage, Kitting, and Retrieval Systems [*Tandem Computers*] [*Navy*]
ASKC........ ASK Corporation [*NASDAQ symbol*] (NQ)
ASKG........ Archiv fuer Schlesische Kirchengeschichte [*A publication*]
ASKI .... ASK Computer Systems, Incorporated [*NASDAQ symbol*] (NQ)
ASKS .... Automatic Station Keeping System
ASKS .... Sydney [*Australia*] [*ICAO location identifier*] (ICLI)
ASKT........ Akkadische Keilschrifttexte [*A publication*] (BJA)
ASKT........ American Society of Knitting Technologists (EA)
ASL............ A-Strain Spontaneous Leukemia [*Type of cell line*]
ASL............ Abbe's Sine Law
ASL............ Above Sea Level
ASL............ Acceptable Supplier List
A S e L ...... Acta Semiotica et Linguistica [*A publication*]
ASL............ Acting Sub-Lieutenant [*Navy*] [*British*]
ASL............ Activity Safety Level (AFIT)
AS & L .... Administrative Support and Logistic Company [*Military*]
ASL............ Advanced Student in Law [*British*] (ROG)
ASL............ Advanced Systems Laboratory
ASL............ Aeronautical Structures Laboratory [*Navy*]
ASL............ Aircraft Specialties Lines
ASL............ Aircraft Summary List

ASL .... Alabama Public Library Service, Montgomery, AL [*OCLC symbol*] (OCLC)
ASL .... American Association of State Libraries [*Later, ASCLA*] (EA)
ASL .... American School in London
ASL .... American Shuffleboard Leagues (EA)
ASL .... American Sign Language [*for the deaf*]
ASL .... American Soccer League
ASL .... Annual Survey of Law [*A publication*] (APTA)
ASL .... Antistreptolysin [*Immunology*]
ASL .... Applied Science Laboratory
ASL .... Archivio Storico Lombardo [*A publication*]
ASL .... Arctic Submarine Laboratory [*Navy*] (MSC)
ASL .... Argininosuccinate Lyase [*Also, AL*] [*An enzyme*]
ASL .... Arithmetic Shift Left [*Data processing*]
ASL .... Army Standards Laboratory
ASL .... Association of Standards Laboratories
ASL .... Association for Symbolic Logic (EA)
ASL .... Astigmatic Spectral Line
ASL .... Astro-Space Lab, Inc. (MCD)
ASL .... Astrosurveillance Science Laboratory
ASL .... Atmospheric Sciences Laboratory [*Army Laboratory Command*] [*White Sands Missile Range, NM*]
ASL .... Australian Special Libraries [*A publication*]
ASL .... Authorized Stock Level (CINC)
ASL .... Authorized Stockage List [*Army*]
ASL .... Automated Soft Lander [*Aerospace*] (MCD)
ASL .... Available Space List [*Data processing*]
ASL .... Average Service Life
ASL .... Aviation Systems Laboratory (MCD)
ASL .... Azimuth Steering Line (MCD)
ASL .... Marshall, TX [*Location identifier*] [*FAA*] (FAAL)
ASL .... Smoky Lake Public Library, Alberta [*Library symbol*] [*National Library of Canada*] (NLC)
ASL .... Spurling Aviation [*Seattle, WA*] [*FAA designator*] (FAAC)
ASL .... Submarine Tender (Small) [*Navy ship symbol*] (NATG)
ASLA .... American Savings and Loan Association (EA)
ASLA .... American Society of Landscape Architects (EA)
ASLA .... Association of State Library Agencies [*Formerly, Association of State Libraries*] [*Later, ASCLA*]
ASLA .... Association for the Study of Literature and Alchemy (EA)
As Lab. ...... Asian Labour [*A publication*]
ASLAB ...... Atomic Safety and Licensing Appeal Board (NRCH)
ASLADS .... Automatic Shipboard Launch Aircraft Data System
ASLAMS .... Automated Ship Location and Attitude Measuring System
ASLAP ...... American Society of Laboratory Animal Practitioners (EA)
ASLAP ...... Atomic Safety and Licensing Appeal Panel [*Nuclear Regulatory Commission*]
ASLA Pres Newsl ... Association of State Library Agencies. President's Newsletter [*A publication*]
ASLB .... Atomic Safety and Licensing Board [*Nuclear Regulatory Commission*]
ASLBM ..... Antisubmarine Launched Ballistic Missile
ASLBP ...... Atomic Safety and Licensing Board Panel [*Nuclear Regulatory Commission*]
ASLC .... Adaptive Side-Lobe Canceller [*RADAR*] (MCD)
ASLC .... Australian Securities Law Cases [*A publication*] (APTA)
ASLCM ..... Advanced Sea-Launched Cruise Missile (MCD)
ASLE .... Account Sales
ASLE .... American Society of Lubrication Engineers (EA)
ASLE (Am Soc Lubr Eng) Annu Meet Prepr ... ASLE (American Society of Lubrication Engineers) Annual Meeting. Preprints [*A publication*]
ASLE Annu Meet Prepr ... ASLE [*American Society of Lubrication Engineers*] Annual Meeting. Preprints [*A publication*]
ASLEEP .... Automated Scanning Low-Energy Electron Probe (IEEE)
ASLEF ...... Associated Society of Locomotive Engineers and Firemen [*A union*] [*British*] (DCTA)
ASLE Pap ... ASLE [*American Society of Lubrication Engineers*] Papers [*A publication*]
ASLE Prepr ... ASLE [*American Society of Lubrication Engineers*] Preprints [*A publication*]
ASLET ...... American Society of Law Enforcement Trainers (EA)
ASLE Trans ... ASLE [*American Society of Lubrication Engineers*] Transactions [*A publication*]
ASLF .... Annales de Saint-Louis des Francais [*A publication*]
ASLG .... Academy for State and Local Government (EA)
ASLG .... Atti. Societa Linguistica di Scienze e Lettere di Genova [*A publication*]
ASLH .... American Society for Legal History (EA)
ASLH .... American Society of the Legion of Honor. Magazine [*A publication*]
ASLH .... Lord Howe Island [*Australia*] [*ICAO location identifier*] (ICLI)
ASLHC ...... Association of Scottish Local Health Councils [*British*]
ASLHM .... American Society of the Legion of Honor. Magazine [*A publication*]
ASLI .... American Savings and Loan Institute [*Later, IFE*] (EA)
Aslib .... Association of Special Libraries and Information Bureaux [*Acronym is now organization's official name*]
Aslib Inf ..... Aslib Information [*A publication*]
Aslib Info ... Aslib Information [*A publication*]

Aslib Proc .. Aslib Proceedings [*A publication*]
ASLJD ...... Arizona State Law Journal [*A publication*]
ASLK .... Algemene Spaar- en Lijfrentekas [*State-owned bank*] [*Belgium*] (EY)
ASLL .... Acta Societatis Humaniorum Litterarum Lundensis [*A publication*]
ASLL .... American Savings and Loan League [*Later, ALFI*] (EA)
ASLLP .... Australian Second Language Learning Program
ASLM .... American Society of Law and Medicine (EA)
ASLM .... Slave Lake Municipal Library, Alberta [*Library symbol*] [*National Library of Canada*] (NLC)
ASLMR ..... Assistant Secretary for Labor-Management Relations [*Department of Labor*]
ASLMS .... American Society for Laser Medicine and Surgery (EA)
ASLN .... Australian Special Libraries News [*A publication*] (APTA)
ASLNY ..... Art Students' League of New York (EA)
ASLO .... American Society of Limnology and Oceanography (EA)
ASLO .... American Society of Local Officials (EA)
ASLO .... Antistreptolysin-O [*Also, ASO*] [*Clinical chemistry*]
ASLO .... Associated Scottish Life Offices (EAIO)
ASLO .... Australian Scientific Liaison Office [*Washington, DC*]
ASLOBM .. American Society of Limnology and Oceanography. Special Symposium [*A publication*]
ASLod .... Archivio Storico Lodigiano [*A publication*]
ASLO (London) Rep ... Australian Scientific Liaison Office (London). Report [*A publication*] (APTA)
ASLP .... Association of Special Libraries of the Philippines
ASLP .... Australian Society of Legal Philosophy
ASLP Bul ... Association of Special Libraries of the Philippines. Bulletin [*A publication*]
ASLP Bull ... Association of Special Libraries of the Philippines. Bulletin [*A publication*]
ASLP Bulletin ... Australian Society of Legal Philosophy. Bulletin [*A publication*] (APTA)
ASLP Proceedings ... Australian Society of Legal Philosophy. Proceedings [*A publication*] (APTA)
ASLR .... American Short Line Railroads
ASLR .... Australian Securities Law Reporter [*A publication*] (APTA)
ASLRA ..... American Short Line Railroad Association (EA)
ASLRA ..... Association of State Labor Relations Agencies (EA)
ASLRAU ... Australia. Commonwealth Scientific and Industrial Research Organisation. Land Research Series [*A publication*]
ASL Res Rep ... ASL [*American Scientific Laboratories*] Research Report [*A publication*]
ASLS .... Advocates to Save Legal Services [*Inactive*] (EA)
ASLS .... Association for Scottish Literary Studies [*Aberdeen, Scotland*] (EAIO)
ASLSP .... Atti. Societa Ligure di Storia Patria [*A publication*]
ASLSPCTWA ... American Society of Learned Societies on the Protection of Cultural Treasures in War Areas [*World War II*]
ASLT .... Acting Sub-Lieutenant [*Canadian*]
ASLT .... Advanced Solid Logic Technology [*Data processing*]
ASLT .... Aerial Stores Lift Truck (MCD)
ASLT .... Assault (AFM)
ASLTG ...... Assault Gun (AABC)
ASLU .... Acta Societatis Linguisticae Upsaliensis [*A publication*]
ASLU .... Antenna Select Logic Unit [*NASA*] (NASA)
ASLund ...... Arsbok Utgiven av Seminarierna i Slaviska Sprak, Jamforande Sprakforskning, Finsk-Ugriska Sprak och Ostasiatiska Sprak Vid Lunds Universitet [*A publication*]
ASLV .... Advanced Small Launch Vehicle
ASLV .... Assurance sur la Vie [*Life Insurance*] [*French*]
ASLV .... Augmented Satellite Launch Vehicle [*India*]
ASLVA8 .... Agricultura en El Salvador [*A publication*]
ASM .... Advanced Scatterable Mine [*Air Force*] (MCD)
ASM .... Advanced Servomanipulator
ASM .... Advanced Strategic Missile System [*DoD*]
ASM .... Advanced Surface Missile
ASM .... Aerospace Structural Material
ASM .... After Sales Manager (DCTA)
ASM .... Agency Sales Magazine [*Manufacturers' Agents National Association*] [*A publication*]
ASM .... Air Stagnation Model
ASM .... Air-to-Surface Missile
ASM .... Aircraft Survival Measures Programme [*NATO*]
ASM .... Airlift Simulation Model
ASM .... Alarm and Status Module
ASM .... Algebraic Stress Model (MCD)
Asm .... All India Reporter, Assam Series [*A publication*] (DLA)
ASM .... All-Sky Monitor [*Optics*]
ASM .... American Samoa [*ANSI three-letter standard code*] (CNC)
ASM .... American Society of Mammalogists (EA)
ASM .... American Society for Metals [*Later, ASMI*] (EA)
ASM .... American Society for Microbiology (EA)
ASM .... American Society of Missiology (EA)
ASM .... American Solidarity Movement (EA)
ASM .... American Street Machines (EA)
ASM .... American Swedish Monthly [*A publication*]
ASM .... Angular Second Moment
ASM .... Anhydrous Sodium Metasilicate [*Inorganic chemistry*]

ASM .... Annual Survey of Manufactures [*Department of Commerce*] [*Information service or system*]
ASM .... Antarctica Service Medal [*Military decoration*]
ASM .... Antenna Switching Matrix
ASM .... Antiship Missile   (NVT)
ASM .... Apollo Service Module [*NASA*]   (MCD)
ASM .... Apollo Systems Manual [*A publication*]   (MCD)
ASM .... Application Software Module   (MCD)
ASM .... Archivio Storico Messinese [*A publication*]
ASM .... Area Sales Manager   (DS)
ASM .... Arizona State Museum [*University of Arizona*] [*Research center*]   (RCD)
ASM .... Armament Sergeant Major [*British*]
ASM .... Army System Management
ASM .... Artificer Sergeant Major [*British*]
ASM .... Asama [*Japan*] [*Seismograph station code, US Geological Survey*]   (SEIS)
ASM .... Asamera Minerals, Inc. [*AMEX symbol*] [*Vancouver Stock Exchange symbol*]
AsM .... Asia Major [*A publication*]
ASM .... Asian Music [*A publication*]
ASM .... Asmara [*Ethiopia*] [*Airport symbol*]   (OAG)
asm .... Assamese [*MARC language code*] [*Library of Congress*]   (LCCP)
ASM .... Assembler [*Data processing*]
ASM .... Assistant Staff Meteorologist [*NASA*]   (KSC)
ASM .... Assistant Stage Manager
ASM .... Assistant Station Master [*British*]   (ADA)
ASM .... Associated Society of Moulders [*A union*] [*British*]
ASM .... Association Management [*A publication*]
ASM .... Association and Society Manager [*A publication*]
ASM .... Association for Systems Management   (EA)
AsM .... Astigmatism, Myopic [*Also, AM*] [*Ophthalmology*]
ASM .... Asynchronous State Machine   (IEEE)
ASM .... Attache Support Message   (MCD)
ASM .... Automatic Space Management
ASM .... Autonomous Spacecraft Maintenance   (MCD)
ASM .... Auxiliary Storage Manager [*Data processing*]
ASM .... Available Seat Miles [*Airlines term*]
ASM .... Aviation School of Medicine
ASM .... Aviation Support, Mechanical [*Navy rating*]
ASM .... Avionics Shop Maintenance
ASM .... Strathmore Municipal Library, Alberta [*Library symbol*] [*National Library of Canada*]   (NLC)
ASM-1 .... Annual Survey of Manufacturers. AS-1. General Statistics for Industry Groups and Industries [*A publication*]
ASM-2 .... Annual Survey of Manufacturers. AS-2. Value of Product Shipments [*A publication*]
AsMA .... Aerospace Medical Association   (EA)
ASMA .... American Ski Manufacturers' Association   (EA)
ASMA .... American Society of Marine Artists   (EA)
ASMA .... American Society of Music Arrangers   (EA)
ASMA .... American Squid Marketing Association   (EA)
ASMA .... American Student Media Association   (EA)
ASMA .... Antismooth Muscle Antibody [*Immunology*]
As Ma .... Asia Major [*A publication*]
ASMA .... Association of State Mediation Agencies [*Later, ALRA*]
ASMA .... Australian Adhesives and Sealants Manufacturers' Association
ASMA .... Automotive Services Marketing Association [*Canada*]
ASMA .... Journal. Australian Stipendiary Magistrates' Association [*A publication*]   (APTA)
Asmat Sketch Bk ... Asmat Sketch Book [*A publication*]
ASMB .... Acoustical Standards Management Board
ASMB .... Assembling [*FBI standardized term*]
ASMBD ..... Assembled
ASMC .... Adaptive Static Margin Controller   (MCD)
ASMC .... American Society of Mature Catholics [*Defunct*]   (EA)
ASMC .... American Society of Military Comptrollers   (EA)
ASMC .... American Society of Music Copyists   (EA)
ASMC .... Army Supply and Maintenance Command
ASMC .... AUTODIN Station Maintenance Console   (AABC)
ASMC .... Aviation Surface Material Command   (MCD)
ASMCHCCD ... Association of State Maternal and Child Health and Crippled Children's Directors [*Later, AMCHCCP*]   (EA)
ASMCOM ... Army Supply and Maintenance Command   (MUGU)
ASMCTMA ... Amalgamated Sewing Machine, Cycle, and Tool Makers Association [*A union*] [*British*]
ASMD .... Air-to-Surface Missile Development   (MCD)
ASMD .... Antiship Missile Defense
ASMD .... Associated Medical Devices [*NASDAQ symbol*]   (NQ)
ASMD .... Association of Science Museum Directors   (EA)
ASMD .... Assumed   (FAAC)
ASMDMS ... Antiship Missile Defense Missile System   (MCD)
ASMDT ..... American Society of Master Dental Technologists   (EA)
ASME .... Agricultural Soil Moisture Estimation   (MCD)
ASME .... Airport Surface Movement Equipment
ASME .... American Society of Magazine Editors   (EA)
ASME .... American Society of Mechanical Engineers   (EA)
ASME .... Association des Specialistes de la Mesure en Education [*Association of Specialists in Educational Measures*] [*Canada*]

ASME .... Association for the Study of Medical Education
ASME .... Aviation Support Material and Equipment   (MCD)
ASMEA ..... American Society of Mechanical Engineers Auxiliary   (EA)
ASMEA ..... Archivio per le Scienze Mediche [*A publication*]
ASMEAU ... Archivio per le Scienze Mediche [*A publication*]
ASME Boiler Pressure Vessel Code ... American Society of Mechanical Engineers. Boiler and Pressure Vessel Code [*A publication*]
ASMEIGTI ... ASME [*American Society of Mechanical Engineers*] International Gas Turbine Institute   (EA)
ASME Pap ... American Society of Mechanical Engineers. Papers [*A publication*]
ASME Paper ... American Society of Mechanical Engineers. Papers [*A publication*]
ASME Perform Test Codes ... American Society of Mechanical Engineers. Performance Test Codes [*A publication*]
ASMER ..... Association for the Study of Man-Environment Relations   (EA)
ASMET ..... Accelerated Simulated Mission Endurance Test   (MCD)
ASME Trans ... American Society of Mechanical Engineers. Transactions [*A publication*]
ASME Trans Ser F ... American Society of Mechanical Engineers. Transactions. Series F [*A publication*]
ASME Trans Ser I ... American Society of Mechanical Engineers. Transactions. Series I. [*A publication*]
ASMF .... Area Supply and Maintenance Facility   (MCD)
ASMFC ...... Atlantic States Marine Fisheries Commission   (EA)
ASMFER... ASM [*American Society for Metals*] Foundation for Education and Research [*ASM International*]
ASMG .... Atti e Memorie. Societa Magna Grecia [*A publication*]
ASMHBA ... American Society of Mental Hospital Business Administrators [*Later, AMHA*]   (EA)
ASMHF ..... Association of Sports Museums and Halls of Fame [*Later, IASMHF*]   (EA)
ASMI........ Advanced Semiconductor Materials International NV [*NASDAQ symbol*]   (NQ)
ASMI........ Airfield Surface Movement Indicator [*RADAR*] [*Aviation*]
ASMI........ ASM [*American Society for Metals*] International   (EA)
ASMI........ Association for Services Management International   (EA)
ASMIC ...... American Society of Military Insignia Collectors   (EA)
ASMIEC .... Aspects of Microbiology [*A publication*]
AS Mimeogr Circ LA State Univ Agr Exp Sta ... Animal Science Mimeograph Circular. Louisiana State University. Agricultural Experiment Station [*A publication*]
ASMIS ...... Army Safety Management Information System   (MCD)
ASMIS ...... Army Subordinate Command Management Information System [*Formerly, CARMOCS*]   (AABC)
ASML........ Annual Survey of Massachusetts Law [*A publication*]   (ILCA)
ASML........ [*The*] Atlanta, Stone Mountain & Lithonia Railway Co. [*AAR code*]
ASMLS ...... Marigold Library System, Strathmore, Alberta [*Library symbol*] [*National Library of Canada*]   (NLC)
ASMMA ... American Supply and Machinery Manufacturers Association   (EA)
ASMMA ... Atti. Seminario Matematico e Fisico. Universita di Modena [*A publication*]
ASM M81AS-4 ... Annual Survey of Manufacturers. M81AS-4. Expenditures for Plant and Equipment [*A publication*]
ASM M81AS-5 ... Annual Survey of Manufacturers. M81AS-5. Orgin of Exports of Manufactured Products [*A publication*]
ASMMCC ... Armed Services Medical Material Coordination Committee   (CINC)
ASM News ... American Society for Microbiology. News [*A publication*]
ASMNT..... Assessment
ASMO .... Arab Organization for Standardization and Metrology   (EAIO)
ASMO .... Arab Standardization and Metrology Organization   (DS)
ASMO .... Automatic Standard Magnetic Observatory
ASMO .... Canberra [*Australia*] [*ICAO location identifier*]   (ICLI)
ASMOAQ ... Anales. Sociedad Mexicana de Oftalmologia [*A publication*]
ASMODT ... Analytical Sciences Monographs [*A publication*]
ASMOLV ... Afford Service Member Opportunity to Apply for Ordinary Leave [*Army*]   (AABC)
ASMOR .... Automatic Standard Magnetic Observatory - Remote
ASMP........ Air-Sol Moyenne Portee [*Air-to-ground medium-range missile*] [*French*]
ASMP........ American Society of Magazine Photographers   (EA)
ASMP........ Army Survival Measures Plan   (AABC)
ASMP........ Association of Screen Magazine Publishers [*Defunct*]
ASMPA ..... Armed Services Medical Procurement Agency [*Later, Medical Material Directorate*]
ASMPE ..... American Society of Motion Picture Engineers [*Later, ASMPTE*]
ASMP M... Assumption of Moses [*Apocalyptic book*]
ASMPTE... American Society of Motion Picture and Television Engineers [*Formerly, ASMPE*]
ASMR........ Advanced Short-to-Medium Range
ASMR........ Age Standardized Mortality Ratio
ASMRA..... Adjustment of Scheduled Maintenance Requirements through Analysis   (MCD)
ASMRO .... Armed Services Medical Regulating Office
ASMS........ Advanced Strategic Missile System [*DoD*]   (MCD)
ASMS........ Advanced Surface Missile System
ASMS........ Advanced Synchronous Meteorological Satellite

ASMS........ American Society for Mass Spectrometry (EA)
ASMS........ American Society of Maxillofacial Surgeons (EA)
ASMS........ Associate in Science in Medical Secretarial
ASMS........ Atmosphere Sensing and Maintenance System [*NASA*] (KSC)
ASMS........ Automated Systems Management System (MCD)
ASMSA..... Army Signal Material [*or Missile*] Support Agency
ASMSC..... Army Spectrum Management Steering Committee (MCD)
ASMT........ American Society for Medical Technology (EA)
ASMT........ Antiship Missile Target (MCD)
ASMT........ Assessment
ASMT........ Assortment
ASM Trans Q ... ASM [*American Society for Metals*] Transactions Quarterly [*A publication*]
ASM Trans Quart ... ASM [*American Society for Metals*] Transactions Quarterly [*A publication*]
ASMU .... Automatically Stabilized Maneuvering Unit [*NASA*]
ASMUAA ... Acta Scholae Medicinalis Universitatis in Kioto [*A publication*]
As Music.... Asian Music [*A publication*]
ASMVAD ... Anais. Escola Superior de Medicina Veterinaria [*Lisbon*] [*A publication*]
ASMW ...... Amalgamated Society of Metal Workers [*A union*] [*British*]
ASN .... Advertising Services Network [*Australia*]
ASN .... Airborne Special-Type Navigational Aid (MCD)
ASN .... Alco Standard Corp. [*NYSE symbol*] (SPSG)
ASN .... Allotment Serial Number (AFM)
ASN .... American Society of Naturalists (EA)
ASN .... American Society of Nephrology (EA)
ASN .... American Society for Neurochemistry (EA)
ASN .... American Society of Neuroimaging (EA)
ASN .... American Society of Notaries (EA)
ASN .... Ammonium Sulfate-Nitrate [*Fertilizer*]
ASN .... Annali. Scuola Normale Superiore di Pisa [*A publication*]
ASN .... Arizona Sports Network [*Cable TV programming service*]
ASN .... Army Serial Number
ASN .... Army Service Number
Asn............. Asparagine [*Also, Asp(NH₃), N*] [*An amino acid*]
ASN .... Assistant Secretary of the Navy
ASN .... Associate in Nursing
ASN .... Associate in Nursing Science
asn.............. Associated Name [*MARC relator code*] [*Library of Congress*] (LCCP)
ASN .... Association for the Study of the Nationalities (USSR and East Europe) (EA)
ASN .... Atlantic Satellite Network [*Cable-television system*]
ASN .... Atomic Strike Net (AABC)
ASN .... Authority Sequence Number [*Online bibliographies*]
ASN .... Average Sample Number [*Quality control*]
ASN .... Axially Symmetric Nozzle
ASN .... Talladega, AL [*Location identifier*] [*FAA*] (FAAL)
ASNA .... American SMR [*Special Mobile Radio*] Network Association (EA)
ASNA .... Arctic Slope Native Association
ASNAP...... Automatic Steerable Null Antenna Processor
ASNA Reporter ... ASNA [*Alabama State Nurses' Association*] Reporter [*A publication*]
ASNAUT... Astronautical (MSA)
ASNBAQ... Annales des Sciences Naturelles. Zoologie et Biologie Animale [*A publication*]
ASNC .... Association de Ski Nautique du Canada [*Canadian Water Ski Association*]
ASND .... Ascend (FAAC)
ASNE........ American Society of Naval Engineers (EA)
ASNE........ American Society of Newspaper Editors (EA)
ASNE........ Assistant Secretary for Nuclear Energy
ASNED...... ASIS [*American Society for Information Science*] News [*A publication*]
ASNEE5.... Society for Neuroscience. Abstracts [*A publication*]
ASNEMGE ... Association des Societes Nationales, Europeennes, et Mediterraneennes de Gastroenterologie [*Association of National, European, and Mediterranean Societies of Gastroenterology*] (EAIO)
ASNF........ Norfolk Island [*Australia*] [*ICAO location identifier*] (ICLI)
ASN (FM) ... Assistant Secretary of the Navy (Financial Management)
ASNGA7 ... Abhandlungen. Senckenbergische Naturforschende Gesellschaft [*A publication*]
ASNHS ..... American Society for Neo-Hellenic Studies (EA)
ASNHS ..... Association of School Natural History Societies [*British*]
ASN(I & L) ... Assistant Secretary of the Navy (Installation and Logistics)
ASNLH ..... Association for the Study of Negro Life and History [*Later, Association for the Study of Afro-American Life and History*] (EA)
ASNMAP ... Atti. Societa dei Naturalisti e Matematici di Modena [*A publication*]
ASN(M & RA) ... Assistant Secretary of the Navy (Manpower and Reserve Affairs) (MCD)
ASNOA ...... Astrophysica Norvegica [*A publication*]
ASNOL ..... Assistant Senior Naval Officer Landing [*British and Canadian*] [*World War II*]
ASNP........ Agricultural Society of Nigeria. Proceedings [*A publication*]
ASNP........ American Society for Netherlands Philately (EA)
ASNP........ Annali. Scuola Normale Superiore di Pisa [*A publication*]

ASNP........ Army Student Nurse Program (AABC)
ASNPBZ ... Annali. Istituto Sperimentale per la Nutrizione delle Piante [*A publication*]
ASNPIdentBad ... Army Student Nurse Program Identification Badge (AABC)
ASNR .... American Society of Neuroradiology (EA)
ASN(R & D) ... Assistant Secretary of the Navy (Research and Development)
ASNS......... Archiv fuer das Studium der Neueren Sprachen und Literaturen [*A publication*]
ASNSA...... American Society for Nursing Service Administrators [*Later, AONE*] (EA)
ASNSL ...... Archiv fuer das Studium der Neueren Sprachen und Literaturen [*A publication*]
ASN(S & L) ... Assistant Secretary of the Navy (Shipbuilding and Logistics) (MCD)
ASNSP ...... Annali. Scuola Normale Superiore di Pisa [*A publication*]
ASNT........ American Society for Nondestructive Testing (EA)
ASNT........ Australian School of Nuclear Technology (NRCH)
ASNU .... Acta Seminarii Neotestamentici Upsaliensis [*Uppsala*] [*A publication*]
ASNVAI.... Annales des Sciences Naturelles. Botanique et Biologie Vegetale [*A publication*]
ASNW .... Nowra [*Australia*] [*ICAO location identifier*] (ICLI)
AS of NY.... Australian Society of New York [*Later, Australia-New Zealand Society of New York*] (EA)
ASO .... Accessory Sex Organ [*Anatomy*]
ASO .... Accommodation Sales Order
ASO .... Acid-Soluble Oil [*Petroleum refining*]
ASO .... Acoustic Sensor Operator
ASO .... Administrative Service Office
ASO .... Administrative Service Only
ASO .... Advanced Solar Observatory (DEN)
ASO .... Aeronautics Supply Officer (MUGU)
ASO ,......... Air Signal Officer
ASO .... Air Staff Officer
ASO .... Air Staff Orientation (AFM)
ASO .... Air Support Operations (CAAL)
ASO .... Air Surveillance Officer [*Air Force*]
ASO .... Alarm System Operation
ASO .... Allele-Specific Oligonucleotide [*Genetics*]
ASO .... American Journal of Economics and Sociology [*A publication*]
ASO .... American Society for Oceanography [*Later, MTS*] (EA)
ASO .... American Society of Onomatologists [*Defunct*] (EA)
ASO .... American Society of Orthodontists [*Later, AAO*]
ASO .... American Sokol Educational and Physical Culture Organization (EA)
ASO .... American Symphony Orchestra
ASO .... Ammonia System Operations [*NASA*] (NASA)
ASO .... Ammunition Supply Officer (AFM)
ASO .... AmSouth Bancorporation [*NYSE symbol*] (SPSG)
ASO .... Antistreptolysin-O [*Also, ASLO*] [*Clinical chemistry*]
ASO .... Area of Safe Operation
ASO .... Area Safety Officer
ASO .... Area Supply Officer [*Army*]
ASO .... Armament Supply Officer [*Navy*] [*British*] (DMA)
ASO .... Arteriosclerosis Obliterans [*Medicine*]
ASO .... Ashland Chemical Co., Research Library, Columbus, OH [*OCLC symbol*] (OCLC)
ASO .... Aso [*Japan*] [*Seismograph station code, US Geological Survey*] [*Closed*] (SEIS)
Aso............. Asomante [*A publication*]
ASO .... Asosa [*Ethiopia*] [*Airport symbol*] (OAG)
ASO .... Assistant Secretary's Office [*Navy*]
ASO .... Assistant Section Officer [*Air Force*] [*British*]
ASO .... Association for the Study of Obesity (EAIO)
ASO .... Atlantic Southeast Airlines, Inc. [*Hapeville, GA*] [*FAA designator*] (FAAC)
ASO .... Australian Safeguards Office
ASO .... Australian Space Office
ASO .... Australian Study Opportunities [*A publication*]
ASO .... Auxiliary Switch [*Breaker*] Normally Open [*Electricity*]
ASO .... Aviation Safety Office [*or Officer*] [*Military*] (MCD)
ASO .... Aviation Supply Office [*Philadelphia, PA*] [*Navy*]
ASO .... Southern Region [*FAA*] (FAAC)
ASO .... Washington, DC [*Location identifier*] [*FAA*] (FAAL)
ASOA .... American Society of Ophthalmic Administrators (EA)
ASOA .... Australasian Steamship Owners Association (DS)
ASOA .... Australian Serviced Offices Association
ASOA .... Avicultural Society of America (EA)
ASOAP...... Army Spectrometric Oil Analysis Program (AABC)
ASOC .... Air Support Operations Center [*Air Force*]
ASOC .... Analecta Sacri Ordinis Cisterciensis [*Roma*] [*A publication*]
ASoc........... Annales Sociologiques [*A publication*]
ASoc........... Annee Sociologique [*A publication*]
ASOC .... Antarctica and Southern Oceans Coalition (EA)
ASOC .... Armstrong Siddeley Owners Club (EA)
ASoc........... Arts in Society [*A publication*]
ASOC .... Asociacion [*Association*] [*Spanish*]
ASOC .... ASTRO Satellite Operations Center (MCD)
A Soc Arch Namur ... Annales. Societe Archeologique de Namur [*A publication*]

Asoc Argent Microbiol Rev ... Asociacion Argentina de Microbiologia. Revista [*A publication*]
Asoc Argent Mineral Petrol Sediment Rev ... Asociacion Argentina de Mineralogia, Petrologia, y Sedimentologia. Revista [*A publication*]
ASOCAY... Atti. Societa Italiana di Cardiologia [*A publication*]
Asoc Colombiana Bibl Bol ... Asociacion Colombiana de Bibliotecarios. Boletin [*A publication*]
Asoc Cuba Bibl Bol ... Asociacion Cubana de Bibliotecarios. Boletin [*A publication*]
Asoc Geol Argent Monogr ... Asociacion Geologica Argentina. Monografia [*A publication*]
Asoc Geol Argent Rev ... Asociacion Geologica Argentina. Revista [*A publication*]
Asoc Ing Agron Rev ... Asociacion de Ingenieros Agronomos. Revista [*Uruguay*] [*A publication*]
Asoc Ing Uruguay Rev Ingenieria ... Asociacion de Ingenieros del Uruguay. Revista de Ingenieria [*A publication*]
A Sociol (Milano) ... Annali di Sociologia (Milano) [*A publication*]
Asoc Latinoam Entomol Publ ... Asociacion Latinoamericana de Entomologia. Publicacion [*A publication*]
Asoc Latinoam Prod Anim Mem ... Asociacion Latinoamericana de Produccion Animal. Memoria [*A publication*]
Asoc Mat Espanola ... Asociacion Matematica Espanola [*A publication*]
Asoc Med Argent Rev ... Asociacion Medica Argentina. Revista [*A publication*]
Asoc Med PR ... Asociacion Medica de Puerto Rico [*A publication*]
Asoc Mex Geol Pet Bol ... Asociacion Mexicana de Geologos Petroleros. Boletin [*A publication*]
Asoc Mexicana Geofisicos Explor Bol ... Asociacion Mexicana de Geofisicos de Exploracion. Boletin [*A publication*]
Asoc Mex Tec Ind Celul Pap Bol ... Asociacion Mexicana de Tecnicos de las Industrias de la Celulosa y del Papel. Boletin [*A publication*]
A Soc R ...... American Sociological Review [*A publication*]
A Soc Sci Litt Cannes ... Annales. Societe Scientifique Litteraire de Cannes et de l'Arrondissement de Grasse [*A publication*]
Asoc Venez Geol Min Pet Bol ... Asociacion Venezolana de Geologia Mineria y Petroleo. Boletin [*A publication*]
ASODAS... Augmented Synoptic Oceanographic Data Acquisition System [*Navy*] (MSC)
ASODDS... ASWEPS [*Antisubmarine Warfare Environmental Prediction Service*] Submarine Oceanographic Digital Data System
ASOE .... Amalgamated Society of Operative Engineers [*A union*] [*British*]
ASOFAF ... Assistant Secretary of the Air Force
ASOFDC... Archivos. Sociedad Canaria de Oftalmologia [*A publication*]
ASOG .... Analytical Solution of Groups [*Thermodynamics*]
ASOGUA .. Association in Solidarity with Guatemala (EA)
ASOHAF... Archivos. Sociedad Oftalmologica Hispano-Americana [*A publication*]
ASO/ICP... Aviation Supply Office/Inventory Control Point
ASOJ .... Anti-Standoff Jammer [*Defense system*] (MCD)
ASOL .... American Symphony Orchestra League (EA)
ASOL .... American Symphony Orchestra League. Newsletter [*A publication*]
A-SOL .... Antisolar (KSC)
ASOM .... Academie des Sciences d'Outre-Mer [*A publication*]
ASON .... Aerosonic Corp. [*NASDAQ symbol*] (NQ)
ASOOA ..... American Society of Ophthalmologic and Otolaryngologic Allergy [*Later, AAOA*] (EA)
ASOP .... Analytical Satellite Orbit Predictor (MCD)
ASOP .... Army Strategic Objectives Plan
ASOP .... Atomic Standing Operating Procedures (NATG)
ASOP .... Automated Structural Optimization Program [*Air Force*]
ASOP .... Automatic Scheduling and Operating Program (BUR)
ASOP .... Aviation Supply Office Philadelphia [*Navy*]
ASOPD ...... Army Special Operations Pictorial Detachment
ASOR .... American Schools of Oriental Research (EA)
ASOR .... American Schools of Oriental Research. Newsletter
ASOr .... Asialo-Orosomucoid [*Liver metabolism*]
ASORA ...... Australian Journal of Soil Research [*A publication*]
ASORAB... Australian Journal of Soil Research [*A publication*]
ASOR Bul ... American Schools of Oriental Research. Bulletin [*A publication*]
ASORF ...... Apollo Ship's Operational Readiness Force [*NASA*]
ASORN ...... American Society of Ophthalmic Registered Nurses (EA)
ASOR PJSA ... American Schools of Oriental Research. Publications of the Jerusalem School. Archaeology [*A publication*]
ASOS .... American Society of Oral Surgeons [*Later, AAOMS*] (EA)
ASOS .... American Society of Outpatient Surgeons (EA)
ASOS .... Antimony Trisulfide Oxysulfide
ASOS .... Assistant Supervisor of Shipbuilding [*Navy*]
ASOS .... Australian Society of Orthopaedic Surgeons
ASOS .... Automatic Storm Observation Service [*AFCRL*]
ASOSH ..... Assistant Secretary for Occupational Safety and Health [*Department of Labor*]
ASOSS ...... American Society of Sephardic Studies (EA)
ASOT .... Annual System Operating Time (CAAL)
ASOTBI .... Australia. Commonwealth Scientific and Industrial Research Organisation. Division of Soil Mechanics. Technical Paper [*A publication*]

ASOTS ...... Africa South of the Sahara [*Military*] (EA)
ASOTS ...... Automatic Sparrow Operational Test Systems (MCD)
As Outlook ... Asian Outlook [*A publication*]
ASP............ Accao Socialista Portugues [*Portuguese Socialist Action*] (PPE)
ASP............ Accelerated Surface Post [*British*] (DCTA)
ASP............ Accepte sous Protet [*Accepted under Protest*] [*French*] [*Business term*]
ASP............ Accepte sans Protet [*Accepted without Protest*] [*French*] [*Business term*]
ASP............ Accident Sequence Precursor Study [*Nuclear Regulatory Commission*]
AS/P.......... Acquisition Strategy/Plan [*Military*] (CAAL)
ASP............ Activated Sludge Process
ASP............ Active Site Peptide [*Immunochemistry*]
ASP............ Active SONAR Processor
ASP............ Activity Scheduling Processor [*NASA*]
ASP............ Activity Scheduling Program [*NASA*]
ASP............ Actual Ship Position
ASP............ Additional Secondary Phase [*Navigation*]
ASP............ Administrative Site Procedures [*Nuclear energy*] (NRCH)
ASP............ Advanced Self-Protection [*Jammer*] (MCD)
ASP............ Advanced Signal Processor [*Data processing*]
ASP............ Advanced Study Program
ASP............ Advanced System Planning [*Air Force*] (MCD)
ASP............ Advertising and Sales Promotion [*A publication*]
A & SP .... Advertising and Sales Promotion [*A publication*]
ASP............ Aerospace Plane
ASP............ Aerosurface Position (NASA)
ASP............ Afro-Shirazi Party [*Zanzibar*]
ASP............ After Sale Price
ASP............ Air Stores Park [*British military*] (DMA)
ASP............ Air Superiority Program
ASP............ Airborne Science Program [*NASA*] (NASA)
ASP............ Airborne Sensor Platform (MCD)
ASP............ Airborne Support Platform [*Army*]
ASP............ Aircraft Standard Parts (NATG)
ASP............ Airport System Plan (FAAC)
ASP............ Airspace (FAAC)
ASP............ Airspace Subcommittee [*ACC*]
ASP............ Airspeed
ASP............ ALCOA Smelting Process
ASP............ Alice Springs [*Australia*] [*Airport symbol*] (OAG)
ASP............ Alice Springs [*Australia*] [*Seismograph station code, US Geological Survey*] (SEIS)
ASP............ All-Altitude Spin Projected [*Munition*]
ASP............ Allied Standing Procedure [*NATO*] (NATG)
ASP............ Altitude Sounding Projectile (MUGU)
ASP............ Aluminum Silicate Pigment
ASP............ American Self-Protection Association
ASP............ American Selling Price
ASP............ American Society of Papyrologists (EA)
ASP............ American Society of Parasitologists (EA)
ASP............ American Society of Perfumers (EA)
ASP............ American Society of Periodontists [*Later, AAP*]
ASP............ American Society of Pharmacognosy (EA)
ASP............ American Society for Photobiology (EA)
ASP............ American Society of Photogrammetry [*Later, ASPRS*] (EA)
ASP............ American Society of Photographers (EA)
ASP............ American Society for Plasticulture (EA)
ASP............ American Society of Primatologists (EA)
ASP............ American Studies in Papyrology [*A publication*]
ASP............ Ammunition Sub-Park [*British military*] (DMA)
ASP............ Ammunition Supply Point
ASP............ Amphibious Supply Platform [*Army*]
ASP............ Anglo-Saxon Protestant
ASP............ Anglo-Soviet Pact (DAS)
ASP............ Annual Service Practice [*Firings*] [*Military*]
ASP............ Annual System Practice (MCD)
ASP............ Antiship Phoenix
ASP............ Antisocial Personality [*Psychology*]
ASP............ Antisubmarine Patrol
ASP............ Apollo Simple Penetrometer [*NASA*]
ASP............ AppleTalk Session Protocol [*Apple Computer, Inc.*] (BYTE)
ASP............ Arab Socialist Party [*Al Hizb al Ishtiraki al Arabi*] [*Syria*] [*Political party*] (PPW)
ASP............ Arab Socialist Party [*Egypt*] [*Political party*] (PPW)
ASP............ Arc Spraying [*Welding*]
ASP............ Archiv fuer Slavische Philologie [*A publication*]
ASP............ Archival Security Program [*An association*] [*Defunct*] (EA)
ASP............ Archivio Storico Pratese [*A publication*]
ASP............ Archivio Storico Pugliese [*A publication*]
ASP............ Area Search Program
ASP............ Area Specialist Program [*Air Force training program*]
ASP............ Armed Services Papers
ASP............ Army Standardization Program
ASP............ Army Strategic Plan [*A document*]
ASP............ Army Supply Program
ASP............ Array Signal Processing (MCD)
ASP............ As Soon as Possible
ASP............ Asocial Personality
Asp............ Aspartic Acid [*Also, D*] [*An amino acid*]

ASP............ Aspect (ROG)
ASP............ Aspen Airways [*Denver, CO*] [*FAA designator*] (FAAC)
ASP............ Aspen Exploration Corp. [*Vancouver Stock Exchange symbol*]
ASP............ Asphalt
Asp............. Aspinall's Maritime Law Cases [*1871-1940*] [*England*] [*A publication*] (DLA)
ASP............ Aspirator (NASA)
ASP............ Associate Safety Professional [*Designation awarded by Board of Certified Safety Professionals*]
ASP............ Association of Shareware Professionals [*Canada*]
ASP............ Association for Software Protection (EA)
ASP............ Association-Storing Processor [*Data processing*]
ASP............ Association of Surfing Professionals (EA)
ASP............ Associative String Processor (MCD)
ASP............ Associative Structures Package (BUR)
ASP............ Astronautics Standard Practice (AAG)
ASP............ Astronomical Society of the Pacific (EA)
ASP............ Astronomy Spacelab Payloads [*NASA*] (MCD)
ASP............ Atmosphere Sounding Projectile
ASP............ Atomic Solvation Parameter [*Physical chemistry*]
ASP............ Atomic Strike Plan (AFM)
ASP............ Attached Support Processor [*Data processing*]
ASP............ Augmented Support Period [*or Plan*]
ASP............ Australian Superannuation and Employee Benefits Guide [*A publication*]
ASP............ Australian Superannuation Practice [*A publication*] (APTA)
ASP............ Automated Schedule Procedures
ASP............ Automated Seismic Processor [*Earthquake analyzer*]
ASP............ Automated Spooling Priority [*Data processing*]
ASP............ Automatic Sample Processor (KSC)
ASP............ Automatic Schedule Procedure
ASP............ Automatic Self-Powered [*Cannon*] (MCD)
ASP............ Automatic Services and Products
ASP............ Automatic Servo Plotter
ASP............ Automatic Specimen Positioning
ASP............ Automatic Switching Panel
ASP............ Automatic Synthesis Program
ASP............ Auxiliary Spacecraft Power [*NASA*] (MCD)
ASP............ Average Speech Power
ASP............ Avionics Status Panel (MCD)
ASP............ Office of Aviation Systems Plans [*FAA*] (FAAC)
ASP............ Oscoda, MI [*Location identifier*] [*FAA*] (FAAL)
ASP............ Stony Plain Public Libary, Alberta [*Library symbol*] [*National Library of Canada*] (NLC)
ASP............ [*A*] System for Programmers
ASPA......... Acoustic Ship Positioning - Advanced (MCD)
ASPA......... Advanced Strategic Penetrator Aircraft (MCD)
ASPA......... Air Space
ASPA......... Aluminosilicate Polyacrylate [*Type of dental cement*]
ASPA......... American Salvage Pool Association (EA)
ASPA......... American Self-Protection Association (EA)
ASPA......... American Shrimp Processors Association (EA)
ASPA......... American Society of Pension Actuaries (EA)
ASPA......... American Society for Personnel Administration [*Later, SHRM*] (EA)
ASPA......... American Society of Physician Analysts (EA)
ASPA......... American Society of Podiatric Assistants [*Later, ASPMA*] (EA)
ASPA......... American Society of Practicing Architects
ASPA......... American Society of Professional Appraisers (EA)
ASPA......... American Society for Public Administration (EA)
ASPA......... American Sod Producers' Association (EA)
ASPA......... Armed Services Petroleum Agency
ASPA......... Armed Services Procurement Act
ASPA......... Association of South Pacific Airlines [*Fiji*] (EY)
ASPA......... Atti. Societa Piemontese di Archeologia e Belle Arti [*A publication*]
ASPA......... Australasian Student Philosophy Association
ASPA......... Australian Saddle Pony Association
ASPA......... Australian Sales Promotion Association
ASPA......... Auxiliary Storage and Playback Assembly [*Apollo Telescope Mount*] [*NASA*] (KSC)
ASPAB...... Armed Services Patent Advisory Board [*DoD*]
ASPABA ... Atti. Societa Piemontese di Archeologia e Belle Arti [*A publication*]
ASPAC...... Asian and Pacific Council
ASPACLS ... Australian and South Pacific Association for Comparative Literary Studies
ASPA/I...... American Society for Personnel Administration International (EA)
ASPAN...... American Society of Post-Anesthesia Nurses (EA)
ASPap....... American Studies in Papyrology [*A publication*]
ASPAS...... Acoustic Sensor Pattern Assessment System (MCD)
ASPAU...... African Scholarship Program of American Universities [*Joint undertaking, headquartered in Cambridge, MA, to provide aid to African applicants for admission to American universities*]
ASPB........ American Society of Professional Biologists [*Later, AIBS*] (EA)
ASPB........ Armed Services Petroleum Board
ASPB........ Armored Support Patrol Boat [*Military*]
ASPB........ Assault Support Patrol Boat [*Navy symbol*]
ASPBAE.... Asian South Pacific Bureau of Adult Education (EAIO)

ASPBB3 .... Annales Scientifiques. Universite de Besancon. Physiologie et Biologie Animale [*A publication*]
ASPC......... Academie des Sciences (Paris). Comptes Rendus [*A publication*]
ASPC......... Accepte sous Protet pour Compte [*Accepted under Protest for Account*] [*French*]
ASPC......... Aerojet Solid Propulsion Company
ASPC......... Air Space Paper Core
ASPC......... American Sheep Producers Council [*Later, ASIA*] (EA)
ASPC......... American Shetland Pony Club (EA)
ASPC......... American Society for the Prevention of Crime [*Defunct*] (EA)
ASPC......... Analysis of Spare Parts Change (MCD)
ASPC......... Association of Strategic Planning Consultants (EA)
ASPCA ...... American Society for the Prevention of Cruelty to Animals (EA)
Asp Cas...... Aspinall's Maritime Law Cases [*1871-1940*] [*England*] [*A publication*] (DLA)
ASPCC ...... All Service Postal Chess Club (EA)
ASPCD8 .... Auspicium [*A publication*]
ASPCGA ... Atomic Strike Plan Control Group Alternate (AABC)
ASP Ctrattack ... ASP Counterattack [*A publication*]
ASPD......... Advanced Space Propellant Demonstration (MCD)
ASPD......... American Society of Podiatric Dermatology (EA)
ASPD......... American Society for Preventive Dentistry [*Defunct*]
ASPD......... Aviation Ships Planning Document (MCD)
ASPDA...... American Society of Professional Draftsmen and Artists (EA)
ASPDA...... Association of State Planning and Development Agencies [*Later, SEISMA*] (EA)
ASPDE...... Automatic Shaft-Position Data Encoder
ASPDM..... American Society of Psychosomatic Dentistry and Medicine [*Absorbed by IPI*] (EA)
ASPE .... American Society of Plumbing Engineers (EA)
ASPE .... American Society of Professional Ecologists (EA)
ASPE .... American Society of Professional Estimators (EA)
ASPE .... American Society of Psychopathology of Expression (EA)
ASPE .... Assistant Secretary for Planning and Evaluation [*Department of Health and Human Services*]
ASPE .... Association for Special Education [*British*]
ASPEA ...... Advances in Spectroscopy [*A publication*]
ASPEC ...... Association of Sorbitol Producers in the European Community (EAIO)
ASPEC ...... Automatic Sample Preparation Extraction Column [*Chromatography*]
ASPECT.... Acoustic Short-Pulse Echo Classification Technique (NVT)
ASPECT.... American Study Program for Educational and Cultural Training (EA)
Aspects Adhes ... Aspects of Adhesion [*A publication*]
Aspects Allergy Appl Immunol ... Aspects of Allergy and Applied Immunology [*A publication*]
Aspects of Ed ... Aspects of Education [*A publication*]
Aspects Ed ... Aspects of Education [*A publication*]
Aspects Energy Convers Proc Summer Sch ... Aspects of Energy Conversion. Proceedings of a Summer School [*A publication*]
Aspects Fish Parasitol Symp Br Soc Parasitol ... Aspects of Fish Parasitology. Symposium of the British Society for Parasitology [*A publication*]
Aspects Homogeneous Catal ... Aspects of Homogeneous Catalysis [*A publication*]
Aspects of Math E ... Aspects of Mathematics. E [*A publication*]
Aspects Microbiol ... Aspects of Microbiology [*A publication*]
Aspects Nucl Struct Funct ... Aspects of Nuclear Structure and Function [*A publication*]
Aspects Plant Sci ... Aspects of Plant Sciences [*A publication*]
Aspects Pl Sci ... Aspects of Plant Sciences [*A publication*]
Aspects Statist Region Paris ... Aspects Statistiques de la Region Parisienne [*A publication*]
Asp Educ Technol ... Aspects of Educational Technology [*A publication*]
ASPEICP .. Associated Schools Project in Education for International Cooperation and Peace [*UNESCO*] [*Paris, France*] (EAIO)
ASPEICP .. UNESCO Associated Schools Project in Education for International Cooperation and Peace (EAIO)
ASPEMRCM ... CANMET [*Canada Centre for Mineral and Energy Technology*] Library, Western Research Laboratory, Energy, Mines, and Resources Canada [*Bibliotheque CANMET, Laboratoire de Recherche de l'Ouest, Energie, Mines, et Ressources Canada*], Sherwood Park, Alberta [*Library symbol*] [*National Library of Canada*] (NLC)
ASPEN...... Advanced System for Process Engineering
ASPEN...... American Society for Parenteral and Enteral Nutrition (EA)
Aspen......... Aspen Anthology [*A publication*]
ASPEN...... Automatic Speech Exchange System [*Voice messaging*]
Aspen A...... Aspen Anthology [*A publication*]
Aspen J...... Aspen Journal of the Arts [*A publication*]
ASPEP....... Association of Scientists and Professional Engineering Personnel
ASPER...... Assembly System for Peripheral Processors [*Data processing*]
ASPER...... Assistant Secretary for Policy Evaluation and Research [*Department of Labor*]
ASPERA..... Automatic Space Plasma Experiment with a Rotating Analyser [*Instrumentation*]

ASPERS.... Armed Services Procurement Regulations
As Perspect (H) ... Asian Perspectives (Honolulu) [*A publication*]
As Perspect (S) ... Asian Perspectives (Seoul) [*A publication*]
ASPET ...... American Society for Pharmacology and Experimental Therapeutics (EA)
ASPEW ..... American Society of Professional and Executive Women (EA)
ASPG .... Australasian [*or Australian*] Study of Parliament Group
ASPG J ...... Alberta Society of Petroleum Geologists. Journal [*A publication*]
ASPh.......... Archiv fuer Systematische Philosophie [*A publication*]
ASPH .... Asphalt (KSC)
ASPH .... Association of Schools of Public Health (EA)
ASPHA...... American Saddlebred Pleasure Horse Association [*Later, ASHA*] (EA)
ASPHAK... Archives des Sciences Physiologiques [*A publication*]
Asphalt Inst Constr Ser ... Asphalt Institute. Construction Series [*A publication*]
Asphalt Inst Inf Ser ... Asphalt Institute. Information Series [*A publication*]
Asphalt Inst Q ... Asphalt Institute. Quarterly [*A publication*]
Asphalt Inst Res Ser ... Asphalt Institute. Research Series [*A publication*]
Asphalt Paving Technol ... Asphalt Paving Technology [*A publication*]
Asphalt Teerind Ztg ... Asphalt Teerindustrie. Zeitung [*A publication*]
Asphalt Teer Strassenbautech ... Asphalt und Teer. Strassenbautechnik [*West Germany*] [*A publication*]
ASPHER ... Association of Schools of Public Health in the European Region (EAIO)
ASPHO ..... American Society of Pediatric Hematology/Oncology (EA)
ASPHPF... Asphalt-Plank Floor (MSA)
ASPHRS... Asphalt Roof Shingles [*Technical drawings*]
ASPHV...... Association of State Public Health Veterinarians [*Later, NASPHV*] (EA)
ASPI .... Academy of Sports Psychology International (EA)
ASPI .... Aerosurface Position Indicator (MCD)
ASPI .... American Society for Performance Improvement [*Defunct*] (EA)
ASPI .... Apollo Supplemental Procedural Information [*NASA*] (KSC)
ASPI .... Association of Student and Professional Italian-Americans (EA)
ASPI .... Asynchronous Synchronous Programmable Interface [*Data processing*]
ASPI .... Automatic Sample Processor and Injector
ASPIC .... Armed Services Personnel Interrogation Center (AFM)
Aspin.......... Aspinall's Maritime Law Cases [*1871-1940*] [*England*] [*A publication*] (DLA)
ASPIRE..... Achieve Successful Performance, Intensify Reliability Effort
ASPIRE..... Advanced Special Projects in Radiation Effects
ASPIRE..... Associated Students Promoting Individual Rights for Everyone
Aspirin Relat Drugs Their Actions Uses Proc Symp ... Aspirin and Related Drugs. Their Actions and Uses. Proceedings of the Symposium [*A publication*]
Aspir Rab Nauchno Issled Inst Udobr Insektofungits (Moscow) ... Aspirantskie Raboty Nauchno Issledovatel'skii Institut po Udobrenii i Insektofungitsidam (Moscow) [*A publication*]
ASPJ.......... Advanced Self-Protection Jammer
ASPJ.......... Airborne Self-Protection Jammer (MCD)
ASPL .... American Society for Pharmacy Law (EA)
ASPL .... Approved Spare Parts List (MCD)
ASPL .... Army Standard Program Languages
ASPLP ...... American Society for Political and Legal Philosophy (EA)
ASPM........ Advanced Studies in Pure Mathematics [*Elsevier Book Series*] [*A publication*]
ASPM........ Air Scatterable Antipersonnel Mine (MCD)
ASPM........ American Society of Paramedics (EA)
ASPM........ American Society of Podiatric Medicine (EA)
ASPM........ Armed Services Procurement Manual (MCD)
ASPM........ Armed Services Procurement Medal
ASPMA..... American Smoking Pipe Manufacturers Association [*Defunct*] (EA)
ASPMA..... American Society of Podiatric Medical Assistants (EA)
Asp Mar Law Cas ... Aspinall's Maritime Law Cases [*1871-1940*] [*England*] [*A publication*] (DLA)
Asp Mar L Cas (Eng) ... Aspinall's Maritime Law Cases [*1871-1940*] [*England*] [*A publication*] (DLA)
ASP/MC ... Aspencade Motorcyclists Convention (EA)
Asp MC ..... Aspinall's Maritime Law Cases [*1871-1940*] [*England*] [*A publication*] (DLA)
Asp MCL... Aspinall's Maritime Law Cases [*1871-1940*] [*A publication*] (DLA)
ASPMIS.... Apollo Spacecraft Parts and Materials Information Services [*NASA*] (KSC)
Asp MLC... Aspinall's Maritime Law Cases [*1871-1940*] [*England*] [*A publication*] (DLA)
ASPMM.... Amalgamated Society of Plate and Machine Moulders [*A union*] [*British*]
ASPMS ..... Aircraft Space Position Measurement System (MCD)
ASPN......... American Society for Pediatric Neurosurgery (EA)
ASPN......... American Society for Portuguese Numismatics (EA)
ASPN......... American Society of Precision Nailmakers [*Defunct*]
ASPN......... Archivio Storico per le Provincie Napoletane [*A publication*]
ASPN......... Aspen Exploration Corp. [*NASDAQ symbol*] (NQ)
ASPND7.... Ata Reumatologica Brasileira [*A publication*]

Asp(NH₂) ... Asparagine [*Also, Asn, N*] [*An amino acid*]
ASPNI....... American Society for the Protection of Nature in Israel (EA)
ASPO......... AGORA-SPORTS [*Agence France-Presse*] [*Information service or system*] (CRD)
ASPO......... American Society of Planning Officials [*Later, American Planning Association*] (EA)
ASPO......... American Society of Preventive Oncology (EA)
ASPO......... American Society for Psychoprophylaxis in Obstetrics (EA)
ASPO......... Antisubmarine Systems Project Office [*Navy*]
ASPO......... Apollo Spacecraft Project Office [*NASA*]
ASPO......... Army Space Program Office (MCD)
ASPO......... Avionics System Project Officer
ASPOE...... American Society of Petroleum Operations Engineers (EA)
ASPOL...... [*A*] Simulation Process Oriented Language [*1972*] [*Data processing*] (CSR)
AS/POT .... Agena Systems/Power-On Test [*NASA*] (KSC)
ASPP......... Advanced Satellite Products Project [*Madison, WI*] [*NOAA/NESDIS*] (GRD)
ASPP .... Alloy-Steel Protective Plating
ASPP......... American Society of Picture Professionals (EA)
ASPP......... American Society of Plant Physiologists (EA)
ASPP......... American Society of Polar Philatelists (EA)
ASPP........ Antenna Solar Panel Positioner
ASPP........ Archivio Storico per le Provincie Parmensi [*A publication*]
ASPP......... Asiatic Society of Pakistan. Publication [*A publication*]
ASPP......... Association for Sane Psychiatric Practices (EA)
ASPP......... Atmospheric and Space Plasma Physics [*NASA*] (NASA)
ASPPA ..... Armed Services Petroleum Purchasing Agency
ASPPC....... Accepte sous Protet pour Compte [*Accepted under Protest for Account*] [*French*] [*Business term*]
ASPPF....... Association of Seminary Professors in the Practical Fields [*Later, APT*] (EA)
ASPPI....... Azimuth-Stabilized Plan Position Indicator (DEN)
ASPPO ..... Armed Services Procurement Planning Officer
ASPPO ..... Armed Services Production Planning Officer (MCD)
ASPPP...... American Society for Philatelic Pages and Panels (EA)
ASPPR ...... Association of Sugar Producers of Puerto Rico [*Defunct*] (EA)
ASPR .... Aircraft Structural Integrity Program Recorder
ASPR .... American Society for Psychical Research (EA)
ASPR .... Anglo-Saxon Poetic Records [*A publication*]
ASPR .... Armed Services Procurement Regulation [*Later, DAR*]
ASPR .... Armor Systems Program Review (MCD)
ASPR .... Australasian Small Press Review [*A publication*] (APTA)
ASPR .... Aviation Systems Program Review (MCD)
ASPRC....... Academy of the Street of Puerto Rican Congress (EA)
Asp Rep ..... Aspinall's Maritime Law Cases [*1871-1940*] [*A publication*] (DLA)
ASPRL ...... Armament Systems Personnel Research Laboratory [*Lowry Air Force Base, CO*]
ASPRM ..... Armed Services Procurement Regulation Manual (AABC)
Aspro......... Associate Professor (ADA)
ASPRO...... Associative Processor [*Data processing*] (MCD)
As Profile ... Asian Profile [*A publication*]
ASPRS....... American Society for Photogrammetry and Remote Sensing (EA)
ASPRS....... American Society of Plastic and Reconstructive Surgeons (EA)
ASPRS....... Armed Services Procurement Regulation Supplement (AABC)
ASPRSN... American Society of Plastic and Reconstructive Surgical Nurses (EA)
ASPRT ...... Adjusted Sequential Probability Ratio Test [*Statistics*]
ASPRTR.... Aspirator (MSA)
ASPS .... Acoustic Ship Positioning System
ASPS .... Adaptable Space Propulsion System [*Military*]
ASPS .... African Succulent Plant Society [*Defunct*] (EA)
ASPS .... Alveolar Soft Part Sarcoma [*Oncology*]
ASPS .... American Selling Price System
ASPS .... American Society of Pre-Dental Students (EA)
ASPS .... American Society of Professional Salesmen (EA)
ASPS .... Armed Services Procurement Regulation Supplement
ASPS .... Association Sportive des Professions de Sante (EAIO)
ASPS .... Association of Supervisors in Purchasing and Supply [*British*] (DBQ)
ASPS .... Atti. Societa Italiana per il Progresso delle Scienze [*A publication*]
ASPS .... Automated Small Purchase System [*DoD*]
ASPS .... Automatic Specimen Positioning System
ASPS .... County of Strathcona Library, Sherwood Park, Alberta [*Library symbol*] [*National Library of Canada*] (NLC)
ASPSA....... Atti. Societa Peloritana di Scienze Fisiche, Matematiche, e Naturali [*A publication*]
ASPSAJ .... Atti. Societa Peloritana di Scienze Fisiche, Matematiche, e Naturali [*A publication*]
ASPSC....... Association of State and Provincial Safety Coordinators [*Later, ASPSO*] (EA)
ASPSL....... ASPP [*Atmospheric and Space Plasma Physics*] Sortie Laboratory [*NASA*] (NASA)
ASPSO...... Association of State and Provincial Safety Officials [*Formerly, ASPSC*] (EA)
ASPSPOM ... American Society for the Preservation of Sacred, Patriotic, and Operatic Music (EA)
ASPSU ...... Attitude Sensor Parachute Staging Unit (MCD)

ASPT	Academy of Screen Printing Technology (EA)
ASPT	Advanced Simulator for Pilot Training (MCD)
ASPT	American Society of Plant Taxonomists (EA)
ASPT	Army School of Physical Training [British]
ASPTC	Army Support Center (AABC)
ASPU	Abrupt Symmetrical Pull Up (MCD)
ASPU	Automatic Signal Processing Unit (MCD)
ASPUD	ASAE [American Society of Agricultural Engineers] Publication [A publication]
ASPWBPSA	Association of Sometimes Professional Wiffle Ball Players on the Spaceship Aarde (Earth) (EAIO)
ASPZA	Avtomatizatsiya Staleplavil'nogo Proizvodstva [A publication]
ASQ	Active Singles Quest [Technique] [In book title]
ASQ	Administrative Science Quarterly [A publication]
ASQ	Algebraic Solution for Queues
ASQ	Anxiety Scale Questionnaire [Psychology]
As Q	Asia Quarterly [A publication]
ASQ	Attitude toward School Questionnaire [Test]
ASQ	Austin [Nevada] [Airport symbol] [Obsolete] (OAG)
ASQA	Automatic Sky Quality Assessment (MCD)
ASQBA7	Association Senegalaise pour l'Etude du Quaternaire de l'Ouest Africain. Bulletin de Liaison [A publication]
ASQC	American Society for Quality Control (EA)
ASQDE	American Society of Questioned Document Examiners (EA)
A/SQK	Antisqueak [Automotive engineering]
ASR	Absolute Specular Reflectance [Spectroscopy]
ASR	Acceptance Summary Report
ASRA	Accommodation Sales Requisition
ASR	Accounting Series Release [Securities and Exchange Commission]
ASR	Accumulators Shift Right [Data processing] (BUR)
ASR	Acoustic Stapedius Reflex [Medicine]
ASR	Active Status Register
ASR	Advanced Salvo Rifle (MCD)
ASR	Advanced Surveillance RADAR
ASR	Advanced Systems Requirements
ASR	Advanced Systems Research Proprietary Ltd. [Australia]
ASR	Agricultural Science Review [A publication]
ASR	Air-Sea Rescue
ASR	Air Search RADAR
ASR	Air Staff Requirement
ASR	Air Surveillance RADAR (AFM)
ASR	Airborne Scanning Radiometer
ASR	Airborne Surveillance RADAR (IEEE)
ASR	Airport Surveillance RADAR
ASR	Aldosterone Secretion Rate [Endocrinology]
ASR	All Star Resources [Vancouver Stock Exchange symbol]
ASR	Alternate Supply Rate (MCD)
ASR	Alternate Supply Route
ASR	Altimeter Setting Region [Aviation] (AIA)
ASR	American Iron and Steel Institute. Statistical Report [A publication] (EAAP)
ASR	American River College, Sacramento, CA [OCLC symbol] (OCLC)
ASR	American Saudi Roundtable (EA)
ASR	American-Scandinavian Review [A publication]
ASR	American Slavic Review [A publication]
ASR	American Society of Rocketry
ASR	American Sociological Review [A publication]
ASR	American Southwest Mortgage Investment Co. [AMEX symbol] (SPSG)
ASR	American State Reports [A publication] (DLA)
ASR	Analog Shift Register [Data processing]
ASR	Anisotropic Saturation Recovery [NMR imaging]
ASR	Annales. Societa Retorumantscha [A publication]
ASR	Annual Summary Report
ASR	Approved System Requirement
ASR	Architects for Social Responsibility (EA)
ASR	Archives de Sociologie des Religions [A publication]
ASR	Area Surveillance RADAR
ASR	Arithmetic Shift Right [Data processing]
ASR	Armed Strike Reconnaissance (AABC)
ASR	Army Scripture Reader [British military] (DMA)
ASR	Army Service Reserve [British] (ROG)
ASR	Army Service Ribbon [Military decoration]
ASR	Army Status Report (AABC)
ASR	As Required (MCD)
ASR	Association for the Sociology of Religion (EA)
ASR	Atmospheric Sound Refraction
ASR	Atomic Strike Recording [Air Force]
ASR	Attack, Sustain, Release [Electronic musical instruments]
ASR	Australasian Software Report [A publication] (APTA)
ASR	Australian Securities Law Reporter [A publication] (APTA)
ASR	Australian Synthetic Rubber Company Ltd.
AS/R	Automated Storage/Retrieval [Data processing]
AS/R	Automatic Send/Receive Teletypewriter [Communications equipment]
ASR	Automatic SONAR Readout
ASR	Automatic Speech Recognition
ASR	Automatic Sprinkler Riser [Technical drawings]
ASR	Automatic Step Regulator

ASR	Automatic Surveillance Receiver (MCD)
ASR	Automotive Service Reports [A publication] (EAAP)
ASR	Auxiliary Submarine Rescue Ship [Navy symbol]
ASR	Available Supply Rate
ASR	Aviation Safety Regulation
ASR	Avionics System Review (NASA)
ASR	Avon Science Fiction Reader [A publication]
ASR	Kayseri [Turkey] [Airport symbol] (OAG)
ASR	Submarine Rescue Ship [Navy symbol]
ASRA	ADP [Automatic Data Processing] Systems Resources Analysis
ASRA	American Seafood Retailers Association (EA)
ASRA	American Shropshire Registry Association (EA)
ASRA	American Society of Regional Anesthesia (EA)
ASRA	Applied Science and Research Applications [Program] [Supersedes RANN] [National Science Foundation]
ASRA	Athwartships Reference Axis
ASRA	Automatic Stereo Recording Amplifier
ASRAA	Advanced Short-Range Air-to-Air Missile (MCD)
ASRAAM	Advanced Short-Range Air-to-Air Missile (RDA)
ASRAB	Annales. Societe Royale d'Archeologie de Bruxelles [A publication]
ASRADI	Adaptive Surface-Signal Recognition and Direction Indicator [Navy]
ASRAP	Acoustic Sensor [or SONAR] Range Prediction (NVT)
ASRAPS	Acoustic Sensor [or SONAR] Range Prediction System (NVT)
ASRB	Armed Services Renegotiation Board [Later, RB]
ASRB	Army Security Review Board
ASRBA	American Satin Rabbit Breeders' Association (EA)
ASR Bull INORGA	ASR [Automatizovane Systemy Rizeni] Bulletin INORGA [A publication]
ASRC	Air-Sea Rescue Craft
ASRC	American Synthetic Rubber Corporation
ASRC	Atmospheric Sciences Research Center [State University of New York] [Research center]
ASRD	Advanced Systems Research Department
ASRD	Aircraft Shipment Readiness Date [Army] (AABC)
ASRD	American Society of Retired Dentists (EA)
ASRD	Avionic Subsystem Requirement Document (MCD)
ASRDI	Aerospace Safety Research and Data Institute [Lewis Research Center] [NASA]
ASRDL	Army Signal Research and Development Laboratory
ASRE	Admiralty Signal and RADAR Establishment [British]
ASRE	American Society of Refrigerating Engineers [Later, ASHRAE]
ASREC	American Society of Real Estate Counselors (EA)
ASREFO	Anthony Sharp and Rachael Ellison Family Organization (EA)
ASRF	Advanced Size Reduction Facility (MCD)
ASRF	Air-Sea Rescue Flight [British military] (DMA)
ASRF	American Seed Research Foundation (EA)
ASRF	Sydney [Australia] [ICAO location identifier] (ICLI)
ASRGN	Altimeter Setting Region [Aviation]
ASRHA	American Small and Rural Hospital Association (EA)
ASRHAT	Annales. Societe Royale d'Histoire et d'Archeologie de Tournai [A publication]
ASRI	Agricultural Systems Research Institute [Beltsville, MD] [Department of Agriculture] (GRD)
ASRI	Aluminum Smelters Research Institute [Later, ARA] (EA)
ASRI	Richmond [Australia] [ICAO location identifier] (ICLI)
ASRL	Associate in Science in Recreation Leadership
ASRL	Atmospheric Sciences Research Laboratory [Research Triangle Park, NC] [Environmental Protection Agency] (GRD)
ASRL	Australian Scientific Research Liaison [British]
ASRM	Abort Solid Rocket Motor [NASA] (NASA)
ASRM	Advanced Solid Rocket Motor [Proposed] [NASA]
ASRM	American Society of Range Management [Later, SRM] (EA)
ASRM	Antenna System Readiness Monitor (MCD)
ASRm	Spirit River Municipal Library, Alberta [Library symbol] [National Library of Canada] (NLC)
ASRNDH	Anales. Instituto Nacional de Investigaciones Agrarias. Serie Recursos Naturales [A publication]
ASRNH	American Society for Russian Naval History (EA)
ASRO	Amateur Scientist Research Organization (EA)
ASRO	Assistant Superintendent, Range Operations [NASA] (KSC)
ASRO	Association of Social Research Organisations [British]
ASROC	Antisubmarine Rocket [Navy]
ASR/OPS	Air Surveillance RADAR/Operations Center System
ASRP	African Studies and Research Program [Howard University] [Research center] (RCD)
ASRP	Airborne SIGINT Reconnaissance Program (MCD)
ASRP	Ammunition Stockpile Reliability Program (MCD)
ASRP	Arab Socialist Renaissance Party [Syria]
ASRPA	Army Signal Radio Propagation Agency
ASRPB	Aviation Selected Reserve Programs Branch [BUPERS]
ASRPCM	Australia. Commonwealth Scientific and Industrial Research Organisation. Division of Soils. Report on Progress [A publication]
ASRR	American Society for Reformation Research
ASRRAQ	ASL [American Scientific Laboratories] Research Report [A publication]
ASRS	Adjusted Service Rating Score [Military]
ASRS	Advanced Assembly Sequence Record Sheet (MCD)
ASRS	Advanced Strategic Reconnaissance System [Air Force]

ASRS .... Air Safety Reporting System [*NASA*]
ASRS .... Air-Sea Rescue Service [*British military*]   (DMA)
ASRS .... Airborne Satellite Receiving Station
ASRS .... Amalgamated Society of Railway Servants [*New Zealand*]
ASRS .... American Sable Rabbit Society   (EA)
ASRS .... American Society of Roommate Services   (EA)
ASRS .... Ammunition Stock Recording System
ASRS .... Anglo-Soviet Recognition Signals
ASRS .... Anti-Stoke Stimulated Raman Scattering [*Spectrometry*]   (MCD)
ASRS .... Apollo Simulated Remote Site [*NASA*]   (KSC)
ASRS .... Archivio. Societa Romana di Storia Patria [*A publication*]
ASRS .... Assembly Sequence Record Sheet
ASRS .... Australian Sex Role Scale
ASRS .... Automated Seat Reservation System [*Aviation*]
ASRS .... Automated Shareholder Records System   (MCD)
AS/RS .... Automated Storage/Retrieval Systems   (EA)
ASRS .... Auxiliary Support Reaction System
ASRS .... Aviation Safety Reporting System   (MCD)
ASRSC ...... Armed Services Research Specialists Committee
ASRSC ...... Atlantic Sea Run Salmon Commission   (EA)
ASRSD ...... Advances in Space Research [*A publication*]
ASRSD ...... Ammunition Systems Reliability and Safety Division [*Picatinny Arsenal*] [*Army*]
ASRSOW .. Associated Society of Range Stove and Ornamental Workers [*A union*] [*British*]
ASRSP ...... Archivio. Societa Romana di Storia Patria [*A publication*]
ASRSWS ... Assembly Sequence Record Sheet - Work Sheet
ASRT .... Air Support RADAR Team [*Marine Corps*]
ASRT .... American Society of Radiologic Technologists   (EA)
ASRT .... Assort   (MSA)
ASRU .... Archivio Storico del Risorgimento Umbrio [*A publication*]
ASRWA7 ... Agricultural Science Review. Cooperative State Research Service. US Department of Agriculture [*A publication*]
ASS .... Accessory Supply System
ASS .... Acoustical Society of Scandinavia [*Formerly, Nordic Acoustics Society*]   (EA)
ASS .... Acquisition Sun Sensor   (MCD)
ASS .... Acta Sanctorum [*Acts of the Saints*] [*Latin*]
ASS .... Advanced Space Station
ASSCM ...... Aerosol Sampling System
ASS .... Aerospace Support Systems   (MCD)
ASS .... Aerospace Surveillance System
ASS .... Affective Sensitivity Scale
ASS .... Air Sampling System
ASS .... Air Surveillance System
ASS .... Airborne Surveillance Set
ASS .... Aircraft Security System   (MCD)
ASS .... Airlock Support Subsystem [*NASA*]   (NASA)
ASS .... Airspace Surveillance Station
ASS .... Altitude Sensing System
ASS .... Amalgamated Society of Shuttlemakers [*A union*] [*British*]
ASS .... Amazing Science Stories [*A publication*]
ASS .... Analog Simulation System
ASS .... Anterior Superior Spine [*Anatomy*]
ASS .... Archivio Storico Siciliano [*A publication*]
ASS .... Argenteuil Symposia Series [*Elsevier Book Series*] [*A publication*]
ASS .... Argininosuccinate Synthetase [*An enzyme*]
ASS .... Army Signal School [*British*]
ASS .... Army Special Staff
AsS .... Asiatische Studien [*A publication*]
ASS .... Assassination   (ROG)
Ass .... Assemblee Generale du Contentieux, Conseil d'Etat [*France*]   (ILCA)
ASS .... Assembler Language [*Data processing*]   (CMD)
ASS .... Assembly
Ass .... Assessor [*Assistant. Assessor*] [*German*]
ASS .... Assigns   (ROG)
ASS .... Assistant
ASS .... Assistant Secretary of State   (DAS)
ASS .... Assize Rolls [*British*]
ASS .... Associate in Secretarial Science
ASS .... Associate in Secretarial Studies
ASS .... Association
Ass .... Assurance [*Insurance*] [*French*]   (ILCA)
ASS .... Assyria
ASS .... Australian Social Security Guide [*A publication*]
ASS .... Automatic Stabilization System
ASS .... Automatic Start-Up System [*Reactor*]
ASS .... Autopilot Surface Servo
AS(S) .... Auxiliary Steam (System) [*Nuclear energy*]   (NRCH)
ASS .... Axisymmetric Spiral [*Astronomy*]
Ass .... Liber Assisarum [*Book of Assizes, or pleas of the crown*] [*Pt. 5 of Year Books*] [*A publication*]   (DLA)
ASSA .... Advanced Strategic Standoff Aircraft   (MCD)
ASSA .... Allied Social Science Associations   (EA)
ASSA .... American Shetland Sheepdog Association   (EA)
ASSA .... American Society for the Study of Arteriosclerosis [*Later, CAAHA*]

ASSA .... Anatomical Society of Southern Africa [*Onderstepoort, South Africa*]   (EAIO)
ASSA .... Area Supply Support Activity [*Army*]   (AFIT)
ASSA .... [*The*] Army Signal Supply Agency   (MCD)
ASSA .... Army Signal Support Agency
ASSA .... Cargo Submarine [*Navy symbol*] [*Obsolete*]
ASSAFOET ... Assafoetida [*Pharmacy*]   (ROG)
ASSAL....... Annual Survey of South African Law [*A publication*]
ASSAM ..... Advanced Strategic Standoff Attack Missile   (MCD)
Assam .... All India Reporter, Assam Series [*A publication*]   (DLA)
Assam Rev Tea News ... Assam Review and Tea News [*A publication*]
ASSAP .... Association for the Scientific Study of Anomalous Phenomena
ASSar .... Archivio Storico Sardo [*A publication*]
ASSAS....... Assassination   (ROG)
ASSASSIN ... Automated System for Storing and Subsequently Selecting Information [*Developed by ICI, Inc.*]
ASSAW ..... Aerospace Surveillance and Warning
ASSB .... Anonymous Society of Second Bananas   (EA)
ASSB .... Apollo Site Selection Board [*NASA*]   (KSC)
AS & SB..... Automated Systems and Services Branch [*NTIS*]
ASSB .... Avionics Subsystem for Strategic Bombers
Ass Bibliot Fr Bull Inf ... Association des Bibliothecaires Francais. Bulletin d'Informations [*A publication*]
ASSB & OM ... American Society to Save Biharis and Other Minorities
ASSBT....... American Society of Sugar Beet Technologists   (EA)
ASSBWMM ... Amalgamated Society of Scale Beam and Weighing Machine Makers [*A union*] [*British*]
ASSC .... Air Service Signal Corps
ASSC .... Airborne Systems Support Center
ASSc .... Archivio di Storia della Scienza [*A publication*]
ASSC .... Army Subsistence Supply Center [*Merged with Defense Subsistence Supply Center*]
ASSC .... Australian Social Security Cases [*A publication*]
ASSC .... Savanna Community Library, Silver Valley, Alberta [*Library symbol*] [*National Library of Canada*]   (NLC)
3-A SSC ..... 3-A Sanitary Standards Committee   (EA)
ASSCAS.... Advanced Spacecraft Subsystem Cost Analysis Structure   (MCD)
Assce.......... Assurance [*Insurance*] [*French*]
ASSCI........ American Section of the Societe de Chimie Industrielle   (EA)
ASSCM ..... Avionics Software Support Cost Model   (MCD)
ASSCN ...... Association   (EY)
Ass Com Gen ... Assistant-Commissary-General [*British*]
AssCPHO's ... Association of County Public Health Officers [*British*]
Assd .... Assigned   (DLA)
ASSD........ Associated
ASSD........ Assorted   (ROG)
ASSD........ Assured   (ROG)
ASSDD...... Association of Summer Session Deans and Directors [*Later, AUSS*]   (EA)
AssDipFor ... Associate Diploma in Forestry
ASSDR ...... Alliance for Social Security and Disability Recipients   (EA)
ASSE .... American Society of Safety Engineers   (EA)
ASSE .... American Society of Sanitary Engineering   (EA)
ASSE .... American Society of Swedish Engineers   (EA)
asse .... Assurance [*Insurance*] [*French*]
ASSE .... Automation System for Scientific Experiments
ASSEA ...... Association of Surgeons of South East Asia   (EAIO)
ASSE J ...... ASSE Journal [*A publication*]
ASSEM ..... Assemble   (MSA)
Assem .... Assembly   (DLA)
Assem Autom ... Assembly Automation [*A publication*]
Assembly Eng ... Assembly Engineering [*A publication*]
Assem Eng ... Assembly Engineering [*A publication*]
Assem Fastener Eng ... Assembly and Fastener Engineering [*A publication*]
Assem Gen Comm Int Tech Sucr ... Assemblee Generale. Commission Internationale Technique de Sucrerie [*A publication*]
As SE Monde Insul ... Asie du Sud-Est et Monde Insulindien [*A publication*]
ASSER........ Assessor of Archdeaconry [*Ecclesiastical*]
ASSERON ... Army Service Squadron [*Corresponds to Navy's CASU*]
ASSERT.... Australian Society of Sexual Educators, Researchers, and Therapists
ASSESMT ... Assessment   (KSC)
ASSESS..... Airborne Science Shuttle [*or Spacelab*] Experiment System Simulation [*NASA*]   (MCD)
ASSESS..... Airborne Science Shuttle Experiments System Simulation [*NASA*]   (NASA)
ASSESS..... Analytical Studies of Surface Effects of Submerged Submarines [*Navy*]
Assess Arct Mar Environ Sel Top Symp ... Assessment of the Arctic Marine Environment. Selected Topics. Based on a Symposium Held in Conjunction with Third International Conference on Port and Ocean Engineering under Arctic Conditions [*A publication*]
Assess & Eval in Higher Educ ... Assessment and Evaluation in Higher Education [*A publication*]
Assess J ..... Assessors Journal [*A publication*]
Assessment in Higher Ed ... Assessment in Higher Education [*A publication*]
Assessors J ... Assessors Journal [*A publication*]

Assess Pharmacodyn Eff Hum Pharmacol Symp ... Assessment of Pharmacodynamic Effects in Human Pharmacology. Symposium [*A publication*]

Assess Radioact Contam Man Proc Symp ... Assessment of Radioactive Contamination in Man. Proceedings. Symposium on Assessment of Radioactive Organ and Body Burdens [*A publication*]

ASSET...... Abstracts of Selected Solar Energy Technology [*Japan*] [*A publication*]

ASSET...... Advanced Skewed Sensory Electronic Triad [*Navy*]

ASSET...... Advanced System Synthesis and Evaluation Technique [*Lockheed Aircraft*]

ASSET...... Aerothermodynamic Structural Systems Environmental Test [*Military*]

ASSET...... American Society of Scientific and Engineering Translators

ASSET...... American-South African Study and Educational Trust

ASSET...... Anglo-Scandinavian Study of Early Thrombolysis

ASSET...... Association of Supervisory Staffs, Executives, and Technicians (KSC)

ASSET...... ASW [*Antisubmarine Warfare*] Submarine System Evaluation Technique

ASSET...... Automated Spares Simulation Estimating Technique [*The Boeing Co.*]

ASSET...... Automated System for Sequential Extraction and Tabulation (NVT)

ASSET...... Automated Systems and Software Engineering Technology (MCD)

ASSETS .... [*A*] Survey of Students' Educational Talents and Skills [*Educational test*]

ASSF .... Acta Societatis Scientiarum Fennicae [*A publication*]

ASSF .... Arbetarnas och Smabrukarnas Socialdemokratiska Foerbund [*Social Democratic League of Workers and Smallholders*] [*Finland*] [*Political party*] (PPE)

ASSFJ .... Aleksandr Solzhenitsyn Society for Freedom and Justice (EA)

ASSFN ...... American Society for Stereotactic and Functional Neurosurgery (EA)

Ass Franc Avance Sc C R ... Association Francaise pour l'Avancement des Sciences. Comptes-Rendus [*A publication*]

ASSGB ...... Association of Ski Schools in Great Britain

ASSGT ...... Assignment (ROG)

ASSH......... Advance Space System Hardening (MCD)

ASSH......... American Society for Surgery of the Hand (EA)

ASSIA .... Applied Social Sciences Index and Abstracts [*Information service or system*] (IID)

ASSIBS ..... American Society for the Study of Ideological Belief Systems (EA)

AS Sic .... Archivio Storico Siciliano [*A publication*]

ASSID .... Australian Society for the Study of Intellectual Disability

ASSIDER ... Associazione Industrie Siderurgiche Italiane [*Iron and Steel Industries Association*] [*Italy*] (EY)

ASSIFONTE ... Association de l'Industrie de la Fonte de Fromage de la CEE [*Association of the Processed Cheese Industry of the European Economic Community*]

ASSIG .... Assignation (DSUE)

ASSIG .... Australian Serials Special Interest Group [*Library Association of Australia*]

AS-SIGNAL ... Austast-Synchron-Signal (MCD)

Assign for Crs ... Assignments for Benefits of Creditors [*A publication*] (DLA)

Assignment Chil ... Assignment Children [*A publication*]

Assignment Child ... Assignment Children [*A publication*]

ASSIGT..... Assignment

ASSIM ...... Assimilated

Ass Ind...... Assam, India (ILCA)

ASSINSEL ... Association Internationale des Selectionneurs pour la Protection des Obtentions Vegetales [*International Association of Plant Breeders for the Protection of Plant Varieties - IAPBPPV*] (EAIO)

ASSIST ..... Afloat Supply Systems Improvement and Support Team (MCD)

ASSIST ..... Army System for Standardized Intelligence Support Terminals (MCD)

ASSIST ..... Assistant

Assist .... Assistent [*Assistant*] [*German*]

ASSIST ..... Automation Services - System Improvement - Solution and Tracking (MCD)

ASSIST ..... [*A*] Simple Systematic Integration of Statistical Techniques (BUR)

Assist .... Writ of Assistance [*Legal term*] (DLA)

Assistant Librn ... Assistant Librarian [*A publication*]

Assistenza Soc ... Assistenza Sociale [*A publication*]

Assist Inf.... Assistance Informations [*France*] [*A publication*]

Assist Libn ... Assistant Librarian [*A publication*]

Assist Soc .. Assistenza Sociale [*A publication*]

ASSITEJ... Association Internationale du Theatre pour l'Enfance et de la Jeunesse [*International Association of Theatre for Children and Youth*] (EAIO)

ASSIU .... Avionics Subsystem Interface Unit (MCD)

Assiut Univ Fac Sci Bull ... Assiut University. Faculty of Science. Bulletin [*A publication*]

ASSJ.......... Association for the Sociological Study of Jewry (EA)

Ass Jerus ... Assizes of Jerusalem [*A publication*] (DLA)

ASSL .... Abnormal Steady State Limits (MCD)

AS & SL..... All Ships and Stations Letters

ASSLAD.... Astrophysics and Space Science Library [*A publication*]

ASSLT & B ... Assault and Battery [*Legal term*] (DLA)

ASSM........ Aligned Short Fiber Sheet Molding Compound (MCD)

ASSM........ Antisurface Ship Missile [*NATO*] (MCD)

ASSM........ Assembler [*Data processing*]

AssM .... Associated Microfilming Service, Inc., Mountain Lakes, NJ [*Library symbol*] [*Library of Congress*] (LCLS)

ASSM........ Association of State Supervisors of Mathematics (EA)

ASSM........ Authorization for Sale of Salvage Material

ASSM........ Shannon Municipal Library, Sexsmith, Alberta [*Library symbol*] [*National Library of Canada*] (NLC)

ASSMBH .. Acta Salmanticensia. Serie de Medicina [*A publication*]

AssMos...... Assumption of Moses (Pseudepigrapha) (BJA)

ASSMR ..... American Society for Surface Mining and Reclamation (EA)

ASSMT ..... Assessment [*Business term*]

ASSMT ..... Assignment (ROG)

ASSMT ..... Assortment [*Business term*]

ASSN......... Assign

ASSN......... Association

Assn Am Ag Coll & Exp Pro ... Association of American Agricultural Colleges and Experiment Stations. Proceedings [*A publication*]

Assn Am Col Bul ... Association of American Colleges. Bulletin [*A publication*]

Assn Am Geog Ann ... Association of American Geographers. Annals [*A publication*]

Assn Asian Stud Newsletter ... Association for Asian Studies. Newsletter [*A publication*]

Ass Naz Ing Architetti Ital Quad ... Associazione Nazionale degli Ingegneri ed Architetti Italiani. Quaderni [*A publication*]

Assn Bar City NY Rec ... Association of the Bar of the City of New York. Record [*A publication*]

Assn Bibl Francais Bull Inf ... Association des Bibliothecaires Francais. Bulletin d'Informations [*A publication*]

Assn Canadienne Bibl Langue Francaise Bul ... Association Canadienne des Bibliothecaires de Langue Francaise. Bulletin [*A publication*]

ASSNCE ... Assurance

Assn Comp Mach J ... Association for Computing Machinery. Journal [*A publication*]

Assn Ed Radio J ... Association for Education by Radio. Journal [*A publication*]

Assn of Gov Bds of State Univ & Allied Insts Proc ... Association of Governing Boards of State Universities and Allied Institutions. Proceedings [*A publication*]

Assn Italiana Bibl Boll Inf ... Associazione Italiana Biblioteche. Bollettino d'Informazioni [*A publication*]

Assn Men... Association Men (Rural Manhood) [*A publication*]

Assn Mgt ... Association Management [*A publication*]

Assn Offic Ag Chem J ... Association of Official Agricultural Chemists. Journal [*A publication*]

ASSNS ...... Assigns (ROG)

Assn Sch Bsns Officials US & Canada Proc ... Association of School Business Officials of the United States and Canada. Proceedings [*A publication*]

Assn Stud Teach Yrbk ... Association for Student Teaching. Yearbook [*A publication*]

Assn for Sup & Curric Develop Yearbook ... Association for Supervision and Curriculum Development. Yearbook [*A publication*]

Assn Sup & Curric Devel Yrbk ... Association for Supervision and Curriculum Development. Yearbook [*A publication*]

Ass'n Trial Law Am Newsl ... Association of Trial Lawyers of America. Newsletter [*A publication*] (DLA)

ASSO........ American Society for the Study of Orthodontics (EA)

ASSO......... Archivio Storico per la Sicilia Orientale [*A publication*]

ASSO......... Associate

ASSOC...... Associate [*or Association*] (AFM)

Assoc Am Fert Control Off Off Publ ... Association of American Fertilizer Control Officials. Official Publication [*A publication*]

Assoc Am Geographers Annals ... Association of American Geographers. Annals [*A publication*]

Assoc Am Geographers Comm Coll Geography Resource Paper ... Association of American Geographers. Commission on College Geography. Resource Paper [*A publication*]

Assoc Am Geogr Comm Coll Geogr Publ ... Association of American Geographers. Commission on College Geography. Publication [*A publication*]

Assoc Asphalt Paving Technol ... Association of Asphalt Paving Technologists. Conference [*A publication*]

Assoc Belge Dev Pac Energ At Bull Inf ... Association Belge pour le Developpement Pacifique de l'Energie Atomique. Bulletin d'Information [*A publication*]

Assoc Belge Photogr Cinematogr Bull ... Association Belge de Photographie et de Cinematographie. Bulletin [*A publication*]

Assoc Bibl Francais Bul ... Association des Bibliothecaires Francais. Bulletin d'Informations [*A publication*]

Assoc Biochim Hop Que Bull ... Association des Biochimistes des Hopitaux du Quebec. Bulletin [*A publication*]

Assoc Bras Ind Aliment Setor Aliment Calorico Proteicos Rev ... Associacao Brasileira das Industrias da Alimentacao. Setor de Alimentos Calorico Proteicos. Revista [*A publication*]

Assoc Bras Pesqui Plant Aromat Oleos Essen Bol ... Associacao Brasileira de Pesquisas sobre Plantas Aromaticas e Oleos Essenciais. Boletim [*A publication*]

Assoc Brit IRE ... Associate of the British Institution of Radio Engineers

Assoc Bull Int Assoc Milk Dealers ... Association Bulletin. International Association of Milk Dealers [*A publication*]

Assoc Cadres Dir Industr B ... Association de Cadres Dirigeants de l'Industrie pour le Progres Social et Economique. Bulletin [*A publication*]

Assoc Canadienne-Francaise Av Sci Annales ... Association Canadienne-Francaise pour l'Avancement des Sciences. Annales [*A publication*]

Assoc Can Bibl Lang Fr Bull ... Association Canadienne des Bibliothecaires de Langue Francaise. Bulletin [*A publication*]

ASSOCD ... Associated (EY)

Assoc Demographes Quebec Bul ... Bulletin. Association de Demographes du Quebec [*A publication*]

AssocDip .... Associate Diploma

AssocDipAbStudies ... Associate Diploma in Aboriginal Studies

AssocDipAdmin ... Associate Diploma in Administration

AssocDipAg ... Associate Diploma in Agriculture

AssocDipAHCD ... Associate Diploma in Aboriginal Health and Community Development

AssocDipAppBiol ... Associate Diploma in Applied Biology

AssocDipAppSc ... Associate Diploma in Applied Science

AssocDipArts ... Associate Diploma in Arts

AssocDipBltEnvir ... Associate Diploma Built Environment Technician

AssocDipCart ... Associate Diploma in Cartography (ADA)

AssocDipCHN ... Associate Diploma in Community Health Nursing

AssocDipCivEng ... Associate Diploma in Civil Engineering

AssocDipClinLabTech ... Associate Diploma in Clinical Laboratory Techniques

AssocDipClinNursStud(Gerontol) ... Associate Diploma in Clinical Nursing Studies (Gerontology)

AssocDipCompAppl ... Associate Diploma in Computer Applications

AssocDipDT ... Associate Diploma in Diversional Therapy

AssocDipElecEng ... Associate Diploma in Electrical Engineering

AssocDipLoc&AppHist ... Associate Diploma in Local and Applied History

AssocDipMechEng ... Associate Diploma in Mechanical Engineering

AssocDipNursEd ... Associate Diploma in Nurse Education

AssocDipNursStudies ... Associate Diploma in Nursing Studies

AssocDipRc ... Associate Diploma in Rehabilitation Counselling

AssocDipRec ... Associate Diploma in Recreation

AssocDipSecMgt ... Associate Diploma in Security Management

AssocDipSmallBusMgt ... Associate Diploma in Small Business Management

AssocDipSptSc ... Associate Diploma in Sports Science

Assoc Elettrotec Elettron Ital Rend Riun Annu ... Associazione Elettrotecnica ed Elettronica Italiana. Rendiconti della Riunione Annuale [*A publication*]

Assoc Elettrotec Ital Rend Riun Annu ... Associazione Elettrotecnica Italiana. Rendiconti della Riunione Annuale [*A publication*]

Assoc Eng Geol Ann Meet Program Abstr ... Association of Engineering Geologists. Annual Meeting. Program and Abstracts [*A publication*]

Assoc Eng Geol Annu Mtg Guideb ... Association of Engineering Geologists. Annual Meeting. Guidebook [*A publication*]

Assoc Eng Geol Annu Mtg Guide Field Trips ... Association of Engineering Geologists. Annual Meeting. Guide to Field Trips [*A publication*]

Assoc Eng Geol Bull ... Association of Engineering Geologists. Bulletin [*A publication*]

Assoc Food and Drug Off Q Bull ... Association of Food and Drug Officials. Quarterly Bulletin [*A publication*]

Assoc Fr Chim Ind Cuir Conf ... Association Francaise des Chimistes des Industries du Cuir. Conference [*A publication*]

Assoc Fr Etude Quat Bull ... Association Francaise pour l'Etude du Quaternaire. Bulletin [*A publication*]

Assoc Fr Gemmol Bull ... Association Francaise de Gemmologie. Bulletin [*A publication*]

Assoc Fr Tech Pet Rev ... Association Francaise des Techniciens du Petrole. Revue [*A publication*]

Assoc Geofis Ital Atti Conv Annu ... Associazione Geofisica Italiana. Atti del Convegno Annuale [*Italy*] [*A publication*]

Assoc Geographes Francais Bull ... Association de Geographes Francais. Bulletin [*A publication*]

Assoc Geogr Fr Bull ... Association de Geographes Francais. Bulletin [*A publication*]

Assoc Geol Bassin Paris Bull ... Association des Geologues du Bassin de Paris. Bulletin [*A publication*]

Assoc Geol Bassin Paris Bull Inf ... Association des Geologues du Bassin de Paris. Bulletin d'Information [*A publication*]

Assoc Green Crop Driers Yearb ... Association of Green Crop Driers. Yearbook [*A publication*]

AssociateIElecIE ... Associate of the Institution of Electrical and Electronics Incorporated Engineers [*British*] (DBQ)

Assoc IEE .. Associate of the Institution of Electrical Engineers [*British*]

Assoc I Min E ... Associate of the Institution of Mechanical Engineers [*British*]

Assoc INA ... Associate of the Institution of Naval Architects [*British*]

Assoc Ind Angola Bol ... Associacao Industrial de Angola. Boletim [*A publication*]

Assoc Ing Electr Sortis Inst Electrotech Montefiore Bull ... Association des Ingenieurs Electriciens Sortis de l'Institut Electrotechnique Montefiore. Bulletin [*Belgium*] [*A publication*]

AssocInstAEA ... Associate of the Institute of Automotive Engineer Assessors [*British*] (DBQ)

AssocInstAEA (Body Dvn) ... Associate of the Institute of Automotive Engineer Assessors (Body Division) [*British*] (DBQ)

Assoc Inst MM ... Associate of the Institute of Mining and Metallurgy [*British*]

Assoc Int Cancer Res Symp ... Association for International Cancer Research. Symposia [*A publication*]

Assoc Int Etude Argiles ... Association Internationale pour l'Etude des Argiles [*A publication*]

Assoc Int Geol Ing Bull ... Association Internationale de Geologie de l'Ingenieur. Bulletin [*A publication*]

Assoc Int Limnol Theor Appl Trav ... Association Internationale de Limnologie Theoretique et Appliquee. Travaux [*A publication*]

Assoc Int Odonto Stomatol Infant J ... Association Internationale d'Odonto Stomatologie Infantile. Journal [*A publication*]

Assoc Int Sci Hydrol Publ ... Association Internationale des Sciences Hydrologiques. Publication [*A publication*]

AssocIPHE ... Associate of the Institution of Public Health Engineers [*British*] (DBQ)

Assoc Iron Steel Electr Eng Proc ... Association of Iron and Steel Electrical Engineers. Proceedings [*A publication*]

AssocISI .... Associate of the Iron and Steel Institute [*British*]

Assoc Jpn Portland Cem Eng Rev Gen Meet ... Association of Japanese Portland Cement Engineers. Review of General Meeting [*A publication*]

Assoc Latinoam Entomol Publ ... Asociacion Latinoamericana de Entomologia. Publicacion [*A publication*]

AssocLUA ... Associate of Life Underwriters Association of Australia

Assoc Manage ... Association Management [*A publication*]

AssocMCT ... Associateship of the Manchester College of Technology [*British*]

Assoc Met Sprayers Pap Symp Eng Appl Met Spraying ... Association of Metal Sprayers. Papers. Symposium on Engineering Applications of Metal Spraying [*A publication*]

AssocMIAeE ... Associate Member of the Institution of Aeronautical Engineers [*British*]

Assoc Mine Mangr S Afr Circ ... Association of Mine Managers of South Africa. Circulars [*A publication*]

Assoc Mine Mangr S Afr Pap Discuss ... Association of Mine Managers of South Africa. Papers and Discussions [*A publication*]

Assoc (M) Inst CE ... Associate (Member) of the Institution of Civil Engineers [*British*]

ASSOCN ... Association

Assoc Nat Enseign Agric Public Bull Trimest ... Association des Naturalistes de l'Enseignement Agricole Public. Bulletin Trimestriel [*A publication*]

Assoc News ... Associate News [*A publication*] (APTA)

Assoc Off Anal Chem J ... Association of Official Analytical Chemists. Journal [*A publication*]

Assoc Off Analyt Chemists J ... Association of Official Analytical Chemists. Journal [*A publication*]

Assoc Official Agr Chemists Jour ... Association of Official Agricultural Chemists. Journal [*A publication*]

Assoc Off Seed Anal Proc ... Association of Official Seed Analysts. Proceedings [*A publication*]

ASSOCOMAPLAST ... Associazione Nazionale Costruttori di Macchine per Materie Plastiche e Gomma [*Association of makers of plastic and rubber manufacturing machinery*] [*Italy*] (EY)

Assoc Pacific Coast Geographers Yearbook ... Association of Pacific Coast Geographers. Yearbook [*A publication*]

Assoc Public Analysts J ... Association of Public Analysts. Journal [*A publication*]

Assoc RCATS ... Associate of the Royal College of Advanced Technology [*British*]

Assoc Recor ... Association for Recorded Sound Collections. Journal [*A publication*]

Assoc Reg Etude Sci Bull ... Association Regionale pour l'Etude et la Recherche Scientifiques. Bulletin [*A publication*]

Assoc Res Nerv Ment Dis Res Publ ... Association for Research in Nervous and Mental Disease. Research Publications [*A publication*]

Assoc Res Nerv Ment Dis Ser Res Publ ... Association for Research in Nervous and Mental Disease. Series of Research Publications [*A publication*]

AssocRINA ... Associate of the Royal Institution of Naval Architects [*British*]

Assoc Sc ..... Associate in Science

Assoc Sci Tech Soc S Afr Annu Proc ... Associated Scientific and Technical Societies of South Africa. Annual Proceedings [*A publication*]

Assoc Senegal Etud Quat Ouest Afr Bull Liaison ... Association Senegalaise pour l'Etude du Quaternaire de l'Ouest Africain. Bulletin de Liaison [*A publication*]

AssocSLAET ... Associate of the Society of Licensed Aircraft Engineers and Technologists [*British*] (DBQ)

Assoc Soc Manager ... Association and Society Manager [*A publication*]
Assoc Tech Ind Gaz ... Association Technique de l'Industrie du Gaz en France. Proceedings [*A publication*]
Assoc Univ Programs Health Admin Program Notes ... Association of University Programs in Health Administration. Program Notes [*A publication*]
ASSOFERLEGHE ... Associazione Produttori Italiani di Ferroleghe ed Affini [*Ferro-alloy producers association*] [*Italy*]   (EY)
ASSOFOND ... Associazione Nazionale delle Fonderie [*Foundries association*] [*Italy*]   (EY)
ASSOGLACE ... Association des Artisans Glaciers et des Fabricants de Mix pour Glace des Pays de la CEE [*Association of Home-Made Ice-Cream and Ice-Mix Manufacturers in the European Economic Community*]
Asso & Man ... Asso and Manuel's Institutes of Spanish Civil Law [*A publication*]   (DLA)
ASSOMEP ... Associazione Nazionale Industria dell'Ottica, Meccanica Fine, e di Precisione [*Optical and Precision Instrument Manufacturers Association*] [*Italy*]   (EY)
ASSOMET ... Associazione Nazionale Industrie Metalli Non-Ferrosi [*Non-Ferrous Metal Industries Association*] [*Italy*]   (EY)
ASSOPOMAC ... Association des Obtenteurs de Pommes de Terre du Marche Commun [*Association of Certified Seed Potato Suppliers of the Common Market*]
ASSORECO ... Association des Ressortissants du Haut et du Moyen Congo [*Association of Natives of the Upper and Middle Congo*]
ASSOTW .. Airfield and Seaplane Stations of the World   (MUGU)
ASSP .... Acoustics, Speech, and Signal Processing   (MCD)
ASSP .... Aerospace Systems Security Program   (AFM)
ASSP .... African Social Studies Programme   (EA)
ASSP .... Agence de Surveillance du Secteur Petrolier [*Petroleum Monitoring Agency, Energy, Mines & Resources, Canada*]
ASSP .... Aircrew Station Standardization Panel
ASSP .... Auxiliary Surface Simulator Platform [*Navy*]   (CAAL)
ASSP .... Axially Scattering Spectrometer Probe   (MCD)
ASSP .... Transport, Submarine [*Later, LPSS*] [*Navy symbol*] [*Obsolete*]
ASSPAP .... Australia. Commonwealth Scientific and Industrial Research Organisation. Soil Publication [*A publication*]
ASSPC ...... IEEE Acoustics, Speech, and Signal Processing Society   (EA)
ASSPh ...... Annuaire. Societe Suisse de Philosophie [*A publication*]
ASSPHR ... Anti-Slavery Society for the Protection of Human Rights   (EA)
ASSR .... Airborne Sea/Swell Recorder [*Oceanography*]   (MSC)
ASSR .... American Society for the Study of Religion   (EA)
ASSR .... Archives de Sciences Sociales des Religions [*A publication*]
ASSR .... Autonomous Soviet Socialist Republic
ASSR .... Sydney [*Australia*] [*ICAO location identifier*]   (ICLI)
ASSRA ...... American Single Shot Rifle Association   (EA)
ASSRC ...... Aviation Section Signal Reserve Corps
Ass Reg Da ... Assia Regis David [*A publication*]   (DLA)
ASSRFM ... Alaska Series Special Reports for Management [*A publication*]
ASSRM ..... Air Supplemented Solid Rocket Motor   (MCD)
ASSRON ... Air Service Support Squadron [*Army*]
ASSS .... Aerospace Systems Safety Society   (MCD)
ASSS .... American Society for the Study of Sterility [*Later, AFS*]   (EA)
ASSS .... American Suffolk Sheep Society   (EA)
ASSS .... Assigns   (ROG)
ASSS .... Associate in Science in Secretarial Studies
ASSS .... Sydney [*Australia*] [*ICAO location identifier*]   (ICLI)
AssSeign .... Assemblees du Seigneur [*Bruges*] [*A publication*]
ASS Short-Circuit Test Auth Publ ... Association of Short-Circuit Testing Authorities. Publication [*A publication*]
ASST .... Advanced Supersonic Transport
ASST .... American Society for Steel Treaters [*Later, ASM*]
ASST .... Antiship Surveillance and Targeting [*Navy*]   (NVT)
ASST .... Antisurface Ship Surveillance and Targeting   (MCD)
AsSt .... Asian Student [*A publication*]
ASST .... Assented [*Securities*]
ASST .... Assessment
ASST .... Assignment   (ROG)
ASST .... Assistant   (EY)
ASST .... Association of Social Science Teachers [*Later, ASBS*]   (EA)
ASST .... Assort
ASST .... Automatic System Self-Test [*Aviation*]   (MCD)
ASSTA ...... Acier-Stahl-Steel [*A publication*]
Ass Tax ..... Assessed Taxes (Decisions of Judges) [*A publication*]   (DLA)
ASSTD ...... Associated
ASSTD ...... Assorted
ASSTG ...... Assisting
Asst Libn ... Assistant Librarian [*A publication*]
ASSTN ...... Assistance   (MSA)
ASSTSAS ... Association pour la Sante et la Securite du Travail, Secteur Affaires Sociales [*Association for the Health and Safety of Labour, Social Affairs Sector*] [*Canada*]
ASSU .... Air Support Signal Unit   (NATG)
ASSU .... American Sunday School Union [*Later, AMF*]
ASSUA6 .... Acta Psychiatrica Scandinavica. Supplementum [*A publication*]
ASSUC ...... Association des Organisations Professionnelles du Commerce des Sucres pour les Pays de la Communaute Economique Europeenne [*Association of Sugar Trade Organizations for the European Economic Community Countries*] [*Belgium*]

ASSUD9 .... US Department of Agriculture. Science and Education Administration. Agricultural Research Results. ARR-S [*A publication*]
Assuntos Eur ... Assuntos Europeus [*A publication*]
Assur .... Assurance
Assurb .... Assurbanipal [*King of ancient Assyria*]   (BJA)
ASSURE ... Automated Software System Used for Reliability Evaluation
Assuring Radiat Prot Annu Natl Conf Radiat Control ... Assuring Radiation Protection. Annual National Conference on Radiation Control [*A publication*]
ASSURLUX ... Les Assurances Reunies du Luxembourg [*Insurance agency*] [*Luxembourg*]   (EY)
As Surv ...... Asian Survey [*A publication*]
ASSVB .... Annali. Istituto Sperimentale per la Selvicoltura [*A publication*]
ASSW .... Antisurface Ship Warfare   (MCD)
ASSW .... Associated With [*Aviation*]   (FAAC)
ASSX .... Sydney [*Australia*] [*ICAO location identifier*]   (ICLI)
ASSY .... Assembly
ASSY .... Sydney/Kingsford Smith International [*Australia*] [*ICAO location identifier*]   (ICLI)
Assy Misc .. Assyriological Miscellanies [*A publication*]
ASSYR ...... Assyria
Assyriol Studies ... Assyriological Studies [*A publication*]
Assyr S .... Assyriological Studies [*A publication*]
AssyrSt .... Assyriological Studies [*A publication*]
A St .... Aberystwyth Studies [*A publication*]
AST .... Abort-Scan Table [*NASA*]
AST .... Absolute Sensation Threshold
AST .... Absolute Space-Time
AST .... Accelerated Service Test   (MCD)
AST .... Action Sociale Tchadienne [*Chadian Social Action*]
AST .... Action Speed Tactical
AST .... Add-Subtract Time
AST .... Additional Specialty Training [*Military*]
AST .... Adiabatic Storage Test [*For hazardous chemicals*]
AS & T .... Administrative, Staff, and Technical [*Budget term*]
AST .... Administrative-Supply Technician [*Army*]   (AABC)
AST .... Advanced Simulation Technology [*DoD*]   (IEEE)
AST .... Advanced Supersonic Technology
AST .... Advanced Supersonic Transport
AST .... Advanced System Technology
AS & T .... Advanced Systems and Technology   (MCD)
AST .... Aerial Survey Team   (AFM)
AST .... Aerospace Technologist [*or Technology*] [*NASA*]
AST .... AIM Strategic Income Fund [*AMEX symbol*]   (SPSG)
AST .... Air Staff Target [*Royal Air Force*] [*British*]
AST .... Air Support Tactics
AST .... Air-Supported Threat [*Army*]
AST .... Air Surveillance Technician [*Air Force*]
AST .... Aircraft Systems Trainer   (MCD)
AST .... Airlock Systems Test [*NASA*]   (MCD)
AST .... All Systems Test [*NASA*]   (KSC)
AST .... Allowable Ship Turn
ASt .... Altostratus [*Cloud*] [*Meteorology*]   (AIA)
AST .... American String Teacher [*A publication*]
AST .... Aminosultopride [*Biochemistry*]
AST .... Analecta Sacra Tarraconensia [*A publication*]
AST .... Angiotensin Sensitivity Test [*Medicine*]
AST .... Antisidetone [*Telecommunications*]   (TEL)
AST .... Antisyphilitic Treatment [*Medicine*]
AST .... Applied Science and Technology Index [*A publication*]
AST .... Area Specialist Team [*Army*]
AST .... Arkansas State Library, Little Rock, AR [*OCLC symbol*]   (OCLC)
AST .... Arming System Tester   (MCD)
AST .... Army Satellite Tracking Center
AST .... Army Specialized Training
A e St .... Arte e Storia [*A publication*]
AST .... Artificial Site Tuff [*Geology*]
AST .... Artillery Supply Truck [*British*]
ASt .... Asian Studies [*A publication*]
ASt .... Asiatische Studien [*A publication*]
AST .... Aspartate Aminotransferase [*Also, AAT, ASAT, GOT*] [*An enzyme*]
AST .... Assembly and Structure Test
AST .... Assented [*Economics*]
AST .... Assessment
AST .... Association for Student Teaching [*Later, ATE*]   (EA)
AST .... Association of Surgical Technologists   (EA)
AST .... Association of Swimming Therapy [*British*]
AST .... Astemizole [*Pharmacology*]
Ast .... Astigmatism [*Also, As*] [*Ophthalmology*]
AST .... Astonishing Stories [*A publication*]
AST .... Astoria [*Oregon*] [*Airport symbol*] [*Obsolete*]   (OAG)
AST .... Astrida [*Rwanda*] [*Seismograph station code, US Geological Survey*] [*Closed*]   (SEIS)
AST .... Astro Airways Corp. [*Pine Bluff, AR*] [*FAA designator*]   (FAAC)
AST .... Astrology
AST .... Astronomy   (NASA)
AST .... At Same Time

A ST.......... Atlanta Street Railroad
AST........... Atlantic School of Theology [*Canada*]
AST........... Atlantic Standard Time
AST........... Atmospheric Surveillance Technology   (MCD)
AST........... Atomized Suspension Technique
AST........... Atti e Memorie. Societa Tiburtina di Storia e d'Arte [*A publication*]
AST........... Audiometry Sweep Test
AST........... Augustus Resources Ltd. [*Vancouver Stock Exchange symbol*]
AST........... Automated Speech Technology   (MCD)
ASt............ Automatic Starter
AST........... Average Sampling Time [*Statistics*]
AST........... Ayres Space Test [*Psychology*]
AST........... Stettler Public Library, Alberta [*Library symbol*] [*National Library of Canada*]   (NLC)
ASTA........ Advanced Strategic Transport Aircraft
ASTA........ Aerial Survey and Target Acquisition [*Military*]
ASTA........ Aerospace Technologies of Australia
ASTA........ American Sail Training Association   (EA)
ASTA........ American Seed Trade Association   (EA)
ASTA........ American Society of Travel Agents   (EA)
ASTA........ American Spice Trade Association   (EA)
ASTA........ American String Teachers Association   (EA)
ASTA........ American Surgical Trade Association   (EA)
ASTA........ Anti-alpha-staphylolysin [*Immunology*]
ASTA........ Associate of the Swimming Teachers' Association [*British*]   (DBQ)
ASTA........ AST Research, Inc. [*Irvine, CA*] [*NASDAQ symbol*]   (NQ)
ASTA........ Aviation Systems Test Activity [*Later, AEFA*]   (MCD)
ASTA........ Stavely Public Library, Alberta [*Library symbol*] [*National Library of Canada*]   (NLC)
ASTAA...... Airborne Special-Type Auxiliary Assembly   (MCD)
ASTABS.... Automatic Status Board Subsystem   (MCD)
ASTACC ... Advanced Ship Types and Combatant Craft   (MCD)
ASTACS.... ASW [*Antisubmarine Warfare*] Tactical [*Data or Support*] Center Systems   (MCD)
ASTAN...... American Ski Teachers Association of Natur Teknik   (EA)
ASTAP ...... Acoustic Sensor Training Aids Program [*Navy*]   (CAAL)
ASTAP ...... Advanced Statistical Analysis Program [*Data processing*]   (MCD)
ASTAR ...... Advanced Surveillance and Target Acquisition RADAR
ASTAR ...... Airborne Search Target Attack RADAR   (MCD)
ASTAS ...... AntiRADAR Surveillance and Target Acquisition System
Ast & AstroAb ... Astronomy and Astrophysics. Abstracts [*A publication*]
ASTB........ Advanced Survivability Test Bed [*Military*]   (INF)
ASTB........ And So To Bed [*Commercial firm*] [*British*]
ASTB........ Astable   (MSA)
AStbC .... St. Bernard College, St. Bernard, AL [*Library symbol*] [*Library of Congress*]   (LCLS)
ASTC........ Administrative Section for Technical Cooperation [*United Nations*]
ASTC........ Advanced Satellite Tracking Center
ASTC........ American Sealyham Terrier Club   (EA)
ASTC........ American Shih Tzu Club   (EA)
ASTC........ American Society of Theater Consultants   (EA)
ASTC........ American Society of Trial Consultants   (EA)
ASTC........ Appalachian State Teachers College [*Later, ASU*] [*North Carolina*]
ASTC........ Arkansas State Teachers College [*Later, University of Central Arkansas*]
ASTC........ Aroostook State Teachers College [*Merged with University of Maine*]
ASTC........ Associate of the Sydney Technical College [*Australia*]
ASTC........ Association of Science-Technology Centers   (EA)
ASTC........ Australian Sales Tax Cases [*Australia*]
ASTC........ Automatic Steam-Temperature Control
ASTCC ...... American Sabbath Tract and Communications Council   (EA)
ASTCDPD ... Association of State and Territorial Chronic Disease Program Directors   (EA)
ASTD........ Advanced Space Technology Division [*NASA*]   (NASA)
ASTD........ Advanced Structures Technology Demonstration
ASTD........ Air-Supported Threat Defense [*Army*]   (AABC)
ASTD........ American Society of Teachers of Dancing   (EA)
ASTD........ American Society for Training and Development   (EA)
ASTD........ Antiship Torpedo Defense [*or Device*]   (MCD)
ASTD........ Area Scale Temperature Display
ASTD........ Army Specialized Training Division
ASTD........ Assented [*Investment term*]
ASTD........ Assistant Steward [*British military*]   (DMA)
ASTDD...... Association of State and Territorial Dental Directors   (EA)
ASTDLHS ... Association of State and Territorial Directors of Local Health Services [*Defunct*]   (EA)
ASTDM..... Advanced Smokeless Technology Demonstration Motor   (MCD)
ASTDN...... Association of State and Territorial Directors of Nursing   (EA)
ASTDPHN ... Association of State and Territorial Directors of Public Health Nursing [*Later, ASTDN*]   (EA)
ASTDS ...... Air-Supported Threat Defense System [*Army*]
ASTE........ Aerospace Systems Test Environment
ASTE........ Amalgamated Society of Telephone Employees [*A union*] [*British*]

ASTE......... American Society of Test Engineers   (EA)
ASTE......... American Society of Tool Engineers [*Later, SME*]
ASTE......... Armament System Test Environment   (MCD)
ASTE......... Association for Software Testing and Evaluation   (EA)
ASTE......... Association for the Study of Soviet-Type Economies [*Later, ACES*]   (EA)
ASTE......... Astec Industries, Inc. [*Chattanooga, TN*] [*NASDAQ symbol*]   (NQ)
ASTEC ...... Advanced Solar Turbo-Electric Conversion
ASTEC ...... Advanced Systems Technology   (IEEE)
ASTEC ...... Aerospace System Test and Evaluation Complex   (KSC)
ASTEC ...... American Steamship Traffic Executives Committee
ASTEC ...... Antisubmarine Technical Evaluation Center [*Navy*]
ASTEC ...... Association of Science-Technology Centers
ASTEC ...... Australian Science and Technology Council
ASTEC ...... Avionics System Test Equipment Comparator   (MCD)
ASTED ...... Association pour l'Avancement des Sciences et des Techniques de la Documentation [*Acronym is now organization's official name*]
ASTED ...... Automated Sequential Trace Enrichment of Dialysate
ASTEG ...... All Systems Test Equipment Group
Ast Ent....... Aston's Entries [*1673*] [*A publication*]   (DLA)
ASTEP ...... Algorithm Simulation Test and Evaluation Program [*NASA*]
ASTER ...... Antisubmarine Terrier Missile [*Navy*]
ASTF .... Aeropropulsion Systems Test Facility [*Arnold Air Force Station, TN*] [*Air Force*]   (MCD)
ASTF .... Aerospace Structures Test Facility [*Air Force*]
ASTF .... American Sovereignty Task Force   (EA)
ASTG .... Aerospace Test Group   (NASA)
ASTGO...... Authorization of Special Types General Order [*British*]   (DCTA)
ASTH .... Asthenopia [*Ophthalmology*] [*Medicine*]
ASTHE...... Average Straight Time Hourly Earnings [*Accounting*]
ASTHMA ... Aerotherm Axisymmetric Transient Heating and Material Ablation [*Program*]
ASTHO ..... Association of State and Territorial Health Officials   (EA)
As Thought Soc ... Asian Thought and Society [*A publication*]
ASTI .... Active Sodium Transport Inhibitor [*Biochemistry*]
ASTI .... Annual. Swedish Theological Institute [*A publication*]
ASTI .... Applied Science and Technology Index [*A publication*]
ASTI .... Applied Spectrum Technologies, Inc. [*NASDAQ symbol*]   (NQ)
ASTI .... Applied Statistics Training Institute
ASTI .... Association for Science, Technology, and Innovation   (EA)
ASTI .... Automated System for Transportation Intelligence [*Army*]   (RDA)
ASTI .... Stirling Public Library, Alberta [*Library symbol*] [*National Library of Canada*]   (NLC)
ASTIA .... Armed Services Technical Information Agency [*Later, Defense Documentation Center*]
ASTIB .... Army Scientific and Technical Intelligence Bulletin [*A publication*]
ASTIC .... Algonquian Syllabic Texts in Canadian Repositories [*Bibliographic project*]
ASTic .... Archivio Storico Ticinese [*A publication*]
ASTIG .... Astigmatism [*Electronics*]
ASTIIT...... American Society for Technion-Israel Institute of Technology   (EA)
ASTIN ...... Actuarial Studies in Non-Life Insurance [*of the International Actuarial Association*] [*Brussels, Belgium*]   (EA)
Astin Bull... Astin Bulletin [*Leiden*] [*A publication*]
A S & T Ind ... Applied Science and Technology Index [*A publication*]
ASTINDMAN ... Assistant Industrial Manager [*of Naval District*]   (MUGU)
ASTINFO ... Asian Scientific and Technological Information Network   (EAIO)
ASTIO .... Advanced Systems Technology and Integration Office [*Army*]
ASTIP....... Army Scientific and Technical Information Program   (DIT)
ASTIS........ Arctic Science and Technology Information System [*Arctic Institute of North America*] [*University of Calgary*] [*Information service or system*]   (IID)
ASTIS....... Astronomy Information Service [*Space Telescope Science Institute*] [*Information service or system*]   (IID)
ASTIS....... Australian Science and Technology Information Service
ASTK .... American Software Technology [*NASDAQ symbol*]   (NQ)
ASTL .... American Society of Transportation and Logistics   (EA)
ASTL .... Approved Supplier Tab List
A & StL ...... Atlantic & St. Lawrence Railroad
ASTM........ Advance STOL [*Short Takeoff and Landing*] Transport (Medium) [*Aviation*]   (MCD)
ASTM........ Amalgamated Society of Tobacco Manufacturers [*A union*] [*British*]
ASTM........ American Society for Testing and Materials [*Acronym is now organization's official name*]   (EAIO)
ASTM........ American Standard of Testing Materials
ASTM........ American Standards Test Manual
ASTM........ Australian Stamp Duties [*A publication*]
ASTM........ Standard Municipal Library, Alberta [*Library symbol*] [*National Library of Canada*]   (NLC)
ASTM (Am Soc Test Mater) Data Ser ... ASTM (American Society for Testing and Materials) Data Series [*A publication*]
ASTM Book ASTM Stand ... American Society for Testing and Materials. Book of ASTM Standards [*A publication*]

ASTM Bul ... American Society for Testing and Materials. Bulletin [*A publication*]

ASTMC..... ARS [*American Rocket Society*] Structures and Materials Committee

ASTME...... American Society of Tool and Manufacturing Engineers [*Later, SME*] (EA)

ASTME/ASM West Metal Tool Conf ... American Society of Tool and Manufacturing Engineers. ASTME/ASM Western Metal and Tool Conference [*A publication*]

ASTME Collect Papers ... American Society of Tool and Manufacturing Engineers. ASTME Collected Papers [*A publication*]

ASTME Creative Mfg Semin Tech Papers ... American Society of Tool and Manufacturing Engineers. Creative Manufacturing Seminars. Technical Papers [*A publication*]

ASTM Geotechnical Testing Journal ... American Society for Testing and Materials. Geotechnical Testing Journal [*A publication*]

ASTMH .... American Society of Tropical Medicine and Hygiene (EA)

ASTM J Testing Evaln ... ASTM [*American Society for Testing and Materials*] Journal of Testing and Evaluation [*A publication*]

ASTM Meet Prepr ... American Society for Testing and Materials. Meeting. Preprints [*A publication*]

ASTM Proc ... ASTM [*American Society for Testing and Materials*] Proceedings [*A publication*]

ASTMS ..... Association of Scientific, Technical, and Managerial Staffs [*British*]

ASTM Special Technical Publication ... American Society for Testing and Materials. Special Technical Publication [*A publication*]

ASTM Spec Tech Publ ... ASTM [*American Society for Testing and Materials*] Special Technical Publication [*A publication*]

ASTM Stand N ... ASTM [*American Society for Testing and Materials*] Standardization News [*A publication*]

ASTM Stand News ... ASTM [*American Society for Testing and Materials*] Standardization News [*A publication*]

ASTM Std ... ASTM [*American Society for Testing and Materials*] Standards [*A publication*]

ASTM Stdn News ... ASTM [*American Society for Testing and Materials*] Standardization News [*A publication*]

ASTN......... Air Station [*Air Force*]

ASTN......... Astern

ASTN......... Astronomic (AABC)

ASTN......... Austin McDaniel Corp. [*Kennewick, WA*] [*NASDAQ symbol*] (NQ)

ASTN......... Automotive Satellite Television Network [*Automotive engineering*]

ASTND...... Association of State and Territorial Nutrition Directors

ASTO .... Antistreptolysin [*Immunology*] (DHSM)

ASTO .... Assembly Tool (AAG)

ASTOAR.... Annali di Stomatologia [*A publication*]

ASTOR...... Antiship Torpedo (IEEE)

ASTOR...... Antisubmarine Torpedo (MSA)

ASTOR...... Antisubmarine Torpedo Ordnance Rocket (MCD)

ASTOVL ... Advanced Short Takeoff and Vertical Landing [*Military*]

ASTP .... Advanced Systems and Technology Programme [*European Space Agency*]

ASTP .... American Society of Tax Professionals (EA)

ASTP .... Apollo-Soyuz Test Project [*NASA/USSR*]

ASTP .... Archives Suisses des Traditions Populaires [*A publication*]

ASTP .... Army Specialized Training Program [*World War II*]

ASTP .... Association for Short Term Psychotherapy (EA)

ASTP .... Australian System of Tariff Preferences for Developing Countries

ASTP .... St. Paul Public Library, Alberta [*Library symbol*] [*National Library of Canada*] (NLC)

ASTPCW .. Australia. Commonwealth Scientific and Industrial Research Organisation. Division of Soil Research. Technical Paper [*A publication*]

ASTPHLD ... Association of State and Territorial Public Health Laboratory Directors (EA)

ASTPHND ... Association of State and Territorial Public Health Nutrition Directors (EA)

ASTPO...... Accident Source Term Program Office [*Nuclear energy*] (NRCH)

ASTR......... Addition, Subtraction, Timing, and Ratio

ASTR......... Aerospace Systems Test Reactor [*Formerly, Aircraft Shield Test Reactor*]

ASTR......... American Society for Theatre Research (EA)

ASTR......... American Society of Therapeutic Radiologists [*Later, ASTRO*] (EA)

ASTR......... Astronomy

ASTR......... Astrosystems, Inc. [*NASDAQ symbol*] (NQ)

ASTRA...... Adapted Swimming-Pool Tank Reactor, Austria

ASTRA...... Advanced Static Test Recording Apparatus

ASTRA...... Air Space Transportation

ASTRA...... Air Staff Trainee [*or Training*] [*Air Force*]

ASTRA...... Analysis and Simulation Tool for Resource Allocation (MCD)

ASTRA...... Application of Science and Technology to Rural Areas [*An association*]

ASTRA...... Application of Space Techniques Relating to Aviation [*International Civil Aviation Organization*]

ASTRA...... Applied Space Technology Regional Advancement (KSC)

ASTRA ...... Association in Scotland to Research into Astronautics [*Glasgow*] (EAIO)

ASTRA ...... Astronomical and Space Techniques for Research on the Atmosphere [*National Science Foundation project*]

ASTRA ..... Astronomical Space Telescope Research Assembly (MCD)

ASTRA ..... Australian Space Technology and Research Authority

ASTRA ..... Automatic Scheduling with Time-Integrated Resource Allocation

ASTRA ..... Automatic Sorting, Testing, Recording Analysis

ASTRA ..... Automatic Strobe Tracking (CET)

ASTRAC ... Arizona Statistical Repetitive Analog Computer

ASTRACCS ... Army Strategic Command and Control Systems (MCD)

ASTRAL.... Analog Schematic Translator to Algebraic Language [*Data processing*] (IEEE)

ASTRE ...... Airport Surface Traffic RADAR Equipment (MCD)

ASTRE ...... Applied Science through Research and Engineering

ASTREC.... Atomic Strike Evaluation Center

ASTREC.... Atomic Strike Recording System [*Air Force*]

ASTREX.... Advanced Space Structure Technology Research Experiments (MCD)

ASTRG ..... Air Starting

ASTRID .... Association Scientifique et Technique pour la Recherche en Informatique Documentaire [*Scientific and Technical Association for Research in Documentary Information*] [*Information service or system*] [*Belgium*]

ASTRO...... Advanced Spacecraft Trainer [*or Transport or Truck*] Reusable Orbiter [*NASA*] (MCD)

ASTRO...... Air Space Travel Research Organization

ASTRO...... American Society for Therapeutic Radiology and Oncology (EA)

ASTRO...... America's Sound Transportation Review Organization [*AAR*] [*Defunct*]

ASTRO...... Antarctic Submillimeter Telescope and Remote Observatory Project [*AT & T Bell Labs, Boston University, University of Illinois*]

ASTRO...... Antisubmarine Test Requirement Outline

ASTRO...... Army Strategic and Tactical Reorganization Objective

ASTRO...... Artificial Satellite Time and Radio Orbit (MCD)

ASTRO...... Astronautical

Astro .... Astronomical

ASTRO...... International Association of State Trading Organizations of Developing Countries [*Ljubljana, Yugoslavia*] (EAIO)

Astro Aeron ... Astronautics and Aeronautics [*A publication*]

ASTROC ... Automatic Stellar Tracking, Recognition, and Orientation Computer

ASTROCOM ... Astronaut Communications (MCD)

Astro Ephem ... Astronomical Ephemeris [*A publication*]

Astrofiz ...... Astrofizika [*A publication*]

Astrofiz Issled ... Astrofizicheskie Issledovaniya [*A publication*]

Astrofiz Issled Izv Spets Astrofiz Obs ... Astrofizicheskie Issledovaniya. Izvestiya Spetsial'noi Astrofizicheskoi Observatorii [*A publication*]

ASTROL ... Astrology [*or Astrologer*]

Astrol 77 .... Astrology '77 [*A publication*]

Astrol 78 ... Astrology '78 [*A publication*]

Astrol Now ... Astrology Now [*A publication*]

Astrom Astrofiz ... Astrometriya i Astrofizika [*A publication*]

Astrometriya & Astrofiz ... Astrometriya i Astrofizika [*A publication*]

ASTRON... Astronomer [*or Astronomy*]

Astron .... Astronomy and Astrophysics [*A publication*]

Astron Abhandl Ergaenzungshefte Astron Nachr ... Astronomische Abhandlungen als Ergaenzungshefte zu den Astronomischen Nachrichten [*A publication*]

Astron Astr ... Astronomy and Astrophysics [*A publication*]

Astron & Astrophys ... Astronomy and Astrophysics [*A publication*]

Astron Astrophys ... Astronomy and Astrophysics [*A publication*]

Astron Astrophys Abstr ... Astronomy and Astrophysics Abstracts [*A publication*]

Astron & Astrophys Suppl Ser ... Astronomy and Astrophysics. Supplement Series [*A publication*]

Astron Astrophys Suppl Ser ... Astronomy and Astrophysics. Supplement Series [*A publication*]

Astronaut Acta ... Astronautica Acta [*A publication*]

Astronaut Aeronaut ... Astronautics and Aeronautics [*A publication*]

Astronaut Forschungsber Dtsch Raketen Ges eV ... Astronautische Forschungsberichte. Deutsche Rakete Gesellschaft eV [*A publication*]

Astronaut Forschungsber Hermann Oberth Ges ... Astronautische Forschungsberichte. Hermann Oberth Gesellschaft [*A publication*]

Astronautics Aerospace Eng ... Astronautics and Aerospace Engineering [*A publication*]

Astronaut Sci Rev ... Astronautical Sciences Review [*A publication*]

Astron Circ Acad Sin ... Astronomical Circulars. Academia Sinica [*A publication*]

Astron Her ... Astronomical Herald [*A publication*]

Astron J ...... Astronomical Journal [*A publication*]

Astron Jahresber ... Astronomischer Jahresbericht [*A publication*]

Astron Kal (Moscow) ... Astronomicheskii Kalendar (Moscow) [*A publication*]

Astron (Milwaukee) ... Astronomy (Milwaukee) [*A publication*]

Astronom and Astrophys ... Astronomy and Astrophysics [*A publication*]
Astronom Astrophys Ser ... Astronomy and Astrophysics. Supplement Series [*A publication*]
Astronom J ... Astronomical Journal [*A publication*]
Astronom Nachr ... Astronomische Nachrichten [*A publication*]
Astronom Z ... Akademija Nauk SSSR. Astronomiceskii Zurnal [*A publication*]
Astronom Zh ... Astronomicheskii Zhurnal [*A publication*]
Astron-Opt Inst Univ Turku Inf ... Astronomia-Optika Institucio. Universitato de Turku. Informo [*A publication*]
Astron (Paris) ... Astronomie (Paris) [*A publication*]
Astron (Paris) Suppl ... Astronomie (Paris). Supplement [*A publication*]
Astron Raumfahrt ... Astronomie und Raumfahrt [*A publication*]
Astron Saellsk ... Astronomiska Saellskapet [*A publication*]
Astron Soc Aust Proc ... Astronomical Society of Australia. Proceedings [*A publication*]
Astron Soc India Bull ... Astronomical Society of India. Bulletin [*A publication*]
Astron Soc Jpn Publ ... Astronomical Society of Japan. Publications [*A publication*]
Astron Soc Pacific Pubs ... Astronomical Society of the Pacific. Publications [*A publication*]
Astron Soc Pac Leafl ... Astronomical Society of the Pacific. Leaflet [*A publication*]
Astron & Space ... Astronomy and Space [*A publication*]
Astron Tidsskr ... Astronomisk Tidsskrift [*A publication*]
Astron Tsirk ... Astronomicheskii Tsirkulyar [*USSR*] [*A publication*]
Astron Vestn ... Astronomicheskii Vestnik [*A publication*]
Astron Zh ... Astronomicheskii Zhurnal [*A publication*]
Astroph J S ... Astrophysical Journal. Supplement Series [*A publication*]
Astrophys .. Astrophysics [*A publication*]
Astrophys Gravitation Proc Solvay Conf Phys ... Astrophysics and Gravitation. Proceedings of the Solvay Conference on Physics [*A publication*]
Astrophys J ... Astrophysical Journal [*A publication*]
Astrophys J Lett Ed ... Astrophysical Journal. Letters to the Editor [*A publication*]
Astrophys J Suppl ... Astrophysical Journal. Supplement [*A publication*]
Astrophys J Suppl Ser ... Astrophysical Journal. Supplement Series [*A publication*]
Astrophys L ... Astrophysical Letters [*A publication*]
Astrophys Lett ... Astrophysical Letters [*A publication*]
Astrophys Norv ... Astrophysica Norvegica [*Norway*] [*A publication*]
Astrophys & Space Sci ... Astrophysics and Space Science [*A publication*]
Astrophys Space Sci ... Astrophysics and Space Science [*A publication*]
Astrophys Space Sci Lib ... Astrophysics and Space Science Library [*Reidel, Dordrecht*] [*A publication*]
Astrophys Space Sci Libr ... Astrophysics and Space Science Library [*A publication*]
ASTROS ... Automated Shell Theory for Rotating Structures [*NASA*]
ASTROSPACE ... Astronautics and Space (KSC)
Astro Sp Sc ... Astrophysics and Space Science [*A publication*]
ASTRP ...... Army Specialized Training Reserve Program
Astrux .... Astruxius [*Authority cited in pre-1607 legal work*] (DSA)
ASTS .... Administrative Systems Testing Section [*Social Security Administration*]
ASTS .... Airport Surface Traffic Simulator
ASTS .... American Sabbath Tract Society [*Later, ASTCC*] (EA)
ASTS .... American Society of Transplant Surgeons (EA)
ASTS .... Armament System Test Set (MCD)
ASTS .... Automated Stock Transfer System (MCD)
ASTS .... Avionics System Test Specification (MCD)
ASTSC ...... Annals of Statistics [*A publication*]
ASTSECAF ... Assistant Secretary of the Air Force
ASTSECNAV ... Assistant Secretary of the Navy
ASTSECNAVAIR ... Assistant Secretary of the Navy for Air
ASTSECNAVFIN ... Assistant Secretary of the Navy (Financial Management)
ASTSECNAVINSLOG ... Assistant Secretary of the Navy (Installation and Logistics)
ASTSECNAVRESDEV ... Assistant Secretary of the Navy (Research and Development)
ASTSP .... American-Soviet Textbook Study Project [*An association*] (EA)
ASTSWMO ... Association of State and Territorial Solid Waste Management Officials (EA)
ASTT .... American Society of Traffic and Transportation (EA)
ASTT .... Apollo Special Task Team [*NASA*]
ASTt .... Arctic Small Tool Tradition [*Archeology*]
ASTT .... Associate in Science in Teacher Training
ASTT .... Astarte. Journal of Arctic Biology [*A publication*]
ASTTA8 .... ASTM [*American Society for Testing and Materials*] Special Technical Publication [*A publication*]
ASTTB9 .... Astarte [*A publication*]
ASTTCM .. Amalgamated Society of Telegraph and Telephone Construction Men [*A union*] [*British*]
ASTTE ...... Artillery Siege Train Traction Engine [*British*]
ASTU .... Air Support Test Unit
ASTU .... Air Support Training Units
ASTU .... Army Specialized Training Unit
ASTU .... Automatic Systems Test Unit

ASTUTE ... Association of System 2000 Users for Technical Exchange
ASTV .... American Communications and Television, Inc. [*NASDAQ symbol*] (NQ)
ASTVC ...... American Society of TV Cameramen (EA)
AST/VCE ... Acoustic Shield Thermal/Variable Cycle Engine (MCD)
ASTW .... Tamworth [*Australia*] [*ICAO location identifier*] (ICLI)
ASTWg .... Aerospace Test Wing [*Air Force*] (AFM)
ASTWKT .. Amalgamated Society of Textile Workers and Kindred Trades [*A union*] [*British*] (DCTA)
Asty .... Artistry [*Record label*]
ASTYD ...... Aerosol Science and Technology [*A publication*]
ASTZA5 .... Atti. Simposio Internazionale di Zootecnia [*A publication*]
ASU .... Acknowledgement Signal Unit [*Telecommunications*] (TEL)
ASU .... Acoustic Sensor Unit [*Navy*] (CAAL)
ASU .... Active Service Unit [*Irish Republican Army*] [*Northern Ireland*]
ASU .... Administrative Service Unit
ASU .... Administrative Support Unit
ASU .... Aeromedical Staging Unit (AFM)
ASU .... Air Separation Unit [*For oxygen production*]
ASU .... Aircraft Scheduling Unit
ASU .... Aircraft Starting Unit
ASU .... Aircraft Storage Unit [*Military*] [*British*]
ASU .... Airspur, Inc. [*Los Angeles, CA*] [*FAA designator*] (FAAC)
ASU .... Altitude Sensing Unit [*Aviation*] (AIA)
ASU .... American School and University [*A publication*]
ASU .... American Servicemen's Union (EA)
ASU .... American Snowshoers Union (EA)
ASU .... American Student Union
ASU .... Analog Stimulus Unit
ASu .... Anthroponymica Suecana [*A publication*]
ASU .... Antisurface Ship Warfare [*Navy*] (CAAL)
ASU .... Appalachian State University [*Boone, NC*]
ASU .... Approval for Service Use [*Military*] (NVT)
ASU .... Arab Socialist Union [*Syria*] [*Political party*] (PPW)
ASU .... Arab Socialist Union [*Egypt*] [*Political party*] (PPW)
ASU .... Area Service Unit
ASU .... Area of Substantial Unemployment [*CETA*] [*Department of Labor*]
ASU .... Arizona State University [*Arizona*] [*Seismograph station code, US Geological Survey*] (SEIS)
ASU .... Arkansas State University [*Beebe*]
ASU .... Arkansas State University Library, State University, AR [*OCLC symbol*] (OCLC)
ASU .... Aston Resources Ltd. [*Vancouver Stock Exchange symbol*]
ASU .... Astronomy Study Unit [*American Topical Association*] (EA)
ASU .... Asuncion [*Paraguay*] [*Airport symbol*] (OAG)
ASU .... Automatic Switching Unit [*Telecommunications*]
ASU .... Automotive Study Unit [*American Topical Association*] (EA)
ASU .... Auxiliary Sensor Unit (MCD)
a-su--- .... Saudi Arabia [*MARC geographic area code*] [*Library of Congress*] (LCCP)
As U A .... Annales. Universite d'Abidjan [*A publication*]
ASUBJSCD ... Army Subject Schedule (AABC)
ASU Bus Tchr ... Arizona State University. Business Teacher [*A publication*]
ASUC .... American Society of University Composers (EA)
ASUC .... American Society of University Composers. Proceedings [*A publication*]
ASUC .... Associated Students of the University of California
ASUD .... Aerovia Sud Americana
ASUG .... American Software Users Group (EA)
ASUHA ..... Asufaruto [*A publication*]
ASUI .... American Society of Utility Investors (EA)
ASUI .... Analele Stiintifice ale Universitatii (Iasi) [*A publication*]
ASULAN .... Agrisul [*A publication*]
ASULGC ... Association of State Universities and Land-Grant Colleges (EA)
ASUN .... Sundre Public Library, Alberta [*Library symbol*] [*National Library of Canada*] (NLC)
ASUNB ..... American School and University [*A publication*]
Asuntos Agr ... Asuntos Agrarios [*A publication*]
ASUNW .... Sunwapta Shores Public Library, Alberta [*Library symbol*] [*National Library of Canada*] (NLC)
ASUP .... Air Supply
ASUP .... AUTODIN Switch Upgrade Project (MCD)
ASUPA ...... Aluminium Sulphate Producers Association (EAIO)
ASUPT ...... Advanced Simulator for Undergraduate Pilot Training [*Air Force*]
A/SUPT ..... Assistant Superintendent (DCTA)
ASURS ...... Advanced Surveillance and Reconnaissance Systems
ASUS .... Apostleship of the Sea in the United States (EA)
A/SUSP ..... Air Suspension [*Automotive engineering*]
ASUSSR ..... Academy of Science (Union of Soviet Socialist Republics)
ASUT .... Adapter Subunit Tester
ASUT .... Association Suisse d'Usagers de Telecommunications [*Swiss Association of Telecommunications Users*] [*Zurich*] (TSSD)
ASUTS ...... American Society of Ultrasound Technical Specialists [*Later, SDMS*] (EA)
Asutustoiminnan Aikak ... Asutustoiminnan Aikakauskirja [*A publication*]
ASU-USA ... Amateur Skating Union of the United States of America (EA)

ASUVCW ... Auxiliary to Sons of Union Veterans of the Civil War   (EA)
ASUVDM ... Annales Scientifiques. Universite de Besancon. Biologie Vegetale [*A publication*]
ASUW .... Antiship Underwater Warfare   (MCD)
ASUW .... Antisurface Warfare [*Navy*]
ASUWC..... Antisurface Warfare Commander [*Navy*]
ASV .... Acceleration Switching Valve
ASV .... Adaptive Sensing Vehicle [*Robot*]
ASV .... Advocates for a Safe Vaccine   (EA)
ASV .... Aerospace Vehicle   (KSC)
ASV .... Aerothermodynamic Structural Vehicle [*Air Force*]
ASV .... Air Charter Services [*West Hartford, CT*] [*FAA designator*]   (FAAC)
ASV .... Air Shutoff Valve
ASV .... Air Solenoid Valve
ASV .... Air Suction Valve [*Automotive engineering*]
ASV .... Airborne Surface Vessel Detection [*RADAR device*]
ASV .... Aircraft-to-Surface Vessel [*Navy*]
ASV .... All Systems Vehicle
ASV .... Alpine Silver Ltd. [*Vancouver Stock Exchange symbol*]
ASV .... Aluminum Structured Vehicle [*Automotive engineering*]
ASV .... American Standard Version [*of the Bible, 1901*]
ASV .... Angle Stop Valve [*Technical drawings*]
ASV .... Anode Supply Voltage
ASV .... Anodic Stripping Voltammetry [*Chemical analysis*]
ASV .... Antisnake Venom [*Medicine*]
ASV .... Antisurface Vessel [*Navy*]
ASV .... Arithmetic Simple Variable
ASV .... Armored Security Vehicle [*Army*]
ASV .... Armored Support Vehicle   (MCD)
ASV .... Asset Share Value [*Insurance*]
ASV .... Authorized Standard Version [*of the Bible*] [*A publication*]
ASV .... Autogenous Saphenous Vein (Graft) [*Surgery*]
ASV .... Automatic Self-Verification
ASV .... Automatic Shuttle Valve
ASV .... Auxiliary Survey Vessel [*Oceanography*]   (MSC)
ASV .... Avian Sarcoma Virus [*Same as RSV*]
ASV .... RADAR [*Navy symbol*] [*Obsolete*] [*British*]
ASVA........ Associate of the Incorporated Society of Valuers and Auctioneers [*British*]   (DBQ)
ASVAB..... Armed Services Vocational Aptitude Battery [*Tests*]
A/Svc........ Air Service
ASVC........ Automatic Secure Voice Communications   (CAAL)
ASVD .... Allstar Video, Inc. [*NASDAQ symbol*]   (NQ)
ASVE........ American Society of Veterinary Ethology   (EA)
ASVI......... American Society for Value Inquiry   (EA)
ASVIP .... American Standard Vocabulary for Information Processing   (BUR)
ASVIP .... Atrial Synchronous Ventricular Inhibited Pacemaker [*Cardiology*]
ASVO .... American Society of Veterinary Ophthalmology   (EA)
ASVPP ...... American Society of Veterinary Physiologists and Pharmacologists   (EA)
ASVS .... Airborne Stabilized Viewing System
ASVS .... Automatic Signature Verification System
ASVSA ...... Aansteeklike Siektesvereniging van Suider Afrika [*Infectious Diseases Society of Southern Africa*]   (EAIO)
ASVT........ Applications Systems Verification Test [*NASA*]
ASVT........ Applications Systems Verification and Transfer   (MCD)
ASW .... Absatzwirtschaft Data Bank [*Dusseldorf, Federal Republic of Germany*] [*Database producer*] [*Information service or system*]   (IID)
ASW .... Abstracts for Social Workers [*A publication*]
ASW .... Acoustic Surface Wave
ASW .... Administration in Social Work [*A publication*]
ASW .... Air-to-Surface Weapon
ASW .... Allied Steel and Wire, Ltd. [*British*]
AS & W...... American Steel and Wire Gauge
ASW .... Antisubmarine Warfare
ASW .... Antisubmarine Weapon   (NATG)
ASW .... Applications Software [*Data processing*]
ASW .... Artificial Seawater
AsW .... Asia Watch Committee   (EA)
ASW .... Assistant Secretary of War
ASW .... Aswan [*Egypt*] [*Airport symbol*]   (OAG)
ASW .... Australia Standard White [*Variety of wheat*]
ASW .... Australian Social Welfare [*A publication*]   (ADA)
ASW .... Australian Standard White [*Wheat*]   (ADA)
ASW .... Automotive Specialty Warehouse
ASW .... Auxiliary Switch [*Electricity*]
ASW .... Southwest Region [*FAA*]   (FAAC)
ASW .... Warsaw, IN [*Location identifier*] [*FAA*]   (FAAL)
ASWA .... American Society of Women Accountants   (EA)
ASWA .... American Steel Warehouse Association [*Later, SSCI*]
ASWA .... Assistant Secretary of War for Air [*World War II*]
ASWA .... Audio Switch Assembly [*Ground Communications Facility, NASA*]
A/SWA ...... Aviation/Space Writers Association
ASWAAF .. Arms and Services with the Army Air Forces
ASW/AAW ... Antisubmarine Warfare and Antiair Warfare
ASWAC..... Aerospace Warning and Control   (MCD)

ASWAC..... Antisubmarine Warfare Advisory Committee
ASWACS .. Antisubmarine Warfare Air Control Ship   (NVT)
ASWAF ..... Arms and Services on Duty with Air Force
ASWASP... Antisubmarine Warfare Airborne Simulation Program [*Navy*]   (CAAL)
ASWB........ Antisubmarine Warfare Barriers [*Military*]
ASWBPL... Armed Services Whole Blood Processing Laboratory   (AABC)
ASWC....... Antisubmarine Warfare Center [*NATO*]   (NATG)
ASWC....... Antisubmarine Warfare Commander [*Navy*]   (NVT)
ASWC........ Army Special Warfare Center
ASWC........ ASW [*Antisubmarine Warfare*] Coordinator   (MCD)
ASWCCCS ... Antisubmarine Warfare Centers Command and Control System [*Navy*]   (CAAL)
ASWCCS... Antisubmarine Warfare Command and Control Centers System   (MCD)
ASWCR..... Airborne Surveillance Warning and Control RADAR [*ASD/ADC*]
ASWCRL .. Appalachian Soil and Water Conservation Research Laboratory [*Beckley, WV*] [*Department of Agriculture*]   (GRD)
ASWCS ..... Antisubmarine Warfare Control System [*Navy*]   (CAAL)
ASWCSI... Antisubmarine Warfare Combat System Integration [*Navy*]   (CAAL)
A/SWD...... Antisubmarine War Division [*British*]
ASWD .... Army Special Weapons Depot
ASWDKW ... Amalgamated Society of Wire Drawers and Kindred Workers [*A union*] [*British*]   (DCTA)
ASWE........ Admiralty Surface Weapons Establishment [*British*]
ASWEA ..... Association for Social Work Education in Africa [*See also AESA*]   (EAIO)
ASWEC ..... Antisubmarine Warfare Electronic Countermeasures System   (MCD)
ASWEPS... Antisubmarine Weapons Environmental Prediction Service [*Navy*]
ASWEX..... Antisubmarine Warfare Exercise   (NVT)
ASWF........ [*A*] Special Wish Foundation   (EA)
ASWFCO.. Antisubmarine Warfare Fire Control Officer [*Navy*]   (CAAL)
ASWFORSIXTHF ... Antisubmarine Warfare Force, Sixth Fleet [*Navy*]
ASWG .... American Steel and Wire Gauge
ASWG .... Wagga Wagga [*Australia*] [*ICAO location identifier*]   (ICLI)
ASWGRU ... Antisubmarine Warfare Group
ASWGW ... Anti-Submarine Wire-Guided Weapon [*British military*]   (DMA)
ASWH .... Advise Soldier Write Home
ASWHS..... Advanced Submarine Weapon Handling System   (MCD)
ASWI .... Antisubmarine Warfare Installations [*NATO*]   (NATG)
ASWICS.... Antisubmarine Warfare Integrated Combat System [*Navy*]   (MCD)
ASWILS.... Antisubmarine Warfare Improved Localization System   (NVT)
ASWIPT.... Antisubmarine Warfare Training in Port [*Navy*]   (NVT)
ASWIXS.... Antisubmarine Warfare Information Exchange System [*or Subsystem*] [*Navy*]   (NVT)
ASWL........ Antisubmarine Warfare Laboratory [*Military*]
ASWLC ..... American Shortwave Listeners Club   (EA)
ASW-LR.... Antisubmarine Warning - Long Range   (NATG)
ASWM ...... Antisubmarine Warfare Missile [*Navy*]   (CAAL)
ASWM ...... Association of State Wetland Managers   (EA)
ASWM ...... ASW [*Antisubmarine Warfare*] Module [*Navy*]
ASWM ...... Williamtown [*Australia*] [*ICAO location identifier*]   (ICLI)
ASWO .... Air Stations Weekly Orders [*Navy*]
ASWO .... Antisubmarine Warfare Officer [*Navy*]   (CAAL)
ASWOC .... Antisubmarine Warfare Operations Centers [*Navy*]   (NVT)
ASWOC .... Antisubmarine Warfare Operations Controller [*Navy*]   (CAAL)
ASWORG ... Antisubmarine Warfare Operational Research Group [*World War II*]
ASWPO..... Antisubmarine Warfare Project Office [*Navy*]
ASWPTL... Antisubmarine Warfare Operations Patrol   (NVT)
ASWR........ Antisubmarine Warfare Systems Project Office [*Washington, DC*] [*Navy*]
ASWRC..... Antisubmarine Warfare Research Center [*NATO*]   (NATG)
AS²WRE.... American Society of Senior Wire Rope Engineers   (EA)
ASWRECEN ... Antisubmarine Warfare Research Center [*NATO*]   (NATG)
ASWS .... Advanced Strike Weapon System   (MCD)
ASWS .... Aerospace Surveillance Warning System   (MCD)
ASWS .... Antisubmarine Warfare Systems [*Navy*]
ASWSAG .. Antisubmarine Warfare Systems Analysis Group [*Navy*]
ASWSCCS ... Antisubmarine Warfare Ship Command and Control System   (NVT)
ASW/SOW ... Antisubmarine Warfare Standoff Weapon
ASWSPO .. Antisubmarine Warfare Systems Project Office [*Navy*]
ASW-SR.... Antisubmarine Warning - Short Range   (NATG)
ASWSS...... Antisubmarine Warfare Schoolship [*Navy*]   (NVT)
ASWTACSCOL ... Antisubmarine Warfare Tactical School
ASWTC..... Antisubmarine Warfare Training Center [*Navy*]
ASWTDS .. Antisubmarine Warfare Tactical Data System [*Navy*]   (NVT)
ASWTNS .. Antisubmarine Warfare Tactical Navigation System [*Navy*]   (NG)
ASWTRACEN ... Antisubmarine Warfare Training Center [*Navy*]
ASWTRO ... Antisubmarine Warfare Test Requirement Outline   (MCD)
ASWTU..... Antisubmarine Warfare Training Unit
ASWTV..... Antisubmarine Warfare Target Vehicle   (MCD)
ASWU .... Antisubmarine Warfare Unit [*Navy*]

ASW/UW ...	Antisubmarine Warfare/Underwater Warfare
ASWW	Amalgamated Society of Wood Workers [*British*]
ASX...........	Air South, Inc. [*Mobile, AL*] [*FAA designator*]　(FAAC)
ASX...........	Ashland [*Wisconsin*] [*Airport symbol*] [*Obsolete*]　(OAG)
Asx...........	Aspartic Acid [*or Asparagine*] [*Also, B*] [*An amino acid*]
ASX...........	Australian Stock Exchange　(ADA)
ASXBA8 ...	Archives of Sexual Behavior [*A publication*]
ASXT........	American Society of X-Ray Technicians [*Later, ASRT*]
ASY.........	Advanced Systems, Inc. [*NYSE symbol*]　(SPSG)
ASY...........	Agriculture Statistical Yearbook and Agriculture Sample [*Amman*] [*A publication*]
ASY...........	Ashley, ND [*Location identifier*] [*FAA*]　(FAAL)
ASY...........	Aslib Information [*A publication*]
ASY...........	Association and Society Manager [*A publication*]
ASY...........	Astounding Stories Yearbook [*A publication*]
ASY...........	Asylum
a-sy---	Syria [*MARC geographic area code*] [*Library of Congress*]　(LCCP)
ASYA........	American Stock Yards Association　(EA)
ASYG........	Assistant Secretary General　(NATG)
ASYL........	Asylum
ASYL........	Sylvan Lake Public Library, Alberta [*Library symbol*] [*National Library of Canada*]　(NLC)
ASYM......	Association of Synthetic Yarn Manufacturers　(EA)
ASYM.......	Asymmetric　(MSA)
ASYMCA..	Association of Secretaries Young Men's Christian Associations [*Later, YMCA*]
ASYMP.....	Asymptote [*Mathematics*]
ASYN	Asynchronous　(MSA)
ASYNBA...	Association des Syndicats du Benin [*Employers' organization*] [*Benin*]　(EY)
ASYNC......	Asynchronous
ASYNCH ..	Asynchronous
ASYS	Amtech Systems, Inc. [*NASDAQ symbol*]　(NQ)
ASYSTD....	Advanced System Time Domain
ASZ...........	Allgemeine Sport-Zeitung [*A publication*]
ASZ...........	American Society of Zoologists　(EA)
ASZ...........	Ashizuri [*Japan*] [*Seismograph station code, US Geological Survey*]　(SEIS)
ASZ...........	Assistenz [*Germany*] [*A publication*]
ASZBAI.....	Archivum Societatis Zoologicae-Botanicae Fennicae "Vanamo" [*A publication*]
ASZD........	American Society for Zero Defects [*Later, American Society for Performance Improvement*]
A Szekely Nemz Muz ...	A Szekely Nemzeti Muzeum Ertesitoeje [*A publication*]
A Szekely Nemz Muz Ertes ...	A Szekely Nemzeti Muzeum Ertesitoeje [*A publication*]
AS Zg........	Aerztliche Sachverstaendigen-Zeitung [*A publication*]
ASZOAN ..	Annales Scientifiques. Universite de Besancon. Zoologie [*A publication*]
AT	A Tempo [*In Strict Time*] [*Music*]
AT	Absolute Threshold
AT	Absolute Title [*Business term*]
AT.............	Acceptance Tag　(NRCH)
AT.............	Acceptance Test　(NRCH)
AT	[*On-Site*] Acceptance and Training
A & T	Acceptance and Transfer
AT	Acceptance Trials [*Shipbuilding*]
AT	Access Time
AT	Accounting Tabulating [*Card*]　(AAG)
AT.............	Achievement Test
AT.............	Achilles Tendon [*Anatomy*]
AT.............	Across Tape [*Curve*]
AT.............	Act Together　(EA)
AT.............	Action Taken
A/T	Action Time [*Air Force*]
AT.............	Active Training [*Army*]
AT.............	Adapter, Tee
AT.............	Address Translator [*Data processing*]
AT.............	Adjunctive Therapy [*Medicine*]
AT.............	Administrative Trainee [*Civil Service*] [*British*]
AT.............	Advanced Technology [*In PC AT, model name of a computer*] [*IBM Corp.*]
AT.............	Advanced Trainer [*Air Force*]
AT	Aerial Tape Armor [*Telecommunications*]　(TEL)
AT	Aerial Torpedo
AT	Aerial Tours [*Australia*]
AT.............	Africa Today [*A publication*]
A & T	Agricultural and Technical [*In a college name*]
AT.............	Agronomie Tropicale [*A publication*]
AT.............	Air Technician [*Air National Guard*]　(AFM)
AT	Air Temperature
AT	Air Traffic Service [*of FAA*] [*Also known as AAT, ATS*]　(FAAC)
AT	Air Transmit
AT	Air Transport [*Military*]
AT	Airtight [*Technical drawings*]
AT	[*The*] Alalakh Tablets　(BJA)
AT	Alcadd Test [*Psychology*]
AT	Alcohol and Tobacco Tax Division [*Internal Revenue Service*] [*United States*]　(DLA)
AT	All Together　(EA)
AT	Allergen Tachyphylaxis [*Immunology*]
A/T	Allowance Type [*Military*]　(AFIT)
AT	ALLTEL Corp. [*Formerly, Allied Telephone Co.*] [*NYSE symbol*]　(SPSG)
AT	Alternative Technology
AT	Altes Testament [*Old Testament*] [*German*]
AT	Amateur Station [*ITU designation*]
AT	Ambient Temperature
AT	American Terms [*Business term*]
AT	American Translation [*of the Bible*]
AT	American Turners　(EA)
AT	Aminotransferase [*An enzyme*]
AT	Amitriptyline [*Also, AMI*] [*Antidepressant compound*]
AT	Ammunition Technician [*British military*]　(DMA)
AT	Amount Tendered
A-T	Ampere-Turn [*Technical drawings*]
A/T	Amperes per Terminal
AT	Analecta Tarraconensia [*A publication*]
A/T	Analog to Time　(MCD)
AT	Analysis Time
AT	Anaphylatoxin [*Immunology*]
AT	Ancien Testament [*Old Testament*] [*French*]
AT	Angle Template
A/T	Angle Tracker　(MUGU)
AT	Angle of Train
AT	Animal Transport [*British and Canadian*] [*World War II*]
AT	Annual Tour
AT	Annual Training [*Military*]　(AFM)
AT	Antennas, Simple [*JETDS nomenclature*] [*Military*]　(CET)
AT	Anterior Tibial (Muscle) [*Anatomy*]
AT	Antik Tanulmanyok [*A publication*]
AT	Antitank [*Also, ATk*]
AT	Antithrombin [*Hematology*]
AT	Antitorpedo [*Navy*]
AT	Antitrypsin [*Biochemistry*]
AT	Antur Teifi [*Teifi Valley Business Centre*] [*British*]
AT	Appalachian Trail
AT	Apparent Time　(ADA)
AT	Appeal Tribunal　(DLA)
AT	Applanation Tonometry [*Ophthalmology*]
AT	Apply Template　(MCD)
AT	Appropriate Technology
AT	Aptitude Test
AT	Arch-Treasurer
AT	Archeolgrafo Triestino [*A publication*]
AT	Arizona Territory [*Obsolete*]　(ROG)
AT	Armament Test
AT	Armoured Tractor [*British*]
AT	Armoured Train [*British*]
AT	Army Telegraph [*Stamp surcharge*] [*British*]　(ROG)
AT	Army of Tennessee, CSA [*An association*]　(EA)
AT	Army Transport [*British military*]　(DMA)
AT	Arrival Time　(AABC)
AT	Artillery　(CINC)
AT	Artillery Tractor [*British*]
AT	ASCAP [*American Society of Composers, Authors, and Publishers*] in Action [*A publication*]
AT	Aspartocin [*Endocrinology*]
AT	Asphalt Tile [*Technical drawings*]
AT	Assay Ton
A & T	Assemble and Test
A/T	Assembly and Test [*Aerospace*]　(AAG)
AT	Associate in Technology
AT	Assortment
At	Astatine [*Chemical element*]
AT	Astern Flag [*Navy*] [*British*]
AT	Astronomical Time
AT	Ataxia Telangiectasia [*Genetic disease*]
At	Atenea [*A publication*]
AT	Athlone Resources Ltd. [*Vancouver Stock Exchange symbol*]
AT	Atlantic Ocean
At	Atlantic Reporter [*A publication*]　(DLA)
AT	Atlantic Standard Time
At	Atlantida [*A publication*]
AT	Atlas Chemical Industries, Inc. [*Research code symbol*]
AT	Atlin News Miner [*A publication*]
at	Atmosphere, Technical [*Unit of pressure*]
AT	Atomic
AT	Atomic Time
AT	Atopic Dermatitis [*Medicine*]
A/T	Attack Teacher
AT	Attenuation　(DEN)
AT	Audit Trail
AT	Aufbereitungs-Technik [*A publication*]
AT	Auroral Time [*Geophysics*]
at	Australia [*MARC country of publication code*] [*Library of Congress*]　(LCCP)
AT	Austria [*ANSI two-letter standard code*]　(CNC)

AT	Author's Time [Publishing]
AT	Autogenic Training [Influencing the body through autosuggestion]
AT	Automated [or Automatic] Teller Machine (ADA)
AT	Automatic TAEM [Terminal Area Energy Management] [NASA] (NASA)
AT	Automatic Test
AT	Automatic Ticketing
AT	Automatic Translation
A/T	Automatic Transmission [Automotive engineering]
AT	Automatic Transmitter
A/T	Autothrottle [Aerospace]
AT	Autumn [A publication]
AT	Auxiliary Timer
AT	Available Time
AT	Aviation Electronics Technician [Navy rating]
AT	Awaiting Transportation (AFM)
AT	[The] Bible - An American Translation (1935) [A publication] (BJA)
AT	Royal Air Maroc - Compagnie Nationale de Transports Aeriens [Morocco] [ICAO designator] (FAAC)
AT	Simple Antenna (MCD)
at-----	Tienshan Mountain Region [MARC geographic area code] [Library of Congress] (LCCP)
AT	Tug, Ocean-Going [Navy symbol]
AT1	Aviation Electronics Technician, First Class [Navy rating]
AT1	West Kanaga [Alaska] [Seismograph station code, US Geological Survey] [Closed] (SEIS)
AT2	Aviation Electronics Technician, Second Class [Navy rating]
AT2	South Tanaga [Alaska] [Seismograph station code, US Geological Survey] [Closed] (SEIS)
AT³	Advanced Technology Tactical Transport [Proposed low-altitude long-range airlifter] [Military]
AT3	Appropriate Technology in the Third World [G. V. Olsen Associates] [Information service or system] (CRD)
AT3	Aviation Electronics Technician, Third Class [Navy rating]
AT3	North Tanaga [Alaska] [Seismograph station code, US Geological Survey] [Closed] (SEIS)
AT-10	Anti-Tetany Substance 10 [Same as DHT, Dihydrotachysterol] [Pharmacology]
AT40	America's Top 40 [Radio program]
ATA	Abort Time Assembly [NASA] (NASA)
ATA	Abstracts on Tropical Agriculture [Information service or system] [A publication]
ATA	Academic Travel Abroad (EA)
ATA	Actoma Resources Ltd. [Vancouver Stock Exchange symbol]
ATA	Actual Time of Arrival
ATA	Additional Training Assemblies
ATA	Administrative Telecommunications Agency [Canada]
ATA	Admission Temporaire/Temporary Admission [Customs] (IMH)
ATA	Advanced Tactical Aircraft [Army]
ATA	Advanced Test Accelerator [Lawrence Livermore National Laboratory]
ATA	Advanced Transport Aircraft (MCD)
ATA	Advertising Typographers Association (EA)
ATA	Africa Travel Association (EA)
ATA	Agence des Telecommunications Administratives [Administrative Telecommunications Agency] [Canada]
ATA	Aid to Artisans (EA)
ATA	Air-to-Air
ATA	Air Force Training Auxiliary [British]
ATA	Air Training Advisor (NATG)
ATA	Air Transport Association of America (EA)
ATA	Air Transport Auxiliary [British] [World War II]
ATA	Air Turbine Alternator
ATA	Airborne Target Augmenter
ATA	Aircraft Development Test Activity [Army] (MCD)
ATA	Airport Traffic Area (MCD)
ATA	Albanian Telegraphic Agency [News agency] (EY)
ATA	Alimentary Toxic Aleukia
ATAAC	Aloe Technology Association (EA)
ATA	Alpha Tau Alpha (EA)
ATA	Alternative to Amniocentesis [Medicine]
ATAM	Alternative Technology Association [Australia]
ATA	Alttestamentliche Abhandlungen [Muenster] [A publication]
ATA	Amateur Television Association (EA)
ATA	Amateur Trapshooting Association (EA)
ATA	American Tarentaise Association (EA)
ATA	American Taxation Association (EA)
ATA	American Taxicab Association [Later, ITA] (EA)
ATA	American Taxpayers Association
ATA	American Teachers Association [Later, NEA] (EA)
ATA	American Teilhard Association (EA)
ATA	American Telemarketing Association [Deerfield, IL] (EA)
ATA	American Tennis Association (EA)
ATA	American Theatre Annual [A publication]
ATA	American Theatre Association [Defunct] (EA)
ATA	American Thyroid Association (EA)
ATA	American Tinnitus Association (EA)
ATA	American Title Association [Later, ALTA]
ATA	American Topical Association (EA)
ATA	American Traffic Association
ATA	American Trainers Association (EA)
ATA	American Trakehner Association (EA)
ATA	American Transit Association [Later, APTA] (EA)
ATA	American Translators Association (EA)
ATA	American Transplant Association (EA)
ATA	American Travel Association [Later, ATI]
ATA	American Tree Association
ATA	American Trucking Associations (EA)
ATA	American Tube Association/FMA (EA)
ATA	American Tunaboat Association (EA)
ATA	Aminotriazole [Herbicide]
ATA	Angling Trade Association (EAIO)
ATA	Annee Theologique Augustinienne [A publication]
ATA	Anta [Peru] [Airport symbol] (OAG)
ATA	Antarctica [ANSI three-letter standard code] (CNC)
AT/A	Antiquity. A Quarterly Review of Archaeology. Antiquity Trust [A publication]
ATA	Antithyroglobulin Antibody [Immunochemistry]
ATA	Appropriation Transfer Account (AFM)
ATA	ARCNET Trade Association (EA)
ATA	Army Transportation Association
ATA	Artra Group, Inc. [NYSE symbol] (SPSG)
ATA	Assembly and Test Area [NASA] (KSC)
ATA	Associate Technical Aide
ATA	Associate in Technical Arts
ATA	Association for Academic Travel Abroad (EA)
ATA	Association of Talent Agents (EA)
ATA	Association of Technical Artists [Later, IG]
ATA	Association des Technologistes Agricoles [Association of Agricultural Technologists] [Canada]
ATA	Association des Technologistes Agro-Alimentaires [Association of Subsistence Agriculture Technologists] [Canada]
ATA	Association du Traite Atlantique [Atlantic Treaty Association] (EAIO)
ATA	Association des Tremblay d'Amerique [Tremblay (Family) Association of America] [Canada]
ATA	Asynchronous Terminal Adapter [Telecommunications]
ATA	Atar [Djibouti] [Seismograph station code, US Geological Survey] (SEIS)
ATA	Atlanta, TX [Location identifier] [FAA] (FAAL)
ATA	Atlantic Treaty Association (EA)
ATA	Atmosphere, Absolute
ATA	Auditor of Traffic Accounts
ATA	Australian Taxpayers' Association
ATA	Australian Trainers Association
ATA	Australian Transcontinental Airways
ATA	Authorization for Temporary Admission [Customs]
ATA	Auto-Throttle Actuator (MCD)
ATA	Automated Testing Analyzer [Data processing]
ATA	Automatic Target Acquisition (MCD)
ATA	Automatic Terrain Avoidance [Air Force]
ATA	Automatic Track Acquisition
ATA	Automatic Tracking Antenna
ATA	Automatic Trouble Analysis (TEL)
ATA	Automotive Technicians Association International (EA)
ATA	Auxiliary Ocean Tug [Navy symbol]
ATA	Auxiliary Timer Assembly
ATA	Average T-Matrix Approximation (MCD)
ATA	Average Turnaround [Data processing]
ATA	Aviation Training Aids
ATA	Avionics Test Article (NASA)
ATA	Azimuth Torquer Amplifier
ATA	Taber Public Library, Alberta [Library symbol] [National Library of Canada] (NLC)
ATAA	Air Transport Association of America
ATAA	Aminothiazoleneacetic Acid [Biochemistry]
ATAA	Army Theatre Arts Association (EA)
ATAA	Assembly of Turkish American Associations (EA)
ATAA	Auto-Throttle Actuator Assembly (MCD)
ATAAC	Air-to-Air Aftercooling System [Pronounced "attack"]
ATAAD	Antitank Assault Air Defense (MCD)
ATAADS	Antitank/Assault/Air Defense System (MCD)
ATAAM	Advanced Tactical Air-to-Air Missile (MCD)
ATABCS	Airborne Tactical Air Battle Control System
ATABE	Automatic Target and Battery Evaluation [Military]
At Absorpt Newsl	Atomic Absorption Newsletter [A publication]
ATABW	American Trade Association for British Woolens (EA)
ATAC	Abbreviated Transportation Accounting Classification [Army]
ATAC	Advanced Tactical
ATAC	Advanced Tanker Cargo [Aircraft] (MCD)
ATAC	Air Transport Advisory Council [British]
ATAC	Air Transport Association of Canada
ATAC	Air Transportable Acoustic Communications (CAAL)
ATAC	Airborne Tactical Air Coordinator [Navy] (NVT)
ATAC	Airborne Two-Way Acoustic and Control System (MCD)
ATAC	All Tariffs Computerized [Project]
ATAC	American Transportation Advisory Council
ATAC	Applied Technology Advanced Computer
ATAC	Army Tank-Automotive Center [or Command] [Warren, MI]

ATAC .... Australian Time Assignment Committee
At Acad Med S Paulo ... Atos. Academia de Medicina de Sao Paulo [*A publication*]
ATACAP ... Antenna to Antenna Compatibility Analysis Program   (MCD)
ATAC (Asoc Tec Azucar Cuba) ... ATAC (Asociacion de Tecnicos Azucareros de Cuba) [*A publication*]
ATACC...... Airborne Tactical Air Control Capability [*Air Force*]   (AFM)
ATACC...... Automatic Tactical Air Control Center   (MCD)
ATACC7.... ATAC (Asociacion de Tecnicos Azucareros de Cuba) [*A publication*]
ATACCIS ... Army Tactical Command and Control/Information System   (MCD)
ATACC J ... ATACC [*Alberta Teachers' Association, Computer Council*] Journal [*A publication*]
ATACCO... Aviation Tactical Coordinator [*Navy*]   (NVT)
ATACCS ... Advanced Tactical Air Command and Control System   (MCD)
ATACM .. Army Tactical Missile System   (MCD)
ATACMS.. Army Tactical Missile System   (RDA)
ATACNET ... Analysis of Tactical Single Channel Net Radios   (MCD)
ATACO ..... Air Tactical Control Officer   (NVT)
ATACO ..... Air Tactical Control Operator
ATACO ..... Assistant Tactical Officer [*Navy*]   (CAAL)
ATAC Rev Bimest Asoc Tec Azucar Cuba ... ATAC. Revista Bimestral. Asociacion de Tecnicos Azucareros de Cuba [*A publication*]
ATACS ...... Advanced Tactical Air Combat Simulation
ATACS ...... Airborne Target Acquisition Control System   (MCD)
ATACS ...... Analyst-to-Analyst Communications Service   (MCD)
ATACS ...... Army Tactical Communications System
ATAD .... Absent on Temporary Additional Duty [*Navy*]
ATAD .... Atlanta Army Depot [*Georgia*]   (AABC)
ATAD .... Automatic Target Acquisition, Detection   (MCD)
ATAD .... Automatic Target Designation
ATADSIA ... Allied Tactical Data Systems Interoperability Agency [*NATO*]   (NATG)
ATAE........ American Trade Association Executives [*Later, ASAE*]
ATAE........ Associated Telephone Answering Exchanges [*Formerly, ATE*]   (EA)
ATAE........ Association of Tutors in Adult Education [*British*]
ATAE...... Automotive Trade Association Executives   (EA)
ATAEBC .. Agronomie Tropicale. Serie Agronomie Generale. Etudes Scientifiques [*A publication*]
ATAF........ Agricultural Technical Assistance Foundation [*Defunct*]   (EA)
ATAF........ Allied Tactical Air Force [*NATO*]
ATAFCS ... Airborne Target Acquisition and Fire Control System   (MCD)
ATAFM..... American Teilhard Association for the Future of Man [*Later, ATA*]   (EA)
ATAG .... Air Training Advisory Group
ATAGAS... Air-to-Air Gunnery Assessment   (MCD)
ATAGDK .. Atualidades Agronomicas [*Sao Paulo*] [*A publication*]
ATAIRS .... Army Tactical Requirements for Infrared Systems   (MCD)
ATAKDW ... Allattenyesztes es Takarmanyozas [*Animal Breeding and Feeding*] [*A publication*]
ATALA...... Association for Automatic Language Processing [*Paris, France*]   (EA)
Atalanta Norv ... Atalanta Norvegica [*A publication*]
ATALARS ... Advanced Tactical Aircraft Launch and Recovery System   (MCD)
ATAM .... Automotive Trade Association Managers [*Later, ATAE*]
ATA Mag .. ATA [*Alberta Teachers Association*] Magazine [*A publication*]
ATAMS..... Advanced Tactical Attacks/Manned System   (IEEE)
ATAN........ Airman, Aviation Electronics Technician [*Navy rating*]
ATA Newsletter ... Alberta Teachers Association. Newsletter [*A publication*]
ATANT ..... Abhandlungen zur Theologie des Alten und Neuen Testaments [*Zurich*] [*A publication*]
ATAO .... Das Alte Testament im Lichte des Alten Orients [*A publication*]   (BJA)
ATAP......... Active Tuition Assistance Plan [*UAW-General Motors Corp.*]
ATAP......... Apollo Telemetry Aircraft Project [*NASA*]
ATAPAA... Annales de Technologie Agricole [*Paris*] [*A publication*]
ATAPS ...... Advanced Tactical Aircraft Program System
ATAQ .... Association des Traducteurs Anglophones du Quebec [*Association of Anglophone Translators of Quebec*]
ATAR .... Above Transmitted as Received   (FAAC)
ATAR .... Acquisition Tracking and Recognition [*Aviation*]
ATAR .... Advanced Tactical Avionics RADAR
ATAR .... Air-to-Air Recovery [*Air Force*]   (AFM)
ATAR .... Air-to-Air Visual Recognition [*Aviation*]
ATAR .... Airborne Tracking, Acquisition, and Recognition
ATAR .... Antitank Aircraft Rocket
ATAR .... Automated Travel Agents Reservation
Ata Reumatol Bras ... Ata Reumatologica Brasileira [*A publication*]
ATARRS ... [*The*] Army Training Requirements and Resource System
ATARS...... Advanced Tactical Airborne Reconnaissance System [*Air Force*]   (MCD)
ATARS...... Aircraft Traffic Advisory Resolution System
ATARS...... Antiterrain Avoidance RADAR System   (MCD)
ATARS...... Army Tactical Airspace Regulation System   (MCD)
ATARS...... Automated Traffic Advisory and Resolution Service [*Collision-avoidance system*] [*Aviation*]
ATAS......... Academy of Television Arts and Sciences   (EA)

ATAS......... Advanced Tactical Attack System   (MCD)
ATAS......... Advanced Target Acquisition Sensor [*Air Force*]   (MCD)
ATAS......... Advanced Target Acquisition System [*Air Force*]
ATAS......... Air-to-Air Stinger   (MCD)
ATAS......... Air Traffic (Area) Supervisor   (FAAC)
ATAS......... Air Transport Auxiliary Service [*British*] [*World War II*]
ATAS......... Association of Telephone Answering Services   (EA)
ATAS......... Automatic Terminal Approach System   (MCD)
ATAS....... Automatic Terrain Avoidance System [*Military*]
ATAS......... Automatic Test Analysis System
ATAS......... Automatic Three-Axis Stabilization
ATAS......... Automatic Tracking Antenna System
ATASCII .... Atari-Version American Standard Code for Information Interchange [*Character code*]
Atas Inst Micol Univ Fed Pernambuco ... Atas. Instituto de Micologia da Universidade Federal de Pernambuco [*A publication*]
ATASMA ... Advanced Tactical Attack System Mission Analysis   (MCD)
Atas Soc Biol Rio De J ... Atas. Sociedade de Biologia do Rio De Janeiro [*A publication*]
ATAT........ Advanced Technology Airfoil Tests   (MCD)
ATaT .... Talladega College, Talladega, AL [*Library symbol*] [*Library of Congress*]   (LCLS)
At At Eng... Atomics and Atomic Engineering [*A publication*]
At At Technol ... Atomics and Atomic Technology [*A publication*]
AT/AV....... Antitank/Antivehicle   (MCD)
ATAVJ ...... Art Teachers Association of Victoria. Journal [*A publication*]   (APTA)
ATAV News ... Art Teachers Association of Victoria. News Sheet [*A publication*]   (APTA)
ATAV News Sheet ... Art Teachers Association of Victoria. News Sheet [*A publication*]   (APTA)
ATAW .... Advanced Tactical Assault Weapon
ATAWDS ... Advanced Terminal Aerial Weapon Delivery Simulation   (MCD)
ATAWS..... Autonomous Tactical All-Weather Strike   (MCD)
ATAX .... America First Tax Exempt Mortgage Fund [*NASDAQ symbol*]   (NQ)
ATB .... Access Type BIT [*Binary Digit*] [*Data processing*]
ATB .... Acetylene-Terminated Bisphel [*Organic chemistry*]
ATB .... Across the Board
ATB .... Added Thermal Barrier   (CAAL)
ATB .... Address Translation Buffer [*Telecommunications*]   (TEL)
AT(B)......... Administration of Territories Committee (Balkans) [*World War II*]
ATB .... Advanced Technology Bomber [*Air Force*]
ATB .... Advanced Test Battery [*Aptitude and skills test*]
ATB .... Advanced Torsion Bar   (MCD)
ATB .... Aeration Test Burner [*Heating*]
ATB .... Age at Time of Bomb [*Of survivors at Hiroshima*]
ATB .... Air Technical Battalion   (MCD)
ATB .... Air Transport Bureau [*ICAO*]
ATB .... Air Transportation Board
ATB .... Airborne Test Bed
ATB .... Aircraft Technical Bulletin
ATB .... All-Terrain Bike
ATB .... All Trunks Busy [*Telecommunications*]
ATB .... Altdeutsche Textbibliothek [*A publication*]
ATB .... Alternate-Top-Bevel Teeth [*Saw blades*]
ATB .... Amphibious Training Base [*Navy*]
ATB .... Anterior Tibialis [*Anatomy*]
ATB .... Antitactical Ballistic Missile   (MCD)
ATB .... Antitank Battery [*Military*]
ATB .... Aptitude Test Battery [*Educational test*]
ATB .... Arctic Test Branch [*Army*]   (MCD)
ATB .... Army Training Board
ATB .... Army Transportation Board   (MCD)
ATB .... Articulated Total Body   (MCD)
ATB .... Artillery Test Board [*Army*]
ATB .... Asphalt-Tile Base [*Technical drawings*]
ATB .... Association for Tropical Biology   (EA)
ATB .... Atbara [*Sudan*] [*Airport symbol*]   (OAG)
ATB .... Australian Tobacco Board
ATB .... Automated Ticket and Boarding Pass [*Travel industry*]
ATB .... Automobile Transporters Tariff Bureau, Inc., Southfield MI [*STAC*]
ATB .... Average Time of Burning
ATBA......... American Transportation Bowling Association   (EA)
ATBA......... American Truckers Benevolent Association [*Crest Hill, IL*]   (EA)
ATBA......... Association of Theatre Benefit Agents [*Defunct*]   (EA)
ATBA......... Automatic Test Break and Access [*Telecommunications*]   (TEL)
ATBAN ..... Atomic Bargain Analysis Report   (CINC)
ATBC......... Association of Trial Behavior Consultants [*Later, ASTC*]   (EA)
ATBC......... Atlantic Bancorporation [*Vorhees, NJ*] [*NASDAQ symbol*]   (NQ)
A & TBCB ... Architectural and Transportation Barriers Compliance Board [*Office of Human Development Services*] [*Washington, DC*]

ATBCB ...... Architectural and Transportation Barriers Compliance Board [*Office of Human Development Services*] [*Washington, DC*]

ATBD .... Automatic Torque Biasing Differential [*Automotive engineering*]

ATBI .... Allied Trades of the Baking Industry (EA)

ATBL .... Bliss [*A. T.*] & Co. [*NASDAQ symbol*] (NQ)

ATBM .... Advanced Tactical Ballistic Missile [*AMC - Missile*]

ATBM .... Antitactical Ballistic Missile

ATBM .... Average Time between Maintenance

ATBMC.... Airborne Test Bed Mode Control

ATBN .... Antitank Battalion [*Marine Corps*]

ATBT .... Acoustic Telemetry Bathythermometer

ATBT .... Airborne Test Bed Turret

ATC .... Ablative Thrust Chamber [*NASA*]

ATC .... Ablative Thrust Control (MCD)

ATC .... Achilles Track Club (EA)

ATC .... Acoustical Test Chamber

ATC .... Acoustical Tile Ceiling [*Technical drawings*]

ATC .... Action Taken Code (MCD)

ATC .... Action Training Coalition [*Defunct*] (EA)

ATC .... Activated Thymus Cell[*s*] [*Immunochemistry*]

ATC .... Active Thermal Control

ATC .... Active Transfer Command

ATC .... Address Translation Chip

ATC .... Adiabatic Toroidal Compressor [*Nuclear energy*]

ATC .... Advanced Technology Center [*Aerospace*]

ATC .... Advanced Technology Components [*Program*] [*Army, Navy*] (RDA)

ATC .... Advanced Telecommunications Corporation [*Atlanta, GA*] (TSSD)

ATC .... Advanced Training Command (MCD)

ATC .... Advertising Training Center [*New York, NY*]

ATC .... Aerial Tuning Condenser

ATC .... Aetna Telecommunications Consultants [*Centerville, MA*] [*Telecommunications*] (TSSD)

ATC .... After Top Center [*Valve position*]

ATC .... Agence Transcongolaise des Communications [*Congo Railways*] (DCTA)

ATC .... Agricultural Trade Council (EA)

ATC .... Air Target Chart (CINC)

ATC .... Air Temperature Control (IEEE)

ATC .... Air Traffic Conference of America [*Defunct*] (EA)

ATC .... Air Traffic Control

ATC .... Air Training Command [*Randolph Air Force Base, TX*]

ATC .... Air Training Corps [*RAF*] [*British*]

ATC .... Air Transport Command [*Air Force*]

ATC .... Air Transport Committee [*ICAO*]

ATC .... Air Transportable Clinic (MCD)

ATC .... Air Travel Card [*Airline notation*]

ATC .... Airborne Test Conductor (MUGU)

ATC .... Aircraft Technical Committee [*Aerospace Industries Association*] (MCD)

ATC .... Airline Travel Clubs (EA)

ATC .... Airport [*or Airway*] Traffic Control

AT C .... Airtight Containers [*Freight*]

ATC .... All-Terrain Carrier [*Roscoe Brown Corp.*]

ATC .... All-Terrain Cycle

ATC .... All Things Considered [*Radio program*]

ATC .... Allergic to Combat [*A play on the initialism for the Air Transport Command*]

ATC .... Allied Telecommunications Committee [*Allied Control Commission for Italy*]

ATC .... Allied Textiles Companies [*British*]

ATC .... Alpine Tourist Commission [*See also TGA*] [*Switzerland*] (EAIO)

ATC .... American Television & Communications Corp. [*Cable TV operator*]

ATC .... American Textbook Council (EA)

ATC .... American Trade Consortium

ATC .... Analog Technology Company

ATC .... Annotated Tax Cases [*A publication*]

ATC .... Annular Turbojet Combustor

ATC .... Anterior Trabeculae Carneae [*Heart anatomy*]

ATC .... Anti-Torpedo Craft [*British military*] (DMA)

ATC .... Antigen-Transporting Cell [*Immunology*]

ATC .... Antiseparation Tailored Contour (MCD)

ATC .... Any-to-Come [*Type of wager where any cash forthcoming from earlier bets finances further bets*] [*British*]

ATC .... Apollo Time Conditioner [*NASA*]

ATC .... Appalachian Trail Conference (EA)

ATC .... Applied Technology Council (EA)

ATC .... Apprenticeship and Training Conference [*Bureau of Apprenticeship and Training*] [*Department of Labor*]

ATC .... Approved Type Certificate [*Governmental airworthiness certification for planes*]

ATC .... Architecture Technology Corporation [*Minneapolis, MN*] [*Information service or system*] [*Telecommunications*] (TSSD)

ATC .... Arctic Test Center [*Army*]

ATC .... Armament Test Center [*Military*]

ATC .... Armored Troop Carrier [*Army*]

ATC .... Army Tactical Command (NVT)

ATC .... Army Terminal Command

ATC .... Army Topographic Command [*Formerly, Army Map Service*]

ATC .... Army Training Center

ATC .... Army Transportation Corps

ATC .... Arnold Transit Company [*Later, ATCO*] [*AAR code*]

ATC .... Around the Clock [*Medicine*]

ATC .... Art Teacher's Certificate [*British*]

ATC .... Arthur's Town [*Bahamas*] [*Airport symbol*] (OAG)

ATC .... Artificial Top Component [*Virology*]

ATC .... Aspartate Transcarbamylase [*Also, ATCase*] [*An enzyme*]

ATC .... Assembly Text Chip [*Data processing*]

ATC .... Assessed Tax Case (DLA)

ATC .... Assistant Test Chief

ATC .... Assistant Test Conductor

ATC .... Assistant Town Clerk [*British*]

ATC .... Assistant Transmission Controller

ATC .... Assistant Trial Counsel

ATC .... Associated Technology Company [*Information service or system*] (IID)

ATC .... Associated Traffic Clubs of America [*Later, TCI*] (EA)

ATC .... Association of Tax Consultants (EA)

ATC .... Asynchronous Terminal Concentrator [*Telecommunications*] (TSSD)

ATC .... Atari Corporation [*AMEX symbol*] (SPSG)

ATC .... ATE Computer (MCD)

ATC .... Atlantic Coast Copper Corp. Ltd. [*Toronto Stock Exchange symbol*]

ATC .... Atlantic Richfield Co., R and D Library, Dallas, TX [*OCLC symbol*] (OCLC)

ATC .... Attachie [*British Columbia*] [*Seismograph station code, US Geological Survey*] [*Closed*] (SEIS)

ATC .... Australian Tax Cases [*A publication*] (APTA)

ATC .... Australian Tonnage Committee

ATC .... Australian Trade Commission (EA)

ATC .... Austrian Trade Commission (EA)

ATC .... Automated Technical Control [*System*] [*Honeywell, Inc.*] [*Army*] (RDA)

ATC .... Automated Telecommunications Center (MCD)

ATC .... Automatic Tap Changing

ATC .... Automatic Target Counting

ATC .... Automatic Temperature Compensation

ATC .... Automatic Temperature Control

ATC .... Automatic Threshold Circuit (MCD)

ATC .... Automatic Timing Corrector

ATC .... Automatic Tone Correction

ATC .... Automatic Tool Changer

ATC .... Automatic Tracking Control (MSA)

ATC .... Automatic Traction Control [*Automotive engineering*]

ATC .... Automatic Traffic Control

ATC .... Automatic Train Control

ATC .... Automatic Tuning Control

ATC .... Automatic Turbidity Compensation Hemoglobin Test

ATC .... Automation Training Center (MCD)

ATC .... Automotive Transportation Center [*Purdue University*] [*Research center*] (RCD)

ATC .... Average Total Cost

ATC .... Aviation Electronics Technician, Chief [*Navy rating*]

ATC .... Aviation Training Center

ATC .... Mini Armored Troop Carrier [*Navy symbol*]

ATC .... National Council of Athletic Training [*Acronym is based on former name, Athletic Training Council*] (EA)

ATC .... Project ASTIC [*UTLAS symbol*]

ATCA .... Advanced Tanker Cargo Aircraft

ATCA .... Air Traffic Conference of America [*Defunct*] (EA)

ATCA .... Air Traffic Control Association (EA)

ATCA .... Air Training Corps of America

ATCA .... Airedale Terrier Club of America (EA)

ATCA .... Allied Tactical Communications Agency [*Brussels, Belgium*] [*NATO*] (NATG)

ATCA .... American Teilhard de Chardin Association [*Later, ATAFM*]

ATCA .... American Theatre Critics Association (EA)

ATCA .... American Transit Collectors' Association (EA)

ATCA .... Antique Telephone Collectors Association [*Later, TCI*] (EA)

ATCA .... Antique Toy Collectors of America (EA)

ATCA .... Antique Truck Club of America (EA)

ATCA .... Atlantic Tuna Convention Act of 1975

ATCA .... Attitude and Translation Control Assembly [*Aviation*] (MCD)

ATCA .... Australian Terrier Club of America (EA)

ATCAA ..... Air Traffic Control Assigned Airspace (FAAC)

ATCAA ..... Automatica [*United States*] [*A publication*]

ATCAC ..... Air Traffic Control Advisory Committee [*Department of Transportation*]

ATCAP ..... Air Traffic Control Automation Panel [*International Civil Aviation Organization*]

ATCAP ..... Army Telecommunications Center Automatic Programming (MCD)

ATCAS ..... Air Traffic Control Automatic System [*Sweden*]

ATCase ..... Aspartate Transcarbamylase [*Also, ATC*] [*An enzyme*]

ATCBGS ... Air Traffic Control Beacon Ground Station

ATCBI....... Air Traffic Control Beacon Interrogator
ATCC........ Aerial Target Control Central   (NG)
ATCC........ Aerospace Traffic Control Center
ATCC........ Air Traffic Control Center [*Air Force*]
ATCC........ Air Traffic Control Communication
ATCC.... Air Training Corps Cadet [*British*]
ATCC........ AirTran Corp. [*NASDAQ symbol*]   (SPSG)
ATCC........ American Type Culture Collection   (EA)
ATCC........ Association of Transport Coordinating Officers   (DCTA)
ATCC........ Atlantic Division Transport Control Center [*Military*]
ATCCBG... Acta Cancerologica [*A publication*]
ATCCC... Advanced Tactical Command and Control Capabilities
ATCCEJ... Adjuvant Therapy of Cancer [*A publication*]
ATCC (L)... Allied Tanker Coordinating Committee in London
ATCCS...... Army Tactical Command and Control System
ATCC (W) ... Allied Tanker Coordinating Committee in Washington
ATCDE...... Association of Teachers in Colleges and Departments of Education [*British*]
ATCE........ Ablative Thrust Chamber Engine [*NASA*]
ATCE........ Air Threat to Central Europe
ATCE........ ATC Environmental, Inc. [*NASDAQ symbol*]   (NQ)
ATCE........ Attitude and Translation Control Electronics
ATCE........ Automatic Test and Checkout Equipment   (AFM)
ATCEI....... Angiotensin Converting Enzyme Inhibitor [*Biochemistry*]
ATCEU...... Air Traffic Control Evaluation Unit [*British*]
ATCF........ After Tax Cash Flow
ATCF........ Air Traffic Control Facility
ATCFAS.... Air Traffic Control Flight Advisory Service   (MCD)
ATCH........ ASW [*Antisubmarine Warfare*] Torpedo-Carrying Helicopter
Atch........... Atchison. English Navigation and Trade Reports [*A publication*]   (DLA)
ATCH........ Attach [*or Attachment*]   (AFM)
ATCHD...... Attached
Atch EC ..... Atcheson's Election Cases [*England*] [*A publication*]   (DLA)
ATCHEMPI ... Attach on Morning Report the Following Named EM [*Enlisted Man*] Who Has Been Authorized to Report to Your Station upon Expiration of Leave. Retain Him/Her Pending Further Instructions   (AABC)
ATCHMT ... Attachment   (MUGU)
ATCK........ Attack   (MSA)
ATCL........ Acceleration-Type Control Law
ATCL........ Air Traffic Control Line   (AFM)
ATCL........ Associate of Trinity College of Music, London [*British*]
ATCL........ Atlin Claim [*A publication*]
ATCLO...... Amphibious Training Command Liaison Officer [*Navy*]
ATCM ...... Advanced Technology Cruise Missile   (MCD)
ATCM ...... Air Training Command Manual [*Air Force*]
ATCM .... American Television & Communications Corp. [*Englewood, CO*] [*NASDAQ symbol*]   (NQ)
ATCM ...... Associate of the Toronto Conservatory of Music
ATCM ...... Associate, Trinity College of Music [*Canadian*]
ATCM ...... Aviation Electronics Technician, Master Chief [*Navy rating*]
ATCMD ..... Advance Transportation Control and Movement Document
ATCMU .... Associated Third Class Mail Users [*Later, TCMA*]   (EA)
ATCNB...... Air Traffic Control and Navigation Board
ATCO .... Active Token Collectors Organization   (EA)
ATCO .... Air Taxi-Commercial Operator
ATCO .... Air Traffic Control Office [*or Operations*] [*Air Force*]
ATCO .... Air Traffic Coordinating Officer
ATCO .... Air Transportation Coordination Office   (CINC)
ATCO .... Arnold Transit Company [*Formerly, ATC*] [*AAR code*]
ATCO .... Atcor, Inc. [*NASDAQ symbol*]   (NQ)
ATCOGS... Army Telecommunications Combat Theater and General Support [*5 Year Plan*]   (MCD)
ATCOM .... Air Traffic Communications   (MCD)
ATCOM .... Atoll Commander [*In Pacific operations*] [*World War II*]
ATCOPS... Atlantis Commodities Purchasing Service
ATCOR ..... Air Traffic Control Operations Representative   (FAAC)
ATCOR ..... Air Traffic Coordinator
ATCOREU ... Air Traffic Coordinator Europe
ATCORUS ... Air Transport Coordinator for the United States
ATCOS...... Atmospheric Composition Satellite [*NASA*]
ATCP........ Advanced Technology Crew Protection   (MCD)
ATCP........ Air Traffic Control Procedures
ATCP........ Air Training Command Pamphlet [*Air Force*]
ATCP........ Antarctic Treaty Consultative Parties
ATCPA...... Air Taxi and Commercial Pilots Association   (EA)
ATCPS...... Audio Tape Cassette Player Set
ATCQ .... Air Travel Card of High Credit [*Airline notation*]
ATCR........ Air Training Command Regulation [*Air Force*]
ATCR........ Authenticolor, Inc. [*NASDAQ symbol*]   (NQ)
ATCRB...... Air Traffic Control RADAR Beacon
ATCRBS.... Air Traffic Control RADAR Beacon System
ATCRS...... Air Traffic Control RADAR System
ATCRU ..... Air Traffic Control RADAR Unit   (AFM)
ATCS........ Active Thermal Control Subsystem [*NASA*]   (MCD)
ATCS........ Advanced Tactical Control System   (MCD)
ATCS........ Advanced Train Control System [*Union Pacific Railroad Co.*]
ATCS........ Air Traffic Communication System [*NASA*]   (KSC)
ATCS........ Air Traffic Communications Service   (MCD)

ATCS........ Air Traffic Communications Station
ATCS........ Air Traffic Control Specialist   (FAAC)
ATCS........ Airborne Tactical Command System [*Formerly, ATDS*]   (MCD)
ATCS........ Aircraft Tactical Control System
ATCS........ Attitude and Translation Control System   (MCD)
ATCS........ Aviation Electronics Technician, Senior Chief [*Navy rating*]
ATCSCC.... Air Traffic Control Systems Command Center   (FAAC)
ATCSD...... Annual Technical Conference. American Electroplaters' Society [*A publication*]
ATCSF....... Air Traffic Control Simulation Facility
ATCSS....... Air Traffic Control Signaling System
ATCSS....... Army Tactical Communication System Simulator   (MCD)
ATCT........ Air [*or Airport*] Traffic Control Tower
ATCT........ Air Traffic Control Transponder
ATCU .... Air Transportable Communications Unit   (NVT)
ATCU .... Attitude and Translation Control Unit
ATCV....... Australian Trust for Conservation Volunteers
ATCYA...... Appropriate Technology [*A publication*]
ATD .... Absent on Temporary Duty [*Navy*]
ATD .... Absolutely to Die [*Slang*]
ATD .... Acceptance and Takeover Date [*Telecommunications*]   (TEL)
ATD .... Accession Treaty and Decision Concerning the European Coal and Steel Community [*A publication*]   (DLA)
ATD .... Acta Theologica Danica [*A publication*]
ATD .... Actual Time of Departure
ATD .... Advanced Technology Demonstration
ATD .... Advanced Technology Developments   (MCD)
ATD .... Advanced Torpedo Decoy   (CAAL)
ATD .... Aerospace Technology Division [*Formerly, Aerospace Information Division; later, ARP*] [*Library of Congress*]
ATD .... Air Transportable Dispensary   (AFM)
ATD .... Air Turbine Drive   (NG)
ATD .... Aircrew Training Device   (MCD)
ATD .... Airlift and Training Division [*Air Force*]   (MCD)
ATD .... Alzheimer Type Dementia [*Medicine*]
ATD .... American Truck Dealers   (EA)
ATD .... Analog to Time to Digital [*Data processing*]
ATD .... Androstatrienedione [*Organic chemistry*]
ATD .... Annual Training Deployment   (MCD)
ATD .... Annual Training Duty [*Marine Corps*]
ATD .... Anthropomorphic Test Dummy
ATD .... Armor Training Devices   (RDA)
ATD .... Art Teacher's Diploma [*British*]
ATD .... Asphyxiating Thoracic Dystrophy [*Medicine*]
ATD .... Assistant Test Director
ATD .... Association for Theatre and Disability   (EA)
ATD .... Association of Tongue Depressors   (EA)
ATD .... Asynchronous Time Division [*Telecommunications*]
ATD .... Audio Tone Decoder
ATD .... Australasian Tax Decisions [*A publication*]   (APTA)
ATD .... Australian Tax Decisions [*A publication*]   (APTA)
ATD .... Australian Teacher of the Deaf [*A publication*]   (APTA)
ATD .... Automated Ticket Dispenser
ATD .... Automatic Tape Degausser
ATD .... Automatic Target Designation
ATD .... Automatic Target Detection   (MCD)
ATD .... Automatic Teaching Device
ATD .... Dayton, OH [*Location identifier*] [*FAA*]   (FAAL)
ATD .... [*A*] Touch of Days [*An association*]   (EA)
ATDA .... Advanced Technology Demonstration Aircraft
ATDA .... Alternate Target Docking Adapter [*NASA*]   (MCD)
ATDA .... American Train Dispatchers Association   (EA)
ATDA .... Army Training Device Agency [*Orlando, FL*]   (AABC)
ATDA .... Augmented Target Docking Adapter [*Gemini*] [*NASA*]
At Data ...... Atomic Data [*Later, Atomic Data and Nuclear Data Tables*] [*A publication*]
At Data Nucl Data Tables ... Atomic Data and Nuclear Data Tables [*A publication*]
ATDB .... ACE Target Data Base   (MCD)
ATDB .... Aerothermodynamic Data Book [*NASA*]   (NASA)
ATDC .... After Top Dead Center [*Valve position*]
ATDC .... Association of Thalidomide-Damaged Children
ATDC .... Austin Ten Drivers Club [*High Wycombe, Buckinghamshire, England*]   (EAIO)
ATDD .... Asynchronous Time Diversity Device   (MCD)
ATDDL ..... Apollo Technical Documentation Distribution List [*NASA*]   (KSC)
ATDE .... Advanced Technology Demonstrator Engine
ATDG .... Automated Test Data Generator [*Data processing*]
ATDI .... Advanced Terminal Defense Interceptor   (MCD)
At Diffus Semicond ... Atomic Diffusion in Semiconductors [*A publication*]
ATDip....... Art Teacher's Diploma [*British*]
ATDL .... Atmospheric Turbulence and Diffusion Laboratory [*Oak Ridge, Tennessee*]
ATD/LC .... Aerospace Technology Division [*Formerly, Aerospace Information Division; later, ARP*]/Library of Congress   (AFM)
ATDLG...... Advanced Technology Demonstration LASER Gyro   (MCD)
ATDLP...... Apollo Trajectory Decision Logic Prototype [*NASA*]
ATDLP...... Army-Wide Training and Doctrinal Literature Program

ATDM	Asynchronous Time-Division Multiplexing [*Data processing*]
ATDMA	Advanced Time-Division Multiple Access (IEEE)
ATDNT	Attendant (MUGU)
ATDO	Airways Technical District Office [*FAA*]
ATDP	Air Traffic Data Processor
ATDP	Attitudes toward Disabled Persons [*Psychology*]
ATDPS	Airborne Tactical Data Processing System
ATDR	Aeronautical Technical Directive Requirement [*Obsolete*]
ATDS	Air Tactical Data System (MCD)
ATDS	Airborne Tactical Data System [*Later, ATCS*]
ATDS	Airways Technical District Supervisor [*FAA*]
ATDS	Association of Teachers of Dramatic Science [*British*]
ATDS	Automatic Telemetry Decommutation System
ATDS	Automatic Transient Detection System (MCD)
ATDS	Aviation Tactical Data System
ATDSAY	ASTM [*American Society for Testing and Materials*] Data Series [*A publication*]
ATDT	Attendant
ATDU	Air Transport Development Unit [*British*]
ATDU	Aircraft Torpedo Development Unit [*British*]
ATE	Above Target Elevation (MCD)
ATE	Acceptance Test Equipment (MCD)
ATE	Acquisition and Tracking Electronics (MCD)
A & TE	Acquisition and Tracking Electronics (MCD)
AT(E)	Administration of Territories Committee (Europe) [*World War II*]
ATE	Advanced Technology Engine (MCD)
ATE	Advanced Textbooks in Economics [*Elsevier Book Series*] [*A publication*]
ATE	Advanced Turbofan Engine
ATE	Aerospace Test Equipment
ATE	Air Turbo Exchanger
ATE	Airborne Teletypewriter Equipment
ATE	Airborne Test Equipment (MCD)
ATE	Altitude Transmitting Equipment [*FAA*]
ATE	Aluminum Triethyl [*Organic chemistry*]
ATE	Anti-Terrorismo ETA [*Anti-ETA Terrorism*] [*Spanish*] (PPE)
ATE	Approximation to English
ATE	Area Test Equipment
ATE	Associate in Technical Education
ATE	Associated Telephone Exchanges [*Later, ATAE*]
ATE	Association of Teacher Educators (EA)
ATE	Association for the Therapeutic Education [*British*]
ATE	ATE Management Service Co., Inc., Cincinnati, OH [*OCLC symbol*] (OCLC)
Ate	Atenea [*A publication*]
ATE	Atlantic Energy [*NYSE symbol*] (SPSG)
ATE	Atlantis Enterprise [*Vancouver Stock Exchange symbol*]
ATE	Autographic Theme Extraction [*System*]
ATE	Automated Test Equipment
ATE	Automatic Test Equipment (NASA)
ATE	Bedrijfsvoering; Tijdschrift voor Organisatiekunde en Arbeidskunde, Produktie, Onderhoud, Inkoop, en Logistiek [*A publication*]
ATE	Mobile, AL [*Location identifier*] [*FAA*] (FAAL)
ATEA	American Technical Education Association (EA)
ATEA	American Toy Export Association (EA)
A-TEAM	Acquisition Team [*Army*] (RDA)
ATEC	Agency for Tele-Education in Canada
ATEC	Allison Transmission Electronic Control [*Detroit Diesel Allison*]
ATEC	Army Test and Evaluation Command [*AMC*]
ATEC	AT & E Corporation [*NASDAQ symbol*] (NQ)
ATEC	Atlantic Treaty Education Committee [*NATO*] (NATG)
ATEC	Automated Technical Control [*System*] [*Honeywell, Inc.*] [*Army*]
ATEC	Automatic Test Equipment Complex (MCD)
ATEC	Aviation Technician Education Council (EA)
ATECO	Automatic Telegram Transmission with Computers [*Telecommunications*] (TEL)
ATECOM	Army Test and Evaluation Command [*AMC*] (MUGU)
ATECP	Army Training Extension Course Program
AT-ECT	Atrial Ectopy [*Cardiology*]
ATEE	Acetyltyrosine Ethyl Ester [*Biochemistry*]
ATEE	Association for Teacher Education in Europe (EAIO)
ATEE	Association of Teachers of Electrical Engineering [*British*]
ATEE	ATE Enterprises, Inc. [*NASDAQ symbol*] (NQ)
ATEED	Advanced Technology Energy Efficient Demonstrator (MCD)
ATEGG	Advanced Turbine Engine Gas Generator [*Air Force*]
ATEHA6	Agrotecnia [*A publication*]
ATEI	Amusement Trades Exhibition International [*Great Britain*] (ITD)
ATE/ICE	Automatic Test Equipment for Internal Combustion Engines (MCD)
ATEK	Amertek, Inc. [*Woodstock, ON*] [*NASDAQ symbol*] (NQ)
ATEL	Advanced Telecommunications Corp. [*NASDAQ symbol*] (NQ)
ATEL	Audio Techniques and Evaluation Laboratory [*NASA*]
ATEL	Aviation Traders Engineering Limited [*British*]
A Telecom	Annales des Telecommunications [*A publication*]
At Elektr Stn	Atomnye Elektricheskie Stantsii [*USSR*] [*A publication*]

Atelier	Atelier des Photographen [*A publication*]
A Tem	A Tempo [*In Strict Time*] [*Music*]
ATEM	Advanced Technical Engagement Model (MCD)
ATEM	Aircraft Test Equipment Modification
ATEM	Analytical Transmission Electron Microscope
ATEM	Automatic Test Equipment, Missile (MCD)
A TEMP	A Tempo [*In Strict Time*] [*Music*]
Atemswegs- Lungenkr	Atemswegs- und Lungenkrankheiten [*A publication*]
ATEN	Atmospheric Environment [*A publication*]
At En	Atomnaja Energija [*A publication*]
ATENE	Association for Theological Education in the Near East [*Later, A TIME*]
Ateneo LJ	Ateneo Law Journal [*A publication*] (DLA)
Ateneo Parmense Acta Bio-Med	Ateneo Parmense. Acta Bio-Medica [*A publication*]
Ateneo Parmense Acta Nat	Ateneo Parmense. Acta Naturalia [*A publication*]
Ateneo Parmense Sez 1	Ateneo Parmense. Sezione 1. Acta Bio-Medica [*A publication*]
Ateneo Parmense Sez 2	Ateneo Parmense. Sezione 2. Acta Naturalia [*Italy*] [*A publication*]
At Energ	Atomnaya Energiya [*USSR*] [*A publication*]
At Energ Itogi Nauki Tekh	Atomnaya Energetika Itogi Nauki i Tekhniki [*A publication*]
At Energiya (USSR)	Atomnaya Energiya (USSR) [*A publication*]
At Energ Prilozh	Atomnaya Energiya Prilozhenie [*A publication*]
At Energy Aust	Atomic Energy in Australia [*A publication*]
At Energy Board (Repub S Afr) Rep	Atomic Energy Board (Republic of South Africa). Report [*A publication*]
At Energy Bull	Atomic Energy Bulletin [*Japan*] [*A publication*]
At Energy Can Ltd AECL (Rep)	Atomic Energy of Canada Limited. AECL (Report) [*A publication*]
At Energy Establ Winfrith Memo	Atomic Energy Establishment Winfrith. Memorandum [*A publication*]
At Energy Establ Winfrith Rep	Atomic Energy Establishment Winfrith. Report [*A publication*]
At Energy Law J	Atomic Energy Law Journal [*A publication*]
At Energy Law Rep	Atomic Energy Law Reports [*A publication*]
At Energy Miner Cent (Pak) Rep	Atomic Energy Minerals Centre (Pakistan). Report [*A publication*]
At Energy Res Establ GB Mem	Atomic Energy Research Establishment, Great Britain. Memorandum [*A publication*]
At Energy Res Establ GB Rep	Atomic Energy Research Establishment, Great Britain. Report [*A publication*]
At Energy Res Q Rep	Atomic Energy Research. Quarterly Report [*Japan*] [*A publication*]
At Energy Rev	Atomic Energy Review [*A publication*]
At Energy Rev Spec Issue	Atomic Energy Review. Special Issue [*A publication*]
At Energy (Sydney)	Atomic Energy (Sydney) [*Australia*] [*A publication*]
At Enerj Kom (Turkey) Bilimsel Yayin Seri	Atom Enerjisi Komisyonu (Turkey) Bilimsel Yayinlar Seri [*A publication*]
At Eng	Atomic Energy in Australia [*A publication*] (APTA)
At Eng Tech	Atomics. Engineering and Technology [*A publication*]
At Eng Technol	Atomic Engineering Technology [*A publication*]
At En Newsl	Atomic Energy Newsletter [*A publication*]
At En Rev	Atomic Energy Review [*A publication*]
At En Yb	Atomic Energy Yearbook [*A publication*]
ATEOS	Airborne Toxic Elements and Organic Species
ATEP	Advanced Technical Education Program
ATEP	Annual Training Equipment Pools (AABC)
ATEP	Association of Training and Employment Professionals (EA)
ATEP	Augmented Thermally Electric Propulsion
ATEPS	Advanced Techniques for Electrical Power Management, Control, and Distribution Systems [*Army*] (RDA)
ATER	Association of Theaters of Emilia and Romagna [*Ballet company*]
Ate R	Atene e Roma [*A publication*]
ATER	Automatic Testing, Evaluation, and Reporting
ATERB	Australian Telecommunications and Electronics Research Board
ATERD	Archiwum Termodynamiki [*A publication*]
ATERM	Air Terminal
ATES	Aquifer Thermal Energy Storage
ATES	Army Test and Evaluation Seminar
ATES	Automated Tactical Environmental System
ATESD8	Aristoteleion Panepistemion Thessalonikis Epistimoniki Epetiris Geoponikis kai Dasologikis Skolis [*A publication*]
ATESEA	Association for Theological Education in South East Asia (EAIO)
ATESL	Association of Teachers of English as a Second Language (EA)
ATES Newsl	ATES [*Aquifer Thermal Energy Storage*] Newsletter [*A publication*]
ATESS	Automated Tactical Environmental System (MCD)
AT(E)SSS	Administration of Territories Committee (Europe), Shipping and Supply Subcommittee [*World War II*]
ATET	Advanced Technical Experimental Transportation (MCD)
Atetra P	Adenosine Tetraphosphate [*Biochemistry*]
ATEWA	Automatic Target Evaluator and Weapon Assignor
ATEWS	Advanced Tactical Electronic Warfare System (AFM)
ATEX	Atlantic Express, Inc. [*NASDAQ symbol*] (NQ)

ATEX.........	Atlantic Tradewind [*or Tropical*] Experiment [*National Science Foundation*]
ATF............	Acceptance Test Facility [*Nuclear energy*]
ATF............	Accounting and Finance [*A publication*]
ATF............	Accounting Tabulating Form (AAG)
ATF............	Actual Time of Fall
ATF............	Advanced Tactical Fighter [*Air Force*] (MCD)
ATF............	Advanced Toroidal Facility [*Oak Ridge National Laboratory*]
ATF............	After the Fact (MCD)
ATF............	Air Task Force
ATF............	Air Traffic Flow [*Later, ATIF*] (MCD)
ATF............	Algebraic Technological Function [*Data processing*]
ATF............	American Tennis Federation (EA)
ATF............	American Trails Foundation (EA)
ATF............	American Typecasting Fellowship (EA)
ATF............	Amphibious Task Force [*Navy*] (NVT)
ATF............	Angiotensin-II-Ferritin [*Biochemistry*]
ATF......	Antarctic Task Force
ATF......	Antelope Resources [*Vancouver Stock Exchange symbol*]
ATF............	Antenna Test Facility
ATF............	Armed Tactical Fighter [*General Dynamics Corp.*] (ECON)
ATF............	Army Training Film
ATF............	As Trustee For [*Banking*]
ATF............	Asphalt-Tile Floor [*Technical drawings*]
ATF............	Associate Administrator for Air Traffic and Airway Facilities [*FAA*] (FAAC)
ATF............	Auditorium and Training Facility [*NASA*] (NASA)
ATF............	Australian Task Force
ATF............	Australian Tax Forum
ATF............	Automatic Target Follow
ATF............	Automatic Terrain Following [*Military*] (MCD)
ATF............	Automatic Text Formatter
ATF............	Automatic Track Finding [*System*] [*Video technology*]
ATF............	Automatic Tracking Feature (NVT)
ATF............	Automatic Transmission Fluid
ATF............	Autotumorolytic Factor [*Oncology*]
ATF............	Aviation Turbine Fuel
ATF............	Bureau of Alcohol, Tobacco, and Firearms [*Department of the Treasury*]
ATF............	Bureau of Alcohol, Tobacco, and Firearms Laboratory, Washington, DC [*OCLC symbol*] (OCLC)
ATF............	Equity Income Fund First Exchange Series [*AMEX symbol*] (SPSG)
ATF............	Fleet Ocean Tug [*Navy symbol*]
ATF............	French Southern and Antarctic Lands [*ANSI three-letter standard code*] (CNC)
ATFAC......	American Turpentine Farmers Association Cooperative (EA)
ATFAP......	Arson Task Force Assistance Program
ATF/ATA ...	Automatic Terrain Following/Automatic Terrain Avoidance [*Military*]
ATFC.........	Account Traffic (FAAC)
ATFC.........	Air Task Force Commander (MUGU)
ATFC.........	Atico Financial Corporation [*NASDAQ symbol*] (NQ)
ATFCA......	Asian Track and Field Coaches Association (EAIO)
ATFCB......	Alcohol, Tobacco, and Firearms Cumulative Bulletin [*A publication*] (DLA)
ATFCC......	ATF Colada [*A publication*]
ATFCNN...	Allied Task Force Commander, North Norway [*NATO*] (NATG)
ATFD.........	Automated Tactical Fusion Division
ATFE.........	Advanced Thermal Flight Experiment (MCD)
ATFERO...	Atlantic Ferry Organization [*Based in Canada under Ministry of Aircraft Production*] [*British*] [*World War II*]
ATFI..........	Automated Tariff Filing and Information System [*Washington, DC*] (EGAO)
AT FIB......	Atrial Fibrillation [*Cardiology*]
ATFMA.....	Advanced Tactical Fighter Mission Analysis (MCD)
ATFMG.....	Alliance Telecommunications Frequency Management Group [*Telecommunications service*] (TSSD)
ATFO	Airways Technical Field Office [*FAA*]
ATFOS......	Alignment and Test Facility for Optical Systems [*Navy*]
ATFP.........	Alliance of Television Film Producers [*Later, Association of Motion Picture and Television Producers*] (EA)
ATFR.........	Arlin Test of Formal Reasoning [*Intelligence test*]
ATFR.........	Automatic Terrain-Following RADAR [*Military*]
ATFRAM..	Airborne Time/Frequency Range/Altitude Monitor (MCD)
ATF Rep	Australian Teachers' Federation. Report [*A publication*] (APTA)
ATFS	Association of Track and Field Statisticians [*London, England*] (EAIO)
ATFX.........	Fleet Tug [*Navy symbol*] (MCD)
ATG..........	Accordion Teachers' Guild (EA)
ATG..........	Advanced Technology Group [*Navy*]
ATG..........	Agence des Telecommunications Gouvernementales [*Government Telecommunications Agency*] [*Canada*]
ATG..........	Air-to-Ground [*Photos, missiles, etc.*]
ATG..........	Air Transport Group [*Australia*]
ATG..........	Air Turbine Generator
ATG..........	Alaskan Territorial Guard
ATG..........	Alcatel Thomson Gigadisc [*Optical disk*]
ATG..........	All Test Go (MCD)

ATG..........	American Traders Group (EA)
ATG..........	Ammonium Thioglycolate
ATG..........	Antenna Test Group [*Army*] (AABC)
ATG..........	Antigua-Barbuda [*ANSI three-letter standard code*] (CNC)
ATG..........	Antitank Gun [*Military*]
ATG..........	Antithymocyte Globulin [*Immunochemistry*]
ATG..........	Archivo Teologico Granadino [*A publication*]
ATG..........	Association of Teachers of Geology [*British*]
ATG..........	Association of Teachers of German [*British*]
ATG..........	Atlanta Gas Light Co. [*NYSE symbol*] (SPSG)
ATG..........	Australian Income Tax Guide [*A publication*] (APTA)
ATG..........	Automated Test-Case Guidance [*Data processing*]
ATG..........	Automatic Test Grading
ATGA.......	American Toy Goat Association (EA)
ATGAAT..	Antropologica [*Caracas*] [*A publication*]
ATGAF......	Advanced Technology Ground Attack Fighter [*Air Force*]
ATGAM.....	Antithymocyte Gamma-Globulin [*Immunology*]
ATGAR	Antitank Guided Air Rocket
ATGER	Association of Teachers of German [*British*]
ATGIN	Atomic Ground Intercept (MCD)
ATGL........	Antitank Grenade Launcher (AABC)
ATGM.......	Antitank Guided Missile
ATGS........	Advanced Terminal Guidance System
ATGSB	Admission Test for Graduate Study in Business
ATGW	Antitank Guided Weapon (MCD)
ATH..........	Above the Horizon
ATH..........	Air Transportable Hospital (AFM)
ATH..........	Alumina Trihydrate [*Inorganic chemistry*]
ATH..........	Antitank Helicopter (MCD)
ATH..........	Arapahoe Mining [*Vancouver Stock Exchange symbol*]
ATh..........	Arbeiten zur Theologie [*Stuttgart*] [*A publication*]
ATH..........	Artificial Time History [*Nuclear energy*] (NRCH)
A Th..........	Associate in Theology
ATh..........	Associate in Therapy
ath	Athapascan [*MARC language code*] [*Library of Congress*] (LCCP)
Ath	Athenaeum [*A publication*]
Ath	Athenaeus [*First century AD*] [*Classical studies*] (OCD)
Ath	Athene. The American Magazine of Hellenic Thought [*A publication*]
ATH..........	Athens [*Greece*] [*Later, PEN*] [*Geomagnetic observatory code*]
ATH..........	Athens [*Greece*]
ATH..........	Athens [*Greece*] [*Airport symbol*] (OAG)
ATH..........	Athens Observatory [*Greece*] [*Seismograph station code, US Geological Survey*] (SEIS)
ATH..........	Athletic (MUGU)
ATH..........	Athlone Industries, Inc. [*NYSE symbol*] (SPSG)
ATH..........	Athwartships
ATH..........	August Thyssen-Huette Aktiengesellschaft [*August Thyssen Foundry Joint Stock Company*] [*Federal Republic of Germany*]
ATH..........	Autonomous Terminal Homing [*Air Force*]
a-th---..........	Thailand [*MARC geographic area code*] [*Library of Congress*] (LCCP)
ATHA.......	American Turkey Hunters Association (EA)
ATHAA.....	Albrecht-Thaer-Archiv [*A publication*]
ATHABZ...	Applied Scientific Research Corporation of Thailand. Annual Report [*A publication*]
Ath Adm	Athletic Administration [*A publication*]
AThANT ...	Abhandlungen zur Theologie des Alten und Neuen Testaments [*Zurich*] [*A publication*]
ATHAS	Advanced Thermal Analysis (MCD)
AThAug.....	Annee Theologique Augustinienne [*A publication*]
ATHBA	Acta Radiologica. Therapy, Physics, Biology [*Later, Acta Radiologica. Series Two. Oncology, Radiation, Physics, and Biology*] [*A publication*]
ATHBA3 ...	Acta Radiologica. Therapy, Physics, Biology [*Later, Acta Radiologica. Series Two. Oncology, Radiation, Physics, and Biology*] [*A publication*]
AthBE........	Athletes for a Better Education
Ath Bus	Athletic Business [*A publication*]
ATHC........	Association of Thrift Holding Companies [*Washington, DC*] (EA)
Ath Coach ...	Athletics Coach [*A publication*]
ATHCOM ...	Australasian Tertiary Handbook Collection on Microfiche [*A publication*] (APTA)
AThD.........	Acta Theologica Danica [*Copenhagen*] [*A publication*]
ATHE.........	Association for Theatre in Higher Education (EA)
ATHELO ..	Attack Helicopter Organization [*Military*]
Athenae......	Athenaeum. Studi Periodici di Letteratura e Storia dell'Antichita. Universita di Pavia [*A publication*]
Athenaeum Pavia ...	Athenaeum. Studi Periodici di Letteratura e Storia dell'Antichita. Universita di Pavia [*A publication*]
Atherogenesis Proc Int Symp ...	Atherogenesis. Proceedings of the International Symposium [*A publication*]
Atheroscler ...	Atherosclerosis [*A publication*]
Atheroscler Coron Heart Dis Hahnemann Symp ...	Atherosclerosis and Coronary Heart Disease. Hahnemann Symposium [*A publication*]
Atheroscler Drug Discovery ...	Atherosclerosis Drug Discovery [*A publication*]

Atheroscler Proc Int Symp ... Atherosclerosis. Proceedings. International Symposium on Atherosclerosis [*A publication*]
Atheroscler Rev ... Atherosclerosis Reviews [*A publication*]
ATHESA... Automatic Three-Dimensional Electronics Scanning Array (MUGU)
ATHI .... Two Hills Public Library, Alberta [*Library symbol*] [*National Library of Canada*] (NLC)
AThijmG.... Annalen van het Thijmgenootschap [*A publication*]
Ath J .... Athletic Journal [*A publication*]
ATHL .... Athletic
Athl Adm ... Athletic Administration [*A publication*]
Athl Coach ... Athletics Coach [*A publication*]
Athl Educ Rep ... Athletic Educator's Report [*A publication*]
Athletic J ... Athletic Journal [*A publication*]
Athl J ...... Athletic Journal [*A publication*]
Athlr.......... Aethelred [*King of England*] (ILCA)
Athl Train ... Athletic Training [*A publication*]
A Th M ...... Archeion Thessalikon Meleton [*A publication*]
ATHM...... Three Hills Municipal Library, Alberta [*Library symbol*] [*National Library of Canada*] (NLC)
Ath Mar Set ... Atherley on Marriage Settlements [*A publication*] (DLA)
Ath Mitt..... Mitteilungen. Deutsches Archaeologische Institut. Abteilung Athens [*A publication*]
Ath Mitt-BH ... Athenische Mitteilungen. Beiheft [*A publication*]
ATHOC..... Automatic Target Handoff Computer (MCD)
ATHODYD ... Aerothermodynamic Duct
ATHOM.... Thorhild Municipal Library, Alberta [*Library symbol*] [*National Library of Canada*] (NLC)
ATHP .... Autonomous Terminal Homing Program (MCD)
ATHPB..... Advances in Theoretical Physics [*A publication*]
Ath Pur and Fac ... Athletic Purchasing and Facilities [*A publication*]
AThR......... Anglican Theological Review [*A publication*]
ATHRS..... Air Transportation Hydrant Refueling System (AFIT)
ATHS .... American Truck Historical Society (EA)
ATHS .... Australian Theatre Historical Society
ATHSAK... Annals of Thoracic Surgery [*A publication*]
ATHSC..... Atherosclerosis [*Medicine*]
Ath Train ... Athletic Training [*A publication*]
ATI .... Above-Threshold Ionization (MCD)
ATI .... Acetylene-Terminated Imide [*Polymer technology*]
ATI .... Actual Time of Interception
ATI .... Advanced Terminal Interceptor
ATi .... Advanced Turbocharged Intercooled [*Truck engineering*]
ATI .... Aerial Tuning Inductance
ATI .... Aero Transporti Italiani SpA [*Airline*] [*Italy*] (EY)
ATI .... Aerosol Techniques, Incorporated
ATI .... Air Target Indicator
ATI .... Air Technical Index [*Air Force*]
ATI .... Air Technical Information [*Used by Armed Services Technical Information Agency - later, Defense Documentation Center - to accession and identify documents*]
ATI .... Air Technical Intelligence [*Air Force*]
ATI .... American Technology & Information, Inc. [*Vancouver Stock Exchange symbol*]
ATI .... American Telco, Inc. [*Telecommunications service*] (TSSD)
ATI .... American Travel Inns (EA)
ATI .... Appropriate Technology International (EA)
ATI .... Aptitude-Treatment Interactions [*Education*]
ATI .... Armored Transportation Institute (EA)
ATI .... Army Training Instruction
ATI .... Artigas [*Uruguay*] [*Airport symbol*] (OAG)
ATI .... Artillery Target Intelligence (MCD)
ATI .... Asbestos Textile Institute (EA)
ATI .... Associate of the Textile Institute [*British*]
ATI .... Associated Telemanagement, Incorporated [*Newburyport, MA*] [*Telecommunications*] (TSSD)
ATI .... Association of Teachers of Italian [*British*]
ATI .... Association of Technical Institutions (EY)
ATI .... Association of Thai Industries (DS)
ATI .... ATI Medical [*AMEX symbol*] (SPSG)
ATI .... Atico [*Peru*] [*Seismograph station code, US Geological Survey*] (SEIS)
ATI .... AtLANta Technologies, Incorporated [*Atlanta, GA*] [*Telecommunications service*] (TSSD)
ATI .... Atomwirtschaft Atomtechnik [*A publication*]
ATI .... Attitudes toward Industrialization [*Psychology*]
ATI .... Audiometer Telephone Interface [*for the hearing-impaired*]
ATI .... Australian Transport Index [*A publication*] (APTA)
ATI .... Automated Technical Information (MCD)
ATI .... Automatic Target Identification
ATI .... Automatic Track Initiation
ATI .... Automation Techniques, Incorporated
ATI .... Average Total Inspection [*QCR*]
ATI .... Tilley Public Library, Alberta [*Library symbol*] [*National Library of Canada*] (NLC)
ATIAA5..... Acta. Institut d'Anesthesiologie [*A publication*]
ATIAD8..... Anuario Tecnico. Instituto de Pesquisas Zootecnicas "Francisco Osorio" [*A publication*]
ATIB .... Army Tactical Intelligence Agency Blueprint (MCD)
ATIBA8..... Antibiotica [*Bilingual Edition*] [*A publication*]

ATIBT .... Association Technique Internationale des Bois Tropicaux [*International Technical Tropical Timber Association*] (EAIO)
ATIC......... Adaptable Terminal Interface Configuration [*Military*] (MCD)
ATIC......... Aerospace Technical Intelligence Center
ATIC......... Air Technical Intelligence Center
ATIC......... Army Tactical Intelligence Committee (MCD)
ATIC......... Army Tactical Intelligence Concept (MCD)
ATIC......... Association Technique de l'Importation Charbonniere (EA)
ATIC......... Atlantic Business [*A publication*]
ATID .... American Trade and Industrial Development
ATID .... Australian Transport Information Directory [*Australia Bureau of Transport Economics*] [*Information service or system*] (CRD)
ATIEP .... Association of Telephone Information and Entertainment Providers [*British*]
ATIF .... Alpha Trans-Inducing Factor [*Genetics*]
ATIF .... American Tennis Industry Federation (EA)
ATIG .... Alternative Technology Information Group (EAIO)
ATIGS .... Advanced Tactical Inertial Guidance System [*Navy*]
ATII .... Advanced Techniques for Imagery Interpretation (AABC)
ATII .... Associate of the Institute of Taxation [*British*] (DBQ)
ATIL .... Air Target Intelligence Liaison Program [*Air Force*]
ATILH...... Association Technique de l'Industrie des Liants Hydrauliques [*Technical Association for the Hydraulic Binders Industry*] (EISS)
ATIME...... Association of Theological Institutes in the Middle East (EAIO)
ATIMS ..... Automatic Time Interval Measurement System [*Air Force*]
ATIN .... AIDS [*Acquired Immune Deficiency Syndrome*] Targeted Information Newsletter [*Williams & Wilkins*] [*A publication*]
ATIN .... Andean Trade Information Network (EAIO)
At Ind........ Atom Industry [*A publication*]
A T Index... Alternative/Appropriate Technology Index [*A publication*]
At Indones ... Atom Indonesia [*A publication*]
At-Inf........ Atom-Informationen [*A publication*]
At Inn Shell Processes ... Atomic Inner-Shell Processes [*A publication*]
ATIO......... Anguilla Tourist Information Office [*Later, ATIRO*] (EA)
ATIR......... Absolute Terminal Innervation Ratio [*Psychiatry*]
ATIR......... Atlantica and Iceland Review [*A publication*]
ATIRA Tech Dig ... ATIRA [*Ahmedabad Textile Industry's Research Association*] Technical Digest [*A publication*]
ATIRO...... Anguilla Tourist Information and Reservation Office (EA)
ATIS......... Adirondack Trail Improvement Society (EA)
ATIS......... Advanced Thermal Imaging Scanner [*or System*]
ATIS......... Air Technical Intelligence Study [*Air Force*]
ATIS......... Airborne Test Instrumentation System [*Air Force*] (MCD)
ATIS......... Allied Translator and Interpreter Service
ATIS......... Antenna and Transmitter Improvement Study
ATIS......... Association of Teachers in Independent Schools [*Australia*]
ATIS......... Association of Teachers in Independent Schools in New York City and Vicinity (EA)
ATIS......... AT & T Information Systems [*Telecommunications*]
ATIS......... Automatic Terminal Information Service [*Aviation*] (AFM)
ATIS......... Automatic Transmitter Identification System [*Citizens band radio*]
ATISC .... Air Technical Intelligence Services Command [*Air Force*]
ATISNYCV ... Association of Teachers in Independent Schools in New York City and Vicinity (EA)
ATIWG...... Apollo Test Integration Working Groups [*NASA*] (KSC)
ATIX......... Airlantic Transport [*Air carrier designation symbol*]
ATJ........... Association of Teachers of Japanese (EA)
ATJ........... Australasian Typographical Journal [*A publication*]
ATJC......... Annular Turbojet Combustor
ATJL......... Adriatico Tirreno Jonio Ligure [*Shipping*] [*Italy*] (EY)
At Jpn .... Atoms in Japan [*A publication*]
ATJS .... Advanced Tactical Jamming System [*Aircraft*]
ATJS .... Airborne Tactical Jamming System [*Air Force*]
ATJSA....... Atoms in Japan. Supplement [*A publication*]
ATK.......... Alliant Techsystems [*NYSE symbol*] (SPSG)
ATK.......... AMTRAK Library, Washington, DC [*OCLC symbol*] (OCLC)
ATk.......... Antitank [*Also, AT*] (NATG)
ATK.......... Asitka Resources Corp. [*Vancouver Stock Exchange symbol*]
ATK.......... Atkasuk Village, AK [*Location identifier*] [*FAA*] (FAAL)
Atk .... Atkinson's Quarter Sessions Records [*Yorkshire, England*] [*A publication*] (DLA)
Atk .... Atkyn's English Chancery Reports [*1736-55*] [*A publication*] (DLA)
ATK.......... Atqasuk [*Alaska*] [*Airport symbol*] (OAG)
ATK.......... Attack (AABC)
ATK.......... Available Tonne-Kilometer (ADA)
AtKap........ Ateneum Kaplanskie [*Wloclawek, Poland*] [*A publication*]
ATKCARAIRWING ... Attack Carrier Air Wing [*Navy*]
Atk Ch Pr... Atkinson's Chancery Practice [*A publication*] (DLA)
Atk Con...... Atkinson on Conveyancing [*A publication*] (DLA)
ATKHC...... Attack Helicopter Company [*Military*] (AABC)
Atkinson..... Atkinson's Law of Solicitors' Liens [*1905*] [*A publication*] (DLA)
ATKM........ Atek Metals Center, Inc. [*NASDAQ symbol*] (NQ)
ATKN .... Atkinson [*Guy F.*] Company of California [*San Francisco, CA*] [*NASDAQ symbol*] (NQ)

Atk PT .... Atkyn's Parliamentary Tracts [*A publication*] (DLA)
ATKRON .. Attack Squadron [*Navy*] (MUGU)
ATKSC...... Attack Surveillance Committee [*Army*] (AABC)
ATKSC...... Attack Surveillance Coverage [*Army*] (AABC)
Atk Sher... Atkinson on Sheriffs [*A publication*] (DLA)
Atk Titles... Atkinson on Marketable Titles [*A publication*] (DLA)
ATL .... Achilles Tendon Lengthening [*Medicine*]
ATL .... Acoustic Test Laboratory
ATL .... Active Time List [*Data processing*]
ATL .... Actual Total Loss
ATL .... Adult T-Cell Leukemia [*Medicine*]
ATL .... Advanced Technology Laboratory [*Navy*] (MCD)
AT/L.......... Advanced Technology/Libraries [*Information service*]
ATL .... Aeronautical Turbine Laboratory
ATL .... Air Atlantic [*East Boston, MA*] [*FAA designator*] (FAAC)
ATL .... Air Trails, Inc. [*Salinas, CA*] [*FAA designator*] (FAAC)
ATL .... Air Transport Liaison [*Military*] [*British*]
ATL .... American Tariff League [*Later, TRC*]
ATL .... American Theological Library Association, Princeton, NJ
               [*OCLC symbol*] (OCLC)
ATL .... Analog Threshold Logic
ATL .... Antitrust Law
ATL .... Applied Technology Laboratory [*Army*] (GRD)
ATL .... Armament Technology Division [*Air Force*] (MCD)
ATL .... Armywide Training Literature
ATL .... Arranged Total Loss [*Insurance*] (AIA)
ATL .... Artificial Transmission Line
ATL .... Association des Traducteurs Litteraires [*Literary Translators'
               Association*] [*Canada*]
ATL .... Atalanta Sosnoff Capital Corp. [*NYSE symbol*] (SPSG)
ATL .... [*The*] Athenian Tribute Lists [*A publication*] (OCD)
ATL .... Atlanta [*Georgia*] [*Seismograph station code, US Geological
               Survey*] (SEIS)
ATL .... Atlanta [*Georgia*] [*Airport symbol*]
ATL .... Atlantic (AFM)
Atl .... Atlantic [*Record label*]
Atl .... Atlantic Monthly [*A publication*]
Atl .... Atlantico [*A publication*]
ATL .... Atlantis Tank Landing Craft
ATL .... Atlantisch Perspektief [*A publication*]
ATL .... Atlas (ROG)
ATL .... Attempt to Locate
ATL .... Australian Income Tax Legislation [*A publication*]
ATL .... Automated Tape Library
ATL .... Automatic Test Line
ATL .... Automatic Turret Lathe
ATL .... Awaiting Trial
ATL .... Tank Landing Craft [*Navy symbol*] [*Obsolete*]
ATLA.......... Adult T-Cell Leukemia Antigen [*Medicine*]
ATLA......... Air Transport Licensing Authority [*British*]
ATLA......... Alternatives to Laboratory Animals [*A publication*]
ATLA......... American Theological Library Association (EA)
ATLA......... American Theological Library Association, Yale University
               Divinity School, New Haven, CT [*Library symbol*]
               [*Library of Congress*] (LCLS)
ATLA......... Antiquarian Trade List Annual [*A publication*]
ATLA......... Association of Trial Lawyers of America (EA)
Atla .... Atlantis [*A publication*]
ATLA-Alt L ... ATLA-Alternatives to Laboratory Animals [*A publication*]
ATLABL ... Atalanta Norvegica [*A publication*] (MUGU)
Atl Adv...... Atlantic Advocate [*A publication*]
ATLAI........ American Theological Library Association. Indexes
ATLAM..... Antiterritorial Land Mine (MCD)
Atlan .... Atlantic Monthly [*A publication*]
Atlan Adv... Atlantic Advocate [*A publication*]
Atlan Bs C ... Atlanta Business Chronicle [*United States*] [*A publication*]
Atlan Com Q ... Atlantic Community Quarterly [*A publication*]
Atlan Cons ... Atlanta Constitution [*United States*] [*A publication*]
Atlan Insight ... Atlantic Insight [*A publication*]
Atlan Mo.... Atlantic Monthly [*A publication*]
Atlanta Econ R ... Atlanta Economic Review [*A publication*]
Atlanta ER ... Atlanta Economic Review [*A publication*]
Atlanta Hist J ... Atlanta Historical Journal [*A publication*]
Atlanta Jou ... Atlanta Journal/Atlanta Constitution Weekend [*A publication*]
Atlanta M .. Atlanta Magazine [*A publication*]
Atlanta Med ... Atlanta Medicine [*A publication*]
Atlantic...... Atlantic Monthly [*A publication*]
Atlantic Community Q ... Atlantic Community Quarterly [*A publication*]
Atlantic Econ J ... Atlantic Economic Journal [*A publication*]
Atlantic Pap ... Atlantic Papers [*A publication*]
ATLA Pro ... American Theological Library Association. Proceedings [*A
               publication*]
ATLAS ...... Abbreviated Test Language for Avionics Systems
ATLAS ...... Advanced Tactical Lightweight Air Superiority [*RADAR*] [*Air
               Force*] (MCD)
ATLAS ...... Advanced Tactical Lightweight Avionics System
ATLAS ...... Advanced Target Location and Strike
ATLAS ...... Advanced Technology Large Aircraft System [*Air
               Force*] (MCD)
ATLAS ...... ALITALIA, Lufthansa, Air France, Sabena [*Consortium of
               airlines*] (MCD)

ATLAS ...... Antitank LASER-Assisted System [*British*]
ATLAS ...... Argonne Tandem/LINAC Accelerator System [*Department of
               Energy*]
ATLAS ...... Army Tactical, Logistical, and Air Simulation (MCD)
ATLAS ...... Artillery Towing Light Auxiliary System [*Army*] (MCD)
ATLAS ...... Association of Teachers of Latin American Studies (EA)
ATLAS ...... Attendance and Labor System (MCD)
ATLAS ...... Australian Travel and Leisure Automated Systems
ATLAS ...... Automated Tape Label Assignment System (MCD)
ATLAS ...... Automatic Tabulating, Listing, and Sorting System [*Software*]
ATLAS ...... Automatic Tape Load Audit System
ATLAS ...... Automatic Test Equipment Language Standardization (MCD)
ATLAS ...... Automatic Thin-Layer Analytical System
ATLAS ...... [*A*] Tactical, Logistical, and Air Simulation [*NATO*] (NATG)
ATLAS ...... [*A*] Total Library Automation System
Atlas of Aust Resources ... Atlas of Australian Resources [*A
               publication*] (APTA)
Atlas Bin Alloy Period Index ... Atlas of Binary Alloys. A Periodic Index [*A
               publication*]
Atlas Div Fish Oceanogr CSIRO ... Atlas. Division of Fisheries and
               Oceanography. Commonwealth Scientific and Industrial
               Organisation [*A publication*] (APTA)
Atlas Fiz Svoistv Miner Porod Khibinskikh Mestorozhd ... Atlas Fizicheskikh
               Svoistv Mineralov i Porod Khibinskikh Mestorozhdenii [*A
               publication*]
Atlas Jap Fossils ... Atlas of Japanese Fossils [*A publication*]
Atlas Newsl ... Atlas Newsletter [*A publication*] (APTA)
Atlas Protein Sequence Struct ... Atlas of Protein Sequence and Structure [*A
               publication*]
Atlas Radiol Clin ... Atlas de Radiologie Clinique [*France*] [*A publication*]
ATLASS.... Advanced Technology for Large Structural Systems [*National
               Science Foundation*]
Atlas W P Rev ... Atlas World Press Review [*A publication*]
ATLB......... Air Transport Licensing Board
ATLC.......... Atlantic (FAAC)
Atl Comm Q ... Atlantic Community Quarterly [*A publication*] (DLA)
Atl Community Quar ... Atlantic Community Quarterly [*A publication*]
Atl Com Q ... Atlantic Community Quarterly [*A publication*]
ATLD......... Air Transportable Loading Dock (AFM)
Atl 2d .... Atlantic Reporter, Second Series (West) [*A publication*] (DLA)
Atl Econ R ... Atlantic Economic Review [*A publication*]
ATLF......... Atlantic Financial Federal [*NASDAQ symbol*] (NQ)
Atl Fisherman ... Atlantic Fisherman [*A publication*]
ATLG......... [*The*] Atlantic Group, Inc. [*NASDAQ symbol*] (NQ)
ATLGT...... Archeion tou Thrakikou Laographikou kai Glossikou
               Thesaurou [*A publication*]
ATLIS........ Airborne Tracking LASER Identification System
ATLIS........ Army Technical Library Improvement Studies
ATLIS........ Australian Transport Literature Information System [*Australia
               Bureau of Transport Economics*] [*Information service or
               system*] (CRD)
ATLIS........ Automatic Tracking LASER Illumination System (MCD)
ATLIT .... Advanced Technology Light Twin Engine Aircraft (MCD)
ATLIT .... Advanced Technology Light Twin Engine Research Aircraft [*Air
               Force*] (MCD)
ATLJ .... American Trial Lawyers Association. Journal [*A
               publication*] (DLA)
ATLL......... Adult T-Cell Leukemia-Lymphoma [*Medicine*]
ATl L J ...... American Trial Lawyers Journal [*A publication*]
Atl M .... Atlantic Monthly [*A publication*]
Atl Med J... Atlantic Medical Journal [*A publication*]
Atl Mo........ Atlantic Monthly [*A publication*]
Atl Nat ...... Atlantic Naturalist [*A publication*]
ATLNDS... Atalanta [*A publication*]
ATLO .... Acceptance Test and Launch Operations [*NASA*] (MCD)
ATLO .... Air Transport Liaison Officer [*British*]
AtlO.......... Atlantic Ocean
ATLP........ Army-Wide Training Literature Program (AABC)
ATLPA...... Arctic and Alpine Research [*A publication*]
ATLPAV ... Arctic and Alpine Research [*A publication*]
Atl PR .... Atlantic Province Reports [*Information service or system*] [*A
               publication*] (DLA)
Atl Pro Bk R ... Atlantic Provinces Book Review [*A publication*]
Atl Prov...... Atlantic Province Reports [*Information service or system*] [*A
               publication*] (DLA)
Atl R.......... Atlantic Reporter [*A publication*] (DLA)
ATLRD6... Advances in Prostaglandin and Thromboxane and Leukotriene
               Research [*A publication*]
Atl Rep...... Atlantic Reporter [*A publication*] (DLA)
Atl Rep...... Atlantide Report [*A publication*]
Atl Repr .... Atlantic Reporter [*A publication*] (DLA)
ATLRS ..... Aircraft Tube-Launched Recoilless System (MCD)
ATLS .... Advanced Trauma Life Support System
ATLS .... Association of TAFE [*Technical and Further Education*]
               Library Staff [*Australia*]
ATLS .... Australian Transport Literature Information System [*Database*]
Atl Salmon J ... Atlantic Salmon Journal [*A publication*]
ATLSS.... Center for Advanced Technology for Large Structural Systems
               [*Lehigh University*] [*Research center*] (RCD)
ATLU .... Antigua Trades and Labour Union [*Affiliated with the Antigua
               Labour Party*] (EY)

ATLV......... Adult T-Cell Leukemia Virus
ATM.......... Access ATM Network, Inc. [*Toronto Stock Exchange symbol*]
ATM.......... Adoption Triangle Ministries [*Later, AFRC*]   (EA)
ATM.......... Advanced Telescope Mission [*Skylab*] [*NASA*]
ATM.......... Air Atlas/Air Maroc
ATM.......... Air Target Materials [*Military*]
ATM.......... Air Target Mosaic   (MCD)
ATM.......... Air Traffic Management
ATM.......... Air Turbine Motor
ATM.......... Aircraft Thermal Management   (MCD)
ATM.......... Aircrew Training Manual [*A publication*]   (MCD)
ATM.......... Altamira [*Brazil*] [*Airport symbol*]   (OAG)
ATM.......... Aluminum Trimethyl [*Organic chemistry*]
ATM.......... Amici Thomae Mori [*An association*] [*Angers, France*]   (EA)
AT/M......... Ampere-Turn per Meter   (MCD)
ATM.......... Antenna Test Model
ATM.......... Anthem Electronics, Inc. [*NYSE symbol*]   (SPSG)
ATM.......... Antitactical Missile
ATM.......... Antitank Missile [*Army*]
ATM.......... Apollo Telescope Mount [*NASA*]
ATM.......... Arc Tangent Mechanism
ATM.......... Army TMDE Modernization   (RDA)
ATM.......... Army Training Memorandum [*British*]
ATM.......... Assistant Traffic Manager
ATM.......... Associated Tobacco Manufacturers [*Defunct*]   (EA)
ATM.......... Association of Teachers of Management [*British*]
ATM.......... Association of Teachers of Mathematics [*Derby, England*]   (EAIO)
ATM.......... Asynchronous Transfer Mode [*Data processing*]
ATM.......... At the Market [*Market order*] [*Stock exchange term*]
AtM .... Atlantic Monthly [*A publication*]
ATM.......... Atmosphere
atm .... Atmosphere, Standard [*Unit of pressure*]
ATM.......... Atomic Energy of Canada Ltd. Library [*UTLAS symbol*]
ATM.......... Australian Tax Monitor [*A publication*]
ATM.......... Authentication Maneuver [*Aviation*]   (FAAC)
ATM.......... Automated [*or Automatic*] Teller Machine [*Banking*]
ATM.......... Automatic Toning Machine [*Color printing technology*]
ATM.......... Auxiliary Tape Memory [*Spacecraft guidance*]
ATM.......... Axial Turbo Machine
ATM.......... Thorsby Municipal Library, Alberta [*Library symbol*] [*National Library of Canada*]   (NLC)
ATMA ...... Adhesive Tape Manufacturers Association   (EAIO)
ATMA ...... American Textile Machinery Association   (EA)
ATMA ...... American Tour Managers Association   (EA)
ATMAAP ... Atti. Societa Toscana di Scienze Naturali Residente in Pisa. Memorie. Serie A [*A publication*]
ATMAC .... Advanced Technology Microelectronic Array Computer   (MCD)
ATMAC .... Air Traffic Management Automated Center   (AABC)
At Masses Fundam Constants ... Atomic Masses and Fundamental Constants [*A publication*]
At Masses Fundam Constants Proc Int Conf M ... Atomic Masses and Fundamental Constants. Proceedings of the International Conference on Atomic Masses and Fundamental Constants [*A publication*]
ATMAT..... Atmospheric Attenuation of Sound   (MCD)
ATMC ...... Advanced Technology Multimedia Communications   (MCD)
ATMC ...... Air Transport Movement Control Center
ATMC ...... Automotive Training Managers Council   (EA)
ATMCH .... Association of Teachers of Maternal and Child Health   (EA)
ATMC(O) ... Apollo Telescope Mount Console [*NASA*]
ATMCS ..... Army Tactical Multichannel Communications System   (MCD)
ATM-D...... Apollo Telescope Mount - Deployed [*NASA*]   (MCD)
ATMD ...... Attention Medical Co. [*Irving, TX*] [*NASDAQ symbol*]   (NQ)
ATMDA .... Apollo Telescope Mount Deployment Assembly [*NASA*]
ATMDC .... Apollo Telescope Mount Digital Computer [*NASA*]
ATMDS..... Antitank Mine Dispensing System   (MCD)
ATME ...... American Textile Machinery Exhibition - Yarn, Fiber, and Non-Woven Manufacturing Processes   (ITD)
ATME ...... Association of Travel Marketing Executives   (EA)
ATME ...... Atmospheric Transmission Measurement Equipment
ATME ...... Automatic Transmission Measuring Equipment [*Telecommunications*]   (TEL)
ATMED6 .. Atualidades Medicas [*A publication*]
ATMG ...... Angus Telemanagement Group, Inc. [*Pickering, ON*] [*Information service or system*] [*Telecommunications*]   (TSSD)
ATMG ...... Arms Transfer Management Group
ATMG ...... Atomizing
ATMH...... Automatic Test Message Handling   (MCD)
ATMI ...... American Textile Manufacturers Institute   (EA)
ATMI ...... Association for Technology in Music Instruction   (EA)
ATM Mess Pr ... ATM [*Archiv fuer Technisches Messen*] Messtechnische Praxis [*A publication*]
ATMN...... Amalgamated Tin Mines of Nigeria
ATMNA .... Automation [*A publication*]
atmo .... Atentisimo [*Yours Truly*] [*Spanish*] [*Correspondence*]
ATMO...... Atmosphere [*A publication*]
ATMO...... Atmospheric
At Mol Phy ... Atomic and Molecular Physics [*A publication*]

ATMOS..... Atmosphere   (KSC)
ATMOS..... Atmospheric Trace Molecules Observed by Spectroscopy
ATMOS..... Automatic Testing Multiple Operating System   (MCD)
Atmos Chem Air Pollut Semin ... Atmospheric Chemistry and Air Pollution. Seminar [*A publication*]
Atmos Chem Probl Scope ... Atmospheric Chemistry Problems and Scope [*A publication*]
Atmos Elektr Tr Vses Simp ... Atmosfernoe Elektrichestvo Trudy Vsesoyuznogo Simpoziuma po Atmosfernomu Elektrichestvu [*A publication*]
Atmos Env ... Atmospheric Environment [*A publication*]
Atmos Envir ... Atmospheric Environment [*A publication*]
Atmos Environ ... Atmospheric Environment [*A publication*]
Atmos Fiz... Atmosferos Fizika [*A publication*]
Atmos-Ocean ... Atmosphere-Ocean [*Canada*] [*A publication*]
Atmos Oceanic Phys ... Atmospheric and Oceanic Physics [*A publication*]
Atmos Oceanic Phys (Engl Ed) ... Atmospheric and Oceanic Physics (English Edition) [*A publication*]
Atmos Ozone Opt Atmos Sol Radiat (Belsk) ... Atmospheric Ozone Optics of Atmosphere Solar Radiation (Belsk) [*A publication*]
Atmos Pollut Proc Int Colloq ... Atmospheric Pollution. Proceedings of the International Colloquium [*A publication*]
Atmos Qual Improv Tech Bull ... Atmospheric Quality Improvement. Technical Bulletin [*A publication*]
Atmos Technol ... Atmospheric Technology [*A publication*]
ATMP....... Air Target Materials Program [*Military*]   (AFM)
ATMPA2... Annals of Tropical Medicine and Parasitology [*A publication*]
Atm Poll Bull ... Atmosphere Pollution Bulletin [*A publication*]
ATMR ...... Advanced-Technology Medium-Range Transport
ATMS....... Administrative Transport Management Survey   (MCD)
ATMS....... Advanced Text Management System [*IBM Corp.*]
ATMS....... Air Traffic Management System [*Army*]   (AABC)
ATM-S ...... Apollo Telescope Mount - Stowed [*NASA*]   (MCD)
ATMS....... Assembly Tracking and Management System   (MCD)
ATMS....... Association of Telephone Messaging Suppliers   (EA)
ATMS....... Atmospheric Turbulence Measuring Set   (MCD)
ATMS....... Australian Traditional Medicine Society
ATMS....... Automatic Transmission Measuring System [*Terminated*]
ATMS....... Automatic Trunk Measuring System [*Bell System*]
ATMSAB .. Atualidades Medico Sanitarias [*A publication*]
ATMT ...... Antitank Missile Test   (MCD)
ATMT ...... Attempt   (FAAC)
ATMTas.... Adabietsunaslik va Tilsunaslik Masalalari/Voprosy Literaturovedenija i Jazykoznanija (Tasent) [*A publication*]
ATMTC..... Attempt to Contact   (FAAC)
ATMU ...... Aircraft Torpedo Maintenance Unit [*Navy*]
ATMVAK ... Agronomia Tropical (Maracay, Venezuela) [*A publication*]
ATMXAQ ... Agricultura Tecnica en Mexico [*A publication*]
ATN.......... Acton Corp. [*AMEX symbol*]   (SPSG)
ATN.......... Actual Test Number [*NASA*]
ATN.......... Acute Tubular Necrosis [*Nephrology*]
ATN.......... Adaptive Tactical Navigation   (MCD)
ATN.......... Alabama, Tennessee & Northern R. R. [*AAR code*]
ATN.......... Astrogeophysical Transmission Network [*Air Force's Air Weather Service Teletypewriter circuit*]
ATN.......... Atna Resources Ltd. [*Vancouver Stock Exchange symbol*]
ATN.......... Attention
ATN.......... Audio Teleconference Network [*Acadia University*] [*Wolfville, NS*]   (TSSD)
ATN.......... Augmented Transition Network [*Language analysis*]
ATN.......... Australian Television Network
ATN.......... Autonomously Functioning Thyroid Nodule [*Endocrinology*]
ATN.......... Aviation Technician, Navigation
ATN.......... Avionics Technical Note
ATN.......... Helena/Fort Harrison, MT [*Location identifier*] [*FAA*]   (FAAL)
ATN.......... Namatanai [*Papua New Guinea*] [*Airport symbol*]   (OAG)
ATN.......... US Air Transit [*Garland, TX*] [*FAA designator*]   (FAAC)
ATNBAX.... Atti. Societa Toscana di Scienze Naturali. Processi Verbali e Memorie. Serie B [*A publication*]
ATNC .... Atraumatic Normocephalic [*Medicine*]
ATND .... Attend   (FAAC)
ATNED ..... ATES [*Aquifer Thermal Energy Storage*] Newsletter [*A publication*]
ATNG .... AlaTenn Resources, Inc. [*NASDAQ symbol*]   (NQ)
ATNM ...... Alcoholism. The National Magazine [*A publication*]
ATNM ...... Antitank, Nonmetallic
ATNMAW ... Agronomie Tropicale. Serie Riz et Riziculture et Cultures Vivrieres Tropicales [*A publication*]
ATNN....... American Telemedia Network, Inc. [*NASDAQ symbol*]   (NQ)
ATNO....... Atomic Number
ATNR .... Asymmetrical Tonic Neck Reflex
At Nucl En ... Atomics and Nuclear Energy [*A publication*]
At Nucl Energy ... Atomics and Nuclear Energy [*England*] [*A publication*]
ATO.......... Abort-to-Orbit [*NASA*]   (NASA)
ATO.......... Academy of Teachers of Occupations [*Defunct*]   (EA)
ATO.......... Accelerated Take-Off [*British military*]   (DMA)
ATO.......... Action Technical Order
ATO.......... Actual Time Over   (MCD)
ATO.......... Aeronautical Telecommunications Officers   (ADA)
ATO.......... Aeronautical Telecommunications Operator

ATO.......... African Timber Organization   (EAIO)
ATO.......... Agricultural Trade Office [Foreign Agricultural Service]
ATO.......... Air Tactics Officer [Air Force]
ATO.......... Air Targets Officer
ATO.......... Air Tasking Order
ATO.......... Air Terminal Officer [Air Force]
ATO.......... Air Training Officer [Air Force]
ATO.......... Air Transfer Order
ATO.......... Aircraft Technical Order
ATO.......... Aircraft Transfer Order
ATO.......... Allied Travel Office   (NATG)
ATO.......... Alpha Tau Omega [Fraternity]
ATO.......... Ammunition Technical Officer [Ireland]
ATO.......... Antarctic Treaty Organization   (ASF)
ATO.......... Apollo Test Operations [NASA]   (KSC)
ATO.......... Arab Towns Organization [Safat, Kuwait]   (EAIO)
ATO.......... Area Traffic Officer
ATO.......... Army Tank Office   (RDA)
ATO.......... Assisted Takeoff [British aviation and rocket term]
ATO.......... At the Opening [Investment term]
ATO.......... Athenaeum of Ohio, Norwood, OH [OCLC symbol]   (OCLC)
ATO.......... Atmos Energy Corp. [NYSE symbol]   (SPSG)
ATO.......... Aviation Test Office [Edwards Air Force Base, CA] [Army]
ATO.......... Ocean Tug, Old [Navy symbol]
ATO.......... Tomahawk Public Library, Alberta [Library symbol] [National Library of Canada]   (NLC)
ATOA........ Air Transport Operators Association   (EAIO)
ATOA........ American Truck Owners Association [New York, NY]   (EA)
ATOA........ American Tung Oil Association [Defunct]
ATOC........ Air Transport Operation Centre [Military] [British]
ATOC........ Allied Tactical Operations Center [Military]
ATOC........ Average Total Operating Cost   (KSC)
ATOE........ American Theatre Organ Enthusiasts [Later, ATOS]
ATOF........ Tofield Public Library, Alberta [Library symbol] [National Library of Canada]   (NLC)
ATOG........ Abnormal Transient Operational Guidelines [Nuclear energy]   (NRCH)
ATOG........ Air-to-Ground Gunnery   (MCD)
ATOG........ Allowable Takeoff Gross [Weight] [for an aircraft]
ATOG........ Andover Togs, Inc. [New York, NY] [NASDAQ symbol]   (NQ)
ATOG........ Anticipated Transient Operating Guideline [Nuclear energy]   (NRCH)
ATOIA....... Automobil-Industrie [West Germany] [A publication]
ATOIC....... Antiterrorism Operations and Intelligence Cell [Army]
ATOL........ Air Travel Organisers Licence [British]
ATOLL....... Acceptance Test of Launch Language [NASA]
ATOLL....... Atlantic Tropical Oceanic Lower Layer [National Oceanic and Atmospheric Administration]
Atoll Res Bull ... Atoll Research Bulletin [A publication]
ATOLS....... Advanced Takeoff and Landing System   (MCD)
ATOM........ Analog Tree-Organized Multiplexer
ATOM........ Apollo Telescope Orientation Mount Program [NASA]   (MCD)
ATOM........ Arizona Trade-Off Model [State of Arizona and Department of Commerce project to resolve conflicts between economic and environmental goals]
ATOM........ Astronomical Telescope Orientation Mount [NASA]
Atom .... Atomics [A publication]
ATOM........ Automatic Transmission of Mail [Early electronic mail system]
ATOM........ Automatique, Inc. [NASDAQ symbol]   (NQ)
Atom Absorpt Newsl ... Atomic Absorption Newsletter [A publication]
ATOMDEF ... Atomic Defense
ATOMDEV ... Atomic Device [Military]
Atomedia Philipp ... Atomedia Philippines [A publication]
Atom Ener A ... Atomic Energy in Australia [A publication]
Atom Energy LJ ... Atomic Energy Law Journal [A publication]   (DLA)
Atom Ener R ... Atomic Energy Review [A publication]
Atom En L Rep CCH ... Atomic Energy Law Reporter (Commerce Clearing House) [A publication]   (DLA)
Atomic Data ... Atomic Data and Nuclear Data Tables [A publication]
Atomic Energy in Aust ... Atomic Energy in Australia [A publication]   (APTA)
Atomic Energy L J ... Atomic Energy Law Journal [A publication]
Atomic Eng LJ ... Atomic Energy Law Journal [A publication]
Atomic Sci ... Bulletin of the Atomic Scientists [A publication]
Atom Indones ... Atom Indonesia [A publication]
Atomkernene ... Atomkernenergie [A publication]
Atomkerneneg Kerntech ... Atomkernenergie Kerntechnik [A publication]
ATOMKI Kozl ... ATOMKI [Atommag Kutato Intezet] Koezlemenyek [A publication]
Atomnaya En ... Atomnaya Energiya [USSR] [A publication]
Atomn Energ ... Atomnaya Energiya [USSR] [A publication]
Atomo Petrol Elet ... Atomo, Petrol, Elettricita [Italy] [A publication]
Atomprax... Atompraxis [A publication]
ATOMS..... Automated Technical Order Maintenance Sequences [or Systems] [The Boeing Co.]   (MCD)
ATOMSTATSREP ... Atomic Status Report   (NATG)
Atomtech Tajek ... Atomtechnikai Tajekoztato [A publication]
Atomwirtsch ... Atomwirtschaft Atomtechnik [A publication]
Atomwirtsch Atomtech ... Atomwirtschaft Atomtechnik [A publication]
ATON........ Aids to Navigation
ATONU..... Assistance Technique de l'Organisation des Nations Unies

Atoomenerg Haar Toepass ... Atoomenergie en Haar Toepassingen [A publication]
Atoomenerg Toepass ... Atoomenergie en Haar Toepassingen [A publication]
ATOP .... Ambient Temperature Observer/Predictor   (MCD)
ATOP .... Australian Taxation Office Practice [A publication]
ATopPir.... Actas. Primera Reunion de Toponimia Pirenaica [A publication]
ATOPS ...... Advanced Transport Operating System   (MCD)
A Tor......... Atti. Accademia delle Scienze di Torino [A publication]
ATOR .... Australian Torts Reporter [A publication]
ATORP.... Antitorpedo   (MSA)
ATORP...... Atomic Torpedo [Military]
ATOS .... American Theatre Organ Society   (EA)
ATOS .... Assisted Takeoff System
ATOS .... Association of Temporary Office Services
ATOS .... Automated Technical Order System [Air Force]   (MCD)
ATOT .... Actual Time over Target   (AFM)
ATOT .... Angle Track on Target [Military]
ATOVS...... Advanced TIROS [Television Infrared Observation Satellite] Operational Vertical Sounder
ATOWG .... Advanced Technical Objective Working Group
ATP .... Accelerator-Tritium Producer [Nuclear physics]
ATP .... Acceptance Test Plan [or Procedure]
ATP .... Accord Transports Permissables [European agreement on the transport of perishable foodstuffs]
ATP .... Acquisition, Tracking, and Pointing [Military]   (SDI)
ATP .... Activation Test Program   (MCD)
ATP .... Actual Time of Penetration [Aviation]   (FAAC)
ATP .... Adenosine Triphosphate [Biochemistry]
ATP .... Admissions Testing Program
ATP .... Advance Test Plant   (AAG)
ATP .... Advanced Tactical Processor
ATP .... Advanced Technology Program [Military]
ATP .... Advanced Test in Psychology
ATP .... Advanced Tracking Program   (MCD)
ATP .... Advanced Turboprop [Aeronautics]
ATP .... Agence Tchadienne de Presse [Chad Press Agency]
ATP .... Agreement for the International Transport of Perishable Products
ATP .... Aid and Trade Provision [Shipping]   (DS)
ATP .... Air Tactical Publication
ATP .... Air Traffic Procedures
ATP .... Aircraft Technical Publishers [Information service or system]   (IID)
ATP .... Airline Tariff Publishing Co.
ATP .... Airline Transport Pilot [Certificate] [British]   (IEEE)
ATP .... Aitape [Papua New Guinea] [Airport symbol]   (OAG)
ATP .... Alcohol Treatment Program
ATP .... Allied Tactical Publication [Army] [NATO]   (AFIT)
ATP .... Allied Technical Publication [Navy] [NATO]   (NG)
ATP .... Alternate Target Point
ATP .... Alternate Test Procedure [for aviation jet fuels] [Navy]
ATP .... American Telephone & Telegraph Co., Technical Process, Piscataway, NJ [OCLC symbol]   (OCLC)
ATP .... American Theater Productions, Inc.
ATP .... Ammunition Transfer Point   (MCD)
ATP .... Antitorque Pedal
ATP .... AppleTalk Transaction Protocol [Apple Computer, Inc.]
ATP .... Appropriate Technology Project [Maintained by the Volunteers in Asia]
ATP .... Archivio per lo Studio delle Tradizioni Populari [A publication]
ATP .... Army Tank Program   (MCD)
ATP .... Army Training Plan   (MCD)
ATP .... Army Training Program
ATP .... Array Transform Processor
ATP .... Arts et Traditions Populaires [A publication]
A & TP...... Assembly and Test Pit [Nuclear energy]   (NRCH)
ATP .... Association for the Teaching of Psychology [British]
ATP .... Association of Technical Professionals   (EA)
ATP .... Association of Tennis Professionals   (EA)
ATP .... Association of Tequila Producers   (EA)
ATP .... Association for Transpersonal Psychology   (EA)
ATP .... Association of Transportation Practitioners   (EA)
ATP .... Astronautics Test Procedures   (AAG)
ATP .... At (Time or Place) [Aviation]   (FAAC)
ATP .... Augmented Thrust Propulsion
ATP .... Australian Trade Practices Report [A publication]   (APTA)
ATP .... Authority to Participate Card
ATP .... Authority to Proceed   (MCD)
ATP .... Authorization to Purchase [Food stamp card] [Department of Agriculture]
ATP .... Automated Test Plan   (BUR)
ATP .... Auxiliary Tool Production   (MCD)
ATPA....... Alpha Temperature Probe Assembly [NASA]   (MCD)
ATPA....... Auxiliary Turbopump Assembly
ATPAC...... Air Traffic Procedures Advisory Committee   (FAAC)
ATPAD9.... Annals of Tropical Paediatrics [A publication]
ATPAM.... Association of Theatrical Press Agents and Managers   (EA)
At Parm ..... Ateneo Parmense [A publication]
ATPAS ...... Association of Teachers of Printing and Allied Subjects [British]

ATP-ASCP ... Army Transportation Plan in Support of the Army Strategic Capabilities Plan   (AABC)
ATPase ...... Adenosine Triphosphatase [*An enzyme*]
ATPC .... Association of Temporary Personnel Contractors
ATPC .... Association of Tin Producing Countries   (EAIO)
ATPC .... Athey Products Corporation [*Raleigh, NC*] [*NASDAQ symbol*]   (NQ)
ATPCC ...... Attitudes toward Parental Control of Children [*Psychology*]
ATPD .... Aid to the Totally and Permanently Disabled [*Social Security Administration*]   (OICC)
ATPD .... Ambient Temperature and Pressure, Dry [*Medicine*]
ATPDC ...... Advances in Tumor Prevention, Detection, and Characterization [*Elsevier Book Series*] [*A publication*]
ATPDC ...... Atomic Transition Probabilities Data Center
ATPE .... Association of Teachers in Penal Establishments [*British*]
ATPF .... Armament Test Preparation Facility
ATP-FC ..... Acquisition, Tracking, Pointing, and Fire Control [*Military*]   (SDI)
ATPFS .... Air Transportable Pantograph Fueling System   (MCD)
ATPG .... Automatic Test Pattern [*or Program*] Generation   (MCD)
At Phys ..... Atomic Physics [*A publication*]
ATPI .... Advanced Tobacco Products, Incorporated [*San Antonio, TX*] [*NASDAQ symbol*]   (NQ)
ATPI .... American Textbook Publishers Institute [*Later, AAP*]   (EA)
ATPI .... American Transfer Printing Institute [*Later, ITPI*]   (EA)
ATPL .... Airline Transport Pilot's Licence [*British*]   (DBQ)
ATPLO ...... Army of Tripura People's Liberation Organization [*India*]   (PD)
ATPM .... Association of Teachers of Preventive Medicine   (EA)
ATPO .... Associate Technical Project Officer
ATPOS ...... Atomic Post-Strike Analysis Report
At Power .... Atomic Power [*A publication*]
At Pow R .... Atomic Power Review [*A publication*]
ATPQ .... Acetylene-Terminated Phenylquinoxaline [*Polymer technology*]
ATPR .... Advanced Triga Prototype Reactor
ATPR .... Annual Technical Progress Report
ATPR .... Australian Trade Practices Reporter [*A publication*]
ATPR (Com) ... Australian Trade Practices Reporter. Commission Decisions [*A publication*]
ATPR (Digest) ... Australian Trade Practices Reporter. Cases and Decisions Digest [*A publication*]
At Processes Appl ... Atomic Processes and Applications [*A publication*]
ATPS .... Alternate Thermal Protection System   (MCD)
ATPS .... Ambient Temperature and Pressure, Saturated [*Medicine*]
ATPS .... Automatic Type Placement System
ATPSD ...... ACM [*Association for Computing Machinery*] Transactions on Programming Languages and Systems [*A publication*]
ATPU .... Air Transport Pressurizing Unit
ATPW .... Air Transit of the Printed Word [*Australia*]
ATQ .... American Transcendental Quarterly [*A publication*]
ATQ .... Amritsar [*India*] [*Airport symbol*]   (OAG)
ATQK .... Atuaqunik. Newsletter of Northern Quebec [*A publication*]
At Quart ..... Art Quarterly [*A publication*]
ATR .... Acceptance Test Report   (MCD)
ATR .... Achates Resources Ltd. [*Vancouver Stock Exchange symbol*]
ATR .... Achilles Tendon Reflex [*Neurology*]
ATR .... Advance Technical Requirements   (MCD)
ATR .... Advanced Tactical RADAR [*Army*]   (MCD)
ATR .... Advanced Telecommunication Research
ATR .... Advanced Test Reactor [*Nuclear energy*]
ATR .... Advanced Thermal Reactor
ATR .... African Trade Review [*A publication*]
ATR .... Aided Target Recognition [*Army*]
ATR .... Air-Launched Trainer Rocket   (AFM)
ATR .... Air Traffic Regulations
ATR .... Air Transport of Radiation
ATR .... Air Transport Radio [*NASA*]   (NASA)
ATR .... Air Transport Rating [*NASA*]   (FAAC)
ATR .... Air Transportation Rack [*NASA*]   (NASA)
ATR .... Air Turbo Rocket
ATR .... Aircraft Trouble Report
ATR .... Alliance Tire & Rubber Co. Ltd. [*AMEX symbol*]   (SPSG)
ATR .... Ambient Temperature Range
ATR .... Americans for Tax Reform   (EA)
ATR .... Analog Tape Recorder
ATR .... Angle, Time, Range [*Data processing*]
ATR .... Anglican Theological Review [*A publication*]
ATR .... Answering Time Recorder [*Telecommunications*]   (TEL)
ATR .... Anti-Torture Research [*An association*] [*Copenhagen, Denmark*]   (EAIO)
ATR .... Anti-Transmit-Receive
ATR .... Antitank Regiment [*Military*]
ATR .... Apollo Test Requirements [*NASA*]   (KSC)
ATR .... Apprenticeship and Training Representative [*Bureau of Apprenticeship and Training*] [*Department of Labor*]
ATR .... Art Therapist, Registered
ATR .... Association of Teachers of Russian [*British*]
ATR .... Atar [*Mauritania*] [*Airport symbol*]   (OAG)
At R .... Atene e Roma [*A publication*]
ATR .... Atlantic Richfield Co., Geoscience Library, Dallas, TX [*OCLC symbol*]   (OCLC)

ATR .... Atlantic Tracking Range [*NASA*]
ATR .... Atlas Airlines [*Muncie, IN*] [*FAA designator*]   (FAAC)
ATR .... Atresia [*Medicine*]
ATR .... Attenuated Total Reflectance [*Instrumentation*]
ATR .... Attribute
ATR .... Audio Tape Recording
ATR .... Austin Trumbull Radio [*Air transport radio prior to April 15, 1967*]   (MCD)
ATR .... Australasian Tax Reports [*A publication*]   (APTA)
ATR .... Australian Tax Reports (Butterworths) [*A publication*]   (DLA)
ATR .... Australian Technology Resources
ATR .... Australian Telecommunication Research [*A publication*]   (APTA)
ATR .... Automatic Target Recognition
ATR .... Automatic Trunk Routiner   (MCD)
ATR .... Automotive Test Rig [*Military*]   (RDA)
ATR .... Aviation Technician, RADAR
ATR .... Aviation Training Record
ATR .... Rescue Ocean Tug [*Navy symbol*]
ATR .... Waterloo, DE [*Location identifier*] [*FAA*]   (FAAL)
ATRA .... Advanced Transit Association   (EA)
A-TRA .... Akhal-Teke Registry of America   (EA)
ATRA .... All-Terrain Racing Association   (EA)
ATRA .... American Therapeutic Recreation Association   (EA)
ATRA .... American Tort Reform Association   (EA)
ATRA .... American Toy Retailers Association   (EA)
ATRA .... Atratech, Inc. [*NASDAQ symbol*]   (NQ)
ATRA .... Australian Tape Recordist Association
ATRA .... Automatic Tracking Razor Action [*The Gillette Co.*]
ATRA .... Automatic Transmission Rebuilders Association   (EA)
At Radiat .... Atomes et Radiations [*A publication*]
ATRAN ..... Automatic Terrain Recognition and Navigation Guidance System
A/TRANS ... Automatic Transmission [*Automotive engineering*]
ATR Aust Telecommun Res ... ATR: Australian Telecommunication Research [*A publication*]   (APTA)
ATRAX ...... Air Transportable Communications Complex
Atrazine Inform Sheet Geigy Agr Chem Atrazine Herbic ... Atrazine Information Sheet. Geigy Agricultural Chemicals. Atrazine Herbicides [*A publication*]
ATRC .... Advanced Test Reactor Critical Facility [*Nuclear energy*]
ATRC .... Air Traffic Regulation Center   (AFM)
ATRC .... Air Training Command [*Air Force*]
ATRC .... Antitracking Control
ATRC .... Arizona Transportation Research Center [*Arizona State University*] [*Research center*]   (RCD)
ATRC .... Army Transportation Research Command
ATRC .... Atlantic Research Corporation [*NASDAQ symbol*]   (NQ)
ATRCA .... Atlas de Radiologie Clinique [*A publication*]
ATRCE ...... Advanced Test Reactor Critical Experiment [*Nuclear energy*]
ATRCV .... All-Terrain Remote Control Vehicle   (MCD)
ATRD .... Automatic Target Recognition Device
ATRDB ...... Army Terrain Requirements Data Base
ATREDV .... Annals of Tropical Research [*A publication*]
ATren .... Archivio Trentino [*A publication*]
ATREP .... Air Traffic Representative   (FAAC)
At Rep .... Atlantic Reporter [*A publication*]   (DLA)
At Res B ..... Atoll Research Bulletin [*A publication*]
AT Rev .... Australian Tax Review [*A publication*]   (APTA)
ATREX ...... Astrophysics Transient Explorer
ATRF .... Australian Tax Research Foundation
ATRHTRBAA ... Association to Remind Husbands to Remember Birthdays and Anniversaries [*Probably mythical*]
ATRI .... Air Transportable Radio Installations
ATRI .... Artists Technical Research Institute   (EA)
A Trial Law Am LJ ... Association of Trial Lawyers of America. Law Journal [*A publication*]
ATRIB .... Average Transfer Rate of Information BITS [*Binary Digits*] [*Data processing*]   (IEEE)
ATRID .... Automatic Target Recognition, Identification, and Detection
ATriest ...... Archeolgrafo Triestino [*A publication*]
ATRIF .... Air Transportation Research International Forum   (MCD)
ATRIMA ..... As Their Respective Interests May Appear [*Legal term*]   (ADA)
ATRIP .... Asociacion Internacional para el Progreso de la Ensenanza y de la Investigacion de la Propiedad Intelectual [*International Association for the Advancement of Teaching and Research in Intellectual Property*]   (EAIO)
ATRIP .... Australian Transport Research in Progress [*Australia Bureau of Transport Economics*] [*Information service or system*]   (CRD)
ATRIP .... International Association for the Advancement of Teaching and Research in Intellectual Property   (EA)
ATRIS .... Air Traffic Regulation Identification System [*Army*]
ATRIS .... Air Transportation Research Information Service [*National Academy of Sciences*] [*Information service or system*]
ATRJ .... Association of Teachers of Russian. Journal [*A publication*]
ATRL .... Antitank Rocket Launcher Imagery Interpretation   (AABC)
ATRLS .... Actual Time of Release [*Aviation*]
ATRM .... Acute Transient Radiation Myelopathy [*Oncology*]
ATRM .... After Torpedo Room
ATRM .... American Tax Reduction Movement   (EA)

ATRM .... Trochu Municipal Library, Alberta [*Library symbol*] [*National Library of Canada*]   (NLC)
ATRMA .... Advances in Tracer Methodology [*A publication*]
ATRN .... Army Tactical Requirements for National Reconnaissance   (MCD)
ATRN .... Austron, Inc. [*NASDAQ symbol*]   (NQ)
ATRO .... Acting Transportation Officer
ATRO .... Actual Time of Return to Operation   (AFM)
ATRO .... Astronics Corp. [*NASDAQ symbol*]   (NQ)
At Roma ..... Atene e Roma [*A publication*]
ATRON ...... Atlantic Squadron
A Trop........ Acta Tropica [*A publication*]
ATrP .... Allied Training Publications [*NATO*]   (NATG)
ATRP .... American Tax Reform Project   (EA)
ATRR........ Allocated Transfer Risk Reserve [*Banking*]
ATRR........ Antitrust and Trade Regulation Report [*Bureau of National Affairs*]
ATRRS ...... Army Training Requirements and Resources System
ATRS......... Advanced Tactical Reconnaissance System   (MCD)
ATRS......... Advanced Technology Rotor System   (MCD)
ATRS .... Assembly Test Recording System
ATRS......... Automatic Temporary Roof Support [*Mining industry*]
ATRSC ...... American Tan Rabbit Specialty Club   (EA)
ATRSO...... Accepts Transfer as Offered   (NOAA)
ATRT........ Anti-Transmit-Receive Tube
ATrT .... Troy State University, Troy, AL [*Library symbol*] [*Library of Congress*]   (LCLS)
ATrT-N ..... Troy State University, School of Nursing, Montgomery, AL [*Library symbol*] [*Library of Congress*]   (LCLS)
ATRU .... Australian Income Tax Rulings [*A publication*]
ATS .... Absolute Temperature Scale
ATS........... Academically Talented Student
ATS........... Acceptance Test Specification [*DoD*]
ATS........... Acetylene-Terminated Sulfone [*Organic chemistry*]
ATS........... Acoustic Target Sensor
ATS........... Acoustic Telemetry Subsystem   (MCD)
ATS........... Acoustic Transmission System
ATS........... Acquisition Target and Search
ATS........... Acquisition and Tracking System
ATS........... Active Television System   (MCD)
ATS........... Administrative Terminal System [*IBM Corp.*]
ATS........... Advanced Tactical Strike   (MCD)
ATS........... Advanced Technology Satellite
ATS........... Advanced Technology Spacecraft [*NASA*]   (MCD)
ATS........... Advanced Technology Systems, Inc. [*Arlington, VA*] [*Telecommunications*]   (TSSD)
ATS........... Aeronautical Training Society
ATS........... Aerospace Test System   (MCD)
ATS........... Agence Telegraphique Suisse [*Swiss News Agency*] [*Berne, Switzerland*]
ATS........... Air-to-Surface [*Missiles*]   (MCD)
ATS........... Air Tactical School [*Air Force*]
ATS........... Air Traffic Section   (AFM)
ATS........... Air Traffic Service [*of FAA*] [*Also known as AAT, AT*]
ATS........... Air Transport Service [*Navy*]
ATS........... Air Transport Squadron [*Air Force*]   (MCD)
ATS........... Air Transportable SONAR
ATS........... Air Turbine Starter   (NG)
ATS........... Aircraft Trouble-Shooting System   (MCD)
ATS........... Aircrew Training System   (MCD)
ATS........... Alarm Termination Subsystem [*Telecommunications*]   (TEL)
ATS........... Alexis De Tocqueville Society   (EA)
ATS........... Alliance for Traffic Safety   (EA)
ATS........... Alliance of Transylvanian Saxons [*Cleveland, OH*]   (EA)
ATS........... American Tarantula Society [*Defunct*]   (EA)
ATS........... American Teachers' Series [*A publication*]
ATS........... American Technical Society
ATS........... American Temperance Society [*Later, AHTS*]   (EA)
ATS........... American Tentative Society
ATS........... American Theatre Society [*Commercial firm*]   (EA)
ATS........... American Theological Society - Midwest Division   (EA)
ATS........... American Therapeutic Society [*Later, American Society for Clinical Pharmacology and Therapeutics*]   (EA)
ATS........... American Thermographic Society [*Later, American Academy of Thermology*]   (EA)
ATS........... American Thesaurus of Slang
ATS........... American Thoracic Society   (EA)
ATS........... American Tolkien Society   (EA)
ATS........... American Tract Society   (EA)
ATS........... American Trauma Society   (EA)
ATS........... American Trudeau Society [*Later, American Thoracic Society*]
ATS........... American-Turkish Society   (EA)
ATS........... Ammonium Thiosulfate [*Fertilizer*]
ATS........... Analog Tone Signal   (MCD)
ATS........... Angle Tracking System [*NASA*]
ATS........... Animal-Tub-Sized [*Paper*]
ATS........... Antitetanus Serum [*Medicine*]
ATS........... Antithymocyte Serum [*Immunochemistry*]
ATS........... Anxiety Tension State [*Psychology*]
ATS........... Apparent Time at Ship   (DS)
ATS........... Application Transfer Study [*IBM problem solving process*]

ATS........... Applications Technology Satellite [*Communications satellite*] [*NASA*]
ATS........... Arabic Translation Series [*A publication*]
ATS........... Arbeiten und Texte zur Slavistik [*A publication*]
ATS........... Army Technical School [*British military*]   (DMA)
ATS........... Army Topographic Station   (AABC)
ATS........... Army Transport Service [*Obsolete*] [*Later, Military Sea Transportation Service, then Military Sealift Command*]
ATS........... Artesia, NM [*Location identifier*] [*FAA*]   (FAAL)
ATS........... Arturo Toscanini Society   (EA)
ATS........... Assistant Traffic Supervisor   (DCTA)
ATS........... Associate of Theological Study [*British*]
ATS........... Associated Technical Services, Inc. [*Glen Ridge, NJ*] [*Information service or system*]
ATS........... Association of Theological Schools   (EA)
ATS........... Association for Transarmament Studies [*Later, CBDA*]   (EA)
ATS........... Astronomical Time Switch
ATS........... Asymptotic Threshold Shift [*Hearing*]
ATS........... Asynchronous Task Storage [*NASA*]   (NASA)
ATS........... At the Suit Of
ATS........... AT & T Transfer System [*Telecommunications*]
ATS........... Atlantic Shopping Centres Ltd. [*Toronto Stock Exchange symbol*]
ATS........... Atlantic Tracking Ship [*NASA*]   (KSC)
ATS........... Atlantic Trade Study
ATS........... Attitude Thrustor System
ATS........... Attitude Transfer System   (MCD)
ATS........... Australian Treaty Series [*A publication*]   (APTA)
ATS........... Automated Time Standards   (MCD)
ATS........... Automated Titles System [*Australia*]
ATS........... Automated Trading System [*NYSE computer*]
ATS........... Automatic Telemetry System
ATS........... Automatic Telephone Set
ATS........... Automatic Terminal System [*NASA*]   (NASA)
ATS........... Automatic Test Scoring
ATS........... Automatic Test System
ATS........... Automatic Throttle/Speed Control System   (MCD)
ATS........... Automatic Transfer of Savings [*Banking*]
ATS........... Automatic Transfer Service [*Banking*]
ATS........... Automatic Trunk Synchronizer [*Telecommunications*]   (TEL)
ATS........... Automatic Tuning System
ATS........... Auxiliary Territorial Service [*Later, WRAC*] [*British women's service*] [*World War II*]
ATS........... Avionic Test Set   (MCD)
ATS........... Avionics Test Station   (MCD)
ATS........... Salvage and Rescue Ship [*Navy symbol*]
a-ts--- .... Trucial States [*United Arab Emirates*] [*MARC geographic area code*] [*Library of Congress*]   (LCCP)
ATS............ [*A*] Tutorial System [*1971*] [*Data processing*]   (CSR)
ATS............ United States Army Troop Support and Aviation Material Readiness Command, St. Louis, MO [*OCLC symbol*]   (OCLC)
ATSA........ Aerial Transport of South Australia
ATSA........ Aero Transportes Sociedad Anonima [*Mexican airline*]
ATSA........ American Tarpan Studbook Association   (EA)
ATSA........ American Traffic Services Association [*Later, ATSSA*]   (EA)
ATSA........ American Tramp Shipowners Association   (EA)
ATSA........ Association of Technical Studies Advisers [*British*]
ATSAAL ... Associated Scientific and Technical Societies of South Africa. Annual Proceedings [*A publication*]
ATSAC...... Association of Theatre Screen Advertising Companies [*Defunct*]
ATS/AD..... Air Turbine Starter/Accessory Drive   (MCD)
ATSB......... Advanced Tactical Support Base [*Navy*]   (NVT)
ATSB......... Airborne Test Safety Board   (MCD)
ATSC......... Advanced TV Systems Committee   (EA)
ATSC......... Air Technical Service Command [*Air Force*]
ATSC......... Air Turbine Starter, Cartridge   (MCD)
ATSC......... American Torah Shelemah Committee   (EA)
ATSC......... Army Technical Service Corps
ATSC......... Army Training Support Center [*Fort Eustis, VA*]
ATSC......... Associate in the Technology of Surface Coatings [*British*]   (DBQ)
ATSC......... Atlanta Service Center [*IRS*]
ATSCCP ... Air Traffic Service Contingency Command Post [*of FAA*]   (FAAC)
At Sci J ...... Atomic Scientists Journal [*A publication*]
At Sci News ... Atomic Scientists News [*A publication*]
ATSCV....... Air Turbine Starter Control Value   (MCD)
ATSD........ Airborne Traffic Situation Display [*FAA*]
ATSD........ Arctic Tent Stake Driver   (MCD)
ATSD........ Assembly Type Supply Directive [*Military*]   (AFIT)
ATSDA...... American Tang Soo Do Association   (EA)
ATSD (AE) ... Assistant to the Secretary of Defense (Atomic Energy)
ATSDR...... Agency for Toxic Substances and Disease Registry [*Atlanta, GA*] [*Department of Health and Human Services*]
ATSD(R & O) ... Assistant to the Secretary of Defense (Review and Oversight)
ATSE......... Advanced Throttling Slurry Engine   (KSC)
ATSED2..... Annales. Tabac. Section 2 [*A publication*]
ATSER ...... Agency for Toxic Substances and Emergency Response
ATSES....... Assembly Time Standard Estimating Sheet   (MCD)

AtSetBib .... Atti della Settimana Biblica [*A publication*]   (BJA)
AT & SF ..... [*The*] Atchison, Topeka & Santa Fe Railway Co. [*Also known as Santa Fe*]
ATSF .... [*The*] Atchison, Topeka & Santa Fe Railway Co. [*Also known as Santa Fe*] [*AAR code*]
ATSF .... Automatic Target Selection File   (CINC)
AT & SFR ... [*The*] Atchison, Topeka & Santa Fe Railway Co. [*Also known as Sante Fe*]
ATSFSD .... Air Traffic Service Flight Services Division [*of FAA*]
ATSG .... Acoustic Test Signal Generator   (CAAL)
ATSI .... Association of Telemessaging Services International   (EA)
ATSIC ...... Aboriginal and Torres Strait Islander Commission [*Australia*]
ATSIC .... Aboriginal and Torres Strait Islander Curriculum Information [*Australia*]
ATSIT .... Automatic Techniques for Selection and Identification of Targets [*Army/Air Force*]   (MCD)
ATSJEA .... Automatic Test System Jet Engine Accessories
ATS List Transl ... Associated Technical Services, Inc. List of Translations [*A publication*]
ATSM .... Advanced Tactical Stand-Off Missile   (MCD)
ATS(M) .... Air Transportation Squadron (Medium)
ATSM .... ATS Money Systems, Inc. [*NASDAQ symbol*]   (NQ)
ATSM .... Automated Technique for Spacecraft Monitoring [*NASA*]
ATSO .... Advanced Telecommunications Sciences Office [*STRATCOM*] [*Army*]   (RDA)
ATSOA ...... American Truck Stop Operators Association   (EA)
ATSOCC ... Applications Technology Satellite Operations Control Center [*NASA*]
ATSP .... Association of Teachers of Spanish and Portuguese [*British*]
ATSP .... Association of Technical and Supervisory Professionals   (EA)
At Spectrosc ... Atomic Spectroscopy [*A publication*]
At Spektrosk Spekr Anal Mater Resp Soveshch ... Atomnaya Spektroskopiya i Spektral'nyi Analiz. Materialy Respublikanskogo Soveshchaniya [*A publication*]
ATSq .... Air Transport Squadron [*Air Force*]
ATSQMC ... Army Transport Service Quartermaster Corps [*Obsolete*]
ATSR .... Activity Time Status Report   (MCD)
ATSR .... Along-Track Scanning Radiometer
ATSR .... Argonne Thermal Source Reactor
ATSS .... Acquisition and Tracking Subsystem   (MUGU)
ATSS .... Association of Teachers of Social Studies [*British*]
ATSS .... Association of Track and Structure Suppliers [*Later, REMSA*]   (EA)
ATSS .... Augmented Target Screening Subsystem   (MCD)
ATSS .... Auto Tracking Scan System [*for television video quality*] [*Sony Corp.*]
ATSS .... Automatic Target Scoring Systems   (MCD)
ATSS .... Automatic Telecommunications Switching System
ATSS .... Automatic Telegraph Subsystem [*Navy*] [*British*]   (MCD)
ATSS .... Automatic Test Support Systems   (RDA)
ATSS .... Auxiliary Training Submarine [*Navy symbol*]
ATSSA ...... American Traffic Safety Services Association   (EA)
ATSSS ...... Air Transportable SONAR Surveillance System
Atst .... Artist [*Record label*]
ATST .... Atlantic Standard Time
At Stolknoveniya ... Atomnye Stolknoveniya [*A publication*]
ATS Trans ... Danish Academy of Technical Sciences. Transactions [*A publication*]
At Strom .... Atom und Strom [*A publication*]
At und Strom ... Atom und Strom [*A publication*]
At Struct Mech Prop Met ... Atomic Structure and Mechanical Properties of Metals [*A publication*]
ATSU .... Air Travel Security Unit
ATSU .... Association of Time-Sharing Users [*Later, ACU*]   (EA)
ATSUDG ... Archives of Toxicology. Supplement [*A publication*]
ATSVA ...... Avtomatika, Telemekhanika, i Svyaz [*A publication*]
ATSZA ...... Automazione e Strumentazione [*A publication*]
ATT .... Accelerated Test Technology
ATT .... Acceptance Thermal Test [*or Testing*] [*NASA*]   (NASA)
ATT .... Advanced Technician's Test   (MCD)
ATT .... Advanced Technology Transport
ATT .... Advanced Transonic Technology   (MCD)
ATT .... Air Terminal Team
ATT .... Air Traffic Transponder
ATT .... Air Training Team   (NATG)
ATT .... All Thrust Termination   (MUGU)
AT & T ...... American Telephone & Telegraph Co. [*New York, NY*]
ATT .... American Telephone & Telegraph Co. [*New York, NY*]
ATT .... American Telephone & Telegraph Co., Long Lines, Bedminister, NJ [*OCLC symbol*]   (OCLC)
ATT .... Amphibian Technology Tested
ATT .... Application Transfer Teams [*IBM Corp.*]
ATT .... Arginine Tolerance Test [*Endocrinology*]
ATT .... Army Training Test
ATT .... Artillery Tactical Terminal
ATT .... Associated Talmud Torahs [*A publication*]   (BJA)
ATT .... Association Technique du Tourisme [*Tourism Technique Association*] [*Canada*]
ATT .... Atmautluak [*Alaska*] [*Airport symbol*]   (OAG)
ATT .... Attach   (KSC)
ATT .... Attache

ATT .... Attachment [*Telecommunications*]   (TEL)
ATT .... Attempted [*FBI standardized term*]
ATT .... Attempts
ATT .... Attendant   (MSA)
ATT .... Attended Public Telephone [*Telecommunications*]   (TEL)
ATT .... Attending
ATT .... Attention
ATT .... Attenuation [*Instrumentation*]
ATT .... Attic [*Greek dialect*]   (ROG)
ATT .... Attica [*New York*] [*Seismograph station code, US Geological Survey*] [*Closed*]   (SEIS)
Att .... Atticus [*of Nepos*] [*Classical studies*]   (OCD)
ATT .... Attitude
ATT .... Attorney
ATT .... Augmented Transition Tree   (MCD)
ATT .... Automatic Target Tracking   (MCD)
ATT .... Automatic Toll Ticketing   (TEL)
ATT .... Automatic Turbine Tester   (NRCH)
ATT .... Avalanche Transit Time
ATT .... Average Task Time
Att .... Epistulae ad Atticum [*of Cicero*] [*Classical studies*]   (OCD)
ATT .... Tuskegee Institute, Tuskegee, AL [*Library symbol*] [*Library of Congress*]   (LCLS)
ATTA .... Advanced Training Technology Associates [*Commercial firm*] [*British*]
ATTA .... American Tin Trade Association   (EA)
ATTAC ...... Advanced Technologies for Tactical Aircraft   (MCD)
ATTACHT ... Attachment
Att ANL R F ... Atti. Accademia Nazionale dei Lincei. Rendiconti. Classe di Scienze Fisiche, Matematiche, e Naturali [*A publication*]
ATTAS .... Advanced Technologies Testing Aircraft System [*NASA*]
Att Ass Gen ... Atti. Associazione Genetica Italiana [*A publication*]
Att Ber .... Die Attische Beredsamkeit [*A publication*]   (OCD)
ATTC .... Advanced Technical Training Center [*Military*]   (MUGU)
ATTC .... Advanced Television Test Center [*Telecommunications*]   (TSSD)
ATTC .... Army Tropic Test Center   (MCD)
ATTC .... Atlantic Transportation Terminal Command [*Army*]
ATTC .... Auto-Trol Technology Corporation [*NASDAQ symbol*]   (NQ)
ATTC .... Automatic Transmission Test and Control [*Telecommunications*]   (TEL)
ATTC .... Aviation Technical Training Center
ATTCE ...... Attendance   (ROG)
AT & T Co Com L ... American Telephone & Telegraph Company Commission. Leaflets [*A publication*]   (DLA)
ATTCOM ... AT & T Communications [*Telecommunications*]   (TSSD)
AT & T Co TC ... American Telephone & Telegraph Company Commission Telephone Cases [*A publication*]   (DLA)
ATTCS .... Automatic Takeoff Thrust Control System   (IEEE)
ATTD .... Alcohol and Tobacco Tax Division [*Internal Revenue Service*]
ATTD .... Attend   (ROG)
ATTD .... Attitude   (KSC)
ATTD .... Avalanche Transit Time Diode
ATTE .... Automatic Transistor Test Equipment
At Tekh Rubezhom ... Atomnaya Tekhnika za Rubezhom [*A publication*]
Attempt Sedimentol Charact Carbonate Deposits ... Attempt at Sedimentological Characterization of Carbonate Deposits [*A publication*]
ATTEN ...... Attention
ATTEN ...... Attenuator   (KSC)
ATTESTG ... Attesting   (ROG)
ATTESTN ... Attestation
ATTF .... Advanced Technical Training Facility [*Military*]
ATTF .... Amphibious Tanker Terminal Facility [*Navy*]
ATTG .... Attending
ATTG .... Automated Tactical Target Graphic
ATTGEN .... Attorney General   (ADA)
ATTI .... American Telephone & Telegraph Co. International   (TEL)
ATTI .... Association of Teachers in Technical Institutions [*British*]
Atti .... Atti. Congresso Internazionale di Estetica [*A publication*]
Atti Accad Crusca ... Atti. Reale Accademia della Crusca [*A publication*]
Atti Accad Fisiocrit Siena ... Atti. Accademia dei Fisiocritici in Siena [*A publication*]
Atti Accad Fisiocrit Siena Sez Agrar ... Atti. Accademia dei Fisiocritici in Siena. Sezione Agraria [*A publication*]
Atti Accad Fisiocrit Siena Sez Med-Fis ... Atti. Accademia dei Fisiocritici in Siena. Sezione Medico-Fisica [*A publication*]
Atti Accad Fis-Med-Statist Milano ... Atti. Accademia Fisio-Medico-Statistica di Milano [*A publication*]
Atti Accad Geografili ... Atti. Reale Accademia dei Geografili di Firenze [*A publication*]
Atti Accad Gioenia Sci Nat Catania ... Atti. Accademia Gioenia di Scienze Naturali in Catania [*A publication*]
Atti Accad Ital Mem Cl Sci Fis Mat Natur ... Atti. Reale Accademia d'Italia. Memorie. Classe di Scienze Fisiche, Matematiche, e Naturali [*A publication*]
Atti Accad Ital Mem Cl Sci Morali Stor Filol ... Atti. Reale Accademia d'Italia. Memorie. Classe di Scienze Morali, Storiche, e Filologiche [*A publication*]

Atti Accad Ital Rendic Cl Sci Fis Mat Natur ... Atti. Reale Accademia d'Italia. Rendiconti. Classe di Scienze Fisiche, Matematiche, e Naturali [*A publication*]

Atti Accad Ital Rendic Cl Sci Morali Stor Filol ... Atti. Reale Accademia d'Italia. Rendiconti. Classe di Scienze Morali, Storiche, e Filologiche [*A publication*]

Atti Accad Ligure Sci & Lett ... Atti. Accademia Ligure di Scienze e Lettere [*A publication*]

Atti Accad Ligure Sci Lett ... Atti. Accademia Ligure di Scienze e Lettere [*A publication*]

Atti Accad Lincei Mem Cl Sci Fis Mat Natur ... Atti. Reale Accademia dei Lincei. Memorie. Classe di Scienze Fisiche, Matematiche, e Naturali [*A publication*]

Atti Accad Lincei Mem Cl Sci Morali Stor Filol ... Atti. Reale Accademia dei Lincei. Memorie. Classe di Scienze Morali, Storiche, e Filologiche [*A publication*]

Atti Accad Lincei Rendic Cl Sci Fis Mat Natur ... Atti. Reale Accademia dei Lincei. Rendiconti. Classe di Scienze Fisiche, Matematiche, e Naturali [*A publication*]

Atti Accad Lincei Rendic Cl Sci Morali Stor Filol ... Atti. Reale Accademia dei Lincei. Rendiconti. Classe di Scienze Morali, Storiche, e Filologiche [*A publication*]

Atti Accad Lincei Rendic Sedute Solenni ... Atti. Reale Accademia dei Lincei. Rendiconti delle Sedute Solenni [*A publication*]

Atti Accad Med Chir (Napoli) ... Atti. Reale Accademia Medico-Chirurgica (Napoli) [*A publication*]

Atti Accad Med Lomb ... Atti. Accademia Medica Lombarda [*A publication*]

Atti Accad Med Lombarda ... Atti. Accademia Medica Lombarda [*A publication*]

Atti Accad Naz Ital Entomol Rend ... Atti. Accademia Nazionale Italiana di Entomologia. Rendiconti [*Italy*] [*A publication*]

Atti Accad Naz Lincei ... Atti. Accademia Nazionale dei Lincei [*A publication*]

Atti Accad Naz Lincei Cl Sci Fis Mat Nat Rend ... Atti. Accademia Nazionale dei Lincei. Classe di Scienze Fisiche, Matematiche, e Naturali. Rendiconti [*A publication*]

Atti Accad Naz Lincei Mem Cl Sci Fis Mat Nat ... Atti. Accademia Nazionale dei Lincei. Memorie. Classe di Scienze Fisiche, Matematiche, e Naturali [*A publication*]

Atti Accad Naz Lincei Mem Cl Sci Fis Mat Nat Sez 2a ... Atti. Accademia Nazionale dei Lincei. Memorie. Classe di Scienze Fisiche, Matematiche, e Naturali. Sezione 2a. Fisica, Chimica, Geologia, Paleontologia, e Mineralogia [*A publication*]

Atti Accad Naz Lincei Mem Cl Sci Fis Mat Nat Sez 3a ... Atti. Accademia Nazionale dei Lincei. Memorie. Classe di Scienze Fisiche, Matematiche, e Naturali. Sezione 3a. Botanica, Zoologia, Fisiologia, Patologia [*A publication*]

Atti Accad Naz Lincei Mem Cl Sci Fis Mat Natur ... Atti. Reale Accademia Nazionale dei Lincei. Memorie. Classe di Scienze Fisiche, Matematiche, e Naturali [*A publication*]

Atti Accad Naz Lincei Mem Cl Sci Fis Mat Natur Sez 1a ... Atti. Accademia Nazionale dei Lincei. Memorie. Classe di Scienze Fisiche, Matematiche, e Naturali. Sezione 1a. Matematica, Meccanica, Astronomia, Geodesia, e Geofisica [*A publication*]

Atti Accad Naz Lincei Rend Cl Sci Fis Mat & Nat ... Atti. Accademia Nazionale dei Lincei. Rendiconti. Classe di Scienze Fisiche, Matematiche, e Naturali [*A publication*]

Atti Accad Naz Lincei Rend Cl Sci Fis Mat Natur ... Atti. Accademia Nazionale dei Lincei. Rendiconti. Classe di Scienze Fisiche, Matematiche, e Naturali [*A publication*]

Atti Accad Naz Lincei Rend Cl Sci Fis Mat Natur (8) ... Atti. Accademia Nazionale dei Lincei. Rendiconti. Classe di Scienze Fisiche, Matematiche, e Naturali (Serie 8) [*A publication*]

Atti Accad Naz Lincei Rendic Cl Sci Fis Mat Natur ... Atti. Reale Accademia Nazionale dei Lincei. Rendiconti. Classe di Scienze Fisiche, Matematiche, e Naturali [*A publication*]

Atti Accad Naz Lincei Rendic Cl Sci Morali Stor Filol ... Atti. Reale Accademia Nazionale dei Lincei. Rendiconti. Classe di Scienze Morali, Storiche, e Filologiche [*A publication*]

Atti Accad Naz Lincei Rendic Sedute Solenni ... Atti. Reale Accademia Nazionale dei Lincei. Rendiconti delle Sedute Solenni [*A publication*]

Atti Accad Naz Lincei (Serie Ottava) ... Atti. Accademia Nazionale dei Lincei (Serie Ottava) [*A publication*]

Atti Accad Peloritana ... Atti. Reale Accademia Peloritana [*A publication*]

Atti Accad Peloritana Cl Sci Fis Mat Biol ... Atti. Reale Accademia Peloritana. Classe di Scienze Fisiche, Matematiche, e Biologiche PB

Atti Accad Peloritana Pericolanti Cl Sci Fis Mat Nat ... Atti. Accademia Peloritana dei Pericolanti. Classe di Scienze Fisiche, Matematiche, e Naturali [*A publication*]

Atti Accad Peloritana Pericolanti Cl Sci Fis Mat Natur ... Atti. Accademia Peloritana dei Pericolanti. Classe di Scienze Fisiche, Matematiche, e Naturali [*A publication*]

Atti Accad Peloritana Pericolanti Cl Sci Med Biol ... Atti. Accademia Peloritana dei Pericolanti. Classe di Scienze Medico-Biologiche [*A publication*]

Atti Accad Pontaniana ... Atti. Accademia Pontaniana [*A publication*]

Atti Accad Roveretana Agiati ... Atti. Accademia Roveretana degli Agiati [*A publication*]

Atti Accad Sci Ferrara ... Atti. Accademia delle Scienze di Ferrara [*A publication*]

Atti Accad Sci Fis Mat Napoli ... Atti. Accademia delle Scienze Fisiche e Matematiche di Napoli [*A publication*]

Atti Accad Sci Ist Bologna Cl Sci Fis Mem ... Atti. Accademia delle Scienze. Istituto di Bologna. Classe di Scienze Fisiche. Memorie [*A publication*]

Atti Accad Sci Ist Bologna Cl Sci Fis Mem Ser IV ... Atti. Accademia delle Scienze. Istituto di Bologna. Classe di Scienze Fisiche. Memorie. Serie IV [*A publication*]

Atti Accad Sci Ist Bologna Cl Sci Fis Rend ... Atti. Accademia delle Scienze. Istituto di Bologna. Classe di Scienze Fisiche. Rendiconti [*A publication*]

Atti Accad Sci Ist Bologna Cl Sci Fis Rend Ser XIII ... Atti. Accademia delle Scienze. Istituto di Bologna. Classe di Scienze Fisiche. Rendiconti. Serie XIII [*A publication*]

Atti Accad Sci Ist Bologna Ren ... Atti. Accademia delle Scienze. Istituto di Bologna. Rendiconti [*A publication*]

Atti Accad Sci Istit Bologna Cl Sci Fis Rend XIII ... Atti. Accademia delle Scienze. Istituto di Bologna. Classe di Scienze Fisiche. Rendiconti. Serie XIII [*A publication*]

Atti Accad Sci Lett Arti Palermo ... Atti. Accademia di Scienze, Lettere, ed Arti di Palermo [*A publication*]

Atti Accad Sci Lett Arti Palermo Parte I ... Atti. Accademia di Scienze, Lettere, ed Arti di Palermo. Parte Prima. Scienze [*A publication*]

Atti Accad Sci Lett Arti di Palermo Parte I ... Atti. Accademia di Scienze, Lettere, ed Arti di Palermo. Parte Prima. Scienze [*A publication*]

Atti Accad Sci Lett Arti Palermo Parte I 4 ... Atti. Accademia di Scienze, Lettere, ed Arti di Palermo. Parte Prima. Scienze. Serie Quarta [*A publication*]

Atti Accad Sci Lett Arti Palermo Ser Quarta Sci ... Atti. Accademia di Scienze, Lettere, ed Arti di Palermo. Scienze. Serie Quarta [*A publication*]

Atti Accad Sci Med Chir (Napoli) ... Atti. Reale Accademia delle Scienze Medico-Chirurgiche (Napoli) [*A publication*]

Atti Accad Sci Siena Fisiocrit ... Atti. Accademia delle Scienze di Siena. Detta de Fisiocritici [*A publication*]

Atti Accad Sci Torino ... Atti. Accademia delle Scienze di Torino [*A publication*]

Atti Accad Sci Torino Cl Sci Fis Mat Nat ... Atti. Accademia delle Scienze di Torino. Classe di Scienze Fisiche, Matematiche, e Naturali [*A publication*]

Atti Accad Sci Torino Cl Sci Fis Mat Natur ... Atti. Accademia delle Scienze di Torino. Classe di Scienze Fisiche, Matematiche, e Naturali [*A publication*]

Atti Accad Sci Torino Cl Sci Morali Stor Filol ... Atti. Reale Accademia delle Scienze di Torino. Classe di Scienze Morali, Storiche, e Filologiche [*A publication*]

Atti Accad Sci Torino I ... Atti. Accademia delle Scienze di Torino. I [*A publication*]

Atti Accad Sci Torino I Cl Sci Fis Mat Nat ... Atti. Accademia delle Scienze di Torino. I. Classe di Scienze Fisiche, Matematiche, e Naturali [*A publication*]

Atti Accad Sci Veneto-Trentino-Istriana ... Atti. Accademia Scientifica Veneto-Trentino-Istriana [*A publication*]

Atti Acc Arch N ... Atti. Reale Accademia di Archeologia, Lettere, e Belle Arti di Napoli [*A publication*]

Atti Acc Lig ... Atti. Accademia Ligure di Scienze e Lettere [*A publication*]

Atti Acc Linc ... Atti. Reale Accademia dei Lincei [*A publication*]

Atti Acc Med Lomb ... Atti. Accademia Medica Lombarda [*A publication*]

Atti Acc (Nap) ... Atti. Accademia Nazionale di Scienze Morali e Politiche (Napoli) [*A publication*]

Atti Acc Olimp ... Atti. Accademia Olimpica [*A publication*]

Atti Acc Pel ... Atti. Accademia Peloritana [*A publication*]

Atti Acc Sci Torino ... Atti. Accademia delle Scienze di Torino [*A publication*]

Atti Acc Stor Arte San ... Atti e Memorie. Accademia di Storia dell'Arte Sanitaria [*A publication*]

Atti Ac Torino ... Atti. Accademia delle Scienze di Torino [*A publication*]

Atti Ac Udine ... Atti. Accademia di Scienze, Lettere, ed Arti di Udine [*A publication*]

Atti Ass Genet Ital ... Atti. Associazione Genetica Italiana [*A publication*]

Atti Ass Ital Aerotec ... Atti. Associazione Italiana di Aerotecnica [*A publication*]

Atti Assoc Genet Ital ... Atti. Associazione Genetica Italiana [*A publication*]

Atti C Ant Cl ... Atti. Centro Ricerche e Documentazione sull'Antichita Classica [*A publication*]

Atti Cent Naz Mecc Agr ... Atti. Centro Nazionale Meccanico Agricolo [*A publication*]

Atti C It Rom ... Atti. Centro Studi e Documentazione sull'Italia Romana [*A publication*]

Atti Clin Odont ... Atti. Clinica Odontoiatrica e Societa Napolitana di Stomatologia [*A publication*]

Atti Clin Odontoi Soc Napolitana Stomatol ... Atti. Clinica Odontoiatrica e Societa Napolitana di Stomatologia [*A publication*]

Atti Clin Oto-Rino-Laringoiatr Univ Palermo ... Atti. Clinica Oto-Rino-Laringoiatrica. Universita di Palermo [*A publication*]

Atti Coll Ing Milano ... Atti. Collegio degl ie Ingegneri di Milano [*A publication*]

Atti Cong Nat Ital ... Atti. Congresso del Naturalis i Italiani [*A publication*]

Atti Congr Geogr Ital ... Atti. Congresso Geografico Italiano [*A publication*]
Atti Congr Int Amer ... Atti. Congresso Internazionale degli Americanisti [*A publication*]
Atti Congr Int Elettron ... Atti. Congresso Internazionale per l'Elettronica [*A publication*]
Atti Congr Int Fil ... Atti. Congresso Internazionale di Filosofia [*A publication*]
Atti Congr Int Mat ... Atti. Congresso Internazionale dei Matematici [*A publication*]
Atti Congr Int Mater Plast ... Atti. Congresso Internazionale delle Materie Plastiche [*A publication*]
Atti Congr Int Stor Med ... Atti. Congresso Internazionale di Storia della Medicina [*A publication*]
Atti Congr Int Stud Bizantini ... Atti. Congresso Internazionale dei Studi Bizantini [*A publication*]
Atti Congr Naz Apic Ital ... Atti. Congresso Nazionale della Sezione Apicultori Italiani [*A publication*]
Atti Congr Naz Chim Ind ... Atti. Congresso Nazionale di Chimica Industriale [*A publication*]
Atti Congr Naz Chim Pura Appl ... Atti. Congresso Nazionale di Chimica Pura ed Applicata [*A publication*]
Atti Congr Naz Ital Entomol ... Atti. Congresso Nazionale Italiano di Entomologia [*A publication*]
Atti Congr Naz Soc Ital Biol Mar Riass ... Atti. Congresso Nazionale della Societa Italiana di Biologia Marina Riassunti [*A publication*]
Atti Congr Soc Ital Ortod ... Atti del Congresso. Societa Italiana di Ortodonzia [*A publication*]
Atti Congr Unione Mat Ital ... Atti. Congresso dell'Unione Matematica Italiana [*A publication*]
Atti Convegi Lincei ... Atti. Convegni Lincei [*Rome*] [*A publication*]
Atti Conv Int Grano Duro ... Atti. Convegno Internazionale del Grano Duro [*A publication*]
Atti Conv Naz Apic ... Atti. Convegno Nazionale della Apicultori [*A publication*]
Atti Conv Naz Tec Nav ... Atti. Convegno Nazionale di Tecnica Navale [*A publication*]
Atti Conv Prev Soc ... Atti. Convegno "Fiscalizzazione Oneri Sociala e Riforma della Previdenza Sociale" [*A publication*]
Atti Conv Salute ... Atti. VI Convegno della Salute [*A publication*]
Atti C St R ... Atti. Congresso Nazionale di Studi Romani [*A publication*]
ATTID....... AT Times [*A publication*]
Atti Fac Ing Univ Bologna ... Atti. Facolta d'Ingegneria. Universita di Bologna [*A publication*]
Atti Fond Giorgio Ronchi ... Atti. Fondazione Giorgio Ronchi [*A publication*]
Atti Fond Giorgio Ronchi & Contrib Ist Naz Ottica ... Atti. Fondazione Giorgio Ronchi e Contributi dell'Istituto Nazionale di Ottica [*A publication*]
Atti Fond Ronchi ... Atti. Fondazione Giorgio Ronchi [*A publication*]
Atti Giornate Fitopatol ... Atti della Giornate Fitopatologiche [*A publication*]
Atti Ist Bot Lab Crittogam Univ Pavia ... Atti. Istituto di Botanica. Laboratorio Crittogamico. Universita di Pavia [*A publication*]
Atti Ist Bot Labor Crittog Univ Pavia ... Atti. Istituto Botanico e Laboratorio Crittogamico. Universita di Pavia [*A publication*]
Atti Ist Bot Univ Pavia ... Atti. Istituto Botanico. Universita di Pavia [*A publication*]
Atti Ist Geol Univ Genova ... Atti. Istituto di Geologia. Universita di Genova [*A publication*]
Atti Ist Geol Univ Pavia ... Atti. Istituto Geologico. Universita di Pavia [*A publication*]
Atti Istr ...... Atti e Memorie. Societa Istriana di Archeologia e Storia Patria [*A publication*]
Atti Ist Veneto ... Atti. Istituto Veneto di Scienze, Lettere, ed Arti [*A publication*]
Atti Ist Veneto Sci Lett Arti ... Atti. Istituto Veneto di Scienze, Lettere, ed Arti [*A publication*]
Atti Ist Veneto Sci Lett Arti Cl Sci Mat Nat ... Atti. Istituto Veneto di Scienze, Lettere, ed Arti. Classe di Scienze Matematiche e Naturali [*A publication*]
Atti Mem Accad Agric Sci Lett (Verona) ... Atti e Memorie. Accademia di Agricoltura, Scienze, e Lettere (Verona) [*A publication*]
Atti Mem Accad Naz Sci Lett Arti (Modena) ... Atti e Memorie. Accademia Nazionale di Scienze, Lettere, ed Arti (Modena) [*A publication*]
Atti Mem Accad Patavina Sci Lett Arti ... Atti e Memorie. Accademia Patavina di Scienze, Lettere, ed Arti [*A publication*]
Atti Mem Accad Patav Sci Lett Arti ... Atti e Memorie. Accademia Patavina di Scienze, Lettere, ed Arti [*A publication*]
Atti Mem Accad Petrarca Lett Arti Sci ... Atti e Memorie. Reale Accademia Petrarca di Lettere, Arti, e Scienze [*A publication*]
Atti Mem Accad Sci Lett Arti Modena ... Atti e Memorie. Reale Accademia di Scienze, Lettere, ed Arti de Modena [*A publication*]
Atti Mem Accad Sci Lett Arti Padova ... Atti e Memorie. Reale Accademia di Scienze, Lettere, ed Arti in Padova [*A publication*]
Atti Mem Accad Stor Arte Sanit ... Atti e Memorie. Accademia di Storia dell'Arte Sanitaria [*A publication*]
Atti Mem Accad Virgiliana Mantova ... Atti e Memorie. Accademia Virgiliana di Mantova [*A publication*]
Atti Mem Acc Virg ... Atti e Memorie. Reale Accademia Virgiliana [*A publication*]

Atti Mem Deputazione Stor Antiche Prov Modenesi ... Atti e Memorie. Deputazione di Storia Patria per le Antiche Provincie Modenesi [*A publication*]
Atti Mem Deputazione Stor Emilia Romagna ... Atti e Memorie. Reale Deputazione di Storia Patria per l'Emilia e la Romagna [*A publication*]
Atti Mem Deputazione Stor Modenesi ... Atti e Memorie. Reale Deputazione di Storia Patria per le Provincie Modenesi [*A publication*]
Atti Mem Deputazione Stor Modenesi Parmensi ... Atti e Memorie. Reale Deputazione di Storia Patria per le Provincie Modenesi e Parmensi [*A publication*]
Atti Mem Deputazione Stor Patria Antiche Prov Modenesi ... Atti e Memorie. Deputazione di Storia Patria per le Antiche Provincie Modenesi [*A publication*]
Atti Mem Deputazione Stor Romagna ... Atti e Memorie. Reale Deputazione di Storia Patria per le Provincie di Romagna [*A publication*]
Atti Mem M ... Atti e Memorie. Reale Accademia di Mantova [*A publication*]
Atti Mem Modena ... Atti e Memorie. Deputazione di Storia Patria per le Antiche Provincie Modenesi [*A publication*]
Atti Memo Acad Agric Sci Lett (Verona) ... Atti e Memorie. Accademia di Agricoltura, Scienze, e Lettere (Verona) [*A publication*]
Atti Mem Soc Istriana ... Atti e Memorie. Societa Istriana di Archeologia e Storia Patria [*A publication*]
Atti Mem Soc Mag Gr ... Atti e Memorie. Societa Magna Grecia [*A publication*]
Atti Mem Soc Magna Grecia ... Atti e Memorie. Societa Magna Grecia [*A publication*]
Atti Mem Soc Tiburtina ... Atti e Memorie. Societa Tiburtina di Storia e d'Arte [*A publication*]
Atti M Grecia ... Atti e Memorie. Societa Magna Grecia [*A publication*]
Atti Mod .... Atti e Memorie. Reale Accademia di Scienze, Lettere, ed Arti de Modena [*A publication*]
Atti Mus Civ Stor Nat Triesti ... Atti. Museo Civico di Storia Naturale di Triesti [*A publication*]
Atti Mus Trieste ... Atti. Civici Musei di Storia ed Arte di Trieste [*A publication*]
Atti Not Assoc Ital Metall ... Atti Notizie. Associazione Italiana di Metallurgia [*A publication*]
Atti Ortop Traum ... Atti di Ortopedia e Traumatologia [*A publication*]
Atti Palermo ... Atti. Accademia di Scienze, Lettere, ed Arti di Palermo [*A publication*]
Atti Parl ..... Atti Parlamentari [*Parliamentary Acts*] [*Italian*]   (ILCA)
Atti Pont Acc ... Atti. Pontificia Accademia Romana di Archeologia [*A publication*]
Atti Pontif Accad Sci ... Atti. Pontificia Accademia delle Scienze [*A publication*]
Atti Pontif Accad Sci Nuovi Lincei ... Atti. Pontificia Accademia delle Scienze. Nuovi Lincei [*A publication*]
Atti R Accad Fisiocrit Siena ... Atti. Regia Accademia dei Fisiocritici in Siena [*A publication*]
Atti R Accad Geografili ... Atti. Reale Accademia dei Geografili [*A publication*]
Atti R Accad Ital Rend Cl Sci Fis Mat Nat ... Atti. Reale Accademia d'Italia. Rendiconti. Classe di Scienze Fisiche, Matematiche, e Naturali [*A publication*]
Atti R Accad Lincei Mem Cl Sc Fis Mat e Nat ... Atti. Reale Accademia dei Lincei. Memorie. Classe di Scienze Fisiche, Matematiche, e Naturali [*A publication*]
Atti R Accad Lincei Rendic Cl Sc Fis Mat e Nat ... Atti. Reale Accademia dei Lincei. Rendiconti. Classe di Scienze Fisiche, Matematiche, e Naturali [*A publication*]
Atti R Accad Lincei (Roma) Mem Cl Sc Fis Mat e Nat ... Atti. Reale Accademia dei Lincei (Roma). Memorie. Classe di Scienze Fisiche, Matematiche, e Naturali [*A publication*]
Atti R Accad Lincei (Roma) Rendic Cl Sc Fis Mat e Nat ... Atti. Reale Accademia dei Lincei (Roma). Rendiconti. Classe di Scienze Fisiche, Matematiche, e Naturali [*A publication*]
Atti R Accad Naz Lincei (Roma) ... Atti. Reale Accademia Nazionale dei Lincei (Roma) [*A publication*]
Atti R Accad Peloritana ... Atti. Reale Accademia Peloritana [*A publication*]
Atti R Accad Peloritana Cl Sci Fis Mat Biol ... Atti. Reale Accademia Peloritana. Classe di Scienze Fisiche, Matematiche, e Biologiche [*A publication*]
Atti R Accad Sci Torino Cl Sci Fis Mat Nat ... Atti. Reale Accademia delle Scienze di Torino. Classe di Scienze Fisiche, Matematiche, e Naturali [*A publication*]
Atti Rend Accad Naz Lincei Cl Sci Fis Mat Natur ... Atti. Rendiconti. Accademia Nazionale dei Lincei. Classe di Scienze Fisiche, Matematiche, e Naturali [*A publication*]
Atti R Univ Genova ... Atti. Reale Universita di Genova [*A publication*]
ATTIS .... American Telephone & Telegraph Co. Information Systems (TEL)
ATTIS .... AT & T Information Systems [*Telecommunications*] (TSSD)
Atti Sci Soc Elv Sci Nat ... Atti Scientifici. Societa Elvetica di Scienze Naturali [*A publication*]
Atti Semin Mat & Fis Univ Modena ... Atti. Seminario Matematico e Fisico. Universita di Modena [*A publication*]
Atti Sem Mat Fis Univ Modena ... Atti. Seminario Matematico e Fisico. Universita di Modena [*A publication*]

Atti Simp Conferme Prospettive Uso Calcitonina ... Atti. Simposio Conferme e Prospettive nell'Uso della Calcitonina [*A publication*]
Atti Simp Int Agrochim ... Atti. Simposio Internazionale di Agrochimica [*A publication*]
Atti Simp Int Zootec ... Atti. Simposio Internazionale di Zootecnia [*A publication*]
Atti Sind Ing Lombardia ... Atti. Sindacati Ingegneri di Lombardia [*A publication*]
Atti Soc Astron Ital ... Atti. Societa Astronomica Italiana [*A publication*]
Atti Soc Cultori Sc Med e Nat Cagliari ... Atti. Societa fra i Cultori delle Scienze Mediche e Naturali in Cagliari [*A publication*]
Atti Soc Elv Sci Nat Parte Sci ... Atti. Societa Elvetica di Scienze Naturali. Parte Scientifica [*A publication*]
Atti Soc Friuli ... Atti. Societa per la Preistoria e Protostoria della Regione Friuli-Venezia Giulia [*A publication*]
Atti Soc Ital Anat ... Atti. Societa Italiana di Anatomia [*A publication*]
Atti Soc Ital Cardiol ... Atti. Societa Italiana di Cardiologia [*A publication*]
Atti Soc Ital Progr Sci ... Atti. Societa Italiana per il Progresso delle Scienze [*A publication*]
Atti Soc Ital Prog Sci ... Atti. Societa Italiana per il Progresso delle Scienze [*A publication*]
Atti Soc Ital Sci Nat ... Atti. Societa Italiana di Scienze Naturali. Museo Civile di Storia Naturale [*A publication*]
Atti Soc Ital Sci Nat Mus Civ Stor Nat Milano ... Atti. Societa Italiana di Scienze Naturali. Museo Civico di Storia Naturale di Milano [*A publication*]
Atti Soc Ital Sci Vet ... Atti. Societa Italiana delle Scienze Veterinarie [*A publication*]
Atti Soc Ital Sc Nat (Milano) ... Atti. Societa Italiana di Scienze Naturali (Milano) [*A publication*]
Atti Soc Ital Stor Crit Sci Med Natur ... Atti. Societa Italiana di Storia Critica delle Scienze Mediche e Naturali [*A publication*]
Atti Soc Lig Stor Patria ... Atti. Societa Ligure di Storia Patria [*A publication*]
Atti Soc Ligust Sc Nat e Geogr ... Atti. Societa Ligustica di Scienze Naturali e Geografiche [*A publication*]
Atti Soc Lomb Sci Med Biol ... Atti. Societa Lombarda di Scienze Mediche e Biologiche [*A publication*]
Atti Soc Med-Chir Padova Fac Med Chir Univ Padova ... Atti. Societa Medico-Chirurgica di Padova e Facolta di Medicina e Chirurgia della Universita di Padova [*A publication*]
Atti Soc Nat Mat Modena ... Atti. Societa dei Naturalisti e Matematici di Modena [*A publication*]
Atti Soc Oftalmol Lomb ... Atti. Societa Oftalmologica Lombarda [*A publication*]
Atti Soc Peloritana Sci Fis Mat e Nat ... Atti. Societa Peloritana di Scienze Fisiche, Matematiche, e Naturali [*A publication*]
Atti Soc Peloritana Sci Fis Mat Nat ... Atti. Societa Peloritana di Scienze Fisiche, Matematiche, e Naturali [*A publication*]
Atti Soc Peloritana Sci Fis Mat Natur ... Atti. Societa Peloritana di Scienze Fisiche, Matematiche, e Naturali [*A publication*]
Atti Soc Peloritan Sci Fis Mat e Nat ... Atti. Societa Peloritana di Scienze Fisiche, Matematiche, e Naturali [*A publication*]
Atti Soc Salernitana Med Chir ... Atti. Societa Salernitana di Medicina e Chirurgia [*A publication*]
Atti Soc Tiburtina ... Atti e Memorie. Societa Tiburtina di Storia e d'Arte [*A publication*]
Atti Soc Toscana Sci Nat Pisa Mem ... Atti. Societa Toscana di Scienze Naturali Residente in Pisa. Memorie [*A publication*]
Atti Soc Toscana Sci Nat Pisa P V ... Atti. Societa Toscana di Scienze Naturali Residente in Pisa. Processi Verbali [*A publication*]
Atti Soc Toscana Sci Nat Pisa P V Mem Ser A ... Atti. Societa Toscana di Scienze Naturali Residente in Pisa. Processi Verbali e Memorie. Serie A [*A publication*]
Atti Soc Toscana Sci Nat P V Mem Ser B ... Atti. Societa Toscana di Scienze Naturali. Processi Verbali e Memorie. Serie B [*A publication*]
Atti Soc Toscana Sci Nat Resid Pisa Mem Ser A ... Atti. Societa Toscana di Scienze Naturali Residente in Pisa. Memorie. Serie A [*A publication*]
ATTITB..... Air Transport and Travel Industry Training Board [*British*]　(AIA)
Atti Tor...... Atti. Reale Accademia delle Scienze di Torino [*A publication*]
Atti Ven...... Atti. Istituto Veneto di Scienze, Lettere, ed Arti [*A publication*]
Atti V Simp Int Agrochim "Zolfo in Agricoltura" ... Atti. V Simposio Internazionale di Agrochimica su "Lo Zolfo in Agricoltura" [*A publication*]
ATTIX...... American Telephone & Telegraph Co. Interexchange Carrier　(TEL)
ATTK........ Attack
ATTLA...... Air Transportability Test Loading Agency
ATTM....... At This Time
ATTM .... Authorization to Transfer Material
ATTMA...... Advanced Transport Technology Mission Analysis　(MCD)
ATTMCA ... Association of Tile, Terrazzo, Marble Contractors and Affiliates [*Later, NTCA*]　(EA)
ATTN........ Attain　(ROG)
ATTN........ Attention　(AFM)
ATTN......... Attenuator
Attn............ Austroton [*Austria, Germany, etc.*] [*Record label*]
ATTND..... Attendant　(AABC)
ATTNDIR ... Attention Director　(MCD)

ATTNG ..... Attending
ATTNINV ... Attention Invited　(MCD)
Atto y SS.... Atento y Seguro Servidor [*(Yours) Very Truly*] [*Spanish*] [*Correspondence*]
ATTPO...... Advanced Transport Technology Program Office [*NASA*]
ATTR........ All Thrust Terminate Relay　(MUGU)
ATTR........ Audit Technical Time Report [*IRS*]
ATTR........ Average Time to Repair　(MCD)
ATTRA...... Automatic Telemetry Tracking Receiving Antenna
ATTRAS ..... Automatic Telemetry Tracking Antenna System　(MCD)
ATTREF ..... Attitude Reference Program [*NASA*]
ATTRIB.... Attribute
ATTRIB .... Attributed
ATTRP...... Australian Travel Training Review Panel
ATTS........ American Tax Token Society　(EA)
ATTS........ American Time Travel Society [*Defunct*]　(EA)
ATTS........ Antitank Target System [*Military*]　(INF)
ATTS........ Army Training Target System　(MCD)
ATTS........ Automatic Tank Target System [*Military*]　(INF)
ATTS........ Automatic Telemetry Tracking System [*NASA*]
ATTSq...... Aircrew Training and Test Squadron [*Air Force*]
ATTT........ Advanced Technology Tactical Transport [*Proposed low-altitude long-range airlifter*] [*Military*]　(MCD)
ATTT........ American Telephone & Telegraph Co. Technologies　(TEL)
Attual Chemioter ... Attualita di Chemioterapia [*A publication*]
Attual Lab ... Attualita di Laboratorio [*A publication*]
Attual Med ... Attualita Medica [*A publication*]
Attual Ostet Ginecol ... Attualita di Ostetricia e Ginecologia [*A publication*]
Attual Zool ... Attualita Zoologiche [*A publication*]
ATTUD ..... Advances in Tunnelling Technology and Subsurface Use [*A publication*]
ATTW .... Association of Teachers of Technical Writing　(EA)
ATTW .... Attwoods PLC [*NASDAQ symbol*]　(NQ)
ATTY......... Attorney　(AFM)
Att'y Gen Ann Rep ... Attorney General's Annual Report [*A publication*]　(DLA)
Att'y Gen LJ ... Attorney General's Law Journal [*A publication*]　(DLA)
Atty Gen Op ... Attorney General's Opinions [*A publication*]　(DLA)
Atty Gen Op NY ... Attorney General's Opinions [*A publication*]　(DLA)
Att'y Gen Rep ... United States Attorneys-General Reports [*A publication*]　(DLA)
ATU.......... Advanced Training Unit
ATU.......... Alcohol Tax Unit [*Department of the Treasury*]
ATU.......... Alliance of Independent Telephone Unions [*Later, TIU*]
ATU.......... Altorientalische Texte und Untersuchungen [*Leiden*] [*A publication*]
ATU.......... Altus Flying Service [*Altus, OK*] [*FAA designator*]　(FAAC)
ATU.......... Amalgamated Transit Union　(EA)
ATU.......... American Technological University　(MCD)
ATU.......... Antenna Tuning Unit　(MSA)
ATU.......... Application Terminal Unit [*Telecommunications*]　(TEL)
ATU.......... Arab Telecommunications Union　(EA)
ATU.......... Arthurian Resources Ltd. [*Vancouver Stock Exchange symbol*]
ATU.......... Athens University [*Greece*] [*Seismograph station code, US Geological Survey*]　(SEIS)
ATU.......... Attu, AK [*Location identifier*] [*FAA*]　(FAAL)
ATU.......... Audio Terminal Unit　(NASA)
ATU.......... Audio Thermal Unit　(MCD)
ATU.......... Augsburg Transmission Upgrade　(MCD)
ATU.......... Automatic Tracking Unit
ATU.......... Autonome Transfer Unit [*Data processing*]　(DIT)
ATU.......... Auxiliary Test Unit
ATu........... Friedman Library (Hugo Friedman Memorial), Tuscaloosa, AL [*Library symbol*] [*Library of Congress*]　(LCLS)
a-tu--- .... Turkey [*MARC geographic area code*] [*Library of Congress*]　(LCCP)
Atual Agron ... Atualidades Agronomicas [*A publication*]
Atual Agron (Sao Paulo) ... Atualidades Agronomicas (Sao Paulo) [*A publication*]
Atual Agropecu ... Atualidades Agropecuarias [*A publication*]
Atual Agrovet ... Atualidades Agroveterinarias [*A publication*]
Atual Med ... Atualidades Medicas [*A publication*]
Atual Med Sanit ... Atualidades Medico Sanitarias [*A publication*]
Atual Vet.... Atualidades Veterinarias [*A publication*]
Atual Vet (Sao Paulo) ... Atualidades Veterinarias (Sao Paulo) [*A publication*]
ATUC........ Aden Trade Union Congress
ATUC .... African Trade Union Confederation [*Confederation Syndicale Africaine*] [*Later, OATUU*]
ATUC........ Average Total Unit Cost
ATUCH..... American Trade Union Council for Histadrut　(EA)
ATUC(SR) ... African Trades Union Congress of Southern Rhodesia
ATUF........ Austrian Trade Union Federation
ATUG........ Australian Telecommunications Users Group　(TSSD)
AT-UK....... Appropriate Technology - United Kingdom Unit [*ITDG*] [*British*]
ATUR .... Automatic Telephone Using Radio [*Telecommunications service*]　(TEL)
ATURF...... Airborne TOW [*Tube-Launched, Optically Tracked, Wire-Guided Weapon*] USAREUR [*United States Army, Europe*] Repair Facility　(MCD)
ATURM .... Amphibious Training Unit, Royal Marines [*British*]

ATURS......	Automatic Traffic Usage Recording System (TEL)
ATUS........	Advanced Technology Upper Stage (MCD)
ATuS.........	Stillman College, Tuscaloosa, AL [Library symbol] [Library of Congress] (LCLS)
ATuV	United States Veterans Administration Hospital, Tuscaloosa, AL [Library symbol] [Library of Congress] (LCLS)
ATV	Advanced Television [See also HDTV]
ATV	Advanced Test Vehicle (MCD)
ATV	Aerodynamic Test Vehicle (MCD)
ATV	Agena Target Vehicle [NASA] (KSC)
ATV	Air Test Vehicle
ATV	Aircraft Trailing Vortices
ATV	Akademiet for de Tekniska Videnskaber [Academy of Technical Sciences] [Denmark]
ATV	All-Terrain Vehicle
ATV	Amateur Television (MSA)
ATV	ARC International Corp. [AMEX symbol] [Toronto Stock Exchange symbol] (SPSG)
ATV	Armored Transport Vehicle (NATG)
ATV	Associated Television Ltd. [British independent, commercial television company]
AtV...........	Ateneo Veneto [A publication]
ATV	Automatic Threshold Variation
ATV	Automatic Ticket Vendors (ADA)
ATV	Turner Valley Public Library, Alberta [Library symbol] [National Library of Canada] (NLC)
ATV	United States Veterans Administration Hospital, Tuskegee, AL [Library symbol] [Library of Congress] (LCLS)
ATVA	Tennessee Valley Authority, Technical Library, Muscle Shoals, AL [Library symbol] [Library of Congress] (LCLS)
ATVC	American Travellers Corporation [Warrington, PA] [NASDAQ symbol] (NQ)
ATVC.........	Ascent Thrust Vector Control [or Controller] [NASA] (MCD)
ATVC.........	Automatic Thrust Vector Control [NASA]
ATVCD........	Ascent Thrust Vector Control Driver [NASA] (MCD)
ATVED......	Atualidades Veterinarias [A publication]
ATVEDH ..	Atualidades Veterinarias [Sao Paulo] [A publication]
ATVM	Attenuator-Thermoelement Voltmeter
ATVMA4 .	Annals. Transvaal Museum [A publication]
ATVS.........	Advanced Television Seeker (MCD)
ATVS.........	ATV Systems [NASDAQ symbol] (NQ)
ATVSC	Advanced TV Systems Committee (EA)
ATVWS.....	Airport Trailing Vortex Warning System
ATW	Advanced Technology Workstation [Computer system]
ATW	Aerospace Test Wing [Air Force]
ATW	Ahead-Throwing Weapon [Antisubmarine]
ATW	Air Transport Wing [Air Force]
ATW	Air Transport World [A publication]
ATW	Aircraft Tail Warning
ATW	American Theatre Wing (EA)
ATW	Antitank Weapon (NATG)
ATW	Appleton [Wisconsin] [Airport symbol] (OAG)
ATW	Approved Tank Wagon
ATW	AT & E Corp. [AMEX symbol] (SPSG)
ATW	Atlantic & Western Railway Co. [AAR code]
ATW	Atmospheric Tactical Warning (MCD)
AT/W	Atomic Hydrogen Weld
ATW	Atwater Library of the Mechanics' Institute of Montreal [UTLAS symbol]
Atw...........	Atwater's Reports [1 Minnesota] [A publication] (DLA)
ATW	Aviation Electronics Technician Airborne CIC [Combat Information Center] Equipment
ATWA	Association of Third World Affairs (EA)
ATWAR	Assessment of Theater Warfare [Model] (MCD)
Atwater	Atwater's Reports [1 Minnesota] [A publication] (DLA)
ATWD.......	Atwood Oceanics, Inc. [NASDAQ symbol] (NQ)
ATWDDS ...	Automated Terminal Weather Dissemination Display System (MCD)
At Weapons Res Establ (UK) Rep O ...	Atomic Weapons Research Establishment (United Kingdom). Report. Series O [A publication]
ATWESS...	Antitank Weapons Effect Signature Simulator [Army] (INF)
ATWg........	Air Transport Wing [Air Force] (AFM)
At World	Atomic World [A publication]
ATWS........	Adjustable Thermal Wire Stripper
ATWS........	Anticipated Transient without Scram [Physics]
ATWS........	Association of Third World Studies (EA)
ATWS........	Automatic Track-while-Scan [Radar]
ATWT	As the World Turns [A television program]
ATWT	Atmospheric Thermonuclear Weapons Testing
ATWT	Atomic Weight
ATWTFC ..	As the World Turns Fan Club (EA)
ATWU	Amalgamated Textile Workers' Union [British] (DCTA)
ATX	Abingdon, VA [Location identifier] [FAA] (FAAL)
ATX	Ameritex Resources Ltd. [Vancouver Stock Exchange symbol]
ATX	Australian Sales Tax Guide [A publication] (APTA)
ATX	Automatic TELEX Exchange [Telecommunications] (TEL)
ATX	Automatic Transaxle
ATX	Business. The Magazine of Managerial Thought and Action [A publication]
ATX	Cross [A. T.] Co. [AMEX symbol] (SPSG)

ATXPL	Atomic Explosion
ATY	Automatie, Maandblad voor Meettechniek en Regeltechniek, Mechanisering, en Automatisering [Baarn] [A publication]
ATY	Watertown [South Dakota] [Airport symbol] (OAG)
ATYBAK ...	Annales. Universitatis Turkuensis. Series A-II. Biologica-Geographica-Geologica [A publication]
ATYPI	Association Typographique Internationale [International Typographic Association]
Atyp Mycobacteria Proc Symp ...	Atypical Mycobacteria. Proceedings. Symposium [A publication]
ATZ	Acquisition Trigger at Zero Beat
ATZ	Aerodrome Traffic Zone
ATZOAU ..	Attualita Zoologiche [A publication]
AU.............	Absorbance Unit [Physical chemistry]
AU.............	Accounting Unit (NATG)
AU.............	Ad Usum [According to Custom] [Pharmacy]
AU.............	Address Unit [Data processing]
AU.............	Afrika und Uebersee [A publication]
AU.............	Air University [Maxwell Air Force Base, AL]
AU.............	Airborne Unit
AU.............	Alignment Unit
AU.............	All Up (ADA)
AU.............	Alma Urbis [Beloved City] [Rome]
AU.............	Almost Uncirculated [Condition of coins] [Numismatics]
AU.............	Alternate Uses [Personality research] [Psychology]
AU.............	Amax Gold, Inc. [NYSE symbol] (SPSG)
AU.............	American University [Washington, DC]
AU.............	Americana Unit [American Topical Association] (EA)
AU.............	Analyzer Unit (CAAL)
AU.............	Angstrom Unit [Also, A]
AU.............	Annals of the University [Grenoble] [A publication]
AU.............	Anno Urbis [In the Year of the City of Rome] [Latin]
AU.............	Anson Unit [Of hydrolytic enzyme activity]
AU.............	Anti-U-Boat Warfare [British] [World War II]
AU.............	Antitoxin Unit [Immunology]
AU.............	Apprentices Union [British]
au-----	Arabian Sea and Area [MARC geographic area code] [Library of Congress] (LCCP)
AU.............	Arbitrary Unit
A & U	Architecture and Urbanism [A publication]
AU.............	Arithmetic Unit [Data processing]
AU.............	Army Unit
AU.............	Astronomical Unit [Equal to average distance from earth to sun]
AU.............	Astronomy Unit [Later, ASU] [American Topical Association] (EA)
AU.............	Atheists United (EA)
AU.............	Atlantic Union (DAS)
AU.............	Atomic Units (MCD)
AU.............	Attachment Unit (MCD)
Au.............	Auberger [Blood group]
AU.............	Auburn University [Alabama]
Au.............	Audio [A publication]
AU.............	Audit
AU.............	Augmitto Explorations Ltd. [Toronto Stock Exchange symbol]
AU.............	August
AU.............	Aunes [French Ells]
AU.............	Aures Unitas [Both Ears] [Latin]
AU.............	Auris Uterque [Each Ear] [Latin]
Au.............	Aurum [Gold] [Chemical element]
Au.............	Ausonia [A publication]
AU.............	Austral Lineas Aereas [Argentina] [ICAO designator] (FAAC)
AU.............	Australia [ANSI two-letter standard code] (CNC)
Au.............	Australia Antigen [Immunology]
AU.............	Austria
au.............	Austria [MARC country of publication code] [Library of Congress] (LCCP)
AU.............	Author [Online database field identifier] [Data processing]
AU.............	Authorized User (DCTA)
AU.............	Automobile
AU.............	Autopsy [Also, AUT] [Medicine]
Au.............	Autumn
AU.............	Auxiliary Unit
AU.............	Der Altsprachliche Unterricht [A publication]
Au.............	National Library of Australia, Canberra, Australia [Library symbol] [Library of Congress] (LCLS)
AU.............	University of Alabama, University, AL [Library symbol] [Library of Congress] (LCLS)
AUA..........	Alkylation Unit Acid [Petroleum refining]
AUA..........	Allied Underwear Association (EA)
AUA..........	American Underground-Space Association (EA)
AUA..........	American Unitarian Association
AUA..........	American Urological Association (EA)
AuA..........	Anglistik und Amerikanistik [A publication]
AUA..........	Annals. Ukrainian Academy of Arts and Sciences in the US [A publication]
Au A	Antike und Abendland [A publication]
AUA..........	Argonne Universities Association
AUA..........	Arithmetic Underachievers [Education]
AUA..........	Aruba [Netherlands Antilles] [Airport symbol]
AUA..........	Asamera Minerals Ltd. [Toronto Stock Exchange symbol]

AUA.......... Associated Unions of America [*Later, OPEIU*] (EA)

AUA.......... Association des Universites Africaines [*Association of African Universities - AAU*] (EAIO)

AUA.......... Association of University Anesthetists (EA)

AUA.......... Association of University Architects (EA)

AUA.......... Australian Ultralight Association

AUA.......... Austrian Airways [*Oesterreichische Luftverkehrs AG*]

AUA.......... Automated Universal Array (MCD)

AUAA....... American Urological Association Allied (EA)

AUAA....... Artists United Against Apartheid (EA)

AUAA J..... AUAA [*American Urological Association Allied*] Journal [*A publication*]

AUAEAI.... Annales. Universite d'Abidjan. Serie E. Ecologie [*A publication*]

AUAF........ Association of University Affiliated Facilities [*Later, AAUAP*] (EA)

AUAFA..... Acta Universitatis Agriculturae. Facultas Silviculturae. Series C [*A publication*]

AUAIP....... Aeronautics Upper Atmosphere Impact Program [*NASA*]

AUAMCA ... Annales. Universite d'Abidjan. Serie B. Medecine [*A publication*]

AuAP........ Parliamentary Library, Parliament House, Adelaide, SA, Australia [*Library symbol*] [*Library of Congress*] (LCLS)

AuAr......... Armidale City and Dumarasq Shire War Memorial Library, Armidale, NSW, Australia [*Library symbol*] [*Library of Congress*] (LCLS)

AuArA ...... Armidale Newspaper Co. Ltd., Armidale, NSW, Australia [*Library symbol*] [*Library of Congress*] (LCLS)

AUARAN.. Arkansas. Agricultural Experiment Station. Special Report [*A publication*]

AUARBO .. Australia. Commonwealth Scientific and Industrial Research Organisation. Division of Animal Physiology. Annual Report [*A publication*]

AuArU ...... University of New England, Armidale, NSW, Australia [*Library symbol*] [*Library of Congress*] (LCLS)

AUAS .... Academy of Underwater Arts and Sciences (EA)

AuASA...... Public Library of South Australia, Adelaide, SA, Australia [*Library symbol*] [*Library of Congress*] (LCLS)

AUASAM ... Automatic Aimpoint Selection and Maintenance (MCD)

AUASAQ .. Annals. Ukrainian Academy of Arts and Sciences in the US [*A publication*]

AuAU........ University of Adelaide, Adelaide, SA, Australia [*Library symbol*] [*Library of Congress*] (LCLS)

AUAW....... Amalgamated Union of Asphalt Workers [*British*] (DCTA)

AUB........... Aft Utility Bridge (NASA)

AUB........... American University of Beirut [*Lebanon*]

AUB........... Analele. Universitatii Bucuresti [*A publication*]

AUB........... Annales Universitatis Scientiarum Budapestensis de Rolando Eoetvoes Nominatae [*A publication*]

AUB........... Annales. Universite de Besancon [*A publication*]

A d U B ..... Annales. Universite de Brazzaville [*A publication*]

AuB............ Autour de la Bible [*Paris*] [*A publication*]

AUBADE .. Annales Scientifiques. Universite de Besancon. Biologie Animale [*A publication*]

AUBBER... Associated University Bureaus of Business and Economic Research [*Later, AUBER*]

AUBC........ Association of Universities of the British Commonwealth

AUBCB...... Analele. Universitatii Bucuresti. Chimie [*A publication*]

AUBCBI.... Analele. Universitatii Bucuresti. Chimie [*A publication*]

AUBEAN .. Acta Urologica Belgica [*A publication*]

AUBER...... Association for University Business and Economic Research [*University, AL*] (EA)

AUBFF...... Arquivos. Universidade de Bahia. Faculdade de Filosofia [*A publication*]

AUBG........ Acta Universitatis Upsaliensis [*A publication*]

AuBh.......... Broken Hill Municipal Library, Broken Hill, NSW, Australia [*Library symbol*] [*Library of Congress*] (LCLS)

AuBiR....... Australian Biblical Review [*Melbourne*] [*A publication*]

AUBKA7 ... Archives. Union Medicale Balkanique [*A publication*]

AuBL......... LaTrobe University, Bundoora, V, Australia [*Library symbol*] [*Library of Congress*] (LCLS)

AUB-LCO ... Analele. Universitatii Bucuresti. Limbi Clasice si Orientale [*A publication*]

AUB-LG .... Analele. Universitatii Bucuresti. Limbi Germanice [*A publication*]

AUBLL...... Analele. Universitatii Bucuresti. Limba si Literatura Romana [*A publication*]

AUB-LLR ... Analele. Universitatii Bucuresti. Limba Literara [*A publication*]

AUBLR...... Analele. Universitatii Bucuresti. Limbi Romanice [*A publication*]

AUB-LUC ... Analele. Universitatii Bucuresti. Literatura Universala Comparata [*A publication*]

AuBpF........ Flinders University of South Australia, Bedford Park, SA, Australia [*Library symbol*] [*Library of Congress*] (LCLS)

AUBRCC... Australian Uniform Building Regulations Co-Ordinating Council

AuBrP........ Queensland Parliamentary Library, Parliament House, Brisbane, QLD, Australia [*Library symbol*] [*Library of Congress*] (LCLS)

AuBrS........ State Library of Queensland, Brisbane, QLD, Australia [*Library symbol*] [*Library of Congress*] (LCLS)

AuBrS-O.... State Library of Queensland, Oxley Memorial Library, Brisbane, QLD, Australia [*Library symbol*] [*Library of Congress*] (LCLS)

AuBrU .... University of Queensland, St. Lucia, Brisbane, QLD, Australia [*Library symbol*] [*Library of Congress*] (LCLS)

AUBud....... Annales Universitatis Scientiarum Budapestensis de Rolando Eoetvoes Nominatae. Sectio Philologica [*A publication*]

Auburn Univ Eng Exp Stn Bull ... Auburn University. Engineering Experiment Station. Bulletin [*A publication*]

AuBut........ Butterworths Proprietory Ltd., Chatswood, NSW, Australia [*Library symbol*] [*Library of Congress*] (LCLS)

AUBV .... Air University Board of Visitors

AUC.......... Acta Universitatis Carolinae [*A publication*]

AUC.......... Air Users' Committee [*British*]

AUC.......... American University of Cairo

AUC.......... American University of the Caribbean

AUC.......... Ammonium Uranyl Carbonate [*Inorganic chemistry*]

AUC.......... Anales. Universidad de Chile [*A publication*]

AUC.......... Anno Urbis Conditae [*In the Year from the Building of the City (Rome)*] [*753 BC*] [*Latin*]

AUC.......... Anuarul. Universitatea Cluj [*A publication*]

AUC.......... Apple University Consortium

AUC.......... Arauca [*Colombia*] [*Airport symbol*] (OAG)

AUC.......... Area under Plasma Concentration Curve [*Hematology*]

AUC.......... Asociacion de Universidades del Caribe [*Association of Caribbean Universities and Research Institutes*] (EAIO)

AUC.......... Association of Uptown Converters (EA)

AUC.......... Atlantic Union College [*South Lancaster, MA*]

AUC.......... Au Courant [*A publication*]

AUC.......... Auckland [*New Zealand*] [*Seismograph station code, US Geological Survey*] (SEIS)

AUC.......... Auteursrecht [*A publication*]

AUC.......... Coeur D'Alene, ID [*Location identifier*] [*FAA*] (FAAL)

AUCA........ American Unitarian Christian Association (EA)

AUCal........ Annali. Facolta di Lettere, Filosofia, e Magistero. Universita di Cagliari [*A publication*]

AUCANUKUS ... Australia, Canada, United Kingdom, United States (ADA)

AuCaRec.... Australasian Catholic Record [*Manly, NSW*] [*A publication*]

AUCAS...... Association of University Clinical Academic Staff [*British*]

AUCBE...... Advisory Unit for Computer Based Education [*Hatfield, England*] [*Information service or system*] [*Telecommunications*] (TSSD)

AUCBM .... Arab Union for Cement and Building Materials [*See also UACMC*] (EAIO)

AUCC........ Annuario. Universita Cattolica del Sacro Cuore [*A publication*]

AUCC........ Association of Universities and Colleges of Canada [*Association des Universites et Colleges du Canada*]

AUCCCD .. Association of University and College Counseling Center Directors (EA)

AUCCTU .. All Union Central Council of Trade Unions [*USSR*]

AUCE .... Anales. Universidad Central del Ecuador [*A publication*]

AUCE .... Association of University and College Employees [*See also AEUC*] [*Canada*]

AUCEN ..... Association Universitaire Canadienne d'Etudes Nordiques [*Association of Canadian Universities for Northern Studies*]

AUCF .... Americans United to Combat Fluoridation [*Later, AUDF*] (EA)

AuCF.......... Federal Capital Press of Australia, Canberra, ACT, Australia [*Library symbol*] [*Library of Congress*] (LCLS)

AUCG-B.... Acta Universitatis Carolinae. Geographica [*A publication*]

Auch.......... Auchinleck's Manuscript Cases, Scotch Court of Session [*A publication*] (DLA)

AuChr .... Antike und Christentum [*A publication*]

AUCII........ Archivio Unione Comunita Israelitiche Italiane [*A publication*]

Auckland U L Rev ... Auckland University. Law Review [*A publication*]

Auckland Univ L Rev ... Auckland University. Law Review [*A publication*]

Auck ULR ... Auckland University. Law Review [*A publication*]

Auck UL Rev ... Auckland University. Law Review [*A publication*]

AuClM....... Monash University, Clayton, V, Australia [*Library symbol*] [*Library of Congress*] (LCLS)

AUCM....... Automated Urease-Chromous Method [*Analytical chemistry*]

AUCMB .... Acta Universitatis Carolinae. Medica. Monographia [*A publication*]

AUCN....... Auction (ROG)

AuCNL ...... Commonwealth National Library, Parliament House, Canberra, ACT, Australia [*Library symbol*] [*Library of Congress*] (LCLS)

AUCOA..... Association of United Contractors of America [*Defunct*] (EA)

AUCP .... Acta Universitatis Carolinae Pragensis [*A publication*]

AUCPD ..... Annual UMR-DNR [*University of Missouri, Rolla - Department of Natural Resources*] Conference on Energy. Proceedings [*A publication*]

AUC Ph ..... Acta Universitatis Carolinae. Philologica [*A publication*]

AUCS .... Advanced UHF Communication System (MCD)

auct........... Auctorum [*Of Authors*] [*Biology, taxonomy*]

AuCT .... Auxiliary Current Transformer

AUCTNR .. Auctioneer

AUCTNRG ... Auctioneering

Auct Reg & L Chron ... Auction Register and Law Chronicle [*A publication*] (DLA)

AuCU .... Australian National University, Canberra, ACT, Australia [*Library symbol*] [*Library of Congress*]   (LCLS)
AUD .... Acta et Commentationes Universitatis Dorpatensis [*A publication*]
AUD .... Aktionsgemeinschaft Unabhaengiger Deutscher [*Action Group of Independent Germans*] [*Federal Republic of Germany*] [*Political party*]   (PPE)
AUD .... Association for Union Democracy   (EA)
AUD .... Association to Unite the Democracies   (EA)
Aud .... Audience [*A publication*]
AUD .... Audio [*or Audible or Audiology*]   (MSA)
AUD .... Audit [*or Auditor*]   (AFM)
Aud .... Audubon [*A publication*]
AUD .... Augustus Downs [*Australia*] [*Airport symbol*] [*Obsolete*]   (OAG)
AUD .... Australian Dollar [*Monetary unit*]   (ADA)
AUD .... Automatic Data Processing, Inc. [*NYSE symbol*]   (SPSG)
AudA .... Audio Archives [*Record label*]
AUDACIOUS ... Automatic Direct Access to Information with the On-Line UDC [*Universal Decimal Classification*] System [*American Institute of Physics*] [*Information retrieval*]
AUDAR .... Autodyne Detection and Ranging
AUDB .... Arming Unit Distribution Box [*Army*]   (MCD)
AUDBAO ... Australia. Commonwealth Scientific and Industrial Research Organisation. Division of Building Research. Technical Paper [*A publication*]
AudC .... Audio Collectors [*Record label*]
AuDDa .... Department of Aboriginal Affairs, Darwin, NT, Australia [*Library symbol*] [*Library of Congress*]   (LCLS)
AUDELCO ... Audience Development Committee   (EA)
AUDET .... Associatie van Uitgevers van Dagbladen en Tijdschriften [*Netherlands*]   (ECON)
AUDGENAV ... Auditor General of the Navy
AUDI .... Arab Urban Development Institute   (EA)
AUDI .... Societe Internationale d'Audiologie
AUDINET ... American Electric Power Co., Inc. Unified Dial Network   (TEL)
Audio Engg ... Audio Engineering [*A publication*]
Audio Eng Soc J ... Audio Engineering Society. Journal [*A publication*]
Audio Eng Soc Prepr ... Audio Engineering Society. Preprint [*A publication*]
Audiol .... Audiology [*A publication*]
Audiol Akust ... Audiologische Akustik [*A publication*]
Audiol (Jap) ... Audiology (Japan) [*A publication*]
Audio Scene Can ... Audio Scene Canada [*A publication*]
Audiov Commun ... Audio Visual Communications [*A publication*]
Audio Video Can ... Audio Video Canada [*A publication*]
Audiov Instr ... Audiovisual Instruction [*A publication*]
Audiovis Instr ... Audiovisual Instruction [*A publication*]
Audio Visual G ... Audio Visual Guide [*A publication*]
Audio-Visual Language J ... Audio-Visual Language Journal [*A publication*]
Audio Visual Lib ... Audio Visual Librarian [*A publication*]
Audiov Libr ... Audiovisual Librarian [*A publication*]
AUDIT ...... Aircraft Unitized Diagnostic Inspection and Test [*Boeing*]
AUDIT ...... Army Uniform Data Inquiry Technique
AUDIT ...... Auditory Input Task [*Data processing*]
AUDIT ...... Automatic Unattended Detection Inspection Transmitter [*Raytheon Co.*]
Auditor .... Internal Auditor [*A publication*]
AUDITRPT ... Audit Trail Report [*Military*]
AUDJDK ... Audiology [*Japan*] [*A publication*]
AUDLA ..... Audiology [*A publication*]
AUDLAK .. Audiology [*Basel*] [*A publication*]
Audn .... Audience [*A publication*]
AuDpAr ..... Queensland State Archives, Dutton Park, QLD, Australia [*Library symbol*] [*Library of Congress*]   (LCLS)
AUDPC ...... Area under the Disease Progress Curve [*Botany*]
Aud Q .... Audita Querela [*A publication*]   (DLA)
AudR .... Audio Rarities [*Record label*]
AUDREY .. Audio Reply [*IEEE*]
AUDREY .. Automatic Digit Recognition
AUDRI ...... Automated Drug Identification
AUDTCF ... Ankara Universitesi Dil ve Tarih-Cografya Fakultesi. Dergisi [*Ankara*] [*A publication*]
AUDTCFY ... Ankara Universitesi Dil ve Tarih-Cografya Fakultesi. Yayinlari [*A publication*]
AUDTR .... Auditor   (MSA)
AUDUA ..... Audio [*A publication*]
AUDUAD ... Audubon [*A publication*]
Audubon Mag ... Audubon Magazine [*A publication*]
Audubon Soc RI Bull ... Audubon Society of Rhode Island. Bulletin [*A publication*]
AUDYA ..... Autodynamics Cl A [*NASDAQ symbol*]   (NQ)
AuE .... Arheologija un Etnografija [*A publication*]
AUE .... Army User Equipment   (MCD)
AUE .... Association des Universitaires d'Europe
AUE .... Au Resources Ltd. [*Vancouver Stock Exchange symbol*]
AUE .... Aurora High School PRECIS Project [*UTLAS symbol*]
AUE .... Sebring, FL [*Location identifier*] [*FAA*]   (FAAL)
AUEA .... Auxiliary Utility Equipment Area   (NRCH)
AUEBF ..... All-Ukrainian Evangelical Baptist Fellowship   (EA)
AUEC .... Association of University Evening Colleges [*Later, ACHE*]   (EA)

AUEFW ..... Amalgamated Union of Engineering and Foundry Workers [*British*]
AUEHSC ... Association of University Environmental Health/Sciences Centers   (EA)
AUELA ..... Automatica si Electronica [*A publication*]
AUENA ..... Automobile Engineer [*England*] [*A publication*]
Auerbach Data Base Manage ... Auerbach Data Base Management [*A publication*]
Auerbach Rep ... Auerbach Reporter [*A publication*]
AUET .... Armored, Universal Engineer Tractor
AUEW .... Amalgamated Union of Engineering Workers [*British*]   (DCTA)
AUEW(C) ... Amalgamated Union of Engineering Workers - Constructional [*British*]   (DCTA)
AUEW(E) ... Amalgamated Union of Engineering Workers - Engineering [*British*]   (DCTA)
AUEW(F) .. Amalgamated Union of Engineering Workers - Foundry [*British*]   (DCTA)
AUEW-TASS ... Amalgamated Union of Engineering Workers - Technical and Supervisory [*British*]   (DCTA)
AUF .... Archiv fuer Urkundenforschung [*A publication*]
AUF .... Augustine Island [*Alaska*] [*Seismograph station code, US Geological Survey*]   (SEIS)
AUF .... Australian Ultralight Federation
AUF .... Average Utilization Factor
AUFB-A ...... Aufbau [*A publication*]
AUFBE4 .... Annali. Universita di Ferrara. Nuova Serie. Sezione XX. Biologia [*A publication*]
Aufbereit .... Aufbereitungs-Technik [*A publication*]
Aufbereit-Tech ... Aufbereitungs-Technik [*A publication*]
Aufbereitungs-Tech ... Aufbereitungs-Technik [*A publication*]
Aufer .... [*Etienne*] d'Aufrere [*Flourished, 15th century*] [*Authority cited in pre-1607 legal work*]   (DSA)
Auff .... Auffuehrung [*Performance*] [*German*]
Aufg .... Aufgabe [*Task*] [*German*]
AuFirGS .... Church of Jesus Christ of Latter-Day Saints, Genealogical Society Library, Adelaide Stake Branch, Firle, SA, Australia [*Library symbol*] [*Library of Congress*]   (LCLS)
AUFL .... Auflage [*Edition*] [*German*]
AUFM .... Asociacion Universal de Federalistas Mundiales [*World Association of World Federalists*]
AUFNA2 ... Audubon Field Notes [*A publication*]
Aufre .... [*Etienne*] d'Aufrere [*Flourished, 15th century*] [*Authority cited in pre-1607 legal work*]   (DSA)
AUFS .... Absorbance Units Full Scale [*Physical chemistry*]
AUFS .... American Universities Field Staff [*Later, UFSI-IWA*]   (EA)
AUFS .... American Universities Field Staff. Reports Series [*A publication*]
Aufs .... Aufsatz [*Essay*] [*German*]
Aufschluss Sonderh ... Aufschluss Sonderheft [*A publication*]
AUFS EA .. American Universities Field Staff. Reports. East Asia Series [*A publication*]
AUFS-IWA ... American Universities Field Staff - Institute of World Affairs [*Later, UFSI-IWA*]   (EA)
AUFSRS .... American Universities Field Staff. Reports Series [*A publication*]
AUFS SA ... American Universities Field Staff. Reports. South Asia Series [*A publication*]
AUFS SEA ... American Universities Field Staff. Reports. Southeast Asia Series [*A publication*]
Auftr .... Auftrag [*Order*] [*German*]
Au Fu .... Ausgrabungen und Funde [*A publication*]
AUFW .... Amalgamated Union of Foundry Workers [*British*]
AUFWPA ... Association of University Fisheries and Wildlife Program Administrators   (EA)
Aufz .... Aufzeichnung [*Note*] [*German*]
AUG .... Adenine, Uracil, Guanine [*Biochemistry*]
AUG .... Amdahl Users Group   (EA)
AUG .... Anales. Universidad de Guayaquil [*A publication*]
AUG .... Annales. Universite de Grenoble [*A publication*]
AUG .... Augat, Inc. [*NYSE symbol*]   (SPSG)
AUG .... Augdome Corp. [*Vancouver Stock Exchange symbol*]
AUG .... Augere [*Increase*] [*Pharmacy*]
AUG .... Augment   (AABC)
Aug .... Augmentation [*Music*]
AUG .... August   (EY)
AUG .... Augusta [*Maine*] [*Airport symbol*]   (OAG)
AUG .... Augusta Railroad Co. [*AAR code*]
Aug .... [*Saint*] Augustine [*Deceased, 430*] [*Authority cited in pre-1607 legal work*]   (DSA)
Aug .... Augustine   (BJA)
Aug .... Augustiniana [*A publication*]
Aug .... [*Antonius*] Augustinus [*Deceased, 1586*] [*Authority cited in pre-1607 legal work*]   (DSA)
AUG .... Australian United Gold No Liability
Aug .... Divus Augustus [*of Suetonius*] [*Classical studies*]   (OCD)
AUG .... University of Maine at Augusta, Augusta, ME [*OCLC symbol*]   (OCLC)
Aug Bero .... Augustinus Berous [*Deceased, 1554*] [*Authority cited in pre-1607 legal work*]   (DSA)
AUGC .... Americans United for God and Country   (EA)
AugLv .... Augustiniana (Louvain) [*A publication*]

Augm.......... Augmentation [*Music*]
AUGM....... Augmentative
AugMad..... Augustinus (Madrid) [*A publication*]
AUGRA ..... Authority Granted (NOAA)
AugRom ..... Augustinianum (Rome) [*A publication*]
AUGT .... August (ROG)
AUGU........ Augmenting Unit [*Navy*]
Augu............ [*Saint*] Augustine [*Deceased, 430*] [*Authority cited in pre-1607 legal work*] (DSA)
Augu............ Augustinus Berous [*Deceased, 1554*] [*Authority cited in pre-1607 legal work*] (DSA)
August........ Augustine [*354-430AD*] [*Classical studies*] (OCD)
Augustana Libr Pub ... Augustana Library Publications [*A publication*]
Augustin Stud ... Augustinian Studies [*A publication*]
AUH .... Abu Dhabi [*United Arab Emirates*] [*Airport symbol*] (OAG)
AUH .... Anales. Universidad Hispalense [*A publication*]
AUH .... Aurora, NE [*Location identifier*] [*FAA*] (FAAL)
AuHaA....... Australian Council for Educational Research, Hawthorn, V, Australia [*Library symbol*] [*Library of Congress*] (LCLS)
AUHC........ Adelaide University History Club [*Australia*]
AUHisp ...... Anales. Universidad Hispalense [*A publication*]
AUHJ .... Australian Journal for Health, Physical Education, and Recreation [*A publication*]
AuH₂O....... Goldwater, Barry [*Chemical symbols for gold and water; used to refer to the 1964 Republican presidential candidate*]
AuHP......... Parliamentary Library, Parliament House, Hobart, TAS, Australia [*Library symbol*] [*Library of Congress*] (LCLS)
AUHPAI ... Australian Journal of Hospital Pharmacy [*A publication*]
AuHS......... State Library of Tasmania, Hobart, TAS, Australia [*Library symbol*] [*Library of Congress*] (LCLS)
AuHU .... University of Tasmania, Hobart, TAS, Australia [*Library symbol*] [*Library of Congress*] (LCLS)
AUI............ Action d'Urgence Internationale [*International Emergency Action - IEA*] [*Paris, France*] (EAIO)
AUI............ Analele. Universitatii Al. I. Cuza (Iasi) [*A publication*]
AUI............ Applied Urbanetics, Incorporated [*Information service or system*] (IID)
AUI............ Asociacion Universitaria Interamericana [*Interamerican University Association*] [*Spanish*]
AUI............ Associacao Universitaria Interamericana [*Interamerican University Association*] [*Portuguese*]
AUI............ Associated Universities, Incorporated (EA)
AUI............ Association Universitaire Interamericaine [*Interamerican University Association*] [*France*]
AUI............ Aua [*Papua New Guinea*] [*Airport symbol*] (OAG)
AUI............ Augustine Island [*Alaska*] [*Seismograph station code, US Geological Survey*] (SEIS)
AUI............ Las Vegas, NV [*Location identifier*] [*FAA*] (FAAL)
AUIBA....... Analele Stiintifice ale Universitatii Al. I. Cuza din Iasi. Sectiunea 2a. Biologie [*A publication*]
AUID......... Association of University Interior Designers (EA)
AUIN......... Automotive Industries, Inc. [*NASDAQ symbol*] (NQ)
AUINA...... Automotive Industries [*A publication*]
AuIpQT...... Queensland Times Proprietory Ltd., Ipswich, QLD, Australia [*Library symbol*] [*Library of Congress*] (LCLS)
AUIRAT.... Australia. Commonwealth Scientific and Industrial Research Organisation. Irrigation Research Stations. Technical Paper [*A publication*]
AUIUSA..... Americans for Undivided Israel USA (EA)
AUJ .... Aberdeen University. Journal [*A publication*]
AUJ .... Air-to-Umbilical Junction Box
AUJ .... Ambunti [*Papua New Guinea*] [*Airport symbol*] (OAG)
AUJ .... Atigaru Point, AK [*Location identifier*] [*FAA*] (FAAL)
AUJ .... Aujourd'hui [*Today*] [*French*]
AUJDDT... Australian Journal of Developmental Disabilities [*A publication*]
Aujourd'hui ... Aujourd'hui: Art et Architecture [*A publication*]
AUJR......... Agra University. Journal of Research [*A publication*]
AUJS......... Advanced Universal Jamming System
AUJSA....... Australian Journal of Statistics [*A publication*]
AUJW .... Allgemeine Unabhaengige Juedische Wochenzeitung (BJA)
AUK.......... Alakanuk [*Alaska*] [*Airport symbol*] (OAG)
AUK.......... Auckland Explorations Ltd. [*Vancouver Stock Exchange symbol*]
AUK.......... Auki [*Solomon Islands*] [*Seismograph station code, US Geological Survey*] (SEIS)
AuKirGS.... Church of Jesus Christ of Latter-Day Saints, Genealogical Society Library, Sydney South Branch, Sutherland Ward Chapel, Kirrawee, NSW, Australia [*Library symbol*] [*Library of Congress*] (LCLS)
AUKOI...... Association of United Kingdom Oil Independents
AuKU......... University of New South Wales, Kensington, NSW, Australia [*Library symbol*] [*Library of Congress*] (LCLS)
AUL.......... Acta Universitatis Latviensis [*A publication*]
AUL.......... Acta Universitatis Lundensis [*A publication*]
AUL.......... Acute Undifferentiated Leukemia [*Hematology*]
AUL.......... Air University Library
AUL.......... Americans United for Life (EA)
AUL.......... Annales. Universite de Lyon [*A publication*]
AUL.......... Annali. Universita di Lecce [*A publication*]
AUL.......... Athabasca University Library [*UTLAS symbol*]

AUL........... Aur [*Marshall Islands*] [*Airport symbol*] (OAG)
AUL........... Average Useful Life
AUL........... Bulletin. Association des Amis de l'Universite de Liege [*A publication*]
AU-L.......... University of Alabama, Law Library, University, AL [*Library symbol*] [*Library of Congress*] (LCLS)
Aul Gell Noct Att ... Aulus Gellius. Noctes Atticae [*A publication*] (DLA)
AULJA ...... Australian Library Journal [*A publication*]
AULLA...... Australasian Universities Language and Literature Association (EAIO)
AULLDF ... Americans United for Life Legal Defense Fund (EA)
AULR .... American University Law Review [*A publication*]
AULR .... Attrition, Utilization, and Loss Rate (AFM)
AU-LS .... University of Alabama, Library Sciences School, University, AL [*Library symbol*] [*Library of Congress*] (LCLS)
AULT .... Ault, Inc. [*NASDAQ symbol*] (NQ)
Ault .... Court Rolls of Ramsey Abbey [*1928*] [*England*] [*A publication*] (DLA)
AUM......... Adelaide University. Magazine [*A publication*] (APTA)
AUM......... Advanced Underwater Missile
AUM......... Air-to-Underwater Missile [*Air Force*]
AUM......... Anales. Universidad de Murcia [*A publication*]
AUM......... Andrews University. Monographs [*A publication*]
AUM......... Animal-Unit Month
AUM......... Association of Umbrella Manufacturers and Suppliers [*Defunct*] (EA)
AUM......... Association for the Understanding of Man (EA)
AUM......... Augustine Island [*Alaska*] [*Seismograph station code, US Geological Survey*] (SEIS)
AUM......... Austin, MN [*Location identifier*] [*FAA*] (FAAL)
AUM......... Auto Marine Electric Ltd. [*Vancouver Stock Exchange symbol*]
AU-M........ University of Alabama, Medical Center, Birmingham, AL [*Library symbol*] [*Library of Congress*] (LCLS)
AUM......... University of Massachusetts-Amherst, Amherst, MA [*OCLC symbol*] (OCLC)
AuMacD.... Daily Mercury, Mackay, QLD, Australia [*Library symbol*] [*Library of Congress*] (LCLS)
AUMACY ... Australian Mammalogy [*A publication*]
AUMCA4.. Archivos Uruguayos de Medicina, Cirujia, y Especialidades [*A publication*]
AUMCS..... Annales Universitatis Mariae Curie-Sklodowska. Sectio F. Nauki Filozoficzne i Humanistyczne [*A publication*]
AUMDC.... Automedica [*A publication*]
AuMDS ..... David Syme & Co. Ltd., Melbourne, V, Australia [*Library symbol*] [*Library of Congress*] (LCLS)
AUMGAG ... Audubon Magazine [*A publication*]
AUMIA ..... Australian Mineral Industry [*A publication*]
AUMID ...... Australian Miner [*A publication*]
AUMKA .... Annales Universitatis Mariae Curie-Sklodowska. Sectio D. Medicina [*A publication*]
AUML .... Automated Medical Laboratories [*NASDAQ symbol*] (NQ)
AUMLA ..... Australasian Universities Modern Language Association. Journal [*A publication*]
AUMLGC ... Affirmation: United Methodists for Lesbian/Gay Concerns (EA)
AUMMAY ... Australian Museum. Magazine [*A publication*]
AUMNA.... Australian Mining [*A publication*]
AuMP........ Parliamentary Library of Victoria, Parliament House, Melbourne, V, Australia [*Library symbol*] [*Library of Congress*] (LCLS)
AuMS .... State Library of Victoria, Melbourne, V, Australia [*Library symbol*] [*Library of Congress*] (LCLS)
AUMTA .... Automatisme [*A publication*]
AuMU........ University of Melbourne, Melbourne, V, Australia [*Library symbol*] [*Library of Congress*] (LCLS)
AuMuU...... Murdoch University, Murdoch, WA, Australia [*Library symbol*] [*Library of Congress*] (LCLS)
AUN .... Absque Ulla Nota [*Without Any Marking or Note*] [*Latin*]
AUN .... Annali. Facolta di Lettere e Filosofia. Universita di Napoli [*A publication*]
AUN .... Auburn, CA [*Location identifier*] [*FAA*] (FAAL)
Au N........... Aufstieg und Niedergang der Roemischen Welt [*A publication*]
AUNAB4... Annales. Universite et ARERS [*Association Regional pour l'Etude et la Recherche Scientifiques*] [*A publication*]
AuNaG....... Griffith University, Nathan, QLD, Australia [*Library symbol*] [*Library of Congress*] (LCLS)
AuNc.......... Newcastle Public Library, Civic Center, Newcastle, NSW, Australia [*Library symbol*] [*Library of Congress*] (LCLS)
AuNcU....... University of Newcastle, Newcastle, NSW, Australia [*Library symbol*] [*Library of Congress*] (LCLS)
AUND .... American Underwriters Group, Inc. [*NASDAQ symbol*] (NQ)
AUNED ...... Australian Uranium News [*A publication*]
AuNeU........ University of Western Australia, Nedlands, WA, Australia [*Library symbol*] [*Library of Congress*] (LCLS)
AUNHA .... Australian Natural History [*A publication*]
A Univ Abidjan Ethnosociologie ... Annales. Universite d'Abidjan. Ethnosociologie [*A publication*]
A Univ Abidjan Histoire ... Annales. Universite d'Abidjan. Histoire [*A publication*]
A Univ Abidjan Lettres ... Annales. Universite d'Abidjan. Lettres [*A publication*]

A Univ Abidjan Linguist ... Annales. Universite d'Abidjan. Linguistique [*A publication*]
A Univ Abidjan Ser A Dr ... Annales. Universite d'Abidjan. Serie A. Droit [*A publication*]
A Univ Madagascar Ser Dr Sci Econ ... Annales. Universite de Madagascar. Serie de Droit et des Sciences Economiques [*A publication*]
A Univ M Curie-Sklodowska ... Annales Universitatis Mariae Curie-Sklodowska [*A publication*]
A Univ M Curie-Sklodowska Oecon ... Annales Universitatis Mariae Curie-Sklodowska. Sectio Oeconomica [*A publication*]
A Univ Sci Budapest Sect Geogr .... Annales Universitatis Scientiarum Budapestensis de Rolando Eoetvoes Nominatae. Sectio Geographica [*A publication*]
A Univ Sci Soc Toulouse ... Annales. Universite des Sciences Sociales de Toulouse [*A publication*]
AUNL........ Advertising Unlimited, Inc. [*NASDAQ symbol*] (NQ)
AUNMA5 ... Australian Museum [*Sydney*]. Memoirs [*A publication*]
AuNocGS... Church of Jesus Christ of Latter-Day Saints, Genealogical Society Library, Melbourne Branch, Northcote, V, Australia [*Library symbol*] [*Library of Congress*] (LCLS)
AuNqIT ..... Queensland Institute of Technology, North Quay, QLD, Australia [*Library symbol*] [*Library of Congress*] (LCLS)
AuNrM ...... Macquarie University, North Ryde, NSW, Australia [*Library symbol*] [*Library of Congress*] (LCLS)
AUNS........ Al'manakh Ukraiens'koho Narodnoho Soiuzu [*A publication*]
AUNT........ Alliance for Undesirable but Necessary Tasks [*From book title, "The Woman from AUNT"*]
AUNT........ Automatic Universal Translator
AUNVAW ... Avhandlinger Utgitt av Norsk Videnskaps-Akademi I Oslo. Matematisk-Naturvidenskapelig Klasse [*A publication*]
AUO .... Administratively Uncontrollable Overtime
AUO .... Amulet Resources Corp. [*Vancouver Stock Exchange symbol*]
AUO .... Amyloid of Unknown Origin [*Medicine*]
AUO .... Area Utilization Office [*GSA*]
AUO .... Auburn/Opelika [*Alabama*] [*Airport symbol*] (OAG)
AUOASRN ... Acta Universitatis Ouluensis. Series A. Scientiae Rerum Naturalium [*A publication*]
AUOD .... Alliance Universelle des Ouvriers Diamantaires [*Universal Alliance of Diamond Workers - UADW*] [*Antwerp, Belgium*] (EAIO)
AUOF .... Americans United to Outlaw Fluoridation (EA)
AUONAD ... Collected Reports. Natural Science Faculty. Palacky University [*Olomouc*] [*A publication*]
AUO-Ph ..... Acta Universitatis Palackianae Olomucensis. Facultas Philosophica. Philologica [*A publication*]
AUP.......... Actual Unit Price [*Billing*] (MCD)
AUP.......... African Union of Physics [*See also UAP*] (EAIO)
AUP.......... Aguan [*Papua New Guinea*] [*Airport symbol*] (OAG)
AUP.......... Air University Press
AUP.......... Annales. Universite de Paris [*A publication*]
AUP.......... Athletes United for Peace (EA)
AUP.......... Australian United Press
AUP.......... AUTODIN Upgrade Program (MCD)
AU/P .... Phylon. Atlanta University [*A publication*]
AUPA .... Association of Unclaimed Property Administrators [*Later, NAUPA*]
AuPaE........ Economic Society of Australia and New Zealand, Melbourne University, Parkville, V, Australia [*Library symbol*] [*Library of Congress*] (LCLS)
AuPaU .... University of Melbourne, Baillieu Library, Parkville, V, Australia [*Library symbol*] [*Library of Congress*] (LCLS)
AUPE .... Amalgamated Union of Public Employees [*Singapore*]
AUPELF ... Association des Universites Partiellement ou Entierement de Langue Francaise [*Association of Wholly or Partially French Language Universities*] [*Montreal, PQ*] (EA)
AUP(Fr)..... Association of University Professors (French) [*British*]
AUPG .... American University Publishers Group Ltd.
AUPHA..... Association of University Programs in Health Administration (EA)
AUPHAY .. Australasian Journal of Pharmacy [*A publication*]
AUPHB ...... Australian Physicist [*A publication*]
AUPJB .... Australian Paediatric Journal [*A publication*]
AuPL.......... Library Board of Western Australia, State Bibliographical Centre, Perth, WA, Australia [*Library symbol*] [*Library of Congress*] (LCLS)
AUPMDI... Australasian Physical and Engineering Sciences in Medicine [*A publication*]
AUPO........ Acta Universitatis Palackianae Olomucensis [*A publication*]
AUPO........ Association of University Professors of Ophthalmology (EA)
AUPOHS .. Association of University Programs in Occupational Health and Safety (EA)
AUPRD ..... AUTOTESTCON [*Automatic Testing Conference*] Proceedings [*A publication*]
AUPS......... American University Press Services, Inc. [*Information service or system*] (IID)
AuPT .... Auxiliary Potential Transformer
AUQ .... Atuona [*Marquesas Islands*] [*Airport symbol*] (OAG)
AUQ .... Aurogin Resources [*Vancouver Stock Exchange symbol*]
AUR........... Aberdeen University. Review [*A publication*]
AUR........... Accomplishment Utilization Report
AUR........... Aircraft Utilization Report

AUR........... All Up Round (MCD)
AUR........... Association of University Radiologists (EA)
AUR........... AUR Resources, Inc. [*Toronto Stock Exchange symbol*]
AUR........... Aurakhmat [*USSR*] [*Seismograph station code, US Geological Survey*] [*Closed*] (SEIS)
AUR........... Aural
AUR........... Auricular [*or Auricle*] [*Also, A*] [*Medicine*]
Aur .... Auriga [*Constellation*]
AUR........... Aurillac [*France*] [*Airport symbol*] [*Obsolete*] (OAG)
AUR........... Auris [*Ear*] [*Latin*]
Aur .... Aurora [*A publication*]
AUR........... Aurora High School PRECIS Project [*UTLAS symbol*]
AUR........... Aurora, NC [*Location identifier*] [*FAA*] (FAAL)
AUR........... Aurum [*Gold*] [*Latin*]
AUR........... Automatisering Gids [*A publication*]
AUR........... York Region Board of Education [*UTLAS symbol*]
AURA .... Adventure Unlimited Retail Association [*Commercial firm*] (EA)
AURA .... American University Institute for Risk Analysis [*American University*] [*Research center*] (RCD)
AURA .... Army Unit Resiliancy Analysis [*Data processing*] (RDA)
AURA .... Association of Universities for Research in Astronomy (EA)
AURA .... Audience Reaction Assessment [*Television ratings*] [*British*]
AURA .... Aura Systems, Inc. [*NASDAQ symbol*] (NQ)
AURA .... Australian Rock Art Research Association
AURANT .. Auranteum [*Orange (Rind)*] [*Pharmacy*] (ROG)
AURBO....... Aurora Borealis
AURCA ...... Automation and Remote Control [*A publication*]
AURDAW ... Australasian Radiology [*A publication*]
AURE .... Aurora Environmental, Inc. [*NASDAQ symbol*] (NQ)
Aurel .... Aurelian [*of Scriptores Historiae Augustae*] [*Classical studies*] (OCD)
Aurel Corbul ... Aurelius Corbulus [*Flourished, 16th century*] [*Authority cited in pre-1607 legal work*] (DSA)
AUREQ ...... Authority Is Requested (NOAA)
AURF .... Americans United Research Foundation (EA)
Auri .... Auriga [*Constellation*]
AURIN........ Aurinarium [*Ear Cone*] [*Pharmacy*]
AURIS....... Aberdeen University Research & Industrial Services Ltd. [*United Kingdom*] (IRUK)
AURIST ..... Auristillae [*Ear Drops*] [*Pharmacy*]
AURISTILL ... Auristillae [*Ear Drops*] [*Pharmacy*]
AUROAV .. Annales d'Urologie [*A publication*]
AURPO ..... Association of University Radiation Protection Officers [*British*]
AURRP....... Association of University Related Research Parks (EA)
AURS .... Automated Unit Reference Sheets (MCD)
AUS........... Actum ut Supra [*Done as Above*] [*Latin*]
AUS........... Advanced Underwriting Service [*Database*] [*R & R Newkirk*] [*Information service or system*] (CRD)
AUS........... Air US [*Denver, CO*] [*FAA designator*] (FAAC)
AUS........... Ambassador of the United States
AUS........... American Union of Students (EA)
AUS........... Annales Universitatis Saraviensis [*A publication*]
AUS........... Annuaire. Universite de Sofia. Faculte des Lettres [*A publication*]
AuS .... Arbeit und Sitte in Palaestina [*A publication*] (BJA)
AUS........... Army of the United States
AUS........... Assistant Under-Secretary (ADA)
AUS........... Augusta & Summerville Railroad Co. [*AAR code*]
Aus .... [*Saint*] Augustine [*Deceased, 430*] [*Authority cited in pre-1607 legal work*] (DSA)
AUS........... Ausimont NV [*NYSE symbol*] (SPSG)
Aus .... Ausonia [*A publication*]
AUS........... Austin [*Texas*] [*Seismograph station code, US Geological Survey*] [*Closed*] (SEIS)
AUS........... Austin [*Texas*] [*Airport symbol*] (OAG)
AUS........... Austin Resources, Inc. [*Vancouver Stock Exchange symbol*]
AUS........... Australia [*ANSI three-letter standard code*] (CNC)
Aus............ [*The*] Australian [*A publication*] (ADA)
AUS........... Australian Coal Report [*A publication*]
AUS........... Austria
AUS........... Automated Ultrasonic Scanner (MCD)
AuS .... Auxiliary Switch [*Electricity*]
AuS .... City of Sydney Public Library, Sydney, NSW, Australia [*Library symbol*] [*Library of Congress*] (LCLS)
AUSA .... American Underground-Space Association (EA)
AUSA .... Association of the United States Army (EA)
Aus Ab St... Australian Aboriginal Studies [*A publication*]
AUSAEW ... Annale. Universiteit van Stellenbosch. Serie A-3. Landbouwetenskappe [*A publication*]
AUS AG & R ... Acta Universitatis Szegediensis. Acta Germanica et Romanica [*A publication*]
AUS AHLH ... Acta Universitatis Szegediensis de Attila Jozsef Nominatae. Sectio: Acta Historiae Litterarum Hungaricarum [*A publication*]
AuSAJ .... Department of the Attorney General and of Justice, Sydney, NSW, Australia [*Library symbol*] [*Library of Congress*] (LCLS)
Ausb.......... Ausbildung [*Education*] [*German*]

AUSB......... Australian Business [*Australian Consolidated Press*] [*Information service or system*]

AUSBC...... ASEAN [*Association of South East Asian Nations*] - United States Business Council [*Bangkok, Thailand*] (EAIO)

AUSBCM ... Apollo Unified S-Band Circuit Margin [*Program*] [*NASA*]

AUSBDY... Annale. Universiteit van Stellenbosch. Serie A-4. Bosbou [*A publication*]

AusBiR ...... Australian Biblical Review [*Melbourne*] [*A publication*]

Aus BR....... Australian Biblical Review [*A publication*] (APTA)

Ausbreitungsrechn Messverfahren Luftueberwach ... Ausbreitungsrechnung und Messverfahren zur Luftueberwachung [*A publication*]

AuSbW ...... West Australian Institute of Technology, South Bentley, WA, Australia [*Library symbol*] [*Library of Congress*] (LCLS)

AUSC .... Austin Service Center [*IRS*]

AUSCANUKUS ... Australia, Canada, United Kingdom, United States (MCD)

AUSCJ .... Association of US Chess Journalists [*Later, CJA*] (EA)

AUSC-NA ... Association of Ukrainian Sports Clubs in North America (EA)

Aus Comp Bul ... Australian Computer Bulletin [*A publication*]

Aus Comp J ... Australian Computer Journal [*A publication*]

AUSCOR... Automatic Scanning Correlator

AusCR....... Australian Catholic Record [*Sydney*] [*A publication*]

Aus C Rec .. Australasian Catholic Record [*A publication*] (APTA)

AusCRec.... Australian Catholic Record [*Sydney*] [*A publication*]

AUSCS ...... Americans United for Separation of Church and State (EA)

Ausdex .... Australian Defence Export Group

AUSDIL .... Australian Dangerously Ill List [*Scheme*]

Aus Ed Res ... Australian Education Researcher [*A publication*]

Aus Educ Ind ... Australian Education Index [*A publication*]

AUS E & L ... Acta Universitatis Szegediensis de Attila Jozsef Nominatae. Sectio: Ethnographica et Linguistica [*A publication*]

AUSem St ... Andrews University. Seminary Studies [*A publication*]

AUSEX...... Acoustic Underwater Sound Experiment (MCD)

AUSFS ...... Americans United for a Smoke Free Society (EA)

AUS(G)....... Assistant Under-Secretary, General [*Air Ministry*] [*British*]

AUSG....... Ausgabe [*Edition*] [*German*]

Aus Geo...... Australian Geographer [*A publication*]

Ausgrab Fun ... Ausgrabungen und Funde [*A publication*]

Ausgr Fu .... Ausgrabungen und Funde. Nachrichtenblatt fuer Vor- und Fruehgeschichte [*A publication*]

AuSGS....... Church of Jesus Christ of Latter-Day Saints, Genealogical Society Library, Sydney Branch, Sydney, NSW, Australia [*Library symbol*] [*Library of Congress*] (LCLS)

Aus G Stud ... Australian Geographical Studies [*A publication*]

AUSHAF... Acta Physica et Chemica [*A publication*]

Aushandel ... Nachrichten fuer Aussenhandel [*A publication*]

AUSINET ... Australian Information Network

AusJBibArch ... Australian Journal of Biblical Archaeology [*Sydney*] [*A publication*]

AUS J HPER ... Australian Journal for Health, Physical Education, and Recreation [*A publication*]

Aus J Lin ... Australian Journal of Linguistics [*A publication*]

Aus J Phil.. Australasian Journal of Philosophy [*A publication*]

Aus J Screen Theory ... Australian Journal of Screen Theory [*A publication*]

Aus J Sport Sci ... Australian Journal of Sport Sciences [*A publication*]

Aus J Sports Med ... Australian Journal of Sports Medicine [*A publication*]

AusL .... Australian Letters [*A publication*]

Aus Leg Mon Dig ... Australian Legal Monthly Digest [*A publication*]

AUSLOAN ... AUSLOAN: Australian Inter-Library Loans Manual [*A publication*] (APTA)

Aus L Rev .. Australian Left Review [*A publication*]

AUSM .... Advanced Upper Stage Motor (MCD)

AUSMBV ... Australia. Commonwealth Scientific and Industrial Research Organisation. Soil Mechanics Section. Technical Paper [*A publication*]

AUSMIISL ... Association of US Members of the International Institute of Space Law (EA)

AUSMIMPS ... Australian Standard Material Issue and Movement Priority System

Aus Mo Motor Manual ... Australian Monthly Motor Manual [*A publication*] (APTA)

AuSN .... Library of New South Wales, Sydney, NSW, Australia [*Library symbol*] [*Library of Congress*] (LCLS)

Aus Nat...... Aus der Natur [*A publication*]

AuSN-M.... Library of New South Wales, Mitchell Library, Sydney, NSW, Astralia [*Library symbol*] [*Library of Congress*] (LCLS)

AUSNVM ... Association of United States Night Vision Manufacturers (EA)

Auson .... Ausonius [*Fourth century AD*] [*Classical studies*] (OCD)

Aus Outl..... Australian Outlook [*A publication*]

AuSP .... Parliamentary Library, Parliament House, Sydney, NSW, Australia [*Library symbol*] [*Library of Congress*] (LCLS)

Aus PAIS... Australian Public Affairs Information Service [*Information service or system*] [*A publication*]

AUS-PEAS ... Acta Universitatis Szegediensis de Attila Jozsef Nominatae. Papers in English and American Studies [*A publication*]

Aus Psych .. Australian Psychologist [*A publication*]

AusQ .... Australian Quarterly [*A publication*]

AUSQA ..... Australian Quarterly [*A publication*]

Aus Quart .. Australian Quarterly [*A publication*]

AUSRA...... Records. Australian Academy of Science [*A publication*]

AUSRAPID ... Australian Sport and Recreation Association for People with an Intellectual Disability

Aus Rep...... Austin's Appeal Reports [*Ceylon*] [*A publication*] (ILCA)

AUSS......... Advanced Underwater Search System (MCD)

AUSS......... American Union of Swedish Singers (EA)

AUSS......... Andrews University. Seminary Studies [*A publication*]

AUSS......... Assistant Under-Secretary of State (DAS)

AUSS......... Association of University Summer Sessions (EA)

AUSSAT ... Australian Domestic Communications Satellite

Aus Sci Ind ... Australian Science Index [*Information service or system*] [*A publication*]

Aussenpol .. Aussenpolitik [*A publication*]

Aussenpoli ... Aussenpolitik [*A publication*]

Aussenwirt ... Aussenwirtschaft [*A publication*]

ausserd....... Ausserdem [*Furthermore*] [*German*]

Aus Soc ...... Australian Society [*A publication*]

Aus Soc W .. Australian Social Work [*A publication*]

Aus Speleo Abstr ... Australian Speleo Abstracts [*A publication*]

Ausst.......... Ausstellung [*Exhibition*] [*German*]

AUSSTOCK ... Australian Stock Exchanges Share Prices [*Database*]

Aust............ Austin's English County Court Cases [*1867-69*] [*A publication*] (DLA)

Aust............ [*The*] Australian [*A publication*] (APTA)

AUST........ Australian

AUST........ Austria

AusT .... Austrian Telefunken [*Record label*]

AUSTA...... Australian Studies Association

Aust Aborig ... Australian Aborigines Annual Bibliography [*A publication*] (APTA)

Aust Acacias ... Australian Acacias [*A publication*] (APTA)

Aust Acad H ... Australian Academy of the Humanities. Proceedings [*A publication*]

Aust Acad and Res Lib ... Australian Academic and Research Libraries [*A publication*]

Aust Acad Res Libr ... Australian Academic and Research Libraries [*A publication*] (APTA)

Aust Acad Res Libs ... Australian Academic and Research Libraries [*A publication*]

Aust Acad Sci Rep ... Australian Academy of Science. Reports [*A publication*] (APTA)

Aust Acad Sci Sci Ind Forum Forum Rep ... Australian Academy of Science. Science and Industry Forum. Forum Report [*A publication*] (APTA)

Aust Acc..... Australian Accountant [*A publication*]

Aust Accnt ... Australian Accountant [*A publication*] (APTA)

Aust Accountancy Progress ... Australian Accountancy Progress [*A publication*] (APTA)

Aust Accountancy Student ... Australian Accountancy Student [*A publication*] (APTA)

Aust Accountant ... Australian Accountant [*A publication*] (APTA)

Aust Account Student ... Australian Accountancy Student [*A publication*] (APTA)

Aust Acct ... Australian Accountant [*A publication*] (APTA)

Aust Acctnt ... Australian Accountant [*A publication*]

Aust Acct Stud ... Australian Accountancy Student [*A publication*] (APTA)

Aust Adv Vet Sci ... Australian Advances in Veterinary Science [*A publication*] (APTA)

Aust AEC AAEC/E Rep ... Australian Atomic Energy Commission. AAEC/E. Report [*A publication*]

Aust AEC AAEC/TM Rep ... Australian Atomic Energy Commission. AAEC/TM. Report [*A publication*]

Aust AEC Inf Pap ... Australian Atomic Energy Commission. Information Paper [*A publication*] (APTA)

Aust AEC Res Establ AAEC/E ... Australian Atomic Energy Commission Research Establishment. AAEC/E [*A publication*]

Aust AEC Res Establ Rep AAEC/S ... Australian Atomic Energy Commission. Research Establishment. Report AAEC/S [*A publication*] (APTA)

Aust AEC TRG Rep ... Australian Atomic Energy Commission. TRG Report [*A publication*] (APTA)

Aust Aeronaut Comm Rep ACA ... Australian Aeronautical Research Committee. Report ACA [*A publication*] (APTA)

Aust Aeronaut Res Comm Rep ... Australian Aeronautical Research Committee. Report [*A publication*] (APTA)

Aust Aeronaut Res Comm Rep ACA ... Australian Aeronautical Research Committee. Report ACA [*A publication*]

Aust Aeronaut Res Lab Aerodyn Rep ... Australia. Aeronautical Research Laboratories. Aerodynamics Report [*A publication*]

Aust Aeronaut Res Lab Guided Weapons Note ... Australia. Aeronautical Research Laboratories. Guided Weapons Note [*A publication*]

Aust Aeronaut Res Lab Mater Note ... Australia. Aeronautical Research Laboratories. Materials Note [*A publication*] (APTA)

Aust Aeronaut Res Lab Mater Rep ... Australia. Aeronautical Research Laboratories. Materials Report [*A publication*] (APTA)

Aust Aeronaut Res Lab Mech Eng Note ... Australia. Aeronautical Research Laboratories. Mechanical Engineering Note [*A publication*]

Aust Aeronaut Res Lab Mech Eng Rep ... Australia. Aeronautical Research Laboratories. Mechanical Engineering Report [*A publication*]

Aust Aeronaut Res Lab Metall Note ... Australia. Aeronautical Research Laboratories. Metallurgy Note [*A publication*]

Aust Aeronaut Res Lab Metall Rep ... Australia. Aeronautical Research Laboratories. Metallurgy Report [*A publication*]

Aust Aeronaut Res Lab Metall Tech Mem ... Australia. Aeronautical Research Laboratories. Metallurgy Technical Memorandum [*A publication*]

Aust Aeronaut Res Lab Rep MET ... Australia. Aeronautical Research Laboratories. Report MET (Metallurgy) [*A publication*]

Aust Aeronaut Res Lab Struct ... Australia. Aeronautical Research Laboratories. Structures and Materials Note [*A publication*] (APTA)

Aust Aeronaut Res Lab Struct Mater Note ... Australia. Aeronautical Research Laboratories. Structures and Materials Note [*A publication*]

Aust Aeronaut Res Lab Struct Mater Rep ... Australia. Aeronautical Research Laboratories. Structures and Materials Report [*A publication*]

Aust Aeronaut Res Lab Struct Note ... Australia. Aeronautical Research Laboratories. Structures Note [*A publication*] (APTA)

Aust Aeronaut Res Lab Struct Rep ... Australia. Aeronautical Research Laboratories. Structures Report [*A publication*] (APTA)

Aust Agric News ... Australian Agricultural Newsletter [*A publication*] (APTA)

Aust Amateur Mineral ... Australian Amateur Mineralogist [*A publication*] (APTA)

Aust Amateur Mineralogist ... Australian Amateur Mineralogist [*A publication*] (APTA)

Aust Amat Miner ... Australian Amateur Mineralogist [*A publication*] (APTA)

Aust-American Assn Canb News Bul ... Australian-American Association in Canberra. News Bulletin [*A publication*] (APTA)

Aust-American J ... Australian-American Journal [*A publication*] (APTA)

Aust Ann of Med ... Australasian Annals of Medicine [*A publication*] (APTA)

Aust Ann Med ... Australasian Annals of Medicine [*A publication*] (APTA)

Aust Arab Horse News ... Australian Arabian Horse News [*A publication*] (APTA)

Aust Argus L Rep ... Australian Argus Law Reports [*A publication*]

Aust Army J ... Australian Army Journal [*A publication*] (APTA)

Aust Aronaut Lab Struct Mater Rep ... Australia. Aeronautical Research Laboratories. Structures and Materials Report [*A publication*] (APTA)

Aust Aronaut Res Lab Metall Tech Memo ... Australia. Aeronautical Research Laboratories. Metallurgy Technical Memorandum [*A publication*] (APTA)

Aust Assoc Neurol Proc ... Australian Association of Neurologists. Proceedings [*A publication*] (APTA)

AUSTAT ... Australian Society of Teachers, Alexander Technique

Aust At Energy Symp Proc ... Australian Atomic Energy Symposium. Proceedings of a Symposium on the Peaceful Uses of Atomic Energy. University of Sydney, June 2-6, 1958 [*A publication*] (APTA)

Austauschbarkeit Gasen Vortr Semin ... Austauschbarkeit von Gasen. Vortraege zum Seminar [*A publication*]

Aust Auth ... Australian Author [*A publication*] (APTA)

Aust Automobile Trade J ... Australian Automobile Trade Journal [*A publication*] (APTA)

Aust Automot Eng & Equip ... Australian Automotive Engineering and Equipment [*A publication*] (APTA)

Aust Aviation Newsletter ... Australian Aviation Newsletter [*A publication*] (APTA)

Aust Aviat Newsl ... Australian Aviation Newsletter [*A publication*] (APTA)

Aust Aviat Yb ... Australian Aviation Yearbook [*A publication*] (APTA)

Aust Avicult ... Australian Aviculture [*A publication*] (APTA)

Aust Baker ... Australian Baker and Millers' Journal [*A publication*] (APTA)

Aust Bank .. Australian Banker [*A publication*]

Aust Bankr Cas ... Australian Bankruptcy Cases [*A publication*] (APTA)

Aust Baptist ... Australian Baptist [*A publication*] (APTA)

Aust Bar Gaz ... Australian Bar Gazette [*A publication*] (APTA)

Aust Bar Rev ... Australian Bar Review [*A publication*]

Aust Bee J ... Australian Bee Journal [*A publication*] (APTA)

Aust Bib R ... Australian Biblical Review [*A publication*]

Aust Bird Bander ... Australian Bird Bander [*A publication*] (APTA)

Aust Birdwatcher ... Australian Birdwatcher [*A publication*] (APTA)

Aust BL ... Australian Bulletin of Labour [*A publication*]

Aust Bldg Forum ... Australia Building Forum [*A publication*]

Aust Bldr ... Australian Builder [*A publication*] (APTA)

Aust Boating ... Australian Boating [*A publication*] (APTA)

Aust Book Auction Rec ... Australian Book Auction Records [*A publication*] (APTA)

Aust Book R ... Australian Book Review [*A publication*] (APTA)

Aust Book Rev ... Australian Book Review [*A publication*] (APTA)

Aust Book Rev Children's Book & Ed Suppl ... Australian Book Review. Children's Books and Educational Supplement [*A publication*] (APTA)

Aust Brewing & Wine J ... Australian Brewing and Wine Journal [*A publication*] (APTA)

Aust Brewing Wine J ... Australian Brewing and Wine Journal [*A publication*] (APTA)

Aust Build ... Australian Builder [*A publication*]

Aust Builder ... Australian Builder [*A publication*] (APTA)

Aust Build Forum ... Australian Building Forum [*A publication*] (APTA)

Aust Build Sci Technol ... Australian Building Science and Technology [*A publication*] (APTA)

Aust Build Technol ... Australian Building Technology [*A publication*] (APTA)

Aust Bull Labour ... Australian Bulletin of Labour [*A publication*] (APTA)

Aust Bur Miner Resour Geol Geophys BMR J Aust Geol Geophys ... Australia. Bureau of Mineral Resources. Geology and Geophysics. BMR Journal of Australian Geology and Geophysics [*A publication*] (APTA)

Aust Bur Miner Resour Geol Geophys Bull ... Australia. Bureau of Mineral Resources. Geology and Geophysics. Bulletin [*A publication*]

Aust Bur Miner Resour Geol Geophys Pam ... Australia. Bureau of Mineral Resources. Geology and Geophysics. Pamphlet [*A publication*]

Aust Bur Miner Resour Geol Geophys Rep ... Australia. Bureau of Mineral Resources. Geology and Geophysics. Report [*A publication*]

Aust Bus ..... Australian Business [*A publication*]

Aust Bus Brief ... Australian Business Brief [*A publication*]

Aust Bus Cond Bull ... Australasian Business Conditions Bulletin [*A publication*]

Aust Bush Nursing J ... Australian Bush Nursing Journal [*A publication*] (APTA)

Aust Business L Rev ... Australian Business Law Review [*A publication*] (APTA)

Aust Bus Law R ... Australian Business Law Review [*A publication*] (APTA)

Aust Bus Law Rev ... Australian Business Law Review [*A publication*]

Aust Bus Lawyer ... Australian Business Lawyer [*A publication*]

Aust Bus L Rev ... Australian Business Law Review [*A publication*] (APTA)

Aust Bus Rev ... Australian Business Law Review [*A publication*]

Aust Camera ... Australian Camera and Cine [*A publication*] (APTA)

Aust Canegrow ... Australian Canegrower [*A publication*] (APTA)

Aust Canning Convention ... Australian Canning Convention. Proceedings [*A publication*] (APTA)

Aust Canning Convention Procs ... Australian Canning Convention. Proceedings [*A publication*] (APTA)

Aust Cath Hist Soc J ... Australian Catholic Historical Society. Journal [*A publication*] (APTA)

Aust Catholic D ... Australian Catholic Digest [*A publication*] (APTA)

Aust Catholic Truth Soc Rec ... Australian Catholic Truth Society. Record [*A publication*] (APTA)

Aust Ceram Conf Proc ... Australian Ceramic Conference. Proceedings [*A publication*] (APTA)

Aust Chem Abstr ... Australian Chemical Abstracts [*A publication*]

Aust Chem Eng ... Australian Chemical Engineering [*A publication*]

Aust Chem Eng Conf ... Australian Chemical Engineering. Conference [*A publication*] (APTA)

Aust Chem Engineering ... Australian Chemical Engineering [*A publication*] (APTA)

Aust Chem Engng ... Australian Chemical Engineering [*A publication*] (APTA)

Aust Chem Inst J Proc ... Australian Chemical Institute. Journal and Proceedings [*A publication*]

Aust Chem Proc ... Australian Chemical Processing [*A publication*] (APTA)

Aust Chem Process ... Australian Chemical Processing [*A publication*]

Aust Chem Process Eng ... Australian Chemical Processing and Engineering [*A publication*]

Aust Chem Process Engng ... Australian Chemical Processing and Engineering [*A publication*] (APTA)

Aust Chem Processing ... Australian Chemical Processing [*A publication*] (APTA)

Aust Child Family Welf ... Australian Child and Family Welfare [*A publication*]

Aust Child Fam Welfare ... Australian Child and Family Welfare [*A publication*] (APTA)

Aust Child Limited ... Australian Children Limited [*A publication*] (APTA)

Aust Child Ltd ... Australian Children Limited [*A publication*] (APTA)

Aust Children Ltd ... Australian Children Limited [*A publication*] (APTA)

Aust Children TV Com Newsl ... Australian Children's Television Committee. Newsletter [*A publication*]

Aust Christian ... Australian Christian [*A publication*] (APTA)

Aust Church Q ... Australian Church Quarterly [*A publication*] (APTA)

Aust Church Rec ... Australian Church Record [*A publication*] (APTA)

Aust Citizen Ltd ... Australian Citizen Limited [*A publication*] (APTA)

Aust Citrus News ... Australian Citrus News [*A publication*] (APTA)

Aust Civ Eng ... Australian Civil Engineering [*A publication*]

Aust Civ Engng ... Australian Civil Engineering [*A publication*] (APTA)

Aust Civ Engng Constr ... Australian Civil Engineering and Construction [*A publication*] (APTA)

Aust Civil Eng Construc ... Australian Civil Engineering and Construction [*A publication*] (APTA)

Aust Civil Engng Constr ... Australian Civil Engineering and Construction [*A publication*] (APTA)

Aust Climatol Summ ... Australian Climatological Summary [*A publication*] (APTA)

Aust Clin Rev ... Australian Clinical Review [*A publication*]

Aust CL Rev ... Australian Current Law Review [*A publication*] (APTA)

Aust Coal Ass (Res) Rep ... Australian Coal Association (Research) Limited. Report [*A publication*] (APTA)

Aust Coal & Harbour ... Australian Coal, Shipping, Steel, and the Harbour [*A publication*] (APTA)

Aust Coalmining ... Australian Coalmining and Mine Mechanisation [*A publication*] (APTA)

Aust Coin ... Australian Coin Review [*A publication*] (APTA)

Aust Coll Educ Vic Chapter Newsl ... Australian College of Education. Victorian Chapter. Newsletter [*A publication*] (APTA)

Aust Coll Speech Ther J ... Australian College of Speech Therapists. Journal [*A publication*] (APTA)

Aust Commonw Advis Counc Sci Ind Bull ... Australia. Commonwealth Advisory Council of Science and Industry. Bulletin [*A publication*]

Aust Commonw Advis Counc Sci Ind Pam ... Australia. Commonwealth Advisory Council of Science and Industry. Pamphlet [*A publication*]

Aust Commonw Counc Sci Ind Res Bull ... Australia. Commonwealth Council for Scientific and Industrial Research. Bulletin [*A publication*] (APTA)

Aust Commonw Counc Sci Ind Res Pam ... Australia. Commonwealth Council for Scientific and Industrial Research. Pamphlet [*A publication*] (APTA)

Aust Commonw Dep Supply Aeronaut Res Comm Rep ACA ... Australia. Commonwealth Department of Supply. Aeronautical Research Committee. Report ACA [*A publication*] (APTA)

Aust Commonw Dep Supply Aeronaut Res Consult Comm Rep ACA ... Australia. Commonwealth Department of Supply. Aeronautical Research Consultative Committee. Report ACA [*A publication*] (APTA)

Aust Commonw Dep Supply Aeronaut Res Guided Weapons Note ... Australia. Commonwealth Department of Supply. Aeronautical Research Laboratories. Guided Weapons Note [*A publication*] (APTA)

Aust Commonw Dep Supply Aeronaut Res Lab Metall Note ... Australia. Commonwealth Department of Supply. Aeronautical Research Laboratories. Metallurgy Note [*A publication*] (APTA)

Aust Commonw Dep Supply Aeronaut Res Lab Metall Tech Memo ... Australia. Commonwealth Department of Supply. Aeronautical Research Laboratories. Metallurgy Technical Memorandum [*A publication*] (APTA)

Aust Commonw Dep Supply Aeronaut Res Lab Rep MET ... Australia. Commonwealth Department of Supply. Aeronautical Research Laboratories. Report MET (Metallurgy) [*A publication*] (APTA)

Aust Commonw Dep Supply Aeronaut Res Lab Rep SM ... Australia. Commonwealth Department of Supply. Aeronautical Research Laboratories. Report SM [*Structures and Materials*] [*A publication*] (APTA)

Aust Commonw Dep Supply Def Res Lab Rep ... Australia. Commonwealth Department of Supply. Defence Research Laboratories. Report [*A publication*]

Aust Commonw Dep Supply Def Res Lab Report ... Australia. Commonwealth Department of Supply. Defence Research Laboratories. Report [*A publication*] (APTA)

Aust Commonw Dep Supply Def Res Lab Tech Note ... Australia. Commonwealth Department of Supply. Defence Research Laboratories. Technical Note [*A publication*]

Aust Commonw Dep Supply Def Stand Lab Rep ... Australia. Commonwealth Department of Supply. Defence Standards Laboratories. Report [*A publication*] (APTA)

Aust Commonw Dep Supply Def Stand Lab Tech Note ... Australia. Commonwealth Department of Supply. Defence Standards Laboratories. Technical Note [*A publication*] (APTA)

Aust Commonw Dep Supply Res Lab Tech Note ... Australia. Commonwealth Department of Supply. Defence Research Laboratories. Technical Note [*A publication*] (APTA)

Aust Commonw Dept Supply Aeronaut Res Comm Rep ... Australia. Commonwealth Department of Supply. Aeronautical Research Committee. Report [*A publication*]

Aust Commonw Inst Sci Ind Bull ... Australia. Commonwealth Institute of Science and Industry. Bulletin [*A publication*] (APTA)

Aust Commonw Inst Sci Ind Pam ... Australia. Commonwealth Institute of Science and Industry. Pamphlet [*A publication*]

Aust Commonw Sci Ind Res Organ Div Metrol Tech Pap ... Australia. Commonwealth Scientific and Industrial Research Organisation. Division of Metrology. Technical Paper [*A publication*] (APTA)

Aust Comp Law Cases ... Australian Company Law Cases [*A publication*] (APTA)

Aust Comput Bull ... Australian Computer Bulletin [*A publication*] (APTA)

Aust Comput J ... Australian Computer Journal [*A publication*]

Aust Comput Sci Commun ... Australian Computer Science Communications [*A publication*] (APTA)

Aust Conf Chem Eng ... Australian Conference on Chemical Engineering [*A publication*] (APTA)

Aust Conf Nucl Tech Anal Proc ... Australian Conference on Nuclear Techniques of Analysis. Proceedings [*A publication*] (APTA)

Aust Conf Nucl Tech Anal Summ Proc ... Australian Conference on Nuclear Techniques of Analysis. Summary of Proceedings [*A publication*] (APTA)

Aust Con LR ... Australian Construction Law Reporter [*A publication*]

Aust Conserv Found Newsl ... Australian Conservation Foundation. Newsletter [*A publication*] (APTA)

Aust Conv .. Australian Conveyancer and Solicitors' Journal [*A publication*] (APTA)

Aust Conveyancer ... Australian Conveyancer and Solicitors' Journal [*A publication*] (APTA)

Aust Conv Sol J ... Australian Conveyancer and Solicitors' Journal [*A publication*]

Aust Cordial Maker ... Australian Cordial Maker, Brewer, and Bottler's Gazette [*A publication*] (APTA)

Aust Corr Eng ... Australian Corrosion Engineering [*A publication*] (APTA)

Aust Corros Eng ... Australian Corrosion Engineering [*A publication*]

Aust Corros Engng ... Australian Corrosion Engineering [*A publication*] (APTA)

Aust Corrosion Eng ... Australian Corrosion Engineering [*A publication*] (APTA)

Aust Cott Grow ... Australian Cotton Grower [*A publication*] (APTA)

Aust Cott Grow Fmr Dairym ... Australian Cotton Grower, Farmer, and Dairyman [*A publication*] (APTA)

Aust Counc Aeronaut Rep ACA ... Australian Council for Aeronautics. Report ACA [*A publication*] (APTA)

Aust Country ... Australian Country Magazine [*A publication*] (APTA)

Aust Country Mag ... Australian Country Magazine [*A publication*] (APTA)

AustCP ...... Australian Country Party [*Political party*] (ADA)

Aust Credit Unions Mag ... Australian Credit Unions Magazine [*A publication*]

Aust CSIRO Abstr Publ Pap List Transl ... Australia. Commonwealth Scientific and Industrial Research Organisation. Abstracts of Published Papers and List of Translations [*A publication*]

Aust CSIRO Anim Res Lab Tech Pap ... Australia. Commonwealth Scientific and Industrial Research Organisation. Animal Research Laboratories. Technical Paper [*A publication*]

Aust CSIRO Annu Rep ... Australia. Commonwealth Scientific and Industrial Research Organisation. Annual Report [*A publication*]

Aust CSIRO Bull ... Australia. Commonwealth Scientific and Industrial Research Organisation. Bulletin [*A publication*]

Aust CSIRO Chem Res Lab Tech Pap ... Australia. Commonwealth Scientific and Industrial Research Organisation. Chemical Research Laboratories. Technical Paper [*A publication*] (APTA)

Aust CSIRO Coal Res Div Locat Rep ... Australia. Commonwealth Scientific and Industrial Research Organisation. Coal Research Division. Location Report [*A publication*] (APTA)

Aust CSIRO Coal Res Div Misc Rep ... Australia. Commonwealth Scientific and Industrial Research Organisation. Coal Research Division. Miscellaneous Report [*A publication*] (APTA)

Aust CSIRO Coal Res Div Tech Commun ... Australia. Commonwealth Scientific and Industrial Research Organisation. Coal Research Division. Technical Communication [*A publication*] (APTA)

Aust CSIRO CSIRO Wildl Res ... Australia. Commonwealth Scientific and Industrial Research Organisation. CSIRO Wildlife Research [*A publication*] (APTA)

Aust CSIRO Div Anim Genet Res Rep ... Australia. Commonwealth Scientific and Industrial Research Organisation. Division of Animal Genetics. Research Report [*A publication*]

Aust CSIRO Div Anim Health Annu Rep ... Australia. Commonwealth Scientific and Industrial Research Organisation. Division of Animal Health. Annual Report [*A publication*]

Aust CSIRO Div Anim Health Prod Tech Pap ... Australia. Commonwealth Scientific and Industrial Research Organisation. Division of Animal Health and Production. Technical Paper [*A publication*]

Aust CSIRO Div Anim Physiol Annu Rep ... Australia. Commonwealth Scientific and Industrial Research Organisation. Division of Animal Physiology. Annual Report [*A publication*]

Aust CSIRO Div Appl Chem Annu Rep ... Australia. Commonwealth Scientific and Industrial Research Organisation. Division of Applied Chemistry. Annual Report [*A publication*]

Aust CSIRO Div Appl Chem Tech Pap ... Australia. Commonwealth Scientific and Industrial Research Organisation. Division of Applied Chemistry. Technical Paper [*A publication*]

Aust CSIRO Div Appl Geomech Tech Memo ... Australia. Commonwealth Scientific and Industrial Research Organisation. Division of Applied Geomechanics. Technical Memorandum [*A publication*]

Aust CSIRO Div Appl Geomech Tech Pap ... Australia. Commonwealth Scientific and Industrial Research Organisation. Division of Applied Geomechanics. Technical Paper [*A publication*]

Aust CSIRO Div Appl Geomech Tech Rep ... Australia. Commonwealth Scientific and Industrial Research Organisation. Division of Applied Geomechanics. Technical Report [*A publication*]

Aust CSIRO Div Appl Org Chem Res Rep ... Australia. Commonwealth Scientific and Industrial Research Organisation. Division of Applied Organic Chemistry. Research Report [*A publication*]

Aust CSIRO Div Appl Org Chem Tech Pap ... Australia. Commonwealth Scientific and Industrial Research Organisation. Division of Applied Organic Chemistry. Technical Paper [*A publication*] (APTA)

Aust CSIRO Div Atmos Phys Tech Pap ... Australia. Commonwealth Scientific and Industrial Research Organisation. Division of Atmospheric Physics. Technical Paper [*A publication*]

Aust CSIRO Div Build Res Annu Rep ... Australia. Commonwealth Scientific and Industrial Research Organisation. Division of Building Research. Annual Report [*A publication*]

Aust CSIRO Div Build Res Tech Pap ... Australia. Commonwealth Scientific and Industrial Research Organisation. Division of Building Research. Technical Paper [*A publication*] (APTA)

Aust CSIRO Div Chem Eng Rep ... Australia. Commonwealth Scientific and Industrial Research Organisation. Division of Chemical Engineering. Report [*A publication*]

Aust CSIRO Div Chem Phys Annu Rep ... Australia. Commonwealth Scientific and Industrial Research Organisation. Division of Chemical Physics. Annual Report [*A publication*]

Aust CSIRO Div Chem Technol Res Rev ... Australia. Commonwealth Scientific and Industrial Research Organisation. Division of Chemical Technology. Research Review [*A publication*]

Aust CSIRO Div Chem Technol Tech Pap ... Australia. Commonwealth Scientific and Industrial Research Organisation. Division of Chemical Technology. Technical Paper [*A publication*] (APTA)

Aust CSIRO Div Coal Res Locat Rep ... Australia. Commonwealth Scientific and Industrial Research Organisation. Division of Coal Research. Location Report [*A publication*]

Aust CSIRO Div Coal Res Misc Rep ... Australia. Commonwealth Scientific and Industrial Research Organisation. Division of Coal Research. Miscellaneous Report [*A publication*]

Aust CSIRO Div Coal Res Ref LR ... Australia. Commonwealth Scientific and Industrial Research Organisation. Division of Coal Research. Reference LR [*Location Report*] [*A publication*] (APTA)

Aust CSIRO Div Coal Res Tech Commun ... Australia. Commonwealth Scientific and Industrial Research Organisation. Division of Coal Research. Technical Communication [*A publication*]

Aust CSIRO Div Dairy Res Annu Rep ... Australia. Commonwealth Scientific and Industrial Research Organisation. Division of Dairy Research. Annual Report [*A publication*]

Aust CSIRO Div Entomol Annu Rep ... Australia. Commonwealth Scientific and Industrial Research Organisation. Division of Entomology. Annual Report [*A publication*]

Aust CSIRO Div Entomol Tech Pap ... Australia. Commonwealth Scientific and Industrial Research Organisation. Division of Entomology. Technical Paper [*A publication*]

Aust CSIRO Div Fish Oceanogr Annu Rep ... Australia. Commonwealth Scientific and Industrial Research Organisation. Division of Fisheries and Oceanography. Annual Report [*A publication*]

Aust CSIRO Div Fish Oceanogr Circ ... Australia. Commonwealth Scientific and Industrial Research Organisation. Division of Fisheries and Oceanography. Circular [*A publication*]

Aust CSIRO Div Fish Oceanogr Fish Synop ... Australia. Commonwealth Scientific and Industrial Research Organisation. Division of Fisheries and Oceanography. Fisheries Synopsis [*A publication*]

Aust CSIRO Div Fish Oceanogr Rep ... Australia. Commonwealth Scientific and Industrial Research Organisation. Division of Fisheries and Oceanography. Report [*A publication*] (APTA)

Aust CSIRO Div Fish Oceanogr Tech Pap ... Australia. Commonwealth Scientific and Industrial Research Organisation. Division of Fisheries and Oceanography. Technical Paper [*A publication*]

Aust CSIRO Div Fish Tech Pap ... Australia. Commonwealth Scientific and Industrial Research Organisation. Division of Fisheries. Technical Paper [*A publication*]

Aust CSIRO Div Food Preserv Rep Res ... Australia. Commonwealth Scientific and Industrial Research Organisation. Division of Food Preservation. Report of Research [*A publication*]

Aust CSIRO Div Food Preserv Tech Pap ... Australia. Commonwealth Scientific and Industrial Research Organisation. Division of Food Preservation. Technical Paper [*A publication*]

Aust CSIRO Div Food Preserv Transp Tech Pap ... Australia. Commonwealth Scientific and Industrial Research Organisation. Division of Food Preservation and Transport. Technical Paper [*A publication*] (APTA)

Aust CSIRO Div Food Res Rep Res ... Australia. Commonwealth Scientific and Industrial Research Organisation. Division of Food Research. Report of Research [*A publication*]

Aust CSIRO Div Food Res Tech Pap ... Australia. Commonwealth Scientific and Industrial Research Organisation. Division of Food Research. Technical Paper [*A publication*]

Aust CSIRO Div For Prod For Prod Newsl ... Australia. Commonwealth Scientific and Industrial Research Organisation. Division of Forest Products. Forest Products Newsletter [*A publication*] (APTA)

Aust CSIRO Div For Prod Technol Pap ... Australia. Commonwealth Scientific and Industrial Research Organisation. Division of Forest Products. Technological Paper [*A publication*]

Aust CSIRO Div For Res Annu Rep ... Australia. Commonwealth Scientific and Industrial Research Organisation. Division of Forest Research. Annual Report [*A publication*]

Aust CSIRO Div Hortic Res Rep ... Australia. Commonwealth Scientific and Industrial Research Organisation. Division of Horticulture. Research Report [*A publication*]

Aust CSIRO Div Ind Chem Tech Pap ... Australia. Commonwealth Scientific and Industrial Research Organisation. Division of Industrial Chemistry. Technical Paper [*A publication*]

Aust CSIRO Div Irrig Res Annu Rep ... Australia. Commonwealth Scientific and Industrial Research Organisation. Division of Irrigation Research. Annual Report [*A publication*]

Aust CSIRO Div Irrig Res Rep ... Australia. Commonwealth Scientific and Industrial Research Organisation. Division of Irrigation. Research Report [*A publication*]

Aust CSIRO Div Land Resour Manage Tech Pap ... Australia. Commonwealth Scientific and Industrial Research Organisation. Division of Land Resources Management. Technical Paper [*A publication*] (APTA)

Aust CSIRO Div Land Res Reg Surv Tech Pap ... Australia. Commonwealth Scientific and Industrial Research Organisation. Division of Land Research and Regional Survey. Technical Paper [*A publication*]

Aust CSIRO Div Land Res Tech Pap ... Australia. Commonwealth Scientific and Industrial Research Organisation. Division of Land Research. Technical Paper [*A publication*]

Aust CSIRO Div Land Use Res Tech Pap ... Australia. Commonwealth Scientific and Industrial Research Organisation. Division of Land Use Research. Technical Paper [*A publication*]

Aust CSIRO Div Math Stat Tech Pap ... Australia. Commonwealth Scientific and Industrial Research Organisation. Division of Mathematical Statistics. Technical Paper [*A publication*] (APTA)

Aust CSIRO Div Mech Eng Annu Rep ... Australia. Commonwealth Scientific and Industrial Research Organisation. Division of Mechanical Engineering. Annual Report [*A publication*]

Aust CSIRO Div Meteorol Phys Tech Pap ... Australia. Commonwealth Scientific and Industrial Research Organisation. Division of Meteorological Physics. Technical Paper [*A publication*]

Aust CSIRO Div Metrol Tech Pap ... Australia. Commonwealth Scientific and Industrial Research Organisation. Division of Metrology. Technical Paper [*A publication*] (APTA)

Aust CSIRO Div Mineral Tech Commun ... Australia. Commonwealth Scientific and Industrial Research Organisation. Division of Mineralogy. Technical Communication [*A publication*] (APTA)

Aust CSIRO Div Miner Chem Invest Rep ... Australia. Commonwealth Scientific and Industrial Research Organisation. Division of Mineral Chemistry. Investigation Report [*A publication*] (APTA)

Aust CSIRO Div Miner Chem Locat Rep ... Australia. Commonwealth Scientific and Industrial Research Organisation. Division of Mineral Chemistry. Location Report [*A publication*]

Aust CSIRO Div Miner Chem Tech Commun ... Australia. Commonwealth Scientific and Industrial Research Organisation. Division of Mineral Chemistry. Technical Communication [*A publication*]

Aust CSIRO Div Nutr Biochem Res Rep ... Australia. Commonwealth Scientific and Industrial Research Organisation. Division of Nutritional Biochemistry. Research Report [*A publication*]

Aust CSIRO Div Plant Ind Annu Rep ... Australia. Commonwealth Scientific and Industrial Research Organisation. Division of Plant Industry. Annual Report [*A publication*]

Aust CSIRO Div Plant Ind Field Stn Rec ... Australia. Commonwealth Scientific and Industrial Research Organisation. Division of Plant Industry. Field Station Record [*A publication*]

Aust CSIRO Div Plant Ind Tech Pap ... Australia. Commonwealth Scientific and Industrial Research Organisation. Division of Plant Industry. Technical Paper [*A publication*]

Aust CSIRO Div Soil Mech Tech Pap ... Australia. Commonwealth Scientific and Industrial Research Organisation. Division of Soil Mechanics. Technical Paper [*A publication*]

Aust CSIRO Div Soil Res Tech Pap ... Australia. Commonwealth Scientific and Industrial Research Organisation. Division of Soil Research. Technical Paper [*A publication*]

Aust CSIRO Div Soils Div Rep ... Australia. Commonwealth Scientific and Industrial Research Organisation. Division of Soils. Divisional Report [*A publication*]

Aust CSIRO Div Soils Notes Soil Tech ... Australia. Commonwealth Scientific and Industrial Research Organisation. Division of Soils. Notes on Soil Techniques [*A publication*] (APTA)

Aust CSIRO Div Soils Rep Prog ... Australia. Commonwealth Scientific and Industrial Research Organisation. Division of Soils. Report on Progress [*A publication*]

Aust CSIRO Div Soils Soils Land Use Ser ... Australia. Commonwealth Scientific and Industrial Research Organisation. Division of Soils. Soils and Land Use Series [*A publication*]

Aust CSIRO Div Soils Tech Pap ... Australia. Commonwealth Scientific and Industrial Research Organisation. Division of Soils. Technical Paper [*A publication*]

Aust CSIRO Div Text Ind Rep ... Australia. Commonwealth Scientific and Industrial Research Organisation. Division of Textile Industry. Report [*A publication*]   (APTA)

Aust CSIRO Div Trop Agron Annu Rep ... Australia. Commonwealth Scientific and Industrial Research Organisation. Division of Tropical Agronomy. Annual Report [*A publication*]

Aust CSIRO Div Trop Agron Tech Pap ... Australia. Commonwealth Scientific and Industrial Research Organisation. Division of Tropical Agronomy. Technical Paper [*A publication*]

Aust CSIRO Div Trop Crops Pastures Tech Pap ... Australia. Commonwealth Scientific and Industrial Research Organisation. Division of Tropical Crops and Pastures. Technical Paper [*A publication*]

Aust CSIRO Div Trop Crops Pastures Trop Agron Tech Memo ... Australia. Commonwealth Scientific and Industrial Research Organisation. Division of Tropical Crops and Pastures. Tropical Agronomy. Technical Memorandum [*A publication*]   (APTA)

Aust CSIRO Div Trop Pastures Annu Rep ... Australia. Commonwealth Scientific and Industrial Research Organisation. Division of Tropical Pastures. Annual Report [*A publication*]

Aust CSIRO Div Trop Pastures Tech Pap ... Australia. Commonwealth Scientific and Industrial Research Organisation. Division of Tropical Pastures. Technical Paper [*A publication*]

Aust CSIRO Div Water Land Resour Div Rep ... Australia. Commonwealth Scientific and Industrial Research Organisation. Division of Water and Land Resources. Divisional Report [*A publication*]

Aust CSIRO Div Water Land Resour Nat Resour Ser ... Australia. Commonwealth Scientific and Industrial Research Organisation. Division of Water and Land Resources. Natural Resources Series [*A publication*]

Aust CSIRO Div Water Resour Div Rep ... Australia. Commonwealth Scientific and Industrial Research Organisation. Division of Water Resources. Divisional Report [*A publication*]

Aust CSIRO Div Wildl Rangelands Res Tech Pap ... Australia. Commonwealth Scientific and Industrial Research Organisation. Division of Wildlife and Rangelands Research. Technical Paper [*A publication*]

Aust CSIRO Div Wildl Res Rep ... Australia. Commonwealth Scientific and Industrial Research Organisation. Division of Wildlife Research. Report [*A publication*]

Aust CSIRO Div Wildl Res Tech Pap ... Australia. Commonwealth Scientific and Industrial Research Organisation. Division of Wildlife Research. Technical Paper [*A publication*]

Aust CSIRO Food Preserv Q ... Australia. Commonwealth Scientific and Industrial Research Organisation. Food Preservation Quarterly [*A publication*]

Aust CSIRO Food Res Q ... Australia. Commonwealth Scientific and Industrial Research Organisation. Food Research Quarterly [*A publication*]

Aust CSIRO For Prod Lab Div Appl Chem Technol Pap ... Australia. Commonwealth Scientific and Industrial Research Organisation. Forest Products Laboratory. Division of Applied Chemistry. Technological Paper [*A publication*]

Aust CSIRO For Prod Lab Div Build Res Technol Pap ... Australia. Commonwealth Scientific and Industrial Research Organisation. Forest Products Laboratory. Division of Building Research. Technological Paper [*A publication*]   (APTA)

Aust CSIRO For Prod Lab Technol Pap ... Australia. Commonwealth Scientific and Industrial Research Organisation. Forest Products Laboratory. Technological Paper [*A publication*]   (APTA)

Aust CSIRO Inst Biol Resour Div Water Land Resour Tech Memo ... Australia. Commonwealth Scientific and Industrial Research Organisation. Institute of Biological Resources. Division of Water and Land Resources. Technical Memorandum [*A publication*]

Aust CSIRO Inst Nat Resour Environ Div Water Resour Tech Mem ... Australia. Commonwealth Scientific and Industrial Research Organisation. Institute of Natural Resources and Environment. Division of Water Resources. Technical Memorandum [*A publication*]

Aust CSIRO Irrig Res Stn Techn Pap ... Australia. Commonwealth Scientific and Industrial Research Organisation. Irrigation Research Stations. Technical Paper [*A publication*]   (APTA)

Aust CSIRO Irrig Res Stn Tech Pap ... Australia. Commonwealth Scientific and Industrial Research Organisation. Irrigation Research Stations. Technical Paper [*A publication*]

Aust CSIRO Land Resour Lab Div Soils Bienn Rep ... Australia. Commonwealth Scientific and Industrial Research Organisation. Land Resources Laboratories. Division of Soils. Biennial Report [*A publication*]

Aust CSIRO Land Resour Manage Tech Pap ... Australia. Commonwealth Scientific and Industrial Research Organisation. Land Resources Management Technical Paper [*A publication*]

Aust CSIRO Land Res Ser ... Australia. Commonwealth Scientific and Industrial Research Organisation. Land Research Series [*A publication*]

Aust CSIRO Mar Biochem Unit Annu Rep ... Australia. Commonwealth Scientific and Industrial Research Organisation. Marine Biochemistry Unit. Annual Report [*A publication*]

Aust CSIRO Mar Lab Rep ... Australia. Commonwealth Scientific and Industrial Research Organisation. Marine Laboratories Report [*A publication*]

Aust CSIRO Min Dep Univ Melbourne Ore Dressing Invest Rep ... Australia. Commonwealth Scientific and Industrial Research Organisation. Mining Department. University of Melbourne. Ore Dressing Investigations. Report [*A publication*]   (APTA)

Aust CSIRO Mineragraphic Invest Tech Pap ... Australia. Commonwealth Scientific and Industrial Research Organisation. Mineragraphic Investigations. Technical Paper [*A publication*]

Aust CSIRO Miner Res Lab Annu Rep ... Australia. Commonwealth Scientific and Industrial Research Organisation. Minerals Research Laboratories. Annual Report [*A publication*]

Aust CSIRO Miner Res Lab Invest Rep ... Australia. Commonwealth Scientific and Industrial Research Organisation. Minerals Research Laboratories. Investigation Report [*A publication*]

Aust CSIRO Natl Meas Lab Bienn Rep ... Australia. Commonwealth Scientific and Industrial Research Organisation. National Measurement Laboratory. Biennial Report [*A publication*]

Aust CSIRO Natl Meas Lab Tech Pap ... Australia. Commonwealth Scientific and Industrial Research Organisation. National Measurement Laboratory. Technical Paper [*A publication*]

Aust CSIRO Natl Stand Lab Bienn Rep ... Australia. Commonwealth Scientific and Industrial Research Organisation. National Standards Laboratory. Biennial Report [*A publication*]

Aust CSIRO Natl Stand Lab Tech Pap ... Australia. Commonwealth Scientific and Industrial Research Organisation. National Standards Laboratory. Technical Paper [*A publication*]

Aust CSIRO Nat Stand Lab Tech Pap ... Australia. Commonwealth Scientific and Industrial Research Organisation. National Standards Laboratory. Technical Paper [*A publication*]   (APTA)

Aust CSIRO Soil Mech Sect Tech Memo ... Australia. Commonwealth Scientific and Industrial Research Organisation. Soil Mechanics Section. Technical Memorandum [*A publication*]

Aust CSIRO Soil Mech Sect Tech Pap ... Australia. Commonwealth Scientific and Industrial Research Organisation. Soil Mechanics Section. Technical Paper [*A publication*]

Aust CSIRO Soil Publ ... Australia. Commonwealth Scientific and Industrial Research Organisation. Soil Publication [*A publication*]

Aust CSIRO Soils Land Use Ser ... Australia. Commonwealth Scientific and Industrial Research Organisation. Soils and Land Use Series [*A publication*]

Aust CSIRO Trop Crops Pastures Ann Rep ... Australia. Commonwealth Scientific and Industrial Research Organisation. Tropical Crops and Pastures. Annual Report [*A publication*]

Aust CSIRO Trop Crops & Pastures Div Rep ... Australia. Commonwealth Scientific and Industrial Research Organisation. Tropical Crops and Pastures. Divisional Report [*A publication*]

Aust CSIRO Wheat Res Unit Annu Rep ... Australia. Commonwealth Scientific and Industrial Research Organisation. Wheat Research Unit. Annual Report [*A publication*]

Aust CSIRO Wildl Res ... Australia. Commonwealth Scientific and Industrial Research Organisation. Wildlife Research [*A publication*]

Aust CSIRO Wildl Surv Sect Tech Pap ... Australia. Commonwealth Scientific and Industrial Research Organisation. Wildlife Survey Section. Technical Paper [*A publication*]

Aust Ctry Mag ... Australian Country Magazine [*A publication*]   (APTA)

Aust Culturist ... Australian Culturist [*A publication*]   (APTA)

Aust Curr Law Rev ... Australian Current Law Review [*A publication*]   (APTA)

Aust Curr L Rev ... Australian Current Law Review [*A publication*]

Aust Dairy R ... Australian Dairy Review [*A publication*]   (APTA)

Aust Dairy Rev ... Australian Dairy Review [*A publication*]   (APTA)

Aust D 2d ... Australian Digest, Second Edition [*A publication*]   (DLA)

Aust Def Res Lab Paint Notes ... Australia. Defence Research Laboratories. Paint Notes [*A publication*]

Aust Def Res Lab Plat Notes ... Australia. Defence Research Laboratories. Plating Notes [*A publication*]

Aust Def Sci Serv Mater Res Lab Tech Note ... Australian Defence Scientific Service. Materials Research Laboratory. Technical Note [*A publication*]   (APTA)

Aust Def Sci Serv Weapons Res Est Tech Note ... Australian Defence Scientific Service. Weapons Research Establishment. Technical Note [*A publication*]   (APTA)

Aust Def Sc Serv ARL Report ... Australian Defence Scientific Service. Aeronautical Research Laboratories. Report [*A publication*]

Aust Def Stand Lab Rep ... Australia. Defence Standards Laboratories. Report [*A publication*]

Aust Def Stand Lab Tech Mem ... Australia. Defence Standards Laboratories. Technical Memorandum [*A publication*]

Aust Def Stand Lab Tech Memo ... Australia. Defence Standards Laboratories. Technical Memorandum [*A publication*]   (APTA)
Aust Def Stand Lab Tech Note ... Australia. Defence Standards Laboratories. Technical Note [*A publication*]
Aust Demographic R ... Australian Demographic Review [*A publication*]   (APTA)
Aust Dental J ... Australian Dental Journal [*A publication*]   (APTA)
Aust Dent J ... Australian Dental Journal [*A publication*]
Aust Dent Mirr ... Australian Dental Mirror [*A publication*]   (APTA)
Aust Dent Summ ... Australian Dental Summary [*A publication*]   (APTA)
Aust Dep Agric Biol Branch Tech Pap ... Australia. Department of Agriculture. Biology Branch. Technical Paper [*A publication*]
Aust Dep Def Mater Res Lab Rep ... Australia. Department of Defence. Materials Research Laboratories. Report [*A publication*]   (APTA)
Aust Dep Def Mater Res Lab Tech Note ... Australia. Department of Defence. Materials Research Laboratories. Technical Note [*A publication*]   (APTA)
Aust Dep Def Weapons Res Establ Tech Rep ... Australia. Department of Defence. Weapons Research Establishment. Technical Report [*A publication*]   (APTA)
Aust Dep Health Aust Radiat Lab Tech Rep ARL/TR ... Australia. Department of Health. Australian Radiation Laboratory. Technical Report Series ARL/TR [*A publication*]   (APTA)
Aust Dep Health Aust Radiat Lab Tech Rep Ser ARL/TR ... Australia. Department of Health. Australian Radiation Laboratory. Technical Report Series ARL/TR [*A publication*]   (APTA)
Aust Dep Munitions Paint Notes ... Australia. Department of Munitions. Paint Notes [*A publication*]   (APTA)
Aust Dep Supply Aeronaut Res Lab Mech Eng Note ... Australia. Department of Supply. Aeronautical Research Laboratories. Mechanical Engineering Note [*A publication*]   (APTA)
Aust Dep Supply Aeronaut Res Lab Struct Mater Note ... Australia. Department of Supply. Aeronautical Research Laboratories. Structures and Materials Note [*A publication*]   (APTA)
Aust Dep Supply Def Res Lab Paint Notes ... Australia. Department of Supply. Defence Research Laboratories. Paint Notes [*A publication*]   (APTA)
Aust Dep Supply Def Res Lab Plat Notes ... Australia. Department of Supply. Defence Research Laboratories. Plating Notes [*A publication*]   (APTA)
Aust DFA Treaty Series ... Australia. Department of Foreign Affairs. International Treaties and Conventions [*A publication*]
Aust Digest ... Australian Digest [*A publication*]   (APTA)
Aust Dir ..... Australian Director [*A publication*]   (APTA)
Aust Director ... Australian Director [*A publication*]   (APTA)
Aust Dirt Bike ... Australasian Dirt Bike [*A publication*]
AUSTDK ... Austrobaileya [*A publication*]
Aust Draftsmen ... Australian Draftsmen [*A publication*]   (APTA)
Aust Dried Fruit News ... Australian Dried Fruit News [*A publication*]   (APTA)
Aust Early Child Resource Booklets ... Australian Early Childhood Resource Booklets [*A publication*]   (APTA)
Aust Econ ... Australian Economic Papers [*A publication*]
Aust Econ H ... Australian Economic History Review [*A publication*]
Aust Econ Hist R ... Australian Economic History Review [*A publication*]   (APTA)
Aust Econ Hist Rev ... Australian Economic History Review [*A publication*]   (APTA)
Aust Econ News Dig ... Australian Economic News Digest [*A publication*]   (APTA)
Aust Econ P ... Australian Economic Papers [*A publication*]
Aust Econ Pap ... Australian Economic Papers [*A publication*]
Aust Econ R ... Australian Economic Review [*A publication*]
Aust Econ Rev ... Australian Economic Review [*A publication*]   (APTA)
Aust Ed Res ... Australian Education Researcher [*A publication*]
Aust Ed Rev ... Australian Education Review [*A publication*]
Aust Educ Index ... Australian Education Index [*A publication*]
Aust Educ R ... Australian Education Review [*A publication*]   (APTA)
Aust Educ Res ... Australian Education Researcher [*A publication*]   (APTA)
Aust Educ Rev ... Australian Education Review [*A publication*]   (APTA)
AUSTEL ... Australian Telecommunications Authority
Aust Electrochem Conf ... Australian Electrochemistry Conference [*A publication*]   (APTA)
Aust Electron Bull ... Australian Electronics Bulletin [*A publication*]   (APTA)
Aust Electron Eng ... Australian Electronics Engineering [*A publication*]
Aust Electron Engng ... Australian Electronics Engineering [*A publication*]   (APTA)
Aust Electr World ... Australian Electrical World [*A publication*]
Aust Elect Wld ... Australian Electrical World [*A publication*]   (APTA)
Aust Elec World ... Australian Electrical World [*A publication*]   (APTA)
Aust Encycl ... Australian Encyclopaedia [*A publication*]   (APTA)
Aust Endeavourer ... Australian Endeavourer [*A publication*]   (APTA)
Aust Engineer ... Australasian Engineer [*A publication*]   (APTA)
Aust Engr ... Australasian Engineer [*A publication*]   (APTA)
Aust Ent Mag ... Australian Entomological Magazine [*A publication*]
Aust Entomol Mag ... Australian Entomological Magazine [*A publication*]
Aust Entomol Soc J ... Australian Entomological Society. Journal [*A publication*]   (APTA)

Aust Entomol Soc Misc Publ ... Australian Entomological Society. Miscellaneous Publication [*A publication*]
Aust Exporter ... Australian Exporter [*A publication*]   (APTA)
Aust External Terr ... Australian External Territories [*A publication*]   (APTA)
Aust Ext Terr ... Australian External Territories [*A publication*]   (APTA)
Aust Fact .... Australian Factory [*A publication*]   (APTA)
Aust Factory ... Australian Factory [*A publication*]   (APTA)
Aust Fam Physician ... Australian Family Physician [*A publication*]
Aust Fam Safe ... Australian Family Safety [*A publication*]
Aust Fashion News ... Australian Fashion News [*A publication*]   (APTA)
Aust Fd Manuf ... Australian Food Manufacturer and Distributor [*A publication*]   (APTA)
Aust Fd Mf ... Australian Food Manufacturer and Distributor [*A publication*]
Aust Fd Mfr ... Australian Food Manufacturer and Distributor [*A publication*]   (APTA)
Aust Fed Police ... Australian Federal Police [*A publication*]
Aust Financial R ... Australian Financial Review [*A publication*]   (APTA)
Aust Financial Rev ... Australian Financial Review [*A publication*]   (APTA)
Aust Financial Times ... Australian Financial Times [*A publication*]   (APTA)
Aust Financ Rev ... Australian Financial Review [*A publication*]
Aust Finish ... Australian Finishing [*A publication*]
Aust Finish Rev ... Australian Finishing Review [*A publication*]   (APTA)
Aust Fin Rev ... Australian Financial Review [*A publication*]   (APTA)
Aust Fish ... Australian Fisheries [*A publication*]
Aust Fish Educ Leafl ... Australian Fisheries Education Leaflet [*A publication*]   (APTA)
Aust Fisheries ... Australian Fisheries [*A publication*]
Aust Fish Newsl ... Australian Fisheries Newsletter [*A publication*]   (APTA)
Aust Fish Pap ... Australian Fisheries Paper [*A publication*]   (APTA)
Aust Fm Mgmt J ... Australian Farm Management Journal [*A publication*]   (APTA)
Aust Food Manuf ... Australian Food Manufacturer and Distributor [*A publication*]   (APTA)
Aust Food Manuf Distrib ... Australian Food Manufacturer and Distributor [*A publication*]
Aust Food Mfr Distrib ... Australian Food Manufacturer and Distributor [*A publication*]
Aust For ..... Australian Forestry [*A publication*]
Aust For Aff R ... Australian Foreign Affairs Record [*A publication*]   (APTA)
Aust For Aff Rec ... Australian Foreign Affairs Record [*A publication*]
Aust Foreign Aff Rec ... Australian Foreign Affairs Record [*A publication*]
Aust Forest ... Australian Forest Research [*A publication*]
Aust Forester ... Australian Forester [*A publication*]   (APTA)
Aust Forest Grower ... Australian Forest Grower [*A publication*]
Aust Forest Inds J ... Australian Forest Industries Journal [*A publication*]
Aust Forest Res ... Australian Forest Research [*A publication*]
Aust Forestry ... Australian Forestry [*A publication*]   (APTA)
Aust For Grow ... Australian Forest Grower [*A publication*]   (APTA)
Aust For Ind J ... Australian Forest Industries Journal [*A publication*]
Aust For Ind J Aust Log ... Australian Forest Industries Journal and Australian Logger [*A publication*]
Aust For J ... Australian Forest Journal [*A publication*]   (APTA)
Aust For (Perth) ... Australian Forestry (Perth) [*A publication*]   (APTA)
Aust For Res ... Australian Forest Research [*A publication*]
Aust For Resour ... Australian Forest Resources [*A publication*]   (APTA)
Aust For Tree Nutr Conf Contrib Pap ... Australian Forest Tree Nutrition Conference. Contributed Papers [*A publication*]   (APTA)
Aust Foundry Trade J ... Australian Foundry Trade Journal [*A publication*]   (APTA)
Aust Found Trade J ... Australian Foundry Trade Journal [*A publication*]   (APTA)
Aust Fract Group Conf Proc ... Australian Fracture Group Conference. Proceedings [*A publication*]   (APTA)
Aust Furn Trade J ... Australian Furnishing Trade Journal [*A publication*]   (APTA)
Aust Gas Bull ... Australian Gas Bulletin [*A publication*]
Aust Gas J ... Australian Gas Journal [*A publication*]
Aust Gem ... Australian Gem and Treasure Hunter [*A publication*]
Aust Gemmol ... Australian Gemmologist [*A publication*]
Aust Gemmologist ... Australian Gemmologist [*A publication*]   (APTA)
Aust Gems ... Australian Gems and Crafts [*A publication*]   (APTA)
Aust Geneal ... Australian Genealogist [*A publication*]   (APTA)
Aust Genealogist ... Australian Genealogist [*A publication*]   (APTA)
Aust Geog .. Australian Geographer [*A publication*]   (APTA)
Aust Geogr ... Australian Geographer [*A publication*]
Aust Geographer ... Australian Geographer [*A publication*]   (APTA)
Aust Geog Rec ... Australian Geographical Record [*A publication*]   (APTA)
Aust Geog Record ... Australian Geographical Record [*A publication*]   (APTA)
Aust Geogr Rec ... Australian Geographical Record [*A publication*]   (APTA)
Aust Geogr Stud ... Australian Geographical Studies [*A publication*]   (APTA)
Aust Geogr Studies ... Australian Geographical Studies [*A publication*]   (APTA)
Aust Geog S ... Australian Geographical Studies [*A publication*]
Aust Geog Stud ... Australian Geographical Studies [*A publication*]   (APTA)
Aust Geog Studies ... Australian Geographical Studies [*A publication*]   (APTA)
Aust Geol ... Australian Geologist [*A publication*]   (APTA)
Aust Geomechanics J ... Australian Geomechanics Journal [*A publication*]   (APTA)
Aust Geomech J ... Australian Geomechanics Journal [*A publication*]

Aust Gliding ... Australian Gliding [*A publication*]   (APTA)
Aust Goat World ... Australian Goat World [*A publication*]   (APTA)
Aust Gourmet ... Australian Gourmet [*A publication*]   (APTA)
Aust Gov Anal Lab Rep Invest ... Australian Government Analytical Laboratories. Report of Investigations [*A publication*]   (APTA)
Aust Gov Publ ... Australian Government Publications [*A publication*]   (APTA)
Aust Grade Teach ... Australian Grade Teacher [*A publication*]   (APTA)
Aust Grapegr ... Australian Grapegrower [*Later, Australian Grapegrower and Winemaker*] [*A publication*]   (APTA)
Aust Grapegrow ... Australian Grapegrower and Winemaker [*A publication*]   (APTA)
Aust Hand Weaver ... Australian Hand Weaver and Spinner [*A publication*]   (APTA)
Aust Hardware J ... Australian Hardware Journal [*A publication*]   (APTA)
Aust Her ... Australia's Heritage [*A publication*]
Aust Hereford A ... Australian Hereford Annual [*A publication*]   (APTA)
Aust Hereford Ann ... Australian Hereford Annual [*A publication*]   (APTA)
Aust Hereford Annu ... Australian Hereford Annual [*A publication*]   (APTA)
Aust Hereford J ... Australian Hereford Journal [*A publication*]   (APTA)
Aust Hereford Soc Q ... Hereford Quarterly. Australian Hereford Society [*A publication*]   (APTA)
Aust Hi-Fi ... Australian Hi-Fi [*A publication*]   (APTA)
Aust Highway ... Australian Highway [*A publication*]   (APTA)
Aust Hist Bibl ... Australian Historical Bibliography [*A publication*]
Aust Hist Stud ... Australian Historical Studies [*A publication*]
Aust Hist Teach ... Australian History Teacher [*A publication*]   (APTA)
Aust Home Beaut ... Australian Home Beautiful [*A publication*]   (APTA)
Aust Home J ... Australian Home Journal [*A publication*]   (APTA)
Aust Homemaker ... Australian Homemaker [*A publication*]   (APTA)
Aust Hosp ... Australian Hospital [*A publication*]
Aust Hospital ... Australian Hospital [*A publication*]   (APTA)
Aust House Gard ... Australian House and Garden [*A publication*]   (APTA)
Aust House and Garden ... Australian House and Garden [*A publication*]   (APTA)
Aust Housing ... Australian Housing [*A publication*]   (APTA)
Aust Human Res Cncl A Rept ... Australian Humanities Research Council. Annual Report [*A publication*]   (APTA)
Aust Hwy ... Australian Highway [*A publication*]   (APTA)
Aust Immigr Consol Stat ... Australian Immigration: Consolidated Statistics [*A publication*]   (APTA)
Austin .... Austin's Reports [*Ceylon*] [*A publication*]   (DLA)
Austin BJ ... Austin Business Journal [*A publication*]
Austin CC .. Austin's English County Court Reports [*A publication*]   (DLA)
Austin (Ceylon) ... Austin's Ceylon Reports [*A publication*]   (DLA)
Aust Ind Dev Assoc Dir Repts ... Australian Industries Development Association. Director Reports [*A publication*]   (APTA)
Aust Ind Development Assn Director Report ... Australian Industries Development Association. Director Reports [*A publication*]   (APTA)
Aust Ind LR ... Australian Industrial Law Review [*A publication*]   (APTA)
Aust Ind Min Stand ... Australian Industrial and Mining Standard [*A publication*]   (APTA)
Austin Sem Bul ... Austin Seminary Bulletin. Faculty Edition [*A publication*]
Aust Inst Internat Aff NSW Br ... Australian Institute of International Affairs. New South Wales Branch [*A publication*]   (APTA)
Aust Inst Mar Sci Monogr Ser ... Australian Institute of Marine Science. Monograph Series [*A publication*]
Aust Intercollegian ... Australian Intercollegian [*A publication*]   (APTA)
Aust Irrig ... Australasian Irrigator and Pasture Improver [*A publication*]   (APTA)
Aust Irrig Past Improver ... Australasian Irrigator and Pasture Improver [*A publication*]   (APTA)
Aust J .... Australian Journal [*A publication*]   (APTA)
Aust J Adult Ed ... Australian Journal of Adult Education [*A publication*]   (APTA)
Aust J Adult Educ ... Australian Journal of Adult Education [*A publication*]   (APTA)
Aust J Adv Ed ... Australian Journal of Advanced Education [*A publication*]
Aust J Adv Nurs ... Australian Journal of Advanced Nursing [*A publication*]
Aust J Ag E ... Australian Journal of Agricultural Economics [*A publication*]
Aust J Ag Econ ... Australian Journal of Agricultural Economics [*A publication*]   (APTA)
Aust J Agr ... Australian Journal of Agricultural Research [*A publication*]
Aust J Ag R ... Australian Journal of Agricultural Research [*A publication*]   (APTA)
Aust J Agr Econ ... Australian Journal of Agricultural Economics [*A publication*]   (APTA)
Aust J Ag Res ... Australian Journal of Agricultural Research [*A publication*]   (APTA)
Aust J Agric Econ ... Australian Journal of Agricultural Economics [*A publication*]   (APTA)
Aust J Agric Res ... Australian Journal of Agricultural Research [*A publication*]
Aust J Agr Res ... Australian Journal of Agricultural Research [*A publication*]
Aust J Alcohol & Drug Depend ... Australian Journal of Alcohol and Drug Dependence [*A publication*]   (APTA)
Aust J Appl Sci ... Australian Journal of Applied Science [*A publication*]
Aust J Arch & Arts ... Australian Journal of Architecture and Arts [*A publication*]   (APTA)

Aust J Biblical Archaeol ... Australian Journal of Biblical Archaeology [*A publication*]   (APTA)
Aust J Biol ... Australian Journal of Biological Sciences [*A publication*]
Aust J Biol Sci ... Australian Journal of Biological Sciences [*A publication*]
Aust J Bot ... Australian Journal of Botany [*A publication*]
Aust J Botany ... Australian Journal of Botany [*A publication*]   (APTA)
Aust J Bot Supplry Ser Suppl ... Australian Journal of Botany. Supplementary Series. Supplement [*A publication*]   (APTA)
Aust J Bot Suppl Ser ... Australian Journal of Botany. Supplementary Series [*A publication*]
Aust J Bot Suppl Ser Suppl ... Australian Journal of Botany. Supplementary Series. Supplement [*A publication*]   (APTA)
Aust J Chem ... Australian Journal of Chemistry [*A publication*]
Aust J Chem Eng ... Australian Journal of Chemical Engineers [*A publication*]   (APTA)
Aust J Clin Exp Hypn ... Australian Journal of Clinical and Experimental Hypnosis [*A publication*]
Aust J Coal Min Technol Res ... Australian Journal of Coal Mining Technology and Research [*A publication*]
Aust J Dair ... Australian Journal of Dairy Technology [*A publication*]
Aust J Dairy Tech ... Australian Journal of Dairy Technology [*A publication*]   (APTA)
Aust J Dairy Technol ... Australian Journal of Dairy Technology [*A publication*]
Aust J Dairy Technology ... Australian Journal of Dairy Technology [*A publication*]   (APTA)
Aust J Dairy Technol Suppl ... Australian Journal of Dairy Technology. Supplement [*A publication*]   (APTA)
Aust J Dent ... Australian Journal of Dentistry [*A publication*]   (APTA)
Aust J Dentistry ... Australian Journal of Dentistry [*A publication*]   (APTA)
Aust J Derm ... Australasian Journal of Dermatology [*A publication*]
Aust J Derm ... Australian [*later, Australasian*] Journal of Dermatology [*A publication*]   (APTA)
Aust J Dermatol ... Australasian Journal of Dermatology [*A publication*]   (APTA)
Aust J Dermatol ... Australian [*later, Australasian*] Journal of Dermatology [*A publication*]
Aust J Dev Disabil ... Australian Journal of Developmental Disabilities [*A publication*]
Aust J Dev Disabilities ... Australian Journal of Developmental Disabilities [*A publication*]   (APTA)
Aust J Early Child ... Australian Journal of Early Childhood [*A publication*]   (APTA)
Aust J Earth Sci ... Australian Journal of Earth Sciences [*A publication*]
Aust J Ecol ... Australian Journal of Ecology [*A publication*]
Aust J Ed ... Australian Journal of Education [*A publication*]   (APTA)
Aust J Educ ... Australian Journal of Education [*A publication*]
Aust Jewish Herald ... Australian Jewish Herald [*A publication*]   (APTA)
Aust Jewish Hist Soc J & Proc ... Australian Jewish Historical Society. Journal and Proceedings [*A publication*]   (APTA)
Aust Jewish Hist Soc J Proc ... Australian Jewish Historical Society. Journal and Proceedings [*A publication*]   (APTA)
Aust Jewish News ... Australian Jewish News [*A publication*]   (APTA)
Aust Jewish Outlook ... Australian Jewish Outlook [*A publication*]   (APTA)
Aust J Ex A ... Australian Journal of Experimental Agriculture and Animal Husbandry [*A publication*]   (APTA)
Aust J Ex B ... Australian Journal of Experimental Biology and Medical Science [*A publication*]
Aust J Exp Agr Anim Husb ... Australian Journal of Experimental Agriculture and Animal Husbandry [*A publication*]
Aust J Exp Agric ... Australian Journal of Experimental Agriculture [*A publication*]
Aust J Exp Agric An Husb ... Australian Journal of Experimental Agriculture and Animal Husbandry [*A publication*]   (APTA)
Aust J Exp Agric & Anim Husb ... Australian Journal of Experimental Agriculture and Animal Husbandry [*A publication*]   (APTA)
Aust J Exp Agric Anim Husb ... Australian Journal of Experimental Agriculture and Animal Husbandry [*A publication*]
Aust J Exp B ... Australian Journal of Experimental Biology and Medical Science [*A publication*]   (APTA)
Aust J Exp Biol ... Australian Journal of Experimental Biology and Medical Science [*A publication*]   (APTA)
Aust J Exp Biol Med Sci ... Australian Journal of Experimental Biology and Medical Science [*A publication*]
Aust J Exper Agric ... Australian Journal of Experimental Agriculture [*A publication*]
Aust J Exper Agric ... Australian Journal of Experimental Agriculture and Animal Husbandry [*A publication*]   (APTA)
Aust J Expl Biol Med Sci ... Australian Journal of Experimental Biology and Medical Science [*A publication*]   (APTA)
Aust J Fam Ther ... Australian Journal of Family Therapy [*A publication*]   (APTA)
Aust J Foren Sci ... Australian Journal of Forensic Sciences [*A publication*]
Aust J Forensic Sci ... Australian Journal of Forensic Sciences [*A publication*]
Aust J For Sci ... Australian Journal of Forensic Sciences [*A publication*]   (APTA)
Aust J French Stud ... Australian Journal of French Studies [*A publication*]   (APTA)
Aust J Fr S ... Australian Journal of French Studies [*A publication*]

Aust J Fr Stud ... Australian Journal of French Studies [*A publication*] (APTA)
Aust J Geod Photogramm and Surv ... Australian Journal of Geodesy, Photogrammetry, and Surveying [*A publication*]
Aust J Health Phys Educ Recreation ... Australian Journal for Health, Physical Education, and Recreation [*A publication*] (APTA)
Aust J Health Phys Edu Recreation ... Australian Journal for Health, Physical Education, and Recreation [*A publication*] (APTA)
Aust J Higher Ed ... Australian Journal of Higher Education [*A publication*] (APTA)
Aust J Higher Educ ... Australian Journal of Higher Education [*A publication*] (APTA)
Aust J Hlth Phys Ed Rec ... Australian Journal of Health, Physical Education, and Recreation [*A publication*]
Aust J Hosp Pharm ... Australian Journal of Hospital Pharmacy [*A publication*]
Aust J Inst ... Australian Journal of Instrumentation and Control [*A publication*]
Aust J Instrum Control ... Australian Journal of Instrumentation and Control [*A publication*] (APTA)
Aust J Instrum & Control ... Australian Journal of Instrumentation and Control [*A publication*]
Aust J Instrument Tech ... Australian Journal of Instrument Technology [*A publication*] (APTA)
Aust J Instrument Technology ... Australian Journal of Instrument Technology [*A publication*] (APTA)
Aust J Instrum Tech ... Australian Journal of Instrument Technology [*A publication*] (APTA)
Aust J Instrum Technol ... Australian Journal of Instrument Technology [*A publication*] (APTA)
Aust J Inst Trans ... Australian Journal. Institute of Transport [*A publication*] (APTA)
Aust J Inst Transp ... Australian Journal. Institute of Transport [*A publication*]
Aust JLS .... Australian Journal of Law and Society [*A publication*]
Aust JL & Soc ... Australian Journal of Law and Society [*A publication*] (APTA)
Aust JM ..... Australian Journal of Management [*A publication*]
Aust J Manage ... Australian Journal of Management [*A publication*] (APTA)
Aust J Mar ... Australian Journal of Marine and Freshwater Research [*A publication*]
Aust J Mar Freshwater Res ... Australian Journal of Marine and Freshwater Research [*A publication*]
Aust J Mar Freshwat Res ... Australian Journal of Marine and Freshwater Research [*A publication*] (APTA)
Aust J Mar Freshw Res ... Australian Journal of Marine and Freshwater Research [*A publication*]
Aust J Med Lab Sci ... Australian Journal of Medical Laboratory Science [*A publication*] (APTA)
Aust J Med Technol ... Australian Journal of Medical Technology [*A publication*]
Aust J Ment Retard ... Australian Journal of Mental Retardation [*A publication*] (APTA)
Aust J Mgmt ... Australian Journal of Management [*A publication*]
Aust J Music Ed ... Australian Journal of Music Education [*A publication*] (APTA)
Aust J Music Educ ... Australian Journal of Music Education [*A publication*] (APTA)
Aust Jnl of Forensic Sciences ... Australian Journal of Forensic Sciences [*A publication*] (APTA)
Aust Jnl of Social Issues ... Australian Journal of Social Issues [*A publication*]
Aust J Ophthalmol ... Australian Journal of Ophthalmology [*A publication*]
Aust J Optom ... Australian Journal of Optometry [*A publication*]
Aust J Optometry ... Australian Journal of Optometry [*A publication*] (APTA)
Aust J Pharm ... Australian Journal of Pharmacy [*A publication*]
Aust J Pharmacy ... Australian Journal of Pharmacy [*A publication*] (APTA)
Aust J Pharm Sci ... Australian Journal of Pharmaceutical Sciences [*A publication*]
Aust J Pharm Suppl ... Australian Journal of Pharmacy. Supplement [*A publication*] (APTA)
Aust J Phil ... Australasian Journal of Philosophy [*A publication*]
Aust J Phys ... Australian Journal of Physics [*A publication*]
Aust J Phys Astrophys Suppl ... Australian Journal of Physics. Astrophysical Supplement [*A publication*]
Aust J Phys Ed ... Australian Journal of Physical Education [*A publication*] (APTA)
Aust J Phys Educ ... Australian Journal of Physical Education [*A publication*] (APTA)
Aust J Physical Educ ... Australian Journal of Physical Education [*A publication*] (APTA)
Aust J Physiother ... Australian Journal of Physiotherapy [*A publication*] (APTA)
Aust J Physiotherapy ... Australian Journal of Physiotherapy [*A publication*] (APTA)
Aust J Plan ... Australian Journal of Plant Physiology [*A publication*] (APTA)
Austl J Plant Physiol ... Australian Journal of Plant Physiology [*A publication*]
Austl J Pl Physiol ... Australian Journal of Plant Physiology [*A publication*]
Aust J Pol Hist ... Australian Journal of Politics and History [*A publication*]

Aust J Pol and Hist ... Australian Journal of Politics and History [*A publication*] (APTA)
Aust J Poli ... Australian Journal of Politics and History [*A publication*]
Aust J Poli & Hist ... Australian Journal of Politics and History [*A publication*] (APTA)
Aust J Polit Hist ... Australian Journal of Politics and History [*A publication*] (APTA)
Aust J Politics Hist ... Australian Journal of Politics and History [*A publication*] (APTA)
Aust J Politics & History ... Australian Journal of Politics and History [*A publication*] (APTA)
Aust J Ps Phil ... Australasian Journal of Psychology and Philosophy [*A publication*] (APTA)
Aust J Psyc ... Australian Journal of Psychology [*A publication*]
Aust J Psych ... Australian Journal of Psychology [*A publication*] (APTA)
Aust J Psychol ... Australian Journal of Psychology [*A publication*]
Aust J Psychological Research ... Australian Journal of Psychological Research [*A publication*] (APTA)
Aust J Psychology ... Australian Journal of Psychology [*A publication*] (APTA)
Aust J Psych Res ... Australian Journal of Psychological Research [*A publication*] (APTA)
Aust J Pub Admin ... Australian Journal of Public Administration [*A publication*]
Aust J Publ ... Australian Journal of Public Administration [*A publication*] (APTA)
Aust J Publ Admin ... Australian Journal of Public Administration [*A publication*]
Aust Jr .... Austin's Lectures on Jurisprudence [*A publication*] (DLA)
Austl Jr .... Australian Jurist [*A publication*]
Austl J Reading ... Australian Journal of Reading [*A publication*] (APTA)
Aust J Rem Educ ... Australian Journal of Remedial Education [*A publication*] (APTA)
Aust Jr R .... Australian Jurist Reports [*A publication*]
Aust J Sci ... Australian Journal of Science [*A publication*]
Aust J Science ... Australian Journal of Science [*A publication*] (APTA)
Aust J Scientific Research ... Australian Journal of Scientific Research [*A publication*] (APTA)
Aust J Scient Res ... Australian Journal of Scientific Research [*A publication*] (APTA)
Aust J Sci Res B ... Australian Journal of Scientific Research. Series B. Biological Sciences [*A publication*]
Aust J Sci Res Ser A ... Australian Journal of Scientific Research. Series A. Physical Sciences [*A publication*]
Aust J Sci Res Ser B ... Australian Journal of Scientific Research. Series B [*A publication*] (APTA)
Aust J of Screen Th ... Australian Journal of Screen Theory [*A publication*]
Aust J Soc ... Australian Journal of Social Issues [*A publication*]
Aust J Social Iss ... Australian Journal of Social Issues [*A publication*] (APTA)
Aust J Social Issues ... Australian Journal of Social Issues [*A publication*] (APTA)
Austl Social Work ... Australian Journal of Social Work [*A publication*] (APTA)
Aust J Soc Is ... Australian Journal of Social Issues [*A publication*]
Aust J Soc Issues ... Australian Journal of Social Issues [*A publication*] (APTA)
Aust J Soc Work ... Australian Journal of Social Work [*A publication*] (APTA)
Aust J Soil ... Australian Journal of Soil Research [*A publication*]
Aust J Soil Res ... Australian Journal of Soil Research [*A publication*]
Austl J Spec Ed ... Australian Journal of Special Education [*A publication*]
Aust J Stat ... Australian Journal of Statistics [*A publication*]
Aust J Statist ... Australian Journal of Statistics [*A publication*] (APTA)
Aust J Stats ... Australian Journal of Statistics [*A publication*] (APTA)
Aust J Teach Ed ... Australian Journal of Teacher Education [*A publication*]
Aust J Teach Educ ... Australian Journal of Teacher Education [*A publication*] (APTA)
Aust J Teach Pract ... Australian Journal of Teaching Practice [*A publication*] (APTA)
Aust Junior Farmer ... Australian Junior Farmer [*A publication*] (APTA)
Aust Jur ..... Austin's Lectures on Jurisprudence [*A publication*] (ILCA)
Aust Jur ..... Australian Jurist [*A publication*] (APTA)
Aust Jur ..... Australian Jurist Reports [*A publication*] (APTA)
Aust Jur Abr ... Austin's Lectures on Jurisprudence, Abridged [*A publication*] (DLA)
Aust Jur R ... Australian Jurist Reports [*A publication*] (ILCA)
Aust Jur Rep ... Australian Jurist Reports [*A publication*]
Aust J Zool ... Australian Journal of Zoology [*A publication*]
Aust J Zool Supplry Ser ... Australian Journal of Zoology. Supplementary Series [*A publication*] (APTA)
Aust J Zool Supplry Ser Suppl ... Australian Journal of Zoology. Supplementary Series. Supplement [*A publication*] (APTA)
Aust J Zool Suppl Ser ... Australian Journal of Zoology. Supplementary Series [*A publication*]
Aust KA ..... Austin's Kandran Appeals [*Ceylon*] [*A publication*] (DLA)
AUSTL ...... Australia
Austl Acts .. Acts of the Australian Parliament [*A publication*] (DLA)
Austl AD ..... Australian Annual Digest [*A publication*] (DLA)
Aust Lapidary ... Australian Lapidary Magazine [*A publication*]

Austl Argus LR ... Australian Argus Law Reports [*A publication*]
Aust Law.... Australian Lawyer [*A publication*]
Aust Law J ... Australian Law Journal [*A publication*]
Aust Law News ... Australian Law News [*A publication*]   (APTA)
Aust Law Rev ... Australian Law Review [*A publication*]   (APTA)
Aust Lawyer ... Australian Lawyer [*A publication*]   (APTA)
Austl Bankr Cas ... Australian Bankruptcy Cases [*A publication*]
Austl Bus L Rev ... Australian Business Law Review [*A publication*]
Austl C Acts ... Commonwealth Acts (Australia) [*A publication*]   (DLA)
Austl Cap Terr Subs Leg ... Subsidiary Legislation of the Australian Capital
    Territory [*A publication*]   (DLA)
Austl Com J ... Australian Commercial Journal [*A publication*]
Austl Convey & Sol J ... Australian Conveyancer and Solicitors' Journal [*A
    publication*]   (DLA)
Austl Current L Rev ... Australian Current Law Review [*A
    publication*]   (DLA)
Austl D...... Australian Digest [*A publication*]   (DLA)
Aust Leather J ... Australian Leather Journal. Boot and Shoe Recorder [*A
    publication*]   (APTA)
Aust Leath Footwear Rev ... Australasian Leather and Footwear Review [*A
    publication*]   (APTA)
Aust Leath J ... Australian Leather Journal. Boot and Shoe Recorder [*A
    publication*]   (APTA)
Aust Leath Tr Rev ... Australian Leather Trades Review [*A
    publication*]   (APTA)
Aust Left R ... Australian Left Review [*A publication*]
Aust Left Rev ... Australian Left Review [*A publication*]
Aust Leg Mon Dig ... Australian Legal Monthly Digest [*A publication*]
Austl Engy ... Forecasts of Energy Demand and Supply (Australia) [*A
    publication*]
Aust Lett .... Australian Letters [*A publication*]   (APTA)
Aust Liberal ... Australian Liberal [*A publication*]   (APTA)
Aust Lib J .. Australian Library Journal [*A publication*]
Aust Libr J ... Australian Library Journal [*A publication*]
Aust Libr J Suppl ... Australian Library Journal. Supplement [*A
    publication*]   (APTA)
Aust Libr News ... Australian Library News [*A publication*]
AUSTLIT ... Australian Literary Database
Aust Literary Letter ... Australian Literary Letter [*A publication*]   (APTA)
Aust Lit S... Australian Literary Studies [*A publication*]   (APTA)
Aust Lit St ... Australian Literary Studies [*A publication*]
Aust Lit Stud ... Australian Literary Studies [*A publication*]   (APTA)
Aust L J ..... Australian Law Journal [*A publication*]
Austl J For Sci ... Australian Journal of Forensic Sciences [*A publication*]
Austl JL Soc'y ... Australian Journal of Law and Society [*A
    publication*]   (DLA)
Austl J Phil ... Australasian Journal of Philosophy [*A publication*]
Austl Jr...... Australian Jurist [*A publication*]   (DLA)
Aust LJ Rep ... Australian Law Journal. Reports [*A publication*]
Austl Jur R ... Australian Jurist Reports [*A publication*]
Austl Law... Australian Lawyer [*A publication*]   (DLA)
Austl LJ ..... Australian Law Journal [*A publication*]
Austl LJ Rep ... Australian Law Journal. Reports [*A publication*]
Austl LMD ... Australian Legal Monthly Digest [*A publication*]   (DLA)
Austl LR ... Australian Law Reports [*A publication*]   (DLA)
Austl L Times ... Australian Law Times [*A publication*]   (DLA)
Aust LN ..... Australian Law News [*A publication*]   (APTA)
Austl and NZJ Criminology ... Australian and New Zealand Journal of
    Criminology [*A publication*]
Aust L Rep ... Australian Law Reports [*A publication*]
Austl Stat R Consol ... Statutory Rules Consolidation, Australian Parliament
    [*A publication*]   (DLA)
Aust LT...... Australian Law Times [*A publication*]   (APTA)
Austl Tax ... Australian Tax Decisions [*A publication*]
Austl Tax Rev ... Australian Tax Review [*A publication*]
Austl YB Int'l L ... Australian Yearbook of International Law [*A publication*]
Aust Machinery & Prod Eng ... Australian Machinery and Production
    Engineering [*A publication*]   (APTA)
Aust Mach Prod Eng ... Australian Machinery and Production Engineering [*A
    publication*]
Aust Mach Prod Engng ... Australian Machinery and Production Engineering
    [*A publication*]   (APTA)
Aust Mag ... Australian Magazine [*A publication*]   (APTA)
Aust Mammal ... Australian Mammalogy [*A publication*]
Aust Man... Australian Manager [*A publication*]   (APTA)
Aust Manager ... Australian Manager [*A publication*]   (APTA)
Aust Manag R ... Australian Management Review [*A publication*]   (APTA)
Aust Manuf ... Australasian Manufacturer [*A publication*]   (APTA)
Aust Mar Sci Bull ... Australian Marine Sciences Bulletin [*A publication*]
Aust Mar Sci Newsl ... Australian Marine Sciences Newsletter [*A
    publication*]   (APTA)
Aust Marxist Rev ... Australian Marxist Review [*A publication*]   (APTA)
Aust Mater Res Lab Rep ... Australia. Materials Research Laboratories.
    Report [*A publication*]   (APTA)
Aust Mater Res Lab Tech Note ... Australia. Materials Research Laboratories.
    Technical Note [*A publication*]   (APTA)
Aust Math Soc Bul ... Australian Mathematical Society. Bulletin [*A
    publication*]
Aust Math Soc Bull ... Australian Mathematical Society. Bulletin [*A
    publication*]
Aust Math Soc J ... Australian Mathematical Society. Journal [*A publication*]

Aust Math Soc J Ser A ... Australian Mathematical Society. Journal. Series A
    [*A publication*]
Aust Maths Teach ... Australian Mathematics Teacher [*A
    publication*]   (APTA)
Aust Math Teach ... Australian Mathematics Teacher [*A
    publication*]   (APTA)
Aust Mech Eng ... Australian Mechanical Engineering [*A
    publication*]   (APTA)
Aust Mech Engng ... Australian Mechanical Engineering [*A
    publication*]   (APTA)
Aust Mech Engr ... Australian Mechanical Engineering [*A
    publication*]   (APTA)
Aust Med J ... Australian Medical Journal [*A publication*]   (APTA)
Aust Merino Wool Campaign ... Australian Merino Wool Campaign [*A
    publication*]   (APTA)
Aust Meteorol Mag ... Australian Meteorological Magazine [*A publication*]
Aust Methodist Hist Soc J Proc ... Australasian Methodist Historical Society.
    Journal and Proceedings [*A publication*]   (APTA)
Aust Methods Eng ... Australian Methods Engineer [*A publication*]   (APTA)
Aust Met Mag ... Australian Meteorological Magazine [*A
    publication*]   (APTA)
Aust Mger ... Australian Manager [*A publication*]
Aust Mgr ... Australian Manager [*A publication*]   (APTA)
Aust Milk Dairy Prod J ... Australian Milk and Dairy Products Journal [*A
    publication*]   (APTA)
Aust Min.... Australian Mining [*A publication*]
Aust Min Counc Newsl ... Australian Mining Council. Newsletter [*A
    publication*]   (APTA)
Aust Min Dev Lab Bull ... Australian Mineral Development Laboratories
    [*AMDEL*]. Bulletin [*A publication*]   (APTA)
Aust Min Dev Labs Bull ... Australian Mineral Development Laboratories
    [*AMDEL*]. Bulletin [*A publication*]   (APTA)
Aust Min Engng Rev ... Australian Mining and Engineering Review [*A
    publication*]   (APTA)
Aust Min Eng Rev ... Australian Mining and Engineering Review [*A
    publication*]   (APTA)
Aust Miner Dev Lab Bull ... Australian Mineral Development Laboratories
    [*AMDEL*]. Bulletin [*A publication*]   (APTA)
Aust Miner Dev Lab Rep ... Australian Mineral Development Laboratories
    [*AMDEL*]. Report [*A publication*]   (APTA)
Aust Miner Ind ... Australian Mineral Industry [*A publication*]
Aust Miner Ind Annu Rev ... Australian Mineral Industry. Annual Review [*A
    publication*]
Aust Miner Ind Q ... Australian Mineral Industry. Quarterly [*A publication*]
Aust Miner Ind Rev ... Australian Mineral Industry. Review [*A
    publication*]   (APTA)
Aust Miner Ind Stat ... Australian Mineral Industry. Statistics [*A
    publication*]   (APTA)
Aust Min Ind ... Australian Mineral Industry [*A publication*]
Aust Min Ind Stat ... Australian Mineral Industry. Statistics [*A
    publication*]   (APTA)
Aust Mining ... Australian Mining [*A publication*]   (APTA)
Aust Min Pet Law J ... Australian Mining and Petroleum Law Journal [*A
    publication*]
Aust Min Stand ... Australian Mining Standard [*A publication*]   (APTA)
Aust Min Year Book ... Australian Mining Year Book [*A publication*]
Aust Mod Rail ... Australian Model Railway Magazine [*A publication*]
Aust Mon Mag ... Australian Monthly Magazine [*A publication*]
Aust Mon Weath Rep ... Australian Monthly Weather Report and
    Meteorological Abstract [*A publication*]   (APTA)
Aust Mot Cycle News ... Australian Motor Cycle News [*A
    publication*]   (APTA)
Aust Motorist ... Australian Motorist [*A publication*]   (APTA)
Aust Motor Sports ... Australian Motor Sports [*A publication*]   (APTA)
Aust Munic J ... Australian Municipal Journal [*A publication*]   (APTA)
Aust Museum Mag ... Australian Museum. Magazine [*A publication*]   (APTA)
Aust Musical News & D ... Australian Musical News and Musical Digest [*A
    publication*]
Aust Mus Mag ... Australian Museum. Magazine [*A publication*]
Aust Mus Rec ... Australian Museum. Records [*A publication*]
Aust Mus (Syd) Mem ... Australian Museum (Sydney). Memoir [*A
    publication*]
Aust Mus (Sydney) Mem ... Australian Museum (Sydney). Memoirs [*A
    publication*]
Austn Amer ... Austin American-Statesman [*A publication*]
Aust Nat..... Australian Naturalist [*A publication*]   (APTA)
Aust Nat Bibliogr ... Australian National Bibliography [*A
    publication*]   (APTA)
Aust Nat Clay ... Australian National Clay [*A publication*]   (APTA)
Aust Nat H ... Australian Natural History [*A publication*]   (APTA)
Aust Nat Hist ... Australian Natural History [*A publication*]
Aust Natl Meas Lab Tech Pap ... Australia. National Measurement
    Laboratory. Technical Paper [*A publication*]
Aust Natl Univ Res Sch Phys Sci Dep Eng Phys Publ ... Australian National
    University. Research School of Physical Sciences.
    Department of Engineering Physics. Publication [*A
    publication*]   (APTA)
Aust Natn Clay ... Australian National Clay [*A publication*]   (APTA)
Aust Natn Rev ... Australian National Review [*A publication*]
Aust Nat Univ News ... Australian National University. News [*A
    publication*]   (APTA)

Aust Nat Univ Res Sch Pacif Stud Geog Pub ... Australian National University. Research School of Pacific Studies. Department of Geography. Publication [*A publication*]   (APTA)
Aust Natural History ... Australian Natural History [*A publication*]   (APTA)
Aust Natur His ... Australian Natural History [*A publication*]   (APTA)
Aust Natur Hist ... Australian Natural History [*A publication*]
Aust Neigh ... Australia's Neighbours [*A publication*]   (APTA)
Aust Neighb ... Australia's Neighbours [*A publication*]   (APTA)
Aust Neighbours ... Australia's Neighbours [*A publication*]
Aust News ... Austral News [*A publication*]   (APTA)
Aust News (Johannesburg) ... Austral News (Johannesburg) [*A publication*]   (APTA)
Aust News (Montreal) ... Austral News (Montreal) [*A publication*]   (APTA)
Aust News R ... Australian News Review [*A publication*]   (APTA)
Aust News (Singapore) ... Austral News (Singapore) [*A publication*]   (APTA)
Aust News (Wellington) ... Austral News (Wellington) [*A publication*]   (APTA)
Aust New Zeal Environ Rep ... Australian and New Zealand Environmental Report [*A publication*]   (APTA)
Aust Now ... Australia Now [*A publication*]   (APTA)
Aust Nucl Sci Technol Organ Rep ... Australian Nuclear Science and Technology Organisation. Report [*A publication*]
Aust Numismatic J ... Australian Numismatic Journal [*A publication*]   (APTA)
Aust Numismatic Soc Rep ... Australian Numismatic Society. Report [*A publication*]   (APTA)
Aust Num J ... Australian Numismatic Journal [*A publication*]   (APTA)
Aust Num Meteor Res Centr (Melb) Ann Rep ... Australian Numerical Meteorology Research Centre (Melbourne). Annual Report [*A publication*]   (APTA)
Aust Num Soc Rept ... Australian Numismatic Society. Report [*A publication*]   (APTA)
Aust Nurses J ... Australian Nurses' Journal [*A publication*]   (APTA)
Aust Nurses J (Melbourne) ... Australian Nurses' Journal (Melbourne) [*A publication*]
Aust NZ Assoc Adv Sci Congr Pap ... Australian and New Zealand Association for the Advancement of Science. Congress. Papers [*A publication*]   (APTA)
Aust NZ Conf Geomech Proc ... Australian-New Zealand Conference on Geomechanics. Proceedings [*A publication*]
Aust & NZ Environ Rep ... Australian and New Zealand Environmental Report [*A publication*]   (APTA)
Aust & NZ General Practitioner ... Australian and New Zealand General Practitioner [*A publication*]   (APTA)
Aust NZ Gen Practnr ... Australian and New Zealand General Practitioner [*A publication*]   (APTA)
Aust NZ J C ... Australian and New Zealand Journal of Criminology [*A publication*]
Aust & NZJ Crim ... Australian and New Zealand Journal of Criminology [*A publication*]
Aust & NZ J Criminol ... Australian and New Zealand Journal of Criminology [*A publication*]   (APTA)
Aust NZ J Dev Disabil ... Australian and New Zealand Journal of Developmental Disabilities [*A publication*]
Aust NZ Jl Criminol ... Australian and New Zealand Journal of Criminology [*A publication*]
Aust NZ Jl Sociol ... Australian and New Zealand Journal of Sociology [*A publication*]
Aust NZ Jl Surgery ... Australian and New Zealand Journal of Surgery [*A publication*]
Aust NZ J M ... Australian and New Zealand Journal of Medicine [*A publication*]
Aust & NZ J Med ... Australian and New Zealand Journal of Medicine [*A publication*]   (APTA)
Aust NZ J Med ... Australian and New Zealand Journal of Medicine [*A publication*]
Aust NZ J Med Suppl ... Australian and New Zealand Journal of Medicine. Supplement [*A publication*]   (APTA)
Aust NZ J O ... Australian and New Zealand Journal of Obstetrics and Gynaecology [*A publication*]
Aust NZ J Obstet Gynaec ... Australian and New Zealand Journal of Obstetrics and Gynaecology [*A publication*]   (APTA)
Aust NZ J Obstet Gynaecol ... Australian and New Zealand Journal of Obstetrics and Gynaecology [*A publication*]
Aust & NZ J Obstet & Gynaecol ... Australian and New Zealand Journal of Obstetrics and Gynaecology [*A publication*]   (APTA)
Aust NZ J Obstet Gynaecol (Suppl) ... Australian and New Zealand Journal of Obstetrics and Gynaecology (Supplement) [*A publication*]
Aust NZ J Ophthalmol ... Australian and New Zealand Journal of Ophthalmology [*A publication*]
Aust NZ J P ... Australian and New Zealand Journal of Psychiatry [*A publication*]
Aust NZ J Psychiat ... Australian and New Zealand Journal of Psychiatry [*A publication*]
Aust NZ J Psychiatry ... Australian and New Zealand Journal of Psychiatry [*A publication*]
Aust & NZ J Psychiatry ... Australian and New Zealand Journal of Psychiatry [*A publication*]   (APTA)
Aust NZ J S ... Australian and New Zealand Journal of Surgery [*A publication*]

Aust & NZ J Soc ... Australian and New Zealand Journal of Sociology [*A publication*]   (APTA)
Aust NZ J Soc ... Australian and New Zealand Journal of Sociology [*A publication*]   (APTA)
Aust & NZ J Sociol ... Australian and New Zealand Journal of Sociology [*A publication*]   (APTA)
Aust NZ J Sociol ... Australian and New Zealand Journal of Sociology [*A publication*]
Aust NZ J Surg ... Australian and New Zealand Journal of Surgery [*A publication*]
Aust & NZ J Surgery ... Australian and New Zealand Journal of Surgery [*A publication*]   (APTA)
Aust NZ Rose A ... Australian and New Zealand Rose Annual [*A publication*]   (APTA)
Aust NZ Soc ... Australian and New Zealand Journal of Sociology [*A publication*]
Aust & NZ W ... Australian and New Zealand Weekly [*A publication*]   (APTA)
Aust NZ W ... Australian and New Zealand Weekly [*A publication*]   (APTA)
Aust OCCA Proc News ... Australian OCCA [*Oil and Colour Chemists Association*] Proceedings and News [*A publication*]   (APTA)
Aust Occupational Ther J ... Australian Occupational Therapy Journal [*A publication*]   (APTA)
Aust Occup Ther J ... Australian Occupational Therapy Journal [*A publication*]   (APTA)
Aust Off J Pat ... Australian Official Journal of Patents [*A publication*]
Aust Off J Pat ... Australian Official Journal of Patents, Trade Marks, and Designs [*A publication*]   (APTA)
Aust Off J Pat Trade Marks Des Pat Abr Suppl ... Australian Official Journal of Patents, Trade Marks, and Designs. Patent Abridgments Supplement [*A publication*]
Aust Oil Colour Chem Assoc Proc News ... Australian Oil and Colour Chemists Association. Proceedings and News [*A publication*]   (APTA)
Aust Oil Gas J ... Australasian Oil and Gas Journal [*A publication*]   (APTA)
Aust Oil Seed Gr ... Australian Oil Seed Grower [*A publication*]   (APTA)
Aust Orchid Rev ... Australian Orchid Review [*A publication*]   (APTA)
Aust Orthod J ... Australian Orthodontic Journal [*A publication*]
Aust Out .... Australian Outlook [*A publication*]   (APTA)
Aust Outdoors ... Australian Outdoors [*A publication*]
Aust Outl ... Australian Outlook [*A publication*]   (APTA)
Aust Outloo ... Australian Outlook [*A publication*]
Aust Outlook ... Australian Outlook [*A publication*]
Aust & Pac Book Prices Curr ... Australian and Pacific Book Prices Current [*A publication*]   (APTA)
Aust Packaging ... Australian Packaging [*A publication*]   (APTA)
Aust Paedia ... Australian Paediatric Journal [*A publication*]
Aust Paediat J ... Australian Paediatric Journal [*A publication*]   (APTA)
Aust Paediatric J ... Australian Paediatric Journal [*A publication*]   (APTA)
Aust Paediatr J ... Australian Paediatric Journal [*A publication*]
Aust Paint J ... Australian Paint Journal [*A publication*]
Aust Paint J Aust Finish Rev ... Australian Paint Journal. Incorporating the Australian Finishing Review [*A publication*]
Aust Paint J Suppl ... Australian Paint Journal. Supplement [*A publication*]
Aust Parks ... Australian Parks [*Later, Australian Parks and Recreation*] [*A publication*]
Aust Parks ... Australian Parks and Recreation [*A publication*]   (APTA)
Aust Parks Recreat ... Australian Parks and Recreation [*A publication*]
Aust Parks & Recreat ... Australian Parks and Recreation [*A publication*]   (APTA)
Aust Parl Deb House Rep ... Australia. House of Representatives. Parliamentary Debates [*A publication*]   (APTA)
Aust Parl Deb Senate ... Australia. Parliament. Senate. Parliamentary Debates [*A publication*]   (APTA)
Aust Parl H of R Parl Deb ... Australia. Parliament. House of Representatives. Parliamentary Debates [*A publication*]   (APTA)
Aust Parl Paper ... Australian Parliamentary Paper [*A publication*]
Aust Parl Sen Parl Deb ... Australia. Parliament. Senate. Parliamentary Debates [*A publication*]   (APTA)
Aust Past ... Australian Pastoralist [*A publication*]   (APTA)
Aust Pat Doc ... Australian (Patent Document) [*A publication*]   (APTA)
Aust Pat Off Aust Off J Pat ... Australia. Patent Office. Australian Official Journal of Patents [*A publication*]
Aust Pat Off Aust Off J Pat Trade Marks Des ... Australia. Patent Office. Australian Official Journal of Patents, Trade Marks, and Designs [*A publication*]   (APTA)
Aust Pet Explor Assoc J ... Australian Petroleum Exploration Association. Journal [*A publication*]   (APTA)
Aust Phot ... Australian Photography [*A publication*]
Aust Photogr J ... Australian Photographic Journal [*A publication*]   (APTA)
Aust Phys ... Australian Physicist [*A publication*]
Aust Physicist ... Australian Physicist [*A publication*]   (APTA)
Aust Physiol Pharmacol Soc Proc ... Australian Physiological and Pharmacological Society. Proceedings [*A publication*]   (APTA)
Aust Pl .... Australian Plants [*A publication*]
Aust Plan Inst J ... Australian Planning Institute. Journal [*A publication*]   (APTA)
Aust Plann Inst J ... Australian Planning Institute. Journal [*A publication*]   (APTA)
Aust Plant Dis Rec ... Australian Plant Disease Recorder [*A publication*]

Aust Plant Introd Rev ... Australian Plant Introduction Review [*A publication*] (APTA)
Aust Plant Pathol Soc Newsl ... Australian Plant Pathology Society. Newsletter [*A publication*] (APTA)
Aust Plants ... Australian Plants [*A publication*]
Aust Plas Rubb J ... Australian Plastics and Rubber Journal [*A publication*] (APTA)
Aust Plast .. Australian Plastics [*A publication*]
Aust Plast All Trades Rev ... Australian Plastics and Allied Trades Review [*A publication*] (APTA)
Aust Plastics J ... Australian Plastics Journal [*A publication*] (APTA)
Aust Plastics & Rubber J ... Australian Plastics and Rubber Journal [*A publication*] (APTA)
Aust Plastics Yrbk ... Australian Plastics Year Book [*A publication*] (APTA)
Aust Plast J ... Australian Plastics Journal [*A publication*] (APTA)
Aust Plast Rubb ... Australian Plastics and Rubber [*A publication*]
Aust Plast Rubber ... Australian Plastics and Rubber [*A publication*]
Aust Plast & Rubber ... Australian Plastics and Rubber [*A publication*] (APTA)
Aust Plast & Rubber Buy Guide ... Australian Plastics and Rubber Buyers Guide [*A publication*] (APTA)
Aust Plast Rubber J ... Australian Plastics and Rubber Journal [*A publication*]
Aust Plast Yb ... Australian Plastics Year Book [*A publication*] (APTA)
Aust Pl Dis Rec ... Australian Plant Disease Recorder [*A publication*] (APTA)
Aust Police J ... Australian Police Journal [*A publication*] (APTA)
Aust Pol J .. Australian Police Journal [*A publication*]
Aust Pop Phot ... Australian Popular Photography [*A publication*]
Aust Post Office Res Lab Rep ... Australian Post Office Research Laboratories. Report [*A publication*] (APTA)
Aust Power Eng ... Australian Power Engineering [*A publication*] (APTA)
Aust Pr....... Australian Printer [*A publication*] (APTA)
Aust Presb Life ... Australian Presbyterian Life [*A publication*]
Aust Pre-School Assn Biennial Conf ... Australian Pre-School Association. Biennial Conference [*A publication*] (APTA)
Aust Pre-School Q ... Australian Pre-School Quarterly [*A publication*] (APTA)
Aust Pre-School Quart ... Australian Pre-School Quarterly [*A publication*] (APTA)
Aust Presch Q ... Australian Pre-School Quarterly [*A publication*]
Aust Pre-Sch Quart ... Australian Pre-School Quarterly [*A publication*] (APTA)
Aust Press Statement ... Australia. Government Public Relations Office. Ministerial Press Statements [*A publication*] (APTA)
Aust Printer ... Australasian Printer [*A publication*] (APTA)
Aust Process Eng ... Australian Process Engineering [*A publication*]
Aust Processs Engng ... Australian Process Engineering [*A publication*] (APTA)
Aust Prod... Australia. Commonwealth Bureau of Census and Statistics. Monthly Bulletin of Production Statistics [*A publication*] (APTA)
Aust Prod Action ... Australian Productivity Action [*A publication*]
Aust Psych ... Australian Psychologist [*A publication*] (APTA)
Aust Psychl ... Australian Psychologist [*A publication*]
Aust Psychol ... Australian Psychologist [*A publication*]
Aust Public Aff Inf Serv ... Australian Public Affairs Information Service [*A publication*]
Aust Publ Libr Issues ... Australian Public Library Issues [*A publication*]
Aust Pulp Pap Ind Tech Assoc Proc ... Australian Pulp and Paper Industry Technical Association. Proceedings [*A publication*] (APTA)
Aust Pump J ... Australian Pump Journal [*A publication*] (APTA)
Aust Pwr Engng ... Australian Power Engineering [*A publication*] (APTA)
Aust Q........ Australian Quarterly [*A publication*]
Aust Qly..... Australian Quarterly [*A publication*] (APTA)
Aust Quart ... Australian Quarterly [*A publication*]
AUSTR...... Australia
Aust R .... Australian Review [*A publication*]
Aus Trade .. Austrian Trade News [*A publication*]
Aust Radiat Lab Tech Rep ARL/TR ... Australian Radiation Laboratory. Technical Report ARL/TR [*A publication*] (APTA)
Aust Radiat Lab Tech Rep Ser ARL/TR ... Australian Radiation Laboratory. Technical Report Series ARL/TR [*A publication*] (APTA)
Aust Radiat Rec ... Australian Radiation Records [*A publication*] (APTA)
Aust Radio ... Australasian Radiology [*A publication*] (APTA)
Aust Radiol ... Australasian Radiology [*A publication*]
Aust Railway Hist Soc Bul ... Australian Railway Historical Society. Bulletin [*A publication*] (APTA)
AUSTRAL ... Australasian (ROG)
AUSTRAL ... Australia
Australas Ann Med ... Australasian Annals of Medicine [*A publication*]
Australas Baker ... Australasian Baker and Millers' Journal [*A publication*] (APTA)
Australas Baker Millers J ... Australasian Baker and Millers' Journal [*A publication*]
Australas Beekpr ... Australasian Beekeeper [*A publication*] (APTA)
Australas Bull Med Phys Biophy ... Australasian Bulletin of Medical Physics and Biophysics [*A publication*] (APTA)
Australas Bull Med Phys Biophys ... Australasian Bulletin of Medical Physics and Biophysics [*A publication*]
Australas Cath Rec ... Australasian Catholic Record [*A publication*]

Australas Chem Metall ... Australasian Chemist and Metallurgist [*A publication*] (APTA)
Australas Conf Heat Mass Transfer Proc ... Australasian Conference on Heat and Mass Transfer. Proceedings [*A publication*] (APTA)
Australas Corros ... Australasian Corrosion Engineering [*A publication*] (APTA)
Australas Corros Assoc Prepr Pap Annu Conf ... Australasian Corrosion Association. Preprinted Papers of the Annual Conference [*A publication*] (APTA)
Australas Corros Assoc Tech Pap Annual Conf ... Australasian Corrosion Association. Technical Paper of the Annual Conference [*A publication*] (APTA)
Australas Corros Eng ... Australasian Corrosion Engineering [*A publication*]
Australas Corros Engng ... Australasian Corrosion Engineering [*A publication*] (APTA)
Australas Eng ... Australasian Engineer [*A publication*]
Australas Engng Mach ... Australasian Engineering and Machinery [*A publication*] (APTA)
Australas Engr ... Australasian Engineer [*A publication*] (APTA)
Australas Environ ... Australasian Environment [*A publication*] (APTA)
Australas Hardware Machinery ... Australasian Hardware and Machinery [*A publication*] (APTA)
Australas Herb News ... Australasian Herbarium News [*A publication*]
Australasian Ann Med ... Australasian Annals of Medicine [*A publication*]
Australasian As Rp ... Australasian Association for the Advancement of Science. Reports [*A publication*]
Australasian Bk News ... Australasian Book News and Library Journal [*A publication*] (APTA)
Australas IMM Conf ... Australasian Institute of Mining and Metallurgy. Conference [*A publication*] (APTA)
Australas Inst Met Annu Conf ... Australasian Institute of Metals. Annual Conference [*A publication*] (APTA)
Australas Inst Met J ... Australasian Institute of Metals. Journal [*A publication*] (APTA)
Australas Inst Met Met Congr ... Australasian Institute of Metals. Metals Congress [*A publication*] (APTA)
Australas Inst Mining Met Proc ... Australasian Institute of Mining and Metallurgy. Proceedings [*A publication*]
Australas Inst Min Metall Conf ... Australasian Institute of Mining and Metallurgy. Conference [*A publication*] (APTA)
Australas Inst Min Metall Conf Ser ... Australasian Institute of Mining and Metallurgy. Conference Series [*A publication*]
Australas Inst Min Metall Monogr Ser ... Australasian Institute of Mining and Metallurgy. Monograph Series [*A publication*]
Australas Inst Min Metall Proc ... Australasian Institute of Mining and Metallurgy. Proceedings [*A publication*]
Australas Inst Min Metall Symp Ser ... Australasian Institute of Mining and Metallurgy. Symposia Series [*A publication*] (APTA)
Australas Insur Banking Rec ... Australasian Insurance and Banking Record [*A publication*]
Australas Insur J ... Australasian Insurance Journal [*A publication*]
Australas Irrig ... Australasian Irrigator and Pasture Improver [*A publication*] (APTA)
Australas J Dermatol ... Australasian Journal of Dermatology [*A publication*]
Australas J Med Technol ... Australasian Journal of Medical Technology [*A publication*] (APTA)
Australas J Phar ... Australasian Journal of Pharmacy [*A publication*] (APTA)
Australas J Pharm ... Australasian Journal of Pharmacy [*A publication*]
Australas J Pharm Sci Suppl ... Australasian Journal of Pharmacy. Science Supplement [*A publication*]
Australas Leath Footwear Rev ... Australasian Leather and Footwear Review [*A publication*] (APTA)
Australas Leath Trades Rev ... Australasian Leather Trades Review [*A publication*] (APTA)
Australas Manuf ... Australasian Manufacturer [*A publication*]
Australas Manuf Eng ... Australasian Manufacturing Engineer [*A publication*]
Australas Med Congr ... Australasian Medical Congress. Transactions [*A publication*] (APTA)
Australas Med Gaz ... Australasian Medical Gazette [*A publication*] (APTA)
Australas Mfr ... Australasian Manufacturer [*A publication*] (APTA)
Australas Mfr Plast Rev ... Australasian Manufacturer. Plastics Review [*A publication*] (APTA)
Australas Nurses J ... Australasian Nurses Journal [*A publication*]
Australas Nurs J (Port Adelaide) ... Australasian Nursing Journal (Port Adelaide) [*A publication*]
Australas Oil Gas J ... Australasian Oil and Gas Journal [*A publication*] (APTA)
Australas Oil & Gas Rev ... Australasian Oil and Gas Review [*A publication*] (APTA)
Australas Oil Gas Rev ... Australasian Oil and Gas Review [*A publication*]
Australas Past Rev ... Australasian Pastoralists' Review [*A publication*] (APTA)
Australas Pharm Notes News ... Australasian Pharmaceutical Notes and News [*A publication*] (APTA)
Australas Photogr Rev ... Australasian Photographic Review [*A publication*] (APTA)
Australas Photo Rev ... Australasian Photo Review [*A publication*] (APTA)
Australas Photo Review ... Australasian Photo Review [*A publication*] (APTA)

Australas Phys and Eng Sci Med ... Australasian Physical and Engineering Sciences in Medicine [*A publication*]
Australas Phys Eng Sci Med ... Australasian Physical and Engineering Sciences in Medicine [*A publication*]
Australas Phys Sci Med ... Australasian Physical Sciences in Medicine [*Later, Australasian Physical and Engineering Sciences in Medicine*] [*A publication*]
Australas Plant Pathol ... APP. Australasian Plant Pathology [*A publication*] (APTA)
Australas Plat Finish ... Australasian Plating and Finishing [*A publication*] (APTA)
Australas Print ... Australasian Printer [*A publication*] (APTA)
Australas Printer ... Australasian Printer [*A publication*] (APTA)
Australas Radiol ... Australasian Radiology [*A publication*]
Australas Schoolmaster ... Australasian Schoolmaster and Literary Review [*A publication*]
Australas Trade Rev ... Australasian Trade Review and Manufacturers Journal [*A publication*] (APTA)
Australas Typogr J ... Australasian Typographical Journal [*A publication*] (APTA)
Austral Comput J ... Australian Computer Journal [*A publication*]
Austral Econ Hist R ... Australian Economic History Review [*A publication*] (APTA)
Austral Econ Pap ... Australian Economic Papers [*A publication*] (APTA)
Austral Fam Physician ... Australian Family Physician [*A publication*]
Austral For Aff Rec ... Australian Foreign Affairs Record [*A publication*]
Australian Acad and Res Lib ... Australian Academic and Research Libraries [*A publication*] (APTA)
Australian Econ Hist R ... Australian Economic History Review [*A publication*]
Australian Econ Pas ... Australian Economic Papers [*A publication*]
Australian Econ R ... Australian Economic Review [*A publication*]
Australian For Affairs Rec ... Australian Foreign Affairs Record [*A publication*]
Australian For J ... Australian Forestry Journal [*A publication*]
Australian Garden History Soc Jnl ... Australian Garden History Society. Journal [*A publication*]
Australian Inst Libn Proc ... Australian Institute of Librarians. Proceedings [*A publication*] (APTA)
Australian J Mgt ... Australian Journal of Management [*A publication*]
Australian J Mus Ed ... Australian Journal of Music Education [*A publication*]
Australian J Psychol ... Australian Journal of Psychology [*A publication*]
Australian J Statis ... Australian Journal of Statistics [*A publication*]
Australian Lib J ... Australian Library Journal [*A publication*]
Australian Math Teacher ... Australian Mathematics Teacher [*A publication*]
Australian Mineral Industry Q ... Australian Mineral Industry. Quarterly [*A publication*]
Australian M J ... Australian Medical Journal [*A publication*]
Australian and New Zealand Assoc Adv Sci Rept ... Australian and New Zealand Association for the Advancement of Science. Report [*A publication*]
Australian New Zeal J Obstet Gynaecol ... Australian and New Zealand Journal of Obstetrics and Gynaecology [*A publication*]
Australian New Zeal J Surg ... Australian and New Zealand Journal of Surgery [*A publication*]
Australian and NZ J Sociol ... Australian and New Zealand Journal of Sociology [*A publication*]
Australian Offic J Pat Pat Abridgments Suppl ... Australian Official Journal of Patents, Trade Marks, and Designs. Patent Abridgments Supplement [*A publication*]
Australian Soc Explor Geophys Bull ... Australian Society of Exploration Geophysicists. Bulletin [*A publication*]
AUSTRALIS ... Australian Technical, Research, and Library Information Service [*CSIRO*]
Austral J Agr Econ ... Australian Journal of Agricultural Economics [*A publication*] (APTA)
Austral J Agric Econ ... Australian Journal of Agricultural Economics [*A publication*]
Austral J Biol Sci ... Australian Journal of Biological Sciences [*A publication*]
Austral J Bot ... Australian Journal of Botany [*A publication*]
Austral J Chem ... Australian Journal of Chemistry [*A publication*]
Austral J High Educ ... Australian Journal of Higher Education [*A publication*] (APTA)
Austral J Hum Commun Dis ... Australian Journal of Human Communication Disorders [*A publication*]
Austral J Phys ... Australian Journal of Physics [*A publication*]
Austral J Polit Hist ... Australian Journal of Politics and History [*A publication*]
Austral J Soc Issues ... Australian Journal of Social Issues [*A publication*]
Austral J Statist ... Australian Journal of Statistics [*A publication*] (APTA)
Austral M .. Australian Mining [*A publication*] (APTA)
Austral Math Soc Gaz ... Australian Mathematical Society. Gazette [*A publication*]
Austral Med J ... Australian Medical Journal [*A publication*]
Austral N ... Australia Now [*A publication*]
Austral N Zealand J Sociol ... Australian and New Zealand Journal of Sociology [*A publication*] (APTA)
Austral O ... Australian Outlook [*A publication*]

Austral Off J Pat ... Australian Official Journal of Patents [*A publication*] (APTA)
Austral Outlook ... Australian Outlook [*A publication*]
Austral Paint J ... Australian Paint Journal [*A publication*]
Austral Pkg ... Australian Packaging [*A publication*]
Austral Plan Inst J ... Australian Planning Institute. Journal [*A publication*]
Austral Publ Aff Inform Serv ... Australian Public Affairs Information Service [*Information service or system*] [*A publication*] (APTA)
Austral Quart ... Australian Quarterly [*A publication*]
Austral Sci Index ... Australian Science Index [*Information service or system*] [*A publication*]
Austral Teacher Deaf ... Australian Teacher of the Deaf [*A publication*]
Austr BC .... Australian Bankruptcy Cases [*A publication*] (DLA)
Austr Beek ... Australasian Beekeeper [*A publication*] (APTA)
Austr Brew Wi J ... Australian Brewing and Wine Journal [*A publication*] (APTA)
Austr Bus LR ... Australian Business Law Review [*A publication*]
Austr Chem Abstr ... Australian Chemical Abstracts [*A publication*] (APTA)
Austr Chem Inst J Pr ... Australian Chemical Institute. Journal and Proceedings [*A publication*] (APTA)
Austr Chem Met ... Australasian Chemist and Metallurgist [*A publication*] (APTA)
Austr Civ Eng Constr ... Australian Civil Engineering and Construction [*A publication*] (APTA)
Austr CLR ... Australia. Commonwealth Law Reports [*A publication*] (DLA)
Austr Cott Grow ... Australian Cotton Grower [*A publication*] (APTA)
Austr Cott Grow Farm Dairym ... Australian Cotton Grower, Farmer, and Dairyman [*A publication*] (APTA)
Austr Dent J ... Australian Dental Journal [*A publication*] (APTA)
Austr Dent Mirr ... Australian Dental Mirror [*A publication*] (APTA)
Aust Rd Index ... Australian Road Index [*A publication*]
Aust Rd Res ... Australian Road Research [*A publication*]
Aust Rd Res Progress ... Australian Road Research in Progress [*A publication*]
Aust Rd Res Rep ... Australian Road Research. Reports [*A publication*]
AUSTRE ... Australian Scientific and Technological Reports [*A publication*] (APTA)
AUSTRE on COM ... Australian Scientific and Technological Reports on COM [*A publication*] (APTA)
Aust Red Cross Q ... Australian Red Cross Quarterly [*A publication*] (APTA)
Aust Refrig Air Cond & Heat ... Australian Refrigeration, Air Conditioning, and Heating [*A publication*] (APTA)
Aust Refrig Air Cond Heat ... Australian Refrigeration, Air Conditioning, and Heating [*A publication*]
Aust Refrig Air Condit ... Australian Refrigeration, Air Conditioning, and Heating [*A publication*]
Aust Refrig Air Condit Heat ... Australian Refrigeration, Air Conditioning, and Heating [*A publication*]
Aust Refrig Air Con Heat ... Australian Refrigeration, Air Conditioning, and Heating [*A publication*]
Aust Refrig Rev ... Australian Refrigeration Review [*A publication*] (APTA)
Austr Eng ... Australasian Engineer [*A publication*] (APTA)
Aust Rep .... Australian Reporter [*A publication*] (APTA)
Aust Represent Basins Program Rep Ser Rep ... Australian Representative Basins Program Report. Series Report [*A publication*]
Aust Reptile Park Rec ... Australian Reptile Park. Records [*A publication*] (APTA)
Austr For .... Australian Forestry [*A publication*] (APTA)
Austr For J ... Australian Forestry Journal [*A publication*] (APTA)
Austr Geogr ... Australian Geographer [*A publication*] (APTA)
Austr Geogr Soc Rep ... Australian Geographical Society. Report [*A publication*] (APTA)
Austr Herb News ... Australasian Herbarium News [*A publication*] (APTA)
Aust Rhodes R ... Australian Rhodes Review [*A publication*]
Austria Geol Bundesanst Verh ... Austria. Geologische Bundesanstalt. Verhandlungen [*A publication*]
Austria Geol Bunesanst Jahrb ... Austria. Geologische Bundesanstalt. Jahrbuch [*A publication*]
Austria Mach Steel ... Austria. Machinery and Steel [*A publication*]
Austrian Ital Yugosl Chem Eng Conf Proc ... Austrian-Italian-Yugoslav Chemical Engineering Conference. Proceedings [*A publication*]
Austrian J Oncol ... Austrian Journal of Oncology [*A publication*]
Austria Zentralanst Meteorol Geodynamik Arb ... Austria. Zentralanstalt fuer Meteorologie und Geodynamik. Arbeiten [*A publication*]
Austr Inst Aborig Stud Newsletter ... Australian Institute of Aboriginal Studies. Newsletter [*A publication*]
Austr J Agric Res ... Australian Journal of Agricultural Research [*A publication*] (APTA)
Austr J Appl Sci ... Australian Journal of Applied Science [*A publication*] (APTA)
Austr J Biol Sci ... Australian Journal of Biological Sciences [*A publication*] (APTA)
Austr J Bot ... Australian Journal of Botany [*A publication*] (APTA)
Austr J Chem ... Australian Journal of Chemistry [*A publication*] (APTA)
Austr J Dent ... Australian Journal of Dentistry [*A publication*] (APTA)
Austr J Derm ... Australian [*later, Australasian*] Journal of Dermatology [*A publication*]
Austr J Exp Biol Med Sci ... Australian Journal of Experimental Biology and Medical Science [*A publication*] (APTA)

Austr J Instr Techn ... Australian Journal of Instrument Technology [*A publication*]   (APTA)
Austr J Mar Freshwat Res ... Australian Journal of Marine and Freshwater Research [*A publication*]   (APTA)
Austr J Pharm ... Australian Journal of Pharmacy [*A publication*]   (APTA)
Austr J Phys ... Australian Journal of Physics [*A publication*]   (APTA)
Austr J Psychol ... Australian Journal of Psychology [*A publication*]   (APTA)
Austr J Sci ... Australian Journal of Science [*A publication*]   (APTA)
Austr J St... Australian Journal of Statistics [*A publication*]
Austr Jur.... Australian Jurist [*A publication*]
Austr J Zool ... Australian Journal of Zoology [*A publication*]   (APTA)
Austr Leath J ... Australian Leather Journal [*A publication*]   (APTA)
Austrl Fin... Australian Financial Review [*A publication*]
Austr LJ..... Australian Law Journal [*A publication*]
Austr LT .... Australian Law Times [*A publication*]
Austr Mach Prod Eng ... Australian Machinery and Production Engineering [*A publication*]   (APTA)
Austr Mech Eng ... Australian Mechanical Engineering [*A publication*]   (APTA)
Austr Med Gaz ... Australasian Medical Gazette [*A publication*]   (APTA)
Austr Med J ... Australian Medical Journal [*A publication*]   (APTA)
Austr Min Ind Rev ... Australian Mineral Industry. Review [*A publication*]   (APTA)
Austr Min Ind Stat ... Australian Mineral Industry. Statistics [*A publication*]   (APTA)
Austr Mth Weath Rep ... Australian Monthly Weather Report [*A publication*]   (APTA)
Austr Mus Mag ... Australian Museum. Magazine [*A publication*]   (APTA)
Austr Nat... Australian Naturalist [*A publication*]   (APTA)
Austr Neighb ... Australia's Neighbours [*A publication*]   (APTA)
Austr NZ Gen Pract ... Australian and New Zealand General Practitioner [*A publication*]   (APTA)
Austr NZ J Obst Gynaec ... Australian and New Zealand Journal of Obstetrics and Gynaecology [*A publication*]   (APTA)
Austr NZ J Surg ... Australian and New Zealand Journal of Surgery [*A publication*]   (APTA)
Aust Road Haulage J ... Australian Road Haulage Journal [*A publication*]   (APTA)
Aust Road Res ... Australian Road Research [*A publication*]
Aust Road Res Bd Bull ... Australian Road Research Board. Bulletin [*A publication*]   (APTA)
Aust Road Res Board ARR Rep ... Australian Road Research Board. ARR Reports [*A publication*]   (APTA)
Aust Road Res Board Bull ... Australian Road Research Board. Bulletin [*A publication*]
Aust Road Res Board Conf ... Australian Road Research Board. Conference [*A publication*]   (APTA)
Aust Road Res Board Proc Conf ... Australian Road Research Board. Proceedings of the Conference [*A publication*]   (APTA)
Aust Road Res Bp Spec Rep ... Australian Road Research Board. Special Report [*A publication*]   (APTA)
Aust Road Research ... Australian Road Research [*A publication*]   (APTA)
Austr Off J Pat ... Australian Official Journal of Patents, Trade Marks, and Designs [*A publication*]   (APTA)
Aust Rose A ... Australian Rose Annual [*A publication*]   (APTA)
Aust Rose Annu ... Australian Rose Annual [*A publication*]   (APTA)
Austr Past ... Australian Pastoralist [*A publication*]   (APTA)
Austr Past Rev ... Australasian Pastoralists' Review [*A publication*]   (APTA)
Austr Photogr J ... Australian Photographic Journal [*A publication*]   (APTA)
Austr Plast ... Australian Plastics [*A publication*]   (APTA)
Austr Plast All Trade Rev ... Australian Plastics and Allied Trades Review [*A publication*]   (APTA)
Austr Plast Rubb J ... Australian Plastics and Rubber Journal [*A publication*]   (APTA)
Austr Pl Dis Rec ... Australian Plant Disease Recorder [*A publication*]   (APTA)
Austr Q ...... Australian Quarterly [*A publication*]   (APTA)
Austr Rad Rec ... Australian Radiation Records [*A publication*]   (APTA)
Austr Sci Abstr ... Australian Science Abstracts [*A publication*]   (APTA)
Austr Sci Ind ... Australian Science Index [*Information service or system*] [*A publication*]   (APTA)
Austr Stand Q ... Australian Standards Quarterly [*A publication*]   (APTA)
Austr Statesm Min Stand ... Australian Statesman and Mining Standard [*A publication*]   (APTA)
Austr Sug J ... Australian Sugar Journal [*A publication*]   (APTA)
Austr Surv ... Australian Surveyor [*A publication*]   (APTA)
Austr Tax... Australian Tax Decisions [*A publication*]   (DLA)
Austr Tax D ... Australian Tax Decisions [*A publication*]
Austr Tax R ... Australian Tax Review [*A publication*]
Austr Terr ... Australian Territories [*A publication*]   (APTA)
Austr Timb J ... Australian Timber Journal [*A publication*]   (APTA)
Austr Tob J ... Australian Tobacco Journal [*A publication*]   (APTA)
Aust Rubber ... Australian Rubber [*A publication*]   (APTA)
Austr Vet J ... Australian Veterinary Journal [*A publication*]   (APTA)
Austr Weld Eng ... Australian Welding Engineer [*A publication*]   (APTA)
Austr Wild Life ... Australian Wild Life [*A publication*]   (APTA)
Aust Saf N ... Australian Safety News [*A publication*]
Aust Saf News ... Australian Safety News [*A publication*]
Aust Sch L ... Australian School Librarian [*A publication*]   (APTA)
Aust Sch Lib ... Australian School Librarian [*A publication*]   (APTA)
Aust Sch Libr ... Australian School Librarian [*A publication*]   (APTA)

Aust Sch Librn ... Australian School Librarian [*A publication*]
Aust School Libn ... Australian School Librarian [*A publication*]
Aust School Libr ... Australian School Librarian [*A publication*]   (APTA)
Aust Sci... Australian Scientist [*A publication*]
Aust Sci Abstr ... Australian Science Abstracts [*A publication*]   (APTA)
Aust Science Teachers J ... Australian Science Teachers' Journal [*A publication*]   (APTA)
Aust Scient ... Australian Scientist [*A publication*]   (APTA)
Aust Scientist ... Australian Scientist [*A publication*]   (APTA)
Aust Sci Index ... Australian Science Index [*Information service or system*] [*A publication*]   (APTA)
Aust Sci Newsl ... Australian Science Newsletter [*A publication*]
Aust Sci Teach J ... Australian Science Teachers' Journal [*A publication*]
Aust Seacraft ... Australian Seacraft Magazine [*A publication*]   (APTA)
Aust Seacraft ... Australian Seacraft, Power, and Sail [*A publication*]   (APTA)
Aust Seacraft Mag ... Australian Seacraft Magazine [*A publication*]   (APTA)
Aust Shell News ... Australian Shell News [*A publication*]   (APTA)
Aust's Heritage ... Australia's Heritage [*A publication*]   (APTA)
Aust Shorthorn ... Australian Shorthorn [*A publication*]   (APTA)
AUSTSIA ... Australasia   (ADA)
Aust Ski ..... Australian Ski Year Book [*A publication*]   (APTA)
Aust Ski YB ... Australian Ski Year Book [*A publication*]   (APTA)
AUSTSN... Australasian   (ADA)
Austsn Cath Rec ... Australasian Catholic Record [*A publication*]   (APTA)
Austsn J Pharm ... Australasian Journal of Pharmacy [*A publication*]   (APTA)
Austsn J Philos ... Australasian Journal of Philosophy [*A publication*]   (APTA)
Austsn Meth Hist Soc J ... Australasian Methodist Historical Society. Journal and Proceedings [*A publication*]   (APTA)
Austsn Pr ... Australasian Printer [*A publication*]   (APTA)
Aust Soc ..... Australian Society [*A publication*]   (APTA)
Aust Soc Accountants SA Convention ... Australian Society of Accountants. South Australian Division. Convention Reports [*A publication*]   (APTA)
Aust Soc Anim Prod NSW Branch Bull ... Australian Society of Animal Production. New South Wales Branch. Bulletin [*A publication*]
Aust Soc Anim Prod Victorian Branch Fed Counc Bull ... Australian Society of Animal Production. Victorian Branch. Federal Council. Bulletin [*A publication*]
Aust Soc Dairy Technol Tech Pub ... Australian Society of Dairy Technology. Technical Publication [*A publication*]   (APTA)
Aust Soc Dairy Technol Tech Publ ... Australian Society of Dairy Technology. Technical Publication [*A publication*]
Aust Soc Dairy Techn Tech Publ ... Australian Society of Dairy Technology. Technical Publication [*A publication*]   (APTA)
Aust Soc Dairy Tech Tech Pub ... Australian Society of Dairy Technology. Technical Publication [*A publication*]   (APTA)
Aust Soc Explor Geophys Bull ... Australian Society of Exploration Geophysicists. Bulletin [*A publication*]
Aust Soc Study Lab Hist Bull ... Australian Society for the Study of Labour History. Bulletin [*A publication*]   (APTA)
Aust Soc Sugar Cane Technol Proc Conf ... Australian Society of Sugar Cane Technologists. Proceedings of the Conference [*A publication*]   (APTA)
Aust Soc Welf ... Australian Social Welfare [*A publication*]
Aust Soc Welfare ... Australian Social Welfare [*A publication*]   (APTA)
Aust Soc Welf Impact ... Australian Social Welfare Impact [*A publication*]
Aust Soc Work ... Australian Social Work [*A publication*]
Aust South Dep Mines Geol Sur Bull ... South Australia. Department of Mines. Geological Survey. Bulletin [*A publication*]   (APTA)
Aust South Dep Mines Geol Surv Rep Invest ... South Australia. Department of Mines. Geological Survey. Report of Investigations [*A publication*]   (APTA)
Aust South Dep Mines Min Rev ... South Australia. Department of Mines. Mining Review [*A publication*]   (APTA)
Aust Spec Libr News ... Australian Special Libraries News [*A publication*]
Aust Stamp Bull ... Australian Stamp Bulletin [*A publication*]   (APTA)
Aust Stamp M ... Australian Stamp Monthly [*A publication*]   (APTA)
Aust Stamp Mo ... Australian Stamp Monthly [*A publication*]   (APTA)
Aust Stand ... Australian Standard [*Sydney*] [*A publication*]
Aust Stand Q ... Australian Standards Quarterly [*A publication*]   (APTA)
Aust Stand Specif ... Australian Standard Specifications [*A publication*]   (APTA)
Aust Stand Specif Stand Ass Aust ... Australian Standard Specifications. Standards Association of Australia [*A publication*]   (APTA)
Aust Statesm Min Stand ... Australian Statesman and Mining Standard [*A publication*]   (APTA)
Aust Stock Exchange J ... Australian Stock Exchange Journal [*A publication*]   (APTA)
Aust Stock Exch J ... Australian Stock Exchange Journal [*A publication*]
Aust Stud ... Australian Student [*A publication*]
Aust Stud & Farm M ... Australian Stud and Farm Monthly [*A publication*]   (APTA)
Aust Stud Legal Philos ... Australian Studies in Legal Philosophy [*A publication*]   (APTA)
Aust Sugar J ... Australian Sugar Journal [*A publication*]   (APTA)
Aust Sugar Yr Bk ... Australian Sugar Year Book [*A publication*]   (APTA)
Aust Sug J ... Australian Sugar Journal [*A publication*]   (APTA)
Aust Sug Yb ... Australian Sugar Yearbook [*A publication*]   (APTA)

Aust Surv ... Australian Surveyor [*A publication*]
Aust Survey ... Australian Surveyor [*A publication*]   (APTA)
Aust Surveyor ... Australian Surveyor [*A publication*]   (APTA)
AUSTSWIM ... Australian Council for the Teaching of Swimming and Water
   Safety
Aust Syst Bot ... Australian Systematic Botany [*A publication*]
Aust TAFE Teach ... Australian TAFE [*Department of Technical and Further
   Education*] Teacher [*A publication*]   (APTA)
Aust Tax D ... Australasian Tax Decisions [*A publication*]   (APTA)
Aust Tax Rev ... Australasian Tax Review [*A publication*]   (APTA)
Aust Tax Rev ... Australian Tax Review [*A publication*]
Aust T Deaf ... Australian Teacher of the Deaf [*A publication*]   (APTA)
Aust Teach ... Australian Teacher [*A publication*]   (APTA)
Aust Teach Deaf ... Australian Teacher of the Deaf [*A publication*]   (APTA)
Aust Teacher of the Deaf ... Australian Teacher of the Deaf [*A
   publication*]   (APTA)
Aust Teach Fed Rep ... Australian Teachers' Federation. Report [*A
   publication*]   (APTA)
Aust Teach J ... Australian Technical Journal [*A publication*]   (APTA)
Aust Telecomm Res ... Australian Telecommunication Research [*A
   publication*]   (APTA)
Aust Telecomm Research ... Australian Telecommunication Research [*A
   publication*]   (APTA)
Aust Telecommun Dev Assoc ... Australian Telecommunications
   Development Association. Annual Report [*A
   publication*]   (APTA)
Aust Telecommun Res ... Australian Telecommunication Research [*A
   publication*]   (APTA)
Aust Terr ... Australian Territories [*A publication*]   (APTA)
Aust Territ ... Australian Territories [*A publication*]   (APTA)
Aust Territories ... Australian Territories [*A publication*]   (APTA)
Aust Theatre Yrbk ... Australian Theatre Yearbook [*A publication*]   (APTA)
Aust Timber J ... Australian Timber Journal [*A publication*]   (APTA)
Aust Timb J ... Australian Timber Journal [*A publication*]
Aust Timb J ... Australian Timber Journal and Building Products
   Merchandiser [*A publication*]   (APTA)
Aust Tobacco J ... Australian Tobacco Journal [*A publication*]   (APTA)
Aust Tob Grow Bull ... Australian Tobacco Grower's Bulletin [*A publication*]
Aust Tob J ... Australian Tobacco Journal [*A publication*]   (APTA)
Aust Today ... Australia Today [*A publication*]   (APTA)
Aust Torts Reports ... Australian Torts Reports [*A publication*]
Aust Tract Test ... Australian Tractor Test [*A publication*]   (APTA)
Aust Tract Test Comm Aust Tract Test ... Australian Tractor Testing
   Committee. Australian Tractor Test [*A
   publication*]   (APTA)
Aust Trade Chronicle ... Australian Trade Chronicle [*A publication*]   (APTA)
Aust Transp ... Australian Transport [*A publication*]
Aust Transport ... Australian Transport [*A publication*]   (APTA)
Aust Travel Goods ... Australian Travel Goods and Handbags and Accessories
   [*A publication*]   (APTA)
Aust Traveller ... Australian Traveller [*A publication*]   (APTA)
Aust Univ ... Australian University [*A publication*]   (APTA)
Aust Uranium News ... Australian Uranium News [*A publication*]
Aust Urban Stud ... Australian Urban Studies [*A publication*]   (APTA)
Aust Vet J ... Australian Veterinary Journal [*A publication*]
Aust Vet Pr ... Australian Veterinary Practitioner [*A publication*]   (APTA)
Aust Vet Pract ... Australian Veterinary Practitioner [*A publication*]
Aust Waste Conf ... Australian Waste Conference [*A publication*]   (APTA)
Aust Waste Disposal Conf ... Australian Waste Disposal Conference [*A
   publication*]   (APTA)
Aust Waste Manage Control Conf Pap ... Australian Waste Management and
   Control Conference. Papers [*A publication*]   (APTA)
Aust Water Resour Counc Conf Ser ... Australian Water Resources Council.
   Conference Series [*A publication*]
Aust Water Resour Counc Hydrol Ser ... Australian Water Resources Council.
   Hydrological Series [*A publication*]
Aust Water Resour Counc Stream Gauging Inf ... Australian Water Resources
   Council. Stream Gauging Information [*A publication*]
Aust Water Resour Counc Tech Pap ... Australian Water Resources Council.
   Technical Paper [*A publication*]
Aust Water Resour Coun Tech Pap ... Australian Water Resources Council.
   Technical Paper [*A publication*]   (APTA)
Aust Water Wastewater Assoc Fed Conv ... Australian Water and Wastewater
   Association. Federal Convention [*A publication*]   (APTA)
Aust Water Wastewater Assoc Summer Sch ... Australian Water and
   Wastewater Association. Summer School [*A
   publication*]   (APTA)
Aust Water Well J ... Australasian Water Well Journal [*A
   publication*]   (APTA)
Aust Wat Resour Coun Hydrol Ser ... Australian Water Resources Council.
   Hydrological Series [*A publication*]   (APTA)
Aust Weapons Res Establ Tech Rep ... Australia. Weapons Research
   Establishment. Technical Report [*A publication*]   (APTA)
Aust Weed ... Australian Weeds [*A publication*]
Aust Weed Control Handb ... Australian Weed Control Handbook [*A
   publication*]   (APTA)
Aust Weeds ... Australian Weeds [*A publication*]
Aust Weeds Conf Proc ... Australian Weeds Conference. Proceedings [*A
   publication*]   (APTA)
Aust Weld ... Australian Welder [*A publication*]   (APTA)
Aust Weld Engr ... Australian Welding Engineer [*A publication*]   (APTA)

Aust Welding J ... Australian Welding Journal [*A publication*]   (APTA)
Aust Weld J ... Australian Welding Journal [*A publication*]
Aust Weld Res ... Australian Welding Research [*A publication*]
Aust Weld Res Ass Bull ... Australian Welding Research Association. Bulletin
   [*A publication*]
Aust West Dep Mines Annu Rep Geol Surv ... Western Australia. Department
   of Mines. Annual Report of the Geological Survey [*A
   publication*]
Aust West Dep Mines Bull ... Western Australia. Department of Mines.
   Bulletin [*A publication*]   (APTA)
Aust (West) Dep Mines Rep Mineral Anal Chem ... Australia (Western).
   Department of Mines. Report of the Mineralogist, Analyst,
   and Chemist [*A publication*]
Aust West Geol Surv Bull ... Western Australia. Geological Survey. Bulletin [*A
   publication*]   (APTA)
Aust (West) Geol Surv Miner Resour Bull ... Australia (Western). Geological
   Survey. Mineral Resources Bulletin [*A publication*]
Aust (West) Rep Dir Gov Chem Lab ... Australia (Western). Report of the
   Director of Government Chemical Laboratories [*A
   publication*]
Aust Wildl Res ... Australian Wildlife Research [*A publication*]
Aust Wild R ... Australian Wildlife Research [*A publication*]   (APTA)
Aust Wine Brewing Spir Rev ... Australian Wine, Brewing, and Spirit Review
   [*A publication*]   (APTA)
Aust Wine Brewing and Spir Rev ... Australian Wine, Brewing, and Spirit
   Review [*A publication*]   (APTA)
Aust Wine Brew Spirit Rev ... Australian Wine, Brewing, and Spirit Review [*A
   publication*]   (APTA)
Aust Womens W ... Australian Women's Weekly [*A publication*]   (APTA)
Aust Wool Bd Rep ... Australian Wool Board. Report [*A publication*]   (APTA)
Aust Wool Bur Wool Stat Service ... Australian Wool Bureau. Wool Statistical
   Service [*A publication*]   (APTA)
Aust Wool Bur Wool Stat Service Aust Wool Stat Analysis ... Australian Wool
   Bureau. Wool Statistical Service. Australian Wool.
   Statistical Analysis [*A publication*]   (APTA)
Aust Wool Stat Analysis ... Australian Wool. Statistical Analysis [*A
   publication*]   (APTA)
Aust Wool Test Auth Text Test Bull ... Australian Wool Testing Authority.
   Textile Testing Bulletin [*A publication*]   (APTA)
Aust Workshop Coal Hydrogenation ... Australian Workshop on Coal
   Hydrogenation [*A publication*]   (APTA)
Aust YB Intl L ... Australian Yearbook of International Law [*A
   publication*]   (APTA)
Aust Yearbook Int L ... Australian Yearbook of International Law [*A
   publication*]
Aust Y Int L ... Australian Yearbook of International Law [*A
   publication*]   (DLA)
Aust Yr Bk IL ... Australian Yearbook of International Law [*A publication*]
Aust Yr Book Int Law ... Australian Yearbook of International Law [*A
   publication*]   (APTA)
Aust Zoo .... Australian Zoologist [*A publication*]   (APTA)
Aust Zool ... Australian Zoologist [*A publication*]
Aust Zoologist ... Australian Zoologist [*A publication*]   (APTA)
AuSU .... University of Sydney, Sydney, NSW, Australia [*Library
   symbol*] [*Library of Congress*]   (LCLS)
AUSUDIAP ... Association of US University Directors of International
   Agricultural Programs [*Later, AIARD*]   (EA)
Aus Unterricht Forsch ... Aus Unterricht und Forschung. Korrespondenzblatt
   der Hoeheren Schulen Wuertembergs. Neue Folge [*A
   publication*]
Ausw .... Auswaertiges [*Nonresident*] [*German*]
Ausw .... Auswahl [*Choice*] [*German*]
Aus Walde Mitt Niedersaechs Landesforstverwalt ... Aus dem Walde.
   Mitteilungen aus der Niedersaechsischen
   Landesforstverwaltung [*A publication*]
Auszuege Auslegeschr Patentschr ... Auszuege Auslegeschriften
   Patentschriften [*A publication*]
Auszuege Europ Patentschr ... Auszuege aus den Europaeischen
   Patentschriften [*A publication*]
AUT .... Advanced Unit Training [*Army*]
AUT .... Advanced User Terminal [*Navy*]   (MCD)
AUT .... Ammonium Uranyl Tricarbonate [*Inorganic chemistry*]
AUT .... Analele. Universitatii din Timisoara. Seria Stiinte Filologice [*A
   publication*]
AUT .... Annales Universitatis Turkuensis [*A publication*]
AUT .... Annali. Universita Toscane [*A publication*]
AUT .... Asian University [*EDUCATSS*] [*UTLAS symbol*]
AUT .... Association of University Teachers [*A union*] [*British*]
AUT .... Au Tau [*Hong Kong*] [*Later, HKO*] [*Geomagnetic observatory
   code*]
AUT .... Austria [*ANSI three-letter standard code*]   (CNC)
Aut .... Authentic Science Fiction [*A publication*]
Aut .... Authenticum [*A publication*]   (DSA)
AUT .... Author [*Online database field identifier*] [*Data processing*]
AUT .... Authority
AUT .... Auto + Motortechniek [*A publication*]
AUT .... Autograph
AUT .... Automatic
AUT .... Autonomous
AUT .... Autopsy [*Also, AU*] [*Medicine*]
AUT .... Autrex, Inc. [*Toronto Stock Exchange symbol*]

AUT.......... Autumn
AUTA....... Association of University Teachers in Accounting [British]
AUTDEX... Author Index
AUTEC.... Atlantic Undersea Test and Evaluation Center [Navy] [Acronym also used to refer to device for detection, amplification, and transmission of undersea noise]
Aut Eng...... Automotive Engineering [A publication]
AUTFAE.... Ankara Universitesi. Tip Fakultesi. Mecmuasi [A publication]
AUTH....... Authentic
AUTH....... Author
AUTH....... Authority (AFM)
AUTH....... Authorization [or Authorized] (EY)
AUTH....... Authorized Version [or King James Version of the Bible, 1611] (ROG)
AUTHAB.. Authorized Abbreviation (MCD)
AUTHAB.. Authorized About
AUTHBUPERSMAN ... Authorized in Bureau of Naval Personnel Manual
AUTHD..... Authorized (ROG)
AUTHEN ... Authentic (AABC)
Authen .... Authenticum [A publication] (DSA)
AUTHEXANDO ... Authority Granted to Execute Acceptance and Oath of Office for ____
AUTHGR ... Authority Granted [Army]
AUTHGRA ... Authority Granted [Military] (NVT)
AUTHN..... Authentication (AFM)
AUTHPROBOUT ... Authorized to Proceed On or About [Date] [Military]
AUTHY..... Authority
AUTIMPEX ... China National Automotive Industry Import/Export Corporation [People's Republic of China] (IMH)
AuTJC .... James Cook University of North Queensland, Townsville, QLD, Australia [Library symbol] [Library of Congress] (LCLS)
AUT/KY.... Automation Co. of Kentucky [McDonnell Douglas Corp.]
AUTM....... Automatic
AUTMA.... Automatizace [A publication]
AUTMV .... Automotive (MUGU)
AUTM WTR CK ... Automatic Water Check [Freight]
AuTNQ...... North Queensland Newspaper Co. Ltd., Townsville, QLD, Australia [Library symbol] [Library of Congress] (LCLS)
AUTO........ AutoInfo, Inc. [Lake Success, NY] [NASDAQ symbol] (NQ)
AUTO........ Automatic (AFM)
Auto .... Automatic Coupling [Music]
AUTO........ Automobile
Auto Age .... Automotive Age [A publication]
AUTOBUS ... Automated Budget System
Auto C........ Automobile Cases [Commerce Clearing House] [A publication] (DLA)
AUTOCAP ... Automated Continuous Acceptance of Propellants (MCD)
AUTOCAP ... Automotive Consumer Action Program (EA)
Auto Cas .... Automobile Cases [Commerce Clearing House] [A publication] (DLA)
Auto Cas 2d ... Automobile Cases, Second Series [Commerce Clearing House] [A publication] (DLA)
AUTOCAT ... Automatic Communication Relay (NVT)
AUTOCAT ... Automatic Control of Air Transmissions (NATG)
Auto Chn S ... Automotive Chain Store [A publication]
AUTOCOM ... Automated Combustor [Computer code]
Auto and Con ... Automation and Control [A publication]
AUTO CV ... Automatic Check Valve (MSA)
AUTODIN ... Automatic Digital Network [DoD]
Auto Eng.... Automobile Engineer [A publication]
AUTOFAC .... AUTODIN Facility (MCD)
AUTO-FETS ... Automated Field Evaluation and Test System (MCD)
AUTOFLOW ... Automatic Flowcharting
AUTOG..... Autograph
Autogene Metallbearb ... Autogene Metallbearbeitung [A publication]
Autogestion et Social ... Autogestion et Socialisme [A publication]
AUTO-GOSS ... Automated Ground Operations Scheduling System [Also, AGOSS] (MCD)
AUTOGRAF ... [A] programming language [1972] (CSR)
Autograph Collect J ... Autograph Collectors Journal [A publication]
AUTOGRP ... Automatic Grouping System [Hospital records] (DHSM)
Auto Highwy ... Automotive Industries. Truck and Off Highway [A publication]
Auto Housg ... Automation in Housing and Systems Building News [A publication]
AutoICS..... Automated Immunochemistry System
Auto ID...... Automatic Identification [Data processing]
Auto Ind..... Automotive Industries [A publication]
Auto Ind Rep ... Autotransaction Industry Report [A publication]
Auto Ins Cas ... Automobile Insurance Cases [Commerce Clearing House] [A publication] (DLA)
AutoKo....... Automatic Corps [Communications System] [General Electric Co.]
Autoko .... Automatische Korpsstamunetz [Tactical Communications System] [Federal Republic of Germany]
AUTOLABS ... Automatic Low-Altitude Bombing System (MCD)
AUTOLAND ... Automatic Landing [NASA] (NASA)
AUTOLING ... Automated Linguistic Fieldworker [Data processing] (DIT)
Auto L Rep ... Automobile Law Reporter [Commerce Clearing House] [A publication] (DLA)

Auto L Rep CCH ... Automobile Law Reports. Commerce Clearing House [A publication]
AUTOM.... Automotive (MSA)
AUTOMAN ... European Automated Manufacturing Exhibition and Conference [British Robot Association] (TSPED)
Autom Anal Drugs Other Subst Pharm Interest ... Automated Analysis of Drugs and Other Substances of Pharmaceutical Interest [A publication]
AUTOMAP ... Automatic Machining Program
AUTOMASIA ... South East Asian International Automated Manufacturing Technology and Robotics Show and Conference (TSPED)
AUTOMAST ... Automatic Mathematical Analysis and Symbolic Translation [Data processing]
AUTOMAT ... Automated Material System (MCD)
Automat Control and Computer Sci ... Automatic Control and Computer Sciences [A publication]
Automat Control Comput Sci ... Automatic Control and Computer Sciences [A publication]
Automat Control Theory Appl ... Automatic Control Theory and Applications [A publication]
Automat Data Process Inform B ... Automatic Data Processing Information Bulletin [A publication]
Automat Document and Math Linguistics ... Automatic Documentation and Mathematical Linguistics [A publication]
Automat Elec Tech J ... Automatic Electric Technical Journal [A publication]
Automatica-J IFAC ... Automatica: The Journal of IFAC [International Federation of Automatic Control] [A publication]
Automatic Control Theory Appl ... Automatic Control Theory and Applications [A publication]
Automation (Cleve) ... Automation (Cleveland) [A publication]
Automatisierungspraxis ... Automatisierungspraxis fuer Grundlagen Geratebau und Betriebserfahrungen [A publication]
Automat Monit Mea ... Automatic Monitoring and Measuring [A publication]
Automat Programming ... Automatic Programming [A publication]
Automat Remote Contr ... Automation and Remote Control [USSR] [A publication]
Automat Remote Control ... Automation and Remote Control [A publication]
Automat Welding (USSR) ... Automatic Welding (USSR) [A publication]
Autom Control ... Automatic Control [Japan] [A publication]
Autom and Control ... Automation and Control [A publication]
Autom Control Comput Sci ... Automatic Control and Computer Sciences [A publication]
Autom Control and Comput Sci ... Automatic Control and Computer Sciences [A publication]
Autom Control Comput Sci (Engl Transl) ... Automatic Control and Computer Sciences (English Translation) [A publication]
Autom Control Theory & Appl ... Automatic Control Theory and Applications [A publication]
Autom Data Process Inf Bull ... Automatic Data Processing Information Bulletin [A publication]
Autom Doc Math Linguist ... Automatic Documentation and Mathematical Linguistics [A publication]
Autom Doc Rech Reflexions ... Automatisation Documentaire. Recherches et Reflexions [A publication]
Autom Elec Tech J ... Automatic Electric Technical Journal [A publication]
Autom si Electron ... Automatica si Electronica [A publication]
Auto Merch ... Auto Merchandising News [A publication]
AUTOMET ... Automatic Meteorological Correction [A missile guidance technique]
AUTOMEX ... Automatic Message Exchange Service
Autom et Inf Ind ... Automatique et Informatique Industrielles [A publication]
Autom Mach ... Automatic Machining [A publication]
Autom Microbiol Immunol Pap Symp ... Automation in Microbiology and Immunology. Papers. Symposium on Rapid Methods and Automation in Microbiology [A publication]
Autom Monit and Meas ... Automatic Monitoring and Measuring [A publication]
Autom Monit Meas (Engl Transl) ... Automatic Monitoring and Measuring (English Translation) [A publication]
AUTOMN ... Automation (MSA)
Automobile Abs ... Automobile Abstracts [A publication]
Automobiltech Z ... Automobiltechnische Zeitschrift [A publication]
Automob Q ... Automobile Quarterly [A publication]
Automob Technol ... Automobile Technology [Japan] [A publication]
Automot Abstr ... Automotive Abstracts [A publication]
Automot Aviat Ind ... Automotive and Aviation Industries [A publication]
Automot Des Eng ... Automotive Design Engineering [A publication]
Automot Eng ... Automotive Engineering [A publication]
Automot Eng (Lond) ... Automotive Engineer (London) [A publication]
Automot Engng ... Automotive Engineering [A publication]
Automot Eng (Pittsb) ... Automotive Engineering (Pittsburgh) [A publication]
Automot Engr ... Automotive Engineer [A publication]
Automot Ind ... Automotive Industries [A publication]
Automotive & Aviation Ind ... Automotive and Aviation Industries [A publication]
Automotive Eng ... Society of Automotive Engineers. Journal of Automotive Engineering [A publication]
Automotive Ind ... Automotive Industry [A publication] (APTA)
Automot N ... Automotive News [A publication]
Automot News ... Automotive News [A publication]
Automot Serv News ... Automotive Service News [Japan] [A publication]

Automot Top ... Automotive Topics [*A publication*]   (APTA)
Autom & Remote Control ... Automation and Remote Control [*USSR*] [*A publication*]
Autom Remote Control ... Automation and Remote Control [*USSR*] [*A publication*]
Autom Strum ... Automazione e Strumentazione [*A publication*]
Autom & Strum ... Automazione e Strumentazione [*A publication*]
Autom Subj Citation Alert ... Automatic Subject Citation Alert [*A publication*]
Autom Syst Rizeni ... Automatizovane Systemy Rizeni - Bulletin INORGA [*A publication*]
AUTOMV ... Automotive   (AABC)
Autom Weld ... Automatic Welding [*USSR*] [*A publication*]
AUTON..... Automation   (AFM)
AUTONET ... Automatic Network Display
Auto News ... Automotive News [*A publication*]
AuTooT...... Toowoomba Newspapers Publishers Ltd., Toowoomba, QLD, Australia [*Library symbol*] [*Library of Congress*]   (LCLS)
AUTOP ..... Automatic Pistol
Auto PA ..... Automatic Personal Accident [*Insurance*]   (AIA)
AUTOPARTAC ... International Automotive Parts and Accessories Trade Show [*British*]   (ITD)
AUTOPIC ... Automatic Personal Identification Code [*IBM Corp.*]
AUTOPLOT ... Automatic Plotting Routine   (ADA)
AUTOPOD ... Automatic Proof of Delivery
AUTOPROBE ... Automated Programming, Budgeting, and Operational Evaluation [*Army*]
AUTO PROG ... Automatic Programming [*Data processing*]
AUTOPROMT ... Automatic Programming of Machine Tools [*IBM Corp.*]
AUTOPSY ... Automatic Operating System [*IBM Corp.*]
AUTO PTS ... Automobile Parts [*Freight*]
AUTOQEST ... Automatic Generation of Requests [*Data processing*]   (DIT)
Auto Rbldr ... Automotive Rebuilder [*A publication*]
AUTOROS ... Automated Retail Outlet System   (MCD)
AUTOSAG ... Ad Universiterrarum Orbis Summi Architecti Gloriam [*To the Glory of the Grand Architect of the Universe*] [*Latin*] [*Freemasonry*]
AUTOSATE ... Automated System Analysis Technique
AUTOSCRIPT ... Automated System for Composing, Revising, Illustrating, and Phototypesetting
AUTO S & CV ... Automatic Stop and Check Valve   (AAG)
AUTOSERVCEN ... Automated Service Center
AUTOSEVCOM ... Automatic Secure Voice Communications
AUTOSEVOCOM ... Automatic Secure Voice Communications   (NVT)
AUTOSEVOCON ... Automatic Secure Voice Communications Network
AUTOSPEC ... Automated Specifications [*Data processing*]   (DIT)
AUTOSPOT ... Automatic System for Positioning Tools
AUTOSTIF ... Automatic Stiffening   (MSA)
AUTOSTRAD ... Automated System for Transportation Data [*Military*]
AUTOSTRT ... Automatic Starter
AUTOSTRTG ... Automatic Starting
AUTOSYN ... Automatically Synchronous [*Remote-indicating system*] [*Trade name*] [*Western Electric Co.*]
Auto Tech .. Auto Technik [*A publication*]
AUTOTR .. Autotransformer
AUTOTRAN ... Automatic Translation
AUTOVON ... Automatic Voice Network [*DoD*]
Aut Pand.... Authenticis Pandectis [*Latin*]   (DSA)
AUTR .... Autotrol Corp. [*NASDAQ symbol*]   (NQ)
AUTRA ...... Automobile Utility Trailer Rental Association   (EA)
AUTRAN ... Automatic Target Recognition Analysis
AUTRAN .. Automatic Utility Translator   (IEEE)
AUTRB...... Australian Transport [*A publication*]
Aut Remot (R) ... Automation and Remote Control (USSR) [*A publication*]
AUTS........ Automatic Update Transaction System [*DoD*]
AUT/TEX ... Automation Co. of Texas [*McDonnell Douglas Corp.*]
AUTUA...... Annales Universitatis Turkuensis. Series A-I. Astronomica-Chemica-Physica-Mathematica [*A publication*]
Aut Weld R ... Automatic Welding (USSR) [*A publication*]
AuU............ Afrika und Uebersee [*A publication*]
AUU .... Americans for the Universality of UNESCO   (EA)
AUU .... Association of Urban Universities   (EA)
AUU .... Atlanta University Center, Atlanta, GA [*OCLC symbol*]   (OCLC)
AUU .... Aurukun Mission [*Australia*] [*Airport symbol*]   (OAG)
AuU............ Australian National University, Canberra, ACT, Australia [*Library symbol*] [*Library of Congress*]   (LCLS)
AUUA....... Americas UNIVAC [*Universal Automatic Computer*] Users Association [*Formerly, USE, UUA*]   (EA)
AUUASLU ... Acta Universitatis Upsaliensis. Acta Societatis Linguisticae Upsaliensis [*A publication*]
AUUHL..... Acta Universitatis Upsaliensis. Historia Litterarum [*A publication*]
AUUNBA ... Acta Universitatis Upsaliensis. Nova Acta Regiae Societatis Scientiarum Upsaliensis. Series VC [*A publication*]
AuUqP....... University of Queensland Press, Microform Division, St. Lucia, Brisbane, QLD, Australia [*Library symbol*] [*Library of Congress*]   (LCLS)
Auus.......... [*Saint*] Augustine [*Deceased, 430*] [*Authority cited in pre-1607 legal work*]   (DSA)
AUUSAU .. Acta Universitatis Upsaliensis. Studia Anglistica Upsaliensia [*A publication*]

AUUSEU .. Acta Universitatis Upsaliensis. Studia Ethnologica Upsaliensia [*A publication*]
AUUSGU .. Acta Universitatis Upsaliensis. Studia Germanistica Upsaliensia [*A publication*]
AUUSRU .. Acta Universitatis Upsaliensis. Studia Romanica Upsaliensia [*A publication*]
AUUUDX .. Acta Universitatis Upsaliensis. Symbolae Botanicae Upsalienses [*A publication*]
AUV.......... Administrative Use Vehicle [*Military*]   (AABC)
AUV.......... Anales. Universidad de Valencia [*A publication*]
AUV.......... Ardmore, OK [*Location identifier*] [*FAA*]   (FAAL)
AUV.......... Armored Utility Vehicle
AUV.......... Autonomous Underwater Vehicle [*Navy*]
Auvergne Litt ... L'Auvergne Litteraire, Artistique, et Historique [*A publication*]
AUVJA...... Australian Veterinary Journal [*A publication*]
AUVL .... Airborne Ultraviolet LASER
AUVMIS... Administrative Use Vehicle Management Information System [*Military*]   (MCD)
AUVS .... Association for Unmanned Vehicle Systems   (EA)
AUW.......... Acta Universitatis Wratislaviensis [*A publication*]
AUW.......... Advanced Underseas Weapons [*Army*]
AUW.......... Airframe Unit Weight
AUW.......... All Up Weight [*Aviation*]   (FAAC)
AUW.......... Antiunderwater Warfare [*Navy*]   (CINC)
AUW.......... Aussenwirtschaft. Zeitschrift fuer Internationale Wirtschaftsbeziehungen [*A publication*]
AUW.......... Wausau [*Wisconsin*] [*Airport symbol*]   (OAG)
AUWC....... Advanced Underseas Weapons Circuitry
AUWE .... Admiralty Underwater Weapons Establishment [*British*]
AUWEA .... Automatic Welding (English Translation) [*A publication*]
AUWEDT ... Australian Weeds [*A publication*]
AUWJA...... Australian Welding Journal [*A publication*]
AUWMD... ASCE [*American Society of Civil Engineers*] Urban Water Resources Research Program. Technical Memorandum IHP [*International Hydrological Programme*] [*A publication*]
AuWol........ Wollongong Public Library, Wollongong, NSW, Australia [*Library symbol*] [*Library of Congress*]   (LCLS)
AUWPET ... Agricultural University (Wageningen). Papers [*A publication*]
AUWS .... Automatic Unmanned Weather Station
AUWTB .... ASCE [*American Society of Civil Engineers*] Urban Water Resources Research Program. Technical Memorandum [*A publication*]
AuWWA .... Australian Water and Wastewater Association
AUX.......... Araguaina [*Brazil*] [*Airport symbol*]   (OAG)
AUX.......... Auxiliary   (AFM)
Aux............. Auxiliary Light [*Navigation signal*]
AUXCP....... Auxiliary Airborne Command Post   (MCD)
Aux Front Spectrosc Laser Ec Ete Phys Theor ... Aux Frontieres de la Spectroscopie Laser. Ecole d'Ete de Physique Theorique [*A publication*]
AUXGCS... Auxiliary Ground Control Station [*NASA*]   (KSC)
AUXIL....... Auxiliary
AUXOPS... Auxiliary Operational Members [*Coast Guard*]
AUXOSC... Auxiliary Oscillator
AUXR......... Auxiliary Register
AUXRC ..... Auxiliary Recording Control [*Circuit*] [*Bell System*]
AUXT .... Auxton Computer Enterprises, Inc. [*NASDAQ symbol*]   (NQ)
AUXTRAC ... Auxiliary Track   (MUGU)
AUY.......... Aneityum [*Vanuata*] [*Airport symbol*]   (OAG)
AUY.......... Audrey Resources, Inc. [*Toronto Stock Exchange symbol*]
AUZ.......... Australian Packaging [*Sydney*] [*A publication*]
AUZ.......... Authorize   (FAAC)
AUZCA ..... Analele Stiintifice ale Universitatii Al. I. Cuza din Iasi. Sectiunea 1c. Chimie [*A publication*]
AUZFA...... Analele Stiintifice ale Universitatii Al. I. Cuza din Iasi. Sectiunea 1b. Fizica [*A publication*]
AUZMA .... Analele Stiintifice ale Universitatii Al. I. Cuza din Iasi. Sectiunea 1a. Matematica [*A publication*]
AUZOA3... Australian Zoologist [*A publication*]
AV.............. Abnormal Voltage
aV.............. Abvolt [*Unit of electromotive force*]
AV.............. Acid Value [*Chemistry*]
AV.............. Actual Value
AV.............. Actual Velocity
AV.............. Ad Valorem [*According to the Value*] [*Latin*] [*Business term*]
AV.............. Adriamycin, Vincristine [*Antineoplastic drug regimen*]
AV.............. Advanced Voyager
AV.............. Aerospace Vehicle   (AFM)
AV.............. Air-Cushion Vehicle built by Air Vehicles [*England*] [*Usually used in combination with numerals*]
AV.............. Air Vent
AV.............. Allgemeine Verwaltungsvorschrift [*or Vorschrift*] [*General Administrative Regulation*] [*German*]   (ILCA)
AV.............. Alternative Vote
AV.............. American Vegetarian   (EA)
AV.............. American Viewpoint [*Later, ERC*]
AV.............. Anglo-Vernacular
AV.............. Angular Velocity   (MCD)
AV.............. Animal-Vues   (EA)

AV	Annales Valaisannes [*A publication*]
AV	Anno Vixit [*He Lived (a given number of) Years*] [*Latin*]
AV	Annual Value (ADA)
AV	[*The*] Answering Voice [*A publication*]
AV	Anterior Ventral Neuron [*Neurophysiology*]
AV	Anteversion [*Medicine*]
A/V	Anti-Vermin [*Battle dress*] [*British and Canadian*] [*World War II*]
AV	Anti-Vivisection Party [*British*]
AV	Anticipated Vacancy [*Civil Service*]
AV	Antivehicle [*Munitions*]
AV	Aonde Vamos (BJA)
AV	Aortic Valve [*Cardiology*]
AV	Arbeitsverwendungsfaehig [*Fit for labor duty only*] [*German military - World War II*]
AV	Archaeologische Veroeffentlichungen. Deutsches Archaeologisches Institut Cairo [*A publication*]
AV	Archivio Veneto [*A publication*]
AV	Area Weapon Verify (MCD)
AV	Arheoloski Vestnik [*A publication*]
AV	Armored Vehicle (MCD)
AV	Arteriovenous [*Medicine*]
AV	Artha Vijnana [*A publication*]
AV	Artillery Volunteers
AV	Asparagus Virus
AV	Association Value [*Psychometrics*]
AV	Ateneo Veneto [*A publication*]
AV	Atomic Value (ADA)
AV	Atrioventricular [*Cardiology*]
AV	Audio Visual [*A publication*]
AV	Audiovisual
AV	Auriculoventricular [*Medicine*]
AV	Aurum [*Gold*] [*Numismatics*]
AV	Aus Aachens Vorzeit [*A publication*]
AV	Austere Version (MCD)
AV	Authorized Version [*or King James Version of the Bible, 1611*]
AV	Autophagic Vacuole [*Botany*]
AV	AUTOVON (MCD)
AV	Auxiliary Vessel (NOAA)
AV	AV Communication Review [*A publication*]
AV	Available [*or Availability*] [*Online database field identifier*] [*Data processing*]
AV	Avenue [*Correspondence*] (EY)
AV	Average
AV	Average Value (NASA)
AV	Average Variability
Av	Aves [*Birds*] [*of Aristophanes*] [*Classical studies*] (OCD)
Av	Avesta [*Language, etc.*]
AV	AVIANCA [*Colombia*] [*ICAO designator*] (FAAC)
AV	Aviation
AV	Aviation [*Special duties officer*] [*British*]
AV	Avionics (NASA)
AV	Avoir [*Credit*] [*French*]
AV	Avoirdupois
AV	Hawker Siddeley Aviation Ltd. [*Great Britain*] [*ICAO aircraft manufacturer identifier*] (ICAO)
AV	Seaplane Tender [*Navy symbol*]
AV	Vimy Public Library, Alberta [*Library symbol*] [*National Library of Canada*] (NLC)
AVA	Absolute Virtual Address [*Data processing*]
AVA	Academy of Veterinary Allergy (EA)
AVA	Activity Vector Analysis [*Psychology*]
AVA	Adult Video Association (EA)
AVA	American Vaulting Association (EA)
AVA	American Vecturist Association (EA)
AVA	American Ventilation Association [*Defunct*] (EA)
AVA	American Veterans Alliance (EA)
AVA	American Victims of Abortion (EA)
AVA	American Video Association (EA)
AVA	American Vocational Association (EA)
AVA	American Volkssport Association (EA)
AVA	Apovincaminic Acid [*Biochemistry*]
AVA	Arteriovenous Anastomosis [*Medicine*]
AVA	Asbestos Victims of America (EA)
AVA	ASEAN [*Association of South East Asian Nations*] Valuers Association [*Kuala Lumpur, Malaysia*] (EAIO)
AVA	Association of Veterinary Anaesthetists [*British*]
AVA	Association for Volunteer Administration (EA)
AVA	Auctioneers and Valuers Association of Australia
AVA	Audio/Video Affiliates, Inc. [*NYSE symbol*] (SPSG)
AVA	Audiovisual Annunciator
AVA	Automated Vision Association [*Later, AIA*] (EA)
AVA	Automatic Voice Answering [*Computer-generated recording unit for telephone directory assistance*]
AVA	Avance International, Inc. [*Vancouver Stock Exchange symbol*]
ava	Avaric [*MARC language code*] [*Library of Congress*] (LCCP)
AVA	Average Alarm
AVA	Azimuth Versus Amplitude
AVA	Grand Forks, ND [*Location identifier*] [*FAA*] (FAAL)

AVA	Vauxhall Public Library, Alberta [*Library symbol*] [*National Library of Canada*] (NLC)
AVAA	American Viticultural Area Association (EA)
AVAC	Audio-Visual Aids Committee [*British*]
AVAC	Automated Vacuum
AVAC	Automated Vacuum-Assisted Collection System [*Disney World trash disposal system*]
AVAC	Avacare [*NASDAQ symbol*] (NQ)
'Avad	'Avadim (BJA)
Av Adj Assoc Dig	Digest of Reports of the Average Adjusters Association [*1895*] [*A publication*] (DLA)
AVADS	Advanced Vulcan Air Defense System (MCD)
AVADS	Autotrack Vulcan Air Defense System
AVAE	Association for Voluntary Action in Europe [*See also AVE*] (EAIO)
AVAGA	Avvenire Agricolo [*A publication*]
AVAIL	Available [*or Availability*] (KSC)
AVAK	Avantek, Inc. [*NASDAQ symbol*] (NQ)
AVAL	Available [*or Availability*] (AFM)
Av Aliment Mejora Anim	Avances en Alimentacion y Mejora Animal [*A publication*]
Av Aliment Mejora Anim Supl	Avances en Alimentacion y Mejora Animal. Suplemento [*A publication*]
AVANA	Altitude Reservation Void for Aircraft Not Airborne by _____ [*Aviation*] (FAAC)
Avances Aliment Mejora Anim	Avances en Alimentacion y Mejora Animal [*A publication*]
A Van Leeuw	Antonie Van Leeuwenhoek Journal of Microbiology and Serology [*A publication*]
AVANT	Association of Voluntary Agencies on Narcotics Treatment
Avant Sc C	Avant-Scene Cinema [*A publication*]
Avant Scene	Avant-Scene Cinema [*A publication*]
Avant Sc Th	Avant Scene Theatre [*A publication*]
AVAP	Airport Vicinity Air Pollution
AVAPA	Archivio "De Vecchi" per l'Anatomia Patologica e la Medicina Clinica [*A publication*]
AVAR	Asymptomatic Variance
AVAR	Regional Office, Alberta Agriculture, Vermilion, Alberta [*Library symbol*] [*National Library of Canada*] (NLC)
AVAS	Association of Voluntary Action Scholars [*Later, ARNOVA*] (EA)
AVASAX	Acta Veterinaria. Academiae Scientiarum Hungaricae [*A publication*]
AVASI	Abbreviated Visual Approach Slope Indicator [*Aviation*]
AVASIS	Abbreviated Visual Approach Slope Indicator System [*Aviation*]
AVASS	Association of Voluntary Aided Secondary Schools [*British*]
AVATI	Asphalt and Vinyl Asbestos Tile Institute [*Later, RFCI*] (EA)
AV-AWOS	Aviation Automated Weather Observation System (NOAA)
AV-AWOS-T	Aviation-Automatic/Weather Observing System Developmental Model (T) (MCD)
AVB	Advanced Aviation Base Ship [*Navy symbol*] [*Obsolete*]
AVB	Allgemeine Versicherungsbedingungen [*General conditions of insurance*] [*German*] (ILCA)
AVB	Analog Video Bandwidth
AVB	Association of Volunteer Bureaus [*Later, NVC*] (EA)
AVB	Aviation Baseship
AVB	Avionics Bulletin (MCD)
AVBAAI	Agronomia y Veterinaria [*A publication*]
AVBAD	Army Aviator Badge [*Military decoration*]
AVBAT	Aviation Battalion [*Army*]
AVBAY	Avionics Bay (MCD)
AVBIB	Advances in the Biosciences [*A publication*]
AVBIDB	Avian Biology [*A publication*]
AVBL	Available [*or Availability*]
AVBLTY	Availability
AVBNA	Arhiv Bioloskih Nauka [*A publication*]
AVBNAN	Arhiv Bioloskih Nauka [*A publication*]
AVBS	Absolute Value BIT [*Binary Digit*] Synchronizer
AVBWKN	Annalen der Vereeniging tot het Hevorderen van de Beoefening der Wetenschap Onder de Katholieken in Nederland [*A publication*]
AVC	Abdominal Vena Cava [*Medicine*]
AVC	Academy of Veterinary Cardiology (EA)
AVC	Acceleration Vector Control
AVC	Additional Voluntary Contribution [*Employee's wage contribution toward a company pension plan*]
AVC	AddValue Communications [*Telecommunications service*] (TSSD)
AVC	Adriamycin, Vincristine, Cyclophosphamide [*Antineoplastic drug regimen*]
AVC	Aeronautical Video Charts (MCD)
AVC	Aireworth Volunteer Corps [*British military*] (DMA)
AVC	Altitude Velocity Chart
AVC	American Values Center (EA)
AVC	American Veterans Committee (EA)
AVC	American Video Channels, Inc. [*New York, NY*] [*Telecommunications*] (TSSD)
AVC	American Viewcard Club (EA)
AVC	Appraisal & Valuation Consultants Ltd. [*British*]
AVC	Arc Vacuum Cast

AVC .... Arivaca Silver Mines Ltd. [*Vancouver Stock Exchange symbol*]
AVC .... Army Veterinary Corps [*Facetious translation during World War I "All Very Cushy"*] [*Later, RAVC*] [*British*]
AVC .... Army Volunteers Corps [*British*]
AVC .... Artillery Volunteer Corps [*British*]
AVC .... Association of Visual Communicators (EA)
AVC .... Association of Vitamin Chemists (EA)
AVC .... Associative Visual Cortex [*Anatomy*]
AVC .... Atrioventricular Canal [*Cardiology*]
AVC .... Automatic Valve Control (IEEE)
AVC .... Automatic Vent Control (IEEE)
AVC .... Automatic Vibration Control
AVC .... Automatic Voltage Control (NATG)
AVC .... Automatic Volume Control [*Telecommunications*]
AVC .... Avco-Everett Research Laboratory, Everett, MA [*OCLC symbol*] (OCLC)
AVC .... Average Variable Costs
AVC .... Avionics Change (MCD)
AVC .... Lakeland College, Vermilion, Alberta [*Library symbol*] [*National Library of Canada*] (NLC)
AVC .... Large Catapult Lighter [*Navy symbol*] [*Obsolete*]
AVC .... Victorian Conveyancing Law and Practice [*Australia*] [*A publication*]
AVCA .... American Volleyball Coaches Association (EA)
AVCAD .... Aviation Cadet [*Navy*]
AVCAL ..... Aviation Calibration Equipment (MCD)
AVCAL ..... Aviation Consolidated Allowance List [*Military*] (NVT)
AVCARS .. Augmented Visual Carrier Aircraft Recovery System (MCD)
Av Cas .... Aviation Cases [*Commerce Clearing House*] [*A publication*] (DLA)
AVCAT ..... Aviation Fuel, High-Flash Point [*NATO*]
AVCC .... Acorn Venture Capital Corp. [*NASDAQ symbol*] (NQ)
AVCC .... Association of Venture Capital Clubs (EA)
AVCCOA .. Audiovisual, Computer, and Communication Office Automation
AVCG .... Automatic Vapor Crystal Growth [*Materials processing*]
AVCH .... Assistant Vice Chancellor (DLA)
AVCI .... Audio-Visual Credit Interchange [*Defunct*] (EA)
AVCM ...... Master Chief Avionics Technician [*Navy rating*]
AVCM ...... Valhalla Centre Municipal Library, Alberta [*Library symbol*] [*National Library of Canada*] (NLC)
AVCMF .... Arivaca Silver Mines Ltd. [*NASDAQ symbol*] (NQ)
AVCN .... Anteroventral Cochlear Nucleus
AVCO .... Average Cost [*Accounting term*]
Avco Corp Res Rep ... Avco Corporation. Research Reports [*A publication*]
AV Comm R ... AV Communication Review [*A publication*]
AV Commun Rev ... AV Communication Review [*A publication*]
AVCP .... Victoria Civil Procedure Updater [*Australia*] [*A publication*]
AVCPAY ... Advances in Clinical Pharmacology [*A publication*]
AVCR .... AV Communication Review [*A publication*]
AVCRAD.. Aviation Classification Repair Activity Depot [*Army*] (RDA)
AVCS .... Advanced Vidicon Camera System
AVCS .... Assistant Vice Chief of Staff
AVCS .... Atrioventricular Conduction System [*Cardiology*]
AVC of SA ... Assistant Vice Chief of Staff, Army [*Later, AVCSA*] (AABC)
AVCSA ...... Assistant Vice Chief of Staff, Army [*Formerly, AVC of SA*] (AABC)
AVD .... Aerospace Vehicle Detection
AVD .... Air Vehicle Detection (MCD)
AVD .... Air Velocity Detector
AVD .... Alternate Voice Data
AVD .... Anode Voltage Drop
AVD .... Antivehicle Device [*Air Force*] (MCD)
AVD .... Apparent Volume of Distribution [*Clinical chemistry*]
AVD .... Army Veterinary Department [*British*]
AVD .... Army Victualling Department [*British*]
AVD .... Atmospheric Vehicle Detection
AVD .... Automatic Voice Data (MCD)
AVD .... Automatic Voltage Digitizer
AVD .... Aviation Training Devices (Provisional) [*Army*] (RDA)
AVD .... Avondale Resources, Inc. [*Vancouver Stock Exchange symbol*]
AVD .... Seaplane Tender, Destroyer [*Navy symbol*] [*Obsolete*]
AVDA .... American Venereal Disease Association (EA)
AVDA .... American Veterinary Distributors Association (EA)
AVDA .... Associated Video Dealers of America [*Defunct*] (EA)
AVDA .... Avenida [*Avenue*] (EY)
AVDAC ..... Aviation Data Analysis Center (MCD)
AVDC .... Acoustics and Vibration Data Center (MCD)
AVDD .... Advanced Vehicle Design Department
Av-Dev ..... Aviation Developments [*Australia*]
AVDIA ...... Avian Diseases [*A publication*]
AVDL .... Avondale Industries, Inc. [*NASDAQ symbol*] (NQ)
AVDLRS ... Aviation Depot Level Repairables (MCD)
AVDM ...... Axial Vector Dominance Model
AVDO .... Aerospace Vehicle Distribution Office [*or Officer*] [*Air Force*] (AFM)
AVDP .... Aided Visual Development Program
AVDP .... Alaska Village Demonstration Project [*Environmental Protection Agency*]
AVDP .... Avoirdupois (KSC)
AVDPS ...... Avoirdupois

AVDS .... American Veterinary Dental Society (EA)
AVDS .... Audiovisual Distribution System (MCD)
AVDTH..... Average Depth (NOAA)
AVDU .... Audiovisual Display Unit
AVE .... Ad Valorem [*According to the Value*] Equivalent
AVE .... Aerospace Vehicle Electronics (MCD)
AVE .... Aerospace [*or Airborne*] Vehicle Equipment
AVE .... Airborne Vehicle Equipment
AVE .... Aortic Valve Echophonocardiogram [*Cardiology*]
AVE .... Asocio de Verduloj Esperantistaj [*Association of Esperantist Greens - AEG*] (EAIO)
AVE .... Association pour le Volontariat a l'Acte Gratuit en Europe [*Association for Voluntary Action in Europe - AVAE*] (EAIO)
AVE .... Atmospheric Variability Experiment [*NASA*]
AVE .... Automated Voltammetric Electrode [*Electrochemistry*]
AVE .... Automatic Volume Expansion
AVE .... AVEMCO Corp. [*NYSE symbol*] (SPSG)
AVE .... Avenal, CA [*Location identifier*] [*FAA*] (FAAL)
AVE .... Avenue [*Correspondence*] (AFM)
AVE .... Avenue Resources, Inc. [*Vancouver Stock Exchange symbol*]
AVE .... Average
AVE .... Averroes [*Morocco*] [*Geomagnetic observatory code*]
AVE .... Averroes [*Morocco*] [*Seismograph station code, US Geological Survey*] (SEIS)
ave .... Avesta [*MARC language code*] [*Library of Congress*] (LCCP)
AVE .... Vegreville Public Library, Alberta [*Library symbol*] [*National Library of Canada*] (NLC)
AVEA .... American Veterinary Exhibitors' Association (EA)
AVEA .... National Adult Vocational Education Association (EA)
AVEBD...... Average Blank Data [*Data processing*]
AVEC........ Allen Video-Enhanced Contrast [*Microscopy*]
AVEC........ Association of Poultry Processors and Poultry Import- and Export-Trade in the EEC Countries (EAIO)
AVEC........ Automatic Vibration Exciter Control
AVEE........ Alberta Environment Centre, Vegreville, Alberta [*Library symbol*] [*National Library of Canada*] (NLC)
AVEIA ...... Archivio Veterinario Italiano [*A publication*]
AVEIAN.... Archivio Veterinario Italiano [*A publication*]
AVEL........ Aircraft Velocity (MCD)
AVEM ...... Association of Vacuum Equipment Manufacturers (EA)
A Ven .... Archeologia Veneta [*A publication*]
AVen .... Archivio Veneto [*A publication*]
Avenir Agr ... Avenir Agriculture [*A publication*]
Avenir Med ... Avenir Medical [*A publication*]
AVENS...... Audiovisual Education in Neurosurgery
AVENSA... Aerovias Venezolanas Sociedad Anonima [*Airline*] [*Venezuela*]
Av Ensenanza Invest Esc Nac Agric (Chapingo) ... Escuela Nacional de Agricultura (Chapingo). Avances en la Ensenanza y la Investigacion [*A publication*]
AVEOS...... Advanced Visual [*Near Visual*] Electro-Optic Sensor [*Simulator*] (MCD)
AVEP........ Average Visual Evoked Potential [*Neurophysiology*]
AVEPDA... American Vocational Education Personnel Development Association (EA)
AVER .... Assistant Veterans Employment Representative [*Department of Labor*]
AVER .... Average
AVER .... Vermilion Public Library, Alberta [*Library symbol*] [*National Library of Canada*] (NLC)
AVERA...... American Vocational Education Research Association (EA)
AVERAGE ... Adrian Van Reypen Egerton [*Near-acronym used as shortened first name of detective-story character Average Jones, in stories by Samuel Hopkins Adams*]
Averbach Acci Cas ... Averbach on Handling Accident Cases [*A publication*] (DLA)
AVERDISROP ... Avert Disruption of Operation
AVERE...... Association Europeenne des Vehicules Electriques Routiers [*European Electric Road Vehicle Association*] (EAIO)
AVERT...... AIDS Virus Education and Research Trust [*British*]
AVERT...... Association of Volunteer Emergency Radio Teams
AVERT...... Automatic Verification, Evaluation, and Readiness Tester
Avery Ind Archit Per ... Avery Index to Architectural Periodicals of Columbia University [*A publication*]
Avery Index Archit Period ... Avery Index to Architectural Periodicals [*A publication*]
Avery Index Archit Period Second Ed Revis Enlarged Suppl ... Avery Index to Architectural Periodicals. Second Edition. Revised and Enlarged. Supplement [*A publication*]
AVES........ Air Vane Erection System (MCD)
A Ves.......... Arheoloski Vestnik [*Ljubljana*] [*A publication*]
AVES........ Automatic Vertical Electrophoresis System [*Instrumentation*]
Avesta Stainless Bull ... Avesta Stainless Bulletin [*A publication*]
AVETD...... Atomno-Vodorodnaya Energetika i Tekhnologiya [*A publication*]
AVEXS...... Aviation Electronic Equipment Information Exchange System (MCD)
AVEZA6.... Acta Vitaminologica et Enzymologica [*A publication*]
AVF .... All-Volunteer Force [*Army*]
AVF .... America Victory Force (EA)
AVF .... American Vineyard Foundation (EA)

AVF .... America's Victory Force [*An association*]   (EA)
AVF .... Antiviral Factor
AVF .... Archivos Venezolanos de Folklore [*A publication*]
AVF .... Arteriovenous Fistula [*Medicine*]
AVF .... Association of Venture Founders   (EA)
AVF .... Augmented V Lead, Left Leg [*Electrocardiogram*] [*Medicine*]
AVF .... Availability Factor
AVF .... Avril Sur Loire [*France*] [*Seismograph station code, US Geological Survey*]   (SEIS)
AVF .... Azimuthally Varying Field
AVFC .... AmVestors Financial Corporation [*Topeka, KS*] [*NASDAQ symbol*]   (NQ)
AVFG .... Air Vehicle Functional Group [*Military*]
AVFMER .. Air Vehicle Field Maintenance Evaluation Requirement   (MCD)
AVFP .... Activate VFR [*Visual Flight Rules*] Flight Plan [*Aviation*]   (FAAC)
AVFPNO .. Pilot Failed to Activate VFR/DVFR Flight Plan [*Aviation*]   (FAAC)
AVFR .... Available for Reassignment
AVFSAO .. Archiv fuer Fischereiwissenschaft [*A publication*]
AVFUEL ... Aviation Fuel   (MSA)
AVG .... Advanced Growth Systems, Inc. [*Vancouver Stock Exchange symbol*]
AVG .... Air Ventilation Garment [*NASA*]
AVG .... Aircraft Escort Vessel [*Navy symbol*] [*Obsolete*]
AVG .... American Volunteer Group [*Flying Tigers*] [*World War II*]
AVG .... Aminoethoxyvinylglycine [*Organic chemistry*]
AVG .... Angestelltenversicherungsgesetz [*Unemployment Insurance*] [*German*]
AVG .... Average   (AFM)
AVG .... Educational Screen and Audiovisual Guide [*Later, AV Guide: The Learning Media Magazine*] [*A publication*]
AVG .... Goals-Against Average [*Hockey*]
AVGA .... Avant-Garde Computing, Inc. [*NASDAQ symbol*]   (NQ)
AVGAS ...... Aviation Gasoline
AVGE .... Average   (ADA)
AVGP .... Armored Vehicle General Purpose [*General Motors armored car*] [*Canada*]
AVGS .... Adaptive Video Guidance System   (MCD)
AVGSAP ... Automated Viscoelastic Grain Structural Analysis Program   (MCD)
AVH .... Acute Viral Hepatitis [*Medicine*]
AVH .... Adventure Vehicle [*Vancouver Stock Exchange symbol*]
AVH .... Aircraft Rescue Boat [*Navy symbol*]
AVH .... Allamvedelmi Hivatal [*Hungarian secret police*]
AVH .... Average Heading
Av & HBL .. Avery and Hobb's Bankrupt Law [*A publication*]   (DLA)
Av Hist Soc Aust J ... Aviation Historical Society of Australia. Journal [*A publication*]   (APTA)
AVHMA .... American Veterinary Holistic Medical Association [*Later, AHVMA*]   (EA)
Avh Norsk Vid-Akad Oslo I NS ... Avhandlinger Utgitt av Norsk Videnskaps-Akademi I Oslo. I. Matematisk-Naturvidenskapelig Klasse. Ny Serie [*A publication*]
Avh Nor Vidensk-Akad Oslo I ... Avhandlinger Utgitt av Norsk Videnskaps-Akademi I Oslo. I. Matematisk-Naturvidenskapelig Klasse [*A publication*]
AVHOM ... Aided Visual Homing Missile   (MCD)
AVHRR ..... Advanced Very-High-Resolution Radiometer [*NASA*]
AVHUEA ... Acta Veterinaria Hungarica [*A publication*]
Avh Utgitt Nor Vidensk-Akad Oslo Mat-Naturvidensk Kl ... Avhandlinger Utgitt av Norsk Videnskaps-Akademi I Oslo. Matematisk-Naturvidenskapelig Klasse [*A publication*]
AVI .... Active Vibration Isolator   (MCD)
AVI .... Acuvision Systems, Inc. [*Vancouver Stock Exchange symbol*]
AVI .... Air Velocity Index
AVI .... Airborne Vehicle Identification
AVI .... American Veterans of Israel   (EA)
AVI .... American Video Institute [*Rochester Institute of Technology*] [*Research center*]   (RCD)
AVI .... Anglovaal Industries Ltd. [*South Africa*]
AVI .... Appalachian Volunteers, Incorporated   (EA)
AVI .... Association Universelle d'Aviculture Scientifique [*World's Poultry Science Association - WPSA*]   (EAIO)
AVI .... Association of Veterinary Inspectors
Av I .... Audiovisual Instruction [*A publication*]
AVI .... Australian Veterinarians in Industry
AVI .... Aviation   (DLA)
AVI .... Avoid Verbal Instructions [*DoD*]   (MCD)
AVI .... Vilna Public Library, Alberta [*Library symbol*] [*National Library of Canada*]   (NLC)
AVI .... Waterville, ME [*Location identifier*] [*FAA*]   (FAAL)
AVIA .... Adult Video Industry Association of Australia
AVIA .... Aviation Pay [*Navy*]
AVIAA ...... Aviation Age [*A publication*]
AVIAC ...... Aviation Industry Advisory Council   (ADA)
AVIACO ... Aviacion y Comercio SA [*Aviation and Trade Corporation*] [*Airline*] [*Spain*]
Avian Biol .. Avian Biology [*A publication*]

AVIANCA ... Aerovias Nacionales de Colombia [*Colombian National Airways*]
Avian Dis ... Avian Diseases [*A publication*]
Avian Pathol ... Avian Pathology [*A publication*]
Avian Res ... Avian Research [*A publication*]
Aviat Age ... Aviation Age [*A publication*]
AVIATECA ... Empresa Guatemalteca de Aviacion [*Airline*] [*Guatemala*]
Aviation Da ... Aviation Daily [*A publication*]
Aviation N ... Aviation News [*A publication*]
Aviation Q ... United States Aviation Quarterly [*A publication*]   (DLA)
Aviation W ... Aviation Week [*A publication*]
Aviat Kosmonavt ... Aviatsiya i Kosmonavtika [*USSR*] [*A publication*]
Aviat Med ... Aviation Medicine [*A publication*]
Aviat Res Monogr ... Aviation Research Monographs [*A publication*]
Aviat Rev ... Aviation Review [*A publication*]
Aviats Khim ... Aviatsiya i Khimiya [*A publication*]
Aviat Space Environ Med ... Aviation, Space, and Environmental Medicine [*A publication*]
Aviat Spac Environ Med ... Aviation, Space, and Environmental Medicine [*A publication*]
Aviat Sp En ... Aviation, Space, and Environmental Medicine [*A publication*]
Aviats Promst ... Aviatsionnaya Promyshlennost [*A publication*]
Aviat Week Space Technol ... Aviation Week and Space Technology [*A publication*]
Avia Week ... Aviation Week and Space Technology [*A publication*]
Avic Mag ... Avicultural Magazine [*A publication*]
Avicult Mag ... Avicultural Magazine [*A publication*]
Avicult Tec ... Avicultura Tecnica [*A publication*]
AVID .... Advanced Visual Information Display
AVID .... Aerospace Vehicle Interactive Design   (MCD)
AVID .... Agriculture Victoria-Library Catalogue [*Victoria Department of Agriculture and Rural Affairs*] [*Australia*] [*Information service or system*]   (IID)
AVID .... Airborne Vehicle Identification   (AABC)
AVID .... American Video Teleconferencing Corp. [*Farmingdale, NY*] [*NASDAQ symbol*]   (NQ)
AVID .... Automated Vibration Diagnostic System   (MCD)
AVIEN .... Aviation Engineering Corp.   (MCD)
AVIK .... Viking Public Library, Alberta [*Library symbol*] [*National Library of Canada*]   (NLC)
AVIM .... Aviation Intermediate Maintenance [*Army*]   (MCD)
AVINB .... Advances in Instrumentation [*A publication*]
A-V Ind ...... Audio-Visual Index [*A publication*]
AV Inst ...... Audiovisual Instruction [*A publication*]
Av Instr ...... Audiovisual Instruction [*A publication*]
AVIOB .... Aviation Observation   (NOAA)
AVIONICS ... Aviation Electronics
AVIOS .... American Voice Input/Output Society   (EA)
AVIP .... Association of Viewdata Information Providers   (EA)
AVIRA2 ..... Acta Virologica [*Prague*] [*English Edition*] [*A publication*]
AVIRIS ...... Airborne Visible-Infrared Imaging Spectrometer
AVIS .... Active Vibration Isolation System
AVIS .... Audiovisual Information System
AVIS .... Automatic Visual Inspection System [*NASA*]
AVISD .... Avishkar [*A publication*]
AVISPA ..... Aerovias Interamericanas de Panama SA
AVISURS ... Aerospace Vehicle Inventory, Status, and Utilization Reporting System
AVIT .... Audiovisual Instructional Technology [*Military*]   (AABC)
A Viva .... Archeologia Viva [*A publication*]
AVJ .... Antivibration Joint
AVJC .... Antelope Valley Junior College [*Later, Antelope Valley College*] [*Lancaster, CA*]
AV J-C ...... Avant Jesus-Christ [*Before Christ*] [*French*]
AVK .... Alva, OK [*Location identifier*] [*FAA*]   (FAAL)
AVK .... Audiovisual Kit [*Army*]
AVKO .... Audio, Visual, Kinesthetic, and Oral [*Teaching techniques*]   (EA)
AVKOA ...... Aviatsiya i Kosmonavtika [*A publication*]
AVKOERF ... AVKO Educational Research Foundation   (EA)
AVL .... Address Validity   (MCD)
AVL .... Adelson-Velskii and Landis Trees [*Data processing*]
AVL .... Allegheny College, Meadville, PA [*OCLC symbol*]   (OCLC)
AVL .... Allport-Vernon-Lindzey [*Study of values*]
AVL .... Angle Versus Length [*Data processing*]
AVL .... Approved Vendors List
AVL .... Armored Vehicle Launched [*Military*]   (MCD)
AVL .... Aroostook Valley Railroad Co. [*AAR code*]
AVL .... Asheville [*North Carolina*] [*Airport symbol*]   (OAG)
AVL .... Associated Veterinary Laboratories [*Defunct*]   (EA)
AVL .... Audio Visual Library, University of Toronto [*UTLAS symbol*]
AVL .... Augmented V Lead, Left Arm [*Electrocardiogram*] [*Medicine*]
AVL .... Automatic Vehicle Location   (IEEE)
AVL .... Avalon Corp. [*NYSE symbol*]   (SPSG)
AVL .... Avionics Verification Laboratory   (MCD)
AVLA .... Audio-Visual Language Association [*British*]
AVLABS ..... Aviation Laboratories [*Army*]
AVLB .... Armored Vehicle Launched Bridge [*Military*]   (INF)
AVLBL ...... Available [*or Availability*]   (MSA)
AVLF .... Airborne Very-Low-Frequency   (NG)

AVLF......... Alberta Fire Training School, Alberta Labour, Vermilion, Alberta [*Library symbol*] [*National Library of Canada*] (NLC)
AVLH....... Assam Valley Light Horse [*British military*] (DMA)
AV Libn ..... Audiovisual Librarian [*A publication*]
AVLINE.... Audiovisuals On-Line [*National Library of Medicine*] [*Rockville Pike, MD*] [*Database*]
AVLIS ...... Atomic Vapor LASER Isotope Separation
A-V L J...... Audio-Visual Language Journal [*A publication*]
AVLM .... Antivehicle Land Mine
AVLO........ Audiovisual Liaison Officer [*Army*]
AVLOC...... Airborne Visible-LASER Optical-Communications
AVLOC ..... Aviation Logistics Officer Course [*Army*] (INF)
Av L Rep.... Aviation Law Reporter [*Commerce Clearing House*] [*A publication*] (DLA)
Av L Rep CCH ... Aviation Law Reports. Commerce Clearing House [*A publication*]
AVLSI ...... Advanced Very-Large-Scale Integration [*Electronics*]
AVLUB...... Aviation Lubricant (MUGU)
AVM......... Acoustic Velocity Meter (NOAA)
AVM......... Acute Viral Meningitis [*Medicine*]
AVM......... Air Velocity Meter
AVM......... Air Vice-Marshal [*British*]
AVM......... Airborne Vibration Monitor (NG)
AVM......... Anterior Ventral Microtubule [*Anatomy*]
AVM......... Antivehicle Mine
AVM......... Arteriovenous Malformation [*Medicine*]
AVM......... Audiovisual Modulator
AVM......... Automatic Vehicle Monitoring [*Antihijack device*]
AVM......... Automatic Voting Machine
AVM......... Ave Maria
AVM......... Aviation Medical
AVM......... Guided Missile Ship [*Navy symbol*]
AVM......... Veteran Municipal Library, Alberta [*Library symbol*] [*National Library of Canada*] (NLC)
AVMA...... American Veterinary Medical Association (EA)
AVMA...... Audio-Visual Management Association (EA)
AVMC...... Association for Vertical Market Computing (EA)
AVMC...... AVM Corporation [*NASDAQ symbol*] (NQ)
AVMCS.... Ambient Air Ventilation Microclimate System [*Army*] (RDA)
AVMDA.... Amusement and Vending Machine Distributors Association (EA)
AVMEBI... Avtometriia [*A publication*]
AVMED.... Aviation Medicine [*A publication*]
A-V Media ... Audio-Visual Media [*A publication*]
AVMF ...... Aviatsiya Voenno Morskogo Flota [*Aviation - Naval Fleet*] [*USSR*]
AVMGAN ... Avicultural Magazine [*A publication*]
AVMH...... Available Manhours (AFM)
AVMHB.... Archives of Mechanics [*Archiwum Mechaniki Stosowanej*] [*A publication*]
AVMI ...... Automated Video Maintenance Information (MCD)
AVMP ...... Audio Video Market Place [*A publication*]
AVMPAG ... Archivos Venezolanos de Medicina Tropical y Parasitologia Medica [*A publication*]
AVMR ...... Association of Visual Merchandise Representatives (EA)
AVMR ...... Avino Mines & Resources Ltd. [*NASDAQ symbol*] (NQ)
AVMRI..... Arctic Vessel and Marine Research Institute [*National Research Council of Canada*] [*Later, Institute of Marine Dynamics*] [*Research center*] (RCD)
AVMS....... Administration de la Voie Maritime du Saint-Laurent [*St. Lawrence Seaway Authority - SLSA*] [*Canada*]
AVMS....... Advanced Manufacturing Systems, Inc. [*NASDAQ symbol*] (NQ)
AVMS....... Annulus Vacuum Maintenance System [*Nuclear energy*] (NRCH)
AVMS....... Automatic Vehicle Monitoring System [*Army*] (MCD)
AVMS....... Naval Aviation [*USSR designation*]
AVN......... Atrioventricular Node [*Cardiology*]
AVN......... Avanti Productions, Inc. [*Vancouver Stock Exchange symbol*]
AVN......... AVIANCA [*Aerovias Nacionales de Colombia SA*] [*Colombian airline*]
AVN......... Aviation (AFM)
AVN......... Aviation News [*A publication*]
AVN......... Avignon [*France*] [*Airport symbol*] (OAG)
AVN......... Rochester, NY [*Location identifier*] [*FAA*] (FAAL)
a-vn---....... Vietnam, North [*MARC geographic area code*] [*Library of Congress*] (LCCP)
AVNA....... American Veterinary Neurology Association (EA)
AVNAG..... Annalen des Vereins fuer Nassauische Altertumskunde und Geschichtsforschung [*A publication*]
AVNAKGF ... Annalen des Vereins fuer Nassauische Altertumskunde und Geschichtsforschung [*A publication*]
AVNB........ Avascular Necrosis of Bone [*Medicine*]
AVNC........ Aviation Center [*Army*]
AVN(CM) ... Aviation Pay (Crewmember) [*Navy*]
AVNDA..... Avtomobil'nye Dorogi [*A publication*]
AVNDTA .. Aviation Development Test Activity [*Test and Evaluation Command*] [*Army*] (RDA)
AVNEC ..... Army Aviation Employment Conference
AVNENGRBN ... Aviation Engineer Battalion [*Marine Corps*]

AVNL........ Automatic Video Noise Leveling [*or Limiting*]
AVNMED ... Aviation Medicine [*Military*] (AABC)
AVN(NCM) ... Aviation Pay (Non-Crewmember) [*Navy*]
AVNP........ Arviap Nipinga. Eskimo Point [*A publication*]
AVNR........ Atrioventricular Nodal Reentry [*Cardiology*]
AVNS .... Aviation School [*Army*]
AVNSAFCEN ... Naval Aviation Safety Center
AVNSBV... Advances in Neurosurgery [*A publication*]
AVNSCOLCOM ... Naval Aviation School Command
AVNU........ Aviation Unit [*Marine Corps*]
AVNUA2... Archivos Venezolanos de Nutricion [*A publication*]
AVO.......... Administrative Veterinary Officer [*British military*] (DMA)
AVO.......... Avino Mines & Resources Ltd. [*Vancouver Stock Exchange symbol*]
AVO.......... Avoid Verbal Orders [*Military*]
AVO.......... Avon [*Australia*] [*Seismograph station code, US Geological Survey*] (SEIS)
AVO.......... Avon Park, FL [*Location identifier*] [*FAA*] (FAAL)
Avocado Grow ... Avocado Grower [*A publication*]
AVOCON ... Automated Vocabulary Control [*Subsystem of PLIS*] [*Data processing*]
AVOID...... Accelerated View of Input Data
AVOID...... Airfield Vehicle Obstacle Indication Device
AVOIDS.... Avionic Observation of Intruder Danger Systems [*Army*]
AVOIL...... Aviation Oil [*Military*]
AVOIR...... Avoirdupois
AVOLO..... Automatic Voice Link Observation
AVOMBI... Advances in Ophthalmology [*A publication*]
AVON....... Avon Rent-a-Car & Truck Corp. [*NASDAQ symbol*] (NQ)
AVOZVOTS ... Average Australian Voters
AVP.......... Actinomycin D, Vincristine, Platinol [*Cisplatin*] [*Antineoplastic drug regimen*]
AVP.......... Adaptive Video Processor
AVP.......... Address Verification Pulse (KSC)
AVP.......... Aeronautical Video Plates (MCD)
AVP.......... Aktionsgemeinschaft Vierte Partei [*Fourth Party Action Group*] [*Federal Republic of Germany*] [*Political party*] (PPW)
AvP.......... Alterntuemer von Pergamon [*A publication*]
AVP.......... Alvin W. Vogtle, Jr. Plant [*Nuclear energy*] (NRCH)
AVP.......... Antiviral Protein [*Immunology*]
AVP.......... Arginine Vasopressin [*Antidiuretic hormone*]
AVP.......... Army Validation Program
AVP.......... Arubaanse Volks Partij [*Aruban People's Party*] [*Netherlands Antilles*] [*Political party*] (PPW)
AVP.......... Assistant Vice President
AVP.......... Association of Volleyball Professionals (EA)
AVP.......... Automatic Variable Perforating
AVP.......... Avcorp Industries, Inc. [*Toronto Stock Exchange symbol*]
AVP.......... Aviation Publication (MCD)
AVP.......... Avoirdupois (ADA)
AVP.......... Avon Products, Inc. [*NYSE symbol*] (SPSG)
AVP.......... Office of Aviation Policy [*FAA*] (FAAC)
AVP.......... Small Seaplane Tender [*Navy symbol*] [*Obsolete*]
AVP.......... Wilkes-Barre/Scranton [*Pennsylvania*] [*Airport symbol*] [*Derived from location of airport: Avoca, Pennsylvania*]
AVPA....... American Veneer Package Association (EA)
AVPA....... Australian Veterinary Poultry Association
AVPADN ... Avian Pathology [*A publication*]
AVPBC .... Advances in Psychobiology [*A publication*]
AVPBCP ... Advances in Psychobiology [*A publication*]
AVPC....... Association of Vice-Principals in Colleges [*British*]
AVPCA ..... Advances in Pharmacology and Chemotherapy [*A publication*]
AVPCCS.... Archiv foer Pharmaci og Chemi. Scientific Edition [*A publication*]
AVPI........ Agricultural and Veterinary Products Index [*A publication*]
AVPL....... Average Picture Level (MSA)
AVPMAM ... American Veterinary Medical Association. Scientific Proceedings of the Annual Meeting [*A publication*]
AVPOOL... Available Labor Pool Model (MCD)
AVPPAV ... Archivos Venezolanos de Puericultura y Pediatria [*A publication*]
AVPRA..... Avtomobil'naya Promyshlennost [*A publication*]
Av Prod Anim ... Avances en Produccion Animal [*A publication*]
AVPTA9.... Archivos Venezolanos de Patologia Tropical y Parasitologia Medica [*A publication*]
AVPUG ..... AV [*Audiovisual*] Pansophic Users Group (EA)
AVPZAR ... Archiv fuer Pflanzenschutz [*A publication*]
AVR......... Advance Murgor [*Vancouver Stock Exchange symbol*]
AVR......... Agent's Vehicle Record (DS)
AVR......... Aircraft [*or Aviation*] Rescue Vessel [*Navy symbol*] [*Obsolete*]
AVR......... American Ventures [*Vancouver Stock Exchange symbol*]
AVR......... Aortic Valve Replacement [*Cardiology*]
AVR......... Arkansas River Valley Regional Library, Dardanelle, AR [*OCLC symbol*] (OCLC)
AVR......... Armoured Vehicle, Reconnaissance [*British military*] (DMA)
AVR......... Army Veterinary and Remount Services [*British*]
AVR......... Army Volunteer Reserve [*British*]
AVR......... Augmented V Lead, Right Arm [*Electrocardiogram*] [*Medicine*]
AVR......... Australian Video Review [*A publication*] (APTA)
AVR......... Automatic Voice Relay
AVR......... Automatic Voltage Regulator

AVR .... Automatic Volume Recognition (MCD)
AVR .... Aviator (AABC)
AVR .... Avirulence
AVR .... Axial Velocity Ratio
AVRAD ..... Altitude Variation Rate and Displacement
AVRADA .. Avionics Research and Development Activity [*Fort Monmouth, NJ*] [*Army*] (GRD)
AVRADCOM ... Army Aviation Research and Development Command [*Fort Monmouth, NJ*] (MCD)
AVRD .... Audio Video Review Digest [*A publication*]
AVRDC ..... Asian Vegetable Research and Development Center (EA)
AVRE .... Armoured Vehicle, Royal Engineers [*British and Canadian*] [*World War II*]
AVRE .... Assault Vehicle, Royal Engineers [*British*]
AVRHS ..... Association for Vital Records and Health Statistics (EA)
AVRI......... Animal Virus Research Institute [*British*] (ARC)
AVRLSS... Arkansas Valley Regional Library Service System [*Library network*]
AVRO .... A. V. Roe & Co. Ltd. [*Acronym used as designation for a British aircraft and is formed from the name of the aircraft's manufacturer*]
AVROC ..... Aviation Reserve Officers Candidate Program
AVRS........ American Veterinary Radiology Society [*Defunct*] (EA)
AVRS........ Army Veterinary and Remount Services [*British military*] (DMA)
AVRS........ Atrial Vascular Relaxant Substance [*Biochemistry*]
AVRS........ Audio-Video Recording System [*Air Force*]
AVRTAJ ... Acta Vertebratica [*A publication*]
AVRV .... Avian Retrovirus
AVRY .... Avery, Inc. [*New York, NY*] [*NASDAQ symbol*] (NQ)
AVS+ .... Address Verification System Plus [*Information Design, Inc.*] [*Information service or system*] (IID)
AVS .... Adjustable Voltage Screwdown
AVS .... Advance in Schedule (KSC)
AVS .... Advanced V/STOL [*Vertical/Short Takeoff and Landing*] Weapon System (MCD)
AVS .... Advanced Vertical Strike Fighter (MCD)
AVS .... Advanced Vortex System (MCD)
AVS .... Aerospace Vehicle System (MCD)
AVS .... Aided Visual System
AVS .... Air Valve Silencer
AVS .... Air Vehicle Specification (MCD)
AVS .... Airborne V/STOL [*Vertical/Short Takeoff and Landing*] Simulator (MCD)
AVS .... Airborne Viewing System
AVS .... Altitude-Vertical Scale
AVS .... American Vacuum Society (EA)
AVS .... American Vegan Society (EA)
AVS .... American Videotext Services, Inc. [*Peekskill, NY*] [*Telecommunications*] (TSSD)
AVS .... American Viola Society (EA)
AVS .... Anti-Vivisection Society [*Absorbed by VIL*] (EA)
AVS .... Applied Videotex Systems, Inc. [*Telecommunications service*] (TSSD)
AVS .... Army Veterinary Service [*British*] (DAS)
AVS .... Arteriovenous Shunt [*Cardiology*]
AVS .... Association for Voluntary Sterilization, Inc. [*New York, NY*] [*Research center*]
AVS .... Automated Verification System [*Data processing*] (MCD)
AVS .... Aviation Supply Ship [*Navy symbol*]
AVS .... Aviva Resources, Inc. [*Vancouver Stock Exchange symbol*]
a-vs--- .... Vietnam, South [*MARC geographic area code*] [*Library of Congress*] (LCCP)
AVSA........ African Violet Society of America (EA)
A/VSA........ Altimeter/Velocity Sensor Antenna
AVSA......... Australian Victorian Studies Association
AVSAB ..... American Veterinary Society of Animal Behavior (EA)
AVSC........ Association for Voluntary Surgical Contraception (EA)
AVSC........ Audiovisual Support Center [*Army*] (AABC)
AVSCA7.... Acta Veterinaria Scandinavica [*A publication*]
AVSCB ..... Advances in Veterinary Science and Comparative Medicine [*A publication*]
AVSCM..... American Veterinary Society for Computer Medicine (EA)
AVSCOM ... Aviation and Surface Material Command [*Air Force*]
AVSCOM ... Aviation Systems Command [*St. Louis, MO*] [*Army*]
AVSD .... Avco Systems Development (MCD)
AVSECOM ... Aviation Security Command [*Philippines*]
AVSEP ...... Audiovisual Superimposed Electrocardiogram Presentation
AVSER ...... Aviation Safety Engineering and Research (KSC)
AVSF........ Advanced Vertical Strike Fighter
AVSI......... Advanced Vertical Speed Indicator
AVSIM...... Avionic System Simulation (MCD)
AVSL .... Association of Visual Science Librarians (EA)
AVSLK ..... Archiv des Vereins fuer Siebenbuergische Landeskunde [*A publication*]
AVsLund.... Vetenskaps-Societeten i Lund. Aarsbok [*A publication*]
AVSM........ Auxiliary Video Switching Matrix
AVSN .... Automatic Voice Switching Network (AFIT)
AVSPAC ... Acta Veterinaria Scandinavica. Supplementum [*A publication*]
AVSq .... Audiovisual Squadron [*Air Force*]
AVSR......... Avionics Verification Status Room [*NASA*] (NASA)

AVSRCK ... Advances in Sleep Research [*A publication*]
AVSS .... Aided Visual Sensor System
AVSS .... Apollo Vehicle Systems Section [*NASA*] (KSC)
AVSS .... Automated Vendor Selection System (NRCH)
AVSS .... Automatic Video Scoring System [*Army*] (INF)
AVST .... Advanced Vehicle Simulation Technique
AVST......... Australian Investment Planning Guide [*A publication*]
AVST......... Automated Visual Sensitivity Tester
AVSTA ..... Advances in Space Science and Technology [*A publication*]
AVSV......... Aortic Valve Stroke Volume [*Cardiology*]
AVSVA ..... Avtomaticheskaya Svarka [*A publication*]
AVSYCOM ... Aviation Systems Command [*Army*] (MCD)
AVSYN....... Air Vehicle Synthesis [*Program*]
AVT .... Acceptance Vibration Testing [*NASA*] (NASA)
AVT .... Ad Valorem Tax [*Added Value Tax*]
AVT .... Adult Vocational Training [*HEW*]
AVT .... Advanced Video Terminal
AVT .... Air Velocity Transducer
AVT .... Air Vibrating Table
AVT .... All Vehicle Test
AVT .... All Volatile Treatment [*Nuclear energy*] (NRCH)
AVT .... Apollo Validation Test [*NASA*] (KSC)
AVT .... Applications Vertical Test Program [*Communication Satellite program*]
AVT .... Applied Voice Technology [*Telecommunications service*] (TSSD)
AVT .... Archivio Veneto-Tridentino [*A publication*]
AVT .... Arginine Vasotocin [*Endocrinology*]
AVT .... Audiovisual-Tutorial [*Instruction*] [*Media System Corp.*]
AVT .... Austin Area Vocational-Technology Institute, Austin, MN [*OCLC symbol*] (OCLC)
AVT .... Autovend Technology Corp. [*Vancouver Stock Exchange symbol*]
AVT .... Auxiliary Aircraft Training Ship
AVT .... Auxiliary Aircraft Transport [*Navy symbol*] [*Obsolete*]
AVT .... Available Time (AFM)
AVT .... Aviation Medicine Technician [*Navy*]
AVT .... Avnet, Inc. [*NYSE symbol*] (SPSG)
AVT .... Spokane, WA [*Location identifier*] [*FAA*] (FAAL)
AVT .... Training Carrier
a-vt--- .... Vietnam [*MARC geographic area code*] [*Library of Congress*] (LCCP)
AVTAG ..... Aviation Fuel [*Gasoline/Kerosene*] [*NATO*]
AVTAS ..... Advanced Visual Target Acquisition System (MCD)
AVTC........ American Video Teleconferencing Corporation [*Farmingdale, NY*] [*Telecommunications*] (TSSD)
AVTE........ Adult, Vocational, and Technical Education
AVTEA ..... Avtomatika i Telemekhanika [*A publication*]
AVThRw.... Aufsaetze und Vortraege zur Theologie und Religionswissenschaft [*Berlin*] [*A publication*]
AVTMP..... Average Temperature (NOAA)
Avtodorozhnik Ukr ... Avtodorozhnik Ukrainy [*A publication*]
Avtog Delo ... Avtogennoe Delo [*A publication*]
Avtomatika ... Akademija Nauk Ukrainskoi RSR. Institut Elektrotehniki Avtomatika [*Kiev*] [*A publication*]
Avtomat Izchisl Tekhn ... Avtomatika i Izchislitelna Tekhnika [*A publication*]
Avtomat Sistemy Upravlen ... Leningradskii Gosudarstvennyi Universitet Avtomatizirovannye Sistemy Upravlenija [*A publication*]
Avtomat Sistemy Upravlenija i Pribory Avtomat ... Avtomatizirovannye Sistemy Upravlenija i Pribory Avtomatiki [*A publication*]
Avtomat i Telemeh ... Akademija Nauk SSSR. Avtomatika i Telemehanika [*Moscow*] [*A publication*]
Avtomat i Telemekh ... Akademiya Nauk SSSR. Avtomatika i Telemekhanika [*A publication*]
Avtomat Upravlenie i Vychisl Tekhn ... Avtomaticheskoe Upravlenie i Vychislitel'naya Tekhnika [*A publication*]
Avtomat Upravl i Vycisl Tehnika ... Avtomaticeskoe Upravlenie i Vycislitel'naja Tehnika [*A publication*]
Avtomat i Vychisl Tekhn ... Avtomatika i Vychislitel'naya Tekhnika. Akademiya Nauk Latviiskoi SSR [*A publication*]
Avtomat i Vycisl Tekhn ... Avtomatika i Vychislitel'naya Tekhnika. Minskii Radiotekhnicheskii Institut [*A publication*]
Avtomat i Vycisl Tehnika (Minsk) ... Avtomatika i Vycislitel'naja Tehnika (Minsk) [*Minskii Radiotekhnicheskii Institut*] [*A publication*]
Avtomat i Vycisl Tehn (Riga) ... Avtomatika i Vycislitel'naja Tehnika (Riga) [*Akademija Nauk Latviiskoi SSR*] [*A publication*]
Avtometrija ... Avtometrija Akademija Nauk SSSR [*A publication*]
Avtom Khim Proizvod (Kiev) ... Avtomatizatsiya Khimicheskikh Proizvodstv (Kiev) [*A publication*]
Avtom Khim Proizvod (Moscow) ... Avtomatizatsiya Khimicheskikh Proizvodstv (Moscow) [*A publication*]
Avtom Khim Promsti ... Avtomatizatsiya Khimicheskoi Promyshlennosti [*A publication*]
Avtom Kompleksn Mekh Khim Tekhnol Protsessov ... Avtomatizatsiya i Kompleksnaya Mekhanizatsiya Khimiko Tekhnologicheskikh Protsessov [*A publication*]
Avtom Nauchn Issled Khim ... Avtomatizatsiya Nauchnykh Issledovanii v Khimii [*A publication*]
Avtomob Dorogi ... Avtomobil'nye Dorogi [*A publication*]

Avtomob Dorogi Dorozhne Budiv ... Avtomobil ni Dorogi i Dorozhne Budivnitstvo [*A publication*]
Avtomob Prom-St ... Avtomobil'naya Promyshlennost [*USSR*] [*A publication*]
Avtomob Traktorostr ... Avtomobile- i Traktorostroenie [*A publication*]
Avtomob Trakt Promst ... Avtomobil'naya i Traktornaya Promyshlennost [*A publication*]
Avtomob Transp (Kiev) ... Avtomobil'nyi Transport (Kiev) [*A publication*]
Avtomob Transp (Moscow) ... Avtomobil'nyi Transport (Moscow) [*A publication*]
Avtomon Transp Kaz ... Avtomobil'nyi Transport Kazakhstana [*Kazakh SSR*] [*A publication*]
Avtom Priborostr ... Avtomatizatsiya i Priborostroenie [*A publication*]
Avtom Priborostr Inf Nauchno Tekh ... Avtomatika i Priborostroenie. Informasionnyi Nauchno-Tekhnicheskii [*A publication*]
Avtom Proizvod Protsessov ... Avtomatizatsiya Proizvodstvennykh Protsessov [*A publication*]
Avtom Proizvod Protsessov Mashinostr Priborostr (Lvov) ... Avtomatizatsiya Proizvodstvennykh Protsessov v Mashinostroenii i Priborostroenii (Lvov) [*A publication*]
Avtom Sist Upr Prib Avtom ... Avtomatizirovannye Sistemy Upravlenija i Pribory Avtomatiki [*A publication*]
Avtom Staleplavil'n Proizvod ... Avtomatizatsiya Staleplavil'nogo Proizvodstva [*USSR*] [*A publication*]
Avtom Svarka ... Avtomaticheskaya Svarka [*A publication*]
Avtom & Telemekh ... Avtomatika i Telemekhanika [*A publication*]
Avtom Telemekh ... Avtomatika i Telemekhanika [*A publication*]
Avtom Telemekh Svyaz ... Avtomatika, Telemekhanika, i Svyaz [*A publication*]
Avtom Tsitol Diagn Opukholei ... Avtomatizatsiya Tsitologicheskoi Diagnostiki Opukholei [*A publication*]
Avtom & Vychisl Tekh ... Avtomatika i Vychislitel'naya Tekhnika [*A publication*]
Avtotrakt Delo ... Avtotraktornoe Delo [*A publication*]
AVTP........ Adult Vocational Training Program [*HEW*]
AVTR .... Advanced Video Tape Recorder
AVTR .... Airborne Video Tape Recorder   (MCD)
AVTR .... Analog Video Tape Recorder   (MCD)
AVTR .... Avatar Holdings, Inc. [*NASDAQ symbol*]   (NQ)
AVTRA...... Avtomobil'nyi Transport [*A publication*]
AVTRW..... Association of Veterinary Teachers and Research Workers [*British*]
AVTS........ Advanced Visual Technology System [*NASA*]
AVTSS ...... Automated Video Target Scoring System
AVTUR ..... Aviation Turbine Fuel   (ADA)
AVU........... Adventura Energy [*Vancouver Stock Exchange symbol*]
AVU........... American Vegetarian Union [*Defunct*]   (EA)
AVU........... Avu Avu [*Solomon Islands*] [*Airport symbol*]   (OAG)
AVU........... Vulcan Public Library, Alberta [*Library symbol*] [*National Library of Canada*]   (NLC)
Avulso Div Fom Prod Miner (Braz) ... Avulso. Divisao de Fomento da Producao Mineral (Brazil) [*A publication*]
AVUM....... Aviation Unit Maintenance [*Army*]   (MCD)
AVUM....... Avionics Unit Maintenance   (MCD)
AVUS .... Automobil Versuchs- und Untersuchungs Strecke [*Automobile Test Track*] [*Department of Energy*]
AVUSAV... Aberdeen University. Studies [*A publication*]
AVV........... Algemeen Vrijzinning Vakverbond in Nederland [*General Liberal Labor Federation*] [*Netherlands*]
AVV........... Avinda Video, Inc. [*Toronto Stock Exchange symbol*]
AVV........... Avvocato [*Solicitor*] [*Italian*]   (EY)
AV 3V........ Anteroventral Portion of the Third Ventricle [*Neuroanatomy*]
Avven Agr .. Avvenire Agricolo [*A publication*]
AVVI......... Altimeter Vertical Velocity Indicator [*NASA*]   (MCD)
AVVI......... Altitude-Vertical Velocity Indicator [*NASA*]   (MCD)
AVVM....... Valleyview Municipal Library, Alberta [*Library symbol*] [*National Library of Canada*]   (NLC)
AVVOS...... Oscar Adolphson Primary School, Valleyview, Alberta [*Library symbol*] [*National Library of Canada*]   (BIB)
AVVTA...... Avtomatika i Vychislitel'naya Tekhnika (1961-66) [*A publication*]
AVVTS ...... Twilight Colony School, Valleyview, Alberta [*Library symbol*] [*National Library of Canada*]   (BIB)
AVW.......... Average Width
AVW.......... Victorian Accident Compensation Practice Guide [*Australia*] [*A publication*]
AVWWA ... Australian Vietnam Women's Welfare Association
AVX........... Avalon, CA [*Location identifier*] [*FAA*]   (FAAL)
AVX........... AVX Corp. [*NYSE symbol*]   (SPSG)
AVX........... Catalina Island [*California*] [*Airport symbol*]   (OAG)
AVY........... Angavokely [*Madagascar*] [*Seismograph station code, US Geological Survey*]   (SEIS)
AVY........... Avery Dennison Corp. [*NYSE symbol*]   (SPSG)
AVZ........... Avocet Ventures, Inc. [*Vancouver Stock Exchange symbol*]
'AvZar....... 'Avodah Zarah   (BJA)
AW............. A. A. Weinman [*Designer's mark, when appearing on US coins*]
AW............. Above Waist [*Medicine*]
AW............. Above Water
A/W........... Accordance With   (MSA)
AW............. Acid Waste
AW............. Acoustic Warfare   (NVT)

AW............. Actual Weight [*Business term*]
A-W.......... Addison-Wesley [*Publisher*]
AW............. Advanced WESTAR   (MCD)
AW............. Africa Watch [*An association*]   (EA)
AW............. [*The*] Ahnapee & Western Railway Co. [*Later, AHW*] [*AAR code*]
AW............. Air Niger [*ICAO designator*]   (FAAC)
AW............. Air Warning
AW............. Air-to-Water
AW............. Air Weapon [*British military*]   (DMA)
AW............. Air Wonder Stories [*A publication*]
AW............. Air-World Co.
AW............. Airlock Wall   (MCD)
AW............. Airways
AW............. Airwork Ltd. [*British*]
A/W........... Airworthy   (ADA)
AW............. Alignment Window
A & W........ Alive and Well
AW............. All-Alaska Weekly [*A publication*]
AW............. All Water
AW............. All-Weather [*As applied to fighter aircraft, etc.*]
AW............. All Widths [*Lumber*]
A & W........ Allen and Wright [*Root beer*] [*Initialism also used as name of franchised drive-in restaurants*]
AW............. Allgemeine Wochenzeitung der Juden in Deutschland [*A publication*]
AW............. Alliance Witness [*A publication*]
AW............. Alternate Weapon
AW............. Altertumswissenschaft   (BJA)
AW............. American Waste Services Class A [*NYSE symbol*]   (SPSG)
AW............. American West [*A publication*]
AW............. American Wildlands   (EA)
AW............. Americas Watch   (EA)
AW............. Amit Women   (EA)
AW............. Amphibious Warfare [*British military*]   (DMA)
AW............. Annals of Wyoming [*A publication*]
AW............. Antike Welt [*A publication*]
AW............. Antiwear
AW............. Arc Welding
AW............. Arcana Workshops [*Teaches philosophy of Alice A. Bailey toward human relations*]   (EA)
AW............. Arm Width
AW............. Arming Wire [*Bombs*]
AW............. Army-Wide
AW............. Articles of War
AW............. Aruba [*ANSI two-letter standard code*]   (CNC)
aw----- .... Asia, Southwestern [*MARC geographic area code*] [*Library of Congress*]   (LCCP)
AW............. Assembly Week   (MCD)
AW............. Assembly Workstand [*NASA*]   (NASA)
AW............. Atomic Warfare
AW............. Atomic Weight
AW............. Augmentor-Wing [*Aviation*]
AW............. Aussenwirtschaft [*Foreign Economic Relations*] [*German*]
AW............. Australian Workman [*A publication*]
AW............. Automatic Weapons
AW............. Automatic Welding
AW............. Auxiliary Winding
AW............. Average Wage
AW............. Aviation ASW [*Antisubmarine Warfare*] Operator [*Navy rating*]
AW............. Aviation Week [*A publication*]
AW............. Axial Width
AW............. Distilling Ship [*Navy symbol*]
AW............. Wander AG [*Switzerland*] [*Research code symbol*]
AW............. Wetaskiwin Public Library, Alberta [*Library symbol*] [*National Library of Canada*]   (NLC)
AW1.......... Aviation ASW [*Antisubmarine Warfare*] Operator, First Class [*Navy rating*]
AW2.......... Aircraftwoman, Second Class [*Canadian*]
AW2.......... Aviation ASW [*Antisubmarine Warfare*] Operator, Second Class [*Navy rating*]
AW3.......... Aviation ASW [*Antisubmarine Warfare*] Operator, Third Class [*Navy rating*]
AWA.......... Acoustic Wave Analysis
AWA.......... Advise When Able   (FAAC)
AWA.......... Aerobic Way Association [*Commercial firm*]   (EA)
AWA.......... Air Warfare Analysis Section [*British*]
AWA.......... Air Weather Association   (EA)
AWA.......... Air West Airlines Ltd. [*Richmond, BC*] [*FAA designator*]   (FAAC)
AWA.......... All Wave Antenna
AWA.......... All-Weather Attack
AWA.......... Alliance of Women in Architecture   (EA)
AWA.......... Aluminum Wares Association [*Later, CMA*]
AWA.......... Amalgamated Wireless Australasia Ltd. [*Telecommunications service*]   (TSSD)
AWA.......... Ambulate with Assistance [*Medicine*]
A/WA......... Amchitka [*Alaska*] [*Seismograph station code, US Geological Survey*] [*Closed*]   (SEIS)
AWA.......... American Warehousemen's Association   (EA)

AWA......... American Watch Association   (EA)
AWA......... American Waterfowl Association
AWA......... American Welders Association   (EA)
AWA......... American Whitewater Affiliation   (EA)
AWA......... American Wilderness Alliance [*Later, AW*]   (EA)
AWA......... American Wine Association   (EA)
AWA......... American Woman's Association [*Defunct*]   (EA)
AWA......... Anglian Water Authority [*British*]   (DCTA)
AWA......... Antique Wireless Association   (EA)
AWA......... Assist Work Authorization
AWA......... Association of Women in Architecture   (EA)
AWA......... Atmospheric Winds Aloft
AWA......... Audio Warning Amplifier   (AAG)
AWA......... Audio Wave Analyzer
AWA......... Aviation/Space Writers Association   (EA)
awa............ Awadhi [*MARC language code*] [*Library of Congress*]   (LCCP)
AWA......... Away without Authorization
AWA......... Warburg Public Library, Alberta [*Library symbol*] [*National Library of Canada*]   (NLC)
AWAA....... Airman Apprentice, Aviation ASW [*Antisubmarine Warfare*] Operator, Striker [*Navy rating*]
AWAAM... All-Weather Air-to-Air Missile   (MCD)
AWAAPM ... Advanced Wide-Area Antipersonnel Mine   (MCD)
AWAAS..... All-Weather Attack Avionics System   (MCD)
AWAC....... Airborne Weapon and Control
AWAC....... Auto Workers Action Caucus   (EA)
AWACS..... Advanced Warning Airborne Command System
AWACS..... Advanced Warning and Control System   (IEEE)
AWACS..... Airborne [*or Aircraft*] Warning and Control System [*Air Force*]
AWACS..... Chipewyan Lake School, Wabasca, Alberta [*Library symbol*] [*National Library of Canada*]   (BIB)
AWAD....... Dairy Division, Alberta Agriculture, Wetaskiwin, Alberta [*Library symbol*] [*National Library of Canada*]   (NLC)
AWADM... Advanced Wide Area Defense Missile   (MCD)
AWADS .... Adverse Weather [*or All-Weather*] Aerial Delivery System [*Ordnance delivery method*]
AWADS .... Army Wartime Asset Distribution Study
AWAE ...... Automotive Wholesalers Association Executives   (EA)
AWAFC.... American West African Freight Conference   (EA)
AWAG...... Actors Working for an Actors Guild   (EA)
AWAG...... All-Weather Aircraft Guided Missile   (MCD)
AWAG...... American Wit and Gags [*Book title*]
AWAG...... Australian Writers-Authors Group
AWAIC..... Abused Women's Aid in Crisis   (EA)
AWAIC..... Wainwright Community Library, Alberta [*Library symbol*] [*National Library of Canada*]   (NLC)
AWAL ...... America West Airlines, Inc. [*NASDAQ symbol*]   (NQ)
AWAM...... Advanced Wide-Area Missile   (MCD)
Awamia Rev Rech Agron Maroc ... Awamia. Revue de la Recherche Agronomique Marocaine [*A publication*]
AWAN....... Airman, Aviation ASW [*Antisubmarine Warfare*] Operator, Striker [*Navy rating*]
AWAN....... AWA [*Alberta Wilderness Association*] Newsletter [*A publication*]
AWANS .... Aviation Weather and Notice to Airmen System   (MCD)
AWANS .... Wanham School, Alberta [*Library symbol*] [*National Library of Canada*]   (BIB)
AWAPA .... Academy of Wind and Percussion Arts   (EA)
AWAR ...... Area Weighted Average Resolution [*Photography*]
AWAR ...... Warner Public Library, Alberta [*Library symbol*] [*National Library of Canada*]   (NLC)
AWARDS ... Aircraft Wide-Angle Reflective Display System [*Singer Co., Link Division*]
Awards Nucl Med Radiopharmacol ... Awards in Nuclear Medicine and Radiopharmacology [*A publication*]
AWARE .... Adirondack World Affairs Resources for Education
AWARE .... Advanced Weapon/Aircraft Requirements Evaluation   (MCD)
AWARE ... Airborne Warning and Recording Equipment
AWARE ... All Women's Archaeological Research Expedition
AWARE .... Association for Women's Active Return to Education [*Defunct*]
AWARE .... Association for Women's AIDS [*Acquired Immune Deficiency Syndrome*] Research and Education
AWARE .... Australian Wildlife Ambulance Rescue and Emergency Service
AWARS..... Airborne Weather and Reconnaissance System   (MCD)
AWAS .... Acoustic Wave Analysis System
AWAS .... Air Warfare Analysis Section [*British*]
AWAS .... American Waldensian Aid Society [*Later, AWS*]   (EA)
AWAS .... Ansett Worldwide Aviation Services [*Australia*]   (ADA)
AWAS .... Automated Work Authorization System   (MCD)
Awas.......... Awasis [*A publication*]
AWAS .... Waskatenau Public Library, Alberta [*Library symbol*] [*National Library of Canada*]   (NLC)
AWASP..... Advance Weapon Ammunition Support Point
AWASTS .. St. Theresa School, Wabasca, Alberta [*Library symbol*] [*National Library of Canada*]   (BIB)
AWAT .... Archiv fuer Wissenschaftliche Erforschung des Alten Testaments [*Halle*] [*A publication*]
AWAT .... Area Weighted Average T-Number   (IEEE)
AWA Tech Rev ... AWA [*Amalgamated Wireless Australasia*] Technical Review [*A publication*]
AWAVS..... Aviation Wide-Angle Visual System   (MCD)

AWB......... Afrikaner Weerstandsbeweging [*Afrikaner Resistance Movement*] [*South Africa*] [*Political party*]   (ECON)
AWB......... Agricultural Wages Board [*British*]
AWB......... Air Waybill [*Shipping*]
AWB......... Alliance of Women Bikers   (EA)
AWB......... Association of Women Broadcasters
AWB......... Average White Back [*Football*]
AWB......... [*The*] Average White Band [*Rock music group*]
AWBA ...... American Wheelchair Bowling Association   (EA)
AWBA ...... American Wholesale Booksellers Association   (EA)
AWBAbh ... Koeniglich-Preussische Akademie der Wissenschaften (Berlin). Abhandlungen [*A publication*]
AWBC ...... American Women Buyers Club   (EA)
AWBE ...... Automatic Weather Broadcast Equipment   (FAAC)
AWBMA ... Archiwum Budowy Maszyn [*A publication*]
AWBMS... Amalgamated Welded Boiler Makers Society [*A union*] [*British*]
AWBR ...... Australian Women's Book Review [*A publication*]
AWBSb.... Koeniglich-Preussische Akademie der Wissenschaften (Berlin). Sitzungsberichte [*A publication*]
AWC .... Absolute Worst Case
AWC .... Acting Wing-Commander [*British*]
AWC .... Affiliated Warehouse Companies   (EA)
AWC .... Agricultural Wages Committee [*British*]   (DAS)
AWC .... Air War College [*Maxwell Air Force Base, AL*]
AWC .... Air Warfare Co-Ordination [*British military*]   (DMA)
AWC .... Air Warfare Control   (MCD)
AWC .... Air Weapons Controller
AWC .... Air Wing Commander
AWC .... Airborne Weapons Control
AWC .... Algemeen Weekblad voor Christendom en Cultuur [*A publication*]
AWC .... Allied Works Council [*World War II*]
AWC .... Alma White College [*New Jersey*]
AWC .... American Watershed Council   (EA)
AWC .... American Whippet Club   (EA)
AWC .... American Women Composers   (EA)
AWC .... American Wood Council   (EA)
AWC .... American Wool Council   (EA)
AWC .... Amphibians and Watercraft [*Army*]   (RDA)
AWC .... Amphibious Warfare Communications [*Navy*]   (MCD)
AWC .... Amphibious and Watercraft   (MCD)
AWC .... Angelic Warfare Confraternity [*Defunct*]   (EA)
AWC .... Arab Women's Council   (EA)
AWC .... Army War College
AWC .... Army Weapons Command [*AMC*]
AWC .... Assisting Work Center
AWC .... Association for Women in Computing   (EA)
AWC .... Association of World Citizens   (EA)
AWC .... Astronauts' Wives Club
AWC .... Atlantic Waterfowl Council   (EA)
AWC .... Australian Wildlife Club
AWC .... Australian Wool Commission
AWC .... Available Water-Holding Capacity [*Soil science*]
AWC .... United States Army War College, Carlisle Barracks, PA [*OCLC symbol*]   (OCLC)
AWC .... Wanham Community Library, Alberta [*Library symbol*] [*National Library of Canada*]   (NLC)
AWCA ...... American Women's Clergy Association   (EA)
AWCA ...... Wetaskiwin City Archives, Alberta [*Library symbol*] [*National Library of Canada*]   (BIB)
AWCAP..... Air War College Associate Program   (AFM)
AWCAP..... Airborne Weapons Corrective Action Program   (MCD)
AWCAS..... Adverse Weather Close Air Support [*Military*]   (MCD)
AWCC...... Active Well Coincidence Counter [*Nuclear energy*]   (NRCH)
AWCCD.... Australian Worker's Compensation Case Digests [*A publication*]
AWCCS.... Army War College Correspondence Studies   (MCD)
AWCCSC... Army War College Corresponding Studies Course   (INF)
AWCCV.... Advanced Weapons Carriage Configured Vehicle   (MCD)
AWCEA...... American Wood Chip Export Association   (EA)
AWCH NSW Newsletter ... Association for the Welfare of Children in Hospital. New South Wales. Newsletter [*A publication*]   (APTA)
AWCI .... Aircraft and Weapons Control Interceptor
AWCI .... American Wire Cloth Institute   (EA)
AWCI .... Association of the Wall and Ceiling Industries - International   (EA)
AWCI .... [*A*] Wellness Center, Incorporated   (EA)
AWCIS...... Aircraft and Weapons Control Interceptor System
AWCIT...... Advanced Weapon Carriage Integration Technology   (MCD)
AWCLS..... All-Weather Carrier Landing System [*Navy*]
AWCM...... Aviation ASW [*Antisubmarine Warfare*] Operator, Master Chief [*Navy rating*]
AWCMA ... American Window Covering Manufacturers Association   (EA)
AWCO...... Air Warfare Control Officer
AWCO....... Area Wage and Classification Office
AWCO....... Assistant Weapons Control Officer
AWCOA .... American Wrestling Coaches and Officials Association [*Later, NWCA*]   (EA)
AWC-PM .. Amphibians and Watercraft Product Manager [*Army*]   (RDA)

AWCRC.....   Adam Walsh Child Resource Center   (EA)
AWCS.......   Agency-Wide Coding Structure [*Military*]
AWCS.......   Air Weapons Control System [*Air Force*]
AWCS........   Airborne Weapon Control System   (MCD)
AWCS........   Automatic Warning and Control System
AWCS.......   Automatic Weapons Control System
AWCS........   Automatic Work Control System [*Military*]   (MCD)
AWCS........   Aviation ASW [*Antisubmarine Warfare*] Operator, Senior Chief [*Navy rating*]
AWCS........   AW Computer Systems, Inc. [*NASDAQ symbol*]   (NQ)
AWCSq......   Airborne Warning and Control Squadron [*Air Force*]
AWCU......   Association of World Colleges and Universities [*Later, AWE*]
AWD..........   Abbey Woods Development [*Vancouver Stock Exchange symbol*]
AWD..........   Advanced Workshop Detachment [*British and Canadian*] [*World War II*]
AWD..........   Air Warfare Division [*Navy*]
AWD..........   Alive with Disease [*Medicine*]
AWD..........   All-Wheel Drive [*Automotive engineering*]
AWD..........   American War Dads   (EA)
AWD..........   Association for Women in Development   (EA)
AWD..........   Association for Workplace Democracy [*Defunct*]   (EA)
AWD..........   Astrogeodetic World Datum
AWD..........   Aussenwirtschaftsdienst des Betriebsberaters [*German*] [*A publication*]   (DLA)
AWD..........   Average Working Depth
AWD..........   Award   (AABC)
AWD..........   Awning Deck [*of a ship*]   (DS)
AWD..........   Recht der Internationalen Wirtschaft Aussenwirtschaftsdienst des Betriebsberaters [*A publication*]
AWD..........   Worsley and District Library Society, Alberta [*Library symbol*] [*National Library of Canada*]   (BIB)
AWDA......   Automotive Warehouse Distributors Association   (EA)
AWDATS ...   Artillery Weapons Data Transmission System   (MCD)
AWDD......   American Wholesalers and Distributors Directory [*Pronounced "awed"*] [*A publication*]
AWDEA ....   Admiralty Works Department Employees Association [*A union*] [*British*]
AWDI.......   Automated Worthless Document Index
AWDISCOM ...   Awaiting Disciplinary Action This Command [*Army*]
AWDR.......   Advanced Weapon Delivery RADAR
AWDS ......   Automated Weather Distribution System   (MCD)
AWDS ......   Automated Wire Data System
AWDS ......   Automatic Waveform Digitizing System   (MCD)
AWDS ......   Automatic Wire Data System   (MCD)
AWE..........   Accepted Weight/Estimate [*Ships*]
AWE..........   Advise When Established [*Aviation*]   (FAAC)
AWE..........   All-Weather Electronics
AWE..........   Alliance of Women for Equality
AWE..........   America West Airlines, Inc. [*Tempo, AZ*] [*FAA designator*]   (FAAC)
AWE..........   Association of Women Executives [*Canada*]
AWE..........   Association for World Education   (EA)
AWE..........   Association for World Evangelism   (EA)
AWE..........   Australian Work Ethic Scale
AWE..........   Average Weekly Earnings
AWE..........   Awesome Resources Ltd. [*Vancouver Stock Exchange symbol*]
AWE..........   Tazewell, TN [*Location identifier*] [*FAA*]   (FAAL)
AWE..........   Western Region [*FAA*]   (FAAC)
AWEA ......   American Wind Energy Association   (EA)
AWECOM ...   Army Weapons Command [*AMC*]   (MCD)
AWECS .....   Advanced Wind Energy Conversion System   (MCD)
AWED.......   American Woman's Economic Development Corp.   (EA)
AWeldI .....   Associate of the Welding Institute [*British*]   (DBQ)
AWEMS....   Wembley Elementary School, Alberta [*Library symbol*] [*National Library of Canada*]   (BIB)
AWES.......   Association of West European Shipbuilders [*London, England*]   (EAIO)
AWES.......   Westlock Public Library, Alberta [*Library symbol*] [*National Library of Canada*]   (NLC)
AWESS .....   Automatic Weapons Effect Signature Simulator   (MCD)
AWEUS.....   Association of Women Employees of the University of Sydney [*Australia*]
AWF..........   Acceptable Workload Factor [*Management*]
AWF..........   Adjoint Wave Function
AWF..........   Adrenal Weight Factor [*Endocrinology*]
AWF..........   African Wildlife Foundation   (EA)
AWF..........   All-Weather Flare
AWF..........   Alliance of Warehouses and Federations   (EA)
AWF..........   Alliance World Fellowship   (EA)
AWF..........   Australian Wheatgrowers' Federation
AWF..........   Aviation Weather Facility
AWFC.......   Andy Williams Fan Club   (EA)
AWFI........   American Wood Fabric Institute
AWFSR .....   Automation of Wartime Functional Supply Requirements   (MCD)
AWG..........   Activation Working Group [*Military*]   (MCD)
AWG..........   All-Weather Guidance
AWG..........   American Wire Gauge [*Standard*]
AWG..........   Arctic Working Group [*University of Toronto*] [*Research center*]   (RCD)

AWG........   Art Workers Guild   (EAIO)
AWG........   Association of Women Gemologists [*Defunct*]   (EA)
AWG........   Association for Women Geoscientists   (EA)
AWG.........   Astro-Wing Airlines [*Dallas, TX*] [*FAA designator*]   (FAAC)
AWG.........   Washington, IA [*Location identifier*] [*FAA*]   (FAAL)
A & W Gai ...   Abdy and Walker's Gaius and Ulpian [*A publication*]   (DLA)
Awgie........   Australian Writers' Guild Award
AWGN......   Additive White Gaussian Noise [*Telecommunications*]   (TEL)
AWG Phk ...   Akademie der Wissenschaften in Goettingen. Philologisch-Historische Klasse [*A publication*]
awgz--- ....   Gaza Strip [*MARC geographic area code*] [*Library of Congress*]   (LCCP)
AWH ....   American Women's Hospitals [*Later, AWHS*]
AWH ....   Association of Western Hospitals [*Later, HCF*]
AWH ....   Whitecourt Public Library, Alberta [*Library symbol*] [*National Library of Canada*]   (NLC)
AWHA......   American Walking Horse Association   (EA)
AWHA......   Australian Women's Home Army
AWHDA....   American Wholesale Horticultural Dealers Association [*Later, HDA*]   (EA)
AWHE......   American Women's Himalayan Expeditions
AWHRC....   American Women's Hospital Reserve Corps [*British*]   (DAS)
AWHS ....   American Women's Hospitals Service [*Formerly, AWH*] [*Later, AWHS/AMWA*]   (EA)
AWHS ....   Whitelaw School, Alberta [*Library symbol*] [*National Library of Canada*]   (BIB)
AWHS/AMWA ...   American Women's Hospitals Service Committee of AMWA [*American Medical Women's Association*]   (EA)
AWHSL.....   Association of Women Highway Safety Leaders
AWHT.......   Helen E. Taylor School, Wembley, Alberta [*Library symbol*] [*National Library of Canada*]   (BIB)
AWHV......   Aircraft Weapons Handling Vehicle
AWI ....   Accommodation Weight Investigation   (KSC)
AWI ....   Air Warfare Instructor [*Navy*] [*British*]
AWI ....   Air Wisconsin [*Appleton, WI*] [*FAA designator*]   (FAAC)
AWI ....   Aircraftwoman, First Class [*Canadian*]
AWI ....   All-Weather Interceptor
AWI ....   America and West Indies [*Obsolete*] [*British*]
AWI ....   American Watchmakers Institute   (EA)
AWI ....   American Welding Institute   (EA)
AWI ....   Animal Welfare Institute   (EA)
AWI ....   Antigua [*Antigua*] [*Seismograph station code, US Geological Survey*] [*Closed*]   (SEIS)
AWI ....   Architectural Woodwork Institute   (EA)
AWI ....   Arm Width Index
AWI ....   Asian Women's Institute   (EAIO)
A & WI......   Atlantic and West Indies
AWI ....   Australia Wide Industries
AWI ....   Winfield Public Library, Alberta [*Library symbol*] [*National Library of Canada*]   (NLC)
AWIA ......   American Wood Inspection Agency
AWIC ....   Animal Welfare Information Center [*Department of Agriculture*] [*Information service or system*]   (IID)
AWIC ....   Australian Wool Industry Council
AWID ....   Association for Women in Development   (EA)
AWIFA......   Angewandte Informatik/Applied Informatics [*A publication*]
AWIL........   Willingdon Public Library, Alberta [*Library symbol*] [*National Library of Canada*]   (NLC)
AWILD.....   Wildwood Public Library, Alberta [*Library symbol*] [*National Library of Canada*]   (NLC)
AWIN ....   Association of Women in Natural Foods   (EA)
AWIPS ......   Advanced Weather Interactive Processing System [*National Oceanic and Atmospheric Administration*]
AWIPS-90 ...   Advanced Weather Interactive Processing System of the 1990's [*National Oceanic and Atmospheric Administration*]
AWIR ....   ADCOM Weekly Intelligence Review Support   (MCD)
AWIR ....   Ankole-Watusi International Registry   (EA)
AWIR ....   Annual Worldwide Industry Review   (IMH)
AWIRA.....   American Wax Importers and Refiners Association
AWIS........   All-Weather Identification Sensor
AWIS........   Association for Women in Science   (EA)
AWIU ....   Aluminum Workers International Union [*Later, ABCWIU*]   (EA)
awiu--- ....   Israel-Syria Demilitarized Zones [*MARC geographic area code*] [*Library of Congress*]   (LCCP)
AWIU(I).....   Allied Workers International Union (Independent)
awiw--- ....   Israel-Jordan Demilitarized Zones [*MARC geographic area code*] [*Library of Congress*]   (LCCP)
awiy--- ....   Iraq-Saudi Arabia Neutral Zone [*MARC geographic area code*] [*Library of Congress*]   (LCCP)
AWJ..........   Allgemeine Wochenzeitung der Juden in Deutschland [*A publication*]
AWJD.......   Allgemeine Wochenzeitung der Juden in Deutschland [*A publication*]
AWJSRA...   Augmenter Wing Jet STOL [*Short Takeoff and Landing*] Research Aircraft
A & W Just ...   Abdy and Walker's Justinian [*A publication*]   (DLA)
AWK..........   American Water Works Co., Inc. [*NYSE symbol*]   (SPSG)
AWK..........   Americans Want to Know [*Defunct*]   (EA)
AWK..........   Arwick International Resources Ltd. [*Vancouver Stock Exchange symbol*]

AWK.........	Australian Worker's Compensation Guide [*A publication*]
AWK.........	Awkward Expression or Construction [*Used in correcting manuscripts, etc.*]
AWK.........	Water Tankers [*Navy symbol*] (MUGU)
AWL.........	Absent with Leave [*Military*]
AWL.........	Absent without Leave [*Military*] [*British*]
AWL.........	Administrative Weight Limitation [*Military*] (AABC)
AWL.........	Agarwal Resources Ltd. [*Vancouver Stock Exchange symbol*]
AWL.........	All-Weather Landing
AWL.........	Anti-War League [*Australia*]
AWL.........	Artificial White Light
AWL.........	Association for a World Language (EA)
AWL.........	Automated Wire List [*NASA*] (NASA)
AWL.........	Average Work Load
AWLA......	American Weight Lifting Association (EA)
AWLA......	Australian Women's Land Army
AWLAR.....	All-Weather Low-Altitude Route [*Aviation*] (FAAC)
AWLF........	African Wildlife Leadership Foundation
AWLMA9 ...	Akademie der Wissenschaften und der Literatur in Mainz. Abhandlungen der Mathematisch-Naturwissenschaftlichen Klasse [*A publication*]
AWLM AGSK ...	Akademie der Wissenschaften und der Literatur in Mainz. Abhandlungen der Geistes- und Sozialwissenschaftlichen Klasse [*A publication*]
AWLMGS ...	Akademie der Wissenschaften und der Literatur in Mainz. Abhandlungen der Geistes- und Sozialwissenschaftlichen Klasse [*A publication*]
AWLML....	Akademie der Wissenschaften und der Literatur in Mainz. Klasse der Literatur [*A publication*]
AWLOG....	Army Wholesale Logistic System (AABC)
AWLRAO ...	Australian Wildlife Research [*A publication*]
AWLRF.....	All-Weather Long-Range Fighter
AWLS........	All-Weather Landing System [*Also, ALS*]
AWLU.......	Aural Warning Logic Unit (MCD)
AWM........	Air and Waste Management (OICC)
AWM........	American War Mothers (EA)
AWM........	Appliance Wiring Material
AWM........	Arc Welding Machine
AWM........	Association for Women in Mathematics (EA)
AWM........	Auskunftsblatt [*Bern*] [*A publication*]
AWM........	Automatic Writing Machine
AWM........	Awaiting Maintenance (AFM)
AWM........	West Memphis, AR [*Location identifier*] [*FAA*] (FAAL)
AWMA......	Aluminum Window Manufacturers Association [*Later, Architectural Aluminum Manufacturers Association*]
AWMA......	American Walnut Manufacturers Association [*Later, FHAWA*]
AWMA......	Automatic Welding Machinery Association [*Defunct*] (EA)
AWMAbh ...	Akademie der Wissenschaften in Muenchen. Abhandlungen [*A publication*]
AWMADF ...	Agricultural Water Management [*A publication*]
AWMC......	Army Weapons and Mobility Command
AWMC......	Association of Workers for Maladjusted Children [*British*]
AWMCS.....	Aviation Weapons Movement Control System (MCD)
AWMG......	American Wooden Money Guild (EA)
AWMIA2 ..	Awamia. Revue de la Recherche Agronomique Marocaine [*A publication*]
AWMMAE ...	Akademie der Wissenschaften und der Literatur in Mainz. Mathematisch-Naturwissenschaftlichen Klasse. Mikrofauna des Meeresbodens [*A publication*]
AWMSb	Akademie der Wissenschaften in Muenchen. Philosophisch-Historische Klasse. Sitzungsberichte [*A publication*]
AWN.........	Activation Work Notice
AWN.........	Air Weather Network
AWN.........	Allahabad Weekly Notes [*India*] [*A publication*] (DLA)
AWN.........	Alton Downs [*Australia*] [*Airport symbol*] [*Obsolete*] (OAG)
AWN.........	Aston Whole Number [*Chemistry*]
AWN.........	Automated Weather Network [*Air Force*]
AWN.........	Awning (MSA)
AWNCS.....	Automated Weather Network Coordinating Station [*Air Force*]
AWND.......	Aspen Wind, Inc. [*NASDAQ symbol*] (NQ)
AWNDLS ...	Anchor Windlass
AWNMC...	Automated Weather Network Management Center [*Military*]
AWNY.......	Advertising Women of New York [*New York, NY*] (EA)
AWO.........	Accounting Work Order
AWO.........	Admiralty Weekly Order [*British military*] (DMA)
AWO.........	Afrique Industrie Infrastructures [*A publication*]
AWO.........	Agricultural Workers' Organization
AWO.........	Alterio Resources Ltd. [*Toronto Stock Exchange symbol*]
AWO.........	American Waterways Operators (EA)
AWO.........	Arlington, WA [*Location identifier*] [*FAA*] (FAAL)
AWO.........	Army Welfare Officer [*British*]
AWO.........	Average Monthly Weather Outlook [*A publication*]
AWOA......	American West Overseas Association (EA)
AWOC......	Agricultural Workers Organizing Committee [*Later, UFWA*] [*AFL-CIO*]
AWOC......	All-Weather Operations Committee [*ATA*]
AWOD......	All-Weather Operations Division [*ICAO*] (MCD)
AWOIS......	Automated Wreck and Obstruction Information System [*National Oceanic and Atmospheric Administration*] [*Information service or system*] (IID)
AWOL.......	Absent without Official Leave [*Military*]
AWOL.......	After Women or Liquor [*Slang*]
AWOL.......	[A] Wolf on the Loose [*Slang*]
AWOP......	Absent without Pay (MCD)
AWOP......	All-Weather Operations Panel [*International Civil Aviation Organization*]
AWORS	Worsley School, Alberta [*Library symbol*] [*National Library of Canada*] (BIB)
AWOS......	Automatic Weather Observing/Reporting System (FAAC)
AWOS......	Woking School, Alberta [*Library symbol*] [*National Library of Canada*] (BIB)
AWOT......	Adsorption Wall Open Tubular Column [*Chromatography*]
AWP.........	Actual Working Pressure
AWP.........	Airway Pressure [*Pulmonary ventilation*]
AWP.........	Albania Workers' Party [*Political party*]
AWP.........	ALCAN [*Aluminum Co. of Canada Ltd.*] World Price [*Obsolete*] (FEA)
AWP.........	Allied Weather Publications [*NATO*] (NATG)
AWP.........	Amusement with Prizes [*Pinball machines*] [*British*]
AWP.........	Annual Work Plan
AWP.........	Anthology of World Poetry [*A publication*]
AWP.........	Antisubmarine Warfare Programs [*Navy*] (MCD)
AWP.........	Arbeitsgemeinschaft fuer Wissenschaft und Politik [*Association for Sciences and Politics*] [*Innsbruck, Austria*] (EAIO)
AWP.........	Army Warranty Program
AWP.........	Associated Writing Programs (EA)
AWP.........	Association for Women in Psychology (EA)
AWP.........	Association for World Peace [*Founded in 1951*] [*Defunct*] [*British*]
AWP.........	Atlanta & West Point Rail Road Co. [*AAR code*]
A & WP....	Atlanta & West Point Rail Road Co.
AW & P.....	Authority, Worldliness, and Power
AWP.........	Automatic Wage Payments (MCD)
AWP.........	Automatic Withdrawal Prohibit [*Nuclear energy*] (NRCH)
AWP.........	Average Wholesale Price
AWP.........	Awaiting Parts (AFM)
AWPA......	American Walking Pony Association (EA)
AWPA......	American Wire Producers Association (EA)
AWPA......	American Women Playwrights Association (EA)
AWPA......	American Wood Preservers' Association (EA)
AWPA......	American Word Processing Association (EA)
AWPA......	Australian Women Pilots Association
AWPA......	Angewandte Parasitologie [*A publication*]
AWPB......	American Wood Preservers Bureau (EA)
AWPDS.....	Attack Warning Processing and Display System (MCD)
AWPE.......	Abstracts of Working Papers in Economics [*Cambridge University Press*] [*Information service or system*] (IID)
AWPI.......	American Wood Preservers Institute (EA)
AWPOA	Air and Water Pollution [*A publication*]
AWPOAZ ...	Air and Water Pollution [*A publication*]
AWPPW.....	Association of Western Pulp and Paper Workers (EA)
A/WPR......	Air/Water Pollution Report [*Business Publishers, Inc.*] [*Information service or system*] (CRD)
AWPS.......	American Welara Pony Society (EA)
AWR........	Actual Weight Report
AWR........	Adaptive Waveform Recognition
AWR........	Advanced Weather RADAR (MCD)
AWR........	Allahabad Weekly Reporter [*India*] [*A publication*] (DLA)
AWR........	American Warmblood Registry (EA)
AWR........	Ammunition War Reserve (CINC)
AWR........	Anglo-Welsh Review [*A publication*]
AWR........	Annual Wage Reporting [*Social Security Administration*]
AWR........	Army War Room (AABC)
AWR........	Arrowhead Resources Ltd. [*Vancouver Stock Exchange symbol*]
AWR........	Association for the Study of the World Refugee Problem [*Vaduz, Liechtenstein*] (EAIO)
AWR........	Association of Western Railways [*Later, WRA*]
AWR........	Automated Work Request (NVT)
AWR........	Wandering River Public Library, Alberta [*Library symbol*] [*National Library of Canada*] (NLC)
AWR........	Window Rock, AZ [*Location identifier*] [*FAA*] (FAAL)
AWRA......	American Water Resources Association (EA)
AWRA......	Augmentor Wing Research Aircraft [*Aviation*] (MCD)
AWRAM ...	Reynolds Alberta Museum, Wetaskiwin, Alberta [*Library symbol*] [*National Library of Canada*] (BIB)
AWRD......	Air Warfare Research Department [*Navy*] (MCD)
AWRE	Atomic Weapons Research Establishment [*British*]
AWRF......	Associated Wire Rope Fabricators (EA)
AWRHA	Australian Water Resources Council. Hydrological Series [*A publication*]
AWRIS......	Army War Room Information System
AWRL.......	Ammo War Reserve Level (CINC)
AWRN......	Awareness (KSC)
AWRNCO ...	Aircraft Warning Company [*Marine Corps*]
AWRO......	Atomic Weapon Retrofit Order
AWRRC.....	Arkansas Water Resources Research Center [*University of Arkansas*] [*Research center*] (RCD)
AWRS......	Airborne Weather RADAR System
AWRS......	Airborne Weather and Reconnaissance System (MCD)
AWRS......	Aircraft Weapons Release Set [*or System*] (NG)
AWRS......	All-Weather Reconnaissance System

AWRS....... Anti-Whole Rabbit Serum [Immunology]
AWRS....... Australian War Records Section
AWRS....... Aviation Weather Reporting Station
AWRT...... American Women in Radio and Television (EA)
AWRTAQ ... Australian Water Resources Council. Technical Paper [A publication]
AWRU....... Aircraft Weapons Release Unit [DoD] (MCD)
AWS .... Acoustic Warfare System [Navy] (MCD)
AWS .... Adjustable Wire Stripper
AWS .... Advanced Warning System
AWS .... Advanced Weapons System (MCD)
AWS .... African Writers Series [A publication]
AWS .... Air Warning Squadron [Marine Corps]
AWS .... Air Warning System
AWS .... Air Weapon Systems [Air Force]
AWS .... Air Weather Service [Scott Air Force Base, IL]
AWS .... Air Wing Staff [Air Force]
AWS .... Air Wonder Stories [A publication]
AWS .... Aircraft Warning Service [Military]
AWS .... Alba-Waldensian, Inc. [AMEX symbol] (SPSG)
AWS .... All-Weather System (MCD)
AWS .... Alston Wilkes Society (EA)
AWS .... Altitude Warning System (MCD)
AWS .... American Waldensian Society (EA)
AWS .... American War Standards [DoD]
AWS .... American Warmblood Society (EA)
AWS .... American Watercolor Society (EA)
AWS .... American Welding Society (EA)
AWS .... American Wine Society (EA)
AWS .... Annual Wage Survey (OICC)
AWS .... Area Wage Survey (OICC)
AWS .... Area Working Standards
AWS .... Army Weather Service (NATG)
AWS .... Army Welfare Services [British]
AWS .... Association of Winery Suppliers (EA)
AWS .... Astronaut Work Station [NASA]
AWS .... Attack Warning System [Civil Defense]
AWS .... Australian Warships Systems Pty. Ltd.
AWS .... Automated Wiring System (MCD)
AWS .... Automatic Weather Station
AWS .... Automatic Welding System
AWS .... Aviation Weather Service [of National Weather Service]
AWS .... Awaiting Sentence [of court-martial]
AWS .... Columbus, GA [Location identifier] [FAA] (FAAL)
AWSA .... Air Warfare Systems Analysis
AWSA .... Airborne Waveguide Slotted Array
AWSA .... American Water Ski Association (EA)
AWSA .... Arab Women Solidarity Association (EAIO)
AWSA .... Australian Wool Surveillance Authority
AWSAA..... Airborne Waveguide Slotted Array Antenna
AWSACS .. All-Weather Standoff Attack Control System (MCD)
AWSC....... Agricultural Weather Service Center [National Oceanic and Atmospheric Administration]
AWSC....... Air Warfare Simulation Complex (MCD)
AWSC....... American Waterways Shipyard Conference (EA)
AWSCOM ... Advanced Weapons Support Command [Army] (AABC)
AWSCPA .. American Woman's Society of Certified Public Accountants [Chicago, IL]
AWSEF ..... American Water Ski Educational Foundation (EA)
AWSF........ Alpha Waste Storage Facility [Nuclear energy]
AWSG .... Army Work Study Group
AW & SHG ... American Warmblood and Sport Horse Guild (EA)
AW-SHORADS ... All-Weather Short-Range Air Defense Missile System (MCD)
AWSI........ Adaptive Wafer Scale Integration (MCD)
AWSI........ Alliance Well Service, Inc. [NASDAQ symbol] (NQ)
AWSI........ American Friends of the Association for Welfare of Soldiers in Israel (EA)
AWSJ .... Asian Wall Street Journal [A publication]
AWSM ...... Acoustic Warfare Support Measures (NVT)
AWSM ...... Air Weapons Systems Management
AWSM ...... Air Weather Service Manual
AWSO .... All-Weather Sleepout (ADA)
AWSO .... Assembly Work Schedule Order
AWSOS..... Army Women's Services Officers School [British military] (DMA)
AWSP........ Air Weapons Systems Plan
AWSP........ Army-Wide Signature Program (MCD)
AWSP........ Automatic Weapons (Self-Propelled) [Military]
AWSS........ Association of Women Soil Scientists (EA)
AWST....... American Western Corp. [NASDAQ symbol] (NQ)
AWST....... Australian Western Standard Time
AWSTA..... All-Weather Station
AWSTA..... Aviation Week and Space Technology [A publication]
AWSTAS .. All-Weather Sea Target Acquisition System [Navy] (MCD)
AWSTG..... Air Weather Service Training Guide
AWSTL..... Air Weather Service Technical Library [Air Force] [Information service or system] (IID)
AWSWO ... Air Weather Service Office
AWT .... Actual Work Time [Bell System]
AWT .... Advanced Waste Treatment [of water]

AWT .... Aeroelastic Wind Tunnel
AWT .... Air & Water Technologies Corp. Class A [AMEX symbol] (SPSG)
AWT .... Altitude Wind Tunnel
AWT .... Anechoic Water Tank
AWT .... Arc-Jet Wind Tunnel
AWT .... Arctic Warfare Training [British military] (DMA)
AWT .... Associate in Wildlife Technology
AWT .... Association of Wind Teachers [British]
AWT .... Average Work Time
AWT .... Await
AWT .... Awaiting Trial [by court-martial]
AWTA .... American Working Terrier Association (EA)
AWTAO.... Association of Water Transportation Accounting Officers [New York, NY] (EA)
AWTAS.... Automated Weapons Test Analysis System
AWTB .... All-Weather Test Bed (MCD)
AWTBS.... All-Weather Tactical Bombing System
AWTC .... Association of Women Tax Clerks [A union] [British]
AWTCE.... Association of World Trade Chamber Executives (EA)
AWTD....... Air Warfare Training Division [Navy] [British]
AWTE ...... Association for World Travel Exchange (EA)
AWTEA.... Allgemeine Waermetechnik [A publication]
AWTF....... American Writers Theatre Foundation (EA)
AWTG...... Atomic Weapons Training Group [DASA]
AWTI........ Air Weapons Training Installation (NATG)
AWTL....... Advanced Waste Treatment Laboratory [National Environmental Research Center]
AWTMS.... All-Weather Topographic Mapping System [Army]
AWTR ...... Assistant Writer [British military] (DMA)
AWTS ...... Army-Wide Training Support (AABC)
AWTSS.... All-Weather Tactical Strike System [Air Force] (MCD)
AWTSS .... Army-Wide Training Support System
AWTT ...... Above Water Thrown Torpedo [Navy] (CAAL)
AWTT ...... Above Water Torpedo Tube [Navy] (NVT)
AWTTP..... Apollo Wind-Tunnel Testing Program [NASA]
AWU......... Agricultural Workers' Union (DAS)
AWU......... Aluminum Workers International Union [Later, ABCWIU]
AWU......... Associated Western Universities [Department of Energy] [Salt Lake City, UT]
AWU......... Associated Workers' Union [Philippines]
AWU......... Association for the World University (EA)
AWU......... Atomic Weight Unit
AWU......... Australian Workers' Union
AWV......... American Lightwave [Vancouver Stock Exchange symbol]
AWV......... Association for Women Veterinarians (EA)
AWV......... Atmospheric Wind Velocity
AWV......... Water Valley Public Library, Alberta [Library symbol] [National Library of Canada] (NLC)
AWVA ...... Another World Viewer Alliance (EA)
AWVS....... American Women's Voluntary Services [World War II] (EA)
AWW........ Above Water Warfare [Navy] (NVT)
AWW........ Advanced Wild Weasel [RADAR warning system]
AWW........ Algers, Winslow & Western Railway Co. [AAR code]
AWW........ All's Well That Ends Well [Shakespearean work]
AWW........ American Westwater Technology Group Ltd. [Vancouver Stock Exchange symbol]
AWW........ Association of Women Welders [A union] [British]
AWW........ Australian Women's Weekly [A publication] (APTA)
AWW........ Australian Writer's Workshop [A publication] (APTA)
AWW........ Winchester, IN [Location identifier] [FAA] (FAAL)
AWWA ...... American Water Works Association (EA)
AWWA ...... Armenian Women's Welfare Association (EA)
AWWBT.... Association of Women Workers in the Bedstead Trade [A union] [British]
AWWC...... Association of Workshop Way Consultants (EA)
AWWDs.... Koenigliche Akademie der Wissenschaften (Wien). Denkschriften [A publication]
AWWI ...... American Wash and Wear Institute
AWWM..... Automatic Wire Wrap Machine
AWWMCCS ... Army Worldwide Military Command and Control Information Systems (RDA)
AWWP ...... Amphibious Warfare Working Party (NATG)
AWWPA ... American Wire Weavers Protective Association
AWWR ...... Alaska Wildlife Watcher's Report [A publication]
AWWS ...... Automated Want and Warrant System [Data processing system used in police work]
AWWSb .... Akademie der Wissenschaften in Wien. Sitzungsberichte [A publication]
AWWU...... American Watch Workers Union
AWX......... Account Weather [Aviation] (FAAC)
AWX......... All-Weather Aircraft [Air Force] (NATG)
AWX......... Andaurex Resources, Inc. [Vancouver Stock Exchange symbol]
AWX(F)..... All-Weather Fighter
AWX(I)...... All-Weather Intruder
AWY......... Airway
AWY......... Erie, PA [Location identifier] [FAA] (FAAL)
AWYDC .... All-Weather Yaw Damper Computer
AWZ......... Ahwaz [Iran] [Airport symbol] [Obsolete] (OAG)
AWZ......... Merced, CA [Location identifier] [FAA] (FAAL)
AX.............. Abnormal Xylem Elements [Botany]

AX .... Aged, Adrenalectomized Animals [*Endocrinology*]
AX .... Air Togo [*ICAO designator*] (FAAC)
AX .... Altex Resources Ltd. [*Toronto Stock Exchange symbol*]
AX .... American Exploration Co. [*AMEX symbol*] (SPSG)
AX .... American Express Co. (ADA)
AX .... Armpit [*Medicine*] (DHSM)
AX .... Attack Experimental [*Air Force*] (MCD)
AX .... Aviation ASW [*Antisubmarine Warfare*] Technician [*Navy rating*]
AX .... Axillary [*Medicine*]
AX .... Axiom
AX .... Axis (AAG)
AX .... Axle Housing Cover Gasket [*Automotive engineering*]
AX .... Quarterdeck [*i.e., "after castle," by analogy with FX - forecastle*] [*Navy*] [*British*]
AX1 .... Aviation ASW [*Antisubmarine Warfare*] Technician, First Class [*Navy rating*]
AX2 .... Aviation ASW [*Antisubmarine Warfare*] Technician, Second Class [*Navy rating*]
AX3 .... Aviation ASW [*Antisubmarine Warfare*] Technician, Third Class [*Navy rating*]
AXA .... Alexa Ventures, Inc. [*Vancouver Stock Exchange symbol*]
AXA .... Algona, IA [*Location identifier*] [*FAA*] (FAAL)
AXA .... Anguilla [*West Indies*] [*Airport symbol*] (OAG)
AXAA .... Airman Apprentice, Aviation ASW [*Antisubmarine Warfare*] Technician, Striker [*Navy rating*]
AXAF .... Advanced X-Ray Astrophysics Facility [*Great Observatory Program*] [*NASA*]
AXAN .... Airman, Aviation ASW [*Antisubmarine Warfare*] Technician, Striker [*Navy rating*]
AXB .... Artha Vijnana [*A publication*]
AXB .... Auxiliary Boiler [*of a ship*] (DS)
AXBS .... Auxiliary Boiler Survey [*of a ship*] (DS)
AXBT .... Airborne Expendable Bathythermograph
AXC .... Alpine Exploration [*Vancouver Stock Exchange symbol*]
AXC .... Aramac [*Australia*] [*Airport symbol*] (OAG)
AXC .... Aviation ASW [*Antisubmarine Warfare*] Technician, Chief [*Navy rating*]
AXCM .... Aviation ASW [*Antisubmarine Warfare*] Technician, Master Chief [*Navy rating*]
AXCS .... Aviation ASW [*Antisubmarine Warfare*] Technician, Senior Chief [*Navy rating*]
AXD .... Alexandroupolis [*Greece*] [*Airport symbol*] (OAG)
AXD .... Alpha Xi Delta [*Sorority*]
AXD .... Auxiliary Drum (CET)
AXE .... American Resource [*Vancouver Stock Exchange symbol*]
Axel Heiberg Isl Res Geol McGill Univ ... Axel Heiberg Island Research Reports. Geology. McGill University [*A publication*]
AXF .... AABBAX International Financial [*Vancouver Stock Exchange symbol*]
AXF .... Advanced X-Ray Facility
AXFBS .... Auxiliary Fire Tube Boiler Survey [*of a ship*] (DS)
AXFL .... Axial Flow
AXFMR ...... Automatic Transformer (IEEE)
AXFTB .... Auxiliary Fire Tube Boiler [*of a ship*] (DS)
AXFTBS .... Auxiliary Fire Tube Boiler Survey [*of a ship*] (DS)
AXG .... Amax Gold, Inc. [*Toronto Stock Exchange symbol*]
AXH .... Arcola, TX [*Location identifier*] [*FAA*] (FAAL)
AXI .... Air Express International Airlines, Inc. [*Atlanta, GA*] [*FAA designator*] (FAAC)
AXI .... Argonex International Ltd. [*Vancouver Stock Exchange symbol*]
AXI .... Mount Airy, NC [*Location identifier*] [*FAA*] (FAAL)
AXICS .... Apollo XI Collector Society [*Defunct*] (EA)
AXIM .... Axiom Systems, Inc. [*NASDAQ symbol*] (NQ)
AXIS .... Atmospheric X-Ray Imaging Spectrometer (MCD)
AXIS .... Automatic X-Ray Inspection (MCD)
AXIS .... Auxiliary System for Interactive Statistics [*Sweden*] [*Information service or system*] (IID)
AXIS .... Z-Axis Corp. [*NASDAQ symbol*] (NQ)
AXL .... Anderson Exploration Ltd. [*Toronto Stock Exchange symbol*]
AXL .... Arc Xenon Lamp
AXL .... Cartonnages et Emballages Modernes [*A publication*]
AXLN .... Axlon, Inc. [*Sunnyvale, CA*] [*NASDAQ symbol*] (NQ)
AXM .... Acetoxycycloheximide [*Biochemistry*]
AXM .... Armenia [*Colombia*] [*Airport symbol*] (OAG)
AXM .... United States Army Materiel Command, Alexandria, VA [*OCLC symbol*] (OCLC)
AXMIN ..... Axminster [*England*]
AXN .... Alexandria [*Minnesota*] [*Airport symbol*] [*Obsolete*] (OAG)
AXN .... Alexis Nihon Finance, Inc. [*Toronto Stock Exchange symbol*]
AXO .... Aaxico Air Lines
AXO .... Alamco, Inc. [*AMEX symbol*] (SPSG)
AXO .... Alberta Exploration [*Vancouver Stock Exchange symbol*]
AXO .... Assistant Experimental Officer [*Ministry of Agriculture, Fisheries, and Food*] [*Also, AEO, AExO*] [*British*]
AXP .... Allied Exercise Publications [*NATO*]
AXP .... American Express Co. [*NYSE symbol*] [*Toronto Stock Exchange symbol*] (SPSG)
AXP .... Axial Pitch (IEEE)
AXP .... Spring Point [*Bahamas*] [*Airport symbol*] (OAG)

AXPS .... Air Express
AXQ .... JIB Incorporated D/B/A Action Air Charter and Action Airlines [*East Haddam, CT*] [*FAA designator*] (FAAC)
AXR .... AMREP Corp. [*NYSE symbol*] (SPSG)
AXR .... Argentex Resource Exploration Corp. [*Vancouver Stock Exchange symbol*]
AXR .... Automatic X-Ray Radiograph
AXROS ...... Automated X-Ray Orientation System (MCD)
AXS .... Access
AXS .... Altus [*Oklahoma*] [*Airport symbol*] (OAG)
AXS .... Altus, OK [*Location identifier*] [*FAA*] (FAAL)
AxS .... Anxiety Sign [*Psychology*]
AXSIGCOMM ... Axis [*or Axes*] of Signal Communication [*Army*]
AXT .... Address to Index, True
AXT .... Akita [*Japan*] [*Airport symbol*] (OAG)
AXT .... Alternating Exotropia [*Ophthalmology*]
AXT .... Australian Sales Tax Guide [*A publication*]
AXU .... Axum [*Ethiopia*] [*Airport symbol*] (OAG)
AXV .... Alexis Nihon Finance, Inc. [*Vancouver Stock Exchange symbol*]
AXV .... Wapakoneta, OH [*Location identifier*] [*FAA*] (FAAL)
AXVMA .... Archiv fuer Experimentelle Veterinaermedizin [*A publication*]
AXVMAW ... Archiv fuer Experimentelle Veterinaermedizin [*A publication*]
AXWHB ..... Auxiliary Waste Heat Boiler [*of a ship*] (DS)
AXWHBS ... Auxiliary Waste Heater Boiler Survey [*of a ship*] (DS)
AXWTB ..... Auxiliary Water Tube Boiler [*of a ship*] (DS)
AXWTBS .. Auxiliary Waste Tube Boiler Survey [*of a ship*] (DS)
AXX .... Axiom International Development Corp. [*Formerly, Axiom Explorations, Inc.*] [*Vancouver Stock Exchange symbol*]
AXXN .... Action Auto Rental, Inc. [*NASDAQ symbol*] (NQ)
AXXX .... Artel Communications Corp. [*NASDAQ symbol*] (NQ)
AY .... Abundantly Yours (EA)
AY .... Academic Year (MCD)
AY .... Aeritalia SpA [*Italy*] [*ICAO aircraft manufacturer identifier*] (ICAO)
AY .... Agency
AY .... Allied Youth [*Later, AYFCC*]
AY .... Alsatian Yiddish (BJA)
AY .... Annual Yield [*Business term*]
ay................ Antarctica [*MARC country of publication code*] [*Library of Congress*] (LCCP)
AY .... Aster Yellows [*A plant disease*]
AY .... Atlas Yellowknife Resources Ltd. [*Toronto Stock Exchange symbol*]
AY .... Ayerst Laboratories [*Research code symbol*]
AY .... Ayrshire Yeomanry [*British military*] (DMA)
AY .... Finnair Oy [*Finland*] [*ICAO designator*] (FAAC)
ay----- .... Yellow Sea and Area [*MARC geographic area code*] [*Library of Congress*] (LCCP)
AYA .... American Yachtsmen's Association [*Later, BOAT/US*] (EA)
AYA .... American Yankee Association (EA)
AYA .... American Yoga Association (EA)
AYA .... Awana Youth Association (EA)
AYA .... Ayagualo [*El Salvador*] [*Seismograph station code, US Geological Survey*] [*Closed*] (SEIS)
AYB .... Accessory Bulletin (MCD)
AYB .... Avrupa Yatirim Bankasi [*European Investment Bank*] [*Turkish*]
AYBIL .... Australian Yearbook of International Law [*A publication*] (APTA)
AYC .... Accessory Change (MCD)
AYC .... Aerodynamic Yaw Coupling
AYC .... American Yorkshire Club (EA)
AYC .... American Youth Congress
AYC .... Australian Youth Choir
AYC .... Automatic Yaw Control
AYCA .... Afghan Youth Council in America (EA)
AYCC .... American Yugoslav Claims Committee (EA)
AYCC .... Australian Yugoslav Community Centre
Ayck Ch F ... Ayckbourn's Chancery Forms [*A publication*] (DLA)
Ayck Ch Pr ... Ayckbourn's Chancery Practice [*A publication*] (DLA)
Ayck Jur .... Ayckbourn's Jurisdiction of the Supreme Court of Judicature [*A publication*] (DLA)
AYCP........ Aerodynamic Yaw Coupling Parameters
AYD .... Alleged Year Disability Began [*Social Security Administration*] (OICC)
AYD .... American Youth for Democracy
AYD .... Associate of Youth Development [*British*] (DBQ)
AYD .... Association of Yarn Distributors (EA)
AYD .... Average Yarding Distance [*Forestry*]
AYD .... Aydin Corp. [*NYSE symbol*] (SPSG)
AYE .... Alcohol Education for Youth [*An association*]
AYE .... Argyll Energy Corp. [*Toronto Stock Exchange symbol*]
AYE .... Ayenquera [*Peru*] [*Seismograph station code, US Geological Survey*] (SEIS)
AYE .... Fort Devens (Ayer), MA [*Location identifier*] [*FAA*] (FAAL)
a-ye--- .... Yemen (Sanaa) [*MARC geographic area code*] [*Library of Congress*] (LCCP)
AYF .... American Youth Foundation (EA)
AYF .... Antiyeast Factor [*Medicine*]

AYF .... Armenian Youth Federation of America - Youth Organization of the ARF [*Armenian Revolutionary Federation of America*] (EA)
AYFCC ...... Allied Youth and Family Counseling Center (EA)
AYFYRA ... American Y-Flyer Yacht Racing Association (EA)
AYG .... Yuguara [*Colombia*] [*Airport symbol*] (OAG)
AYGA .... Goroka [*Papua New Guinea*] [*ICAO location identifier*] (ICLI)
AYH .... American Youth Hostels (EA)
AYI .... Academic Year Institute [*National Science Foundation*]
AYI .... Angle of Yaw Indicator
AYI .... Antony Resources [*Vancouver Stock Exchange symbol*]
AYI .... Kiln, MS [*Location identifier*] [*FAA*] (FAAL)
AYI .... Yari [*Colombia*] [*Airport symbol*] (OAG)
AYJUSA ... Association of Yugoslav Jews in the USA (EA)
AYK .... Ayerok Petroleum [*Vancouver Stock Exchange symbol*]
AYL .... As You Like It [*Shakespearean work*]
AYLA .... Lae [*Papua New Guinea*] [*ICAO location identifier*] (ICLI)
AYLB........ Aylesbeare [*England*]
AYLB........ Aylesbury [*England*]
Ayl Char .... Ayliffe's Calendar of Ancient Charters [*1774*] [*A publication*] (DLA)
Ayliffe .... Ayliffe's Pandects [*A publication*] (DLA)
Ayliffe .... Ayliffe's Parergon Juris Canonici Anglicani [*A publication*] (DLA)
Ayl Int........ Ayliffe's Introduction to the Calendar of Ancient Charters [*A publication*] (DLA)
Ayl Pan ...... Ayliffe's Pandect of the Roman Civil Law [*A publication*] (DLA)
Ayl Pand .... Ayliffe's Pandect of the Roman Civil Law [*A publication*] (DLA)
Ayl Par...... Ayliffe's Parergon Juris Canonici Anglicani [*A publication*] (DLA)
AYLR........ Aylesford Review [*A publication*]
AYM.......... Ancient York Mason [*Freemasonry*]
AYM.......... Anglican Youth Movement [*Canada*]
AYM.......... Assistant Yard Master [*Railroads*] [*British*]
aym............ Aymara [*MARC language code*] [*Library of Congress*] (LCCP)
Aym........... Aymo Cravetta [*Deceased, 1569*] [*Authority cited in pre-1607 legal work*] (DSA)
AYM.......... Youngstown Municipal Library, Alberta [*Library symbol*] [*National Library of Canada*] (NLC)
AYMD....... Madang [*Papua New Guinea*] [*ICAO location identifier*] (ICLI)
AYMH....... Mount Hagen [*Papua New Guinea*] [*ICAO location identifier*] (ICLI)
AYN.......... Abercynon [*Cardiff*] [*Welsh depot code*]
AYN.......... Watsonville, CA [*Location identifier*] [*FAA*] (FAAL)
AYNZ........ Nadzab [*Papua New Guinea*] [*ICAO location identifier*] (ICLI)
AYO.......... Albany Corp. [*Toronto Stock Exchange symbol*]
AYO.......... Area Youth Office [*British*]
AYP .... Alaska Yukon Pioneers (EA)
AYP .... Allegheny Power System, Inc. [*NYSE symbol*] (SPSG)
AYP .... Allentown Public Library, Allentown, PA [*OCLC symbol*] (OCLC)
AYP .... Ayacucho [*Peru*] [*Airport symbol*] (OAG)
AYPA........ Anglican Young People's Association [*British*]
AYPY........ Port Moresby [*Papua New Guinea*] [*ICAO location identifier*] (ICLI)
AYQ.......... Ayers Rock [*Australia*] [*Airport symbol*] (OAG)
AYQ.......... Ponca City, OK [*Location identifier*] [*FAA*] (FAAL)
AYR .... American Year Review [*A publication*]
Ayr............ Ayr's Registration Cases [*Scotland*] [*A publication*] (DLA)
AYRB........ Rabaul [*Papua New Guinea*] [*ICAO location identifier*] (ICLI)
AYRCGA... All Year Round Chrysanthemum Growers' Association (EAIO)
Ayr Land Tr ... Ayrton's Land Transfer Act [*A publication*] (DLA)
AYRS........ Amateur Yacht Research Society [*Turnchapel, Plymouth, England*] (EAIO)
AYRS........ Ayrshire [*County in Scotland*]
Ayrshire Archaeol Natur Hist Collect 2 Ser ... Ayrshire Archaeological and Natural History Collections. Series 2 [*A publication*]
Ayr & Wig ... Ayr and Wigton's Registration Cases [*Scotland*] [*A publication*] (DLA)
AYS........... Agni Yoga Society (EA)
AYS........... At Your Service
a-ys---........ Southern Yemen (Aden) [*MARC geographic area code*] [*Library of Congress*] (LCCP)
AYS........... Waycross [*Georgia*] [*Airport symbol*] (OAG)
AYS........... Waycross, GA [*Location identifier*] [*FAA*] (FAAL)
AYSA......... American Yarn Spinners Association (EA)
A2YSC....... Associated Two-Year Schools in Construction (EA)
AYSO .... American Youth Soccer Organization (EA)
AYSS .... Allegheny & South Side [*AAR code*]
AYT........... Antalya [*Turkey*] [*Airport symbol*] (OAG)
AYT .... Army Youth Team [*British*]
AYU........... Aiyura [*Papua New Guinea*] [*Airport symbol*] [*Obsolete*]
AYW.......... Archives of Yad Washem [*A publication*] (BJA)
AYWC ...... American Youth Work Center (EA)
AYWK ...... Wewak [*Papua New Guinea*] [*ICAO location identifier*] (ICLI)
AZ............. Aboda Zara (BJA)
AZ............. Abscission Zone [*Botany*]

AZ............. Academy of Zoology [*Uttar Pradesh, India*] (EA)
AZ............. Active Zone
AZ............. Air Zero
AZ............. Airship Tender [*Navy symbol*] [*Obsolete*]
AZ............. ALITALIA [*Aerolinee Italiane Internazionali*] [*Italian airline*] [*ICAO designator*]
AZ............. Alpha Zeta (EA)
AZ............. Aluminium-Zentrale e V
AZ............. Archaeologische Zeitung [*A publication*]
AZ............. Archivalische Zeitschrift [*A publication*]
AZ............. Arizona [*Postal code*]
AZ............. Arizona Reports [*A publication*]
Az............. Arizona State Department of Library and Archives, Phoenix, AZ [*Library symbol*] [*Library of Congress*] (LCLS)
AZ............. Atlas Corp. [*NYSE symbol*] (SPSG)
AZ............. Auf Zeit [*On Credit*] [*German*]
AZ............. Aviation Maintenance Administrationman [*Navy rating*]
AZ............. Azathioprine [*Also, AZA, AZT*] [*Immunosuppressive drug*]
AZ............. Azimuth (AFM)
Az............. [*Jacobus*] d'Azo [*Flourished, 1191-1220*] [*Authority cited in pre-1607 legal work*] (DSA)
AZ............. Azores Islands
AZ............. Azote [*Nitrogen*] [*French*]
AZ............. Azure [*Heraldry*] [*Philately*]
AZ1 .... Aviation Maintenance Administrationman, First Class [*Navy rating*]
AZ2 .... Aviation Maintenance Administrationman, Second Class [*Navy rating*]
AZ3 .... Aviation Maintenance Administrationman, Third Class [*Navy rating*]
AZA .... Ahavah, Zedakah, Ahdut (BJA)
AZA .... Aleph Zadik Aleph [*Society*]
AZA .... ALZA Corp. [*AMEX symbol*] (SPSG)
AZA .... American Zombie Association (EA)
AZ A .... Arizona Court of Appeals Reports [*A publication*] (DLA)
AZA .... Arizona Golden Pacific [*Vancouver Stock Exchange symbol*]
AZA .... Azacytidine [*or Azacitidine*] [*Also, AC, Aza-C*] [*Antineoplastic drug*]
AZA .... Azathioprine [*Also, AZ, AZT*] [*Immunosuppressive drug*]
AZA .... University of Arizona, Health Sciences Center Library, Tucson, AZ [*OCLC symbol*] (OCLC)
AZAA........ Airman Apprentice, Aviation Maintenance Administrationman, Striker [*Navy rating*]
Azabu Juika Daigaku Kenkyu Hokoku Bull ... Azabu Juika Daigaku Kenkyu Hokoku/Bulletin. Azabu Veterinary College [*A publication*]
Aza-C .... Azacytidine [*or Azacitidine*] [*Also, AC, AZA*] [*Antineoplastic drug*]
AZAN......... Airman, Aviation Maintenance Administrationman, Striker [*Navy rating*]
AZAP........ Agence Zaire-Presse [*Zaire Press Agency*]
AZAPO ..... Azanian People's Organization [*South Africa*] (PPW)
AZAR .... Adjustable Zero, Adjustable Range
AZARAO .. Arizona. Agricultural Experiment Station. Research Report [*A publication*]
AZATAU... Arizona. Agricultural Experiment Station. Technical Bulletin [*A publication*]
AZB .... Amazon Bay [*Papua New Guinea*] [*Airport symbol*] (OAG)
AZB .... Arizona Commerce Bank [*AMEX symbol*] (SPSG)
AZB .... Arizona Motor Tariff Bureau, Inc., Phoenix AZ [*STAC*]
AzB .... Copper Queen Library, Bisbee, AZ [*Library symbol*] [*Library of Congress*] (LCLS)
AzBe........... Benson Public Library, Benson, AZ [*Library symbol*] [*Library of Congress*] (LCLS)
Az-BPH ...... Arizona Regional Library for the Blind and Physically Handicapped, Phoenix, AZ [*Library symbol*] [*Library of Congress*] (LCLS)
AZBTAZ .... Annotationes Zoologicae et Botanicae [*A publication*]
AzBu .... Buckeye Public Library, Buckeye, AZ [*Library symbol*] [*Library of Congress*] (LCLS)
AZBUD7 ... Acta Zoologica Bulgarica [*A publication*]
AZBW........ Arizona Bancwest Corp. [*NASDAQ symbol*] (NQ)
AZC .... American Zionist Council [*Later, AZF*] (EA)
AZC .... Arizona State University, College of Law Library, Tempe, AZ [*OCLC symbol*] (OCLC)
AZC .... Aviation Maintenance Administrationman, Chief [*Navy rating*]
AzCc........... Cave Creek Public Library, Cave Creek, AZ [*Library symbol*] [*Library of Congress*] (LCLS)
AZCC .... Zama City Community Library, Alberta [*Library symbol*] [*National Library of Canada*] (NLC)
AzCg .... Casa Grande Public Library, Casa Grande, AZ [*Library symbol*] [*Library of Congress*] (LCLS)
AzCh .... Chandler Public Library, Chandler, AZ [*Library symbol*] [*Library of Congress*] (LCLS)
AzCH......... Chinle High School Library, Chinle, AZ [*Library symbol*] [*Library of Congress*] (LCLS)
AZCM .... Aviation Maintenance Administrationman, Master Chief [*Navy rating*]
AzCN .... Navajo Community College, Chinle, AZ [*Library symbol*] [*Library of Congress*] (LCLS)
AZCO .... Aztec Resources Corporation [*NASDAQ symbol*] (NQ)

AzCo .... Coolidge Public Library, Coolidge, AZ [*Library symbol*] [*Library of Congress*] (LCLS)
AzCoC .... Central Arizona College, Instructional Materials Center, Coolidge, AZ [*Library symbol*] [*Library of Congress*] (LCLS)
AzCot .... Cottonwood Public Library, Cottonwood, AZ [*Library symbol*] [*Library of Congress*] (LCLS)
AZCRAY ... Acta Zoologica Cracoviensia [*A publication*]
AZCS .... Aviation Maintenance Administrationman, Senior Chief [*Navy rating*]
AZD .... Scottsdale Public Library, Scottsdale, AZ [*OCLC symbol*] (OCLC)
AZD .... Yazd [*Iran*] [*Airport symbol*] (OAG)
AzDC .... Cochise College, Douglas, AZ [*Library symbol*] [*Library of Congress*] (LCLS)
AZDJ .... Allgemeine Zeitung des Judentums [*A publication*]
AZDU .... Azidodideoxyuridine [*Antiviral*]
AZE .... American Maize-Products Co. [*AMEX symbol*] (SPSG)
aze .... Azerbaijani [*MARC language code*] [*Library of Congress*] (LCCP)
AZE .... Hazlehurst, GA [*Location identifier*] [*FAA*] (FAAL)
AZEAAR ... Annales de Zoologie - Ecologie Animale [*A publication*]
AZEGAB ... Archives de Zoologie Experimentale et Generale [*A publication*]
AZEL .... Azimuth and Elevation (MSA)
Azerbaidzan Gos Univ Ucen Zap ... Azerbaidzanskii Gosudarstvennyi Universitet Imeni M. Kirova. Ucenye Zapiski [*A publication*]
Azerbaidzan Gos Univ Ucen Zap Ser Fiz-Mat Nauk ... Azerbaidzanskii Gosudarstvennyi Universitet Imeni S. M. Kirova. Ucenye Zapiski. Serija Fiziko-Matematiceskih Nauk [*A publication*]
Azerbaidzhan Med Zhurnal ... Azerbaidzhanskii Meditsinskii Zhurnal [*A publication*]
Azerb Ak Heberleri ... Azerbajdzan SSR Elmler Akademijasynyn Herberleri. Izvestija Akademii Nauk Azerbajdzanskoj SSR [*A publication*]
Azerb Gos Med Inst Mater Nauchn Konf ... Azerbaidzhanskii Gosudarstvennyi Meditsinskii Institut Materialy Nauchnoi Konferentsii [*A publication*]
Azerb Khim Zh ... Azerbaidzhanskii Khimicheskii Zhurnal [*A publication*]
Azerb Med Zh ... Azerbaidzhanskii Meditsinskii Zhurnal [*A publication*]
Azerb Nauchno-Issled Inst Oftalmol Sb Tr ... Azerbaidzhanskii Nauchno-Issledovatel'skii Institut Oftal'mologii. Sbornik Trudov [*A publication*]
Azerb Neft Khoz ... Azerbajdzhanskoe Neftyanoe Khozyajstvo [*A publication*]
AzerSSR .... Azerbaydzhani Soviet Socialist Republic
AZEU .... Azido(ethyl)dideoxyuridine [*Antiviral*]
AZF .... American Zionist Federation (EA)
AzF .... Flagstaff City-Coconino County Public Library, Flagstaff, AZ [*Library symbol*] [*Library of Congress*] (LCLS)
AZFC .... Alexander Zonjic Fan Club (EA)
AZFEAA ... Acta Zoologica Fennica [*A publication*]
AzFGS .... Church of Jesus Christ of Latter-Day Saints, Genealogical Society Library, Flagstaff Branch, Flagstaff, AZ [*Library symbol*] [*Library of Congress*] (LCLS)
AzFhA .... United States Army, Technical Reference Division Library, Fort Huachuca, AZ [*Library symbol*] [*Library of Congress*] (LCLS)
AzFlCo .... Pinal County Public Library, Florence, AZ [*Library symbol*] [*Library of Congress*] (LCLS)
AzFlP .... Arizona State Prison Library, Florence, AZ [*Library symbol*] [*Library of Congress*] (LCLS)
AzFM .... Museum of Northern Arizona, Flagstaff, AZ [*Library symbol*] [*Library of Congress*] (LCLS)
AzFU .... Northern Arizona University, Flagstaff, AZ [*Library symbol*] [*Library of Congress*] (LCLS)
AZG .... Australian Gold [*Vancouver Stock Exchange symbol*]
AzG .... Velma Teague Library, Glendale, AZ [*Library symbol*] [*Library of Congress*] (LCLS)
AzGAF .... United States Air Force, Luke Air Force Base Library, Glendale, AZ [*Library symbol*] [*Library of Congress*] (LCLS)
AzGaH .... Ganado High School Library, Ganado, AZ [*Library symbol*] [*Library of Congress*] (LCLS)
AzGC .... Glendale Community College, Glendale, AZ [*Library symbol*] [*Library of Congress*] (LCLS)
AzGi .... Gilbert Public Library, Gilbert, AZ [*Library symbol*] [*Library of Congress*] (LCLS)
AzGoU ...... UMC Industries, Unidynamics Phoenix, Inc. Library, Goodyear, AZ [*Library symbol*] [*Library of Congress*] (LCLS)
AzGrcN ...... United States National Park Service, Grand Canyon National Park Library, Grand Canyon, AZ [*Library symbol*] [*Library of Congress*] (LCLS)
AZGS .... Azusa Ground Station
AzHA .... Hayden Public Library, Hayden, AZ [*Library symbol*] [*Library of Congress*] (LCLS)
AzHGS ...... Church of Jesus Christ of Latter-Day Saints, Genealogical Society Library, Holbrook Branch, Holbrook, AZ [*Library symbol*] [*Library of Congress*] (LCLS)
AzHH .... Holbrook High School Library, Holbrook, AZ [*Library symbol*] [*Library of Congress*] (LCLS)

AZHIA ...... Arizona Highways [*A publication*]
AzHP .... Petrified Forest National Park, Painted Desert Library, Holbrook, AZ [*Library symbol*] [*Library of Congress*] (LCLS)
AZHUE4 ... Acta Zoologica Hungarica [*A publication*]
AZI .... American Zellter, Incorporated
AZI .... American Zinc Institute [*Later, ZI*] (EA)
AZi .... American Zionist (BJA)
AZI .... Association Zen Internationale [*International Zen Association - IZA*] (EAIO)
AZI .... Azidothymidine [*Later, ZDV*] [*Antiviral*]
AZIC .... Arizona Instrument Corp. [*NASDAQ symbol*] (NQ)
AZIH .... Archiwum Zydowskiego Instytutu Historycznego [*A publication*]
AZII .... American Zinc Institute, Incorporated [*Later, ZI*] (MCD)
AZIMDI .... Arnoldia Zimbabwe [*A publication*]
AZIN .... Aztech International Ltd. [*NASDAQ symbol*] (NQ)
AZJ .... Allgemeine Zeitung des Judentums [*A publication*]
AZK .... Arizako Mines Ltd. [*Vancouver Stock Exchange symbol*]
AzKaH .... Monument Valley High School Library, Kayenta, AZ [*Library symbol*] [*Library of Congress*] (LCLS)
AzKiM .... Kingman City-Mohave County Library, Kingman, AZ [*Library symbol*] [*Library of Congress*] (LCLS)
AzKiMC .... Mohave Community College, Resource Center, Kingman, AZ [*Library symbol*] [*Library of Congress*] (LCLS)
AZKZA ..... Azerbaidzhanskii Khimicheskii Zhurnal [*A publication*]
AZL .... Arizona Land Income Corp. Class A [*AMEX symbol*] (SPSG)
AZ L .... Arizona Law Review [*A publication*]
AZL .... University of Arizona College of Law, Library, Tucson, AZ [*OCLC symbol*] (OCLC)
AzLa .... Lakeside Public Library, Lakeside, AZ [*Library symbol*] [*Library of Congress*] (LCLS)
AZLD .... Azure Laid (ADA)
AZLGAC ... Annals of Zoology [*Agra*] [*A publication*]
AzLhc .... Lake Havasu City Public Library, Lake Havasu City, AZ [*Library symbol*] [*Library of Congress*] (LCLS)
AzLp .... Litchfield Park Public Library, Litchfield Park, AZ [*Library symbol*] [*Library of Congress*] (LCLS)
AZ LR .... Arizona Law Review [*A publication*]
AZM .... Assumption College, Worcester, MA [*OCLC symbol*] (OCLC)
AZM .... Azimuth
AZM .... Azora Minerals [*Vancouver Stock Exchange symbol*]
AZM .... Azoxymethane [*A carcinogen*]
AzM .... Mesa Public Library, Mesa, AZ [*Library symbol*] [*Library of Congress*] (LCLS)
AzMa .... Mammoth Public Library, Mammoth, AZ [*Library symbol*] [*Library of Congress*] (LCLS)
Az Mar Law ... Azuni's Maritime Law [*A publication*] (DLA)
AzMC .... Mesa Community College, Mesa, AZ [*Library symbol*] [*Library of Congress*] (LCLS)
AzMGS ..... Church of Jesus Christ of Latter-Day Saints, Genealogical Society Library, Mesa Branch, Mesa, AZ [*Library symbol*] [*Library of Congress*] (LCLS)
AzMi .... Miami Memorial-Gila County Library, Miami, AZ [*Library symbol*] [*Library of Congress*] (LCLS)
AzML .... Latter-Day Saints Genealogical Library, Mesa, AZ [*Library symbol*] [*Library of Congress*] (LCLS)
AzMo .... Morenci Public Library, Morenci, AZ [*Library symbol*] [*Library of Congress*] (LCLS)
AZMXAY ... Acta Zoologica Mexicana [*A publication*]
AZMZA ..... Azerbaidzhanskii Meditsinskii Zhurnal [*A publication*]
AzN .... Nogales Public Library, Nogales, AZ [*Library symbol*] [*Library of Congress*] (LCLS)
AZN .... Northern Arizona University, Flagstaff, AZ [*OCLC symbol*] (OCLC)
AZN .... St. Joseph, MO [*Location identifier*] [*FAA*] (FAAL)
AzNPHi ..... Pimeria Alta Historical Society Museum, Nogales, AZ [*Library symbol*] [*Library of Congress*] (LCLS)
AZO .... Allgemeine Zionistische Organisation [*A publication*]
AZO .... Allgemeine Zollordnung [*German General Customs Regulations*] [*A publication*] (DLA)
AZO .... Alpha Zeta Omega [*Fraternity*]
AZO .... Kalamazoo [*Michigan*] [*Airport symbol*] (OAG)
AzO .... Oracle Public Library, Oracle, AZ [*Library symbol*] [*Library of Congress*] (LCLS)
AZOCAF ... Acta Zoologica Cracoviensia [*English Translation*] [*A publication*]
AZOF .... Annales Zoologica Fennici [*A publication*]
AZOFAO .. Annales Zoologici Fennici [*A publication*]
AZOGAR ... Annales Zoologici [*Warsaw*] [*A publication*]
AZOGB ..... Australian and New Zealand Journal of Obstetrics and Gynaecology [*A publication*]
AZOIAX ... Archivio Zoologico Italiano [*A publication*]
AZOJA2 .... Annotationes Zoologicae Japonenses [*A publication*]
AZOLA8 ... Acta Zoologica Lilloana [*A publication*]
AZON .... Azimuth Only
AZOOAH ... Annales de Zootechnie [*Paris*] [*A publication*]
AZOSAT ... Acta Zoologica [*Stockholm*] [*A publication*]
AZOTAW ... Archivos de Zootecnia [*A publication*]
Azotul Agric ... Azotul in Agricultura [*A publication*]

AZOV .... Aufschlagzuender ohne Verzoegerung [*Nondelay fuze*] [*German military - World War II*]

AZP .... Archiv fuer die Zivilistische Praxis [*A publication*]   (ILCA)

AZP .... Arizona Department of Library Archives, Tempe, AZ [*OCLC symbol*]   (OCLC)

AzP .... Page Public Library, Page, AZ [*Library symbol*] [*Library of Congress*]   (LCLS)

AzPa............ Colorado River Indian Tribes Public Library, Parker, AZ [*Library symbol*] [*Library of Congress*]   (LCLS)

AzPh .... Phoenix Public Library, Phoenix, AZ [*Library symbol*] [*Library of Congress*]   (LCLS)

AzPhDA .... United States Department of Agriculture, Water Conservation Laboratory Library, Phoenix, AZ [*Library symbol*] [*Library of Congress*]   (LCLS)

AzPhF .... First National Bank Library, Phoenix, AZ [*Library symbol*] [*Library of Congress*]   (LCLS)

AzPhGS..... Church of Jesus Christ of Latter-Day Saints, Genealogical Society Library, Phoenix Arizona North Branch, Phoenix, AZ [*Library symbol*] [*Library of Congress*]   (LCLS)

AzPhH .... Honeywell Information Systems, Phoenix, AZ [*Library symbol*] [*Library of Congress*]   (LCLS)

AzPhM .... Maricopa County Free Library, Phoenix, AZ [*Library symbol*] [*Library of Congress*]   (LCLS)

AzPhMC.... Maricopa County Community College, Phoenix, AZ [*Library symbol*] [*Library of Congress*]   (LCLS)

AzPhML.... Maricopa County Law Library, Phoenix, AZ [*Library symbol*] [*Library of Congress*]   (LCLS)

AzPhMM .. Maricopa County Medical Society, Phoenix, AZ [*Library symbol*] [*Library of Congress*]   (LCLS)

AzPhMo .... Motorola, Inc., Semiconductor Products Division Library, Phoenix, AZ [*Library symbol*] [*Library of Congress*]   (LCLS)

AzPhWGS ... Church of Jesus Christ of Latter-Day Saints, Genealogical Society Library, Phoenix Arizona West Branch, Phoenix, AZ [*Library symbol*] [*Library of Congress*]   (LCLS)

AzPr .... Prescott City-Yavapai County Library, Prescott, AZ [*Library symbol*] [*Library of Congress*]   (LCLS)

AzPrGS...... Church of Jesus Christ of Latter-Day Saints, Genealogical Society Library, Prescott Branch, Prescott, AZ [*Library symbol*] [*Library of Congress*]   (LCLS)

AzPrP .... Prescott College, Prescott, AZ [*Library symbol*] [*Library of Congress*]   (LCLS)

AzPrSH ..... Sharlott Hall Museum, Prescott Historical Society, Prescott, AZ [*Library symbol*] [*Library of Congress*]   (LCLS)

AzPrV .... United States Veterans Administration Center, Prescott, AZ [*Library symbol*] [*Library of Congress*]   (LCLS)

AzPrY .... Yavapai College, Prescott, AZ [*Library symbol*] [*Library of Congress*]   (LCLS)

AzPrY-V .... Yavapai College, Verde Campus, Clarkdale, AZ [*Library symbol*] [*Library of Congress*]   (LCLS)

AzQ .... Arizona Quarterly [*A publication*]

AZQ .... Aziridinyl Benzoquinone [*Organic chemistry*]

AZR .... Adrar [*Algeria*] [*Airport symbol*]   (OAG)

AZR .... Armour Research Center, Scottsdale, AZ [*OCLC symbol*]   (OCLC)

AZR .... Azure Resources [*Vancouver Stock Exchange symbol*]

AZRAN ..... Azimuth and Range

AZRD .... Arizona Road Dust [*Environmental chemistry*]

AZRNG ..... Azimuth and Range   (MSA)

AzRou .... Rough Rock Public Library, Rough Rock, AZ [*Library symbol*] [*Library of Congress*]   (LCLS)

AZRU .... Aztec Ruins National Monument

AZS............ Alloyed Zinc Sheet

AZS............ Alumina-Zirconia-Silica [*Inorganic chemistry*]

AZS............ Arizona Star Resource Corp. [*Vancouver Stock Exchange symbol*]

AZS............ Arizona State University, Tempe, AZ [*OCLC symbol*]   (OCLC)

AZS............ Automatic Zero Set [*Military*]

AZS............ Charlottesville, VA [*Location identifier*] [*FAA*]   (FAAL)

AzS............ Scottsdale Public Library, Scottsdale, AZ [*Library symbol*] [*Library of Congress*]   (LCLS)

AzSaf .... Safford City-Graham County Public Library, Safford, AZ [*Library symbol*] [*Library of Congress*]   (LCLS)

AzSafGS .... Church of Jesus Christ of Latter-Day Saints, Genealogical Society Library, Safford Branch, Safford, AZ [*Library symbol*] [*Library of Congress*]   (LCLS)

AzSArm ..... Armour Research Center Library, Scottsdale, AZ [*Library symbol*] [*Library of Congress*]   (LCLS)

AzSe .... Sedona Public Library, Sedona, AZ [*Library symbol*] [*Library of Congress*]   (LCLS)

AzSh .... Show Low Public Library, Show Low, AZ [*Library symbol*] [*Library of Congress*]   (LCLS)

AZSHAG .. Acta Zoologica. Academiae Scientiarum Hungaricae [*A publication*]

AzShGS ..... Church of Jesus Christ of Latter-Day Saints, Genealogical Society Library, Show Low Branch, Show Low, AZ [*Library symbol*] [*Library of Congress*]   (LCLS)

AZSITE..... Archaeological Sites Data Base [*Tucson*] [*Information service or system*]   (IID)

AzSj .... Saint Johns Public Library, Saint Johns, AZ [*Library symbol*] [*Library of Congress*]   (LCLS)

AzSjGS ...... Church of Jesus Christ of Latter-Day Saints, Genealogical Society Library, St. Johns Branch, Stake Center, St. Johns, AZ [*Library symbol*] [*Library of Congress*]   (LCLS)

AzSnGS ..... Church of Jesus Christ of Latter-Day Saints, Genealogical Society Library, Snowflake Branch, Snowflake, AZ [*Library symbol*] [*Library of Congress*]   (LCLS)

AzSo........... Somerton Public Library, Somerton, AZ [*Library symbol*] [*Library of Congress*]   (LCLS)

AzSp........... Springerville Public Library, Springerville, AZ [*Library symbol*] [*Library of Congress*]   (LCLS)

AZSPA6 .... Arquivos de Zoologia do Estado de Sao Paulo [*A publication*]

AzStdGS .... Church of Jesus Christ of Latter-Day Saints, Genealogical Society Library, St. David Arizona Stake Branch, St. David, AZ [*Library symbol*] [*Library of Congress*]   (LCLS)

AzSu........... Sun City Public Library, Sun City, AZ [*Library symbol*] [*Library of Congress*]   (LCLS)

AZT .... Ascheim-Zondek Test [*Medicine*]

AZT .... Azathioprine [*Also, AZ, AZA*] [*Immunosuppressive drug*]

AZT .... Azidodeoxythymidine [*Biochemistry*]

AZT .... Azidothymidine [*Later, ZDV*] [*Antiviral*]

AZT .... Azusa Transponder

AZT .... Tucson Public Library, Tucson, AZ [*OCLC symbol*]   (OCLC)

AzT .... Tucson Public Library, Tucson, AZ [*Library symbol*] [*Library of Congress*]   (LCLS)

AzTAM...... Arizona Medical Center, University of Arizona, Tucson, AZ [*Library symbol*] [*Library of Congress*]   (LCLS)

AzTAP ...... Aerial Phenomena Research Organization, Inc., Information Services Division, Tucson, AZ [*Library symbol*] [*Library of Congress*]   (LCLS)

AZTC........ Aztec Manufacturing Co. [*NASDAQ symbol*]   (NQ)

AZTC........ Azusa Transponder Coherent

AzTCM...... Walter Chiles Cox Memorial Foundation, Tucson, AZ [*Library symbol*] [*Library of Congress*]   (LCLS)

AzTe........... Tempe Public Library, Tempe, AZ [*Library symbol*] [*Library of Congress*]   (LCLS)

AzTeS .... Arizona State University, Tempe, AZ [*Library symbol*] [*Library of Congress*]   (LCLS)

AzTeS-Hi... Arizona Historical Foundation, Arizona State University, Tempe, AZ [*Library symbol*] [*Library of Congress*]   (LCLS)

AzTeS-L .... Arizona State University, College of Law, Tempe, AZ [*Library symbol*] [*Library of Congress*]   (LCLS)

AzTGS ...... Church of Jesus Christ of Latter-Day Saints, Genealogical Society Library, Tucson Branch, Tucson, AZ [*Library symbol*] [*Library of Congress*]   (LCLS)

AZTh .... Arbeiten zur Theologie [*Stuttgart/Berlin*] [*A publication*]

AzThE........ Eastern Arizona College, Thatcher, AZ [*Library symbol*] [*Library of Congress*]   (LCLS)

AzTK........ Kitt Peak National Observatory, Tucson, AZ [*Library symbol*] [*Library of Congress*]   (LCLS)

AzTo.......... Tombstone-Cochise County Library, Tombstone, AZ [*Library symbol*] [*Library of Congress*]   (LCLS)

AzTol .... Tolleson Public Library, Tolleson, AZ [*Library symbol*] [*Library of Congress*]   (LCLS)

AzTP.......... Arizona Historical Society, Tucson, AZ [*Library symbol*] [*Library of Congress*]   (LCLS)

AzTPC ...... Pima College, Tucson, AZ [*Library symbol*] [*Library of Congress*]   (LCLS)

AZT-TP..... Azidothymidine-Triphosphate [*Biochemistry*]

AzTu .... Tuba City Public Library, Tuba City, AZ [*Library symbol*] [*Library of Congress*]   (LCLS)

AzTV.......... United States Veterans Administration Hospital, Tucson, AZ [*Library symbol*] [*Library of Congress*]   (LCLS)

azu............. Arizona [*MARC country of publication code*] [*Library of Congress*]   (LCCP)

AZU .... Azul [*Race of maize*]

AZU .... Azurin

AzU .... University of Arizona, Tucson, AZ [*Library symbol*] [*Library of Congress*] [*OCLC symbol*]   (LCLS)

AzU-L .... University of Arizona, College of Law, Tucson, AZ [*Library symbol*] [*Library of Congress*]   (LCLS)

AzU-M....... University of Arizona, Health Sciences Center, Tucson, AZ [*Library symbol*] [*Library of Congress*]   (LCLS)

Azuni Mar Law ... Azuni's Maritime Law [*A publication*]   (DLA)

AZUSA...... Azimuth, Speed, Altitude

AZWBAI ... Arizona. Game and Fish Department. Wildlife Bulletin [*A publication*]

AzWhr .... Whiteriver Public Library, Whiteriver, AZ [*Library symbol*] [*Library of Congress*]   (LCLS)

AzWi.......... Williams Public Library, Williams, AZ [*Library symbol*] [*Library of Congress*]   (LCLS)

AzWic .... Wickenburg Public Library, Wickenburg, AZ [*Library symbol*] [*Library of Congress*]   (LCLS)

AzWin........ Roxanne Whipple Memorial Library, Winslow, AZ [*Library symbol*] [*Library of Congress*]   (LCLS)

AZWO .... Azure Wove   (ADA)

AzWr.......... Window Rock Public Library, Window Rock, AZ [*Library symbol*] [*Library of Congress*]   (LCLS)

AZXNAP... Archives de Zoologie Experimentale et Generale. Notes et Revue [*A publication*]

AZY .... Arizona Western College, Yuma, AZ [*OCLC symbol*]   (OCLC)

AzY .... Yuma City-County Public Library, Yuma, AZ [*Library symbol*]
                 [*Library of Congress*]   (LCLS)
AzYAW ..... Arizona Western College, Yuma, AZ [*Library symbol*] [*Library
                 of Congress*]   (LCLS)
AZYC......... American Zionist Youth Council   (EA)
AZYF......... American Zionist Youth Foundation   (EA)
AzYGS....... Church of Jesus Christ of Latter-Day Saints, Genealogical
                 Society Library, Yuma Branch, Yuma, AZ [*Library
                 symbol*] [*Library of Congress*]   (LCLS)
AzYo .... Youngtown Public Library, Youngtown, AZ [*Library symbol*]
                 [*Library of Congress*]   (LCLS)
AZZFAB ... Annales Zoologici. Societatis Zoologicae-Botanicae Fennicae
                 "Vanamo" [*A publication*]

B

B .... Air Force Training Category [*24 inactive duty training periods and 15 days active duty training per year*]
B .... Air Route Traffic Control Center Clearance Delivered [*Symbol*]   (FAAC)
B .... All India Reporter, Bombay Series [*A publication*]   (DLA)
B .... Aspartic Acid [*or Asparagine*] [*Also, Asx*] [*An amino acid*] [*Symbol*]
B .... Baccalaureate
B .... Bachelor
B .... Bacillus [*Bacteriology*]
B .... Back
B .... Backward Edge [*Skating*]
B .... Bag [*Shipping*]
B .... Bagarottus dei Corradi da Bologna [*Flourished, 1200-42*] [*Authority cited in pre-1607 legal work*]   (DSA)
B .... Baht [*Monetary unit*] [*Thailand*]
B .... Bailie [*British*]   (ROG)
B .... Bajocian [*Geology*]
B .... Baker [*Phonetic alphabet*] [*World War II*]   (DSUE)
B .... Balanced
B .... Balanced Fund [*Investment term*]
B .... Balboa [*Monetary unit*] [*Panama*]
B .... [*Jacobus*] Balduini [*Deceased, 1235*] [*Authority cited in pre-1607 legal work*]   (DSA)
B .... Baldus de Ubaldis [*Deceased, 1400*] [*Authority cited in pre-1607 legal work*]   (DSA)
B .... Bale [*Shipping*]
B .... Ball
B .... Ballinger Publishing Co.
B .... Ballistic
B .... Balloon Ceiling [*Meteorology*]   (FAAC)
B .... Balneum [*Bath*] [*Medicine*]
B .... Bancus [*Common Bench*] [*Legal*] [*British*]   (ROG)
B .... Band
B .... Bands (Civilian and Military) [*Public-performance tariff class*] [*British*]
B .... Bandwidth [*Frequency range*]
B .... Bani [*Monetary unit*] [*Romania*]
B .... Bank
B .... Banker [*A publication*]
B .... Baptist
B .... Bar
B .... Barber [*Charles E.*] [*Designer's mark, when appearing on US coins*]
B .... Barber's Gold Law [*South Africa*] [*A publication*]   (DLA)
B .... Barbour's New York Reports [*A publication*]   (DLA)
B .... Barcelona [*A publication*]
B .... Barge
B .... Baritone [*Music*]
b .... Barn [*Area of nuclear cross-section*]
B .... Barnes Group, Inc. [*NYSE symbol*]   (SPSG)
B .... Barometric Pressure Correction [*Symbol*]
B .... Baron
B .... Baroness Publications Ltd., Inc. [*Publisher*]
B .... Barrel [*Shipping*]
B .... Bartholomaeus Brixiensis [*Deceased circa 1258*] [*Authority cited in pre-1607 legal work*]   (DSA)
B .... Bartholomaeus de Capua [*Deceased, 1328*] [*Authority cited in pre-1607 legal work*]   (DSA)
B .... Bartolus de Sassoferrato [*Deceased, 1357*] [*Authority cited in pre-1607 legal work*]   (DSA)
B .... Base
B .... Basin [*of a river*] [*Geology*]
B .... Basophil [*Hematology*]
B .... Bass [*or Basso*] [*Music*]
B .... Bassoon [*Music*]   (ROG)
B .... Bastard [*Slang*]   (DSUE)
B .... Bat
B .... Batch [*Data processing*]

B .... Bath
B .... Batsman   (ADA)
B .... Battery
B .... Battle
B .... Baud [*Unit of data transmission speed*]   (MCD)
B .... Baume   (GPO)
b .... Bavli [*or Babylonian Talmud*]   (BJA)
B .... Bay [*Maps and charts*]
B .... Bay [*Thoroughbred racing*]
B .... Bayou [*Maps and charts*]
B .... Bazianus [*Deceased, 1197*] [*Authority cited in pre-1607 legal work*]   (DSA)
B .... BCE, Inc. [*Formerly, Bell Canada Enterprises*] [*Vancouver Stock Exchange symbol*]
B .... BCE, Inc. [*Formerly, Bell Canada Enterprises*] [*Toronto Stock Exchange symbol*]
B .... Beacon [*Aviation*]
B .... Beak
B .... Beam [*of a ship*]
B .... Bearing [*Angle*]
b .... Beauty [*or Bottom*] (Quark) [*Atomic physics*]
B .... Beavan's English Rolls Court Reports [*A publication*]   (DLA)
B .... Beaver [*On lead tokens used as payment in the Canadian fur trade during the 1700's*]
B .... Beco [*Lane*] [*Portuguese*] [*Correspondence*]
b .... Bed [*Medicine*]
B .... Beda [*Deceased, 735*] [*Authority cited in pre-1607 legal work*]   (DSA)
B .... Bedroom   (ROG)
B .... Beer [*Phonetic alphabet*] [*Pre-World War II*]   (DSUE)
B .... Before
B .... Beginning of Precipitation [*Meteorology*]   (FAAC)
B .... Bei [*At, With*] [*German*]
B .... Beiaard [*A publication*]
B .... Bel [*Ten decibels*]
B .... Belga [*Monetary unit*] [*Belgium*]
B .... Belgium [*IYRU nationality code*]
B .... Bell Canada Enterprises, Inc. [*Toronto Stock Exchange symbol*] [*Vancouver Stock Exchange symbol*]
b .... Ben   (BJA)
B .... Benediction
B .... Benedictus de Isernia [*Flourished, 1221-52*] [*Authority cited in pre-1607 legal work*]   (DSA)
b .... Benefice [*Profit*] [*French*]
B .... Benzedrine
B .... Bering Standard Time   (FAAC)
B .... Bernardus de Bottone de Parma [*Deceased, 1266*] [*Authority cited in pre-1607 legal work*]   (DSA)
B .... Bernardus Compostellanus, Junior [*Deceased, 1267*] [*Authority cited in pre-1607 legal work*]   (DSA)
B .... Bernardus Compostellanus, Senior [*Flourished, 1198-1216*] [*Authority cited in pre-1607 legal work*]   (DSA)
B .... Bernardus de Pavia [*Deceased, 1213*] [*Authority cited in pre-1607 legal work*]   (DSA)
B .... Bernoulli Number [*Mathematics*]
B .... Bertrandus de Montefaventino [*Deceased, 1342*] [*Authority cited in pre-1607 legal work*]   (DSA)
B .... Beta
B .... Beva [*A prefix meaning multiplied by one billion; same as "giga"*]
b .... Bi-Monthly
B .... Bias [*Telecommunications*]
B .... Bible
B .... Biblical   (ROG)
B .... Bibliofilia [*A publication*]
B .... Bibliotekarz [*A publication*]
B .... Bicuspid [*Dentistry*]
B .... Bid [*Stock exchange term*]   (SPSG)
B .... Biekorf [*A publication*]
B .... Biennial
B .... Bigaku [*A publication*]

B	Bight
B	Bilateral School [British]
b	Billet [Bill] [French]
B/	Billet a Ordre [Promissory Note] [French]
B	Billion (MCD)
B	Bills (ROG)
B	Bin-Tainer [Shipping] (DCTA)
B	Binary (BUR)
B	Binding Chain [Toxin]
B	Bioactive
B	Biology [Secondary school course] [British]
B	Biomass [Biology]
B	Biopsy [Medicine]
B	Biosedra [France] [Research code symbol]
B	Biotin
B	Biplane
B	Birth
B	Bis [Twice] [Pharmacy]
B	Bishop [Ecclesiastical]
B	Bishop [Chess]
B	BIT [Binary Digit] [Data transmission speed] [Data processing] (DIT)
B	Bitch
B	Black [Pencils]
B	Black [Buoy]
B	Black [Philately]
B	Black and White [Photography, television, etc.]
B	Blank (BUR)
B	Blend
B	Bleomycin [Also, Bl, Bleo, BLM] [Antineoplastic drug]
B	Blessed
B	Blinkers [Horse racing]
b	Block (Copolymerized) [Organic chemistry]
B	Bloody [Slang] [British] (DSUE)
B	Blue [Philately]
B	Blue [Aviation] (FAAC)
B	Blue Return [Round trip fare] [British]
B	Blue Sky (ROG)
B	Board
B	Boarding [Schools or pupils]
B	Boat
B	Boatswain
B	Boatyard [British Waterways Board sign]
B	Body
B	[The] Boeing Co. [ICAO aircraft manufacturer identifier] (ICAO)
B	Boiler
B	Boilermaker [Navy]
B	Boils At
B	Bolivar [Monetary unit] [Venezuela]
B	Boliviano [Monetary unit] [Bolivia]
B	Bomb (NG)
B	Bombardier
B	Bomber [Designation for US military aircraft]
B	Bomber Field
B	Bond [Investment term]
B	Bonded
B	Bone-Marrow Derived [Hematology]
B	Book
B	Boolean [Mathematics]
B	Booster
b	Booster Pump [Liquid gas carriers]
B	Born
B	Boron [Chemical element]
B	Boston Stock Exchange
B	Bottom
B	Bound (ADA)
B	Bowled [Cricket]
B	Bowled Out
B	Box Van [Shipping] (DCTA)
B	Boys School [British]
B	Brace [Medicine]
B	Brake Horsepower
B	Bravo [International phonetic alphabet] (DSUE)
B	Brazda [A publication]
B	Brazing
B	Breadth
B	Break [Electronics]
B	Breaking [FBI standardized term]
B	Breezing [Horse racing]
B	Brewster [Unit] [Physics]
B	Bridge [Shipping]
B	Brief [Currency] [German]
B	Brightness
B	Bristol [France] [Research code symbol]
B	Bristol [Board/paper]
B	British
b------	British Commonwealth [MARC geographic area code] [Library of Congress] (LCCP)
B	Broad [Also, BR] [Spectral]
B	Broadcasting
B	Broadcasting [A publication]
B	Broke [Rough finish of paper]
B	Broken
B	Broken Sea [Navigation]
B	Broker [London Stock Exchange]
B	Bromouridine [One-letter symbol; see BrUrd]
B	Bronchodilator [Medicine]
B	Brooke's Abridgment [England] [A publication] (DSA)
B	Brother [or Brotherhood]
B	Brought Down [Horse racing]
B	Brucella [Bacteriology]
B	Bruder [Brother] [German] [Freemasonry] (ROG)
B	Brunswick [Record label] [Great Britain]
B	Buccal [Pertaining to the cheek]
B	Buchanan's Supreme Court Reports, Cape Of Good Hope [1868-79] [South Africa] [A publication] (DLA)
B	Buckingham [Electrostatic measure]
B	Budget (DLA)
B	Buffer [Data processing] (TEL)
B	Bug (DSUE)
B	Bugler [British military] (DMA)
B	Building (ADA)
B	Built for British [As suffix to plane designation]
B	Bulb
B	Bulgarus de Bulgarinis [Deceased, 1166] [Authority cited in pre-1607 legal work] (DSA)
B	Bulletin
B	[The] Bulletin [A publication] (APTA)
B	Buoyancy
B	Burchardus Wormatiensis [Deceased, 1025] [Authority cited in pre-1607 legal work] (DSA)
B	Burgerlijk Wetboek [Civil Code] [Netherlands] (DLA)
B	Buried (ROG)
B	Burned [Ecology]
B	Bursa Cells [Of thymus or lymph nodes]
B	Bursitis [Medicine]
B	Bus [Data processing]
B	Bust (ADA)
B	Butcher [Navy]
B	Butter [Phonetic alphabet] [Royal Navy] [World War I] (DSUE)
B	Buyer
B	By (ROG)
B	Bye [Cricket]
B	Byte [Usually 8 BITS] [Data processing]
B	Called to the Bar [British] (ROG)
B	China [Aircraft nationality and registration mark] (FAAC)
B	Class "B" Preferred or Common Stock [Investment term]
B	Codex Vaticanus (BJA)
B	Common Bench [Legal term] (DLA)
°B	Degrees Baume
B	Excursion [Also, BE] [Airline fare code]
B	Farbenfabriken Bayer [Germany] [Research code symbol]
B	Flammable Liquids [Fire classification]
B	Human Being Detail [Rorschach] [Psychology]
B	Hydrogen Burning (IEEE)
B	Indian Law Reports, Bombay Series [A publication] (DLA)
B	Kelco Co. [Research code symbol]
B	Laake Oy [Finland] [Research code symbol]
B	Lack Characteristics of Desirable Investment [Moody's bond rating] [Investment term]
b	Magnetic Flux Density
B	Magnetic Induction (DAS)
B	Mean Barometric Pressure [Symbol]
B	Medium [Women's shoe width]
B	Multiple [Missile launch environment symbol]
B	Narrow [Men's shoe width]
B	Polar Radius of Earth [Symbol]
B	Series "B" Bonds or Debentures [Investment term]
B	Speculative [Standard & Poor's bond rating] [Investment term]
B	Susceptance [Symbol] [IUPAC]
B	Takeda Pharm. Industries [Japan] [Research code symbol]
B	Usually Reliable Source of Intelligence Information [Military]
B	Weekly Law Bulletin [Ohio] [A publication] (DLA)
1B	First Base [or Baseman] [Baseball]
1B	One-Base Hit [Baseball]
B²	Brooks Brothers [Clothing store]
2B	Second Base [or Baseman] [Baseball]
2-B	Selective Service Class [for Man Deferred or Deferrable from Military Service Because of His Necessity to War Production] [Obsolete]
2B	Two-Base Hit [Baseball]
2B	Two-Box [Oceanography]
3B	Third Base [or Baseman] [Baseball]
3B	Three-Base Hit [Baseball]
B4	Before
B4	Block of Four [Philately]
4-B	Selective Service Class [for Public Officials Deferred by Law]
5B	Bald with Bridgework, Bifocals, Baywindow, and Bunions [A humorous unofficial Selective Service Class]
5B	Cyprus [Aircraft nationality and registration mark] (FAAC)

B 26	Bulk Carrier of 26,000 Deadweight Tons [*Shipping*] (DS)
B 30	Bulk Carrier of 30,000 Deadweight Tons [*Shipping*] (DS)
B-52............	Stratofortress strategic bomber [*Boeing Co.*]
3B's	[*Johann Sebastian*] Bach, [*Ludwig van*] Beethoven, and [*Johannes*] Brahms [*Classical composers*]
3B's	Beer, Bum, and Bacca [*Nautical*] [*Slang*] [*British*] (DSUE)
3B's	Boheme, Butterfly, and Barber of Seville [*Frequently performed operas*]
3B's	Brief, Bright, Brotherly [*Religion*] (DSUE)
3B's	Bull Baffles Brains [*Bowdlerized version*] (DSUE)
3B's	Burn, Bash, and Bury [*The camper's code for cleanup*] [*Slang*] [*Australian*] (DSUE)
B-52's	Popular music group
B (School) ..	Business School
B (Test)	Breath Test [*For determining whether or not an auto driver is legally drunk*] [*British*]
Ba	Babel. International Journal of Translation [*Budapest*] [*A publication*]
BA	Baccalaureus Artium [*Bachelor of Arts*] [*Latin*]
BA	Bach [*A publication*]
B des A	Bachelier des Arts [*Bachelor of Arts*] [*French*]
BA	Bachelor of Agriculture
BA	Bachelor of Arts
BA	Backache [*Medicine*]
BA	Backlash Allowance (MSA)
BA	Backup Aerospace Vehicle [*or Aircraft*]
Ba	Baconiana [*A publication*]
Ba	Bagarottus dei Corradi da Bologna [*Flourished, 1200-42*] [*Authority cited in pre-1607 legal work*] (DSA)
BA	Bahamas [*IYRU nationality code*] (IYR)
ba	Bahrain [*MARC country of publication code*] [*Library of Congress*] (LCCP)
BA	Balkan Archiv [*A publication*]
BA	Ball
BA	Balneum Arenae [*Sand Bath*] [*Medicine*]
Ba	Bandinus Familiatus de Pisa [*Deceased, 1218*] [*Authority cited in pre-1607 legal work*] (DSA)
BA	Bands of America (EA)
BA	Bank Acceptance
BA	Bank Administration [*Bank Administration Institute*] [*A publication*]
BA	Bank of America
B of A	Bank of America
BA	Bank Angle
BA	BankAmericard [*Later, Visa*] [*Credit card*]
B & A	Banning and Arden's Patent Reports [*United States*] [*A publication*] (DLA)
BA	Baptized
BA	Bar [*Freight*]
Ba	Barium [*Chemical element*]
B & A	Barnewall and Adolphus' English King's Bench Reports [*109-110 English Reprint*] [*1830-34*] [*A publication*] (DLA)
B & A	Barnewall and Alderson's English King's Bench Reports [*1817-22*] [*A publication*] (DLA)
BA	Barometric Altimeter (MCD)
BA	Baron (ROG)
BA	Barremian-Aptian [*Paleontology*]
B & A	Barron and Arnold's English Election Cases [*1843-46*] [*A publication*] (DLA)
B & A	Barron and Austin's English Election Cases [*1842*] [*A publication*] (DLA)
B&A	Barros & Associates Ltd. [*Information service or system*] (IID)
Ba	Baruch [*Book of the Bible*] (BJA)
BA	Base Activation
BA	Base Assembly
BA	Basic Agreement
BA	Basic Authorization
BA	Basilar Artery [*Anatomy*]
BA	Basion [*Craniometric point*]
BA	Batterers Anonymous (EA)
BA	Battery Adjust (AABC)
BA	Batting Average [*Baseball*]
BA	Battle of Atlantic [*World War II*]
BA	Baume
BA	Beach Abort
B/A	Beam Approach (DEN)
BA	Bedstead Alliance [*A union*] [*British*]
BA	Beitraege zur Assyriologie und Semitischen Sprachwissenschaft [*A publication*]
BA	Bell Aerosystems Co. (KSC)
BA	Belt Association (EA)
BA	Benzanthracene [*Also, BzAnth*] [*Organic chemistry*]
BA	Benzyladenine [*Biochemistry*]
BA	Beta Activity [*Measure of radioactivity*]
BA	Biblical Aramaic (BJA)
BA	Biblical Archaeologist [*A publication*]
B of A	Bibliography of Agriculture [*Oryx Press*] [*Phoenix, AZ*] [*A publication*]
B & A	Bid and Asked [*Investment term*]
BA	Bifidus Acidophilus Live [*Health-food product*]
BA	Bikes for Africa (EA)

B/A	Billed At [*Commerce*]
BA	Binary Add [*Data processing*]
BA	Biography Almanac [*Later, Almanac of Famous People*] [*A publication*]
BA	Biological Abstracts [*A publication*]
BA	Biological Activity
BA	Blanket Agreement
BA	Blasting Agent (MCD)
BA	Blind Approach [*Aviation*]
BA	Blood Agar [*Growth medium*]
BA	Blue Anchor, Inc. [*Formerly, CFE*] [*Later, BAI*] [*An association*]
BA	Bnei Akiva (BJA)
B & A	Boat and Aircraft (CAAL)
BA	[*The*] Boeing Co. [*NYSE symbol*] (SPSG)
BA	Bollettino d'Arte [*A publication*]
BA	Bolt Action [*British military*] (DMA)
B/A	Bomb-Aimer [*British military*] (DMA)
BA	Bone Age [*Medicine*]
B > A	Bone Greater Than Air [*Conduction*]
BA	Book of Awards [*New Zealand*] [*A publication*]
BA	Books Abroad [*A publication*]
BA	Booksellers Association of Great Britain and Ireland (EAIO)
BA	Boolean Algebra [*Mathematics*]
BA	Boric Acid [*Inorganic chemistry*]
BA	Boston & Albany Railroad [*AAR code*]
B & A	Boston & Albany Railroad
BA	Brachial Artery [*Anatomy*]
BA	Braking Action [*Aviation*] (FAAC)
BA	Braniff Airways, Inc. [*of Braniff International Corp.*]
BA	Breaks Above
BA	Breathing Air (MCD)
BA	Breathing Apparatus
BA	Bridge Amplifier
B/A	Bridle Arrester (MCD)
BA	Brith Abraham (BJA)
BA	British Academy
BA	British Admiralty
BA	British Aerospace PLC
BA	British Aircraft Corp. Ltd. [*ICAO aircraft manufacturer identifier*] (ICAO)
BA	British Airtours Ltd. [*Airline*]
BA	British Airways [*United Kingdom*] [*ICAO designator*] (ICDA)
BA	British Aluminium Co. Ltd.
BA	British America
BA	British Army
BA	British Artists [*A publication*]
BA	British Association Screw Thread
BA	Brodmann's Areas [*Brain anatomy*]
BA	Bromoacetone [*War gas*]
BA	Bromoacetyl [*Organic chemistry*]
BA	Bronchial Asthma [*Medicine*]
BA	Bronsted Acid [*Biochemistry*]
BA	Bronze Age
BA	Brucellus Abortus [*Bacteriology*]
BA	Brymon Airways [*British*]
BA	Buccoaxial [*Dentistry*]
BA	Budget Activity [*Navy*]
BA	Budget Authority [*Office of Management and Budget*]
BA	Budget Authorization [*Air Force*] (AFM)
BA	Buenos Aires [*A publication*]
BA	Buenos Aires [*Argentina*]
BA	Buffer Amplifier [*Data processing*]
BA	Buffoons of America (EA)
BA	Bugger All [*Slang*] [*British*] (DSUE)
BA	Building Advisor [*Red Cross Disaster Services*]
BA	Building Application [*Australia*]
BA	Buisson Ardent [*The Burning Bush*] [*Freemasonry*]
BA	Bulletin des Assurances [*A publication*] (ILCA)
BA	Bundesanwalt [*Public Prosecutor or Attorney General*] [*German*] (ILCA)
BA	Bundesanwaltschaft [*The Office of Public Prosecutor*] [*German*] (ILCA)
BA	Bureau of Accounts [*Department of the Treasury*]
B/A	Bureau of Aeronautics [*Later, Naval Air Systems Command*]
BA	Burglar Alarm
BA	Burmese Army (CINC)
BA	Burned Area [*Ecology*]
BA	Bus Available [*Data processing*]
BA	Business Acronyms [*A publication*]
BA	Business Administration [*A publication*]
BA	Busted Aristocrat [*A cadet officer reduced to the ranks*] [*Military slang*]
BA	Butyl Acrylate [*Organic chemistry*]
Ba	Ciba-Geigy AG [*Switzerland*] [*Research code symbol*]
BA	Die Botschaft des Alten Testaments [*Stuttgart*] [*A publication*]
BA	Graduate in Arts
BA	Primary Type Battery [*JETDS nomenclature*] [*Military*] (CET)
Ba	Siegfried AG [*Switzerland*] [*Research code symbol*]
Ba	Speculative Elements [*Moody's bond rating*] [*Investment term*]
B of AA	Bachelor of Aeronautical Administration

BAA .... Bachelor of Applied Arts
BAA .... Bachelor of Art and Architecture (ADA)
BAA .... Backup Aerospace Vehicle [*or Aircraft*] Authorization
BAA .... Bank of America Australia
BAA .... Barber, Albert P., Kenosha WI [*STAC*]
BAA .... Battlefield Automation Appraisal (MCD)
BAA .... Benzoylarginine Amide [*Biochemistry*]
BAA .... Bialla [*Papua New Guinea*] [*Airport symbol*] (OAG)
BAA .... Billeting and Accommodations Advisory [*Military communications*]
BAA .... BO-S-AIRE Airlines, Inc. [*Anderson, SC*] [*FAA designator*] (FAAC)
BAA .... Branched-Chain Amino Acid [*Biochemistry*]
BAA .... Braunschweiger Anglistische Arbeiten [*A publication*]
BAA .... Brewers Association of America (EA)
BAA .... Brigade Administrative Area [*Military*] [*British*]
BAA .... British Agrochemicals Association
BAA .... British Airports Authority
BAA .... British Anodising Association
BAA .... British Archaeological Abstracts [*A publication*]
BAA .... British Archaeological Association
BAA .... British Astronomical Association
BAA .... Broadband Active Analyzer
BAA .... Budget Activity Account [*Army*] (AABC)
BAA .... Buenos Aires [*Argentina*] [*Seismograph station code, US Geological Survey*] (SEIS)
BAA .... Bulletin d'Archeologie Algerienne [*A publication*]
BAA .... Bulletin des Archives d'Anvers [*A publication*]
BAA .... Bureau of African Affairs [*Department of State*]
BAA .... Butylacetanilide [*Organic chemistry*]
Baa .... Lower Medium [*Moody's bond rating*]
Baa .... Technisch Weekblad [*A publication*]
BAAA .... British American Arts Association (EA)
BAAAC..... Bulletin. Association des Amis de l'Art Copte [*A publication*]
BAAB. ...... British Amateur Athletic Board
BAABL...... Boletin. Academia Argentina de Buenas Letras [*A publication*]
BAAC .... Basic Army Administrative Course
BAAF .... Brigade Airborne Alert Force [*Military*]
BAAF........ Butts Army Airfield [*Fort Carson, CO*]
BAAFB ..... Bulletin. Academie des Sciences Agricoles et Forestieres (Bucharest) [*A publication*]
BAAFBT ... Bulletin. Academie des Sciences Agricoles et Forestieres [*A publication*]
BAAFLP.... Bulletin. Association Amicale des Anciens Eleves de la Faculte des Lettres de Paris [*A publication*]
BAAG .... British Army Aid Group [*China*] [*World War II*]
BAAI......... Bollettino. Associazione degli Africanisti Italiani [*A publication*]
BAAJ .... British Archaeological Association. Journal [*A publication*]
BAAL....... Black Academy of Arts and Letters [*Defunct*] (EA)
BAAL....... Boletin. Academia Argentina de Letras [*A publication*]
BAAL....... British Association of Applied Linguists [*British*]
BAALA...... Societe des Agricultures d'Algerie. Bulletin [*A publication*]
BA Alger... Bulletin d'Archeologie Algerienne [*A publication*]
BAALPE ... British Association of Advisers and Lecturers in Physical Education
BAAM ...... Basic Administration and Management
BAAN ...... Budget Authorization Account Number [*Air Force*] (AFM)
BAAP........ Badger Army Ammunition Plant (AABC)
BAAPA...... Bulletin. American Association of Petroleum Geologists [*A publication*]
BAAPS ..... British Association of Aesthetic Plastic Surgeons (EAIO)
BAAR .... Board for Aviation Accident Research [*Army*]
BAAR .... Bollettino. Associazione Archeologica Romana [*A publication*]
BAAR .... British Acupuncture Association and Register [*British*]
BAARD ..... Bulletin. Association des Amis de Rabelais et de la Deviniere [*A publication*]
BAARINC ... Booz-Allen Applied Research, Incorporated
BAAS........ British Association for the Advancement of Science
BAAS........ British Association for American Studies (EA)
BAAS........ Broadband Acoustic Array Section
BAASB ..... British Association for American Studies. Bulletin [*A publication*]
BA in A & Sci ... Bachelor of Arts in Arts and Sciences
BA(AsianStudies) ... Bachelor of Arts (Asian Studies)
BAAT .... British Association of Art Therapists Ltd.
BAAT........ Bromoacetylmono(azobenzenearsonic Acid)-L-tyrosine [*Biochemistry*]
BAATC..... Bay Area Army Terminal Center
BAB .... Academie Royale de Belgique. Bulletin. Classe des Lettres et des Sciences Morales et Politiques [*A publication*]
BAB .... Babbing [*Fishing for eels*]
BAB .... Babbitt [*Metallurgy*]
BAB .... Babinski [*Reflex*] [*Medicine*]
BAB .... Babson College, Babson Park, MA [*OCLC symbol*] (OCLC)
Bab........... Babylonia (BJA)
Bab........... Babyloniaca. Etudes de Philologie Assyro-Babylonienne [*Paris*] [*A publication*]
Bab........... Babylonian Talmud (BJA)
Ba & B........ Ball and Beatty's Irish Chancery Reports [*1807-14*] [*A publication*] (ILCA)

BAB .... Beni-Abbes [*Algeria*] [*Seismograph station code, US Geological Survey*] (SEIS)
BAB .... Black Americans for Bush (EA)
BAB .... Blood Agar Base [*Growth medium*]
BAB .... Booster Assembly Building [*NASA*]
BAB .... Branch and Bound [*Algorithm*]
BAB .... British Airways ADS [*NYSE symbol*] [*Toronto Stock Exchange symbol*] (SPSG)
BAB .... British Airways Board (AIA)
BAB .... Marysville, CA [*Location identifier*] [*FAA*] (FAAL)
BA in BA... Bachelor of Arts in Business Administration
BABA........ Boletin. Academia de Bellas Artes de Valladolid [*A publication*]
BABA........ Boys' Apparel Buyers Association (EA)
BABA........ Burma-America Buddhist Association (EA)
BABAB..... Bauplanung-Bautechnik [*A publication*]
BABA LTD ... British Anaerobic & Biomass Association Ltd.
BA Barcel... Bulleti Informatiu. Institut de Prehistoria i Arqueologia. Diputacio Provincial de Barcelona [*A publication*]
BABAT...... Boletin. Academia de Bellas Artes y Ciencias Historicas de Toledo [*A publication*]
Bab Auc...... Babington's Law of Auctions [*A publication*] (DLA)
BABC........ Black American Baptist Churchmen [*An association*] (EA)
BABC........ Boletin. Academia de Bellas Artes de Cordoba [*A publication*]
BA in B & E ... Bachelor of Arts in Business and Economics
Ba & Be...... Ball and Beatty's Irish Chancery Reports [*1807-14*] [*A publication*] (DLA)
B Aberdeen Univ Afr Stud Group ... Bulletin. Aberdeen University. African Studies Group [*A publication*]
B A Besch .. Bulletin van de Vereeniging tot Bevordering der Kennis van de Antike Beschaving [*A publication*]
BABF........ British Amateur Baseball Federation
BABF........ Fraser Valley Regional Library, Abbotsford, British Columbia [*Library symbol*] [*National Library of Canada*] (NLC)
BABFVL.... Library Technician Program, Fraser Valley College, Abbotsford, British Columbia, [*Library symbol*] [*National Library of Canada*] (NLC)
BABIEC .... Biotechnology and Applied Biochemistry [*A publication*]
BABIM..... Bis(amidino-benzimidazolyl)methane [*Biochemistry*]
Bab J A ...... Babel. Journal of the Australian Federation of Modern Language Teachers Association [*Darlinghurst, New South Wales*] [*A publication*]
BABL........ Boletin. Real Academia de Buenas Letras de Barcelona [*A publication*]
BABLB ...... Boletin. Real Academia de Buenas Letras de Barcelona [*A publication*]
BABM .... Alert Bay Public Library and Museum, British Columbia [*Library symbol*] [*National Library of Canada*] (NLC)
BAB MTL ... Babbitt Metal [*Freight*]
BABN .... Bollettino. Archivio Storico del Banco di Napoli [*A publication*]
BaBo .... [*The*] Ballad Book [*A publication*]
BAbPr........ Beitraege zum Altbabylonischen Privatrecht [*A publication*] (BJA)
BABS......... [*The*] Babbage Society (EA)
BABS......... Beam Approach Beacon System [*Aviation*] (KSC)
BABS........ Biosynthetic Antibody Binding Site [*Biochemistry*]
BABS......... Blind Approach Beacon System [*Aviation*]
BABS......... Book Acquisition and Bibliographic Service [*National Book Centre*] [*Canada*]
BABS......... British Association of Barbershop Singers (EAIO)
BABS........ British Association for Brazing and Soldering
BABSD........ South African Bureau of Standards. Bulletin [*A publication*]
Bab Set-Off ... Babington's Law of Set-Off [*A publication*] (DLA)
BABT........ British Approvals Board for Telecommunications
BABT........ Brotherhood of Associated Book Travelers (EA)
BA Bull LA ... Bar Association Bulletin, Los Angeles [*A publication*] (DLA)
BABY........ Fertility & Genetics Research, Inc. [*Chicago, IL*] [*NASDAQ symbol*] (NQ)
Baby J........ Baby John [*A publication*]
BABYL...... Babylonia [*or Babylonian*]
BAC .... Bacau [*Romania*] [*Seismograph station code, US Geological Survey*] (SEIS)
BAC .... Baccalaureate Exam [*France*]
BAC .... Baccalaureus
B Ac .... Bachelor of Accounts
BAc .... Bachelor of Acupuncture [*British*] (DBQ)
BAC .... Back Association of Canada
BAC .... Bacterial Adherent Colonies
BAC .... Bacterial Antigen Complex [*Immunochemistry*]
BAC .... Bacteriological
BAC .... Banister Continental Ltd. [*Toronto Stock Exchange symbol*]
BAC .... BankAmerica Corporation [*NYSE symbol*] (SPSG)
BAC .... BankAmericard [*Later, Visa*] [*Credit card*]
BAC .... BAPTA [*Bearing and Power Transfer Assembly*] Accelerometer and Conditioner [*Aerospace*]
BAC .... Barclays Review [*A publication*]
BAC .... Barometric Altitude Control
BAC .... Base Area Commandant
BAC .... Beech Aircraft Corporation (KSC)
BAC .... Bell Aerospace Company
BAC .... Bell Aircraft Corporation (MCD)
BAC .... Belmont Abbey College [*North Carolina*]

BAC .... Below All Clouds [*Aviation*]
BAC .... Bendix Aviation Corporation [*Later, Bendix Corp.*]
BAC .... Benzalkonium Chloride [*Organic chemistry*]
BAC .... Biblioteca de Autores Cristianos [*A publication*]
BAC .... Bile Acid Concentration [*Gastroenterology*]
BAC .... Binary-Analog Conversion [*Data processing*]   (DIT)
BAC .... Binary Asymmetric Channel
BAC .... Biological Activated Carbon [*Water treatment*]
BAC .... Bipolar Active-Plastic Cell
BAC .... Bird Airplane Club   (EA)
BAC .... Bird Association of California   (EA)
BAC .... Bis(acryloyl)cystamine [*Organic chemistry*]
BAC .... Black Affairs Center [*Later, BACTOD*]   (EA)
BAC .... Blood Alcohol Concentration [*or Content*] [*Sobriety test*]
BAC .... Blower Access Cover
BAC .... Board of the Army Council
BAC .... Boating Anti-Pollution Council   (EA)
BAC .... Boeing Aerospace [*or Aircraft*] Corp.   (MCD)
BAC .... Boletin. Academia Colombiana [*A publication*]
BAC .... Boletin. Real Academia de Cordoba [*A publication*]
BAC .... Bollettino di Archeologia Cristiana [*A publication*]   (BJA)
BAC .... Booster Assembly Contractor [*NASA*]   (NASA)
BAC .... Boric Acid Concentrator   (NRCH)
BAC .... Born-Again Christian
BAC .... Breath Alcohol Concentration
BAC .... Bristol Aeroplane Company   (MCD)
BAC .... British Air Commission [*Washington*]
BAC .... British Aircraft Corp. Ltd.
BAC .... British Archives Council   (DIT)
BAC .... British Association of Chemists
BAC .... British Association for Counselling
BAC .... British Atlantic Committee   (EAIO)
BAC .... British Atomic Committee
BAC .... Bromacetylcellulose [*or Bromoacetycellulose*] [*Organic chemistry*]
BAC .... Bronchial Allergen Challenge [*Immunology*]
BAC .... Bronchoalveolar Cells [*Medicine*]
BAC .... Brotherhood of Anglican Churchmen [*Canada*]
BAC .... Buccoaxiocervical [*Dentistry*]
BAC .... Buchanan's Appeal Court Reports, Cape Of Good Hope [*A publication*]   (DLA)
BAC .... Budget Advisory Committee [*Army*]
BAC .... Budget at Completion   (MCD)
BAC .... Buffalo Aeronautical Corporation [*Buffalo, NY*] [*FAA designator*]   (FAAC)
BAC .... Buffer Access Card [*Data processing*]   (NASA)
BAC .... Building Access Card [*Issued to Senate staff members to ensure security in the Capitol*]
BAC .... Bulletin Archeologique. Comite des Travaux Historiques et Archeologiques [*A publication*]
BAC .... Bureau of Air Commerce [*Later, Civil Aeronautics Authority*]
BAC .... Burma Airways Corporation [*Rangoon*]   (EY)
BAC .... Business Advisory Council [*Later, Business Council*]
BAC .... Business Archives Council [*British*]
BAC .... Buy a Car [*Slogan during automobile sales slump of 1974-75*]
BAC .... International Union of Bricklayers and Allied Craftsmen   (EA)
Ba de Ca ..... Bartholomaeus de Capua [*Deceased, 1328*] [*Authority cited in pre-1607 legal work*]   (DSA)
BACA .... British Advisory Committee for Aeronautics
BACA .... British Association of Clinical Anatomists
BACA .... British Association of Concert Agents
BACA .... Bulleti. Associacio Catalana d'Antropologia [*A publication*]
BACAA ...... Bacardi Corp. Cl A [*NASDAQ symbol*]   (NQ)
Bac Ab .... Bacon's Abridgment [*1736-1832*] [*A publication*]   (DLA)
Bac Abr ...... Bacon's Abridgment [*1736-1832*] [*A publication*]   (DLA)
B Acad Roy Belg ... Bulletin. Classe des Lettres et des Sciences Morales et Politiques. Academie Royale de Belgique [*A publication*]
B Acad Sci ... Bulletin. Academy of Sciences of the USSR. Division of Chemical Science [*A publication*]
BACAIC .... Boeing Airplane Company [*later, The Boeing Co.*] Algebraic Interpretive Computing System
BACAN ..... British Association for the Control of Airport Noise
Bac Aph ..... [*Sir Francis*] Bacon's Aphorisms [*A publication*]   (DLA)
Bac Aphorisms ... [*Sir Francis*] Bacon's Aphorisms [*A publication*]   (DLA)
BACAS ...... Biological Agent Casualty Assessment System   (MCD)
BACAT ...... Barge Aboard Catamaran
Bac Ben Soc ... Bacon on Benefit Societies and Life Insurance [*A publication*]   (DLA)
BACBLNAC ... Boletin. Academia de Ciencias, Bellas Letras, y Nobles Artes de Cordoba [*A publication*]
BACC .... Baccalaureate
B Acc .... Bachelor of Accountancy
BACC .... Brazilian-American Chamber of Commerce   (EA)
BACC .... British-American Chamber of Commerce   (EA)
BACC .... British-American Collectors' Club   (EA)
BACC .... British-American Coordinating Committee [*Turkey*]
BACC .... Building and Construction Council [*Australia*]
Bac Ca .... Bacon's Case of Treason [*1641*] [*A publication*]   (DLA)
BACCC ...... Base Activation Central Control Committee
Bacch .... Bacchae [*of Euripides*] [*Classical studies*]   (OCD)
Bacch .... Bacchides [*of Plautus*] [*Classical studies*]   (OCD)

Bac Chanc ... Bacon's Chancery Cases [*England*] [*A publication*]   (DLA)
BACCHUS ... Boost Alcohol Consciousness Concerning the Health of University Students [*In association name BACCHUS of the US*]   (EA)
BACCHUS ... British Aircraft Corp. Ltd. Commercial Habitat under the Sea
Bacchyl ...... Bacchylides [*Fifth century BC*] [*Classical studies*]   (OCD)
Bac Comp Arb ... Bacon's Complete Arbitrator [*A publication*]   (DLA)
B Acc's .... Bachelor of Accounts
BACD .... Ballet America Concert Dancers
BACD .... Basic Alteration Class Drawing [*Navy*]   (CAAL)
BA on CD .... Biological Abstracts on Compact Disc [*A publication*]
Bac Dec ...... Bacon's Decisions (Ritchie) [*England*] [*A publication*]   (DLA)
Bac Dig ...... Bacon's Georgia Digest [*A publication*]   (DLA)
BACE........ Bachelor of Air Conditioning Engineering
BACE........ Basic Automatic Checkout Equipment
BACE........ British Association of Consulting Engineers
Bac El........ Bacon's Elements of the Common Law [*A publication*]   (DLA)
BAC Eng..... Bachelor of Air Conditioning Engineering
BACER ...... Biological and Climatic Effects Research
BA in Cer A ... Bachelor of Arts in Ceramic Art
BACG .... British Association of Crystal Growth
Bac Gov...... Bacon on Government [*A publication*]   (DLA)
BACH .... Bachelor
Bach .... Bach's Reports [*19-21 Montana*] [*A publication*]   (DLA)
BACHAD .. Brit Chalutzim Datiyim   (BJA)
Bach of Arts ... Bachelor of Arts [*A publication*]
BA Chem ... Bachelor of Applied Chemistry
Bache Pa Just ... Bache's Pennsylvania Justice's Manual [*A publication*]   (DLA)
B Ac Hist ... Boletin. Real Academia de la Historia [*A publication*]
BachJb....... Bach-Jahrbuch [*A publication*]
BACHR....... Bachelor
BACI......... Brazilian-American Cultural Institute   (EA)
BACIE .... British Association for Commercial and Industrial Education   (DCTA)
BACIE J .... BACIE [*British Association for Commercial and Industrial Education*] Journal [*A publication*]
Bac Ins .... Bacon on Benefit Societies and Life Insurance [*A publication*]   (DLA)
BACIS .... Budget Accounting Information System [*IBM Corp.*]
BACK........ Backwardation [*Commodity futures trading*]   (ROG)
BACK........ Boublik, Alder, Chen, Kreglewski Equation [*Physical chemistry*]
Backgr Collect ... Background to Collecting [*A publication*]   (APTA)
Backgr Notes ... Background Notes [*A publication*]
Background Migraine Migraine Symp ... Background to Migraine. Migraine Symposium [*A publication*]
Background Pap Workshop Tropospheric Transp Pollut Ocean ... Background Papers for a Workshop on the Tropospheric Transport of Pollutants to the Ocean [*A publication*]
Back Notes ... Background Notes on the Countries of the World. US Department of State [*A publication*]
Back Sher .. Backus on Sheriffs [*A publication*]   (DLA)
Backyard.... Your Big Backyard [*A publication*]
BACL........ Boletin. Academia Cubana de la Lengua [*A publication*]
BA Class.... Bachelor of Arts - Classical
Bac Law Tr ... [*Sir Francis*] Bacon's Law Tracts [*A publication*]   (DLA)
Bac Law Tracts ... [*Sir Francis*] Bacon's Law Tracts [*A publication*]   (DLA)
Bac Lease ... Bacon on Leases and Terms of Years [*A publication*]   (DLA)
Bac Lib Reg ... Bacon's Liber Regis, vel Thesaurus Rerum Ecclesiasticarum [*A publication*]   (DLA)
BACLIN.... Baroclinic   (FAAC)
BAClLg..... Bulletin Semestriel. Association des Classiques de l'Universite de Liege [*A publication*]
BACM ...... BACM Industries Ltd. [*Formerly, British-American Construction & Materials Ltd.*]
BACM .... British Association of Colliery Management   (DCTA)
BACM .... Bulletin. Academie pour l'Histoire de la Culture Materielle [*A publication*]
Bac Max .... [*Sir Francis*] Bacon's Maxims of the Law [*A publication*]   (DLA)
BACMI...... British Aggregate Construction Materials Industry
BACO .... Base Activation Change Order
BACO .... Beck/Arnley Corporation [*NASDAQ symbol*]   (NQ)
BACOAV... Bulletin. Agricultural Chemical Society of Japan [*A publication*]
BACOD..... Bleomycin, Adriamycin, Cyclophosphamide, Oncovin [*Vincristine*], Dexamethasone [*Antineoplastic drug regimen*]
BACol .... Boletin. Academia Colombiana [*A publication*]
BA Coll Agric Mag ... BA [*Bansilal Amritlal*] College of Agriculture Magazine [*India*] [*A publication*]
BACON ..... Backfile Conversion Project [*European Patent Office*]
Bacon .... Bacon. Arguments in Law [*A publication*]   (DLA)
Bacon .... Bacon on Government [*A publication*]   (DLA)
Bacon .... Bacon on Leases and Terms of Years [*A publication*]   (DLA)
Bacon .... Bacon's Abridgment [*1736-1832*] [*A publication*]   (DLA)
Bacon .... [*Sir Francis*] Bacon's Aphorisms [*A publication*]   (DLA)
Bacon .... Bacon's Complete Arbitrator [*A publication*]   (DLA)
Bacon .... Bacon's Elements of the Common Law [*A publication*]   (DLA)
Bacon .... Bacon's Essay on Uses [*A publication*]   (DLA)
Bacon .... [*Sir Francis*] Bacon's Law Tracts [*A publication*]   (DLA)

Bacon .... Bacon's Liber Regis [*A publication*]   (DLA)
Bacon .... [*Sir Francis*] Bacon's Maxims of the Law [*A publication*]   (DLA)
BACON ..... Bleomycin, Adriamycin, CCNU [*Lomustine*], Oncovin [*Vincristine*], Nitrogen Mustard [*Antineoplastic drug regimen*]
Bacon Max Reg ... [*Sir Francis*] Bacon's Maxims of the Law [*A publication*]   (DLA)
BACOP...... Bleomycin, Adriamycin, Cyclophosphamide, Oncovin [*Vincristine*], Prednisone [*Antineoplastic drug regimen*]
BA Copt ..... Bulletin. Societe d'Archeologie Copte [*A publication*]
BACP .... Business Advisory Committee on Procurement [*DoD*]
BACR........ British Association for Cancer Research
Bac Read Uses ... [*Sir Francis*] Bacon. Reading upon the Statute of Uses [*A publication*]   (DLA)
Bac Rep...... Bacon's Decisions (Ritchie) [*England*] [*A publication*]   (DLA)
B A Crist .... Bullettino di Archeologia Cristiana [*A publication*]
BACS........ Backup Acquisition System
BACS........ Bankers' Automated Clearing Services [*British*]   (DCTA)
BACS......... Bay Area Cryonics Society [*Later, American Cryonics Society*]   (EA)
BACS........ Ben Asia Container Services   (DS)
BACS........ Bibliographic Access and Control System [*Washington University*] [*Information service or system*]   (IID)
BACS........ Black American Cinema Society   (EA)
BACS........ Bloomington Academic Computer Services [*Indiana University*] [*Research center*]   (RCD)
BACS........ Body Axis Coordinate System   (MCD)
BACS........ British Association for Canadian Studies
BACS........ British Association for Chemical Specialities
BACS........ British Association of Cosmetic Surgeons
BACSA ...... British Association for Cemeteries in South Asia
BACSEB.... BUWEPS [*Bureau of Naval Weapons, now obsolete*] Aviation Clothing and Survival Equipment Bulletin   (MCD)
Bac St Uses ... [*Sir Francis*] Bacon. Reading upon the Statute of Uses [*A publication*]   (DLA)
BACT........ Bacteria [*or Bacteriology*]
BACT........ BCNU [*Carmustine*], ara-C, Cyclophosphamide, Thioguanine [*Antineoplastic drug regimen*]
B Act .... Bellum Actiacum [*of Ausonius*] [*Classical studies*]   (OCD)
BACT........ Best Available Control Technology [*Environmental Protection Agency*]
BACT........ British Association of Conference Towns
Bact Bacteriophages Fungi ... Bacteria, Bacteriophages, and Fungi [*A publication*]
Bac TE .... Bacon's Liber Regis, vel Thesaurus Rerum Ecclesiasticarum [*A publication*]   (DLA)
BACTER ... Bacteriology
Bacteriol Proc ... Bacteriological Proceedings [*A publication*]
Bacteriol Rev ... Bacteriological Reviews [*A publication*]
Bacteriol Virusol Parazitol Epidemiol (Buchar) ... Bacteriologia, Virusologia, Parazitologia, Epidemiologia (Bucharest) [*A publication*]
BACTH ..... Bulletin Archeologique. Comite des Travaux Historiques et Scientifiques [*Paris*] [*A publication*]
BACTHS.... Bulletin Archeologique. Comite des Travaux Historiques et Scientifiques [*Paris*] [*A publication*]
BACTLGY ... Bacteriology
BACTM..... Bifurcation Analysis and Catastrophy Theory Methodology   (MCD)
BACTOD... Black Affairs Center for Training and Organizational Development   (EA)
Bact Proc.... Bacteriological Proceedings [*A publication*]
Bac Tr .... [*Sir Francis*] Bacon's Law Tracts [*A publication*]   (DLA)
Bact R .... Bacteriological Reviews [*A publication*]
Bact Rev ..... Bacteriological Reviews [*A publication*]
Bact Rs....... Bacteriological Reviews [*A publication*]
BACU .... Battle Area Control Unit [*Military*]
BACUP...... British Association of Cancer United Patients
Bac Uses .... Bacon's Essay on Uses [*A publication*]   (DLA)
BACV........ Budget at Completion Variance   (MCD)
Bac Works ... [*Sir Francis*] Bacon's Works [*A publication*]   (DLA)
BAD.......... Bangkok Bank. Monthly Review [*A publication*]
BAD.......... Bank Account Debits Tax   (ADA)
B & Ad ...... Barnewall and Adolphus' English King's Bench Reports [*109-110 English Reprint*] [*1830-34*] [*A publication*]   (DLA)
BAD.......... Base Ammunition Depot   (NATG)
BAD.......... Berlin Airlift Device [*Military decoration*]
BAD.......... Biological Aerosol Detection [*Army*]   (MCD)
BAD.......... British Admiralty Delegation [*to Washington*]
BAD.......... British Association of Dermatologists [*or Dermatology*]   (EAIO)
BAD.......... Buzz Attenuation Device   (CAAL)
BAD.......... Department of Bantu Administration and Development [*An agency of South African government*]
BAD.......... Magazine of Bank Administration [*A publication*]
BAD.......... Shreveport, LA [*Location identifier*] [*FAA*]   (FAAL)
BADA .... Base Air Depot Area [*Air Force*]
BADA .... British Antique Dealers' Association
Badan Fizjogr Pol Zachod ... Badania Fizjograficzne nad Polska Zachodnia. B. Biologia [*A publication*]
BADAS...... Binary Automatic Data Annotation System

BADB .... Badbury [*England*]
BADB .... Boating Accident Data Base [*Coast Guard*] [*Database*]
BADB .... Bromoacetyl-DNP-Diamino-L-Butyric Acid [*Biochemistry*]
BADC .... Binary Asymmetric Dependent Channel
BADCT...... Best Available Demonstrated Control Technology [*Environmental Protection Agency*]
BADE .... Bromoacetyl-DNP-Ethylenediamine [*Biochemistry*]
BADESUL ... Banco de Desenvolvimento do Estado do Rio Grande Do Sul SA [*Brazil*]   (EY)
BADF........ Bile Acid-Dependent Fraction [*Medicine*]
BADGE ..... Base Air Defense Ground Environment [*Air Force*]
BADGE ..... Bekesy Ascending Descending Gap Evaluation
Badger Pharm ... Badger Pharmacist. Wisconsin Pharmaceutical Association [*A publication*]
Bad Hersfelder Jh ... Bad Hersfelder Jahresheft [*A publication*]
BADIC....... Biological Analysis Detection Instrumentation and Control
Badische Hist Komm Neujahrsbl ... Badische Historische Kommission. Neujahrsblaetter [*A publication*]
BADL .... Badlands National Monument [*South Dakota*]
BADL .... Bonner Arbeiten zur Deutschen Literatur [*A publication*]
BADL .... Bromoacetyl-DNP-L-Lysine [*Biochemistry*]
BADLG...... British Archaeologists and Developers Liaison Group
B Adm .... Bachelor of Administration
Bad M .... Badminton Magazine [*A publication*]
B Adm Eng ... Bachelor of Administrative Engineering
BADMEP ... Burlington Atmospheric Density Model Evaluation Program [*IBM Corp.*]
BAdmin...... Bachelor of Administration
BADO .... Bromoacetyl-DNP-L-Ornithine [*Biochemistry*]
BADS........ Biological Agent Decontamination Simulant   (MCD)
BADSA ...... Backup Air Data Sensor Assembly   (MCD)
BADT........ Bank Account Debits Tax   (ADA)
B of Adv Art & Des ... Bachelor of Advertising Arts and Design
BADWS..... Bayerische Akademie der Wissenschaften. Philosophisch-Historische Klasse. Sitzungsberichte [*A publication*]
B of AE ...... Bachelor of Aeronautical Engineering
BAE .... Bachelor of Aeronautical Engineering
B Ae .... Bachelor of Aeronautics
BAE .... Bachelor of Agricultural Engineering
BAE .... Bachelor of Architectural Engineering
BAE .... Bachelor of Art Education
BAE .... Bachelor of Arts in Education
BAE .... Back-Action Evasion [*Physics*]
BAE .... Badminton Association of England   (EAIO)
BAE .... Bank of Jamaica. Bulletin [*A publication*]
BaE .... Barium Enema [*Medicine*]
BAE .... Barrier Tech [*Vancouver Stock Exchange symbol*]
BAE .... Beacon Antenna Equipment
BAE .... Biblioteca de Autores Espanoles [*A publication*]
BAE .... Boletin. Real Academia Espanola [*A publication*]
BAE .... Bovine Aortic Endothelium
BAE .... Brasilia [*Brazil*] [*Seismograph station code, US Geological Survey*]   (SEIS)
BAE .... British Admiralty Establishment
BAe .... British Aerospace PLC
BAE .... British Antarctic Expedition
BAE .... British Association of Electrologists
BAE .... Bureau for Africa and Europe [*AID*]
BAE .... Bureau of Agricultural Economics [*Functions dispersed, 1953*] [*Department of Agriculture*]
BAE .... Bureau of American Ethnology [*of the Smithsonian Institution*]
BAE .... Milwaukee, WI [*Location identifier*] [*FAA*]   (FAAL)
BAEA........ British Actors' Equity Association [*A union*]   (DCTA)
BAEA........ British Atomic Energy Authority
BAEAD2.... Alabama. Agricultural Experiment Station. Bulletin (Auburn University) [*A publication*]
BA in E & B ... Bachelor of Arts in Economics and Business
BAEB........ Bituminous and Aggregate Equipment Bureau   (EA)
BAEC........ Bangladesh Atomic Energy Commission   (EY)
BAEC........ Bollettino. Amicizia Ebraico-Cristiana di Firenze [*A publication*]
BAEC........ Bovine Artery Endothelial Cell [*Cytology*]
BAEC........ British Agricultural Export Council
BAEC........ Bulletin. Association des Amis des Eglises et de l'Art Coptes [*A publication*]
BAECE...... [*The*] British Association for Early Childhood Education
BA (Econ) .. Bachelor of Arts (Economics)
BA Ed .... Bachelor of Art Education
BA Ed .... Bachelor of Arts in Education
BAEDS ..... Best Alternative Equally Effective Data System
BA(Educ)... Bachelor of Arts (Education)
B Ae E .... Bachelor of Aeronautical Engineering
BAEE........ Benzoylarginine Ethyl Ester [*Biochemistry*]
BAEE........ British Army Equipment Exhibition   (MCD)
BA in E Ed ... Bachelor of Arts in Elementary Education
B Ae Eng.... Bachelor of Aeronautical Engineering
BAEF........ Belgian American Educational Foundation   (EA)
BAEF........ British American Educational Foundation   (EA)
B Aegypt .... Carmen de Bello Aegyptiaco sive Actiaco [*of Ausonius*] [*Classical studies*]   (OCD)
BAEO .... Boletin. Asociacion Espanola de Orientalistas [*A publication*]

BAEP......... Brainstem Auditory Evoked Potential [*Neurophysiology*]
BAEPE...... Boletin. Asociacion Europea de Profesores de Espanol [*A publication*]
BAER......... Brainstem Auditory Evoked Response [*Neurophysiology*]
Baer Berl.... Baer von Berlin [*A publication*]
B/AERE .... British Atomic Energy Research Establishment
B Aero E .... Bachelor of Aeronautical Engineering
B Ae S ...... Bachelor of Aeronautical Science
B Ae Sc ...... Bachelor of Aeronautical Science
Baessler-Arch ... Baessler-Archiv. Beitraege zur Voelkerkunde [*A publication*]
Baetica .... Baetica; Estudios de Arte, Geografia, e Historia [*A publication*]
BaEV......... Baboon Endogenous Virus
BAF........... Backup Alert Force
BAF........... Baffle [*Regulating device*]   (KSC)
BAF........... Balance Fixture   (MCD)
BAF........... Bamberger Abhandlungen und Forschungen [*A publication*]
BAF........... Barrier Reef Resources [*Vancouver Stock Exchange symbol*]
BAF........... Belacker [*France*] [*Seismograph station code, US Geological Survey*]   (SEIS)
BAF........... Belgian Air Force
BAF........... Bioaccumulation Factor [*Nuclear energy*]   (NRCH)
BAF........... Brith Abraham Foundation [*Later, BZ*]   (EA)
BAF........... British Air Ferries Ltd.
BAF........... British Air Force
BAF........... British Aqueous Fusion Process   (MCD)
BA & F ...... Budget, Accounting, and Finance   (AFM)
BAF........... Bulletin. Association des Amis de Flaubert [*A publication*]
BAF........... Bunker Adjustment Factor [*Business term*]
BAF........... Burmese Air Force   (CINC)
BAF........... Westfield, MA [*Location identifier*] [*FAA*]   (FAAL)
BAFA........ Boletin. Asociacion Folklorica (Argentina) [*A publication*]
BAFA........ Bul Bul Academy of Fine Arts [*Dacca, Pakistan*]
BAFC........ Bryan Adams Fan Club   (EA)
BAFCOM ... Basic Armed Forces Communication Plan
BAFE........ British Approvals for Fire Equipment
BAFF........ British Air Forces in France [*World War II*]
BAFG........ British Air Forces in Greece [*British military*]   (DMA)
BAFISUD ... Banco Financiero Sudamericano [*South American Financial Bank*]
BAFL........ Baltic American Freedom League   (EA)
BAFM....... British Association in Forensic Medicine
BAFM....... British Association of Friends of Museums
BAFO .... Base Accounting and Finance Office [*Air Force*]   (AFM)
BAfO........ Beiheft. Archiv fuer Orientforschung [*Graz*] [*A publication*]
BAFO .... Best and Final Offer [*DoD*]   (MCD)
BAFO .... British Air Forces of Occupation [*Military*]
BAFO .... British Army Forces Overseas
BAFOEG... Biotechnology in Agriculture and Forestry [*A publication*]
BAFPD....... Biogas and Alcohol Fuels Production [*A publication*]
BAFPE ...... Bay Area Functional Performance Evaluation [*Personality research*] [*Psychology*]
B Afr .... Bellum Africum [*of Ausonius*] [*Classical studies*]   (OCD)
BAFS .... [*The*] British Academy of Forensic Sciences
BAFSM ..... Basic Artillery Force Simulation Model   (MCD)
BAFSV ...... British Armed Forces Special Vouchers [*British military*]   (DMA)
BAFT .... Bankers Association for Foreign Trade [*Washington, DC*]   (EA)
BAFTA ...... British Academy of Film and Television Arts
BAFV .... British Armed Forces Voucher [*Pronounced "baff"*] [*Paper money used on military bases*]   (DSUE)
BAFVC ...... Bids Accepted for the Following Vacancies   (FAAC)
B Ag .... Bachelor of Agriculture
BAG .... Bag All Garbage
Bag............. Bagarottus dei Corradi da Bologna [*Flourished, 1200-42*] [*Authority cited in pre-1607 legal work*]   (DSA)
BAG .... Baggage   (AFM)
BAG .... Baguio [*Philippines*] [*Seismograph station code, US Geological Survey*]   (SEIS)
BAG .... Baguio [*Philippines*] [*Airport symbol*]   (OAG)
BAG .... Baguio [*Philippines*] [*Geomagnetic observatory code*]
BAG .... Ballistic Attack Game
bag............. Basque [*MARC language code*] [*Library of Congress*]   (LCCP)
BAG .... Battalion Artillery Group   (MCD)
BAG .... Behavioral Assessment Grid
BAG .... Beitraege zur Alten Geschichte [*A publication*]
BAG .... Beta Absorption Gauge
BAG .... Black Action Group [*Australia*]
BAG .... Bloc Africain de Guinee [*African Bloc of Guinea*]
BAG .... Boletin. Academia Gallega [*A publication*]
BAG .... Book Arts Guild   (EA)
BAG .... Bovagblad [*A publication*]
BAG .... British Artists in Glass
BAG .... Buccoaxiogingival [*Dentistry*]
BAG .... Bundesarbeitsgericht [*Federal Supreme Labour Court*] [*German*]   (DLA)
BAGA .... British Amateur Gymnastics Association
BAGAG .... Research Station, Agriculture Canada [*Station de Recherches, Agriculture Canada*] Agassiz, British Columbia [*Library symbol*] [*National Library of Canada*]   (NLC)
BAGAIR.... [*Number of Pounds Indicated*] - Baggage to Accompany Passenger Authorized for Air Travel Outside Continental US

BAGB .... Bulletin. Association Guillaume Bude [*A publication*]
BAGB SC .. Bulletin. Association Guillaume Bude. Supplement Critique [*A publication*]
BAGC .... Business Alliance on Government Competition   (EA)
Bag Ch Pr .. Bagley's Practice at Chambers [*1834*] [*A publication*]   (DLA)
B Ag E........ Bachelor of Agricultural Engineering
BAgEc........ Bachelor of Agricultural Economics   (ADA)
B Agenc Int Energie Atom ... Bulletin. Agence Internationale de l'Energie Atomique [*A publication*]
Bag Eng Const ... Bagehot. English Constitution [*8th ed.*] [*1904*] [*A publication*]   (DLA)
Bag Engl Const ... Bagehot. English Constitution [*8th ed.*] [*1904*] [*A publication*]   (DLA)
BA(GenStud) ... Bachelor of Arts in General Studies [*British*]   (DBQ)
BAGF .... Bulletin. Association des Geographes Francais [*A publication*]
BAGG .... Buffered Azide Glucose Glycerol [*Broth*] [*Microbiology*]
Baghdad Univ Coll Sci Bull ... Baghdad University. College of Science. Bulletin [*A publication*]
BaghMitt ... Baghdader Mitteilungen des Deutschen Archaeologischen Instituts. Abteilung Baghdad [*Berlin*] [*A publication*]
BAGI .... Backscatter/Absorption Gas Imaging   (MCD)
Bagl........... Bagley's Reports [*16 California*] [*A publication*]   (DLA)
Bagl (Cal)... Bagley's Reports [*16-19 California*] [*A publication*]   (DLA)
Bagl & H .... Bagley and Harman's Reports [*17-19 California*] [*A publication*]   (DLA)
Bagl & Har ... Bagley and Harman's Reports [*17-19 California*] [*A publication*]   (DLA)
Bagl & Har (Cal) ... Bagley and Harman's Reports [*17-19 California*] [*A publication*]   (DLA)
BAGMA .... British Agricultural and Garden Machinery Association
BAGO........ Bloque Antiguerrillero del Oriente [*Eastern Anti-Guerrilla Bloc*] [*El Salvador*]   (PD)
B Agr.......... Bachelor of Agriculture
BAGR .... Bureau of Aeronautics General Representative [*Obsolete*] [*Navy*]
B Agr E ...... Bachelor of Agricultural Engineering
BAGRED... Bureau of Aeronautics General Representative, Eastern District [*Obsolete*] [*Navy*]
BAgri .... Bachelor of Agriculture
BAgric........ Bachelor of Agriculture [*British*]
B Agr S ...... Bachelor of Agricultural Science
B Agr Sc.... Bachelor of Agricultural Science
BAGRWD ... Bureau of Aeronautics General Representative, Western District [*Obsolete*] [*Navy*]
BAGS........ Bachelor of Arts in General Studies
BAGS........ Bombing and Gunnery School [*British*]   (DMA)
BAGS........ Bulletin. American Geographical Society [*A publication*]
BAGS........ Bullpup All-Weather Guidance System [*Naval Ordnance Systems Command*]
BAGS........ Pacad, Inc. [*NASDAQ symbol*]   (NQ)
BAgSc........ Bachelor of Agricultural Science   (ADA)
BAH........... Baha Resources Ltd. [*Vancouver Stock Exchange symbol*]
BAH........... Bahamas   (ROG)
BAH........... Bahrain Islands [*Airport symbol*]   (OAG)
BAH........... Barrette [*Hawaii*] [*Seismograph station code, US Geological Survey*] [*Closed*]   (SEIS)
BAH........... Basic Adaptive Hardware
BAH........... Biological Agriculture and Horticulture [*A publication*]
BAH........... Boletin. Academia de la Historia [*A publication*]
BAH........... Bulletin. Academie d'Hippone [*A publication*]
BAH........... Business Archives and History [*A publication*]
BAHAD..... Bulletin of Animal Health and Production in Africa [*A publication*]
Bahamas LRC ... Law Revision Committee, Bahamas   (DLA)
BAHC........ Baptist Association of Hospital Chaplains   (EA)
BAHD........ Bulletin d'Archeologie et d'Histoire Dalmate [*A publication*]
Bahia Bal E ... Bahia. Balanco Energetico Consolidado [*A publication*]
Bahia Cent Pesqui Desenvolvimento Bol Tec ... Bahia. Centro de Pesquisas e Desenvolvimento. Boletim Tecnico [*A publication*]
Bahia Ener ... Bahia. Annuario Energetico [*A publication*]
BAHID...... Basic and Applied Histochemistry [*A publication*]
BAHIFAI .. Bibliotheque Archeologique et Historique de l'Institut Francais d'Archeologie d'Istanbul [*A publication*]
BAHist....... Boletin. Real Academia de la Historia [*A publication*]
Bah LR...... Bahamas Law Reports [*A publication*]   (DLA)
BAHODP.. Bangladesh Horticulture [*A publication*]
BAHOH ... British Association of the Hard of Hearing
BAHP .... British Association of Homoeopathic Pharmacists
BAHR........ Bahrain
BAH Re ..... Bachelor of Arts in Human Relations
BAHRGNY ... Bar Association for Human Rights of Greater New York   (EA)
BAHS .... British Agricultural History Society
BAHT .... Basic Attack Helicopter Team [*Army*]   (RDA)
BAHVS...... British Association of Homoeopathic Veterinary Surgeons
BAI .... Baccalaureus in Arte Ingeniaria [*Bachelor of Engineering*]   (EY)
BAI .... Backup Aerospace Vehicle [*or Aircraft*] Inventory
BAI .... Baika Women's College [*EDUCATSS*] [*UTLAS symbol*]
BAI .... Baikonur [*Satellite launch complex*] [*USSR*]
Bai............. Bailey's Law Reports [*South Carolina*] [*A publication*]   (DLA)
BAI .... Baird-Associates, Incorporated   (MCD)

BAI .... Balch Institute Library, Philadelphia, PA [*OCLC symbol*] (OCLC)
BAI .... Bank Administration Institute (EA)
BAI .... Bari [*Italy*] [*Seismograph station code, US Geological Survey*] [*Closed*] (SEIS)
BAI .... Barometric Altitude Indicator (NASA)
BAI .... Basal Area Increment [*Forestry*]
BAI .... Base Activation Instruction
BAI .... Battlefield Air Interdiction (MCD)
BAI .... Bearing Altitude Indicator [*Aerospace*]
BAI .... Behavior Analysis in Ireland (EAIO)
BAI .... Biological and Agricultural Index [*A publication*]
BAI .... Blue Anchor, Incorporated [*An association*] (EA)
BAI .... Bnos Agudath Israel (EA)
BAI .... Bulletin. American Institute of Swedish Arts, Literature, and Science [*A publication*]
BAI .... Bureau of Animal Industry [*Department of Agriculture*]
BAIB .... Bailey Corp. [*NASDAQ symbol*] (CTT)
BAIBL .... Bulletin. Academie des Inscriptions et Belles-Lettres [*A publication*]
BAIC .... Bahamas Agricultural and Industrial Corporation (EY)
BAIC .... Binary Asymmetric Independent Channel
BAIC .... British Aviation Insurance Co. (AIA)
BAIC .... Bureau of Agricultural and Industrial Chemistry [*Department of Agriculture*]
BAICF .... Bile Acid-Independent Canalicular Fraction [*Medicine*]
BAID .... Black Americans Information Directory [*A publication*]
BAID .... Boolean Array Identifier [*Mathematics*]
Bai Eq .... Bailey's Equity Reports [*South Carolina*] [*A publication*] (DLA)
BAIF .... Bile Acid-Independent Fraction [*Medicine*]
BAII .... Banque Arabe et Internationale d'Investissement [*France*]
Bail.......... Bailey's Law Reports [*South Carolina*] [*A publication*] (DLA)
BAIL .... Boundary and Interior Layer (MCD)
Bail CC ...... Bail Court Cases [*A publication*]
Bail CC ...... Lowndes and Maxwell's English Bail Court Cases [*1852-54*] [*A publication*] (DLA)
Bail Cr Rep ... Lowndes and Maxwell's English Bail Court Cases [*1852-54*] [*A publication*] (DLA)
Bail Ct Cas ... Lowndes and Maxwell's English Bail Court Cases [*1852-54*] [*A publication*] (DLA)
Bail Ct R .... Bail Court Reports (Saunders and Cole) [*England*] [*A publication*] (DLA)
Bail Ct Rep ... Lowndes and Maxwell's English Bail Court Cases [*1852-54*] [*A publication*] (DLA)
Bail Ct Rep ... Saunders and Cole's English Bail Court Reports [*1846-48*] [*A publication*] (DLA)
Baild.......... Baildon's Select Cases in Chancery [*Selden Society Publication, Vol. 10*] [*A publication*] (DLA)
Bail Dig...... Bailey's North Carolina Digest [*A publication*] (DLA)
Bail Eq .... Bailey's Equity Reports [*South Carolina*] [*A publication*] (DLA)
Bail Eq (SC) ... Bailey's Equity Reports [*South Carolina*] [*A publication*] (DLA)
Bailey .... Bailey's Equity Reports [*South Carolina*] [*A publication*] (DLA)
Bailey .... Bailey's Law Reports [*South Carolina*] [*A publication*] (DLA)
Bailey Ch ... Bailey's Chancery Reports [*South Carolina*] [*A publication*] (DLA)
Bailey Dict ... Nathan Bailey's English Dictionary [*A publication*] (DLA)
Bailey Eq.... Bailey's Equity Reports, South Carolina Court of Appeals [*A publication*] (DLA)
Bailey Mast Liab ... Bailey's Law of Master's Liability for Injuries to Servant [*A publication*] (DLA)
Bail L .... Bailey's Law Reports [*South Carolina*] [*A publication*] (DLA)
Baill Dig..... Baillie's Digest of Mohammedan Law [*A publication*] (DLA)
Baill Inher ... Baillie's Mohammedan Law of Inheritance [*A publication*] (DLA)
Bail L (SC) ... Bailey's Law Reports [*South Carolina*] [*A publication*] (DLA)
Bailm......... Bailment [*Legal term*] (DLA)
BAIMR...... United States Bureau of Animal Industry. Monthly Record [*A publication*] (DLA)
BAINB....... Bulletin. Astronomical Institutes of the Netherlands. Supplement Series [*A publication*]
Bainb Mines ... Bainbridge on Mines and Minerals [*A publication*] (DLA)
Bainb M & M ... Bainbridge on Mines and Minerals [*A publication*] (DLA)
BAINS....... Basic Advanced Integrated Navigation System
BAIO......... Brigade Artillery Intelligence Officer [*Military*] [*British*]
BAIR......... Braniff, Inc. [*Dallas, TX*] [*NASDAQ symbol*] (NQ)
BAIR......... Breathing Air (NASA)
BAIR......... British Airports Information Retrieval [*System*]
BAIR......... Bureau for the Advancement of Independent Retailing (EA)
BAIR......... Bureau of Aeronautics Industrial Reserve [*Obsolete*] [*Navy*]
BAIS......... Battlefield Airborne Illumination System (CINC)
BAIS......... British Association for Irish Studies
BAIS......... Bulletin Articles Information Subsystem [*Data processing*]
BAIT......... Bacterial Automated Identification Technique
BAIT......... Black Awareness in Television (EA)
BAIU......... Bulletin. Alliance Israelite Universelle [*A publication*]
BAIX......... Buckeye Airways International [*Air carrier designation symbol*]
BAJ........... Bachelor of Arts in Journalism

BA in J .... Bachelor of Arts in Journalism
BAJ....... Bali [*Papua New Guinea*] [*Airport symbol*] (OAG)
BAJ........... BJ Aero Freight, Inc. [*Oskaloosa, IA*] [*FAA designator*] (FAAC)
BAJ........... Sterling, CO [*Location identifier*] [*FAA*] (FAAL)
BAK .... Backer Resources [*Vancouver Stock Exchange symbol*]
BAK .... Backup File [*Data processing*]
BAK .... Baker Industries, Inc. [*AMEX symbol*] (SPSG)
BAK .... Bakery
BAK .... Bakker. Actueel Vakblad voor de Broodbakkerij. Banketbakkerij [*Nijmegen*] [*A publication*]
BAK .... Baku [*USSR*] [*Airport symbol*] (OAG)
BAK .... Baku [*USSR*] [*Seismograph station code, US Geological Survey*] (SEIS)
bak .... Bashkir [*MARC language code*] [*Library of Congress*] (LCCP)
BAK .... Blackhawk Airways, Inc. [*Janesville, WI*] [*FAA designator*] (FAAC)
BAK .... British Cargo Ship
BAK .... Broadband Antenna Kit
BAK .... Columbus, IN [*Location identifier*] [*FAA*] (FAAL)
Bak Bur...... Baker on the Law Relating to Burials [*A publication*] (DLA)
Bak Corp.... Baker's New York Corporation Laws [*A publication*] (DLA)
Bakelite Rev ... Bakelite Review [*A publication*]
Baker Calif ... Bakersfield Californian [*A publication*]
Baker J T Chem Co Prod Bull ... Baker, J. T., Chemical Company. Product Bulletin [*A publication*]
Baker Millers J ... Baker and Millers' Journal [*A publication*] (APTA)
Baker Millr J ... Baker and Millers' Journal [*A publication*] (APTA)
Baker Prod ... Bakery Production and Marketing [*A publication*]
Baker Quar ... Baker's Law of Quarantine [*A publication*] (DLA)
Baker's...... Baker's Digest [*A publication*]
Baker's Dig ... Baker's Digest [*A publication*]
BakerSJ..... Baker Street Journal [*A publication*]
Baker's Rev ... Baker's Review [*A publication*]
Baker's Tech Dig ... Baker's Technical Digest [*A publication*]
Bak Health L ... Baker's Health Laws [*A publication*] (DLA)
Bak Highw ... Baker's Law of Highways [*A publication*] (DLA)
Baking Ind ... Baking Industry [*A publication*]
Baking Technol ... Baking Technology [*A publication*]
Bakish Mater Corp Publ ... Bakish Materials Corporation. Publication [*A publication*]
Bakkerij Wet ... Bakkerij Wetenschap [*A publication*]
Bak Quar ... Baker's Law of Quarantine [*A publication*] (DLA)
BAKR .... Baker Communications, Inc. [*NASDAQ symbol*] (NQ)
BAKS........ Barracks
BAKUP...... Banking Users' Group [*British*]
BAL .... Balance [*Accounting*] (AFM)
Bal............ Balance [*Balance*] [*Accounting*] [*French*]
Bal............ Balasingham's Reports [*Ceylon*] [*A publication*] (DLA)
BAL .... Balcor Resources Corp. [*Vancouver Stock Exchange symbol*]
Bal............ Baldus de Ubaldis [*Deceased, 1400*] [*Authority cited in pre-1607 legal work*] (DSA)
BAL .... Baldwin Securities Corp. [*AMEX symbol*] (SPSG)
BAL .... Ballistic [*or Ballistics*] (MSA)
Bal............ Balmoral Shoe [*Orthosis*]
BAL .... Balsamic [*Mild, Healing*] [*Medicine*] (ROG)
bal .... Baluchi [*MARC language code*] [*Library of Congress*] (LCCP)
BAL .... Base Allowance List (MUGU)
BAL .... Base Authorization List
BAL .... Basic Assembly Language [*Programming language*] [*Sperry UNIVAC*] [*Data processing*]
BAL .... Berichte. Verhandlungen der Saechsischen Akademie der Wissenschaften zu Leipzig [*Berlin*] [*A publication*]
BAL .... Berul Associates Limited [*Information service or system*] (IID)
BAL .... Bibliography of American Literature [*A publication*]
BAL .... Biological Assessment Laboratory
BAL .... Blood Alcohol Level [*Medicine*]
BAL .... Boat Allowance List [*Navy*] (CAAL)
BAL .... Bohn's Artist's Library [*A publication*]
BAL .... Boston Australia Limited [*Australia*]
BAL .... British Anti-Lewisite [*Also, DMP: Dimercapto, propanol*] [*Detoxicant*]
BAL .... British Architectural Library [*Royal Institute of British Architects*] [*Information service or system*] (IID)
BAL .... Broad Absorption Line [*Quasar*] [*Astrophysics*]
BAL .... Bronchoalveolar Lavage [*Medicine*]
BAL .... Buenos Aires Literaria [*A publication*]
BAL .... Bulletin des Antiquites Luxembourgeoises [*A publication*]
BAL .... Business Application Language
BAL .... Butler Area Librarians [*Library network*]
BAL .... University of Baltimore, Baltimore, MD [*OCLC symbol*] (OCLC)
BALA....... Bulletin. American Library Association [*A publication*]
BALA........ Bulletin. Association Lyonnaise de Recherches Archeologiques [*A publication*]
BALAC....... Bulletin d'Ancienne Litterature et d'Archeologie Chretienne [*A publication*]
BALAD..... Bleachable Absorber LASER Amplifier and Detector
BA(Lan)..... Bachelor of Languages [*British*] (DBQ)
BALANCE ... Basic and Logically Applied Norms - Civil Engineering (AFM)

Bal Ann Codes ... Ballinger's Annotated Codes and Statutes [*Washington*] [*A publication*] (DLA)

BAL ARENAE ... Balneum Arenae [*Sand Bath*] [*Medicine*]

Balas .... Balasingham's Supreme Court Reports [*Ceylon*] [*A publication*] (DLA)

BALAS ...... Business Association of Latin American Studies (EA)

Balasingham Rep ... Balasingham's Reports of Cases [*Ceylon*] [*A publication*] (ILCA)

Balas NC .... Balasingham's Notes of Cases [*Ceylon*] [*A publication*] (DLA)

Balasov Gos Ped Inst Ucen Zap ... Balasovkii Gosudarstvennyi Pedagogiceskii Institut. Ucenye Zapiski [*A publication*]

Balas RC .... Balasingham's Reports of Cases [*1904-09*] [*Ceylon*] [*A publication*] (DLA)

BALAST .... Balloon Astronomy

Balaton Symp Part Phys ... Balaton Symposium on Particle Physics [*A publication*]

BA(Law) .... Bachelor of Arts in Law

BALB .... Boletin. Real Academia de Buenas Letras de Barcelona [*A publication*]

Balb .... Pro Balbo [*of Cicero*] [*Classical studies*] (OCD)

BALC .... Balcony [*Classified advertising*] (ADA)

BALC .... Brotherhood of the American Lutheran Church [*Later, American Lutheran Church Men*] (EA)

BALC .... Bulletin d'Ancienne Litterature Chretienne Latine [*Maredosous*] [*A publication*]

BALCE ...... Balance [*Accounting*] (ROG)

balce .... Balance [*Balance*] [*Accounting*] [*French*]

Bald .... Baldasseroni on Maritime Law [*A publication*] (DLA)

Bald .... Baldus (Commentator on the Code) [*A publication*] (DLA)

Bald .... Baldwin's United States Circuit Court Reports [*A publication*] (DLA)

B & Ald ...... Barnewall and Alderson's English King's Bench Reports [*A publication*] (DLA)

Bald App .... Appendix to 11 Peters, United States Reports [*A publication*] (DLA)

Bald App 11 Pet ... Baldwin. Appendix to 11 Peters [*A publication*] (DLA)

BALDAS ... Ballistic Data Acquisition System (MCD)

Bald Bank .. Baldwin. Law of Bankruptcy [*11th ed.*] [*1915*] [*A publication*] (DLA)

Bald CC ..... Baldasseroni on Maritime Law [*A publication*] (DLA)

Bald CC ..... Baldus (Commentator on the Code) [*A publication*] (DLA)

Bald CC ..... Baldwin's United States Circuit Court Reports [*A publication*] (DLA)

Bald Cir C ... Baldwin's United States Circuit Court Reports [*A publication*] (DLA)

Bald Conn Dig ... Baldwin's Connecticut Digest [*A publication*] (DLA)

Bald Const ... Baldwin's View of the United States Constitution with Opinions [*A publication*] (DLA)

Baldev PC .. Baldeva Ram Dave. Privy Council Judgment [*India*] [*A publication*] (DLA)

BALDICER ... Balanced Diet Certificates [*Economics simulation game*]

Bald Novell ... Baldus Bartolinus Novellus [*Deceased, 1490*] [*Authority cited in pre-1607 legal work*] (DSA)

BALDNY ... Ballistic Density

Bald Op ...... Baldwin's View of the United States Constitution with Opinions [*A publication*] (DLA)

Bald Pat Cas ... Baldwin's Patent, Copyright, Trade-Mark Cases [*A publication*] (DLA)

Bald Pat Etc Cas ... Baldwin's Patent, Copyright, Trade-Mark Cases [*A publication*] (DLA)

Bald Rep .... Baldwin's United States Circuit Court Reports [*A publication*] (DLA)

Balduin .... [*Franciscus*] Balduinus [*Deceased, 1572*] [*Authority cited in pre-1607 legal work*] (DSA)

Bald US Sup Ct Rep ... United States Supreme Court Reports, Photo Reproduction Set by Baldwin [*A publication*] (DLA)

Baldw .... Baldwin's United States Circuit Court Reports [*A publication*] (DLA)

Baldw Dig .. Baldwin's Connecticut Digest [*A publication*] (DLA)

Baldwin ...... Baldwin on Bankruptcy [*A publication*] (DLA)

Baldwin's CC US Rep ... Baldwin's United States Circuit Court Reports [*A publication*] (DLA)

Baldwin's Rep ... Baldwin's United States Circuit Court Reports [*A publication*] (DLA)

BA(LeisureStud) ... Bachelor of Arts (Leisure Studies)

B Alex .... Bellum Alexandrinum [*of Ausonius*] [*Classical studies*] (OCD)

Balf .... Balfour's Practice Laws of Scotland [*A publication*] (DLA)

BALF .... Black American Literature Forum [*A publication*]

BALF .... Blue Army of Our Lady of Fatima [*Later, World Apostolate of Fatima - WAF*] (EA)

BALF .... Bulletin. Academie Royale de Langue et de Litterature Francaises [*A publication*]

Balf Pr .... Balfour's Practice Laws of Scotland [*A publication*] (DLA)

BALFRAN ... Balanced Force Requirements Analysis (MCD)

Balgarska M ... Balgarska Muzyka [*A publication*]

BALGOL ... Burroughs Algebraic Compiler (IEEE)

BALH .... British Association for Local History

BALI .... Bali Jewelry Ltd. [*NASDAQ symbol*] (NQ)

BALI .... Bollettino dell'Atlante Linguistico Italiano [*A publication*]

BALI .... British Association of Landscape Industries

BALIA .... Biotin-Avidin-Linked Immunoassay [*Immunochemistry*]

BA(LibSc) ... Bachelor of Arts (Library Science)

BALIC .... Board of Action on Letter of Intent Conversion [*Navy*]

B A Liege ... Bulletin. Institut Archeologique Liegeois [*A publication*]

BAL IS .... Balearic Islands

BALIS .... Bayerisches Landwirtschaftliches Informationssystem [*Bavarian Agricultural Information System*] [*Federal Republic of Germany*] [*Databank*] (IID)

Bal Isls .... Balearic Islands

BALit .... Biblioteka Analiz Literackich [*A publication*]

BALITAC ... Basic Literal Automatic Coding

Balkan Stud ... Balkan Studies [*A publication*]

BalkE .... Balkansko Ezikoznanije [*A publication*]

Balk St .... Balkan Studies [*A publication*]

Balk Stud .... Balkan Studies [*A publication*]

B-ALL .... B-Cell Leukemia [*Medicine*]

Ball .... Ballard's Somerton Court Rolls [*Oxford Archaeological Society, No. 50*] [*England*] [*A publication*] (DLA)

BALL .... Ballast (KSC)

BALL .... Ballistic (AFM)

BALLAD ... Ballistic LORAN Assist Device

Ballade .... Ballade Tidsskrift for Ny Musikk [*A publication*]

BA/LLB ..... Bachelor of Arts/Bachelor of Laws (ADA)

Ball & B ..... Ball and Beatty's Irish Chancery Reports [*1807-14*] [*A publication*] (DLA)

Ball Banks ... Ball on National Banks [*A publication*] (DLA)

Ball Bear J ... Ball Bearing Journal [*A publication*]

Ball & Beatty ... Ball and Beatty's Irish Chancery Reports [*1807-14*] [*A publication*] (DLA)

Ball & B (Ir) ... Ball and Beatty's Irish Chancery Reports [*1807-14*] [*A publication*] (DLA)

Ball Conv .... Ball's Popular Conveyancer [*A publication*] (DLA)

Ball Dig .... Ball's Digest of the Common Law [*A publication*] (DLA)

Ballentine ... Ballentine's Law Dictionary [*A publication*] (DLA)

Ballentine's Law Dict ... Ballentine's Self Pronouncing Law Dictionary [*A publication*] (DLA)

Ballet N ...... Ballet News [*A publication*]

Ballet Rev .... Ballet Review [*A publication*]

Ball Ind .... Ball's Index to Irish Statutes [*A publication*] (DLA)

Ballinger's Ann Codes & St ... Ballinger's Annotated Codes and Statutes [*Washington*] [*A publication*] (DLA)

Ball Lim ..... Ballantine. Statute of Limitations [*1810*] [*A publication*] (DLA)

Balloon Res Technol Symp ... Balloon Research and Technology Symposium [*A publication*]

BALLOTS ... Bibliographic Automation of Large Library Operations Using a Time-Sharing System [*Later, RLIN*] [*Stanford University*]

Ball Roller Bear Eng ... Ball and Roller Bearing Engineering [*A publication*]

Ball & Roller Bear Engng ... Ball and Roller Bearing Engineering [*A publication*]

Ball State J ... Ball State Journal for Business Educators [*A publication*]

Ball St Bus Rev ... Ball State Business Review [*A publication*]

Ball St Guide ... Ball's Student Guide to the Bar [*A publication*] (DLA)

Ball St Uni ... Ball State University Forum [*A publication*]

BALLUTE ... Balloon Parachute

BALLWIN ... Ballistic Wind

BALM .... Block and List Manipulator [*Data processing*] (CSR)

BALM .... Bollettino dell'Atlante Linguistico Mediterraneo [*A publication*]

BAL MAR ... Balneum Mariae [*Salt-Water Bath*] [*Medicine*]

BALMI .... Ballistic Missile (MUGU)

BALN .... Balneum [*Bath*] [*Medicine*] (ROG)

BALN CAL ... Balneum Calidum [*Warm Bath*] [*Medicine*] (ROG)

Balneo Bohem ... Balneologia Bohemica [*A publication*]

Balneol Pol ... Balneologia Polska [*A publication*]

Balneol Soc Japan Jour ... Balneological Society of Japan. Journal [*A publication*]

Bal Notes ... Balasingham's Notes of Cases [*Ceylon*] [*A publication*] (ILCA)

Bal Novel ... Baldus Bartolinus Novellus [*Deceased, 1490*] [*Authority cited in pre-1607 legal work*] (DSA)

BALO .... Bulletin des Annonces Legales Obligatoires [*Official Gazette for Legal Notice*] [*A publication*] (ILCA)

BALOE ...... British/American Light Opera Exchange

BALOG ...... Base Logistical Command

BALOP ...... Balopticon (IEEE)

BALPA ...... Balance of Payments [*Accounting*]

BALPA ...... British Airline Pilots Association

Bal Pak .... Baluchistan, Pakistan (ILCA)

BALPAY ... International Balance of Payments [*Economics simulation game*]

Bal Pay't Rep ... Balance of Payments Report [*A publication*] (DLA)

Bal R .... Baltic Review [*A publication*]

Ba LR .... University of Baltimore. Law Review [*A publication*]

Bal RD .... Baldeva Ram Dave. Privy Council Judgment [*India*] [*A publication*] (DLA)

Bal Rep ...... Balasingham's Reports of Cases [*Ceylon*] [*A publication*] (ILCA)

BALRHEO ... Balancing Rheostat

BALS .... Balancing Set (IEEE)

Bals .... Balboas [*Monetary unit*] [*Panama*]

BALS .... Balsamum [*Balsam*] [*Pharmacy*]

BALS .... Blind Approach Landing System [*Aviation*]

BALSA ...... Black American Law Students Association (EA)

Bal Sheet....   Balance Sheet [*A publication*]
BALSPACON ... Balance of Space to Space Control Agencies
Bal St .... Balkan Studies [*A publication*]
BALT............ Baltimore [*Maryland*]
BALT......... Barometric Altitude   (MCD)
BALT........ British Association for Language Teaching
BALT........ Bronchus Associated Lymphoid Tissue
BALTAP ... Allied Forces Baltic Approaches [*NATO*]
Balt C Rep ... Baltimore City Reports [*A publication*]   (DLA)
BALTHUM ... Balloon Temperature and Humidity [*Sonde*] [*Meteorology*]
Baltic Sea Environ Proc ... Baltic Sea Environment. Proceedings [*A publication*]
Baltimore B of Ed ... Baltimore Bulletin of Education [*A publication*]
Baltimore Mus Art N ... Baltimore Museum of Art. News [*A publication*]
Baltimore Mus N ... Baltimore Museum of Art. News [*A publication*]
Baltim BJ ... Baltimore Business Journal [*A publication*]
Balt LT...... Baltimore Law Transcript [*A publication*]   (DLA)
Balt L Tr .... Baltimore Law Transcript [*A publication*]   (DLA)
Baltmr Sun ... Sun (Baltimore) [*A publication*]
BALTO...... Baltimore [*Maryland*]
BALTRAC ... Ballastable Tractor
BALUN ..... Balanced-to-Unbalanced Line Transformer [*Telecommunications*]   (TEL)
BALUN ...... Balancing Unit [*Radio*]
BA Lux...... Bulletin d'Archeologie Luxembourgeoise [*A publication*]
BAL VAP .. Balneum Vaporis [*Vapor Bath*] [*Medicine*]
Balwant Vidyapeeth J Agric Sci Res ... Balwant Vidyapeeth Journal of Agricultural and Scientific Research [*A publication*]
Balwant Vidyapeeth J Agr Sci Res ... Balwant Vidyapeeth Journal of Agricultural and Scientific Research [*A publication*]
BALWND ... Ballistic Wind
BAM.......... Bachelor of Applied Mathematics
BAM.......... Bachelor of Arts in Music
BAM.......... Bachelor of Ayurvedic Medicine
BAM.......... Bacteriological Analytical Manual [*A publication*]
BaM........... Baghdader Mitteilungen [*Berlin*] [*A publication*]
BAM.......... Baikal-Amur Mainline [*USSR railroad in Siberia*]
BAM.......... Ballistic Advanced Missile   (MCD)
bam .... Bambara [*MARC language code*] [*Library of Congress*]   (LCCP)
BAM.......... Band Approximation Method   (MCD)
BaM........... Barium Meal [*Medicine*]
BAM.......... Base Automotive Maintenance
BAM.......... Basic Access Method [*Data processing*]
BAM.......... Battle Mountain [*Nevada*] [*Airport symbol*] [*Obsolete*]   (OAG)
BAM.......... Battlefield Automation Management   (MCD)
BAMN....... Belize Action Movement   (PD)
BAM.......... Bikers Against Manslaughter   (EA)
BAM.......... Binary Angular Measurement [*Military*]   (CAAL)
BAM.......... Black Action Movement
BAM.......... Block Access Method [*Data processing*]
BaM........... Boite-a-Musique, Paris [*Record label*] [*France*]
BAM.......... Book About Me [*Psychological testing*]
BAM........... Booker Aircraft Museum [*Wycombe Air Park, Booker, Buckinghamshire, England*]
BAM.......... Bowling Apparel Manufacturers of America   (EA)
BAM.......... Bradley Aberration Method
BAM......... British Air Ministry
BAM.......... Broad Anatomy Marine [*See also HAM*] [*Slang term for female marines*] [*Bowdlerized version*]
BAM.......... Broadcasting Amplitude Modulation
BAMG....... Brooklyn Academy of Music
BAM.......... Brothers to All Men [*An association*]
BAM.......... Buenos Aires Musical [*A publication*]
BAM.......... Bulk Airmail
BAM.......... Bulletin d'Archeologie Marocaine [*A publication*]
BAM......... Bundesanstalt fuer Materialforschung und -Pruefung [*Federal Institute for Materials Research and Testing*] [*Federal Republic of Germany*] [*Database producer*] [*Information retrieval*]   (IID)
BAM.......... Bundesanstalt fuer Materialprufung Unter den Eichen [*International Association for Structural Mechanics in Reactor Technology*]   (EAIO)
BAM.......... Bureau of Aviation Medicine   (KSC)
BAM........ Bus Access Module
BAM......... Bus Arbitration Module [*Motorola, Inc.*]
BAM.......... Business Air Services Ltd. [*Toronto, ON, Canada*] [*FAA designator*]   (FAAC)
BAM.......... Business America [*A publication*]
BAM.......... Matsqui-Sumas-Abbotsford Museum, Abbotsford, British Columbia [*Library symbol*] [*National Library of Canada*]   (NLC)
BAMA ...... Boys and Young Men's Apparel Manufacturers Association   (EA)
BAMA ...... British Aerosol Manufacturers Association
BAMA ...... British Army Motoring Association [*British military*]   (DMA)
BAMA ...... British Automobile Manufacturers Association   (EA)
BAMA ...... Brotherhood Association of Military Airmen
BAMAB..... Battery Man [*A publication*]
BAMalgache ... Bulletin. Academie Malgache [*A publication*]
BAM Amtsbl Mitteilungsbl ... BAM Berlin Amtsblatt und Mitteilungsblatt der Bundesanstalt fuer Materialpruefung [*A publication*]

B Am Anth A ... Bulletin. American Anthropological Association [*A publication*]
BA Maroc .. Bulletin d'Archeologie Marocaine [*A publication*]
BAMB .... Bureau of Administrative Management and Budget [*United Nations Development Program*]
BAMBAM ... Bookline Alert: Missing Books and Manuscripts [*Information service or system*] [*A publication*]
BAM-Ber... BAM-Berichte. Forschung und Entwicklung in der Bundesanstalt fuer Materialpruefung [*A publication*]
Bamber....... Report of Mining Cases Decided by the Railway and Canal Commission [*A publication*]   (DLA)
BAMBI...... Ballistic Missile Bombardment [*or Boost*] Interceptor [*Military*]
BAMBI...... Bayesian Analysis Modified by Inspection [*Data processing*]
BAMBY..... Bran and Multiple Vitamins and Minerals, B-Complex Vitamins, and Yogurt [*A nutritional plan*]
BAMC .... Brooke Army Medical Center
BAMCO ..... British Air Ministry Control Office
BAMD........ Bis(acetatomercurimethyl)dioxane [*Organic chemistry*]
BAME .... Benzoylarginine Methyl Ester [*Biochemistry*]
BA in M Ed ... Bachelor of Arts in Music Education
BAMEG .... Bulletin Annuel. Musee d'Ethnographie de la Ville de Geneve [*A publication*]
BAMEO .... Base Aircraft Maintenance and Engineering Organization [*Canadian Navy*]
Bamer........ Banco de America [*Bank of America*] [*Nicaragua*]   (GEA)
B Amer School Orient ... Bulletin. American Schools of Oriental Research [*A publication*]
BAMG .... Browning Aircraft Machine Gun
B Am Hist Col ... Bulletin. American Historical Collection [*A publication*]
BAMI .... Basic American Medical, Incorporated [*NASDAQ symbol*]   (NQ)
BAMI .... Brothers to All Men International   (EA)
BAMIA...... Bulletin. American Meteorological Society [*A publication*]
BAmicEbrCr ... Bollettino. Amicizia Ebraico-Cristiana di Firenze [*A publication*]
Bamidgeh Bull Fish Cult Isr ... Bamidgeh. Bulletin of Fish Culture in Israel [*A publication*]
BAMIRAC ... Ballistic Missile Radiation Analysis Center
BAMM ...... Balloon Altitude Mosaic Measurements   (MCD)
BAMM ...... Bangor America, Inc. [*Wallington, NJ*] [*NASDAQ symbol*]   (NQ)
BAMM ...... Basic Acrylic Monomer Manufacturers Association   (EA)
BAMM .... British Association of Manipulative Medicine
B Am Math S ... Bulletin. American Mathematical Society [*A publication*]
B Am Meteor ... Bulletin. American Meteorological Society [*A publication*]
BAMN ...... By Any Means Necessary
BAMO....... Bureau of Aeronautics Material Officer [*Obsolete*] [*Navy*]
BAMOA ..... Bulletin. American Mathematical Society [*A publication*]
BAMON..... Bleomycin, Adriamycin, Methotrexate, Oncovin [*Vincristine*], Nitrogen mustard [*Antineoplastic drug regimen*]
BAMP....... Bampton [*England*]
BAMP....... Battlefield Automation Management Plan [*or Program*]   (MCD)
BAMP....... Build Ada Main Program [*Data processing*]
B Am Pal.... Bulletins of American Paleontology [*A publication*]
B Am Phys S ... Bulletin. American Physical Society [*A publication*]
B Am Pr Hist Res ... Bulletin. American School of Prehistoric Research [*A publication*]
BAMR .... Bureau of Aeronautics Maintenance Representative [*Obsolete*] [*Navy*]
BAMRAM ... Bulletin. Academie de Medecine de Roumanie [*A publication*]
BAMRG .... British Agricultural Marketing Research Group
BAMRO .... Bureau of Aeronautics Maintenance Repair Officer [*Obsolete*] [*Navy*]
BAMRRO ... Bureau of Aeronautics Maintenance Resident Representative Office [*Obsolete*] [*Navy*]
BAMS .... Base Automated Mobility System   (MCD)
BAMS........ Bell Atlantic Mobile Systems [*Telecommunications*]
BAMS........ British American Minesweeper [*British military*]   (DMA)
BAMS........ Broadcast to Allied Merchant Ships
BAMS........ Bulletin. American Mathematical Society [*A publication*]
BAMS........ Bulletin. American Musicological Society [*A publication*]
BAMSL..... Bar Association of Metropolitan St. Louis. Bankruptcy Reporter [*A publication*]   (DLA)
B Am Soc P ... Bulletin. American Society of Papyrologists [*A publication*]
B Am S Pap ... Bulletin. American Society of Papyrologists [*A publication*]
BAMSR..... British Admiralty Maintenance and Supply Representative
BAMT .... Boric Acid Mix Tank [*Nuclear energy*]   (NRCH)
BA (Mus).. Bachelor of Arts (Music)
BAN.......... Andover Newton Theological School, Newton Center, MA [*OCLC symbol*]   (OCLC)
BAN.......... Banbury [*British depot code*]
Ban............ Bandinus Familiatus de Pisa [*Deceased, 1218*] [*Authority cited in pre-1607 legal work*]   (DSA)
BAN.......... Banff [*Alberta*] [*Seismograph station code, US Geological Survey*] [*Closed*]   (SEIS)
BAN.......... Bangor [*City in Wales*]   (ROG)
BAN.......... Banished   (ROG)
BAN.......... Banister, Inc. [*AMEX symbol*]   (SPSG)
BAN.......... Banking Law Journal [*A publication*]
Ban............ Banner [*Record label*]

BAN.......... Banyon Air Service [*Ft. Lauderdale, FL*] [*FAA designator*] (FAAC)
BAN.......... Base Activation Notice
BAN.......... Best Asymptotically Normal [*Estimates*] [*Econometrics*]
BAN.......... Bionics Adaptive Network
BAN.......... Blacks Against Nukes (EA)
BAN.......... Bond Anticipation Note [*Banking*]
BAN.......... British American Bank Note, Inc. [*Toronto Stock Exchange symbol*] [*Vancouver Stock Exchange symbol*]
BAN.......... British Approved Name
BAN.......... Budget Allocation Notice (MCD)
BAN.......... Bulletin de l'Afrique Noire [*A publication*]
Ban & A ..... Banning and Arden's Patent Cases [*United States*] [*A publication*] (DLA)
BANA........ Benzoylargininenaphthylamide
BA of NA ... Bnei Akiva of North America (EA)
BANA........ Braille Authority of North America (EA)
Banach Center Publ ... Banach Center. Publications [*Warsaw*] [*A publication*]
BANAGAS ... Bahrain National Gas Co. [*State enterprise*] (EY)
BANAIM... Bureau d'Amenagement du Nouvel Aeroport International de Montreal [*New Montreal International Airport Project Office - NMIAPO*] [*Canada*]
B Analyt Hist Rom ... Bulletin Analytique d'Histoire Romaine [*A publication*]
BANAMEX ... Banco Nacional de Mexico [*National Bank of Mexico*]
BANANAS ... Benevolent Association for Naming All Nonentities After Schools
Banaras LJ ... Banaras Law Journal [*India*] [*A publication*] (DLA)
Banaras Metall ... Banaras Metallurgist [*A publication*]
BA Narb..... Bulletin. Commission Archeologique de Narbonne [*A publication*]
BANAZ ..... Boletin. Academia Aragonesa de Nobles y Bellas Artes de San Luis de Zaragoza [*A publication*]
Banb Erev Hamal ... Banber Erevani Hamalsarani-Vestnik Erevanskogo Universiteta [*A publication*]
Ban Br........ [*Sir Orlando*] Bridgman's English Common Pleas Reports, Edited by Bannister [*124 English Reprint*] [*1660-67*] [*A publication*] (DLA)
Banbury (Eng) ... Banbury. English Exchequer Reports [*145 English Reprint*] [*A publication*] (DLA)
Banbury Rep ... Banbury Report [*A publication*]
BANC........ British Association of Nature Conservationists
Banca Borsa Tit Cred ... Banca, Borsa, e Titoli di Credito [*A publication*] (ILCA)
Banca d'Italia Bol ... Banca d'Italia. Bollettino [*A publication*]
Banca Nazionale del Lavoro Q R ... Banca Nazionale del Lavoro. Quarterly Review [*A publication*]
Banca Naz Lav Quart R ... Banca Nazionale del Lavoro. Quarterly Review [*A publication*]
B Anc Lit.... Bulletin d'Ancienne Litterature et d'Archeologie Chretienne [*A publication*]
Banco Angola Bol Trim ... Banco de Angola. Boletim Trimestral [*A publication*]
Banco Brasil Bol Trim ... Banco do Brasil. Boletim Trimestral [*A publication*]
BANCOBU ... Banque Commerciale du Burundi (EY)
Banco Central Bolivia Bol Estadistico ... Banco Central de Bolivia. Boletin Estadistico [*A publication*]
Banco Nacl ... Banco Nacional de Comercio Exterior, SA, Mexico. Annual Report [*A publication*]
B Anc Or Mus ... Bulletin. Ancient Orient Museum [*Tokyo*] [*A publication*]
Banco Roma ... Banco Roma. Review of the Economic Conditions in Italy [*A publication*]
BANCS...... Bell Administrative Network Communication System [*Telecommunications*] (TEL)
BANC SUP ... Bancus Superior [*King's Bench*] [*British*] [*Legal term*] (ROG)
BAND....... Bandelier National Monument
Band.......... Bandinus Familiatus de Pisa [*Deceased, 1218*] [*Authority cited in pre-1607 legal work*] (DSA)
BAND....... Bandolier
BAND....... Book Action for Nuclear Disarmament [*British*]
BANDES... National Bank for Social and Economical Development [*Cuba*]
BANDMR ... Bandmaster [*Military*] [*British*] (ROG)
BANDR ...... Bandmaster [*Military*] [*British*] (ROG)
BANE .... Bible and the Ancient Near East [*A publication*]
BANESTO ... Banco Espanol de Credito [*Spain*]
BANEWS ... British Army News Service [*British military*] (DMA)
BANEXI.... Banque pour l'Expansion Industrielle [*Industrial Development Bank*] [*France*] (EY)
BANF .... Bilateral Acoustic Neurofibromatosis [*Medicine*]
B-ANF .... Biological Receptors - Atrial Natriuretic Factor
BANF .... Business Account Number File [*IRS*]
BANG........ Angle at Leaf Base [*Botany*]
Bang.......... Bangladesh (ILCA)
BANG........ Bangor Hydro-Electric Co. [*NASDAQ symbol*] (NQ)
BANGA ..... Bauingenieur [*A publication*]
Bangabasi College Mag ... Bangabasi College Magazine [*Calcutta*] [*A publication*]
Bangabasi Morning College Mag ... Bangabasi Morning College Magazine [*Calcutta*] [*A publication*]
Bangalore Th F ... Bangalore Theological Forum [*A publication*]
B (Angers) ... Bulletin. Centre de Recherches et d'Enseignement de l'Antiquite (Angers) [*A publication*]

Bangkok Bank Mo R ... Bangkok Bank. Monthly Review [*A publication*]
Bangkok R ... Monthly Review (Bangkok) [*A publication*]
BANGLA... Bangladash
Bangladesh Acad Sci J ... Bangladesh Academy of Sciences. Journal [*A publication*]
Bangladesh Agric Sci Abstr ... Bangladesh Agricultural Sciences Abstracts [*A publication*]
Bangladesh Agr Sci Abstr ... Bangladesh Agricultural Sciences Abstracts [*A publication*]
Bangladesh Devel Stud ... Bangladesh Development Studies [*A publication*]
Bangladesh Geol Surv Rec ... Bangladesh Geological Survey. Records [*A publication*]
Bangladesh Hortic ... Bangladesh Horticulture [*A publication*]
Bangladesh J Agric ... Bangladesh Journal of Agriculture [*A publication*]
Bangladesh J Agric Sci ... Bangladesh Journal of Agricultural Sciences [*A publication*]
Bangladesh J Anim Sci ... Bangladesh Journal of Animal Sciences [*A publication*]
Bangladesh J Biol Agric Sci ... Bangladesh Journal of Biological and Agricultural Sciences [*Later, Bangladesh Journal of Biological Sciences*] [*A publication*]
Bangladesh J Biol Sci ... Bangladesh Journal of Biological Sciences [*A publication*]
Bangladesh J Bot ... Bangladesh Journal of Botany [*A publication*]
Bangladesh J Sci & Ind Res ... Bangladesh Journal of Scientific and Industrial Research [*A publication*]
Bangladesh J Sci Ind Res ... Bangladesh Journal of Scientific and Industrial Research [*A publication*]
Bangladesh J Sci Res ... Bangladesh Journal of Scientific Research [*A publication*]
Bangladesh J Zool ... Bangladesh Journal of Zoology [*A publication*]
Bangladesh Med Res Counc Bull ... Bangladesh Medical Research Council. Bulletin [*A publication*]
Bangladesh Pharm J ... Bangladesh Pharmaceutical Journal [*A publication*]
Bangladesh Vet J ... Bangladesh Veterinary Journal
Bangla Dev Stud ... Bangladesh Development Studies [*A publication*]
Bangla Hist Stud ... Bangladesh Historical Studies [*A publication*]
BANGLE... Angle at Leaf Base [*Botany*]
Bang LR..... Bangala Law Reporter [*India*] [*A publication*] (DLA)
Bangor Dail ... Bangor Daily News [*A publication*]
BANHC...... Bengal Army Native Hospital Corps [*British military*] (DMA)
BANHCAFE ... Banco Hondureno del Cafe [*Honduras*] (EY)
BANHQ..... Boletin. Academia Nacional de la Historia (Quito) [*A publication*]
BAnimSc.... Bachelor of Animal Science
BANIR...... Bombing and Navigation Inertial Reference
Bank.......... Bankers' Magazine [*A publication*]
Bank.......... Bankruptcy [*Legal term*] (DLA)
Bank.......... Bankruptcy Court [*Legal term*] (DLA)
Bank Admin ... Magazine of Bank Administration [*A publication*]
Bank Ad News ... Bank Advertising News [*A publication*]
BANKANAL ... Bank Analysis System [*Robinson-Humphrey Co.*] [*Defunct*] [*Information service or system*] (CRD)
Bank-Betr... Bank-Betrieb [*A publication*]
Bank C....... Banking Code [*A publication*] (DLA)
Bank Can R ... Bank of Canada. Review [*A publication*]
Bank Cas.... Banking Cases [*A publication*] (DLA)
Bank Ct Rep ... American Law Times, Bankruptcy Reports [*A publication*] (DLA)
Bank Ct Rep ... Bankrupt Court Reporter [*New York*] [*A publication*] (DLA)
BANKCY... Bankruptcy
Bank England Q Bul ... Bank of England. Quarterly Bulletin [*A publication*]
Bank Eng QB ... Bank of England. Quarterly Bulletin [*A publication*]
Bank Eng Q Bull ... Bank of England. Quarterly Bulletin [*A publication*]
Banker-F... Banker-Farmer [*A publication*]
Bankers Bus ... Banker's Business [*A publication*]
Bankers J... Bankers' Journal [*A publication*] (APTA)
Banker's LJ ... Banker's Law Journal [*A publication*] (DLA)
Bankers' M ... Bankers' Magazine [*A publication*]
Bankers M ... Bankers' Monthly [*A publication*]
Bankers' Mag ... Bankers' Magazine [*A publication*]
Bankers Mag ... Bankers Magazine of Australasia [*A publication*] (APTA)
Bankers Mag A'sia ... Bankers Magazine of Australasia [*A publication*] (APTA)
Bankers Mag Aust ... Bankers Magazine of Australasia [*A publication*] (APTA)
Bankers Mag Australas ... Bankers Magazine of Australasia [*A publication*] (APTA)
Bankers M Australasia ... Bankers Magazine of Australasia [*A publication*]
Bankers' Mo ... Bankers' Monthly [*A publication*]
Bankers' Mon ... Bankers' Monthly [*A publication*]
Bank Finland Mo Bul ... Bank of Finland. Monthly Bulletin [*A publication*]
Bank Finland Mthly B ... Bank of Finland. Monthly Bulletin [*A publication*]
Bank Gaz ... Bankruptcy Gazette [*A publication*] (DLA)
Bank I .... Bankter's Institutes of Scottish Law [*A publication*] (DLA)
Banking...... ABA [*American Bankers Association*] Banking Journal [*A publication*]
Banking Am Bankers Assn ... Banking. American Bankers Association [*A publication*]
Banking Law J ... Banking Law Journal [*A publication*]
Banking LJ ... Banking Law Journal [*A publication*]

Bank & Ins ... Bankruptcy and Insolvency Reports [*1853-55*] [*England*] [*A publication*] (DLA)

Bank & Insol Rep ... Bankruptcy and Insolvency Reports [*1853-55*] [*England*] [*A publication*] (DLA)

Bank Insol Rep ... Bankruptcy and Insolvency Reports [*1853-55*] [*England*] [*A publication*] (DLA)

Bank & Ins R ... Bankruptcy and Insolvency Reports [*1853-55*] [*England*] [*A publication*] (DLA)

Bank Inst ... Bankter's Institutes of Scottish Law [*A publication*] (DLA)

Bank Law J ... Banking Law Journal [*A publication*]

Bank Law J Dig Fed Sup ... Banking Law Journal Digest. Federal Supplement [*A publication*]

Bank Lit Index ... American Bankers Association. Banking Literature Index [*A publication*]

Bank LJ ..... Banking Law Journal [*A publication*]

Bank London South Amer R ... Bank of London and South America. Review [*A publication*]

Bank London and South Am R ... Bank of London and South America. Review [*A publication*]

Bank Mag ... Bankers' Magazine [*A publication*]

Bank Mag A/sia ... Bankers Magazine of Australasia [*A publication*] (APTA)

Bank Mark ... Bank Marketing [*A publication*]

Bank Mktg M ... Bank Marketing Magazine [*A publication*]

Bank Mktg R ... Bank Marketing Report [*A publication*]

Bank M (L) ... Bankers' Magazine (London) [*A publication*]

Bank M (Lond) ... Bankers' Magazine (London) [*A publication*]

Bank M (NY) ... Bankers' Magazine (New York) [*A publication*]

Bank Montreal Bus R ... Bank of Montreal. Business Review [*A publication*]

Bank Nova Scotia Mo R ... Bank of Nova Scotia. Monthly Review [*A publication*]

Bank NSW Circular ... Bank of New South Wales. Circular [*A publication*]

Bank NSW R ... Bank of New South Wales. Review [*A publication*] (APTA)

Bank of NSW R ... Bank of New South Wales. Review [*A publication*] (APTA)

Bank NSW Re ... Bank of New South Wales. Review [*A publication*] (APTA)

Bank NSW Rev ... Bank of New South Wales. Review [*A publication*] (APTA)

BANKPAC ... Banking Profession Political Action Committee [*Acronym now used as official name of organization*] (EA)

Bankr .... Bankruptcy [*Legal term*] (DLA)

Bankr Act ... Bankruptcy Act [*Legal term*] (DLA)

Bankr B Bull ... Bankruptcy Bar Bulletin [*A publication*] (DLA)

Bankr Ct Dec ... Bankruptcy Court Decisions [*A publication*] (DLA)

Bank Reg ... Bankruptcy Register [*A publication*] (DLA)

Bank Rep ... American Law Times, Bankruptcy Reports [*A publication*] (DLA)

Bankr Form ... Bankruptcy Forms [*A publication*] (DLA)

Bankr Ins R ... Bankruptcy and Insolvency Reports [*1853-55*] [*England*] [*A publication*] (DLA)

Bankr L Rep ... Bankruptcy Law Reports [*Commerce Clearing House*] [*A publication*] (DLA)

Bankr R ...... Rules of Bankruptcy and Official Forms [*A publication*] (DLA)

Bankr Reg ... National Bankruptcy Register [*New York*] [*A publication*] (DLA)

Bankr Rule ... Rules of Bankruptcy and Official Forms [*A publication*] (DLA)

Banks .... Banks' Reports [*1-5 Kansas*] [*A publication*] (DLA)

Bank Sierra Leone Econ R ... Bank of Sierra Leone. Economic Review [*A publication*]

Bank Sudan Ec Fin Bull ... Bank of Sudan. Economic and Financial Bulletin [*A publication*]

Bank Sys ... Bank Systems and Equipment [*A publication*]

Bank Syst and Equip ... Bank Systems and Equipment [*A publication*]

Bankt .... Macdowall's Institute of Laws of Scotland [*3 vols.*] [*1751-53*] [*A publication*] (DLA)

Bank Thailand Mo Bul ... Bank of Thailand. Monthly Bulletin [*A publication*]

Bank Thailand Q Bul ... Bank of Thailand. Quarterly Bulletin [*A publication*]

Bankt I .... Bankter's Institutes of Scottish Law [*A publication*] (DLA)

BANLE ...... Boletin. Academia Norteamericana de la Lengua Espanola [*A publication*]

Ban LJ .... Banaras Law Journal [*India*] [*A publication*] (DLA)

Ban LJ .... Banking Law Journal [*A publication*]

BANMAC ... Bulletin. Academie Nationale de Medecine [*Paris*] [*A publication*]

Bann .... Bannister's Reports, English Common Pleas [*A publication*]

Bann & A ... Banning and Arden's Patent Cases [*United States*] [*A publication*] (DLA)

Bann & A Pat Cas ... Banning and Arden's Patent Cases [*United States*] [*A publication*] (DLA)

Bann & Ard ... Banning and Arden's Patent Cases [*United States*] [*A publication*] (DLA)

Bann Br ...... Bannister's Edition of Orlando Bridgman's English Common Pleas Reports [*A publication*] (DLA)

Bann Lim ... Banning. Limitations of Actions [*3rd ed.*] [*1906*] [*A publication*] (DLA)

B Ann Mus Ferr ... Bollettino Annuale. Musei Ferraresi [*A publication*]

B Annu Mus Ethnogr Geneve ... Bulletin Annuel. Musee d'Ethnographie de la Ville de Geneve [*A publication*]

BANOCO ... Bahrain National Oil Company [*State enterprise*] (EY)

BA Non-Class ... Bachelor of Arts - Non-Classical

BANP .... [*The*] Book of American Negro Poetry [*A publication*]

Banq .... Banque [*Bank*] [*French*]

BANQ .... Biblionews and Australian Notes and Queries [*A publication*]

BANQ .... Burritt InterFinancial Bancorporation [*NASDAQ symbol*] (NQ)

Banque Centrale Etats Afr Ouest Notes Info et Statis ... Banque Centrale des Etats de l'Afrique de l'Ouest. Notes d'Information et Statistiques [*A publication*]

Banque Centrale Madagascar Bul Mensuel Statis ... Banque Centrale de Madagascar. Bulletin Mensuel de Statistiques [*A publication*]

Banque Etats Afr Centrale Etud et Statis ... Banque des Etats de l'Afrique Centrale. Etudes et Statistiques [*A publication*]

Banque Fr Bul Trim ... Banque de France. Bulletin Trimestriel [*A publication*]

Banque Marocaine du Commerce Exterieur Mo Info R ... Banque Marocaine du Commerce Exterieur. Monthly Information Review [*A publication*]

Banque Nat Belgique Bul ... Banque Nationale de Belgique. Bulletin [*A publication*]

Banque Nationale de Belgique Bul ... Banque Nationale de Belgique. Bulletin [*A publication*]

Banque Nat Paris R Econ ... Banque Nationale de Paris. Revue Economique [*A publication*]

Banque Repub Burundi Bul Mensuel ... Banque de la Republique du Burundi. Bulletin Mensuel [*A publication*]

Banque Repub Burundi Bul Trim ... Banque de la Republique du Burundi. Bulletin Trimestriel [*A publication*]

Banque Zaire Bul Trim ... Banque du Zaire. Bulletin Trimestriel [*A publication*]

BANS .... Back, Arm, Neck, Scalp [*Medicine*]

BANS .... British Association of Numismatic Societies

BANSDOC ... Bangladesh National Scientific and Technical Documentation Centre [*Information service or system*] (IID)

BANSHEE ... Balloon and Nike Scaled High Explosive Experiment (KSC)

Bansilal Amritlal Agric Coll Mag ... Bansilal Amritlal Agricultural College. Magazine [*A publication*]

Bansk Obz ... Bansky Obzor [*A publication*]

Banta's Greek Exch ... Banta's Greek Exchange [*A publication*]

B Ant Fr ..... Bulletin. Societe Nationale des Antiquaires de France [*A publication*]

B Anthropol Inst ... Bulletin. Anthropological Institute [*Nagoya*] [*A publication*]

B Ant Lux .. Bulletin des Antiquites Luxembourgeoises [*A publication*]

BANW .... Business Alert to Nuclear War (EA)

BANWYS ... Black and Non-White YMCA Staffs [*An association*] [*Defunct*] (EA)

Banyasz Kohasz Lap Banyasz ... Banyaszati es Kohaszati Lapok. Banyaszat [*A publication*]

Banyasz Kohasz Lapok ... Banyaszati es Kohaszati Lapok [*A publication*]

Banyasz Kohasz Lapok Banyasz ... Banyaszati es Kohaszati Lapok. Banyaszat [*A publication*]

Banyasz Kohasz Lapok Banyasz Kulonszam ... Banyaszati es Kohaszati Lapok. Banyaszat Kulonszam [*A publication*]

Banyasz Kohasz Lapok Koeolaj Foeldgaz ... Banyaszati es Kohaszati Lapok. Koeolaj es Foeldgaz [*A publication*]

Banyasz Kohasz Lapok Kohasz ... Banyaszati es Kohaszati Lapok. Kohaszat [*A publication*]

Banyasz Kohasz Lapok Ontode ... Banyaszati es Kohaszati Lapok. Ontode [*A publication*]

Banyasz Kut Intez Kozl ... Banyaszati Kutato Intezet Kozlemenyei [*A publication*]

Banyasz Kut Intez Kozlem ... Banyaszati Kutato Intezet Kozlemenyei [*Hungary*] [*A publication*]

Banyasz Lapok ... Banyaszati Lapok [*A publication*]

BANYB ...... Banyaszat [*A publication*]

BAnz .... Bundesanzeiger [*Federal Reporter*] [*A publication*] (ILCA)

BANZ Antarct Exped Rep Ser B ... BANZ [*British-Australian-New Zealand*] Antarctic Research Expedition. Report. Series B [*A publication*] (APTA)

BANZARE ... British-Australian-New Zealand Antarctic Research Expedition [*1929-31*]

BAO .... Bachelor of the Art of Obstetrics

BAO .... Bachelor of Art of Oratory

BAO .... Bankruptcy Annulment Order [*Legal term*] (DLA)

BAO .... Banque d'Afrique Occidentale [*Bank of French West Africa*]

BAO .... Bardine Oils Ltd. [*Vancouver Stock Exchange symbol*]

BAO .... Basal Acid Output [*Medicine*]

BAO .... Base of Air Operations

BAO .... Basic Attack Option (MCD)

BAO .... Batavia Area Office [*Energy Research and Development Administration*]

BAO .... Battalion Administration Officer (MCD)

B & AO ...... Body and Assembly Operation [*Ford Motor Co.*]

BAO .... Brasilia Array [*Brazil*] [*Seismograph station code, US Geological Survey*] (SEIS)

BAO .... British Army of Occupation [*World War II*]

BAO .... British Association of Orthodontists

BAO .... British Association of Otolaryngologists

BAO .... Brookhaven Area Office [*Energy Research and Development Administration*]

BAO .... Budget and Accounting Officer [*Military*]

BAO .... Burlington Area Office [*Energy Research and Development Administration*]
BAOPS ...... Base Operations
BAOR .... British Army of the Rhine [*NATO/NORTHAG*]
BAOS .... British Association of Oral and Maxillo-Facial Surgeons
BAOT .... British Association of Occupational Therapists
BAP .... BA Resources [*Vancouver Stock Exchange symbol*]
BAP .... Bacterial Alkaline Phosphatase [*or Bacterial Alkaline Phosphomonoesterase*] [*An enzyme*]
BAP .... Baibara [*Papua New Guinea*] [*Airport symbol*]   (OAG)
BAP .... Ballistic Aimpoint [*Military*]   (CAAL)
BAP .... Band Amplitude Product
BAP .... Bankers Association of the Philippines   (DS)
BAP .... Baptist
BAP .... Baptized
BAP .... Barometric Absolute Pressure [*Automotive engineering*]
BAP .... Basaltic Achondrite Parent [*Planetary body*]
BAP .... Base Auxiliary Power   (KSC)
BAP .... Basic Assembler Program [*Data processing*]
BAP .... Beacon Aircraft Position   (MUGU)
BaP .... Benzo(a)pyrene
BAP .... Benzyl-Aminophenol [*Organic chemistry*]
BAP .... Benzylaminopurine [*Biochemistry*]
BAP .... Best Adaptive Path [*NASA*]
BAP .... Beta Alpha Psi   (EA)
BAP .... Billet a Payer [*Bill Payable*] [*French*] [*Business term*]
BAP .... Biotechnology Action Programme [*A publication*]
BAP .... Bleed Air Precooler
BAP .... Blood Agar Plate [*Microbiology*]
BAP .... Boeing Associated Products   (MCD)
BAP .... [*The*] Book of American Poetry [*A publication*]
BAP .... Born Again Pagans   (EA)
BAP .... Brachial Artery Pressure [*Medicine*]
BAP .... Branch Arm Piping [*Nuclear energy*]   (NRCH)
BAP .... Brief Adaptive Psychotherapy [*Psychology*]
BAP .... British Association for Psychopharmacology
BAP .... Bromoform-Triallyl Phosphate [*Flame retardant*]
BAP .... Bulgarian Agrarian Party [*Political party*]   (PPW)
BAP .... Bulletin de l'Administration des Prisons [*A publication*]
BAP .... Business Automobile Policy [*Insurance*]
BAP .... Butte, Anaconda & Pacific Railway Co. [*AAR code*]
BAPA .... Benzoylarginine p-Nitroanilide [*Also, BAPNA*] [*Biochemistry*]
BA (Paris) ... Bulletin Archeologique. Comite des Travaux Historiques et Scientifiques (Paris) [*A publication*]
BAPBAN ... Bulletin. Academie Polonaise des Sciences. Serie des Sciences Biologiques [*A publication*]
BAPC .... British Aircraft Preservation Council
BAPC .... Bulletin. Academie Polonaise de Cracovie [*A publication*]
BAPCT ...... Bachelor of Arts in Practical Christian Training
BAPE .... Balloon Atmospheric Propagation Experiment [*NASA*]
BAPE .... Baseplate [*Technical drawings*]
BAPE .... Boletim. Academia Portuguesa do Ex-Libris [*A publication*]
BAPE .... Branch Arm Piping Enclosure [*Nuclear energy*]   (NRCH)
BAPEL ...... Boletim. Academia Portuguesa do Ex-Libris [*A publication*]
BAPERS .... Battalion Automated Personnel System
BAPG .... Business Applications Programming Guide   (MCD)
BAPHR ..... Bay Area Physicians for Human Rights   (EA)
BAPI .... Barcelona, Spain - Pisa, Italy [*Submarine cable*] [*Telecommunications*]   (TEL)
BAPI .... Bollettino. Archivio Paleografico Italiano [*A publication*]
BAPI .... British Alternative Press Index [*A publication*]
BAPL .... Bettis Atomic Power Laboratory [*AEC*]   (MCD)
BAPN .... Beta-Aminopropionitrile [*Organic chemistry*]
BAPNA ...... Benzoylarginine p-Nitroanilide [*Also, BAPA*] [*Biochemistry*]
BAPO .... British Army Post Office [*British military*]   (DMA)
BAPP .... Beta-Amyloid Precursor Protein
BAPP .... Bis(aminopropyl)piperazine [*Organic chemistry*]
BAPP .... Bulgarian Agrarian People's Party [*Political party*]   (PPW)
BAPP .... Bureau Arabe de Presse et de Publications [*Paris*]   (BJA)
BAppEc ...... Bachelor of Applied Economics   (ADA)
B Applied Sc ... Bachelor of Applied Science
BAppSc ...... Bachelor of Applied Science   (ADA)
BAppSc-BltEnvir ... Bachelor of Applied Science - Built Environment
BAppSc-Comptg ... Bachelor of Applied Science - Computing
BAppSc-ConstMgmt ... Bachelor of Applied Science - Construction Management
BAppSc-ElectSysComptg ... Bachelor of Applied Science - Electronic Systems and Computing
BAppSci(Nsg) ... Bachelor of Applied Science (Nursing)   (ADA)
BAppSc-Optom ... Bachelor of Applied Science - Optometry
BAppSc-QuantSurv ... Bachelor of Applied Science - Quantity Surveying
BAppSc-Surv ... Bachelor of Applied Science - Surveying
BAPREPT ... Beds and Patients Report
BA Prov ..... Bulletin Archeologique de Provence [*A publication*]
BAPS .... Bovine Albumin Phosphate Saline [*Physiology*]
BAPS .... Branch Arm Piping Shielding [*Nuclear energy*]   (NRCH)
BAPS .... British Association of Paediatric Surgeons   (EAIO)
BAPS .... British Association of Plastic Surgeons
BAPS .... Bureau of Air Pollution Sciences
BAPSA ...... Bulletin. American Physical Society [*A publication*]

BAPSL ...... Bulletin. Academie Polonaise des Sciences et des Lettres [*A publication*]
BAPT .... Baptist
BAPT .... Baptized
BAPT .... Basic Avionics Procedure Trainer [*British military*]   (DMA)
BAPT .... [*Incorporated*] British Association for Physical Training
BAPTA ..... Bearing and Power Transfer Assembly [*Aerospace*]
BAPTA ..... Bis(aminophenoxy)ethanetetraacetic Acid [*Organic chemistry*]
Bapt B .... Baptist Bulletin [*A publication*]
Bapt H Heri ... Baptist History and Heritage [*A publication*]
Bapt Hist and Heritage ... Baptist History and Heritage [*A publication*]
Bapt Q .... Baptist Quarterly [*London*] [*A publication*]
Bapt Q .... Baptist Quarterly Review [*London*] [*A publication*]
Bapt Ref R ... Baptist Reformation Review [*A publication*]
BAPXB ..... Baupraxis [*A publication*]
BAQ .... Bachelor Airmen's Quarters [*Air Force*]
BAQ .... Barclays Review [*A publication*]
BAQ .... Barranquila [*Colombia*] [*Airport symbol*]   (OAG)
BAQ .... Basic Allowance for Quarters [*Military*]
BAQ .... Bibliotheque Administrative du Quebec [*UTLAS symbol*]
BAQ(AC)... Basic Allowance for Quarters for Adopted Child [*Military*]
BAQ(DIS RET) ... Basic Allowance for Quarters Pending Disability Retirement [*Military*]
BAQ(F)...... Basic Allowance for Quarters for Father [*Military*]
BAQ(H)..... Basic Allowance for Quarters for Husband [*Military*]
BAQ(LC)... Basic Allowance for Quarters for Legitimate Children [*Military*]
BAQ(M) .... Basic Allowance for Quarters for Mother [*Military*]
BAQ(SC)... Basic Allowance for Quarters for Stepchildren [*Military*]
BAQ(W).... Basic Allowance for Quarters for Wife [*Military*]
BAR .... Babinet Absorption Rule
B Ar .... Bachelor of Architecture
BAR .... Bacille Acido-Resistant [*Acid-Fast Bacillus*] [*Medicine*]
BAR .... Bailed Aircraft Repairables   (MCD)
BAR .... Baker Analyzed Reagent [*Chemistry*]
BAR .... Banco Resources Ltd. [*Vancouver Stock Exchange symbol*]
B & AR..... Bangor & Aroostook Railroad Co.
BAR .... Bangor & Aroostook Railroad Co. [*AAR code*]
BAR .... Banner Aerospace [*NYSE symbol*]   (SPSG)
BAR .... Banner Elk, NC [*Location identifier*] [*FAA*]   (FAAL)
Bar .... Bar Reports in All Courts [*England*] [*A publication*]   (DLA)
Bar .... Barber's Reports [*14-42 Arkansas*] [*A publication*]   (DLA)
Bar .... Baretti [*A publication*]
BAR .... Baritone [*Music*]
Bar .... Barleycorn [*Unit of weight*] [*Obsolete*] [*British*]   (ROG)
Bar .... Barnardiston's English King's Bench Reports [*A publication*]   (DLA)
BAR .... Barometer [*or Barometric*]
BAR .... Barque [*Bark, Boat*] [*French*]   (ROG)
BAR .... Barrel [*Shipping*]
BAR .... Barrett [*California*] [*Seismograph station code, US Geological Survey*]   (SEIS)
BAR .... Barrier   (NVT)
Bar .... Barrister [*A publication*]
bar .... Barrister   (ADA)
BAR .... Barron's [*A publication*]
Bar .... Barrows' Reports [*18 Rhode Island*] [*A publication*]   (DLA)
Bar .... Bartholomaeus Brixiensis [*Deceased circa 1258*] [*Authority cited in pre-1607 legal work*]   (DSA)
Bar .... Bartholomaeus de Saliceto [*Deceased, 1411*] [*Authority cited in pre-1607 legal work*]   (DSA)
Bar .... Bartolus de Sassoferrato [*Deceased, 1357*] [*Authority cited in pre-1607 legal work*]   (DSA)
Bar .... Baruch [*Book of the Bible*]
BAR .... Base Address Register [*Data processing*]   (BUR)
BAR .... Battery Acquisition RADAR
BAR .... Biblical Archaeologist Reader [*A publication*]   (BJA)
BAR .... Biblical Archaeology Review [*A publication*]
BAR .... Biblioteca dell'Archivum Romanicum [*A publication*]
BAR .... Billet a Recevoir [*Bill Receivable*] [*French*] [*Business term*]
BAR .... Blade Area Ratio
BAR .... Blueprint Analysis Report   (MCD)
BAR .... Board of Airline Representatives [*Australia*]
BAR .... Board of Appeals and Review [*Later, ARB*] [*Civil Service Commission*]   (AFM)
BAR .... Bone Apposition Rate [*Physiology*]
BAR .... Book Arts Review [*A publication*]
BAR .... Book Auction Records [*A publication*] [*British*]
BAR .... British Army Review [*A publication*]
BAR .... British Association for the Retarded
BAR .... Broadcast Advertisers Reports [*Information service or system*] [*Defunct*]
BAR .... Browning Automatic Rifle
BAR .... Budget Adjustment Request
BAR .... Buffer Address Register [*Data processing*]
BAR .... Bulletin. Association des Amis de Rabelais et de la Deviniere [*A publication*]
BAR .... Bureau of Aeronautics Representative [*Obsolete*] [*Navy*]
BAR .... Bureau of Automotive Regulation
BAR .... One-Ninety-Five Broadway Corp. [*Morristown, NY*] [*FAA designator*]   (FAAC)

BARAB...... Bulletin. Academie Royale d'Archeologie de Belgique [*A publication*]
BARAC...... Black American Response to the African Crisis   (EA)
Bar & Ad.... Barnewall and Adolphus' English King's Bench Reports [*109-110 English Reprint*] [*1830-34*] [*A publication*]   (DLA)
Bar & Al..... Barnewall and Alderson's English King's Bench Reports [*A publication*]   (DLA)
Bar Anc Stat ... Barrington's Observations upon the Statutes from Magna Charta to 21 James I [*A publication*]   (DLA)
Bar Ar........ Bartholomaeus Archamonus [*Authority cited in pre-1607 legal work*]   (DSA)
Bar Archa .. Bartholomaeus Archamonus [*Authority cited in pre-1607 legal work*]   (DSA)
Bar & Arn .. Barron and Arnold's English Election Cases [*1843-46*] [*A publication*]   (DLA)
Barat R....... Barat Review [*A publication*]
Bar & Au.... Barron and Austin's English Election Cases [*1842*] [*A publication*]   (DLA)
Bar & Aust ... Barron and Austin's English Election Cases [*1842*] [*A publication*]   (DLA)
BARB........ Ballast Aerating Retrieval Boom   (MCD)
BARB........ Barbados   (ROG)
Barb .... [*Andreas*] Barbatia [*Deceased, 1480*] [*Authority cited in pre-1607 legal work*]   (DSA)
Barb........ Barber Greene Co. [*NASDAQ symbol*]   (NQ)
Barb .... Barber's Gold Law [*South Africa*] [*A publication*]   (DLA)
Barb .... Barber's Reports [*14-42 Arkansas*] [*A publication*]   (DLA)
BARB........ Barbette [*Military*]
barb........... Barbiturate [*Pharmacology*]
Barb .... Barbour's Supreme Court Reports [*New York*] [*A publication*]   (DLA)
BARB........ British Angular Rate Bombsight
BARB........ British Association of Rose Breeders
BARB........ Broadcasters Audience Research Board [*British*] [*Information service or system*]
BARB........ Bulletin. Academie Royale de Belgique [*Brussels*] [*A publication*]
BARB........ Button at Right Bottom [*Telephone touch-tone dial*]
Barba .... [*Andreas*] Barbatia [*Deceased, 1480*] [*Authority cited in pre-1607 legal work*]   (DSA)
Barb Abs .... Barbour's Abstracts of Chancellor's Decisions [*New York*] [*A publication*]   (DLA)
Barbados Annu Rep Dep Sci Agric ... Barbados. Annual Report. Department of Science and Agriculture [*A publication*]
Barbados Nurs J ... Barbados Nursing Journal [*A publication*]
Barb App Dig ... Barber's Digest [*New York*] [*A publication*]   (DLA)
Barb Ark .... Barber's Reports [*14-42 Arkansas*] [*A publication*]   (DLA)
Barbat .... [*Andreas*] Barbatia [*Deceased, 1480*] [*Authority cited in pre-1607 legal work*]   (DSA)
Barb Ch ...... Barbour's Chancery Reports [*New York*] [*A publication*]   (DLA)
Barb Chancery Rep ... Barbour's Chancery Reports [*New York*] [*A publication*]   (DLA)
Barb Ch (NY) ... Barbour's Chancery Reports [*New York*] [*A publication*]   (DLA)
Barb Ch Pr ... Barbour's Chancery Practice [*New York*] [*A publication*]   (DLA)
Barb Ch Rep ... Barbour's Chancery Reports [*New York*] [*A publication*]   (DLA)
Barb & C KY St ... Barbour and Carroll's Kentucky Statutes [*A publication*]   (DLA)
Barb Cr L... Barbour's Criminal Law [*A publication*]   (DLA)
Barb Cr Law ... Barbour's Criminal Law [*A publication*]   (DLA)
Barb Cr P... Barbour's Criminal Pleadings [*A publication*]   (DLA)
Barb Cr P... Barbour's Criminal Practice [*A publication*]   (DLA)
Barb Dig ..... Barber's Digest of Kentucky [*A publication*]   (DLA)
Barbe.......... Barber's Reports [*14-42 Arkansas*] [*A publication*]   (DLA)
Barber .... Barber's Gold Law [*South Africa*] [*A publication*]   (DLA)
Barber .... Barber's Reports [*14-42 Arkansas*] [*A publication*]   (DLA)
BArbG........ Bundesarbeitsgericht [*Federal Labor Court*] [*German*]   (ILCA)
Barb Gro ..... Barbeyrac's Edition of Grotius on War and Peace [*A publication*]   (DLA)
Barb Ins .... Barber on Insurance [*A publication*]   (DLA)
Barb LR ..... Barbados Law Reports [*A publication*]   (DLA)
Barb (NY) SCR ... Barbour's Supreme Court Reports [*New York*] [*A publication*]   (DLA)
Barbour...... Barbour's Supreme Court Reports [*New York*] [*A publication*]   (DLA)
Barbour (NY) ... Barbour's Supreme Court Reports [*New York*] [*A publication*]   (DLA)
Barbour's Ch R .. Barbour's Chancery Reports [*New York*] [*A publication*]   (DLA)
Barbour's Sup Court Rep ... Barbour's Supreme Court Reports [*New York*] [*A publication*]   (DLA)
Barb Par..... Barbour on Parties in Law and Equity [*A publication*]   (DLA)
Barb Puf..... Barbeyrac's Edition of Puffendorf's Law of Nature and Nations [*A publication*]   (DLA)
Barb R........ Barbour's Supreme Court Reports [*New York*] [*A publication*]   (DLA)
Bar Brix ..... Bartholomaeus Brixiensis [*Deceased circa 1258*] [*Authority cited in pre-1607 legal work*]   (DSA)

Bar Brixi .... Bartholomaeus Brixiensis [*Deceased circa 1258*] [*Authority cited in pre-1607 legal work*]   (DSA)
Bar Brixien ... Bartholomaeus Brixiensis [*Deceased circa 1258*] [*Authority cited in pre-1607 legal work*]   (DSA)
Barb SC ..... Barbour's Supreme Court Reports [*New York*] [*A publication*]   (DLA)
Barb SCR... Barbour's Supreme Court Reports [*New York*] [*A publication*]   (DLA)
Barb Set-Off ... Barbour on the Law of Set-Off [*A publication*]   (DLA)
Barb Sup Ct ... Barbour's Supreme Court Reports [*New York*] [*A publication*]   (DLA)
Barb Sup Ct Reports ... Barbour's Supreme Court Reports [*New York*] [*A publication*]   (DLA)
BarBu......... University of the West Indies, Cave Hill Campus, Bridgetown, Barbados [*Library symbol*] [*Library of Congress*]   (LCLS)
BarBU-L...... University of the West Indies, Law Library, St. Michael, Barbados [*Library symbol*] [*Library of Congress*]   (LCLS)
Bar Bull Boston ... Bar Bulletin of the Boston Bar Association [*A publication*]
Bar Bull (NY County La) ... Bar Bulletin, New York County Lawyers' [*A publication*]   (DLA)
Bar Bull (NY County Law A) ... New York County Lawyers Association. Bar Bulletin [*A publication*]
BARC........ Barge, Amphibious, Resupply, Cargo
BARC......... Barrett Resources Corporation [*Denver, CO*] [*NASDAQ symbol*]   (NQ)
Bar de C ..... Bartholomaeus de Capua [*Deceased, 1328*] [*Authority cited in pre-1607 legal work*]   (DSA)
BARC........ Bay Area Reference Center [*San Francisco Public Library*] [*San Francisco, CA*] [*Library network*]
BARC........ Bay Area Religious Channel [*Cable TV programming service*]
BARC......... Beltsville Agricultural Research Center [*Maryland*] [*Department of Agriculture*]
BARC......... Bhabha Atomic Research Centre [*India*] [*Research center*]
BARC......... Bikini Atoll Rehabilitation Committee [*Federal government*]
BARC........ British Aeronautical Research Committee
BARC......... British American Repertory Company
BARC......... British Automobile Racing Club
Bar de Ca ... Bartholomaeus de Capua [*Deceased, 1328*] [*Authority cited in pre-1607 legal work*]   (DSA)
BARCAP ... Barrier Combat Air Patrol [*Navy*]
Bar de Cap ... Bartholomaeus de Capua [*Deceased, 1328*] [*Authority cited in pre-1607 legal work*]   (DSA)
Barc Dig..... Barclay's Missouri Digest [*A publication*]   (DLA)
Barc Dig Law Sc ... Barclay's Digest of the Law of Scotland [*A publication*]   (DLA)
B Arc E ...... Bachelor of Architectural Engineering
B Arch........ Bachelor of Architecture
Bar Ch........ Barnardiston's English Chancery Reports [*A publication*]   (DLA)
BArchAlex ... Bulletin. Societe Archeologique d'Alexandrie [*A publication*]
B Arch (Arch) ... Bachelor of Architecture in Architecture
B Arch (ArchE) ... Bachelor of Architecture in Architectural Engineering
B Arch in City Pl ... Bachelor of Architecture in City Planning
B Arch Des ... Bachelor of Architectural Design
B Arch Eng ... Bachelor of Architectural Engineering
BArchHist ... Bachelor of Architectural History
Barc High .. Barclay's Law of Highways [*A publication*]   (DLA)
BArchTech ... Bachelor of Architectural Technology
BArch & TP ... Bachelor of Architecture and Town Planning   (ADA)
Bar Chy...... Barnardiston's English Chancery Reports [*A publication*]   (DLA)
Barc Inst Invest Geol Publ ... Barcelona. Instituto de Investigaciones Geologicas. Publicaciones [*A publication*]
Barc Inst Prov Paleontol Actividades ... Barcelona. Instituto Provincial de Paleontologia. Actividades [*A publication*]
Barc Inst Prov Paleontol Bol Inf ... Barcelona. Instituto Provincial de Paleontologia. Boletin Informativo [*Sabadell*] [*A publication*]
Barc Inst Prov Paleontol Paleontol Evol ... Barcelona. Instituto Provincial de Paleontologia. Paleontologia y Evolucion [*A publication*]
Barclays R ... Barclays Review [*A publication*]
Barclays Rev ... Barclays Review [*A publication*]
Barc Mo Dig ... Barclay's Missouri Digest [*A publication*]   (DLA)
Bar & Cr... Barnewall and Cresswell's English King's Bench Reports [*A publication*]   (DLA)
BARCS...... Battlefield Area Reconnaissance System [*RADAR*] [*Army*]
Barc Univ Fac Cienc Misc Alcobe ... Barcelona Universidad. Facultad de Ciencias. Miscellanea Alcobe [*A publication*]
Barc Univ Inst Geol Mem Commun ... Barcelona Universidad. Instituto Geologia. Memorias y Communicaciones [*A publication*]
BARD .... Barden Corp. [*NASDAQ symbol*]   (NQ)
Bard .... [*Marcus Antonius*] Bardus [*Flourished, 16th century*] [*Authority cited in pre-1607 legal work*]   (DSA)
BARD .... Binational Agricultural Research and Development Fund [*Research center*] [*US-Israeli*]   (IRC)
BARD .... Bulletin. Association des Amis de Rabelais et de la Deviniere [*A publication*]
Bar Dig....... Barclay's Digest of the Law of Scotland [*A publication*]   (DLA)
BARDOC .. Barrier Doctrine [*Military*]   (NVT)
Bardsey Obs Rep ... Bardsey Observatory Report [*A publication*]
B Ar E .... Bachelor of Architectural Engineering

BAREA...... Bacteriological Reviews [*A publication*]
BAREA...... Basal Leaf Area [*Botany*]
BA in Rel Ed ... Bachelor of Arts in Religious Education
Bar Eq........ Barton's Suit in Equity [*A publication*]   (DLA)
BA Rev....... Black Academy Review [*A publication*]
Bar Exam... Bar Examiner [*A publication*]
Bar Ex Ann ... Bar Examination Annual [*1893-94*] [*A publication*]   (DLA)
Bar Ex Guide ... Bar Examination Guide [*1895-99*] [*A publication*]   (DLA)
Bar Ex J ... Bar Examination Journal [*A publication*]   (DLA)
Bar Ex Jour ... Bar Examination Journal [*A publication*]   (DLA)
BARF........ Burning Anomaly Rate Factor   (MCD)
BARFO...... Best and Revised Final Offer [*DoD*]
BARG....... Bargain   (ADA)
Bargaining Rep ... Bargaining Report [*A publication*]
Bar Gaz..... Bar Gazette [*A publication*]   (APTA)
BARGN..... Bargain   (ROG)
Barh Pre Ex ... Barham's Student's Guide to the Preliminary Examinations [*A publication*]   (DLA)
BARIDN.... Agricultural Research Council. Meat Research Institute [*Bristol*]. Biennial Report [*A publication*]
B Ariege..... Bulletin. Societe Prehistorique de l'Ariege [*A publication*]
Bar Int Pr R ... Bar. Das Internationale Privat-und-Strafrecht [*A publication*]   (DLA)
barit........... Baritone [*Music*]   (ADA)
BARITT .... Barrier Injection Transit Time [*Physics*]
BARK........ Barking [*Borough in England*]
B-ARK....... Beta-Androgenic Receptor Kinase [*An enzyme*]
BARKTH... Bark Thickness [*Botany*]
BARLANT ... Atlantic Barrier Patrol [*Eastern seaward extension of the DEW Line*] [*Obsolete*]
Bar & Leg W ... Bar and Legal World [*England*] [*A publication*]   (DLA)
Barl Just .... Barlow. Justice of Peace [*1745*] [*A publication*]   (DLA)
BARLLF.... Bulletin. Academie Royale de Langue et de Litterature Francaises [*A publication*]
BARM........ British Admiralty Repair Mission
Bar Mag..... Barrington's Magna Charta [*A publication*]   (DLA)
BARMAW ... Bulletin. Academie Royale de Medecine de Belgique [*A publication*]
Bar Mus Hist Soc J ... Barbados Museum and Historical Society. Journal [*A publication*]
Barn .... Barnabites [*Also, CRSP*] [*Roman Catholic men's religious order*]
Barn .... Barnardiston's English King's Bench Reports [*A publication*]   (DLA)
Barn .... Barnes' English Common Pleas Reports [*A publication*]   (DLA)
Bar N .... Barnes' Notes of Cases of Practice in Common Pleas [*94 English Reprint*] [*A publication*]   (DLA)
Barn .... Barnfield's Reports [*19-20 Rhode Island*] [*A publication*]   (DLA)
B & Arn...... Barron and Arnold's English Election Cases [*1843-46*] [*A publication*]   (DLA)
B Arn.......... Bibliotheca Arnamagnaeana [*A publication*]
BARN .... Biological Agricultural Reactor of the Netherlands
BARN .... Body Awareness Resource Network
BARN .... Bombing and Reconnaissance Navigation
Barn & A ... Barnewall and Adolphus' English King's Bench Reports [*109-110 English Reprint*] [*1830-34*] [*A publication*]   (DLA)
Barn & A .... Barnewall and Alderson's English King's Bench Reports [*A publication*]   (DLA)
Barn & Ad ... Barnewall and Adolphus' English King's Bench Reports [*109-110 English Reprint*] [*A publication*]   (DLA)
Barn & Ad (Eng) ... Barnewall and Adolphus' English King's Bench Reports [*109-110 English Reprint*] [*A publication*]   (DLA)
Barn & Adol ... Barnewall and Adolphus' English King's Bench Reports [*109-110 English Reprint*] [*1830-34*] [*A publication*]   (DLA)
Barn & Ald ... Barnewall and Alderson's English King's Bench Reports [*A publication*]   (DLA)
Barn & Ald (Eng) ... Barnewall and Alderson's English King's Bench Reports [*A publication*]   (DLA)
Barnard...... Barnardiston's English King's Bench Reports [*A publication*]   (DLA)
Barnard...... Barnardiston's Tempore Hardwicke Reports, Chancery [*1740-41*] [*England*] [*A publication*]   (DLA)
Barnard Ch ... Barnardiston's English Chancery Reports [*1740-41*] [*A publication*]   (DLA)
Barnard Ch (Eng) ... Barnardiston's English Chancery Reports [*1740-41*] [*A publication*]   (DLA)
Barnard Ch Rep ... Barnardiston's English Chancery Reports [*1740-41*] [*A publication*]   (DLA)
Barnardiston CC ... Barnardiston's English Chancery Cases [*1740-41*] [*A publication*]   (DLA)
Barnard KB ... Barnardiston's English King's Bench Reports [*A publication*]   (DLA)
Barnaul Gos Ped Inst Ucen Zap ... Barnaul'skii Gosudarstvennyi Pedagogiceskii Institut. Ucenye Zapiski [*A publication*]
Barn C........ Barnardiston's English Chancery Reports [*1740-41*] [*A publication*]   (DLA)
Barn & C .... Barnewall and Cresswell's English King's Bench Reports [*107-109 English Reprint*] [*A publication*]   (DLA)

Barn & C (Eng) ... Barnewall and Cresswell's English King's Bench Reports [*107-109 English Reprint*] [*A publication*]   (DLA)
Barn Ch...... Barnardiston's English Chancery Reports [*1740-41*] [*A publication*]   (DLA)
Barn & Cr... Barnewall and Cresswell's English King's Bench Reports [*107-109 English Reprint*] [*A publication*]   (DLA)
Barn & Cress ... Barnewall and Cresswell's English King's Bench Reports [*107-109 English Reprint*] [*A publication*]   (DLA)
Barn Eq Pr ... Barnes' Equity Practice [*A publication*]   (DLA)
Barnes .... Barnes' Notes of Cases of Practice in Common Pleas [*94 English Reprint*] [*A publication*]   (DLA)
Barnes NC ... Barnes' Notes of Cases of Practice in Common Pleas [*94 English Reprint*] [*A publication*]   (DLA)
Barnes Notes ... Barnes' Notes of Cases of Practice in Common Pleas [*94 English Reprint*] [*A publication*]   (DLA)
Barnes Notes (Eng) ... Barnes' Notes of Cases of Practice in Common Pleas [*94 English Reprint*] [*A publication*]   (DLA)
Barnes's Fed Code ... Barnes's Federal Code [*A publication*]   (DLA)
Barnet .... Barnet's English Central Criminal Courts Reports [*27-92*] [*A publication*]   (DLA)
Barnf & S ... Barnfield and Stiness' Reports [*20 Rhode Island*] [*A publication*]   (DLA)
Barn KB ..... Barnardiston's English King's Bench Reports [*A publication*]   (DLA)
Barn No ..... Barnes' Notes of Cases of Practice in Common Pleas [*94 English Reprint*] [*A publication*]   (DLA)
Barn Nob Cr ... Barnes and Noble Critical Study Series [*A publication*]
Barn Pr M ... Barnstaple's Printed Minutes and Proceedings [*A publication*]   (DLA)
Barn Sh...... Barnes' Exposition of the Law Respecting Sheriff [*1816*] [*A publication*]   (DLA)
BARNST ... Barnstaple [*Municipal borough in England*]
Barnw Dig ... Barnwall's Digest of the Year Books [*A publication*]   (DLA)
BARO........ Barometer   (AABC)
BARO........ Barostat   (KSC)
Bar Obs St ... Barrington's Observations upon the Statutes from Magna Charta to 21 James I [*A publication*]   (DLA)
Bar Ob Stat ... Barrington's Observations upon the Statutes from Magna Charta to 21 James I [*A publication*]   (DLA)
Baroda J Nutr ... Baroda Journal of Nutrition [*A publication*]
Baroda LR ... Baroda Law Reports [*India*] [*A publication*]   (DLA)
Baroid News Bull ... Baroid News Bulletin [*A publication*]
Baron .... Barony of Urie Court Records [*1604-1747*] [*Scotland*] [*A publication*]   (DLA)
Baron Ch Mort ... Baron on Chattel Mortgages [*A publication*]   (DLA)
BAROPS ... Barrier Operations [*Military*]   (NVT)
Barossa Hist Bull ... Barossa Historical Bulletin [*A publication*]   (APTA)
BARPAC ... Pacific Barrier Patrol [*Western seaward extension of the DEW Line*] [*Obsolete*]
Bar Prec Conv ... Barton's Modern Precedents in Conveyancing [*A publication*]   (DLA)
BARR........ Barratry [*FBI standardized term*]
BARR........ Barrier   (MSA)
BARR........ Barringer Resources, Inc. [*NASDAQ symbol*]   (NQ)
BARR........ Barrister
Barr .... Barrows' Reports [*18 Rhode Island*] [*A publication*]   (DLA)
Barr .... Barr's Reports [*1-10 Pennsylvania*] [*A publication*]   (DLA)
B & ARR.... Boston & Albany Railroad
BARR........ British Association for Rheumatology and Rehabilitation
BARR........ Bureau of Aeronautics Resident Representative [*Obsolete*] [*Navy*]
BARR........ Bureau on Agriculture and Renewable Resources
Barr & Arn ... Barron and Arnold's English Election Cases [*1843-46*] [*A publication*]   (DLA)
Barr & Aus ... Barron and Austin's English Election Cases [*1842*] [*A publication*]   (DLA)
Barr Ch Pr ... Barroll. Chancery Practice [*Maryland*] [*A publication*]   (DLA)
Bar Re........ Bar Reports in All Courts [*England*] [*A publication*]   (DLA)
Bar Rep...... Bar Reports [*1865-71*] [*A publication*]   (DLA)
Barring Obs St ... Barrington's Observations upon the Statutes from Magna Charta to 21 James I [*A publication*]   (DLA)
Barring St .. Barrington's Observations upon the Statutes from Magna Charta to 21 James I [*A publication*]   (DLA)
Barr M .... Barradall. Manuscript Reports [*Virginia*] [*A publication*]   (DLA)
BA/RRM... Biological Abstracts/Reports, Reviews, Meetings [*Formerly, BIOI*] [*A publication*]
Barr MSS .. Barradall. Manuscript Reports [*Virginia*] [*A publication*]   (DLA)
Barr Ob...... Barrington's Observations upon the Statutes from Magna Charta to 21 James [*A publication*]   (DLA)
Barr Obs St ... Barrington's Observations upon the Statutes from Magna Charta to 21 James I [*A publication*]   (DLA)
Barron & H Fed Pr & Proc ... Barron and Holtzoff's Federal Practice and Procedure [*A publication*]   (DLA)
Barron Mir ... Barron's Mirror of Parliament [*A publication*]   (DLA)
Barrows...... Barrows' Reports [*18 Rhode Island*] [*A publication*]   (DLA)
Barrows (RI) ... Barrows' Reports [*18 Rhode Island*] [*A publication*]   (DLA)
Barrow (W J) Res Lab Publ ... Barrow (W. J.) Research Laboratory. Publication [*A publication*]
Barr (PA) ... Barr's Reports [*1-10 Pennsylvania*] [*A publication*]   (DLA)

Barr St .... Barrington's Observations upon the Statutes from Magna Charta to 21 James I [*A publication*] (DLA)
Barr Ten ..... Barry on Tenures [*A publication*] (DLA)
Barry Build Soc ... Barry on Building Societies [*A publication*] (DLA)
Barry Ch Jur ... Barry. Statutory Jurisdiction of Chancery [*1861*] [*A publication*] (DLA)
Barry Ch Pr ... Barry. Statutory Jurisdiction of Chancery [*1861*] [*A publication*] (DLA)
Barry Conv ... Barry. Practice of Conveyancing [*1865*] [*A publication*] (DLA)
Barry Forms Conv ... Barry on Forms and Precedents in Conveyancing [*A publication*] (DLA)
Barry Ten ... Barry on Tenures [*A publication*] (DLA)
BARS .... Armstrong-Spallumcheen Museum and Archives Society, Armstrong, British Columbia [*Library symbol*] [*National Library of Canada*] (NLC)
BARS .... Backup Attitude Reference System
BARS .... Ballistic Analysis Research System
BARS .... Baryon-Isobar Rest System
BARS .... Baseline Accounting and Reporting System (NASA)
BARS .... Behaviorally Anchored Rating Scale
BARS .... Bell Audit Relate System [*Bell Laboratories*]
BARS .... Boating Accident Reports System [*Coast Guard*] [*Information service or system*] (IID)
B-ARS .... British-American Rhykenological Society (EA)
BARS .... Budget Analysis Reporting System (MCD)
Bar de Sa .... Bartholomaeus de Saliceto [*Deceased, 1411*] [*Authority cited in pre-1607 legal work*] (DSA)
BARSA ...... Billing, Accounts Receivable, Sales Analysis (IBMDP)
Bar de Sal .. Bartholomaeus de Saliceto [*Deceased, 1411*] [*Authority cited in pre-1607 legal work*] (DSA)
Bar de Sali ... Bartholomaeus de Saliceto [*Deceased, 1411*] [*Authority cited in pre-1607 legal work*] (DSA)
B Ar Sc .... Bachelor of Arts and Sciences
Bar SC Rep ... Barbour's Supreme Court Reports [*New York*] [*A publication*] (DLA)
BARSDJ .... North Carolina. Agricultural Research Service. Bulletin [*A publication*]
BARS-F ..... Bomber Air Relay System - Fly Along (MCD)
BARSTUR ... Barking Sands Tactical Underwater Range [*Naval Oceanographic Office*]
BARS-X ..... Bomber Air Relay System - Extension (MCD)
BART .... Baronet [*British*]
Bart .... Bartolus de Sassoferrato [*Deceased, 1357*] [*Authority cited in pre-1607 legal work*] (DSA)
BART .... Barton Industries, Inc. [*NASDAQ symbol*] (NQ)
BART .... Baseline Armor Reliability Test [*Army*] (MCD)
BART .... Basic Armor Reliability Test (MCD)
BART .... Bay Area Rapid Transit [*San Francisco area, California*]
BART .... Best Available Retrofit Technology [*Environmental Protection Agency*]
BART .... Bio-Automated Roving Target [*Gun-like toy*]
BART .... Brooklyn Army Terminal
BARTAP ... Barge Transportation Appraisal Program [*Military*] (MCD)
Bart Bri ...... Bartholomaeus Brixiensis [*Deceased circa 1258*] [*Authority cited in pre-1607 legal work*] (DSA)
Bart de Cap ... Bartholomaeus de Capua [*Deceased, 1328*] [*Authority cited in pre-1607 legal work*] (DSA)
Bart Cepol ... Bartholomaeus Cepolla [*Deceased, 1477*] [*Authority cited in pre-1607 legal work*] (DSA)
Bart Cong Election Cases ... Bartlett's Congressional Election Cases [*A publication*] (DLA)
Bart Conv ... Barton's Science of Conveyancing [*2nd ed.*] [*1810-22*] [*A publication*] (DLA)
Bart El Cas ... Bartlett's Congressional Election Cases [*A publication*] (DLA)
Bart Elec Cas ... Bartlett's Congressional Election Cases [*A publication*] (DLA)
Bart Eq .... Barton's Suit in Equity [*A publication*] (DLA)
Barth .... Bartholomaeus Brixiensis [*Deceased circa 1258*] [*Authority cited in pre-1607 legal work*] (DSA)
Barth Belenz ... Bartholomaeus Belenzinus de Modena [*Deceased, 1478*] [*Authority cited in pre-1607 legal work*] (DSA)
Barth Brix ... Bartholomaeus Brixiensis [*Deceased circa 1258*] [*Authority cited in pre-1607 legal work*] (DSA)
Bartho Belenz ... Bartholomaeus Belenzinus de Modena [*Deceased, 1478*] [*Authority cited in pre-1607 legal work*] (DSA)
Barthol .... Bartholomaeus de Exeter [*Flourished, 12th century*] [*Authority cited in pre-1607 legal work*] (DSA)
Bartholoman ... Bartholoman's Reports, Yorkshire Lent Assize [*March 9, 1911*] [*England*] [*A publication*] (DLA)
Bartho Mutinen ... Bartholomaeus Belenzinus (Mutinensis) [*Deceased, 1478*] [*Authority cited in pre-1607 legal work*] (DSA)
Bartho de Sali ... Bartholomaeus de Saliceto [*Deceased, 1411*] [*Authority cited in pre-1607 legal work*] (DSA)
Bart Ind ...... Bartlett's Index of the Laws of Rhode Island [*A publication*] (DLA)
Bartlett Tree Res Lab Bull ... Bartlett Tree Research Laboratory. Bulletin [*A publication*]
Bart L Pr .... Barton's Law Practice [*A publication*] (DLA)
Bart Max ... Barton's Maxims in Conveyancing [*A publication*] (DLA)
Bart Mines ... Bartlett's Law of Mining [*1850*] [*A publication*] (DLA)
Barto .... Bartholomaeus [*Authority cited in pre-1607 legal work*] (DSA)

Barto .... Bartolus de Sassoferrato [*Deceased, 1357*] [*Authority cited in pre-1607 legal work*] (DSA)
Bartol Camer ... Bartholomaeus Camerarius [*Deceased, 1564*] [*Authority cited in pre-1607 legal work*] (DSA)
Bart Prec Conv ... Barton's Modern Precedents in Conveyancing [*3rd ed.*] [*1826*] [*A publication*] (DLA)
BART REG ... Barton Regis [*England*]
BARTS ...... St. Bartholomew's Hospital [*London*]
Bart Socin .. Bartholomaeus Socinus [*Deceased, 1507*] [*Authority cited in pre-1607 legal work*] (DSA)
B Art Tournus ... Bulletin. Amis des Arts et des Sciences de Tournus [*A publication*]
BARTU ...... Bureau of Aeronautics Training Unit [*Obsolete*] [*Navy*]
BARU .... Barometric Altitude Reference Unit
BARUK ...... Board of Airline Representatives in the United Kingdom
BARV .... Beach Armored Recovery Vehicle
BARY .... Barry's Jewelers, Inc. [*Duarte, CA*] [*NASDAQ symbol*] (NQ)
Baryon Reson Conf ... Baryon Resonances. Conference [*A publication*]
BARZREX ... Bartok Archives Z-Symbol Rhythm Extraction [*Data processing*]
BAS .... Bachelor of Agricultural Science
BAS .... Bachelor of Applied Science
BAS .... Bachelor of Architectural Science
BAS .... Bachelor of Arts and Sciences
BAS .... Bachelor of Arts in Speech
BAS .... Balalae [*Solomon Islands*] [*Airport symbol*] (OAG)
BAS .... Bancaria [*A publication*]
BAS .... Base (DCTA)
BAS .... Basel [*Bale*] [*Switzerland*] [*Seismograph station code, US Geological Survey*] (SEIS)
BAS .... Basic [*Rate*] [*Value of the English pound*]
BAS .... Basic Airspeed [*Aviation*]
BAS .... Basic Allowance for Subsistence [*Military*]
BAS .... Basic Angle System
BAS .... BASIC [*Beginner's All-Purpose Symbolic Instruction Code*] Program File [*Data processing*]
Bas .... Basophils [*Hematology*]
BAS .... Bass ADS [*NYSE symbol*] (SPSG)
BAS .... Basso [*Music*]
BAS .... Bastard [*Slang*] (DSUE)
BAS .... Battlefield Automated Systems [*Data processing*] [*Military*] (RDA)
BAS .... Bay Area Library and Information System, Hayward, CA [*OCLC symbol*] (OCLC)
Bas .... Bazianus [*Deceased, 1197*] [*Authority cited in pre-1607 legal work*] (DSA)
BAS .... Behavioral Approach Scale [*Psychology*]
BAS .... Bell Audit System [*Bell Laboratories*]
BAS .... Bendix Antiskid System [*Automotive engineering*]
BAS .... Benzylantiserotonin [*Pharmacology*]
BAS .... Bioactive Aortic Substance [*Biochemistry*]
BAS .... Bioanalytical Systems
BAS .... Biological Agent Simulant (MCD)
BAS .... Biological Anthropological Section (EA)
BAS .... Bleed Air System
BAS .... Blind Approach System [*Aviation*] (MCD)
BAS .... Block Automation System [*NYSE trading computer*]
BAS .... Bochumer Anglistische Studien [*A publication*]
BAS .... Bomb Alarm System [*Air Force*]
BAS .... Bomb Assembly Spares (NG)
BAS .... Book of Alternative Services [*Ecclesiastical*]
BAS .... Books-Across-the-Sea [*Project*]
BAS .... Boolean Assignment Statement [*Mathematics*]
BAS .... Brazilian-American Society [*Defunct*] (EA)
BAS .... Brazilian American Survey [*A publication*]
BAS .... British Acoustical Society
BAS .... British Allergy Society
BAS .... British Antarctic Survey [*Research center*] (IRC)
BAS .... British Army Staff
BAS .... British Association of Settlements and Social Action Centres
BAS .... Budget Allocation Sheets (MCD)
BAS .... Budget Allocation Summary (MCD)
BAS .... Bulletin of the Atomic Scientists [*A publication*]
BAS .... Bureau of Analyzed Samples [*British*]
BAS .... Business Air Service Ltd. [*Airline*] [*Canada*]
BAS .... Business and Society [*A publication*]
BASA .... British Adhesive and Sealants Association
BASA .... British Association of Seed Analysts
Bas Adv Tra ... Basic Advance Training
BASAF ...... British and South African Forum
BASA Mag ... BASA [*British Australian Studies Association*] Magazine [*A publication*]
BASATA ... British and South Asian Trade Association [*British Overseas Trade Board*] (DS)
BASB .... British Antarctic Survey. Bulletin [*A publication*]
BASBWE .. British Association of Symphonic Bands and Wind Ensembles (EAIO)
BA Sc .... Bachelor of Agricultural Science
BA Sc .... Bachelor of Applied Science
BASC .... Base Activation Statistical Control
BASC .... Berlin Air Safety Center

BASC........ British Association for Shooting and Conservation
BASCA...... British Academy of Songwriters, Composers, and Authors
BASCD...... British Association for the Study of Community Dentistry
BAS CON ... Basso Continuo [Continued Bass] [Music]   (ROG)
BASCOP ... Base Communications Plan [United States Army Communications Command]   (MCD)
BASD........ Basic Active Service Date   (AABC)
BASD........ Bollettino di Archeologia e Storia Dalmata [A publication]
BASD........ British Antarctic Survey. Data [A publication]
BASE........ BankAmericard Service Exchange
BASE........ Base Ten Systems, Inc. [NASDAQ symbol]   (NQ)
BASE........ Basic Army Strategic Estimate [A document]
BASE........ Basic Automation Systems Elements
BASE........ Basic Semantic Element [Data processing]   (DIT)
BASE........ Battlefield Surveillance [RADAR] Electronics   (MCD)
BASE........ Behavioral Academic Self-Esteem [Student personality test] [Psychology]
BASE........ Beta-Alumina Solid Electrolyte
BASE........ Brokerage Accounting System Elements [IBM computer program]
BASE........ Buildings, Antennas, Spans, and Earth Formations [Fixed-object parachuting]
BASE........ Buyer Attitudes and Sales Experiences [LIMRA]
BASEC...... Base Section [Military]
BASecStud ... Bachelor of Arts in Secretarial Studies   (ADA)
BASEDEV ... Base Development Report
BASEEFA ... British Approvals Service for Electrical Equipment in Flammable Atmospheres [General Council of British Shipping]   (DS)
BASEFOR ... Base Force
Basel Inst Immunol Annu Rep ... Basel Institute for Immunology. Annual Report [A publication]
BASEMAG ... Base de Datos Geomagneticos [Instituto Geografico Nacional] [Database]
BASEOPS ... Base Operations
BASES...... Beam Approach Seeker Evaluation System [Air Force]   (MCD)
BASES...... British Anti-Smoking Education Society
BASESERVUNIT ... Base Service Unit [Navy]
BASF........ Badische Anilin- und Sodafabrik AG [Baden Aniline and Soda Factory] [Federal Republic of Germany]
BASF Inf ... BASF [Badische Anilin- und Sodafabrik] Information [A publication]
BASF Rev .. BASF [Badische Anilin- und Sodafabrik] Review [A publication]
BASH .... Baroque All Style High [Acronym is title of silk screen by sculptor Eduardo Paolozzi]
BASH .... Bird Aircraft Strike Hazard
BASH .... Body Acceleration Synchronous with the Heartbeat [Cardiology]
BASH .... Booksellers' Association Service House [British]
BashSSR.... Bashkir Soviet Socialist Republic
BASI .... Bulletin. American Swedish Institute [A publication]
BASI .... Bureau of Air Safety Investigation [Australia]
B Asian Schol ... Bulletin of Concerned Asian Scholars [A publication]
BASIC .... Banking and Securities Industry Committee [Inactive]
BASIC .... Basic Algebraic Symbolic Interpretive Compiler   (IEEE)
BASIC .... Basic Appraisal System for Incoming Components
BASIC .... Basic Automatic Stored Instruction Computer   (BUR)
BASIC .... Battle Area Surveillance and Integrated Communications System [Marine Corps]
BASIC .... Bedell Advertising Selling Improvement Corporation
BASIC .... Beginner's All-Purpose Symbolic Instruction Code [Programming language invented by T. E. Kurtz and J. G. Kemeny at Dartmouth College in 1963-64]
BASIC .... Biological Abstracts' Subjects in Context [A publication]
BASIC .... Bridge and Structures Information Center [University of Pittsburgh Department of Civil Engineering] [Information service or system]   (IID)
BASIC .... Bulletin. American Society for Information Science [A publication]
Basic Appl Histochem ... Basic and Applied Histochemistry [A publication]
Basic Biol Color Ser ... Basic Biology in Color Series [A publication]
Basic Clin Aspects Neurosci ... Basic and Clinical Aspects of Neuroscience [A publication]
Basic Clin Endocrinol ... Basic and Clinical Endocrinology [A publication]
Basic and Clin Immunol ... Basic and Clinical Immunology [A publication]
Basic Clin Nutr ... Basic and Clinical Nutrition [A publication]
Basic Doc World Fertil Surv ... Basic Documentation/World Fertility Survey [A publication]
BASIC (English) ... British-American Scientific International Commercial English
Basic Life Sci ... Basic Life Sciences [A publication]
Basic Neurochem 2nd Ed ... Basic Neurochemistry. 2nd Edition [A publication]
BASICPAC ... BASIC [Beginner's All-Purpose Symbolic Instruction Code] Processor and Computer
BASICPAC ... Battle Area Surveillance and Integrated Communications System Processor and Computer [Marine Corps]
Basic Pharmacol Ther ... Basic Pharmacology Therapeutics [Japan] [A publication]

Basic Rec Rep LA Dep Public Works ... Basic Records Report. Louisiana Department of Public Works [A publication]
Basic Rec Rep US Dep Inter Geol Surv ... Basic Record Report. United States Department of Interior. Geological Survey [A publication]
Basic Res Cardiol ... Basic Research in Cardiology [A publication]
BASICS..... Battle Area Surveillance and Integrated Communications System [Marine Corps]   (IEEE)
Basic Sci Princ Nucl Med ... Basic Science Principles of Nuclear Medicine [A publication]
Basic Sleep Mech ... Basic Sleep Mechanisms [A publication]
BASICTNG ... Basic Training [Military]   (NVT)
BASIDS..... Biologiski Aktivo Savienojumu Kimijas Tehnologija Rigas Politehniskaja Instituta [A publication]
Basin Plann Rep Allegheny Basin Reg Water Resour Plann Board ... Basin Planning Report. Allegheny Basin Regional Water Resources Planning Board [A publication]
Basin Plann Rep NY State Dep Environ Conserv ORB ... Basin Planning Report. New York State Department of Environmental Conservation. Series ORB [A publication]
Basin Plann Rep NY State Dept Environ Conserv ARB ... Basin Planning Report. New York State Department of Environmental Conservation. Series ARB [A publication]
Basin Plann Rep NY State Water Resour Comm ENB ... Basin Planning Report. New York State Water Resources Commission. Series ENB [A publication]
BASIS........ Bank Automated Service Information System   (BUR)
BASIS........ Base-Stored Image Sensor
BASIS........ Basic Achievement Skills Individual Screener [Educational test]
BASIS........ Battelle Automated Search Information System [Database management system] [Battelle Memorial Institute] [Information service or system]
BASIS........ Bay Area Spatial Information System [Geogroup Corp.] [Information service or system]   (IID)
BASIS........ Biological and Agricultural Sciences Information Service [University of Minnesota, St. Paul] [Information service or system]   (IID)
BASIS........ Booking and Sampling for Indirect Standards [British]
BASIS........ Budgetary and Scheduling Information System   (MCD)
BASIS........ Bulletin. American Society for Information Science [A publication]
BASIS........ Bureau of Accreditation and School Improvement Studies [University of Michigan] [Research center]   (RCD)
BASIS........ Burroughs Advanced Statistical Inquiry System [Data processing]   (BUR)
BASIS........ Burroughs and Sperry Information Systems [Suggested name for the corporation formed by the Burroughs/Sperry merger]
BASJE....... Bolivian Air-Shower Joint Experiment
BASKAV ... Baskerville Chemical Journal [A publication]
Baskerville Chem J ... Baskerville Chemical Journal [A publication]
Baskir Gos Univ Ucen Zap ... Baskirskii Gosudarstvennyi Universitet. Ucenye Zapiski [A publication]
BASL .... Bochumer Arbeiten zur Sprach- und Literaturwissenschaft [A publication]
BASLAY.... Bulletin. Academie et Societe Lorraines des Sciences [A publication]
Basler Beitr Chir ... Basler Beitraege zur Chirurgie [A publication]
Basler Beitr Ethnol ... Basler Beitraege zur Ethnologie [A publication]
Basler Beitr Geogr ... Basler Beitraege zur Geographie [A publication]
Basler Veroeffentl Gesch Med Biol ... Basler Veroeffentlichungen zur Geschichte der Medizin und der Biologie [A publication]
Basler Z Gesch & Altertumsk ... Basler Zeitschrift fuer Geschichte und Altertumskunde [A publication]
BASLP....... Bulletin. Australian Society of Legal Philosophy [A publication]
BASM........ Ashcroft Museum, British Columbia [Library symbol] [National Library of Canada]   (NLC)
BASM........ Bachelor of Arts, Master of Science
BASM........ Bachelor of Arts in Sacred Music   (BJA)
BASM........ Bollettino. Associazione per gli Studi Mediterranei [A publication]
BASM........ British Association of Sport Medicine
BASO .... Base Accountable Supply Officer [Air Force]
BASO .... Basophil [Hematology]   (DHSM)
BASO .... Brigade Air Support Officer [Military] [British]
BASO .... British Association of Surgical Oncology
BASO .... Bulletin. American Schools of Oriental Research in Jerusalem and Bagdad [A publication]
BASO .... Bureau of Aeronautics Shipment Order [Obsolete] [Navy]
BASOC..... Brigade Air Support Operations Centre [Military] [British]
BASOIS..... Base Operating Information System [Formerly, COCOAS]
BASOPS..... Base Operations Office
BASOPS (SMS) ... Base Operating Information System (Supply Management System)
BASOR...... Bulletin. American Schools of Oriental Research [A publication]
BASORSS ... Bulletin. American Schools of Oriental Research. Supplementary Series [A publication]
BA in Sp... Bachelor of Arts in Speech
BASP......... Bollettino. Reale Accademia di Scienze, Lettere, e Belle Arti di Palermo [A publication]
BASP........ British Association of Social Psychiatry

BASP......... Bulletin. Academie de Science de St. Petersbourg [*A publication*]
BASP......... Bulletin. American Society of Papyrologists [*A publication*]
BASPA...... British Amateur Strand Pulling Association
BASPM..... Basic Planning Memorandum (NATG)
BASPR...... Bulletin. American School of Prehistoric Research [*A publication*]
BASR........ Bulletin. Academie des Sciences de Russie [*A publication*]
BASR........ Bureau of Applied Social Research [*Columbia University*] (IID)
BASRA...... British American Scientific Research Association
Basrah Nat Hist Mus Publ ... Basrah Natural History Museum. Publication [*A publication*]
Bas R Card ... Basic Research in Cardiology [*A publication*]
B/ASRE..... British Admiralty Signal RADAR Establishment
B As S ...... Bachelor of Association Science
BASS........ Backup Avionics Subsystem Software (MCD)
BASS........ Base Augmentation Support Set
BASS........ Bass Anglers Sportsman Society (EA)
BASS........ Battlefield Area Surveillance System (MCD)
BASS........ Behavioral and Social Sciences
BASS........ Beitraege zur Assyriologie und Semitischen Sprachwissenschaft [*A publication*]
BASS........ Belgian Archives for the Social Sciences [*Information service or system*] (IID)
BASS........ Benthic Acoustic Stress Sensor [*Oceanographic instrument*]
BASS........ Best Available Shelter Survey [*of fallout shelters*] [*Civil Defense*]
BASS........ British Airways Shuttle Services
BASS........ British Australian Settlers Society
BASS........ Broadband Analysis SONAR Surveillance (MCD)
BASSAC... British Association of Settlements and Social Action Centres
BAssBude .. Bulletin. Association Guillaume Bude [*Paris*] [*A publication*]
B As Sc....... Bachelor of Association Science
BASS CON ... Basso Continuo [*Continued Bass*] [*Music*]
BASS CONT ... Basso Continuo [*Continued Bass*] [*Music*]
Bass Crim Pl ... Bassett's Illinois Criminal Pleading and Practice [*A publication*] (DLA)
B Ass Geogr Franc ... Bulletin. Association des Geographes Francais [*A publication*]
B Ass Mos Ant ... Bulletin d'Information. Association Internationale pour l'Etude de la Mosaique Antique [*A publication*]
B Assoc Cadres Dir Industr Progres Soc Econ ... Bulletin. Association de Cadres Dirigeants de l'Industrie pour le Progres Social et Economique [*A publication*]
B Ass Pro Aventico ... Bulletin. Association Pro Aventico [*A publication*]
BASSR....... British Antarctic Survey. Scientific Reports [*A publication*]
Bass Sound ... Bass Sound Post [*A publication*]
BAST........ Bastard (DLA)
BAST........ Bastardy [*FBI standardized term*]
BAST........ Best Available and Safest Technology
BAST........ Board on Army Science and Technology [*National Research Council, Academies of Science and Engineering, and Institute of Medicine*]
BAST........ Boric Acid Storage Tank (IEEE)
BASt......... Bundesanstalt fuer Strassenwesen [*Federal Highway Research Institute*] [*Database producer*] (IID)
B Astr I Cz ... Bulletin. Astronomical Institutes of Czechoslovakia [*A publication*]
BASTUR ... Baking Sands Tactical Underwater Range [*Oahu, HI*]
BASU........ Balkan Studies [*A publication*]
BA Sud Est Eur ... Bulletin d'Archeologie Sud-Est Europeenne [*A publication*]
BASURSS ... Bulletin. Academie des Sciences de l'URSS [*A publication*]
BASW....... Bell Alarm Switch (AAG)
BASW....... British Army Staff, Washington (MCD)
BASW....... British Association of Social Workers
BASX........ Basler Airlines, Inc. [*Air carrier designation symbol*]
BASYS...... Basic System (IEEE)
BAT .... Bachelor of Arts in Teaching
bat .... Baltic [*MARC language code*] [*Library of Congress*] (LCCP)
BAT .... Basic Air Temperature
BAT .... Basic Armor Training (MCD)
BAT .... Bataille [*A publication*]
BAT .... Batch File [*Data processing*]
BAT .... Batean [*Ship's rigging*] (ROG)
BAT .... Bathurst Paper Ltd. [*Toronto Stock Exchange symbol*]
BAT .... Battalion
BAT .... Battalion Antitank Recoilless Rifle
BAT .... Batter
BAT .... Battery (AAG)
BAT .... Battle (AABC)
BAT .... Battleship (MUGU)
BAT .... Bayram-Ali [*USSR*] [*Seismograph station code, US Geological Survey*] [*Closed*] (SEIS)
BAT .... Beam Approach Training [*Military*]
BAT .... Behavioral Avoidance Test [*Psychometrics*]
BAT .... Bell Advanced Tilt Rotor (MCD)
BAT .... Benzilic Acid Tropine Ester [*Also, BETE, BTE*] [*Pharmacology*]
BAT .... Best Available Technology
BAT .... Best Available Treatment (MCD)
BAT .... Bioassay Tank [*Spacecraft*] [*NASA*]

BAT .... Biological Abstracts on Tape [*Biosciences Information Service*] [*Information service or system*]
BAT .... Biomedical Application Teams [*NASA*]
BAT .... Blackstone Advantage Term Trust [*NYSE symbol*] (SPSG)
BAT .... Blind Approach Training [*Air Force*]
BAT .... Bloom Analogies Test [*Intelligence test*]
BAT .... Boeing Air Transport
BAT .... Boletin Arqueologico de Tarragona [*A publication*]
BAT .... Bolshoi Alt-Azimuth Telescope [*USSR*]
BAT .... Bore Autonomic Tester
BAT .... Boric Acid Tank [*Nuclear energy*] (NRCH)
BAT .... Boric Acid Transfer [*Nuclear energy*] (NRCH)
BAT .... Boston Athenaeum, Boston, MA [*OCLC symbol*] (OCLC)
BAT .... Branch Assistance Team [*Military*] (AABC)
BAT .... Break-Away Torque [*Automotive engineering*]
BAT .... British Aerial Transport Ltd.
BAT .... British-American Tobacco Co.
BAT .... British Antarctic Territory
BAT .... Bromoacetamidothymidine [*Antineoplastic drug*]
BAT .... Brown Adipose Tissue [*Physiology*]
BAT .... Bureau of Air Transport [*Philippines*] (DS)
BAT .... Bureau of Apprenticeship and Training [*Department of Labor*]
BAT .... Bureau de l'Assistance Technique [*Technical Assistance Bureau*]
BAT .... Buses and Trucks
BAT .... Bushwaster Armored Turret (MCD)
BAT .... Butler Air Transport Ltd.
BATA........ Black American Travel Association [*Defunct*]
BATAB...... Baker and Taylor's Automated Buying System [*Teleordering system*] [*Baker & Taylor Companies*] [*Information service or system*] (IID)
BaTaSYSTEMS ... Baker & Taylor Electronic Book Ordering Service [*Baker & Taylor Companies*] [*Trademark*]
BATBAMS ... British Antitank Bar Mine System (MCD)
BAT-C...... Behavioral Assertiveness Test for Children
BATC........ Big Apple Triathlon Club (EA)
BATC........ Boeing Atlantic Test Center (KSC)
BATC........ British Amateur Television Club
BATC........ British-American Tobacco Co.
BATC........ Burnside-Ott Aviation Training Center [*Florida*]
BAT CHG ... Battery Charger [*Military*] (MSA)
Batch Mfg Cor ... Batchelder's Law of Massachusetts Manufacturing Corporations [*A publication*] (DLA)
BATCRULANT ... Battleships and Cruisers, Atlantic Fleet
BATCRUPAC ... Battleships and Cruisers, Pacific Fleet
BATCS ...... Breakdown Air Traffic Control Services (FAAC)
Bat Dig....... Battle's Digest [*North Carolina*] [*A publication*] (DLA)
BATDIV.... Battleship Division
BATE........ Base Activation Test Equipment
BATEA...... Best Available Technology Economically Achievable [*Wastewater treatment*]
Bate Ag ...... Bateman on Agency [*A publication*] (DLA)
BATEAM ... Biomedical Technology Transfer Team
Bate Auct ... Bateman. Law of Auctions [*11th ed.*] [*1953*] [*A publication*] (DLA)
Bate Com L ... Bateman's Commercial Law [*A publication*] (DLA)
Bate Const ... Bateman's United States Constitutional Law [*A publication*] (DLA)
Bate Exc..... Bateman. General Laws of Excise [*2nd ed.*] [*1840*] [*A publication*] (DLA)
BATELCO ... Bahamas Telecommunications Corporation [*Telecommunications service*] (TSSD)
BATELCO ... Bahrain Telecommunications Company (TSSD)
Bateman E ... Bateman Eichler and Hill Richards. News Release [*A publication*]
Bateman E ... Bateman Eichler and Hill Richards. Research Report [*A publication*]
BATES ...... Ballistic Test and Evaluation Systems (KSC)
Bates .... Bates' Delaware Chancery Reports [*A publication*] (DLA)
BATES ...... Battlefield Artillery Target Engagement System (MCD)
Bates' Ann St ... Bates' Annotated Revised Statutes [*Ohio*] [*A publication*] (DLA)
Bates Ch..... Bates' Delaware Chancery Reports [*A publication*] (DLA)
Bates' Dig .. Bates' Digest [*Ohio*] [*A publication*] (DLA)
Bateson ...... Leicester Records [*Municipal Courts, 1103-1603*] [*England*] [*A publication*] (DLA)
Bates Part .. Bates' Law of Partnership [*A publication*] (DLA)
BA in Text ... Bachelor of Science in Textiles
BATF........ Beam Approach Training Flight [*British military*] (DMA)
BATF........ Biological Aerosol Test Facility [*Army*]
BATF........ Boletin. Asociacion Tucumana de Folklore [*A publication*]
BATF........ Bureau of Alcohol, Tobacco, and Firearms [*Department of the Treasury*]
BATFOR ... Battle Force
BATH........ Back Again to Hoover [*Slogan during 1974 economic downturn*]
BATH........ Best Available True Heading (MCD)
BA Theo..... Bachelor of Arts in Theology
BATHRM ... Bathroom [*Classified advertising*] (ADA)
Baths Bath Eng ... Baths and Bath Engineering [*A publication*]

Baths Serv Rec Mgmt ... Baths Service and Recreation Management [*A publication*]
BATHY ..... Bathythermograph [*Oceanography*] (MSC)
Batim Int.... Batiment International [*France*] [*A publication*]
Batim Int Build Res Pract ... Batiment International/Building Research and Practice [*A publication*]
BATL........ Business Apprentices Training Limited [*Australia*]
BATLANT ... Battleships, Atlantic Fleet
BATLSK.... British Army Training Liaison Staff, Kenya
BATM .... Atlin Historical Museum, British Columbia [*Library symbol*] [*National Library of Canada*] (NLC)
BATM .... Baird Corp. [*NASDAQ symbol*] (NQ)
BATM .... British Admiralty Technical Mission [*World War II*]
BATM .... Bureau of Air Traffic Management
BATMA..... Bulletin. Association Technique Maritime et Aeronautique [*A publication*]
BATN .... Battalion (ROG)
BATNEEC ... Best Available Technology Not Entailing Excessive Costs [*British*]
BATO .... Balloon-Assisted Takeoff [*Air Force*]
BATOD ..... British Association of Teachers of the Deaf
B Atom Sci ... Bulletin of the Atomic Scientists [*A publication*]
Baton Rou B ... Greater Baton Rouge Business Report [*A publication*]
BATP........ Boric Acid Transfer Pump (IEEE)
BATP .... Bridge Across the Pond Tom Jones Fan Club (EA)
BATPAC ... Battleships, Pacific Fleet
BATRA...... Battelle Technical Review [*A publication*]
BATRAM ... Battery Random Access Memory [*External storage system*] [*Data processing*]
BATRON .. Battleship Squadron
BATROP... Baratropic (FAAC)
BATRS ...... British Amateur Tape Recording Society
BATRY ...... Battery
BATS .... Ballistic Aerial Target System
BATS .... Basic Additional Teleprocessing Support [*Data processing*] (BUR)
BATS .... Beta Alternating Transmission System (MCD)
BATS .... Bulk Filtering Acquisition and Tracking System (MCD)
BATS .... Business Air Transport Service
BATSE ...... Burst and Transient Source Experiment [*Gamma Ray Observatory satellite data collection*]
BATSHIP ... Battleship
BATSHIPSBATFORPAC ... Battleships, Battle Force, Pacific Fleet
BATSHIPSLANT ... Battleships, Atlantic Fleet
BATSHIPSPAC ... Battleships, Pacific Fleet
Bat Sp Perf ... Batten. Specific Performance on Contracts [*1849*] [*A publication*] (DLA)
BATSS....... Battlefield Automated Tactical Support System (MCD)
Bat Stan ... Batten on the Stannaries Act [*A publication*] (DLA)
Bat Stat...... Battle's Revised Statutes of North Carolina [*1873*] [*A publication*] (DLA)
BATT........ Barry All the Time (EA)
BATT........ Battalion
BATT........ Batten (KSC)
BATT........ Battery (KSC)
BATT........ Battery [*FBI standardized term*]
Batt .... Batty's Irish King's Bench Reports [*A publication*] (DLA)
BATT........ British Army Training Team
BATTDW ... Batteries [*New York*] [*A publication*]
Battelle Inf (Frankfurt) ... Battelle Information (Frankfurt) [*A publication*]
Battelle Inst Mater Sci Colloq ... Battelle Memorial Institute. Materials Science Colloquia [*A publication*]
Battelle Mem Inst Battelle Inst Mater Sci Colloq ... Battelle Memorial Institute. Battelle Institute Materials Science Colloquia [*A publication*]
Battelle Mem Inst DCIC Rep ... Battelle Memorial Institute. Defense Ceramic Information Center. DCIC Report [*A publication*]
Battelle Mem Inst DMIC Memo ... Battelle Memorial Institute. Defense Metals Information Center. DMIC Memorandum [*A publication*]
Battelle Mem Inst DMIC Rep ... Battelle Memorial Institute. Defense Metals Information Center. DMIC Report [*A publication*]
Battelle Mg ... Battelle Monographs [*A publication*]
Battelle Res Outlook ... Battelle Research Outlook [*A publication*]
Battelle T ... Battelle Today [*A publication*]
Battelle Tech R ... Battelle Technical Review [*A publication*]
Battel R & D ... Battelle Memorial Institute. Probable Levels of R and D Expenditures [*A publication*]
Battery Bimon ... Battery Bimonthly [*A publication*]
Battery Counc Int Conv Proc ... Battery Council. International Convention. Proceedings [*A publication*]
Battery Mn ... Battery Man [*A publication*]
BATTLE.... Battalion Analyzer and Tactical Trainer for Local Engagements (MCD)

Battle's Revisal ... Battle's Revised Statutes of North Carolina [*1873*] [*A publication*] (DLA)
BATTN...... Battalion (ADA)
Batts' Ann St ... Batts' Annotated Revised Civil Statutes [*Texas*] [*A publication*] (DLA)
Batts' Rev St ... Batts' Annotated Revised Civil Statutes [*Texas*] [*A publication*] (DLA)
BATTY ...... Battery
Batty (Ir).... Batty's Irish King's Bench Reports [*A publication*] (DLA)
BATU .... Brotherhood of Asian Trade Unionists (EAIO)
BATUS...... British Army Training Unit, Suffield [*British military*] (DMA)
BATV........ Boilerplates Aerodynamic Test Vehicle (MCD)
BATV........ Bureau for Adult Thalidomide Victims [*West Germany*]
BAU .... Baseband Assembly Unit
BAU .... Bauru [*Brazil*] [*Airport symbol*] (OAG)
BAU .... Bay Resources [*Vancouver Stock Exchange symbol*]
BAU .... Beau Canada Exploration Ltd. [*Toronto Stock Exchange symbol*]
BAU .... Bombing Analysis Unit [*Supreme Headquarters, Allied Expeditionary Force*] [*World War II*]
BAU .... British Absolute Unit
BAU........... Business as Usual
BAUA .... Business Aircraft Users' Association [*British*]
BAUADE .. US Department of Agriculture. Science and Education Administration. Bibliographies and Literature of Agriculture [*A publication*]
Bau Betr ..... Bau und Betrieb [*A publication*]
B Auckland Inst Mus ... Bulletin. Auckland Institute and Museum [*A publication*]
BAUD........ Baudot Code
B Au E........ Bachelor of Automobile Engineering
Bauelem Elektrotech ... Bauelemente der Elektrotechnik [*A publication*]
B Au Eng.... Bachelor of Automobile Engineering
Bauen Landwirtsch ... Bauen fuer die Landwirtschaft [*A publication*]
BAUF........ Budget Authorization and Updating Form (MCD)
BAUFO ..... Bauforschungsprojekte [*Building Research Projects*] [*Fraunhofer Society*] [*Information service or system*] (IID)
BAUGA ..... Buecherei des Augenarztes [*A publication*]
Bauginia Z Basler Botan Ges ... Bauginia. Zeitschrift. Basler Botanische Gesellschaft [*A publication*]
Bauinf Wiss Tech ... Bauinformation. Wissenschaft und Technik [*East Germany*] [*A publication*]
Bauing Prax ... Bauingenieur Praxis [*A publication*]
BAUK .... Baukol-Noonan, Inc. [*Minot, ND*] [*NASDAQ symbol*] (NQ)
BAUMA .... Baumeister [*A publication*]
Baumasch Bautech ... Baumaschine und Bautechnik [*A publication*]
Baum B ...... Baum Bugle [*A publication*]
BaumB ...... Baum Bugle: A Journal of Oz [*A publication*]
Bauplanung Bautech ... Bauplanung-Bautechnik [*A publication*]
B Aur.......... Boletin Auriense [*A publication*]
BAUS........ British Association of Urological Surgeons
B & Aust .... Barron and Austin's English Election Cases [*1842*] [*A publication*] (DLA)
B & Aust Cases (Eng) ... Barron and Austin's English Election Cases [*1842*] [*A publication*] (DLA)
Baustoffind Ausg B ... Baustoffindustrie. Ausgabe B. Bauelemente [*A publication*]
Bautech-Arch ... Bautechnik-Archiv [*A publication*]
Bautechnik Ausg A ... Bautechnik. Ausgabe A [*A publication*]
Bauteile Rep ... Bauteile Report [*A publication*]
B Automatn ... Business Automation [*A publication*]
BAUVA ..... Bauverwaltung [*A publication*]
Bau & Werk ... Baukunst und Werkform [*A publication*]
BAV .... Bachelier en Arts Visuels [*Bachelor of Visual Arts*] [*French*]
BAV .... Baotou [*China*] [*Airport symbol*] (OAG)
BAV .... Bavaria [*State in West Germany*] (ROG)
BAV .... Bavarian Lion Industries Ltd. [*Vancouver Stock Exchange symbol*]
Bav .... [*Marcus Antonius*] Baverius [*Flourished, 16th century*] [*Authority cited in pre-1607 legal work*] (DSA)
BAV .... Blacksburg [*Virginia*] [*Seismograph station code, US Geological Survey*] (SEIS)
BAV .... Boletin. Academia Venezolana [*A publication*]
BAV .... Bolivar, TN [*Location identifier*] [*FAA*] (FAAL)
BAV .... [*A*] Book of American Verse [*A publication*]
BAVA .... Byelorussian-American Veteran Association (EA)
BAVED..... Bayerische Verwaltungsblaetter [*A publication*]
Baver.......... [*Marcus Antonius*] Baverius [*Flourished, 16th century*] [*Authority cited in pre-1607 legal work*] (DSA)
BA Vexin ... Bulletin Archeologique du Vexin Francais [*A publication*]
BAVF........ Blinded American Veterans Foundation (EA)
BAVFAV... Bulletin. Academie Veterinaire de France [*A publication*]
BAVIP....... Bleomycin, Adriamycin, Vinblastine, Imidazole carboxamide [*Dacarbazine*], Prednisone [*Antineoplastic drug regimen*]
BAVIP....... British Association of Viewdata Information Providers
BAVTE...... Bureau of Adult, Vocational, and Technical Education (OICC)
BAW .... Banco Central. Boletin Informativo [*Madrid*] [*A publication*]
BAW .... Bare Aluminum Wire
BAW .... Baywest Capital [*Vancouver Stock Exchange symbol*]
BAW .... Bronchoalveolar Wash Fluids [*Medicine*]

BAW .... Bulk Acoustic Wave [*Physics*]
BAW .... Butanol/Acetic Acid/Water [*Solvent system*]
BAWA .... Burley Auction Warehouse Association   (EA)
BAWA .... Byelorussian-American Women Association   (EA)
BAWA .... Unitarian Universalists for Black and White Action   (EA)
BaWb .... Beitraege zum Assyrischen Woerterbuch [*A publication*]   (BJA)
BAWB .... Bomber Activity Weekly Brief   (MCD)
BAWHA ..... Bide-a-Wee Home Association   (EA)
BAWLA ..... British Amateur Weight Lifters' Association
BAWOA ..... Bauen und Wohnen [*A publication*]
BAWPE ..... Biased Antiworld Paw Entry [*Testing of left and right laterality in mice*]
BAW PHK ... Bayerische Akademie der Wissenschaften. Philosophisch-Historische Klasse. Sitzungsberichte [*A publication*]
BAWRA .... British Australian Wool Realization Association
BAWS........ Basic Acoustic Warfare System   (MCD)
BAWS........ Bayerische Akademie der Wissenschaften. Philosophisch-Historische Klasse. Sitzungsberichte [*A publication*]
BAWTA ..... Bauwelt [*A publication*]
BAWTR...... Babcock & Wilcox Test Reactor
BAX .... Bad Axe, MI [*Location identifier*] [*FAA*]   (FAAL)
BAX .... Baxter International [*NYSE symbol*]   (SPSG)
BAX .... Baxter Laboratories, Inc. [*of Baxter Travenol Laboratories, Inc.*] [*Research code symbol*]
Bax .... Baxter's Reports [*60-68 Tennessee*] [*A publication*]   (DLA)
BAX .... Management Facetten [*A publication*]
BAX .... Travenol Laboratories [*of Baxter Travenol Laboratories, Inc.*] [*Research code symbol*]
Bax Jud Acts ... Baxter on Judicature Acts and Rules [*A publication*]   (DLA)
Bax S.......... Arnold Bax Society. Bulletin [*A publication*]
Baxt.......... Baxter's Reports [*60-68 Tennessee*] [*A publication*]   (DLA)
Baxter .... Baxter's Reports [*60-68 Tennessee*] [*A publication*]   (DLA)
Baxt (Tenn) ... Baxter's Reports [*60-68 Tennessee*] [*A publication*]   (DLA)
BAY .... Baia Mare [*Romania*] [*Airport symbol*]   (OAG)
BAY .... Bay Financial Corp. [*NYSE symbol*]   (SPSG)
BAY .... Bay Mills Ltd. [*Toronto Stock Exchange symbol*]
BAY .... Bayandai [*USSR*] [*Seismograph station code, US Geological Survey*] [*Closed*]   (SEIS)
BAY .... Bayonet   (MSA)
Bay .... Bay's Reports [*1-3, 5-8 Missouri*] [*A publication*]   (DLA)
Bay .... Bay's South Carolina Reports [*1783-1804*] [*A publication*]   (DLA)
BAY .... Coos Bay Public Library, Coos Bay, OR [*OCLC symbol*]   (OCLC)
BAY .... Farbenfabriken Bayer [*Germany*] [*Research code symbol*]
BAYA .... [*The*] Federal Savings Bank of Puerto Rico [*NASDAQ symbol*]   (NQ)
Bay Bills .... Bayley on Bills and Notes [*A publication*]   (DLA)
BAYC........ Bay Area Recovery Centers, Inc. [*NASDAQ symbol*]   (NQ)
BAYC........ Bayonet Candelabra
BAYCANDDC ... Bayonet Candelabra Double Contact
BAYCANDSC ... Bayonet Candelabra Single Contact
Bay Cons.... Bayard on the Constitution of the United States [*A publication*]   (DLA)
Bay Dig Ind ... Baylies' Digested Index of English and American Reports [*A publication*]   (DLA)
Bay Dom Serv ... Baylies on Domestic Servants [*A publication*]   (DLA)
BAYED...... Bayerland [*A publication*]
Bayer Aerztebl ... Bayerisches Aerzteblatt [*A publication*]
Bayer Akad Wiss Jahrb ... Bayerische Akademie der Wissenschaften. Jahrbuch [*A publication*]
Bayer Akad Wiss Math-Natur Kl Abh ... Bayerische Akademie der Wissenschaften. Mathematisch-Naturwissenschaftliche Klasse. Abhandlungen [*A publication*]
Bayer Akad Wiss Math-Natur Kl Abh NF ... Bayerische Akademie der Wissenschaften. Mathematisch-Naturwissenschaftliche Klasse. Abhandlungen. Neue Folge [*Munich*] [*A publication*]
Bayer Akad Wiss Math-Natur Kl S-B ... Bayerische Akademie der Wissenschaften. Mathematisch-Naturwissenschaftliche Klasse. Sitzungsberichte [*A publication*]
Bayer Akad Wiss Math-Natur Kl Sitzungsber ... Bayerische Akademie der Wissenschaften. Mathematisch-Naturwissenschaftliche Klasse. Sitzungsberichte [*A publication*]
Bayer Akad Wiss Math-Naturw Abt Abh ... Bayerische Akademie der Wissenschaften. Mathematisch-Naturwissenschaftliche Abteilung. Abhandlungen [*A publication*]
Bayer Akad Wiss Math-Naturwiss Kl Abh ... Bayerische Akademie der Wissenschaften. Mathematisch-Naturwissenschaftliche Klasse. Abhandlungen [*A publication*]
Bayer Akad Wiss Math-Naturwiss Kl Sitzungsber ... Bayerische Akademie der Wissenschaften. Mathematisch-Naturwissenschaftliche Klasse. Sitzungsberichte [*A publication*]
Bayer Akad Wiss Philos-Hist Abt Abh ... Bayerische Akademie der Wissenschaften. Philosophisch-Historische Abteilung. Abhandlungen [*A publication*]
Bayer Akad d Wiss Philos-Philol u Hist Kl Abhandl ... Bayerische Akademie der Wissenschaften. Philosophisch-Philologische und Historiche Klasse. Abhandlungen [*A publication*]
Bayer Bienenztg ... Bayerische Bienen-Zeitung [*A publication*]
Bayer Bildungswesen ... Bayerisches Bildungswesen [*A publication*]

Bayer Color ... Bayer Colorist [*A publication*]
Bayer Farben Rev Spec Ed (USA) ... Bayer Farben Revue. Special Edition (USA) [*A publication*]
Bayerische Akad Wiss Jahrbuch ... Bayerische Akademie der Wissenschaften. Jahrbuch [*A publication*]
Bayerische Volksm ... Bayerische Volksmusik [*A publication*]
Bayer Landwirt Jahrb ... Bayerisches Landwirtschaftliches Jahrbuch [*A publication*]
Bayer Landwirtschaftsrat Vierteljahresschr ... Bayerischer Landwirtschaftsrat Vierteljahresschrift [*A publication*]
Bayer Landwirtsch Jahrb ... Bayerisches Landwirtschaftliches Jahrbuch [*A publication*]
Bayer Landwirtsch Jahrb Sonderh ... Bayerisches Landwirtschaftliches Jahrbuch. Sonderheft [*A publication*]
Bayer Landw Jb ... Bayerisches Landwirtschaftliches Jahrbuch [*A publication*]
Bayer Mitt Gummi Ind (Engl Transl) ... Bayer Mitteilungen fuer die Gummi Industrie (English Translation) [*A publication*]
Bayer Sitzb ... Bayerische Akademie der Wissenschaften. Sitzungsberichte [*A publication*]
Bayer Staatssamml Palaeontol Hist Geol Mitt ... Bayerische Staatssammlung fuer Palaeontologie und Historische Geologie. Mitteilungen [*A publication*]
Bayer Staatsztg Bayer Staatsanz ... Bayerische Staatszeitung und Bayerischer Staatsanzeiger [*A publication*]
Bayer-Symp ... Bayer-Symposium [*A publication*]
Bayer Verwaltungsbl ... Bayerische Verwaltungsblaetter [*A publication*]
Bayer Vorgeschbl ... Bayerische Vorgeschichtsblaetter [*A publication*]
Bayer Z Vermessungswesen ... Bayerische Zeitschrift fuer Vermessungswesen [*A publication*]
Bay Ev........ Bayard on Evidence [*A publication*]   (DLA)
BAYL......... Bayly Corp. [*NASDAQ symbol*]   (NQ)
Bayl B .... Bayley on Bills [*A publication*]   (DLA)
Bayl Ch Pr ... Bayley's Commentaries on the Laws of England [*A publication*]   (DLA)
Bayl F & R ... Bayley on Fines and Recoveries [*A publication*]   (DLA)
Baylles Sur ... Baylles on Sureties and Guarantors [*A publication*]   (DLA)
Baylor Bus Studies ... Baylor Business Studies [*A publication*]
Baylor Dent J ... Baylor Dental Journal [*A publication*]
Baylor Geol Stud Bull ... Baylor Geological Studies. Bulletin [*A publication*]
Baylor Law ... Baylor Law Review [*A publication*]
Baylor Law R ... Baylor Law Review [*A publication*]
Baylor L Rev ... Baylor Law Review [*A publication*]
Baylor Nurs Educ ... Baylor Nursing Educator [*A publication*]
Bayl Q & A ... Bayley's Questions and Answers for Students [*A publication*]   (DLA)
Bay LR....... Baylor Law Review [*A publication*]
BAYM .... Bayless [*A. J.*] Markets, Inc. [*NASDAQ symbol*]   (NQ)
BaYMV ...... Barley Yellow Mosaic Virus
BAYO .... Byelorussian-American Youth Organization   (EA)
Bayreuth Math Schr ... Bayreuther Mathematische Schriften [*A publication*]
BAYS........ Bayswater Realty & Capital Corp. [*NASDAQ symbol*]   (NQ)
BAYSAH... Bayer-Symposium [*A publication*]
BAYSK...... Bayonet Skirted
Bay State Libn ... Bay State Librarian [*A publication*]
Bay State Mo ... Bay State Monthly [*A publication*]
Bay St Librn ... Bay State Librarian [*A publication*]
BAYU .... Bayou International Ltd. [*NASDAQ symbol*]   (NQ)
Bay Vg Bl... Bayerische Vorgeschichtsblaetter [*A publication*]
BAYWA .... Bayerische Warenvermittlung Landwirtschaftlicher Genossenschaften Aktiengesellschaft [*Bavarian Commodity Supply and Agricultural Association*] [*Federal Republic of Germany*]
Bay Workr ... Bay Area Worker [*A publication*]
Baz .... Bazianus [*Deceased, 1197*] [*Authority cited in pre-1607 legal work*]   (DSA)
Baz .... Bazianus de Baldone de Vaude [*Flourished, 13th century*] [*Authority cited in pre-1607 legal work*]   (DSA)
BAZ .... Bazil [*Red sheep*] [*Bookbinding*]   (ROG)
BAZ .... New Braunfels, TX [*Location identifier*] [*FAA*]   (FAAL)
Baza .... Bazianus [*Deceased, 1197*] [*Authority cited in pre-1607 legal work*]   (DSA)
Bazan .... Bazianus [*Deceased, 1197*] [*Authority cited in pre-1607 legal work*]   (DSA)
BAZE........ Bayesian Zero-Failure [*Data processing*]   (MCD)
Bazele Fiz Chim Intaririi Liantilor Anorg ... Bazele Fizico-Chimice ale Intaririi Liantilor Anorganici [*A publication*]
BAZTA...... Bauzeitung [*A publication*]
B & B....... B & B Productions [*New Jersey*] [*Record label*]
BB .... B and Better [*Lumber*]
BB .... Baba Bathra [*or Bava Batra*]   (BJA)
Bb.............. Babbitt [*Metallurgy*]
BB .... Baby Bond [*Investment term*]
B/B........... Baby Incendiary Bomb
BB .... Babylonische Briefe aus der Zeit der Hammurapi Dynastie [*A publication*]   (BJA)
BB .... Babylonische Busspsalmen [*A publication*]   (BJA)
BB .... Bachelor of Bacteriology
B to B .... Back to Back [*Technical drawings*]
B of B .... Back of Board   (MSA)
BB .... Backboard [*Telecommunications*]   (TEL)
BB .... Backbord [*Portside*] [*German military*]

BB	Bad Breath
BB	Bail Bond (DLA)
BB	Balair SA [Switzerland] [ICAO designator] (FAAC)
BB	Balanced Budget
BB	Ball Bearing [Technical drawings]
B & B	Ball and Beatty's Irish Chancery Reports [1807-14] [A publication] (DLA)
BB	Ball on National Banks [A publication] (DLA)
B & B	Balled and Burlapped [Plant industry]
BB	Balloon Barrage
BB	Banco de Bilbao [Spain]
BB	Bank Book
BB	Bank Building & Equipment Corp. of America [AMEX symbol] (SPSG)
BB	Bank Burglary
B & B	Banks & Barns [Commercial firm] [British]
BB	Barbadensis [Pharmacy] (ROG)
bb	Barbados [MARC country of publication code] [Library of Congress] (LCCP)
BB	Barbados [ANSI two-letter standard code] (CNC)
BB	Barclaycard [Credit card] (ADA)
BB	Bare Base [Air Force] (AFM)
BB	Barrel Bulk [Shipping] (ROG)
BB	Barrels [or Boxes] [Freight]
BB	Barry's Babes [Later, BGR] (EA)
BB	Base Burning (MCD)
BB	Baseband (AAG)
BB	Bases on Balls [Baseball]
BB	Basketball (ADA)
B & B	Bath and Basin [Classified advertising] (ADA)
BB	Bats Both Right-Handed and Left-Handed [Baseball]
BB	Battleship [Navy symbol]
BB	Bayley on Bills [A publication] (DLA)
BB	Bayreuther Blaetter [A publication]
BB	Bearer Bond [Investment term] (ADA)
BB	Beautiful Books [A publication]
BB	Bed Bath [Medicine]
B & B	Bed and Breakfast [Tourist accommodations]
BB	Bedspread Blanket
BB	Begin Bracket [Indicator] [Data processing] (IBMDP)
B & B	Bell and Bell [Technical drawings]
BB	Below Bridges [Navigation]
B & B	Bench and Bar [A publication]
B & B	Benedictine and Brandy
BB	Bennington Bunch [An association] (EA)
B & B	Benton & Bowles [Advertising agency]
BB	Beobachtung [Observation] [German]
BB	Berlin Brigade
BB	Bernard Berenson [American art critic, 1865-1959]
BB	Beslissingen in Belastingzaken [Reports of Tax Cases] [A publication] (ILCA)
BB	Best Black [Pencil leads] (ROG)
BB	Best of Breed
BB	Bezzenbergers Beitraege [A publication]
Bb	Biblica [A publication] (BJA)
BB	Bibliographie de Belgique [A publication]
BB	Biblische Beitraege [A publication]
BB	Biceps Brachii [A muscle]
B & B	Biculturalism and Bilingualism [Canada]
BB	Big Board [The New York Stock Exchange, Inc.] [Slang]
BB	Big Brother [From George Orwell's novel, "1984"]
Bb	Bijblad op het Staatsblad [A publication]
BB	Bill Blass [Couturier]
BB	Bill Book [Shipping]
BB	Billboard [A publication]
BB	Billion Barrels [Shipping]
BB	Birmingham Belt R. R. [AAR code]
BB	Bishops (ADA)
BB	BIT [Binary Digit]/Byte Conversion [Telecommunications] (TEL)
BB	Bitter and Burton [British] (DSUE)
BB	Black-Bordered [Stationery]
BB	Blanket Bath [Medicine]
BB	Block Brazing
BB	Blocking Back [Football]
BB	Blood Bank
b & b	Blood and Bone (ADA)
BB	Bloody Bastard [British slang]
BB	Blowback
BB	Blue-Black
BB	Blue Bomber [Valium tablet] [Slang]
BB	Blue Book [Directory of proprietaries]
BB	Bluebird [Division of Victor] [Record label]
BB	B'nai B'rith [Later, BBI] (EA)
BB	Body Burden [of radiation]
BB	Bomb (MUGU)
BB	Bomb Bay [of an aircraft]
BB	Bomber [Russian aircraft symbol]
BB	Bonner Beitraege [A publication]
BB	Bonner-Bibel (BJA)
BB	Books and Bookmen [A publication]
B & B	Books and Bookmen [A publication]
BB	Booster Battery
BB	Bossche Bijdragen [A publication]
B/B	Both-to-Blame [Shipping]
BB	Both Bones [With reference to fractures] [Medicine]
B/B	Bottled in Bond [Wines and spirits]
BB	Bottom Bounce [SONAR propagation mode] [Navy] (NG)
BB	Bought Book [Tea trade] (ROG)
B & B	Bowler and Bowers' United States Comptroller's Decisions [2, 3] [A publication] (DLA)
BB	Boys' Brigade [London, England]
BB	Branch Bill
B or B	Brass or Bronze [Top] [Freight]
BB	Breadboard [NASA] (KSC)
BB	Break Bulk [Shipping]
BB	Breaker Block
BB	Breaks Below
BB	Breakthrough Bleeding [Medicine]
BB	Breast Biopsy [Medicine]
BB	Brigitte Bardot [French actress]
BB	British Blue [A British sailor]
BB	British Business [A publication]
BB	Broadband [Communications channel description] (IEEE)
BB	Broadcast Bureau [of FCC]
B & B	Broderip and Bingham's English Common Pleas Reports [A publication] (DLA)
BB	Bronsted Base [Biochemistry]
B & B	Brown & Bigelow
BB	Brown Sedge Growth with Brown Sedge [Ecology]
BB	Brownish-Black
BB	Brush Border [of intestinal epithelial cell] [Cell physiology]
B & B	Buffet and Bull [Slang for a political dinner]
BB	Building Block (KSC)
BB	Bulk Burning (IEEE)
BB	Bulletin of Bibliography [A publication]
BB	Bulletin du Bibliophile et du Bibliothecaire [A publication]
BB	Bulletin Board [Computer online message system]
BB	Bum Boy [Slang] [British] (DSUE)
BB	Bunching Block (MSA)
BB	Bundesblatt [Switzerland] [A publication]
BB	Bureau of Biologics [Also, BOB] [FDA]
BB	Bureau of the Budget [Later, OMB]
BB	Burgan Bank [Kuwait]
BB	Burnaby Public Library, British Columbia [Library symbol] [National Library of Canada] (NLC)
BB	Burning Bush [Freemasonry]
BB	Burroughs Bibliophiles (EA)
BB	Burton and Bitter [Drink served in British public houses]
BB	Bus-Bar Layout Drawing [Data processing] (TEL)
BB	Bust Bodice [Early name for brassiere]
B-B	Butane-Butene Fraction
B & B	Buttons and Bows [Magazine in Judith Krantz's novel "I'll Take Manhattan"]
BB	Buy Back [Investment term]
BB	Double Black [Pencil]
BB	Hawker Siddeley Aviation Ltd. [Great Britain] [ICAO aircraft manufacturer identifier] (ICAO)
BB	Lower Medium [Standard & Poor's bond rating] [Investment term]
B & B	National Block and Bridle Club (EA)
BB	Secondary Type Battery [JETDS nomenclature] [Military] (CET)
BBA	Bachelor of Business Administration
BBA	Balmaceda [Chile] [Airport symbol] (OAG)
BBA	Banque Belge d'Afrique [Belgian African Bank]
BBA	Beclobrinic Acid [Biochemistry]
BBA	Berliner Byzantinistische Arbeiten [A publication]
BBA	Bermuda Benevolent Association
BBA	Betaling by Aflewering [Cash on Delivery] [Afrikaans]
BBA	Big Brothers of America [Later, BB/BSA] (EA)
BBA	Biochimica et Biophysica Acta [A publication]
BBA	Bishop Baraga Association (EA)
BBA	Black Business Alliance (EA)
BBA	Bluetick Breeders of America (EA)
BBA	Bogart-Brociner Associates [Information service or system] (IID)
BBA	Bombay Co. [AMEX symbol] (SPSG)
BBA	Born before Arrival [of mother at hospital] [Medicine]
BBA	Brain & Brown Airfreighters [Australia]
BBA	British Bankers' Association
BBA	British Bloodstock Agency
BBA	British Board of Agreement [Department of the Environment] (IRUK)
BBA	British Bobsleigh [or Bobsled] Association (EAIO)
BBA	British Business Association [Singapore] (DS)
BBA	Broadband Antenna
BBA	Bureau of the Budget Approval [Obsolete]
BBA	Burnaby Art Gallery, British Columbia [Library symbol] [National Library of Canada] (NLC)
BBAA	Barzona Breeders Association of America (EA)
BBAA	Big Band Academy of America (EA)

BBAA......... Boletin Bibliografico de Antropologia Americana [*A publication*]
BBAA......... Bridal and Bridesmaids Apparel Association   (EA)
B Bac......... Bachelor of Bacteriology
BBAC........ British Balloon and Airship Club
BBAC........ Bus-to-Bus Access Circuit [*Bell System*]
BBACA...... Biochimica et Biophysica Acta [*A publication*]
BB Ad .... Bachelor of Business Administration
BB Adm .... Bachelor of Business Administration
BBAE........ Bulletin. Bureau of American Ethnology [*A publication*]
BBAH....... Basic Resources International (Bahamas) Ltd. [*NASDAQ symbol*]   (NQ)
BBA Libr ... BBA [*Biochimica et Biophysica Acta*] Library [*A publication*]
BBAM .... Bamfield Marine Station, Bamfield, British Columbia [*Library symbol*] [*National Library of Canada*]   (BIB)
B Banque Nat Belgique ... Bulletin. Banque Nationale de Belgique [*A publication*]
BBAR........ Bass Baritone [*Music*]
B Bar......... Bench and Bar [*A publication*]
B & Bar ..... Bench and Bar [*A publication*]
BBAS........ Balloon-Borne Astronomical Studies   (MCD)
BBASA6.... Chung Yang Yen Chiu Yuan Chih Wu Hsueh Hui K'an [*A publication*]
B Baud ...... Bulletin Baudelairien [*A publication*]
BBB........... [*Johann Sebastian*] Bach, [*Ludwig van*] Beethoven, and [*Johannes*] Brahms [*Classical composers*]
BBB........... Bags, Barrels, or Boxes [*Freight*]
BBB........... Baltimore Bancorp [*NYSE symbol*]   (SPSG)
BBB........... Bankers' Blanket Bond [*Investment term*]
BBB........... Banque de France. Bulletin Trimestriel [*A publication*]
BBB........... Baseband Breadboard
BBB........... Basic Boxed Base
BBB........... Bed, Breakfast, and Bath [*Tourist accommodations*]
BBB........... Beecham Bovril Brands [*Commercial firm*] [*British*]
BBB........... Benson, MN [*Location identifier*] [*FAA*]   (FAAL)
BBB........... Best Berlin Broadcast [*Radio program broadcast from Berlin by Robert H. Best, former South Carolina journalist*] [*World War II*]
BBB........... Better Business Bureau
BBB........... Blood Brain Barrier [*Neurology*]
BBB........... B'nai B'rith Bulletin [*A publication*]   (ADA)
BBB........... Body Bound Bolts   (MSA)
BBB........... Boletin de Bibliotecas y Bibliografia [*A publication*]
BBB........... Bonner Biblische Beitraege [*A publication*]
BBB........... Bulletin du Bibliophile et du Bibliothecaire [*A publication*]
BBB........... Bundle Branch Block [*Cardiology*]
BBB........... Medium [*Standard & Poor's bond rating*] [*Investment term*]
BBB........... Treble Black [*Pencil*]
BBBB........ Bilateral Bundle Branch Block [*Cardiology*]
BBBC....... British Boxing Board of Control
BBBCM..... British Columbia Microelectronics, Burnaby, British Columbia [*Library symbol*] [*National Library of Canada*]   (NLC)
BBBM........ British Columbia Museum of Mining, Britannia Beach, British Columbia [*Library symbol*] [*National Library of Canada*]   (NLC)
BBBMB ..... Biochimica et Biophysica Acta. M. Biomembranes [*A publication*]
BBBNS ...... Biblioteca Bio-Bibliografica della Terra Santa. Nova Serie [*A publication*]
BBBr .... Boletim Bibliografico Brasileiro [*A publication*]
BBBRD ...... BBR. Brunnenbau, Bau von Wasserwerken, Rohrleitungsbau [*A publication*]
BB/BSA.... Big Brothers/Big Sisters of America   (EA)
BBBT........ Bisbutoxybenzylidenebitoluidine [*Organic chemistry*]
BB Bul....... BB [*B'nai Brith in Australia*] Bulletin [*A publication*]   (APTA)
BBC.......... Bachelor of Beauty Culture
BBC.......... Bachelor of Building Construction
B of BC....... Bachelor of Building Construction
BBC.......... Backup Bus Controller [*Data processing*]
BBC.......... Bank of British Columbia [*Toronto Stock Exchange symbol*] [*Vancouver Stock Exchange symbol*]
BBC.......... Barrels, Boxes, or Crates [*Freight*]
BBC.......... Basic Building Code
BBC.......... Battery Booster Cable
BBC.......... BC [*British Columbia*] Bancorp [*Toronto Stock Exchange symbol*] [*Vancouver Stock Exchange symbol*]
BBC.......... Beam-to-Beam Correlation   (NVT)
BBC.......... Before Bottom Center [*Valve position*]
BBC.......... Before Business Clearance   (NASA)
BBC.......... Belfast Banking Company [*Ireland*]
BBC.......... Bergen Brunswig Corporation [*AMEX symbol*]   (SPSG)
BBC.......... Bermuda Base Command [*World War II*]
BBC.......... Big Bear [*California*] [*Seismograph station code, US Geological Survey*] [*Closed*]   (SEIS)
BBC.......... Billionaire Boys Club   (EA)
BBC.......... Biplabi Bangla Congress [*India*] [*Political party*]   (PPW)
BBC.......... Blade-Brake Clutch [*on lawn mowers*]
BBC.......... Blockhouse Battery Charger [*NASA*]
BBC.......... British Broadcasting Corporation [*State-operated radio and television*]
BBC.......... Broadband Conducted   (IEEE)

BBC.......... Bromobenzyl Cyanide [*Tear gas*]
BBC.......... Brooks Bird Club   (EA)
BBC.......... Brown, Boveri & Company Ltd. [*Switzerland*]
BBC.......... Browne, Bortz & Coddington, Inc. [*Denver, CO*] [*Telecommunications*]   (TSSD)
BBC.......... Brush Beryllium Company   (MCD)
BBC.......... Buffered Block Channel   (MCD)
BBC.......... Building Block Concept [*Army-ROAD concept*]
BBC.......... Davenport, IA [*Location identifier*] [*FAA*]   (FAAL)
BBCAU...... British Borneo Civil Affairs Unit [*World War II*]
BBCBB ...... Berichte Biochemie und Biologie [*A publication*]
BBCC........ Big Bands Collectors' Club   (EA)
BBC Eng .... BBC [*British Broadcasting Corporation*] Engineering [*A publication*]
BBC Eng Div Monogr ... BBC [*British Broadcasting Corporation*] Engineering Division. Monograph [*A publication*]
BB & CIRly ... Bombay, Baroda, and Central India Railway
BBCJC....... Genealogical Society Library, Church of Jesus Christ of Latter-Day Saints, Burnaby, British Columbia [*Library symbol*] [*National Library of Canada*]   (NLC)
BBCM........ Bella Coola Museum, British Columbia [*Library symbol*] [*National Library of Canada*]   (NLC)
BBCNA...... BBC [*Brown, Boveri & Cie.*] Nachrichten [*A publication*]
BBC Nachr ... BBC [*Brown, Boveri & Cie.*] Nachrichten [*A publication*]
BBCP........ (Benzyl)benzylidenecyclopentanone [*Organic chemistry*]
BBCRN...... West Kootenay District Nursing Archives, Registered Nurses Association of British Columbia, Blueberry Creek, British Columbia [*Library symbol*] [*National Library of Canada*]   (NLC)
BB-CS....... British Beer-Mat Collectors' Society   (EA)
BBCS........ British Butterfly Conservation Society
BBCS .... Bulletin. Board of Celtic Studies [*A publication*]
BBCS-DIAG ... Bracken Basic Concept Scale - Diagnostic Scale [*Educational development test*]
BBCSO...... British Broadcasting Corporation Symphony Orchestra
BBCSSO.... British Broadcasting Corporation Scottish Symphony Orchestra
BBCT........ Broad-Based Consumption Tax   (ADA)
BBCW....... Bare Beryllium Copper Wire
BBD .... Baby Born Dead [*Medicine*]
BBD .... Blackboard
BBD .... Bombardier, Inc. [*Toronto Stock Exchange symbol*]
BBD .... Brady, TX [*Location identifier*] [*FAA*]   (FAAL)
BBD .... Bucket-Brigade Device [*Electronics*]
BBD .... Bulletin Board [*Technical drawings*]
BBDAA...... Bulletin d'Information. Association Belge pour le Developpement Pacifique de l'Energie Atomique [*A publication*]
BBDC........ Before Bottom Dead Center [*Valve position*]
B Bd Celt S ... Bulletin. Board of Celtic Studies/Bwletin y Bwrdd Gwybodau Celtaidd [*A publication*]
BBDE........ Berlin Brigade
BBDI......... Bulletin of Bibliography and Dramatic Index [*A publication*]
BB DL........ Baby or Doll [*Freight*]
BBD & O ... Batten, Barton, Durstine & Osborn [*Advertising agency*]
BBDO........ BBDO International, Inc. [*NASDAQ symbol*]   (NQ)
BBDR .... Best Buy Drugs, Inc. [*Riviera Beach, FL*] [*NASDAQ symbol*]   (NQ)
Bbds .... Barbadensis [*Pharmacy*]   (ROG)
BBE........... Bacteroids Bile Esculin [*Agar*] [*Microbiology*]
BBE........... Belden & Blake Energy Co. [*AMEX symbol*]   (SPSG)
BBE........... Bradbury International Equity [*Vancouver Stock Exchange symbol*]
BB & EA .... British Building and Engineering Appliances
BB Ed........ Bachelor of Business Education
BBEDCRA ... Balanced Budget and Emergency Deficit Control Reaffirmation Act [*1987*]
B Bel Art .... Boletin de Bellas Artes [*Seville*] [*A publication*]
B Belg Anthrop ... Bulletin. Societe Royale Belge d'Anthropologie et de Prehistoire [*A publication*]
BB & EM .... Bed, Breakfast, and Evening Meal [*Tourist accommodations*]
BBER........ Bureau of Business and Economic Research [*Old Dominion University*] [*Norfolk, VA*] [*Research center*]   (RCD)
BBEUMCS ... Bureau of the Budget in Exile Unrequited Marching and Chowder Society   (EA)
BBEZA ...... Biochimica et Biophysica Acta. Enzymology [*A publication*]
BBF........... Bacus/B'Gosh Families [*An association*]   (EA)
BBF........... Balloon-Borne Filter
BBF........... Better Boys Foundation   (EA)
BBF........... Beyond Baroque Foundation   (EA)
BBF........... Boron-Based Fuel
BBF........... Brother's Brother Foundation   (EA)
BBF........... Bulletin des Bibliotheques de France [*A publication*]
BBF........... International Brotherhood of Boilermakers, Iron Shipbuilders, Blacksmiths, Forgers, and Helpers
BBFC........ Bama Band Fan Club   (EA)
BBFC........ Barry Bostwick Fan Club   (EA)
BBFC........ Bellamy Brothers Fan Club   (EA)
BBFC........ Bibi Besch Fan Club   (EA)
BBFC........ Billy Blanton Fan Club   (EA)
BBFC........ Bobby Bare Fan Club   (EA)
BBFC........ Bobby Blue Fan Club   (EA)

BBFC......... Boris Becker Fan Club (EA)
BBFC......... British Board of Film Classification
BBFC......... Bruce Boxleitner Fan Club (EA)
BBFC......... Buford's Boosters Fan Club (EA)
BBFC......... Slim and Steve: the Bogart and Bacall Fan Club (EA)
BBFFL....... Barbara Bush Foundation for Family Literacy (EA)
BBFI......... Baptist Bible Fellowship International (EA)
BBFLP....... Billy Barty Foundation for Little People (EA)
BBFR....... Balloon-Borne Filter Radiometer
BBFU....... Beach Boys Freaks United (EA)
BBG .... Banbury Gold Mines [Vancouver Stock Exchange symbol]
BBG .... Basler Beitraege zur Geschichtswissenschaft [A publication]
BBG .... Benziger, Bruce & Glencoe, Inc.
BBG .... Berlin Border Guard [East Germany]
BBG .... Big Big Gastrin [Endocrinology]
BBG .... Blaetter fuer das Bayerische Gymnasialschulwesen [A publication]
BBG .... Board of Broadcast Governors [Later, Canadian Radio-Television Commission]
BBG .... [Governor's] Bodyguard, Bombay [British military] (DMA)
BBG .... Bouncing-Ball Generator
BBG .... Brooklyn Botanic Garden [Brooklyn, NY]
BBG .... Butaritari [Kiribati] [Airport symbol] (OAG)
BBG .... Guided Missile Capital Ship [Navy symbol] [Obsolete]
BBGA .... Belgian Begonia Growers Association [Defunct] (EA)
BBGG .... Bollettino della Badia Greca di Grottaferrata [A publication]
BBGKY...... Bogoliubov-Born-Green-Kirkwood-Yvon [Plasma kinetic theory hierarchy]
BBGS........ Babbage's, Inc. [NASDAQ symbol] (NQ)
B BGS .... Barrels or Bags [Freight]
BBGSB ...... Biochimica et Biophysica Acta. G. General Subjects [A publication]
BBGV .... Greater Vancouver Regional District, Burnaby, British Columbia [Library symbol] [National Library of Canada] (BIB)
BBGVL...... Greater Vancouver Library Federation, Burnaby, British Columbia [Library symbol] [National Library of Canada] (NLC)
BBH .... Al-Baha [Saudi Arabia] [Airport symbol] (OAG)
BBH .... Bartle Bogle Hegarty [Commercial firm] [British]
BBH .... Battalion Beachhead [Army]
BBH .... Bowdoin College, Brunswick, ME [OCLC symbol] (OCLC)
BBH .... Bulletin Analytique de Bibliographie Hellenique [A publication]
BBH .... Notities over Europa [A publication]
BBH .... Paris, ID [Location identifier] [FAA] (FAAL)
BBHC....... Buffalo Bill Historical Center (EA)
BBHCD ..... Bangason Bango Hakhoe Chi [A publication]
BBHF....... B'nai B'rith Hillel Foundations (EA)
BBHFC..... Boston Bruins Hockey Fan Club (EA)
BBHOAM ... Board of Brethren Homes and Older Adult Ministries [Later, BHOAM] (EA)
BBHP .... Barkerville Historic Park, British Columbia [Library symbol] [National Library of Canada] (NLC)
BBHS........ Australian Business Brief and Hansard Service [Australian Chamber of Commerce] [Information service or system] [Defunct] (IID)
BBHS........ British Buddy Holly Society (EAIO)
BBHW .... Baseboard Hot Water [Heating system] [Classified advertising]
BBI........... Barbecue Briquet Institute [Later, BIA]
BBI........... Barnett Banks, Inc. [NYSE symbol] (SPSG)
BBI........... Beauty and the Beast International [An association] (EA)
BBI........... Behavioral Books Institute [Book club]
BBI........... Bhubaneswar [India] [Airport symbol] (OAG)
BBI........... Big Bend [Idaho] [Seismograph station code, US Geological Survey] (SEIS)
BBI........... Biomedical Business International [A publication]
BBI........... Bis(benzimidazole) [Organic chemistry]
BBI........... Biscuit Bakers Institute [Absorbed by B & CMA] (EA)
BBI........... Blue Blazes Irregulars (EA)
BBI........... B'nai B'rith International (EA)
BBI........... Bowen Island Public Library, British Columbia [Library symbol] [National Library of Canada] (BIB)
BBI........... Brandeis - Bardin Institute (EA)
BBI........... Broadband Interneuron [Neuroanatomy]
BBI........... Brother to Brother International (EA)
BBI........... Brown Bag Institute (EA)
BBI........... Buxom Belles, International (EA)
BBIA .... Billiard and Bowling Institute of America (EA)
BBib .... Beschreibende Bibliographien [A publication]
B Bib Arts .. Bachelor of Biblical Arts
BBibl .... Bulletin du Bibliophile [A publication]
BBICAJE .. B'nai B'rith International Commission on Adult Jewish Education [Later, BBICCJE] (EA)
BBICAW ... BSBI [Botanical Society of the British Isles] Conference Reports [A publication]
BBICCJE .. B'nai B'rith International Commission on Continuing Jewish Education (EA)
B Bi Ch ...... Bachelor of Biological Chemistry
B Bi Chem .. Bachelor of Biological Chemistry
B Bi E........ Bachelor of Biological Engineering
B Bi Eng..... Bachelor of Biological Engineering

BBII.......... Brass and Bronze Ingot Institute (EA)
BBIJM....... B'nai B'rith International Jewish Monthly [A publication]
BBIM........ Buoyant Ballistic Inertial Missile (MCD)
B Bimestr Soc Comptabil France ... Bulletin Bimestriel. Societe de Comptabilite de France [A publication]
BBIP.......... British Books in Print [Whitaker & Sons, Ltd.] [Information service or system] (IID)
B Bi Phy..... Bachelor of Biological Physics
B Bi S........ Bachelor of Biological Sciences
B Bi Sc ...... Bachelor of Biological Sciences
BBISCHC ... B'nai B'rith International Senior Citizens Housing Committee (EA)
BBIT.......... British Columbia Institute of Technology, Burnaby, British Columbia [Library symbol] [National Library of Canada] (NLC)
BBJ .... Ball Bearing Joint
BBJ .... Boston Bar Journal [A publication]
BBK .... Bank of Bahrain and Kuwait [Bahrain] (EY)
BBK .... Bargmann Bowen and Kemp, Inc. [Telecommunications service] (TSSD)
B of BK....... Baronet of British Kingdom [Initials used by Arthur Orton in his diary] (ROG)
BBK .... Berliner Beitraege zur Keilschriftforschung [A publication] (BJA)
BBK .... Bezirksbankkontor [District Banking Office] [German]
BBK .... BFS Bancorp [AMEX symbol] (SPSG)
BBK .... Bibliotekininkystes ir Bibliografijos Klausimai [A publication]
BBK .... Big Bar Gold Corp. [Vancouver Stock Exchange symbol]
BBK .... Breadboard Kit [NASA]
BBK .... Business Review (Bangkok) [A publication]
BBK .... Kingsway Branch, Burnaby Public Library, British Columbia [Library symbol] [National Library of Canada] (NLC)
BBKC....... Boycott Burger King Coalition [Defunct] (EA)
BBKCA.... Bruns' Beitraege zur Klinischen Chirurgie [A publication]
BBKCA8.... Bruns' Beitraege zur Klinischen Chirurgie [A publication]
BBKG .... Beitraege zur Bayerischen Kirchengeschichte [A publication]
BB/KR...... Brown, Boveri-Krupp Reaktorbau [Germany]
BBKS .... Bobbie Brooks, Inc. [NASDAQ symbol] (NQ)
BBL.......... Baltimore Biological Laboratory
BBL.......... Barrel (AFM)
BBL.......... Basic Business Language [Data processing] (IEEE)
BBL.......... Bed and Breakfast League (EA)
Bbl........... Biblica [Rome] [A publication]
BBL.......... Biblioteksbladet [A publication]
BBl........... [Henry] Blackstone's English Common Pleas Reports [1788-96] [A publication] (ILCA)
BBL.......... Brampton Brick Ltd. [Toronto Stock Exchange symbol]
BBL.......... Branch Back and Load [Data processing]
BBL.......... Brooklyn Business Library
BBL.......... Buys Ballot Law
BBL.......... Lenkurt Electric Co., Burnaby, British Columbia [Library symbol] [National Library of Canada] (NLC)
BBLA .... Audiobook Service to the Handicapped, British Columbia Library Services Branch, Burnaby [Library symbol] [National Library of Canada] (NLC)
BBLA .... Beitraege zur Biblischen Landes- und Altertumskunde [A publication]
BBLAK ...... Beitraege zur Biblischen Landes- und Altertumskunde [A publication]
BBLC........ Boston Biomedical Library Consortium [Library network]
bbl/d.......... Barrels per Day (IMH)
BBldg .... Bachelor of Building (ADA)
BBldSc .... Bachelor of Building Science (ADA)
BBLG .... Basler Beitraege zur Deutschen Literatur- und Geistesgeschichte [A publication]
BBLG........ Bovine Beta-Lactoglobulin [Biochemistry]
BBLIP........ Base Burning/Lateral Injection Propulsion (MCD)
BBLL .... Banner Blade Length [Botany]
BBLM........ Lakes District Museum, Burns Lake, British Columbia [Library symbol] [National Library of Canada] (NLC)
BBLMV ..... Blueberry Leaf Mottle Virus
BBLS .... Barrels [Shipping]
BBLT .... Bus Block Transfer
BBM .... Bachelor of Business Management
BBM .... Basic Brazeau Medium [Culture media]
BBM .... Betriebs-Berater. Zeitschrift fuer Recht und Wirtschaft [A publication]
BBM .... Big Bend [Montana] [Seismograph station code, US Geological Survey] [Closed] (SEIS)
BBM .... Boletin Bibliografico Mexicano [A publication]
BBM .... Books by Mail
BBM .... Bread, Butter, and Marmalade [Slang]
BBM .... Break-Before-Make
BBM .... Building Block Monochromator
BBM .... Bulk Biomass Model [Pisciculture]
BBM .... Bulk Rate Business Mail
BBM .... Bulletin. Brooklyn Museum [A publication]
BBMB........ Bank Bumiputra Malaysia Berhad (FEA)
BBMB........ Bulletin Bibliographique. Musee Belge [A publication]
BBME........ British Bank of the Middle East
BBMIP ...... Branch-Bound Mixed Integer Programming [Data processing]

BBML........ Bottle-Baby Meal [*Airline notation*]
BBMLC..... Bring Back Mark Lindsay Campaign   (EA)
BBMO........ Bis(bromomethyl)oxetane [*Organic chemistry*]
BBMP........ Boletin. Biblioteca de Menendez Pelayo [*A publication*]
BBMPG....... Baroda Museum and Picture Gallery. Bulletin [*A publication*]
BBMRA..... British Brush Manufacturers Research Association   (IRUK)
BBMS........ Brace Bit Makers Society [*A union*] [*British*]
BBMT........ Technical Library, Microtel Pacific Research Ltd., Burnaby, British Columbia [*Library symbol*] [*National Library of Canada*]
BBMV .... Blueberry Mottle Virus
BBN .... Babylon, NY [*Location identifier*] [*FAA*]   (FAAL)
BBN .... Balloon-Borne Nephelometer
BBN .... Bario [*Malaysia*] [*Airport symbol*]   (OAG)
BBN .... Berliner Beitraege zur Namenforschung [*A publication*]
BBN .... Big Brand Names [*i.e., well-established writers*] [*Publishing slang*]
BBN .... Black Butte [*New Mexico*] [*Seismograph station code, US Geological Survey*] [*Closed*]   (SEIS)
BBN .... Bolt, Beranek & Newman, Inc. [*NYSE symbol*]   (SPSG)
BBN .... Borabicyclononane [*Organic chemistry*]
BBN .... British Book News [*A publication*]
BBN .... Bromobenzylnitrile [*Toxic compound*]
BBN .... Bulletin d'Information et de Documentation. Banque Nationale [*A publication*]
BBNK .... BayBanks, Inc. [*NASDAQ symbol*]   (NQ)
BBNL........ Boletin. Biblioteca National (Lima) [*A publication*]
BBNM....... Boletin. Biblioteca National (Mexico) [*A publication*]
BBNPA...... Biochimica et Biophysica Acta. Nucleic Acids and Protein Synthesis [*A publication*]
BBO .... Berbera [*Somalia*] [*Airport symbol*]   (OAG)
BBO .... Billion Barrels of Oil
BBO .... Bis(biphenylyl)oxazole [*Organic chemistry*]
BBO .... British Ballet Organization
BBO .... Morgantown, WV [*Location identifier*] [*FAA*]   (FAAL)
BBOD....... Bis(biphenyl)oxadiazole [*Organic chemistry*]
BB/ODT..... Bottom Bounce/Omnidirectional Transmission [*Navy*]
BBOE .... Billions of Barrels of Oil Equivalent   (MCD)
BBOJ........ Berks, Bucks, and Oxon. Archaeological Journal [*A publication*]
B-BOP .... Bristol Bay Oceanographic Processes
BBOT .... Bis(tert-butylbenzoxazolyl)thiophene [*Organic chemistry*]
BBP........... Bank of Papua New Guinea. Quarterly Economic Bulletin [*A publication*]
BBP........... Bavarian Border Police [*Germany*]
BBP........... Bennettsville, SC [*Location identifier*] [*FAA*]   (FAAL)
BBP........... Bilin-Binding Protein [*Biochemistry*]
BBP........... Boletim de Bibliografia Portuguesa [*A bibliographic publication*] [*Portugal*]
BBP........... Border Boundary Police [*Thailand*]   (CINC)
BBP........... Boxes, Barrels, or Packages [*Freight*]
BBP........... Break Bulk Point [*Transportation*]
BBP........... Building Block Principle
BBP........... Butyl Benzyl Phthalate [*Organic chemistry*]
BBPAD...... Bano Biggyan Patrika [*A publication*]
BBPCA...... Berichte. Bunsengesellschaft fuer Physikalische Chemie [*A publication*]
BBPCT ...... Blocking, Bracing, Packing, Crating, and Tiedown Materials [*Military*]   (INF)
BBPI .... Blau [*Barry*] & Partners, Incorporated [*Fairfield, CT*] [*NASDAQ symbol*]   (NQ)
BBPM........ Bralorne Pioneer Museum, British Columbia [*Library symbol*] [*National Library of Canada*]   (NLC)
BBPMAT .. Buletin Balai Penelitian Perkebunan Bedan [*A publication*]
BBPMB...... Bulletin Bibliographique. Musee Belge [*A publication*]
BBPN........ Balloon-Borne Polar Nephelometer
BBPS .... Behavior-Based Personnel Systems
BBPS .... Build and Blood Pressure Study [*Society of Actuaries*]
BBPTB ...... Biochimica et Biophysica Acta. P. Protein Structure [*A publication*]
BBQ .... Barbecue   (ADA)
BBQ .... Barbuda [*West Indies*] [*Airport symbol*]   (OAG)
BBQ .... Brooklyn, Bronx, and Queens [*New York City slang for nightclub or restaurant that has fallen out of favor with the pacesetters*]
BBQC .... British Board of Quality Control
BBR .... Balloon-Borne Radio
BBR .... Basse-Terre [*Guadeloupe*] [*Airport symbol*]   (OAG)
BBR .... Baylor Business Review [*A publication*]
BBR .... BB Real Estate Investment Corp. [*AMEX symbol*]   (SPSG)
BBR .... Beebe Ranch [*California*] [*Seismograph station code, US Geological Survey*]   (SEIS)
BBR .... Beitraege zur Kenntnis der Babylonischen Religion [*A publication*]
BBR .... Black Body Radiator
BBr............. Books at Brown [*A publication*]
BBR .... Bothnian Bay Reports [*A publication*]
B & BR...... Bristol and Birmingham Railway   (ROG)
BBR .... Broadband Radiated   (IEEE)
BBR .... Buletinul Bibliotecii Romane [*A publication*]
BBR .... Bureau of Biological Research [*Rutgers University*] [*Research center*]   (RCD)

BBR .... Bureau of Business Research [*University of Texas, Austin*] [*Information service or system*]   (IID)
BBR .... Bureau of Business Research [*Ball State University*] [*Research center*]   (RCD)
BBRC........ Ball Brothers Research Corp.
BBRC........ Burr-Brown Corporation [*NASDAQ symbol*]   (NQ)
BBRCA...... Biochemical and Biophysical Research Communications [*A publication*]
BBRG........ Ball Bearing
B Bri........... Bartholomaeus Brixiensis [*Deceased circa 1258*] [*Authority cited in pre-1607 legal work*]   (DSA)
BBRI .... Boston Biomedical Research Institute [*Research center*]   (RCD)
BBRI .... Brain Behaviour Research Institute [*Australia*]
B Brix........ Bartholomaeus Brixiensis [*Deceased circa 1258*] [*Authority cited in pre-1607 legal work*]   (DSA)
B/BRK...... Booster Brake [*Automotive engineering*]
BBRM........ British Bombing Research Mission [*World War II*]
BBROA...... Baender, Bleche, Rohre [*A publication*]
BBRP......... Berliner Beitraege zur Romanischen Philologie [*A publication*]
B Br Psycho ... Bulletin. British Psychological Society [*A publication*]
BBRR........ Brookhaven Beam Research Reactor
BBRS .... Balloon-Borne Radio System
BBRS .... Blair Bell Research Society [*British*]
BBS........... Bachelor of Business Science
BBS........... Bachelor of Business Studies
BBS........... Barber Blue Sea [*Commercial firm*]   (DS)
BBS........... Barber Suggestibility Scale [*Psychology*]
BBS........... Bardet-Beidl Syndrome [*Medicine*]
BBS........... Bare Base Set [*Air Force*]
BBS........... Below Bridges [*Transportation*]
BBS........... Berean Bible Society   (EA)
BBS........... Best of a Bad Situation
BBS........... Betriebsberufsschule [*Factory Training School*] [*Germany*]
BBS........... Biological, Behavioral, and Social Sciences [*Directorate*]
BBS........... Bombesin [*Biochemistry*]
BBS........... Books for Bible Students [*A publication*]
BBS........... Britannia Building Society [*British*]
BBS........... British Biophysical Society
BBS........... British Bone Society
BBS........... British Bryological Society
BBS........... Brittany Base Section [*World War II*]
BBS........... Brittle Bone Society [*British*]
BBS........... Brunei Broadcasting Service
BBS........... Building Block System
BBS........... Bulletin of Baltic Studies [*A publication*]
BBS........... Bulletin Board Systems [*Personal computer message network system*]
BBSA .... Bridge and Building Supply Association [*Defunct*]
BBSAJ....... Bulletin. British School of Archaeology, Jerusalem [*1922-25, after 1927 included in PEFOS*] [*A publication*]
BBSc .... Bachelor of Behavioural Science
BB Sc .... Bachelor of Business Science
BBSCDH ... Behavioral and Brain Sciences [*A publication*]
BBSFC....... Beach Boys Stomp Fan Club   (EAIO)
BBSI .... Beauty and Barber Supply Institute   (EA)
BBSIA .... Bulletin Bibliographique. Societe Internationale Arthurienne [*A publication*]
BBSJ......... Ball Bearing Swivel Joint
BBSL .... Bee Biology and Systematics Laboratory [*Department of Agriculture*] [*Research center*]   (RCD)
BBSO .... Big Bear Solar Observatory [*California Institute of Technology*] [*Research center*]   (RCD)
BBSP .... Balloon-Borne Solar Pointer
BBSP .... Bare Base Support Package   (MCD)
BBSP .... Botetourt Bibliographical Society. Publications [*A publication*]
BBSPA ..... Biochimica e Biologia Sperimentale [*A publication*]
BBSSV...... Blueberry Shoestring Virus
BBST .... Bibliotheque Bonaventurienne. Series "Textes" [*A publication*]
BBSU........ Bid Bond Service Undertaking
BBSU........ British Bombing Survey Units [*World War II*]
BBT........... Backlight Burtek Trainer
BBT........... Ball Bearing Torque
BBT........... Barbados Board of Tourism   (EA)
BBT........... Basal Body Temperature [*Medicine*]
BBT........... BBC Realty Investors [*Toronto Stock Exchange symbol*] [*Vancouver Stock Exchange symbol*]
BBT........... Betar Brith Trumpeldor   (EA)
BBT........... Black Ball Transport, Inc. [*AAR code*]
BBT........... Bombardment   (KSC)
BB/T.......... Bottom Bounce/Track [*Navy*]
BBT........... Brotherhood of Book Travelers [*Later, ABT*]   (EA)
BBT........... Buck-Boost Transformer
BBT........... Bulletin of Black Theatre [*A publication*]
BBTA........ British Bureau of Television Advertising
BBTF .... BB & T Financial Corp. [*NASDAQ symbol*]   (NQ)
BBTL .... Baby Brother Tender Love [*Doll manufactured by Mattel, Inc.*]
BBTR........ Battle Bridge Tier [*Shipping*]   (ROG)
BBTU........ Barge Builders Trade Union [*British*]
BBU........... Beefmaster Breeders Universal   (EA)
BBU........... BIT [*Binary Digit*] Buffer Unit [*Data processing*]   (CET)
B & BU....... Bond and Burglary

BBU	British Business [*A publication*]
BBU	Bucharest [*Romania*] Banesa Airport [*Airport symbol*] (OAG)
BBUC	British Columbia Union Catalogue, Burnaby, British Columbia [*Library symbol*] [*National Library of Canada*] (NLC)
B Buddhist Cult Inst Ryukoku Univ	Bulletin. Buddhist Cultural Institute. Ryukoku University [*A publication*]
BBude	Bulletin. Association Guillaume Bude [*Paris*] [*A publication*]
BBuild	Bachelor of Building (ADA)
BBUL	Burns Lake Public Library, British Columbia [*Library symbol*] [*National Library of Canada*] (NLC)
B Bull	Bar Bulletin [*A publication*] (DLA)
B(Burgos)	Boletin. Institucion Fernan-Gonzalez (Burgos) [*A publication*]
BBus	Bachelor of Business (ADA)
BBus-Accy	Bachelor of Business - Accountancy
BBusAd	Bachelor of Business Administration (ADA)
BBus-Comn	Bachelor of Business - Communication
BBus-Comptg	Bachelor of Business - Computing
BBus-HealthAdmin	Bachelor of Business - Health Administration
BBus-Mgt	Bachelor of Business - Management
BBus-PubAdmin	Bachelor of Business - Public Administration
BBV	Banco Bilbao Vizcaya SA [*NYSE symbol*] (CTT)
BBV	Black Beetle Virus
BBV	[*The*] Boy's Book of Verse [*A publication*]
BBVM	Burnaby Village Museum, British Columbia [*Library symbol*] [*National Library of Canada*] (NLC)
BBVS	B'nai B'rith Vocational Service [*Later, B'nai B'rith Career and Counseling Services*] (EA)
BBW	Bare Brass Wire
BB/W	Biobreeding/Worcester [*Rat variety*]
BBW	B'nai B'rith Women (EA)
BBW	Broken Bow, NE [*Location identifier*] [*FAA*] (FAAL)
BBWA	Bright Belt Warehouse Association (EA)
BBWAA	Baseball Writers Association of America (EA)
BBWC	Broadband Waveguide Circulator
BBWI	Black Business Women - International [*French*] (EAIO)
BBWR	Bezpartyjny Blok Wspolpracy z Rzadem [*Non-Party Bloc of Cooperation with the Government*] [*Poland*] [*Political party*] (PPE)
BBWV	Broad Bean Wilt Virus [*Plant pathology*]
B Bx	Bartholomaeus Brixiensis [*Deceased circa 1258*] [*Authority cited in pre-1607 legal work*] (DSA)
BBX	Blue Bell [*Pennsylvania*] [*Airport symbol*] (OAG)
B Bx	Breast Biopsy [*Medicine*]
BBY	Bankbedrijf en Effectenbedrijf [*A publication*]
BBY	Best Buy Co. [*Bloomington, MN*] [*NYSE symbol*] (SPSG)
BBY	Britannica Book of the Year [*A publication*]
BBYCY	Bow Buoyancy
BBYO	B'nai B'rith Youth Organization (EA)
BBYP	Birinci Bes Yillik Plani [*First Five-Year Plan*]
BByzA	Berliner Byzantinistische Arbeiten. Deutsche Akademie der Wissenschaften zu Berlin [*A publication*]
BByzI	Bulletin. Byzantine Institute [*A publication*]
BBZ	Baylor Business Studies [*A publication*]
BBz	Bearing Bronze [*Metallurgy*]
BbZ	Biblische Zeitschrift [*A publication*]
BBZ	Zambezi [*Zambia*] [*Airport symbol*] (OAG)
BC	Baccalaureus Chirurgiae [*Bachelor of Surgery*]
BC	Bach Choir [*Record label*]
BC	Bachelor of Chemistry
BC	Bachelor of Classics
BC	Bachelor of Commerce
BC	Back to the City [*An association*] [*Defunct*] (EA)
BC	Back-Connected [*Technical drawings*]
BC	Back Course [*Aviation*] (FAAC)
BC	Backpackers Club [*Reading, Berkshire, England*] (EAIO)
BC	Backward Chaining [*Psychology*]
BC	Bad Character
BC	Bad Check [*Banking*]
BC	Bad Conduct [*British military*] (DMA)
BC	Bail Court [*Legal term*] (DLA)
B/C	Bales of Cotton [*Shipping*]
B & C	Ball and Chain [*Slang for a wife*]
BC	Ball Change [*Dance terminology*]
BC	Ballistic Camera
BC	Balloon Command (DAS)
Bc	Banc [*Bank*] [*French*]
BC	Band Corporal
BC	Bank of Canada [*Banque du Canada*]
BC	Bank Clearing [*Business term*] (ADA)
BC	Bank for Cooperatives
BC	Bankcard
BC	Bankers Committee (EA)
B & C	Banking and Currency Committee [*US Senate*]
BC	Bankruptcy Cases [*A publication*] (DLA)
BC	Bankruptcy Court [*Legal term*] (DAS)
BC	Bar (Handle) Control [*Early automobiles*] (ROG)
BC	Bare Copper
BC	Barge Cargo (AAG)
BC	Barium Crown
BC	Barleycorn [*Unit of weight*] [*Obsolete*] [*British*] (ROG)
B & C	Barnewall and Cresswell's English King's Bench Reports [*107-109 English Reprint*] [*A publication*] (DLA)
BC	Barrel Coating
BC	Barrick-Cullaton Gold Trust Units [*Toronto Stock Exchange symbol*]
BC	Barrier Coat (MSA)
BC	Barter Clubs (EA)
B de C	Bartholomaeus de Capua [*Deceased, 1328*] [*Authority cited in pre-1607 legal work*] (DSA)
BC	Base Collector
BC	Base Command
BC	Basel Club (EAIO)
BC	Basic Control [*Mode*] [*Data processing*]
BC	Basic Copy [*Genetics*]
BC	Bass Clarinet
BC	Basso Continuo [*Continued Bass*] [*Music*]
BC	Bathyconductograph
BC	Battalion Commander (MCD)
BC	Battery Charger [*Military*]
BC	Battery Commander [*Army*]
BC	Battle Cruiser [*Navy*]
BC	Battle Cruiser Flag [*Navy*] [*British*]
BC	Bayonet Cap
BC	Beacon College [*Inactive*] (EA)
BC	Beam Collimator
BC	Beatles Connection [*An association*] (EA)
B & C	Bed and Chair [*Rest*] [*Medicine*]
BC	Before Calculators
BC	Before Casinos
BC	Before Christ
BC	Before Cloning [*Cytology*]
BC	Before Commercialism
BC	Before Computer
BC	Before the Crash [*i.e., before the 1929 stock market collapse*] [*Slang*]
BC	Before Credit Cards [*Slang*]
BC	Before Croonery [*Musical slang*]
BC	Beginning Climb [*Aviation*] (FAAC)
BC	Behavior Cards [*Psychological testing*]
BC	Bell Canada [*Toronto Stock Exchange symbol*]
BC	Bell Cord [*Technical drawings*]
BC	Bellanca Contact (EA)
BC	Bell's Commentaries on the Laws of Scotland [*A publication*] (DLA)
B/C	Bench Check (NASA)
B-C	Benefit-Cost [*Ratio*]
BC	Bengal Cavalry [*British military*] (DMA)
BC	Bereavement Center (EA)
BC	Berlin Command [*Allied German Occupation Forces*]
BC	Between Centers [*Technical drawings*]
BC	Biblical Colloquium (EA)
BC	Bibliographia Cartographica [*A publication*]
BC	Bibliographic Classification [*System of library classification devised by Henry Evelyn Bliss*]
BC	Bibliotheca Celtica [*A publication*]
BC	Bicomponent [*Laboratory tubing*]
BC	Bile Canaliculi [*Anatomy*]
B/C	Bill for Collection
BC	Billing Cease Date (TEL)
BC	Binary Code
BC	Binary Counter
BC	Binding Capacity
BC	Biological and Chemical
BC	Biological and Chemical Warfare (NATG)
B & C	Biopsy and Curettage [*Gynecology*]
BC	Bipolar Cell [*In the retina*]
BC	Birth Certificate
BC	Birth Control
BC	Bisexual Center (EA)
BC	Black-Capped Chickadee [*Ornithology*]
BC	Black Code [*Law passed after the Civil War limiting the rights of Negroes in the South*]
BC	Black Colt (ROG)
BC	[*Y*] Blaengwyr Cenedlaethol [*The National Resurgence Party of the peoples of Britain*]
BC	Blastodermal Cell [*Insect embryology*]
BC	Blind Child [*Social Security Administration*] (OICC)
BC	Bliss Classification
BC	Block Count [*Data processing*]
BC	Blood Culture [*Medicine*]
BC	Bloomsday Club (EA)
BC	Blue Card (EA)
BC	Blue Chip [*Investment term*]
BC	Blue Crescent [*Later, BCI*] [*An association*] (EAIO)
BC	Blue Cross [*Health insurance plan*]
BC	Board of Control [*British*] (ROG)
BC	Boat Club
BC	Body-Centered [*Crystallography*]
BC	Body Count [*Military*] (CINC)
BC	Bogus Check [*Banking*]
BC	Bohemian Club (EA)

BC .... Boletim Cultural. Camara Municipal do Porto [*A publication*]
BC .... Bollettino della Capitale [*A publication*]
BC .... Bolometric Correction
BC .... Bolt Circle [*Technical drawings*]
BC .... Bombay Cavalry [*British military*]   (DMA)
BC .... Bomber Command
BC .... Bonded Single Cotton [*Wire insulation*]   (MSA)
BC .... Bone Conduction [*Medicine*]
BC .... Book Collector [*A publication*]
BC .... Bookcase   (MSA)
BC .... Boom Controller   (MCD)
BC .... Boresight Camera
BC .... Born in Colony [*British*]   (ADA)
BC .... Borocarbon
BC .... Borough Constituency
BC .... Borough Council
BC .... Boston College [*Chestnut Hill, MA*]
BC .... Bottom Center [*Valve position*]
BC .... Bottom Chord
BC .... Bottom Contour [*Navy*] [*British*]
BC .... Box Core [*Marine geology*]
BC .... Boxes or Crates [*Freight*]
BC .... Boyle-Conway Solution [*Neurophysiology*]
BC .... Brachium [*Neurology*]
BC .... Brachium Conjunctivum [*Neuroanatomy*]
BC .... Brachycardia [*Cardiology*]
BC .... Bradford College [*Formerly, BJC*] [*Massachusetts*]
BC .... Bradley Commander [*Army*]   (INF)
BC .... Breguet Cruise [*SST*]
BC .... Brightness Contrast
BC .... Brisbane Courier [*A publication*]   (APTA)
BC .... Bristol Channel [*British*]
BC .... British Columbia [*Canadian province*] [*Postal code*]
BC .... British Columbia Law Reports [*Canada*] [*A publication*]   (DLA)
BC .... British Commissioner [*Salvation Army*]
BC .... British Commonwealth
B & C .... British & Commonwealth [*Company*]
B & C .... British & Commonwealth Holdings [*Commercial firm*]   (ECON)
BC .... British Corporation
BC .... British Council
BC .... Brixton College [*London, England*]
B/C .... Broadcast   (NATG)
BC .... Broadcast Control
B/C .... Broadcasting [*A publication*]
BC .... Broadcasting   (MCD)
BC .... Broadcasting Program [*Association of Independent Colleges and Schools specialization code*]
BC .... Broadcasting Station [*ITU designation*]   (CET)
BC .... Bronchial Carcinoid
BC .... Bronchiectatic Cyst [*Pulmonary medicine*]
BC .... Brotherhood Commission   (EA)
BC .... Brunswick Corporation [*NYSE symbol*]   (SPSG)
BC .... Bubble Chamber
BC .... Bubble Column [*Engineering*]
BC .... Bubble Curtain [*Pisciculture*]
BC .... Buccal Cartilage [*Dentistry*]
BC .... Buccal Commissure [*Dentistry*]
BC .... Buccocervical [*Dentistry*]
BC .... Budget Center   (MCD)
BC .... Budget Code [*Air Force*]   (AFIT)
BC .... Budgetary Control   (DCTA)
BC .... Budgeted Cost   (ADA)
BC .... Buecker Flugzeugbau GmbH & Hagglund-Soner [*Federal Republic of Germany*] [*ICAO aircraft manufacturer identifier*]   (ICAO)
B & C .... Building and Contents [*Insurance*]
BC .... Bulbocavernosus [*Muscle group*]
BC .... Bulkhead Connector
BC .... Bulletin of the Comediantes [*A publication*]
BC .... Bulletin Critique [*A publication*]
BC .... Bulletin de Nos Communautes [*A publication*]
BC .... Buoyancy Compensators
BC .... Buoyant Capsule   (MCD)
BC .... Burden Center
BC .... Bureau of the Census [*Department of Commerce*]   (MCD)
BC .... Bureau of Consultation [*Federal Trade Commission*]
BC .... Bureau of Customs [*Later, US Customs Service*] [*Department of the Treasury*]
BC .... Burro Club [*Democratic political organization*] [*Defunct*]   (EA)
BC .... Burroughs Corporation
BC .... Bursting Charge [*Military*]
BC .... Bus Controller   (MCD)
BC .... Bus Coupler [*Data processing*]   (MCD)
BC .... Business Census
BC .... Business Council   (EA)
BC .... Butacaine [*Topical anesthetic*]
Bc .... Conjugated Bilirubin [*Chemistry*]
BC .... Coquitlam Public Library, British Columbia [*Library symbol*] [*National Library of Canada*]   (NLC)

BC .... European Air Transport [*Belgium*] [*ICAO designator*]   (FAAC)
BC .... New South Wales Bankruptcy Cases [*A publication*]
BC .... Sandoz AG [*Switzerland*] [*Research code symbol*]
BC .... Y Blaengwyr Cenedlaethol [*The National Resurgence Party of the Peoples of Britain*]
B3C .... Beverage Container Control Coalition [*Later, WCFR*]   (EA)
BCA .... Bachelor of Commercial Arts
BCA .... Bachelor of Creative Arts
BCA .... Bangladesh Cultural Association   (EA)
BCA .... Baracoa [*Cuba*] [*Airport symbol*]   (OAG)
BCA .... Barca [*Ship's rigging*]   (ROG)
BCA .... Barium Chloranilate [*Organic chemistry*]
B de Ca .... Bartholomaeus de Capua [*Deceased, 1328*] [*Authority cited in pre-1607 legal work*]   (DSA)
BCA .... Base Closure Action   (MCD)
BCA .... Basenji Club of America   (EA)
BCA .... Battery Control Area [*Army*]
BCA .... Battlefield Commanders' Aid [*Army*]
BCA .... BCA Credit Information [*Later, Broadcast Credit Association*]   (EA)
BCA .... Beale Cypher Association   (EA)
BCA .... Benefit Cost Analysis [*Accounting*]
BCA .... Benzenecarboxylic Acid [*Organic chemistry*]
BCA .... Best Copy Available
BCA .... Best Cruise Altitude
BCA .... Bicinchoninic Acid [*Organic chemistry*]
BCA .... Bicycle Club of America   (EA)
BCA .... Bilderberg Continuum Atmosphere
BCA .... Billiard Congress of America   (EA)
BCA .... Blaetter fuer Christliche Archaeologie und Kunst [*A publication*]
BCA .... Bliss Classification Association [*London, England*]
BCA .... Blood Color Analyzer [*Medicine*]
BCA .... Blue Cross Association [*Later, BCBSA*]   (EA)
BCA .... Board of Certification in Anesthesiology   (EA)
BCA .... Board of Contract Appeals [*Energy Research and Development Administration*]
BCA .... Book Club Associates [*British*]
BCA .... Booster Change Assembly   (MCD)
BCA .... Bovine Carbonic Anhydrase [*An enzyme*]
BCA .... Boy Clerks Association [*A union*] [*British*]
BCA .... Boys' Clubs of America   (EA)
BCA .... Brascade Resources, Inc. [*Toronto Stock Exchange symbol*]
BCA .... Briard Club of America   (EA)
BCA .... British Caledonian Airways Ltd.
BCA .... British Car Auctions
BCA .... British Cement Association [*Also, an information service or system*]   (IID)
BCA .... British Central Africa [*Pre-World War II*]
BCA .... British Chief Administrator
BCA .... British Chiropractors' Association
BCA .... British College of Accountancy, Ltd.
B/C of A ..... British College of Aeronautics
BCA .... British Colonial Airlines, Inc.
BCA .... British Commonwealth Alliance   (ADA)
BCA .... Broadcast Control Authority   (NVT)
BCA .... Broadcast Credit Association   (EA)
BCA .... Buddhists Concerned for Animals [*Inactive*]   (EA)
BCA .... Buick Club of America   (EA)
BCA .... Building Code of Australia
BCA .... Bulbocavernosus Activity [*Physiology*]
BCA .... Bulldog Club of America   (EA)
BCA .... Bullseye Class Association   (EA)
BCA .... Bureau of Co-Ordination of Arabization   (EA)
BCA .... Business Committee for the Arts   (EA)
BCA .... Business Council of Australia
BCAA .... Branched-Chain Amino Acid [*Biochemistry*]
BCAA .... Bristol Centre for the Advancement of Architecture [*British*]   (CB)
BCABP ...... British Campaign Against Book Piracy
BCABP ...... Bureau of Competitive Assessment and Business Policy [*Department of Commerce*]
BCAC .... Bollettino. Commissione Archeologica Comunale di Roma [*A publication*]
BCAC .... Breast Cancer Advisory Center   (EA)
BCAC .... British Conference on Automation and Computation
BCA CCH ... Board of Contract Appeals Decisions. Commerce Clearing House [*A publication*]
BCACR ...... Bollettino. Commissione Archeologica Comunale di Roma [*A publication*]
BC Admin .. British Columbia Administrator [*A publication*]
BCAFBWA ... Buddhist Churches of America Federation of Buddhist Women's Associations   (EA)
B Cal .... British Caledonian Airways   (DCTA)
BCALA ...... Black Caucus of the American Library Association   (EA)
BCALA ...... Black Librarians Caucus   (EA)
BCAM .... Bulletin. Cercle Archeologique, Litteraire, et Artistique de Malines [*A publication*]
B Camuno St Pr Istor ... Bollettino. Centro Camuno di Studi Preistorici [*A publication*]

BCAN .... Bulletin. Commission Archeologique de Narbonne [*A publication*]

BCAN .... Bureau Control Activity Number

BCANA ..... Bulletin. International Union Against Cancer [*A publication*]

B Cancer .... Bulletin du Cancer [*Paris*] [*A publication*]

BCA News ... BCA [*Business Committee for the Arts*] News [*A publication*]

B Can L ...... Bachelor of Canon Law

BCAO .... Branch Cultural Affairs Officer [*United States Information Service*]

BCAP........ Bipartite Civil Aviation Panel [*Post-World War II, Germany*]

BCAP........ Budget/Cost Account Plan   (MCD)

BCAPT ...... Braverman-Chevigny Auditory Projective Test [*Psychology*]

BCAR........ Bollettino. Commissione Archeologica Comunale di Roma [*A publication*]

BCAR........ British Civil Airworthiness Requirements

BCAR........ British Civil Aviation Regulations   (MCD)

BCAR........ British Council for Aid to Refugees

BCARDD... Connecticut Arboretum Bulletin [*A publication*]

BC Art Teach Assn J ... British Columbia Art Teachers' Association. Journal [*A publication*]

BCAS......... Barclay Classroom Assessment System [*Student personality test*]

BCAS........ Base Contracting Automated System [*Data processing*]

BCAS........ Beacon Collision Avoidance System [*Aviation*]

BCAS........ British Compressed Air Society

BCA (Sic)... Beni Culturali e Ambientali (Sicilia) [*A publication*]

BCASSI News ... British Columbia Association of School Supervisors of Instruction. News [*A publication*]

Bcast .... Broadcast [*United Kingdom*] [*A publication*]

BCATF....... Bearcat Explorations Ltd. [*NASDAQ symbol*]   (NQ)

BCATP ...... British Commonwealth Air Training Plan [*World War II*]

BCAVE....... Bleomycin, CCNU [*Lomustine*], Adriamycin, Vinblastine [*Antineoplastic drug regimen*]

BC-B .... Bacteriochlorophyll-B [*Biochemistry*]

BCB........... Ballet Contemporani de Barcelona

BCB........... Battery Control Building [*Army*]

BCB........... BC [*British Columbia*] Business [*A publication*]

BCB........... Big Creek Baldy [*Montana*] [*Seismograph station code, US Geological Survey*] [*Closed*]   (SEIS)

BCB........... Binary Code Box

BCB........... BIT [*Binary Digit*] Control Block [*Data processing*]   (IBMDP)

BCB........... Blacksburg, VA [*Location identifier*] [*FAA*]   (FAAL)

BCB........... Boletin Cultural y Bibliografico [*Bogota*] [*A publication*]

BCB........... Brilliant Cresyl Blue [*Biological stain*]

BCB........... Brinkman's Cumulatieve Catalogus van Boeken in Nederland en Vlaanderen Uitgegeven of Herdrukt met Aanvullingen over Voorafgaande Jaren [*A publication*]

BCB........... British Consultants Bureau   (CB)

BCB........... Broadcast Band

BCB........... Broadcasting Corporation of the Bahamas

BCB........... Business Corporation Board

BCB........... Button Cell Battery

BCB........... Cott Beverages Ltd. [*Toronto Stock Exchange symbol*]

BCBA........ Academie Royale de Belgique. Bulletin. Classe des Beaux-Arts [*A publication*]

BCBC........ Being for Carter before the Convention [*One of the Carter Administration's criteria for appointment of federal judges*]

BCBC........ Brooklyn Center for the Performing Arts at Brooklyn College

BCBG........ Bon Chic, Bon Genre [*Good Style, Good Family*] [*Initialism used to denote French Yuppies*] [*Lifestyle classification*]

BCBIEQ .... Biochemistry and Cell Biology [*A publication*]

BCBJ .... Monthly Bulletin. Central Bank of Jordan [*A publication*]

BCBL........ Bulletin. Cercle Belge de Linguistique [*A publication*]

BC Branch Lectures ... British Columbia Branch Lectures [*A publication*]   (DLA)

BC/BS ...... Blue Cross/Blue Shield [*Health insurance plan*]

BCBSA...... Blue Cross and Blue Shield Association [*Chicago, IL*]   (EA)

BC Bus Ed Assn News ... British Columbia Business Educators' Association. Newsletter [*A publication*]

BC Bus Mag ... BC [*British Columbia*] Business Magazine [*A publication*]

BCC .... Bail Court Cases [*Legal*] [*British*]

BCC .... Bail Court Reports (Saunders and Cole) [*England*] [*A publication*]   (DLA)

BCC .... Balanced Colorimeter Chamber   (MCD)

BCC .... Ballistic Camera Control   (KSC)

BCC .... Baltimore College of Commerce [*Maryland*]

BCC .... Basal Cell Carcinoma [*Medicine*]

BCC .... Basic Cryptanalysis Course

BCC .... Battery Control Central [*Army*]

BCC .... Baylor Computing Center [*Baylor College of Medicine*] [*Research center*]   (RCD)

BCC .... Beam Coupling Coefficient

BCC .... Bear Creek, AK [*Location identifier*] [*FAA*]   (FAAL)

BCC .... Behavior Classification Checklist [*Psychology*]

BCC .... Benard Convection Cell

BCC .... Bentall Capital Corp. [*Toronto Stock Exchange symbol*]

BCC .... Berkshire Community College [*Pittsfield, MA*]

BCC .... Best Candidate Committee   (EA)

BCC .... Bethune-Cookman College [*Daytona Beach, FL*]

BCC .... Birth Control Clinic

BCC .... Blank Carbon Copy

BCC .... Blind Carbon Copy

BCC .... Block Check Character [*Data processing*]

BCC .... Blocked Calls Cleared [*Telecommunications*]

BCC .... Body-Centered Cubic [*Also, BCCUB*] [*Crystallography*]

BCC .... Boise Cascade Corporation [*NYSE symbol*]   (SPSG)

BCC .... Boone and Crockett Club   (EA)

BCC .... Branch Conditionally [*Data processing*]

BCC .... Brazilian Chamber of Commerce   (DS)

BCC .... Brevard Community College [*Florida*]   (KSC)

BCC .... Briar Cliff College [*Sioux City, IA*]

BCC .... British Chamber of Commerce   (DS)

BCC .... British Clothing Industry Productivity and Technology Centre   (CB)

BCC .... British Colour Council

bcc .... British Columbia [*MARC country of publication code*] [*Library of Congress*]   (LCCP)

BCC .... British Columbia Reports [*A publication*]   (DLA)

BCC .... British Copyright Council   (ILCA)

BCC .... British Council of Churches

BCC .... British Crafts Centre   (CB)

BCC .... British Crown Colony

BCC .... Broadcast Control Center

BCC .... Broadcasting Corporation of China

BCC .... Bronx Community College [*New York*]

BCC .... Brookdale Community College, Lincroft, NJ [*OCLC symbol*]   (OCLC)

BCC .... Brown's Chancery Cases [*England*] [*A publication*]   (DLA)

BCC .... Budget Classification Code   (NVT)

BCC .... Buick Compact Club   (EA)

BCC .... Bureau Central de Compensation [*Central Bureau of Compensation - CBC*]   (EAIO)

BCC .... Bureau of Community Corrections   (OICC)

BCC .... Bus and Coach Council [*British*]

BCC .... Business Communications Company, Inc. [*Norwalk, CT*] [*Information service or system*] [*Telecommunications*]   (TSSD)

BCC .... Colson Canyon [*California*] [*Seismograph station code, US Geological Survey*]   (SEIS)

BCC .... Family History Library, Church of Jesus Christ of Latter-Day Saints, Cranbrook, British Columbia [*Library symbol*] [*National Library of Canada*]   (BIB)

BCC-52 ...... BASIC-52 Computer/Controller

BCCA........ Bearded Collie Club of America   (EA)

BCCA........ Beer Can Collectors of America   (EA)

BCCA........ Buick Collector's Club of America [*Defunct*]

BCCA........ Buick Compact Club of America [*Later, BCC*]   (EA)

BCCA........ Byelorussian Congress Committee of America   (EA)

BCCB........ British Chamber of Commerce, Bangkok   (DS)

BCCB........ Columbia Bible College, Clearbrook, British Columbia [*Library symbol*] [*National Library of Canada*]   (BIB)

BCCC........ Ballistic Compressor Computer Code

BCCC........ Bullseye Cancel Collectors Club

BCCCA...... Biscuit, Cake, Chocolate, and Confectionery Alliance   (EAIO)

BCCCD..... Biweekly Cryogenics Current Awareness Service [*A publication*]

BCCCN...... Bollettino. Commemorazione del XVI Centenario del Concilio di Nicea [*A publication*]

BCCD .... Bulk-Channel Charge-Coupled Device [*Electronics*]   (TEL)

BCCE........ British Cleaning Council Exhibition   (ITD)

BCCF .... Bollettino Critico di Cose Francescane [*A publication*]

BCCFC....... Billy "Crash" Craddock Fan Club   (EA)

BCCFSUA ... Barn Cleaner, Cattle Feeder, and Silo Unloader Association [*Later, FEA*]   (EA)

BCCI......... Bank of Credit & Commerce International   (ECON)

BCCI......... Business Card Collectors International   (EA)

BCCL........ Birkbeck College Computation Laboratory [*British*]

BCCMP..... Boletim Cultural. Camara Municipal do Porto [*A publication*]

BCCO........ Base Consolidation Control Office   (AFM)

B & C Comp ... Bellinger and Cotton's Annotated Codes and Statutes [*Oregon*] [*A publication*]   (DLA)

BC Couns... British Columbia Counsellor [*A publication*]

BCCP........ Biotin Carboxyl Carrier Protein [*Biochemistry*]

BCCS......... Barber Coin Collector Society   (EA)

BC/CS ...... Bottle Cleaning/Charging Station

BCCT........ [*The*] Bible in Current Catholic Thought [*A publication*]

BCCT........ Break Control Command Transducers   (NASA)

BCCT........ British Columbia Coast Terminals [*Canada*]

BCCUB...... Body-Centered Cubic [*Also, BCC*] [*Crystallography*]

BCCUS...... Belgian Chamber of Commerce in the United States [*Later, Belgian American Chamber of Commerce in the United States*]

BCCW........ Bare Copper-Clad Wire

BCD .... Bacolod [*Philippines*] [*Airport symbol*]   (OAG)

BCD .... Bad Conduct Discharge [*Military*]

BCD .... Bank fuer Gemeinwirtschaft. Aussenhandelsdienst [*A publication*]

BCD .... Bankruptcy Court Decisions [*A publication*]

B & CD...... Barrier and Countersurveillance Division [*Army*]   (RDA)

BCD .... Battle Correlator Display

BCD .... Behind Completion Date

BCD .... Beta-Cyclodextrin [*Organic chemistry*]

BCD.......... Between Comfort and Discomfort
BCD.......... Binary-Coded Data [*or Decimal*] [*Data processing*]
BCD.......... Bleomycin, Cyclophosphamide, Dactinomycin [*Antineoplastic drug regimen*]
BCD.......... Blocked Calls Delayed [*Telecommunications*]
BCd.......... Blood Cadmium Level
BCD.......... Bramalea Ltd. [*Toronto Stock Exchange symbol*]
BCD.......... Brill, C. D., Washington DC [*STAC*]
BCD.......... Burst Cartridge Detection
BCD.......... Business Conditions Digest [*A publication*]
BCD.......... Business Cycle Developments [*Bureau of the Census*] [*A publication*]
BCD.......... Casitas Dam [*California*] [*Seismograph station code, US Geological Survey*] (SEIS)
BCD.......... Castlegar and District Public Library, Castlegar, British Columbia [*Library symbol*] [*National Library of Canada*] (NLC)
BCDA .... Barge and Canal Development Association [*British*]
BCDA .... Biscuit and Cracker Distributors Association (EA)
BCD/B....... Binary-Coded Decimal/Binary (DEN)
BCDC .... Benzylcinchonidinium Chloride [*Organic chemistry*]
BCDC .... Binary-Coded Decimal Counter
BCDC .... Black Country Development Corporation [*Department of Environment*] [*British*]
BCDC .... Breast Cancer Detection Center [*University of Michigan*] [*Research center*] (RCD)
BCDD .... Base Construction Depot Detachment [*Navy*]
BCDDP...... Breast Cancer Detection Demonstration Project [*NCI/ACS cosponsored project*]
BCDE........ Bulk-Cohesion-Dipolarity-Elasticity [*Factor analysis of physical property data of liquid compounds*]
BC Dep Mines Bull ... British Columbia. Department of Mines. Bulletin [*A publication*]
BC Dep Mines Non Met Miner Invest Rep ... British Columbia. Department of Mines. Non Metallic Mineral Investigations Report [*A publication*]
BC Dep Mines Pet Resour Bull ... British Columbia. Department of Mines and Petroleum Resources. Bulletin [*A publication*]
BC Dep Recreat Conserv Annu Rep ... British Columbia. Department of Recreation and Conservation. Annual Report [*A publication*]
BCDF........ B-Cell Differentiation Factor [*Immunology*]
BCDI........ Black Child Development Institute [*Later, NBCDI*] (EA)
BCDI........ Bollettino della Carta dei Dialetti Italiani [*A publication*]
BCDIC .... Binary-Coded Decimal Interchange Code (IEEE)
BCDMOS ... Bipolar-CMOS-DMOS (MCD)
BCDP........ Battery Control Data Processor [*Army*]
BCD/Q .... Binary-Coded Decimal/Quaternary (DEN)
BCDR .... Beta-Cedrene
BCDVM .... Doukhobor Village Museum, Castelgar, British Columbia [*Library symbol*] [*National Library of Canada*] (NLC)
BCE.......... Bachelor of Chemical Engineering
BCE.......... Bachelor of Christian Education
BCE.......... Bachelor of Civil Engineering
BCE.......... Backup Control Electronics (MCD)
bce .... Balance [*Balance*] [*French*] [*Accounting*]
BCE.......... Barium Cloud Experiment [*NASA*]
BCE.......... Basal Cell Epithelioma [*Obsolete*] [*Medicine*]
BCE.......... Base Civil Engineer [*Military*] (AFM)
BCE.......... Base Level Commercial Equipment [*DoD*]
BCE.......... Baseline Cost Estimate (AABC)
BCE.......... Battle Coordination Element [*Army*] (MCD)
BCE.......... BCE, Inc. [*Formerly, Bell Canada Enterprises*] [*NYSE symbol*] (SPSG)
BCE.......... Beam Collimation Error (MUGU)
BCE.......... Before Christian Era
BCE.......... Before the Common Era [*Jewish equivalent of BC*]
BCE.......... Bench Checkout Equipment
BCE.......... Board of Customs and Excise [*British*]
BCE.......... Boston Computer Exchange
BCE.......... Bovine Capillary Endothelial [*Cytology*]
BCE.......... Brace Resources Ltd. [*Vancouver Stock Exchange symbol*]
BCE.......... Bradley Crew Evaluator [*Army*] (INF)
BCE.......... British Coal Enterprise
BCE.......... British Columbia Hydro and Power Authority [*Formerly, British Columbia Electric Co. Ltd.*] [*AAR code*]
BCE.......... British Commonwealth and Empire
BCE.......... Bryce Canyon, UT [*Location identifier*] [*FAA*] (FAAL)
BCE.......... Bubble Chamber Experiment
B & CE....... Building and Civil Engineer [*British*]
BCE.......... Bulletin des Communautes Europeennes [*A publication*]
BCE.......... Bus Control Electronics (MCD)
BCE.......... Bus Control Element (MCD)
BCEC........ Blue-Collar Ethnic Catholic [*Political demography*]
B CECA ..... Bulletin. Communaute Europeenne du Charbon et de l'Acier [*A publication*]
BCECC ...... British-Central-European Chamber of Commerce (DAS)
BCECC ...... Bulletin de Cultures Ethniques et de Civilisations Comparees [*A publication*]
BCECF ...... Bis(carboxyethyl)carboxyfluorescein [*Organic chemistry*]
BCECRS.... Base Civil Engineering Course [*Air Force*]

BC Ed........ Bachelor of Commercial Education
BCED........ Bibliography of the Computer in Environmental Design [*A publication*]
BCEDLFB ... Bulletin. Centre d'Etudes et de Discussion de Litterature Francaise. Universite de Bordeaux [*A publication*]
B Ce Eng.... Bachelor of Cement Engineering
BCEFCU ... Bankers Committee to Eliminate Favoritism to Credit Unions (EA)
BCEI......... Base Closing Economic Injury [*Loan*]
BCEI......... Bureau Canadien de l'Education Internationale [*Canadian Bureau for International Education - CBIE*]
BCEIA .... Bishops' Committee for Ecumenical and Interreligious Affairs (EA)
BCEL........ British Commonwealth Ex-Services League [*Formerly, British Empire Services League*] [*London, England*]
BCEL........ Business Council for Effective Literacy (EA)
BCELA .... British Communications and Electronics [*A publication*]
B Celt St.... Bulletin. Board of Celtic Studies [*A publication*]
BCEM........ Bureau of Community Environmental Management [*Terminated, 1973*] [*HEW*]
BCEN .... Banque Commerciale pour l'Europe du Nord [*Commercial Bank for North Europe*] [*French*]
BCEN .... Black College Educational Network (TSSD)
BC Engl Teach J ... British Columbia English Teachers' Association. Journal [*A publication*]
BCent........ Bible du Centenaire [*A publication*] (BJA)
B Centre Docum Et Jur Econ Soc ... Bulletin. Centre de Documentation d'Etudes Juridiques, Economiques, et Sociales [*A publication*]
B Centre Europ Cult ... Bulletin. Centre Europeen de la Culture [*A publication*]
B Centre Inform Et Credit ... Bulletin. Centre d'Information et d'Etude du Credit [*A publication*]
BC Env Aff LR ... Boston College. Environmental Affairs Law Review [*A publication*]
BC Environ Aff Law R ... Boston College. Environmental Affairs Law Review [*A publication*]
BC Envtl Aff L Rev ... Boston College. Environmental Affairs Law Review [*A publication*]
BCEP........ Book of Classic English Poetry [*A publication*]
BCEPS....... Butoxycarbonylethyl Polysulfide [*Organic chemistry*]
BCER........ Bank of China. Economic Review [*A publication*]
B Ceram RA Spec Publ ... British Ceramic Research Association. Special Publications [*A publication*]
B Ceram RA Tech Note ... British Ceramic Research Association. Technical Notes [*A publication*]
B Cercle Num ... Bulletin. Cercle d'Etudes Numismatiques [*A publication*]
B Cer E...... Bachelor of Ceramic Engineering
B Cer Eng... Bachelor of Ceramic Engineering
BCES .... Bis(chloroethyl)sulfide [*Biochemistry*]
BCESCH ... Base Civil Engineering School [*Air Force*]
BCESS....... Bibliotheque des Centres d'Etudes Superieures Specialisees [*A publication*]
BCETB ...... Bulletin d'Information. CETAMA [*A publication*]
BCETCEHRS ... Bibliotheque des Centres d'Etudes Superieures Specialisees. Travaux du Centre d'Etudes Superieures Specialisees d'Histoire de Religions de Strasbourg [*A publication*]
BCEX........ Bundle Controlled Expansion
BCF.......... Bachelor of City Forestry
BCF.......... Bandpass Crystal Filter
BCF.......... Basic Control Frequency
BCF.......... Basophil Chemotactic Factor [*Hematology*]
BCF.......... Battle Cruiser Force [*British military*] (DMA)
BCF.......... Beam Correction Factor
BCF.......... Before Columbus Foundation (EA)
BCF.......... Belfast Car Ferries Ltd. (DS)
BCF.......... Billion Conductor Feet [*Telecommunications*] (TEL)
BCF.......... Billion Cubic Feet
BCF.......... Bioconcentration Factor [*of chemicals by living organisms*]
BCF.......... Blood Cancer Foundation (EA)
BCF.......... Body/Caudal Fin [*Ichthyology*]
BCF.......... Boletim Trimestral Subcomissao Catarinense de Folclore da Comissao Nacional Brasileira de Folclore do Instituto Brasileiro de Educacao, Ciencia, e Cultura [*A publication*]
BCF.......... British Commonwealth Forces
BCF.......... British Cycling Federation
BCF.......... Bromochlorodifluoromethane [*Fire extinguishing agent*] [*Organic chemistry*] (ADA)
BCF.......... Budgetaire, Comptable, et Financier [*Budget, Accounting, and Finance - BA & F*]
BCF.......... Bulk Continuous Filament [*Textile science*]
BCF.......... Bulked Continuous Fiber [*or Filament*] [*Textile*]
BCF.......... Bureau of Commercial Fisheries [*Later, National Marine Fisheries Service*]
BCF.......... Burlington Coat Factory Warehouse Corp. [*NYSE symbol*] (SPSG)
BCF.......... Business China [*A publication*]
BCF.......... FM Broadcasting Station [*ITU designation*] (CET)
BCFAG ...... Bouguer Corrected Free-Air Gradient [*Geophysics*]
B-CFC....... B-Colony Forming Cells
BCFC........ Billy Cate Fan Club (EA)

BCFC .... Bobby "C" Fan Club (EA)
BCFC .... Brandon Call Fan Club (EA)
BCFC .... Buddy Clark Fan Club (EA)
BCFC .... Business Coalition for Fair Competition (EA)
BCFD .... Billions of Cubic Feet per Day [of gas]
BCFESR .... British Commonwealth Far East Strategic Reserve
BCFF .... Bulletin. Comite Flamand de France [A publication]
BCFG .... Fog Patches [Aviation code] (FAAC)
BCFK .... British Commonwealth Forces, Korea [British
          military] (DMA)
BCFLS ...... Best Commercial Flight Line Test Set (MCD)
BCFM .... Black Citizens for a Fair Media (EA)
BCFM .... Broken Corn and Foreign Material [Quality measure for grain]
BCFMA ...... Broadcast Cable Financial Management Association (EA)
BC For Serv Annu Rep ... British Columbia. Forest Service. Annual Report [A
          publication]
BC For Serv Can For Serv Jt Rep ... British Columbia Forest Service-
          Canadian Forestry Service. Joint Report [A publication]
BC For Serv For Res Rev ... British Columbia. Forest Service. Forest Research
          Review [A publication]
BC For Serv Res Notes ... British Columbia. Forest Service. Research Notes
          [A publication]
BC For Serv Tech Publ ... British Columbia. Forest Service. Technical
          Publication [A publication]
BCFP .... Breast-Cyst Fluid Protein [Immunochemistry]
BCFSK ...... Binary Code Frequency Shift Keying [SAGE]
BCFTE ...... British Commonwealth Forest Translation Exchange
BCFVA ...... Fraser Valley Antique Farm Machinery Association,
          Clearbrook, British Columbia [Library symbol] [National
          Library of Canada] (NLC)
BCG .... Bacillus Calmette-Guerin [TB vaccine] (GPO)
BCG .... Ballistocardiogram [Medicine]
BCG .... Battalion Control Group [Army]
BCG .... Bemichi [Guyana] [Airport symbol] (OAG)
BCG .... Bicolor Guaiac [Test] [Medicine]
BCG .... Bidirectional Categorical Grammar
BCG .... Block-Connected Graph [Mathematics] [Used in GPRS]
BCG .... Blue-Collar Guy [Lifestyle classification]
BCG .... Blue Compact Galaxy [Astronomy]
BCG .... Board for Certification of Genealogists (EA)
BCG .... Body-Cooling Garment [NASA] (MCD)
BCG .... Boston Consulting Group (ECON)
BCG .... Bromcresol Green [An indicator] [Chemistry]
BCG .... Bucking Current Generator
BC Gaz ...... British Columbia Gazette [A publication]
BCGC .... Bradley Commander/Gunner Certification Test [Army] (INF)
BCGD .... Background
BCGF .... B-Cell Growth Factor [Biochemistry]
BCGN .... BCI Geonetics, Inc. [NASDAQ symbol] (NQ)
BCGuineP ... Boletim Cultural da Guine Portuguesa [A publication]
B Ch .... Baccalaureus Chirurgiae [Bachelor of Surgery]
B Ch .... Bachelor of Chemistry
B Ch .... Barbour's Chancery Reports [New York] [A
          publication] (DLA)
BCH .... Basal Cell Hyperplasia [Medicine]
BCH .... Beach (MCD)
BCh .... Ben Chajim (BJA)
BCH .... Bids per Circuit per Hour [Telecommunications]
BCH .... Binary-Coded Hexadecimal (MCD)
BCH .... Binary-Coded Hollerith
BCH .... Block Control Header [Data processing] (IBMDP)
BCH .... Blocked Calls Held [Telecommunications]
BCH .... Bomber Command Headquarters [British military] (DMA)
BCH .... Booksellers Clearing House [Commercial firm] [British]
BCH .... Bose-Chaudhuri-Hocquenghem [Cyclic codes]
          [Telecommunications] (MCD)
BCH .... Branch (ADA)
B/CH .... Bristol Channel [British]
BCH .... Bulletin. Commission Royale d'Histoire [A publication]
BCH .... Bulletin de Correspondance Hellenique [A publication]
BCH .... Chilliwack Public Library, British Columbia [Library symbol]
          [National Library of Canada] (NLC)
BCHAC ...... Bulletin. Cercle Historique et Archeologique de Courtrai [A
          publication]
BCHCM ...... Board of Certified Hazard Control Management (EA)
B Ch D ...... Baccalaureus Chirurgiae Dentium [Bachelor of Dental Surgery]
B Ch E ...... Bachelor of Chemical Engineering
BCHE .... Chetwynd Public Library, British Columbia [Library symbol]
          [National Library of Canada] (NLC)
B Chem ..... Bachelor of Chemistry
B Chem E... Bachelor of Chemical Engineering
B Chem S J ... Bulletin. Chemical Society of Japan [A publication]
B Ch Eng.... Bachelor of Chemical Engineering
BCHF .... Fraser Valley College, Chilliwack, British Columbia [Library
          symbol] [National Library of Canada] (NLC)
BCHG .... Bunching (MSA)
BCHG .... Test a BIT [Binary Digit] and Change [Data processing]
B Chir ...... Baccalaureus Chirurgiae [Bachelor of Surgery]
BC His Q ... British Columbia Historical Quarterly [A publication]
BChl.......... Bacteriochlorophyll [Biochemistry]
BCHL .... Bond Corporation Holdings Ltd. [Australia]

BCHM .... Chilliwack Museum, British Columbia [Library symbol]
          [National Library of Canada] (NLC)
B-CHOP.... Bleomycin, Cyclophosphamide, Hydroxydaunomycin
          [Adriamycin], Oncovin [Vincristine], Prednisone
          [Antineoplastic drug regimen]
B Chr Ed .... Bachelor of Christian Education
BChrom ..... Bachelor of Chromatics
BCHS .... Bing Crosby Historical Society (EA)
BCHS .... Bulletin. Cincinnati Historical Society [A publication]
BCHS .... Bureau of Community Health Services [Health Services
          Administration]
BCH Supp ... Bulletin de Correspondance Hellenique. Supplement [A
          publication]
BCHW .... Black Caucus of Health Workers (EA)
BCI............ Banca Commerciale Italiana [Italy]
BC & I .... Banca Popolare Commercio & Industria [People's Bank of
          Commerce & Industry] [Italy]
BCI............ Barcaldine [Australia] [Airport symbol] (OAG)
BCI............ Barro Colorado Island [Canal Zone] [Site of Smithsonian
          Tropical Research Institute]
BCI............ Basic Concepts Inventory [Psychology]
BCI............ Basic Cost Information (AFIT)
BCI............ Bat Conservation International (EA)
BCI............ Battery Condition Indicator (MCD)
BCI............ Battery Council International (EA)
BCI............ Bell Canada International, Inc. [Ottawa, ON]
          [Telecommunications] (TSSD)
BCI............ Bidirectional Computer Interface Program
BCI............ Binary-Coded Information
BCI............ Biomedical Communications Inventory [National Library of
          Medicine]
BCI............ BIT [Binary Digit] Count Integrity
          [Telecommunications] (TEL)
BCI............ Bituminous Coal Institute [Absorbed by NCA]
BCI............ Blue Circle Industries [British]
BCI............ Blue Crescent International (EAIO)
BCI............ Bluff Creek Industries R. R. [AAR code]
BCI............ Bond Corporation International [Hong Kong]
BCI............ Bonsai Clubs International (EA)
BCI............ Brazilian Coffee Institute (EA)
BCI............ British Columbia Institute of Technology Library [UTLAS
          symbol]
BCI............ British Columbia Resources Investment Corp. [Toronto Stock
          Exchange symbol] [Vancouver Stock Exchange symbol]
BCI............ Broadcast Interference [Telecommunications]
BCI............ Budgetary Cost Information [Accounting]
BCI............ Bureau of Contract Information [Defunct] (EA)
BCI............ International Broadcasting Station [ITU designation] (DEN)
BCI............ Nederlandse Chemische Industrie [A publication]
BCIA......... [A] Critical Introduction to the Apocrypha [L. H. Brockinton]
          [A publication]
BCIE .... Banco Centroamericano de Integracion Economica [Central
          American Bank of Economic Integration] [Teguciagalpa,
          Honduras]
B & Cie....... Bordier & Compagnie [Bank] [Switzerland]
BCIE .... British Channel Island Ferries
BCIF .... British Channel Island Ferries
BCII .... Business Computing [NASDAQ symbol] (NQ)
BCIIS........ Bulletin. Christian Institutes of Islamic Studies [A publication]
BCIL .... Bond Corp. International Ltd. [Hong Kong] (ECON)
BCIL .... Bulk/Common Items List (MCD)
BCIM........ Beyond Capacity of Intermediate Maintenance [Army] (MCD)
BCIM........ Bureau of Catholic Indian Missions (EA)
BC Ind Com'l L Rev ... Boston College. Industrial and Commercial Law
          Review [A publication]
BC Ind & Com L R ... Boston College. Industrial and Commercial Law Review
          [A publication]
BC Ind & Com L Rev ... Boston College. Industrial and Commercial Law
          Review [A publication]
BC Indus & Com L Rev ... Boston College. Industrial and Commercial Law
          Review [A publication]
BC Int'l and Comp LJ ... Boston College. International and Comparative Law
          Journal [A publication]
BC Int'l and Comp L Rev ... Boston College. International and Comparative
          Law Review [A publication]
BCIP .... Belgian Centre for Information Processing
BCIR......... Bomber Command Intelligence Report
BCIRA .... British Cast Iron Research Association
BCIRA Abstr Foundry Lit ... BCIRA [British Cast Iron Research Association]
          Abstracts of Foundry Literature [A publication]
BCIRA Abstr Int Foundry Lit ... BCIRA [British Cast Iron Research
          Association] Abstracts of International Foundry Literature
          [A publication]
BCIRA Abstr Int Lit Metal Cast Prod ... BCIRA [British Cast Iron Research
          Association] Abstracts of International Literature on Metal
          Castings Production [A publication]
BCIRA J ... BCIRA [British Cast Iron Research Association] Journal [A
          publication]
B Circ Num Nap ... Bollettino. Circolo Numismatico Napoletano [A
          publication]

BCN..........	Bilateral Cortical Necrosis [*Medicine*]
BCN..........	Biomedical Communications Network [*Proposed*] [*National Library of Medicine*]
BCN..........	Boulder City [*Nevada*] [*Seismograph station code, US Geological Survey*] [*Closed*] (SEIS)
BCN..........	Breakdown Control Number (MCD)
BCN..........	Brecon [*Welsh depot code*]
BCN..........	British Commonwealth of Nations
BCN..........	Broadband Communication Network (BUR)
BCN..........	Bureau Control Number
BCN..........	Business Computer Network, Inc. [*San Antonio, TX*] [*Telecommunications*] (TSSD)
BCNC........	Benzylcinchoninium Chloride [*Organic chemistry*]
BCNC........	Black Christian Nationalist Church
BC (Newspr) (Q) ...	Brisbane Courier Reports (Newspaper) (Queensland) [*A publication*] (APTA)
BCNJ........	Bancorp New Jersey, Inc. [*NASDAQ symbol*] (NQ)
BCNO........	British College of Naturopathy and Osteopathy
BCNR.......	Board for Correction of Naval Records
BC (NSW) ...	New South Wales Bankruptcy Cases [*A publication*] (APTA)
BCNU.......	Bis(chloroethyl)nitrosourea [*Carmustine*] [*Also, BiCNU*] [*Antineoplastic drug regimen*]
BCNUDJ...	Basic and Clinical Nutrition [*A publication*]
BCNY.......	Bond Club of New York [*New York, NY*] (EA)
BCNY.......	Brazilian Center of New York (EA)
BCNZ.......	Broadcasting Corporation of New Zealand
Bco...........	Banco [*Bank*] [*Italian*]
bco...........	Banco [*Bank*] [*French*]
Bco...........	Banco [*Bank*] [*Spanish*]
Bco...........	Banco [*Bank*] [*Portuguese*]
BCO..........	Base Contracting Officer [*Military*]
BCO..........	Battery Control Officer [*Army*] (AABC)
BCO..........	Battery Cutoff [*Telecommunications*] (TEL)
BCO..........	Bibliotheca Classica Orientalis [*A publication*]
BCO..........	Bill in Care Of [*Telecommunications*] (TEL)
BCO..........	Binary-Coded Octal [*Data processing*]
BCO..........	Blessings Corporation [*AMEX symbol*] (SPSG)
BCO..........	Booster Engine Cutoff [*Rocketry*]
BCO..........	Bridge Cutoff (IEEE)
BCOA.......	Basenji Club of America (EA)
BCOA.......	Bituminous Coal Operators' Association (EA)
BCOA.......	Borzoi Club of America (EA)
BCOB.......	Booster Cutoff Backup
BCOB.......	Broken Clouds or Better (MUGU)
BCOD.......	BC [*British Columbia*] Outdoors [*Canada*] [*A publication*]
BCOE.......	Bench Checkout Equipment
BCOF........	British Commonwealth Occupation Force [*Military*]
BCOI	British Central Office of Information
BCol	Book Collector [*A publication*]
BCOL	British Columbia Railway Co. [*AAR code*]
B Co Leg J'nal ...	Beaver County Legal Journal [*Pennsylvania*] [*A publication*]
B Com	Bachelor of Commerce
B Com	Bulletin of the Comediantes [*A publication*]
BCOM	Burroughs Computer Output to Microfilm (IEEE)
BCOM	Courtenay and District Museum, Courtenay, British Columbia [*Library symbol*] [*National Library of Canada*] (NLC)
B Com Adm ...	Bachelor of Commercial Administration
BCombStuds ...	Bachelor of Combined Studies [*British*] (DBQ)
B Comediant ...	Bulletin of the Comediantes [*A publication*]
BComEtSulp ...	Bulletin. Comite des Etudes. Compagnie de S. Sulpice [*Paris*] [*A publication*]
B Comm	Bachelor of Commerce
B Commun Europ ...	Bulletin des Communautes Europeennes [*A publication*]
BCOMN....	North Island College, Courtenay, British Columbia [*Library symbol*] [*National Library of Canada*] (NLC)
B Compos...	Bernardus Compostellanus [*Authority cited in pre-1607 legal work*] (DSA)
BComSc	Bachelor of Commercial Science
BCON........	British Commonwealth Occupation News [*A publication*] (APTA)
B Con As Sc ...	Bulletin of Concerned Asian Scholars [*A publication*]
B Concern As Schol ...	Bulletin of Concerned Asian Scholars [*A publication*]
B Concerned Asian Scholars ...	Bulletin of Concerned Asian Scholars [*A publication*]
B/CONF....	Bearing/Confidence
B Conjonct Region ...	Bulletin de Conjoncture Regionale [*A publication*]
B Conjoncture Suppl ...	Bulletin de Conjoncture Regionale. Supplement [*A publication*]
BCOO.......	Bomber Command Operational Order
BCOO.......	British College of Ophthalmic Opticians (DBQ)
BCOP	BCNU [*Carmustine*], Cyclophosphamide, Oncovin [*Vincristine*], Prednisone [*Antineoplastic drug regimen*]
B Copyrgt S ...	Bulletin. Copyright Society of the USA [*A publication*]
BCORP......	Business Council on the Reduction of Paperwork (EA)
BCOS.........	British Chiefs of Staff
BCP..........	Bachelor of City Planning
BCP..........	Bag Cell Peptide [*Biochemistry*]
BCP..........	Ballast Control Panel
BCP..........	Barrincorp Industries, Inc. [*Toronto Stock Exchange symbol*]
BCP..........	Base Condemnation Percent (NASA)
BCP..........	Basotho Congress Party [*Lesotho*] [*Political party*] (PPW)
BCP..........	Battery Command Post
BCP..........	BCNU [*Carmustine*], Cyclophosphamide, Prednisone [*Antineoplastic drug regimen*]
BCP..........	Beam Candlepower
BCP..........	Behavioral Characteristics Progression [*Scale*]
BCP..........	Bench Mark Control Point (NASA)
BCP..........	Bereaved Children's Program [*Later, BC*] (EA)
BCP..........	Bing Crosby Productions
BCP..........	BIT [*Binary Digit*] Control Panel [*Data processing*] (MCD)
BCP..........	Blanket Crime Policy [*Insurance*]
BCP..........	Blended Credit Program [*Federal government*]
BCP..........	Blue Cross Plan [*Health insurance*]
BCP..........	Board of Certification in Pedorthics (EA)
BCP..........	Book of Common Prayer [*Episcopalian*]
BCP..........	Bootstrap Commissioning Program [*Air Force*]
BCP..........	Borden Chemicals/Plastics [*NYSE symbol*] (SPSG)
BCP..........	British Commonwealth Pacific Airlines Ltd. (ADA)
BCP..........	Bromcresol Purple [*An indicator*] [*Chemistry*]
BCP..........	Bruccoli-Clark Publishers
BCP..........	Budget Change Proposal [*Accounting*]
BCP..........	Built-Up Cast Iron Propeller [*of a ship*] (DS)
BCP..........	Bulgarian Communist Party [*Bulgarska Komunisticheska Partiia*] [*Political party*] (PPW)
BCP..........	Bund-Communist Party [*Political party*] (BJA)
BCP..........	Burma Communist Party [*"White Flag" party*] [*Political party*] (PD)
BCP..........	Byte Control Protocol [*Data processing*]
BCPA........	Boys Club Professional Association [*Later, ABGCP*] (EA)
BCPA........	British Commonwealth Pacific Airlines Ltd.
BCPAA......	Beitraege zur Chemischen Physiologie und Pathologie [*A publication*]
BCPC........	Bradley Commander Proficiency Course [*Army*] (INF)
BCPC........	British Crop Protection Council
BCPCA.....	Biochemical Pharmacology [*A publication*]
BCPCB7	Buletinul de Cercetari Piscicole [*A publication*]
BCPD.......	Branch Circuit Protection Device
BCPDA.....	Bis(chlorosulfophenyl)phenanthrolinedicarboxylic Acid [*Organic chemistry*]
BCPE.........	Bollettino. Centro Internazionale per lo Studio dei Papiri Ercolanesi [*Cronache Ercolanesi*] [*Napoli*] [*A publication*]
BCPE.........	Bulletin. Centre Protestant d'Etudes [*A publication*]
BCPEA......	British Columbia Professional Engineer [*A publication*]
BCPF	Bishops' Committee on Priestly Formation (EA)
BCPG........	Bulletin of Canadian Petroleum Geology [*A publication*]
BCPGA.....	Bulletin of Canadian Petroleum Geology [*A publication*]
BcPh ....:...	Benzo(c)phenanthrene [*Organic chemistry*]
BCPHBM ...	British Journal of Clinical Pharmacology [*A publication*]
BCPI	Beef Cattle Price Index
BCPL	Basic Combined Programming Language
BCPL.........	Bootstrap Combined Programming Language [*Data processing*] (CSR)
BCPN........	Boletin. Comision Provincial de Monumentos de Navarra [*A publication*]
BCPO........	Boletin. Comision Provincial de Monumentos de Orense [*A publication*]
BCPO	British Commonwealth Producers' Organization
BCPOrense ...	Boletin. Comision Provincial de Monumentos de Orense [*A publication*]
BCPPAB....	Buletinul. Institutului de Cercetari si Proiectari Piscicole [*A publication*]
B & C Pr Cas ...	British and Colonial Prize Cases [*A publication*] (DLA)
BC Prof Eng ...	British Columbia Professional Engineer [*A publication*]
BC Prov Mus Nat Hist Anthropol Handb ...	British Columbia Provincial Museum of Natural History and Anthropology. Handbook [*A publication*]
BC Prov Mus Nat Hist Anthropol Rep ...	British Columbia Provincial Museum of Natural History and Anthropology. Report [*A publication*]
BCPS	Beam Candlepower Seconds
BCPSG	British Caribbean Philatelic Study Group (EA)
BCPSM	Board of Certified Product Safety Management (EA)
BCPTA	British Chemical Engineering and Process Technology [*A publication*]
BCQ...........	Book Collector's Quarterly [*A publication*]
B Cr............	Bachelor of Criminology
BCR	Bail Court Cases (Lowndes and Maxwell) [*England*] [*A publication*] (DLA)
BCR	Bail Court Reports [*Legal*] [*British*]
BCR	Bail Court Reports (Saunders and Cole) [*England*] [*A publication*] (DLA)
BCR	Bank Cash Ratio (ADA)
BCR	Bank Cash Reserve (ADA)
BCR	Bar Chart Report (MCD)
BCR	Bard [*C. R.*], Inc. [*NYSE symbol*] (SPSG)
BCR	Battery Charge Regulator
BCR	Battery Control RADAR [*Army*]
BCR	Battlefield Communications Review
BCR	Benefit-Cost Ratio [*Finance*]
BCR	Bibliographical Center for Research, Denver, CO [*OCLC symbol*] (OCLC)

BCR .... Bibliographical Center for Research, Rocky Mountain Region [*Library network*]
BCR .... Billing-Collecting-Remitting [*Accounting*] (TEL)
BCR .... Bituminous Coal Research (EA)
BCR .... Blocked Calls Released [*Telecommunications*]
BCR .... Bollettino. Commissione Archeologica Comunale di Roma [*A publication*]
BCR .... Borocarbon Resistor (CET)
BCR .... Bragg Cell Receiver (MCD)
BCR .... British Columbia Reports [*A publication*] (DLA)
BCR .... Brown's Chancery Cases [*England*] [*A publication*] (DLA)
BCR .... Bucaramanga [*Colombia*] [*Seismograph station code, US Geological Survey*] (SEIS)
BCR .... Budget Change Request [*Accounting*] (MCD)
BCr............. Bulletin Critique du Livre Francais [*A publication*]
BCR .... Business Communications Review [*A publication*]
BCR .... Community Bureau of Reference [*Belgium*]
BCR .... Cranbrook Public Library, British Columbia [*Library symbol*] [*National Library of Canada*] (NLC)
B & CR....... Reports of Bankruptcy and Companies Winding-Up Cases [*1918-41*] [*England*] [*A publication*] (DLA)
BCRA........ British Cave Research Association
BCRA........ Bureau Central des Renseignements et d'Action [*French Resistance organization*]
BCRAA...... Bulletin. Commissions Royales d'Art et d'Archeologie [*A publication*]
BCRAD..... BCRA [*British Carbonization Research Association*] Review [*A publication*]
BCRA/EE ... Ensayos Economicos. Banco Central de la Republica Argentina [*A publication*]
BCRA Rev ... BCRA [*British Carbonization Research Association*] Review [*A publication*]
BCRBD...... Boletim. Casa Regional da Beira-Douro [*A publication*]
BCRC......... Beef Cattle Research Center [*Michigan State University*] [*Research center*] (RCD)
BCRC......... Blissymbolics Communication Resource Centre [*British*] (CB)
BCRCA...... Boletim. Comissao Reguladora de Cereais do Arquipelago dos Acores [*A publication*]
BCRD .... Basic Consolidated Requirements Document (NASA)
BCRE......... Creston Public Library, British Columbia [*Library symbol*] [*National Library of Canada*] (NLC)
BCREA...... Bulletin. Centre de Recherches et d'Essais de Chatou [*A publication*]
B & C Rec... Brick and Clay Record [*A publication*]
BCRED...... Bulletin. Centres de Recherches Exploration-Production ELF [*Essences et Lubrifiants de France*] - Aquitaine [*A publication*]
BCREK...... East Kootenay Community College, Cranbrook, British Columbia [*Library symbol*] [*National Library of Canada*] (NLC)
BC Rep....... Bail Court Cases (Lowndes and Maxwell) [*England*] [*A publication*]
BC Rep....... Bail Court Reports (Saunders and Cole) [*England*] [*A publication*] (DLA)
BC Rep....... British Columbia Reports [*A publication*] (DLA)
BC Rep....... Brown's Chancery Cases [*England*] [*A publication*] (DLA)
BCREQ...... Broadcast Requested (FAAC)
BC Res ...... BC [*British Columbia*] Research [*A publication*]
BC Res .... British Columbia Research [*A publication*]
BC Res Counc Annu Rep ... British Columbia. Research Council. Annual Report [*A publication*]
BC Res Counc Tech Bull ... British Columbia. Research Council. Technical Bulletin [*A publication*]
B C Res Mus ... Bulletin. Council for Research in Music Education [*A publication*]
BC Rev Stat ... British Columbia Revised Statutes [*Canada*] [*A publication*] (DLA)
BC Rev Stat ... Revised Statutes of British Columbia [*A publication*]
BCRH........ Bulletin. Commission Royale d'Histoire [*A publication*]
BCRK .... Bear Creek Corp. [*NASDAQ symbol*] (NQ)
B/CRK....... Bell Crank [*Automotive engineering*]
BCRLSB.... Library Services Branch, Ministry of Provincial Secretary and Government Services, Cranbrook, British Columbia [*Library symbol*] [*National Library of Canada*] (NLC)
BCR & M ... Burlington, Cedar Rapids & Minnesota Railroad
BCRM .... Campbell River Museum and Archives, British Columbia [*Library symbol*] [*National Library of Canada*] (NLC)
BCR & N.... Burlington, Cedar Rapids & Northern Railway
BCRNL...... BCR [*Bituminous Coal Research*] National Laboratory (EA)
BCROS....... Black Crossover Vote [*Political science*]
BCRR........ Boyne City Railroad Co. [*AAR code*]
BCRR......... Bureau du Coordonnateur, Reforme de la Reglementation [*Office of the Coordinator, Regulatory Reform*] [*Canada*]
BCRR......... Railway Museum, Cranbrook, British Columbia [*Library symbol*] [*National Library of Canada*] (NLC)
BCRRR...... Buddhist Council for Refugee Rescue and Resettlement (EA)
BCRST ...... Bibliography on Cold Regions Science and Technology [*A publication*]
BCRT........ Binary-Coded Range Time (MUGU)
BCRT......... Bright Cathode-Ray Tube (DEN)

BCRTD...... Bulletin. Commission Royale de Toponymie et de Dialectologie [*A publication*]
BCRTS ..... Binary-Coded Range Time Signal (MUGU)
BCRUD5 ... Biology of Crustacea [*A publication*]
BCRV......... Blunt Conical Reentry Vehicle
BCS........... Bachelor of Chemical Science
BCS........... Bachelor of College Studies
BCS........... Bachelor of Commercial Science
BCS........... Bachelor of Computer Science
BCS........... Backup Control System
BCS........... Banque Centrale de Syrie [*Central Bank of Syria*] (BJA)
BCS........... Barclays PLC [*NYSE symbol*] (SPSG)
BCS........... Bardeen-Cooper-Schrieffer Theory [*Theoretical physics*]
BCS........... Basic Contract Specification
BCS........... Basic Control System [*For satellites*] (MDG)
BCS........... Battered Child Syndrome
BCS........... Battery Computer System (MCD)
BCS........... Battle Cruiser Squadron [*Navy*]
BCS........... Battlefield Computer System
BCS CR...... BC [*British Columbia*] Sugar Refinery Ltd. [*Toronto Stock Exchange symbol*]
BCS........... Beam Communications Set
BCS........... Beam Control Subsystem (MCD)
BCS........... Belleek Collector's Society [*Commercial firm*] (EA)
BCS........... Bengal Civil Service [*British*]
BCS........... Biblical Creation Society [*British*]
BCS........... Bibliographic Control System (ADA)
BCS........... Bidirectional Category System
BCS........... Biomedical Computing Society [*Later, SIGBIO*] (BUR)
BCS........... Black Country Society [*British*]
BCS........... Blip Counter System
BCS........... Block Control Sheet [*Data processing*]
BCS........... Block Control Signal [*Telecommunications*] (TEL)
BCS........... Blood Cell Separator [*Medicine*]
BCS........... Board of Certification in Surgery (EA)
BCS........... Boeing Computer Services Co. [*Information service or system*] (IID)
BCS........... Bombing Computer Set
BCS........... Book Communications System [*Information service*]
BCS........... Boston Computer Society (EA)
BCS........... Branch if Carry Set
BCS........... British Calibration Service [*Research center*] (IRC)
BCS........... British Cartographic Society
BCS........... British Ceramic Society
BCS........... British Chiefs of Staff
BCS........... British Computer Society [*London*]
BCS........... Broadcast Communications System
BCS........... Brothers of Charity of Spokane [*Roman Catholic religious order*]
BCS........... Bucknell Computer Services [*Bucknell University*] [*Research center*] (RCD)
BCS........... Budd-Chiari Syndrome [*Medicine*]
BCS........... Bulletin of Chinese Studies [*A publication*]
BCS........... Burst Communications Systems (MCD)
BCS........... Business Communications Service [*British Telecommunications International*] [*London*] (TSSD)
BCS........... Business Communications Systems [*Telecommunications*] (TEL)
BCS........... Business Computer Systems [*A publication*]
BCS........... Business Control System
BCS........... Business Customer Services [*Telecommunications*] (TEL)
BCS........... Office of Buildings and Community Systems [*Department of Energy*]
BCS........... Selkirk College, Castlegar, British Columbia [*Library symbol*] [*National Library of Canada*] (NLC)
BCSA........ British Colleges Sports Association
BCSA........ British Commonwealth Sugar Agreement
B CSAR Belg ... Bulletin. Classe des Sciences. Academie Royale de Belgique [*A publication*]
BC Sc .... Bachelor of Commercial Science
BCSC........ British Council of Shopping Centres
BCSCA...... Bibliotheca Cardiologica (Switzerland) [*A publication*]
BC Sch Couns News ... British Columbia School Counsellors' Association. Newsletter [*A publication*]
BC Sci Teach ... BC [*British Columbia*] Science Teacher [*A publication*]
BCSD........ Blank Corrected Sample Data [*Data processing*]
BC Se .... Bachelor of Commercial Service
BCSE .... Board of US Civil Service Examiners
BCSFLS .... Bollettino. Centro di Studi Filologici e Linguistici Siciliani [*A publication*]
BCSH .... Barat College of the Sacred Heart [*Later, Barat College*] [*Lake Forest, IL*]
BCSH .... British Committee for Standards in Haematology
BCSI .... Biometric Computer Service, Incorporated
BCSI .... Breast Cancer Screening Indicator
BCSI .... Built-In Cleaning Systems Institute [*Defunct*] (EA)
BCSI .... Business Computer Solutions [*Miami, FL*] [*NASDAQ symbol*] (NQ)
BCSic .... Bollettino. Centro di Studi Filologici e Linguistici Siciliani [*A publication*]
BCSJA....... Bulletin. Chemical Society of Japan [*A publication*]

BCSLA R... BCSLA [*British Columbia School Librarians' Association*] Reviews [*A publication*]

BCSLA Reviews ... BC [*British Columbia*] School Librarians Association. Reviews [*A publication*]

BCSM........ British Control Supply Mission [*World War II*]

BCSMC..... British Columbia Sports Medicine Clinic [*University of British Columbia*] [*Research center*] (RCD)

BCSO........ Bollettino. Centro di Studi Onomastici [*G. D. Serra*] [*A publication*]

BCSO........ British Commonwealth Scientific Office

BCSO(NA) ... British Commonwealth Scientific Office (North America) [*Washington, DC*]

BCSP .... Board of Certified Safety Professionals (EA)

BCSP .... Bollettino. Centro di Studi di Poesia Italiana e Straniera [*Roma*] [*A publication*]

BCSP .... Built-Up Cast Steel Propeller [*of a ship*] (DS)

BCSR .... Bubble Column Slurry Reactor [*Chemical engineering*]

BCSS .... Bishops' Committee for the Spanish Speaking [*Later, SHA*]

BCSS .... Bollettino. Centro di Studi Filologici e Linguistici Siciliani [*A publication*]

BCSS .... Breast Cancer Support Service [*Australia*]

BCST .... BC [*British Columbia*] Studies [*Canada*] [*A publication*]

BCST .... Broadcast [*Information transmission*] (AFM)

BCSTA ...... Bulletin. Calcutta School of Tropical Medicine [*A publication*]

BC Stat ..... British Columbia Statutes [*Canada*] [*A publication*] (DLA)

BCSTB....... Biochemical Society. Transactions [*A publication*]

BCSTG....... Broadcasting

BCSTN ...... Broadcast Station (FAAC)

BCSTR ...... Broadcaster

BC St Stor Archit ... Bollettino. Centro di Studi per la Storia dell'Architettura [*A publication*]

BCSV .... Bollettino. Centro di Studi Vichiani [*A publication*]

BCSWS ..... Battalion Close Support Weapon System (MCD)

BCSYDM .. Bristol-Myers Cancer Symposia [*A publication*]

BCT........... Bachelor of Christian Training

BCT........... Bandwidth Compression Technique

BCT........... Banque des Connaissances et des Techniques [*Knowledge and Technique Bank*] [*National Agency for the Promotion of Research*] [*Information service or system*] (IID)

BCT........... Basic Combat Training [*Army*] [*Later, BT*]

BCT........... Battalion Combat Team

BCT........... Battery Control Trailer (NATG)

BCT........... Bell. Competing Titles [*Scotland*] [*A publication*] (DLA)

BCT........... Best Conventional Technology [*Environmental Protection Agency*]

BCT........... Between Commands Testing [*Data processing*]

BCT........... Block-Cutpoint-Tree [*Mathematics*] [*Used in ASAMS*]

BCT........... Boca Raton, FL [*Location identifier*] [*FAA*] (FAAL)

BCT........... Body-Centered Tetragonal [*Crystallography*]

BCT........... Booklet Category Test [*Brain dysfunction test*]

BCT........... Boulangerie, Confiserie, Tabac [*Bakery, Confectionary, and Tobacco*] [*Canadian Union*]

BCT........... Briefcase Terminal [*Army*] (INF)

BCT........... British Caspian Trust

BCT........... British Columbia Telephone Co. [*Toronto Stock Exchange symbol*] [*Vancouver Stock Exchange symbol*]

BCT........... Brookfield [*Connecticut*] [*Seismograph station code, US Geological Survey*] (SEIS)

BCT........... Bus Configuration Table (MCD)

BCT........... Bushing Current Transformer (KSC)

BCT........... Gordon-Conwell Theological Seminary, South Hamilton, MA [*OCLC symbol*] (OCLC)

BCT........... Television Broadcasting Station [*ITU designation*] (CET)

BCTA........ British Children's Theatre Association

BC Tax Rep (CCH) ... British Columbia Tax Reporter (Commerce Clearing House) [*A publication*] (DLA)

BCTC........ British Carpet Technical Centre (CB)

BCTD........ Building and Construction Trades Department [*AFL-CIO*]

BCTD........ Bulletin. Commission Royale de Toponymie et de Dialectologie [*A publication*]

BCTE........ Bankers Committee for Tax Equality [*of the National Tax Equality Association*] (EA)

BCTF .... Breast Cancer Task Force [*National Cancer Institute*]

BCTF News ... British Columbia Teachers' Federation. Newsletter [*A publication*]

BCTH .... Bulletin Archeologique. Comite des Travaux Historiques [*A publication*]

BCTH .... Bulletin. Comite des Travaux Historiques et Scientifiques [*A publication*]

BC Third World LJ ... Boston College. Third World Law Journal [*A publication*] (DLA)

BCTIC .... Biomedical Computing Technology Information Center [*Oak Ridge National Laboratory*] [*Department of Energy*] (IID)

BCTKA...... Bromatologia i Chemia Toksykologiczna [*A publication*]

BCTKAG.... Bromatologia i Chemia Toksykologiczna [*A publication*]

BCTMP..... Bleached Chemi-Thermomechanical Pulp

BCTN .... Baja California - Territorio Norte

BCTOS ...... Bicentennial Council of the Thirteen Original States [*Later, CTOS*] (EA)

BCTP......... Battle Command Training Program [*Army*]

BCTPC ...... Bomber Command Tactical Planning Committee

BCTRD6..... Breast Cancer Research and Treatment [*A publication*]

BCTS........ Baja California - Territorio Sur

BCTU .... Basutoland Congress of Trade Unions

BCTV .... Berks Community Television [*Reading, PA*] [*Telecommunications*] (TSSD)

BCTV .... Bibliography on Cable Television [*A publication*] (TSSD)

BCTWIU... Bakery, Confectionary, and Tobacco Workers' International Union (EA)

BCU .... Ballistics Computer Unit

BCU .... Basic Computer Unit

BCU .... Battery/Coolant Unit (RDA)

BCU .... Bay Cabinet Unit

BCU .... Bayamon Central University, Bayamon, PR [*OCLC symbol*] (OCLC)

BCU .... BCU Industries, Inc. [*Toronto Stock Exchange symbol*]

BCU .... Bear Canyon [*Utah*] [*Seismograph station code, US Geological Survey*] [*Closed*] (SEIS)

BCU .... Bible Christian Union (EA)

BCU .... Big Close-Up [*A photograph or motion picture sequence taken from a short distance*]

BCU .... Binary Counting Unit (IEEE)

BCU .... Block Control Unit [*Data processing*] (IBMDP)

BCu .... Boletim Cultural [*A publication*]

BCU .... Bombardment Control Unit

BCU .... Boom Control Unit (MCD)

BCU .... B'rith Christian Union [*Later, FSJ*] (EA)

BCU .... British Canoe Union

BCU .... British Commonwealth Union (ADA)

BCU .... Buffer Control Unit [*Data processing*] (CET)

BCU .... Bus Control Unit (KSC)

BCU .... Hyannis, MA [*Location identifier*] [*FAA*] (FAAL)

BCUBAS ... Biological Sciences Curriculum Study. Bulletin [*A publication*]

BCUICE .... British Canoe Union International Canoeing Exhibition [*London, England*]

BCUM .... Cumberland Museum, British Columbia [*Library symbol*] [*National Library of Canada*] (NLC)

BCUN........ Business Council for the United Nations (EA)

BC Univ Dep Geol Rep ... British Columbia University. Department of Geology. Report [*A publication*]

BCURA ..... British Coal Utilisation Research Association

BCURA ..... British Coal Utilisation Research Association. Monthly Bulletin [*A publication*]

BCURA Gaz ... BCURA [*British Coal Utilization Research Association*] Gazette [*A publication*]

B Current L ... Butterworth's Current Law [*A publication*] (DLA)

BCUSA...... Buddhist Center of the United States of America (EA)

BCV .... Ball Check Valve

BCV .... Bancroft Convertible Fund, Inc. [*AMEX symbol*] (SPSG)

BCV .... Barge Carrying Vessel

BCV .... Barrel Cactus Virus

BCV .... Basal Cerebral Vigilance [*Sleep*]

BCV .... Battery Control Van (NATG)

BCV .... Battle Casualty Vietnam

BCV .... Bishop's Committee on Vocations (EA)

BCV .... Brightness Contrast Value

BCVM .... Creston Valley Museum, Creston, British Columbia [*Library symbol*] [*National Library of Canada*] (NLC)

BCVP .... BCNU [*Carmustine*], Cyclophosphamide, Vincristine, Prednisone [*Antineoplastic drug regimen*]

BCVPP ...... BCNU [*Carmustine*], Cyclophosphamide, Vinblastine, Procarbazine, Prednisone [*Antineoplastic drug regimen*]

BCVTP ...... Buciclovir Triphosphate [*Antiviral*]

BCVX........ Biconvex

BCW .... Bakery and Confectionery Workers' International Union of America [*Later, BCTWIU*]

BCW .... Bare Copper Wire

BCW .... Becor Western, Inc. [*NYSE symbol*] (SPSG)

BCW .... Biological and Chemical Warfare

BCW .... Bobbin Coil Winder

bcw .... Bogie Cattle Wagon [*Australian*] (ADA)

BCW .... Buffer Control Word [*Data processing*]

BCW .... Bury Cooper Whitehead Ltd. [*British*] (IRUK)

BC Water Waste Assoc Proc Annu Conf ... British Columbia Water and Waste Association. Proceedings of the Annual Conference [*A publication*]

BCWD .... Biological and Chemical Warfare Division [*DoD*]

BCWIU of A ... Bakery and Confectionery Workers' International Union of America [*Later, BCTWIU*] (EA)

BCWL .... Bulletin of Canadian Welfare Law [*A publication*]

BCWP........ Beam Candle Watt Power (MCD)

BCWP........ Budgeted Cost for Work Performed

BCWS........ Beam Candle Watt Seconds (MCD)

BCWS........ Budgeted Cost for Work Scheduled

BCX .... BCE Mobile Communications, Inc. [*Toronto Stock Exchange symbol*]

BC-X Can For Serv Pac For Res Cent ... BC-X. Canadian Forestry Service. Pacific Forest Research Centre [*A publication*]

BCY .... Banco Central [*Toronto Stock Exchange symbol*]

Bcy .... Bankruptcy [*Legal term*] (DLA)

BCY .... Boise City, OK [*Location identifier*] [*FAA*] (FAAL)

BCYCD...... BioCycle [*A publication*]
BCZ .... Barracuda Resources Ltd. [*Vancouver Stock Exchange symbol*]
BCZ .... Berlin Control Zone [*Allied German Occupation Forces*]
BCZ .... Butler, AL [*Location identifier*] [*FAA*]   (FAAL)
BD............. Bachelor of Divinity
BD............. Back Dividends
BD............. Backward Diode
BD............. Bad Delivery [*Investment term*]
B & D .... Bad and Doubtful Debt   (DCTA)
BD............. Bahrain Dinar [*Monetary unit*]   (BJA)
BD............. Balfour Declaration [*1917*] [*For protection of the Jewish
               settlement of Palestine*]   (BJA)
BD............. Balloon Destroyer [*British*]
BD............. Band [*Volume*] [*German*]
BD............. Band   (KSC)
BD............. Bande Dessinee [*Comic strip*] [*French*]
BD............. Bangladesh [*ANSI two-letter standard code*]   (CNC)
BD............. Bank Draft
BD............. Bar Draft [*Depth of water over a bar*]
BD............. Bark Dieback [*Plant pathology*]
B & D .... Barker & Dobson [*British*]
BD............. Barkley Dam [*TVA*]
BD............. Barrack Department [*British military*]   (DMA)
BD............. Barrels per Day
BD............. Base Deficit
BD............. Base Detonating
BD............. Base Diameter
BD............. Base-Down (Prism) [*Ophthalmology*]
BD............. Basic Democrats [*Pakistan*]
BD............. Basophilic Degeneration [*Hematology*]
BD............. Batten's Disease [*Medicine*]
BD............. Battle Dress [*Military*]
Bd.............. Baud [*Unit of data transmission speed*]   (CET)
BD............. BCE Development Corp. [*Toronto Stock Exchange symbol*]
               [*Vancouver Stock Exchange symbol*]
BD............. Beam Degrader
BD............. Beaver Defenders   (EA)
B-D............ Becton, Dickinson & Co. [*Initialism used in titles of a series of
               technical publications*]
BD............. Before Divestiture [*AT & T*]   (IT)
BD............. Beginning Descent [*Aviation*]   (FAAC)
BD............. Behavior Disorder
BD............. Behavioral Differential
BD............. Behcet's Disease [*Medicine*]
BD............. Belladonna [*Deadly Nightshade (or its medicinal extract)*]
BD............. Below Deck [*of a ship*]   (DS)
BD............. Bend Down
B & D .... Benloe and Dalison's English Common Pleas Reports [*A
               publication*]   (DLA)
BD............. Benzoylated DEAE [*Diethylaminoethyl*] [*Organic chemistry*]
BD............. Berger's Disease [*Medicine*]
BD............. Berlin District [*Allied German Occupation Forces*]
BD............. Bernoulli Disk
BD............. Best Delay [*Audiometry*]
BD............. Bible Dictionary [*A publication*]   (BJA)
BD............. Big Deal [*An association*]   (EA)
BD............. Bile Duct [*Medicine*]
BD............. Billing Day   (DCTA)
BD............. Bills Discounted
B/D............ Binary to Decimal [*Data processing*]
BD............. Binary Decoder [*Data processing*]
BD............. Binary Digit [*Data processing*]   (MCD)
BD............. Binary Discrete   (MCD)
BD............. Binary Divide
BD............. Binocular Deprivation [*Optics*]
BD............. Biographical Dictionaries and Related Works [*A publication*]
BD............. Bis in Die [*Twice a Day*] [*Pharmacy*]
BD............. BIT [*Binary Digit*] Density [*Data processing*]
BD............. Black Death [*1348-49*]
B & D .... Black & Decker Manufacturing Co.
BD............. Block Design [*Psychometrics*]
BD............. Blowdown [*Nuclear energy*]   (NRCH)
BD............. Blowing Dust [*Meteorology*]   (FAAC)
BD............. Board
BD............. Bodansky Unit [*Clinical chemistry*]
BD............. Bold   (ADA)
BD............. Bomb Disposal
BD............. Bond [*Investment term*]
B & D .... Bondage and Discipline
BD............. Bone Dry
BD............. Bonner Durchmusterung [*Star chart*]
BD............. Boom Defence [*Navy*] [*British*]
BD............. Booster Development
BD............. Borderline Dull [*Medicine*]
BD............. Bottle Drainage
BD............. Boulevard   (EY)
BD............. Bound
BD............. Box Diffusion [*Oceanography*]
b & d.......... Brandy and Dry Ginger   (ADA)
BD............. British Midland Airways Ltd. [*ICAO designator*]   (FAAC)
BD............. Broad   (ADA)

BD............. Broadband Distributive Services [*Telecommunications*]
B/D............ Broker-Dealer
BD............. Brought Down [*Accounting*]
BD............. Buccodistal [*Dentistry*]
BD............. Bulletin du Cange [*A publication*]
BD............. Bundle   (MCD)
BD............. Bureau of Drugs [*Later, Center for Drugs and Biologics*] [*FDA*]
BD............. Buried   (ROG)
BD............. Bursal Dependent [*Cells*] [*Immunology*]
bd .... Burundi [*MARC country of publication code*] [*Library of
               Congress*]   (LCCP)
BD............. Character in "Doonesbury" comic strip, named for Yale
               quarterback Brian Dowling
BD............. [*The*] Egyptian Book of the Dead   (BJA)
B7D............ Buyer Has Seven Days to Take Up [*Securities brokerage*]
               [*Investment term*]
BDA .... Bachelor of Domestic Arts
BDA .... Bachelor of Dramatic Art
BDA .... Backup Drive Amplifier   (MCD)
BDA .... Battle Damage Assessment
BDA .... Beer Drinkers of America   (EA)
BDA .... Bermuda [*Airport symbol*]   (OAG)
BDA .... Bermuda Island   (NASA)
BDA .... Bermuda Resources Ltd. [*Vancouver Stock Exchange symbol*]
BDA .... Bermuda Tracking Station [*NASA*]   (KSC)
BDA .... Beth Din of America   (EA)
BDA .... Binary Discriminant Analysis [*Statistics*]
BDA .... Blast Danger Area   (NASA)
BDA .... Bleed Door Actuator
BDA .... Block Decoder Assembly [*Space Flight Operations Facility,
               NASA*]
BDA .... Bollettino d'Arte [*A publication*]
BDA .... Bomb Damage Assessment
BDA .... Booster-Distribution Amplifier
BDA .... Boulder Dam [*Arizona*] [*Seismograph station code, US
               Geological Survey*] [*Closed*]   (SEIS)
BDA .... British Dental Association
BDA .... British Diabetic Association   (IRUK)
BDA .... [*The*] British Dietetic Association
BDA .... British Dyslexia Association
BDA .... Broadcast Designers Association   (EA)
BDA .... Burma Defense Army [*Later, BNA*] [*World War II*]
BDA .... Hamilton [*Bermuda*] [*Airport symbol*]
BDAA .... Balalaika and Domra Association of America   (EA)
BDAA .... Bio-Dynamic Agricultural Association [*British*]
BDAC .... Bureau of Drug Abuse Control [*Absorbed by Bureau of
               Narcotics and Dangerous Drugs of Department of Justice*]
BDAE .... Banque de Developpement de l'Afrique de l'Est [*East African
               Development Bank - EADB*]   (EAIO)
BDAE .... Boston Diagnostic Aphasia Examination
Bd Agric and Fish Ann Rep Proc Dis Anim Acts (London) ... Board of
               Agriculture and Fisheries. Annual Reports of Proceedings
               under the Diseases of Animals Acts (London) [*A
               publication*]
BDAI .... Bird Dog Association, International   (EA)
BDAL .... Biographical Dictionary of Australian Librarians [*A
               publication*]
BDAM .... Basic Direct Access Method [*IBM Corp.*] [*Data
               processing*]   (BUR)
BDAM .... Basic Disk Access Method   (MCD)
BDAPC....... Bulletin. Debating Association of Pennsylvania Colleges [*A
               publication*]
BDAR .... Battlefield Damage Assessment and Repair [*Technical manual*]
               [*Army*]   (RDA)
BDART...... Battle Damage Assessment and Reporting Team
BDAS........ Buddy DeFranco Appreciation Society   (EA)
BDASI....... Bulletin. Department of Antiquities of the State of Israel [*A
               publication*]
BDAT .... Best Demonstrated Available Technology
BDATS...... Biological Detection and Alarm Training Simulant   (MCD)
BDB .... Bagneres De Bigorre [*France*] [*Seismograph station code, US
               Geological Survey*]   (SEIS)
BDB .... Base Development Board [*Military*]   (AABC)
BDB .... Bibliographic Database
BDB .... Big Dumb Booster Rocket
BDB .... Bis-diazotized Benzidine [*Hematology*]
BDB .... Bjerrum Double Band [*Physics*]
BDB .... Borsenblatt fuer den Deutschen Buchhandel [*A publication*]
BDB .... Broadcasters Database [*Houston, TX*] [*Information service or
               system*]   (IID)
BDB .... Bundaberg [*Australia*] [*Airport symbol*]   (OAG)
BDB .... [*A*] Hebrew and English Lexicon of the Old Testament (Brown,
               Driver, and Briggs) [*A publication*]   (BJA)
BDBAD ..... Baumaschinendienst [*A publication*]
BDBBDB... Departement de Biologie. College Bourget Rigaud. Bulletin [*A
               publication*]
BDBD .... Bureau of Domestic Business Development [*Department of
               Commerce*]
BDBHA ..... Boersenblatt fuer den Deutschen Buchhandel [*A publication*]
BDBJ .... Board of Deputies of British Jews

BDC .... Bachelier en Droit Canonique [*Bachelor of Canon Law*] [*French*]
BDC .... Backup Digital Computer
BDC .... Batch Data Class [*Telecommunications*]
BDC .... Before Dead Center [*Valve position*]
BDC .... Benedict College, Columbia, SC [*OCLC symbol*] (OCLC)
BDC .... Beneficiary Developing Country [*Trade status*]
BDC .... Bentley Drivers Club (EA)
BDC .... Benzenediazonium Chloride [*Organic chemistry*]
BDC .... Berlin Document Center [*Allied German Occupation Forces*]
BDC .... Bi-Directional Converter (NASA)
BDC .... Binary Decimal Counter [*Data processing*]
BDC .... Block Downconverter [*Satellite communications*]
BDC .... Bomb Data Center [*International Association of Chiefs of Police*]
BDC .... Bonded Double Cotton [*Wire insulation*] (KSC)
BDC .... Book Development Council [*British*]
BDC .... Bottom Dead Center [*Engineering*]
BDC .... Bridge Display Console
BDC .... Brigade Data Center [*Military*] (AABC)
BDC .... Bulleti de Dialectologia Catalana [*A publication*]
BDC .... Bulletin. Deccan College Research Institute [*A publication*]
BDC .... Bureau of Domestic Commerce [*Formerly, Business and Defense Services Administration and Office of Field Services*] [*Department of Commerce*] [*Terminated, 1977, functions transferred to Domestic and International Business Administration*]
BDC .... Bureau International de Documentation des Chemins de Fer [*International Office of Railway Documentation*]
BDC .... Burn-Dressing Change [*Medicine*]
BDC .... Burndy Corporation [*NYSE symbol*] (SPSG)
BDC .... Business Development Consultants International, Ltd. [*British*]
BDC .... Dawson Creek Public Library, British Columbia [*Library symbol*] [*National Library of Canada*] (NLC)
BDCB .... Buffered Data and Control Bus
BDCC/ME ... British Defence Coordination Committee, Middle East (NATG)
BDCDA ..... Bulletin de Documentation. Centre d'Information du Chrome Dur [*A publication*]
BDCF .... Baseline Data Collection Facility (MCD)
BDCGA ..... Berichte. Deutsche Chemische Gesellschaft [*A publication*]
BDCGS ..... Birth Defect and Clinical Genetic Society (EA)
BDCL .... Library Advisory Council, Dawson Creek, British Columbia [*Library symbol*] [*National Library of Canada*] (NLC)
BDCLSB.... Library Services Branch, Ministry of Provincial Secretary and Government Services, Dawson Creek, British Columbia [*Library symbol*] [*National Library of Canada*] (NLC)
BDCNB ..... Bulletin. Centre de Compilation de Donnees Neutroniques [*A publication*]
BDCNL...... Northern Lights College, Dawson Creek, British Columbia [*Library symbol*] [*National Library of Canada*] (NLC)
Bd Cont App Dec ... Board of Contract Appeals Decisions [*Commerce Clearing House*] [*A publication*] (DLA)
Bd/Cpl .... Band Corporal [*British military*] (DMA)
BDCR .... Baseline Document Change Request (MCD)
BDCSB ...... Building Design and Construction [*A publication*]
Bd/CSgt..... Band Colour Sergeant [*British military*] (DMA)
BDCT........ Bradford Durfee College of Technology [*Later, Southeastern Massachusetts Technical Institute*]
BDCWW ... Walter Wright Pioneer Village, Dawson Creek, British Columbia [*Library symbol*] [*National Library of Canada*] (NLC)
BDD........... Balzac Deflection Door
BDD........... Bantam, Doubleday, Dell Publishing Group
BDD........... Baseline Definition Document (NASA)
BDD........... Binary-to-Decimal Decoder [*Data processing*]
BDD........... Binary Digital Data [*Data processing*]
bdd .... Binding Designer [*MARC relator code*] [*Library of Congress*] (LCCP)
BDD........... Blanket Delivery Date [*Military*] (AABC)
BDD........... Boom Defence Depot [*Navy*] [*British*]
BDD........... British Defence Directory [*Brassey's Defence Publishers Ltd.*] [*Information service or system*] (IID)
BDD........... Brodsky, David, New York NY [*STAC*]
BDD........... Brookport, IL [*Location identifier*] [*FAA*] (FAAL)
BDD........... Bureau of Dangerous Drugs [*Canada*]
BDD........... Business Dateline Database [*Information service or system*] (IT)
BDDA .... Butanediol Diacetate [*Organic chemistry*]
BDDB .... Baseline Design Data Book (MCD)
BDDI .... Beading Die
BD D & M .. Board of Decorations and Medals [*Navy*]
BDDV........ Beading Device [*Tool*] (AAG)
BDDV........ Biocular Display Driver's Viewer
BD in E ...... Bachelor of Divinity in Education
BDE .... Baende [*Volumes*] [*German*]
BDE .... Barnhart Dictionary of Etymology [*A publication*]
BDE .... Basic Design Engineering (MCD)
BDE .... Baudette, MN [*Location identifier*] [*FAA*] (FAAL)
BDE .... Beta Disintegration Energy
BDE .... Bile Duct Examination [*Medicine*]

BDE .... Boletin de Dialectologia Espanola [*A publication*]
BDE .... Bond Dissociation Energy [*Chemistry*]
BDE .... Brigade (AABC)
BDE .... Bright Display Equipment
BDE .... British Destroyer Escort
BDE .... British Document Exchange
BDE .... Brown, Durbin, and Evans [*Statisticians*]
BDE .... Bundesverband Deutscher Eisenbahnen [*Union of Non-Federal Railways, Bus-Services, and Cable-Ways*] [*Federal Republic of Germany*] (EY)
BDE .... Buyer Designated Equipment (MCD)
BDEAAK... Estacion Experimental Agropecuaria Pergamino. Boletin de Divulgacion [*A publication*]
BDEAF...... British Columbia Chapter, American Foundrymen's Society Archives and Museum, Delta, British Columbia [*Library symbol*] [*National Library of Canada*] (NLC)
BDEC........ Black Dome Energy Corporation [*NASDAQ symbol*] (NQ)
BDEC........ Bulletin. Department of English (Calcutta) [*A publication*]
BD/ECC .... Blowdown/Emergency Core Cooling [*Nuclear energy*] (NRCH)
B Deccan Coll Res Inst ... Bulletin. Deccan College Research Institute [*A publication*]
BDECW.... Pacific & Yukon Region, Canadian Wildlife Service, Environment Canada [*Service Canadien de la Faune de la Region du Pacifique et du Yukon, Environnement Canada*] Delta, British Columbia [*Library symbol*] [*National Library of Canada*] (NLC)
BDEF........ Base Detonating Fuze (MCD)
BDEGL...... Banque de Developpement des Etats du Grand Lac [*Development Bank of the Great Lakes States*] (EAIO)
BDEL........ Bank of Delaware Corp. [*NASDAQ symbol*] (NQ)
BDELT...... Brigade Landing Team [*Army*] (AABC)
BDEM .... Delta Museum and Archives, British Columbia [*Library symbol*] [*National Library of Canada*] (NLC)
BDentSc..... Bachelor in Dental Science [*British*]
BDEOA ...... British Columbia Orchard Archives Society, Delta, British Columbia [*Library symbol*] [*National Library of Canada*] (NLC)
BDEP........ Banponce Corp. [*Formerly, Banco De Ponce*] [*NASDAQ symbol*] (NQ)
B Dept Ag (Trinidad) ... Bulletin. Department of Agriculture (Trinidad and Tobago) [*A publication*]
B Dept Archaeol Anthropol ... Bulletin. Department of Archaeology and Anthropology [*Taipei*] [*A publication*]
B Dept Sociol (Okinawa) ... Bulletin. Department of Sociology (Okinawa) [*A publication*]
B Des.......... Bachelor of Design
B Des A Ed ... Bachelor of Design in Art Education
BDEV......... BLOC Development Corp. [*NASDAQ symbol*] (NQ)
BDEVDI..... Brain and Development [*A publication*]
BDF .... 1838 Bond-Debenture Trading [*Formerly, Drexel Bond-Debenture Trading Fund*] [*NYSE symbol*] (SPSG)
BDF .... Barclay's Development Fund [*Barclay's Bank*] [*British*]
BDF .... Base Defense Force [*Military*] (NVT)
BDF .... Base Detonating Fuse
BDF .... BCE Place Finance Corp. [*Toronto Stock Exchange symbol*] [*Vancouver Stock Exchange symbol*]
BDF .... Black Development Foundation
BDF .... Blocked Data Format (MCD)
BdF .... Boletim de Filologia [*A publication*]
BDF .... Bradford, IL [*Location identifier*] [*FAA*] (FAAL)
BDF .... Brasilia [*Brazil*] [*Seismograph station code, US Geological Survey*] (SEIS)
BDF .... British Digestive Foundation (IRUK)
BDFA........ Basic Daily Food Allowance (AABC)
BDFC........ Bob Dylan Fan Club (EA)
BDFC........ Bobby Darin Fan Club (EA)
BDFGA..... Bio-Dynamic Farming and Gardening Association (EA)
BDFJ .... Biographical Dictionary of Federal Judiciary [*A publication*]
BDFS........ Bachelor Degrees for Soldiers [*Program*]
BDFS........ Base Development Feasibility Study [*Navy*]
B/DFT .... Bank Draft (DS)
BD-FT....... Board-Foot (MUGU)
BDG.......... Badger Mountain [*Washington*] [*Seismograph station code, US Geological Survey*] (SEIS)
BDG.......... Bandag, Inc. [*NYSE symbol*] (SPSG)
BDG.......... Bilirubin Diglucuronide [*Biochemistry*]
BDG.......... Binding (MSA)
BDG.......... Blanding [*Utah*] [*Airport symbol*] (OAG)
BDG.......... Blanding, UT [*Location identifier*] [*FAA*] (FAAL)
BDG.......... Bloc Democratique Gabonais [*Gabonese Democratic Bloc*] [*Later, PDG*]
BDG.......... Blue Diamond Growers [*An association*] (EA)
BDG.......... Bridge [*Board on Geographic Names*] (KSC)
BDG.......... Bridger Resources, Inc. [*Vancouver Stock Exchange symbol*]
BDG.......... Bridging [*Graphics*]
BDG.......... Buffered Deoxycholate Glucose [*Broth*] [*Microbiology*]
BDG.......... Building (ADA)
BdG.......... Bundesgesetz [*Federal Act or Statute*] [*German*] (ILCA)
BDG.......... Scandinavian Economies. A Business Economic Report on Denmark, Finland, Norway, and Sweden [*A publication*]
BDGAA ..... Bilten Dokumentacije [*A publication*]

BDGAB ..... Boletin. Direccion General de Archivos y Bibliotecas [*A publication*]
BDGC .... Bad Conduct Discharge, General Court-Martial, after Confinement in Prison [*Navy*]
BDGE .... Bridge (ADA)
BDGE .... Butanediol Diglycidyl Ether [*Organic chemistry*]
BdGes .... Bundesgesetz [*Federal Act or Statute*] [*German*] (ILCA)
BDGF .... Bile Duct Growth Factor [*Biochemistry*]
BDGF .... Bone-Derived Growth Factor [*Genetics*]
BDGF .... Bovine Derived Growth Factor [*Biochemistry*]
BDGF .... Brain Derived Growth Factor [*Biochemistry*]
BDGH....... Binding Head
BDGHA..... Bundesgesundheitsblatt [*A publication*]
BDGI .... Bad Conduct Discharge, General Court-Martial, Immediate [*Navy*]
BDGNA..... Bavarian Dance Group of North America (EA)
BDGP .... Bad Conduct Discharge, General Court-Martial, after Violation of Probation [*Navy*]
BDGT .... Budget Rent a Car Corp. [*NASDAQ symbol*] (NQ)
BDH........... Bandar Lengeh [*Iran*] [*Airport symbol*] (OAG)
BDH........... Bearing, Distance, and Heading
BDH........... British Drug Houses Ltd. [*Research code symbol*]
BDHA........ British Dental Hygienists Association
BDHCA..... Belgian Draft Horse Corporation of America (EA)
BDHI .... Bearing, Distance, and Heading Indicator
BDHSA...... Bomb Director High-Speed Aircraft
BDHT........ Blowdown Heat Transfer [*Nuclear energy*]
BDi............ Bachelor of Didactics
BDI .... Bank Descriptor Index [*Data processing*]
BDI .... Base Diffusion Isolation
BDI .... Bearing Deviation Indicator [*Aerospace*]
BDI .... Beck Depression Inventory [*Psychology*]
BDI .... Beyond Infinity [*A publication*]
BDI .... Biological Damage Indicator
BDI .... Bird Island [*Seychelles Islands*] [*Airport symbol*] (OAG)
BdI .... Bollettino. Istituto di Corrispondenza Archeologica [*A publication*]
BDI .... Both Dates Inclusive [*Business term*]
BDI .... Bullet Dispersion Indicator
BDI .... Bundesverband der Deutschen Industrie [*Federation of German Industries*]
BDI .... Bureau of Dairy Industry [*Department of Agriculture*] [*Functions transferred to ARS, 1953*]
BDI .... Bureau of Disability Insurance [*Social Security Administration*]
BDI .... Burundi [*ANSI three-letter standard code*] (CNC)
BDIA .... Base Diameter
BDIAC....... Battelle - Defense Information Analysis Center [*Battelle Memorial Institute*]
BDial......... Balgarska Dialektologija [*A publication*]
BDIC.......... Battelle - Defense Information Center [*Battelle Memorial Institute*] (MCD)
BDIC.......... Binary-Coded Decimal Interchange Code
B Did.......... Bachelor of Didactics
BDID .... Bystander Dominates Initial Dominant [*Sociology*]
B Di E .... Bachelor of Diesel Engineering
B Di Eng .... Bachelor of Diesel Engineering
BDIPD....... Blaetter fuer Deutsche und Internationale Politik [*A publication*]
B Dipl......... Bachelor of Diplomacy
BDIR.......... Bus Direction [*Data processing*] (TEL)
BDIS.......... Birth Defects Information System [*Center for Birth Defects Information Services, Inc.*] [*Information service or system*] (IID)
BDIS.......... Bis((dimethylaminoethyl)indole)sulfide [*Biochemistry*]
B Divis Hum Relat ... Bulletin. Division of Human Relations [*A publication*]
BDJ............ American Adjustable Rate Term Trust 1996 [*NYSE symbol*] (SPSG)
BDJ............ Banjarmasin [*Indonesia*] [*Airport symbol*] (OAG)
BdJ............ Barre du Jour [*A publication*]
BDJ............ Boulder Junction, WI [*Location identifier*] [*FAA*] (FAAL)
BDJ............ Brans-Dicke-Jordan [*Scalar-tensor theory*]
BDJOA...... British Dental Journal [*A publication*]
BDK........... Bedrock Resources Ltd. [*Vancouver Stock Exchange symbol*]
BDK........... Beitraege zur Deutschen Klassik [*A publication*]
BDK........... Black & Decker Corp. [*NYSE symbol*] (SPSG)
BDK........... Bondoukou [*Ivory Coast*] [*Airport symbol*] (OAG)
BDKA .... Beitraege zur Deutschen Klassik. Abhandlungen [*A publication*]
BDKGA .... Berichte. Deutsche Keramische Gesellschaft [*A publication*]
BDL .... Bachelor of Divine Literature
BDL .... Bad Data Lister
BDL .... Banque de Donnees Locales [*Local Area Data Bank*] [*National Institute of Statistics and Economic Studies*] [*Information service or system*] (IID)
BDL .... Base of Dorsal Lip
BDL .... Baseline Demonstration LASER (MCD)
BDL .... Battery Data Link [*Air Force*]
BDL .... Beach Discharge Lighter
BDL .... Beleid en Maatschappij [*A publication*]
BDL .... Below the Detectable Limit
BDL .... Bennett, D. L., Wheeling WV [*STAC*]
BDL .... Best Dressed List

BDL .... Building Description Language
BDL .... Bundle
BDL .... Burndale Resources Ltd. [*Vancouver Stock Exchange symbol*]
BDL .... Flanigan's Enterprises, Inc. [*Formerly, Big Daddy's Lounges, Inc.*] [*AMEX symbol*] (SPSG)
BDL .... Hartford [*Connecticut*]/Springfield [*Massachusetts*] [*Airport symbol*] [*Derived from name of airport: Bradley Field*]
BDL .... Windsor Locks, CT [*Location identifier*] [*FAA*] (FAAL)
BDLC........ Burroughs Data Link Control [*Data processing*] (BUR)
BDLE........ Bundle
BDLG .... Blaetter fuer Deutsche Landesgeschichte [*A publication*]
BDLI .... Bundesverband der Deutschen Luftfahrt-, Raumfahrt- und Ausruestungsindustrie eV [*Aerospace industries association*] [*Federal Republic of Germany*] (EY)
BDLIC ...... Bolleti del Diccionari de la Llengua Catlana [*A publication*]
BDLM .... Bibliographien zur Deutschen Literatur des Mittelalters [*A publication*]
BDLR......... Bandolier (MSA)
BDLS .... Battery Data Link System [*Air Force*]
BDLS......... Bundles
BDLTEA ... Burley and Dark Leaf Tobacco Export Association (EA)
BDM.......... Ballistic Defense Missile
BDM.......... Banque de Donnees Macroeconomiques [*Macroeconomic Data Bank*] [*National Institute of Statistics and Economic Studies*] [*Information service or system*]
BDM.......... BDM International, Inc. [*AMEX symbol*] (SPSG)
BDM.......... Binary Delta Modulation
BDM.......... Binary Digital Multiplier [*Data processing*]
BDM.......... Births, Deaths, and Marriages
BDM.......... Blackdome Mining Corp. [*Toronto Stock Exchange symbol*] [*Vancouver Stock Exchange symbol*]
BDM.......... Bollettino del Domus Mazziniana [*A publication*]
BDM.......... Bomber Defense Missile [*Air Force*]
BDM.......... Bubble Domain Memory
BDMA .... Benzyldimethylamine [*Organic chemistry*]
BDMA .... Butylene Dimethacrylate [*Organic chemistry*]
BDMHL .... Bachelor of Divinity and Master of Hebrew Literature (BJA)
BDMI .... Biographical Dictionaries Master Index [*A publication*]
BDMS........ Bactometer Data Management System
BDMS........ Bulk Direct Mail Service (ADA)
BDMSC...... BDM Service Co. (MCD)
BDN........... Badana [*Saudi Arabia*] [*Airport symbol*] [*Obsolete*] (OAG)
BDN........... Bank Draft Number (TEL)
BDN........... Bausteine zum Deutschen Nationaltheater [*A publication*]
BDN........... Bell Data Network [*Telecommunications*]
BDN........... Bend Down
BDN........... Bodon [*USSR*] [*Seismograph station code, US Geological Survey*] (SEIS)
BDN........... Bulletin d'Information. Office de Commercialisation [*A publication*]
B DNA .... Deoxyribonucleic Acid, Traditional Form [*DNA with right-handed helix*] [*Biochemistry, genetics*]
BDNF .... Brain-Derived Neurotrophic Factor [*Neurochemistry*]
BDNG........ Bedding (MSA)
BDNI.......... Builders Design, Inc. [*NASDAQ symbol*] (NQ)
BDNKA ..... Busushchee Nauki [*A publication*]
BDNMSSS ... Board of Directors NATO Maintenance Supply Service System (NATG)
BDO........... Bandung [*Indonesia*] [*Airport symbol*] (OAG)
BDO........... Base de Donnees des Obligations Francaises [*DAFSA*] [*Database*]
BDO........... Bile Duct Obstruction [*Medicine*]
BD & O ...... Blackham, Dundas, and Osborne's Irish Nisi Prius Reports [*1846-48*] [*A publication*] (DLA)
BDO........... Blanket Delivery Order (MCD)
BDO........... Boom Defense Officer
BDO........... Bottom Dropped Out [*Investment term*]
BDO........... Bow Door
BDO........... Budoia [*Papua New Guinea*] [*Seismograph station code, US Geological Survey*] (SEIS)
BDO........... Business Eastern Europe [*A publication*]
B Docum Prat Secur Soc Legisl Trav ... Bulletin de Documentation Pratique de Securite Sociale et de Legislation du Travail [*A publication*]
B/DOE ...... Barrels per Day Oil Equivalent
BDOGA ..... Bericht. Deutsche Ophthalmologische Gesellschaft [*A publication*]
B-DOPA ..... Bleomycin, Dacarbazine, Oncovin [*Vincristine*], Prednisone, Adriamycin [*Antineoplastic drug regimen*]
BDOS .... Basic Disk Operating System
BDOS .... Batch Disk Operating System
BDOT .... British Department of Transport
BDOZER.... Bulldozer [*Freight*]
BDP .... Bahamian Democratic Party [*Political party*] (PPW)
BDP .... Base Development Plan (AABC)
BDP .... Battlefield Development Plan (RDA)
BDP .... BCED Capital Investment Corp. [*Toronto Stock Exchange symbol*] [*Vancouver Stock Exchange symbol*]
BDP .... Beach Discharge Point (MCD)
BDP .... Beclomethasone Dipropionate [*Pharmacology*]
BDP .... Beitraege zur Deutschen Philologie [*A publication*]

BDP .... Bhadrapur [*Nepal*] [*Airport symbol*] (OAG)
BDP .... Bonded Double Paper [*Wire insulation*] (KSC)
BDP .... Boogie Down Productions [*Rap recording group*]
BDP .... Bophuthatswana Democratic Party [*Political party*] (PPW)
BDP .... Botswana Democratic Party [*Political party*] (PPW)
BDP .... Bottom Dead Point
BDP .... Bridge Display Panel [*Navy*] (CAAL)
BDP .... Brine Disposal Program [*Environmental Data and Information Service*] (MSC)
BDP .... British Democratic Party [*Political party*]
BDP .... Broad Pass [*Alaska*] [*Seismograph station code, US Geological Survey*] [*Closed*] (SEIS)
BDP .... Brookes Deflection Potentiometer
BDP .... Bundle Drawing Process [*Metal fiber technology*]
BDP .... Business Data Processing
BDPA .... Black Data Processing Associates (EA)
BDPA .... Bureau of Data Processing and Accounts [*Social Security Administration*]
BDPE........ Bromodiphenyl(ethylphenyl)ethylene [*Endocrinology*]
BDPEC...... Bureau of Disease Prevention and Environmental Control
BDPH .... Blaetter fuer Deutsche Philosophie. Zeitschrift der Deutsche Philosophische Gesellschaft [*A publication*]
BDPI.......... Base Data Processing Installation
BDPN........ Bedpan (MSA)
BDPO........ Business Data Processing Operation
BDPS......... Brigade Data Processing System
BDPSK...... Binary Differential Phase-Shift Keying [*Telecommunications*] (TEL)
BDQ........... Vadodara [*India*] [*Airport symbol*] (OAG)
B en Dr....... Bachelier en Droit [*Bachelor of Laws*] [*French*]
BDR .... Bad Demographic Risk [*Television*]
BDR .... Bandmaster [*Military*] [*British*] (ROG)
BDR .... Bank Descriptor Registers [*Data processing*]
BDR .... Battle Damage Repair [*Army*] (RDA)
BDR .... Beardmore Resources [*Vancouver Stock Exchange symbol*]
BDR .... Bearer Depositary Receipt [*Investment term*]
BDR .... Bedrijfsdocumentaire; Magazine op het Gebied van Praktisch Management [*A publication*]
BDR .... Bell Doesn't Ring [*Telecommunications*] (TEL)
BDR .... Best Depth Range [*Military*] (NVT)
BDR .... Bi-Duplexed Redundancy [*Telecommunications*]
BDR .... Binary Dump Routine
BDR .... Binder (MSA)
BDR .... Bomb Damage Repair
BDR .... Bombardier
BDR .... Border (FAAC)
BDR .... Bridgeport [*Connecticut*] [*Airport symbol*] (OAG)
BDR .... Bridgewater State College, Bridgewater, MA [*OCLC symbol*] (OCLC)
BDR .... Brigadier
B Dr Art ..... Bachelor of Dramatic Art
BDRC .... Barwon Disability Resource Council [*Australia*]
BDRC .... Becton, Dickinson & Co. Research Center
B/DR/F/I .. Ballantine/Del Rey/Fawcett/Ivy [*Publishing group*]
BDRI.......... Bright Display RADAR Indicator
BDRL........ Biological Defense Research Laboratory
BDRM .... Bedroom
BDRM .... Boardroom Business Products, Inc. [*NASDAQ symbol*] (NQ)
BDRN .... [*The*] Bank of Darien [*Darien, CT*] [*NASDAQ symbol*] (NQ)
BDRP........ Business Directory of Registered Plumbers [*A publication*]
BDRS........ Business Development Report System [*Department of Commerce*] [*Database*]
BDRT .... Baud Rate [*Data transmission speed*] [*Data processing*]
B Dr Tchecosl ... Bulletin de Droit Tchecoslovaque [*A publication*]
BDRY .... Boundary (AABC)
BDS .... Bachelor of Dental Surgery
BDS .... Ballistics Dispensing System (MCD)
BDS .... Barbados [*Seismograph station code, US Geological Survey*] (SEIS)
BDS .... Bard Silver & Gold [*Vancouver Stock Exchange symbol*]
BDS .... Base Data System (AFM)
BDS .... Base Development Survey (MCD)
BDS .... Base Distribution System [*Air Force*] (AFM)
BDS .... Base Divider Strip (AAG)
BDS .... Battle Dressing Station [*Military*] (NVT)
BDS .... Battlefield Data System
BDS .... Beitraege zur Danziger Statistik [*Danzig*]
BDS .... Bibliographic Database Search Service [*University of Wyoming Libraries*] (OLDSS)
BDS .... Binary Decode Scaler [*Data processing*]
BDS .... Bindings [*Publishing*]
BDS .... Biographical Dictionaries and Related Works. Supplement [*A publication*]
BDS .... Biological Defense System
BDS .... Biological Detection System
BDS .... Bis in Die Sumendus [*To Be Taken Twice a Day*] [*Pharmacy*]
BDS .... Bloc Democratique Senegalais [*Senegal*] [*Political party*] (PPW)
BDS .... Blood Derived Serum
BDS .... Boards
BDS .... Bomb Damage Survey

BDS .... Bomb Director Set [*or System*] [*Army*]
BDS .... Bomb-Disposal Squad
BDS .... Bonded Double Silk [*Wire insulation*]
BDS .... Bound in Boards
BDS .... Brass Divider Strip [*Technical drawings*]
BDS .... Brindisi [*Italy*] [*Airport symbol*] (OAG)
BDS .... British Deer Society
BDS .... British Defence Staff
BDS .... Broker's Daily Statement
BDS .... Bulk Data Switching
BDS .... Butanediol Succinate [*Organic chemistry*]
BDSA........ Bis(dimethylsilyl)acetamide [*Organic chemistry*]
BDSA........ Business and Defense Services Administration [*Later, BDC*] [*Department of Commerce*]
BD Sc .... Bachelor of Dental Science
BDSD .... Base Detonating, Self-Destroying
BDSekt ...... Bjulleten Dialektologiceskogo Sektora Instituta Russkogo Jazyka [*A publication*]
BDSF........ Bone-Marrow-Derived Suppressor Factor [*Immunology*]
Bd/Sgt....... Band Sergeant [*British military*] (DMA)
BDSI........ Bad Conduct Discharge, Sentence of Summary Court-Martial, Immediate [*Navy*]
BDSI.......... Basic Direct Shipping Instructions
BDSLD .... Bids Solicited (FAAC)
BDSM....... Bandsman [*Military*] [*British*]
BDSMN .... Bandsman [*Military*] [*British*]
BDSP .... Bad Conduct Discharge, Summary Court-Martial, after Violation of Probation [*Navy*]
BDSP........ Basic Data Set Project [*National Science Foundation*]
BDSPU...... Bollettino. Deputazione di Storia Patria per l'Umbria [*A publication*]
BDST........ Bed Depth Service Time [*Wastewater treatment*]
BDST......... British Double Summer Time
BDSW....... British Defence Staff, Washington, DC [*Also, BDSWASHDC*] (NATG)
BDSWASHDC ... British Defence Staff, Washington, DC [*Also, BDSW*] (NATG)
BDSY .... Baron Data Systems [*NASDAQ symbol*] (NQ)
BDT .... Back Door Trot [*i.e., a call of nature*] [*Obsolete slang*]
BDT .... Bado Lite [*Zaire*] [*Airport symbol*] (OAG)
BDT .... Ballistic Damage Tolerance (MCD)
BDT .... Beam Deflection Tube
BDT .... Bhumibol Dam [*Thailand*] [*Seismograph station code, US Geological Survey*] (SEIS)
BDT .... Binary-to-Decimal Transmitter [*Data processing*] (NOAA)
BDT .... Binary Deck-to-Tape [*Data processing*]
BDT .... Block Data Transfer (MCD)
BDT .... Bone-Dried Ton
BDT .... Burdett Resources Ltd. [*Vancouver Stock Exchange symbol*]
BDT .... Bureau of Domestic Trade [*Philippines*] (DS)
BDT .... Burst Delay Timer (MCD)
BDTC .... British Dependent Territories Citizen [*Hong Kong*]
BDTD .... Balanced Digital Transmission Device [*Army*]
BDTF......... Bomber Defence Training Flight [*British military*] (DMA)
BDTN .... Beam-Driven Thermonuclear (MCD)
Bd Trade Metropolitan Toronto J ... Journal. Board of Trade of Metropolitan Toronto [*A publication*]
BDTS........ Batch Data Transmission System
BDTS........ Brass Dressers Trade Society [*A union*] [*British*]
BDTS......... Buffered Data Transmission Simulator
BDTS........ Bulk Data Transfer Subsystem [*Telecommunications*] (TEL)
BDU........... Banque de Donnees Urbaines de Paris et de la Region d'Ile-De-France [*Urban Data Bank of Paris and the Paris Region*] [*Paris Office of Urbanization*] [*France*] [*Information service or system*] (IID)
BDU........... Bardufoss [*Norway*] [*Airport symbol*] (OAG)
BDU........... Barograph Display Unit
BDU........... Baseband Distribution Unit
BDU........... Basic Device Unit [*Data processing*] (IBMDP)
BDU........... Basic Display Unit [*Data processing*]
BDU........... Battery Display Unit [*Army*]
BDU........... Battle Dress Uniform [*Military*]
BDU........... Big Dutch Hollow [*Utah*] [*Seismograph station code, US Geological Survey*] (SEIS)
BDU........... Biomedical Display Unit (KSC)
BDU........... Bomb-Disposal Unit
BDU........... Bomb, Dummy Unit (AFM)
BDU........... Bombing Development Unit
BDU........... Bradsue Resources [*Vancouver Stock Exchange symbol*]
BDU........... Bromodeoxyuridine [*Also, BDUR, BrDU*] [*Biochemistry*]
BDUCVM ... Cowichan Valley Museum, Duncan, British Columbia [*Library symbol*] [*National Library of Canada*] (NLC)
BDUFM .... British Columbia Forest Museum, Duncan, British Columbia [*Library symbol*] [*National Library of Canada*] (NLC)
BDUMAY ... Duke University. Marine Station Bulletin [*A publication*]
BDUR .... Bromodeoxyuridine [*Also, BDU, BrDU*] [*Biochemistry*]
BDUZD8 ... Universidad Nacional de Tucuman. Facultad de Agronomia y Zootecnia. Boletin de Divulgacion [*A publication*]
BDV .... Bend-Down Virginia [*A picked-up stub of a cigarette*]
BDV .... Best Dark Virginia [*Tobacco*] [*British*] (ROG)
BDV .... Binary Divide (MSA)

BDV .... Blow-Down Valve [*Railroad term*]
BDV .... Boom Defence Vessel [*Navy*] [*British*]
BDV .... Breakdown Voltage [*Telecommunications*]   (TEL)
BDV .... Bremen Demokratische Volkspartei [*Bremen Democratic People's Party*] [*Federal Republic of Germany*] [*Political party*]   (PPE)
BDV .... Brussels Definition of Value   (IMH)
BDV .... Budkov [*Czechoslovakia*] [*Geomagnetic observatory code*]
BDVA .... Beitraege zur Deutschen Volks- und Altertumskunde [*A publication*]
BDVG .... Bow Diving
BDW .... Bank Descriptor Word [*Data processing*]
BDW .... Beach, Dewey W., Denver CO [*STAC*]
BDW .... Blunted Delta Wing
BDW .... Boulder [*Wyoming*] [*Seismograph station code, US Geological Survey*]   (SEIS)
BDW .... Buffered Distilled Water [*Chemistry*]
BDW .... Bulletin du Dictionnaire Wallon [*A publication*]
BDW .... Buried Distribution Wire [*Telecommunications*]   (TEL)
BDWPHGS ... Beauty, Divinity, Wisdom, Power, Honor, Glory, Strength [*Freemasonry*]   (ROG)
BDWTU .... British Diamond Workers Trade Union
BDWY .... Broadway [*A street name*]
BDX .... Becton, Dickinson & Co. [*NYSE symbol*]   (SPSG)
BDX .... Bendix Aviation Corp. [*Later, Bendix Corp.*]   (MCD)
BDX .... Bourdeaux Resources Ltd. [*Vancouver Stock Exchange symbol*]
BDX .... Broadus, MT [*Location identifier*] [*FAA*]   (FAAL)
BDXR .... Block Demultiplexer [*Ground Communications Facility, NASA*]
BDY .... Betty Lake, AK [*Location identifier*] [*FAA*]   (FAAL)
BDY .... Body
BDY .... Boundary   (KSC)
BDY .... Broadway [*A street name*] [*British*]
BDYFLP.... Body Flap   (NASA)
Bdy Mon ... Boundary Monument [*Control point*] [*Nautical charts*]
BDYN .... American Biodynamics, Inc. [*NASDAQ symbol*]   (NQ)
BDY or RF ... Body or Roof [*Freight*]
BDZ .... Business Europe. A Weekly Report to Managers. Europe, Middle-East, and Africa [*A publication*]
BDZR .... Bulldozer   (MSA)
BE .... Aero B Venezuela [*Venezuela*] [*ICAO designator*]   (FAAC)
BE .... [*The*] Babylonian Expedition of the University of Pennsylvania. Series A: Cuneiform Texts [*A publication*]
BE .... Bachelor of Education
BE .... Bachelor of the Elements
BE .... Bachelor of Elocution
BE .... Bachelor of Engineering
BE .... Bachelor of English
BE .... Bachelor of Expression
BE .... Back End   (MSA)
BE .... Backscattered Electron   (MCD)
BE .... Bacterial Endocarditis [*Medicine*]
BE .... Bale
BE .... Balgarski Ezik [*A publication*]
BE .... Baltimore & Eastern Railroad Co. [*Absorbed into Consolidated Rail Corp.*] [*AAR code*]
BE .... Band Elimination
B of E .... Bank of England
BE .... Bank of England
BE .... Bank Error
BE .... Barium Enema [*Medicine*]
BE .... Baron of Exchequer [*British*]   (ROG)
BE .... Barrett's Esophagus [*Medicine*]
BE .... Base Ejection
BE .... Base Excess [*Medicine*]
BE .... Basic Education [*A publication*]
BE .... Basic Encyclopedia [*Army*]   (AABC)
BE .... Basic English
BE .... Battlefield Environment   (MCD)
Be .... [*Degree*] Baume
BE .... Bazillenemulsion [*Bacillary emulsion*] [*Immunology*]
BE .... Beacon Explorer [*Satellite*] [*NASA*]
Be .... Bealoideas [*A publication*]
BE .... Bearing Error [*Military*]   (CAAL)
Be .... Becker [*Blood group*]
Be .... Beda [*Deceased, 735*] [*Authority cited in pre-1607 legal work*]   (DSA)
BE .... Bedrijfseconoom [*A publication*]
BE .... Beech Aircraft Corp. [*ICAO aircraft manufacturer identifier*]   (ICAO)
B & E .... Beginning and Ending   (ADA)
BE .... Belgium [*ANSI two-letter standard code*]   (CNC)
be .... Belgium [*MARC country of publication code*] [*Library of Congress*]   (LCCP)
Be .... Belgrade [*A publication*]
BE .... Bell End
BE .... Below Elbow [*Medicine*]
Be .... Benedictus de Isernia [*Flourished, 1221-52*] [*Authority cited in pre-1607 legal work*]   (DSA)
BE .... Benguet Corp. [*NYSE symbol*]   (SPSG)
BE .... Berkeley Exchange   (EA)

Be .... Beryllium [*Chemical element*]
BE .... Best Estimate Model   (NRCH)
BE .... Biblical Essays [*A publication*]   (BJA)
BE .... Biblical Evangelism   (EA)
BE .... Bibliografia Espanola [*Spain*] [*A publication*]
Be .... Bibliotheque Royale d'Albert 1er, Bruxelles, Belgium [*Library symbol*] [*Library of Congress*]   (LCLS)
BE .... Biennial
BE .... Bile Esculin [*Medicine*]
B/E .... Bill of Entry [*Shipping*]
BE .... Bill of Exchange [*Accounting*]
BE .... Binding Edge   (ADA)
BE .... Binding Energy
BE .... Biplane Experimental [*Aircraft*] [*World War I*]
BE .... Black Elegance [*A publication*]
BE .... Black Enamelled
BE .... Black English [*Dialect*]
BE .... Black Enterprise [*A publication*]
BE .... Bleriot Experimental [*British military*]   (DMA)
BE .... Bluie East [*US air bases in Greenland*] [*World War II*]
BE .... Board of Education
B of E .... Board of Education
BE .... Bombing Encyclopedia   (CINC)
BE .... Booster Engine [*Rocketry*]
B/E .... Boy Entrant [*British military*]   (DMA)
B/E .... Break-Even Point [*Accounting*]
BE .... Breaker End   (MSA)
B & E .... Breaking and Entering
BE .... Brief Entry
BE .... British Element
B/E .... British Embassy   (DS)
BE .... British Empire
BE .... Bronchoesophagology [*Medicine*]
BE .... Bucyrus-Erie Co.
BE .... Buddhist Era
B & E .... Building and Engineering [*British*]
BE .... Bull Elephants   (EA)
BE .... Bureau of Economics [*Federal Trade Commission*]
BE .... Bureau of Explosives [*Later, HMS (BOE)*]
BE .... Business Economist [*A publication*]
BE .... Business Equipment
b/e .... By-Election [*Politics*]
BE .... Excursion [*Also, B*] [*Airline fare code*]
B³E .... Balancing the Budget on the Backs of the Elderly [*Political charge*]
BEA .... Background Equivalent Activity
BEA .... Barn Equipment Association [*Later, FEA*]   (EA)
BE-A .... Beacon Explorer A [*Satellite*] [*NASA*]
BEA .... Beatty [*Nevada*] [*Seismograph station code, US Geological Survey*] [*Closed*]   (SEIS)
Bea .... Beaver [*Record label*] [*Canada*]
BEA .... Beaver College, Glenside, PA [*OCLC symbol*]   (OCLC)
BEA .... Beeville, TX [*Location identifier*] [*FAA*]   (FAAL)
BEA .... Beginning Education Assessment [*Educational development test*]
BEA .... Bereina [*Papua New Guinea*] [*Airport symbol*]   (OAG)
BEA .... BEST [*Beneficial Employees Security Trust*] Employers Association   (EA)
BEA .... Bills of Exchange Act [*1882*] [*British*]
BEA .... Binary Encounter Approximation [*Nuclear physics*]
BEA .... Boletin de Estudios Asturianos [*A publication*]
BEA .... Break Even Analysis [*Accounting*]
BEA .... British East Africa
BEA .... British Electricity Authority
BEA .... British Engineers Association
BEA .... British Epilepsy Association
BEA .... British European Airways Corp. [*Later, British Airways*]
BEA .... Broadcast Education Association   (EA)
BEA .... Budget Enforcement Act [*1990*]
BEA .... Building Economic Alternatives [*Co-Op America*] [*A publication*]
BEA .... Bulletin des Etudes Arabes [*A publication*]
BEA .... Bureau of Economic Affairs [*Later, Bureau of Economic and Business Affairs*] [*Department of State*]
BEA .... Bureau of Economic Analysis [*Department of Commerce*] [*Washington, DC*]   (IID)
BEA .... Bureau of European Affairs [*Department of State*]
BEAA........ Business Education Adminstrators Association [*Defunct*]   (EA)
BEAB........ British Electrical Approvals Board
Bea Bank.... Beames' Commitments in Bankruptcy [*A publication*]   (DLA)
BEAC......... Banque des Etats de l'Afrique Centrale [*Bank of Central African States*]
BEAC......... Beaconsfield [*Urban district in England*]
BEAC......... Boeing Engineering Analog Computer   (IEEE)
BEAC......... British European Airways Corporation [*Later, British Airways*]
Bea CE....... Beames' Costs in Equity [*A publication*]   (DLA)
Beach Contrib Neg ... Beach on Contributory Negligence [*A publication*]   (DLA)
Beach Eq Prac ... Beach's Modern Practice in Equity [*A publication*]   (DLA)
Beach Inj.... Beach on Injunctions [*A publication*]   (DLA)

Beach Mod Eq Jur ... Beach's Commentaries on Modern Equity Jurisprudence [*A publication*]   (DLA)
Beach Priv Corp ... Beach on Private Corporations [*A publication*]   (DLA)
Beach Pub Corp ... Beach on Public Corporations [*A publication*]   (DLA)
Beach Rec .. Beach on the Law of Receivers [*A publication*]   (DLA)
BEACON .. British European Airways Corp. [*later, British Airways*] Computerized Office Network
Bea Costs ... Beames' Costs in Equity [*A publication*]   (DLA)
BEACOTRON ... Beam Coupling Tube   (NATG)
BEAD (Ankara Turkey) ... Bati Edebiyatlari Arastirma Dergisi (Ankara, Turkey) [*A publication*]
Bead J .... Bead Journal [*A publication*]
Bea Eq Pl ... Beames' Equity Pleading [*A publication*]   (DLA)
BEAFA .... Biomass Energy and Alcohol Fuels Act of 1980
BE(Ag) .... Bachelor of Engineering (Agriculture)
BEAG .... Bateria de Examenes de Aptitud General [*General Aptitude Test Battery*] [*Spanish*]
BEAIRA .... British Electrical and Allied Industries Research Association   (MCD)
BEA J .... Business Education Association of Metropolitan New York. Journal [*A publication*]
BEAJA ...... BEAMA [*British Electrical and Allied Manufacturers Association*] Journal [*A publication*]
BEAL .... Banco Europeu para a America Latina [*Bank*] [*Portuguese*]   (EY)
BEAL .... Banque Europeenne pour l'Amerique Latine [*Bank*] [*French*]   (EY)
BEAM ...... Beaminster [*England*]
Be-Am .... Bibliotheque Royale d'Albert 1er, American Studies Center, Bruxelles, Belgium [*Library symbol*] [*Library of Congress*]   (LCLS)
BEAM ...... Brain Electrical Activity Mapping
BEAM ...... Building Equipment Accessories and Materials [*Program*] [*Canada*]
BEAM ...... Burroughs Electronic Accounting Machine   (BUR)
BEAM ...... Summit Technology, Inc. [*NASDAQ symbol*]   (NQ)
BEAMA ...... British Electrical and Allied Manufacturers Association
BEAMA J ... BEAMA [*British Electrical and Allied Manufacturers Association*] Journal [*A publication*]
Beames Glanv ... Beames' Glanville [*A publication*]   (DLA)
Beam Foil Spectros ... Beam Foil Spectroscopy [*A publication*]
Beam Foil Spectros Proc Int Conf ... Beam Foil Spectroscopy. Proceedings of the International Conference on Beam Foil Spectroscopy [*A publication*]
BEAMOS ... Beam Addressed Metal Oxide Semiconductor [*Memory technology*]
BEAMS ..... Base Engineering Automated Management System   (AFM)
BEAMS ..... Basic Education Assistance Material Service [*National Multimedia Center for Adult Basic Education*]   (IID)
BEAMS ..... Budget Execution Appropriation Maintenance System [*Military*]
BEAN .... Bloc d'Esquerra d'Alliberament Nacional [*Left Bloc for National Liberation*] [*Spain*]   (PPW)
BEAN .... Republic Resources, Inc. [*NASDAQ symbol*]   (NQ)
Bea Ne Ex ... Beames on the Writ of Ne Exeat Regno [*A publication*]   (DLA)
Bea Ord ...... Beames' Orders in Chancery [*England*] [*A publication*]   (DLA)
BEAP .... British East Africa Protectorate [*British government*]
BEAPA ...... Bureau of East Asian and Pacific Affairs [*Formerly, Bureau of Far Eastern Affairs*] [*Department of State*]
Bea Pl Eq ... Beames' Pleas in Equity [*A publication*]   (DLA)
BEAR .... Beacon Experiment and Auroral Research
BEAR .... Beam Experiment Aboard Rocket   (MCD)
BEAR .... Bear Automotive Service Equipment Co. [*Milwaukee, WI*] [*NASDAQ symbol*]   (NQ)
BEAR .... Biological Effects of Atomic Radiation
BEAR .... Bonus, Extension, and Reenlistment [*Army*]   (INF)
BeAR .... Rijksuniversitaire Centrum te Antwerpen [*State University Center of Antwerp*], Antwerpen, Belgium [*Library symbol*] [*Library of Congress*]   (LCLS)
BEARA ...... British Electronic and Applied Research Association   (MCD)
BEARS ...... Breadboard of an Electrochemical Air Revitalization System [*NASA*]
Bears Bluff Lab Prog Rep ... Bears Bluff Laboratories. Progress Report [*A publication*]
Bear Steels Rating Nonmet Inclusion Symp ... Bearing Steels; The Rating of Nonmetallic Inclusion. Symposium [*A publication*]
BEART ...... Beaver Army Terminal [*Oregon*]
Bear Tithes ... Bearblock. Treatise upon Tithes [*6th ed.*] [*1832*] [*A publication*]   (DLA)
Beas .... Beasley's New Jersey Chancery Reports [*A publication*]   (DLA)
Beas .... Beasley's New Jersey Equity Reports [*12-13*] [*A publication*]   (DLA)
BEAS .... British Executive Air Services
Beasl .... Beasley's New Jersey Equity Reports [*A publication*]   (DLA)
BEAST ...... Brookings Economics and Statistical Translator [*Data processing*]
BEAST ...... Business, Engineering, Appropriate Technology, and Skilled Trades [*Peace Corps program*]
Beat .... Beatty's Irish Chancery Reports [*1814-36*] [*A publication*]   (DLA)
BEAT .... Best Execution Analysis Tabulation [*Data processing*]

BEAT .... Breaking and Entering and Auto Theft [*Police crime computer*]
BEATS ...... Both Ends, All Time Saved [*Shipping*]
Beatt .... Beatty's Irish Chancery Reports [*1814-36*] [*A publication*]   (DLA)
Beatty .... Beatty's Irish Chancery Reports [*1814-36*] [*A publication*]   (DLA)
Beatty Ir Ch ... Beatty's Irish Chancery Reports [*1814-36*] [*A publication*]   (DLA)
beau .... Bordereau [*Statement*] [*French*] [*Business term*]
Beau Bills ... Beaumont. Bills of Sale [*1855*] [*A publication*]   (DLA)
Beaufortia Ser Misc Publ Zool Mus Univ Amsterdam ... Beaufortia Series of Miscellaneous Publications. Zoological Museum. University of Amsterdam [*A publication*]
Beau Ins ..... Beaumont. Life and Fire Insurance [*2nd ed.*] [*1846*] [*A publication*]   (DLA)
Beaur Org .. Beauregard. Organisation de la Famille [*A publication*]   (DLA)
BeAUSI ..... Universitaire Faculteiten Sint-Ignatius te Antwerpen, Antwerp, Belgium [*Library symbol*] [*Library of Congress*]   (LCLS)
Beaux-Arts Inst Des Bul ... Beaux-Arts Institute of Design. Bulletin [*A publication*]
Beav .... Beavan's English Rolls Court Reports [*A publication*]   (DLA)
BEAV .... Beaver [*Canada*] [*A publication*]
Beavan Ch ... Beavan's English Rolls Court Reports [*A publication*]   (DLA)
Beav (Eng) ... Beavan's English Rolls Court Reports [*A publication*]   (DLA)
BEAVER ... Be Ever Alert, Vigilant/Error Removal [*United States Air Force Security System's acronym for the Zero Defects Program*]
Beaver .... Beaver County Legal Journal [*Pennsylvania*] [*A publication*]
Beaver County LJ ... Beaver County Legal Journal [*Pennsylvania*] [*A publication*]
Beaver County LJ (PA) ... Beaver County Legal Journal (Pennsylvania) [*A publication*]
Beav OC ..... Beavan's Ordines Cancellariae [*A publication*]   (DLA)
Beav R & C ... Beavan. Railway and Canal Cases [*England*] [*A publication*]   (DLA)
Beav R & C Cas ... English Railway and Canal Cases, by Beavan and Others [*A publication*]   (DLA)
Beav & W ... Beavan and Walford's Railway and Canal Cases [*England*] [*A publication*]   (DLA)
Beav & Wal ... Beavan and Walford's Railway and Canal Cases [*England*] [*A publication*]   (DLA)
Beav & Wal Ry Cas ... Beavan and Walford's Railway and Canal Cases [*England*] [*A publication*]   (DLA)
Beav & W Ry Cas ... Beavan and Walford's Railway and Canal Cases [*England*] [*A publication*]   (DLA)
Beaw .... Beawes' Lex Mercatoria [*England*] [*A publication*]   (DLA)
Beawes' Lex Merc ... Beawes' Lex Mercatoria [*England*] [*A publication*]   (DLA)
Beaw Lex Mer ... Beawes' Lex Mercatoria [*England*] [*A publication*]   (DLA)
BEB .... Beach Erosion Board [*Army*]
BE-B .... Beacon Explorer B [*Satellite*] [*NASA*]
BEB .... Benbecula [*Hebrides Islands*] [*Airport symbol*]   (OAG)
BEB .... Benign Essential Blepharospasm [*Medicine*]   (EA)
BEB .... Best Ever Bottled [*Wines and spirits*]
BEB .... Bridge Erection Boat
BEBA .... Beeba's Creations, Inc. [*San Diego, CA*] [*NASDAQ symbol*]   (NQ)
BEBA .... Bilingual Education Bibliographic Abstracts [*National Clearinghouse for Bilingual Education*] [*Rosslyn, VA*] [*Database*]
BEBA .... Bring 'Em Back Alive [*AAA Holiday News Service*]
BEBA .... Bureau of Economic and Business Affairs [*Formerly, Bureau of Economic Affairs*] [*Department of State*]
BEBC .... Big European Bubble Chamber [*Nuclear particle detector*]
BEBEBP ...... Bioelectrochemistry and Bioenergetics [*A publication*]
BEBI .... Breast Examination Bras, Incorporated
BEBIM ...... Bulletin of Experimental Biology and Medicine [*A publication*]
BEBMA ...... Byulleten' Eksperimental'noi Biologii i Meditsiny [*A publication*]
BEBO .... Bond-Energy Bond-Order [*Chemical kinetics*]
BEBR .... Bechtel Briefs [*A publication*]
BEBR .... Bureau of Economic and Business Research [*University of Delaware*] [*Research center*]   (RCD)
BEBR .... Bureau of Economic and Business Research [*University of Florida*] [*Gainesville*] [*Information service or system*]   (IID)
BEBRF .... Benign Essential Blepharospasm Research Foundation   (EA)
B Ec .... Bachelor of Economics
BEC .... Bachelor of Engineering Construction
BEC.../..... Background Equivalent Concentration [*Data processing*]
BEC .... Banque Europeenne de Credit [*Belgium*]
BEC .... Barbecon, Inc. [*Toronto Stock Exchange symbol*]
BEC .... Barnes Engineering Co.   (KSC)
BEC .... Base Equipment Container
BEC .... Base Extension Course
BEC .... Because   (ADA)
BEC .... Beckman Instruments, Inc. [*NYSE symbol*]   (CTT)
BEC .... Beech Aircraft Corp. [*Wichita, KS*] [*FAA designator*]   (FAAC)
BEC .... Beginning of Equilibrium Cycle [*Nuclear energy*]   (NRCH)
BEC .... Berkeley Enthusiasts Club [*Woking, Surrey, England*]   (EAIO)
BEC .... Bermuda-Columbia [*Bermuda*] [*Seismograph station code, US Geological Survey*]   (SEIS)

BEC............ Bibliotheque de l'Ecole des Chartes [*A publication*]
BEC............ Big East Conference   (EA)
BEC............ Big Eight Conference   (EA)
BEC............ Bio-Energy Council   (EA)
BEC............ Bioelectrochemistry
BEC............ Blood Ethanol Concentration [*Medicine*]
BEC............ Boeing Engineering Company   (MCD)
BEC............ Boletim de Estudos Classicos [*A publication*]
BEC............ Books on Egypt and Chaldea [*A publication*]
BEC............ Bowles Engineering Corporation
BEC............ Brevard Engineering College [*Florida*]   (KSC)
BE & C........ British Empire and Commonwealth
BEC............ British Employers' Confederation
BEC............ British Engineers Club
BEC............ Bromoergocryptine [*Organic chemistry*]
BEC............ Brown Engineering Company   (KSC)
BEC............ Building Employers' Confederation [*A union*] [*British*]
BEC............ Bureau of Employees' Compensation [*Later, OWCP*]
     [*Department of Labor*]
BEC............ Bureau Europeen de Coordination des Organisations
     Internationales de Jeunesse [*European Coordination
     Bureau for International Youth Organizations -
     ECB*]   (EAIO)
BEC............ Burst Error Correction [*Encoder/decoder*]   (MCD)
BEC............ Business Economics [*A publication*]
BEC............ Business Education Connection   (OICC)
BEC............ Business Education Council
BEC............ Business Electronics Computer [*Used in training*]
BEC............ Riverview Hospital, Port Coquitlam, British Columbia [*Library
     symbol*] [*Library network*]   (NLC)
BEC............ Wichita, KS [*Location identifier*] [*FAA*]   (FAAL)
BECA........ Bureau of Educational and Cultural Affairs [*Later Known as
     USIA, then as ICA or USICA, then again as USIA*]
BECAMP.. Ballistic Environmental Characteristics and Measurement
     Program [*Army*]   (AABC)
BECAN...... Biomedical Engineering Current Awareness Notification
     [*Database, publication*] [*Brunel University*] [*Information
     service or system*]   (CRD)
BECBSG... Big Eight Council on Black Student Government   (EA)
BECC......... Biomass Energy Coordinating Committee [*Department of
     Energy*]
BECC......... British Empire Cancer Council
BECCA...... Business Espionage Controls and Countermeasures
     Association   (EA)
B Ec Cam Commerc Ravenna ... Bollettino Economico. Camera di
     Commercio. Industria, Artigianato, e Agricoltura de
     Ravenna [*A publication*]
BECCE...... Basic Engineering Casualty Control Exercise [*Military*]   (NVT)
B Ecc L....... Burn's Ecclesiastical Law [*A publication*]   (DLA)
Bec Cr .... Beccaria on Crimes and Punishments [*A publication*]   (DLA)
BECD......... Behavioural Sciences and Community Development [*A
     publication*]
BECE........ Bachelor of Electro-Chemical Engineering
BECEG...... Bureau Europeen de Controle et d'Etudes Generales
Be (Ceylon) ... Beven's Ceylon Reports [*A publication*]   (DLA)
BECG........ Bipartite Economics Control Group [*Post-World War II,
     Germany*]
BECGF...... British Empire and Commonwealth Games Federation
BECH .... Beecham Group PLC [*NASDAQ symbol*]   (NQ)
BECh .... Bibliotheque de l'Ecole des Chartes [*A publication*]
BEChem... Bachelor of Chemical Engineering   (ADA)
Bech Hist ... Bechard. Histoire du Droit Municipal [*A publication*]   (DLA)
BeCHS...... Berks County Historical Society. Papers [*A publication*]
Bechuanaland Prot Geol Surv Dep Miner Resour Rep ... Bechuanaland
     Protectorate. Geological Survey Department. Mineral
     Resources Report [*A publication*]
BECI.......... Bibliografia Espanola de Ciencias de la Informacion [*Database*]
     [*Universidad Complutense de Madrid*] [*Spanish*]
     [*Information service or system*]   (CRD)
Beck .... Beck's Colorado Reports [*12-16 Colorado and 1 Colorado Court
     of Appeals*] [*A publication*]   (DLA)
Beckacite Nachr ... Beckacite Nachrichten [*A publication*]
Beck (Colo) ... Beck's Colorado Reports [*12-16 Colorado and 1 Colorado
     Court of Appeals*] [*A publication*]   (DLA)
BeckettC .... Beckett Circle [*A publication*]
Beck Isoliertech ... Beck Isoliertechnik [*A publication*]
Beckman Bull ... Beckman Bulletin [*A publication*]
Beckman Instrum Inc Tech Rep ... Beckman Instruments, Incorporated.
     Technical Report [*A publication*]
Beckman Rep ... Beckman Report [*A publication*]
Beck Med Jur ... Beck's Medical Jurisprudence [*A publication*]   (DLA)
BECKTRAN ... Beckman Translation [*Programming language*] [*Beckman
     Instruments, Inc.*]
BEc/LLB ... Bachelor of Economics/Bachelor of Laws   (ADA)
BECM........ British Electrical Conduit Manufacturers
BECO .... Beaman Corporation [*NASDAQ symbol*]   (NQ)
BECO .... Booster Engine Cutoff [*Rocketry*]
BECO .... Brown Engineering Company   (KSC)
B Ecole Fr Ex Or ... Bulletin. Ecole Francaise d'Extreme-Orient [*A
     publication*]
BEcon......... Bachelor of Economics

B Econ Europe ... Bulletin Economique pour l'Europe [*A publication*]
B Econ Res ... Bulletin of Economic Research [*A publication*]
B Econ Soc Maroc ... Bulletin Economique et Social du Maroc [*A publication*]
BECR......... Bercor, Inc. [*La Mirada, CA*] [*NASDAQ symbol*]   (NQ)
BECRB ...... Beckman Report [*A publication*]
BECS .... Basic Error Control System
BECSB....... Bulletin. European Communities. Supplement [*A publication*]
BEc(SocSc) ... Bachelor of Economics (Social Sciences)
BECTA ...... Bulletin of Environmental Contamination and Toxicology [*A
     publication*]
BECTO ...... British Electric Cable Testing Organisation   (MCD)
BECUN ..... Battelle's Educational Computer User's Network [*Battelle
     Memorial Institute*] [*Information service or system*]   (IID)
BE & CWLC ... British Empire and Commonwealth Weight-Lifting Council
B Ed .... Bachelor of Education
BED .... Bachelor of English Divinity
BED .... Bald Eagle [*District of Columbia*] [*Seismograph station code,
     US Geological Survey*] [*Closed*]   (SEIS)
BED .... Basic Engineering Development
BED .... Bedford [*Massachusetts*] [*Airport symbol*]   (OAG)
BED .... Bedford, MA [*Location identifier*] [*FAA*]   (FAAL)
BED .... Block Error Detector   (MCD)
BED .... Blue Diamond Energy [*Vancouver Stock Exchange symbol*]
BEd .... Board of Education
BED .... Board of Educational Development [*University of California,
     Berkeley*]
BED .... Box External Data
BED .... Bridge-Element Delay   (IEEE)
BED .... Bureau of Energy Development [*Philippines*]   (DS)
BED .... Bureau of Export Development [*Department of Commerce*]
BEDA .... Bureau of European Designers Associations   (EA)
BEDAC...... Burst Error Detection and Correlation
BEDBA..... Berichte. Deutsche Botanische Gesellschaft [*A publication*]
BEDCE ...... Basic Engineering Damage Control Exercise [*Military*]   (NVT)
Bed Dr Comm ... Bedarride. Droit Commercial [*A publication*]   (DLA)
Bedell .... Bedell's Reports [*163-191 New York*] [*A publication*]   (DLA)
BEDF........ Bedford Computer Corp. [*NASDAQ symbol*]   (NQ)
BEDFD..... Bedford [*Borough and county in England*]
Bedfordshire Archaeol J ... Bedfordshire Archaeological Journal [*A
     publication*]
Bedi Kart.... Bedi Kartlisa [*A publication*]
BEDM .... Builders Exchange of Detroit and Michigan   (EA)
B Ednl Research J ... British Educational Research Journal [*A publication*]
BEDOC ...... Beds Occupied
Bedrijfsontwikkeling Ed Akkerbouw ... Bedrijfsontwikkeling. Editie
     Akkerbouw. Maandblad voor Agrarische Produktie.
     Verwerking en Afzet [*A publication*]
Bedrijfsontwikkeling Ed Tuinbouw ... Bedrijfsontwikkeling. Editie Tuinbouw
     [*A publication*]
Bedrijfsontwikkeling Ed Veehouderij ... Bedrijfsontwikkeling. Editie
     Veehouderij [*A publication*]
BEDRM..... Bedroom [*Classified advertising*]   (ADA)
BEDS......... Basic Education Development System   (OICC)
BEDS......... Bedfordshire [*County in England*]
BEDS......... Beitraege zur Erforschung der Deutschen Sprache [*A
     publication*]
BEdSc .... Bachelor of Educational Science   (ADA)
BEdSt........ Bachelor of Educational Studies   (ADA)
BEdStud..... Bachelor of Educational Studies
BEDT......... Brooklyn Eastern District Terminal [*AAR code*]
BEDT-TTF ... Bis(ethylenedithiolo)tetrathiafulvalene [*Organic chemistry*]
BEE........... Bachelor of Electrical Engineering
BEE........... Band Edge Energy
BE & E .... Basic Electricity and Electronics
BEE........... Beecham Products-Western Hemisphere Research, Parsippany,
     NJ [*OCLC symbol*]   (OCLC)
Bee .... Bee's United States District Court Reports [*A
     publication*]   (DLA)
BEE.......... Benton, IL [*Location identifier*] [*FAA*]   (FAAL)
BEE.......... Berichten over de Buitenlandse Handel [*A publication*]
BEE.......... Books for Equal Education [*An association*] [*Defunct*]
BEE.......... Bulletin of Environmental Education [*A publication*]
BEE........... Bureau of Educational Evaluation [*Research center*]   (RCD)
BEE........... Bureau Europeen de l'Environnement [*European
     Environmental Bureau*] [*Research center*]
     [*Belgium*]   (IRC)
BEE.......... Business Efficiency Exhibition [*British*]   (DIT)
BEEA........ British Educational Equipment Association   (DS)
Bee Adm..... Bee's Admiralty. An Appendix to Bee's District Court Reports
     [*A publication*]   (DLA)
Bee Anal..... Beebee's Analysis of Common Law Practice [*A
     publication*]   (DLA)
Beebe Cit.... Beebe's Ohio Citations [*A publication*]   (DLA)
BEEC......... Binary Error Erasure Channel   (IEEE)
Bee CCR .... Bee's English Crown Cases Reserved [*A publication*]   (DLA)
B of EE (Com Opt) ... Bachelor of Electrical Engineering, Communication
     Option
BEEF .... Base Engineer Emergency Force [*Air Force*]   (AFM)
BEEF .... Business and Engineering Enriched FORTRAN [*Programming
     language*] [*Sperry UNIVAC*]
Beef Cattle Sci Handb ... Beef Cattle Science Handbook [*A publication*]

Beef Res Rep ... Beef Research Report [*A publication*] (APTA)
Beef Res Rep (Bur Agric Econ) ... Beef Research Report (Bureau of Agricultural Economics) [*A publication*] (APTA)
BEEFS....... Bypass Electronic Emergency Fuel System
Bee Genet Inf Bull ... Bee Genetics Information Bulletin [*A publication*]
BEEIA .... Edison Electric Institute. Bulletin [*A publication*]
Beekeep A ... Bee-Keeping Annual [*A publication*]
Beekeep Div Leafl (Tanganyika) ... Beekeeping Division Leaflet. Forest Department (Tanganyika) [*A publication*]
Beekeep Inf Coop Ext Serv (Ohio) ... Beekeeping Information. Cooperative Extension Service (Ohio) [*A publication*]
Beekeep (QD) ... Beekeeping (Queensland) [*A publication*]
Bee Kingdom Leafl ... Bee Kingdom Leaflet [*A publication*]
Beekprs Bull ... Beekeepers Bulletin [*A publication*]
Beekprs Mag ... Bee-Keepers Magazine [*A publication*]
Beekprs News ... Bee-Keepers News [*A publication*]
Beekprs Rec ... Bee-Keepers Record [*A publication*]
Beeler........ Beeler's Reports [*Tennessee*] [*A publication*] (DLA)
BEEM........ Beech Mountain Railroad Co. [*AAR code*]
BEEM........ Bureau Electronics Equipment Model [*Navy*] (MCD)
BEEMA..... Association des Ingenieurs Electriciens Sortis de l'Institut Electrotechnique Montefiore. Bulletin [*A publication*]
BEENA...... Bergbau und Energiewirtschaft [*A publication*]
BEEO .... Battlefield Electromagnetic Environment Office [*Fort Huachuca, AZ*] [*United States Electronic Proving Ground*] (GRD)
BEEP........ Battalion Equipment Evaluation Program [*DoD*]
BEEP........ Black Executive Exchange Program [*of The National Urban League*] (EA)
BEEP........ Bureau Europeen de l'Education Populaire [*European Bureau of Adult Education - EBAE*] (EAIO)
BEEP........ Roadrunner Enterprises, Inc. [*Albuquerque, NM*] [*NASDAQ symbol*] (NQ)
B of EE (Power Opt) ... Bachelor of Electrical Engineering, Power Option
BEER........ Biological Effects [*of Nonionizing*] Electromagnetic Radiation (MCD)
BEER........ Bombardment Enhanced Etch Rate
BEER........ Brief Easy Editing Routine (ADA)
BEES........ Battlefield Environmental Effects Software [*Army*]
BEET........ Best-Estimated Evaluation Trajectory [*NASA*] (KSC)
BeethovenJb ... Beethoven-Jahrbuch [*A publication*]
Bee Wld ..... Bee World [*A publication*]
BEF........... Band Elimination Filter
BEF........... Bank of England. Quarterly Bulletin [*A publication*]
BEF........... Battalion Expeditionary Force (CINC)
BEF........... Baughan, E. F., Baltimore MD [*STAC*]
BEF........... Before
BEF........... Best Excitatory Frequency [*Neurophysiology*]
BEF........... Blunt End Forward (KSC)
BEF........... Boletin Eclesiastico de Filipinas [*A publication*]
BEF........... Bonus Expeditionary Force
BEF........... Brazilian Expeditionary Force
BEF........... British Empire Forces
BEF........... British Expeditionary Force
BEF........... Buffered Emitter Follower
BEF........... Bulletin des Etudes Francaises [*A publication*]
BEFAP ...... Bell Laboratories FORTRAN Assembly Program [*Data processing*] (IEEE)
BEFAR ...... Bibliotheque des Ecoles Francaises d'Athenes et de Rome [*A publication*]
BEFBAZ.... Berichte. Naturforschende Gesellschaft (Freiburg Im Breisgau) [*A publication*]
BEFC........ Bob Everhart Fan Club (EA)
BEFE........ Before
BEFEMENTD... Before Mentioned [*Legal*] [*British*] (ROG)
BEFEO....... Bulletin. Ecole Francaise d'Extreme-Orient [*A publication*]
BEFLIX..... Bell FLICKS [*Programming language*] [*1973*] (CSR)
BEFM........ Bending Form [*Tool*] (AAG)
BEFourragere ... Belgian Fourragere [*Military decoration*]
BEFPA....... Bollettino. Istituto di Entomologia Agraria e Osservatorio di Fitopatologia di Palermo [*A publication*]
BEFT .... Beaufort Bulletin. Dome Petroleum Ltd. [*A publication*]
BEFT .... Bureau of Education for Fair Trade
BEG .... Beginning
BEG .... Being (ROG)
BEG .... Belgische Kleding [*A publication*]
BEG .... Belgrade [*Yugoslavia*] [*Airport symbol*] (OAG)
BEG .... Boletin de Estudios Germanicos [*A publication*]
BEG .... Brigade Engineer Group [*Marine Corps*] (CINC)
BEG .... Budget Estimate Guidance [*Military*]
BEGAA...... Bergbau-Archiv [*A publication*]
BEGBA...... Bulletin. Eidgenoessisches Gesundheitsamt. Beilage B [*A publication*]
Begg Code .. Begg. Conveyancing Code [*Scotland*] [*A publication*] (DLA)
Begg J Orthod Theory Treat ... Begg Journal of Orthodontic Theory and Treatment [*A publication*]
Begg L Ag .. Begg. Law Agents [*Scotland*] [*A publication*] (DLA)
BEGHA ..... Bulletin of Engineering Geology and Hydrogeology [*English Translation*] [*Yugoslavia*] [*A publication*]
BEGIA .... Bulletin. Institution of Engineers (India) [*A publication*]
BEGL......... Begleitung [*Accompaniment*] [*Music*]

BEGMA .... Beitraege zur Gerichtlichen Medizin [*A publication*]
BEGOA ..... Gerlands Beitraege zur Geophysik [*A publication*]
BEGR........ Bore Erosion Gauge Reading
BEGS........ British and European Geranium Society (EAIO)
BEGUB...... Bulletin EGU [*A publication*]
BEH.......... Beheaded (ROG)
beh............. Behozatal [*Import, Imports*] [*Hungarian*]
BEH.......... Benton Harbor [*Michigan*] [*Airport symbol*] (OAG)
BEH.......... Bibliografia General Espanola e Hispanoamericana [*A bibliographic publication*] [*Spain*]
BEH.......... Bureau of Education for the Handicapped [*Office of Education*] [*Later, SEP*]
BEHA .... British Export Houses' Association (DS)
Behandl Industrieabwaessern ... Behandlung von Industrieabwaessern [*A publication*]
Behandl Rheumatoiden Arthritis D-Penicillamin Symp ... Behandlungen der Rheumatoiden Arthritis mit D-Penicillamin. Symposion [*A publication*]
Behandl Verwert Kommunaler Abwasserschlaemme ... Behandlung und Verwertung Kommunaler Abwasserschlaemme [*A publication*]
Behari .... Revenue Reports of Upper Provinces [*India*] [*A publication*] (DLA)
BEHAV ..... Behavioral
Behav .... Behaviour [*A publication*]
Behav Abstr ... Behavioural Abstracts [*A publication*]
Behav Assess ... Behavioral Assessment [*A publication*]
Behav Biol ... Behavioral Biology [*A publication*]
Behav Brain Res ... Behavioural Brain Research [*A publication*]
Behav Chem State Irradiat Ceram Fuels Proc Panel ... Behaviour and Chemical State of Irradiated Ceramic Fuels. Proceedings. Panel [*A publication*]
Behav Ecol Sociobiol ... Behavioral Ecology and Sociobiology [*A publication*]
Behav Genet ... Behavior Genetics [*A publication*]
Behav and Inf Technol ... Behaviour and Information Technology [*A publication*]
Behavioral Bio ... Behavioral Biology [*A publication*]
Behavioral Sci ... Behavioral Science [*A publication*]
Behavioral & Social Sci Libn ... Behavioral and Social Sciences Librarian [*A publication*]
Behavior Sci Notes ... Behavior Science Notes [*A publication*]
Behavior Ther ... Behavior Therapy [*A publication*]
Behaviour Inf Tech ... Behaviour and Information Technology [*A publication*]
Behaviour Res & Ther ... Behaviour Research and Therapy [*A publication*]
Behav Med Abstr ... Behavioral Medicine Abstracts [*A publication*]
Behav Modif ... Behavior Modification [*A publication*]
Behav Neural Biol ... Behavioral and Neural Biology [*A publication*]
Behav Neurochem ... Behavioral Neurochemistry [*A publication*]
Behav Neuropsychiatry ... Behavioral Neuropsychiatry [*A publication*]
Behav Neurosci ... Behavioral Neuroscience [*A publication*]
Behav Pharmacol ... Behavioral Pharmacology [*A publication*]
Behav Pharmacol Curr Status ... Behavioral Pharmacology. The Current Status [*A publication*]
Behav Processes ... Behavioural Processes [*A publication*]
Behav Psychother ... Behavioural Psychotherapy [*A publication*]
Behav Res M ... Behavior Research Methods and Instrumentation [*A publication*]
Behav Res Methods & Instrum ... Behavior Research Methods and Instrumentation [*A publication*]
Behav Res Methods Instrum ... Behavior Research Methods and Instrumentation [*A publication*]
Behav Res Methods Instrum & Comput ... Behavior Research Methods, Instruments, and Computers [*A publication*]
Behav Res Severe Dev Disabil ... Behavior Research of Severe Developmental Disabilities [*A publication*]
Behav Res T ... Behaviour Research and Therapy [*A publication*]
Behav Res Ther ... Behaviour Research and Therapy [*A publication*]
Behav Sc ... Behavioral Science [*A publication*]
Behav Sci ... Behavioral Science [*A publication*]
Behav Sci Com Dev ... Behavioural Sciences and Community Development [*A publication*]
Behav Sci Community Develop ... Behavioural Sciences and Community Development [*A publication*]
Behav Sci & L ... Behavior Sciences and the Law [*A publication*] (DLA)
Behav Sci N ... Behavior Science Notes [*A publication*]
Behav Sci R ... Behavior Science Research [*A publication*]
Behav and Soc Sci Libr ... Behavioral and Social Sciences Librarian [*A publication*]
Behav Soc Sci Libr ... Behavioral and Social Sciences Librarian [*A publication*]
Behav Ther ... Behavior Therapy [*A publication*]
Behav Today ... Behavior Today [*A publication*]
Behav Toxicol ... Behavioral Toxicology [*A publication*]
BEHD........ Behind (ROG)
BEHE .... Bibliotheque de l'Ecole des Hautes Etudes Belfagor [*A publication*]
BEHF........ Behalf (ROG)
BEHMA .... Berg- und Huettenmaennische Monatshefte. Montanistische Hochschule in Leoben [*A publication*]
BEHP .... Bis(ethylhexyl) Phthalate [*Organic chemistry*]

Behring Inst Mitt ... Behring Institute Mitteilungen [*West Germany*] [*A publication*]
Behring Inst Res Commun ... Behring Institute. Research Communications [*A publication*]
Behringwerk Mitt ... Behringwerk Mitteilungen [*A publication*]
BEHSA...... Behavioral Science [*A publication*]
BEHSDV... Behavioral Assessment [*A publication*]
BEHVL...... Behavioral (AFM)
BEI............ Banca Europea degli Investimenti [*European Investment Bank - EIB*] [*Italian*]
BEI............ Banco Europeo de Inversion [*European Investment Bank - EIB*] [*Spanish*]
BEI............ Banque Europeenne d'Investissement [*European Investment Bank - EIB*] [*French*]
BEI............ Banque d'Expansion Industrielle [*Industrial Development Bank*] [*Canada*]
BEI............ Bear River Range [*Idaho*] [*Seismograph station code, US Geological Survey*] (SEIS)
Bei............ Beiblatt zur Anglia [*A publication*]
BEI............ Beica [*Ethiopia*] [*Airport symbol*] (OAG)
BEI............ Benchmark Electronics, Inc. [*AMEX symbol*] (SPSG)
BEI............ Benefit Eligibility Interview [*Unemployment insurance*] (OICC)
BEI............ Benefits International [*A publication*]
BEI............ Biological Exposure Index
BEI............ Bridgeport Engineering Institute [*Connecticut*]
BEI............ British Education Index [*Bibliographic database*] [*British Library*] [*A publication*]
BEI............ Budget Enactment Instruction
BEI............ Budget Executives Institute [*Later, PEI*] (EA)
BEI............ Butanol-Extractable Iodine [*Clinical chemistry*]
BEI............ Review of the Economic Conditions in Italy [*A publication*]
BEIA......... Bureau d'Education Ibero-Americain
BEIB......... Biomedical Engineering and Instrumentation Branch [*National Institutes of Health*]
Beibl.......... Beiblatt zur Anglia [*A publication*]
Beibl Ann Phys ... Beiblaetter zu den Annalen der Physik [*A publication*]
Beiblatt ...... Beiblatt zur Anglia [*A publication*]
BEICIP...... Bureau d'Etudes Industrielles et de Cooperation, Institut Francais du Petrole [*Office of Industrial Studies and Cooperation, French Institute of Petroleum*] [*Canada*]
BEID......... Behavioral Effects of Infectious Diseases [*Army*]
BEIF .... Beifolgend [*Herewith*] [*German*]
BEIFC........ Barbara Eden International Fan Club (EA)
BEIH .... BEI Holdings Ltd. [*NASDAQ symbol*] (NQ)
Beih Ber Naturhist Ges Hannover ... Beihefte. Berichten der Naturhistorischen Gesellschaft zu Hannover [*A publication*]
Beihefte Arch Schiffs- u Tropen-Hyg ... Beihefte. Archiv fuer Schiffs und Tropen-Hygiene [*A publication*]
Beihefte Elem Math ... Beihefte. Zeitschrift Elemente der Mathematik [*A publication*]
Beih Int Z Vitam-Ernaehrungsforsch ... Beiheft. Internationale Zeitschrift fuer Vitamin- und Ernaehrungsforschung [*A publication*]
Beih Schweiz Bienenztg ... Beihefte. Schweizerische Bienenzietung [*A publication*]
Beih Sydowia Ann Mycol Ser II ... Beihefte. Sydowia Annales. Mycologici. Serie II [*A publication*]
Beih Tueb Atlas Vorderen Orients Reihe A Naturwiss ... Beihefte. Tuebinger Atlas des Vorderen Orients. Reihe A. Naturwissenschaften [*A publication*]
Beih Zentralbl Gewerbehyg Unfallverhuet ... Beihefte. Zentralblatt fuer Gewerbehygiene und Unfallverhuetung [*A publication*]
Beih Z Schweiz Forstver ... Beiheft. Zeitschriften des Schweizerischen Forstvereins [*A publication*]
BEII .... BEI Electronics, Inc. [*NASDAQ symbol*] (NQ)
Beijing R ... Beijing Review [*A publication*]
BEIND....... Beratende Ingenieure [*A publication*]
BEIR .... Biological Effects of Ionizing Radiation
BEISP........ Beispiel [*Example*] [*Music*]
Beispiele Angew Forsch Ges Foerd Angew Forsch ... Beispiele Angewandter Forschung. Fraunhofer Gesellschaft zur Foerderung der Angewandten Forschung [*A publication*]
BEITA .... Business Equipment and Information Technology Association [*British*]
BEITC .... Business Energy Investment Tax Credit [*IRS*]
Beitr .... Beitraeg [*or Beitraege*] [*Contribution, Share*] [*German*] (OCD)
Beitr .... Beitraege zur Geschichte der Deutschen Sprache und Literatur [*Halle*] [*A publication*]
Beitraege Algebra Geom ... Beitraege zur Algebra und Geometrie [*A publication*]
Beitraege Anal ... Beitraege zur Analysis [*A publication*]
Beitraege Gesch Buchw ... Beitraege zur Geschichte des Buchwesens [*A publication*]
Beitraege Namen ... Beitraege zur Namenforschung [*A publication*]
Beitraege Numer Math ... Beitraege zur Numerischen Mathematik [*A publication*]
Beitrage Bf ... Beitraege zur Aegyptischen Bauforschung und Altertumskunde [*Cairo*] [*A publication*]
Beitr Agrarwiss ... Beitraege zur Agrarwissenschaft [*A publication*]

Beitr Allg A ... Beitraege zur Allgemeinen und Vergleichenden Archaeologie [*A publication*]
Beitr Biol Pfl ... Beitraege zur Biologie der Pflanzen [*A publication*]
Beitr Biol Pflanz ... Beitraege zur Biologie der Pflanzen [*A publication*]
Beitr Chem Physiol Pathol ... Beitraege zur Chemischen Physiologie und Pathologie [*West Germany*] [*A publication*]
Beitr Datenverarb Unternehmensforsch ... Beitraege Datenverarbeitung und Unternehmensforschung [*A publication*]
Beitr Deutsch Volks Altertumskunde ... Beitraege zur Deutschen Volks- und Altertumskunde [*A publication*]
Beitr Engl u Nordamerikas ... Beitraege zur Erforschung der Sprache und Kultur Englands und Nordamerikas [*A publication*]
Beitr Ent .... Beitraege zur Entomologie [*A publication*]
Beitr Entomol ... Beitraege zur Entomologie [*A publication*]
Beitr Entwicklungsmech Anat Pflanz ... Beitraege zur Entwicklungsmechanischen Anatomie der Pflanzen [*A publication*]
Beitr Forschungstech ... Beitraege zur Forschungstechnologie [*Berlin*] [*A publication*]
Beitr Forschungstechnol ... Beitraege zur Forschungstechnologie [*A publication*]
Beitr Forstwirtsch ... Beitraege fuer die Forstwirtschaft [*West Germany*] [*A publication*]
Beitr Geobot Landesaufn Schweiz ... Beitraege Geobotanischen Landesaufnahme der Schweiz [*A publication*]
Beitr Geol Karte Schweiz ... Beitraege zur Geologischen Karte der Schweiz [*A publication*]
Beitr Geol Schweiz Geotech Ser ... Beitraege zur Geologie der Schweiz. Geotechnische Serie [*A publication*]
Beitr Geol Schweiz Kleinere Mitt ... Beitraege zur Geologie der Schweiz. Kleinere Mitteilungen [*A publication*]
Beitr Geol Thueringen ... Beitraege zur Geologie von Thueringen [*A publication*]
Beitr Geoph ... Beitraege zur Geophysik [*A publication*]
Beitr Geophysik ... Beitraege zur Geophysik [*A publication*]
Beitr Gerichtl Med ... Beitraege zur Gerichtlichen Medizin [*A publication*]
Beitr Gesch Dtsch Sprache ... Beitraege zur Geschichte der Deutschen Sprache und Literatur [*A publication*]
Beitr Gesch Landwirtschaftswiss ... Beitraege zur Geschichte der Landwirtschaftswissenschaften [*A publication*]
Beitr Gesch Moenchtums Benediktinerordens ... Beitraege zur Geschichte des Alten Moenchtums und des Benediktinerordens [*A publication*]
Beitr Gesch Pharm ... Beitraege zur Geschichte der Pharmazie [*A publication*]
Beitr Gesch Pharm Ihrer Nachbargeb ... Beitraege zur Geschichte der Pharmazie und Ihrer Nachbargebiete [*A publication*]
Beitr Gesch Phil Mittelalters ... Beitraege zur Geschichte der Philosophie und Theologie des Mittelalters [*A publication*]
Beitr Gesch Tech Ind ... Beitraege zur Geschichte der Technik und Industrie. Jahrbuch des Vereines Deutscher Ingenieure [*A publication*]
Beitr Gesch Univ Erfurt ... Beitraege zur Geschichte der Universitaet Erfurt [*A publication*]
Beitr Gesch Univ Halle-Wittenberg ... Beitraege zur Geschichte der Universitaet Halle-Wittenberg [*A publication*]
BeitrHistTh ... Beitraege zur Historischen Theologie [*Tuebingen*] [*A publication*]
Beitr Hyg Epidemiol ... Beitraege zur Hygiene und Epidemiologie [*A publication*]
Beitr Infusionsther Klin Ernaehr ... Beitraege zur Infusionstherapie und Klinische Ernaehrung [*A publication*]
Beitr Infusionsther Klin Ernaehr Forsch Prax ... Beitraege zur Infusionstherapie und Klinische Ernaehrung. Forschung und Praxis [*A publication*]
Beitr Inkunabelk ... Beitraege zur Inkunabelkunde. Gesellschaft fuer Typenkunde des 15 Jahrhunderts-Wiegendruck-Gesellschaft [*A publication*]
Beitr Int Kongr Gesch Wiss ... Beitraege zum Internationalen Kongress fuer Geschichte der Wissenschaft [*A publication*]
Beitr Klin Chir ... Beitraege zur Klinischen Chirurgie [*A publication*]
Beitr Klin Erforsch Tuberk Lungenkr ... Beitraege zur Klinik und Erforschung der Tuberkulose und der Lungenkrankheiten [*A publication*]
Beitr Klin Neurol Psychiatr ... Beitraege zur Klinischen Neurologie und Psychiatrie [*A publication*]
Beitr Klin Tuberk Spezif Tuber-Forsch ... Beitraege zur Klinik der Tuberkulose und Spezifischen Tuberkulose-Forschung [*A publication*]
Beitr Konfl ... Beitraege zur Konfliktforschung [*A publication*]
Beitr Konfliktforsch ... Beitraege zur Konfliktforschung [*A publication*]
Beitr Kryptogamenflora Schweiz ... Beitraege zur Kryptogamenflora der Schweiz [*A publication*]
Beitr Krystallogr Mineral ... Beitraege zur Krystallographie und Mineralogie [*A publication*]
Beitr z Land u Volk v Elsass-Loth ... Beitraege zur Landes und Volkeskunde von Elsass-Lothringen [*A publication*]
Beitr Math Informatik Nachrichtentech ... Beitraege zur Mathematik, Informatik, und Nachrichtentechnik [*A publication*]
Beitr Math-Naturwiss Unterr ... Beitraege zum Mathematisch-Naturwissenschaftlichen Unterricht [*A publication*]
Beitr Meer ... Beitraege zur Meereskunde [*A publication*]

Beitr Mineralogie u Petrographie ... Beitraege zur Mineralogie und Petrographie [*A publication*]
Beitr Miner Petrogr ... Beitraege zur Mineralogie und Petrographie [*A publication*]
Beitr Musik ... Beitraege zur Musikwissenschaft [*A publication*]
BeitrMw ..... Beitraege zur Musikwissenschaft [*DDR*] [*A publication*]
Beitr Nam F ... Beitraege zur Namenforschung [*A publication*]
Beitr Naturkd Forsch Suedwestdtsch ... Beitraege zur Naturkundlichen Forschung in Suedwestdeutschland [*A publication*]
Beitr Naturkd Forsch Suedwestdtsch Beih ... Beitraege zur Naturkundlichen Forschung in Suedwestdeutschland. Beihefte [*A publication*]
Beitr Naturkd Forsch Suedwestdtschl ... Beitraege zur Naturkundlichen Forschung in Suedwestdeutschland [*A publication*]
Beitr Naturkd Niedersachsens ... Beitraege zur Naturkunde Niedersachsens [*A publication*]
Beitr Naturk Forsch Suedwdtl ... Beitraege zur Naturkundlichen Forschung in Suedwestdeutschland [*A publication*]
Beitr Neotrop Fauna ... Beitraege zur Neotropischen Fauna [*A publication*]
Beitr Neurochir ... Beitraege zur Neurochirurgie [*A publication*]
Beitr Numer Math ... Beitraege zur Numerischen Mathematik [*A publication*]
Beitr Onkol ... Beitraege zur Onkologie [*A publication*]
Beitr Orthop Traumatol ... Beitraege zur Orthopaedie und Traumatologie [*A publication*]
Beitr Path .. Beitraege zur Pathologie [*A publication*]
Beitr Path Anat u Allg Path ... Beitraege zur Pathologischen Anatomie und zur Allgemeinen Pathologie [*A publication*]
Beitr Pathol ... Beitraege zur Pathologie [*A publication*]
Beitr Pathol Anat Allg Pathol ... Beitraege zur Pathologischen Anatomie und zur Allgemeinen Pathologie [*A publication*]
Beitr Phys Atmos ... Beitraege zur Physik der Atmosphaere [*A publication*]
Beitr Plasmaphys ... Beitraege aus der Plasmaphysik [*A publication*]
Beitr Pl Physik ... Beitraege aus der Plasmaphysik [*A publication*]
Beitr Radioastron ... Beitraege zur Radioastronomie [*A publication*]
Beitr Rheumatol ... Beitraege zur Rheumatologie [*A publication*]
Beitr Sexualforsch ... Beitraege zur Sexualforschung [*A publication*]
Beitr Silikose-Forsch ... Beitraege zur Silikose-Forschung [*A publication*]
Beitr Silikose-Forsch (Pneumokoniose) ... Beitraege zur Silikose-Forschung (Pneumokoniose) [*A publication*]
Beitr Silikose-Forsch Sonderb ... Beitraege zur Silikose-Forschung. Sonderband [*A publication*]
Beitr Tabakforsch ... Beitraege zur Tabakforschung [*A publication*]
Beitr Tabakforsch Int ... Beitraege zur Tabakforschung International [*A publication*]
Beitr Trop Landwirtsch Veterinaermed ... Beitraege zur Tropischen Landwirtschaft und Veterinaermedizin [*A publication*]
Beitr Trop Subtrop Landwirtsch Tropenveterinaermed ... Beitraege zur Tropischen und Subtropischen Landwirtschaft und Tropenveterinaermedizin [*A publication*]
Beitr Vogelkd ... Beitraege zur Vogelkunde [*A publication*]
Beitr Wuerttemb Apothekengesch ... Beitraege zur Wuerttembergischen Apothekengeschichte [*A publication*]
Beit Sonderschulwesen Rehabilitationspaedagog ... Beitraege zum Sonderschulwesen und zur Rehabilitationspaedagogik [*A publication*]
BEJ .... Bannon, E. J., Buffalo NY [*STAC*]
bej .... Beja [*MARC language code*] [*Library of Congress*] (LCCP)
bej .... Bejegyzett [*Registered, Incorporated*] [*Hungarian*]
BEJ .... Berau [*Indonesia*] [*Airport symbol*] (OAG)
Be Jb .... Beethoven-Jahrbuch [*A publication*]
BEJE .... Bureau Europeen de la Jeunesse et de l'Enfance
BEJUA .... Behavioral Engineering [*A publication*]
BEK .... Becker Milk Co. Ltd. [*Toronto Stock Exchange symbol*]
BEK .... Beli, AK [*Location identifier*] [*FAA*] (FAAL)
BEK .... Butyl Ethyl Ketene [*Organic chemistry*]
BEKDDR ... Bund der Evangelischen Kirchen in der Deutschen Demokratischen Republik [*Federation of Protestant Churches in the German Democratic Republic*] (EY)
Bekes Koezl ... A Bekes Megyei Muzeumok Koezlemenyei [*A publication*]
Beke es Szocial ... Beke es Szocializmus [*A publication*]
BEKOA ..... Berichte. Gesellschaft fuer Kohlentechnik [*A publication*]
BEKULA ... Berliner Kraft- und Licht (Bewag)-Aktiengesellschaft [*Berlin Power and Light Joint Stock Company*] [*Federal Republic of Germany*]
B El .... Bachelor of Elocution
BEL .... Bachelor of English Literature
BEL .... Bahaa Esperanto-Ligo (EA)
BEL .... Balgarski Ezik i Literatura [*A publication*]
BEL .... Basic Equipment List (MCD)
BEL .... Beleaguered (AABC)
BEL .... Belem [*Brazil*] [*Airport symbol*] (OAG)
Bel .... Belfagor [*A publication*]
BEL .... Belgium [*ANSI three-letter standard code*] (CNC)
Bel .... Beling's Ceylon Reports [*A publication*] (DLA)
BEL .... Bell Atlantic Corp. [*NYSE symbol*] (SPSG)
BEL .... Bell Character [*Keyboard*]
BEL .... Bell Journal of Economics [*A publication*]
BEL .... Bellasis. Bombay Reports [*A publication*] (DLA)
Bel .... Bellewe's English King's Bench Reports Tempore Richard II [*1378-1400*] [*A publication*] (DLA)
Bel .... Bellinger's Reports [*4-8 Oregon*] [*A publication*] (DLA)

bel .... Belorussian [*MARC language code*] [*Library of Congress*] (LCCP)
BEL .... Below [*Technical drawings*]
BEL .... Belsk [*Poland*] [*Geomagnetic observatory code*]
BEL .... Belsk [*Poland*] [*Seismograph station code, US Geological Survey*] [*Closed*] (SEIS)
Bel .... [*Jacobus de*] Belvisio [*Deceased, 1335*] [*Authority cited in pre-1607 legal work*] (DSA)
BEL .... Book of English Literature [*A publication*]
BEL .... British Empire League
BEL .... Bureau Equipment List (MCD)
BEL .... Bus-Earth Tracking Station Link [*NASA*]
BEL .... Mededelingen. Verbond van Belgische Ondernemingen [*A publication*]
BEL .... United States Army, TRADOC, Fort Belvoir, Van Noy Post Library, Fort Belvoir, VA [*OCLC symbol*] (OCLC)
BELA .... Black Entertainment Lawyers Association [*Later, BESLA*] (EA)
BELAIR ..... Belgian Air Staff [*NATO*] (NATG)
Belarusk Med Dumka ... Belaruskaia Medychnaia Dumka [*A publication*]
Belastungsgrenzen Kunstst Bauteilen ... Belastungsgrenzen von Kunststoff Bauteilen [*A publication*]
BELC .... Black Employees of the Library of Congress (EA)
Bel Cas T R II ... Bellewe's Cases Tempore Richard II [*1378-1400*] [*A publication*] (ILCA)
Bel Ca T H VIII ... Bellewe's Cases Tempore Henry VIII [*Brooke's New Cases*] [*England*] [*A publication*] (DLA)
BELCH ...... Belchamp [*England*]
BELCRK ... Bell Crank [*Automotive engineering*]
BELD .... Battlefield Environment LASER Designator [*MIRADCOM*] (MCD)
Bel and Dr ... Bel and the Dragon [*Old Testament book*] [*Apocrypha*]
BEL AND DRAGON ... [*The*] History of the Destruction of Bel and the Dragon [*Apocrypha*]
BELDWSS ... Battlefield Environment LASER Designator/Weapon System Simulation [*MIRADCOM*] (RDA)
B Ele .... Bachelor of Elements
Beleid en Mij ... Beleid en Maatschappij [*A publication*]
Bel Ex .... Bell on Excise [*A publication*] (DLA)
BELF .... Bel Fuse, Inc. [*NASDAQ symbol*] (NQ)
BELF .... Belfast [*City in Northern Ireland*] (ROG)
BELF .... Bicyclists Educational and Legal Foundation (EA)
BELG .... Belgium
BelgAE .... Belgian Antarctic Expedition [*1897-99, 1957-58*]
Belg Apic ... Belgique Apicole [*A publication*]
Belg Chem Ind ... Belgische Chemische Industrie [*A publication*]
Belg Commr ... Statistiques du Commerce Exterieur. Union Economique Belgo-Luxembourgeoise [*A publication*]
Belg Econ ... Belgium. Economic and Technical Information. English Edition [*A publication*]
Belg E & T ... Belgium Economy and Technique [*A publication*]
BELGF ...... Belgium Standard Ltd. [*NASDAQ symbol*] (NQ)
Belgian R Internat Law ... Belgian Review of International Law [*A publication*]
Belgicatom Bull ... Belgicatom Bulletin [*Belgium*] [*A publication*]
Belgicatom Bull Inf ... Belgicatom Bulletin d'Information [*A publication*]
Belg Inst Verbetering Beit Driemaand Publ ... Belgisch Institut tot Verbetering van de Beit Driemaandelijkse Publikatie [*A publication*]
Belgique Med ... Belgique Medicale [*A publication*]
Belg J Food Chem Biotechnol ... Belgian Journal of Food Chemistry and Biotechnology [*A publication*]
Belg Jud ..... Belgique Judiciaire [*A publication*] (ILCA)
Belg Memo ... Business Memo from Belgium [*A publication*]
Belg Ned Tijdschr Oppervlatke Tech Met ... Belgisch-Nederlands Tijdschrift voor Oppervlatketechnieken van Metalen [*A publication*]
Belg P .... Belgium Pharmacopoeia [*A publication*]
Belg Plast ... Belgian Plastics [*A publication*]
Belgra .... Belgravia [*A publication*]
Belg Rev ..... Belgian American Trade Review [*A publication*]
Belg Rev Int'l L ... Belgian Review of International Law [*A publication*] (DLA)
Belg Serv Geol Mem ... Belgium. Service Geologique. Memoire [*A publication*]
Belg Serv Geol Prof Pap ... Belgium. Service Geologique. Professional Paper [*A publication*]
Belg Stat A ... Annuaire Statistique de la Belgique [*A publication*]
Belg Tijdschr Geneeskd ... Belgisch Tijdschrift voor Geneeskunde [*A publication*]
Belg Tijdschr Radiol ... Belgisch Tijdschrift voor Radiologie [*A publication*]
Belg Tijdschr Reumatol Fys Geneeskd ... Belgisch Tijdschrift voor Reumatologie en Fysische Geneeskunde [*A publication*]
Belg Tijds Soc Zekerh ... Belgisch Tijdschrift voor Sociale Zekerheid [*A publication*]
BELINDIS ... Belgian Information and Dissemination Service [*European host database system*] [*Ministry of Economic Affairs*] (IID)
Beling .... Beling's Ceylon Reports [*A publication*] (DLA)
Beling & Van ... Beling and Vanderstraaten's Ceylon Reports [*A publication*] (DLA)
BelJud .... Bellum Judaicum [*Josephus*] [*Classical studies*] (BJA)
BELK .... Elkford Public Library, British Columbia [*Library symbol*] [*National Library of Canada*] (NLC)

Bel L.......... Belaruskaja Linhvistyka [*A publication*]
Bell............ Bell. Calcutta Reports [*A publication*] (DLA)
BELL......... Bell National Corp. [*NASDAQ symbol*] (NQ)
Bell............ Bellasis. Bombay Reports [*A publication*] (DLA)
Bell............. Bellewe's English King's Bench Reports [*A publication*] (DLA)
Bell............ Bellinger's Reports [*4-8 Oregon*] [*A publication*] (DLA)
Bell............ Bell's Cases in the Scotch Court of Session [*A publication*] (DLA)
Bell............ Bell's English Crown Cases Reserved [*169 English Reprint*] [*A publication*] (DLA)
Bell............ Bell's Scotch Appeal Cases [*A publication*] (DLA)
BELL......... Binary Envelope Locked Loop (MCD)
Bell............ Brooke's New Cases (Collected by Bellewe) [*A publication*] (DLA)
BELL......... Bulletin. Societe des Etudes de Lettres (Lausanne) [*A publication*]
BELLAD ... Belladonna [*Deadly Nightshade (or its medicinal extract)*] (ROG)
BELLADON ... Belladonna [*Deadly Nightshade (or its medicinal extract)*] (ROG)
Bellam........ [*Egidius*] Bellamera [*Deceased, 1407*] [*Authority cited in pre-1607 legal work*] (DSA)
Bell Ap Ca ... Bell's Scotch Appeal Cases [*A publication*] (DLA)
Bell App..... Bell's House of Lords Scotch Appeal Cases [*1842-50*] [*A publication*] (DLA)
Bell App Bell (SC) ... Bell's House of Lords Scotch Appeal Cases [*1842-50*] [*A publication*] (DLA)
Bell App Cas ... Bell's House of Lords Scotch Appeal Cases [*1842-50*] [*A publication*] (DLA)
Bell Arb...... Bell's Law of Arbitration in Scotland [*A publication*] (DLA)
Bellas .... Bellasis. Civil Cases [*Bombay*] [*A publication*] (DLA)
Bellas .... Bellasis. Criminal Cases [*Bombay*] [*A publication*] (DLA)
Bellasis ...... Bombay Sadr Diwani Adalat Reports [*A publication*] (DLA)
Bell Aw....... Bell's Law of Awards [*A publication*] (DLA)
Bell C .... Bell's Reports, Court of Session [*1790-92*] [*Scotland*] [*A publication*] (DLA)
Bell Cas...... Bell's Cases in the Scotch Court of Session [*A publication*] (DLA)
Bell Cas T Hen VIII ... Brooke's New Cases, English King's Bench [*1515-58*] [*A publication*] (DLA)
Bell Cas T H VIII ... Brooke's New Cases (Collected by Bellewe) [*A publication*] (DLA)
Bell Cas T Rich II ... Bellewe's English King's Bench Reports Tempore Richard II [*1378-1400*] [*A publication*] (DLA)
Bell Cas T R II ... Bellewe's English King's Bench Reports Tempore Richard II [*1378-1400*] [*A publication*] (DLA)
Bell CC...... Bellasis. Civil Cases [*Bombay*] [*A publication*] (DLA)
Bell CC...... Bellasis. Criminal Cases [*Bombay*] [*A publication*] (DLA)
Bell CC...... Bell's English Crown Cases Reserved [*169 English Reprint*] [*A publication*] (DLA)
Bell CC (Eng) ... Bell's English Crown Cases Reserved [*169 English Reprint*] [*A publication*] (DLA)
Bell CHC ... Bell's Reports, High Court of Calcutta [*India*] [*A publication*] (DLA)
Bell Comm ... Bell's Commentaries on the Laws of Scotland [*A publication*] (DLA)
Bell Convey ... Bell. Lecture on Conveyancing [*Scotland*] [*A publication*] (DLA)
Bellcore...... Bell Communications Research, Inc. [*Livingston, NJ*] (TSSD)
Bell Cr C .... Beller's Criminal Cases [*Bombay*] [*A publication*] (DLA)
Bell Cr C .... Bell's English Crown Cases [*A publication*] (DLA)
Bell Cr Ca .. Beller's Criminal Cases [*Bombay*] [*A publication*] (DLA)
Bell Cr Ca .. Bell's English Crown Cases [*A publication*] (DLA)
Bell Cr Cas ... Beller's Criminal Cases [*Bombay*] [*A publication*] (DLA)
Bell Cr Cas ... Bell's English Crown Cases [*A publication*] (DLA)
Bell CT...... Bell. Competing Titles [*Scotland*] [*A publication*] (DLA)
Bell Ct of Sess ... [*R.*] Bell's Decisions, Scotch Court of Session [*A publication*] (DLA)
Bell Ct of Sess Fol R ... Bell's Decisions, Scotch Court of Session [*A publication*] (DLA)
Bell Deeds ... Bell. System of the Forms of Deeds [*Scotland*] [*A publication*] (DLA)
Bell Del ...... Beller's Delineations of Universal Law [*A publication*] (DLA)
Bell Dict..... Bell's Dictionary and Digest of the Laws of Scotland [*A publication*] (DLA)
Bell Dict Dec ... Bell's Dictionary of Decisions, Scotch Court of Session [*A publication*] (DLA)
Belle Glade AREC Res Rep EV Fla Univ Agric Res Educ Cent ... Belle Glade AREC. Research Report EV. Florida University. Agricultural Research and Education Center [*A publication*]
Bell Elec..... Bell. Election Law of Scotland [*A publication*] (DLA)
Beller.......... Bellerophon [*of Euripides*] [*Classical studies*] (OCD)
Belleten...... Belleten Turk Tarih Kurumu [*A publication*]
Belle W Baruch Libr Mar Sci ... Belle W. Baruch Library in Marine Science [*A publication*]
Bellewe....... Bellewe's English King's Bench Reports [*A publication*] (DLA)
Bellewe (Eng) ... Bellewe's English King's Bench Reports [*A publication*] (DLA)
Bellewe's Ca Temp Hen VIII ... Brooke's New Cases, English King's Bench [*1515-58*] [*A publication*] (DLA)

Bellewe's Ca Temp R II ... Bellewe's Cases Tempore Richard II [*1378-1400*] [*A publication*] (DLA)
Bellewe T H VIII ... Brooke's New Cases (Collected by Bellewe) [*A publication*] (DLA)
Bell Exp Test ... Bell on Expert Testimony [*A publication*] (DLA)
Bell Fol....... Bell's Folio Reports, Scotch Court of Session [*1794-95*] [*A publication*] (DLA)
Bell Folio.... [*R.*] Bell's Decisions, Scotch Court of Session [*A publication*] (DLA)
Bell HC...... Bell's Reports, High Court of Calcutta [*India*] [*A publication*] (DLA)
Bell HL ...... Bell's House of Lords Scotch Appeal Cases [*1842-50*] [*A publication*] (DLA)
Bell HL Sc ... Bell's House of Lords Scotch Appeal Cases [*1842-50*] [*A publication*] (DLA)
Bell HW..... Bell. Property as Arising from the Relation of Husband and Wife [*1849*] [*A publication*] (DLA)
Bell Illus .... Bell's Illustrations of Principles [*A publication*] (DLA)
Bell (In)...... Bell's Reports, High Court of Calcutta [*India*] [*A publication*] (DLA)
Bellinger .... Bellinger's Reports [*4-8 Oregon*] [*A publication*] (DLA)
Bellingh Tr .. Report of Bellingham's Trial [*A publication*] (DLA)
Belli's Mod Trials ... Belli's Modern Trials [*A publication*] (DLA)
Bell J Econ ... Bell Journal of Economics [*A publication*]
Bell J Econ and Manage Sci ... Bell Journal of Economics and Management Science [*Later, Bell Journal of Economics*] [*A publication*]
Bell J Econ Manage Sci ... Bell Journal of Economics and Management Science [*Later, Bell Journal of Economics*] [*A publication*]
Bell J Econom ... Bell Journal of Economics [*A publication*]
BellJud....... De Bello Judaico [*Josephus*] (BJA)
Bell Lab Re ... Bell Laboratories Record [*A publication*]
Bell Lab Rec ... Bell Laboratories Record [*A publication*]
Bell Leas .... Bell on Leases [*Scotland*] [*A publication*] (DLA)
Bell L & T .. Bell on Landlord and Tenant [*Bengal*] [*A publication*] (DLA)
BELLMATIC ... Bell Laboratories Machine-Aided Technical Information Center (DIT)
Bell Med LJ ... Bell's Medico-Legal Journal [*A publication*] (DLA)
Bell No....... Bell's Supplemented Notes to Hume on Crimes [*A publication*] (DLA)
Bello........... [*Nicolaus*] Bellonus [*Flourished, 1542-47*] [*Authority cited in pre-1607 legal work*] (DSA)
Bell Oct...... Bell's Octavo Reports, Scotch Court of Sessions [*1790-92*] [*A publication*] (DLA)
Bellon......... [*Nicolaus*] Bellonus [*Flourished, 1542-47*] [*Authority cited in pre-1607 legal work*] (DSA)
Bell (Or)..... Bellinger's Reports [*4-8 Oregon*] [*A publication*] (DLA)
Bell PC....... Bell's Cases in Parliament: Scotch Appeals [*A publication*] (DLA)
Bell Prin..... Bell's Principles of the Law of Scotland [*10 eds.*] [*1829-99*] [*A publication*] (DLA)
Bell Put Mar ... Bell's Putative Marriage Case [*Scotland*] [*A publication*] (DLA)
BELLREL ... Bell Laboratories Library Real-Time Loan System
Bell S.......... Bell. Sale of Food and Drugs [*14th ed.*] [*1968*] [*A publication*] (DLA)
Bell Sale..... Bell. Sale of Food and Drugs [*14th ed.*] [*1968*] [*A publication*] (DLA)
Bell's App .. Bell's House of Lords Scotch Appeal Cases [*1842-50*] [*A publication*] (DLA)
Bell Sc App ... Bell's Appeals to House of Lords from Scotland [*A publication*] (DLA)
Bell Sc App Cas ... Bell's Scotch Appeal Cases [*A publication*] (DLA)
Bell Sc Cas ... Bell's Cases in the Scotch Court of Session [*A publication*] (DLA)
Bell Sc Dig ... Bell's Scottish Digest [*A publication*] (DLA)
Bell's Comm Bell's ... Commentaries on Laws of Scotland [*7 eds.*] [*1800-70*] [*A publication*] (DLA)
Bell Scot Dig ... Bell's Scottish Digest [*A publication*] (DLA)
Bell's Dict .. Bell's Dictionary of Decisions, Scotch Court of Session [*A publication*] (DLA)
Bell Ses Cas ... Bell's Cases in the Scotch Court of Session [*A publication*] (DLA)
Bell Sty ...... Bell. System of the Forms of Deeds (Styles) [*Scotland*] [*A publication*] (DLA)
Bell System Tech J ... Bell System Technical Journal [*A publication*]
Bell Syst T ... Bell System Technical Journal [*A publication*]
Bell Syst Tech J ... Bell System Technical Journal [*A publication*]
Bell TD ...... Bell. Testing of Deeds [*Scotland*] [*A publication*] (DLA)
BELLTEL ... Bell Telephone
Bell Telephone Mag ... Bell Telephone Magazine [*A publication*]
Bell Teleph Syst Tech Publ Monogr ... Bell Telephone System. Technical Publications. Monographs [*A publication*]
Bell UL ...... Beller's Delineation of Universal Law [*A publication*] (DLA)
Bell 8vo ...... Bell's Octavo Reports, Scotch Court of Sessions [*1790-92*] [*A publication*] (DLA)
BELNAV ... Belgian Naval Staff [*NATO*] (NATG)
Beloit.......... Beloit Poetry Journal [*A publication*]
Beloit Poet ... Beloit Poetry Journal [*A publication*]
Beloruss Nauchno Issled Inst Melior Vodn Khoz Tr ... Belorusskii Nauchno-Issledovatel'skii Institut Melioratsii i Vodnogo Khozyaistva. Trudy [*A publication*]

Beloruss Nauchno Issled Kozhno Venerol Inst Sb Nauchn Tr ... Belorusskii Nauchno-Issledovatel'skii Kozhno-Venerologicheskii Institut. Sbornik Nauchnykh Trudov [*A publication*]

BELP .... Belknap, Inc. [*NASDAQ symbol*] (NQ)

Belper .... [*Petrus de*] Bellapertica [*Deceased, 1308*] [*Authority cited in pre-1607 legal work*] (DSA)

Belperti ...... [*Petrus de*] Bellapertica [*Deceased, 1308*] [*Authority cited in pre-1607 legal work*] (DSA)

Bel Po J ..... Beloit Poetry Journal [*A publication*]

Bel Prob ..... Belknap's Probate Law of California [*A publication*] (DLA)

BELR .... Bell Laboratories Record [*A publication*]

BELRA ...... British Empire Leprosy Relief Association

BeLS .... [*The*] Best Love Story Poems [*A publication*]

BelSSR ...... Byelorussian Soviet Socialist Republic

Belt Bro ...... Belt's Edition of Brown's Chancery Reports [*1778-94*] [*A publication*] (DLA)

Belt's Supp (Eng) ... Belt's Supplement to Vesey, Senior's, English Chancery Reports [*1746-56*] [*A publication*] (DLA)

Belt Sup ..... Belt's Supplement to Vesey, Senior's, English Chancery Reports [*1746-56*] [*A publication*] (DLA)

Belt Supp ... Belt's Supplement to Vesey, Senior's, English Chancery Reports [*1746-56*] [*A publication*] (DLA)

Belt Sup Ves ... Belt's Supplement to Vesey, Senior's, English Chancery Reports [*1746-56*] [*A publication*] (DLA)

Beltsville Symp Agric Res ... Beltsville Symposia in Agricultural Research [*A publication*]

Belt Ves Sen ... Belt's Edition of Vesey, Senior's, English Chancery Reports [*A publication*] (DLA)

BeLU .... Universite de Liege, Liege, Belgium [*Library symbol*] [*Library of Congress*] (LCLS)

Belvis .... [*Jacobus de*] Belvisio [*Deceased, 1335*] [*Authority cited in pre-1607 legal work*] (DSA)

BELW .... Bellwether Exploration Co. [*NASDAQ symbol*] (NQ)

BEM .... Bachelor of Engineering of Mines

BEM .... Bachelor of Mining Engineering

BEM .... Ballistic Evaluation Motor (MCD)

bem .... Bemba [*MARC language code*] [*Library of Congress*] (LCCP)

BEM .... Bergstrom Capital [*AMEX symbol*] (SPSG)

BEM .... British Empire Medal

BEM .... Bug-Eyed Monster [*Science fiction or fantastic literature which makes great use of monsters in its storyline or illustrations*]

BEM .... Bulletin Economique et Social du Maroc [*A publication*]

BEM .... Bureau of Executive Manpower [*Civil Service Commission*]

BEM .... Business Executives Move for New National Priorities [*An association*] (EA)

BEM .... Buthylethylmagnesium [*Organic chemistry*]

BEM .... Enderby and District Museum, Enderby, British Columbia [*Library symbol*] [*National Library of Canada*] (NLC)

BEM .... Montreal City & District Savings Bank [*Toronto Stock Exchange symbol*]

BEMA ...... Bakery Equipment Manufacturers Association (EA)

BEMA ...... Business Equipment Manufacturers Association [*Later, CBEMA*]

BEMAC .... British Exports Marketing Advisory Committee [*Defunct*]

BEMAR ..... Backlog of Essential Maintenance and Repair (AFM)

BEMB .... Bituminous Equipment Manufacturers Bureau [*Later, BAEB*] (EA)

BEMBA ...... Boletin de Estudios Medicos y Biologicos [*A publication*]

BE-ME ...... Bachelor of Engineering in Mechanical Engineering

BEME .... Brigade Electrical and Mechanical Engineer [*Military*] [*British*]

BEMF .... Back Electromotive Force (DEN)

BEMI .... Biciklista Esperantista Movado Internacia [*International Movement of Esperantist Bicyclists - IMEB*] (EAIO)

BEMI .... Bio-Electro-Magnetics Institute (EA)

BEMID ..... Bulletin. Electron Microscope Society of India [*A publication*]

BeMMR ..... Besseler. Musik des Mittelalters und der Renaissance [*A publication*]

BEMO .... Base Equipment Management Office [*Air Force*] (AFM)

BEMP .... Bubble Electromagnetic Pulse

BEMS .... Bioelectromagnetics Society (EA)

BEMS .... British Energy Management Systems

BEM SIG .... Bioelectromagnetics Special Interest Group (EA)

BEMT .... Bureau of Health Professions Education and Manpower Training [*HEW*]

BEMTA ..... Berliner und Muenchener Tieraerztliche Wochenschrift [*A publication*]

BEn .... Bachelor of Engineering

B En .... Bachelor of English

BEN .... Bene [*Well*] [*Pharmacy*]

Ben .... Benedictina [*A publication*]

BEN .... Benedictio [*Blessing*] [*Latin*] (ADA)

Ben .... Benedict's United States District Court Reports [*A publication*] (DLA)

BEN .... Benelux [*A publication*]

Ben .... Bengal Law Reports [*India*] [*A publication*] (DLA)

ben .... Bengali [*MARC language code*] [*Library of Congress*] (LCCP)

BEN .... Benghazi [*Libya*] [*Airport symbol*] (OAG)

BEN .... Benin [*ANSI three-letter standard code*] (CNC)

Ben .... Benloe's English King's Bench and Common Pleas Reports [*A publication*] (DLA)

BEN .... Bennett College, Greensboro, NC [*OCLC symbol*] (OCLC)

BEN .... Bennington Aviation [*Bennington, VT*] [*FAA designator*] (FAAC)

BEN .... Bermuda - Navy [*Bermuda*] [*Seismograph station code, US Geological Survey*] [*Closed*] (SEIS)

BEn .... Black Enterprise [*A publication*]

BEN .... Bull's-Eye News [*A publication*]

Ben .... De Beneficiis [*of Seneca the Younger*] [*Classical studies*] (OCD)

BEN .... Franklin Resources, Inc. [*NYSE symbol*] (SPSG)

BENA ...... Belgian Engineers in North America [*Defunct*] (EA)

BENA ...... British Empire Naturalist Association

Ben Adm .... Benedict's American Admiralty Practice [*A publication*] (DLA)

Ben Adm Prac ... Benedict's American Admiralty Practice [*A publication*] (DLA)

Ben Av .... Stephen and Benecke on Average [*A publication*] (DLA)

Bench & B ... Bench and Bar [*A publication*]

Bench and B Minn ... Bench and Bar of Minnesota [*A publication*]

Benchmark Pap Biochem ... Benchmark Papers in Biochemistry [*A publication*]

Benchmark Pap Ecol ... Benchmark Papers in Ecology [*A publication*]

Benchmark Pap Energy ... Benchmark Papers on Energy [*A publication*]

Benchmark Papers Electrical Engrg Comput Sci ... Benchmark Papers in Electrical Engineering and Computer Science [*A publication*]

Benchmark Pap Genet ... Benchmark Papers in Genetics [*A publication*]

Benchmark Pap Geol ... Benchmark Papers in Geology [*A publication*]

Benchmark Pap Hum Physiol ... Benchmark Papers in Human Physiology [*A publication*]

Benchmark Pap Microbiol ... Benchmark Papers in Microbiology [*A publication*]

Benchmark Pap Opt ... Benchmark Papers in Optics [*A publication*]

Benchmark Pap Syst Evol Biol ... Benchmark Papers in Systematic and Evolutionary Biology [*A publication*]

BENCOM ... Beneficial Communications [*Computer system*] [*Beneficial Management Corp.*]

BEN CS ..... Bengal Civil Service [*British*] (ROG)

Ben & D ..... Benloe and Dalison's English Common Pleas Reports [*A publication*] (DLA)

B-END .... Beta-Endorphin [*Biochemistry*]

Ben & Dal .. Benloe and Dalison's English Common Pleas Reports [*A publication*] (DLA)

BENDEX ..... Beneficiary Data Exchange System [*between state welfare agencies and the Social Security Administration*]

Bendix Tech J ... Bendix Technical Journal [*A publication*]

Bendl .... Bendloe's [*or Benloe's*] English Common Pleas [*1531-1628*] [*A publication*] (DLA)

Bendloe ...... Bendloe's [*or Benloe's*] Reports, English Common Pleas [*Edition of 1661*] [*A publication*] (DLA)

BENDS ...... Both Ends

BENE .... Benedict Nuclear Pharmaceuticals, Inc. [*NASDAQ symbol*] (NQ)

Bene .... Benedict's United States District Court Reports [*A publication*] (DLA)

Bene .... Benedictus de Isernia [*Flourished, 1221-52*] [*Authority cited in pre-1607 legal work*] (DSA)

BENE .... Beneficiary

BENECHAN ... BENELUX [*Belgium, Netherlands, Luxembourg*] Subarea Channel [*NATO*] (NATG)

BENED ...... Benedictine

Bened .... Benedict's United States District Court Reports [*A publication*] (DLA)

Benedict ...... Benedict's United States District Court Reports [*A publication*] (DLA)

BENEDJ ... Behavioral Neuroscience [*A publication*]

BENEF .... Beneficiary (AFM)

Benefit Series UCIS ... United States Social Security Board Unemployment Compensation Interpretation Service. Benefit Series [*A publication*] (DLA)

BENEFL ...... Beneficial (ROG)

BENEFY ... Beneficiary (ROG)

BENELUX ... Belgium, Netherlands, Luxembourg [*Economic union*]

Benelux (The Hague) ... Union Economique Benelux (The Hague) [*A publication*]

Benet Ct-M ... Benet on Military Law and Courts-Martial [*A publication*] (DLA)

BENEV .... Benevolent (ROG)

BENF .... Benafuels, Inc. [*NASDAQ symbol*] (NQ)

Ben FB .... Full Bench Rulings, High Court [*Fort William, Bengal*] [*A publication*] (DLA)

Ben FI Cas ... Bennett's Fire Insurance Cases [*A publication*] (DLA)

B Eng .... Bachelor of Engineering

BENG .... Bengal

Beng .... Bengal Law Reports [*India*] [*A publication*] (DLA)

BENG .... Bengali [*Language, etc.*] (ROG)

BENG .... Best Energy Systems, Inc. [*NASDAQ symbol*] (NQ)

B Eng A .... Bachelor of Agricultural Engineering

Bengal Agric J ... Bengal Agricultural Journal [*A publication*]

Bengal P P ... Bengal Past and Present [*A publication*]

Bengal Public Health J ... Bengal Public Health Journal [*A publication*]

Bengal Vet ... Bengal Veterinarian [*A publication*]

BEng/BBus ... Bachelor of Engineering/Bachelor of Business

BEng-Civil ... Bachelor of Engineering - Civil
BEngE .... Bachelor of Electrical Engineering
BEng-Elec ... Bachelor of Engineering - Electrical
BEng-Elect ... Bachelor of Engineering - Electrical
Beng LR ..... Bengal Law Reports [*India*] [*A publication*]   (DLA)
Beng LR App Cas ... Bengal Law Reports, Appeal Cases [*India*] [*A publication*]   (DLA)
Beng LRPC ... Bengal Law Reports, Privy Council [*India*] [*A publication*]   (DLA)
Beng LR Supp ... Bengal Law Reports, Supplement [*India*] [*A publication*]   (DLA)
BEng and Man ... Bachelor of Mechanical Engineering, Manufacture, and Management [*British*]   (DBQ)
BEng-Mech ... Bachelor of Engineering - Mechanical
BEngSc ...... Bachelor of Engineering Science   (ADA)
Beng SDA .. Bengal Sadr Diwani Adalat Cases [*India*] [*A publication*]   (DLA)
B Eng (Tech) ... Bachelor of Engineering (Technology)
Beng Zillah ... Decisions of the Zillah Courts, Lower Provinces [*India*] [*A publication*]   (DLA)
BENH .... BankEast Corp. [*NASDAQ symbol*]   (NQ)
Ben & HLC ... Bennett and Heard's Leading Criminal Cases [*England*] [*A publication*]   (DLA)
BENHS ..... British Entomological and Natural History Society
Benin R .... Benin Review [*A publication*]
Ben Ins .... Benecke on Marine Insurance [*A publication*]   (DLA)
Ben Ins Cas ... Bennett's Insurance Cases [*A publication*]   (DLA)
BENJ .... [*The*] Benjamin Franklin Savings & Loan Association [*Portland, OR*] [*NASDAQ symbol*]   (NQ)
Benj .... Benjamin on Sales of Personal Property [*1868-1955*] [*A publication*]   (DLA)
Benj .... Benjamin's New York Annotated Cases [*A publication*]   (DLA)
Benj Chalm Bills & N ... Benjamin's Chalmer's Bills and Notes [*A publication*]   (DLA)
Benj Sa .... Benjamin on Sales of Personal Property [*1868-1955*] [*A publication*]   (DLA)
Benj Sales .. Benjamin on Sales of Personal Property [*1868-1955*] [*A publication*]   (DLA)
Ben Just ..... Benedict's New York Civil and Criminal Justice [*A publication*]   (DLA)
Ben in Keil ... Benloe's English King's Bench Reports [*73 English Reprint*] [*1531-1628*] [*A publication*]   (DLA)
Benl .... Benloe and Dalison's English Common Pleas Reports [*A publication*]   (DLA)
Benl .... Benloe's English King's Bench Reports [*73 English Reprint*] [*1531-1628*] [*A publication*]   (DLA)
Benl in Ashe ... Benloe at the End of Ashe's Tables [*A publication*]   (DLA)
Benl & D .... Benloe and Dalison's English Common Pleas Reports [*A publication*]   (DLA)
Benl & Dal ... Benloe and Dalison's English Common Pleas Reports [*A publication*]   (DLA)
Benl & D (Eng) ... Benloe and Dalison's English Common Pleas Reports [*A publication*]   (DLA)
Benl (Eng) ... Benloe's English King's Bench Reports [*73 English Reprint*] [*1531-1628*] [*A publication*]   (DLA)
Benl KB ...... Benloe's English King's Bench Reports [*73 English Reprint*] [*1531-1628*] [*A publication*]   (DLA)
Benl in Keil ... Benloe in Keilway's Reports [*A publication*]   (DLA)
Benl New .... Benloe's English King's Bench and Common Pleas Reports [*A publication*]   (DLA)
Benloe .... Benloe's English King's Bench Reports [*73 English Reprint*] [*1531-1628*] [*A publication*]   (DLA)
Benl Old ..... Benloe and Dalison's English Common Pleas Reports [*A publication*]   (DLA)
BenM .... Benediktinische Monatsschrift [*A publication*]   (BJA)
Ben Monroe ... Ben Monroe's Kentucky Reports [*A publication*]   (DLA)
Benn .... Bennett's Reports [*16-21 Missouri*] [*A publication*]   (DLA)
Benn .... Bennett's Reports [*1 California*] [*A publication*]   (DLA)
Benn .... Bennett's Reports [*1 Dakota*] [*A publication*]   (DLA)
Benn Cal .... Bennett's Reports [*1 California*] [*A publication*]   (DLA)
Benn (Dak) ... Bennett's Dakota Cases [*A publication*]   (DLA)
Benne .... Reporter of Vol. 7, Modern Reports [*England*] [*A publication*]   (DLA)
Bennett ...... Bennett's Reports [*1 California*] [*A publication*]   (DLA)
Bennett ...... Bennett's Reports [*1 Dakota*] [*A publication*]   (DLA)
Bennett ...... Bennett's Reports [*16-21 Missouri*] [*A publication*]   (DLA)
Benn Farm ... Bennett's Rights and Liabilities of Farmers [*A publication*]   (DLA)
Benn FI Cas ... Bennett's Fire Insurance Cases [*A publication*]   (DLA)
Benn & H Cr Cas ... Bennett and Heard's Leading Criminal Cases [*England*] [*A publication*]   (DLA)
Benn & H Dig ... Bennett and Heard's Massachusetts Digest [*A publication*]   (DLA)
Benn & H Lead Crim Cas ... Bennett and Heard's Leading Criminal Cases [*England*] [*A publication*]   (DLA)
BEN NI ...... Bengal Native Infantry [*Military*] [*British*]   (ROG)
Benn (MO) ... Bennett's Missouri Cases [*A publication*]   (DLA)
Benn Pr MC ... Bennett's Dissertation on Practice of Masters in Chancery [*A publication*]   (DLA)
Benn Rec ..... Bennett on Receivers [*A publication*]   (DLA)
BENNY SUGG ... Beneficial Suggestions [*Program*]

Ben Ord ..... Benevolent Orders   (DLA)
BENPD ...... Building Energy Progress [*A publication*]
BENREP ... Big Ben Report [*World War II*]
Ben Rev Bd Serv MB ... Benefits Review Board Service. Matthew Bender [*A publication*]
BENS .... Bounded Error Navigation System   (MCD)
BENS .... Business Executives for National Security   (EA)
BEN SC ...... Bengal Staff Corps [*Military*] [*British*]   (ROG)
BENSD ...... Biomass Energy Institute. Newsletter [*A publication*]
Ben & S Dig ... Benjamin and Slidell's Louisiana Digest [*A publication*]   (DLA)
BENS/ED ... Business Executives for National Security Education Fund   (EA)
B Ent .... Bachelor of Entomology
BENT .... Beginning Evening Nautical Twilight
Bent .... Bentley's Irish Chancery Reports [*A publication*]   (DLA)
B Ent .... Black Enterprise [*A publication*]
BENT .... Breast Exposure National Trends [*Study*] [*FDA*]
Bent Abr ..... Benton's Abridgement of the Debates of Congress [*A publication*]   (DLA)
Bent Cod .... Bentham's Codification [*A publication*]   (DLA)
Bent Const Code ... Bentham's Constitutional Code for All Nations [*A publication*]   (DLA)
Bent Ev ...... Bentham's Judicial Evidence [*A publication*]   (DLA)
Benth Ev .... Bentham on Rationale of Judicial Evidence [*A publication*]   (DLA)
Benth Jud Ev ... Bentham on Rationale of Judicial Evidence [*A publication*]   (DLA)
Benth Jud Ev ... Bentham's Judicial Evidence [*A publication*]   (DLA)
Bent Jud Ev ... Bentham's Judicial Evidence [*A publication*]   (DLA)
Bentl Atty-Gen ... Bentley's Reports [*13-19 Attorneys-General's Opinions*] [*A publication*]   (DLA)
Bentley .... Bentley's Miscellany [*A publication*]
Bent Mor Leg ... Bentham's Principles of Morals and Legislation [*A publication*]   (DLA)
Bent Mor & Leg ... Bentham's Principles of Morals and Legislation [*A publication*]   (DLA)
Bent Pack Jur ... Bentham's Act of Packing as Applied to Special Juries [*1821*] [*A publication*]   (DLA)
B & ENT & PL ... Breaking and Entering in Nighttime and Petty Larceny
Bent Pun ..... Bentham's Rationale of Punishment [*A publication*]   (DLA)
Bent Q .... Bentley's Quarterly Review [*A publication*]
B Ent Res ... Bulletin of Entomological Research [*A publication*]
Bent The Leg ... Bentham's Theory of Legislation [*A publication*]   (DLA)
BENV .... Built Environment [*A publication*]
B Envir Con ... Bulletin of Environmental Contamination and Toxicology [*A publication*]
BEnvSc ...... Bachelor of Environmental Science
BEnvSci ..... Bachelor of Environmental Science
BENZ .... Benzidine [*Carcinogen*]
Benzene Its Ind Deriv ... Benzene and Its Industrial Derivatives [*A publication*]
Benzene Work Environ ... Benzene in the Work Environment [*A publication*]
Benzole Dig ... Benzole Digest [*A publication*]
Benzole Prod Ltd Inf Circ ... Benzole Producers Limited. Information Circular [*A publication*]
Benzole Prod Ltd Res Pap ... Benzole Producers Limited. Research Paper [*A publication*]
BEO .... Banquet Event Order [*Food service industry*]
BEO .... Basque Educational Organization   (EA)
BEO .... Belmont [*Australia*] [*Airport symbol*]
BEO .... Belmont Resources [*Vancouver Stock Exchange symbol*]
BEO .... Beograd [*Belgrade*] [*Yugoslavia*] [*Seismograph station code, US Geological Survey*]   (SEIS)
BEO .... Black Elected Official
BEO .... Broadcast Engineering Officer   (ADA)
BEO .... Bulletin d'Etudes Orientales [*A publication*]
BEO .... Newcastle Belmont Airport [*Australia*] [*Airport symbol*]   (OAG)
BEOA .... British and European Osteopathic Association [*Sutton, Surrey, England*]   (EAIO)
BEOC .... Battery Echelon Operating Control   (AFM)
BEOD .... Bulletin d'Etudes Orientales (Damascus) [*A publication*]
BEOG .... Basic Educational Opportunity Grants [*Office of Education*]
BEOL .... Bent's Old Fort National Historic Site
BEOP .... Best Estimate of Orbital Parameters
Beor .... Queensland Law Reports (Beor) [*A publication*]
BEOVF ...... Belmont Resources [*NASDAQ symbol*]   (NQ)
B of EP .... Bachelor of Engineering Physics
BEP .... Bachelor of Engineering Physics
BEP .... Back-End Processor [*Computer*]   (TSSD)
BEP .... Beitraege zur Englischen Philologie [*A publication*]
Bep .... Bepaling [*Provision in statute or contract*] [*Netherlands*]   (ILCA)
BEP .... Beppu [*Japan*] [*Seismograph station code, US Geological Survey*] [*Closed*]   (SEIS)
BEP .... Best Efficiency Point   (KSC)
BEP .... Bet PLC ADS [*NYSE symbol*] [*Toronto Stock Exchange symbol*]   (SPSG)
BEP .... Biological Effects Program [*IDOE project*] [*Terminated, 1978*]   (MSC)

BEP.......... BIT [*Binary Digit*] Error Probability [*Data processing*]   (KSC)
BEP.......... Bleomycin, Etoposide, Platinol [*Cisplatin*] [*Antineoplastic drug regimen*]
BEP.......... Brain Evoked Potential [*Neurophysiology*]
BEP.......... British Equestrian Promotions, Ltd.
BEP.......... Budget Execution Plan [*Army*]
BEP.......... Bulletin des Etudes Parnassiennes [*A publication*]
BEP.......... Bulletin des Etudes Portugaises et de l'Institut Francais au Portugal [*A publication*]
BEP.......... Bureau of Engraving and Printing [*Department of the Treasury*]
BEP.......... Perry, GA [*Location identifier*] [*FAA*]   (FAAL)
BEPA........ Bald Eagle Protection Act [*1940*]
BEPC........ Beijing Electron-Positron Collider [*High-energy physics*] [*China*]
BEpc........ Blood Erythrocytes Particle Counter [*Medicine*]
BEPC........ British Electrical Power Convention   (MCD)
BEPD........ Basic Entry Pay Date
BEPD........ Bureau of Educational Personnel Development [*HEW*]
BEPFA...... Beitraege zur Biologie der Pflanzen [*A publication*]
BEPh....... Beitraege zur Englischen Philologie [*A publication*]
BE Phy...... Bachelor of Engineering Physics
BEPI........ Budget Estimates Presentation Instructions   (AFM)
BEPIF....... Bulletin des Etudes Portugaises et de l'Institut Francais au Portugal [*A publication*]
BePJ......... Beautiful Poems on Jesus [*A publication*]
BEPN........ Defence Research Establishment Pacific, Canada Department of National Defence [*Centre de Recherches pour la Defense Pacifique, Ministere de la Defense Nationale*] Esquimalt, British Columbia [*Library symbol*] [*National Library of Canada*]   (NLC)
BEPO........ British Experimental Pile Operation [*Nuclear reactor*]   (DEN)
BEPOC...... Burroughs Electrographic Printer-Plotter for Ordnance Computing
BEPQ........ Bureau of Entomology and Plant Quarantine [*Department of Agriculture*] [*Functions transferred to ARS, 1953*]
BEPRD...... Bulletin Europeen de Physiopathologie Respiratoire [*A publication*]
BEPS........ Building Energy Performance Standards
BEQ.......... Bachelor Enlisted Quarters
BEQ.......... Bessemer, AL [*Location identifier*] [*FAA*]   (FAAL)
BEQ.......... Binary Encoded Quaternary   (MCD)
BEQB........ Bank of England. Quarterly Bulletin [*A publication*]
BEQD........ Bequeathed [*Legal term*]
BEQIDC.... Bulletin. Equine Research Institute [*A publication*]
BEQT........ Bequest
BEQTH..... Bequeath [*Legal term*]   (ROG)
BEQTHD.. Bequeathed [*Legal term*]
BER.......... Basal Energy Requirement [*Nutrition*]
BER.......... Basic Electrical Rhythm [*Neurophysiology*]
BER.......... Bearings, Inc. [*NYSE symbol*]   (SPSG)
BeR.......... Before the Romantics [*A publication*]
Ber.......... Berakhot [*or Berakot*]   (BJA)
ber.......... Berber [*MARC language code*] [*Library of Congress*]   (LCCP)
BER.......... Bergen [*Norway*] [*Seismograph station code, US Geological Survey*]   (SEIS)
BER.......... Bergen Community College, Paramus, NJ [*OCLC symbol*]   (OCLC)
Ber.......... Berichte. Deutsche Chemische Gesellschaft [*A publication*]
Ber.......... Berichtigung [*Settlement (of an account), Adjustment (of a bill), Correction*] [*German*] [*Business term*]
BeR.......... Berkeley Review [*A publication*]
BER.......... Berlin [*West Germany*] [*Airport symbol*]   (OAG)
BER.......... Bern Resources Ltd. [*Vancouver Stock Exchange symbol*]
Ber.......... Bernardus de Bottone de Parma [*Deceased, 1266*] [*Authority cited in pre-1607 legal work*]   (DSA)
Ber.......... Bernardus Compostellanus, Senior [*Flourished, 1198-1216*] [*Authority cited in pre-1607 legal work*]   (DSA)
Ber.......... Berton's New Brunswick Reports [*A publication*]   (DLA)
BER.......... Beyond Economical Repair   (MCD)
BER.......... Biological Energy Research [*Department of Energy*]
BER.......... Biological and Environmental Research Program [*Department of Energy*]
BER.......... BIT [*Binary Digit*] Effectiveness Report   (CAAL)
BER.......... BIT [*Binary Digit*] Error Rate [*Data processing*]
BER.......... Blue Emerald Resources [*Vancouver Stock Exchange symbol*]
BER.......... Bremerton, WA [*Location identifier*] [*FAA*]   (FAAL)
BER.......... Budget Execution Review [*Army*]   (AABC)
BER.......... Bulletin of Economic Research [*A publication*]
BER.......... Bureau of Economic Regulation [*of CAB*]
BER.......... Bureau of Equipment and Recruiting [*Navy*] [*Abolished, 1914*]
BER.......... Business and Economic Review [*A publication*]
BERA........ Biomass Energy Research Association   (EA)
BERA........ British Educational Research Association
BERA........ Business Education Research of America [*Hato Rey, PR*]   (EA)
Ber Abwassertech Ver ... Berichte. Abwassertechnische Vereinigung [*A publication*]
BerADev .... Berlin Airlift Device [*Military decoration*]   (AABC)
Ber Afd Trop Prod K Inst Trop ... Berichten. Afdeling Tropische Producten van het Koninklijke Institut por de Tropen [*A publication*]
Ber Akad Wiss Wien ... Sitzungsberichte. Akademie der Wissenschaften in Wien [*A publication*]

Ber Alg Proefst AVROS ... Bericht. Algemeen Proefstation der AVROS [*A publication*]
Berar .... Berar Law Journal [*India*] [*A publication*]   (DLA)
Ber Arbeitsgem Ferromagn ... Berichte. Arbeitsgemeinschaft Ferromagnetismus [*A publication*]
Ber Arbeitsgem Saechs Bot ... Berichte. Arbeitsgemeinschaft Saechsischer Botaniker [*A publication*]
Ber Arbeitstag Arbeitsgem Saatzuchtleiter ... Bericht. Arbeitstagung der Arbeitsgemeinschaft der Saatzuchtleiter [*A publication*]
Beratende Ing ... Beratende Ingenieure [*West Germany*] [*A publication*]
Ber Bayer Bot Ges Erforsch Heim Flora ... Berichte. Bayerische Botanische Gesellschaft zur Erforschung der Heimischen Flora [*A publication*]
Ber Biochem Biol ... Berichte Biochemie und Biologie [*A publication*]
BERBOH .. British Examining and Registration Board in Occupational Hygiene
Ber Bun Ges ... Berichte. Bunsengesellschaft fuer Physikalische Chemie [*A publication*]
Ber Bunsen Ges ... Berichte. Bunsengesellschaft fuer Physikalische Chemie [*A publication*]
Ber Bunsenges Phys Chem ... Berichte. Bunsengesellschaft fuer Physikalische Chemie [*A publication*]
BERC........ Bartlesville Energy Research Center [*Department of Energy*]
Berc.......... Berceo [*A publication*]
BERC........ Biomedical Engineering Research Corporation [*Illinois*]
BERC........ Black Economic Research Center   (EA)
BERC........ Black Educational Resources Center [*Later, BMCERC*]   (EA)
BERC........ Business and Economic Research Center [*Middle Tennessee State University*] [*Research center*]   (RCD)
BERCOMB ... Berlin Commission British [*Post-World War II*]
Ber Compos ... Bernardus Compostellanus [*Authority cited in pre-1607 legal work*]   (DSA)
BERCON... Berlin Contingency [*NATO*]   (NATG)
BERD .... Bureau of Economic Research and Development [*Virginia State University*] [*Research center*]   (RCD)
BERD .... East European Development Bank [*Acronym is based on foreign phrase*]
BERD .... Office of Buildings Energy Research and Development [*Department of Energy*]
Ber Deu Bot ... Berichte. Deutsche Botanische Gesellschaft [*A publication*]
Ber Deut Ausschusses Stahlbau ... Berichte. Deutscher Ausschuss fuer Stahlbau [*A publication*]
Ber Deut Bot Ges ... Berichte. Deutsche Botanische Gesellschaft [*A publication*]
Ber Deut Chem Ges ... Berichte. Deutsche Chemische Gesellschaft [*A publication*]
Ber Deut Keram Gesell ... Berichte. Deutsche Keramische Gesellschaft [*A publication*]
Ber Deut Pharm Ges ... Bericht der Deutschen Pharmazeutischen Gesellschaft [*A publication*]
Ber Deut Wetterdienst ... Berichte. Deutscher Wetterdienst [*A publication*]
BERDEV... Berlin Airlift Device [*Military decoration*]
Ber Dt Bot Ges ... Berichte. Deutsche Botanische Gesellschaft [*A publication*]
Ber Dt Chem Ges ... Berichte. Deutsche Chemische Gesellschaft [*A publication*]
Ber Dtsch Bot Ges ... Berichte. Deutsche Botanische Gesellschaft [*A publication*]
Ber Dtsch Chem Ges ... Berichte. Deutsche Chemische Gesellschaft [*West Germany*] [*A publication*]
Ber Dtsch Chem Ges A ... Berichte. Deutsche Chemische Gesellschaft. Abteilung A. Vereins Nachriften [*A publication*]
Ber Dtsch Chem Ges B ... Berichte. Deutsche Chemische Gesellschaft. Abteilung B. Abhandlungen [*A publication*]
Ber Dtsch Ges Geol Wiss Reihe A ... Berichte. Deutsche Gesellschaft fuer Geologische Wissenschaften. Reihe A. Geologie und Palaeontologie [*A publication*]
Ber Dtsch Ges Geol Wiss Reihe B ... Berichte. Deutsche Gesellschaft fuer Geologische Wissenschaften. Reihe B. Mineralogie und Lagerstaettenforschung [*A publication*]
Ber Dtsch Ges Holzforsch ... Bericht. Deutsche Gesellschaft fuer Holzforschung [*A publication*]
Ber Dtsch Keram Ges ... Berichte. Deutsche Keramische Gesellschaft [*A publication*]
Ber Dtsch Landeskd ... Bericht zur Deutschen Landeskunde [*A publication*]
Ber Dtsch Ophthalmol Ges ... Bericht. Deutsche Ophthalmologische Gesellschaft [*West Germany*] [*A publication*]
Ber Dtsch Pharm Ges ... Berichte. Deutsche Pharmazeutische Gesellschaft [*A publication*]
Ber Dtsch Phys Ges ... Berichte. Deutsche Physikalische Gesellschaft [*A publication*]
Ber Dtsch Wetterdienstes ... Berichte. Deutscher Wetterdienst [*A publication*]
Ber Dtsch Wiss Komm Meeresforsch ... Berichte. Deutscher Wissenschaftliche Kommission fuer Meeresforschung [*A publication*]
Ber Durum Teigwaren Tag Vortr ... Bericht ueber die Durum-Teigwaren-Tagung. Vortraege [*A publication*]
Ber D W Meer ... Berichte. Deutsche Wissenschaftliche Kommission fuer Meeresforschung [*A publication*]
Berdyanskii Opytn Neftemaslozavod Tr ... Berdyanskii Opytnyi Neftemaslozavod. Trudy [*A publication*]
BERE........ Bureau of Educational Research and Evaluation [*Mississippi State University*] [*Research center*]   (RCD)

BEREA...... Bulletin of Entomological Research [*A publication*]
Ber Eidg Anst Forstl Versuchswes ... Berichte. Eidgenoessische Anstalt fuer das Forstliche Versuchswesen [*A publication*]
Ber Ernst-Mach-Inst ... Bericht. Ernst-Mach-Institut [*Freiburg*] [*A publication*]
Beret Faellesudvalget Statens Mejeri Husdyrbrugsfors (Den) ... Beretning-Faellesudvalget for Statens Mejeri- og Husdyrbrugsforsoeg (Denmark) [*A publication*]
Beret Faellesudvalget Statens Planteavls- Husdyrbrugsfors ... Beretning fra Faellesudvalget foer Statens Planteavls- og Husdyrbrugsforsog [*A publication*]
Beret Forsoegslab Statens Husdyrbrugsudvalg ... Beretning fra Forsoegslaboratoriet Udgivet af Statens Husdyrbrugsudvalg [*A publication*]
Beret Forsogslab ... Beretning fra Forsogslaboratoriet [*A publication*]
Beretn Statsfrokontr (Denmark) ... Beretning fra Statsfrokontrollen (Denmark) [*A publication*]
Beret Statens Forogsmejeri ... Beretning fra Statens Forogsmejeri [*A publication*]
Beret Statens Husdyrbrugsfors ... Beretning fra Statens Husdyrbrugsforsog [*A publication*]
BERF........ Business Education Research Foundation (EA)
Ber Fachausschuesse Dtsch Glastech Ges ... Berichte der Fachausschuesse. Deutsche Glastechnische Gesellschaft [*A publication*]
Ber Forschungsinst Cech Zuckerind Prag ... Bericht. Forschungsinstitut der Cechoslavakischen Zuckerindustrie in Prag [*A publication*]
Ber Forschungsinst Zuckerind Boehm Machren Prag ... Bericht. Forschungsinstitut der Zuckerindustrie fuer Boehmen und Machren in Prag [*A publication*]
Ber Forschungsstelle Nedri As Hveragerdi Isl ... Berichte aus der Forschungsstelle Nedri As Hveragerdi Island [*A publication*]
Berg........... Bergonum [*A publication*]
BERGA...... Bergakademie [*A publication*]
Bergbau-Arch ... Bergbau-Archiv [*West Germany*] [*A publication*]
Bergbau Energiewirtsch ... Bergbau und Energiewirtschaft [*West Germany*] [*A publication*]
Bergbau Rohst Energ ... Bergbau Rohstoffe Energie [*A publication*]
Bergbau Rundsch ... Bergbau Rundschau [*A publication*]
Bergbau Wirtsch ... Bergbau und Wirtschaft [*A publication*]
Bergbauwiss ... Bergbauwissenschaften [*A publication*]
Bergbauwissen Verfahrenstech Bergbau Huettenwes ... Bergbauwissenschaften und Verfahrenstechnik im Bergbau und Huettenwesen [*A publication*]
Bergbauwiss Verfahrenstech Bergbau Huettenwes ... Bergbauwissenschaften und Verfahrenstechnik im Bergbau und Huettenwesen [*A publication*]
BERGD...... Bergbau [*A publication*]
Bergens Mus Arbok Naturvitensk Rekke ... Bergens Museums. Aarbok. Naturvitenskapelig Rekke [*A publication*]
Bergens Mus Skr ... Bergens Museums. Skrifter [*A publication*]
Ber Geobot Forschungsinst Ruebel Zuerich ... Bericht. Geobotanische Forschungsinstitut Ruebel in Zuerich [*A publication*]
Ber Geobot Inst Eidg Tech Hochsch Stift Ruebel Zuer ... Berichte. Geobotanische Institut der Eidgenoessischen Technischen Hochschule Stiftung Ruebel Zuerich [*A publication*]
Ber Geol Ges DDR Gesamtgeb Geol Wiss ... Berichte. Geologische Gesellschaft in der Deutschen Demokratischen Republik fuer das Gesamtgebiet der Geologischen Wissenschaft [*A publication*]
Ber Geol Ges Dtsch Demokrat Repub Gesamtgeb Geol Wiss ... Berichte. Geologische Gesellschaft in der Deutschen Demokratischen Republik fuer das Gesamtgebiet der Geologischen Wissenschaft [*East Germany*] [*A publication*]
Ber Gesamte Physiol Exp Pharmakol ... Berichte ueber die gesamte Physiologie und Experimentelle Pharmakologie [*A publication*]
Ber Gesellsch Math Datenverarb ... Berichte der Gesellschaft fuer Mathematik und Datenverarbeitung [*A publication*]
Ber Ges Inn Med DDR ... Bericht. Gesellschaft fuer Innere Medizin der Deutschen Demokratischen Republik [*A publication*]
Ber Ges Kohlentech ... Berichte. Gesellschaft fuer Kohlentechnik [*East Germany*] [*A publication*]
Ber Getreidechem-Tag (Detmold) ... Bericht ueber die Getreidechemiker-Tagung (Detmold) [*West Germany*] [*A publication*]
Ber Getreidetag (Detmold) ... Bericht ueber die Getreidetagung (Detmold) [*A publication*]
Berg Huettenmaenn Jahrb Montan Hochsch Leoben ... Berg- und Huettenmaennisches Jahrbuch. Montanistische Hochschule in Leoben [*A publication*]
Berg Huettenmaenn Monatsh ... Berg- und Huettenmaennische Monatshefte [*A publication*]
Berg Huettenmaenn Monatsh Montan Hochsch Leoben ... Berg- und Huettenmaennische Monatshefte. Montanistische Hochschule in Leoben [*Austria*] [*A publication*]
Berg Huettenmaenn Monatsh Suppl ... Berg- und Huettenmaennische Monatshefte. Supplementum [*A publication*]
Berg u Huettenm Ztg ... Berg- und Huettenmaennische Zeitung [*A publication*]
Berg Huttenmann Monatsh ... Berg- und Huettenmaennische Monatshefte [*Austria*] [*A publication*]

Bergmann Schaefer Lehrb Experimentalphys ... Bergmann Schaefer Lehrbuch der Experimentalphysik [*A publication*]
Berg Tech... Berg Technik [*A publication*]
BERH .... Board of Engineers for Rivers and Harbors [*Army*]
BERH-RSP ... Board of Engineers for Rivers and Harbors Resident Scholar Program [*Fort Belvoir, VA*] [*Army*]
BERI .... Bernadia [*Italy*] [*Seismograph station code, US Geological Survey*] (SEIS)
BERI .... Business Environment Risk Information [*Information service or system*] (IID)
Berichte...... Berichte. Deutsche Chemische Gesellschaft [*A publication*]
Berichte...... Muenzen- und Medaillensammler Berichte aus allen Gebieten der Geld-, Muenzen-, und Medaillenkunde [*A publication*]
Berichte Dtsch Wiss Komm Meeresforsch ... Berichte. Deutsche Wissenschaftliche Kommission fuer Meeresforschung [*A publication*]
Ber Inf Europ Gem ... Berichte und Informationen. Europaeische Gemeinschaften [*A publication*]
Ber Inf KEG ... Berichte und Informationen. Kommission der Europaeischen Gemeinschaften [*A publication*]
Bering Sea Oceanogr ... Bering Sea Oceanography [*A publication*]
Ber Inst Festkoerpermech Fraunhofer-Ges ... Bericht. Institut fuer Festkoerpermechanik der Fraunhofer-Gesellschaft [*A publication*]
Ber Inst Hochenergiephys (Wien) ... Bericht. Institut fuer Hochenergiephysik. Oesterreichische Akademie der Wissenschaften (Wien) [*A publication*]
Ber Inst Tabakforsch (Dresden) ... Berichte. Institut fuer Tabakforschung (Dresden) [*East Germany*] [*A publication*]
Ber Inst Tabakforsch Wohlsdorf-Biendorf ... Berichte. Institut fuer Tabakforschung. Wohlsdorf-Biendorf [*A publication*]
Ber Inst Tex Faserforsch (Stuttgart) ... Berichte. Institut fuer Textil und Faserforschung (Stuttgart) [*A publication*]
Ber Intern Kongr Phot ... Berichte. Internationale Kongress fuer Photographie [*A publication*]
Ber Int Ges Getreidechem ... Berichte. Internationale Gesellschaft fuer Getreidechemie [*A publication*]
Ber Int Kongr Grenzflaechenaktive Stoffe ... Berichte vom Internationalen Kongress fuer Grenzflaechenaktive Stoffe [*A publication*]
Ber Int Semin Kernstrukturphys Autom ... Bericht ueber das Internationale Seminar Kernstrukturphysik und Automatisierung [*A publication*]
Berita Biol ... Berita Biologi [*A publication*]
Ber Jahrestag Dtsch Ges Arbeitsmed ... Bericht ueber die Jahrestagung der Deutschen Gesellschaft fuer Arbeitsmedizin [*A publication*]
BERJAYA ... Bersatu Rakyat Jelata Sabah [*Sabah People's Union*] [*Malaysia*] [*Political party*] (PPW)
Ber J Soc.... Berkeley Journal of Sociology [*A publication*]
Berk .... Berkeley [*A publication*]
BERK........ Berkeley [*England*]
BERK........ [*The*] Berkline Corp. [*NASDAQ symbol*] (NQ)
Berkala Ilmu Kedokt ... Berkala Ilmu Kedokteran [*Journal of the Medical Sciences*] [*Indonesia*] [*A publication*]
Berkala Ilmu Kedokt Gadjah Mada ... Berkala Ilmu Kedokteran [*Journal of the Medical Sciences*] [*A publication*]
Berk Bud St ... Berkeley Buddhist Studies Series [*A publication*]
Berk Co LJ ... Berks County Law Journal [*A publication*]
Berkeley J Sociol ... Berkeley Journal of Sociology [*A publication*]
Ber Kernforschungsanlage Juelich ... Berichte. Kernforschungsanlage Juelich [*A publication*]
Ber Kernforschungszentr Karlsruhe ... Bericht. Kernforschungszentrum Karlsruhe [*A publication*]
Ber Kfa Juelich ... Berichte. Kernforschungsanlage Juelichgesellschaft mit Beschraenkter Haftung [*A publication*]
Ber Kongr Dt Ges Psychol ... Berichte ueber den 24 Kongress der Deutschen Gesellschaft fuer Psychologie [*A publication*]
Ber Kontaktstud Werkstoffkd Eisen Stahl ... Berichte. Gehalten im Kontaktstudium "Werkstoffkunde Eisen und Stahl" [*A publication*]
Berk Relig ... Berkeley Religious Studies Series [*A publication*]
Berks.......... Berks County Law Journal [*A publication*]
BERKS........ Berkshire [*County in England*]
Berks Co .... Berks County Law Journal [*A publication*]
BerksCoHS ... Berks County Historical Society. Papers [*A publication*]
Berkshire A J ... Berkshire Archaeological Journal [*A publication*]
Berkshire Archaeol J ... Berkshire Archaeological Journal [*A publication*]
Berkshire Arch J ... Berkshire Archaeological Journal [*A publication*]
Berkshire Hist Sc Soc ... Berkshire Historical and Scientific Society [*A publication*]
BERL......... Berlin (ROG)
BERL......... Beryl [*Jewelry*] (ROG)
BERLA........ Bericht ueber Landwirtschaft [*A publication*]
Berl Abh..... Abhandlungen der Preussische Akademie der Wissenschaften zu Berlin [*A publication*] (OCD)
Ber Landwirt Bundes Min Ernaehr Landwirt Forsten ... Berichte ueber Landwirtschaft. Bundes Ministerium fuer Ernaehrung, Landwirtschaft, und Forsten [*A publication*]
Ber Landwirt N F ... Berichte ueber Landwirtschaft. Neue Folge [*A publication*]
Ber Landwirtsch ... Berichte ueber Landwirtschaft [*A publication*]

Ber Landwirtsch Sonderh ... Berichte ueber Landwirtschaft. Sonderheft [*A publication*]
Berl Beitr Archaeom ... Berliner Beitraege zur Archaeometrie [*A publication*]
Berl Ent Z .. Berliner Entomologische Zeitschrift [*A publication*]
Berl Freie Univ FU Pressedienst Wiss ... Berlin Freie Universitaet. FU Pressedienst Wissenschaft [*A publication*]
Berl Geowissenschaftliche Abh Reihe A ... Berliner Geowissenschaftliche Abhandlungen. Reihe A [*A publication*]
Ber Limnol Flusst Freudenthal Munden ... Berichte. Limnologische Flusstation Freudenthal Munden [*A publication*]
Berliner Med Z ... Berliner Medizinische Zeitschrift [*A publication*]
Berliner Num Z ... Berliner Numismatische Zeitschrift [*A publication*]
Berliner Philol Wochenschr ... Berliner Philologische Wochenschrift [*A publication*]
Berliner Statis ... Berliner Statistik [*A publication*]
Berliner Tieraerztl Wochenschr ... Berliner Tieraerztliche Wochenschrift [*A publication*]
Berl Jahrb Pharm ... Berlinisches Jahrbuch fuer die Pharmacie [*A publication*]
Berl Klin Wchnschr ... Berliner Klinische Wochenschrift [*A publication*]
Berl Muench Tieraerztl Wochenschr ... Berliner und Muenchener Tieraerztliche Wochenschrift [*A publication*]
Berl Muench Tieraerztl Wschr ... Berliner und Muenchener Tieraerztliche Wochenschrift [*A publication*]
Berl Mus .... Berliner Museen [*A publication*]
Berl Stat ..... Berliner Statistik [*A publication*]
Berl Tieraerztl Wchnschr ... Berliner Tieraerztliche Wochenschrift [*A publication*]
Berl Wetterkarte Suppl ... Berliner Wetterkarte. Supplement [*West Germany*] [*A publication*]
Berl Winck Prog ... Berlin. Winckelmannsprogramm der Archaeologischen Gesellschaft [*A publication*]
BERM........ Basic Encyclopedic Redundancy Media (IEEE)
BERM........ Bermuda (DLA)
BERM........ Biological and Environmental Reference Materials
BERM........ BIT [*Binary Digit*] Error Rate Monitor
Ber Math-Statist Sekt Forschungszentrum (Graz) ... Berichte. Forschungszentrum. Mathematisch-Statistische Sektion (Graz) [*A publication*]
Ber Max-Planck-Inst Stroemungsforsch ... Bericht. Max-Planck-Institut fuer Stroemungsforschung [*West Germany*] [*A publication*]
Ber May ..... Bernardus Maynardi [*Authority cited in pre-1607 legal work*] (DSA)
Berm Hist Q ... Bermuda. Historical Quarterly [*A publication*]
Ber MPI Kernphys (Heidelberg) ... Bericht. Max-Planck-Institut fuer Kernphysik (Heidelberg) [*A publication*]
Ber MPI Phys Astrophys Inst Extraterr Phys ... Bericht. Max-Planck-Institut fuer Physik und Astrophysik. Institut fuer Extraterrestrische Physik [*A publication*]
Ber MPI Plasmaphys Garching ... Bericht. Max-Planck-Institut fuer Plasmaphysik. Garching bei Muenchen [*A publication*]
Ber MPI Stroemungsforsch ... Bericht. Max-Planck-Institut fuer Stroemungsforschung [*A publication*]
Bermuda Biol Stn Res Spec Publ ... Bermuda. Biological Station for Research. Special Publication [*A publication*]
Bermuda LRC ... Law Reform Committee, Bermuda (DLA)
Bermuda Rep Dir Agric Fish ... Bermuda. Report of the Director of Agriculture and Fisheries [*A publication*]
Bern........... Bernard's Church Cases [*Ireland*] [*A publication*] (DLA)
Bern........... Bernardus de Bottone de Parma [*Deceased, 1266*] [*Authority cited in pre-1607 legal work*] (DSA)
Bernar .... Bernardus de Bottone de Parma [*Deceased, 1266*] [*Authority cited in pre-1607 legal work*] (DSA)
Ber Naturforsch Ges (Augsb) ... Berichte. Naturforschende Gesellschaft (Augsburg) [*A publication*]
Ber Naturforsch Ges (Bamberg) ... Berichte. Naturforschende Gesellschaft (Bamberg) [*A publication*]
Ber Naturforsch Ges (Freiburg) ... Berichte. Naturforschende Gesellschaft (Freiburg) [*A publication*]
Ber Naturforsch Ges (Freiburg Breisgau) ... Berichte. Naturforschende Gesellschaft (Freiburg Im Breisgau) [*A publication*]
Ber Naturhist Ges Hannover ... Bericht. Naturhistorische Gesellschaft zu Hannover [*A publication*]
Ber Naturwiss-Med Ver Innsb ... Berichte. Naturwissenschaftlich-Medizinischer Verein in Innsbruck [*A publication*]
Ber Naturwiss Ver Regensburg ... Berichte des Naturwissenschaftlichen Vereins zu Regensburg [*A publication*]
Ber Naturw Med Ver Innsbruck ... Berichte. Naturwissenschaftlich-Medizinischer Verein in Innsbruck [*A publication*]
Bern Ch Cas ... Bernard's Church Cases [*Ireland*] [*A publication*] (DLA)
BERND ..... Bio-Energy Re-News [*A publication*]
Berner Beitr Gesch Med Naturwiss ... Berner Beitraege zur Geschichte der Medizin und der Naturwissenschaften [*A publication*]
Ber Neth Plantenziektenkundige Dienst ... Berichte. Netherlands. Plantenziektenkundige Dienst [*A publication*]
Bernice Pauahi Bishop Museum Bull ... Bernice Pauahi Bishop Museum. Bulletin [*A publication*]
Bernice Pauahi Bishop Museum Bull Special Pub ... Bernice Pauahi Bishop Museum. Bulletin. Special Publication [*A publication*]
Bernice Pauahi Bishop Mus Oc P ... Bernice Pauahi Bishop Museum. Occasional Papers [*A publication*]

Bernice P Bishop Mus Spec Publ ... Bernice Pauahi Bishop Museum. Special Publication [*A publication*]
Bero............ [*Augustinus*] Berous [*Deceased, 1554*] [*Authority cited in pre-1607 legal work*] (DSA)
BEROA ..... Better Roads [*A publication*]
Ber Oberhess Ges Nat Heikd Giessen Naturwiss Abt ... Bericht. Oberhessische Gesellschaft fuer Natur und Heilkunde zu Giessen. Naturwissenschaftliche Abteilung [*A publication*]
Ber Oesterr Studienges Atomenerg ... Berichte. Oesterreichische Studiengesellschaft fuer Atomenergie [*A publication*]
Ber Offenbacher Vereins Naturkd ... Bericht des Offenbacher Vereins fuer Naturkunde [*A publication*]
Ber Ohara Inst Landw Biol ... Berichte. Ohara Institut fuer Landwirtschaftliche Biologie [*A publication*]
Ber Ohara Inst Landwirtsch Biol Okayama Univ ... Berichte. Ohara Institut fuer Landwirtschaftliche Biologie. Okayama Universitaet [*A publication*]
Ber Ohara Inst Landwirtsch Forsch Kurashiki ... Berichte. Ohara Institut fuer Landwirtschaftliche Forschungen in Kurashiki [*A publication*]
Ber Ohara Inst Landwirtsch Forsch Okayama Univ ... Berichte. Ohara Institut fuer Landwirtschaftliche Forschungen. Okayama Universitaet [*A publication*]
BERP........ British Experimental Rotor Program
Ber Pet Ind ... Berichte ueber die Petroleum Industrie [*A publication*]
Ber Phys Chem Unters Rheinwassers ... Bericht ueber die Physikalisch-Chemische Untersuchung des Rheinwassers [*A publication*]
Ber Physiol Lab Versuchsanst Landwirtsch Inst Univ Halle ... Berichte. Physiologisches Laboratorium und der Versuchsanstalt des Landwirtschaftlichen Instituts der Universitaet Halle [*A publication*]
Ber Phys-Med Ges Wuerzb ... Berichte. Physikalisch-Medizinische Gesellschaft zu Wuerzburg [*A publication*]
BERPM ..... Basic Exchange Rate Planning Model [*Telecommunications*] (TEL)
BerRabb ..... Bereshit Rabba (BJA)
Ber Rassenkeuze ... Bericht ueber Rassenkeuze [*A publication*]
Ber Raumforsch und Raumplanung ... Berichte zur Raumforschung und Raumplanung [*A publication*]
Ber RGK ... Bericht. Roemisch-Germanische Kommission [*A publication*]
Ber Rijksd Oudh Bod ... Berichten. Rijksdienst voor het Oudheidkundige Bodemonderzoek [*A publication*]
Berry .... Berry's Reports [*1-28 Missouri Appeals*] [*A publication*] (DLA)
BERRY F V ... Berry, Fruit, or Vegetable [*Freight*]
BERS........ Beres Industries, Inc. [*NASDAQ symbol*] (NQ)
B & ERS..... Boat and Engine Repair Shop [*Coast Guard*]
BERS........ Bureau of Educational Research and Service [*Memphis State University*] [*Research center*] (RCD)
BERS........ Bureau of Educational Research and Service [*University of Tennessee at Knoxville*] [*Research center*] (RCD)
Ber Saarland ... Bericht. Staatliche Denkmalpflege im Saarland [*A publication*]
Ber Sachs Ges Wiss ... Berichte. Verhandlungen der Saechsischen Gesellschaft der Wissenschaften zu Leipzig [*A publication*] (OCD)
Ber Schweiz Bot Ges ... Berichte. Schweizerische Botanische Gesellschaft [*A publication*]
Ber Schweiz Bot Ges Bull Soc Bot Suisse ... Berichte. Schweizerische Botanische Gesellschaft/Bulletin de la Societe Botanique Suisse [*A publication*]
BERSEAPAT ... Bering Sea Patrol [*Navy*]
Ber Senckenberg Naturforsch Ges ... Bericht der Senckenbergischen Naturforschenden Gesellschaft [*A publication*]
Ber Staat Denkmaf Saarland ... Bericht. Staatliche Denkmalpflege im Saarland. Beitraege zur Archaeologie und Kunstgeschichte [*A publication*]
Ber Studiengruppe Systemforsch (Heidelberg) ... Bericht. Studiengruppe fuer Systemforschung (Heidelberg) [*A publication*]
BERT........ Basic Energy Reduction Technology (IEEE)
Bert .... Berton's New Brunswick Reports [*A publication*] (DLA)
Bert .... Bertrandus [*Authority cited in pre-1607 legal work*] (DSA)
BERT........ BIT [*Binary Digit*] Error-Rate Test [*Data processing*]
Bertach....... [*Johannes*] Bertachinus [*Deceased, 1497*] [*Authority cited in pre-1607 legal work*] (DSA)
Ber Taetigkeit Naturwiss Ges Isis Bautzen ... Bericht ueber die Taetigkeit der Naturwissenschaftlichen Gesellschaft Isis. Bautzen [*A publication*]
Ber Tag Baeckerei-Technol Vortr Tag ... Berichte ueber die Tagung fuer Baeckerei-Technologie. Vortraege, gehalten Anlaesslich der Tagung der Arbeitsgemeinschaft Getreideforschung [*A publication*]
Ber Tag Muellerei Technol ... Bericht ueber die Tagung fuer Muellerei Technologie [*A publication*]
Ber Tag Muellerei-Technol Vortr Tag ... Bericht ueber die Tagung fuer Muellerei-Technologie. Vortraege Gehalten Anlaesslich der Tagung der Arbeitsgemeinschaft Getreideforschung [*A publication*]
Ber Tag Nordwestdtsch Forstver ... Berichte ueber die Tagung im Nordwestdeutscher Forstverein [*A publication*]

Ber Tech Akad Wuppertal ... Berichte. Technische Akademie Wuppertal [*A publication*]
Ber Tech Wiss Abt Verb Keram Gewerke Dtschl ... Berichte. Technisch Wissenschaftliche Abteilung des Verbandes Keramischer Gewerke in Deutschland [*A publication*]
BERTH...... Berthing
Bertr.......... Bertrandus de Montefaventino [*Deceased, 1342*] [*Authority cited in pre-1607 legal work*]   (DSA)
Bertran....... Bertrandus [*Authority cited in pre-1607 legal work*]   (DSA)
BERUA...... Berufs-Dermatosen [*A publication*]
BERUAG... Dermatoses Professionnelles [*A publication*]
Berufs-Derm ... Berufs-Dermatosen [*A publication*]
Ber Ukr Wiss Forsch Inst Phys Chem ... Berichte. Ukrainische Wissenschaftliche Forschungs Institut fuer Physikalische Chemie [*A publication*]
Ber Univ Jyvaeskyla Math Inst ... Bericht. Jyvaeskylae Universitaet. Mathematisches Institut [*A publication*]
Ber Verhandl Saechs Akad Wiss Leipzig Math Naturwiss Kl ... Berichte. Verhandlungen der Saechsischen Akademie der Wissenschaften zu Leipzig. Mathematisch-Naturwissenschaftliche Klasse [*A publication*]
Ber Verhandl Saechs Akad Wiss Leipzig Philol Hist Kl ... Berichte. Verhandlungen der Saechsischen Akademie der Wissenschaften zu Leipzig. Philologisch-Historische Klasse [*A publication*]
Ber Verhandl Saechs Ges Wiss Leipzig Philol Hist ... Berichte. Verhandlungen der Saechsischen Gesellschaft der Wissenschaften zu Leipzig. Philologisch-Historische Klasse [*A publication*]
Ber Verh Saechs Akad Wiss Leipzig Math-Naturwiss Kl ... Berichte. Verhandlungen der Saechsischen Akademie der Wissenschaften zu Leipzig. Mathematisch-Naturwissenschaftliche Klasse [*East Germany*] [*A publication*]
Ber Verh Saechs Akad Wiss Leipzig Math Phys Kl ... Berichte. Verhandlungen der Saechsischen Akademie der Wissenschaften zu Leipzig. Mathematisch-Physische Klasse [*A publication*]
Berwicks .... Berwickshire [*County in England*]
Ber Wiss Biol ... Berichte ueber die Wissenschaftliche Biologie [*A publication*]
Ber Wissenschaftsgesch ... Berichte zur Wissenschaftsgeschichte [*A publication*]
Berytus....... Berytus Archaeological Studies [*A publication*]
Ber Zusammenkunft Dtsch Ophthalmol Ges ... Bericht ueber die Zusammenkunft der Deutschen Ophthalmologischen Gesellschaft [*A publication*]
BES............ Bachelor of Engineering Sciences
BES............ Bachelor of Environmental Studies
BES............ Bachelor of Science in Engineering
BES............ Balanced Electrolyte Solution [*Physiology*]
BES............ Basic Energy Sciences Program [*Department of Energy*] [*Washington, DC*]
BES............ Basic Executive System [*Honeywell, Inc.*]
BES............ Behavior Evaluation Scale [*Educational testing*]
BES............ Bennettsville, SC [*Location identifier*] [*FAA*]   (FAAL)
Bes .... Besah   (BJA)
BES............ Besancon [*France*] [*Seismograph station code, US Geological Survey*]   (SEIS)
BES............ Best Products Co., Inc. [*NYSE symbol*]   (SPSG)
BES............ Bet 'Eked Sefarim   (BJA)
BES............ Binocular Earth Sensor   (MCD)
BES............ Bioelectrochemical Society   (EA)
BES............ Biological Engineering Society [*British*]
BES............ Biomass Energy Systems Program [*Department of Energy*]
BES............ Bis(hydroxyethyl)aminoethanesulfonic Acid [*A buffer*] [*Organic chemistry*]
BES............ Black Enamel Slate   (MSA)
BES............ Booster Exhaust Stream
BES............ Bose-Einstein Statistics
BE & S .... Break, Enter, and Steal   (ADA)
BES............ Brest [*France*] [*Airport symbol*]   (OAG)
BES............ British Ecological Society
BES............ British Empire Series [*A publication*]
BES............ British Endodontic Society
BES............ Bromoethanesulfonic Acid [*Organic chemistry*]
BES............ Budget Estimate Submission [*DoD*]
BES............ Buildings and Equipment Section [*Library Administration and Management Association*]
BES............ Bulletin d'Epigraphie Semitique [*A publication*]   (BJA)
BES............ Bureau of Employment Security [*Later, US Employment Service*] [*Department of Labor*]
BES............ Business Expansion Scheme [*British*]
BES............ Saskatoon Board of Education [*UTLAS symbol*]
BESA......... Bank Export Services Act [*1982*]
BESA......... British Engineering Standards Association
BESA......... Building Energy Systems Analysis Project [*Public Works Canada*]
BESAC...... Basic Energy Sciences Committee [*Department of Energy*] [*Washington, DC*]   (EGAO)
Besancon Univ Ann Sci Ser 3 ... Besancon Universite. Annales Scientifiques. Serie 3. Geologie [*A publication*]

BESc.......... Bachelor of Engineering Science
Besch.......... Beschikking [*Decree*] [*Netherlands*]   (ILCA)
BESD......... Basic Enlisted Service Date   (AABC)
BESE......... Bureau of Elementary and Secondary Education [*Office of Education*]
BESEP....... Base Electronics System Engineering Plan   (NG)
BESERL.... Behavior and Systems Research Laboratory [*Army*]
BESEX ...... Bering Sea Expedition [*or Experiment*]
BESI .... Besicorp Group, Inc. [*NASDAQ symbol*]   (NQ)
BESI .... BioProcess Engineering Society International   (EA)
BESI .... Black Educational Services, Incorporated
BESID........ BS. Betriebssicherheit [*Austria*] [*A publication*]
Beskontaktn Elektr Mash ... Beskontaktnye Elektricheskiye Mashiny [*A publication*]
Besl .... Besluit [*Decree or Resolution*] [*Netherlands*]   (ILCA)
BESL .... British Empire Service League
BESLA ...... Black Entertainment and Sports Lawyers Association   (EA)
BESM........ Bovine Embryo Skeletal Muscle
BESM........ Bulletin Economique et Social du Maroc [*A publication*]
BESMEX... Bering Sea Marine Mammal Experiment [*National Oceanic and Atmospheric Administration*]   (MSC)
BESO......... Bank of England Staff Organisation
BESO......... British Executive Service Overseas [*Overseas Development Administration*]   (DS)
BESOM...... Brookhaven Energy System Optimization Model   (MCD)
BESP .... Basic Energy Sciences Program [*Department of Energy*] [*Washington, DC*]
B Esp A ...... Boletin. Asociacion Espanola de Amigos de la Arqueologia [*A publication*]
B Esp Or .... Boletin. Asociacion Espanola de Orientalistas [*A publication*]
BESRL....... Behavior and Systems Research Laboratory [*Arlington, VA*] [*Army*]   (IEEE)
BESS .... Beneficiary Evaluation Survey Service [*LIMRA*]
Bess........... Bessarione [*A publication*]
BESS .... Bessemer [*Metallurgy*]
BESS .... Binary Electromagnetic Signal Signature
BESS .... Biomedical Experiment Scientific [*or Support*] Satellite [*NASA*]   (NASA)
BESS .... Bolton Environmental Sensing System   (NOAA)
BESS .... Bottom Environmental Sensing System
Bess Prec ... Besson's New Jersey Precedents [*A publication*]   (DLA)
BESSY....... Berlin Electron Storage Ring for Synchrotron Radiation
BEST .... Ballastable Earthmoving Sectionalized Tractor [*Formerly, UET*] [*Army*]
BEST .... Ballistic Evaluation Static Test   (MCD)
BEST .... Basic Educational Skills Test
BEST .... Basic Essential Skills Testing
BEST .... Battery Energy Storage Test
BEST .... Beginning Entrepreneurial Support Team
BEST .... Behavioral Skills Training [*Navy*]
Best .... Best Sellers [*A publication*]
BEST .... Bestway Rental, Inc. [*NASDAQ symbol*]   (NQ)
BEST .... Better Electronic Service Technicians
BEST .... Black Efforts for Soul in Television
BEST .... Board of Environmental Studies and Toxicology [*NRC*]
BEST .... Booster Exhaust Study Test [*NASA*]   (NASA)
BEST .... Breast Examination through Simultaneous Temperature Evaluation
BEST .... British Expertise in Science and Technology [*Longman Cartermill Ltd.*] [*Scotland*] [*Information service or system*]   (IID)
BEST .... Broad-Based Enhanced Savings Tax
BEST .... Bureau of Evaluative Studies and Testing [*Indiana University*] [*Research center*]   (RCD)
BEST .... Business EDP [*Electronic Data Processing*] Systems Technique [*NCR Corp.*]   (IEEE)
BEST .... Business Equipment Software Techniques [*Data processing*]
BESTA ...... Beton- und Stahlbetonbau [*A publication*]
Best Beg & Rep ... Best on the Right to Begin and Reply [*A publication*]   (DLA)
Best Ev .... Best on Evidence [*A publication*]   (DLA)
Best Jur Tr ... Best on Trial by Jury [*A publication*]   (DLA)
Best Law Dic ... Best's Law Dictionary [*A publication*]   (DLA)
Best Life..... Best's Review. Life/Health Insurance Edition [*A publication*]
Best Nr....... Bestellnummer [*Order Number*] [*German*]
Best Pres.... Best on Presumptions of Law and Fact [*A publication*]   (DLA)
Best Presumptions ... Best on Presumptions of Law and Fact [*A publication*]   (DLA)
BESTS........ Belgian Educational Student Travel Service
Best & S ..... Best and Smith's English Queen's Bench Reports [*A publication*]   (DLA)
Best Sell..... Best Sellers [*A publication*]
Best & S (Eng) ... Best and Smith's English Queen's Bench Reports [*A publication*]   (DLA)
Best's Ins N ... Best's Insurance News [*A publication*]
Best's Life.. Best's Review. Life/Health Insurance Edition [*A publication*]
Best & Sm .. Best and Smith's English Queen's Bench Reports [*A publication*]   (DLA)
Bests Prop ... Best's Review. Property/Liability Edition [*A publication*]
Bests R .... Best's Review. Life/Health Insurance Edition [*A publication*]

Best's Rev Life Health Insur Ed ... Best's Review. Life/Health Insurance Edition [*A publication*]

Best's Rev Prop/Casualty Insur Ed ... Best's Review. Property/Casualty Insurance Edition [*A publication*]

Bests R Life Ed ... Best's Review. Life/Health Insurance Edition [*A publication*]

Bests R Prop Ed ... Best's Review. Property/Liability Edition [*A publication*]

Best's R Property Ed ... Best's Review. Property/Liability Edition [*A publication*]

besz .... Beszerzes [*Purchase*] [*Hungarian*]

Beszamolo Vizgazdalkodasi Tud Kut Intez Munkajarol ... Beszamolo a Vizgazdalkodasi Tudomanyos Kutato Intezet Munkajarol [*A publication*]

BET .... Bachelor of Engineering Technology

BET .... Background Elimination Technique   (MCD)

BET .... Balanced Expansion Technique   (MCD)

BET .... Basic Economics Test [*Educational test*]

BET .... Bedrijf en Techniek [*Amsterdam*] [*A publication*]

BET .... Beltec Enterprises Ltd. [*Vancouver Stock Exchange symbol*]

BET .... Bennett's Transport [*Commercial firm*] [*British*]

BET .... Bentley College, Waltham, MA [*OCLC symbol*]   (OCLC)

BET .... Best Estimate of Trajectory [*Apollo*] [*NASA*]

BET .... Bethel [*Alaska*] [*Seismograph station code, US Geological Survey*] [*Closed*]   (SEIS)

BET .... Bethel [*Alaska*] [*Airport symbol*]   (OAG)

BET .... Bethlehem Corp. [*AMEX symbol*]   (SPSG)

BET .... Between   (KSC)

BET .... Billet [*Bill*] [*French*] [*Business term*]   (ROG)

BET .... Binary Encoded Ternary   (MCD)

BET .... Black Entertainment Television [*Cable-television system*]

BET .... Blow-Out Emergency Team [*British government*]

BET .... Bridge Educational Trust Ltd. [*British*]

BET .... [*The*] British Electric Traction Co. Ltd.

BET .... Brunauer-Emmett-Teller [*Adsorption equation*]

BET .... Business English Test [*Vocational guidance test*]

BETA .... Babcock Easy Terminal Access System   (MCD)

BETA .... Battlefield Exploitation and Target Acquisition   (MCD)

BETA .... Beta Phase, Inc. [*Menlo Park, CA*] [*NASDAQ symbol*]   (NQ)

BETA .... Birth Education, Training, and Acceptance

BETA .... Boeing Engineering Thermal Analyzer   (MCD)

BETA .... Broadcasting and Entertainment Trades Alliance [*A union*] [*British*]   (EAIO)

BETA .... Business Equipment Trade Association [*London, England*]

Beta Adrenerge Blocker Hochdruck Int Symp ... Beta Adrenerge Blocker und Hochdruck Internationales Symposion [*A publication*]

Beta Adrenergic Blockers Hypertens ... Beta Adrenergic Blockers and Hypertension [*A publication*]

Betablocker Ggw Zukunft Int Symp ... Betablocker Gegenwart und Zukunft Internationales Symposium [*A publication*]

Beta Blocker Hypertonie Behandl ... Beta Blocker in der Hypertonie Behandlung [*A publication*]

Beta Blockers Present Status Future Prospects Int Symp ... Beta Blockers. Present Status and Future Prospects. An International Symposium [*A publication*]

Beta Phi Research Exch ... Beta Phi Research Exchange [*A publication*]

BETC .... Bartlesville Energy Technology Center [*Later, NIPER*] [*Department of Energy*] [*Bartlesville, OK*] [*Information service or system*]   (GRD)

BETE .... Benzilic Acid Tropine Ester [*Also, BAT, BTE*] [*Pharmacology*]

BETFOR ... Headquarters British Element Trieste Forces

Beth Hamikra ... Beth Hamikra. Bulletin of the Israel Society for Biblical Research and the World Jewish Biblical Society [*A publication*]

Beth Israel Hosp Semin Med ... Beth Israel Hospital. Seminars in Medicine [*A publication*]

Beth Isr Hosp Semin Med ... Beth Israel Hospital. Seminars in Medicine [*A publication*]

Bet Hom & Gard ... Better Homes and Gardens [*A publication*]

BETKA ...... Bergbautechnik [*A publication*]

Bet Libns .... Between Librarians [*A publication*]

BETN .... Between   (ROG)

BETNET ... Bilingual Education Telecommunications Network [*National Clearinghouse for Bilingual Education*] [*Wheaton, MD*]   (TSSD)

Betongtek Publ ... Betongtekniske Publikasjoner [*A publication*]

Beton Herstellung Verwend ... Beton, Herstellung, Verwendung [*A publication*]

Betons Ind ... Betons Industriels [*France*] [*A publication*]

Betonstein Zig ... Betonstein Zeitung [*A publication*]

Betontech Ber ... Betontechnische Berichte [*West Germany*] [*A publication*]

Betonwerk Fertigteil-Tech ... Betonwerk und Fertigteil-Technik [*West Germany*] [*A publication*]

B Et Or .... Bulletin d'Etudes Orientales [*A publication*]

B Et Orient ... Bulletin d'Etudes Orientales [*A publication*]

BETR .... Betreffend [*Referring To*] [*German*]

Betr-Berat ... Betriebs-Berater. Zeitschrift fuer Recht und Wirtschaft [*A publication*]

BETRC ...... British Engine Technical Reports [*A publication*]

BETRD ...... Betrieb (Duesseldorf) [*A publication*]

Betr Erz ...... Betrifft Erziehung [*West Germany*] [*A publication*]

Betriebswirt Mitt Wirtberater ... Betriebswirtschaftliche Mitteilungen fuer den Wirtschaftsberater [*A publication*]

Betriebswirtsch Forsch Praxis ... Betriebswirtschaftliche Forschung und Praxis [*A publication*]

Betriebswirtsch Mitt Wirtschaftsberat ... Betriebswirtschaftliche Mitteilungen fuer den Wirtschaftsberater [*A publication*]

BETRO ...... British Export Trade Research Organisation

Betr-Oekon ... Betriebs-Oekonom [*A publication*]

BetrRG .... Betriebsrategesetz [*Law on Works Councils*] [*German*]   (ILCA)

Betr-Tech ... Betriebs-Technik [*A publication*]

BetrVG .... Betriebsverfassungsgesetz [*Law on the Representation of Workers and Works Councils*] [*German*]   (ILCA)

BETS .... Bulletin. Evangelical Theological Society [*Later, Journal. Evangelical Theological Society*] [*A publication*]

BEtSS .... Better Education thru Simplified Spelling   (EA)

BETT .... Bolt Extrusion Thrust Termination   (MCD)

BETT .... British Education and Training Technology Exhibition   (ITD)

BETT .... Buildings Energy Technology Transfer Program [*Canada*]

Betterave Ind Agr ... Betterave et les Industries Agricoles [*A publication*]

Better Bus ... Better Business [*New Zealand*] [*A publication*]

Better F .... Better Farming [*A publication*]

Betts' Adm Pr ... Betts' Admiralty Practice [*A publication*]   (DLA)

Betts' Dec ... Blatchford and Howland's United States District Court Reports [*A publication*]   (DLA)

Bett's Dec ... Olcott's United States District Court Reports [*A publication*]   (DLA)

BETUA ...... Toyama Daigaku Kogakubu Kiyo [*A publication*]

BETV .... Bald Eagle Total Value

BETW .... Between   (ROG)

Betw Libns ... Between Librarians [*A publication*]

BETZ .... Betz Laboratories, Inc. [*NASDAQ symbol*]   (NQ)

Betz Indic ... Betz Indicator [*A publication*]

BEU .... Basic Encoding Unit

BEU .... Bedourie [*Australia*] [*Airport symbol*] [*Obsolete*]   (OAG)

BEU .... Bellevue Oil & Minerals [*Vancouver Stock Exchange symbol*]

BEU .... BENELUX Economische Union [*BENELUX Economic Union*] [*Brussels, Belgium*]   (EAIO)

BEU .... British Empire Union

BEU .... Independent Bakery Employees Union

BEUC .... Bureau Europeen des Unions de Consommateurs [*European Bureau of Consumers' Unions*]   (EAIO)

BEUL .... Building Energy Utilization Laboratory [*Iowa State University*] [*Research center*]   (RCD)

BEUP .... [*The*] Babylonian Expedition of the University of Pennsylvania: Cuneiform Texts [*A publication*]

B Eur S Hum ... Bulletin. European Society of Human Genetics [*A publication*]

Beurteilungskriterien Chemother ... Beurteilungskriterien fuer Chemotherapeutika [*A publication*]

BEV .... Baboon Endogenous Virus

BEV .... Beersheba [*Israel*] [*Airport symbol*] [*Obsolete*]   (OAG)

BEV .... Bevatron

BEV .... Bevel

BEV .... Beverage

BEV .... Beverley [*Jamaica*] [*Seismograph station code, US Geological Survey*] [*Closed*]   (SEIS)

BEV .... Beverly Enterprises [*NYSE symbol*]   (SPSG)

BeV .... Billion Electron Volts

BEV .... Black English Vernacular [*Dialect*]

BEV .... Bovine Enterovirus

BEV .... Broadway Beverages [*Vancouver Stock Exchange symbol*]

BEVA .... British Exhibition Venues Association

BEVALAC ... Bevatron/Super-HILAC [*Combination of accelerators*]

Bev Ann ... Beverage Industry Annual Manual [*A publication*]

Bev Ceylon ... Beven's Ceylon Reports [*A publication*]   (ILCA)

Bev Emp L ... Bevin on Employer's Liability for Negligence of Servants [*A publication*]   (DLA)

Beven .... Beven on Negligence in Law [*1889-1928*] [*A publication*]   (DLA)

Beven .... Beven's Ceylon Reports [*A publication*]   (DLA)

Beverage ... Beverage Industry [*A publication*]

Beverage Ind ... Beverage Industry [*A publication*]

Bev Hills BAJ ... Beverly Hills Bar Association. Journal [*A publication*]   (DLA)

Bev Hom ... Bevil on Homicide [*A publication*]   (DLA)

Bev & M ..... Bevin and Mill's Reports [*Ceylon*] [*A publication*]   (DLA)

BEVOA ..... Beitraege zur Vogelkunde [*A publication*]

Bev Pat .... Bevill's Patent Cases [*England*] [*A publication*]   (DLA)

BEVSA ...... Berichte. Verhandlungen der Saechsischen Akademie der Wissenschaften zu Leipzig. Mathematisch-Naturwissenschaftliche Klasse [*A publication*]

Bev & Sieb ... Beven and Siebel's Reports [*Ceylon*] [*A publication*]   (DLA)

BEvTh .... Beitraege zur Evangelischen Theologie [*Munich*] [*A publication*]

BEvTSoc .... Bulletin. Evangelical Theological Society [*Wheaton, IL*] [*Later, Journal. Evangelical Theological Society*] [*A publication*]

Bev Wld ..... Beverage World [*A publication*]

Bev Wld 100 ... Beverage World 100 [*A publication*]

Bev Wld P ... Beverage World Periscope. Late Breaking News and Analysis [*A publication*]

BEW .... Beira [*Mozambique*] [*Airport symbol*]   (OAG)

BEW	Board of Economic Warfare [*World War II*]
BEW	British Electronics Week [*Trade show*] (ITD)
BEW	Butanol/Ethanol/Water [*Solvent system*]
BEWA	British Effluent and Water Association [*Trade association*]
Bewirtsch Fester Abfaelle Ber Int Kongr	Bewirtschaftung Fester Abfaelle Berichte Internationaler Kongress [*A publication*]
BeWiU	Universitaire Instelling Antwerpen, Wilrijk, Belgium [*Library symbol*] [*Library of Congress*] (LCLS)
Bew & N Pr	Bewley and Naish on Common Law Procedure [*A publication*] (DLA)
BEWT	Bureau of East-West Trade [*Department of Commerce*]
B Ex	Bachelor of Expression
BEX	Baden Explorations [*Vancouver Stock Exchange symbol*]
BEX	Bexhill Museum [*British*]
BEX	Bloomfield, IA [*Location identifier*] [*FAA*] (FAAL)
BEX	Board of Examiners for the Foreign Service [*Department of State*]
BEX	Broadband Exchange [*Western Union communication system*]
BEXA	Business Efficiency Exhibition [*Business Equipment Association of South Africa*] (TSPED)
B Exam	Bar Examiner [*A publication*]
B Exam J	Bar Examination Journal [*A publication*] (DLA)
BEXBA	Bulletin of Experimental Biology and Medicine [*English Translation*] [*A publication*]
BEXBB	Biochemistry and Experimental Biology [*A publication*]
BEXEC	Budget Execution [*Army*] (AABC)
B Exp B Med	Bulletin of Experimental Biology and Medicine [*A publication*]
BEY	Beirut [*Lebanon*] [*Airport symbol*] (OAG)
BEY	Butte, MT [*Location identifier*] [*FAA*] (FAAL)
Bey B	Beyond Baroque [*A publication*]
BEYN	Beynhurst [*England*]
BEZ	Baldor Electric Co. [*NYSE symbol*] (SPSG)
B Ez	Balkansko Ezikoznanije [*A publication*]
BEZ	Beru [*Kiribati*] [*Airport symbol*] (OAG)
Bez	Bezah (BJA)
BEZ	Bezueglich [*In Regard To, With Reference To*] [*German*]
BEZ	Loris, SC [*Location identifier*] [*FAA*] (FAAL)
BEZEA	Betonstein Zeitung [*A publication*]
Bez G	Bezirksgericht [*District Court*] [*German*] (DLA)
Bez Ger	Bezirksgericht [*District Court*] [*German*] (DLA)
BEZHDK	Beton i Zhelezobeton [*Tiflis*] [*A publication*]
Bezop Gorn Rab	Bezopasnost Gornykh Rabot [*A publication*]
Bezop Tr Proizvod Issled Ispyt Sprav Posobie 2-e Izd	Bezopasnost Truda na Proizvodstve Issledovaniya i Ispytaniya Spravochnoe Posobie 2-e Izdanie [*A publication*]
Bezop Tr Prom-St	Bezopasnost Truda v Promyshlennosti [*A publication*]
BEZW	Beziehungsweise [*Respectively*] [*German*]
BF	Alaska International Air, Inc. [*ICAO designator*] (FAAC)
BF	Bachelor of Finance
BF	Bachelor of Forestry
BF	Back Fat [*Animal husbandry*]
BF	Back-Feed
BF	Back Focal
BF	Back Folded [*Freight*]
BF	Backdoor Financing [*Public debt transactions*] [*Investment term*]
BF	Backface (MSA)
BF	Backup Force
bf	Bahamas [*MARC country of publication code*] [*Library of Congress*] (LCCP)
BF	Bandpass Filter
BF	Bankruptcy Fee (ADA)
BF	Banque de France [*Bank of France*]
BF	Banqueting/Catered Functions [*Public-performance tariff class*] [*British*]
BF	Bark Forager [*Ornithology*]
BF	Barren Foundation (EA)
BF	Barrier Filter [*Medicine*]
BF	Basal Fold
BF	Base File
BF	Base Frequency (ADA)
BF	Base Funded (AFM)
BF	Base Fuze
BF	Batch Fabrication
BF	Battle Fatigue (INF)
BF	Bayonet Fighting
BF	Beam Forming
BF	Beat-Frequency
BF	Beaten Favourite [*Horse racing*] [*British*]
BF	Beef (ROG)
BF	Beer Firkin
BF	Before Flight (MCD)
BF	Belgian Fourragere [*Military decoration*]
B & F	Bell and Flange [*Technical drawings*]
BF	Bellerive Foundation (EAIO)
BF	Bengal Fusiliers [*British military*] (DMA)
BF	Bentonite Flocculation [*Test*]
B/F	Best and Final Offer
BF	Best Friend [*Initialism used by author E. B. White to describe his wife*]

BF	Beverly Foundation (EA)
BF	Bibelforskaren (BJA)
BF	Bibliofilia [*A publication*]
BF	Bibliographie de la France [*A publication*]
BF	Bibliotherapy Forum [*Association of Specialized and Cooperative Library Agencies*]
BF	Bile Flow [*Physiology*]
BF	Black Female
BF	Black Filly [*Horse racing*] (ROG)
BF	Blank Flange
BF	Blast Furnace [*Ironmaking*]
BF	Blastogenic Factor [*Immunochemistry*]
BF	Bleeding Frequency [*Medicine*]
B/F	Blip/Frame (CET)
BF	Blocking Factor
BF	Blood Flow [*Medicine*]
BF	Bloody Fool [*British slang*]
BF	Blue Affirmative Flag [*Navy*] [*British*]
BF	Blues Foundation (EA)
BF	Board-Foot
BF	Boiler Feed [*Technical drawings*]
BF	Bold Face [*Printing term*]
BF	Boletin de Filologia [*A publication*]
BF	Bona Fide [*In Good Faith*] [*Latin*]
BF	Bonae Feminae [*To the Good Woman*] [*Latin*]
BF	Bond Fund [*Finance*]
BF	Bone Formation
BF	Bonum Factum [*A Good or Proper Act, Deed, or Decree*] [*Latin*] [*Legal term*] (DLA)
BF	Book Forum [*A publication*]
BF	Books from Finland [*A publication*]
BF	Boring Fixture (MCD)
BF	Born Fool (DAS)
BF	Borough Fiscal [*British*] (ROG)
B & F	Boston & Fitchburg Railroad
BF	Both Faces [*Technical drawings*]
BF	Bottom Face [*Technical drawings*]
BF	Bouillon Filtre [*Bouillon Filtrate*]
B/F	Bound/Free [*Ratio*] [*Biochemistry*]
BF	Boyfriend [*Slang*]
B & F	Branch and Flow [*Diagram*]
BF	Branching Filter [*Telecommunications*] (TEL)
BF	Brandon Films, Inc.
BF	Breadalbane Fencibles [*British military*] (DMA)
BF	Breakthrough Foundation (EA)
BF	Breast Fed [*Medicine*]
B & F	Breslich & Foss [*British*]
BF	Bridge/Forecastle [*of a ship*] (DS)
BF	Brief
Bf	Brief [*Currency*] [*German*]
BF	Bristol Fighter [*Aircraft*] [*World War I*]
BF	British Forces (DMA)
B & F	Broderick and Freemantle's English Ecclesiastical Reports [*1840-64*] [*A publication*] (DLA)
BF	Bronze Floors [*On ships*]
BF	Broth Filtrate [*Microbiology*]
BF	Brought Forward [*Business term*]
BF	Buffered [*Medicine*]
BF	Burkina Faso [*ANSI two-letter standard code*] (CNC)
BF	Burnup Fraction [*of fuel in plasma*] (MCD)
B & F	Business and Farm [*IRS*]
BF	Disputation between Bird and Fish (BJA)
BF	Fernie Public Library, British Columbia [*Library symbol*] [*National Library of Canada*] (NLC)
BF	Franc [*Monetary unit*] [*Belgium*]
BF1	Virus Isolated from Bovine Feces [*Medicine*]
2-B-F	Selective Service Class [*for Man Physically Disqualified for Military Service but Necessary to War Production*] [*Obsolete*]
BFA	Bachelor of Fine Arts
BFA	Bacon Families Association (EA)
BFA	Balloon Federation of America (EA)
BFA	Banque Franco-Allemande SA
BFA	Barrel Futurities of America (EA)
BFA	Before Flight Abort [*NASA*] (MCD)
BFA	Benelumat Revue [*A publication*]
BFA	Benzylfurylmethyl Alcohol [*Organic chemistry*]
BF of A	Bicycle Federation of America (EA)
BFA	Bicycle Federation of Australia
BFA	Bilingual Foundation of the Arts (EA)
BFA	Blackburn Family Association (EA)
BFA	Blank Firing Adaptor [*Army*] (MCD)
BFA	Blank Firing Attachment (MCD)
BFA	Board, Family, and Associates [*Company stockholders*]
BFA	Boyne Falls, MI [*Location identifier*] [*FAA*] (FAAL)
BFA	Bream Fishermen Association
BFA	Brefeldin A [*Biochemistry*]
BFA	British First Army
BFA	Broadcasting Foundation of America (EA)
BFA	Bulletin. Faculty of Arts. University of Egypt [*Cairo*] [*A publication*]

BFA............ Bulletin. Federation des Avoues de Belgique [*A publication*]
BFA............ Bureau of Finance and Administration [*US Postal Service*] (MCD)
BFA............ Burkina Faso [*ANSI three-letter standard code*] (CNC)
BFA............ Category B Flying Accident [*British military*] (DMA)
BFAC......... Bulletin. Faculty of Arts. University of Egypt (Cairo) [*A publication*]
B-FACT..... Booster Flight-Acceptance Composite Test [*NASA*]
BFAD........ British First Airborne Division
BFA in DA ... Bachelor of Fine Arts in Dramatic Art
BFA in Ed ... Bachelor of Fine Arts in Education
BfAi........... Bundesstelle fuer Aussenhandelsinformation [*Federal Office of Foreign Trade Information*] [*German Ministry of Economics*] [*Cologne, Federal Republic of Germany*] [*Information service or system*] (IID)
BFALA...... Bachelor of Fine Arts in Landscape Architecture
BFAM....... Budget Formulation and Appropriation Model (MCD)
BFAM....... Bulletin. Fogg Art Museum [*A publication*]
BFA in Mus ... Bachelor of Fine Arts in Music
BFAP........ British Forces, Arabian Peninsula [*British military*] (DMA)
BFA in PS .. Bachelor of Fine Arts in Painting and Sculpture
BFAR........ British Foundation for Age Research (IRUK)
BFAS........ Basic File Access System
BFA in Sp .. Bachelor of Fine Arts in Speech
B'FAST..... Breakfast [*Classified advertising*] (ADA)
BFAWU..... Bakers' Food and Allied Workers' Union [*British*] (DCTA)
BFB.......... Biofeedback
BFB.......... British Flight Battalion
BFB.......... Broad-Flanged Beam
BFBS .... British Forces Broadcasting Service [*or Station*]
BFBS .... British and Foreign Bible Society
BFBS .... Brookfield Bancshares Corp. [*NASDAQ symbol*] (NQ)
BFBU........ Beaufort Bulletin. Dome Petroleum Ltd. [*A publication*]
BFBV........ Beaver Valley Public Library, Fruitvale, British Columbia [*Library symbol*] [*National Library of Canada*] (NLC)
BFC........... Backup Flight Control (MCD)
BFC........... Badfinger Fan Club (EA)
BFC........... Balance Forward Master (MCD)
BFC........... Bangles Fan Club [*Later, Bangles n' Mash International*] (EA)
BFC........... BankAtlantic Financial [*AMEX symbol*] (SPSG)
BFC........... Banque Francaise pour le Commerce [*French Commercial Bank*]
BFC........... Base des Forces Canadiennes [*Canadian Forces Base - CFB*]
BFC........... Bellefonte Central Railroad Co. [*AAR code*]
BFC........... Bending Feedback Control
BFC........... Berlin Fan Club (EA)
BFC........... Board of Fire Commissioners [*New South Wales, Australia*]
BFC........... Body Flap Control (MCD)
BFC........... Bohr Frequency Condition
BFCT.......... Bold Face Capitals [*Printing term*]
BFC........... Boletin. Instituto de Filologia. Universidad de Chile [*A publication*]
BFC........... Bollettino di Filologia Classica [*A publication*]
BFC........... British Free Corps [*Corps formed by Germans among POW's and civil internees*] [*World War II*]
BFC........... Broadcasting and Film Commission [*Later, CC*] (EA)
BFC........... Budget and Forecast Calendarization [*Accounting*]
BFC........... Bureau of Foreign Commerce [*Abolished, 1961*] [*Department of Commerce*]
BFC........... Bureau International du Film des Chemins de Fer [*International Railway Film Bureau*]
BFCA........ Benzylfurancarboxylic Acid [*Organic chemistry*]
BFCA........ Bichon Frise Club of America (EA)
BFCC........ British Foreign and Colonial Corporation [*Finance*]
BFCD........ Bureau of Flood Control and Drainage [*Philippines*] (DS)
BFCE........ Banque Francaise du Commerce Exterieur [*French state-owned bank*]
BFCF .... Bremerton Freight Car Ferry [*AAR code*]
BFChTh..... Beitraege zur Foerderung Christlicher Theologie [*Guetersloh*] [*A publication*]
BFCL .... Bulletin. Facultes Catholiques de Lyon [*A publication*]
BFCLD ...... Union Canadienne des Travailleurs Unis des Brasseries, Farines, Cereales, Liqueurs Douces, et Distilleries [*International Union of United Brewery, Flour, Cereal, Soft Drink, and Distillery Workers of America - BFCSD*]
BFCO........ Band Filter Cutoff (MSA)
BFCO........ Bloomfield Savings & Loan Association, FA [*NASDAQ symbol*] (NQ)
BFCP .... Broadway Financial Corporation [*NASDAQ symbol*] (NQ)
BFCS .... Backup Flight Control System [*NASA*] (NASA)
BFCS .... Bing's Friends and Collectors Society (EA)
BFCS .... British Friesian Cattle Society of Great Britain and Ireland
BFCSD ...... International Union of United Brewery, Flour, Cereal, Soft Drink, and Distillery Workers of America [*Later, Brewery and Soft Drink Workers Conference - USA and Canada*]
BFCT .... Boiler Feed Compound Tank [*Technical drawings*]
BFCTL....... Bibliotheque de la Faculte Catholique de Theologie de Lyon [*A publication*]
BFCU........ Bureau of Federal Credit Unions [*Later, NCUA*] [*Social Security Administration*]
BFCY .... Beneficiary

BFCY-P ..... Best-Fit Central Y-Plane
BFD .... Back Focal Distance (MSA)
BFD .... Banque Federale de Developpement [*Federal Business Development Bank - FBDB*] [*Canada*]
BFD .... Basic Floppy Disk
BFD .... Battery Firing Device (MCD)
BFD .... Battlefield Day (RDA)
BFD .... Beaufield Resources, Inc. [*Toronto Stock Exchange symbol*]
BFD .... Bellfield [*Australia*] [*Seismograph station code, US Geological Survey*] (SEIS)
BFD .... Big Fine Deal
BFD .... Binary-Floating-Decimal [*Data processing*]
BFD .... Blank Film Door
BFD .... Blind Fire Director (NATG)
BFD .... Bookform Drawing (MSA)
BFD .... Boolean Function Designator [*Mathematics*]
BFD .... Bradford [*Pennsylvania*] [*Airport symbol*] (OAG)
BFD .... Budget Formulation Directive [*Military*] (AABC)
BFD .... Bulletin for International Fiscal Documentation [*A publication*]
BFDC........ Battalion Fire Distribution Center (AABC)
BFDC........ Bureau of Foreign and Domestic Commerce [*Functions later dispersed*] [*Department of Commerce*]
BFDK........ Before Dark (FAAC)
BFDL........ Blue Force Data Link [*Military*] (CAAL)
BFDS........ Board of Faculty of Dental Surgery [*British*]
BFE.......... Bachelor of Forest Engineering
BFE.......... Battlefield Estimate
BFE.......... Beam-Forming Electrode
BFE.......... Board for Fundamental Education (EA)
BFE.......... Boletin de Filologia Espanola [*A publication*]
BFE.......... Bromotrifluoroethylene [*Organic chemistry*]
BFE.......... Brownfield, TX [*Location identifier*] [*FAA*] (FAAL)
BFE.......... BTL [*Bell Telephone Laboratories*] Furnished Equipment (MCD)
BFE.......... Buyer Furnished Equipment (MCD)
BFEA .... Bureau of Far Eastern Affairs [*Department of State*]
BFEC........ Bendix Field Engineering Corporation [*of Bendix Corp.*]
BFEC........ British Food Export Council (DS)
BFEEC ...... Banking Federation of the European Economic Community (EAIO)
BFEEE....... Bureau Federal d'Examen des Evaluations Environnementales [*Federal Environmental Assessment Review Office*] [*Canada*]
BFEL........ Buffelsfontein Gold Mining Co. Ltd. [*NASDAQ symbol*] (NQ)
BFEN........ BF Enterprises, Inc. [*NASDAQ symbol*] (NQ)
BF Eng...... Bachelor of Forest Engineering
BFEP........ Bicentennial Futures Education Project [*Australia*]
BFES .... British Families Education Service
BFF .... Beyond Fiction [*A publication*]
BFF .... Black Filmmaker Foundation (EA)
BFf........... Blodau'r Ffair [*A publication*]
BFF .... Bovine Follicular Fluid
BFF .... Budget Furniture Forum [*Later, ROFF*] (EA)
BFF .... Buffalo - Larkin [*New York*] [*Seismograph station code, US Geological Survey*] [*Closed*] (SEIS)
BFF .... Buffered Flip-Flop [*Data processing*]
BFF .... Bundesforschungsanstalt fuer Fischerei [*Database producer*] [*Federal Republic of Germany*]
BFF .... Burma Frontier Force [*British military*] (DMA)
BFF .... Scottsbluff [*Nebraska*] [*Airport symbol*] (OAG)
BFFA .... British Film Fund Agency
BFFC .... Bill Farrar Fan Club (EA)
BFFEIFC... Bobby Fuller Four-Ever International Fan Club [*Defunct*] (EA)
BFFRAM .. British Columbia. Ministry of Forests. Forest Research Review [*A publication*]
BFFS........ British Federation of Film Societies
BFG .... B. F. Goodrich Co.
BfG........... Bank fuer Gemeinwirtschaft [*Frankfurt, Germany*]
BFG .... Big Friendly Giant [*In the children's bestseller "The BFG" by Roald Dahl*]
BFG .... Binary Frequency Generator (IEEE)
BFG .... Briefing (AABC)
BFG .... British Forces Germany [*NATO*]
BFG .... Brute Force Gyro
BFG .... Buffing (MSA)
BFGF........ Basic Fibroblast Growth Factor [*Biochemistry*]
BFH .... Bouwmarkt [*A publication*]
BFH .... British Field Hospital [*British military*] (DMA)
BFH .... Bundesfinanzhof [*Federal Supreme Fiscal Court*] [*German*] (DLA)
BFHA .... Bulletin. Friends Historical Association [*A publication*]
BFHE........ Entscheidungen des Bundesfinanzhofs [*German*] (DLA)
BFHFI....... Black Filmmakers Hall of Fame, Incorporated (EA)
BFHP........ Base Fuze Hole Plug
BFI........... Baltic Freight Index [*of spot market rates*] [*Shipping*] (DS)
BFI........... Battlefield Interdiction (MCD)
BFI........... Bearing Frequency Indicator (NVT)
BFI........... Betriebsforschungsinstitut [*Institute for Industrial Research*] [*German Iron and Steel Engineers Association*] [*Dusseldorf*] [*Information service or system*] (IID)
BFI............ British Film Institute

BFI............ Browning-Ferris Industries, Inc. [*NYSE symbol*]   (SPSG)
BFI............ Buckminster Fuller Institute   (EA)
BFI............ Business Forms Institute [*Defunct*]
BFI............ Seattle, WA [*Location identifier*] [*FAA*]   (FAAL)
BFIAS........ Ballistics Force Integrator and Analyzer System   (MCD)
BFID......... Boolean Function Identifier [*Mathematics*]
BFIF.......... Bulletin Folklorique d'Ile-De-France [*A publication*]
BFIFC........ Bureau of Foods Irradiated Foods Committee [*Food and Drug Administration*]
B Fil........... Boletin de Filologia [*A publication*]
B Fil Gr Padova ... Bollettino. Istituto di Filologia Greca. Universita di Padova [*A publication*]
B Fil Ling Sic ... Bollettino. Centro di Studi Filologici e Linguistici Siciliani [*A publication*]
BFinAdmin ... Bachelor of Financial Administration   (ADA)
BFJ............ B. F. Jones Memorial Library, Aliquippa, PA [*OCLC symbol*]   (OCLC)
BFJ............ Ba [*Fiji*] [*Airport symbol*]   (OAG)
BFJ............ Booster Fuel Jacket
BFJSC....... Benjamin Franklin Junior Stamp Club [*Later, BFSC*]   (EA)
BFK........... Buffalo, OK [*Location identifier*] [*FAA*]   (FAAL)
BFL........... Bachelor of Family Life
BFL........... Back Focal Length [*Optics*]
BFL........... Bakersfield [*California*] [*Airport symbol*]   (OAG)
BFL........... Bakersfield, CA [*TACAN station*]   (NASA)
BFL........... BancFlorida Financial Corp. [*NYSE symbol*]   (SPSG)
BFL........... Baptists for Life   (EA)
BFL........... Bird-Fanciers Lung [*Medicine*]
BFL........... Bomb Fall Line [*Military*]   (NVT)
BFL........... Books for Libraries [*Program*]
BFL........... Books for Libraries Micropublications, Freeport, NY [*Library symbol*] [*Library of Congress*]   (LCLS)
BFL........... Brackenridge Field Laboratory [*University of Texas at Austin*] [*Research center*]   (RCD)
BFL........... British Foreign Legion [*British military*]   (DMA)
BFL........... Buffered FET [*Field Effect Transistor*] Logic [*Integrated circuitry*]
BFL........... Bulletin. Faculte des Lettres de Lille [*A publication*]
BFL........... Bunzl Flexpack Limited [*British*]
BFL........... United States Food and Drug Administration, Bureau of Food, Washington, DC [*OCLC symbol*]   (OCLC)
BFLAV ...... Bulletin. Foreign Language Association of Virginia [*A publication*]
BFLCM ..... Langley Centennial Museum and National Exhibition Centre, Fort Langley, British Columbia [*Library symbol*] [*National Library of Canada*]   (NLC)
BFLD......... Bluefield Supply Co. [*NASDAQ symbol*]   (NQ)
BFLFMM ... British Columbia Farm Machinery Museum, Fort Langley, British Columbia [*Library symbol*] [*National Library of Canada*]   (NLC)
BFLMS...... Benjamin Franklin Literary and Medical Society   (EA)
BFLO......... Buffalo, Inc. [*NASDAQ symbol*]   (NQ)
BFLOPS..... Billion Floating-Point Operations per Second [*Data processing*]
BFLPC....... Fort Langley National Historic Park, Parks Canada [*Parc Historique National de Fort Langley, Parcs Canada*] British Columbia [*Library symbol*] [*National Library of Canada*]   (NLC)
BFLS......... Bulletin. Faculte des Lettres de Strasbourg [*A publication*]
BFM .... Barium Ferrite Magnet
BFM .... Basic Field Manual [*Military*]
BFM .... Basic Fighter Maneuver [*Air Force*]   (MCD)
BFM .... Basic Flight Maneuver [*Aviation*]   (FAAC)
BFM .... Before Full Moon [*Freemasonry*]   (ROG)
BFM .... Bessel Function Model   (MCD)
BFM .... Bethany Fellowship Missions   (EA)
BFM .... Boletin de Filologia (Montevideo) [*A publication*]
BFM .... British Food Mission [*World War II*]
BFM .... Broadcast Financial Management Association [*Later, BCFMA*]   (EA)
BFM .... Business Conditions Digest [*A publication*]
BFM .... Fernie Museum, British Columbia [*Library symbol*] [*National Library of Canada*]   (NLC)
BFM .... Mobile, AL [*Location identifier*] [*FAA*]   (FAAL)
BFMA........ Business Forms Management Association   (EA)
BFMB........ Bank of Finland. Monthly Bulletin [*A publication*]
BFMDS..... Base Flight Management Data System   (AFM)
BFMF .... British Federation of Musical Festivals
BFMF .... British Footwear Manufacturers' Federation
BFMI .... Business Firms Master Index [*A publication*]
BFMIRA ... British Food Manufacturing Industries Research Association   (ARC)
BFMO .... Base Fuels Management Officer [*Air Force*]   (AFM)
BFMP .... British Federation of Master Printers [*A union*]
BFN .... Beam-Forming Network
BFN .... Bloemfontein [*South Africa*] [*Airport symbol*]   (OAG)
BFN .... British Forces Network
BFN .... Fort Nelson Public Library, British Columbia [*Library symbol*] [*National Library of Canada*]   (NLC)
BFNC......... Benign Familial Neonatal Convulsions [*Medicine*]

BFNJ .... Bijdragen Uitgegeven door en Philosophische en Theologische Faculteiten der Noord- en Zuid-Nederlandse Jezuieten [*A publication*]
BFNP........ Browns Ferry Nuclear Plant   (NRCH)
BFNPP........ Browns Ferry Nuclear Power Plant   (NRCH)
BFNS........ Black Fox Nuclear Station   (NRCH)
BFO .... Balanced Forearm Orthosis [*Medicine*]
BFO .... Baruch-Foster Corp. [*AMEX symbol*]   (SPSG)
BFO .... Beat-Frequency Oscillator
BFo............ Biuletyn Fonograficzny [*A publication*]
BFO .... Buffalo Range [*Zimbabwe*] [*Airport symbol*]   (OAG)
BFO .... Bunker Fuel Oil   (DS)
BFO .... Business Forum [*A publication*]
BFO .... Steel News [*A publication*]
BFOL......... Beaufort Outlook. Newsletter from the Northern Office of the Beaufort Sea Alliance [*A publication*]
B Fon.......... Biuletyn Fonograficzny [*A publication*]
BFOO .... Berichte. Forschungsinstitut fuer Osten und Orient [*Vienna*] [*A publication*]
BFOODAB ... Budget Formulation Office, Office of the Director of the Army Budget
BFOQ .... Bona Fide Occupational Qualification
B For .... Bachelor of Forestry   (ADA)
BFORM..... Budget Formulation [*Army*]   (AABC)
BForSc....... Bachelor of Forestry Science   (ADA)
B Forum ..... Book Forum [*A publication*]
BFOV........ Broad Field of View   (MCD)
BFOZ-P..... Best-Fit Optic Z-Plane
BFP........... Balco Industries [*Toronto Stock Exchange symbol*] [*Vancouver Stock Exchange symbol*]
BFP........... Batters Faced by Pitcher [*Baseball*]
BFP........... Battlefield Period   (MCD)
BFP........... Bayes Fixed Sample-Size Procedure [*Statistics*]
BFP........... Beaver Falls [*Pennsylvania*] [*Airport symbol*]   (OAG)
BFP........... Biological False Positive [*Clinical chemistry*]
BFP........... Boiler Feed Pump [*Technical drawings*]
BFP........... Bona Fide Purchaser [*Legal term*]   (DLA)
BFP........... Bottom Finding Pinger
BFP........... Bureau of Freelance Photographers [*British*]   (CB)
BFP........... UCLA Business Forecasting Project [*Information service or system*]   (IID)
BFPA .... British Fluid Power Association   (EAIO)
BFPDDA ... Binary Floating-Point Digital Differential Analyzer   (IEEE)
BFPEA ...... British Fireboard Packaging Employers' Association
BFPhLL.... Bibliotheque de la Faculte de Philosophie et Lettres de l'Universite de Liege [*A publication*]
BFPLUL.... Bibliotheque de la Faculte de Philosophie et Lettres de l'Universite de Liege [*A publication*]
BFP/MAP ... Books for Professionals/Miller Accounting Publications [*Harcourt, Brace, Jovanovich, Inc.*]
BFPMS...... British Federation of Printing Machinery and Supplies
BFPO........ British Field Post Office [*World War II*]
BFPO........ British Forces Post Office
BFPPE2..... Bulletin Francais de la Peche et de la Pisciculture [*A publication*]
BFPPS ...... Bureau of Foods, Pesticides, and Product Safety [*FDA*]
BFPQ......... Block Floating Point Quantitizer   (MCD)
BFPV .... Bona Fide Purchaser for Value [*of a security, or other negotiable instrument*] [*Legal term*]
BFR .... Barrier Film Rectifier
BFR .... Beauford Resources Ltd. [*Vancouver Stock Exchange symbol*]
BFR .... Bedford, IN [*Location identifier*] [*FAA*]   (FAAL)
BFR .... Before   (MSA)
BFR .... Before Flight Reliability   (MCD)
BFR .... Bibliotheque Francaise et Romane [*A publication*]
BFR .... Biennial Flight Review [*Department of Aviation*] [*Australia*]
BFR .... Bile Flow Rate [*Physiology*]
BFR .... Black, Female Republican
BFR .... Blast Furnace Research, Inc. [*Defunct*]   (EA)
BFR .... Blip-Frame Ratio   (MSA)
BFR .... Block Format Recording
BFR .... Blood Flow Rate [*Medicine*]
BFR .... Boletin de Filologia (Rio De Janeiro) [*A publication*]
BFR .... Bone Formation Rate [*Medicine*]
BFR .... Bridged Frequency Ringing [*Telecommunications*]   (TEL)
BFR .... Briefer
BFR .... Buffer [*Data processing*]   (MSA)
BFR .... Buffered Ringer's Solution [*Medicine*]
BFRE......... Break-Free Corp. [*NASDAQ symbol*]   (NQ)
BFRL........ Basic Facility Requirements List [*Navy*]
BFRL........ Fraser Lake Public Library, British Columbia [*Library symbol*] [*National Library of Canada*]   (NLC)
BFRNA2.... British Columbia. Ministry of Forests. Research Note [*A publication*]
BFRO......... Black Family Research Organization   (EA)
BFRP......... Boron Fiber Reinforced Plastics   (NASA)
BFRPD ...... Biofuels Report [*A publication*]
BFRS .... Bio-Feedback Research Society [*Later, BSA*]   (EA)
BFS .... Bachelor of Foreign Service
BFS .... Backup Flight System   (MCD)
BFS........... Band Filter Set

BFS .... Base Facilities for SACLANT [*NATO*]   (NATG)
BFS .... Battlefield Functional System   (MCD)
BFS .... Beam-Foil Spectroscopy
BFS .... Bedford Software Ltd. [*Toronto Stock Exchange symbol*]
BFS .... Beef Friesian Society   (EA)
BFS .... Belfast [*Northern Ireland*] [*Airport symbol*]   (OAG)
BFS .... Ben Franklin Society   (EA)
BFS .... Best Fit Sphere   (MCD)
BFS .... Bird Friends Society [*Defunct*]   (EA)
BFS .... Black Fox Station [*Nuclear energy*]   (NRCH)
BFS .... Blast Furnace Slag
BFS .... Board of Foreign Scholarships [*Department of State*] [*Washington, DC*]
BFS .... Bonney-Fessenden Sociograph [*Psychology*]
BFS .... Border-Fault System [*Geology*]
BFS .... Brute Force [*Unregulated*] Supply   (IEEE)
BFS .... Bulletin. Faculte des Lettres de Strasbourg [*A publication*]
BFS .... Bundesamt fur Statistik [*Federal Statistical Office*] [*Information service or system*]   (IID)
BFS .... Bureau of Family Services [*of SSA*]
BFS .... Bureau of Flight Standards   (KSC)
BFS .... Saul [*B. F.*] Real Estate Investment Trust [*NYSE symbol*]   (SPSG)
BFSA .... Behaviorists for Social Action   (EA)
BFSc .... Bachelor of Fisheries Science
BFSC .... Battlefield Functional System Concept   (MCD)
BFSC .... Benjamin Franklin Stamp Club   (EA)
BF Set .... British Field [*Wireless*] Set [*British military*]   (DMA)
BFSGA ...... Bulletin. Federation des Societes de Gynecologie et d'Obstetrique de Langue Francaise [*A publication*]
BFSH .... Bovine Follicle-Stimulating Hormone [*Biochemistry*]
BFSI .... BFS Bankorp, Inc. [*NASDAQ symbol*]   (NQ)
BFSJ .... Fort St. John Public Library, British Columbia [*Library symbol*] [*National Library of Canada*]   (NLC)
BFSJA ...... Fort St. James Public Library, British Columbia [*Library symbol*] [*National Library of Canada*]   (NLC)
BFSJHS .... Fort St. James National Historic Site [*Parc Historique National Fort St.-James*], British Columbia [*Library symbol*] [*National Library of Canada*]   (NLC)
BFSL .... Burma Five Star Line   (DS)
BFSLYC .... British Federation of Sand and Land Yacht Clubs
BFSO .... Base Fuels Supply Officer [*Air Force*]   (AFM)
BFSP .... Best Fixed-Sample Procedure [*Statistics*]
BFSP .... British Foreign and State Papers [*A publication*]   (DLA)
BFSPHP.... Fort Steele Provincial Historic Park, British Columbia [*Library symbol*] [*National Library of Canada*]   (NLC)
BFSS .... British Field Sports Society
BFSW .... Buffered Filtered Seawater
BFT .... Bachelor of Foreign Trade
BFT .... Bank for Foreign Trade of the USSR
BFT .... Basic Fitness Test [*British military*]   (DMA)
BFT .... Batch Fabrication Technique
BFT .... Beaufort [*South Carolina*] [*Airport symbol*]   (OAG)
BFT .... Biofeedback Training [*Physiology*]
BFT .... Bizarre Fantasy Tales [*A publication*]
BFT .... Bulgarian Foreign Trade [*A publication*]
BFT .... Bureau of Foreign Trade [*Philippines*]   (DS)
BFT .... Cleveland, OH [*Location identifier*] [*FAA*]   (FAAL)
BFTA .... Bulk Fuel Tank Assembly   (MCD)
BFTADA ... Bulletin. Fruit Tree Research Station. Series E [*Akitsu*] [*A publication*]
BFTB .... Better Fabrics Test Bureau
BFTD .... Battalion Field Training Days   (MCD)
BFTh .... Beitraege zur Foerderung Christlicher Theologie [*Guetersloh*] [*A publication*]
BFTM .... Ballistic Flight Test Missile   (MCD)
BFTMB ..... Bundesministerium fuer Forschung und Technologie. Mitteilungen [*A publication*]
BFTP .... Bailment Flight Test Program
BFTPA ...... British Film and Television Producers' Association
BFTRA ...... Bois et Forets des Tropiques [*A publication*]
BFTS .... Bomber Fighter Training System   (MCD)
BFTSC .... Brassboard Fault Tolerant Spaceborne Computer   (MCD)
BFTSS .... Bohemian Free Thinking School Society   (EA)
BFTT .... British Federation of Textile Technicians   (DCTA)
BFTV .... Birdfinder Corp. [*Sarasota, FL*] [*NASDAQ symbol*]   (NQ)
BFU .... Benjamin Franklin University [*Washington, DC*]
BFU .... Boletin de Filologia. Instituto de Estudios Superiores del Uruguay [*A publication*]
BFU .... Burst-Forming Unit
BFU .... Franc [*Monetary unit*] [*Burundi*]
BFUA........ Banking, Finance, and Urban Affairs   (DLA)
BFUCH ..... Boletin de Filologia. Instituto de Filologia. Universidade de Chile [*A publication*]
BFUe.......... Burst-Forming Unit erythroid [*Hematology*]
BFUP......... Board of Fire Underwriters of the Pacific [*Later, ISO*]
BFUSA ...... Basketball Federation of the United States of America [*Defunct*]
BFUSA ...... Beach Front USA [*An association*]   (EA)
BFUW .... British Federation of University Women
BFV........... Ballast Flood Valve
BFV........... Bradley Fighting Vehicle [*Army*]

BfV .... Bundesamt fuer Verfassungsschutz [*Federal Office for the Protection of the Constitution*] [*West German counterintelligence agency*]
BFV............ Clinton, OK [*Location identifier*] [*FAA*]   (FAAL)
BFVA .... Bradley Fighting Vehicle Armament [*Army*]   (RDA)
BFVMTL... Baseline Flight Vehicle Mission Time Line
BFVS .... Bradley Fighting Vehicle Systems [*Army*]   (RDA)
BFW........... Baw Faw Mountain [*Washington*] [*Seismograph station code, US Geological Survey*]   (SEIS)
BFW........... Bibles for the World   (EA)
BFW........... Boiler Feed Water [*Technical drawings*]
BFW........... Bread for the World   (EA)
BfW........... Buero fuer Wirtschaftsfragen [*Office of Economic Affairs*] [*German*]
BFWTT ..... Boilerwater/Feedwater Test and Treatment
BFX........... Bafoussam [*Cameroon*] [*Airport symbol*]   (OAG)
BFX........... Buffton Corp. [*AMEX symbol*]   (SPSG)
BFX........... Overseas Business Reports [*A publication*]
BFXC........ BFI Communications [*NASDAQ symbol*]   (NQ)
BFY........... Budget Fiscal Year
BFY........... Library and Resource Collection, Yoho National Park, Field, British Columbia [*Library symbol*] [*National Library of Canada*]   (NLC)
BFZ........... Branch of Fall Zero
BFZ........... Huntsville, AL [*Location identifier*] [*FAA*]   (FAAL)
BG .... [*The*] Babylonian Genesis [*A publication*]   (BJA)
BG .... Bacillus globigii [*Biological warfare with bacteria*]
BG .... Back Gear [*Technical drawings*]
BG .... Background [*Low-priority processing*] [*Data processing*]
BG .... Bag
bg............. Bangladesh [*MARC country of publication code*] [*Library of Congress*]   (LCCP)
BG .... Bangladesh Biman [*ICAO designator*]   (FAAC)
B of G .... Bank of Ghana
BG .... Barge
B & G .... Barton & Guestier [*Wine*]
BG .... Basal Groove
BG .... Battle Group
BG .... Bay Gelding [*Horse*]
BG .... Beach Group
BG .... Bearing
BG .... Bearing Pennant [*Navy*] [*British*]
BG .... Before Girls [*i.e., before women became part of armed forces*] [*Military*]
BG .... Before Goetz [*A reference to "vigilante" Bernhard Goetz, who shot four youths on a New York subway in 1984 after allegedly being threatened by them*] [*See also AG*]
BG .... Being
BG .... Belastinggids [*A publication*]
BG .... [*David*] Ben-Gurion [*First prime minister of Israel*]   (BJA)
B-G........... Bender-Gestalt Test [*Psychology*]
BG .... Benny Goodman [*Clarinetist*]
BG .... Benzylideneglucose [*Biochemistry*]
BG .... Berufungsgericht [*Court of Appeal*] [*German*]   (ILCA)
BG .... Beta-Gamma
BG .... Bevel Gear
BG .... Bicolor Guaiac [*Test*] [*Medicine*]
BG .... Big
BG .... Bijdragen tot de Geschiedenis [*A publication*]
BG .... Billing Group [*Telecommunications*]   (TEL)
BG .... Binders' Guild   (EA)
BG .... Birmingham Gauge
BG .... Black Gelding [*Horse racing*]   (ROG)
BG .... Black Giant Mines Ltd. [*Vancouver Stock Exchange symbol*]
BG .... Blast Gauge   (MUGU)
B/G........... Blood/Gas [*Clinical chemistry*]
BG .... Blood Glucose [*Medicine*]
BG .... Blood Group   (ADA)
BG .... Blood and Guts [*Code name used to refer to Oliver North, National Security Council aide during Reagan administration*]
BG .... Blue Guitar [*A publication*]
BG .... Bluegill [*Ichthyology*]
BG .... Bluish Green
BG .... Board of Governors
BG .... Board of Guardians [*British*]   (ROG)
BG .... Body Guard [*Special Air Service*] [*British*]
Bg............. Bogen [*Bow*] [*Music*]
BG .... Bogoslovski Glasnik [*A publication*]
BG .... Bond International Gold, Inc. [*Toronto Stock Exchange symbol*]
B/G........... Bonded Goods [*International trade*]
BG .... Bone Graft [*Orthopedics*]
BG .... Bordet-Gengou [*Bacillus*] [*Microbiology*]
BG .... Botanic Garden
BG .... Breeding Gain
BG .... Breguet-Dassault [*Societe Anonyme des Ateliers d'Aviation Louis Breguet*] [*France*] [*ICAO aircraft manufacturer identifier*]   (ICAO)
BG .... Bren Gun [*or Gunner*] [*British military*]   (DMA)
BG .... Brig [*Ship*]   (ROG)

BG............	Brigade of Gurkhas [*British military*] (DMA)
BG............	Brigadier General
BG............	Brilliant Green [*An indicator*] [*Chemistry*]
BG............	British Gauge [*Metal industry*]
BG............	British Grenadiers
BG............	British Guiana
BG............	British Guiana Law Reports [*A publication*] (DLA)
BG............	Brown Group, Inc. [*NYSE symbol*] (SPSG)
B & G.......	Brownlow and Goldesborough's Nisi Prius Reports [*1569-1624*] [*England*] [*A publication*] (DLA)
BG............	Buccogingival [*Dentistry*]
BG............	Bulgaria [*ANSI two-letter standard code*] (CNC)
BG............	Bundesgericht [*Federal Supreme Court*] [*German*] (DLA)
BG............	Bundesgesetz [*Federal Act or Statute*] [*German*] (ILCA)
BG............	Bungaku [*A publication*]
BG............	Burg
BG............	Butylene Glycol [*Organic chemistry*]
BG............	Buying [*Rate*] [*Value of the English pound*]
BGA.........	American Belted Galloway Cattle Breeders' Association [*Later, BGS*] (EA)
BGA.........	Barre Granite Association (EA)
BGA.........	Behavior Genetics Association (EA)
BGA.........	Bernard Geis Associates [*Publisher*] [*Obsolete*]
BGA.........	Better Government Association (EA)
BGA.........	Blood Gas Analyzer [*Physiology*]
BGA.........	Blue-Green Algae [*Water purification*]
BGA.........	Brigade Resources, Inc. [*Vancouver Stock Exchange symbol*]
BGA.........	British Gliding Association (MCD)
BGA.........	Bucaramanga [*Colombia*] [*Airport symbol*] (OAG)
BGA.........	Bundesgesundheitsamt [*Database producer*]
BGAD.......	Bluegrass Army Depot
BGAL.......	Bengal Oil & Gas Co. [*NASDAQ symbol*] (NQ)
BGal........	Betagalactoside
BGAL.......	British Guiana Airways Ltd. [*A national airline*]
BGall.......	Bellum Gallicum [*of Caesar*] [*Classical studies*] (OCD)
BGAM......	Angmagssalik [*Greenland*] [*ICAO location identifier*] (ICLI)
BGAOAT ..	Breviora Geologica Asturica [*A publication*]
BGAS.......	Angissoq [*Greenland*] [*ICAO location identifier*] (ICLI)
BGAS.......	Berkshire Gas Co. [*NASDAQ symbol*] (NQ)
BGAS.......	Bulolo Goldfields Aeroplane Service [*Australia*]
BGAT.......	Aputiteq [*Greenland*] [*ICAO location identifier*] (ICLI)
BGB.........	Bat Groups of Britain (EAIO)
BGB.........	Big Ben Resources, Inc. [*Vancouver Stock Exchange symbol*]
BGB.........	[*Governor's*] Bodyguard, Bengal [*British military*] (DMA)
BGB.........	Booksellers of Great Britain
BGB.........	Booue [*Gabon*] [*Airport symbol*] (OAG)
BGB.........	Brilliant Green Bile [*Microorganism growth medium*]
BGB.........	Bubble-Gum Brigade [*Preteens*]
BGB.........	Buergerliches Gesetzbuch [*German Civil Code*] (DLA)
BGB.........	Builders of Greater Britain [*A publication*]
BGB.........	Bulletin. Association Guillaume Bude [*A publication*]
BGB.........	Bulletin. Groupe Belge des Auditeurs. Academie de Droit International de La Haye [*A publication*]
BGBA.......	Boys' and Girls' Brigades of America (EA)
BGBH.......	Bijdragen voor de Geschiedenis van het Bisdom van Haarlem [*A publication*]
BGBL.......	Bundesgesetzblatt [*Federal Law Gazette*] [*A publication*] (ILCA)
BGBR.......	Big Bear, Inc. [*NASDAQ symbol*] (NQ)
BGBT.......	Big Bite, Inc. [*NASDAQ symbol*] (NQ)
BGBW......	Narssarssuaq [*Greenland*] [*ICAO location identifier*] (ICLI)
BGBWD....	Blaetter fuer Grundstuecks, Bau-, und Wohnungsrecht [*A publication*]
BGC.........	Bailiff Grand Cross
BGC.........	Bank Giro Credit [*British*] (DCTA)
BGC.........	Bay State Gas Company [*NYSE symbol*] (SPSG)
BGC.........	Black Gold Cooperative Library System, Ventura, CA [*OCLC symbol*] (OCLC)
BGC.........	Blood Group Class
BGC.........	Board of Green Cloth (ROG)
BGC.........	Boat Group Commander [*Navy*] (NVT)
BGC.........	Bolinger Road [*California*] [*Seismograph station code, US Geological Survey*] (SEIS)
BGC.........	Braganca [*Portugal*] [*Airport symbol*] (OAG)
BGC.........	Bren Gun Carrier [*British military*] (DMA)
BGC.........	British Gas Corporation
BGCC.......	Bowling Green College of Commerce [*Later, a division of Western Kentucky State College*]
BG/CDR....	Battle Group Commander (MCD)
BGCG.......	Battery Guidance Command Group
BGCH.......	Christianshab [*Greenland*] [*ICAO location identifier*] (ICLI)
BGCO.......	Constable Point [*Greenland*] [*ICAO location identifier*] (ICLI)
BGCPS.....	British Gas Corporation Pension Scheme
BGCTH	Bulletin. Section de Geographie. Comite des Travaux Historiques et Scientifiques [*A publication*]
BGD.........	Bangladesh [*ANSI three-letter standard code*] (CNC)
BGD.........	BGM Diversified Energy, Inc. [*Vancouver Stock Exchange symbol*]
BGD.........	Billion Gallons per Day
BGD.........	Bogdanovka [*USSR*] [*Seismograph station code, US Geological Survey*] [*Closed*] (SEIS)

BGD.........	Borger, TX [*Location identifier*] [*FAA*] (FAAL)
BGD.........	Bulolo Gold Dredging [*Australia*]
BGD.........	Golden and District Museum, Golden, British Columbia [*Library symbol*] [*National Library of Canada*] (NLC)
BGDA......	Bluegrass Depot Activity [*Army*] (AABC)
BGDB......	Daneborg [*Greenland*] [*ICAO location identifier*] (ICLI)
BGDE......	Brigade
BGDH......	Danmarkshavn [*Greenland*] [*ICAO location identifier*] (ICLI)
BGDN......	Butylene Glycol Dinitrate [*Organic chemistry*]
BGDSL......	Beitraege zur Geschichte der Deutschen Sprache und Literatur [*Halle*] [*A publication*]
BGDSLH...	Beitraege zur Geschichte der Deutschen Sprache und Literatur (Halle) [*A publication*]
BGDSLT ...	Beitraege zur Geschichte der Deutschen Sprache und Literatur (Tuebingen) [*A publication*]
BGDU.......	Dundas [*Greenland*] [*ICAO location identifier*] (ICLI)
BGE.........	Bachelor of Geological Engineering
BGE.........	Bainbridge, GA [*Location identifier*] [*FAA*] (FAAL)
BGE.........	Baltimore Gas & Electric Co. [*NYSE symbol*] (SPSG)
BGE.........	Barge (ROG)
BGE.........	Booker Gold Explorations [*Vancouver Stock Exchange symbol*]
BGE.........	Bull General Electric
BGE.........	Butyl Glycidyl Ether [*Organic chemistry*]
BGE.........	Entscheidungen des Schweizerischen Bundesgerichtes [*Switzerland*] (DLA)
BGEA.......	Bill Glass Evangelistic Association (EA)
BGEA.......	Billy Graham Evangelistic Association (EA)
B Ge E......	Bachelor of Geological Engineering
B Ge Eng...	Bachelor of Geological Engineering
BGEM......	Egedesminde [*Greenland*] [*ICAO location identifier*] (ICLI)
BGEN......	Biogen, Inc. [*NASDAQ symbol*] (NQ)
BGEN......	Brigadier General
BGENA.....	Biologie et Gastro-Enterologie [*A publication*]
B Gen Ed....	Bachelor of General Education
BGES........	Board of Governors of the European Schools [*Brussels, Belgium*] (EAIO)
BGF.........	Bangui [*Central African Republic*] [*Airport symbol*] (OAG)
BGF.........	Bobby Goldsmith Foundation [*Australia*]
B & GF.....	Bombing and Gunnery Flight [*British military*] (DMA)
BGF.........	Grand Forks Public Library, British Columbia [*Library symbol*] [*National Library of Canada*] (NLC)
BGF.........	Winchester, TN [*Location identifier*] [*FAA*] (FAAL)
BGFBM.....	Boundary Museum, Grand Forks, British Columbia [*Library symbol*] [*National Library of Canada*] (NLC)
BGFC.......	Bobby Goldsboro Fan Club (EA)
BGFD.......	Frederiksdal [*Greenland*] [*ICAO location identifier*] (ICLI)
BGFE........	Boston Grain and Flour Exchange (EA)
BGFH.......	Frederikshab [*Greenland*] [*ICAO location identifier*] (ICLI)
BGFMA.....	Bridge Grid Flooring Manufacturers Association (EA)
BGFND.....	Bulletin. Groupe Francais d'Humidimetrie Neutronique [*A publication*]
BGFO.......	Bureau of Government Financial Operations [*Department of Treasury*]
BGFRS......	Board of Governors, Federal Reserve System
BGG.........	Black Granite Gauge
BGG.........	Booster Gas Generator
BGG.........	Bovine Gamma Globulin [*Immunology*]
BGG.........	Briggs & Stratton Corp. [*NYSE symbol*] (SPSG)
BGG.........	Burg Eltz [*Federal Republic of Germany*] [*Seismograph station code, US Geological Survey*] (SEIS)
BGGD......	Gronnedal [*Greenland*] [*ICAO location identifier*] (ICLI)
BGGH......	Godthab [*Greenland*] [*ICAO location identifier*] (ICLI)
BGGL.......	Sondrestrom [*Greenland*] [*ICAO location identifier*] (ICLI)
BGGN......	Godhavn [*Greenland*] [*ICAO location identifier*] (ICLI)
BGGPB.....	Biofeedback and Self-Regulation [*A publication*]
BGGUA....	Bulletin. Groenlands Geologiske Undersoegelse [*A publication*]
BGH.........	Bear Gulch [*California*] [*Seismograph station code, US Geological Survey*] (SEIS)
BGH.........	Beleggers Belangen [*A publication*]
BGH.........	Borough (ROG)
BGH.........	Bovine Growth Hormone [*Endocrinology*]
BGH.........	British General Hospital
BGH.........	Bundesgerichtshof [*Federal Supreme Court*] [*German*] (DLA)
BGHB.......	Bijdragen tot de Geschiedenis Bijzonderlijk van het Aloude Hertogdom Brabant [*A publication*]
BGHB.......	Holsteinsborg [*Greenland*] [*ICAO location identifier*] (ICLI)
BGHD......	Bulletin de Geographie Historique et Descriptive [*A publication*]
BGHS........	Squamish Valley Museum, Garibaldi Highlands, British Columbia [*Library symbol*] [*National Library of Canada*] (NLC)
BGHSt.......	Entscheidungen des Bundesgerichtshof in Strafsachen [*Reports of the Federal Supreme Court in Criminal Matters*] [*A publication*] (ILCA)
BGHZ.......	Entscheidungen des Bundesgerichtshof in Zivilsachen [*Reports of the Federal Supreme Court in civil cases*] [*A publication*] (ILCA)
BGI...........	Barbados [*Airport symbol*] (OAG)
BGI...........	Beaver Resources, Inc. [*Toronto Stock Exchange symbol*] [*Vancouver Stock Exchange symbol*]
BGI...........	Borland Graphics Interface [*Borland International*] (BYTE)

BGI .... British Gas International
BGI .... Gibsons Public Library, British Columbia [*Library symbol*] [*National Library of Canada*] (NLC)
BGIFH .... Boys and Girls International Floor Hockey (EA)
BGIGA .... Biuletyn Glownego Instytutu Gornictwa [*A publication*]
BGIPM .... Ephinstone Pioneer Museum, Gibsons, British Columbia [*Library symbol*] [*National Library of Canada*] (NLC)
BGIRA .... British Glass Industry Research Association [*Research center*] (IRC)
BGIS .... Isortoq [*Greenland*] [*ICAO location identifier*] (ICLI)
BGIT .... Ivigtut [*Greenland*] [*ICAO location identifier*] (ICLI)
BGJ .... Borgarfjordur [*Iceland*] [*Airport symbol*] (OAG)
BGJH .... Julianehab [*Greenland*] [*ICAO location identifier*] (ICLI)
BGJN .... Jakobshavn [*Greenland*] [*ICAO location identifier*] (ICLI)
BGK .... Bhatnagar-Gross-Krook [*Equation*]
BGKD .... Kap Dan [*Greenland*] [*ICAO location identifier*] (ICLI)
BGKK .... Kulusuk [*Greenland*] [*ICAO location identifier*] (ICLI)
BGKM .... Kungmiut [*Greenland*] [*ICAO location identifier*] (ICLI)
BGKT .... Kap Tobin [*Greenland*] [*ICAO location identifier*] (ICLI)
BGL .... Bachelor of General Laws (DLA)
BGL .... Baglung [*Nepal*] [*Airport symbol*] (OAG)
BGL .... Betriebsgewerkschaftsleitung [*Factory Union Headquarters*] [*Germany*]
BGL .... Brooke Group Ltd. [*NYSE symbol*] (SPSG)
BGLA .... British Growers' Look Ahead International Exhibition (ITD)
BGLA .... Business Group for Latin America [*Later, COA*]
BGLE .... Bangladesh Development Studies [*A publication*]
BGLE .... British Graham Land Expedition [*1934-37*]
BGLR .... British Guiana Law Reports (Old and New Series) [*A publication*] (DLA)
BGLR .... Bugler
BGLRK .... Beitraege zur Geschichte und Lehre der Reformierten Kirche [*Neukirchen*] [*A publication*]
BGLS .... Bausteine zur Geschichte der Literatur bei den Slaven [*A publication*]
BGLT .... Battle Group Landing Team
BGLY .... Begley Co. [*NASDAQ symbol*] (NQ)
BGM .... Basegram [*Navy*]
BGM .... Benelux Group on Mortality (EAIO)
BGM .... Biennial General Meeting
BGM .... Binghamton [*New York*] [*Airport symbol*] (OAG)
BGM .... British Gallantry Medal
BGM .... Buglemaster [*Navy*]
BGM .... Greenwood Museum, British Columbia [*Library symbol*] [*National Library of Canada*] (NLC)
BGMA .... British Gear Manufacturers Association (MCD)
BGMA .... British Guiana Militia Artillery [*British military*] (DMA)
381 BGMA ... 381st Bomb Group Memorial Association (EA)
BGMC .... BOCES [*Boards of Cooperative Educational Services*] Geneseo Migrant Center (EA)
BGMGAV ... Background to Migraine. Migraine Symposium [*A publication*]
BGMI .... Biography and Genealogy Master Index [*A publication*]
BGMIA .... Boletin Geologico y Minero [*A publication*]
BGMM .... Marmorilik [*Greenland*] [*ICAO location identifier*] (ICLI)
BGMRAO ... Balance General Mobilization Reserve Acquisition Objective [*DoD*]
BGMSTR .. Buglemaster
BGMTS ..... Bradley Gunnery and Missile Target System [*Army*] (INF)
BGMV .... Bean Golden Mosaic Virus
BGMV .... Mesters Vig [*Greenland*] [*ICAO location identifier*] (ICLI)
BGN .... Begin (FAAC)
BGN .... Berglynn Resources [*Vancouver Stock Exchange symbol*]
BGN .... Big Creek [*Nevada*] [*Seismograph station code, US Geological Survey*] [*Closed*] (SEIS)
BGN .... Bijdragen voor de Geschiedenis der Nederlanden [*A publication*]
BGN .... Board on Geographic Names [*Defense Mapping Agency*] [*Washington, DC*]
BGN .... Branchioganglionic Neuron [*Neurology*]
BGN .... Brigantine [*Ship*]
BGN .... North Platte, NE [*Location identifier*] [*FAA*] (FAAL)
BGNN .... Nanortalik [*Greenland*] [*ICAO location identifier*] (ICLI)
BGNS .... Narssaq [*Greenland*] [*ICAO location identifier*] (ICLI)
BGNSA .... Berufsgenossenschaft [*A publication*]
BGO .... Bema Gold Ltd. [*Toronto Stock Exchange symbol*] [*Vancouver Stock Exchange symbol*]
BGO .... Bergen [*Norway*] [*Airport symbol*] (OAG)
BGO .... Bismuth Germanate [*Inorganic chemistry*]
BGO .... Bowling Green [*Ohio*] [*Seismograph station code, US Geological Survey*] (SEIS)
BGOC .... Black Giant Oil Company [*NASDAQ symbol*] (NQ)
BGOS .... Orssuiorssuaq [*Greenland*] [*ICAO location identifier*] (ICLI)
BGP .... Bagra [*Pakistan*] [*Seismograph station code, US Geological Survey*] (SEIS)
BGP .... Barrier, Grease Proof (MSA)
BGP .... Barrington Properties Ltd. [*Toronto Stock Exchange symbol*] [*Vancouver Stock Exchange symbol*]
B of GP ...... Board of General Purposes [*Freemasonry*]
BGPA .... Bateria General de Preubas de Aptitud [*General Aptitude Test Battery*] [*Spanish*]

BGPC .... Prins Christian Sund [*Greenland*] [*ICAO location identifier*] (ICLI)
BGPDC ...... Brouwer General Perturbations Differential Correction Program (MCD)
BGPH .... Bishop Graphics, Inc. [*NASDAQ symbol*] (NQ)
Bg Pis .... [*Johannes*] Burgundio Pisanus [*Deceased, 1194*] [*Authority cited in pre-1607 legal work*] (DSA)
BGPMN .... Bijdragen voor de Geschiedenis van de Provincie der Minderbroeders in de Nederlanden [*A publication*]
BGPP .... Beneficiary Government Production Program
BGPTM ..... Beiträge zur Geschichte der Philosophie und Theologie des Mittelalters [*A publication*]
BGPW .... Bare Gold-Plated Wire
BGQ .... Big Lake, AK [*Location identifier*] [*FAA*] (FAAL)
BGQS .... Qutdligssat [*Greenland*] [*ICAO location identifier*] (ICLI)
BGR .... Bailey, G. R., Escanaba MI [*STAC*]
BGR .... Bangor [*Maine*] [*Airport symbol*] (OAG)
BGR .... Barry Gibb Record (EA)
BGR .... Basal Granule
BGR .... Bombing and Gunnery Range
BGR .... British Gas Region
BGR .... Bulgaria [*ANSI three-letter standard code*] (CNC)
BGR .... Bundesanstalt fuer Geowissenschaften und Rohstoffe [*Federal Institute for Geosciences and Natural Resources*] [*Federal Republic of Germany*] [*Information service or system*] (IID)
BGR .... Granisle Public Library, British Columbia [*Library symbol*] [*National Library of Canada*] (NLC)
17th BGRA ... 17th Bomb Group Reunion Association (EA)
BGRE .... Greenwood Public Library, British Columbia [*Library symbol*] [*National Library of Canada*] (NLC)
BGRG .... British Geomorphological Research Group
BGRM .... Groundbirch Museum, British Columbia [*Library symbol*] [*National Library of Canada*] (NLC)
BGRNS ...... Nootka Sound Historical Society, Gold River, British Columbia [*Library symbol*] [*National Library of Canada*] (NLC)
BGROD ...... Bundesgesetzblatt fuer die Republik Oesterreich [*A publication*]
B Group Seine Marne ... Bulletin. Groupement Archeologique de Seine-Et-Marne [*A publication*]
BGRR .... Brookhaven Graphite Research Reactor
BGRS .... Bungaku Ronshu [*Studies on Literature*] [*A publication*]
BGRS .... Bureau of Governmental Research and Service [*University of Oregon*] [*Research center*] (RCD)
BGRS .... Ravns Storo [*Greenland*] [*ICAO location identifier*] (ICLI)
BGRSA ...... Bulletin. Groupement International pour la Recherche Scientifique en Stomatologie [*A publication*]
BGRV .... Boost Glide Reentry Vehicle [*Air Force*]
BGS .... Bachelor of General Studies
BGS .... Backup Gimbal Servo
BGS .... Backup Guidance System [*NASA*]
BGS .... Bags
BGS .... Bailly Generating Station [*Nuclear energy*] (NRCH)
BGS .... Belted Galloway Society (EA)
BGS .... Beta Gamma Sigma
BGS .... Big Spring, TX [*Location identifier*] [*FAA*] (FAAL)
BGS .... Blood Group Substances [*Hematology*]
BGS .... Bluegrass Petroleum, Inc. [*Vancouver Stock Exchange symbol*]
BGS .... Boeing Ground Support (KSC)
BGS .... Bombing and Gunnery School [*British*]
BGS .... Brigadier, General Staff [*Army*] [*British*]
BGS .... British Gas Corp. [*Toronto Stock Exchange symbol*]
BGS .... British Geological Survey
BGS .... British Geotechnical Society
BGS .... British Geriatrics Society
BGS .... British Glaciological Society (NOAA)
BGS .... British Goat Society
BGS .... British Grassland Society
BGS .... Brothers of the Good Shepherd [*Roman Catholic religious order*]
BGS .... Bundesgrenzschutz [*Military*] [*West Germany*] (NATG)
BGS .... Business Grant Services [*Information service or system*]
BGS .... Gulf Islands Secondary School, Ganges, British Columbia [*Library symbol*] [*Library network*] (NLC)
BGSA .... British Gas Staff Association [*A union*]
BGSA .... Bulletin. Geological Society of America [*A publication*]
BGSC .... Scoresbysund [*Greenland*] [*ICAO location identifier*] (ICLI)
BGSCA ...... Buick GS [*Gran Sport*] Club of America (EA)
BGSF .... Sondre Stromfjord [*Greenland*] [*ICAO location identifier*] (ICLI)
BGSG .... Sermiligaq [*Greenland*] [*ICAO location identifier*] (ICLI)
BGSGB ...... Bibliotheca Gastroenterologica [*A publication*]
BGSI .... Mary Hawkins Memorial Library, Saltspring Island Public Library, Ganges, British Columbia [*Library symbol*] [*National Library of Canada*] (NLC)
BGSPD .... Bulgarsko Geofizichno Spisanie [*A publication*]
BGSPS .... British Gas Staff Pension Scheme
BGSR .... British Gas PLC American Depository Receipts [*Toronto Stock Exchange symbol*]
BGSS .... Battalion Ground Surveillance Section [*Army*] (AABC)
BGSS .... BGS Systems, Inc. [*NASDAQ symbol*] (NQ)

BGSSE....... Beitraege zur Geschichte von Stadt und Stift Essen [*A publication*]
BGST........ Bradley Gunnery Skills Test [*Army*]   (INF)
BGST........ Sukkertoppen [*Greenland*] [*ICAO location identifier*]   (ICLI)
BGSTB...... Biologist [*Champaign, IL*] [*A publication*]
BGSU....... Bowling Green State University [*Ohio*]
BGT.......... Bender-Gestalt Test [*Psychology*]
BGT.......... Bight   (ROG)
BGT.......... Blackstone Strategic Term Trust [*NYSE symbol*]   (SPSG)
BGT.......... Bodensee-Geraetetechnik   (MCD)
BGT.......... Bought   (ROG)
BGT.......... Bungarotoxin [*Also, BTX, BuTx*] [*Biochemistry*]
BGTB........ Brazilian Government Trade Bureau   (EA)
BGTD........ Beigetretene Teile Deutschlands [*Newly Adhered Parts of Germany*] [*Name given to former East German territory after unification*]   (ECON)
BGTL........ Thule Air Base [*Greenland*] [*ICAO location identifier*]   (ICLI)
BGTM....... Tingmiarmiut [*Greenland*] [*ICAO location identifier*]   (ICLI)
BGTN....... Tiniteqilaq [*Greenland*] [*ICAO location identifier*]   (ICLI)
BGTO....... Bonaire Government Tourist Office   (EA)
BGTS....... British Geotechnical Society
BGU.......... Ben-Gurion University   (BJA)
BGU.......... Berliner Griechische Urkunden [*A publication*]   (OCD)
BGU.......... Bluegrass Unlimited [*A publication*]
BGU.......... Bowling Green State University, Bowling Green, OH [*OCLC symbol*]   (OCLC)
BGU.......... Bridge Resources Ltd. [*Vancouver Stock Exchange symbol*]
BGU.......... British Guiana
BGUM....... Unanak [*Greenland*] [*ICAO location identifier*]   (ICLI)
BGUP....... Upernavik [*Greenland*] [*ICAO location identifier*]   (ICLI)
BGV.......... Bac-Giang [*Vietnam*] [*Seismograph station code, US Geological Survey*]   (SEIS)
BGVF........ British Guiana Volunteer Force [*British military*]   (DMA)
BGW......... Baghdad [*Iraq*] [*Airport symbol*]   (OAG)
BGW......... Battlefield Guided Weapon   (MCD)
BGWK....... Boekenschouw voor Godsdienst, Wetenschap en Kunst [*A publication*]
BGWVAO ... George Washington University. Bulletin [*A publication*]
BGX.......... Bage [*Brazil*] [*Airport symbol*]   (OAG)
BGX.......... Biologix (BC) Ltd. [*Vancouver Stock Exchange symbol*]
BGY.......... Bergamo [*Italy*] [*Airport symbol*]   (OAG)
BGYF........ Bright Greenish Yellow Fluorescence [*A fungal metabolite property*]
BGZ.......... Brasil Gold Resources [*Vancouver Stock Exchange symbol*]
BGZ.......... Kansas City, KS [*Location identifier*] [*FAA*]   (FAAL)
BH............. Bachelor of Hamburgerology [*McDonald's Corp. Hamburger University*]
BH............. Bachelor of Hebrew
BH............. Bachelor of Humanics
Bh............. Bachelor's Degree (Honours) [*British*]
BH............. Bahamasair Holding Ltd. [*Bahamas*] [*ICAO designator*]   (FAAC)
BH............. Bahrain [*ANSI two-letter standard code*] [*IYRU nationality code*]   (CNC)
B of H........ Band of Hope [*British*]
BH............. Bank Holiday
BH............. Barker-Henderson [*Theory*] [*Chemical physics*]
B/H............ Base-Height Ratio
BH............. Base Hospital [*Military*]
BH............. Baskets or Hampers [*Freight*]
BH............. Bath & Hammondsport Railroad Co. [*AAR code*]
BH............. Beach   (ADA)
BH............. Bear Hills Native Voice [*Hobbema, Alberta*] [*A publication*]
B & H........ Becker & Hayes, Inc. [*Information service or system*]   (IID)
BH............. Beer House   (ROG)
BH............. Bell & Howell Co.
BH............. Beni Hasan [*Egyptology*]   (ROG)
BH............. Benjamin Harrison [*US president, 1833-1901*]
B & H........ Benson & Hedges   (ADA)
bh .... Benzhydryl [*As substituent on nucleoside*] [*Biochemistry*]
BH............. Biblia Hebraica   (BJA)
BH............. Biblical Hebrew   (BJA)
BH............. Bibliografia Hispanica [*A publication*]
BH............. Bibliographia Huntiana [*Computer-based bibliography*]
BH............. Bibliotheque Historique [*A publication*]
BH............. Bill of Health
BH............. Binary to Hexadecimal   (BUR)
BH............. Birthday Honours [*Titles conferred on the sovereign's birthday*] [*British*]
BH............. Black Hawk [*Military*]   (MCD)
BH............. Blasthole
B & H........ Blatchford and Howland's United States District Court Reports [*A publication*]   (DLA)
BH............. Block Handler [*Data processing*]
BH............. Blockhouse [*NASA*]   (KSC)
BH............. Bloody Hell [*British slang*]
BH............. Blue Hills Power Plant [*Nuclear energy*]   (NRCH)
B of H........ Board of Health
BH............. Boiler House [*Technical drawings*]
BH............. Books for the Heart [*A publication*]
BH............. Boosey & Hawkes [*Record label*] [*Great Britain, USA*]

B & H........ Boosey & Hawkes [*Record label*] [*Great Britain, USA*]   (ADA)
B/H............ Bordeaux-Hamburg Inclusive [*Shipping*]
BH............. Borehole
BH............. Both Hands [*Psychometrics*]
BH............. Brain Hormone [*Endocrinology*]
BH............. Branch Head
BH............. Breath-Hold Diving
B & H........ Breitkopf & Haertel [*Music*]
BH............. Brigade Headquarters [*Army*]
BH............. Brinell Hardness Number [*Also, BHN, BHNo, HB*]
bh............. British Honduras [*MARC country of publication code*] [*Library of Congress*]   (LCCP)
BH............. British Honduras
BH............. British Hovercraft
BH............. Brookhaven Office [*AEC*]
BH............. Buestenhalter [*Brassiere*] [*German slang*]
BH............. Bulk Head
BH............. Bulletin Hispanique [*A publication*]
BH............. Bung-Hole [*i.e., cheese*] [*British slang*]
BH............. Buried History: Quarterly Journal of the Australian Institute of Archaeology [*A publication*]   (APTA)
BH............. Business History [*A publication*]
BH............. Flux Density Versus Magnetizing Force [*Symbol*]   (MCD)
BH............. Houston Public Library, British Columbia [*Library symbol*] [*National Library of Canada*]   (NLC)
BH............. Turks & Caicos Airways Ltd. [*ICAO designator*] [*Obsolete*]   (OAG)
1BH........... One-Base Hit [*Baseball*]
2BH........... Two-Base Hit [*Baseball*]
3BH........... Three-Base Hit [*Baseball*]
BH$_4$......... Tetrahydrobiopterin [*Biochemistry*]
B2H2.......... Ball-Burton-Hill-Hatch Plan [*Senate resolution calling for international cooperation in waging war, planning postwar rehabilitation, etc. Introduced after World War II by Senators Joseph Ball, Harold Burton, Lester Hill, and Carl Hatch*]
BHA.......... Bachelor of Hospital Administration
BHA.......... Bahama Resources Ltd. [*Vancouver Stock Exchange symbol*]
BHA.......... Bankcard Holders of America   (EA)
BHA.......... Baptist Hospital Association   (EA)
BHA.......... Base Helix Angle [*NASA*]
BHA.......... Bengal Horse Artillery [*British military*]   (DMA)
BHA.......... Better Hearing Australia [*An association*]   (EAIO)
BHA.......... Bioinstrumentation Harness Assembly
BHA.......... Biscayne Holdings, Inc. A [*AMEX symbol*]   (SPSG)
BHA.......... Blazer Horse Association   (EA)
BHA.......... Bleed Hose Assembly
BHA.......... Bombay Horse Artillery [*British military*]   (DMA)
BHA.......... Brennan & Hargraves, Inc. [*Rocky Hill, CT*] [*FAA designator*]   (FAAC)
BHA.......... British Homeopathic Association
BHA.......... British Humanist Association
BHA.......... British Hypnotherapy Association
BHA.......... Broken Hill [*Kabwe*] [*Zambia*] [*Seismograph station code, US Geological Survey*]   (SEIS)
BHA.......... Bulk Handling Authority [*Australia*]
BHA.......... Bureau of Hearings and Appeals [*Social Security Administration*]
BHA.......... Bus History Association   (EA)
BHA.......... Butylated Hydroxyanisole [*Antioxidant*]
BHA.......... Harvard Divinity School, Cambridge, MA [*OCLC symbol*]   (OCLC)
BHA.......... Hazelton Public Library, British Columbia [*Library symbol*] [*National Library of Canada*]   (NLC)
BHAB........ British Helicopter Advisory Board   (AIA)
BHAD....... Beachhead Air Defense   (MCD)
BHAD....... Black Hills Army Depot
BHAD....... Broach Adapter
BH Adm..... Bachelor of Hospital Administration
BHAG........ BHA Group, Inc. [*Kansas City, MO*] [*NASDAQ symbol*]   (NQ)
BHAG........ Bulletin. Societe d'Histoire et d'Archeologie de Gand [*A publication*]
BHAGA..... Bhagirath [*A publication*]
Bhagirath Irrig Power Q ... Bhagirath. The Irrigation and Power Quarterly [*A publication*]
BHAM....... Beecham Group PLC [*NASDAQ symbol*]   (NQ)
BHAM....... Birmingham [*City, county borough, and university in England*]
B'ham Post ... Birmingham Post [*A publication*]
BHAR........ Bulletin. Section Historique. Academie Roumaine [*A publication*]
Bhar Ma Q ... Bharata Manisha Quarterly [*A publication*]
BHAS........ Burroughs Hospital Administrative System [*Data processing*]   (BUR)
BHAT........ Beta-Blocker Heart Attack Trial [*Cardiology*]
Bhavan's J ... Bhavan's Journal [*A publication*]
BHB.......... Bar Harbor [*Maine*] [*Airport symbol*]   (OAG)
BHB.......... Blue Horizontal Branch
BHB.......... Butropium Bromide [*Pharmacology*]
BHB.......... Nouvelles Economiques de Suisse [*A publication*]
BHBLA...... Behavioral Biology [*A publication*]
B & H Black ... Broom and Hadley's Blackstone [*A publication*]   (DLA)

BHBN........ Butyl(hydroxybutyl)nitrosamine [*Organic chemistry*]
BHBR........ Boat Harbor
BHBSA....... Harvard Business School. Bulletin [*A publication*]
BHC.......... Ballistic Height Correction
BHC.......... Baltimore Hebrew College   (BJA)
BHC.......... Bank Holding Company
BHC.......... Beam-Heated Cathode
BHC.......... Bell Helicopter Company   (MCD)
BHC.......... Benedictine Heights College [*Oklahoma*]
BHC.......... Benzene Hexachloride [*Also, GBH, HCH*] [*Insecticide*]
BHC.......... Better Health Commission [*Australia*]
BHC.......... Better Heating-Cooling Council [*Later, HI*]   (EA)
BHC.......... BHC Communications Class A [*AMEX symbol*]   (SPSG)
BHC.......... Blockhouse Computer [*NASA*]   (KSC)
BHC.......... Body Heat Content
BHC.......... Bombay High Court Reports [*1862-75*] [*India*] [*A publication*]   (DLA)
BHC.......... Borehole Capsule
BHC.......... Borehole Compensated [*Sonic log*]
BHC.......... Born-Haber Cycle [*Physics*]
BHC.......... Boston Hebrew College   (BJA)
BHC.......... British High Commissioner
BHC.......... British Hovercraft Corporation
BHC.......... Brotherhood of the Holy Cross [*Anglican religious community*]
BHC.......... Bullhead City [*Arizona*]/Laughlin [*Nevada*] [*Airport symbol*]   (OAG)
BHC.......... Burst Height Compensator [*Military*]   (CAAL)
BHC.......... Business History Conference   (EA)
BHC.......... Business in Thailand [*A publication*]
BHC.......... Busy Hour Call [*Telecommunications*]   (TEL)
BHC.......... Holy Cross Greek Orthodox School of Theology, Brookline, MA [*OCLC symbol*]   (OCLC)
BHC.......... Journeymen Barbers, Hairdressers, Cosmetologists and Proprietors' International Union of America
BHCA....... Basset Hound Club of America   (EA)
BHCA....... Busy Hour Call Attempts [*Telecommunications*]
BHCDA...... Bureau of Health Care Delivery and Assistance [*Department of Health and Human Services*]
BHCEC...... British Health-Care Export Council   (DS)
BHCFC...... Buddy Holly and the Crickets Fan Club   (EAIO)
BHCNU...... Bis(hydroxycyclohexyl)nitrosourea [*Antineoplastic drug*]
BHCPJ...... Bombay High Court Printed Judgments [*1869-1900*] [*India*] [*A publication*]   (DLA)
BHCR....... Bombay High Court Reports [*1862-75*] [*India*] [*A publication*]   (DLA)
B & H Cr Cas ... Bennett and Heard's Leading Criminal Cases [*England*] [*A publication*]   (DLA)
B & H Crim Cas ... Bennett and Heard's Leading Criminal Cases [*England*] [*A publication*]   (DLA)
BHCT........ Bottom Hole Circulating Temperature [*Oil well borehole*]
BHD.......... BCNU [*Carmustine*], Hydroxyurea, Dacarbazine [*Antineoplastic drug regimen*]
BHD.......... Beachhead   (AFM)
BHD.......... Belfast [*Northern Ireland*] Harbour [*Airport symbol*]   (OAG)
BHD.......... Berhad [*Public Limited Company*] [*Malaysian*]   (FEA)
BHD.......... Beta-Hydroxysteroid Dehydrogenase [*An enzyme*]
BHD.......... Bighorn Development Corp. [*Vancouver Stock Exchange symbol*]
BHD.......... Binary Homing Device
BHD.......... Birkenhead [*British depot code*]
Bhd.......... Brotherhood   (ILCA)
BHD.......... Bulkhead   (AAG)
BHDEA..... Bulletin of the History of Dentistry [*A publication*]
B & H Dig .. Bennett and Heard's Massachusetts Digest [*A publication*]   (DLA)
BHDL....... Bulletin Historique. Diocese de Lyon [*A publication*]
BHDP........ Baltimore Huntington's Disease Project [*Johns Hopkins University*] [*Research center*]   (RCD)
BHDV........ BCNU [*Carmustine*], Hydroxyurea, Dacarbazine, Vincristine [*Antineoplastic drug regimen*]
BHE.......... Bachelor of Household Economics
B He.......... Baltische Hefte [*A publication*]
BHE.......... Barid Hollanda [*A publication*]
BHE.......... Biharmonic Equation
BHE.......... Blenheim [*New Zealand*] [*Airport symbol*]   (OAG)
BHE.......... Bolton-Hunter Reagent-Labeled Eledoisin [*Analytical biochemistry*]
BHE.......... Bureau of Higher Education [*Later, Bureau of Higher and Continuing Education*] [*Office of Education*]
BHEAT..... Bulletin d'Histoire et Exegese de l'Ancien Testament [*Louvain*] [*A publication*]
BH Ec........ Bachelor of Home Economics
BHEC....... British Hospitals Export Council [*Later, BHCEC*]   (DS)
BHED........ Bis(hydroxyethyl)dimerate [*Organic chemistry*]
BHEDC ..... British Hospital Equipment Display Centre   (CB)
B-HEF....... Business-Higher Education Forum [*Washington, DC*]   (EA)
BHEL .... Bharat Heavy Electricals Limited [*India*]
BHEP .... Bis(hydroxyethyl)piperazine [*Organic chemistry*]
B Hesbaye-Condroz ... Bulletin. Cercle Archeologique Hesbaye-Condroz [*A publication*]
BHET........ (Beta-Hydroxyethyl)theophylline [*Biochemistry*]

BHET .... Bis(hydroxyethyl)terephthalate [*Organic chemistry*]
BHET .... Bulletin d'Histoire et Exegese de l'Ancien Testament [*Louvain*] [*A publication*]
BHEW....... Bulletin. Societe pour l'Histoire des Eglises Wallonnes [*A publication*]
BHF.......... Background Heat Flux
BHF.......... Berliner Handels- & Frankfurter Bank [*Berlin & Frankfurt Bank*]
BHF.......... Blues Heaven Foundation   (EA)
BHF.......... Bonner Historische Forschungen [*A publication*]
BHF.......... Business History Foundation [*Defunct*]   (EA)
BHFC .... Bob Hastings Fan Club [*Inactive*]   (EA)
BHFC .... Bob Homan Fan Club   (EA)
BHFC .... Bonnie Hartle Fan Club   (EA)
BHFC .... Boyce and Hart Fan Club   (EA)
BHFC .... Brice Henderson Fan Club   (EA)
BHFCBV ... Baseball Hall of Fame Committee on Baseball Veterans   (EA)
BHFIA....... Bulletin. Haffkine Institute [*A publication*]
BHFX .... Broach Fixture
BHG.......... Bad Reichenhall [*Federal Republic of Germany*] [*Seismograph station code, US Geological Survey*]   (SEIS)
BH & G ..... Better Homes and Gardens [*Information service or system*] [*A publication*]   (IID)
BHG.......... Blackwood Hodge (Canada) Ltd. [*Toronto Stock Exchange symbol*]
BHG.......... Booth-Henry-Gorin [*Equations for calculation of net charge and valence of molecule*]
BHG.......... Sulphur Springs, TX [*Location identifier*] [*FAA*]   (FAAL)
BHGA....... British Hang Gliding Association
BHGDA..... Better Homes and Gardens [*A publication*]
BHGNA..... Behavior Genetics [*A publication*]
BHH .... Baptist History and Heritage [*A publication*]
BHH .... Biblisch-Historisches Handwoerterbuch [*A publication*]   (BJA)
BHH .... Bisha [*Saudi Arabia*] [*Airport symbol*]   (OAG)
BHH .... Broken Hill Holdings Ltd. [*Australia*]
BHH .... Hudson Hope Public Library, British Columbia [*Library symbol*] [*National Library of Canada*]   (NLC)
BHHI........ Black Hawk Holdings, Inc. [*NASDAQ symbol*]   (NQ)
BHHI........ British Home and Hospital for Incurables
BHHM ...... Hudson Hope Museum, British Columbia [*Library symbol*] [*National Library of Canada*]   (NLC)
BHHMC.... Board of Hospitals and Homes of the Methodist Church [*Later, National Association of Health and Welfare Ministries of the United Methodist Church*]   (EA)
BHHS....... British Hosta and Hemerocallis Society   (EAIO)
BHHW ...... Biblisch-Historisches Handwoerterbuch [*A publication*]   (BJA)
BHI .... Bahia Blanca [*Argentina*] [*Airport symbol*]   (OAG)
BHI .... Baker Hughes, Incorporated [*NYSE symbol*]   (SPSG)
BHI .... Bertha Hill [*Idaho*] [*Seismograph station code, US Geological Survey*] [*Closed*]   (SEIS)
BHI .... Better Hearing Institute   (EA)
BHI .... Binaural Hearing Impairment
BHI .... Biosynthetic Human Insulin [*Medicine*]
BHI .... Brain-Heart Infusion [*Growth medium*]
BHI .... British Horological Institute
BHI .... British Humanities Index [*Library Association Publishing Ltd.*] [*London*] [*A publication*]
BHI .... Bullet Hit Indicator   (MCD)
BHi........... Bulletin Hispanique [*A publication*]
BHI .... Bureau of Health Insurance [*Social Security Administration*]
BHI .... Bureau Hydrographique International [*International Hydrographic Organization*]   (EAIO)
BHI .... Burst-Height Indicator
BHI .... Business History [*A publication*]
BHI .... Europe Outremer. Revue Internationale [*A publication*]
BHI-Ac...... Brain-Heart Infusion [*Broth*] with Acetone [*Growth medium*]
BHIB .... Beef Heart Infusion Broth [*Microbiology*]
BHIBA...... Brain-Heart Infusion Blood Agar [*Growth medium*]
BHIF........ Better Highways Information Foundation [*Later, ARTBA*]
BHIJA ...... Bulletin. Heart Institute (Japan) [*A publication*]
BHis.......... Biblioteca Hispana [*A publication*]
BHIS.......... Brain-Heart Infusion Supplemented [*Broth or agar*] [*Growth medium*]
BHisp........ Bibliografia Hispanica [*A publication*]
BHisp........ Bulletin Hispanique [*A publication*]
B Hispan ... Bulletin Hispanique [*A publication*]
B Hispan S ... Bulletin of Hispanic Studies [*A publication*]
B Hist Med ... Bulletin of the History of Medicine [*A publication*]
BHJ .... Bhuj [*India*] [*Airport symbol*]   (OAG)
BHJ .... Bulkhead Jack
BHJL......... Jack Lynn Memorial Museum, Horsefly, British Columbia [*Library symbol*] [*National Library of Canada*]   (NLC)
BHK.......... Baby Hamster Kidney
BHK.......... Bhakra [*India*] [*Seismograph station code, US Geological Survey*]   (SEIS)
BHK.......... Biblia Hebraica (R. Kittel) [*A publication*]   (BJA)
BHK.......... Black Hawk Mining, Inc. [*Toronto Stock Exchange symbol*]
BHK.......... Bukhara [*USSR*] [*Airport symbol*]   (OAG)
BHKIM ..... Ksan Indian Village and Museum, Haselton, British Columbia [*Library symbol*] [*National Library of Canada*]   (NLC)
BHL.......... Bachelor of Hebrew Letters

BHL.......... Bachelor of Hebrew Literature
BHL.......... Bachelor of Humane Letters
BHL.......... Bernard-Henri Levy [*French writer and philosopher*]
BHL.......... Better Humanity League [*Commercial firm*]   (EA)
BHL.......... Biblical History and Literature   (BJA)
BHL.......... Biological Half-Life
BHL.......... Bunker Hill Income Securities, Inc. [*NYSE symbol*]   (SPSG)
BHL.......... Busy Hour Load [*Telecommunications*]   (TEL)
BHLA....... Ben Hur Life Association [*Crawfordsville, IN*]   (EA)
B & H Lead Ca ... Bennett and Heard's Leading Criminal Cases [*England*] [*A publication*]   (DLA)
B & H Lead Cas ... Bennett and Heard's Leading Criminal Cases [*England*] [*A publication*]   (DLA)
BHLF......... Blair House Library Foundation   (EA)
BHLH........ Agassiz-Harrison Historical Society, Agassiz, British Columbia [*Library symbol*] [*National Library of Canada*]   (BIB)
BHLS........ Below/Hook Lifters Section of the Material Handling Institute   (EA)
BHlthSc..... Bachelor of Health Science
BHM......... B & H Maritime Carriers Ltd. [*AMEX symbol*]   (CTT)
BHM......... Bible Holiness Movement   (EA)
BHM......... Bibliography of the History of Medicine [*A publication*]
BHM......... Birmingham [*Alabama*] [*Airport symbol*]
BHM......... Bulletin of the History of Medicine [*A publication*]
BHM......... Bulletin. Societe Francaise d'Histoire de la Medecine [*A publication*]
BHM......... Bureau of Health Manpower [*Later, Health Resources Administration*] [*HEW*]
BHM......... Busy Hour Model [*Data processing*]
BHM......... Hope Museum, British Columbia [*Library symbol*] [*National Library of Canada*]   (NLC)
BHM......... National Institute of Health - Health Manpower, Bethesda, MD [*OCLC symbol*] [*Inactive*]   (OCLC)
BHMA....... Bald-Headed Men of America   (EA)
BHMA....... British Hard Metal Association
BHMA....... British Herbal Medicine Association
BHMA....... British Holistic Medical Association [*British*]
BHMA....... Builders' Hardware Manufacturers Association   (EA)
BHM Berg u Huttenm Mh ... BHM. Berg- und Huttenmaennische Monatshefte [*A publication*]
BHMC....... Bell & Howell/Mamiya Company
BHME....... Bureau of Health Manpower Education [*National Institutes of Health*]
BHMF....... Bis(hydroxymethyl)ferrocene [*Organic chemistry*]
BHMF....... Bis(hydroxymethyl)furan [*Organic chemistry*]
BHMH...... Butylazo(hydroxy)(methyl)hexane [*Organic chemistry*]
BHMHFC ... Bret "Hit Man" Hart Fan Club   (EA)
BHMK....... Kilby Provincial Historic Park, Harrison Mills, British Columbia [*Library symbol*] [*National Library of Canada*]   (NLC)
BHMMA... Berg- und Huettenmaennische Monatshefte [*A publication*]
BHMNAFWB ... Board of Home Missions of the National Association of Free Will Baptists   (EA)
BHMO...... Blue Hill Meteorological Observatory [*Harvard University*]   (MCD)
BHMP....... Bis(hydroxymethyl)peroxide [*Organic chemistry*]
BH/MP..... Breather Hose/Mouthpiece   (MCD)
BHMR....... Barclays Home Mortgage Rate [*British*]   (DCTA)
BHMS...... Bachelor of Human Movement Studies
BHMS...... Bishop's Home Mission Society [*Australia*]
BHMS...... British Holistic Medical Society
BHMS...... Buddy Holly Memorial Society   (EA)
BHN .... Basic Human Needs
BHN .... Brinell Hardness Number [*Also, BH, BHNo, HB*]
BHN .... Brotherhood of the Holy Name
BHN .... Fort Leonard Wood, MO [*Location identifier*] [*FAA*]   (FAAL)
BHND .... Behind   (FAAC)
BHNHE...... Bureau of Human Nutrition and Home Economics [*Department of Agriculture*] [*Functions transferred to ARS, 1953*]
BHNNA .... Societe d'Histoire Naturelle de l'Afrique du Nord. Bulletin [*A publication*]
BHNo........ Brinell Hardness Number [*Also, BH, BHN, HB*]
BHNRC..... Beltsville Human Nutrition Research Center [*Department of Agriculture*]
BHO .... B & H Ocean Carriers Ltd. [*AMEX symbol*]   (CTT)
BHO .... Barkhor Resources, Inc. [*Vancouver Stock Exchange symbol*]
BHO .... Bartley Herbarium, Ohio University [*Athens, OH*]
bho .... Bhojpuri [*MARC language code*] [*Library of Congress*]   (LCCP)
BHO .... Bhopal [*India*] [*Airport symbol*]   (OAG)
BHO .... Black Hole Ocarina   (MCD)
BHO .... Branch Hydrographic Office [*Navy*]
BHO .... Business Horizons [*A publication*]
BHOAM.... Brethren Homes and Older Adult Ministries [*An association*]   (EA)
B Ho Ec...... Bachelor of Household Economy
Bhop.......... All India Reporter, Bhopal Series [*A publication*]   (DLA)
B Hor .... Bachelor of Horticulture
B Hor .... Business Horizons [*A publication*]
BHort........ Bachelor of Horticulture
BHortSc..... Bachelor of Horticultural Science

B Ho Sc...... Bachelor of Household Science
BHP.......... Balboa Heights [*Canal Zone*] [*Seismograph station code, US Geological Survey*]   (SEIS)
BHP.......... Basic Health Profile
BHP.......... Beverly Hills Public Library, Beverly Hills, CA [*OCLC symbol*]   (OCLC)
BHP.......... Bhojpur [*Nepal*] [*Airport symbol*]   (OAG)
BHP.......... Biological Hazard Potential [*Atomic energy*]
BHP.......... Bishop
BHP.......... Bishop's University Library [*UTLAS symbol*]
BHP.......... Boiler Horsepower
BHP.......... Bottom Hole Pressure [*Oil well borehole*]
BHP.......... Brake Horsepower
BHP.......... Brashear-Hastings Prism
BHP.......... British Horsepower
BHP.......... Broken Hill Proprietary ADR [*NYSE symbol*]   (SPSG)
BHP.......... Butyl Hydroperoxide [*Organic chemistry*]
BHPAS...... Bulletin. National Research Institute of History and Philology. Academia Sinica [*A publication*]
BHPCTHS ... Bulletin Historique et Philologique. Comite des Travaux Historiques et Scientifiques [*A publication*]
BHPF........ Bulletin Historique et Litteraire. Societe de l'Histoire du Protestantisme Francais [*A publication*]
BHP-HR..... Brake Horsepower-Hour   (AAG)
BHP J........ BHP [*Broken Hill Proprietary Ltd.*] Journal [*A publication*]   (APTA)
BHP Jl....... BHP [*Broken Hill Proprietary Ltd.*] Journal [*A publication*]   (APTA)
BHP Jo ...... BHP [*Broken Hill Proprietary Ltd.*] Journal [*A publication*]   (APTA)
B H Points ... Bulletin of High Points [*A publication*]
BHP R .... BHP [*Broken Hill Proprietary Ltd.*] Review [*A publication*]   (APTA)
BHPRD ..... Bureau of Health Planning and Resource Development [*Later, Bureau of Health Planning*] [*HEW*]
BHP Res Div Inf Circ ... Broken Hill Proprietary Ltd. Research Division. Information Circular [*A publication*]   (APTA)
BHP Rev .... BHP [*Broken Hill Proprietary Ltd.*] Review [*A publication*]   (APTA)
BHPRIC.... Bishopric
BHPSO...... Bulletin. Historical and Philosophical Society of Ohio [*A publication*]
BHPT .... (Beta-Hydroxypropyl)theophylline [*Biochemistry*]
BHP Tech Bull ... BHP [*Broken Hill Proprietary Ltd.*] Technical Bulletin [*A publication*]   (APTA)
BHQ .... Battalion Headquarters [*British military*]   (DMA)
BHQ .... Brigade Headquarters [*Army*]
BHQ .... Broken Hill [*Australia*] [*Airport symbol*]   (OAG)
BHR......... Bahrain [*ANSI three-letter standard code*]   (CNC)
BHR......... Basal Heart Rate [*Medicine*]
BHR......... Bharatpur [*Nepal*] [*Airport symbol*] [*Obsolete*]   (OAG)
BHR......... Bibliotheque d'Humanisme et Renaissance [*A publication*]
BHR......... Biotechnology and Human Research
BHR......... Black Hill Resources Ltd. [*Vancouver Stock Exchange symbol*]
BHR......... Block Handler Routine [*Data processing*]   (BUR)
BHR......... Block Header Record [*Data processing*]
BHR......... Brandl, H. R., Chicago IL [*STAC*]
BHR......... British Hotelier and Restaurateur [*A publication*]
BHR......... Bulkhead Receptacle
BHR......... Business History Review [*A publication*]
BHRA....... British Hydromechanics Research Association [*Later, BHRA Ltd.*]
BHRA....... British Hypnosis Research Association
BHRC....... Beverly Hills Racquets Club [*Book title*]
BHRI .... Brewers Hop Research Institute [*Later, USBA*]
BHS.......... Bachelor of Health Science
BHS.......... Bachelor of Home Science
BHS.......... Bahamas [*ANSI three-letter standard code*]   (CNC)
BHS.......... [*The*] Baptist Historical Society [*British*]
BHS.......... Base Heat Shield
BHS.......... Baseball Hall of Shame   (EA)
BHS.......... Basic Hole System
BHS.......... Bathurst [*Australia*] [*Airport symbol*]   (OAG)
BHS.......... Bernard Herrmann Society   (EA)
BHS.......... Beta-Hemolytic Streptococcus [*Medicine*]
BHS.......... Biblia Hebraica Stuttgartensia [*A publication*]   (BJA)
BHS.......... Biuletyn Historii Sztuki [*A publication*]
BHS.......... Black Hills State College, Spearfish, SD [*OCLC symbol*]   (OCLC)
BHS.......... Blue Hills Station [*Nuclear energy*]   (NRCH)
BHS.......... Bonhomie & Hattiesburg Southern R. R. [*AAR code*]
BHS.......... Borehole Seismometer
BHS.......... British Heritage Society   (EA)
BHS.......... British Herpetological Society
BHS.......... British Home Stores [*Retail chain*]
BHS.......... Bulletin of Hispanic Studies [*A publication*]
BHS.......... Bureau of Health Services [*Public Health Service*]
BHS.......... Burlesque Historical Society   (EA)
BHSAM .... Bulletin Historique. Societe des Antiquitaires de la Morinie [*A publication*]
BHSc......... Bachelor of Household Science
BHSCS...... Bone Haft and Scale Cutters Society [*A union*] [*British*]

BHSDO ..... Been Here Since Day One [*Group of Reagan administration staffers*]
BHSK .... Bolton-Hunter Reagent-Labeled Substance K [*Analytical biochemistry*]
BHSL........ Beverly Hills Savings & Loan [*NASDAQ symbol*]   (NQ)
BHSM .... Bulletin. Historical Society of Montgomery County [*A publication*]
BHSMCo... Bulletin. Historical Society of Montgomery County [*A publication*]
BHSR .... Balanced Half-Sample Replication [*Statistics*]
BHST........ Bottom Hole Static Temperature [*Oil well borehole*]
BHT .... Babylonian Historical Texts Relating to the Capture and Downfall of Babylon [*A publication*]   (BJA)
BHT.......... Backhoe Trench [*Archeology*]
BHT.......... Baht [*Monetary unit*] [*Thailand*]
BH & T ..... Ballistic Hull and Turret Vehicle   (MCD)
BHT.......... Bell Helicopter Textron, Inc.
BHT.......... Bob Hope Theatre [*London, England*]
BHT.......... Bottom Hole Temperature [*Oil well borehole*]
BHT.......... Breath-Hold Time
BHT.......... Breath Hydrogen Test
BHT.......... Brotherhood of the Holy Trinity
BHT.......... Butylated Hydroxytoluene [*Also, DBPC*] [*Antioxidant*]
BHTC .... Black Hills Teachers College [*Later, Black Hills State College*] [*South Dakota*]
BHTC .... Book House Training Centre [*British*]
BHTD .... Bureau of Hygiene and Tropical Diseases [*Database producer*]
BHTh........ Beitraege zur Historischen Theologie [*Tuebingen*] [*A publication*]
BH(T)P ..... Bottom Hole (Treating) Pressure [*Oil well borehole*]
BHTP .... Bulletin d'Histoire du Theatre Portugais [*A publication*]
BHTPA...... Best Holiday Trav-L-Park Association   (EA)
BHTV .... Borehole Televiewer [*Drilling technology*]
B Hu......... Bachelor of Humanities
BHU .... Bhavnagar [*India*] [*Airport symbol*]   (OAG)
Bhu........... Bhutan
BHU .... Latrobe, PA [*Location identifier*] [*FAA*]   (FAAL)
BHUA....... Banking, Housing, and Urban Affairs   (DLA)
BHUT........ Bhutan
BhV.......... Bharatiya Vidya [*A publication*]
BHV.......... Book of Heroic Verse [*A publication*]
BHV.......... Business History Review [*A publication*]
BHVBamberg ... Bericht. Historischer Verein fuer das Fuerstbistum (Bamberg) [*A publication*]
BHVFB...... Bericht. Historischer Verein fuer das Fuerstbistum (Bamberg) [*A publication*]
BHW......... Bell & Howell Co. [*NYSE symbol*]   (SPSG)
BHW......... West Branch, MI [*Location identifier*] [*FAA*]   (FAAL)
BHWR...... Boiling Heavy Water Reactor
BHX .... Birmingham [*England*] [*Airport symbol*]   (OAG)
BHXU...... Brayton Heat Exchanger Unit
B Hy......... Bachelor of Hygiene
BHY......... Belding Heminway Co., Inc. [*NYSE symbol*]   (SPSG)
B HYG ...... Bachelor of Hygiene
BHZ......... Belo Horizonte [*Brazil*] [*Airport symbol*]   (OAG)
BHZ......... Berliner Handelszentrale [*Berlin Trade Center*] [*German*]
BHZ......... Business Horizons [*A publication*]
BI .... Background Information   (MCD)
BI .... Background Investigation
BI .... Backward Indicator [*Telecommunications*]   (TEL)
BI .... Bacteriologic Index [*Clinical microbiology*]
BI .... Balch Institute [*Philadelphia, PA*]
BI .... Balearic Islands
B & I........ Bankruptcy and Insolvency Cases [*Legal*] [*British*]
B & I........ Bankruptcy and Insolvency Reports [*1853-55*] [*England*] [*A publication*]   (DLA)
BI .... Base Composite Price Index   (MCD)
BI .... Base Ignition
BI .... Base-In (Prism) [*Ophthalmology*]
B & I........ Base and Increment [*Technical drawings*]
BI .... Basic Infantry
BI .... Battalion Infantry   (CINC)
BI .... Batted In [*Short form for RBI, Runs Batted In*] [*Baseball*]
BI .... Battery Inverter   (AAG)
BI .... Battlefield Illumination   (AABC)
BI .... Battlefield Interdiction   (MCD)
BI .... Bearing Indicator   (MCD)
BI .... Beer Institute   (EA)
BI .... Befrienders International [*Later, BISW*]   (EAIO)
BI .... Behavioral Inventory
BI .... Bell Industries, Inc. [*NYSE symbol*]   (SPSG)
BI .... Bermuda Islands
BI .... Beth Israel   (BJA)
Bi............. Biblica [*A publication*]
Bi............. Bibliofilia [*A publication*]
Bi............. Bibliografia Italiana [*A publication*]
BI .... Bibliographic Instruction [*Library science*]
Bi............. Bibliotheca Islamica [*A publication*]
Bi............. Biblos [*A publication*]
Bi.............. Bicolor
Bi............... Bijdragen [*A publication*]

Bi............... Bile [*Blood group*]
B & I.......... Billeting and Inventory [*Military*]
BI .... Billing Instructions [*Telecommunications*]   (TEL)
BI .... Biological Indicator [*Microbiology*]
BI .... Biological Inventory
BI .... Biology   (DSUE)
Bi............. Biot [*Also, aA*] [*Unit of electric current*]
Bi............. Bipolar Cell [*In the retina*]
BI .... Bisexual   (DSUE)
Bi............. Bismuth [*Chemical element*]
BI .... Bismuth Institute [*Brussels, Belgium*]   (EAIO)
BI .... Black Information [*Banking*] [*British*]
BI .... Black Iron
BI .... Blanking Input   (IEEE)
BI .... Blind Individual [*Social Security Administration*]   (OICC)
BI .... Block-In   (MCD)
BI .... Bnai Israel   (BJA)
BI .... Bobov in Israel [*An association*]   (EA)
BI .... Bobs International [*An association*]   (EAIO)
BI .... Bodily Injury [*Insurance*]
B(I)........... Bomber (Intruder) [*British military*]   (DMA)
BI .... Bone Injury [*Medicine*]
BI .... Books at Iowa [*A publication*]
BI .... Boring Institute   (EA)
BI .... Boston Irish
BI .... Braille Institute   (EA)
BI .... Branch Immaterial
B or I .... Brass or Iron [*Freight*]
BI .... Bricklin International   (EA)
BI .... Brief Introduction
B & I.......... Brilliant and Ivory [*Jewelry*]   (ROG)
BI .... British India
bi .... British Indian Ocean Territory [*MARC country of publication code*] [*Library of Congress*]   (LCCP)
BI .... British Industry [*Vancouver Stock Exchange symbol*]
BI .... British Institution   (ROG)
BI .... British-Israel World Federation
Bi............. [*Petrus*] Brito [*Flourished, 13th century*] [*Authority cited in pre-1607 legal work*]   (DSA)
BI .... Broadcast Intercept   (MCD)
BI .... Brookings Institution   (EA)
BI .... Browning Institute   (EA)
BI .... Buffer Index [*Data processing*]
B/I........... Built-In [*Classified advertising*]   (ADA)
BI .... Bulk Issue   (ADA)
BI .... Bulletin Italien [*A publication*]
BI .... Bureau Inlichtingen [*Netherlands Information Office*] [*World War II*]
BI .... Bureau of Investigation [*Federal Trade Commission*]
BI .... Burn Index [*Medicine*]
BI .... Burundi [*ANSI two-letter standard code*]   (CNC)
B/I........... Bus Interface [*Data processing*]
BI .... Business Index [*A publication*]
BI .... Business Insurance [*A publication*]
BI .... Business International Corp.
BI .... Business Interruption [*Insurance*]
BI .... Input Blocking Factor [*Data processing*]   (IBMDP)
BI .... Royal Brunei Airlines [*Airlines code*]   (FAAC)
BI1 .... Barter Island [*Alaska*] [*Seismograph station code, US Geological Survey*]   (SEIS)
BI2 .... Barter Island [*Alaska*] [*Seismograph station code, US Geological Survey*]   (SEIS)
BI3 .... Barter Island [*Alaska*] [*Seismograph station code, US Geological Survey*]   (SEIS)
BI4 .... Barter Island [*Alaska*] [*Seismograph station code, US Geological Survey*]   (SEIS)
BI's........... Buergerinitiativen [*Citizens' action groups*] [*Federal Republic of Germany*]
BIA .... Administrative Decisions under Immigration and Nationality Laws of the United States [*A publication*]   (DLA)
BIA .... Bachelor of Industrial Arts
BIA .... Bangor International Airport
BIA .... Barbecue Industry Association   (EA)
BIA .... Bastia [*Corsica*] [*Airport symbol*]   (OAG)
BIA .... Bee Industries Association   (EA)
BiA .... Biblical Archaeologist [*A publication*]
BIA .... Bicycle Institute of America [*Defunct*]   (EA)
BIA .... Binding Industries of America   (EA)
BIA .... Biogenic Institutes of America [*Later, AHMI*]   (EA)
BIA .... Board of Immigration Appeals [*Department of Justice*]
BIA .... Boating Industry Association [*Later, NMMA*]
BIA .... Bollettino. Reale Istituto di Archeologia e Storia dell'Arte [*A publication*]
BIA .... Boost, Insertion, and Abort [*Aerospace*]
BIA .... Booster Interstage Assembly [*Aerospace*]
BIA .... Bouraq Indonesia Airlines   (FEA)
BIA .... Braille Institute of America [*Later, BI*]   (EA)
BIA .... Brazilian International Airlines
BIA .... Briana Resources Ltd. [*Vancouver Stock Exchange symbol*]
BIA .... Brick Institute of America   (EA)
BIA .... Bridal Industry Association   (EA)

BIA .... British Insurance Association
BIA .... British and International Addressing Post [*A publication*]
BIA .... British Island Airways Ltd.
BIA .... Broadcasting in Australia [*A publication*]
BIA .... Bulletin. Institute of Archaeology [*A publication*]
BIA .... Bureau of Indian Affairs [*Department of the Interior*]
BIA .... Bureau of Insular Affairs [*Originally, part of War Department; functions transferred to Department of Interior, 1939*]
BIA .... Bureau of International Affairs   (MCD)
BIA .... Bureau International Afghanistan   (EA)
BIA .... Bureau Issues Association   (EA)
BIA .... Burma Independence Army [*Fighting on the side of the Japanese*] [*World War II*]
BIA .... Buses International Association   (EA)
BIA .... Business Improvement Area
BIA .... Real-Aerovias Brasil [*Brazilian international airline*]
BIAA .... Bollettino. Reale Istituto di Archeologia e Storia dell'Arte [*A publication*]
BIAA .... Bureau of Inter-American Affairs [*Department of State*]
BIAAD4 ..... Buletinul. Institutului Agronomic Cluj-Napoca. Seria Agricultura [*A publication*]
BIAB .... Brief Index of Adaptive Behavior [*Educational development test*]
BIAB .... Bulletin. Institut Archeologique Bulgare [*A publication*]
BIABE .... Biomass Abstracts [*A publication*]
BIA Bulg.... Bulletin. Institut Archeologique Bulgare [*A publication*]
BIAC .... BI, Inc. [*NASDAQ symbol*]   (NQ)
BIAC .... Bioinstrumentation Advisory Council [*Defunct*]
BIAC .... Business and Industry Advisory Committee [*NATO*]   (NATG)
BIACC .... Basic Integrated Aircraft Command and Control [*Navy*]
BIACDA .... Buletinul. Institutului Agronomic Cluj-Napoca [*A publication*]
BIAD .... Bureau International d'Anthropologie Differentielle [*International Bureau of Differential Anthropology*]
BIADDD .... Biotechnology Advances [*A publication*]
Biafra R...... Biafra Review [*A publication*]
BIAHA ...... Bulletin. International Association of Scientific Hydrology [*A publication*]
BIAL......... Bulletin. Institut Archeologique Liegeois [*A publication*]
BIAL......... Bulletin. Institute of Archaeology. University of London [*A publication*]
BIALB .... Boletim. Instituto de Tecnologia de Alimentos [*Campinas, Brazil*] [*A publication*]
BIALL .... British and Irish Association of Law Librarians   (DLA)
BIAM .... Banque d'Informations Automatisees sur les Medicaments [*Data Bank for Medicaments*] [*Information service or system*]   (IID)
BIAMA...... Bulletin International. Academie Polonaise des Sciences et des Lettres. Classe des Sciences Mathematiques et Naturelles. Serie A. Sciences Mathematiques [*A publication*]
Biamp........ Biamperometric [*Electromagnetics*]
BIANA ...... Bibliotheca Anatomica [*A publication*]
Bian & Nero ... Bianco e Nero [*A publication*]
BIAO .... Bulletin. Institut Francais d'Archeologie Orientale [*A publication*]
BIAP......... Bulletin International. Academie Polonaise des Sciences et des Lettres [*A publication*]
BIAP......... Bureau International d'Audiophonologie [*International Office for Audiophonology - IOA*] [*Brussels, Belgium*]   (EA)
BIAPS....... Battery Inverter Accessory Power Supply
BIAPSL..... Bulletin International. Academie Polonaise des Sciences et des Lettres [*A publication*]
BIAR......... Akureyri [*Iceland*] [*ICAO location identifier*]   (ICLI)
BIAR......... Base Installation Action Requirements
BI(A)R....... Board of Inquiry (Army) Rules [*British military*]   (DMA)
BI Arch ..... Bachelor of Interior Architecture
BI Arch E... Bachelor of Interior Architectural Engineering
BI Arch Eng ... Bachelor of Interior Architectural Engineering
BIAS......... Battlefield Illumination Airborne System   (AFM)
BIAS......... Broadcast Industry Automation System [*Data Communications Corp.*] [*Information service or system*]   (IID)
BIAS......... Brooklyn Institute of Arts and Sciences
BIAS......... Bulletin in Applied Statistics [*A publication*]
BIAS......... Buoy Integrated Antenna Submarine [*or System*]   (MCD)
BIAS......... Byelorussian Institute of Arts and Science   (EA)
BIASILL ... Basic Iron Aluminum Silicate [*Du Pont trademark*]
BIAT......... British Institute of Architectural Technicians   (EAIO)
BIAT......... Burn-In/Aging Tester
BIAT......... Business Information Analysis and Integration Technique [*Data processing*]
BIATA ...... British Independent Air Transport Association
BIATBP..... Estacion Experimental Agricola de Tucuman. Boletin [*A publication*]
BIAVDX.... Buletinul. Institutului Agronomic Cluj-Napoca. Seria Zootehnie si Medicina Veterinara [*A publication*]
BIB......... Baby Incendiary Bomb
BIB......... Backward Indicator BIT [*Binary Digit*] [*Telecommunications*]   (TEL)
BIB......... Bag in Box [*Packaging*]
BIB......... Balanced Incomplete Block [*Statistical design*]
BIB......... Bank of Israel. Bulletin [*Jerusalem*] [*A publication*]
BIB......... Bibe [*Drink*] [*Pharmacy*]

BIB............. Bible
BIB............. Bible Grove, IL [*Location identifier*] [*FAA*]   (FAAL)
Bib............. Bibletone [*Record label*]
Bib............. Biblica [*A publication*]
BIB............. Biblical   (ROG)
BIB............. Bibliography   (ROG)
Bib............. Biblos [*A publication*]
B & IB .... Billing and Instruction Book
BIB............. Biographical Information Blank
BIB............. Bipartite Board [*Post-World War II, Germany*]
BIB............. Board for International Broadcasting [*Independent government agency*]
BIB............. Boat Information Book [*Navy*]   (CAAL)
BIB............. Bottled in Bond [*Wines and spirits*]
BIB............. Broadcast Information Bureau, Inc.
BIB............. Brunel Institute for Bioengineering [*Brunel University*] [*Information service or system*]   (IID)
BIB............. Bulletin. Institut International de Bibliographie [*A publication*]
BIB............. Open; Vaktijdschrift voor Bibliothecarissen, Literatuuronderzoekers, Bedrijfsarchivarissen, en Documentalisten [*A publication*]
BIBA .... Babson Institute of Business Administration [*Massachusetts*]
Bib A .... Biblical Archeologist [*A publication*]
BIBA .... British Insurance Brokers' Association   (DLA)
BibAg......... Bibliography of Agriculture [*A publication*]
BIBAM...... Bibliography of Australian Medicine and Health Services [*A publication*]
Bib Am Ling Am Soc Am ... Bibliographie Americaniste. Linguistique Amerindienne. Societe des Americanistes [*A publication*]
Bib Arch..... Biblical Archaeologist [*A publication*]
Bib Arch R ... Biblical Archaeology Review [*A publication*]
Bib Arch Rev ... Biblical Archaeology Review [*A publication*]
BIBB .... Bibb Co. [*NASDAQ symbol*]   (NQ)
Bibb............ Bibb's Kentucky Reports [*4-7 Kentucky*] [*1808-17*] [*A publication*]   (DLA)
Bibb (KY)... Bibb's Kentucky Reports [*4-7 Kentucky*] [*1808-17*] [*A publication*]   (DLA)
BIBD......... Balanced Incomplete Block Design [*Mathematics*]
BIBDATA ... Bibliographic Data   (ADA)
BIBE......... Big Bend National Park
BIBEDL..... Biologie du Comportement [*A publication*]
Bib Hist Am ... Bibliografia de Historia de America [*A publication*]
BI & BI...... Biculturalism and Bilingualism [*Canada*]
BIBIA .... Biotechnology and Bioengineering [*A publication*]
BIBIC........ British Institute for Brain Injured Children
Bib Inz Oprogram ... Biblioteka Inzynierii Oprogramowania [*A publication*]
Bibl............. Biblica [*Rome*] [*A publication*]
BIBL .... Biblical
BIBL .... Bibliografia Espanola [*Ministerio de Cultura*] [*Spain*] [*Information service or system*]   (CRD)
Bibl............. Bibliographic Index [*A publication*]
Bibl............. Bibliographie Linguistique [*A publication*]
BIBL .... Bibliography
Bibl............. Bibliotheca [*of Apollodorus*] [*Classical studies*]   (OCD)
Bibl............. Bibliotheca [*of Photius*] [*Classical studies*]   (OCD)
BIBL .... Bibliotheca [*Library*] [*Latin*]
BIBL .... Blonduos [*Iceland*] [*ICAO location identifier*]   (ICLI)
Bibl A .... Biblical Archaeologist [*A publication*]
Bibl Anat.... Bibliotheca Anatomica [*A publication*]
Bibl Anatom ... Bibliotheca Anatomica [*A publication*]
Bibl Arch ... Biblical Archaeologist [*A publication*]
Bibl Archaeolo ... Biblical Archaeologist [*A publication*]
Bibl Archeol ... Biblical Archeologist [*A publication*]
Bibl Arch Roman Ser II Linguistica ... Biblioteca dell'Archivum Romanicum. Serie II. Linguistica [*A publication*]
Bibl Asiatica ... Bibliographia Asiatica [*A publication*]
BIBLB....... Boletim Internacional de Bibliografia Luso-Brasileira [*Lisboa*] [*A publication*]
Bibl Biotheor ... Bibliotheca Biotheoretica [*A publication*]
Bibl Br Sci Arts ... Bibliotheque Britannique. Sciences et Arts [*A publication*]
Bibl Cardio ... Bibliotheca Cardiologica [*A publication*]
Bibl Cardiol ... Bibliotheca Cardiologica [*A publication*]
Bibl Dedalo ... Biblioteca Dedalo [*A publication*]
Bibl Docum Terminology ... Bibliography, Documentation, Terminology [*A publication*]
Bibl Ec Chartes ... Bibliotheque de l'Ecole des Chartes [*A publication*]
Bibl Ec Franc ... Bibliotheque des Ecoles Francaises d'Athenes et de Rome [*A publication*]   (OCD)
Bibl Ecole Chartes ... Bibliotheque de l'Ecole des Chartes [*A publication*]
Bibl Engl Lang & Lit ... Bibliography of English Language and Literature [*A publication*]
Bible T .... Bible Today [*A publication*]
bibl-f.......... Bibliographical Footnotes
Bibl Filol.... Bibliografia Filologica do Centro de Estudos Filologica de Lisboa [*A publication*]
Bibl Gastro ... Bibliotheca Gastroenterologica [*A publication*]
Bibl Gastroenterol ... Bibliotheca Gastroenterologica [*A publication*]
BiblGeo...... Bibliography and Index of Geology [*A publication*]
Bibl Gesch Dt Arbeiterbewegung ... Bibliographie zur Geschichte der Deutschen Arbeiterbewegung [*A publication*]
Bibl Gynaecol ... Bibliotheca Gynaecologica [*A publication*]

Bibl Haem ... Bibliotheca Haematologica [*A publication*]
Bibl Haemat ... Bibliotheca Haematologica [*A publication*]
Bibl Haematol ... Bibliotheca Haematologica [*A publication*]
Bibl Hist Sueo-Gothica ... Bibliotheca Historica Sueo-Gothica [*A publication*]
Bibl Hist Vaudoise ... Bibliotheque Historique Vaudoise [*A publication*]
BiblH & R ... Bibliotheque d'Humanisme et Renaissance [*A publication*]
Bibl Hum R ... Bibliotheque d'Humanisme et Renaissance [*A publication*]
Bibl Hum Renaissance ... Bibliotheque d'Humanisme et Renaissance [*A publication*]
Biblical Rev ... Biblical Review [*A publication*]
Bibl Ind ...... Bibliographic Index [*A publication*]
Bibl & Ind Geol ... Bibliography and Index of Geology [*A publication*]
Biblio. ...... Bibliofilia [*A publication*]
BIBLIO ..... Bibliographical Note   (DSUE)
BIBLIO-DATA ... National Bibliographic Data Base [*Deutsche Bibliothek*] [*Database*]
Biblio France ... Bibliographie de la France [*A publication*]
Bibliog .... Bibliographer [*A publication*]
BIBLIOG .. Bibliography
Bibliog Doc Terminology ... Bibliography, Documentation, Terminology [*A publication*]
Bibliogr Agric ... Bibliography of Agriculture [*A publication*]
Bibliogr Annu Madagascar ... Bibliographie Annuelle de Madagascar [*A publication*]
Bibliogr Bestrahlung Lebensm ... Bibliographie zur Bestrahlung von Lebensmitteln [*West Germany*] [*A publication*]
Bibliogr Bibl Conmem Orton Inst Interamer Cienc Agr ... Bibliografias. Biblioteca Conmemorativa Orton. Instituto Interamericano de Ciencias Agricolas [*A publication*]
Bibliogr Bras Odontol ... Bibliografia Brasileira Odontologia [*A publication*]
Bibliogr Bur Soils ... Bibliography. Commonwealth Bureau of Soils [*A publication*]
Bibliogr Carto ... Bibliographia Cartographica [*A publication*]
Bibliogr Chim ... Bibliographia Chimica [*A publication*]
Bibliogr Econ Geol ... Bibliography of Economic Geology [*A publication*]
Bibliogr Engl Lit ... Bibliography of English Language and Literature [*A publication*]
Bibliogr Farm ... Bibliografica Farmaceutica [*A publication*]
Bibliogr For Bur (Oxf) ... Annotated Bibliography. Commonwealth Forestry Bureau (Oxford) [*A publication*]
Bibliogr Genet ... Bibliographia Genetica [*A publication*]
Bibliogr Genet Med ... Bibliographica Genetica Medica [*A publication*]
Bibliogr Geol Lit At Energy Raw Mater ... Bibliography of Geological Literature on Atomic Energy Raw Materials [*A publication*]
Bibliogr Geol Pol ... Bibliografia Geologiczna Poliski [*A publication*]
Bibliogr High Temp Chem Phys Gases Plasmas ... Bibliography on the High Temperature Chemistry and Physics of Gases and Plasmas [*A publication*]
Bibliogr High Temp Chem Phys Mater ... Bibliography on the High Temperature Chemistry and Physics of Materials [*A publication*]
Bibliogr High Temp Chem Phys Mater Condens State ... Bibliography on the High Temperature Chemistry and Physics of Materials in the Condensed State [*A publication*]
Bibliogr Hist Med ... Bibliography of the History of Medicine [*A publication*]
Bibliogr Index ... Bibliographic Index [*A publication*]
Bibliogr Index Geol ... Bibliography and Index of Geology [*A publication*]
Bibliogr Index Geol Exclus North Am ... Bibliography and Index of Geology Exclusive of North America [*A publication*]
Bibliogr Index Health Educ Period ... Bibliographic Index of Health Education Periodicals. BIHEP [*A publication*]
Bibliogr Index Micropaleontology ... Bibliography and Index of Micropaleontology [*A publication*]
Bibliogr Irradiat Foods ... Bibliography in Irradiation of Foods [*West Germany*] [*A publication*]
Bibliogr Lit Agric US Dep Agric Econ Stat Serv ... Bibliographies and Literature of Agriculture. United States Department of Agriculture. Economics and Statistics Service [*A publication*]
Bibliogr Med Biol ... Bibliografia Medico-Biologica [*A publication*]
Bibliogr North Am Geol ... Bibliography of North American Geology [*A publication*]
Bibliogr Paint Technol ... Bibliographies in Paint Technology [*A publication*]
Bibliogr Phytosociol Syntaxon ... Bibliographia Phytosociologica Syntaxonomica [*A publication*]
Bibliogr Reihe Kernforschungsanlage Juelich ... Bibliographische Reihe der Kernforschungsanlage Juelich [*A publication*]
Bibliogr Repert Inst Chret ... RIC. Repertoire Bibliographique des Institutions Chretiennes [*A publication*]
Bibliogr Reprod ... Bibliography of Reproduction [*A publication*]
Bibliogr Rev Chem ... Bibliography of Reviews in Chemistry [*A publication*]
Bibliogr Sci Ind Rep ... Bibliography of Scientific and Industrial Reports [*A publication*]
Bibliogr Ser IAEA ... Bibliographical Series. International Atomic Energy Agency [*A publication*]
Bibliogr Ser Inst Pap Chem ... Bibliographic Series. Institute of Paper Chemistry [*A publication*]
Bibliogr Ser Ore For Res Lab ... Bibliographical Series. Oregon State University. Forest Research Laboratory [*A publication*]
Bibliogr Stud ... Bibliographien und Studien [*A publication*]

Bibliogr Subj Index S Afr Geol ... Bibliography and Subject Index of South African Geology [*A publication*]
Bibliogr Tech Rep ... Bibliography of Technical Reports [*A publication*]
Bibliogr Umweltradioakt Lebensm ... Bibliographie zur Umweltradioaktivitaet in Lebensmitteln [*West Germany*] [*A publication*]
Bibliog Soc Am Pa ... Bibliographical Society of America. Papers [*A publication*]
Biblio Ital Educ Sordi ... Bibliografia Italiana sull'Educazione dei Sordi [*A publication*]
Biblio Sci Nat Helv ... Bibliographia Scientiae Naturalis Helvetica [*Bern*] [*A publication*]
Biblio Soc Am ... Bibliographical Society of America. Papers [*A publication*]
Biblioteca Nac Jose Marti R ... Biblioteca Nacional Jose Marti. Revista [*A publication*]
Biblioth Med Cassel ... Bibliotheca Medica Cassel [*A publication*]
Bibliot Vrach ... Biblioteka Vracha [*A publication*]
Bibl Jose Jeronimo Triana ... Biblioteca Jose Jeronimo Triana [*A publication*]
Bibl Laeger ... Bibliotek for Laeger [*A publication*]
Bibl Liberta ... Biblioteca della Liberta [*A publication*]
Bibl Mat ..... Biblioteka Matematyczna [*A publication*]
Bibl Med Can ... Bibliotheca Medica Canadiana [*A publication*]
Bibl Meridionale ... Bibliotheque Meridionale [*A publication*]
Bibl Microbiol ... Bibliotheca Microbiologica [*A publication*]
Bibl Nutr D ... Bibliotheca Nutrito et Dieta [*A publication*]
Bibl Nutr Dieta ... Bibliotheca Nutrito et Dieta [*A publication*]
Bibl Ophthalmol ... Bibliotheca Ophthalmologica [*A publication*]
BiblOr .... Bibliotheca Orientalis [*A publication*]   (BJA)
Bibl Orient ... Bibliotheca Orientalis [*A publication*]
Bibl Oto-Rhino-Laryngol ... Bibliotheca Oto-Rhino-Laryngologica [*A publication*]
Bibl Paediatr ... Bibliotheca Paediatrica [*A publication*]
Bibl Pflanz ... Bibliographie der Pflanzenschutzliteratur [*A publication*]
Biblphical Bull US Dep Agric Libr ... Bibliographical Bulletin. United States Department of Agriculture. Library [*A publication*]
Biblphical Contr US Dep Agric Libr ... Bibliographical Contributions. United States Department of Agriculture. Library [*A publication*]
Biblphie Anat ... Bibliographie Anatomique [*A publication*]
Biblphien Dt Wetterd ... Bibliographien des Deutschen Wetterdienstes [*A publication*]
Bibl Phonet ... Bibliotheca Phonetica [*A publication*]
Bibl Phonetica ... Bibliotheca Phonetica [*A publication*]
Biblphy Agric (Wash) ... Bibliography of Agriculture (Washington) [*A publication*]
Biblphy Bee Research Ass ... Bibliography. Bee Research Association [*A publication*]
Bibl Phycol ... Bibliotheca Phycologica [*A publication*]
Biblphy Int Bee Res Ass ... Bibliography. International Bee Research Association [*A publication*]
Bibl Primatol ... Bibliotheca Primatologica [*A publication*]
Bibl Problemow ... Biblioteka Problemow [*A publication*]
Bibl Psych ... Bibliotheca Psychiatrica [*A publication*]
Bibl Psychiatr ... Bibliotheca Psychiatrica [*A publication*]
Bibl Psychiatr Neurol ... Bibliotheca Psychiatrica et Neurologica [*A publication*]
Bibl Radiol ... Bibliotheca Radiologica [*A publication*]
Bibl Repro ... Bibliography of Reproduction [*A publication*]
BiblRes ...... Biblical Research. Papers of the Chicago Society of Biblical Research [*Amsterdam*] [*A publication*]
Bibl Sac ...... Bibliotheca Sacra [*A publication*]
Bibl Selective Pubns Officielles Fr ... Bibliographie Selective des Publications Officielles Francaises [*A publication*]
Bibl Sel'sk Profsoiuznogo Akt ... Bibliotechka Sel'skogo Profsoiuznogo Aktivista [*A publication*]
Bibl Soc Am Pa ... Bibliographical Society of America. Papers [*A publication*]
Bibl Stor T ... Biblioteca Storica Toscana. Sezione di Storia del Risorgimento [*A publication*]
BiblStud ..... Biblische Studien [*Neukirchen*] [*A publication*]
Bibl Topogr ... Bibliographie Topographique des Principales Cites Grecques de l'Italie Meridionale et de la Sicile dans l'Antiquite [*A publication*]   (OCD)
Bibl Tuberc ... Bibliotheca Tuberculosea [*A publication*]
Bibl Tuberc Med Thorac ... Bibliotheca Tuberculosea et Medicinae Thoracalis [*A publication*]
Bibl Tub Me T ... Bibliotheca Tuberculosea et Medicinae Thoracalis [*A publication*]
Bibl Universelle Rev Suisse ... Bibliotheque Universelle et Revue Suisse [*A publication*]
Bibl Univers Geneve ... Bibliotheque Universelle de Geneve [*A publication*]
Bibl Univers Rev Gen ... Bibliotheque Universelle et Revue de Geneve [*A publication*]
Bibl Univers Rev Suisse ... Bibliotheque Universelle et Revue Suisse [*A publication*]
Bibl Univers Rev Suisse Etrang Nouv Periode ... Bibliotheque Universelle et Revue Suisse et Etrangere. Nouvelle Periode [*A publication*]
Bibl Univers Sci B L Arts Sci Arts ... Bibliotheque Universelle des Sciences, Belles Lettres, et Arts. Sciences et Arts [*A publication*]
Bibl "Vita Hum" ... Bibliotheca "Vita Humana" [*A publication*]
Bibl Wirtschaftspresse ... Bibliographie der Wirtschaftspresse [*A publication*]
BiblZ .... Biblische Zeitschrift [*A publication*]

BIBM......... Bureau International du Beton Manufacture [*International Bureau for Precast Concrete*] (EAIO)

BIBNET .... Bibliographic Network [*OCLC retrieval system*] [*Data processing*]

Bib Not....... Biblische Notizen. Beitraege zur Exegetischen Diskussion [*A publication*]

BibO........... Bibbia e Oriente Fossano, Cuneo (BJA)

BibO........... Bibliotheca Orientalis [*A publication*]

BIBO.......... Bureau of International Business Operations [*Department of Commerce*] [*Abolished, 1963*]

Bib Or .... Bibbia e Oriente [*A publication*]

Bib Padagog ... Bibliographie Padagogik [*A publication*]

Bib R .... Biblical Review [*A publication*]

BIBR........... Bulletin. Institut Historique Belge de Rome [*A publication*]

BIBRA .... British Industrial Biological Research Association (ARC)

BIBRA Bull ... BIBRA [*British Industrial Biological Research Association*] Bulletin [*A publication*]

Bib Res....... Biblical Research [*A publication*]

BIBS .... Built-In Breathing System

Bib Sac...... Bibliotheca Sacra [*A publication*]

Bib Sacra ... Bibliotheca Sacra [*A publication*]

Bibs of Aust Writers ... Bibliographies of Australian Writers [*State Library of South Australia*] [*A publication*] (APTA)

Bib Soc Am ... Bibliographical Society of America. Papers [*A publication*]

BibTB .... Biblical Theology Bulletin [*Rome*] [*A publication*]

Bib Th Bul ... Biblical Theology Bulletin [*A publication*]

Bib Tr No 1 No 3 ... Bible Translator. Technical Papers. Numbers 1 and 3 [*A publication*]

Bib Tr No 2 No 4 ... Bible Translator. Practical Papers. Numbers 2 and 4 [*A publication*]

Bib Tr P ..... Bible Translator. Practical Papers [*A publication*]

Bib Tr T ..... Bible Translator. Technical Papers [*A publication*]

BI Bulg....... Bulletin. Institut Archeologique Bulgare [*A publication*]

Bib World ... Biblical World [*A publication*]

Bib Z .... Biblische Zeitschrift [*A publication*]

BIC............. Baha'i International Community

BIC............. Balkan Intelligence Centre [*British*] [*World War II*]

BIC............. Bank Investment Contract

BIC............. Barium Ion Cloud [*NASA*]

BIC............. Battery Interconnecting Cables (NATG)

BIC............. Battlefield Information Center [*Army*] (AABC)

BIC............. Bayes Information Criterion

BIC............. Beatles Information Center (EAIO)

BIC............. Beef Industry Council (EA)

BIC............. Benefices Industriels et Commerciaux [*Industrial and Business Profits*] [*French*]

BIC............. Bibas in Christo [*May You Live in Christ*] [*Latin*]

BIC............. Bic Corp. [*AMEX symbol*] (SPSG)

BIC............. Bicuculline [*Organic chemistry*]

BIC............. Biodeterioration Information Centre [*British*]

BIC............. Biographical Inventory Creativity

BIC............. Biomedical Instrumentation Consultant

BIC............. Bombardment-Induced Conductivity

BICL............ Books in Canada [*A publication*]

BIC............. Braniff International Council [*Club for frequent flyers*] (EA)

BIC............. British Importers' Confederation (DS)

BIC............. British Insulated Cables

BIC............. Broadband Interface Controller [*Motorola, Inc.*]

BIC............. Building Information Centre [*Cauldon College of Further and Higher Education*] [*British*] (CB)

BIC............. Bulletin Interieur des Cadres [*A publication*]

BIC............. Bureau International de la Chaussure et du Cuir

BIC............. Bureau International du Cinema [*International Cinematograph Bureau*]

BIC............. Bureau of International Commerce [*Department of Commerce*] [*Functions transferred to Domestic and International Business Administration*]

BIC............. Bureau International des Containers [*International Container Bureau*] [*Paris, France*] (EAIO)

BIC............. Bus Interface Circuit [*Data processing*] (MDG)

BIC............. Business in the Community [*British*]

B-I-C.......... Business Intelligence Center [*SRI International*] [*Information service or system*] (IID)

BIC............. Business and Investments Centre [*British*]

BIC............. Butec International Chemical Corp. [*Formerly, Tay River Petroleum Ltd.*] [*Vancouver Stock Exchange symbol*]

BIC............. Butter Information Council [*British*]

BIC............. Butyl Isocyanate [*Organic chemistry*]

BIC............. Byte Input Control [*Data processing*]

BICA.......... Bighorn Canyon National Recreation Area

BICA.......... Bollettino. Istituto di Corrispondenza Archeologica [*A publication*]

BICA.......... Reykjavik [*Iceland*] [*ICAO location identifier*] (ICLI)

BICAER .... Bulletin. International Committee on Urgent Anthropological and Ethnological Research [*A publication*]

BICARB .... Bicarbonate

BICARSA ... Billing, Inventory Control, Accounts Receivable, Sales Analysis (IBMDP)

BI/CAS...... Business International Country Assessment Service [*Business International Corp.*] [*Defunct*] [*Information service or system*] (CRD)

BICB.......... Institut Royal Colonial Belge. Bulletin des Seances [*A publication*]

BICByz ...... Bulletin d'Information et de Coordination. Association Internationale des Etudes Byzantines [*A publication*]

BICC.......... Battlefield Information Communications Center (MCD)

BICC.......... Battlefield Information Control Center [*Army*] (AABC)

BICC.......... Battlefield Integration Coordination Center

BICC.......... Boletin. Instituto Caro y Cuervo [*A publication*]

BICC.......... Boston International Choreography Competition

BICC.......... British Insulated Callender's Cable

BICC.......... Bureau d'Interventions Cliniques et Communautaires [*Office of Clinical and Communal Operations*] [*Canada*]

BICC.......... Reykjavik [*Iceland*] [*ICAO location identifier*] (ICLI)

BICE.......... Banca Internationala de Colaborare Economica [*International Bank for Economic Cooperation - IBEC*] [*Romanian*]

BICE.......... Banca Internazionale per la Cooperazione Economica [*International Bank for Economic Cooperation - IBEC*] [*Italian*]

BICE.......... Bureau International Catholique de l'Enfance [*International Catholic Child Bureau - ICCB*] [*Geneva, Switzerland*] (EA)

BICEB .... Bulletin d'Information des Centrales Electriques [*A publication*]

BICED .... Biologie Cellulaire [*A publication*]

BICEMA ..... British Internal Combustion Engine Manufacturers' Association

BICEP .... British Industrial Collaborative Exponential Program

BICEPS ..... Basic Inservice Computer Education for Primary Schools [*Australia*]

BICEPT..... Book Indexing with Context and Entry Points from Text [*Indexing method*] [*Data processing*] (DIT)

BICERI...... British Internal Combustion Engine Research Institute Ltd. (IRUK)

BICFET...... Bipolar Inversion Channel Field Effect Transistor (MCD)

Bic Forum .. Bicycle Forum [*A publication*]

BICH.......... Bulletin. International Committee of Historical Sciences [*A publication*]

BICHA ...... Biochemistry [*A publication*]

BICHB....... Bioinorganic Chemistry [*A publication*]

Bich Crim Proc ... Bishop on Criminal Procedure [*A publication*] (DLA)

BICHS....... Bulletin. International Committee of Historical Sciences [*A publication*]

BICINE ..... Bis(hydroxyethyl)glycine [*A buffer*] [*Organic chemistry*]

BICIV .... Bipartite Civil Service Advisors [*Post-World War II, Germany*]

Bick........... Bicknell and Hawley's Reports [*10-20 Nevada*] [*A publication*] (DLA)

Bick Civ Pr ... Bicknell's Indiana Civil Practice [*A publication*] (DLA)

Bick Cr Pr ... Bicknell's Indiana Criminal Practice [*A publication*] (DLA)

Bickel C M N ... Bickel's Coin and Medal News. Munt en Medaljenuus [*A publication*]

Bick & H .... Bicknell and Hawley's Reports [*10-20 Nevada*] [*A publication*] (DLA)

Bick & Hawl ... Bicknell and Hawley's Reports [*10-20 Nevada*] [*A publication*] (DLA)

Bick (In)..... Bicknell's Reports [*India*] [*A publication*] (DLA)

BICL........... Biocell Technology [*NASDAQ symbol*] (NQ)

BICMA...... Bulletin. Institute of Chemistry. Academia Sinica [*Taiwan*] [*A publication*]

BICMG...... Brothers of the Immaculate Conception of the Mother of God [*See also CBH*] [*Huybergen, Netherlands*] (EAIO)

BiCNU ...... Bis(chloroethyl)nitrosourea [*Carmustine*] [*Also, BCNU*] [*Antineoplastic drug regimen*]

BICO .... Biocontrol Technology, Inc. [*Indiana, PA*] [*NASDAQ symbol*] (NQ)

BICO .... Bipartite Control Office [*Post-World War II, Germany*]

B & ICO..... British and Irish Communist Organization [*Irish*]

BICOB....... Biological Conservation [*A publication*]

BICOM ..... Bipartite Communications Panel [*Post-World War II, Germany*]

BICOM ..... Brunel Institute of Computational Mathematics [*British*] (IRUK)

BICOND ... Biconditional

BICORD ... Bistatic Coherent RADAR Display (MCD)

BICP .... Biomedical Interdisciplinary Curriculum Project [*National Science Foundation*]

BICR.......... Bollettino. Istituto Centrale di Restauro [*A publication*]

BICRA .... Bulletin. Institute for Chemical Research. Kyoto University [*A publication*]

BICRAM ... Beijer Institute Centre for Resource Assessment and Management [*British*] (IRUK)

BICS .... [*The*] British Institute of Cleaning Science

BICS .... Building Industry Consulting Service [*Telecommunications*] (TEL)

BICS .... Bulletin. Institute of Classical Studies. University of London [*A publication*]

BICS .... Burroughs Inventory Control System [*Data processing*] (BUR)

BICSA .... British Industry Committee on South Africa

BICSC .... British Institute of Cleaning Science

BICSI......... Building Industry Consulting Service International [*Tampa, FL*] [*Telecommunications service*]

BIC/SVP ... Business Information Centre/SVP [*Information service or system*] (IID)

BICTA .... Bibliotheca Tuberculosea [*A publication*]

BICTA .... British Investment Casting Trade Association
BICWM ..... Brethren in Christ World Missions (EA)
BICYA .... Biological Cybernetics [*A publication*]
Bicycles Bull ... Bicycles Bulletin [*A publication*]
BID .... Bachelor of Industrial Design
B of ID ...... Bachelor of Interior Design
BID .... Background Information Document [*Environmental Protection Agency*]
BID .... Bacterial Identification
BID .... Banco Interamericano de Desarrollo [*Inter-American Development Bank*] [*Spanish*]
BID .... Banque Interamericaine de Developpement [*Inter-American Development Bank*] [*French*]
BID .... Bellevue Index of Depression
Bid .... Bidder's Court of Referees Reports [*England*] [*A publication*] (DLA)
Bid .... Bidder's Locus Standi Reports [*England*] [*A publication*] (DLA)
BID .... Biddy [*Slang*] (DSUE)
BID .... Bidston [*England*] [*Seismograph station code, US Geological Survey*] [*Closed*] (SEIS)
BID .... Big I Development Ltd. [*Vancouver Stock Exchange symbol*]
BID .... Bis in Die [*Twice a Day*] [*Pharmacy*]
BID .... Blast-Induced Distortion (MCD)
BID .... Block Island [*Rhode Island*] [*Airport symbol*] (OAG)
BID .... Blockade Intelligence Department [*Ministry of Economic Warfare*] [*British*] [*World War II*]
BID .... Blow in Door
BID .... Brazilian Infantry Division [*World War II*]
BID .... British Investors Database
BID .... Brought in Dead [*Medicine*]
BID .... Bureau, Institute, and Division [*National Institutes of Health*]
BID .... Bureau of Institutional Development [*Office of Education*]
BID .... Inter-American Development Bank, Washington, DC [*OCLC symbol*] (OCLC)
BID .... Sotheby's Holdings, Inc. Class A [*NYSE symbol*] (SPSG)
bi7d .... Bis in Septem Diebus [*Twice a Week*] [*Pharmacy*]
BIDAP .... Bibliographic Data Processing Program [*For keyword indexing*] [*Information retrieval software*]
BIDCO ...... Business and Industrial Development Corporation [*Generic term for a for-profit investment company*]
BIDCUS .... Bibliotheque de l'Institut de Droit Canonique de l'Universite de Strasbourg [*A publication*]
Bidd .... Bidder's Locus Standi Reports, I [*1820-36*] [*A publication*] (DLA)
Biddie .... [*Baby*] Boomer in Debt [*Lifestyle classification*]
BIDE .... Built-In Diagnostic Equipment [*Analytical chemistry*]
BIDEC .... Binary-to-Decimal Converter [*Data processing*]
BIDEC .... Bipartite Decartelization Commission [*Berlin*] [*Post-World War II, Germany*]
BIDEF .... Bideford [*Municipal borough in England*]
BIDESC .... Bipartite Decartelization Sub-Commission [*Minden*] [*Post-World War II, Germany*]
BIDFD .... Bulletin. International Dairy Federation [*A publication*]
BIDI .... Business and Industrial Development Institute [*Saginaw Valley State College*] [*Database search service*] (OLDSS)
BIDICS ...... Bond Index to the Determination of Inorganic Crystal Structures [*McMaster University, Canada*]
BIDICS (Bond Index Determinations Inorg Cryst Struct) ... BIDICS (Bond Index to the Determinations of Inorganic Crystal Structures) [*A publication*]
BIDID .... Biosources Digest [*A publication*]
BIDIEA ..... Bibliotheca Diatomologica [*A publication*]
Bid Ins ...... Biddle on Insurance [*A publication*] (DLA)
BIDO .... British Industrial Development Office [*Through foreign branches, encourages investments in Britain from abroad*]
BIDOPS .... Bi-Doppler Scoring System (MCD)
BIDP .... Basic Institutional Development Program [*Under Title III of the Higher Education Act*]
BIDR .... Bollettino. Istituto di Diritto Romano [*A publication*]
Bid Retr Leg ... Biddle on Retrospective Legislation [*A publication*] (DLA)
BIDS .... Base Intrusion Detection System (MCD)
BIDS .... Battlefield Information Distribution System (MCD)
BIDS .... Bendix Integrated Data System
BIDS .... Boiler Information Data System [*Southwest Research Institute*]
BIDS .... Building Industry Development Services
BIDS .... Moody's Bond Information Database Service [*Moody's Investors Service, Inc.*] [*Information service or system*] (CRD)
Bid Tab Stat ... Biddle's Table of Statutes [*A publication*] (DLA)
BIDV .... Djupivogur [*Iceland*] [*ICAO location identifier*] (ICLI)
Bid War Sale Chat ... Biddle on Warranties in Sale of Chattels [*A publication*] (DLA)
BIDZD ...... Boei Ika Daigakko Zasshi [*A publication*]
BIE .... Bachelor of Industrial Engineering
BIE .... Beatrice, NE [*Location identifier*] [*FAA*] (FAAL)
BIE .... Binaural Intensity Effect
BIE .... Bio-Electron Systems Class A [*AMEX symbol*] (SPSG)
BIE .... Blackout Restrictions in Industrial Establishments [*British*] [*World War II*]
BIE .... Boletin. Instituto de las Espanas [*A publication*]

BIE .... Boletin. Instituto Espanol de Londres [*A publication*]
BIE .... Boundary Integral Equation (MCD)
BIE .... British Institute of Embalmers
BIE .... British Institute of Engineers (MCD)
BIE .... Bulletin. Institut d'Egypte [*A publication*]
BIE .... Bureau of Industrial Economics [*Department of Commerce*]
BIE .... Bureau International d'Education [*International Bureau of Education - IBE*] (EAIO)
BIE .... Bureau International des Expositions [*International Bureau of Exhibitions*] (EAIO)
BIE .... Business-Industry-Education [*Days*] [*Usually sponsored by chambers of commerce*]
BIEA .... Boletin. Instituto de Estudios Asturianos [*A publication*]
BIECO ...... Bipartite Economic Panel [*Post-World War II, Germany*]
BIECO/RAIL ... Bipartite Economic Panel Railway Supplies Committee [*Post-World War II, Germany*]
Biedermanns Zentralbl ... Biedermanns Zentralblatt [*A publication*]
Biedermanns Zentralbl Abt A ... Biedermanns Zentralblatt. Abteilung A. Allgemeiner und Referierender Teil [*A publication*]
Biedermanns Zentralbl Abt B ... Biedermanns Zentralblatt. Abteilung B. Tierernaehrung [*A publication*]
BIEE .... British Institute of Electrical Engineers
BIEG .... Egilsstadir [*Iceland*] [*ICAO location identifier*] (ICLI)
BIEGB ...... Bulletin. International Association of Engineering Geology [*A publication*]
BIEH .... Boletin. Instituto de Estudios Helenicos [*A publication*]
BIEM .... Bureau International de l'Edition Mecanique
bien .... Biennial [*Botany*]
BIEN .... Billings Corp. [*NASDAQ symbol*] (NQ)
BIEN .... Business Information Exchange Network [*Databank*] [*Canada*]
Bienenbl Bundesgebiet ... Bienen-Blatt fuer des Bundesgebiet [*A publication*]
Bienenw Zbl ... Bienenwirtschaftliches Zentralblatt [*A publication*]
Bienen Ztg ... Bienen-Zeitung [*A publication*]
Bien-Etre Soc Canadien ... Bien-Etre Social Canadien [*A publication*]
BI Eng ...... Bachelor of Industrial Engineering
BIENN ...... Biennial
Bienn Conf Carbon Ext Abstr Program ... Biennial Conference. Carbon. Extended Abstracts and Program [*A publication*]
Bienn Congr Int Deep Drawing Res Group ... Biennial Congress. International Deep Drawing Research Group [*A publication*]
Biennial Rep Iowa Att'y Gen ... Biennial Report of the Attorney General of the State of Iowa [*A publication*] (DLA)
Biennial Rep & Op W Va Atty's Gen ... Biennial Report and Official Opinions of the Attorney General of the State of West Virginia [*A publication*] (DLA)
Biennial Rep SD Att'y Gen ... Biennial Report of the Attorney General of the State of South Dakota [*A publication*] (DLA)
Biennial Rep VT Att'y Gen ... Biennial Report of the Attorney General of the State of Vermont [*A publication*] (DLA)
Bienn Int CODATA Conf ... Biennial International CODATA [*Committee on Data for Science and Technology*] Conference [*A publication*]
Bienn Rep Hawaii Geophys ... Biennial Report. Hawaii Institute of Geophysics [*A publication*]
Bienn Rep Hawaii Inst Geophys ... Biennial Report. Hawaii Institute of Geophysics [*A publication*]
Bienn Rev Anthropol ... Biennial Review of Anthropology [*A publication*]
Bienn Studi Stor Arte Med ... Biennial. Studi Storia Arte Medicina [*A publication*]
Bien Rep Hawaii Agr Exp Sta ... Biennial Report. Hawaii Agricultural Experiment Station [*A publication*]
Bien Rep Iowa Book Agr ... Biennial Report. Iowa. Book of Agriculture. Iowa State Department of Agriculture [*A publication*]
Bien Rep Nev State Dept Agr ... Biennial Report. Nevada State Department of Agriculture [*A publication*]
BieOr .... Bibbia e Oriente Fossano, Cuneo (BJA)
BIEPR .... Bureau of International Economic Policy and Research [*Department of Commerce*]
BIES .... Bulletin. Israel Exploration Society [*Formerly, BJPES*] [*Jerusalem*] [*A publication*]
BIET .... Basic Initial Entry Test (MCD)
BIET .... Basic Initial Entry Training (MCD)
BietOr .... Biblica et Orientalia. Sacra Scriptura Antiquitatibus Orientalibus Illustrata [*Rome*] [*A publication*] (BJA)
BIF .... Balanced Income & Growth Fund Trust Units [*Toronto Stock Exchange symbol*]
BIF .... Banded Iron Formation [*Geology*]
BIF .... Bank Insurance Fund
BIF .... Basic in Flow (NRCH)
BIF .... Basic Imagery File (MCD)
BIF .... Beef Improvement Federation (EA)
BIF .... Best Inhibitory Frequency [*Neurophysiology*]
BIF .... Boletin. Instituto Frances [*A publication*]
BIF .... Bombardier's Information File
BIF .... British Industries Fair
BIF .... British Industries Federation
BIF .... Budget Information Form (OICC)
BIF .... El Paso, TX [*Location identifier*] [*FAA*] (FAAL)
BIF & A ..... Bipartite Food and Agriculture Panel [*Post-World War II, Germany*]

BIFAD .... Board for International Food and Agricultural Development [*Agency for International Development*] [*Washington, DC*]

BIFAO .... Bulletin. Institut Francais d'Archeologie Orientale [*A publication*]

BIFD .... Bulletin for International Fiscal Documentation [*A publication*]

BIFF .... Battlefield Identification Friend or Foe   (MCD)

BIFF .... Bistatic Identification, Friend or Foe   (MCD)

BIFFEX ..... Baltic International Freight Futures Exchange [*London, England*]

BIFG .... Boletin. Institucion Fernan-Gonzalez [*A publication*]

BIFG .... Bollettino. Istituto di Filologia Greca. Universita di Padova [*A publication*]

BIFIN .... Bipartite Finance Panel [*Post-World War II, Germany*]

BIFL .... Biflyx [*NASDAQ symbol*]   (NQ)

BIFLTA ..... Bulletin. Illinois Foreign Language Teachers Association [*A publication*]

BIFM......... Fagurholsmyri [*Iceland*] [*ICAO location identifier*]   (ICLI)

BIFMA ...... Business and Institutional Furniture Manufacturers Association   (EA)

BIFP .... Boletin. Instituto de Investigaciones Folkloricas. Universidad Interamericana (Panama) [*A publication*]

BIFP .... Bulletin et Memoires. Institut des Fouilles de Provence et des Prealpes [*A publication*]

BIFR .... Before Encountering Instrument Flight Rules Conditions   (FAAC)

BIFR .... Buletinul. Institutului de Filologie Romaina "Alexandru Philippide" [*Iasi*] [*A publication*]

BIFRI .... Buletinul. Institutului de Filologie Romaina "Alexandru Philippide" (Iasi) [*A publication*]

BIFU .... Banking Insurance and Finance Union [*Formerly, National Union of Bank Employees - NUBE*] [*British*]   (DCTA)

BIFV .... Boletin. Instituto de Folklore [*A publication*]

BIFV .... Bradley Infantry Fighting Vehicle [*Army*]   (INF)

BIG .... BCS [*Boeing Computer Services*] Interactive Graphics

BIG .... Best in Group

BIG .... Bicycle-Motocross Industrial Guild   (EA)

BIG .... Big, Intrusive Government

BIG .... Big Mountain [*Alaska*] [*Seismograph station code, US Geological Survey*]   (SEIS)

Big............. Bignell's Reports [*India*] [*A publication*]   (DLA)

BIG .... Bigstone Minerals [*Vancouver Stock Exchange symbol*]

BIG .... Biological Isolation Garment [*NASA*]

BIG .... Blacks in Government   (EA)

BIG .... Bond International Gold, Inc. [*NYSE symbol*]

BIG .... Business Information Group [*Information service or system*]   (EISS)

BIG .... Business Investment Game

BIG .... Delta Junction/Fort Greely, AK [*Location identifier*] [*FAA*]   (FAAL)

BIG .... Melbourne Business Information Guide [*A publication*]   (APTA)

BIGB......... Big B, Inc. [*NASDAQ symbol*]   (NQ)

BIGBA .... Buletinul. Institutului Politehnic "Gheorghe Gheorghiu-Dej" Bucuresti [*A publication*]

Big B & B ... Bigelow's Bench and Bar of New York [*A publication*]   (DLA)

Big B & N... Bigelow's Cases on Bills and Notes [*A publication*]   (DLA)

Big Cas...... Bigelow's Cases, William I to Richard I [*A publication*]   (DLA)

Big Cas B & N ... Bigelow's Cases on Bills and Notes [*A publication*]   (DLA)

Big Cas Torts ... Bigelow's Leading Cases on Torts [*A publication*]   (DLA)

Big D......... Big Deal [*A publication*]

BIGEB .... Biochemical Genetics [*A publication*]

Bigelow Estop ... Bigelow on Estoppel [*A publication*]   (DLA)

Bigelow Lead Cas ... Bigelow's Leading Cases on Bills and Notes, Torts, or Wills [*A publication*]   (DLA)

BIGENA.... Bibliography and Index of Geology Exclusive of North America [*A publication*]

Big Eng Proc ... Bigelow's English Procedure [*A publication*]   (DLA)

Big Eq .... Bigelow on Equity [*A publication*]   (DLA)

Big Est .... Bigelow on Estoppel [*A publication*]   (DLA)

Big Farm Manage ... Big Farm Management [*A publication*]

BIGFET..... Bipolar Insulated Gate Field-Effect Transistor [*Bell Laboratories*]

Big Fr .... Bigelow on Frauds [*A publication*]   (DLA)

Bigg Cr L ... Bigg's Criminal Law [*A publication*]   (DLA)

BIGGL .... Biggleswade [*Urban district in England*]

Bigg RR Acts ... Biggs on Acts Relating to Railways [*A publication*]   (DLA)

BIGI.......... Brougher Insurance Group, Incorporated [*Greenwood, IN*] [*NASDAQ symbol*]   (NQ)

Big Jarm Wills ... Bigelow's Edition of Jarman on Wills [*A publication*]   (DLA)

BIGLA....... Bioloski Glasnik [*A publication*]

Big L & A Ins Cas ... Bigelow's Life and Accident Insurance Cases [*A publication*]   (DLA)

Big L & A Ins Rep ... Bigelow's Life and Accident Insurance Reports [*A publication*]   (DLA)

Big Lead Cas ... Bigelow's Leading Cases on Bills and Notes, Torts, or Wills [*A publication*]   (DLA)

Big Ll Cas ... Bigelow's Life and Accident Insurance Cases [*A publication*]   (DLA)

Big Mama .. Big Mama Rag [*A publication*]

Bign........... Bignell's Reports [*India*] [*A publication*]   (DLA)

BIGO .... Big O Tires, Inc. [*NASDAQ symbol*]   (NQ)

Big Ov Cas ... Bigelow's Overruled Cases [*United States, England, Ireland*] [*A publication*]   (DLA)

Big Plac..... Bigelow's Placita Anglo-Normanica [*A publication*]   (DLA)

Big Proc ..... Bigelow's English Procedure [*A publication*]   (DLA)

BIGR......... Grimsey [*Iceland*] [*ICAO location identifier*]   (ICLI)

BIGS......... Booster Inertial Guidance System [*Aerospace*]

Big Sky Econ Mont Stat Univ Coop Ext Serv ... Big Sky Economics. Montana State University. Cooperative Extension Service [*A publication*]

BIGT......... Big Turtle, Inc. [*NASDAQ symbol*]   (NQ)

Big Torts .... Bigelow on Torts [*A publication*]   (DLA)

BIH .... Benign Intracranial Hypertension [*Medicine*]

BiH .... Bibliografia Hispanica [*A publication*]

BIH .... Bishop [*California*] [*Airport symbol*]   (OAG)

BIH .... Built-In Hold [*of countdown*] [*NASA*]   (KSC)

BIH .... Bureau International de l'Heure [*International Time Bureau*]   (EAIO)

BIHAA ...... Bibliotheca Haematologica [*A publication*]

Bihang K Svensk Vetensk-Akad Handl (Stockholm) ... Bihang till Kongliga Svenska Vetenskaps-Akademiens Handlingar (Stockholm) [*A publication*]

Bihar Acad Agr Sci Proc ... Bihar Academy of Agricultural Sciences. Proceedings [*A publication*]

BIHBR....... Bulletin. Institut Historique Belge de Rome [*A publication*]

BIHC .... Boat Inlet/High-Capacity [*Analytical combustion system*]

BIHEP....... Bibliographic Index of Health Education Periodicals [*Information service or system*] [*A publication*]

B I Hist R... Bulletin. Institute of Historical Research [*A publication*]

Bih LJ Rep ... Bihar Law Journal Reports [*India*] [*A publication*]   (DLA)

BIHN......... Hofn/Hornafjordur [*Iceland*] [*ICAO location identifier*]   (ICLI)

BIHO......... Big Hole National Battlefield

BI Hochschultaschenb ... BI [*Bibliographisches Institut*] Hochschultaschenbuecher [*A publication*]

BIHOR ...... Bihorium [*During Two Hours*] [*Pharmacy*]

BIHP .... Bulletin. Institute of History and Philology. Academia Sinica [*A publication*]

BiHR .... Bibliotheque d'Humanisme et Renaissance [*A publication*]

BIHR .... British Institute of Human Rights   (DLA)

BIHR .... Bulletin. Institute of Historical Research [*A publication*]

Bih Rep ..... Bihar Reports [*India*] [*A publication*]   (DLA)

BIHU......... Husavik [*Iceland*] [*ICAO location identifier*]   (ICLI)

BII .... Background Illumination Intensity

BII............. Ballen Booksellers International, Incorporated [*UTLAS symbol*]

BII............. Banca Internationala de Investitii [*International Investment Bank*]

BII............. Banque d'Information Industrielle [*Industrial Information Data Base*] [*Industrial Research Center of Quebec*] [*Information service or system*]   (IID)

BII............. Basic Issue Items [*Army*]   (AABC)

BII............. Battery Information Index [*Battelle Memorial Institute*]   (IID)

BII............. BII Enterprises, Inc. [*Toronto Stock Exchange symbol*]

BII............. Biosophical Institute, Incorporated [*Defunct*]

BII............. Biotechnica International, Inc.

BI & I .... Boiler Inspection and Insurance

BII............. British Institute of Innkeeping

BII............. Bulletin. Iranian Institute of America [*A publication*]

BII............. Business Interruption Insurance

BIIA .... British Institute of Industrial Art

BIIB .... Basic Imagery Interpretation Brief   (MCD)

BIIBA .... British Insurance and Investment Brokers' Association

BIIC .... Battlefield Integrated Information Center   (MCD)

BIICC .... Bureau International d'Information des Chambres de Commerce

BIICL........ British Institute of International and Comparative Law

BIIDD........ Bulletin. Institute for Industrial and Social Development [*South Korea*] [*A publication*]

BIIH .... Boletin. Instituto de Investigaciones Historicas [*A publication*]

BIIL .... Basic Issue Items List [*Army*]   (AABC)

BIIL .... Boletin. Instituto de Investigaciones Literarias [*A publication*]

BIINA....... Biuletyn. Instytutu Naftowego [*A publication*]

BIINVD..... Battlefield Illumination Integrated Night Vision Devices   (MCD)

BIIPAM-CTIF ... Banque d'Information Industrielle de Pont-A-Mousson et du CTIF [*Centre Technique des Industries de la Fonderie*] [*French*] [*Information service or system*]   (CRD)

BIIR .... Basic Imagery Interpretation Report   (MCD)

BIIRHT ..... Bulletin d'Information. Institut de Recherche et d'Histoire des Textes [*A publication*]

BIIS .... Isafjordur [*Iceland*] [*ICAO location identifier*]   (ICLI)

BIIT .... British Institute of Industrial Therapy

BIIZDH.... Instytut Zootechnik. Biuletyn Informacyjny [*A publication*]

BIJ .... Born in Japan

Bijbl I E.... Bijblad bij de Industriele Eigendom [*A publication*]

Bijdr.......... Bijdragen. Tijdschrift voor Filosofie en Theologie [*Nijmegen/ Brugge*] [*A publication*]

Bijdragen ... Bijdragen tot de Taal-Land- en Volkenkunde [*A publication*]

Bijdragen Dialectencommissie ... Bijdragen en Mededeelingen der Dialectencommissie van de Koninklijke Akademie van Wetenschappen te Amsterdam [*A publication*]
Bijdragen Nederl-Indie ... Bijdragen tot de Taal-Land- en Volkenkunde van Nederlandsche-Indie [*A publication*]
Bijdrag Taal-Land- Volkenk ... Bijdragen tot de Taal-Land- en Volkenkunde [*A publication*]
Bijdr Dierk ... Bijdragen tot de Dierkunde [*A publication*]
Bijdr Gesch Geneesk ... Bijdragen tot de Geschiedenis der Geneeskunde. Nederlandsche Maatschappij tot Bevordering der Geneeskunst [*A publication*]
Bijdr Gesch Ndl ... Bijdragen voor de Geschiedenis der Nederlanden [*A publication*]
Bijdr Taal- Land-en Volkenk Nederl-Indie ... Bijdragen tot de Taal-Land- en Volkenkunde van Nederlandsche-Indie [*A publication*]
BijdrTLV ... Bijdragen tot de Taal-Land- en Volkenkunde [*A publication*]
bijl .... Bijlage [*Annex*] [*Netherlands*]   (ILCA)
BIJOA ...... Biochemical Journal [*A publication*]
BIJS .... Bulletin. Institute of Jewish Studies [*A publication*]
Bijv Stb ...... Bijvoegsel tot het Staatsblad [*A publication*]
BIK .... Biak [*Indonesia*] [*Airport symbol*]
BIK .... Biergrosshandel. Zeitschrift fuer den Gesamten Biergrosshandel und Getrankegrosshandel [*A publication*]
BIK .... Bikitaite [*A zeolite*]
BIKE .... Bicycle   (ROG)
Biken J ...... Biken Journal [*A publication*]
BIKF .... Keflavik [*Iceland*] [*ICAO location identifier*]   (ICLI)
BIKHD ...... Bioorganicheskaya Khimiya [*A publication*]
BiKi .... Bibel und Kirche [*Stuttgart*] [*A publication*]
BIKJA .... Biken Journal [*A publication*]
BIKLEK .... Biopolimery i Kletka [*A publication*]
BIKOA ...... Biologiai Koezlemenyek [*A publication*]
BIKP .... Kopasker [*Iceland*] [*ICAO location identifier*]   (ICLI)
BIKR .... Saudarkrokur [*Iceland*] [*ICAO location identifier*]   (ICLI)
BIL .... Basic Impulse Insulation Level [*Electronics*]
BIL .... Bilateral
bil .... Bilingual [*Texts*]   (BJA)
BIL .... Bill of Lading
BIL .... Billet   (AABC)
BIL .... Billikin Resources, Inc. [*Vancouver Stock Exchange symbol*]
BIL .... Billings [*Montana*] [*Airport symbol*]   (OAG)
BIL .... Billion
Bil. .... Bilychnis [*A publication*]
BIL .... Block Input Length [*Data processing*]   (BUR)
BIL .... Blue Indicator Light
BIL .... Bollettino Internazionale di Informazioni sul Latino [*A publication*]
BIL .... Brother-in-Law   (ADA)
BIL .... Bulk Items List
BILA .... Battelle Institute Learning Automation [*Battelle Memorial Institute*]   (IEEE)
BILA .... Bible Institute of Los Angeles
BILA .... British Insurance Law Association   (DLA)
BILA .... Bureau of International Labor Affairs [*Department of Labor*]
BILA Bull .. British Insurance Law Association. Bulletin [*A publication*]   (DLA)
BILAL .... Bulletin d'Information. Laboratoire d'Analyse Lexicologique [*A publication*]
Bilas .... All India Reporter, Bilaspur Series [*A publication*]   (DLA)
Bil Aspects Inorg Chem Symp ... Biological Aspects of Inorganic Chemistry. Symposium [*A publication*]
BILAT ...... Bilateral
Bil Aw ...... Billing. Law of Awards and Arbitration [*1845*] [*A publication*]   (DLA)
BILB .... Built-In Light Beacon
Bilb Ord ..... Ordinances of Bilboa [*A publication*]   (DLA)
BILC .... Boletim. Instituto Luis de Camoes [*A publication*]
BILC .... British International Law Cases [*A publication*]   (DLA)
BILD .... Bibliographic Index of Library Documents [*Helsinki School of Economics*] [*Database*]
BILDG .... Bill of Lading [*Shipping*]   (NOAA)
Bild Wiss ... Bild der Wissenschaft [*A publication*]
BILE .... Balanced Inductor Logical Element
BILE .... Bollettino. Istituto di Lingue Estere [*Genova*] [*A publication*]
Bile Acid Meet Proc ... Bile Acid Meeting. Proceedings [*A publication*]
Bile Acid Metab Health Dis Proc Bile Acid Meet ... Bile Acid Metabolism in Health and Disease. Proceedings of the Bile Acid Meeting [*A publication*]
BiLeb .... Bibel und Leben [*Duesseldorf*] [*A publication*]
BILEG .... Bollettino. Istituto di Lingue Estere (Genova) [*A publication*]
BILEUG .... Bollettino. Istituto di Lingue Estere (Genoa) [*A publication*]
BILI .... Basic Issue List Items [*Army*]
bili .... Bilirubin [*Clinical chemistry*]
BILIA .... Biologicke Listy [*A publication*]
Biling Ed Pap Ser ... Bilingual Education Paper Series [*A publication*]
Biling Rev ... Bilingual Review/Revista Bilingue [*A publication*]
Bilirubin Metab Newborn Int Symp ... Bilirubin Metabolism in the Newborn. International Symposium [*A publication*]
BiLit .... Bibel und Liturgie [*Klosterneuburg, Austria*] [*A publication*]
Biljeske Inst Oceanogr Ribar (Split) ... Biljeske. Institut za Oceanografiju i Ribarstvo (Split) [*A publication*]

BILL .... Before Infantry Light and Lethal [*Antitank*]   (MCD)
BILL .... Billericay [*England*]
BILL .... Billiards
BILLA .... Billboard [*A publication*]
BILLD .... Billiard [*Freight*]
Billings Geol Soc Annu Field Conf Guideb ... Billings Geological Society. Annual Field Conference. Guidebook [*A publication*]
Billot Extrad ... Billot. Traite de l'Extradition [*A publication*]   (DLA)
Bill & Pr Pat ... Billing and Prince's Law and Practice of Patents [*A publication*]   (DLA)
Bill of Rights J ... Bill of Rights Journal [*A publication*]   (DLA)
Bill Rights J ... Bill of Rights Journal [*A publication*]   (DLA)
Bill Rights Rev ... Bill of Rights Review [*A publication*]   (DLA)
Bill Rts J ... Bill of Rights Journal [*A publication*]   (DLA)
BILLS .... Current Commonwealth Bills [*Database*] [*Australia*]
B Ill Wall ... Bulletin Illustre de la Wallonie [*A publication*]
BILPatr ...... Bulletin d'Information et de Liaison. Association Internationale des Etudes Patristiques [*A publication*]
Bil Pews ..... Billing. Law Relating to Pews [*1845*] [*A publication*]   (DLA)
BILS .... British International Law Society   (DLA)
BILT .... MicroBilt Corp. [*Atlanta, GA*] [*NASDAQ symbol*]   (NQ)
Bilt Dok ..... Bilten Dokumentacije [*Yugoslavia*] [*A publication*]
Bilten Drushtvo Mat Fiz Nar Repub Makedonija ... Bilten. Drushtvo na Matematicharite i Fizicharite od Narodna Republika Makedonija [*A publication*]
Bilt Farm Drus Maked ... Bilten za Farmaceutskoto Drustvo za Makedonija [*A publication*]
Bilt Farm Drus Soc Repub Makedonija ... Bilten za Farmaceutskoto Drustvo za Socijalisticka Republika Makedonija [*A publication*]
Bilt Hematol Transfuz ... Bilten za Hematologiju i Transfuziju [*A publication*]
Bilt Hmelj Sirak ... Bilten za Hmelj i Sirak [*A publication*]
Bilt Hmelj Sirak Lek Bilje ... Bilten za Hmelj Sirak i Lekovito Bilje [*A publication*]
Bilt Sojuzot Zdruzenijata Farm Farm Teh SR Maked ... Bilten za Sojuzot za Zdruzenijata za Farmacevtite i Farmacevtskite Tehnicari za SR Makedonija [*A publication*]
BILU .... Bet Ya'akov Lekhu ve-Nelkhah   (BJA)
B of IM ...... Bachelor of Industrial Management
BIM .... Bachelor of Industrial Management
BIM .... Banco Industrial del Mediterraneo [*Industrial Bank of the Mediterranean*] [*Spain*]
BIM .... Basic Industrial Materials [*Program*] [*Navy*]
BIM .... Beginning of Information Marker [*Data processing*]
BIM .... Best in Match
BIM .... Big M Petroleum, Inc. [*Vancouver Stock Exchange symbol*]
BIM .... Bimini [*Bahamas*] [*Airport symbol*]   (OAG)
BI-M .... Bimonthly
BIM .... Biographical Inventory for Medicine
BIM .... Biologically Induced Mineralization [*Microbial metabolism*]
BIM .... BIT [*Binary Digit*] Image Memory [*Data processing*]
BIM .... Blade Inspection Method
BIM .... Board of International Ministries   (EA)
BIM .... Branch If Multiplexer
BIM .... British Institute of Management
BIM .... Brookings Papers on Economic Activity [*A publication*]
BIM .... Bubble Interfacial Microlayer Sampler [*Oceanography*]   (MSC)
BIM .... Bus Interface Module
BIM .... Bus Interrupter Module [*Motorola, Inc.*]
BIM .... ICN Biomedicals [*AMEX symbol*]   (SPSG)
BIMA .... Business and Industry Management Abstracts [*A publication*]
BIMAC .... Bistable Magnetic Core [*Data processing*]
BIMAG .... Bistable Magnetic Core [*Data processing*]
Bi-M Bull N Dak Agric Exp Stn ... Bi-Monthly Bulletin. North Dakota Agricultural Experiment Station [*A publication*]
BIMC .... Monthly Circular. Baltic and International Maritime Conference [*A publication*]
BIMCAM ... British Industrial Measuring and Control Apparatus Manufacturers' Association
BIMCO ..... Baltic and International Maritime Conference [*Copenhagen, Denmark*]   (EAIO)
BIMDA ..... Biochemical Medicine [*A publication*]
BIMDB ...... Biomedicine [*A publication*]
BIME .... Bath Institute of Medical Engineering [*University of Bath*] [*British*]   (IRUK)
BIMEA ..... Biologie Medicale [*A publication*]
BIMEB ..... Biomedical Engineering [*A publication*]
BIMH .... British Institute of Mental Handicap
BIMHEI ..... Butterworths International Medical Reviews. Hematology [*A publication*]
BIMOA ..... Biologiya Morya [*Kiev*] [*A publication*]
Bi-Mo L Rev ... Bi-Monthly Law Review. University of Detroit [*A publication*]   (DLA)
BiMOS ...... Bipolar Metal-Oxide Semiconductor   (IEEE)
BIMRAB ... BUWEPS [*Bureau of Naval Weapons, now obsolete*] - Industry Material Reliability Advisory Board
Bi-M Res Notes Canada Dep For ... Bi-Monthly Research Notes. Canada Department of Forestry [*A publication*]
BIMS .... Battlefield Integration Management System [*Army*]
BIMS .... Blade Inspection Method System   (MCD)
BIMS .... Bubble Interfacial Microlayer Sampler [*Oceanography*]
BIMS .... Bus Ion Mass Spectrometer [*Space science instrumentation*]

BIMYDY...   Bibliotheca Mycologica [*A publication*]

BIN ....   Babylonian Inscriptions in the Collection of James B. Nies   (BJA)

BIN ....   Bamian [*Afghanistan*] [*Airport symbol*] [*Obsolete*]   (OAG)

BIN ....   Bank Identification Number

BIN ....   Bell Information Network

BIN ....   Billboard Information Network [*Billboard Publications, Inc.*] [*Information service or system*]   (IID)

BIN ....   Binary   (AFM)

BIN ....   Binks Manufacturing Co. [*AMEX symbol*]   (SPSG)

Bin.............   Binney's Pennsylvania Reports [*1799-1814*] [*A publication*]   (DLA)

BIN ....   Binza [*Leopoldville*] [*Zaire*] [*Geomagnetic observatory code*]

BIN ....   Binza [*Leopoldville*] [*Zaire*] [*Seismograph station code, US Geological Survey*]   (SEIS)

BIN ....   Bis in Noctus [*Twice a Night*] [*Pharmacy*]

BIN ....   Boise Interagency Fire Center [*Boise, ID*] [*FAA designator*]   (FAAC)

BIN ....   Bollettino Italiano di Numismatica [*A publication*]

BIN ....   BOMARC [*Boeing-Michigan Aeronautical Research Center*] Interceptor

BIN ....   Bullion Range Exploration [*Vancouver Stock Exchange symbol*]

BIN ....   Business Information Network [*Billboard Publications, Inc.*] [*New York, NY*] [*Telecommunications*]   (TEL)

BIN ....   Invermere Public Library, British Columbia [*Library symbol*] [*National Library of Canada*]   (NLC)

BINAC......   Binary Automatic Computer [*Eckert-Maudely Computer Corp.*]

BINAGRI ..   Biblioteca Nacional de Agricultura [*National Library of Agriculture*] [*Brazil*] [*Information service or system*]   (IID)

BINC ....   Biospherics, Incorporated [*NASDAQ symbol*]   (NQ)

BINC ....   Black Incumbent

BINCOS....   Binder Control Subsystem

B Ind ....   Bachelor of Industry

BIND ....   Bacterial Ice Nucleation Diagnosis [*DNA Plant Technology Corp. test*]

BIND ....   Binding   (ROG)

BIND ....   Bindley Western Industries, Inc. [*NASDAQ symbol*]   (NQ)

B Ind E ......   Bachelor of Industrial Engineering

B Ind Ed.....   Bachelor of Industrial Education

BINDEX....   Book Indexing

Bin Dig.......   Binmore's Index-Digest of Michigan Reports [*A publication*]   (DLA)

BINDIS .....   Binomial Probability Distributions   (MCD)

B Ind Mgt ..   Bachelor of Industrial Management

B Indo Econ Stud ...   Bulletin of Indonesian Economic Studies [*A publication*]

B Indones Econ Stud ...   Bulletin of Indonesian Economic Studies [*A publication*]

BIndTech...   Bachelor of Industrial Technology

BINEA.......   Biologia Neonatorum [*Later, Biology of the Neonate*] [*A publication*]

BINEAA....   Biologia Neonatorum [*Later, Biology of Neonate*] [*A publication*]

BINED.......   BIOP [*Board on International Organizations and Programs*] Newletter [*United States*] [*A publication*]

BINET.......   Bicentennial Information Network [*American Revolution Bicentennial Administration*]

B Inf ....   Bulletin d'Information. Institut d'Etude Economique et Sociale des Classes Moyennes [*A publication*]

BINF.........   Nordfjordur [*Iceland*] [*ICAO location identifier*]   (ICLI)

B Inform Centre Docum Educ Europe ...   Bulletin d'Information. Centre de Documentation pour l'Education en Europe [*A publication*]

B Inform C N C ...   Bulletin d'Information. Centre National de la Cinematographie [*A publication*]

B Inform Dept Econ Sociol Rur ...   Bulletin d'Information. Departement d'Economie et de Sociologie Rurales [*A publication*]

B Inform Econ ...   Bulletin d'Informations Economiques [*A publication*]

B Inform Econ Caisse Nat Marches Etat ...   Bulletin d'Information Economique de la Caisse Nationale des Marches de l'Etat [*A publication*]

B Inform Haut Comite Et Inform Alcool ...   Bulletin d'Information. Haut Comite d'Etude et d'Information sur l'Alcoolisme [*A publication*]

B Inform Region Champagne-Ardenne ...   Bulletin d'Information Regionale Champagne-Ardenne [*A publication*]

B Inform Region Paris ...   Bulletin d'Information de la Region Parisienne [*A publication*]

BInfoTech ...   Bachelor of Information Technology and Communication

B Inf Zak Narod ...   Biuletyn Informacyjny. Zakladu Narodowego Ossolinskich Biblioteki Polskiej Akademii Nauk [*A publication*]

Bing............   Bingham's English Common Pleas Reports [*130-131 English Reprint*] [*A publication*]   (DLA)

BING ....   [*The*] Binghamton Savings Bank [*Binghamton, NY*] [*NASDAQ symbol*]   (NQ)

BING ....   Federation of European Rigid Polyurethane Foam Associations   (EAIO)

Bing Act & Def ...   Bingham's Actions and Defences in Real Property [*A publication*]   (DLA)

Bing & Colv Rents ...   Bingham and Colvin on Rents [*A publication*]   (DLA)

Bing Des ....   Bingham on the Laws of Descent [*A publication*]   (DLA)

Bing (Eng) ...   Bingham's English Common Pleas Reports [*130-131 English Reprint*] [*A publication*]   (DLA)

Bing Ex ......   Bingham. Judgments and Executions [*1815*] [*A publication*]   (DLA)

Bing Ex Cont ...   Bingham's Executory Contracts, Etc. [*A publication*]   (DLA)

Bing Inf......   Bingham. Infancy and Coveture [*1826*] [*A publication*]   (DLA)

Bing Judg...   Bingham. Judgments and Executions [*1815*] [*A publication*]   (DLA)

Bing L & T ...   Bingham. Landlord and Tenant [*1820*] [*A publication*]   (DLA)

Bing NC .....   Bingham. New Cases, English Common Pleas [*131-133 English Reprint*] [*A publication*]   (DLA)

Bing N Cas ...   Bingham. New Cases, English Common Pleas [*131-133 English Reprint*] [*A publication*]   (DLA)

Bing NC (Eng) ...   Bingham. New Cases, English Common Pleas [*131-133 English Reprint*] [*A publication*]   (DLA)

BINGO ......   Beacon Instrumented Guided Ordnance   (MCD)

BINGO ......   Bearing Indicator and Navigator to Grounded Operator   (MCD)

BI/NGO ....   Bilateral/Non-Governmental Organization   (ADA)

Bing RP......   Bingham on the Law of Real Property [*A publication*]   (DLA)

BINL.........   Basic Inventory of Natural Language [*Test*]

BINL.........   Blinder International Enterprises, Inc. [*Englewood, CO*] [*NASDAQ symbol*]   (NQ)

Binm Ind ....   Binmore's Index-Digest of Michigan Reports [*A publication*]   (DLA)

Binn...........   Binney's Pennsylvania Supreme Court Reports [*1799-1814*] [*A publication*]   (DLA)

Binnenschiffahrts-Nachr ...   Binnenschiffahrts-Nachrichten ... [*A publication*]

Binn Jus .....   Binns' Pennsylvania Justice [*A publication*]   (DLA)

Binn (PA)...   Binney's Pennsylvania Reports [*1799-1814*] [*A publication*]   (DLA)

Binns' Just ...   Binns' Pennsylvania Justice [*A publication*]   (DLA)

BINOCS....   Binoculars [*Slang*] [*British*]   (DSUE)

BINOMEXP ...   Binomial Expansion [*Mathematics*]

B Inostr Kommerc Inform Priloz ...   Bjulleten Inostrannoj Kommerceskoj Informacii Prilozenie [*A publication*]

BINOVC....   Break in Overcast [*Meteorology*]

BINR ....   Basic Intrinsic Noise Ratio   (CET)

B In Sci T...   Bulletin d'Informations Scientifiques et Techniques. Commissariat a l'Energie Atomique [*A publication*]

BINSCS.....   Boreal Institute for Northern Studies. Contribution Series [*A publication*]

BINSOP.....   Boreal Institute for Northern Studies. Occasional Publication [*A publication*]

BINSS ....   Binary to Seven Segment [*Data processing*]

B Inst A (London) ...   Bulletin. Institute of Archaeology (London) [*A publication*]

BInstArch ..   Bulletin. Institute of Archaeology [*London*] [*A publication*]

B Inst Archaeol ...   Bulletin. Institute of Archaeology. University of London [*A publication*]

B Inst Communication Res ...   Bulletin. Institute of Communication Research [*A publication*]

B Inst Develop Stud ...   Bulletin. Institute of Development Studies [*A publication*]

B Inst Est Hel ...   Boletin. Instituto de Estudios Helenicos. Universidad de Barcelona. Facultad de Filosofia y Letras [*A publication*]

B Inst Ethnol Acad Sinica ...   Bulletin. Institute of Ethnology. Academia Sinica [*A publication*]

B Inst Fondam Afr Noire ...   Bulletin. Institut Fondamental d'Afrique Noire [*A publication*]

B Inst Franc Et Andines ...   Bulletin. Institut Francais d'Etudes Andines [*A publication*]

B Inst Hist Belg Rom ...   Bulletin. Institut Historique Belge de Rome [*A publication*]

B Inst Hist Med (Hyderabad) ...   Bulletin. Institute of History of Medicine (Hyderabad) [*A publication*]

B Inst Hist Philol Acad Sinica ...   Bulletin. Institute of History and Philology. Academia Sinica [*A publication*]

B Inst Int Adm Publ ...   Bulletin. Institut International d'Administration Publique [*A publication*]

B Inst Mod Hist Acad Sinica ...   Bulletin. Institute of Modern History. Academia Sinica [*A publication*]

BInst NDT ...   British Institute of Non-Destructive Testing   (EAIO)

B Inst Rech Econ ...   Bulletin. Institut de Recherches Economiques [*A publication*]

B Inst Trad Cult ...   Bulletin. Institute of Traditional Culture [*A publication*]

BINSUM...   Brief Intelligence Summary   (NATG)

Binsurance ...   Business Insurance [*A publication*]

BIntArch...   Bachelor in Interior Architecture

B Int Assoc Educ Vocat Guidance ...   Bulletin. International Association for Educational and Vocational Guidance [*A publication*]

B Int Committee on Urg Anthropol Ethnol Res ...   Bulletin. International Committee on Urgent Anthropological and Ethnological Research [*A publication*]

B Int Committee Urgent Anthro Ethno Res ...   Bulletin. International Committee on Urgent Anthropological and Ethnological Research [*A publication*]

BIntDesign ...   Bachelor in Interior Design

B Interminist Rational Choix Budget ...   Bulletin Interministeriel pour la Rationalisation des Choix Budgetaires [*A publication*]

B Interparl ...   Bulletin Interparlementaire [*A publication*]

B Int Fisc Docum ... Bulletin for International Fiscal Documentation [*A publication*]
B Int Fis D ... Bulletin for International Fiscal Documentation [*A publication*]
B Int L........ Bachelor of International Law
BINUA ...... Bulletin d'Instrumentation Nucleaire [*A publication*]
BIO .... Base Installation Officer
BIO .... Bedford Institute of Oceanography [*Canada*]   (MSC)
BiO............ Bibbia e Oriente [*A publication*]
BIO .... Bilbao [*Spain*] [*Airport symbol*]   (OAG)
BIO .... Bio-Rad Laboratories, Inc. [*AMEX symbol*]   (SPSG)
BIO .... Bio-Research Module   (MCD)
BIO .... Biographics   (AABC)
BIO .... Biography   (DSUE)
BIO .... Biological Information-Processing Organization [*Later, SIGBIO*]
BIO .... Biological Research Module [*NASA*]   (NASA)
BIO .... Biology [*or Biological*]   (KSC)
BIO .... Biophysics   (ADA)
BIO .... Biorka [*Alaska*] [*Seismograph station code, US Geological Survey*] [*Closed*]   (SEIS)
BIO .... Bioscope [*The cinema*] [*Obsolete*] [*British*]   (DSUE)
BIO .... Biotechnology Investment Opportunities [*Database*] [*High Tech Publishing Co.*] [*Information service or system*]   (CRD)
BIO .... Branch Intelligence Officer [*Military*] [*British*]
BIO .... Brit Ivrit Olamit [*World Association for Hebrew Language and Culture*]   (EAIO)
BIO .... British Imperial Oil Co. Ltd. [*Australia*]
BIOA .... Bureau of International Organization Affairs [*Department of State*]
BioAb........ Biological Abstracts [*A publication*]
BioAg........ Biological and Agricultural Index [*A publication*]
BIOALRT ... Bioastronautics Laboratory Research Tool   (IEEE)
Bioantioksidant Luchevom Porazhenii Zlokach Roste ... Bioantioksidanty v Luchevom Porazhenii i Zlokachestvennom Roste [*A publication*]
Biobehav Rev ... Biobehavioral Reviews [*A publication*]
BIOBUND ... Computerized Biology Data and Program Bank at the University of Notre Dame [*Information service or system*] [*Defunct*]   (IID)
BIOC .... Biochem International, Inc. [*NASDAQ symbol*]   (NQ)
BioC .... Biologia Culturale [*A publication*]
BIOCAS .... BIOSIS/CAS [*BioSciences Information Service/Chemical Abstracts Service*] Registry Number Concordance [*American Chemical Society*] [*Information service or system*]   (CRD)
Bioc Biop A ... Biochimica et Biophysica Acta [*A publication*]
Bioc Biop R ... Biochemical and Biophysical Research Communications [*A publication*]
BIOCC....... Bedford Institute of Oceanography. Collected Contributions [*A publication*]
BIOCC....... Branch Immaterial Officer Candidate Course
BIOCHEM ... Biochemical [*or Biochemistry*]
Biochem ..... Biochemistry [*A publication*]
Biochem Actions Horm ... Biochemical Actions of Hormones [*A publication*]
Biochem Acute Allerg React Int Symp ... Biochemistry of the Acute Allergic Reactions. International Symposium [*A publication*]
Biochem Adenosylmethionine Proc Int Symp ... Biochemistry of Adenosylmethionine. Proceedings of an International Symposium on the Biochemistry of Adenosylmethionine [*A publication*]
Biochem Anal Membr ... Biochemical Analysis of Membranes [*A publication*]
Biochem Anima Dev ... Biochemistry of Animal Development [*A publication*]
Biochem Arch ... Biochemical Archives [*A publication*]
Biochem Aspects Plant Parasite Relat Proc Symp ... Biochemical Aspects of Plant Parasite Relationships. Proceedings of the Symposium [*A publication*]
Biochem Bact Growth 2nd Ed ... Biochemistry of Bacterial Growth. 2nd Edition [*A publication*]
Biochem Befunde Differentialdiag Inn Kr ... Biochemische Befunde in der Differentialdiagnose Innerer Krankheiten [*A publication*]
Biochem Biophys Perspect Mar Biol ... Biochemical and Biophysical Perspectives in Marine Biology [*A publication*]
Biochem Biophys Res Commun ... Biochemical and Biophysical Research Communications [*A publication*]
Biochem Bull (NY) ... Biochemical Bulletin (New York) [*A publication*]
Biochem Cell Biol ... Biochemistry and Cell Biology [*A publication*]
Biochem Cell Differ ... Biochemistry of Cell Differentiation [*A publication*]
Biochem Cell Differ Fed Eur Biochem Soc Meet ... Biochemistry of Cell Differentiation. Federation of European Biochemical Societies. Meeting [*A publication*]
Biochem Centralbl ... Biochemisches Centralblatt [*A publication*]
Biochem Clin ... Biochemical Clinics [*A publication*]
Biochem Clin Aspects Pteridines ... Biochemical and Clinical Aspects of Pteridines [*A publication*]
Biochem Clin Bohemoslov ... Biochemia Clinica Bohemoslovaca [*A publication*]
Biochem Collagen ... Biochemistry of Collagen [*A publication*]
Biochem Correl Brain Struct Funct ... Biochemical Correlates of Brain Structure and Function [*A publication*]

Biochem Cutaneous Epidermal Differ Proc Jpn US Semin ... Biochemistry of Cutaneous Epidermal Differentiation. Proceedings of the Japan-US Seminar on Biochemistry of Cutaneous Epidermal Differentiation [*A publication*]
Biochem Cytol Plant Parasite Interact Symp ... Biochemistry and Cytology of Plant Parasite Interaction Symposium [*A publication*]
Biochem Dev ... Biochemistry of Development [*A publication*]
Biochem Developing Brain ... Biochemistry of the Developing Brain [*A publication*]
Biochem Dis ... Biochemistry of Disease [*A publication*]
Biochem Dis (NY) ... Biochemistry of Disease (New York) [*A publication*]
Biochem Educ ... Biochemical Education [*England*] [*A publication*]
Biochem Eff Environ Pollut ... Biochemical Effects of Environmental Pollutants [*A publication*]
Biochem Endocrinol ... Biochemical Endocrinology [*A publication*]
Biochem Exercise Proc Int Symp ... Biochemistry of Exercise. Proceedings of the International Symposium on Exercise Biochemistry [*A publication*]
Biochem Exp Biol ... Biochemistry and Experimental Biology [*A publication*]
Biochem Folic Acid Relat Pteridines ... Biochemistry of Folic Acid and Related Pteridines [*A publication*]
Biochem Gen ... Biochemical Genetics [*A publication*]
Biochem Genet ... Biochemical Genetics [*A publication*]
Biochem Int ... Biochemistry International [*A publication*]
Biochem Interact Plants Insects ... Biochemical Interaction between Plants and Insects [*A publication*]
Biochemistry (Engl Transl Biokhimiya) ... Biochemistry (English Translation of Biokhimiya) [*A publication*]
Biochemistry Ser One ... Biochemistry. Series One [*A publication*]
Biochem J .. Biochemical Journal [*A publication*]
Biochem Med ... Biochemical Medicine [*A publication*]
Biochem Med Metab Biol ... Biochemical Medicine and Metabolic Biology [*A publication*]
Biochem Membr Transp ... Biochemistry of Membrane Transport [*A publication*]
Biochem Methods Monit Risk Pregnancies ... Biochemical Methods for Monitoring Risk Pregnancies [*A publication*]
Biochem Neurol Dis ... Biochemistry and Neurological Disease [*A publication*]
Biochem Parasites Host Parasite Relat Proc Int Symp ... Biochemistry of Parasites and Host Parasite Relationships. Proceedings of the International Symposium on the Biochemistry of Parasites and Host Parasite Relationships [*A publication*]
Biochem Pathol Connect Tissue ... Biochemistry and Pathology of Connective Tissue [*A publication*]
Biochem Pharmac ... Biochemical Pharmacology [*A publication*]
Biochem Pharmacol ... Biochemical Pharmacology [*A publication*]
Biochem Physiol Pflanz ... Biochemie und Physiologie der Pflanzen [*A publication*]
Biochem Prep ... Biochemical Preparations [*A publication*]
Biochem Probl Lipids Proc Int Conf ... Biochemical Problems of Lipids. Proceedings. International Conference [*A publication*]
Biochem Rev (Bangalore) ... Biochemical Reviews (Bangalore) [*A publication*]
Biochem Sens Funct ... Biochemistry of Sensory Functions [*A publication*]
Biochem Ser Monogr ... Biochemistry: a Series of Monographs [*A publication*]
Biochem Smooth Muscle Proc Symp ... Biochemistry of Smooth Muscle. Proceedings of the Symposium [*A publication*]
Biochem Soc Spec Publ ... Biochemical Society. Special Publications [*A publication*]
Biochem Soc Symp ... Biochemical Society. Symposia [*A publication*]
Biochem Soc Trans ... Biochemical Society. Transactions [*A publication*]
Biochem SSR ... Biochemistry-USSR [*A publication*]
Biochem Syst ... Biochemical Systematics [*Later, Biochemical Systematics and Ecology*] [*A publication*]
Biochem Syst Ecol ... Biochemical Systematics and Ecology [*A publication*]
Biochem Women Clin Concepts ... Biochemistry of Women. Clinical Concepts [*A publication*]
Biochem Women Methods Clin Invest ... Biochemistry of Women. Methods for Clinical Investigation [*A publication*]
Biochem Z ... Biochemische Zeitschrift [*A publication*]
Biochim Appl ... Biochimica Applicata [*A publication*]
Biochim Biol Sper ... Biochimica e Biologia Sperimentale [*A publication*]
Biochim Biophys Acta ... Biochimica et Biophysica Acta [*A publication*]
Biochim Biophys Acta B ... Biochimica et Biophysica Acta. B. Bioenergetics [*A publication*]
Biochim Biophys Acta Bioenerg ... Biochimica et Biophysica Acta. B. Bioenergetics [*A publication*]
Biochim Biophys Acta Biomembranes ... Biochimica et Biophysica Acta. M. Biomembranes [*A publication*]
Biochim Biophys Acta BR ... Biochimica et Biophysica Acta. BR. Reviews on Bioenergetics [*A publication*]
Biochim Biophys Acta Enzymol ... Biochimica et Biophysica Acta. Enzymology [*A publication*]
Biochim Biophys Acta G ... Biochimica et Biophysica Acta. G. General Subjects [*A publication*]
Biochim Biophys Acta General Subjects ... Biochimica et Biophysica Acta. G. General Subjects [*A publication*]
Biochim Biophys Acta Libr ... Biochimica et Biophysica Acta. Library [*A publication*]
Biochim Biophys Acta Lipids Lipid Metab ... Biochimica et Biophysica Acta. Lipids and Lipid Metabolism [*A publication*]

Biochim Biophys Acta M ... Biochimica et Biophysica Acta. M. Biomembranes [*A publication*]
Biochim Biophys Acta MR ... Biochimica et Biophysica Acta. MR. Reviews on Biomembranes [*A publication*]
Biochim Biophys Acta Nucl Acids Protein Synth ... Biochimica et Biophysica Acta. Nucleic Acids and Protein Synthesis [*A publication*]
Biochim Biophys Acta P ... Biochimica et Biophysica Acta. P. Protein Structure [*A publication*]
Biochim Biophys Acta Protein Struct ... Biochimica et Biophysica Acta. P. Protein Structure [*A publication*]
Biochim Ter Sper ... Biochimica e Terapia Sperimentale [*A publication*]
Bioch Pharm ... Biochemical Pharmacology [*A publication*]
Bioch Soc T ... Biochemical Society. Transactions [*A publication*]
Bioclimat Numero Spec ... Bioclimat Numero Special [*A publication*]
Biocomplex Invest Kaz ... Biocomplex Investigation in Kazakhstan [*A publication*]
BIOCORE ... Biological Cosmic Ray Experiment   (MCD)
Bioc Phy Pf ... Biochemie und Physiologie der Pflanzen [*A publication*]
BIOD .... Battalion Input/Output Device   (MCD)
BIOD .... Biotechnology Development Corp. [*NASDAQ symbol*]   (NQ)
BIODA .... Biodynamica [*A publication*]
BIODEF .... Biological Defense [*Military*]
Biodeterior Invest Tech ... Biodeterioration Investigation Techniques [*A publication*]
BIOEA .... Biomedical Engineering [*English Translation*] [*A publication*]
Bioelectr B ... Bioelectrochemistry and Bioenergetics [*A publication*]
Bioelectrochem Bioenerg ... Bioelectrochemistry and Bioenergetics [*A publication*]
BIOENG ... Bioengineering
Bioeng Abstr ... Bioengineering Abstracts [*A publication*]
BIOENVMT ... Bioenvironmental
BIOETHICSLINE ... Bioethics Online [*Database*]
Bioethics Q ... Bioethics Quarterly [*A publication*]
BIOFA .... Biofizika [*A publication*]
BIOFDL .... Annual Research Reviews. Biofeedback [*A publication*]
Biofeedback Self-Regul ... Biofeedback and Self-Regulation [*A publication*]
Biofeedback and Self-Regul ... Biofeedback and Self-Regulation [*A publication*]
Biofiz .... Biofizika [*A publication*]
Biofiz Biokhim Myshechnogo Sokrashcheniya ... Biofizika i Biokhimiya Myshechnogo Sokrashcheniya [*A publication*]
Biofiz Radiobiol ... Biofizika i Radiobiologiya [*A publication*]
Biofiz Rast Mater Vses Simp Mol Prikl Biofiz Rast ... Biofizika Rastenii. Materialy Vsesoyuznogo Simpoziuma po Molekulyarnoi i Prikladnoi Biofizike Rastenii [*A publication*]
Biofiz Zhivoi Kletki ... Biofizika Zhivoi Kletki [*A publication*]
Biofuels Rep ... Biofuels Report [*A publication*]
BIOG .... Bio-Gas of Colorado, Inc. [*NASDAQ symbol*]   (NQ)
BIOG .... Biografias [*Database*] [*Ministerio de Cultura*] [*Spanish*] [*Information service or system*]   (CRD)
BIOG .... Biographer (ROG)
BIOG .... Biography
Biog Amine ... Biogenic Amines [*A publication*]
Biog Amines ... Biogenic Amines [*A publication*]
Biogas Alcohol Fuels Prod ... Biogas and Alcohol Fuels Production [*A publication*]
Biogeochem Devils Lake ND ... Biogeochemistry of Devils Lake, North Dakota [*A publication*]
Biogeochemi ... Biogeochemistry [*A publication*]
BIOGEOG ... Biogeography (ADA)
Biogeogr Nauchn Konf Mater ... Biogeograficheskaya Nauchnaya Konferentsiya Materialy [*A publication*]
Biogeokhim Diageneza Osadkov Okeana ... Biogeokhimiya Diageneza Osadkov Okeana [*A publication*]
Biog Ind ..... Biography Index [*A publication*]
Biogr Hervorragender Naturwiss Tech Med ... Biographien Hervorragender Naturwissenschaftler, Techniker, und Mediziner [*A publication*]
Biogr Index ... Biography Index [*A publication*]
Biogr Mem Fellows Roy Soc ... Biographical Memoirs of Fellows of the Royal Society [*A publication*]
Biogr Mem Fellows R Soc ... Biographical Memoirs of Fellows of the Royal Society [*A publication*]
Biogr Mem Nat Acad Sci (USA) ... Biographical Memoirs. National Academy of Sciences (United States of America) [*A publication*]
Biogr Mem Natl Acad Sci ... Biographical Memoirs. National Academy of Sciences [*A publication*]
Biogr Nat Acad Roy Belg ... Biographie Nationale. Academie Royale des Sciences, des Lettres, et des Beaux-Arts de Belgique [*A publication*]
BIOHA ...... Biokhimiya [*Moscow*] [*A publication*]
BioI .... Biography Index [*A publication*]
BIOI .... BioResearch Index [*Later, BA/RRM*] [*A publication*]
Bioinorg Ch ... Bioinorganic Chemistry [*A publication*]
Bioinorg Chem ... Bioinorganic Chemistry [*A publication*]
BIOJA .... Biophysical Journal [*A publication*]
Bio-Joule Newsl ... Bio-Joule Newsletter [*Canada*] [*A publication*]
BIOKA .... Biometrika [*A publication*]
Biokhim ...... Biokhimiya [*A publication*]

Biokhim Aspekty Introd Otdalennoi Gibrid Filogenii Rast ... Biokhimicheskie Aspekty Introduktsii Otdalennoi Gibridizatsii i Filogenii Rastenii [*A publication*]
Biokhim Chain Prozvod ... Biokhimiya Chainogo Proizvodstva [*A publication*]
Biokhim Issled Protsesse Sel Kukuruzy ... Biokhimicheskie Issledovaniya v Protsesse Selektsii Kukuruzy [*A publication*]
Biokhim Kul't Rast Mold ... Biokhimiya Kul'turnykh Rastenii Moldavu [*A publication*]
Biokhim Nasekomykh ... Biokhimiya Nasekomykh [*A publication*]
Biokhim Plodov Ovoshchei ... Biokhimiya Plodov i Ovoshchei [*A publication*]
Biokhim Rast ... Biokhimiya Rastenii [*A publication*]
Biokhim Tekhnol Protsessy Pishch Promsti ... Biokhimicheskie i Tekhnologicheskie Protsessy v Pishchevoi Promyshlennosti [*A publication*]
Biokhim Vinodel ... Biokhimiya Vinodeliya [*A publication*]
Biokhim Zerna Khlebopeeh ... Biokhimiya Zerna i Khlebopeeheniya [*A publication*]
Biokhim Zh ... Biokhimichna Zhurnal [*A publication*]
Biokompleksnye Issled Kaz ... Biokompleksnye Issledovaniya v Kazakhstane [*A publication*]
Biokon Rep ... Biokon Reports [*A publication*]
BIOL .... Bio Logicals, Inc. (ens) [*NASDAQ symbol*]   (NQ)
Biol .... Biologia [*A publication*]
BIOL .... Biological (ROG)
BIOL .... Biology (EY)
Biol .... O Biologico [*A publication*]
Biol Abh ..... Biologische Abhandlungen [*A publication*]
Biol Abs ..... Biological Abstracts [*A publication*]
Biol Abstr .... Biological Abstracts [*A publication*]
Biol Abstr RRM ... Biological Abstracts/RRM [*Reports, Reviews, Meetings*] [*A publication*]
Biol Actinomycetes Relat Org ... Biology of the Actinomycetes and Related Organisms [*A publication*]
Biol Actions Dimethyl Sulfoxide ... Biological Actions of Dimethyl Sulfoxide [*A publication*]
Biol Afr ...... Biologia Africana [*A publication*]
Biol Aging Dev ... Biology of Aging and Development [*A publication*]
Biol Agric & Hortic ... Biological Agriculture and Horticulture [*A publication*]
Biol Agric Index ... Biological and Agricultural Index [*A publication*]
Biol & Agr Ind ... Biological and Agricultural Index [*A publication*]
Biol Akklim Obez'yan Mater Simp ... Biologiya i Akklimatizatsiya Obez'yan. Materialy Simpoziuma [*A publication*]
Biol Akt Nek Aminotiolov Aminosul'fidov ... Biologicheskaya Aktivnost Nekotorykh Aminotiolov i Aminosul'fidov [*A publication*]
Biol Akt Veshchestva Mikroorg ... Biologicheski Aktivnye Veshchestva Mikroorganizmov [*A publication*]
Biol Akt Veshchestva Mikroorg Ikh Ispol'z ... Biologicheski Aktivnye Veshchestva Mikroorganizmov i Ikh Ispol'zovanie [*A publication*]
Biol Amplification Syst Immunol ... Biological Amplification Systems in Immunology [*A publication*]
Biol Appl Electron Spin Reson ... Biological Applications of Electron Spin Resonance
Biol Artif Membr Desalin Water Proceed Study Week ... Biological and Artificial Membranes and Desalination of Water. Proceedings of the Study Week [*A publication*]
Biol B .... Biological Bulletin [*A publication*]
Biol Baltic Sea ... Biology of the Baltic Sea [*A publication*]
Biol Balt Morya ... Biologiya Baltiiskogo Morya [*A publication*]
Biol Basis Clin Eff Bleomycin ... Biological Basis of Clinical Effect of Bleomycin [*A publication*]
Biol Behav ... Biology of Behaviour [*A publication*]
Biol Board Can Bull ... Biological Board of Canada. Bulletin [*A publication*]
Biol Brain Dysfunct ... Biology of Brain Dysfunction [*A publication*]
Biol Brain Dysfunction ... Biology of Brain Dysfunction [*A publication*]
Biol (Bratislava) ... Biologia (Bratislava) [*A publication*]
Biol Bul ...... Biological Bulletin [*A publication*]
Biol Bull ...... Biological Bulletin [*A publication*]
Biol Bull Acad Sci USSR ... Biology Bulletin. Academy of Sciences of the USSR [*A publication*]
Biol Bull Dep Biol Coll Sci Tunghai Univ ... Biological Bulletin. Department of Biology. College of Science. Tunghai University [*A publication*]
Biol Bull India ... Biological Bulletin of India [*A publication*]
Biol Bull Mar Biol Lab (Woods Hole) ... Biological Bulletin. Marine Biological Laboratory (Woods Hole) [*Massachusetts*] [*A publication*]
Biol Bull (Woods Hole) ... Biological Bulletin (Woods Hole) [*A publication*]
Biol Cancer 2nd Ed ... Biology of Cancer. 2nd Edition [*A publication*]
Biol Carbohydr ... Biology of Carbohydrates [*A publication*]
Biol Cell ..... Biologie Cellulaire [*A publication*]
Biol Cell ..... Biology of the Cell [*A publication*]
Biol Cephalopods Proc Symp ... Biology of Cephalopods. Proceedings of a Symposium [*A publication*]
Biol Chem Eucaryotic Cell Surf Proc Miami Winter Symp ... Biology and Chemistry of Eucaryotic Cell Surfaces. Proceedings. Miami Winter Symposia [*A publication*]
Biol Chem Hoppe-Seyler ... Biological Chemistry Hoppe-Seyler [*A publication*]
Biol Chem Zivocisne Vyroby Vet ... Biologizace a Chemizace Zivocisne Vyroby-Veterinaria [*A publication*]

Biol Clin Aspects Fetus ... Biological and Clinical Aspects of the Fetus [*A publication*]
Biol Clin Basis Radiosensitivity Rep Proc Conf ... Biological and Clinical Basis of Radiosensitivity. Report. Proceedings. Conference [*A publication*]
Biol Comport ... Biologie du Comportement [*A publication*]
Biol Conf "Oholo" Annu Meet ... Biological Conference "Oholo." Annual Meeting [*A publication*]
Biol Conser ... Biological Conservation [*A publication*]
Biol Conserv ... Biological Conservation [*A publication*]
Biol Contemp ... Biologia Contemporanea [*A publication*]
Biol Control Soil-Borne Plant Pathog Int Symp ... Biology and Control of Soil-Borne Plant Pathogens. International Symposium on Factors Determining the Behavior of Plant Pathogens in Soil [*A publication*]
Biol Counc Ser Drug Action Mol Level ... Biological Council Series. Drug Action at the Molecular Level [*A publication*]
Biol Crist Cours Dev Senescence Colloq ... Biologie de Cristallin au Cours de Developpement et de la Senescence. Colloque [*A publication*]
Biol Crustacea ... Biology of Crustacea [*A publication*]
Biol Culturale ... Biologia Culturale [*A publication*]
Biol Cybern ... Biological Cybernetics [*A publication*]
Biol Cybernet ... Biological Cybernetics [*A publication*]
Biol Cybernetics ... Biological Cybernetics [*A publication*]
Biol Cytoplasmic Microtubules Pap Conf ... Biology of Cytoplasmic Microtubules. Papers. Conference [*A publication*]
BIOLD5..... Biologia [*Budapest*] [*A publication*]
BIOLDEF ... Biological Defense [*Military*] (AABC)
Biol Deistvie Bystrykh Neitronov ... Biologicheskoe Deistvie Bystrykh Neitronov [*A publication*]
Biol Deistvie Gig Znach Atmos Zagryaz ... Biologicheskoe Deistvie i Gigienicheskoe Znachenie Atmosfernykh Zagryaznenii [*A publication*]
Biol Deistvie Radiats ... Biologicheskoe Deistvie Radiatsii [*Ukrainian SSR*] [*A publication*]
Biol Deistvie Ul'trafiolet Izluch Dokl Vses Soveshch ... Biologicheskoe Deistvie Ul'trafioletovogo Izlucheniya. Doklady Vsesoyuznoi Soveshchanii [*A publication*]
Biol Diag Brain Disord Proc Int Conf ... Biological Diagnosis of Brain Disorders. Proceedings. International Conference [*A publication*]
Biol Diatoms ... Biology of Diatoms [*A publication*]
Biol Dig...... Biology Digest [*A publication*]
Biol Eff Asbestos Proc Work Conf ... Biological Effects of Asbestos. Proceedings. Working Conference [*A publication*]
Biol Eff Neutron Irradiat Proc Symp ... Biological Effects of Neutron Irradiation. Proceedings. Symposium. Effects of Neutron Irradiation upon Cell Function [*A publication*]
Biol Eff Nonioniz Radiat Conf ... Biological Effects of Nonionizing Radiation. Conference [*A publication*]
Biol Environ Eff Low Level Radiat Proc Symp ... Biological and Environmental Effects of Low Level Radiation. Proceedings of a Symposium on Biological Effects of Low Level Radiation Pertinent to Protection of Man and His Environment [*A publication*]
Biol Flora Mosk Obl ... Biologicheskaia Flora Moskovskoi Oblasti [*A publication*]
Biol Gabonica ... Biologia Gabonica [*A publication*]
Biol Gallo-Hell ... Biologia Gallo-Hellenica [*A publication*]
Biol Gallo-Hellenica ... Biologia Gallo-Hellenica [*A publication*]
Biol Gastro ... Biologie et Gastro-Enterologie [*A publication*]
Biol Gastro-Enterol ... Biologie et Gastro-Enterologie [*A publication*]
Biol Gen..... Biologia Generalis [*A publication*]
Biol Glas..... Bioloski Glasnik [*A publication*]
Biol Handb ... Biological Handbooks [*A publication*]
Biol Heilkunst ... Biologische Heilkunst [*A publication*]
Biol Hum Aff ... Biology and Human Affairs [*A publication*]
Biol Hum Fetal Growth ... Biology of Human Fetal Growth [*A publication*]
Biol Hystricomorph Rodents Proc Symp ... Biology of Hystricomorph Rodents. Proceedings of a Symposium [*A publication*]
Biol Identif Comput Proc Meet ... Biological Identification with Computers. Proceedings of a Meeting [*A publication*]
Biol Implic Met Environ Proc Annu Hanford Life Sci Symp ... Biological Implications of Metals in the Environment. Proceedings of the Annual Hanford Life Sciences Symposium [*A publication*]
Biol Ind ...... Biologia et Industria [*A publication*]
Biol Int....... Biology International [*A publication*]
Biol Issled Sev Vostoke Evr Chasti SSSR ... Biologicheskie Issledovaniya na Severo Vostoke Evropeiskoi Chasti SSSR [*A publication*]
Biol J.......... Biological Journal [*A publication*]
Biol Jaarb .. Biologisch Jaarboek [*A publication*]
Biol Jb........ Biologisch Jaarboek [*Gent*] [*A publication*]
Biol J Linn ... Biological Journal. Linnean Society [*A publication*]
Biol J Linn Soc ... Biological Journal. Linnean Society [*A publication*]
Biol J Linn Soc Lond ... Biological Journal. Linnean Society of London [*A publication*]
Biol J Nara Women's Univ ... Biological Journal. Nara Women's University [*A publication*]

Biol J Okayama Univ ... Biological Journal. Okayama University [*A publication*]
Biol Khim... Biologiya i Khimiya [*A publication*]
Biol Koezl... Biologiai Koezlemenyek [*A publication*]
Biol Koezlem ... Biologiai Koezlemenyek [*A publication*]
Biol Lab Rabbit ... Biology of the Laboratory Rabbit [*A publication*]
Biol Lab Zhivotn ... Biologiya Laboratornykh Zhivotnykh [*A publication*]
Biol Lat...... Biologica Latina [*A publication*]
Biol Listu ... Biologickych Listu [*A publication*]
Biol Listy ... Biologicke Listy [*A publication*]
Biol Luchistykh Gribkov ... Biologiya Luchistykh Gribkov [*A publication*]
Biol Macromol ... Biological Macromolecules [*A publication*]
Biol Macromol Assem ... Biological Macromolecules and Assemblies [*A publication*]
Biol Medd K Dan Vidensk Selsk ... Biologiske Meddelelser Kongelige Danske Videnskabernes Selskab [*A publication*]
Biol Meddr ... Biologiske Meddelelser [*A publication*]
Biol Med Milano Ed Ital ... Biologie Medical Milano. Edizione per l'Italia [*Milano*] [*A publication*]
Biol Med (Niteroi Brazil) ... Biologia Medica (Niteroi, Brazil) [*A publication*]
Biol Med (Paris) ... Biologie Medicale (Paris) [*A publication*]
Biol Mem ... Biological Memoirs [*A publication*]
Biol Memb ... Biologicheskie Membrany [*A publication*]
Biol Membr ... Biological Membranes [*A publication*]
Biol Membr ... Biologicheskie Membrany [*A publication*]
Biol Mikroorg Ikh Ispol'z Nar Khoz ... Biologiya Mikroorganizmov i Ikh Ispol'zovanie v Narodnom Khozyaistve [*A publication*]
Biol Monit Water Effluent Qual Symp ... Biological Monitoring of Water and Effluent Quality. Symposium [*A publication*]
Biol Moria ... Biologiia Moria [*A publication*]
Biol Morya ... Biologiya Morya [*A publication*]
Biol Morya (Vladivost) ... Biologiya Morya (Vladivostok) [*A publication*]
Biol Nauka Sel'sk Lesn Khoz ... Biologicheskaya Nauka. Sel'skomu i Lesnomu Khozyatsteu [*A publication*]
Biol Nauki ... Biologicheskie Nauki [*Moscow*] [*A publication*]
Biol Neonat ... Biology of the Neonate [*A publication*]
Biol Neonatorum ... Biologia Neonatorum [*Later, Biology of the Neonate*] [*A publication*]
Biol Nitrogen Fixation ... Biology of Nitrogen Fixation [*A publication*]
Biol Nocardiae ... Biology of the Nocardiae [*A publication*]
Biol Notes Ill Nat Hist Surv ... Biological Notes. Illinois Natural History Survey [*A publication*]
Biol Oceanic Pac Proc Annu Biol Colloq ... Biology of the Oceanic Pacific. Proceedings. Annual Biology Colloquium [*A publication*]
Biol Oceanogr ... Biological Oceanography [*A publication*]
Biologia Bratisl ... Biologia. Casopis Slovenskej Akademie vied Bratislava [*A publication*]
Biologia Pl ... Biologia Plantarum [*A publication*]
Biologica Lat ... Biologica Latina [*A publication*]
Biol Osn Bor'by Obrastaniem ... Biologicheskie Osnovy Bor'by s Obrastaniem [*A publication*]
Biol Osn Povysh Prod Skh Rast ... Biologicheskie Osnovy Povysheniya Produktivnosti Sel'skokhozyaistvennykh Rastenii [*A publication*]
Biol Pap Univ Alaska ... Biological Papers. University of Alaska [*A publication*]
Biol Pap Univ Alaska Spec Rep ... Biological Papers. University of Alaska. Special Report [*A publication*]
Biol Penguins ... Biology of Penguins [*A publication*]
Biol Pesq.... Biologia Pesquera [*A publication*]
Biol & Philos ... Biology and Philosophy [*A publication*]
Biol Plant... Biologia Plantarum [*A publication*]
Biol Plant (Prague) ... Biologia Plantarum (Prague) [*A publication*]
Biol Pr........ Biologicke Prace [*A publication*]
Biol Probl Sev Tezisy Dokl Simp ... Biologicheskie Problemy Severa Tezisy Dokladov Simpozium [*A publication*]
Biol Prod Protsessy Basseine Volgi ... Biologicheskie Produktsionnye Protsessy v Basseine Volgi [*A publication*]
Biol Prop Mamm Surf Membr Symp ... Biological Properties. Mammalian Surface Membrane. Symposium [*A publication*]
Biol Protsessy Miner Obmen Pochvakh Kol'sk Poluostrova ... Biologicheskie Protsessy i Mineral'nyi Obmen v Pochvakh Kol'skogo Poluostrova [*A publication*]
Biol Psych Bul ... Biological Psychology Bulletin [*A publication*]
Biol Psychi ... Biological Psychiatry [*A publication*]
Biol Psychiatry ... Biological Psychiatry [*A publication*]
Biol Psychol ... Biological Psychology [*A publication*]
Biol Psychol Bull (Okla City) ... Biological Psychology Bulletin (Oklahoma City) [*A publication*]
Biol R......... Biological Reviews [*A publication*]
Biol Rdsch ... Biologische Rundschau [*A publication*]
Biol React Intermed Proc Int Conf ... Biological Reactive Intermediates, Formation Toxicity, and Inactivation. Proceedings of an International Conference on Active Intermediates, Formation Toxicity, and Inactivation [*A publication*]
Biol Reprod ... Biology of Reproduction [*A publication*]
Biol Reprod Kletok ... Biologiya Reprodakisii Kletok [*A publication*]
Biol Reprod Suppl ... Biology of Reproduction. Supplement [*A publication*]
BIOLREPT ... Biological Report (AABC)

Biol Resour Nat Cond Mong People's Repub ... Biological Resources and Natural Conditions. Mongolian People's Republic [*A publication*]

Biol Res Pregnancy Perinatol ... Biological Research in Pregnancy and Perinatology [*A publication*]

Biol Res Rep Univ Jyvaeskylae ... Biological Research Reports. University of Jyvaeskylae [*A publication*]

Biol Resur Bodoemov Mold ... Biologicheskie Resursy Bodoemov Moldavii [*A publication*]

Biol Resur Prir Usloviya Mong Nar Resp ... Biologicheskie Resursy i Prirodnye Usloviya Mongol'skoi Narodnoi Respubliki [*A publication*]

Biol Rev ...... Biological Reviews. Cambridge Philosophical Society [*A publication*]

Biol Rev Camb Philos Soc ... Biological Reviews. Cambridge Philosophical Society [*A publication*]

Biol Rev Cambridge Phil Soc ... Biological Reviews. Cambridge Philosophical Society [*A publication*]

Biol Rev City Coll NY ... Biological Review. City College of New York [*A publication*]

Biol Rhythms Neuroendocr Act ... Biological Rhythms in Neuroendocrine Activity [*A publication*]

Biol Role Porphyrins Relat Struct Pap Conf ... Biological Role of Porphyrins and Related Structures. Papers. Conference [*A publication*]

Biol Roles Sialic Acid ... Biological Roles of Sialic Acid [*A publication*]

Biol Rol Mikroelem Ikh Primen Sel'sk Khoz Med ... Biologicheskaya Rol Mikroelementov i Ikh Primenenie v Sel'skom Khozyaistve i Meditsine [*A publication*]

Biol Rs .... Biological Reviews [*A publication*]

BIOLRSCH ... Biological Research   (AABC)

Biol Rundsch ... Biologische Rundschau [*A publication*]

Biol Rundschau ... Biologische Rundschau [*A publication*]

Biol Sci .... Biological Science [*A publication*]

Biol Sci Curric Study Bull ... Biological Sciences Curriculum Study Bulletin [*A publication*]

Biol Sci Curriculum Study Bull ... Biological Sciences Curriculum Study. Bulletin [*A publication*]

Biol Sci (Tokyo) ... Biological Science (Tokyo) [*A publication*]

Biol Seal Proc Symp ... Biology of the Seal. Proceedings of the Symposium [*A publication*]

Biol Shk ..... Biologiya Shkole [*A publication*]

Biol Signals Proc Symp ... Biological Signals. Proceedings of a Symposium [*A publication*]

Biol Soc ...... Biology and Society [*A publication*]

Biol Soc Nev Mem ... Biological Society of Nevada. Memoirs [*A publication*]

Biol Soc Nev Occas Pap ... Biological Society of Nevada. Occasional Papers [*A publication*]

Biol Soc Pak Monogr ... Biological Society of Pakistan. Monograph [*A publication*]

Biol Soc Washington Proc ... Biological Society of Washington. Proceedings [*A publication*]

Biol Soc Wash Proc ... Biological Society of Washington. Proceedings [*A publication*]

Biol Sol ...... Biologie du Sol. Bulletin International d'Informations [*A publication*]

Biol Sol Microbiol ... Biologie du Sol. Microbiologie [*A publication*]

Biol Struct Morphog ... Biological Structures and Morphogenesis [*A publication*]

Biol Svoistva Khim Soedin ... Biologicheskie Svoistva Khimicheskikh Soedinenii [*A publication*]

Biol Symp .. Biological Symposia [*A publication*]

Biol Trab Inst Biol "Juan Noe" Fac Med Univ Chile ... Biologica. Trabajos. Instituto de Biologia "Juan Noe." Facultad de Medicina de la Universidad de Chile [*A publication*]

Biol Trace Elem Res ... Biological Trace Element Research [*A publication*]

Biol Unserer Zeit ... Biologie in Unserer Zeit [*A publication*]

Biol Uterus ... Biology of the Uterus [*A publication*]

Biol Vestn .. Bioloski Vestnik [*A publication*]

Biol Vnutr Vod ... Biologiya Vnutrennykh Vod [*A publication*]

Biol Vnutr Vod Inf Byull ... Biologiya Vnutrennykh Vod. Informatsionnyi Byulleten [*A publication*]

Biol Vses Inst Eksp Vet ... Biologicheskii i Vsesoyuzni Institut Eksperimental'noi Veterinarii [*A publication*]

BIOLWPN ... Biological Weapons [*Military*]   (AABC)

BIOLWPNSYS ... Biological Weapons System [*Military*]   (AABC)

Biol Zakl Pol'nohospod ... Biologicke Zaklad Pol'nohospodarstvo [*A publication*]

Biol Zbl ...... Biologisches Zentralblatt [*A publication*]

Biol Zb L'viv Derzh Univ ... Biologichnii Zbirnik. L'vivs'kii Derzhaenii Universitet [*A publication*]

Biol Zentralbl ... Biologisches Zentralblatt [*A publication*]

Biol Zh .... Biologicheskii Zhurnal [*A publication*]

Biol Zh Arm ... Biologicheskii Zhurnal Armenii [*A publication*]

Biol Zh Armeni ... Biologicheskii Zhurnal Armenii [*A publication*]

Biom .... Biometrics [*A publication*]

Biom .... Biometrika [*A publication*]

BIOM .... Buffer Input-Output Memory [*Data processing*]

BIOMA ...... Biometrics [*A publication*]

BIOMASS ... Biological Investigation of Marine Antarctic Systems and Stocks Program [*Texas A & M University*] [*Research center*]   (RCD)

Biomass Dig ... Biomass Digest [*A publication*]

Biomass Energy Inst Newsl ... Biomass Energy Institute. Newsletter [*Canada*] [*A publication*]

Biomater Med Dev Artif Organs ... Biomaterials, Medical Devices, and Artificial Organs [*A publication*]

Biomater Med Devices Artif Organs ... Biomaterials, Medical Devices, and Artificial Organs [*A publication*]

Biomater Med Devices and Artif Organs ... Biomaterials, Medical Devices, and Artificial Organs [*A publication*]

Bio-Math ... Bio-Mathematics [*A publication*]

Biomat Med ... Biomaterials, Medical Devices, and Artificial Organs [*A publication*]

Biom Bull ... Biometrae Bulletin [*A publication*]

Biomech Symp Jt Appl Mech Fluids Eng Bioeng Conf ... Biomechanics Symposium Presented at the Joint Applied Mechanics Fluids Engineering and Bioengineering Conference [*A publication*]

BIOMED ... Biological Medicine

Biomed Appl ... Biomedical Applications [*A publication*]

Biomed Appl Gas Chromatogr ... Biomedical Applications of Gas Chromatography [*A publication*]

Biomed Appl Immobilized Enzymes Proteins ... Biomedical Applications of Immobilized Enzymes and Proteins [*A publication*]

Biomed Appln Polym ... Biomedical Applications of Polymers [*A publication*]

Biomed Biochim Acta ... Biomedica Biochimica Acta [*A publication*]

Biomed Clin Aspects Coenzyme Q Proc Int Symp ... Biomedical and Clinical Aspects of Coenzyme Q. Proceedings of the International Symposium [*A publication*]

Biomed Commun ... Biomedical Communications [*A publication*]

Biomed Eng ... Biomedical Engineering [*New York*] [*A publication*]

Biomed Eng (Berl) ... Biomedical Engineering (Berlin) [*A publication*]

Biomed Eng (Engl Transl) ... Biomedical Engineering (English Translation) [*A publication*]

Biomed Eng (Engl Transl Med Tekh) ... Biomedical Engineering (English Translation of Meditsinskaya Tekhnika) [*A publication*]

Biomed Eng (Lond) ... Biomedical Engineering (London) [*A publication*]

Biomed Engng Curr Aware Notif ... Biomedical Engineering Current Awareness Notification [*A publication*]

Biomed Eng (NY) ... Biomedical Engineering (New York) [*A publication*]

Biomed Eng (USSR) ... Biomedical Engineering (USSR) [*A publication*]

Biomed Environ Mass Spectrom ... Biomedical and Environmental Mass Spectrometry [*A publication*]

Biomed Expr ... Biomedicine Express [*Paris*] [*A publication*]

Biomed Express (Paris) ... Biomedicine Express (Paris) [*A publication*]

Bio Med Instrum ... Bio Medical Instrumentation [*A publication*]

Biomed Instrum Technol ... Biomedical Instrumentation and Technology [*A publication*]

Biomed Mass ... Biomedical Mass Spectrometry [*A publication*]

Biomed Mass Spectrom ... Biomedical Mass Spectrometry [*A publication*]

Biomed Mater Symp ... Biomedical Materials Symposium [*A publication*]

Biomed Pharmacother ... Biomedicine and Pharmacotherapy [*A publication*]

Biomed & Pharmacother ... Biomedicine and Pharmacotherapy [*A publication*]

Bio-Med Purv ... Bio-Medical Purview [*A publication*]

Bio-Med Rep 406 Med Lab ... Bio-Medical Reports of the 406 Medical Laboratory [*A publication*]

Biomed Res ... Biomedical Research [*A publication*]

Biomed Sci Instrum ... Biomedical Sciences Instrumentation [*A publication*]

Biomed Sci (Tokyo) ... Biomedical Sciences (Tokyo) [*A publication*]

Biomed Tech ... Biomedizinische Technik [*Berlin*] [*A publication*]

Biomed Tech (Berlin) ... Biomedizinische Technik (Berlin) [*A publication*]

Biomed Tech Biomed Eng ... Biomedizinische Technik. Biomedical Engineering [*A publication*]

Biomembr Lipids Proteins Recept Proc NATO Adv Study Inst ... Biomembranes, Lipids, Proteins, and Receptors. Proceedings of a NATO Advanced Study Institute [*A publication*]

BIOMET ... Biometry

Biometeorol Czlowieka ... Biometeorologia Czlowieka [*A publication*]

Biometeorol Res Cent (Leiden) Monogr Ser ... Biometeorological Research Centre (Leiden). Monograph Series [*A publication*]

Biomet-Praximet ... Biometrie-Praximetrie [*A publication*]

Biometrical J ... Biometrical Journal [*A publication*]

Biometrie Hum ... Biometrie Humaine [*A publication*]

Biometr-Praxim ... Biometrie-Praximetrie [*A publication*]

Biometr Z ... Biometrische Zeitschrift [*A publication*]

Biom Hum ... Biometrie Humaine [*A publication*]

Biom J .... Biometrical Journal [*A publication*]

Biom J .... Biometrical Journal. Journal of Mathematical Methods of Biosciences [*A publication*]

BIOMOD .. Biochemical Modeling [*Data processing*]

Biom Z .... Biometrische Zeitschrift [*A publication*]

Biom Zeit ... Biometrische Zeitschrift [*A publication*]

BION .... Believe It or Not

BION .... BioAnalogics, Inc. [*NASDAQ symbol*]   (NQ)

BIONICS .. Biological Electronics   (IEEE)

Bionika Mat Model Biol ... Bionika i Matematicheskoe Modelirovanie v Biologii [*A publication*]

BIONUCL ... Bionucleonics

Bioorg Chem ... Bioorganic Chemistry [*A publication*]

Bioorg Khim ... Bioorganicheskaya Khimiya [*A publication*]

Bioorg Mar Chem ... Bioorganic Marine Chemistry [*A publication*]
BIOP......... Bioplasty, Inc. [*NASDAQ symbol*] (NQ)
BIOPA....... Biophysics [*English Translation*] [*A publication*]
BIOPACK ... Biological Packs (NG)
BIOPAE ..... Biophysics [*English Translation of Biofizika*] [*A publication*]
BIOPEI ..... Biology and Philosophy [*A publication*]
Biopharm Drug Dispos ... Biopharmaceutics and Drug Disposition [*A publication*]
BioPharm Manuf ... BioPharm Manufacturing [*A publication*]
Biophys...... Biophysics [*A publication*]
Biophys Centralbl ... Biophysikalisches Centralblatt [*A publication*]
Biophys Ch ... Biophysical Chemistry [*A publication*]
Biophys Chem ... Biophysical Chemistry [*A publication*]
Biophysics (Engl Transl Biofizika) ... Biophysics (English Translation of Biofizika) [*A publication*]
Biophys J ... Biophysical Journal [*A publication*]
Biophys J Suppl ... Biophysical Journal. Supplement [*A publication*]
Biophys Soc Annu Meet Abstr ... Biophysical Society. Annual Meeting. Abstracts [*A publication*]
Biophys Soc Symp ... Biophysical Society. Symposium [*A publication*]
Biophys Str ... Biophysics of Structure and Mechanism [*A publication*]
Biophys Struct & Mech ... Biophysics of Structure and Mechanism [*A publication*]
Biophys Struct Mech ... Biophysics of Structure and Mechanism [*A publication*]
BIOP Newsl ... BIOP [*Board of International Organizations and Programs*] Newsletter [*A publication*]
Biopolym Symp ... Biopolymers Symposia [*A publication*]
Bioquim Clin ... Bioquimica Clinica [*A publication*]
Bioquim Clini ... Bioquimica Clinica [*A publication*]
BIOQUIP ... DECHEMA [*Deutsche Gesellschaft fuer Chemisches Apparatewesen, Chemische Technik, und Biotechnologie eV*] Biotechnology Equipment Suppliers [*Frankfurt Am Main, Federal Republic of Germany*] [*Information service or system*] (IID)
BiOr .... Bibliotheca Orientalis [*A publication*]
BIOR .... Bio-Response, Inc. [*NASDAQ symbol*] (NQ)
BIOR .... Business Input/Output Rerun [*UNIVAC compiling system*] [*Data processing*]
BIORA....... Biochemistry [*English Translation*] [*A publication*]
Bior & D Laws ... Bioren and Duane's United States Laws [*A publication*] (DLA)
BIOREP .... Biological Report
BIOREP/CHEMREP ... Biological/Chemical Attack Report
BioRes Index ... BioResearch Index [*Later, BA/RRM*] [*A publication*]
Biorheol Suppl ... Biorheology. Supplement [*A publication*]
BIORS....... Bedford Institute of Oceanography. Report Series [*A publication*]
BIOS.......... Basic Input-Output System [*IBM Corp.*]
BIOS.......... Biological Investigation of Space [*NASA*]
BIOS.......... Biological Orbiting Satellite (MCD)
BIOS.......... Biological Satellite
BIOS.......... Biosonics, Inc. [*NASDAQ symbol*] (NQ)
BIOS.......... British Intelligence Objectives Subcommittee
BIOSAT .... Biological Satellite (KSC)
BioSci......... BioScience [*A publication*]
Biosci Commun ... Biosciences Communications [*A publication*]
Bioscience & Ind ... Bioscience and Industry [*A publication*]
Biosci Rep ... Bioscience Reports [*A publication*]
Biosci Rep Abo Akad ... Bioscience Report. Abo Akademi [*A publication*]
BIOSE........ Bio-Sciences [*A publication*]
Biosfera Chel Mater Vses Simp ... Biosfera i Chelovek Materialy Vsesoyuznogo Simpoziuma [*A publication*]
Biosint Sostoyanie Khlorofillov Rast ... Biosintez i Sostoyanie Khlorofillov v Rastenii [*A publication*]
BIOSIS...... BioSciences Information Service [*Database producer*] [*Philadelphia, PA*]
BIOSOMA ... Biological, Social, Machine [*Combination*]
Biosources Dig ... Biosources Digest [*A publication*]
BIOSPEX ... Biological Space Experiments (MCD)
BIOSTAT ... Biostatistics
BIOSW...... BIOS. Baffin Island Oil Spill Project Working Report [*A publication*]
Biosynth Antibiot ... Biosynthesis of Antibiotics [*A publication*]
Biosynth Prod Cancer Chemother ... Biosynthetic Products for Cancer Chemotherapy [*A publication*]
Bio Syst...... Bio Systems [*A publication*]
BIOT.......... Biotechnica International, Inc. [*NASDAQ symbol*] (NQ)
BIOT.......... British Indian Ocean Territory
BIOTA....... Biological Institute of Tropical America (EA)
BIOTEC .... Biotechnology
Biotech .... Biotechnology International. Trends and Perspectives [*A publication*]
Biotech Bio ... Biotechnology and Bioengineering [*A publication*]
Biotech Bioeng ... Biotechnology and Bioengineering [*A publication*]
Biotechnol ... Bio/Technology. The International Monthly for Industrial Biology [*A publication*]
Biotechnol Adv ... Biotechnology Advances [*A publication*]
Biotechnol Agric For ... Biotechnology in Agriculture and Forestry [*A publication*]

Biotechnol Appl Biochem ... Biotechnology and Applied Biochemistry [*A publication*]
Biotechnol Bioeng ... Biotechnology and Bioengineering [*A publication*]
Biotechnol Bioeng Symp ... Biotechnology and Bioengineering. Symposium [*A publication*]
Biotechnol Genet Eng Rev ... Biotechnology and Genetic Engineering Reviews [*A publication*]
Biotechnol & Genet Eng Rev ... Biotechnology and Genetic Engineering Reviews [*A publication*]
Biotechnol Law Rep ... Biotechnology Law Report [*A publication*]
Biotechnol Lett ... Biotechnology Letters [*England*] [*A publication*]
Biotechnol Monogr ... Biotechnology Monographs [*A publication*]
Biotechnol Prog ... Biotechnology Progress [*A publication*]
Biotechnol Ser ... Biotechnology Series [*A publication*]
Biotelemetr ... Biotelemetry [*Later, Biotelemetry and Patient Monitoring*] [*A publication*]
Biotelem Patient Monit ... Biotelemetry and Patient Monitoring [*A publication*]
Biotest Bull ... Biotest Bulletin [*A publication*]
BIOTEX .... Bio-Technology Exhibition (TSPED)
BIOT GR SCH ... Biotite Granite Schist [*Geology*]
Bioticheskie Komponenty Nazemn Ekosistem Tyan Shanya ... Bioticheskie Komponenty Nazemnykh Ekosistem Tyan Shanya [*A publication*]
BIOTROP ... Regional Center for Tropical Biology [*SEAMEO*] [*Research center*] [*Indonesia*] (IRC)
BioV .... Bioloski Vestnik [*A publication*]
BIOVD ...... Biovigyanam [*A publication*]
BIOW .... Banks of Iowa, Inc. [*NASDAQ symbol*] (NQ)
BIOWAR... Biological Warfare
BIOXF .... Bionex Corp. [*NASDAQ symbol*] (NQ)
BIOZ .... Biostim, Inc. [*NASDAQ symbol*] (NQ)
BIP............. Baggage Improvement Program [*IATA*] (DS)
BIP............. Balanced Indigenous Population
BIP............. Balanced in Plane (IEEE)
BIP............. Balloon Interrogation Package
BIP............. Banco Industrial del Peru [*Industrial Bank of Peru*]
BIP............. Banque International de Placement
BIP............. Basic Information Package
BIP............. BASIC Interpreter Package
BIP............. Best's Review. Property/Casualty Insurance Edition [*A publication*]
BIP............. Bi-Petro Resources [*Vancouver Stock Exchange symbol*]
BIP............. Binary Image Processor [*Data processing*]
BIP............. Bipropellant (KSC)
BIP............. Bismuth Iodoform Paraffin [*Medicine*]
BIP............. Block Improvement Program [*for M1A1 tank*] [*Army*]
BIP............. Blue Cross Interim Payment [*Insurance*]
BIP............. Books in Print [*Bibliographic database*] [*R. R. Bowker Co.*] [*A publication*]
BIP............. Botswana Independence Party [*Political party*] (PPW)
BIP............. Budget Increment Package [*DoD*]
BIP............. Buergerinitiative Parlament [*Citizens' Parliamentary Initiative*] [*Austria*] [*Political party*] (EY)
BIP............. Bulimba [*Australia*] [*Airport symbol*] [*Obsolete*] (OAG)
BIP............. Bulletin de l'Industrie Petroliere [*A publication*]
BIP............. Bureau d'Information et de Presse [*Circulated Allied propaganda in France and informed Allies of resistance activities*] [*World War II*]
BIP............. Bureau of International Programs [*Department of Commerce*]
B-I-P .... Business Intelligence Program Research Catalog [*SRI International*] [*Information service or system*] (IID)
BIPA.......... Banque d'Informations Politiques et d'Actualite [*Political and Current Events Information Bank*] [*Database*] [*Telesystems - Questel*] [*Information service or system*] (IID)
BIPA.......... Patreksfjordur [*Iceland*] [*ICAO location identifier*] (ICLI)
BIPAA .... Bulletin. Institut Pasteur [*Paris*] [*A publication*]
BIPAC .... Business-Industry Political Action Committee (EA)
BIPAD....... Binary Pattern Detector
BIPAD....... Bureau of Independent Publishers and Distributors (EA)
BIPADB .... Instituto de Pesquisas Agronomicas. Boletim Tecnico [*A publication*]
BIPAR .... Bureau International des Producteurs d'Assurances et de Reassurances [*International Association of Insurance and Reinsurance Intermediaries - IAIRI*] [*Paris, France*] (EAIO)
BIPASS ..... Burroughs Inventory Planning Analysis and Simulation System [*Data processing*] (BUR)
B I Pasteur ... Bulletin. Institut Pasteur [*Paris*] [*A publication*]
BIPCA .... Bureau International Permanent de Chimie Analytique pour les Matieres Destinees a l'Alimentation de l'Homme et des Animaux [*Permanent International Bureau of Analytical Chemistry of Human and Animal Food*]
BIPCB .... Biological Psychiatry [*A publication*]
BIPCO....... Built-in-Place Component [*Electronics*]
BIPD.......... Biparting Door
BI/PD .... Bodily Injury and Property Damage [*Insurance*]
BIPE .... Bureau d'Informations et de Previsions Economiques [*Office of Economic Information and Forecasting*] [*Information service or system*] (IID)

BIPED .... Buletinul. Institutului Politehnic "Gheorghe Gheorghiu-Dej" Bucuresti. Seria Electrotehnica [*A publication*]
BIPEX .... British International Postcard Exhibition
BIPG .... Bulletin. Institut de Phonetique de Grenoble [*A publication*]
BIPGA .... Buletinul. Institutului de Petrol, Gaze, si Geologie [*A publication*]
BIPHDW ... Bibliotheca Phycologica [*A publication*]
BIPHEX ..... Biomedicine and Pharmacotherapy [*A publication*]
BIPID .... Bits and Pieces [*A publication*]
BIPL .... Biopool International, Inc. [*NASDAQ symbol*]   (NQ)
BIPM .... Benzimidazolylphenylmaleimide [*Organic chemistry*]
BIPM .... Bureau International des Poids et Mesures [*International Bureau of Weights and Measures*] [*Sevres, France*]   (EA)
BIPMA ...... Biopolymers [*A publication*]
BIPNA .... Bibliotheca Phonetica [*A publication*]
BIPO .... British Institute of Public Opinion
BIPOLT .... Bulk Inland Petroleum, Oil, and Lubrication Transport   (NATG)
BIPP .... Bismuth Iodoform and Paraffin Paste [*Medicine*]
BIPP .... Bureau of Intergovernmental Personnel Programs
BIPS .... Banking Information Processing System [*Data processing*]   (BUR)
BIPS .... Billion Instructions per Second [*Computing power measurement*] [*Data processing*]
BIPS .... Branch Information Processing System [*Data processing*]
BIPS .... Brayton Isotope Power System
BIPY .... Bipyridine [*Also, BPY*] [*Organic chemistry*]
BIQ .... Base Inspection Questionnaire [*Air Force*]
BIQ .... Biarritz [*France*] [*Airport symbol*]   (OAG)
BIQ .... Flint, MI [*Location identifier*] [*FAA*]   (FAAL)
BIQH .... Bureau Independant pour les Questions Humanitaires [*Independent Bureau for Humanitarian Issues*]   (EAIO)
BIR .... Banco de Intercambio Regional [*Argentina*]
BIR .... Banque d'Information sur les Recherches [*INSERM Research Information Bank*] [*National Institute for Health and Medical Research*] [*Information service or system*]   (IID)
BIR .... Basic Incidence Rate [*Medicine*]
BIR .... [*Classified on the*] Basis of Information Revealed
BIR .... Before Initial Release [*Information system*]   (MCD)
B-IR .... Bell-Independent Relations [*Telecommunications*]   (TEL)
BiR .... Biblical Research [*Chicago*] [*A publication*]
BIR .... Bibliography on Incineration of Refuse and Waste [*Air Pollution Control Association*] [*A publication*]
BIR .... Biratnagar [*Nepal*] [*Airport symbol*]   (OAG)
BIR .... Birmingham Steel Corp. [*NYSE symbol*]   (SPSG)
BIR .... Board of Inland Revenue [*British*]
BIR .... Break-In Relay
BIR .... British Institute of Radiology   (DEN)
BIR .... Bureau of Immigration Research [*Australia*]
BIR .... Bureau of Intelligence and Research [*Department of State*]
BIR .... Bureau of Internal Revenue [*Department of the Treasury*] [*Later, Internal Revenue Service*]
BIR .... Bureau International de la Recuperation [*International Bureau of Recuperation*] [*Brussels, Belgium*]   (EA)
BIRAG ...... Big Island Rainforest Action Group   (EA)
B Iran Inst ... Bulletin. Iranian Institute [*A publication*]
BIRAP .... Balloon Infrared Astronomy Platform
Birbal Sahni Inst Palaeobot Birbal Sahni Mem Lect ... Birbal Sahni Institute of Palaeobotany. Birbal Sahni Memorial Lecture [*Luchnow*] [*A publication*]
Birbal Sahni Inst Palaeobot Spec Publ ... Birbal Sahni Institute of Palaeobotany. Special Publication [*A publication*]
BIR Bull .... BIR [*British Institute of Radiology*] Bulletin [*A publication*]
BIRC .... Bio-Integral Resource Center   (EA)
BIRD .... Banque d'Information Robert Debre [*Centre International de l'Enfance*] [*Database*]
BIRD .... Banque Internationale pour la Reconstruction et le Developpement [*International Bank for Reconstruction and Development; also known as the World Bank*] [*French*]
BIRD .... Base d'Information Robert Debre [*Robert Debre Information Base*] [*International Children's Center*] [*Information service or system*]   (IID)
BIRD .... Bird Corp. [*NASDAQ symbol*]   (NQ)
BIRDL .... Centre for Brain Injury Rehabilitation and Development [*British*]   (CB)
BIRD .... Reykjavik [*Iceland*] [*ICAO location identifier*]   (ICLI)
Bird-Band .. Bird-Banding [*A publication*]
Bird Behav ... Bird Behaviour [*A publication*]
Bird Conv ... Bird. New Pocket Conveyancer [*5th ed.*] [*1830*] [*A publication*]   (DLA)
Bird E .... Bird Effort [*A publication*]
BIRDIE ..... Battery Integration and RADAR Display Equipment [*Air defense system*]
BIRDIE ..... Battery Integration Routing Display Equipment   (MCD)
Bird Keeping ... Bird Keeping in Australia [*A publication*]
Bird L .... Bird Lore [*Pennsylvania*] [*A publication*]
Bird L & T ... Bird. Laws Respecting Landlords, Tenants, and Lodgers [*11th ed.*] [*1833*] [*A publication*]   (DLA)
BIRDS .... Bangladesh Integrated Rural Development Services   (EAIO)

Bird Sol Pr ... Bird. Solution of Precedents of Settlements [*1800*] [*A publication*]   (DLA)
Birds St ...... Birdseye's Statutes [*New York*] [*A publication*]   (DLA)
Bird Supp ... Bird's Supplement to Barton's Conveyancing [*A publication*]   (DLA)
Birdw .... Birdwood's Printed Judgments [*India*] [*A publication*]   (DLA)
B Ir E .... Bachelor of Irrigation Engineering
BIRE .... British Institute of Radio Engineers
BIREB .... Biology of Reproduction [*A publication*]
B Ir Eng ..... Bachelor of Irrigation Engineering
BiRes .... Biblical Research [*Chicago*] [*A publication*]
BIRES .... Broadband Isotropic Real-Time Electric Field Sensor   (MCD)
BIRESUL ... Bulletin. Institut de Recherches Economiques et Sociales. Universite de Louvain [*A publication*]
Biret Vocab ... Biret. Vocabulaire des Cinq Codes, ou Definitions Simplifiees des Termes de Droit et de Jurisprudence Exprimes dan ces Codes [*1862*] [*A publication*]   (DLA)
BIRF .... Banco Internacional de Reconstruccion y Fomento [*International Bank for Reconstruction and Development; also known as World Bank*] [*Spanish*]
BIRF .... Brewing Industry Research Foundation [*British*]
BIRG .... Raufarhofn [*Iceland*] [*ICAO location identifier*]   (ICLI)
BIRI .... Brainerd International, Inc. [*Minnetonka, MN*] [*NASDAQ symbol*]   (NQ)
BIRI .... Brewing Industries Research Institute [*Defunct*]   (EA)
BIRISPT ... Bureau International de Recherche sur les Implications Sociales du Progres Technique
BIRK .... Reykjavik Airport [*Iceland*] [*ICAO location identifier*]   (ICLI)
Birk J .... Birkenhead's Judgments, House of Lords [*1919-22*] [*England*] [*A publication*]   (DLA)
BIRL .... Beneficial Insects Research Laboratory [*Department of Agriculture*] [*Newark, DE*]   (GRD)
Birla Archaeol Cult Res Inst Res Bull ... Birla Archaeological and Cultural Research Institute. Research Bulletin [*A publication*]
BIRLS .... Beneficiary Identification Records Location Subsystem   (MCD)
BIRM .... Birmingham [*City, county borough, and university in England*]
BIRMA ...... Birmingham University. Chemical Engineer [*A publication*]
BIRMAS ... Boeing Infrared Missile Attack Simulation   (MCD)
Birmingham Ph Soc Pr ... Birmingham [*England*] Philosophical Society. Proceedings [*A publication*]
Birmingham Univ Chem Eng ... Birmingham University. Chemical Engineer [*A publication*]
Birmingham Univ Hist ... Birmingham University. Historical Journal [*A publication*]
BIRO .... Base Industrial Relations Office [*or Officer*] [*Military*]
BIRODT .... Butterworths International Medical Reviews. Otolaryngology [*A publication*]
BIRPA .... Bulletin. Institut Royal du Patrimoine Artistique [*A publication*]
BIRPI .... Bureaux Internationaux Reunis pour la Protection de la Propriete Intellectuelle [*United International Bureau for the Protection of Intellectual Property*] [*Later, WIPO*]
BIRPS .... British Institutions Reflection Profiling Syndicate [*Seismic profiling*]
BIRS .... Baptist Information Retrieval System [*Southern Baptist Convention*] [*Nashville, TN*] [*Library network*] [*Defunct*]
BIRS .... Basic Indexing and Retrieval System [*Data processing*]   (DIT)
BIRS .... Biology Information Retrieval System [*Marine science*]   (MSC)
BIRS .... British Institute of Recorded Sound
BIRS .... British Institute of Recorded Sound. Bulletin [*A publication*]
BIRSC .... Bulletin. Institut de Recherches Scientifiques au Congo [*A publication*]
BIRT .... Birtcher Medical Systems [*NASDAQ symbol*]   (NQ)
BIRT .... Bolt Installation and Removal Tool
BIRT .... Bulletin d'Information. Institut de Recherche et d'Histoire des Textes [*A publication*]
Birth Defects ... Birth Defects. Original Article Series [*A publication*]
Birth Defects Orig Artic Ser ... Birth Defects. Original Article Series [*A publication*]
Birth Family J ... Birth and the Family Journal [*A publication*]
Birth Fam J ... Birth and the Family Journal [*A publication*]
BIRUA ...... Biologische Rundschau [*A publication*]
BIS .... Bachelor of Interdisciplinary Studies
BIS .... Bank for International Settlements [*Basel, Switzerland*]
BIS .... Banking Information Service [*British*]
BIS .... Barrister Information Systems Corp. [*AMEX symbol*]   (SPSG)
BIS .... Baseline Intelligence Summary Supplement   (MCD)
BIS .... Battlefield Illumination System
BIS .... Bechtel Information Services   (IID)
BIS .... Best in Show [*Dog show term*]
BIS .... Bibliographic Instruction Section [*Association of College and Research Libraries*]
BIS .... Bibliotheks- und Informationssystem [*Library and Information System*] [*German*]
BIS .... Biocide Injection System   (MCD)
BIS .... Biographical Inventory for Students [*Psychology*]
BIS .... Biomedical Information Service [*University of Minnesota, Minneapolis*] [*Information service or system*]   (IID)
BIS .... Bishop College, Dallas, TX [*OCLC symbol*] [*Inactive*]   (OCLC)
BIS .... Bishop Resources Development Ltd. [*Vancouver Stock Exchange symbol*]

BIS............. Bismarck [*North Dakota*] [*Airport symbol*]　(OAG)
BIS............. Bismuth [*Chemical element*] [*Symbol is Bi*]　(ROG)
Bis .... Bissell's United States Circuit Court Reports [*A publication*]　(DLA)
BIS............. Bissextile Year [*Leap Year*]　(ROG)
BIS............. Bistre [*Yellowish Brown*]　(ROG)
BIS............. Board of Inspection and Survey [*Navy*]
BIS............. Books in Series [*A publication*]
BIS............. Bounty Information Service　(EA)
BIS............. Brain Information Service　(EA)
BIS............. Bremsstrahlung Isochromat Spectroscopy　(MCD)
BIS............. British Ichthyological Society
BIS............. British Imperial System
BIS............. British Information Services
BIS............. British Interplanetary Society
BIS............. British Iris Society　(EAIO)
BIS............. British and Irish Skeptic　(EAIO)
BIS............. Brought into Service [*Telecommunications*]　(TEL)
BIS............. Browning Institute. Studies [*A publication*]
BIS............. Bulletin of Indonesian Economic Studies [*A publication*]
BIS............. Bulletin. Institute for the Study of the USSR [*A publication*]
BIS............. Bureau of Inspection and Survey
BIS............. Bureau Interafricain des Sols et de l'Economie Rurale [*Inter-African Bureau of Soils and Rural Economy*]
BIS............. Bureau International du Scoutisme
BIS............. Burn-In Screening
BIS............. Business Information Service [*Financial Times Business Information Ltd.*] [*British*] [*Information service or system*]　(IID)
BIS............. Business Information Services [*Control Data Corp.*] [*Information service or system*]　(IID)
BIS............. Business Information Systems [*Bell System*]
BIS............. Business Insurance [*A publication*]
BIS............. Business Intelligence Services Ltd. [*British*]
BISA .... Bibliographic Information on Southeast Asia [*University of Sydney Library*] [*Database*] [*Information service or system*]　(IID)
BISA .... Biographical Index of South Australians [*A publication*]　(APTA)
BISAC .... Book Industry Systems Advisory Committee [*Book Industry Study Group*] [*New York, NY*]
BISAD .... Business Information Systems Analysis and Design [*Bell System*]　(DIT)
BISAHR ... Bistatic Synthetic Aperture Harmonic RADAR　(MCD)
BI-SAL ...... Bi-State Academic Libraries [*Library network*]
BISAM ...... Basic Indexed Sequential Access Method [*IBM Corp.*] [*Data processing*]
BISC .... Biscayan
BISC .... British Iron and Steel Corp.
BISC .... Bulletin. International Seismological Centre [*A publication*]
BISchk .... Buletin i Institutit te Shkencave [*A publication*]
BISCLANT ... Bay of Biscay Subarea [*NATO*]
BISCOM ... Business Information Systems Communications [*Bell System*]
BISCUS..... Business Information Systems Customer Service [*Bell System*]
BISCUS/FACS ... Business Information Systems Customer Service/Facilities Assignment and Control System [*Bell System*]　(MCD)
BIS in D ..... Bis in Die [*Twice a Day*] [*Pharmacy*]　(ROG)
BISD.......... Bowker's International Serials Database [*R. R. Bowker Co.*] [*Information service or system*]　(IID)
BIS in 7 D .. Bis in Septem Dies [*Twice in Seven Days*] [*Pharmacy*]　(ROG)
BISDN....... Broadband Integrated Services Digital Network [*Telecommunications*]
BISDP .... Boletin Informativo. Seminario de Derecho Politico [*A publication*]
BISDSL..... Britische und Irische Studien zur Deutschen Sprache und Literatur [*A publication*]
BISEC........ Bipartite Secretariat [*Post-World War II, Germany*]
BISF........... Bolton Institute for a Sustainable Future　(EA)
BISF........... British Iron and Steel Federation
BISFA........ British Industrial and Scientific Film Association
BISFA........ Bureau International pour la Standardisation de la Rayonne et des Fibres Synthetiques [*International Bureau for the Standardisation of Manmade Fibres*]　(EAIO)
BISG.......... Bockus International Society of Gastroenterology　(EA)
BISG.......... Book Industry Study Group　(EA)
BISGM...... Boletin Informativo. Secretaria General del Movimiento [*A publication*]
BIS-GMA ... Bisphenol A-Glycidyl Methacrylate [*Organic chemistry*]
BISH.......... Bishop　(DSUE)
BISH.......... Bishop, Inc. [*NASDAQ symbol*]　(NQ)
Bish Burr ... Bishop's Edition of Burrill on Assignments [*A publication*]　(DLA)
Bish Con .... Bishop on Contracts [*A publication*]　(DLA)
Bish Cont ... Bishop on Contracts [*A publication*]　(DLA)
Bish Cr Law ... Bishop on Criminal Law [*A publication*]　(DLA)
Bish Cr Proc ... Bishop on Criminal Procedure [*A publication*]　(DLA)
Bish First Bk ... Bishop. First Book of the Law [*A publication*]　(DLA)
Bish Ins...... Bishop on Insolvent Debtors [*A publication*]　(DLA)
Bish Mar & Div ... Bishop on Marriage and Divorce [*A publication*]　(DLA)
Bish Mar Div & Sep ... Bishop on Marriage, Divorce, and Separation [*A publication*]　(DLA)

Bish Mar Wom ... Bishop on Married Women [*A publication*]　(DLA)
Bish New Cr Law ... Bishop's New Criminal Law [*A publication*]　(DLA)
Bish New Cr Proc ... Bishop's New Criminal Procedure [*A publication*]　(DLA)
Bish Noll Pros ... Bishop's Law of Nolle Prosequi [*A publication*]　(DLA)
Bish Non-Cont Law ... Bishop on Non-Contract Law, Rights, and Torts [*A publication*]　(DLA)
Bishop Dig ... Bishop's Digest [*Montana*] [*A publication*]　(DLA)
BIS HOR... Bis Horis [*Every Two Hours*] [*Pharmacy*]　(ROG)
Bish Stat Cr ... Bishop on Statutory Crimes [*A publication*]　(DLA)
Bish St Crimes ... Bishop on Statutory Crimes [*A publication*]　(DLA)
Bish Wr L .. Bishop on Written Law [*A publication*]　(DLA)
BISI .... Bollettino. Istituto Storico Italiano [*A publication*]
BISI .... Siglufjordur [*Iceland*] [*ICAO location identifier*]　(ICLI)
BISIAM..... Bollettino. Istituto Storico Italiano e Archivio Muratoriano [*A publication*]
BISIMAM ... Bollettino. Istituto Storico Italiano per il Medioevo e Archivio Muratoriano [*A publication*]
BISITS ...... British Iron and Steel Industry Translation Service
BISLDP..... Sociedad Mexicana de Lepidopterologia. Boletin Informativo [*A publication*]
BISM........ Business Information Systems Management [*Mountain View, CA*] [*Telecommunications service*]　(TSSD)
BISMAC ... Business Machine Computer
BISMAPS ... Business Information Systems Modeling and Planning System [*Bell System*]
BISMPL.... BITs [*Binary Digits*] per Sample　(MCD)
BISMRA ... Bureau of Inter-Industrial Statistics and Multiple Regression Analysis　(MCD)
Bismuth Inst Bull (Brussels) ... Bismuth Institute. Bulletin (Brussels) [*A publication*]
BISN.......... British India Steam Navigation Co.
BISNA ...... BioScience [*A publication*]
BISNC ...... British India Steam Navigation Company　(ROG)
BISNET..... Bank Information System Network
BISO.......... Bulletin. Institut pour l'Etude de l'Europe Sud-Orientale [*A publication*]
BISON...... Belo Information Systems Online Network [*A. H. Belo Corp.*] [*Discontinued service*] [*Information service or system*]　(IID)
BISp .... Between Ischial Spines [*Pelvic measurement*] [*Gynecology*]
bisp............ Bispinous [*or Interspinous*] [*Gynecology*]
BISP .... British Institute of Sewage Purification
BISp .... Bundesinstitut fuer Sportwissenschaft [*Federal Institute for Sports Science*] [*Federal Republic of Germany*]　(IID)
BISP .... Business Information Systems Programs [*Bell System*]
BISPE........ Board of Inspection and Survey, Preliminary Evaluation [*Navy*]
Bisp Eq...... Bispham's Principles of Equity [*A publication*]　(DLA)
Bisph Eq ... Bispham's Principles of Equity [*A publication*]　(DLA)
BISQ.......... Bank for International Settlements, Quarterly [*Database*] [*I. P. Sharp Associates*] [*Information service or system*]　(CRD)
BISRA .... Belize Institute of Social Research and Action
BISRA .... British Iron and Steel Research Association
BISRA/BS ... Belizean Studies. Belizean Institute of Social Research and Action and St. John's College [*A publication*]
BISRD .... Boletim Informativo. Sociedade Brasileira de Radiologia [*A publication*]
BISS.......... Bank for International Settlements, Semi-Annual [*Database*] [*I. P. Sharp Associates*] [*Information service or system*]　(CRD)
BISS.......... Base and Installation Security System [*Military*]
BISS.......... Base Intrusion Surveillance System　(MCD)
BISS.......... Battlefield Identification System Study [*NATO*]　(NATG)
BISS.......... Bibliographie Internationale des Sciences Sociales [*A publication*]
BISS.......... Bioisolator Suit System [*NASA*]　(MCD)
BISS.......... Biological Isolator Suit System　(MCD)
Biss .... Bissell's United States Circuit Court Reports [*A publication*]　(DLA)
BISS.......... Boletin. Institucion Sancho el Sabio [*A publication*]
BISS.......... Sandskeid [*Iceland*] [*ICAO location identifier*]　(ICLI)
BISSC .... Baking Industry Sanitation Standards Committee　(EA)
Bissell .... Bissell's United States Circuit Court Reports, Seventh Circuit [*A publication*]　(DLA)
Biss Est...... Bissett on Estates for Life [*A publication*]　(DLA)
Bissett Est ... Bissett on Estates for Life [*A publication*]　(DLA)
Biss Part .... Bisset's Partnership and Joint Stock Companies [*1847*] [*A publication*]　(DLA)
Biss & Sm .. Bissett and Smith's Digest [*South Africa*] [*A publication*]　(DLA)
Biss Stat..... Bissell's Minnesota Statutes [*A publication*]　(DLA)
Biss (US).... Bissell's United States Circuit Court Reports, Seventh Circuit [*A publication*]　(DLA)
BIST .... British Institute of Surgical Technologists
BIST .... Built-In Self-Test
BIST .... Stykkisholmur [*Iceland*] [*ICAO location identifier*]　(ICLI)
BISTA .... Bureau of International Scientific and Technological Affairs [*Department of State*]
BISTAR..... Bistatic Thinned Array RADAR　(MCD)
B Ist Sier.... Bollettino. Istituto Sieroterapico Milanese [*A publication*]

BISTSS...... Business Information System/Trunks and Special Services [*Telecommunications*] (TEL)
BISU.......... Boeing Interface Surveillance Unit (KSC)
BISV.......... Bollettino. Istituto di Storia della Societa e dello Stato Veneziano [*A publication*]
BISW........ Befrienders International Samaritans Worldwide (EA)
BISWA...... Biuletyn. Instytuta Spawalnictwa. Gliwice [*A publication*]
BISYNC .... Binary Synchronous Transmission [*Data processing*]
BIT............ Bachelor of Industrial Technology
BIT............ Baitadi [*Nepal*] [*Airport symbol*] (OAG)
BIT............ Band Ignitor Tube
BIT............ Bendigo Institute of Technology [*Australia*]
BIT............ Bilateral Investment Treaty
BIT............ Binary Digit [*Data processing*]
BIT............ Biotechnica International, Inc.
BIT............ Bituminous [*Technical drawings*]
BIT............ Boric Acid Injection Tank (IEEE)
BIT............ Born-Infeld Theory [*Physics*]
BIT............ Boron Injection Tank [*Nuclear energy*] (NRCH)
BIT............ Built-In Test [*or Testing*] [*Data processing*]
BIT............ Bureau International du Travail [*International Labour Office*] [*French*]
BIT............ Business Information Technology
BIT............ Business Insurance Trust (DLA)
BITA.......... British Industrial Truck Association
BITA.......... Reykjavik [*Iceland*] [*ICAO location identifier*] (ICLI)
BITAA...... Bitumen, Teere, Asphalte, Peche [*A publication*]
BItal.......... Bulletin Italien [*A publication*]
B Ital Biol .. Bollettino. Societa Italiana di Biologia Sperimentale [*A publication*]
BIT/BITE ... Built-In Test/Built-In Test Equipment [*Military*] (RDA)
BITBLT..... BIT [*Binary Digit*]-Block Transfer
BITC.......... Base Information Transfer Center [*Military*]
BITC.......... Brain Injury Therapy Centre [*Australia*]
BITC.......... Bulletin. Institute of Traditional Cultures [*A publication*]
BITCH....... Black Intelligence Test of Cultural Homogeneity [*Sometimes facetiously translated "Black Intelligence Test to Counter Honkeyism"*]
BITDOC.... BITNET [*Because It's Time Network*] Development and Operations Center
BITE.......... Backward Interworking Telephony Event [*Telecommunications*] (TEL)
BITE.......... Built-In Test Equipment
BITE.......... Thingeyri [*Iceland*] [*ICAO location identifier*] (ICLI)
BITEJ........ Bureau International pour le Tourisme et les Echanges de la Jeunesse [*International Bureau for Youth Tourism and Exchanges*] (EAIO)
BiTerS....... Bible et Terre Sainte (Nouvelle Serie) [*Paris*] [*A publication*]
BITEST..... Binomial Proportion Test (MCD)
BITG.......... Bureau International Technique des Gelatines (EAIO)
BITH......... Thorshofn [*Iceland*] [*ICAO location identifier*] (ICLI)
BITIFP...... Bureau International Technique des "Inorganic Feed Phosphates" [*Inorganic Feed Phosphates International Technical Bureau - IFPITB*] (EAIO)
BITJA........ Journal. Birla Institute of Technology and Science [*A publication*]
Bitki Koruma Buelt ... Bitki Koruma Bulteni [*A publication*]
Bitki Koruma Bul ... Bitki Koruma Bulteni [*A publication*]
Bitki Koruma Bul Ek Yayin ... Bitki Koruma Bulteni. Ek Yayin [*A publication*]
Bitki Koruma Bul Plant Prot Bull ... Bitki Koruma Bulteni. Plant Protection Bulletin [*A publication*]
BITL.......... Bureau International Technique de l'ABS [*Acronitrile-Butadiene-Styrene*] [*of the European Council of Chemical Manufacturers' Federations*] (EAIO)
BITLC .... Baking Industry and Teamster Labor Conference (EA)
BITM......... Bureau International Technique du Methanol [*of the European Council of Chemical Manufacturers' Federations*] (EAIO)
BITN......... Bilateral Iterative Network
BITN......... Bitumen
BITNET .... Because It's Time Network [*Interuniversity communications network*]
Bit Nord Tidskr Informationsbehandl ... Bit Nordisk Tidskrift fuer Informationsbehandling [*A publication*]
BITNSC.... BITNET [*Because It's Time Network*] Network Support Center
BITO......... Burnishing Tool
BITOA....... Bild und Ton [*A publication*]
BiTod .... Bible Today [*A publication*]
BITP......... Bureau International Technique des Polyesters (EAIO)
BITPI........ Bureau International Technique des Polyesters Insatures [*of the European Council of Chemical Manufacturers' Federations*] (EAIO)
Bit Prac Cas ... Bittleston's Practice Cases under Judicature Acts [*England*] [*A publication*] (DLA)
BiTr.......... Bible Translator [*A publication*]
BiTrans...... Bible Translator [*A publication*]
BITS .... Binary Intersystem Transmission Standard
BITS .... BIOSIS [*BioSciences Information Service*] Information Transfer Service
BITS .... BIOSIS [*BioSciences Information Service*] Information Transfer System [*A publication*]

BITS .... Birla Institute of Technology and Science [*Pilani, India*]
BITS .... Boeing Intelligent Terminal System [*Boeing Computer Services Co.*] [*Information service or system*] (IID)
BITS .... Built-In Test System [*Military*] (CAAL)
BITS .... Bureau International du Tourisme Social [*International Bureau of Social Tourism - IBST*] (EAIO)
Bitt .... Bittleston's Reports in Chambers, Queen's Bench Division [*England*] [*A publication*] (DLA)
Bitt Ch .... Bittleston's Reports in Chambers, Queen's Bench Division [*England*] [*A publication*] (DLA)
Bitt Cha Cas ... Bittleston's Chamber Cases [*1883-84*] [*A publication*] (DLA)
Bitt Chamb Rep ... Bittleston's Reports in Chambers, Queen's Bench Division [*England*] [*A publication*] (DLA)
Bitt Ch Cas ... Bittleston's Reports in Chambers, Queen's Bench Division [*England*] [*A publication*] (DLA)
Bitt PC .... Bittleston's Practice Cases under Judicature Acts [*England*] [*A publication*] (DLA)
Bitt Prac Cas ... Bittleston's Practice Cases [*A publication*] (ILCA)
Bitt Pr Cas ... Bittleston's Practice Cases under Judicature Acts [*England*] [*A publication*] (DLA)
Bitt Pr Case ... Bittleston's Practice Cases under Judicature Acts [*England*] [*A publication*] (DLA)
Bitt Rep in Ch ... Bittleston's Reports in Chambers, Queen's Bench Division [*England*] [*A publication*] (DLA)
Bitt W & P ... Bittleston, Wise, and Parnell's Reports [*2, 3 New Practice Cases*] [*England*] [*A publication*] (DLA)
BITU.......... Benzyl-Iso-Thiourea [*Organic chemistry*]
BITU.......... Bitco Corp. [*NASDAQ symbol*] (NQ)
BITUA....... Bitumen [*A publication*]
BITUM...... Bituminous (MSA)
Bitum Coal Res Inc Tech Rep ... Bituminous Coal Research, Incorporated. Technical Report [*A publication*]
BITUMD... Bituminized [*Freight*]
Bitumen Teere Asphalte Peche ... Bitumen, Teere, Asphalte, Peche, und Verwandte Stoffe [*A publication*]
Bitum Low Medium Level Radioact Wastes Proc Semin ... Bituminization of Low and Medium Level Radioactive Wastes. Proceedings of a Seminar [*A publication*]
Bit & Wise ... Bittleston and Wise. New Magistrates' Cases [*England*] [*A publication*] (DLA)
BITX.......... Response Technologies, Inc. [*NASDAQ symbol*] (NQ)
BITYA .... Byulleten' Informatsionnogo Tsentra po Yadernym Dannym [*A publication*]
BIU .... Bar-Ilan University (BJA)
BIU .... Basic Information Unit (BUR)
BIU .... Battery Interface Unit (MCD)
BIU .... Bildudalur [*Iceland*] [*Airport symbol*] (OAG)
BIU .... Biological Indicator Unit [*Food testing*]
BIU .... Buffer Interface Unit [*Data processing*] (NASA)
BIU .... Bureau International des Universites
BIU .... Bus Interface Unit [*Data processing*]
BIUGA ..... Biuletyn. Instytutu Geologicznego [*A publication*]
Biul Geol.... Biuletyn Geologiczny [*A publication*]
Biul Gl Bot Sada (Leningrad) ... Biulleten Glavnogo Botanicheskogo Sada (Leningrad) [*A publication*]
Biul Gl Inst Gorn ... Biuletyn Glownego Instytutu Gornictwa [*Poland*] [*A publication*]
Biul Gos Nikitsk Bot Sad ... Biulleten Gosudarstvennyi Nikitskii Botanicheskii Sad [*A publication*]
Biul IB........ Biuletyn. Instytutu Bibliograficznego [*A publication*]
Biul IGS.... Biuletyn Gospodarstwa Spolecznego [*A publication*]
Biul Inf Geol Geofiz Ekon Tech Prac Geol ... Biuletyn Informacyjny. Geologia. Geofizyka oraz Ekonomika i Technika Prac Geologicznych [*A publication*]
Biul Inf Inst Badaw Proj Przem Farb Lakierow ... Biuletyn Informacyjny. Instytut Badawezo Projektowy Przemyslu Farb i Lakierow [*A publication*]
Biul Inf Inst Farb Lakierow ... Biuletyn Informacyjny. Instytut Farb i Lakierow [*A publication*]
Biul Inf Inst Lekow ... Biuletyn Informacyjny. Instytutu Lekow [*A publication*]
Biul Inf Inst Mater Ogniotrwalych ... Biuletyn Informacyjny. Instytutu Materialow Ogniotrwalych [*A publication*]
Biul Inf Inst Przem Tworzyw Farb ... Biuletyn Informacyjny. Instytut Przemyslu Tworzyw i Farb [*A publication*]
Biul Inf Inst Przem Wiazacych Mater Budow (Krakow) ... Biuletyn Informacyjny. Instytut Przemyslu Wiazacych Materialow Budowlanych (Krakow) [*A publication*]
Biul Inf Inst Zbozowego Warszawie ... Biuletyn Informacyjny. Instytutu Zbozowego w Warszawie [*A publication*]
Biul Inf Mater Ogniotrwalych ... Biuletyn Informacyjny. Materialow Ogniotrwalych [*A publication*]
Biul Inf Nauk Tech Inst Tech Budow ... Biuletyn Informacyjny. Naukowo Technicznej. Instytut Techniki Budowlanej [*A publication*]
Biul Inform Inst Zboz Warszawie ... Biuletyn Informacyjny. Instytutu Zbozowego w Warszawie [*A publication*]
Biul Inf Przem Farb Lakierow ... Biuletyn Informacyjny Przemyslu Farb i Lakierow [*A publication*]
Biul Inst Energ ... Biuletyn. Instytutu Energetyki [*A publication*]

Biul Inst Genet Hodowli Zwierzat Pol Akad Nauk ... Biuletyn. Instytutu Genetyki i Hodowli Zwierzat Polskiej Akademii Nauk [*Poland*] [*A publication*]
Biul Inst Geol (Warsaw) ... Biuletyn. Instytut Geologiczny (Warsaw) [*A publication*]
Biul Inst Hodowli Aklimat Ros (Warszawa) ... Biuletyn. Instytutu Hodowli i Aklimatyzacji Roslin (Warszawa) [*A publication*]
Biul Inst Hodowli Aklim Rosl ... Biuletyn. Instytutu Hodowli i Aklimatyzacji Roslin [*A publication*]
Biul Inst Mech Precyz ... Biuletyn. Instytutu Mechaniki Precyzyjnej [*A publication*]
Biul Inst Med Morsk Gdansk ... Biuletyn. Instytutu Medycyny Morskiej w Gdansku [*A publication*]
Biul Inst Med Morsk Trop Gdyni ... Biuletyn. Instytutu Medycyny Morskiej i Tropikalne w Gdyni [*A publication*]
Biul Inst Met Niezelaz ... Biuletyn. Instytut Metali Niezelaznych [*A publication*]
Biul Inst Naftowego ... Biuletyn. Instytutu Naftowego [*A publication*]
Biul Inst Ochr Rosl ... Biuletyn. Instytutu Ochrony Roslin [*Poznan*] [*A publication*]
Biul Inst Rosl Lecz ... Biuletyn. Instytutu Roslin Leczniezych [*A publication*]
Biul Inst Spawalnictwa ... Biuletyn. Instytutu Spawalnictwa [*A publication*]
Biul Inst Spawalnictwa (Gliwice) ... Biuletyn. Instytutu Spawalnictwa (Gliwice) [*A publication*]
Biul Inst Tech Drewna ... Biuletyn. Instytutu Technologii Drewna [*A publication*]
Biul Inst Weglowego Komun ... Biuletyn. Instytutu Weglowego. Komunikat [*A publication*]
Biul Inst Wlok ... Biuletyn. Instytutu Wlokiennictwa [*A publication*]
Biul Inst Ziemniaka ... Biuletyn. Instytutu Ziemniaka [*A publication*]
Biul Kwarant Ochr Ros Min Roln (Warszawa) ... Biuletyn. Kwarantanny i Ochrony Roslin Ministerstwo Rolnictwa (Warszawa) [*A publication*]
Biull Eksp Biol Med ... Biulleten Eksperimentalnoi Biologii i Meditsiny [*A publication*]
Biull Gl Bot Sada ... Biulleten Glavnogo Botanicheskogo Sada [*A publication*]
Biull Izobret ... Biulleten Izobretenii [*USSR*] [*A publication*]
Biul Lubel Towarz Nauk Mat Fiz Chem ... Biuletyn Lubelskiego Towarzystwa Naukowego. Matematyka, Fizka, Chemia [*A publication*]
Biul Lubel Tow Nauk Biol ... Biuletyn Lubelskiego Towarzystwa Naukowego Biologia [*A publication*]
Biul Lubel Tow Nauk Sect A-D Suppl ... Biuletyn Lubelskiego Towarzystwa Naukowego. Sectio A-D. Supplement [*A publication*]
Biul Lubel Tow Nauk Wydz 2 ... Biuletyn Lubelskiego Towarzystwa Naukowego. Wydzial 2. Biologia [*A publication*]
Biul Lubel Tow Nauk Wydz 3 ... Biuletyn Lubelskiego Towarzystwa Naukowego. Wydzial 3. Geografia [*A publication*]
Biull Vses Nauchno-Issled Inst Kukuruzy ... Biulleten Vsesoiuznogo Nauchno-Issledovatel'skogo Instituta Kukuruzy [*A publication*]
Biul Nauchno Tekh Inf Agron Fiz ... Biulleten Nauchno-Tekhnicheskoi Informatsii po Agronomicheskoi Fizike [*A publication*]
Biul Nauchno Tekh Inf Maslichn Kult ... Biulleten Nauchno-Tekhnicheskoi Informatsii po Maslichnym Kul'turam [*A publication*]
Biul Nauchno-Tekh Inf Vses Nauchno-Issled Inst Risa ... Biulleten Nauchno-Tekhnicheskoi Informatsii Vsesoiuznyi Nauchno-Issledovatel'skii Instituta Risa [*A publication*]
Biul Nauchn Rabot Vses Nauchno Issled Inst Zhivotnovod ... Biulleten Nauchnykh Rabot. Vsesoiuznyi Nauchno-Issledovatel'skii Institut Zhivotnovodstva [*A publication*]
Biul Panst Inst Nauk Leczn Surow Ros Poznaniu ... Biuletyn Panstwowy Instytut Naukowy Leczniczych Surowcow Roslinnych w Poznaniu [*A publication*]
Biul Peryglac ... Biuletyn Peryglacjalny [*A publication*]
Biul PIK ... Biuletyn Panstwowego Instytutu Ksiazki [*A publication*]
Biul Prod Pieczarek ... Biuletyn Producenta Pieczarek [*A publication*]
Biul Sluzby Sanit Epidemiol Wojewodztwa Katowickiego ... Biuletyn Sluzby Sanitarno Epidemiologiczej Wojewodztwa Katowickiego [*A publication*]
Biul Tech Elektrownie Elektrocieplownie ... Biuletyn Techniczny, Elektrownie, i Elektrocieplownie [*Poland*] [*A publication*]
Biul Vses Inst Gel'mintol ... Biulleten. Vsesoiuznyi Institut Gel'mintologii [*A publication*]
Biul Vses Nauchno Issled Inst Zashch Rast ... Biulleten Vsesoiuznyi Nauchno-Issledovatel'skii Institut Zashchity Rastenii [*A publication*]
Biul Warzywniczy ... Biuletyn Warzywniczy [*A publication*]
Biul Wojsk Akad Med ... Biuletyn Wojskowej Akademii Medycznej [*A publication*]
Biul Wojsk Akad Tech ... Biuletyn Wojskowej Akademii Technicznej Imienia Jaroslawa Dabrowskiego [*A publication*]
Biul Zakl Badan Nauk Gornoslask Okregu Przem Pol Akad Nauk ... Biuletyn Zaklad Badan Naukouyeh Gornoslaskiego Okregu Przemyslowego Polskiej Akademii Nauk [*A publication*]
Biul Zakl Ochr Srodowiska Reg Przem Pol Akad Nauk ... Biuletyn Zaklad Ochrony Srodowiska Regionow Przemyslowych Polskiej Akademii Nauk [*A publication*]
Biul Zydowskiego Inst Hist ... Biuletyn Zydowskiego Instytutu Historycznego [*A publication*]
Biul Zydowskiego Inst Hist Pol ... Biuletyn Zydowskiego Instytutu Historycznego w Polsci [*A publication*]

BIUNA ...... Biologieunterricht [*A publication*]
BIV .... Banco Industrial de Venezuela [*Industrial Bank of Venezuela*]
BIV .... Big V Supermarkets, Inc. [*AMEX symbol*] (SPSG)
BIV .... Bivouac (AABC)
BIV .... Boletin Indigenista Venezolano [*A publication*]
BIV .... Bovine Immunodeficiency Virus
BIV .... Built-In Variance (MCD)
BIVA .... British Interactive Video Association [*Information service or system*] (IID)
BIVAR ...... Bivariant Function Generator (DEN)
BiViChr ..... Bible et Vie Chretienne [*Maredsous*] [*A publication*]
BiVieChr ..... Bible et Vie Chretienne [*Maredsous*] [*A publication*]
BIVM .... Vestmannaeyjar [*Iceland*] [*ICAO location identifier*] (ICLI)
BIVO .... Vopnafjordur [*Iceland*] [*ICAO location identifier*] (ICLI)
BIW .... Battle Injury or Wound
Bi W .... Biblical World [*A publication*]
BI-W .... Biweekly
BIW .... Business Information Wire [*Database*] [*The Canadian Press*] [*Information service or system*] (CRD)
BIWAA9 .... Bulletin of Vegetable Crops Research Work [*A publication*]
BIWC .... BIW Cable Systems, Inc. [*NASDAQ symbol*] (NQ)
BiWelt .... Die Bibel in der Welt [*Ruhr*] [*A publication*]
BIWF .... British-Israel World Federation
BIWIA .... Bild der Wissenschaft [*A publication*]
Biwkly Cryog Curr Aware Serv ... Biweekly Cryogenics Current Awareness Service [*A publication*]
BiWM .... Bisexual White Male
BIX .... Biloxi, MS [*Location identifier*] [*FAA*] (FAAL)
BIX .... Binary Information Exchange
BIX .... BYTE Information Exchange [*Electronic conferencing system provided by McGraw-Hill's Byte magazine*]
BIY .... Bedfordshire Imperial Yeomanry [*British military*] (DMA)
BIZ .... Bank fuer Internationalen Zahlungsausgleich [*Bank for International Settlements*] [*German*]
BiZ .... Biblische Zeitschrift [*A publication*]
BIZ .... Bicaz [*Romania*] [*Seismograph station code, US Geological Survey*] (SEIS)
BIZ .... Billings Gazette [*A publication*]
Biz .... Bizarre Mystery Magazine [*A publication*]
BIZ .... Business [*Slang*] (DSUE)
BIZEA ...... Biochemische Zeitschrift [*A publication*]
BIZEB ...... Biometrische Zeitschrift [*A publication*]
BIZFORC ... Business Forecasting (MCD)
BIZNA ...... Biologisches Zentralblatt [*A publication*]
BIZNET .... American Business Network [*US Chamber of Commerce*] [*Washington, DC*] [*Cable-television system*] [*Telecommunications*] (TSSD)
B I Zool AS ... Bulletin. Institute of Zoology. Academia Sinica [*Taipei*] [*A publication*]
BIZYAS ..... Chung Yang Yen Chiu Yuan T'ung Wu Yen Chiu So Chi K'an [*A publication*]
B-J .... Bach Jahrbuch [*A publication*]
BJ .... Bachelor of Journalism
BJ .... Bachelor of Jurisprudence
BJ .... Back Judge [*Football*]
BJ .... Bakhtar Afghan Airlines [*Afghanistan*] [*ICAO designator*] (FAAC)
bj .... Ball-Jointed [*Body*] [*Doll collecting*]
BJ .... Barrage Jammers [*RADAR*]
B & J .... Barrie & Jenkins [*Publisher's imprint*]
BJ .... Bellum Judaicum [*Josephus*] [*Classical studies*] (OCD)
BJ .... Bence Jones [*As in Bence Jones protein, Bence Jones reaction, etc.*] [*Named for Henry Bence Jones, 19th century London physician*]
BJ .... Benin [*ANSI two-letter standard code*] (CNC)
BJ .... Bharatiya Janata Party [*Indian People's Party*] [*Political party*]
BJ .... Bibliotheca Judaica [*A publication*] (BJA)
BJ .... Biceps Jerk [*Neurology*]
BJ .... Black Jumbo [*Diplomatic codes*] [*World War II*]
BJ .... Blue Jeans Magazine [*A publication*]
BJ .... Bonding Jig (MCD)
B & J .... Bone and Joint [*Medicine*]
BJ .... Bone and Joint [*Medicine*]
BJ .... Bonner Jahrbuecher [*A publication*]
BJ .... Bookman's Journal [*A publication*]
BJ .... Break Jaw (MSA)
BJ .... Bulkhead Jack
BJ .... La Sainte Bible. Traduit en Francais sous la Direction de l'Ecole Biblique de Jerusalem [*A publication*]
BJ's .... Blue-Johnnies [*Australian slang for "delirium tremens"*]
BJA .... Ball Joint Actuator
BJA .... Basic Journal Abstracts [*A publication*]
BJA .... Bejaia [*Algeria*] [*Airport symbol*] (OAG)
BJA .... British Journal of Administrative Management [*A publication*]
BJA .... British Journal of Aesthetics [*A publication*]
BJA .... British Judo Association
BJA .... Bund Juedischer Akademiker (BJA)
BJA .... Bureau of Justice Assistance
BJA .... Burlap and Jute Association (EA)
BJAL .... British Journal of Administrative Law [*A publication*] (DLA)
BJANA ...... British Journal of Anaesthesia [*A publication*]

B Jap S S F ... Bulletin. Japanese Society of Scientific Fisheries [*A publication*]
BJAY......... Blue Jay [*A publication*]
BJAYAC.... British Journal of Audiology [*A publication*]
B JB........... Bach-Jahrbuch [*A publication*]
B Jb........... Bonner Jahrbuecher des Rheinischen Landesmuseums in Bonn und des Vereins von Altertumsfreunden im Rheinlande [*A publication*]
BJB........... Burnham, J. B., Chicago IL [*STAC*]
BJBE........ Bulletin. Jardin Botanique de l'Etat a Bruxelles [*A publication*]
BjBI........... Balkan-ji-Bari International [*Children's Own Garden International - COGI*] (EAIO)
BJBNDL ... Boletin. Jardin Botanico Nacional [*A publication*]
BJBTB....... Bangladesh Journal of Botany [*A publication*]
BJC........... Babinet Jamin Compensator
BJC........... Baltimore Junior College [*Maryland*]
BJC........... Beijing Jeep Corp. (ECON)
BJC........... Bennett Junior College [*New York*]
BJC........... Bismarck Junior College [*North Dakota*]
BJC........... Boise Junior College [*Idaho*]
BJC........... Boone Junior College [*Iowa*]
BJC........... Bradford Junior College [*Later, BC*] [*Massachusetts*]
BJC........... British Jewish Cockney
BJC........... Brotherhood of the Jungle Cock (EA)
BJC........... Denver, CO [*Location identifier*] [*FAA*] (FAAL)
BJCAAI..... British Journal of Cancer [*A publication*]
BJCB........ British Joint Communications Board [*British military*] (DMA)
BJCC........ Bicentennial Junior Committees of Correspondence [*American Revolution Bicentennial Administration, US Postal Service, and National Association of Elementary School Principals*]
BJCE........ Bibliography of Jewish Communities in Europe [*Catalog at General Archives for the History of the Jewish People, Jerusalem*] [*A publication*] (BJA)
BJCEA...... Boletin. Junta do Control de Energia Atomica [*A publication*]
BJCEB....... British Joint Communications-Electronics Board [*Military*]
BJCO........ British Joint Communications Office (NATG)
BJCPA...... Baptist Joint Committee on Public Affairs (EA)
BJCPB...... British Journal of Social and Clinical Psychology [*A publication*]
BJCPBU.... British Journal of Social and Clinical Psychology [*A publication*]
BJCPDW... British Journal of Clinical Psychology [*A publication*]
BJ Crim ..... British Journal of Criminology [*A publication*]
B J Criminology ... British Journal of Criminology [*A publication*]
BJCT........ Bioject Medical Systems Ltd. [*NASDAQ symbol*] (NQ)
BJD........... Bakkafjordur [*Iceland*] [*Airport symbol*] (OAG)
bjd............. Bookjacket Designer [*MARC relator code*] [*Library of Congress*] (LCCP)
BJDCA...... British Journal of Diseases of the Chest [*A publication*]
BJDCAT ... British Journal of Diseases of the Chest [*A publication*]
BJDEAZ.... British Journal of Dermatology [*A publication*]
BJDEB...... British Journal of Disorders of Communication [*A publication*]
BJ Delinq... British Journal of Delinquency [*A publication*]
BJDIAD .... Bijdragen tot de Dierkunde [*A publication*]
B J Disorders of Communication ... British Journal of Disorders of Communication [*A publication*]
BJDPE4..... British Journal of Developmental Psychology [*A publication*]
BJDSA9 ..... British Journal of Dermatology. Supplement [*A publication*]
BJE........... Bachelor of Jewish Education (BJA)
BJE........... Books-on-Japan-in-English [*A publication*]
BJE........... Britannica Junior Encyclopedia [*A publication*]
BJE........... Bureau of Jewish Education
BJEBA...... British Journal of Experimental Biology [*A publication*]
BJEC........ Blue Jay Energy Corporation [*NASDAQ symbol*] (NQ)
BJECD ...... Bell Journal of Economics [*A publication*]
BJ Ed......... Bachelor of Jewish Education
B J Ednl Psych ... British Journal of Educational Psychology [*A publication*]
B J Ednl Studies ... British Journal of Educational Studies [*A publication*]
B J Ednl Technology ... British Journal of Educational Technology [*A publication*]
BJEMA...... Bell Journal of Economics and Management Science [*Later, Bell Journal of Economics*] [*A publication*]
BJEMA...... British Journal of Aesthetics [*A publication*]
BJEP......... British Journal of Educational Psychology [*A publication*]
BJEP......... Bureau on Jewish Employment Problems (EA)
BJEPA...... British Journal of Experimental Pathology [*A publication*]
BJEPA5..... British Journal of Experimental Pathology [*A publication*]
BJer.......... Bible de Jerusalem [*A publication*] (BJA)
BJES......... British Journal of Educational Studies [*A publication*]
BJESA....... British Journal of Educational Psychology [*A publication*]
BJESAE .... British Journal of Educational Psychology [*A publication*]
B Jeun Fr ... Bulletin. Jeunesse Prehistorique et Geologique de France [*A publication*]
B Jew Pal Soc ... Bulletin. Jewish Palestine Exploration Society [*A publication*]
BJewPES... Bulletin. Jewish Palestine Exploration Society [*A publication*]
BJF........... Ball Joint Fitting
BJF........... Batch Job Foreground [*Data processing*]
BJF........... Batsfjord [*Norway*] [*Airport symbol*] (OAG)
BJF........... Biblioteka Juznoslovenskog Filologa [*A publication*]

BJF............ Black, James F., Baltimore MD [*STAC*]
BJFBE6..... Belgian Journal of Food Chemistry and Biotechnology [*A publication*]
BJFPDD.... British Journal of Family Planning [*A publication*]
BJG........... Bank of Japan. Monthly Economic Review [*A publication*]
BJG........... Bestand Juedischer Gemeinden in Staatsarchiv Hamburg [*A publication*] (BJA)
BJG........... [*The*] Book of Joshua in Greek [*A publication*] (BJA)
BJGL......... Blaetter fuer Juedische Geschichte und Literatur [*A publication*]
B J Guidance & Counseling ... British Journal of Guidance and Counselling [*A publication*]
BJGZ......... Berliner Juedische Gemeinde-Zeitung [*A publication*]
BJH........... Bajhang [*Nepal*] [*Airport symbol*] (OAG)
BJH........... Brown, James H., Atlanta GA [*STAC*]
BJHEA...... British Journal of Haematology [*A publication*]
BJHEAL ... British Journal of Haematology [*A publication*]
BJHIL....... Bibliographie zur Juedisch-Hellenistischen und Intertestamentarischen Literatur [*A publication*]
BJHMA..... British Journal of Hospital Medicine [*A publication*]
BJHMAB ... British Journal of Hospital Medicine [*A publication*]
BJHS......... British Journal for the History of Science [*A publication*]
BJHSAT.... British Journal for the History of Science [*A publication*]
BJI........... Bemidji [*Minnesota*] [*Airport symbol*] (OAG)
BJI........... British Journal of Industrial Relations [*A publication*]
BJI........... Bulletin des Juridictions Indigenes [*A publication*]
BJI2.......... Peking [*Republic of China*] [*Seismograph station code, US Geological Survey*] (SEIS)
BJIC.......... Ben & Jerry's Homemade, Incorporated [*Waterbury, VT*] [*NASDAQ symbol*] (NQ)
BJIC.......... Black-Jewish Information Center [*Defunct*] (EA)
BJIMA...... British Journal of Industrial Medicine [*A publication*]
BJIMAG ... British Journal of Industrial Medicine [*A publication*]
BJ Ind Rel ... British Journal of Industrial Relations [*A publication*]
BJIR......... British Journal of Industrial Relations [*A publication*]
BJJ........... Wooster, OH [*Location identifier*] [*FAA*] (FAAL)
BJJTEC..... Biblioteca Jose Jeronimo Triana [*A publication*]
BJK & E..... Bozell, Jacobs, Kenyon & Eckhardt [*Advertising agency*] [*New York, NY*]
BJL........... Bachelor of Jewish Literature (BJA)
BJL........... Banjul [*Gambia*] [*Airport symbol*] (OAG)
BJL........... Beeler, J. L., Los Angeles CA [*STAC*]
BJ Lea....... Lea's Tennessee Reports [*A publication*] (DLA)
BJLS......... British Journal of Law and Society [*A publication*]
BJM........... Between Job Monitor [*Data processing*]
BJM........... Bioject Medical Systems Ltd. [*Vancouver Stock Exchange symbol*]
BJM........... Bluejacket's Manual [*Navy*]
BJM........... Bones, Joints, Muscles [*Medicine*]
BJM........... Bujumbura [*Burundi*] [*Airport symbol*] (OAG)
BJM........... Metropolitan Toronto Business Journal [*A publication*]
B J Ma St Ps ... British Journal of Mathematical and Statistical Psychology [*A publication*]
B J Math & Stat Psych ... British Journal of Mathematical and Statistical Psychology [*A publication*]
BJMEAC.... British Journal of Medical Education [*A publication*]
BJMEDF... British Journal of Sexual Medicine [*A publication*]
BJ Mental Subnormality ... British Journal of Mental Subnormality [*A publication*]
BJMPA ..... British Journal of Medical Psychology [*A publication*]
BJMPAB... British Journal of Medical Psychology [*A publication*]
BJMPs...... British Journal of Medical Psychology [*A publication*]
BJMRDK .. Brazilian Journal of Medical and Biological Research [*A publication*]
BJMSA ...... British Journal of Mathematical and Statistical Psychology [*A publication*]
BJMSBL ... British Journal of Mental Subnormality [*A publication*]
BJMTD...... British Journal of Music Therapy [*A publication*]
BJN........... Bear Island [*Formerly, Bjornoya*] [*Norway*] [*Geomagnetic observatory code*]
B/JNT....... Ball Joint [*Automotive engineering*]
BJNTA...... British Journal of Non-Destructive Testing [*A publication*]
BJNUA...... British Journal of Nutrition [*A publication*]
BJNUAV... British Journal of Nutrition [*A publication*]
BJO........... Banjo
BJO........... Saint John's Seminary, Brighton, MA [*OCLC symbol*] (OCLC)
BJOADD... Bangladesh Journal of Agriculture [*A publication*]
BJOCA ..... British Journal of Occupational Safety [*A publication*]
BJOGA ..... British Journal of Obstetrics and Gynaecology [*A publication*]
BJOGAS ... British Journal of Obstetrics and Gynaecology [*A publication*]
BJOH .... Bureau des Jeux Olympiques d'Hiver de 1988, Gouvernement du Canada [*Office of the 1988 Winter Olympic Games, Government of Canada*]
B John Ryl ... Bulletin. John Rylands Library. University of Manchester [*A publication*]
BJOPA ...... British Journal of Ophthalmology [*A publication*]
BJOPAL.... British Journal of Ophthalmology [*A publication*]
BJOSA ...... British Journal of Sociology [*A publication*]
BJOSB....... British Journal of Oral Surgery [*Later, British Journal of Oral and Maxillofacial Surgery*] [*A publication*]

BJOSBV.... British Journal of Oral Surgery [*Later, British Journal of Oral and Maxillofacial Surgery*] [*A publication*]

BJOSEY.... British Journal of Oral and Maxillofacial Surgery [*A publication*]

BJOTA...... Begg Journal of Orthodontic Theory and Treatment [*A publication*]

BJP............ Bachelor of Jewish Pedagogy

BJP............ Bharatiya Janata Party [*Indian People's Party*] [*Political party*]   (PPW)

BJP............ British Journal of Photography [*A publication*]

BJP............ British Journal of Psychology [*A publication*]

BJP............ Business Japan [*A publication*]

BJP............ Indianapolis, IN [*Location identifier*] [*FAA*]   (FAAL)

BJPCA....... British Journal of Pharmacology and Chemotherapy [*Later, British Journal of Pharmacology*] [*A publication*]

BJPCAL.... British Journal of Pharmacology and Chemotherapy [*Later, British Journal of Pharmacology*] [*A publication*]

BJPCB...... British Journal of Pharmacology [*A publication*]

BJPCBM... British Journal of Pharmacology [*A publication*]

BJPEBS..... British Journal of Physical Education [*A publication*]

BJPES....... Bulletin. Jewish Palestine Exploration Society [*A publication*]

B J Physical Ed ... British Journal of Physical Education [*A publication*]

BJPIA5...... British Journal for the Philosophy of Science [*A publication*]

BJPOAN... British Journal of Physiological Optics [*A publication*]

BJPs......... British Journal of Psychology [*A publication*]

BJPSA....... British Journal of Plastic Surgery [*A publication*]

BJPSAZ ... British Journal of Plastic Surgery [*A publication*]

BJPSB...... British Journal of Psychiatry [*A publication*]

BJPSB2.... British Journal of Psychiatry. Special Publication [*A publication*]

B J Psych ... British Journal of Psychology [*A publication*]

BJ Psychiatry ... British Journal of Psychiatry [*A publication*]

BJPVA....... British Journal of Preventive and Social Medicine [*A publication*]

BJPVAA.... British Journal of Preventive and Social Medicine [*A publication*]

BJPYA...... British Journal of Psychiatry [*A publication*]

BJPYAJ ... British Journal of Psychiatry [*A publication*]

BJR........... Bahar Dar [*Ethiopia*] [*Airport symbol*]   (OAG)

BJR........... Barch, John R., New York NY [*STAC*]

BJR........... Bulletin des Jeunes Romanistes [*A publication*]

BJR........... Bulletin. John Rylands Library. University of Manchester [*A publication*]

BJRAA...... British Journal of Radiology [*A publication*]

BJRAAP... British Journal of Radiology [*A publication*]

BJ Religious Ed ... British Journal of Religious Education [*A publication*]

BJRHDF ... British Journal of Rheumatology [*A publication*]

BJRL........ Bulletin. John Rylands Library. University of Manchester [*A publication*]

BJRLM ..... Bulletin. John Rylands Library. University of Manchester [*A publication*]

BJRSAB.... British Journal of Radiology. Supplement [*A publication*]

BJS........... Bell Jar System

BJS........... BJ Services Co. [*NYSE symbol*]   (SPSG)

BJS........... British Joint Services

BJS........... British Journal of Sociology [*A publication*]

BJS........... Bureau of Justice Statistics [*Department of Justice*] [*Also, an information service or system*]   (IID)

BJSCP....... British Journal of Social and Clinical Psychology [*A publication*]

BJSFC ...... Billie Jo Spears Fan Club   (EA)

BJSGA ...... British Journal of Psychology. General Section [*A publication*]

BJSGAE ... British Journal of Psychology [*A publication*]

BJSIB........ Bangladesh Journal of Scientific and Industrial Research [*A publication*]

BJSIBL...... Bangladesh Journal of Scientific and Industrial Research [*A publication*]

BJSM .... British Joint Services Mission [*Later, SUKLO*]

BJSM .... British Joint Staff Mission [*World War II*]

BJSMAW ... British Journal of Social Medicine [*A publication*]

B JSME..... Bulletin. JSME [*Japan Society of Mechanical Engineers*] [*A publication*]

B J Social and Clinical Psych ... British Journal of Social and Clinical Psychology [*A publication*]

B J Sociology ... British Journal of Sociology [*A publication*]

BJSPDA ... British Journal of Social Psychology [*A publication*]

BJSRDG... Bangladesh Journal of Scientific Research [*A publication*]

B J Stat Psych ... British Journal of Statistical Psychology [*A publication*]

BJSUA ...... British Journal of Surgery [*A publication*]

BJSUAM .. British Journal of Surgery [*A publication*]

BJT........... Bed Joint [*Technical drawings*]

BJT........... Bipolar Junction Transistor [*Electronics*]

BJTBA4.... British Journal of Tuberculosis [*A publication*]

BJ Teach Ed ... British Journal of Teacher Education [*A publication*]

BJTFC...... B. J. Thomas Fan Club   (EA)

BJTUAR ... British Journal of Tuberculosis and Diseases of the Chest [*A publication*]

BJU........... Beach Jumper Unit

BJU........... Beatrice, NE [*Location identifier*] [*FAA*]   (FAAL)

BJU........... Bob Jones University [*South Carolina*]

Bjull Akad Nauk Uz SSR ... Bjulleten Akademiji Nauk Uzbekskoj SSR [*A publication*]

Bjull Glavn Bot Sada ... Bjulleten Glavnogo Botaniceskogo Sada [*A publication*]

Bjull Gos Nikit Bot Sada ... Bjulleten Gosudarstvennogo Nikitskogo Botaniceskogo Sada [*A publication*]

Bjull Inst Teoret Astronom ... Bjulletin Instituta Teoreticeskoi Astronomii. Akademija Nauk Sojuza Sovetskih Socialisticeskih Respublik [*A publication*]

Bjull Mosk Obsc Ispyt Prir Otd Biol ... Bjulleten Moskovskogo Obscestva Ispytatelej Prirody. Otdel Biologiceskij [*A publication*]

B Jur .... Baccalaureus Juris [*Bachelor of Law*]   (DLA)

BJURA...... British Journal of Urology [*A publication*]

BJURAN... British Journal of Urology [*A publication*]

B.Juris...... Bachelor of Jurisprudence

B Jur & Soc S ... Bachelor of Juridical and Social Sciences   (DLA)

B Just........ Burn's Justice of the Peace [*England*] [*A publication*]   (DLA)

BJV............ Berliner Jahrbuch fuer Vor- und Fruehgeschichte [*A publication*]

BJV............ Braswell, J. V., Dallas TX [*STAC*]

BJVDA...... British Journal of Venereal Diseases [*A publication*]

BJVDAK... British Journal of Venereal Diseases [*A publication*]

BJVN........ Dokumentationszentrum des Bundes Judischer Verfolgter des Naziregimes [*Jewish Documentation Centre - JDC*]   (EAIO)

BJW.......... Bajawa [*Indonesia*] [*Airport symbol*]   (OAG)

BJZ............ Badajoz [*Spain*] [*Airport symbol*]   (OAG)

BK .... Baba Kama [*or Bava Kamma*]   (BJA)

BK .... Back [*Dance terminology*]

BK .... Backwardation [*Commodity futures trading*]

BK .... Balks [*Baseball*]

BK .... Bank

Bk............. Bank [*Bank*] [*Dutch*]

bk............. Bank [*Bank*] [*Hungarian*]

Bk............. Bank [*Bank*] [*Swedish*]

BK .... Bank Book

BK .... Bank of New York Co., Inc. [*NYSE symbol*]   (SPSG)

Bk............. Banke [*Bank*] [*Danish*]

BK .... Bankers' [*Rate*] [*Value of the English pound*]

BK .... Bar Keel [*Shipping*]   (DS)

BK .... Barge, Knockdown   (MSA)

BK .... Bark [*or Barque*]   (ROG)

BK .... Barque

BK .... Bart Resources Ltd. [*Vancouver Stock Exchange symbol*]

BK .... Bedi Kartlisa [*A publication*]

BK .... Beekeeper

BK .... Behavioral Kinesiology [*Book title*]

BK .... Below Knee [*Medicine*]

BK .... Bent Knees [*Doll collecting*]

Bk............. Berkelium [*Chemical element*]

BK .... Berlin Kommandatura

BK .... Berliner Konferenz Europaeischer Katholiken [*Berlin Conference of European Catholics*]   (EAIO)

B u K .... Bibel und Kirche [*A publication*]

BK .... Biblischer Kommentar zum Alten Testament [*A publication*]   (BJA)

BK .... Black

Bk............. Black's United States Supreme Court Reports [*66-67 United States Reports*] [*A publication*]   (DLA)

BK .... Blendkoerper [*Frangible-glass smoke grenade*] [*German military - World War II*]

BK .... Blue Knights International Law Enforcement Motorcycle Club   (EA)

BK .... Book   (AAG)

BK .... Book-Keeper   (ADA)

BK .... Bookcase[s] [*Freight*]

Bk............. Bookman [*A publication*]

BK .... Bradykinin [*Biochemistry*]

BK .... Brake   (KSC)

BK .... Break Signal [*Used to interrupt a transmission in progress*] [*Communications*]   (FAAC)

BK .... Brick [*Classified advertising*]   (ADA)

BK .... British Knights [*Brand name of athletic shoe*]

BK .... Bulk Containers [*Shipping*]   (DCTA)

Bk............. Bulk Tainers [*Shipping*]   (DS)

BK .... Bundeskanzler [*Federal Chancellor*] [*German*]   (ILCA)

BK .... Bundeskanzleramt [*Federal Chancery*] [*German*]   (ILCA)

BK .... Burger King Corp.

BK .... Israel Aircraft Industries Ltd. [*ICAO designator*]   (FAAC)

BK .... Kamloops Public Library, British Columbia [*Library symbol*] [*National Library of Canada*]   (NLC)

BKA .... Bank fuer Kredit und Aussenhandel AG [*Bank for Credit and Export Trade*] [*German*]

Bka........... Banka [*Bank*] [*Russian*]

BKA .... Bankair, Inc. [*West Columbia, SC*] [*FAA designator*]   (FAAC)

BKA .... Bee Keepers Association

BKA .... Below Knee Amputation [*Medicine*]

BKA .... Blackmist Resources, Inc. [*Vancouver Stock Exchange symbol*]

BKA .... Bradykinin Antagonist [*Medicine*]

BKA .... Broadband Klystron Amplifier

BKA .... Bundeskartellamt [*Federal Cartel Office*] [*German*]   (ILCA)

BKA .... Bundeskriminalamt [*Federal Criminal Police Bureau*] [*Federal Republic of Germany*]
BKA .... Sitka, AK [*Location identifier*] [*FAA*] (FAAL)
Bk Abroad ... Books Abroad [*A publication*]
BKAG .... Research Station, Agriculture Canada [*Station de Recherches, Agriculture Canada*] Kamloops, British Columbia [*Library symbol*] [*National Library of Canada*] (NLC)
BKAS .... Technical Library, Alcan Smelters Chemicals Ltd., Kitimat, British Columbia [*Library symbol*] [*National Library of Canada*] (NLC)
BKASL ...... Kaslo Public Library, British Columbia [*Library symbol*] [*National Library of Canada*] (NLC)
BKAT .... Biblischer Kommentar. Altes Testament [*A publication*]
BKAV .... Boarding Kennels Association of Victoria [*Australia*]
BKB .... Bank of Boston Corp. [*NYSE symbol*] (SPSG)
BKB .... Bank of Israel. Economic Review [*A publication*]
BKB .... Braunschweigische Kohlen-Bergwerke AG [*Federal Republic of Germany*] (ECON)
BKB .... Kirbyville, TX [*Location identifier*] [*FAA*] (FAAL)
BKBCB ...... Bulletin. Boris Kidric Institute of Nuclear Sciences. Chemistry [*A publication*]
BKBGA4.... Brooklyn Botanic Garden. Annual Report [*A publication*]
Bkbinding & Bk Production ... Bookbinding and Book Production [*A publication*]
Bkbird .... Bookbird [*A publication*]
Bk & Bkmen ... Books and Bookmen [*A publication*]
BKBPT ...... Brotherhood of Knights of the Black Pudding Tasters (EA)
BKBR .... Beitraege zur Kenntnis der Babylonischen Religion [*A publication*]
Bk Buyer .... Book Buyer [*Later, Lamp*] [*A publication*]
BKC .... American Bank of Connecticut [*AMEX symbol*] (SPSG)
BKC .... Black Cliff Mines Ltd. [*Toronto Stock Exchange symbol*]
BKC .... Brookwood Reservoir [*California*] [*Seismograph station code, US Geological Survey*] (SEIS)
BKC .... Buckland [*Alaska*] [*Airport symbol*] (OAG)
BKCC .... Cariboo College, Kamloops, British Columbia [*Library symbol*] [*National Library of Canada*] (NLC)
BKCM ...... Kitimat Centennial Museum, British Columbia [*Library symbol*] [*National Library of Canada*] (NLC)
Bk Coll ...... Book Collector [*A publication*]
Bk Collec.... Book Collector [*A publication*]
Bk Collecting & Lib Mo ... Book Collecting and Library Monthly [*A publication*]
Bk Collector ... Book Collector [*A publication*]
BKCSD ...... Bulletin. Korean Chemical Society [*South Korea*] [*A publication*]
BKCT .... Cariboo-Thompson Nicola Library System, Kamloops, British Columbia [*Library symbol*] [*National Library of Canada*] (NLC)
BKCY .... Bankruptcy
BKD .... Blackboard (MSA)
bkd .... Book Designer [*MARC relator code*] [*Library of Congress*] (LCCP)
BKD .... Breckenridge, TX [*Location identifier*] [*FAA*] (FAAL)
BKDI .... Brake Die
BKDN .... Breakdown (MSA)
BKDNDIO ... Breakdown Diode [*Electronics*]
BKE .... Baker, OR [*Location identifier*] [*FAA*] (FAAL)
BKE .... Bankeno Resources Ltd. [*Toronto Stock Exchange symbol*]
Bk Egypt A ... Central Bank of Egypt. Annual Report [*A publication*]
BKEJA ...... Berichte. Kernforschungsanlage Juelich [*A publication*]
BKEM ...... Keremeos Museum, British Columbia [*Library symbol*] [*National Library of Canada*] (NLC)
BK ENG.... Break Engage (CAAL)
BKEP .... Boosted Kinetic Energy Penetrator [*Proposed submunition*]
BKESVM .. Similkameen Valley Museum, Keremeos, British Columbia [*Library symbol*] [*National Library of Canada*] (NLC)
BKEX .... Brock Exploration Corp. [*NASDAQ symbol*] (NQ)
BKF .... Baker, Fentress & Co. [*NYSE symbol*] (CTT)
BKF .... Blocking Factor (CMD)
BKF .... Denver, CO [*Location identifier*] [*FAA*] (FAAL)
Bk Forum ... Book Forum [*A publication*]
BKFSD ...... Bulletin. Korean Fisheries Technological Society [*South Korea*] [*A publication*]
bkfst .... Breakfast
BKG .... Baker Gold Ltd. [*Vancouver Stock Exchange symbol*]
BKG .... Banking
BKG .... Bookkeeping
BKG .... Utica, NY [*Location identifier*] [*FAA*] (FAAL)
BKGD .... Background
BKGDF ...... Baker Gold Ltd. [*NASDAQ symbol*] (NQ)
BKGP .... Blaetter fuer Kirchengeschichte Pommerns [*A publication*]
BKGRD ...... Background [*Low-priority processing*] [*Data processing*]
BKH .... Baksteen. Tweemaandelijks Tijdschrift Gewijd aan de Technische en Esthetische Eigenschappen van Gebakken Kleiprodukten [*A publication*]
BKH .... Black Hills Corp. [*NYSE symbol*] (SPSG)
BKH .... [*The*] Book House [*ACCORD*] [*UTLAS symbol*]
BKH .... Kekaha, HI [*Location identifier*] [*FAA*] (FAAL)
Bk Hawaii ... Bank of Hawaii. Monthly Review [*A publication*]
Bkhd .... Bulkhead

BKHS .... Blockhouse [*NASA*] (AAG)
Bki .... Banki [*Russian*]
BKI .... Bering [*Komandorsky Islands*] [*USSR*] [*Seismograph station code, US Geological Survey*] (SEIS)
BKI .... Better Kitchens Institute (EA)
BKI .... Break-In [*Telecommunications*] (TEL)
BKI .... Kimberley Public Library, British Columbia [*Library symbol*] [*National Library of Canada*] (NLC)
BKI .... Kota Kinabalu [*Malaysia*] [*Airport symbol*] (OAG)
BkIA .... Books at Iowa [*A publication*]
BKIF .... Business Name and Address Key Index File [*IRS*]
BKIHM ..... Kimberley and District Heritage Museum, Kimberley, British Columbia [*Library symbol*] [*National Library of Canada*] (NLC)
BKISA .... Bulletin. Boris Kidric Institute of Nuclear Sciences. Supplement [*A publication*]
BKIT .... Kitimat Public Library, British Columbia [*Library symbol*] [*National Library of Canada*] (NLC)
BKIWW..... Beker Industries Corp. Wts [*NASDAQ symbol*] (NQ)
BKJ .... Beitraege zur Kinder- und Jugendliteratur [*A publication*]
BK JUB ..... Book of Jubilees [*Apocalyptic book*]
Bk Judg..... Book of Judgments, by Townshend [*A publication*] (DLA)
BKK .... Bangkok [*Thailand*] [*Airport symbol*] (OAG)
BKK .... Expovisie. Beurzen, Tentoonstellingen, Congressen, Hotellerie [*A publication*]
BKKA .... Diocese of Kootenay Archives, Kelowna, British Columbia [*Library symbol*] [*National Library of Canada*] (NLC)
BKL .... Bakel [*Senegal*] [*Seismograph station code, US Geological Survey*] (SEIS)
B Kl .... Bass Klarinette [*Bass Clarinet*] [*Music*]
Bkl .... Booklist [*A publication*]
BkL .... Bookman (London) [*A publication*]
BKL .... Cleveland [*Ohio*] Burke Lakefront [*Airport symbol*] (OAG)
BKLA .... BKLA Bancorp [*Formerly, Bank of Los Angeles*] [*NASDAQ symbol*] (NQ)
BKLE .... Buckle (ROG)
Bklegger .... Booklegger Magazine [*A publication*]
Bklist .... Booklist and Subscription Books Bulletin [*Later, Booklist*] [*A publication*]
Bk LJ .... Banking Law Journal [*A publication*]
BKLKB ...... Banyaszati es Kohaszati Lapok. Kohaszat [*A publication*]
BKLM .... Bank Leumi Le-Israel BM [*NASDAQ symbol*] (NQ)
BKLN .... Brooklyn
BKLR .... Black Letter [*Printing*]
BKLT .... Booklet (AFM)
BKLY .... Berkley [*W. R.*] Corp. [*NASDAQ symbol*] (NQ)
BKM .... Bakalalan [*Malaysia*] [*Airport symbol*] (OAG)
BKM .... Bankers' Monthly [*A publication*]
BKM .... Battelle Memorial Institute, Columbus, OH [*OCLC symbol*] (OCLC)
BKM .... Buckram (ADA)
BKM .... Kamloops Museum, British Columbia [*Library symbol*] [*National Library of Canada*] (NLC)
Bkman (Lond) ... Bookman (London) [*A publication*]
Bkmark...... Bookmark [*A publication*]
Bkmark (Idaho) ... Bookmark. University of Idaho [*A publication*]
BKMD .... Bank Maryland Corp. [*NASDAQ symbol*] (NQ)
BKME ...... Bank of Kuwait & the Middle East (ECON)
BKME ...... Bleached Kraft Mill Effluent [*Pulp and paper processing*]
BKMGA ...... Blackwood's Magazine [*A publication*]
BKMR .... Beitraege zur Kulturgeschichte des Mittelalters und der Renaissance [*A publication*]
BKN .... Bank Negara Malaysia. Quarterly Economic Bulletin [*A publication*]
BKN .... Barquentine [*Ship*]
BKN .... Belkin, Inc. [*Toronto Stock Exchange symbol*]
BKN .... Broken
BKN .... Buckhorn, Inc. [*AMEX symbol*] (SPSG)
Bk-News .... Book-News [*A publication*]
BKNG .... Banknorth Group, Inc. [*NASDAQ symbol*] (NQ)
Bk Nigeria ... Central Bank of Nigeria. Annual Report and Statement of Accounts [*A publication*]
BKNT .... Banker's Note, Inc. [*NASDAQ symbol*] (NQ)
BKNW .... British Columbia Native Women's Society, Kamloops, British Columbia [*Library symbol*] [*National Library of Canada*] (NLC)
BKO .... Baker International Corp. [*Formerly, Baker Oil Tools, Inc.*] [*NYSE symbol*] (SPSG)
BKO .... Bamako [*Mali*] [*Airport symbol*] (OAG)
BKO .... Bank of Korea. Quarterly Economic Review [*A publication*]
BKO .... Barkhausen-Kurz Oscillator
BKO .... Beitraege zur Kenntnis des Orients [*A publication*]
BKO .... Okanagan Regional Library, Kelowna, British Columbia [*Library symbol*] [*National Library of Canada*] (NLC)
BKOAA ..... Byulleten' Komissii po Opredeleniyu Absolyutnogo Vozrasta Geologicheskikh Formatsii [*A publication*]
BKOC .... Okanagan College, Kelowna, British Columbia [*Library symbol*] [*National Library of Canada*] (NLC)
BKOCH ..... Ocelot Chemicals, Kitimat, British Columbia [*Library symbol*] [*National Library of Canada*] (NLC)

BKOM .... Kelowna Centennial Museum and Archives, British Columbia [*Library symbol*] [*National Library of Canada*] (NLC)
B Konan Women Coll ... Bulletin. Konan Women's College [*A publication*]
BKP .... Bayerische Koenigpartei [*Bavarian Royalist Party*] [*Pre-World War II*]
BKP .... Black Pearl Resources Ltd. [*Vancouver Stock Exchange symbol*]
BkP .... Brookhaven Press, Washington, DC [*Library symbol*] [*Library of Congress*] (LCLS)
BKP .... Bulgarska Komunisticheska Partiia [*Bulgarian Communist Party*] [*Political party*] (PPE)
BKP .... Burger King Investors [*NYSE symbol*] (SPSG)
BKPG .... Bookkeeping (MUGU)
BKPT .... Bankrupt (ROG)
BKQ .... Bakery Production and Marketing [*A publication*]
BKQ .... Bakra Resources Ltd. [*Vancouver Stock Exchange symbol*]
BKQ .... Blackall [*Australia*] [*Airport symbol*] (OAG)
BKR .... Baker [*Michael*] Corp. [*AMEX symbol*] (SPSG)
BKR .... Bakuriani [*USSR*] [*Seismograph station code, US Geological Survey*] (SEIS)
BKR .... Banker [*A publication*]
BKR .... Bankit Resource Corp. [*Vancouver Stock Exchange symbol*]
BKR .... Breaker (KSC)
BKR .... Broker [*Business term*]
BKR .... Civil Air Patrol, South Carolina Wing [*Columbia, SC*] [*FAA designator*] (FAAC)
BKRC .... Bulletin. Korean Research Center [*A publication*]
Bkr-Dir ...... Directory of Bankruptcy Attorneys [*Information service or system*] (EISS)
Bk Reg .... National Bankruptcy Register Reports [*A publication*] (DLA)
Bk Rev Dig ... Book Review Digest [*Information service or system*] [*A publication*]
Bk Rev Ind ... Book Review Index [*A publication*]
Bk Rev Mo ... Book Reviews of the Month [*A publication*]
BKRM .... Kettle Valley Railway Museum, Kelowna, British Columbia [*Library symbol*] [*National Library of Canada*] (NLC)
BKRP .... Bankruptcy File [*Canada Systems Group*] [*Ottawa, ON*] [*Information service or system*] (IID)
BKRPCY ... Bankruptcy (ADA)
BKRPT ...... Bankrupt
BKRPTCY ... Bankruptcy
BKRS .... BSI Holdings, Inc. [*Formerly, Brokers Securities, Inc.*] [*NASDAQ symbol*] (NQ)
BKRUPT ... Bankrupt (ROG)
BKRY .... Bakery (AABC)
BKS .... Barracks (AABC)
BKS .... Bengkulu [*Indonesia*] [*Airport symbol*] (OAG)
BKS .... Berkeley-Byerly [*California*] [*Seismograph station code, US Geological Survey*] (SEIS)
BKS .... Berkley Resources, Inc. [*Vancouver Stock Exchange symbol*]
BKS .... Blutkorpersenkung [*Blood Sedimentation Rate*] [*German*] [*Medicine*]
BKS .... Bohr-Kramers-Slater [*Quantum theory*]
bks .... Books (DLA)
BKS .... Broadcast Keying Station (NVT)
BKS .... Falfurrias, TX [*Location identifier*] [*FAA*] (FAAL)
Bks Abroad ... Books Abroad [*A publication*]
Bks & Bkmn ... Books and Bookmen [*A publication*]
BKSC .... [*The*] Bank of South Carolina [*NASDAQ symbol*] (NQ)
BKSCA .... Black Scholar [*A publication*]
Bks in Can ... Books in Canada [*A publication*]
BKSLF .... Back Shelf
Bks & Libs ... Books and Libraries at the University of Kansas [*A publication*]
BKSO .... Bank South Corp. [*NASDAQ symbol*] (NQ)
BKSP .... Backspace Character [*Keyboard*] [*Data processing*] (BUR)
BKSSM ..... S. S. Moyie Museum, Kaslo, British Columbia [*Library symbol*] [*National Library of Canada*] (NLC)
BKST .... Backstamp
BKST .... Bank of Stamford [*Stamford, CT*] [*NASDAQ symbol*] (NQ)
Bks Today ... Books Today [*Sunday Chicago Tribune*] [*A publication*]
BKSTS .... British Kinematography, Sound, and Television Society
BKSTS J .... BKSTS [*British Kinematograph Sound and Television Society*] Journal [*A publication*]
BKT .... Bakertalc, Inc. [*Toronto Stock Exchange symbol*]
BKT .... Basket
BKT .... Berliner Klassikertexte [*A publication*] (OCD)
BKT .... Blackstone Income Trust [*NYSE symbol*] (SPSG)
BKT .... Blackstone, VA [*Location identifier*] [*FAA*] (FAAL)
BKT .... Blinker Tube
BKT .... Bracket
BKT .... British Trades Union Congress [*TUC*]
BKT .... Bucket
BKTCY ...... Bankruptcy
BK Tech Rev ... BK Technical Review [*A publication*]
BKTL .... Blessed Kateri Tekakwitha League (EA)
BKTLA ...... Book Trolley [*A publication*]
Bk Trolley ... Book Trolley [*A publication*]
BKU .... Baker, MT [*Location identifier*] [*FAA*] (FAAL)
BKU .... Betioky [*Madagascar*] [*Airport symbol*] (OAG)
BKUN .... BankUnited, a Saving Bank [*NASDAQ symbol*] (NQ)
BKUP .... Backup (KSC)
BKV .... Bibliothek der Kirchenvaeter [*A publication*]

BKV .... Bibliothek der Kirchenvater (BJA)
BKV .... Brookmere Ventures [*Vancouver Stock Exchange symbol*]
BKV .... Brooksville, FL [*Location identifier*] [*FAA*] (FAAL)
BKV .... Brotherhood of the Knights of the Vine (EA)
BKVT .... BankVermont Corp. [*NASDAQ symbol*] (NQ)
BKW .... Bakkerswereld [*A publication*]
BKW .... Beckley [*West Virginia*] [*Airport symbol*] (OAG)
BKW .... Bible Key Words [*London, 1949-1965*] [*A publication*] (BJA)
BKW .... [*A*] Book of Weird Tales [*A publication*]
BkW .... Book World [*A publication*]
BKW .... Breakwater
BKWD .... Backward (KSC)
Bk Wk .... Book Week [*A publication*]
Bk World ... Book World [*A publication*]
BKWS........ BKW Inc. [*NASDAQ symbol*] (NQ)
BKX .... Brookings [*South Dakota*] [*Airport symbol*] (OAG)
BKY .... Bankruptcy
BKY .... Berkey, Inc. [*NYSE symbol*] (SPSG)
BKY .... Bluesky Oil & Gas [*Toronto Stock Exchange symbol*] [*Vancouver Stock Exchange symbol*]
BKY .... Bukavu [*Zaire*] [*Airport symbol*] (OAG)
BKY .... St. Louis, MO [*Location identifier*] [*FAA*] (FAAL)
BKZ .... Brinkley, AR [*Location identifier*] [*FAA*] (FAAL)
BKZ .... Bukoba [*Tanzania*] [*Airport symbol*] (OAG)
B des L .... Bachelier des Lettres [*Bachelor of Letters*] [*French*]
BL .... Bachelor of Laws
BL .... Bachelor of Letters
BL .... Bachelor of Literature
BL .... Background Listening [*Music*]
BL .... Backlash (MSA)
BL .... Badminton Library [*A publication*]
BL .... Bale
BL .... Ball Lightning
BL .... Bank Larceny
BL .... Barrel (MCD)
BL .... Barrister-at-Law
BL .... Basal Lamina [*Neuroanatomy*]
BL .... Baseline
BL .... Basic Load [*Ammunition*] (AABC)
BL .... Basolateral [*Anatomy*]
BL .... Basutoland
BL .... Bath Road [*Bristol*] [*British depot code*]
BL .... Bats Left-Handed [*Baseball*]
BL .... Beak Line
BL .... Bell (IEEE)
BL .... Bell on Leases [*A publication*] (DLA)
BL .... Bellanca Aircraft Corp. [*ICAO aircraft manufacturer identifier*] (ICAO)
B & L .... Bellar & Lichtenberg [*Device*]
BL .... Bend Line (MSA)
BL .... Bengal Lancers [*British military*] (DMA)
BL .... Between Layers [*Aviation*] (FAAC)
BL .... Bibel und Leben [*Duesseldorf*] [*A publication*]
BL .... Bibel-Lexikon [*A publication*] (BJA)
BL .... Bibel und Liturgie [*A publication*] (BJA)
BL .... Bible League (EA)
BL .... Bibliographie Linguistique [*A publication*]
BL .... Bibliotheekleven [*A publication*]
BL .... Bilevel (MCD)
BL .... Bill of Lading [*Shipping*]
BL .... Bill Lodged [*British*] (ADA)
BL .... Billet (MSA)
BL .... Biological Laboratory [*Army*] (MCD)
BL .... Bioluminescence
BL .... Black
BL .... Black Leghorn [*Poultry*]
BL .... Black Letter [*Printing*]
BL .... Black Light
BL .... Black Liquor [*Pulp and paper technology*]
Bl. .... Black Lung [*Social Security Administration*] (OICC)
BL .... Black Perspective in Music [*A publication*]
Bl. .... Blackford's Indiana Reports [*1817-47*] [*A publication*] (DLA)
Bl. .... Black's United States Supreme Court Reports [*66-67 United States Reports*] [*A publication*] (DLA)
Bl. .... Blackstone's Commentaries on the Laws of England [*A publication*] (DLA)
Bl. .... [*Henry*] Blackstone's English Common Pleas Reports [*1788-96*] [*A publication*] (DLA)
Bl. .... [*Sir William*] Blackstone's English King's Bench Reports [*1746-80*] [*A publication*] (DLA)
BL .... Blade (MSA)
BL .... Blair Corp. [*AMEX symbol*] (SPSG)
BL .... Blank [*Microtiter plate*]
BL .... Blank Line [*Data processing*]
BL .... Blanking (DEN)
BL .... Blaser [*Blower*] [*Wind instrument player*]
Bl. .... Blasinstrumente [*Wind Instruments*] [*Music*]
BL .... Blast
Bl. .... Blatchford's United States Circuit Court Reports [*A publication*] (DLA)
Bl. .... Blatt [*Newspaper, Sheet*] [*German*] (BJA)

BL .... Bleed (MSA)
Bl .... Bleomycin [*Also, B, Bleo, BLM*]
BL .... Blessed
BL .... Bloch & Co., Cleveland, OH [*Library symbol*] [*Library of Congress*] (LCLS)
BL .... Block
BL .... Block Length
BL .... Blood
BL .... Bloom [*or Blossom*] (ROG)
Bl .... Blount's Law Dictionary [*A publication*] (DLA)
BL .... Blower
BL .... Blowline
BL .... Blue (KSC)
BL .... Blue Line (MCD)
BL .... Blue Pennant [*Navy*] [*British*]
BL .... Boat Lanes
BL .... Bodleian Library (DAS)
BL .... Bombline
BL .... Bone-Marrow-Derived Lymphocyte [*Hematology*]
BL .... Book List. Society for Old Testament Studies [*Manchester*] [*A publication*]
BL .... Booklist [*A publication*]
BL .... Border Line
BL .... Borderline Lepromatous [*Medicine*]
BL .... Bottom Layer [*Technical drawings*]
BL .... Boundary Layer
B and L....... Brain and Language [*A publication*]
BL .... Brascan Limited [*Toronto Stock Exchange symbol*]
bl .... Brazil [*MARC country of publication code*] [*Library of Congress*] [*IYRU nationality code*] (LCCP)
BL .... Breadth-Length
BL .... Breech-Loading [*Weapon*]
B/L.............. Bridgelayer [*British military*] (DMA)
BL .... Bristol Laboratories
BL .... British Legion
BL .... British Leyland [*Later, BL Ltd., then Rover Group*] [*Auto manufacturing company*]
BL .... British Library [*Formerly, The British Museum Reading Room*]
BL .... British Lion [*Motion picture company*]
B & L.......... Browning and Lushington's English Admiralty Reports [*1863-65*] [*A publication*] (DLA)
BL .... Buccolingual [*Dentistry*]
BL .... Building Line [*Technical drawings*]
B & L.......... Building and Loan
B & L.......... Building and Loan Association (DLA)
B & L.......... Bullen and Leake's Precedents of Pleading [*A publication*] (ILCA)
BL .... Bulletin des Lettres [*A publication*]
BL .... Bulletin Linguistique. Faculte des Lettres de Bucarest [*A publication*]
BL .... Bullock Ridge Splitting [*Agriculture*]
BL .... Bundelkund Legion [*British military*] (DMA)
BL .... Bureau of Litigation [*Federal Trade Commission*]
BL .... Burkitt's Lymphoma [*Medicine*]
BL .... Business Lawyer [*A publication*]
BL .... Business Licence [*British*] (ADA)
BL .... Butt Line [*Technical drawings*]
BL .... Buttock Line [*Engineering*]
BL .... By-Line [*Publishing*]
BL .... Graduate in Letters
BL .... Leadair Jet Service [*France*] [*ICAO designator*] (FAAC)
BL .... South Africa [*Formerly, FY*] [*License plate code assigned to foreign diplomats in the US*]
BLA .... Air Polynesia, Inc. [*Honolulu, HI*] [*FAA designator*] (FAAC)
BLA .... Bachelor of Landscape Architecture
BLA .... Bachelor of Law and Administration
BLA .... Bachelor of Liberal Arts
BLA .... Bagala [*Ship's rigging*] (ROG)
BLA .... [*The*] Baltimore & Annapolis Railroad Co. [*AAR code*]
BLA .... Baptist Life Association [*Buffalo, NY*] (EA)
BLA .... Barcelona [*Venezuela*] [*Airport symbol*] (OAG)
BLA .... Base Loaded Antenna
BLA .... Bear Lake Resources Ltd. [*Vancouver Stock Exchange symbol*]
BLA .... Belgian Linen Association [*Later, ILPC*] (EA)
BLA .... Bilateral Agreements
BLA .... Bills of Lading Act
BLA .... Binary Logical Association
BLA .... Bird Lovers Anthology [*A publication*]
BLA .... Black Art [*London*] [*A publication*]
BLA .... Black Liberation Army (EA)
BLA .... Black Lung Association (EA)
bla .... Blackfoot [*MARC language code*] [*Library of Congress*] (LCCP)
BLA .... Blacksburg [*Virginia*] [*Seismograph station code, US Geological Survey*] (SEIS)
BLA .... Blocking Acknowledgment [*Telecommunications*] (TEL)
BLA .... Bracket and Linkage Assembly
BLA .... British Land of America, Inc. [*NYSE symbol*] (SPSG)
BLA .... British Legal Association (DLA)
BLA .... British Liberation Army [*Later, British Army of the Rhine*]
BLA .... Brown Lung Association (EA)

BLA .... Bureau for Latin America [*Agency for International Development*]
BLA .... Bureau de Liaison des Syndicats Europeens (CEE) des Produits Aromatiques [*Liaison Bureau of the European and EEC Unions of Aromatic Products*] (EAIO)
BLA .... Business Latin America [*A publication*]
BLA .... Byelorussian Literary Association (EA)
BLA .... Graduate in Liberal Arts
BLA .... Grammatik des Biblische-Aramaeischen [*H. Bauer and P. Leander*] [*A publication*] (BJA)
B Labor Mus Louvre ... Bulletin. Laboratoire du Musee de Louvre [*A publication*]
BLAC........ British Light Aviation Center (MCD)
Bla Ch....... Bland's Maryland Chancery Reports [*A publication*] (DLA)
Black......... Blackerby's Magistrates' Reports [*1327-1716*] [*England*] [*A publication*] (DLA)
Black......... Blackford's Indiana Reports [*1817-47*] [*A publication*] (DLA)
Black......... Black's Reports [*30-53 Indiana*] [*A publication*] (DLA)
Black......... Black's United States Supreme Court Reports [*66-67 United States Reports*] [*A publication*] (DLA)
Black......... [*Henry*] Blackstone's English Common Pleas Reports [*1788-96*] [*A publication*] (DLA)
Black......... [*Sir William*] Blackstone's English King's Bench Reports [*1746-80*] [*A publication*] (DLA)
Black......... [*Sir William*] Blackstone's Reports in King's Bench Tempore George II and III and Common Pleas, George III [*1746-80*] [*A publication*] (DLA)
Black......... Blackwood's Magazine [*A publication*]
Black Abr... Blackstone's Commentaries on the Laws of England, Abridged [*A publication*] (DLA)
Black Am L ... Black American Literature Forum [*A publication*]
Black Anal ... Blackstone's Analysis of the Laws of England [*A publication*] (DLA)
Blackb........ Blackburn on Sales [*A publication*] (DLA)
Black Bk Adm ... Twiss. Black Book of the Admiralty [*A publication*] (DLA)
Blackb Sales ... Blackburn on Sales [*A publication*] (DLA)
Black Bus News ... Black Business News [*A publication*]
BlackCh..... Black Church [*A publication*]
Black Col ... Black Collegian [*A publication*]
Black Coll .. Black Collegian [*A publication*]
Black Com ... Blackstone's Commentaries on the Laws of England [*A publication*] (DLA)
Black Cond ... Blackwell's Condensed Illinois Reports [*A publication*] (DLA)
Black Cond Rep ... Blackwell's Condensed Illinois Reports [*A publication*] (DLA)
Black Const Law ... Black on Constitutional Law [*A publication*] (DLA)
Black Const Prohib ... Black's Constitutional Prohibitions [*A publication*] (DLA)
Black Dict.. Black's Law Dictionary [*A publication*] (DLA)
Black D & O ... Blackham, Dundas, and Osborne's Irish Nisi Prius Reports [*1846-48*] [*A publication*] (DLA)
Black Emp Li ... Black on Employer's Liability [*A publication*] (DLA)
Black Ent ... Black Enterprise [*A publication*]
Black Enterp ... Black Enterprise [*A publication*]
Black F....... Black Forum [*A publication*]
Blackf.......... Blackford's Indiana Reports [*1817-47*] [*A publication*] (DLA)
Blackf (Ind) ... Blackford's Indiana Reports [*1817-47*] [*A publication*] (DLA)
Blackford's Ia R ... Blackford's Indiana Reports [*1817-47*] [*A publication*] (DLA)
Black Fox Mag ... Black Fox Magazine [*A publication*]
Black H...... [*Henry*] Blackstone's English Common Pleas Reports [*1788-96*] [*A publication*] (DLA)
Black Hills Eng ... Black Hills Engineer [*A publication*]
BlackI .... Black Images: A Critical Quarterly on Black Arts and Culture [*A publication*]
BlackIC...... Black I: A Canadian Journal of Black Expression [*A publication*]
Black Inf Index ... Black Information Index [*A publication*]
Black Interp Laws ... Black on Construction and Interpretation of Laws [*A publication*] (DLA)
Black Intox Liq ... Black on the Laws Regulating the Manufacture and Sale of Intoxicating Liquors [*A publication*] (DLA)
Black Judg ... Black on Judgments [*A publication*] (DLA)
Black Judgm ... Black on Judgments [*A publication*] (DLA)
Black Jus ... Blackerby's Justices' Cases [*England*] [*A publication*] (DLA)
Black Just ... Blackerby's Justices' Cases [*England*] [*A publication*] (DLA)
Black Law Dict ... Black's Law Dictionary [*A publication*] (DLA)
Black LD.... Black's Law Dictionary [*A publication*] (DLA)
Black L J ... Black Law Journal [*A publication*]
Black L Tr ... Blackstone's Law Tracts [*A publication*] (DLA)
BLACKM.. Blackmore [*England*]
Black Mag ... Blackwood's Magazine [*A publication*]
Black Mag Ch ... Blackstone on Magna Charta [*A publication*] (DLA)
Black Mus Jazz Rev ... Black Music and Jazz Review [*A publication*]
Black N Dig ... Black News Digest [*A publication*]
Black Per M ... Black Perspective in Music [*A publication*]
Black Perspective M ... Black Perspective in Music [*A publication*]
Black Pol Econ ... Review of Black Political Economy [*A publication*]
BlackR .... Black Review [*A publication*]
Black R ...... Blackford's Indiana Reports [*1817-47*] [*A publication*] (DLA)

Black R ...... Black's United States Supreme Court Reports [*66-67 United States Reports*] [*A publication*] (DLA)

Black R ...... [*Sir William*] Blackstone's English King's Bench Reports [*1746-80*] [*A publication*] (DLA)

Black Rep... Black's United States Supreme Court Reports [*66-67 United States Reports*] [*A publication*] (DLA)

Black Rock For Bull ... Black Rock Forest. Bulletin [*A publication*]

Black Rock For Pap ... Black Rock Forest. Papers [*A publication*]

Black Sal.... Blackburn on Sales [*A publication*] (DLA)

Black Sch... Black Scholar [*A publication*]

Black Ship Ca ... Black's Decisions in Shipping Cases [*A publication*] (DLA)

Black's Law Dict ... Black's Law Dictionary [*A publication*] (DLA)

Black Soc ... Black Sociologist [*A publication*]

Blackst ...... [*Sir William*] Blackstone's Reports in King's Bench Tempore George II and III and Common Pleas, George III [*1746-80*] [*A publication*] (DLA)

Black St Const ... Black on Construction and Interpretation of Laws [*A publication*] (DLA)

Blackstone's Commen ... Blackstone's Commentaries on the Laws of England [*A publication*] (DLA)

Blackst R ... [*Sir William*] Blackstone's English King's Bench Reports [*1746-80*] [*A publication*] (DLA)

Black Tax Tit ... Blackwell's Tax Titles [*A publication*] (ILCA)

Black W ... Black World [*A publication*]

Black W ... [*Sir William*] Blackstone's English King's Bench Reports [*1746-80*] [*A publication*] (DLA)

Blackw ...... Blackwood's Magazine [*A publication*]

Blackw Cond ... Blackwell's Condensed Illinois Reports [*A publication*] (DLA)

Blackwood's Mag ... Blackwood's Magazine [*A publication*]

Blackw Sc Act ... Blackwell's Scotch Acts [*A publication*] (DLA)

Blackw Tax Titles ... Blackwell's Tax Titles [*A publication*] (DLA)

Blackw TT ... Blackwell's Tax Titles [*A publication*] (DLA)

Bla Com ..... Blackstone's Commentaries on the Laws of England [*A publication*] (DLA)

Bla Comm .. Blackstone's Commentaries on the Laws of England [*A publication*] (ILCA)

BLAD .... Borderline Left-Axis Deviation [*Cardiology*]

BLADE...... Basic Level Automation of Data through Electronics

BLADE...... Bell Laboratories Automatic Device

BLADES ... Bell Laboratories Automatic Design System [*Computer program*]

BLADING ... Bill of Lading [*Shipping*]

BLADS ...... Bell Laboratories Automatic Design System [*Computer program*]

Blaett Dtsche u Int Polit ... Blaetter fuer Deutsche und Internationale Politik [*A publication*]

Blaett Technikgesch ... Blaetter fuer Technikgeschichte [*A publication*]

BLAG........ Benign Lymphocytic Angiitis and Granulomatosis [*Medicine*]

Blagoveshch Gos Med Inst Tr ... Blagoveshchenskii Gosudarstvennyi Meditsinskii Institut. Trudy [*A publication*]

Bl Agric Chem Soc Jap ... Bulletin. Agricultural Chemical Society of Japan [*A publication*]

Bla H.......... [*Henry*] Blackstone's English Common Pleas Reports [*1788-96*] [*A publication*] (DLA)

BLAI.......... Bernstein/Leibstone Associates, Inc. [*NASDAQ symbol*] (NQ)

Blair .... Blair. Manual for Scotch Justices of the Peace [*A publication*] (DLA)

Blair Co...... Blair County Law Reports [*Pennsylvania*] [*A publication*] (DLA)

Blair Co LR ... Blair County Law Reports [*Pennsylvania*] [*A publication*] (DLA)

Blair Co LR (PA) ... Blair County Law Reports [*Pennsylvania*] [*A publication*] (DLA)

Blair & Ketchum's ... Blair and Ketchum's Country Journal [*A publication*]

BLAIS........ Battlefield Location and Information System [*Army*] (RDA)

BLAISE..... British Library Automated Information Service [*European host database system*] (IID)

BLAK........ Black Industries, Inc. [*NASDAQ symbol*] (NQ)

Blake.......... Blake's Reports [*1-3 Montana*] [*A publication*] (DLA)

Blake & H ... Blake and Hedges' Reports [*2-3 Montana*] [*A publication*] (DLA)

Blake Ill Q ... Blake; an Illustrated Quarterly [*A publication*]

BlakeN...... Blake Newsletter [*A publication*]

Blake Q...... Blake; an Illustrated Quarterly [*A publication*]

BlakeS ...... Blake Studies [*A publication*]

Blake Stud ... Blake Studies [*A publication*]

B La L ...... Bachelor of Latin Letters

Bla Life Ass ... Blayney. Life Assurance [*1837*] [*A publication*] (DLA)

BLAM....... Ballistically Launched Aerodynamic Missile

BLAM....... Boletin Latino-Americano de Musica [*A publication*]

BLAM....... Boundary Layer Acoustic Monitor (MCD)

BLAM....... Bulletin. Librairie Ancienne et Moderne [*A publication*]

Bl Amer Lit Forum ... Black American Literature Forum [*A publication*]

Bl Am Phys Soc ... Bulletin. American Physical Society [*A publication*]

BLAN .... Bridge Communications, Inc. [*Mountain View, CA*] [*NASDAQ symbol*] (NQ)

Blanc & WLC ... Blanchard and Weeks' Leading Cases on Mines [*A publication*] (DLA)

Bland.......... Bland's Maryland Chancery Reports [*A publication*] (DLA)

BLandArch ... Bachelor in Landscape Architecture

Bland Ch (MD) ... Bland's Maryland Chancery Reports [*A publication*] (DLA)

Bland Ch R ... Bland's Maryland Chancery Reports [*A publication*] (DLA)

BLANDF... Blandford [*England*]

Bland's Ch ... Bland's Maryland Chancery Reports [*A publication*] (DLA)

Bland's Ch R ... Bland's Maryland Chancery Reports [*A publication*] (DLA)

Bland's Chy Rep ... Bland's Maryland Chancery Reports [*A publication*] (DLA)

Blan Lim .... Blanshard. Statutes of Limitations [*A publication*] (DLA)

Blansh Lim ... Blanshard. Statutes of Limitations [*A publication*] (DLA)

Blan & W Lead Cas ... Blanchard and Weeks' Leading Cases on Mines [*A publication*] (DLA)

BLAPL ...... Belgian and Luxembourg Association of Penal Law (EAIO)

BL Arch ...... Bachelor of Landscape Architecture

BLAS .... Basic Linear Algebra Subroutines (MCD)

BLAS .... Blasius Industries, Inc. [*NASDAQ symbol*] (NQ)

BLAS .... Blasphemy (DLA)

BLASA ...... Belgian-Luxembourg American Studies Association [*Brussels, Belgium*] (EAIO)

Blash Juries ... Blashfield. Instructions to Juries [*A publication*] (DLA)

Bl Assoc Chim ... Bulletin. Association des Chimistes [*A publication*]

BLAST ...... Black Legal Action for Soul in Television [*Student legal action organization*]

BLAST ...... Building Loads Analysis and System Thermodynamics [*Computer program*]

Blast F & Steel Pl ... Blast Furnace and Steel Plant [*A publication*]

Blast Furn Coke Oven Raw Mater Proc ... Blast Furnace, Coke Oven, and Raw Materials. Proceedings [*A publication*]

Blast Furn Steel Plant ... Blast Furnace and Steel Plant [*A publication*]

BLAT........ Blind Learning Aptitude Test [*Education*]

BLAT........ British Life Assurance Trust

Blat CCR.... Blatchford's United States Circuit Court Reports [*A publication*] (DLA)

Blatch........ Blatchford's United States Circuit Court Reports [*A publication*] (DLA)

Blatchf .... Blatchford's United States Circuit Court Reports [*A publication*] (DLA)

Blatchf CC ... Blatchford's United States Circuit Court Reports [*A publication*] (DLA)

Blatchf CC Rep ... Blatchford's United States Circuit Court Reports [*A publication*] (DLA)

Blatchf & H ... Blatchford and Howland's United States District Court Reports [*A publication*] (DLA)

Blatchford & H ... Blatchford and Howland's Reports [*United States*] [*A publication*] (DLA)

Blatchf Pr Cas ... Blatchford's Prize Cases [*United States*] [*A publication*] (DLA)

Blatchf Prize Cas ... Blatchford's Prize Cases [*United States*] [*A publication*] (DLA)

Blatchf (US Circ Ct) ... Blatchford's United States Circuit Court Reports [*A publication*] (DLA)

Blatch & H ... Blatchford and Howland's United States District Court Reports [*A publication*] (DLA)

Blatch (US Cir Ct) ... Blatchford's United States Circuit Court Reports [*A publication*] (DLA)

BLATS ...... Built-Up Low-Cost Advanced Titanium Structures (MCD)

BLAU .... Blau [*Barry*] & Partners, Inc. [*NASDAQ symbol*] (NQ)

B-LAV .... B-Cell-Lymphadenopathy Associated Virus

BLAV........ British Latin America Volunteers [*British military*] (DMA)

Bla W .... [*Sir William*] Blackstone's English King's Bench Reports [*1746-80*] [*A publication*] (DLA)

Blax Eng Co ... Blaxland's Codex Legum Anglicanum [*A publication*] (DLA)

Blay Ann.... Blayney. Life Annuities [*1817*] [*A publication*] (DLA)

Blay Life Ins ... Blayney. Life Assurance [*1837*] [*A publication*] (DLA)

B Lazio Merid ... Bollettino. Istituto di Storia e di Arte del Lazio Meridionale [*A publication*]

BLB............ Banking Law Bulletin [*Australia*] [*A publication*]

BLB............ Big Little Book [*of comic strips*]

BLB............ Black Label Resources, Inc. [*Vancouver Stock Exchange symbol*]

BLB............ Black Light Blue [*Source for near ultraviolet radiation*]

BLB............ Bloembollenexport [*A publication*]

BLB............ Blood Banking [*Medical specialty*] (DHSM)

BLB............ [*Mask designed by*] Boothby, Lovelace, and Bulbulian [*of Mayo Clinic*] [*Medicine*]

BLB............ Boy's Life Brigade

BLB............ British Linen Bank

BLB............ Bulletin Linguistique. Faculte des Lettres de Bucarest [*A publication*]

BLBA........ Black Lung Benefits Act [*1972*]

Bl B Adm ... Twiss. Black Book of the Admiralty [*A publication*] (DLA)

BLBCCA ... Big Little Book Collector's Club of America (EA)

BLBD........ Babylonian Legal and Business Documents [*A publication*] (BJA)

BLBD........ Binary Light Beam Deflector

Bl Belt Mag ... Black Belt Magazine [*A publication*]

Bl Bergshandteringens Vaenner ... Blad foer Bergshandteringens Vaenner [*A publication*]

BLBFC....... Bonnie Lou Bishop Fan Club (EA)

BLBG......... Biological Laboratory, Brunswick, Georgia [*US Bureau of Commercial Fisheries; later, National Marine Fisheries Service*]
BLBHAE... Balneologia Bohemica [*A publication*]
BLBI......... Bulletin. Leo Baeck Institute [*A publication*]
BLBIA...... Bluegrass [*A publication*]
Bl Bks B..... Black Books Bulletin [*A publication*]
BLBP......... Blind Loaded and Blind Plugged [*Projectile*] (MCD)
BLBS......... British Library Bibliographic Services [*London, England*]
BLBSB...... Better Light Better Sight Bureau [*Defunct*] (EA)
BLC........... Backlight Compensation [*Photography*]
BLC........... Baker Lake [*Northwest Territories*] [*Geomagnetic observatory code*]
BLC........... Baker Lake [*Northwest Territories*] [*Seismograph station code, US Geological Survey*] (SEIS)
BLC........... Bali [*Cameroon*] [*Airport symbol*] (OAG)
BLC........... Barrier Layer Cell
BLC........... Baseband Level Control (MCD)
BLC........... Baseline Configuration
BLC........... Battery Level Computer (MCD)
BLC........... Belo [*A. H.*] Corporation [*NYSE symbol*] (SPSG)
BLC........... Ben Line Containers Ltd. (DS)
BLC........... Bengal Light Cavalry [*British military*] (DMA)
BLC........... Black Literature Criticism [*A publication*]
BLC........... Blackberry Gold Resources, Inc. [*Vancouver Stock Exchange symbol*]
Bl C........... Blood Culture [*Medicine*]
BLC........... Blue Line Copy
BLC........... Bluffton College, Bluffton, OH [*OCLC symbol*] (OCLC)
BLC........... Bollettino di Legislazione Comparata [*A publication*] (ILCA)
BLC........... Bombay Light Cavalry [*British military*] (DMA)
BLC........... Boundary Layer Control
BLC........... British Leather Confederation (IRUK)
BLC........... British Library General Catalogue of Printed Books [*A publication*]
BLC........... British Lighting Council [*Defunct*]
BLC........... Broadband Latching Circulator
BLC........... Bulletin de Litterature Chretienne [*A publication*]
BLC........... Burlington Liars Club (EA)
BLCA........ Black Canyon of the Gunnison National Monument
BLCC......... Balchem Corporation [*Slate Hill, NY*] [*NASDAQ symbol*] (NQ)
BLCC......... Belo-Luxembourg Chamber of Commerce (DS)
Bl CC......... Blatchford's United States Circuit Court Reports [*A publication*] (DLA)
Bl CCR...... Blatchford's United States Circuit Court Reports [*A publication*] (DLA)
BLCE......... Balance (ADA)
BLCE......... Baseline Calibration Equipment
BLCED...... Blood Cells [*A publication*]
BLCHD...... Bleached [*Freight*]
Bl Chem Soc Jap ... Bulletin. Chemical Society of Japan [*A publication*]
BLCHG...... Bleaching [*Freight*]
Bl Chr R..... Bland's Chancery Reports [*A publication*] (DLA)
Bl Chy Pr... Blake. Chancery Practice [*A publication*] (DLA)
BLCK......... Black Angus Systems, Inc. [*NASDAQ symbol*] (NQ)
BLCK......... Block (BUR)
BLCK......... Kaatza Historical Museum, Lake Cowichan, British Columbia [*Library symbol*] [*National Library of Canada*] (NLC)
BLCL......... B-Lymphoblastoid Cell Line [*Biochemistry*]
Bl Com...... Blackstone's Commentaries on the Laws of England [*A publication*] (DLA)
Bl Comm.... Blackstone's Commentaries on the Laws of England [*A publication*] (DLA)
BLCR......... Belcor, Inc. [*Irvine, CA*] [*NASDAQ symbol*] (NQ)
BLCT......... Basic Language Concepts Test [*Child development test*]
BLD........... Bachelor of Landscape Design [*British*] (DBQ)
BLD........... Balance Resources Ltd. [*Vancouver Stock Exchange symbol*]
BLD........... Balanced Line Driver (MSA)
BLD........... Baldwin Technology Corp. [*AMEX symbol*] (SPSG)
BLDN......... Balled [*Freight*]
BLD........... Baseline Documentation (MCD)
BLD........... Beam-Lead Device (IEEE)
BLD........... Below Limit of Detection
BLD........... Bharatiya Lok Dal [*India*] [*Political party*] (PPW)
BLD........... Billion Liters per Day
BLD........... Blinder (MSA)
bld............. Blood [*Philately*]
Bl D........... Blount's Law Dictionary [*A publication*] (DLA)
BLD........... Blue-Laid [*Paper*]
BLD........... Bold (ADA)
Bld............ Boulder [*Maps and charts*]
BLD........... Boulder City, NV [*Location identifier*] [*FAA*] (FAAL)
BLD........... Boulevard (EY)
BLD........... Building (NATG)
BLD........... Bulletin Legislatif Dalloz [*A publication*] (ILCA)
BLDCS...... Bureau of Laundry and Dry Cleaning Standards (EA)
BL Des....... Bachelor of Landscape Design
Bl Deut Phil ... Blaetter fuer Deutsche Philosophie [*A publication*]
Bl Deutsche Landesgesch ... Blaetter fuer Deutsche Landesgeschichte [*A publication*]

Bldg........... Building [*A publication*]
BLDG........ Building (AFM)
BLDGA...... Buildings [*A publication*]
Bldg Age.... Building Age and National Builder [*A publication*]
Bldg Conserv ... Building Conservation [*A publication*]
Bldg Conservation ... Building Conservation [*A publication*]
Bldg Contr ... Building and Construction Contracts [*A publication*] (DLA)
Bldg Des..... Building Design [*A publication*]
Bldg Desgn ... Building Design and Construction [*A publication*]
Bldg Design ... Building Design [*A publication*]
Bldg E........ Building Engineer
Bldg Econ... Building Economist [*A publication*] (APTA)
Bldg Economist ... Building Economist [*A publication*]
Bldg Env ... Building and Environment [*A publication*]
Bldg Envir ... Building and Environment [*A publication*]
Bldg Environ ... Building and Environment [*A publication*]
Bldg & Environment ... Building and Environment [*A publication*]
Bldg Forum ... Building Forum [*A publication*] (APTA)
Bldg Mater ... Building Materials [*A publication*]
Bldg Mater ... Building Materials and Equipment [*A publication*] (APTA)
Bldg Mats List ... Building Materials List [*A publication*]
Bldg Mgmt Abs ... Building Management Abstracts [*A publication*]
Bldg Opr .... Building Operating Management [*A publication*]
Bldg Products ... Building Products [*A publication*]
Bldg Refurb ... Building Refurbishment [*A publication*]
Bldg Refurbishment & Maintenance ... Building Refurbishment and Maintenance [*A publication*]
Bldg Research Assocn New Zealand Bldg Information Bull ... Building Research Association of New Zealand. Building Information Bulletin [*A publication*]
Bldg Research & Practice ... Building Research and Practice [*A publication*]
Bldg Res Practice ... Building Research and Practice [*A publication*]
Bldg Res (Washington DC) ... Building Research (Washington, DC) [*A publication*]
Bldgs.......... Buildings: The Construction and Building Management Journal [*A publication*]
Bldg Sci...... Building Science [*A publication*]
Bldg Serv ... Building Services [*A publication*]
Bldg Serv Engr ... Building Services Engineer [*A publication*]
Bldg Serv Environ Engr ... Building Services and Environmental Engineer [*A publication*]
Bldg Services ... Building Services [*A publication*]
Bldg Services Engineer ... Building Services Engineer [*A publication*]
Bldg Services Environ Engnr ... Building Services and Environmental Engineer [*A publication*]
Bldg Services & Environmental Engineer ... Building Services and Environmental Engineer [*A publication*]
Bldg S Home ... Building Supply and Home Centers [*A publication*]
Bldg SN ..... Building Supply News [*A publication*]
Bldg Soc Gaz ... Building Societies Gazette [*A publication*]
Bldg Specif ... Building Specification [*A publication*]
Bldg Specification ... Building Specification [*A publication*]
Bldg with Steel ... Building with Steel [*A publication*]
Bldg Study Div Bldg Res CSIRO ... Building Study. Division of Building Research. Commonwealth Scientific and Industrial Research Organisation [*A publication*] (APTA)
Bldg Systems Design ... Building Systems Design [*A publication*]
Bldg Systm ... Building Systems Design [*A publication*]
Bldg Tech File ... Building Technical File [*A publication*]
Bldg Tech Mgmt ... Building Technology and Management [*A publication*]
Bldg Technol Mgmt ... Building Technology and Management [*A publication*]
Bldg Trades J ... Building Trades Journal [*A publication*]
Bldg Trades Jnl ... Building Trades Journal [*A publication*]
BLDG WDWRK ... Building Woodwork [*Freight*]
BLDI......... Blank Die
BLDIA....... Black Diamond [*A publication*]
Bl Dict........ Black's Law Dictionary [*A publication*] (DLA)
BLDIS .... Blood Information Service [*Information service or system*] (IID)
Bl D Lg....... Blaetter fuer Deutsche Landesgeschichte [*A publication*]
BLDN......... Blowdown (NASA)
Bl D & O..... Blackham, Dundas, and Osborne's Irish Nisi Prius Reports [*1846-48*] [*A publication*] (DLA)
Bl D & Osb ... Blackham, Dundas, and Osborne's Irish Nisi Prius Reports [*1846-48*] [*A publication*] (DLA)
Bl D Ph ...... Blaetter fuer Deutsche Philosophie [*A publication*]
BLDR......... Bleeder (MSA)
BLDR......... Builder
Bld Res Prac ... Building Research and Practice [*A publication*]
BLDS......... Blinds [*Classified advertising*] (ADA)
Blds............ Boulders [*Quality of the bottom*] [*Maps and charts*]
BLDSC...... British Library Document Supply Centre (CB)
Bld Serv Enging Res Tech ... Building Services Engineering Research and Technology [*A publication*]
BLDT......... Balloon-Launched Decelerator Test [*Air Force*]
Bld Technol Mgmnt ... Building Technology and Management [*A publication*]
Bl Dte Philos ... Blaetter fuer Deutsche Philosophie [*A publication*]
Bl Dt und Internat Pol ... Blaetter fuer Deutsche und Internationale Politik [*A publication*]
Bl Dtsch Int Polit ... Blaetter fuer Deutsche und Internationale Politik [*A publication*]

BLDUP...... Buildup [*Meteorology*] (FAAC)
BLE............ Bachelor of Library Economics
BLE............ Ballatar Explorations [*Vancouver Stock Exchange symbol*]
BLE............ Basal Level Element [*Genetics*]
BLE............ Basal Level Enhancer [*Genetics*]
B & LE...... Bessemer & Lake Erie Railroad Co.
BLE............ Bessemer & Lake Erie Railroad Co. [*AAR code*]
BLE............ Binary Logic Element [*Data processing*] (BUR)
BlE............ Black Experience [*A publication*]
BLE............ Blacks in Law Enforcement [*An association*] (EA)
BLE............ Blake Resources Ltd. [*Toronto Stock Exchange symbol*]
BLE............ Blunt Leading Edge
BLE............ Bombardment-Induced Light Emission [*Physics*]
BLE............ Borlange [*Sweden*] [*Airport symbol*] (OAG)
B of LE...... Brotherhood of Locomotive Engineers
BLE............ Buddhist League of Esperantists [*Baiersbronn, Federal Republic of Germany*] (EAIO)
BLE............ Budhana Ligo Esperantista [*Buddhist League of Esperantists - BLE*] (EAIO)
BLE............ Bulletin Linguistique et Ethnologique [*A publication*]
BLE............ Bulletin de Litterature Ecclesiastique [*A publication*]
BLe............ Grammatik des Biblische-Aramaeischen [*H. Bauer and P. Leander*] [*A publication*] (BJA)
BLE............ Lake Providence, LA [*Location identifier*] [*FAA*] (FAAL)
Bleacher Finish Tex Chem ... Bleacher, Finisher, and Textile Chemist [*A publication*]
B Leader..... Bar Leader [*A publication*] (DLA)
BL Ec........ Bachelor of Library Economics
BLEC........ Business Law Education Centre [*Australia*]
Bleck......... Bleckley's Reports [*34, 35 Georgia*] [*A publication*] (DLA)
Bleckley..... Bleckley's Reports [*34, 35 Georgia*] [*A publication*] (DLA)
BLED........ Bledisloe [*England*]
BLEDCO... Brooklyn Local Economic Development Corporation
BLEDE...... Backscattered LASER Energy Digitizing Equipment (MCD)
BLegS....... Bachelor of Legal Studies (ADA)
Bl Emp L.... Black on Employer's Liability [*A publication*] (DLA)
BLEND...... Black Enterprise [*A publication*]
BL Eng...... Bachelor of Landscape Engineering
Bleo........... Bleomycin [*Also, B, Bl, BLM*] [*Antineoplastic drug*]
BLEO-COMF ... Bleomycin, Cyclophosphamide, Oncovin [*Vincristine*], Methotrexate, Fluorouracil [*Antineoplastic drug regimen*]
BLERT...... Block Error Rate Test
BLESA...... Bollettino. Laboratorio di Entomologia Agraria "Filippo Silvestri" di Portici [*A publication*]
BLESAS.... Bollettino. Laboratorio di Entomologia Agraria "Filippo Silvestri" de Portici [*A publication*]
BLESMA... British Limbless Ex-Service Men's Association
BLESSED ... Bell Little Electrodata Symbolic System for the Electrodata [*Symbolic assembly program*]
BLESTO-VIII ... Bears, Lions, Eagles, Steelers, Vikings, Colts, Dolphins, and Bills [*Computerized scouting combine for professional football teams; name comprises membership teams*]
BLET........ Bletsoe [*England*]
BLET........ Bureau of Libraries and Educational Technology [*Later, BLLR*] [*HEW*]
BLEU........ Belgium-Luxembourg Economic Union [*Political party*] (PPE)
BLEU........ Blind Landing Experimental Unit [*Aviation*]
BLEVE...... Boiling Liquid Expanding Vapor Explosion [*Chemical engineering*]
BLEWS...... Baseline Electronic Warfare System (MCD)
B Lezoux .... Bulletin. Comite Archeologique de Lezoux [*A publication*]
BLF........... Baluchistan Liberation Front [*Pakistan*] [*Political party*] (PD)
BLF........... Bank of London and South America. Review [*A publication*]
BLF........... Baryta Light Fling (MSA)
BLF........... Bee Line Airlines [*Houston, TX*] [*FAA designator*] (FAAC)
BLF........... Bloemfontein [*South Africa*] [*Seismograph station code, US Geological Survey*] (SEIS)
BLF........... Bluefield [*West Virginia*] [*Airport symbol*] (OAG)
BLF........... Bluff
BLF........... Boundary Layer Flow
BLF........... Busy Lamp Field [*Phone console*] [*Bell System*]
BLF........... Byelorussian Liberation Front (EA)
BLFC........ Brenda Lee Fan Club (EA)
BLFE........ Brotherhood of Locomotive Firemen and Enginemen [*Later, United Transportation Union*] [*AFL-CIO*]
BLFSA...... Blast Furnace and Steel Plant [*A publication*]
BLFSB...... Basic Life Sciences [*A publication*]
BLFST...... Belfast [*City in Northern Ireland*]
BLG .... Bachelor Lake Gold Mines, Inc. [*Toronto Stock Exchange symbol*]
BLG .... Belaga [*Malaysia*] [*Airport symbol*] (OAG)
BLG .... Beluga, AK [*Location identifier*] [*FAA*] (FAAL)
BLG .... Beta-Lactoglobulin [*Biochemistry*]
BlG............ [*The*] Blue and the Gray [*A publication*]
BLG .... Breech Loading Gun
BLG .... Building
BLG .... Business Leader Group [*Washington, DC*] (EA)
BLG .... Laguna Peak [*California*] [*Seismograph station code, US Geological Survey*] (SEIS)

Bl Gesch Tech ... Blaetter fuer Geschichte der Technik. Oesterreichisches Forschungsinstitut fuer Geschichte der Technik [*A publication*]
BLGR........ Blue Grass Breeders, Inc. [*NASDAQ symbol*] (NQ)
Bl Grundstuecks Bau-Wohnungsrecht ... Blaetter fuer Grundstuecks, Bau-, und Wohnungsrecht [*West Germany*] [*A publication*]
BLGTB...... Biologist [*London*] [*A publication*]
Bl Gymnasialschulwesen ... Blaetter fuer das Bayerische Gymnasialschulwesen [*A publication*]
BLH.......... Band-Limited Hiss [*NASA*]
BLH.......... Best's Review. Life/Health Insurance Edition [*A publication*]
BLH.......... Bihar Light Horse [*British military*] (DMA)
Bl H.......... [*Henry*] Blackstone's English Common Pleas Reports [*1788-96*] [*A publication*] (DLA)
BLH.......... Blade Loading Harmonics [*Helicopter*]
Bl & H....... Blake and Hedges' Reports [*2-3 Montana*] [*A publication*] (DLA)
Bl & H....... Blatchford and Howland's United States District Court Reports [*A publication*] (DLA)
BLH.......... Blue Horizon Travel Club [*Cincinnati, OH*] [*FAA designator*] (FAAC)
BLH.......... Blythe [*California*] [*Airport symbol*] (OAG)
BLH.......... Boletin de Estudios Latinoamericanos y del Caribe [*A publication*]
BL-H......... Bristol Laboratories [*Research code symbol*]
BLH.......... British Legion Headquarters
BlH........... Bulletin Hispanique [*A publication*]
BLH .... Historische Grammatik der Hebraeischen Sprache [*H. Bauer and P. Leander*] [*A publication*] (BJA)
Bl Heimatkd ... Blaetter fuer Heimatkunde [*A publication*]
Bl & How ... Blatchford and Howland's United States District Court Reports [*A publication*] (DLA)
BLHS........ Ballistic LASER Holographic System (MCD)
BLI........... Bachelor of Literary Interpretation
BLI........... Bank Leumi Le-Israel
BLI........... Banking Law Institute (EA)
BLI........... Basic Learning Institute
BLI........... Beitraege zur Linguistik und Informationsverarbeitung [*A publication*]
BLI........... Bellingham [*Washington*] [*Airport symbol*] (OAG)
BLI........... Bible Literature International (EA)
Bli........... Bligh's English House of Lords Reports [*A publication*] (DLA)
BLI........... Bondell Industries, Inc. [*Vancouver Stock Exchange symbol*]
BLI........... Brazil Labor Information and Resource Center (EA)
BLI........... Businessland, Incorporated [*NYSE symbol*] (SPSG)
BLI........... Butterfly Lovers International (EA)
BLI........... Buyers Laboratory, Incorporated
B Liaison Inform Adm Centr Econ Finances ... Bulletin de Liaison et d'Information. Administration Centrale de l'Economie et des Finances [*A publication*]
BLib.......... Bachelor of Library Science (ADA)
BLibSc....... Bachelor in Library Science (ADA)
BLIC......... Bureau de Liaison des Industries du Caoutchouc de la CEE [*Rubber Industries Liaison Bureau of the EEC*] [*Belgium*]
BLICD3..... Bibliotheca Lichenologica [*A publication*]
Blick Mus .. Blick ins Museum. Mitteilungen aus den Staatlichen Wissenschaftlichen Museen Dresden [*A publication*]
Blick Rev.... Blickenaderfer. Law Student's Review [*A publication*] (DLA)
Bligh .... Bligh's English House of Lords Reports, Old Series [*1819-21*] [*A publication*] (DLA)
Bligh NS (Eng) ... Bligh's English House of Lords Reports, New Series [*1827-37*] [*A publication*] (DLA)
BLIHS....... Hawkshaw Ranch, Lasqueti Island Historical Society, British Columbia [*Library symbol*] [*National Library of Canada*] (NLC)
BLII.......... Britton Lee, Incorporated [*Los Gatos, CA*] [*NASDAQ symbol*] (NQ)
BLIJ.......... Burma Law Institute. Journal [*A publication*] (DLA)
BLIM......... Lillooet Museum, British Columbia [*Library symbol*] [*National Library of Canada*] (NLC)
B Limousin ... Bulletin. Societe Archeologique et Historique du Limousin [*A publication*]
BLIMP...... Boundary Layer Integral Matrix Procedure (KSC)
BLIMPRON ... Blimp Squadron [*Navy*]
BLIN......... Budget Line Item Number (MCD)
Blind Vis Impair Deaf Blind ... Blindness, Visual Impairment, Deaf-Blindness [*A publication*]
BLing........ Bachelor of Linguistics, University of Manchester [*British*] (DBQ)
BLING....... Bladed Ring [*Turbine component*]
Bli NS....... Bligh's English House of Lords Reports, New Series [*1827-37*] [*A publication*] (DLA)
Bli (OS)..... Bligh's English House of Lords Reports, Old Series [*1819-21*] [*A publication*] (DLA)
BLIP .... Background-Limited Infrared Photography
BLIP .... Boundary Layer Instrumentation Package [*Meteorology*]
BLIP .... Brookhaven Linac Isotope Producer [*Nuclear energy*]
BLIPS....... Basic Learning in Primary Schools [*Australia*]
BLIS .... Baffle/Liner Interface Seal [*Nuclear energy*] (NRCH)
BLIS .... Base Level Inquiry System
BLIS .... Bell Laboratories Interpretive System [*Computer program*]

BLIS	Bliss & Laughlin Industries, Inc. [*NASDAQ symbol*] (CTT)
BLIS	Boundary Layer Instrumentation System [*Meteorology*]
BLIS	Business Lead Identification System [*Timeplace, Inc.*] [*Database*]
BLISK.......	Bladed Disc [*Turbine component*]
BLISS.......	Balloon-Borne LASER In-Situ Sensor [*Spectrometer*]
BLISS.......	Basic Language for the Implementation of System Software [*Data processing*]
BLISS.......	Basic Library Inquiry Subsystem [*Data processing*]
BLISS.......	Betriebswirtschaftliches Literatursuchsystem [*Business Literature Search System*] [*Society for Business Information*] [*Information service or system*] (IID)
BLISS.......	Bibliographic and Library Information Search Service [*Louisiana State University*]
BLISS.......	Bibliographic and Library Instruction for Secondary Schools
BLISS.......	Boundary Layer Induction Stack Suppressor (CAAL)
Bliss	Delaware County Reports [*Pennsylvania*] [*A publication*] (DLA)
Bliss Co Pl ...	Bliss on Code Pleading [*A publication*] (DLA)
Bliss Ins	Bliss on Life Insurance [*A publication*] (DLA)
Bliss NY Co ...	Bliss' New York Code [*A publication*] (DLA)
Bliss NY Code ...	Bliss' New York Code, Annotated [*A publication*] (DLA)
B Lit	Bachelor of Letters
B Lit	Bachelor of Literature
B Lit E	Bulletin de Litterature Ecclesiastique [*A publication*]
B Litt........	Bachelor of Letters
B Litt........	Bachelor of Literature
BLittComm ...	Bachelor of Literature and Communication
BLIX..........	Bleach-Fix [*Photography*]
BLJ	Bachelor of Letters in Journalism
BLJ	Bellabon Resources [*Vancouver Stock Exchange symbol*]
BLJ	Bihar Law Journal Reports [*India*] [*A publication*] (DLA)
BLJ	British Library Journal [*A publication*]
BLJ	Bumper Lift Jack
BLJ	Burma Law Journal [*A publication*] (DLA)
Bl Judgm....	Black on Judgments [*A publication*] (DLA)
BLK..........	Benign Lichenoid Keratosis [*Medicine*]
BLK..........	Black (KSC)
BLK..........	Black [*Thoroughbred racing*]
BLK..........	Black Butte [*Montana*] [*Seismograph station code, US Geological Survey*] [*Closed*] (SEIS)
BLK..........	Black Diamond Resources [*Vancouver Stock Exchange symbol*]
BLK..........	Blackpool [*England*] [*Airport symbol*] (OAG)
BLK..........	Blank (MSA)
BLK..........	Block [*Unit of data*]
BLK..........	Bulk
BLK..........	Bulk Carriers Conference, Arlington VA [*STAC*]
BLK..........	Burrell-Lawrence-Kennedy [*Vacuum milking device*]
BLK B	Bulk in Barrels [*Freight*]
BLK CAR ..	Bulk Carrier [*Shipping*] (DS)
BLKD........	Blocked
BLKD........	Bulkhead (MUGU)
BLKG........	Blanking (MSA)
BLKG........	Blocking (MSA)
BLKGD......	Blanking Die
BLKHD	Bulkhead (KSC)
Blk Lib	Black Liberation [*A publication*]
BLKM.......	Black Mesa & Lake Powell [*AAR code*]
BLKN	Blacken
BLKNG	Blackening
Blk Panth...	Black Panther [*A publication*]
BLKS........	Blocks [*Freight*]
Blk Schol ...	Black Scholar [*A publication*]
BLKSTP....	Blackstrap [*Freight*]
BLKT........	Blanket (MSA)
BLL...........	Baccalaureus Legum [*Bachelor of Laws*]
BLL...........	Bachelor of Latin Letters
BLL...........	Ball Corp. [*NYSE symbol*] (SPSG)
BLL...........	Barrels (ROG)
BLL...........	Base of Lateral Lip
BLL...........	Belaruskaia Litaratura [*A publication*]
BLL...........	Bellevue Public Library, Bellevue, NE [*OCLC symbol*] (OCLC)
BLL...........	Bellingham [*Washington*] [*Seismograph station code, US Geological Survey*] [*Closed*] (SEIS)
BLL...........	Below Lower Limit (IEEE)
BLL...........	Bibliographie Linguistischer Literatur [*Bibliography of Linguistic Literature*] [*Stadt- und Universitatbibliothek Frankfurt*] [*Information service or system*] [*Information service or system*] (CRD)
BLL...........	Billund [*Denmark*] [*Airport symbol*] (OAG)
BLL...........	Boch & Limoges [*Vancouver Stock Exchange symbol*]
BLL...........	Bovine Lung Lipids [*Biochemistry*]
BLL...........	British Library Lending Division
Bl Law Tracts ...	Blackstone's Law Tracts [*A publication*] (DLA)
Bl LD	Black's Law Dictionary [*A publication*] (DLA)
Bl LD	Blount's Law Dictionary [*A publication*] (DLA)
BLLD........	British Library Lending Division
BLLE........	Balanced Line Logical Element
BLLIAX....	Bratislavske Lekarske Listy [*A publication*]
Bl LJ	Black Law Journal [*A publication*]
BLLN.........	Bullion (ROG)
BLLR........	Bureau of Libraries and Learning Resources [*Formerly, BLET*] [*HEW*]
BLL Rev.....	BLL [*British Library Lending Division*] Review [*A publication*]
BLL Review ...	British Library. Lending Division. Review [*A publication*]
BLLS	Boundary Layer LIDAR System (MCD)
Bl LT.........	Blackstone's Law Tracts [*A publication*] (DLA)
Bll Univ Tenn Agr Exp Sta ...	Bulletin. University of Tennessee. Agricultural Experiment Station [*A publication*]
BLLW........	Bell [*W.*] & Co., Inc. [*NASDAQ symbol*] (NQ)
BLM	Bachelor of Landscape Management
BLM	Basic Language Machine [*Computer*] (BUR)
BLM	Belmac Corp. [*AMEX symbol*] (SPSG)
BLM	Belmar/Farmingdale, NJ [*Location identifier*] [*FAA*] (FAAL)
BLM	Beso la Mano [*(I Kiss Your Hand) Respectfully*] [*Spanish*] [*Correspondence*]
BLM	Best Loiter Mach Number [*Aviation*]
BLM	Bilayer Lipid Membrane [*Physical chemistry*]
BLM	Bimolecular Lipid Membrane
BLM	Bleomycin [*Also, B, Bl, Bleo*] [*Antineoplastic drug*]
BLM	Blinking Light Monitor
BLM	Blue Mountain [*Alaska*] [*Seismograph station code, US Geological Survey*] (SEIS)
BLM	Bolletini di Litteratura Moderna [*A publication*]
BLM	Bonniers Litteraera Magasin [*A publication*]
BLM	Book League Monthly [*A publication*]
BLM	Book-Library-Management [*System*]
BLM	Boundary Layer Model (MCD)
BLM	Bureau of Land Management [*Department of the Interior*]
BLMag.......	Bonniers Litteraera Magasin [*A publication*]
BLMB........	Benzoyl Leuco Methylene Blue [*Organic chemistry*]
BLM (Bon Lit) ...	BLM (Bonniers Litterara Magasin) [*A publication*]
BLMC........	British League of Male Chauvinists (EAIO)
BLMCS	Base Level Maintenance Cost System (AFIT)
Blm Neg.....	Bloomfield's Manumission (or Negro) Cases [*New Jersey*] [*A publication*] (DLA)
BLMNR.....	Bureau of Land Management. Alaska. News Release [*A publication*]
BLMP........	Airship International Ltd. [*New York, NY*] [*NASDAQ symbol*] (NQ)
BLMPS	Base Level Military Personnel System
BLMR........	Bureau of Labor - Management Reports [*Department of Labor*]
BLMRA	British Leather Manufacturers Research Association
BLMRA J ...	BLMRA [*British Leather Manufacturers' Research Association*] Journal [*A publication*]
BLMRCP ..	Bureau of Labor - Management Relations and Cooperative Programs [*Department of Labor*]
BLMTH	Bellmouth [*Design engineering*]
BLN	Balloon (AFM)
BLN	Banca Nazionale del Lavoro. Quarterly Review [*A publication*]
BLN	Blend (MSA)
BLN	Blyn Mountain [*Washington*] [*Seismograph station code, US Geological Survey*] (SEIS)
BLN	Bottomline [*A publication*]
BLN	Bullion (ROG)
BLND	Reading Material for the Blind and Physically Handicapped [*Library of Congress*] [*Information service or system*] (CRD)
BLNDMSA ...	Black Top and National Delaine Merino Sheep Association (EA)
BLNE........	Beeline, Inc. [*NASDAQ symbol*] (NQ)
BLNG	Belling
BLNKT......	Blanket (AAG)
Bl NS	Bligh's English House of Lords Reports, New Series [*A publication*] (DLA)
BLO	Base Level Operations
BLO	Bellco Energy Corp. [*Vancouver Stock Exchange symbol*]
BLO	Below
BLO	Below Clouds [*Aviation code*]
BLO	Black Liquor Oxidation [*For pollution control in paper mills*]
BLO	Blocking [*Telecommunications*] (TEL)
BLO	Blonduos [*Iceland*] [*Airport symbol*] (OAG)
BLO	Bloomfield College, Bloomfield, NJ [*OCLC symbol*] (OCLC)
BLO	Bloomington [*Indiana*] [*Seismograph station code, US Geological Survey*] (SEIS)
BLO	Blower (KSC)
BLO	Bombardment Liaison Officer [*Navy*]
BLO	British Liaison Officer
BLO	Building Liaison Officer (ADA)
BLO	Laconia, NH [*Location identifier*] [*FAA*] (FAAL)
BLOAA	Biologia [*Bratislava*] [*A publication*]
BLOB........	Binary Large Object [*Data processing*]
BLOC	Battalion Logistical Operations Center [*Military*] (INF)
BLOC	Block Drug Co., Inc. [*NASDAQ symbol*] (NQ)
BLOC	Block-Oriented Compiler
BLOC	Blockade (AABC)
BLOC	Blockage
BLOC	Booth Library On-Line Circulation [*Data processing system*] [*Eastern Illinois University*] [*Charleston, IL*]
BLODI.......	Block Diagram Compiler
BLODIB....	Block Diagram Compiler B (IEEE)
BLOEMF ..	Bloemfontein [*South Africa*] (ROG)

BLOKOPS ... Blockade Operations [*Military*] (NVT)
BLOM .... Booster Lift-Off Mass [*NASA*] (KSC)
Blood Bank Technol 2nd Ed ... Blood Bank Technology. 2nd Edition [*A publication*]
Blood Purif ... Blood Purification [*A publication*]
Blood Ther J .. Blood Therapy Journal [*A publication*]
Blood Vess ... Blood Vessels [*A publication*]
Bloom Man ... Bloomfield's Manumission (or Negro) Cases [*New Jersey*] [*A publication*]
Bloom Man Neg Cas ... Bloomfield's Manumission (or Negro) Cases [*New Jersey*] [*A publication*] (DLA)
BLOOP...... Benevolent and Loyal Order of Pessimists (EA)
Bl Orcl ...... Black Oracle [*A publication*]
BLOS......... Beyond Line of Sight (MCD)
BLOSSOM ... Basic Liberation of Smokers and Sympathizers of Marijuana
BLOT......... Book List. Society for Old Testament Studies [*A publication*]
BLOT......... British Library of Tape
Blount .... Blount's Law Dictionary [*A publication*] (DLA)
Blount Frag Ant ... Blount. Fragmenta Antiquitatis [*A publication*] (DLA)
Blount LD .. Blount's Law Dictionary [*A publication*] (DLA)
Blount Ten ... Blount on Tenures [*A publication*] (DLA)
Blount Tr ... Blount's Impeachment Trial [*A publication*] (DLA)
BLOW...... Booster Lift-Off Weight [*NASA*] (KSC)
BLOWS...... British Library of Wildlife Sound
BLP........... Back Loading Point [*Military*] [*British*]
BLP........... Ball Lock Pin
BLP........... Barbados Labor Party
BLP........... Basic Launch Plan [*NASA*] (KSC)
BLP........... Basket Loading Pool [*Nuclear energy*] (NRCH)
BLP........... Bela Lyons Pratt [*Designer's mark, when appearing on US coins*]
BLP........... Bilevel Pulse (MCD)
BLP........... Blaettchenpulver [*Flake powder*] [*German military - World War II*]
BL & P .... Blind Loaded and Plugged [*Projectile*]
BLP........... Blood Pressure [*Medicine*]
BLP........... Blue Line Print
BLP........... Bombesin-Like Peptide [*Biochemistry*]
BLP........... Bombing Landplane
BLP........... Bonded Laminates Profiled PLC [*British*]
BLP........... Book of Living Poems [*A publication*]
BLP........... Botswana Liberal Party [*Political party*] (PPW)
BLP........... Boundary Layer Profile [*Meteorology*]
BLP........... Bypass Label Processing [*Data processing*]
BLP........... Lompoc [*California*] [*Seismograph station code, US Geological Survey*] (SEIS)
BLPA........ Barley Leaf Piece Agar [*Microbiology*]
BLPA........ Best Loved Poems of the American People [*A publication*]
BLPC........ Backward Limit Photocell
Blpc........... Blood Lymphocytes Particle Counter [*Instrumentation*] [*Medicine*]
BLPES....... British Library of Political and Economic Science [*London School of Economics*]
BLP L & M Cas ... Brainard's Legal Precedents in Land and Mining Cases [*United States*] [*A publication*] (DLA)
BL/PP........ Bumper Limiter/Protective Plates (MCD)
BLPPD9 .... Bulletin Lembaga Penelitian Peternakan [*A publication*]
B & L Pr..... Bullen and Leake's Precedents of Pleading [*A publication*] (DLA)
Bl Pr Cas..... Blatchford's Prize Cases [*United States*] [*A publication*] (DLA)
Bl Prize ...... Blatchford's Prize Cases [*United States*] [*A publication*] (DLA)
BLPYA ...... Biological Psychology [*A publication*]
BLPZZ ...... Bent Logarithmically Periodic Zig-Zags
BLQ .... Blue Gold Resources [*Vancouver Stock Exchange symbol*]
BLQ .... Bologna [*Italy*] [*Airport symbol*] (OAG)
BLR........... Bahamas Law Reports [*A publication*] (DLA)
BLR........... Bangalore [*India*] [*Airport symbol*] (OAG)
BLR........... Barbados Law Reports [*A publication*] (DLA)
BLR........... Barrier Layer Rectifier
BLR........... Baseline Restorer (IEEE)
BLR........... Baylor Law Review [*A publication*]
BLR........... Belorussian Review [*Munich*] [*A publication*]
BLR........... Below Layer Range (NVT)
BLR........... Bengal Law Reports, High Courts [*India*] [*A publication*] (DLA)
BLR........... Bermuda Law Reports [*A publication*] (DLA)
BLR........... Beyond Local Repair [*Weaponry*] [*British*]
BLR........... Black Rapids [*Alaska*] [*Seismograph station code, US Geological Survey*] (SEIS)
Bl R .... [*Sir William*] Blackstone's English King's Bench Reports [*1746-80*] [*A publication*] (DLA)
BLR........... Blower (NVT)
BLR........... Bodleian Library Record [*A publication*]
BLR........... Boiler (AAG)
BLR........... Bolar Pharmaceutical Co. [*AMEX symbol*] (SPSG)
BLR........... Bombay Law Reporter [*India*] [*A publication*] (DLA)
BLR........... Breech-Loading Rifle
BLR........... Business Law Reports [*A publication*]
BLR........... Business and Law Review [*Corporate Agents, Inc.*] [*Information service or system*] (CRD)
BLR........... Business Law Review [*A publication*]

BLRAC...... Bengal Law Reports, Appeal Cases [*India*] [*A publication*]
BLRCA...... Bell Laboratories Record [*A publication*]
B L Rev ...... Bluegrass Literary Review [*A publication*]
BLRG......... Blue Ridge Real Estate Co./Big Boulder Corp. [*NASDAQ symbol*] (NQ)
BLRG........ Breech-Loading Rifled Guns
BLRI......... Blue Ridge Parkway [*National Park Service designation*]
BLRP......... Best Loved Religious Poems [*A publication*]
BLRPC...... Bengal Law Reports, Privy Council [*India*] [*A publication*] (DLA)
BLR Suppl Vol ... Bengal Law Reports, Supplemental Volume, Full Bench Rulings [*India*] [*A publication*] (DLA)
BLR Sup Vol ... Bengal Law Reports, Supplemental Volume, Full Bench Rulings [*India*] [*A publication*] (ILCA)
BLRT......... Brotherly Love, Relief, and Truth [*Freemasonry*]
BLS......... Bachelor of Liberal Studies
BLS......... Bachelor of Library and Information Studies
BLS......... Bachelor of Library Science
BLS......... Balanced Line System
BLS......... Balloon Launching Station
BLS......... Band-Limited Signal
BLS......... Barrels [*Shipping*]
BLS......... Basic Life Support [*System*]
BLS......... Bel-Air Resources [*Vancouver Stock Exchange symbol*]
BLS......... Bela Lugosi Society (EA)
BLS......... Bell Log System
BLS......... BellSouth Corp. [*NYSE symbol*] (SPSG)
BLS......... Benevolenti Lectori Salutem [*Greeting to the Well-Wishing Reader*] [*Latin*]
BLS........... Black Liquor Solids [*Pulp and paper technology*]
BlS........... Black Scholar [*A publication*]
BLS........... Blood and Lymphatic System [*Medicine*]
Bl S........... Blood Sugar [*Medicine*]
Bls........... Bolivares [*Monetary unit*] [*Venezuela*]
BLS........... Botswana, Lesotho, Swaziland
BLS........... Bottom Left Side (MCD)
BLS........... Boundary Layer Separation
BLS........... Branch Line Society [*British*]
BLS........... Broadband Latching Switch
BLS........... Brooklyn Law School [*New York, NY*]
BLS........... Bureau of Labor Standards [*Absorbed by OSHA*] [*Department of Labor*] [*Washington, DC*]
BLS........... Bureau of Labor Statistics [*Washington, DC*] [*Department of Labor*]
BLS........... Burst Limit Switch (MCD)
BLS........... Business Lawyer. Special Issue [*A publication*]
BLS........... Employee Relations [*A publication*]
BLS 1892 ... Labor and Material Requirements for Private Multi-Family Housing Construction. BLS Bulletin 1892. US Bureau of Labor Statistics [*A publication*]
BLS 2070 ... Handbook of Labor Statistics. BLS Bulletin 2070. US Bureau of Labor Statistics [*A publication*]
BLS 2121 ... Economic Projections to 1990. BLS Bulletin 2121. US Bureau of Labor Statistics [*A publication*]
BLS 2128 ... Productivity Measures for Selected Industries, 1954-80. BLS Bulletin 2128. US Bureau of Labor Statistics [*A publication*]
BLS 2175 ... Handbook of Labor Statistics. BLS Bulletin 2175. US Bureau of Labor Statistics [*A publication*]
BLS 2197 ... Employment Projections for 1995. BLS Bulletin 2197. US Bureau of Labor Statistics [*A publication*]
BLS 2202 ... Occupational Projections and Training. BLS Bulletin 2202. US Bureau of Labor Statistics [*A publication*]
BLS 2224 ... Productivity Measures for Selected Industries, 1954-83. BLS Bulletin 2224. US Bureau of Labor Statistics [*A publication*]
BLS 2253 ... Employment Projections for 1995; Data and Methods. BLS Bulletin 2253. US Bureau of Labor Statistics [*A publication*]
BLS 2256 ... Productivity Measures for Selected Industries, 1958-84. BLS Bulletin 2256. US Bureau of Labor Statistics [*A publication*]
BLSA........ Black Law Student Association (EA)
BLSA........ British Legal Services Agency (DLA)
BLSB....... Ball-Lock Separation Bolt
BLS Bull ..... Bureau of Labor Statistics. Bulletin [*A publication*] (DLA)
BL Sc .... Bachelor of Library Science
BLSC......... Bio-Logic Systems Corporation [*NASDAQ symbol*] (NQ)
BlSch......... Black Scholar [*A publication*]
BLS CPI .... CPI [*Consumer Price Index*] Detailed Report. US and City Averages. US Bureau of Labor Statistics [*A publication*]
BLSCR....... Bollettino Linguistico per la Storia e la Cultura Regionale [*A publication*]
BLSG........ Brigade Logistic Support Group [*Marine Corps*] (CINC)
BLSJICP ... Beam Lead Sealed Junction Integrated Circuit Package (AABC)
Bl Soc Chim Belg ... Bulletin. Societe Chimique de Belgique [*A publication*]
Bl Soc Chim Ind ... Bulletin. Societe de Chimie Industrielle [*A publication*]
BL & SP..... Butter, Lard, and Salt Provisions
BLS PPI..... United States. Bureau of Labor Statistics. Producer Prices and Price Indexes [*A publication*]

BLS PPIA ... Producer Prices and Price Indexes [*later, Producer Price Indexes*]. Supplement to Data for 1983. US Bureau of Labor Statistics [*A publication*]
BLS Review ... United States. Bureau of Labor Statistics. Monthly Labor Review [*A publication*]
BLSS.......... Base Level Self-Sufficiency [*Air Force*]
BLST .... Ballast (MSA)
BLST .... Bankson Language Screening Test [*Child development test*]
BL/ST........ Bluestone [*Inferior gin or whiskey*] [*Slang*] (ADA)
BLSTL....... Billet Steel (MSA)
BLS Whole ... Wholesale Prices and Price Indexes. US Bureau of Labor Statistics [*A publication*]
BLS Whole A ... Wholesale Prices and Price Indexes. Supplement. US Bureau of Labor Statistics [*A publication*]
B Lt .... Bachelor of Literature
BLT........... Bacon, Lettuce, and Tomato Sandwich
BLT........... Baltic Aviation, Inc. [*Denver, CO*] [*FAA designator*] (FAAC)
BLT........... Baltimore Law Transcript [*A publication*] (DLA)
BLT........... BASIC [*Beginner's All-Purpose Symbolic Instruction Code*] Language Translator [*Data processing*] (MCD)
BLT........... Battalion Landing Team [*Military*]
BLT........... Belgie/Economische en Handelsvoorlichting [*A publication*]
BLT........... Bert Leston Taylor [*American columnist, 1866-1921*] [*Initials used as pseudonym*]
BLT........... Biltrite Nightingale, Inc. [*Toronto Stock Exchange symbol*]
BLT........... Blackwater [*Australia*] [*Airport symbol*] (OAG)
BL & T .... Blind Loaded and Traced [*Projectile*]
BLT........... Block Transfer [*Data processing*]
BLT........... Blood-Clot Lysis Time [*Medicine*]
Bl T .... Blood Type [*Medicine*]
BLT........... Bloomer Learning Test [*Intelligence test*]
BLT........... Blount, Inc. [*AMEX symbol*] (SPSG)
BLT........... Boat Landing Team
BLT........... Bolt (MSA)
BLT........... Borrowed Light (KSC)
BLT........... Break-Loose Torque [*Automotive engineering*]
BLT........... Brethren Life and Thought [*A publication*]
BLT........... Built (FAAC)
BLT........... Bureau of Land Transport [*Philippines*] (DS)
BLT........... Burma Law Times [*A publication*] (DLA)
BLT........... But Less Than
BLTBAI..... Folia Societatis Scientiarum Lublinensis. Biologia [*A publication*]
BLTC........ Bottom-Loading Transfer Cask [*Nuclear energy*] (NRCH)
BLTDA...... Burley Leaf Tobacco Dealers Association (EA)
Bl Technikgesch ... Blaetter fuer Technikgeschichte. Forschungsinstitut fuer Technikgeschichte in Wien [*A publication*]
BLTG........ Belting [*Freight*]
BLTI.......... Better Lawn and Turf Institute (EA)
Bl Ti.......... Block on Tithes [*A publication*] (DLA)
BLTIN....... Built-In
BLTLEX.... Battalion Landing Exercise [*Military*] (NVT)
BLTM........ Battalion Level Training Model [*DoD*]
BLTND..... [*The*] Bulletin [*A publication*]
BLTSG ...... Bulletin. Lutheran Theological Seminary [*Gettysburg*] [*A publication*]
Bl TT......... Blackwell's Tax Titles [*A publication*] (DLA)
BLTVC ..... Boundary Layer Thrust Vector Control (MCD)
BLTW........ Trinity Western College, Langley, British Columbia [*Library symbol*] [*National Library of Canada*] (NLC)
BLU .... Basic Link Unit [*Data processing*] (BUR)
BLU .... Basic Logic Unit (IEEE)
BLU .... Blue (KSC)
BLU .... Blue Chip Value Fund [*NYSE symbol*] (SPSG)
Blu............ Bluett's Advocate's Note Book, Isle Of Man [*1720-1846*] [*A publication*] (DLA)
BLU .... Bomb Line Unit (MCD)
BLU .... Bomb, Live Unit (AFM)
BLU .... Emigrant Gap, CA [*Location identifier*] [*FAA*] (FAAL)
BLUD........ Immucor, Inc. [*Norcross, GA*] [*NASDAQ symbol*] (NQ)
BLUE........ Best Linear Unbiased Estimator [*Statistics*]
Blue Chip ... Blue Chip Economic Indicators [*A publication*]
Blue Cross Assoc Res Ser ... Blue Cross Association. Research Series [*A publication*]
Blue Cross Rep ... Blue Cross Reports [*A publication*]
Bluegrass ... Bluegrass Unlimited [*A publication*]
Blues .... Blues Unlimited [*A publication*]
Blue Sky L Rep ... Blue Sky Law Reporter [*Commerce Clearing House*] [*A publication*] (DLA)
Blue Sky L Rep CCH ... Blue Sky Law Reports. Commerce Clearing House [*A publication*]
Bluett .... Bluett's Isle Of Man Cases [*A publication*] (DLA)
B Lugo........ Boletin. Comision Provincial de Monumentos Historicos y Artisticos de Lugo [*A publication*]
BLUMA .... Bollettino. Unione Matematica Italiana [*A publication*]
Blum B'k'cy ... Blumenstiel on Bankruptcy [*A publication*] (DLA)
B Lund .... Bulletin. Societe de Lettres de Lund [*A publication*]
Blunt Mod Volk ... Bluntschli. Das Moderne Voelkerrecht [*A publication*] (DLA)
BLUP........ Best Linear Unbiased Prediction [*Genetics*]
BLUSF ...... Blue Sky Oil & Gas [*NASDAQ symbol*] (NQ)

BLux .... Bulletin Linguistique et Ethnologique. Institut Granducal (Luxembourg) [*A publication*]
BLV............ Bailadores [*Venezuela*] [*Seismograph station code, US Geological Survey*] (SEIS)
BLV............ Belleville, IL [*Location identifier*] [*FAA*] (FAAL)
BLV............ Belvedere Corp. [*AMEX symbol*] (SPSG)
BLV............ Bleed Valve (MCD)
BLV............ [*The*] Book of Living Verse [*A publication*]
BLV............ Bovine Leukemia Virus
BLV............ British Legion Village
BLV............ Scott Air Force Base Library, Scott AFB, IL [*OCLC symbol*] (OCLC)
BLVD........ Boulevard (EY)
BLVD........ Boulevard Bancorp, Inc. [*Chicago, IL*] [*NASDAQ symbol*] (NQ)
BLVS......... Bibliothek des Literarischen Vereins (Stuttgart) [*A publication*]
BLW .... Bellwether Resources [*Vancouver Stock Exchange symbol*]
BLW .... Below (MSA)
BL W .... Black World [*A publication*]
Bl W .... [*Sir William*] Blackstone's English King's Bench Reports [*1746-80*] [*A publication*] (DLA)
BLW .... Boiling Light Water [*Nuclear energy*]
BLW .... Business Lawyer [*A publication*]
BLW .... Waimanalo, HI [*Location identifier*] [*FAA*] (FAAL)
BLWC........ Bread Loaf Writers Conference (EA)
BLWDN..... Blowdown [*Chemical engineering*]
B/LWL........ Beam to Waterline Length
Bl & W Mines ... Blanchard and Weeks' Leading Cases on Mines [*A publication*] (DLA)
BLWR........ Blower (KSC)
BLWS......... Bellows (MSA)
BLWT........ Blowout
BLWT........ Blowtorch
Bl Wuerttemb Kirchengesch ... Blaetter fuer Wuerttembergische Kirchengeschichte [*A publication*]
bl x .... Bleeding Time [*Clinical chemistry*]
BLY............ Bally Manufacturing Corp. [*NYSE symbol*] (SPSG)
BLY............ Banja Luka [*Yugoslavia*] [*Seismograph station code, US Geological Survey*] (SEIS)
BLY............ Bell Molybdenum Mines [*Vancouver Stock Exchange symbol*]
BLY............ Milwaukee, WI [*Location identifier*] [*FAA*] (FAAL)
BLYH .... Blyth Holdings, Inc. [*NASDAQ symbol*] (NQ)
BLYM........ Bursal Lymphomas [*Oncology*]
BLYP......... Bernstein, Lee, Yang, Primakoff [*Physicists*]
Bly Us .... Blydenburgh. Law of Usury [*1844*] [*A publication*] (DLA)
BLYV......... Blyvooruitzicht Gold Mining Co. Ltd. [*NASDAQ symbol*] (NQ)
BLZ........... Belize [*ANSI three-letter standard code*] (CNC)
blz.............. Bladzijde [*Page*] [*Netherlands*] (ILCA)
BLZ........... Blantyre [*Malawi*] [*Airport symbol*] (OAG)
BLZ........... Bolzano [*Italy*] [*Seismograph station code, US Geological Survey*] (SEIS)
BLZ........... Boundary Layer Zone
BLZD........ Blizzard [*Meteorology*] (FAAC)
Bl Zuckerruebenbau ... Blaetter fuer Zuckerruebenbau [*A publication*]
BM............ Baba Mezi'a [*or Bava Mezi'a*] (BJA)
BM............ Bachelor of Mathematics
BM............ Bachelor of Medicine
BM............ Bachelor of Music
BM............ Bachelor of Physic
BM............ Back Marker [*Aviation*]
BM............ Backmixing [*Chemical engineering*]
BM............ Baghdader Mitteilungen [*A publication*]
BM............ Balance of Material (MCD)
BM............ Ballistic Missile (AFM)
BM............ Balneum Mariae [*Salt-Water Bath*] [*Medicine*] (ROG)
BM............ Balneum Marinum [*Sea-Water Bath*] [*Medicine*]
BM............ Baltische Monatsschrift [*A publication*]
BM............ Banber Matenadarani [*A publication*]
BM............ Banca Mondiale [*World Bank*] [*Italian*]
BM............ Banco Mundial [*World Bank*] [*Spanish*]
BM............ Bandmaster (ROG)
BM............ Bankers' Magazine [*A publication*]
BM............ Bar Mitzvah (BJA)
BM............ Basal Medium [*Microbiology*]
BM............ Basal Metabolism [*Medicine*]
BM............ Base Maintenance [*Air Force*] (AFM)
BM............ Basement Membrane [*Medicine*]
BM............ Basilar Membrane [*Ear anatomy*]
BM............ Battle Management [*Military*] (SDI)
BM............ Be-'eravon Mugbal (BJA)
BM............ Beachmaster
BM............ Beam (KSC)
BM............ Beam Monitor
BM............ Bear Market [*Investment term*]
BM............ Beata Maria [*The Blessed Virgin*] [*Latin*]
BM............ Beatae Memoriae [*Of Blessed Memory*] [*Latin*]
BM............ Before Marriage
BM............ Before Midnight (ROG)
BM............ Beit Mikra (BJA)
BM............ Ben Marcato [*Well Marked*] [*Music*] (ROG)

BM............ Ben Monroe's Kentucky Reports [*A publication*] (DLA)
BM............ Bench Maintenance [*NASA*] (KSC)
BM............ Bench Mark Control Point [*Nautical charts*]
BM............ Benchmark [*Computer system evaluation*]
BM............ Bending Moment [*Aerospace*]
BM............ Bene Merenti [*To the Well-Deserving*] [*Latin*]
BM............ Benediktinische Monatshefte [*Beuron*] [*A publication*]
BM............ Bermuda [*ANSI two-letter standard code*] (CNC)
bm............ Bermuda [*MARC country of publication code*] [*Library of Congress*] (LCCP)
BM............ Beth Mikra [*A publication*]
BM............ Bibliotheca Mathematica [*Elsevier Book Series*] [*A publication*]
BM............ Bibliotheque du Museon (BJA)
BM............ Bill of Materials [*Manufacturing*] (MUGU)
BM............ Billet Master [*Military*] [*British*] (ROG)
BM............ Bimonthly
BM............ Binary Multiply
BM............ Binding Margin [*Bookbinding*] (ADA)
BM............ Biomatrix
BM............ Bishop and Martyr [*Church calendars*]
BM............ Black Male
BM............ Black Mountain [*California*]
BM............ Black Muslim
BM............ Blackwood's Magazine [*A publication*]
BM............ Blasius de Morcono [*Flourished, 14th century*] [*Authority cited in pre-1607 legal work*] (DSA)
BM............ Blind Matching [*Parapsychology*]
BM............ Blow Molding [*Bottle manufacturing*]
BM............ Blue Mountains [*Australia*]
BM............ Bluegrass Music News [*A publication*]
BM............ Blume [*Federal Republic of Germany*] [*ICAO aircraft manufacturer identifier*] (ICAO)
BM............ Board Measure [*Lumber*]
BM............ Board's Minute [*Custom house*] [*British*] (ROG)
BM............ Boatswain's Mate [*Navy rating*]
BM............ Body Mass [*Medicine*]
BM............ Body Mounted (MCD)
BM............ Bohr Magneton [*Atomic physics*]
B & M .... Boiler and Machinery
BM............ Boilermaker [*Military*] [*British*]
BM............ Bonae Memoriae [*Of Happy Memory*] [*Latin*]
BM............ Bond Maturity [*Investment term*]
BM............ Bone Marker [*Aviation*]
BM............ Bone Marrow
BM............ Bonniers Maenadstidning [*Stockholm*] [*A publication*]
Bm............ Bookman [*A publication*]
B of M .... Books of the Month [*A publication*]
BM............ Boom (DS)
BM............ Bordmechaniker [*Flight engineer*] [*German military - World War II*]
B & M .... Boston & Maine Corp.
BM............ Boston & Maine Corp. [*AAR code*]
BM............ Boundary Marker (MCD)
BM............ Bowel Movement [*Medicine*]
BM............ Brake Electromagnet
BM............ Branch Manager (MCD)
BM............ Branch Material [*Military*] (AABC)
BM............ Branch Memorandum
BM............ Branch on Minus
BM............ Bravery Medal (ADA)
BM............ Breakdown Maintenance
BM............ Brecon and Merthyr Railway [*Wales*]
BM............ Breech Mechanism [*of a weapon*]
BM............ Brigade Major
BM............ Brightness Merit
B-M............ Bristol-Myers Co.
BM............ British Midland Airways Ltd.
BM............ British Movement [*Political party*]
BM............ British Museum [*London*]
BM............ British Museum. Quarterly [*A publication*]
BM............ Broad Measure (ADA)
BM............ Bronze Medal
B and M ..... Brown Ale and Mild Bitters [*British*] (DSUE)
B & M .... Browne and MacNamara's Railway Cases [*A publication*] (DLA)
BM............ Bubble Memory [*Data storage device*] [*Data processing*] (BUR)
BM............ Buccal Mass [*Dentistry*]
BM............ Buccomesial [*Dentistry*]
B/M............ Buffer Module [*Data processing*]
B/M............ Buffer/Multiplexer [*Data processing*] (CET)
BM............ Bulk Mail
BM............ Bulletin Monumental [*A publication*]
BM............ Bulletin Monumental. Societe Francaise d'Archeologie [*A publication*]
BM............ Bureau of Medicine [*of FDA*]
BM............ Bureau of Mines [*Department of the Interior*]
B of M .... Bureau of Mines [*Department of the Interior*]
BM............ Bureau of the Mint [*Department of the Treasury*]
BM............ Burgomaster
BM............ Burlington Magazine [*A publication*]

BM............ Burrow's Reports Tempore Mansfield [*England*] [*A publication*] (DLA)
BM............ Business Machine
BM............ Business Manager (MCD)
BM............ Business Monitor. Monthly Statistics [*A publication*]
BM............ Butts Master [*British and Canadian*] [*World War II*]
BM............ Buyers' Market [*Investment term*]
BM............ Monitor [*Ship*] [*Navy*] (MCD)
BM............ Moore's Reports [*England*] [*A publication*] (DLA)
BM............ Societa Aero Trasporti Italiani SpA [*Italy*] [*ICAO designator*] (ICDA)
BM1.......... Boatswain's Mate, First Class [*Navy rating*]
BM2.......... Boatswain's Mate, Second Class [*Navy rating*]
BM3.......... Boatswain's Mate, Third Class [*Navy rating*]
BMA .... Bachelor of Municipal Administration
BMA .... Backup Maintenance Activity (MCD)
BMA .... Bahrain Monetary Agency (IMH)
BMA .... Balanced Magnetic Amplifier
BMA .... Bangkok Metropolitan Administration [*Thailand*] (DS)
BMA .... Bangladesh Medical Association of North America (EA)
BMA .... Bank Marketing Association [*Chicago, IL*] (EA)
BMA .... Basic Maintenance Allowance
BMA .... Beach Maintenance Area [*British and Canadian*] [*World War II*]
BMA .... Bergens Museums. Aarbok [*A publication*]
BMA .... Bermuda Monetary Authority (GEA)
BMA .... Bible Memory Association, International (EA)
BMA .... Bicycle Manufacturers Association of America (EA)
BMA .... Biomedical Marketing Association (EA)
BMA .... Black Music Association (EA)
BMA .... Boat Manufacturers Association [*Later, NMMA*] (EA)
BMA .... Body-Mounted Accelerometer
BMA .... Brahma Resources, Inc. [*Vancouver Stock Exchange symbol*]
BMA .... Brigade Maintenance Area [*British military*] (DMA)
BMA .... British Medical Association
BMA .... British Midland Airways Ltd.
BMA .... British Military Administration
BMA .... British Military Authority
BMA .... (Bromobenzoyl)methyladamantylamine [*Biochemistry*]
BMA .... Butyl Methacrylate [*Organic chemistry*]
BMA .... Stockholm [*Sweden*] Bromma Airport [*Airport symbol*] (OAG)
BMAA .... Barracks Master-at-Arms
BM Aa .... Bergens Museums. Aarbok [*A publication*]
BMAA ...... Beta-Methylamino-alanine [*An amino acid*]
BMAA ...... Beverage Manufacturers' Agents Association (EA)
BMAA ...... British Marine Aquarist Association
BMAAA .... Byulleten' Mezhdunarodnykh Agenstv Atomnoi Energii [*A publication*]
BMAB ...... Butyl(methoxy)azobenzene [*Organic chemistry*]
BMA(BB).. British Military Administration, British Borneo
BMAC ...... Basic Memory Access Controller [*Memory management unit*] [*Data processing*]
BMAC ...... BMA Corp. [*NASDAQ symbol*] (NQ)
BMAC ...... Boeing Military Airplane Company
B & Mac..... Browne and MacNamara's Railway Cases [*A publication*] (DLA)
B-MAC...... Multiplexed Analogue Component, Type B [*Satellite television*]
B & Macn... Browne and MacNamara. Railway Cases [*A publication*] (DLA)
B Mad .... Bulletin de Madagascar [*A publication*]
BMAD....... Bulletin Mensuel. Academie Delphinale [*A publication*]
BMadagascar ... Bulletin de Madagascar [*A publication*]
BMADO.... Boeing Military Airplane Development Organization
B Madras Dev Sem Ser ... Bulletin. Madras Development Seminar Series [*A publication*]
B Ma E....... Bachelor of Marine Engineering
BMAEA7... Montana. Agricultural Experiment Station. Bulletin [*A publication*]
B Ma Eng... Bachelor of Marine Engineering
BMAG ...... Body-Mounted Attitude Gyro (KSC)
BMAGNY ... Box Manufacturers Association of Greater New York (EA)
BMAH....... Bulletin. Musees Royaux d'Art et d'Histoire [*A publication*]
BMAIU ..... Bulletin Mensuel. Alliance Israelite Universelle [*A publication*]
B Maj........ Brigade Major (DAS)
BMALDV ... Bollettino Malacologico [*A publication*]
BMAP....... BITmap Images
BMAP....... BMA [*British Medical Association*] Press Cuttings Database [*Information service or system*] (IID)
BMAP....... Boost Measurement and Analysis Program (MCD)
BMAP....... [*The*] Brooklyn Museum Aramaic Papyri [*A publication*] (BJA)
BMAP....... Buffer Map [*Data processing*] (NASA)
BMAPS .... Bexley-Maudsley Automated Psychological Screening [*Test*]
BMAR ...... Backlog of Maintenance and Repair (MCD)
BMAR ...... Ballistic Missile Acquisition RADAR
BMAR ...... Base Maintenance and Repair
BMARB.... Bergens Museums. Aarbok [*A publication*]
B Mar E ..... Bachelor of Marine Engineering
B Marin Sci ... Bulletin of Marine Science [*A publication*]
BMAS....... Barium-Magnesia-Alumina-Silicate [*Inorganic chemistry*]
BMAS....... British Medical Acupuncture Society

BMASDI ...   Mississippi. Agricultural and Forestry Experiment Station.
                  Bulletin [*A publication*]
BMASR ....   Bureau of Military Application of Scientific Research   (NATG)
BMAT ....   Basic Motor Ability Test [*Education*]
BMAT ....   Beginning Morning Astronomical Twilight
                  [*Navigation*]   (MCD)
BMath ....   Bachelor of Mathematics
B Math Biol ...   Bulletin of Mathematical Biology [*A publication*]
B Math Stat ... Bulletin of Mathematical Statistics [*A publication*]
BMAT/S .....   Ballistic Missile Analyst Technician-Specialist
BMAW ......   Bare Metal Arc Welding
B May ....   Bernardus Maynardi [*Authority cited in pre-1607 legal
                  work*]   (DSA)
BMB ....   Bahrain Middle East Bank
BMB ....   Ballistic Missile Branch
BMB ....   Baltic Marine Biologists   (EAIO)
BMB ....   Barclays Merchant Bank [*British*]
BMB ....   Barry Melton Band [*Pop music group*]
BMB ....   Base Maintenance Building   (MCD)
BMB ....   Biomedical Belt [*NASA*]
BMB ....   BMB Compuscience Canada Ltd. [*Toronto Stock Exchange
                  symbol*]
BMB ....   Boehringer Mannheim Biochemicals
BMB ....   Bomber [*Military*]
BMB ....   Boston Museum. Bulletin [*A publication*]
BMB ....   British Medical Bulletin [*A publication*]
BMB ....   British Metrication Board
BMB ....   Broadcast Measurement Bureau
BMB ....   Bulletin Bibliographique. Musee Belge [*A publication*]
BMB ....   Bulletin. Musee Basque [*A publication*]
BMB ....   Bulletin. Musee de Beyrouth [*A publication*]
BMB ....   Bumba [*Zaire*] [*Airport symbol*]   (OAG)
BMB ....   McBride Public Library, British Columbia [*Library symbol*]
                  [*National Library of Canada*]   (NLC)
BMBA ....   British Merchant Banking and Securities Houses
                  Association   (EAIO)
BMBAB .....   Bulletin. Musees Royaux des Beaux-Arts de Belgique [*A
                  publication*]
BMBDR .....   Bombardier   (AFM)
BM Beyrouth ... Bulletin. Musee de Beyrouth [*A publication*]
BMBIA ....   Bulletin of Mathematical Biophysics [*A publication*]
BMBL ....   Berliner Munzblaetter [*A publication*]
BMBR ....   Bomber [*Air Force*]   (AFM)
BMBS ....   Bachelor of Medicine and Bachelor of Surgery
BMBSq .....   Bombardment Squadron [*Air Force*]
BMBT ....   Bis(methyloxybenzylidene)bitoluidine [*Organic chemistry*]
BMBTA .....   Baumaschine und Bautechnik [*A publication*]
BMBTAN ..   Baumaschine und Bautechnik [*A publication*]
BMBUA ....   British Medical Bulletin [*A publication*]
BMBUAQ ...   British Medical Bulletin [*A publication*]
BMC ....   Ballistic Missile Center [*Air Materiel Command*] [*Obsolete*]
BMC ....   Basic Military Compensation   (MCD)
BMC ....   Basic Missile Checker   (NATG)
BMC ....   Battelle Monte Carlo [*Data processing*]
BMC ....   Bearing Mounted Clutch
BMC ....   Biel's Microfilm Company, West Seneca, NY [*Library symbol*]
                  [*Library of Congress*]   (LCLS)
BMC ....   Billing Memo Charge [*Business term*]
BMC ....   Binary Magnetic Core
BMC ....   Biomedical Chromatography [*A publication*]
BMC ....   Biomedical Computer
BMC ....   Black Mountain College [*1933-1956*]
BMC ....   Blind Mating Connector   (MCD)
BMC ....   Block Multiplexer Channel
BMC ....   Blue Mountain College [*Mississippi*]
BMC ....   BMC Industries, Inc. [*NYSE symbol*]   (SPSG)
BMC ....   Boatswain's Mate, Chief [*Navy rating*]
BMC ....   Boehringer Mannheim Corporation [*Chemical industry
                  supplier*]
BMC ....   Bone Marrow Cell [*Cytology*]
BMC ....   Bone Mineral Content [*Medicine*]
BMC ....   Book Marketing Council [*British*]
BMC ....   Boycott McDonald's Coalition   (EA)
BMC ....   Brethren/Mennonite Council for Lesbian and Gay
                  Concerns   (EA)
BMC ....   Brigham City, UT [*Location identifier*] [*FAA*]   (FAAL)
BMC ....   British Medical Council
BMC ....   British Motor Corporation Ltd.
BMC ....   British Mountaineering Council
BMC ....   British Museum Catalogue
BMC ....   Brittle Matrix Composite [*Materials science*]
BMC ....   Broker Management Council   (EA)
BMC ....   Bryn Mawr College [*Pennsylvania*]
BMC ....   Bryn Mawr College, Bryn Mawr, PA [*OCLC symbol*]   (OCLC)
BMC ....   Bubble Memory Controller [*Data processing*]
BMC ....   Bulk Mail Center [*Postal Service*]
BMC ....   Bulk Media Conversion
BMC ....   Bulk Molding Compound
BMC ....   Bullnose Morris Club   (EA)
BMC ....   Bureau of Motor Carriers [*ICC*]
BMC ....   Burst Multiplexer Channel [*Telecommunications*]

BMC ....   Joint Brazil-United States Military Commission
BM/C3 ....   Battle Management/Command, Control,
                  Communications   (MCD)
BMC/AMC ...   Ballistic Missile Center, Air Materiel Command [*Obsolete*]
BMCBB .....   Boatswain's Mate, Construction Battalion, Boatswain [*Navy
                  rating*]
BMCBS .....   Boatswain's Mate, Construction Battalion, Stevedore [*Navy
                  rating*]
BMCC ....   Bando McGlocklin Capital Corp. [*NASDAQ symbol*]   (NQ)
BMCCC .....   Bishop Method of Clothing Construction Council   (EA)
BMCE ....   Banque Marocaine du Commerce Exterieur [*Morocco*]
BMCERC ..   Black and Multiethnic Christian Education Resources
                  Center   (EA)
BMCET/S ...   Ballistic Missile Checkout Equipment Technician-Specialist
BM/C3I .....   Battle Management/Command, Control, Communications, and
                  Intelligence [*Military*]
BMCL ....   Bulletin of Medieval Canon Law [*A publication*]
BMCM ....   Boatswain's Mate, Master Chief [*Navy rating*]
BMCMEB ...   Boletin. Museo de Ciencias Naturales y Antropologicas Juan
                  Cornelio Moyano [*A publication*]
BMCN ....   Book of the Month Club. News [*A publication*]
BMCO ......   Ballistic Missile Construction Office
BMCO ....   Biomechanical Combined Oxidation [*Water treatment*]
B M Coins Rom Emp ... British Museum Catalogue of Coins of the Roman
                  Empire [*A publication*]   (OCD)
BMCR ....   Black Methodists for Church Renewal   (EA)
BMCR ....   Bollettino. Museo della Civilta Romana [*A publication*]
BMCS ....   BMC Software, Inc. [*NASDAQ symbol*]   (NQ)
BMCS ....   Boatswain's Mate, Senior Chief [*Navy rating*]
BMCS ....   Bureau of Motor Carrier Safety [*Department of Transportation*]
BMCT ....   Beginning Morning Civil Twilight [*Navigation*]
BMCT ....   Bennett Mechanical Comprehension Test [*Mechanical ability
                  test*]
BMC/W .....   Bone Mineral Content/Width [*Medicine*]
BMD ....   AL Laboratories, Inc. [*NYSE symbol*]   (SPSG)
BMD ....   Bacitracin Methylene Disalicylate [*Animal antibiotic*]
BMD ....   Ballistic Missile Defense
BMD ....   Ballistic Missile Division [*Ballistic Research Laboratory*]
BMD ....   Base Maintenance Division [*Navy*]
BMD ....   Becker Muscular Dystrophy [*Medicine*]
BMD ....   Belo [*Madagascar*] [*Airport symbol*]   (OAG)
BMD ....   Benchmark Monitor Display System [*Sperry UNIVAC*]
BMD ....   Bengal Medical Department [*British military*]   (DMA)
BMD ....   Big Mahogany Desk
BMD ....   Bijdragen en Mededeelingen der Dialectencommissie van de
                  Koninklijke Akademie van Wetenschappen te Amsterdam
                  [*A publication*]
BMD ....   Biomedical
B & MD .....   Boat & Motor Dealer [*A publication*]
BMD ....   Bone Mineral Density [*Medicine*]
BMD ....   British Medical [*Vancouver Stock Exchange symbol*]
BMD ....   Brittle Materials Design   (MCD)
BMD ....   Bronevaya Mashina Destany [*Soviet airborne combat
                  vehicle*]   (INF)
BMD ....   Bubble Memory Device [*Data processing*]
BMD ....   Bureau of Medical Devices [*Food and Drug Administration*]
BMD ....   United States Food and Drug Administration, Bureau of
                  Medical Devices Library, Silver Spring, MD [*OCLC
                  symbol*]   (OCLC)
BMDA ....   Blue Military Damage Assessment
BMDADS ...   Biomedical Data Analysis and Display System [*NASA*]
BMDATC ...   Ballistic Missile Defense Advanced Technology Center   (AABC)
BMDC ....   Ballistic Missile Defense Center   (MCD)
BMDC ....   Ballistic Missile Defense Committee
BMDC ....   Biomedical Dynamics Corp. [*NASDAQ symbol*]   (NQ)
BMDCA ....   Bernese Mountain Dog Club of America   (EA)
BMDCP ....   Ballistic Missile Defense Command Post   (AABC)
BMDCP ....   Battalion Mortar and Davy Crockett Platoon [*Army*]   (AABC)
BMDDP .....   Bureau of Medical Devices and Diagnostic Products [*FDA*]
BMDEAR ...   Ballistic Missile Defense Emergency Action Report   (AABC)
BMDF ....   Black Mesa Defense Fund   (EA)
BMDIA ....   Bulletin. Mount Desert Island Biological Laboratory [*A
                  publication*]
BMDial ......   Bijdragen en Mededeelingen der Dialectencommissie van de
                  Koninklijke Akademie van Wetenschappen te Amsterdam
                  [*A publication*]
BMDITP ...   Ballistic Missile Defense Integrated Training Plan   (AABC)
BMDJA ......   Burma Medical Journal [*A publication*]
BMDMB .....   Ballistic Missile Defense Missile Battalion   (AABC)
BMDMCS ...   (Bromomethyl)dimethyl Chlorosilane [*Organic chemistry*]
BMDMP .....   Ballistic Missile Defense Master Plan   (AABC)
BMDMPO ...   Ballistic Missile Defense Materials Program Office   (MCD)
BMD-NEAT ...   Ballistic Missile Defense - Nuclear Effects and Threat
                  Committee   (AABC)
BMDNS ....   Basic Mission, Design Number, and Series [*Aircraft*]   (AFM)
BMDO ....   Ballistic Missile Defense Operations   (AABC)
BMDO ....   Bomb and Mine Disposal Officer [*British military*]   (DMA)
BMDOA ......   Ballistic Missile Defense Operations Activity   (AABC)
BMDOA ....   Biomaterials, Medical Devices, and Artificial Organs [*A
                  publication*]
BMDPM ...   Ballistic Missile Defense Program Manager   (AABC)

BMDPO .... Ballistic Missile Defense Program Office (AABC)
BMDR ...... Bombardier
BMDS .... Ballistic Missile Defense System
BMDS .... Base Mail Distribution Scheme [Air Force] (AFM)
BMDS .... Base Manager Data System
BMDS .... Base Manpower Data System [Air Force] (OAG)
BMDS .... Bio-Medicus, Inc. [NASDAQ symbol] (NQ)
BMDSB ..... Ballistic Missile Defense Surveillance Battalion (AABC)
BMDSCOM ... Ballistic Missile Defense Systems Command (AABC)
BME .... Bachelor of Mechanical Engineering
BME .... Bachelor of Mining Engineering
BME .... Bachelor of Music Education
BME .... Bachelor of Music in Education
BME .... Barrage Mansour Eddahbi [Morocco] [Seismograph station code, US Geological Survey] (SEIS)
BME .... Beaver, Meade & Englewood [AAR code]
BME .... Belmoral Mines Ltd. [Toronto Stock Exchange symbol]
BME .... Bench Maintenance Equipment [NASA] (KSC)
BME .... Beta-Mercaptoethanol [Organic chemistry]
BME .... Biomedical Electronics (MCD)
BME .... Biomedical Engineering Program [Carnegie-Mellon University] [Research center] (RCD)
BME .... Born-Mayer Equation [Physics]
BME .... British Museum Expeditions to Middle Egypt [London] [A publication] (BJA)
BM/E .... Broadcast Management/Engineering [A publication]
BME .... Broome [Australia] [Airport symbol] (OAG)
BME .... Brotherhood of Marine Engineers [Later merged with MEBA]
BME .... Buck Memory Element (MCD)
BME .... Bueromaschinen-Export [Office Machinery Export Foreign Trade Enterprise] [German Democratic Republic]
BME .... Division of Biomedical Engineering [University of Virginia] [Research center] (RCD)
BMEA .... Building Maintenance Employers Association [Later, SEA] (EA)
BMEA .... Building Material Exhibitors Association [Defunct] (EA)
BME (Aero Option) ... Bachelor of Mechanical Engineering (Aeronautical Option)
BMEC .... Ball Manufacturers Engineers Committee (EA)
BMEC .... British Marine Equipment Council (DS)
B Mech ...... Bachelor of Mechanics
B Mech E ... Bachelor of Mechanical Engineering
B Med .... Bachelor of Medicine
BM Ed .... Bachelor of Music Education
BMED .... Ballard Medical Products [NASDAQ symbol] (NQ)
B Med Biol ... Bachelor of Medical Biology
BMedLabSc ... Bachelor of Medical Laboratory Science
B Med Lib A ... Bulletin. Medical Library Association [A publication]
BMEDS ..... Base Management Engineering Data System
B Med Sc ... Bachelor of Medical Sciences
B Med Sci ... Bachelor of Medical Sciences
BMEE .... Belmoral Mines Ltd. [NASDAQ symbol] (NQ)
BMEEB ..... Bulletin of Mechanical Engineering Education [A publication]
BMEG .... Building Materials Export Group [United Kingdom] (DS)
BMEGA ..... Bulletin. Mechanical Engineering Laboratory of Japan [A publication]
BMEMDK ... Biological Memoirs [A publication]
B Mem Soc Anthr ... Bulletins et Memoires. Societe d'Anthropologie de Paris [A publication]
B Mem Soc Arch Bordeaux ... Bulletin et Memoires. Societe Archeologique de Bordeaux [A publication]
BM Eng ..... Bachelor of Mechanical Engineering
B Menninger ... Bulletin. Menninger Clinic [A publication]
B Mens Statist Trav Suppl ... Bulletin Mensuel des Statistiques du Travail. Supplement [A publication]
B Mens Stat O-Mer ... Bulletin Mensuel de Statistique d'Outre-Mer [A publication]
BMEO .... British Middle East Office
BMEP .... [The] Book of Modern English Poetry [A publication]
BMEP .... Brake Mean Effective Pressure
BMEPAQ ... British Museum (Natural History). Economic Series [A publication]
BMES .... Biomedical Engineering Society (EA)
B Met .... Bachelor of Metallurgy
BMET .... Biomedical Equipment Technology
BMET .... Biomet, Inc. [NASDAQ symbol] (NQ)
B Metal E .. Bachelor of Metallurgical Engineering
B Met E ...... Bachelor of Metallurgical Engineering
B Met Eng ... Bachelor of Metallurgical Engineering
BMETO .... Ballistic Missiles European Task Organization [Military]
B Metr Mus ... Bulletin. Metropolitan Museum of Art [A publication]
B Metr Mus A ... Bulletin. Metropolitan Museum of Art [New York] [A publication]
BMEU .... Biomedical Engineering Unit [McGill University] [Canada] [Research center] (RCD)
BMEW ...... Ballistic Missile Early Warning [System]
BMEWS.... Ballistic Missile Early Warning System
BMF .... B-Cell Maturation Factor [Immunology]
BMF .... Basic Main Frame (NATG)
BMF .... Basic Mobile Facility (MCD)
BMF .... Beautiful Music Friends (EA)

BMF .... Bending Mode Filters
BMF .... Bene Merenti Fecit [He Erected This to the Well-Deserving] [Latin]
BMF .... BMO II Financial Corp. [Toronto Stock Exchange symbol]
BMF .... Board Measurement Feet
BMF .... Boron Metal Fiber
BMF .... Building Merchants' Federation [British]
BMF .... Bulletin. Musees de France [A publication]
BMF .... Business Mail Foundation [Later, DMMA] (EA)
BMF .... Business Master File [OMB]
BMFA .... Boston Museum of Fine Arts
BMFA .... Bulletin. Museum of Fine Arts [Boston] [A publication]
BMFAAK .. British Museum (Natural History). Fossil Mammals of Africa [A publication]
BMFC .... Barry Morse Fan Club (EA)
BMFC .... Big Man's Fan Club (EA)
BMFC .... Buddy Max Fan Club (EA)
BMFC .... Bunnie Mills Fan Club (EA)
BMFEA ..... Bulletin. Museum of Far Eastern Antiquities [Stockholm] [A publication]
BMFJ .... Bulletin. Maison Franco-Japonais [A publication]
BMFL .... Bidders Master File Listing [DoD]
BMFPRA ... BMO II Financial Pr [Toronto Stock Exchange symbol]
BMFR .... Blaetter fuer Muenzfreunde [A publication]
BMFT .... Bundesministerium fuer Forschung und Technologie [Ministry for Research and Technology] [Information service or system] (IID)
BMFT .... German D-1 Spacelaboratory Payload
BMFT Mitt ... BMFT [Bundesministerium fuer Forschung und Technologie] Mitteilungen [A publication]
BMFT Mitteilungen ... Bonn. Pressereferat des Bundesministeriums fuer Forschung und Technologie. Mitteilungen [A publication]
BMG .... Baader-Meinhof Group [Revolutionary group] [Federal Republic of Germany]
BMG .... Battle Mountain Gold Co. [Toronto Stock Exchange symbol] [NYSE symbol]
BMG .... Benign Monoclonal Gammopathy [Immunochemistry]
BMG .... Bilirubin Monoglucuronide [Biochemistry]
BMG .... Bloomington [Indiana] [Airport symbol] (OAG)
BMG .... British Measures Group
BMG .... British Military Government
BMG .... Browning Machine Gun
BMG .... Budget and Manpower Guidance [Military] (AABC)
BMG .... Business Machines Group [Burroughs Corp.]
BMG .... Business Management Game
BMGA .... British Machine Guarding Authority
BMGC .... British Museum. General Catalogue of Printed Books [A publication]
BMGeire .... Bijdragen en Mededeelingen Uitgegeven door de Vereeniging Geire [A publication]
BMGHA .... Bamidgeh [A publication]
BMGJW .... Bijdragen en Mededeelingen van het Genootschap voor de Joodsche Wetenschap in Nederland [A publication]
BMGLA..... Bulletin. Societe des Sciences Medicales du Grand-Duche de Luxembourg [A publication]
BMGR .... Bone Marrow Granulocyte Reserve [Physiology]
BMGS........ Byzantine and Modern Greek Studies [A publication]
B Mgt E .... Bachelor of Management Engineering
BMH.......... Bank Mees & Hope NV
BMH.......... Beaufort & Morehead Railroad Co. [AAR code]
BMH.......... Benign Monoclonal Hypergammaglobulinemia [Medicine]
BMH.......... Bomai [Papua New Guinea] [Airport symbol] (OAG)
BMH.......... British Military Hospital
BMH.......... British Motor Holdings
BMH.......... Bulletin. Museum Haaretz [Tel Aviv] [A publication]
BMH.......... Handelsvoorlichting Bank Mees en Hope [A publication]
BMHA....... Bulletin pour la Conservation des Monuments Historiques d'Alsace [A publication]
BMHBA .... Bulletin. Musee Hongrois des Beaux Arts [A publication]
BMHDA.... Beta-Methylheptadecanoic Acid [Organic chemistry]
BMHG....... Bijdragen en Mededeelingen van het Historisch Genootschap [A publication]
BMHIA ..... Black Military History Institute of America (EA)
BMHM...... Bulletin. Musee Historique de Mulhouse [A publication]
BMHNAZ ... Museo Nacional de Historia Natural. Boletin [Santiago] [A publication]
BMHP....... Bromomercurihydroxypropane [Clinical chemistry]
BMHS ...... British Morgan Horse Society
BMHS ...... Bulletin. Missouri Historical Society [A publication]
BMHS/J ... Journal. Barbados Museum and Historical Society [A publication]
BMI .... Badger Meter, Incorporated [AMEX symbol] (SPSG)
BMI .... Ballistic Missile Interceptor
BMI .... Bangles n' Mash International (EA)
BMI .... Barley and Malt Institute (EA)
BMI .... Battelle Memorial Institute (EA)
BMI .... Bay Microfilm, Incorporated, Palo Alto, CA [Library symbol] [Library of Congress] (LCLS)
BMI .... Biography Master Index [Gale Research, Inc.] [Information service or system] [A publication] (IID)
BMI .... Bismaleimide [Organic chemistry]

BMI .... Bloomington [*Illinois*] [*Airport symbol*]   (OAG)
BMI .... BMI: The Many Worlds of Music [*A publication*]
BMI .... Body Mass Index [*Medicine*]
BMI .... Book Manufacturers Institute   (EA)
BMI .... Bravais-Miller Indices [*Physics*]
BMI .... British Ministry of Information   (DAS)
BMI .... Broadcast Music, Incorporated
BMIB .... Bank Markazi Iran. Bulletin [*A publication*]
B Mic .... Bachelor of Microbiology
BMIC......... British Music Information Centre   (CB)
BMIC......... Bureau of Mines. Information Circular [*Department of the Interior*] [*A publication*]
BMIC 8900 ... Future Trends and Prospects for the Australian Mineral Processing Sector. Bureau of Mines Information Circular [*A publication*]
BMIC 8917 ... Aluminum Availability - Market Economy Countries. Bureau of Mines Information Circular [*A publication*]
B Midwest M .. Bulletin. Midwest Modern Language Association [*A publication*]
B Mi E .... Bachelor of Mining Engineering
B Mi Eng ... Bachelor of Mining Engineering
BMIGT/M ... Ballistic Missile Inertial Guidance Technician-Mechanic
BMILS ...... Bottom-Mounted Impact Locations System [*Missile technology*]
BMIM .... Mayne Island Museum, British Columbia [*Library symbol*] [*National Library of Canada*]   (NLC)
BMin......... Bachelor of Ministry
BMiningE ... Bachelor of Mining Engineering
B Min Inter ... Bulletin. Ministere de l'Interieur [*A publication*]
BMIP......... Basic Medical Insurance Plan [*UN Food and Agriculture Organization*]
BMIR......... Bollettino. Museo dell'Impero Romano [*A publication*]
BMIS......... Bank Management Information System
B Miss Hist Soc ... Bulletin. Missouri Historical Society [*A publication*]
BMITA...... British Malaysian Industry and Trade Association   (DS)
BMIU .... Bricklayers, Masons Independent Union of Canada
BMJ.......... Baramita [*Guyana*] [*Airport symbol*]   (OAG)
BMJ.......... British Medical Journal [*A publication*]
BMJ.......... Bundesminister der Justiz [*Federal Minister of Justice*] [*German*]   (ILCA)
BMJA....... Bulletin. Museum of Jewish Antiquities [*A publication*]
BMJE .... British Medical Journal Epitome [*A publication*]
BMJF .... BMJ Financial Corp. [*Bordentown, NJ*] [*NASDAQ symbol*]   (NQ)
BMJH .... Boletin. Museo de Motivos Populares Argentinos Jose Hernandez [*A publication*]
BMJOA..... British Medical Journal [*A publication*]
BMJOAE.. British Medical Journal [*A publication*]
BMK .... Baby Mouse Kidney Cells
BMK .... Borkum [*West Germany*] [*Airport symbol*]   (OAG)
BMK .... Mackenzie Public Library, British Columbia [*Library symbol*] [*National Library of Canada*]   (NLC)
BMKR ...... Boilermaker   (MSA)
BMKRM ... Kettle River Museum, Midway, British Columbia [*Library symbol*] [*National Library of Canada*]   (NLC)
BML .... Bachelor of Modern Languages
BML .... Balfour Maclaine Corp. [*AMEX symbol*]   (SPSG)
BML .... Belfast & Moosehead Lake Railroad Co. [*AAR code*]
BML .... Ben May Laboratory for Cancer Research [*University of Chicago*] [*Research center*]   (RCD)
BML .... Berlin, NH [*Location identifier*] [*FAA*]   (FAAL)
BML .... Bible Meditation League [*Later, BLI*]   (EA)
BML .... Bibliotheque du Museon (Louvain) [*A publication*]
BML .... Blue Mountain Lake [*New York*] [*Seismograph station code, US Geological Survey*] [*Closed*]   (SEIS)
BML .... Bodega Marine Laboratory [*University of California*] [*Research center*]   (RCD)
BML .... Bone-Marrow Leucocyte [*Physiology*]
BML .... Bren-Mar Resources [*Vancouver Stock Exchange symbol*]
BML .... British Museum Library [*London*]
BML .... Bulk Material Length   (NRCH)
BML .... Business Modeling Language   (MCD)
BMLA....... British Maritime Law Association
BMLA....... British Medical LASER Association
BMLA....... Bulletin. Medical Library Association [*A publication*]
BML-BS.... British Matchbox Label and Booklet Society
BMLET/R ... Ballistic Missile Launch Equipment Technician-Repairman
BMLO ...... Ballistic Missile Logistics Office
BMLS ...... Balloon-Borne Microwave Limb Sounder [*Atmospheric research*]
BMLS ...... Burke Mills, Inc. [*NASDAQ symbol*]   (NQ)
BMLUS..... Business Men's League of the United States   (EA)
BMM........ Bachelor of Mining and Metallurgy
BMM........ Ballistic Missile Manager
BMM........ Baptist Mid-Missions   (EA)
BMM........ Belaruskaia Mova. Mizhvuzauski Zbornik [*A publication*]
BMM........ Benthic Metabolism Measurement
BMM........ Bibliography of Manichaean Materials [*A publication*]
BMM........ Biblioteca Moderna Mondadori [*A publication*]
BMM........ Big Maria Mountains [*California*] [*Seismograph station code, US Geological Survey*]   (SEIS)

BMM........ Bitam [*Gabon*] [*Airport symbol*]   (OAG)
BMM........ Bohr and Mottleson Model [*of nuclear structure*]
BMM........ Bone-Marrow-Derived Macrophage [*Biochemistry*]
BMM........ Borrowed Military Manpower
BMM........ British Military Mission
BMM........ Bulletin. Metropolitan Museum of Art [*A publication*]
BMM........ Butler Mountain Minerals [*Vancouver Stock Exchange symbol*]
BMM........ Mission Museum and Archives, British Columbia [*Library symbol*] [*National Library of Canada*]   (NLC)
BMMA ..... Bacon and Meat Manufacturers' Association [*British*]
BMMA ..... Beverage Machinery Manufacturers Association   (EA)
BMMA ..... Bulletin. Metropolitan Museum of Art [*A publication*]
BMMBES ... Biochemical Medicine and Metabolic Biology [*A publication*]
BMMCDC ... Binary Metal and Metalloid Constitution Data Center [*Illinois Institute of Technology*]
BMMD...... Birmingham & Midland Motor Omnibus Co. Ltd. [*British*]   (DCTA)
BMMD...... Body Mass Measurements Device   (KSC)
BMMF....... Beatrice M. Murphy Foundation   (EA)
BMMF....... Bible and Medical Missionary Fellowship [*Later, BMMFI/ USA*]   (EA)
BMMFF .... British Man-Made Fibres Federation
BMMFI ..... BMMF [*Bible and Medical Missionary Fellowship*] International [*Later, IUSA*]   (EA)
BMMFI/USA ... BMMF [*Bible and Medical Missionary Fellowship*] International/USA [*Later, IUSA*]   (EA)
BMMG...... British Micro Manufacturer Group
BMMLA..... Bulletin. Midwest Modern Language Association [*A publication*]
BMMP ...... Barge-Mounted Methanol Plant [*Chemical industry*]
BMN.......... Base Manager's Notice
BMN.......... Battle Mountain [*Nevada*] [*Seismograph station code, US Geological Survey*]   (SEIS)
BMN.......... Benzylidenemalononitrile [*Organic chemistry*]
BMN.......... BMO NT Financial Corp. [*Toronto Stock Exchange symbol*]
BMN.......... British Merchant Navy
BMN.......... Building Material News [*A publication*]
BMNA ...... Baptist Mission of North America   (EA)
BMNADT ... Bulletin. Museum National d'Histoire Naturelle. Section A. Zoologie, Biologie, et Ecologie Animales [*A publication*]
BMNB ...... Bulletin. Musee National de Burgas [*A publication*]
BMNBDW ... Bulletin. Museum National d'Histoire Naturelle. Section B. Adansonia Botanique. Phytochimie [*A publication*]
BMNE .... Bulletin. Museum of Mediterranean and Near Eastern Antiquities [*A publication*]
BMNH ...... British Museum (Natural History) [*London*]
BMNLF..... Bangsa Moro National Liberation Front [*Political party*] [*Philippines*]   (FEA)
BMNMDV ... Bulletin. Museum National d'Histoire Naturelle. Section C. Sciences de la Terre. Paleontologie, Geologie, Mineralogie [*A publication*]
BMNPA3 .. British Museum (Natural History). Publication [*A publication*]
BMNPD6 .. Bulletin. Museum National d'Histoire Naturelle. Section B. Botanique, Biologie, et Ecologie Vegetales. Phytochimie [*A publication*]
BmNPV ..... Bombyx mori Nuclear Polyhedrosis Virus
BMNRBA ... British Museum (Natural History). Report [*A publication*]
BMNT .... Beginning Morning Nautical Twilight [*Navigation*]
BMNV .... Nicola Valley Museum-Archives, Merritt, British Columbia [*Library symbol*] [*National Library of Canada*]   (NLC)
BMO.......... Ballistic Missile Office [*Norton Air Force Base, CA*] [*United States Air Force Systems Command*]   (GRD)
BM & O ..... Baltimore, Maryland, and Ohio
BMO.......... Bank of Montreal [*Toronto Stock Exchange symbol*] [*Vancouver Stock Exchange symbol*]
BMO.......... Base Maintenance Operation   (MCD)
BMO.......... Battalion Maintenance Officer [*Army*]   (INF)
BMO.......... Beach Modulator Oscillator
BMO.......... Bhamo [*Burma*] [*Airport symbol*]   (OAG)
BMO.......... Blue Mountains Array [*Oregon*] [*Seismograph station code, US Geological Survey*] [*Closed*]   (SEIS)
BMO.......... Bond Molecular Orbitals
BMO.......... Book Marketing Opportunities Database [*Ad-Lib Publications*] [*Information service or system*]   (CRD)
BMO.......... British Meteorological Office   (MCD)
BMO.......... Brotherhood of Marine Officers   (EA)
BMOC....... Ballistic Missile Orientation Course
BMOC....... Big Machine on Campus [*Computer*]
BMOC....... Big Man on Campus [*Slang*]
B-MOD ..... Behavior Modification [*Psychology*]
BMod .... Bibliographie Moderne [*A publication*]
BMOGA.... Bollettino delle Malattie dell'Orecchio, della Gola, del Naso [*A publication*]
BMOM...... Base Maintenance and Operations Model
B Mon .... Ben Monroe's Kentucky Supreme Court Reports [*A publication*]   (DLA)
BMON...... Bio-Monitor, Inc. [*NASDAQ symbol*]   (NQ)
B Mon .... Bulletin Monumental [*A publication*]
B de Monfa .. Bertrandus de Montefaventino [*Deceased, 1342*] [*Authority cited in pre-1607 legal work*]   (DSA)
B Mon (KY) ... Ben Monroe's Kentucky Reports [*A publication*]   (DLA)

B Mon Mus Pont ... Bollettino Monumenti. Musei e Gallerie Pontificie [*A publication*]
B Monr....... Ben Monroe's Kentucky Reports [*A publication*] (DLA)
B Monr....... Burrow's Reports Tempore Mansfield [*England*] [*A publication*] (DLA)
B Monr....... Moore's Reports [*England*] [*A publication*] (DLA)
B (Montreal) ... Business Review (Montreal) [*A publication*]
B Monument ... Bulletin Monumental [*A publication*]
B Moore..... Bayly Moore. English Common Pleas Reports [*A publication*] (DLA)
BMOPDB ... Butterworths International Medical Reviews. Ophthalmology [*A publication*]
B-MOPP ... Bleomycin, Mustargen, Oncovin [*Vincristine*], Procarbazine, Prednisone [*Antineoplastic drug regimen*]
B Morbihan ... Bulletin Mensuel. Societe Polymatique de Morbihan [*A publication*]
BMORDH ... Butterworths International Medical Reviews. Orthopaedics [*A publication*]
B/MOS..... British Ministry of Supply (AAG)
BMOTR ..... Ballistic Missile Operational Training Readiness
BMP .... Background Measurements Program (MCD)
BMP .... BCNU [*Carmustine*], Methotrexate, Procarbazine [*Antineoplastic drug regimen*]
BMP .... Best Management Practice [*Environmental Protection Agency*]
BMP .... Biomass Protein
BMP .... Birmingham Post [*A publication*]
BMP .... Blind-Made Products
BMP .... BMP Technologies Ltd. [*Vancouver Stock Exchange symbol*]
BMP .... Boletim Mensal. Sociedade de Lingua Portuguesa [*A publication*]
BMP .... Bone Morphogenetic Protein
BMP .... Brake Mean Power
BMP .... Brampton Island [*Australia*] [*Airport symbol*] (OAG)
BMP .... Bricklayers, Masons, and Plasterers' International of America [*Later, BAC*]
BMP .... Bureau of Mines, Pittsburg (MCD)
BMP .... Burma Military Police [*British military*] (DMA)
BMP .... Burnham American Properties [*AMEX symbol*] (SPSG)
BMP .... National Council of Building Material Producers [*A union*] [*British*]
BMPA....... Broadband Microwave Power Amplifier
BMPAE6... Boletim. Museu Paraense Emilio Goeldi. Serie Antropologia [*A publication*]
BMPAP..... Bone Marrow Prostatic Acid Phosphatase
BMPBA ..... British Columbia. Department of Mines and Petroleum Resources. Bulletin [*A publication*]
BMPBE9 ... Boletim. Museu Paraense Emilio Goeldi. Serie Botanica [*A publication*]
BMPC........ Bone Marrow Plasmacytosis [*Oncology*]
BMPEAE ... Boletim. Museu Paraense Emilio Goeldi [*A publication*]
BMPGA..... Byulleten' Moskovskogo Obshchestva Ispytatelei Prirody Otdel Geologicheskii [*A publication*]
BMPI........ Biosearch Medical Products, Incorporated [*NASDAQ symbol*] (NQ)
BMPMB.... Bibliotheca Microbiologica [*A publication*]
BMPR....... Bimonthly Progress Report
BMPR....... Bumper [*Automotive engineering*]
BMPSEQ .. Brunner/Mazel Psychosocial Stress Series [*A publication*]
BMPZED .. Boletim. Museu Paraense Emilio Goeldi. Serie Zoologia [*A publication*]
BMQ......... Bamburi [*Kenya*] [*Airport symbol*] [*Obsolete*] (OAG)
BMQ......... Boston Medical Quarterly [*A publication*]
BMQ......... British Museum. Quarterly [*A publication*]
BMQ......... Burnet, TX [*Location identifier*] [*FAA*] (FAAL)
BMQT .... Brigade Major of the Queen's Troops [*British*] (ROG)
BM Qu...... British Museum. Quarterly [*A publication*]
BMR .... Bank Marketing [*A publication*]
BMR .... Basal Metabolic Rate [*Medicine*]
BMR .... Basic Military Requirement
BMR .... Beachmaster
BMR .... Bearingless Main Rotor (RDA)
BMR .... Bihar Mounted Rifles [*British military*] (DMA)
BMR .... Black Music Research Journal [*A publication*]
BMR .... Bomber (AABC)
BMR .... Border Mounted Rifles [*British military*] (DMA)
BMR .... Boulder Mountain Resources [*Vancouver Stock Exchange symbol*]
BMR .... Brookhaven Medical Reactor
BMR .... Bureau of Market Research [*South African*]
BMR .... Bureau of Mineral Resources [*Australia*] (NRCH)
BMR .... Monthly Bibliography of Medical Reviews [*A publication*]
BMRA .... Biomerica, Inc. [*NASDAQ symbol*] (NQ)
BMRA .... Brigade Major, Royal Artillery [*British and Canadian*]
BMRAH.... Bulletin. Musees Royaux d'Art et d'Histoire [*A publication*]
BMRB........ British Market Research Bureau Ltd. [*Information service or system*] (IID)
BMRBA..... Bulletin. Musees Royaux des Beaux-Arts [*A publication*]
BMRC .... British Medical Research Council
BMRC .... Brookhaven Medical Research Center
BMRCDL ... Butterworths International Medical Reviews. Cardiology [*A publication*]

BMR & ECG ... Basic Metabolism Rate and Electrocardiogram [*Medicine*]
BMRED..... Bureau of Mines. Research [*United States*] [*A publication*]
BMRG .... BMR Finance Group, Inc. [*NASDAQ symbol*] (NQ)
BMRG .... British Micropalaeontological Research Group
BMRI........ Base Maintenance Removal Interval [*Air Force*] (AFIT)
BMR J Aust Geol & Geophys ... BMR [*Australia. Bureau of Mineral Resources. Geology and Geophysics*] Journal of Australian Geology and Geophysics [*A publication*] (APTA)
BMR J Aust Geol Geophys ... BMR [*Australia. Bureau of Mineral Resources. Geology and Geophysics*] Journal of Australian Geology and Geophysics [*A publication*] (APTA)
BMRK .... Bullion Monarch Co. [*NASDAQ symbol*] (NQ)
BMRM ...... Maple Ridge Museum, British Columbia [*Library symbol*] [*National Library of Canada*] (NLC)
BMRMO ... Balance Mobilization Reserve Materiel Objective [*Army*] (AABC)
BMRN .... Bimonthly Research Notes. Canada Department of Environment [*A publication*]
BMRNDK ... Butterworths International Medical Reviews. Neurology [*A publication*]
BMRNEL ... Museo Regionale di Scienze Naturali. Bollettino [*A publication*]
BMRODN ... Butterworths International Medical Reviews. Obstetrics and Gynecology [*A publication*]
BMRP........ Pacific Vocational Institute, Maple Ridge, British Columbia [*Library symbol*] [*Obsolete*] [*National Library of Canada*] (NLC)
B & MRR... Boston & Maine Railroad [*Later, Boston & Maine Corp.*]
BMRR .... Brookhaven Medical Research Reactor (NRCH)
BMRS........ Ballistic Missile Reentry System
BMRSA ...... Bulletin of Marine Science [*A publication*]
BMRSYS... Ballistic Missile Reentry System (AABC)
BMS......... Babylonian Magic and Sorcery [*A publication*]
BMS......... Bachelor of Marine Science
BMS......... Bachelor of Mechanical Science
BMS......... Bachelor of Medical Science
BMS......... Background Mapping Sensor
BMS......... Background Measurement Satellite (NASA)
BMS......... Ballistic Missile Ship [*Navy*]
BMS......... Baptist Mission Society
BMS......... Basic Mapping Support [*Data processing*]
BMS......... Basic Meteorological Services (FAAC)
BMS......... Battalion Maintenance Sergeant [*Military*] (INF)
BMS......... Battlefield Management System [*Military*] (INF)
BMS......... Behavior Monitor System
BMS......... Below Minimum Standards [*TV ratings*]
BMS......... Bemis Co., Inc. [*NYSE symbol*] (SPSG)
BMS......... Benedictiner Monatsschrift [*A publication*]
BMS......... Berlin Mills [*AAR code*]
BMS......... Bill of Material System (MCD)
BMS......... Biomedical Monitoring System
BMS......... Biomedical Studies Section [*Oak Ridge National Laboratory*] (IID)
BMS......... Biowaste Monitoring System (MCD)
BMS......... Bloc des Masses Senegalaises [*Bloc of the Senegalese Masses*]
BMS......... Blow Molding System
BMS......... Boeing Materials Specification
BMS......... Bomb Maintenance Spares
BMS......... Bondi-Metzner-Sachs [*Physics*]
BMS......... Borane Methyl Sulfide [*Organic chemistry*]
BMS......... Boron Management System [*Nuclear energy*] (NRCH)
BM(S)........ Boron Measurement (System) [*Nuclear energy*] (NRCH)
BMS......... Breathing Metabolic Simulator [*IBM Corp.*]
BMS......... British Manufacture and Research
BMS......... British Ministry of Supply
BMS......... British Music Society
BMS......... British Mycological Society
BMS......... Brumado [*Brazil*] [*Airport symbol*] (OAG)
BMS......... Brunswick Mining & Smelting Corp. Ltd. [*Toronto Stock Exchange symbol*]
BMS........... Building Material Series [*National Institute of Standards and Technology*]
BMS......... Building Monitoring System (ADA)
BMS......... Bureau of Medical Services [*Public Health Service*]
BMS......... Bureau of Medicine and Surgery [*Later, Naval Medical Command*] [*Navy*]
BMS......... Bureau Militaire de Standardisation [*Military Agency for Standardization*] [*NATO*]
BMS......... Burst Measuring System
BMS......... Business Management System (BUR)
BMS......... Bypass Monochrome Signal
BMSA....... Bulletins et Memoires. Societe d'Anthropologie [*A publication*]
BMSA....... Seaman Apprentice, Boatswain's Mate, Striker [*Navy rating*]
B M S Anthr ... Bulletins et Memoires. Societe d'Anthropologie de Paris [*A publication*]
BMSAO..... Bulletin et Memoires. Societe des Antiquaires de l'Ouest [*A publication*]
BMSB........ Bis(methylstyryl)benzene [*Organic chemistry*]
BM Sc....... Bachelor of Mechanical Science
BMSc........ Bachelor of Medical Science, University of Dundee [*United Kingdom*] (DBQ)
BMSC........ Ballistic Missile Systems Command [*Army*] (RDA)

BMSD........ Bendix Missile Systems Division   (MCD)
BMSF........ Ballistic Missile Surface Force
BMSIA ...... Biomedical Sciences Instrumentation [*A publication*]
BM & SIAL ... Bureau of Medicine and Supply Integrated Allowance List
BMSL........ Boomsail [*Ship's rigging*]   (ROG)
BMSLP ..... Boletim Mensal. Sociedade de Lingua Portuguesa [*A publication*]
BMSM....... British Merchant Shipping Mission
BMSM....... British Military Supply Mission [*World War II*]
BMSMA.... Bulletins et Memoires. Societe Medicale des Hopitaux de Paris [*A publication*]
BMSN .... Seaman, Boatswain's Mate, Striker [*Navy rating*]
BMSO ...... Base Medical Supply Office [*or Officer*] [*Air Force*]   (AFM)
BMSO ...... Blue Mountain Seismological Observatory
BMSQ ...... Boston Medical and Surgical Quarterly [*A publication*]
BMSR....... Bench Model Solar Receiver   (MCD)
BMSRC.... Boatswain's Mate, Ship Repair, Crane Operator [*Navy rating*]
BMSRDE.. British Ministry of Supply Research and Development Establishment
BMSRR..... Boatswain's Mate, Ship Repair, Rigger [*Navy rating*]
BMSRS ..... Boatswain's Mate, Ship Repair, Canvasman [*Navy rating*]
BMSS .... British Model Soldier Society
BMSS .... Buoy Messenger
BMSS .... Butterfly and Moth Stamp Society   (EA)
BMSSB..... Bulletin Mathematique [*Romania*] [*A publication*]
B Ms Sc ..... Bachelor of Mechanical Sciences
BMSSD ...... Biomass Digest [*A publication*]
BMST........ Business Management System Team [*Air Force*]   (MCD)
BMSTA ..... Transactions. British Mycological Society [*A publication*]
BMSTR ..... Bandmaster
BMSTRG .. Beamsteering   (MSA)
BMSYA ..... Biomedical Mass Spectrometry [*A publication*]
BMT .... Bachelor of Medical Technology
BMT .... Basic Military Training
BMT .... Basic Motion-Time Study
BMT .... Battalion Maintenance Technician [*Military*]   (INF)
BMT .... Beaumont, TX [*Location identifier*] [*FAA*]   (FAAL)
BMT .... Beginning of Magnetic Tape [*Data processing*]   (MDG)
BMT .... Beginning Morning Nautical Twilight [*Navigation*]   (CINC)
BMT .... Bene Merenti [*To the Well-Deserving*] [*Latin*]
BMT .... Bet Midrash le Torah   (BJA)
BMT .... Bibliography of Medical Translations [*A publication*]
BMT .... Biomagnetic Technologies, Inc. [*AMEX symbol*]   (SPSG)
BMT .... Biomedical Technology Information Service [*A publication*]
BMT .... Bone Marrow Transplant [*Medicine*]
BMT .... British Maritime Technology Ltd. [*Research center*]   (IRC)
BMT .... British Mean Time   (DAS)
BMT .... Brooklyn-Manhattan Transit Corp. [*A New York City subway line*]
BMTA ...... Bangkok Mass Transit Authority [*Thailand*]   (DS)
BMTBA.... Bulletin of Mathematical Biology [*A publication*]
BMTC....... British Mass Transit Consultants [*Commercial firm*]
BMTC........ Bryn Mawr Bank Corporation [*Bryn Mawr, PA*] [*NASDAQ symbol*]   (NQ)
BMTD ...... Ballistic Missile Terminal Defense
BMTF........ Bench Mark Test Files   (MCD)
BMTFA..... Buletinul. Institutului Politehnic din Iasi. Sectia I. Matematica, Mecanica Teoretica, Fizica [*A publication*]
BMTI........ Block Mode Terminal Interface [*Data processing*]
BMTLC..... Bimetallic
BMTP........ Bureau of Mines Technical Paper
BMTS .... Ballistic Missile Target System   (MCD)
BMTS .... Ballistic Missile Test System   (IEEE)
BMTS .... Basic Military Training School
BMTV .... Ballistic Missile Test Vessel
BMTV .... British Medical Television
B Mu .... Bachelor of Music
BMU .... Beach Master Unit [*Navy*]
B Mu .... Berliner Museen [*A publication*]
BMU......... Bermuda [*ANSI three-letter standard code*]   (CNC)
BMU......... Bima [*Indonesia*] [*Airport symbol*]   (OAG)
BMU......... Board for Mission and Unity [*Church of England*]
BMU......... Bureau of Manpower Utilization [*World War II*]
BMU......... Bus Monitor Unit   (MCD)
BMU......... University of Massachusetts, Boston, Boston, MA [*OCLC symbol*]   (OCLC)
BMUG....... Berkeley Macintosh Users' Group   (EISS)
BmuHB...... Bermuda Library, Hamilton, Bermudas [*Library symbol*] [*Library of Congress*]   (LCLS)
B Mus .... Bachelor of Music
BMus .... Berliner Museen [*A publication*]
BMUS .... British Medical Ultrasound Society   (EAIO)
BMusA ...... Bachelor of Applied Music
B Mus Anthropol Prehist ... Bulletin. Musee d'Anthropologie Prehistorique [*A publication*]
B Mus Art ... Bulletin. Musees Royaux d'Art et d'Histoire [*Bruxelles*] [*A publication*]
BMusB...... Bulletin. Museum of Fine Arts (Boston) [*A publication*]
BMusBeyr... Bulletin. Musee de Beyrouth [*A publication*]
B Mus E..... Bachelor of Music Education
B Mus Ed... Bachelor of Music in Education

BMusEd..... Bachelor of Music Education
B Mus F A ... Bulletin. Museum of Fine Arts [*Boston*] [*A publication*]
B Mus Far East Antiq ... Bulletin. Museum of Far Eastern Antiquities [*A publication*]
BMusFr ..... Bulletin. Musees de France [*A publication*]
BMusHongr ... Bulletin. Musee Hongrois des Beaux Arts [*A publication*]
B Mus Imp ... Bollettino. Museo dell'Impero Romano [*A publication*]
B Mus (Monaco) ... Bulletin. Musee d'Anthropologie Prehistorique (Monaco) [*A publication*]
B Mus Mon Lyon ... Bulletin des Musees et Monuments Lyonnais [*A publication*]
B Mus Mulhouse ... Bulletin. Musee Historique de Mulhouse [*A publication*]
B Mus Natur Verona ... Bollettino. Museo Civico di Storia Naturale di Verona [*A publication*]
B Mus Padova ... Bollettino. Museo Civico di Padova [*A publication*]
B Mus (PSM) ... Bachelor of Music in Public School Music
B Mus Vars ... Bulletin. Musee National de Varsovie [*A publication*]
B Muz .... Belgarsko Muzikoznanie [*A publication*]
BMV .... Base Mount Valve
BMV .... Beata Maria Virgo [*Blessed Mary the Virgin*] [*Latin*]
BMV .... Bistable Multivibrator
BMV .... Blessed Mary the Virgin   (DAS)
BMV .... Bromegrass Mosaic Virus
BMVA .... Sorores Franciscanae Beatae Mariae Virginis Angelorum [*Franciscan Sisters of Our Lady of the Holy Angels*] [*Roman Catholic religious order*]
BMvD .... Bureau Marcel van Dijk, SA [*Information service or system*]   (IID)
BMVP........ Barrier, Moisture Vapor Proof   (MSA)
BMW .... Bare Molybdenum Wire
BMW .... Bayerische Motoren Werke [*Bavarian Motor Works*] [*German automobile manufacturer; initialism used as name of its cars and motorcycles*]
BMW .... Beamwidth   (MSA)
B Mw .... Beitraege zur Musikwissenschaft [*A publication*]
BMW-ACA ... BMW [*Bavarian Motor Works*] Automobile Club of America   (EA)
BMWAS.... Building and Monument Workers Association of Scotland [*A union*]
BMWCCA ... BMW [*Bavarian Motor Works*] Car Club of America   (EA)
BMW-CCC ... BMW [*Bavarian Motor Works*] Car Club of Canada   (EAIO)
BMWE ...... Brotherhood of Maintenance of Way Employes   (EA)
BMWEJ .... Brotherhood of Maintenance of Way Employees. Journal [*A publication*]
BMWRA .... BMW [*Bavarian Motor Works*] Riders Association   (EA)
BMWS....... Ballistic Missiles Weapon System
BMWT ...... British Ministry of War Transport [*World War II*]
BMWVCA ... BMW [*Bavarian Motor Works*] Vintage Club of America   (EA)
BMX .... Bicycle Motocross
BMXR ...... Batch Mixer
BMXR .... Block Multiplexer [*Ground Communications Facility, NASA*]
BMY .... Belep [*New Caledonia*] [*Airport symbol*]   (OAG)
BMY .... Black Marlin Energy [*Vancouver Stock Exchange symbol*]
BMY .... Bristol-Myers Squibb Co. [*NYSE symbol*]   (SPSG)
BMYBA ..... British Mycological Society. Bulletin [*A publication*]
BMYSD2... British Mycological Society. Symposium [*A publication*]
BMZ .... Balance Magnetometric Zero   (NOAA)
BMZ .... Bamu [*Papua New Guinea*] [*Airport symbol*]   (OAG)
BMZ .... Basement Membrane Zones [*Anatomy*]
BMZTA..... Biomedizinische Technik [*A publication*]
BN............. All Between _____ and _____ [*Message handling*]   (FAAC)
BN............. Bachelor of Nursing
BN............. Balancing Network
BN............. Ballistic Number   (MCD)
BN............. Banknote
BN............. Barn
BN............. Baron
BN............. Barons Oil Ltd. [*Toronto Stock Exchange symbol*]
BN............. Bassoon [*Music*]
BN............. Battalion   (AFM)
BN............. Bauxite & Northern Railway Co. [*Later, BXN*] [*AAR code*]
BN............. Beacon
BN............. Becklin-Neugebauer [*Astronomy*]
BN............. Been
BN............. Beitraege zur Namenforschung [*A publication*]
BN............. Ben Naphtali   (BJA)
Bn............. Benedictus de Isernia [*Flourished, 1221-52*] [*Authority cited in pre-1607 legal work*]   (DSA)
BN............. Benelux Nieuws [*Belgium*] [*A publication*]
Bn............. Benzyl [*Organic chemistry*]
BN............. Bet Nahrain   (BJA)
BN............. Beta-Naphthol [*Organic chemistry*]
BN............. Beverage Network [*An association*]   (EA)
BN............. Bibliotheque Nationale [*A publication*]
BN............. Bibliotheque Norbertine [*A publication*]
BN............. Bicycle Network   (EA)
BN............. Billion
B & N .... Bills and Notes [*Legal term*]   (DLA)
BN............. Bills and Notes
BN............. Binary Number [*Data processing*]
BN............. Biography News [*A publication*]

BN............ Biuletyn Numizmatyczny [*A publication*]
BN............. Blind Navigation
BN............. Bloody Nuisance [*British slang*]
BN............. Blowing Sand [*Meteorology*]   (FAAC)
Bn............. Blue Nose Minnow [*Ichthyology*]
BN............. Bolt and Nut
BN............. Bombardier-Navigator   (MUGU)
Bn............. Bombesin [*Biochemistry*]
B/N........... Bombing/Navigation   (NG)
BN............. Bond Number [*Chemistry*]
BN............. Book Notes [*A publication*]
BN............. Borden, Inc. [*NYSE symbol*] [*Wall Street slang name: "Moo Moo"*]   (SPSG)
BN............. Born   (ADA)
BN............. Boron Nitride [*Inorganic fiber*]
BN............. Borsen [*A publication*]
BN............. Branch on Nonzero
BN............. Braniff Airways, Inc. [*of Braniff International Corp.*] [*ICAO designator*]   (OAG)
BN............. Brazilian Navy
BN............. Brigantine [*Ship*]   (ROG)
BN........... Britten Norman (Bembridge) Ltd. [*Great Britain*] [*ICAO aircraft manufacturer identifier*]   (ICAO)
BN............. Brown Norway [*Rat variety*]
BN............. Browning Newsletter [*A publication*]
B'n............. Bruedern [*Brethren*] [*German*] [*Freemasonry*]
BN............. Brunei Darussalam [*ANSI two-letter standard code*]   (CNC)
BN............. Brussels Nomenclature [*Standard customs nomenclature published by the Customs Cooperation Council*]
BN............. Bulimia Nervosa [*Medicine*]
BN............. Bull Nose
B/N........... Bulletin with Newsweek [*A publication*]   (APTA)
BN............. Bureau of Narcotics [*Department of the Treasury*] [*Absorbed by BNDD of Department of Justice*]
BN............. Burke's Newsletter [*A publication*]
BN............. Burlington Northern, Inc. [*AAR code*]
BN............. Burmese Navy   (CINC)
BN............. But Not
B Na........... Bachelor of Navigation
BNA........... Banca Nazionale dell'Agricoltura [*National Bank of Agriculture*] [*Italy*]   (ECON)
BNA........... Bangladesh News Agency
BNA........... Baromedical Nurses Association   (EA)
BNA........... Basle Nomina Anatomica [*Basel Anatomical Nomenclature*] [*Medicine*]
BNA........... Beta-Naphthylamine [*Organic chemistry*]
BNA........... Blackwell North America, Inc. [*New Jersey*] [*ACCORD*] [*UTLAS symbol*]
B/NA......... Blackwell North America, Inc. [*Information service or system*]   (IID)
BNA........... Boeing Network Architecture [*Telecommunications*]   (TSSD)
BNA........... Botswana National Airways
BNA........... Brazil Nut Association
BNA........... British Naval Attache   (NATG)
BNA........... British North America
BNA........... British North Atlantic   (DS)
BNA........... Bunia-Ruampara [*Zaire*] [*Geomagnetic observatory code*]
BNA........... Bureau of National Affairs   (EA)
BNA........... Burma National Army [*Formerly, BDA*]
BNA........... Nakusp Public Library, British Columbia [*Library symbol*] [*National Library of Canada*]   (NLC)
BNA........... Nashville [*Tennessee*] [*Airport symbol*] [*Derived from Berry Field-Nashville*]
BNA........... Tijdschrift. Nationale Bank van Belgie [*A publication*]
BNAA......... British North American Act
BNAC....... British-North American Committee   (EA)
BNAF....... Brazil Nut Advertising Fund [*Defunct*]   (EA)
BNAF....... British North Africa Force
BNAF....... Business Name and Address File [*IRS*]
BNAKM.... Nakusp Museum, British Columbia [*Library symbol*] [*National Library of Canada*]   (NLC)
BNAM....... Naramata Museum, British Columbia [*Library symbol*] [*National Library of Canada*]   (NLC)
BNAMC.... Bulletin. National Association for Music Therapy [*A publication*]
BNAP....... Bulletin. National Association of Secondary-School Principals [*A publication*]
BNAPM..... British National Association of Perry Makers
BNAPS..... British North America Philatelic Society   (EA)
BN Arch..... Bachelor of Naval Architecture
B Narcotics ... Bulletin on Narcotics [*A publication*]
BNAS........ British Naval Air Service
BNAS......... British Naval Air Staff
BNA Sec Reg ... Securities Regulation and Law Reports (Bureau of National Affairs) [*A publication*]
BNASS...... Biennial National Atomic Spectroscopy Symposium
B Nat Geogr Soc India ... Bulletin. National Geographical Society of India [*A publication*]
BNatRes .... Bachelor of Natural Resources   (ADA)

B Nauk Inst Nauk Ekon Univ Warszaw ... Biuletyn Naukowy Instytutu Nauk Ekonomicznych Universytetu Warszawskiego [*A publication*]
BNB........... Banque Nationale de Belgique [*National Bank of Belgium*]
BNB........... Baton Broadcasting, Inc. [*Toronto Stock Exchange symbol*]
BNB........... Beslissingen Nederlandse Belastingrechtspraak [*Tax Case Reports*] [*A publication*]   (ILCA)
BNB........... Bikes Not Bombs   (EA)
BNB........... Boende [*Zaire*] [*Airport symbol*]   (OAG)
BNB........... Bracton's Note Book Tempore Henry III [*A publication*]   (DLA)
BNB........... Brazilian News Briefs [*A publication*]   (EAAP)
BNB........... British National Bibliography [*A publication*]
BNB........... British North Borneo
BNBC....... British National Book Centre
BNBC....... Broad National Bancorporation [*NASDAQ symbol*]   (NQ)
BNBE....... Bibliografia Extranjera Depositada en la Biblioteca Nacional [*Ministerio de Cultura*] [*Spain*] [*Information service or system*]   (CRD)
BNBE....... Economic Bulletin. National Bank of Egypt [*A publication*]
BNBG....... Bull & Bear Group, Inc. [*NASDAQ symbol*]   (NQ)
BNBGAP... Bulletin. National Botanic Garden [*Lucknow*] [*A publication*]
BN Bian Ner ... BN. Bianco e Nero [*A publication*]
BNBID...... Behavioral and Neural Biology [*A publication*]
BNBM...... British Nuclear Ballistic Missile
BNB/REN ... Revista Economica do Nordeste. Banco do Nordeste do Brasil. Departamento de Estudos Economicos do Nordeste [*A publication*]
BNBRF...... British National Bibliography Research Fund
BNBSA..... British National Bibliographical Staff Association
BNBUD..... Baroid News Bulletin [*A publication*]
BNC........... Baby "N" Connector   (IEEE)
BNC........... Barcan Communications, Inc. [*Vancouver Stock Exchange symbol*]
BNC........... Base Neutralizing Capacity [*Chemistry*]
BNC........... Benzoylated-Naphthoylated (DEAE) [*Diethylaminoethyl*]-Cellulose [*Analytical biochemistry*]
BNC........... Bethany Nazarene College [*Oklahoma*]
BNC........... Bibliotheque Nationale du Canada [*National Library of Canada - NLC*]
BNC........... Bingham. New Cases, English Common Pleas [*A publication*]   (DLA)
BNC........... Board of Navy Commissioners [*1815-1842*]
BNC........... Brand Name Contract   (AABC)
BNC........... Brasenose College [*Oxford*]
BNC........... British National Committee on Surface Active Agents
BNC........... Brooke's New Cases, English King's Bench [*1515-58*] [*A publication*]   (DLA)
BNC........... Bulgarian National Committee   (EA)
BNC........... Busbee's North Carolina Law Reports [*A publication*]   (DLA)
BNC........... Business and Finance [*A publication*]
BNC........... Regional Financial Shares Investment Fund, Inc. [*NYSE symbol*]   (SPSG)
BNCA........ Buccaneer National Class Association   (EA)
BNCA........ Bureau of National Capital Airports [*of FAA*]
Bnc Angola ... Boletin Trimestral. Banco de Angola [*A publication*]
BNCAR..... British National Committee on Antarctic Research
BNCC........ BUIC [*Backup Interceptor Control*] NOPAD Control Center
BNCDST ... British National Committee on Data for Science and Technology   (DIT)
BNCE/CE ... Comercio Exterior. Banco Nacional de Comercio Exterior [*A publication*]
Bnc Espana ... Banco de Espana [*A publication*]
BNCF........ Biblioteca Nazionale Centrale, Florence [*Italy*]
BNCH........ Bench   (MSA)
BNCHBD.. Benchboard   (KSC)
BNC/ICC .. British National Committee of the International Chamber of Commerce   (DS)
BNCL........ Binnacle   (MSA)
Bnc Lavoro ... Italian Trends. Banco Lavoro [*A publication*]
BNCLR...... Binocular   (MSA)
BNCM...... British National Committee on Materials
BNCM....... Nanaimo Centennial Museum, British Columbia [*Library symbol*] [*National Library of Canada*]   (NLC)
BNCO........ British Non-Commissioned Officer [*British military*]   (DMA)
BNCOC .... Basic Noncommissioned Officer Course [*Army*]   (INF)
BNCOE ..... British National Committee on Ocean Engineering
BNCOQ..... Bachelor Noncommissioned Officers' Quarters [*Air Force*]   (AFM)
BNCOR..... British National Committee on Research
B & NCR... Belfast and North Counties Railway [*British*]   (ROG)
BNCRC...... Bethesda National Christian Resource Center   (EA)
BNCS........ British Numerical Control Society   (MCD)
BNCSR...... British National Committee on Space Research
BNCT .... Boron Neutron Capture Therapy
BNCW...... Bare Nickel Chrome Wire
BND........... Bachelor of Nutrition and Dietetics
BND........... Band   (KSC)
BND........... Bandar Abbas [*Iran*] [*Airport symbol*]   (OAG)
BND........... Bandung [*Indonesia*] [*Seismograph station code, US Geological Survey*] [*Closed*]   (SEIS)

BND.......... Bend
BND.......... Benzoylated-Naphthoylated DEAE [*Diethylaminoethyl*]
bnd .... Binder [*MARC relator code*] [*Library of Congress*] (LCCP)
BND.......... Bond (ROG)
BND.......... Bonded (MSA)
BND.......... Bound (FAAC)
BND.......... Brenda Mines Ltd. [*Toronto Stock Exchange symbol*] [*Vancouver Stock Exchange symbol*]
BND.......... Bundesnachrichtendienst [*Federal Intelligence Service*] [*Federal Republic of Germany*]
BNDC........ British Nuclear Design and Construction
BNDD........ Bureau of Narcotics and Dangerous Drugs [*Formerly, Bureau of Narcotics and Bureau of Drug Abuse Control; later, Drug Enforcement Administration*] [*Department of Justice*]
BNDDIS.... Band Display
BNDE........ Banco Nacional do Desenvolvimento Economico [*National Economic Development Bank*] [*Brazil*]
BNDG........ Bonding
BNDL........ Bundle
BndM........ Benediktinische Monatsschrift [*A publication*]
BNDO........ Bureau National des Donnees Oceaniques [*National Bureau for Ocean Data*] [*European host database system*] [*France*] [*Information service or system*] (IID)
BNDP .... Bet-Nahrain Democratic Party [*Political party*] (BJA)
BNDP .... Brunei National Democratic Party [*Political party*] (FEA)
Bndr .... Bandmaster [*Military*] [*British*] (DMA)
BNDR........ Binder
BNDRY ..... Boundary (AFM)
BNDS .... Silvery Slocan Historical Museum, New Denver, British Columbia [*Library symbol*] [*National Library of Canada*] (NLC)
BNDSA...... Bibliotheca Nutrito et Dieta (Switzerland) [*A publication*]
BNDSD ..... Bundesarbeitsblatt [*A publication*]
BNDSMN ... Bondsman
BNDY .... Brandywine Savings and Loan Association [*NASDAQ symbol*] (NQ)
BNDZ .... Bonderize
BNE .... Bachelor of Naval Engineering
Bne .... Bartone [*Record label*]
BNE .... Bathymetric Navigation Equipment
BNE .... Board of National Estimates [*Terminated*] [*CIA*]
BNE .... Board of Nurse Examiners
BNE .... Bowne & Co., Inc. [*AMEX symbol*] (SPSG)
BNE .... Brisbane [*Australia*] [*Airport symbol*] (OAG)
BNE .... Burnie High School [*Tasmania*] [*Seismograph station code, US Geological Survey*] (SEIS)
BNE .... But Not Exceeding
BNE .... Nelson Public Library, British Columbia [*Library symbol*] [*National Library of Canada*] (BIB)
BNE .... Richmond, VA [*Location identifier*] [*FAA*] (FAAL)
BNEC .... British National Export Council
BNEC .... British Nuclear Energy Conference
BN Ed .... Bachelor of Nursing Education
BNEM .... Nelson Museum, British Columbia [*Library symbol*] [*National Library of Canada*] (NLC)
BNEMRL ... Battelle New England Marine Research Laboratory [*Battelle Memorial Institute*] [*Research center*] (RCD)
BN Eng ...... Bachelor of Naval Engineering
BNEOB .... Biology of the Neonate [*A publication*]
BNEP........ Basic Naval Establishment Plan
BNEPB ..... Behavioral Neuropsychiatry [*A publication*]
BNER .... Brenner Companies, Inc. [*NASDAQ symbol*] (NQ)
BNES........ British Nuclear Energy Society
BNESAA ... Bureau of Near Eastern and South Asian Affairs [*Department of State*]
BNF .... Backus Naur [*or Normal*] Form [*ALGOL*] [*Data processing*] (BUR)
BNF .... Baranof, AK [*Location identifier*] [*FAA*] (FAAL)
BNF .... Beitraege zur Namenforschung [*A publication*]
BNF .... Beta-Naphthoflavone [*Organic chemistry*]
BNF .... Big Name Fan [*of science fiction or fantastic literature*] [*See also LNF*]
BNF .... Biological Nitrogen Fixation [*Agriculture*]
BNF .... Bomb Nose Fuze
BNF .... Boolean Normal Form [*Mathematics*]
BNF .... Boron Nitride Fiber [*Inorganic fiber*]
BNF .... Botswana National Front [*Political party*] (PPW)
BNF .... Brand Names Foundation (EA)
BNF .... Braniff International Corp. [*ICAO designator*]
BNF .... British National Formulary [*A publication*]
BNF .... British Non-Ferrous Metals Abstracts [*BNF Metals Technology Centre*] [*Information service or system*] (CRD)
BNF .... British Nuclear Forum
BNF .... British Nuclear Fuels Ltd.
BNF .... British Nutrition Foundation
BNF .... Bulgarian National Front (EA)
BNFC........ British National Film Catalogue (DIT)
BNFEX..... Battalion Field Exercise [*Military*] (NVT)
BNFL........ British Nuclear Fuels Ltd.
BNFMRA ... British Non-Ferrous Metals Research Association
BNFMTC.. BNF Metals Technology Centre (EAIO)

BNF Nutr Bull ... BNF [*British Nutrition Foundation*] Nutrition Bulletin [*A publication*]
BNFP........ Barnwell Nuclear Fuel Plant (NRCH)
BNG.......... Bangui [*Central African Republic*] [*Seismograph station code, US Geological Survey*] (SEIS)
BNG.......... Bangui [*Central African Republic*] [*Geomagnetic observatory code*]
BNG.......... Banning, CA [*Location identifier*] [*FAA*] (FAAL)
BNG.......... Bending (MSA)
BNG.......... Benetton Group SpA [*NYSE symbol*] (SPSG)
BNG.......... Branch No Group [*Data processing*] (MDG)
BNG.......... British New Guinea (ADA)
BNG.......... Broadland Noise Generator
BNG.......... Bureau of Natural Gas [*of FPC*]
BNG.......... State University of New York at Binghamton, Binghamton, NY [*OCLC symbol*] (OCLC)
B Ng Jb..... Byzantinisch-Neugriechische Jahrbuecher [*A publication*]
BNGM....... British Naval Gunnery Mission [*British military*] (DMA)
BNGO....... Bingo King Co., Inc. [*NASDAQ symbol*] (NQ)
BNGrJb..... Byzantinisch-Neugriechische Jahrbuecher [*A publication*]
BNGS .... Bomb Navigation Guidance System
BNH .... Berlin [*New Hampshire*] [*Seismograph station code, US Geological Survey*] (SEIS)
BNH .... Brenham, TX [*Location identifier*] [*FAA*] (FAAL)
BNH .... Bunker Hill Mining [*Vancouver Stock Exchange symbol*]
BNH .... Burnish (KSC)
BNHB....... BNH Bancshares, Inc. [*New Haven, CT*] [*NASDAQ symbol*] (NQ)
BNHC........ Bank of New Hampshire Corporation [*Manchester, NH*] [*NASDAQ symbol*] (NQ)
BNHI........ Bancorp Hawaii, Incorporated [*NASDAQ symbol*] (NQ)
BNHMB6 ... Bulletin. Natural History Museum in Belgrade [*A publication*]
BNHN....... Benihana National Corp. [*NASDAQ symbol*] (NQ)
BNHPDH ... Basrah Natural History Museum. Publication [*A publication*]
BNHQ....... Battalion Headquarters [*Marine Corps*]
BNHS....... British Natural Hygiene Society
BNHSC ..... Boston National Historic Sites Commission [*Government agency, discontinued, 1960*]
BNI .... Bank van de Nederlandse Antillen. Quarterly Bulletin [*A publication*]
BNI .... Bengal Native Infantry [*Military*] [*British*]
BNI .... Benin City [*Nigeria*] [*Airport symbol*] (OAG)
BNI .... Bibliografia Nazionale Italiana [*A publication*]
BNI .... Borkin Industries Corp. [*Vancouver Stock Exchange symbol*]
BNI .... Burlington Northern, Incorporated [*NYSE symbol*] (SPSG)
BNIAA ...... Norinsho Kachiku Eisei Shikenjo Kenkyu Hokoku [*A publication*]
B Nimes ..... Bulletin. Societe d'Etude des Sciences Naturelles de Nimes [*A publication*]
BNIO .... British National Institute of Oceanography
BNIST .... Bureau National de l'Information Scientifique et Technique [*National Scientific and Technical Information Bureau*] [*France*] [*Information service or system*] (IID)
BNIST Rapp Annu ... BNIST [*Bureau National de l'Information Scientifique et Technique*] Rapport Annuel [*A publication*]
BNJ........... Bonn [*West Germany*] [*Airport symbol*] (OAG)
BNJ........... British Numismatic Journal, Including the Proceedings of the British Numismatic Society [*A publication*]
BNJ........... Business News. Facts, Analysis, Information [*A publication*]
BNJ........... Byzantinisch-Neugriechische Jahrbuecher [*A publication*]
B NJ Acad S ... Bulletin. New Jersey Academy of Science [*A publication*]
BNK .... ABA [*American Bankers Association*] Banking Journal [*A publication*]
BNK .... Ballina [*Australia*] [*Airport symbol*]
BNK .... Bank (ROG)
BNK .... Bank Reports [*A publication*]
BNKAB .... Bionika [*A publication*]
BNKF........ Bankers First Corp. [*Augusta, GA*] [*NASDAQ symbol*] (NQ)
BNKG....... Banking (ADA)
BNKM....... Marine Bank [*Board on Geographic Names*]
BNKRB..... Banker [*A publication*]
BNKS......... United New Mexico Finance Corp. [*Formerly, Bank Securities, Inc.*] [*NASDAQ symbol*] (NQ)
BNKW .... BankWorcester Corp. [*NASDAQ symbol*] (NQ)
BNL .... Background Noise Level (CAAL)
BNL .... Banca Nazionale del Lavoro. Quarterly Review [*A publication*]
BNL .... Barnwell, SC [*Location identifier*] [*FAA*] (FAAL)
BNL .... Battelle Northwest Laboratories
BNL .... Beitraege zur Neueren Literaturgeschichte [*A publication*]
BNL .... Beneficial Corp. [*Wall Street slang name: "Big Nose Louie"*] [*NYSE symbol*] (SPSG)
BNL .... Benthic Nepheloid Layer [*Oceanography*]
BNL .... Berkeley Nuclear Laboratories [*England*]
BNL .... Brookhaven National Laboratory [*Department of Energy*] [*Upton, NY*]
BNLO........ British Naval Liaison Officer
BNLUS..... British Naval Liaison [*Office*] US Navy [*London*]
BNLVAI.... Brookhaven National Laboratory. Lectures in Science. Vistas in Research [*A publication*]
BNM......... Bank Marketing [*A publication*]
BNM.......... Before New Moon [*Freemasonry*] (ROG)

BNM......... Board of National Ministries (EA)
BNM......... Bodinumu [*Papua New Guinea*] [*Airport symbol*] (OAG)
BNM......... Malaspina College, Nanaimo, British Columbia [*Library symbol*] [*National Library of Canada*] (NLC)
BNMB....... Bank Negara Malaysia. Bulletin [*A publication*]
BNMBL..... MacMillan Bloedel Ltd., Nanaimo, British Columbia [*Library symbol*] [*National Library of Canada*] (NLC)
BNMFDC ... New Mexico. Department of Game and Fish. Bulletin [*A publication*]
BNML........ Bitter National Magnet Laboratory
BNML....... Burlington Northern (Manitoba) Limited [*AAR code*]
BNMRA .... British Non-Ferrous Metals Research Association
BNMS .... Bus Neutral Mass Spectrometer [*Space science instrumentation*]
BNMSE..... Brief Neuropsychological Mental Status Examination
BNN.......... Banner Entertainment [*Vancouver Stock Exchange symbol*]
BNN.......... Bronnoysund [*Norway*] [*Airport symbol*] (OAG)
BNN.......... Buggalo Nam Newsletter [*A publication*]
BNND........ Learning Resources Centre, David Thompson Library, Nelson, British Columbia [*Library symbol*] [*National Library of Canada*] (BIB)
BNNT .... Barnes' Notes on the New Testament [*A publication*]
BN Nursing Studies ... Bachelor of Nursing, Nursing Studies, University of Southampton [*British*] (DBQ)
BNO.......... Backus Normal Form [*ALGOL*] [*Data processing*]
BNo........... Biblische Notizen [*A publication*]
BNO.......... Bipartite News Office [*Post-World War II, Germany*]
BNO.......... Biuletyn Nauczyciela Opolskiego [*A publication*]
BNO.......... Bladder Neck Obstruction [*Medicine*]
BNO.......... Bowels Not Opened [*Medicine*]
BNO.......... Burns, OR [*Location identifier*] [*FAA*] (FAAL)
BNOA....... Beta-Naphthoxyacetic Acid [*Plant growth compound*]
BNOA....... British Naturopathic and Osteopathic Association
BNOB....... Bulletin. Nederlandse Oudheidkundige Bond [*A publication*]
BNOC....... Barbados National Oil Company [*State-owned*] (EY)
BNOC....... Basic Noncommissioned Officer Course [*Army*]
BNOC....... British National Oil Corporation [*Pronounced "bee-knock"*] [*Nationalized industry*] [*London, England*]
BNOC....... British National Opera Company
BNOTA ..... Belgisch-Nederlands Tijdschrift voor Oppervlaktetechnieken van Metalen [*A publication*]
BNOV....... But Not Over
BNP.......... Background Noise Power
BNP.......... Bangladesh National Party [*Bangladesh Jatiyabadi Dal*] (PPW)
BNP.......... Bannu [*Pakistan*] [*Airport symbol*] (OAG)
BNP.......... Banque Nationale de Paris [*National Bank of Paris*] [*France*]
BNP.......... Basotho National Party [*Lesotho*] [*Political party*] (PPW)
BNP.......... Bellefonte Nuclear Plant (NRCH)
BNP.......... Boddie-Noell Restaurant Properties [*AMEX symbol*] (SPSG)
BNP.......... Brain Natriuretic Peptide [*Biochemistry*]
BNP.......... British National Party (PPW)
BNP.......... Buller's Law of Nisi Prius [*England*] [*A publication*] (DLA)
BNP.......... Bureau of Naval Personnel [*Also, BUPERS, NAVPERS*]
BNP.......... Pacific Biological Station, Fisheries and Oceans Canada [*Station Biologique du Pacifique, Peches et Oceans Canada*] Nanaimo, British Columbia [*Library symbol*] [*National Library of Canada*] (NLC)
BNPA .... Beta-Nitropropionic Acid [*Organic chemistry*]
BNPCL...... Bureau of Naval Personnel Circular Letters
BNPE........ Bis(nitrophenyl)ethyl [*Organic radical*]
BNPEOC... Bis(nitrophenyl)ethyloxycarbonyl [*Organic radical*]
BNPF........ Beginning, Negative, Positive, Finish [*ASCII subset*]
BNPG-PSG ... Bloque Nacional Popular de Galicia - Partido Socialista Gallego [*Popular National Bloc of Galicia - Galician Socialist Party*] [*Political party*] (PPW)
BNPL........ Bulletin. New York Public Library [*A publication*]
BNPM .... Bureau of Naval Personnel Manual
BNPP........ Barisan Nasional Penbebasan Pattani [*Political party*] [*Thailand*]
BNQ.......... Bibliotheque Nationale du Quebec [*UTLAS symbol*]
BNR.......... Bank Note Reporter [*A publication*]
BNR.......... Bell Northern Research [*Telecommunications*] (TEL)
BNR.......... Billed but Not Received (AFIT)
BNR.......... Bladder Neck Resection [*Medicine*]
BNR.......... Bond Negative Resistor
BN & R ...... Botswana Notes and Records [*A publication*]
BNR.......... Botswana Notes and Records [*A publication*]
BNR.......... Brand Name Resale (AABC)
BNR.......... Brassey's Naval Record [*Brassey's Defence Publishers Ltd.*] [*Information service or system*] [*No longer maintained*] (IID)
BNR.......... Broulan Resources, Inc. [*Toronto Stock Exchange symbol*]
BNR.......... Burner (MSA)
BNR.......... Findlay, OH [*Location identifier*] [*FAA*] (FAAL)
BNRID....... Basic Net Radio Interface Device (MCD)
BNRMAS ... Bolt, Nut, and Rivet Makers Association of Scotland [*A union*]
BNRVR ..... Bengal-Nagpore Railway Volunteer Rifles [*British military*] (DMA)
BNRY....... Bonray Drilling Corp. [*NASDAQ symbol*] (NQ)
BNS .... Bachelor of Naval Science
BNS .... Bachelor of Nursing Science

BNS .... Bangong-Nujiang Suture [*Paleogeography*]
BNS .... Bank of Nova Scotia [*Toronto Stock Exchange symbol*] [*Vancouver Stock Exchange symbol*]
BNS .... Banque Nationale Suisse. Bulletin Mensuel [*A publication*]
BNS .... Barinas [*Venezuela*] [*Airport symbol*] (OAG)
BNS .... Bell Number Screening [*Telecommunications*] (TEL)
BNS .... Bensberg [*Federal Republic of Germany*] [*Seismograph station code, US Geological Survey*] (SEIS)
BNS .... Biblical Numismatic Society (EA)
BNS .... Binary Number System [*Data processing*]
BNS .... Biological Nuclear Solvent [*Physiology*]
BNS .... Bombing-Navigation System (AFM)
BNS .... Bonus (ADA)
BNS .... Boston Naval Shipyard
BNS .... British Naval Staff
BNS .... British Neuropathological Society
BNS .... British Numismatic Society
BNS .... Broadcasters Nonprofit Satellite Service [*Ford Foundation*]
BNS .... Brown & Sharpe Manufacturing Co. [*NYSE symbol*] (SPSG)
BNS .... Bureau of Naval Ships [*Obsolete*] (MCD)
BNS .... Sheridan, WY [*Location identifier*] [*FAA*] (FAAL)
BN Sc....... Bachelor of Nursing Science
BNSC........ British National Space Centre
BNSCDX... Braunschweiger Naturkundliche Schriften [*A publication*]
BNSDA...... Bulletin. New York State Society of Dentistry for Children [*A publication*]
BNSFCP.... Battalion Shore Fire Control Party
BNSH .... Burnish (MSA)
BNSIFCO ... Brian Nolan Spradlin International Fan Club Organization (EA)
BNSIG....... Behavioral Neuropsychology Special Interest Group (EA)
BNSKA...... Bunseki Kagaku [*A publication*]
BNSMR..... Bank of Nova Scotia. Monthly Review [*A publication*]
BNSO .... Bonso Electronics International, Inc. [*NASDAQ symbol*] (NQ)
BNSP .... Basic National Security Police (MCD)
BNSS .... Baroness (ROG)
BNSV....... Vocational Division, Selkirk College, Nelson, British Columbia [*Library symbol*] [*National Library of Canada*] (NLC)
BNSY....... Boston Naval Shipyard
BNT .... Bank of Alberta [*Toronto Stock Exchange symbol*]
BNT .... Bennington College, Bennington, VT [*OCLC symbol*] (OCLC)
BNT .... Bent
BNT .... Bonnet (MSA)
BNT .... Boreal Northern Titles [*Database*] [*Boreal Institute for Northern Studies*] [*Information service or system*] (CRD)
BNT .... Broadband Network Termination [*Telecommunications*]
BNT .... Brussels Tariff Nomenclature (ILCA)
BNT .... Bundi [*Papua New Guinea*] [*Airport symbol*] (OAG)
BNT .... Burnt (ROG)
BNT .... Salt Lake City, UT [*Location identifier*] [*FAA*] (FAAL)
BNTA .... Banta Corp. [*NASDAQ symbol*] (NQ)
BNTA .... British Numismatic Trade Association
BNTF........ Battalion Task Force (MCD)
BNTH....... Beneath (FAAC)
BNTN....... Benton Oil & Gas Co. [*NASDAQ symbol*] (NQ)
BNTO....... Bonding Tool (AAG)
BNTY....... Bounty Group, Inc. [*NASDAQ symbol*] (NQ)
BNU.......... Basic Networking Utilities
BNU.......... Basic Notch Unit
BNU.......... Benson Needham Univas [*International advertising network*]
BNUI........ Bio-Nutrionics, Incorporated [*New York, NY*] [*NASDAQ symbol*] (NQ)
B Num....... Bulletin de Numismatique [*A publication*]
B Num (Paris) ... Bulletin. Societe Francaise de Numismatique (Paris) [*A publication*]
BNUNA..... Bulletin on Narcotics [*Switzerland*] [*A publication*]
BNurs........ Bachelor of Nursing, University of Manchester [*British*] (DBQ)
BNursing ... Bachelor of Nursing
BNV.......... Benevento [*Italy*] [*Seismograph station code, US Geological Survey*] [*Closed*] (SEIS)
BNV.......... Business Asia. Weekly Report to Managers of Asia/Pacific Operations [*A publication*]
BNV.......... North Vancouver City Library, British Columbia [*Library symbol*] [*National Library of Canada*] (NLC)
BNVBR...... Ballard Research, Inc., North Vancouver, British Columbia [*Library symbol*] [*National Library of Canada*] (NLC)
BNVD........ District of North Vancouver Library, British Columbia [*Library symbol*] [*National Library of Canada*] (NLC)
BNVHRTVG ... Bedside Network of the Veterans Hospital Radio and TV Guild [*Later, VBN*] (EA)
BNVI .... Vancouver Island Regional Library, Nanaimo, British Columbia [*Library symbol*] [*National Library of Canada*] (NLC)
BNVIC....... Insurance Corp. of British Columbia, North Vancouver [*Library symbol*] [*National Library of Canada*] (BIB)
BNVPM .... Pacific Marine Training Institute, North Vancouver, British Columbia [*Library symbol*] [*National Library of Canada*] (NLC)
BNVSL...... Special Libraries Cataloguing, Inc., North Vancouver, British Columbia [*Library symbol*] [*National Library of Canada*] (NLC)

BNVTW .... Western Regional Library, Transport Canada [*Bibliotheque Regionale de l'Ouest, Transports Canada*], North Vancouver, British Columbia [*Library symbol*] [*National Library of Canada*]

BNVUDY .. Bericht des Naturwissenschaftlichen Vereins fuer Bielefeld und Umgegend EV [*A publication*]

BNW .... Barnwell Industries, Inc. [*Toronto Stock Exchange symbol*]

BNW .... Blackwell North America, Inc. [*Oregon*] [*ACCORD*] [*UTLAS symbol*]

BNW .... Boone, IA [*Location identifier*] [*FAA*]   (FAAL)

BNW .... Bureau of Naval Weapons [*Obsolete*]

BNW .... New Westminster Public Library, British Columbia [*Library symbol*] [*National Library of Canada*]   (NLC)

BNWAG .... Agricultural Development Branch, Agriculture Canada [*Direction Generale du Developpement Agricole, Agriculture Canada*], New Westminster, British Columbia [*Library symbol*] [*National Library of Canada*] [*Obsolete*]   (BIB)

BNWB .... British Columbian, New Westminster, British Columbia [*Library symbol*] [*National Library of Canada*]   (NLC)

BNWCR ..... CanOcean Resources Ltd., New Westminster, British Columbia [*Library symbol*] [*National Library of Canada*]   (NLC)

BNWD .... Douglas College, New Westminster, British Columbia [*Library symbol*] [*National Library of Canada*]   (NLC)

BNWHC .... New Westminster Historic Centre and Museum, British Columbia [*Library symbol*] [*National Library of Canada*]   (NLC)

BNWL .... Battelle Northwest Laboratories   (KSC)

BNWL .... Lower Mainland Regional Planning Board, New Westminster, British Columbia [*Library symbol*] [*National Library of Canada*]   (NLC)

BNWLH .... Canadian Lacrosse Hall of Fame, New Westminster, British Columbia [*Library symbol*] [*National Library of Canada*]   (NLC)

BNWLP ..... Lockheed Petroleum Services Ltd., New Westminster, British Columbia [*Library symbol*] [*National Library of Canada*]   (NLC)

BNWRC .... Royal Columbian Hospital, New Westminster, British Columbia [*Library symbol*] [*National Library of Canada*]   (NLC)

B & NW RY BN ... Bengal & North-Western Railway Battalion [*British military*]   (DMA)

BNWSP ..... Stuart Plastics Ltd., New Westminster, British Columbia [*Library symbol*] [*National Library of Canada*]   (NLC)

BNX .... British Nuclear Export Executives [*Group to promote export of nuclear power stations of British design*]

BNX .... Falmouth, MA [*Location identifier*] [*FAA*]   (FAAL)

BNY .... Bank of New York Co., Inc.   (ADA)

BNY .... Bellona Island [*Solomon Islands*] [*Airport symbol*]   (OAG)

BNY .... Binghamton [*New York*] [*Seismograph station code, US Geological Survey*]   (SEIS)

BNY .... Bundy Corp. [*NYSE symbol*]   (SPSG)

BNY .... Burney, CA [*Location identifier*] [*FAA*]   (FAAL)

B NY Ac Med ... Bulletin. New York Academy of Medicine [*A publication*]

BNYD .... Boston Navy Yard [*Later, Boston Naval Shipyard*]

BNYD .... Bureau of Navy Yards and Docks [*Later, NFEC*]

BNYLS ..... Bulletin. New York C. S. Lewis Society [*A publication*]

BNYPL ...... Bulletin. New York Public Library [*A publication*]

BNYVV ..... Beet Necrotic Yellow Vein Virus

BNZ .... Bank of New Zealand

BNZ .... BANZ [*British-Australian-New Zealand*] [*Papua New Guinea*] [*Airport symbol*] [*Obsolete*]   (OAG)

BNZ .... Bonanza Resources Ltd. [*Toronto Stock Exchange symbol*]

BNZA .... Bonanza International, Inc. [*NASDAQ symbol*]   (NQ)

BNZED ..... Bulletin. New Zealand National Society for Earthquake Engineering [*A publication*]

BNZS .... Bulgarski Naroden Zemedelski Suiuz [*Bulgarian National Agrarian Union*]   (PPE)

BO .... Bachelor of Oratory

BO .... Bachelor of Osteopathy

BO .... Back Order

BO .... Bad Order [*i.e., requiring repair*]

BO .... Bail Out

B & O .... [*The*] Baltimore & Ohio Railroad Co. [*Chessie System, Inc.*]

B & O .... Band and Orchestra [*Musical slang*]

BO .... Banker's Order

BO .... Barkhausen-Kurz Oscillator

BO .... Base Order

BO .... Base-Out (Prism) [*Ophthalmology*]

BO .... Basioccipital [*Anatomy*]

BO .... Battalion Orders [*British military*]   (DMA)

BO .... Beat Oscillator

B & O .... Belladonna and Opium [*Toxicology*]

BO .... Bench Order

BO .... Beneficial Occupancy

BO .... Benzoyloxime [*Organic chemistry*]

BO .... Best Offer [*Classified advertising*]

B e O .... Bibbia e Oriente [*A publication*]

BO .... Bibbia e Oriente [*A publication*]   (BJA)

BO .... Bibliotheca Orientalis [*A publication*]

BO .... Binary to Octal [*Data processing*]   (BUR)

BO .... Bingo Clubs and Halls [*Public-performance tariff class*] [*British*]

BO .... Biological Origin

BO .... Black Orpheus [*A publication*]

BO .... Blackout

BO .... Blanking Oscillator   (MCD)

BO .... Blockhouse Operation [*NASA*]

BO .... Blocking Oscillator

BO .... Blockout

BO .... Blowoff

BO .... Board of Ordnance

BO .... Board's Order [*British*]   (ROG)

BO .... Bob Oscar Plenty [*Character in "Dick Tracy" comic strip*]

Bo .... Bodenstein Number

BO .... Body Odor [*Slang*]

Bo .... Boghazkoi-Sammlung des Berliner Museum   (BJA)

Bo .... Boghazkoy [*Museum of the Ancient Orient, Istanbul*]   (BJA)

B-O .... Boil-Off

BO .... Boiled [*Linseed*] Oil

BO .... Boiler Manufacturer   (DS)

Bo .... Bolivar [*A publication*]

bo .... Bolivia [*MARC country of publication code*] [*Library of Congress*]   (LCCP)

BO .... Bolivia [*ANSI two-letter standard code*]   (CNC)

BO .... Bolt

BO .... Bolton [*Craniometric point*]

Bo .... Bonaguida de Aretio [*Flourished, 1251-58*] [*Authority cited in pre-1607 legal work*]   (DSA)

Bo .... Bond Number

BO .... Bonding

BO .... Book Order

BO .... Booking Office [*British*]   (ROG)

B/O .... Booster Orbiter   (MCD)

BO .... Born

BO .... Born-Oppenheimer Method [*Physical chemistry*]

BO .... Borough

Bo .... Boston Records [*Record label*]

BO .... Botanical Origin

BO .... Bottom

Bo .... Bottu [*France*] [*Research code symbol*]

BO .... Bought

BO .... Bought Off   (MCD)

BO .... Bowel [*Medicine*]

BO .... Bowel Obstruction [*Medicine*]

BO .... Bowels Opened [*Medicine*]

BO .... Box Office [*Theatrical slang*]

BO .... Branch Office

B/O .... Breakout   (NASA)

BO .... Breakout Box   (MCD)

BO .... Breakover [*Electronics*]

BO .... British Officer [*British military*]   (DMA)

BO .... Broker's Order [*Finance*]

B/O .... Brought Over [*Business term*]

BO .... Bucco-Occlusal [*Dentistry*]

B/O .... Budget Obligation [*or Overlay*]   (NRCH)

BO .... Bug Off [*Slang*]

BO .... Bureau of Ordnance [*Functions transferred to Bureau of Naval Weapons, 1960, and later to Naval Ordnance Systems Command*] [*Navy*]

BO .... Burnout   (KSC)

B-O .... Buy-Off

BO .... Buy Order [*Investment term*]

BO .... Buyer's Option [*Business term*]

BO .... Delta Air Regionalluftverkehr GmbH & Co. [*Germany*] [*ICAO designator*]   (FAAC)

BO .... MBB-UV [*Messerschmitt-Boelkow-Blohm*] [*Federal Republic of Germany*] [*ICAO aircraft manufacturer identifier*]   (ICAO)

BO .... Output Blocking Factor [*Data processing*]   (IBMDP)

BO1 .... Boulder [*Colorado*] [*Seismograph station code, US Geological Survey*] [*Closed*]   (SEIS)

BOA .... Basic Ordering Agreement

BOA .... Benzoic Acid [*Organic chemistry*]

BOA .... Bibliography of Agriculture [*A publication*]

BOA .... Bipolar Operational Amplifier

BOA .... Boaco [*Nicaragua*] [*Seismograph station code, US Geological Survey*]   (SEIS)

Boa .... Boatinus de Mantua [*Deceased, 1300*] [*Authority cited in pre-1607 legal work*]   (DSA)

BOA .... Borcan Resources [*Vancouver Stock Exchange symbol*]

BOA .... Born on Arrival [*of mother at hospital*] [*Medicine*]

BOA .... Boulder Valley School District, Boulder, CO [*OCLC symbol*]   (OCLC)

BOA .... Break-Off Altitude [*Aviation*]   (AFM)

BOA .... British Olympic Association

BOA .... British Optical Association

BOA .... British Orthopaedic Association

BOA .... British Osteopathic Association

BOA .... British Overseas Airways Corp. [*Later, British Airways*]

BOA .... Broad Ocean Area

BOA .... Brush Owner's Association   (EA)

BOA	Butoxyacetanilide [*Pharmacology*]
BOAA	Beta-Oxalylamino-alanine [*An amino acid*]
BoAb	Boating Abstracts [*A publication*]
BOAC	Billed Office Account Code [*Army*] (AFIT)
BOAC	British Overseas Airways Corporation [*Humorously interpreted as "Better on a Camel"*] [*Later, British Airways*]
BOAD	Banque Ouest Africaine de Developpement [*West African Development Bank - WADB*] (EAIO)
BOAD	Business Organizations and Agencies Directory [*Later, BOAPD*] [*A publication*]
BOADICEA	British Overseas Airways Corp. [*later, British Airways*] Digital Information Computer for Electronic Automation
BOAE	Bureau of Occupational and Adult Education [*Office of Education*]
BOAFG	British Order of Ancient Free Gardeners
BOAG	British Overseas Aid Group (DS)
BOAM	Bell Owned and Maintained [*Telecommunications*] (TEL)
BOA-MILS	Broad Ocean Area - Missile Impact Locating System [*Navy*] (NG)
BOAMP	Bulletin Officiel des Annonces des Marches Publics [*Direction des Journaux Officiels*] [*Database*]
BOAP	Bleomycin, Oncovin [*Vincristine*], Adriamycin, Prednisone [*Antineoplastic drug regimen*]
BOAPD	Business Organizations, Agencies, and Publications Directory [*Formerly, BOAD*] [*A publication*]
BOAR	Board of Action on Redetermination [*Navy*]
Board Environ Stud Res Pap Univ Newcastle	University of Newcastle. Board of Environmental Studies. Research Paper [*A publication*] (APTA)
Board Mfr	Board Manufacture and Practice [*A publication*]
Board of Review Decisions	Decisions. Income Tax Board of Review [*A publication*] (APTA)
Boardroom	Boardroom Reports [*A publication*]
BOAS	Bulletin. School of Oriental and African Studies [*A publication*]
BOASI	Bureau of Old-Age and Survivors Insurance [*Social Security Administration*]
BOAT	Basics of Adult Teaching (OICC)
Boat	Boatinus de Mantua [*Deceased, 1300*] [*Authority cited in pre-1607 legal work*] (DSA)
BOAT	Boatmen's Bankshares, Inc. [*NASDAQ symbol*] (NQ)
Boat Bus	Boating Business [*A publication*]
BOATS	BMT [*British Maritime Technology Ltd.*] Abstracts Online [*Wallsend, Tyne, and Wear, England*] [*Information service or system*] (IID)
BOAT/US	Boat Owners Association of the United States (EA)
BOB	Barges on Board [*Shipping*]
BOB	Berner Oberland-Bahnen [*Bernese Overland Railways*]
BOB	Best on Best (MCD)
BOB	Best of Breed
BOB	Bibliography of Bioethics [*A publication*]
BOB	Bobbin (KSC)
Bo B	Bok og Bibliotek [*A publication*]
BOB	Bora-Bora [*French Polynesia*] [*Airport symbol*] (OAG)
BOB	Brains on Board [*Robot*] [*Androbot, Inc.*]
BOB	Bureau of Biologics [*Also, BB*] [*FDA*]
BOB	Bureau of the Budget [*Later, OMB*]
BOB	Business Opportunity Bank [*Institute for New Enterprise Development*]
BOB	By og Bygd. Norsk Folkemuseums Arbok [*A publication*]
BOB's	Blitter Objects [*Amiga computer hardware*]
B & O Bd of Rev	Selected Decisions of the Board of Revenue, Bihar and Orissa [*A publication*] (DLA)
BOBE	Bob Evans Farms, Inc. [*NASDAQ symbol*] (NQ)
BOBELE	Boris Becker of Leimen [*Acronym also refers to pretzel produced by German bakers in recognition of this tennis player*]
BOBO	Big Oil Bail Out [*Reference by Rep. James H. Scheuer (NY) to a particular toxic waste clean-up bill*]
BOBR	Boring Bar
BOBS	Beacon Only Bombing System
BO/BS	Bolted-on-Base
BOBS	Bruininks-Oseretsky Balance Subtest [*Occupational therapy*]
BOC	Back Office Crunch [*Business term*]
BOC	Bacterial Organic Carbon [*Water chemistry*]
BOC	Bank of China [*People's Republic of China*] (IMH)
BOC	Bank of Communications [*China*] (ECON)
BOC	Battalion Operations Center (AABC)
BOC	Battalion Orderly Corporal [*British and Canadian*]
BOC	Battery Operations Center [*Air Force*]
BOC	Bayes Operating Characteristic
BOC	Beard Oil Co. [*AMEX symbol*] (SPSG)
BOC	Beginning of Cycle (NRCH)
BOC	Bell Operating Company [*Also, BSOC*] [*Post-divestiture division of American Telephone & Telegraph Co.*]
BOC	Best Operational Capability
BOC	Bevitron Orbit Code
BOC	Billet Occupational Code [*Military*] (CAAL)
BOC	Bingham Oceanographic Collection
BOC	Block-Oriented Computer
BOC	Blowout Coil
BOC	Blue Oyster Cult [*Rock music group*]

BOC	Board of Customs [*British*] (DAS)
BOC	Bocas Del Toro [*Panama*] [*Airport symbol*] (OAG)
BOC	Bochum [*Federal Republic of Germany*] [*Seismograph station code, US Geological Survey*] (SEIS)
BOC	Body-on-Chassis [*Technical drawings*]
BOC	Borgward Owners' Club (EA)
BOC	Bottom of Conduit (NRCH)
BOC	Breach of Contract [*Legal term*]
BOC	Bristol Owners' Club (EA)
BOC	Bristol Owners Club, US Branch (EA)
BOC	British Ornithologists' Club
BOC	British Overseas Citizenship
BOC	British Oxygen Company [*Later, BOC Group*]
BOC	Brittany Oceanological Center
BOC	Brought on Charge (MCD)
BOC	Buick-Oldsmobile-Cadillac Group [*General Motors Corp.*]
BOC	Build Out Capacitor [*Telecommunications*] (TEL)
BOC	Bulletin Officiel des Chemins de Fer [*A publication*]
BOC	Bureau of Customs [*Later, US Customs Service*] [*Department of the Treasury*]
BOC	Butoxycarbonyl [*Also, Boc*] [*Organic chemistry*]
BOC	Byte Output Control [*Data processing*]
BOCA	Benelli Owner's Club of America (EA)
BOCA	Boat Owners Council of America [*Defunct*]
BOCA	Boca Raton Capital Corp. [*NASDAQ symbol*] (NQ)
BOCA	Building Officials and Code Administrators International (EA)
BOCA	Building Officials Conference of America, Inc.
BOCA	Mariner Corp. [*NASDAQ symbol*] (NQ)
BOCAAD Bull Comput Aided Archit Des	BOCAAD. Bulletin of Computer-Aided Architectural Design [*A publication*]
BoCaPo	[*The*] Book of Canadian Poetry [*A publication*]
BOCB	Buffets, Inc. [*NASDAQ symbol*] (NQ)
BOCC	Boccaccio [*Italian author, 1313-1375*] (ROG)
BOCC	Branch Officer Candidate Course [*DoD*]
BOCCA	Board for Coordination of Civil Aviation [*NATO*]
BOccThy	Bachelor of Occupational Therapy (ADA)
BOCDA	Building Official and Code Administrator [*United States*] [*A publication*]
BOCES	Boards of Cooperative Educational Services
BOCES XVIII	Boletin. Centro de Estudios del Siglo XVIII, Oviedo [*A publication*]
BOCF	Bureau of Commercial Fisheries [*Later, National Marine Fisheries Service*] (MCD)
BoChLi	[*A*] Book of Children's Literature [*A publication*]
BOCKA	Bochu Kagaku [*A publication*]
BOCLE	Ball-on-Cylinder Wear Test
BOCM	Bailey Oil Content Monitor [*Ship ballast discharge*]
BOCM	British Oil and Cake Mills
BOCO	Bogota [*Colombia*] [*Seismograph station code, US Geological Survey*] (SEIS)
BOCOL	Basic Operating Consumer-Oriented Language [*Data processing*]
BOCS	Bendix Optimum Configuration Satellite (IEEE)
BOCS	Box-Office Computer System
B & OCT	[*The*] Baltimore & Ohio Chicago Terminal Railroad Co.
BOCT	[*The*] Baltimore & Ohio Chicago Terminal Railroad Co. [*AAR code*]
BOCVA	Boletin. Academia de Ciencias Fisicas, Matematicas, y Naturales (Caracas, Venezuela) [*A publication*]
BOD	Bacteriological Oxygen Demand [*Water pollution*]
BOD	Base Operations Division [*NASA*] (KSC)
BOD	Base Ordnance Depot
BOD	Basic Operational Data
BOD	Battery Operated Device
BOD	Beneficial Occupancy Date
BOD	Bid Opening Date
BOD	Biochemical Oxygen Demand
BOD	Biological Oxygen Demand
BOD	Bistable Optical Device
BOD	Blackout Door [*Military*]
BOD	Board of Directors (NATG)
BOD	Bodansky Unit [*Clinical chemistry*]
BOD	Bodaybo [*USSR*] [*Seismograph station code, US Geological Survey*] (SEIS)
Bod	[*Jean*] Bodin [*Deceased, 1596*] [*Authority cited in pre-1607 legal work*] (DSA)
BOD	Body [*Slang*] (DSUE)
BOD	Boeing on Dock
BOD	Booksellers Order Distribution [*British*]
BOD	Bordeaux [*France*] [*Airport symbol*] (OAG)
BOD	Boston Ordnance District [*Military*] (AAG)
BOD	Bowman, ND [*Location identifier*] [*FAA*] (FAAL)
BOD	Broad Ocean Deployment
BOD	Broad Ocean Development (MCD)
BOD	Buy-Off Date
BOD	Buyer's Option to Double (ROG)
BODA	Bistable Optical Differential Amplifier (MCD)
BoDaBa	[*A*] Book of Danish Ballads [*A publication*]
Bod Denkm Pfl Mecklenb	Jahrbuch der Bodendenkmalpflege in Mecklenburg [*A publication*]
BODEA	Bodenkultur [*A publication*]

Bodenbiol Microbiol ... Bodenbiologie Microbiologie [*A publication*]
Bodenkd Pflanzenernachr ... Bodenkunde und Pflanzenernachrung [*A publication*]
BODEPE... Boiler Design and Performance
Bodleian Lib Rec ... Bodleian Library Record [*A publication*]
Bodleian Libr Rec ... Bodleian Library Record [*A publication*]
Bodleian Quart Rec ... Bodleian Quarterly Record [*A publication*]
Bodl Libr Rec ... Bodleian Library Record [*A publication*]
BODM....... Bodmin [*Municipal borough in England*]
BODN....... Bowdon Railway Co. [*AAR code*]
BODO....... Bauobjektdokumentation [*Buildings Documentation*] [*Fraunhofer Society*] [*Federal Republic of Germany*] [*Information service or system*] (IID)
BODS .... British Oceanographic Data Service
BoDS....... [*A*] Second Book of Danish Verse [*A publication*]
BODU .... Bureau of Ordnance Design Unit [*Obsolete*] [*Navy*]
Body Pol..... Body Politic [*A publication*]
BOE .... Bachelor of Oral English
BOE .... Barrels of Oil Equivalent
BOE .... Blackout Exit Time
BOE .... Blanket Open End [*Contract*] [*Business term*] (MCD)
BOE .... Boeing Commercial Airplane Group [*Seattle, WA*] [*FAA designator*] (FAAC)
Boe .... [*Petrus*] Boherius [*Deceased, 1388*] [*Authority cited in pre-1607 legal work*] (DSA)
BOE .... Boletin Oficial del Estado [*Official Gazette of Spain*] [*Information service or system*] (IID)
BOE.......... Bottom of Edge
BOE.......... Boundji [*Congo*] [*Airport symbol*] (OAG)
BOE.......... Break of Entry (NASA)
BOE .... Bulletin of Economic Research [*United Kingdom*] [*A publication*]
BOE .... Bureau of Enforcement
BOE .... Bureau of Explosives [*A publication*] (EAAP)
BOEA .... British Offshore Equipment Association (DS)
BOEC .... Beginning of Equilibrium Cycle [*Nuclear energy*] (NRCH)
BOEC .... British Oil Equipment Credits Ltd.
BOED .... Barrels of Oil Equivalent per Day
BOEIA .... Boei Eisei [*A publication*]
Boek .... Het Boek [*A publication*]
BoekOT ..... Boeken van het Oude Testament [*Roermond/Maaseik*] [*A publication*] (BJA)
BOEMA .... Boletin. Instituto de Estudios Medicos y Biologicos. Universidad Nacional Autonoma de Mexico [*A publication*]
Boer............ [*Petrus*] Boherius [*Deceased, 1388*] [*Authority cited in pre-1607 legal work*] (DSA)
Boergyogy Venerol Sz ... Boergyogyaszati es Venerologiai Szemle [*A publication*]
Boeri............ [*Petrus*] Boherius [*Deceased, 1388*] [*Authority cited in pre-1607 legal work*] (DSA)
Boersenbl Dtsch Buchhandel ... Boersenblatt fuer den Deutschen Buchhandel [*East Germany*] [*A publication*]
Boersen-Ztg ... Boersen-Zeitung [*A publication*]
Boet............ [*Anicius Manlius Severinus*] Boethius [*Flourished, 480-524*] [*Authority cited in pre-1607 legal work*] (DSA)
BOF .... Bank of Finland. Monthly Bulletin [*A publication*]
BOF .... Bank of San Francisco [*AMEX symbol*] (SPSG)
BOF .... Barium Oxide Ferrite
BOF .... Basic Oxygen Furnace [*Steelmaking*]
BOF .... Beginning of File (NASA)
BOF .... Beurre, Oeufs, Fromages [*Butter, Eggs, Cheese*] [*French*]
BOF .... Bias Oscillator Frequency
BOF .... Billing and Ordering Forum [*Exchange Carriers Standards Association*] [*Telecommunications*]
BOF .... Binary Oxide Film [*Memory*]
BOF .... Bio-Feed Industries Ltd. [*Vancouver Stock Exchange symbol*]
BOF .... Body-over-Frame [*Automotive engineering*]
BOF .... Boring Old Fart [*Slang*] (DSUE)
BOF .... British Organic Farmers
BOF .... Building Owners Federation of Mutual Insurance Companies [*Defunct*] (EA)
BOF .... Washington, DC [*Location identifier*] [*FAA*] (FAAL)
BOFADS ... Business Office Force Administration Data System [*Bell System*]
BOFC......... Buck Owens Fan Club (EA)
B Offic Ch Com (Bruxelles) ... Bulletin Officiel. Chambre de Commerce (Bruxelles) [*A publication*]
B Off Int..... Bulletin. Office International des Instituts d'Archeologie et d'Histoire de l'Art [*A publication*]
B Off Int Vitic ... Bulletin. Office International de la Viticulture [*A publication*]
Bo Fi Cl...... Bollettino di Filologia Classica [*A publication*]
BOFR........ Bank of Redlands [*NASDAQ symbol*] (NQ)
BoFr.......... [*The*] Book of Friendship [*A publication*]
BOFS........ Black Oil Finish Slate (MSA)
BOFSA ...... Bureau of Oceans, Fisheries, and Scientific Affairs [*Department of State*]
B Of San Pa ... Boletin. Oficina Sanitaria Panamericana [*A publication*]
BOFX........ Boring Fixture (AAG)
BOG.......... Board of Governors [*Federal Reserve System*]

BOG.......... Bogota [*Colombia*] [*Airport symbol*] (OAG)
BOG.......... Bogota [*Colombia*] [*Seismograph station code, US Geological Survey*] (SEIS)
BOG.......... Boil-Off Gas [*Petroleum product transportation*]
BOG.......... Boiling
BOG.......... Brigade of Guards
Bogert Trusts ... Bogert on Trusts and Trustees [*A publication*] (DLA)
Boghazkoei Stud ... Boghazkoei-Studien [*Vorderasiatische Aegyptische Gesellschaft*] [*A publication*]
BOGIA ...... Bollettino. Societa Geologica Italiana [*A publication*]
BOGN....... Bogen Corp. [*NASDAQ symbol*] (NQ)
BOGO........ Bogert Oil Co. [*NASDAQ symbol*] (NQ)
BOGSAAT ... [*A*] Bunch of Guys Sitting around a Table Method [*Facetious description of a decision-making process*]
BOGSAT ... [*A*] Bunch of Guys Seated around a Table Method [*Facetious description of a decision-making process*]
BogSmot .... Bogoslovska Smotra [*Zagreb*] [*A publication*] (BJA)
BogVest...... Bogoslovni Vestnik [*Ljubljana*] [*A publication*] (BJA)
BOH .... Band of Hope [*British*] (DAS)
BOH .... Beautiful Old House
BOH .... Beta-Hydroxyethylhydrazine [*Plant growth compound*]
Boh........... Bohairic Version of the Bible (BJA)
BOH .... Bohemia
BOH .... Bohemian [*Language, etc.*] (ROG)
BOH .... Bottom of Hole [*Geology*]
BOH .... Bournemouth [*England*] [*Airport symbol*] (OAG)
BOH .... Break-Off Height [*Aviation*] (FAAC)
BOH .... Bureau of Ordnance and Hydrography [*Obsolete*] [*Navy*]
BOH .... Oliver Heritage Society Museum and Archives, British Columbia [*Library symbol*] [*National Library of Canada*] (NLC)
Boh Att...... Bohun. Practising Attorney [*A publication*] (DLA)
Boh Curs Can ... Bohun's Cursus Cancellariae (ILCA)
Boh Dec...... Bohun's Declarations and Pleadings [*A publication*] (DLA)
Boh Eccl Jur ... Bohun. Ecclesiastical Jurisdiction [*A publication*] (DLA)
BOHEM...... Bohemian [*Language, etc.*] (ROG)
Boh Eng L ... Bohun. English Lawyer [*A publication*] (DLA)
BOHI......... Bancohio Corp. [*NASDAQ symbol*] (NQ)
Boh Inst Leg ... Bohun's Institutio Legalis (ILCA)
BOHM........ Bohemia, Inc. [*NASDAQ symbol*] (NQ)
Boh Priv Lond ... Bohun. Privilegia Londini [*A publication*] (DLA)
BoHrPo...... [*A*] Book of Historical Poems [*A publication*]
Bohrtech Ztg ... Bohrtechniker Zeitung [*A publication*]
BOHS........ British Occupational Hygiene Society (EAIO)
Boh Ti .... Bohun. Titles [*A publication*] (DLA)
Bohun........ Bohun's Election Cases [*England*] [*A publication*] (DLA)
Bohun Curs Canc ... Bohun's Cursus Cancellariae [*A publication*] (DLA)
Bohun Inst Leg ... Bohun's Institutio Legalis [*A publication*] (DLA)
BOHUNK ... Bohemian-Hungarian [*Slang*]
BoHV........ [*The*] Book of Humorous Verse [*A publication*]
BOI .... Basis of Issue [*Army*]
BOI .... Blackout Initiation Time
BOI .... Board of Investments [*Generic term*]
BOI .... Boise [*Idaho*] [*Airport symbol*] (OAG)
BOI .... Bolt-On Intelligence [*Proposed use for the biochip*]
BOI .... Branch Operating Instruction [*Air Force*]
BOI .... Branch Output Interrupt [*Data processing*] (MDG)
BOI .... Break of Inspection
BOI .... Break of Integrity (NASA)
BOI .... Bulletins of Ordnance Information
BOIA .... Bulletin. Office International des Instituts d'Archeologie et d'Histoire de l'Art [*A publication*]
BOIA .... Bureau of Indian Affairs [*Better known as BIA*] [*Department of the Interior*] (MCD)
BOIID........ Boletin IIE [*Instituto de Investigaciones Electricas*] [*A publication*]
Boiler Eng ... Boiler Engineer [*Japan*] [*A publication*]
Boiler Maker Plate Fabr ... Boiler Maker and Plate Fabricator [*A publication*]
BOIMARS ... Basis of Issue Monitoring and Recording System [*Army*] (AABC)
BOIP......... Basis of Issue Plan [*Army*]
BOIP-C...... Basis of Issue Plan - Complete [*Army*]
BOIPFD ..... BOIP [*Basis of Issue Plan*] Feeder Data [*DoD*]
BOIP II....... Basis of Issue Plan II [*Army*] (AABC)
BOIP-T...... Basis of Issue Plan - Tentative [*Army*]
BOIS......... Basis of Issue System [*Army*]
Bois Forets Trop ... Bois et Forets des Tropiques [*A publication*]
Bois For Trop ... Bois et Forets des Tropiques [*A publication*]
BOJ........... Bank of Japan
BOJ........... Booster Jettison
BOJ........... Bourgas [*Bulgaria*] [*Airport symbol*] (OAG)
BOJAAK... Boletim. Museu Nacional (Rio De Janeiro). Geologia [*A publication*]
BOJODV... Biological Oceanography [*A publication*]
BOK.......... Boekverkoper [*A publication*]
BOK.......... Bokaro [*India*] [*Seismograph station code, US Geological Survey*] (SEIS)
BOK.......... Brookings, OR [*Location identifier*] [*FAA*] (FAAL)
Bok og Bibl ... Bok og Bibliotek [*A publication*]
BOKC........ BancOklahoma Corporation [*NASDAQ symbol*] (NQ)
BOL.......... Bachelor of Oriental Language

BOL .... Basics of Language [*Method*]
BOL .... Bausch & Lomb, Inc. [*NYSE symbol*]   (SPSG)
BOL .... Be On the Lookout [*Police term*]
BOL .... Bearing-Only Launch [*Navy*]   (CAAL)
BOL .... Beginning of Life
BoL .... Bill of Lading [*Shipping*]
BOL .... Bingham Oceanographic Laboratory   (NOAA)
BOL .... Biotechnology Orbital Laboratory   (KSC)
BOL .... Bolito [*Race of maize*]
Bol .... Bolivar [*A publication*]
BOL .... Bolivia [*ANSI three-letter standard code*]   (CNC)
BOL .... Bolivia
BOL .... Bologna [*Italy*] [*Seismograph station code, US Geological Survey*]   (SEIS)
BOL .... Bolus [*Large Pill*] [*Pharmacy*]
BoL .... [*A*] Book of Lullabies [*A publication*]
BOL .... Branch Office London [*ONR*]
BOL .... Build Out Lattice [*Telecommunications*]   (TEL)
BOLA .... Bank Official Loan Act [*1933*]
Bol Acad Buenas Letras Barcelona ... Boletin. Real Academia de Buenas Letras de Barcelona [*A publication*]
Bol Acad Cienc Exactas Fis Nat ... Boletin. Academia de Ciencias Exactas, Fisicas, y Naturales [*A publication*]
Bol Acad Cienc Fis Mat Nat (Caracas) ... Boletin. Academia de Ciencias Fisicas, Matematicas, y Naturales (Caracas, Venezuela) [*A publication*]
Bol Acad Cienc Fis Mat Natur ... Boletin. Academia de Ciencias Fisicas, Matematicas, y Naturales [*Caracas, Venezuela*] [*A publication*]
Bol Acad Hist ... Boletin. Real Academia de la Historia [*Madrid*] [*A publication*]
Bol Acad Nac Cienc (Cordoba) ... Boletin. Academia Nacional de Ciencias (Cordoba) [*A publication*]
Bol Acad Nac Farm ... Boletim. Academia Nacional de Farmacia [*A publication*]
Bol Acad Nac Med ... Boletim. Academia Nacional de Medicina [*A publication*]
Bol Acad Nac Med (B Aires) ... Boletin. Academia Nacional de Medicina (Buenos Aires) [*A publication*]
Bol Acad Nac Med (Braz) ... Boletim. Academia Nacional de Medicina (Brazil) [*A publication*]
Bol Acad Nac Med (Rio De J) ... Boletim. Academia Nacional de Medicina (Rio De Janeiro) [*A publication*]
Bol Ac Hist ... Boletin. Real Academia de la Historia [*A publication*]
Bol Agencia Geral Colon ... Boletin. Agencia Geral das Colonias [*A publication*]
Bol Agr....... Boletin de Agricultura, Mineria, e Industrias [*A publication*]
Bol Agr Dept Prod Veg (Minas Gerais) ... Boletim de Agricultura. Departamento de Producao Vegetal (Minas Gerais) [*A publication*]
Bol Agr Dir Publ Agr (Sao Paulo) ... Boletim de Agricultura. Directoria de Publicidade Agricola (Sao Paulo) [*A publication*]
Bol Agric.... Boletin Agricola. Sociedad Antioquena de Agricultores [*A publication*]
Bol Agric Asoc Agric Rio Culiacan ... Boletin Agricola. Asociacion de Agricultores del Rio Culiacan [*A publication*]
Bol Agric (Belo Horizonte Brazil) ... Boletim de Agricultura (Belo Horizonte, Brazil) [*A publication*]
Bol Agric Zootech e Vet Bello Horizonte ... Boletim de Agricultura, Zootechnia, e Veterinaria. Bello Horizonte [*A publication*]
Bol Agro-Pec ... Boletin Agro-Pecuario [*A publication*]
Bol Agropecu Com Colomb Aliment Lacteos ... Boletin Agropecuario. Compania Colombiana de Alimentos Lacteos [*A publication*]
Bol Argent For ... Boletin Argentino Forestal [*A publication*]
Bol Arq....... Boletin Arqueologico de Tarragona [*A publication*]
Bol Asoc Argent Electrotec ... Boletin. Asociacion Argentina de Electrotecnicos [*A publication*]
Bol Asoc Argent Odontol Ninos ... Boletin. Asociacion Argentina de Odontologia para Ninos [*A publication*]
Bol Asoc Chil Prot Fam ... Boletin. Asociacion Chilena de Proteccion de la Familia [*A publication*]
Bol Asoc Esp Entomol ... Boletin. Asociacion Espanola de Entomologia [*A publication*]
Bol Asoc Med PR ... Boletin. Asociacion Medica de Puerto Rico [*A publication*]
Bol Asoc Med Puerto Rico ... Boletin. Asociacion Medica de Puerto Rico [*A publication*]
Bol Asoc Mex Geofis Explor ... Boletin. Asociacion Mexicana de Geofisicos de Exploracion [*A publication*]
Bol Asoc Mex Geol Pet ... Boletin. Asociacion Mexicana de Geologos Petroleros [*A publication*]
Bol Asoc Mex Geol Petrol ... Boletin. Asociacion Mexicana de Geologos Petroleros [*A publication*]
Bol Asoc Nac Ing Agron ... Boletin. Asociacion Nacional de Ingenieros Agronomos [*A publication*]
Bol Asoc Nac Ingen Agron ... Boletin. Asociacion Nacional de Ingenieros Agronomos [*A publication*]
Bol Asoc Urug Prog Cienc ... Boletin. Asociacion Uruguaya para el Progreso de la Ciencia [*A publication*]

Bol Asoc Venez Enferm Prof ... Boletin. Asociacion Venezolana de Enfermeras Profesionales [*A publication*]
Bol Asoc Venez Geol Min Pet ... Boletin. Asociacion Venezolana de Geologia, Mineria, y Petroleo [*A publication*]
Bol Assist Med Indigen (Luanda) ... Boletim de Assistencia Medicaos Indigenas e da Luta Contra a Moleatia do Sono (Luanda) [*A publication*]
Bol Assoc Bras Fis Med ... Boletim. Associacao Brasileira de Fisicos em Medicina [*Brazil*] [*A publication*]
Bol Assoc Bras Pesqui Plant Aromat Oleos Essen ... Boletim. Associacao Brasileira de Pesquisas sobre Plantas Aromaticas e Oleos Essenciais [*A publication*]
Bol Assoc Bras Quim ... Boletim. Associacao Brasileira de Quimica [*A publication*]
Bol Assoc Filos Nat (Portugal) ... Boletim. Associacao de Filosofia Natural (Portugal) [*A publication*]
Bol AVGMP ... Boletin. AVGMP [*Asociacion Venezolana de Geologia, Mineria, y Petroleo*] [*A publication*]
Bol Azucar Mex ... Boletin Azucarero Mexicano [*A publication*]
Bol Bibl...... Boletin Bibliografico Forestal [*Chile*] [*A publication*]
Bol Bibl Agric ... Boletin para Bibliotecas Agricolas [*A publication*]
Bol Bibl Antropol Amer ... Boletin Bibliografico de Antropologia Americana [*A publication*]
Bol Bibliog Geofisica y Oceanografia Am ... Boletin Bibliografico de Geofisica y Oceanografia Americanas [*A publication*]
Bol Bibliogr Fac Agron Univ Cent Venez ... Boletin Bibliografico. Facultad de Agronomia. Universidad Central de Venezuela [*A publication*]
Bol Biblio (Peru) ... Boletin Bibliografico (Peru) [*A publication*]
Bol Biblioteca ... Boletin de Biblioteca [*A publication*]
Bol Bibl Menendez Pelayo ... Boletin. Biblioteca de Menendez Pelayo [*A publication*]
Bol Bioestat Epidem ... Boletim de Bioestatistica e Epidemiologia [*A publication*]
Bol Biol...... Boletin Biologico [*A publication*]
Bol Biol (S Paulo) ... Boletim Biologica (Sao Paulo) [*A publication*]
Bol Cam Com (Caracas) ... Boletin. Camara de Comercio (Caracas) [*A publication*]
Bol Cear Agron ... Boletim Cearense de Agronomia [*A publication*]
Bol Cent Estud Hosp Servidores Estado (Rio De J) ... Boletim. Centro de Estudos do Hospital dos Servidores do Estado (Rio De Janeiro) [*A publication*]
Bol Cent Invest Biol Univ Zulia ... Boletin. Centro de Investigaciones Biologicas. Universidad del Zulia [*A publication*]
Bol Cent Nav ... Boletin. Centro Naval [*A publication*]
Bol Cent Panam Fiebre Aftosa ... Boletin. Centro Panamericano de Fiebre Aftosa [*A publication*]
Bol Chil Parasitol ... Boletin Chileno de Parasitologia [*A publication*]
Bol Cia Adm Guano ... Boletin. Compania Administradora del Guano [*A publication*]
Bol Ciencias Econs ... Boletim de Ciencias Economicas [*A publication*]
Bol Ciencias Pol y Socs ... Boletin de Ciencias Politicas y Sociales [*A publication*]
Bol Cienc Mar ... Boletim de Ciencias do Mar [*A publication*]
Bol Cienc Tecnol Dep Asuntos Cult Union Panam ... Boletin de Ciencia y Tecnologia. Departamento de Asuntos Culturales. Union Panamericana [*A publication*]
Bol Clin Endocrinol Metab ... Boletin. Clinica de Endocrinologia y Metabolismo [*A publication*]
Bol Clin Hosp Civis Lisb ... Boletim Clinico dos Hospitals Civis de Lisboa [*A publication*]
Bol Col Prof Enferm PR ... Boletin. Colegio de Profesionales de la Enfermeria de Puerto Rico [*A publication*]
Bol Col Quim PR ... Boletin. Colegio de Quimicos de Puerto Rico [*A publication*]
Bol Combust Petroquim ... Boletin de Combustibles y Petroquimica [*A publication*]
Bol Com Geogr Geol Estado Sao Paulo ... Boletim. Comissao Geografica e Geologica do Estado de Sao Paulo [*A publication*]
Bol Com Nac Energ Nucl (Braz) ... Boletim. Comissao Nacional de Energia Nuclear (Brazil) [*A publication*]
Bol Comp Admin Guano ... Boletin. Compania Administradora del Guano [*A publication*]
Bol Cons Nac Pesqui (Brazil) ... Boletim. Conselho Nacional de Pesquisas (Brazil) [*A publication*]
Bol Cuerpo Ing Minas Peru ... Boletin. Cuerpo de Ingenieros de Minas del Peru [*A publication*]
Bol Cult Guine Portug ... Boletim Cultural da Guine Portuguesa [*A publication*]
BOLD .... Bibliographic On-Line Display [*Document storage and retrieval system*] [*Data processing*]
BOLD .... Bleomycin, Oncovin [*Vincristine*], Lomustine, Dacarbazine [*Antineoplastic drug regimen*]
BOLD .... Blind Outdoor Leisure Development   (EA)
BOLD .... Bomb LASER Directed   (MCD)
Bol Demografico (Brazil) ... Boletim Demografico (Brazil) [*A publication*]
Bol Dent Oper ... Boletim de Dentistica Operatoria [*A publication*]
Bol Dent Urug ... Boletin Dental Uruguayo [*A publication*]
Bol Dep For (Uruguay) ... Boletin. Departamento Forestal (Montevideo, Uruguay) [*A publication*]

Bol Dep Geol Uni Son ... Boletin. Departamento de Geologia. Universidad de Sonora [*A publication*]
Bol Dep Nac Prod Miner (Brasil) ... Boletim. Departamento Nacional da Producao Mineral (Brasil) [*A publication*]
Bol Dep Quim Inst Tecnol Estud Super (Monterrey) ... Boletin. Departamento de Quimica. Instituto Tecnologico y de Estudios Superiores (Monterrey) [*A publication*]
Bol Dept Eng Quim Esc Politec Univ Sao Paulo ... Boletim. Departamento de Engenharia Quimica da Escola Politecnica. Universidade de Sao Paulo [*A publication*]
Bol Dermatol Sanit ... Boletin Dermatologico Sanitario [*A publication*]
Bol Didat Esc Agron Eliseu Maciel (Pelotas Brazil) ... Boletim Didatico da Escola de Agronomia Eliseu Maciel (Pelotas, Brazil) [*A publication*]
Bol Dir Agric Ganad (Peru) ... Boletin. Direccion de Agricultura y Ganaderia (Peru) [*A publication*]
Bol Dir Gen Odontol (Santa Fe) ... Boletin de la Direccion General de Odontologia (Santa Fe) [*A publication*]
Bol Dir Malariol Saneamiento Ambiental ... Boletin. Direccion de Malariologia y Saneamiento Ambiental [*A publication*]
Bol Dir Nac Geol Min (Argent) ... Boletin. Direccion Nacional de Geologia y Mineria (Argentina) [*A publication*]
Bol Div Fom Prod Miner (Braz) ... Boletin. Divisao de Fomento da Producao Mineral (Brazil) [*A publication*]
Bol Div Nac Dermatol Sanit ... Boletin. Divisao Nacional de Dermatologia Sanitaria [*A publication*]
Bol Div Nac Lepra ... Boletim. Divisao Nacional de Lepra [*A publication*]
Bol Divulg Inst Nac Invest For (Mex) ... Boletin Divulgativo. Instituto Nacional de Investigaciones Forestales (Mexico) [*A publication*]
Bol Divulg Inst Oleos (Rio De Janeiro) ... Boletim de Divulgacao. Instituto de Oleos (Rio de Janeiro) [*A publication*]
Bol Divulg Minist Agric Ganad ... Boletin Divulgativo. Ministerio de Agricultura y Ganaderia [*A publication*]
Bol Divulg Tec Inst Patol Veg (B Aires) ... Boletin de Divulgacion Tecnica. Instituto de Patologia Vegetal (Buenos Aires) [*A publication*]
Bol Docum Fondo Invest Econ Soc ... Boletin de Documentacion. Fondo para la Investigacion Economica y Social [*A publication*]
BOLDS ...... Burroughs Optical Lens Docking System (MCD)
Bol Eclesias Fil ... Boletin Eclesiastico de Filipinas [*A publication*]
Bol Econ Pubblica ... Bollettino dell'Economia Pubblica [*A publication*]
Bol Entomol Venez ... Boletin de Entomologia Venezolana [*A publication*]
Bol Epidemiol ... Boletin Epidemiologico [*A publication*]
Bol Epidemiol (Rio De J) ... Boletim Epidemiologico (Rio De Janeiro) [*A publication*]
Bol Equipe Odontol Sanit ... Boletim da Equipe de Odontologia Sanitaria [*A publication*]
Bol Esc Farm (Coimbra) ... Boletim. Escola de Farmacia (Coimbra) [*A publication*]
Bol Esc Farm Univ Coimbra Ed Cien ... Boletim. Escola de Farmacia. Universidade de Coimbra. Edicao Cientifica [*A publication*]
Bol Esc Farm Univ Coimbra Ed Didact Not Farm ... Boletim. Escola de Farmacia. Universidade de Coimbra. Edicao Didactica. Noticias Farmaceuticas [*A publication*]
Bol Esc Nac Agr (Lima) ... Boletin. Escuela Nacional de Agricultura (Lima) [*A publication*]
Bol Esc Super Agric "Luiz De Queiroz" Univ Sao Paulo ... Boletim. Escola Superior de Agricultura "Luiz De Queiroz." Universidade de Sao Paulo [*A publication*]
Bol Esc Super Farm Univ Lisboa ... Boletim. Escola Superior de Farmacia. Universidade de Lisboa [*A publication*]
Bol Estac Biol Mar Univ Fed Ceara ... Boletim. Estacao de Biologia Marinha. Universidade Federal do Ceara [*A publication*]
Bol Estac Cent Ecol ... Boletin. Estacion Central de Ecologia [*A publication*]
Bol Estac Cent Ecol (Spain) ... Boletin. Estacion Central de Ecologia (Spain) [*A publication*]
Bol Estac Exp Agric "La Molina" ... Boletin. Estacion Experimental Agricola "La Molina" [*A publication*]
Bol Estac Exp Agric Tucuman ... Boletin. Estacion Experimental Agricola de la Provincia de Tucuman [*A publication*]
Bol Estac Exp Agr "La Molina" ... Boletin. Estacion Experimental Agricola "La Molina" [*A publication*]
Bol Estac Exp Agropec Pres Roque Saenz Pena (Argentina) ... Boletin. Estacion Experimental Agropecuaria de Presidencia Roque Saenz Pena (Argentina) [*A publication*]
Bol Estac Exp Agr "Tingo Maria" ... Boletin. Estacion Experimental Agricola "Tingo Maria" [*A publication*]
Bol Estadistica ... Boletin de Estadistica [*A publication*]
Bol Estadistico Trim (Argentina) ... Boletin Estadistico Trimestral (Argentina) [*A publication*]
Bol Estadistico Trim (Bolivia) ... Boletin Estadistico Trimestral (Bolivia) [*A publication*]
Bol Estud Econ ... Boletin de Estudios Economicos [*A publication*]
Bol Estud Geogr Univ Nac Cuyo ... Boletin de Estudios Geograficos. Universidad Nacional de Cuyo [*A publication*]
Bol Estud Latinoam y Caribe ... Boletin de Estudios Latinoamericanos y del Caribe [*A publication*]
Bol Estud Latinoamer ... Boletin de Estudios Latinoamericanos y del Caribe [*A publication*]

Bol Estud Med Biol ... Boletin de Estudios Medicos y Biologicos [*A publication*]
Bol Estud Med Biol Univ Nac Auton Mex ... Boletin de Estudios Medicos y Biologicos. Universidad Nacional Autonoma de Mexico [*A publication*]
Bol Estud Pesca ... Boletim de Estudos de Pesca [*A publication*]
Bol Estud Supt Desenvolvimento Nordeste Div Geol (Braz) ... Boletim de Estudos. Superintendencia do Desenvolvimento do Nordeste. Divisao de Geologia (Brazil) [*A publication*]
Boletin IF ... Boletin. Instituto de Folklore [*A publication*]
Bol Exp Serv Agric Interam (La Paz) ... Boletin Experimental. Servicio Agricola Interamericano (La Paz) [*A publication*]
Bolex Rep ... Bolex Reporter [*A publication*]
BOLF .... Barge Off Loading Facility
Bol Fac Agron Univ San Carlos Guatemala ... Boletin. Facultad de Agronomia. Universidad de San Carlos de Guatemala [*A publication*]
Bol Fac Cienc Agrar Para ... Boletim. Faculdade de Ciencias Agrarias do Para [*A publication*]
Bol Fac Cienc For Univ Los Andes ... Boletin. Facultad de Ciencias Forestales. Universidad de Los Andes [*A publication*]
Bol Fac Der Cienc Soc (Cordoba) ... Boletin. Facultad de Derecho y Ciencias Sociales (Cordoba) [*A publication*]
Bol Fac Dir (Coimbra) ... Boletim. Faculdade de Direito (Coimbra) [*A publication*]
Bol Fac Farm Coimbra (Coimbra) ... Boletim. Faculdade de Farmacia. Universidade de Coimbra (Coimbra) [*A publication*]
Bol Fac Farm Univ Coimbra Ed Cient ... Boletim. Faculdade de Farmacia. Universidade de Coimbra. Edicao Cientifica [*A publication*]
Bol Fac Farm Univ Coimbra Ed Didact Not Farm ... Boletim. Faculdade de Farmacia. Universidade de Coimbra. Edicao Didactica. Noticias Farmaceuticas [*A publication*]
Bol Fac Farm Univ Lisboa ... Boletim. Faculdade de Farmacia. Universidade de Lisboa [*A publication*]
Bol Fac Filos Cienc Let Univ Sao Paulo Ser Bot ... Boletim. Faculdade de Filosofia, Ciencias, e Letras. Universidade de Sao Paulo. Serie Botanica [*A publication*]
Bol Fac Filos Cienc Let Univ Sao Paulo Ser Zool ... Boletim. Faculdade de Filosofia, Ciencias, e Letras. Universidade de Sao Paulo. Serie Zoologia [*A publication*]
Bol Fac Ing Agrimens Univ Repub ... Boletin. Facultad de Ingenieria y Agrimensura. Universidad de la Republica [*A publication*]
Bol Fac Ing y Agrimensura Montevideo ... Boletin. Facultad de Ingenieria y Agrimensura de Montevideo [*A publication*]
Bol Fac Ing Agrimensura Montevideo ... Boletin. Facultad de Ingenieria y Agrimensura de Montevideo [*A publication*]
Bol Fac Ing Montevideo ... Boletin. Facultad de Ingenieria de Montevideo [*A publication*]
Bol Fac Ing Univ Repub ... Boletin. Facultad de Ingenieria. Universidad de la Republica [*A publication*]
Bol Fac Odontol Piracicaba Univ Estadual Campinas ... Boletim. Faculdade de Odontologia de Piracicaba. Universidade Estadual de Campinas [*A publication*]
Bol Farm Mil ... Boletin de Farmacia Militar [*A publication*]
Bol Fed Med Ecuador ... Boletin. Federacion Medica del Ecuador [*A publication*]
Bol Fisiol Anim (Sao Paulo) ... Boletim de Fisiologia Animal (Sao Paulo) [*A publication*]
Bol Fitossanit ... Boletim Fitossanitario [*A publication*]
Bol For Ind For Amer Lat FAO ... Boletin Forestal y de Industrias Forestales para America Latina. Oficina Forestal Regional de la FAO [*Food and Agriculture Organization*] [*A publication*]
Bol Fund Goncalo Moniz ... Boletim. Fundacao Goncalo Moniz [*A publication*]
Bol Genet ... Boletin Genetico [*A publication*]
Bol Geo Dir Geol (Venez) ... Boletin de Geologia. Direccion de Geologia (Venezuela) [*A publication*]
Bol Geog .... Boletim Geografico [*A publication*]
Bol Geogr ... Boletim Geografico [*A publication*]
Bol Geol (Caracas) ... Boletin de Geologia (Caracas) [*A publication*]
Bol Geol (Caracas) Publ Espec ... Boletin de Geologia (Caracas). Publicacion Especial [*A publication*]
Bol Geol Dir Geol (Venez) ... Boletin de Geologia. Direccion de Geologia (Venezuela) [*A publication*]
Bol Geol Miner ... Boletin Geologico y Minero [*A publication*]
Bol Geol Min (Esp) ... Boletin Geologico y Minero (Espana) [*A publication*]
Bol Geol Publ Espec ... Boletin de Geologia. Publicacion Especial [*A publication*]
Bol Geol Publ Espec Dir Geol (Venez) ... Boletin de Geologia. Publicacion Especial. Direccion de Geologia (Venezuela) [*A publication*]
Bol Geol Univ Ind Santander ... Boletin de Geologia. Universidad Industrial de Santander [*A publication*]
Bol GEOMINAS ... Boletin. GEOMINAS [*A publication*]
Bolg Fiz Zh ... Bolgarskii Fizicheskii Zhurnal [*Bulgaria*] [*A publication*]
Bol Hig Epidemiol ... Boletin de Higiene y Epidemiologia [*A publication*]
Bol Hist Nat Soc "Felipe Poey" ... Boletin de Historia Natural. Sociedad "Felipe Poey" [*A publication*]
Bol Historia Nat ... Boletin de Historia Natural [*A publication*]

Bol Hosp Civ San Juan De Dios (Quito) ... Boletin. Hospital Civil de San Juan De Dios (Quito) [*A publication*]
Bol Hosp Clin Fac Med Univ Bahia ... Boletim. Hospital das Clinicas. Faculdade de Medicina. Universidade da Bahia [*A publication*]
Bol Hosp Fac Med Univ Bahia ... Boletim. Hospital da Faculdade de Medicina. Universidade da Bahia [*A publication*]
Bol Hosp Oftalmol Nuestra Senora de la Luz ... Boletin. Hospital Oftalmologico de Nuestra Senora de la Luz [*A publication*]
Bol Iberoam Cult Tec ... Boletin Iberoamericano de Cultura Tecnica [*A publication*]
Bol IG Univ Sao Paulo Inst Geocien ... Boletim IG. Universidade de Sao Paulo. Instituto de Geociencias [*A publication*]
Bol Ind Anim ... Boletim de Industria Animal [*A publication*]
Bol Inf Asoc Venez Geol Min Pet ... Boletin Informativo. Asociacion Venezolana de Geologia, Mineria, y Petroleo [*A publication*]
Bol Inf Bromatol ... Boletin de Informacion Bromatologica [*A publication*]
Bol Inf Cent Nac Invest Cafe ... Boletin Informativo. Centro Nacional de Investigaciones de Cafe [*A publication*]
Bol Inf Cient Nac ... Boletin de Informaciones Cientificas Nacionales [*A publication*]
Bol Inf Cir Farm ... Boletin Informativo de Circular Farmaceutica [*A publication*]
Bol Inf Dent (Madr) ... Boletin de Informacion Dental (Madrid) [*A publication*]
Bol Inf Estac Exp Agri Tucuman ... Boletin Informativo. Estacion Experimental Agricola de Tucuman [*A publication*]
Bol Inf Inst Biol Marit ... Boletim Informativo. Instituto de Biologia Maritima [*A publication*]
Bol Inf Inst Bot ... Boletin Informativo. Instituto de Botanica [*A publication*]
Bol Inf Inst Cubano Invest Tecnol ... Boletin Informativo. Instituto Cubano de Investigaciones Tecnologicas [*A publication*]
Bol Inform Inst Cacau Bahia ... Boletim Informativo. Instituto de Cacau da Bahia [*A publication*]
Bol Inform Inst For (Chile) ... Boletin Informativo. Instituto Forestal (Santiago-De-Chile) [*A publication*]
Bol Inform Inst Nac Tec Agropec Inst Fitotec ... Boletin Informativo. Instituto Nacional de Tecnologia Agropecuaria. Instituto de Fitotecnia [*A publication*]
Bol Inform Minist Agric (Madrid) ... Boletin de Informacion. Ministerio de Agricultura (Madrid) [*A publication*]
Bol Inform Tec Asoc Invest Tec Ind Madera ... Boletin de Informacion Tecnica. Asociacion de Investigacion Tecnica de las Industrias de la Madera y Corcho [*A publication*]
Bol Inf Parasit Chil ... Boletin de Informaciones Parasitarias Chilenas [*A publication*]
Bol Inf Pet ... Boletin de Informaciones Petroleras [*A publication*]
Bol Inf Soc Bras Radiol ... Boletim Informativo. Sociedade Brasileira de Radiologia [*A publication*]
Bol Inf Tec Dep Met No Ferreos CSIC (Spain) ... Boletin de Informacion Tecnica. Departamento de Metales No Ferreos. Consejo Superior de Investigaciones Cientificas (Spain) [*A publication*]
Bol INPA Bot ... Boletim. INPA [*Instituto Nacional de Pesquisas da Amazonia*]. Botanica [*A publication*]
Bol INPA Patol Trop ... Boletim. INPA [*Instituto Nacional de Pesquisas da Amazonia*]. Patologia Tropical [*A publication*]
Bol INPA Pat Trop ... Boletim. INPA [*Instituto Nacional de Pesquisas da Amazonia*]. Patologia Tropical [*A publication*]
Bol INPA Pesqui Florestais ... Boletim. INPA [*Instituto Nacional de Pesquisas da Amazonia*]. Pesquisas Florestais [*A publication*]
Bol INPA Tecnol ... Boletim. INPA [*Instituto Nacional de Pesquisas da Amazonia*]. Tecnologia [*A publication*]
Bol Inseminacao Artif ... Boletim de Inseminacao Artificial [*A publication*]
Bol Inst Agric Trop Univ PR ... Boletin. Instituto de Agricultura Tropical. Universidad de Puerto Rico [*A publication*]
Bol Inst Agron Campinas ... Boletim. Instituto Agronomico Campinas [*A publication*]
Bol Inst Angola ... Boletim. Instituto de Angola [*A publication*]
Bol Inst Antropol Univ Antioquia Medellin ... Boletin. Instituto de Antropologia. Universidad de Antioquia, Medellin [*A publication*]
Bol Inst Azeite Prod Oleaginosos ... Boletim. Instituto do Azeite e Produtos Oleaginosos [*A publication*]
Bol Inst Bacteriol Chile ... Boletin. Instituto Bacteriologico de Chile [*A publication*]
Bol Inst Biol Bahia ... Boletim. Instituto Biologico da Bahia [*A publication*]
Bol Inst Biol Mar (Mar Del Plata) ... Boletin. Instituto de Biologia Marina (Mar Del Plata) [*A publication*]
Bol Inst Biol Mar Univ Fed Rio Grande Do Norte ... Boletim. Instituto de Biologia Marinha. Universidade Federal do Rio Grande Do Norte [*A publication*]
Bol Inst Boliv Pet ... Boletin. Instituto Boliviano del Petroleo [*A publication*]
Bol Inst Bot (Sao Paulo) ... Boletin. Instituto de Botanica (Sao Paulo) [*A publication*]
Bol Inst Bot Univ Quito ... Boletin. Instituto Botanica. Universidade de Quito [*A publication*]
Bol Inst Cent Biocienc Ser Bot ... Boletim. Instituto Central de Biociencias. Serie Botanica [*A publication*]

Bol Inst Cienc Biol Geocienc Commun Malacol ... Boletin. Instituto de Ciencias Biologicas e de Geociencias. Communicacoes Malacologicas [*A publication*]
Bol Inst Cienc Nat Univ Cent Ecuador ... Boletin. Instituto de Ciencias Naturales. Universidad Central del Ecuador [*A publication*]
Bol Inst Cienc Nat Univ Rio Grande Do Sul ... Boletin. Instituto de Ciencias Naturais. Universidade do Rio Grande Do Sul [*A publication*]
Bol Inst Clin Quir ... Boletin. Instituto de Clinica Quirurgica [*A publication*]
Bol Inst Ecol Exp Agric ... Boletim. Instituto de Ecologia e Experimentacao Agricolas [*A publication*]
Bol Inst Esp Oceanogr ... Boletin. Instituto Espanol de Oceanografia [*A publication*]
Bol Inst Estud Med Biol ... Boletin. Instituto de Estudios Medicos y Biologicos [*A publication*]
Bol Inst Estud Med Biol Univ Nac Mex ... Boletin. Instituto de Estudios Medicos y Biologicos. Universidad Nacional de Mexico [*A publication*]
Bol Inst Estud Polit ... Boletin. Instituto de Estudios Politicos [*A publication*]
Bol Inst For Invest Exp (Madrid) ... Boletin. Instituto Forestal de Investigaciones y Experiencias (Madrid) [*A publication*]
Bol Inst For Lat-Am Invest Capac ... Boletin. Instituto Forestal Latino-Americano de Investigacion y Capacitacion [*A publication*]
Bol Inst For Latino-Am Invest Capac ... Boletin. Instituto Forestal Latino-Americano de Investigacion y Capacitacion [*A publication*]
Bol Inst Genet Soc Nac Agrar (Lima) ... Boletin. Instituto de Genetica. Sociedad Nacional Agraria (Lima) [*A publication*]
Bol Inst Geocienc Astron Univ Sao Paulo ... Boletim. Instituto de Geociencias e Astronomia. Universidade de Sao Paulo [*A publication*]
Bol Inst Geogr Geol (Sao Paulo State) ... Boletim. Instituto Geografico e Geologico (Sao Paulo State) [*A publication*]
Bol Inst Geol ... Boletin. Instituto de Geologia [*A publication*]
Bol Inst Geol (Mex) ... Boletin. Instituto de Geologia (Mexico) [*A publication*]
Bol Inst Geol Min Esp ... Boletin. Instituto Geologico y Minero de Espana [*A publication*]
Bol Inst Geol Univ Nac Auton Mex ... Boletin. Instituto de Geologia. Universidad Nacional Autonoma de Mexico [*A publication*]
Bol Inst Geol Univ Recife Mineral ... Boletim. Instituto de Geologia. Universidade de Recife. Mineralogia [*A publication*]
Bol Inst Hist Nat Curitiba Bot ... Boletim. Instituto de Historia Natural Curitiba Botanica [*A publication*]
Bol Inst Int Am Prot Infanc ... Boletin. Instituto Internacional Americano de Proteccion a la Infancia [*A publication*]
Bol Inst Interam Nino ... Boletin. Instituto Interamericano del Nino [*A publication*]
Bol Inst Invest Bibliogr ... Boletin. Instituto de Investigaciones Bibliograficas [*A publication*]
Bol Inst Invest Cient Angola ... Boletim. Instituto de Investigacao Cientifica de Angola [*A publication*]
Bol Inst Invest Cient Univ Nuevo Leon ... Boletin. Instituto de Investigaciones Cientificas. Universidad de Nuevo Leon [*A publication*]
Bol Inst Invest Geol (Chile) ... Boletin. Instituto de Investigaciones Geologicas (Chile) [*A publication*]
Bol Inst Investig Cient Angola ... Boletin. Instituto de Investigacao Cientifica de Angola [*A publication*]
Bol Inst Invest Recur Mar (Callao) ... Boletin. Instituto de Investigacion de los Recursos Marinos (Callao) [*A publication*]
Bol Inst Invest Vet (Maracay) ... Boletin. Instituto de Investigaciones Veterinarias (Maracay) [*A publication*]
Bol Inst Mar Peru (Callao) ... Boletin. Instituto del Mar del Peru (Callao) [*A publication*]
Bol Inst Mat Astron Fis ... Boletin. Instituto de Matematica, Astronomia, y Fisica [*A publication*]
Bol Inst Med Exp Estud Trat Cancer (Buenos Aires) ... Boletin. Instituto de Medicina Experimental para el Estudio y Tratamiento del Cancer (Buenos Aires) [*A publication*]
Bol Inst Microbiol Univ Fed Rio Grande Do Sul ... Boletim. Instituto de Microbiologia. Universidade Federal do Rio Grande Do Sul [*A publication*]
Bol Inst Nac Antropol Hist Mexico ... Boletin. Instituto Nacional de Antropologia e Historia de Mexico [*A publication*]
Bol Inst Nac Hig Alfonso XIII ... Boletin. Instituto Nacional de Higiene de Alfonso XIII [*A publication*]
Bol Inst Nac Hig (Caracas) ... Boletin. Instituto Nacional de Higiene (Caracas) [*A publication*]
Bol Inst Nac Invest Agron (Madr) ... Boletin. Instituto Nacional de Investigaciones Agronomicas (Madrid) [*A publication*]
Bol Inst Nac Invest Exper Agron For ... Boletin. Instituto Nacional de Investigaciones y Experiencias Agronomicas y Forestales [*A publication*]
Bol Inst Nac Neumol (Mex) ... Boletin. Instituto Nacional de Neumologia (Mexico) [*A publication*]
Bol Inst Nac Pesqui Amazonia Pesqui Florestais ... Boletim. Instituto Nacional de Pesquisas da Amazonia. Pesquisas Florestais [*A publication*]
Bol Inst Nac Pesqui Amazonia Tecnol ... Boletim. Instituto Nacional de Pesquisas da Amazonia. Tecnologia [*A publication*]

Bol Inst Num Hist San Nicolas ... Boletin. Instituto de Numismatica e Historia de San Nicolas de los Arroyos [*Argentina*] [*A publication*]
Bol Inst Oceanogr ... Boletim. Instituto Oceanografico [*A publication*]
Bol Inst Oceanogr Univ Oriente ... Boletin. Instituto Oceanografico. Universidad de Oriente [*A publication*]
Bol Inst Oceanogr Univ Oriente (Cumana) ... Boletin. Instituto Oceanografico. Universidad de Oriente (Cumana) [*A publication*]
Bol Inst Patol Med (Madrid) ... Boletin. Instituto de Patologia Medica (Madrid) [*A publication*]
Bol Inst Pesqui Cir (Rio De J) ... Boletim. Instituto de Pesquisas Cirurgicas (Rio De Janeiro) [*A publication*]
Bol Inst Pesqui Vet "Desiderio Finamor" ... Boletim. Instituto de Pesquisas Veterinarias "Desiderio Finamor" [*A publication*]
Bol Inst Prod Florestais Cortica ... Boletim. Instituto dos Produtos Florestais - Cortica [*A publication*]
Bol Inst Quim Agric (Rio De Janeiro) ... Boletim. Instituto de Quimica Agricola (Rio De Janeiro) [*A publication*]
Bol Inst Quim Mexico ... Boletin. Instituto de Quimica. Universidad Nacional Autonoma de Mexico [*A publication*]
Bol Inst Quim Univ Nac Auton Mex ... Boletin. Instituto de Quimica. Universidad Nacional Autonoma de Mexico [*A publication*]
Bol Inst Salud Publica Chile ... Boletin. Instituto de Salud Publica de Chile [*A publication*]
Bol Inst Sudam Pet (Montevideo) ... Boletin. Instituto Sudamericano del Petroleo (Montevideo) [*A publication*]
Bol Inst Tecnol Aliment ... Boletim. Instituto de Tecnologia de Alimentos [*A publication*]
Bol Inst Tecnol (Rio Grande Sul) ... Boletim. Instituto Tecnologico (Rio Grande Do Sul) [*A publication*]
Bol Inst Tecnol Rural Univ Ceara ... Boletim. Instituto de Tecnologia Rural. Universidade do Ceara [*A publication*]
Bol Inst Tonantzintla ... Boletin. Instituto de Tonantzintla [*A publication*]
Bol Interamer M ... Boletin Interamericano de Musica/Inter-American Music Bulletin [*A publication*]
Bol IPA PSM ... Boletim. IPA [*Instituto de Pesquisas Agronomicas*]. PSM [*Programa de Sorgo e Milheto*] [*A publication*]
Bol Ist Pato Lib ... Bollettino. Istituto di Patologia del Libro [*A publication*]
Bol Ist Stud Verdiani ... Bollettino. Istituto di Studi Verdiani [*A publication*]
BOLiVe ...... [*The*] Book of Living Verse [*A publication*]
Bolivia Dep Nac Geol Bol ... Bolivia. Departamento Nacional de Geologia. Boletin [*A publication*]
Bol Junta Control Energ At ... Boletin. Junta do Control de Energia Atomica [*Peru*] [*A publication*]
Bol Junta Geral Distr Auton Ponta Delgada ... Boletim. Junta Geral Distrito Autonomo Ponta Delgada [*A publication*]
Bol Junta Nac Cortica ... Boletim. Junta Nacional da Cortica [*A publication*]
Boll d A ...... Bollettino d'Arte [*A publication*]
Bol Lab Clin "Luis Razetti" ... Boletin. Laboratorio de la Clinica "Luis Razetti" [*A publication*]
Bol Lab Paleontol Vertebr ... Boletin. Laboratorio de Paleontologia de Vertebrados [*A publication*]
Bol Lab Prod Miner (Braz) ... Boletim. Laboratorio de Producao Mineral (Brazil) [*A publication*]
Bol Lab Quim Nac (Colombia) ... Boletin. Laboratorio Quimico Nacional (Colombia) [*A publication*]
Boll Accad Med-Chir Bologna ... Bollettino. Accademia Medico-Chirurgica di Bologna [*A publication*]
Boll Accad Med Genova ... Bollettino. Accademia Medica de Genova [*A publication*]
Boll Accad Med Pistoiese Filippo Pacini ... Bollettino. Accademia Medica Pistoiese Filippo Pacini [*A publication*]
Boll Accad Svizz Sci Med ... Bollettino. Accademia Svizzera delle Scienze Mediche [*A publication*]
Bolland .... Select Bills in Eyre [*Selden Society Publication No. 30*] [*England*] [*A publication*] (DLA)
Boll Arte .... Bollettino d'Arte [*A publication*]
Boll d'Arte MPI ... Bollettino d'Arte. Ministero della Pubblica Istruzione [*A publication*]
Boll Ass It Dir Mar ... Bollettino d'Informazioni. Associazione Italiana di Diritto Marittimo [*A publication*]
Boll Ass Med March ... Bollettino. Associazione Medica Marchigiana [*A publication*]
Boll Ass Med Trid ... Bollettino. Associazione Medica Tridentina [*A publication*]
Boll Ass Med Triest ... Bollettino. Associazione Medica Triestina [*A publication*]
Boll Ass Min Ital ... Bollettino. Associazione Mineraria Italiana [*A publication*]
Boll Assoc African Ital ... Bollettino. Associazione degli Africanisti Italiani [*A publication*]
Boll Assoc Ital Chim Tess Color ... Bollettino. Associazione Italiana de Chimica Tessile e Coloristica [*A publication*]
Boll Assoc Ital Ind Zucchero Alcool ... Bollettino. Associazione Italiana delle Industrie dello Zucchero e dell'Alcool [*A publication*]
Boll Assoc Ital Piante Med Aromat Altre Piante Utili ... Bollettino. Associazione Italiana pro Piante Medicinali Aromatiche ed Altre Piante Utili [*A publication*]
Boll Assoc Rom Entomol ... Bollettino. Associazione Romana di Entomologia [*A publication*]

Boll Ass Ott Ital ... Bollettino. Associazione Ottica Italiana [*A publication*]
Boll Atti Accad Med Roma ... Bollettino ed Atti. Accademia Medica di Roma [*A publication*]
Boll Atti Soc Ital Endocrinol ... Bollettino ed Atti. Societa Italiana de Endocrinologia [*A publication*]
Boll Bibl ..... Bollettino Biblico [*Associazione Biblica Italiana*] [*A publication*]
Boll Bibliogr Stor Sci Mat ... Bollettino di Bibliografia e Storia delle Scienze Matematiche [*A publication*]
Boll Centro Camuno ... Bollettino. Centro Camuno di Studi Preistorici [*A publication*]
Boll Centro Stud Vichiani ... Bollettino. Centro di Studi Vichiani [*A publication*]
Boll Chim Farm ... Bollettino Chimico Farmaceutico [*A publication*]
Boll Chim Ig Parte Sci ... Bollettino dei Chimici Igienisti. Parte Scientifica [*A publication*]
Boll Chim Unione Ital Parte Sci ... Bollettino dei Chimici. Unione Italiana dei Laboratori Provinciali. Parte Scientifica [*A publication*]
Boll Circ Num Napoletano ... Bollettino. Circolo Numismatico Napoletano [*A publication*]
Boll Class ... Bollettino dei Classici [*A publication*]
Boll Clin ..... Il Bollettino delle Cliniche [*A publication*]
Boll Com .... Bollettino. Comitato per la Preparazione dell'Edizione Nazionale dei Classici Greci e Latini [*A publication*]
Boll Com Arch ... Bollettino. Commissione Archeologica Comunale in Roma [*A publication*] (OCD)
Boll Comm ... Bollettino. Commissione Archeologica Comunale di Roma [*A publication*]
Boll della Comm Arch Com di Roma ... Bollettino. Commissione Archeologica Comunale di Roma [*A publication*]
Boll Com Prep Ed Naz Class Greci Lat ... Bollettino. Comitato per la Preparazione dell'Edizione Nazionale dei Classici Greci e Latini [*A publication*]
Boll Cons Cagliari ... Bollettino Economico. Consiglio Provinciale delle Corporazioni di Cagliari [*A publication*]
Boll Cost Parl ... Bollettino d'Informazioni Costituzionali e Parlamentari [*A publication*]
Boll Coton ... Bollettino della Cotoniera [*A publication*]
Boll Dem Met ... Bollettino Demografico-Meteorico [*A publication*]
Bol Leit ...... Boletim do Leite e Seus Derivados [*Rio De Janeiro*] [*A publication*]
Bol Leite ..... Boletim do Leite [*A publication*]
Bol Leite Seus Deriv ... Boletim do Leite e Seus Derivados [*A publication*]
Boll Epizooz ... Bollettino delle Epizoozie [*A publication*]
Boll F Cl ... Bollettino di Filologia Classica [*A publication*]
Boll Fed Miner ... Bollettino. Federazione Mineraria [*A publication*]
Boll Fil Class ... Bollettino di Filologia Classica [*A publication*] (OCD)
Boll Fond Sen Pascale Cent Diagn Cura Tumori ... Bollettino. Fondazione Sen Pascale Centro per la Diagnosi e la Cura dei Tumori [*A publication*]
Boll For ...... Bollettino Forense [*A publication*]
Boll Geodes ... Bollettino di Geodesia e Scienze Affini [*A publication*]
Boll Geod Sci Affini ... Bollettino di Geodesia e Scienze Affini [*Florence*] [*A publication*]
Boll Geofis Teor Appl ... Bollettino di Geofisica Teorica ed Applicata [*A publication*]
Boll Geofis Teorica Appl ... Bollettino di Geofisica Teorica ed Applicata [*A publication*]
Boll Geof Teor Appl ... Bollettino di Geofisica Teorica ed Applicata. Osservatorio Geofisico [*A publication*]
Boll Gov ..... Bollettino. Commissione Archeologica de Governatorato di Roma [*A publication*]
Bol Liga Cancer ... Boletin. Liga Contra el Cancer [*A publication*]
Boll Inf Ind Olearia Sapon ... Bollettino d'Informazioni per l'Industria Olearia e Saponiera [*A publication*]
Boll Int Opere Sci Med ... Bollettino Internazionale delle Opere Scientifiche Medicina [*A publication*]
Boll Ist Agrar Scandicci ... Bollettino. Istituto Agrario di Scandicci [*A publication*]
Boll Ist Aliment Dietol ... Bollettino. Istituto di Alimentazione e Dietologia [*A publication*]
Boll Ist Dir Rom ... Bollettino. Istituto di Diritto Romano [*A publication*] (OCD)
Boll Ist Ent Agr Oss Fitopat Palermo ... Bollettino. Istituto di Entomologia Agraria e Osservatorio di Fitopatologia di Palermo [*A publication*]
Boll Ist Entomol ... Bollettino. Istituto di Entomologia [*A publication*]
Boll Ist Entomol Agrar Osse Fitopatol Palermo ... Bollettino. Istituto di Entomologia Agraria e Osservatorio di Fitopatologia di Palermo [*A publication*]
Boll Ist Entomol Agrar Oss Fitopatol Palermo ... Bollettino. Istituto di Entomologia Agraria e Osservatorio di Fitopatologia di Palermo [*A publication*]
Boll Ist Entomol Univ Studi Bologna ... Bollettino. Istituto dei Entomologia. Universita degli Studi di Bologna [*A publication*]
Boll Ist Ent Univ Bologna ... Bollettino. Istituto di Entomologia. Universita degli Studi di Bologna [*A publication*]
Boll Ist Patol Libr ... Bollettino. Istituto di Patologia del Libro Alfonso Gallo [*A publication*]
Boll Ist Patol Libro ... Bollettino. Istituto di Patologia del Libro [*A publication*]

Boll Ist Patologia Lib ... Bollettino. Istituto di Patologia del Libro [*A publication*]

Boll Ist Restauro ... Bollettino. Istituto Centrale del Restauro [*A publication*]

Boll Ist Sieroter Milan ... Bollettino. Istituto Sieroterapico Milanese [*A publication*]

Boll Ist Stor Cult Arma Genio ... Bollettino. Istituto Storico e di Cultura dell'Arma del Genio [*A publication*]

Boll Ist Stor It ... Bollettino. Istituto Storico Italiano per il Medioevo e Archivio Muratoriano [*A publication*]

Boll Ist Stor Ital Arte Sanit ... Bollettino. Istituto Storico Italiano dell'Arte Sanitaria [*A publication*]

Boll Ist Tumori Napoli ... Bollettino. Istituto dei Tumori di Napoli [*A publication*]

Boll Lab Chim Prov ... Bollettino. Laboratori Chimici Provinciali [*A publication*]

Boll Lab Entol Agr ... Bollettino. Laboratorio di Entomologia Agraria [*A publication*]

Boll Lab Entomol Agrar Portici ... Bollettino. Laboratorio di Entomologia Agraria "Filippo Silvestri" di Portici [*Italy*] [*A publication*]

Boll Laboratori Chim Prov ... Bollettino. Laboratori Chimici Provinciali [*A publication*]

Boll Laniera ... Bollettino della Laniera [*A publication*]

Boll Malacol ... Bollettino Malacologico [*A publication*]

Boll Mal Orecch Gola Naso ... Bollettino delle Malattie dell'Orecchio, della Gola, del Naso [*A publication*]

Boll Mal Orecchio Gola Naso ... Bollettino delle Malattie dell'Orecchio, della Gola, del Naso [*Italy*] [*A publication*]

Boll Mat..... Bollettino di Matematica [*A publication*]

Boll Mathesis ... Bollettino. Associazione Mathesis. Societa Italiana di Matematica [*A publication*]

Boll MC..... Bollettino dei Musei Comunali di Roma [*A publication*]

Boll Med Svizz ... Bollettino del Medici Svizzeri [*A publication*]

Boll Mem Soc Piemont Chir ... Bollettino e Memorie. Societa Piemontese de Chirurgia [*A publication*]

Boll Mem Soc Tosco Umbro Emiliana Med Interna ... Bollettino e Memorie. Societa Tosco Umbro Emiliana di Medicina Interna [*A publication*]

Boll Mens Cam Com Ind Agr (Perugia) ... Bollettino Mensile. Camera di Commercio Industria e Agricoltura (Perugia) [*A publication*]

Boll Mens Inform Notiz Sta Patol Vegetale Roma ... Bollettino Mensile d'Informazioni e Notizie. Reale Stazione di Patologia Vegetale di Roma e Reale Osservatorio Fitopatologico per la Provincia di Roma e gli Abruzzi [*A publication*]

Boll Metallogr ... Bollettino Metallografico [*A publication*]

Boll Meteorol Idrol Agrar ... Bollettino di Meteorologia e di Idrologia Agraria [*A publication*]

Boll Mus Civico Padova ... Bollettino. Museo Civico di Padova [*A publication*]

Boll Mus Civ Stor Nat Ven ... Bollettino. Museo Civico di Storia Naturale di Venezia [*A publication*]

Boll Mus Civ Stor Nat Venezia ... Bollettino. Museo Civico di Storia Naturale di Venezia [*A publication*]

Boll Mus Civ Stor Nat Verona ... Bollettino. Museo Civico di Storia Naturale di Verona [*A publication*]

Boll dei Mus Is Biol Univ Genova ... Bollettino. Musei e Istituti Biologici. Universita di Genova [*A publication*]

Boll Mus Ist Biol Univ Genova ... Bollettino. Musei e Istituti Biologici. Universita di Genova [*A publication*]

Boll Mus Zool Univ Torino ... Bollettino. Museo di Zoologia. Universita di Torino [*A publication*]

BollN.......... Bollettino Numismatico di Luigi Simonetti [*A publication*]

Boll Oceanol Teor ed Appl ... Bollettino di Oceanologia Teorica ed Applicata [*A publication*]

Boll Ocul.... Bollettino d'Oculistica [*A publication*]

Boll Pal...... Bollettino Paleontologico Italiano [*A publication*]

Boll Pesca Piscic Idrobiol ... Bollettino di Pesca, Piscicoltura, e Idrobiologia [*A publication*]

Boll Psicol App ... Bollettino di Psicologia Applicata [*A publication*]

Boll Psicol Appl ... Bollettino di Psicologia Applicata [*A publication*]

Boll Psicol Appl Inserto ... Bollettino di Psicologia Applicata. Inserto [*A publication*]

Boll R Accad Med Roma ... Bollettino. Reale Accademia Medica di Roma [*A publication*]

Boll Regia Stn Sper Ind Carta Stud Fibre Tess Veg ... Bollettino. Regia Stazione Sperimentale per l'Industria della Carta e lo Studio delle Fibre Tessili Vegetali [*A publication*]

Boll Regia Stn Sper Ind Pelli Mater Concianti Napoli ... Bollettino. Regia Stazione Sperimentale per l'Industria delle Pelli e delle Materie Concianti Napoli [*A publication*]

Boll Regio Is Super Agrar Pisa ... Bollettino. Regio Istituto Superiore Agrario di Pisa [*A publication*]

Boll Ric Inf Cent Reg Sper Ind Enol F Paulsen (Marsala) ... Bollettino di Ricerche e Informazioni. Centro Regionale Sperimentale per l'Industria Enologia F. Paulsen (Marsala) [*A publication*]

Boll Ric Reg Sicil Cent Sper Enol F Paulsen (Marsala) ... Bollettino di Ricerche. Regione Siciliana. Centro Sperimentale Enologia F. Paulsen (Marsala) [*A publication*]

Boll Riv ...... Bollettino delle Riviste [*A publication*]

Boll Schermogr ... Bollettino Schermografico [*A publication*]

Boll Scient ... Bollettino Scientifico [*A publication*]

Boll Sci Fac Chim Ind Bologna ... Bollettino Scientifico. Facolta di Chimica Industriale di Bologna [*Italy*] [*A publication*]

Boll Sci Med ... Bollettino delle Scienze Mediche [*A publication*]

Boll Sc Med Bologna ... Bollettino delle Scienze Mediche di Bologna [*A publication*]

Boll Sedute Accad Gioenia Sci Nat Catania ... Bollettino. Sedute della Accademia Gioenia di Scienze Naturali in Catania [*A publication*]

Boll Senese Stor Patria ... Bollettino Senese di Storia Patria [*A publication*]

Boll Serv Geol Ital ... Bollettino. Servizio Geologico d'Italia [*A publication*]

Boll Soc Adriat Sci (Trieste) ... Bollettino. Societa Adriatica di Scienze (Trieste) [*A publication*]

Boll Soc Adriat Sci (Trieste) Suppl ... Bollettino. Societa Adriatica di Scienze (Trieste). Supplemento [*A publication*]

Boll Soc Biol Sper ... Bollettino. Societa di Biologia Sperimentale [*A publication*]

Boll Soc Ent Ital ... Bollettino. Societa Entomologica Italiana [*A publication*]

Boll Soc Entomol Ital ... Bollettino. Societa Entomologica Italiana [*A publication*]

Boll Soc Eustachiana ... Bollettino. Societa Eustachiana [*A publication*]

Boll Soc Geog ... Bollettino. Societa Geografica Italiana [*A publication*]

Boll Soc Geogr Ital ... Bollettino. Societa Geografica Italiana [*A publication*]

Boll Soc Geol Ital ... Bollettino. Societa Geologica Italiana [*A publication*]

Boll Soc Ital Biol Sper ... Bollettino. Societa Italiana di Biologia Sperimentale [*A publication*]

Boll Soc Ital Cardiol ... Bollettino. Societa Italiana di Cardiologia [*A publication*]

Boll Soc Ital Ematol ... Bollettino. Societa Italiana di Ematologia [*A publication*]

Boll Soc Ital Farm Osp ... Bollettino. Societa Italiana di Farmacia Ospedaliera [*A publication*]

Boll Soc Ital Fis ... Bollettino. Societa Italiana di Fisica [*A publication*]

Boll Soc Ital Patol ... Bollettino. Societa Italiana di Patologia [*A publication*]

Boll Soc Med Chir (Cremona) ... Bollettino. Societa Medico-Chirurgica (Cremona) [*A publication*]

Boll Soc Med-Chir Osp Prov Cremona ... Bollettino. Societa Medico-Chirurgica e Ospedali Provincia di Cremona [*A publication*]

Boll Soc Med-Chir Pavia ... Bollettino. Societa Medico-Chirurgica di Pavia [*A publication*]

Boll Soc Med Chir Pisa ... Bollettino. Societa Medico-Chirurgica di Pisa [*A publication*]

Boll Soc Med Lazzaro Spallanzani Reggio Emilia ... Bollettino. Societa Medica Lazzaro Spallanzani con Sede in Reggio Emilia [*A publication*]

Boll Soc Nat Napoli ... Bollettino. Societa di Naturalisti di Napoli [*A publication*]

Boll Soc Paleontol Ital ... Bollettino. Societa Paleontologica Italiana [*A publication*]

Boll Soc Rom Stud Zool ... Bollettino. Societa Romana per gli Studi Zoologici [*A publication*]

Boll Soc Sarda Sci Nat ... Bollettino. Societa Sarda di Scienze Naturali [*A publication*]

Boll Soc Zool Ital ... Bollettino. Societa Zoologica Italiana [*A publication*]

Boll S P ...... Bollettino Storico Piacentino [*A publication*]

Boll Sta Patol Veg ... Bollettino. Stazione di Patologia Vegetale di Roma [*A publication*]

Boll Sta Patol Vegetale ... Bollettino. Reale Stazione di Patologia Vegetale di Roma [*A publication*]

Boll St Cremonese ... Bollettino Storico Cremonese [*A publication*]

Boll Stn Patol Veg Roma ... Bollettino. Stazione di Patologia Vegetale di Roma [*A publication*]

Boll Stor Cat ... Bollettino Storico Catanese [*A publication*]

Boll Storia Sci Mat ... Bollettino di Storia delle Scienze Matematiche [*A publication*]

Boll Stor Svizz Ital ... Bollettino Storico della Svizzera Italiana [*A publication*]

Boll St Piacentino ... Bollettino Storico Piacentino [*A publication*]

Boll Stran..... Bollettino Universitario Italiano per Stranieri [*A publication*]

Boll Tec FINSIDER ... Bollettino Tecnico FINSIDER [*Societa Finanziaria Siderurgica*] [*Italy*] [*A publication*]

Boll Tec Regio Ist Sper Coltiv Tab Leonardo Angeloni ... Bollettino Tecnico. Regio Istituto Sperimentale per la Coltivazione dei Tabacchi Leonardo Angeloni [*A publication*]

Boll Uffic Cam Com Ind Agr Udine ... Bollettino Ufficiale. Camera di Commercio, Industria, e Agricoltura di Udine [*A publication*]

Boll Uffic Regia Stn Sper Seta (Italy) ... Bollettino Ufficiale. Regia Stazione Sperimentale per la Seta (Italy) [*A publication*]

Boll Uffic Stn Sper Ind Essenze Deriv Agrumi Reggio Calabria ... Bollettino Ufficiale. Stazione Sperimentale per l'Industria delle Essenze e dei Derivati degli Agrumi in Reggio Calabria [*A publication*]

Boll Unione Mat Ital ... Bollettino. Unione Matematica Italiana [*A publication*]

Boll Unione Mat Ital Ser IV ... Bollettino. Unione Matematica Italiana. Series IV [*Italy*] [*A publication*]

Boll Un Mat Ital ... Bollettino. Unione Matematica Italiana [*A publication*]

Boll Un Mat Ital A ... Bollettino. Unione Matematica Italiana. A [*A publication*]

Boll Un Mat Ital A V ... Unione Matematica Italiana. Bollettino. A. Serie V [*Bologna*] [*A publication*]
Boll Un Mat Ital A VI ... Unione Matematica Italiana. Bollettino. A. Serie VI [*A publication*]
Boll Un Mat Ital B ... Bollettino. Unione Matematica Italiana. B [*A publication*]
Boll Un Mat Ital B VI ... Unione Matematica Italiana. Bollettino. B. Serie VI [*A publication*]
Boll Un Mat Ital C 5 ... Bollettino. Unione Matematica Italiana. C. Serie V. Analisi Funzionale e Applicazioni [*A publication*]
Boll Un Mat Ital Suppl ... Unione Matematica Italiana. Bollettino. Supplemento [*A publication*]
Boll Zool .... Bollettino di Zoologia [*A publication*]
Boll Zool Agrar Bachic ... Bollettino di Zoologia Agraria e di Bachicoltura [*A publication*]
Boll Zool Agrar Bachicolt ... Bollettino di Zoologia Agraria e di Bachicoltura [*A publication*]
Boll Zool Agr Bachic ... Bollettino di Zoologia Agraria e di Bachicoltura [*A publication*]
Boll Zool Agr Bachicolt ... Bollettino di Zoologia Agraria e di Bachicoltura [*A publication*]
Boll Zool (Napoli) ... Bollettino di Zoologia (Napoli) [*A publication*]
BOLM .... Bureau of Land Management [*Department of the Interior*] (MCD)
Bolm Apic .. Boletim Apicola [*A publication*]
Bol Mat ...... Boletin de Matematicas [*A publication*]
Bol Mat ...... Boletin Matematico [*A publication*]
Bol Mat Dent ... Boletin de Materias Dentarios [*A publication*]
Bol Mat Estat Fis (Araraquara Brazil) ... Boletim de Matematica, Estatistica, e Fisica (Araraquara, Brazil) [*A publication*]
Bol Mat Estatist Fis ... Boletim de Matematica, Estatistica, e Fisica [*A publication*]
Bol Med Brit ... Boletin Medico Britanico [*A publication*]
Bol Med Chile ... Boletin Medico de Chile [*A publication*]
Bol Med Cirug y Farm (Madrid) ... Boletin de Medicina, Cirugia, y Farmacia (Madrid) [*A publication*]
Bol Med Hosp Inf ... Boletin Medico. Hospital Infantil [*A publication*]
Bol Med Hosp Infant Mex ... Boletin Medico. Hospital Infantil de Mexico [*A publication*]
Bol Med Inf ... Boletin Medico Informativo [*A publication*]
Bol Med Inst Mex Seg Soc ... Boletin Medico. Instituto Mexicano del Seguro Social [*A publication*]
Bol Med Quir ... Boletin Medico-Quirurgico [*A publication*]
Bol Med Soc ... Boletin Medico-Social. Caja de Seguro Obligatorio [*A publication*]
Bol Med Univ Auton Guadalajara ... Boletin Medico. Universidad Autonoma de Guadalajara [*A publication*]
Bol Med Univ Guad ... Boletin Medico. Universidad Autonoma de Guadalajara [*A publication*]
Bol Mensal Estatistica (Portugal) ... Boletim Mensal de Estatistica (Portugal) [*A publication*]
Bol Mens Estad Agri ... Boletin Mensual de Estadisticas Agricolas [*A publication*]
Bol Mens Estadist ... Boletin Mensual de Estadistica [*A publication*]
Bol Mensile Statis ... Bollettino Mensile di Statistica [*A publication*]
Bol Mens Obs Ebro ... Boletin Mensual. Observatorio del Ebro [*A publication*]
Bol Mensual Estadistica ... Boletin Mensual de Estadistica [*A publication*]
Bol Mensual Estadistica Agraria ... Boletin Mensual de Estadistica Agraria [*A publication*]
Bol Mensual Estadisticas Agrics ... Boletin Mensual de Estadisticas Agricolas [*A publication*]
Bolm Esc Agric "Luiz Queiroz" ... Boletim. Escola Agricola "Luiz De Queiroz" [*A publication*]
Bol Met (Ecuad) ... Boletin Meteorologico (Ecuador) [*A publication*]
Bol Met Seism ... Boletin Meteorologico y Seismologico [*A publication*]
Bol Mexic Der Comp ... Boletin Mexicano de Derecho Comparado [*A publication*]
Bol Mex Reumatol ... Boletin Mexicano de Reumatologia [*A publication*]
Bol Minas .. Boletin de Minas [*A publication*]
Bol Minas y Energia ... Boletin de Minas y Energia [*A publication*]
Bol Minas y Petroleo ... Boletin de Minas y Petroleo [*A publication*]
Bol Minas (Port Dir-Geral Minas Serv Geol) ... Boletin de Minas (Portugal Direccao-Geral de Minas e Servicos Geologicos) [*A publication*]
Bolm Ind Anim ... Boletim de Industria Animal [*A publication*]
Bol Mineral ... Boletim Mineralogico [*A publication*]
Bol Minero ... Boletin Minero [*A publication*]
Bol Min Ind ... Boletin Minero e Industrial [*A publication*]
Bol Minist Sanid Asist Soc (Venez) ... Boletim. Ministerio de Sanidad y Asisteneta Social (Venezuela) [*A publication*]
Bol Min Justica ... Boletim. Ministerio de Justica [*Portugal*] [*A publication*] (DLA)
Bol Min Petr ... Boletin de Miras y Petroleo [*Chile*] [*A publication*]
Bolm Inst Angola ... Boletim. Instituto de Angola [*A publication*]
BOLMM ... Brothers of Our Lady, Mother of Mercy [*Tilburg, Netherlands*] (EAIO)
Bolm Mus Para Emilio Goeldi Bot ... Boletim. Museu Paraense Emilio Goeldi. Nova Serie. Botanica [*A publication*]
Bolm Real Soc Esp Hist Nat Secc ... Boletim. Real Sociedade Espanola de Historia Natural. Seccion Biologica [*A publication*]

Bolm Soc Bras Ent ... Boletim. Sociedade Brasileira de Entomologia [*A publication*]
Bolm Soc Broteriana ... Boletim. Sociedade Broteriana [*A publication*]
Bolm Soc Cearense Agron ... Boletim. Sociedade Cearense de Agronomia [*A publication*]
Bolm Tec Inst Agron N ... Boletim Tecnico. Instituto Agronomico do Norte [*A publication*]
Bolm Tec Inst Pesq Exp Agropecuar N ... Boletim Tecnico. Instituto de Pesquisas e Experimentacao Agropecuarias do Norte [*A publication*]
Bolm Univ Parana Zool ... Boletim. Universidade Federal do Parana. Zoologia [*A publication*]
Bol Mus Bot Munic (Curitiba) ... Boletim. Museu Botanico Municipal (Curitiba) [*A publication*]
Bol Mus Cienc Nat ... Boletin. Museo de Ciencias Naturales [*A publication*]
Bol Mus Cienc Nat Antropol Juan Cornelio Moyano ... Boletin. Museo de Ciencias Naturales y Antropologicas Juan Cornelio Moyano [*A publication*]
Bol Museo Civico Padova ... Bollettino. Museo Civico di Padova [*A publication*]
Bol Mus Hist Nat UFMG Bot ... Boletim. Museu de Historia Natural UFMG [*Universidade Federal de Minas Gerais*]. Botanica [*A publication*]
Bol Mus Hist Nat UFMG Geol ... Boletim. Museu de Historia Natural UFMG [*Universidade Federal de Minas Gerais*]. Geologia [*A publication*]
Bol Mus Hist Nat UFMG Zool ... Boletim. Museu de Historia Natural UFMG [*Universidade Federal de Minas Gerais*]. Zoologia [*A publication*]
Bol Mus Lab Mineral Geol Fac Cienc Univ Lisboa ... Boletim. Museu e Laboratorio Mineralogico e Geologicao. Faculdade de Ciencias. Universidade de Lisboa [*A publication*]
Bol Mus Munic Funchal ... Boletim. Museu Municipal do Funchal [*A publication*]
Bol Mus Nac (Rio De Janeiro) ... Boletim. Museu Nacional (Rio De Janeiro) [*A publication*]
Bol Mus Nac (Rio De Janeiro) Geol ... Boletim. Museu Nacional (Rio De Janeiro). Geologia [*A publication*]
Bol Mus Nac (Rio De J) Antropol ... Boletim. Museu Nacional (Rio De Janeiro). Antropologia [*A publication*]
Bol Mus Nac (Rio De J) Bot ... Boletim. Museu Nacional (Rio De Janeiro). Botanica [*A publication*]
Bol Mus Nac Rio De J Nova Ser Geol ... Boletim. Museu Nacional de Rio De Janeiro. Nova Serie. Geologia [*A publication*]
Bol Mus Nac (Rio De J) Zool ... Boletim. Museu Nacional (Rio De Janeiro). Zoologia [*A publication*]
Bol Mus Para Emilio Goeldi Nova Ser Antropol ... Boletim. Museu Paraense Emilio Goeldi. Nova Serie. Antropologia [*A publication*]
Bol Mus Para Emilio Goeldi Nova Ser Bot ... Boletim. Museu Paraense Emilio Goeldi. Nova Serie. Botanica [*A publication*]
Bol Mus Para Emilio Goeldi Nova Ser Geol ... Boletim. Museu Paraense Emilio Goeldi. Nova Serie. Geologia [*A publication*]
Bol Mus Para Emilio Goeldi Nova Ser Zool ... Boletim. Museu Paraense Emilio Goeldi. Nova Serie. Zoologia [*A publication*]
Bol Mus Para Emilio Goeldi Ser Antropol ... Boletim. Museu Paraense Emilio Goeldi. Serie Antropologia [*A publication*]
Bol Mus Para Emilio Goeldi Ser Bot ... Boletim. Museu Paraense Emilio Goeldi. Serie Botanica [*A publication*]
Bol Mus Para Emilio Goeldi Ser Zool ... Boletim. Museu Paraense Emilio Goeldi. Serie Zoologia [*A publication*]
Bol Mus Paraense Emilio Goeldi ... Boletim. Museu Paraense Emilio Goeldi [*A publication*]
Bol Mus Paraense Emilio Goeldi Nova Ser Antropol ... Boletim. Museu Paraense Emilio Goeldi. Nova Serie. Antropologia [*A publication*]
Bol Mus Paraense Emilio Goeldi Nova Ser Bot ... Boletim. Museu Paraense Emilio Goeldi. Nova Serie. Botanica [*A publication*]
Bol Mus Paraense Emilio Goeldi Nova Ser Geol ... Boletim. Museu Paraense Emilio Goeldi. Nova Serie. Geologia [*A publication*]
Bol Mus Soc Argent ... Boletin. Museo Social Argentino [*A publication*]
Bol Mus Soc Arqueol la Serena ... Boletin. Publicaciones del Museo y de la Sociedad Arqueologica de la Serena [*A publication*]
Bol Mus Valp ... Boletin. Museo de Valparaiso [*A publication*]
Bolm Zool Univ S Paulo ... Boletim de Zoologia. Universidade de Sao Paulo [*A publication*]
BOLN .... Bowline Corp. [*NASDAQ symbol*] (NQ)
Bol Nac Minas ... Boletin Nacional de Minas [*A publication*]
Boln Divulg Ganad ... Boletin de Divulgacion Ganaderia [*A publication*]
Boln Divulg (Pergamino) ... Boletin de Divulgacion (Pergamino) [*A publication*]
Boln Estac Exp Agric "Tingo Maria" ... Boletin. Estacion Experimental Agricola "Tingo Maria" [*A publication*]
Boln Geol (Bogota) ... Boletin Geologico. Instituto Geologico Nacional (Bogota, Colombia). [*A publication*]
Boln Mus Hist Nat Javier Prado ... Boletin. Museo de Historia Natural "Javier Prado" [*A publication*]
Boln Mus Nac Hist Nat (Chile) ... Boletin. Museo Nacional de Historia Natural (Chile) [*A publication*]
Boln Of Estado ... Boletin Oficial del Estado [*A publication*]
Bol Not Inst Fom Algodonero (Bogota) ... Boletin de Noticias. Instituto de Fomento Algodonero (Bogota) [*A publication*]

Boln Patol Veg Ent Agric ... Boletin de Patologia Vegetal y Entomologia Agricola [*A publication*]
Boln R Soc Esp Hist Nat ... Boletin. Real Sociedad Espanola de Historia Natural [*A publication*]
Boln Rur Inst Nac Tecnol Agropec ... Boletin Rural. Instituto Nacional de Tecnologia Agropecuaria [*A publication*]
Boln Soc Venez Cienc Nat ... Boletin. Sociedad Venezolana de Ciencias Naturales [*A publication*]
Boln Tec Fac Agron Univ Chile ... Boletin Tecnico. Facultad de Agronomia. Universidad de Chile [*A publication*]
Bol Nucl ..... Boletin Nucleo [*A publication*]
Bol Num (Brasil) ... Boletim de Numismatica (Brasil) [*A publication*]
Boln Univ Montevideo Fac Agron ... Boletin. Universidad de la Republica. Faculdad de Agronomia (Montevideo) [*A publication*]
BOLO .... Be On the Lookout [*Police term*]
Bol Obras Sanit Nac (Argent) ... Boletin de Obras Sanitarias de la Nacion (Argentina) [*A publication*]
Bol Obs Ebro Ser A ... Boletin. Observatorio del Ebro. Serie A [*A publication*]
Bol Oceanogr Pesc ... Boletin de Oceanografia y Pescas [*A publication*]
Bol Odont ... Boletin de Odontologia [*A publication*]
Bol Odont Mex ... Boletin Odontologico Mexicano [*A publication*]
Bol Odontol (Bogota) ... Boletin de Odontologia (Bogota) [*A publication*]
Bol Odontol Mex ... Boletin Odontologico Mexicano [*A publication*]
Bol Odont Paul ... Boletim Odontologico Paulista [*A publication*]
Bol Of Asoc Tec Azucar Cuba ... Boletin Oficial. Asociacion de Tecnicos Azucareros de Cuba [*A publication*]
Bol Of Col Quim PR ... Boletin Oficial. Colegio Quimicos de Puerto Rico [*A publication*]
Bol Of Estado ... Boletin Oficial del Estado [*Spain*] [*A publication*]
Bol Ofic Sanit Panam Engl Ed ... Boletin. Oficina Sanitaria Panamericana. English Edition [*A publication*]
Bol Ofic Sanit Panamer ... Boletin. Oficina Sanitaria Panamericana [*A publication*]
Bol Of Sanit Panam ... Boletin. Oficina Sanitaria Panamericana [*A publication*]
Bol Of Sanit Panam Engl Ed ... Boletin. Oficina Sanitaria Panamericana. English Edition [*A publication*]
Bol Oftal .... Boletin Oftalmologico [*A publication*]
Bologna Med ... Bologna Medica [*A publication*]
Bolognet ..... [*Johannes*] Bolognetus [*Deceased, 1575*] [*Authority cited in pre-1607 legal work*] (DSA)
Bologni .... [*Ludovicus*] Bologninus [*Deceased, 1508*] [*Authority cited in pre-1607 legal work*] (DSA)
Bol Oncol ... Boletim de Oncologia [*A publication*]
Bol Ord Med ... Boletim. Ordem dos Medicos [*A publication*]
BOLOVAC ... Bolometric Voltage and Current [*Voltage measurement*] [*National Institute of Standards and Technology*]
Bol Paleontol B Aires ... Boletin Paleontologico de Buenos Aires [*A publication*]
Bol Parana Geocienc ... Boletim Paranaense de Geociencias [*A publication*]
Bol Parana Geogr ... Boletim Paranaense de Geografia [*A publication*]
Bol Par Geogr ... Boletim Paranaense de Geografia [*A publication*]
Bol Patol Med (Madr) ... Boletin de Patologia Medica (Madrid) [*A publication*]
Bol Patol Veg Entomol Agric ... Boletin de Patologia Vegetal y Entomologia Agricola [*A publication*]
Bol Paul Geogr ... Boletim Paulista de Geografia [*A publication*]
Bol Pecuar Dir Geral Serv Pecuar (Portugal) ... Boletim Pecuario. Direccao Geral dos Servicos Pecuarios (Portugal) [*A publication*]
Bol Pecu (Lisb) ... Boletim Pecuario (Lisbon) [*A publication*]
Bol Petroleo ... Boletin del Petroleo [*A publication*]
Bol Planificacion ... Boletin de Planificacion [*A publication*]
Bol Popular Min Agric (Guatemala) ... Boletin Popular. Direccion General de Agricultura de Guatemala. Ministerio de Agricultura (Guatemala) [*A publication*]
Bol Prod Anim ... Boletin de Produccion Animal [*A publication*]
Bol Prod Fom Agric ... Boletin de Produccion y Fomento Agricola [*A publication*]
Bol Protes .. Boletin de Protesis [*A publication*]
Bol Psicol ... Boletim de Psicologia [*A publication*]
Bol Psiquiatr ... Boletim de Psiquiatria [*A publication*]
Bol Quim Peru ... Boletin del Quimico Peruano [*A publication*]
Bol R Ac Hist ... Boletin. Real Academia de la Historia [*Madrid*] [*A publication*]
Bol Radiact ... Boletin de Radiactividad [*A publication*]
Bol Real Ac ... Boletin. Real Academia de la Historia [*A publication*]
Bol Real Soc Geogr ... Boletin. Real Sociedad de Geografia [*Madrid*] [*A publication*]
Bol Resenas Ser Ganad ... Boletin de Resenas. Serie Ganaderia (Havana) [*A publication*]
Bol Rev Peru Pediat ... Boletin. Revista Peruana de Pediatria [*A publication*]
Bol R Soc Espan Hist Nat ... Boletin. Real Sociedad Espanola de Historia Natural [*A publication*]
Bol R Soc Esp Hist Nat ... Boletin. Real Sociedad Espanola de Historia Natural [*A publication*]
Bol R Soc Esp Hist Nat Secc Biol ... Boletin. Real Sociedad Espanola de Historia Natural. Seccion Biologica [*A publication*]
Bol R Soc Esp Hist Nat Secc Geol ... Boletin. Real Sociedad Espanola de Historia Natural. Seccion Geologica [*A publication*]
BOLS .... Bolster (KSC)

BOLS .... Boreales. Revue du Centre de Recherches Inter-Nordiques [*A publication*]
BOLS .... Bur Oak Library System [*Library network*]
BOLSA ...... Bank of London and South America
BOLSA ...... Bank of London and South America. Review [*A publication*]
Bol Salubr Hig ... Boletin de Salubridad e Higiene [*A publication*]
Bol Salud Publica ... Boletin de Salud Publica [*A publication*]
Bol Sanat (Sao Lucas) ... Boletim do Sanatorio (Sao Lucas) [*A publication*]
Bol Secr Sal Publ ... Boletin Administrativo. Secretaria de Salud Publica de la Nacion [*A publication*]
Bol Ser D Estud Espec Inst Geol Miner Repub Peru ... Boletin. Serie D. Estudios Especiales. Instituto de Geologia y Mineria. Republica del Peru [*Lima*] [*A publication*]
Bol Serv Def Contra Plagas Inspeccion Fitopatol (Spain) ... Boletin. Servicio de Defensa Contra Plagas e Inspeccion Fitopatologica (Spain) [*A publication*]
Bol Serv Geol Minas (Mocambique) ... Boletim dos Servicos de Geologia e Minas (Mocambique) [*A publication*]
Bol Serv Geol Nac Nicaragua ... Boletin. Servicio Geologico Nacional de Nicaragua [*A publication*]
Bol Serv Med Nac Empl (Ch) ... Boletin. Servicio Medico Nacional de Empleados (Chile) [*A publication*]
Bol Serv Nac Sal (Ch) ... Boletin. Servicio Nacional de Salud (Chile) [*A publication*]
Bol Serv Odontol Sanit (Porto Alegre) ... Boletim. Servico de Odontologia Sanitaria. Secretaria da Saude. Rio Grande do Sul (Porto Alegre) [*A publication*]
Bol Serv Plagas For ... Boletin. Servicio de Plagas Forestales [*A publication*]
Bol Soc Arg Angiol ... Boletines. Sociedad Argentina de Angiologia [*A publication*]
Bol Soc Arg Bot ... Boletin. Sociedad Argentina de Botanica [*A publication*]
Bol Soc Arg Ciruj ... Boletines y Trabajos. Sociedad Argentina de Cirujanos [*A publication*]
Bol Soc Argent Angiol ... Boletin. Sociedad Argentina de Angiologia [*A publication*]
Bol Soc Argent Bot ... Boletin. Sociedad Argentina de Botanica [*A publication*]
Bol Soc Arg Est Gaea ... Boletin. Sociedad Argentina de Estudios Geograficos Gaea [*A publication*]
Bol Soc Astr Mex ... Boletin. Sociedad Astronomica de Mexico [*A publication*]
Bol Soc Biol Concepcion ... Boletin. Sociedad de Biologia de Concepcion [*A publication*]
Bol Soc Boliv Pediat ... Boletin. Sociedad Boliviana de Pediatria [*A publication*]
Bol Soc Bot Estado Jalisco ... Boletin. Sociedad Botanica del Estado de Jalisco [*A publication*]
Bol Soc Bot Mex ... Boletin. Sociedad Botanica de Mexico [*A publication*]
Bol Soc Bras Agron ... Boletim. Sociedade Brasileira de Agronomia [*A publication*]
Bol Soc Bras Ent ... Boletim. Sociedade Brasileira de Entomologia [*A publication*]
Bol Soc Bras Geol ... Boletim. Sociedade Brasileira de Geologia [*A publication*]
Bol Soc Brasil Mat ... Boletim. Sociedade Brasileira de Matematica [*A publication*]
Bol Soc Bras Mat ... Boletim. Sociedade Brasileira de Matematica [*A publication*]
Bol Soc Bras Med Vet ... Boletim. Sociedade Brasileira de Medicina Veterinaria [*A publication*]
Bol Soc Bras Tuberc ... Boletim. Sociedade Brasileira de Tuberculose [*A publication*]
Bol Soc Broteriana ... Boletim. Sociedade Broteriana [*A publication*]
Bol Soc Castell Cult ... Boletin. Sociedad Castellonense de Cultura [*A publication*]
Bol Soc Cast Leon Pediat ... Boletin. Sociedad Castellanoleonesa de Pediatria [*A publication*]
Bol Soc Catal Pediat ... Boletin. Sociedad Catalana de Pediatria [*A publication*]
Bol Soc Cear Agron ... Boletin. Sociedade Cearense de Agronomia [*A publication*]
Bol Soc Cearense Agron ... Boletim. Sociedade Cearense de Agronomia [*A publication*]
Bol Soc Chil Obstet Ginec ... Boletin. Sociedad Chilena de Obstetricia y Ginecologia [*A publication*]
Bol Soc Chil Obstet Ginecol ... Boletin. Sociedad Chilena de Obstetricia y Ginecologia [*A publication*]
Bol Soc Chil Quim ... Boletin. Sociedad Chilena Quimica [*A publication*]
Bol Soc Chim Sao Paulo ... Boletim. Sociedade de Chimica de Sao Paulo [*A publication*]
Bol Soc Cient Hispano-Marroqui ... Boletin. Sociedad Cientifica Hispano-Marroqui de Alcazarquivir [*A publication*]
Bol Soc Cirug Chile ... Boletin. Sociedad de Cirugia de Chile [*A publication*]
Bol Soc Cirug Cord ... Boletines y Trabajos. Sociedad de Cirugia de Cordoba [*A publication*]
Bol Soc Cirug Urug ... Boletin. Sociedad de Cirugia del Uruguay [*A publication*]
Bol Soc Cir Urug ... Boletin. Sociedad de Cirugia del Uruguay [*A publication*]
Bol Soc Col Cienc Nat ... Boletin. Sociedad Colombiana de Ciencias Naturales [*A publication*]

Bol Soc Colomb Quim Farm ... Boletin. Sociedad Colombiana de Quimicos Farmaceuticos [*A publication*]

Bol Soc Cubana Dermatol Sifilogr ... Boletin. Sociedad Cubana de Dermatologia y Sifilografia [*A publication*]

Bol Soc Cub Derm Sif ... Boletin. Sociedad Cubana de Dermatologia y Sifilografia [*A publication*]

Bol Soc Dent Guatem ... Boletin. Sociedad Dental de Guatemala [*A publication*]

Bol Soc Eng Rio Grande Do Sul ... Boletim. Sociedade de Engenharia do Rio Grande Do Sul [*A publication*]

Bol Soc Esp Ceram ... Boletin. Sociedad Espanola de Ceramica [*A publication*]

Bol Soc Esp Ceram Vidrio ... Boletin. Sociedad Espanola de Ceramica y Vidrio [*A publication*]

Bol Soc Esp Hist Farm ... Boletin. Sociedad Espanola de Historia de la Farmacia [*A publication*]

Bol Soc Esp Hist Med ... Boletin. Sociedad Espanola de Historia de la Medicina [*A publication*]

Bol Soc Fom Fabril ... Boletin. Sociedad de Fomento Fabril [*A publication*]

Bol Soc Geogr Lisboa ... Boletim. Sociedade de Geografia de Lisboa [*A publication*]

Bol Soc Geogr (Madrid) ... Boletin. Real Sociedad de Geografia (Madrid) [*A publication*]

Bol Soc Geol Boliv ... Boletin. Sociedad Geologica Boliviana [*A publication*]

Bol Soc Geol Mex ... Boletin. Sociedad Geologica Mexicana [*A publication*]

Bol Soc Geol Peru ... Boletin. Sociedad Geologica del Peru [*A publication*]

Bol Soc Geol Port ... Boletim. Sociedade Geologica de Portugal [*A publication*]

Bol Soc Ital Fis ... Bollettino. Societa Italiana di Fisica [*A publication*]

Bol Soc Mat Mexicana ... Boletin. Sociedad Matematica Mexicana [*A publication*]

Bol Soc Mat Mexicana 2 ... Boletin. Sociedad Matematica Mexicana. Segunda Serie [*Mexico City*] [*A publication*]

Bol Soc Med Cent Materno Infant Gral Maximino Avila Camacho ... Boletin. Sociedad Medica del Centro Materno Infantil Gral Maximino Avila Camacho [*Mexico*] [*A publication*]

Bol Soc Med e Cirug S Paulo ... Boletim. Sociedade de Medicina e Cirugia de Sao Paulo [*A publication*]

Bol Soc Mex Hist Filos Med ... Boletin. Sociedad Mexicana de Historia y Filosofia de la Medicina [*A publication*]

Bol Soc Mex Micol ... Boletin. Sociedad Mexicana de Micologia [*A publication*]

Bol Soc Nac Mineria Petrol ... Boletin. Sociedad Nacional de Mineria y Petroleo [*A publication*]

Bol Soc Paran Mat 2 ... Boletim. Sociedade Paranaense de Matematica. 2 Serie [*Panama*] [*A publication*]

Bol Soc Paul Med Vet ... Boletim. Sociedade Paulista de Medicina Veterinaria [*A publication*]

Bol Soc Port Cienc Nat ... Boletim. Sociedade Portuguesa de Ciencias Naturais [*A publication*]

Bol Soc Port Entomol ... Boletim. Sociedade Portuguesa de Entomologia [*A publication*]

Bol Soc Quim Peru ... Boletin. Sociedad Quimica del Peru [*A publication*]

Bol Soc St Vald ... Bollettino. Societa di Studi Valdesi [*A publication*]

Bol Soc Valencia Pediatr ... Boletin. Sociedad Valenciana de Pediatria [*A publication*]

Bol Soc Venez Cienc Nat ... Boletin. Sociedad Venezolana de Ciencias Naturales [*A publication*]

Bol Soc Venez Cir ... Boletin. Sociedad Venezolana de Cirugia [*A publication*]

Bol Soc Venez Espeleol ... Boletin. Sociedad Venezolana de Espeleologia [*A publication*]

Bol Soc Venez Geol ... Boletin. Sociedad Venezolana de Geologos [*A publication*]

Bol Suelos Deriv Cenizas Volcanicas ... Boletin sobre Suelos Derivados de Cenizas Volcanicas [*A publication*]

Bol Supt Serv Cafe (Sao Paulo) ... Boletim. Superintendencia dos Servicos do Cafe (Sao Paulo) [*A publication*]

BOLT......... Basic Occupational Language Training

BOLT......... Basic Occupational Literacy Test

BOLT......... Beam of Light Transistor (MSA)

BOLT......... Beam of Light Transmitter

BOLT......... Bolt Technology Corp. [*NASDAQ symbol*] (NQ)

BOLT......... Bomb LASER Tracking (MCD)

Bol Tec Arpel ... Boletin Tecnico Arpel [*A publication*]

Bol Tec Asoc Interam Bibl Doc Agric ... Boletin Tecnico. Asociacion Interamericana de Bibliotecarios y Documentalistas Agricolas [*A publication*]

Bol Tec Braz Dep Nac Obras Contra Secas ... Boletim Tecnico. Brazil Departamento Nacional de Obras Contra as Secas [*A publication*]

Bol Tec Cent Pesqui Desenvolvimento (Estado Bahia) ... Boletim Tecnico. Centro de Pesquisas e Desenvolvimento (Estado da Bahia) [*A publication*]

Bol Tec Cent Tecnol Agric Aliment ... Boletim Tecnico. Centro de Tecnologia Agricola e Alimentar [*A publication*]

Bol Tec Cent Tecnol Agric Aliment (Rio De Janeiro) ... Boletim Tecnico. Centro de Tecnologia Agricola e Alimentar (Rio De Janeiro) [*A publication*]

Bol Tec Dep Nac Obras Contra Secas ... Boletim Tecnico. Departamento Nacional de Obras Contra as Secas [*A publication*]

Bol Tec Dep Prod Veg Secr Agric Parana ... Boletim Tecnico. Departamento de Producao Vegetal Secretaria de Agricultura do Parana [*A publication*]

Bol Tec Dept Invest Agr Min Agr Dir Agr Pesca (Chile) ... Boletin Tecnico. Departamento de Investigacion Agricola. Ministerio de Agricultura. Direccion de Agricultura y Pesca (Chile) [*A publication*]

Bol Tec Div Tecnol Agric Aliment (Brazil) ... Boletim Tecnico. Divisao de Tecnologia Agricola e Alimentar (Brazil) [*A publication*]

Bol Tec Equipe Pedol Fertil Solo (Brazil) ... Boletim Tecnico. Equipe de Pedologia e Fertilidade do Solo (Brazil) [*A publication*]

Bol Tec Esc Ingen For Univ Chile ... Boletin Tecnico. Escuela de Ingenieria Forestal. Universidad de Chile [*A publication*]

Bol Tec Esc Nac Agr Chapingo ... Boletin Tecnico. Escuela Nacional de Agricultura Chapingo [*A publication*]

Bol Tec Esc Super Agric Antonio Narro Univ Coahuila Saltillo ... Boletin Tecnico. Escuela Superior de Agricultura "Antonio Narro." Universidad de Coahuila (Saltillo) [*A publication*]

Bol Tec Es Super Agric Antonio Narro Univ Coahuila Saltillo ... Boletin Tecnico. Escuela Superior de Agricultura "Antonio Narro." Universidad de Coahuila (Saltillo) [*A publication*]

Bol Tec Feder Nac Cafeteros (Colombia) ... Boletin Tecnico. Federacion Nacional de Cafeteros (Colombia) [*A publication*]

Bol Tec Inst Agron ... Boletim Tecnico. Instituto Agronomico [*A publication*]

Bol Tec Inst Agron Leste (Cruz Das Almas) ... Boletim Tecnico. Instituto Agronomico do Leste (Cruz Das Almas) [*A publication*]

Bol Tec Inst Agron Nordeste ... Boletim Tecnico. Instituto Agronomico do Nordeste [*A publication*]

Bol Tec Inst Agron Norte ... Boletim Tecnico. Instituto Agronomico do Norte [*A publication*]

Bol Tec Inst Agron Norte Belem ... Boletim Tecnico. Instituto Agronomico do Norte Belem [*A publication*]

Bol Tec Inst Agron Sul ... Boletim Tecnico. Instituto Agronomico do Sul [*A publication*]

Bol Tec Inst Agron Sul (Pelotas) ... Boletim Tecnico. Instituto Agronomico do Sul (Pelotas) [*A publication*]

Bol Tec Inst Agron Sul (Pelotas Brazil) ... Boletim Tecnico. Instituto Agronomico do Sul (Pelotas, Brazil) [*A publication*]

Bol Tec Inst Fom Algodonero (Bogota) ... Boletim Tecnico. Instituto de Fomenta Algodonero (Bogota) [*A publication*]

Bol Tec Inst For Chile ... Boletin Tecnico. Instituto Forestal. Santiago-De-Chile [*A publication*]

Bol Tec Inst Nac Invest For (Mex) ... Boletin Tecnico. Instituto Nacional de Investigaciones Forestales (Mexico) [*A publication*]

Bol Tec Inst Pesqui Exp Agropecu Norte ... Boletim Tecnico. Instituto Pesquisas e Experimentacao Agropecuarias do Norte [*A publication*]

Bol Tec Inst Prov Agropecu (Mendoza) ... Boletin Tecnico. Instituto Provincial Agropecuario (Mendoza) [*A publication*]

Bol Tec IPEAN ... Boletim Tecnico. Instituto Pesquisas e Experimentacao Agropecuarias do Norte [*A publication*]

Bol Tec Min Agr (Colombia) ... Boletin Tecnico. Ministerio de Agricultura (Colombia) [*A publication*]

Bol Tec Min Agr (Guatemala) ... Boletin Tecnico. Ministerio de Agricultura (Guatemala) [*A publication*]

Bol Tec Minist Agric Ganad (Costa Rica) ... Boletin Tecnico. Ministerio de Agricultura y Ganaderia (Costa Rica) [*A publication*]

Bol Tec Minist Agric Ind (San Jose Costa Rica) ... Boletin Tecnico. Ministerio de Agricultura e Industrias (San Jose, Costa Rica) [*A publication*]

Bol Tec Peru Serv Invest Promoc Agr ... Boletin Tecnico. Peru. Servicio de Investigacion y Promocion Agraria [*A publication*]

Bol Tec PETROBRAS ... Boletim Tecnico. PETROBRAS [*Petroleo Brasileiro SA*] [*Centro de Pesquisas e Desenvolvimento*] [*A publication*]

Bol Tec Serv Nac Levantamento Conserv Solos ... Boletim Tecnico. Servico Nacional de Levantamento e Conservacao de Solos [*A publication*]

Bol Tec Univ Chile Fac Cienc For ... Boletin Tecnico. Universidad de Chile. Facultad de Ciencias Forestales [*A publication*]

BOLTOP... Better on Lips than on Paper [*Put at the end of a letter with kisses*] [*British*]

Bol Trab Soc Argent Cir ... Boletines y Trabajos. Sociedad Argentina de Cirujanos [*A publication*]

Bol y Trab Soc Cirug Buenos Aires ... Boletines y Trabajos. Sociedad de Cirugia de Buenos Aires [*A publication*]

Bol Univ Chile ... Boletin. Universidad de Chile [*A publication*]

Bol Univ Fed Parana Bot ... Boletim. Universidade Federal do Parana. Botanica [*A publication*]

Bol Univ Fed Parana Fis Teor ... Boletim. Universidade Federal do Parana. Fisica Teorica [*Brazil*] [*A publication*]

Bol Univ Fed Parana Zool ... Boletim. Universidade Federal do Parana. Zoologia [*A publication*]

Bol Univ Parana Farm ... Boletim. Universidade do Parana. Farmacognosia [*A publication*]

Bol Univ Parana Farmacogn ... Boletim. Universidade do Parana. Farmacognosia [*A publication*]

Bol Univ Parana Geol ... Boletim. Universidade do Parana. Geologia [*A publication*]

Bol Univ Sao Paulo Inst Geocien Astron ... Boletim. Universidade de Sao Paulo. Instituto de Geociencias e Astronomia [*A publication*]
Bol Univ Sao Paulo Inst Geocienc ... Boletim. Universidade de Sao Paulo. Instituto de Geociencias [*A publication*]
Bol Urug Sociol ... Boletin Uruguayo de Sociologia [*A publication*]
BOLY .... Bolyard Oil & Gas Ltd. [*NASDAQ symbol*] (NQ)
Bol Zool ..... Boletim de Zoologia [*A publication*]
Bol Zool Biol Mar ... Boletim de Zoologia e Biologia Marinha [*Later, Boletim de Zoologia*] [*A publication*]
Bol Zool Biol Mar (Nova Ser) ... Boletim de Zoologia e Biologia Marinha (Nova Serie) [*A publication*]
Bol Zool Mus Para Emilio Goeldi ... Boletim de Zoologia. Museu Paraense Emilio Goeldi [*A publication*]
BOM......... Base Operation Manager
BOM......... Basic Operating Monitor
BOM......... Beginning of Month [*Accounting*] (NASA)
BOM......... Bill of Materials [*Digital Dynamics Ltd.*] [*Software package*]
BOM......... Binary Order of Magnitude [*Data processing*]
BOM......... BIT [*Binary Digit*]-Oriented Message (RDA)
BOM......... Board on Medicine [*of the National Academy of Sciences*] [*Later, IOM*] (EA)
BOM......... Bombardier
BOM......... Bombay [*India*] [*Airport symbol*] (OAG)
BOM......... Bombay [*Colaba*] [*India*] [*Seismograph station code, US Geological Survey*] (SEIS)
BOM......... Bombay [*India*] [*Later, ABG*] [*Geomagnetic observatory code*]
Bom......... Bombay High Court Reports [*1862-75*] [*India*] [*A publication*] (DLA)
BOM......... Bombing (AABC)
BOM......... Born-Oppenheimer Method [*Physical chemistry*]
BOM......... Bottom Ocean Monitor [*Marine science*] (MSC)
BOM......... Bowmar Instrument Corp. [*AMEX symbol*] (SPSG)
BOM......... British Oil and Mineral
BOM......... Builders Old Measurement
BOM......... Bureau of Mines [*Department of the Interior*]
BOM......... Business Office Must [*Copy that must be printed*] [*Publishing*]
BOM......... Butyl(octyl)magnesium [*Organic chemistry*]
BOM......... Buying on Margin [*Investment term*]
BOM......... By Other Means (NVT)
BOM......... Osoyoos Museum, British Columbia [*Library symbol*] [*National Library of Canada*] (NLC)
BOMA...... Banks of Mid-America, Inc. [*Oklahoma City, OK*] [*NASDAQ symbol*] (NQ)
BOMA...... Building Owners and Managers Association International (EA)
Bom AC ..... Bombay Reports, Appellate Juris [*India*] [*A publication*] (DLA)
BOMAI ..... Building Owners and Managers Association International
BOMAP ... Barbados Oceanographic and Meteorological Analysis Project
BOMAP ... BOMEX [*Barbados Oceanographic and Meteorological Experiment*] Analysis Program (NOAA)
BOMARC ... Boeing-Michigan Aeronautical Research Center
BOMB ...... Bombardier [*British*] (ROG)
BOMB ...... Bombardment
BOMB ...... Bombardon [*Musical instrument*]
BOMB ...... British Overseas Media Bureau
Bomb......... Indian Law Reports, Bombay Series [*A publication*] (DLA)
Bombay Geogr Mag ... Bombay Geographical Magazine [*A publication*]
Bombay Hosp J ... Bombay Hospital Journal [*A publication*]
Bombay LJ ... Bombay Law Journal [*India*] [*A publication*] (DLA)
Bombay Technol ... Bombay Technologist [*A publication*]
BOMBB ...... Biomembranes [*A publication*]
Bomb Cr Cas ... Bombay Reports, Crown Cases [*India*] [*A publication*] (DLA)
Bomb Cr Rul ... Bombay High Court Criminal Rulings [*India*] [*A publication*] (DLA)
BOMBDR ... Bombardier
BOMBEX ... Bombing Exercise [*Military*] (NVT)
Bomb HC... Bombay High Court Reports [*1862-75*] [*India*] [*A publication*] (DLA)
Bomb H Ct ... Bombay High Court Reports [*1862-75*] [*India*] [*A publication*] (DLA)
Bomb Hg Ct ... Bombay High Court Reports [*1862-75*] [*India*] [*A publication*] (DLA)
Bomb LR.... Bombay Law Reporter [*India*] [*A publication*] (DLA)
Bomb SC.... Bombay Staff Corps [*British military*] (DMA)
Bomb Sel Cas ... Bombay Select Cases, Sadr Diwani Adalat [*India*] [*A publication*] (DLA)
Bomb Ser ... Indian Law Reports, Bombay Series [*A publication*] (DLA)
BOMC...... Baronial Order of Magna Charta (EA)
BOMC....... Bomaine Corporation [*NASDAQ symbol*] (NQ)
BOMC...... Book-of-the-Month Club, Inc.
BOMCOM ... Bomber Command [*Army*]
Bom Cr Cas ... Bombay Reports, Crown Cases [*India*] [*A publication*] (ILCA)
BOMD...... BoMed Medical Manufacturing Ltd. [*NASDAQ symbol*] (NQ)
BOMDD.... Bio Med [*A publication*]
Bome S-Afr ... Bome in Suid-Afrika [*A publication*]
BOMEX .... Barbados Oceanographic and Meteorological Experiment [*National Oceanic and Atmospheric Administration*]

BOMFOG ... [*The*] Brotherhood of Man under the Fatherhood of God [*Journalistic slang for political platitudes; said to be taken from a speech by Hubert H. Humphrey*]
Bom HCR .. Bombay High Court Reports [*1862-75*] [*India*] [*A publication*] (DLA)
BOMI .... Box Office Management International [*An association*] (EA)
BOMID ..... Branch Office, Military Intelligence Division [*Army*]
BOMINE .. Bomb Mine (MCD)
BOMIS ...... Bottom-Mounted Instrumentation System (MCD)
Bom LJ ...... Bombay Law Journal [*India*] [*A publication*] (DLA)
Bom LR...... Bombay Law Reporter [*India*] [*A publication*] (DLA)
Bom L Rep ... Bombay Law Reports [*India*] [*A publication*] (DLA)
Bom LRJ ... Bombay Law Reporter [*India*] [*A publication*] (DLA)
BOMO...... Bomb or Missile Optics (MCD)
Bom OC ..... Bombay Reports, Oudh Cases [*India*] [*A publication*] (DLA)
BOMP...... Base Organization and Maintenance Processor (IEEE)
BOMP...... Bill of Material Processor
BOMREP ... Bombing Report
BOMREPT ... Bombing Report (NATG)
BOMROC ... Bombardment Rocket (KSC)
BOMRON ... Bombing Squadron
BOMS .... Bancorp of Mississippi, Inc. [*Tupelo, MS*] [*NASDAQ symbol*] (NQ)
BOMS .... Bill of Material Status (MCD)
BOMS .... Bureau for Overseas Medical Service [*British*] (CB)
BOMST...... Bombsight (AABC)
Bom Unrep Cr C ... Bombay Unreported Criminal Cases [*1862-98*] [*India*] [*A publication*] (DLA)
BOMXA .... Boletin. Asociacion Mexicana de Geologos Petroleros [*A publication*]
Bon............ Apud Bonifacium [*Latin*] (DSA)
BON.......... Balance of Need Campaign [*Red Cross fund-raising*]
BON.......... Baron (ROG)
BON.......... Beta-Oxynaphthoic Acid [*Also, BONA*] [*Organic chemistry*]
BON.......... Bibliography of Newfoundland, Memorial University [*UTLAS symbol*]
BON.......... Blending Octane Number [*Petroleum technology*]
BON.......... Bonaire [*Netherland Antilles*] [*Airport symbol*] (OAG)
BON.......... Bonanza Airlines Co. [*Torrance, CA*] [*FAA designator*] (FAAC)
BON.......... Bonar, Inc. [*Toronto Stock Exchange symbol*]
BoN............ [*The*] Book of Nonsense [*A publication*]
BON........... Bristol, TN [*Location identifier*] [*FAA*] (FAAL)
BONA........ Bachad Organization of North America (EA)
BONA........ Beta-Oxynaphthoic Acid [*Also, BON*] [*Organic chemistry*]
Bona.......... Bonaguida de Aretio [*Flourished, 1251-58*] [*Authority cited in pre-1607 legal work*] (DSA)
BONAC...... Broadcasting Organizations of Non-Aligned Countries (EY)
Bonacoss ... [*Hippolytus*] Bonacossa [*Deceased, 1591*] [*Authority cited in pre-1607 legal work*] (DSA)
Bonag .... Bonaguida de Aretio [*Flourished, 1251-58*] [*Authority cited in pre-1607 legal work*] (DSA)
B-ONALS ... Type "B" Off-Network Access Lines [*Telecommunications*] (TEL)
BONC........ Broadcasting Organizations of Non-Aligned Countries [*Belgrade, Yugoslavia*] (EAIO)
Bond.......... Bond's United States Circuit Reports [*A publication*] (DLA)
Bond LR..... Bond Law Review [*A publication*]
Bond MD App ... Proceedings of Court of Appeal of Maryland [*In American Legal Records, 1*] [*A publication*] (DLA)
Bone Metab ... Bone Metabolism [*Japan*] [*A publication*]
Bone Miner ... Bone and Mineral [*A publication*]
BONENT .. Board of Nephrology Examiners for Nursing and Technology
Bone Prec... Bone. Precedents in Conveyancing [*1838-40*] [*A publication*] (DLA)
Bones Jt ..... Bones and Joints [*A publication*]
Bon Ins....... Bonney on Insurance [*A publication*] (DLA)
BONIS...... Bibliography of Old Norse-Icelandic Studies [*A publication*]
Boni VIII ... [*Pope*] Boniface VIII [*Deceased, 1303*] [*Authority cited in pre-1607 legal work*] (DSA)
BONM...... Bulletin. Office National Meteorologique [*France*] [*A publication*]
BONMOT ... Sinnspruche, Aphorismen, und Lebensweisheiten [*Mottos, Aphorisms, and Witticisms*] [*Society for Business Information*] [*Information service or system*] (IID)
BONNA..... Bollettino. Societa di Naturalisti di Napoli [*A publication*]
Bonn Car.... Bonney's Railway Carriers [*A publication*] (DLA)
Bonner Arbeiten ... Bonner Arbeiten zur Deutschen Literatur [*A publication*]
Bonner Energ-Rep ... Bonner Energie-Report [*A publication*]
Bonner Jahrb ... Bonner Jahrbuecher [*A publication*] (OCD)
Bonner Jb .. Bonner Jahrbuecher [*A publication*]
Bonner Math Schriften ... Bonner Mathematische Schriften [*Bonn*] [*A publication*]
Bonner Rechtswiss Abh ... Bonner Rechtswissenschaftliche Abhandlungen [*A publication*]
Bonnetti Ital Dict ... Bonnetti's Italian Dictionary [*A publication*] (DLA)
Bonn Geogr Abh ... Bonner Geographische Abhandlungen [*A publication*]
Bonn Hefte Vg ... Bonner Hefte zur Vorgeschichte [*A publication*]
Bonnier E des Preuves ... [*E.*] Bonnier. Traite des Preuves [*1852*] [*A publication*]
Bonn Ins..... Bonney on Insurance [*A publication*] (DLA)

Bonn Jb ...... Bonner Jahrbuecher [*A publication*]
Bonn Litt Mag ... Bonniers Litteraera Magasin [*A publication*]
Bonn Math Schr ... Bonner Mathematische Schriften [*A publication*]
Bonn Zool Beitr ... Bonner Zoologische Beitraege [*A publication*]
Bonn Zool Monogr ... Bonner Zoologische Monographien [*A publication*]
BONP .... Bleomycin, Oncovin [*Vincristine*], Natulan [*Procarbazine hydrochloride*], Prednisolone [*Antineoplastic drug regimen*]
Bon RR Car ... Bonney's Railway Carriers [*A publication*]   (DLA)
Bonsai J ..... Bonsai Journal [*A publication*]
BoNT .... Botulinum Neurotoxin
BONUS ..... Boiling Nuclear Superheat Reactor
BONUS-CX ... Boiling Nuclear Superheat Critical Experiment   (NRCH)
BOO .... Banco de Guatemala. Informe Economico [*A publication*]
BOO .... Bodo [*Norway*] [*Airport symbol*]   (OAG)
Boo .... Bootes [*Constellation*]
BOO .... Brigade Ordnance Officer [*British*]
BOOB .... Block out of Balance [*Data processing*]
BOOB .... Bolt Out of the Blue [*Surprise nuclear attack*]
BOOBOISIE ... Boob and Bourgeoisie [*H. L. Mencken's portmanteau for the American middle class*]
BOOC .... Barcelona Olympic Organizing Committee [*Barcelona, Spain*]   (EAIO)
BOOCA ..... Bollettino d'Oculistica [*A publication*]
BOOK .... Bibliographic On-Line Organized Knowledge [*Data processing*]   (KSC)
Book .... Book Records [*Record label*]
BOOK .... Built-In Orderly Organized Knowledge [*Learning device*]
BOOK .... [*The*] Village Green Bookstore, Inc. [*Rochester, NY*] [*NASDAQ symbol*]   (NQ)
Book Abstr Int Conf At Spectrosc ... Book of Abstracts. International Conference on Atomic Spectroscopy [*A publication*]
Book ASTM Stand ... Book of ASTM [*American Society for Testing and Materials*] Standards [*A publication*]
BOOKB ...... Bookbinding   (ROG)
Book Collec ... Book Collector [*A publication*]
Book Collect ... Book Collector [*A publication*]
Book of Judg ... Book of Judgments [*England*] [*A publication*]   (DLA)
BOOKK ...... Bookkeeping   (ROG)
Bookleger ... Booklegger [*A publication*]
Bookl For Comm (Lond) ... Booklet. Forestry Commission (London) [*A publication*]
Booklist ...... American Library Association. Booklist [*A publication*]
Booklist ...... Booklist and Subscription Books Bulletin [*Later, Booklist*] [*A publication*]
Booklist and SBB ... Booklist and Subscription Books Bulletin [*Later, Booklist*] [*A publication*]
Booklover's M ... Booklover's Magazine [*A publication*]
Bookl Timb Pres Assoc Aust ... Booklet. Timber Preservers' Association of Australia [*A publication*]   (APTA)
Bookm .... Bookman [*A publication*]
Bookmark .... Bookmark. New York State Library [*A publication*]
Bookm (Lond) ... Bookman (London) [*A publication*]
Book Pap Int Tech Conf Am Assoc Tex Chem Color ... Book of Papers. International Technical Conference. American Association of Textile Chemists and Colorists [*A publication*]
Book Pap Natl Tech Conf AATCC ... Book of Papers. National Technical Conference. AATCC [*American Association of Textile Chemists and Colorists*] [*A publication*]
Book Pap Natl Tech Conf Am Assoc Text Chem Color ... Book of Papers. National Technical Conference. American Association of Textile Chemists and Colorists [*A publication*]
Book Prod .. Book Production Industry [*A publication*]
Book R .... Book Reviews [*A publication*]
Book Rev Digest ... Book Review Digest [*A publication*]
Book Revi Index ... Book Review Index [*A publication*]
Book Rev Index Soc Sci Period ... Book Review Index to Social Science Periodicals [*A publication*]
Book Rev Mon ... Book Reviews of the Month [*A publication*]
BOOKS ..... Bookselling   (ROG)
Books .... New York Herald Tribune Books [*A publication*]
Books Earth Sci Relat Top ... Books in the Earth Sciences and Related Topics [*A publication*]
Books in Library and Information Sci ... Books in Library and Information Science [*New York*] [*A publication*]
Books S ...... Books of Sederunt [*A publication*]   (DLA)
Books in Scot ... Books in Scotland [*A publication*]
Books Sed .. Books of Sederunt [*A publication*]   (DLA)
Book Suppl J Child Psychol Psychiatr ... Book Supplement. Journal of Child Psychology and Psychiatry [*A publication*]
BOOL .... Boole & Babbage, Inc. [*Sunnyvale, CA*] [*NASDAQ symbol*]   (NQ)
BOOL .... Boolean [*Mathematics*]
BOOM .... Becoming One's Own Man [*Psychology*]
BOOM .... Explosive Fabricators, Inc. [*NASDAQ symbol*]   (NQ)
BOON .... Boonton Electronics Corp. [*NASDAQ symbol*]   (NQ)
Boone Corp ... Boone on Corporations [*A publication*]   (DLA)
Boor .... Booraem's Reports [*6-8 California*] [*A publication*]   (DLA)
BOOR .... Bureau of Outdoor Recreation [*Terminated, 1978, functions transferred to Heritage Conservation and Recreation Service*] [*Department of the Interior*]   (MCD)

Boo R Act ... Booth on Real Actions [*A publication*]   (DLA)
Booraem ...... Booraem's Reports [*6-8 California*]   (DLA)
BOOS .... Burners Out of Service [*Combustion emission control*]
BOOST ...... Bettering Oregon's Opportunity for Saving Talent [*Educational project*]   (EA)
BOOST ...... Broadened Opportunities for Officer Selection and Training [*Navy*]   (NVT)
Boot .... Bootes [*Constellation*]
BOOT .... Bootstrap [*Data processing*]
Boote .... Boote's Suit at Law [*A publication*]   (DLA)
Boote Act ... Boote. Action at Law [*A publication*]   (ILCA)
Boote Ch Pr ... Boote. Chancery Practice [*A publication*]   (DLA)
Boote SL .... Boote's Suit at Law [*A publication*]   (DLA)
Booth .... Chester Palatine Courts [*1811*] [*England*] [*A publication*]   (DLA)
Booth In Of ... Booth. Indictable Offences [*A publication*]   (DLA)
Booth R Act ... Booth on Real Actions [*A publication*]   (DLA)
Booth Real Act ... Booth on Real Actions [*A publication*]   (DLA)
Booth Wills ... Booth's Law of Wills [*A publication*]   (DLA)
BOOTS ...... Basic Organizing/Optimizing Training Schedules   (MCD)
BOP .... Association for Balance of Political Power   (EA)
BOP .... Balance of Payments [*International trade*]
BOP .... Balance of Plant [*Nuclear energy*]   (NRCH)
BOP .... Balance of Power   (IEEE)
BOP .... Bands-of-Performance   (MCD)
BOP .... Base of Preference Program [*for reenlisting airmen*]
BOP .... Baseline Operations Plan   (MCD)
BOP .... Basic Occupational Preparation
BOP .... Basic Operation Plan [*Army*]
BOP .... Basic Oxygen Process [*Steelmaking*]
BOP .... Bathyscaphe Oceanographic Program
BOP .... BCNU [*Carmustine*], Oncovin [*Vincristine*], Prednisone [*Antineoplastic drug regimen*]
BOP .... Beginning of Period
BOP .... Bibliographique Officiel des Imprimes Publies en Pologne. Bulletin [*A publication*]
BOP .... Binary Output Program
BOP .... Biocompatible Orthopedic Polymer [*Medicine*]
BOP .... Bipolar Operational Power
BOP .... BIT [*Binary Digit*]-Oriented Protocol
BOP .... Blowout Preventer [*or Prevention*]
BOP .... Book-on-Payment [*Travel industry*]
BOP .... Bouwbedrijf [*A publication*]
BOP .... [*The*] Boy's Own Paper [*Late nineteenth- and early twentieth-century periodical*] [*British*]
BOP .... Breach of Peace
BOP .... Broken Orange Pekoe [*Tea*]
BOP .... Bronco Petroleum Ltd. [*Vancouver Stock Exchange symbol*]
BOP .... Buick-Oldsmobile-Pontiac [*General Motors Corp.*]
BOP .... Building Optimization Program [*Data processing*]
BOP .... Bureau of Operations and Programming [*United Nations Development Program*]
BOP .... Bureau of Post [*Philippines*]   (DS)
BOP .... Burnout Proof
BOP .... Businessowners Policy [*Insurance*]
BOPA .... Balance of Payments Act [*International trade*]   (AABC)
BOPACE ... Boeing Plastic Analysis Capability for Engines [*Data processing*] [*NASA*]
BOPAM .... Bleomycin, Oncovin [*Vincristine*], Prednisone, Adriamycin, Mustargen [*Nitrogen mustard*], Methotrexate [*Antineoplastic drug regimen*]
BOPAT ...... Border Patrol
BOPD .... Bataan Ocean Petroleum Depot   (CINC)
BO PEEP ... Bangor [*Wales*] Orange Position Estimating Equipment for Pastures [*Electronic beeper to be attached to sheep*]
BOPF .... Broken Orange Pekoe Fannings [*Tea*]
BOPP .... Balance of Payments Programmed [*International trade*]   (AABC)
BOPP .... BCNU [*Carmustine*], Oncovin [*Vincristine*], Procarbazine, Prednisone [*Antineoplastic drug regimen*]
BOPP .... Biaxially-Oriented Polypropylene [*Plastics technology*]
BOPP .... Boronated Protoporphyrin [*Organic chemistry*]
BOPRESS ... Boiler Pressure
BOPS .... Balance of Payments Statistics [*Information service or system*] [*A publication*]
BOPS .... Banking On-Line Package System   (BUR)
BOPS .... Bomber Operations [*Air Ministry*] [*British*] [*World War II*]
BOPSA ...... Bibliotheca Ophthalmologica [*A publication*]
BOPSSAR ... Balance of Plant Standard Safety Analysis Report [*Nuclear energy*]   (NRCH)
B Opt .... Bachelor of Optometry
BOptom ..... Bachelor of Optometry   (ADA)
BOPTT .... Boom Operator Part Task Trainer   (MCD)
BOPTTS .... Boom Operator Part Task Training Simulator
BOPWG .... Backorder Problem Working Group [*DoD*]
BOQ .... Bachelor Officers' Quarters [*Army*]
BOQ .... Beginning of Quarter [*Accounting*]
BOQ .... Boku [*Papua New Guinea*] [*Airport symbol*] [*Obsolete*]   (OAG)
BOR .... Babylonian and Oriental Record [*A publication*]
B Or .... Bachelor of Oratory
BOR .... Battalion Orderly Room [*British*]

BOR .... Belady Optimum Replacement [*Algorithm*] [*Data processing*]
BOR .... Belfort [*France*] [*Airport symbol*]   (OAG)
BOr .... Bibbia e Oriente [*A publication*]   (BJA)
BOR .... Biserica Orthodoxa Romana [*A publication*]
BOR .... Board of Review [*Army*]
BOR .... Bolero Resources, Inc. [*Vancouver Stock Exchange symbol*]
BoR .... [*A*] Book of Russian Verse [*A publication*]
BOR .... Borg-Warner Corp. [*NYSE symbol*]   (SPSG)
Bor .... Borneo
BOR .... Boron [*Chemical element*] [*Symbol is B*]   (ROG)
BOR .... Borough
BOR .... Borrowings [*Banking*]
BOR .... Borzhomi [*USSR*] [*Seismograph station code, US Geological Survey*] [*Closed*]   (SEIS)
BOR .... Branch Officer Roster [*Army*]
BOR .... British Other Ranks
BOR .... Bureau of Operating Rights [*ICC*]
BOR .... Bureau of Outdoor Recreation [*Terminated, 1978, functions transferred to Heritage Conservation and Recreation Service*] [*Department of the Interior*]
BOR .... Bureau of Reclamation [*Later, WPRS*] [*Department of the Interior*]   (MCD)
BOR .... Bus Out Register [*Data processing*]
BOR .... Business Owner [*A publication*]
BORACS ... Bureau of Research and Community Services [*Duquesne University*] [*Research center*]   (RCD)
BORAL...... Boron-Aluminum
BORAM .... Block-Oriented Random-Access Memory [*Data processing*]
BOran .... Bulletin Trimestriel des Antiquites Africaines Recueillies par les Soins de la Societe de Geographie et d'Archeologie de la Province d'Oran [*A publication*]
BORAX ..... Boiling Reactor Experiments [*Nuclear energy*]
Borch.......... [*Johannes*] Borcholten [*Deceased, 1593*] [*Authority cited in pre-1607 legal work*]   (DSA)
Borcholt ..... [*Johannes*] Borcholten [*Deceased, 1593*] [*Authority cited in pre-1607 legal work*]   (DSA)
Bor Cipotech ... Bor es Cipotechnika [*A publication*]
BORD........ Bordereau [*Statement*] [*French*] [*Business term*]   (AIA)
Bordeaux Chir ... Bordeaux Chirurgicale [*France*] [*A publication*]
Bordeaux Med ... Bordeaux Medical [*A publication*]
Borden's Rev Nutr Res ... Borden's Review of Nutrition Research [*A publication*]
Borderl Neurol ... Borderlands of Neurology [*A publication*]
Borderl Psychiatry ... Borderland of Psychiatry [*A publication*]
Bord Med... Bordeaux Medical [*A publication*]
BORE .... Beryllium Oxide Reactor Experiment [*Formerly, EBOR*] [*Nuclear energy*]
Boreal Inst North Stud Univ Alberta Annu Rep ... Boreal Institute for Northern Studies. University of Alberta. Annual Report [*A publication*]
Boreal Inst North Stud Univ Alberta Occas Publ ... Boreal Institute for Northern Studies. University of Alberta. Occasional Publication [*A publication*]
Borehole Water J ... Borehole Water Journal [*A publication*]
BORF......... Bill of Rights Foundation   (EA)
Borgnin Cavalcan ... Borgninus Cavalcanus [*Flourished, 16th century*] [*Authority cited in pre-1607 legal work*]   (DSA)
Borgyogy Venerol Sz ... Borgyogyaszati es Venerologiai Szemle [*A publication*]
B & ORHS ... Baltimore & Ohio Railroad Historical Society   (EA)
BORI .... Bordano [*Italy*] [*Seismograph station code, US Geological Survey*]   (SEIS)
B Orient ..... Bachelor of Oriental Studies
BORIS....... Board of Realty Information Systems [*Professional Guidance Systems, Inc.*] [*Information service or system*]   (IID)
BORIS....... Box-Office Reservation and Information Service
BORL .... Boreal [*A publication*]
BORM....... Bureau of Raw Materials for American Vegetable Oils and Fats Industries   (EA)
BORN FREE ... Build Options, Renew Norms, Free Roles through Educational Equity [*National project to help students choose appropriate future careers*]
Bornholm Sam ... Bornholmske Samlinger [*A publication*]
BORO .... Borough   (ROG)
B & O RR... [*The*] Baltimore & Ohio Railroad Co. [*Chessie System, Inc.*]
Borr............ Borradaile's Civil Cases, Bombay [*1800-24*] [*India*] [*A publication*]   (DLA)
Bor Res B .. Borneo Research Bulletin [*A publication*]
BoRS......... [*A*] Second Book of Russian Verse [*A publication*]
B Or Sc ...... Bachelor of the Science of Oratory
BORSCHT ... Battery, Overvoltage Protection, Ringing, Supervision, Coding, Hybrids, Testing [*Seven basic functions performed by line circuits*] [*Telecommunications*]
Borsod Szle ... Borsodi Szemle [*A publication*]
Borth .... Borthwick. Modes of Prosecuting for Libel [*1830*] [*A publication*]   (DLA)
BORU........ Boat Operating and Repair Unit [*Navy*]
BORU........ Bulletin Officiel de Ruanda-Urundi [*A publication*]
BoRv .... Book Review Digest [*Information service or system*] [*A publication*]
BOS .... Back-Off System

BOS .... Background Operating System   (IEEE)
BOS .... Backup Operating System   (NASA)
BOS .... Balance of State [*Department of Labor*]
BOS .... Balance-of-System [*Power plant efficiency*]
BOS .... Base Operating Service [*Contract*] [*DoD*]
BOS .... Base Operating Supplies
BOS .... Base Operating Support   (AFM)
BOS .... Basic Oblate Spheroid
BOS .... Basic Operating System [*IBM Corp.*] [*Data processing*]
BOS .... Basic Oxygen Steel [*Steelmaking*]
BOS .... Batch Operating System [*Data processing*]
BOS .... Battalion Orderly Sergeant [*British and Canadian*]
BOS .... Bell Operating System [*Telecommunications*]   (TEL)
BOS .... Best Opposite Sex (to Best of Breed) [*Dog show term*]
BOS .... Bicycles on Stamps [*Study unit*] [*American Topical Association*]   (EA)
BOS .... Blended Old Scotch [*Whiskey*]   (ROG)
BOS .... Boise Creek Resources [*Vancouver Stock Exchange symbol*]
BOS .... Bonner Orientalistische Studien [*A publication*]
BOS .... Book Order and Selection [*Data processing*]
BOS .... Bookseller's Order Service [*For-profit subsidiary of American Booksellers Association*] [*Defunct*]
BOS .... Bosque Alegre [*Argentina*] [*Seismograph station code, US Geological Survey*] [*Closed*]   (SEIS)
BOS .... Boston [*Massachusetts*] [*Airport symbol*]
BOS .... Boston Celtics [*NYSE symbol*]   (SPSG)
BOS .... Boston University, Boston, MA [*OCLC symbol*]   (OCLC)
Bos .... Bosworth's New York Superior Court Reports [*A publication*]   (DLA)
BOS .... Breed of Sire
BOS .... Bright Object Sensor   (MCD)
BOS .... British Origami Society
BOS .... British Orthoptic Society
BOS .... Building Out Section
BOS .... Business Office Supervisor [*Telecommunications*]   (TEL)
BOSA .... Board on Ocean Science Affairs [*National Academy of Science*]   (MSC)
BoSA......... [*A*] Book of South African Verse [*A publication*]
BOSA .... Boston Acoustics, Inc. [*NASDAQ symbol*]   (NQ)
BOSAC...... Bofors Spent Acid Concentration [*Chemical industry*]
Bosbou S-Afr ... Bosbou in Suid-Afrika [*A publication*]
Bosbouwproefstn TNO Korte Meded ... Bosbouwproefstation TNO. Korte Mededeling [*A publication*]
Bosb Suid-Afr ... Bosbou in Suid-Afrika [*A publication*]
BOSCA...... British Oil Spill Control Association   (ASF)
Bosc Con .... Boscawen on Convictions [*A publication*]   (DLA)
Bosch Tech Ber ... Bosch Technische Berichte [*A publication*]
BOSDET ... Boating Safety Detachment [*Coast Guard*]
Bos & D Lim ... Bosanquet and Darby's Limitations [*A publication*]   (DLA)
BOSEY ...... Board of Supply, Executive Yuan [*Responsible for removing surplus US war material to China from Guam*]
BOSFA ...... Bollettino. Societa Italiana di Fisica [*A publication*]
BOSFW ..... Bureau of Sport Fisheries and Wildlife [*Superseded by US Fish and Wildlife Service*] [*Department of the Interior*]   (MCD)
BOSGA...... Bollettino. Servizio Geologico d'Italia [*A publication*]
BOSH .... Bottom-Oriented Shrimp Harvester
BOSN .... Boatswain   (KSC)
Bos N R...... Bosanquet and Puller's New Reports, English Common Pleas [*1804-07*] [*A publication*]   (ILCA)
BOSNYWASH ... Boston, New York, Washington [*Proposed name for possible "super-city" formed by growth and mergers of other cities*]
BOSO .... Bureau of Ordnance Shipment Order [*Obsolete*] [*Navy*]
BOSOR ..... Buckling of Shells of Revolution [*Computer program*] [*NASA*]   (MCD)
BOSOX ..... Boston Red Sox [*Baseball team*]
BOSP .... Bioastronautics Orbital Space Program [*Air Force*]
Bos & P ...... Bosanquet and Puller's English Common Pleas Reports [*126, 127 English Reprint*] [*A publication*]   (DLA)
Bos & P (Eng) ... Bosanquet and Puller's English Common Pleas Reports [*126, 127 English Reprint*] [*A publication*]   (DLA)
Bos Pl......... Bosanquet's Rules of Pleading [*A publication*]   (DLA)
Bos & PNR ... Bosanquet and Puller's New Reports, English Common Pleas [*1804-07*] [*A publication*]   (DLA)
Bos & PNR (Eng) ... Bosanquet and Puller's New Reports, English Common Pleas [*1804-07*] [*A publication*]   (DLA)
Bos Pol Rep ... Boston Police Court. Reports [*A publication*]   (DLA)
Bos & Pu.... Bosanquet and Puller's English Common Pleas Reports [*126, 127 English Reprint*] [*A publication*]   (DLA)
Bos Pub Lib Q ... Boston Public Library. Quarterly [*A publication*]
Bos & Pul ... Bosanquet and Puller's English Common Pleas Reports [*126, 127 English Reprint*] [*A publication*]   (DLA)
Bos & Pul NR ... Bosanquet and Puller's New Reports, English Common Pleas [*1804-07*] [*A publication*]   (DLA)
BOSS......... Ballistic Offense Suppressive System [*Military*]
BOSS......... Base Operating Supply System
BOSS......... Basic Operating System Software [*Toshiba Corp.*] [*Japan*]
BOSS......... Batch Operating Software System
BOSS......... Battalion Operated Surveillance System [*Army*]   (INF)
BOSS......... Behavior of Offshore Structures [*Conference*]
BOSS......... Berkeley-Oakland Service System [*Library network*]

BOSS........ Bioastronautic Orbiting Space Station [*or System*] (MUGU)
BOSS........ Block-Oriented Systems Simulator [*Computer software*]
BOSS........ Boeing Operational Supervisory System
BOSS........ Bomb Orbital Strategic System
BOSS........ Book of the Season Scheme [*British*]
BOSUN ...... Broad Ocean Scoring System [*Missiles*]
BOSS........ Bureau of State Security [*Later, Department of National Security*] [*South Africa*]
BOSS........ Business Opportunities Sourcing System [*Information service or system*] [*Canada*]
BOSS....... Business Organizer Scheduling System
BOSS........ Business-Oriented Search Service [*Information service or system*] (EISS)
BOSS........ Business-Oriented Software System [*Digital Equipment Corp.*] [*Data processing*] (BUR)
BOSSCO ... Boeing Shaped Scan Correlator (MCD)
BOSS-WEDGE ... Bomb Orbital Strategic System - Weapon Development Glide Entry
BoSt .... Boghazkoi-Studien [*Leipzig, 1916-1924*] [*A publication*] (BJA)
BOST........ Boston [*Massachusetts*]
BOST........ Boston Digital Corp. [*NASDAQ symbol*] (NQ)
Bost .... Bostonian [*A publication*]
Bost Coll Ind L Rev ... Boston College. Industrial and Commercial Law Review [*A publication*]
BOSTI ...... Buffalo Organization for Social and Technological Innovation (EA)
BOSTID .... Board on Science and Technology for International Development [*National Academy of Sciences*]
Bost Law Rep ... Boston Law Reporter [*A publication*] (DLA)
Bost LR...... Boston Law Reporter [*A publication*] (DLA)
Bost Mo ..... Boston Monthly Magazine [*A publication*]
Bostn Glbe ... Boston Globe [*A publication*]
Boston BJ .. Boston Bar Journal [*A publication*]
Boston Bsn ... Boston Business Journal [*A publication*]
Boston Col Environmental Affairs Law R ... Boston College. Environmental Affairs Law Review [*A publication*]
Boston Col Ind Com L Rev ... Boston College. Industrial and Commercial Law Review [*A publication*]
Boston Col Ind and Commer Law R ... Boston College. Industrial and Commercial Law Review [*A publication*]
Boston Col Int Comp L Rev ... Boston College. International and Comparative Law Review [*A publication*]
Boston Col Internat and Comparative Law R ... Boston College. International and Comparative Law Review [*A publication*]
Boston Col Int'l & Comp LJ ... Boston College. International and Comparative Law Journal [*A publication*]
Boston Col Law R ... Boston College. Law Review [*A publication*]
Boston College L Rev ... Boston College. Law Review [*A publication*] (DLA)
Boston Coll Environ Aff Law Rev ... Boston College. Environmental Affairs Law Review [*A publication*]
Boston Col Stud Phil ... Boston College. Studies in Philosophy [*A publication*]
Boston J N H ... Boston Journal of Natural History [*A publication*]
Boston J Ph ... Boston Journal of Philosophy and the Arts [*A publication*]
Boston M ... Boston Magazine [*A publication*]
Boston Med Q ... Boston Medical Quarterly [*A publication*]
Boston Med and S J ... Boston Medical and Surgical Journal [*A publication*]
Boston Med Surg J ... Boston Medical and Surgical Journal [*A publication*]
Boston Mus Bul ... Boston Museum of Fine Arts. Bulletin [*A publication*]
Boston Pub Lib Quar ... Boston Public Library. Quarterly [*A publication*]
Boston R .... Boston Review [*A publication*]
Boston Soc C E J ... Boston Society of Civil Engineers. Journal [*A publication*]
Boston Soc of Nat Hist Memoirs ... Boston Society of Natural History. Memoirs [*A publication*]
Boston Soc of Nat Hist Occ Papers ... Boston Society of Natural History. Occasional Papers [*A publication*]
Boston Soc of Nat Hist Proc ... Boston Society of Natural History. Proceedings [*A publication*]
Boston State Hosp Monogr Ser ... Boston State Hospital. Monograph Series [*A publication*]
Boston Studies Philos Sci ... Boston Studies in the Philosophy of Science [*A publication*]
Boston Stud Philos Sci ... Boston Studies in the Philosophy of Science [*A publication*]
Boston U LR ... Boston University. Law Review [*A publication*]
Boston UL Rev ... Boston University. Law Review [*A publication*]
Boston Univ Law R ... Boston University. Law Review [*A publication*]
Boston U St ... Boston University. Studies in Philosophy and Religion [*A publication*]
Bost Pol Rep ... Boston Police Court. Reports [*A publication*] (DLA)
Bost Q .... Boston Quarterly [*A publication*]
Bost R .... Boston Review [*A publication*]
Bost Soc Natur Hist Occ Pa ... Boston Society of Natural History. Occasional Papers [*A publication*]
Bost Soc Natur Hist Proc ... Boston Society of Natural History. Proceedings [*A publication*]
Bost Sym.... Boston Symphony Orchestra. Program Notes [*A publication*]
Bost Sym Concert Bul ... Boston Symphony Orchestra. Concert Bulletin [*A publication*]
Bo Stud ...... Bonner Studien zur Englischen Philologie [*A publication*]
Bost UL Rev ... Boston University. Law Review [*A publication*]
Bost Univ Bus Rev ... Boston University. Business Review [*A publication*]

Bost Univ St Engl ... Boston University. Studies in English [*A publication*]
BOSU .... Bioastronautics Operational Support Unit (MCD)
BOSUAN .. Forestry in South Africa [*A publication*]
Bos U J ...... Boston University. Journal [*A publication*]
Bos U Law Rev ... Boston University. Law Review [*A publication*]
BOSUN...... Boatswain
BOSVA...... British Offshore Support Vessels Association (DS)
BO & SW... Baltimore, Ohio & Southwestern Railway
Bosw.......... Boswell's Reports, Scotch Court of Sessions [*A publication*] (DLA)
Bosw.......... Bosworth's New York Superior Court Reports [*A publication*] (DLA)
BOSWASH ... Boston to Washington [*Proposed name for possible "super-city" formed by growth and mergers between these two*]
BOSX........ BO-S-AIRE Corp. [*Air carrier designation symbol*]
BOSYA...... Bulletin. Ophthalmological Society of Egypt [*A publication*]
BOT .... Bachelor of Occupational Therapy
BOT .... Balance of Trade [*International trade*]
BOT .... Beginning of Tape [*Data processing*]
BOT .... Board of Thailand (DS)
BOT .... Board of Trade [*Shipping*]
BOT .... Board of Transport [*NATO*] (NATG)
BOT .... Board of Trustees
BOT .... Books on Tape
BOT .... Books of the Times [*A publication*]
BOT .... Boom Operator Trainer
BOT .... Botany
BOT .... Botswana [*Spaceflight Tracking and Data Network*] [*NASA*]
BOT .... Bottle
BOT .... Bottom (KSC)
BOT .... Botulinum Toxin
BOT .... Bought
BOT .... Bright Old Thing [*A member of established society in Washington, DC*]
BOT .... Build, Operate, Transfer [*Business term*]
BOT .... Burst-on-Target (MCD)
BOT .... De Boeken van het Oude Testament [*Roermond/Maaseik*] [*A publication*] (BJA)
Bot Abh...... Botanische Abhandlungen aus dem Gebiet der Morphologie und Physiologie [*A publication*]
Bot Abstr... Botanical Abstracts [*A publication*]
BOTAC...... British Overseas Trade Advisory Committee
BOTAN..... Botanical
Botan B A S ... Botanical Bulletin. Academia Sinica [*A publication*]
Botan Gaz .. Botanical Gazette [*A publication*]
Botan J Lin ... Botanical Journal. Linnean Society [*London*] [*A publication*]
Botan Mag ... Botanical Magazine [*Tokyo*] [*A publication*]
Botan Marin ... Botanica Marina [*A publication*]
Botan Notis ... Botaniska Notiser [*A publication*]
Botan Rev... Botanical Review [*A publication*]
Botan Tids ... Botanisk Tidsskrift [*A publication*]
Bot Arch..... Botanisches Archiv [*A publication*]
BOTB........ Basic Officers Training Battalion [*Army*] (INF)
BOTB........ British Overseas Trade Board
Bot Bull Acad Sinica ... Botanical Bulletin. Academia Sinica [*A publication*]
Bot Bull Acad Sinica Inst Bot New Ser ... Botanical Bulletin. Academia Sinica. Institute of Botany. New Series [*A publication*]
Bot Bull Acad Sin (Taipei) ... Botanical Bulletin. Academia Sinica (Taipei) [*A publication*]
Bot Bull Ac Sin ... Botanical Bulletin. Academia Sinica [*A publication*]
Bot Centralbl Beih 2 Abt ... Botanisches Centralblatt. Beihefte. Zweite Abteilung-Systematik. Pflanzengeographie. Angewandte Botanik [*A publication*]
BOTEX...... British Office for Training Exchange
B & OTF.... Bulletins and Orders Task Force [*Nuclear Regulatory Commission*] (NRCH)
Bot Gard (Singapore) Annu Rep ... Botanic Gardens (Singapore). Annual Report [*A publication*]
Bot Gaz ...... Botanical Gazette [*A publication*]
BOTGI....... British Overseas Trade Group for Israel (DS)
Bot Gothob Acta Univ Gothob ... Botanica Gothoburgensia. Acta Universitatis Gothoburgensis [*A publication*]
BOTH........ Bombing over the Horizon
BOTH........ Booth, Inc. [*NASDAQ symbol*] (NQ)
Bot Haves Virksomhed Beret ... Botanisk Haves Virksomhed Beretning [*A publication*]
Bot Helv..... Botanica Helvetica [*A publication*]
Bot Issled Beloruss Otd Vses Bot O-Va ... Botanika. Issledovaniya. Belorusskoe Otdelenie Vsesoyuznogo Botanicheskogo Obshchestva [*A publication*]
Bot J.......... Botanical Journal [*A publication*]
Bot Jaarb ... Botanisch Jaarboek [*A publication*]
Bot Jahrb Syst Pflanzengesch Pflanzengeogr ... Botanische Jahrbuecher fuer Systematik Pflanzengeschichte und Pflanzengeographie [*A publication*]
BOTJAT ... British Orthoptic Journal [*A publication*]
Bot Jb........ Botanische Jahrbuecher fuer Systematik Pflanzengeschichte und Pflanzengeographie [*A publication*]
Bot J Linn Soc ... Botanical Journal. Linnean Society [*London*] [*A publication*]

Bot J Linn Soc (Lond) ... Botanical Journal. Linnean Society (London) [*A publication*]

BOT Jo ...... Board of Trade Journal [*A publication*]   (DLA)

Bot Klausimai ... Botanikos Klausimai [*A publication*]

Bot Koezl .... Botanikai Koezlemenyek [*A publication*]

Bot Koezlem .... Botanikai Koezlemenyek [*A publication*]

BOTLA ...... Bollettino. Societa Italiana di Cardiologia [*A publication*]

Bot Mag (Tokyo) ... Botanical Magazine (Tokyo) [*A publication*]

Bot Mar ...... Botanica Marina [*A publication*]

Bot Mar Suppl ... Botanica Marina. Supplement [*A publication*]

Bot Mater Gerb Bot Inst Akad Nauk ... Botanicheskie Materialy Gerbariya Botanicheskogo Instituta. Akademii Nauk [*A publication*]

Bot Mater Gerb Inst Bot Akad Nauk Kaz ... Botanicheskie Materialy Gerbariya Instituta Botaniki. Akademii Nauk Kazakhskoi [*A publication*]

Bot Mater Gerb Inst Bot Akad Nauk Kaz SSR ... Botanicheskie Materialy Gerbariya Instituta Botaniki. Akademii Nauk Kazakhskoi SSR [*A publication*]

BOTMG .... Bottoming   (MSA)

Bot Monogr (New Delhi) ... Botanical Monographs (New Delhi) [*A publication*]

Bot Monogr (Oxf) ... Botanical Monographs (Oxford) [*A publication*]

BOTMP ..... Bruininks-Oseretsky Test of Motor Proficiency [*Occupational therapy*]

Bot Mus Leafl ... Botanical Museum Leaflets. Harvard University [*A publication*]

Bot Mus Leafl Harv Univ ... Botanical Museum Leaflets. Harvard University [*A publication*]

BOTN .... Bouton Corp. [*NASDAQ symbol*]   (NQ)

BOT (New York) ... Books of the Times (New York) [*A publication*]

Bot Not ...... Botaniska Notiser [*A publication*]

Bot Notis .... Botaniska Notiser [*A publication*]

Bot Notiser ... Botaniska Notiser [*A publication*]

Bot Not Suppl ... Botaniska Notiser. Supplement [*A publication*]

Bot Oecon ... Botanica Oeconomica [*A publication*]

BOTOSS ... Bottom Topography Survey System [*Naval Oceanographic Office*]

BoTP .... [*The*] Book of a Thousand Poems [*A publication*]

BOTP .... Both of This Parish

Bot R .... Botanical Review [*A publication*]

BOTRA ..... Beitraege zur Orthopaedie und Traumatologie [*A publication*]

Bot Rev ...... Botanical Review [*A publication*]

Bot Rhedonica Ser A ... Botanica Rhedonica. Serie A [*A publication*]

BOTS .... Botswana

Bot Soc Edinb Trans ... Botanical Society of Edinburgh. Transactions [*A publication*]

Bot Soc Edinburgh Trans ... Botanical Society of Edinburgh. Transactions [*A publication*]

Bot Stud ..... Botanische Studien [*A publication*]

Bot Surv S Afr Mem ... Botanical Survey of South Africa. Memoir [*A publication*]

Botswana Geol Sur Dep Miner Resour Rep ... Botswana. Geological Survey Department. Mineral Resources Report [*A publication*]

Botswana Geol Surv Dist Mem ... Botswana. Geological Survey. District Memoir [*A publication*]

Botswana Geol Surv Mines Dep Annu Rep ... Botswana. Geological Survey and Mines Department. Annual Report [*A publication*]

Botswana Mag ... Botswana Magazine [*A publication*]

Botswana Notes Rec ... Botswana Notes and Records [*A publication*]

Bott .... Bott's Poor Law Settlement Cases [*A publication*]   (DLA)

Bot Tidsskr ... Botanisk Tidsskrift [*A publication*]

Bott PL .... Bott's Poor Laws [*A publication*]   (DLA)

Bott PL Cas ... Bott's Poor Law Cases [*1560-1833*] [*England*] [*A publication*]   (DLA)

Bott PL Const ... Const's Edition of Bott's Poor Law Cases [*A publication*]   (DLA)

Bott Poor Law Cas ... Bott's Poor Law Settlement Cases [*A publication*]   (DLA)

BOTTS ...... Busy Tone Trunks [*Telecommunications*]   (TEL)

Bott Set Cas ... Bott's Poor Law Settlement Cases [*A publication*]   (DLA)

Bott's PL ..... Bott's Poor Law Cases [*1560-1833*] [*England*] [*A publication*]   (DLA)

BOTU .... Board of Trade Unit [*Military*] [*British and Canadian*]

BoTU .... Die Boghazkoi-Texte im Umschrift [*A publication*]   (BJA)

BOTU(FW) ... Basic Operational Training Unit (Fixed Wing)

BOTU(RW) ... Basic Operational Training Unit (Rotary Wing)

BOTVAL .... Bottom Value

Bot Ver Ham EV Ber ... Botanischer Verein zu Hamburg EV. Berichte [*A publication*]

Bot Z .... Botaniceskij Zurnal [*A publication*]

Bot Zblt ...... Botanisches Zentralblatt [*A publication*]

Bot Zh (Kiev) ... Botanichnyi Zhurnal (Kiev) [*A publication*]

Bot Zh (Leningr) ... Botanicheskii Zhurnal (Leningrad) [*A publication*]

Bot Zh (Moscow) ... Botanicheskii Zhurnal (Moscow) [*A publication*]

Bot Zh (SSSR) ... Botanicheskii Zhurnal (SSSR) [*A publication*]

Bot Ztg .... Botanische Zeitung [*A publication*]

BOU .... Boat Operating Unit [*Navy*]

BOU .... Bonus Petroleum Corp. [*Vancouver Stock Exchange symbol*]

BOU .... Boulder [*Colorado*] [*Seismograph station code, US Geological Survey*] [*Closed*]   (SEIS)

BOU .... Boulder [*Colorado*] [*Geomagnetic observatory code*]

BOU .... British Ornithologists' Union

BOU (Br Ornithol Union) Check-List ... BOU (British Ornithologists' Union) Check-List [*A publication*]

Bouch Ins Dr Mar ... Boucher's Instituts au Droit Maritime [*A publication*]   (DLA)

Bouch Inst .... Boucher's Instituts au Droit Maritime [*A publication*]   (DLA)

Bou Dic ...... Bouvier's Law Dictionary [*A publication*]   (DLA)

Bou Inst ...... Bouvier's Institutes of American Law [*A publication*]   (DLA)

BOUIS .... Bulletin. Oxford University. Institute of Statistics [*A publication*]

BOUL .... Boulevard

Bould .... Bouldin's Reports [*119 Alabama*] [*A publication*]   (DLA)

Bouln .... Boulnois' Reports [*Bengal*] [*A publication*]   (DLA)

Boulnois ..... Boulnois' Reports [*Bengal*] [*A publication*]   (DLA)

Boul P Dr Com ... Boulay-Paty. Droit Commun [*A publication*]   (DLA)

BOUMAC ... Boulder Laboratory Macrosystem [*National Institute of Standards and Technology*]

Bound .... Boundary 2 [*A publication*]

Boundary-Layer Meteorol ... Boundary-Layer Meteorology [*A publication*]

Bound Two ... Boundary Two [*A publication*]

Bourd LT ... Bourdin on the Land Tax [*A publication*]   (DLA)

Bourg Med ... Bourgogne Medicale [*A publication*]

Bourke .... Bourke's Reports, Calcutta High Court [*India*] [*A publication*]   (DLA)

Bourke Lim ... Bourke on the Indian Law of Limitations [*A publication*]   (DLA)

Bourke PP ... Bourke's Parliamentary Precedents [*1842-56*] [*England*] [*A publication*]   (DLA)

Bourne Soc Local Hist Rec ... Bourne Society. Local History Records [*A publication*]

Bousq Dict de Dr ... Bousquet. Dictionnaire de Droit [*A publication*]   (DLA)

BOuT .... De Boeken van het Oude Testament [*Roermond/Maaseik*] [*A publication*]   (BJA)

Bout Man ... Boutwell's Manual of the United States Tax System [*A publication*]   (DLA)

Bouv .... Bouvier's Law Dictionary [*A publication*]   (DLA)

Bouvier .... Bouvier's Law Dictionary [*A publication*]   (DLA)

Bouv Inst .... Bouvier's Institutes of American Law [*A publication*]   (DLA)

Bouv Law Dict ... Bouvier's Law Dictionary [*A publication*]   (DLA)

Bouv L Dict ... Bouvier's Law Dictionary [*A publication*]   (DLA)

Bouwsteenen J V N M ... Bouwsteenen. Jaarboek der Vereeniging voor Nederlandsche Muziekgeschiedenis [*A publication*]

Bouwstenen ... Bouwstenen voor een Geschiedenis der Toonkunst in de Nederlanden [*A publication*]

BOV .... Blending Octane Value

BOV .... Boang [*Papua New Guinea*] [*Airport symbol*]   (OAG)

BoV .... Bockernas Varld [*A publication*]

BOV .... Bogong [*Victoria*] [*Seismograph station code, US Geological Survey*] [*Closed*]   (SEIS)

BOV .... Boolarra Virus

BOV .... Brown Oil of Vitriol

BOV .... Burnout Velocity

BOVC .... Base of Overcast [*Meteorology*]

BOVESPA ... Bolsa de Valores de Sao Paulo [*Sao Paulo Stock Exchange*] [*Brazil*]

Bovine Pract ... Bovine Practitioner [*A publication*]

BOVNDK .. Bericht des Offenbacher Vereins fuer Naturkunde [*A publication*]

Bov Pat Ca ... Bovill's Patent Cases [*A publication*]   (DLA)

BOW .... Bag of Waters [*Medicine*]

BOW .... Bartow, FL [*Location identifier*] [*FAA*]   (FAAL)

BOW .... Base Ordnance Workshop [*British and Canadian*]

BOW .... Beryllium Oxide Washer

BOW .... Bill of Work   (NASA)

BOW .... Blackout Window [*Military*]

BoW .... Book of the Winter [*A publication*]

BOW .... Bow Valley Resource Services Ltd. [*Toronto Stock Exchange symbol*]

BOW .... Bowater, Inc. [*NYSE symbol*]   (SPSG)

Bow .... Bowler and Bowers' United States Comptroller's Decisions [*2, 3*] [*A publication*]   (DLA)

Bow .... Bowler's London Session Records [*1605-85*] [*A publication*]   (DLA)

BOW .... Bowman [*South Carolina*] [*Seismograph station code, US Geological Survey*]   (SEIS)

BOW .... Breach of Warranty [*Insurance*]   (AIA)

BOW .... Kappersbondsnieuws [*A publication*]

BOWA ...... Booker T. Washington National Monument

BOWASH ... Boston-to-Washington Corridor

BOWC .... Brethren of the White Cross [*Book written by James De Mille (1873)*]

Bow Civ Law ... Bowyer's Modern Civil Law [*A publication*]   (DLA)

Bow Com .... Bowyer. Commentaries on Universal Public Law [*1854*] [*A publication*]   (DLA)

Bow Cons Law ... Bowyer. Commentaries on the Constitutional Law of England [*2nd ed.*] [*1846*] [*A publication*]   (DLA)

BOWD .... Budget Office, War Department [*World War II*]

Bowen Pol Econ ... Bowen's Political Economy [*A publication*]   (DLA)

BOWI .... Bibliographie zur Offentlichen Unternehmung und Verwaltung [*Bibliography of Public Management and Administration*] [*NOMOS Datapool*] [*Information service or system*]

Bow Int....... Bowyer. Introduction to the Study and Use of the Civil Law [*1874*] [*A publication*] (DLA)
Bowker Ann ... Bowker Annual of Library and Book Trade Information [*A publication*]
Bowler's First Comp Dec ... Decisions of the First Comptroller of the United States Treasury [*A publication*] (DLA)
Bowl Gr St ... Bowling Green Studies in Applied Philosophy [*A publication*]
Bowl Lib..... Bowles on Libel [*A publication*] (DLA)
BOWO....... Brigade Ordnance Warrant Officer [*British*]
BOWP .... Black Ordinary Working People
Bow Pub Law ... Bowyer. Commentaries on Universal Public Law [*1854*] [*A publication*] (DLA)
BOWR....... Boiler Water
BOWS .... [*The*] Barretts of Wimpole Street [*A play by Rudolf Besier*]
Bowstead.... Bowstead on Agency [*1896-1951*] [*A publication*] (DLA)
Bowyer Mod Civil Law ... Bowyer's Modern Civil Law [*A publication*] (DLA)
BOX.......... Bilirubin Oxidase [*An enzyme*]
BOX.......... Borok [*USSR*] [*Geomagnetic observatory code*]
Box........... Boxspring [*A publication*]
BOX.......... Houston, TX [*Location identifier*] [*FAA*] (FAAL)
Boxbrd Con ... Boxboard Containers [*A publication*]
B Oxf Univ Inst Statist ... Bulletin. Oxford University. Institute of Statistics [*A publication*]
BOY.......... Beginning of Year [*Accounting*]
BOY.......... Bobo-Dioulasso [*Upper Volta*] [*Airport symbol*] (OAG)
BOY.......... Boysen Reservoir, WY [*Location identifier*] [*FAA*] (FAAL)
Boyce......... Boyce's Delaware Supreme Court Reports [*1909-19*] [*A publication*] (DLA)
Boyce Thompson Inst Contrib ... Boyce Thompson Institute. Contributions [*A publication*]
Boyce Thompson Inst Plant Res Prof Pap ... Boyce Thompson Institute for Plant Research. Professional Papers [*A publication*]
Boyce US Pr ... Boyce's Practice in the United States Courts [*A publication*] (DLA)
Boy Char.... Boyle. Charities [*1837*] [*A publication*] (DLA)
Boyd Adm .. Boyd's Admiralty Law [*Ireland*] [*A publication*] (DLA)
Boyd Jus .... Boyd. Justice of the Peace [*A publication*] (DLA)
Boyd Sh...... Boyd. Merchant Shipping Laws [*1876*] [*A publication*] (DLA)
Boyer Mus Coll ... Boyer Museum Collection [*A publication*]
Boyle Act.... Boyle's Precis of an Action at Common Law [*A publication*] (DLA)
Boyle Char ... Boyle. Charities [*1837*] [*A publication*] (DLA)
Boys Cor .... Boys on Coroners [*A publication*] (DLA)
BoZ........... Bote aus Zion (BJA)
BOZ.......... Bozeman [*Montana*] [*Seismograph station code, US Geological Survey*] [*Closed*] (SEIS)
BOZ.......... Sterling Rockfalls, IL [*Location identifier*] [*FAA*] (FAAL)
BOZAA ..... Bollettino di Zoologia Agraria e di Bachicoltura [*A publication*]
Bozart........ Bozart and Contemporary Verse [*A publication*]
BOZED ...... Boersen-Zeitung [*A publication*]
BOZZ .... Bozzuto's, Inc. [*NASDAQ symbol*] (NQ)
BP .... Air Botswana Pty. [*ICAO designator*] (FAAC)
BP .... Bachelor of Painting
BP .... Bachelor of Pedagogy
BP .... Bachelor of Pharmacy
BP .... Bachelor of Philosophy
Bp .... Bachelor's Degree (Pass) [*British*]
BP .... Bacillus Pumilis [*Bacteriology*]
BP .... Back Plane (MCD)
BP .... Back Plaster [*Technical drawings*]
BP .... Back Pressure
BP .... Back Projection (DEN)
BP .... Backpack
BP .... Baghdad Pact (CINC)
B-of-P........ Balance of Payments [*International trade*]
BP .... Balance of Payments [*International trade*]
BP .... Ballistic Processor [*Military*] (CAAL)
BP .... Banasthali Patrika [*A publication*]
BP .... Bandpass
BP .... Baptized
BP .... Barber Pole (KSC)
BP .... Barometric Pressure
BP .... Barrier Preparation (MCD)
BP .... Basal Period
BP .... Base Pairs in DNA [*Genetics*]
BP .... Base Pay [*Military*]
BP .... Base Percussion
BP .... Base Pioneer [*Cell neuron*]
BP .... Base Pitch (MSA)
BP .... Base Point
BP .... Base Pointer [*Data processing*]
BP .... Base Position [*Phylogenetic analysis*]
BP .... Base Procured (AFM)
BP .... Base Protein
BP .... Baseplate [*Technical drawings*]
BP .... Basic Pay
BP .... Basic Protein [*Immunology*]
BP .... Basilar Papilla [*Anatomy*]
BP .... Basse Pression [*Low Pressure*] [*French*]
BP .... Bassposaune [*Bass Trombone*] [*Music*]
BP .... Batch Processing

BP .... Bathophenanthroline [*Organic chemistry*]
BP .... Bathroom Privileges [*Medicine*]
BP .... Battery Package
BP .... Battery-Powered (ADA)
BP .... Batting Practice [*Baseball*]
BP .... Battle Position (AABC)
BP .... Bayernpartei [*Bavarian Party*] [*Federal Republic of Germany*] [*Political party*] (PPE)
BP .... BCNU [*Carmustine*], Prednisone [*Antineoplastic drug regimen*]
BP .... Beach Party
BP .... Beacon Point
BP .... Beacon Press [*Publisher*]
BP .... Beatissime Pater [*Most Holy Father*] [*Latin*]
BP .... Beautiful People [*Slang for the wealthy, world-traveling, partying set*]
BP .... Bedpan
BP .... Before the Present
BP .... Beginning Period (AABC)
BP .... Behavior Pattern (ADA)
BP .... Beitraege zur Philosophie [*A publication*]
Bp .... [*Petrus de*] Bellapertica [*Deceased, 1308*] [*Authority cited in pre-1607 legal work*] (DSA)
BP .... Below Proof
BP .... Benedictines for Peace (EA)
BP .... Benefit Principles (DLA)
BP .... Benzopyrene [*or Benzpyrene*] [*Also, BZ*] [*Carcinogen*]
BP .... Benzoyl Peroxide [*Also, BPO*] [*Organic chemistry*]
BP .... Betriebspreis [*Enterprise Price*] [*German*]
BP .... Between Perpendiculars [*Technical drawings*]
BP .... Bibliographie de la Philosophie [*A publication*]
BP .... Bibliotheque du Parlement [*Library of Parliament*] [*Canada*]
B de P........ Bibliotheque de la Pleiade [*A publication*]
B & P........ Bid and Proposal
BP .... Bijdragen van de Philosophische en Theologische Faculteiten der Nederlandsche Jezuieten [*A publication*]
BP .... Bill of Parcels
BP .... Bills Payable [*Business term*]
BP .... Binding Post (KSC)
BP .... Binding Protein [*Biochemistry*]
BP .... Bioassay Program
BP .... Biopack [*NASA*] (KSC)
BP .... Biophysical Society
BP .... Bioregional Project (EA)
BP .... Bioscience Program [*NASA*]
BP .... Biotic Potential
BP .... Biparietal Diameter [*Gynecology*]
BP .... Birthplace
BP .... Bishop
BP .... Biuletyn Polonistyczny [*A publication*]
BP .... Bizarre People [*Extension of BP - Beautiful People*] [*Slang*]
BP .... Black Powder
BP .... Blackout Preparedness
BP .... Blacky Pictures [*Psychological testing*]
BP .... Blast Propagation (AAG)
BP .... Blind Purchase
BP .... Blister Pack
BP .... Block Parity [*Error checking method*] [*Telecommunications*] (TEL)
B/P............ Blood Precautions [*Isolation*] [*Medicine*]
BP .... Blood Pressure [*Medicine*]
BP .... Blood Program [*Red Cross*]
BP .... Blueprint
B & P........ Blueprints and Plans (MCD)
BP .... Board of Parole [*Abolished, 1976, functions transferred to United States Parole Commission*] [*Department of Justice*]
B/P............ Board President
BP .... Boeren Partij [*Farmers' Party*] [*Netherlands*] [*Political party*] (PPE)
BP .... Boiler Plate
BP .... Boiler Pressure
BP .... Boiling Point
BP .... Boite Postale [*Post Office Box*] [*French*]
BP .... Bollard Pull [*Shipping*] [*British*]
BP .... Bolted Plate [*Technical drawings*]
BP .... Bond and Preferred [*Business term*]
BP .... Bonum Publicum [*The Public Good*] [*Latin*]
BP .... Bonus Points
BP .... Book Profit [*Investment term*]
BP .... Book Publishing
BP .... Booklet Pane [*Philately*]
BP .... Bookplates [*A publication*]
BP .... Boost Pump (MCD)
BP .... Border Patrol
BP .... Boring Party (EA)
BP .... Boron Plastic
B & P......... Bosanquet and Puller's English Common Pleas, Exchequer, and House of Lords Reports [*1796-1804*] [*A publication*] (DLA)
BP .... Bottom Plane (MSA)

BP	Box Project (EA)
B of P	Breach of Peace [*FBI standardized term*]
B of P	Breach of Promise [*Legal term*]
B and P	Bread and Puppet Theater [*Vermont*]
BP	Breakpoint [*Telecommunications*] (TEL)
BP	Brick Protected [*Insurance classification*]
BP	Bristol Polytechnic [*Bristol, England*]
BP	British Patent
BP	British Petroleum Co. [*London*]
BP	British Petroleum Co. [*NYSE symbol*] [*Toronto Stock Exchange symbol*] (SPSG)
BP	British Pharmacopoeia [*A publication in pharmacy*]
BP	British Pound [*Monetary unit*]
BP	British Public [*Slang*]
bp	British Solomon Islands [*MARC country of publication code*] [*Library of Congress*] (LCCP)
BP	Broadcast Pioneers (EA)
BP	Bronchopleural [*Medicine*]
BP	Buccopulpal [*Dentistry*]
BP	Buckingham Palace [*British*]
BP	Budget Project [*Navy*] (CAAL)
B & P	Budgetary and Planning (NASA)
BP	Budgetary Policy
BP	Buergerpartei [*Citizens' Party*] [*Federal Republic of Germany*] [*Political party*] (PPE)
BP	Buffered Printing
BP	Bullet Path [*Ballistics*]
BP	Bullous Pemphigoid [*Medicine*]
BP	Bureau of Power [*of FPC*]
BP	Bureau of Prisons [*Department of Justice*]
BP	Burry Port [*Welsh depot code*]
BP	Butt Plane
BP	By Procuration [*In power of attorney*] [*Legal term*]
BP	Bypass
BP	La Bible et les Peres [*A publication*] (BJA)
BP	Penticton Public Library, British Columbia [*Library symbol*] [*National Library of Canada*] (NLC)
B³P	Balancing the Budget on the Backs of the Poor [*Political charge*]
B Pa	Bachelor of Painting
BPA	Bachelor of Professional Arts
BPA	Bachelor of Public Administration
BPA	Back Pain Association [*British*] [*Research center*] (EAIO)
BPA	Bahn Post Amt [*Railway Post Office*] [*German*]
BPA	Balanced Parametric Amplifier
BPA	Balloon Platoon of America [*Later, HBC*] (EA)
BPA	Baltimore Publishers Association (EA)
BPA	Basic Pressure Altitude
BPA	Basic Purchase Agreement (MCD)
BPA	Beam Plasma Amplification (MCD)
B Pa	Bernardus Papiensis [*Deceased, 1213*] [*Authority cited in pre-1607 legal work*] (DSA)
BPA	Bethpage, NY [*Location identifier*] [*FAA*] (FAAL)
BPA	Billiard Players Association of America
BPA	Biological Photographic Association (EA)
BPA	Bioprocessing Aid
BPA	Bioshield Power Assembly [*NASA*]
BPA	Biphenylamine [*Organic chemistry*]
BPA	Black Psychiatrists of America (EA)
BPA	Blanket Purchase Agreement (KSC)
BPA	Blanket Purchase Authority
BPA	Blood Pressure Assembly (KSC)
BPA	Bonneville Power Administration [*Department of Energy*] [*Portland, OR*]
BPA	Border Patrol Academy
BPA	Bottom Pumparound [*Drilling technology*]
BPA	Bovine Plasma Albumin
BPA	Brazil Philatelic Association (EA)
BPA	British Paediatric Association
BPA	British Pantomime Association
BPA	British Parachute Association
BPA	British Parking Association
BPA	British Peace Assembly
BPA	British Pilots Association [*A union*]
BPA	British Ports Association (DS)
BPA	Broadcasters' Promotion Association [*Later, BPME*] (EA)
BPA	Budget Project Account [*Military*] (AABC)
BPa	Buergerpartei [*Citizens' Party*] [*Federal Republic of Germany*] [*Political party*] (PPW)
BPA	Buffered Pyrophosphatase Activity [*Chemistry*]
BPA	Bullous Pemphigoid Antigen [*Immunology*]
BPA	Bureau of Pension Advocates [*Canada*]
BPA	Bureau of Public Administration [*University of Tennessee at Knoxville*] [*Research center*] (RCD)
BPA	Bureau of Public Assistance [*Later, BFS*] [*Social Security Administration*]
BPA	Burst-Promoting Activity [*Cytology*]
BPA	Bush Pilots Airways Ltd. [*Australia*] (ADA)
BPA	Business Publications Audit of Circulation (EA)
BPA	Major League Baseball Players Association
BPAA	Bowling Proprietors' Association of America (EA)
B/PAA	Business/Professional Advertising Association [*New York, NY*] (EA)
BPAAA	Beitraege zur Pathologischen Anatomie und zur Allgemeinen Pathologie [*A publication*]
BPAA-DAD	Bowling Proprietors' Association of America - Duckpin Activities Department [*Defunct*] (EA)
BPAB	Biotinyl-para-aminobenzoate [*Biochemistry*]
BPABA	Biologia Plantarum [*Prague*] [*A publication*]
BPABAJ	Biologia Plantarum [*Prague*] [*A publication*]
BPABDM	Benchmark Papers in Biochemistry [*A publication*]
BPAC	Better Packaging Advisory Council (EA)
BPAC	Book Publishers' Association of Canada
BPAC	Budget Program Activity Code
BP Accel	BP [*British Petroleum*] Accelerator [*A publication*] (APTA)
BPAC/MPC	Budget Program Activity Code Material Program Code (MCD)
BPAD	Bowker's Publisher Authority Database [*R. R. Bowker Co.*] [*Information service or system*] (CRD)
BPADA	Alberni District Archives, Port Alberni, British Columbia [*Library symbol*] [*National Library of Canada*] (BIB)
BP Adm	Bachelor of Public Administration
BPaed	Bachelor of Paediatrics (ADA)
BPaed	Bachelor of Pedagogy
BPAH	Bulletin. Pan American Health Organization [*A publication*]
BPAHA3	Boletin. Oficina Sanitaria Panamericana. English Edition [*A publication*]
BPAIA	Bulletin of Pathology (Chicago, Illinois) [*A publication*]
BPAM	Alberni Valley Museum, Port Alberni, British Columbia [*Library symbol*] [*National Library of Canada*] (NLC)
BPAM	Basic Partitioned Access Method [*IBM Corp.*] [*Data processing*]
BPAO	Baldwin Piano & Organ Co. [*Loveland, OH*] [*NASDAQ symbol*] (NQ)
BPAO	Branch Public Affairs Officer [*United States Information Service*]
BPAP	Benzoyl(Phenylalanyl)Proline [*Biochemistry*]
B Parl	Bulletin. Societe des Parlers de France [*A publication*]
BPAS	Benzoyl-para-aminosalicylate [*Pharmacology*]
B Pas De Calais	Bulletin. Commission Departementale de Monuments Historiques du Pas-De-Calais [*A publication*]
BPA-SDI	Bonneville Power Administration Selective Dissemination of Information [*Department of the Interior*]
BPAU	Bulletin. Pan American Union [*A publication*]
BPB	Bachelor of Physical Biology
BP-B	Bacteriopheophytin-B [*Biochemistry*]
BPB	Baltimore Photo & Blue Print Co., Baltimore, MD [*Library symbol*] [*Library of Congress*] (LCLS)
BPB	Bank Pass Book (ROG)
BPB	Bank Post Bill [*Business term*]
BPB	BIOS [*Basic Input-Output System*] Parameter Block [*Data processing*] (PCM)
BPB	Black Pigmented Bacteria [*Microbiology*]
BPB	Blanket Position Bond [*Insurance*]
BPB	Boom Patrol Boat [*British Marines' Special Forces*] [*World War II*]
BPB	Bromphenol [*or Bromophenol*] Blue [*A dye*]
BPB	[*J.*] Buller's Paper Books, Lincoln's Inn Library [*A publication*] (DLA)
BPB	Business Planning Board [*Later, BTPB*] (EA)
BPBD	International Alliance of Bill Posters, Billers, and Distributors of US and Canada [*Defunct*] (EA)
BPBIRA	British Paper and Board Industry Research Association
BPBW	Bare Phosphor Bronze Wire
BPC	Back-Pressure Control
BPC	Bandpass Crystal
BPC	Base Point Configuration (AAG)
BPC	Basic Peripheral Channel
BPC	Battery Park City [*New York City*]
BPC	Beach Patrol Craft [*British military*] (DMA)
BPC	Beagle Pup Club [*British*]
BPC	Binding Post Chamber [*Telecommunications*] (TEL)
BPC	Biomaterials Profiling Center [*University of Utah*] [*Research center*] (RCD)
BPC	Black People's Convention [*South Africa*] (PD)
BPC	Black Protest Committee [*Australia*]
BPC	Bonded Phase Chromatography
BPC	Book Prices Current [*1887-1956*] [*A publication*] [*British*]
BPC	Boost Protective Cover [*Apollo*] [*NASA*]
BPC	BP Canada, Inc. [*Toronto Stock Exchange symbol*] [*Vancouver Stock Exchange symbol*]
BPC	Bradmar Petroleum Corp. [*AMEX symbol*] (SPSG)
BPC	British Pharmaceutical Codex [*A publication in pharmacy*]
BPC	British Printing Corporation [*Later, BPCC*]
BPC	British Productivity Council
BPC	British Purchasing Commission
BPC	Brown's Cases in Parliament [*A publication*] (DLA)
BPC	Bulk Petrol Company [*Military*] [*British and Canadian*]
BPC	Bureau of Provisions and Clothing [*See also BSA*] [*Navy*]
BPC	Port Coquitlam Public Library, British Columbia [*Library symbol*] [*National Library of Canada*] (NLC)

BPCA......... Bioshield Pyrotechnic Control Assembly [*for Mariner Venus-Mercury Project spacecraft*] [*NASA*]

BP Calv...... Bulletin des Parlers du Calvados [*A publication*]

BPCBAT.... Biological Psychology Bulletin [*Oklahoma City*] [*A publication*]

BPCC......... Balloon Post Collectors Club   (EA)

BPCC......... Better Postcard Collectors' Club [*Later, D of A*]   (EA)

BPCC......... British Printing & Communication Corporations [*Later, MCC*]

BPCCDZ ... Biosynthetic Products for Cancer Chemotherapy [*A publication*]

BPCD........ Barrels per Calendar Day

BPCDI...... Brookhaven Portable Cesium Developmental Irradiator Unit [*Nuclear energy*]

BPCF .... Bandpass Crystal Filter

BPCH .... Craig Heritage Park, Parksville, British Columbia [*Library symbol*] [*National Library of Canada*]   (NLC)

BPCI.......... Bulk Packaging and Containerization Institute [*Later, CII*]   (EA)

BPCI.......... ISI Infosearch, Port Coquitlam, British Columbia [*Library symbol*] [*National Library of Canada*]   (NLC)

BPCMUS .. Bulletin. Post-Graduate Committee in Medicine. University of Sydney [*A publication*]   (APTA)

BPCO .... Bonneville Pacific Corporation [*Salt Lake City, UT*] [*NASDAQ symbol*]   (NQ)

BP/CP .... Base Procured/Central Procured   (AFM)

BPC/RE..... Revista de Economia. Banco de la Provincia de Cordoba [*A publication*]

BPCS .... Business Periodicals Circulation Services [*Harcourt Brace Jovanovich*]

BPCT........ Best Practicable Control Technology [*Wastewater treatment*]

BPCTCA ... Best Practicable Control Technology Currently Available   (MCD)

BPCTH...... Bulletin Philologique et Historique. Comite des Travaux Historiques et Scientifiques [*Paris*] [*A publication*]

B Pd .... Bachelor of Pedagogy [*or Pedagogics*]

BPD .... Bachelor of Planning and Design

BPD .... Barrels per Day

BPD .... Baseline Program Document   (NASA)

BPD .... Basic Planning Document [*Military*]   (AABC)

BPD .... Basic Point Defense [*Military*]   (NVT)

BPD .... Battlefield Plan Development   (MCD)

BPD .... Beach Party Division [*Navy*]   (NVT)

BPD .... Beaupre Explorations [*Vancouver Stock Exchange symbol*]

BPD .... Biparietal Diameter [*Gynecology*]

BPD .... Blood Program Directives [*Red Cross*]

BPD .... Book Publisher's Directory [*Later, PD*] [*A publication*]

bpd .... Bookplate Designer [*MARC relator code*] [*Library of Congress*]   (LCCP)

BPD .... British Society of Poster Designers

BPD .... Bronchopulmonary Dysplasia [*Medicine*]

BPD .... Bureau of the Public Debt [*Department of the Treasury*]

BPD .... Bushing Potential Device   (MSA)

BPD .... Business Periodicals Directory [*A publication*]

BPD .... Doctor of Bio-Psychology

BPDC........ Bardon Professional Development Centre [*Australia*]

BPDC........ Berkeley Particle Data Center

BPDE........ Benzopyrenedihydrodiolepoxide [*Organic chemistry*]

BPDG .... Berkeley Particle Data Group [*Lawrence Radiation Laboratory*]

BPDMS.... Basic Point Defense Missile System   (MCD)

BPDNA2 ... SUDENE [*Superintendencia do Desenvolvimento do Nordeste*] GCDP [*Grupo Coordenador do Desenvolvimento da Pesca*] Boletim de Estudos de Pesca [*A publication*]

BPDP........ Book Publishing Development Program [*Canada*]

BPDP......... Brotherhood of Painters, Decorators, and Paperhangers of America [*Later, IBPAT*]

B of PDPH of A ... Brotherhood of Painters, Decorators, and Paperhangers of America [*Later, IBPAT*]   (EA)

BPDS........ Basic Point Defense System   (MCD)

BPDS........ Bathophenanthroline Disulphonate [*Organic chemistry*]

BPDSMS... Basic Point Defense Surface Missile System   (NVT)

B Pe............ Bachelor of Pedagogy

BPE .... Bachelor of Physical Education

BPE .... Back Porch Effect

BPE .... Bacterial Phosphatidylethanolamine [*Physiological chemistry*]

BPE .... Beauchamp Exploration, Inc. [*Vancouver Stock Exchange symbol*]

BPE .... Best Preliminary Estimate   (AFM)

BPE .... Binaural Phase Effect

BPE .... BIT [*Binary Digit*]-Plane Encoding [*Data processing*]

BPE .... Boiling Point Elevation

BPE .... Bovine Pituitary Extract

BPE .... Bremen Port of Embarkation [*West Germany*]

BPE .... Brookings Papers on Economic Activity [*A publication*]

BPE .... Budget Program Estimate   (MCD)

BPE .... Bureau of Postsecondary Education [*Later, Bureau of Higher and Continuing Education*] [*Office of Education*]

BPE .... Butyl Phenyl Ether [*Organic chemistry*]

BPEA .... Brookings Papers on Economic Activity [*A publication*]

B Peace Propos ... Bulletin of Peace Proposals [*A publication*]

BPEAD...... Brookings Papers on Economic Activity [*A publication*]

BPEAOA... Bureau of Professional Education of the American Osteopathic Association   (EA)

BPEC .... Bollettino. Comitato per la Preparazione dell'Edizione Nazionale dei Classici Greci e Latini [*A publication*]

BPEC .... Bovine Pulmonary Artery Endothelium Cell [*Cell line*]

BPEC .... Building Products Executives Conference

BPECDB .. Benchmark Papers in Ecology [*A publication*]

B Ped .... Bachelor of Pedagogy [*or Pedagogics*]

BP Ed....... Bachelor of Physical Education

BPED......... Basic Pay Entry Date

B Pe E .... Bachelor of Petroleum Engineering

B Pe Eng .... Bachelor of Petroleum Engineering

BPEFA....... Buletinul. Institutului Politehnic din Brasov. Seria B. Economie Forestiera [*A publication*]

BPE-LCA .. Board of Parish Education, Lutheran Church in America   (EA)

BPEM....... Peachland Museum, British Columbia [*Library symbol*] [*National Library of Canada*]   (NLC)

BPEMM.... Pemberton Museum, British Columbia [*Library symbol*] [*National Library of Canada*]   (NLC)

BPEO........ Best Practicable Environmental Option   (ECON)

BPerfArts... Bachelor of Performing Arts

B Perigord ... Bulletin. Societe Historique et Archeologique du Perigord [*A publication*]

BPES .... Bibliotheca Patrum Ecclesiasticorum Selectissima [*A publication*]

BPES .... Bulletin. Palestine Exploration Society [*A publication*]

BPET .... Burkhart Petroleum Corp. [*Tulsa, OK*] [*NASDAQ symbol*]   (NQ)

B Pet E .... Bachelor of Petroleum Engineering

BPEX .... Business Passenger's Extra Option [*Proposed*] [*Travel industry*]

BPF .... Bandpass Filter

BPF .... Baptist Peace Fellowship   (EA)

BPF .... Base Productivity Factor   (MCD)

BPF .... Bicycling Parking Foundation   (EA)

BPF .... Biliary Protein Fraction

BPF .... Blue Print Files   (NRCH)

BPF .... Bon pour Francs [*Value in Francs*] [*French*]

BPF .... Books for the People Fund   (EA)

BPF .... Bottom Pressure Fluctuation

BPF .... Brethren Peace Fellowship [*Inactive*]   (EA)

BPF .... British Pacific Fleet [*Obsolete*]

BPF .... British Plastics Federation

BPF .... British Polio Fellowship [*British*]

BPF .... Bromine Pentafluoride [*Corrosive compound*]

BPF .... Bronchopleural Fistula [*Anatomy*]

BPF .... Buddhist Peace Fellowship   (EA)

BPF .... Bulletin du Protestantisme Francais [*A publication*]

BPF .... Burst-Promoting Factor [*Endocrinology; hematology*]

BPF(I)....... Ball-Pass Frequency, Inner Race [*Machinery*]

BPFILO..... British Pacific Fleet Intelligence Liaison Officer

BPFLO...... British Pacific Fleet Liaison Officer

B Pfl Z....... Beitraege zur Pflanzenzucht [*A publication*]

BPFM....... Bypass Flow Module [*Nuclear energy*]   (NRCH)

BPF(O)...... Ball-Pass Frequency, Outer Race [*Machinery*]

BPFP .... Botswana Protectorate Federal Party

BPFRAO ... Boletim. Universidade do Parana. Farmacognosia [*A publication*]

BPFS......... Bulk Petroleum Facilities and Systems

BPFT .... Basic Physical Fitness Test   (MCD)

BPG .... Beach Party Group [*Navy*]   (NVT)

BPG .... Beach Party Guard [*Navy*]   (NVT)

BPG .... Benzathine Penicillin G [*Antibacterial*]

BPG .... Big Plasma Glucagon [*Endocrinology*]

BPG .... Blood Pressure Gauge [*Medicine*]

BPG .... Boron Pyrolytic Graphite

BPG .... Break Pulse Generator   (CET)

BPG .... Prince George Public Library, British Columbia [*Library symbol*] [*National Library of Canada*]   (NLC)

BPGAAC... Boletim. Museu Paraense Emilio Goeldi. Nova Serie. Antropologia [*A publication*]

BPGAG...... Experimental Farm, Agriculture Canada [*Ferme Experimentale, Agriculture Canada*], Prince George, British Columbia [*Library symbol*] [*National Library of Canada*]   (BIB)

BPGC........ Bearing per Gyro Compass [*Navigation*]

BPGC........ Bricks, Pottery, Glass, Cement [*Department of Employment*] [*British*]

BPGC........ College of New Caledonia, Prince George, British Columbia [*Library symbol*] [*National Library of Canada*]   (NLC)

BPGEDR ... Benchmark Papers in Genetics [*A publication*]

BPGEES.... Benchmark Papers in Geology [*A publication*]

BPGGA...... Bulletin. Academie Polonaise des Sciences. Serie des Sciences Geologiques et Geographiques [*A publication*]

BPGLSB.... Library Services Branch, Ministry of Provincial Secretary and Government Services, Prince George, British Columbia [*Library symbol*] [*National Library of Canada*]   (NLC)

BPGMD .... Buletinul. Institutului Politehnic "Gheorghe Gheorghiu-Dej" Bucuresti. Seria Mecanica [*A publication*]

BPGRG...... British Plant Growth Regulator Group   (EAIO)

BPGRM..... Fraser - Fort George Regional Museum, Prince George, British Columbia [*Library symbol*] [*National Library of Canada*]   (NLC)

BPGV........ Burry Port & Gwendraeth Valley Railway [*Wales*]

B Ph .... Bachelor of Philosophy

BPH .... Bachelor of Public Health
BPH .... Barrels per Hour
BPH .... Benign Prostatic Hyperplasia [*Medicine*]
BPH .... Benign Prostatic Hypertrophy [*Medicine*]
BPh .... Bibliographie de la Philosophie [*A publication*]
BPH .... Biopharmaceuticals [*AMEX symbol*] (SPSG)
BPH .... Bislig [*Philippines*] [*Airport symbol*] (OAG)
B-P-H .... Botanico-Periodicum-Huntianum [*Book title*]
BPH .... Brown Planthopper [*Entomology*]
BPH .... Bulletin Philologique et Historique [*A publication*]
BPH .... Bump Protection Hat
BPHA .... Benzoylphenylhydroxylamine (NRCH)
B Pharm..... Bachelor of Pharmacy
BPHBA...... BHP [*Broken Hill Proprietary Ltd.*] Technical Bulletin
             (Australia) [*A publication*]
B Ph C........ Bachelor of Pharmaceutical Chemistry
BPhC .... Bibliotheca Philologica Classica [*A publication*]
BPHCTHS ... Bulletin Philologique et Historique. Comite des Travaux
             Historiques et Scientifiques [*Paris*] [*A publication*]
B Ph DI...... Beitraege zur Philosophie des Deutschen Idealismus [*A
             publication*]
BPHE .... Bachelor of Physical and Health Education
BPHE .... Bachelor of Public Health Engineering
Bphe........... Bacteriopheophytin [*Biochemistry*]
BPH Ed...... Bachelor of Public Health Education
BPH Eng.... Bachelor of Public Health Engineering
BPheo......... Bacteriopheophytin [*Biochemistry*]
B Ph Fr A.... Beitraege zur Physik der Freien Atmosphaere [*A publication*]
BPHI .... Boost Phase Intercept (AABC)
B Phil........ Bachelor of Philosophy
B Phila Mus ... Bulletin. Philadelphia Museum of Art [*A publication*]
BPhil(Ed)... Bachelor of Philosophy (Education), University of Birmingham
             [*British*] (DBQ)
B Phil Woch ... Berliner Philologische Wochenschrift [*A publication*] (OCD)
BPHist....... Bulletin Philologique et Historique [*A publication*]
BPHJA ... British Phycological Journal [*A publication*]
BPHJAA ... British Phycological Journal [*A publication*]
B Phl .... Beitraege zur Physiologie [*A publication*]
BPhM .... Bulletin. Societe Internationale pour l'Etude de la Philosophie
             Medievale [*A publication*]
BPHN........ Bachelor of Public Health Nursing
B Pho .... Bachelor of Photography
BPHP......... Bulletin Philologique et Historique. Comite des Travaux
             Historiques et Scientifiques (Paris) [*A publication*]
BPHPDV... Benchmark Papers in Human Physiology [*A publication*]
BPHR .... Bureau of Ports, Harbors, and Reclamation [*Philippines*] (DS)
B Ph S........ Bachelor of Physical Science
BPhSC .... Bulletin. Philological Society of Calcutta [*A publication*]
BPhSJ........ Bulletin. Phonetic Society of Japan [*A publication*]
BPhty .... Bachelor of Physiotherapy (ADA)
BPHUED ... Buletin Penelitian Hutan [*A publication*]
BPhW .... Berliner Philologische Wochenschrift [*A publication*]
B Phy .... Bachelor of Physics
BPhysHlthEd ... Bachelor of Physical Health Education
B Physiopa ... Bulletin de Physiopathologie Respiratoire [*A publication*]
BPI............. Bachelor of Planning, University of Manchester [*British*]
BPI............. Bamberger Polymers, Incorporated [*AMEX symbol*] (SPSG)
BPI............. Bangladesh Press International
BPI............. Big Piney, WY [*Location identifier*] [*FAA*] (FAAL)
BPI............. Billboard Publications, Incorporated
BPI............. Bio-Degradable Plastics, Incorporated
BPI............. Biochemical Process Industry
BPI............. Bipolar Psychological Inventory [*Personality development test*]
             [*Psychology*]
BPI............. BITs [*Binary Digits*] per Inch [*Data density measurement*]
             [*Data processing*]
BPI............. Bituminous Pipe Institute [*Defunct*] (EA)
BPI............. Board of Patent Interferences [*of Patent Office*]
BPI............. Bollettino Paleontologico Italiano [*A publication*]
BPI............. Bollettino delle Pubblicazioni Italiane Ricevute per Diritto di
             Stampa [*A publication*]
BPI............. Bollettino delle Publicazione Italiane [*A publication*]
BPI............. Book Production Industry [*A publication*]
BPI............. Bookman's Price Index [*A reference publication listing rare
             books and their list prices*]
BPI............. Boost Phase Intercept
BPI............. BPI ...A Growers Organization (EA)
BPI............. Break-Point Instruction
BPI............. British Phonographic Industry
BPI............. Bureau of Plant Industry [*Later, BPISAE*] [*Department of
             Agriculture*]
BPI............. Bureau of Public Inquiries
BPI............. Burma Pharmaceutical Industry (DS)
BPI............. Business People, Incorporated [*Minneapolis, MN*]
             [*Telecommunications service*] (TSSD)
BPI............. Business Periodicals Index [*H. W. Wilson Co.*] [*Bronx, NY*] [*A
             publication*]
BPI............. Business Publishers, Incorporated [*Silver Spring, MD*]
             [*Information service or system*] (IID)
BPI............. Buying Power Index
BPI............. Bytes per Inch [*Data processing*]

BPIA .... Business Publications Index and Abstracts [*A publication*]
BPIAS........ Bulletin. Polish Institute of Arts and Sciences in America [*A
             publication*]
BPICA .... Bureau Permanent International des Constructeurs
             d'Automobiles [*International Permanent Bureau of Motor
             Manufacturers*] (EAIO)
BPICM ...... Bureau Permanent International des Constructeurs de
             Motocycles [*Permanent International Bureau of
             Motorcycle Manufacturers*] (EAIO)
BPICS........ British Production and Inventory Control Society (DBQ)
B-PID .... Book-Physical Inventory Difference [*AEC*]
BPIEC .... Beijing Publications Import & Export Corporation
BPIF .... British Printing Industries' Federation (DCTA)
BPIF .... Brunei People's Independence Front [*Political party*] (FEA)
BPII .... BPI Systems, Incorporated [*NASDAQ symbol*] (NQ)
BPIL .... Basic Petroleum International Ltd. [*NASDAQ symbol*] (NQ)
BPIN .... Big Piney Oil & Gas Co. [*NASDAQ symbol*] (NQ)
BPIRF........ BPI Resources Ltd. [*NASDAQ symbol*] (NQ)
BPISAE...... Bureau of Plant Industry, Soils, and Agricultural Engineering
             [*Formerly, BPI*] [*Functions transferred to ARS, 1953*]
             [*Department of Agriculture*]
BPITT........ Bureau Permanent Interafricain de la Tse-Tse et de la
             Trypanosomiase
BPJ .... Balanced Pressure Joint
BPJ .... Beloit Poetry Journal [*A publication*]
BPJ .... Best Professional Judgment [*Environmental Protection Agency*]
BPJC .... Bay Path Junior College [*Longmeadow, MA*]
BPJSA .... Biophysical Journal. Supplement [*A publication*]
Bpk........... Beperk [*Limited*] [*South African*] [*Business term*]
BPK .... Berichte. Preussische Kunstsammlungen [*Berlin*] [*A
             publication*]
BPK .... Black Peak [*Arizona*] [*Seismograph station code, US Geological
             Survey*] [*Closed*] (SEIS)
BPK .... Black Photo Corp. Ltd. [*Toronto Stock Exchange symbol*]
bPKC .... Bovine Protein Kinase C [*An enzyme*]
BPKG........ Blaetter fuer Pfaelzische Kirchengeschichte [*A publication*]
BPKS........ Berichte. Preussische Kunstsammlungen [*A publication*]
BPKT........ Basic Programming Knowledge Test (MCD)
BPKUD...... BP [*Benzin und Petroleum AG Hamburg*] Kurier [*A
             publication*]
BP Kur .... BP [*Benzin und Petroleum AG Hamburg*] Kurier [*A
             publication*]
BPL........... Bachelor of Patent Law
BPL........... Band Pressure Level
BPL........... Barrington Petroleum Ltd. [*Formerly, Barrington Properties
             Ltd.*] [*Toronto Stock Exchange symbol*]
BPL........... Baseplate [*Technical drawings*]
BPL........... Basic Parts List
BPL........... Bearing Plate [*Technical drawings*]
BPL........... Beta-Propriolactone [*Organic chemistry*]
BPL........... Binary Program Loader
BPL........... Birmingham Public Library [*Alabama*]
BPL........... Birthplace
BPL........... Block Proof List [*Data processing*]
BPL........... Blood-Products Laboratory [*British*]
BPL........... Bohn's Philosophical Library [*A publication*]
BPL........... Bone Phosphate of Lime
B/PL.......... Bookplate [*Bibliography*]
BPL........... Bott's Poor Law Cases [*1560-1833*] [*England*] [*A
             publication*] (DLA)
BPL........... Brass Pounders League [*Unit of American Radio Relay League*]
BPL........... Brooklyn Public Library [*NYSE symbol*]
BPL........... Buckeye Partnership [*NYSE symbol*] (SPSG)
BPL........... Burst Position Locator
BPl........... La Bible. Bibliotheque de la Pleiade [*A publication*] (BJA)
BPL........... Veterans Memorial Public Library, Bismarck, ND [*OCLC
             symbol*] (OCLC)
BPLA........ Bow Plane
B Plastics ... British Plastics [*Later, European Plastics News*] [*A publication*]
BPL Cas..... Bott's Poor Law Cases [*1560-1833*] [*England*] [*A
             publication*] (DLA)
BPL Cases ... Bott's Poor Law Cases [*1560-1833*] [*England*] [*A
             publication*] (DLA)
BP Lit........ Boletin de Pastoral Liturgica [*A publication*]
B-PLL........ B-Cell Prolymphocytic Leukemia
BPLNME .. Bibliography of Periodical Literature on the Near and Middle
             East [*A publication*]
BPLQ......... Boston Public Library. Quarterly [*A publication*]
BPM .... Balanced Property Management (ADA)
BPM .... Ballistic Particle Manufacturing [*Desktop manufacturing*]
BPM .... Barbuda People's Movement [*Antigua*] [*Political party*] (PD)
BPM .... Barrels per Minute
BPM .... Batch Processing Monitor [*Xerox Corp.*] [*Data
             processing*] (MCD)
BPM .... Beam Positioning Magnet
BPM .... Beats per Minute [*Cardiology*]
BPM .... Best Practical Means [*Business term*] (DCTA)
BPM .... Bible Protestant Missions (EA)
BPM .... Bipiperidyl Mustard [*Pharmacology*]
BPM .... BITs [*Binary Digits*] per Minute [*Data transmission speed*]
             [*Data processing*]

BPM .... Breaths per Minute
BPM .... Brompheniramine Maleate [*Antihistamine*]
BPM .... Bulletin. Palestine Museum [*A publication*]
BPM .... Penticton Museum and Archives, British Columbia [*Library symbol*] [*National Library of Canada*] (NLC)
BPMA .... Barrier Paper Manufacturers Association [*Defunct*] (EA)
BPMA .... Bio-Technology Purchasing Management Association (EA)
BPMC .... Bertelsmann Printing & Manufacturing Corporation
BPME .... Broadcast Promotion and Marketing Executives (EA)
BPMEL ..... Base Precision Measurement Equipment Laboratories (AFM)
BPMF .... British Postgraduate Medical Federation
BPMGA ..... Berichte. Physikalisch-Medizinische Gesellschaft zu Wuerzburg [*A publication*]
BPMH .... Brompton Park Military Hospital [*British military*] (DMA)
BPMI .... Badger Paper Mills, Incorporated [*Peshtigo, WI*] [*NASDAQ symbol*] (NQ)
BPMIDZ ... Benchmark Papers in Microbiology [*A publication*]
BPMM ...... BITs [*Binary Digits*] per Millimeter [*Data density measurement*] [*Data processing*]
BPMM ...... Port Moody Station Museum, British Columbia [*Library symbol*] [*National Library of Canada*] (NLC)
BPMP .... Port Moody Public Library, British Columbia [*Library symbol*] [*National Library of Canada*] (NLC)
BPMS .... Blood Plasma Measuring System [*Medicine*]
BPMTG ..... [*The*] British Puppet and Model Theatre Guild
BPMV .... Bean Pod Mottle Virus
BPN .... Balikpapan [*Indonesia*] [*Airport symbol*] (OAG)
BPN .... Balloon-Borne Polar Nephelometer
BPN .... Bandpass Network
BPN .... Bloody Public Nuisance [*British slang*]
BPN .... Breakdown Pulse Noise (KSC)
BPN .... British Poets of the Nineteenth Century [*A publication*]
BPN .... Budget Project Number [*Navy*] (NG)
BPN .... Building Products News [*A publication*] (APTA)
BPN .... Bureau Politique National [*National Political Bureau*]
BPNA .... British Petroleum North America
BPNL .... Battelle Pacific Northwest Laboratories [*Nuclear energy*] (NRCH)
B & PNR .... Bosanquet and Puller's New Reports, English Common Pleas [*1804-07*] [*A publication*] (DLA)
BPNR .... Bosanquet and Puller's New Reports, English Common Pleas [*1804-07*] [*A publication*] (DLA)
BPNSA ...... Bibliotheca Psychiatrica et Neurologica (Switzerland) [*A publication*]
BPNSAX ... Aktuelle Fragen der Psychiatrie und Neurologie [*A publication*]
BPNSB ...... Bulletin. Psychonomic Society [*A publication*]
BPO .... Bartlesville Project Office [*Bartlesville, OK*] [*Department of Energy*] (GRD)
BPO .... Base Post Office
BPO .... Base Procurement Office [*Air Force*] (AFM)
BPO .... Basic Postflight (MCD)
BPO .... Benzoyl Peroxide [*Also, BP*] [*Organic chemistry*]
BPO .... Benzylpenicilloyl [*Organic chemistry*]
BPO .... Berlin Philharmonic Orchestra
BPO .... Bicycling Promotion Organization [*Later, BIA*] (EA)
BPO .... (Biphenylyl)phenyloxazole [*Organic chemistry*]
BPO .... British Post Office
BPO .... Bromoperoxidase [*An enzyme*]
BPO .... Business Periodicals Ondisc [*UMI/Data Courier*] [*Information service or system*] (CRD)
BPO .... Oneida, TN [*Location identifier*] [*FAA*] (FAAL)
BPOC .... Before Proceeding on Course [*Aviation*]
BPOC .... Pouce Coupe Public Library, British Columbia [*Library symbol*] [*National Library of Canada*] (NLC)
BPOE .... Benevolent and Protective Order of Elks (EA)
BPOEA ...... British Power Engineering [*A publication*]
BPOJA ...... British Polymer Journal [*A publication*]
B Pol .... Biblioteka Polska [*A publication*]
B Pol .... Biuletyn Prasowy Polonia [*A publication*]
B Pol Biol... Bulletin. Academie Polonaise des Sciences. Serie des Sciences Biologiques [*A publication*]
B Pol Chim .. Bulletin. Academie Polonaise des Sciences. Serie des Sciences Chimiques [*A publication*]
B Pol Math ... Bulletin. Academie Polonaise des Sciences. Serie des Sciences Mathematiques, Astronomiques, et Physiques [*A publication*]
B Pol Sc...... Bachelor of Political Science
B Pol Sci T ... Bulletin. Academie Polonaise des Sciences. Serie des Sciences de la Terre [*A publication*]
B Pol Techn ... Bulletin. Academie Polonaise des Sciences. Serie des Sciences Techniques [*A publication*]
BPOP........ BanPonce Corp. [*NASDAQ symbol*] (NQ)
BPOPD...... British Public Opinion [*A publication*]
BPOR .... Biopore, Inc. [*NASDAQ symbol*] (NQ)
BPORH ..... Powell River Historical Museum, British Columbia [*Library symbol*] [*National Library of Canada*] (NLC)
BPOSA ...... British Poultry Science [*A publication*]
BPOSA4..... British Poultry Science [*A publication*]
BPP .... Beacon Portable Packset
BPP .... Beitraege zur Philosophie und Psychologie [*A publication*]
BPP .... Bengal Past and Present [*A publication*]

BPP .... Bhutan People's Party [*Political party*] (ECON)
BPP .... Biblioteka Pisarzy Polskich i Obcych [*A publication*]
BPP .... Biochemie und Physiologie der Pflanzen [*A publication*]
BPP .... Black Panther Party [*Defunct*] [*Political party*]
BPP .... Black People's Party [*South Africa*] [*Political party*] (PPW)
BPP .... [*A*] Book of Personal Poems [*A publication*]
BPP .... Border Patrol Police [*Thailand*]
BPP .... Borge Prien Prove [*Danish intelligence test*]
BPP .... Botswana People's Party [*Political party*] (PPW)
BPP .... Bovine Pancreatic Polypeptide
BPP .... Bubble Pulse Period
BPP .... Bulk Polymerization Process [*Plastics technology*]
BPP .... Burnham Pacific Properties [*NYSE symbol*] (SPSG)
BPP .... Bursting Pacemaker Potential [*Electrophysiology*]
BPP .... Buyer Protection Plan [*Sales*]
BPPG .... Bureau Planned Procurement Guide [*Navy*]
BPPHA ...... Beitraege aus der Plasmaphysik [*A publication*]
BPPM .... Princeton and District Museum and Archives, Princeton, British Columbia [*Library symbol*] [*National Library of Canada*] (NLC)
BPPMA ..... British Power Press Manufacturers Association (MCD)
BPPO........ Buckingham Palace Press Office [*British*]
BPPRA ..... Bulletin de Physiopathologie Respiratoire [*A publication*]
BPPRD ..... Bulletin of Peace Proposals [*A publication*]
BPPSJ ...... Balanced Pressure Plane Swivel Joint
BPQ .... British Columbia Packers Ltd. [*Vancouver Stock Exchange symbol*]
BPQ .... Budgetary and Planning Quotations (MCD)
BPQP........ Boise Peace Quilt Project (EA)
BPR .... American Book Publishing Record [*A publication*]
BPR .... Banana Plug Resistor
BPR .... Battery Plotting Room
BPR .... Battery-Powered Recorder
BPR .... Berry Pseudorotation
BPR .... Beryllium Physics Reactor (NRCH)
BPR .... Bimonthly Progress Report
BPR .... Block Proof Record [*Data processing*]
BPR .... Blood Pressure Recorder [*Medicine*]
BPR .... Bloque Popular Revolucionario [*Popular Revolutionary Bloc*] [*El Salvador*] (PD)
BPR .... Boiling Point Rise
BPR .... Book Publishing Record (DIT)
B Pr .... Books in Print [*A publication*]
BPR .... Bramalea Properties, Inc. [*Toronto Stock Exchange symbol*]
BPR .... Bridge Plotting Room [*Navy*]
BPR .... Bridgeport, TX [*Location identifier*] [*FAA*] (FAAL)
BP & R ...... British Plastics and Rubber [*A publication*]
BPR .... Bromopyrogallol Red [*An indicator*] [*Chemistry*]
BPR .... Brown's Parliamentary Reports [*England*] [*A publication*] (DLA)
BPR .... Budapesti Regisegei [*A publication*]
BPR .... Building Products Register [*American Institute of Architects*]
BPR .... Bulletin of Prosthetics Research [*A publication*]
BPR .... Bureau of Public Relations [*War Department*] [*World War II*]
BPR .... Bureau of Public Roads [*Department of Transportation*]
BPR .... Burnable Poison Rod [*Nuclear energy*] (NRCH)
BPR .... Butterworth's Property Reports [*A publication*] (APTA)
BPR .... Bypass Ratio
BPR .... Prince Rupert Public Library, British Columbia [*Library symbol*] [*National Library of Canada*] (NLC)
BPRA .... Baptist Public Relations Association
BPRA .... Burnable Poison Rod Assembly [*Nuclear energy*] (NRCH)
BPRA .... Prince Rupert Regional Archives, Prince Rupert, British Columbia [*Library symbol*] [*National Library of Canada*] (NLC)
BPRACS.... Synod Office, Diocese of Caledonia, Anglican Church of Canada, Prince Rupert, British Columbia [*Library symbol*] [*National Library of Canada*] (NLC)
BPRB .... Beef Promotion and Research Board (EA)
BPRC........ American Bloodpressure Center [*NASDAQ symbol*] (NQ)
BPRC........ Battery Protection and Reconditioning Circuit (MCD)
BPRC........ Byrd Polar Research Center [*Ohio State University*] [*Information service or system*] (IID)
BPRCCS.... Byrd Polar Research Center [*A publication*]
BPRD........ Powell River District Libraries, British Columbia [*Library symbol*] [*National Library of Canada*] (NLC)
BPRDP...... Powell River District Public Library Association, British Columbia [*Library symbol*] [*National Library of Canada*] (NLC)
BPRF .... Birds of Prey Rehabilitation Foundation (EA)
BPRF .... Bulletproof [*Army*] (AABC)
BPRFA ...... Britannia Petite Rabbit Fanciers Association (EA)
B Pr Hist Fr ... Bulletin. Societe Prehistorique Francaise. Etudes et Travaux [*A publication*]
BPRI .... British Polarographic Research Institute
B Prince of Wales Mus West India ... Bulletin. Prince of Wales Museum of Western India [*A publication*]
BPRM........ Museum of Northern British Columbia, Prince Rupert, British Columbia [*Library symbol*] [*National Library of Canada*] (NLC)
BPRMA..... Bank Public Relations and Marketing Association [*Later, BMA*]

BPRMA..... Bibliotheca Primatologica [*A publication*]
BPRO .... Blind Persons Resettlement Officer [*Department of Employment*] [*British*]
BPRO .... Branch Public Relations Office
B Proc .... Baccalaureus Procurationis   (DLA)
B (Providence) ... Bulletin. Rhode Island School of Design. Museum Notes (Providence) [*A publication*]
BPRRB ...... Bulletin of Prosthetics Research [*A publication*]
BPRS .... Brief Psychiatric Rating Scale
BPRS .... National Black Public Relations Society   (EA)
BPR-THM ... Bureau of Public Roads Transport Highway Mobilization [*Federal emergency order*]
BPS........... Bachelor of Professional Studies
B Ps........... Bachelor of Psychology
BPS........... Ballistic Protected Shelter   (MCD)
BPS........... Base Postal Section [*Air Force*]   (AFM)
BPS........... Basic Programming Support [*IBM Corp.*]   (BUR)
BPS........... Basic Programming System
BPS........... Basic Psychological Study   (MCD)
BPS........... Batch Processing System
BPS........... Beacon Processing System
BPS........... Bearing Procurement Specification   (MSA)
BPS........... Beats per Second [*Cardiology*]
BPS........... Behavioral Pharmacology Society   (EA)
BPS........... Beijing Proton Synchrotron [*China*]
BPS........... Belgium Philatelic Society   (EA)
BPS........... Benelux Phlebology Society   (EA)
BPS........... Bhutan Philatelic Society   (EA)
BPS........... Biblical and Patristic Studies [*A publication*]
BPS........... Binary Program Space [*Data processing*]
BPS........... Biophysical Society   (EA)
BPS........... Birmingham Photographic Society. Journal [*A publication*]
BPS........... BITs [*Binary Digits*] per Second [*Data transmission speed*] [*Data processing*]
BPS........... Blanked Picture Signal
BPS........... Bloc Populaire Senegalais [*Senegal*]   (PPW)
BPS........... Blowout Pipe System
BPS........... Book Promotion Society [*Canada*]
BPS........... Booklet Pane Society [*Defunct*]   (EA)
BPS........... Boost Pump Start   (MCD)
BPS........... Brain Protein Solvent [*Biochemistry*]
BPS........... Breaths per Second
BPS........... British Pharmacological Society
BPS........... British Photobiology Society
BPS........... British Phycological Society
BPS........... British Plain Spirits
BPS........... British Postmark Society   (EA)
BPS........... British Psychological Society   (EAIO)
BPS........... Bulletin. Psychonomic Society [*A publication*]
BPS........... Buoy Power Supply
BPS........... Bureau of Product Safety [*FDA*]
BPS........... Business and Professional Software [*Software publisher*]
BPS........... Bytes per Second [*Data processing*]   (BUR)
BPS........... Episcopal Divinity School, Cambridge, MA [*OCLC symbol*]   (OCLC)
BPS........... Porto Seguro [*Brazil*] [*Airport symbol*]   (OAG)
BPSA......... Bachelor of Public School Art
BPSBA7 .... British Pteridological Society. Bulletin [*A publication*]
BPSBDA ... Benchmark Papers in Systematic and Evolutionary Biology [*A publication*]
BPSC .... Bearing per Standard Compass [*Navigation*]
BPSC .... Bulletin. Philological Society of Calcutta [*A publication*]
BPSD......... Barrels per Stream Day [*Also, BSD*]
BPSH......... Border Patrol Sector Headquarters
BP Shield Int ... BP [*British Petroleum*] Shield International [*A publication*]
BPSI .... Bank Personnel Selection Inventory [*Test*]
BPSI .... Bell Petroleum Services, Incorporated [*NASDAQ symbol*]   (NQ)
BPSI .... BITs [*Binary Digits*] per Square Inch [*Data density measurement*] [*Data processing*]
B Psic Appl ... Bollettino di Psicologia Applicata [*A publication*]
BPSJ......... Balanced Pressure Swivel Joint
BPSK .... Binary Phase-Shift Keying [*Data processing*]   (IEEE)
BPSM .... Bachelor of Public School Music
BPSM .... Bulk Presorted Mail   (ADA)
BPSMLA... Bulletin. Pennsylvania State Modern Language Association [*A publication*]
BPSN........ Budget Project Symbol Number   (AFM)
BPSO........ Base Personnel Staff Officer [*Air Force*] [*British*]
BPSP .... Bollettino. Societa Pavese di Storia Patria [*A publication*]
BPSS......... Barge-Mounted Production and Storage System   (DS)
BPSS......... Base Perimeter Security System
BPSS......... Base Procurement Service Stores [*Air Force*]   (AFM)
BPSS......... Biopack Subsystem [*NASA*]   (KSC)
B Ps Sc....... Bachelor of Psychic Sciences
BPSTBS.... Bulletin. Academie Polonaise des Sciences. Serie des Sciences de la Terre [*A publication*]
BPSTGC.... Bearing per Steering Gyro Compass [*Navigation*]
B Ps Th...... Bachelor of Psychotherapy
BPsych....... Bachelor of Psychology
B Psychol... Bulletin de Psychologie [*A publication*]

B Psychon S ... Bulletin. Psychonomic Society [*A publication*]
BPSYDB.... Bibliographia Phytosociologica Syntaxonomica [*A publication*]
BPsys .... Blood Pressure, Systolic
BPT........... Bachelor of Physical Therapy
BPT........... Balanced Property Trust   (ADA)
BPT........... Bandpass Transformer
BPT........... Base Point
BPT........... Bathophenanthroline [*Analytical chemistry*]
BPT........... Battle Practice Target [*Obsolete*] [*Navy*] [*British*]
BPT........... Beach Party Team [*Navy*]   (NVT)
BPT........... Beaumont/Port Arthur [*Texas*] [*Airport symbol*]   (OAG)
BPT........... Beginning Procedure Turn [*Aviation*]   (FAAC)
BPT........... Best Practicable Technology [*Environmental Protection Agency*]
BPT........... BGR Precious Metals, Inc. [*Toronto Stock Exchange symbol*]
BPT........... Bipost
BPT........... Bis(pyridiniumtrimethylene) [*Dichloride*] [*Biochemistry*]
BPT........... Blade Passage Tone [*Aviation*]
BPT........... Body Point   (MCD)
BPT........... Boiling Point
BPT........... Borderline Pumping Temperature [*Automotive engineering*]
BPT........... BP Prudhoe Bay Royalty [*NYSE symbol*]   (SPSG)
BPT........... Breakpoint
BPT........... Bridgeport [*Connecticut*] [*Seismograph station code, US Geological Survey*] [*Closed*]   (SEIS)
BPT........... Bridgeport Public Library, Bridgeport, CT [*OCLC symbol*]   (OCLC)
BPT........... Bronchial Provocation Test [*Medicine*]
BPT........... Journal of Contemporary Business [*A publication*]
BPTEU...... Bombay Port Trust Employees' Union [*India*]
BP Th........ Beitraege zur Praktischen Theologie [*A publication*]
bPTH .... Bovine Parathyroid Hormone [*Endocrinology*]
BPTI .... Bovine Pancreatic Trypsin Inhibitor [*Biochemistry*]
BPTJ......... Biuletyn Polskiego Towarzystwa Jezykoznawczego [*A publication*]
BPTO........ BMEWS [*Ballistic Missile Early Warning System*] Performance Test Outline
BPU .... Base Production Unit [*Army*]   (AABC)
BPU .... Basic Pole Unit
BPU .... Basic Processing Unit   (CET)
BPU .... Beijing Polytechnic University [*China*]
BPU .... BITBLT [*Binary Digit-Block Transfer*] Processing Unit
BPU .... Botswana Progressive Union
BPU .... Bountiful Peak [*Utah*] [*Seismograph station code, US Geological Survey*] [*Closed*]   (SEIS)
BPUA .... Biological Papers. University of Alaska [*A publication*]
BPUASR ... Biological Papers. University of Alaska. Special Report [*A publication*]
BPUPBQ ... Bilten Poslovnog Udruzenja Proizvodaca Biljnih Ulja i Masti [*A publication*]
BPV........... Bipropellant Valve   (MCD)
B + PV ...... Boiler and Pressure Vessel [*Nuclear energy*]   (NRCH)
BPV........... Bordetella Pertussis Vaccine
BPV........... Bovine Papillomavirus [*Veterinary medicine*]
BPV........... Bovine Papillomavirus Vaccine [*Veterinary medicine*]
BPV........... Bypass Valve   (NRCH)
BPVA........ Bay of Pigs Veterans Association   (EA)
BP(Vet)...... British Pharmacopoeia (Veterinary)
BPW .... Bare Platinum Wire
BPW .... Berliner Philologische Wochenschrift [*A publication*]
BPW .... Board of Public Works
BPW .... Business and Professional Women's Foundation
BPWC....... Black Political Women's Caucus
BPWF .... Business and Professional Women's Foundation   (EA)
BPWMA.... Buff and Polishing Wheel Manufacturers Association [*Defunct*]
BPWR....... Burnable Poison Water Reactor   (IEEE)
BPWR....... Compania Boliviana de Energia Electrica SA [*NASDAQ symbol*]   (NQ)
BPWS .... Banked Position Withdrawal Sequence   (IEEE)
BPW/USA ... National Federation of Business and Professional Women's Clubs   (EA)
B Py .... Bachelor of Pedagogy
BPY........... Besalampy [*Madagascar*] [*Airport symbol*]   (OAG)
BPY........... Bipyridine [*Also, BIPY*] [*Organic chemistry*]
BPY........... BPI Resources Ltd. [*Vancouver Stock Exchange symbol*]
BPYBA3 ... British Phycological Bulletin [*Later, British Phycological Journal*] [*A publication*]
BPYCA ..... Rikagaku Kenkyusho Iho [*A publication*]
BPYKA ..... Biophysik [*Berlin*] [*A publication*]
BPZ........... Berufspaedagogische Zeitschrift [*A publication*]
BPZBA ..... Bulletin. Societe des Amis des Sciences et des Lettres de Poznan. Serie B. Sciences Mathematiques et Naturelles [*A publication*]
BQ............. Baba Qama [*or Bava Qamma*]   (BJA)
BQ............. Back-Up Quantity
BQ............. Banknote Quarterly [*A publication*]
BQ............. Baptist Quarterly [*A publication*]
BQ............. Bearque [*Bark, Boat*] [*French*]
B & Q .... Barracks and Quarters [*Army*]
BQ............. Base Quota
BQ............. Basis Quote [*Investment term*]

Bq .... Becquerel [*Symbol*] [*SI unit of activity of ionizing radiation source*]
BQ .... Before Queues [*Referring to pre-World War II period*] [*Slang*] [*British*]
BQ .... Bene Quiescat [*May He, or She, Rest Well*] [*Latin*]
BQ .... Bioquant
BQ .... Briquet
BQ .... Empresa Aeromar [*Dominican Republic*] [*ICAO designator*]   (FAAC)
BQ .... Quesnel Library, British Columbia [*Library symbol*] [*National Library of Canada*]   (BIB)
BQA .... Bureau of Quality Assurance [*HEW*]
BQAP .... Bilevel Quality Assurance Program [*NASA*]   (KSC)
BQC .... Charlotte, NC [*Location identifier*] [*FAA*]   (FAAL)
BQC .... Qantel Corp. [*NYSE symbol*]   (SPSG)
BQCM .... Queen Charlotte Islands Museum, Queen Charlotte, British Columbia [*Library symbol*] [*National Library of Canada*]   (NLC)
BQE .... Toledo, OH [*Location identifier*] [*FAA*]   (FAAL)
BQG .... Woodbridge, VA [*Location identifier*] [*FAA*]   (FAAL)
BQK .... Brunswick [*Georgia*] [*Airport symbol*]   (OAG)
BQK .... Brunswick, GA [*Location identifier*] [*FAA*]   (FAAL)
BQL .... Bank Markazi Iran. Bulletin [*A publication*]
BQL .... Basic Query Language [*Data processing*]   (BUR)
BQL .... Batch Query Language [*Programming language*]
BQL .... Boulia [*Australia*] [*Airport symbol*]   (OAG)
BQLI .... Brooklyn, Queens, Long Island [*Section of New York Times*]
BQM .... Airborne Drone Missile Target [*DOD missile designation*]   (MCD)
BQM .... Base Quartermaster [*Marine Corps*]
BQM .... Becker Junior College, Worcester, MA [*OCLC symbol*] [*Inactive*]   (OCLC)
BQM .... Louisville, KY [*Location identifier*] [*FAA*]   (FAAL)
BQM .... Quesnel and District Museum, Quesnel, British Columbia [*Library symbol*] [*National Library of Canada*]   (NLC)
BQMS .... Battery Quartermaster-Sergeant [*British*]
BQN .... Aguadilla [*Puerto Rico*] [*Airport symbol*]   (OAG)
BQO .... Belgian Business [*A publication*]
BQO .... Bouna [*Ivory Coast*] [*Airport symbol*]   (OAG)
BQP .... Bastrop, LA [*Location identifier*] [*FAA*]   (FAAL)
BQQ .... Barra [*Brazil*] [*Airport symbol*]   (OAG)
BQR .... Bodleian Quarterly Record [*A publication*]
BQR .... Quick & Reilly Group, Inc. [*NYSE symbol*]   (SPSG)
BQRP .... Bulletin des Questions et Reponses Parlementaires [*A publication*]
BQS .... Bright QUASAR Survey [*Astronomy*]
BQSI .... Brooklyn-Queens-Staten Island Health Sciences Group [*Library network*]
BQU .... Bangladesh Bank. Bulletin [*A publication*]
BQU .... Business Quarterly [*A publication*]
Bque .... Banque [*Bank*] [*French*]
BQUE .... Barque [*Bark, Boat*] [*French*]
BQV .... Bartlett Cove, AK [*Location identifier*] [*FAA*]   (FAAL)
bR .... Bacteriorhodopsin [*Biochemistry*]
B or R .... Bales or Rolls [*Freight*]
BR .... Ballast Rack   (MCD)
BR .... Baltic Review [*New York*] [*A publication*]
BR .... Baltimore City Reports [*A publication*]   (DLA)
BR .... Banco Regis [*or Reginae*] [*The King's (or Queen's) Bench*] [*Latin*]
BR .... Bank Rate [*Banking*]
BR .... Bank Robbery
BR .... Bankroll [*Slang*]
BR .... Bankruptcy Register [*A publication*]   (DLA)
BR .... Bankruptcy Reports [*A publication*]   (DLA)
BR .... Bar
BR .... Baron   (ROG)
BR .... Barrage Rocket   (NATG)
BR .... Barrel Roll   (CINC)
BR .... Barry Railway [*Wales*]
BR .... Base Reclamation [*of critical materials*]   (AAG)
BR .... Base Register   (CMD)
BR .... Basic Research
BR .... Bathroom
BR .... Bats Right-Handed [*Baseball*]
BR .... Bayerische Rundfunk [*Radio network*] [*West Germany*]
BR .... Beam Ride   (AAG)
BR .... Bed Rest [*Medicine*]
BR .... Bedroom
BR .... Bedroom Steward [*In the first class aboard an ocean liner*]
BR .... Beevers-Ross [*Beta-alumina crystallography*]
BR .... Belgian Reactor
BR .... Belorussian Review [*A publication*]
BR .... Bend Radius   (MCD)
BR .... Benedictine Review [*A publication*]
BR .... Bennington Review [*A publication*]
BR .... Bereshit Rabba   (BJA)
BR .... Biblia Rabbinica [*A publication*]   (BJA)
BR .... Biblical Research [*A publication*]
BR .... Biblical Review [*A publication*]

Br .... Biblioteca Nacional, Rio De Janeiro, Brazil [*Library symbol*] [*Library of Congress*]   (LCLS)
BR .... Bibliotheca Romana [*A publication*]
BR .... Biblisches Reallexikon [*A publication*]   (BJA)
BR .... Bilateral Impedance Rheograph [*Instrumentation*]
BR .... Bilirubin [*Biochemistry*]
BR .... Bill of Rights
BR .... Bills Receivable [*Business term*]
BR .... Binder
BR .... Bioassay Reagent
BR .... Biographical Register [*Australian National University*]
bR .... Biological Reagent [*Peptide grade*]
BR .... Biological Research   (NVT)
BR .... Bioresmethrin [*Biochemistry*]
BR .... Bird Resistant [*Sorghum variety*]
BR .... Birmingham Repair [*British military*]   (DMA)
BR .... Birmingham Revision [*of BNA*] [*Medicine*] [*British*]
BR .... Birthrate
BR .... BIT [*Binary Digit*] Rate [*Data transmission speed*] [*Data processing*]   (MCD)
BR .... Blackout Restrictions [*British*] [*World War II*]
BR .... Blade Rate   (NVT)
BR .... Block Replacement
BR .... Board of Rabbis
BR .... Board of Review [*Army*]
BR .... Body Rot of Papaya [*Plant pathology*]
BR .... Boiler Room
BR .... Boilermaker [*Navy rating*]
BR .... Boiling Range
BR .... Bombardier [*British*]   (ADA)
BR .... Bomber Reconnaissance Aircraft
BR .... Bond Rating [*Investment term*]
BR .... Bone Resorption
BR .... Book Rack   (MSA)
BR .... Book of Reference
BR .... Book Report [*A publication*]
BR .... Book Review
BR .... Booster-Regulator [*NASA*]
B/R .... Bordeaux or Rouen [*Shipping*]   (ROG)
BR .... Border Regiment [*British*]
BR .... Botanical Review [*A publication*]
BR .... Bottom Reflection [*Navy*]   (NVT)
BR .... Braced and Racked [*Freight*]
BR .... Brake Relay
BR .... Bralorne Resources Ltd. [*Toronto Stock Exchange symbol*]
BR .... Branch   (EY)
BR .... Branch Report
BR .... Brass
BR .... Bratschen [*Viola*]
BR .... Brazil [*ANSI two-letter standard code*]   (CNC)
BR .... Brazilian Register [*Ship Classification Society of Brazil*]   (DS)
B & R .... Bread and Roses   (EA)
BR .... Break Request [*Data processing*]   (MDG)
bR .... Breakdown [*Electronics*]
BR .... Breath [*Medicine*]
BR .... Breathing Reserve   (ADA)
BR .... Breeder Reactor
BR .... Breeding Ratio [*Nuclear energy*]   (NRCH)
BR .... Brick Construction
BR .... Bridge [*Interconnects computer networks*]
BR .... Bridging Key [*on Dial Assistance Switchboard*]   (CET)
br .... Brief
BR .... Briefing Room [*Navy*]
BR .... Brig
BR .... Brigadas Revolucionarias [*Revolutionary Brigades*] [*Portugal*] [*Political party*]   (PPE)
Br .... Brigadier [*British military*]   (DMA)
BR .... Brigate Rosse [*Red Brigades*] [*Italy*]   (PD)
BR .... Britain   (ROG)
BR .... British
BR .... British Aircraft Corp. Ltd. [*ICAO aircraft manufacturer identifier*]   (ICAO)
BR .... British Caledonian Airways Ltd. [*ICAO designator*]   (OAG)
BR .... British Railways
BR .... British Revision [*of BNA*] [*Medicine*]
BR .... Broad [*Also, B*] [*Spectral*]
BR .... Broadcasting Reports [*Australia*] [*A publication*]
BR .... Broche [*Sewn*] [*Of books*] [*French*]
Br .... Bromine [*Chemical element*]
br .... Bromo [*As substituent on nucleoside*] [*Biochemistry*]
Br .... Bromocriptine [*Pharmacology*]
Br .... Bronchitis [*Medicine*]
BR .... Bronze
Br .... Brooke's Abridgment [*England*] [*A publication*]   (DSA)
BR .... Brooklyn Law Review [*A publication*]
BR .... Brother
BR .... Brown [*Thoroughbred racing*]
BR .... Brown
Br .... Bruce's Scotch Court of Session Reports [*1714-15*] [*A publication*]   (DLA)
BR .... Brush   (MSA)

BR .... Brymon Airways [*British*]
BR .... Bucimul Romanu [*A publication*]
BR .... Bucknell Review [*A publication*]
BR .... Budapest Regisegei [*A publication*]
B & R .... Budget and Reporting   (NRCH)
BR .... Buffer Register [*Data processing*]
BR .... Bugler
BR .... Builder's Risk [*Insurance*]
B and R ...... Building and Repair [*Red Cross Disaster Services*]
BR .... Bulgarian Register of Shipping   (DS)
BR .... Bulkhead Receptacle
BR .... Bullarium Romanum [*A publication*]
BR .... Bureau of Reclamation [*Later, WPRS*] [*Department of the Interior*]
BR .... Burlington Resources, Inc. [*NYSE symbol*]   (SPSG)
br .... Burma [*MARC country of publication code*] [*Library of Congress*] [*IYRU nationality code*]   (LCCP)
BR .... Business Review [*A publication*]   (APTA)
BR .... Business Review Weekly [*A publication*]   (ADA)
BR .... Business Roundtable   (EA)
BR .... Butadiene Rubber
BR .... Mist [*Meteorology*]   (FAAC)
Br .... Quebec Official Reports, Queen's Bench [*1892-1900*] [*Canada*] [*A publication*]   (DLA)
BR .... Rossland Public Library, British Columbia [*Library symbol*] [*National Library of Canada*]   (BIB)
BR .... United States Bankruptcy Court   (DLA)
BR .... West's Bankruptcy Reporter [*A publication*]   (DLA)
BR1 .... Boilermaker, First Class [*Navy rating*]
BR2 .... Boilermaker, Second Class [*Navy rating*]
BR3 .... Boilermaker, Third Class [*Navy rating*]
BRA .... Asheville, NC [*Location identifier*] [*FAA*]   (FAAL)
BRA .... Bacterial Releasing Agent [*Microbiology*]
BRA .... Bankruptcy Reform Act [*1978*]
BRA .... Barreiras [*Brazil*] [*Airport symbol*]   (OAG)
BRA .... Barrier Reef Airways [*Australia*]
BRA .... Base Rate Area [*Telecommunications*]   (TEL)
BRA .... Beam Ride Actuator
BRA .... Bee Research Association [*Later, IBRA*]
BRA .... Beitraege zur Religionsgeschichte des Altertums [*Halle/S.*] [*A publication*]
BRA .... Bench Replaceable Assembly   (MCD)
BRA .... Bennett, Richard A., Stockton CA [*STAC*]
BRA .... Beta-Resorcylic Acid [*Organic chemistry*]
BRA .... Biomira, Inc. [*Toronto Stock Exchange symbol*]
BRA .... Bombing Restriction Area [*British military*]   (DMA)
BRA .... Booster Release Actuator   (MCD)
BRA .... Boston Redevelopment Authority
BRA .... Bracciera [*Ship's rigging*]   (ROG)
Bra .... Bracton. De Legibus Angliae [*A publication*]   (DLA)
Bra .... Brady's English History [*1648*] [*A publication*]   (DLA)
BRA .... Brain Research Association [*British*]
bra .... Braj [*MARC language code*] [*Library of Congress*]   (LCCP)
BRA .... Branch Address
BRA .... Branch Always [*Data processing*]
BrA .... Brasil Acucareiro [*A publication*]
BRA .... Brassiere   (DSUE)
BRA .... Bratislava [*Czechoslovakia*] [*Seismograph station code, US Geological Survey*] [*Closed*]   (SEIS)
BRA .... Brazil [*ANSI three-letter standard code*]   (CNC)
BRA .... Brigadier, Royal Artillery [*British*]
BRA .... British Records Association
BRA .... British Resorts Association
BRA .... British Robot Association Ltd.
Br-A .... Bromoamiloride [*Biochemistry*]
BRA .... Building Renovating Association
BRA .... Burden Rate Adjustment   (MCD)
BRA .... Business Rankings Annual [*A publication*]
BRA .... Butterworth's Rating Appeals [*1913-31*] [*England*] [*A publication*]   (DLA)
BRA(AA)... Brigadier, Royal Artillery (Antiaircraft Artillery) [*British and Canadian*]
BRAAT...... Base Recovery After Attack   (MCD)
BRAB........ Brabazon Aircraft [*British*]   (DSUE)
BRAB........ Building Research Advisory Board [*Later, ABBE*] [*National Academy of Sciences*]
Brabantse Folkl ... De Brabantse Folklore [*A publication*]
BRABLB ... Boletin. Real Academia de Buenas Letras de Barcelona [*A publication*]
Br Abr .... Brooke's Abridgment [*England*] [*A publication*]   (DLA)
Br Abstr ..... British Abstracts [*A publication*]
Br Abstr A1 ... British Abstracts A1. General, Physical, and Inorganic Chemistry [*A publication*]
Br Abstr A2 ... British Abstracts A2. Organic Chemistry [*A publication*]
Br Abstr A3 ... British Abstracts A3. Physiology and Biochemistry [*A publication*]
Br Abstr B1 ... British Abstracts B1. Chemical Engineering, Fuels, Metallurgy, Applied Electrochemistry, and Industrial Inorganic Chemistry [*A publication*]
Br Abstr B2 ... British Abstracts B2. Industrial Organic Chemistry [*A publication*]

Br Abstr B3 ... British Abstracts B3. Agriculture, Foods, Sanitation [*A publication*]
Br Abstr C ... British Abstracts C. Analysis and Apparatus [*A publication*]
Br Abstr Med Sci ... British Abstracts of Medical Sciences [*A publication*]
BRAC........ Boletin. Real Academia de Cordoba [*A publication*]
BRAC........ Bomb Release Angle Computer   (MCD)
BRAC........ Bonneville Regional Advisory Council [*Terminated, 1978*] [*Department of Energy*]   (EGAO)
Brac.......... Bracton. De Legibus et Consuetudinibus Angliae [*England*] [*A publication*]   (DLA)
Brac.......... Bracton's Note Book, King's Bench [*1217-40*] [*A publication*]   (DLA)
BrAC......... Breath-Alcohol Concentration [*Sobriety test*]
BRAC........ Britannica Reading Achievement Center
BRAC........ Brotherhood of Railway, Airline, and Steamship Clerks; Freight Handlers; Express and Station Employes   (EA)
BRAC........ Building Regulations Advisory Committee [*British*]
BRACA2.... Brasil Acucareiro [*A publication*]
Brac Aug .... Bracara Augusta. Revista Cultural de Camara Municipal de Braga [*A publication*]
BRACH ..... Brachio [*To the Arm*] [*Pharmacy*]
BRACHS... Institute for Bronx Regional and Community History Studies [*Lehman College of City University of New York*] [*Research center*]
Bra Cit ...... Brady's Historical Treatise on Cities [*A publication*]   (DLA)
Brackish Water Factor Dev ... Brackish Water as a Factor in Development [*A publication*]
Brack Misc ... Brackenridge's Miscellanies [*A publication*]   (DLA)
Brack Tr..... Brackenridge on the Law of Trusts [*A publication*]   (DLA)
Brac LJ ...... Bracton Law Journal [*A publication*]
BRACOB.... Blast Response and Collapse of Buildings   (MCD)
BRA Cor ..... Boletin. Real Academia de Ciencias, Bellas Letras, y Nobles Artes de Cordoba [*A publication*]
BRA Cord .. Boletin. Real Academia de Ciencias, Bellas Letras, y Nobles Artes de Cordoba [*A publication*]
BRACS ...... Blast Resistant Artillery Camouflage Screen   (MCD)
BRACS ...... Broadcasting for Remote Aboriginal Communities Scheme [*Australia*]
BR Act .... Booth on Real Actions [*A publication*]   (DLA)
Bract .... Bracton. De Legibus et Consuetudinibus Angliae [*England*] [*A publication*]   (DLA)
Bract .... Digest of Maxims, by James S. Bracton [*A publication*]   (DLA)
Bracton....... Bracton. De Legibus et Consuetudinibus Angliae [*England*] [*A publication*]   (DLA)
Bracton LJ ... Bracton Law Journal [*A publication*]
BRAD .... Bradens, Inc. [*NASDAQ symbol*]   (NQ)
Brad .... Bradford's New York Surrogate's Court Reports [*A publication*]
Brad .... Bradford's Reports [*1838-41*] [*Iowa*] [*A publication*]   (DLA)
Brad .... Bradford's Somerset Star Chamber [*A publication*]   (DLA)
Brad .... Bradwell's Illinois Appellate Reports [*A publication*]   (DLA)
Brad .... Brady's History of the Succession of the Crown of England [*A publication*]   (DLA)
BRAD .... British Rate and Data
BRAD .... Bureau of Research and Development   (KSC)
Bradb .... Bradbury's Pleading and Practice Reports [*New York*] [*A publication*]   (DLA)
Brad Dis..... Bradby on Distresses [*A publication*]   (DLA)
Bradea Bol Herb Bradeanum ... Bradea. Boletim do Herbarium Bradeanum [*A publication*]
BRADF..... Bradfield [*England*]
Bradf .... Bradford's New York Surrogate's Court Reports [*A publication*]   (DLA)
Bradf .... Bradford's Proceedings in the Court of Star Chamber [*Somerset Record Society Publications, Vol. 27*] [*A publication*]   (DLA)
Bradf .... Bradford's Reports [*1838-41*] [*Iowa*] [*A publication*]   (DLA)
Brad Fight ... Bradley Fighting Vehicle. US Army White Paper, 1986 [*A publication*]
Bradford..... Bradford's Iowa Supreme Court Reports [*1839-41*] [*A publication*]   (DLA)
Bradford Antiq ... Bradford Antiquary [*A publication*]
Bradford's R ... Bradford's New York Surrogate's Court Reports [*A publication*]   (DLA)
Bradford's Sur R ... Bradford's New York Surrogate's Court Reports [*A publication*]   (DLA)
Bradf Rep... Bradford's New York Surrogate's Court Reports [*A publication*]   (DLA)
Bradf Sur ... Bradford's New York Surrogate's Court Reports [*A publication*]   (DLA)
Bradf Surr ... Bradford's New York Surrogate's Court Reports [*A publication*]   (DLA)
Bradf Sur R ... Bradford's New York Surrogate's Court Reports [*A publication*]   (DLA)
Bradl .... Bradley's Rhode Island Reports [*A publication*]   (DLA)
Bradl PB .... Bradley's Point Book [*A publication*]   (DLA)
Bradl (RI) .. Bradley's Rhode Island Reports [*A publication*]   (DLA)
Brad R........ Bradford's New York Surrogate's Court Reports [*A publication*]   (DLA)
Brad Sur..... Bradford's New York Surrogate's Court Reports [*A publication*]   (DLA)

Bradw......... Bradwell's Illinois Appellate Reports [*A publication*]   (DLA)
Brady Ind ... Brady's Index, Arkansas Reports [*A publication*]   (DLA)
Brady's Tr ... Brady's Treatise upon Cities and Boroughs [*A publication*]   (DLA)
B Ra E........ Bachelor of Radio Engineering
BRAE......... Boletin. Real Academia Espanola [*A publication*]
BRAE......... BRAE Corp. [*NASDAQ symbol*]   (NQ)
BrAE......... British Antarctic Expedition [*1898-1900, 1907-09, 1910-13*]
B Ra Eng.... Bachelor of Radio Engineering
BRAF......... Braking Action Fair [*Aviation*]   (FAAC)
BRAFD...... BRL Enterprises, Inc. [*NASDAQ symbol*]   (SPSG)
BRAG .... Black Radical Action Group
BRAG .... Braking Action Good [*Aviation*]   (FAAC)
Br Agric Bull ... British Agricultural Bulletin [*A publication*]
BRAGS...... Bioelectrical Repair and Growth Society   (EA)
BRAH........ Bioengineering and Research to Aid the Handicapped Program [*Washington, DC*] [*National Science Foundation*]   (GRD)
BRAH........ Boletin. Real Academia de la Historia [*A publication*]
Brahms-Stud ... Brahms-Studien [*A publication*]
BRAIA...... Brain. Journal of Neurology [*A publication*]
BRAID....... Bidirectional Reference Array, Internally Derived [*Data processing*]   (DIT)
BRAID....... Buying, Receiving, and Accounts Payable Integrated Data   (MCD)
BRAIN....... Baruch Retrieval of Automated Information for Negotiations [*City University of New York*] [*Information service or system*]   (IID)
BRAIN....... Basic Research in Adaptive Intelligence [*EEC*]
BRAIN....... Bay-Area Random Access Information Network [*Defunct*]   (TSSD)
Brain Behav ... Brain, Behavior, and Evolution [*A publication*]
Brain Behav Evol ... Brain, Behavior, and Evolution [*A publication*]
Brain Behav Res Monogr Ser ... Brain and Behavior Research Monograph Series [*A publication*]
Brain Dev ... Brain and Development [*A publication*]
Bra Ind Soc ... Brabrook. Industrial and Provident Societies [*1869*] [*A publication*]   (DLA)
Brain Dysfunct ... Brain Dysfunction [*A publication*]
Brain Dysfunct Infant Febrile Convulsions Symp ... Brain Dysfunction in Infantile Febrile Convulsions. Symposium [*A publication*]
Brain Lang ... Brain and Language [*A publication*]
Brain LP .... Brainard's Legal Precedents in Land and Mining Cases [*United States*] [*A publication*]   (DLA)
Brain/Mind ... Brain/Mind Bulletin [*A publication*]
Brain Pep ... Brain Peptides [*A publication*]
Brain Res ... Brain Research [*A publication*]
Brain Res Bull ... Brain Research Bulletin [*A publication*]
Brain Res Rev ... Brain Research Reviews [*A publication*]
BRAINS .... Behavior Replication by Analog Instruction of the Nervous System [*Electrical stimulation of the brain*]
Brain Stimul Reward Collect Pap Int Conf ... Brain Stimulation Reward. Collection of Papers Prepared for the International Conference [*A publication*]
BRAINT .... Braintree [*Urban district in England*]
Brain Topogr ... Brain Topography [*A publication*]
Braith........ Jamaica Law Reports (Braithwaite) [*A publication*]   (DLA)
Braith Chy ... Braithwaite. Times of Procedure in Chancery [*1864*] [*A publication*]   (DLA)
Braith Oaths ... Braithwaite. Oaths in Chancery [*2nd ed.*] [*1864*] [*A publication*]   (DLA)
Braith Oaths ... Braithwaite. Oaths in the Supreme Court [*4th ed.*] [*1881*] [*A publication*]   (DLA)
Braith Pr.... Braithwaite. Record and Writ Practice of the Court of Chancery [*1858*] [*A publication*]   (DLA)
Brake FE.... Brake and Front End [*A publication*]
Br Alma Comp ... British Almanac Companion [*A publication*]
BRALUP ... Bureau of Resource Assessment and Land Use Planning
BRAM ...... Blocked Random Access Method   (MCD)
B Ramakr Miss Inst ... Bulletin. Ramakrishna Mission Institute of Culture [*A publication*]
B Rama Miss Inst Cult ... Bulletin. Ramakrishna Mission Institute of Culture [*A publication*]
BRAMATEC ... Brain Mapping Technique
Brame........ Brame's Reports [*66-72 Mississippi*] [*A publication*]   (DLA)
BRAN ...... Braking Action Nil [*Aviation*]   (FAAC)
BRAN ...... [*The*] Brand Companies, Inc. [*NASDAQ symbol*]   (NQ)
BRANA ..... Bumper Recycling Association of North America   (EA)
Branch ...... Branch's Reports [*1 Florida*] [*A publication*]   (DLA)
Branch Max ... Branch's Maxims [*A publication*]   (DLA)
Branch Pr... Branch's Principia Legis et Equitatis [*Maxims*] [*A publication*]   (DLA)
Branch Princ ... Branch's Principia Legis et Equitatis [*Maxims*] [*A publication*]   (DLA)
BRANCHYDRO ... Branch Hydrographic Office [*Navy*]
Brand .... Brandenburg's Reports [*21 Opinions Attorneys-General*] [*A publication*]   (DLA)
Brande........ Brande's Dictionary of Science, Etc. [*A publication*]   (DLA)
Brandenburg Bankr ... Brandenburg's Bankruptcy Digest [*A publication*]   (DLA)
Brandenburg Dig ... Brandenburg's Bankruptcy Digest [*A publication*]   (DLA)
Brand F Attachm ... Brandon on Foreign Attachment [*A publication*]   (DLA)

Brand For Att ... Brandon on Foreign Attachment [*A publication*]   (ILCA)
Brand For Attachm ... Brandon on Foreign Attachment [*A publication*]   (DLA)
Brand May Ct ... Brandon. Practice of the Mayor's Court [*1864*] [*A publication*]   (DLA)
BRANDS... Bright Alphanumeric Display System   (CAAL)
Brandschutz Dtsch Feuerwehrztg ... Brandschutz Deutsche Feuerwehrzeitung [*A publication*]
Brandstofnavorsingsinst S Afr Bull ... Brandstofnavorsingsinstituut van Suid-Afrika. Bulletin [*A publication*]
Brandt Sur ... Brandt on Suretyship and Guaranty [*A publication*]   (DLA)
BRANE...... Bombing RADAR Navigation Equipment
Branntweinwirt ... Branntweinwirtschaft [*A publication*]
Brans Dig... Branson's Digest [*Bombay*] [*A publication*]   (DLA)
Brant......... Brantly's Reports [*80-90 Maryland*] [*A publication*]   (DLA)
Br Antarct Surv Bull ... British Antarctic Survey. Bulletin [*A publication*]
Br Antarct Surv Sci Rep ... British Antarctic Survey. Scientific Reports [*A publication*]
Brantly .... Brantly's Reports [*80-90 Maryland*] [*A publication*]   (DLA)
BRAP........ Braking Action Poor [*Aviation*]   (FAAC)
BRAR........ British Rheumatism and Arthritis Association. Review [*A publication*]
Br Archaeol Abstr ... British Archaeological Abstracts [*A publication*]
BRA Rev .... BRA [*British Rheumatic Association*] Review [*A publication*]
BRAS........ Ballistic Rocket Air Suppression
Bras............ Brasilia [*A publication*]
BRAS........ Brassiere   (DSUE)
BRAS........ Building Research Advisory Service [*Building Research Establishment*] [*Department of Industry*] [*British*]   (DS)
Bras Acucareiro ... Brasil Acucareiro [*A publication*]
BRASC ...... Brotherhood of Railway, Airline, and Steamship Clerks; Freight Handlers; Express and Station Employees
BRASCAN ... Brasil [*Portuguese spelling*] and Canada [*In company name "Brascan Ltd."*]
BRASF ...... Bras D'Or Mines Ltd. [*NASDAQ symbol*]   (NQ)
Bras Flores ... Brasil Florestal [*A publication*]
BRASH...... Behavioral Research Aspects of Safety and Health Working Group [*University of Kentucky*] [*Research center*]   (RCD)
Brasil Acucar ... Brasil Acucareiro [*A publication*]
Brasil Apic ... Brasil Apicola [*A publication*]
Bras-Med... Brasil-Medico [*A publication*]
BRASO...... Branch Aviation Supply Office [*Navy*]
Bras Odont ... Brasil Odontologico [*A publication*]
BRASS....... BEEF [*Base Engineer Emergency Forces*] Reporting, Analysis, and Status System [*Air Force*]   (AFM)
BRASS...... Bistatic RADAR System   (MCD)
BRASS...... Bottom Reflection Active SONAR System
BRASS...... Bridge Rating and Analysis Structural System   (MCD)
BRASS...... Business Reference and Services Section [*American Library Association*]
Brass Ann Arm Forc Yb ... Brassey's Annual and Armed Forces Yearbook [*A publication*]
Brass B....... Brass Bulletin [*A publication*]
Brass Founder Finish ... Brass Founder and Finisher [*A publication*]
Brass Fr ...... Brasseur Francais [*A publication*]
Brass Malt ... Brasserie et Malterie [*A publication*]
Brass Nav A ... Brassey's Naval Annual [*A publication*]
Brass W ...... Brass World and Plater's Guide [*A publication*]
Brass & Wood Q ... Brass and Woodwind Quarterly [*A publication*]
Bras Text ... Brasil Textil [*A publication*]
Br Astron Assoc Circ ... British Astronomical Association. Circular [*A publication*]
BRAT........ Bananas, Rice Cereal, Applesauce, and Toast [*Bland diet*] [*Medicine*]
BRAT......... Bi-Drive Recreational All-Terrain Transporter [*Subaru automobile*]
Bratisl Lek Listy ... Bratislavske Lekarske Listy [*A publication*]
Bra Tr Un ... Brabrook's Law of Trade Unions [*A publication*]   (DLA)
BRATS...... Bottom Refraction Acoustic Telemetry System   (MCD)
Brauerei Wiss Beil ... Brauerei. Wissenschaftliche Beilage [*A publication*]
Brau Ind.... Brau Industrie [*A publication*]
Brau Maelzer ... Brauer und Maelzer [*A publication*]
Brau Malzind ... Brau- und Malzindustrie [*A publication*]
BRAUN ..... Braunton [*England*]
Braunk .... Braunkohle [*A publication*]
Braunkohle Waerme Energ ... Braunkohle, Waerme, und Energie [*A publication*]
Braunschweiger Naturkd Schr ... Braunschweiger Naturkundliche Schriften [*A publication*]
Braunschweig Wiss Ges Abh ... Braunschweigische Wissenschaftliche Gesellschaft. Abhandlungen [*A publication*]
Braunschw Jb ... Braunschweigisches Jahrbuch [*A publication*]
Braunschw Konserv Z ... Braunschweigische Konserven-Zeitung [*A publication*]
Brauwiss...... Brauwissenschaft [*A publication*]
BRAVC...... Baker River Audiovisual Center [*Library network*]
BRAVO ..... Best Range of Aging Verified Oscillator   (MUGU)
BRAVO ..... Business Risk and Value of Operation in Space [*NASA*]   (NASA)
BRAXP...... Braking Action Extremely Poor [*Aviation*]   (FAAC)
Bray .... Brayton's Reports [*Vermont*] [*A publication*]   (DLA)

Bray R........ Brayton's Reports [*Vermont*] [*A publication*]   (DLA)
Brayt .... Brayton's Reports [*Vermont*] [*A publication*]   (ILCA)
Brayton's Rep ... Brayton's Reports [*Vermont*] [*A publication*]   (DLA)
Brayton (VT) ... Brayton's Reports [*Vermont*] [*A publication*]   (DLA)
Brayt Rep... Brayton's Reports [*Vermont*] [*A publication*]   (DLA)
BRAZ........ Brazier   (MSA)
BRAZ........ Brazil
Braz Com Nac Energ Nucl Bol ... Brazil. Comissao Nacional de Energia
    Nuclear. Boletim [*A publication*]
Braz Dep Nac Obras Secas Serv Piscic Publ Ser 1 C ... Brazil. Departamento
    Nacional de Obras Contra as Secas. Servico de Piscicultura.
    Publicacao. Serie 1 C [*A publication*]
Braz Dep Nac Prod Miner Anu Miner Bras ... Brazil. Departamento Nacional
    da Producao Mineral. Anuario Mineral Brasileiro [*A
    publication*]
Braz Dep Nac Prod Miner Bol ... Brazil. Departamento Nacional da Producao
    Mineral. Boletim [*A publication*]
Braz Dep Nac Prod Miner Div Aguas ... Brazil. Departamento Nacional da
    Producao Mineral. Divisao de Aguas. Boletim [*A
    publication*]
Braz Dep Nac Prod Miner Lab Prod Miner Bol ... Brazil. Departamento
    Nacional da Producao Mineral. Laboratorio da Producao
    Mineral. Boletim [*A publication*]
Braz Div Fom Prod Miner Avulso ... Brazil. Divisao de Fomento da Producao
    Mineral. Avulso [*A publication*]
Braz Div Fom Prod Miner Bol ... Brazil. Divisao de Fomento da Producao
    Mineral. Boletim [*A publication*]
Braz Div Fom Prod Miner Mem ... Brazil. Divisao de Fomento da Producao
    Mineral. Memoria [*A publication*]
Braz Div Geol Mineral Avulso ... Brazil. Divisao de Geologia e Mineralogia.
    Avulso [*A publication*]
Braz Div Geol Mineral Notas Prelim Estud ... Brazil. Divisao de Geologia e
    Mineralogia. Notas Preliminares e Estudos [*A publication*]
Braz Econ... Brazilian Economy. Trends and Perspectives [*A publication*]
Braz Econ Stud ... Brazilian Economic Studies [*A publication*]
Braz Escritorio Pesqui Exp Equipe Pedol Fertil Solo Bol Tec ... Brazil.
    Escritorio de Pesquisas e Experimentacao. Equipe de
    Pedologia e Fertilidade da Solo. Boletim Tecnico [*A
    publication*]
Braz Fund Serv Saude Publica Rev ... Brazil. Fundacao Servicos de Saude
    Publica. Revista [*A publication*]
BRAZH ..... Brazier Head
Brazil Camara Deput Bibl Bol ... Brazil. Camara dos Deputados. Biblioteca.
    Boletim [*A publication*]
Brazil Cons Nac Petrol Relat ... Brazil. Conselho Nacional do Petroleo.
    Relatorio [*A publication*]
Brazil Dep Nac Prod Miner Lab Prod Miner Avulso ... Brazil. Departamento
    Nacional da Producao Mineral. Laboratorio da Producao
    Mineral. Avulso [*A publication*]
Brazil Div Geol Mineral Bol ... Brazil. Divisao de Geologia e Mineralogia.
    Boletim [*A publication*]
Brazil Div Geol Mineral Notas Prelim Estud ... Brazil. Divisao de Geologia e
    Mineralogia. Notas Preliminares e Estudos [*A publication*]
Brazilian Bus ... Brazilian Business [*A publication*]
Brazilian Econ Studies ... Brazilian Economic Studies [*A publication*]
Brazil-Med ... Brazil-Medico [*A publication*]
Brazil Minist Minas Energ Dep Nac Prod Miner Bol ... Brazil. Ministerio das
    Minas e Energia. Departamento Nacional da Producao
    Mineral. Boletim [*A publication*]
Brazil S ...... Brazilian Studies [*A publication*]
Braz Inst Agron Nordeste Bol Tec ... Brazil. Instituto Agronomico da
    Nordeste. Boletim Tecnico [*A publication*]
Braz Inst Oleos Bol ... Brazil. Instituto de Oleos. Boletim [*A publication*]
Braz J Bot .. Brazilian Journal of Botany [*A publication*]
Braz J Genet ... Brazilian Journal of Genetics [*A publication*]
Braz J Med Biol Res ... Brazilian Journal of Medical and Biological Research
    [*A publication*]
Braz J Vet Res ... Brazilian Journal of Veterinary Research [*A publication*]
Braz Lab Prod Miner Avulso ... Brazil. Laboratorio da Producao Mineral.
    Avulso [*A publication*]
Braz Lab Prod Miner Bol ... Brazil. Laboratorio da Producao Mineral. Boletim
    [*A publication*]
Braz Minist Agric Cent Tecnol Agric Aliment Bol Tec ... Brazil. Ministerio da
    Agricultura. Centro de Tecnologia Agricola e Alimentar.
    Boletim Tecnico [*A publication*]
Braz Minist Agric Dep Nac Prod Miner Div Fom Prod Miner Bol ... Brazil.
    Ministerio da Agricultura. Departamento Nacional da
    Producao Mineral. Divisao do Fomento da Producao
    Mineral. Boletim [*A publication*]
Braz Minist Agric Dep Nac Prod Miner Lab Prod Miner Bol ... Brazil.
    Ministerio da Agricultura. Departamento Nacional da
    Producao Mineral. Laboratorio da Producao Mineral.
    Boletim [*A publication*]
Braz Serv Espec Saude Publica Rev ... Brazil. Servico Especial de Saude
    Publica. Revista [*A publication*]
Braz Serv Fom Prod Miner Avulso ... Brazil. Servico de Fomento da Producao
    Mineral. Avulso [*A publication*]
Braz Serv Fom Prod Miner Bol ... Brazil. Servico de Fomento da Producao
    Mineral. Boletim [*A publication*]
Braz Serv Inf Agric Estud Tee ... Brazil. Servico de Informacao Agricola.
    Estudos Teemcos [*A publication*]

Braz Supt Desenvolvimento Nordeste Div Geol Bol Estud ... Brazil.
    Superintendencia do Desenvolvimento do Nordeste.
    Divisao de Geologia. Boletim de Estudos [*A publication*]
Braz Supt Desenvolvimento Nordeste Div Geol Ser Geol Econ ... Brazil.
    Superintendencia do Desenvolvimento do Nordeste.
    Divisao de Geologia. Serie Geologia Economica [*A
    publication*]
Braz Supt Desenvolvimento Nordeste Div Geol Ser Geol Espec ... Brazil.
    Superintendencia do Desenvolvimento do Nordeste.
    Divisao de Geologia. Serie Geologia Especial [*A
    publication*]
BRB .... Babe Ruth Baseball   (EA)
BRB .... Ballistic Recoverable Booster   (MCD)
BRB .... Ballistic Reentry Body
BRB .... Barbados [*Seismograph station code, US Geological Survey*]
    [*Closed*]   (SEIS)
BRB .... Barbados [*ANSI three-letter standard code*]   (CNC)
BRB .... Base Rate Boundary [*Telecommunications*]   (TEL)
BRB .... Benefits Review Board [*Department of Labor*]   (OICC)
BRB .... Biopharmaceutics Research Branch [*Washington, DC*]
    [*Department of Health and Human Services*]   (GRD)
BRB .... Brick Brewing Co. Ltd. [*Toronto Stock Exchange symbol*]
BRB .... Bright Red Blood [*Medicine*]
BRB .... British Railways Board
Br & B .... Broderip and Bingham's English Common Pleas Reports [*A
    publication*]   (DLA)
BRB .... Bryant College, Smithfield, RI [*OCLC symbol*]   (OCLC)
BRB .... Building Research Board   (EA)
BRBC........ Burro Red Blood Cells
BRBEBE..... Brain, Behavior, and Evolution [*A publication*]
Br Bee J ..... British Bee Journal [*A publication*]
BrBEV........ [*The*] Broadway Book of English Verse [*A publication*]
BRBF .... Babe Ruth Birthplace Foundation   (EA)
BRBI......... Bulletin. Reserve Bank of India [*A publication*]
BRBIDS..... Bryophytorum Bibliotheca [*A publication*]
Br Birds ..... British Birds [*A publication*]
BRBK......... Brenton Banks, Inc. [*NASDAQ symbol*]   (NQ)
Br Bks Print ... British Books in Print [*A publication*]
Br Bl .... Bremer Archaeologische Blaetter [*A publication*]
BRBOA ..... Brown Boveri Review [*A publication*]
BRBQ .... Checkers Restaurant Group, Inc. [*NASDAQ symbol*]   (NQ)
BRBR......... Big Red Bike Ride [*Fundraising event*] [*British*]
Br Br .... Brunn-Bruckmann [*A publication*]
Br Brev Jud ... Brownlow's Brevia Judicialia, Etc. [*1662*] [*A
    publication*]   (DLA)
Br Brev Jud & Ent ... Brownlow's Brevia Judicialia, Etc. [*1662*] [*A
    publication*]   (DLA)
BRBS .... Benefits Review Board Service (Matthew Bender) [*A
    publication*]   (DLA)
BRBUD ..... Brain Research Bulletin [*A publication*]
BRBUDU .. Brain Research Bulletin [*A publication*]
BR BUR .... British Burma   (DLA)
Br Bus .... British Business [*England*] [*A publication*]
Br Business ... British Business [*A publication*]
BRBY......... Bribery [*FBI standardized term*]
BRBZC ...... Brass, Bronze, or Copper [*Freight*]
BRC .... Banco de la Republica. Revista [*A publication*]
BRC .... Barley Canyon [*New Mexico*] [*Seismograph station code, US
    Geological Survey*]   (SEIS)
BRC .... Baroid Corp. [*NYSE symbol*]   (SPSG)
BRC .... Barrick Resources Corporation [*Toronto Stock Exchange
    symbol*]
BRC .... Base Recovery Course [*Military*]   (NVT)
BRC .... Base Repair Cycle   (MCD)
BRC .... Base Residence Course
BRC .... Behavioral Research Council   (EA)
BRC .... Below Regulatory Concern [*Waste classification*]
BR of C....... [*The*] Belt Railway Co. of Chicago
BRC .... [*The*] Belt Railway Co. of Chicago [*AAR code*]
BRC .... Beveren Rabbit Club [*Defunct*]   (EA)
BRC .... Biological Radio Communications
BRC .... Biological Records Centre [*Institute of Terrestrial Ecology*]
    [*Information service or system*]   (IID)
BRC .... Biological Research Center [*Philippines*]
BRC .... Biomass Research Center [*University of Arkansas*]
BRC .... Biomedical Recovery Capsule   (MUGU)
BRC .... Black Rock Coalition   (EA)
BRC .... Blue Ribbon Coalition [*An association*]   (EA)
BRC .... Boilermaker, Chief [*Navy rating*]
BRC .... Brace   (MSA)
BRC .... Branch Conditional
BRC .... Breeder Reactor Corporation
BRC .... Bristol Community College, Fall River, MA [*OCLC
    symbol*]   (OCLC)
BRC .... British Ruling Cases [*A publication*]   (DLA)
BRC .... Broadcast Rating Council [*Later, EMRC*]
BRC .... Brooks Resources Corp. [*Vancouver Stock Exchange symbol*]
BRC .... Brotherhood of Railway Carmen of America [*Later, BRC of US
    & C*] [*AFL-CIO*]
BRC .... Brownstone Revival Committee   (EA)
BRC .... Budget Review Committee

BRC .... Burlingame Research Center (MCD)
BRC .... Burroughs Corporation (AAG)
BRC .... Business Reply Card [Advertising]
BRC .... Business Research Corporation [Boston, MA] [Information service or system] (IID)
BRC .... Royal Roads Military College, Victoria, British Columbia [Library symbol] [National Library of Canada] (NLC)
BRC .... San Carlos De Bariloche [Argentina] [Airport symbol] (OAG)
BRC of A.... Brotherhood of Railway Carmen of America [Later, BRC of US & C] [AFL-CIO] (EA)
BRCA........ Bryce Canyon National Park
Br Cactus & Succulent J ... British Cactus and Succulent Journal [A publication]
Br Cast Iron Res Assoc Jrna Res Dev ... British Cast Iron Research Association. Journal of Research and Development [A publication]
Br Cave Res Assoc Trans ... British Cave Research Association. Transactions [A publication]
BRCC........ Barwon Regional Consultative Council [Australia]
BRCC........ Bovine Research Center at Cornell [Cornell University] [Research center] (RCD)
BRCC........ Bristol Research Corp. [NASDAQ symbol] (NQ)
Br CC .... British [or English] Crown Cases [A publication] (DLA)
Br CC .... Brown's Chancery Cases [England] [A publication] (DLA)
BRCD .... Braced
BRCE........ Bureau de Recherche et de Consultation en Education [Bureau of Research and Consultation in Education] [Canada]
Br Ceram Abstr ... British Ceramic Abstracts [A publication]
Br Ceram Rev ... British Ceramic Review [England] [A publication]
Br Cer Res Assoc Spec Publ ... British Ceramic Research Association. Special Publications [A publication]
BRCH .... Branch (ADA)
Br Ch.......... Brennstoff-Chemie [A publication]
BRCH .... Broach (MSA)
Br Chem Abstr A ... British Chemical Abstracts. A. Pure Chemistry [A publication]
Br Chem Abstr B ... British Chemical Abstracts. B. Applied Chemistry [A publication]
Br Chem Eng ... British Chemical Engineering [A publication]
Br Chem Engng ... British Chemical Engineering [A publication]
Br Chem Engng Process Technol ... British Chemical Engineering and Process Technology [A publication]
Br Chem Eng Process Technol ... British Chemical Engineering and Process Technology [A publication]
BRCI.......... Bulletin. Research Council of Israel [A publication]
Br Claywkr ... British Clayworker [A publication]
BRCM .... Boilermaker, Master Chief [Navy rating]
BRCN .... [An] Elizabeth Barrett Browning Concordance [A publication]
BRCO .... Brady [W. H.] Company [Milwaukee, WI] [NASDAQ symbol] (NQ)
Br Coal Util Res Ass Mon Bull ... British Coal Utilisation Research Association. Monthly Bulletin [A publication]
Br Col........ Brevet-Colonel
Br & Col...... British and Colonial Prize Cases [A publication] (DLA)
Br Col........ British Columbia (ILCA)
Br Colon Drug ... British and Colonial Druggist [A publication]
Br & Col Pr Cas ... British and Colonial Prize Cases [A publication] (DLA)
Br Columbia Med J ... British Columbia Medical Journal [A publication]
Br Columb Libr Q ... British Columbia Library Quarterly [A publication]
Br Com....... Broom. Common Law [9th ed.] [1896] [A publication] (DLA)
Br Commun Electron ... British Communications and Electronics [England] [A publication]
Br Cons Law ... Broom. Constitutional Law [3rd ed.] [1885] [A publication] (DLA)
Br Constr Eng ... British Constructional Engineer [A publication]
Br Corrosion J ... British Corrosion Journal [A publication]
Br Corros J ... British Corrosion Journal [A publication]
Br Council News ... British Council News [A publication]
Br Coy........ Bearer Company [British military] (DMA)
BRCP........ Business Records Holding Corp. [NASDAQ symbol] (SPSG)
BRCPA...... Biological Reviews. Cambridge Philosophical Society [A publication]
BRCR........ Brices Crossroads National Battlefield Site
Br Cr Ca..... British [or English] Crown Cases [A publication] (DLA)
Br Cr Cas ... British [or English] Crown Cases [A publication] (DLA)
Br Crop Prot Counc Monogr ... British Crop Protection Council. Monograph [A publication]
BRCS........ Bahamas Red Cross Society (EAIO)
BRCS........ Basic Reference Coordinate System (MCD)
BRCS......... BMEWS [Ballistic Missile Early Warning System] Rearward Communications System (AFM)
BRCS........ Boilermaker, Senior Chief [Navy rating]
BRCS........ British Red Cross Society
BRCSDT ... Australia. Commonwealth Scientific and Industrial Research Organisation. Land Resources Laboratories. Division of Soils. Biennial Report [A publication]
BRCT........ Burlington Randomized Controlled Trial [Criterion for medical evaluation]
BRC of US & C ... Brotherhood of Railway Carmen of the United States and Canada [AFL-CIO] (EA)
BRD .... Ball Reduction Drive

BRD .... Base Remount Depot [British military] (DMA)
BRD .... Base [or Basic] Retirement Date [Air Force]
BRD .... Bellofram Rolling Diaphragm
BRD .... Binary Rate Divider
BRD .... Blank Recording Disc
BRD .... Board
BRD .... Bomb Release Distance [Army] (AABC)
BRD .... Book Review Digest [Information service or system] [A publication]
BRD .... Booster Requirements Document
BRD .... Borderline
BRD .... Bradner Resources Ltd. [Vancouver Stock Exchange symbol]
BRD .... Braid (KSC)
BRD .... Brainerd [Minnesota] [Airport symbol] (OAG)
BRD .... Brake Die (MCD)
Brd .... Bread [Dietetics]
BRD .... Bridge (ROG)
BRD .... Broadband Subsystem
BRD .... Brodart Co. [ACCORD] [UTLAS symbol]
BRD .... Brooder[s] [Freight]
BRD .... Bundesrepublik Deutschland [Federal Republic of Germany]
BRD .... Ragan [Brad], Inc. [AMEX symbol] (SPSG)
BRDA .... Boxboard Research and Development Association (EA)
BRDAA ...... Beitraege zur Radioastronomie [A publication]
BRDAA ...... Bicycle Ride Directors Association of America (EA)
BRDAC...... Building Research and Development Advisory Committee [Australia]
BRDC .... Bare Refractory, Double Containment [Boiler] [NASA]
BRDC .... Bureau of Research and Development Center [FAA] (AAG)
BRDCST ... Broadcast
Brdcstng...... Broadcasting [A publication]
BRDEC...... Belvoir Research, Development, and Engineering Center [Fort Belvoir, VA] [Army] (RDA)
Br Decorator ... British Decorator [A publication]
Br Den Annu ... British Dental Annual [A publication]
Br Dental J ... British Dental Journal [A publication]
Br Dent J ... British Dental Journal [A publication]
Br Dent Surg Assist ... British Dental Surgery Assistant [A publication]
Brd Ex....... Bread Exchange [Dietetics]
BRDF........ Biomedical Research Defense Fund (EA)
BRDG .... Biomedical Research Development Grants
BRDG .... Breeding
BRDG .... Bridge (KSC)
BRDGAT.... Brewers Digest [A publication]
BRDGSCIT ... Bridge Excitation
BRDIA...... Bulletin on Rheumatic Diseases [A publication]
BRDL........ Brendle's, Inc. [Elkin, NC] [NASDAQ symbol] (NQ)
BRDM .... Soviet Amphibious Armored Reconnaissance Vehicle (MCD)
BRDN .... Brandon Systems Corp. [NASDAQ symbol] (NQ)
BRDP........ Blue Ribbon Defense Panel
BRDR .... Breeder
BRDSPL.... Bollettino. Regia Deputazione di Storia Patria per la Liguria [A publication]
BRDSPU ... Bollettino. Regia Deputazione di Storia Patria per l'Umbria [A publication]
BRDT .... Bayesian Reliability Demonstration Test [Data processing]
BRDTH ..... Breadth
BrDU .... Bromodeoxyuridine [Also, BDU, BDUR] [Biochemistry]
BRDY .... Brandywine Sports, Inc. [NASDAQ symbol] (NQ)
B Re........... Bachelor of Religion
BRE .... Bachelor of Religious Education
BRE .... Beam Ride Error
BRe .... Biblia Revuo [A publication] (BJA)
BRe .... Biblical Research [A publication] (BJA)
BRE .... Bore [Freight]
BRE .... BRE Properties Cl A [NYSE symbol] (SPSG)
BRE .... Bremen [West Germany] [Airport symbol] (OAG)
BRE .... Breslau [Wroclaw] [Poland] [Seismograph station code, US Geological Survey] [Closed] (SEIS)
bre .... Breton [MARC language code] [Library of Congress] (LCCP)
BRE .... Brewsterite [A zeolite]
BRE .... British Rail Engineering
BRE .... Brower Exploration, Inc. [Vancouver Stock Exchange symbol]
BRE .... Building Research Establishment [Research center] [British] (IRC)
BRE .... Bulletin of Export Registration [Export license] [Portugal] (IMH)
BRE .... Bureau of Railway Economics [Later, AAR]
BRE .... Bureau of Recruiting and Examining [Civil Service Commission]
BRE .... Bureau of Research and Engineering [US Postal Service]
BRE .... Business Reply Envelope [Advertising]
BR & EA .... Banking Research and Economic Analysis [Unit] [Department of the Treasury] (GRD)
BREACH... Battlefield Related Evaluation of Countermeasure Hardware [Model] (MCD)
Bread Manuf WA ... Bread Manufacturer and Pastrycook of Western Australia [A publication] (APTA)
B Real Acad ... Boletin. Real Academia de la Historia [A publication]
Breast Cancer Res Treat ... Breast Cancer Research and Treatment [A publication]

Breast Dis Breast ... Breast. Diseases of the Breast [*A publication*]
Breast Feed Mother ... Breast Feeding and the Mother [*A publication*]
BREATHE ... Breathers for the Reduction of Atmospheric Hazards to the Environment [*Student legal action organization*]
BREC......... Bills Recoverable [*Business term*]   (ADA)
BREC......... Brooks Resources Corp. [*NASDAQ symbol*]   (NQ)
Brech.......... [*Johannes*] Brechaeus [*Flourished, 16th century*] [*Authority cited in pre-1607 legal work*]   (DSA)
BRECH PROM ... Breach of Promise [*Legal term*]   (DLA)
BrechtH .... Brecht Heute - Brecht Today [*A publication*]
Brecht J .... Brecht-Jahrbuch [*A publication*]
BRECK...... Brecknockshire [*County in Wales*]   (ROG)
Br Ecol Soc Symp ... British Ecological Society. Symposium [*A publication*]
BRECOM ...... Broadcast Radio Emergency Communication [*Air Force*]
BRECONS ...... Brecknockshire [*County in Wales*]   (ROG)
BR Ed......... Bachelor of Religious Education
Brederod .... [*Petrus Cornelius de*] Brederode [*Flourished, 16th century*] [*Authority cited in pre-1607 legal work*]   (DSA)
BRE Dig..... BRE [*Building Research Establishment*] Digest [*A publication*]
Br Educ Index ... British Education Index [*A publication*]
Br Educ Res J ... British Educational Research Journal [*A publication*]
B Re E......... Bachelor of Refrigeration Engineering
Breeder's Gaz ... Breeder's Gazette [*A publication*]
BREEMA .. British Radio and Electronic Equipment Manufacturers Association   (DS)
B Re Eng.... Bachelor of Refrigeration Engineering
Breese .... Breese's Illinois Reports [*1 Illinois*] [*A publication*]   (DLA)
Breese .... Breese's Illinois Supreme Court Reports [*1 Illinois*] [*1819-31*] [*A publication*]   (DLA)
BREF .... Book Review Editors File [*University Press of New England*] [*Information service or system*]   (IID)
B Reg.......... Bankrupt Register [*A publication*]   (DLA)
BREL......... Boeing Radiation Effect Laboratory
BREMA..... British Radio and Electronic Equipment Manufacturers Association [*Formerly, British Radio Equipment Manufacturers Association*]
Brem A Bl .. Bremer Archaeologische Blaetter [*A publication*]
Bremer Beitr Naturwiss ... Bremer Beitraege zur Naturwissenschaft [*A publication*]
Bremer Briefe Chem ... Bremer Briefe zur Chemie [*A publication*]
BREN .... Bare Reactor Experiment at Nevada
BREN .... Brenco, Inc. [*NASDAQ symbol*]   (NQ)
BREN .... Brno-Enfield [*Machine gun*]
Br Engine Tech Rep ... British Engine Technical Reports [*A publication*]
Br Eng Tech Rep ... British Engine Technical Reports [*A publication*]
Brennerei Ztg ... Brennerei Zeitung [*A publication*]
Brennst-Chem ... Brennstoff-Chemie [*A publication*]
Brennst-Waerme-Kraft ... Brennstoff-Waerme-Kraft [*Fuel, Heat, Power*] [*A publication*]
Brennst Waermewirtsch ... Brennstoff- und Waermewirtschaft [*East Germany*] [*A publication*]
Brenns-Waerme-Kraft ... Brennstoff-Waerme-Kraft [*Fuel, Heat, Power*] [*A publication*]
Brenn-Waerme ... Brennstoff-Waerme-Kraft [*Fuel, Heat, Power*] [*A publication*]
Bren-S........ Brenner-Studien [*A publication*]
B Rens Agr ... Bulletin de Renseignements Agricoles [*A publication*]
Br Ent.......... Brownlow's Entries [*A publication*]   (DLA)
Brent Unempl Bull ... Brent Unemployment Bulletin [*A publication*]
BRENTW ... Brentwood [*Urban district in England*]
BREPAIR ... Bolted Repair [*Composite structures*]   (MCD)
BRER.......... Basic Radiation Effects Reactor
BRERD..... Brain Research Reviews [*A publication*]
BRERD2.... Brain Research Reviews [*A publication*]
BResCIsr ... Bulletin. Research Council of Israel [*Jerusalem*] [*A publication*]
B Res Council Isr ... Bulletin. Research Council of Israel [*A publication*]
BRESD...... Biomedical Research [*A publication*]
B Res Hum ... Bulletin of Research in the Humanities [*A publication*]
Bresl AK ...... Zeitschrift der Anwaltskammer Breslau [*A publication*]
Bresl Phil Abh ... Breslauer Philologische Abhandlungen [*A publication*]   (OCD)
BRESTCHAN ... Brest Subarea, Channel [*NATO*]
BRET........ Beilstein Registry Connection Tables [*Chemistry*]
BRET........ Bistatic Reflected Energy Target   (MCD)
BRET........ Breton [*Language, etc.*]   (ROG)
BRET........ Burning Rate Extraction Technique   (MCD)
B Rethel ..... Bulletin Archeologique, Historique, et Folklorique. Musee du Rethelois et du Porcien [*A publication*]
Breth Life... Brethren Life and Thought [*A publication*]
Brett Ca Eq ... Brett's Cases in Modern Equity [*A publication*]   (DLA)
Brev.......... Brevard's South Carolina Reports [*1793-1816*] [*A publication*]   (DLA)
BREV........ Brevet [*Military*]
BREV........ Brevete [*Patent*] [*French*]
BREV........ Breveted [*Military*] [*British*]   (ROG)
BREV........ Brevier
Brev Dig..... Brevard's Digest of the Public Statute Law, South Carolina [*A publication*]   (DLA)
Breviora Geol Asturica ... Breviora Geologica Asturica [*A publication*]
Brev Ju...... Brevia Judicialia [*Judicial Writs*] [*Latin*] [*Legal term*]   (DLA)
Brev-Maj.... Brevet-Major

Brev Sel...... Brevia Selecta [*Choice Writs*] [*Latin*] [*Legal term*]   (DLA)
Brew.......... Brewer's Reports [*19-26 Maryland*] [*A publication*]   (DLA)
BREW......... Brewing   (ROG)
Brew Dig..... Brewers Digest [*A publication*]
Brew Distill Int ... Brewing and Distilling International [*A publication*]
Brewer........ Brewer's Reports [*19-26 Maryland*] [*A publication*]   (DLA)
Brew Guardian ... Brewers' Guardian [*A publication*]
Brew Guild J ... Brewers' Guild Journal [*A publication*]
Brew J .... Brewers Journal [*A publication*]
Brew (MD) ... Brewer's Reports [*19-26 Maryland*] [*A publication*]   (DLA)
Brew Rev ...... Brewing Review [*A publication*]
BREWS ..... Battlefield Related Electronic Warfare Simulator   (MCD)
Brews .... Brewster's Pennsylvania Reports [*A publication*]   (DLA)
Brews (PA) ... Brewster's Pennsylvania Reports [*A publication*]   (DLA)
Brewst .... Brewster's Pennsylvania Reports [*A publication*]   (DLA)
Brewster ..... Brewster's Pennsylvania Reports [*A publication*]   (DLA)
Brewst PA Dig ... Brewster's Pennsylvania Digest [*A publication*]   (DLA)
Brew Tech Rev ... Brewers Technical Review [*A publication*]
Brew Trade Rev ... Brewing Trade Review [*A publication*]
BREX......... Banner Reflex [*Botany*]
BRF........... Baltic Research Foundation   (EAIO)
BRF........... Baptist Revival Fellowship [*British*]
BRF........... Bass Research Foundation   (EA)
BRF........... Bell Rings Faintly [*Telecommunications*]   (TEL)
BRF........... Best Replacement Factor   (CAAL)
BRF........... Bible Reading Fellowship [*British*]
BRF........... Bioprocessing Research Facility [*Oak Ridge, TN*] [*Oak Ridge National Laboratory*] [*Department of Energy*]   (GRD)
BRF........... Bioresources Research Facility [*University of Arizona*] [*Research center*]   (RCD)
BRF........... Blood Research Foundation   (EA)
BRF........... Borman's, Inc. [*Formerly, Borman Food Stores*] [*NYSE symbol*]   (SPSG)
BRF........... Brain Research Foundation   (EA)
BRF........... Branchial Filament
BRF........... Brewing Research Foundation [*British*]
BRF........... Brief   (FAAC)
BRF........... Brigades Revolutionnaires Francaises [*Revolutionary French Brigades*] [*French*]   (PD)
BRF........... Broach Fixture   (MCD)
BRF........... Bulletin. Rabinowitz Fund for the Exploration of Ancient Synagogues [*A publication*]
BRF........... Short [*Used to indicate the type of approach desired or required*] [*Aviation code*]   (FAAC)
BRFA........ Fireman Apprentice, Boilermaker, Striker [*Navy rating*]
Br Farmer Stockbreed ... British Farmer and Stockbreeder [*A publication*]
BRFC........ Buddy Rich Fan Club   (EA)
BRFC........ Burt Reynolds Fan Club   (EA)
BRFD........ Branford Steam Railroad [*AAR code*]
Br & F Ecc ... Broderick and Freemantle's Ecclesiastical Cases [*1840-64*] [*A publication*]   (DLA)
Br Fed Dig ... Brightly's Federal Digest [*A publication*]   (DLA)
Br Fern Gaz ... British Fern Gazette [*A publication*]
BRFG........ Briefing   (KSC)
BRFM........ British Retail Footwear Market
BRFN........ Fireman, Boilermaker, Striker [*Navy rating*]
Br Food J ... British Food Journal [*A publication*]
Br Foundryman ... British Foundryman [*A publication*]
BRFP........ Baseline Reference Flight Plan   (KSC)
Br & Fr....... Broderick and Freemantle's Ecclesiastical Cases [*1840-64*] [*A publication*]   (DLA)
BRG .... Baud Rate Generator [*Data processing*]
BRG .... Bearing   (AFM)
BRG .... Berggiesshubel [*German Democratic Republic*] [*Seismograph station code, US Geological Survey*]   (SEIS)
BRG .... Blackwell Retail Group [*Great Britain*]
BRG .... Blaetter der Rilke-Gesellschaft [*A publication*]
BRG .... Blue Ridge Resources Ltd. [*Vancouver Stock Exchange symbol*]
BRG .... Bridge [*or Bridging*] [*Telecommunications*]   (TEL)
BRG .... Bridge   (AABC)
BRG .... Brig [*Shipping*]   (ROG)
BRG .... British Gas ADS [*NYSE symbol*]   (SPSG)
BRG .... British Racing Green   (ADA)
Br & G........ Brownlow and Goldesborough's English Common Pleas Reports [*A publication*]   (DLA)
BRG .... Whitesburg, KY [*Location identifier*] [*FAA*]   (FAAL)
BRGBLN... Barrage Balloon
Br Geol...... British Geologist [*A publication*]
Br Geol Lit New Ser ... British Geological Literature. New Series [*A publication*]
BRGHD...... Bridgehead   (MSA)
BRGIAG..... Brewers' Guild Journal [*A publication*]
BRGK .... Bericht. Roemisch-Germanische Kommission [*A publication*]
BRGM .... Bureau de Recherches Geologiques et Minieres [*Bureau of Geological and Mining Research*] [*Information service or system*]   (IID)
Br & Gold... Brownlow and Goldesborough's English Common Pleas Reports [*A publication*]   (DLA)
Br Grassl Soc Occas Symp ... British Grassland Society. Occasional Symposium [*A publication*]
BRgt.......... Besluit van de Regent [*A publication*]

BRGT......... Bright (FAAC)
BRGTAF ... Bragantia [*A publication*]
BRGUAI.... Brewers' Guardian [*A publication*]
Br Guiana Geol Surv Dep Bull ... British Guiana. Geological Survey
    Department. Bulletin [*A publication*]
Br Guiana Geol Surv Dep Miner Resour Pam ... British Guiana. Geological
    Survey Department. Mineral Resources Pamphlet [*A
    publication*]
BRGW .... Brake Release Gross Weight
BRH........... Berry, R. H., San Leandro CA [*STAC*]
BRH........... Birch Hill [*Alaska*] [*Seismograph station code, US Geological
    Survey*] [*Closed*] (SEIS)
BRH........... Bridgehead (AABC)
BRH........... Brohm Resources, Inc. [*Toronto Stock Exchange symbol*]
    [*Vancouver Stock Exchange symbol*]
BRH........... Brush Holder
BRH........... Bulletin of Research in the Humanities [*A publication*]
BRH........... Bureau of Radiological Health [*FDA*]
BRH........... Bureau of Radiological Health, Rockville, MD [*OCLC
    symbol*] (OCLC)
BRH........... Cases in King's Bench Tempore Hardwicke [*1733-38*] [*England*]
    [*A publication*] (DLA)
Br & Had ... Broom and Hadley's Commentaries on the Laws of England [*A
    publication*] (DLA)
BRH Bull ... BRH [*Bureau of Radiological Health*] Bulletin [*A publication*]
Br Heart J ... British Heart Journal [*A publication*]
BRHF .... BR Communications [*NASDAQ symbol*] (NQ)
BRHG .... Breaching (MSA)
Br H I.......... British Humanities Index [*A publication*]
Br Hist Illus ... British History Illustrated [*A publication*]
BRHLA ...... Biorheology [*England*] [*A publication*]
bRHOD ..... Bovine Rhodopsin [*Physiology*]
Br Honduras Dep Agric Annu Rep ... British Honduras. Department of
    Agriculture. Annual Report [*A publication*]
Br Honduras Dep Agric Fish Annu Rep ... British Honduras. Department of
    Agriculture and Fisheries. Annual Report [*A publication*]
Br Humanit Index ... British Humanities Index [*A publication*]
BRI............. Banque des Reglements Internationaux [*Bank for International
    Settlements*]
BRI............. Bari [*Italy*] [*Airport symbol*] (OAG)
BRI............. Bearing and Range Indicator
BRI............. Behavior Research Institute (EA)
BRI............. Bellairs Research Institute [*Canada*] (MSC)
BRI............. Benefit Rights Interview [*Unemployment insurance*]
BRI............. Biomedical Research Institute [*American Foundation for
    Biological Research*] [*Research center*] (RCD)
BRI............. Bionetics Research Institute [*Rockville, MD*]
BRI............. BioResearch Index [*Later, BA/RRM*] [*A publication*]
BRI............. Biosystematics Research Institute [*Canada*] (ARC)
BRI............. Biotechnology Research Institute [*Montreal, PQ*] [*Canada*]
BRI............. Bombesin-Releasing Immunoreactivity
BRI............. Book Review Index [*Gale Research, Inc.*] [*Detroit, MI*]
    [*Information service or system*] [*A publication*]
BRI............. Brain Research Institute [*UCLA*] [*Research center*]
BRI............. Brand Rating Index Corp.
BRI............. Breakdown of Recoverable Items (MCD)
BRI............. Brican Resources [*Vancouver Stock Exchange symbol*]
BRI............. Bridge
BRI............. Brig [*Switzerland*] [*Seismograph station code, US Geological
    Survey*] [*Closed*] (SEIS)
BRI............. Brightness (KSC)
BRI............. British Journal of Industrial Relations [*United Kingdom*] [*A
    publication*]
BRI............. British Library, London, England [*OCLC symbol*] (OCLC)
BRI............. Broker Report Index [*Australia*]
BRI............. Buddhist Research Information [*A publication*]
BRI............. Building Research Institute [*Later, BRAB, ABBE*] (EA)
BRI............. Bureau of Retirement and Insurance [*Civil Service
    Commission*]
B-RI .... Burlington-Rock Island Railroad Co.
BRI............. Business Risks International, Inc. [*Database producer*] (IID)
BRI............. Richmond Public Library, British Columbia [*Library symbol*]
    [*National Library of Canada*] (NLC)
BRIA.......... Beef Research and Information Act [*1976*]
BRIA.......... Bioradioimmunoassay
BRIAAC.... Behavior Rating Instrument for Autistic and Other Atypical
    Children [*Child development test*] [*Psychology*]
BRIAG....... Animal Pathology Laboratory, Food Production and Inspection
    Branch, Agriculture Canada [*Laboratoire de Pathologie
    Veterinaire, Direction Generale de la Production et de
    l'Inspection des Aliments, Agriculture Canada*],
    Richmond, British Columbia [*Library symbol*] [*National
    Library of Canada*] (BIB)
Briar Q....... Briarcliff Quarterly [*A publication*]
BRIB.......... Ballarat and Western Victoria Regional Information Bureau
    [*Australia*]
BRIB.......... Bribery (DLA)
BRIC.......... Black Resources and Information Centre [*Canada*]
BRICA....... Bulletin. Research Council of Israel. Section C. Technology [*A
    publication*]
Brice Ult V ... Brice's Ultra Vires [*A publication*] (DLA)

Brick Ala Dig ... Brickell's Digest [*Alabama*] [*A publication*] (DLA)
Brickb .... Brickbuilder [*A publication*]
Brick Bull... Brick Bulletin [*A publication*]
Brick Clay Rec ... Brick and Clay Record [*A publication*]
Brick Dev Res Inst Tech Notes Clay Prod ... Brick Development Research
    Institute. Technical Notes on Clay Products [*A
    publication*] (APTA)
Brick Dig ... Brickell's Digest [*Alabama*] [*A publication*] (DLA)
Brick Tech Note ... Brick Technical Note [*A publication*] (APTA)
BRICLAW ... British Institute of International and Comparative Law (EA)
BRICS .... Black Resources Information Coordinating Services
    [*Information service or system*] (IID)
BRI-Cum ... Book Review Index Annual Cumulation [*A publication*]
BRID.......... Bridgford Foods Corp. [*NASDAQ symbol*] (NQ)
BRID.......... Bridlington [*Yorkshire resort town*] [*England*] (DSUE)
BRIDG....... Bridgettines [*Roman Catholic religious order*]
Bridg .... [*Sir John*] Bridgman's English Common Pleas Reports [*123
    English Reprint*] [*A publication*] (DLA)
Bridg Conv ... Bridgman on Conveyancing [*A publication*] (DLA)
Bridg Dig Ind ... Bridgman's Digested Index [*A publication*] (DLA)
Bridg Eq Ind ... Bridgman. Index to Equity Cases [*A publication*] (DLA)
BRIDGEX ... Bridge Construction Exercise [*Military*] (NVT)
Bridg J .... [*Sir John*] Bridgman's English Common Pleas Reports [*123
    English Reprint*] [*A publication*] (DLA)
Bridg Leg Bib ... Bridgman. Legal Bibliography [*1801*] [*A publication*] (DLA)
Bridg O ...... Orlando Bridgman's English Common Pleas Reports [*A
    publication*] (DLA)
Bridg Ref.... Bridgman. Reflections on the Study of the Law [*1804*] [*A
    publication*] (DLA)
Bridg Thes ... Bridgman's Thesaurus Juridicus [*A publication*] (DLA)
BRIDP ...... Bridport [*Municipal borough in England*]
BRIE.......... Berkeley Roundtable on the International Economy [*University
    of California*]
Brief .... Brief of the Phi Delta Phi [*Menasha, Wisconsin*] [*A
    publication*] (DLA)
Brief .... Law Society of Western Australia. Brief [*A publication*] (DLA)
Brief Case ... Legal Aid Brief Case [*A publication*]
Brief Clin Lab Observations ... Brief Clinical and Laboratory Observations [*A
    publication*]
Briefing CVCP ... Briefing. Committee of Vice-Chancellors and Principals [*A
    publication*]
BRIEX .... British Railway Industry Export Group
BRIFB........ Berichte und Informationen. Europaeische Gemeinschaften [*A
    publication*]
BRIG.......... Brigade
BRIG.......... Brigadier (EY)
BRIGAND ... Bistatic RADAR Intelligence Generation and Analysis
    System (NVT)
Brigant .... Brigantium. Museo Arqueologico e Historico [*A publication*]
BRIGARTY ... Brigade Artillery [*Army*] (INF)
BRIGEN.... Brigadier General
BRIG GEN ... Brigadier General (AFM)
Briggs Ry Acts ... Brigg's General Railway Acts [*A publication*] (DLA)
BRIGH ...... Brighton [*County borough in England*]
Brigham You ... Brigham Young University. Studies [*A publication*]
Brigham Young U L Rev ... Brigham Young University. Law Review [*A
    publication*]
Brigham Young Univ Geol Stud ... Brigham Young University. Geology
    Studies [*A publication*]
Brigham Young Univ L Rev ... Brigham Young University. Law Review [*A
    publication*]
Brigham Young Univ Res Stud Geol Ser ... Brigham Young University.
    Research Studies. Geology Series [*A publication*]
Brigham Young Univ Sci Bull Biol Ser ... Brigham Young University. Science
    Bulletin. Biological Series [*A publication*]
Brigham YULR ... Brigham Young University. Law Review [*A publication*]
BRIGHED ... Brigade Headquarters [*Army*]
Bright .... Brightly's Pennsylvania Nisi Prius Reports [*A
    publication*] (DLA)
Bright Bank Law ... Brightly's Annotated Bankrupt Law [*A
    publication*] (DLA)
Bright Costs ... Brightly on the Law of Costs in Pennsylvania [*A
    publication*] (DLA)
Bright Dig ... Brightly's Analytical Digest of the Laws of the United States [*A
    publication*] (DLA)
Bright Dig ... Brightly's Digest [*New York*] [*A publication*] (DLA)
Bright Dig ... Brightly's Digest [*Pennsylvania*] [*A publication*] (DLA)
Bright EC... Brightly's Leading Election Cases [*Pennsylvania*] [*A
    publication*] (DLA)
Bright Elec Cas ... Brightly's Leading Election Cases [*Pennsylvania*] [*A
    publication*] (DLA)
Bright Eq Jur ... Brightly's Equitable Jurisdiction [*Pennsylvania*] [*A
    publication*] (DLA)
Bright Fed Dig ... Brightly's Federal Digest [*A publication*] (DLA)
Bright H & W ... Bright. Husband and Wife [*3rd ed.*] [*1849*] [*A
    publication*] (DLA)
Brightly...... Brightly's Pennsylvania Nisi Prius Reports [*A
    publication*] (DLA)
Brightly Dig ... Brightly's Analytical Digest of the Laws of the United States [*A
    publication*] (DLA)
Brightly Dig ... Brightly's Digest [*New York*] [*A publication*] (DLA)

Brightly Dig ... Brightly's Digest [*Pennsylvania*] [*A publication*] (DLA)
Brightly El ... Brightly's Leading Election Cases [*Pennsylvania*] [*A publication*] (DLA)
Brightly El Cas ... Brightly's Leading Election Cases [*Pennsylvania*] [*A publication*] (DLA)
Brightly Elect Cas ... Brightly's Leading Election Cases [*Pennsylvania*] [*A publication*] (DLA)
Brightly Election Cas (PA) ... Brightly's Leading Election Cases [*Pennsylvania*] [*A publication*] (DLA)
Brightly NP ... Brightly's Pennsylvania Nisi Prius Reports [*A publication*] (DLA)
Brightly's Elec Cas ... Brightly's Leading Election Cases [*Pennsylvania*] [*A publication*] (DLA)
Brightly's Rep ... Brightly's Pennsylvania Nisi Prius Reports [*A publication*] (DLA)
Bright NP .. Brightly's Pennsylvania Nisi Prius Reports [*A publication*] (DLA)
Bright NY Dig ... Brightly's New York Digest [*A publication*] (DLA)
Bright (PA) ... Brightly's Pennsylvania Nisi Prius Reports [*A publication*] (DLA)
Bright PA Dig ... Brightly's Pennsylvania Digest [*A publication*] (DLA)
Bright Purd ... Brightly's Edition of Purdon's Digest of Pennsylvania Laws [*A publication*] (DLA)
Bright Pur Dig ... Brightly's Edition of Purdon's Digest of Pennsylvania Laws [*A publication*] (DLA)
Bright Tr & H Pr ... Brightly's Edition of Troubat and Haly's Practice [*A publication*] (DLA)
Bright US Dig ... Brightly's Analytical Digest of the Laws of the United States [*A publication*] (DLA)
BRIGHTW BAR ... Brightwells Barrow [*England*]
BRIGLEX ... Brigade Landing Exercise [*Military*] (NVT)
Brig Yo ULR ... Brigham Young University. Law Review [*A publication*]
BRII .... Brican Resources Ltd. [*NASDAQ symbol*] (NQ)
BRIK .... Brinkmann Instruments, Inc. [*NASDAQ symbol*] (NQ)
BRIL .... Brilliance (KSC)
bril .... Brilliant [*Philately*]
BRIL .... Brilund Ltd. [*NASDAQ symbol*] (NQ)
BRILAB ... Bribery-Labor [*FBI undercover investigation*]
BRILL .... Brillante [*Brilliantly*] [*Music*]
BRILL .... Brilliant [*British*] [*Slang*]
BRIMAFEX ... British Manufacturers of Malleable Tube Fittings Export Group
BRI-MC ..... Book Review Index Master Cumulations [*A publication*]
BRIMD7 .... Brimleyana [*A publication*]
BRIN .... Broadcast International, Inc. [*NASDAQ symbol*] (NQ)
BRINC .... Basic Research, Incorporated (EA)
BRINDEX ... Association of British Independent Oil Exploration Companies
Br Ind Finish (Leighton Buzzard Engl) ... British Industrial Finishing (Leighton Buzzard, England) [*A publication*]
Brink Boeken ... Brinkman's Cumulatieve Catalogus van Boeken [*A publication*]
Br Ink Mkr ... British Ink Maker [*A publication*]
Br Int Law ... British Yearbook of International Law [*A publication*]
BRI Occ Rep ... BRI [*Building Research Institute*] Occasional Report [*A publication*]
BRI-PR ...... Book Review Index: Periodical Reviews, 1976-1984 [*A publication*]
Bri Pub Wor ... Brice. Law Relating to Public Worship [*1875*] [*A publication*] (DLA)
BRIQ .... Briquette (ADA)
BRI-RB ...... Book Review Index: Reference Books, 1965-1984 [*A publication*]
BRIS .... Brisbane [*Australia*] (DSUE)
BRIS .... Bristol [*City and county borough in England*] (ROG)
BRISB .... Brisbane [*Australia*] (ROG)
Brisbin ...... Brisbin's Reports [*1 Minnesota*] [*A publication*] (DLA)
Brisb Minn ... Brisbin's Reports [*1 Minnesota*] [*A publication*] (DLA)
BRISCC ..... British Iron and Steel Consumers' Council
BRISFIT .... Bristol Fighter [*British aircraft*] (DSUE)
Br Isles Bee Breeders' News ... British Isles Bee Breeders' Association. News [*A publication*]
BRISQ .... Business Reference and Information Service Queensland [*Australia*]
Briss .... [*Barnabas*] Brissonius [*Deceased, 1591*] [*Authority cited in pre-1607 legal work*] (DSA)
Brisson ...... [*Barnabas*] Brissonius [*Deceased, 1591*] [*Authority cited in pre-1607 legal work*] (DSA)
Brissonius .. Brissonius. De Verborum Significatione [*A publication*] (DLA)
Bristol Med-Chir J ... Bristol Medico-Chirurgical Journal [*A publication*]
Bristol-Myers Cancer Symp ... Bristol-Myers Cancer Symposia [*A publication*]
Bristol-Myers Nutr Symp ... Bristol-Myers Nutrition Symposia [*A publication*]
Bristol Univ Dep Agric Hortic Bull ... Bristol University. Department of Agriculture and Horticulture. Bulletin [*A publication*]
Bristol Univ Spelaeol Soc Proc ... Bristol University. Spelaeological Society. Proceedings [*A publication*]
BRIT .... Britain [*or British*]
BRIT .... Britannia
BRIT .... Britannica
BRIT .... British (DLA)

Brit .... Britton's Ancient Pleas of the Crown [*A publication*] (DLA)
Brit AA ...... British Archaeological Abstracts [*A publication*]
Brit Abstr Med Sci ... British Abstracts of Medical Sciences [*A publication*]
Brit Acad Proc ... British Academy, London. Proceedings [*A publication*]
Brit Agric Bull ... British Agricultural Bulletin [*A publication*]
BRITAIR ... Brittany Air International [*Airline*] [*France*]
Britannica R For Lang Educ ... Britannica Review of Foreign Language Education [*A publication*]
Brit Arch Ab ... British Archaeological Abstracts [*A publication*]
Brit Archaeol Rep ... British Archaeological Reports [*A publication*]
Brit As Rp ... British Association for the Advancement of Science. Report [*A publication*]
Brit Assoc Am Studies Bull ... British Association for American Studies. Bulletin [*A publication*]
Brit Bee J ... British Bee Journal and Beekeepers' Adviser [*A publication*]
Brit Birds ... British Birds [*A publication*]
Brit Bk N ... British Book News [*A publication*]
Brit Bk N C ... British Book News. Children's Supplement [*A publication*]
Brit Bk News ... British Book News [*A publication*]
Brit Bk Yr .. Britannica Book of the Year [*A publication*]
Brit Bull Spectrosc ... British Bulletin of Spectroscopy [*A publication*]
Brit Burm ... British Burma (ILCA)
Brit Busin ... British Business [*A publication*]
Brit Busn .... British Business [*A publication*]
Brit Cave Res Ass Trans ... British Cave Research Association. Transactions [*A publication*]
Brit Cer Abstr ... British Ceramic Abstracts [*A publication*]
Brit Chem Abstr ... British Chemical Abstracts [*A publication*]
Brit Chem Abstr Coll Ind ... British Chemical Abstracts. Collective Index [*A publication*]
Brit Chem Eng ... British Chemical Engineering [*A publication*]
Brit Chem Phys Abstr ... British Chemical and Physiological Abstracts [*A publication*]
Brit Clayw ... British Clayworker [*A publication*]
BRIT COL ... British Columbia (DLA)
Brit Col (Can) ... British Columbia, Canada (ILCA)
BritColl ...... Britannia Royal Naval College
Brit Col Med J ... British Columbia Medical Journal [*A publication*]
Brit Colon Pharm ... British and Colonial Pharmacist [*A publication*]
Brit & Col Pr Cas ... British and Colonial Prize Cases [*A publication*] (DLA)
Brit Columbia Dep Mines Petrol Resour Bull ... British Columbia. Department of Mines and Petroleum Resources. Bulletin [*A publication*]
Brit Columbia Lib Q ... British Columbia Library Quarterly [*A publication*]
Brit Constr Steelworks Ass Publ ... British Constructional Steelworks Association. Publications [*A publication*]
Brit Corrosion J ... British Corrosion Journal [*A publication*]
Brit Corros J ... British Corrosion Journal [*A publication*]
Brit Cr Cas ... British [*or English*] Crown Cases [*A publication*] (DLA)
Brit Deaf News ... British Deaf News [*A publication*]
Brit Def T ... British Defence Technology [*A publication*]
Brit Dent J ... British Dental Journal [*A publication*]
BRITDOC ... British Document Exchange
BRITE .... Bright RADAR Indicator-Tower Equipment
BRITEC ..... British Information Technology Exhibition and Conference on Engineering Software [*Computational Mechanics Institute*] (TSPED)
Brit Ecol Soc Symp ... British Ecological Society. Symposium [*A publication*]
BritEdI .... British Education Index [*A publication*]
Brit Eng ..... British Engineer [*A publication*]
Brit Eng ..... British Engineering [*A publication*]
Brit Engine Boiler Elec Ins Co Tech Rep ... British Engine, Boiler, and Electrical Insurance Company. Technical Report [*A publication*]
Brit Europ Airw Mag ... British European Airways Magazine [*A publication*]
Brit Food J ... British Food Journal and Hygienic Review [*Later, British Food Journal*] [*A publication*]
Brit & For Evang R ... British and Foreign Evangelical Review [*A publication*]
Brit & For R ... British and Foreign Review [*A publication*]
Brit Foundrym ... British Foundryman [*A publication*]
Brit Gas Corp Ext Rep Res Commun MRS Rep ... British Gas Corporation External Reports. Research Communications and Midlands Research Station Reports [*A publication*]
Brit Granite Whinstone Fed J ... British Granite and Whinstone Federation. Journal [*A publication*]
Brit Grassland Soc J ... British Grassland Society. Journal [*A publication*]
Brit Gui ...... British Guiana (ILCA)
Brit Gui Med Ann ... British Guiana Medical Annual and Hospital Reports [*A publication*]
Brit Gyn J .. British Gynaecological Journal [*A publication*]
BritH .... British Heritage [*A publication*]
Brit Heart J ... British Heart Journal [*A publication*]
Brit Hond ... British Honduras (ILCA)
Brit Hosp Soc Serv J ... British Hospital and Social Service Journal [*A publication*]
Brit Hum .... British Humanities Index [*A publication*]
Brit Ink Maker ... British Ink Maker [*A publication*]
BRITIRE ... British Institution of Radio Engineers
British Archaeological Assocn Conference Trans ... British Archaeological Association. Conference Transactions [*A publication*]

British Ceramic Soc Trans ... British Ceramic Society. Transactions [*A publication*]
British Columbia Dept Mines Ann Rept Bull ... British Columbia. Department of Mines. Annual Report. Bulletin [*A publication*]
British Columbia Univ Dept Geology Rept ... British Columbia University. Department of Geology. Report [*A publication*]
British J Math Statist Psych ... British Journal of Mathematical and Statistical Psychology [*A publication*]
British J Math Statist Psychology ... British Journal of Mathematical and Statistical Psychology [*London*] [*A publication*]
British J Philos Sci ... British Journal for the Philosophy of Science [*A publication*]
British J Pol Science ... British Journal of Political Science [*A publication*]
British Mus (Nat History) Bull Geology ... British Museum (Natural History). Bulletin. Geology [*A publication*]
British Nat Biblio ... British National Bibliography [*London*] [*A publication*]
British R Econ Issues ... British Review of Economic Issues [*A publication*]
British Reports Transl & Theses ... British Reports, Translations, and Theses [*A publication*]
British Tax R ... British Tax Review [*A publication*]
Brit J Addict ... British Journal of Addiction [*A publication*]
Brit J Admin Law ... British Journal of Administrative Law [*A publication*]   (DLA)
Brit J Adm L ... British Journal of Administrative Law [*A publication*]   (DLA)
Brit J Aes ... British Journal of Aesthetics [*A publication*]
Brit J Aesth ... British Journal of Aesthetics [*A publication*]
Brit J Aesthetics ... British Journal of Aesthetics [*A publication*]
Brit J Anaesth ... British Journal of Anaesthesia [*A publication*]
Brit J Ap Phys ... British Journal of Applied Physics [*A publication*]
Brit J Appl Phys ... British Journal of Applied Physics [*A publication*]
Brit J Audiol ... British Journal of Audiology [*A publication*]
Brit J Cancer ... British Journal of Cancer [*A publication*]
Brit J Child Dis ... British Journal of Children's Diseases [*A publication*]
Brit J Clin Pract ... British Journal of Clinical Practice [*A publication*]
Brit J Crim ... British Journal of Criminology [*A publication*]
Brit J of Crimin ... British Journal of Criminology [*A publication*]
Brit J Criminol ... British Journal of Criminology [*A publication*]
Brit J Criminology ... British Journal of Criminology [*A publication*]
Brit J Delinq ... British Journal of Delinquency [*A publication*]
Brit J Dermat ... British Journal of Dermatology [*A publication*]
Brit J Dermatol ... British Journal of Dermatology [*A publication*]
Brit J Dis Chest ... British Journal of Diseases of the Chest [*A publication*]
Brit J Dis Commun ... British Journal of Disorders of Communication [*A publication*]
Brit J Disord Commun ... British Journal of Disorders of Communication [*A publication*]
Brit J Ed Psychol ... British Journal of Educational Psychology [*A publication*]
Brit J Ed Studies ... British Journal of Educational Studies [*A publication*]
Brit J Educ Psychol ... British Journal of Educational Psychology [*A publication*]
Brit J Educ Stud ... British Journal of Educational Studies [*A publication*]
Brit J Exper Path ... British Journal of Experimental Pathology [*A publication*]
Brit J Haemat ... British Journal of Haematology [*A publication*]
Brit J Hist Sci ... British Journal for the History of Science [*A publication*]
Brit J Hosp Med ... British Journal of Hospital Medicine [*A publication*]
Brit J Ind Med ... British Journal of Industrial Medicine [*A publication*]
Brit J Ind Rel ... British Journal of Industrial Relations [*A publication*]
Brit J Indust Med ... British Journal of Industrial Medicine [*A publication*]
Brit J Industr Med ... British Journal of Industrial Medicine [*A publication*]
Brit J Industr Relat ... British Journal of Industrial Relations [*A publication*]
Brit J Int'l L ... British Journal of International Law [*A publication*]   (DLA)
Brit J Int Stud ... British Journal of International Studies [*A publication*]
Brit J Law & Soc ... British Journal of Law and Society [*A publication*]
Brit Jl Photogr ... British Journal of Photography [*A publication*]
Brit J L & Soc ... British Journal of Law and Society [*A publication*]
Brit JL & Soc'y ... British Journal of Law and Society [*A publication*]
Brit J Math & Stat Psychol ... British Journal of Mathematical and Statistical Psychology [*A publication*]
Brit J Med Psychol ... British Journal of Medical Psychology [*A publication*]
Brit J Ment Subnorm ... British Journal of Mental Subnormality [*A publication*]
Brit J M Psychol ... British Journal of Medical Psychology [*A publication*]
Brit J Non-Destruct Test ... British Journal of Non-Destructive Testing [*A publication*]
Brit J Nutr ... British Journal of Nutrition [*A publication*]
Brit J Nutr Proc Nutr Soc ... British Journal of Nutrition. Proceedings of the Nutrition Society [*A publication*]
Brit J Ophth ... British Journal of Ophthalmology [*A publication*]
Brit Jour Radiol ... British Journal of Radiology [*A publication*]
Brit Jour Sociol ... British Journal of Sociology [*A publication*]
Brit J Pharmacol ... British Journal of Pharmacology [*A publication*]
Brit J Pharmacol ... British Journal of Pharmacology and Chemotherapy [*A publication*]
Brit J Pharmacol Chemother ... British Journal of Pharmacology and Chemotherapy [*Later, British Journal of Pharmacology*] [*A publication*]
Brit J Philos Sci ... British Journal for the Philosophy of Science [*A publication*]

Brit J Phil Sci ... British Journal for the Philosophy of Science [*A publication*]
Brit J Phot ... British Journal of Photography [*A publication*]
Brit J Photo ... British Journal of Photography [*A publication*]
Brit J Plast Surg ... British Journal of Plastic Surgery [*A publication*]
Brit J Pol Sci ... British Journal of Political Science [*A publication*]
Brit J Prev Soc Med ... British Journal of Preventive and Social Medicine [*A publication*]
Brit J Psychiat ... British Journal of Psychiatry [*A publication*]
Brit J Psychol ... British Journal of Psychology [*A publication*]
Brit J Psych Soc Work ... British Journal of Psychiatric Social Work [*A publication*]
Brit J Radiol ... British Journal of Radiology [*A publication*]
Brit J Soc ... British Journal of Sociology [*A publication*]
Brit J Social & Clin Psychol ... British Journal of Social and Clinical Psychology [*A publication*]
Brit J Social Psychiat ... British Journal of Social Psychiatry [*A publication*]
Brit J Sociol ... British Journal of Sociology [*A publication*]
Brit J Soc Work ... British Journal of Social Work [*A publication*]
Brit J Surg ... British Journal of Surgery [*A publication*]
Brit J Tuberc ... British Journal of Tuberculosis [*A publication*]
Brit J Urol ... British Journal of Urology [*A publication*]
Brit J Ven Dis ... British Journal of Venereal Diseases [*A publication*]
Brit J Vener Dis ... British Journal of Venereal Diseases [*A publication*]
Brit Kinemat ... British Kinematography [*A publication*]
Brit Kinematogr Sound Telev ... British Kinematography, Sound, and Television [*A publication*]
Brit Kinemat Sound and Telev ... British Kinematography, Sound, and Television [*A publication*]
Brit Lib Assoc ... Library Association of the United Kingdom. Monthly Notes [*A publication*]
Brit Lib J ... British Library Journal [*A publication*]
Brit Lib Res Dev Newsletter ... British Library Research and Development Newsletter [*A publication*]
Brit M Bull ... British Medical Bulletin [*A publication*]
Brit Med J ... British Medical Journal [*A publication*]
Brit MJ ... British Medical Journal [*A publication*]
Brit Mus (Nat Hist) Econom Ser ... British Museum (Natural History). Economic Series [*A publication*]
Brit Mus Q ... British Museum. Quarterly [*A publication*]
Brit Mus Quart ... British Museum. Quarterly [*A publication*]
Brit Mus Quarterly ... British Museum. Quarterly [*A publication*]
Brit Mus Subj Index ... British Museum. Subject Index [*A publication*]
Brit Mus Yearb ... British Museum. Yearbook [*A publication*]
Brit Mycol Soc Trans ... British Mycological Society. Transactions [*A publication*]
Brit Numis J ... British Numismatic Journal [*A publication*]
Brit Orth J ... British Orthoptic Journal [*A publication*]
Brit Osteop J ... British Osteopathic Journal [*A publication*]
Brit Osteop Rev ... British Osteopathic Review [*A publication*]
Brit Overs Pharm Yb ... British and Overseas Pharmacist's Yearbook [*A publication*]
Brit Pat Abs Sect CH Chem ... British Patent Abstracts. Section CH. Chemical [*A publication*]
Brit Petr Equipm ... British Petroleum Equipment [*A publication*]
Brit Petr Equipm Ne ... British Petroleum Equipment News [*A publication*]
Brit Plast.... British Plastics [*Later, European Plastics News*] [*A publication*]
Brit Plast Rubb ... British Plastics and Rubber [*A publication*]
Brit Plast Yb ... British Plastics Yearbook [*A publication*]
Brit Polit Sociol Yb ... British Political Sociology. Yearbook [*A publication*]
Brit Polym J ... British Polymer Journal [*A publication*]
Brit Poultry Sci ... British Poultry Science [*A publication*]
Brit Poult Sci ... British Poultry Science [*A publication*]
Brit Prac Int'l L ... British Practice in International Law [*A publication*]   (DLA)
Brit Printer ... British Printer [*A publication*]
Brit Psychol Soc Bull ... Bulletin. British Psychological Society [*A publication*]
Brit Q .... British Quarterly Review [*A publication*]
Brit Quar Rev ... British Quarterly Review [*A publication*]
Brit Repts Transl Theses ... British Reports, Translations, and Theses [*A publication*]
Brit Rheum Ass Rev ... British Rheumatic Association. Review [*A publication*]
Brit Rul Cas ... British Ruling Cases [*A publication*]   (DLA)
Brit Sch Athens Ann ... British School at Athens. Annual [*A publication*]
Brit Sch at Rome Papers ... British School at Rome. Papers [*A publication*]
Brit Sci News ... British Science News [*A publication*]
Britsh Ink .. British Ink Maker [*A publication*]
Brit Ship L ... British Shipping Laws [*A publication*]   (DLA)
Brit Stand .. British Standard Specification [*A publication*]
Brit Stand Inst Brit Stand ... British Standards Institution. British Standard [*A publication*]
Brit Steelmaker ... British Steelmaker [*A publication*]
Brit Stud Mon ... British Studies Monitor [*A publication*]
Brit Sug Beet Rev ... British Sugar Beet Review [*A publication*]
BRITT .... Bandwidth Reduction and Intelligence Target Tracking   (MCD)
BRITT .... Britannarium [*Of All the Britains*] [*Coin inscription*]   (ROG)
Britt .... Britton's Ancient Pleas of the Crown [*A publication*]   (DLA)
Brit Tax Rev ... British Tax Review [*A publication*]
Brit Techl ... British Technology Index [*Later, Current Technology Index*] [*A publication*]
Brit Telec ... British Telecom Journal [*A publication*]

Brit TS .... British Treaty Series [*A publication*]   (DLA)
Brit Vet J ... British Veterinary Journal [*A publication*]
Brit Weld J ... British Welding Journal [*A publication*]
Brit Yb Int Law ... British Yearbook of International Law [*A publication*]
Brit Yb Int'l L ... British Yearbook of International Law [*A publication*]
Brit Y Book ... British Year Book of International Law [*A publication*]
Brit Yearbook Int L ... British Yearbook of International Law [*A publication*]
Bri Ult V .... Brice's Ultra Vires [*A publication*]   (DLA)
BRIX .... BRIntec Corp. [*Willimantic, CT*] [*NASDAQ symbol*]   (NQ)
BRJ .... Barco Rotary Joint
BRJ .... Beijing Royal Jelly [*Biochemistry*]
BRJ .... Bill of Rights Journal [*A publication*]   (DLA)
BRJ .... Black River [*Jamaica*] [*Seismograph station code, US
    Geological Survey*] [*Closed*]   (SEIS)
BRJ .... Blind Riveted Joint
BRJ .... Braner Resources [*Vancouver Stock Exchange symbol*]
BRJ .... Martinsville, VA [*Location identifier*] [*FAA*]   (FAAL)
Br J Actinother Physiother ... British Journal of Actinotherapy and
    Physiotherapy [*A publication*]
Br J Addict ... British Journal of Addiction [*A publication*]
Br J Adm L ... British Journal of Administrative Law [*A publication*]
Br J Aesth ... British Journal of Aesthetics [*A publication*]
Br J Alcohol Alcohol ... British Journal on Alcohol and Alcoholism [*A
    publication*]
Br J Anaest ... British Journal of Anaesthesia [*A publication*]
Br J Anaesth ... British Journal of Anaesthesia [*A publication*]
Br J Anim Behav ... British Journal of Animal Behaviour [*A publication*]
Br J Appl Phys ... British Journal of Applied Physics [*A publication*]
Br J Appl Phys Suppl ... British Journal of Applied Physics. Supplement [*A
    publication*]
Br J Audiol ... British Journal of Audiology [*A publication*]
Br J Audiology ... British Journal of Audiology [*A publication*]
Br J Audiol Suppl ... British Journal of Audiology. Supplement [*A
    publication*]
Br Jb .... Bremisches Jahrbuch [*A publication*]
Br J Canc ... British Journal of Cancer [*A publication*]
Br J Cancer ... British Journal of Cancer [*A publication*]
Br J Cancer Suppl ... British Journal of Cancer. Supplement [*A publication*]
BR-JC (Army) ... Board of Review and Judicial Council of the Army   (DLA)
Br J Clin Equip ... British Journal of Clinical Equipment [*A publication*]
Br J Clin P ... British Journal of Clinical Practice [*A publication*]
Br J Clin Pharmacol ... British Journal of Clinical Pharmacology [*A
    publication*]
Br J Clin Prat ... British Journal of Clinical Practice [*A publication*]
Br J Clin Psychol ... British Journal of Clinical Psychology [*A publication*]
Br J Cl Ph ... British Journal of Clinical Pharmacology [*A publication*]
Br J Crimin ... British Journal of Criminology [*A publication*]
Br J Dent Sci Prosthetics ... British Journal of Dental Science and Prosthetics
    [*A publication*]
Br J Derm.. British Journal of Dermatology [*A publication*]
Br J Dermatol ... British Journal of Dermatology [*A publication*]
Br J Dermatol Suppl ... British Journal of Dermatology. Supplement [*A
    publication*]
Br J Dermatol Syph ... British Journal of Dermatology and Syphilis [*A
    publication*]
Br J Dev Psychol ... British Journal of Developmental Psychology [*A
    publication*]
Br J Dis Ch ... British Journal of Diseases of the Chest [*A publication*]
Br J Dis Chest ... British Journal of Diseases of the Chest [*A publication*]
Br J Dis Co ... British Journal of Disorders of Communication [*A publication*]
Br J Ed Psy ... British Journal of Educational Psychology [*A publication*]
Br J Educ Psychol ... British Journal of Educational Psychology [*A
    publication*]
Br J Educ S ... British Journal of Educational Studies [*A publication*]
Br J Educ Stud ... British Journal of Educational Studies [*A publication*]
Br J Educ T ... British Journal of Educational Technology [*A publication*]
Br J Educ Tech ... British Journal of Educational Technology [*A publication*]
Br J Eighteenth Century Stud ... British Journal for Eighteenth Century
    Studies [*A publication*]
Br J Ex Pat ... British Journal of Experimental Pathology [*A publication*]
Br J Exp Bio ... British Journal of Experimental Biology [*A publication*]
Br J Exp Biol ... British Journal of Experimental Biology [*A publication*]
Br J Exp Path ... British Journal of Experimental Pathology [*A publication*]
Br J Exp Pathol ... British Journal of Experimental Pathology [*A publication*]
BRJFA....... British Journal of Photography [*A publication*]
Br J Fam Plann ... British Journal of Family Planning [*A publication*]
Br J Guid Couns ... British Journal of Guidance and Counseling [*A
    publication*]
Br J Guid Couns ... British Journal of Guidance and Counselling [*A
    publication*]
Br J Haem ... British Journal of Haematology [*A publication*]
Br J Haematol ... British Journal of Haematology [*A publication*]
Br J Hist S ... British Journal for the History of Science [*A publication*]
Br J Hist Sci ... British Journal for the History of Science [*A publication*]
Br J Hosp Med ... British Journal of Hospital Medicine [*A publication*]
Br J Ind Me ... British Journal of Industrial Medicine [*A publication*]
Br J Ind Med ... British Journal of Industrial Medicine [*A publication*]
Br J Ind Medicine ... British Journal of Industrial Medicine [*A publication*]
Br J Ind Saf ... British Journal of Industrial Safety [*A publication*]
Br J Inebriety ... British Journal of Inebriety [*A publication*]
Br J Inserv Educ ... British Journal of Inservice Education [*A publication*]

Br J Int Stud ... British Journal of International Studies [*A publication*]
Br J Law Soc ... British Journal of Law and Society [*A publication*]
Br J Math S ... British Journal of Mathematical and Statistical Psychology [*A
    publication*]
Br J Med Educ ... British Journal of Medical Education [*A publication*]
Br J Med Ps ... British Journal of Medical Psychology [*A publication*]
Br J Med Psychol ... British Journal of Medical Psychology [*A publication*]
Br J Ment S ... British Journal of Mental Subnormality [*A publication*]
Br J Ment Subnorm ... British Journal of Mental Subnormality [*A
    publication*]
BRJNA ...... Building Research [*A publication*]
Br J Non-Destr Test ... British Journal of Non-Destructive Testing [*A
    publication*]
Br J Nutr.... British Journal of Nutrition [*A publication*]
Br J Obstet Gynaecol ... British Journal of Obstetrics and Gynaecology [*A
    publication*]
Br J Obst G ... British Journal of Obstetrics and Gynaecology [*A publication*]
Br J Occup Saf ... British Journal of Occupational Safety [*A publication*]
Br J Ophth ... British Journal of Ophthalmology [*A publication*]
Br J Ophthalmol ... British Journal of Ophthalmology [*A publication*]
Br J Oral Maxillofac Surg ... British Journal of Oral and Maxillofacial Surgery
    [*A publication*]
Br J Oral & Maxillofac Surg ... British Journal of Oral and Maxillofacial
    Surgery [*A publication*]
Br J Oral S ... British Journal of Oral Surgery [*Later, British Journal of Oral
    and Maxillofacial Surgery*] [*A publication*]
Br J Oral Surg ... British Journal of Oral Surgery [*Later, British Journal of
    Oral and Maxillofacial Surgery*] [*A publication*]
Br J Orthod ... British Journal of Orthodontics [*A publication*]
Br J Pharm ... British Journal of Pharmacology [*A publication*]
Br J Pharmac ... British Journal of Pharmacology [*A publication*]
Br J Pharmac Chemother ... British Journal of Pharmacology and
    Chemotherapy [*Later, British Journal of Pharmacology*] [*A
    publication*]
Br J Pharmacol ... British Journal of Pharmacology [*A publication*]
Br J Pharmacol Chemother ... British Journal of Pharmacology and
    Chemotherapy [*Later, British Journal of Pharmacology*] [*A
    publication*]
Br J Philos Sci ... British Journal for the Philosophy of Science [*A
    publication*]
Br J Phil S ... British Journal for the Philosophy of Science [*A publication*]
Br J Photogr ... British Journal of Photography [*A publication*]
Br J Photogr Ann ... British Journal of Photography. Annual [*A publication*]
Br J Phys Ed ... British Journal of Physical Education [*A publication*]
Br J Physiol Opt ... British Journal of Physiological Optics [*A publication*]
Br J Phys Med ... British Journal of Physical Medicine [*A publication*]
Br J Phys O ... British Journal of Physiological Optics [*A publication*]
Br J Plast Surg ... British Journal of Plastic Surgery [*A publication*]
Br J Pl Sur ... British Journal of Plastic Surgery [*A publication*]
Br J Poli S ... British Journal of Political Science [*A publication*]
Br J Polit Sci ... British Journal of Political Science [*A publication*]
Br J Prev S ... British Journal of Preventive and Social Medicine [*A
    publication*]
Br J Prev Soc Med ... British Journal of Preventive and Social Medicine [*A
    publication*]
Br J Psychi ... British Journal of Psychiatry [*A publication*]
Br J Psychiatry ... British Journal of Psychiatry [*A publication*]
Br J Psychiatry Spec Publ ... British Journal of Psychiatry. Special Publication
    [*A publication*]
Br J Psycho ... British Journal of Psychology [*A publication*]
Br J Psychol ... British Journal of Psychology [*A publication*]
Br J Radiol ... British Journal of Radiology [*A publication*]
Br J Radiol Suppl ... British Journal of Radiology. Supplement [*A
    publication*]
Br J Rheumatol ... British Journal of Rheumatology [*A publication*]
BRJS......... Brajdas Corp. [*NASDAQ symbol*]   (NQ)
Br J Sex Med ... British Journal of Sexual Medicine [*A publication*]
Br J Soc ..... British Journal of Sociology [*A publication*]
Br J Soc Cl ... British Journal of Social and Clinical Psychology [*A
    publication*]
Br J Soc Clin Psychol ... British Journal of Social and Clinical Psychology [*A
    publication*]
Br J Sociol ... British Journal of Sociology [*A publication*]
Br J Sociol Educ ... British Journal of the Sociology of Education [*A
    publication*]
Br J Soc Med ... British Journal of Social Medicine [*A publication*]
Br J Soc Ps ... British Journal of Social Psychiatry [*A publication*]
Br J Soc Psychol ... British Journal of Social Psychology [*A publication*]
Br J Soc W ... British Journal of Social Work [*A publication*]
Br J Soc Wk ... British Journal of Social Work [*A publication*]
Br J Sports Med ... British Journal of Sports Medicine [*A publication*]
Br J Surg..... British Journal of Surgery [*A publication*]
Br J Tuberc ... British Journal of Tuberculosis [*A publication*]
Br J Tuberc Dis Chest ... British Journal of Tuberculosis and Diseases of the
    Chest [*A publication*]
Br J Urol.... British Journal of Urology [*A publication*]
Br J Ven Dis ... British Journal of Venereal Diseases [*A publication*]
Br J Vener Dis ... British Journal of Venereal Diseases [*A publication*]
BRK .... Baby Rat Kidney [*Immunology*]
BRK .... Berkeley-Haviland [*California*] [*Seismograph station code, US
    Geological Survey*]   (SEIS)

BRK .... Berkshire Hathaway, Inc. [*NYSE symbol*]   (CTT)
BRK .... Bourke [*Australia*] [*Airport symbol*]   (OAG)
BRK .... Bracknell Resources Ltd. [*Toronto Stock Exchange symbol*]
BRK .... Brake [*Automotive engineering*]
BRK .... Break   (KSC)
BRK .... Brecknockshire [*County in Wales*]   (ROG)
BRK .... Brick   (MSA)
BRK .... Brockway, Inc. [*NYSE symbol*]   (SPSG)
brk............. Broken [*Quality of the bottom*] [*Nautical charts*]
BRK .... Brook   (MCD)
BRKBD...... Brakeband   (MSA)
BRKF .... Breakfast
BRKG .... Breaking
BRKHIC.... Breaks in Higher Overcast [*Meteorology*]   (FAAC)
BRKIA ...... British Kinematography [*A publication*]
Br Kinematogr ... British Kinematography, Sound, and Television [*A publication*]
Br Kinematogr Sound and Telev ... British Kinematography, Sound, and Television [*A publication*]
BRKKV...... Algemene Bond van Rooms Katholieke Kiesverenigingen [*General League of Roman Catholic Election Societies*] [*Netherlands*]   (PPE)
BRKN .... Broken
BRKN .... [*The*] Broken Hill Proprietary Co. Ltd. [*NASDAQ symbol*]   (NQ)
Br Knitting Ind ... British Knitting Industry [*A publication*]
BRKR........ Breaker
BRKS .... Breakers [*Freight*]
BRKS .... Brecknockshire [*County in Wales*]
BRKT........ Bracket   (KSC)
BRL............ Babe Ruth League   (EA)
BRL............ Balance Return Loss [*Telecommunications*]   (TEL)
BRL............ Ballistic Research Laboratory [*Army*] [*Aberdeen Proving Ground, MD*]
BRL............ Barr Laboratories, Inc. [*AMEX symbol*]   (SPSG)
BRL............ Barrel
BRL............ Beecham Research Laboratories Ltd. [*Great Britain*] [*Research code symbol*]
BRL............ Behavioral Research Laboratories
BRL............ Bell Resources Limited [*Australia*]
BRL............ Berle Resources Limited [*Vancouver Stock Exchange symbol*]
BRL............ Berlin - Free University [*West Germany*] [*Seismograph station code, US Geological Survey*]   (SEIS)
BRL............ Bethesda Research Laboratories [*Life Technologies, Inc.*] [*Gaithersburg, MD*]
BRL............ Biological Research Laboratories [*Syracuse University*] [*Research center*]   (RCD)
BRL........ Bomb Release Line
BRL............ Braille Revival League   (EA)
BR/L......... Brown Line Positive
Br & L .... Browning and Lushington's English Admiralty Reports [*1863-65*] [*A publication*]   (DLA)
BRL............ Buffalo Rat Liver [*Cytology*]
BRL............ Building Research Laboratory [*Ohio State University*] [*Research center*]   (RCD)
BRL............ Bulletin. John Rylands Library. University of Manchester [*A publication*]
BRL............ Burlington [*Iowa*] [*Airport symbol*]   (OAG)
BRL/EEP .. Bomb Release Line/End Exercise Point   (FAAC)
Br Leg Max ... Broom's Legal Maxims [*A publication*]   (DLA)
BRLESC.... Ballistic Research Laboratories Electronic Scientific Computer
BRLG....... Bomb, Radio, Longitudinal, Generator-Powered
BRLGA....... Brain and Language [*A publication*]
BRLI.......... Bio-Reference Laboratories, Inc. [*NASDAQ symbol*]   (NQ)
Br Lib Inf Sci ... British Librarianship and Information Science [*A publication*]
Br Libr News ... British Library News [*A publication*]
BRLN .... [*The*] Brooklyn Savings Bank [*NASDAQ symbol*]   (NQ)
BRLO .... British Routing Liaison Officer [*World War II*]
BRLP .... Burlap
Br LR .... Brooklyn Law Review [*A publication*]
BRLS .... Barrier Ready Light System   (MSA)
BRLTD...... Bulletin. Research Laboratory for Nuclear Reactors. Tokyo Institute of Technology [*A publication*]
Br & Lush .. Browning and Lushington's English Admiralty Reports [*1863-65*] [*A publication*]   (DLA)
BRM .... Babylonian Records in the Library of J. Pierpont Morgan   (BJA)
BRM .... Barandium Resources [*Vancouver Stock Exchange symbol*]
BRM .... Barometer   (FAAC)
BRM .... Barquisimeto [*Venezuela*] [*Airport symbol*]   (OAG)
BRM .... Baseline Reference Mission   (MCD)
BRM .... Basic Rifle Maintenance
BRM .... Basic Rifle Marksmanship [*Program of instruction*] [*Army*]   (INF)
B'RM .... Bedroom [*Classified advertising*]   (ADA)
BRM .... Bernie [*Missouri*] [*Seismograph station code, US Geological Survey*] [*Closed*]   (SEIS)
BRM .... Biological Reference Materials
BRM .... Biological Research Module [*NASA*]   (NASA)
BRM .... Biological Response Modifier Technology [*Biotechnology*]

BRM .... Biological Response Modifiers Program [*National Cancer Institute*]
BRM .... Biological Response Modulator
BRM .... Bras D'Or Mines [*Vancouver Stock Exchange symbol*]
BRM .... Brimstone R. R. [*AAR code*]
BRM .... British Racing Motors
BRM .... Bulletin. Council for Research in Music Education [*A publication*]
BRM .... Business Reply Mail [*Advertising*]
BRM .... Rossland Historical Museum, British Columbia [*Library symbol*] [*National Library of Canada*]   (NLC)
BRMA .... Board of Registration of Medical Auxiliaries [*British*]
BRMA .... Braided Rug Manufacturers Association [*Defunct*]   (EA)
BRMA ...... British Rubber Manufacturers' Association   (EAIO)
BRMA .... Business Records Manufacturers Association [*Later, ABPM*]   (EA)
BRMA .... Richmond Museum and Archives, British Columbia [*Library symbol*] [*National Library of Canada*]   (NLC)
BRMA Rev ... BRMA [*British Rubber Manufacturers' Association Ltd.*] Review [*A publication*]
Br Max....... Broom's Legal Maxims [*A publication*]   (DLA)
Br MB .... Brooklyn Museum. Bulletin [*A publication*]
BRMC .... British Royal Marine Corps   (CINC)
BRMCEW ... Behavior Research Methods [*A publication*]
BRMD .... MacDonald, Dettwiler & Associates Ltd., Richmond, British Columbia [*Library symbol*] [*National Library of Canada*]   (NLC)
BRMEA..... Bruxelles Medical [*A publication*]
BRMEAY ... Bruxelles Medical [*A publication*]
Br Med B ... British Medical Bulletin [*A publication*]
Br Med Bull ... British Medical Bulletin [*A publication*]
Br Med J... British Medical Journal [*A publication*]
Br Med J Pract Obs ... British Medical Journal. Practice Observed Edition [*A publication*]
BRMIA...... Behavior Research Methods and Instrumentation [*A publication*]
BRMIC...... Ramarkrishna Mission Institute of Culture [*Calcutta*]. Bulletin [*A publication*]
Br Min .... British Mining [*A publication*]
BRMM ...... British Raw Materials Mission [*World War II*]
BRMMLA ... Bulletin. Rocky Mountain Modern Language Association [*A publication*]
BRMNA .... British Railway Modellers of North America [*Canada*]
BRMP........ Biological Response Modifiers Program [*National Cancer Institute*]
BrMQ .... British Museum. Quarterly [*A publication*]
Br MQ .... Brooklyn Museum. Quarterly [*A publication*]
Br M Qu..... British Museum. Quarterly [*A publication*]
BRMRA5... Brasil-Medico [*A publication*]
Br Mus (Nat Hist) Bull ... British Museum (Natural History). Bulletin. Geology [*A publication*]
Br Mus (Nat Hist) Bull Geol ... British Museum (Natural History). Bulletin. Geology [*A publication*]
Br Mus (Nat Hist) Bull Zool ... British Museum (Natural History). Bulletin. Zoology [*A publication*]
Br Mus (Nat Hist) Econ Ser ... British Museum (Natural History). Economic Series [*A publication*]
Br Mus (Nat Hist) Fossil Mammals Afr ... British Museum (Natural History). Fossil Mammals of Africa [*A publication*]
Br Mus (Nat Hist) Mineral Leafl ... British Museum (Natural History). Mineralogy Leaflet [*A publication*]
Br Mus (Nat Hist) Palaeontol Leafl ... British Museum (Natural History). Palaeontology Leaflet [*A publication*]
Br Mus (Nat Hist) Publ ... British Museum (Natural History). Publication [*A publication*]
Br Mus (Nat Hist) Rep ... British Museum (Natural History). Report [*A publication*]
Br Mus Yearbook ... British Museum. Yearbook [*A publication*]
BRMY .... Burmah Castrol PLC ADR [*NASDAQ symbol*]   (SPSG)
Br Mycol Soc Symp ... British Mycological Society. Symposium [*A publication*]
Br Mycol Soc Trans ... British Mycological Society. Transactions [*A publication*]
BRN .... Barisan Revolusi Nasional [*Political party*] [*Thailand*]
BRN .... Barnwell Industries, Inc. [*AMEX symbol*]   (SPSG)
BRN .... Basal Retinal Neuron [*Neurology*]
BRN .... Berlin [*West Germany*] [*Seismograph station code, US Geological Survey*]   (SEIS)
BRN .... Berne [*Switzerland*] [*Airport symbol*]   (OAG)
BRN .... Board of Registered Nursing
BRN .... Brinco Ltd. [*Toronto Stock Exchange symbol*]
BRN .... Broadcast Net   (NATG)
BRN .... Brown   (KSC)
BRN .... Brown & Root-Northrop
BRN .... Brunei Darussalam [*ANSI three-letter standard code*]   (CNC)
BRN .... Mountain Home, ID [*Location identifier*] [*FAA*]   (FAAL)
BrNAE....... British National Antarctic Expedition [*1901-04*]
Br Nat Bibliography ... British National Bibliography [*A publication*]
Br NB......... Bracton's Note Book, King's Bench [*1217-40*] [*A publication*]   (DLA)
BRNC .... Britannia Royal Naval College

Br NC......... Brooke's New Cases, English King's Bench [*1515-58*] [*A publication*] (DLA)

Br N Cas .... Brooke's New Cases, English King's Bench [*1515-58*] [*A publication*] (DLA)

BRNG........ Burning

BRNLDT... Australia. Commonwealth Scientific and Industrial Research Organisation. National Measurement Laboratory. Biennial Report [*A publication*]

BRNNRC .. Building Research News. National Research Council of Canada [*A publication*]

BRNO........ Bruno's, Inc. [*NASDAQ symbol*] (NQ)

Br Non Ferrous Met Res Assoc Ann Rep ... British Non-Ferrous Metals Research Association. Annual Report [*A publication*]

Br Non Ferrous Met Res Assoc Res Monogr ... British Non-Ferrous Metals Research Association. Research Monograph [*A publication*]

Br Not .... Brooke's Office and Practice of a Notary [*A publication*] (DLA)

Brno Univ Prirod Fak Scr Geol ... Brno. Universita. Prirodovedecka Fakulta. Scripta Geologia [*A publication*]

BRNR .... Brenner International, Inc. [*Dallas, TX*] [*NASDAQ symbol*] (NQ)

BRNR .... Burner

BRNSBE ... Brenesia [*A publication*]

brnsh........... Brownish [*Philately*]

BRNSHR.... Burnisher (MSA)

brnt............. Burnt [*Philately*]

Br Numismatic J ... British Numismatic Journal [*A publication*]

BRNWA ..... Brennstoff- und Waermewirtschaft [*A publication*]

brnz............. Bronze [*Philately*]

BRO............ Base Requirements Overseas (CINC)

BRO............ Brigade Routine Order [*British*]

BRO............ British Routing Office

BRO............ BRO Resources Ltd. [*Vancouver Stock Exchange symbol*]

BRO...... Broach (KSC)

BRO........ Broad, Inc. [*NYSE symbol*] (SPSG)

BRO........ Broadband Remote Oculometer (KSC)

Bro .... [*W. G.*] Brooke's Ecclesiastical Reports [*1850-72*] [*A publication*] (DLA)

BRO............ Brother

BRO........... Brower Flight Service [*Fort Madison, IA*] [*FAA designator*] (FAAC)

Bro .... Browne's Reports [*Ceylon*] [*A publication*] (DLA)

Bro .... Browne's Reports [*Pennsylvania*] [*A publication*] (DLA)

Bro .... Brown's English Chancery Reports [*28, 29 English Reprint*] [*A publication*] (DLA)

Bro .... Brown's Michigan Nisi Prius Reports [*A publication*] (DLA)

Bro .... Brown's Parliamentary Cases [*England*] [*A publication*] (DLA)

Bro .... Brown's Reports [*53-65, 80-136 Missouri*] [*A publication*] (DLA)

BRO............ Brownsville [*Texas*] [*Airport symbol*] (OAG)

BRO............ Brush-Off [*Slang*]

BRO............ Revelstoke Branch, Okanagan Regional Library, British Columbia [*Library symbol*] [*National Library of Canada*] (BIB)

Bro Ab........ Brooke's Abridgment [*England*] [*A publication*] (DLA)

Bro Abr ...... Brooke's Abridgment [*England*] [*A publication*] (DLA)

Bro Abr in Eq ... Browne's New Abridgment of Cases in Equity [*A publication*] (DLA)

Bro Ac........ Browne. Actions at Law [*1843*] [*A publication*] (DLA)

Bro (A) CL ... Arthur Brown's Compendious View of the Civil Law [*A publication*] (DLA)

Bro Act........ Browne. Actions at Law [*1843*] [*A publication*] (DLA)

Broad .... Broadside Series [*A publication*]

Broadcast... Broadcasting Magazine [*A publication*]

Broadcast Equip Today ... Broadcast Equipment Today [*A publication*]

Broadcasting Bus ... Broadcasting Business [*A publication*] (APTA)

Broadcast Syst and Oper ... Broadcasting Systems and Operations [*A publication*]

Broadcast Technol ... Broadcast Technology [*A publication*]

Bro Adm..... Brown's United States Admiralty Reports [*A publication*] (DLA)

Broadw....... Broadway [*A publication*]

Broad Way Clin Suppl ... Broad Way Clinical Supplement [*England*] [*A publication*]

BROADWOODW ... Broadwoodwidger [*England*]

Bro Ag........ Brown on Agency and Trust [*A publication*] (DLA)

Bro Ag........ Brown. Agency and Trusts [*1868*] [*A publication*] (ILCA)

Bro A & R .. Brown's United States District Court Reports (Admiralty and Revenue Cases) [*A publication*] (DLA)

BROB........ Berichten. Rijksdienst voor het Oudheidkundige Bodemonderzoek [*A publication*]

BROBA ..... Brookings Bulletin [*A publication*]

BROC........ Brigade Rouge d'Occitanie [*Red Brigade of Occitania*] [*France*] (PD)

Bro C & AL ... Browne's Civil and Admiralty Law [*A publication*] (DLA)

Bro Car ..... Browne. Law of Carriers [*1873*] [*A publication*] (DLA)

Bro CC ...... Brown's Chancery Cases [*A publication*]

Bro CC .... Brown's English Chancery Cases [*or Reports*] [*A publication*] (DLA)

Bro Ch......... Brown's English Chancery Reports [*28, 29 English Reprint*] [*A publication*] (DLA)

Bro Ch Cas ... Brown's English Chancery Reports [*28, 29 English Reprint*] [*A publication*] (DLA)

Bro Ch Pr... Browne's Practice of the High Court of Chancery [*A publication*] (DLA)

Bro Ch R .... Brown's English Chancery Reports [*28, 29 English Reprint*] [*A publication*] (DLA)

Bro Civ Law ... Browne's Civil and Admiralty Law [*A publication*] (DLA)

Bro Civ Proc ... Broughton's Indian Civil Procedure [*A publication*] (DLA)

Brock.......... Brockenbrough's Marshall's Decisions, United States Circuit Court [*A publication*] (DLA)

Brock Cas .. Brockenbrough. Virginia Cases [*A publication*] (DLA)

Brock CC ... Brockenbrough's Marshall's Decisions, United States Circuit Court [*A publication*] (DLA)

Brock & H ... Brockenbrough and Holmes. Virginia Cases [*A publication*] (DLA)

Brock & Ho ... Brockenbrough and Holmes. Virginia Cases [*A publication*] (DLA)

Brock & Hol ... Brockenbrough and Holmes. Virginia Cases [*A publication*] (DLA)

Brock & Hol Cas ... Brockenbrough and Holmes. Virginia Cases [*A publication*] (DLA)

Brock Marsh ... Brockenbrough's Marshall's Decisions, United States Circuit Court [*A publication*] (DLA)

Brock Univ Dep Geol Sci Res Rep Ser ... Brock University. Department of Geological Sciences. Research Report Series [*A publication*]

Bro Co Act ... Browne on the Companies' Acts [*A publication*] (DLA)

Bro Com..... Broom's Commentaries on the Common Law [*A publication*] (DLA)

Brod .... Broderick and Freemantle's Ecclesiastical Cases [*1840-64*] [*A publication*] (DLA)

Brodae........ [*Johannes*] Brodaeus [*Deceased, 1563*] [*Authority cited in pre-1607 legal work*] (DSA)

Brod & B .... Broderip and Bingham's English Common Pleas Reports [*A publication*] (DLA)

Brod & Bing ... Broderip and Bingham's English Common Pleas Reports [*129 English Reprint*] [*A publication*] (DLA)

Brod & F .... Broderick and Freemantle's Ecclesiastical Cases [*1840-64*] [*A publication*] (DLA)

Brod & F Ecc Cas ... Broderick and Freemantle's Ecclesiastical Cases [*1840-64*] [*A publication*] (DLA)

Brod & Fr.... Broderick and Freemantle's Ecclesiastical Cases [*1840-64*] [*A publication*] (DLA)

Brod & Fr Ecc Cas ... Broderick and Freemantle's Ecclesiastical Cases [*1840-64*] [*A publication*] (DLA)

Brod & Frem ... Broderick and Freemantle's Ecclesiastical Cases [*1840-64*] [*A publication*] (DLA)

Bro Dig Div ... Browne's Digest of Decisions on Divorce and Alimony [*A publication*] (DLA)

Brodil'naya Prom ... Brodil'naya Promyshlennost [*A publication*]

Bro Div Pr... Browne's Divorce Court Practice [*A publication*] (DLA)

Brodix Am & Eng Pat Cas ... Brodix's American and English Patent Cases [*A publication*] (DLA)

Brodix Am & E Pat Cas ... Brodix's American and English Patent Cases [*A publication*] (DLA)

Brod Stair .. Brodie's Notes and Supplement to Stair's Institutions [*Scotland*] [*A publication*] (DLA)

Bro Ecc...... Brooke's Six Ecclesiastical Judgments [*A publication*] (DLA)

Bro Ent...... Brownlow's Latine Redivivus [*or Entries*] [*A publication*] (DLA)

Bro Ent...... Brown's Entries [*A publication*] (DLA)

Bro & F ...... Broderick and Freemantle's Ecclesiastical Cases [*1840-64*] [*A publication*] (DLA)

BROFICON ... Broadcast Fighter Control [*Military*]

Bro Fix....... Brown on Fixtures [*A publication*] (DLA)

Bro For....... Brown on Forestalling, Regrating, and Monopolizing, with Cases [*A publication*] (DLA)

Bro For....... Brown's Forum [*A publication*] (DLA)

Bro Form.... Brown's Formulae Bene Placitandi [*A publication*] (DLA)

Bro & Fr..... Broderick and Freemantle's Ecclesiastical Cases [*1840-64*] [*A publication*] (DLA)

Bro Fr......... Browne on the Statute of Frauds [*A publication*] (DLA)

Bro & G...... Brownlow and Goldesborough's English Common Pleas Reports [*A publication*] (DLA)

Bro & H...... Brown and Hemingway's Reports [*53-58 Mississippi*] [*A publication*] (DLA)

Bro Hered .. Browne. Law of Rating of Hereditaments [*2nd ed.*] [*1886*] [*A publication*] (DLA)

BROI .... Branch Operating Instruction [*Air Force*] (AFM)

Broil Grow ... Broiler Growing [*A publication*]

Bro Ins .... Browne's Medical Jurisprudence of Insanity [*A publication*] (DLA)

Bro Just ..... Broun's Reports, Scotch Justiciary Court [*1842-45*] [*A publication*] (DLA)

BROK .... Brokerage (ROG)

Bro & L ...... Browning and Lushington's English Admiralty Reports [*1863-65*] [*A publication*] (DLA)

Bro Law Dic ... Brown's Law Dictionary [*A publication*] (DLA)

Bro Leg Max ... Broom's Legal Maxims [*A publication*] (DLA)

Brolga R..... Brolga Review [*A publication*] (APTA)

Bro Lim ...... Brown. Limitations as to Real Property [*1869*] [*A publication*] (DLA)
Bro & Lush ... Browning and Lushington's English Admiralty Reports [*1863-65*] [*A publication*] (DLA)
Bro & Lush M & D ... Browning and Lushington on Marriage and Divorce [*A publication*] (DLA)
BROM .... Bromide [*Chemistry*] (ADA)
Bro & M ..... Brown and McCall's Yorkshire Star Chamber [*Yorkshire Archaeological Society Record, Series 44, 45, 51, 70*] [*A publication*] (DLA)
Bro & M ..... Browne and MacNamara's Railway Cases [*A publication*] (DLA)
BROM .... Bulletin. Royal Ontario Museum. Art and Archaeology Division [*A publication*]
Bro & Mac ... Browne and MacNamara's Railway Cases [*A publication*] (DLA)
Bromatol Chem Toksykol ... Bromatologia i Chemia Toksykologiczna [*A publication*]
Bro Max ..... Broom's Legal Maxims [*A publication*] (DLA)
Bro M & D ... Browning on Marriage and Divorce [*A publication*] (DLA)
Bromley Local Hist ... Bromley Local History [*A publication*]
Bromma Hembygds-Foren Arsskr ... Bromma Hembygds-Forenings Arsskrift [*A publication*]
Brompt Hosp Rep ... Brompton Hospital Reports [*A publication*]
BRON .... Bronchial
BRON .... Bronchoscopy [*Medicine*]
BRONA ..... Bronches [*A publication*]
BRONA3 ..... Bronches [*A publication*]
Bro NB Cas ... Browne's National Bank Cases [*A publication*] (DLA)
Bro NC .... Brooke's New Cases, English King's Bench [*1515-58*] [*A publication*] (DLA)
Bronch .... [*Everhardus*] Bronchorst [*Deceased, 1627*] [*Authority cited in pre-1607 legal work*] (DSA)
BRONCH ... Bronchoscopy [*Medicine*]
Bro Not ...... Brooke on the Office of a Notary in England [*A publication*] (DLA)
Bro NP .... Brown's English Nisi Prius Cases [*A publication*] (DLA)
Bro NP .... Brown's Michigan Nisi Prius Reports [*A publication*] (DLA)
Brook Abr ... Brooke's Abridgment [*England*] [*A publication*] (DLA)
Brook Bul ... Brookings Bulletin [*A publication*]
Brooke .... Brooke's Ecclesiastical Cases [*1850-72*] [*England*] [*A publication*] (DLA)
Brooke .... Brooke's New Cases, English King's Bench [*1515-58*] [*A publication*] (DLA)
Brooke Abr ... Brooke's Abridgment [*England*] [*A publication*] (DLA)
Brooke Bib Leg ... Brooke's Bibliotheca Legum Angliae [*A publication*] (DLA)
Brooke Ch W ... Brooke's Churchwarden's Guide [*A publication*] (DLA)
Brooke Eccl ... Brooke's Six Ecclesiastical Judgments [*A publication*] (DLA)
Brooke Eccl Judg ... Brooke's Ecclesiastical Judgments [*A publication*] (DLA)
Brooke Lim ... Brooke's Reading on the Statute of Limitations [*A publication*] (DLA)
Brooke NC ... Brooke's New Cases, English King's Bench [*1515-58*] [*A publication*] (DLA)
Brooke Not ... Brooke's Office and Practice of a Notary [*A publication*] (DLA)
Brooke (Petit) ... Brooke's New Cases, English King's Bench [*1515-58*] [*A publication*] (DLA)
Brooke Six Judg ... Brooke's Six Ecclesiastical Judgments [*A publication*] (DLA)
Brookhaven Natl Lab Lect Sci Vistas Res ... Brookhaven National Laboratory. Lectures in Science. Vistas in Research [*A publication*]
Brookhaven Symp Biol ... Brookhaven Symposia in Biology [*A publication*]
Brookh Symp Biol ... Brookhaven Symposia in Biology [*A publication*]
Brookings ... Brookings Papers on Economic Activity [*A publication*]
Brookings Bull ... Brookings Bulletin [*A publication*]
Brookings P ... Brookings Papers on Economic Activity [*A publication*]
Brookings Pa Econ Activ ... Brookings Papers on Economic Activity [*A publication*]
Brookings Pas Econ Activity ... Brookings Papers on Economic Activity [*A publication*]
Brookings R ... Brookings Review [*A publication*]
Brook J Int L ... Brooklyn Journal of International Law [*A publication*]
Brookl Bot Gard Rec ... Brooklyn Botanic Garden. Record [*A publication*]
Brookl J Int L ... Brooklyn Journal of International Law [*A publication*]
Brookl L Rev ... Brooklyn Law Review [*A publication*]
Brookl Med J ... Brooklyn Medical Journal [*A publication*]
Brookl Mus Ann ... Brooklyn Museum. Annual [*A publication*]
Brookl Mus Bull ... Brooklyn Museum. Bulletin [*A publication*]
Brookl Mus J ... Brooklyn Museum. Journal [*A publication*]
Brookl Mus Quart ... Brooklyn Museum. Quarterly [*A publication*]
Brook Lodge Conf Lung Cells Dis Proc ... Brook Lodge Conference on Lung Cells in Disease. Proceedings [*A publication*]
Brook LR ... Brooklyn Law Review [*A publication*]
Brookl Rec ... Brooklyn Daily Record [*A publication*] (DLA)
Brooklyn Bar ... Brooklyn Barrister [*A publication*]
Brooklyn Bot Gard Annu Rep ... Brooklyn Botanic Garden. Annual Report [*A publication*]
Brooklyn Bot Gard Mem ... Brooklyn Botanic Garden. Memoirs [*A publication*]

Brooklyn Bot Gard Rec ... Brooklyn Botanic Garden. Record [*A publication*]
Brooklyn Bot Gard Rec Plants Gard ... Brooklyn Botanic Garden. Record. Plants and Gardens [*A publication*]
Brooklyn Daily Rec ... Brooklyn Daily Record [*A publication*] (DLA)
Brooklyn Hosp J ... Brooklyn Hospital. Journal [*A publication*]
Brooklyn J Int L ... Brooklyn Journal of International Law [*A publication*]
Brooklyn J Intl L ... Brooklyn Journal of International Law [*A publication*]
Brooklyn Law R ... Brooklyn Law Review [*A publication*]
Brooklyn L Re ... Brooklyn Law Review [*A publication*]
Brooklyn L Rev ... Brooklyn Law Review [*A publication*]
Brooklyn Mus Ann ... Brooklyn Museum. Annual [*A publication*]
Brooklyn Mus Bul ... Brooklyn Institute of Arts and Sciences. Museum Bulletin [*A publication*]
Brook Mus Q ... Brooklyn Museum. Quarterly [*A publication*]
Brook N Cas ... Brooke's New Cases, English King's Bench [*1515-58*] [*A publication*] (DLA)
Brookng R ... Brookings Review [*A publication*]
Brook Pap Econ Act ... Brookings Papers on Economic Activity [*A publication*]
Brooks .... Brooks' Reports [*106-119 Michigan*] [*A publication*] (DLA)
Brook S Bio ... Brookhaven Symposia in Biology [*A publication*]
Brookville Soc N H B ... Brookville Society of Natural History. Bulletin [*A publication*]
BROOM .... Ballistic Recovery of Orbiting Man (KSC)
Broom .... Broom's Legal Maxims [*A publication*] (DLA)
Broom CL .. Broom's Commentaries on the Common Law [*A publication*] (DLA)
Broom Com Law ... Broom's Commentaries on the Common Law [*A publication*] (DLA)
Broom Const L ... Broom. Constitutional Law [*3rd ed.*] [*1885*] [*A publication*] (DLA)
Broom & H Com ... Broom and Hadley's Commentaries on the Laws of England [*A publication*] (DLA)
Broom & H Comm ... Broom and Hadley's Commentaries on the Laws of England [*A publication*] (DLA)
Broom Leg Max ... Broom's Legal Maxims [*A publication*] (DLA)
Broom Max ... Broom's Legal Maxims [*A publication*] (DLA)
Broom Part ... Broom on Parties to Actions [*A publication*] (DLA)
Broom Ph Law ... Broom. Philosophy of Law [*3rd ed.*] [*1883*] [*A publication*] (DLA)
Bro PA .... Browne's Pennsylvania Reports [*1801-14*] [*A publication*] (DLA)
Bro Parl Cas ... Brown's Cases in Parliament [*A publication*] (DLA)
Bro Pat Pr ... Browne's Patent Office Practice [*A publication*] (DLA)
Bro PC .... Brown's English Parliamentary Cases [*A publication*] (DLA)
BROPD ..... Bjulleteni Rukopisnogo Otdela Puskinskogo Doma [*A publication*]
Bro Prac ..... Brown's Practice (Praxis) [*or Precedents*] in Chancery [*A publication*] (DLA)
Bro Prob Pr ... Browne's Probate Practice [*A publication*] (DLA)
BROR .... Brother (ROG)
BRORAF ... Broteria. Serie Trimestral. Ciencias Naturais [*A publication*]
Bro Read ..... Brooke's Reading on the Statute of Limitations [*A publication*] (DLA)
Bro Reg Act ... Browne's Parliamentary and Municipal Registration Act [*A publication*] (DLA)
Bro RPL ..... Brown. Limitations as to Real Property [*1869*] [*A publication*] (DLA)
Br Orthopt J ... British Orthoptic Journal [*A publication*]
BROS .... Brothers
Bro Sal .... Brown. Treatise on Law of Sale [*Scotland*] [*A publication*] (DLA)
Bro Sp .... [*David Paul*] Brown's Speeches [*A publication*] (DLA)
Bro St .... Brodie's Notes and Supplement to Stair's Institutions [*Scotland*] [*A publication*] (DLA)
Bro Stair .... Brodie's Notes and Supplement to Stair's Institutions [*Scotland*] [*A publication*] (DLA)
Bro St Fr .... Browne on the Statute of Frauds [*A publication*] (DLA)
Bro Sup to Mor ... Brown's Supplement to Morison's Dictionary of Decisions, Scotch Court of Sessions [*A publication*] (DLA)
Bro Supp .... Brown's Supplement to Morison's Dictionary, Scotch Court of Sessions [*A publication*] (DLA)
Bro Syn ...... Brown's Synopsis of Decisions, Scotch Court of Sessions [*1540-1827*] [*A publication*] (DLA)
Bro Synop .. Brown's Synopsis of Decisions, Scotch Court of Sessions [*1540-1827*] [*A publication*] (DLA)
Brot .... Broteria [*A publication*]
BROT .... Brought (ADA)
BROTA ...... Brot und Gebaeck [*A publication*]
BROTAL .... Brot und Gebaeck [*A publication*]
Broteria Ser Cienc Nat ... Broteria. Serie de Ciencias Naturais [*A publication*]
Broteria Ser Trimest Cienc Nat ... Broteria. Serie Trimestral. Ciencias Naturais [*A publication*]
Bro Tr M .... Browne on Trade Markets [*A publication*] (DLA)
BROTS ...... Beneficial Rays of the Sun [*In reference to suntanning, supposedly occuring between 10am and 2pm*] [*See also SROTS*]
Brough Civ Pro ... Broughton's Indian Civil Procedure [*A publication*] (DLA)
Brough Elec ... Brough's Law of Elections [*A publication*] (DLA)
Broun .... Broun's Reports, Scotch Justiciary Court [*1842-45*] [*A publication*] (DLA)

Broun Just ... Broun's Reports, Scotch Justiciary Court [*1842-45*] [*A publication*]   (DLA)
Bro Us & Cus ... Browne's Law of Usages and Customs [*A publication*]   (DLA)
Bro VM ...... Brown's Vade Mecum [*A publication*]   (DLA)
Brow Brev .. Brownlow's Brevia Judicialia, Etc. [*1662*] [*A publication*]   (DLA)
Brown .... Brownlow and Goldesborough's English Common Pleas Reports [*A publication*]   (DLA)
Brown .... Brown's English Chancery Reports [*28, 29 English Reprint*] [*A publication*]   (DLA)
Brown .... Brown's English Parliamentary Cases [*A publication*]   (DLA)
Brown .... Brown's Law Dictionary [*A publication*]   (DLA)
Brown .... Brown's Law Dictionary and Institute [*1874*] [*A publication*]   (DLA)
Brown .... Brown's Michigan Nisi Prius Reports [*A publication*]   (DLA)
Brown .... Brown's Reports [*4-25 Nebraska*] [*A publication*]   (DLA)
Brown .... Brown's Reports [*53-65 Mississippi*] [*A publication*]   (DLA)
Brown .... Brown's Reports [*80-137 Missouri*] [*A publication*]   (DLA)
Brown .... Brown's Scotch Reports [*A publication*]   (DLA)
Brown .... Brown's United States Admiralty Reports [*A publication*]   (DLA)
Brown .... Brown's United States District Court Reports [*A publication*]   (DLA)
Brown Adm ... Brown's United States Admiralty Reports [*A publication*]   (DLA)
Brown Am ... Brown American [*A publication*]
Brown A & R ... Brown's United States District Court Reports (Admiralty and Revenue Cases) [*A publication*]   (DLA)
Brown Boveri Mitt ... Brown Boveri Mitteilungen [*Brown Boveri Review*] [*A publication*]
Brown Boveri Rev ... Brown Boveri Review [*A publication*]
Brown Boveri Symp Nonemissive Electroopt Disp ... Brown Boveri Symposium on Nonemissive Electrooptic Displays [*A publication*]
Brown Bov R ... Brown Boveri Review [*A publication*]
Brown C ..... Brown's English Chancery Cases [*or Reports*] [*A publication*]   (DLA)
Brown CC ... Brown's English Chancery Cases [*or Reports*] [*A publication*]   (DLA)
Brown Ch ... Brown's Chancery Cases Tempore Lord Thurlow [*England*] [*A publication*]   (DLA)
Brown Ch C ... Brown's Chancery Cases Tempore Lord Thurlow [*England*] [*A publication*]   (DLA)
Brown Dict ... Brown's Law Dictionary [*A publication*]   (DLA)
Brown Div Pr ... Browning's Divorce Court Practice [*A publication*]   (DLA)
Browne .... Browne's Civil Procedure Reports [*New York*] [*A publication*]   (DLA)
Browne .... Browne's Reports [*Ceylon*] [*A publication*]   (DLA)
Browne .... Browne's Reports [*Massachusetts*] [*A publication*]   (DLA)
Browne .... Browne's Reports [*Pennsylvania*] [*A publication*]   (DLA)
Browne Act ... Browne. Actions at Law [*1843*] [*A publication*]   (DLA)
Browne Bank Cas ... Browne's National Bank Cases [*A publication*]   (DLA)
Browne Car ... Browne on Carriers [*A publication*]   (DLA)
Brown Ecc ... Brown's English Ecclesiastical Reports [*A publication*]   (DLA)
Browne Civ L ... Browne's Civil and Admiralty Law [*A publication*]   (DLA)
Browne Civ Law ... Browne's Civil and Admiralty Law [*A publication*]   (DLA)
Browne Div ... Browne's Divorce Court Practice [*A publication*]   (DLA)
Browne Div Pr ... Browne. Practice in Divorce and Matrimonial Causes [*11th ed.*] [*1931*] [*A publication*]   (DLA)
Browne Fr .. Browne on the Statute of Frauds [*A publication*]   (DLA)
Browne & G ... Browne and Gray's Reports [*A publication*]   (DLA)
Browne & Gray ... Browne and Gray's Reports [*A publication*]   (DLA)
Browne Jud Interp ... Browne's Judicial Interpretation of Common Words and Phrases [*A publication*]   (DLA)
Browne & MacN ... Browne and MacNamara's English Railway and Canal Cases [*A publication*]   (DLA)
Browne NBC ... Browne's National Bank Cases [*A publication*]   (DLA)
Brown Ent ... Brownlow's Entries [*A publication*]   (DLA)
Browne (PA) ... Browne's Reports [*Pennsylvania*] [*A publication*]   (DLA)
Browne PA R ... Browne's Reports [*Pennsylvania*] [*A publication*]   (DLA)
Browne Prob ... Browne's Probate Practice [*A publication*]   (ILCA)
Browne Prob Pr ... Browne's Probate Practice [*A publication*]   (DLA)
Browne's Rep ... Browne's Reports [*Pennsylvania*] [*A publication*]   (DLA)
Browne St Frauds ... Browne on the Statute of Frauds [*A publication*]   (DLA)
Browne & Th Railw ... Browne and Theobald. Railways [*4th ed.*] [*1911*] [*A publication*]   (DLA)
Browne Tr M ... Browne on Trade Markets [*A publication*]   (DLA)
Browne Us ... Browne on Usages and Customs [*A publication*]   (DLA)
Brown GA Pl & Pr Anno ... Browne. Georgia Pleading and Practice and Legal Forms, Annotated [*A publication*]   (DLA)
Brown & G (Eng) ... Brownlow and Goldesborough's English Common Pleas Reports [*A publication*]   (DLA)
Brown & Gold ... Brownlow and Goldesborough's English Common Pleas Reports [*A publication*]   (DLA)
Brown & H ... Brown and Hemingway's Reports [*53-58 Mississippi*] [*A publication*]   (DLA)
Brown & Hemingway ... Brown and Hemingway's Reports [*53-58 Mississippi*] [*A publication*]   (DLA)
Browning In ... Browning Institute. Studies [*A publication*]
Browning Inst Stud ... Browning Institute. Studies [*A publication*]

Brown & L ... Browning and Lushington's English Admiralty Reports [*1863-65*] [*A publication*]   (DLA)
Brownl .... Brownlow and Goldesborough's English Common Pleas Reports [*A publication*]   (DLA)
Brownl Brev ... Brownlow's Brevia Judicialia, Etc. [*1662*] [*A publication*]   (DLA)
Brown & L (Eng) ... Browning and Lushington's English Admiralty Reports [*1863-65*] [*A publication*]   (DLA)
Brownl Ent ... Brownlow's Entries [*A publication*]   (DLA)
Brownl & G ... Brownlow and Goldesborough's English Common Pleas Reports [*A publication*]   (DLA)
Brownl & Gold ... Brownlow and Goldesborough's English Common Pleas Reports [*A publication*]   (DLA)
Brownl Redv ... Brownlow's Latine Redivivus [*or Entries*] [*A publication*]   (DLA)
Brown & Lush ... Browning and Lushington's English Admiralty Reports [*1863-65*] [*A publication*]   (DLA)
Brown & Lush M & D ... Browning and Lushington on Marriage and Divorce [*A publication*]   (DLA)
Brown & MacN ... Browne and MacNamara's Railway Cases [*A publication*]   (DLA)
Brown M & D ... Browning on Marriage and Divorce [*A publication*]   (DLA)
Brown NP .. Brown's Michigan Nisi Prius Reports [*A publication*]   (DLA)
Brown NP Cas ... Brown's English Nisi Prius Cases [*A publication*]   (DLA)
Brown NP (Mich) ... Brown's Michigan Nisi Prius Reports [*A publication*]   (DLA)
Brown Parl ... Brown's House of Lords Cases [*England*] [*A publication*]   (DLA)
Brown Parl Cas ... Brown's House of Lords Cases [*England*] [*A publication*]   (DLA)
Brown PC ... Brown's House of Lords Cases [*England*] [*A publication*]   (DLA)
Brown & R ... Brown and Rader's Reports [*137 Missouri*] [*A publication*]   (DLA)
BROWNS ... Brownshall [*England*]
Brown's Adm App ... Brown's United States Admiralty Reports (Appendix) [*A publication*]   (DLA)
Brownson ... Brownson's Quarterly Review [*A publication*]
Brown's (Penn) ... Browne's Reports [*Pennsylvania*] [*A publication*]   (DLA)
Brown's Penn Rep ... Browne's Reports [*Pennsylvania*] [*A publication*]   (DLA)
Brown's Roman Law ... Brown's Epitome and Analysis of Savigny's Treatise on Obligations in Roman Law [*A publication*]   (DLA)
Brown Sup ... Brown's Supplement to Morison's Dictionary, Scotch Court of Sessions [*A publication*]   (DLA)
Brown Sup Dec ... Brown's Supplement to Morison's Dictionary, Scotch Court of Sessions [*A publication*]   (DLA)
Brown Syn ... Brown's Synopsis of Decisions, Scotch Court of Sessions [*1540-1827*] [*A publication*]   (DLA)
BROWRO ... Brouwer-Lyddane Orbit Generation Routine
BROWSER ... Browsing On-Line with Selective Retrieval
BRP .... Barrier Pressure [*Medicine*]
BRP .... Bathroom Privileges [*Medicine*]
BRP .... Beacon Ranging Pulse
BRP .... Behavior Rating Profile [*Educational testing*]
BRP .... Beitraege zur Romanischen Philologie [*A publication*]
BRP .... Biaru [*Papua New Guinea*] [*Airport symbol*]   (OAG)
BRP .... Bollettino. Reale Universita Italiana per Stranieri di Perugia [*A publication*]
BRP .... Brain Retraction Pressure [*Neurophysiology*]
BRP .... Brakes Release Point   (ADA)
BRP .... British Patent
BR & P ...... Buffalo, Rochester & Pittsburgh Railroad
BRP .... Bulgarska Rabotnicheska Partiia [*Bulgarian Workers Party*] [*Political party*]   (PPE)
BRP .... Bureau of Radiation Protection   (NRCH)
BRP .... Business Reply Post [*British*]   (ADA)
BRPA .... British Radiological Protection Association   (DEN)
Br Pap Board Makers Assoc Proc Tech Sect ... British Paper and Board Makers Association. Proceedings of the Technical Section [*A publication*]
Br Par .... Brown's Parties to Actions [*A publication*]   (DLA)
BRPB .... British Rail Property Board
Br PC .... Brown's Chancery Cases [*England*] [*A publication*]   (DLA)
BRPC .... Parks Canada [*Parcs Canada*] Revelstoke, British Columbia [*Library symbol*] [*National Library of Canada*]   (NLC)
Br Pet Equip News ... British Petroleum Equipment News [*A publication*]
BRPF .... Bertrand Russell Peace Foundation   (EA)
BRPFD ...... Blech, Rohre, Profile [*A publication*]
BRPGDO .. Brooklyn Botanic Garden. Record. Plants and Gardens [*A publication*]
BRPh .... Beitraege zur Romanischen Philologie [*A publication*]
Br Phil Law ... Broom. Philosophy of Law [*3rd ed.*] [*1883*] [*A publication*]   (DLA)
Br Phycol Bull ... British Phycological Bulletin [*Later, British Phycological Journal*] [*A publication*]
Br Phycol J ... British Phycological Journal [*A publication*]
BrPI .... Instituto Zimotecnico, Piracicaba, Brazil [*Library symbol*] [*Library of Congress*]   (LCLS)
BRPLA ...... British Plastics [*Later, European Plastics News*] [*A publication*]
Br Plast ...... British Plastics [*Later, European Plastics News*] [*A publication*]

Br Plastics Rubber ... British Plastics and Rubber [*A publication*]
Br Plast Moulded Prod Trader ... British Plastics and Moulded Products Trader [*A publication*]
Br Plast Rubber ... British Plastics and Rubber [*A publication*]
BRPM........ Breath Rate per Minute   (MCD)
BRPNDB... Broncho-Pneumologie [*A publication*]
BRPNP...... Big Rock Point Nuclear Plant   (NRCH)
Br Polym J ... British Polymer Journal [*A publication*]
Br Portland Cem Res Assoc Pam ... British Portland Cement Research Association. Pamphlets [*A publication*]
Br Poult Sc ... British Poultry Science [*A publication*]
Br Poult Sci ... British Poultry Science [*A publication*]
Br Power Eng ... British Power Engineering [*England*] [*A publication*]
BRPPDH... Biological Research in Pregnancy and Perinatology [*A publication*]
BRPRA...... British Rubber Products Research Association   (MCD)
BRPRA Techn Bull ... BRPRA [*British Rubber Producers' Research Association*] Technical Bulletin [*A publication*]
BRPRD...... Bulletin of Radiation Protection [*A publication*]
Br Print...... British Printer [*A publication*]
BR & PRY ... Buffalo, Rochester & Pittsburg Railway [*Terminated*]
BRPS.......... British Retinitis Pigmentosa Society
Br Psych Soc Bull ... British Psychological Society. Bulletin [*A publication*]
BRPT......... Briarpatch. Saskatchewan's Independent Monthly Newsmagazine [*Canada*] [*A publication*]
Br Pteridol Soc Bull ... British Pteridological Society. Bulletin [*A publication*]
Br Public Opin ... British Public Opinion [*A publication*]
BRQ.......... Baroque Resources Ltd. [*Vancouver Stock Exchange symbol*]
BRQ.......... Book Research Quarterly [*A publication*]
BRQ.......... Brno [*Czechoslovakia*] [*Airport symbol*]   (OAG)
BRQM....... Brigade Quartermaster [*Marine Corps*]
BRR.......... Balanced Repeated Replication [*Statistics*]
BRR.......... Barra [*Hebrides Islands*] [*Airport symbol*]   (OAG)
BRR.......... Barron's Financial Weekly [*A publication*]
BRR.......... Basic Recommended Reading   (ADA)
BRR.......... Battelle Research Reactor
BRR.......... Bearer
BRR.......... Belton Railroad Co. [*AAR code*]
BRR.......... Berryman [*Missouri*] [*Seismograph station code, US Geological Survey*] [*Closed*]   (SEIS)
BRR.......... Biological Research Resources
BRR.......... Brazilian Economic Studies [*A publication*]
BRR.......... Bridge Receiving Room [*Navy*]
BrR........... Bridled with Rainbows [*A publication*]
BRR.......... Brigade Receiving Room
BRR.......... Brookhaven Research Reactor
Br & R....... Brown and Rader's Reports [*137 Missouri*] [*A publication*]   (DLA)
Br R.......... Browne's Reports [*Ceylon*] [*A publication*]   (DLA)
BRR.......... Bruncor, Inc. [*Toronto Stock Exchange symbol*]
BRR.......... Bureau of Rural Resources [*Australia*]
BRR.......... Lake Jackson, TX [*Location identifier*] [*FAA*]   (FAAL)
BRR.......... Mountain Air Service, Inc. [*Big Bear City, CA*] [*FAA designator*]   (FAAC)
BRRAB...... Brain Research Bulletin [*A publication*]
Br Rayon Silk J ... British Rayon and Silk Journal [*A publication*]
BR/RB....... Bilingual Review/Revista Bilingue [*A publication*]
BRRD........ Barred
BRREA....... Brain Research [*A publication*]
BRREAP.... Brain Research [*A publication*]
Br Reg....... Braithwaite's Register [*A publication*]   (DLA)
Br Reg Geol ... British Regional Geology [*A publication*]
Br Rep Transl Theses ... British Reports, Translations, and Theses [*A publication*]
BrRF.......... Fundacao Casa de Rui Barbosa, Rio De Janeiro, Brazil [*Library symbol*] [*Library of Congress*]   (LCLS)
BRRG........ Barring
BR/RL....... Bomb Rack/Rocket Launcher   (NG)
BRRL......... British Road Research Laboratory
BRRPC...... Rogers Pass Centre, Revelstoke, British Columbia [*Library symbol*] [*National Library of Canada*]   (NLC)
BRRS......... Banana River Repeater Station [*NASA*]   (KSC)
BRRS......... Barris Industries, Inc. [*NASDAQ symbol*]   (NQ)
BRRUD...... Brauerei-Rundschau [*A publication*]
Br Rul Cas ... British Ruling Cases [*A publication*]   (DLA)
BRS........... B-Mode Receiving Station [*Telecommunications*]   (TEL)
BRS........... Ballistic Recording System
BRS........... Balloon Radio System
BRS........... Bartok Recording Studio [*Record label*]
BRS........... Beacon-Radio Set
BRS........... Bertrand Russell Society   (EA)
BRS........... Bible Research Systems [*Information service or system*]   (IID)
BRS........... Bibliographic Retrieval Services, Inc. [*Database host system*] [*Scotia, NY*]
BRS........... Binary Ring Sequence
BRS........... Biofeedback Research Society [*Later, BSA*]   (EA)
BRS........... Biomedical Research Support Program [*Bethesda, MD*] [*National Institutes of Health*]   (GRD)
BRS........... Birch, Raymond Sr., Southampton PA [*STAC*]
BRS........... Block Received Signal [*Telecommunications*]   (TEL)
BRS........... Body Restraint System

BRS........... Boron Recycle System [*Nuclear energy*]   (NRCH)
BRS........... Bottom Right Side   (MCD)
BRS........... Brascan Ltd. [*AMEX symbol*]   (SPSG)
BRS........... Brass   (KSC)
BRS........... Brass Ring Society   (EA)
BRS........... Brazos Petroleum [*Vancouver Stock Exchange symbol*]
BRS........... Break Request Signal [*Data processing*]
BrS........... Breath Sounds [*Medicine*]
BRS........... Brisbane [*Australia*] [*Seismograph station code, US Geological Survey*]   (SEIS)
BRS........... Bristol [*England*] [*Airport symbol*]   (OAG)
BRS........... British Record Society
BRS........... British Research Station
BRS........... British Road Services
B of RS...... Brotherhood of Railroad Signalmen   (EA)
B of RS...... Brotherhood of Railroad Signalmen   (EA)
BRS........... Building Research Station [*British*]
BRS........... Building Research Station News [*A publication*]
BRS........... Bureau of Railroad Safety [*Department of Transportation*]
BRS........... Bureau of Rural Science [*Australia*]
BRS........... Business Radio Service
Br S Afr Co Publ Mazoe Citrus Exp Stn ... British South Africa Company. Publication. Mazoe Citrus Experimental Station [*A publication*]
BRS Bull .... BRS [*Bibliographic Retrieval Services*] Bulletin [*A publication*]
BRSc......... Bachelor of Religious Sciences
BRSC......... Brotherhood of Railway and Steamship Clerks, Freight Handlers, Express and Station Employees [*Later, BRAC*]   (EA)
BRSCB...... Building Research Station. Current Papers [*A publication*]
BRSCC...... British Racing and Sport Car Club
Br Sci News ... British Science News [*A publication*]
BRSE......... Bibliography of Research Studies in Education, 1926-1940 [*A publication*]
BRSF......... Biafra Relief Services Foundation   (EA)
BRSG......... Biomedical Research Support Grants
BRSG......... Boletin. Real Sociedad Geografica [*A publication*]
BRSGI....... Bollettino. Reale Societa Geografica Italiana [*A publication*]
BRSI.......... Ballistic Recovery Systems, Inc. [*NASDAQ symbol*]   (NQ)
BRSI.......... Bureau of Retirement Survivors Insurance [*Social Security Administration*]
BRSIT........ Boresight   (MSA)
BRSL......... Bristol Corp. [*NASDAQ symbol*]   (NQ)
BrSM......... British Studies Monitor [*A publication*]
BRSM........ Steveston Museum, Richmond, British Columbia [*Library symbol*] [*National Library of Canada*]   (NLC)
Br Small Anim Vet Assoc Congr Proc ... British Small Animal Veterinary Association. Congress. Proceedings [*A publication*]
BRSNAN... Feddes Repertorium. Specierum Novarum Regni Vegetabilis. Beihefte [*A publication*]
BRSO........ Bermuda Range Safety Officer [*NASA*]   (KSC)
BRSOA....... British Steel Corporation. Open Report [*A publication*]
Br Soap Manuf ... British Soap Manufacturer [*A publication*]
Br Soc Cell Biol Symp ... British Society for Cell Biology. Symposium [*A publication*]
BRSRA...... Bibliotheca Radiologica [*Switzerland*] [*A publication*]
BRSS......... Breema Rug Study Society [*Later, CRSS*]   (EA)
BRST......... Bristol Holdings, Inc. [*NASDAQ symbol*]   (NQ)
BRST......... Broadcast   (MUGU)
BRST......... Burst
Br Stan Yrbk ... British Standards Yearbook [*A publication*]
BRSTB....... British Steel [*A publication*]
Br Steel ..... British Steel [*A publication*]
Br Steel Corp Open Rep ... British Steel Corporation. Open Report [*A publication*]
Br Steel Corp Rep ... British Steel Corporation. Reports [*A publication*]
Br Steelmaker ... British Steelmaker [*A publication*]
BRSTL....... Bristol [*City and county borough in England*]
BRSTR....... Burster
Br Stud Monit ... British Studies Monitor [*A publication*]
BrSU.......... Universidade de Sao Paulo, Sao Paulo, Brazil [*Library symbol*] [*Library of Congress*]   (LCLS)
BRSUAA... British Sugar Beet Review [*A publication*]
Br Sugar Beet Rev ... British Sugar Beet Review [*A publication*]
Br Sug Beet Rev ... British Sugar Beet Review [*A publication*]
BrSU-H..... Universidade de Sao Paulo, Faculdade de Higiene e Saude Publica, Sao Paulo, Brazil [*Library symbol*] [*Library of Congress*]   (LCLS)
Br Sulphur Corp Q Bull ... British Sulphur Corporation. Quarterly Bulletin [*A publication*]
BrSU-MV ... Universidade de Sao Paulo, Faculdade de Medicina Veterinaria, Sao Paulo, Brazil [*Library symbol*] [*Library of Congress*]   (LCLS)
Br Sup........ Brown's Supplement to Morison's Dictionary, Scotch Court of Sessions [*A publication*]   (DLA)
BrSU-P...... Universidade de Sao Paulo, Escola Politecnica, Sao Paulo, Brazil [*Library symbol*] [*Library of Congress*]   (LCLS)
BrSU-Q...... Universidade de Sao Paulo, Conjucto das Quimicas, Sao Paulo, Brazil [*Library symbol*] [*Library of Congress*]   (LCLS)
BRSV......... Boletin. Real Sociedad Vascongada de Amigos del Pais [*A publication*]

Br Syn .... Brown's Synopsis of Decisions, Scotch Court of Sessions [*1540-1827*] [*A publication*]   (DLA)
Brs Z .... Breslauer Zeitung [*A publication*]
BRT .... Base Resistance Transistor
BRT .... Bathurst Island [*Australia*] [*Airport symbol*]   (OAG)
BRT .... Bayrak Radyo-Televisyon [*Bayrak Radio-Television*]
BRT .... Behavior Research and Therapy [*A publication*]
BRT .... Belgische Radio en Televisie [*Belgian Radio and Television - Dutch Service*]
BRT .... Bend Radius Template   (MCD)
BRT .... Bilateration Ranging Transponder   (MCD)
BRT .... Binary Run Tape [*Data processing*]   (BUR)
BRT .... BioResearch Titles   (DIT)
BRT .... Biotechnical Research Technology [*NIH*]
BRT .... Bolt Removal Tool
BRT .... Bright   (MSA)
BRT .... Bright [*T. G.*] & Co. Ltd. [*Toronto Stock Exchange symbol*]
BRT .... British   (ROG)
BRT .... Brooklyn Rapid Transit Co. [*A New York City subway line*] [*Became BMT*]
BRT .... Brotherhood of Railroad Trainmen [*Later, United Transportation Union*]   (EA)
BRT .... Brought
BRT .... BRT Realty Trust SBI [*NYSE symbol*]   (SPSG)
BRT .... Bruttoregistertonne [*Gross Registered Ton*] [*German*]
BRTA .... Bureau of Resources and Trade Assistance [*Department of Commerce*]
BRTAAN... Brittonia [*A publication*]
BR Tax R ... British Tax Review [*A publication*]
BR & TC .... Better Roads and Transportation Council   (EA)
BRTD .... Bright RADAR Tube Display   (AAG)
BRTE .... Bachelor of Radio and Television Engineering
Br Technol Index ... British Technology Index [*Later, Current Technology Index*] [*A publication*]
Br Telecom Engng ... British Telecommunications Engineering [*A publication*]
Br Telecom J ... British Telecom Journal [*A publication*]
Br Telecommun Eng ... British Telecommunications Engineering [*A publication*]
BRT Eng.... Bachelor of Radio and Television Engineering
Br Territ Borneo Annu Rep Geol Sur Dep ... British Territories in Borneo. Annual Report. Geological Survey Department [*A publication*]
Br Territ Borneo Geol Surv Dep Rep ... British Territories in Borneo. Geological Survey Department. Report [*A publication*]
BRTH .... Breathe   (MSA)
BRTHA ..... Behavior Research and Therapy [*A publication*]
Br Thorac Tuber Assoc Rev ... British Thoracic and Tuberculosis Association. Review [*A publication*]
BRTHR ..... Breather   (MSA)
Brt Lgts...... Bright Lights [*A publication*]
BRTP........ Bachelor of Regional and Town Planning   (ADA)
BRTP........ Biomedical Research Technology Program [*Bethesda, MD*] [*National Institutes of Health*]   (GRD)
BRTRA...... Regional Air Traffic Services School, Transport Canada [*Ecole Regionale des Services de la Circulation Aerienne, Transports Canada*], Richmond, British Columbia [*Library symbol*] [*National Library of Canada*]   (NLC)
Br Travel News ... British Travel News [*A publication*]
BRTRD...... Integrated Barter International [*NASDAQ symbol*]   (NQ)
BRTS .... Bilateration Ranging Transponder System   (MCD)
BRTS .... Bioradiotelemetric System
BRTT .... British Reports, Translations, and Theses [*A publication*]
BRTT........ Britt Tech Corp. [*NASDAQ symbol*]   (NQ)
BRTTS ..... British Roll Tuners Trade Society [*A union*]   (DCTA)
BRTVIA ..... Vancouver International Airport, Transport Canada [*Aeroport International de Vancouver, Transports Canada*], Richmond, British Columbia [*Library symbol*] [*National Library of Canada*]   (NLC)
BRU .... Atlanta, GA [*Location identifier*] [*FAA*]   (FAAL)
BRU .... Babylonische Rechtsurkunden aus der Regierungszeit Artaxerxes I und Darius II [*A publication*]   (BJA)
BRU .... Basic Resolution Unit [*Data processing*]
BRU .... Battery Replacement Unit   (MCD)
BRU .... Bilevel Response Unit
BRU .... Boat Repair Unit [*Navy*]
BRU .... Bomb Rack Unit
BRU .... Boresight Reticle Unit   (MCD)
BRU .... Branch Unconditionally
BRU .... Brayton Rotating Unit
Bru .... Bruce's Scotch Court of Session Reports [*1714-15*] [*A publication*]   (DLA)
BRU .... Brussels [*Belgium*] [*Airport symbol*]   (OAG)
BRUC .... Robert Bruce Industries, Inc. [*Philadelphia, PA*] [*NASDAQ symbol*]   (NQ)
Bruce.......... Bruce's Scotch Court of Session Reports [*1714-15*] [*A publication*]   (DLA)
B Ru E........ Bachelor of Rural Engineering
Bruel & Kjaer Tech Rev ... Bruel and Kjaer Technical Review [*A publication*]
B Ru Eng.... Bachelor of Rural Engineering
BRUFMA ... British Rigid Urethane Foam Manufacturers Association

BRuG .... Bundesrueckerstattungsgesetz [*A publication*]   (BJA)
BRUIN ...... Brown University Interpreter [*Data processing*]
Bruker Rep ... Bruker Report [*A publication*]
Br Ult V ..... Brice's Ultra Vires [*A publication*]   (ILCA)
Bru ML....... Bruce's Military Law [*A publication*]   (DLA)
BRUN........ Brunei
Brun .... [*Albertus*] Brunus [*Deceased, 1541*] [*Authority cited in pre-1607 legal work*]   (DSA)
BRUNCH ... Breakfast and Lunch [*Refers to a late morning or early afternoon meal*]
Brun Col Cas ... Brunner's Collected Cases [*United States*] [*A publication*]   (DLA)
BRUND2... Brunonia [*A publication*]
BR UNESCO ... Bulletin. Commission Nationale de la Republique Populaire Roumaine pour l'UNESCO [*A publication*]
Brunk Ir Dig ... Brunker's Irish Common Law Digest [*A publication*]   (DLA)
Brun Mus J ... Brunei Museum. Journal [*A publication*]
Brunn Col Cas (F) ... Brunner's Collected Cases [*United States*] [*A publication*]   (DLA)
Brunn Coll Cas ... Brunner's Collected Cases [*United States*] [*A publication*]   (DLA)
BRUNNEL ... Bridge-Tunnel [*Proposed English Channel link between Britain and France*]
Brunnenbau Bau Rohrleitungsbau ... Brunnenbau Bau von Wasserwerken Rohrleitungsbau [*A publication*]
Brunner Col Cas ... Brunner's Collected Cases [*United States*] [*A publication*]   (DLA)
Brunner/Mazel Psychosoc Stress Ser ... Brunner/Mazel Psychosocial Stress Series [*A publication*]
Brunner Sel Cas ... Brunner's Selected Cases, United States Circuit Courts [*A publication*]   (DLA)
Brunn Sel Cas ... Brunner's Selected Cases [*United States*] [*A publication*]   (DLA)
Bruns' Beitr Klin Chir ... Bruns' Beitraege zur Klinischen Chirurgie [*A publication*]
Brun Sel Cas ... Brunner's Selected Cases [*United States*] [*A publication*]   (DLA)
Brunskill.... Brunskill's Land Cases [*Ireland*] [*A publication*]   (DLA)
Bruns LC.... Brunskill's Land Cases [*Ireland*] [*A publication*]   (DLA)
BRUNSW ... Brunswick [*Australia*]   (ROG)
Bru Princip ... Bruce, Principia Juris Feudalis [*A publication*]   (DLA)
BRUPT...... Bankrupt [*or Bankruptcy*]   (DCTA)
BrUrd........ Bromouridine [*Also, B*] [*A nucleoside*]
BRurSc....... Bachelor of Rural Science   (ADA)
BRUSA....... British-United States Agreement [*Signed May 17, 1943; formalized cooperation between the communications intelligence agencies of Great Britain and the United States*]
BRUSEI .... US Fish and Wildlife Service. Biological Report [*A publication*]
Brush & P .. Brush and Pencil [*A publication*]
Brus Museum ... Brussels Museum of Musical Instruments. Bulletin [*A publication*]
Brus Mus Roy Beaux Arts Bull ... Brussels. Musees Royaux des Beaux-Arts Belgiques. Bulletin [*A publication*]
B Russell Mem Lect Phil Sci ... Bertrand Russell Memorial Lecture in Philosophy and Science [*A publication*]   (APTA)
Brussels Museum M Instruments Bul ... Brussels Museum of Musical Instruments. Bulletin [*A publication*]
Brussels Mus Roy Bul ... Brussels. Musees Royaux d'Art et d'Histoire. Bulletin [*A publication*]
BRUSTA ... Bureau Regional de l'UNESCO pour la Science et la Technologie en Afrique [*UNESCO Regional Office for Science and Technology in Africa - UNESCO-ROSTA*] [*Nairobi, Kenya*]   (EAIO)
Brut .... Brutus [*of Plutarch*] [*Classical studies*]   (OCD)
Brut .... Brutus or De Claris Oratoribus [*of Cicero*] [*Classical studies*]   (OCD)
Bru & Wil Adm ... Bruce and Williams. Admiralty Jurisdiction [*A publication*]   (DLA)
BRUX .... Bruxelles [*Brussels*] [*City in Belgium*]   (ROG)
Bruxelles Med ... Bruxelles Medical [*A publication*]
Brux Med... Bruxelles Medical [*A publication*]
Bruzard ...... Mauritius Reports, by Bruzard [*1842-45*] [*A publication*]
BRV .... Ballistic Reentry Vehicle
BRV .... Bill of Rights of Virginia [*A publication*]   (DLA)
BRV .... Bremerhaven [*West Germany*] [*Airport symbol*]   (OAG)
BRV .... Brooke, VA [*Location identifier*] [*FAA*]   (FAAL)
BRV .... Brookings Review [*A publication*]
Br Vest .... Bratskij Vestnik [*A publication*]
Br Vet J...... British Veterinary Journal [*A publication*]
BRVMA..... British Radio Valve Manufacturers' Association
BRVRAG.... Breviora [*A publication*]
BRVWA..... Business Review. University of Washington [*A publication*]
BRW .... Barrow [*Alaska*] [*Geomagnetic observatory code*]
BRW .... Barrow [*Alaska*] [*Seismograph station code, US Geological Survey*] [*Closed*]   (SEIS)
BRW .... Barrow [*Alaska*] [*Airport symbol*]   (OAG)
BRW .... Black River & Western Corp. [*AAR code*]
BRW .... Business Review [*Australia*] [*A publication*]
BRW .... Business Review Weekly [*A publication*]   (APTA)

Br Wat Supply ... British Water Supply [*A publication*]
BRWD .... Brentwood Instruments, Inc. [*Torrance, CA*] [*NASDAQ symbol*]   (NQ)
BRWE........ Business Review Weekly [*Financial Review Information Service*] [*Information service or system*] [*A publication*]
BRWJA ..... British Welding Journal [*A publication*]
BRWM ...... Board on Radioactive Waste Management   (EA)
BRWPF ..... Black Revolutionary War Patriots Foundation   (EA)
BRX .... Barahona [*Dominican Republic*] [*Airport symbol*]   (OAG)
BRX .... Benton Resources Ltd. [*Vancouver Stock Exchange symbol*]
BRX .... Brazil. A Monthly Publication on Trade and Industry [*A publication*]
BRY .... Bardstown, KY [*Location identifier*] [*FAA*]   (FAAL)
BRY .... Barry [*Cardiff*] [*Welsh depot code*]
BrY .... Belorussian Yiddish   (BJA)
BRY .... Berry Petroleum Co. Class A [*NYSE symbol*]   (SPSG)
BRY .... Bryology
Bryce Civ L ... Bryce's Study of the Civil Law [*A publication*]   (DLA)
Bryce Tr M ... Bryce. Registration of Trade Marks [*A publication*]   (DLA)
BRYGAW ... Brygmesteren [*A publication*]
BRYOA ..... Bryologist [*A publication*]
BRYOAM ... Bryologist [*A publication*]
Bryol .... Bryologist [*A publication*]
BRYOL...... Bryology   (ROG)
Bryophytorum Bibl ... Bryophytorum Bibliotheca [*A publication*]
Bry & Str Com L ... Bryant and Stratton. Commercial Law [*A publication*]   (DLA)
BRZ .... Better Resources Ltd. [*Vancouver Stock Exchange symbol*]
BRZ .... Braze
BRZ .... Bronze   (KSC)
BRZ .... Wittman, AZ [*Location identifier*] [*FAA*]   (FAAL)
BrzA .... Brazilian Angel [*Record label*]
BrzC.......... Brazilian Columbia [*Record label*]
BrzCont....... Brazilian Continental [*Record label*]
BrzEli......... Brazilian Elite [*Record label*]
BRZG .... Brazing   (KSC)
BrzMGM... Brazilian MGM [*Record label*]
BrzOd........ Brazilian Odeon [*Record label*]
BRZT......... Burst Agritech, Inc. [*NASDAQ symbol*]   (NQ)
BrzV.......... Brazilian Victor [*Record label*]
B des S ...... Bachelier des Sciences [*Bachelor of Science*] [*French*]
BS .... Bachelor of Science
BS .... Bachelor of Science in Pure Science
BS .... Bachelor of Surgery
B & S.......... Bachelors' and Spinsters' Dance   (ADA)
BS .... Back Spread [*Investment term*]
BS .... Backspace Character [*Keyboard*] [*Data processing*]
BS .... Backstage   (ADA)
BS .... Backstairs [*Gossip*]
BS .... Backward Signaling [*Telecommunications*]   (TEL)
BS .... Bahamas [*ANSI two-letter standard code*]   (CNC)
BS .... Balance Sheet [*Accounting*]
BS .... Ballistic Shell
BS .... Bancus Superior [*King's Bench*] [*British*] [*Legal term*]   (DLA)
BS .... Bank-Switching [*Computer technology*]
BS .... Bantock Society   (EA)
BS .... Bantu Studies [*A publication*]
BS .... Baroswitch
B & S.......... Bartholin and Skene [*Glands*] [*Medicine*]
BS .... Base Salvage   (AAG)
BS .... Base Section [*Military*]
BS .... Base Shell
BS .... Base Skirt
BS .... Base Supply   (KSC)
BS .... Basic Sediment [*Petroleum*]
BS .... Basilian Salvatorian Fathers [*Roman Catholic religious order*]
BS .... Basisphenoid [*Anatomy*]
Bs .... Bass [*or Basso*] [*Music*]
BS .... Battery Simulator
BS .... Battle Star
BS .... Battlefield Surveillance   (MCD)
BS .... Battleship
BS .... Battleship Flag [*Navy*] [*British*]
BS .... Battleship Squadron
BS .... Be Specific
BS .... Bead Society   (EA)
BS .... Beam Splitter [*Instrumentation*]
BS .... Beam Steering
BS .... Beam Stop
B & S.......... Beams and Stringers [*Technical drawings*]
BS .... Bedside [*Medicine*]
B/S .... Behind Schedule
BS .... Belinfante-Swihart [*Theory*]
B & S.......... Bell and Spigot [*Technical drawings*]
BS .... Bellwether Stock [*Investment term*]
B/S .... Bench Stock [*Air Force*]   (AFIT)
Bs .... Benedictus [*Blessed*] [*Latin*]
BS .... Beneficial Suggestion   (MCD)
BS .... Berlin Sector [*Allied German Occupation Forces*]
BS .... Best Sellers [*A publication*]

B & S......... Best and Smith's English Queen's Bench Reports [*A publication*]   (DLA)
BS .... Beta Spectrometer
BS .... Bethlehem Steel Corp. [*NYSE symbol*] [*Wall Street slang name: "Bessie"*]   (SPSG)
B & S......... Beven and Siebel's Reports [*Ceylon*] [*A publication*]   (DLA)
B and S....... Bible and Spade [*A publication*]
BS .... Bibliographical Society [*British*]   (DIT)
BS .... Biblioteka Slovesnika [*A publication*]
BS .... Bibliotheca Sacra [*A publication*]
BS .... Bile Salts [*Biochemistry*]
BS .... Bill of Sale
BS .... Bill of Sight [*Customs*]
BS .... Bill of Store
BS .... Binary Scale   (AAG)
BS .... Binary Subtract
BS .... Binder Aviatik, Scheibe-Bruns, Schleicher-Bruns [*Federal Republic of Germany*] [*ICAO aircraft manufacturer identifier*]   (ICAO)
BS .... Biochemical Society [*London, England*]   (EAIO)
BS .... Biometric Society
BS .... Biophysical Society   (MCD)
BS .... Biosystematic Code [*Online database field identifier*]
BS .... Birmingham Southern Railroad Co. [*AAR code*]
BS .... Birmingham Standard [*Wire gauge*]
BS .... Bishop Suffragan
Bs .... [*Simon de*] Bisignano [*Flourished, 1174-79*] [*Authority cited in pre-1607 legal work*]   (DSA)
BS .... Bismuth Subsalicylate [*Antidiarrhea agent*]
B/S .... Bistable   (NRCH)
BS .... BIT [*Binary Digit*] Sync [*Data processing*]
B/S .... BITs [*Binary Digits*] per Second [*Data transmission speed*] [*Data processing*]   (CET)
BS .... Black Scale   (MSA)
BS .... Blessed Sacrament
BS .... Blind Sports [*Later, LBSF*]   (EA)
BS .... Blind Spouse [*Title XVI*] [*Social Security Administration*]   (OICC)
B/S .... Blip/Scan   (MUGU)
BS .... Block Sale [*Investment term*]
BS .... Block Specification   (MCD)
BS .... Blood Sugar [*Medicine*]
BS .... Bloom Syndrome [*Medicine*]
BS .... Blowing Snow [*Meteorology*]   (FAAC)
BS .... Blue Shade [*Paper*]
BS .... Blue Shield [*Health insurance plan*]
BS .... Blue Steel [*Guns*]
B/S .... Board of Inspection and Survey [*Navy*]
BS .... Board Secretary
BS .... Body Shell
BS .... Body Station   (MCD)
BS .... Bogoslovska Smotra [*A publication*]
BS .... Boiler Survey
BS .... Bollettino Senese [*A publication*]
BS .... Bollingen Series [*A publication*]
BS .... Bomb Service
BS .... Bomb Sight
BS .... Bomber Support
BS .... Bonded Single Silk [*Wire insulation*]   (MSA)
BS .... Bonifay Sand [*A soil type*]
BS .... Bookplate Society [*London, England*]   (EAIO)
B & S......... Booster and Sustainer
BS .... Border Surveillance [*Military*]
BS .... Borescope   (MSA)
BS .... Boresight   (KSC)
BS .... Bostonian Society   (EA)
BS .... Botanische Studien [*A publication*]
BS .... Both Sides [*Technical drawings*]
bs................ Botswana [*MARC country of publication code*] [*Library of Congress*]   (LCCP)
BS .... Bottom Sediment [*Maps and charts*]
BS .... Bottom Settlings [*of crude oil in storage*]
BS .... Boundary Stimulus [*To light*]
BS .... Bow Shock [*Astrophysics*]
BS .... Bow and Stern Thruster [*of a ship*]   (DS)
BS .... Bowel Sounds [*Medicine*]
BS .... Boy Scouts
BS .... Brada-Svejda [*Tumor*] [*Medicine*]
BS .... Braidwood Station [*Nuclear energy*]   (NRCH)
BS .... Branch Stack
B and S....... Brandy and Soda
BS .... Breaking Strain [*Of fishing lines or casts*]
BS .... Breath Sounds [*Medicine*]
BS .... Brewster Society   (EA)
BS .... Brickmakers Society [*A union*] [*British*]
B & S......... Briggs & Stratton Corp.
BS .... Brith Sholom   (EA)
BS .... British Shipbuilders
BS .... British Standard
BS .... Brixia Sacra [*A publication*]
BS .... Broadcast Satellite [*Japan*]

BS .... Broadcasting Station
BS .... Brocades-Stheeman [*Netherlands*] [*Research code symbol*]
BS .... Bromeliad Society   (EA)
BS .... Bronte Society   (EA)
B & S .... Brown and Sharpe [*Wire gauge*]
BS .... Brown's Supplement to Morison's Dictionary of Decisions, Scotch Court of Sessions [*A publication*]   (DLA)
BS .... Building Science [*A publication*]
BS .... Bukowiner Schule [*A publication*]
BS .... Bull Session [*Slang for a random conversation*]
BS .... Bulletin Signaletique [*A publication*]
BS .... Bulletin. Sommaires des Periodiques Francais et Etrangers [*A publication*]
BS .... Bullsling [*or Bullslinger*] [*Bowdlerized version*]
BS .... Bur-Sin   (BJA)
BS .... Bureau of Ships [*Later, Naval Sea Systems Command*]
B of S .... Bureau of Standards
BS .... Bureau of Standards
BS .... Bureaucratic Syndrome [*In book title "B.S.: The Bureaucratic Syndrome"*]
BS .... Burned, Shaded [*Ecology*]
BS .... Burns and Schreiber Comedy Hour [*Television program*] [*Obsolete*]
BS .... Business Administration, Management, and/or Marketing Programs [*Association of Independent Colleges and Schools specialization code*]
BS .... Business Systems and Equipment [*A publication*]
BS .... Busy Bee of Norway A/S [*Norway*] [*ICAO designator*]   (FAAC)
BS .... Butterfly Spread [*Investment term*]
BS .... Button Switch
BS .... Byron Society   (EA)
BS .... Byron Station   (NRCH)
BS .... Byzantino-Slavica [*A publication*]
BS .... Graduate in Science
BS .... Nederlandse Binnenlandse Strijdkrachten [*Netherlands Forces of the Interior, 1944*]
BS .... Smithers Public Library, British Columbia [*Library symbol*] [*National Library of Canada*]   (NLC)
B1S .... Beaded One Side [*Lumber*]
B2S .... Beaded Two Sides [*Lumber*]
BS 101 .... Bulletin Signaletique 101. Sciences de l'Information. Documentation [*A publication*]
BSA .... Bachelier en Sciences Administratives [*Bachelor in Administrative Sciences*] [*French*]
BSA .... Bachelor of Science in Agriculture
BSA .... Bachelor of Scientific Agriculture
BSA .... Bank Stationers Association [*Later, FSA*]   (EA)
B de Sa .... Bartholomaeus de Saliceto [*Deceased, 1411*] [*Authority cited in pre-1607 legal work*]   (DSA)
BSA .... Basic Standardization Agreement [*Military*]
BSA .... Basic Stock Allowance [*Military*]
BSA .... Battlefield System Architecture   (MCD)
BSA .... Beach Support Area   (CINC)
BSA .... Bearing Specialists Association   (EA)
BSA .... Benzenesulfonic Acid [*Organic chemistry*]
BSA .... Betonvereniging van Suidelike Africa [*Concrete Society of South Africa*]   (EAIO)
BSA .... Bible Sabbath Association   (EA)
BSA .... Bible-Science Association   (EA)
BSA .... Bibliographical Society of America   (EA)
BSa .... Bibliotheca Sacra [*A publication*]
BSA .... Biofeedback Society of America [*Later, AAPB*]   (EA)
BSA .... Birmingham Small Arms, Inc.   (MCD)
BSA .... Bis(trimethylsilyl)acetamide [*Organic chemistry*]
BSA .... BIT [*Binary Digit*] Sync Acquisition [*Data processing*]
BSA .... Black Stuntmen's Association   (EA)
BSA .... Blind Service Association   (EA)
BSA .... Blue Shield Association [*Later, BCBSA*]   (EA)
BSA .... Board of Scientific Affairs
BSA .... Boarding School Allowance [*Government scholarship*] [*British*]
BSA .... Body Surface Area
BSA .... Bohr-Sommerfeld Atom
BSA .... Borrows, S. A., Detroit MI [*STAC*]
BSA .... Bosaso [*Somalia*] [*Airport symbol*]   (OAG)
BSA .... Boston Shipping Association   (EA)
BSA .... Botanical Society of America   (EA)
BSA .... Bovine Serum Albumin [*Immunology*]
BSA .... Boy Scouts of America   (EA)
BSA .... Brecht Society of America   (EA)
BSA .... Brief Stop for Ammunition Lift [*Military*]   (NVT)
BSA .... Brigade Support Area [*Military*]   (AABC)
BSA .... Brisa International [*Toronto Stock Exchange symbol*]
BSA .... British School of Archaeology in Jerusalem
BSA .... British School at Athens. Annual [*A publication*]
BSA .... British Social Attitudes [*Survey*]
BSA .... British Society of Aesthetics
BSA .... British Society of Audiology
BSA .... [*The*] British Sociological Association
BSA .... British South Africa
BSA .... British Surfing Association
BSA .... Brotherhood of Saint Andrew   (EA)

BSA .... Bruckner Society of America   (EA)
BSA .... Building Societies Act [*British*]
BSA .... Building Societies Association [*British*]
BSA .... Bureau of Supplies and Accounts [*Later, NSUPSC*] [*Navy*]
BSA .... Business Aircraft Corp. [*Stratford, CT*] [*FAA designator*]   (FAAC)
BSA .... Business Software Association   (EA)
BSA .... Byrd [*Antarctica*] [*Seismograph station code, US Geological Survey*] [*Closed*]   (SEIS)
BSA .... Salmo Public Library, British Columbia [*Library symbol*] [*National Library of Canada*]   (NLC)
BSAA .... Boletin. Seminario de Estudios de Arte y Arqueologia [*A publication*]
BSAA .... British South American Airways Corp.
BSAA .... Bulletin Signaletique. Art et Archeologie [*A publication*]
BSAA .... Bulletin. Societe Archeologique d'Alexandrie [*A publication*]
BSAAC ..... British South American Airways Corp. [*Later absorbed by BOAC*]
BSA Adm ... Bachelor of Science in Agricultural Administration
BSAAF ...... Boy Scouts of America Alumni Family [*Defunct*]   (EA)
BSA Al .... Bulletin. Societe d'Archeologie d'Alexandrie [*A publication*]
BSAAM .... Salmon Arm Museum and Heritage Association, British Columbia [*Library symbol*] [*National Library of Canada*]   (NLC)
BSAAV ...... Boletin. Seminario de Estudios de Arte y Arqueologia. Universidad de Valladolid [*A publication*]
BSAB .... Balthazar Scales of Adaptive Behavior [*Psychology*]
BSAB .... Bulletin. Societe d'Anthropologie (Brussels) [*A publication*]
BSAB .... Bulletin. Societe Archeologique de Bordeaux [*A publication*]
BSAB .... Bulletin. Societe Archeologique Bulgare [*A publication*]
BSAC .... British Society for Antimicrobial Chemotherapy
BSAC .... British South Africa Company   (ROG)
BSAC .... British South Africa Corps
BSAC .... Brotherhood of Shoe and Allied Craftsmen   (EA)
BSAC .... Bulletin. Societe d'Archeologie Copte [*A publication*]
BS (Acc) .... Bachelor of Science in Accounting
BS in Acc .. Bachelor of Science in Accounting
BSACI .... British Society for Allergy and Clinical Immunology
BSACorreze ... Bulletin. Societe Archeologique de la Correze [*A publication*]
BS in AD.... Bachelor of Science in Agricultural Education
BSAD......... British Sports Association for the Disabled
BS Adv ...... Bachelor of Science in Advertising
BS in AE .... Bachelor of Science in Administrative Engineering
BSAE .... Bachelor of Science in Aeronautical Engineering
BS in AE .... Bachelor of Science in Aeronautical Engineering
BSAE .... Bachelor of Science in Architectural Engineering
BS in AE .... Bachelor of Science in Architectural Engineering
BSAE .... British School of Archaeology in Egypt. Publications [*A publication*]
BSAE .... Bulletin der Schweizerischen Gesellschaft fuer Anthropologie und Ethnologie [*A publication*]
BS Ae E...... Bachelor of Science in Aeronautical Engineering
BS in Ae E ... Bachelor of Science in Aeronautical Engineering
BSAE-E ..... Bachelor of Science in Aeronautical Engineering - Electronics Major
BS (Ae Elec) ... Bachelor of Science with Aeronautical Engineering Electives
BS in Aero Adm ... Bachelor of Science in Aeronautical Administration
BS in Aero E ... Bachelor of Science in Aeronautical Engineering
BS (Aero E) ... Bachelor of Science in Aeronautical Engineering
BSAF .... Bids Solicited as Follows
BSAF .... Bulletin. Societe Nationale des Antiquaires de France [*A publication*]
BSAFrance ... Bulletin. Societe Nationale des Antiquaires de France [*A publication*]
BS in Ag..... Bachelor of Science in Agriculture
BS Ag........ Bachelor of Science in Agriculture
BSAG........ Bristol Social Adjustment Guides [*Psychology*]
BSAG........ Research Station, Agriculture Canada [*Station de Recherches, Agriculture Canada*] Sidney, British Columbia [*Library symbol*] [*National Library of Canada*]   (NLC)
BS in Ag (DM) ... Bachelor of Science in Agriculture in Dairy Manufacturing
BS in Ag E ... Bachelor of Science in Agricultural Engineering
BS Ag E ..... Bachelor of Science in Agricultural Engineering
BS in Ag & Ed ... Bachelor of Science in Agriculture and Education
BS Agr .... Bachelor of Science in Agriculture
BS in Agr & Chem ... Bachelor of Science in Agriculture and Chemistry
BS in Agr E ... Bachelor of Science in Agricultural Engineering
BS in Agr Ed ... Bachelor of Science in Agricultural Education
BS in Agr Eng ... Bachelor of Science in Agricultural Engineering
BSAHDL... Bulletin. Societe d'Art et d'Histoire du Diocese de Liege [*A publication*]
BSAHL...... Bulletin. Societe Archeologique et Historique du Limousin [*A publication*]
BSAH Liege ... Bulletin. Societe d'Art et d'Histoire du Diocese de Liege [*A publication*]
BSAHLimousin ... Bulletin. Societe Archeologique et Historique du Limousin [*A publication*]
BSAHNantes ... Bulletin. Societe Archeologique et Historique de Nantes et de Loire-Atlantique [*A publication*]
BSAIO....... Boletin. Sociedad Argentina de Investigacion Operativa [*A publication*]

BSA/J........ Journal. British Sociological Association [*A publication*]
BSAL........ Base Spares Allowance List   (MCD)
BSAL........ Basic Stock Allowance List [*Military*]   (NVT)
BSAL........ Block Structured Assembly Language
BSAL........ Bolleti. Societat Arqueologica Lubliana [*A publication*]
BSAL........ Bulletin. Societe d'Anthropologie (Lyon) [*A publication*]
BSAL........ Bulletin. Societe Archeologique du Limousin [*A publication*]
BSALS...... British Society for Agricultural Labour Science
BS in AM... Bachelor of Science in Agricultural Administration
BSAM....... Basic Sequential Access Method [*IBM Corp.*] [*Data processing*]
BSAM....... Bulletin. Societe des Amis de Montaigne [*A publication*]
BSAM....... Bulletin. Societe Archeologique du Midi de la France [*A publication*]
BSAM....... Bulletin Trimestriel. Societe Academique des Antiquaires de la Morinie [*A publication*]
BSAMA..... Bulletin. Schweizerische Akademie der Medizinischen Wissenschaften [*A publication*]
BSAMA5... Bulletin. Academie Suisse des Sciences Medicales [*A publication*]
BS (A Math) ... Bachelor of Science in Applied Mathematics
BSAME..... Bachelor of Science in Aircraft Maintenance Engineering
BSAMorinie ... Bulletin Trimestriel. Societe Academique des Antiquaires de la Morinie [*A publication*]
BS in AN.... Bachelor of Science in Agricultural Engineering
BSAN........ Bulletin. Societe des Antiquaires de Normandie [*A publication*]
BSANormandie ... Bulletin. Societe des Antiquaires de Normandie [*A publication*]
B Sante P ... Bulletin de la Sante Publique [*A publication*]
BSAO .... Bulletin. Societe des Antiquaires de l'Ouest et des Musees de Poitiers [*A publication*]
BSAOuest ... Bulletin. Societe des Antiquaires de l'Ouest et des Musees de Poitiers [*A publication*]
BSAP .... Basic Skills Assessment Program [*Academic achievement and aptitude test*]
BSAP .... Bibliographical Society of America. Papers [*A publication*]
BSAP .... British Society of Animal Production
BSAP .... British Society of Australian Philately
BSAP .... British South Africa Police
BSAP .... Bulletin. Societe des Amis de Marcel Proust et de Combray [*A publication*]
BSAP .... Bulletin Trimestriel. Societe des Antiquaires de Picardie [*A publication*]
BSAPicardie ... Bulletin Trimestriel. Societe des Antiquaires de Picardie [*A publication*]
B Sapo........ Bernardus Saporis [*Flourished, 1327-36*] [*Authority cited in pre-1607 legal work*]   (DSA)
B Sapor ...... Bernardus Saporis [*Flourished, 1327-36*] [*Authority cited in pre-1607 legal work*]   (DSA)
BSAPR ...... Bulletin. Societe des Amis de Port-Royal [*A publication*]
BS in Arch ... Bachelor of Science in Architecture
BS Arch (Arch) ... Bachelor of Science in Architecture in Architecture
BS Arch (Arch E) ... Bachelor of Science in Architecture in Architectural Engineering
BS Arch E ... Bachelor of Science in Architectural Engineering
BSARPR...... Buletin Stiintific. Academia Republicii Populare Romine [*A publication*]
BS Art Ed .. Bachelor of Science in Art Education
BSAS .... British Ship Adoption Society
BSAS .... Bulletin. Societe Archeologique de Sens [*A publication*]
B Sa Sc....... Bachelor of Sacred Sciences
BSASD ...... Bulletin. Societe Archeologique et Statistique de la Drome [*A publication*]
BSAT .... Bachelor of Science in Air Transportation
BSAT .... Bulletin. Societe Archeologique de Touraine [*A publication*]
BSA Touraine ... Bulletin Trimestriel. Societe Archeologique de Touraine [*A publication*]
BSAUD...... British Society of Audiology
BSAV......... Boletin. Seminario de Estudios de Arte y Arqueologia. Universidad de Valladolid [*A publication*]
BSAVA ...... British Small Animal Veterinary Association   (EAIO)
BSAW........ Berichte. Verhandlungen der Saechsischen Akademie der Wissenschaften [*A publication*]
BSAWL ..... Berichte ueber die Verhandlungen der Saechsischen Gesellschaft der Wissenschaft zu Leipzig [*A publication*]
BSB........... Bachelor of Science in Business
BSB........... Ball State Business Review [*A publication*]
BSB........... Bangladesh Shilpa Bank [*Industrial Development Bank*]   (EY)
BSB........... Baseband   (MUGU)
BSB........... Body Surface Burned [*Medicine*]
BSB........... Both Sideband
BSB........... Brasilia [*Brazil*] [*Airport symbol*]   (OAG)
BSB........... British Satellite Broadcasting [*Telecommunications*]
BSB........... British Savings Bond
BSB........... British Standard Beam [*Engineering*]
BSB........... British Supply Board [*Ottawa*] [*World War II*]
BS in BA ... Bachelor of Science in Business Administration
BSBA .... Bachelor of Science in Business Administration
BSBA .... British Shingon Buddhist Association   (EAIO)
BS in B Ad ... Bachelor of Science in Business Administration
BSB Ad ...... Bachelor of Science in Business Administration

BSBB .... Bulletin. Societe des Bibliophiles Belges Seant a Mons [*A publication*]
BSBBM ..... Bulletin. Societe des Bibliophiles Belges Seant a Mons [*A publication*]
BSBC .... Branford Savings Bank [*Branford, CT*] [*NASDAQ symbol*]   (NQ)
BSBC .... British Social Biology Council
BSBC .... Buffalo Sabres Booster Club   (EA)
BS in B Ed ... Bachelor of Science in Business Education
BSB Ed ...... Bachelor of Science in Business Education
BSBF .... Bulletin. Societe des Bibliolatres de France [*A publication*]
BSBFA....... Bulletin. Societe Botanique de France [*A publication*]
BSBG .... Berichte. Schweizerische Botanische Gesellschaft [*A publication*]
BSBGA ...... Berichte. Schweizerische Botanische Gesellschaft [*A publication*]
BSBGD ...... Bulletin. Societe Belge de Geologie [*A publication*]
BSBI .... Botanical Society of the British Isles
BSBIA .... Brookhaven Symposia in Biology [*A publication*]
BSBIAW..... Brookhaven Symposia in Biology [*A publication*]
BSBI Conf Rep ... BSBI [*Botanical Society of the British Isles*] Conference Reports [*A publication*]
BS Biol....... Bachelor of Science in Biology
BS in Biomed Eng ... Bachelor of Science in Biomedical Engineering
BSBK .... Beverly Savings Bank [*Beverly, MA*] [*NASDAQ symbol*]   (NQ)
BSBL .... Bulletin. Societe des Bibliophiles Liegeois [*A publication*]
BS Bl.......... Bundessteuerblatt [*A publication*]
BSBL .... [*The*] Score Board, Inc. [*NASDAQ symbol*]   (NQ)
BS in BMS ... Bachelor of Science in Basic Medical Sciences
BSBN........ BSB Bancorp, Inc. [*NASDAQ symbol*]   (NQ)
B S Bot Fr I ... Bulletin. Societe Botanique de France. Premiere Partie [*A publication*]
BSBPA ...... Bulletin. Societe Belge de Geologie, de Paleontologie, et d'Hydrologie [*Later, Bulletin. Societe Belge de Geologie*] [*A publication*]
BSBPP....... Bulletin. Societe Bibliographique des Publications Populaires [*A publication*]
BSBQA...... Bulletin. Societes Chimiques Belges [*A publication*]
BSBR .... Bollettino Sistematico di Bibliografia Romana [*A publication*]
BSBS .... Bollettino Storico-Bibliografico Subalpino [*A publication*]
BS BSF ...... Boot or Shoes, or Boot or Shoe Findings [*Freight*]
BSB Subalpino ... Bollettino Storico-Bibliografico Subalpino [*A publication*]
BS Bus .... Bachelor of Science in Business
BS in Bus ... Bachelor of Science in Business
BS in Bus Ad ... Bachelor of Science in Business Administration
BS Bus Ad ... Bachelor of Science in Business Administration
BS in Bus Ed ... Bachelor of Science in Business Education
BSBusEd.... Bachelor of Science in Business Education
BS (Bus-MR) ... Bachelor of Science in Business - Medical Records
BSBW........ Backer Spielvogel Bates Worldwide [*Commercial firm*] [*British*]   (ECON)
BSBX .... Bell Savings Holdings, Inc. [*NASDAQ symbol*]   (NQ)
B Sc........... Baccalaureus Scientiae [*Bachelor of Science*] [*Latin*]
B es SC....... Bachelier es Sciences [*Bachelor of Science*] [*French*]   (ROG)
BSC.......... Bachelor of Christian Science
B Sc........... Bachelor of Science
BS in C....... Bachelor of Science in Chemistry
BS in C....... Bachelor of Science in Commerce
BSC.......... Bachelor of Science in Commerce
BSC.......... Backspace Contact
BSC.......... Bahia Solano [*Colombia*] [*Airport symbol*]   (OAG)
BSC.......... Balkan Supply Center [*Navy*]
BSC.......... Bangladesh Shipping Corp.   (DS)
BSC.......... Baptist Students Concerned [*Defunct*]   (EA)
BSC.......... Barber-Scotia College [*Concord, NC*]
BSC.......... Base Security Council [*Air Force*]   (AFM)
BSC.......... Base Statistical Control   (AAG)
BSC.......... Basic   (MUGU)
BSC.......... Basic Message Switching Center [*Data processing*]
BSC.......... Battle Simulation Center   (MCD)
BSC.......... Bear Stearns Companies, Inc. [*NYSE symbol*]   (SPSG)
BSC.......... Belgian Shippers Council   (DS)
BSC.......... Beltsville Space Center [*Later, Goddard Space Flight Center*] [*NASA*]
BSC.......... Bemidji State College [*Later, Bemidji State University*] [*Minnesota*]
BSC.......... Bench Scale Calorimeter
BSC.......... Benevolent Society of Coachmakers [*British*]
BSC.......... Bengal Staff Corps [*British*] [*Military*]
BSC.......... Benzylselenocyanate [*Antineoplastic drug*]
BSC.......... Better Sleep Council [*National Association of Bedding Manufacturers*]   (EA)
BSC.......... Bibliographic Systems Center [*Case Western Reserve University*]   (IID)
BSC.......... Bibliotheque de Sociologie Contemporaine [*A publication*]
BSC.......... Bicycle Stamps Club   (EA)
BSC.......... Billet Sequence Code
BSC.......... Binary Symmetric Channel [*Data processing*]
BSC.......... Binary Synchronous Communication [*IBM Corp.*] [*Data processing*]
BSC.......... Biological Stain Commission   (EA)

BSC........... Biomedical Sciences Corps [*Air Force*] (AFM)
BSC........... Biomedical Signal Conditioner
BSC........... Birmingham Southern College [*Alabama*]
BSC........... Bis(trimethylsilyl)carbamate [*Organic chemistry*]
BSC........... Bisync [*Protocol*] (PCM)
BSC........... BIT [*Binary Digit*] Scan Command [*Data processing*]
BSC........... Blip-Scan Counter
BSC........... Bluefield State College [*West Virginia*]
BSC........... Body Support Cradle
BSC........... Boeing Systems Coordinator (MUGU)
BSC........... Bollettino Storico Catanese [*A publication*]
BSC........... Bollettino Storico Cremonese [*A publication*]
BSC........... Bolted Separable Connector
BSC........... Boresight Camera (MUGU)
BSC........... Borosilicate Crown (MSA)
B/SC......... Brake Skid Control [*or Controller*] (NASA)
BSC........... Brethren Service Commission [*Later, World Ministries Commission*] (EA)
BSC........... Brief Stop for Cargo Lift [*or Delivery*] [*Military*] (NVT)
BSC........... Brighton & South Coast Railway [*British*] (ROG)
BSC........... British Safety Council
BSC........... British Security Coordination [*World War II*]
BSC........... British Shippers Council (DS)
BSC........... British Shoe Corporation
BSC........... British Steel Corporation
BSC........... British Sugar Corporation
BSC........... British Supply Council
BSC........... Bronfman Science Center [*Williams College*] [*Research center*] (RCD)
BSC........... Brookhaven Service Center [*IRS*]
BSC........... Building Services Corporation [*New South Wales, Australia*]
BSC........... Building Societies' Commission [*British*]
BSC........... Bulletin. Societe Chateaubriand [*A publication*]
BSC........... Burley Stabilization Corporation (EA)
BSC........... Business Service Center
BSC........... Cincinnati Bible Seminary, Cincinnati, OH [*OCLC symbol*] (OCLC)
BSC........... Coqualeetza Archives, Sardis, British Columbia [*Library symbol*] [*National Library of Canada*] (NLC)
B Sc........... Graduate in Science
B Sc........... Mistress of Science
BSC........... Santa Cruz Island [*California*] [*Seismograph station code, US Geological Survey*] (SEIS)
BScA.......... Bachelier es Sciences Appliquees [*Bachelor of Applied Science*] [*French*]
BScA.......... Bachelor of Science in Agriculture
BSCA.......... Belgian Sheepdog Club of America (EA)
BSCA.......... Binary Synchronous Communications Adapter [*Data processing*]
BSCA.......... Building Service Contractors Association International (EA)
BSCAA........ Basal Starch Cycloheximide Antibiotic Agar [*Microbiology*]
BScAg........ Bachelor of Science in Agriculture
B Sc Agr..... Bachelor of Science in Agriculture
B Sc in Agr Engr ... Bachelor of Science in Agricultural Engineering
BScAgri..... Bachelor of Science in Agriculture
BScAgric.... Bachelor of Science in Agriculture
BSc(AgricEng) ... Bachelor of Science in Agricultural Engineering
BSc(AH)..... Bachelor of Science (Animal Husbandry) (ADA)
B Sc Ak Med ... Bulletin. Schweizerische Akademie der Medizinischen Wissenschaften [*A publication*]
BSCAM..... Bulletin des Seances. Cercle Archeologique de Mons [*A publication*]
BScApp...... Bachelor of Applied Science (ADA)
BSc(Arch).. Bachelor of Science (Architecture)
BS in Cart .. Bachelor of Science in Cartography
BSCat........ Bollettino Storico Catanese [*A publication*]
BSCB........ British Society for Cell Biology
BS in C & BA ... Bachelor of Science in Commercial and Business Administration
BSCBA...... Brown Swiss Cattle Breeders Association of the USA (EA)
B Sc in Bact ... Bachelor of Science in Bacteriology
BSCC........ Billiards and Snooker Control Council [*An association*] (EAIO)
BSCC........ Bioassay Systems Corporation [*Woburn, MA*] [*NASDAQ symbol*] (NQ)
BSCC........ Biotechnology Science Coordinating Committee [*An interagency governmental group*] [*Washington, DC*]
BSCC........ Boletin. Sociedad Castellonense de Cultura [*A publication*]
BSCC........ Boston Sickle Cell Center [*Boston City Hospital*] [*Research center*] (RCD)
BSCC........ British Shell Collectors Club
BSCC........ British Society for Clinical Cytology
BSCC........ British-Soviet Chamber of Commerce (DS)
BSCC........ Brunei State Chamber of Commerce (DS)
B Sc in CE ... Bachelor of Science in Civil Engineering
BSc(ChemEng) ... Bachelor of Science, Chemical Engineering (ADA)
BSCCO...... Bismuth, Strontium, Calcium, Copper, Oxide [*Inorganic chemistry*]
BScCom..... Bachelor of Commercial Science
BSCD........ Bradley Subcaliber Device [*Army training device*] (INF)
BSc (Dent) ... Bachelor of Science in Dentistry
BSc(DesStud) ... Bachelor of Science (Design Studies)

B Sc (Dn) ... Bachelor of Science in Dianoetics
B Sc (Dom Sc) ... Bachelor of Science (Domestic Science)
BS in CE .... Bachelor of Science in Chemical Engineering
BS in CE .... Bachelor of Science in Civil Engineering
BSCE .... Bachelor of Science in Civil Engineering
BSCE .... Bird Strike Committee Europe (EAIO)
BS in C & Ec ... Bachelor of Science in Commerce and Economics
B Sc Econ .. Bachelor of Science in Economics
BScEd .... Bachelor of Science in Education
BSc(Educ) .. Bachelor of Science (Education)
B Sc in EE ... Bachelor of Science in Electrical Engineering
BScElEd .... Bachelor of Science in Elementary Education (ADA)
BS in CE - Music ... Bachelor of Science in Christian Education - Music
BSc(Eng) ... Bachelor of Science (Engineering) (EY)
BSc(Engg) ... Bachelor of Science (Engineering)
BSc(Engin) ... Bachelor of Science (Engineering)
BS in Cer.... Bachelor of Science in Ceramics
BS in Cer E ... Bachelor of Science in Ceramic Engineering
BS (Cer E) ... Bachelor of Science in Ceramic Engineering
BS in Cer Tech ... Bachelor of Science in Ceramic Technology
B Sc (Est Man) ... Bachelor of Science (Estate Management)
B Sc F........ Bachelor of Science in Forestry
BSCFA...... Bulletin. Societe Chimique de France [*A publication*]
B Sc For ..... Bachelor of Science in Forestry
BSc(Forestry) ... Bachelor of Science (Forestry)
BSc(GenSc) ... Bachelor of Science (General Science) (ADA)
BSCh......... Bachelor of Science in Chemistry
BS in Ch.... Bachelor of Science in Chemistry
B Sch......... Black Scholar [*A publication*]
B-SCH .... Bomber [*Russian aircraft symbol*]
BS in Ch E ... Bachelor of Science in Chemical Engineering
BS Ch E ..... Bachelor of Science in Chemical Engineering
B Sc in HE ... Bachelor of Science in Home Economics
BSc(HEc).. Bachelor of Science in Home Economics
BS (Ch E Elect) ... Bachelor of Science with Chemical Engineering Electives
BS in Chem E ... Bachelor of Science in Chemical Engineering
BS Chem E ... Bachelor of Science in Chemical Engineering
BS in Chem Tech ... Bachelor of Science in Chemical Technology
BS Ch Eng ... Bachelor of Science in Chemical Engineering
BS in Ch Eng ... Bachelor of Science in Chemical Engineering
B S Ch Fr I ... Bulletin. Societe Chimique de France. Premiere Partie [*A publication*]
B S Ch Fr II ... Bulletin. Societe Chimique de France. Deuxieme Partie [*A publication*]
B S Chim Be ... Bulletin. Societes Chimiques Belges [*A publication*]
BS in Chm ... Bachelor of Science in Chemistry
BS in Chm E ... Bachelor of Science in Chemical Engineering
B Sch Mus ... Bachelor of School Music
BSc(HomeSc) ... Bachelor of Science (Home Science)
BSc(HomeSci) ... Bachelor of Science (Home Science)
BSc(HomeScience) ... Bachelor of Science in Home Science
B Sch Or Afr Stud ... Bulletin. School of Oriental and African Studies [*A publication*]
B Sch Orien ... Bulletin. School of Oriental and African Studies [*A publication*]
B Sch Orient Afr Stud ... Bulletin. School of Oriental and African Studies [*A publication*]
BSc(Hort).. Bachelor of Science in Horticulture
BSci........... Behavioral Science [*A publication*]
BSCIA ...... Bulletin. Societe de Chimie Biologique [*A publication*]
B Sci Math ... Bulletin des Sciences Mathematiques [*A publication*]
BSc(IndArts) ... Bachelor of Science (Industrial Arts)
BSCJ......... Bachelor of Science in Criminal Justice
BSCJ......... Ball State Commerce Journal [*A publication*]
BSCJA...... Bristol Chamber of Commerce. Journal [*A publication*]
B Sc L........ Bachelor of the Science of Law
BSCL........ Bell System Common Language [*Telecommunications*] (TEL)
BSCL........ Business Service Checklist [*A publication*]
BSCLA ...... Bulletin Annuel. Societe Suisse de Chronometrie et Laboratoire Suisse de Recherches Horlogeres [*A publication*]
BSCM....... Binary Synchronous Communications Macro
B Sc in ME ... Bachelor of Science in Mechanical Engineering
BScME ...... Bachelor of Science in Mining Engineering (DAS)
BSc(Med).. Bachelor of Science (Medical)
B Sc in Med ... Bachelor of Science in Medicine
B Sc (Med Sci) ... Bachelor of Science (Medical Science)
B Sc in Med Tech ... Bachelor of Science in Medical Technology
B Sc Met ... Bachelor of Science in Metallurgy
BScMin...... Bachelor of Science in Mining (ADA)•
BSc(MLS) ... Bachelor of Science in Medical Laboratory Science (ADA)
BS in CN... Bachelor of Science in Chemical Engineering
BScN......... Bachelor of Science in Nursing
B Scn......... Bachelor of Scientology
BSCN........ BIT [*Binary Digit*] Scan [*Data processing*] (BUR)
BSCNA...... Bulletin. Societe de Chimie Industrielle [*A publication*]
B Sc Nat..... Bulletin des Sciences Naturelles et de Geologie [*A publication*]
B Sc in Nurs ... Bachelor of Science in Nursing
BSc(Nursing) ... Bachelor of Science (Nursing)
BSc(Nutr).. Bachelor of Science (Nutrition)
BSCNY...... Burns Society of the City of New York (EA)
B Sc O........ Bachelor of the Science of Oratory

BSCO......... Burnham Service Corporation [*NASDAQ symbol*]   (NQ)
B Sc in Occ Ther ... Bachelor of Science in Occupational Therapy
BS in Com ... Bachelor of Science in Commerce
BS Com .... Bachelor of Science in Communications
BS in Com & Bus ... Bachelor of Science in Commerce and Business
BS in Com Ed ... Bachelor of Science in Commercial Education
BS in Comm ... Bachelor of Science in Commerce
BS in Comm Rec ... Bachelor of Science in Community Recreation
BSCompSci ... Bachelor of Science in Computer Science
B Sc in Opt ... Bachelor of Science in Optometry
BSc(OT).... Bachelor of Science (Occupational Therapy)
BScP .... Bachelor of Science in Pharmacy   (DAS)
BSCP .... Biological Sciences Communication Project [*American Institute of Biological Sciences*]
BSCP .... British Standard Code of Practice
BSCP Commun ... BSCP [*Biological Sciences Communication Project*] Communique [*A publication*]
BSc(PEd)... Bachelor of Science in Physical Education   (ADA)
B Sc in Phar ... Bachelor of Science in Pharmacy
BSc(Pharm) ... Bachelor of Science in Pharmacy
B Sc in Phys ... Bachelor of Science in Physics
B Sc in Phys Ther ... Bachelor of Science in Physical Therapy
BSc (P & OT) ... Bachelor of Science in Physical and Occupational Therapy
BSc(PT)..... Bachelor of Science (Physical Therapy)
BSc(QS)..... Bachelor of Science in Quantity Surveying   (ADA)
BSCR......... Brighton & South Coast Railway [*British*]   (ROG)
BSCRA ...... British Steel Castings Research Association [*Later, SCRATA*]   (EA)
BS Cr E... Bachelor of Science in Ceramic Engineering
B Sc in Rest Mgt ... Bachelor of Science in Restaurant Management
BSc(RS)..... Bachelor of Science in Rural Science)   (ADA)
BScRT .... Bachelor of Science in Radiologic Technology   (ADA)
BSCS .... Biological Sciences Curriculum Study [*Colorado College*] [*Research center*] [*National Science Foundation*]
BSCS .... Blip-Scan Counter System
BSCSD2... British Society for Cell Biology. Symposium [*A publication*]
B Sc (Soc)... Bachelor of Science (Sociology)
BScSoc....... Bachelor of Social Science
B Sc in Soc Adm ... Bachelor of Science in Social Administration
BSc(Social Science) ... Bachelor of Science (Social Science), University of Edinburgh [*British*]
BSc(Social Sciences) ... Bachelor of Science in the Social Sciences, University of Southampton [*British*]
BSc(SocSc) ... Bachelor of Science (Social Sciences)
BScSS .... Bachelor of Science in Secretarial Studies   (ADA)
BSC/SS ..... Binary Synchronous Communications/Start-Stop
BSC Stat .... British Sulphur Corporation Ltd. Statistical Supplement [*A publication*]
BScSur....... Bachelor of Science in Land Surveying   (ADA)
B Sc Tchg... Bachelor of Science in Teaching   (ADA)
BSc(TE)..... Bachelor of Science in Textile Engineering   (ADA)
BSCTE....... Bell System Center for Technical Education
B Sc (Tech) ... Bachelor of Science (Technology)
B Sc Tech... Bachelor of Technical Science
BSc(Text)... Bachelor of Science in Textiles   (ADA)
BSc(Town & Regional Planning) ... Bachelor of Science (Town and Regional Planning), University of Dundee [*British*]   (DBQ)
BSCU......... Background Storage and Control Unit
BSc(Vet)..... Bachelor of Science (Veterinary)
BSD .... Baccalaureus Scientiae Didacticae [*Bachelor of Didactic Science*]
BSD .... Bachelor of Science in Dentistry   (ADA)
BSD .... Bachelor of Science in Design
BSD .... Ballistic Systems Division [*Norton Air Force Base, CA*]
BSD .... Bangladesh Samajtantrik Dal [*Bangladesh Socialist Party*]   (PPW)
BSD .... Baoshan [*China*] [*Airport symbol*]   (OAG)
BSD .... Barrels per Stream Day [*Also, BPSD*]
BSD .... Barsand Resources, Inc. [*Vancouver Stock Exchange symbol*]
BSD .... Base Supply Depot
BSD .... Battlefield Surveillance Devices   (MCD)
BSD ...... Beam Steering Device
BSD ...... Bedside Drainage [*Medicine*]
BSD ...... Berkeley Standard Distribution [*Data processing*]   (BYTE)
BSD .... Besonders [*Particularly*] [*German*]
BSD .... BIT [*Binary Digit*] Storage Density [*Data processing*]
BSD .... Blast Suppression Device
BSD .... British Society for Dermatopathology   (EAIO)
BSD .... [*The*] British Society of Dowsers
BSD .... British Standard Dimension
BSD .... BSD Bancorp., Inc. [*AMEX symbol*]   (SPSG)
BSD .... Building Societies Database [*British*]
BSD .... Building Systems Division [*Washington, DC*] [*Department of Energy*]   (GRD)
BSD .... Bulk Storage Device   (IEEE)
BSD .... Burst Slug Detection
BSD .... Business Software Database [*Information Sources, Inc.*] [*Information service or system*]   (CRD)
BSDB......... British Society for Developmental Biology
BSDC......... Binary Symmetric Dependent Channel [*Data processing*]

BSDC......... Boundary-Layer Sub-Programme Data Centre [*GARP Atlantic Tropical Experiment*]   (MSC)
BSDC......... British Space Development Company
BSDC......... British Standard Data Code   (BUR)
BSDE......... British Society for Digestive Endoscopy
BS in Dent ... Bachelor of Science in Dentistry
BS Des .... Bachelor of Science in Design
BS Des (Dec Des) ... Bachelor of Science in Design in Decorative Design
BSDF .... Beet Sugar Development Foundation   (EA)
BSDG........ Basic Structural Design Gross Weight   (MCD)
BS in DH ... Bachelor of Science in Dental Hygiene
BSD Hyg ... Bachelor of Science in Dental Hygiene
BS Di......... Bachelor of Scientific Didactics
BSDL......... Boresight Datum Line [*Military*]
BSDM....... BSD Medical Corp. [*NASDAQ symbol*]   (NQ)
BSDP......... Boost Stage Discharge Pressure   (MCD)
BSDP......... Bulgarska Socialdemokraticheska Partiia [*Bulgarian Social Democratic Party*] [*Political party*]   (PPE)
BSDS .... Bartholomew Sales & Distribution Services [*British*]
BSDSL...... Basler Studien zur Deutschen Sprache und Literatur [*A publication*]
BSDU......... Bomber Support Development Unit
BSE............ Bachelor of Sanitary Engineering
BS in E ..... Bachelor of Science in Education
BSE............ Bachelor of Science in Education
BSE............ Bachelor of Science in Engineering
BS in E ..... Bachelor of Science in Engineering
BSE............ Backscatter Electron
BSE............ Bank Systems and Equipment [*A publication*]
BSE............ Basaba Enterprises, Inc. [*Vancouver Stock Exchange symbol*]
BSE............ Base Support Equipment [*Military*]
BSE............ Basis Set Extension [*Physical chemistry*]
BSE............ Bethe-Salpeter Equation [*Physics*]
BSE............ Bilateral Sphenoethmoidectomy [*Medicine*]
BSE............ Birmingham & Southeastern R. R. [*AAR code*]
BSE............ Black Sea Expedition [*1969*] [*Turkey, US*]   (MSC)
BSE............ Boise [*Idaho*] [*Seismograph station code, US Geological Survey*]   (SEIS)
BSE............ Booster Systems Engineer [*NASA*]   (KSC)
BSE............ Boston Edison Co. [*NYSE symbol*]   (SPSG)
BSE............ Boston Stock Exchange [*Massachusetts*]
BSE............ Bovine Spongiform Encephalopathy [*Veterinary medicine*]
BSE............ Breast Self-Examination [*for cancer*] [*Medicine*]
BSE............ Brno Studies in English [*A publication*]
BSE............ Broadband Switching Element [*Telecommunications*]
BSE............ Broadcasting Satellite Experimental [*Japan*]   (MCD)
BSE............ Building and Safety Engineering
BSE............ Building Service Employees' International Union [*Later, SEIU*]   (EA)
BSE............ Bureau of Steam Engineering [*Navy*]
BSE............ Recherches Economiques de Louvain [*A publication*]
BSE............ Sechelt Public Library, British Columbia [*Library symbol*] [*National Library of Canada*]   (NLC)
BSE............ Sodium Barbital-Sucrose EDTA Buffer
B Se A .... Bachelor of Secretarial Arts
BSEA .... Boletin. Seminario de Estudios de Arte y Arqueologia [*A publication*]
BSEU......... British School of Egyptian Archaeology
BSEAA ...... Boletin. Seminario de Estudios de Arte y Arqueologia [*A publication*]
BSE (Ae E) ... Bachelor of Science in Engineering in Aeronautical Engineering
B Seances Acad Roy Sci O-Mer ... Bulletin des Seances. Academie Royale des Sciences d'Outre-Mer [*A publication*]
BSE Bourbonn ... Bulletin. Societe d'Emulation du Bourbonnais [*A publication*]
BSEBourbonnais ... Bulletin. Societe d'Emulation du Bourbonnais [*A publication*]
BS in Ec ..... Bachelor of Science in Economics
BS Ec .... Bachelor of Science in Economics
B/sec .... BITs [*Binary Digits*] per Second [*Data transmission speed*] [*Data processing*]   (NASA)
BSE (CE)... Bachelor of Science in Engineering and Civil Engineering
BSE (Ch E) ... Bachelor of Science in Engineering in Chemical Engineering
B Secretar .. Boletin del Secretariado Tecnico [*A publication*]
BSECS........ British Society for Eighteenth Century Studies
B Sec Sc ..... Bachelor of Secretarial Science
B Sect Geogr Soc Sav ... Bulletin. Section de Geographie. Actes du 96e Congres National des Societes Savantes [*A publication*]
BS in Ed..... Bachelor of Science in Education
BS Ed......... Bachelor of Science in Education
BSED......... Ballistic Systems Education Division [*Air University*] [*Air Force*]
BSED......... Bulletin. Societe d'Etudes Dantesques. Centre Universitaire Mediterraneen [*A publication*]
BSEDEIS .. Bulletin SEDEIS [*Societe d'Etudes et de Documentation Economiques, Industrielles, et Sociales*] [*A publication*]
BS in EE .... Bachelor of Science in Electrical Engineering
BSEE .... Bachelor of Science in Electrical Engineering
BSEE .... Bachelor of Science in Elementary Education
BSE & E..... Bachelor of Science in Engineering and Economics
BSEE .... Boletin. Sociedad Espanola de Excursiones [*A publication*]

BSEEAZ.... Bulletin. Entomological Society of Egypt [*A publication*]
BSE (EE)... Bachelor of Science in Engineering in Electrical Engineering
BSE (EM) ... Bachelor of Science in Engineering in Engineering Mechanics
BSEE-ME ... Bachelor of Science in Electrical and Mechanical Engineering
BSEF .... Boletim. Sociedade de Estudios Filologicos [*A publication*]
BSE (Geod & Surv) ... Bachelor of Science in Engineering in Geodesy and Surveying
BSEIC........ Bulletin. Societe des Etudes Indochinoises [*A publication*]
BSE (Ind E) ... Bachelor of Science in Engineering in Industrial Engineering
B Seis S Am ... Bulletin. Seismological Society of America [*A publication*]
BSEL .... Bachelor of Science and English Literature
BSELB........ Berita Selulosa [*A publication*]
BSELCH ... Buffered Selector Channel
BS El E ...... Bachelor of Science in Electronic Engineering
BS in Elect Eng ... Bachelor of Science in Electronic Engineering
BS El Ed ... Bachelor of Science in Elementary Education
BS Elem..... Bachelor of Science in Elementary Education
BS in Elem Ed ... Bachelor of Science in Elementary Education
BSELot ...... Bulletin. Societe des Etudes Litteraires, Scientifiques, et Artistiques du Lot [*A publication*]
BS in EM ... Bachelor of Science in Engineering of Mines
BSEM........ Bachelor of Science in Engineering of Mines
BSEM........ Backscattered Electron Microscopy
BSEM........ British Society for Electronic Music
BSE (Mat E) ... Bachelor of Science in Engineering in Materials Engineering
BS in E Math ... Bachelor of Science in Engineering Mathematics
BSE (ME) ... Bachelor of Science in Engineering in Mechanical Engineering
BSE (Met E) ... Bachelor of Science in Engineering in Metallurgical Engineering
BSE (M & Ind E) ... Bachelor of Science in Engineering in Mechanical and Industrial Engineering
BSE (Nav Arch & Mar E) ... Bachelor of Science in Engineering in Naval Architecture and Marine Engineering
BSEND...... Building Services and Environmental Engineer [*A publication*]
BS Eng ...... Bachelor of Sanitary Engineering
BS in Eng... Bachelor of Science in Engineering
BS Engr Ad ... Bachelor of Science in Engineering Administration
BS Engr Phys ... Bachelor of Science in Engineering Physics
BS Engr Sci ... Bachelor of Science in Engineering Science
BS Eng Sci ... Bachelor of Science in Engineering Sciences
BSEO........ Bulletin. Societe d'Etudes Oceaniennes [*A publication*]
BS in EP ... Bachelor of Science in Engineering Physics
BSEP .... Bachelor of Science in Engineering Physics
BSEP .... Basic Skills Education Program [*Army*]
BSEP .... Brunswick Steam Electric Plant (NRCH)
BSEPC....... Bulletin. Societe d'Etudes de la Province de Cambrai [*A publication*]
BSEPE4..... Baltic Sea Environment. Proceedings [*A publication*]
BS in E Phys ... Bachelor of Science in Engineering Physics
BSE Phys... Bachelor of Science in Engineering Physics
BSEPT....... Bulletin Scientifique. Ecole Polytechnique de Timisoara [*A publication*]
BSEQA...... Business Systems and Equipment [*A publication*]
BSER .... Brainstem-Evoked Response [*Neurophysiology*]
BSER .... Bulletin. Societe Ernest Renan [*A publication*]
BSERBN ... Base Service Battalion [*Marine Corps*]
BSerSoc ..... Bachelier en Service Social [*Bachelor of Social Work*] [*French*]
B Serv Carte Geol ... Bulletin. Service de la Carte Geologique de la France [*A publication*]
B Serv Carte Geol Alg ... Bulletin. Service de la Carte Geologique de l'Algerie [*A publication*]
B Serv Carte Phytogeogr ... Bulletin. Service de la Carte Phytogeographique [*A publication*]
B Serv Soc Caisses Assur Malad ... Bulletin. Service Social des Caisses d'Assurance Maladie [*A publication*]
B Serv Tunis Statist ... Bulletin. Service Tunisien des Statistiques [*A publication*]
BS in ES..... Bachelor of Science in Engineering Sciences
BSES .... Bachelor of Science in Engineering Sciences
BSES .... British Schools Exploration Society
BSE Sc ...... Bachelor of Science in Engineering Sciences
BSESD ...... Bulletin. School of Engineering and Architecture of Sakarya [*A publication*]
BSES News ... British Schools Exploring Society. News [*A publication*]
B Se St ...... Bachelor of Secretarial Studies
BSET .... Bachelor of Science in Engineering Technology (IEEE)
BSET .... Bassett Furniture Industries, Inc. [*NASDAQ symbol*] (NQ)
BSET .... Test a BIT [*Binary Digit*] and Set [*Data processing*]
BSF .... B-Cell Stimulatory Factor [*Biochemistry*]
BSF .... Bachelor of Science in Forestry
BSF .... Back Surface Field [*Photovoltaic energy systems*]
BSF .... Backspace File (BUR)
BSF .... Ball Spin Frequency [*Machinery*]
BSF .... Ball Spinning Friction
BSF .... Ballon De Servance [*France*] [*Seismograph station code, US Geological Survey*] (SEIS)
BSF .... Baltic Student Federation
BSF .... Bandwidth Shape Factor
BSF .... Benign Senescent Forgetfulness [*Medicine*]
BSF .... Bis(trimethylsilyl)formamide [*Organic chemistry*]
BSF .... Blade Slap Factor [*Helicopter*]

BSF .... Boresight Fixture (MCD)
BSF .... Brief Stop for Fuel [*Military*] (NVT)
BSF .... British Salonica Force
BSF .... British Shipping Federation (DS)
BSF .... British Slag Federation [*A union*]
BSF .... British Society of Flavourists
BSF .... British Standard Fine Thread
BSF .... Bulk Shielding Facility [*ORNL*]
BSF .... Bulletin. Societe Francaise d'Archeologie Classique [*A publication*]
BSF .... Busulfan [*Also, BUS*] [*Antineoplastic drug*]
BSF .... Camp Pohakuloa, HI [*Location identifier*] [*FAA*] (FAAL)
BSF .... US-Israel Binational Science Foundation (EA)
BSFA .... British Science Fiction Association Ltd.
BSFA Bull ... BSFA [*British Steel Founders' Association*] Bulletin [*A publication*]
BSFB .... British Ski Federation (EAIO)
BSFC .... Brake Specific Fuel Consumption
BSFCA....... Bollettino Scientifico. Facolta di Chimica Industriale di Bologna [*A publication*]
BSFE .... Bulletin. Societe Francaise d'Egyptologie [*Paris*] [*A publication*]
BSFEA ...... Bulletin. Societe Francaise des Electriciens [*A publication*]
BSFEM ...... Bulletin. Societe Francaise d'Etudes Mariales [*A publication*]
BSFF......... Bollettino. Societa Filologica Friulana [*A publication*]
BSFF......... Buffer Stock Financing Facility [*International Monetary Fund*]
BSFIA .... Bulletin. Sport Fishing Institute [*A publication*]
BS (Fin) ..... Bachelor of Science in Finance
BS in Fin ... Bachelor of Science in Finance
BSFL......... Bandstop Filter (MSA)
BSFM........ Bachelor of Science in Forest Management
BSF Mgt ... Bachelor of Science in Fisheries Management
BSFN......... Bulletin. Societe Francaise de Numismatique [*A publication*]
BS For........ Bachelor of Science in Forestry
BS in For.... Bachelor of Science in Forestry
BSFP......... Bulletin. Societe Francaise de Philosophie [*A publication*]
BSFR......... Bollettino. Societa Filologica Romana [*A publication*]
B S Fr Cer ... Bulletin. Societe Francaise de Ceramique [*A publication*]
B S Fr D Sy ... Bulletin. Societe Francaise de Dermatologie et de Syphiligraphie [*A publication*]
B S Fr Min ... Bulletin. Societe Francaise de Mineralogie et de Cristallographie [*A publication*]
BSFS......... Bachelor of Science in Foreign Service
BS in FS..... Bachelor of Science in Foreign Service
BS Fsty ...... Bachelor of Science in Forestry
BSFT .... Bachelor of Science in Fuel Technology
BSFW .... Bureau of Sport Fisheries and Wildlife [*Superseded by US Fish and Wildlife Service*] [*Department of the Interior*]
BS in Fy ..... Bachelor of Science in Forestry
BSG........... Base Spares Group
BSG........... Bay St. George Community College [*UTLAS symbol*]
BSG........... Beam Steering Group
BSG........... BIT [*Binary Digit*] Sync Generator [*Data processing*]
BSG........... Brass Ring Resources [*Vancouver Stock Exchange symbol*]
BSG........... Brewer's Spent Grain
BSG........... British Society of Gastroenterology
BSG........... British Standard Gauge [*Telecommunications*] (TEL)
B & SG ...... Brown and Sharpe Gauge
BSG........... Buffered-Saline/Glucose [*Clinical chemistry*]
BSG........... Buletinul. Societatii Geografice Romine [*A publication*]
BSG........... Bulletin. Societe de Geographie [*A publication*]
BSG........... Bundessozialgericht [*Federal Court of Social Security*] [*German*] (ILCA)
BSG........... Business Strategy Group [*of ABT Associates, Inc.*] [*Cambridge, MA*] [*Telecommunications service*] (TSSD)
BSG........... Buyers Screening Guide
BSG........... Entscheidungen des Bundessozialgerichts [*Reports of the Federal Court of Social Security*] [*A publication*] (ILCA)
BSGAE...... Boletin. Sociedad General de Autores de Espana [*A publication*]
BSGAO...... Bulletin. Societe de Geographie et d'Archeologie d'Oran [*A publication*]
BSGB........ Brewer's Spent Grain Bran
BSGDG...... Brevete sans Garantie du Gouvernement [*Patent without Government Guarantee*] [*French*]
BS in GE .... Bachelor of Science in General Engineering
BSGE......... Bachelor of Science in General Engineering
BSGE......... Bulletin. Societe de Geographie d'Egypte [*A publication*]
BS in Ge E ... Bachelor of Science in Geological Engineering
BS in Gen Bus ... Bachelor of Science in General Business
BS Gen Ed ... Bachelor of Science in General Education
BS in Gen Eng ... Bachelor of Science in General Engineering
BS in Gen Nurs ... Bachelor of Science in General Nursing
BS in Gen Sci ... Bachelor of Science in General Science
BS in Gen Std ... Bachelor of Science in General Studies
BS in Geod & Surv ... Bachelor of Science in Geodesy and Surveying
BS (Geog)... Bachelor of Science in Geography
BS (Geol)... Bachelor of Science in Geology
BS in Geol E ... Bachelor of Science in Geological Engineering
BS Geol E .. Bachelor of Science in Geological Engineering
BSGF......... Bulletin. Societe Geologique de France [*A publication*]
BS Ggr .... Bachelor of Science in Geography

BSGI .... Bancserve Group, Incorporated [*Rockford, IL*] [*NASDAQ symbol*] (NQ)
BSGI .... Bollettino. Societa Geografica Italiana [*A publication*]
BSGIA .... Bollettino. Societa Geografica Italiana [*A publication*]
BS Gl .... Bachelor of Science in Geology
BS Gl E ...... Bachelor of Science in Geological Engineering
BSG Mgt ...... Bachelor of Science in Game Management
BSGP .... Bachelor of Science in Geology and Physics
BSGP .... Base Support Group [*Air Force*]
BSGP .... Boletim. Sociedade Geologica de Portugal [*A publication*]
BS Gph ...... Bachelor of Science in Geophysics
BS in Gph E ... Bachelor of Science in Geophysical Engineering
BSGR .... Buletinul. Societatii de Geografie al Romaniei [*A publication*]
BS in GS .... Bachelor of Science in General Studies
BSGS .... Base Support Group System [*Air Force*]
BS in GSM ... Bachelor of Science in General Science and Mathematics
BSGW .... Berichte. Verhandlungen der Saechsischen Gesellschaft der Wissenschaften [*Berlin*] [*A publication*]
BS in GWE ... Bachelor of Science in Group Work Education
BSH .... Benzenesulfonohydrazide [*Organic chemistry*]
BSH .... British Columbia Hydro and Power Authority, Surrey, British Columbia [*Library symbol*] [*National Library of Canada*] (NLC)
BSH .... British Pacific [*Vancouver Stock Exchange symbol*]
BSH .... British Shipbuilding Hydrodynamics
BSH .... British Society for Haematology
BSH .... British Society of Hypnotherapists
BSH .... British Standard Handful [*Slang*] (DSUE)
BSH .... Bush Industries, Inc. [*AMEX symbol*] (SPSG)
BSH .... Bushel (ROG)
BSHA .... Bachelor of Science in Hospital Administration
BSHA .... British Social Hygiene Association
BSHAF .... Bulletin. Societe de l'Histoire de l'Art Francais [*A publication*]
BSHA Geneve ... Bulletin. Societe d'Histoire et d'Archeologie de Geneve [*A publication*]
BSHAP ...... Bulletin. Societe Historique et Archeologique du Perigord [*A publication*]
BSHAP ...... Provincia. Bulletin de la Societe d'Histoire et d'Archeologie de Marseille et de la Provence [*A publication*]
BSHAP ...... Shape of Base of Leaf [*Botany*]
BSHAPerigord ... Bulletin. Societe Historique et Archeologique du Perigord [*A publication*]
BSHAR ...... Bulletin. Section Historique. Academie Roumaine [*A publication*]
BS in HD ... Bachelor of Science in Home Economics Education
BSHE......... Bachelor of Science in Health Education
BSHE......... Bachelor of Science in Hebrew Education (BJA)
BSHE......... Bachelor of Science in Home Economics
BS in HE.... Bachelor of Science in Home Economics
BS in H Ec ... Bachelor of Science in Home Economics
BS H Ec ..... Bachelor of Science in Home Economics
BS in H Econ ... Bachelor of Science in Home Economics
BS in H Ed ... Bachelor of Science in Health Education
BSHEW....... Bulletin. Societe pour l'Histoire des Eglises Wallonnes [*A publication*]
BSHF......... Building and Social Housing Foundation [*British*]
BSHG .... Bushing (MSA)
BSHM ...... Bulletin. Societe d'Histoire de la Medecine [*A publication*]
BSHM ...... Bulletin. Societe d'Histoire Moderne [*A publication*]
BSHMA .... Basket, Skip, and Hamper Makers Association [*A union*] [*British*]
BSH Maroc ... Bulletin. Societe d'Histoire du Maroc [*A publication*]
BSHMC..... Bulletin. Section d'Histoire Moderne et Contemporaine [*A publication*]
BSHNAN.. Bulletin. Societe d'Histoire Naturelle de l'Afrique du Nord [*A publication*]
BSHP......... Beginning Standard Holding Procedure [*Aviation*] (FAAC)
BSHP......... Bishop
BSHP......... British Society for the History of Pharmacy
BSHP......... Bulletin. Societe de l'Histoire du Protestantisme Francais [*A publication*]
BS in HPE ... Bachelor of Science in Health and Physical Education
BS in H & PE ... Bachelor of Science in Health and Physical Education
BSHPF ...... Bulletin. Societe de l'Histoire du Protestantisme Francais [*A publication*]
BSHPIF..... Bulletin. Societe Historique de Paris et de l'Ile de France [*A publication*]
BS in H & RA ... Bachelor of Science in Hotel and Restaurant Administration
BSHS......... [*The*] British Society for the History of Science
BSHS......... Bulletin. Societe d'Histoire et de Geographie de la Region de Setif [*A publication*]
BSHSL ...... Bulletin Signaletique. Histoire et Science de la Litterature [*A publication*]
BSHST ...... Bulletin Signaletique. Histoire des Sciences et des Techniques [*A publication*]
BSHY .... Bulletin. Societe des Sciences Historiques de l'Yonne [*A publication*]
BSI .... Baker Street Irregulars (EA)
BSI .... Banca della Svizzera Italiana [*Swiss-Italian Bank*] [*Switzerland*]
BSI .... Basic Shipping Instructions (NASA)
BSI .... Battery Status Indicator (NATG)

BSI .... Battlefield Systems Integration (MCD)
BSI .... Behavior Status Inventory [*Personality development test*] [*Psychology*]
BSI .... Biogenic Silica [*In water sediments*]
BSI .... Blairsville, PA [*Location identifier*] [*FAA*] (FAAL)
BSI .... Boeing Services International, Inc. (MCD)
BSI .... Bollettino Storico della Svizzera Italiana [*A publication*]
BSI .... Book Services International [*ACCORD*] [*UTLAS symbol*]
BSI .... Booster Situation Indicator
BSI .... Bound Serum Iron [*Serology*]
BSI .... Branch and Store Instruction [*Data processing*] (MDG)
BSI .... Brief Symptom Inventory [*Personality development test*] [*Psychology*]
BSI .... [*The*] British Society for Immunology
BSI .... British Solomon Islands
BSI .... British Standards Institution (ARC)
BSI .... British Studies Intelligencer (EA)
BSI .... Broadcast Satellite International, Inc. [*Dallas, TX*] [*Telecommunications service*] (TSSD)
BSI .... Broker Services, Incorporated [*Englewood, CO*] [*Information service or system*] (IID)
BSI .... Building Stone Institute (EA)
BSI .... Building Systems Institute (EA)
BSI .... Bulletin Social des Industriels [*A publication*]
BSI .... Bulletin. Societe des Etudes Indochinoises [*A publication*]
BSI .... Bureau Socialiste International [*Brussels*]
BS in IA .... Bachelor of Science in Industrial Arts
BSIA .... Bead and Stone Importers Association (EA)
BSIAD ...... Bulletin. South African Institute of Assayers and Analysts [*A publication*]
BSIAP....... Beginning Straight-In Approach [*Aviation*] (FAAC)
BSIB .... Boy Scouts International Bureau
BSIB .... British Society for International Bibliography [*Later, Aslib*]
BSIBA ...... Bollettino. Societa Italiana di Biologia Sperimentale [*A publication*]
BSIC .... Basic Earth Science Systems, Inc. [*NASDAQ symbol*] (NQ)
BSIC .... Binary Symmetric Independent Channel [*Data processing*]
BSIC .... Bulletin. Societe des Etudes Indochinoises [*A publication*]
BSICEN ... Battlefield System Integration Center (MCD)
BSID .... Bayley Scales of Infant Development
BSIE .... Bachelor of Science in Industrial Education
BS in IE ... Bachelor of Science in Industrial Engineering
BSIE .... Bachelor of Science in Industrial Engineering
BSIE .... Banking Systems Information Exchange
BSIE .... Bio-Sciences Information Exchange [*Smithsonian Institution*]
BS in IE & M ... Bachelor of Science in Industrial Engineering and Management
B Sign......... Bulletin Signaletique [*A publication*]
BSignHum ... Bulletin Signaletique. Sciences Humaines, Etc. [*Paris*] [*A publication*]
BSII .... Bionomic Sciences International, Incorporated [*Fenton, MO*] [*NASDAQ symbol*] (NQ)
BSII .... Bollettino degli Studi Inglesi in Italia [*A publication*]
BSIM......... Bachelor of Science in Industrial Management
BS in IM .... Bachelor of Science in Industrial Management
BSIM......... Broadband Service Integration Multiplexer [*Telecommunications*]
BSIM......... Bulletin Francais. Societe Internationale de Musique [*A publication*]
BSIM......... Burnup & Sims, Inc. [*NASDAQ symbol*] (NQ)
BSIN......... Bastian Industries [*NASDAQ symbol*] (NQ)
BSINA .... BSI [*British Standards Institution*] News [*A publication*]
BS in Ind Art ... Bachelor of Science in Industrial Art
BS in Ind Ch ... Bachelor of Science in Industrial Chemistry
BS in Ind E ... Bachelor of Science in Industrial Engineering
BSIndEd .... Bachelor of Science in Industrial Education
BS in Ind Ed ... Bachelor of Science in Industrial Education
BS Ind Eng ... Bachelor of Science in Industrial Engineering
BS Ind Mgt ... Bachelor of Science in Industrial Management
BSIndTech .... Bachelor of Science in Industrial Technology
BSI News... BSI [*British Standards Institution*] News [*A publication*]
BSinRE...... Bachelor of Science in Religious Education (BJA)
BSIP .... British Solomon Islands Protectorate (ADA)
BSIPA........ Buletinul Stiintific. Institutului Politehnic [*Cluj*] [*A publication*]
BSIR .... Bachelor of Science in Industrial Relations
BSIRA ...... British Scientific Instrument Research Association
BSIS .... Bulletin. Society for Italian Studies [*A publication*]
BSI Sales Bull ... BSI [*British Standards Institution*] Sales Bulletin [*A publication*]
BSIT .... Bachelor of Science in Industrial Technology
BSIT .... Bipolar-Mode Static Induction Transistor (MCD)
BSIT .... Building Supply Institute of Technology [*Canada*]
BS in J .... Bachelor of Science in Journalism
BSJ .... Bachelor of Science in Journalism
BSJ .... Bairnsdale [*Australia*] [*Airport symbol*] [*Obsolete*] (OAG)
BSJ .... Baker Street Journal [*A publication*]
BSJ .... Balanced Swivel Joint
BSJ .... Ball and Socket Joint
BSJ .... Bureau of Ships Journal [*Obsolete*] [*Navy*]
BSJC.......... British Seafarers' Joint Council (DS)

BSJE.........	Bachelor of Science in Jewish Education (BJA)
BS Jr.........	Bachelor of Science in Journalism
BSJS.........	Bachelor of Science in Judaic Studies (BJA)
BSK.........	Back Shunt Keying
BSK.........	Backpack Survival Kit (MCD)
BSK.........	Basket
BSK.........	Biskra [Algeria] [Airport symbol] (OAG)
bSK.........	Bovine Substance K
BSK.........	British Silbak Premier Mines [Vancouver Stock Exchange symbol]
BSKC.........	Kwantlen College, Surrey, British Columbia [Library symbol] [National Library of Canada] (NLC)
BSKG.........	Beitraege zur Saechsischen Kirchengeschichte [A publication]
BSKT.........	Basket (KSC)
BSL.........	Bachelor of Sacred Literature
BSL.........	Bachelor of Science in Languages
BSL.........	Bachelor of Science in Law
BSL.........	Bachelor of Science in Linguistics
BSL.........	Back Stage Left [A stage direction]
BSL.........	Bar Resources Ltd. [Vancouver Stock Exchange symbol]
BSL.........	Basel/Mulhouse [Switzerland] [Airport symbol] (OAG)
BSL.........	Baselined Software Library (MCD)
BSL.........	Behavioral Sciences Laboratory [University of Cincinnati] [Information service or system] (IID)
BSL.........	Benign Symmetric Lipomatosis [Medicine]
BSL.........	Best Straight Line [Mathematics]
BSL.........	Bile-Salt Limited Lipase [An enzyme]
BSL.........	Billet Split Lens
BSL.........	Biologic Safety Level
BSL.........	Biot-Savart Law [Physics]
BSL.........	BIT [Binary Digit] Serial Link
BSL.........	Blood Sugar Level [Clinical chemistry]
BSL.........	Blue Sky Laws
BSL.........	Bohn's Standard Library [A publication]
BSL.........	Bollettino Storico Livornese [A publication]
bsl.........	Bookseller [MARC relator code] [Library of Congress] (LCCP)
BSL.........	Botanical Society, London
BSL.........	Brotherhood of St. Laurence [Australia]
BSL.........	Bucknall Steamship Lines Ltd. (ROG)
BSL.........	Building Service League [Later, SEA] (EA)
BSL.........	Bulk Semiconductor Limiter
BSL.........	Bulletin. Societe de Linguistique de Paris [A publication]
BSL.........	Bulletin. Societe Scientifique et Litteraire du Limbourg [A publication]
BSL.........	Byzantino-Slavica [A publication]
BSLA.........	Bachelor of Science in Landscape Architecture
BSLA.........	Bible Study League of America (EA)
BS Lab Rel ...	Bachelor of Science in Labor Relations
BSL Arch...	Bachelor of Science in Landscape Architecture
BS in Lat...	Bachelor of Science in Latin
BSLELEP ...	Bulletin. Societe Lorraine des Etudes Locales dans l'Enseignement Public [A publication]
BSLF.........	Bulgarian Socialist Labor Federation [Defunct] (EA)
BSLHS.........	Shawinigan Lake Historical Society, British Columbia [Library symbol] [National Library of Canada] (NLC)
BSLLW.........	Bulletin. Societe de Langue et Litterature Wallonnes [A publication]
BSLM.........	Bachelor of Science in Landscape Management
BS in LP.....	Bachelor of Science in Land Planning
BSLP.........	Bulletin. Societe Linguistique de Paris [A publication]
BSLR.........	Bus Selector [Data processing]
BS in L & S ...	Bachelor of Science in Letters and Science
BSLS.........	Bachelor of Science in Library Science
BS in LS.....	Bachelor of Science in Library Service
BSLSS.........	Buddy Secondary Life Support System [Aerospace]
BS in LT ...	Bachelor of Science in Laboratory Technology
BSL & W ...	Beaumont, Sour Lake & Western Railway Co.
BSM.........	Austin, TX [Location identifier] [FAA] (FAAL)
BSM.........	Bachelor of Sacred Music
BSM.........	Bachelor of School Music
BSM.........	Bachelor of Science in Medicine
BSM.........	Bachelor of Science in Music
BSM.........	Balsam Resources, Inc. [Vancouver Stock Exchange symbol]
BSM.........	Basic Storage Module (MCD)
BSM.........	Basic Subsystem Module
BSM.........	Basic System Memory [Data processing] (BUR)
BSM.........	Battery Sergeant-Major
BSM.........	Battery Shop Maintenance [NASA] (KSC)
BSM.........	Beitraege zur Schweizerdeutschen Mundartforschungen [A publication]
BSM.........	Beso Sus Manos [With Great Respect] [Spanish] [Correspondence]
BSM.........	Bilingual Syntax Measure [English and Spanish test]
BSM.........	Bistable Multivibrator
BSM.........	Blue Star Mothers of America (EA)
BSM.........	Bollettino Storico Mantovano [A publication]
BSM.........	Bollettino di Studi Mediterranei [A publication]
BSM.........	Booster Separation Motors [NASA] (NASA)
BSM.........	Bottom SONAR Marker
BSM.........	Braked Servomotor
BSM.........	British Studies Monitor [A publication]

BSM.........	British Supply Mission [World War II]
BSM.........	Bronze Star Medal [Military decoration]
BSM.........	Bulletin des Sciences Mathematiques [A publication]
BSM.........	Bulletin Statistique Mensuel [Beirut] [A publication]
BSM.........	San Miguel Island [California] [Seismograph station code, US Geological Survey] (SEIS)
BS in MA...	Bachelor of Science in Mechanical Arts
BSMA.........	Bram Stoker Memorial Association (EA)
bsman.....	Businessman
BSMAS.....	Bond Strength Model of Active Sites
BS in Math ...	Bachelor of Science in Applied Mathematics
B S Math Fr ...	Bulletin. Societe Mathematique de France [A publication]
BS in Math Stat ...	Bachelor of Science in Mathematical Statistics
BSMC.........	Bachelor of Science in Mathematics and Chemistry
BSMC.........	Black Silent Majority Committee of the USA (EA)
BSMCP.........	Blue Shield Medical Care Plans [Later, BSA] [An association]
BS in Md...	Bachelor of Science in Medical Technology
BSMD.........	Bulk Store Memory Device (MCD)
BSME.........	Bachelor of Science in Mechanical Engineering
BS in ME...	Bachelor of Science in Mechanical Engineering
BSME.........	Bachelor of Science in Mining Engineering
BSME.........	Bachelor of Science in Music Education
BS in Mech ...	Bachelor of Science in Engineering Mechanics
BS in Mech ...	Bachelor of Science in Mechanics
BS in Mech Eng ...	Bachelor of Science in Mechanical Engineering
BS in Mech Ind ...	Bachelor of Science in Mechanical Industries
BS in Med ...	Bachelor of Science in Medicine
BSM Ed.....	Bachelor of Science in Music Education
BS in Med Rec ...	Bachelor of Science in Medical Records
BS in Med Rec Lib ...	Bachelor of Science in Medical Records Librarianship
BS in Med S ...	Bachelor of Science in Basic Medical Science
BS in Med Sc ...	Bachelor of Science in Medical Secretarial Science
BS Med T ..	Bachelor of Science in Medical Technology
BS in Med Tech ...	Bachelor of Science in Medical Technology
BS Med Tech ...	Bachelor of Science in Medical Technology
BS in M Educ ...	Bachelor of Science in Music Education
BS (ME Elect) ...	Bachelor of Science with Mechanical Engineering Electives
BS in M Engr ...	Bachelor of Science in Mechanical Engineering
BS in Met...	Bachelor of Science in Metallurgy
BS in Met...	Bachelor of Science in Meteorology
BS Met.........	Bachelor of Science in Meteorology
BS in Met E ...	Bachelor of Science in Metallurgical Engineering
BS Met E ...	Bachelor of Science in Metallurgical Engineering
BS Met Eng ...	Bachelor of Science in Metallurgical Engineering
BS in Met Engin ...	Bachelor of Science in Metallurgical Engineering
BSMF.........	BIT [Binary Digit] Sync Matched Filter [Data processing]
BS Mg E ...	Bachelor of Science in Mining Engineering
BS in Mgt Engr ...	Bachelor of Science in Management Engineering
BS in Mgt Sc ...	Bachelor of Science in Management Science
BSMHA	Bulletins et Memoires. Societe Medicale des Hopitaux de Paris [A publication]
BSMHB.....	Biophysics of Structure and Mechanism [A publication]
BSMI.........	Bureau of Small and Medium Industries [Philippines] (DS)
BS in Min ..	Bachelor of Science in Mineralogy
BS in Min ..	Bachelor of Science in Mining
BS in Min E ...	Bachelor of Science in Mining Engineering
BS in Min E ...	Bachelor of Science in Mining Engineering
BS in Min Eng ...	Bachelor of Science in Mining Engineering
BSMITH...	Blacksmith
BSMMDY ...	Boletin. Sociedad Mexicana de Micologia [A publication]
BS Mng E ...	Bachelor of Science in Mining Engineering
BSMO	Base Supply Management Office [Air Force] (AFM)
BSMP.........	Brussels Sprouts Marketing Program (EA)
B/SMPL...	BITs [Binary Digits] per Sample (NASA)
BS in MRL ...	Bachelor of Science in Medical Record Library Science
BS in MS ...	Bachelor of Science in Military Science
BSMSP.....	Bernoulli Society for Mathematical Statistics and Probability [Voorburg, Netherlands] (EA)
BSMT.........	Bachelor of Science in Medical Technology
BS in MT ...	Bachelor of Science in Medical Technology
BSMT.........	Basement (MSA)
BSMT.........	Board of Schools of Medical Technology [Later, NAACLS] (EA)
BSMT.........	British Society for Music Therapy
BS/MTAR ...	Battlefield Surveillance/Moving Target Acquisition Plan (MCD)
BS Mt E.......	Bachelor of Science in Metallurgical Engineering
BS Mu.......	Bachelor of Sacred Music
BS in Mu Ed ...	Bachelor of Science in Music Education
BS Mus......	Bachelor of Sacred Music
BS Mus......	Bachelor of School Music
BS Mus......	Bachelor of Science in Music
BS Mus Ed ...	Bachelor of Science in Music Education
BS in Mus Ed ...	Bachelor of Science in Musical Education
BSMV.........	Barley Stripe Mosaic Virus
BSMV.........	Bistable Multivibrator (MUGU)
BSN	Bachelor of Science in Nursing
BS in N ...	Bachelor of Science in Nursing
BSN	Backward Sequence Number [Telecommunications] (TEL)
BSN	Barium Sodium Niobate [Crystal]
BSN	Basin [Board on Geographic Names]

BSN .... Basin Petroleum Resources Ltd. [*Vancouver Stock Exchange symbol*]
Bsn .... Bassoon [*Music*]
BSN .... Bibliotheque Scientifique Nationale [*National Science Library*] [*Canada*]
BSN .... Bisegmental Neuron [*Neurology*]
BSN .... Bowel Sounds Normal [*Medicine*]
BSN .... Brine Shrimp Nauplii [*Ichthyology*]
BSN .... British Standard Number
BSN .... Broadband Switching Network [*Telecommunications*]
BSN .... BSN Corp. [*AMEX symbol*] (SPSG)
BSN .... Buletinul. Societatii Numismatice Romane [*A publication*]
BSN .... Novotech Services Ltd., Sidney, British Columbia [*Library symbol*] [*National Library of Canada*] (NLC)
BSN .... San Nicolas Island [*California*] [*Seismograph station code, US Geological Survey*] (SEIS)
BSNA .... Bachelor of Science in Nursing Administration
BSNA .... Bulletin. Societe Nationale des Antiquaires de France [*A publication*]
BSNA .... Bureau of Salesmen's National Associations (EA)
BSNAF ...... Bulletin. Societe Nationale des Antiquaires de France [*A publication*]
BS in Nat G Engin ... Bachelor of Science in Natural-Gas Engineering
BS in Nat Hist ... Bachelor of Science in Natural History
Bsn Atlant ... Business Atlanta [*A publication*]
BSNDT .... British Society for Non-Destructive Testing (MCD)
BS in NE .... Bachelor of Science in Nursing Education
BSNE .... Bachelor of Science in Nursing Education
BS in N Ed ... Bachelor of Science in Nursing Education
BSN Ed ...... Bachelor of Science in Nursing Education
BSNG .... Bulletin des Sciences Naturelles et de Geologie [*A publication*]
BSNG .... Bulletin. Societe Neuchatelloise de Geographie [*A publication*]
BSNM .... British Society of Nutritional Medicines
BSNotes ..... Browning Society. Notes [*A publication*]
BS in Nr ..... Bachelor of Science in Nursing
BSNR .... Biosensor Corp. [*NASDAQ symbol*] (NQ)
BSNR .... Buletinul Societatii Naturalistilor din Romania [*A publication*]
BSNR .... Buletinul. Societatii Numismatice Romane [*A publication*]
BSNRB .... Binnenschiffahrts-Nachrichten [*A publication*]
Bsn Record ... Business Record [*A publication*]
BS in NS .... Bachelor of Science in Natural Science
BSNS .... Bollettino della Sezione di Novara della Regia Deputazione Subalpina di Storia Patria [*A publication*]
Bsns Abroad ... Business Abroad [*A publication*]
Bsns Automation ... Business Automation [*A publication*]
BS in N Sc ... Bachelor of Science in Natural Science
BSNSDN ..... Boletim Tecnico. Servico Nacional de Levantamento e Conservacao de Solos [*A publication*]
Bsns Ed Forum ... Business Education Forum [*A publication*]
Bsns Ed World ... Business Education World [*A publication*]
Bsns Hist R ... Business History Review [*A publication*]
Bsns Lit ...... Business Literature [*A publication*]
Bsns Mgt .... Business Management [*A publication*]
Bsns Mgt (London) ... Business Management (London) [*A publication*]
Bsns Revw ... Business Review [*A publication*]
Bsns & Tech Sources ... Business and Technology Sources [*A publication*]
Bsns W .... Business Week [*A publication*]
Bsns W .... Business World [*A publication*]
Bsn SW Fla ... Business View of Southwest Florida [*A publication*]
BS in Nurs ... Bachelor of Science in Nursing
BS Nurs ..... Bachelor of Science in Nursing
BS Nurs Ed ... Bachelor of Science in Nursing Education
BS in Nurs Ed ... Bachelor of Science in Nursing Education
BSNY .... Bible Seminary in New York
BSO .... Bachelor of the Science of Oratory
B So .... Bachelor of Sociology
BSO .... Baluchi Students' Organization [*Pakistan*] (PD)
BSO .... Basco [*Philippines*] [*Airport symbol*] (OAG)
BSO .... Base Salvage Officer (MCD)
BSO .... Base Supply Officer [*Navy*]
BSO .... Benzene-Soluble Organics [*Pollutant*]
BSO .... Bilateral Salpingo-Oophorectomy [*Gynecology*]
BSO .... Biological Safety Officer [*National Institutes of Health*]
BSO .... Black September Organization [*Israel*]
BSO .... Blue Stellar Object [*Astronomy*]
BSO .... Bomb Safety Officer [*Navy*]
BSO .... Boston Symphony Orchestra
BSO .... British School of Osteopathy
BSO .... British Statistics Office
BSO .... British Supply Office
BSO .... Broad System of Ordering (MCD)
BSO .... Business Owner [*A publication*]
BSO .... Business Statistics Office [*Department of Trade and Industry*] [*Information service or system*] (IID)
BSO .... Buthionine Sulfoximine [*Biochemistry*]
BSO .... Buy Support Objective (AFIT)
BSO .... Monthly Bulletin of Statistics [*A publication*]
BSO .... National Security Organization [*Royal Thai Government*] (CINC)
BSO .... Squamish Public Library, British Columbia [*Library symbol*] [*National Library of Canada*] (NLC)

BSOA .... Bulletin. School of Oriental and African Studies [*A publication*]
BSOAL .... Bank-Share Owners Advisory League [*Inactive*]
BSOAS .... Bulletin. School of Oriental and African Studies [*A publication*]
BSOC .... Bell System Operating Company [*Also, BOC*] [*Post-divestiture division of American Telephone & Telegraph Co.*]
BSOCA ...... British Sociological Associates
BSocAdmin ... Bachelor of Social Administration
B Soc Anthropol Paris ... Bulletins et Memoires. Societe d'Anthropologie de Paris [*A publication*]
B Soc Archeol Hist Limousin ... Bulletin. Societe Archeologique et Historique du Limousin [*A publication*]
B Soc Arch Eure-Et-Loir ... Bulletin. Societes Archeologiques d'Eure-Et-Loir [*A publication*]
B Soc Arch HCH ... Bulletin. Societe Archeologique et Historique des Hauts Cantons de l'Herault [*A publication*]
B Soc Belge Et Exp ... Bulletin. Societe Belge d'Etudes et d'Expansion [*A publication*]
B Soc Belge Et Geogr ... Bulletin. Societe Belge d'Etudes Geographiques [*A publication*]
B Soc Belge Geol Paleont Hydrol ... Bulletin. Societe Belge de Geologie, de Paleontologie, et d'Hydrologie [*Later, Bulletin. Societe Belge de Geologie*] [*A publication*]
B Soc Bulg ... Bulletin. Societe Archeologique Bulgare [*A publication*]
BS in Occ Ther ... Bachelor of Science in Occupational Therapy
BS in Ocean ... Bachelor of Science in Oceanography
B Soc Ethnogr Limousin Marche ... Bulletin. Societe d'Ethnographie du Limousin et de la Marche [*A publication*]
B Soc Et Indoch ... Bulletin. Societe des Etudes Indochinoises [*A publication*]
B Soc Et Indochinoises ... Bulletin. Societe des Etudes Indochinoises [*A publication*]
B Soc Et Ocean ... Bulletin. Societe d'Etudes Oceaniennes [*A publication*]
B Soc Et Sci Aude ... Bulletin. Societe d'Etudes Scientifiques de l'Aude [*A publication*]
B Soc Franc Sociol ... Bulletin. Societe Francaise de Sociologie [*A publication*]
BSocFrEg ... Bulletin. Societe Francaise d'Egyptologie [*Paris*] [*A publication*]
B Soc Fr Min Crist ... Bulletin. Societe Francaise de Mineralogie et de Cristallographie [*A publication*]
B Soc Geogr Eg ... Bulletin. Societe de Geographie d'Egypte [*A publication*]
B Soc Geogr Hellen ... Bulletin. Societe de Geographie Hellenique [*A publication*]
B Soc Geol Belg ... Bulletin. Societe Geologique de Belgique [*A publication*]
B Soc Geol Fr ... Bulletin. Societe Geologique de France [*A publication*]
B Soc Langued Gegr ... Bulletin. Societe Languedocienne de Geographie [*A publication*]
B Soc Linguist Paris ... Bulletin. Societe de Linguistique de Paris [*A publication*]
B Soc Linn ... Bulletin. Societe Linneenne [*A publication*]
B Soc Litt Hist Brie ... Bulletin. Societe Litteraire et Historique de la Brie [*A publication*]
B Soc Myth Franc ... Bulletin. Societe de Mythologie de France [*A publication*]
B Soc Neuch Geogr ... Bulletin. Societe Neuchatelloise de Geographie [*A publication*]
B Soc Prehist Fr ... Bulletin. Societe Prehistorique Francaise [*A publication*]
B Soc Prehist Franc C R Mens ... Bulletin. Societe Prehistorique Francaise. Comptes Rendus Mensuels [*A publication*]
B Soc Roy Belge Anthropol ... Bulletin. Societe Royale Belge d'Anthropologie [*A publication*]
B Soc Roy For Belge ... Bulletin. Societe Royale Forestiere Belge [*A publication*]
BSocSc .... Bachelor of Social Sciences
B Soc Sci Nat Tunisie ... Bulletin. Societe des Sciences Naturelles de Tunisie [*A publication*]
BSocSt .... Bachelor of Social Studies (ADA)
BSocStud ... Bachelor of Social Studies (ADA)
B Soc Suisse Am ... Bulletin. Societe Suisse des Americanistes [*A publication*]
B Soc Suisse American ... Bulletin. Societe Suisse des Americanistes [*A publication*]
B Soc Thanatologie ... Bulletin. Societe de Thanatologie [*A publication*]
B Soc Vosg ... Bulletin. Societe Philomatique Vosgienne [*A publication*]
BSocW .... Bachelor of Social Work
BSocWk ..... Bachelor of Social Work
BS in OH ... Bachelor of Science in Ornamental Horticulture
BSOIW ...... International Association of Bridge, Structural, and Ornamental Iron Workers
BSOM .... Sointula Museum, British Columbia [*Library symbol*] [*National Library of Canada*] (NLC)
BSONA ...... Byulleten' Stantsii Opticheskogo Nablyudeniya Iskusstvennykh Sputnikov Zemli [*A publication*]
BSOO .... Berlin State Opera Orchestra
BS in Opt ... Bachelor of Science in Optics
BS (Opt) ..... Bachelor of Science in Optometry
BS in Opt ... Bachelor of Science in Optometry
BSORM ..... Sooke Region Museum, Sooke, British Columbia [*Library symbol*] [*National Library of Canada*] (NLC)
BS Orn Hort ... Bachelor of Science in Ornamental Horticulture
BS in Ortho ... Bachelor of Science in Orthoptics
BSOS .... Building Societies Ombudsman Scheme [*British*]
BSOS .... Bulletin. School of Oriental Studies [*A publication*]
B So Sc .... Bachelor of Social Science
B So Se .... Bachelor of Social Service

BS in OT....	Bachelor of Science in Occupational Therapy
BSOT........	Bachelor of Science in Occupational Therapy
BSOT........	Boston School of Occupational Therapy [*Tufts University*]
BSOTH	Bilateral Salpingo-Oophorectomy with Hysterectomy [*Medicine*]
B So W	Bachelor of Social Work
B Soz G	Bundessozialgericht [*Federal Supreme Social Security Court*] [*German*] (DLA)
BSP............	Bachelor of Science in Pharmacy
B Sp...........	Bachelor of Speech
BSP......	Bacterial Secondary Production [*Water chemistry*]
BSP......	Ballstop (MSA)
BSP......	Baltimore Steam Packet Co. [*AAR code*]
BSP......	Bank Settlement Plan (ADA)
BSP......	Baseline Schedule Plan (MCD)
BSP......	Bayerische Staatspartei [*Bavarian State Party*] [*Federal Republic of Germany*] (PPW)
BSP......	Bayes Sequential Procedure [*Statistics*]
BSP......	Belgian Socialist Party
BSP......	Belgische Socialistische Partij [*Belgian Socialist Party*] (PPW)
BSP......	Bell System Practices
BSP......	Benchmark Soils Project [*University of Hawaii, University of Puerto Rico*]
BSP......	Bensbach [*Papua New Guinea*] [*Airport symbol*] (OAG)
BSP............	Bibliographical Society of America. Papers [*A publication*]
BSP............	Bibliographical Society [*London*]. Publications [*A publication*]
BSP......	Bills Payable [*Business term*]
BSP......	Bison Petroleum & Minerals [*Vancouver Stock Exchange symbol*]
BSP............	BMEWS [*Ballistic Missile Early Warning System*] Specification (AFM)
BSP............	Bollettino Storico Piacentino [*A publication*]
BSP......	Bollettino Storico Pistoiese [*A publication*]
BSP......	Border Security Police [*NATO*] (NATG)
BSP............	Brief Stop for Embarking or Debarking Personnel [*Military*] (NVT)
BSP............	Bright Source Protection [*Optics*]
BSP......	British Socialist Party
BSP......	British Society of Periodontology
BSP......	[*The*] British Society for Phenomenology
BSP......	British Space Fiction Magazine [*A publication*]
BSP......	British Standard Pipe Thread
BSP......	Broad Street Pneumonia [*Center for Disease Control*]
BSP......	Bromosulfophthalein [*Clinical chemistry*]
BSp......	Bronchospasm [*Medicine*]
BSP......	Brunei Shell Petroleum Co. Ltd. (DS)
BSP............	Burroughs Scientific Processor [*Data processing*] (BUR)
BSP......	Business Strategy Panel [*Military*]
BSP......	Business System Planning
BS in PA	Bachelor of Science in Practical Arts
BS in PA	Bachelor of Science in Public Administration
BSPA	Bachelor of Science in Public Administration
BSPA	Black Students Psychological Association
BSPA	Bollettino. Societa Piemontese di Archeologia [*A publication*]
BSPA	Brushmakers of Scotland Protection Association [*A union*]
BSPA	Sparwood Public Library, British Columbia [*Library symbol*] [*National Library of Canada*] (NLC)
BSPABA....	Bollettino. Societa Piemontese di Archeologia e Belle Arti [*A publication*]
BS in PAL ...	Bachelor of Science in Practical Arts and Letters
BSPBA	Bulletin. Societe de Pharmacie de Bordeaux [*A publication*]
BS in PE ...	Bachelor of Science in Petroleum Engineering
BSPE	Bachelor of Science in Physical Education
BS in PE	Bachelor of Science in Physical Education
BSPEA	Bulletin. Societe de Pathologie Exotique et de Ses Filiales [*A publication*]
BSpecEd	Bachelor of Special Education
BS in P Ed ...	Bachelor of Science in Physical Education
BSpEd.......	Bachelor of Special Education
BSPEEQ....	Boletim. Sociedade Portuguesa de Entomologia [*A publication*]
BS (Per & Ind Rel) ...	Bachelor of Science in Personnel and Industrial Relations
BS in Pet	Bachelor of Science in Petroleum
BS in Pet Engin ...	Bachelor of Science in Petroleum Engineering
BS in Petr E ...	Bachelor of Science in Petroleum Engineering
BSPF........	Bulletin. Societe Prehistorique Francaise [*A publication*]
BS in Ph.....	Bachelor of Science in Pharmacy
BS Ph........	Bachelor of Science in Pharmacy
BSPH........	Bachelor of Science in Public Health
B S Ph........	Bulletin. Societe Francaise de Philosophie [*A publication*]
BS in Phar ...	Bachelor of Science in Pharmacy
BS Phar	Bachelor of Science in Pharmacy
BSPharm ...	Bachelor of Science in Pharmacy
BSPHN......	Bachelor of Science in Public Health Nursing
BS in PHN ...	Bachelor of Science in Public Health Nursing
BS in PHPM ...	Bachelor of Science in Public Health and Preventative Medicine
BS Ph Th ...	Bachelor of Science in Physical Therapy
BS in Phy Ed ...	Bachelor of Science in Physical Education
BS Phys	Bachelor of Science in Physics
BS in Phys Ed ...	Bachelor of Science in Physical Education
BS in Phys Th ...	Bachelor of Science in Physical Therapy
BS in Phys Ther ...	Bachelor of Science in Physical Therapy
BSPi..........	Bollettino Storico Pistoiese [*A publication*]
BSPIA........	Bollettino. Societa Paleontologica Italiana [*A publication*]
BSPiac	Bollettino di Storia Piacentina [*A publication*]
BSPis	Bollettino Storico Pisano [*A publication*]
BSPL........	Behavioral Science Programming Language [*Data processing*]
BS/PL........	Bile Salts/Phospholipid [*Ratio*]
BSPL........	Bulletin. Societe Polonaise de Linguistique [*A publication*]
BSPM	Battlefield Systems Project Management
BSPM	Bulletin. Societe de Prehistoire du Maroc [*A publication*]
BSPMC	Brake System Parts Manufacturers Council (EA)
BSPN........	Bollettino Storico per la Provincia de Novara [*A publication*]
BSPO.........	BMEWS [*Ballistic Missile Early Warning System*] System Program Office (AFM)
BSPP	British Society for Plant Pathology
BSPP	Burma Socialist Programme Party (PPW)
BS in Prac Arts ...	Bachelor of Science in Practical Arts
BS in Pr Ge ...	Bachelor of Science in Professional Geology
BS in Pr Met ...	Bachelor of Science in Professional Meteorology
BSPS.........	Bollettino. Societa Pavese di Storia Patria [*A publication*]
BSPS.........	British Society for the Philosophy of Science
BS in PSM ...	Bachelor of Science in Public School Music
BSPSM......	Saanich Pioneer Society Museum, Saanichton, British Columbia [*Library symbol*] [*National Library of Canada*] (NLC)
BSPSP	Bollettino. Societa Pavese di Storia Patria [*A publication*]
BSPT	Bachelor of Science in Physical Therapy
BS in PT	Bachelor of Science in Physical Therapy
BSPTA	Buletinul Stiintific si Tehnic. Institutului Politehnic (Timisoara) [*A publication*]
BSpThy......	Bachelor of Speech Therapy (ADA)
BSPTR.......	Beaufort Sea Project. Technical Report [*A publication*]
BSPU.........	Bollettino. Regia Deputazione di Storia Patria per l'Umbria [*A publication*]
BSPW	Bare Silver-Plated Wire
BSQ	Bachelor Sergeant Quarters [*Air Force*]
BSQ	Bisbee [*Arizona*] [*Airport symbol*] (OAG)
BSQ	Business Quarterly [*Canada*] [*A publication*]
BSQ	Myrtle Beach, SC [*Location identifier*] [*FAA*] (FAAL)
BSR..........	Bachelor of Science in Recreation
BSR..........	Back Stage Right [*A stage direction*]
BSR..........	Back Surface Reflectance [*Photovoltaic energy systems*]
BSR..........	Backspace Recorder
BSR..........	Ballistic Simulated Round (MCD)
BSR..........	Balloon Supported Rocket
BSR..........	Basal [*or Baseline*] Skin Resistance [*Medicine*]
BSR..........	Basic System Release (MCD)
BSR..........	Battle Short Relay
BSR..........	Battlefield Surveillance RADAR (MCD)
BSR..........	Best Speed Rating [*of a horse*]
BSR..........	Big Sur, CA [*Location identifier*] [*FAA*] (FAAL)
BSR..........	BIT [*Binary Digit*] Slippage Rate [*Data processing*]
BSR..........	BITE [*Built-In Test Equipment*] Status Register (MCD)
BSR..........	Blip-Scan Ratio
BSR..........	Blood Sedimentation Rate [*Medicine*]
BSR..........	Blue Streak Request [*Military*]
BSR..........	Board of Standards Review [*American National Standards Institute*]
BSR..........	Boilermaker, Ship Repair [*Navy rating*]
BSR..........	Bottom Simulating Reflector [*Oceanography*]
BSR..........	Brain Stimulation Reinforcement [*Electrophysiology*]
BSR..........	Branch to Subroutine [*Data processing*]
BSR..........	Bresea Resources Ltd. [*Vancouver Stock Exchange symbol*]
BSR..........	Bristol Simplified Reheat [*Aircraft*] (NATG)
BSR..........	British School of Archaeology at Rome. Papers [*A publication*]
BSR..........	British School at Rome [*Italy*]
BSR..........	British Society for Rheumatology (EAIO)
BSR..........	British [*formerly, Birmingham*] Sound Reproduction [*Initialism is now name of company and brand name of its products*]
BSR..........	Brown Stem Rot [*Plant pathology*]
BSR..........	Buffered Send/Receive
BSR..........	Buletinul Statistic al Romaniei [*A publication*]
BSR..........	Bulk Shielding Reactor
BSR..........	Butane Secondary Refrigerant
BSRA........	British Ship Research Association [*Research center*] (IRC)
BSRA........	British Shipbuilding Research Association
BSRH........	British Society for Research on Ageing (EAIO)
BSRAA	Bulletin. Societe Royale d'Archeologie d'Alexandrie [*A publication*]
BS in RAH ...	Bachelor of Science in Range Animal Husbandry
BSRAP	Beginning Standard Range Approach [*Aviation*] (FAAC)
BSRBB	Bulletin. Societe Royale de Botanique de Belgique [*A publication*]
BSRC.........	Biological Sciences Research Center [*University of North Carolina at Chapel Hill*] [*Research center*] (RCD)
BSRC.........	British Ship Research Council
BSRD........	British Society of Restorative Dentistry
BS in Rec ...	Bachelor of Science in Recreation
BS Rec	Bachelor of Science in Recreation

BS in Rec Lead ... Bachelor of Science in Recreation Leadership
BS Ret........ Bachelor of Science in Retailing
BSRF .... Borderland Sciences Research Foundation   (EA)
BSRFS....... Bell System Reference Frequency Standard
        [*Telecommunications*]   (TEL)
BSRGE ...... Bulletin. Societe Royale de Geographie d'Egypte [*A publication*]
BSRI .... Bem Sex-Role Inventory [*Research test*] [*Psychology*]
BSRIA .... Building Services Research and Information Association
        [*Information service or system*]   (IID)
BSRIA .... Southern Research Institute. Bulletin [*United States*] [*A
        publication*]
BSRL .... Boeing Scientific Research Laboratories
BSRM........ Boeing Small Research Module [*NASA*]
BSRM........ Booster Solid Rocket Motor [*NASA*]   (NASA)
BSRMA ..... Bulletin. Institut National de la Sante et de la Recherche
        Medicale [*A publication*]
BSRO......... Begin Standard Refuel Orbit [*Formerly, BSRRO*]
        [*Aviation*]   (FAAC)
BSRO......... Beitraege zur Statistik der Republik Oesterreich [*Austria*]
BSRP .... Papers. British School at Rome [*A publication*]
BSRRO...... Begin Standard RADAR Refuel Orbit [*Later, BSRO*]
        [*Aviation*]   (FAAC)
BSRS .... Bell System Repair Specification [*Telecommunications*]   (TEL)
BS in RT .... Bachelor of Science in Radiological Technology
BSRT .... Bachelor of Science in Radiological Technology
BSRV-L ..... Bulletin. Societe Royale de Vieux-Liege [*A publication*]
BS in Ry ME ... Bachelor of Science in Railway and Mechanical Engineering
BSS .... Bachelor of Sanitary Science
BSS .... Bachelor of Science in Science
BSS .... Bachelor of Secretarial Science
BSS .... Bachelor of Social Science
BSS .... Bachelor of Special Studies
BSS .... Backup System Services [*NASA*]   (NASA)
BSS .... Balanced Salt Solution [*Cell incubation medium*]
BSS .... Bangladesh Sanwad Sanstha [*News agency*]
BSS .... Baroness   (ROG)
BSS .... Base Service Store [*Air Force*]   (AFIT)
BSS .... Basic Shaft System
BSS .... Beam Steering System
BSS .... Before Stephen Sondheim [*A reference to simpler, less
        sophisticated, and more sentimental musicals*]
BSS .... Behavioral and Social Sciences
BSS .... Beitraege zur Semitischen Sprachwissenschaft [*A
        publication*]   (BJA)
BSS .... Bell's Science Series [*A publication*]
BSS .... Bernard Shaw Society   (EA)
BSS .... Bernard-Soulier Syndrome [*Hematology*]
BSS .... Bessie Smith Society   (EA)
BSS .... Bibliographic Search Services [*University of
        Minnesota*]   (OLDSS)
BSS .... Bibliographical Services Section [*of a library*]
BSS .... Bibliography of Soil Science [*A publication*]
BSS .... Birger Sjoberg Sallskapet [*A publication*]
BSS .... Bistatic SONAR   (CAAL)
BSSC .... Bisymmetric Spiral [*Astronomy*]
BSS .... Black Silk Suture [*Medicine*]
BSS .... BOMARC [*Boeing-Michigan Aeronautical Research Center*]
        Squadron Simulator
BSS .... Bond and Share Society   (EA)
BSS .... Bram Stoker Society   (EA)
BSS .... British Standard Specification
BSS .... Broadcast Satellite Service
BSS .... Bronze Service Star [*Military decoration*]   (AFM)
BSS .... Building Science Series [*National Institute of Standards and
        Technology*]
BSS .... Buletin per Shkencat Shoqerore [*A publication*]
BSS .... Bulk Storage System
BSS .... Bulletin of Spanish Studies [*A publication*]
BSS .... Bulletin de Statistique Suisse [*A publication*]
BSS .... Bureau of School Systems [*Office of Education*]
BSS .... Bureau of State Services [*of Public Health Service*]
BSS .... Bureau of Student Support [*Office of Education*]
BSS .... Business and Society [*A publication*]
BSS .... Business Systems Services   (MCD)
BSS .... School District 88, Skeena-Terrace, British Columbia [*Library
        symbol*] [*National Library of Canada*]   (NLC)
BSSA .... Bachelor of Science in Secretarial Administration
BSSAD ...... Business SA [*South Africa*] [*A publication*]
BS in San E ... Bachelor of Science in Sanitary Engineering
BSSanE ..... Bachelor of Science in Sanitary Engineering
BS in San Sci ... Bachelor of Science in Sanitary Science
BSSAR....... Babcock & Wilcox Standard Safety Analysis Report [*Nuclear
        energy*]   (NRCH)
BSSAT....... Bollettino di Studi Storici ed Archeologici di Tivoli e Regione
        [*A publication*]
BSSBG....... British Society of Social and Behavioural Gerontology
BS Sc.......... Bachelor of Sanitary Science
BS Sc.......... Bachelor of Social Science
BS Sc E ...... Bachelor of Science in Science Engineering
BS Sci Ed ... Bulletin Signaletique. Sciences de l'Education [*A publication*]
BS Sci L..... Bulletin Signaletique. Sciences du Langage [*A publication*]

B S Sci Med ... Bulletin. Societe des Sciences Medicales du Grand-Duche de
        Luxembourg [*A publication*]
BS Sci R..... Bulletin Signaletique. Sciences Religieuses [*A publication*]
BSSE .... Bachelor of Science in Secondary Education
BSSE .... Basis Set Superposition Error [*Physical chemistry*]
BS Sec........ Bachelor of Science in Secondary Education
BS (Sec Adm) ... Bachelor of Science in Secretarial Administration
BS Sec Ed .. Bachelor of Science in Secondary Education
BS in Sec Ed ... Bachelor of Science in Secondary Education
BS in Sec Sc ... Bachelor of Science in Secretarial Science
BS in Sec Sci ... Bachelor of Science in Secretarial Science
BSSG .... British Society of Scientific Glassblowers
BSSGC ...... Buletinul. Societatii de Stiinte Geologice din Republica
        Socialista Romania [*A publication*]
BSSHNY ... Bulletin. Societe des Sciences Historiques et Naturelles de
        l'Yonne [*A publication*]
BSSI.......... Basic School Skills Inventory [*Education*]
BSSI.......... Bollettino Storico della Svizzera Italiana [*A publication*]
BSSIA........ Byulleten' Sovet po Seismologii [*A publication*]
BSSI-D ...... Basic School Skills Inventory - Diagnostic
BSSI-S....... Basic School Skills Inventory - Screen
BSSL.......... Bibliographien zum Studium der Deutschen Sprache und
        Literatur [*A publication*]
BSSL.......... Bulletin. Societe des Sciences et des Lettres de Lodz [*A
        publication*]
BSSLL .... Bulletin. Societe Scientifique et Litteraire du Limbourg [*A
        publication*]
BSSM .... British Society for Strain Measurement
BSSMA ..... Business Systems and Security Marketing Association   (EA)
BSSMS...... British Society for the Study of Mental Subnormality
BSSNB ...... National Bureau of Standards. Building Science Series [*A
        publication*]
BS Soc Ethn ... Bulletin Signaletique. Sociologie - Ethnologie [*A publication*]
BS in Soc Serv ... Bachelor of Science in Social Service
BS in Soc St ... Bachelor of Science in Social Studies
BS (Soc Wk) ... Bachelor of Science in Social Work
BS Sp .... Bachelor of Science in Speech
BSSP.......... Benevolent Society of St. Patrick
BSSP.......... Bollettino Senese di Storia Patria [*A publication*]
BSSP.......... Broadband Solid-State Preamplifier
BSSPD....... British Society for the Study of Prosthetic Dentistry
BS in Spec Flds ... Bachelor of Science in Special Fields
BSSR .... Bureau of Social Sciences Research, Inc.   (MCD)
BSSR .... Byelorussian Soviet Socialist Republic
BSSRS....... British Society for Social Responsibility in Science
BSSRS....... Bureau of Safety and Supply Radio Services
BSSS .... Bachelor of Science in Secretarial Studies
BSSS .... Bachelor of Science in Social Science
BS in SS..... Bachelor of Science in Social Science
BSSS.......... Bathymetric Swath Survey System [*National Ocean
        Survey*]   (MSC)
BSSS.......... British Society of Soil Science
BSSS.......... Bulletin Mensuel. Societe des Sciences de Semur [*A publication*]
BS in S Sc .. Bachelor of Science in Social Science
BSSSC....... Behavioral and Social Sciences Survey Committee   (EA)
BSS Sci ...... Bachelor of Science in Secretarial Science
BS in Stat... Bachelor of Science in Statistics
BS in Struc E ... Bachelor of Science in Structural Engineering
BSSU......... Bench Stock Support Unit [*Military*]
BSSUI .... Benefit Service Series, Unemployment Insurance [*Department
        of Labor*] [*A publication*] [*A publication*]   (DLA)
BSSW .... Bare Stainless-Steel Wire
BSSY .... Bulletin. Societe des Sciences Historiques de l'Yonne [*A
        publication*]
BSSYA....... Biochemical Society. Symposia [*A publication*]
BST .... Bachelor of Sacred Theology
BSt............. Bachelor of Science in Teaching
B St .... Bachelor of Statistics
B St .... Balkan Studies [*A publication*]
BST .... Base Shop Tester
BST .... Beam Steering Transducer
BST .... Beam-Switching Tube
BST .... Belfast, ME [*Location identifier*] [*FAA*]   (FAAL)
BST .... Beobachtungsstelle [*Observation post*] [*German military -
        World War II*]
BST .... Bereitschaftsstellung [*Line of support*] [*German military -
        World War II*]
BST .... Best   (ROG)
BST .... Best Airlines, Inc. [*Detroit, MI*] [*FAA designator*]   (FAAC)
BST .... Best Resources, Inc. [*Vancouver Stock Exchange symbol*]
BSt .... Biblische Studien [*Neukirchen*] [*A publication*]
B/ST .... Bill of Sight [*Customs*]
BST .... Bleed Storage Tank [*Nuclear energy*]   (NRCH)
BST .... Blood Serological Test [*Medicine*]
BS & T .... Blood, Sweat, and Tears [*Rock music group*]
BST .... Blowdown Suppression Tank [*Nuclear energy*]   (NRCH)
BST .... Booster   (MUGU)
BST .... Booster Test Department [*NASA*]   (KSC)
BST .... Boresight Tower   (MUGU)
BST .... Boron Storage Tank [*Nuclear energy*]   (NRCH)

BST............ Boston State College Library, Boston, MA [*OCLC symbol*] (OCLC)

BST............ Bovine Somatotropin [*Endocrinology*]

BST............ Brief Stimulus Therapy [*Psychology*]

BST............ Brief Systems Test [*NASA*] (KSC)

BST............ British Standard Time (NATG)

BST............ British Steel PLC [*NYSE symbol*] (CTT)

BST............ British Summer Time

BST............ Bronte Society. Transactions [*A publication*]

BST............ Business Systems Technology, Inc.

BST............ Stamp Behaviour Study Technique [*Psychology*]

BSTANY ... Boot and Shoe Travelers Association of New York (EA)

BSTAR ...... Battlefield Surveillance and Target Acquisition RADAR (MCD)

B Statist (Bruxelles) ... Bulletin de Statistique (Bruxelles) [*A publication*]

B Stat M .... Bollettino Mensile di Statistica [*A publication*]

BSTB .... Blackie's Science Text Books [*A publication*]

BSTBA ...... Benzoyl(sulfamoyl)(thenyloxy)benzoic Acid [*Biochemistry*]

BStBl .... Bundessteuerblatt [*Federal Tax Gazette*] [*A publication*] (ILCA)

BSTC .... Ball State Teachers College [*Later, Ball State University*] [*Indiana*]

BSTCA ...... Bulletin. Standard Oil Company of California [*A publication*]

BSTCF .... Ball State Teachers College Forum [*Later, Ball State University Forum*] [*A publication*]

BSTD......... Bastard [*Size or material*]

BS in TE.... Bachelor of Science in Textile Engineering

B St E........ Bachelor of Structural Engineering

BSTEA ...... British Steelmaker [*A publication*]

BSTEC .... Bulletin. Societe Toulousaine d'Etudes Classiques [*A publication*]

BSTech ...... Bachelor of Science in Technology

B St Eng.... Bachelor of Structural Engineering

BSTF .... Base Shop Test Facility [*Military*]

BSt(F)........ Biblische Studien (Freiburg) [*A publication*]

BSTFA .... Bis(trimethylsilyl)trifluoroacetamide [*Organic chemistry*]

BSTG......... Bulletin. Societe Theophile Gautier [*A publication*]

BSTGA ...... Bulletin. South Texas Geological Society [*A publication*]

BS in Th.... Bachelor of Science in Physical and Occupational Therapy

BSTHM...... Stewart Historical Museum, British Columbia [*Library symbol*] [*National Library of Canada*] (NLC)

BST & IE... Bachelor of Science in Trade and Industrial Engineering

BSTIS........ Biweekly Scientific and Technical Intelligence Summary [*A publication*]

BSTJ.......... Bell System Technical Journal [*A publication*]

BSTJA .... Bell System Technical Journal [*A publication*]

B St KPA ... Berliner Studien fuer Klassische Philologie und Archeologie [*A publication*]

BSTL .... Bistaple

B St Lat..... Bollettino di Studi Latini [*A publication*]

BSTM........ Biaxial Shock Test Machine [*CERL*] [*Army*] (RDA)

BStM .... Bollettino. Associazione Internazionale degli Studi Mediterranei [*A publication*]

BSTN......... Boston Technology, Inc. [*NASDAQ symbol*] (NQ)

BSTR .... Booster [*Military*] (AFM)

BS Trans.... Bachelor of Science in Transportation

B-Strep...... [*Group*] B Streptococci [*Medicine*]

BSTRK ...... Bomb Service Truck (MUGU)

BSTS .... Benefit Systems Testing Section [*Social Security Administration*]

BSTS .... Boost Surveillance and Tracking System [*Satellite*] [*Military*]

BStud Lat... Bollettino di Studi Latini [*A publication*]

B Stupefiants ... Bulletin des Stupefiants [*A publication*]

BSU .... Basankusu [*Zaire*] [*Airport symbol*] (OAG)

BSU .... Base Service Unit [*Navy*]

BSU .... Baseband Separation Unit (MCD)

BSU .... Basic Sounding Unit [*Telecommunications*] (TEL)

BSU .... Bicycle Study Unit [*American Topical Association*] (EA)

BSU .... Bilevel Stimulus Unit

BSU .... Bis(trimethylsilyl)urea [*Organic chemistry*]

BSU .... Black Students Union

BSU .... Blood Supply Unit [*Military*] [*British*]

BSU .... Boat Support Unit (CINC)

BSU .... British Seafarers' Union

BSU .... Broadband Switching Unit [*Telecommunications*]

BSU .... Business Service Unit [*Telecommunications*] (TEL)

BSU .... Transport Echo. The Benelux Transport Magazine [*A publication*]

BSUAG...... Research Station, Agriculture Canada [*Station de Recherches, Agriculture Canada*] Summerland, British Columbia [*Library symbol*] [*National Library of Canada*] (NLC)

BSUB......... Ball and Socket Upper Bearing

BSUCA ...... Buletinul Stiintific al Universitatii Craiova [*A publication*]

BSUCNY ... British Schools and Universities Club of New York (EA)

BSUF........ Ball State University Forum [*A publication*]

BSUF........ British Schools and Universities Foundation (EA)

BSUG........ Bedford Systems Users Group (EA)

BSUI......... Benefit Service Series, Unemployment Insurance [*Department of Labor*] [*A publication*]

BSUM .... Summerland Museum, British Columbia [*Library symbol*] [*National Library of Canada*] (NLC)

B Sur .... Bachelor of Surgery

BSUR........ Surrey Public Library, British Columbia [*Library symbol*] [*National Library of Canada*] (NLC)

BSURCM .. Surrey Centennial Museum, British Columbia [*Library symbol*] [*National Library of Canada*] (NLC)

BSURCW .. Canada West Gold Rush Museum, Surrey, British Columbia [*Library symbol*] [*National Library of Canada*] (NLC)

BSURE...... Barking Sands Underwater Range Expansion [*Naval Oceanographic Office*] (MCD)

BSurv .... Bachelor of Surveying

BSurvSc .... Bachelor of Surveying Science

BSUS .... Bolivarian Society of the United States (EA)

BSUSSR.... Bulletin. Institute for the Study of the USSR [*A publication*]

BSUT......... Beam Steering Ultrasonic Transducer

BSUV........ Bibliographical Society of the University of Virginia (EA)

B & SV ..... Barkston Ashe and Skyrac Volunteers [*British military*] (DMA)

BSV........... Beach Support Vehicle [*Navy*] (CAAL)

BSV........... Binocular Single Vision [*Ophthalmology*]

BSV........... Black Sheep Ventures, Inc. [*Vancouver Stock Exchange symbol*]

BSV........... Bogie Sheep Van [*Australian*] (ADA)

BSV........... [*A*] Book of Scottish Verse [*A publication*]

BSV........... Boolean Simple Variable [*Mathematics*]

BSV........... Briggs, OH [*Location identifier*] [*FAA*] (FAAL)

BSVAH...... Bulletin. Societe Vervietoise d'Archeologie et d'Histoire [*A publication*]

BSVasc ...... Boletin. Real Sociedad Vascongada de Amigos del Pais [*A publication*]

BS in Voc Ag ... Bachelor of Science in Vocational Agriculture

BS in Voc Ed ... Bachelor of Science in Vocational Education

BSVPB....... Bulletin. Slovenskej Pol'nohospodarskej Akademie. Vyskumneho Ustavu Potravinarskeho [*A publication*]

BSVSAQ ... Kongelige Danske Videnskabernes Selskab. Biologiske Skrifter [*A publication*]

BSW.......... Bachelor of Social Work

BSW.......... Bank of New South Wales. Review [*A publication*]

BSW.......... Bank Street Writer [*A computer program manufactured by Bank Street and Intentional Educations, Inc.*]

BSW.......... Bare Steel Wire

BS & W ...... Basic Sediment and Water [*in crude oil*]

BSW.......... Black Swan Gold Mines Ltd. [*Vancouver Stock Exchange symbol*]

BSW.......... Boot and Shoe Workers' Union [*Later, UFCWIU*]

BSW.......... Bottom Sediment and Water [*in crude oil*]

BSW.......... British Standard Whitworth (MCD)

BSW.......... Brown Stock Washer [*Pulp and paper technology*]

BSWB........ Boy Scouts World Bureau [*Later, WSB*]

BSWC....... British Subject without Citizenship

BSWG....... British Standard Wire Gauge

BSWM....... Bureau of Solid Waste Management [*Environmental Protection Agency*]

Bs Worcstr ... Business Worcester [*A publication*]

BSX........... Bassein [*Burma*] [*Airport symbol*] (OAG)

BSY........... Bank Systems and Equipment [*A publication*]

BSY........... Big Sky Airlines [*Billings, MT*] [*FAA designator*] (FAAC)

BSY........... Biscayne Bay, FL [*Location identifier*] [*FAA*] (FAAL)

BSY........... Busy

BSYM........ Boy Savior Youth Movement [*Defunct*] (EA)

BSYN........ Biosynergy, Inc. [*NASDAQ symbol*] (NQ)

BSYSA....... Bulletin Scientifique. Conseil des Academies des Sciences et des Arts de la RSF de Yougoslavie. Section A. Sciences Naturelles, Techniques, et Medicales [*A publication*]

B Sy Th ...... Bachelor of Systematic Theology

BSZ........... Ballistic Systems Zeus [*Aerospace*]

BSZ........... Battlesight Zero (MCD)

B S Zool Fr ... Bulletin. Societe Zoologique de France [*A publication*]

BS in ZS..... Bachelor of Science in Zoological Sciences

BT .... American Association of Behavioral Therapists (EA)

BT .... Babylonian Talmud (BJA)

BT .... Babylonische Texte [*A publication*] (BJA)

BT .... Bachelor of Teaching

BT .... Bachelor of Technology

BT .... Bachelor of Theology

BT .... Bacillus thuringiensis [*Also, Bt*] [*Bacteriology*]

BT .... Back, Training [*Parachute*]

B & T......... Baker & Taylor Co.

B-of-T .... Balance of Trade [*International trade*]

BT .... Balanced, Total [*Business term*]

B & T......... Ball and Tube [*Photography*]

B & T......... Bank and Trust

BT .... Bankers Trust New York Corp. [*NYSE symbol*] (SPSG)

BT .... Barge, Training (MSA)

BT .... Baronet (EY)

BT .... Base Target (MCD)

BT .... Basic Technique [*Parapsychology*]

BT .... Basic Trainer [*Air Force*]

BT .... Basic Training [*Military*]

BT .... Bateau Torpilleur [*Torpedo Boat*] [*French*]

BT .... Bathythermal Traces

BT .... Bathythermograph [*Oceanography*]

BT .... Battery Target [*Military*] [*British and Canadian*]

BT .... Bea dan Tjukai [*Duties and Customs, Customs Service*] [*Indonesian*]
BT .... Beam-Rider Tail Control
BT .... Beam-Rider Terrier [*Missile*] (MCD)
BT .... Bearing Technology
BT3 .... Beat
BT .... Bedtime
BT .... Before Touching [*Parapsychology*]
BT .... Begin Transmission, Break
BT .... Bellini-Tose System
Bt............. Benedict's United States District Court Reports [*A publication*] (DLA)
BT .... Benefit (ADA)
BT .... Bent (MSA)
BT .... Benzothiophene [*Organic chemistry*]
BT .... Benzoyltyrosine [*Biochemistry*]
BT .... Berlingske Tidende [*A publication*]
BT .... Berth Terms [*Shipping*]
bt .... Bhutan [*MARC country of publication code*] [*Library of Congress*] (LCCP)
BT .... Bhutan [*ANSI two-letter standard code*] (CNC)
BT .... Bias Temperature
BT .... Bible Today [*A publication*]
BT .... Bible Translator [*A publication*]
BT .... Biblical Theologians (EA)
BT .... Bibliotheque de Theologie [*A publication*]
BT .... Biceps Tendon [*Anatomy*]
BT .... Big Table [*A publication*]
BT .... Bill Tomorrow [*Business term*]
bt .... Billet [*Bill*] [*French*] [*Business term*]
BT .... Bio/Technology [*A publication*]
BT .... Biologist's Toolbox
BT .... Bioprocessing Technology [*Technical Insights, Inc.*] [*Information service or system*] (CRD)
BT .... Biotechnology
BT .... Bishop's Transcript [*British*] (ROG)
BT .... Bitemporal (ROG)
BT .... Black Times [*A publication*]
BT .... Bladder Tumor [*Medicine*]
BT .... Blalock-Taussig [*Cardiology*]
BT .... Blanchi-Backlund Transformation [*Engineering*]
BT .... Bleaching Treatment [*Dentistry*]
BT .... Bleeding Time [*Clinical chemistry*]
BT .... Blind Toss
BT .... Block Template
BT .... Blue Tetrazolium [*A dye*]
BT .... Board of Trade [*Shipping*]
B of T .... Board of Trade [*Shipping*]
BT .... Boat (AABC)
BT .... Body Temperature [*Medicine*]
BT .... Boilerman [*Navy rating*]
BT .... Boiling Transition [*Nuclear energy*] (NRCH)
BT .... Bomber Transport [*Air Force*]
BT .... Borderline Tuberculoid [*Medicine*]
BT .... Bottle (MCD)
BT .... Bought
BT .... Boundary Trap
BT .... Bow Thruster [*of a ship*] (DS)
BT .... Brain Tumor [*Medicine*]
BT .... Break Transmission (NVT)
BT .... Breakdown Truck [*British*]
BT .... Breakfast Time [*Early morning television program*] [*BBC*]
BT .... Breakthrough
BT .... Breast Tumor [*Medicine*]
BT .... Breath Test
BT .... Brevet [*Military*]
BT .... Brick and Tile (ADA)
B and T ...... Bridges and Tunnels Crowd [*Derogatory reference to people who reach Manhattan via these routes*]
BT .... Bridging Truck [*British*]
B & T .... Brief and Time [*Photography*]
BT .... British Telecom [*or Telecommunications*] [*Common carrier*]
BT .... British Tissues, Ltd.
BT .... Broadcasting Station, Television [*ITU designation*]
BT .... Broader Term [*Cross-reference*] [*Indexing*]
bt .... Brut [*Gross (as in produce); Rough, Raw*] [*French*]
BT .... Builder's Trials [*Shipbuilding*]
BT .... Built (ROG)
B & T .... Bulb and Time [*Photography*]
BT .... Buried Tape Armor [*Telecommunications*] (TEL)
BT .... Burn Time [*NASA*]
BT .... Burnt (ROG)
BT .... Burnthrough (NVT)
BT .... Bus Tie [*Technical drawings*]
BT .... Business Traveler Magazine [*National Association of Business Travel Agents*] [*A publication*]
BT .... Busy Tone [*Telecommunications*] (TEL)
BT .... Rolls-Royce Ltd. [*Bristol Engine Division*] [*ICAO designator*] (FAAC)
BT .... Scottish Aviation Ltd. [*ICAO aircraft manufacturer identifier*] (ICAO)

BT .... Separative Sign [*Morse telephony*] (FAAC)
BT .... Trail Public Library, British Columbia [*Library symbol*] [*National Library of Canada*] (NLC)
BT1 .... Boilerman, First Class [*Navy rating*]
BT2 .... Boilerman, Second Class [*Navy rating*]
BT3 .... Boilerman, Third Class [*Navy rating*]
BTA .... Balkan Turks of America [*Later, BTAA*] (EA)
BTA .... Ballistic Track Assignor (AAG)
BTA .... Bankers Trust Australia Ltd.
BTA .... Barrier Teachers' Association [*Australia*]
BTA .... Basic Travel Allowance
BTA .... Beam Transfer Area [*LASER technology*]
BTA .... Been to America [*Slang*] [*British*]
BTA .... Behavioral Task Analysis (MCD)
BTA .... Benzotriazole [*Organic chemistry*]
BTA .... Benzoyltrifluoroacetone [*Organic chemistry*]
BTA .... Bertoua [*Cameroon*] [*Airport symbol*] (OAG)
BTA .... Best Technical Approach [*Military*] (AABC)
BTA .... Best Times Available [*Television*]
BTA .... Better than Average
BTA .... Bicycle Transportation Action (EA)
BTA .... Big Thicket Association (EA)
BTA .... Black Theater Alliance (EA)
BTA .... Blood Transfusion Association (EA)
BTA .... Board of Tax Appeals
BTA .... Brith Trumpeldor of America (EA)
BTA .... British Theatre Association
BTA .... British Tinnitus Association
BTA .... British Tourist Authority (EA)
BTA .... British Transport Advertising
BTA .... British Troops, Austria [*World War II*]
BTA .... Britt Airlines, Inc. [*Terre Haute, IN*] [*FAA designator*] (FAAC)
BTA .... Bruce Trail Association (EA)
BTA .... Bulgarian Telegraph Agency [*News agency*]
BTA .... Bulgarska Telegrafna Agentsiya [*Bulgarian News Agency*]
BTA .... Burlington, WA [*Location identifier*] [*FAA*] (FAAL)
BTA .... Business Travel Accident [*Insurance*]
BTA .... Business Trend Analysts, Inc. [*Commack, NY*] [*Information service or system*] (IID)
BTA .... Bute Resources [*Vancouver Stock Exchange symbol*]
BTA .... United States Board of Tax Appeals Reports [*A publication*] (DLA)
BTAA........ Balkan Turks of America Association (EA)
BTACCH... Board of Tax Appeals Decisions (Commerce Clearing House) [*A publication*] (DLA)
BTAED...... BMWI Tagesnachrichten [*A publication*]
BTAF........ British Tactical Air Force
BTA J .... Business Teachers Association of New York State. Journal [*A publication*]
BTAM ...... Basic Tape Access Method [*Data processing*]
BTAM ...... Basic Telecommunications Access Method [*IBM Corp.*] [*Data processing*]
BTAM ...... Basic Teleprocessing Access Method
BTAM ...... Basic Terminal Access Method [*Data processing*]
BTAM ...... Bulletin de Theologie Ancienne et Medievale [*A publication*]
BTAM (P-H) ... Board of Tax Appeals Memorandum Decisions (Prentice-Hall, Inc.) [*A publication*] (DLA)
BTAMS..... British Trans-Atlantic Air Mail Service
BTAO .... Bureau of Technical Assistance Operations [*UN*]
BTAP........ Bond Trade Analysis Program [*IBM Corp.*]
BTAPB ..... Bitumen, Teere, Asphalte, Peche, und Verwandte Stoffe [*A publication*]
BTAPH...... Board of Tax Appeals Decisions (Prentice-Hall, Inc.) [*A publication*] (DLA)
BTAQAO .. Universidade de Sao Paulo. Escola Superior de Agricultura Luiz De Queiroz. Boletim Tecnico Cientifico [*A publication*]
BTAS........ Band Training and Advisory Services Branch [*Canada, Indian and Inuit Affairs Program*] [*Canada*]
BTAS........ Bulletin. Texas Archaeological Society [*A publication*]
BTB........... Basic Test Battery [*Navy*]
BTB........... Biblical Theology Bulletin [*A publication*]
BTB........... Bone-Patellar Tendon-Tubercle Bone [*Graft*]
BTB........... Braided Tube Bundle
BTB........... Breakthrough Bleeding [*Medicine*]
BTB........... Bromthymol [*or Bromothymol*] Blue [*A dye*]
BTB........... Bumper to Bumper
BTB........... Bus Tie Breaker
BTBA........ British Tenpin Bowling Association, Ltd.
BTBC........ Boehm Test of Basic Concepts [*Psychology*]
BTBCA...... Bulletin. Torrey Botanical Club [*A publication*]
BTBib .... Bulletin de Theologie Biblique [*Rome*] [*A publication*]
B & TBL ... Braille and Talking Book Library (ADA)
BTBPE ..... Bis(tribromophenoxy)ethane [*Flame retardant*] [*Organic chemistry*]
BTBS .... Book Trade Benevolent Society [*British*]
BTBT........ BT Shipping Ltd. [*NASDAQ symbol*] (NQ)
BTBVA...... Bulletin Technique. Bureau Veritas [*France*] [*A publication*]
B of TC...... Bachelor of Textile Chemistry
BTC........... Bachelor of Textile Chemistry
BTC........... Bahrain Tourism Company (EY)
BTC........... Basic Technical Course [*Military*]

BTC............ Basic Training Center [Military]
BTC............ Battery Training Corps [British]
BTC............ Baxter Technologies Corporation [Toronto Stock Exchange symbol]
BTC............ Before Top Center [Valve position]
BTC............ Begin Telemetry Cycle
BTC............ Below Threshold Change [Air Force]
BTC............ Bench Test Console
BTC............ Beryllium Thrust Chamber
BTC............ Bicycle Touring Club [British]
BTC............ Binary Time Code (MCD)
BTC............ BIT [Binary Digit] Time Counter [Data processing]
BTC............ Block Transfer Controller [Data processing]
BTC............ Blood Transfusion Centre [British]
BTC............ Boilerman, Chief [Navy rating]
BTC............ Boys Town Center for the Study of Youth Development, Omaha, NE [OCLC symbol] (OCLC)
BTC............ Brands and Their Companies [Formerly, TND] [A publication]
BTC............ British Technical Council [of the Motor and Petroleum Industries]
BTC............ British Textile Confederation (DCTA)
BTC............ British Transport Commission
BTC............ Brown Trout Club (EA)
BTC............ Bus Tie Contractor (MCD)
BTC............ Business and Technology Center [Control Data Corp.] [British]
BTC............ Business Telecommunications Corporation [Chicago, IL] (TSSD)
BTC............ Business Training College
BTC............ Butembo [Zaire] [Seismograph station code, US Geological Survey] (SEIS)
BTC............ Central Technical Library, Cominco Ltd., Trail, British Columbia [Library symbol] [National Library of Canada] (NLC)
BTC............ Organon Laboratories Ltd. [Great Britain] [Research code symbol]
BTCA........ Basic Tables of Commissioning Allowances [Navy]
BTCA........ Bedlington Terrier Club of America (EA)
BTCA........ Big Thicket Conservation Association (EA)
BTCA........ Border Terrier Club of America (EA)
BTCA........ Boston Terrier Club of America (EA)
BTCA........ Bull Terrier Club of America (EA)
BTCA........ Butanetetracarboxylic Acid [Organic chemistry]
BTCA........ Trail City Archives, British Columbia [Library symbol] [National Library of Canada] (NLC)
BTCAB...... Boletim Tecnico. Centro de Tecnologia Agricola e Alimentar (Brazil) [A publication]
BTCC........ Big Thicket Coordinating Committee [Defunct] (EA)
B of TCC.... Board of Trade of the City of Chicago
BTCC........ Broome Technical Community College [New York]
BTCCDT ... Centro Nacional de Investigaciones de Cafe. Boletin Tecnico [Chinchina] [A publication]
BTCE........ Bureau of Transport and Communications Economics [Austria] [Also, an information service or system] (IID)
BTCE........ Bureau of Transport and Communications Electronics [Australia]
BTCG........ Bipartite Transport Control Group [Post-World War II, Germany]
BT Ch .... Bachelor of Textile Chemistry
BTCHDA .. Bio-Technology [New York] [A publication]
BTCI.......... Brown Transport Company, Incorporated [Atlanta, GA] [NASDAQ symbol] (NQ)
BTCM........ Boilerman, Master Chief [Navy rating]
BTCMPI ... British Technical Council of Motor and Petroleum Industries
BTCO .... Boston Terminal Company [AAR code]
Bt-Col......... Brevet-Colonel
BTCP........ British Transport Commission Police
BTCR........ Butcher (MSA)
BTCS........ Boilerman, Senior Chief [Navy rating]
BTCV........ British Trust for Conservation Volunteers
BTD .... Bachelor of Textile Dyeing
BTD .... Balanced Tape Drive
BTD .... Bank of Thailand. Monthly Bulletin [A publication]
BTD .... Bathythermal Data (MCD)
BTD .... Bell. Testing of Deeds [Scotland] [A publication] (DLA)
BTD .... Bias Telegraph Distortion
BTD .... Binary to Decimal [Data processing] (BUR)
BTD .... Bitec Development Corp. [Vancouver Stock Exchange symbol]
BTD .... Bomb Testing Device
BTD .... Bond Test Device (MCD)
BTD .... Brief Task Description (AAG)
BTD .... Bulk Tape Degausser
BTD .... Bulletin. Commission Royale de Toponymie et de Dialectologie [A publication]
BTD .... Burn to Depletion [NASA] (KSC)
BTDA........ Benzophenonetetracarboxylic Dianhydride [Organic chemistry]
BTDB........ British Transport Docks Board
BTDC........ Before Top Dead Center [Valve position]
BTDCPF.... Bathythermographic Data Collection and Processing Facility [Oceanography]
BTDE........ Benzophenonetetracarboxylic Diethylester [Organic chemistry]
BT Des .... Bachelor of Textile Design

BTDL......... Basic Transient Diode Logic [Data processing] (BUR)
BTDMSBA ... Black-Top Delaine Merino Sheep Breeders' Association (EA)
BTDO........ British Trade Development Office [Later, BTIO] (EA)
BTDPAF ... Bathythermographic Data Processing and Analysis Facility [Oceanography]
BTE.......... Bachelor of Textile Engineering
B of TE....... Bachelor of Textile Engineering
BTE.......... Baker & Taylor Co. [ACCORD] [UTLAS symbol]
BTE.......... Battery Terminal Equipment
BTE.......... Battery Timing Equipment (AAG)
BTE.......... Battle Energy Corp. [Vancouver Stock Exchange symbol]
BTE.......... Behind the Ear [Hearing aid] [Audiology]
BTE.......... Belfast Telegraph [A publication]
Bte........... Benedicite [Bless You] [Latin]
BTE.......... Benzilic Acid Tropine Ester [Also, BAT, BETE] [Pharmacology]
BTE.......... Better than Expected [Politics]
BTE.......... Bidirectional Transceiver Element [Telecommunications]
BTE.......... Blunt Trailing Edge
BTE.......... Boite [Box, Post Office Box] [French] [Correspondence]
BTE.......... Boltzmann Transport Equation [Physics]
BTE.......... Bonthe [Sierra Leone] [Airport symbol] (OAG)
BTE.......... Bord Telecom Eireann [Nationalized industry] [Ireland] (EY)
BTE.......... Bourdon Tube Element
BTE.......... Brayton Turboelectric Engine
BTE.......... Brevete [Patent] [French]
BTE.......... British Troops in Egypt [World War II]
BTE.......... Bulk Tape Eraser
B of TE....... Bureau of Ordnance Fleet Test Equipment [Obsolete] [Navy]
BTE.......... Bureau of Transport Economics [Australia] [Information service or system] (IID)
BTE.......... Business Telecommunications Equipment [Canada]
BTE.......... Business Terminal Equipment [Telecommunications] (TEL)
BTE.......... Terrace Public Library, British Columbia [Library symbol] [National Library of Canada] (NLC)
BTEA........ British Textile Employers' Association (EAIO)
BTEC........ BancTec, Inc. [NASDAQ symbol] (NQ)
BTEC........ Blanket Tool Expenditure Control (MCD)
BTEC........ Brucellosis and Tuberculosis Eradication Committee [Australia]
BTEC........ Business and Technician Education Council [British]
B Tech........ Bachelor of Technology
BTechInfSys ... Bachelor of Technology in Information Systems
BTEE......... Benzoyltyrosine Ethyl Ester [Biochemistry]
BTEE......... Brayton Turboelectric Engine
BTEK........ Baltek Corp. [NASDAQ symbol] (NQ)
BTEKA...... Byulleten' Tekhniko-Ekonomicheskoi Informatsii [A publication]
BTelE........ Bachelor of Telecommunications Engineering (ADA)
BT Eng....... Bachelor of Textile Engineering
BTENW..... North West College, Terrace, British Columbia [Library symbol] [National Library of Canada] (NLC)
BTERD....... Biological Trace Element Research [A publication]
BTE & S..... Bureau of Transport Economics and Statistics [ICC]
BTESM ..... Building Thermal Envelope Systems and Materials
BText .... Bachelor of Textiles
B Textil Anc ... Bulletin de Liaison. Centre International d'Etude des Textiles Anciens [A publication]
BTF........... Ballet Theatre Foundation (EA)
BTF........... Ballistic Test Facility [Air Research and Development Command] (AAG)
BTF........... Beam Rider Tail Control Fragmentation [Missile] (MCD)
BTF........... Bench Test Fixture
BTF........... Benzotrifuroxan [Organic chemistry]
BTF........... Betriebswirtschaftliche Forschung und Praxis [A publication]
BTF........... Bidirectional Test Fixture (MCD)
BTF........... Bomb Tail Fuse
BTF........... Bountiful, UT [Location identifier] [FAA] (FAAL)
BTF........... Brazilian Tourism Foundation (EA)
BTF........... Breakthrough Foundation (EA)
BTF........... British Pacific Financial, Inc. [Formerly, British Pacific Resources, Inc.] [Vancouver Stock Exchange symbol]
BTF........... British Trawler Federation
BTF........... Bulk Transfer Facility
BTFA........ Basic and Traditional Food Association [Inactive] (EA)
BTFA........ Benzoyltrifluoroacetone [Organic chemistry] (NRCH)
BTFA........ Bilinear Target Factor Analysis [Mathematics]
BTFA........ Bistrifluoroacetamide [Organic chemistry]
BTFA........ Fireman Apprentice, Boilerman, Striker [Navy rating]
BTFC........ Billy Troy Fan Club (EA)
BTFC........ BT Financial Corporation [Johnstown, PA] [NASDAQ symbol] (NQ)
BTFCA ...... Bulletin Technique. Societe Francaise des Constructions Babcock et Wilcox [A publication]
BTFFA...... Bulletin Technique des Mines de Fer de France [A publication]
BTFHA...... British Touch for Health Association
BTFIA .... Bollettino Tecnico FINSIDER [Societa Finanziaria Siderurgica] [A publication]
BTFL .... Butterfly (MSA)
BTFN........ Fireman, Boilerman, Striker [Navy rating]
BTG .... Ball Tooth Gear

BTG .... Battery Timing Group
BTG .... Beacon Trigger Generator
BTG .... Beating [*FBI standardized term*]
BTG .... Beating the Gun [*Investment term*]
BTG .... Becoming the Gift [*Religious education test*]
BTG .... Beta Thickness Gauge (DEN)
BTG .... Beta-Thromboglobulin [*Hematology*]
BTG .... Blood Triacylglycerol [*Hematology*]
BTG .... Brent Resources Group Ltd. [*Vancouver Stock Exchange symbol*]
BTG .... British Technology Group
BTG .... British Troops in Germany (DMA)
BTG .... Burst Transmission Group
BTGC...... Bio-Technology General Corporation [*NASDAQ symbol*] (NQ)
BTGCA..... Burley Tobacco Growers Cooperative Association (EA)
BTGJ ...... Ball Tooth Gear Joint
B Th .... Bachelor of Theology
BTH .... Basic Transmission Header [*Data processing*] (IBMDP)
BTH.......... Bath (ADA)
BTH............ Bathroom (ADA)
BTH............ Batu Besar [*Indonesia*] [*Airport symbol*] (OAG)
BTH.......... Berth (MSA)
BTH.......... Bethlehem Resources Corp. [*Toronto Stock Exchange symbol*] [*Vancouver Stock Exchange symbol*]
BTH.......... Beyond the Horizon (MCD)
BTH........... Bibliotheque de Theologie Historique [*A publication*]
BTH.......... Birth (ADA)
BTH.......... Bis(benzylidene)thiocarbohydrazone [*Organic chemistry*]
BTH.......... British Thomson-Houston Co.
BTH.......... British Transport Hotels [*Commercial firm*]
BTH.......... Bulk Transfer Hose
BTh.......... Bulletin de Theologie Ancienne et Medievale [*A publication*]
BTHA .... British Travel and Holidays Association [*Later, British Travel Association*]
BTHDA ..... Birth Defects. Original Article Series [*A publication*]
BThE .... Brake Thermal Efficiency
BTHG........ Business Traveler Hotel Guide [*National Association of Business Travel Agents*] [*A publication*]
BTHL .... Bethel Bancorp [*NASDAQ symbol*] (NQ)
BTHM ..... Bethlehem Resources Corp. [*NASDAQ symbol*] (NQ)
Bthol .... Bartholomaeus Brixiensis [*Deceased circa 1258*] [*Authority cited in pre-1607 legal work*] (DSA)
BThom ...... Bulletin Thomiste [*A publication*]
BTHRM ... Bathroom [*Classified advertising*] (ADA)
BTHU....... British Thermal Unit
BTHW ...... Biblisch-Theologisches Handwoerterbuch [*A publication*] (BJA)
BTI............ Bacillus thuringiensis israelensis [*Bacteriology*]
BTI............ Bank and Turn Indicator [*Aviation*]
BTI............ Barter Island [*Alaska*] [*Airport symbol*] (OAG)
BTI............ BAT Industries Ltd. [*AMEX symbol*] (SPSG)
BTI............ Bilateral Tubal Interruption [*Gynecology*]
BTI............ Biotechnica International, Inc.
BTI............ Boston Theological Institute (EA)
BTI............ Boston Theological Institute, Cambridge, MA [*OCLC symbol*] (OCLC)
BTI............ Boston Theological Institute Library [*Library network*]
BTI............ Boys' Towns of Italy (EA)
BTI............ Bridged Tap Isolator (IEEE)
BTI............ British Technology Index [*Later, Current Technology Index*] [*A publication*]
BTI............ British Theatre Institute (EA)
BTI............ British Tobacco Industry
BTI............ British Troops in Iraq (DMA)
BTI............ British Tutorial Institute
BTI............ BTI Computer Systems [*Formerly, Basic Timesharing, Inc.*]
BTI............ Buddhist Text Information [*A publication*]
BTI............ Burst Time Indicator (MCD)
BTI............ Business Traveler International [*A publication*]
BTIAL .... Bulletin Trimestriel. Institut Archeologique du Luxembourg [*A publication*]
BTIALux ... Bulletin Trimestriel. Institut Archeologique du Luxembourg [*A publication*]
B Tibetol .... Bulletin of Tibetology [*A publication*]
BTIC.......... Bomb Targets Information Committee [*Air Ministry*] [*British*] [*World War II*]
BTID........ Bis Terve in Die [*Two or Three Times a Day*] [*Pharmacy*]
BTIDA...... Byulleten' Tsentra po Yadernym Dannym [*A publication*]
BTIF .... Business Taxpayer Information File [*IRS*]
BTIIA6 ...... Bulletin Technique d'Information des Ingenieurs des Services Agricoles [*A publication*]
B'TINE...... Brigantine [*Ship*] (ADA)
BTIO........ British Trade and Investment Office (EA)
BTIPAR.... Instituto de Pesquisa Agropecuaria do Norte [*IPEAN*]. Boletim Tecnico [*A publication*]
BTIS .... Bankers Trust Information Service [*Database producer*]
BTIS .... Bureau of Transportation and International Services [*US Postal Service*] (MCD)
BTITA .... Bulletin. Tokyo Institute of Technology [*A publication*]

BTJ .... American Friends of Boys Town of Jerusalem [*Superseded by BTJFA*] (EA)
BTJ .... Ball Tooth Joint
BTJ .... Banda Aceh [*Indonesia*] [*Airport symbol*] (OAG)
BTJ .... Bibliotekstjanst AB [*Library Service Ltd.*] [*Sweden*] [*Information service or system*] (IID)
BTJ .... British Business [*A publication*]
BTJ .... British Trade Journal [*A publication*] (ROG)
BTJ .... Brotherhood of Traveling Jewelers (EA)
BTJE .... Bypass Turbojet Engine Noise
BTJFA .... Boys Town Jerusalem Foundation of America (EA)
BTK .... Big Strike Resources [*Vancouver Stock Exchange symbol*]
BTK .... Bratsk [*USSR*] [*Airport symbol*] (OAG)
B of TKC... Board of Trade of Kansas City [*Missouri*]
BTL........... Battle Creek [*Michigan*] [*Airport symbol*] (OAG)
BTL........... Beacon Tracking Level (KSC)
BTL........... Beginning Tape Label [*Data processing*] (BUR)
BTL........... Behind the Line [*Air Force*]
BTL........... Bell Telephone Laboratories, Inc. [*Murray Hill, NJ*]
BTL........... Bell Telephone Laboratories, Inc., Holmdel, NJ [*OCLC symbol*] (OCLC)
BTL........... Below the Line [*Budget*]
BTL........... Bend Tangency Line (MCD)
BTL........... Between Layers [*Aviation*] (FAAC)
BTL........... Bilateral Tubal Ligation [*Gynecology*]
BTL........... Birmingham Technology Ltd. at Aston Science Park [*British*] (IRUK)
BTL........... Bitolterol [*Pharmacology*]
BTL........... Bottle
BTL........... Bottomline [*A publication*]
BTL........... BTL Corp. [*Formerly, Butler Brothers*]
BTL........... Butler International, Inc. [*NYSE symbol*] (SPSG)
BTLEX ...... Battalion Landing Team Landing Exercise [*Military*] (NVT)
BTL ILUM-L ... Battlefield Illumination L System (MCD)
BTLL .... Bottom Lead Left (MSA)
BTLR......... Bottom Lead Right (MSA)
BTLR......... Butler Manufacturing Co. [*NASDAQ symbol*] (NQ)
BTLS .... Breadboard Terminal Landing System [*NASA*] (KSC)
BTLV........ Bijdragen tot de Taal-Land- en Volkenkunde [*A publication*]
BTLVNI.... Bijdragen tot de Taal-Land- en Volkenkunde van Nederlandsche-Indie [*A publication*]
B of TM ..... Bachelor of Textile Management
BTM .... Ballast Tank Meter
BTM .... Batch Time-Sharing Monitor [*Xerox Corp.*] [*Data processing*] (MCD)
BTM .... Battalion Training Model [*Military*]
BTM .... Bell Telephone Manufacturing Co. [*Telecommunications*]
BTM .... Bellows Tankage Module
Btm............ Benzylthiomethyl [*Biochemistry*]
BTM .... Benzyltrimethylammonium Chloride [*Also, TMBAC*] [*Organic chemistry*]
BTM .... Biochemical Test Monitor
BTM .... Blast Test Missile (NG)
BTM .... Blast Test Motor (MCD)
BTM .... Bottom
BTM .... British Trade Mission
BTM .... Broadband Trunk Module [*Telecommunications*]
BTM .... Bromotrifluoromethane [*Fire extinguishing agent*] [*Organic chemistry*] (ADA)
BTM .... Brushless Torque Motor
BTM .... Bulling the Market [*Investment term*]
BTM .... Butte [*Montana*] [*Airport symbol*] (OAG)
BTM .... Trail Museum, British Columbia [*Library symbol*] [*National Library of Canada*] (NLC)
BTMA .... Basic Telecommunication (MCD)
BTMA .... Boat Trailer Manufacturers Association [*Later, TMA*] (EA)
BTMA .... Bow Tie Manufacturers Association (EA)
BTMA .... Braided Trimming Manufacturers Association [*Later, EFMCNTA*] (EA)
BTMA .... British Textile Machinery Association (DS)
BTMC....... British Tabulating Machinery Company
BTMC....... British Telecom Mobile Communications
BTMD ...... Batten-Turner Muscular Dystrophy [*Syndrome*] [*Medicine*]
BTMDA .... Bulletin. Tokyo Medical and Dental University [*A publication*]
BTME........ Babcock Test of Mental Efficiency [*Psychology*]
BTMF........ Block Type Manipulation Facility
BTMG .... Blaetter der Thomas Mann Gesellschaft [*A publication*]
BTMNA ..... Bitamin [*A publication*]
BTMS........ Battalion Training Management System [*Army*] (INF)
BTMS........ Body Temperature Measuring System
BTMS........ Brake Temperature Monitoring System (MCD)
BTMSA ...... Bis(trimethylsilyl)acetylene [*Organic chemistry*]
BTMSD ..... Bio Times [*A publication*]
BTN .... Baptist Telecommunications Network [*Nashville, TN*] [*Cable-television system*]
BTN .... Battalion
BTN .... Beam-Riding Tail-Controlled Nuclear Missile
BTN .... Beam Tracking Nuclear [*Military*] (CAAL)
BTN .... Between
BTN .... Bhutan [*ANSI three-letter standard code*] (CNC)
BTN .... Billing Telephone Number [*Telecommunications*] (TEL)

BTN .... British Travel News [*A publication*]
BTN .... Britton, SD [*Location identifier*] [*FAA*]   (FAAL)
BTN .... Brussels Tariff Nomenclature [*See also CCCN*] [*EEC*]
BTN .... Button   (AAG)
BTN .... Butuan [*Philippines*] [*Seismograph station code, US Geological Survey*] [*Closed*]   (SEIS)
BTNA ...... British Troops in North Africa [*World War II*]
BTNEC...... Bis(trinitroethyl)carbonate [*An explosive*]
BTNEN ..... Bis(trinitroethyl)nitramine [*An explosive*]
BTNHD.... Button Head
BTNKA ..... Biotechniek [*The Netherlands*] [*A publication*]
BTNQA ..... Botanique [*A publication*]
BTO .... Bachman-Turner Overdrive [*Rock music group*]
Bto............. Bartolus de Sassoferrato [*Deceased, 1357*] [*Authority cited in pre-1607 legal work*]   (DSA)
BTO .... Battalion Transport Officer [*British military*]   (DMA)
BTO .... Belgian Tourist Office   (EA)
BTO .... Big-Time Operator [*Slang*]
BTO .... Blanket Tool Order
BTO .... Blanket Travel Order   (MCD)
BTO .... Blocking-Tube Oscillator
BTO .... Bombing through Overcast [*By means of RADAR equipment*]
BTO .... Botopasie [*Surinam*] [*Airport symbol*]   (OAG)
BTO .... Branch Transportation Office [*or Officer*] [*Army*]
BTO .... Brazil Tourism Office   (EA)
BTO .... Brief Task Outline   (AAG)
BTO .... Brigade Transport Officer [*British*]
BTO .... Britcol Resource Development [*Vancouver Stock Exchange symbol*]
BTO .... British Trust for Ornithology
BTO .... Brussels Treaty Organization [*Later, Western European Union*]
BTO .... Translation Bureau Library, Secretary of State [*UTLAS symbol*]
BTOC .... Brigade Tactical Operations Center
BTOF....... British Trawler Officers Federation [*A union*]
BTOGW .... Basic Takeoff Gross Weight [*Aviation*]   (MCD)
BTOMM ... West Coast Maritime Museum, Tofino, British Columbia [*Library symbol*] [*National Library of Canada*]   (NLC)
BTON ...... Brighton   (ROG)
BTONA ..... Beton, Herstellung, Verwendung [*A publication*]
B Tor Bot C ... Bulletin. Torrey Botanical Club [*A publication*]
BTP........... Bachelor of Town Planning
BTP........... Batch Transfer Program
BTP........... Beam Tape Packaging [*Data processing*]
BTP........... Bibliotheque des Textes Philosophiques [*A publication*]
BTP........... Bis Tris Propane [*Biological buffer*]
BTP........... Black Thunder Petroleum [*Vancouver Stock Exchange symbol*]
BTP........... BMEWS [*Ballistic Missile Early Warning System*] Test Procedure   (AFM)
BTP........... [*A*] Book of Treasured Poems [*A publication*]
BTP........... Bovine Trophoblast Protein [*Biochemistry*]
BTP........... Braille Technical Press [*Defunct*]   (EA)
BTP........... Branch Technical Position [*Nuclear energy*]   (NRCH)
BTP........... British Telecom Phonecards [*Prepaid cards for use in noncoin pay telephones*]
BTP........... Butler, PA [*Location identifier*] [*FAA*]   (FAAL)
BT PABA... Benzoyl-Tyrosyl Para-Aminobenzoic Acid [*Organic chemistry*]
BTPC........ Brussels Treaty Permanent Commission   (NATG)
BTPC........ Bulletin des Tribunaux de Police Congolais [*A publication*]
BTPD........ Body Temperature, [*Ambient*] Pressure, Dry [*Medicine*]
BTPD........ Busy Tax Practitioner's Digest [*Australia*] [*A publication*]
BTPGA...... Beitraege zur Pathologie [*A publication*]
BTPII........ Boston Tea Party II [*An association*]   (EA)
BTPS .... Body Temperature, [*Ambient*] Pressure, Saturated [*with water*] [*Medicine*]
BTQ .... Banque de Terminologie du Quebec [*Terminology Bank of Quebec*] [*French Language Board*] [*Information service or system*]   (IID)
BTQ-7........ Brisbane TV Ltd. [*Queensland, Australia*] [*Telecommunications service*]   (TSSD)
BTQSA...... Bulletin Technique de la Suisse Romande [*A publication*]
BTR .... Back Tape Reader
BTR .... Ballast Tube Resistor
BTR .... Barrel-Tile Roof [*Technical drawings*]
BTR .... Baton Rouge [*Louisiana*] [*Airport symbol*]   (OAG)
BTR .... Bearing Time Recorder
BTR .... Behind Tape Reader   (MCD)
BTR .... Betrust Investments [*Vancouver Stock Exchange symbol*]
BTR .... Better   (FAAC)
B Tr............ Bishop's Trial [*A publication*]   (DLA)
BTR .... Blanket Tritium Recovery [*Subsystem*]   (MCD)
BTR .... Block Tape Recorder
BTR .... BMEWS [*Ballistic Missile Early Warning System*] Test Report   (AFM)
BTR .... Boom Time Remaining   (NASA)
BTR .... Bradley Real Estate Trust [*AMEX symbol*]   (SPSG)
BTR .... Brewing Trade Review Licensing Law Reports [*England*] [*A publication*]   (DLA)
BTR .... British Tax Review [*A publication*]
BTR .... Broadcast and Television Receivers   (MCD)
BTR .... Broneje Transporter [*Soviet Armored Personnel Carrier*]
BTR .... Bureau of Tourism Research [*Australia*]

BTR .... Bureau of Trade Regulation [*Department of Commerce*]
BTR .... Burn Time Remaining   (MCD)
BTR .... Bus Transfer   (AAG)
BTR .... Business Technology Research, Inc. [*Telecommunications service*]   (TSSD)
BTR .... Business Trends. A Concise and Systematic Weekly Report to Management on the Argentine Economy [*A publication*]
BTR .... Butare [*Astrida*] [*Rwanda*] [*Seismograph station code, US Geological Survey*] [*Closed*]   (SEIS)
BTR .... Sunbelt Airlines [*Camden, AR*] [*FAA designator*]   (FAAC)
BTR .... Tumbler Ridge Public Library, British Columbia [*Library symbol*] [*National Library of Canada*]   (BIB)
Btran .... Bertrandus [*Authority cited in pre-1607 legal work*]   (DSA)
BTRC........ Brain Tumor Research Center [*University of California, San Francisco*] [*Research center*]   (RCD)
BTRG........ Bullet-Trap Rifle Grenade [*Army*]   (INF)
BTRI......... BTR Realty, Inc. [*NASDAQ symbol*]   (NQ)
B Trim Banque France ... Bulletin Trimestriel. Banque de France [*A publication*]
B Trim Ecole Nat Sante Publ ... Bulletin Trimestriel. Ecole Nationale de la Sante Publique [*A publication*]
B Tr Int Ch Fer ... Bulletin des Transports Internationaux par Chemins de Fer [*A publication*]
BTRL......... Biotech Research Laboratories, Inc. [*NASDAQ symbol*]   (NQ)
BTRLR ...... Brewing Trade Review Law Reports [*A publication*]   (DLA)
BTRMLK.. Buttermilk [*Freight*]
BTROA ..... Biotropica [*A publication*]
BTRP......... Bachelor of Town and Regional Planning   (ADA)
BT & RP ... Bachelor of Town and Regional Planning   (ADA)
BTRS .... Behavior Therapy and Research Society   (EA)
BTRS .... Boron Thermal Regeneration System [*Nuclear energy*]   (NRCH)
BTRY .... Battery   (AFM)
BTS .... Bachelor of Technological Science
BTS .... Bairnsdale Technical School [*Australia*]
BTS .... Balloon Transport System
BTS .... Barrier Terminal Strip
BTS .... Base of Terminal Service [*for airmen*]
BTS .... Basic Training School
BTS .... Batch Terminal Simulator [*Data processing*]
BTS .... Bates College, Lewiston, ME [*OCLC symbol*]   (OCLC)
BTS .... Battery Test Set
BTS .... Beacon Tracking System
BTS .... Beam Transport System
BTS .... Bellini-Tose System
BTS .... Bench Test Specification
BTS .... Bible et Terre Sainte [*A publication*]   (BJA)
BTS .... Biomet Tech, Inc. [*Vancouver Stock Exchange symbol*]
BTS .... Biotelemetry System
BTS .... Bithionol Sulfoxide [*Pharmacology*]
BTS .... Black Turtle Soup
BTS .... Blessed Trinity Society [*Defunct*]
BTS .... Blood Transfusion Service [*Medicine*]
BTS .... Blue Tool Steel   (MSA)
BTS .... Board of Thoracic Surgery [*Later, American Board of Thoracic Surgery*]   (EA)
BTS .... Boeing Test Support [*NASA*]   (KSC)
BTS .... Boolean Time Sequence [*Mathematics*]
BTS .... Boys Technical School [*British military*]   (DMA)
BTS .... Bratislava [*Czechoslovakia*] [*Airport symbol*]   (OAG)
BTS .... Brazilian Thorium Sludge
BTS .... British Telecommunications Systems Ltd.   (TEL)
BTS .... [*The*] British Thoracic Society
BTS .... British Transplantation Society
BTS .... British Trolleybus Society   (DCTA)
BTS .... Broadcast Transmission Systems   (MCD)
BTS .... Budget Tracking System
BTS .... Bus Tie Relay   (MCD)
BTS .... Business Telecommunications Services   (ADA)
BTS .... Business Times. An Economic and Business Review [*A publication*]
BTS........... IEEE Broadcast Technology Society   (EA)
BTSAAM .. Bulletin Trimestriel. Societe Academique des Antiquaires de la Morinie [*A publication*]
BTSAP ...... Bulletin Trimestriel. Societe des Antiquaires de Picardie [*A publication*]
BTSB .... Bound to Stay Bound Books, Inc.
BTSB .... [*The*] Braintree Savings Bank [*Braintree, MA*] [*NASDAQ symbol*]   (NQ)
BTSC .... Ban the Soviets Coalition   (EA)
BTSC .... Bankers Trust of South Carolina [*NASDAQ symbol*]   (NQ)
BTSCB...... Bulletin Technique de Securite et Salubrite. Institut National des Industries Extractives [*A publication*]
BTSEAA.... El Salvador. Direccion General de Investigaciones Agronomicas. Seccion de Entomologia. Boletin Tecnico [*A publication*]
BTSF .... Black Tennis and Sports Foundation   (EA)
BTSG........ Brain Tumor Study Group [*National Cancer Institute*]
BTSH........ Bovine Thyroid-Stimulating Hormone [*Endocrinology*]
BTSM........ Ballistic Test Submodule   (RDA)

BTSN......... Book Trade Systems Network [*Publishers' Association*] [*British*]
BTSS .... Basic Time-Sharing System   (BUR)
BTSS .... Braille Time-Sharing System
BTST .... Ballistic Test Site Terminal   (MCD)
BTST .... BIT [*Binary Digit*] Test [*Data processing*]
BTST .... Bootstrap   (MSA)
BTST .... Busy-Tone Start Lead
BTSU......... Biblical Topics Study Unit [*American Topical Association*]   (EA)
BTSWN...... Boatswain   (AABC)
BTT........... Bachelor of Textile Technology
BTT........... Bank to Turn [*Aviation*]   (MCD)
BTT........... Beginning to Tape Test
BTT........... Bettles [*Alaska*] [*Airport symbol*]   (OAG)
BTT........... Bitterroot Resources Ltd. [*Vancouver Stock Exchange symbol*]
BTT........... Blackstone Target Term Trust, Inc. [*NYSE symbol*]   (CTT)
BTT........... Brainstem Transmission Time [*Neurophysiology*]
BTT........... British Tea Table Co.   (ROG)
BTT........... Business Transfer Tax [*Proposed*] [*Canada*]
BTT........... Business Turnover Tax   (IMH)
BTT........... Busy Tone Trunk [*Telecommunications*]
BTTA........ British Thoracic and Tuberculosis Association
BTTA........ Journal. British Thoracic and Tuberculosis Association [*A publication*]
BTTA Rev ... BTTA [*British Thoracic and Tuberculosis Association*] Review [*Scotland*] [*A publication*]
BTTCA9.... Inter-American Tropical Tuna Commission. Bulletin [*A publication*]
BTTN .... Butanetriol Trinitrate [*An explosive*]
Btto .... Brutto [*Gross (as in produce)*] [*German*] [*Business term*]
BTTP......... British Towing Tank Panel   (MCD)
BTTS .... Buddhist Text Translation Society   (EA)
BTU .... Basic Transmission Unit [*Data processing*]
BTU .... Basutoland Congress of Trade Unions
BTU .... Bateaux Resources, Inc. [*Vancouver Stock Exchange symbol*]
BTU .... Bintulu [*Malaysia*] [*Airport symbol*]   (OAG)
BTU .... Board of Trade Unit [*British*]
BTU .... British Thermal Unit
BTU .... Bus Terminal Unit   (MCD)
BTU .... Pyro Energy Corp. [*NYSE symbol*]   (SPSG)
BTUC .... British Telecom Unions Committee
BTUC .... Burma Trade Union Congress
BTU/h .... British Thermal Units per Hour   (MCD)
BTUI......... BTU International, Inc. [*NASDAQ symbol*]   (CTT)
BTUPA...... Bulletin. Union des Physiciens [*A publication*]
BTURN ..... Black Turnout [*Political science*]
BTV .... Basic Transportation Vehicle
BTV .... Batavia [*Indonesia*] [*Later, TNG*] [*Geomagnetic observatory code*]
BTV .... Beance Tubaire Volontaire [*Voluntary opening of eustachian tubes*] [*Deep-sea diving*] [*French*]
BTV .... Blast Test Vehicle   (NG)
BTV .... Buoyancy Transport Vehicle   (MCD)
BTV .... Burlington [*Vermont*] [*Airport symbol*]   (OAG)
BTVOR...... [*Weather*] Broadcast Terminal Very-High-Frequency Omnirange
BTVP........ British Tertiary Volcanic Province [*Geology*]
BTVVA...... Bulletin Technique Vevey [*A publication*]
BTW .... Backward Traveling Wave
BTW .... Bare Tungsten Wire
BTW .... Belasting op Toegevoegde Waarde [*Value-Added Tax*] [*Dutch*]
BTW .... Between
BTW .... Bimetal Turbine Wheel
BTW .... Bitterwater Creek [*California*] [*Seismograph station code, US Geological Survey*]   (SEIS)
BTW .... Boat Wave
BTWF........ Booker T. Washington Foundation   (EA)
BTWLD..... Butt Welded
BTWN ...... Between   (AABC)
BTWO ...... Bancshares 2000, Inc. [*NASDAQ symbol*]   (NQ)
BTWS....... Buried Trench Weapons System   (MCD)
BTWSM... Board of Trade of the Wholesale Seafood Merchants   (EA)
BTX .... Banctexas Group, Inc. [*NYSE symbol*]   (SPSG)
BTX .... Barytex Resources Corp. [*Vancouver Stock Exchange symbol*]
BTX .... Batrachotoxin [*Biochemistry*]
BTX .... Benzene, Toluene, and Xylene
BTX .... Bildschirmtext [*Viewdata system*] [*Federal Ministry of Posts and Telecommunications*] [*Federal Republic of Germany*]   (TSSD)
BTX .... Bungarotoxin [*Also, BGT, BuTx*] [*Biochemistry*]
BTX .... Butadiene Extraction [*Chemical engineering*]
BTX-B........ Brevetoxin-B [*Biochemistry*]
BTY .... Battery
BTY .... Beatty [*Nevada*] [*Seismograph station code, US Geological Survey*] [*Closed*]   (SEIS)
BTY .... Beatty, NV [*Location identifier*] [*FAA*]   (FAAL)
BTY .... British Telecommunications Ltd. [*NYSE symbol*] [*Toronto Stock Exchange symbol*]   (SPSG)
BTYCF ...... Beauty Counselors International [*NASDAQ symbol*]   (NQ)
BTZ........... Berlitz International [*NYSE symbol*]   (SPSG)

BTZ........... Bursa [*Turkey*] [*Airport symbol*] [*Obsolete*]   (OAG)
BTZBA ...... Beton i Zhelezobeton [*A publication*]
BU............. Backup   (KSC)
BU............. Baptist Union
BU............. Base Unit
BU............. Base-Up (Prism) [*Ophthalmology*]
BU............. Bath Unit [*Military*] [*British and Canadian*]
BU............. Beatles Unlimited   (EA)
BU............. Bend Up
BU............. Biblische Untersuchungen [*A publication*]   (BJA)
BU............. Binding Unit   (IEEE)
BU............. Biology Unit [*American Topical Association*]   (EA)
Bu............. Blue
BU............. Blues Unlimited [*A publication*]
BU............. Boatowners Unlimited [*An association*]   (EA)
BU............. Boston University [*Massachusetts*]
BU............. Bottom Up
BU............. Braathens South-American and Far East Airtransport [*Norway*] [*ICAO designator*]   (FAAC)
BU............. Brandeis University [*Waltham, MA*]   (BJA)
B/U........... Breaking Up   (ADA)
BU............. Breath Units
BU............. Brick Unprotected [*Insurance classification*]
BU............. Brilliant Uncirculated [*Condition of coins*] [*Numismatics*]
BU............. Bromouracil [*Biochemistry*]
BU............. Brooklyn Union Gas Co. [*Wall Street slang name: "Bug"*] [*NYSE symbol*]   (SPSG)
BU............. Brown University [*Rhode Island*]
BU............. Builder [*Navy rating*]
BU............. Buildup   (KSC)
bu .... Bulgaria [*MARC country of publication*] [*Library of Congress*]   (LCCP)
BU............. Bulgaria [*IYRU nationality code*]
BU............. Bulgarian Register of Shipping   (DS)
Bu............. Bulgarus de Bulgarinis [*Deceased, 1166*] [*Authority cited in pre-1607 legal work*]   (DSA)
BU............. Bulk [*Substrate*] [*Electron device*]   (MSA)
BU............. Bulk Freight Containers [*Shipping*]   (DCTA)
BU............. Buoy Boat
BU............. Bureau   (AABC)
BU............. Burglary
BU............. Buried   (ROG)
BU............. Burma [*ANSI two-letter standard code*]   (CNC)
BU............. Burn Unit [*Medicine*]
BU............. Burnup
BU............. Bus Unit [*Data processing*]
BU............. Bushel
BU............. Bushmaster Aircraft Corp. [*ICAO aircraft manufacturer identifier*]   (ICAO)
Bu............. Butyl [*Organic chemistry*]
BU............. Buzzer   (IEEE)
BU............. USAF [*United States Air Force*] Specification Bulletin   (MCD)
BU1........... Builder, First Class [*Navy rating*]
BU2........... Builder, Second Class [*Navy rating*]
BU3........... Builder, Third Class [*Navy rating*]
BuA........... Babylonien und Assyrien [*A publication*]   (BJA)
BUA........... Bollettino Ufficiale della Valle d'Aosta [*Official Gazette of the Valle d'Aosta*] [*A publication*]   (ILCA)
BUA........... Booster Umbilical Assembly
BUA........... British United Airways
BUA........... Buffalo, SD [*Location identifier*] [*FAA*]   (FAAL)
BUA........... Buka Island [*Papua New Guinea*] [*Airport symbol*]   (OAG)
BUA........... Bulletin. Universite l'Aurore [*A publication*]
BUAC........ British Universities Accommodation Consortium
BUAER...... Bureau of Aeronautics [*Later, Naval Air Systems Command*] [*Obsolete*]
BUAMD.... Business America [*A publication*]
BUAS........ Border Union Agricultural Society [*British*]
BUAS........ British Universities Association of Slavists
BUAV .... British Union for the Abolition of Vivisection
BUB .... Backup Block   (MCD)
BUB .... Bubble   (KSC)
BuB .... Buch und Bibliothek [*A publication*]
BUB .... Buchberg [*Switzerland*] [*Seismograph station code, US Geological Survey*]   (SEIS)
BuB .... Buecherei und Bildung [*A publication*]
BuB .... Bureau of the Budget [*Later, OMB*]
BUB .... Burwell, NE [*Location identifier*] [*FAA*]   (FAAL)
BUBBA...... Bundesbaublatt [*A publication*]
BUBEA...... Bulletin Belgicatom [*A publication*]
BUBFA...... Bulletin Biologique de la France et de la Belgique [*A publication*]
BUBMEM ... Bubble Memory [*Data storage device*] [*Data processing*]   (MSA)
BUBUD..... Bureau of the Budget [*Later, OMB*]
BUC.......... Backup Computer   (CET)
BUC.......... Backup Controller   (MCD)
BUC.......... Bucharest [*Romania*] [*Later, SUR*] [*Geomagnetic observatory code*]
BUC.......... Bucharest [*Romania*] [*Seismograph station code, US Geological Survey*]   (SEIS)

BUC .... Buckhorn, California [*Spaceflight Tracking and Data Network*] [*NASA*]
BUC .... Bucks County Community College, Newtown, PA [*OCLC symbol*]   (OCLC)
BUC .... Burketown [*Australia*] [*Airport symbol*]   (OAG)
BUC .... Chief Builder [*Navy rating*]
BUC1 .... Bucharest [*Romania*] [*Seismograph station code, US Geological Survey*]   (SEIS)
BUC2 .... Bucharest [*Romania*] [*Seismograph station code, US Geological Survey*]   (SEIS)
BUCA .... Constructionman Apprentice, Builder, Striker [*Navy rating*]
BUCAB...... Bulletin du Cancer [*A publication*]
BUCC .... Buccaneer Aircraft ["*Banana Bomber*"] [*British*]   (DSUE)
BUCDA ..... Bulletin. Georgia Academy of Science [*A publication*]
Buch .... Buchanan's Cape Of Good Hope Reports [*A publication*]   (DLA)
Buch .... Buchanan's Court of Session [*1800-13*] [*Scotland*] [*A publication*]   (DLA)
Buch .... Buchanan's New Jersey Equity Reports [*A publication*]   (DLA)
Buch .... Buchanan's Supreme Court Reports [*Cape Colony*] [*A publication*]   (DLA)
Buch AC..... Buchanan's Appeal Court Reports, Cape Of Good Hope [*A publication*]   (DLA)
Buchan .... Buchanan's New Jersey Equity Reports [*A publication*]   (DLA)
Buchanan ... Buchanan's Reports, Court of Session and Justiciary [*Scotland*] [*A publication*]   (DLA)
Buch App Cas ... Buchanan's Appeal Court Reports, Cape Of Good Hope [*A publication*]   (DLA)
Buchar- Univ- An Geol ... Bucharest. Universitatea. Analele. Geologie [*A publication*]
Buchar Univ An Ser Stiint Nat ... Bucharest. Universitatea. Analele. Seria Stiintele Naturii [*A publication*]
Buch und Bibl ... Buch und Bibliothek [*A publication*]
Buch Cas.... Buchanan's Remarkable Criminal Cases [*Scotland*] [*A publication*]   (DLA)
Buch Ct Ap Cape GH ... Buchanan's Appeal Court Reports, Cape Of Good Hope [*A publication*]   (DLA)
Buch Ct App Cape G H ... Buchanan's Appeal Court Reports, Cape Of Good Hope [*A publication*]   (ILCA)
BuChE .... Butyrylcholinesterase [*An enzyme*]
Buch E Cape GH ... Buchanan's Cape Of Good Hope Reports [*A publication*]   (DLA)
Buch ED Cape GH ... [*Eben J. or James*] Buchanan's Eastern District Reports, Cape Of Good Hope [*A publication*]   (DLA)
Buch Eq (NJ) ... Buchanan's New Jersey Equity Reports [*A publication*]   (DLA)
Buchh......... Buchhalter [*Bookkeeper, Accountant*] [*German*]
Buch J Cape GH ... Buchanan's Reports, Cape Of Good Hope [*A publication*]   (DLA)
Buch Lien Law ... Buchan's California Lien Laws [*A publication*]   (DLA)
Buch Pr Pl ... Buchanan's Precedents of Pleading [*A publication*]   (DLA)
Buchr Atomkernenerg ... Buchreihe Atomkernenergie [*A publication*]
Buch Rep.... Buchanan's Cape Of Good Hope Reports [*A publication*]   (DLA)
BuCHS ...... Bucks County Historical Society. Papers [*A publication*]
Buch SC Rep ... Buchanan's Supreme Court Reports, Cape Of Good Hope [*1868-79*] [*South Africa*] [*A publication*]   (DLA)
Buch Tr ...... Buchanan's Remarkable Criminal Cases [*Scotland*] [*A publication*]   (DLA)
BUCK .... Buckingham [*Municipal borough in England*]
BUCK .... Buckland [*England*]
BUCK .... Buckram [*Fabric*]
Buck .... Buck's English Cases in Bankruptcy [*1816-20*] [*A publication*]   (DLA)
Buck .... Buck's Reports [*7-8 Montana*] [*A publication*]   (DLA)
BUCK .... Currency Technology Corp. [*NASDAQ symbol*]   (NQ)
Buck Bankr (Eng) ... Buck's English Cases in Bankruptcy [*1816-20*] [*A publication*]   (DLA)
Buck Cas.... Buck's English Cases in Bankruptcy [*1816-20*] [*A publication*]   (DLA)
Buck Comp Act ... Buckley on the Companies Acts [*1873-1949*] [*A publication*]   (DLA)
Buck Cooke ... Bucknill's Cooke's Cases of Practice, Common Pleas [*England*] [*A publication*]   (DLA)
Buck Dec.... Buckner's Decisions [*in Freeman's Mississippi Chancery Reports, 1839-43*] [*A publication*]   (DLA)
Buck Eccl Law ... Buck's Massachusetts Ecclesiastical Law [*A publication*]   (DLA)
Buck Ins..... Bucknill. Care of the Insane [*1880*] [*A publication*]   (DLA)
Buckl.......... Buckley on the Companies Acts [*1873-1949*] [*A publication*]   (DLA)
Buck Lun.... Bucknill on Lunacy [*A publication*]   (DLA)
Bucknell Re ... Bucknell Review [*A publication*]
Bucknell Rev ... Bucknell Review [*A publication*]
BUCKS...... Buckinghamshire [*County in England*]
Bucks .... Bucks County Law Reporter [*Pennsylvania*] [*A publication*]   (DLA)
BucksCoHS ... Bucks County Historical Society. Papers [*A publication*]
Bucks Co L Rep ... Bucks County Law Reporter [*Pennsylvania*] [*A publication*]   (DLA)

Bucks Co LR (PA) ... Bucks County Law Reporter [*Pennsylvania*] [*A publication*]   (DLA)
BUCM .... Master Chief Builder [*Navy rating*]
BUCO........ Build-Up Control Organization [*Established to supervise flow of personnel and equipment to the Continent, immediately following Normandy invasion*] [*British*] [*World War II*]
BUCO........ Buildings Control Officer
BUCON..... Bureau of Construction and Repair [*Until 1940*] [*Navy*]
BUCOP ..... British Union Catalogue of Periodicals [*A publication*]
BUC & R... Bureau of Construction and Repair [*Until 1940*] [*Navy*]
BUCS........ American Franchise Group, Inc. [*NASDAQ symbol*]   (NQ)
BUCS........ Backup Control System   (MCD)
BUCS........ Senior Chief Builder [*Navy rating*]
BUCS/ST.. BUCS [*Backup Control System*] Self Test   (MCD)
BUCU .... Burring Cutter
BUD......... Anheuser-Busch Companies, Inc. [*NYSE symbol*]   (SPSG)
BUD......... Basic Underwater Demolition Team [*Marine Corps*]
BUD......... Beneficial Use Date
BUD......... British Urban Development
Bud............ [*Guillelmus*] Budaeus [*Deceased, 1540*] [*Authority cited in pre-1607 legal work*]   (DSA)
BUD......... Budapest [*Hungary*] [*Airport symbol*]   (OAG)
BUD......... Budapest [*Hungary*] [*Seismograph station code, US Geological Survey*]   (SEIS)
BUD......... Budd Canada, Inc. [*Toronto Stock Exchange symbol*]
BUD......... Budget   (AFM)
BUD......... Budget Office [*Army*]
BUD......... Marion, OH [*Location identifier*] [*FAA*]   (FAAL)
Budae........ [*Guillelmus*] Budaeus [*Deceased, 1540*] [*Authority cited in pre-1607 legal work*]   (DSA)
Budapesti Musz Egy Elemiszerkem Tansz Kozl ... Budapesti Muszaki Egyetem Elemiszerkemiai Tanszekenek Kozlemenyei [*A publication*]
Budapesti Musz Egy Mezogazd Kem Technol Tansz Evk ... Budapesti Muszaki Egyetem Mezogazdasagi Kemiai Technologiai Tanszekenek Evkonyve [*A publication*]
Budapesti Musz Egy Mezogazd Kem Technol Tansz Kozl ... Budapesti Muszaki Egyetem Mezogazdasagi Kemiai Technologiai Tanszekenek Kozlemenyei [*A publication*]
Budapest Reg ... Budapest Regisegei [*A publication*]
Budavox Telecommun Rev ... Budavox Telecommunication Review [*A publication*]
BUDC........ Backup Digital Computer
BUDD........ Buddhism
BUDFIN.... Budget and Finance Division [*NATO*]   (NATG)
Budget........ Budget of the US Government [*A publication*]
Budget Program Newsl ... Budget and Program Newsletter [*A publication*]
Budget SA ... Budget of the US Government. Special Analyses [*A publication*]
Budiv Mater Konstr ... Budivel'ni Materialy i Konstruktsii [*A publication*]
BUDL .... Budleigh [*England*]
BUDOCKS ... Bureau of Yards and Docks [*Later, NFEC*] [*Washington, DC*] [*Navy*]
Budownictwo Roln ... Budownictwo Rolnicze [*A publication*]
BUdR .... Bromouracildeoxyriboside [*Antineoplastic drug*]
Bud Reg...... Budapest Regisegei [*A publication*]
BUDS .... Backup Digital System
BUD/S........ Basic Underwater Demolition/SEAL [*Sea, Air, and Land Capability*] Training Department [*Navy*]
BUDWSR ... Brown University Display for Working Set References
BUE .... Banque de l'Union Europeenne [*European Union Bank*] [*France*]
BUE .... Bilateral Upper Extremity [*Occupational therapy*]
BUE .... Buddhist Union of Europe   (EAIO)
BUE .... Buell Industries, Inc. [*AMEX symbol*]   (SPSG)
BUE .... Buenos Aires [*Argentina*] [*Airport symbol*]   (OAG)
BUE .... Built-Up Edge   (MCD)
BUE .... Bulletin. Faculty of Arts. University of Egypt [*Cairo*] [*A publication*]
BUEC .... Backup Emergency Communications
BUECD ..... Bulletin d'Ecologie [*A publication*]
Buech Augenarzt ... Buecherei des Augenarztes [*A publication*]
Buecher Arch Bienenk ... Buecher des Archiv fuer Bienenkunde [*A publication*]
Buecherei Bienenk ... Buecherei fuer Bienenkunde [*A publication*]
Buecher Wirt ... Buecher fuer die Wirtschaft [*A publication*]
BUENG ..... Bureau of Engineering [*Obsolete*] [*Navy*]
Buenos Aires M ... Buenos Aires Musical [*A publication*]
Buenos Aires Mus ... Buenos Aires Musical [*A publication*]
Buenos Aires (Prov) Com Invest Cient Monogr ... Buenos Aires (Province). Comision de Investigaciones Cientificas. Monografias [*A publication*]
Buerotech... Buerotechnik [*A publication*]
Buerotech Autom & Organ ... Buerotechnik Automation und Organisation [*A publication*]
Buerotech und Org ... Buerotechnik und Organisation [*A publication*]
BUESD...... Buerger im Staat [*A publication*]
BUF .... Backup Facility [*Nuclear war games*]
BUF .... Black United Front [*South Africa*]   (PD)
BUF .... British Union of Fascists
BUF .... Buffalo [*Rat variety*]
BUF .... Buffalo [*New York*] [*Airport symbol*]

BUF .... Buffalo [*New York*] [*Seismograph station code, US Geological Survey*] [*Closed*] (SEIS)
BUF .... Buffalo Resources [*Vancouver Stock Exchange symbol*]
BUF .... Buffer [*Data processing*]
BUF .... State University of New York at Buffalo, Buffalo, NY [*OCLC symbol*] (OCLC)
BUFCS ...... Backup Flight Control System (MCD)
BUFF .... Big Ugly Fat Fellow [*Nickname for B-52 bomber*]
BUFF .... Brothers United for Future Foreskins (EA)
BUFF .... Buffer (NASA)
Buffalo Gal Notes ... Buffalo Fine Arts Academy. Albright Art Gallery. Notes [*A publication*]
Buffalo Hist Soc Publ ... Buffalo Historical Society. Publications [*A publication*]
Buffalo L Rev ... Buffalo Law Review [*A publication*]
Buffalo Nw ... Buffalo News [*A publication*]
Buffalo Phil ... Buffalo Philharmonic. Program Notes [*A publication*]
Buffalo Soc Nat Sci Bull ... Buffalo Society of Natural Sciences. Bulletin [*A publication*]
Buffalo Soc N Sc B ... Buffalo Society of Natural Sciences. Bulletin [*A publication*]
BUFFB ...... Boletim. Universidade Federal do Parana. Fisica Teorica (Brazil) [*A publication*]
Buff Law R ... Buffalo Law Review [*A publication*]
Buff LR ...... Buffalo Law Review [*A publication*]
Buff L Rev ... Buffalo Law Review [*A publication*]
Buff Super Ct ... Sheldon's Superior Court Reports [*Buffalo, New York*] [*A publication*] (DLA)
Buff Super Ct (NY) ... Sheldon's Superior Court Reports [*Buffalo, New York*] [*A publication*] (DLA)
BUFLY ...... Butterfly [*Stroke*] [*Swimming*]
BUFORA... British UFO Research Association (EAIO)
BUFORA... British Unidentified Flying Objects Research Association
BUFSA ...... Bulletin. Association Francaise pour l'Etude du Sol [*A publication*]
BUFVC ...... British Universities Film and Video Council [*Information service or system*] (IID)
BUG .... Benguela [*Angola*] [*Airport symbol*] (OAG)
BUG .... Bochum - University [*Federal Republic of Germany*] [*Seismograph station code, US Geological Survey*] (SEIS)
BUG .... Boletin. Universidad de Granada [*A publication*]
BUG .... Bottom-Up Greedy
BUG .... Brooklyn Union Gas Co.
BUG .... Buccal Ganglion [*Dentistry*]
BUG .... Bugatti [*Automobile*]
BUG .... Bugler [*Navy*]
BUG ...... Business User Group [*Data processing*]
BUGGA ...... Bulletin. Geological Survey of Great Britain [*A publication*]
BUGINAR ... Buginarium [*Nasal Bougie*] [*Pharmacy*]
BUGMAF ... Geological Society of America. Bulletin [*A publication*]
BUGS .... Backup Guidance System [*NASA*]
BUGS .... Brown University Graphic System
BUGSYS ... [*A*] programming language (CSR)
BUGTA ..... Bulletin of Grain Technology [*India*] [*A publication*]
BUGX .... Barrier Science & Technology, Inc. [*Port Jervis, NY*] [*NASDAQ symbol*] (NQ)
BUH .... Bucharest [*Romania*] [*Airport symbol*] (OAG)
BUH .... Buehlerhoehe [*Federal Republic of Germany*] [*Seismograph station code, US Geological Survey*] (SEIS)
BUH .... Builder, Heavy [*Navy rating*]
BUI .... Badminton Union of Ireland (EAIO)
BUI .... Bokoudini [*Indonesia*] [*Airport symbol*] (OAG)
BUI .... Brain Uptake Index [*Physiology*]
BUI .... Knoxville, TN [*Location identifier*] [*FAA*] (FAAL)
BUI .... Nederland USSR Instituut. Maandberichten [*A publication*]
BUIA .... British United Island Airways
BUIAA .... Bulletin d'Informations Scientifiques et Techniques. Commissariat a l'Energie Atomique [*France*] [*A publication*]
BUIC .... Backup Interceptor Control [*System*] [*Air Force*]
BUIC .... Bureau [*of Naval Personnel*] Unit Identification Code
BUICS .... Backup Interceptor Control System [*Air Force*]
BUIDD ...... Building Ideas [*A publication*]
BUII .... Buia [*Italy*] [*Seismograph station code, US Geological Survey*] (SEIS)
BUILD .... Base for Uniform Language Definition [*Data processing*] (IEEE)
Build .... Builder [*A publication*] (APTA)
Build .... Building [*A publication*] (APTA)
BUILD ...... Building (ROG)
Build & Archit ... Building and Architecture [*A publication*] (APTA)
Build Briefs Div Build Res CSIRO ... Building Briefs. Division of Building Research. Commonwealth Scientific and Industrial Research Organisation [*A publication*] (APTA)
Build & Cons ... Building and Construction [*A publication*] (APTA)
Build & Cons (VIC) ... Building and Construction and Cazaly's Contract Reporter (Melbourne, Victoria) [*A publication*] (APTA)
Build Decorating Mat ... Building and Decorating Materials [*A publication*] (APTA)
Build & Decorating Materials ... Building and Decorating Materials [*A publication*] (APTA)

Build Des Constr ... Building Design and Construction [*A publication*]
Build Dig .... Building Digest [*A publication*]
Build Econ ... Building Economist [*A publication*] (APTA)
Build En Conserv ... Buildings Energy Conservation [*A publication*]
Build Energy Prog ... Building Energy Progress [*A publication*]
Build & Eng ... Building and Engineering [*A publication*] (APTA)
Build Environ ... Building and Environment [*England*] [*A publication*]
Builder (NSW) ... Builder (New South Wales) [*A publication*] (APTA)
Builders Timber Merchants J ... Builders and Timber Merchants Journal [*A publication*]
Build Forum ... Building Forum [*A publication*] (APTA)
Build (Hobart) ... Building (Hobart) [*A publication*] (APTA)
Build Ideas ... Building Ideas [*A publication*]
Build Inf Bull ... Building Information Bulletin [*New Zealand*] [*A publication*]
Building & Arch ... Building and Architecture [*A publication*] (APTA)
Building Ltg and Engng ... Building, Lighting, and Engineering [*A publication*] (APTA)
Building Ltg Engng ... Building, Lighting, and Engineering [*A publication*] (APTA)
Building Sci Ser Nat Bur Stand US ... Building Science Series. United States National Bureau of Standards [*A publication*]
Build Int (Engl Ed) ... Build International (English Edition) [*A publication*]
Build J .... Builders' Journal [*A publication*]
Build Light Eng ... Building, Lighting, and Engineering [*A publication*] (APTA)
Build Ltg Engng ... Building, Lighting, and Engineering [*A publication*] (APTA)
Build Maint ... Building Maintenance [*A publication*]
Build & Manuf ... Building and Manufacturing [*A publication*] (APTA)
Build Mat... Building Materials, Components, and Equipment [*A publication*]
Build Mat Dig ... Building Materials Digest [*A publication*]
Build Mater ... Building Materials [*Sydney*] [*A publication*] (APTA)
Build Mater & Equip ... Building Materials and Equipment [*A publication*] (APTA)
Build Mater Equip (Syd) ... Building Materials and Equipment (Sydney) [*A publication*] (APTA)
Build Materials ... Building Materials [*A publication*] (APTA)
Build Mater Mag ... Building Materials Magazine [*Australia*] [*A publication*]
Build NSW ... Builder NSW [*New South Wales*] [*A publication*] (APTA)
Build Off Code Adm ... Building Official and Code Administrator [*United States*] [*A publication*]
Build Oper Manage ... Building Operating Management [*A publication*]
Build Perm .... Building-Permit Activity [*Florida*] [*A publication*]
Build Prod News ... Building Products News [*A publication*] (APTA)
Build Res .... Building Research [*A publication*]
Build Res Establ Dig ... Building Research Establishment. Digest [*A publication*]
Build Res Estab (Sta) Digest ... Building Research Establishment (Station). Digest [*A publication*]
Build Res Pract ... Building Research and Practice [*A publication*]
Build Res Stn Curr Pap ... Building Research Station. Current Papers [*England*] [*A publication*]
Build Sci .... Building Science [*A publication*]
Build Sci Ser Natl Bur Stand ... Building Science Series. United States National Bureau of Standards [*A publication*]
Build Sci Ser Natl Bur Stand US ... Building Science Series. United States National Bureau of Standards [*A publication*]
Build Seals Sealants ... Building Seals and Sealants [*A publication*]
Build Serv ... Building Services [*A publication*]
Build Serv Eng ... Building Services Engineer [*A publication*]
Build Serv Eng Res ... Building Services Engineering Research and Technology [*A publication*]
Build Serv Eng Res and Technol ... Building Services Engineering Research and Technology [*A publication*]
Builds Serv Environ Eng ... Building Services and Environmental Engineer [*England*] [*A publication*]
Build Stand ... Building Standards [*United States*] [*A publication*]
Build Steel ... Building with Steel [*A publication*]
Build Syst Des ... Building Systems Design [*A publication*]
Build Technol Manage ... Building Technology and Management [*England*] [*A publication*]
Build Worker ... Building Worker [*A publication*] (APTA)
Built Env .... Built Environment [*A publication*]
Built Envir ... Built Environment [*A publication*]
Built Environ ... Built Environment [*A publication*]
BUIMB ...... Bollettino. Unione Matematica Italiana. Series IV [*A publication*]
BUIND ...... Business India [*A publication*]
BU Int'l LJ ... Boston University. International Law Journal [*A publication*] (DLA)
BUIRA .... British Universities Industrial Relations Association
BUIS .... Barrier Up Indicator System (MSA)
BUIS .... Buck Island Reef National Monument
BUISYS .... Barrier Up Indicator System
BUJ .... Baccalaureus Utriusque Juris [*Bachelor of Both Laws; i.e., Canon and Civil Laws*]
BUJ .... Blue Ridge, TX [*Location identifier*] [*FAA*] (FAAL)
BUJ .... Boston University. Journal [*A publication*]
BUJ .... Business Japan [*A publication*]

BUJPA ...... Bulletin. Japan Petroleum Institute [*A publication*]
Bujq Soc ..... Bujqesia Socialiste [*A publication*]
BUK .... Albuq [*Yemen*] [*Airport symbol*] (OAG)
BUK .... Aspen, CO [*Location identifier*] [*FAA*] (FAAL)
BUKEA ..... Busseiron Kenkyu [*A publication*]
BUKKA ..... Bunko Kenkyu [*A publication*]
BUKN .... Bucknell Industries, Inc. [*Farmingdale, NY*] [*NASDAQ symbol*] (NQ)
BUL .... B + U. Bouw en Uitvoering van Gemeentewerken; Maandblad voor Functionarissen van de Diensten van Publieke en Openbare Werken [*A publication*]
BUL .... Boston University. Law Review [*A publication*]
BUL .... Brandon University Library [*UTLAS symbol*]
BUL .... Builder, Light [*Navy rating*]
BUL .... Bulawayo [*Zimbabwe*] [*Seismograph station code, US Geological Survey*] (SEIS)
bul .... Bulgarian [*MARC language code*] [*Library of Congress*] (LCCP)
Bul .... Bulgarus de Bulgarinis [*Deceased, 1166*] [*Authority cited in pre-1607 legal work*] (DSA)
BUL .... Bullet Group, Inc. [*Formerly, Bullet Energy Limited*] [*Vancouver Stock Exchange symbol*]
Bul .... [*The*] Bulletin [*A publication*] (APTA)
BUL .... Bulletin (AFM)
BUL .... Bulletin. Universite de Lyon [*A publication*]
BUL .... Bulolo [*Papua New Guinea*] [*Airport symbol*] (OAG)
BUL .... Miami, FL [*Location identifier*] [*FAA*] (FAAL)
Bul Admin Penitentiaire ... Bulletin. Administration Penitentiaire [*A publication*]
Bul Afr Noire ... Bulletin de l'Afrique Noire [*A publication*]
Bul Akad Stiince RSS Moldoven ... Buletinul Akademiei. Stiince a RSS Moldovenest [*A publication*]
Bul ALO .... Bulletin. Commission Royale des Anciennes Lois et Ordonnances de Belgique [*A publication*]
Bul Am Acad Psy and L ... Bulletin. American Academy of Psychiatry and the Law [*A publication*]
Bul/AMQ .. Bulletin. Association Mathematique du Quebec [*A publication*]
Bul Am Repub ... Bulletin. International Bureau of the American Republics [*A publication*]
Bul Analytique Docum ... Bulletin Analytique de Documentation Politique, Economique, et Sociale Contemporaine [*A publication*]
Bul Anthro Surv India ... Bulletin. Anthropological Survey of India [*A publication*]
Bul Arch Maroc ... Bulletin d'Archeologie Marocaine [*A publication*]
Bul Art Inst Chic ... Bulletin. Art Institute of Chicago [*A publication*]
Bul Assoc Lit Ling Comp ... Bulletin. Association for Literary and Linguistic Computing [*A publication*]
Bul Atomic Sci ... Bulletin of the Atomic Scientists [*A publication*]
Bul Aust Asian Assn of Vic ... Bulletin. Australian-Asian Association of Victoria [*A publication*] (APTA)
Bul Aust Assn Occupational Therapists ... Bulletin. Australian Association of Occupational Therapists [*A publication*] (APTA)
Bul Aust Ind ... Bulletin for Australian Industry [*A publication*] (APTA)
Bul Aust Industry ... Bulletin for Australian Industry [*A publication*] (APTA)
Bul Aust Soc Stud Lab Hist ... Bulletin. Australian Society for the Study of Labour History [*A publication*] (APTA)
Bul B .... Bulletin of Bibliography [*A publication*]
BULB .... Melridge, Inc. [*NASDAQ symbol*] (NQ)
Bul Belg ..... Bulletin. Banque Nationale de Belgique [*A publication*]
Bul Bibl ...... Bulletin Bibliographique [*A publication*]
Bul Bibl de France ... Bulletin des Bibliotheques de France [*A publication*]
Bul Bibliog ... Bulletin of Bibliography [*A publication*]
Bul of Bibliography ... Bulletin of Bibliography and Dramatic Index [*A publication*]
Bul Black Theatre ... Bulletin of Black Theatre [*A publication*]
Bul BN .... Bulletin d'Information et de Documentation. Banque Nationale [*A publication*]
Bul Bude .... Bulletin. Association Guillaume Bude [*A publication*]
Bul Build Assoc India ... Bulletin. Builders Association of India [*A publication*]
Bul Bus Research Ohio State Univ ... Bulletin of Business Research. Ohio State University [*A publication*]
Bul Cent Bank Ceylon ... Bulletin. Central Bank of Ceylon [*A publication*]
Bul Cercet Piscic ... Buletinul de Cercetari Piscicole [*A publication*]
Bul Chambre Com Francaise ... Bulletin. Chambre de Commerce Francaise et Organe Officiel du Tourisme Francaise en Australie [*A publication*] (APTA)
Bul Child Bks ... Bulletin. Center for Children's Books [*A publication*]
Bul Chr Inst Islamic St ... Bulletin. Christian Institutes of Islamic Studies [*A publication*]
Bul Christ Assoc Psych Stud ... Bulletin. Christian Association for Psychological Studies [*A publication*]
Bul Cl Lo .... Bulletin. Institute of Classical Studies. University of London [*A publication*]
Bul Corresp Hellenique ... Bulletin de Correspondance Hellenique [*A publication*]
Bul Cult Tutun ... Buletinul Culturii Tutunului [*A publication*]
BULDB .... Building [*A publication*]
Bul D Cpr ... Bulletin. Institut Belge de Droit Compare [*A publication*]

Bul Doc Bibliog ... Bulletin de Documentation Bibliographique [*A publication*]
Bul Docum ... Bulletin de Documentation [*A publication*]
Bul Docum Econ ... Bulletin de Documentation Economique [*A publication*]
Bul Ec .... Bulletin. Institut des Sciences Economiques [*A publication*]
Bul Econ et Fin ... Bulletin Economique et Financier [*A publication*]
Bul Econ Research (England) ... Bulletin of Economic Research (England) [*A publication*]
Bul Econ et Soc Maroc ... Bulletin Economique et Social du Maroc [*A publication*]
Bul Enf .... Bulletin. Association Internationale pour la Protection de l'Enfance [*A publication*]
Bulet Cluj ... Buletinul. Societatii de Stiinte din Cluj [*A publication*]
Buletin Univ Shtet Tiranes Shkencat Nat ... Buletin. Universiteti Shteteror te Tiranes. Seria Shkencat Natyrore [*A publication*]
Bul Fac Agron Cluj ... Buletinul Facultatii de Agronomie din Cluj [*A publication*]
Bul Fac Sti Cernauti ... Buletinul Facultatii de Stiinte din Cernauti [*A publication*]
Bul Fac Stiinte Cernauti ... Buletinul Facultatii de Stiinte din Cernauti [*A publication*]
Bul Fiz .... Buletin Fizik [*A publication*]
BULG .... Bulgaria
Bulg .... Bulgarus de Bulgarinis [*Deceased, 1166*] [*Authority cited in pre-1607 legal work*] (DSA)
Bulg .... Radioprom & Orfei (Bulgaria) [*Record label*]
Bulg Acad Sci Commun Dep Chem ... Bulgarian Academy of Sciences. Communications. Department of Chemistry [*A publication*]
Bulg Akad Nauk Dokl ... Bulgarska Akademiya na Naukite. Doklady [*A publication*]
Bulg Akad Nauk Geol Inst Izv Ser Inzh Geol Khidrogeol ... Bulgarska Akademiya na Naukite. Geologicheski Institut. Izvestiya. Seriya Inzhenerna Geologiya i Khidrogeologiya [*A publication*]
Bulg Akad Nauk Geol Inst Izv Ser Paleontol ... Bulgarska Akademiya na Naukite. Geologicheski Institut. Izvestiya. Seriya Paleontologiya [*A publication*]
Bulg Akad Nauk Inst Okeanogr Ribno Stop Izv ... Bulgarska Akademiya na Naukite. Institut po Okeanografiya i Ribno Stopanstvo Izvestiya [*A publication*]
Bulg Akad Nauk Zool Inst Muz Izv ... Bulgarska Akademiya na Naukite. Otdeleniye za Biologichni Nauki. Zoologicheski Institut si Muzey. Izvestiya [*A publication*]
Bulgar J Phys ... Bulgarian Journal of Physics [*A publication*]
Bulgar Math Monographs ... Bulgarian Mathematical Monographs [*A publication*]
Bulgar Muz ... Bulgarska Muzika [*A publication*]
Bul Geol Tutkimuslaitos (Fin) ... Bulletin. Geologinen Tutkimuslaitos (Finland) [*A publication*]
Bulg Ez ...... Bulgarski Ezik [*A publication*]
Bulg F .... Bulgarian Films [*A publication*]
Bulg Geofiz Spis ... Bulgarsko Geofizichno Spisanie [*Bulgaria*] [*A publication*]
Bulg Geol Druzh Spis ... Bulgarsko Geologichesko Druzhestvo. Spisanie [*A publication*]
Bulg Hist .... Bulgarian Historical Review/Revue Bulgare d'Histoire [*A publication*]
Bulg J Phys ... Bulgarian Journal of Physics [*A publication*]
Bulg Tiutiun ... Bulgarski Tiutiun [*A publication*]
Bul Hel .... Bulletin de Correspondance Hellenique [*A publication*]
BULI .... [*The*] Bulletin [*Database*] [*Australia*]
BULIB .... Bulletin on Inventions [*A publication*]
BULID .... Business Librarian [*A publication*]
Bul Indonesian Econ Studies ... Bulletin of Indonesian Economic Studies [*A publication*]
Bul Ind Psychol ... Bulletin for Industrial Psychology and Personnel Practice [*A publication*] (APTA)
Bul Inf Lab Cent Color ... Buletin Information. Laboratorul Central Coloristic [*A publication*]
Bul Info ...... Bulletin d'Information. Departement d'Economie et de Sociologie Rurales [*Paris*] [*A publication*]
Bul Info Region Parisienne ... Bulletin d'Information de la Region Parisienne [*A publication*]
Bul Inst Agron Cluj Napoca ... Buletinul. Institutului Agronomic Cluj-Napoca [*A publication*]
Bul Inst Agron Cluj Napoca Inst Agron Dr Petru Groza ... Buletinul. Institutului Agronomic Cluj-Napoca. Institutul Agronomic "Dr. Petru Groza" [*A publication*]
Bul Inst Agron Cluj Napoca Ser Agric ... Buletinul. Institutului Agronomic Cluj-Napoca. Seria Agricultura [*A publication*]
Bul Inst Cercet Proiect Piscic ... Buletinul. Institutului de Cercetari si Proiectari Piscicole [*A publication*]
Bul Inst Pet Gaze Geol ... Buletinul. Institutului de Petrol, Gaze, si Geologie [*Romania*] [*A publication*]
Bul Inst Polit Brasov Ser B Econ For ... Buletinul. Institutului Politehnic din Brasov. Seria B. Economie Forestiera [*A publication*]
Bul Inst Politeh Brasov A ... Buletinul. Institutului Politehnic din Brasov. Seria A. Mecanica [*A publication*]
Bul Inst Politeh Bucur ... Buletinul. Institutului Politehnic Bucuresti [*A publication*]

Bul Inst Politeh Bucuresti ... Buletinul. Institutului Politehnic Bucuresti [*A publication*]

Bul Inst Politeh Bucuresti Ser Chim Metal ... Buletinul. Institutului Politehnic "Gheorghe Gheorghiu-Dej" Bucuresti. Seria Chimie-Metalurgie [*A publication*]

Bul Inst Politeh Bucuresti Ser Mec ... Buletinul. Institutului Politehnic "Gheorghe Gheorghiu-Dej" Bucuresti. Seria Mecanica [*A publication*]

Bul Inst Politeh (Chim-Metal) ... Buletinul. Institutului Politehnic "Gheorghe Gheorghiu-Dej" Bucuresti. Seria Chimie-Metalurgie [*A publication*]

Bul Inst Politeh Gheorghe Gheorghiu Dej Bucur ... Buletinul. Institutului Politehnic "Gheorghe Gheorghiu-Dej" Bucuresti [*A publication*]

Bul Inst Politeh Gheorghe Gheorghiu Dej Bucuresti ... Buletinul. Institutului Politehnic "Gheorghe Gheorghiu-Dej" Bucuresti [*A publication*]

Bul Inst Politeh Gheorghe Gheorghiu Dej Bucuresti Ser Chim ... Buletinul. Institutului Politehnic "Gheorghe Gheorghiu-Dej" Bucuresti. Seria Chimie [*A publication*]

Bul Inst Politeh Gheorghe Gheorghiu Dej Bucuresti Ser Mec ... Buletinul. Institutului Politehnic "Gheorghe Gheorghiu-Dej" Bucuresti. Seria Mecanica [*A publication*]

Bul Inst Politeh Gheorghe Gheorghiu Dej Chim-Metal ... Buletinul. Institutului Politehnic "Gheorghe Gheorghiu-Dej." Seria Chimie-Metalurgie [*Romania*] [*A publication*]

Bul Inst Politeh Gheorghe Gheorghiu Dej Electroteh ... Buletinul. Institutului Politehnic "Gheorghe Gheorghiu-Dej." Seria Electrotehnica [*Romania*] [*A publication*]

Bul Inst Politeh Gheorghe Gheorghiu Dej Mec ... Buletinul. Institutului Politehnic "Gheorghe Gheorghiu-Dej." Seria Mecanica [*Romania*] [*A publication*]

Bul Inst Politeh Iasi ... Buletinul. Institutului Politehnic din Iasi [*A publication*]

Bul Inst Politeh Iasi I ... Buletinul. Institutului Politehnic din Iasi. Sectia I. Matematica, Mecanica Teoretica, Fizica [*A publication*]

Bul Inst Politeh Iasi III ... Buletinul. Institutului Politehnic din Iasi. Sectia III. Electrotehnica, Electronica Automatizari [*A publication*]

Bul Inst Politeh Iasi Sect I ... Buletinul. Institutului Politehnic din Iasi. Sectia I. Matematica, Mecanica Teoretica, Fizica [*A publication*]

Bul Inst Politeh Iasi Sect II ... Buletinul. Institutului Politehnic din Iasi. Sectia II. Chimie [*A publication*]

Bul Inst Politeh Iasi Sect III ... Buletinul. Institutului Politehnic din Iasi. Sectia III. Electrotehnica, Electronica Automatizari [*A publication*]

Bul Inst Politeh Iasi Sect IV ... Buletinul. Institutului Politehnic din Iasi. Sectia IV. Mecanica Tehnica [*A publication*]

Bul Inst Politeh Iasi Sect V ... Buletinul. Institutului Politehnic din Iasi. Sectia V [*A publication*]

Bul Inst Politeh (Mec) ... Buletinul. Institutului Politehnic "Gheorghe Gheorghiu-Dej" Bucuresti. Seria Mecanica [*A publication*]

Bul Inst Politehn Bucuresti ... Buletinul. Institutului Politehnic Bucuresti [*A publication*]

Bul Inst Politehn Bucuresti Ser Chim-Metal ... Buletinul. Institutului Politehnic "Gheorghe Gheorghiu-Dej" Bucuresti. Seria Chimie-Metalurgie [*Bucharest*] [*A publication*]

Bul Inst Politehn Bucuresti Ser Electrotehn ... Buletinul. Institutului Politehnic "Gheorghe Gheorghiu-Dej" Bucuresti. Seria Electrotehnica [*A publication*]

Bul Inst Politehn Bucuresti Ser Mec ... Institutului Politehnic Gheorghe Gheorghiu Dej Bucuresti. Buletinul. Seria Mecanica [*Bucharest*] [*A publication*]

Bul Inst Politehn Iasi ... Buletinul. Institutului Politehnic din Iasi. Seria Noua [*A publication*]

Bul Inst Politehn Iasi NS ... Buletinul. Institutului Politehnic din Iasi. Seria Noua [*A publication*]

Bul Inst Politehn Iasi Sect I ... Institutului Politehnic din Iasi. Buletinul. Sectia I [*Iasi*] [*A publication*]

Bul Inst Stud si Project Energ ... Buletinul. Institutului de Studii si Projectari Energetice [*A publication*]

Bul Inst Stud & Proj Energ ... Buletinul. Institutului de Studii si Projectari Energetice [*A publication*]

Bul Internat Fiscal Docum ... Bulletin for International Fiscal Documentation [*A publication*]

Bul Internat Fiscal Documentation ... Bulletin for International Fiscal Documentation [*A publication*]

Bul Int Fiscal Doc ... Bulletin for International Fiscal Documentation [*A publication*]

BULIT .... Bulimia Test [*Personality development test*] [*Psychology*]

Bul J Rylands ... Bulletin. John Rylands Library. University of Manchester [*A publication*]

Bul Jur I..... Bulletin des Juridictions Indigenes du Droit Coutumier [*A publication*]

BULK .... B & H Bulk Carriers, Ltd. [*NASDAQ symbol*]   (NQ)

Bul Kebun Raya Bot Gard Indones ... Buletin Kebun Raya. Botanical Gardens of Indonesia [*A publication*]

Bulk Solids Handl ... Bulk Solids Handling [*A publication*]

Bulk Syst Int ... Bulk Systems International [*A publication*]

BULL......... Bull Run Gold Mines Ltd. [*NASDAQ symbol*]   (NQ)

BULL......... Bulletin

BULL......... Bulliat [*Let It Boil*] [*Pharmacy*]

Bull A Ariz Univ Ext Serv ... Bulletin A. University of Arizona. Extension Service [*A publication*]

Bull Aberd N Scotl Coll Agric ... Bulletin. Aberdeen and North of Scotland College of Agriculture [*A publication*]

Bul Lab Etud Polit Admin ... Bulletin. Laboratoire d'Etudes Politiques et Administratives [*A publication*]

Bul Laborat ... Buletinul Laboratoarelor [*A publication*]

Bull ABTPL ... Bulletin. Association of British Theological and Philosophical Libraries [*A publication*]

Bull Acad Chir Dent (Paris) ... Bulletin. Academie de Chirurgie Dentaire (Paris) [*A publication*]

Bull Acad Dent Handicap ... Bulletin. Academy of Dentistry for the Handicapped [*A publication*]

Bull Acad Dent (Paris) ... Bulletin. Academie Dentaire (Paris) [*A publication*]

Bull Acad Ebroic ... Bulletin. Academie Ebroicienne [*A publication*]

Bull Acad Gen Dent ... Bulletin. Academy of General Dentistry [*A publication*]

Bull Acad Imp Sc St Petersb ... Bulletin. Academie Imperiale des Sciences de St. Petersbourg [*A publication*]

Bull Acad Int ... Bulletin. Academie Internationale de Geographie Botanique [*A publication*]

Bull Acad M ... Bulletin. American Academy of Medicine [*A publication*]

Bull Acad Malgache ... Bulletin. Academie Malgache [*A publication*]

Bull Acad Med Belg ... Bulletin. Academie Royale de Medecine de Belgique [*Mededeelingen van de Koninklijke Belgische Academie voor Geneeskunde*] [*A publication*]

Bull Acad Med (Paris) ... Bulletin. Academie de Medecine (Paris) [*A publication*]

Bull Acad Med Roum ... Bulletin. Academie de Medecine de Roumanie [*A publication*]

Bull Acad Med Tol ... Bulletin. Academy of Medicine of Toledo [*A publication*]

Bull Acad Med Toledo ... Bulletin. Academy of Medicine of Toledo and Lucas County [*Ohio*] [*A publication*]

Bull Acad Med Tor ... Bulletin. Academy of Medicine of Toronto [*A publication*]

Bull Acad Med Toronto ... Bulletin. Academy of Medicine of Toronto [*A publication*]

Bull Acad Natl Med ... Bulletin. Academie Nationale de Medecine [*Paris*] [*A publication*]

Bull Acad Natl Med (Paris) ... Bulletin. Academie Nationale de Medecine (Paris) [*A publication*]

Bull Acad Nat Med ... Bulletin. Academie Nationale de Medecine [*France*] [*A publication*]

Bull Acad Polon Sci Ser Sci Biol ... Bulletin. Academie Polonaise des Sciences. Serie des Sciences Biologiques [*A publication*]

Bull Acad Polon Sci Ser Sci Math ... Academie Polonaise des Sciences. Bulletin. Serie des Sciences Mathematiques [*A publication*]

Bull Acad Polon Sci Ser Sci Math Astronom Phys ... Bulletin. Academie Polonaise des Sciences. Serie des Sciences Mathematiques, Astronomiques, et Physiques [*A publication*]

Bull Acad Polon Sci Ser Sci Phys Astronom ... Academie Polonaise des Sciences. Bulletin. Serie des Sciences Physiques et Astronomiques [*Warsaw*] [*A publication*]

Bull Acad Polon Sci Ser Sci Tech ... Bulletin. Academie Polonaise des Sciences. Serie des Sciences Techniques [*A publication*]

Bull Acad Pol Sci ... Bulletin. Academie Polonaise des Sciences [*A publication*]

Bull Acad Pol Sci Biol ... Bulletin. Academie Polonaise des Sciences. Serie des Sciences Biologiques [*A publication*]

Bull Acad Pol Sci Cl 2 ... Bulletin. Academie Polonaise des Sciences. Classe 2. Agrobiologie, Biologie, Sciences Medicales [*A publication*]

Bull Acad Pol Sci Ser Sci Biol ... Bulletin. Academie Polonaise des Sciences. Serie des Sciences Biologiques [*A publication*]

Bull Acad Pol Sci Ser Sci Chim ... Bulletin. Academie Polonaise des Sciences. Serie des Sciences Chimiques [*A publication*]

Bull Acad Pol Sci Ser Sci Chim Geol Geogr ... Bulletin. Academie Polonaise des Sciences. Serie des Sciences Chimiques, Geologiques, et Geographiques [*A publication*]

Bull Acad Pol Sci Ser Sci Geol Geogr ... Bulletin. Academie Polonaise des Sciences. Serie des Sciences Geologiques et Geographiques [*A publication*]

Bull Acad Pol Sci Ser Sci Math Astron et Phys ... Bulletin. Academie Polonaise des Sciences. Serie des Sciences Mathematiques, Astronomiques, et Physiques [*A publication*]

Bull Acad Pol Sci Ser Sci Math Astron Phys ... Bulletin. Academie Polonaise des Sciences. Serie des Sciences Mathematiques, Astronomiques, et Physiques [*A publication*]

Bull Acad Pol Sci Ser Sci Phys et Astron ... Bulletin. Academie Polonaise des Sciences. Serie des Sciences Physiques et Astronomiques [*A publication*]

Bull Acad Pol Sci Ser Sci Phys Astron ... Bulletin. Academie Polonaise des Sciences. Serie des Sciences Physiques et Astronomiques [*A publication*]

Bull Acad Pol Sci Ser Sci Tech ... Bulletin. Academie Polonaise des Sciences. Serie des Sciences Techniques [*A publication*]

Bull Acad Pol Sci Ser Sci Terre ... Bulletin. Academie Polonaise des Sciences. Serie des Sciences de la Terre [*A publication*]

Bull Acad R Belg Cl Sci ... Bulletin. Academie Royale de Belgique. Classe des Sciences [*A publication*]

Bull Acad R Med Belg ... Bulletin. Academie Royale de Medecine de Belgique [*A publication*]

Bull Acad Roy Belg Cl ... Bulletin. Academie Royale de Belgique. Classe des Sciences [*A publication*]

Bull Acad Roy Belg Cl Beaux Arts ... Bulletin. Academie Royale de Belgique. Classe des Beaux-Arts [*A publication*]

Bull Acad Roy Belg Cl Lett ... Bulletin. Academie Royale de Belgique. Classe des Lettres et des Sciences Morales et Politiques [*A publication*]

Bull Acad Roy Med Belgique ... Bulletin. Academie Royale de Medecine de Belgique [*A publication*]

Bull Acad Roy Med (Paris) ... Bulletin. Academie Royale de Medicine (Paris) [*A publication*]

Bull Acad Sci Agric For ... Bulletin. Academie des Sciences Agricoles et Forestieres [*A publication*]

Bull Acad Sci Ga SSR ... Bulletin. Academy of Sciences of the Georgian SSR [*A publication*]

Bull Acad Sci Lett Montpellier ... Bulletin. Academie des Sciences et Lettres de Montpellier [*A publication*]

Bull Acad Sci Math Nat Acad R Serbe A ... Bulletin. Academie des Sciences Mathematiques et Naturelles. Academie Royale Serbe. Serie A. Sciences Mathematiques et Physiques [*A publication*]

Bull Acad Sci Math Nat Acad R Serbe B ... Bulletin. Academie des Sciences Mathematiques et Naturelles. Academie Royale Serbe. Serie B. Sciences Naturelles [*A publication*]

Bull Acad Sci Math Natur (Belgrade) A ... Bulletin. Academie des Sciences Mathematiques et Naturelles. Academie Royale Serbe. Serie A. Sciences Mathematiques et Physiques (Belgrade) [*A publication*]

Bull Acad Sci St Louis ... Bulletin. Academy of Sciences of St. Louis [*A publication*]

Bull Acad Sci United Prov Agra Oudh India ... Bulletin. Academy of Sciences of the United Provinces of Agra and Oudh, India [*A publication*]

Bull Acad Sci URSS ... Bulletin. Academie des Sciences de l'URSS [*A publication*]

Bull Acad Sci USSR Div Chem Sci ... Bulletin. Academy of Sciences of the USSR. Division of Chemical Science [*A publication*]

Bull Acad Sci USSR Geol Ser ... Bulletin. Academy of Sciences of the USSR. Geologic Series [*A publication*]

Bull Acad Sci USSR Phys Sci ... Bulletin. Academy of Sciences of the USSR. Physical Sciences [*A publication*]

Bull Acad Sci USSR Phys Ser ... Bulletin. Academy of Sciences of the USSR. Physical Series [*A publication*]

Bull Acad Sci USSR Phys Ser (Columbia Tech Transl) ... Bulletin. Academy of Sciences of the USSR. Physical Series (Columbia Technical Translations) [*A publication*]

Bull Acad Serbe Sci Arts Classe Sci Tech ... Bulletin. Academie Serbe des Sciences et des Arts. Classe des Sciences Techniques [*Belgrade*] [*A publication*]

Bull Acad Serbe Sci Arts Cl Sci Math Nat ... Bulletin. Academie Serbe des Sciences et des Arts. Classe des Sciences Mathematiques et Naturelles [*A publication*]

Bull Acad Serbe Sci Arts Cl Sci Math Nat Sci Nat ... Bulletin. Academie Serbe des Sciences et des Arts. Classe des Sciences Mathematiques et Naturelles. Sciences Naturelles [*A publication*]

Bull Acad Serbe Sci Arts Cl Sci Math Natur ... Bulletin. Academie Serbe des Sciences et des Arts. Classe des Sciences Mathematiques et Naturelles [*A publication*]

Bull Acad Serbe Sci Arts Cl Sci Math Natur NS ... Bulletin. Academie Serbe des Sciences et des Arts. Classe des Sciences Mathematiques et Naturelles. Nouvelle Serie [*Belgrade*] [*A publication*]

Bull Acad Serbe Sci Arts Cl Sci Math Natur Sci Math ... Bulletin. Academie Serbe des Sciences et des Arts. Classe des Sciences Mathematiques et Naturelles. Sciences Mathematiques [*A publication*]

Bull Acad Serbe Sci Arts Cl Sci Med ... Bulletin. Academie Serbe des Sciences et des Arts. Classe des Sciences Medicales [*Belgrade*] [*A publication*]

Bull Acad Serbe Sci et Arts Cl Sci Tech ... Bulletin. Academie Serbe des Sciences et des Arts. Classe des Sciences Techniques [*A publication*]

Bull Acad Serbe Sci Cl Sci Math Nat ... Bulletin. Academie Serbe des Sciences. Classe des Sciences Mathematiques et Naturelles [*A publication*]

Bull Acad Soc Lorraines Sci ... Bulletin. Academie et Societe Lorraines des Sciences [*A publication*]

Bull Acad Sui Sci Med ... Bulletin. Academie Suisse des Sciences Medicales [*A publication*]

Bull Acad Suisse Sci Med ... Bulletin. Academie Suisse des Sciences Medicales [*A publication*]

Bull Acad Vet Fr ... Bulletin. Academie Veterinaire de France [*A publication*]

Bull Acad Vet France ... Bulletin. Academie Veterinaire de France [*A publication*]

Bull ACLS ... Bulletin. American Council of Learned Societies [*A publication*]

Bull Ac Malg ... Bulletin. Academie Malgache [*A publication*]

Bull Ac Polon Sci ... Bulletin. Academie Polonaise des Sciences [*A publication*]

Bull Act Inst Geol Subsurf Res ... Bulletin. Activity of the Institute for Geology and Subsurface Research [*Athens*] [*A publication*]

Bull Adler Mus Hist Med ... Bulletin. Adler Museum of the History of Medicine [*A publication*]

Bull Advis Counc Sci Ind Res (Can) ... Bulletin. Advisory Council for Scientific and Industrial Research (Canada) [*A publication*]

Bull Aeronaut Res Inst Univ Tokyo ... Bulletin. Aeronautical Research Institute. University of Tokyo [*A publication*]

Bull AFG ... Bulletin. Association Francaise de Gemmologie [*A publication*]

Bull Afghan Geol Miner Surv ... Bulletin. Afghan Geological and Mineral Survey [*A publication*]

Bull Agence Gen Colon (Fr) ... Bulletin. Agence Generale des Colonies (France) [*A publication*]

Bull Agr CB ... Bulletin Agricole du Congo Belge [*A publication*]

Bull Agr Chem Soc Jap ... Bulletin. Agricultural Chemical Society of Japan [*A publication*]

Bull Agr Congo ... Bulletin Agricole du Congo [*A publication*]

Bull Agric Chem Insp Stn ... Bulletin. Agricultural Chemicals Inspection Station [*A publication*]

Bull Agric Chem Insp Stn (Tokyo) ... Bulletin. Agricultural Chemicals Inspection Station (Tokyo) [*A publication*]

Bull Agric Chem Soc Jpn ... Bulletin. Agricultural Chemical Society of Japan [*A publication*]

Bull Agric Cong Belg ... Bulletin Agricole du Congo Belge [*A publication*]

Bull Agric Congo Belg ... Bulletin Agricole du Congo Belge [*A publication*]

Bull Agric Dep (Assam) ... Bulletin. Agricultural Department (Assam) [*A publication*]

Bull Agric Dep (Tasm) ... Bulletin. Agricultural Department (Tasmania) [*A publication*]

Bull Agric Exp Stn (Rehovoth) ... Bulletin. Agricultural Experiment Station (Rehovoth) [*A publication*]

Bull Agric Exp Stn (Tahreer Prov) ... Bulletin. Agricultural Experiment Station (Tahreer Province) [*A publication*]

Bull Agric Hort ... Bulletin de l'Agriculture et de l'Horticulture [*A publication*]

Bull Agric Mech Coll Texas ... Bulletin. Agricultural and Mechanical College of Texas [*A publication*]

Bull Agric Res Inst Kanagawa Prefect ... Bulletin. Agricultural Research Institute of Kanagawa Prefecture [*A publication*]

Bull Agric Rwanda ... Bulletin Agricole du Rwanda [*A publication*]

Bull Agri Eng Res Stn ... Bulletin. Agricultural Engineering Research Station. Nogyo Doboku Shikenjo Hokou [*Japan*] [*A publication*]

Bull Agron Inst Rech Agron Trop Cult Vivrieres ... Bulletin Agronomique. Institut de Recherches Agronomiques Tropicales et des Cultures Vivrieres [*A publication*]

Bull Agr Res Inst (Pusa) ... Bulletin. Agricultural Research Institute (Pusa) [*A publication*]

Bull Agr Res Sta (Rehovat) ... Bulletin. Agricultural Research Station (Rehovat) [*A publication*]

Bull Aichi Agr Exp Sta ... Bulletin. Aichi Agricultural Experiment Station [*A publication*]

Bull Aichi Environ Res Cent ... Bulletin. Aichi Environmental Research Center [*A publication*]

Bull Aichi Gakugei Univ ... Bulletin. Aichi Gakugei University [*A publication*]

Bull Aichi Inst Technol ... Bulletin. Aichi Institute of Technology [*A publication*]

Bull Aichi Univ Ed Natur Sci ... Bulletin. Aichi University of Education. Natural Science [*Kariya*] [*A publication*]

Bull AIEMA ... Bulletin d'Information. Association Internationale pour l'Etude de la Mosaique Antique [*A publication*]

Bull AI Et SE Eur ... Bulletin. Association Internationale d'Etudes du Sud-Est Europeen [*A publication*]

Bull Akita Prefect Coll Agric ... Bulletin. Akita Prefectural College of Agriculture [*A publication*]

Bull Akron Dent Soc ... Bulletin. Akron [*Ohio*] Dental Society [*A publication*]

Bull Ala Agr Exp Sta ... Bulletin. Alabama Agricultural Experiment Station. Auburn University [*A publication*]

Bull Ala Agric Exp Sta ... Bulletin. Alabama Agricultural Experiment Station. Auburn University [*A publication*]

Bull Ala Agric Exp Stn ... Bulletin. Alabama Agricultural Experiment Station. Auburn University [*A publication*]

Bull Alameda-Contra Costa Med Assoc ... Bulletin. Alameda-Contra Costa Medical Association [*California*] [*A publication*]

Bull Alameda Cty Dent Soc ... Bulletin. Alameda County Dental Society [*A publication*]

Bull Alaska Agr Exp Sta ... Bulletin. Alaska Agricultural Experiment Station [*A publication*]

Bull Alaska Agric Exp Stn ... Bulletin. Alaska Agricultural Experiment Station [*A publication*]

Bull Alex .... Bulletin. Societe Archeologique d'Alexandrie [*A publication*]

Bull Alexandria Fac Med ... Bulletin. Alexandria Faculty of Medicine [*A publication*]

Bull Alexandria Univ Fac Arts ... Bulletin. Faculty of Arts. Alexandria University [*Majallat Kulliyat al-Adab. Jami'at al-Iskandaruyah*] [*A publication*]

Bull Alger Carcinol ... Bulletin Algerien de Carcinologie [*A publication*]

Bull Allegheny County Med Soc ... Bulletin. Allegheny County Medical Society [*Pennsylvania*] [*A publication*]

Bull ALLF ... Bulletin. Academie Royale de Langue et de Litterature Francaises [*A publication*]

Bull Alloy Phase Diagrams ... Bulletin of Alloy Phase Diagrams [*A publication*]

Bull Allyn Mus ... Bulletin. Allyn Museum [*A publication*]

Bull Am Acad Dermatol ... Bulletin. American Academy of Dermatology [*A publication*]
Bull Am Acad Orthopaedic Surg ... Bulletin. American Academy of Orthopaedic Surgeons [*A publication*]
Bull Am Acad Psychiatr Law ... Bulletin. American Academy of Psychiatry and the Law [*A publication*]
Bull Am Acad Psychiatry Law ... Bulletin. American Academy of Psychiatry and the Law [*A publication*]
Bull Am Acad Psych & L ... Bulletin. American Academy of Psychiatry and the Law [*A publication*]   (DLA)
Bull Am Acad Rel ... Bulletin. American Academy of Religion [*A publication*]
Bull Am Anthr Ass ... Bulletin. American Anthropological Association [*A publication*]
Bull Am Assoc Bot Gard Arboreta ... Bulletin. American Association of Botanical Gardens and Arboreta [*A publication*]
Bull Am Assoc Dent Ed ... Bulletin. American Association of Dental Editors [*A publication*]
Bull Am Assoc Hosp Dent ... Bulletin. American Association of Hospital Dentists [*A publication*]
Bull Am Assoc Nurse Anesth ... Bulletin. American Association of Nurse Anesthetists [*A publication*]
Bull Am Assoc Pet Geol ... Bulletin. American Association of Petroleum Geologists [*A publication*]
Bull Am Assoc Variable Star Obs ... Bulletin. American Association of Variable Star Observers [*A publication*]
Bull Am Ass Petrol Geol ... Bulletin. American Association of Petroleum Geologists [*A publication*]
Bull Am Ass Publ Hlth Dent ... Bulletin. American Association of Public Health Dentists [*A publication*]
Bull Am Ass Publ Hlth Phys ... Bulletin. American Association of Public Health Physicians [*A publication*]
Bull Am Ass Univ Prof ... Bulletin. American Association of University Professors [*A publication*]
Bull Am Astron Soc ... Bulletin. American Astronomical Society [*A publication*]
Bull Am Cancer Soc ... Bulletin. American Cancer Society [*A publication*]
Bull Am Ceram Soc ... Bulletin. American Ceramic Society [*A publication*]
Bull Am Cer Soc ... Bulletin. American Ceramic Society [*A publication*]
Bull Am Coll Nurse Midwifery ... Bulletin. Americana College of Nurse-Midwifery [*A publication*]
Bull Am Coll Physicians ... Bulletin. American College of Physicians [*A publication*]
Bull Am Coll Surg ... Bulletin. American College of Surgeons [*A publication*]
Bull Am Dahlia Soc ... Bulletin. American Dahlia Society [*A publication*]
Bull Am Dent Ass ... Bulletin. American Dental Association [*A publication*]
Bull Amer Acad Arts Sci ... Bulletin. American Academy of Arts and Sciences [*A publication*]
Bull Amer Counc Learned Soc ... Bulletin. American Council of Learned Societies [*A publication*]
Bull Amer Math Soc ... Bulletin. American Mathematical Society [*A publication*]
Bull Amer Math Soc NS ... Bulletin. American Mathematical Society. New Series [*A publication*]
Bull Amer Meteorol Soc ... Bulletin. American Meteorological Society [*A publication*]
Bull Amer Sch Orient Res ... Bulletin. American Schools of Oriental Research [*A publication*]
Bull Amer Soc Bakery Eng ... Bulletin. American Society of Bakery Engineers [*A publication*]
Bull Am Foundrymen's Assoc ... Bulletin. American Foundrymen's Association [*A publication*]
Bull Am Game Protect Ass ... Bulletin. American Game Protective Association [*A publication*]
Bull Am Group IIC ... Bulletin. American Group. International Institute for Conservation of Historic and Artistic Works [*A publication*]
Bull Am Hosta Soc ... Bulletin. American Hosta Society [*A publication*]
Bull Am Inst Min Metall Eng ... Bulletin. American Institute of Mining and Metallurgical Engineers [*A publication*]
Bull Am Malacol Union Inc ... Bulletin. American Malacological Union, Incorporated [*A publication*]
Bull Am Math Soc ... Bulletin. American Mathematical Society [*A publication*]
Bull Am Meteorol Soc ... Bulletin. American Meteorological Society [*A publication*]
Bull Am Mus Nat Hist ... Bulletin. American Museum of Natural History [*A publication*]
Bull Am Orchid Soc ... Bulletin. American Orchid Society [*A publication*]
Bull Am Paleontol ... Bulletins of American Paleontology [*A publication*]
Bull Am Paleontology ... Bulletins of American Paleontology [*A publication*]
Bull Am Pharm Assoc ... Bulletin. American Pharmaceutical Association [*A publication*]
Bull Am Phys Soc ... Bulletin. American Physical Society [*A publication*]
Bull Am Prot Hosp Assoc ... Bulletin. American Protestant Hospital Association [*A publication*]
Bull Am Sch Prehist Res ... Bulletin. American School of Prehistoric Research [*A publication*]
Bull Am Sch Prehist Research ... Bulletin. American School of Prehistoric Research [*A publication*]
Bull Am Soc Hosp Pharm ... Bulletin. American Society of Hospital Pharmacists [*A publication*]

Bull Am Soc Inform Sci ... Bulletin. American Society for Information Science [*A publication*]
Bull Am Soc Inf Sci ... Bulletin. American Society for Information Science [*A publication*]
Bull Am Soc Pap ... Bulletin. American Society of Papyrologists [*A publication*]
Bull Am Soc Vet Clin Pathol ... Bulletin. American Society of Veterinary Clinical Pathologists [*A publication*]
Bull Am Zinc Inst ... Bulletin. American Zinc Institute [*A publication*]
Bull Anal Ent Med Vet ... Bulletin Analytique d'Entomologie Medical et Veterinaire [*A publication*]
Bull Anal Entomol Med Vet ... Bulletin Analytique d'Entomologie Medicale et Veterinaire [*A publication*]
Bull Anal Test ... Bulletin of Analysis and Testing [*A publication*]
Bull Anc Eleves Ec Fr Meun ... Bulletin. Anciens Eleves de l'Ecole Francaise de Meunerie [*A publication*]
Bull Anciens Eleves Ecole Franc Meun ... Bulletin. Anciens Eleves de l'Ecole Francaise de Meunerie [*A publication*]
Bull Anglo-Sov LA ... Bulletin. Anglo-Soviet Law Association [*A publication*]   (DLA)
Bull Anim Behav ... Bulletin of Animal Behavior [*A publication*]
Bull Anim Health Prod Afr ... Bulletin of Animal Health and Production in Africa [*A publication*]
Bull Annls Soc R Ent Belg ... Bulletin et Annales. Societe Royale Entomologique de Belgique [*A publication*]
Bull Ann Soc Entomol Belg ... Bulletin et Annales. Societe Entomologique de Belgique [*A publication*]
Bull Ann Soc R Belge Entomol ... Bulletin et Annales. Societe Royale Belge d'Entomologie [*A publication*]
Bull Ann Soc R Entomol Belg ... Bulletin et Annales. Societe Royale d'Entomologie de Belgique [*A publication*]
Bull Ann Soc Roy Entomol Belg ... Bulletin et Annales. Societe Royale d'Entomologie de Belgique [*A publication*]
Bull Ann Soc Suisse Chronom et Lab Suisse Rech Horlogeres ... Bulletin Annuel. Societe Suisse de Chronometrie et Laboratoire Suisse de Recherches Horlogeres [*A publication*]
Bull Annu Soc Suisse Chronom Lab Suisse Rech Horlog ... Bulletin Annuel. Societe Suisse de Chronometrie et Laboratoire Suisse de Recherches Horlogeres [*A publication*]
Bull Ant Fr ... Bulletin. Societe Nationale des Antiquaires de France [*A publication*]
Bull Antivenin Inst Am ... Bulletin. Antivenin Institute of America [*A publication*]
Bull Aomori Agr Exp Sta ... Bulletin. Aomori Agricultural Experiment Station [*A publication*]
Bull Aomori Agric Exp Stn ... Bulletin. Aomori Agricultural Experiment Station [*A publication*]
Bull Aomori Apple Exp Stn ... Bulletin. Aomori Apple Experiment Station [*A publication*]
Bull A Phys Soc ... Bulletin. American Physical Society [*A publication*]
Bull Apic.... Bulletin Apicole [*A publication*]
Bull Apic Doc Sci Tech Inf ... Bulletin Apicole de Documentation Scientifique et Technique et d'Information [*A publication*]
Bull APM Forests ... Bulletin. APM [*Australian Paper Manufacturers*] Forests Proprietary Ltd. [*A publication*]   (APTA)
Bull Aquat Biol ... Bulletin of Aquatic Biology [*A publication*]
BullArch .... Bulletin Archeologique. Comite des Travaux Historiques et Scientifiques [*Paris*] [*A publication*]
Bull Arch Alg ... Bulletin d'Archeologie Algerienne [*A publication*]
Bull Archeol ... Bulletin Archeologique, Historique, et Artistique. Societe Archeologique de Tarn-et-Garonne [*A publication*]
Bull Arch Maroc ... Bulletin d'Archeologie Marocaine [*A publication*]
Bull ARERS ... Bulletin. Association Regionale pour l'Etude et la Recherche Scientifiques [*A publication*]
Bull Argic Exp Stn N Carol St Univ ... Bulletin. Agricultural Experiment Station. North Carolina State University [*A publication*]
Bull Ariz Agr Exp Sta ... Bulletin. Arizona Agricultural Experiment Station [*A publication*]
Bull Ariz Agr Exp Sta Coop Ext Serv ... Bulletin. Arizona Agricultural Experiment Station. Cooperating Extension Service [*A publication*]
Bull Ariz Agric Exp Stn ... Bulletin. Arizona Agricultural Experiment Station [*A publication*]
Bull Ark Agr Exp Sta ... Bulletin. Arkansas Agricultural Experiment Station [*A publication*]
Bull Ark Agric Exp Stn ... Bulletin. Arkansas Agricultural Experiment Station [*A publication*]
Bull Arkansas Agric Exp Stn ... Bulletin. Arkansas Agricultural Experiment Station [*A publication*]
Bull Arts Sci Div Univ Ryukyus Math Natur Sci ... Bulletin. Arts and Science Division. University of the Ryukyus. Mathematics and Natural Sciences [*A publication*]
Bull Ass...... Bulletin des Assurances [*A publication*]
Bull Ass Anat (Paris) ... Bulletin. Association des Anatomistes (Paris) [*A publication*]
Bull Ass Can Bibliot Lang Fr ... Bulletin. Association Canadienne des Bibliothecaires de Langue Francaise [*A publication*]
Bull Ass Dipl Microbiol Nancy ... Bulletin. Association des Diplomes de Microbiologie. Faculte de Pharmacie de Nancy [*A publication*]

Bull Ass Diplomes Microbiol Fac Pharm Nancy ... Bulletin. Association des Diplomes de Microbiologie. Faculte de Pharmacie de Nancy [*A publication*]

Bull Ass Franc Avance Sci ... Bulletin. Association Francaise pour l'Avancement des Sciences [*A publication*]

Bull Ass Franc Canc ... Bulletin. Association Francaise pour l'Etude du Cancer [*A publication*]

Bull Ass Fr Etude Sol ... Bulletin. Association [Francaise pour l'Etude du Sol [*A publication*]

Bull Ass Geogr Fr ... Bulletin. Association des Geographes Francais [*A publication*]

Bull Ass Guillaume Bude ... Bulletin. Association Guillaume Bude [*A publication*]

Bull Ass Int Hydrol Scient ... Bulletin. Association Internationale d'Hydrologie Scientifique [*A publication*]

Bull Ass Int Sec Soc ... Bulletin. Association Internationale de la Securite Sociale [*A publication*]

Bull Ass Jur Eur ... Bulletin. Association des Juristes Europeens [*A publication*]

Bull Ass Med Corp ... Bulletin. Association Medicale Corporative [*A publication*]

Bull Ass Med Hait ... Bulletin. Association Medicale Haitienne [*A publication*]

Bull Ass Med Lang Fr ... Bulletin. Association des Medecins de Langue Francaise [*A publication*]

Bull Assoc Anat ... Bulletin. Association des Anatomistes [*A publication*]

Bull Assoc Anat (Nancy) ... Bulletin. Association des Anatomistes (Nancy) [*A publication*]

Bull Assoc Anc Eleves Inst Ind Ferment Bruxelles ... Bulletin. Association des Anciens Eleves de l'Institut des Industries de Fermentation de Bruxelles [*Belgium*] [*A publication*]

Bull Assoc Anc Eleves Super Ferment Gand ... Bulletin. Association des Anciens Eleves de l'Institut Superieur des Fermentations de Gand [*A publication*]

Bull Assoc Anc Etud Brass Univ Louv ... Bulletin. Association des Anciens Etudiants de l'Ecole Superieure de Brasserie de l'Universite de Louvain [*A publication*]

Bull Assoc Anc Etud Ec Super Brass Univ Louv ... Bulletin. Association des Anciens Etudiants de l'Ecole Superieure de Brasserie de l'Universite de Louvain [*A publication*]

Bull Assoc Anc Etud Ec Super Brass Univ Louvain ... Bulletin. Association des Anciens Etudiants de l'Ecole Superieure de Brasserie de l'Universite de Louvain [*A publication*]

Bull Assoc Anciens Eleves Ecole Fr Meun ... Bulletin. Association des Anciens Eleves de l'Ecole Francaise de Meunerie [*France*] [*A publication*]

Bull Assoc Biochim Hop Que ... Bulletin. Association des Biochimistes des Hopitaux du Quebec [*A publication*]

Bull Assoc Chim ... Bulletin. Association des Chimistes [*A publication*]

Bull Assoc Chim Sucr Distill Fr Colon ... Bulletin. Association des Chimistes de Sucrerie et de Distillerie de France et des Colonies [*A publication*]

Bull Assoc Chim Sucr Distill Ind Agric Fr Colon ... Bulletin. Association des Chimistes de Sucrerie, de Distillerie, et des Industries Agricoles de France et des Colonies [*A publication*]

Bull Assoc Diplomes Microbiol Fac Pharm Nancy ... Bulletin. Association des Diplomes de Microbiologie. Faculte de Pharmacie de Nancy [*A publication*]

Bull Ass Oceanogr Phys ... Bulletin. Association d'Oceanographie Physique [*A publication*]

Bull Assoc Eng Geol ... Bulletin. Association of Engineering Geologists [*A publication*]

Bull Assoc Engng Geol ... Bulletin. Association of Engineering Geologists [*A publication*]

Bull Assoc Enseign Math Ser B ... Bulletin. Association des Enseignants de Mathematiques. Serie B [*Rabat*] [*A publication*]

Bull Assoc Fr Chim Ind Cuir Doc Sci Tech Ind Cuir ... Bulletin de l'Association Francaise des Chimistes des Industries du Cuir et Documents Scientifiques et Techniques des Industries du Cuir [*A publication*]

Bull Assoc Fr Etude Cancer ... Bulletin. Association Francaise pour l'Etude du Cancer [*A publication*]

Bull Assoc Fr Etude Sol ... Bulletin. Association Francaise pour l'Etude du Sol [*A publication*]

Bull Assoc Fr Etud Sol ... Bulletin. Association Francaise pour l'Etude du Sol [*A publication*]

Bull Assoc Fr Ing Chim Tech Ind Cuir Doc Inf Cent Tech Cuir ... Bulletin. Association Francaise des Ingenieurs, Chimistes, et Techniciens des Industries du Cuir et Documents et Informations du Centre Technique du Cuir [*A publication*]

Bull Assoc Fr Ing Tech Cinema ... Bulletin. Association Francaise des Ingenieurs et Techniciens du Cinema [*A publication*]

Bull Assoc Fr Tech Pet ... Bulletin. Association Francaise des Techniciens du Petrole [*France*] [*A publication*]

Bull Assoc Guillaume Bude ... Bulletin. Association Guillaume Bude [*A publication*]

Bull Assoc Int Doc Tech Inf ... Bulletin. Association Internationale des Documentalistes et Techniciens de l'Information [*A publication*]

Bull Assoc Int Geol Ing ... Bulletin. Association Internationale de Geologie de l'Ingenieur [*A publication*]

Bull Assoc Kinet India ... Bulletin. Association of Kineticists of India [*A publication*]

Bull Assoc Minn Entomol ... Bulletin. Association of Minnesota Entomologists [*A publication*]

Bull Assoc Perm Congr Belg Route ... Bulletin. Association Permanente des Congres Belges de la Route [*A publication*]

Bull Assoc R Anc Etud Brass Univ Louv ... Bulletin. Association Royal des Anciens Etudiants en Brasserie de l'Universite de Louvain [*A publication*]

Bull Assoc Reg Etude Rech Sci ... Bulletin. Association Regionale pour l'Etude et la Recherche Scientifiques [*A publication*]

Bull Assoc State Eng Soc ... Bulletin. Associated State Engineering Societies [*A publication*]

Bull Assoc Suisse Electr ... Bulletin. Association Suisse des Electriciens [*A publication*]

Bull Assoc Tech Fonderie ... Bulletin. Association Technique de Fonderie [*A publication*]

Bull Assoc Tech Mar Aeronaut ... Bulletin. Association Technique Maritime et Aeronautique [*France*] [*A publication*]

Bull Assoc Tech Marit Aeronaut ... Bulletin. Association Technique Maritime et Aeronautique [*A publication*]

Bull Assoc Trop Biol ... Bulletin. Association for Tropical Biology [*A publication*]

Bull Ass Oper Millers ... Bulletin. Association of Operative Millers [*A publication*]

Bull Ass Philomath Alsace et Lorraine ... Bulletin. Association Philomathique d'Alsace et de Lorraine [*A publication*]

Bull Ass Suisse El ... Bulletin. Association Suisse des Electriciens [*A publication*]

Bull Ass Suisse Elec ... Bulletin. Association Suisse des Electriciens [*A publication*]

Bull Ass Tech Fo ... Bulletin. Association Technique de Fonderie [*A publication*]

Bull Ass Tech Ind Pap ... Bulletin. Association Technique de l'Industrie Papetiere [*A publication*]

Bull Astr .... Bulletin Astronomique [*A publication*]

Bull Astr Inst Neth ... Bulletin. Astronomical Institutes of the Netherlands [*A publication*]

Bull Astron ... Bulletin Astronomique [*France*] [*A publication*]

Bull Astron Inst Czech ... Bulletin. Astronomical Institutes of Czechoslovakia [*A publication*]

Bull Astron Inst Neth ... Bulletin. Astronomical Institutes of the Netherlands [*A publication*]

Bull Astron Inst Neth Suppl Ser ... Bulletin. Astronomical Institutes of the Netherlands. Supplement Series [*A publication*]

Bull Astron Observ Belg ... Bulletin Astronomique. Observatoire Royale de Belgique [*A publication*]

Bull Astronom Inst of Czechoslovakia ... Bulletin. Astronomical Institutes of Czechoslovakia [*A publication*]

Bull Astron Soc India ... Bulletin. Astronomical Society of India [*A publication*]

Bull At Energy Res Inst Korea ... Bulletin. Atomic Energy Research Institute of Korea [*A publication*]

Bull Atmos Radioactiv ... Bulletin of Atmospheric Radioactivity [*Japan*] [*A publication*]

Bull Atom Sci ... Bulletin of the Atomic Scientists [*A publication*]

Bull Atom Scient ... Bulletin of the Atomic Scientists [*A publication*]

Bull At Sci ... Bulletin of the Atomic Scientists [*A publication*]

Bull Auckl Inst Mus ... Bulletin. Auckland Institute and Museum [*A publication*]

Bull Audiophonol ... Bulletin d'Audiophonologie [*A publication*]

Bull Aust Ind Devt Ass ... Australian Industries Development Association. Bulletin [*A publication*]

Bull Aust Math Soc ... Bulletin. Australian Mathematical Society [*A publication*]

Bull Aust Miner Dev Lab ... Bulletin. Australian Mineral Development Laboratories [*A publication*]

Bull Australas Inst Min Metall ... Bulletin. Australasian Institute of Mining and Metallurgy [*A publication*]

Bull Austral Math Soc ... Bulletin. Australian Mathematical Society [*A publication*]

Bull Aust Road Res Bd ... Bulletin. Australian Road Research Board [*A publication*] (APTA)

Bull Aust Soc Explor Geophys ... Bulletin. Australian Society of Exploration Geophysicists [*A publication*]

Bull Aust Soc Stud Lab Hist ... Bulletin. Australian Society for the Study of Labour History [*A publication*] (APTA)

Bull Aust Weld Res Assoc ... Bulletin. Australian Welding Research Association [*A publication*] (APTA)

Bull Av .... Bulletin. Federation des Avoues [*A publication*]

Bull Ayer Clin Lab PA Hosp ... Bulletin. Ayer Clinical Laboratory of the Pennsylvania Hospital [*A publication*]

Bull Azabu Univ Vet Med ... Bulletin. Azabu University of Veterinary Medicine [*A publication*]

Bull Azabu Vet Coll ... Bulletin. Azabu Veterinary College [*A publication*]

Bull BA ...... Bulletin. Musee National Hongrois des Beaux-Arts [*A publication*]

Bull Balai Penelitian Perkebunan Medan ... Bulletin Balai Penelitian Perkebunan Medan [*A publication*]

Bull Basic Sci Res ... Bulletin of Basic Science Research [*A publication*]

Bull Basrah Nat Hist Mus ... Bulletin. Basrah Natural History Museum [*A publication*]

Bull Bas Sci Res ... Bulletin of Basic Science Research [*A publication*]

Bull & B Bank ... Buller and Bund's Manual of Bankruptcy [*A publication*] (DLA)

Bull Belgicatom ... Bulletin Belgicatom [*A publication*]

Bull Belg Metrol ... Bulletin Belge de Metrologie [*Service de la Metrologie*] [*A publication*]

Bull Belg Phys Soc ... Bulletin. Belgian Physical Society [*A publication*]

Bull Bell Mus Pathobiol ... Bulletin. Bell Museum of Pathobiology [*A publication*]

Bull Benelux ... Bulletin. Benelux [*A publication*]

Bull Bergen Cty Dent Soc ... Bulletin. Bergen County Dental Society [*A publication*]

Bull Bernice P Bishop Mus ... Bulletin. Bernice P. Bishop Museum [*A publication*]

Bull Bibl ..... Bulletin of Bibliography [*A publication*]

Bull Bibl Fr ... Bulletin des Bibliotheques de France [*A publication*]

Bull Bibl de France ... Bulletin des Bibliotheques de France [*A publication*]

Bull Bibl France ... Bulletin des Bibliotheques de France [*A publication*]

Bull Bibliog ... Bulletin of Bibliography [*A publication*]

Bull Bibliogr Mag Notes ... Bulletin of Bibliography and Magazine Notes [*A publication*]

Bull Biblioth Fr ... Bulletin des Bibliotheques de France [*A publication*]

Bull Bibl Natl ... Bulletin. Bibliotheque Nationale [*A publication*]

Bull Biblphique Pedol ORSTOM ... Bulletin Bibliographique de Pedologie. Office de la Recherche Scientifique et Technique d'Outre-Mer [*A publication*]

Bull Bibl Soc Rencesvals ... Bulletin Bibliographique. Societe Rencesvals [*A publication*]

Bull Bime ... Bulletin Bimestriel [*A publication*]

Bull Bimest INACOL ... Bulletin Bimestriel. INACOL [*Institut National pour l'Amelioration des Conserves de Legumes*] [*A publication*]

Bull Bimest Inst Natl Amelior Conserves Legumes (Belg) ... Bulletin Bimestriel. Institut National pour l'Amelioration des Conserves de Legumes (Belgium) [*A publication*]

Bull Bingham Oceanogr Collect Yale Univ ... Bulletin. Bingham Oceanographic Collection. Yale University [*A publication*]

Bull Biogeogr Soc Jpn ... Bulletin. Biogeographical Society of Japan [*A publication*]

Bull Biol Board Can ... Bulletin. Biological Board of Canada [*A publication*]

Bull Biol France et Belgique ... Bulletin Biologique de la France et de la Belgique [*A publication*]

Bull Biol Fr Belg ... Bulletin Biologique de la France et de la Belgique [*A publication*]

Bull Biol Pharm ... Bulletin des Biologistes Pharmaciens [*A publication*]

Bull Biol Res Cent (Baghdad) ... Bulletin. Biological Research Centre (Baghdad) [*A publication*]

Bull Biol Res Cent Publ (Baghdad) ... Bulletin. Biological Research Centre. Publication (Baghdad) [*A publication*]

Bull Biol Soc Wash ... Bulletin. Biological Society of Washington [*A publication*]

Bull Bismuth Inst ... Bulletin. Bismuth Institute [*A publication*]

Bull BN ...... Bulletin. Banque Nationale [*A publication*]

Bull BNL ... Bulletin. Benelux [*A publication*]

Bull Board Celtic Stud ... Bulletin. Board of Celtic Studies [*A publication*]

Bull Board Sci Art (NZ) ... Bulletin. Board of Science and Art (New Zealand) [*A publication*]

Bull B Okla Agric Exp Stn ... Bulletin B. Oklahoma Agricultural Experiment Station [*A publication*]

Bull Boris Kidric Inst Nucl Sci ... Bulletin. Boris Kidric Institute of Nuclear Sciences [*A publication*]

Bull Boris Kidric Inst Nucl Sci Biol ... Bulletin. Boris Kidric Institute of Nuclear Sciences. Biology [*A publication*]

Bull Boris Kidric Inst Nucl Sci Ceram Metall ... Bulletin. Boris Kidric Institute of Nuclear Sciences. Ceramics and Metallurgy [*A publication*]

Bull Boris Kidric Inst Nucl Sci Chem ... Bulletin. Boris Kidric Institute of Nuclear Sciences. Chemistry [*A publication*]

Bull Boris Kidric Inst Nucl Sci Electron ... Bulletin. Boris Kidric Institute of Nuclear Sciences. Electronics [*A publication*]

Bull Boris Kidric Inst Nucl Sci Nucl Eng ... Bulletin. Boris Kidric Institute of Nuclear Sciences. Nuclear Engineering [*A publication*]

Bull Boris Kidric Inst Nucl Sci Phys ... Bulletin. Boris Kidric Institute of Nuclear Sciences. Physics [*A publication*]

Bull Boris Kidric Inst Nucl Sci Suppl ... Bulletin. Boris Kidric Institute of Nuclear Sciences. Supplement [*A publication*]

Bull Bot Gard Buitenzorg ... Bulletin. Botanic Gardens of Buitenzorg [*A publication*]

Bull Bot Soc Bengal ... Bulletin. Botanical Society of Bengal [*A publication*]

Bull Bot Soc Coll Sci (Nagpur) ... Bulletin. Botanical Society. College of Science (Nagpur) [*A publication*]

Bull Bot Soc Gov Sci Coll (Jabalpur (MP) India) ... Bulletin. Botanical Society. Government Science College (Jabalpur (MP) India) [*A publication*]

Bull Bot Soc Univ Saugar ... Bulletin. Botanical Society. University of Saugar [*A publication*]

Bull Bot Surv India ... Bulletin. Botanical Survey of India [*A publication*]

Bull B Psych Soc ... Bulletin. British Psychological Society [*A publication*]

Bull Brackishwater Aquacult Dev Cent ... Bulletin. Brackishwater Aquaculture Development Centre [*A publication*]

Bull Br Antarct Surv ... Bulletin. British Antarctic Survey [*Cambridge*] [*A publication*]

Bull Br Arachnol Soc ... Bulletin. British Arachnological Society [*A publication*]

Bull Br Beekprs Ass Res Comm ... Bulletin. British Bee-Keepers Association. Research Committee [*A publication*]

Bull Br Cast Iron Res Assoc ... Bulletin. British Cast Iron Research Association [*A publication*]

Bull Brew Sci ... Bulletin of Brewing Science [*A publication*]

Bull Br Hydromech Res Ass ... Bulletin. British Hydromechanics Research Association [*A publication*]

Bull Br Interplanet Soc ... Bulletin. British Interplanetary Society [*A publication*]

Bull Brit Mus Natur Hist ... Bulletin. British Museum (Natural History) [*A publication*]

Bull Brit Mus Natur Hist Geol ... Bulletin. British Museum (Natural History). Geology [*A publication*]

Bull Brit Psychol Soc ... Bulletin. British Psychological Society [*A publication*]

Bull Brit Soc Hist Sci ... Bulletin. British Society for the History of Science [*A publication*]

Bull Br Mus (Nat Hist) Bot ... Bulletin. British Museum (Natural History). Botany [*A publication*]

Bull Br Mus (Nat Hist) Entomol ... Bulletin. British Museum (Natural History). Entomology [*A publication*]

Bull Br Mus (Nat Hist) Entomol Suppl ... Bulletin. British Museum (Natural History). Entomology. Supplement [*A publication*]

Bull Br Mus (Nat Hist) Geol ... Bulletin. British Museum (Natural History). Geology [*A publication*]

Bull Br Mus (Nat Hist) Geol Suppl ... Bulletin. British Museum (Natural History). Geology. Supplement [*A publication*]

Bull Br Mus (Nat Hist) Hist Ser ... Bulletin. British Museum (Natural History). Historical Series [*A publication*]

Bull Br Mus Nat Hist Mineral ... Bulletin. British Museum (Natural History). Mineralogy [*A publication*]

Bull Br Mus (Nat Hist) Zool ... Bulletin. British Museum (Natural History). Zoology [*A publication*]

Bull Br Mus (Nat Hist) Zool Suppl ... Bulletin. British Museum (Natural History). Zoology. Supplement [*A publication*]

Bull Br Mycol Soc ... Bulletin. British Mycological Society [*A publication*]

Bull Bronx Cty Dent Soc ... Bulletin. Bronx County Dental Society [*A publication*]

Bull Brooklyn Entomol Soc ... Bulletin. Brooklyn Entomological Society [*A publication*]

Bull Brooklyn Ent Soc ... Bulletin. Brooklyn Entomological Society [*A publication*]

Bull Br Ornithol Club ... Bulletin. British Ornithologists' Club [*A publication*]

Bull Br Soc Rheol ... Bulletin. British Society of Rheology [*A publication*]

Bull Buffalo Gen Hosp ... Bulletin. Buffalo General Hospital [*A publication*]

Bull Buffalo Soc Nat Sci ... Bulletin. Buffalo Society of Natural Sciences [*A publication*]

Bull Bur Agric Intell Plant Des ... Bulletin. Bureau of Agricultural Intelligence and Plant Diseases [*A publication*]

Bull Bur Bio Technol ... Bulletin. Bureau of Bio Technology [*A publication*]

Bull Bur Chem US Dep Agric ... Bulletin. Bureau of Chemistry. United States Department of Agriculture [*A publication*]

Bull Bureau Animal Indust US Dept Agric ... Bulletin. Bureau of Animal Industry. United States Department of Agriculture [*A publication*]

Bull Bur Ent US Dep Agric ... Bulletin. Bureau of Entomology. United States Department of Agriculture [*A publication*]

Bull Bur Geol Topogr (NJ) ... Bulletin. Bureau of Geology and Topography (New Jersey) [*A publication*]

Bull Bur Miner Resour Geol Geophys ... Australia. Bureau of Mineral Resources. Geology and Geophysics. Bulletin [*A publication*] (APTA)

Bull Bur Miner Resour Geol Geophys (Aust) ... Bulletin. Bureau of Mineral Resources. Geology and Geophysics (Australia) [*A publication*]

Bull Bur Mines Geol (State Montana) ... Bulletin. Bureau of Mines and Geology (State of Montana) [*A publication*]

Bull Bur Rech Geol Min ... Bulletin. Bureau de Recherches Geologiques et Minieres [*A publication*]

Bull Bur Rech Geol Minieres ... Bulletin. Bureau de Recherches Geologiques et Minieres [*France*] [*A publication*]

Bull Bur Rech Geol Minieres Deuxieme Ser Sect 2 ... Bulletin. Bureau de Recherches Geologiques et Minieres. Deuxieme Serie. Section 2. Geologie des Gites Mineraux [*A publication*]

Bull Bur Rech Geol Minieres Deuxieme Ser Sect 3 ... Bulletin. Bureau de Recherches Geologiques et Minieres. Deuxieme Serie. Section 3. Hydrogeologie - Geologie de l'Ingenieur [*A publication*]

Bull Bur Rech Geol Minieres (Fr) Sect 1 ... Bulletin. Bureau de Recherches Geologiques et Minieres (France). Section 1. Geologie de la France [*A publication*]

Bull Bur Rech Geol Minieres (Fr) Sect 2 ... Bulletin. Bureau de Recherches Geologiques et Minieres (France). Section 2. Geologie Appliquee [*A publication*]

Bull Bur Rech Geol Minieres (Fr) Sect 3 ... Bulletin. Bureau de Recherches Geologiques et Minieres (France). Section 3. Hydrogeologie - Geologie de l'Ingenieur [*A publication*]

Bull Bur Rech Geol Minieres (Fr) Sect 4 ... Bulletin. Bureau de Recherches Geologiques et Minieres (France). Section 4. Geologie Generale [*A publication*]

Bull Bur Rech Geol Minieres Sec 2 Geol Appl ... Bulletin. Bureau de Recherches Geologiques et Minieres (France). Section 2. Geologie Appliquee [*A publication*]

Bull Bur Rech Geol Minieres Ser 2 Sect 1 ... Bulletin. Bureau de Recherches Geologiques et Minieres. Serie 2. Section 1 [*A publication*]

Bull Bur Rech Geol Minieres Ser 2 Sect 2 ... Bulletin. Bureau de Recherches Geologiques et Minieres. Serie 2. Section 2 (France) [*A publication*]

Bull Bur Rech Geol Minieres Ser 2 Sect 4 ... Bulletin. Bureau de Recherches Geologiques et Minieres. Serie 2. Section 4 [*A publication*]

Bull Bur Rech Geol Min Sect 3 (Fr) ... Bulletin. Bureau de Recherches Geologiques et Minieres. Section 3. Hydrogeologie - Geologie de l'Ingenieur (France) [*A publication*]

Bull Bur Rech Geol Min Sect 2 Geol Appl Chron Mines (Fr) ... Bulletin. Bureau de Recherches Geologiques et Minieres. Section 2. Geologie Appliquee. Chronique des Mines (France) [*A publication*]

Bull Bur Rech Geol Min Sect 2 Geol Appl (Fr) ... Bulletin. Bureau de Recherches Geologiques et Minieres. Section 2. Geologie Appliquee (France) [*A publication*]

Bull Bur Rech Geol Min Sect 2 Geol Gites Miner (Fr) ... Bulletin. Bureau de Recherches Geologiques et Minieres. Section 2. Geologie des Gites Mineraux (France) [*A publication*]

Bull Bus Archs Coun Aust ... Business Archives Council of Australia. Bulletin [*A publication*]   (APTA)

Bull Bus Hist Soc ... Bulletin. Business Historical Society [*A publication*]

Bull Bussey Inst ... Bulletin. Bussey Institution [*A publication*]

Bull B Wyo Agric Exp Stn ... Bulletin B. Wyoming Agricultural Experiment Station [*A publication*]

Bull Calcutta Math Soc ... Bulletin. Calcutta Mathematical Society [*A publication*]

Bull Calcutta Sch Trop Med ... Bulletin. Calcutta School of Tropical Medicine [*A publication*]

Bull Calif Agr Exp Sta ... Bulletin. California Agricultural Experiment Station [*A publication*]

Bull Calif Agric Exp Stn ... Bulletin. California Agricultural Experiment Station [*A publication*]

Bull Calif Dep Agric ... Bulletin. California Department of Agriculture [*A publication*]

Bull Calif Dept Agr ... Bulletin. California Department of Agriculture [*A publication*]

Bull Calif Insect Surv ... Bulletin of the California Insect Survey [*A publication*]

Bull Calif State Min Bur ... Bulletin. California State Mining Bureau [*A publication*]

Bull Canada Dept Agric ... Bulletin. Dominion of Canada. Department of Agriculture [*A publication*]

Bull Cancer ... Bulletin du Cancer [*Paris*] [*A publication*]

Bull Cancer Inst Okayama Univ Med Sch ... Bulletin. Cancer Institute. Okayama University Medical School [*A publication*]

Bull Cancer (Paris) ... Bulletin du Cancer (Paris) [*A publication*]

Bull Can Pet Geol ... Bulletin of Canadian Petroleum Geology [*A publication*]

Bull Can Petrol Geol ... Bulletin of Canadian Petroleum Geology [*A publication*]

Bull Can Welfare L ... Bulletin of Canadian Welfare Law [*A publication*]

Bull Can Welfare Law ... Bulletin of Canadian Welfare Law [*A publication*]   (DLA)

Bull Can Wheat Board ... Bulletin. Canadian Wheat Board [*A publication*]

Bull Caoutch Inst Fr Outre Mer ... Bulletin. Caoutchoucs de l'Institut Francais d'Outre-Mer [*A publication*]

Bull Carnegie Mus Nat Hist ... Bulletin. Carnegie Museum of Natural History [*A publication*]

Bull Carte Veg Provence Alpes Sud ... Bulletin de la Carte et de la Vegetation de la Provence et des Alpes du Sud [*A publication*]

Bull CCB .... Bulletin. Center for Children's Books [*A publication*]

Bull & C Dig ... Bullard and Curry's Louisiana Digest [*A publication*]   (DLA)

Bull Cent Build Res Inst (Roorkee India) ... Bulletin. Central Building Research Institute (Roorkee, India) [*A publication*]

Bull Cent Compilation Donnees Neutroniques ... Bulletin. Centre de Compilation de Donnees Neutroniques [*France*] [*A publication*]

Bull Cent Etud Rech Sci (Biarritz) ... Bulletin. Centre d'Etudes et de Recherches Scientifiques (Biarritz) [*A publication*]

Bull Cent Food Technol Res Inst (Mysore) ... Bulletin. Central Food Technological Research Institute (Mysore) [*A publication*]

Bull Cent Insp Inst Weights Meas (Tokyo) ... Bulletin. Central Inspection Institute of Weights and Measures (Tokyo) [*A publication*]

Bull Cent Int Engrais Chim ... Bulletin. Centre International des Engrais Chimiques [*A publication*]

Bull Cent Leather Res Inst (Madras) ... Bulletin. Central Leather Research Institute (Madras) [*A publication*]

Bull Cent Mar Fish Res Inst ... Bulletin. Central Marine Fisheries Research Institute [*A publication*]

Bull Cent Phys Nucl Univ Lib Bruxelles ... Bulletin. Centre de Physique Nucleaire. Universite Libre de Bruxelles [*A publication*]

Bull Cent Phys Nucl Univ Libre Bruxelles ... Bulletin. Centre de Physique Nucleaire. Universite Libre de Bruxelles [*A publication*]

Bull Central Res Lab OIT ... Bulletin. Central Research Laboratory. Osaka Institute of Technology [*A publication*]

Bull Cent Rech Essais Chatou ... Bulletin. Centre de Recherches et d'Essais de Chatou [*France*] [*A publication*]

Bull Cent Rech Explor ELF Aquitaine ... Bulletin. Centres de Recherches Exploration-Production ELF [*Essences et Lubrifiants de France*] - Aquitaine [*A publication*]

Bull Cent Rech Explor Prod ELF Aquitaine ... Bulletin. Centres de Recherches Exploration-Production ELF [*Essences et Lubrifiants de France*] - Aquitaine [*A publication*]

Bull Cent Rech Pau ... Bulletin. Centre de Recherches de Pau [*A publication*]

Bull Centre Pol Rech Sci Paris ... Bulletin. Centre Polonais de Recherches Scientifiques de Paris [*A publication*]

Bull Cent Res Inst Univ Kerala (India) Ser C Nat Sci ... Bulletin. Central Research Institute. University of Kerala (India). Series C. Natural Science [*A publication*]

Bull Cent Res Inst Univ Kerala (Trivandrum) Ser C ... Bulletin. Central Research Institute. University of Kerala (Trivandrum). Series C. Natural Science [*A publication*]

Bull Cent Res Inst Univ Trav ... Bulletin. Central Research Institute. University of Travancore [*A publication*]

Bull Centres Rech Explor-Prod ELF-Aquitaine ... Bulletin. Centres de Recherches Exploration-Production ELF [*Essences et Lubrifiants de France*] - Aquitaine [*A publication*]

Bull Cent Text Controle Rech Sci ... Bulletin. Centre Textile de Controle et de Recherche Scientifique [*A publication*]

BullCER .... Bulletin. Cercle Ernest Renan [*Paris*] [*A publication*]

Bull Cerc Arch Hesbaye-Condroz ... Bulletin. Cercle Archeologique Hesbaye-Condroz [*A publication*]

Bull Cerc Benel Hist Pharm ... Bulletin. Cercle Benelux d'Histoire de la Pharmacie [*A publication*]

Bull Cercle Benelux Hist Pharm ... Bulletin. Cercle Benelux d'Histoire de la Pharmacie [*A publication*]

Bull Cercle Etud Met ... Bulletin. Cercle d'Etudes des Metaux [*A publication*]

Bull Cercle Etud Metaux ... Bulletin. Cercle d'Etudes des Metaux [*A publication*]

Bull Cercle Zool Congolais ... Bulletin. Cercle Zoologique Congolais [*A publication*]

Bull des Cereales Plant Fecule ... Bulletin des Cereales et des Plantes a Fecule [*A publication*]

Bull CETA ... Bulletin. Centres d'Etudes Techniques Agricoles [*A publication*]

Bull CETIOM Cent Tech Interprof Ol Metrop ... Bulletin CETIOM. Centre Technique Interprofessionnel des Oleagineux Metropolitains [*A publication*]

Bull Ceyl Fish ... Bulletin. Ceylon Fisheries. Ceylon Department of Fisheries [*A publication*]

Bull CFL .... Bulletin. Cercle Francois Laurent [*A publication*]

Bull Chem Res Inst Non-Aqueous Solutions Tohoku Univ ... Bulletin. Chemical Research Institute of Non-Aqueous Solutions. Tohoku University [*Japan*] [*A publication*]

Bull Chem Soc Jap ... Bulletin. Chemical Society of Japan [*A publication*]

Bull Chem Soc Japan ... Bulletin. Chemical Society of Japan [*A publication*]

Bull Chem Technol Macedonia ... Bulletin. Chemists and Technologists of Macedonia [*A publication*]

Bull Chem Thermodyn ... Bulletin of Chemical Thermodynamics [*A publication*]

Bull Chest Dis Res Inst Kyoto Univ ... Bulletin. Chest Disease Research Institute. Kyoto University [*A publication*]

Bull Chiba Agric ... Bulletin. Chiba College of Agriculture [*A publication*]

Bull Chiba-Ken Agr Exp Sta ... Bulletin. Chiba-ken Agricultural Experiment Station [*A publication*]

Bull Chiba Prefect Agri Exp Stn ... Bulletin. Chiba Prefecture Agricultural Experiment Station [*Japan*] [*A publication*]

Bull Chic Acad Sci ... Bulletin. Chicago Academy of Sciences [*A publication*]

Bull Chic Herpetol Soc ... Bulletin. Chicago Herpetological Society [*A publication*]

Bull Chichibu Mus Nat Hist ... Bulletin. Chichibu Museum of Natural History [*A publication*]

Bull Chin Assoc Adv Sci ... Bulletin. Chinese Association for the Advancement of Science [*A publication*]

Bull Chin Bot Soc ... Bulletin. Chinese Botanical Society [*A publication*]

Bull Chin Mater Med ... Bulletin of Chinese Materia Medica [*A publication*]

Bull Chir Accid Trav ... Bulletin Chirurgical des Accidents du Travail [*A publication*]

Bull Chubu Inst Technol ... Bulletin. Chubu Institute of Technology [*A publication*]

Bull Chugoku Agr Exp Sta ... Bulletin. Chugoku National Agricultural Experiment Station [*A publication*]

Bull Chugoku Agr Exp Sta Ser A Ser D Ser E ... Bulletin. Chugoku Agricultural Experiment Station. Series A, D, and E [*A publication*]

Bull Chugoku Natl Agric Exp Stn Ser A ... Bulletin. Chugoku National Agricultural Experiment Station. Series A (Crop Division) [*A publication*]

Bull Chugoku Natl Agric Exp Stn Ser A (Crop Div) ... Bulletin. Chugoku National Agricultural Experiment Station. Series A (Crop Division) [*A publication*]

Bull Chugoku Natl Agric Exp Stn Ser B ... Bulletin. Chugoku National Agricultural Experiment Station. Series B (Livestock Division) [*A publication*]

Bull Chugoku Natl Agric Exp Stn Ser B (Livest Div) ... Bulletin. Chugoku National Agricultural Experiment Station. Series B (Livestock Division) [*A publication*]

Bull Chugoku Natl Agric Exp Stn Ser E ... Bulletin. Chugoku National Agricultural Experiment Station. Series E (Environment Division) [*A publication*]

Bull Chugoku Natl Agric Exp Stn Ser E (Environ Div) ... Bulletin. Chugoku National Agricultural Experiment Station. Series E (Environment Division) [*A publication*]

Bull Chukyo Women's Coll ... Bulletin. Chukyo Women's College [*A publication*]

Bull Chukyo Women's Univ ... Bulletin. Chukyo Women's University [*A publication*]

Bull Chungking Inst Ind Res ... Bulletin. Chungking Institute of Industrial Research [*A publication*]

Bull CIMAB ... Bulletin. Centre d'Information du Material et des Articles de Bureau [*A publication*]

Bull Cinci Dent Soc ... Bulletin. Cincinnati Dental Society [*A publication*]

Bull City Hosp Akr ... Bulletin. City Hospital of Akron [*United States*] [*A publication*]

Bull Civ ...... Bulletin des Arrets de la Cour de Cassation. Chambres Civiles [*A publication*] (DLA)

Bull Civ II .. Bulletin des Arrets de la Cour de Cassation. Chambres Civiles. Deuxieme Section Civile [*A publication*]

Bull Civ III ... Bulletin des Arrets de la Cour de Cassation. Chambres Civiles. Troisieme Section Civile [*France*] [*A publication*]

Bull Classe Sci Acad Roy Belg ... Bulletin. Classe des Sciences. Academie Royale de Belgique [*A publication*]

Bull Clemson Agr Exp Sta ... Bulletin. Clemson Agricultural Experiment Station [*A publication*]

Bull Cleve Dent Soc ... Bulletin. Cleveland Dental Society [*A publication*]

Bull Cleveland Med Libr ... Bulletin. Cleveland Medical Library [*A publication*]

Bull Cleveland Museum ... Bulletin. Cleveland Museum of Art [*A publication*]

Bull Cleveland Sci Tech Inst ... Bulletin. Cleveland Scientific and Technical Institution [*A publication*]

Bull Cleve Med Libr Assoc ... Bulletin. Cleveland Medical Library Association [*A publication*]

Bull Clin Neurosci ... Bulletin of Clinical Neurosciences [*A publication*]

Bull Cl Phys Math Acad Imp Sci St Petersbourg ... Bulletin. Classe Physico-Mathematique. Academie Imperiale des Sciences de St. Petersbourg [*A publication*]

Bull Cl Sci Acad R Belg ... Bulletin. Classe des Sciences. Academie Royale de Belgique [*A publication*]

Bull Cl Sci Acad R Belg 5e Ser ... Bulletin. Classe des Sciences. Academie Royale de Belgique. 5e Serie [*A publication*]

Bull Cl Sci Acad Royale Belg ... Bulletin. Classe des Sciences. Academie Royale de Belgique [*A publication*]

Bull Cocon Res Inst (Cey) ... Bulletin. Coconut Research Institute (Ceylon) [*A publication*]

Bull Cocon Res Inst (Ceylon) ... Bulletin. Coconut Research Institute (Ceylon) [*A publication*]

Bull Coll Agr Forest Univ Nanking ... Bulletin. College of Agriculture and Forestry. University of Nanking [*A publication*]

Bull Coll Agric Res Cent Wash State Univ ... Bulletin. College of Agriculture. Research Center. Washington State University [*A publication*]

Bull Coll Agric Res Cent Wash St Univ ... Bulletin. College of Agriculture. Research Center. Washington State University [*A publication*]

Bull Coll Agric Sci (Mosonmagyarovar Hung) ... Bulletin. College of Agricultural Sciences (Mosonmagyarovar, Hungary) [*A publication*]

Bull Coll Agric Tokyo Imp Univ ... Bulletin. College of Agriculture. Tokyo Imperial University [*A publication*]

Bull Coll Agric Univ Teheran ... Bulletin. College of Agriculture. University of Teheran [*A publication*]

Bull Coll Agric Utsunomiya Univ ... Bulletin. College of Agriculture. Utsunomiya University [*A publication*]

Bull Coll Agric Vet Med Nihon Univ ... Bulletin. College of Agriculture and Veterinary Medicine. Nihon University [*A publication*]

Bull Coll Agr Utsunomiya Univ ... Bulletin. College of Agriculture. Utsunomiya University [*A publication*]

Bull Coll Art Ass ... Bulletin. College Art Association of America [*A publication*]

Bull College Sci (Baghdad) ... Bulletin. College of Science (Baghdad) [*A publication*]

Bull College Sci Univ Ryukyus ... University of the Ryukyus. College of Science. Bulletin [*Naha*] [*A publication*]

Bull Coll Eng Hosei Univ ... Bulletin. College of Engineering. Hosei University [*A publication*]

Bull Coll Eng Natl Taiwan Univ ... Bulletin. College of Engineering. National Taiwan University [*A publication*]

Bull Coll Foreign Stud (Yokohama) Nat Sci ... Bulletin. College of Foreign Studies (Yokohama). Natural Science [*A publication*]

Bull Coll Gen Educ Nagoya City Univ Nat Sci Sect ... Bulletin. College of General Education. Nagoya City University. Natural Science Section [*A publication*]

Bull Coll Sci 1 ... Bulletin. College of Science. Part 1 [*Baghdad*] [*A publication*]

Bull Coll Sci Univ Baghdad ... Bulletin. College of Science. University of Baghdad [*A publication*]

Bull Coll Sci Univ Ryukyus ... Bulletin. College of Science. University of the Ryukyus [*A publication*]

Bull Coll Wm & Mary ... William and Mary College. Bulletin [*A publication*] (DLA)

Bull Colo Agr Exp Sta ... Bulletin. Colorado Agricultural Experiment Station [*A publication*]

Bull Colo Agric Exp Stn ... Bulletin. Colorado Agricultural Experiment Station [*A publication*]

Bull Colo Dept Agr ... Bulletin. Colorado Department of Agriculture [*A publication*]

Bull Colo State Univ Agr Exp Sta ... Bulletin. Colorado State University. Agricultural Experiment Station [*A publication*]

Bull Colo State Univ Exp Stn ... Bulletin. Colorado State University. Experiment Station [*A publication*]

Bull Colo St Univ Agric Exp Stn ... Bulletin. Colorado State University. Agricultural Experiment Station [*A publication*]

Bull Colo Vet Med Ass ... Bulletin. Colorado Veterinary Medical Association [*A publication*]

Bull Colo Vet Med Assoc ... Bulletin. Colorado Veterinary Medical Association [*A publication*]

BullComEt ... Bulletin. Comite d'Etudes [*Paris*] [*A publication*]

Bull Com For ... Bulletin. Comite des Forets [*A publication*]

Bull Comite Centr Ind ... Bulletin. Comite Central Industriel de Belgique [*A publication*]

Bull Comite Etud Hist Sci Afr Occident Franc ... Bulletin. Comite d'Etudes Historiques et Scientifiques de l'Afrique Occidentale Francaise [*A publication*]

Bull Comm Arch Narbonne ... Bulletin. Commission Archeologique de Narbonne [*A publication*]

Bull Comm Geol Finl ... Bulletin. Commission Geologique de Finlande [*A publication*]

Bull Comm Hist Archeol Mayenne ... Bulletin. Commission Historique et Archeologique de la Mayenne [*A publication*]

Bull Commonw Bur Past Fld Crops ... Bulletin. Commonwealth Bureau of Pastures and Field Crops [*A publication*]

Bull Commonw Bur Pastures Field Crops ... Bulletin. Commonwealth Bureau of Pastures and Field Crops [*A publication*]

Bull Commonw Scient Ind Res Org ... Bulletin. Commonwealth Scientific and Industrial Research Organisation [*A publication*]

Bull Commonw Sci Ind Res Org ... Bulletin. Commonwealth Scientific and Industrial Research Organisation [*A publication*]

Bull Commonw Sci Industr Res Organ (Aust) ... Bulletin. Commonwealth Scientific and Industrial Research Organisation (Australia) [*A publication*]

Bull Comp L ... American Bar Association. Comparative Law Bureau. Bulletin [*A publication*] (DLA)

Bull Comp Lab Rel ... Bulletin of Comparative Labour Relations [*A publication*] (DLA)

Bull Compr Gas Man Ass ... Bulletin. Compressed Gas Manufacturers Association [*United States*] [*A publication*]

Bull of Computer Aided Archtl Design ... Bulletin of Computer Aided Architectural Design [*A publication*]

Bull Conn Agr Exp Sta ... Bulletin. Connecticut Agricultural Experiment Station [*A publication*]

Bull Conn Agric Exp Stn ... Bulletin. Connecticut Agricultural Experiment Station [*A publication*]

Bull Conn Hist Soc ... Bulletin. Connecticut Historical Society [*A publication*]

Bull Conn St Geol Nat Hist Surv ... Bulletin. Connecticut State Geological and Natural History Survey [*A publication*]

Bull Contr .. Bulletin des Contributions [*A publication*]

Bull Contrib Dir ... Bulletin des Contributions Directes [*A publication*]

Bull Co-Op Ext Serv Coll Agric Univ Idaho ... Bulletin. Co-Operative Extension Service. College of Agriculture. University of Idaho [*A publication*]

Bull Coop Ext Serv Colo State Univ ... Bulletin. Cooperative Extension Service. Colorado State University [*A publication*]

Bull Coop Ext Serv Montana State Univ ... Montana State University. Cooparative Extension Service. Bulletin [*A publication*]

Bull Coop Ext Serv Mont State Univ ... Bulletin. Cooperative Extension Service. Montana State University [*A publication*]

Bull Coop Ext Serv Ohio St Univ ... Bulletin. Cooperative Extension Service. Ohio State University [*A publication*]

Bull Coop Ext Serv Univ Conn ... Bulletin. Cooperative Extension Service. University of Connecticut [*A publication*]

Bull Coop Ext Serv Univ GA Coll Agric ... Bulletin. Cooperative Extension Service. University of Georgia. College of Agriculture [*A publication*]

Bull Copper Brass Res Assoc ... Bulletin. Copper and Brass Research Association [*A publication*]

Bull Cop Soc ... Bulletin. Copyright Society of the USA [*A publication*]

Bull Copte .. Bulletin. Societe d'Archeologie Copte [*A publication*]

Bull Copyright Soc'y ... Bulletin. Copyright Society of the USA [*A publication*]

Bull Copyright Soc'y USA ... Bulletin. Copyright Society of the USA [*A publication*]

Bull Cornell Univ Agric Exp Stn ... Bulletin. Cornell University. Agricultural Experiment Station [*A publication*]

Bull Cornell Univ Eng Exp St ... Bulletin. Cornell University. Engineering Experiment Station [*A publication*]

Bull Corresp Hellen ... Bulletin de Correspondance Hellenique [*A publication*]

Bull Corr Hell ... Bulletin de Correspondance Hellenique [*A publication*]

Bull Council Res Mus Educ ... Bulletin. Council for Research in Music Education [*A publication*]

Bull C'right Soc'y ... Bulletin. Copyright Society of the USA [*A publication*]

Bull Crim ... Bulletin des Arrets de la Chambre Criminelle de la Cour de Cassation [*A publication*] (ILCA)

Bull Crimean Astrophys Obs ... Bulletin. Crimean Astrophysical Observatory [*A publication*]

Bull Cr Soc ... Bulletin. Copyright Society of the USA [*A publication*]

Bull CSIRO ... Australia. Commonwealth Scientific and Industrial Research Organisation. Bulletin [*A publication*] (APTA)

Bull & Cur Dig ... Bullard and Curry's Louisiana Digest [*A publication*] (DLA)

Bull Curr Doc ... Bulletin of Current Documentation [*A publication*]

Bull Czech L ... Bulletin of Czechoslovak Law [*A publication*] (DLA)

Bull Czech Med Ass Great Brit ... Bulletin. Czechoslovak Medical Association in Great Britain [*A publication*]

Bull Daito Bunka Univ ... Bulletin. Daito Bunka University [*Japan*] [*A publication*]

Bull Deccan Coll Res Inst ... Bulletin. Deccan College Research Institute [*A publication*]

Bull Del Agric Exp Stn ... Bulletin. Delaware Agricultural Experiment Station [*A publication*]

Bull Delaware County Med Soc ... Bulletin. Delaware County Medical Society [*Pennsylvania*] [*A publication*]

Bull Dent.... Bulletin Dentaire [*A publication*]

Bull Dent Guid Counc Cereb Palsy ... Bulletin. Dental Guidance Council for Cerebral Palsy [*A publication*]

Bull Dep Agric (Br Columb) ... Bulletin. Department of Agriculture (British Columbia) [*A publication*]

Bull Dep Agric (Ceyl) ... Bulletin. Department of Agriculture (Ceylon) [*A publication*]

Bull Dep Agric (Cyp) ... Bulletin. Department of Agriculture (Cyprus) [*A publication*]

Bull Dep Agric (Dom Can) ... Bulletin. Department of Agriculture (Dominion of Canada) [*A publication*]

Bull Dep Agric For (Un S Afr) ... Bulletin. Department of Agriculture and Forestry (Union of South Africa) [*A publication*]

Bull Dep Agric (Madras) ... Bulletin. Department of Agriculture (Madras) [*A publication*]

Bull Dep Agric NW Terr ... Bulletin. Department of Agriculture. North-West Territories [*A publication*]

Bull Dep Agric (NZ) ... Bulletin. Department of Agriculture (New Zealand) [*A publication*]

Bull Dep Agric (Queb) ... Bulletin. Department of Agriculture (Quebec) [*A publication*]

Bull Dep Agric Res R Trop Inst (Amsterdam) ... Bulletin. Department of Agricultural Research. Royal Tropical Institute (Amsterdam) [*A publication*]

Bull Dep Agric Res Trop Inst (Amst) ... Bulletin. Department of Agricultural Research. Royal Tropical Institute (Amsterdam) [*A publication*]

Bull Dep Agric (Tas) ... Bulletin. Department of Agriculture (Tasmania) [*A publication*] (APTA)

Bull Dep Agric (Tasm) ... Bulletin. Department of Agriculture (Tasmania) [*A publication*] (APTA)

Bull Dep Agric Tech Serv (S Afr) ... Bulletin. Department of Agricultural Technical Services (South Africa) [*A publication*]

Bull Dep Agric Tech Serv (Transv) ... Bulletin. Department of Agricultural Technical Services (Transvaal) [*A publication*]

Bull Dep Agric (West Aust) ... Bulletin. Department of Agriculture (Western Australia) [*A publication*]

Bull Dep Civ Engng QD Univ ... Bulletin. Department of Civil Engineering. University of Queensland [*A publication*] (APTA)

Bull Dep Civ Eng Queensl Univ ... Bulletin. Department of Civil Engineering. University of Queensland [*A publication*] (APTA)

Bull Dep Ent Kans St Univ ... Bulletin. Department of Entomology. Kansas State University [*A publication*]

Bull Dep For (S Afr) ... Bulletin. Department of Forestry (Pretoria, South Africa) [*A publication*]

Bull Dep For Univ Ibadan ... Bulletin. Department of Forestry. University of Ibadan [*A publication*]

Bull Dep Gen Educ Tokyo Med Dent Univ ... Bulletin. Department of General Education. Tokyo Medical and Dental University [*A publication*]

Bull Dep Geol Heb Univ (Jerusalem) ... Bulletin. Department of Geology. Hebrew University (Jerusalem) [*A publication*]

Bull Dep Mines (Br Columbia) ... Bulletin. Department of Mines (British Columbia) [*A publication*]

Bull Dep Sci Ind Res (NZ) ... Bulletin. Department of Scientific and Industrial Research (New Zealand) [*A publication*]

Bull Dept Agr Econ Univ Manchester ... Bulletin. Department of Agricultural Economics. University of Manchester [*A publication*]

Bull Dept Agric and Indust (West Australia) ... Bulletin. Department of Agriculture and Industries (Western Australia) [*A publication*]

Bull Dept Agr (Mysore) Entomol Ser ... Bulletin. Department of Agriculture (Mysore State). Entomology Series [*A publication*]

Bull Dept Agron Mosonmagyarovar Coll Agr Sci ... Bulletin. Department of Agronomy. Mosonmagyarovar College of Agricultural Sciences [*A publication*]

Bull Dept Agr (Tanganyika) ... Bulletin. Department of Agriculture (Tanganyika) [*A publication*]

Bull Dept Agr Tech Serv (Repub S Afr) ... Bulletin. Department of Agricultural Technical Services (Republic of South Africa) [*A publication*]

Bull Dept Gen Ed College Sci Tech Nihon Univ ... Bulletin. Department of General Education. College of Science and Technology. Nihon University [*A publication*]

Bull Dept Gen Educ Nagoya City Univ Nat Sci Sect ... Bulletin. Department of General Education. Nagoya City University. Natural Science Section [*A publication*]

Bull Dep Zool Univ Panjab (New Ser) ... Bulletin. Department of Zoology. University of the Panjab (New Series) [*A publication*]

Bull Dep Zool Univ Punjab ... Bulletin. Department of Zoology. University of the Punjab [*A publication*]

Bull Dir Bel ... Bulletin van de Directe Belastingen [*A publication*]

Bull Direction Etudes Recherches Ser C Math Informat ... Bulletin. Direction des Etudes et Recherches. Serie C. Mathematiques. Informatique [*A publication*]

Bull Direction Etudes Rech Ser C Math Inform ... Electricite de France. Bulletin de la Direction des Etudes et Recherches. Serie C. Mathematiques-Informatique [*Grenoble*] [*A publication*]

Bull Dir Etud & Rech A ... Bulletin. Direction des Etudes et Recherches. Serie A [*A publication*]

Bull Dir Etud & Rech B ... Bulletin. Direction des Etudes et Recherches. Serie B [*A publication*]

Bull Dir Etud & Rech C ... Bulletin. Direction des Etudes et Recherches. Serie C [*A publication*]

Bull Dir Etud Rech Electr Fr Ser A ... Bulletin. Direction des Etudes et Recherches. Electricite de France. Serie A. Nucleaire, Hydraulique, Thermique [*A publication*]

Bull Dir Etud & Rech Ser A ... Bulletin. Direction des Etudes et Recherches. Serie A [*A publication*]

Bull Dir Etud & Rech Ser B ... Bulletin. Direction des Etudes et Recherches. Serie B [*A publication*]

Bull Dir Etud & Rech Ser C ... Bulletin. Direction des Etudes et Recherches. Serie C [*A publication*]

Bull Dir Mines Geol (Afr Equa) ... Bulletin. Direction des Mines et de la Geologie (Afrique Equatoriale) [*A publication*]

Bull Dis...... Buller's Law of Distress for Rent [*A publication*] (DLA)

Bull Div Miner Resour (VA) ... Bulletin. Division of Mineral Resources (Virginia) [*A publication*]

Bull Div Plant Ind NSW Dept Agr ... Bulletin. Division of Plant Industry. New South Wales Department of Agriculture [*A publication*]

Bull Div Silv Dep For Papua & N Guinea ... Bulletin. Division of Silviculture. Department of Forests of Papua and New Guinea [*A publication*]

Bull Div Veg Physiol Path US Dep Agric ... Bulletin. Division of Vegetable Physiology and Pathology. United States Department of Agriculture [*A publication*]

Bull Doc Bibliog ... Bulletin de Documentation Bibliographique [*A publication*]

Bull Doc Cent Inf Chrome Dur ... Bulletin de Documentation. Centre d'Information du Chrome Dur [*France*] [*A publication*]

Bull Doc Int Superphosphate Mfr Ass Agr Comm ... Bulletin of Documentation. International Superphosphate Manufacturers Association. Agricultural Committee [*A publication*]

Bull Docum Ass Int Fabr Superphos ... Bulletin de Documentation. Association Internationale des Fabricants de Superphosphates [*A publication*]

Bull Dosente ... Bulletin vir Dosente [*A publication*]

Bull de Droit Nucl ... Bulletin de Droit Nucleaire [*A publication*]

Bull Droit Nucl ... Bulletin de Droit Nucleaire [*A publication*]

Bull de Droit Tchecoslovaque ... Bulletin de Droit Tchecoslovaque [*A publication*]

Bull Duke Univ Sch For ... Bulletin. Duke University School of Forestry [*A publication*]

Bull Earth Miner Sci Exp Sta PA State Univ ... Bulletin. Earth and Mineral Sciences Experiment Station. Pennsylvania State University [*A publication*]

Bull Earth Miner Sci Exp Stn PA State Univ ... Bulletin. Earth and Mineral Sciences Experiment Station. Pennsylvania State University [*A publication*]

Bull Earthquake Res Inst Univ Tokyo ... Bulletin. Earthquake Research Institute. University of Tokyo [*A publication*]

Bull Earth Sci Fac Ege Univ (Izmir) ... Bulletin. Earth Science Faculty. Ege University (Izmir) [*A publication*]

Bull East Scotl Coll Agric ... Bulletin. East of Scotland College of Agriculture [*A publication*]

Bull Eccl..... Bullingbroke's Ecclesiastical Law [*A publication*] (DLA)

Bull Ec Meun Belge ... Bulletin. Ecole de la Meunerie Belge [*A publication*]

Bull Ec Natl Super Agron Ind Aliment ... Bulletin. Ecole Nationale Superieure d'Agronomie et des Industries Alimentaires [*A publication*]

Bull Ec Natl Super Agron Nancy ... Bulletin. Ecole Nationale Superieure Agronomique de Nancy [*A publication*]

Bull Ec Natn Sup Agron Nancy ... Bulletin. Ecole Nationale Superieure Agronomique de Nancy [*A publication*]
Bull Ec Nat Super Agron Ind Aliment ... Bulletin. Ecole Nationale Superieure d'Agronomie et des Industries Alimentaires [*A publication*]
Bull Ecol .... Bulletin d'Ecologie [*A publication*]
Bull Ecole Franc Extreme-Orient ... Bulletin. Ecole Francaise d'Extreme-Orient [*Hanoi*] [*A publication*]
Bull Ecole Nat Super Agron Nancy ... Bulletin. Ecole Nationale Superieure Agronomique de Nancy [*A publication*]
Bull Ecole Super Agr Tunis ... Bulletin. Ecole Superieure d'Agriculture de Tunis [*A publication*]
Bull Ecol Res Comm-NFR (Statens Naturvetensk Forskningsrad) ... Bulletins. Ecological Research Committee-NFR (Statens Naturvetenskapliga Forskningsrad) [*A publication*]
Bull Ecol Soc Amer ... Bulletin. Ecological Society of America [*A publication*]
Bull Econom ... Bulletin Economique Mensuelle [*A publication*]
Bull Edinburgh Sch Agr ... Bulletin. Edinburgh School of Agriculture [*A publication*]
Bull Educ Dev & Res ... Bulletin of Educational Development and Research [*A publication*]
Bull Educ Res Inst Fac Educ Univ Kagoshima ... Bulletin. Educational Research Institute. Faculty of Education. University of Kagoshima [*A publication*]
Bull Egypt Univ Fac Arts ... Bulletin. Faculty of Arts. Egyptian University [*A publication*]
Bull Ehime Agr Exp Sta ... Bulletin. Ehime Agricultural Experiment Station [*A publication*]
Bull Ehime Prefect Agric Exp Stn ... Bulletin. Ehime Prefectural Agricultural Experiment Station [*A publication*]
Bull Ehime Univ For ... Bulletin. Ehime University Forest [*A publication*]
Bull Eidgenoess Gesundh Beil B ... Bulletin. Eidgenoessisches Gesundheitsamt. Beilage B [*Switzerland*] [*A publication*]
Bulleid Mem Lect ... Bulleid Memorial Lectures [*A publication*]
Bull Eighth Dist Dent Soc ... Bulletin. Eighth District Dental Society [*Kenmore, New York*] [*A publication*]
Bull Electron Microsc Soc India ... Bulletin. Electron Microscope Society of India [*A publication*]
Bull Electrotech Lab ... Bulletin. Electrotechnical Laboratory [*Japan*] [*A publication*]
Bull Electrotech Lab (Tokyo) ... Bulletin. Electrotechnical Laboratory (Tokyo) [*A publication*]
Bull Eleventh Dist Dent Soc NY ... Bulletin. Eleventh District Dental Society [*Jamaica, New York*] [*A publication*]
Bull Endem Dis ... Bulletin of Endemic Diseases [*A publication*]
Bull Endem Dis (Baghdad) ... Bulletin of Endemic Diseases (Baghdad) [*A publication*]
Bull Endemic Diseases ... Bulletin of Endemic Diseases [*A publication*]
Bull Eng Geol Hydrogeol (Engl Transl) ... Bulletin of Engineering Geology and Hydrogeology (English Translation) [*Yugoslavia*] [*A publication*]
Bull Engrais ... Bulletin des Engrais [*A publication*]
Bull Eng Res Inst Kyoto Univ ... Bulletin. Engineering Research Institute of Kyoto University [*Japan*] [*A publication*]
Bull Enseign Public Gouvernement Cherifien ... Bulletin. Enseignement Public du Gouvernement Cherifien [*A publication*]
Bull Entomol ... Bulletin of Entomology [*A publication*]
Bull Entomol Res ... Bulletin of Entomological Research [*A publication*]
Bull Entomol Soc Am ... Bulletin. Entomological Society of America [*A publication*]
Bull Entomol Soc Amer ... Bulletin. Entomological Society of America [*A publication*]
Bull Entomol Soc Egypt ... Bulletin. Entomological Society of Egypt [*A publication*]
Bull Entomol Soc Egypt Econ Ser ... Bulletin. Entomological Society of Egypt. Economic Series [*A publication*]
Bull Entomol Soc Nigeria ... Bulletin. Entomological Society of Nigeria [*A publication*]
Bull Ent Res ... Bulletin of Entomological Research [*A publication*]
Bull Ent Soc Am ... Bulletin. Entomological Society of America [*A publication*]
Bull Ent Soc Egypt Econ Ser ... Bulletin. Entomological Society of Egypt. Economic Series [*A publication*]
Bull Envir Contam Toxic ... Bulletin of Environmental Contamination and Toxicology [*A publication*]
Bull Environ Contam ... Bulletin of Environmental Contamination and Toxicology [*A publication*]
Bull Environ Contam Toxicol ... Bulletin of Environmental Contamination and Toxicology [*A publication*]
Bull Environ Pollut Control Res Cent Shizuoka Prefect ... Bulletin. Environmental Pollution Control and Research Center. Shizuoka Prefecture [*A publication*]
Bull Environ Sci ... Bulletin of Environmental Sciences [*South Korea*] [*A publication*]
Bull Environ Sci ... Bulletin of Environmental Sciences. Hanyang University [*Republic of Korea*] [*A publication*]
Bull Epizoot Dis Afr ... Bulletin of Epizootic Diseases of Africa [*A publication*]
Bull Equine Res Inst ... Bulletin. Equine Research Institute [*A publication*]
Buller MSS ... [*J.*] Buller's Paper Books, Lincoln's Inn Library [*A publication*]   (DLA)
Buller NP ... Buller's Law of Nisi Prius [*England*] [*A publication*]   (DLA)
Bull Escher Wyss ... Bulletin Escher Wyss [*A publication*]

Bull Essex Cty Dent Soc ... Bulletin. Essex County [*New Jersey*] Dental Society [*A publication*]
BullETHS ... Bulletin. Evangelical Theological Society [*Wheaton, IL*] [*Later, Journal. Evangelical Theological Society*] [*A publication*]
Bulletin-AQQUA ... Bulletin. Association Quebecoise pour l'Etude du Quaternaire [*A publication*]
Bulletin Comp L ... Bulletin. Comparative Law Bureau [*A publication*]   (DLA)
Bulletin de Liaison ... Bulletin de Liaison. Centre d'Etudes des Peintures Murales Romaines [*A publication*]
Bulletin Singapore Natl Inst Chem ... Bulletin. Singapore National Institute of Chemistry [*A publication*]
Bull Etud Commun Mediter ... Bulletin de l'Etude en Commun de la Mediterranee [*A publication*]
Bull Etud Orient ... Bulletin d'Etudes Orientales [*A publication*]
Bull Etud Rech Tech ... Bulletin d'Etudes et de Recherches Techniques [*A publication*]
Bull Eur Assoc Theor Comput Sci ... Bulletin. European Association for Theoretical Computer Science [*A publication*]
Bull Eur Chiro Union ... Bulletin. European Chiropractors' Union [*A publication*]
Bull Eur Communities ... Bulletin. European Communities [*Luxembourg*] [*A publication*]
Bull Eur Communities Suppl ... Bulletin. European Communities. Supplement [*Luxembourg*] [*A publication*]
Bull Eur Physiopathol Respir ... Bulletin Europeen de Physiopathologie Respiratoire [*A publication*]
Bull Eur South Obs ... Bulletin. European Southern Observatory [*West Germany*] [*A publication*]
Bull Exp Biol Med ... Bulletin of Experimental Biology and Medicine [*A publication*]
Bull Exp Biol Med (Eng Transl Byull Eksp Biol Med) ... Bulletin of Experimental Biology and Medicine (English Translation of Byulleten' Eksperimental'noi Biologii i Meditsiny) [*A publication*]
Bull Exp Farm Coll Agr Ehime Univ ... Bulletin. Experimental Farm College of Agriculture. Ehime University [*A publication*]
Bull Exp Fms Brch Dep Agric (Can) ... Bulletin. Experimental Farms Branch. Department of Agriculture (Canada) [*A publication*]
Bull Exp For Tokyo Univ Agric Technol ... Bulletin of the Experiment Forest. Tokyo University of Agriculture and Technology [*A publication*]
Bull Exp Stn Horse Breed (Slatinany) ... Bulletin. Experimental Station for Horse Breeding (Slatinany) [*A publication*]
Bull Fac Agric Cairo Univ ... Bulletin. Faculty of Agriculture. Cairo University [*A publication*]
Bull Fac Agric Hirosaki Univ ... Bulletin. Faculty of Agriculture. Hirosaki University [*A publication*]
Bull Fac Agric Kagoshima Univ ... Bulletin. Faculty of Agriculture. Kagoshima University [*A publication*]
Bull Fac Agric Meiji Univ ... Bulletin. Faculty of Agriculture. Meiji University [*A publication*]
Bull Fac Agric Mie Univ ... Bulletin. Faculty of Agriculture. Mie University [*A publication*]
Bull Fac Agric Miyazaki Univ ... Bulletin. Faculty of Agriculture. Miyazaki University [*A publication*]
Bull Fac Agric Niigata Univ ... Bulletin. Faculty of Agriculture. Niigata University [*A publication*]
Bull Fac Agric Saga Univ ... Bulletin. Faculty of Agriculture. Saga University [*A publication*]
Bull Fac Agric Sci (Mosonmagyarovar Hung) ... Bulletin. Faculty of Agricultural Sciences (Mosonmagyarovar, Hungary) [*A publication*]
Bull Fac Agric Shimane Univ ... Bulletin. Faculty of Agriculture. Shimane University [*A publication*]
Bull Fac Agric Shizuoka Univ ... Bulletin. Faculty of Agriculture. Shizuoka University [*A publication*]
Bull Fac Agric Tamagawa Univ ... Bulletin. Faculty of Agriculture. Tamagawa University [*A publication*]
Bull Fac Agric Tokyo Univ Agric Technol ... Bulletin. Faculty of Agriculture. Tokyo University of Agriculture and Technology [*A publication*]
Bull Fac Agric Tottori Univ ... Bulletin. Faculty of Agriculture. Tottori University [*A publication*]
Bull Fac Agric Univ Miyazaki ... Bulletin. Faculty of Agriculture. University of Miyazaki [*A publication*]
Bull Fac Agric Yamaguti Univ ... Bulletin. Faculty of Agriculture. Yamaguti University [*A publication*]
Bull Fac Agr Kagoshima Univ ... Bulletin. Faculty of Agriculture. Kagoshima University [*A publication*]
Bull Fac Agr Meiji Univ ... Bulletin. Faculty of Agriculture. Meiji University [*A publication*]
Bull Fac Agr Niigata Univ ... Bulletin. Faculty of Agriculture. Niigata University [*A publication*]
Bull Fac Agr Shimane Univ ... Bulletin. Faculty of Agriculture. Shimane University [*A publication*]
Bull Fac Agr Shizuoka Univ ... Bulletin. Faculty of Agriculture. Shizuoka University [*A publication*]
Bull Fac Agr Univ Miyazaki ... Bulletin. Faculty of Agriculture. University of Miyazaki [*A publication*]
Bull Fac Agr Yamaguchi Univ ... Bulletin. Faculty of Agriculture. Yamaguchi University [*A publication*]

Bull Fac Bioresour Mie Univ ... Bulletin. Faculty of Bioresources. Mie University [*A publication*]

Bull Fac Ed Kagoshima Univ Natur Sci ... Bulletin. Faculty of Education. Kagoshima University. Natural Science [*A publication*]

Bull Fac Educ Chiba Univ ... Bulletin. Faculty of Education. Chiba University [*A publication*]

Bull Fac Educ Hirosaki Univ ... Bulletin. Faculty of Education. Hirosaki University [*A publication*]

Bull Fac Educ Hiroshima Univ ... Bulletin. Faculty of Education. Hiroshima University [*A publication*]

Bull Fac Educ Hiroshima Univ Part 3 (Sci Tech) ... Bulletin. Faculty of Education. Hiroshima University. Part 3 (Science and Technology) [*A publication*]

Bull Fac Educ Kanazawa Univ Nat Sci ... Bulletin. Faculty of Education. Kanazawa University. Natural Science [*A publication*]

Bull Fac Educ Kobe Univ ... Bulletin. Faculty of Education. Kobe University [*A publication*]

Bull Fac Educ Kochi Univ Ser 3 ... Bulletin. Faculty of Education. Kochi University. Series 3 [*A publication*]

Bull Fac Educ Univ Kagoshima Nat Sci ... Bulletin. Faculty of Education. University of Kagoshima. Natural Science [*A publication*]

Bull Fac Educ Utsunomiya Univ Sect 2 ... Bulletin. Faculty of Education. Utsunomiya University. Section 2 [*A publication*]

Bull Fac Educ Wakayama Univ Nat Sci ... Bulletin. Faculty of Education. Wakayama University. Natural Science [*A publication*]

Bull Fac Educ Yamaguchi Univ ... Bulletin. Faculty of Education. Yamaguchi University [*A publication*]

Bull Fac Ed Univ Kagoshima ... Bulletin. Faculty of Education. University of Kagoshima [*A publication*]

Bull Fac Ed Utsunomiya Univ Sect 2 ... Bulletin. Faculty of Education. Utsunomiya University. Section 2 [*A publication*]

Bull Fac Ed Wakayama Univ Natur Sci ... Wakayama University. Faculty of Education. Bulletin. Natural Science [*A publication*]

Bull Fac Eng Alexandria Univ ... Bulletin. Faculty of Engineering. Alexandria University [*Egypt*] [*A publication*]

Bull Fac Eng Cairo Univ ... Bulletin. Faculty of Engineering. Cairo University [*A publication*]

Bull Fac Eng Hiroshima Univ ... Bulletin. Faculty of Engineering. Hiroshima University [*A publication*]

Bull Fac Eng Hokkaido Univ ... Bulletin. Faculty of Engineering. Hokkaido University [*A publication*]

Bull Fac Eng Ibaraki Univ ... Bulletin. Faculty of Engineering. Ibaraki University [*A publication*]

Bull Fac Eng Miyazaki Univ ... Bulletin. Faculty of Engineering. Miyazaki University [*A publication*]

Bull Fac Engrg Hiroshima Univ ... Bulletin. Faculty of Engineering. Hiroshima University [*A publication*]

Bull Fac Engrg Miyazaki Univ ... Bulletin. Faculty of Engineering. Miyazaki University [*A publication*]

Bull Fac Eng Tokushima Univ ... Bulletin. Faculty of Engineering. Tokushima University [*A publication*]

Bull Fac Eng Toyama Univ ... Bulletin. Faculty of Engineering. Toyama University [*Japan*] [*A publication*]

Bull Fac Eng Univ Alexandria Chem Eng ... Bulletin. Faculty of Engineering. University of Alexandria. Chemical Engineering [*Egypt*] [*A publication*]

Bull Fac Eng Univ Alexandria Eng Chem Eng ... Bulletin. Faculty of Engineering. University of Alexandria. Engineering. Chemical Engineering [*A publication*]

Bull Fac Eng Yokohama Natl Univ ... Bulletin. Faculty of Engineering. Yokohama National University [*A publication*]

Bull Fac Eng Yokohama Univ ... Bulletin. Faculty of Engineering. Yokohama University [*A publication*]

Bull Fac Fish Hokkaido Univ ... Bulletin. Faculty of Fisheries. Hokkaido University [*A publication*]

Bull Fac Fish Mie Univ ... Bulletin. Faculty of Fisheries. Mie University [*A publication*]

Bull Fac Fish Nagasaki Univ ... Bulletin. Faculty of Fisheries. Nagasaki University [*Japan*] [*A publication*]

Bull Fac For Univ BC ... Bulletin. Faculty of Forestry. University of British Columbia [*A publication*]

Bull Fac Gen Ed Gifu Univ ... Gifu University. Faculty of General Education. Bulletin [*A publication*]

Bull Fac Gen Educ Utsunomiya Univ Sect 2 ... Bulletin. Faculty of General Education. Utsunomiya University. Section 2 [*A publication*]

Bull Fac Home Life Sci Fukuoka Women's Univ ... Bulletin. Faculty of Home Life Science. Fukuoka Women's University [*A publication*]

Bull Fac Lib Arts Ibaraki Univ (Nat Sci) ... Bulletin. Faculty of Liberal Arts. Ibaraki University (Natural Science) [*A publication*]

Bull Fac Med Istanbul ... Bulletin. Faculte de Medecine d'Istanbul [*A publication*]

Bull Fac Pharm Cairo Univ ... Bulletin. Faculty of Pharmacy. Cairo University [*A publication*]

Bull Fac Pharm Kinki Univ ... Bulletin. Faculty of Pharmacy. Kinki University [*A publication*]

Bull Fac Sch Educ Hiroshima Univ Part I ... Bulletin. Faculty of School Education. Hiroshima University. Part I [*A publication*]

Bull Fac Sch Educ Hiroshima Univ Part II ... Bulletin. Faculty of School Education. Hiroshima University. Part II [*A publication*]

Bull Fac School Ed Hiroshima Univ Part II ... Bulletin. Faculty of School Education. Hiroshima University. Part II [*A publication*]

Bull Fac Sci Alexandria Univ ... Bulletin. Faculty of Science. Alexandria University [*A publication*]

Bull Fac Sci Assiut Univ ... Bulletin. Faculty of Science. Assiut University [*A publication*]

Bull Fac Sci (Cairo) ... Bulletin. Faculty of Science (Cairo) [*A publication*]

Bull Fac Sci Cairo Univ ... Bulletin. Faculty of Science. Cairo University [*A publication*]

Bull Fac Sci Eng Chuo Univ ... Bulletin. Faculty of Science and Engineering. Chuo University [*A publication*]

Bull Fac Sci Engrg Chuo Univ ... Bulletin. Faculty of Science and Engineering. Chuo University [*A publication*]

Bull Fac Sci Ibaraki Univ Ser A ... Bulletin. Faculty of Science. Ibaraki University. Series A. Mathematics [*A publication*]

Bull Fac Sci Ibaraki Univ Series A ... Bulletin. Faculty of Science. Ibaraki University. Series A. Mathematics [*A publication*]

Bull Fac Sci King Abdul Aziz Univ ... Bulletin. Faculty of Science. King Abdul Aziz University [*A publication*]

Bull Fac Sci Riyad Univ ... Bulletin. Faculty of Science. Riyad University. Series II [*A publication*]

Bull Fac Sci Univ Fr Chin Peiping ... Bulletin. Faculte des Sciences. Universite Franco-Chinoise de Peiping [*A publication*]

Bull Fac Textile Fibers Kyoto Univ Ind Arts Textile Fibers ... Bulletin. Faculty of Textile Fibers. Kyoto University of Industrial Arts and Textile Fibers [*A publication*]

Bull Far Eastern Antiquities ... Bulletin. Museum of Far Eastern Antiquities [*Stockholm*] [*A publication*]

Bull Farm Manage Land Util Ser H ... Bulletin. Farm Management and Land Utilization. Series H [*A publication*]

Bull Farouk I Univ Fac Arts ... Bulletin. Farouk I University. Faculty of Arts [*Cairo*] [*A publication*]

Bull Far Seas Fish Res Lab (Shimizu) ... Bulletin. Far Seas Fisheries Research Laboratory (Shimizu) [*A publication*]

Bull Fed Belg Soc Sci ... Bulletin. Federation Belge des Societes de Sciences Mathematiques, Physiques, Chimiques, Naturelles, Medicales, et Appliquees [*A publication*]

Bull Fed Ind Chim Bel ... Bulletin. Federation des Industries Chimiques de Belgique [*A publication*]

Bull Fed Int Assoc Chim Text Couleur ... Bulletin. Federation Internationale des Associations des Chimistes du Textile et de la Couleur [*A publication*]

Bull Fed Min Agr (Salisbury) ... Bulletin. Federal Ministry of Agriculture (Salisbury) [*A publication*]

Bull Fed Soc Gynecol Obstet Lang Fr ... Bulletin. Federation des Societes de Gynecologie et d'Obstetrique de Langue Francaise [*A publication*]

Bull Fed Soc Hist Nat Franche-Comte ... Bulletin. Federation des Societes d'Histoire Naturelle de Franche-Comte [*A publication*]

Bull Field Geol Club South Aust ... Bulletin. Field Geology Club of South Australia [*A publication*]

Bull Fifth Dist Dent Soc (Fresno) ... Bulletin. Fifth District Dental Society (Fresno) [*California*] [*A publication*]

Bull Fifth Dist Dent Soc State NY ... Bulletin. Fifth District Dental Society of the State of New York [*Syracuse, NY*] [*A publication*]

Bull Fil Soc Biol Paris ... Bulletin. Filiales de la Societe de Biologie de Paris [*A publication*]

Bull First Agron Div Tokai-Kinki Nat Agr Exp Sta ... Bulletin. First Agronomy Division. Tokai-Kinki National Agricultural Experiment Station [*A publication*]

Bull First Agron Div Tokai-Kinki Natl Agric Exp Stn ... Bulletin. First Agronomy Division. Tokai-Kinki National Agricultural Experiment Station [*A publication*]

Bull Fish Exp Stn Gov Gen Chosen Ser B ... Bulletin. Fishery Experiment Station. Government General of Chosen. Series B [*A publication*]

Bull Fish Res Board Can ... Bulletin. Fisheries Research Board of Canada [*A publication*]

Bull Fish Res Dev ... Bulletin of Fisheries Research and Development [*A publication*]

Bull Fish Res Stn (Ceylon) ... Bulletin. Fisheries Research Station (Ceylon) [*A publication*]

Bull Fla Agr Exp Sta ... Bulletin. Florida Agricultural Experiment Station [*A publication*]

Bull Fla Agric Exp Stn ... Bulletin. Florida Agricultural Experiment Station [*A publication*]

Bull Fla Agric Ext Serv ... Bulletin. Florida Agricultural Extension Service [*A publication*]

Bull Fla Dep Agric ... Bulletin. Florida Department of Agriculture [*A publication*]

Bull Fla Dept Agr Div Plant Ind ... Bulletin. Florida Department of Agriculture. Division of Plant Industry [*A publication*]

Bull Fla State Mus Biol Sci ... Bulletin. Florida State Museum. Biological Sciences [*A publication*]

Bull Fla Univ Agr Exp Sta ... Bulletin. Florida University. Agricultural Experiment Station [*A publication*]

Bull Fogg Art Mus ... Bulletin. Fogg Art Museum [*A publication*]

Bull Fonds Rech For Univ Laval ... Bulletin. Fonds de Recherches Forestieres. Universite Laval [*A publication*]

Bull Food Ind Exp Stn Hiroshima Prefect ... Bulletin. Food Industrial Experiment Station. Hiroshima Prefecture [*A publication*]

Bull For Comm (Lond) ... Bulletin. Forestry Commission (London) [*A publication*]
Bull For Comm Tasm ... Bulletin. Forestry Commission of Tasmania [*A publication*]
Bull For Comm Vict ... Bulletin. Forests Commission of Victoria [*A publication*]
Bull For Dep (Uganda) ... Bulletin. Forest Department. Kampala (Uganda) [*A publication*]
Bull For Dep W Aust ... Bulletin. Forests Department of Western Australia [*A publication*]
Bull For Dep West Aust ... Bulletin. Forests Department of Western Australia [*A publication*]
Bull Ford For Cent ... Bulletin. Ford Forestry Center [*A publication*]
Bull Forest Comm Vict ... Bulletin. Forests Commission of Victoria [*A publication*] (APTA)
Bull Forest Dep WA ... Bulletin. Forests Department of Western Australia [*A publication*] (APTA)
Bull Forests Comm Tasm ... Bulletin. Forests Commission of Tasmania [*A publication*] (APTA)
Bull Forests Dep West Aust ... Bulletin. Forests Department of Western Australia [*A publication*] (APTA)
Bull For Exp Sta (Meguro) ... Bulletin. Government Forest Experiment Station (Meguro) [*A publication*]
Bull For For Prod Res Inst ... Bulletin. Forestry and Forest Products Research Institute [*A publication*]
Bull For Prod Res (Lond) ... Bulletin. Forest Products Research. Ministry of Technology (London) [*A publication*]
Bull For Timb Bur ... Bulletin. Forestry and Timber Bureau [*A publication*] (APTA)
Bull For Timb Bur (Aust) ... Bulletin. Forestry and Timber Bureau (Canberra, Australia) [*A publication*]
Bull Fouad I Univ Fac Arts ... Bulletin. Fouad I University. Faculty of Arts [*Giza*] [*A publication*]
Bull Foundry Abstr Br Cast Iron Res Assoc ... Bulletin and Foundry Abstracts. British Cast Iron Research Association [*A publication*]
Bull Franc Piscicult ... Bulletin Francais de Pisciculture [*A publication*]
Bull Freshwater Fish Res Lab (Tokyo) ... Bulletin. Freshwater Fisheries Research Laboratory (Tokyo) [*A publication*]
Bull Freshw Fish Res Lab (Tokyo) ... Bulletin. Freshwater Fisheries Research Laboratory (Tokyo) [*A publication*]
Bull Friends Hist Ass ... Bulletin. Friends Historical Association [*A publication*]
Bull Frnds Hist Assn ... Bulletin. Friends Historical Association [*Philadelphia*] [*A publication*]
Bull Fr Piscic ... Bulletin Francais de Pisciculture [*A publication*]
Bull Fruit Tree Res Stn Minist Agric For Ser E (Akitsu) ... Bulletin. Fruit Tree Research Station. Ministry of Agriculture and Forestry. Series E (Akitsu) [*A publication*]
Bull Fruit Tree Res Stn Ser A (Hiratsuka) ... Bulletin. Fruit Tree Research Station. Series A (Hiratsuka) [*A publication*]
Bull Fruit Tree Res Stn Ser A (Yatabe) ... Bulletin. Fruit Tree Research Station. Series A (Yatabe) [*A publication*]
Bull Fruit Tree Res Stn Ser B (Okitsu) ... Bulletin. Fruit Tree Research Station. Series B (Okitsu) [*A publication*]
Bull Fruit Tree Res Stn Ser C (Morioka) ... Bulletin. Fruit Tree Research Station. Series C (Morioka) [*A publication*]
Bull Fruit Tree Res Stn Ser D (Kuchinotsu) ... Bulletin. Fruit Tree Research Station. Series D (Kuchinotsu) [*A publication*]
Bull Fruit Tree Res Stn Ser E (Akitsu) ... Bulletin. Fruit Tree Research Station. Series E (Akitsu) [*A publication*]
Bull Ft Wayne Med Soc ... Bulletin. Fort Wayne Medical Society [*Indiana*] [*A publication*]
Bull Fuel Res Inst S Afr ... Bulletin. Fuel Research Institute of South Africa [*A publication*]
Bull Fuji Women's Coll ... Bulletin. Fuji Women's College [*A publication*]
Bull Fukuoka Agr Exp Stn ... Bulletin. Fukuoka Agricultural Experiment Station [*A publication*]
Bull Fukuokaken For Exp Sta ... Bulletin. Fukuokaken Forest Experiment Station [*A publication*]
Bull Fukuoka Pref Agr Exp Sta ... Bulletin. Fukuoka Prefectural Agricultural Experiment Station [*A publication*]
Bull Fukuoka Ringyo Shikenjo ... Bulletin. Fukuoka. Ringyo Shikenjo [*A publication*]
Bull Fukuoka Univ Ed 3 ... Bulletin. Fukuoka University of Education. Part 3. Natural Sciences [*A publication*]
Bull Fukuoka Univ Educ Part III Math Nat Sci Technol ... Bulletin. Fukuoka University of Education. Part III. Mathematics, Natural Sciences, and Technology [*A publication*]
Bull Fukuoka Univ Educ Part 3 Nat Sci ... Bulletin. Fukuoka University of Education. Part 3. Natural Sciences [*A publication*]
Bull Fukushima Prefect Fish Exp Stn ... Bulletin. Fukushima Prefectural Fisheries Experimental Station [*A publication*]
Bull GA Acad Sci ... Bulletin. Georgia Academy of Science [*A publication*]
Bull GA Agr Exp Sta ... Bulletin. Georgia Agricultural Experiment Station [*A publication*]
Bull GA Agric Exp Stn ... Bulletin. Georgia Agricultural Experiment Station [*A publication*]
Bull Galenica ... Bulletin Galenica [*A publication*]
Bull Gard Club Amer ... Bulletin. Garden Club of America [*A publication*]
Bull GB For Prod Res ... Bulletin. Great Britain Forest Products Research [*A publication*]

Bull Geisinger Med Cent ... Bulletin. Geisinger Medical Center [*A publication*]
Bull Gen Ed Dokkyo Univ School Medicine ... Bulletin of General Education. Dokkyo University. School of Medicine [*A publication*]
Bull Genessee County Med Soc ... Bulletin. Genessee County Medical Society [*Michigan*] [*A publication*]
Bull Genet ... Bulletin of Genetics [*China*] [*A publication*]
Bull Gen Therap (Paris) ... Bulletin General de Therapeutique Medicale, Chirurgicale, et Obstetricale (Paris) [*A publication*]
Bull Geochem Soc India ... Bulletin. Geochemical Society of India [*A publication*]
Bull Geod ... Bulletin Geodesique [*A publication*]
Bull Geodesique ... Bulletin Geodesique [*A publication*]
Bull Geogr Hist ... Bulletin de Geographie Historique et Descriptive [*A publication*]
Bull Geogr Soc Phila ... Bulletin. Geographical Society of Philadelphia [*A publication*]
Bull Geogr Surv Inst ... Bulletin. Geographical Survey Institute [*A publication*]
Bull Geol Inst Bulg Acad Sci Ser Geotecton ... Bulletin. Geological Institute. Bulgarian Academy of Sciences. Series Geotectonics [*A publication*]
Bull Geol Inst Univ Upps ... Bulletin. Geological Institutions of the University of Uppsala [*A publication*]
Bull Geol Inst Univ Ups ... Bulletin. Geologiska Institut. Universitet Upsala [*A publication*]
Bull Geol Miner Resour Dep (Sudan) ... Bulletin. Geological and Mineral Resources Department (Sudan) [*A publication*]
Bull Geol Min Metall Soc India ... Bulletin. Geological, Mining, and Metallurgical Society of India [*A publication*]
Bull Geol Min Metall Soc Liberia ... Bulletin. Geological, Mining, and Metallurgical Society of Liberia [*A publication*]
Bull Geol Soc Am ... Bulletin. Geological Society of America [*A publication*]
Bull Geol Soc Amer ... Bulletin. Geological Society of America [*A publication*]
Bull Geol Soc Am Part 1 ... Bulletin. Geological Society of America. Part 1 [*A publication*]
Bull Geol Soc China ... Bulletin. Geological Society of China [*A publication*]
Bull Geol Soc Den ... Bulletin. Geological Society of Denmark [*A publication*]
Bull Geol Soc Denmark ... Bulletin. Geological Society of Denmark [*A publication*]
Bull Geol Soc Finl ... Bulletin. Geological Society of Finland [*A publication*]
Bull Geol Soc Malays ... Bulletin. Geological Society of Malaysia [*A publication*]
Bull Geol Soc Turk ... Bulletin. Geological Society of Turkey [*A publication*]
Bull Geol Surv Can ... Bulletin. Geological Survey of Canada [*A publication*]
Bull Geol Surv Dep (Botswana) ... Bulletin. Geological Survey Department (Republic of Botswana) [*A publication*]
Bull Geol Surv Dep (Malawi) ... Bulletin. Geological Survey Department (Malawi) [*A publication*]
Bull Geol Surv Div (Jamaica) ... Bulletin. Geological Survey Division (Jamaica) [*A publication*]
Bull Geol Surv Div (Solomon Isl) ... Bulletin. Geological Survey Division (Solomon Islands) [*A publication*]
Bull Geol Surv G ... Bulletin. Geological Survey of Georgia [*A publication*]
Bull Geol Surv GB ... Bulletin. Geological Survey of Great Britain [*A publication*]
Bull Geol Surv Georgia ... Bulletin. Geological Survey of Georgia [*United States*] [*A publication*]
Bull Geol Surv Gr Brit ... Bulletin. Geological Survey of Great Britain [*A publication*]
Bull Geol Surv Greenland ... Bulletin. Geological Survey of Greenland [*A publication*]
Bull Geol Surv Guyana ... Bulletin. Geological Survey of Guyana [*A publication*]
Bull Geol Surv India A ... Bulletin. Geological Survey of India. Series A. Economic Geology [*A publication*]
Bull Geol Surv India Ser B ... Bulletins. Geological Survey of India. Series B. Engineering Geology and Ground Water [*A publication*]
Bull Geol Surv Indones ... Bulletin. Geological Survey of Indonesia [*A publication*]
Bull Geol Surv Irel ... Bulletin. Geological Survey of Ireland [*A publication*]
Bull Geol Surv Israel ... Bulletin. Geological Survey of Israel [*A publication*]
Bull Geol Surv Jap ... Bulletin. Geological Survey of Japan [*A publication*]
Bull Geol Surv Jpn ... Bulletin. Geological Survey of Japan [*A publication*]
Bull Geol Surv NSW ... Bulletin. Geological Survey of New South Wales [*A publication*]
Bull Geol Surv Prague ... Bulletin. Geological Survey of Prague [*A publication*]
Bull Geol Surv Rhod ... Bulletin. Geological Survey of Rhodesia [*A publication*]
Bull Geol Surv S Afr ... Bulletin. Geological Survey of South Africa [*A publication*]
Bull Geol Surv S Aust ... Bulletin. Geological Survey of South Australia [*A publication*]
Bull Geol Surv South Aust ... Geological Survey of South Australia. Bulletin [*A publication*] (APTA)
Bull Geol Surv Taiwan ... Bulletin. Geological Survey of Taiwan [*A publication*]
Bull Geol Surv Tanz ... Bulletin. Geological Survey of Tanzania [*A publication*]

Bull Geol Surv Tas ... Geological Survey of Tasmania. Bulletin [*A publication*] (APTA)

Bull Geol Surv Tasm ... Geological Survey of Tasmania. Bulletin [*A publication*] (APTA)

Bull Geol Surv Vic ... Geological Survey of Victoria. Bulletin [*A publication*] (APTA)

Bull Geol Surv Vict ... Geological Survey of Victoria. Bulletin [*A publication*] (APTA)

Bull Geol Surv West Aust ... Bulletin. Geological Survey of Western Australia [*A publication*]

Bull Geophys ... Bulletin de Geophysique [*A publication*]

Bull Geophys Obs Haile Sellassie I Univ ... Bulletin. Geophysical Observatory. Haile Sellassie I University [*Ethiopia*] [*A publication*]

Bull Georgetown Univ Med Cent ... Bulletin. Georgetown University Medical Center [*A publication*]

Bull Geotherm Resour Counc (Davis Calif) ... Bulletin. Geothermal Resources Council (Davis, California) [*A publication*]

Bull Ghana Geol Surv ... Bulletin. Ghana Geological Survey [*A publication*]

Bull Gifu College E ... Bulletin. Gifu College of Education [*A publication*]

Bull Gifu College Ed ... Bulletin. Gifu College of Education [*A publication*]

Bull Gov Chem Lab West Aust ... Western Australia. Government Chemical Laboratories. Bulletin [*A publication*] (APTA)

Bull Gov For Exp Stn (Tokyo) ... Bulletin. Government Forest Experiment Station (Tokyo) [*A publication*]

Bull Gov Ind Res Inst (Osaka) ... Bulletin. Government Industrial Research Institute (Osaka) [*A publication*]

Bull Govt Chem Labs West Aust ... Western Australia. Government Chemical Laboratories. Bulletin [*A publication*] (APTA)

Bull Govt Forest Expt Sta ... Bulletin. Government Forest Experiment Station [*Tokyo*] [*A publication*]

Bull Grain Technol ... Bulletin of Grain Technology [*A publication*]

Bull Greene County Med Soc ... Bulletin. Greene County Medical Society [*Missouri*] [*A publication*]

Bull Greenville County Med Soc ... Bulletin. Greenville County Medical Society [*South Carolina*] [*A publication*]

Bull Groenl Geol Unders ... Bulletin. Groenlands Geologiske Undersoegelse [*Denmark*] [*A publication*]

Bull Gronl Geol Unders ... Bulletin. Groenlands Geologiske Undersoegelse [*A publication*]

Bull Groupe Fr Argiles ... Bulletin. Groupe Francais des Argiles [*A publication*]

Bull Groupe Fr Humidimetrie Neutron ... Bulletin. Groupe Francais d'Humidimetrie Neutronique [*A publication*]

Bull Groupe Fr Humidimetrie Neutronique ... Bulletin. Groupe Francais d'Humidimetrie Neutronique [*France*] [*A publication*]

Bull Groupe Trav Etud Equilibre Foret-Gibier ... Bulletin. Groupe de Travail pour l'Etude de l'Equilibre Foret-Gibier [*A publication*]

Bull Group Eur Rech Sci Stomatol Odontol ... Bulletin. Groupement Europeen pour la Recherche Scientifique en Stomatologie et Odontologie [*A publication*]

Bull Group Int Rech Sci Stomatol ... Bulletin. Groupement International pour la Recherche Scientifique en Stomatologie [*A publication*]

Bull Group Int Rech Sci Stomatol Odontol ... Bulletin. Groupement International pour la Recherche Scientifique en Stomatologie et Odontologie [*A publication*]

Bull Grpe Fr Argiles ... Bulletin. Groupe Francais des Argiles [*A publication*]

Bull GTV (Group Tech Vet) Dossiers Tech Vet ... Bulletin des GTV (Groupements Techniques Veterinaires). Dossiers Techniques Veterinaires [*A publication*]

Bull Guerre Biol Pharm ... Bulletin de Guerre des Biologistes Pharmaciens [*A publication*]

Bull Haffkine Inst ... Bulletin. Haffkine Institute [*A publication*]

Bull Harvard Med Alumni Ass ... Bulletin. Harvard Medical Alumni Association [*A publication*]

Bull Hatano Tob Exp Stn ... Bulletin. Hatano Tobacco Experiment Station [*A publication*]

Bull Hear Inst (Jpn) ... Bulletin. Heart Institute (Japan) [*A publication*]

Bull Heart Inst (Jpn) ... Bulletin. Heart Institute (Japan) [*A publication*]

Bull Hell Vet Med Soc ... Bulletin. Hellenic Veterinary Medical Society [*A publication*]

Bull Hennepin County Med Soc ... Bulletin. Hennepin County Medical Society [*Minnesota*] [*A publication*]

Bull Highw Res Bd ... Bulletin. Highway Research Board [*A publication*]

Bull Hiroshima Agric Coll ... Bulletin. Hiroshima Agricultural College [*A publication*]

Bull Hiroshima Food Res Inst ... Bulletin. Hiroshima Food Research Institute [*A publication*]

Bull Hiroshima Jogakuin Coll ... Bulletin. Hiroshima Jogakuin College [*A publication*]

Bull Hiroshima Prefect Agric Exp Stn ... Bulletin. Hiroshima Prefectural Agricultural Experiment Station [*A publication*]

Bull Hiroshima Prefect Inst Public Health ... Bulletin. Hiroshima Prefectural Institute of Public Health [*A publication*]

Bull Hisp ... Bulletin Hispanique [*A publication*]

Bull Hispanique ... Bulletin Hispanique [*A publication*]

Bull Hist Dent ... Bulletin of the History of Dentistry [*A publication*]

Bull Hist Med ... Bulletin of the History of Medicine [*A publication*]

Bull Hist Metal Group ... Bulletin. Historical Metallurgy Group [*A publication*]

Bull Histol Appl ... Bulletin d'Histologie Appliquee [*A publication*]

Bull Hoblitzelle Agric Lab Tex Res Found ... Bulletin. Hoblitzelle Agricultural Laboratory. Texas Research Foundation [*A publication*]

Bull Hoblitzelle Agr Lab Tex Res Found ... Bulletin. Hoblitzelle Agricultural Laboratory. Texas Research Foundation [*A publication*]

Bull Hokkaido For Exp Stn ... Bulletin. Hokkaido Forest Experiment Station [*A publication*]

Bull Hokkaido Pref Agr Exp Sta ... Bulletin. Hokkaido Prefectural Agricultural Experiment Station [*A publication*]

Bull Hokkaido Prefect Agric Exp Stn ... Bulletin. Hokkaido Prefectural Agricultural Experiment Station [*A publication*]

Bull Hokkaido Reg Fish Res Lab ... Bulletin. Hokkaido Regional Fisheries Research Laboratories [*A publication*]

Bull Hokkaido Underground Resour Invest ... Bulletin of Hokkaido Underground Resource Investigation [*Japan*] [*A publication*]

Bull Hokuriku Natl Agric Exp Stn ... Bulletin. Hokuriku National Agricultural Experiment Station [*A publication*]

Bull Hortic (Liege) ... Bulletin Horticole (Liege) [*A publication*]

Bull Hortic Res Stn (Minist Agric For) Ser A (Hiratsuka) ... Bulletin. Horticultural Research Station (Ministry of Agriculture and Forestry). Series A (Hiratsuka) [*A publication*]

Bull Hortic Res Stn (Minist Agric For) Ser B (Okitsu) ... Bulletin. Horticultural Research Station (Ministry of Agriculture and Forestry). Series B (Okitsu) [*A publication*]

Bull Hortic Res Stn (Minist Agric For) Ser C (Morioka) ... Bulletin. Horticultural Research Station (Ministry of Agriculture and Forestry). Series C (Morioka) [*A publication*]

Bull Hortic Res Stn (Minist Agric For) Ser D (Kurume) ... Bulletin. Horticultural Research Station (Ministry of Agriculture and Forestry). Series D (Kurume) [*A publication*]

Bull Hosp Joint Dis ... Bulletin. Hospital for Joint Diseases [*A publication*]

Bull Hosp Jt Dis ... Bulletin. Hospital for Joint Diseases [*A publication*]

Bull Hosp Jt Dis Orthop Inst ... Bulletin. Hospital for Joint Diseases. Orthopaedic Institute [*A publication*]

Bull Hot Spring Res Inst Kanagawa Prefect ... Bulletin. Hot Spring Research Institute. Kanagawa Prefecture [*A publication*]

Bull Hudson Cty Dent Soc ... Bulletin. Hudson County Dental Society [*A publication*]

Bull Hum Body Meas ... Bulletin of Human Body Measurement [*A publication*]

Bull Hunan Med Coll ... Bulletin. Hunan Medical College [*A publication*]

Bull Hydrobiol Res ... Bulletin of Hydrobiological Research [*A publication*]

Bull Hyg ..... Bulletin of Hygiene [*A publication*]

Bull Hyg Lab US Mar Hosp Serv ... Bulletin. Hygienic Laboratory. United States Marine Hospital Service [*A publication*]

Bull Hyg Lab US Pub Health and Mar Hosp Serv ... Bulletin. Hygienic Laboratory. United States Public Health and Marine Hospital Service [*A publication*]

Bull Hyg Lab US Pub Health Serv ... Bulletin. Hygienic Laboratory. United States Public Health Service [*A publication*]

Bull Hyg Prof ... Bulletin de l'Hygiene Professionnelle [*A publication*]

Bull Hyogo Pref Agr Exp Sta ... Bulletin. Hyogo Prefectural Agricultural Experiment Station [*A publication*]

Bull Hyogo Prefect Agric Cent Exp Ext Educ ... Bulletin. Hyogo Prefectural Agricultural Center for Experiment, Extension, and Education [*A publication*]

Bull Hyogo Prefect Agric Inst ... Bulletin. Hyogo Prefectural Agricultural Institute [*A publication*]

Bull Hyogo Prefect For Exp Stn ... Bulletin. Hyogo Prefectural Forest Experiment Station [*A publication*]

Bul Liaison et Info ... Bulletin de Liaison et d'Information [*A publication*]

Bull IBA ..... Bulletin. International Bar Association [*A publication*] (DLA)

Bull Ibaraki Prefect For Exp Stn ... Bulletin. Ibaraki Prefectural Forest Experiment Station [*A publication*]

Bull ICID ... Bulletin. International Commission on Irrigation and Drainage [*A publication*]

Bull ICJ ..... Bulletin. International Commission of Jurists [*A publication*] (DLA)

Bull Idaho Agr Exp Sta ... Bulletin. Idaho Agricultural Experiment Station [*A publication*]

Bull Idaho Bur Mines Geol ... Bulletin. Idaho Bureau of Mines and Geology [*A publication*]

Bull Idaho For Wildl Range Exp Stn ... Bulletin. Idaho Forest, Wildlife, and Range Experiment Station [*A publication*]

Bull Idaho Oreg Wash Agr Exp Sta US Dept Agr ... Bulletin. Idaho, Oregon, and Washington Agricultural Experiment Stations and US Department of Agriculture [*A publication*]

BULLIENT ... Bullientis [*Boiling*] [*Pharmacy*] (ROG)

Bull IFAL .. Bulletin. Institut Francais d'Amerique Latine [*A publication*]

Bull IFAN ... Bulletin. Institut Francais d'Afrique Noire [*A publication*]

Bull IFAO ... Bulletin. Institut Francais d'Archeologie Orientale [*A publication*]

Bull III .... Bulletin. Institut Intermediaire International [*A publication*] (DLA)

Bull Ill Agr Exp Sta ... Bulletin. Illinois Agricultural Experiment Station [*A publication*]

Bull Ill Agric Exp Sta ... Bulletin. University of Illinois. Agricultural Experiment Station [*A publication*]

Bull Ill Coop Crop Rep Serv ... Bulletin. Illinois Cooperative Crop Reporting Service [*A publication*]

Bull Ill State Geol Surv ... Bulletin. Illinois State Geological Survey [*A publication*]
Bull Ill St Geol Surv ... Bulletin. Illinois State Geological Survey [*A publication*]
Bull Ill St Lab Nat Hist ... Bulletin. Illinois State Laboratory of Natural History [*A publication*]
Bull Imp Bur Pastures Forage Crops ... Bulletin. Imperial Bureau of Pastures and Forage Crops [*A publication*]
Bull Imp Inst ... Bulletin. Imperial Institute [*London*] [*A publication*]
Bull Imp Inst (London) ... Bulletin. Imperial Institute (London) [*A publication*]
Bull Imp Seric Stn (Tokyo) ... Bulletin. Imperial Sericultural Station (Tokyo) [*A publication*]
Bull Indep Biol Lab (Kefar-Malal) ... Bulletin. Independent Biological Laboratories (Kefar-Malal) [*A publication*]
Bull Indian Coun Agric Res ... Bulletin. Indian Council of Agricultural Research [*A publication*]
Bull Indian Geol Ass ... Bulletin. Indian Geologists' Association [*A publication*]
Bull Indian Ind Res ... Bulletins. Indian Industrial Research [*A publication*]
Bull Indian Inst Hist Med ... Bulletin. Indian Institute of the History of Medicine [*A publication*]
Bull Indian Natl Sci Acad ... Bulletin. Indian National Science Academy [*A publication*]
Bull Indian Phytopathol Soc ... Bulletin. Indian Phytopathological Society [*A publication*]
Bull Indian Soc Earthqu Technol ... Bulletin. Indian Society of Earthquake Technology [*A publication*]
Bull Indian Soc Malar Commun Dis ... Bulletin. Indian Society for Malaria and Other Communicable Diseases [*A publication*]
Bull Indian Soc Soil Sci ... Bulletin. Indian Society of Soil Science [*A publication*]
Bull India Sect Electrochem Soc ... Bulletin. India Section. Electrochemical Society [*A publication*]
Bull Ind Res Cent Ehime Prefect ... Bulletin. Industrial Research Center of Ehime Prefecture [*A publication*]
Bull Ind Res Inst Ehime Prefect ... Bulletin. Industrial Research Institute of Ehime Prefecture [*A publication*]
Bull Ind Res Inst Kanagawa Prefect ... Bulletin. Industrial Research Institute of Kanagawa Prefecture [*Japan*] [*A publication*]
Bull Ind Techn ... Bulletin of Industrial Technology [*A publication*]
Bull Inf Appl Ind Radioelem ... Bulletin d'Information sur les Applications Industrielles des Radioelements [*A publication*]
Bull Inf Assoc Belge Dev Pac Energ At ... Bulletin d'Information. Association Belge pour le Developpement Pacifique de l'Energie Atomique [*Belgium*] [*A publication*]
Bull Inf Assoc Nat Serv Eau (Belg) ... Bulletin d'Information. Association Nationale des Services d'Eau (Belgium) [*A publication*]
Bull Inf Assoc Tech Energ Nucl ... Bulletin d'Information. Association Technique pour l'Energie Nucleaire [*A publication*]
Bull Inf Ass Tech Prod Util Energ Nucl ... Bulletin d'Information. Association Technique pour la Production et l'Utilisation de l'Energie Nucleaire [*A publication*]
Bull Inf ATEN ... Bulletin d'Information. ATEN [*Association Technique pour l'Energie Nucleaire*] [*France*] [*A publication*]
Bull Inf ATEN Suppl ... Bulletin d'Information. ATEN [*Association Technique pour l'Energie Nucleaire*]. Supplement [*France*] [*A publication*]
Bull Inf Bibliogr ... Bulletin d'Information et de Bibliographie [*A publication*]
Bull Inf Bur Natl Metrol ... Bulletin d'Information. Bureau National de Metrologie [*A publication*]
Bull Inf Cent Electr ... Bulletin d'Information des Centrales Electriques [*France*] [*A publication*]
Bull Inf Cent Natl Exploit Oceans ... Bulletin d'Information. Centre National pour l'Exploitation des Oceans [*France*] [*A publication*]
Bull Inf Centre Donnees Stellaires ... Bulletin d'Information. Centre de Donnees Stellaires [*A publication*]
Bull Inf CNEEMA (Cent Natl Etud Exp Mach Agric) ... Bulletin d'Information. CNEEMA (Centre National d'Etudes et d'Experimentation de Machinisme Agricole) [*A publication*]
Bull Inf Generateurs Isot ... Bulletin d'Information sur les Generateurs Isotopiques [*A publication*]
Bull Inf INEAC ... Bulletin d'Information. Institut National pour l'Etude Agronomique du Congo Belge [*A publication*]
Bull Inf Inst Text Fr Nord ... Bulletin d'Information. Institut Textile de France - Nord [*A publication*]
Bull Infirm Cathol Can ... Bulletin. Infirmieres Catholiques du Canada [*A publication*]
Bull Inf ITF Nord ... Bulletin d'Information. ITF [*Institut Textile de France*] Nord [*A publication*]
Bull Inf Minist Agric ... Bulletin d'Information. Ministere de l'Agriculture [*A publication*]
Bull Inform Inst Nat Etud Agron Congo (INEAC) ... Bulletin d'Information. Institut National pour l'Etude Agronomique du Congo Belge (INEAC) [*A publication*]
Bull Inform Inst Rebois Tunis ... Bulletin d'Information. Institut de Reboisement de Tunis [*A publication*]
Bull Inform Tech Centre Tech Bois ... Bulletin d'Informations Techniques. Centre Technique du Bois [*A publication*]

Bull Inf Rizic Fr ... Bulletin d'Information des Riziculteurs de France [*A publication*]
Bull Inf Sci Tech ... Bulletin d'Informations Scientifiques et Techniques [*A publication*]
Bull Inf Sci Tech Commis Energ At ... Bulletin d'Informations Scientifiques et Techniques. Commissariat a l'Energie Atomique [*France*] [*A publication*]
Bull Inf Sci & Tech (Paris) ... Bulletin d'Informations Scientifiques et Techniques (Paris) [*A publication*]
Bull Inf Stn Exp Avic Ploufragan ... Bulletin d'Information. Station Experimentale d'Aviculture de Ploufragan [*A publication*]
Bull Inf Tech Charbon Fr ... Bulletin d'Informations Techniques. Charbonages de France [*A publication*]
Bull Inf UGGI ... Bulletin d'Information. UGGI [*Union Geodesique et Geophysique Internationale*] [*A publication*]
Bull Inst Agric Res Rolling Land (Tokyo) ... Bulletin. Institute for Agricultural Research on Rolling Land (Tokyo) [*A publication*]
Bull Inst Agric Res Tohoku Univ ... Bulletin. Institute for Agricultural Research. Tohoku University [*A publication*]
Bull Inst Agron Gembloux ... Bulletin. Institut Agronomique et Stations de Recherches de Gembloux [*Belgium*] [*A publication*]
Bull Inst Agron Sta Rech Gembloux ... Bulletin. Institut Agronomique et Stations de Recherches de Gembloux [*A publication*]
Bull Inst Agron Stn Rech Gembloux ... Bulletin. Institut Agronomique et Stations de Recherches de Gembloux [*A publication*]
Bull Inst Agron Stn Rech Gembloux Hors Ser ... Bulletin. Institut Agronomique et Stations de Recherches de Gembloux. Hors Serie [*A publication*]
Bull Inst Agron Stns Rech Gembloux ... Bulletin. Institut Agronomique et Stations de Recherches de Gembloux [*A publication*]
Bull Inst Agr Res Tohoku Univ ... Bulletin. Institute for Agricultural Research. Tohoku University [*A publication*]
Bull Inst Appl Geol King Abdulaziz Univ ... Bulletin. Institute of Applied Geology. King Abdulaziz University [*Jeddah*] [*A publication*]
Bull Inst Arch ... Bulletin. Institute of Archaeology [*A publication*]
Bull Inst Archaeol Univ London ... Bulletin. Institute of Archaeology. University of London [*A publication*]
Bull Inst Archeol Liegeois ... Bulletin. Institut Archeologique Liegeois [*A publication*]
Bull Inst Arch Liegeois ... Bulletin. Institut Archeologique Liegeois [*A publication*]
Bull Inst At Energ Kyoto Univ ... Bulletin. Institute of Atomic Energy. Kyoto University [*Japan*] [*A publication*]
Bull Inst At Energy Kyoto Univ ... Bulletin. Institute of Atomic Energy. Kyoto University [*A publication*]
Bull Inst Balneother ... Bulletin. Institute of Balneotherapeutics [*Japan*] [*A publication*]
Bull Inst Basic Sci Inha Univ ... Bulletin. Institute for Basic Science. Inha University [*A publication*]
Bull Inst Chem Acad Sin ... Bulletin. Institute of Chemistry. Academia Sinica [*Taiwan*] [*A publication*]
Bull Inst Chem Res Kyoto Univ ... Bulletin. Institute for Chemical Research. Kyoto University [*A publication*]
Bull Inst Classic Stud ... Bulletin. Institute of Classical Studies. University of London [*A publication*]
Bull Inst Class Studies ... Bulletin. Institute of Classical Studies [*A publication*]
Bull Inst Cl St ... Bulletin. Institute of Classical Studies. University of London [*A publication*]
Bull Inst Const Med Kumamoto Univ ... Bulletin. Institute of Constitutional Medicine. Kumamoto University [*A publication*]
Bull Inst Corros Sci Technol ... Bulletin. Institute of Corrosion Science and Technology [*A publication*]
Bull Inst Desert Egypte ... Bulletin. Institut du Desert d'Egypte [*A publication*]
Bull Inst Egypt ... Bulletin. Institut d'Egypte [*A publication*]
Bull Inst Egypte ... Bulletin. Institut d'Egypte [*A publication*]
Bull Inst Email Vitrifie ... Bulletin. Institut de l'Email Vitrifie [*A publication*]
Bull Inst Eng ... Bulletin. Institution of Engineers [*A publication*]
Bull Inst Eng (India) ... Bulletin. Institution of Engineers (India) [*A publication*]
Bull Inst Filip Geol ... Bulletin. Institute of Filipino Geologists [*A publication*]
Bull Inst Fondam Afr Noire Ser A Sci Nat ... Bulletin. Institut Fondamental d'Afrique Noire. Serie A. Sciences Naturelles [*A publication*]
Bull Inst Fr Afr Noire ... Bulletin. Institut Francais d'Afrique Noire [*A publication*]
Bull Inst Fr Afr Noire Ser A Sci Nat ... Bulletin. Institut Francais d'Afrique Noire. Serie A. Sciences Naturelles [*A publication*]
Bull Inst Franc Archeol Orient ... Bulletin. Institut Francais d'Archeologie Orientale [*Cairo*] [*A publication*]
Bull Inst Fr Archeol Orient ... Bulletin. Institut Francais d'Archeologie Orientale [*A publication*]
Bull Inst Fr Cafe Cacao ... Bulletin. Institut Francais du Cafe et du Cacao [*A publication*]
Bull Inst Gas Technol ... Bulletin. Institute of Gas Technology [*A publication*]
Bull Inst Gen Psychol ... Bulletin. Institut General Psychologique [*A publication*]
Bull Inst Geol Bassin Aquitaine ... Bulletin. Institut de Geologie du Bassin d'Aquitaine [*A publication*]

Bull Inst Geol Geophys Res (Belgrade) Ser A ... Bulletin. Institute for Geological and Geophysical Research (Belgrade). Series A. Geology [*A publication*]

Bull Inst Geol Geophys Res (Belgrade) Ser B ... Bulletin. Institute for Geological and Geophysical Research (Belgrade). Series B. Engineering Geology and Hydrogeology [*A publication*]

Bull Inst Geol Geophys Res (Belgrade) Ser C ... Bulletin. Institute for Geological and Geophysical Research (Belgrade). Series C. Applied Geophysics [*A publication*]

Bull Inst Geol Geophys Res Ser A (Engl Transl) ... Bulletin. Institute for Geological and Geophysical Research. Series A. Geology (English Translation) [*A publication*]

Bull Inst Geol Geophys Res Ser B (Engl Trans) ... Bulletin. Institute for Geological and Geophysical Research. Series B. Engineering Geology and Hydrogeology (English Translation) [*A publication*]

Bull Inst Geol Geophys Res Ser C (Eng Trans) ... Bulletin. Institute for Geological and Geophysical Research. Series C. Applied Geophysics (English Translation) [*A publication*]

Bull Inst Geol Sci ... Bulletin. Institute of Geological Sciences [*A publication*]

Bull Inst Geol Univ Louis Pasteur Strasbourg ... Bulletin. Institut de Geologie. Universite Louis Pasteur de Strasbourg [*A publication*]

Bull Inst Geophys Natl Cent Univ ... Bulletin. Institute of Geophysics. National Central University [*Taiwan*] [*A publication*]

Bull Inst Hist Belge ... Bulletin. Institut Historique Belge de Rome [*A publication*]

Bull Inst Hist Belg Rome ... Bulletin. Institut Historique Belge de Rome [*A publication*]

Bull Inst Hist Med ... Bulletin. Institute of History of Medicine [*A publication*]

Bull Inst Hist Med Johns Hopk Univ ... Bulletin. Institute of History of Medicine. Johns Hopkins University [*A publication*]

Bull Inst Hist Res ... Bulletin. Institute of Historical Research [*A publication*]

Bull Inst Immunol Sci Hokkaido Univ ... Bulletin. Institute of Immunological Science. Hokkaido University [*A publication*]

Bull Inst Ind Soc Dev ... Bulletin. Institute for Industrial and Social Development [*South Korea*] [*A publication*]

Bull Inst Int Bibliogr ... Bulletin. Institut International de Bibliographie [*A publication*]

Bull Inst Internat Statist ... Bulletin. Institut International de Statistique [*A publication*]

Bull Inst Int Froid ... Bulletin. Institut International du Froid [*A publication*]

Bull Inst Int Froid Annexe ... Bulletin. Institut International du Froid. Annexe [*France*] [*A publication*]

Bull Inst Int Stat ... Bulletin. Institut International de Statistique [*A publication*]

Bull Inst Jam Sci Ser ... Bulletin. Institute of Jamaica. Science Series [*A publication*]

Bull Inst Jew St ... Bulletin. Institute of Jewish Studies [*A publication*]

Bull Inst Marit Trop Med Gdynia ... Bulletin. Institute of Maritime and Tropical Medicine in Gdynia [*A publication*]

Bull Inst Mar Med Gdansk ... Bulletin. Institute of Marine Medicine in Gdansk [*A publication*]

Bull Inst Mar Trop Med Gdynia ... Bulletin. Institute of Maritime and Tropical Medicine in Gdynia [*A publication*]

Bull Inst Math Acad Sinica ... Bulletin. Institute of Mathematics. Academia Sinica [*A publication*]

Bull Inst Math Appl ... Bulletin. Institute of Mathematics and Its Applications [*A publication*]

Bull Inst Med ... Bulletin. Instituts de Medecine [*A publication*]

Bull Inst Med Exp ... Bulletin. Institut de Medecine Experimentale [*A publication*]

Bull Inst Med Research FMS ... Bulletin. Institute for Medical Research. Federated Malay States [*A publication*]

Bull Inst Med Res (Kuala Lumpur) ... Bulletin. Institute for Medical Research (Kuala Lumpur) [*A publication*]

Bull Inst Med Res Malaya ... Bulletin. Institute for Medical Research of Malaya [*A publication*]

Bull Inst Med Res Univ Madr ... Bulletin. Institute for Medical Research. University of Madrid [*A publication*]

Bull Inst Met ... Bulletin. Institute of Metals [*A publication*]

Bull Inst Met Finish ... Bulletin. Institute of Metal Finishing [*A publication*]

Bull Inst Miner Deposits Chin Acad Geol Sci ... Bulletin. Institute of Mineral Deposits. Chinese Academy of Geological Sciences [*Beijing*] [*A publication*]

Bull Inst Min Metall ... Bulletin. Institution of Mining and Metallurgy [*A publication*]

Bull Inst Nat Educ Shiga Heights ... Bulletin. Institute of Natural Education in Shiga Heights [*A publication*]

Bull Inst Nat Genevois ... Bulletin. Institut National Genevois [*A publication*]

Bull Inst Natl Hyg (Paris) ... Bulletin. Institut National d'Hygiene (Paris) [*A publication*]

Bull Inst Natl Sante Rech Med (Paris) ... Bulletin. Institut National de la Sante et de la Recherche Medicale (Paris) [*A publication*]

Bull Inst Natl Sci Rech Oceanogr Peche ... Bulletin. Institut National Scientifique et Technique d'Oceanographie et de Peche [*A publication*]

Bull Inst Natl Sci Tech Oceanogr Peche Salammbo ... Bulletin. Institut National Scientifique et Technique d'Oceanographie et de Peche de Salammbo [*A publication*]

Bull Inst Nutr Bulg Acad Sci ... Bulletin. Institute of Nutrition. Bulgarian Academy of Sciences [*A publication*]

Bull Inst Obs Phys Globe Puy De Dome ... Bulletin. Institut et Observatoire Physique du Globe du Puy De Dome [*A publication*]

Bull Inst Oceanogr Fish ... Bulletin. Institute of Oceanography and Fisheries [*A publication*]

Bull Inst Oceanogr (Monaco) ... Bulletin. Institut Oceanographique (Monaco) [*A publication*]

Bull Inst Pap Chem ... Bulletin. Institute of Paper Chemistry [*A publication*]

Bull Inst Pasteur ... Bulletin. Institut Pasteur [*Paris*] [*A publication*]

Bull Inst Pasteur (Paris) ... Bulletin. Institut Pasteur (Paris) [*A publication*]

Bull Inst Peches Marit Maroc ... Bulletin. Institut des Peches Maritimes du Maroc [*A publication*]

Bull Inst Phys Chem Res ... Bulletin. Institute of Physical and Chemical Research [*A publication*]

Bull Inst Phys (Lond) ... Bulletin. Institute of Physics (London) [*A publication*]

Bull Inst Phys (Malays) ... Bulletin. Institute of Physics (Malaysia) [*A publication*]

Bull Inst Phys Univ Libre Bruxelles ... Bulletin. Institut de Physique. Universite Libre de Bruxelles [*Belgium*] [*A publication*]

Bull Inst Pin ... Bulletin. Institut du Pin [*A publication*]

Bull Inst Post Grad Med Educ Res ... Bulletin. Institute of Post Graduate Medical Education and Research [*A publication*]

Bull Inst Prov Coop Agr ... Bulletin. Institut Provincial de Cooperation Agricole [*A publication*]

Bull Inst Public Health (Tokyo) ... Bulletin. Institute of Public Health (Tokyo) [*A publication*]

Bull Inst Radiat Breed ... Bulletin. Institute of Radiation Breeding [*Japan*] [*A publication*]

Bull Inst R Sci Nat Belg ... Bulletin. Institut Royal des Sciences Naturelles de Belgique [*A publication*]

Bull Inst R Sci Nat Belg Biol ... Bulletin. Institut Royal des Sciences Naturelles de Belgique. Biologie [*A publication*]

Bull Inst R Sci Nat Belg Entomol ... Bulletin. Institut Royal des Sciences Naturelles de Belgique. Entomologie [*A publication*]

Bull Inst R Sci Nat Belg Sci Terre ... Bulletin. Institut Royal des Sciences Naturelles de Belgique. Sciences de la Terre [*A publication*]

Bull Instrum Nucl ... Bulletin d'Instrumentation Nucleaire [*A publication*]

Bull Inst Sanit Eng ... Bulletin. Institution of Sanitary Engineers [*A publication*]

Bull Inst Sci Natur Belg ... Bulletin. Institut Royal des Sciences Naturelles de Belgique [*A publication*]

Bull Inst Sociol Solvay ... Bulletin. Institut de Sociologie Solvay [*A publication*]

Bull Inst Space Aeronaut Sci Univ Tokyo ... Bulletin. Institute of Space and Aeronautical Science. University of Tokyo [*A publication*]

Bull Inst Space & Aeronaut Sci Univ Tokyo A ... Bulletin. Institute of Space and Aeronautical Science. University of Tokyo. A [*A publication*]

Bull Inst Space & Aeronaut Sci Univ Tokyo B ... Bulletin. Institute of Space and Aeronautical Science. University of Tokyo. B [*A publication*]

Bull Inst Tech Porc ... Bulletin. Institut Technique du Porc [*A publication*]

Bull Inst Text Fr ... Bulletin. Institut Textile de France [*A publication*]

Bull Inst Tropen Afd Agrar Onderz ... Bulletin. Instituut voor de Tropen Afdeling Agrarisch Onderzoek [*A publication*]

Bull Inst Verre ... Bulletin. Institut du Verre [*A publication*]

Bull Inst Vitreous Enamellers ... Bulletin. Institute of Vitreous Enamellers [*A publication*]

Bull Inst Zool Acad Sin (Taipei) ... Bulletin. Institute of Zoology. Academia Sinica (Taipei) [*A publication*]

Bull Int Acad Pol Sci Lett Cl Sci Math Nat Ser A ... Bulletin International. Academie Polonaise des Sciences et des Lettres. Classe des Sciences Mathematiques et Naturelles. Serie A. Sciences Mathematiques [*Poland*] [*A publication*]

Bull Int Acad Pol Sci Lett Cl Sci Math Nat Ser B ... Bulletin International. Academie Polonaise des Sciences et des Lettres. Classe des Sciences Mathematiques et Naturelles. Serie B. Sciences Naturelles [*A publication*]

Bull Int Acad Pol Sci Lett Cl Sci Math Nat Ser B 1 ... Bulletin International. Academie Polonaise des Sciences et des Lettres. Classe des Sciences Mathematiques et Naturelles. Serie B-1. Botanique [*A publication*]

Bull Int Acad Pol Sci Lett Cl Sci Math Nat Ser B-2 ... Bulletin International. Academie Polonaise des Sciences et des Lettres. Classe des Sciences Mathematiques et Naturelles. Serie B-2. Zoologie [*A publication*]

Bull Int Acad Sci Cracovie ... Bulletin International. Academie des Sciences du Cracovie [*A publication*]

Bull Int Acad Sci Cracovie Cl Sci Math Natur ... Bulletin International. Academie des Sciences du Cracovie. Classe des Sciences Mathematiques et Naturelles [*A publication*]

Bull Int Acad Sci Cracovie Cl Sci Math Natur Ser A ... Bulletin International. Academie des Sciences du Cracovie. Classe des Sciences Mathematiques et Naturelles. Serie A. Sciences Mathematiques [*A publication*]

Bull Int Acad Sci Lett Cracovie ... Bulletin International. Academie des Sciences et des Lettres du Cracovie [*A publication*]

Bull Int Acad Sci Lett Cracovie Ser A ... Bulletin International. Academie des Sciences et des Lettres du Cracovie. Serie A [*A publication*]

Bull Int Acad Yougoslave Cl Sci Math Natur ... Bulletin International. Academie Yougoslave des Sciences et des Beaux-Arts. Classe des Sciences Mathematiques et Naturelles [*A publication*]

Bull Int Acad Yougoslave Sci Beaux-Arts Cl Sci Math Nat ... Bulletin International. Academie Yougoslave des Sciences et des Beaux-Arts. Classe des Sciences Mathematiques et Naturelles [*Yugoslavia*] [*A publication*]

Bull Int Ass Med Mus ... Bulletin. International Association of Medical Museums [*A publication*]

Bull Int Assoc Eng Geol ... Bulletin. International Association of Engineering Geology [*A publication*]

Bull Int Assoc Med Mus ... Bulletin. International Association of Medical Museums [*A publication*]

Bull Int Assoc Sci Hydrol ... Bulletin. International Association of Scientific Hydrology [*A publication*]

Bull Int Assoc Shell Spat Struct ... Bulletin. International Association for Shell and Spatial Structures [*A publication*]

Bull Int Ass Sci Hydrol ... Bulletin. International Association of Scientific Hydrology [*A publication*]

Bull Int Ass Shell Struct ... Bulletin. International Association for Shell Structures [*A publication*]

Bull Int Ass Wood Anatomists ... Bulletin. International Association of Wood Anatomists [*A publication*]

Bull Int Comm Hist Sci ... Bulletin. International Committee of Historical Sciences [*A publication*]

Bull Intern Assocn Paper Hist ... Bulletin. International Association of Paper Historians [*A publication*]

Bull for Internat Fiscal Docum ... Bulletin for International Fiscal Documentation [*A publication*]

Bull Int Fisc Doc ... Bulletin for International Fiscal Documentation [*A publication*]

Bull Int Inst Ref ... International Institute of Refrigeration. Bulletin [*Paris*] [*A publication*]

Bull Int Inst Refrig ... Bulletin. International Institute of Refrigeration [*A publication*]

Bull for Int'l Fisc Doc ... Bulletin for International Fiscal Documentation [*A publication*]

Bull Int Off Epizoot ... Bulletin. International Office of Epizootics [*A publication*]

Bull Int Peat Soc ... Bulletin. International Peat Society [*A publication*]

Bull Int Potash Inst ... Bulletin. International Potash Institute [*A publication*]

Bull Int Ry Congr Ass ... Bulletin. International Railway Congress Association [*A publication*]

Bull Int Sc Soc ... Bulletin International des Sciences Sociales [*A publication*] (DLA)

Bull Int Ser Sante Armees Terre Mer Air ... Bulletin International. Services de Sante des Armees de Terre, de Mer, et de l'Air [*A publication*]

Bull Int Soc Trop Ecol ... Bulletin. International Society for Tropical Ecology [*A publication*]

Bull Int Tin Res ... Bulletin. International Tin Research and Development Council [*A publication*]

Bull Int Union Cancer ... Bulletin. International Union Against Cancer [*Switzerland*] [*A publication*]

Bull Int Union Tuberc ... Bulletin. International Union Against Tuberculosis [*A publication*]

Bull Int Un Tub ... Bulletin. International Union Against Tuberculosis [*A publication*]

Bull Invent ... Bulletin on Inventions [*United States*] [*A publication*]

Bull Io Agric Exp St ... Bulletin. Iowa Agricultural Experiment Station [*A publication*]

Bull Iowa Agr Exp Sta ... Bulletin. Iowa Agricultural Experiment Station [*A publication*]

Bull Iowa Nurses Assoc ... Bulletin. Iowa Nurses Association [*A publication*]

Bull Iowa State Univ Sci Technol Eng Exp Stn ... Bulletin. Iowa State University of Science and Technology. Engineering Experiment Station [*A publication*]

Bull Iranian Math Soc ... Bulletin. Iranian Mathematical Society [*A publication*]

Bull Iranian Petrol Inst ... Bulletin. Iranian Petroleum Institute [*A publication*]

Bull Iran Pet Inst ... Bulletin. Iranian Petroleum Institute [*A publication*]

Bull Iraq Nat Hist Mus (Univ Baghdad) ... Bulletin. Iraq Natural History Museum (University of Baghdad) [*A publication*]

Bull IRCB .. Bulletin des Seances. Institut Royal Colonial Belge [*A publication*]

Bull IRO (Aust) ... Bulletin. Commonwealth Scientific and Industrial Research Organisation (Australia) [*A publication*]

Bull Iron Steel Inst ... Bulletin. Iron and Steel Institute [*A publication*]

Bull Isaac Ray Med Libr ... Bulletin. Isaac Ray Medical Library [*A publication*]

Bull Ishikawa-Ken Agric Exp Stn ... Bulletin. Ishikawa-Ken Agricultural Experiment Station [*A publication*]

Bull Ishikawa Prefect Coll Agric ... Bulletin. Ishikawa Prefecture College of Agriculture [*A publication*]

Bull (Israel) Res Counc ... Bulletin. Research Council (Israel) [*A publication*]

Bull Isr Phys Soc ... Bulletin. Israel Physical Society [*A publication*]

Bull Isr Soc Spec Libr & Inf Cent ... Bulletin. Israel Society of Special Libraries and Information Centres [*A publication*]

Bull ISSA ... Bulletin. International Social Security Association [*A publication*]

Bull It .... Bulletin Italien [*A publication*]

Bull Iwate-Ken Agr Exp Sta ... Bulletin. Iwate-Ken Agricultural Experiment Station [*A publication*]

Bull Iwate Univ For ... Bulletin. Iwate University Forests [*A publication*]

Bull Jacks Mem Hosp ... Bulletin. Jackson Memorial Hospital and the School of Medicine of the University of Florida [*A publication*]

Bull JAG .... Bulletin. Judge Advocate General of the Army [*United States*] [*A publication*] (DLA)

Bull Jam Geol Surv ... Bulletin. Jamaica Geological Survey [*A publication*]

Bull Japan Pet Inst ... Bulletin. Japan Petroleum Institute [*A publication*]

Bull Japan Soc Mech Engrs ... Bulletin. Japanese Society of Mechanical Engineers [*A publication*]

Bull Japan Soc Precis Engng ... Bulletin. Japan Society of Precision Engineering [*A publication*]

Bull Jap Pet Inst ... Bulletin. Japan Petroleum Institute [*A publication*]

Bull Jap Soc Grinding Eng ... Bulletin. Japan Society of Grinding Engineers [*A publication*]

Bull Jap Soc Mech E ... Japan Society of Mechanical Engineers. Bulletin [*A publication*]

Bull Jap Soc Precis Eng ... Bulletin. Japan Society of Precision Engineering [*A publication*]

Bull Jap Soc Sci Fish ... Bulletin. Japanese Society of Scientific Fisheries [*A publication*]

Bull Jard Bot Buitenzorg ... Bulletin. Jardin Botanique de Buitenzorg [*A publication*]

Bull Jard Bot Etat Brux ... Bulletin. Jardin Botanique de l'Etat a Bruxelles [*A publication*]

Bull Jard Bot Natl Belg ... Bulletin. Jardin Botanique National de Belgique [*A publication*]

Bull Jard Bot Natn Belg ... Bulletin. Jardin Botanique National de Belgique [*A publication*]

Bull Jealott's Hill Res St ... Bulletin. Jealott's Hill Research Station [*A publication*]

Bull Jew Hosp ... Bulletin. Jewish Hospital [*United States*] [*A publication*]

Bull Jew Pal Expl Soc ... Bulletin. Jewish Palestine Exploration Society [*A publication*]

Bull John Rylands Libr ... Bulletin. John Rylands Library [*A publication*]

Bull John Ryl Libr ... John Rylands Library. Bulletin [*A publication*]

Bull Johns Hopk Hosp ... Bulletin. Johns Hopkins Hospital [*A publication*]

Bull Johns Hopkins Hosp ... Bulletin. Johns Hopkins Hospital [*A publication*]

Bull Josai Dent Univ ... Bulletin. Josai Dental University [*A publication*]

Bull Jpn Electron Mater Soc ... Bulletin. Japan Electronic Materials Society [*A publication*]

Bull Jpn Entomol Acad ... Bulletin. Japan Entomological Academy [*A publication*]

Bull Jpn Inst Met ... Bulletin. Japan Institute of Metals [*A publication*]

Bull Jpn Min Ind Assoc ... Bulletin. Japan Mining Industry Association [*A publication*]

Bull Jpn Pet Inst ... Bulletin. Japan Petroleum Institute [*A publication*]

Bull Jpn Sea Reg Fish Res Lab ... Bulletin. Japan Sea Regional Fisheries Research Laboratories [*A publication*]

Bull Jpn Soc Mech Eng ... Bulletin. Japan Society of Mechanical Engineers [*A publication*]

Bull Jpn Soc Phycol ... Bulletin. Japanese Society of Phycology [*A publication*]

Bull Jpn Soc Precis Eng ... Bulletin. Japan Society of Precision Engineering [*A publication*]

Bull Jpn Soc Sci Fish ... Bulletin. Japanese Society of Scientific Fisheries [*A publication*]

Bull Jpn Soc Tuberc ... Bulletin. Japanese Society of Tuberculosis [*A publication*]

Bull J Ryl Libr ... Bulletin. John Rylands Library [*A publication*]

Bull JSAE ... Bulletin. JSAE [*Japan Society of Automotive Engineers*] [*A publication*]

Bull JSME ... Bulletin. JSME [*Japan Society of Mechanical Engineers*] [*A publication*]

Bull Kagawa Agr Exp Sta ... Bulletin. Kagawa Agricultural Experiment Station [*A publication*]

Bull Kagawa Agric Exp Stn ... Bulletin. Kagawa Agricultural Experiment Station [*A publication*]

Bull Kagawa Prefect Agric Exp Stn ... Bulletin. Kagawa Prefecture Agricultural Experiment Station [*A publication*]

Bull Kagoshima Univ For ... Bulletin. Kagoshima University Forest [*A publication*]

Bull Kanagawa Agric Exp Stn ... Bulletin. Kanagawa Agricultural Experiment Station [*A publication*]

Bull Kanagawa Hort Exp Stn ... Bulletin. Kanagawa Horticultural Experiment Station [*A publication*]

Bull Kanagawa Hortic Exp Stn ... Bulletin. Kanagawa Horticultural Experiment Station [*A publication*]

Bull Kanagawa Prefect Mus Nat Sci ... Bulletin. Kanagawa Prefectural Museum of Natural Science [*A publication*]

Bull Kans Agr Exp Sta ... Bulletin. Kansas Agricultural Experiment Station [*A publication*]

Bull Kans Agric Exp Stn ... Bulletin. Kansas Agricultural Experiment Station [*A publication*]

Bull Kansas City Vet Coll Quart ... Bulletin. Kansas City Veterinary College. Quarterly [*A publication*]

Bull Kans Eng Exp Stn ... Bulletin. Kansas Engineering Experiment Station [*A publication*]

Bull Kans St Agric Coll ... Bulletin. Kansas State Agricultural College [*A publication*]

Bull Kans State Geol Surv ... Bulletin. Kansas State Geological Survey [*A publication*]

Bull Karachi Geogr Soc ... Bulletin. Karachi Geographical Society [*A publication*]

Bull K Belg Inst Natuurwet Aardwet ... Bulletin van het Koninklijke Belgische Instituut voor Natuurwetenschappen. Aardwetenschappen [*A publication*]

Bull K Belg Inst Natuurwet Biol ... Bulletin van het Koninklijke Belgische Instituut voor Natuurwetenschappen. Biologie [*A publication*]

Bull K Belg Inst Natuurwet Entomol ... Bulletin van het Koninklijke Belgische Instituut voor Natuurwetenschappen. Entomologie [*A publication*]

Bull Kent Agr Exp St ... Bulletin. Kentucky Agricultural Experiment Station [*A publication*]

Bull Kent Agric Exp St ... Bulletin. Kentucky Agricultural Experiment Station [*A publication*]

Bull Kent County Med Soc ... Bulletin. Kent County Medical Society [*California*] [*A publication*]

Bull Kent Geol Surv ... Bulletin. Kentucky Geological Survey [*A publication*]

Bull Kentucky Geol Surv ... Bulletin. Kentucky Geological Survey [*A publication*]

Bull Kern County Med Soc ... Bulletin. Kern County Medical Society [*California*] [*A publication*]

Bull Kesennuma Miyagi Prefect Fish Exp Stn ... Bulletin. Kesennuma Miyagi Prefectural Fisheries Experiment Station [*A publication*]

Bull King County Med Soc ... Bulletin. King County Medical Society [*Washington*] [*A publication*]

Bull Kisarazu Tech Coll ... Bulletin. Kisarazu Technical College [*A publication*]

Bull Kobayasi Inst Phys Res ... Bulletin. Kobayasi Institute of Physical Research [*A publication*]

Bull Kobe Med Coll ... Bulletin. Kobe Medical College [*A publication*]

Bull Kobe Women's Coll ... Bulletin. Kobe Women's College [*A publication*]

Bull Kobe Women's Coll Domest Sci Dep ... Bulletin. Kobe Women's College. Domestic Science Department [*A publication*]

Bull Kobe Women's Univ Fac Home Econ ... Bulletin. Kobe Women's University. Faculty of Home Economics [*A publication*]

Bull Kochi Tech Coll ... Bulletin. Kochi Technical College [*A publication*]

Bull Korean Chem Soc ... Bulletin. Korean Chemical Society [*South Korea*] [*A publication*]

Bull Korean Fish Soc ... Bulletin. Korean Fisheries Society [*A publication*]

Bull Korean Fish Technol Soc ... Bulletin. Korean Fisheries Technological Society [*A publication*]

Bull Korean Math Soc ... Bulletin. Korean Mathematical Society [*A publication*]

Bull Korea Ocean Res & Dev Inst ... Bulletin. Korea Ocean Research and Development Institute [*A publication*]

Bull Kwasan Observ ... Bulletin. Kwasan Observatory [*A publication*]

Bull KY Agr Exp Sta ... Bulletin. Kentucky Agricultural Experiment Station [*A publication*]

Bull KY Agric Exp Stn ... Bulletin. Kentucky Agricultural Experiment Station [*A publication*]

Bull Kyoto Daigaku Inst Chem Res ... Bulletin. Kyoto Daigaku Institute for Chemical Research [*A publication*]

Bull Kyoto Gakugei Univ Ser B Math Nat Sci ... Bulletin. Kyoto Gakugei University. Series B. Mathematics and Natural Science [*A publication*]

Bull Kyoto Prefect Univ For ... Bulletin. Kyoto Prefectural University Forests [*A publication*]

Bull Kyoto Univ Ed Ser B ... Bulletin. Kyoto University of Education. Series B. Mathematics and Natural Science [*A publication*]

Bull Kyoto Univ Educ Ser B Math Nat Sci ... Bulletin. Kyoto University of Education. Series B. Mathematics and Natural Science [*A publication*]

Bull Kyoto Univ For ... Bulletin. Kyoto University Forests [*A publication*]

Bull Kyo Univ Obs ... Bulletin. Kyoto University Observatory [*A publication*]

Bull Kyushu Agr Exp Sta ... Bulletin. Kyushu Agricultural Experiment Station [*A publication*]

Bull Kyushu Agric Exp Stn ... Bulletin. Kyushu Agricultural Experiment Station [*A publication*]

Bull Kyushu Inst Tech Math Natur Sci ... Bulletin. Kyushu Institute of Technology. Mathematics and Natural Science [*A publication*]

Bull Kyushu Inst Technol ... Bulletin. Kyushu Institute of Technology [*A publication*]

Bull Kyushu Inst Technol Math Nat Sci ... Bulletin. Kyushu Institute of Technology. Mathematics and Natural Science [*A publication*]

Bull Kyushu Inst Technol Sci & Technol ... Bulletin. Kyushu Institute of Technology. Science and Technology [*A publication*]

Bull Kyushu Univ For ... Bulletin. Kyushu University Forests [*A publication*]

Bull Kyus Inst Technol ... Bulletin. Kyushu Institute of Technology [*A publication*]

Bull & L ..... Bullen and Leake's Pleadings on Actions in King's Bench Decisions [*A publication*]   (DLA)

Bull LA Agr Exp Sta ... Bulletin. Louisiana Agricultural Experiment Station [*A publication*]

Bull LA Agric Exp Stn ... Bulletin. Louisiana Agricultural Experiment Station [*A publication*]

Bull Lab Biol Appl (Paris) ... Bulletin. Laboratoire de Biologie Appliquee (Paris) [*A publication*]

Bull Lab Geol Fac Sci Caen ... Bulletin. Laboratoire de Geologie. Faculte des Sciences de Caen [*A publication*]

Bull Lab Geol Mineral Geophys Mus Geol Univ Laus ... Bulletin. Laboratoires de Geologie, Mineralogie, Geophysique, et Musee Geologique. Universite de Lausanne [*A publication*]

Bull Lab Geol Mineral Geophys Mus Geol Univ Lausanne ... Bulletin. Laboratoires de Geologie, Mineralogie, Geophysique, et Musee Geologique. Universite de Lausanne [*A publication*]

Bull Lab Marit Dinard ... Bulletin. Laboratoire Maritime de Dinard [*A publication*]

Bull Lab Prof ... Bulletin du Laboratoire Professionnel [*A publication*]

Bull LA Coop Ext Serv ... Bulletin. Louisiana Cooperative Extension Service [*A publication*]

Bull Landbproefstn Suriname ... Bulletin. Landbouwproefstation in Suriname [*A publication*]

Bull LA Neurol Soc ... Bulletin. Los Angeles Neurological Societies [*A publication*]

Bull Leg...... Bulletin Legislatif Belge [*A publication*]   (DLA)

Bull Legal Devel ... Bulletin of Legal Developments [*A publication*]   (DLA)

Bull Leg D ... Bulletin Legislatif Dalloz [*A publication*]   (DLA)

Bull Leg Dev ... Bulletin of Legal Developments [*A publication*]   (DLA)

Bull Lembaga Penelitian Peternakan ... Bulletin Lembaga Penelitian Peternakan [*A publication*]

Bull Liaison Lab Lab Prof Pein Bitry Thiais (Fr) ... Bulletin de Liaison du Laboratoire. Laboratoire de la Profession des Peintures Bitry Thiais (France) [*A publication*]

Bull Liaison Lab Ponts Chaussees ... Bulletin de Liaison des Laboratoires des Ponts et Chaussees [*A publication*]

Bull Liaison Rech Inform Automat ... Bulletin de Liaison de la Recherche en Informatique et Automatique [*Rocquencourt*] [*A publication*]

Bull Liberia Geol Surv ... Bulletin. Liberia Geological Survey [*A publication*]

Bull Lloyd Libr Bot Pharm Mater Med ... Bulletin. Lloyd Library of Botany, Pharmacy, and Materia Medica [*A publication*]

Bull London Math Soc ... Bulletin. London Mathematical Society [*A publication*]

Bull Los Ang Cty Mus Nat Hist Sci ... Bulletin. Los Angeles County Museum of Natural History. Contributions in Science [*A publication*]

Bull Los Angeles County Med Ass ... Bulletin. Los Angeles County Medical Association [*A publication*]

Bull Los Angeles Dent Soc ... Bulletin. Los Angeles Dental Society [*A publication*]

Bull Los Angeles Neurol Soc ... Bulletin. Los Angeles Neurological Societies [*A publication*]

Bull Los Ang Neurol Soc ... Bulletin. Los Angeles Neurological Societies [*A publication*]

Bull & L Pr ... Bullen and Leake's Precedents of Pleading [*A publication*]   (DLA)

Bull L Science & Tech ... Bulletin of Law, Science, and Technology [*A publication*]   (DLA)

Bull L Sci and Tech ... Bulletin of Law, Science, and Technology [*A publication*]

Bull Madhya Pradesh Agric Dep ... Bulletin. Madhya Pradesh Agriculture Department [*A publication*]

Bull Madras Gov Mus Nat Hist Sect ... Bulletin. Madras Government Museum. Natural History Section [*A publication*]

Bull Maine Life Sci Agric Exp Stn ... Bulletin. Maine Life Sciences and Agriculture Experiment Station [*A publication*]

Bull Malaysian Math Soc ... Bulletin. Malaysian Mathematical Society [*A publication*]

Bull Malaysian Math Soc (2) ... Bulletin. Malaysian Mathematical Society. Second Series [*Kuala Lumpur*] [*A publication*]

Bull Malaysian Min Agric Rural Dev ... Bulletin. Malaysian Ministry of Agriculture and Rural Development [*A publication*]

Bull Malays Kementerian Pertanian ... Bulletin. Malaysia Kementerian Pertanian [*A publication*]

Bull Malays Minist Agric Rural Dev ... Bulletin. Malaysia Ministry of Agriculture and Rural Development [*A publication*]

Bull Manila Med Soc ... Bulletin. Manila Medical Society [*A publication*]

Bull Mar Biol Stn Asamushi ... Bulletin. Marine Biological Station of Asamushi [*A publication*]

Bull Mar Ecol ... Bulletins of Marine Ecology [*A publication*]

Bull Margaret Hague Maternity Hospital ... Bulletin. Margaret Hague Maternity Hospital [*A publication*]

Bull Marine Sci ... Bulletin of Marine Science [*A publication*]

Bull Marine Sci Gulf and Caribbean ... Bulletin of Marine Science of the Gulf and Caribbean [*Later, Bulletin of Marine Science*] [*A publication*]

Bull Mar Sci ... Bulletin of Marine Science [*A publication*]

Bull Mar Sci Gulf Caribb ... Bulletin of Marine Science of the Gulf and Caribbean [*Later, Bulletin of Marine Science*] [*A publication*]

Bull Mason Clinic ... Bulletin. Mason Clinic [*A publication*]

Bull Mass Agr Exp Sta ... Bulletin. Massachusetts Agricultural Experiment Station [*A publication*]
Bull Mass Agric Exp Sta ... Bulletin. Massachusetts Agricultural Experiment Station [*A publication*]
Bull Mass Audubon Soc ... Bulletin. Massachusetts Audubon Society [*A publication*]
Bull Mass Nurses Assoc ... Bulletin. Massachusetts Nurses Association [*A publication*]
Bull Mat Biophys ... Bulletin of Mathematical Biophysics [*A publication*]
Bull Mater Sci ... Bulletin of Materials Science [*India*] [*A publication*]
Bull Mater Sci (India) ... Bulletin of Materials Science (India) [*A publication*]
Bull Math .. Bulletin of Mathematics [*London*] [*A publication*]
Bull Math .. Bulletin Mathematique [*Romania*] [*A publication*]
Bull Math Assoc India ... Bulletin. Mathematical Association of India [*A publication*]
Bull Math Biol ... Bulletin of Mathematical Biology [*A publication*]
Bull Math Biology ... Bulletin of Mathematical Biology [*A publication*]
Bull Math Biophys ... Bulletin of Mathematical Biophysics [*A publication*]
Bull Math Soc Sci Math RS Roumanie ... Bulletin Mathematique. Societe des Sciences Mathematiques de la Republique Socialiste de Roumanie [*A publication*]
Bull Math Soc Sci Math RS Roumanie NS ... Bulletin Mathematique. Societe des Sciences Mathematiques de la Republique Socialiste de Roumanie. Nouvelle Serie [*A publication*]
Bull Math Statist ... Bulletin of Mathematical Statistics [*A publication*]
Bull Matieres Grasses Inst Colon Marseille ... Bulletin des Matieres Grasses. Institut Colonial de Marseille [*A publication*]
Bull Mat Sci ... Bulletin of Materials Science [*India*] [*A publication*]
Bull MD Agr Exp Sta ... Bulletin. Maryland Agricultural Experiment Station [*A publication*]
Bull MD Agric Exp Stn ... Bulletin. Maryland Agricultural Experiment Station [*A publication*]
Bull MD Herpetol Soc ... Bulletin. Maryland Herpetological Society [*A publication*]
Bull Md Off Anim Health Consum Serv ... Bulletin. Maryland Office of Animal Health and Consumer Services [*A publication*]
Bull ME Agric Exp Sta ... Bulletin. Maine University Agricultural Experiment Station [*A publication*]
Bull ME Agric Exp Stn ... Bulletin. Maine Agricultural Experiment Station [*A publication*]
Bull Mech Eng Educ ... Bulletin of Mechanical Engineering Education [*A publication*]
Bull Mech Eng Lab ... Bulletin. Mechanical Engineering Laboratory [*A publication*]
Bull Mech Engng Educ ... Bulletin of Mechanical Engineering Education [*A publication*]
Bull Med Coll V ... Bulletin. Medical College of Virginia [*A publication*]
Bull Med Coll VA ... Bulletin. Medical College of Virginia [*A publication*]
Bull Mediev Canon L ... Bulletin of Medieval Canon Law [*A publication*]   (DLA)
Bull Med Leg Toxicol Med ... Bulletin de Medecine Legale et de Toxicologie Medicale [*A publication*]
Bull Med Libr Ass ... Bulletin. Medical Library Association [*A publication*]
Bull Med Libr Assoc ... Bulletin. Medical Library Association [*A publication*]
Bull Med Nord ... Bulletin Medical du Nord [*A publication*]
Bull Med (Paris) ... Bulletin Medical (Paris) [*A publication*]
Bull Med Res Natl Soc Med Res ... Bulletin for Medical Research. National Society for Medical Research [*A publication*]
Bull Med Staff Methodist Hosp Dallas ... Bulletin. Medical Staff of Methodist Hospitals of Dallas [*A publication*]
Bull Med Suisses ... Bulletin des Medecins Suisses [*A publication*]
Bull ME For Dep ... Bulletin. Maine Forestry Department [*A publication*]
Bull Meiji Coll Pharm ... Bulletin. Meiji College of Pharmacy [*Japan*] [*A publication*]
Bull Mem Acad R Med Belg ... Bulletin et Memoires. Academie Royale de Medecine de Belgique [*A publication*]
Bull Mem Ec Natl Med Pharm Dakar ... Bulletins et Memoires. Ecole Nationale de Medecine et de Pharmacie de Dakar [*A publication*]
Bull Mem Ec Prep Med Pharm Dakar ... Bulletins et Memoires. Ecole Preparatoire de Medecine et de Pharmacie de Dakar [*A publication*]
Bull Mem Fac Med Pharm Dakar ... Bulletins et Memoires. Faculte de Medecine et de Pharmacie de Dakar [*A publication*]
Bull Mem Fac Natl Med Pharm Dakar ... Bulletin et Memoires. Faculte Nationale de Medecine et de Pharmacie de Dakar [*A publication*]
Bull et Mem Soc Anat Paris ... Bulletins et Memoires. Societe Anatomique de Paris [*A publication*]
Bull Mem Soc Anthropol Paris ... Bulletins et Memoires. Societe d'Anthropologie de Paris [*A publication*]
Bull Mem Soc Archeol Hist Charente ... Bulletin et Memoires. Societe Archeologique et Historique de la Charente [*A publication*]
Bull et Mem Soc Centr Med Vet ... Bulletins et Memoires. Societe Centrale de Medecine Veterinaire [*A publication*]
Bull Mem Soc Chir Paris ... Bulletin et Memoires. Societe des Chirurgiens de Paris [*A publication*]
Bull et Mem Soc Chir Paris ... Bulletins et Memoires. Societe de Chirurgie de Paris [*A publication*]
Bull Mem Soc Fr Ophtalmol ... Bulletins et Memoires. Societe Francaise d'Ophtalmologie [*A publication*]

Bull et Mem Soc Med Hop Bucarest ... Bulletins et Memoires. Societe Medicale des Hopitaux de Bucarest [*A publication*]
Bull et Mem Soc Med Hop Paris ... Bulletins et Memoires. Societe Medicale des Hopitaux de Paris [*A publication*]
Bull Mem Soc Med Paris ... Bulletin et Memoires. Societe de Medecine de Paris [*A publication*]
Bull et Mem Soc Nat Chir (Paris) ... Bulletins et Memoires. Societe Nationale de Chirurgie (Paris) [*A publication*]
Bull Mem Soc Natl Chir ... Bulletins et Memoires. Societe Nationale de Chirurgie [*A publication*]
Bull et Mem Soc Therap ... Bulletins et Memoires. Societe de Therapeutique [*A publication*]
Bull Menninger Clin ... Bulletin. Menninger Clinic [*A publication*]
Bull Mens Ecole Super Agr Viticult Angers ... Bulletin Mensuel. Ecole Superieure d'Agriculture et de Viticulture d'Angers [*A publication*]
Bull Mens Inf ... Bulletin Mensuel d'Informations [*Paris*] [*A publication*]
Bull Mens Nat Belg ... Bulletin Mensuel des Naturalistes Belges [*A publication*]
Bull Mens Off Int Hyg Publique ... Bulletin Mensuel. Office International d'Hygiene Publique [*A publication*]
Bull Mens Soc Linn Lyon ... Bulletin Mensuel. Societe Linneenne de Lyon [*A publication*]
Bull Mens Soc Med Mil Fr ... Bulletin Mensuel. Societe de Medecine Militaire Francaise [*A publication*]
Bull Mens Soc Natl Hortic Fr ... Bulletin Mensuel. Societe Nationale d'Horticulture de France [*A publication*]
Bull Mens Soc Natur Luxembourgeois ... Bulletin Mensuel. Societe des Naturalistes Luxembourgeois [*A publication*]
Bull Mens Soc Vet Prat France ... Bulletin Mensuel. Societe Veterinaire Pratique de France [*A publication*]
Bull Met Mus ... Bulletin. Metals Museum [*Japan*] [*A publication*]
Bull Metr Mus ... Bulletin. Metropolitan Museum of Art [*A publication*]
Bull Metrol ... Bulletin de Metrologie [*A publication*]
Bull Metrop Mus Art ... Metropolitan Museum of Art. Bulletin [*New York*] [*A publication*]
Bull Meun Fr ... Bulletin Meunerie Francaise [*A publication*]
Bull Mich Agric Coll ... Bulletin. Michigan Agricultural College [*A publication*]
Bull Mich Agric Coll Exp Stn ... Bulletin. Michigan Agricultural College. Experiment Station [*A publication*]
Bull Mich Dent Hyg Assoc ... Bulletin. Michigan Dental Hygienists Association [*A publication*]
Bull Mich State Dent Soc ... Bulletin. Michigan State Dental Society [*A publication*]
Bull Mich St Univ ... Bulletin. Michigan State University [*A publication*]
Bull Micr Appl ... Bulletin de Microscopie Appliquee [*A publication*]
Bull Microbiol ... Bulletin of Microbiology [*A publication*]
Bull Microscopie Appl ... Bulletin de Microscopie Appliquee [*A publication*]
Bull Microsc Soc Can ... Bulletin. Microscopical Society of Canada [*A publication*]
Bull Millard Fillmore Hosp ... Bulletin. Millard Fillmore Hospital [*A publication*]
Bull Min Agr (Egypt) ... Bulletin. Ministry of Agriculture (Egypt) [*A publication*]
Bull Min Agr Land (Jamaica) ... Bulletin. Ministry of Agriculture and Lands (Jamaica) [*A publication*]
Bull Mineral ... Bulletin de Mineralogie [*France*] [*A publication*]
Bull Mineral Res Explor Inst (Turkey) ... Bulletin. Mineral Research and Exploration Institute (Turkey). Foreign Edition [*A publication*]
Bull Miner Ind Exp Stn PA State Univ ... Bulletin. Mineral Industries Experiment Station. Pennsylvania State University [*A publication*]
Bull Miner Res Explor Inst (Turk) ... Bulletin. Mineral Research and Exploration Institute (Turkey) [*A publication*]
Bull Miner Res Explor Inst (Turk) Foreign Ed ... Bulletin. Mineral Research and Exploration Institute (Turkey). Foreign Edition [*A publication*]
Bull Minist Agric (Egypt) Tech Scient Serv ... Bulletin. Ministry of Agriculture (Egypt) Technical and Scientific Service [*A publication*]
Bull Minist Agric Fish Fd ... Bulletin. Ministry of Agriculture, Fisheries, and Food [*A publication*]
Bull Minist Agric Fish Fd (Lond) ... Bulletin. Ministry of Agriculture, Fisheries, and Food (London) [*A publication*]
Bull Minist Agric Fish Food (GB) ... Bulletin. Ministry of Agriculture, Fisheries, and Food (Great Britain) [*A publication*]
Bull Minist Agric Fish (NZ) ... Bulletin. Ministry of Agriculture and Fisheries (New Zealand) [*A publication*]
Bull Minist Agric (Queb) ... Bulletin. Ministry of Agriculture (Quebec) [*A publication*]
Bull Minist Agric Rural Dev (Malays) ... Bulletin. Ministry of Agriculture and Rural Development (Malaysia) [*A publication*]
Bull Min Met Soc Am ... Bulletin. Mining and Metallurgical Society of America [*A publication*]
Bull Minn Geol Surv ... Bulletin. Minnesota Geological Survey [*A publication*]
Bull Misaki Mar Biol Inst Kyoto Univ ... Bulletin. Misaki Marine Biological Institute. Kyoto University [*A publication*]
Bull Misc Inf (Kew) ... Bulletin of Miscellaneous Information. Royal Botanic Gardens (Kew) [*A publication*]

Bull Misc Inform Roy Bot Gard (Kew) ... Bulletin of Miscellaneous Information. Royal Botanic Gardens (Kew) [*A publication*]
Bull Misc Inf R Bot Gard ... Bulletin of Miscellaneous Information. Royal Botanic Gardens [*A publication*]
Bull Miss Agric Exp Sta ... Bulletin. Mississippi State University. Agricultural Experiment Station [*A publication*]
Bull Miss Agric Exp Stn ... Bulletin. Mississippi Agricultural Experiment Station [*A publication*]
Bull Miss Agric Mech Coll ... Bulletin. Mississippi Agricultural and Mechanical College [*A publication*]
Bull Mississippi Geol Econ Topogr Surv ... Bulletin. Mississippi Geological, Economic, and Topographical Survey [*A publication*]
Bull Miss Sch Min Tech Ser ... Bulletin. Missouri School of Mines. Technical Series [*A publication*]
Bull Miss State Univ Agr Exp Sta ... Bulletin. Mississippi State University. Agricultural Experiment Station [*A publication*]
Bull Miyagi Agr Coll ... Bulletin. Miyagi Agricultural College [*A publication*]
Bull Miyagi Agric Coll ... Bulletin. Miyagi Agricultural College [*A publication*]
Bull Miyazaki Agr Exp Sta ... Bulletin. Miyazaki Agricultural Experiment Station [*A publication*]
Bull Mizunami Fossil Mus ... Bulletin. Mizunami Fossil Museum [*A publication*]
Bull MMA ... Bulletin. Metropolitan Museum of Art [*A publication*]
Bull MO Acad Sci Suppl ... Bulletin. Missouri Academy of Science. Supplement [*A publication*]
Bull MO Bot Gdn ... Bulletin. Missouri Botanical Garden [*A publication*]
Bull MO Hist Soc ... Bulletin. Missouri Historical Society [*A publication*]
Bull Mol Biol Med ... Bulletin of Molecular Biology and Medicine [*A publication*]
Bull Mon.... Bulletin Monumental [*A publication*]
Bull Monaro Conserv Soc ... Monaro Conservation Society. Bulletin [*A publication*]
Bull Monmouth Cty Dent Soc ... Bulletin. Monmouth County [*New Jersey*] Dental Society [*A publication*]
Bull Monroe County Med Soc ... Bulletin. Monroe County Medical Society [*New York*] [*A publication*]
Bull Mont Agr Exp Sta ... Bulletin. Montana Agricultural Experiment Station [*A publication*]
Bull Montana Agric Exp Stn ... Bulletin. Montana Agricultural Experiment Station [*A publication*]
Bull Montg-Bucks Dent Soc ... Bulletin. Montgomery-Bucks Dental Society [*A publication*]
Bull Mont State Coll Coop Ext Serv ... Bulletin. Montana State College. Cooperative Extension Service [*A publication*]
Bull Morioka Tob Exp Stn ... Bulletin. Morioka Tobacco Experiment Station [*A publication*]
Bull Mt Desert Isl Biol Lab ... Bulletin. Mount Desert Island Biological Laboratory [*A publication*]
Bull Mukogawa Women's Univ Nat Sci ... Bulletin. Mukogawa Women's University. Natural Science [*Japan*] [*A publication*]
Bull Murithienne ... Bulletin de la Murithienne [*A publication*]
Bull Mus Anthr Prehist (Monaco) ... Bulletin. Musee d'Anthropologie Prehistorique (Monaco) [*A publication*]
Bull Mus Art Hist Geneve ... Bulletin. Musee d'Art et d'Histoire de Geneve [*A publication*]
Bull Mus Belge ... Bulletin Bibliographique et Pedagogique. Musee Belge [*A publication*]
Bull Mus Comp Zool ... Bulletin. Museum of Comparative Zoology [*A publication*]
Bull Mus Comp Zool Harv ... Bulletin. Museum of Comparative Zoology at Harvard University [*A publication*]
Bull Mus Comp Zool Harv Univ ... Bulletin. Museum of Comparative Zoology at Harvard University [*A publication*]
Bull Musees Royaux ... Bulletin. Musees Royaux d'Art et d'Histoire [*A publication*]
Bull Museum (Boston) ... Bulletin. Museum of Fine Arts (Boston) [*A publication*]
Bull Mus Far East Antiquities ... Bulletin. Museum of Far Eastern Antiquities [*A publication*]
Bull Mus Fi A ... Museum of Fine Arts. Bulletin [*A publication*]
Bull Mus Fine Arts (Boston) ... Bulletin. Museum of Fine Arts (Boston) [*A publication*]
Bull Mus Hist Nat Belg ... Bulletin. Musee Royal d'Histoire Naturelle de la Belgique [*A publication*]
Bull Mus Hist Nat Mars ... Bulletin. Museum d'Histoire Naturelle de Marseille [*A publication*]
Bull Mus Hist Nat Marseille ... Bulletin. Musee d'Histoire Naturelle de Marseille [*A publication*]
Bull Mus Hist Nat Pays Serbe ... Bulletin. Museum d'Histoire Naturelle du Pays Serbe [*A publication*]
Bull Mus Hist Natur Belg ... Bulletin. Musee Royal d'Histoire Naturelle de la Belgique [*A publication*]
Bull Mus Hong ... Bulletin. Musee Hongrois des Beaux-Arts [*A publication*]
Bull Mus Mon Lyonn ... Bulletin des Musees et Monuments Lyonnais [*A publication*]
Bull Mus Nat Hist Nat (Paris) ... Bulletin. Museum National d'Histoire Naturelle (Paris) [*A publication*]
Bull Mus Natl Hist Nat ... Bulletin. Museum National d'Histoire Naturelle [*Paris*] [*A publication*]

Bull Mus Natl Hist Nat Bot ... Bulletin. Museum National d'Histoire Naturelle. Botanique [*Paris*] [*A publication*]
Bull Mus Natl Hist Nat Ecol Gen ... Bulletin. Museum National d'Histoire Naturelle. Ecologie Generale [*Paris*] [*A publication*]
Bull Mus Natl Hist Nat Sci Terre ... Bulletin. Museum National d'Histoire Naturelle. Serie 3. Sciences de la Terre [*Paris*] [*A publication*]
Bull Mus Natl Hist Nat Sect B Andansonia Bot Phytochim ... Bulletin. Museum National d'Histoire Naturelle. Section B. Andansonia Botanique. Phytochimie [*A publication*]
Bull Mus Natl Hist Nat Ser 3 Sci Terre ... Bulletin. Museum National d'Histoire Naturelle. Serie 3. Sciences de la Terre [*Paris*] [*A publication*]
Bull Mus Natl Hist Nat Zool ... Bulletin. Museum National d'Histoire Naturelle. Zoologie [*Paris*] [*A publication*]
Bull Mus R Hist Nat Belg ... Bulletin. Musee Royal d'Histoire Naturelle de la Belgique [*A publication*]
Bull Mus Roy Beaux Arts Belg ... Bulletin. Musees Royaux des Beaux-Arts de Belgique [*A publication*]
Bull Mycol ... Bulletin of Mycology [*A publication*]
Bull Mysore Geol Assoc ... Bulletin. Mysore Geologists Association [*A publication*]
Bull Nagano Agr Exp Sta ... Bulletin. Nagano Agricultural Experiment Station [*A publication*]
Bull Nagaoka Munic Sci Mus ... Bulletin. Nagaoka Municipal Science Museum [*A publication*]
Bull Nagoya City Univ Dep Gen Educ Nat Sci Sect ... Bulletin. Nagoya City University. Department of General Education. Natural Science Section [*A publication*]
Bull Nagoya Inst Tech ... Bulletin. Nagoya Institute of Technology [*A publication*]
Bull Nagoya Inst Technol ... Bulletin. Nagoya Institute of Technology [*A publication*]
Bull Naikai Reg Fish Res Lab ... Bulletin. Naikai Regional Fisheries Research Laboratory [*Japan*] [*A publication*]
Bull N Am Gladiolus Counc ... Bulletin. North American Gladiolus Council [*A publication*]
Bull Naniwa Univ Ser A ... Bulletin. Naniwa University. Series A. Engineering and Natural Sciences [*A publication*]
Bull Naniwa Univ Ser B ... Bulletin. Naniwa University. Series B. Agricultural and Natural Science [*A publication*]
Bull Nanjing Inst Geol Miner Resour ... Bulletin. Nanjing Institute of Geology and Mineral Resources [*A publication*]
Bull Nansei Reg Fish Res Lab ... Bulletin. Nansei Regional Fisheries Research Laboratories [*A publication*]
Bull Nara Univ Ed Natur Sci ... Bulletin. Nara University of Education. Natural Science [*A publication*]
Bull Nara Univ Educ Nat Sci ... Bulletin. Nara University of Education. Natural Science [*A publication*]
Bull Narc ... Bulletin on Narcotics [*A publication*]
Bull Narcotics ... Bulletin on Narcotics [*A publication*]
Bull Nat Assoc Wool Manuf ... Bulletin. National Association of Wool Manufacturers [*A publication*]
Bull Nat Ass Watch Clock Collect ... Bulletin. National Association of Watch and Clock Collectors [*A publication*]
Bull Nat Dist Heat Assoc ... Bulletin. National District Heating Association [*A publication*]
Bull Nat Formul Comm ... Bulletin. National Formulary Committee [*A publication*]
Bull Nat Geophys Res Inst (India) ... Bulletin. National Geophysical Research Institute (India) [*A publication*]
Bull Nat His Mus Belgr Ser A Mineral Geol Paleontol ... Bulletin. Natural History Museum in Belgrade. Series A. Mineralogy, Geology, Paleontology [*A publication*]
Bull Nat Hist Mus ... Bulletin. Natural History Museum, Balboa Park [*United States*] [*A publication*]
Bull Nat Hist Mus Belgr ... Bulletin. Natural History Museum in Belgrade [*A publication*]
Bull Nat Hist Mus Belgrade B ... Bulletin. Natural History Museum in Belgrade. Series B. Biological Sciences [*A publication*]
Bull Nat Hist Mus Belgr Ser B Biol Sci ... Bulletin. Natural History Museum in Belgrade. Series B. Biological Sciences [*A publication*]
Bull Nat Hist Res Cent Univ Baghdad ... Bulletin. Natural History Research Center. University of Baghdad [*A publication*]
Bull Nat Hist Soc New Br ... Bulletin. Natural History Society of New Brunswick [*A publication*]
Bull Nat Inst Anim Ind ... Bulletin. National Institute of Animal Industry [*A publication*]
Bull Nat Inst Geol Min (Bandung Indonesia) ... Bulletin. National Institute of Geology and Mining (Bandung, Indonesia) [*A publication*]
Bull Nat Inst Hyg Sci ... Bulletin. National Institute of Hygienic Sciences [*A publication*]
Bull Nat Inst Sci India ... Bulletin. National Institute of Sciences of India [*A publication*]
Bull Natl Bot Gard ... Bulletin. National Botanic Garden [*Lucknow, India*] [*A publication*]
Bull Natl Bot Gard (Lucknow) ... Bulletin. National Botanic Garden (Lucknow) [*A publication*]
Bull Natl Fish Univ Pusan Nat Sci ... Bulletin of National Fisheries. University of Pusan. Natural Sciences [*A publication*]

Bull Natl Geophys Res Inst (India) ... Bulletin. National Geophysical Research Institute (India) [*A publication*]

Bull Natl Grassl Res Inst ... Bulletin. National Grassland Research Institute [*Japan*] [*A publication*]

Bull Natl Hyg Lab (Tokyo) ... Bulletin. National Hygienic Laboratory (Tokyo) [*A publication*]

Bull Natl Inst Agric Sci Ser A ... Bulletin. National Institute of Agricultural Sciences. Series A (Physics and Statistics) [*A publication*]

Bull Natl Inst Agric Sci Ser A (Phys Stat) ... Bulletin. National Institute of Agricultural Sciences. Series A (Physics and Statistics) (Japan) [*A publication*]

Bull Natl Inst Agric Sci Ser B (Soils Fert) (Japan) ... Bulletin. National Institute of Agricultural Sciences. Series B (Soils and Fertilizers) (Japan) [*A publication*]

Bull Natl Inst Agric Sci Ser C Plant Pathol Entomol ... Bulletin. National Institute of Agricultural Sciences. Series C. Plant Pathology and Entomology [*A publication*]

Bull Natl Inst Agric Sci Ser D (Physiol Genet) (Japan) ... Bulletin. National Institute of Agricultural Sciences. Series D (Physiology and Genetics) (Japan) [*A publication*]

Bull Natl Inst Agric Sci Ser D Plant Physiol Genet Crops Gen ... Bulletin. National Institute of Agricultural Sciences. Series D. Plant Physiology, Genetics, and Crops in General [*A publication*]

Bull Natl Inst Agric Sci Ser G (Anim Husb) ... Bulletin. National Institute of Agricultural Sciences. Series G (Animal Husbandry) (Japan) [*A publication*]

Bull Natl Inst Agri Sci Ser C ... Bulletin. National Institute of Agricultural Sciences. Series C [*Japan*] [*A publication*]

Bull Natl Inst Agrobiol Resour ... Bulletin. National Institute of Agrobiological Resources [*A publication*]

Bull Natl Inst Anim Health (Jpn) ... Bulletin. National Institute of Animal Health (Japan) [*A publication*]

Bull Natl Inst Anim Ind (Chiba) ... Bulletin. National Institute of Animal Industry (Chiba) [*A publication*]

Bull Natl Inst Anim Ind (Ibaraki) ... Bulletin. National Institute of Animal Industry (Ibaraki) [*A publication*]

Bull Natl Inst Hyg Sci (Tokyo) ... Bulletin. National Institute of Hygienic Sciences (Tokyo) [*A publication*]

Bull Natl Inst Oceanogr (India) ... Bulletin. National Institute of Oceanography (India) [*A publication*]

Bull Natl Inst Pollut Resour ... Bulletin. National Research Institute for Pollution and Resources [*Japan*] [*A publication*]

Bull Natl Inst Sci India ... Bulletin. National Institute of Sciences of India [*A publication*]

Bull Natl Med Dent Assoc Natl Advocates Soc ... Bulletin. National Medical and Dental Association and National Advocates Society [*Chicago*] [*A publication*]

Bull Natl Mus (Singapore) ... Bulletin. National Museum (Singapore) [*A publication*]

Bull Natl Pearl Res Lab ... Bulletin. National Pearl Research Laboratory [*Japan*] [*A publication*]

Bull Natl Plant Belg ... Bulletin. Nationale Plantentuin van Belgie [*A publication*]

Bull Natl Res Counc Philipp ... Bulletin. National Research Council of the Philippines [*A publication*]

Bull Natl Res Inst Aquacult ... Bulletin. National Research Institute of Aquaculture [*A publication*]

Bull Natl Res Inst Fish Eng ... Bulletin. National Research Institute of Fisheries Engineering [*A publication*]

Bull Natl Res Inst Tea ... Bulletin. National Research Institute of Tea [*Japan*] [*A publication*]

Bull Natl Res Lab Metrol ... Bulletin. National Research Laboratory of Metrology [*Japan*] [*A publication*]

Bull Natl Res Lab Metrology ... Bulletin. National Research Laboratory of Metrology [*Japan*] [*A publication*]

Bull Natl Sci Found ... Bulletin. National Science Foundation [*A publication*]

Bull Natl Sci Mus Ser A (Zool) ... Bulletin. National Science Museum. Series A (Zoology) (Japan) [*A publication*]

Bull Natl Sci Mus Ser B (Bot) ... Bulletin. National Science Museum. Series B (Botany) (Japan) [*A publication*]

Bull Natl Sci Mus Ser C (Geol) ... Bulletin. National Science Museum. Series C (Geology) [*Later, Bulletin. National Science Museum. Series C. (Geology and Paleontology)*] (Japan) [*A publication*]

Bull Natl Sci Mus Ser C (Geol Paleontol) ... Bulletin. National Science Museum. Series C (Geology and Paleontology) (Japan) [*A publication*]

Bull Natl Sci Mus Ser D (Anthropol) ... Bulletin. National Science Museum. Series D (Anthropology) (Japan) [*A publication*]

Bull Natl Sci Mus (Tokyo) ... Bulletin. National Science Museum (Tokyo) [*A publication*]

Bull Natl Speleol Soc ... Bulletin. National Speleological Society [*United States*] [*A publication*]

Bull Natl Tuberc Assoc ... Bulletin. National Tuberculosis Association [*US*] [*A publication*]

Bull Natl Tuberc Respir Dis Assoc ... Bulletin. National Tuberculosis Respiratory Disease Association [*US*] [*A publication*]

Bull Nat Mons ... Bulletin des Naturalistes de Mons et du Borinage [*A publication*]

Bull Natn Inst Agric Sci (Tokyo) ... Bulletin. National Institute of Agricultural Sciences (Tokyo) [*A publication*]

Bull Natn Inst Hyg Sci (Tokyo) ... Bulletin. National Institute of Hygienic Sciences (Tokyo) [*Japan*] [*A publication*]

Bull Natn Inst Sci India ... Bulletin. National Institute of Sciences of India [*A publication*]

Bull Natn Sci Mus (Tokyo) ... Bulletin. National Science Museum (Tokyo) [*A publication*]

Bull Nat Pearl Res Lab (Jpn) ... Bulletin. National Pearl Research Laboratory (Japan) [*A publication*]

Bull Nat Res Counc (US) ... Bulletin. National Research Council (US) [*A publication*]

Bull Nat Res Lab Metrology ... Bulletin. National Research Laboratory of Metrology [*Japan*] [*A publication*]

Bull Nat Sci Brd ... Bulletin. National Science Board, Philippine Islands [*A publication*]

Bull Nat Sci (Wellington) ... Bulletin of Natural Sciences (Wellington) [*A publication*]

Bull Nat Soc Ind Malar ... Bulletin. National Society of India for Malaria and Other Mosquito Borne Disease [*A publication*]

Bull Nat Spel Soc ... Bulletin. National Speleological Society [*United States*] [*A publication*]

Bull Nat Tax Assoc ... Bulletin. National Tax Association [*A publication*] (DLA)

Bull Nat Tub Ass ... Bulletin. National Tuberculosis Association [*United States*] [*A publication*]

Bull N Carol Dep Conserv Dev ... Bulletin. North Carolina Department of Conservation and Development [*A publication*]

Bull N Carol St Univ Agric Exp Stn ... Bulletin. North Carolina State University. Agricultural Experiment Station [*A publication*]

Bull NC Div Miner Resour ... Bulletin. North Carolina Division of Mineral Resources [*A publication*]

Bull NC Div Resour Plann Eval Miner Resour Sect ... Bulletin. North Carolina Division of Resource Planning and Evaluation. Mineral Resources Section [*A publication*]

Bull N Dak Agr Exp Sta ... Bulletin. North Dakota Agricultural Experiment Station [*A publication*]

Bull N Dak Agric Exp St ... Bulletin. North Dakota Agricultural Experimental Station [*A publication*]

Bull N Dak Agric Exp Stn ... Bulletin. North Dakota Agricultural Experiment Station [*A publication*]

Bull Nebr Agric Exp St ... Bulletin. Nebraska Agricultural Experiment Station [*A publication*]

Bull Neurol Inst NY ... Bulletin. Neurological Institute of New York [*A publication*]

Bull Nev Agr Exp St ... Bulletin. Nevada Agricultural Experiment Station [*A publication*]

Bull Newark Dent Club ... Bulletin. Newark [*New Jersey*] Dental Club [*A publication*]

Bull New Engl Med Cent ... Bulletin. New England Medical Center [*A publication*]

Bull New Hamps Agric Exp Stn ... Bulletin. New Hampshire Agricultural Experiment Station [*A publication*]

Bull New Jers Agric Exp St ... Bulletin. New Jersey Agricultural Experiment Station [*A publication*]

Bull New Jers Agric Exp Stn ... Bulletin. New Jersey Agricultural Experiment Station [*A publication*]

Bull New Jers St Soil Conserv Comm ... Bulletin. New Jersey State Soil Conservation Committee [*A publication*]

Bull New Mex Agric Exp Stn ... Bulletin. New Mexico Agricultural Experiment Station [*A publication*]

Bull New York Acad Med ... Bulletin. New York Academy of Medicine [*A publication*]

Bull NH Agric Exp Stn ... Bulletin. New Hampshire Agricultural Experiment Station [*A publication*]

Bull N Hampshire Agric Exper Station ... Bulletin. New Hampshire Agricultural Experiment Station [*A publication*]

Bull Niger For Dep ... Bulletin. Nigerian Forestry Departments [*A publication*]

Bull Nigerian For Dep ... Bulletin. Nigerian Forestry Departments [*A publication*]

Bull Niigata Univ For ... Bulletin. Niigata University Forests [*A publication*]

Bull Ninth Dist Dent Soc ... Bulletin. Ninth District Dental Society [*White Plains, New York*] [*A publication*]

Bull Nippon Dent Coll Gen Educ ... Bulletin. Nippon Dental College. General Education [*A publication*]

Bull Nippon Dent Univ Gen Educ ... Bulletin. Nippon Dental University. General Education [*A publication*]

Bull Nippon Vet Zootech Coll ... Bulletin. Nippon Veterinary and Zootechnical College [*A publication*]

Bull NJ Acad Sci ... Bulletin. New Jersey Academy of Science [*A publication*]

Bull NJ Agr Exp Sta ... Bulletin. New Jersey Agricultural Experiment Station [*A publication*]

Bull NJ Bur Geol Topogr ... Bulletin. New Jersey Bureau of Geology and Topography [*A publication*]

Bull NJ Soc Dent Child ... Bulletin. New Jersey Society of Dentistry for Children [*A publication*]

Bull N Mex Agr Exp Sta ... Bulletin. New Mexico Agricultural Experiment Station [*A publication*]

Bull Norg Geol Unders ... Bulletin. Norges Geologiske Undersokelse [*A publication*]

Bull North Carolina Bd Health ... Bulletin. North Carolina Board of Health [*A publication*]

Bull North Dist Dent Soc ... Bulletin. Northern District Dental Society [*Atlanta, Georgia*] [*A publication*]

Bull North Scotl Coll Agric ... Bulletin. North of Scotland College of Agriculture [*A publication*]

Bull NP ...... Buller's Law of Nisi Prius [*England*] [*A publication*] (DLA)

Bull NP (Eng) ... Buller's Law of Nisi Prius [*England*] [*A publication*] (DLA)

Bull NRDC ... Bulletin. National Research Development Corporation [*England*] [*A publication*]

Bull N Rhodesia Dept Agr ... Bulletin. Northern Rhodesia Department of Agriculture [*A publication*]

Bull NRLM ... Bulletin. NRLM [*National Research Laboratory of Metrology*] [*A publication*]

Bull N Scot Coll Agr ... Bulletin. North of Scotland College of Agriculture [*A publication*]

Bull N Scotl Coll Agric ... Bulletin. North of Scotland College of Agriculture [*A publication*]

Bull N Scotl Coll Agric Beekeep Dep ... Bulletin. North of Scotland College of Agriculture. Beekeeping Department [*A publication*]

Bull NSW Inst Ed Res ... New South Wales Institute for Educational Research. Bulletin [*A publication*]

Bull NTA ... Bulletin. National Tax Association [*A publication*] (DLA)

Bull Nth Terr Austr ... Bulletin of the Northern Territory of Australia [*A publication*]

Bull Number Theory Related Topics ... Bulletin of Number Theory and Related Topics [*A publication*]

Bull Nutr Inst UAR ... Bulletin. Nutrition Institute of the United Arab Republic [*A publication*]

Bull NY Acad Med ... Bulletin. New York Academy of Medicine [*A publication*]

Bull NY Agr Exp Sta ... Bulletin. New York Agricultural Experiment Station [*A publication*]

Bull NY Cty Dent Soc ... Bulletin. New York County Dental Society [*A publication*]

Bull NY Med Coll Flower Fifth Ave ... Bulletin. New York Medical College. Flower and Fifth Avenue [*A publication*]

Bull NYPL ... Bulletin. New York Public Library [*A publication*]

Bull NY Pub Lib ... Bulletin. New York Public Library [*A publication*]

Bull NY Public Libr ... Bulletin. New York [*City*] Public Library [*A publication*]

Bull NY St Agric Exp St ... Bulletin. New York State Agricultural Experiment Station [*A publication*]

Bull NY St Agric Exp Stn ... Bulletin. New York State Agricultural Experiment Station [*A publication*]

Bull NY State Flower Ind ... Bulletin. New York State Flower Industries [*A publication*]

Bull NY State Mus ... Bulletin. New York State Museum [*A publication*]

Bull NY State Mus Sci Serv ... Bulletin. New York State Museum and Science Service [*A publication*]

Bull NY State Soc Anesthesiol ... Bulletin. New York State Society of Anesthesiologists [*A publication*]

Bull NY St Conserv Dep ... Bulletin. New York State Conservation Department [*A publication*]

Bull NY St Dep Agric ... Bulletin. New York State Department of Agriculture [*A publication*]

Bull NY St Mus ... Bulletin. New York State Museum [*A publication*]

Bull NY St Mus Sci Serv ... Bulletin. New York State Museum and Science Service [*A publication*]

Bull NY Zool Soc ... Bulletin. New York Zoological Society [*A publication*]

Bull NZ Astr Soc ... Bulletin. New Zealand Astronomical Society. Variable Star Section [*A publication*]

Bull NZ Dep Scient Ind Res ... Bulletin. New Zealand Department of Scientific and Industrial Research [*A publication*]

Bull NZ Dept Sci Ind Res ... Bulletin. New Zealand Department of Scientific and Industrial Research [*A publication*]

Bull NZ Geol Surv ... Bulletin. New Zealand Geological Survey [*A publication*]

Bull NZ Geol Surv New Ser ... Bulletin. New Zealand Geological Survey. New Series [*A publication*]

Bull NZ Natl Soc Earthq Eng ... Bulletin. New Zealand National Society for Earthquake Engineering [*A publication*]

Bull NZ Soc Earthquake Eng ... Bulletin. New Zealand Society of Earthquake Engineering [*A publication*]

Bull NZ Soc Periodontol ... Bulletin. New Zealand Society of Periodontology [*A publication*]

Bull O .... Weekly Law Bulletin [*Ohio*] [*A publication*] (DLA)

Bull Obs Puy De Dome ... Bulletin. Observatoire du Puy De Dome [*A publication*]

Bull Oceanogr Inst ... Bulletin. Oceanographical Institute of Taiwan [*A publication*]

Bull Ocean Res Inst Univ Tokyo ... Bulletin. Ocean Research Institute. University of Tokyo [*A publication*]

Bull OEPP ... Bulletin OEPP [*Organisation Europeenne et Mediterraneenne pour la Protection des Plantes*] [*A publication*]

Bull Oerlikon ... Bulletin Oerlikon [*Switzerland*] [*A publication*]

Bull Off Ass Med Dent Fr ... Bulletin Officiel. Association des Medecins Dentistes de France [*A publication*]

Bull Off Dir Rech Sci Ind Inv (Fr) ... Bulletin Officiel. Direction des Recherches Scientifiques et Industrielles et des Inventions (France) [*A publication*]

Bull Offic ... Bulletin Officiel de la Propriete Industrielle [*Berne*] [*A publication*]

Bull Office Exper Stations US Dept Agric ... Bulletin. Office of Experiment Stations. United States Department of Agriculture [*A publication*]

Bull Office Surg Gen US War Dept ... Bulletins. Office of the Surgeon General. United States War Department [*A publication*]

Bull Offic Propriete Ind (Fr) ... Bulletin Officiel de la Propriete Industrielle (France) [*A publication*]

Bull Off Int Epizoot ... Bulletin. Office International des Epizooties [*A publication*]

Bull Off Int Hyg Publ ... Bulletin Mensuel. Office International d'Hygiene Publique [*A publication*]

Bull Off Off Int Cacao Choc ... Bulletin Officiel. Office International du Cacao et du Chocolat [*A publication*]

Bull Off Propr Ind Abr ... Bulletin Officiel de la Propriete Industrielle. Abreges [*A publication*]

Bull Off Propr Ind Brev Invent Abr Listes ... Bulletin Officiel de la Propriete Industrielle. Brevets d'Invention, Abreges, et Listes [*A publication*]

Bull Off Soc Int Psycho Proph Obstet ... Bulletin Officiel. Societe Internationale de Psychoprophylaxie Obstetricale [*A publication*]

Bull Ogata Inst Med Chem Res ... Bulletin. Ogata Institute for Medical and Chemical Research [*A publication*]

Bull (Ohio) ... Weekly Law Bulletin (Ohio) [*A publication*] (DLA)

Bull Ohio Agr Exp Sta ... Bulletin. Ohio Agricultural Experiment Station [*A publication*]

Bull Ohio Agric Exp St ... Bulletin. Ohio Agricultural Experiment Station [*A publication*]

Bull Ohio Agric Exp Stn ... Bulletin. Ohio Agricultural Experiment Station [*A publication*]

Bull Ohio Biol Surv ... Bulletin. Ohio Biological Survey [*A publication*]

Bull Ohio Eng Exp St ... Bulletin. Ohio Engineering Experiment Station [*A publication*]

Bull Ohio St Univ Co-Op Ext Serv ... Bulletin. Ohio State University. Co-Operative Extension Service [*A publication*]

Bull Oil Nat Gas Comm ... Bulletin. Oil and Natural Gas Commission [*India*] [*A publication*]

Bull Oil Natur Gas Comm (India) ... Bulletin. Oil and Natural Gas Commission (India) [*A publication*]

Bull OIV .... Bulletin de l'OIV [*Office International de la Vigne et du Vin*] [*A publication*]

Bull Oji Inst For Tree Impr ... Bulletin. Oji Institute for Forest Tree Improvement [*A publication*]

Bull Okayama Coll Sci ... Bulletin. Okayama College of Science [*A publication*]

Bull Okayama Tob Exp Stn ... Bulletin. Okayama Tobacco Experiment Station [*A publication*]

Bull Okayama Univ Sci ... Bulletin. Okayama University of Science [*A publication*]

Bull Okayama Univ Sci A Nat Sci ... Bulletin. Okayama University of Science. A. Natural Science [*A publication*]

Bull Okayama Univ Sci B Hum Sci ... Bulletin. Okayama University of Science. B. Human Sciences [*A publication*]

Bull Okla Agric Exp St ... Bulletin. Oklahoma Agricultural Experiment Station [*A publication*]

Bull Okla Agric Exp Stn ... Bulletin. Oklahoma Agricultural Experiment Station [*A publication*]

Bull Okla Anthrop Soc ... Bulletin. Oklahoma Anthropological Society [*A publication*]

Bull Okla Dent Ass ... Bulletin. Oklahoma State Dental Association [*A publication*]

Bull Okla Geol Surv ... Bulletin. Oklahoma Geological Survey [*A publication*]

Bull Oklahoma Geol Surv ... Bulletin. Oklahoma Geological Survey [*A publication*]

Bull Okla Ornithol Soc ... Bulletin. Oklahoma Ornithological Society [*A publication*]

Bull Okla State Univ Agr Exp Sta ... Bulletin. Oklahoma State University. Agricultural Experiment Station [*A publication*]

Bull ONAF ... Bulletin. Office National de Coordination des Allocations Familiales [*A publication*]

Bull Ont Agric Coll ... Bulletin. Ontario Agricultural College [*A publication*]

Bull Ont Coll Pharm ... Bulletin. Ontario College of Pharmacy [*A publication*]

Bull Ont Dep Agric ... Bulletin. Ontario Department of Agriculture [*A publication*]

Bull Ont Med Ass ... Bulletin. Ontario Medical Association [*A publication*]

Bull Oper Res Soc Am ... Bulletin. Operations Research Society of America [*A publication*]

Bull Ophthalmol Soc Egypt ... Bulletin. Ophthalmological Society of Egypt [*A publication*]

Bull Ophth Soc Eg ... Bulletin. Ophthalmological Society of Egypt [*A publication*]

Bull Op Res Soc Am ... Bulletin. Operations Research Society of America [*A publication*]

Bull Orange County Med Assoc ... Bulletin. Orange County Medical Association [*California*] [*A publication*]

Bull Ordre Natl Pharm ... Bulletin. Ordre National des Pharmaciens [*A publication*]

Bull Ordre Pharm (Brussels) ... Bulletin. Ordre des Pharmaciens (Brussels) [*A publication*]

Bull Ore Agric Coll ... Bulletin. Oregon Agricultural College [*A publication*]

Bull Ore Agric Exp Stn ... Bulletin. Oregon Agricultural Experiment Station [*A publication*]

Bull Ore Ent Soc ... Bulletin. Oregon Entomological Society [*A publication*]

Bull Ore For Res Lab ... Bulletin. Oregon State University. Forest Research Laboratory [*A publication*]

Bull Oreg Agr Exp Sta ... Bulletin. Oregon Agricultural Experiment Station [*A publication*]

Bull Oreg Agric Exp St ... Bulletin. Oregon Agricultural Experiment Station [*A publication*]

Bull Organ Int Metrol Leg ... Bulletin. Organisation Internationale de Metrologie Legale [*A publication*]

Bull Org Mond Sante ... Bulletin. Organisation Mondiale de la Sante [*A publication*]

Bull Orn Soc NZ ... Bulletin. Ornithological Society of New Zealand [*A publication*]

Bull ORSA ... Bulletin. Operations Research Society of America [*A publication*]

Bull Orton Soc ... Bulletin. Orton Society [*A publication*]

Bull Osaka Agric Res Cent ... Bulletin. Osaka Agricultural Research Center [*A publication*]

Bull Osaka Med Sch ... Bulletin. Osaka Medical School [*A publication*]

Bull Osaka Med Sch Suppl ... Bulletin. Osaka Medical School. Supplement [*A publication*]

Bull Osaka Munic Tech Res Inst ... Bulletin. Osaka Municipal Technical Research Institute [*Japan*] [*A publication*]

Bull Osaka Mus Nat Hist ... Bulletin. Osaka Museum of Natural History [*A publication*]

Bull Osaka Prefect Tech College ... Bulletin. Osaka Prefectural Technical College [*A publication*]

Bull Os Med Sch ... Bulletin. Osaka Medical School [*A publication*]

Bull Otago Catchm Bd ... Bulletin. Otago Catchment Board [*A publication*]

Bull Oxf Univ Inst Stat ... Bulletin. Oxford University. Institute of Statistics [*A publication*]

Bull PA Agr Exp Sta ... Bulletin. Pennsylvania Agricultural Experiment Station [*A publication*]

Bull PA Agric Exp Stn ... Bulletin. Pennsylvania Agricultural Experiment Station [*A publication*]

Bull Pac Coast Soc Orthod ... Bulletin. Pacific Coast Society of Orthodontists [*US*] [*A publication*]

Bull Pacif Orchid Soc Haw ... Bulletin. Pacific Orchid Society of Hawaii [*A publication*]

Bull Pac Orchid Soc Hawaii ... Bulletin. Pacific Orchid Society of Hawaii [*A publication*]

Bull Pac Trop Bot Gard ... Bulletin. Pacific Tropical Botanical Garden [*A publication*]

Bull Pan Am Health Organ ... Bulletin. Pan American Health Organization [*A publication*]

Bull Parenter Drug Assoc ... Bulletin. Parenteral Drug Association [*A publication*]

Bull Passaic Cty Dent Soc ... Bulletin. Passaic County Dental Society [*A publication*]

Bull PA State Univ Agr Exp Sta ... Bulletin. Pennsylvania State University. Agricultural Experiment Station [*A publication*]

Bull Pathol (Chicago) ... Bulletin of Pathology (Chicago, Illinois) [*A publication*]

Bull Patna Sci Coll Philos Soc ... Bulletin. Patna Science College Philosophical Society [*A publication*]

Bull Peab Mus Nat Hist ... Bulletin. Peabody Museum of Natural History [*A publication*]

Bull Peace Propos ... Bulletin of Peace Proposals [*A publication*]

Bull Peak Dist Mines Hist Soc ... Bulletin. Peak District Mines Historical Society [*Matlock Bath*] [*A publication*]

Bull Penns Agric Exp St ... Bulletin. Pennsylvania Agricultural Experiment Station [*A publication*]

Bull Penns St Dent Soc ... Bulletin. Pennsylvania State Dental Society [*A publication*]

Bull Perma Int Ass Navig Congr ... Bulletin. Permanent International Association of Navigation Congresses [*A publication*]

Bull Permanent Int Assoc Navigation Congresses ... Bulletin. Permanent International Association of Navigation Congresses [*A publication*]

Bull Perm Int Assoc Navig Congr ... Bulletin. Permanent International Association of Navigation Congresses [*A publication*]

Bull Pharm ... Bulletin of Pharmacy [*A publication*]

Bull Pharmacol (Beijing) ... Bulletin of Pharmacology (Beijing) [*A publication*]

Bull Pharm (Istanbul) ... Bulletin of Pharmacy (Istanbul) [*A publication*]

Bull Pharm Res Inst (Osaka) ... Bulletin. Pharmaceutical Research Institute (Osaka) [*A publication*]

Bull Pharm Sud Est ... Bulletin de Pharmacie du Sud-Est [*A publication*]

Bull Phila Cty Dent Soc ... Bulletin. Philadelphia County Dental Society [*A publication*]

Bull Philadelphia Astronaut Soc ... Bulletin. Philadelphia Astronautical Society [*A publication*]

Bull Phila Herpetol Soc ... Bulletin. Philadelphia Herpetological Society [*A publication*]

Bull Philipp Biochem Soc ... Bulletin. Philippine Biochemical Society [*A publication*]

Bull Philol Hist ... Bulletin Philologique et Historique [*A publication*]

Bull Phil Soc Wash ... Bulletin. Philosophical Society of Washington [*District of Columbia*] [*A publication*]

Bull Phys Fitness Res Inst ... Bulletin. Physical Fitness Research Institute [*A publication*]

Bull Physio Pathol Respir ... Bulletin de Physio-Pathologie Respiratoire [*A publication*]

Bull Physiopathol Respir (Nancy) ... Bulletin de Physiopathologie Respiratoire (Nancy) [*A publication*]

Bull Pittsb Univ ... Bulletin. Pittsburgh University [*A publication*]

Bull Plankton Soc Jpn ... Bulletin. Plankton Society of Japan [*A publication*]

Bull Plant Bd Fla ... Bulletin. Plant Board of Florida [*A publication*]

Bull Plant Physiol (Beijing) ... Bulletin. Plant Physiology (Beijing) [*A publication*]

Bull P NSW Dep Agric Div Plant Ind ... Bulletin P. New South Wales Department of Agriculture. Division of Plant Industry [*A publication*]

Bull Pol Acad Sci Biol ... Bulletin. Polish Academy of Sciences. Biology [*A publication*]

Bull Pol Acad Sci Biol Sci ... Bulletin. Polish Academy of Sciences. Biological Sciences [*A publication*]

Bull Pol Acad Sci Chem ... Bulletin. Polish Academy of Sciences. Chemistry [*A publication*]

Bull Pol Acad Sci Earth Sci ... Bulletin. Polish Academy of Sciences. Earth Sciences [*A publication*]

Bull Pol Inst Arts Sci Am ... Bulletin. Polish Institute of Arts and Sciences in America [*A publication*]

Bull Pol Inst Arts Sci Amer ... Bulletin. Polish Institute of Arts and Sciences in America [*A publication*]

Bull Pol Med Sci Hist ... Bulletin of Polish Medical Science and History [*A publication*]

Bull Postgrad Inst Med Educ Res (Chandigarh) ... Bulletin. Postgraduate Institute of Medical Education and Research (Chandigarh) [*A publication*]

Bull Poznan Tow Przyjaciol Nauk Ser D ... Bulletin. Poznanskie Towarzystwo Przyjaciol Nauk. Serie D [*A publication*]

Bull Presse- Informationsamt Bundesregier ... Bulletin. Presse- und Informationsamt der Bundesregierung [*A publication*]

Bull Press Exchange Documn Cent Apimondia ... Bulletin. Press Exchange and Documentation Centre of Apimondia [*A publication*]

Bull Primary Tungsten Assoc ... Bulletin. Primary Tungsten Association [*A publication*]

Bull Prosthet Res ... Bulletin of Prosthetics Research [*A publication*]

Bull Prot Veg ... Bulletin de la Protection des Vegetaux [*A publication*]

Bull Psychon Soc ... Bulletin. Psychonomic Society [*A publication*]

Bull Public Health Inst Hyogo Prefect ... Bulletin. Public Health Institute of Hyogo Prefecture [*A publication*]

Bull Puerto Rico Agric Exp Stn Insular Stn (Rio Piedras) ... Bulletin. Puerto Rico Agricultural Experiment Station. Insular Station (Rio Piedras) [*A publication*]

Bull Punjab Agric Univ ... Bulletin. Punjab Agricultural University [*A publication*]

Bull Pure Appl Sci ... Bulletin of Pure and Applied Sciences [*A publication*]

Bull Pusan Fish Coll (Nat Sci) ... Bulletin. Pusan Fisheries College (Natural Sciences) [*A publication*]

Bull Que Soc Crim ... Bulletin. Quebec Society of Criminology [*A publication*] (DLA)

Bull Quezon Inst (Manila) ... Bulletin. Quezon Institute (Manila) [*A publication*]

Bull Radiat Prot ... Bulletin of Radiation Protection [*India*] [*A publication*]

Bull Radio Electr Eng Div Natl Res Counc Can ... Bulletin. Radio and Electrical Engineering Division. National Research Council of Canada [*A publication*]

Bull Radio Electr Eng Div Nat Res Counc Can ... Bulletin. Radio and Electrical Engineering Division. National Research Council of Canada [*A publication*]

Bull Raffles Mus ... Bulletin. Raffles Museum [*A publication*]

Bull R Col Psychiatr ... Bulletin. Royal College of Psychiatrists [*A publication*]

Bull Rech Agron Gembloux ... Bulletin des Recherches Agronomiques de Gembloux [*A publication*]

Bull Reg Res Lab (Jammu) ... Bulletin. Regional Research Laboratory (Jammu) [*A publication*]

Bull Rem Sens Soc Aust ... Remote Sensing Association of Australia. Bulletin [*A publication*] (APTA)

Bull Repub Inst Prot Nat Mus Nat Hist Titograd ... Bulletin. Republic Institution for the Protection of Nature and the Museum of Natural History in Titograd [*A publication*]

Bull Res Coll Agric Vet Sci Nihon Univ ... Bulletin of Research. College of Agriculture and Veterinary Science. Nihon University [*A publication*]

Bull Res Coll Agr Vet Med Nihon Univ ... Bulletin of Research. College of Agriculture and Veterinary Medicine. Nihon University [*A publication*]

Bull Res Counc Isr ... Bulletin. Research Council of Israel [*A publication*]

Bull Res Counc Isr Sect A Chem ... Bulletin. Research Council of Israel. Section A. Chemistry [*A publication*]

Bull Res Counc Isr Sect A Math Phys Chem ... Bulletin. Research Council of Israel. Section A. Mathematics, Physics, and Chemistry [*A publication*]

Bull Res Counc Isr Sect B Biol Geol ... Bulletin. Research Council of Israel. Section B. Biology and Geology [*A publication*]

Bull Res Counc Isr Sect B Zool ... Bulletin. Research Council of Israel. Section B. Zoology [*A publication*]

Bull Res Counc Isr Sect C Technol ... Bulletin. Research Council of Israel. Section C. Technology [*A publication*]

Bull Res Counc Isr Sect D Bot ... Bulletin. Research Council of Israel. Section D. Botany [*A publication*]

Bull Res Counc Isr Sect E Exp Med ... Bulletin. Research Council of Israel. Section E. Experimental Medicine [*A publication*]

Bull Res Counc Isr Sect F ... Bulletin. Research Council of Israel. Section F. Mathematics and Physics [*A publication*]

Bull Res Counc Isr Sect G Geo-Sci ... Bulletin. Research Council of Israel. Section G. Geo-Sciences [*A publication*]

Bull Res Coun Israel ... Bulletin. Research Council of Israel [*A publication*]

Bull Reserve Bank ... Bulletin. Reserve Bank of New Zealand [*A publication*]

Bull Reserve Bank Aust ... Reserve Bank of Australia. Bulletin [*A publication*]

Bull Res Hum ... Bulletin of Research in the Humanities [*A publication*]

Bull Res Humanit ... Bulletin of Research in the Humanities [*A publication*]

Bull Res Inst Appl Electr ... Bulletin. Research Institute of Applied Electricity [*A publication*]

Bull Res Inst Appl Mech Kyushu Univ ... Bulletin. Research Institute for Applied Mechanics. Kyushu University [*Japan*] [*A publication*]

Bull Res Inst Diathetic Med Kumamoto Univ ... Bulletin. Research Institute for Diathetic Medicine. Kumamoto University [*A publication*]

Bull Res Inst Electron Shizuoka Univ ... Bulletin. Research Institute of Electronics. Shizuoka University [*A publication*]

Bull Res Inst Ferment Yamanashi Univ ... Bulletin. Research Institute of Fermentation. Yamanashi University [*Japan*] [*A publication*]

Bull Res Inst Food Sci Kyoto Univ ... Bulletin. Research Institute for Food Science. Kyoto University [*A publication*]

Bull Res Inst Min Dressing Metall ... Bulletin. Research Institute of Mineral Dressing and Metallurgy [*Japan*] [*A publication*]

Bull Res Inst Miner Dressing Metall Tohoku Univ ... Bulletin. Research Institute of Mineral Dressing and Metallurgy. Tohoku University [*Japan*] [*A publication*]

Bull Res Inst Polymers Textiles ... Bulletin. Research Institute for Polymers and Textiles [*A publication*]

Bull Res Inst Sci Meas Tohoku Univ ... Bulletin. Research Institute for Scientific Measurements. Tohoku University [*A publication*]

Bull Res Inst Sumatra Plant Assoc ... Bulletin. Research Institute. Sumatra Plantations Association [*A publication*]

Bull Res Inst Univ Kerala (Trivandrum) Ser A ... Bulletin. Research Institute. University of Kerala (Trivandrum). Series A. Physical Sciences [*A publication*]

Bull Res Lab Nucl React Tokyo Inst Technol ... Bulletin. Research Laboratory for Nuclear Reactors. Tokyo Institute of Technology [*A publication*]

Bull Res Lab Precis Mach Electron ... Bulletin. Research Laboratory of Precision Machinery and Electronics [*A publication*]

Bull Res Lab Precis Mach and Electron ... Bulletin. Research Laboratory of Precision Machinery and Electronics [*A publication*]

Bull Res Lab Precis Mach Electron Tokyo Inst Technol ... Bulletin. Research Laboratory of Precision Machinery and Electronics. Tokyo Institute of Technology [*A publication*]

Bull Rheum Dis ... Bulletin on Rheumatic Diseases [*A publication*]

Bull Rhode Isl Agric Exp Stn ... Bulletin. Rhode Island Agricultural Experiment Station [*A publication*]

Bull RI Agric Exp Stn ... Bulletin. Rhode Island Agricultural Experiment Station [*A publication*]

Bull Richmond County Med Soc ... Bulletin. Richmond County Medical Society [*Georgia*] [*A publication*]

Bull Rijksmus ... Bulletin. Rijksmuseum [*A publication*]

Bull Riverside County Med Assoc ... Bulletin. Riverside County Medical Association [*California*] [*A publication*]

Bull ROM ... Bulletin. Royal Ontario Museum. Art and Archaeology Division [*A publication*]

Bull Roum ... Academie Roumaine. Bulletin de la Section Historique [*A publication*]

Bull Rubber Grow Assoc ... Bulletin. Rubber Growers Association [*A publication*]

Bull Rylands Libr ... Bulletin. John Rylands Library [*A publication*]   (OCD)

Bull S Afr Cult Hist Mus ... Bulletin. South African Cultural History Museum [*A publication*]

Bull S Afr Inst Assayers Anal ... Bulletin. South African Institute of Assayers and Analysts [*A publication*]

Bull Saga Agr Exp Sta ... Bulletin. Saga Agricultural Experiment Station [*A publication*]

Bull Saginaw County Med Soc ... Bulletin. Saginaw County Medical Society [*Michigan*] [*A publication*]

Bull Saitama Hortic Exp Stn ... Bulletin. Saitama Horticultural Experiment Station [*A publication*]

Bull Salesian Polytech ... Bulletin. Salesian Polytechnic [*A publication*]

Bulls Am Paleontology ... Bulletins of American Paleontology [*A publication*]

Bull San Diego Cty Dent Soc ... Bulletin. San Diego County Dental Society [*A publication*]

Bull San Mateo County Med Soc ... Bulletin. San Mateo County Medical Society [*California*] [*A publication*]

Bull San Mateo Cty Dent Soc ... Bulletin. San Mateo [*California*] County Dental Society [*A publication*]

Bull Santa Clara County Med Soc ... Bulletin. Santa Clara County Medical Society [*A publication*]

Bull Sante Prod Anim Afr ... Bulletin des Sante et Production Animales en Afrique [*A publication*]

Bull SC Acad Sci ... Bulletin. South Carolina Academy of Science [*A publication*]

Bull Sch For Mont St Univ ... Bulletin. School of Forestry. Montana State University [*A publication*]

Bull Sch For S F Austin St Coll ... Bulletin. School of Forestry. Stephen F. Austin State College [*A publication*]

Bull Sch Med Univ MD ... Bulletin. School of Medicine. University of Maryland [*A publication*]

Bull School Eng Archit Sakarya ... Bulletin. School of Engineering and Architecture of Sakarya [*A publication*]

Bull Sch Orient Afr Stud ... Bulletin. School of Oriental and African Studies [*A publication*]

Bull Sch Orient Stud ... Bulletin. School of Oriental Studies [*A publication*]

Bull Schweiz Akad Med Wiss ... Bulletin. Schweizerische Akademie der Medizinischen Wissenschaften [*A publication*]

Bull Schweiz Electrotech Ver ... Bulletin. Schweizerischer Elektrotechnischer Verein [*Switzerland*] [*A publication*]

Bull Schweiz Ges Anthropol Ethnol ... Bulletin. Schweizerische Gesellschaft fuer Anthropologie und Ethnologie [*A publication*]

Bull Sci Acad Imp Sci Saint Petersbourg ... Bulletin Scientifique. Academie Imperiale des Sciences de Saint Petersbourg [*A publication*]

Bull Sci Assoc Ing Electr Inst Electrotech (Montefiore) ... Bulletin Scientifique. Association des Ingenieurs Electriciens Sortis de l'Institut Electrotechnique (Montefiore) [*A publication*]

Bull Sci Cons Acad RSF Yougosl ... Bulletin Scientifique. Conseil des Academies de la RSF de Yougoslavie [*A publication*]

Bull Sci Cons Acad RSF Yougosl Sect A Sci Nat Tech Med ... Bulletin Scientifique. Conseil des Academies de la RSF de Yougoslavie. Section A. Sciences Naturelles, Techniques, et Medicales [*A publication*]

Bull Sci Cons Acad Sci Arts RSF Yougosl Sect A ... Bulletin Scientifique. Conseil des Academies des Sciences et des Arts de la RSF de Yougoslavie. Section A. Sciences Naturelles, Techniques, et Medicales [*A publication*]

Bull Sci Conseil Acad RSF Yougoslav Sect A ... Bulletin Scientifique. Conseil des Academies de la RSF de Yougoslavie. Section A [*Zagreb*] [*A publication*]

Bull Sci Ecole Polytech Timisoara ... Bulletin Scientifique. Ecole Polytechnique de Timisoara. Comptes Rendus des Seances. Societe Scientifique de Timisoara [*A publication*]

Bull Sci Econ Bur Rech Minieres Alger ... Bulletin Scientifique et Economique. Bureau de Recherches Minieres de l'Algerie [*A publication*]

Bull Sci Eng Res Lab Waseda Univ ... Bulletin. Science and Engineering Research Laboratory. Waseda University [*A publication*]

Bull Sci Engrg Div Univ Ryukyus Math Natur Sci ... Bulletin. University of the Ryukyus. Science and Engineering Division. Mathematics and Natural Sciences [*A publication*]

Bull Scient France et Belgique ... Bulletin Scientifique de la France et de la Belgique [*A publication*]

Bull Scient Fr Belg ... Bulletin Scientifique de la France et de la Belgique [*A publication*]

Bull Sci Geol ... Bulletin des Sciences Geologiques [*Strasbourg*] [*A publication*]

Bull Sci Hist Auvergne ... Bulletin Scientifique et Historique de l'Auvergne [*A publication*]

Bull Sci Ind Maison Roure Bertrand Fils ... Bulletin Scientifique et Industriel de la Maison Roure Bertrand Fils [*A publication*]

Bull Sci Inst Text Fr ... Bulletin Scientifique. Institut Textile de France [*A publication*]

Bull Sci ITF ... Bulletin Scientifique. Institut Textile de France [*A publication*]

Bull Sci Lab Denison Univ ... Bulletin. Scientific Laboratories of Denison University [*A publication*]

Bull Sci Math ... Bulletin des Sciences Mathematiques [*A publication*]

Bull Sci Math (2) ... Bulletin des Sciences Mathematiques (2e Serie) [*Paris*] [*A publication*]

Bull Sci Pharmacol ... Bulletin des Sciences Pharmacologiques [*A publication*]

Bull Sci Roumain ... Bulletin Scientifique Roumain [*A publication*]

Bull Sci Sect A ... Bulletin Scientifique. Section A. Sciences Naturelles, Techniques, et Medicales [*A publication*]

Bull Sci Tech Doc Cent (Egypt) ... Bulletin. Scientific and Technical Documentation Centre (Egypt) [*A publication*]

Bull Sci Technol Agency ... Bulletin. Science and Technology Agency [*Japan*] [*A publication*]

Bull Sci Terre Univ Poitiers ... Bulletin. Sciences de la Terre. Universite de Poitiers [*A publication*]

Bull Scott Assoc Geogr Teach ... Bulletin. Scottish Association of Geography Teachers [*A publication*]

Bull Scott Georgian Soc ... Bulletin. Scottish Georgian Society [*A publication*]

Bull Scripps Inst Oceanogr Univ Calif ... Bulletin. Scripps Institution of Oceanography of the University of California [*A publication*]

Bull Sc Soc Philomat Paris ... Bulletin des Sciences. Societe Philomathique de Paris [*A publication*]

Bull S Dak Agr Exp Sta ... Bulletin. South Dakota Agricultural Experiment Station [*A publication*]

Bull S Dak Agric Exp St ... Bulletin. South Dakota Agricultural Experiment Station [*A publication*]

Bull SD Geol Surv ... Bulletin. South Dakota Geological Survey [*A publication*]

Bull Seances Acad R Sci Outre-Mer (Brussels) ... Bulletin des Seances. Academie Royale des Sciences d'Outre-Mer (Brussels) [*A publication*]

Bull Seanc Soc Sci Nancy ... Bulletin des Seances. Societe des Sciences de Nancy et Reunion Biologique de Nancy [*A publication*]

Bull Sea View Hosp ... Bulletin. Sea View Hospital [*A publication*]

Bull Sec Agron Div Tokai-Kinki Natl Agric Exp Stn ... Bulletin. Second Agronomy Division. Tokai-Kinki National Agricultural Experiment Station [*A publication*]

Bull Second Agron Div Tokai-Kinki Nat Agr Exp Sta ... Bulletin. Second Agronomy Division. Tokai-Kinki National Agricultural Experiment Station [*A publication*]

Bull Second Dist Dent Soc ... Bulletin. Second District Dental Society [*Brooklyn, New York*] [*A publication*]

Bull Sect Geogr Comite Trav Hist Sci ... Bulletin. Section de Geographie. Comite des Travaux Historiques et Scientifiques. Ministere de l'Instruction Publique et des Beaux Arts. Ministere de l'Education Nationale [*A publication*]

Bull Sect Hist Acad Roumaine ... Bulletin. Section Historique. Academie Roumaine [*A publication*]

Bull Sect Log ... Bulletin. Section of Logic [*A publication*]

Bull Sect Sci Acad Roum ... Bulletin. Section Scientifique. Academie Roumaine [*A publication*]

Bull Seikai Reg Fish Res Lab ... Bulletin. Seikai Regional Fisheries Research Laboratory [*A publication*]

Bull Seishin Igaku Inst ... Bulletin. Seishin Igaku Institute [*A publication*]

Bull Seishin Igaku Inst (Seishin Igaku Kenkyusho Gyosekishu) ... Bulletin. Seishin Igaku Institute (Seishin Igaku Kenkyusho Gyosekishu) [*A publication*]

Bull Seismol Soc Am ... Bulletin. Seismological Society of America [*A publication*]

Bull Seismol Soc Amer ... Bulletin. Seismological Society of America [*A publication*]

Bull Seismol (Warsaw) ... Bulletin Seismologique (Warsaw) [*A publication*]

Bull Seism Soc Am ... Bulletin. Seismological Society of America [*A publication*]

Bull Seoul Natl Univ For Seoul Taehakyo Yonsuplim Pogo ... Bulletin. Seoul National University Forests/Seoul Taehakkyo Yonsuplim Pogo [*A publication*]

Bull Ser C Soc Geol Mineral Bretagne ... Bulletin. Serie C. Societe Geologique et Mineralogique de Bretagne [*A publication*]

Bull Ser Exp Stn Gov Gen Chosen ... Bulletin. Sericultural Experiment Station. Government General of Chosen [*A publication*]

Bull Seric Exp Stn (Tokyo) ... Bulletin. Sericultural Experiment Station (Tokyo) [*A publication*]

Bull Serv Bot Agron Tunis ... Bulletin. Service Botanique et Agronomique de Tunisie [*A publication*]

Bull Serv Carte Geol Alger ... Bulletin. Service de la Carte Geologique de l'Algerie [*A publication*]

Bull Serv Carte Geol Alger Ser 2 ... Bulletin. Service de la Carte Geologique de l'Algerie. Serie 2. Stratigraphie [*A publication*]

Bull Serv Carte Geol Alger Ser 3 ... Bulletin. Service de la Carte Geologique de l'Algerie. Serie 3. Geologie Appliquee [*A publication*]

Bull Serv Carte Geol Alger Ser 5 ... Bulletin. Service de la Carte Geologique de l'Algerie. Serie 5. Petrographie [*A publication*]

Bull Serv Carte Geol Alger Ser 6 ... Bulletin. Service de la Carte Geologique de l'Algerie. Serie 6. Metallogenie [*A publication*]

Bull Serv Carte Geol Als Lorr ... Bulletin. Service de la Carte Geologique d'Alsace et de Lorraine [*A publication*]

Bull Serv Carte Geol Fr ... Bulletin. Service de la Carte Geologique de la France [*A publication*]

Bull Serv Cult Etud Peuplier et Saule ... Bulletin. Service de Culture et d'Etudes du Peuplier et du Saule [*A publication*]

Bull Serv Et ... Bulletin. Service des Etudes et de la Documentation Economiques. Office de la Statistique Generale [*A publication*]

Bull Serv Geol Luxemb ... Bulletin. Service Geologique du Luxembourg [*A publication*]

Bull Serv Geol Rwandaise ... Bulletin. Service Geologique de la Republique Rwandaise [*A publication*]

Bull Serv Instrum Mes ... Bulletin. Service des Instruments de Mesure [*A publication*]

Bull Serv Med Trav ... Bulletin. Service Medical du Travail [*A publication*]

Bull SEV .... Bulletin. Schweizerischer Elektrotechnischer Verein [*A publication*]

Bull Shanghai Sci Inst ... Bulletin. Shanghai Science Institute [*A publication*]

Bull Shemane Agric Exp Stn ... Bulletin. Shemane Agricultural Experiment Station [*A publication*]

Bull Shenyang Inst Geol Miner Resour ... Bulletin. Shenyang Institute of Geology and Mineral Resources [*A publication*]

Bull Shiga Pref Agr Exp Sta ... Bulletin. Shiga Prefectural Agricultural Experiment Station [*A publication*]

Bull Shih Yen Pao Kao Taiwan For Res Inst ... Bulletin. Shih Yen Pao Kao. Taiwan Forest Research Institute [*A publication*]

Bull Shikoku Agr Exp Sta ... Bulletin. Shikoku Agricultural Experiment Station [*A publication*]

Bull Shikoku Agric Exp Stn ... Bulletin. Shikoku Agricultural Experiment Station [*A publication*]

Bull Shikoku Natl Agric Exp Stn ... Bulletin. Shikoku National Agricultural Experiment Station [*A publication*]

Bull Shikoku Natl Agric Exp Stn Extra Issue ... Bulletin. Shikoku National Agricultural Experiment Station. Extra Issue [*A publication*]

Bull Shimane Agr Coll ... Bulletin. Shimane Agricultural College [*A publication*]

Bull Shimane Agr Exp Sta ... Bulletin. Shimane Agricultural Experiment Station [*A publication*]

Bull Shimane Agric Coll ... Bulletin. Shimane Agricultural College [*A publication*]

Bull Shimane Agric Exp Stn ... Bulletin. Shimane Agricultural Experiment Station [*A publication*]

Bull Shimane Univ Nat Sci ... Bulletin. Shimane University. Natural Science [*Japan*] [*A publication*]

Bull Shinshu Univ For ... Bulletin. Shinshu University Forests [*A publication*]

Bull Shizuoka Agr Exp Sta ... Bulletin. Shizuoka Agricultural Experiment Station [*A publication*]

Bull Shizuoka Daigaku Nogaku-Bu ... Bulletin. Shizuoka Daigaku Nogaku-Bu [*A publication*]

Bull Shizuoka Pref Agr Exp Sta ... Bulletin. Shizuoka Prefectural Agricultural Experiment Station [*A publication*]

Bull Shizuoka Prefect Fish Exp Stn ... Bulletin. Shizuoka Prefectural Fisheries Experiment Station [*A publication*]

Bull SHPF ... Bulletin. Societe de l'Histoire du Protestantisme Francais [*A publication*]

Bull Shrimp Cult Res Cent ... Bulletin. Shrimp Culture Research Center [*A publication*]

Bull Signal ... Bulletin Signaletique [*A publication*]

Bull Signal 221 ... Bulletin Signaletique 221. Gitologie Economie Miniere [*A publication*]

Bull Signal Ent Med Vet ... Bulletin Signaletique. Entomologie Medicale et Veterinaire [*A publication*]

Bull Sign Polym Peint Bois Cuirs ... Bulletin Signaletique. Polymeres, Peintures, Bois, Cuirs [*A publication*]

Bull Sinai Hosp Detroit ... Bulletin. Sinai Hospital of Detroit [*A publication*]

Bull SL .... Bulletin. Societe de Linguistique de Paris [*A publication*]

Bull Sloane Hosp Women Columbia-Presbyt Med Cent ... Bulletin. Sloane Hospital for Women in the Columbia-Presbyterian Medical Center [*A publication*]

Bull Slov Pol'nohospod Akad Vysk Ustavu Potravin ... Bulletin. Slovenskej Pol'nohospodarskej Akademie. Vyskumneho Ustavu Potravinarskeho [*A publication*]

Bull Soc Acup ... Bulletin. Societe d'Acupuncture [*A publication*]

Bull Soc Agric Alg ... Bulletin. Societe d'Agriculture d'Alger [*A publication*]

Bull Soc Agric Fr ... Bulletin. Societe des Agriculteurs de France [*A publication*]

Bull Soc Agricrs Fr ... Bulletin. Societe des Agriculteurs de France [*A publication*]

Bull Soc Agr Sci Arts Sarthe ... Bulletin. Societe d'Agriculture, Sciences, et Arts de la Sarthe [*A publication*]

Bull Soc Alsac Constr Mec ... Bulletin. Societe Alsacienne de Construction Mecanique [*A publication*]

Bull Soc Amis Andre-Marie Ampere ... Bulletin. Societe des Amis d'Andre-Marie Ampere [*A publication*]

Bull Soc Amis Sci Lett Poz ... Bulletin. Societe des Amis des Sciences et des Lettres de Poznan [*A publication*]

Bull Soc Amis Sci Lett Poznan Ser B ... Bulletin. Societe des Amis des Sciences et des Lettres de Poznan. Serie B. Sciences Mathematiques et Naturelles [*A publication*]

Bull Soc Amis Sci Lett Poznan Ser C ... Bulletin. Societe des Amis des Sciences et des Lettres de Poznan. Serie C. Medecine [*A publication*]

Bull Soc Amis Sci Lett Poznan Ser D ... Bulletin. Societe des Amis des Sciences et des Lettres de Poznan. Serie D. Sciences Biologiques [*A publication*]

Bull Soc Amis Sci Lett Poznan Ser D Sci Biol ... Bulletin. Societe des Amis des Sciences et des Lettres de Poznan. Serie D. Sciences Biologiques [*A publication*]

Bull Soc Analyt Chem ... Bulletin. Society for Analytical Chemistry [*A publication*]

Bull Soc Anat Paris ... Bulletin. Societe Anatomique de Paris [*A publication*]

Bull Soc Anthropol ... Bulletins et Memoires. Societe d'Anthropologie de Paris [*A publication*]

Bull Soc Antiq Picardie ... Bulletin. Societe des Antiquaires de Picardie [*A publication*]

Bull Soc Antiquaires Ouest ... Bulletin. Societe des Antiquaires de l'Ouest [*A publication*]

Bull Soc Ant Ouest ... Bulletin. Societe des Antiquaires de l'Ouest et des Musees de Poitiers [*A publication*]

Bull Soc Apic Alpes-Marit ... Bulletin. Societe d'Apiculture des Alpes-Maritimes [*A publication*]

Bull Soc Archeol Finistere ... Bulletin. Societe Archeologique du Finistere [*A publication*]

Bull Soc Archeol Hist Artist Vieux Pap ... Bulletin. Societe Archeologique, Historique, et Artistique de Vieux Papier [*A publication*]

Bull Soc Belge Etud Napoleon ... Bulletin. Societe Belge d'Etudes Napoleoniennes [*A publication*]
Bull Soc Belge Geol ... Bulletin. Societe Belge de Geologie [*Belgium*] [*A publication*]
Bull Soc Belge Ing Ind ... Bulletin. Societe Belge des Ingenieurs et des Industriels [*A publication*]
Bull Soc Belge Ophtalmol ... Bulletin. Societe Belge d'Ophtalmologie [*A publication*]
Bull Soc Belge Phys ... Bulletin. Societe Belge de Physique [*A publication*]
Bull Soc Belg Geol Paleontol Hydrol ... Bulletin. Societe Belge de Geologie, de Paleontologie, et d'Hydrologie [*Later, Bulletin. Societe Belge de Geologie*] [*A publication*]
Bull Soc Borda ... Bulletin. Societe de Borda [*A publication*]
Bull Soc Bot Belg ... Bulletin. Societe Royale de Botanique de Belgique [*A publication*]
Bull Soc Bot Fr ... Bulletin. Societe Botanique de France [*A publication*]
Bull Soc Bot France ... Bulletin. Societe Botanique de France [*A publication*]
Bull Soc Bot Fr Lett Bot ... Bulletin. Societe Botanique de France. Lettres Botaniques [*A publication*]
Bull Soc Bot Geneve ... Bulletin. Societe Botanique de Geneve [*A publication*]
Bull Soc Bot N Fr ... Bulletin. Societe de Botanique du Nord de la France [*A publication*]
Bull Soc Bot Nord Fr ... Bulletin. Societe de Botanique du Nord de la France [*A publication*]
Bull Soc Bot Suisse ... Bulletin. Societe Botanique Suisse [*A publication*]
Bull Soc Cent For Belg ... Bulletin. Societe Centrale Forestiere de Belgique [*A publication*]
Bull Soc Centr Med Vet ... Bulletin. Societe Centrale de Medecine Veterinaire [*A publication*]
Bull Soc Chim Belg ... Bulletin. Societes Chimiques Belges [*A publication*]
Bull Soc Chim (Beograd) ... Bulletin. Societe Chimique (Beograd) [*A publication*]
Bull Soc Chim Biol ... Bulletin. Societe de Chimie Biologique [*France*] [*A publication*]
Bull Soc Chim Fr ... Bulletin. Societe Chimique de France [*A publication*]
Bull Soc Chim Fr 1 ... Bulletin. Societe Chimique de France. Premiere Partie. Chimie Analytique, Chimie Minerale, Chimie Physique [*A publication*]
Bull Soc Chim Fr 2 ... Bulletin. Societe Chimique de France. Deuxieme Partie [*A publication*]
Bull Soc Chim France ... Bulletin. Societe Chimique de France [*A publication*]
Bull Soc Chim de France ... Bulletin. Societe Chimique de France [*A publication*]
Bull Soc Chim Fr Doc ... Bulletin. Societe Chimique de France. Documentation [*A publication*]
Bull Soc Chim Fr Mem ... Bulletin. Societe Chimique de France. Memoires [*A publication*]
Bull Soc Chim Fr Part 1 ... Bulletin. Societe Chimique de France. Premiere Partie. Chimie Analytique, Chimie Minerale, Chimie Physique [*A publication*]
Bull Soc Chim Fr Part 2 ... Bulletin. Societe Chimique de France. Deuxieme Partie. Chimie Organique, Biochimie [*A publication*]
Bull Soc Chim Ind ... Bulletin. Societe de Chimie Industrielle [*France*] [*A publication*]
Bull Soc Chir Paris ... Bulletin. Societe de Chirurgie de Paris [*A publication*]
Bull Soc Encour Ind Natl ... Bulletin. Societe d'Encouragement pour l'Industrie Nationale [*A publication*]
Bull Soc Ent Egypte ... Bulletin. Societe Entomologique d'Egypte [*A publication*]
Bull Soc Ent Fr ... Bulletin. Societe Entomologique de France [*A publication*]
Bull Soc Ent Mulhouse ... Bulletin. Societe Entomologique de Mulhouse [*A publication*]
Bull Soc Entomol Egypte ... Bulletin. Societe Entomologique d'Egypte [*A publication*]
Bull Soc Entomol Fr ... Bulletin. Societe Entomologique de France [*A publication*]
Bull Soc Entomol Suisse ... Bulletin. Societe Entomologique Suisse [*A publication*]
Bull Soc Et Legisl ... Bulletin. Societe d'Etudes Legislatives [*A publication*] (ILCA)
Bull Soc Et Lot ... Bulletin. Societe des Etudes du Lot [*A publication*]
Bull Soc Etud Oceaniennes ... Bulletin. Societe d'Etudes Oceaniennes [*A publication*]
Bull Soc For Belg ... Bulletin. Societe Royale Forestiere de Belgique [*A publication*]
Bull Soc For Franche-Comte ... Bulletin. Societe Forestiere de Franche-Comte et Belfort [*A publication*]
Bull Soc For Franche-Comte ... Bulletin Trimestriel. Societe Forestiere de Franche-Comte et des Provinces de l'Est [*Salins-Les-Bains*] [*A publication*]
Bull Soc Franc Hyg ... Bulletin. Societe Francaise d'Hygiene [*A publication*]
Bull Soc Franc Phot ... Bulletin. Societe Francaise de Photographie [*A publication*]
Bull Soc Franc Physiol Veg ... Bulletin. Societe Francaise de Physiologie Vegetale [*A publication*]
Bull Soc Fr Ceram ... Bulletin. Societe Francaise de Ceramique [*A publication*]
Bull Soc Fr Dermatol Syphiligr ... Bulletin. Societe Francaise de Dermatologie et de Syphiligraphie [*A publication*]
Bull Soc Fr Electr ... Bulletin. Societe Francaise des Electriciens [*France*] [*A publication*]

Bull Soc Fr Hist Hop ... Bulletin. Societe Francaise d'Histoire des Hopitaux [*A publication*]
Bull Soc Frib Sci Nat ... Bulletin. Societe Fribourgeoise des Sciences Naturelles [*A publication*]
Bull Soc Fr Micros ... Bulletin. Societe Francaise de Microscopie [*A publication*]
Bull Soc Fr Mineral ... Bulletin. Societe Francaise de Mineralogie [*A publication*]
Bull Soc Fr Mineral et Cristallogr ... Bulletin. Societe Francaise de Mineralogie et de Cristallographie [*A publication*]
Bull Soc Fr Miner Cristallogr ... Bulletin. Societe Francaise de Mineralogie et de Cristallographie [*A publication*]
Bull Soc Fr Mycol Med ... Bulletin. Societe Francaise de Mycologie Medicale [*A publication*]
Bull Soc Fr Phil ... Bulletin. Societe Francaise de Philosophie [*A publication*]
Bull Soc Fr Photogramm ... Bulletin. Societe Francaise de Photogrammetrie [*Later, Bulletin. Societe Francaise de Photogrammetrie et de Teledetection*] [*A publication*]
Bull Soc Fr Photogramm et Teledetect ... Bulletin. Societe Francaise de Photogrammetrie et de Teledetection [*A publication*]
Bull Soc Fr Physiol Veg ... Bulletin. Societe Francaise de Physiologie Vegetale [*A publication*]
Bull Soc Geographie ... Bulletin. Societe de Geographie [*A publication*]
Bull Soc Geol Belg ... Bulletin. Societe Geologique de Belgique [*A publication*]
Bull Soc Geol Fr ... Bulletin. Societe Geologique de France [*A publication*]
Bull Soc Geol France ... Bulletin. Societe Geologique de France [*A publication*]
Bull Soc Geol Fr Suppl ... Bulletin. Societe Geologique de France. Supplement. Compte Rendu Sommaire des Seances [*A publication*]
Bull Soc Geol Mineral Bretagne Ser C ... Bulletin. Societe Geologique et Mineralogique de Bretagne. Serie C [*A publication*]
Bull Soc Geol Normandie ... Bulletin. Societe Geologique de Normandie [*A publication*]
Bull Soc Hist Archeol Perigord ... Bulletin. Societe Historique et Archeologique du Perigord [*A publication*]
Bull Soc Hist Nat Afr Nord ... Bulletin. Societe d'Histoire Naturelle de l'Afrique du Nord [*A publication*]
Bull Soc Hist Nat Doubs ... Bulletin. Societe d'Histoire Naturelle du Doubs [*A publication*]
Bull Soc Hist Nat Metz ... Bulletin. Societe d'Histoire Naturelle de Metz [*A publication*]
Bull Soc Hist Nat Toulouse ... Bulletin. Societe d'Histoire Naturelle de Toulouse [*A publication*]
Bull Soc Hist Natur Afr Nord ... Bulletin. Societe d'Histoire Naturelle de l'Afrique du Nord [*A publication*]
Bull Societe Ind Mulhouse ... Bulletin. Societe Industrielle de Mulhouse [*A publication*]
Bull Soc Imp Nat Moscou ... Bulletin. Societe Imperiale des Naturalistes de Moscou [*A publication*]
Bull Soc Ind ... Bulletin Social des Industriels. Association des Patrons et Ingenieurs Catholiques de Belgique [*A publication*]
Bull Soc Ind Amiens ... Bulletin. Societe Industrielle d'Amiens [*A publication*]
Bull Soc Ind Miner St Etienne ... Bulletin. Societe de l'Industrie Minerale de St. Etienne [*A publication*]
Bull Soc Ind Rouen ... Bulletin. Societe Industrielle de Rouen [*A publication*]
Bull Soc Int Chir ... Bulletin. Societe Internationale de Chirurgie [*A publication*]
Bull Soc Int Crimin ... Bulletin. Societe Internationale de Criminologie [*A publication*] (ILCA)
Bull Soc Int Electr ... Bulletin. Societe Internationale des Electriciens [*A publication*]
Bull Soc Lat Am Stud ... Bulletin. Society for Latin American Studies [*A publication*]
Bull Soc Lepid Fr ... Bulletin. Societe des Lepidopteristes Francais [*A publication*]
Bull Soc Linn Bord ... Bulletin. Societe Linneenne de Bordeaux [*A publication*]
Bull Soc Linn Lyon ... Bulletin. Societe Linneenne de Lyon [*A publication*]
Bull Soc Linn Normandie ... Bulletin. Societe Linneenne de Normandie [*A publication*]
Bull Soc Linn Provence ... Bulletin. Societe Linneenne de Provence [*A publication*]
Bull Soc Lorraine Sci ... Bulletin. Societe Lorraine des Sciences [*A publication*]
Bull Soc Math Belg ... Bulletin. Societe Mathematique de Belgique [*A publication*]
Bull Soc Math Belg Ser A ... Bulletin. Societe Mathematique de Belgique. Serie A [*A publication*]
Bull Soc Math Belg Ser B ... Bulletin. Societe Mathematique de Belgique. Serie B [*A publication*]
Bull Soc Math Fr ... Bulletin. Societe Mathematique de France [*A publication*]
Bull Soc Math France ... Bulletin. Societe Mathematique de France [*A publication*]
Bull Soc Math France Mem ... Societe Mathematique de France. Bulletin, Memoire [*A publication*]
Bull Soc Math France Suppl Mem ... Societe Mathematique de France. Bulletin, Supplement, Memoire [*A publication*]
Bull Soc Math Grece ... Bulletin. Societe Mathematique de Grece [*A publication*]

Bull Soc Math Grece NS ... Bulletin. Societe Mathematique de Grece. Nouvelle Serie [*A publication*]

Bull Soc Math Phys Macedoine ... Bulletin. Societe des Mathematiciens et des Physiciens de la Republique Populaire de Macedoine [*A publication*]

Bull Soc Med Afr Noire ... Bulletin. Societe Medicale d'Afrique Noire de Langue Francaise [*A publication*]

Bull Soc Med Afr Noire Lang Fr ... Bulletin. Societe Medicale d'Afrique Noire de Langue Francaise [*A publication*]

Bull Soc Med-Chir Indo-Chine ... Bulletin. Societe Medico-Chirurgicale de l'Indo-Chine [*A publication*]

Bull Soc Med Hop Lyon ... Bulletin. Societe Medicale des Hopitaux de Lyon [*A publication*]

Bull Soc Med Hop Pa ... Bulletins et Memoires. Societe Medicale des Hopitaux de Paris [*A publication*]

Bull Soc Med Hop Paris ... Bulletins et Memoires. Societe Medicale des Hopitaux de Paris [*A publication*]

Bull Soc Med Par ... Bulletin et Memoires. Societe de Medecine de Paris [*A publication*]

Bull Soc Microsc Can ... Bulletin. Societe de Microscopie du Canada [*A publication*]

Bull Soc Mycol ... Bulletin. Societe Mycologique de Geneve [*A publication*]

Bull Soc Mycol Fr ... Bulletin. Societe Mycologique de France [*A publication*]

Bull Soc Nat Antiq Fr ... Bulletin. Societe Nationale des Antiquaires de France [*A publication*]

Bull Soc Nat Archeol Ain ... Bulletin. Societe des Naturalistes et des Archeologues de l'Ain [*A publication*]

Bull Soc Nat Fr ... Bulletin. Societe Nationale des Antiquaires de France [*A publication*]

Bull Soc Nat Lux ... Bulletin. Societe des Naturalistes Luxembourgeois [*A publication*]

Bull Soc Nat Voroneje ... Bulletin. Societe des Naturalistes de Voroneje [*A publication*]

Bull Soc Nav Archit Mar Eng ... Bulletin. Society of Naval Architects and Marine Engineers [*A publication*]

Bull Soc Neuchatel Sci Nat ... Bulletin. Societe Neuchateloise des Sciences Naturelles [*A publication*]

Bull Soc NZ ... Bulletin. Royal Society of New Zealand [*A publication*]

Bull Soc Obst Gynec ... Bulletin. Societe d'Obstetrique et de Gynecologie de Paris [*A publication*]

Bull Soc Ophtal Egy ... Bulletin. Societe d'Ophtalmologie d'Egypte [*A publication*]

Bull Soc Ophtal Fr ... Bulletin. Societes d'Ophtalmologie de France [*A publication*]

Bull Soc Ophtalmol Fr ... Bulletin. Societes d'Ophtalmologie de France [*A publication*]

Bull Soc Ophtalmol Paris ... Bulletin. Societe d'Ophtalmologie de Paris [*A publication*]

Bull Soc Path Exot ... Bulletin. Societe de Pathologie Exotique [*A publication*]

Bull Soc Path Exot ... Bulletin. Societe de Pathologie Exotique et de Ses Filiales [*A publication*]

Bull Soc Pathol Exot ... Bulletin. Societe de Pathologie Exotique [*A publication*]

Bull Soc Pathol Exot Filiales ... Bulletin. Societe de Pathologie Exotique et de Ses Filiales [*A publication*]

Bull Soc Pediat Paris ... Bulletin. Societe de Pediatrie de Paris [*A publication*]

Bull Soc Pharmacol Environ Pathol ... Bulletin. Society of Pharmacological and Environmental Pathologists [*A publication*]

Bull Soc Pharm Bord ... Bulletin. Societe de Pharmacie de Bordeaux [*A publication*]

Bull Soc Pharm Lille ... Bulletin. Societe de Pharmacie de Lille [*A publication*]

Bull Soc Pharm Mars ... Bulletin. Societe de Pharmacie de Marseille [*A publication*]

Bull Soc Pharm Marseille ... Bulletin. Societe de Pharmacie de Marseille [*A publication*]

Bull Soc Pharm Nancy ... Bulletin. Societe de Pharmacie de Nancy [*A publication*]

Bull Soc Pharm Strasb ... Bulletin. Societe de Pharmacie de Strasbourg [*A publication*]

Bull Soc Philomat Paris ... Bulletin. Societe Philomatique de Paris [*A publication*]

Bull Soc Philom Vosg ... Bulletin. Societe Philomatique Vosgienne [*A publication*]

Bull Soc Photogr Sci Technol Jpn ... Bulletin. Society of Photographic Science and Technology of Japan [*A publication*]

Bull Soc Phycol Fr ... Bulletin. Societe Phycologique de France [*A publication*]

Bull Soc Port Sci Nat ... Bulletin. Societe Portugaise des Sciences Naturelles [*A publication*]

Bull Soc Portugaise Sc Nat ... Bulletin. Societe Portugaise des Sciences Naturelles [*A publication*]

Bull Soc Prehist Fr ... Bulletin. Societe Prehistorique Francaise [*A publication*]

Bull Soc Prof Hist Geogr ... Bulletin. Societe des Professeurs d'Histoire et de Geographie [*A publication*]

Bull Soc Promot Eng Educ ... Bulletin. Society for the Promotion of Engineering Education [*A publication*]

Bull Soc R Belge Electr ... Bulletin. Societe Royale Belge des Electriciens [*A publication*]

Bull Soc R Belge Gynecol Obstet ... Bulletin. Societe Royale Belge de Gynecologie et d'Obstetrique [*A publication*]

Bull Soc R Bot Belg ... Bulletin. Societe Royale de Botanique de Belgique [*A publication*]

Bull Soc R For Belg ... Bulletin. Societe Royale Forestiere de Belgique [*A publication*]

Bull Soc R For Belg Tijdschr K Belg Bosbouwmaatsch ... Bulletin. Societe Royale Forestiere de Belgique/Tijdschrift van de Koninklijke Belgische Bosbouwmaatschappij [*A publication*]

Bull Soc Romande Apic ... Bulletin. Societe Romande d'Apiculture [*A publication*]

Bull Soc Roum Neurol Psychiatr Psychol Endocrinol ... Bulletin. Societe Roumaine de Neurologie, Psychiatrie, Psychologie, et Endocrinologie [*A publication*]

Bull Soc Roy Belg Elec ... Bulletin. Societe Royale Belge des Electriciens [*A publication*]

Bull Soc Roy Sci Liege ... Bulletin. Societe Royale des Sciences de Liege [*A publication*]

Bull Soc R Pharm Bruxelles ... Bulletin. Societe Royale de Pharmacie de Bruxelles [*A publication*]

Bull Soc R Sci Liege ... Bulletin. Societe Royale des Sciences de Liege [*A publication*]

Bull Soc Sci Anc ... Bulletin. Societe des Sciences Anciennes [*A publication*]

Bull Soc Sci Bretagne ... Bulletin. Societe Scientifique de Bretagne [*A publication*]

Bull Soc Scient Bretagne ... Bulletin. Societe Scientifique de Bretagne [*A publication*]

Bull Soc Scient Med Ouest ... Bulletin. Societe Scientifique et Medicale de l'Ouest [*A publication*]

Bull Soc Sci Hyg Aliment Aliment Ration ... Bulletin. Societe Scientifique d'Hygiene Alimentaire et d'Alimentation Rationnelle [*A publication*]

Bull Soc Sci Hyg Aliment Aliment Ration Homme ... Bulletin. Societe Scientifique d'Hygiene Alimentaire et d'Alimentation Rationnelle de l'Homme [*A publication*]

Bull Soc Sci Lett Lodz ... Bulletin. Societe des Sciences et des Lettres de Lodz [*A publication*]

Bull Soc Sci Lett Lodz Cl 4 ... Bulletin. Societe des Sciences et des Lettres de Lodz. Classe 4. Sciences Medicales [*A publication*]

Bull Soc Sci Lettres Lodz ... Bulletin. Societe des Sciences et des Lettres de Lodz [*A publication*]

Bull Soc Sci Med Grand-Duche Luxemb ... Bulletin. Societe des Sciences Medicales du Grand-Duche de Luxembourg [*A publication*]

Bull Soc Sci Med Gr-Duche Luxemb ... Bulletin. Societe des Sciences Medicales du Grand-Duche de Luxembourg [*A publication*]

Bull Soc Sci Nancy ... Bulletin. Societe des Sciences de Nancy [*A publication*]

Bull Soc Sci Nat ... Bulletin. Societe des Sciences Naturelles [*A publication*]

Bull Soc Sci Nat Mar ... Bulletin. Societe des Sciences Naturelles du Maroc [*A publication*]

Bull Soc Sci Nat Maroc ... Bulletin. Societe des Sciences Naturelles du Maroc [*A publication*]

Bull Soc Sci Nat Ouest Fr ... Bulletin. Societe des Sciences Naturelles de l'Ouest de la France [*A publication*]

Bull Soc Sci Nat Phys Mar ... Bulletin. Societe des Sciences Naturelles et Physiques du Maroc [*A publication*]

Bull Soc Sci Nat Phys Maroc ... Bulletin. Societe des Sciences Naturelles et Physiques du Maroc [*A publication*]

Bull Soc Sci Nat Tun ... Bulletin. Societe des Sciences Naturelles de Tunisie [*A publication*]

Bull Soc Sci Nat Tunis ... Bulletin. Societe des Sciences Naturelles de Tunisie [*A publication*]

Bull Soc Sci Photogr Jpn ... Bulletin. Society of Scientific Photography of Japan [*A publication*]

Bull Soc Sci Vet Lyon ... Bulletin. Societe des Sciences Veterinaires de Lyon [*A publication*]

Bull Soc Sci Vet Med Comp Lyon ... Bulletin. Societe des Sciences Veterinaires et de Medecine Comparee de Lyon [*A publication*]

Bull Soc Sc Vet Lyon ... Bulletin. Societe des Sciences Veterinaires de Lyon [*A publication*]

Bull Soc Sea Water Sci (Jpn) ... Bulletin. Society of Sea Water Science (Japan) [*A publication*]

Bull Soc Stiinte Geol Repub Soc Rom ... Buletinul. Societatii de Stiinte Geologice din Republica Socialista Romania [*A publication*]

Bull Soc Vaudoise Sci Nat ... Bulletin. Societe Vaudoise des Sciences Naturelles [*A publication*]

Bull Soc Vaud Sci Nat ... Bulletin. Societe Vaudoise des Sciences Naturelles [*A publication*]

Bull Soc Vector Ecol ... Bulletin. Society of Vector Ecologists [*A publication*]

Bull Soc Vet Hell ... Bulletin. Societe Veterinaire Hellenique [*A publication*]

Bull Soc Vieux Papier ... Bulletin. Societe de Vieux Papier [*A publication*]

Bull Soc Zool Anvers ... Bulletins. Societe de Zoologie d'Anvers [*A publication*]

Bull Soc Zool Fr ... Bulletin. Societe Zoologique de France [*A publication*]

Bull Soc Zool France ... Bulletin. Societe Zoologique de France [*A publication*]

Bull Soil Bur (NZ) ... Bulletin. Soil Bureau Department of Scientific and Industrial Research (New Zealand) [*A publication*]

Bull Soil Surv Gt Br ... Bulletin. Soil Survey of Great Britain [*A publication*]

Bull Sonoma County Med Assoc ... Bulletin. Sonoma County Medical Association [*California*] [*A publication*]

Bull South Calif Acad Sci ... Bulletin. Southern California Academy of Sciences [*A publication*]

Bull South Pac Gen Hosp ... Bulletin. Southern Pacific General Hospital [*A publication*]

Bull South Res Inst ... Bulletin. Southern Research Institute [*A publication*]

Bull South Tex Geol Soc ... Bulletin. South Texas Geological Society [*A publication*]

Bull Spec Astrophys Obs (North Caucasus) ... Bulletin. Special Astrophysical Observatory (North Caucasus) [*A publication*]

Bull Spec Libr Coun Phila ... Bulletin. Special Libraries Council of Philadelphia and Vicinity [*A publication*]

Bull Speleol Soc DC ... Bulletin. Speleological Society of the District of Columbia [*A publication*]

Bull Spokane County Med Soc ... Bulletin. Spokane County Medical Society [*Washington*] [*A publication*]

Bull Sport Fish Inst ... Bulletin. Sport Fishing Institute [*A publication*]

Bull Stand Oil Co Calif ... Bulletin. Standard Oil Company of California [*A publication*]

Bull State Biol Surv Kans ... Bulletin. State Biological Survey of Kansas [*A publication*]

Bull State Fruit Exp Stn Southwest MO State Univ (Mt Grove) ... Bulletin. State Fruit Experiment Station. Southwest Missouri State University (Mountain Grove) [*A publication*]

Bull State Geol Surv Kansas ... Bulletin. State Geological Survey of Kansas [*A publication*]

Bull State Inst Mar Trop Med Gdansk ... Bulletin. State Institute of Marine and Tropical Medicine in Gdansk [*A publication*]

Bull State Plant Board Fla ... Bulletin. State Plant Board of Florida [*A publication*]

Bull State Univ Iowa ... Bulletin. State University of Iowa [*A publication*]

Bull Statist Soc NSW ... Bulletin. Statistical Society of New South Wales [*A publication*]   (APTA)

Bull S Tex Geol Soc ... Bulletin. South Texas Geological Society [*A publication*]

Bull St Francis Hosp Sanat (Roslyn NY) ... Bulletin. St. Francis Hospital and Sanatorium (Roslyn, New York) [*A publication*]

Bull Sth Calif Acad Sci ... Bulletin. Southern California Academy of Sciences [*A publication*]

Bull St Marianna Univ Sch Med Gen Educ ... Bulletin. St. Marianna University. School of Medicine. General Education [*A publication*]

Bull St Mens Com Forg Fr ... Bulletin Statistique Mensuel. Comite des Forges de France [*A publication*]

Bull Stn Exp Agric Hong A ... Bulletin. Stations d'Experimentation Agricole Hongroises. A. Production Vegetale [*A publication*]

Bull Stn Exp Agric Hong C ... Bulletin. Stations d'Experimentation Agricole Hongroises. C. Horticulture [*A publication*]

Bull Stomatol Kyoto Univ ... Bulletin of Stomatology. Kyoto University [*A publication*]

Bull Storrs Agric Exp Stn Univ Conn ... Bulletin. Storrs Agricultural Experiment Station. University of Connecticut [*A publication*]

Bull Sugadaira Biol Lab ... Bulletin. Sugadaira Biological Laboratory [*A publication*]

Bull Sugar Beet Res ... Bulletin of Sugar Beet Research [*A publication*]

Bull Sugar Beet Res Suppl ... Bulletin of Sugar Beet Research. Supplement [*A publication*]

Bull Suicidol ... Bulletin of Suicidology [*A publication*]

Bull Suisse Mycol ... Bulletin Suisse de Mycologie [*A publication*]

Bull Suzugamine Women's Coll Nat Sci ... Bulletin. Suzugamine Women's College. Natural Science [*A publication*]

Bull SW Ass Petrol Geol ... Bulletin. Southwestern Association of Petroleum Geologists [*A publication*]

Bull Swazild Dep Agric ... Bulletin. Swaziland Department of Agriculture [*A publication*]

Bull Synd Apic ... Bulletin. Union Syndicale des Apiculteurs [*A publication*]

Bull Taichung Dist Agric Improv Stn ... Bulletin. Taichung District Agricultural Improvement Station [*A publication*]

Bull Taiwan Agric Res Inst ... Bulletin. Taiwan Agricultural Research Institute [*A publication*]

Bull Taiwan Forestry Res Inst ... Bulletin. Taiwan Forestry Research Institute [*A publication*]

Bull Taiwan For Res Inst ... Bulletin. Taiwan Forestry Research Institute [*A publication*]

Bull Tall Timbers Res Stn ... Bulletin. Tall Timbers Research Station [*A publication*]

Bull Tamagawa-Gakuen Women's Jr Coll ... Bulletin. Tamagawa-Gakuen Women's Junior College [*A publication*]

Bull Tas For Comm ... Tasmanian Forest Commission. Bulletin [*A publication*]   (APTA)

Bull Tea Res Stn Minist Agric For ... Bulletin. Tea Research Station. Ministry of Agriculture and Forestry [*Japan*] [*A publication*]

Bull Tech AIBr ... Bulletin Technique AIBr [*Association des Ingenieurs Sortis de l'Universite Libre de Bruxelles*] [*A publication*]

Bull Tech Api ... Bulletin Technique Apicole [*A publication*]

Bull Tech Bur Veri ... Bulletin Technique. Bureau Veritas [*A publication*]

Bull Tech Chambre Synd Mines Fer Fr ... Bulletin Technique. Chambre Syndicale des Mines de Fer de France [*A publication*]

Bull Tech Dep Genet Anim ... Bulletin Technique. Departement de Genetique Animale [*France*] [*A publication*]

Bull Tech Div Sols Queb Minist Agric ... Bulletin Technique. Division des Sols. Province de Quebec - Ministere de l'Agriculture [*A publication*]

Bull Tech Genie Rural ... Bulletin Technique du Genie Rural [*France*] [*A publication*]

Bull Tech Houille Deriv Inst Natl Ind Charbon ... Bulletin Technique de l'Houille et Derives. Institut National de l'Industrie Charbonniere [*A publication*]

Bull Tech Inf ... Bulletin Technique d'Information [*A publication*]

Bull Tech Inf Ingrs Servs Agric ... Bulletin Technique d'Information des Ingenieurs des Services Agricoles [*A publication*]

Bull Tech Inf Ing Serv Agric ... Bulletin Technique d'Information des Ingenieurs des Services Agricoles [*A publication*]

Bull Tech Inf Min Agric (France) ... Bulletin Technique d'Information. Ministere de l'Agriculture (France) [*A publication*]

Bull Tech Inform Min Agr (France) ... Bulletin Technique d'Information. Ministere de l'Agriculture (France) [*A publication*]

Bull Tech Mines Fer Fr ... Bulletin Technique des Mines de Fer de France [*A publication*]

Bull Techn Soc Stand Petroles ... Bulletin Technique. Societe Standard Francaise des Petroles [*A publication*]

Bull Techn Suisse Rom ... Bulletin Technique de la Suisse Romande [*A publication*]

Bull Tech Secur Salubr Inst Natl Ind Extr ... Bulletin Technique de Securite et Salubrite. Institut National des Industries Extractives [*A publication*]

Bull Tech Soc Fr Constr Babcock Wilcox ... Bulletin Technique. Societe Francaise des Constructions Babcock et Wilcox [*A publication*]

Bull Tech Soc Fr Constr Babcock et Wilcox ... Bulletin Technique. Societe Francaise des Constructions Babcock et Wilcox [*France*] [*A publication*]

Bull Tech Suisse Romande ... Bulletin Technique de la Suisse Romande [*A publication*]

Bull Tech Univ Istanbul ... Bulletin. Technical University of Istanbul [*A publication*]

Bull Tech Valorisation Util Combust Inst Natl Ind Extr ... Bulletin Technique. Valorisation et Utilisation des Combustibles. Institut National des Industries Extractives [*A publication*]

Bull Tech Vevey ... Bulletin Technique Vevey [*A publication*]

Bull Tenn Agric Exp Stn ... Bulletin. Tennessee Agricultural Experiment Station [*A publication*]

Bull Tenn Nurses Assoc ... Bulletin. Tennessee Nurses Association [*A publication*]

Bull Tenth Dist Dent Soc (Rockville Centre) ... Bulletin. Tenth District Dental Society (Rockville Centre) [*New York*] [*A publication*]

Bull Tex Agr Exp Sta ... Bulletin. Texas Agricultural Experiment Station [*A publication*]

Bull Tex Agric Exp St ... Bulletin. Texas Agricultural Experiment Station [*A publication*]

Bull Tex Agric Exp Stn ... Bulletin. Texas Agricultural Experiment Station [*A publication*]

Bull Tex Mem Mus ... Bulletin. Texas Memorial Museum [*A publication*]

Bull Tex Nurses Assoc ... Bulletin. Texas Nurses Association [*A publication*]

Bull Tex Ornithol Soc ... Bulletin. Texas Ornithological Society [*A publication*]

Bull Thermodyn & Thermochem ... Bulletin of Thermodynamics and Thermochemistry [*A publication*]

Bull Tob Res Inst ... Bulletin. Tobacco Research Institute [*A publication*]

Bull Tob Res Inst Taiwan Tob Wine Monop Bur ... Bulletin. Tobacco Research Institute. Taiwan Tobacco and Wine Monopoly Bureau [*A publication*]

Bull Tochigi Agr Exp Sta ... Bulletin. Tochigi Agricultural Experiment Station [*A publication*]

Bull Tohoku Inst Technol Sect B ... Bulletin. Tohoku Institute of Technology. Section B. Sciences [*A publication*]

Bull Tohoku Nat Agr Exp Sta ... Bulletin. Tohoku National Agricultural Experiment Station [*A publication*]

Bull Tohoku Natl Agric Exp Stn ... Bulletin. Tohoku National Agricultural Experiment Station [*A publication*]

Bull Tohoku Natn Agric Exp Stn ... Bulletin. Tohoku National Agricultural Experiment Station [*A publication*]

Bull Tohoku Natol Agr Exp Stn (Morioka) ... Bulletin. Tohoku National Agricultural Experiment Station (Morioka) [*A publication*]

Bull Tohoku Reg Fish Res Lab ... Bulletin. Tohoku Regional Fisheries Research Laboratory [*A publication*]

Bull Tokai-Kinki Agr Exp Sta ... Bulletin. Tokai-Kinki National Agricultural Experiment Station [*A publication*]

Bull Tokai-Kinki Nat Agr Exp Sta ... Bulletin. Tokai-Kinki National Agricultural Experiment Station [*A publication*]

Bull Tokai-Kinki Natl Agric Exp Stn ... Bulletin. Tokai-Kinki National Agricultural Experiment Station [*A publication*]

Bull Tokai Reg Fish Res Lab ... Bulletin. Tokai Regional Fisheries Research Laboratory [*A publication*]

Bull Tokyo Coll Domest Sci ... Bulletin. Tokyo College of Domestic Science [*A publication*]

Bull Tokyo Dent Coll ... Bulletin. Tokyo Dental College [*A publication*]

Bull Tokyo Gakugei Univ ... Bulletin. Tokyo Gakugei University [*A publication*]

Bull Tokyo Gakugei Univ Ser 4 ... Bulletin. Tokyo Gakugei University. Series 4 [*A publication*]

Bull Tokyo Inst Technol ... Bulletin. Tokyo Institute of Technology [*A publication*]

Bull Tokyo Kasei Daigaku ... Bulletin. Tokyo Kasei Daigaku [*A publication*]

Bull Tokyo Med Dent Univ ... Bulletin. Tokyo Medical and Dental University [*A publication*]

Bull Tokyo Metro Rehab Cent Phys Ment Handcp ... Bulletin. Tokyo Metropolitan Rehabilitation Center of the Physically and Mentally Handicapped [*A publication*]

Bull Tokyo Sci Mus ... Bulletin. Tokyo Science Museum [*A publication*]

Bull Tokyo Univ For ... Bulletin. Tokyo University Forests [*A publication*]

Bull Toledo Dent Soc ... Bulletin. Toledo [*Ohio*] Dental Society [*A publication*]

Bull Torr Bot Club ... Bulletin. Torrey Botanical Club [*A publication*]

Bull Torrey Bot Club ... Bulletin. Torrey Botanical Club [*A publication*]

Bull Tottori Agr Exp Sta ... Bulletin. Tottori Agricultural Experiment Station [*A publication*]

Bull Tottori Tree Fruit Exp Stn ... Bulletin. Tottori Tree Fruit Experiment Station [*A publication*]

Bull Tottori Univ For ... Bulletin. Tottori University Forests [*A publication*]

Bull Train .. Bulletin on Training [*A publication*]

Bull Tra Soc Pharm Lyon ... Bulletin des Travaux. Societe de Pharmacie de Lyon [*A publication*]

Bull Trav Soc Pharm Bordeaux ... Bulletin des Travaux. Societe de Pharmacie de Bordeaux [*A publication*]

Bull Tri Cty Dent Soc ... Bulletin. Tri-County Dental Society [*Morristown, New Jersey*] [*A publication*]

Bull Trim Ass Cent Vet ... Bulletin Trimestriel. Association Centrale des Veterinaires [*A publication*]

Bull Trimest INACOL ... Bulletin Trimestriel INACOL [*Institut National pour l'Amelioration des Conserves de Legumes*] [*A publication*]

Bull Trimest Inst Natl Amelior Conserves Legumes (Belg) ... Bulletin Trimestriel. Institut National pour l'Amelioration des Conserves de Legumes (Belgium) [*A publication*]

Bull Trimest Soc Hist Nat Amis Mus Autun ... Bulletin Trimestriel. Societe d'Histoire Naturelle des Amis de la Museum d'Autun [*A publication*]

Bull Trimest Soc Mycol Fr ... Bulletin Trimestriel. Societe Mycologique de France [*A publication*]

Bull Trim Soc Mycol Fr ... Bulletin Trimestriel. Societe Mycologique de France [*A publication*]

Bull Tufts N Engl Med Cent ... Bulletin. Tufts New England Medical Center [*A publication*]

Bull Tufts New Engl Med Cent ... Bulletin. Tufts New England Medical Center [*A publication*]

Bull Tulane Med Fac ... Bulletin. Tulane Medical Faculty [*A publication*]

Bull Tulane Univ Med Fac ... Bulletin. Tulane University Medical Faculty [*A publication*]

Bull Un Int Tub ... Bulletin. Union Internationale Contre la Tuberculose [*A publication*]

Bull Union Agric Egypte ... Bulletin. Union des Agriculteurs d'Egypte [*A publication*]

Bull Union Cty Dent Soc ... Bulletin. Union [*New Jersey*] County Dental Society [*A publication*]

Bull Union Oceanogr Fr ... Bulletin. Union des Oceanographes de France [*A publication*]

Bull Union Physiciens ... Bulletin. Union des Physiciens [*A publication*]

Bull Union Synd Agric Egypte ... Bulletin. Union Syndicale des Agriculteurs d'Egypte [*A publication*]

Bull Union Synd Apic Picards ... Bulletin. Union Syndicale des Apiculteurs Picards [*A publication*]

Bull United Plant Assoc South Ind Sci Dep ... Bulletin. United Planters' Association of Southern India. Scientific Department [*A publication*]

Bull Univ Alberta ... Bulletin. University of Alberta [*A publication*]

Bull Univ Coll Med (Calcutta) ... Bulletin. University College of Medicine (Calcutta) [*A publication*]

Bull Univ Coll Med Calcutta Univ ... Bulletin. University College of Medicine. Calcutta University [*A publication*]

Bull Univ GA Coll Agr Coop Ext Serv ... Bulletin. University of Georgia. College of Agriculture. Cooperative Extension Service [*A publication*]

Bull Univ Idaho Coll Agr Ext Serv ... Bulletin. University of Idaho. College of Agriculture. Extension Service [*A publication*]

Bull Univ Ill Eng Exp Stat ... Bulletin. University of Illinois. Engineering Experiment Station [*A publication*]

Bull Univ Iowa Inst Agr Med ... Bulletin. University of Iowa. Institute of Agricultural Medicine [*A publication*]

Bull Univ KY Off Res Eng Serv ... Bulletin. University of Kentucky. Office of Research and Engineering Services [*A publication*]

Bull Univ MD Coop Ext Serv ... Bulletin. University of Maryland. Cooperative Extension Service [*A publication*]

Bull Univ MD Sch Med ... Bulletin. University of Maryland. School of Medicine [*A publication*]

Bull Univ Miami Sch Med ... Bulletin. University of Miami School of Medicine and Jackson Memorial Hospital [*A publication*]

Bull Univ Miami Sch Med Jackson Mem Hosp ... Bulletin. University of Miami School of Medicine and Jackson Memorial Hospital [*A publication*]

Bull Univ Minn Eng Exp Stat ... Bulletin. University of Minnesota. Institute of Technology. Engineering Experiment Station [*A publication*]

Bull Univ MO Coll Agr Exp Sta ... Bulletin. University of Missouri. College of Agriculture. Experiment Station [*A publication*]

Bull Univ MO Rolla Tech Ser ... Bulletin. University of Missouri at Rolla. Technical Series [*A publication*]

Bull Univ Nebr State Mus ... Bulletin. University of Nebraska State Museum [*A publication*]

Bull Univ Neb St Mus ... Bulletin. University of Nebraska State Museum [*A publication*]

Bull Univ Osaka Prefect Ser A ... Bulletin. University of Osaka Prefecture. Series A. Sakai [*A publication*]

Bull Univ Osaka Prefect Ser B Agric Biol ... Bulletin. University of Osaka Prefecture. Series B. Agriculture and Biology [*A publication*]

Bull Univ Osaka Prefecture Ser A ... Bulletin. University of Osaka Prefecture. Series A. Engineering and Natural Sciences [*A publication*]

Bull Univ Osaka Pref Ser B ... Bulletin. University of Osaka Prefecture. Series B [*A publication*]

Bull Univ RI Agric Exp Stn ... Bulletin. University of Rhode Island. Agricultural Experiment Station [*A publication*]

Bull Univ Wash Eng Exp Stat ... Bulletin. University of Washington. Engineering Experiment Station [*A publication*]

Bull Us .... Bulletin Usuel des Lois et Arretes [*A publication*]   (ILCA)

Bull US Bur Min ... Bulletin. United States Bureau of Mines [*A publication*]

Bull US Bur Mines ... Bulletin. United States Bureau of Mines [*A publication*]

Bull US Cst Geod Surv ... Bulletin. United States Coast and Geodetic Survey [*A publication*]

Bull US Dept Agric ... Bulletin. United States Department of Agriculture [*A publication*]

Bull US Geol Surv ... Bulletin. United States Geological Survey [*A publication*]

Bull US Natl Mus ... Bulletin. United States National Museum [*A publication*]

Bull US Nat Mus ... Bulletin. United States National Museum [*A publication*]

Bull US Natn Mus ... Bulletin. United States National Museum [*A publication*]

Bull Utah Agr Exp Sta ... Bulletin. Utah Agricultural Experiment Station [*A publication*]

Bull Utah Agric Exp Stn ... Bulletin. Utah Agricultural Experiment Station [*A publication*]

Bull Utah Eng Exp Stn ... Bulletin. Utah Engineering Experiment Station [*A publication*]

Bull Utsunomiya Tob Exp Stn ... Bulletin. Utsunomiya Tobacco Experiment Station [*A publication*]

Bull Utsunomiya Univ For ... Bulletin. Utsunomiya University Forests [*A publication*]

Bull Utsunomiya Univ Sect 2 ... Bulletin. Utsunomiya University. Section 2 [*A publication*]

Bull VA Agr Exp Sta ... Bulletin. Virginia Agricultural Experiment Station [*A publication*]

Bull VA Agric Exp Stn ... Bulletin. Virginia Agricultural Experiment Station [*A publication*]

Bull VA Agric Ext Serv ... Bulletin. Virginia Agricultural Extension Service [*A publication*]

Bull VA Geol Surv ... Bulletin. Virginia Geological Survey [*A publication*]

Bull Val Dent Soc ... Bulletin. Valley Dental Society [*Encino, California*] [*A publication*]

Bull Vanc Med Ass ... Bulletin. Vancouver Medical Association [*A publication*]

Bull Vancouver Med Assoc ... Bulletin. Vancouver Medical Association [*A publication*]

Bull VA Polytech Inst Agr Ext Serv ... Bulletin. Virginia Polytechnic Institute. Agricultural Extension Service [*A publication*]

Bull VA Polytech Inst State Univ VA Water Resources Cent ... Bulletin. Virginia Polytechnic Institute and State University. Virginia Water Resources Research Center [*A publication*]

Bull VA Sect Amer Chem Soc ... Bulletin. Virginia Sections of the American Chemical Society [*A publication*]

Bull VA Water Resour Res Cent ... Bulletin. Virginia Water Resources Research Center [*A publication*]

Bull Veg Crops Res Work ... Bulletin. Vegetable Crops Research Work [*A publication*]

Bull Veg Ornamental Crops Res Stn Ser A ... Bulletin. Vegetable and Ornamental Crops Research Station. Series A [*A publication*]

Bull Veg Ornamental Crops Res Stn Ser B (Morioka) ... Bulletin. Vegetable and Ornamental Crops Research Station. Series B (Morioka) [*A publication*]

Bull Veg Ornamental Crops Res Stn Ser C (Kurume) ... Bulletin. Vegetable and Ornamental Crops Research Station. Series C (Kurume) [*A publication*]

Bull Verm Agric Exp St ... Bulletin. Vermont Agricultural Experiment Station [*A publication*]

Bull Ver Schweiz Pet-Geol Ing ... Bulletin. Vereinigung der Schweizerischen Petroleum-Geologen und -Ingenieure [*A publication*]

Bull Ver Schweiz Petrol Geol-Ing ... Bulletin. Vereinigung der Schweizerischen Petroleum-Geologen und -Ingenieure [*A publication*]

Bull Vet Inst Pulawy ... Bulletin. Veterinary Institute in Pulawy [*A publication*]

Bull Vet (Lisb) ... Bulletin Veterinaire (Lisbon) [*A publication*]
Bull Vict Inst Educ Res ... Bulletin. Victorian Institute of Educational Research [*A publication*] (APTA)
Bull Vict Mem Mus ... Bulletin. Victoria Memorial Museum of the Geological Survey of Canada [*A publication*]
Bull Virg Agric Exp St ... Bulletin. Virginia Agricultural Experiment Station [*A publication*]
Bull Virg Dent Ass ... Bulletin. Virginia State Dental Association [*A publication*]
Bull V Luna Gen Hosp Med Soc ... Bulletin V. Luna General Hospital Medical Society [*A publication*]
Bull Volcan ... Bulletin Volcanologique [*A publication*]
Bull Volcanic Eruptions (Tokyo) ... Bulletin of Volcanic Eruptions (Tokyo) [*A publication*]
Bull Volcanol ... Bulletin Volcanologique [*A publication*]
Bull VT Agric Exp Stn ... Bulletin. Vermont Agricultural Experiment Station [*A publication*]
Bull Vysk Ustavu Pap Celul ... Bulletin. Vyskumneho Ustavu Papieru a Celulozy [*A publication*]
Bull Vysk Ustavu Potravin ... Bulletin. Vyskumneho Ustavu Potravinarskeho [*A publication*]
Bull Vysk Ustavu Priem Celul ... Bulletin. Vyskumneho Ustavu Priemyslu Celulozy [*A publication*]
Bull Wagner Free Inst Sci ... Bulletin. Wagner Free Institute of Science [*A publication*]
Bull Wakayama Fruit Tree Exp Stn ... Bulletin. Wakayama Fruit Tree Experiment Station [*A publication*]
Bull War Med ... Bulletin of War Medicine [*A publication*]
Bull Waseda Appl Chem Soc ... Bulletin. Waseda Applied Chemical Society [*A publication*]
Bull Waseda Univ Inst of Comp Law ... Waseda University. Institute of Comparative Law. Bulletin [*Tokyo, Japan*] [*A publication*] (DLA)
Bull Wash Agr Exp Sta ... Bulletin. Washington Agricultural Experiment Station [*A publication*]
Bull Wash Agric Exp St ... Bulletin. Washington Agricultural Experiment Station [*A publication*]
Bull Wash Agric Exp Stn ... Bulletin. Washington Agricultural Experiment Station [*A publication*]
Bull Washington Agric Exp Stn ... Bulletin. Washington Agricultural Experiment Station [*A publication*]
Bull Wash St Coll Ext Serv ... Bulletin. Washington State College Extension Service [*A publication*]
Bull Wat Res Fdn Aust ... Bulletin. Water Research Foundation of Australia [*A publication*] (APTA)
Bull Wds For Dep S Aust ... Bulletin. Woods and Forests Department of South Australia [*A publication*]
Bull Welsh Pl Breed Stn ... Bulletin. Welsh Plant Breeding Station. University College of Wales [*A publication*]
Bull West Soc Eng ... Bulletin. Western Society of Engineers [*A publication*]
Bull WHO ... Bulletin. World Health Organization [*A publication*]
Bull Wildl Dis ... Bulletin. Wildlife Disease Association [*A publication*]
Bull Wildl Dis Assoc ... Bulletin. Wildlife Disease Association [*A publication*]
Bull Wis Agr Exp Sta ... Bulletin. Wisconsin Agricultural Experiment Station [*A publication*]
Bull Wis Agric Exp Stn ... Bulletin. Wisconsin Agricultural Experiment Station [*A publication*]
Bull Wisc Agric Exp St ... Bulletin. Wisconsin Agricultural Experiment Station [*A publication*]
Bull Wld Hlth Org ... Bulletin. World Health Organization [*A publication*]
Bull Wollongong Univ Coll ... Wollongong University College. Bulletin [*A publication*] (APTA)
Bull Wom Aux Amer Med Ass ... Bulletin. Woman's Auxiliary to American Medical Association [*A publication*]
Bull Wood Res Lab VA Polyt Inst ... Bulletin. Wood Research Laboratory. Virginia Polytechnic Institute [*A publication*]
Bull Woods For Dep South Aust ... South Australia. Woods and Forests Department. Bulletin [*A publication*] (APTA)
Bull Woods Forests Dep S Aust ... Bulletin. Woods and Forests Department of South Australia [*A publication*]
Bull Woods Forests Dep S Aust ... South Australia. Woods and Forests Department. Bulletin [*A publication*] (APTA)
Bull World Health Organ ... Bulletin. World Health Organization [*A publication*]
Bull W Scotl Agric Coll ... Bulletin. West of Scotland Agricultural College [*A publication*]
Bull W Va Agric Exp Sta ... Bulletin. West Virginia University. Agricultural Experiment Station [*A publication*]
Bull W Va Univ Agr Exp Sta ... Bulletin. West Virginia University. Agricultural Experiment Station [*A publication*]
Bull Wyo Agr Exp Sta ... Bulletin. Wyoming Agricultural Experiment Station [*A publication*]
Bull Wyo Agric Exp Stn ... Bulletin. Wyoming Agricultural Experiment Station [*A publication*]
Bull Wyo Dept Agr Div Statist Inform ... Bulletin. Wyoming Department of Agriculture. Division of Statistics and Information [*A publication*]
Bull Yale Sch For ... Bulletin. Yale University School of Forestry [*A publication*]
Bull Yamagata Univ Agric Sci ... Bulletin. Yamagata University. Agricultural Science [*A publication*]

Bull Yamagata Univ Eng ... Bulletin. Yamagata University. Engineering [*A publication*]
Bull Yamagata Univ Med Sci ... Bulletin. Yamagata University. Medical Science [*A publication*]
Bull Yamagata Univ Nat Sci ... Bulletin. Yamagata University. Natural Science [*A publication*]
Bull Yamagata Univ Natur Sci ... Bulletin. Yamagata University. Natural Science [*A publication*]
Bull Yamaguchi Agric Exp Stn ... Bulletin. Yamaguchi Agricultural Experiment Station [*A publication*]
Bull Yamaguchi Med Sch ... Bulletin. Yamaguchi Medical School [*A publication*]
Bull Yamaguchi Prefect Poult Breed Stn ... Bulletin. Yamaguchi Prefectural Poultry Breeding Station [*A publication*]
Bull Yamanashi Agric Exp Stn ... Bulletin. Yamanashi Agricultural Experiment Station [*A publication*]
Bull Yamanashi For Exp Sta ... Bulletin. Yamanashi Prefectural Forest Experiment Station [*A publication*]
Bull Yamanashi Pref Agr Exp Sta ... Bulletin. Yamanashi Prefectural Agricultural Experiment Station [*A publication*]
Bull Yichang Inst Geol Miner Resour ... Bulletin. Yichang Institute of Geology and Mineral Resources [*A publication*]
Bull Y Natl Fert Dev Cent (US) ... Bulletin Y. National Fertilizer Development Center (United States) [*A publication*]
Bull (Zagreb) ... Bulletin International. Academie Yougoslave (Zagreb) [*A publication*]
Bull Zimbabwe Geol Surv ... Bulletin. Zimbabwe Geological Survey [*A publication*]
Bull Zool .... Bulletin of Zoology [*A publication*]
Bull Zool Mus Univ Amsterdam ... Bulletin. Zoologisch Museum Universitet van Amsterdam [*A publication*]
Bull Zool Nom ... Bulletin of Zoological Nomenclature [*A publication*]
Bull Zool Nomencl ... Bulletin of Zoological Nomenclature [*A publication*]
Bull Zool Soc Coll Sci (Nagpur) ... Bulletin. Zoological Society College of Science (Nagpur) [*A publication*]
Bull Zool Soc Egypt ... Bulletin. Zoological Society of Egypt [*A publication*]
Bull Zool Surv India ... Bulletin. Zoological Survey of India [*A publication*]
Bul si Mem Soc Med Vet Bucuresti ... Buletinul si Memorie. Societatii de Medicina Veterinaria din Bucuresti [*A publication*]
Bul Mens Bur Relat Pub Ind Sucriere ... Bulletin Mensuel. Bureau des Relations Publiques de l'Industrie Sucriere [*A publication*]
Bul Mensuel Statis (Cameroon) ... Bulletin Mensuel des Statistiques (Cameroon) [*A publication*]
Bul Mensuel Statis (Congo People's Republic) ... Bulletin Mensuel des Statistiques (Congo People's Republic) [*A publication*]
Bul Mensuel Statis (France) ... Bulletin Mensuel de Statistique (France) [*A publication*]
Bul Mensuel Statis (Gabon) ... Bulletin Mensuel de Statistique (Gabon) [*A publication*]
Bul Mensuel Statis (Ivory Coast) ... Bulletin Mensuel de Statistique (Ivory Coast) [*A publication*]
Bul Mensuel Statis (Tunisia) ... Bulletin Mensuel de Statistique (Tunisia) [*A publication*]
Bul Midw MLA ... Bulletin. Midwest Modern Language Association [*A publication*]
Bul Mon Ist ... Buletinul Monumentelor Istorica [*A publication*]
Bul Musashino Academia M ... Bulletin. Musashino Academia Musicae [*A publication*]
Bul Narcotics (UN) ... Bulletin on Narcotics (United Nations) [*A publication*]
Bul Nat Gallery of SA ... Bulletin. National Gallery of South Australia [*A publication*] (APTA)
Bul NHPL ... Bulletin. New Hampshire Public Libraries [*A publication*]
Bul NYPL ... Bulletin. New York Public Library [*A publication*]
Bul Pan Am Union ... Bulletin. Pan American Union [*A publication*]
Bul Penelitian Hutan ... Buletin Penelitian Hutan [*A publication*]
Bul Penelitian Teknol Hasil Pertanian ... Buletin Penelitian Teknologi Hasil Pertanian [*A publication*]
Bul Pol .... Bulletin des Sciences Politiques [*A publication*]
Bul Polit Liberal ... Bulletin sur les Politiques Liberales [*A publication*]
Bul Post-Graduate Ctee in Medicine Univ of Syd ... Bulletin. Post-Graduate Committee in Medicine. University of Sydney [*A publication*]
Bul for Psych ... Bulletin for Psychologists [*A publication*] (APTA)
BULR .... Boston University. Law Review [*A publication*]
BULR .... Buehler International, Inc. [*Lake Bluff, IL*] [*NASDAQ symbol*] (NQ)
Bu LR .... Buffalo Law Review [*A publication*]
BU L Rev ... Boston University. Law Review [*A publication*]
Buls .... Bulstrode's English King's Bench Reports [*1610-25*] [*A publication*] (DLA)
Bul Sci AIM ... Bulletin Scientifique. Association des Ingenieurs Electriciens Sortis de l'Institut Electrotechnique (Montefiore) [*A publication*]
Bul Septuagint St ... Bulletin. International Organization for Septuagint and Cognate Studies [*A publication*]
Bul Shken Bujqesore Tirana Inst Larte Shteteror Bujqesise ... Buletini i Shkencave Bujqesore Tirana. Institute i Larte Shteteror i Bujqesise [*A publication*]
Bul Shkencave Bujqesore ... Buletini i Shkencave Bujqesore [*A publication*]
BulSNTS ... Bulletin. Studiorum Novi Testamenti Societas [*A publication*]

Bul Soc Liegeoise Musicol ... Bulletin. Societe Liegeoise de Musicologie [*A publication*]
Bul Soc Rom Geogr ... Buletinul. Societatii Regale Romane de Geografie [*A publication*]
Bul Soc Stiinte Cluj ... Buletinul. Societatii de Stiinte din Cluj [*A publication*]
Bul S Res Inst ... Bulletin. Southern Research Institute [*A publication*]
Bulst.......... Bulstrode's English King's Bench Reports [*1610-25*] [*A publication*] (DLA)
Bul Stand ... Buletinul de Standardizare [*A publication*]
Bul Stat Agr ... Bulletin des Statistiques Agricoles [*A publication*]
Bul Static ... Bulletin du Static [*A publication*]
Bul Statis Agric ... Bulletin Statistique Agricole [*A publication*]
Bul Statis (Belgium) ... Bulletin de Statistique (Belgium) [*A publication*]
Bul Statis et Docum ... Bulletin de Statistique et de Documentation [*A publication*]
Bul Statis et Econ ... Bulletin Statistique et Economique [*A publication*]
Bul Statis Mensuel (Lebanon) ... Bulletin Statistique Mensuel (Lebanon) [*A publication*]
Bul Statis (Rwanda) ... Bulletin de Statistique (Rwanda) [*A publication*]
Bul Sti Inst Politehn (Cluj) ... Buletinul Stiintific. Institutului Politehnic (Cluj) [*A publication*]
Bul Sti Inst Politehn (Cluj) Ser Construc ... Buletinul Stiintific. Institutului Politehnic (Cluj). Seria Constructii [*A publication*]
Bul Sti Inst Politehn (Cluj) Ser Electromec ... Buletinul Stiintific. Institutului Politehnic (Cluj). Seria Electromecanica [*A publication*]
Bul Sti Inst Politehn (Cluj) Ser Mec ... Buletinul Stiintific. Institutului Politehnic (Cluj). Seria Mecanica [*A publication*]
Bul Stiint Inst Constr (Bucuresti) ... Buletinul Stiintific. Institutul de Constructii (Bucuresti) [*A publication*]
Bul Stiint Inst Pedagog (Baia Mare) Ser B ... Buletin Stiintific. Institutul Pedagogic (Baia Mare). Seria B. Biologie, Fizico- Chimie, Matematica [*A publication*]
Bul Stiint Inst Politeh (Cluj) ... Buletinul Stiintific. Institutului Politehnic (Cluj) [*A publication*]
Bul Stiint Inst Politeh (Cluj-Napoca) ... Buletinul Stiintific. Institutului Politehnic (Cluj-Napoca) [*A publication*]
Bul Stiint Inst Politeh (Cluj) Ser Electromec ... Buletinul Stiintific. Institutului Politehnic (Cluj). Seria Electromecanica [*A publication*]
Bul Stiint Inst Politehn Cluj-Napoca Ser Arhitect-Construc ... Institutului Politehnic Cluj-Napoca. Buletinul Stiintific. Seria Arhitectura-Constructii [*A publication*]
Bul Stiint Inst Politehn Cluj-Napoca Ser Construc Mas ... Institutului Politehnic Cluj-Napoca. Buletinul Stiintific. Seria Constructii de Masini [*A publication*]
Bul Stiint Inst Politehn (Cluj) Ser Electromec ... Buletinul Stiintific. Institutului Politehnic (Cluj). Seria Electromecanica [*A publication*]
Bul Stiint Inst Politehn (Cluj) Ser Mec ... Buletinul Stiintific. Institutului Politehnic (Cluj). Seria Mecanica [*A publication*]
Bul Stiint Teh Inst Politeh (Timisoara) ... Buletinul Stiintific si Tehnic. Institutului Politehnic (Timisoara) [*A publication*]
Bul Stiint Univ Craiova ... Buletinul Stiintific al Universitat. Universitatii Craiova [*Romania*] [*A publication*]
Bul Sti Tehn Inst Politehn "Traian Vuia" (Timisoara) ... Buletinul Stiintific si Tehnic. Institutului Politehnic "Traian Vuia" (Timisoara) [*A publication*]
Bulstr .... Bulstrode's English King's Bench Reports [*1610-25*] [*A publication*] (DLA)
Bul Suicidol ... Bulletin of Suicidology [*A publication*]
Bul Teh Inf Cent Cercet Mater Prot ... Buletin Tehnico-Informativ. Central de Cercetari pentru Materiale de Protectie [*A publication*]
Bul Teh Inf Lab Cent Cercet Lacuri Cerneluri Bucuresti ... Buletin Tehnico-Informativ. Laboratorului Central de Cercetari pentru Lacuri si Cerneluri Bucuresti [*A publication*]
Bulteni Istanbul Tek Univ ... Istanbul Teknik Universitesi Bulteni [*Bulletin of the Technical University of Istanbul*] [*A publication*]
Bul Univ Brasov ... Buletinul. Universitatea din Brasov [*A publication*]
Bul Univ Brasov Ser A Mec Apl ... Buletinul. Universitatii din Brasov. Seria A. Mecanica Aplicata Constructii de Masini [*A publication*]
Bul Univ Brasov Ser C ... Buletinul. Universitatea din Brasov. Seria C [*A publication*]
Bul Univ Brasov Ser C Mat Fiz Chim Sti Natur ... Buletinul. Universitatii din Brasov. Seria C. Matematica, Fizica, Chimie, Stiinte Naturale [*A publication*]
Bul Univ Galati Fasc II Mat Fiz Mec Teoret ... Universitatea din Galati Buletinul Fascicula II Matematica Fizica. Mecanica Teoretica [*A publication*]
Bul Univ Shteteror Tiranes Ser Shkencat Mjekesore ... Buletin. Universiteti Shteteror te Tiranes. Seria Shkencat Mjekesore [*A publication*]
Bul Univ Shteteror Tiranes Ser Shkencat Nat ... Buletin. Universiteti Shteteror te Tiranes. Seria Shkencat Natyrore [*A publication*]
Bul Univ Shteteror Tiranes Shk Nat ... Buletin. Universiteti Shteteror te Tiranes. Fakulteti i Shkencave te Natyres [*A publication*]
Bul Univ V Babes Bolyai (Cluj) Ser Stiint Nat ... Buletinul Universitatilor "V Babes" si "Bolyai" (Cluj). Seria Stiintele Natura [*A publication*]
Bul Un L .... Bulletin. Association des Amis de l'Universite de Liege [*A publication*]

Bul Vie M Belge ... Bulletin. Vie Musicale Belge [*Bulletin van het Belgisch Muziekleven*] [*A publication*]
Bul VIER ... Bulletin. Victorian Institute of Educational Research [*A publication*] (APTA)
BUM.......... Bargaining Unit Member [*of a faculty union*]
BUM.......... Boletin. Universidad de Madrid [*A publication*]
BUM.......... Break-Up Missile (MCD)
BUM.......... Bulletin. Societe "Union Musicologique" [*A publication*]
BuM.......... Bureau of Mines [*Department of the Interior*]
BUM.......... Butler, MO [*Location identifier*] [*FAA*] (FAAL)
Bumagodel Mashinostr ... Bumagodelatel'noe Mashinostroenie [*A publication*]
Bumazh Prom ... Bumazhnaya Promyshlennost [*A publication*]
Bumaz Prom ... Bumazhnaya Promyshlennost [*A publication*]
Bum Derevoobrab Promst ... Bumazhnaya i Derevoobrabatyvayushchaya Promyshlennost [*A publication*]
BUMED ... Bureau of Medicine and Surgery [*Obsolete*] [*Navy*]
BUMEDINST ... Bureau of Medicine and Surgery Instructions [*Navy*]
BUMF .... Bum-Fodder [*Toilet paper*] [*Slang*] [*British*] (DSUE)
BUMINES ... Bureau of Mines [*Department of the Interior*]
BUMMB ... Building Materials Magazine [*Australia*] [*A publication*]
BUMP .... Basic Update Matrix Program
BUMP .... Boston University Marine Program [*Boston University*] [*Research center*]
BUMP .... Bottom-Up Modular Programming
BUMP .... Bumpstead [*England*]
BUMPA ... Bumazhnaya Promyshlennost [*A publication*]
Bump B'k'cy ... Bump on Bankruptcy [*A publication*] (DLA)
Bump Comp ... Bump on Composition in Bankruptcy [*A publication*] (DLA)
Bump Const Dec ... Bump's Notes on Constitutional Decisions [*A publication*] (DLA)
Bump Fed Pr ... Bump. Federal Procedure [*A publication*] (DLA)
Bump Fraud Conv ... Bump on Fraudulent Conveyances [*A publication*] (DLA)
Bump Fr Conv ... Bump on Fraudulent Conveyances [*A publication*] (DLA)
Bump Int Rev ... Bump's Internal Revenue Laws [*A publication*] (DLA)
Bump NC ... Bump's Notes on Constitutional Decisions [*A publication*] (DLA)
Bump Pat ... Bump's Law of Patents, Trade-Marks, Etc. [*A publication*] (DLA)
Bump's Int Rev Law ... Bump's Internal Revenue Laws [*A publication*] (DLA)
Bump St L ... Bump. United States Stamp Laws [*A publication*] (DLA)
BUMS .... Bachelor of Unani Medicine and Surgery
BUM & S... Bureau of Medicine and Surgery [*Navy*]
BUMSD .... Bulletin of Materials Science [*A publication*]
BUMTAW ... Bulletin. Academie Malgache [*A publication*]
BUMYDG ... Bulletin of Mycology [*A publication*]
BUN........... Blood Urea Nitrogen [*Medicine*]
BUN........... Bunnythorpe [*New Zealand*] [*Seismograph station code, US Geological Survey*] [*Closed*] (SEIS)
BUNAC .... British Universities North America Club (EA)
BUNAV ..... Bureau of Navigation [*Later, Bureau of Naval Personnel*] [*Navy*]
BUNB .... Bunbury [*Australia*] (ROG)
Bunb .... Bunbury. English Exchequer Reports [*145 English Reprint*] [*A publication*] (DLA)
BUNCH ..... Burroughs, UNIVAC, NCR, Control Data, Honeywell [*IBM competitors in computer manufacture*]
BUNDD ..... Bundesrat - Drucksache [*A publication*]
Bundesanst Pflanzenschutz Flugbl ... Bundesanstalt fuer Pflanzenschutz Flugblatt [*A publication*]
Bundesanzeiger Beil ... Bundesanzeiger. Beilage [*A publication*]
Bundesarbeitsbl ... Bundesarbeitsblatt [*A publication*]
Bundesges.. Bundesgesundheitsblatt [*West Germany*] [*A publication*]
Bundesgesetzbl Repub Oesterr ... Bundesgesetzblatt fuer die Republik Oesterreich [*A publication*]
Bundesminist Bild Wiss Forschungsber ... Bundesministerium fuer Bildung und Wissenschaft. Forschungsbericht [*A publication*]
Bundesminist Forsch Technol Forschungsber DV ... Bundesministerium fuer Forschung und Technologie. Forschungsbericht DV. Datenverarbeitung [*A publication*]
Bundesminist Forsch Technol Forschungsber K ... Bundesministerium fuer Forschung und Technologie. Forschungsbericht K. Kernforschung [*A publication*]
Bundesminist Forsch Technol Forschungsber M ... Bundesministerium fuer Forschung und Technologie. Forschungsbericht M. Meeresforschung [*A publication*]
Bundesminist Forsch Technol Forschungsber T ... Bundesministerium fuer Forschung und Technologie. Forschungsbericht T. Technologische Forschung und Entwicklung [*A publication*]
Bundesminist Forsch Technol Forschungsber W ... Bundesministerium fuer Forschung und Technologie. Forschungsbericht W. Weltraumforschung [*A publication*]
Bundesminist Forsch Technol Forschungsber Weltraumforsch ... Bundesministerium fuer Forschung und Technologie. Forschungsbericht W. Weltraumforschung [*A publication*]
Bundes Vers Inst Kulturtech Tech Bodenk ... Bundesversuchsinstitut fuer Kulturtechnik und Technische Bodenkunde [*A publication*]

BundJb....... Bunder Jahrbuch [*A publication*]
BUNDMB ... Bundnerisches Monatsblatt [*A publication*]
B UNESCO Reg Off Educ ... Bulletin. UNESCO [*United Nations Educational, Scientific, and Cultural Organization*] Regional Office for Education in Asia [*A publication*]
BUNG........ Bungalow [*Classified advertising*] (ADA)
B Universities Annual ... British Universities Annual [*A publication*]
BUNK........ Bunkum [*Nonsense*] [*Slang*] (DSUE)
BUNO....... Bureau Number [*Aircraft identification*] [*Obsolete*] [*Navy*]
BUNS .... Block Unit Numbers (MCD)
Bunseki Kag ... Bunseki Kagaku [*A publication*]
BUnt .... Biblische Untersuchungen [*Regensburg*] [*A publication*]
BUNT....... British Underground Nuclear Test (MCD)
BUNT....... Bunting, Inc. [*NASDAQ symbol*] (NQ)
BUNY....... Board of Underwriters of New York (EA)
Buny Dom L ... Bunyon. Domestic Law [*1875*] [*A publication*] (DLA)
Buny Fire Ins ... Bunyon. Fire Insurance [*7th ed.*] [*1923*] [*A publication*] (DLA)
Buny Life Ass ... Bunyon on Life Assurance [*A publication*] (DLA)
Buny Life Ins ... Bunyon. Life Insurance [*5th ed.*] [*1914*] [*A publication*] (DLA)
BUO.......... Beaumont, CA [*Location identifier*] [*FAA*] (FAAL)
BUO.......... Bleeding [*or Bruising*] of Undetermined Origin [*Medicine*]
BUO.......... Burao [*Somalia*] [*Airport symbol*] (OAG)
BUOPD..... Osaka Prefecture University (Saikai). Bulletin. Series D [*A publication*]
BUORD..... Bureau of Ordnance [*Functions transferred to Bureau of Naval Weapons, 1960, and later to Naval Ordnance Systems Command*] [*Navy*]
BUORDINST ... Bureau of Ordnance Instructions [*Later, NAVORDINST*]
BUOU....... Backup Optical Unit (NASA)
B/UP .... Back Up [*Automotive engineering*]
BUP .... Backup Plate
BUP .... Basotho Unity Party [*South Africa*] [*Political party*] (PPW)
BUP .... Bend Up [*Technical drawings*]
BUP .... Bristol United Press Ltd., Bristol, United Kingdom [*Library symbol*] [*Library of Congress*] (LCLS)
BUP .... British United Press
BUP .... Bulletin. University of Pittsburgh [*A publication*]
BUP .... Pittsfield, ME [*Location identifier*] [*FAA*] (FAAL)
BUPA........ British United Provident Association (DCTA)
BUPERS.... Bureau of Naval Personnel [*Also, BNP, NAVPERS*]
BUPERSCONINSTRBIL ... Bureau of Naval Personnel Controlled Instructor Billets
BUPFA5.... Commonwealth Bureau of Pastures and Field Crops. Hurley Berkshire Bulletin [*A publication*]
BUPP........ Backup Plate, Perforated
Buppie....... Black Urban Professional [*Lifestyle classification*]
BUPRD..... Budget and Program Newsletter [*United States*] [*A publication*]
BUPS........ Beacon, Ultra Portable "S" Band [*Navy*]
BUQ.......... Bulawayo [*Zimbabwe*] [*Airport symbol*] (OAG)
BUR .... Back Up Register
BUR .... Backup Rate (NASA)
BuR .... Bucknell Review [*A publication*]
BUR .... Builder, Concrete [*Navy rating*]
BUR .... Built-Up Roofing
BUR .... Burbank [*California*] [*Airport symbol*]
BUR .... Bureau (AFM)
BUR .... Bureaucrat [*A publication*]
BUR .... Buried
BUR .... Burlington [*Vermont*] [*Seismograph station code, US Geological Survey*] [*Closed*] (SEIS)
BUR .... Burlington Industries, Inc. [*NYSE symbol*] (SPSG)
BUR .... Burlington Public Library [*UTLAS symbol*]
BUR .... Burma [*ANSI three-letter standard code*] (CNC)
bur .... Burmese [*MARC language code*] [*Library of Congress*] (LCCP)
Bur .... Burnett's Wisconsin Supreme Court Reports [*1841-43*] [*A publication*] (DLA)
BUR .... Burnt Island Gold Ltd. (NPL) [*Vancouver Stock Exchange symbol*]
Bur .... Burrow. English King's Bench Reports [*A publication*] (DLA)
Bur Am Ethn ... Bureau of American Ethnology. Bulletin [*A publication*]
Bur Am Ethnol Annual Report ... Bureau of American Ethnology. Annual Report [*A publication*]
Bur Ass ...... Burrill on Voluntary Assignments [*A publication*] (DLA)
B Urb Pl..... Bachelor of Urban Planning
Bur Chy...... Burrough's History of the Chancery [*A publication*] (DLA)
Bur Circ Ev ... Burrill on Circumstantial Evidence [*A publication*] (DLA)
Burdekin-Townsville Reg QD Resour Ser ... Burdekin-Townsville Region, Queensland. Resource Series [*A publication*] (APTA)
Burdick Crime ... Burdick's Law of Crime [*A publication*] (DLA)
Burdick Roman Law ... Burdick's Principles of Roman Law [*A publication*] (DLA)
BURDS...... Burroughs Distribution Scheduling System [*Data processing*] (BUR)
Bureau of Steel Manuf ... Bureau of Steel Manufacturers of Australia. Paper Presented at the Annual Meeting [*A publication*] (APTA)
BUREC...... Bureau of Reclamation [*Later, WPRS*] [*Department of the Interior*]

Bur Econ Geol Univ Tex Austin Miner Resour Circ ... Bureau of Economic Geology. University of Texas at Austin. Mineral Resource Circular [*A publication*]
Buren Ispyt Gazov Skvazhin Oslozhennykh Usloviyakh Uzb ... Burenie i Ispytanie Neftyanykh i Gazovykh Skvazhin v Oslozhennykh Usloviyakh Uzbekistana [*A publication*]
Burf............ Burford's Reports [*6-18 Oklahoma*] [*A publication*] (DLA)
Bur Farmer ... Bureau Farmer [*A publication*]
Bur Forms ... Burrill's Forms [*A publication*] (DLA)
BURG........ Burgess
BURG........ Burgher (ROG)
BURG........ Burgomaster (ROG)
Burg .... [*Johannes*] Burgundio Pisanus [*Deceased, 1194*] [*Authority cited in pre-1607 legal work*] (DSA)
Burg Col & For Law ... Burge on Colonial and Foreign Law [*A publication*] (DLA)
Burg Dig..... Burgwyn's Digest Maryland Reports [*A publication*] (DLA)
Burge App ... Burge on Appellate Jurisdiction [*1841*] [*A publication*] (DLA)
Burge Col Law ... Burge on Colonial and Foreign Law [*A publication*] (DLA)
Burge Confl Law ... Burge on the Conflict of Laws [*A publication*] (DLA)
Burge Mar Int L ... Burge on Maritime International Law [*A publication*] (DLA)
Burgen........ Burgess' Reports [*16-49 Ohio*] [*A publication*] (DLA)
Burgenlaend Bienenzucht ... Burgenlaendische Bienenzucht [*A publication*]
Burgenl Heimatbl ... Burgenlaendische Heimatblaetter [*A publication*]
Burgenl Heim Bl ... Burgenlaendische Heimatblaetter [*A publication*]
Burgess ...... Burgess' Reports [*16-49 Ohio*] [*A publication*] (DLA)
Burge Sur ... Burge on Suretyship [*A publication*] (DLA)
BurgHb...... Burgenlaendische Heimatblaetter [*A publication*]
BURGL...... Burglary (DLA)
Burg Monographs in Sci ... Burg Monographs in Science [*Basel*] [*A publication*]
Bur & Gres Eq Pl ... Burroughs and Gresson's Irish Equity Pleader [*A publication*] (DLA)
Burgw MD Dig ... Burgwyn's Digest Maryland Reports [*A publication*] (DLA)
Buridava..... Buridava Studii si Materiale [*A publication*]
Bur Inform ... Bureau et Informatique [*A publication*]
Bur Insp Test Commer Commod (China) Bull ... Bureau for Inspecting and Testing Commercial Commodities (China). Bulletin [*A publication*]
BURISA .... British Urban and Regional Information System Association
BURJL...... Bulletin Ustavu Russkeho Jazyka a Literatury [*A publication*]
Burke Cel Tr ... Burke's Celebrated Trials [*A publication*] (DLA)
Burke Cop ... Burke. Copyright [*1842*] [*A publication*] (DLA)
Burke Cr L ... Burke. Criminal Law [*2nd ed.*] [*1845*] [*A publication*] (DLA)
Burke Int Cop ... Burke. International Copyright [*1852*] [*A publication*] (DLA)
Burke Pub Sch ... Burke on the Law of Public Schools [*A publication*] (DLA)
Burke Tr .... Burke's Celebrated Trials [*A publication*] (DLA)
Burks .... Burks' Reports [*91-98 Virginia*] [*A publication*] (DLA)
BURL........ Bradford University Research Ltd. [*British*] (IRUK)
BURL........ Burlesque (ROG)
Burlamaqui ... Burlamaqui's Natural and Political Law [*A publication*] (DLA)
Bur Law Dic ... Burrill's Law Dictionary [*A publication*] (DLA)
Burlesque Reps ... Skillman's New York Police Reports [*A publication*]
Burlington Mag ... Burlington Magazine [*A publication*]
Bur LJ....... Burma Law Journal [*A publication*] (DLA)
Burl M....... Burlington Magazine [*A publication*]
Burl Mag.... Burlington Magazine [*A publication*]
Burl Nat..... Burlamaqui's Natural and Political Law [*A publication*] (DLA)
Burl Natural & Pol Law ... Burlamaqui's Natural and Political Law [*A publication*] (DLA)
Bur LR ...... Burma Law Reports [*A publication*] (DLA)
Bur LT ...... Burma Law Times [*A publication*] (DLA)
Bur M........ Burrow's Reports Tempore Mansfield [*England*] [*A publication*] (DLA)
BURMA .... Be Undressed, Ready, My Angel [*Correspondence*] (DSUE)
Burma Law Inst J ... Burma Law Institute. Journal [*A publication*] (DLA)
Burma L Inst J ... Burma Law Institute. Journal [*A publication*] (DLA)
Burma LR .. Burma Law Reports [*A publication*] (DLA)
Burma Med J ... Burma Medical Journal [*A publication*]
Bur Miner Resour Geol Geophys Bull (Canberra) ... Bureau of Mineral Resources, Geology, and Geophysics. Bulletin (Canberra) [*A publication*]
Bur Miner Resour Geol Geophys Rep (Canberra) ... Bureau of Mineral Resources, Geology, and Geophysics. Report (Canberra) [*A publication*]
Bur Mines Inf Circ ... Bureau of Mines. Information Circular [*United States*] [*A publication*]
Bur Mines Rep Invest ... Bureau of Mines. Report of Investigations [*United States*] [*A publication*]
Bur Mines Res ... Bureau of Mines. Research [*Washington, DC*] [*A publication*]
Bur Mines Technol News ... Bureau of Mines. Technology News [*United States*] [*A publication*]
Burm LJ..... Burma Law Journal [*A publication*] (DLA)
Burm LR .... Burma Law Reports [*A publication*] (DLA)
Burm LT .... Burma Law Times [*A publication*] (DLA)

Burn .... Burnett's Wisconsin Reports [*A publication*] (DLA)
BURN .... Burnham [*England*]
Burn .... High Commission Court [*1865*] [*England*] [*A publication*] (DLA)
Burn .... Star Chamber Proceedings [*England*] [*A publication*] (DLA)
BURN .... Trilling Medical Technologies, Inc. [*NASDAQ symbol*] (NQ)
Burn Att Pr ... Burn's Attorney's Practice [*A publication*] (DLA)
Burn Cr L ... Burnet. Criminal Law of Scotland [*A publication*] (DLA)
Burn Dict ... Burn's Law Dictionary [*A publication*] (DLA)
Burn Eccl ... Burn's Ecclesiastical Law [*A publication*] (DLA)
Burn Ecc Law ... Burn's Ecclesiastical Law [*A publication*] (DLA)
Burnet .... Burnet. Manuscript Decisions, Scotch Court of Session [*A publication*] (DLA)
Burnett .... Burnett's Reports [*20-22 Oregon*] [*A publication*] (DLA)
Burnett .... Burnett's Wisconsin Reports [*A publication*] (DLA)
Burnett's Rep ... Burnett's Wisconsin Reports [*A publication*] (DLA)
Burnett (Wis) ... Burnett's Wisconsin Reports [*A publication*] (DLA)
Burn JP ...... Burn's Justice of the Peace [*England*] [*A publication*] (DLA)
Burn Law Dict ... Burn's Law Dictionary [*A publication*] (DLA)
Burn Mar Ins ... Burn's Marine Insurance [*A publication*] (DLA)
Burns' Ann St ... Burns' Annotated Statutes [*Indiana*] [*A publication*] (DLA)
Burns-Begg ... Southern Rhodesia Reports [*A publication*] (DLA)
Burns Chron ... Burns Chronicle [*A publication*]
Burn's Ecc Law ... Burn's Ecclesiastical Law [*A publication*] (DLA)
Burns Incl Therm Inj ... Burns, Including Thermal Injury [*A publication*]
Burn's JP (Eng) ... Burn's Justice of the Peace [*England*] [*A publication*] (DLA)
Burns Pract ... Burns. Conveyancing Practice [*Scotland*] [*A publication*] (DLA)
Burns' Rev St ... Burns' Annotated Statutes [*Indiana*] [*A publication*] (DLA)
Burn St Job ... Burn on Stock Jobbing [*A publication*] (DLA)
BURP .... Backup Rate of Pitch
Bur Pr .... Burrill's New York Practice [*A publication*] (DLA)
BURR .... Backup Rate of Roll
Burr .... Burrow. English King's Bench Reports Tempore Lord Mansfield [*97, 98 English Reprint*] [*A publication*] (DLA)
Burr Adm ... Burrill's Admiralty Cases [*1584-1839*] [*A publication*] (DLA)
Burr Ass ... Burrill on Assignments [*A publication*] (DLA)
Burr Ch ...... Burroughs' History of the Chancery [*A publication*] (DLA)
Burr Circ Ev ... Burrill on Circumstantial Evidence [*A publication*] (DLA)
Burr Dict ... Burrill's Law Dictionary [*A publication*] (DLA)
Bur Rech Geol Min Bull Sect 2 Geol Gites Miner (Fr) ... Bureau de Recherches Geologiques et Minieres. Bulletin. Section 2. Geologie des Gites Mineraux (France) [*A publication*]
Burrell .... Burrell's Reports, Admiralty, Edited by Marsden [*167 English Reprint*] [*A publication*] (DLA)
Burrell (Eng) ... Burrell's Reports, Admiralty, Edited by Marsden [*167 English Reprint*] [*A publication*] (DLA)
Burr (Eng) ... Burrow. English King's Bench Reports Tempore Lord Mansfield [*97, 98 English Reprint*] [*A publication*] (DLA)
Burr Forms ... Burrill's Forms [*A publication*] (DLA)
Burr & Gr Eq Pl ... Burroughs and Gresson's Irish Equity Pleader [*A publication*] (DLA)
Burrill .... Burrill's Law Dictionary [*A publication*] (DLA)
Burrill Ass ... Burrill on Voluntary Assignments [*A publication*] (DLA)
Burrill Assignm ... Burrill on Assignments [*A publication*] (DLA)
Burrill Circ Ev ... Burrill on Circumstantial Evidence [*A publication*] (DLA)
Burrill Pr ... Burrill's Practice [*A publication*] (DLA)
Bur River .... Burning River News [*A publication*]
Burr Law Dict ... Burrill's Law Dictionary [*A publication*] (DLA)
Burroughs Clear House ... Burroughs Clearing House [*A publication*]
Burrow .... Burrow's Reports, English King's Bench [*A publication*] (DLA)
Burrow Sett Cas ... Burrow's English Settlement Cases [*A publication*] (DLA)
Burr Pr .... Burrill's New York Practice [*A publication*] (DLA)
Burr Pub Sec ... Burroughs on Public Securities [*A publication*] (DLA)
Burr SC ...... Burrow's English Settlement Cases [*A publication*] (DLA)
Burr S Cas ... Burrow's English Settlement Cases [*A publication*] (DLA)
Burr S Cases ... Burrow's English Settlement Cases [*A publication*] (DLA)
Burr Sett Cas ... Burrow's English Settlement Cases [*A publication*] (DLA)
Burr Sett Cas (Eng) ... Burrow's English Settlement Cases [*A publication*] (DLA)
Burr Tax .... Burroughs on Taxation [*A publication*] (DLA)
Burr TM .... Burrow's Reports Tempore Mansfield [*England*] [*A publication*] (DLA)
Burr Tr .... Burr's Trial, Reported by Robertson [*A publication*] (DLA)
Burr Tr Rob ... Burr's Trial, Reported by Robertson [*A publication*] (DLA)
BURS .... Bibliotheque Universelle et Revue Suisse [*A publication*]
BURS .... Burris Individuals, Inc. [*NASDAQ symbol*] (NQ)
BURS .... Bursar
Bursat .... [*Franciscus*] Bursatus [*Flourished, 17th century*] [*Authority cited in pre-1607 legal work*] (DSA)
Bur SC .... Burrow's English Settlement Cases [*A publication*] (DLA)
Bur Stand (US) Cir ... Bureau of Standards (United States). Circular [*A publication*]
Bur Stand US Handb ... US Bureau of Standards. Handbook [*A publication*]
Bur Stand US J Res ... US Bureau of Standards. Journal of Research [*A publication*]
Bur Sugar Exp Stn (Brisbane) Annu Rep ... Bureau of Sugar Experiment Stations (Brisbane). Annual Report [*A publication*]

Bur Sugar Exp St Queensl Tech Commun ... Bureau of Sugar Experiment Stations. Queensland Technical Communications [*A publication*]
Bur Sug Exp Sta Tech Commun ... Queensland. Bureau of Sugar Experiment Stations. Technical Communication [*A publication*] (APTA)
Bur Sug Exp Stat Tech Commun ... Queensland. Bureau of Sugar Experiment Stations. Technical Communication [*A publication*] (APTA)
Bur Tax ...... Burroughs on Taxation [*A publication*] (DLA)
Burt Bank .. Burton on Bankruptcy [*A publication*] (DLA)
Burt Cas ..... Burton's Collection of Cases and Opinions [*England*] [*A publication*] (DLA)
Burt Man ... Burton. Manual of the Laws of Scotland [*A publication*] (DLA)
Burt Parl .... Burton's Parliamentary Diary [*A publication*] (DLA)
Burt Real Prop ... Burton on Real Property [*A publication*] (DLA)
Burt RP ...... Burton on Real Property [*A publication*] (DLA)
Burt Sc Tr .. Burton's Scotch Trials [*A publication*] (DLA)
BURY .... Backup Rate of Yaw
BUS .... Bachelor of Urban Studies
BUS .... Backscatter Ultraviolet Spectrometer
BUS .... Bank of the United States
BUS .... Bartholin's, Urethral, Skene's [*Glands*] [*Medicine*]
BUS .... Batumi [*USSR*] [*Airport symbol*] (OAG)
BUS .... Beilstein Unique Sequence [*Chemistry*]
BUS .... Brown University. Studies [*A publication*]
BUS .... Building Use Studies [*Research firm*] [*British*]
BUS .... Bulletin. Universite de Strasbourg [*A publication*]
BUS .... Burmac Energy Corp. [*Vancouver Stock Exchange symbol*]
BUS .... Bushel
BUS .... Business (AFM)
BUS .... Business Division [*Census*] (OICC)
BUS .... Business and Society Review [*A publication*]
Bus .... Busiris [*of Isocrates*] [*Classical studies*] (OCD)
BUS .... Busulfan [*Also, BSF*] [*Antineoplastic drug*]
BUS .... Industrial Management [*London*] [*A publication*]
BUSa .... Bollettino Ufficiale Regione Sarda [*Official Bulletin of the Regione Sarda*] [*A publication*] (ILCA)
BUSA .... British Universities Society of Arts
BUSAB ...... Business Administration [*England*] [*A publication*]
BUSAC .... Bureau of Ships Analog Computer [*Obsolete*] [*Navy*]
Bus Adm ..... Business Administration [*A publication*]
BUSADMIN ... Business Administration
Bus Admin ... Business Administration [*A publication*]
Bus Admin (Great Britain) ... Business Administration (Great Britain) [*A publication*]
BUSAK ...... Bus Acknowledgement [*Data processing*] (TEL)
Bus Am ..... Business America [*A publication*]
BUSAN ..... Business Analyst Skills Evaluation [*Test*]
BUSANDA ... Bureau of Supplies and Accounts [*Later, NSUPSC*] [*Navy*]
Busan Women's Univ J ... Busan Women's University. Journal [*South Korea*] [*A publication*]
BUSARB ... British-United States Amateur Rocket Bureau
Bus Arch Cncl Aust Bull ... Business Archives Council of Australia. New South Wales Branch. Bulletin [*A publication*] (APTA)
Bus Arch & Hist ... Business Archives and History [*A publication*] (APTA)
Bus Archives Council Aust Bul ... Business Archives Council of Australia. Bulletin [*A publication*] (APTA)
Bus Archives Council Aust Pub ... Business Archives Council of Australia. Publications [*A publication*] (APTA)
Bus Archs Hist ... Business Archives and History [*A publication*] (APTA)
Bus Asia ..... Business Asia [*A publication*]
Busb .... Busbee's North Carolina Law Reports [*A publication*] (DLA)
Bus Barometer ... Business Barometer of Central Florida [*A publication*]
BUSBC .... Brazil-US Business Council (EA)
Busb Cr Dig ... Busbee's Criminal Digest [*North Carolina*] [*A publication*] (DLA)
Busbee Eq (NC) ... Busbee's North Carolina Equity Reports [*A publication*] (DLA)
Busb Eq ...... Busbee's North Carolina Equity Reports [*A publication*] (DLA)
Busb L .... Busbee's North Carolina Law Reports [*A publication*] (DLA)
Bus in Brief ... Business in Brief [*A publication*]
BUSC .... Boletin. Universidad de Santiago de Compostela [*A publication*]
BUSCA ...... Bollettino delle Scienze Mediche [*A publication*]
BUSCB ...... Building Science [*A publication*]
Bus China .. Business China [*A publication*]
BUSCI .... British-United States Convoy Instructions
Bus & Com ... Business and Commerce [*A publication*] (DLA)
Bus Comm ... Business Communications Review [*A publication*]
Bus Comp Sys ... Business Computer Systems [*A publication*]
BUSCON .. Microcomputer Bus Users' Show and Conference [*MultiDynamics, Inc.*] (TSPED)
Bus Cond Dig ... Business Conditions Digest [*A publication*]
Bus Conditions Dig ... Business Conditions Digest [*A publication*]
BUSE .... Boston University. Studies in English [*A publication*]
BUSEB ...... Byulleten' Sovetskoi Antarkticheskoi Ekspeditsii [*A publication*]
Bus Econ .... Business Economics [*A publication*]
Bus and Econ Dim ... Business and Economic Dimensions [*Florida*] [*A publication*]

Bus and Econ Dimensions ... Business and Economic Dimensions [*A publication*]
Bus Economist ... Business Economist [*A publication*]
Bus and Econ Perspectives ... Business and Economic Perspectives [*A publication*]
Bus and Econ R (Univ SC) ... Business and Economic Review (University of South Carolina) [*A publication*]
BUSED ...... Base and User [*A publication*]
Bus Ed Forum ... Business Education Forum [*A publication*]
Bus Ed J ..... Business Education Journal [*A publication*]
Bus Ed News ... Business Education Council. Newsletter [*A publication*]
Bus Ed Observer ... New Jersey Business Education Observer [*A publication*]
Bus Educ Forum ... Business Education Forum [*A publication*]
Bus Educ Ind ... Business Education Index [*A publication*]
Bus Educ Index ... Business Education Index [*A publication*]
Bus Ed World ... Business Education World [*A publication*]
Bus E Eur ... Business Eastern Europe [*A publication*]
BUSEN ...... Beilstein Unique Sequence Number [*Chemistry*]
Bus Eq .... Busbee's North Carolina Equity Reports [*A publication*]   (DLA)
Bus Europe ... Business Europe [*A publication*]
Bus Exch ..... Business Exchange [*A publication*]
BUSF .... British Universities Sports Federation
Bus and Fin (Ireland) ... Business and Finance (Ireland) [*A publication*]
Bus Forum ... Business Forum [*A publication*]
Bus Franchise Guide CCH ... Business Franchise Guide. Commerce Clearing House [*A publication*]
BUSH .... Bush Terminal R. R. [*AAR code*]
BUSH .... Bushel
BUSH .... Bushing   (MSA)
Bush .... Bush's Kentucky Reports [*64-77 Kentucky*] [*A publication*]   (DLA)
BUSH .... Buy United States Here [*Program to procure US-made supplies from overseas subsidiaries of US firms*]   (AFM)
Bush Dig .... Bush's Digest of Florida Laws [*A publication*]   (DLA)
Bus Health ... Business and Health [*A publication*]
Bush Elec ... Bushby. Parliamentary Elections [*5th ed.*] [*1880*] [*A publication*]   (DLA)
BUSHIPS ... Bureau of Ships [*Later, Naval Sea Systems Command*]
Bus Hist ..... Business History [*A publication*]
Bus History ... Business History [*A publication*]
Bus Hist R ... Business History Review [*A publication*]
Bus Hist Rev ... Business History Review [*A publication*]
Bus Hist Soc Bull ... Business History Society. Bulletin [*A publication*]
Bush (KY) .. Bush's Kentucky Reports [*64-77 Kentucky*] [*A publication*]   (DLA)
Bus Horiz ... Business Horizons [*A publication*]
Bus Horizn ... Business Horizons [*A publication*]
Bus Horizons ... Business Horizons [*A publication*]
BUSI .... Bring-Up Security Investigation [*Military*]
BusI .... Business Periodicals Index [*A publication*]
BUSIB .... Bussei [*A publication*]
Bus India .... Business India [*A publication*]
Busin Econ ... Business Economics [*A publication*]
Busin Economist ... Business Economist [*A publication*]
Busines NC ... Business North Carolina [*A publication*]
Busines NJ ... Southern New Jersey Business Digest [*A publication*]
Business Automn ... Business Automation [*A publication*]
Business Equip Dig ... Business Equipment Digest [*A publication*]
Business Insur ... Business Insurance [*A publication*]
Business LJ ... Business Law Journal   (DLA)
Business LR ... Business Law Review [*A publication*]
Business Q ... Business Quarterly [*A publication*]
Business R ... Business Review [*A publication*]   (APTA)
Business Rev ... Business Review [*A publication*]   (APTA)
Bus Inf Technol ... Business Information Technology [*A publication*]
Busin Monitor Rubb ... Business Monitor. Rubber [*A publication*]
Busin Monitor Synth ... Business Monitor. Synthetic Resins and Plastics Materials [*A publication*]
Busin R ...... Business Review [*A publication*]
Busin Soc R ... Business and Society Review [*A publication*]
Bus Insur .... Business Insurance [*A publication*]
Bus Int Mo ... Business International. Money Report [*A publication*]
Bus Intnl .... Business International [*A publication*]
BUSIVISIT ... Business Visit [*Program*] [*United States Travel Service*]
Bus Ja .... Business Japan [*A publication*]
Bus Jap ...... Business Japan [*A publication*]
Bus Japan .. Business Japan [*A publication*]
Bus J (Manila) ... Business Journal (Manila) [*A publication*]
Bus Jpn ...... Business Japan [*A publication*]
Bus Jrl NJ ... Business Journal of New Jersey [*A publication*]
Bus J (San Jose) ... Business Journal (San Jose, California) [*A publication*]
BUSKA ...... Bulletin. Schweizerischer Elektrotechnischer Verein [*A publication*]
BUSKB ...... Bussei Kenkyu [*A publication*]
Busk Pr ...... Buskirk. Indiana Practice [*A publication*]   (DLA)
BUSL .... Boston University School of Law   (DLA)
BUSL .... Buoy Boat, Stern Loading
Bus & L ...... Business and Law [*A publication*]   (DLA)
Bus L .... Business Lawyer [*A publication*]
BUSL .... Business Life [*Canada*] [*A publication*]

BUSLA ...... Bulletin International. Academie Yougoslave des Sciences et des Beaux-Arts. Classe des Sciences Mathematiques et Naturelles [*A publication*]
B Us L Ar ... Bulletin Usuel des Lois et Arretes [*A publication*]
Bus Latin A ... Business Latin America [*A publication*]
Bus Law ..... Business Lawyer [*A publication*]
Bus Law ..... Businessman's Law [*A publication*]
Bus Law R ... Business Law Review [*A publication*]
Bus Lawyer ... Business Lawyer [*A publication*]
Bus LJ .... Business Law Journal   (DLA)
Bus LR .... Business Law Review [*A publication*]
Bus L Rep .. Business Law Reports   (DLA)
Bus L Rev ... Business Law Review [*A publication*]
Bus L Rev (Butterworths) ... Business Law Review (Butterworths) [*A publication*]
BUSM .... British United Shoe Machinery [*Commercial firm*]
Bus Mag ...... Business Magazine [*A publication*]
Bus Mark .... Business Marketing [*A publication*]
Bus Matters ... Business Matters [*A publication*]
Bus Mexico ... Business Mexico [*A publication*]
Bus Mktg ... Business Marketing [*A publication*]
BUSN .... Business North [*Canada*] [*A publication*]
Busn Times ... Business Times [*A publication*]
BUSP .... Butt Splice   (MCD)
Bus Period Index ... Business Periodicals Index [*A publication*]
Bus & Prof ... Business and Professions [*A publication*]   (DLA)
Bus & Prof C ... Business and Professions Code   (DLA)
Bus Prof Ethics J ... Business and Professional Ethics Journal [*A publication*]
Bus and Public Affairs ... Business and Public Affairs [*A publication*]
Bus Q .... Business Quarterly [*A publication*]
BUSRA .... British-United States Routing Agreement [*Shipping*]
BUSRAT ... Battle-Unit Short-Range Antitank Weapon System   (NATG)
Bus R (Bangkok) ... Business Review (Bangkok) [*A publication*]
Bus Reg .... Business Regulation   (DLA)
Bus Reg L Rep ... Business Regulation Law Report [*A publication*]   (DLA)
Bus Rev ...... Business Review [*A publication*]   (APTA)
Bus Rev Kobe Univ ... Business Review. Kobe University [*A publication*]
Bus Rev Wash Univ ... Business Review. Washington University [*A publication*]
BUSRQ ...... Bus Request [*Data processing*]   (TEL)
BUSS .... Backup Scram System [*Nuclear energy*]   (NRCH)
BUSS .... Backup Study Sheets [*Military*]
BUSS .... Balloon-Borne Ultraviolet Stellar Spectrometer
BUSS .... Biomedical Urine Sampling System   (KSC)
BUSS .... Bradford University Software Services Ltd. [*British*]   (IRUK)
BUSS .... Buoy Underwater Sound Signal   (NG)
Bus Scotland ... Business Scotland [*A publication*]
Bus Scr ...... Business Screen [*A publication*]
Bus & Scty ... Business and Society [*A publication*]
Bus & Scty R ... Business and Society Review [*A publication*]
Bus Soc ...... Business and Society [*A publication*]
Bus & Soc ... Business and Society Review [*A publication*]
Bus and Society ... Business and Society [*A publication*]
Bus and Society R ... Business and Society Review [*A publication*]
Bus & Soc R ... Business and Society Review [*A publication*]
Bus Soc Rev ... Business and Society Review [*A publication*]
Bus and Socy Rev ... Business and Society Review [*A publication*]
Bus Stat ...... Business Statistics. US Department of Commerce [*A publication*]
BUS STOP ... Breathers United to Stop Standing Time of Passenger-Buses [*Student legal action organization*]
Bus Syst .... Business Systems [*A publication*]
Bus Syst & Equip ... Business Systems and Equipment [*A publication*]
Bus Taiwan ... Business and Industry Taiwan [*A publication*]
BUSTDS ... Bureau of Standards
Bus Transp ... Bus Transportation [*A publication*]
Bus Venezuela ... Business Venezuela [*A publication*]
Bus W .... Business Week [*A publication*]
Bus Week ... Business Week [*A publication*]
BUSWREC ... Ban Unsafe Schoolbuses Which Regularly Endanger Children [*Student legal action organization*]
Busw & Wol Pr ... Buswell and Wolcott. Massachusetts Practice [*A publication*]   (DLA)
BUT .... Basic Unit Training
BUT .... Bollettino Ufficiale Trentino Alto-Adige [*Official Gazette of the Trentino Alto-Adige*] [*A publication*]   (ILCA)
BUT .... Breakup Time [*Ophthalmology*]
BUT .... British United Traction Co.
BUT .... Buletin. Universiteti Shteteror te Tiranes. Seria Shkencat Shoqerore [*A publication*]
BUT .... Bulletin. Universite de Toulouse [*A publication*]
BUT .... Bureau of University Travel [*Defunct*]
BUT .... Business International [*A publication*]
BUT .... Butanol [*Organic chemistry*]
But .... [*Jacobus*] Butrigarius [*Deceased, 1348*] [*Authority cited in pre-1607 legal work*]   (DSA)
But .... [*Antonius de*] Butrio [*Deceased, 1408*] [*Authority cited in pre-1607 legal work*]   (DSA)
BUT .... Butte [*Montana*] [*Seismograph station code, US Geological Survey*]   (SEIS)
BUT .... Button

BUT .... Butyrum [Butter] [Pharmacy]   (ROG)
BUTC .... Butler [John O.] Company [Chicago, IL] [NASDAQ symbol]   (NQ)
BUTEL ..... Bureau of Telecommunications [Philippines]   (DS)
BUTI .... BeautiControl Cosmetics, Incorporated [Carrollton, TX] [NASDAQ symbol]   (NQ)
Butig .... [Hieronymus] Butigella [Deceased, 1504] [Authority cited in pre-1607 legal work]   (DSA)
BUTL .... Butler National Corp. [NASDAQ symbol]   (NQ)
But Law & Cl ... Butler's Lawyer and Client [A publication]   (DLA)
Butler .... Butler County Legal Journal [Pennsylvania] [A publication]   (DLA)
Butler Co Litt ... Butler's Notes to Coke on Littleton [A publication]   (DLA)
Butler Hor Jur ... Butler's Horae Juridicae [A publication]   (DLA)
Butler Univ Bot Stud ... Butler University Botanical Studies [A publication]
Butl Sec Mat Soc Catalana Cienc Fis Quim Mat ... Butlleti. Seccio de Matematiques. Societat Catalana de Ciencies Fisiques, Quimiques, i Matematiques [A publication]
Butl Soc Catalana Cienc Fis Quim Mat 2 ... Butlleti. Societat Catalana de Ciencies Fisiques, Quimiques, i Matematiques. Segona Epoca [A publication]
BUTM .... Baring Unit Trust Management Service [Finance] [British]
BUTMB ..... Building Technology and Management [A publication]
BUTN .... Butane   (MSA)
BUTPA ...... Butane Propane [A publication]
Butr .... [Jacobus] Butrigarius [Deceased, 1348] [Authority cited in pre-1607 legal work]   (DSA)
BUTR .... Butterfield Equities [NASDAQ symbol]   (NQ)
Butri .... [Jacobus] Butrigarius [Deceased, 1348] [Authority cited in pre-1607 legal work]   (DSA)
Butsuri Phys Soc Jap ... Butsuri. Physical Society of Japan [A publication]
BUTT .... Buttock [Slang]   (DSUE)
Butter & Cheese J ... Butter and Cheese Journal [A publication]
Butter Cheese Milk Prod J ... Butter, Cheese, and Milk Products Journal [A publication]
Butterworths Int Med Rev Cardiol ... Butterworths International Medical Reviews [A publication]
Butterworths Int Med Rev Clin Endocrinol ... Butterworths International Medical Reviews. Clinical Endocrinology [A publication]
Butterworths Int Med Rev Clin Pharmacol Ther ... Butterworths International Medical Reviews. Clinical Pharmacology and Therapeutics [A publication]
Butterworths Int Med Rev Gastroenterol ... Butterworths International Medical Reviews. Gastroenterology [A publication]
Butterworths Int Med Rev Hematol ... Butterworths International Medical Reviews. Hematology [A publication]
Butterworths Int Med Rev Neurol ... Butterworths International Medical Reviews. Neurology [A publication]
Butterworths Int Med Rev Obstet Gynecol ... Butterworths International Medical Reviews. Obstetrics and Gynecology [A publication]
Butterworths Int Med Rev Ophthalmol ... Butterworths International Medical Reviews. Ophthalmology [A publication]
Butterworths Int Med Rev Orthop ... Butterworths International Medical Reviews. Orthopaedics [A publication]
Butterworths Int Med Rev Otolaryngol ... Butterworths International Medical Reviews. Otolaryngology [A publication]
Butterworths Int Med Rev Pediatr ... Butterworths International Medical Reviews. Pediatrics [A publication]
Butterworths Int Med Rev Rheumatol ... Butterworths International Medical Reviews. Rheumatology [A publication]
Butterworths Int Med Rev Surg ... Butterworths International Medical Reviews. Surgery [A publication]
Butterworths Int Med Rev Urol ... Butterworths International Medical Reviews. Urology [A publication]
Butterworth's SA Law Review ... Butterworth's South African Law Review [A publication]   (DLA)
Butterworth's South Afr L Rev ... Butterworth's South African Law Review [A publication]   (DLA)
Butt RA ...... Butterworth's Rating Appeals [1913-31] [England] [A publication]   (DLA)
Butt Rat App ... Butterworth's Rating Appeals [1913-31] [England] [A publication]   (DLA)
Butt SA Law Rev ... Butterworth's South African Law Review [A publication]   (DLA)
Butts Sh ..... Butts' Edition of Shower's English King's Bench Reports [A publication]   (DLA)
Butt WCC .. Butterworth's Workmen's Compensation Cases [A publication]   (DLA)
Butt Work Comp Cas ... Butterworth's Workmen's Compensation Cases [A publication]   (DLA)
BuTx .... Bungarotoxin [Also, BGT, BTX] [Biochemistry]
BUU .... Basic User Unit   (MCD)
BUU .... Burlington, WI [Location identifier] [FAA]   (FAAL)
BUV .... Backscatter Ultraviolet [Spectrometry]   (MCD)
BUV .... Buchan [Australia] [Seismograph station code, US Geological Survey] [Closed]   (SEIS)
BUVOA ..... Bulletin Volcanologique [A publication]
BUVS .... Backscatter Ultraviolet Spectrometer
BUVSA ...... Bulletin. Vereinigung der Schweizerischen Petroleum-Geologen und -Ingenieure [A publication]

BUW .... Bau Bau [Indonesia] [Airport symbol]   (OAG)
BUW .... Business Week [A publication]
BUWEA ..... Business Week [A publication]
BUWEAPS ... Bureau of Weapons [Navy]
BUWEPS .. Bureau of Naval Weapons [Obsolete]
BUWEPSFLEREADREP ... Bureau of Naval Weapons Fleet Readiness Representative [Obsolete]   (MCD)
BUWEPSFLEREADREPCEN ... Bureau of Naval Weapons Fleet Readiness Representative, Central [Obsolete]   (MCD)
BUWEPSFLEREADREPLANT ... Bureau of Naval Weapons Fleet Readiness Representative, Atlantic [Obsolete]   (MCD)
BUWEPSFLEREADREPPAC ... Bureau of Naval Weapons Fleet Readiness Representative, Pacific [Obsolete]   (MCD)
BUWEPSFLTREADREP ... Bureau of Naval Weapons Fleet Readiness Representative [Obsolete]   (MUGU)
BUWEPS FR ... Bureau of Naval Weapons Fleet Readiness [Obsolete]   (MCD)
BUWEPSINST ... Bureau of Naval Weapons Instruction [Obsolete]   (MCD)
BUWEPSNOTE ... Bureau of Naval Weapons Notice [Obsolete]
BUWEPSREP ... Bureau of Naval Weapons Representative [Obsolete]   (MCD)
BUWEPSRESREP ... Bureau of Naval Weapons Resident Representative [Obsolete]
BUWEPSTECHREP ... Bureau of Naval Weapons Technical Representative [Obsolete]   (MUGU)
BUWEPSTLO ... Bureau of Naval Weapons Technical Liaison Office [Obsolete]   (MUGU)
BUWNE ..... Brotherhood of Utility Workers of New England   (EA)
BUX .... Bunia [Zaire] [Airport symbol]   (OAG)
BUX .... Greece's Weekly for Business and Finance [A publication]
Buxton........ Buxton's Reports [123-129 North Carolina] [A publication]   (DLA)
Buxton (NC) ... Buxton's Reports [123-129 North Carolina] [A publication]   (DLA)
BUY .... Bunbury [Australia] [Airport symbol]   (OAG)
BUY .... Burlington, NC [Location identifier] [FAA]   (FAAL)
BUYAC ..... Buying Activity [Air Force]   (AFM)
BUYARD .. Bureau of Yards and Docks [Later, NFEC] [Navy]   (KSC)
BUY & D ... Bureau of Yards and Docks [Later, NFEC] [Navy]
BUYDSDOCKS ... Bureau of Yards and Docks [Later, NFEC] [Navy]
BUYRA ..... Bulletin. Parenteral Drug Association [A publication]
BUZ .... Budakeszi [Hungary] [Later, TYH] [Geomagnetic observatory code]
BUZ .... Bushehr [Iran] [Airport symbol]   (OAG)
BUZ .... Buzzer   (MSA)
BUZ .... Columbus, OH [Location identifier] [FAA]   (FAAL)
BV .... Babylonian Vocalization   (BJA)
BV .... Bacitracin V [Antibacterial compound]
BV .... Back View   (MSA)
BV .... Balanced Voltage
BV .... Balneum Vaporis [Vapor Bath] [Medicine]
BV .... Baltimore Vegetarians [Later, VRG]   (EA)
BV .... Bayerische Vereinsbank [Union Bank of Bavaria] [Munich, West Germany]
BV .... Beata Virgo [Blessed Virgin] [Latin]
BV .... Beatitudo Vestra [Your Holiness] [Latin]
BV .... Before Video
B & V .... Beling and Vanderstraaten's Ceylon Reports [A publication]   (DLA)
BV .... Bellows Valve
BV .... Bene Vale [Farewell] [Latin]
BV .... Bene Vixit [He Lived a Good Life] [Latin]
BV .... Berkeley Version   (BJA)
BV .... Besloten Vennootschap [Private or Closed Limited Company] [Dutch]
BV .... Betamethasone Valerate [Glucocorticoid]
BV .... Beverage   (KSC)
BV .... Bible Version [As opposed to the Prayer Book version of the Psalms]
BV .... Biblical Viewpoint [A publication]
BV .... Biological Value
BV .... Biological Variation
BV .... Birth Visit   (ROG)
BV .... Black Veterans, Inc.   (EA)
BV .... Bleed Valve   (MCD)
BV .... Blessed Virgin
BV .... Blockbuster Entertainment Corp. [NYSE symbol]   (SPSG)
BV .... Blood Vessel [Medicine]
BV .... Blood Volume [Medicine]
BV .... Blow Valve
B-V .... Blue-Visual [Color index]
BV .... Boeing-Vertol Division [The Boeing Co.] [ICAO aircraft manufacturer identifier]   (ICAO)
BV .... Bogens Verden [A publication]
BV .... Bogoslovni Vestnik [A publication]
BV .... Bonnet Valve
BV .... Bons Vivants [An association]   (EA)
BV .... Book Value [Business term]
BV .... Bouvet Island [ANSI two-letter standard code]   (CNC)
bv............ Bouvet Island [MARC country of publication code] [Library of Congress]   (LCCP)

BV .... Breakdown Voltage

BV .... Brick Veneered [*Insurance classification*]

BV .... Bronchovesicular [*Breath sounds*] [*Medicine*]

BV .... Bureau Veritas [*International register for the classification of shipping and aircraft*]

BV .... Bureau Voucher [*Army*]   (AABC)

BV .... Busy Verification [*Telecommunications*]   (TEL)

BV .... Bypass Valve   (MCD)

BV .... Carib Jet (Antigua) Ltd. [*Great Britain*] [*ICAO designator*]   (FAAC)

BV .... Vernon Library, British Columbia [*Library symbol*] [*National Library of Canada*]   (NLC)

BVA .... Bachelor of Vocational Agriculture

BVA .... Best Corrected Visual Acuity [*Ophthalmology*]

BVA .... Biventricular Assistance [*Cardiology*]

BVA .... Blinded Veterans Association   (EA)

BVA .... Board of Veterans Appeals [*Veterans Administration*]

BVA .... Boundary Value Analysis [*Computer program test*]

BVA .... British Veterinary Association

BVA .... British Videogram Association

BVA .... Buena Vista [*Guatemala*] [*Seismograph station code, US Geological Survey*]   (SEIS)

BVA .... Vancouver Public Library, British Columbia [*Library symbol*] [*National Library of Canada*]   (NLC)

BVAA .... Vancouver City Archives, British Columbia [*Library symbol*] [*National Library of Canada*]   (NLC)

BVAABS ... Synod Office, Ecclesiastical Province of British Columbia, Anglican Church of Canada, Vancouver, British Columbia [*Library symbol*] [*National Library of Canada*]   (NLC)

BVAABSA ... Archives, British Columbia Provincial Synod, Anglican Church of Canada, Vancouver, British Columbia [*Library symbol*] [*National Library of Canada*]   (NLC)

BVAAD ..... Alcoholism and Drug Abuse Commission, Vancouver, British Columbia [*Library symbol*] [*National Library of Canada*]   (NLC)

BVAADP... Alcohol and Drug Programs, Vancouver, British Columbia [*Library symbol*] [*National Library of Canada*]   (NLC)

BVAAE...... Associated Engineering Services Ltd., Vancouver, British Columbia [*Library symbol*] [*National Library of Canada*]   (NLC)

BVAAG ..... Agriculture Canada, Vancouver, British Columbia [*Library symbol*] [*National Library of Canada*]   (NLC)

BVAAM .... Fifteenth Field Artillery Regiment, Royal Canadian Artillery Museum and Archives Society, Vancouver, British Columbia [*Library symbol*] [*National Library of Canada*]   (NLC)

BVAAP...... Information Services, Asia Pacific Foundation of Canada, Vancouver, British Columbia [*Library symbol*] [*National Library of Canada*]   (NLC)

BVAB........ Bulletin van de Vereeniging tot Bevordering der Kennis van de Antike Beschaving [*A publication*]

BVABCR ... Corporate Information, BC Rail, Vancouver, British Columbia [*Library symbol*] [*National Library of Canada*]   (NLC)

BVABCS.... British Columbia Sports Hall of Fame and Museum, Vancouver, British Columbia [*Library symbol*] [*National Library of Canada*]   (NLC)

BVABOT... Vancouver Board of Trade Library, British Columbia [*Library symbol*] [*National Library of Canada*]   (NLC)

BVABS...... Brown Strachan Associates, Vancouver, British Columbia [*Library symbol*] [*National Library of Canada*]   (NLC)

BVABSM .. British Columbia Museum, Vancouver, British Columbia [*Library symbol*] [*National Library of Canada*]   (NLC)

BVABT...... British Columbia Telephone Co., Burnaby, British Columbia [*Library symbol*] [*National Library of Canada*]   (NLC)

BVABY...... British Columbia and Yukon Chamber of Mines, Vancouver, British Columbia [*Library symbol*] [*National Library of Canada*]   (NLC)

BVAC........ Capilano College, Vancouver, British Columbia [*Library symbol*] [*National Library of Canada*]   (NLC)

BVACAA... Archives, Archdiocese of Vancouver, Catholic Church, British Columbia [*Library symbol*] [*National Library of Canada*]   (NLC)

BVACBA... CBA Engineering Ltd., Vancouver, British Columbia [*Library symbol*] [*National Library of Canada*]   (NLC)

BVACBV .. VTR Library, Canadian Broadcasting Corp. [*Videotheque, Societe Radio-Canada*], Vancouver, British Columbia [*Library symbol*] [*National Library of Canada*]   (BIB)

BVACCA... Cancer Control Agency of British Columbia, Vancouver, British Columbia [*Library symbol*] [*National Library of Canada*]   (NLC)

BVACCU... British Columbia Central Credit Union, Vancouver, British Columbia [*Library symbol*] [*National Library of Canada*]   (NLC)

BVACF...... Council of Forest Industries of British Columbia, Vancouver, British Columbia [*Library symbol*] [*National Library of Canada*]   (NLC)

BVACG...... Regional Library, Canadian Coast Guard [*Bibliotheque Regionale, Garde Cotiere Canadienne*] North Vancouver, British Columbia [*Library symbol*] [*National Library of Canada*]   (NLC)

BVACI....... Chemetics International Ltd., Vancouver, British Columbia [*Library symbol*] [*National Library of Canada*]   (NLC)

BVACILS .. British Columbia College and Institute Library Services Clearinghouse for the Print Impaired (CILS), Vancouver, British Columbia [*Library symbol*] [*National Library of Canada*]   (NLC)

BVACM..... Centennial Museum, Vancouver, British Columbia [*Library symbol*] [*National Library of Canada*]   (NLC)

BVACOM ... Cominco Ltd., Vancouver, British Columbia [*Library symbol*] [*National Library of Canada*]   (NLC)

BVADC...... Coal Division, Denison Mines Ltd., Vancouver, British Columbia [*Library symbol*] [*National Library of Canada*]   (BIB)

BVAEAE ... Atmospheric Environment Service, Environment Canada [*Service de l'Environnement Atmospherique, Environnement Canada*] Vancouver, British Columbia [*Library symbol*] [*National Library of Canada*]   (NLC)

BVAEC...... British Columbia Energy Commission, Vancouver, British Columbia [*Library symbol*] [*National Library of Canada*]   (NLC)

BVAEN ..... Envirocon Ltd., Vancouver, British Columbia [*Library symbol*] [*National Library of Canada*]   (NLC)

BVAEP...... Environmental Protection Service, Environment Canada/ Pacific Region [*Service de la Protection de l'Environnement, Environnement Canada/Region du Pacifique*] West Vancouver, British Columbia [*Library symbol*] [*National Library of Canada*]   (NLC)

BVAF........ Vancouver Laboratory, Fisheries and Oceans Canada [*Laboratoire de Vancouver, Peches et Oceans Canada*], British Columbia [*Library symbol*] [*Obsolete*] [*National Library of Canada*]   (NLC)

BVAFA...... Fine Arts, Music, and Films Division, Vancouver Public Library, British Columbia [*Library symbol*] [*National Library of Canada*]   (NLC)

BVAFI .... Fisheries Management Regional Library, Fisheries and Oceans Canada [*Bibliotheque Regionale de la Gestion des Pecheries, Peches et Oceans Canada*] Vancouver, British Columbia [*Library symbol*] [*National Library of Canada*]   (NLC)

BVAFP ...... Forintek Canada Corp., Vancouver, British Columbia [*Library symbol*] [*National Library of Canada*]   (NLC)

BVAFV ...... Farris, Vaughan, Wills & Murphy Law Firm, Vancouver, British Columbia [*Library symbol*] [*National Library of Canada*]   (NLC)

BVAG .... Geological Survey of Canada [*Commission Geologique du Canada*] Vancouver, British Columbia [*Library symbol*] [*National Library of Canada*]   (NLC)

BVAGB...... Golder Brawner & Associates Ltd., Vancouver, British Columbia [*Library symbol*] [*National Library of Canada*]   (NLC)

BVAGF...... Staff Medical Library, G. F. Strong Rehabilitation Centre, Vancouver, British Columbia [*Library symbol*] [*National Library of Canada*]   (BIB)

BVAH........ British Columbia Hydro and Power Authority, Vancouver, British Columbia [*Library symbol*] [*National Library of Canada*]   (NLC)

BVAHD..... Vancouver Health Department, British Columbia [*Library symbol*] [*National Library of Canada*]   (NLC)

BVAHE...... British Columbia Hydro Engineering Library, Vancouver, British Columbia [*Library symbol*] [*National Library of Canada*]   (NLC)

BVAHP ..... Historic Photographic Collection, Vancouver Public Library, British Columbia [*Library symbol*] [*National Library of Canada*]   (NLC)

BVAHS...... H. A. Simons Ltd., Vancouver, British Columbia [*Library symbol*] [*National Library of Canada*]   (NLC)

BVAI......... International North Pacific Fisheries, Vancouver, British Columbia [*Library symbol*] [*National Library of Canada*]   (NLC)

BVAIB....... IBIS Information & Research Services, Vancouver, British Columbia [*Library symbol*] [*National Library of Canada*]   (NLC)

BVAINA.... Resource Center, Information Services, Indian and Northern Affairs Canada, British Columbia Region [*Centre de Ressources, Services d'Information, Affaires Indiennes et du Nord Canadien, Bureau Regional de la CB*] Vancouver, British Columbia [*Library symbol*] [*National Library of Canada*]   (NLC)

BVAJ .... Canada Department of Justice [*Ministere de la Justice*] Vancouver, British Columbia [*Library symbol*] [*National Library of Canada*]   (NLC)

BVAJH...... Jewish Historical Society, Vancouver, British Columbia [*Library symbol*] [*National Library of Canada*]   (BIB)

BVAJI .... Justice Institute of British Columbia, Vancouver, British Columbia [*Library symbol*] [*National Library of Canada*]   (NLC)

BVAJR ...... Jewish Resource Centre, Vancouver, British Columbia [*Library symbol*] [*National Library of Canada*]   (BIB)

BVAL........ BC [*British Columbia*] Court House Library Society, Vancouver, British Columbia, [*Library symbol*] [*National Library of Canada*]   (NLC)

BVAL......... Blackman's Volunteer Army of Liberation [*An association*] (EA)

BVALD...... Ladner, Downs, Barristers & Solicitors, Vancouver, British Columbia [*Library symbol*] [*National Library of Canada*] (NLC)

BVALE...... Valemount Public Library, British Columbia [*Library symbol*] [*National Library of Canada*] (NLC)

B Vallad..... Boletin. Seminario de Estudios de Arte y Arqueologia. Universidad de Valladolid [*A publication*]

BVALMW ... L. M. Warren, Inc., Vancouver, British Columbia [*Library symbol*] [*National Library of Canada*] (NLC)

BVALS...... Legal Resource Centre, Legal Services Society, Vancouver, British Columbia [*Library symbol*] [*National Library of Canada*] (NLC)

BVAM....... British Columbia Medical Library Service, Vancouver, British Columbia [*Library symbol*] [*National Library of Canada*] (NLC)

BVAMB..... MacMillan Bloedel Research Ltd., Vancouver, British Columbia [*Library symbol*] [*National Library of Canada*] (NLC)

BVAMBL.. MacMillan Bloedel Ltd., Vancouver, British Columbia [*Library symbol*] [*National Library of Canada*] (NLC)

BVAME..... McElhanney Engineering, Vancouver, British Columbia [*Library symbol*] [*National Library of Canada*] (NLC)

BVAMI...... Employment and Immigration Canada [*Emploi et Immigration Canada*] Vancouver, British Columbia [*Library symbol*] [*National Library of Canada*] (NLC)

BVAMM ... Maritime Museum, Vancouver, British Columbia [*Library symbol*] [*National Library of Canada*] (NLC)

BVAMOE ... Mobil Oil Estates Ltd., Vancouver, British Columbia [*Library symbol*] [*National Library of Canada*] (NLC)

BVAMUM ... British Columbia Museum of Medicine, Vancouver, British Columbia [*Library symbol*] [*National Library of Canada*] (NLC)

BVAMV .... Military Vehicle Historical Society of British Columbia and Museum, Vancouver, British Columbia [*Library symbol*] [*National Library of Canada*] (NLC)

BVAN .... Western Laboratory, National Research Council [*Laboratoire de l'Ouest, Conseil National de Recherches*] Vancouver, British Columbia [*Library symbol*] [*National Library of Canada*] (NLC)

BVANH..... Health Protection Branch, Canada Department of National Health and Welfare [*Direction Generale de la Protection de la Sante, Ministere de la Sante Nationale et du Bien-Etre Social*] Vancouver, British Columbia [*Library symbol*] [*National Library of Canada*] (NLC)

BVANHC.. Northwest History Collection, Vancouver Public Library, British Columbia [*Library symbol*] [*National Library of Canada*] (NLC)

BVAOCA... Oblate Resource Centre and Archives, Vancouver, British Columbia [*Library symbol*] [*National Library of Canada*] (NLC)

BVAOD.... Byulleten' Vil'nyusskoi Astronomicheskoi Observatorii [*A publication*]

BVAOL...... Open Learning Institute, Richmond, British Columbia [*Library symbol*] [*National Library of Canada*] (NLC)

BVAP......... BCNU [*Carmustine*], Vincristine, Adriamycin, Prednisone [*Antineoplastic drug regimen*]

BVAP......... Placer Development Library, Vancouver, British Columbia [*Library symbol*] [*National Library of Canada*] (NLC)

BVAPAD... Product Assurance & Development, British Columbia Packers Ltd., Vancouver, British Columbia [*Library symbol*] [*National Library of Canada*] (NLC)

BVAPC...... Phillips Cables Ltd., Vancouver, British Columbia [*Library symbol*] [*National Library of Canada*] (NLC)

BVAPD...... Planning Development Library, Greater Vancouver Regional District, Vancouver, British Columbia [*Library symbol*] [*National Library of Canada*] (NLC)

BVAPDA... P/DAUM Information Services, Vancouver, British Columbia [*Library symbol*] [*National Library of Canada*] (BIB)

BVAPE...... West Vancouver Laboratory, Fisheries and Oceans Canada [*Laboratoire de West-Vancouver, Peches et Oceans Canada*] British Columbia [*Library symbol*] [*National Library of Canada*] (NLC)

BVAPP...... Pacific Press Library, Vancouver, British Columbia [*Library symbol*] [*National Library of Canada*] (NLC)

BVAPPC ... Pulp and Paper Centre, University of British Columbia, Vancouver, British Columbia [*Library symbol*] [*National Library of Canada*] (NLC)

BVAPPR ... Vancouver Laboratory, Pulp and Paper Research Institute of Canada, British Columbia [*Library symbol*] [*National Library of Canada*] (NLC)

BVAPR...... Resource Centre, Pacific Rim Institute for Tourism, Vancouver, British Columbia [*Library symbol*] [*National Library of Canada*] (BIB) ●

BVAPVI .... Provincial Resource Centre for the Visually-Impaired, Vancouver, British Columbia [*Library symbol*] [*National Library of Canada*] (NLC)

BVAPW..... Price, Waterhouse & Co., Vancouver, British Columbia [*Library symbol*] [*National Library of Canada*] (NLC)

BVAPWP .. Pacific Region Library, Public Works Canada [*Bibliotheque de la Region du Pacifique, Travaux Publics Canada*] Vancouver, British Columbia [*Library symbol*] [*National Library of Canada*] (NLC)

BVAR .... British Columbia Research Council, Vancouver, British Columbia [*Library symbol*] [*National Library of Canada*] (NLC)

BVARD ..... Russell & Dumoulin, Vancouver, British Columbia [*Library symbol*] [*National Library of Canada*] (NLC)

BVARE...... Archives of the Ecclesiastical Province of British Columbia, Vancouver, British Columbia [*Library symbol*] [*National Library of Canada*] (NLC)

BVAREC ... Regent College, Vancouver, British Columbia [*Library symbol*] [*National Library of Canada*] (NLC)

BVARJ ...... Rolf Jensen & Associates Ltd., Vancouver, British Columbia [*Library symbol*] [*National Library of Canada*] (NLC)

BVARN ..... Registered Nurses Association of British Columbia, Vancouver, British Columbia [*Library symbol*] [*National Library of Canada*] (NLC)

BVAS......... Bio-Vascular, Inc. [*NASDAQ symbol*] (NQ)

BVAS......... Simon Fraser University, Burnaby, British Columbia [*Library symbol*] [*National Library of Canada*] (NLC)

BVASA ..... Archives and Special Collections, Simon Fraser University, Burnaby, British Columbia [*Library symbol*] [*National Library of Canada*] (NLC)

BVASC ..... Sandwell & Co., Vancouver, British Columbia [*Library symbol*] [*National Library of Canada*] (NLC)

BVASEC ... British Columbia Securities Commission, Vancouver, British Columbia [*Library symbol*] [*National Library of Canada*] (BIB)

BVASG ...... Simon Fraser Gallery, Simon Fraser University, Burnaby, British Columbia [*Library symbol*] [*National Library of Canada*] (NLC)

BVASLA .... F. F. Slaney & Co. Ltd., Vancouver, British Columbia [*Library symbol*] [*National Library of Canada*] (NLC)

BVASM ..... Map Library, Simon Fraser University, Burnaby, British Columbia [*Library symbol*] [*National Library of Canada*] (NLC)

BVASP ...... Social Planning and Research Council of British Columbia, Vancouver [*Library symbol*] [*National Library of Canada*] (BIB)

BVASPH... Health Sciences Library, St. Paul's Hospital, Vancouver, British Columbia [*Library symbol*] [*National Library of Canada*] (NLC)

BVAST ...... Vancouver School of Theology, British Columbia [*Library symbol*] [*National Library of Canada*] (NLC)

BVASW..... Swan Wooster Engineering Co., Vancouver, British Columbia [*Library symbol*] [*National Library of Canada*] (NLC)

BVAT......... Blood-Stage Variant Antigen Type [*Immunology*]

BVATAN... Noise Library, Air Navigation Systems Requirements, Transport Canada [*Bibliotheque Normes de Bruit, Exigences du Systeme de Navigation Aerienne, Transports Canada*], Vancouver, British Columbia [*Library symbol*] [*National Library of Canada*] (NLC)

BVATAS ... Aviation Safety Programs, Transport Canada [*Programme de la Securite Aerienne, Transports Canada*], Vancouver, British Columbia [*Library symbol*] [*National Library of Canada*] (NLC)

BVATCA ... Air Regional Library (PGSL), Transport Canada [*Bibliotheque Regionale de l'Air (PGSL), Transports Canada*] Vancouver, British Columbia [*Library symbol*] [*National Library of Canada*] (NLC)

BVATE ...... Elizabeth Watson Library, Teck Mining Group Ltd., Vancouver, British Columbia [*Library symbol*] [*National Library of Canada*] (NLC)

BVATF ...... British Columbia Teachers' Federation Resources Centre, Vancouver, British Columbia [*Library symbol*] [*National Library of Canada*] (NLC)

BVATM..... Trans Mountain Pipe Line Co. Ltd., Vancouver, British Columbia [*Library symbol*] [*National Library of Canada*] (NLC)

BVATPF.... Towers, Perrin, Forster & Crosby, Vancouver, British Columbia [*Library symbol*] [*National Library of Canada*] (NLC)

BVATPT ... Professional and Technical Services Library, Transport Canada [*Bibliotheque des Services Professionnels et Techniques, Transports Canada*], Vancouver, British Columbia [*Library symbol*] [*National Library of Canada*] (NLC)

BVAU .... University of British Columbia, Vancouver, British Columbia [*Library symbol*] [*National Library of Canada*] (NLC)

BVAUBCA ... Archives, British Columbia Conference, United Church, Vancouver, British Columbia [*Library symbol*] [*National Library of Canada*] (NLC)

BVAUCA ... Archives, Unitarian Church of Vancouver, British Columbia [*Library symbol*] [*National Library of Canada*] (NLC)

BVAUCC ... Charles Crane Memorial Library, University of British Columbia, Vancouver, British Columbia [*Library symbol*] [*National Library of Canada*] (NLC)

BVAUG ..... Department of Geography, University of British Columbia, Vancouver, British Columbia [*Library symbol*] [*National Library of Canada*] (NLC)

BVAUL...... Law Library, University of British Columbia, Vancouver, British Columbia [*Library symbol*] [*National Library of Canada*] (NLC)

BVAULS ... School of Library, Archival, and Information Studies, University of British Columbia, Vancouver, British Columbia [*Library symbol*] [*National Library of Canada*] (NLC)

BVAUM .... Map Division, University of British Columbia, Vancouver, British Columbia [*Library symbol*] [*National Library of Canada*] (NLC)

BVAUS...... Special Collections Division, University of British Columbia, Vancouver, British Columbia [*Library symbol*] [*National Library of Canada*] (NLC)

BVAUW .... Woodward Biomedical Library, University of British Columbia, Vancouver, British Columbia [*Library symbol*] [*National Library of Canada*] (NLC)

BVAUWGV ... United Way of Greater Vancouver, Vancouver, British Columbia [*Library symbol*] [*National Library of Canada*] (NLC)

BVAVA...... Vancouver Art Gallery, British Columbia [*Library symbol*] [*National Library of Canada*] (NLC)

BVAVCL... Vancouver Community College, Langara Campus, Vancouver, British Columbia [*Library symbol*] [*National Library of Canada*] (NLC)

BVAVCLT ... Library Technician Program, Vancouver Community College, British Columbia [*Library symbol*] [*National Library of Canada*] (NLC)

BVAVSA... [*The*] Emily Carr College of Art, Vancouver, British Columbia [*Library symbol*] [*National Library of Canada*] (NLC)

BVAWC..... Workers Compensation Board of British Columbia, Vancouver, British Columbia [*Library symbol*] [*National Library of Canada*] (NLC)

BVAWCT ... West Coast Transmission Ltd., Vancouver, British Columbia [*Library symbol*] [*National Library of Canada*] (NLC)

BVAWH .... Warnock Hersey International Ltd., Vancouver, British Columbia [*Library symbol*] [*National Library of Canada*] (NLC)

BVB .... Boa Vista [*Brazil*] [*Airport symbol*] (OAG)

BVB .... Bont. Maandblad voor het Bontbedrijf [*A publication*]

BVBC........ Bobby Vinton Booster Club (EA)

BVBRF ...... Blood Vessel of Branchial Filament

BVC .... Bear Valley Observatory [*California*] [*Seismograph station code, US Geological Survey*] [*Closed*] (SEIS)

BVC .... Bible et Vie Chretienne [*Paris*] [*A publication*]

BVC .... Black Varnish Cambric [*Insulation*] (MSA)

BVC .... Boa Vista [*Cape Verde Islands*] [*Airport symbol*] (OAG)

BVC .... Buena Vista College [*Storm Lake, IA*]

BVC .... Bushveldt Carabineers [*British military*] (DMA)

BVCPP ...... BCNU [*Carmustine*], Vinblastine, Cyclophosphamide, Procarbazine, Prednisone [*Antineoplastic drug regimen*]

BVD .... Beacon Video Digitizer

BVD .... Beverly Development, Inc. [*Toronto Stock Exchange symbol*]

BVD .... Bonus Vacation Days [*United Auto Workers*]

BVD .... Bovine Viral Diarrhea

BVD .... BVD Co. [*Initials stand for Bradley, Voorhies, and Day, organizers of the company, and have come to be used as a generic term for underwear*]

BVDH .... Vanderhoof Public Library, British Columbia [*Library symbol*] [*National Library of Canada*] (NLC)

BVDS......... Bleomycin, Vinblastine, Doxorubicin, Streptozocin [*Antineoplastic drug regimen*]

BVDT .... Brief Vestibular Disorientation Test

BVDU .... Bromovinyldeoxyuridine [*Biochemistry*]

BVDV .... Bovine Viral Diarrhea Virus

BVE .... Bachelor of Vocational Education

BVE .... Batallon Vasco Espanol [*Spanish Basque Battalion*] (PD)

BVE .... Binocular Visual Efficiency

BVE .... Bivariate Exponential [*Distribution*] [*Statistics*]

BVE .... Bootheville, LA [*Location identifier*] [*FAA*] (FAAL)

BVE .... Brandevor Enterprises Ltd. [*Toronto Stock Exchange symbol*] [*Vancouver Stock Exchange symbol*]

BVE .... Breadboard Verification Equipment [*NASA*]

BVE .... Brive-La-Gaillarde [*France*] [*Airport symbol*] (OAG)

BVE .... Butyl Vinyl Ether [*Organic chemistry*]

B Verf G..... Bundesverfassungsgericht [*Federal Constitutional Court*] [*German*] (DLA)

BVerfGE.... Entscheidungen des Bundesverfassungsgerichts [*Reports of Decisions of the Federal Constitutional Court*] [*A publication*] (ILCA)

B Verw G.... Bundesverwaltungsgericht [*Federal Supreme Administrative Court*] [*German*] (DLA)

BVetC .... British Veterinary Codex [*A publication*]

B Vet Med ... Bachelor of Veterinary Medicine

BVetSc....... Bachelor of Veterinary Science (ADA)

BVF .... Bua [*Fiji*] [*Airport symbol*] [*Obsolete*] (OAG)

BVFS .... Bay View Capital Corp. [*NASDAQ symbol*] (NQ)

BVG .... Battlefield Visualization Graphics (AABC)

BVG .... Berlevag [*Norway*] [*Airport symbol*] (OAG)

BVG .... Berliner Verkehrs-Gesellschaft [*Later, Berliner Verkehrs-Betriebe*] [*Berlin Transport*] [*West Berlin*]

BVG .... Bijdragen voor Vaderlandsche Geschiedenis en Oudheidskunde [*A publication*]

BVG .... Bureau du Verificateur General du Canada [*Office of the Auditor-General of Canada*]

BVG .... Enterprise, AL [*Location identifier*] [*FAA*] (FAAL)

BVGE .... Beverage (MSA)

BVGO........ Bijdragen voor Vaderlandsche Geschiedenis en Oudheidskunde [*A publication*]

BVGPA...... Boletin Informativo. Asociacion Venezolana de Geologia, Mineria, y Petroleo [*A publication*]

BVH.......... Beaverhead Resources [*Vancouver Stock Exchange symbol*]

BVH.......... Biventricular Hypertrophy [*Cardiology*]

BVHUA...... Bibliotheca "Vita Humana" [*A publication*]

BVI........... Beaver Falls, PA [*Location identifier*] [*FAA*] (FAAL)

BVI........... Better Vision Institute (EA)

BVI........... Birdsville [*Australia*] [*Airport symbol*] (OAG)

BVI........... Bow Valley Industries Ltd. [*AMEX symbol*] [*Toronto Stock Exchange symbol*] (SPSG)

BVI........... British Virgin Islands

BVI........... Greater Victoria Public Library, British Columbia [*Library symbol*] [*National Library of Canada*] (NLC)

BVI........... Venezolaans Nederlandse Kamer van Koophandel en Industrie. Bulletin [*A publication*]

BVIA......... Art Gallery of Greater Victoria, Victoria, British Columbia [*Library symbol*] [*National Library of Canada*] (NLC)

BVIABS..... Synod Office, Diocese of British Columbia, Anglican Church of Canada, Victoria, British Columbia [*Library symbol*] [*National Library of Canada*] (NLC)

BVIADP .... Alcohol and Drug Programs, Victoria, British Columbia [*Library symbol*] [*National Library of Canada*] (BIB)

BVIAGC .... CLEU Library, British Columbia Ministry of Attorney General, Victoria, British Columbia [*Library symbol*] [*National Library of Canada*] (NLC)

BVIAGL .... Law Library, British Columbia, Ministry of the Attorney General, Victoria, British Columbia [*Library symbol*] [*National Library of Canada*] (NLC)

BVIB......... British Columbia Barkerville Restoration Advisory Committee, Victoria, British Columbia [*Library symbol*] [*National Library of Canada*] (NLC)

BVIBA....... Biologiya Vnutrennykh Vod. Informatsionnyi Byulleten [*A publication*]

BVIC......... Camosun College, Victoria, British Columbia [*Library symbol*] [*National Library of Canada*] (NLC)

BVICA....... Victoria City Archives, British Columbia [*Library symbol*] [*National Library of Canada*] (NLC)

B Victoria Mem ... Bulletin. Victoria Memorial Museum of the Geological Survey of Canada [*A publication*]

BVIDE....... British Columbia Ministry of Education, Victoria, British Columbia [*Library symbol*] [*National Library of Canada*] (NLC)

BVIED....... British Columbia Ministry of Industry and Small Business Development, Victoria, British Columbia [*Library symbol*] [*National Library of Canada*] (NLC)

BVIEM...... Institute of Ocean Sciences, Fisheries and Oceans Canada [*Institut des Sciences Oceanographiques, Peches et Oceans Canada*] Sidney, British Columbia [*Library symbol*] [*National Library of Canada*] (NLC)

BVIF......... Pacific Forest Research Centre, Agriculture Canada [*Centre de Recherches Forestieres du Pacifique, Agriculture Canada*] Victoria, British Columbia [*Library symbol*] [*National Library of Canada*] (NLC)

BVIFC ...... Bobby Vinton International Fan Club (EA)

BVIFC ...... British Columbia Ferry Corp., Victoria, British Columbia [*Library symbol*] [*National Library of Canada*] (NLC)

BVIFO...... British Columbia Ministry of Forests, Victoria, British Columbia [*Library symbol*] [*National Library of Canada*] (NLC)

BVIFS....... British Columbia Forest Service, Victoria, British Columbia [*Library symbol*] [*National Library of Canada*] (NLC)

BVIGH ...... Victoria General Hospital, British Columbia [*Library symbol*] [*National Library of Canada*] (NLC)

BVIH .... British Columbia Ministry of Highways and Public Works, Victoria, British Columbia [*Library symbol*] [*National Library of Canada*] (NLC)

BVIHCR.... Ministry Library, Ministry of Municipal Affairs, Recreation, and Culture, Victoria, British Columbia [*Library symbol*] [*National Library of Canada*] (NLC)

BVIHE....... British Columbia Ministry of Health, Victoria, British Columbia [*Library symbol*] [*National Library of Canada*] (NLC)

BVIHRS .... British Columbia Ministry of Human Resources, Vancouver, British Columbia [*Library symbol*] [*National Library of Canada*] (NLC)

BVIHRS .... British Columbia Ministry of Social Services and Housing, Vancouver, British Columbia [*Library symbol*] [*National Library of Canada*] (NLC)

BVIL......... Law Library Foundation, Victoria, British Columbia [*Library symbol*] [*National Library of Canada*] [*Obsolete*] (NLC)

BVILBP..... Lester B. Pearson College of the Pacific, Victoria, British Columbia [*Library symbol*] [*National Library of Canada*] (NLC)

BVILFW.... British Columbia Ministry of Environment, Victoria, British Columbia [*Library symbol*] [*National Library of Canada*] (NLC)

BVILPHP ... Parks Library, Ministry of Parks, Victoria, British Columbia [*Library symbol*] [*National Library of Canada*] (NLC)

BVILSB..... Library Services Branch, Ministry of Provincial Secretary and Governement Services, Victoria, British Columbia [*Library symbol*] [*National Library of Canada*] (NLC)

BVIM........ British Columbia Ministry of Energy, Mines and Petroleum Resources, Victoria, British Columbia [*Library symbol*] [*National Library of Canada*] (NLC)

BVIMH ..... Maltwood Art Museum, University of Victoria, British Columbia [*Library symbol*] [*National Library of Canada*] (NLC)

BVIML...... British Columbia Ministry of Labour, Victoria, British Columbia [*Library symbol*] [*National Library of Canada*] (NLC)

BVIMM..... Maritime Museum of British Columbia, Victoria, British Columbia [*Library symbol*] [*National Library of Canada*] (NLC)

BVIP......... Legislative Library, Victoria, British Columbia [*Library symbol*] [*National Library of Canada*] (NLC)

BVIPA....... Provincial Archives of British Columbia, Victoria, British Columbia [*Library symbol*] [*National Library of Canada*] (NLC)

BVIPM...... British Columbia Provincial Museum, Victoria, British Columbia [*Library symbol*] [*National Library of Canada*] (NLC)

BVIPME ... Ethnology Division, British Columbia Provincial Museum, Victoria, British Columbia [*Library symbol*] [*National Library of Canada*] (NLC)

BVIPR ...... Victoria Press Ltd., British Columbia [*Library symbol*] [*National Library of Canada*] (NLC)

BVIRA....... Byulleten' Vsesoyuznogo Nauchno-Issledovatel'skogo Instituta Rastenievodstva Imeni N. I. Vavilova [*A publication*]

BVIRJ........ Victoria Medical and Hospital Libraries, Royal Jubilee Hospital Site, British Columbia [*Library symbol*] [*National Library of Canada*] (NLC)

BVISC .... British Columbia Systems Corp., Victoria, British Columbia [*Library symbol*] [*National Library of Canada*] (NLC)

BVIT......... Thurber Consultants Ltd., Victoria, British Columbia [*Library symbol*] [*National Library of Canada*] (NLC)

BVITRA .... Thalassa Research Associates, Victoria, British Columbia [*Library symbol*] [*National Library of Canada*] (NLC)

BVIUCN.... Union Catalogue of British Columbia Newspapers, Victoria, British Columbia [*Library symbol*] [*National Library of Canada*] (NLC)

BVIV......... University of Victoria, British Columbia [*Library symbol*] [*National Library of Canada*] (NLC)

BVIVA....... Department of History in Art, University of Victoria, British Columbia [*Library symbol*] [*National Library of Canada*] (NLC)

BVIVG...... Geography Department, University of Victoria, British Columbia [*Library symbol*] [*National Library of Canada*] (NLC)

BVIVL ...... Law Library, University of Victoria, British Columbia [*Library symbol*] [*National Library of Canada*] (NLC)

BVJ.......... British Veterinary Journal [*A publication*]

BVJOA ..... British Veterinary Journal [*A publication*]

BVJOA9 .... British Veterinary Journal [*A publication*]

BVL.......... Bear Valley [*California*] [*Seismograph station code, US Geological Survey*] (SEIS)

BVL.......... Bellevue Ventures Limited [*Vancouver Stock Exchange symbol*]

BVL.......... Beveled [*Technical drawings*]

BVL.......... Bilateral Vas Ligation [*Medicine*]

BVL.......... Bonneville, UT [*Location identifier*] [*FAA*] (FAAL)

BVL.......... BVL [*Bowlers' Victory Legion*] Fund (EA)

BVLA........ British Volunteers, Latin America [*British military*] (DMA)

BVLS........ Battery-Voltage Limit System

BVM .... Bachelor of Veterinary Medicine

BVM .... Beata Virgo Maria [*Blessed Virgin Mary*] [*Latin*]

BVM .... Beau Val Mines [*Vancouver Stock Exchange symbol*]

BVM .... Belmonte [*Brazil*] [*Airport symbol*] (OAG)

BVM .... Bibliotheques Vertes pour le Monde [*Green Library - GL*] [*Saint Egreve, France*] (EAIO)

BVM .... Boussinesq Viscosity Model (MCD)

BVM .... Bureau of Veterinary Medicine [*FDA*]

BVM .... Business Visitors Memorandum [*British Overseas Trade Board*] (DS)

BVM .... Buvoha Mededelingen [*A publication*]

BVM .... Sisters of Charity of the Blessed Virgin Mary [*Roman Catholic religious order*]

BVMA .... Vernon Museum, Archives and Art Gallery, British Columbia [*Library symbol*] [*National Library of Canada*] (NLC)

BVMGT..... Bender Visual-Motor Gestalt Test [*Education*]

BVMS........ Bachelor of Veterinary Medicine and Surgery

BVM & S ... Bachelor of Veterinary Medicine and Surgery

BVN .... Bivariate Normal Mixture [*Statistics*]

BVNLDN .. Berichte des Vereins Natur und Heimat und des Naturhistorischen Museums zu Luebeck [*A publication*]

BVO .... Bartlesville, OK [*Location identifier*] [*FAA*] (FAAL)

BVO .... Bravo Resources [*Vancouver Stock Exchange symbol*]

BVO .... Brominated Vegetable Oil [*Soft drink additive*]

BVocArts ... Bachelor of Vocational Arts

BVocEd...... Bachelor of Vocational Education

BVOR .... [*Weather*] Broadcast Very-High-Frequency Omnirange

BVOR .... O'Keefe Ranch and Interior Heritage Society, Vernon, British Columbia [*Library symbol*] [*National Library of Canada*] (NLC)

BVP............ Bayerische Volkspartei [*Bavarian People's Party*] [*Federal Republic of Germany*] [*Political party*] (PPE)

BVP............ Beacon Video Processor

BVP............ Benzyl(vinyl)pyridinium Bromide [*Organic chemistry*]

BVP............ Blood Vessel of Pinnule

BVP............ Blood Vessel Prosthesis [*Medicine*]

BVP............ Booster Vacuum Pump

BVP............ Boundary Value Problem

BVP............ British Visitor's Passport

BVP............ British Volunteer Programme

BVP............ Burton Public Library, Burton, OH [*OCLC symbol*] (OCLC)

BVP............ Business Venture Profiles [*TECHSTART International, Inc.*] [*Information service or system*] (CRD)

BVP............ Personenvervoer [*A publication*]

BVPP .... BCNU [*Carmustine*], Vincristine, Procarbazine, Prednisone [*Antineoplastic drug regimen*]

BVPP .... Blood Vessel of Palp

BVPS .... Beacon Video Processing System

BVPS .... Beaver Valley Power Station (NRCH)

BVPS .... Booster Vacuum Pump System

BVQ .... Glasgow, KY [*Location identifier*] [*FAA*] (FAAL)

BVR .... Balanced Valve Regulator

BVR .... Bangalore Volunteer Rifles [*British military*] (DMA)

BVR .... Bausteine zur Volkskunde und Religionswissenschaft [*A publication*]

BVR .... Beroepsvervoer [*A publication*]

BVR .... Beyond Visual Range (MCD)

BVR .... Black Void Reactor

BVR .... Bloque de la Vanguardia Revolucionaria [*Bolivia*] [*Political party*] (PPW)

BVR .... Bureau of Vocational Rehabilitation (OICC)

BVR .... Bureaus for Reciprocal Accounts [*Bulgarian*]

BVR .... Byggvaruregistret [*Building Commodity File*] [*Swedish Building Center*] [*Stockholm*] [*Information service or system*] (IID)

BVR .... Clearinghouse [*Banking*]

BVRAAM ... Beyond Visual Range Air-to-Air Missile (MCD)

BVRB......... Bernard van Risenburgh [*Label stamped on works by the master ebeniste*]

BVRM .... Beyond Visual Range Missile (MCD)

BVRO .... Base Vehicle Reporting Officer

BVRR......... Bureau of Veterans Reemployment Rights [*Department of Labor*]

BVRS .... Breadboard Visual Reference System [*NASA*]

BVRT .... Benton Visual Retention Time [*Psychiatry*]

BVS............ Bachelor of Veterinary Science

BVS............ Bachelor of Veterinary Surgery

BVS............ Battery Vehicle Society [*British*]

BVS............ Bevier & Southern Railroad Co. [*AAR code*]

BVS............ Bibliothek-Verbund-System [*Library Network System*] [*Siemens AG*] [*Information service or system*] (IID)

BVS............ Biodegradable Volatile Solids [*Analytical chemistry*]

BVS............ Brethren Volunteer Service (EA)

BVS............ British Vexillological Society

BVS............ Buddhist Vihara Society (EA)

BVS............ Bulk Verification Services [*British*]

BVS............ Buoyant Venus Station [*NASA*]

BVS............ Bureau of Vital Statistics (AFM)

BVSAW ..... Berichte. Verhandlungen der [*Koeniglich*] Saechsischen Akademie der Wissenschaften zu Leipzig [*A publication*]

BVSAWL .. Berichte. Verhandlungen der Saechsischen Akademie der Wissenschaften zu Leipzig [*A publication*]

BVSB .... Broadview Savings Bank [*NASDAQ symbol*] (NQ)

BV Sc .... Bachelor of Veterinary Science

BVSC .... Birdview Satellite Communications, Inc. [*NASDAQ symbol*] (NQ)

BVSc & AH ... Bachelor of Veterinary Science and Animal Husbandry

BVSGW ..... Berichte. Verhandlungen der Saechsischen Gesellschaft der Wissenschaften [*A publication*]

BVSI .... Brite Voice System, Inc. [*NASDAQ symbol*] (NQ)

BVSP .... Basaltic Volcanism Study Project [*Planetary science*]

BVSRJL ..... Bulletin Vysoke Skoly Russkeho Jazyka a Literatury [*A publication*]

BVSV......... Bimetal Vacuum Switching Valve [*Automotive engineering*]

BVT .... Bouvet Island [*ANSI three-letter standard code*] (CNC)

BVT .... Brevet [*Military*]

BVT .... Lafayette, IN [*Location identifier*] [*FAA*] (FAAL)

BVU .... Bellevue, WA [*Location identifier*] [*FAA*] (FAAL)

BVU .... Bromoisovalerylurea [*Pharmacology*]

BVU .... (Bromovinyl)uracil [*Antiviral compound*]

BVUPD ..... Bulletin. Vyskumneho Ustavu Potravinarskeho [*A publication*]

BVV .... Brookhaven, MS [*Location identifier*] [*FAA*] (FAAL)

BVW	Backward Volume Wave [*Telecommunications*] (TEL)
BVW	Binary Voltage Weigher
BVX	Bacitracin V and X [*Antibacterial compound*]
BVX	Batesville [*Arkansas*] [*Airport symbol*] (OAG)
BVX	Batesville, AR [*Location identifier*] [*FAA*] (FAAL)
BVY	Beverly, MA [*Location identifier*] [*FAA*] (FAAL)
BVZ	Berliner Volks-Zeitung [*A publication*]
BVZ	Beverly Springs [*Australia*] [*Airport symbol*] [*Obsolete*] (OAG)
B & W	Babcock & Wilcox Co.
b/w	Backed With [*Used by record companies and trade papers to indicate music on the alternative side of a disk*]
BW	Bacteriological Warfare
BW	Bacteriological Warhead
BW	Baltischer Weltrat [*Baltic World Council*] (EAIO)
BW	Bandwidth [*Frequency range*]
BW	Bango Whiplash [*Military*]
BW	Bankwissenschaft [*A publication*]
BW	Baroclinic Waves [*Astronomy*]
BW	Barrack Warden [*British military*] (DMA)
BW	Basal Web
BW	Beam Width (CET)
BW	Bell Wire
BW	Below Waist [*Medicine*]
BW	Below Watch
BW	Below Water (NG)
BW	Bendix-Westinghouse Automotive Air Brake Co.
BW	Best of Winners [*Dog show term*]
BW	Between Worlds [*A publication*]
BW	Bewusstein [*Consciousness*] [*Psychology*]
BW	Bibles for the World (EA)
BW	Biblical World [*Chicago*] [*A publication*]
BW	Bid Wanted [*Business term*]
BW	Bijbels Woordenboek [*A publication*] (BJA)
B o W	Biochemistry of Wood [*A publication*]
BW	Biological Warfare
BW	Biological Weapons [*Military*]
BW	Birth Weight [*Medicine*]
BW	Biweekly
BW	Black Watch [*Military unit*] [*British*]
BW	Black and White [*Photography, television, etc.*] (KSC)
B & W	Black and White [*Photography, television, etc.*]
BW	Black Writers [*A publication*]
BW	Bladder Washout [*Urology*]
BW	Blick durch die Wirtschaft [*A publication*]
BW	Blood Wassermann [*Medicine*]
BW	Blues World [*A publication*]
BW	Bluie West [*US air bases in Greenland*] [*World War II*]
BW	Blunted Wedge
BW	Board of Works [*British*]
BW	Body Water [*Medicine*]
BW	Body Weight
BW	Body Whorl
BW	Body Wing (KSC)
BW	Bonded Warehouse
BW	Bonded Winery
BW	Book World [*Chicago Tribune*] [*A publication*]
BW	Books and Writers [*A publication*]
BW	Borg-Warner Corp.
BW	Both Ways [*Technical drawings*]
BW	Botswana [*ANSI two-letter standard code*] (CNC)
BW	Bottom Withdrawal [*Tube*]
BW	Bound With (ROG)
BW	Braided Wire Armor (AAG)
BW	Brain Water
BW	Brass and Wind News [*A publication*]
B & W	Bread and Water
BW	Bridgewire (NASA)
BW	British Waterways [*State-owned company*]
BW	British West Indian Airways Ltd. [*ICAO designator*] (OAG)
B & W	Brown & Williamson Tobacco Corp.
BW	Brush Wellman, Inc. [*NYSE symbol*] (SPSG)
BW	Buecherei Winter [*A publication*]
BW	Burgerlijk Wetboek [*Civil Code*] [*Netherlands*] (ILCA)
BW	Buried Wire [*Telecommunications*] (TEL)
BW	Burroughs Wellcome Co.
BW	Burroughs Wellcome Research Institute [*Great Britain*] [*Research code symbol*]
BW	Business Week [*A publication*]
BW	Butler's Wharf [*Shipping*] [*British*] (ROG)
BW	Kurzes Bibelwoerterbuch [*A publication*] (BJA)
BW	Trinidad and Tobago Airways Corp. [*Trinidad and Tobago*] [*ICAO designator*] (ICDA)
BWA	Backward Wave Amplifier
BWA	Baptist World Aid (EA)
BWA	Baptist World Alliance (EA)
BWA	Bedstead Workmens Association [*A union*] [*British*]
BWA	Bent Wire Antenna
BWA	Bhairawa [*Nepal*] [*Airport symbol*] (OAG)
BWA	Black Women's Association (EA)
BWA	Botswana [*ANSI three-letter standard code*] (CNC)
BWA	Boxing Writers Association
BWA	Branch Warehouse Association (EA)
BWA	British Waterworks Association
BWA	British Wildlife Appeal (EAIO)
BWA	Building Waterproofers Association [*Defunct*] (EA)
BWA	Business Venezuela [*A publication*]
BWAA	Baseball Writers Association of America (EA)
BWAA	Bowling Writers Association of America (EA)
BWAid	Baptist World Aid (EA)
BWANT	Beitraege zur Wissenschaft vom Alten und Neuen Testament [*Leipzig/Stuttgart*] [*A publication*]
BWAR	Budget Workload Analysis Report [*Navy*] (NG)
BWARF	Baptist World Relief [*Later, Baptist World Aid*] (EA)
BWAS	Barron-Welsh Art Scale [*Psychology*]
BWAT	Beitraege zur Wissenschaft vom Alten Testament [*A publication*]
BWATA	Biuletyn Wojskowej Akademii Technicznej Imienia Jaroslawa Dabrowskiego [*A publication*]
BWAuNT ..	Beitraege zur Wissenschaft vom Alten und Neuen Testament [*Leipzig/Stuttgart*] [*A publication*]
B'WAY	Broadway [*A street name*]
BWAY	Broadway Holdings, Inc. [*NASDAQ symbol*] (NQ)
BWB	Berliner Wirtschaftsbericht [*A publication*]
BWB	British Waterways Board
BWB	Brooker Wheaton Aviation [*Canada*] [*FAA designator*] (FAAC)
BWB	Bryan, OH [*Location identifier*] [*FAA*] (FAAL)
BWB	Burma Weekly Bulletin [*A publication*]
BWBA	North American District of the Belgian Warmblood Breeding Association (EA)
BWBR	Bureau of Naval Weapons Branch Representative [*Obsolete*] (MCD)
BWC	Backward Wave Converter (CET)
BWC	Baldwin-Wallace College [*Berea, OH*]
BWC	Baltic Women's Council (EA)
BWC	Baltic World Council (EA)
BWC	Basic Weight Controller
BWC	Battle Watch Captain (MCD)
BWC	Beauty without Cruelty USA (EA)
BWC	Biological Weapons Convention
BWC	Board of War Communications [*World War II*]
B/WC	Bomb-to-Warhead Conversion (MCD)
BWC	Bonded Wine Cellar
BWC	Bowhunters Who Care (EA)
BWC	Brawley, CA [*Location identifier*] [*FAA*] (FAAL)
BWC	Bretton Woods Committee (EA)
BWC	British War Cabinet
BWC	Broadband Waveguide Circulator
BWC	Buffer Word Counter [*Data processing*]
BWC	Bureau of Water Carriers
BWC	Bureau Weather Control
BWCA	Boundary Waters Canoe Area [*Minnesota*]
BWCC	Bomb-to-Warhead Conversion Components (CINC)
BWCC	Butterworth's Workmen's Compensation Cases [*A publication*] (DLA)
BWCC (Eng) ...	Butterworth's Workmen's Compensation Cases [*A publication*] (DLA)
BWCO	Bonneville-West Corporation [*Salt Lake City, UT*] [*NASDAQ symbol*] (NQ)
BWCP	Base Wire Communications Program [*Air Force*]
BWCP	Bench Welder Control Panel
BWCR	National Black Women's Consciousness Raising Association (EA)
BWCS	Base Wire Communications System [*Air Force*] (CET)
BWCS	Black Women in Church and Society (EA)
BWCS	Blue Willow Collectors Society (EA)
BWCSA	Broad Way Clinical Supplement [*A publication*]
BW/CW	Biological Warfare/Chemical Warfare (NG)
BWD	Babcock Woodall-Duckham Ltd. [*British*] (IRUK)
BWD	Bacillary White Diarrhea [*Veterinary medicine*]
BWD	Backward [*Telecommunications*] (TEL)
BW(D)	Bacteriological Warfare, Defence [*British*] [*World War II*]
BWD	Biological Warfare Defense
BWD	Bridgewest Development [*Vancouver Stock Exchange symbol*]
BWD	Brownwood [*Texas*] [*Airport symbol*] (OAG)
BWD	Bulk Wet Density
BWDA	Bicycle Wholesale Distributors Association (EA)
BWDEB	Boden Wand und Decke [*A publication*]
B & W Dgns ...	Berkshire and Westminster Dragoons [*British military*] (DMA)
BWE	Bachelor of Welding Engineering
BWE	[*American Association of*] Black Women Entrepreneurs (EA)
BWE	Brewmaster Systems Ltd. [*Vancouver Stock Exchange symbol*]
BWE	Business Week [*A publication*]
BWE	BUWEPS [*Bureau of Naval Weapons, now obsolete*] Evaluation
BWE	Weston School of Theology, Cambridge, MA [*OCLC symbol*] (OCLC)
BWEA	Black Women's Educational Alliance (EA)
BWEA	British Wind Energy Association (IRUK)
BWEM	Westbank Museum, British Columbia [*Library symbol*] [*National Library of Canada*] (NLC)

BWEPRN ... Black Women's Educational Policy and Research Network   (EA)
BWESA ..... Berliner Wetterkarte. Supplement [*A publication*]
BWF .... Bailett Weighting Function
BWF .... Beyond War Foundation   (EA)
BWF .... Biblical Witness Fellowship   (EA)
BWF .... Black World Foundation   (EA)
BWF .... Breit-Wigner Formula
BWF .... Bretton Woods Fund   (EA)
BWF .... British Wool Federation
BWF .... Building Wake Factor [*Nuclear energy*]   (NRCH)
BWF .... Burst Waveform
BWF .... Business Review. Wells Fargo Bank [*A publication*]
BWF .... Butt Welded Filter
BWFC .... Benny Wilson Fan Club   (EA)
BWFC .... Betty White Fan Club   (EA)
BWFCRS ... Brackish Water Fish Culture Research Station [*Australia*]
BWFRR ..... Bureau of Naval Weapons Fleet Readiness Representative [*Obsolete*]   (MCD)
BWFRRCEN ... Bureau of Naval Weapons Fleet Readiness Representative, Central [*Obsolete*]   (MUGU)
BWFRRLANT ... Bureau of Naval Weapons Fleet Readiness Representative, Atlantic [*Obsolete*]   (MUGU)
BWFRRPAC ... Bureau of Naval Weapons Fleet Readiness Representative, Pacific [*Obsolete*]   (MUGU)
BWG .... Biphenyl Work Group   (EA)
BWG .... Birmingham Wire Gauge
BWG .... Bouw. Onafhankelijk Weekblad voor de Bouw [*A publication*]
BWG .... Bowling Green, KY [*Location identifier*] [*FAA*]   (FAAL)
BWGMSB ... Bright Wire Goods Manufacturers Service Bureau [*Defunct*]   (EA)
BWH .... Blower Wheel Housing
BWHB .... Black and White Horizontal Bands [*Navigation markers*]
BWHC .... Heiltsuk Cultural Education Centre, Waglisla, British Columbia [*Library symbol*] [*National Library of Canada*]   (NLC)
B WHO ..... Bulletin. World Health Organization [*A publication*]
BWHP .... Black Women's Health Project [*Later, NBWHP*]   (EA)
BWI .... Baltimore [*Maryland*] [*Airport symbol*] [*Name derived from Baltimore-Washington International Airport*]
B Wi .... Bankwirtschaft [*A publication*]
B Wi .... Bankwissenschaft [*A publication*]
BWI .... Battle Wound Injury   (CINC)
BWI .... Boating Writers International   (EA)
BWI .... British Water International
BWI .... British West Indies [*Later, WI*]
BWI .... Budget Workload Indicators
BWIA .... British West Indian Airways Ltd.
BWIN .... Baldwin & Lyons, Inc. [*NASDAQ symbol*]   (NQ)
BWIP .... Basalt Waste Isolation Project [*Department of Energy*]
BWIP .... Black Women in Publishing   (EA)
BWIR .... Black-White Infrared [*Film*]
B Wirtsch B ... Berliner Wirtschaftsbericht [*A publication*]
BWIU .... Building Workers' Industrial Union [*Australia*]
BWIU .... Building Workers' Industrial Union [*British*]
BWIU & PF ... Building Workers' Industrial Union and Plasterers' Federation [*Australia*]
BWJ .... Butt Welded Joint
BWK .... Batch Weighing Kit
BWK .... Belt Weather Kit   (MCD)
B Wk .... Book Week [*A publication*]
BWK .... Bowker Out of Print Books [*Source file*] [*UTLAS symbol*]
BWK .... Brennstoff-Waerme-Kraft [*Fuel, Heat, Power*] [*A publication*]
BWK .... Brickwork
BWK .... Brillouin-Wentzel-Kramers [*Physics*]
BWK .... Bulwark
BWKG .... Blaetter fuer Wuerttembergische Kirchengeschichte [*A publication*]
BWKR .... Bassett-Walker, Inc. [*NASDAQ symbol*]   (NQ)
BWL .... Belt Work Line
BWL .... Biological Warfare Laboratory
BWL .... Blackwell, OK [*Location identifier*] [*FAA*]   (FAAL)
BWL .... Bouwbelangen [*A publication*]
BWL .... Bowl America, Inc. [*AMEX symbol*]   (SPSG)
BWLC .... Cariboo-Chilcotin Archives, Williams Lake, British Columbia [*Library symbol*] [*National Library of Canada*]   (NLC)
BWLM ...... William Lake Museum, British Columbia [*Library symbol*] [*National Library of Canada*]   (NLC)
BWLT .... Bow Light
BWM .... Backward Wave Magnetron   (MSA)
BWM .... Best Western Motels [*Motel chain*]
BWM .... Block-Write Mode [*Computer graphics*]   (BYTE)
BWM .... Brenwest Mining [*Vancouver Stock Exchange symbol*]
BWM .... British War Medal
BWM .... Bursts with Memory [*Physics*]
BWM .... International Broom and Whisk Makers' Union of America [*Defunct*]   (EA)
BWM .... Wells Museum, British Columbia [*Library symbol*] [*National Library of Canada*]   (NLC)
BWMB ..... British Wool Marketing Board
BWMS .... British Wireless Marine Service   (DEN)
BWN .... Bandar Seri Begawan [*Brunei*] [*Airport symbol*]   (OAG)
BWN .... Benefit Week Number [*Unemployment insurance*]   (OICC)

BWN .... Black Women's Network [*An association*]   (EA)
BWN .... Brown [*Telecommunications*]   (TEL)
BWNIC ...... British Withdrawal from Northern Ireland Campaign
BWO .... Backward Wave Oscillator
BW(O) .... Bacteriological Warfare, Operational Panel [*British*] [*World War II*]
BWO .... Base Work Order   (AAG)
BWO .... Bibliographie der Wirtschaftspresse [*A publication*]
BWO .... Blue-Winged Olive [*Insect*]
BWO .... Bridge Wireless Officer [*British military*]   (DMA)
BWOC .... Big Woman on Campus [*Slang*]
BWOGF .... Bluewater Oil & Gas Ltd. [*NASDAQ symbol*]   (NQ)
BWOS .... Backward Wave Oscillator Synchronizer
BWOT .... Backward Wave Oscillator Tube
BW(P) .... Bacteriological Warfare, Policy Panel [*British*] [*World War II*]
BWP .... Ballistic Wind Plotter
BWP .... Barrier, Waterproof   (MSA)
BWP .... Basic War Plan [*Navy*]
BWP .... Belgische Werkliedenpartij [*Belgian Workers' Party*] [*Later, Belgian Socialist Party*] [*Political party*]   (PPE)
BWP .... Bewani [*Papua New Guinea*] [*Airport symbol*]   (OAG)
BWP .... [*The*] Birds of Western Palearctic [*Book series*] [*British*] [*A publication*]
BWP .... Wahpeton, ND [*Location identifier*] [*FAA*]   (FAAL)
BWPA .... Backward Wave Power Amplifier
BWPA .... British Wood Preserving Association
BWPA News Sheet ... BWPA [*British Wood Preserving Association*] News Sheet [*A publication*]
BWPC .... Blue/White Pottery Club   (EA)
BWPE .... Biased World Paw Entry [*Testing of left and right laterality in mice*]
B W Pr .... Wickelmannsprogramm der Archaeologischen Gesellschaft zu Berlin [*A publication*]
BWPS .... Bus Workers' Protection Society [*A union*] [*British*]
BWQ .... Brass and Woodwind Quarterly [*A publication*]
BWQ .... Brewarrina [*Australia*] [*Airport symbol*]   (OAG)
BWR .... Alpine, TX [*Location identifier*] [*FAA*]   (FAAL)
BWR .... Bandwidth Radio   (MCD)
BWR .... Bandwidth Ratio
bwr .... Belorussian Soviet Socialist Republic [*MARC country of publication code*] [*Library of Congress*]   (LCCP)
BWR .... Benedict-Webb-Rubin [*Equation of state*]
Bw R .... Betriebswirtschaftliche Rundschau [*A publication*]
BWR .... Biweekly Report   (MCD)
BWR .... Black Warrior Review [*A publication*]
BWR .... Boiling Water Reactor
BWR .... Bouwkroniek. Weekblad voor de Bouwvakken en Aanverwante Vakken. Aanbestedingsbulletin voor Alle Werken en Leveringen [*A publication*]
BWR .... Breakwater Resources Ltd. [*Toronto Stock Exchange symbol*] [*Vancouver Stock Exchange symbol*]
BWR .... Bureau of Naval Weapons Representative [*Obsolete*]
BWRA .... British Welding Research Association [*Later, WI*]   (MCD)
BWRL .... Boll Weevil Research Laboratory [*Department of Agriculture*] [*Mississippi State, MS*] [*Research center*]
BWRL .... Breakwater Resources Limited [*NASDAQ symbol*]   (NQ)
BWRL .... Bureau of War Risk Litigation
BWRM ...... City of White Rock Museum and Archives, British Columbia [*Library symbol*] [*National Library of Canada*]   (NLC)
BWROG .... Boiling Water Reactor Owners Group [*Nuclear energy*]   (NRCH)
BWRR .... Bureau of Naval Weapons Resident Representative [*Obsolete*]   (MUGU)
BWRS .... British War Relief Society [*in US*]
BWRU .... Boll Weevil Research Unit [*Mississippi State, MS*] [*Agricultural Research Service*] [*Department of Agriculture*]   (GRD)
BWRVP ..... Black Women's Roundtable on Voter Participation   (EA)
BWRWS ..... Biological Warfare Rapid Warning System [*Army*]
BWS .... Base Weather Station   (MCD)
BWS .... Batch Weighing System
BWS .... Battered Woman [*or Wife*] Syndrome [*Medicine*]
BWS .... Battlefield Weapons System
BWS .... Beaufort Wind Scale
BWS .... Beckwith-Wiedemann Syndrome [*Medicine*]
BWS .... Better World Society   (EA)
BWS .... Beveled Wood Siding [*Technical drawings*]
BWS .... Big White Set [*Type of lush movie set used in 1930's musical-comedy films*]
BWS .... Biological Weapons System [*Military*]
BWS .... Bureau of Water Supply [*Philippines*]   (DS)
BWSC .... Boys of Woodcraft Sportsmen's Clubs [*Later, Woodmen Rangers and Rangerettes*]   (EA)
BWSC .... British War Supplies Committee [*Combined Production and Resources Board*] [*World War II*]
BWSF .... British Water Ski Federation
BWSL .... Battlefield Weapons System Laboratory
BWSO .... Backward Wave Sweep Oscillator
BWSRT ..... Bureau of Naval Weapons Support Representative, Naval Air Training Command [*Obsolete*]   (MUGU)
BWST .... Borated Water Storage Tank [*Nuclear energy*]   (NRCH)
BWSTRN .. Bowstring

BWSTx...... Black Widow Spider Toxin
BWSV........ Black Widow Spider Venom
BWT.......... Backward Wave Tube [*Physics*]
BWT.......... Bermuda-Schwortz Industries, Inc. [*Vancouver Stock Exchange symbol*]
BWT.......... Bestuurswetenschappen [*A publication*]
BWT.......... Birth Weight [*Medicine*]
BWT.......... Boeing Wind Tunnel
BWT.......... Bohr-Wheeler Theory
BWT.......... Both Way Trunk
BWTA....... Boston Wool Trade Association (EA)
BWTA....... British Wood Turners' Association
BWT Bull... Butterworth's Weekly Tax Bulletin [*Australia*] [*A publication*]
BWTF....... Bank Wire Transfer of Funds
BWTP....... Bureau of Work-Training Programs [*Terminated, 1969*] [*Department of Labor*]
BWTR....... Babcock & Wilcox Test Reactor
BWTRY..... Bowater PLC ADR [*NASDAQ symbol*] (SPSG)
BWTS....... Base Wire and Telephone System [*Air Force*] (MCD)
BWTS....... Bayonet Workers' Trade Society [*A union*] [*British*]
BWTSA..... Bauwirtschaft [*A publication*]
BWTSDS... Base Wire and Telephone System Development Schedule [*Air Force*]
BWU......... Blue-Whale-Unit [*Whaling industry*]
BWUJD..... Busan Women's University. Journal [*A publication*]
BWV......... Bach Werke-Verzeichnis [*Music*]
BWV......... Back-Water Valve
BWV......... West Vancouver Memorial Library, British Columbia [*Library symbol*] [*National Library of Canada*] (NLC)
BWVA...... British War Veterans of America (EA)
BWVACET ... Bulletin. West Virginia Association of College English Teachers [*A publication*]
BWVHC.... Hatfield Consultants Ltd., West Vancouver, British Columbia [*Library symbol*] [*National Library of Canada*] (NLC)
BWVS....... Black and White Vertical Stripes [*Navigation markers*]
BWW......... Barter Worldwide, Inc. [*Information service or system*] (IID)
BWW......... Biggers, Whitten, and Whittingham [*Growth medium*] [*Gynecology*]
BWWA...... Business Who's Who of Australia [*R. G. Riddell Pty. Ltd.*] [*Information service or system*] (IID)
BW (WP)... Book World (Washington Post) [*A publication*]
BWWSAP ... Branntweinwirtschaft [*A publication*]
BWX......... Berliner Wirtschaft; Mitteilungen der Industriekammer und Handelskammer zu Berlin [*A publication*]
BWY......... Blast Wave Yield
BWY......... Bouw/Werk. De Bouw in Feiten, Cijfers, en Analyses [*A publication*]
BWY......... Bowes Lyon Resources Ltd. [*Vancouver Stock Exchange symbol*]
BWYV....... Beet Western Yellows Virus
BWZ......... Schooley's Mountain, NJ [*Location identifier*] [*FAA*] (FAAL)
BX............ Bacitracin X [*Antibacterial compound*]
BX............ Base Exchange
BX............ Base Register [*Data processing*]
BX............ Basic Exercises
BX............ Biopsy [*Medicine*]
BX............ Box
bx............ Box Container [*Shipping*] (DS)
BX............ Branch Exchange [*Telecommunications*]
bx............ Brunei [*MARC country of publication code*] [*Library of Congress*] (LCCP)
BX............ Compania SPANTAX (Servicios y Transportes Aereos Air Charter) [*Spain*] [*ICAO designator*] (ICDA)
5BX.......... Five Basic Exercises [*British military*] (DMA)
BXA......... Bogalusa, LA [*Location identifier*] [*FAA*] (FAAL)
BXA......... Bureau of Export Administration [*Department of Commerce*]
BXA......... Burrard Air [*Richmond, BC, Canada*] [*FAA designator*] (FAAC)
BXB......... Babo [*Indonesia*] [*Airport symbol*] (OAG)
BXBX....... Business Exchange, Inc. [*NASDAQ symbol*] (NQ)
BX-C........ Bithorax Complex [*Gene cluster in fruit fly*]
BXCO....... Bracken Explorations Company [*NASDAQ symbol*] (NQ)
BXD......... Bade [*Indonesia*] [*Airport symbol*] (OAG)
BXD......... Boxed
BXD......... Bulletin de Documentation Rhenane [*A publication*]
BXDT....... Boxcar Detector (MSA)
BXE......... Bakel [*Senegal*] [*Airport symbol*] (OAG)
BXE......... Bowtex Energy (Canada) Corp. [*Toronto Stock Exchange symbol*]
BXF......... Box Fin
BXG......... BRX Mining & Petroleum [*Vancouver Stock Exchange symbol*]
BXG......... Waynesboro, GA [*Location identifier*] [*FAA*] (FAAL)
BXH......... Martha's Vineyard, MA [*Location identifier*] [*FAA*] (FAAL)
BXI.......... Boundiali [*Ivory Coast*] [*Airport symbol*] (OAG)
BXK......... Bank Leumi Le-Israel. Economic Review [*A publication*]
BXK......... Broadband X-Band Klystron
BXK......... Buckeye, AZ [*Location identifier*] [*FAA*] (FAAL)
BXL......... Boston College Law School, Newton, MA [*OCLC symbol*] (OCLC)
BXM......... Boston College, Chestnut Hill, MA [*OCLC symbol*] (OCLC)
BXN......... Bauxite & Northern Railway Co. [*AAR code*]

BXN.......... Dallas-Fort Worth, TX [*Location identifier*] [*FAA*] (FAAL)
BXO.......... Bissau [*Portuguese Guinea*] [*Airport symbol*] (OAG)
BXR.......... Barexor Minerals, Inc. [*Vancouver Stock Exchange symbol*]
BXR.......... Siren, WI [*Location identifier*] [*FAA*] (FAAL)
BXS........... Base Excess [*Medicine*]
BXS........... Borrego Springs [*California*] [*Airport symbol*] (OAG)
BXTJA ...... Bendix Technical Journal [*A publication*]
BX/TK....... Boxed or Tanked
BXU.......... Butuan [*Philippines*] [*Airport symbol*] (OAG)
BXV.......... Boxboard Containers [*A publication*]
BXV.......... Breiddalsvik [*Iceland*] [*Airport symbol*] (OAG)
BXY.......... Allentown, PA [*Location identifier*] [*FAA*] (FAAL)
BY .... Bay (ADA)
BY .... Bedfordshire Yeomanry [*British military*] (DMA)
BY .... Billion Years
BY .... Blowing Spray [*Meteorology*] (FAAC)
BY .... Britannia Airways Ltd. [*ICAO designator*] (FAAC)
BY .... British Yearbook of International Law [*A publication*]
BY .... Budget Year (AFM)
BY .... Busy [*Telecommunications*] (TEL)
BY .... Byelorussian Soviet Socialist Republic [*ISO two-letter standard code*] (CNC)
BY1 .... Byrd - Stanford Research Institute [*Antarctica*] [*Seismograph station code, US Geological Survey*] [*Closed*] (SEIS)
BYA .... Bay Ann Resources, Inc. [*Vancouver Stock Exchange symbol*]
BYA .... Beleidsanalyse [*A publication*]
BYA .... Boundary, AK [*Location identifier*] [*FAA*] (FAAL)
BYA .... Byrd Station, Antarctica
BYAA .... Byelorussian Youth Association of America [*Later, BAYO*] (EA)
BYB .... British Yearbook of International Law [*A publication*]
Byb .... Byblian (BJA)
ByB .... Byblos Librairie Bookshop, Beirut, Lebanon [*Library symbol*] [*Library of Congress*] (LCLS)
BYB .... Maandstatistiek Bouwnijverheid [*A publication*]
BYBBA ...... Brigham Young University. Science Bulletin. Biological Series [*A publication*]
BYBBAJ .... Brigham Young University. Science Bulletin. Biological Series [*A publication*]
BYC .... Banyan Corp. [*AMEX symbol*] (SPSG)
BYC .... Bengal Yeomanry Cavalry [*British military*] (DMA)
BYC .... Berkshire Yeomanry Cavalry [*British military*] (DMA)
BYC .... Brewers Yeast Council [*Later, Brewers Yeast and Grains Council*] [*Defunct*] (EA)
BYC .... British Youth Council (EAIO)
BYC .... Yacuiba [*Bolivia*] [*Airport symbol*] (OAG)
BYCM .... Byers Communications [*NASDAQ symbol*] (NQ)
BYD .... Barley Yellow Dwarf [*Plant pathology*]
BYD .... Bayridge Development [*Vancouver Stock Exchange symbol*]
BYD .... Beyond (FAAC)
BYD .... Bicentennial Youth Debates [*National Endowment for the Humanities program*]
BYD .... Bureau of Yards and Docks [*Later, NFEC*] [*Navy*] (MCD)
BYDAA ..... Baylor Dental Journal [*A publication*]
Bydgoskie Tow Nauk Wydz Nauk Tech Pr Ser B ... Bydgoskie Towarzystwo Naukowe Wydzial Nauk Technicznych. Prace. Seria B [*A publication*]
BYDIR....... By Direction (NVT)
BYDV........ Barley Yellow Dwarf Virus
BYE .... Barile-Yaguchi-Eveland [*Growth medium*] [*Microbiology*]
BYE .... Benefit Year Ending [*Unemployment insurance*]
ByF........... Biblia y Fe [*Madrid*] [*A publication*]
BYF........... Bloody Young Fool [*Officer under the age of 30*] [*British*] (DSUE)
BYG .... Buffalo, WY [*Location identifier*] [*FAA*] (FAAL)
BYG .... BYG Natural Resources, Inc. [*Toronto Stock Exchange symbol*]
BYGEA ...... Byggmestern [*A publication*]
BYGGDOK ... Institutet for Byggdokumentation [*Swedish Institute of Building Documentation*] [*Stockholm*] [*Information service or system*] (IID)
Bygnin Medd ... Bygningsstatiske Meddelelser [*A publication*]
BYGSA ...... Brigham Young University. Geology Studies [*A publication*]
BYH.......... Blytheville, AR [*Location identifier*] [*FAA*] (FAAL)
BYH.......... Bulletin. Europese Gemeenschappen. Europese Gemeenschap voor Kolen en Staal, Europese Economische Gemeenschap, Europese Gemeenschap voor Atoomenergie [*A publication*]
BYI............ Burley, ID [*Location identifier*] [*FAA*] (FAAL)
BYIL......... British Yearbook of International Law [*A publication*]
BYILDJ..... Biology International [*A publication*]
ByJ........... Byzantinisch-Neugriechische Jahrbuecher [*A publication*]
BYK .... Bouake [*Ivory Coast*] [*Airport symbol*] (OAG)
BYL.......... Bulletin van de Generale Bankmaatschappij [*A publication*]
Byl Bills .... Byles on Bills of Exchange [*A publication*] (DLA)
Byles .... Byles on Bills of Exchange [*A publication*] (DLA)
Byl Exch ... Byles' Law of Exchange [*A publication*] (DLA)
BYLINE .... Brigham Young Libraries Information Network [*Brigham Young University*] [*Provo, UT*] [*Information service or system*] (IID)
BYLJA...... Bayerisches Landwirtschaftliches Jahrbuch [*A publication*]
By LR....... Baylor Law Review [*A publication*]

Byl Us L..... Byles on the Usury Laws [*A publication*]   (DLA)
BYM .... Bayamo [*Cuba*] [*Airport symbol*]   (OAG)
BYM .... Bell Journal of Economics [*A publication*]
BYM .... Historic Yale Museum, British Columbia [*Library symbol*] [*National Library of Canada*] (NLC)
BYM-AG... Bornu Youth Movement - Action Group Alliance [*Nigeria*]
BYMEA..... Bygningsstatiske Meddelelser [*A publication*]
BYMOA .... Byulleten' Moskovskogo Obshchestva Ispytatelei Prirody Otdel Biologicheskii [*A publication*]
BYMS....... British Yard Motor Minesweepers
BYMUX .... Byte-Multiplexer Channel
BYMV .... Bean Yellow Mosaic Virus
BYN .... Bangor Public Library, Bangor, ME [*OCLC symbol*]   (OCLC)
BYN .... Bryan, OH [*Location identifier*] [*FAA*]   (FAAL)
BYN .... Byron Resources, Inc. [*Vancouver Stock Exchange symbol*]
Bynk.......... Bynkershoek's Quaestionum Juris Publici [*A publication*]   (DLA)
Bynks Obs Jur Rom ... Bynkershoek's Observationum Juris Roman Libri [*A publication*]   (DLA)
BYNT .... Buoyant   (MSA)
Byn War..... Bynkershoek's Law of War [*A publication*]   (DLA)
BYO........... Bring Your Own [*Liquor*] [*Party invitation notation*]
BYOB .... Bring Your Own Beef [*Phrase popularized during 1973 beef shortage*]
BYOB .... Bring Your Own Boat
BYOB .... Bring Your Own Booze [*or Bottle*] [*Party invitation notation*]
BYOG .... Bring Your Own Grog [*British*]   (ADA)
B Yokohama City Univ ... Bulletin. Yokohama City University [*A publication*]
BYOTV...... Bring Your Own TV
BYOU .... Bayou Resources, Inc. [*NASDAQ symbol*]   (NQ)
BYOV .... Bring Your Own Vehicle
BYOW .... Bring Your Own Wine   (ADA)
BYP........... Bypass   (KSC)
BYPU......... Baptist Young People's Union
BYR .... Billion Years
BYR .... Byrd [*Antarctica*] [*Seismograph station code, US Geological Survey*] [*Closed*]   (SEIS)
BYRD .... [*The*] Byrd [*William*] Press, Inc. [*NASDAQ symbol*]   (NQ)
ByrdAE...... Byrd Antarctic Expedition [*1928-30, 1933-35*]
Byrne BS.... Byrne. Bills of Sale [*2nd ed.*] [*1870*] [*A publication*]   (DLA)
Byrne Pat ... Byrne on Patents [*A publication*]   (DLA)
Byron J ..... Byron Journal [*A publication*]
BYRS .... Buyers
BYRS .... Byers, Inc. [*Hingham, MA*] [*NASDAQ symbol*]   (NQ)
Byrsa.......... Cahiers de Byrsa [*A publication*]
BYS........... Barstow, CA [*Location identifier*] [*FAA*]   (FAAL)
BY$........... Base Year Dollars   (MCD)
BYS........... Byelorussian Soviet Socialist Republic [*ISO three-letter standard code*]   (CNC)
Bysl........... Byzantino-Slavica [*A publication*]
BYSTA ...... Byulleten' Stroitel'noi Tekhniki [*A publication*]
ByT .... Barrasiha-Ye Tarikhi [*A publication*]
BYT .... Bentley Resources Ltd. [*Vancouver Stock Exchange symbol*]
BYT .... Bright Young Thing   (DSUE)
BYT .... Bytom [*Poland*] [*Seismograph station code, US Geological Survey*]   (SEIS)
BYTE........ CompuCom Systems, Inc. [*NASDAQ symbol*]   (NQ)
BYTE Spcl ... BYTE. The Small Systems Journal. Special IBM Issue [*A publication*]
Byth Conv .. Bythewood. Precedents in Conveyancing [*4th ed.*] [*1884-90*] [*A publication*]   (DLA)
Byth Prec ... Bythewood. Precedents in Conveyancing [*4th ed.*] [*1884-90*] [*A publication*]   (DLA)
BYTX........ Bytex Corp. [*NASDAQ symbol*]   (NQ)
BYU .... Barksdale, LA [*Location identifier*] [*FAA*]   (FAAL)
BYU .... Bayou
BYU .... Bayreuth [*West Germany*] [*Airport symbol*]   (OAG)
BYU .... Brandy Resources [*Vancouver Stock Exchange symbol*]
BYU .... Brigham Young University [*Utah*]
BYU .... Brigham Young University, Hawaii Campus, Laie, HI [*OCLC symbol*]   (OCLC)
BYU .... Bristol-Myers, Americus (Unit) [*AMEX symbol*]   (SPSG)
BYU .... BYU [*Brigham Young University*] Law Review [*A publication*]
Byul Gl Upr Stroit Voiski (Sofia) ... Byulleten'. Glavno Upravlenie na Stroitelnite Voiski (Sofia) [*A publication*]
Byull Abastumanskaya Astrofiz Obs Akad Nauk Gruz SSR ... Byulleten' Abastumanskaya Astrofizicheskaya Observatoriya Akademiya Nauk Gruzinskoi SSR [*Georgian SSR*] [*A publication*]
Byull Akad Nauk Gruz SSR Abastumanskaya Astrofiz Obs ... Byulleten' Akademiya Nauk Gruzinskoi SSR Abastumanskaya Astrofizicheskaya Observatoriya [*Georgian SSR*] [*A publication*]
Byull Akad Nauk Uzb SSR ... Byulleten' Akademii Nauk Uzbekskoi SSR [*A publication*]
Byull Azerb Nauchno Issled Inst Khlopkovod ... Byulleten' Azerbaidzhanskogo Nauchno Issledovatel'skogo Instituta Khlopkovodstva [*A publication*]
Byull Belogo Morya ... Byulleten' Belogo Morya [*A publication*]

Byull Bot Sada Akad Nauk Arm SSR ... Byulleten' Botanicheskogo Sada Akademii Nauk Armyanskoi SSR [*A publication*]
Byull Bot Sada Erevan ... Byulleten' Botanicheskogo Sada Erevan [*A publication*]
Byull Eksp Biol Med ... Byulleten' Eksperimental'noi Biologii i Meditsiny [*A publication*]
Byull Fiziol Rast ... Byulleten' po Fiziologii Rastenii [*A publication*]
Byull Glavn Bot Sada (Leningr) ... Byulleten' Glavnogo Botanicheskogo Sada (Leningrad) [*A publication*]
Byull Gl Bot Sada ... Byulleten' Glavnogo Botanicheskogo Sada [*Leningrad*] [*A publication*]
Byull Gos Nikitsk Bot Sada ... Byulleten' Gosudarstvennogo Nikitskogo Botanicheskogo Sada [*A publication*]
Byull Inf Tsentra Yad Dannym ... Byulleten' Informatsionnogo Tsentral'nogo po Yadernym Dannym [*A publication*]
Byull Inf Tsentr Genet Lab Im I V Michurina ... Byulleten' Informatsii Tsentralnoi Geneticheskoi Laboratorii Imeni I. V. Michurina [*A publication*]
Byull Inst Astrofiz Akad Nauk Tadzh ... Byulleten' Instituta Astrofiziki Akademiya Nauk Tadzhikskoi SSR [*A publication*]
Byull Inst Astrofiz Akad Nauk Tadzh SSR ... Byulleten' Instituta Astrofiziki Akademiya Nauk Tadzhikskoi SSR [*A publication*]
Byull Inst Biol Akad Nauk Beloruss SSR ... Byulleten Instituta Biologii Akademiya Nauk Belorusskoi SSR [*A publication*]
Byull Inst Biol Akad Nauk B SSR ... Byulleten' Instituta Biologiya Akademiya Nauk Belorusskoi SSR [*A publication*]
Byull Inst Biol Vodokhran ... Byulleten' Instituta Biologii Vodokhranilishcha [*A publication*]
Byull Inst Metallokeram Spets Splavov Akad Nauk Ukr SSR ... Byulleten' Instituta Metallokeramiki i Spetsial'nykh Splavov Akademiya Nauk Ukrainskoi SSR [*A publication*]
Byull Inst Teor Astron ... Byulleten' Instituta Teoreticheskoi Astronomii [*USSR*] [*A publication*]
Byull Inst Teor Astron Akad Nauk SSSR ... Byulleten' Instituta Teoreticheskoi Astronomii Akademiya Nauk SSSR [*A publication*]
Byull Inst Teoret Astronom ... Akademiya Nauk SSSR. Byulleten Instituta Teoreticheskoi Astronomii [*A publication*]
Byull Kavk Inst Miner Syrya ... Byulleten' Kavkazskogo Instituta Mineral'nogo Syr'ya [*A publication*]
Byull Kirgiz Nauch Issled Inst Zemled ... Byulleten' Kirgizskogo Nauchno-Issledovatel'skogo Instituta Zemledeliya [*A publication*]
Byull Kirgiz Nauchno-Issled Inst Zeml ... Byulleten' Kirgizskogo Nauchno-Issledovatel'skogo Instituta Zemledeliya [*A publication*]
Byull Kirg Nauchno Issled Inst Zemled ... Byulleten' Kirgizskogo Nauchno-Issledovatel'skogo Instituta Zemledeliya [*A publication*]
Byull Kom Izuch Chetvertichn Perioda Akad Nauk SSSR ... Byulleten' Komissii po Izucheniyu Chetvertichnogo Perioda Akademiya Nauk SSSR [*A publication*]
Byull Kom Kometam Meteoram Astron Sov Akad Nauk SSSR ... Byulleten' Komissii po Kometam i Meteoram Astronomicheskogo Sovieta Akademii Nauk SSSR [*A publication*]
Byull Kom Opred Absol Geol Form ... Byulleten' Komissii po Opredeleniyu Absolyutnogo Vozrasta Geologicheskikh Formatsii [*USSR*] [*A publication*]
Byull Kom Opred Absol Vozrasta Geol Form Akad Nauk SSSR ... Byulleten' Komissii po Opredeleniyu Absolyutnogo Vozrasta Geologicheskikh Formatsii Akademiya Nauk SSSR [*A publication*]
Byull Leningr Inst Organ Okhr Tr ... Byulleten' Leningradskii Institut Organizatsii i Okhrany Truda [*A publication*]
Byull Leningr Otd Inst Udobr Agropochvoved ... Byulleten' Leningradskogo Otdeleniya Institut Udobrenii i Agropochvovedeniya [*A publication*]
Byull Mezhdunar O-Va Torfu ... Byulleten' Mezhdunarodnogo Obshchestva po Torfu [*A publication*]
Byull Mosk Obshch Ispyt Prir ... Byulleten' Moskovskogo Obshchestva Ispytatelei Prirody Otdel Biologicheskii [*A publication*]
Byull Mosk Ova Ispyt Prir Kalinin Otd ... Byulleten' Moskovskogo Obshchestva Ispytatelei Prirody Kalininskii Otdel [*A publication*]
Byull Mosk Ova Ispyt Prir Otd Biol ... Byulleten' Moskovskogo Obshchestva Ispytatelei Prirody Otdel Biologicheskii [*A publication*]
Byull Mosk Ova Ispyt Prir Otd Geol ... Byulleten' Moskovskogo Obshchestva Ispytatelei Prirody Otdel Geologicheskii [*A publication*]
Byull Nauch-Issled Inst Malyarii Med Parazitol ... Byulleten' Nauchno-Issledovatel'skogo Instituta Malyarii i Meditsinskoi Parazitologii [*A publication*]
Byull Nauchno Issled Inst Malyarii Med Parazitol ... Byulleten' Nauchno Issledovatel'skogo Instituta Malyarii i Meditsinskoi Parazitologii [*A publication*]
Byull Nauchno Issled Khim Farm Inst ... Byulleten' Nauchno Issledovatel'skogo Khimiko Farmatsevticheskogo Instituta [*A publication*]
Byull Nauchno-Tekh Inf ... Byulleten' Nauchno-Tekhnicheskoi Informatsii [*A publication*]
Byull Nauchno-Tekh Inf Agron Fiz ... Byulleten' Nauchno-Tekhnicheskoi Informatsii po Agronomicheskoi Fizike [*A publication*]

Byull Nauchno Tekh Inf Arm Nauchno Issled Inst Zemled ... Byulleten' Nauchno-Tekhnicheskoi Informatsii Armyanskogo Nauchno-Issledovatel'skogo Instituta Zemledeliya [*A publication*]

Byull Nauchno Tekh Inf Beloruss Nauchno Issled Inst Zemled ... Byulleten' Nauchno-Tekhnicheskoi Informatsii Belorusskogo Nauchno-Issledovatel'skogo Instituta Zemledeliya [*A publication*]

Byull Nauchno Tekh Inf Gos Geol Kom SSSR ... Byulleten' Nauchno-Tekhnicheskoi Informatsii Gosudarstvennyi Geologicheskii Komitet SSSR [*A publication*]

Byull Nauchno Tekh Inf Inst ... Byulleten' Nauchno-Tekhnicheskoi Informatsii Nauchno-Issledovatel'skogo Instituta Pchelovodstva [*A publication*]

Byull Nauchno Tekh Inf Litov Nauchno Issled Inst Zhivotnovod ... Byulleten' Nauchno-Tekhnicheskoi Informatsii Litovskogo Nauchno-Issledovatel'skogo Instituta Zhivotnovodstva [*A publication*]

Byull Nauchno Tekh Inf Maslichn Kult ... Byulleten' Nauchno-Tekhnicheskoi Informatsii po Maslichnym Kulturam [*A publication*]

Byull Nauchno Tekh Inf Minist Geol Okhr Nedr SSSR ... Byulleten' Nauchno-Tekhnicheskoi Informatsii Ministerstvo Geologii i Okhrany Nedr SSSR [*A publication*]

Byull Nauchno Tekh Inf Minist Geol SSSR ... Byulleten' Nauchno-Tekhnicheskoi Informatsii Ministerstvo Geologii SSSR [*A publication*]

Byull Nauchno-Tekh Inf S-Kh Mikrobiol ... Byulleten' Nauchno-Tekhnicheskoi Informatsii po Sel'skokhozyaistvennoi Mikrobiologii [*A publication*]

Byull Nauchno-Tekh Inf (Sumskaya Gos Skh Opytn Stn) ... Byulleten' Nauchno-Tekhnicheskoi Informatsii (Sumskaya Gosudarstvennaya Sel'skokhozyaistvennaya Opytnaya Stantsiya) [*A publication*]

Byull Nauchno Tekh Inf Tadzh Nauchno Issled Inst Sel'sk Khoz ... Byulleten' Nauchno-Tekhnicheskoi Informatsii Tadzhikskogo Nauchno-Issledovatel'skogo Instituta Sel'skogo Khozyaistva [*A publication*]

Byull Nauchno Tekh Inf Tsentr Torfobolotnoi Opytn Stant ... Byulleten' Nauchno-Tekhnicheskoi Informatsii Tsentralnoi Torfobolotnoi Opytnoi Stantsii [*A publication*]

Byull Nauchno Tekh Inf Turkm Nauchno Issled Inst Zemled ... Byulleten' Nauchno-Tekhnicheskoi Informatsii Turkmenskogo Nauchno-Issledovatel'skogo Instituta Zemledeliya [*A publication*]

Byull Nauchno Tekh Inf Ukr Nauchno Issled Inst Met ... Byulleten' Nauchno-Tekhnicheskoi Informatsii Ukrainskii Nauchno-Issledovatel'skii Institut Metallov [*A publication*]

Byull Nauchno Tekh Inf Ukr Nauchno Issled Inst Ogneuporov ... Byulleten' Nauchno-Tekhnicheskoi Informatsii Ukrainskogo Nauchno-Issledovatel'skogo Instituta Ogneuporov [*A publication*]

Byull Nauchno Tekh Inf Ukr Nauchno Issled Uglekhim Inst ... Byulleten' Nauchno-Tekhnicheskoi Informatsii Ukrainskii Nauchno-Issledovatel'skii Uglekhimicheskii Institut [*A publication*]

Byull Nauchno Tekh Inf Ural Nauchno Issled Inst Chern Met ... Byulleten' Nauchno-Tekhnicheskoi Informatsii Ural'skogo Nauchno-Issledovatel'skogo Instituta Chernykh Metallov [*A publication*]

Byull Nauchno Tekh Sov Metall Legk Met ... Byulleten' Nauchno-Tekhnicheskogo Soveta po Metallurgii Legkikh Metallov [*A publication*]

Byull Nauchno-Tekh Sov Metall Tyazh Tsvetn Met ... Byulleten' Nauchno-Tekhnicheskogo Soveta po Metallurgii Tyazhilykh Tsvetnykh Metallov [*Poland*] [*A publication*]

Byull Nauchno-Tekh Sov Obogashch Rud Tsvetn Met ... Byulleten' Nauchno-Tekhnicheskogo Soveta po Obogashcheniyu Rud Tsvetnykh Metallov [*Romania*] [*A publication*]

Byull Nauchno-Tekh Sov Obrab Tsvetn Met Vtorichnoi Metall ... Byulleten' Nauchno-Tekhnicheskogo Soveta po Obrabotke Tsvetnykh Metallov i Vtorichnoi Metallurgii [*Czechoslovakia*] [*A publication*]

Byull Nauchn Stud Ova Kaz Gos Univ ... Byulleten' Nauchnogo Studencheskogo Obshchestva Kazakhskii Gosudarstvennyi Universitet [*A publication*]

Byull Obmena Opytom Lakokras Promsti ... Byulleten' Obmena Opytom Lakokrasochnoi Promyshlennosti [*A publication*]

Byull Ova Estestvoispyt Voronezh Gos Univ ... Byulleten' Obshchestva Estestvoispytatelei pri Voronezhskom Gosudarstvennom Universitete [*A publication*]

Byull Pochvoveda ... Byulleten' Pochvoveda [*A publication*]

Byull Sakharotresta ... Byulleten' Sakharotresta [*A publication*]

Byull Sov Antarkt Eksped ... Byulleten' Sovetskoi Antarkticheskoi Ekspeditsii [*USSR*] [*A publication*]

Byull Sov Seismol ... Byulleten' Sovet po Seismologii [*USSR*] [*A publication*]

Byull Sredneaziat Gos Univ ... Byulleten' Sredneaziatskogo Gosudarstvennogo Universiteta [*A publication*]

Byull Stn Opt Nablyudeniya Iskusstvennykh Sputnikov Zemli ... Byulleten' Stantsii Opticheskogo Nablyudeniya Iskusstvennykh Sputnikov Zemli [*USSR*] [*A publication*]

Byull Stroit Tekh ... Byulleten' Stroitel'noi Tekhniki [*USSR*] [*A publication*]

Byull Stud Nauchn Ova Kaz Gos Univ ... Byulleten' Studencheskogo Nauchnogo Obshchestva Kazakhskii Gosudarstvennyi Universitet [*A publication*]

Byull Stud Nauchn Ova Leningr Gos Univ ... Byulleten' Studencheskogo Nauchnogo Obshchestva Leningradskii Gosudarstvennyi Universitet [*A publication*]

Byull Tekh-Ehkon Inf Gos Nauchno-Issled Inst Nauchn Tekh Inf ... Byulleten' Tekhniko-Ehkonomicheskoj Informatsii. Gosudarstvennyj Nauchno-Issledovatel'skij Institut Nauchnoj i Tekhnicheskoj Informatsii [*A publication*]

Byull Tekh Ekon Inf ... Byulleten' Tekhniko-Ekonomicheskoi Informatsii [*A publication*]

Byull Tekh-Ekon Inf Gos Nauchno-Issled Inst Nauchn Tekh Inf ... Byulleten' Tekhniko-Ekonomicheskoi Informatsii Gosudarstvennyi Nauchno-Issledovatel'skii Institut Nauchnoi i Tekhnicheskoi Informatsii [*USSR*] [*A publication*]

Byull Tekh Ekon Inf Mork Flota ... Byulleten' Tekhniko-Ekonomicheskoi Informatsii Morskogo Flota [*A publication*]

Byull Tekh Ekon Inf Sov Nar Khoz B SSR ... Byulleten' Tekhniko-Ekonomicheskoi Informatsii Sovet Narodnogo Khozyaistva Belorusskoi SSR [*A publication*]

Byull Tekh Ekon Inf Sov Nar Khoz Stalinskogo Ekon Adm Raiona ... Byulleten' Tekhniko-Ekonomicheskoi Informatsii Sovet Narodnogo Khozyaistva Stalinskogo Ekonomicheskogo Administrativnogo Raiona [*A publication*]

Byull Tekh Inf Sov Nar Khoz Kursk Ekon Adm Raiona ... Byulleten' Tekhnicheskoi Informatsii Sovet Narodnogo Khozyaistva Kurskogo Ekonomicheskogo Administrativnogo Raiona [*A publication*]

Byull Tekh Inf Stroit ... Byulleten' Tekhnicheskoi Informatsii po Stroitel'stvu [*A publication*]

Byull Tsentra Yad Dannym ... Byulleten' Tsentra po Yadernym Dannym [*USSR*] [*A publication*]

Byull Tsvetn Metall ... Byulleten' Tsvetnoi Metallurgii [*A publication*]

Byull Ural Otd Mosk Ova Ispyt Prir ... Byulleten' Ural'skogo Otdeleniya Moskovskogo Obshchestva Ispytatelei Prirody [*A publication*]

Byull Vil'nyus Astron Obs ... Byulleten' Vil'nyusskoi Astronomicheskoi Observatorii [*Lithuanian SSR*] [*A publication*]

Byull Vost Sib Fenol Kom ... Byulleten' Vostochno Sibirskoi Fenologicheskoi Komissii [*A publication*]

Byull Vses Astron Geod Ova ... Byulleten' Vsesoyuznogo Astronomo-Geodezicheskogo Obshchestva [*A publication*]

Byull Vses Inst Eksp Vet ... Byulleten' Vsesoyuznogo Instituta Eksperimental'noi Veterinarii [*A publication*]

Byull Vses Inst Gel'mintol ... Byulleten' Vsesoyuznogo Instituta Gel'mintologii [*A publication*]

Byull Vses Inst Rastenievod ... Byulleten' Vsesoyuznogo Instituta Rastenievodstva [*A publication*]

Byull Vses Kardiol Nauchn Tsentra AMN SSSR ... Byulleten' Vsesoyuznogo Kardiologicheskogo Nauchnogo Tsentra AMN SSSR [*A publication*]

Byull Vses Koord Kom Mikroelem ... Byulleten' Vsesoyuznoi Koordinatsionnoi Komissee po Mikroelementam [*A publication*]

Byull Vses Nauchno Issled Geol Inst ... Byulleten' Vsesoyuznogo Nauchno-Issledovatel'skogo Geologicheskogo Instituta [*A publication*]

Byull Vses Nauchno-Issled Inst Agrolesomelior ... Byulleten' Vsesoyuznogo Nauchno-Issledovatel'skogo Instituta Agrolesomelioratsii [*A publication*]

Byull Vses Nauchno Issled Inst Chain Promsti ... Byulleten' Vsesoyuznogo Nauchno-Issledovatel'skogo Instituta Chainoi Promyshlennosti [*A publication*]

Byull Vses Nauchno-Issled Inst Chaya Subtrop Kul't ... Byulleten' Vsesoyuznogo Nauchno-Issledovatel'skogo Instituta Chaya i Subtropicheskikh Kul'tur [*A publication*]

Byull Vses Nauchno Issled Inst Eksp Vet Im Ya R Kovalenko ... Byulleten' Vsesoyuznogo Nauchno-Issledovatel'skogo Instituta Eksperimental'noi Veterinarii Imeni Ya. R. Kovalenko [*A publication*]

Byull Vses Nauchno-Issled Inst Fiziol Biokhim Skh Zhivotn ... Byulleten. Vsesoyuznogo Nauchno-Issledovatelskogo Instituta Fiziologii i Biokhimii i Pitaniya Sel'skokhozyaistvennyk Zhivotnyk [*A publication*]

Byull Vses Nauchno-Issled Inst Kukuruzy ... Byulleten' Vsesoyuznogo Nauchno-Issledovatel'skogo Instituta Kukuruzy [*A publication*]

Byull Vses Nauchno-Issled Inst Rastenievod Im N I Vavilova ... Byulleten' Vsesoyuznogo Nauchno-Issledovatel'skogo Instituta Rastenievodstva Imeni N. I. Vavilova [*USSR*] [*A publication*]

Byull Vses Nauchno Issled Inst Tsem ... Byulleten' Vsesoyuznogo Nauchno-Issledovatel'skogo Instituta Tsementov [*A publication*]

Byull Vses Nauchno Issled Inst Udobr Agropochvoved ... Byulleten' Vsesoyuznogo Nauchno-Issledovatel'skogo Instituta Udobrenii i Agropochvovedeniya [*A publication*]

Byull Vses Nauchno-Issled Inst Zashch Rast ... Byulleten' Vsesoyuznogo Nauchno-Issledovatel'skogo Instituta Zashchity Rastenii [*A publication*]

Byull Vses Ordena Lenina Inst Eksp Vet ... Byulleten' Vsesoyuznogo Ordena Lenina Instituta Eksperimental'noi Veterinarii [*A publication*]
Byull Vulkanol Stn Akad Nauk SSSR ... Byulleten' Vulkanologicheskikh Stantsii Akademiya Nauk SSSR [*A publication*]
Byull Vulkanol Stn Kamchatke Akad Nauk SSSR ... Byulleten' Vulkanologicheskikh Stantsii na Kamchatke Akademiya Nauk SSSR [*A publication*]
Byul Nauk Inf Zemlerob ... Byulleten' Naukovoi Informatsii po Zemlerobstvu [*A publication*]
BYU LR ..... Brigham Young University. Law Review [*A publication*]
BYU L Rev ... Brigham Young University. Law Review [*A publication*]
BYUP .... Brigham Young University Press
BYUS .... Brigham Young University. Studies [*A publication*]
BYV .... Beet Yellows Virus
BYW .... Blakely Island [*Washington*] [*Airport symbol*]   (OAG)
BYX .... Barymin Explorations Ltd. [*Toronto Stock Exchange symbol*]
BYX .... Bayou Steel [*AMEX symbol*]   (SPSG)
BYY .... Bay City, TX [*Location identifier*] [*FAA*]   (FAAL)
Byz .... Byzantina [*A publication*]
BYZ .... Byzantine
ByZ .... Byzantinische Zeitschrift [*A publication*]
Byz .... Byzantion [*A publication*]
Byzan .... Byzantine
Byzant .... Byzantion; Revue Internationale des Etudes Byzantines [*A publication*]
Byzantinak ... Byzantina kai Metabyzantina [*A publication*]
Byzantine M ... Byzantine and Modern Greek Studies [*A publication*]
Byzantine S ... Byzantine Studies [*A publication*]
Byzantinische Z ... Byzantinische Zeitschrift [*A publication*]
Byzantinosl ... Byzantino-Slavica [*A publication*]
Byzantin Z ... Byzantinische Zeitschrift [*A publication*]
Byz Arch .... Byzantinisches Archiv [*A publication*]
Byz-Bulg .... Byzantino-Bulgarica [*A publication*]
Byz F .... Byzantinische Forschungen [*A publication*]
Byz Forsch ... Byzantinische Forschungen [*A publication*]
Byz Jb .... Byzantinisch-Neugriechische Jahrbuecher [*A publication*]
Byz-Met ..... Byzantina-Metabyzantina [*A publication*]
ByzMetabyz ... Byzantina-Metabyzantina [*A publication*]
Byz und Neugr Jahrb ... Byzantinisch-Neugriechische Jahrbucher [*A publication*]   (OCD)
Byz-Neugr Jahrb ... Byzantinisch-Neugriechische Jahrbuecher [*A publication*]
BYZNGJB ... Byzantinisch-Neugriechische Jahrbuecher [*A publication*]
BYZOA ..... Byulleten' Izobretenii [*A publication*]
ByzS .... Byzantino-Slavica [*A publication*]
ByzSl .... Byzantino-Slavica [*A publication*]
Byz Slav ..... Byzantino-Slavica. Sbornik pro Studium Byzantskoslovanskych Vztahu [*A publication*]
ByzZ .... Byzantinische Zeitschrift [*A publication*]
Byz Zeitschr ... Byzantinische Zeitschrift [*A publication*]   (OCD)
BZ .... Audible Signal Devices [*JETDS nomenclature*] [*Military*]   (CET)
BZ .... Bairnco Corp. [*NYSE symbol*]   (SPSG)
BZ .... Belize [*ANSI two-letter standard code*]   (CNC)
BZ .... Belousov-Zhabotinskii [*Physical chemistry*]
BZ .... Benzene [*Organic chemistry*]   (ADA)
BZ .... Benzodiazepine [*Also, BZD*] [*Organic chemistry*]
BZ .... Benzopyrene [*or Benzpyrene*] [*Also, BP*] [*Carcinogen*]
Bz .... Benzoyl [*Organic chemistry*]
BZ .... Berliner Zeitung [*A publication*]
Bz .... Bestellzettel [*Order Form*] [*German*]
bz .... Bezahlt [*Paid*] [*German*]
BZ .... Biblische Zeitschrift [*A publication*]
BZ .... Bild Zeitung [*Picture newspaper*] [*German*]
BZ .... Blank when Zero
BZ .... Bnai Zion   (EA)
BZ .... Borsen Zeitung [*A publication*]
BZ .... Brillouin Zone [*Physics*]
BZ .... Brittany Air International [*France*] [*ICAO designator*]   (FAAC)
BZ .... Bronze
BZ .... Byzantinische Zeitschrift [*A publication*]
BZ .... Iraq [*Formerly, TS*] [*License plate code assigned to foreign diplomats in the US*]
BZ .... Quinuclidinyl Benzilate [*Also, QNB*] [*Army symbol*]
Bza .... Benzimidazole [*Biochemistry*]
Bza .... Benzimidazolyl [*Biochemistry*]
BZA .... Berichte ueber Landwirtschaft. Zeitschrift fuer Agrarpolitik und Landwirtschaft [*A publication*]
BZA .... Board of Zoning Adjustment
BZA .... Bombenzielapparat [*Bomb sight*] [*German military - World War II*]
BZA .... British Zeolite Association
BZA .... Yuma, AZ [*Location identifier*] [*FAA*]   (FAAL)
BZAC .... Benzoylacetone [*Organic chemistry*]
BZAC .... Brazing Accessory [*Tool*]   (AAG)
B Zambia Lang Group ... Bulletin of the Zambia Language Group [*A publication*]
BzAnth .... Benzanthracene [*Also, BA*] [*Organic chemistry*]
BZAW .... Beihefte. Zeitschrift fuer die Alttestamentliche Wissenschaft [*Giessen/Berlin*] [*A publication*]
B Zb .... Bayerisches Zahnaerzteblatt [*A publication*]

BZ Bl .... Bayerisches Zahnaerzteblatt [*A publication*]
BZ Bl .... Bundeszollblatt [*A publication*]
BZ & C ...... Bellaire, Zanesville & Cincinnati Railroad [*Nickname: Bent, Zigzagged, and Crooked*]
BZC .... Hyannis, MA [*Location identifier*] [*FAA*]   (FAAL)
BZD .... Benzidine [*Carcinogen*]
BZD .... Benzodiazepine [*Also, BZ*] [*Organic chemistry*]
BZD .... Blizzard Resources, Inc. [*Vancouver Stock Exchange symbol*]
BzDB .... Bibliographien zur Deutsche Barockliteratur [*A publication*]
BZE .... Bankers' Magazine [*A publication*]
BZE .... Belize City [*Belize*] [*Airport symbol*]   (OAG)
BZE .... Bozeman [*Montana*] [*Seismograph station code, US Geological Survey*] [*Closed*]   (SEIS)
BZF .... Biblische Zeitfragen [*Muenster*] [*A publication*]
BZF .... Brazil Fund, Inc. [*NYSE symbol*]   (SPSG)
B Zfr .... Clinton, OK [*Location identifier*] [*FAA*]   (FAAL)
B Zfr .... Biblische Zeitfragen [*A publication*]
BZFX .... Brazing Fixture
BZG .... Basler Zeitschrift fuer Geschichte und Altertumskunde [*A publication*]
BZG .... Beitraege zur Geschichte der Deutschen Arbeiterbewegung [*A publication*]
BZG .... Bombenzielgeraet [*Bomb sight*] [*German military - World War II*]
BZG .... Bydgoszcz [*Poland*] [*Airport symbol*] [*Obsolete*]   (OAG)
BZGA .... Basler Zeitschrift fuer Geschichte und Altertumskunde [*A publication*]
BZGAK ..... Basler Zeitschrift fuer Geschichte und Altertumskunde [*A publication*]
BZGL .... Bezueglich [*In Regard To, With Reference To*] [*German*]
Bzh .... Benzhydryl [*Biochemistry*]
BZHM .... Berliner Zahnaerztliche Halbmonatsschrift [*A publication*]
BZI .... Beam Zero Indication   (MCD)
BZI .... Benyzlimidazole [*Organic chemistry*]
BZIH .... Biuletyn Zydowskiego Instytutu Historycznego [*A publication*]
BZion .... Der Bote aus Zion [*Berlin*] [*A publication*]   (BJA)
BZJ .... Indiantown Gap, PA [*Location identifier*] [*FAA*]   (FAAL)
BzJA .... Beihefte zum Ja [*A publication*]
BZK .... Brookfield, MO [*Location identifier*] [*FAA*]   (FAAL)
Bzl .... Benzyl [*Organic chemistry*]
BZM .... Beit Zeiroth Mizrahi (BJA)
BZM .... Berliner Zeitung am Mittag [*A publication*]
BZM .... Beton, Herstellung, Verwendung [*A publication*]
BZM .... Boston University, School of Theology, Boston, MA [*OCLC symbol*]   (OCLC)
BZM .... Bozeman [*Montana*] [*Seismograph station code, US Geological Survey*] [*Closed*]   (SEIS)
BZM .... Hickory, NC [*Location identifier*] [*FAA*]   (FAAL)
BZMT .... BizMart, Inc. [*NASDAQ symbol*]   (NQ)
BzMW .... Beitraege zur Musikwissenschaft [*A publication*]
BZN .... Beitraege zur Namenforschung [*Heidelberg*] [*A publication*]
BZN .... Bozeman [*Montana*] [*Airport symbol*]   (OAG)
BzNH .... Bizantion-Nea Hellas [*A publication*]
BZNW .... Beihefte. Zeitschrift fuer die Neutestamentliche Wissenschaft und die Kunde der Alteren Kirche [*Giessen/Berlin*] [*A publication*]
BZO .... Bonanza Oil & Gas Ltd. [*Toronto Stock Exchange symbol*]
BZP .... Bizant [*Australia*] [*Airport symbol*] [*Obsolete*]   (OAG)
BZP .... Galena, AK [*Location identifier*] [*FAA*]   (FAAL)
BZPCA ...... British Zone Petroleum Coordinating Authority [*Post-World War II, Germany*]
BZQ .... Benzquinamide [*Pharmacology*]
BZR .... Baz Resources Ltd. [*Vancouver Stock Exchange symbol*]
BZR .... Beazer PLC ADS [*NYSE symbol*]   (SPSG)
BZR .... Beziers [*France*] [*Airport symbol*]   (OAG)
BZR .... Buzzer [*RADAR*]   (FAAC)
BZR Gg ...... Beihefte. Zeitschrift fuer Religions und Geistesgeschichte [*A publication*]
B8ZS .... Bipolar with Eight-Zero Substitution [*Coding*] [*Telecommunications*]
BZ Sc .... Bachelor of Zoological Science
BZStF .... Biblische Zeit-und Streitfragen   (BJA)
BZT .... Brazoria, TX [*Location identifier*] [*FAA*]   (FAAL)
B Ztfr .... Biblische Zeitfragen [*A publication*]
BZThS .... Bonner Zeitschrift fuer Theologie und Seelsorge [*A publication*]
BZTS .... Bonner Zeitschrift fuer Theologie und Seelsorge [*A publication*]
BZU .... Buta [*Zaire*] [*Airport symbol*]   (OAG)
BZV .... Berliner Zionistische Vereinigung [*A publication*]   (BJA)
BZV .... Brazzaville [*People's Republic of the Congo*] [*Airport symbol*]   (OAG)
BZW .... Barclays de Zoete Wedd [*Investment firm*] [*British*]
BZW .... Bare Zirconium Wire
BZW .... Beziehungsweise [*Respectively*] [*German*]
BZWW ...... Beihefte. Zeitschrift Wirkendes Wort [*A publication*]
BZX .... Bank of Tanzania. Economic Bulletin [*A publication*]
BZX .... Bismarck, ND [*Location identifier*] [*FAA*]   (FAAL)

C

C................. [A] programming language [*Bell Telephone Laboratories*] [*1974*] (CSR)
C................. Acceleration Correction
C................. All India Reporter, Calcutta Series [*A publication*] (DLA)
C................. Ampere [*Unit of electric current*] (ROG)
C................. Basso Continuo [*Continued Bass*] [*Music*] (ROG)
C................. Business Class [*Also, J*] [*Airline fare code*]
C................. Byk-Gulden Lomberg [*Germany*] [*Research code symbol*]
C................. Cable
C................. Cactus [*Horticulture*]
C................. Cadet [*British military*] (DMA)
C................. Caecum
C................. Caesar [*100-44BC*] [*Roman general, statesman, and writer*]
C................. Cage Container (DCTA)
C................. Caius (ROG)
C................. Caledonian [*Railway*] [*Scotland*] (ROG)
C................. Calendae [*Calends*] [*The First Day of the Month*] [*Latin*]
C................. California Reports [*A publication*] (DLA)
C................. California State Library, Sacramento, CA [*Library symbol*] [*Library of Congress*] (LCLS)
C................. California Supreme Court Reports [*A publication*] (DLA)
C................. Calling-On [*Railroad signal arm*] [*British*]
C................. Calm [*i.e., no wind*]
C................. Calorie
C................. Calyx [*Botany*] (ROG)
C................. Cambridge [*Municipal borough in England*]
C................. Campaign [*A publication*]
C................. Can [*Buoy*] [*Maps and charts*]
C................. Canada
C................. Canada. Department of the Environment. Fisheries and Marine Service. Technical Report Series [*A publication*]
C................. Canceled
C................. Cancer
C................. Candela [*Formerly, Candlepower*] [*See also cd*] (MDG)
C................. Candela [*A publication*]
C................. Candle [*Illumination*]
C................. Canine [*Deciduous*] [*Dentistry*]
C................. Cannon Street Station [*London*] (ROG)
C................. Canoe
C................. Canon
C................. Canto (ROG)
C................. Capacitance [*Symbol*] [*IUPAC*]
C................. Capacitor (CET)
c................. Capacity [*Medicine*]
C................. Capacity [*Electricity*] (DAS)
C................. Cape [*Maps and charts*]
C................. Cape Provincial Division Reports [*South Africa*] [*A publication*] (DLA)
C................. Capitals [*Printing*]
C................. Capitulum [*Chapter*] [*Latin*] (ROG)
C................. Capo [*The Beginning*] [*Music*]
C................. Captain [*Worn on captain's uniform*] [*Hockey*]
C................. Captain
C................. Caput [*Head*] [*Latin*]
C................. Carat [*Unit of measure for precious stones or gold*]
C................. Carbohydrate [*Dietetics*]
C................. Carbon [*Chemical element*]
C................. Card [*Manuscript descriptions*]
C................. Cargo/Transport [*Designation for all US military aircraft*]
C................. Carnian [*Geology*]
C................. Carrier
C................. Carry
C................. Carton
C................. Case
C/-............. Case Packaging [*Shipping*] (DS)
C................. Cash [*Stock exchange term*] (SPSG)
C................. Cassenne [*France*] [*Research code symbol*]
C................. Cast (AAG)
C................. Castle
C................. Castrum Peregrini [*A publication*]
C................. Casualty [*Insurance*]

C................. Catalog
C................. Catalyst
C................. Catch [*Pisciculture*]
C................. Catcher [*Baseball*]
C................. Catechism
C................. Cathode
C................. Catholic
C................. Cattle (ROG)
C................. Caucasian
C................. Caudal [*Anatomy*]
C................. Caught [*by*] [*In cricket*]
C................. Caught Out
C................. Causa [*Case or Cause*]
C................. Cause
C................. Cavalry [*British military*] (DMA)
C................. Cavern (ROG)
C................. Ceiling [*Hazard limit*]
C................. [*Pope*] Celestine [*Authority cited in pre-1607 legal work*] (DSA)
C................. Cell
C................. Celsius [*Centigrade*] [*Temperature scale*]
C................. Celtic (ROG)
C................. Cenobio [*A publication*]
C................. Cenomanian [*Paleontology*]
C................. Censor (ROG)
C................. Cent [*Monetary unit*]
C................. Centavo [*Monetary unit in many Spanish-American countries*]
C................. Center [*A position in football, lacrosse, basketball*]
c................. Centi [*A prefix meaning divided by 100*] [*SI symbol*]
C................. Centigrade [*Celsius*] [*Temperature scale*]
C................. Centigram
C................. Centime [*Monetary unit*] [*France*]
C................. Centimeter
C................. Centissime (ROG)
C................. Cento [*Composition compiled from other works*]
C................. Central
C................. Central Standard Time (FAAC)
C................. Centrifugal
C................. Centum [*Hundred*]
C................. Century [*A publication*]
C................. Century
C................. Certified (AAG)
C................. Cervical [*Medicine*]
C................. Cervus [*Deer*] (ROG)
C................. Cessna Aircraft Co. [*ICAO aircraft manufacturer identifier*] (ICAO)
C................. Chairman [*or Chairwoman or Chairperson*]
C................. Chancellor
C................. Chancery
C................. Change [*Army*] [*Used in combinations only*] (AABC)
C................. Chapel
C................. Chapter
C................. Character (BUR)
C................. Charge (ROG)
C................. Charge Conjugation [*Atomic physics*]
C................. Charles Curtis [*Genotype of Phlox paniculata*]
C................. Charlie [*Phonetic alphabet*] [*International since 1956*] (DSUE)
C................. Charlotte [*North Carolina*] [*Mint mark, when appearing on US coins*]
c................. Charmed (Quark) [*Atomic physics*]
C................. Chemisches Zentralblatt [*A publication*]
C................. Chemistry [*Secondary school course*] [*British*]
C................. Chest [*Tea trade*] (ROG)
C................. Chest [*Medicine*]
C................. Chief
C................. Child
C................. Chlorambucil [*Also, CHL, CMB*] [*Antineoplastic drug*]
C................. Chloramphenicol [*Antimicrobial compound*]
C................. Choppy, Short, or Cross Sea [*Navigation*]
C................. Christian
C................. Chrominance [*Video monitor*]

C................	Chronium (ROG)
C................	Chronometer Time [*Navigation*]
C................	Chrysler Corp. [*NYSE symbol*] [*Toronto Stock Exchange symbol*] (SPSG)
C................	Church
C................	Churchwarden
C................	Ciba-Geigy AG [*Switzerland*] [*Research code symbol*]
C................	Cibus [*Meal*] [*Latin*]
C................	Cilag-Chemie AG [*Switzerland*] [*Research code symbol*]
C................	Cimetidine [*Pharmacology*]
C................	Cinemas [*Public-performance tariff class*] [*British*]
c................	Circa [*or Circiter or Circum*] [*About (used with dates denoting approximate time)*] [*Latin*] (GPO)
C................	Circle [*Freemasonry*] (ROG)
C................	Circling [*Approach and landing charts*] [*Aviation*]
C................	Circuit
C................	Circular
C................	Circum
C................	Circumference
C................	Circumlocution [*Used in correcting manuscripts, etc.*]
C................	Cirrus [*Meteorology*]
C................	Cited (DLA)
C................	City [*Maps and charts*]
c................	Civil [*Legal term*] (DLA)
C................	Class [*Used with number for Navy rating as: 1c; i.e., first class*]
C................	Class "C" Preferred or Common Stock [*Investment term*]
C................	Classical
C................	Clean
C................	Clear [*Calculators*]
C................	Clearance
C................	Cleverness Factor [*Psychology*]
C................	Cliff (ROG)
C................	Climb [*Aviation*] (FAAC)
C................	Clipped [*Ecology*]
C................	Clock
C................	Clockwise
C................	Clonus
C................	Closed
C................	Closure [*Medicine*]
C................	Cloudy [*Meteorology*]
C................	Club
C................	Coagulase [*An enzyme*]
C................	Coarse [*Agronomy*]
C................	Coarse [*Appearance of bacterial colony*]
C................	Coast Guard [*Military flight identification prefix*] (FAAC)
C................	Coastal-Nonrigid Airship [*Royal Naval Air Service*] [*British*]
C................	Cobalt [*Chemical symbol is Co*]
C................	Cobbly [*Agronomy*]
C................	Cocaine [*Slang*]
C................	Code (DLA)
C................	Codex
C................	Codex Ephaemi [*Ephraem the Syrian*] [*A publication*] (ROG)
C................	Codex Juris Civilis [*A publication*] (ILCA)
C................	Coefficient
C................	Coffin [*Missile launch environment symbol*]
C................	Cognate
C................	Cognitive
C................	Coil [*Genetics*]
C................	Coimbra [*A publication*]
C................	Col [*With The*] [*Music*]
C................	Cold
C................	Colla [*With The*] [*Music*] (ROG)
C................	Collateral
C................	Collector [*Electronics*]
C................	College
C................	Collier's [*A publication*]
C................	Colon [*Monetary unit*] [*Costa Rica, El Salvador*]
C................	Colonel (ROG)
C................	Color
C................	Color Detail [*Rorschach*] [*Psychology*]
C................	Color Index
C................	Colorado [*Dark-colored cigar*]
C................	Colt [*Thoroughbred racing*]
C................	Columbia [*Record Label*] [*Great Britain, Europe, Australia, etc.*]
C................	Columbia Journalism Review [*A publication*]
C................	Combat [*In unit designations and symbols only*]
C................	Command (ROG)
C................	Command Paper
C................	Commandant [*Coast Guard*]
C................	Commander [*Usually in combination, as: CNAB for Commander, Naval Air Bases*]
C................	Commanding Officer
C................	Commerce Department
C................	Commercial Bank (ROG)
C................	Commissary [*Marine Corps*]
C................	Commodore [*Navy*] [*British*] (ROG)
C................	Common [*Ecology*]
C................	Common Entrance [*Examination for entry into public school*] [*British*]
C................	Common Meter [*Music*]
C................	Common (Noun) [*Linguistics*]
C................	Common Time
C................	Commonweal [*A publication*]
C................	Communications
C................	Compact [*Car size*]
C................	Compania [*Company, Society*] [*Spanish*]
C................	Companion
C................	Compass
C................	Compatible
C................	Complement [*Immunochemistry*]
C................	Complement [*Linguistics*]
C................	Complete (NASA)
C................	Complex
C................	Complexity
C................	Compliance
C................	Composite (ROG)
C................	Compositus [*Compound*] [*Pharmacy*]
C................	Compound [*Engines*] [*Lloyd's Register*] [*Shipping*]
C................	Comprehensive School [*British*]
C................	Compression
C................	Compte [*Account*] [*Business term*] [*French*] (GPO)
C................	Comptroller
C................	Compulsory
C................	Compute [*or Computer*] (MDG)
C................	Con [*With*] [*Music*] (ROG)
C................	Concealed [*Ecology*]
C................	Concentration
c................	Concentration by Volume [*Chemistry*]
C................	Concisus [*Cut*] [*Medicine*]
C................	Concurrent
c................	Condemnation [*Legal term*] (DLA)
C................	Condemned
C................	Condemno [*I Condemn*] [*Used by Romans in criminal trials*] [*Latin*]
c................	Condenser
C................	Conditioning [*Neurophysiology*]
C................	Conductivity
C................	Conductor
C................	Confessor
C................	Confidential
C................	Congius [*Gallon*] [*Pharmacy*]
C................	Congregation
C................	Congress
C................	Congressional (ROG)
C................	Conservative [*Politics*]
C................	Consonant [*Linguistics*]
C................	Consortium
C................	Constable
C................	Constant
C................	Constant Region [*Immunochemistry*]
C................	Constructor [*Freemasonry*] (ROG)
C................	Consul [*or Consulate*]
C................	Consul [*License plate code assigned to foreign diplomats in the US*]
C................	Consultant in Dental Surgery [*Medical Officer designation*] [*British*]
C................	Consultation [*Medicine*]
C................	Consumption
C................	Contact
C................	Contact Publishers [*Holland*]
C................	Container (DCTA)
C................	Continental [*Air mass*]
C................	Continuous [*Botany*]
C................	Continuous Operation during Hours Shown [*Broadcasting*]
C................	Conto [*Account*] [*Italian*]
C................	Contra [*Against*] [*Latin*]
C................	Contraction
C................	Contralateral [*Anatomy*]
C................	Contralto [*Music*]
C................	Contrast (ADA)
C................	Control
C................	Control [*Officer's rating*] [*British Royal Navy*]
C................	Controlled [*Currency exchange rate*] [*British*]
C................	Controls [*JETDS nomenclature*] [*Military*] (CET)
C................	Contusus [*Bruised*] [*Medicine*]
C................	Convection (ADA)
C................	Convict (ADA)
C................	Cook [*Ranking title*] [*British Women's Royal Naval Service*]
C................	Cooker
C................	Copper [*Chemical symbol is Cu*]
C................	Coppered
C................	Copy
C................	Copyhold [*British*] [*Legal term*] (ROG)
C................	Copyright
C................	Cord
C................	Cordoba [*Monetary unit*] [*Nicaragua*]
C................	Corinthians [*New Testament book*] (BJA)
C................	Corolla
C................	Corps
C................	Corpus [*Body*] [*Latin*] (DLA)
C................	Correction

C...............	Correspondent [*A publication*]
C...............	Cortex [*Anatomy*]
C...............	Corundum [*CIPW classification*] [*Geology*]
C...............	Cost
C...............	Costa [*Rib*] [*Anatomy*]
C...............	Cotton (AAG)
C...............	Cotyledon [*Botany*]
C...............	Cough [*Medicine*]
C...............	Coulomb [*Symbol*] [*SI unit of electric charge*]
C...............	Councillor (ROG)
C...............	Count
C...............	Counter
C...............	Counter-Tenor [*Music*]
C...............	Country
C...............	County
c...............	Coupon [*Coupon*] [*French*]
C...............	Coupon
c...............	Coupure [*Denomination*] [*Business term*] [*French*]
c...............	Cours [*Quotation, Price*] [*French*]
C...............	Course Angle [*Navigation*]
C...............	Course Winner [*Horse racing*]
C...............	Court
C...............	Cousin
C...............	Cove [*Maps and charts*]
C...............	Cover [*of a magazine*]
C...............	Crane Engines [*Trains*] [*British*]
C...............	Created
C...............	Creosote [*Telecommunications*] (TEL)
C...............	Critica [*A publication*]
c...............	Criticised [*Soundness of decision or reasoning in cited case criticised for reasons given*] [*Used in Shephard's Citations*] [*Legal term*] (DLA)
C...............	Critique [*A publication*]
C...............	Cross (ADA)
C...............	Crossed [*Stereo images*]
C...............	Crowned
C...............	Cruiser
C...............	Crystalline
C...............	Cuba
C...............	Cubic
C...............	Cum [*With*] [*Latin*]
C...............	Cumulus [*Cloud*] [*Meteorology*]
C...............	Cup
C...............	Curacy [*or Curate*]
C...............	Curie [*Unit of radioactivity*] [*See Ci*]
C...............	Currency
C...............	Current
C...............	Current Expenditure [*Economics*]
C...............	Currentis [*Of the Current Month or Year*] [*Latin*]
C...............	Cushion Lift (AAG)
C...............	Cuticle
C...............	Cycle [*Electricity*]
c...............	Cyclic [*Biochemistry*]
C...............	Cyclohexane [*Organic chemistry*]
C...............	Cyclophosphamide [*Cytoxan*] [*Antineoplastic drug*]
C...............	Cylinder
C...............	Cylindrical [*Leaf characteristic*] [*Botany*]
C...............	Cysteine [*One-letter symbol*] [*Also, Cys, CySH*]
C...............	Cytidine [*One-letter symbol; see Cyd*]
C...............	Cytosine [*Also, Cyt*] [*Biochemistry*]
c...............	Deaza [*As substituent on nucleoside*] [*Biochemistry*]
°C...............	Degrees Celsius
C...............	[*Term of reference for the*] Director of Britain's Secret Intelligence Service [*Said to date from the desire for anonymity on the part of the department's first director, Sir Mansfield Cumming*]
C...............	E. R. Squibb & Sons [*Research code symbol*]
C...............	Electrical Equipment [*Fire classification*]
C...............	Fairly Reliable Source of Intelligence Information
C...............	[*Sir Stewart*] Graham [*A British intelligence agent during World War II*]
C...............	Heat Capacity [*Symbol*] [*IUPAC*]
C...............	Imperfect Time [*Represents an incomplete circle and refers to 4/4 time*] [*Music*]
C...............	Income Not Paying Interest [*Standard & Poor's bond rating*]
C...............	Indian Law Reports, Calcutta Series [*A publication*] (DLA)
C...............	Institut Pasteur [*France*] [*Research code symbol*]
c-----	Intercontinental Areas (Western Hemisphere) [*MARC geographic area code*] [*Library of Congress*] (LCCP)
C...............	Lab. Sopharga [*France*] [*Research code symbol*]
C...............	Lord Chancellor (DLA)
C...............	Lowest [*Moody's bond rating*] [*Investment term*]
C...............	Medium Narrow [*Men's shoe width*]
C...............	Medium Wide [*Women's shoe width*]
C...............	Minor league baseball league classification [*Sixth highest rank, for a league composed of teams from cities with aggregate population of 150,000 to 250,000*]
C...............	One Hundred [*Roman numeral*]
C...............	One Hundred Dollar Bill [*C Note*] [*Slang*]
C...............	Protected Cruiser [*Navy symbol*] [*Obsolete*]
C...............	Series "C" Bonds or Debentures [*Investment term*]
C...............	Shape Descriptor [*C-clamp, for example. The shape resembles the letter for which it is named*]
c...............	Specific Heat Capacity [*Symbol*] [*IUPAC*]
c...............	Speed of Light in Vacuum [*Symbol*]
c...............	Velocity of Sound [*Symbol*] [*IUPAC*]
C1...............	Canadian Canoe, Single Person (ADA)
C1...............	Chief Petty Officer, First Class [*Navy*] [*Canadian*]
C-1...............	First Cervical Vertebra [*Second cervical vertebra is C-2, etc., through C-7*] [*Medicine*]
1-C.............	Selective Service Class [*for a Member of Armed Forces of the US, the National Oceanic and Atmospheric Administration, or the Public Health Service*]
1/C.............	Single Conductor [*Wire or cable*]
C2...............	Canadian Canoe, Two Person (ADA)
C2...............	Chief Petty Officer, Second Class [*Navy*] [*Canadian*]
C²...............	Command and Control [*Pronounced "see-squared"*]
2-C.............	Selective Service Class [*for Registrant Deferred from Military Service Because of Agricultural Occupation*]
2/C.............	Two-Conductor [*Wire or cable*]
C³...............	Command and Control Center
C³...............	Command, Control, and Communications [*Pronounced "see-cubed"*]
C3...............	Complement Component Three [*Hematology*]
3C...............	Equatorial Guinea [*Aircraft nationality and registration mark*] (FAAC)
3/C.............	Three-Conductor [*Wire or cable*]
C4...............	Channel 4 [*Television*] [*British*]
C⁴...............	Command, Control, Communications, and Computer Systems (NVT)
C-4.............	Composition-4 [*Explosive*]
C-4.............	Computer-Controlled Catalytic Converter [*General Motors Corp.*]
4C...............	Four Color [*Printing*]
4/C.............	Four-Conductor [*Wire or cable*]
4-C.............	Selective Service Class [*for Aliens Not Currently Liable for Military Service*]
7/C.............	Seven-Conductor [*Wire or cable*] (MSA)
C¹⁴.............	Radioactive Carbon [*Key substance for determination of age of objects by measurement of radioactivity*]
C33.............	Prisoner identification number assigned to Oscar Wilde in Reading Gaol [*Used as pseudonym*]
C63.............	Cinemists 63 (EA)
C77.............	Cinema 77 [*A publication*]
C 83............	Cinema 83 [*A publication*]
C22-83-9	Construction Reports. C22-83-9. Housing Completions [*A publication*]
C25-83-9	Construction Reports. C25-83-9. New One-Family Houses Sold and for Sale [*A publication*]
C40-85-5	Construction Reports. C40-85-5. Housing Units Authorized by Building Permits and Public Contracts [*A publication*]
3C's............	Character, Capacity, Capital [*Accounting*]
4C's............	Cotton, Climate, Cattle, and Citrus [*Traditional elements of Arizona's economy*]
4C's............	Cut, Carat, Clarity, Color [*Factors in determining the value of a diamond*]
5C's............	Character, Capacity, Capital, Collateral, and Conditions [*Credit evaluation*] [*Banking*]
C (Bomb)....	Cobalt Bomb [*Nuclear*]
C (Colds)....	Catarrhal Colds [*Medicine*]
C (Print).....	Color Print [*Publishing*]
C (Section) ...	Caesarean Section [*Medicine*]
CA...............	Assistant Commandant [*Coast Guard*]
CA...............	CA. A Bulletin of Cancer Progress [*A publication*]
CA...............	CA. A Cancer Journal for Clinicians [*A publication*]
CA...............	Cable (MSA)
CA...............	Cable Assembly
CA...............	Cable Authority [*British*]
Ca...............	[*Guillelmus de*] Cabriano [*Deceased, 1201*] [*Authority cited in pre-1607 legal work*] (DSA)
CA...............	Cadmium Association [*London, England*] (EAIO)
CA...............	Caffeic Acid [*Organic chemistry*]
Ca...............	Calcareous [*Quality of the bottom*] [*Nautical charts*]
Ca...............	Calcium [*Chemical element*]
CA...............	Calibrated Altitude [*Navigation*]
CA...............	California [*Postal code*]
CA...............	California Appellate Reports [*A publication*] (DLA)
CA...............	Callable Bond [*Investment term*]
CA...............	Camanachd Association (EA)
CA...............	Cambodian Appeal [*Inactive*] (EA)
CA...............	Canada [*ANSI two-letter standard code*] (CNC)
CA...............	Canadian Army
CA...............	Canamin Resources [*Vancouver Stock Exchange symbol*]
CA...............	Cancer [*or Carcinoma*] [*Medicine*]
Ca...............	Candle
CA...............	Candy Apple [*Bowdlerized version*]
CA...............	Cant [*or Canting*] [*Heraldry*]
CA...............	Cantors Assembly (EA)
CA...............	Cape
CA...............	Capital Account [*Finance*]
CA...............	Capital Airlines, Inc.
CA...............	Capital Appreciation [*Business term*]

CA.............. Capital Asset
CA.............. Car Accountant
CA.............. Car Assembly
ca.............. Carbonate Accumulation [*Archeology*]
CA.............. Carbonic Anhydrase [*An enzyme*]
CA.............. Carcinoma
CA.............. Cardiac Arrest [*Medicine*]
CA.............. Cardinal
CA.............. Cargo Ship
CA.............. Caribbean Area [*Services to the Armed Forces*] [*Red Cross*]
CA.............. Carrier Aircraft (MCD)
CA.............. Carries Ampholytes [*Chemistry*]
CA.............. Carry
CA.............. Cartographic Assistant [*Ministry of Agriculture, Fisheries, and Food*] [*British*]
CA.............. Cascade Amplifier (DEN)
Ca.............. Case [*Legal term*] (ILCA)
CA.............. Case Aide [*Red Cross*]
CA.............. Cash Account [*Banking*]
CA.............. Cashier and Accountant [*British*] (ROG)
CA.............. Castles Association (EA)
CA.............. Cat Allergen [*Immunology*]
CA.............. Catboat Association (EA)
CA.............. Catch per Angler [*Pisciculture*]
CA.............. Catecholamine [*or Catecholaminergic*] [*Biochemistry*]
CA.............. Category
CA.............. Catenarian Arch [*Freemasonry*] (ROG)
CA.............. Caterer [*Military*] [*British*]
CA.............. Catering Accountant [*British military*] (DMA)
CA.............. Cathode
CA.............. Catholic Action
Ca.............. Caudality Scale [*Psychology*]
Ca.............. Causa [*Decretum Gratiani*] [*A publication*] (DSA)
CA.............. Cavan [*County in Ireland*] (ROG)
CA.............. Celiac Axis [*Anatomy*]
CA.............. Cell Attached [*Microbiology*]
CA.............. Cellulose Acetate [*Organic chemistry; plastics*]
CA.............. Census Agglomeration [*Canada*]
CA.............. Centare [*Unit of area in metric system*]
CA.............. Center for Astrophysics [*Harvard-Smithsonian*]
CA.............. Central Airways Corp. (AAG)
CA.............. Central America
CA.............. Central Area
CA.............. Cephalic Artery
CA.............. Cercetari Arheologice [*A publication*]
CA.............. Cerebral Aqueduct [*Brain anatomy*]
CA.............. Cerebrovascular Amyloid [*Medicine*]
C of A........ Certificate of Airworthiness
CA.............. Certificate of Airworthiness
C of A........ Certificate of Analysis
CA.............. Cervicoaxial [*Dentistry*]
CA.............. Chancery Appeal Cases, English Law Reports [*A publication*] (DLA)
CA.............. Chances Accepted [*Baseball*]
CA.............. Change Administration
CA.............. Channel Adapter [*Data processing*] (IBMDP)
CA.............. Charge d'Affaires [*Foreign Service*]
CA.............. Charge Amplifier (NRCH)
CA.............. Chargeable to Accidents (MCD)
CA.............. Chartered Accountant
C/A.............. Chartered Agent [*Business term*]
CA.............. Checks Anonymous
CA.............. Chemical Abstracts [*Chemical Abstracts Service*] [*Database*] [*A publication*]
CA.............. Chemical Addition and Sampling System [*Nuclear energy*] (NRCH)
C A.............. Chemical Age [*A publication*]
C/A.............. Cheque Account [*British*] [*Banking*] (ADA)
C & A........ Chicago & Alton Railroad Co. [*Also known as Alton*]
CA.............. Chief Accountant
CA.............. Chief Advisor
CA.............. Children of the Americas (EA)
CA.............. Chile Alert (EA)
CA.............. Chinese Army (CINC)
CA.............. Chloramphetamine [*Neurochemistry*]
CA.............. Chloranil [*Organic chemistry*]
CA.............. Chlorendic Acid [*Organic chemistry*]
CA.............. Chlorendic Anhydride [*Also, CAN*] [*Organic chemistry*]
CA.............. Choline-Adrenalin [*Test*] [*Medicine*]
CA.............. Christ Alongside (EA)
CA.............. Christian Army (ROG)
CA.............. Chronological Age [*Psychology*]
CA.............. Church Administration [*A publication*]
CA.............. Church Army [*British*]
CA.............. Church Army [*An association*] (EA)
CA.............. Church Association [*British*]
CA.............. Churchman Associates (EA)
ca.............. Circa [*or Circiter or Circum*] [*About (used with dates denoting approximate time)*] [*Latin*]
CA.............. Circular Arc [*Aviation*]
CA.............. cis-Aconityl [*Organic radical*]

CA.............. Citizens Advocacy
CA.............. Citizens for Animals [*Inactive*] (EA)
CA.............. Civic Action
CA.............. Civil Affairs
CA.............. Civil Agency
CA.............. Civil Authorities
CA.............. Civil Aviation
CA.............. Civil Aviation Administration of China - CAAC [*China*] [*ICAO designator*] (FAAC)
CA.............. Claim Agent [*Insurance*]
CA.............. Clamshell Alliance (EA)
CA.............. Classical America (EA)
CA.............. Classical Association (EAIO)
CA.............. Classics of Art [*A publication*]
C & A........ Classification and Audit (AFM)
CA.............. Clear and Add
CA.............. Clear Aperture (MSA)
CA.............. Clerical Aptitude [*Test*]
CA.............. Clerical Assistant [*Civil Service*] [*British*]
CA.............. Clipped and Ash [*Ecology*]
CA.............. Clipping Amplifier
CA.............. Close Annealed [*Metal industry*]
CA.............. Closest Approach [*Aerospace*]
CA.............. Clothing Allowance [*British military*] (DMA)
CA.............. Clowns of America [*Later, CAI*] (EA)
CA.............. Club Anri [*Commercial firm*] (EA)
CA.............. Club Aquarius (EA)
CA.............. Coagulation [*Test*]
CA.............. Coalitions for America (EA)
CA.............. Coarse Alignment
CA.............. Coast Alliance [*Defunct*] (EA)
CA.............. Coast Artillery
C/A.............. Coat of Arms (AABC)
CA.............. Coaxial (AAG)
CA.............. Cocaine Anonymous (EA)
CA.............. Codex Aleppensis (BJA)
CA.............. Cold Acclimated [*Physiology*]
CA.............. Cold Agglutination [*Test*] [*Clinical chemistry*]
CA.............. Cold Air
CA.............. Coll'arco [*With the Bow*] [*Music*]
CA.............. Colloid Antigen [*Immunology*]
CA.............. Colonial Allowance [*British military*] (DMA)
CA.............. Color Association of the United States
CA.............. Combat Aircrew [*or Aircrewman*]
CA.............. Combat Assault
CA.............. Combined Arms (AABC)
CA.............. Command Accountant [*Military*] [*British*]
CA.............. Command Action (NATG)
C & A........ Command and Administration
CA.............. Commandant Assistant [*Coast Guard*]
CA.............. Commercial Activities
CA.............. Commercial Agent
CA.............. Commercial Air
CA.............. Commercial Art Program [*Association of Independent Colleges and Schools specialization code*]
CA.............. Commissioner of Accounts
CA.............. Commissural and Association [*Anatomy*]
CA.............. Commitment Authorization
CA.............. Common Antigen [*Immunochemistry*]
CA.............. Communication Arts [*A publication*]
CA.............. Communications Adapter
CA.............. Communist Activities [*British*]
CA.............. Commutator Assemblies [*SONAR*] (MCD)
Ca.............. Compagnia [*Company*] [*Italian*] (GPO)
Ca.............. Companhia [*Company*] [*Portuguese*]
ca.............. Compania [*Company, Society*] [*Spanish*]
CA.............. Compania Anonima [*Joint Stock Company*] [*Spanish*] (CED)
C & A........ Compartment and Access [*Technical drawings*]
CA.............. Compensation Act [*Forms*]
CA.............. Competent Authority
CA.............. Compressed Air (AAG)
CA.............. Comptroller of Accounts
CA.............. Comptroller of the Army
CA.............. Computer Assembly
CA.............. Computer Associates International, Inc. [*NYSE symbol*] (SPSG)
CA.............. Computer Automation, Inc. [*Richardson, TX*] (TSSD)
CA.............. Computers and Automation (BUR)
CA.............. CONCERN/America (EA)
CA.............. Concert Artist [*Record label*] [*Great Britain*]
CA.............. Conchologists of America (EA)
CA.............. Condylomata Acuminata [*Medicine*]
CA.............. Cone Angle [*NASA*] (NASA)
CA.............. Confederate Army
CA.............. Configuration Alternative (MCD)
CA.............. Configured Article
CA.............. Confirming Authority [*Australia*]
CA.............. Conflict Alert [*Aviation*]
CA.............. Connecting Arrangement [*Telecommunications*]

CA	Conseil d'Administration [*Board of Directors (of a private organization, company, fund, or governmental or other financial body)*] [*Administrative Council (of a political party, university, or non-financial governmental unit)*]
CA	Constant Amplitude
CA	Constituent Assembly [*Vietnam*]
CA	Construction Authorization (NRCH)
CA	Constructionman, Apprentice [*Navy rating*]
CA	Constructive Availability (CAAL)
CA	Consular Agent
CA	Consultant-Adviser
CA	Consultant Agreement (MCD)
CA	Consumer Alert (EA)
CA	Consumers' Association (EAIO)
c/a	Conta Aberta [*Unsettled Account*] [*Business term*] [*Portuguese*]
CA	Contact Adhesive
CA	Contact Area, Articular [*Medicine*]
CA	Contemporary Authors [*A publication*]
CA	Continental Airways (AAG)
CA	Continental Assurance Co.
CA	Contingencies of the Army
CA	Contingency Abort [*NASA*] (NASA)
CA	Continue-Any [*Mode*] [*Data processing*] (IBMDP)
CA	Continuous-Action [*Pharmacy*]
CA	Contract Administration [*or Administrator*] [*DoD*]
CA	Contract Authorization
CA	Contract Award
CA	Contracting Activity
CA	Contractor-Assisted
CA	Control Area [*Data processing*]
CA	Control Armourer [*British military*] (DMA)
CA	Control Assembly
CA	Control Augmentation
CA	Controlled Atmosphere
CA	Controller of Accounts
CA	Convening Authority
CA	Convention Africaine [*African Covenant*]
C & A	Cooke and Alcock's Irish King's Bench Reports [*1833-34*] [*A publication*] (DLA)
CA	Cooperative Agreement
CA	Coopers Appreciation [*An association*] (EA)
CA	Cor Anglais [*English Horn*]
CA	Coracoacromial [*Anatomy*]
CA	Coriolis Absorber
CA	Cornu Ammonis [*Anatomy*]
CA	Coronary Artery [*Medicine*]
CA	Corpora Alata [*Insect anatomy*]
CA	Corpora Amylacea [*Neurology*]
CA	Corps Adjutant [*British military*] (DMA)
C d'A	Corps d'Afrique
C of A	Corps of Armourers [*British military*] (DMA)
CA	Corpus Allatum
CA	Correct [*an error*] or Amplify [*information*] [*US Copyright Office form*]
CA	Corrective Action (MCD)
C/A	Corrente Anno [*Current Year*] [*Italian*]
CA	Correspondence Aid [*A publication*]
CA	Cortisone Acetate [*Endocrinology*]
CA	Cosmopolitan Associates [*Later, OC*]
ca	Cost About
CA	Cost Account [*Accounting*]
CA	Cost Accountant [*Accounting*] (AABC)
C/A	Cost of Arms [*Army*] (AABC)
CA	Council Accepted [*Medicine*]
CA	Council of the Alleghenies (EA)
CA	Counselor Association (EA)
CA	Counter Air (MCD)
C/A	Counterattack
CA	Countryside Act [*Town planning*] [*British*]
CA	County Alderman [*British*]
CA	County Architect [*British*]
CA	County Attorney
CA	Coupons Attached [*Business term*]
CA	Courant Alternatif [*Alternating Current*] [*French*]
CA	Courier Aircrafts Ltd. [*Australia*]
CA	Course Alignment
CA	Court of Appeal
CA	Court of Appeals Reports [*New Zealand*] [*A publication*] (DLA)
CA	Court of Arches [*England*] (DLA)
CA	Court of Customs Appeals Reports [*1919-29*] [*A publication*] (DLA)
CA	Court of Customs and Patent Appeals Reports [*A publication*] (DLA)
CA	Courtship Analysis [*Psychology*]
CA	Cover Aft
CA	Crab Apple (EA)
CA	Cranial Academy (EA)
CA	Crank Angle (MCD)
CA	Credit Account [*Business term*]
CA	Credit Associate [*Designation awarded by Society of Certified Consumer Credit Executives*]
CA	Creel Associates, Inc. [*Oak Brook, IL*] (TSSD)
CA	Critica d'Arte [*A publication*]
CA	Critical Assembly [*Nuclear energy*] (NRCH)
CA	Criticality Analysis (KSC)
CA	Cromwell Association (EA)
CA	Croquet Association [*British*]
CA	Croup-Associated [*Virus*]
CA	Crown Agent
CA	Cruise Altitude [*Aviation*]
CA	Cruising Association [*London, England*] (EAIO)
CA	Ctenidial Analog [*Biology*]
CA	Cuadernos Americanos [*A publication*]
CA	Cuadra Associates, Inc. [*Information service or system*] (IID)
CA	Cuenta Abierta [*Open Account*] [*Spanish*] [*Business term*]
CA	Curates' Alliance [*British*]
CA	Curing Agent
CA	Current Account [*Business term*]
CA	Current Analysis [*Program*] [*Department of State*]
CA	Current Anthropology [*A publication*]
CA	Current Asset [*Business term*]
CA	Curse of Agade (BJA)
CA	Custodian Account [*Banking*]
CA	Customs Act [*Canada*]
CA	Cyanoacrylate Adhesive
CA	Cyclohexenedicarboxylic Acid [*Organic chemistry*]
CA	Cypriote Archaic (BJA)
CA	Cyproterone Acetate [*Endocrinology*]
CA	Cyprus Airways Ltd. (IMH)
CA	Cytarabine [*Cytosine arabinoside*] [*Also, ara-C, CAR*] [*Antineoplastic drug*]
CA	Gun Cruiser [*Navy symbol*]
CA	Office of Congressional Affairs [*Energy Research and Development Administration*] (NRCH)
CA	Recueils de Jurisprudence. Cour d'Appel [*Quebec, Canada*] [*A publication*]
CA	SONAR Commutator Assemblies [*JETDS nomenclature*] [*Military*] (CET)
Ca	Speculative - Often in Default [*Moody's bond rating*]
CA	United States Court of Appeals [*Formerly, United States Circuit Court of Appeals*]
CA: 80's	Congressional Agenda: 80's [*Later, CA: 90's*] (EA)
CA: 90's	Congressional Agenda: 90's (EA)
CAA	Caging Amplifier Assembly
CA A	California Appellate Reports [*A publication*] (DLA)
CAA	Camara de Industria y Comercio Argentino-Alemana [*A publication*]
CAA	Cambridge Acoustical Associates, Inc. (MCD)
CAA	Canadian Acoustical Association
CAA	Canadian Archaeological Association [*SA ACA*]
CAA	Canadian Authors Association
CAA	Canadian Automobile Association
CAA	Canberra [*Australia*] [*Geomagnetic observatory code*]
CAA	Cantors Assembly of America [*Later, CA*] (EA)
CAA	Carriage Association of America (EA)
CAA	Casamino Acids [*Biochemistry*]
CAA	Catear Resources Ltd. [*Vancouver Stock Exchange symbol*]
CAA	Catholic Aid Association (EA)
CAA	Catholic Anthropological Association [*Defunct*] (EA)
CAA	Catholic Art Association [*Defunct*] (EA)
CAA	Cement Admixtures Association (EAIO)
CAA	Center for American Archeology (EA)
CAA	Central African Airways Corp.
CAA	Central American Airways [*Louisville, KY*] [*FAA designator*] (FAAC)
CAA	Central Assets Account [*Finance*]
CAA	Chanaral [*Chile*] [*Seismograph station code, US Geological Survey*] (SEIS)
CAA	Chaplains' Aid Association [*Later, CAA/SEF*] (EA)
CAA	Chemical Agent Alarm
CAA	Chester Alan Arthur [*US president, 1829-1886*]
CAA	Chief Aircraft Artificer [*British military*] (DMA)
CAA	Chief of Army Aviation
CAA	Chile-American Association (EA)
CAA	Chinese for Affirmative Action (EA)
CAA	Chinese Astronomy and Astrophysics [*A publication*]
CAA	Chiropractic Advancement Association [*British*]
CAA	Cigar Association of America (EA)
CAA	Cinema Advertising Association [*British*]
CAA	Circular Aperture Antenna
CAA	Citizens Assessment Administration
CAA	Civil Aeronautics Administration [*Later, part of FAA*]
CAA	Civil Aeronautics Authority Reports [*A publication*] (DLA)
CAA	Civil Affairs Association (EA)
CAA	Civil Air Attache [*British*]
CAA	Civil Aviation Agency [*Australia*]
CAA	Civil Aviation Authority [*British*] [*Australia*]
CAA	Clean Air Act [*1963, 1990*]
CAA	Coalition of Automotive Associations [*Defunct*] (EA)
CAA	Collectors of American Art (EA)

CAA .... College Art Association (EA)
CAA .... Collision Avoidance Aid
CAA .... Colombian American Association (EA)
CAA .... Combined Arms Army (MCD)
CAA .... Comite des Amities Acadiennes [*Acadian Friendship Committee - AFC*] (EAIO)
CAA .... Commission on Art and Antiquities
CAA .... Commonwealth Arbitration Awards and Determinations [*A publication*] (APTA)
CAA .... Commonwealth Archivists Association [*Later, ACARM*] (EA)
CAA .... Commonwealth Association of Architects [*London, England*] (EAIO)
CAA .... Community Action Agencies [*Community Services Administration*]
CAA .... Computer Amplifier Alarm
CAA .... Computer-Assisted Accounting (BUR)
CAA .... Computing Across America [*From book title, "Computing Across America: The Bicycle Odyssey of a High-Tech Nomad" by Steven K. Roberts*]
CAA .... Concept Analysis (MCD)
CAA .... Concepts Analysis Agency [*Bethesda, MD*] [*Army*] (AABC)
CAA .... Conciliation and Arbitration Act [*Australia*] (ADA)
CAA .... Confederation Arabe d'Athletisme [*Arab Amateur Athletic Federation - AAAF*] (EAIO)
CAA .... Conference on Asian Affairs [*Later, AS*] (MCD)
CAA .... Conseil Africain de l'Arachide [*African Groundnut Council*] (EAIO)
CAA .... Constitutional Aplastic Anemia [*Medicine*]
CAA .... Controlled Access Area (MCD)
CAA .... Coronary Artery Aneurysm [*Cardiology*]
CAA .... Correctional Administrators Association of America [*Later, ASCA*] (EA)
CAA .... Council of Association Attorneys (EA)
CAA .... Cowboy Artists of America (EA)
CAA .... Creative Artists Agency
CAA .... Cremation Association of America [*Later, CANA*] (EA)
CAA .... Crime Aboard Aircraft
CAA .... Croatian Academy of America (EA)
CAA .... Crypto Access Authorization [*Military*] (AABC)
CAA .... Cyanoacrylate Adhesive
Caa .... Poor Standing [*Moody's bond rating*]
CAAA .... California Agricultural Aircraft Association (EA)
CAAA .... Canadian Academic Accounting Association [*See also ACPC*]
CAAA .... Chief of Army Audit Agency
CAAA .... Clean Air Act Amendment
CAAA .... Coast Artillery Antiaircraft
CAAA .... College Art Association of America [*Later, CAA*] (EA)
CAAA .... Commuter Airline Association of America [*Later, RAA*] (EA)
CAAA .... Composers, Authors, and Artists of America
CAAA .... Crane Army Ammunition Activity (AABC)
CaAAAR.... Alberta Department of Agriculture, Regional Office, Airdrie, AB, Canada [*Library symbol*] [*Library of Congress*] (LCLS)
CaAAiM .... Airdrie Municipal Library, Airdrie, AB, Canada [*Library symbol*] [*Library of Congress*] (LCLS)
CAAAL...... Classified Abstract Archive of the Alcohol Literature
CaAAM ..... Acme Municipal Library, Acme, AB, Canada [*Library symbol*] [*Library of Congress*] (LCLS)
CAAA-MWD ... Commanding Army Audit Agency - Midwestern District
CAAAP/AP ... Amazonia Peruana. Centro Amazonico de Antropologia y Aplicacion Practica. Departamento de Documentacion y Publicaciones [*A publication*]
CAAAV ..... Coalition Against Anti-Asian Violence (EA)
CaAB .... Banff Library, Banff, AB, Canada [*Library symbol*] [*Library of Congress*] (LCLS)
CAAB .... California Apricot Advisory Board (EA)
CAAB .... California Artichoke Advisory Board (EA)
CAAB .... California Asparagus Advisory Board [*Defunct*] (EA)
CAAB .... California Avocado Advisory Board [*Later, CAC*]
CAAB .... Canadian Advertising Advisory Board
CAAB .... Canadian Archaeological Association. Bulletin [*A publication*]
CAAB .... Commandement Allie des Approches de la Baltique [*Baltic Approaches Allied Command*] [*NATO*] (NATG)
CAAB .... Contract Administration Advisory Board [*DoD*]
CaABA....... Archives of the Canadian Rockies, Banff, AB, Canada [*Library symbol*] [*Library of Congress*] (LCLS)
CaABaAR ... Alberta Department of Agriculture, Regional Office, Barrhead, AB, Canada [*Library symbol*] [*Library of Congress*] (LCLS)
CaABAC.... Alpine Club, Banff, AB, Canada [*Library symbol*] [*Library of Congress*] (LCLS)
CaABAH ... Alberta Horticultural Research Centre, Brooks, AB, Canada [*Library symbol*] [*Library of Congress*] (LCLS)
CaABdM ... Black Diamond Municipal Library, Black Diamond, AB, Canada [*Library symbol*] [*Library of Congress*] (LCLS)
CaABeAg... Canada Department of Agriculture, Research Station, Beaverlodge, AB, Canada [*Library symbol*] [*Library of Congress*] (LCLS)
CaABeM.... Beiseker Municipal Library, Beiseker, AB, Canada [*Library symbol*] [*Library of Congress*] (LCLS)

CaABi .... Bow Island Public Library, Bow Island, AB, Canada [*Library symbol*] [*Library of Congress*] (LCLS)
CaABIDM ... Banff Municipal Library, Improvement District No. 9, Banff, AB, Canada [*Library symbol*] [*Library of Congress*] (LCLS)
CaABPWG ... Peter Whyte Gallery, Banff, AB, Canada [*Library symbol*] [*Library of Congress*] (LCLS)
CaABSFA .. Banff School of Fine Arts, Banff, AB, Canada [*Library symbol*] [*Library of Congress*] (LCLS)
CAABU ..... Council for the Advancement of Arab-British Understanding [*London, England*]
CaAC .... Calgary Public Library, Calgary, AB, Canada [*Library symbol*] [*Library of Congress*] (LCLS)
CAAC .... Center for Academic & Administrative Computing [*George Washington University*] [*Research center*] (RCD)
CAAC .... Chinese American Association of Commerce (EA)
CAAC .... Civil Aviation Administration of China
CAAC .... Civilian Aviation Advisory Committee [*Air Defense Planning Board*] (AAG)
CAAC .... College Admissions Assistance Center [*Defunct*]
CAAC .... Combat Alert Aircrew [*Air Force*]
CAAC .... Committee to Assure the Availability of Casein (EA)
CAAC .... Counseling and Assistance Center [*Military*] (NVT)
CaACAC.... AMOCO Canada Petroleum Co. Ltd., Calgary, AB, Canada [*Library symbol*] [*Library of Congress*] (LCLS)
CaACaCJC ... Church of Jesus Christ of Latter-Day Saints, Genealogical Society Library, Cardston Branch, Cardston, AB, Canada [*Library symbol*] [*Library of Congress*] (LCLS)
CaACAD ... Alcoholism and Drug Abuse Commission, Calgary, AB, Canada [*Library symbol*] [*Library of Congress*] (LCLS)
CaACAE.... Alberta Energy Co., Calgary, AB, Canada [*Library symbol*] [*Library of Congress*] (LCLS)
CaACAEL ... Alsands Energy Ltd., Library and Records Centre, Calgary, AB, Canada [*Library symbol*] [*Library of Congress*] (LCLS)
CaACAG ... Alberta Gas Ethylene Co., Calgary, AB, Canada [*Library symbol*] [*Library of Congress*] (LCLS)
CaACAH ... Alberta Department of Agriculture, Horse Industry Branch, Calgary, AB, Canada [*Library symbol*] [*Library of Congress*] (LCLS)
CaACAI..... Arctic Institute of North America, Calgary, AB, Canada [*Library symbol*] [*Library of Congress*] (LCLS)
CaACAL.... Camrose Lutheran College, Camrose, AB, Canada [*Library symbol*] [*Library of Congress*] (LCLS)
CaACaM ... Canmore Municipal Library, Canmore, AB, Canada [*Library symbol*] [*Library of Congress*] (LCLS)
CaACAO ... Ashland Oil Canada Ltd., Calgary, AB, Canada [*Library symbol*] [*Library of Congress*] (LCLS)
CaACAqE ... Aquatic Environments Ltd., Calgary, AB, Canada [*Library symbol*] [*Library of Congress*] (LCLS)
CaACARC ... Arctec Ltd., Calgary, AB, Canada [*Library symbol*] [*Library of Congress*] (LCLS)
CaACarM ... Carbon Municipal Library, Carbon, AB, Canada [*Library symbol*] [*Library of Congress*] (LCLS)
CaACB....... Brascon Resources Ltd., Calgary, AB, Canada [*Library symbol*] [*Library of Congress*] (LCLS)
CaACBB.... Berean Bible College, Calgary, AB, Canada [*Library symbol*] [*Library of Congress*] (LCLS)
CaACCH ... Calgary Herald, Calgary, AB, Canada [*Library symbol*] [*Library of Congress*] (LCLS)
CaACCJC ... Church of Jesus Christ of Latter-Day Saints, Genealogical Society Library, Calgary Branch, Calgary, AB, Canada [*Library symbol*] [*Library of Congress*] (LCLS)
CaACCL.... Calgary Library Service Centre, Calgary, AB, Canada [*Library symbol*] [*Library of Congress*] (LCLS)
CaACCP.... Canadian Petroleum Association, Calgary, AB, Canada [*Library symbol*] [*Library of Congress*] (LCLS)
CaACCS .... Canadian Superior Oil Ltd., Calgary, AB, Canada [*Library symbol*] [*Library of Congress*] (LCLS)
CaACDG ... Devonian Group of Charitable Foundations, Calgary, AB, Canada [*Library symbol*] [*Library of Congress*] (LCLS)
CaACDP.... Dome Petroleum Ltd., Calgary, AB, Canada [*Library symbol*] [*Library of Congress*] (LCLS)
CAACE...... Christian Association for Adult and Continuing Education [*British*]
CaACeC..... Cessford Community Library, Cessford, AB, Canada [*Library symbol*] [*Library of Congress*] (LCLS)
CaACEC.... Montreal Engineering Company Ltd., Calgary, AB, Canada [*Library symbol*] [*Library of Congress*] (LCLS)
CaACEM... Alberta Education Materials Resources Centre, Calgary, AB, Canada [*Library symbol*] [*Library of Congress*] (LCLS)
CaACEN.... Alberta Department of the Environment, Calgary, AB, Canada [*Library symbol*] [*Library of Congress*] (LCLS)
CaACER.... Alberta Energy Resources Conservation Board, Calgary, AB, Canada [*Library symbol*] [*Library of Congress*] (LCLS)
CaACERC ... ESSO [*Standard Oil*] Resources Canada Ltd., Calgary, AB, Canada [*Library symbol*] [*Library of Congress*] (LCLS)
CaACERI .. ESSO [*Standard Oil*] Resources Canada Ltd., Library Information Center, Calgary, AB, Canada [*Library symbol*] [*Library of Congress*] (LCLS)
CaACerM .. Cereal Municipal Library, Cereal, AB, Canada [*Library symbol*] [*Library of Congress*] (LCLS)

CaACERR ... Energy Resources Research, Calgary, AB, Canada [*Library symbol*] [*Library of Congress*] (LCLS)

CaACES .... City of Calgary Electric System, Resource Centre, Calgary, AB, Canada [*Library symbol*] [*Library of Congress*] (LCLS)

CaACF .... Foothills Pipe Lines (Yukon) Ltd., Calgary, AB, Canada [*Library symbol*] [*Library of Congress*] (LCLS)

CaACG ...... Glenbow Alberta Institute, Calgary, AB, Canada [*Library symbol*] [*Library of Congress*] (LCLS)

CaACGO ... Gulf Oil Canada Ltd., Calgary, AB, Canada [*Library symbol*] [*Library of Congress*] (LCLS)

CaACGP .... Great Plains Development Co. of Canada Ltd., Calgary, AB, Canada [*Library symbol*] [*Library of Congress*] (LCLS)

CaACGTL ... Alberta Gas Trunk Line Co. Ltd., Calgary, AB, Canada [*Library symbol*] [*Library of Congress*] (LCLS)

CaACH ...... Home Oil Co. Ltd., Calgary, AB, Canada [*Library symbol*] [*Library of Congress*] (LCLS)

CaACHaS ... Haverlift Systems Ltd., Calgary, AB, Canada [*Library symbol*] [*Library of Congress*] (LCLS)

CaACHB ... Hudson's Bay Oil & Gas Co. Ltd., Calgary, AB, Canada [*Library symbol*] [*Library of Congress*] (LCLS)

CaAChCU ... Canadian Union College, College Heights, AB, Canada [*Library symbol*] [*Library of Congress*] (LCLS)

CaACHO ... Husky Oil Operation, Calgary, AB, Canada [*Library symbol*] [*Library of Congress*] (LCLS)

CaACHS .... Chevron Standard Ltd., Calgary, AB, Canada [*Library symbol*] [*Library of Congress*] (LCLS)

CaACI .... Imperial Oil Ltd., Calgary, AB, Canada [*Library symbol*] [*Library of Congress*] (LCLS)

CaACIA ..... Canada Department of Indian Affairs and Northern Development, Parks Canada, Western Regional Office, Calgary, AB, Canada [*Library symbol*] [*Library of Congress*] (LCLS)

CaACIPRD ... ESSO [*Standard Oil*] Resources Canada Ltd., Production Research Division, Calgary, AB, Canada [*Library symbol*] [*Library of Congress*] (LCLS)

CaACL .... Law Society of Alberta, Calgary, AB, Canada [*Library symbol*] [*Library of Congress*] (LCLS)

CaACLM ... Cold Lake Municipal Library, Cold Lake, AB, Canada [*Library symbol*] [*Library of Congress*] (LCLS)

CaACLS .... Calgary Public School Board, Calgary, AB, Canada [*Library symbol*] [*Library of Congress*] (LCLS)

CaACM ..... Mobil Oil Canada Ltd., Exploration Library, Calgary, AB, Canada [*Library symbol*] [*Library of Congress*] (LCLS)

CaACMD .. Macleod Dixon Library, Calgary, AB, Canada [*Library symbol*] [*Library of Congress*] (LCLS)

CaACME ... Montreal Engineering Co. Ltd., Monenco Library, Calgary, AB, Canada [*Library symbol*] [*Library of Congress*] (LCLS)

CaACMM ... I. N. McKinnon Memorial Library, Calgary, AB, Canada [*Library symbol*] [*Library of Congress*] (LCLS)

CaACMR ... Mount Royal Junior College, Calgary, AB, Canada [*Library symbol*] [*Library of Congress*] (LCLS)

CaACNE .... Northern Engineering Services Co. Ltd., Calgary, AB, Canada [*Library symbol*] [*Library of Congress*] (LCLS)

CaACNER ... Norcen Energy Resources Ltd., Calgary, AB, Canada [*Library symbol*] [*Library of Congress*] (LCLS)

CaACNP .... Northern Pipeline Agency, Calgary, AB, Canada [*Library symbol*] [*Library of Congress*] (LCLS)

CaACNWS ... Nowsco Well Service Ltd., Calgary, AB, Canada [*Library symbol*] [*Library of Congress*] (LCLS)

CaACoM ... Cochrane Municipal Library, Cochrane, AB, Canada [*Library symbol*] [*Library of Congress*] (LCLS)

CaAConM ... Consort Municipal Library, Consort, AB, Canada [*Library symbol*] [*Library of Congress*] (LCLS)

CaACP .... Pacific Petroleums Ltd., Calgary, AB, Canada [*Library symbol*] [*Library of Congress*] (LCLS)

CaACPC .... Petro-Canada, Calgary, AB, Canada [*Library symbol*] [*Library of Congress*] (LCLS)

CaACPCE ... Petro-Canada Exploration, Calgary, AB, Canada [*Library symbol*] [*Library of Congress*] (LCLS)

CaACPCR ... Petro-Canada, Research Laboratory, Calgary, AB, Canada [*Library symbol*] [*Library of Congress*] (LCLS)

CaACPF .... Plasti-Fab Ltd., Calgary, AB, Canada [*Library symbol*] [*Library of Congress*] (LCLS)

CaACPL .... Planning Library and Resource Centre, City of Calgary, Calgary, AB, Canada [*Library symbol*] [*Library of Congress*] (LCLS)

CaACPMC ... Alberta Petroleum Marketing Commission, Calgary, AB, Canada [*Library symbol*] [*Library of Congress*] (LCLS)

CaACPO .... Panarctic Oils Ltd., Calgary, AB, Canada [*Library symbol*] [*Library of Congress*] (LCLS)

CaACPow .. Calgary Power Ltd., Calgary, AB, Canada [*Library symbol*] [*Library of Congress*] (LCLS)

CaACPP .... PanCanadian Petroleum Ltd., Calgary, AB, Canada [*Library symbol*] [*Library of Congress*] (LCLS)

CaACrM .... Crossfield Municipal Library, Crossfield, AB, Canada [*Library symbol*] [*Library of Congress*] (LCLS)

CaACS .... J. C. Sproule & Associates Ltd., Calgary, AB, Canada [*Library symbol*] [*Library of Congress*] (LCLS)

CaACSA .... Southern Alberta Institute of Technology, Calgary, AB, Canada [*Library symbol*] [*Library of Congress*] (LCLS)

CaACSAA ... Alberta College of Art, Calgary, AB, Canada [*Library symbol*] [*Library of Congress*] (LCLS)

CaACSC .... Shell Canada Ltd., Calgary, AB, Canada [*Library symbol*] [*Library of Congress*] (LCLS)

CaACSDI .. Sulphur Development Institute of Canada, Calgary, AB, Canada [*Library symbol*] [*Library of Congress*] (LCLS)

CaACSO .... Sun Oil Co., Calgary, AB, Canada [*Library symbol*] [*Library of Congress*] (LCLS)

CaACSP .... Institute of Sedimentary and Petroleum Geology, Calgary, AB, Canada [*Library symbol*] [*Library of Congress*] (LCLS)

CaACTBC ... Tom Baker Cancer Centre, Medical Library, Calgary, AB, Canada [*Library symbol*] [*Library of Congress*] (LCLS)

CaACTCP ... Trans-Canada Pipelines, Calgary, AB, Canada [*Library symbol*] [*Library of Congress*] (LCLS)

CaACTCR ... Texaco Canada Resources Ltd., Calgary, AB, Canada [*Library symbol*] [*Library of Congress*] (LCLS)

CaACTE .... Techman Engineering Ltd., Calgary, AB, Canada [*Library symbol*] [*Library of Congress*] (LCLS)

CaACTP .... Total Petroleum (North American) Ltd., Calgary, AB, Canada [*Library symbol*] [*Library of Congress*] (LCLS)

CaACTU .... Transalta Utilities, Calgary, AB, Canada [*Library symbol*] [*Library of Congress*] (LCLS)

CAACU ..... Civilian Anti-Aircraft Co-Operation Unit [*British military*] (DMA)

CaACU ..... University of Calgary, Calgary, AB, Canada [*Library symbol*] [*Library of Congress*] (LCLS)

CaACUAI ... University of Calgary, Arctic Institute of North America, Calgary, AB, Canada [*Library symbol*] [*Library of Congress*] (LCLS)

CaACUCES ... University of Calgary, Research Centre for Canadian Ethnic Studies, Calgary, AB, Canada [*Library symbol*] [*Library of Congress*] (LCLS)

CaACUFE ... University of Calgary, Faculty of Education, Calgary, AB, Canada [*Library symbol*] [*Library of Congress*] (LCLS)

CaACUM .. University of Calgary, Medical Library, Calgary, AB, Canada [*Library symbol*] [*Library of Congress*] (LCLS)

CaACUMA ... University of Calgary, Maps Library, Calgary, AB, Canada [*Library symbol*] [*Library of Congress*] (LCLS)

CaACUMC ... University of Calgary, Department of Education, Materials Centre Library, Calgary, AB, Canada [*Library symbol*] [*Library of Congress*] (LCLS)

CaACUNO ... Union Oil of Canada Ltd., Calgary, AB, Canada [*Library symbol*] [*Library of Congress*] (LCLS)

CaACVC .... Alberta Vocational Centre, Calgary, AB, Canada [*Library symbol*] [*Library of Congress*] (LCLS)

CaACVZS ... V. Zay Smith Associates Ltd., Calgary, AB, Canada [*Library symbol*] [*Library of Congress*] (LCLS)

CaACW ..... Western Canada High School, Calgary, AB, Canada [*Library symbol*] [*Library of Congress*] (LCLS)

CaACWB ... Williams Brothers Canada Ltd., Calgary, AB, Canada [*Library symbol*] [*Library of Congress*] (LCLS)

CaACWRD ... Western Research and Development Ltd., Calgary, AB, Canada [*Library symbol*] [*Library of Congress*] (LCLS)

CAAD .... Computer-Aided Architectural Design (MCD)

CAAD .... Computer Air-Air Dispenser (MCD)

CA A 2d ..... California Appellate Reports, Second Series [*A publication*] (DLA)

CA A 3d ..... California Appellate Reports, Third Series [*A publication*] (DLA)

CaADM ..... Delia Municipal Library, Delia, AB, Canada [*Library symbol*] [*Library of Congress*] (LCLS)

CaADrM .... Drumheller Municipal Library, Drumheller, AB, Canada [*Library symbol*] [*Library of Congress*] (LCLS)

CAADRP ... Civil Aircraft Airworthiness Data Recording Program [*British*] (MCD)

CAAE .... Canadian Association for Adult Education

CaAE .... Edmonton Public Library, Edmonton, AB, Canada [*Library symbol*] [*Library of Congress*] (LCLS)

CaAEA ...... Alberta Historical Resources, Edmonton, AB, Canada [*Library symbol*] [*Library of Congress*] (LCLS)

CaAEacC ... East Coulee Community Library, East Coulee, AB, Canada [*Library symbol*] [*Library of Congress*] (LCLS)

CaAEAD .... Alcoholism and Drug Abuse Commission, Edmonton, AB, Canada [*Library symbol*] [*Library of Congress*] (LCLS)

CaAEAE .... Alberta Department of Advanced Education and Manpower, Edmonton, AB, Canada [*Library symbol*] [*Library of Congress*] (LCLS)

CaAEAg ..... Alberta Department of Agriculture, Edmonton, AB, Canada [*Library symbol*] [*Library of Congress*] (LCLS)

CaAEAgL .. Alberta Department of Agriculture, Laboratory, Edmonton, AB, Canada [*Library symbol*] [*Library of Congress*] (LCLS)

CaAEAME ... Allsopp, Morgan Engineering Ltd., Edmonton, AB, Canada [*Library symbol*] [*Library of Congress*] (LCLS)

CaAEAO ... Alberta Department of Agriculture, O. S. Longman Building, Edmonton, AB, Canada [*Library symbol*] [*Library of Congress*] (LCLS)

CaAEAOS ... Alberta Oil Sands Information Centre, Edmonton, AB, Canada [*Library symbol*] [*Library of Congress*] (LCLS)

CaAEAPA ... Alberta Personnel Administration, Edmonton, AB, Canada [*Library symbol*] [*Library of Congress*] (LCLS)

CaAEASC ... Alberta Securities Commission, Edmonton, AB, Canada [*Library symbol*] [*Library of Congress*] (LCLS)

CaAEAtG .. Alberta Department of the Attorney General, Edmonton, AB, Canada [*Library symbol*] [*Library of Congress*] (LCLS)

CaAEAU ... Athabasca University, Edmonton, AB, Canada [*Library symbol*] [*Library of Congress*] (LCLS)

CaAEAUC ... Alberta Government Union Catalogue, Edmonton Concordia College, Edmonton, AB, Canada [*Library symbol*] [*Library of Congress*] (LCLS)

CaAEC .... Concordia College, Edmonton, AB, Canada [*Library symbol*] [*Library of Congress*] (LCLS)

CaAECA .... Alberta Department of Consumer and Corporate Affairs, Edmonton, AB, Canada [*Library symbol*] [*Library of Congress*] (LCLS)

CaAECC .... Alberta Cancer Clinic, Edmonton, AB, Canada [*Library symbol*] [*Library of Congress*] (LCLS)

CaAECCH ... Charles Camsell Hospital, Peter Wilcock Library, Edmonton, AB, Canada [*Library symbol*] [*Library of Congress*] (LCLS)

CaAECCI .. Cross Cancer Institute, Edmonton, AB, Canada [*Library symbol*] [*Library of Congress*] (LCLS)

CaAECJC ... Church of Jesus Christ of Latter-Day Saints, Genealogical Society Library, Edmonton Branch, Edmonton, AB, Canada [*Library symbol*] [*Library of Congress*] (LCLS)

CaAECL .... Alberta Culture, Edmonton, AB, Canada [*Library symbol*] [*Library of Congress*] (LCLS)

CaAECLS ... Alberta Culture Library Services, Edmonton, AB, Canada [*Library symbol*] [*Library of Congress*] (LCLS)

CaAECS .... Alberta Union of Civil Service Employees, Edmonton, AB, Canada [*Library symbol*] [*Library of Congress*] (LCLS)

CaAECSD ... Edmonton Catholic School District, Edmonton, AB, Canada [*Library symbol*] [*Library of Congress*] (LCLS)

CaAECYR ... Alberta Culture, Edmonton, AB, Canada [*Library symbol*] [*Library of Congress*] (LCLS)

CaAECYRH ... Alberta Culture, Heritage Resources Development, Edmonton, AB, Canada [*Library symbol*] [*Library of Congress*] (LCLS)

CaAEDC .... Alberta Department of Government Services, Computing and Systems Division, Edmonton, AB, Canada [*Library symbol*] [*Library of Congress*] (LCLS)

CaAEDN ... Distribution Networks, Edmonton, AB, Canada [*Library symbol*] [*Library of Congress*] (LCLS)

CaAEE .... Alberta Department of Education, Edmonton, AB, Canada [*Library symbol*] [*Library of Congress*] (LCLS)

CAAEE ...... Coast and Antiaircraft Experimental Establishment [*British*] [*World War II*]

CaAEEA .... City of Edmonton Archives, Edmonton, AB, Canada [*Library symbol*] [*Library of Congress*] (LCLS)

CaAEEAE ... Environment Canada, Atmospheric Environment Service, Edmonton, AB, Canada [*Library symbol*] [*Library of Congress*] (LCLS)

CaAEEAV ... Alberta Department of Education, Audio Visual Services Branch, Edmonton, AB, Canada [*Library symbol*] [*Library of Congress*] (LCLS)

CaAEEC .... Alberta Department of Economic Development, Edmonton, AB, Canada [*Library symbol*] [*Library of Congress*] (LCLS)

CaAEECA ... Environment Council of Alberta, Edmonton, AB, Canada [*Library symbol*] [*Library of Congress*] (LCLS)

CaAEECW ... Canada Department of the Environment, Canadian Wildlife Service, Edmonton, AB, Canada [*Library symbol*] [*Library of Congress*] (LCLS)

CaAEEM ... Alberta Education Materials Resource Centre, Edmonton, AB, Canada [*Library symbol*] [*Library of Congress*] (LCLS)

CaAEEN .... Alberta Department of the Environment, Edmonton, AB, Canada [*Library symbol*] [*Library of Congress*] (LCLS)

CaAEENR ... Alberta Energy and Natural Resources Library, Edmonton, AB, Canada [*Library symbol*] [*Library of Congress*] (LCLS)

CaAEEP .... Edmonton Power Co., Edmonton, AB, Canada [*Library symbol*] [*Library of Congress*] (LCLS)

CaAEEPS ... Environment Canada, Environmental Protection Service, Northwest Region, Edmonton, AB, Canada [*Library symbol*] [*Library of Congress*] (LCLS)

CaAEESE ... Alberta Department of Education, Special Education, Materials Resource Centre, Edmonton, AB, Canada [*Library symbol*] [*Library of Congress*] (LCLS)

CaAEF .... Canada Department of the Environment, Northern Forest Research Centre, Edmonton, AB, Canada [*Library symbol*] [*Library of Congress*] (LCLS)

CaAEFIA ... Alberta Department of Federal and Intergovernmental Affairs, Edmonton, AB, Canada [*Library symbol*] [*Library of Congress*] (LCLS)

CaAEGH ... Edmonton General Hospital, Edmonton, AB, Canada [*Library symbol*] [*Library of Congress*] (LCLS)

CaAEGM .. Grant MacEwan Community College, Edmonton, AB, Canada [*Library symbol*] [*Library of Congress*] (LCLS)

CaAEGS .... Alberta Department of Government Services, Edmonton, AB, Canada [*Library symbol*] [*Library of Congress*] (LCLS)

CaAEGT .... Alberta Government Telephones Commission, Edmonton, AB, Canada [*Library symbol*] [*Library of Congress*] (LCLS)

CaAEHA ... Hardy Associates Ltd., Edmonton, AB, Canada [*Library symbol*] [*Library of Congress*] (LCLS)

CaAEHC ... Alberta Housing Corporation, Edmonton, AB, Canada [*Library symbol*] [*Library of Congress*] (LCLS)

CaAEHCI ... Health Care Insurance Commission, Edmonton, AB, Canada [*Library symbol*] [*Library of Congress*] (LCLS)

CaAEHO ... Alberta Hospital, Oliver, AB, Canada [*Library symbol*] [*Library of Congress*] (LCLS)

CaAEHR ... Alberta Human Rights Commission, Edmonton, AB, Canada [*Library symbol*] [*Library of Congress*] (LCLS)

CaAEHSC ... Hospital Services Commission, Edmonton, AB, Canada [*Library symbol*] [*Library of Congress*] (LCLS)

CaAEHSD ... Alberta Department of Social Services and Community Health, Edmonton, AB, Canada [*Library symbol*] [*Library of Congress*] (LCLS)

CaAEHT ... Alberta Department of Transportation, Edmonton, AB, Canada [*Library symbol*] [*Library of Congress*] (LCLS)

CaAEHTT ... Alberta Department of Transportation, Highways Testing Laboratory, Edmonton, AB, Canada [*Library symbol*] [*Library of Congress*] (LCLS)

CaAEIC ..... Alberta Department of Business Development and Tourism, Edmonton, AB, Canada [*Library symbol*] [*Library of Congress*] (LCLS)

CaAEJ .... Canada Department of Justice, Edmonton, AB, Canada [*Library symbol*] [*Library of Congress*] (LCLS)

CaAELBS ... Alberta Labour-Building Standards Library, Edmonton, AB, Canada [*Library symbol*] [*Library of Congress*] (LCLS)

CaAELF .... Alberta Department of Energy and Natural Resources, Renewable Resources Division, Edmonton, AB, Canada [*Library symbol*] [*Library of Congress*] [*Obsolete*] (LCLS)

CaAELL .... Province of Alberta Law Library System, Edmonton, AB, Canada [*Library symbol*] [*Library of Congress*] (LCLS)

CaAEM ..... Empress Municipal Library, Empress, AB, Canada [*Library symbol*] [*Library of Congress*] (LCLS)

CaAEMA ... Alberta Department of Municipal Affairs, Edmonton, AB, Canada [*Library symbol*] [*Library of Congress*] (LCLS)

CaAEMB ... Multilingual Biblioservice, Edmonton, AB, Canada [*Library symbol*] [*Library of Congress*] (LCLS)

CaAEML ... Alberta Department of Labour, Edmonton, AB, Canada [*Library symbol*] [*Library of Congress*] (LCLS)

CaAEMLOH ... Alberta Department of Labour, Occupational Health and Safety Division, Edmonton, AB, Canada [*Library symbol*] [*Library of Congress*] (LCLS)

CaAEMM ... Alberta Department of Energy and Natural Resources, Edmonton, AB, Canada [*Library symbol*] [*Library of Congress*] [*Obsolete*] (LCLS)

CaAEMT ... Ministry of Transport, Canadian Air Transportation Administration, Edmonton, AB, Canada [*Library symbol*] [*Library of Congress*] (LCLS)

CaAEMTC ... Ministry of Transport, Canadian Air Transportation Administration, Construction Branch, Edmonton, AB, Canada [*Library symbol*] [*Library of Congress*] (LCLS)

CaAEMTCA ... Ministry of Transport, Canadian Air Transportation Administration, Civil Aviation Branch, Edmonton, AB, Canada [*Library symbol*] [*Library of Congress*] (LCLS)

CaAENA ... Northern Alberta Institute of Technology, Edmonton, AB, Canada [*Library symbol*] [*Library of Congress*] (LCLS)

CaAENABC ... North American Baptist College and Divinity School, Edmonton, AB, Canada [*Library symbol*] [*Library of Congress*] (LCLS)

CaAENI ..... Technical Data Control Centre, Edmonton, AB, Canada [*Library symbol*] [*Library of Congress*] (LCLS)

CaAENR .... Alberta Department of Energy and Natural Resources, Edmonton, AB, Canada [*Library symbol*] [*Library of Congress*] (LCLS)

CaAEO ...... Oblate Archives of Alberta-Saskatchewan, Edmonton, AB, Canada [*Library symbol*] [*Library of Congress*] (LCLS)

CaAEOH ... Alberta Worker's Health, Safety, and Compensation, Edmonton, AB, Canada [*Library symbol*] [*Library of Congress*] (LCLS)

CaAEOM .. Alberta Ombudsman, Edmonton, AB, Canada [*Library symbol*] [*Library of Congress*] (LCLS)

CaAEP .... Alberta Legislature Library, Edmonton, AB, Canada [*Library symbol*] [*Library of Congress*] (LCLS)

CaAEP .... Cassell's Anthology of English Poetry [*A publication*]

CaAEPAA ... Provincial Archives of Alberta, Edmonton, AB, Canada [*Library symbol*] [*Library of Congress*] (LCLS)

CaAEPC .... Alberta Provincial Courts, Edmonton, AB, Canada [*Library symbol*] [*Library of Congress*] (LCLS)

CaAEPL .... Edmonton Catholic School District, Professional Library, Edmonton, AB, Canada [*Library symbol*] [*Library of Congress*] (LCLS)

CaAEPRD ... Alberta Department of the Attorney General, Planning, Research, and Development Division, Edmonton, AB, Canada [*Library symbol*] [*Library of Congress*] (LCLS)

CaAEPU .... Alberta Public Utilities Board, Edmonton, AB, Canada [*Library symbol*] [*Library of Congress*] (LCLS)

CaAEPW ... Alberta Department of Housing and Public Works, Edmonton, AB, Canada [*Library symbol*] [*Library of Congress*] (LCLS)

CaAER....... Alberta Research, Edmonton, AB, Canada [*Library symbol*] [*Library of Congress*] (LCLS)

CaAERA.... Royal Alexandra Hospital, Edmonton, AB, Canada [*Library symbol*] [*Library of Congress*] (LCLS)

CaAERC.... Alberta Research Council, Clover Bar Branch, Edmonton, AB, Canada [*Library symbol*] [*Library of Congress*] (LCLS)

CaAERM... R. M. Hardy & Associates Ltd., Edmonton, AB, Canada [*Library symbol*] [*Library of Congress*] (LCLS)

CaAERPW ... Alberta Department of Recreation, Parks, and Wildlife, Edmonton, AB, Canada [*Library symbol*] [*Library of Congress*] (LCLS)

CaAERSWE ... Alberta Research Council, Solar and Wind Energy Research Program Information Centre, Edmonton, AB, Canada [*Library symbol*] [*Library of Congress*] (LCLS)

CaAERU.... Alberta Research Council, University Branch, Edmonton, AB, Canada [*Library symbol*] [*Library of Congress*] (LCLS)

CaAES....... Statistics Canada, Edmonton, AB, Canada [*Library symbol*] [*Library of Congress*] (LCLS)

CaAESAE ... Stanley Associates Engineering Ltd., Edmonton, AB, Canada [*Library symbol*] [*Library of Congress*] (LCLS)

CaAESC .... Syncrude Canada Ltd., Edmonton, AB, Canada [*Library symbol*] [*Library of Congress*] (LCLS)

CaAESD.... Alberta School for the Deaf, Edmonton, AB, Canada [*Library symbol*] [*Library of Congress*] (LCLS)

CaAESG .... Alberta Solicitor General's Department, Edmonton, AB, Canada [*Library symbol*] [*Library of Congress*] (LCLS)

CaAESIS ... Schick Information Systems, Edmonton, AB, Canada [*Library symbol*] [*Library of Congress*] (LCLS)

CaAET....... Alberta Treasury Department, Edmonton, AB, Canada [*Library symbol*] [*Library of Congress*] (LCLS)

CaAETA .... Travel Alberta, Edmonton, AB, Canada [*Library symbol*] [*Library of Congress*] [*Obsolete*] (LCLS)

CaAETATE ... Transport Canada, Canadian Air Transportation Administration, Telecommunications and Electronics, Edmonton, AB, Canada [*Library symbol*] [*Library of Congress*] (LCLS)

CaAETBS ... Alberta Treasury Department, Bureau of Statistics, Edmonton, AB, Canada [*Library symbol*] [*Library of Congress*] (LCLS)

CaAETCT ... Alberta Treasury Department, Corporate Tax Administration, Edmonton, AB, Canada [*Library symbol*] [*Library of Congress*] (LCLS)

CaAEU ...... University of Alberta, Edmonton, AB, Canada [*Library symbol*] [*Library of Congress*] (LCLS)

CaAEUA ... University of Alberta, Archives, Edmonton, AB, Canada [*Library symbol*] [*Library of Congress*] (LCLS)

CaAEUB.... University of Alberta, Boreal Institute for Northern Studies, Edmonton, AB, Canada [*Library symbol*] [*Library of Congress*] (LCLS)

CaAEUL.... University of Alberta, Law Library, Edmonton, AB, Canada [*Library symbol*] [*Library of Congress*] (LCLS)

CaAEULS ... University of Alberta, Faculty of Library Science, Edmonton, AB, Canada [*Library symbol*] [*Library of Congress*] (LCLS)

CaAEUM .. University of Alberta, University Map Collection, Edmonton, AB, Canada [*Library symbol*] [*Library of Congress*] (LCLS)

CaAEUN ... Unifarm Association, Edmonton, AB, Canada [*Library symbol*] [*Library of Congress*] (LCLS)

CaAEUS.... University of Alberta, Special Collections Department, Edmonton, AB, Canada [*Library symbol*] [*Library of Congress*] (LCLS)

CaAEUSJ ... University of Alberta, Faculte Saint-Jean, Edmonton, AB, Canada [*Library symbol*] [*Library of Congress*] (LCLS)

CaAEUT.... Alberta Department of Utilities and Telephones, Edmonton, AB, Canada [*Library symbol*] [*Library of Congress*] (LCLS)

CaAEVC.... Alberta Vocational Centre, Edmonton, AB, Canada [*Library symbol*] [*Library of Congress*] (LCLS)

CaAExC..... Exshaw Community Library, Exshaw, AB, Canada [*Library symbol*] [*Library of Congress*] (LCLS)

CAAF........ Campbell Army Airfield [*Fort Campbell, Kentucky*]

C of AAF... Chief of the Army Air Forces [*World War II*]

CAAF........ Chief of the Army Air Forces [*World War II*]

CAAF........ Combined Allied Air Forces

CAAF........ Conseil Asiatique d'Analystes Financiers [*Asian Council of Securities Analysts - ASAC*] [*Tokyo, Japan*] (EAIO)

CaAFAAR ... Alberta Department of Agriculture, Regional Office, Fairview, AB, Canada [*Library symbol*] [*Library of Congress*] (LCLS)

CaAFAAV ... Alberta Department of Agriculture, Veterinary Laboratory, Fairview, AB, Canada [*Library symbol*] [*Library of Congress*] (LCLS)

CaAFAC.... Fairview College, Fairview, AB, Canada [*Library symbol*] [*Library of Congress*] (LCLS)

CAAFDP ... Central American Association of Families of Disappeared Persons [*See also ACAFADE*] [*San Jose, Costa Rica*] (EAIO)

CaAFk .... Fort Kent Public Library, Fort Kent, AB, Canada [*Library symbol*] [*Library of Congress*] (LCLS)

CaAFmK.... Keyona College, Fort McMurray, AB, Canada [*Library symbol*] [*Library of Congress*] (LCLS)

CaAFmSI... SUNCOR, Inc., Resources Group, Information Centre, Fort McMurray, AB, Canada [*Library symbol*] [*Library of Congress*] (LCLS)

CAAFS ...... Institute of Chemical Analysis, Applications, and Forensic Science [*Northeastern University*] [*Research center*] (RCD)

CaAFSM.... Fort Saskatchewan Municipal Library, Fort Saskatchewan, AB, Canada [*Library symbol*] [*Library of Congress*] (LCLS)

CaAFsSG... Sherritt Gordon Mines Ltd., Fort Saskatchewan, AB, Canada [*Library symbol*] [*Library of Congress*] (LCLS)

CAAG .... Civil Aviation Advisory [*or Assistance*] Group [*FAA*]

CAAGB ...... Canada Agriculture [*A publication*]

CaAGcM ... Grand Centre Municipal Library, Grand Centre, AB, Canada [*Library symbol*] [*Library of Congress*] (LCLS)

CaAGcNL ... Northern Lights Library Co-Operative, Grand Centre, AB, Canada [*Library symbol*] [*Library of Congress*] (LCLS)

CaAGM .... Gleichen Municipal Library, Gleichen, AB, Canada [*Library symbol*] [*Library of Congress*] (LCLS)

CaAGPC.... Grande Prairie College, Grande Prairie, AB, Canada [*Library symbol*] [*Library of Congress*] (LCLS)

CAAGS..... Caseless Ammunition Aerial Gun System (MCD)

CaAGVC.... Alberta Vocational Centre, Grouard, AB, Canada [*Library symbol*] [*Library of Congress*] (LCLS)

CAAH....... Cahiers Alsaciens d'Archeologie, d'Art, et d'Histoire [*A publication*]

CAAH....... Chronology of African-American History [*A publication*]

CAAHA ..... Council on Arteriosclerosis of the American Heart Association (EA)

CaAHM.... Hanna Municipal Library, Hanna, AB, Canada [*Library symbol*] [*Library of Congress*] (LCLS)

CaAHrM ... High River Municipal Library, High River, AB, Canada [*Library symbol*] [*Library of Congress*] (LCLS)

CaAHuM... Hussar Municipal Library, Hussar, AB, Canada [*Library symbol*] [*Library of Congress*] (LCLS)

CaAIr........ Iron River Public Library, Iron River, AB, Canada [*Library symbol*] [*Library of Congress*] (LCLS)

CAAIS ...... Computer-Assisted Action Information System [*NATO*] (NATG)

CAA J .... Civil Aeronautics Administration. Journal [*A publication*]

CaAJ .... Jasper Public Library, Jasper, AB, Canada [*Library symbol*] [*Library of Congress*] (LCLS)

CAAJA ...... Council of Affiliated Associations of Jewelers of America (EA)

CAAK .... Civil Aviation Administration of Korea [*Democratic People's Republic of Korea*]

CAAL........ Canadian Association of Applied Linguistics

CAAL........ COMOPTEVFOR Acronym and Abbreviation List [*A publication*] (CAAL)

CAAL........ Corporate Author Authority List

CaAL .... Lethbridge Public Library, Lethbridge, AB, Canada [*Library symbol*] [*Library of Congress*] (LCLS)

CaALaAF .. Alberta Department of Agriculture, Field Crops Branch, Lacombe, AB, Canada [*Library symbol*] [*Library of Congress*] (LCLS)

CaALaAg... Canada Department of Agriculture, Research Station, Lacombe, AB, Canada [*Library symbol*] [*Library of Congress*] (LCLS)

CaALADR ... Canada Department of Agriculture, Animal Diseases Research Institute (West), Lethbridge, AB, Canada [*Library symbol*] [*Library of Congress*] (LCLS)

CaALAg..... Canada Department of Agriculture, Lethbridge, AB, Canada [*Library symbol*] [*Library of Congress*] (LCLS)

CaALAI..... Alberta Department of Agriculture, Irrigation Division, Lethbridge, AB, Canada [*Library symbol*] [*Library of Congress*] (LCLS)

CaALaP..... Parkland Regional Library, Lacombe, AB, Canada [*Library symbol*] [*Library of Congress*] (LCLS)

CaALAR.... Alberta Department of Agriculture, Regional Office, Lethbridge, AB, Canada [*Library symbol*] [*Library of Congress*] (LCLS)

CaALC....... Lethbridge College, Lethbridge, AB, Canada [*Library symbol*] [*Library of Congress*] (LCLS)

CaALCJC ... Church of Jesus Christ of Latter-Day Saints, Genealogical Society Library, Lethbridge Branch, Stake Center, Lethbridge, AB, Canada [*Library symbol*] [*Library of Congress*] (LCLS)

CaALEn.... Alberta Department of the Environment, Lethbridge, AB, Canada [*Library symbol*] [*Library of Congress*] (LCLS)

CAALG..... Central Australia Adult Literacy Group

CaALiM .... Linden Municipal Library, Linden, AB, Canada [*Library symbol*] [*Library of Congress*] (LCLS)

CAALL...... Canadian Association of Administrators of Labour Legislation

CaALLbVC ... Alberta Vocational Centre, Lac La Biche, AB, Canada [*Library symbol*] [*Library of Congress*] (LCLS)

CaALoM.... Longview Municipal Library, Longview, AB, Canada [*Library symbol*] [*Library of Congress*] (LCLS)

CAALS ...... Consortium on Automated Analytical Laboratory Systems [*National Institute of Standards & Technology*]

CaALU ...... University of Lethbridge, Lethbridge, AB, Canada [*Library symbol*] [*Library of Congress*] (LCLS)

CaALUG ...	University of Lethbridge, Department of Geography, Lethbridge, AB, Canada [Library symbol] [Library of Congress] (LCLS)
CAAM	Civil Aeronautics Administration Manual
CAAM	Conventional Airfield Attack Missile (MCD)
CaAMCH ..	Crescent Heights High School, Medicine Hat, AB, Canada [Library symbol] [Library of Congress] (LCLS)
CaAMe	Medley Public Library, Medley, AB, Canada [Library symbol] [Library of Congress] (LCLS)
CAAMF......	Cowboy Artists of America Museum Foundation (EA)
CaAMG	Medicine Hat General Hospital, Medicine Hat, AB, Canada [Library symbol] [Library of Congress] (LCLS)
CaAMHS ..	Medicine Hat High School, Medicine Hat, AB, Canada [Library symbol] [Library of Congress] (LCLS)
CaAMiC	Millarville Community Library, Millarville, AB, Canada [Library symbol] [Library of Congress] (LCLS)
CaAMM	Medicine Hat College, Medicine Hat, AB, Canada [Library symbol] [Library of Congress] (LCLS)
CaAMoM ..	Morrin Municipal Library, Morrin, AB, Canada [Library symbol] [Library of Congress] (LCLS)
CaAMP......	Medicine Hat Public Library, Medicine Hat, AB, Canada [Library symbol] [Library of Congress] (LCLS)
CAAN	Cambridge Analytical Associates, Inc. [Boston, MA] [NASDAQ symbol] (NQ)
CAAN	Continental Advertising Agency Network [Later, Advertising and Marketing International Network] (EA)
CAAN	Contracting and Acquisition Newsletter [A publication]
CAANA	Comptes Rendus. Association des Anatomistes [A publication]
CAANB	Cahiers d'Anesthesiologie [A publication]
CAANS......	Canadian Association for the Advancement of Netherlandic Studies [See also ACAEN]
CAAO	Canadian Association of Amateur Oarsmen
CaAOAC ...	Olds Agricultural College, Olds, AB, Canada [Library symbol] [Library of Congress] (LCLS)
CaAOAF....	Alberta Department of Agriculture, Farm Business Management Branch, Olds, AB, Canada [Library symbol] [Library of Congress] (LCLS)
CaAOM	Okotoks Municipal Library, Okotoks, AB, Canada [Library symbol] [Library of Congress] (LCLS)
CAA Op	Civil Aeronautics Authority Opinions [A publication] (DLA)
CaAOyM ...	Oyen Municipal Library, Oyen, AB, Canada [Library symbol] [Library of Congress] (LCLS)
CAAP........	Certified Advertising Agency Practitioner
CAAP........	Child and Adolescent Adjustment Profile [Child development test] [Psychology]
CAAP........	Cornhusker Army Ammunition Plant (AABC)
CaAPH	Alberta Hospital, Staff Library, Ponoka, AB, Canada [Library symbol] [Library of Congress] (LCLS)
CaAPrEN ..	Alberta Department of the Environment, Peace River, AB, Canada [Library symbol] [Library of Congress] (LCLS)
CAAPS	Council for Aboriginal Alcohol Program Services [Australia]
Ca Ar.........	Cahiers Archeologiques [A publication]
CAAR	Calgary Archaeologist. University of Calgary [Canada] [A publication]
CAAR	Compressed Air Accumulator Rocket
CAARA	Canadian Architect [A publication]
CAARC......	Commonwealth Advisory Aeronautical Research Council [London, England] (EAIO)
CaARd	Red Deer Public Library, Red Deer, AB, Canada [Library symbol] [Library of Congress] (LCLS)
CaARDAR ...	Alberta Department of Agriculture, Regional Office, Red Deer, AB, Canada [Library symbol] [Library of Congress] (LCLS)
CaARDC....	Red Deer College, Red Deer, AB, Canada [Library symbol] [Library of Congress] (LCLS)
CaARDMC ...	Michener Centre, Red Deer, AB, Canada [Library symbol] [Library of Congress] (LCLS)
CaARI.......	Cyprus American Archaeological Research Institute [Research center] (IRC)
CaARM	Rockyford Municipal Library, Rockyford, AB, Canada [Library symbol] [Library of Congress] (LCLS)
CAARRS ...	Contract Administration Automated Records Retrieval System (MCD)
CaARS.......	Canada Department of National Defence, Defence Research Establishment, Suffield, Ralston, AB, Canada [Library symbol] [Library of Congress] (LCLS)
CaARuM ...	Rumsey Municipal Library, Rumsey, AB, Canada [Library symbol] [Library of Congress] (LCLS)
CAAS........	Canadian Association of African Studies [See also ACEA]
CAAS........	Canadian Association for American Studies (EA)
CAAS........	Center for Afro-American and African Studies [University of Michigan] [Research center] (RCD)
CAAS........	Center for Afro-American Studies [University of California, Los Angeles] [Research center] (RCD)
CAAS........	Ceylon Association for the Advancement of Science (MCD)
CAAS........	Chet Atkins Appreciation Society (EA)
CAAS........	Chinese Association for the Advancement of Science
CAAS........	Combined Arms and Support [Army] (AABC)
CAAS........	Computer-Aided Alerting Subsystem (CAAL)
CAAS........	Computer-Aided Approach Spacing [Aviation]
CAAS........	Computer-Assisted Acquisition System [for libraries]
CAAS........	Contemporary Authors Autobiography Series [A publication]
CAAS........	Contracted Advisory and Assistance Services [DoD]
CAAS........	Council of American Artist Societies (EA)
CAASA	Community Aid Abroad, Southern Africa Group [Australia]
CaASA	St. Albert Public Library, St. Albert, AB, Canada [Library symbol] [Library of Congress] (LCLS)
CaASAMLM ...	MLM Groundwater Engineering, St. Albert, AB, Canada [Library symbol] [Library of Congress] (LCLS)
CAAS Bull ...	Canadian Association for American Studies. Bulletin [A publication]
CAASE......	Computer-Assisted Area Source Emissions [Environmental Protection Agency]
CAA/SEF ..	Chaplains' Aid Association/Seminary Education Fund (EA)
CAASF	Canadian Army Active Service Force
CaASgY	Yellowhead Regional Library, Spruce Grove, AB, Canada [Library symbol] [Library of Congress] (LCLS)
CaASM	Strathmore Municipal Library, Strathmore, AB, Canada [Library symbol] [Library of Congress] (LCLS)
CaASMLS ...	Marigold Library System, Strathmore, AB, Canada [Library symbol] [Library of Congress] (LCLS)
CaASpEMRCM ...	Energy, Mines, and Resources Canada, Western Research Laboratory, CANMET Library, Sherwood Park, AB, Canada [Library symbol] [Library of Congress] (LCLS)
CaASpS	County of Strathcona Library, Sherwood Park, AB, Canada [Library symbol] [Library of Congress] (LCLS)
CAASR	Canadian Association of Applied Social Research [See also ACRSA]
CaAStM	Standard Municipal Library, Standard, AB, Canada [Library symbol] [Library of Congress] (LCLS)
CAAT	Campaign Against Arms Trade [British] (EAIO)
CAAT	Center for Alternatives to Animal Testing [At Johns Hopkins]
CAAT	College of Applied Arts and Technology
CAAT	Computer-Assisted Audit Techniques
CAAT	Computer-Assisted Axial Tomography [Also, CAT, CT] [Roentgenography]
CAATC	Civil Aeronautics Administration Type Certificate
CaAThM ...	Three Hills Municipal Library, Three Hills, AB, Canada [Library symbol] [Library of Congress] (LCLS)
CAATO	Combined Army Air Transport Organization [World War II]
CaATrM....	Trochu Municipal Library, Trochu, AB, Canada [Library symbol] [Library of Congress] (LCLS)
CAAV	Central Association of Agricultural Valuers [British]
CAAV	Civil Aviation Administration of Vietnam
CaAVAR....	Alberta Department of Agriculture, Regional Office, Vermilion, AB, Canada [Library symbol] [Library of Congress] (LCLS)
CaAVC......	Lakeland College, Vermilion, AB, Canada [Library symbol] [Library of Congress] (LCLS)
CaAVeE.....	Alberta Environmental Centre, Vegreville, AB, Canada [Library symbol] [Library of Congress] (LCLS)
CaAVM	Veteran Municipal Library, Veteran, AB, Canada [Library symbol] [Library of Congress] (LCLS)
CAAW	Customer Authorization for Additional Work
CaAW	Wetaskiwin Municipal Library, Wetaskiwin, AB, Canada [Library symbol] [Library of Congress] (LCLS)
CaAWAD ..	Alberta Department of Agriculture, Dairy Division, Wetaskiwin, AB, Canada [Library symbol] [Library of Congress] (LCLS)
CAAWEX ...	Canned Antiair Warfare Exercise (NVT)
CAA-WTS ...	Civil Aviation Authority - War Training Service
CAAX........	Central American Airways [Air carrier designation symbol]
CaAYM	Youngstown Municipal Library, Youngstown, AB, Canada [Library symbol] [Library of Congress] (LCLS)
CAB	Cabalistic (ROG)
CAB	Caballero [Cavalier] [Spanish] (DSUE)
CAB	Cabin (MSA)
CAB	Cabinda [Angola] [Airport symbol] (OAG)
CAB	Cabinet (KSC)
CAB	Cables [Business term]
CAB	Cabletelevision Advertising Bureau [New York, NY] (EA)
CAB	Cabramurra [Australia] [Seismograph station code, US Geological Survey] [Closed] (SEIS)
CAB	Cabriolet (ROG)
CAB	Cahiers d'Archeologie Biblique [A publication]
CAB	Calibrate
CaB	Cambridge Bible for Schools and Colleges [A publication] (BJA)
CAB	Campaign Against US Military Bases in the Philippines (EA)
CAB	Canadian Armoured Brigade
CAB	Canadian Association of Broadcasters
CAB	Capped Argon Bubbling [Steelmaking]
CAB	Captured Air Bubble (MCD)
CAB	Carbon Arc Brazing
CAB	Career Adaptive Behavior Inventory [Vocational guidance test]
CAB	CasaBlanca Industries, Inc. [AMEX symbol] (SPSG)
CAB	Cellulose Acetate Butyrate [Organic chemistry]
CAB	Centralized Accounting and Billing (MCD)
CAB	Ceramic Awareness Bulletin [Defense Ceramic Information Center] [A publication]
CAB	Change Analysis Board
CAB	Citizens' Advice Bureau [British]

CAB .... Citizen's Advisory Board (OICC)
CAB .... Civil Aeronautics Board [*Independent government agency*] [*Terminated, 1984, functions transferred to Department of Transportation*]
CAB .... Civil Aeronautics Board Reports [*A publication*] (DLA)
CAB .... Civil Aeronautics Bulletin
CAB .... Civil Air Branch [*Air Force*]
CAB .... CNO [*Chief of Naval Operations*] Advisory Board
CAB .... Collating and Binding
CAB .... Combat Aviation Battalion [*or Brigade*]
CAB .... Combined Arms Battalion (MCD)
CAB .... Command Advisory Board
CAB .... Commonwealth Agricultural Bureaux [*Database producer*] (EA)
CAB .... Commonwealth Bureau of Soils [*British*]
CAB .... Comprehensive Ability Battery [*Test*]
CAB .... Condor Aviation Ltd. [*Ontario, Canada*] [*FAA designator*] (FAAC)
CAB .... Consequential Arc Back
CAB .... Consumers' Advisory Board
CAB .... Contract Appeals Board [*Veterans Administration*]
CAB .... Controlled Amortization Bond
CAB .... Controlled Atmosphere Brazing [*Metallurgy*]
CAB .... Cooperative Analysis of Broadcasting [*Term used in TV rating*]
CAB .... Coronary Artery Bypass [*Medicine*]
CAB .... Corrective Action Board
CAB .... Corrosion Advice Bureau [*British*]
CAB .... Cost Analysis Brief (MCD)
CAB .... Cost Audit Board (NASA)
CAB .... Critical Air Blast [*Test*]
CAB .... Cultural Association of Bengal (EA)
CAB .... Current Affairs Bulletin [*A publication*] (APTA)
CAB .... Current Awareness Bibliographies [*DTIC*]
CAB .... Current Awareness Bulletin [*A publication*]
CAB .... Cytoplasmic Androgen Binder [*Endocrinology*]
CABA .... Charge Account Bankers Association [*Later, ABA*]
CABA .... Compressed Air Breathing Apparatus
CaBAbF..... Fraser Valley Union Library, Abbotsford, BC, Canada [*Library symbol*] [*Library of Congress*] (LCLS)
CaBAbFV... Fraser Valley College, Abbotsford, BC, Canada [*Library symbol*] [*Library of Congress*] (LCLS)
CABAF...... Currency Adjustment and Bunkering Adjustment Factors [*British*] (DCTA)
CaBAgAg... Canada Department of Agriculture, Research Station, Agassiz, BC, Canada [*Library symbol*] [*Library of Congress*] (LCLS)
CABAL...... Calcium-Boron-Aluminum [*Glasses*]
CABAL...... Clifford, Arlington, Buckingham, Ashley, Lauderdale [*Ministers of Charles II of England*] [*Some claim that the word "cabal" is derived from this acronym; others, that it comes from the Hebrew "cabala"*]
CAB Annot Bibliogr ... Commonwealth Agricultural Bureaux. Annotated Bibliography [*Database*] [*A publication*]
CAB-ATM ... Civil Aeronautics Board Air Transport Mobilization Standby Order
CaBBB......... Burnaby Public Library, Burnaby, BC, Canada [*Library symbol*] [*Library of Congress*] (LCLS)
CABB........ Captured Air Bubble Boat [*Navy*]
CaBBA....... Burnaby Art Gallery, Burnaby, BC, Canada [*Library symbol*] [*Library of Congress*] (LCLS)
CaBBCJC .. Church of Jesus Christ of Latter-Day Saints, Genealogical Society Library, Vancouver Branch, Stake Center, Burnaby, Vancouver, BC, Canada [*Library symbol*] [*Library of Congress*] (LCLS)
CaBBIT ..... British Columbia Institute of Technology, Burnaby, BC, Canada [*Library symbol*] [*Library of Congress*] (LCLS)
CaBBL....... Lenkurt Electric Co., Burnaby, BC, Canada [*Library symbol*] [*Library of Congress*] (LCLS)
CaBBPVI... Pacific Vocational Institute, Burnaby, BC, Canada [*Library symbol*] [*Library of Congress*] (LCLS)
CaBBT ...... British Columbia Telephone Co., Burnaby, BC, Canada [*Library symbol*] [*Library of Congress*] (LCLS)
CaBBUC.... British Columbia Union Catalogue, Burnaby, BC, Canada [*Library symbol*] [*Library of Congress*] (LCLS)
CaBC.......... Caribbean Broadcasting Corporation
CABCD...... Cancer Biochemistry - Biophysics [*A publication*]
CABCD4.... Cancer Biochemistry - Biophysics [*A publication*]
CaBCh .... Chilliwack Public Library, Chilliwack, BC, Canada [*Library symbol*] [*Library of Congress*] (LCLS)
CaBClF...... Fraser Valley College, Clearbrook, BC, Canada [*Library symbol*] [*Library of Congress*] (LCLS)
CaBCoM.... Courtenay and District Museum, Courtenay, BC, Canada [*Library symbol*] [*Library of Congress*] (LCLS)
CaBComN ... North Island College, Comox, BC, Canada [*Library symbol*] [*Library of Congress*] (LCLS)
CaBCrEK... East Kootenay Community College, Cranbrook, BC, Canada [*Library symbol*] [*Library of Congress*] (LCLS)
CaBCS ...... Selkirk College, Castlegar, BC, Canada [*Library symbol*] [*Library of Congress*] (LCLS)
CABD .... Canadian Building Digest [*A publication*]

CaBDC....... Dawson Creek Public Library, Dawson Creek, BC, Canada [*Library symbol*] [*Library of Congress*] (LCLS)
CaBDCL.... Library Advisory Council, Dawson Creek, BC, Canada [*Library symbol*] [*Library of Congress*] (LCLS)
CaBDCNL ... Northern Lights College, Dawson Creek, BC, Canada [*Library symbol*] [*Library of Congress*] (LCLS)
Cab & E.... Cababe and Ellis' Queen's Bench Reports [*1882-85*] [*England*] [*A publication*] (DLA)
CABE........ Canadian Alliance of Black Educators [*See also ACEN*]
CABE........ Canadian Association for Business Economics
CABE........ Christian Association of Business Executives [*British*]
CABE........ Coalition Against Black Exploitation (EA)
CABE........ Companion of the Association of Business Executives [*British*] (DBQ)
CaBEC....... Crease Clinic Library, Essondale, BC, Canada [*Library symbol*] [*Library of Congress*] (LCLS)
Cab & El .... Cababe and Ellis' Queen's Bench Reports [*1882-85*] [*England*] [*A publication*] (DLA)
Cab & El (Eng) ... Cababe and Ellis' Queen's Bench Reports [*1882-85*] [*England*] [*A publication*] (DLA)
Cab & Ell ... Cababe and Ellis' Queen's Bench Reports [*1882-85*] [*England*] [*A publication*] (DLA)
CaBEPN ... Canada Department of National Defence, Defence Research Establishment, Esquimalt, BC, Canada [*Library symbol*] [*Library of Congress*] (LCLS)
CABFM..... Canadian Association for Business Forms Management
CABG .... Coronary Artery Bypass Graft [*Medicine*]
CABGS..... Coronary Artery Bypass Graft Surgery [*Medicine*]
CaBGS....... Gulf Islands Secondary School, Ganges, BC, Canada [*Library symbol*] [*Library of Congress*] (LCLS)
CAB(H) ..... Combined Arms Battalions (Heavy) [*Army*]
CABI......... CAB [*Commonwealth Agricultural Bureaux*] International [*United Kingdom*] [*Research center*] (IRC)
Cab Int ...... Cababe. Interpleader and Attachment of Debts [*1900*] [*A publication*] (ILCA)
CABIOS .... Computer Applications in the Biosciences [*A publication*]
Ca Bi Q ..... Catholic Biblical Quarterly [*A publication*]
CABK........ Colonial American Bankshares Corp. [*NASDAQ symbol*] (NQ)
CaBK .... Kamloops Public Library, Kamloops, BC, Canada [*Library symbol*] [*Library of Congress*] (LCLS)
CaBKAg.... Canada Department of Agriculture, Research Station, Kamloops, BC, Canada [*Library symbol*] [*Library of Congress*] (LCLS)
CaBKAS .... ALCAN Smelters Chemical Ltd., Technical Library, Kitimat, BC, Canada [*Library symbol*] [*Library of Congress*] (LCLS)
CaBKCC .... Cariboo College, Kamloops, BC, Canada [*Library symbol*] [*Library of Congress*] (LCLS)
CaBKCT .... Cariboo-Thompson Nicola Library System, Kamloops, BC, Canada [*Library symbol*] [*Library of Congress*] (LCLS)
CaBKM .... Kamloops Museum, Kamloops, BC, Canada [*Library symbol*] [*Library of Congress*] (LCLS)
CaBKO ...... Okanagan Regional Library, Kelowna, BC, Canada [*Library symbol*] [*Library of Congress*] (LCLS)
CaBKOC.... Okanagan College, Kelowna, BC, Canada [*Library symbol*] [*Library of Congress*] (LCLS)
CaBKOM .. Kelowna Centennial Museum and Archives, Kelowna, BC, Canada [*Library symbol*] [*Library of Congress*] (LCLS)
CAB(L) ..... Combined Arms Battalions (Light) [*Army*]
CABL........ Communication Cable, Inc. [*Siler City, NC*] [*NASDAQ symbol*] (NQ)
CABL........ Consolidation above Battalion Level [*Army*] (RDA)
Cab Lawy... Cabinet Lawyer, by John Wade [*England*] [*A publication*] (DLA)
CABLE...... Consolidation of Administration at Battalion Level [*Army*]
Cablecast Cable TV Eng ... Cablecasting, Cable TV Engineering [*A publication*]
Cable Mktg ... Cable Marketing [*A publication*]
Cable Rpt ... Cable Report [*A publication*]
Cables & Transm ... Cables et Transmission [*A publication*]
Cables Transm ... Cables et Transmission [*A publication*]
Cable Telev Eng ... Cable Television Engineering [*A publication*]
Cable TV Adv ... Cable TV Advertising [*A publication*]
Cable TV B ... Cable Television Business [*A publication*]
Cable TVBD ... Cable Television Business Directory. CATV Suppliers Phone Book [*A publication*]
Cable TV Fin ... Cable TV Finance [*A publication*]
Cable TV Pro ... Cable TV Programming [*A publication*]
Cabl Transm ... Cables et Transmission [*A publication*]
CaBLTW ... Trinity Western College, Langley, BC, Canada [*Library symbol*] [*Library of Congress*] (LCLS)
CABM .... Center for Advanced Biotechnology and Medicine [*Rutgers University*] [*Research center*] (RCD)
C-ABM ...... Chinese-Oriented Antiballistic Missile System (AABC)
CABMA..... Canadian Association of British Manufacturers and Agencies
CABMA..... College Athletic Business Management Association (EA)
CaBMrP .... Pacific Vocational Institute, Maple Ridge, BC, Canada [*Library symbol*] [*Library of Congress*] (LCLS)
CABN .... Caribou News [*Canada*] [*A publication*]

CaBNaMBL ... MacMillan Bloedel Ltd., Nanaimo, BC, Canada [*Library symbol*] [*Library of Congress*] (LCLS)
CaBNM ...... Malaspina College, Nanaimo, BC, Canada [*Library symbol*] [*Library of Congress*] (LCLS)
CaBNND .... David Thompson University Centre [*Formerly, Notre Dame University of Nelson*], Nelson, BC, Canada [*Library symbol*] [*Library of Congress*] (LCLS)
CaBNP .... Canada Department of the Environment, Fisheries and Marine Service, Research and Development Directorate, Pacific Biological Station, Nanaimo, BC, Canada [*Library symbol*] [*Library of Congress*] (LCLS)
CaBNSV .... Selkirk College, Vocational Division, Nelson, BC, Canada [*Library symbol*] [*Library of Congress*] (LCLS)
CABNT ...... Cabinet
CaBNv .... North Vancouver City Library, North Vancouver, BC, Canada [*Library symbol*] [*Library of Congress*] (LCLS)
CaBNvBR ... Ballard Research, Inc., North Vancouver, BC, Canada [*Library symbol*] [*Library of Congress*] (LCLS)
CaBNvD .... District of North Vancouver Library, North Vancouver, BC, Canada [*Library symbol*] [*Library of Congress*] (LCLS)
CaBNVI ..... Vancouver Island Regional Library, Nanaimo, BC, Canada [*Library symbol*] [*Library of Congress*] (LCLS)
CaBNvPM ... Pacific Marine Training Institute, North Vancouver, BC, Canada [*Library symbol*] [*Library of Congress*] (LCLS)
CaBNW ..... New Westminster Public Library, New Westminster, BC, Canada [*Library symbol*] [*Library of Congress*] (LCLS)
CaBNWB... British Columbia Library, New Westminster, BC, Canada [*Library symbol*] [*Library of Congress*] (LCLS)
CaBNWCR ... CanOcean Resources Ltd., New Westminster, BC, Canada [*Library symbol*] [*Library of Congress*] (LCLS)
CaBNWD .. Douglas College, New Westminster, BC, Canada [*Library symbol*] [*Library of Congress*] (LCLS)
CaBNWHC ... New Westminster Historic Centre and Museum, New Westminster, BC, Canada [*Library symbol*] [*Library of Congress*] (LCLS)
CaBNWL... Lower Mainland Regional Planning Board, New Westminster, BC, Canada [*Library symbol*] [*Library of Congress*] (LCLS)
CaBNWLP ... Lockhead Petroleum Services Ltd., New Westminster, BC, Canada [*Library symbol*] [*Library of Congress*] (LCLS)
CaBNWRC ... Royal Columbian Hospital, New Westminster, BC, Canada [*Library symbol*] [*Library of Congress*] (LCLS)
CABO .... Canadian Association of Basketball Officials
CABO .... Cisplatin, Methotrexate, Bleomycin, Oncovin (Vincristine) [*Antineoplastic drug regimen*]
CABO .... Council of American Building Officials (EA)
CABOP....... Cyclophosphamide, Adriamycin, Bleomycin, Oncovin [*Vincristine*], Prednisone [*Antineoplastic drug regimen*]
CaboV .... Cabo Verde [*A publication*]
CABP......... Calcium Binding Protein [*Biochemistry*]
CABP......... Carboxyarabitol Bisphosphate [*Biochemistry*]
CABP......... Conjugate Acid-Base Pair [*Chemistry*]
CaBP.......... Penticton Public Library, Penticton, BC, Canada [*Library symbol*] [*Library of Congress*] (LCLS)
CaBPaM.... Alberni Valley Museum, Port Alberni, BC, Canada [*Library symbol*] [*Library of Congress*] (LCLS)
CaBPc........ Port Coquitlam Public Library, Port Coquitlam, BC, Canada [*Library symbol*] [*Library of Congress*] (LCLS)
CaBPcRH .. Riverview Hospital, Port Coquitlam, BC, Canada [*Library symbol*] [*Library of Congress*] (LCLS)
CaBPG....... Prince George Public Library, Prince George, BC, Canada [*Library symbol*] [*Library of Congress*] (LCLS)
CaBPGC .... College of New Caledonia, Prince George, BC, Canada [*Library symbol*] [*Library of Congress*] (LCLS)
CaBPM...... Penticton Museum and Archives, Penticton, BC, Canada [*Library symbol*] [*Library of Congress*] (LCLS)
CaBPmP .... Port Moody Public Library, Port Moody, BC, Canada [*Library symbol*] [*Library of Congress*] (LCLS)
CaBPO...... Dominion Radio Astrophysical Observatory, Penticton, BC, Canada [*Library symbol*] [*Library of Congress*] (LCLS)
CaBPorH ... Powell River Historical Museum, Powell River, BC, Canada [*Library symbol*] [*Library of Congress*] (LCLS)
CABPP ...... Commission for Acceleration of Black Participation in Psychology
CaBPR....... Prince Rupert Public Library, Prince Rupert, BC, Canada [*Library symbol*] [*Library of Congress*] (LCLS)
CaBPRACS ... Anglican Church of Canada, Diocese of Caledonia, Synod Office, Victoria, BC, Canada [*Library symbol*] [*Library of Congress*] (LCLS)
CaBPrD ..... Powell River District Libraries, Powell, BC, Canada [*Library symbol*] [*Library of Congress*] (LCLS)
CABR......... Cabrillo National Monument
CABR......... Centre for Applied Business Research [*Australia*]
CABR......... Children's Adaptive Behavior Report [*Child development test*] [*Psychology*]
CABRA...... Copper and Brass Research Association [*Later, CDA*]
CaBraDE... Dollman Electronics Ltd., Brampton, ON, Canada [*Library symbol*] [*Library of Congress*] (LCLS)
CaBRC....... Royal Roads Military College, Royal Roads, BC, Canada [*Library symbol*] [*Library of Congress*] (LCLS)
C A Brescia ... Commentari. Accademia di Brescia [*A publication*]

CaBRi .... Richmond Public Library, Richmond, BC, Canada [*Library symbol*] [*Library of Congress*] (LCLS)
CaBRM...... Rossland Historical Museum, Rossland, BC, Canada [*Library symbol*] [*Library of Congress*] (LCLS)
CABS......... Cable Advertising Systems, Inc. [*Austin, TX*] [*NASDAQ symbol*] (NQ)
CABS......... CCNU [*Lomustine*], Adriamycin, Bleomycin, Streptozotocin [*Antineoplastic drug regimen*]
CABS......... Center for the Applied Behavioral Sciences [*St. Louis University*] [*Research center*] (RCD)
CABS......... Children's Assertiveness Behavior Scale
CABS......... Command Automated Budget System [*Army*]
CABS......... Computer-Aided Batch Scheduling
CABS......... Computer-Assisted Bibliographic Service [*University of South Dakota*] (OLDSS)
CABS......... Computerized Annotated Bibliography System [*Alberta University*] [*Canada*]
CABS......... Consolidated Ammunition Bulk Shippers (MCD)
CABS......... Contemporary Authors Bibliographical Series [*A publication*]
CABS......... Coronary Artery Bypass Surgery [*Medicine*]
CABS......... Current Awareness in Biological Sciences [*Pergamon Press*] [*Information service or system*] (IID)
CABSADS ... Computerized, Automated, Bus Spacing and Dispatching System
CABSAF.... Catholic University of America. Biological Studies [*A publication*]
CaBSAg ..... Canada Department of Agriculture, Research Station, Saanichton, BC, Canada [*Library symbol*] [*Library of Congress*] (LCLS)
CaBSH...... British Columbia Hydro and Power Authority, Surrey, BC, Canada [*Library symbol*] [*Library of Congress*] (LCLS)
CaBSIOS... Canada Department of Fisheries and Oceans, Institute of Ocean Studies, Sidney, BC, Canada [*Library symbol*] [*Library of Congress*] (LCLS)
CaBSKC .... Kwantlen College, Surrey, BC, Canada [*Library symbol*] [*Library of Congress*] (LCLS)
CaBSS .... School District 88, Skeena-Terrace, BC, Canada [*Library symbol*] [*Library of Congress*] (LCLS)
CaBSuAg... Canada Department of Agriculture, Research Station, Summerland, BC, Canada [*Library symbol*] [*Library of Congress*] (LCLS)
CABSUS ... Committee of Atomic Bomb Survivors in the US (EA)
CABT......... Cabinet
CaBTC....... Consolidated Mining & Smelting Co., Central Technical Library, Trail, BC, Canada [*Library symbol*] [*Library of Congress*] (LCLS)
CaBTeNW ... North West College, Terrace, BC, Canada [*Library symbol*] [*Library of Congress*] (LCLS)
CABUA ..... Canadian Business [*A publication*]
CA Bull ...... CA. A Bulletin of Cancer Progress [*A publication*]
CA Bull Cancer Prog ... CA. A Bulletin of Cancer Progress [*A publication*]
CABV......... Canadian Association of Business Valuators
CaBV .... Vernon Library, Vernon, BC, Canada [*Library symbol*] [*Library of Congress*] (LCLS)
CaBVa........ Vancouver Public Library, Vancouver, BC, Canada [*Library symbol*] [*Library of Congress*] (LCLS)
CaBVaA.... Vancouver City Archives, Vancouver, BC, Canada [*Library symbol*] [*Library of Congress*] (LCLS)
CaBVaABSA ... Anglican Church of Canada, British Columbia Provincial Synod, Archives, Vancouver, BC, Canada [*Library symbol*] [*Library of Congress*] (LCLS)
CaBVaADP ... Alcohol and Drug Programs, Vancouver, BC, Canada [*Library symbol*] [*Library of Congress*] (LCLS)
CaBVaAE.. Associated Engineering Services Ltd., Vancouver, BC, Canada [*Library symbol*] [*Library of Congress*] (LCLS)
CaBVaAg... Canada Department of Agriculture, Entomological Society of British Columbia Library, Vancouver, BC, Canada [*Library symbol*] [*Library of Congress*] (LCLS)
CaBVaBT .. British Columbia Telephone Co., Vancouver, BC, Canada [*Library symbol*] [*Library of Congress*] (LCLS)
CaBVaBY .. British Columbia and Yukon Chamber of Mines, Vancouver, BC, Canada [*Library symbol*] [*Library of Congress*] (LCLS)
CaBVaC..... Capilano College, Vancouver, BC, Canada [*Library symbol*] [*Library of Congress*] (LCLS)
CaBVaCAA ... Catholic Church, Archdiocese of Vancouver, Archives, Vancouver, BC, Canada [*Library symbol*] [*Library of Congress*] (LCLS)
CaBVaCBA ... CBA Engineering Ltd., Vancouver, BC, Canada [*Library symbol*] [*Library of Congress*] (LCLS)
CaBVaCCU ... BC Central Credit Union, Vancouver, BC, Canada [*Library symbol*] [*Library of Congress*] (LCLS)
CaBVaCF .. Council of Forest Industries of British Columbia, Vancouver, BC, Canada [*Library symbol*] [*Library of Congress*] (LCLS)
CaBVaCI ... Chemetics International Ltd., Vancouver, BC, Canada [*Library symbol*] [*Library of Congress*] (LCLS)
CaBVaCM ... Centennial Museum, Vancouver, BC, Canada [*Library symbol*] [*Library of Congress*] (LCLS)
CaBVaCOM ... Cominco Ltd., Vancouver, BC, Canada [*Library symbol*] [*Library of Congress*] (LCLS)

CaBVaEC .. British Columbia Energy Commission, Vancouver, BC, Canada [*Library symbol*] [*Library of Congress*] (LCLS)

CaBVaEN ... Envirocon Ltd., Vancouver, BC, Canada [*Library symbol*] [*Library of Congress*] (LCLS)

CaBVaEP .. Canada Department of the Environment, Environmental Protection Service, Vancouver, BC, Canada [*Library symbol*] [*Library of Congress*] (LCLS)

CaBVaF ..... Canada Department of the Environment, Fisheries and Marine Service, Research and Development Directorate, Vancouver Laboratory, Vancouver, BC, Canada [*Library symbol*] [*Library of Congress*] (LCLS)

CaBVaFA .. Vancouver Public Library, Fine Arts, Music, and Films Division, Vancouver, BC, Canada [*Library symbol*] [*Library of Congress*] (LCLS)

CaBVaFi.... Canada Department of Fisheries and Oceans, Vancouver, BC, Canada [*Library symbol*] [*Library of Congress*] (LCLS)

CaBVaFP... Canada Department of the Environment, Forest Products Laboratory, Vancouver, BC, Canada [*Library symbol*] [*Library of Congress*] (LCLS)

CaBVaFV .. Farris, Vaughan, Wills & Murphy Law Firm, Vancouver, BC, Canada [*Library symbol*] [*Library of Congress*] (LCLS)

CaBVaG..... Canada Geological Survey, Vancouver, BC, Canada [*Library symbol*] [*Library of Congress*] (LCLS)

CaBVaGB ... Golder, Brawner & Associates Ltd., Vancouver, BC, Canada [*Library symbol*] [*Library of Congress*] (LCLS)

CaBVaH .... British Columbia Hydro and Power Authority [*Formerly, British Columbia Electric Co. Ltd.*], Vancouver, BC, Canada [*Library symbol*] [*Library of Congress*] (LCLS)

CaBVaHE ... British Columbia Hydro Engineering Library, Vancouver, BC, Canada [*Library symbol*] [*Library of Congress*] (LCLS)

CaBVaHP ... Vancouver Public Library, Historic Photographic Collection, Vancouver, BC, Canada [*Library symbol*] [*Library of Congress*] (LCLS)

CaBVaHS ... H. A. Simons Ltd., Vancouver, BC, Canada [*Library symbol*] [*Library of Congress*] (LCLS)

CaBVaI...... International North Pacific Fisheries, Vancouver, BC, Canada [*Library symbol*] [*Library of Congress*] (LCLS)

CaBVaJ ..... Canada Department of Justice, Vancouver, BC, Canada [*Library symbol*] [*Library of Congress*] (LCLS)

CaBVaJI.... Justice Institute of British Columbia, Vancouver, BC, Canada [*Library symbol*] [*Library of Congress*] (LCLS)

CaBVaL..... Law Society of British Columbia, Vancouver, BC, Canada [*Library symbol*] [*Library of Congress*] (LCLS)

CaBVaLMW ... L. M. Warren, Inc., Vancouver, BC, Canada [*Library symbol*] [*Library of Congress*] (LCLS)

CaBVaM.... British Columbia Medical Library Service, Vancouver, BC, Canada [*Library symbol*] [*Library of Congress*] (LCLS)

CaBVaMB ... MacMillan Bloedel Research Limited, Vancouver, BC, Canada [*Library symbol*] [*Library of Cong.ess*] (LCLS)

CaBVaMBL ... MacMillan Bloedel Limited, Vancouver, BC, Canada [*Library symbol*] [*Library of Congress*] (LCLS)

CaBVaMI .. Canada Employment and Immigration Department, Vancouver, BC, Canada [*Library symbol*] [*Library of Congress*] (LCLS)

CaBVaMM ... Maritime Museum, Vancouver, BC, Canada [*Library symbol*] [*Library of Congress*] (LCLS)

CaBVaMOE ... Mobil Oil Estates Ltd., Vancouver, BC, Canada [*Library symbol*] [*Library of Congress*] (LCLS)

CaBVaNH ... Canada Department of National Health and Welfare, Health Protection Branch, Vancouver, BC, Canada [*Library symbol*] [*Library of Congress*] (LCLS)

CaBVaNHC ... Vancouver Public Library, Northwest History Collection, Vancouver, BC, Canada [*Library symbol*] [*Library of Congress*] (LCLS)

CaBVaP ..... Placer Development Library, Vancouver, BC, Canada [*Library symbol*] [*Library of Congress*] (LCLS)

CaBVaPAD ... British Columbia Packers Ltd., Product Assurance and Development, Vancouver, BC, Canada [*Library symbol*] [*Library of Congress*] (LCLS)

CaBVaPC .. Phillips Cables Ltd., Vancouver, BC, Canada [*Library symbol*] [*Library of Congress*] (LCLS)

CaBVaPD .. Greater Vancouver Regional District, Planning Development Library, Vancouver, BC, Canada [*Library symbol*] [*Library of Congress*] (LCLS)

CaBVaPE .. Canada Department of the Environment, Pacific Environment Institute, Vancouver, BC, Canada [*Library symbol*] [*Library of Congress*] (LCLS)

CaBVaR..... British Columbia Research Council, Vancouver, BC, Canada [*Library symbol*] [*Library of Congress*] (LCLS)

CaBVaRB .. Royal Bank of Canada, Vancouver, BC, Canada [*Library symbol*] [*Library of Congress*] (LCLS)

CaBVaRC .. Rayonier Canada, Research Division, Vancouver, BC, Canada [*Library symbol*] [*Library of Congress*] [*Obsolete*] (LCLS)

CaBVaRE .. Archives of the Ecclesiastical Province of British Columbia, Vancouver, BC, Canada [*Library symbol*] [*Library of Congress*] (LCLS)

CaBVaRN ... Registered Nurses Association, Vancouver, BC, Canada [*Library symbol*] [*Library of Congress*] (LCLS)

CaBVaS ..... Simon Fraser University, Vancouver, BC, Canada [*Library symbol*] [*Library of Congress*] (LCLS)

CaBVaSC .. Sandwell & Co., Vancouver, BC, Canada [*Library symbol*] [*Library of Congress*] (LCLS)

CaBVaSG .. Simon Fraser University, Simon Fraser Gallery, Burnaby, BC, Canada [*Library symbol*] [*Library of Congress*] (LCLS)

CaBVaSLA ... F. F. Slaney & Co. Ltd., Vancouver, BC, Canada [*Library symbol*] [*Library of Congress*] (LCLS)

CaBVaSM ... Simon Fraser University, Map Library, Vancouver, BC, Canada [*Library symbol*] [*Library of Congress*] (LCLS)

CaBVaSPH .. Saint Paul's Hospital, Health Sciences Library, Vancouver, BC, Canada [*Library symbol*] [*Library of Congress*] (LCLS)

CaBVaST... Vancouver School of Theology, Vancouver, BC, Canada [*Library symbol*] [*Library of Congress*] (LCLS)

CaBVaSW ... Swan Wooster Engineering Co., Vancouver, BC, Canada [*Library symbol*] [*Library of Congress*] (LCLS)

CaBVaTE .. Teck Mining Group Ltd., Elizabeth Watson Library, Vancouver, BC, Canada [*Library symbol*] [*Library of Congress*] (LCLS)

CaBVaTF .. British Columbia Teachers' Federation Resources Centre, Vancouver, BC, Canada [*Library symbol*] [*Library of Congress*] (LCLS)

CaBVaU .... University of British Columbia, Vancouver, BC, Canada [*Library symbol*] [*Library of Congress*] (LCLS)

CaBVaUBCA ... United Church, British Columbia Conference, Archives, Vancouver, BC, Canada [*Library symbol*] [*Library of Congress*] (LCLS)

CaBVaUCC ... University of British Columbia, Charles Crane Memorial Library, Vancouver, BC, Canada, [*Library symbol*] [*Library of Congress*] (LCLS)

CaBVaUG ... University of British Columbia, Department of Geography, Vancouver, BC, Canada [*Library symbol*] [*Library of Congress*] (LCLS)

CaBVaUL ... University of British Columbia, Law Library, Vancouver, BC, Canada [*Library symbol*] [*Library of Congress*] (LCLS)

CaBVaUM ... University of British Columbia, Map Division, Vancouver, BC, Canada [*Library symbol*] [*Library of Congress*] (LCLS)

CaBVaUS .. University of British Columbia, Special Collections Division, Vancouver, BC, Canada [*Library symbol*] [*Library of Congress*] (LCLS)

CaBVaUW ... University of British Columbia, Woodward Library, Vancouver, BC, Canada [*Library symbol*] [*Library of Congress*] (LCLS)

CaBVaUWGV ... United Way of Greater Vancouver, Vancouver, BC, Canada [*Library symbol*] [*Library of Congress*] (LCLS)

CaBVaVA ... Vancouver Art Gallery, Vancouver, BC, Canada [*Library symbol*] [*Library of Congress*] (LCLS)

CaBVaVCL ... Vancouver City College, Langara, Vancouver, BC, Canada [*Library symbol*] [*Library of Congress*] (LCLS)

CaBVaVSA ... Vancouver School of Art, Vancouver, BC, Canada [*Library symbol*] [*Library of Congress*] (LCLS)

CaBVaWC ... Workers Compensation Board of British Columbia, Vancouver, BC, Canada [*Library symbol*] [*Library of Congress*] (LCLS)

CaBVaWH ... Warnock Hersey International Ltd., Vancouver, BC, Canada [*Library symbol*] [*Library of Congress*] (LCLS)

CaBVaWT ... West Coast Transmission Ltd., Vancouver, BC, Canada [*Library symbol*] [*Library of Congress*] (LCLS)

CaBVi .... Greater Victoria Public Library, Victoria, BC, Canada [*Library symbol*] [*Library of Congress*] (LCLS)

CaBViA ...... Art Gallery of Greater Victoria, Victoria, BC, Canada [*Library symbol*] [*Library of Congress*] (LCLS)

CaBViAGC ... British Columbia Ministry of Attorney General, CLEU Library, Victoria, BC, Canada [*Library symbol*] [*Library of Congress*] (LCLS)

CaBViB ...... British Columbia Barkerville Restoration Advisory Committee, Victoria, BC, Canada [*Library symbol*] [*Library of Congress*] (LCLS)

CaBViBE ... British Columbia Bureau of Economics and Statistics, Business-Finance Library, Victoria, BC, Canada [*Library symbol*] [*Library of Congress*] (LCLS)

CaBViC ...... Camosun College, Victoria, BC, Canada [*Library symbol*] [*Library of Congress*] (LCLS)

CaBViDE ... British Columbia Ministry of Education, Victoria, BC, Canada [*Library symbol*] [*Library of Congress*] (LCLS)

CaBViED ... British Columbia Ministry of Economic Development, Victoria, BC, Canada [*Library symbol*] [*Library of Congress*] (LCLS)

CaBViEM ... Canada Department of the Environment, Institute of Ocean Sciences, Victoria, BC, Canada [*Library symbol*] [*Library of Congress*] (LCLS)

CaBViEP ... British Columbia Ministry of the Environment, Environmental Protection, Pollution Control Branch, Victoria, BC, Canada [*Library symbol*] [*Library of Congress*] (LCLS)

CaBViF ...... Canada Department of the Environment, Forest Research Laboratory, Victoria, BC, Canada [*Library symbol*] [*Library of Congress*] (LCLS)

CaBViFS.... British Columbia Forest Service, Victoria, BC, Canada [*Library symbol*] [*Library of Congress*] (LCLS)

CaBViH ..... British Columbia Ministry of Highways and Public Works, Victoria, BC, Canada [*Library symbol*] [*Library of Congress*] (LCLS)

CaBViHe ... British Columbia Ministry of Health, Victoria, BC, Canada [*Library symbol*] [*Library of Congress*] (LCLS)
CaBViHI ... British Columbia Ministry of Health, Health Information, Victoria, BC, Canada [*Library symbol*] [*Library of Congress*] (LCLS)
CaBViHPP ... British Columbia Ministry of Health, Health Promotion Programmes, Victoria, BC, Canada [*Library symbol*] [*Library of Congress*] (LCLS)
CaBViHRS ... British Columbia Ministry of Human Resources, Staff Development Division, Victoria, BC, Canada [*Library symbol*] [*Library of Congress*] (LCLS)
CaBViL .... Law Library Foundation, Victoria, BC, Canada [*Library symbol*] [*Library of Congress*] (LCLS)
CaBViLBP ... Lester B. Pearson College of the Pacific, Victoria, BC, Canada [*Library symbol*] [*Library of Congress*] (LCLS)
CaBViLC ... Public Library Commission, Victoria, BC, Canada [*Library symbol*] [*Library of Congress*] (LCLS)
CaBViLDC ... Library Development Commission, Victoria, BC, Canada [*Library symbol*] [*Library of Congress*] (LCLS)
CaBViLFW ... British Columbia Ministry of the Environment, Victoria, BC, Canada [*Library symbol*] [*Library of Congress*] (LCLS)
CaBViLPHP ... British Columbia Ministry of Lands, Parks, and Housing, Parks Library, Victoria, BC, Canada [*Library symbol*] [*Library of Congress*] (LCLS)
CaBViLSB ... Ministry of the Provincial Secretary and Government Services, Library Services Branch, Victoria, BC, Canada [*Library symbol*] [*Library of Congress*] (LCLS)
CaBViM .... British Columbia Ministry of Mines and Petroleum Resources, Victoria, BC, Canada [*Library symbol*] [*Library of Congress*] (LCLS)
CaBViMH ... University of Victoria, Maltwood Art Museum, Victoria, BC, Canada [*Library symbol*] [*Library of Congress*] (LCLS)
CaBViMM ... Maritime Museum of British Columbia, Victoria, BC, Canada [*Library symbol*] [*Library of Congress*] (LCLS)
CaBViO ..... Dominion Astrophysical Observatory, Victoria, BC, Canada [*Library symbol*] [*Library of Congress*] (LCLS)
CaBViP ...... Legislative Library, Victoria, BC, Canada [*Library symbol*] [*Library of Congress*] (LCLS)
CaBViPA ... Provincial Archives, Victoria, BC, Canada [*Library symbol*] [*Library of Congress*] (LCLS)
CaBViPME ... British Columbia Provincial Museum, Ethnology Division, Victoria, BC, Canada [*Library symbol*] [*Library of Congress*] (LCLS)
CaBViPR ... Victoria Press Ltd., Victoria, BC, Canada [*Library symbol*] [*Library of Congress*] (LCLS)
CaBViRC ... British Columbia Ministry of Recreation and Conservation, Fish and Game Branch, Victoria, BC, Canada [*Library symbol*] [*Library of Congress*] (LCLS)
CaBViT ...... R. Thuber & Associates, Victoria, BC, Canada [*Library symbol*] [*Library of Congress*] (LCLS)
CaBViV ...... University of Victoria, Victoria, BC, Canada [*Library symbol*] [*Library of Congress*] (LCLS)
CaBViVA ... University of Victoria, Department of History in Art, Victoria, BC, Canada [*Library symbol*] [*Library of Congress*] (LCLS)
CaBViVG ... University of Victoria, Geography Department, Victoria, BC, Canada [*Library symbol*] [*Library of Congress*] (LCLS)
CaBViVL ... University of Victoria, Law Library, Victoria, BC, Canada [*Library symbol*] [*Library of Congress*] (LCLS)
CaBVMA ... Vernon Museum, Archives and Art Gallery, Vernon, BC, Canada [*Library symbol*] [*Library of Congress*] (LCLS)
CAB(WA) ... Citizens' Advice Bureau of Western Australia
CaBWv .... West Vancouver Memorial Library, West Vancouver, BC, Canada [*Library symbol*] [*Library of Congress*] (LCLS)
CaBWvHC ... Hatfield Consultants Ltd., West Vancouver, BC, Canada [*Library symbol*] [*Library of Congress*] (LCLS)
CABx .... Citizens' Advice Bureaux [*British*] (ILCA)
CAC .... Cable Access Cover
CAC .... Cacwhuacintle [*Race of maize*]
CAC .... Calama [*Chile*] [*Seismograph station code, US Geological Survey*] (SEIS)
CAC .... California Air Charter [*Burbank, CA*] [*FAA designator*] (FAAC)
CAC .... California Avocado Commission (EA)
CAC .... California State University and Colleges, Tape Profile, Long Beach, CA [*OCLC symbol*] (OCLC)
CAC .... Canada Art Council [*Conseil des Arts du Canada*]
CAC .... Canadian-American Committee (EA)
CAC .... Canadian Armoured Corps
CAC .... Caravan America-China [*Inactive*] (EA)
CAC .... Carbon Arc Cutting [*Welding*]
CAC .... Cardiac Accelerator Center [*Physiology*]
CAC .... Cardiac Arrest Code [*Medicine*]
CAC .... Career Assistance Counseling [*Air Force*] (AFM)
CAC .... Caribbean Air Command [*Air Force*]
CAC .... Cascadia Mines [*Vancouver Stock Exchange symbol*]
CAC .... Cascavel [*Brazil*] [*Airport symbol*] (OAG)
CAC .... Cathedrals Advisory Committee [*Church of England*]
CAC .... Catholic Anthropological Conference
CAC .... Center Accessory Compartment (MCD)
CAC .... Central Advisory Committee [*British*]

CAC .... Central Air Conditioning [*Classified advertising*]
CAC .... Central American Club of New York (EA)
CAC .... Central Arbitration Committee [*British*] (ILCA)
CAC .... Centre for Advancement of Counselling [*British*]
CAC .... Centre for the Analysis of Conflict [*United Kingdom*] [*Research center*] (IRC)
CAC .... Cessna Aircraft Company
CAC .... Cessna Airmaster Club (EA)
CAC .... Champion Aircraft Company
CAC .... Change Administration Conference
CAC .... Change [*or Changing*] to Approach Control [*Aviation*] (FAAC)
CAC .... Chase Aircraft Company
CAC .... Chemical Abstracts Condensates [*A publication*] (IID)
C of AC ...... Chief of Air Corps [*World War II*]
CAC .... Chief of Air Corps [*World War II*]
CAC .... Chief Artillery Controller (NATG)
CAC .... Children's Advocacy Center (EA)
CAC .... Chloroacetyl Chloride [*Organic chemistry*]
CAC .... Christian Action Council (EA)
CAC .... Cigarette Advertising Code, Inc. (EA)
CAC .... Citizens Advocate Center [*Antipoverty organization*] [*Defunct*]
CAC .... Civic Action Centers [*Military*] (CINC)
CAC .... Civil Administration Committee [*US Military Government, Germany*]
CAC .... Classical Association of Canada [*See also SCEC*]
CAC .... Classroom Adjustment Code
CAC .... Clear All Channels
CAC .... Clerical Administrative Class (ADA)
CAC .... Climate - Altitude Chamber
CAC .... Climate Analysis Center [*National Weather Service*]
CAC .... Coaching Association of Canada
CAC .... Coast Artillery Corps [*Army*]
CAC .... CoastAmerica Corporation [*NYSE symbol*] (SPSG)
CAC .... Collection Advisory Center (MCD)
CAC .... College Admissions Center (EA)
CAC .... Colonial Aircraft Company
CAC .... Combat Air Crew
CAC .... Combat Analysis Capability (MCD)
CAC .... Combined Action Company [*Formerly, Joint Action Company*] [*Military*]
CAC .... Combined Additional Coverage [*Insurance*]
CAC .... Combined Arms Center (AABC)
CAC .... Comite Administratif de Coordination [*Administrative Committee on Coordination - ACC*] [*United Nations*] [*French*] (ASF)
CAC .... Comite Administrativo de Coordinacion [*Administrative Committee on Coordination - ACC*] [*United Nations*] [*Spanish*] (MSC)
CAC .... Command Analysis Center
CAC .... Command and Control (NVT)
CAC .... Commander Air Center
CAC .... Commission of Assembly of the Church of Scotland (DAS)
CAC .... Commission du Codex Alimentarius [*Joint FAO-WHO Codex Alimentarius Commission*] (EAIO)
CAC .... Commonwealth Aircraft Corporation Ltd. [*Australia*] (MCD)
CAC .... Communications Analysis Corporation [*Framingham, MA*] [*Telecommunications*] (TSSD)
CAC .... Community Activity Center (MCD)
CAC .... Commuting Area Candidates [*Civil Service*]
CAC .... Compagnie des Agents de Change [*French stockbrokers society*] [*Paris*] [*Information service or system*] (IID)
CAC .... Complete Address Constant
CAC .... Computer Access Corporation [*Information service or system*] (IID)
CAC .... Computer-Aided Classification
CAC .... Computer-Assisted Counseling [*Proposed for Air Force*]
CAC .... Congressional Arts Caucus (EA)
CAC .... Congressional Automotive Caucus (EA)
CAC .... Conseil des Arts du Canada [*Canada Council*] (EAIO)
CAC .... Consolidated Aircraft Corporation [*Later, General Dynamics Corp.*] (AAG)
CAC .... Consolidated Athletic Commission (EA)
CAC .... Constant Alert Cycle
CAC .... Constitution and Ancient Charges [*Freemasonry*] (ROG)
CAC .... Constitutional Acts of Canada [*Database*] [*Federal Department of Justice*] [*Information service or system*] (CRD)
CAC .... Consumer's Advisory Council
CAC .... Consumers' Association of Canada
CAC .... Contact Approach Control [*Aviation*] (FAAC)
CAC .... Contact Area Commander
CAC .... Containment Atmosphere Control [*Monitor, or System*] [*Nuclear energy*] (IEEE)
CAC .... Continental Air Command
CAC .... Continental Army Command [*See CONARC*]
CAC .... Continuous Aim Correction [*Military*] (CAAL)
CAC .... Continuous Annular Chromatograph
CAC .... Contract Auditor Coordinator
CAC .... Control and Analysis Centers [*ERADCOM*] (RDA)
CAC .... Control and Coordination [*Army*]
CAC .... CONVAIR [*Consolidated-Vultee Aircraft Corp.*] Astronautics Corporation [*Later, General Dynamics Corp.*] (AAG)

CAC .... Cooperation and Coordination
CAC .... Corporate Accounting [*A publication*]
CAC .... Correction Action Committee
CAC .... Corrugated Asbestos Cement (ADA)
CAC .... Cosmetology Accrediting Commission [*Later, NACCAS*] (EA)
CAC .... Cost Account Code [*Accounting*]
CAC .... Council for the Advancement of Citizenship (EA)
CAC .... Crosley Automobile Club (EA)
CAC .... Crown Agents for the Colonies [*British*]
CAC .... Crusade Against Corruption (EA)
CAC .... Currency Adjustment Charge [*Business term*]
CAC .... Current Abstracts of Chemistry [*Institute for Scientific Information*] [*Database*] [*A publication*]
CAC .... Current Actions Center
CAC .... Curriculum Advisory Committee [*American Occupational Therapy Association*]
CAC .... Customer Applicability Code (MCD)
CAC .... Customs Additional Code (DS)
CAC .... Czechoslovak Association of Canada (EAIO)
CAC .... Heavy Cruiser, Guided Missile [*Navy symbol*]
CAC .... Newton, KS [*Location identifier*] [*FAA*] (FAAL)
CACA .... Canadian Agricultural Chemics Association
CACA .... Canadian Amateur Cowboys Association
CACA .... Carlsbad Caverns National Park
CACA .... Central After Care Association [*British*]
CACA .... Chinese American Citizens Alliance (EA)
CACA .... Citizens Association for the Care of Animals (EA)
CACA .... Collision Alert [*Air traffic control*]
CACA .... Computer-Aided Circuit Analysis [*Electronics*]
CACA .... Continuous Accumulation of Coriolis Acceleration [*Bioscience*]
CACA .... Council Against Communist Aggression [*Later, CDF*] (EA)
CACAA ..... Cafe, Cacao, The [*A publication*]
CACAC ..... Civil Aircraft Control Advisory Committee [*British*] (AIA)
CA Cancer J Clin ... CA. A Cancer Journal for Clinicians [*A publication*]
Cacao Choc Suikerwerken ... Cacao Chocolade en Suikerwerken [*A publication*]
Cacao Colomb ... Cacao en Colombia [*A publication*]
CACAS ...... Chemical Agent Casualty Assessment System (MCD)
Cacau Atual ... Cacau Atualidades [*A publication*]
CACB .... Center Aisle Connector Bracket (MCD)
CACB .... Compressed Air Circuit Breaker (MSA)
CACBB ...... Annual Reports on the Progress of Chemistry. Section B. Organic Chemistry [*A publication*]
CACBB4 .... Annual Reports on the Progress of Chemistry. Section B. Organic Chemistry [*A publication*]
CaCC .... Cathodal Closure Contraction [*Also, CCC*] [*Physiology*]
CACC .... Chinese American Civic Council (EA)
CACC .... Christian Anti-Communism Crusade (EA)
CACC .... Civil Aviation Communication Center [*Canada*]
CACC .... Colombian-American Chamber of Commerce (EA)
CACC .... Colonial Life & Accident Insurance Co. [*NASDAQ symbol*] (NQ)
CACC .... Communications and Configuration Console (MCD)
CACC .... Computer Application Control Code
CACC .... Conseil Acadien de Cooperation Culturelle en Atlantique [*Acadian Council of Cultural Cooperation in Atlantic Canada*]
CACC .... Continental Africa Chamber of Commerce (EA)
CACC .... Cossack-American Citizens' Committee (EA)
CACC .... Council for the Accreditation of Correspondence Colleges [*British*]
CACCE ...... Council of American Chambers of Commerce in Europe [*Later, European Council of American Chambers of Commerce*] (EA)
CACCI .... Confederation of Asian-Pacific Chambers of Commerce and Industry [*Taipei, Taiwan*] (EAIO)
Cacciat Ital ... Cacciatore Italiano [*A publication*]
Cacciat Trent ... Cacciatore Trentino [*A publication*]
CACD .... Computer-Aided Circuit Design
CACDA ..... Combined Arms Combat Development Activity [*Fort Leavenworth, KS*] [*Army*] (AABC)
CACE .... Canadian Association of Chairmen of English Departments
CACE .... Counteracting Chromatographic Electrophoresis
CACEED ... Conference of Americans of Central and Eastern European Descent [*Defunct*] (EA)
CACEEG ... Cancer Cells [*Cold Spring Harbor*] [*A publication*]
Ca Celeb..... Causes Celebres [*Quebec Provincial Reports*] [*A publication*] (DLA)
CACEP ...... Congressional Arts Caucus Education Program (EA)
CACEQ ..... Citizens Advisory Committee on Environmental Quality
CACEX...... Carteira de Comercio Exterior [*Foreign Trade Department*] [*Brazil*]
CACF........ Case Assignment Control File [*IRS*]
CACFOA... Chief and Assistant Chief Fire Officers' Association [*British*]
CACGP...... Commission on Atmospheric Chemistry and Global Pollution [*British*]
CACH........ Cache, Inc. [*NASDAQ symbol*] (NQ)
CACH........ Canadian Churchman [*A publication*]
CACH........ Canyon de Chelly National Monument
CACH........ Consumer Affairs Clearinghouse

CaCh.......... Sorores Carmelitae a Caritate [*Carmelite Sisters of Charity*] [*Roman Catholic religious order*]
CACHE ..... Chicago Area Computer Hobbyist Exchange
CACHE ..... Computer Aids for Chemical Engineering Education [*National Academy of Engineering*]
CACHE ..... Computer-Controlled Automated Cargo Handling Envelope
Cacher........ [*Octavianus Osascus*] Cacheranus [*Flourished, 16th century*] [*Authority cited in pre-1607 legal work*] (DSA)
Cacheran... [*Octavianus Osascus*] Cacheranus [*Flourished, 16th century*] [*Authority cited in pre-1607 legal work*] (DSA)
CACI......... CACI International, Inc. [*NASDAQ symbol*] (NQ)
CACI......... Canadian Academic Centre in Italy
CACI......... Catholic Alumni Clubs International (EA)
CACI......... Centre Academique Canedien en Italie [*Canadian Academic Centre in Italy*]
CACI......... Civil Aviation Chaplains International (EAIO)
CACI......... Classic AMX Club International (EA)
CACI......... Community Arts Councils, Incorporated [*Later, American Council for the Arts*] (EA)
CACI......... Consolidated Analysis Centers, Incorporated
CAC & IC .. Current Abstracts of Chemistry and Index Chemicus [*A publication*]
CACL........ Canadian Association of Children's Librarians
CACL........ Canadian Association for Community Living (EAIO)
CACL........ Castle Clinton National Monument
CACL........ Computer and Aerospace Components Limited [*British*]
CACLALS ... Canadian Association for Commonwealth Literature and Language Studies [*See also ACELLC*]
CACLD..... Canadian Association for Children with Learning Disabilities
CACM .... Central American Common Market
CACM .... Communications. ACM [*Association for Computing Machinery*] [*A publication*]
CACM .... Communications. Association for Computing Machinery
CACNB ..... Comite Associe du Code National du Batiment [*Associate Committee of the National Building Code*] [*National Research Council of Canada*]
CACNRWC ... Cuban-American Committee for Normalization of Relations with Cuba (EA)
CACO .... Canadian Conservationist [*A publication*]
CACO .... Cape Cod National Seashore [*National Park Service designation*]
CACO .... Casualty Assistance Calls Officer
CACO .... [*The*] Cato Corp. [*NASDAQ symbol*] (NQ)
CACO .... Corporate Administrative Contracting Officer [*DoD*]
CACOD ..... Canadian Consumer [*A publication*]
CACOM ..... Central American Common Market
CACON .... Cargo Container (KSC)
CACON .... Chemical Abstracts Condensates [*Database*]
CACP........ Cahiers de l'Amitie Charles Peguy [*A publication*]
CACP........ Canadian Association of Chiefs of Police
CACP........ Casualty Assistance Calls Program (CINC)
CACP........ Central Arbitration Control Point (BYTE)
CACP........ Council for the Advancement of Consumer Policy (EA)
CACPAF ... Continental Association of CPA [*Certified Public Accountant*] Firms (EA)
CAC/PL.... Canadian Advisory Committee on Programming Languages
CACR .... Clean Air Car Race
CACR .... Contract Acquisition Cost Report (MCD)
CACR .... Council for Agricultural and Chemurgic Research (EA)
CA/CRL .... Custody Authorization/Custody Receipt Listing
CACS........ California Aqueduct Control System
CACS........ Canada. Climatological Studies [*A publication*]
CACS........ Centralized Alarm and Control System [*Telecommunications*] (TEL)
CACS........ Centre for Applied Colloid Science [*Australia*]
CA/CS .... Change Administration Cover Sheet
CACS........ Commonwealth Accommodation and Catering Services [*Australia*]
CACS........ Computer-Aided [*or -Assisted*] Communication System
CACS........ Content Addressable Computing System
CACS........ Continental Airways and Communications Service [*Air Force*]
CACS........ Core Auxiliary Cooling System [*Nuclear energy*] (NRCH)
CACS........ Corps Area Communications System [*Vietnam*] (MCD)
CACSO..... Central American and Caribbean Sports Organization (EAIO)
CACST..... Central Advisory Council for Science and Technology [*British*]
CACSW..... Citizens' Advisory Council on the Status of Women
CACT........ Civil Air Carrier Turbojet (FAAC)
CACT........ Command Automatic Card Tester
Cact J .... Cactus Journal [*A publication*]
CACTO ..... Cactoblastis [*South American moth brought to Australia to destroy the prickly pear*] (DSUE)
CACTOS ... Computation and Communication Trade-Off Study [*ARPA*]
Cact Succ J ... Cactus and Succulent Journal [*A publication*]
Cact Succ J Gr Br ... Cactus and Succulent Journal of Great Britain [*A publication*]
Cact Suc Mex ... Cactaceas y Suculentas Mexicanas [*A publication*]
Cact Suculentas Mex ... Cactaceas y Suculentas Mexicanas [*A publication*]
Cactus Succ J ... Cactus and Succulent Journal [*United States*] [*A publication*]
Cactus Succ J Gt Br ... Cactus and Succulent Journal of Great Britain [*A publication*]
Cactus Succulent J ... Cactus and Succulent Journal [*A publication*]

Cactus Succulent J GB ... Cactus and Succulent Journal of Great Britain [*A publication*]
Ca Cu .... Boletin. Instituto Caro y Cuervo [*A publication*]
CACUCS ... Conference of Administrators of College and University Counseling Services (EA)
CACUL...... Canadian Association of College and University Libraries
CACUL Newsl ... Canadian Association of College and University Libraries. Newsletter [*A publication*]
CACUSS ... Canadian Association of College and University Student Services
CACV .... Cooperstown & Charlotte Valley Railway Corp. [*AAR code*]
CACW .... Central American Confederation of Workers (EAIO)
CACW .... Chinese-American Composite Wing [*Air Force*]
CAC & W... Continental Aircraft Control and Warning (MUGU)
CACW .... Core Auxiliary Cooling Water [*Nuclear energy*] (NRCH)
CACWS..... Core Auxiliary Cooling Water System [*Nuclear energy*] (NRCH)
CACWV..... Committee to Aid Cold War Veterans (EA)
CACX .... Cancer of the Cervix [*Medicine*]
CACYA4.... Cancer Cytology [*A publication*]
CAD........... Cabling Diagram
Cad............. Cadaver [*Medicine*]
cad............. Caddo [*MARC language code*] [*Library of Congress*] (LCCP)
CAD............ Cadenza [*Cadence*] [*Music*]
CAD............ Cadet
CAD............ Cadger (ROG)
CAD............ Cadillac, MI [*Location identifier*] [*FAA*] (FAAL)
CAD............ Cadiz Railroad Co. [*AAR code*]
CAD............ Cadmium [*Chemical symbol is Cd*] (KSC)
Cad............. Caducee [*A publication*]
Cad............. Caduceo. Revista Grafica Espanola Economico Financiera [*A publication*]
Cad............. Caduceus [*A publication*]
CAD............ Cady Mountains [*California*] [*Seismograph station code, US Geological Survey*] [*Closed*] (SEIS)
CAD............ Canadian Air Division (MCD)
CAD............ Canadian Annual Digest [*A publication*] (DLA)
CAD............ Cartridge-Actuated Device [*Military*] (NVT)
CAD............ Cash Against Documents [*Sales*]
CAD............ Center for Affective Disorders [*University of Wisconsin, Madison*] [*Research center*] (RCD)
CAD............ Center Aiming Disc (NATG)
CAD............ Center Area Discrete [*Channel*] (FAAC)
CAD............ Center for Astronomical Data [*Academy of Sciences of the USSR*] [*Information service or system*] (IID)
CAD............ Central Aircraft Dispatch
CAD............ Central Ammunition Depot (NATG)
C-A-D .... C'Est-a-Dire [*That Is to Say*] [*French*]
CAD............ Character Assemble/Disassemble
CAD............ Chicago Assyrian Dictionary [*A publication*] (BJA)
CAD............ Chief of Air Defense
CAD............ Civil Affairs Division [*Military*]
CAD............ Civil Aviation Department [*Brunei*] (DS)
CAD............ Civil Aviation Department [*Australia*]
CAD............ Collective Address Directory [*Navy*] (NVT)
CAD............ Collision-Activated Dissociation [*Spectrometry*]
CAD............ Collisionally Activated Dissociation
CAD............ Combat Arms Division (INF)
CAD............ Comite d'Aide au Developpement [*OCDE*]
CAD............ Commercial Advance Design [*Reports*] (MCD)
CAD............ Commission for Aboriginal Development [*Australia*]
CAD............ Committee for Agricultural Development [*Iowa State University*] [*Research center*] (RCD)
CAD............ Communications Access Device (CET)
CAD............ Commutated Aerial Direction
CAD............ Company of American Dance
CAD............ Compensated Avalanche Diode
CAD............ Computation and Analysis Division [*NASA*] (MCD)
CAD............ Computer Access Device
CAD............ Computer Adaptor Display
CAD............ Computer-Aided Design
CAD............ Computer-Aided Detection
CAD............ Computer-Aided Drafting
CAD............ Computer Applications Digest [*A publication*]
CAD............ Computer-Assisted Design
CAD............ Computer-Assisted Diagnosis
CAD............ Computer-Assisted Dialog
CAD............ Computer-Associated [*or -Assisted*] Device
CAD............ Concepts and Analysis Division [*US Army Engineer Topographic Laboratories*]
CAD............ Containment Atmosphere Dilution [*Nuclear energy*] (NRCH)
CAD............ Continuous Acceleration Device
CAD............ Contract Action Directive (MCD)
CAD............ Contract Administration Data [*DoD*]
CAD............ Contract Award Date (AAG)
CAD............ Coronary Artery Disease [*Medicine*]
CAD............ Corporate Affairs Department [*Western Australia*]
CAD............ Corps Advisory Detachment
CAD............ Corrective Action Directive [*or Disposition*]
CAD............ Course Administrative Data [*DoD*]
CAD............ Customs Appeals Decisions [*A publication*] (DLA)

CAD.......... Cyclophosphamide, Adriamycin, Dacarbazine [*Antineoplastic drug regimen*]
CAD.......... Cytarabine, Daunorubicin [*Antineoplastic drug regimen*]
CA 2d .... California Appellate Reports, Second Series [*A publication*] (DLA)
CA 3d .... California Appellate Reports, Third Series [*A publication*] (DLA)
CADA .... CAM Data Systems, Inc. [*NASDAQ symbol*] (NQ)
CADA .... Campus Americans for Democratic Action [*Defunct*] (EA)
CADA .... Clear Air Dot Angle
CADA .... Computer-Aided Design and Analysis
CADA .... Computer-Assisted Development Aids
CADA .... Computer-Assisted Distribution and Assignment (NVT)
CADA .... Crossbow Archery Development Association (EAIO)
CADAC ..... Clean Arithmetic with Decimal Base and Controlled Precision (MCD)
CADAI...... Center Apollo Documentation Administration Instructions [*NASA*] (KSC)
CADAL...... Centro di Azione e Documentazione sull'America Latina
CADAM .... Computer-Aided Design and Manufacturing
CADAM .... Computer-Augmented Design and Manufacturing [*Trademark of Cadam, Inc.*] [*Aviation*]
CADAM .... Computer-Graphics-Augmented Design and Manufacturing (MCD)
Cad Amazonia ... Cadernos da Amazonia [*A publication*]
CADAMS ... Laboratory for Computer-Aided Design and Analysis in the Molecular Sciences [*Washington State University*] [*Research center*] (RCD)
CADANCE ... Computer-Aided Design and Numerical Control Effort
CADAPSO ... Canadian Association of Data and Professional Service Organizations [*Information service or system*] (EISS)
CADAR ..... Computer-Aided Design, Analysis, and Reliability (IEEE)
CADAT ..... Computer-Aided Design and Test [*System*]
CADAV ..... Cadaver [*Medicine*] (ROG)
CADB .... Cadbury [*England*]
CADB .... Cadbury Schweppes PLC [*London, England*] [*NASDAQ symbol*] (NQ)
CadB .... Cadernos Brasileiros [*A publication*]
CADB .... Climate Assessment Data Base [*National Meteorological Center*] [*Database*]
CADC .... Cambridge Automatic Digital Computer (IEEE)
CADC .... Canadian Army Dental Corps (DMA)
CADC .... Central Air Data Computer
CADC .... Centro Academico da Democracia Crista [*Academic Center for Christian Democracy*] [*Portugal*] [*Political party*] (PPE)
CADC .... Combined Administrative Committee
CADC .... Continental Air Defense Command [*Discontinued, 1975*]
CADC .... Crown Asset Disposal Corporation [*Canada*]
CADC .... District of Columbia Court of Appeals (DLA)
CAD/CAM ... Computer-Aided Design/Computer-Aided Manufacturing
CAD/CAM Tech ... CAD/CAM [*Computer-Aided Design/Computer-Aided Manufacturing*] Technology [*A publication*]
Cad Cient ... Cadernos Cientificos. Instituto Pasteur de Lisboa [*A publication*]
CADCO..... Core and Drum Corrector
CADCTS ... Central Air Data Computer Test Set
Cadd.......... Cheap Analyzer of Demographic Data [*Term coined by William F. Doescher, publisher of "D & B Reports"*]
CADD........ Combat Air Delivery Division [*Air Force*] (AFM)
CADD........ Computer-Aided Design Development
CADD........ Computer-Aided Design and Drafting [*Software package*] (MCD)
CADD........ Computer-Assisted Drug Design
CADDA..... Computer-Aided Design and Design Automation
CADDAC .. Central Analog Data Distributing and Computing System (KSC)
CADDE ..... Canadian Association of Deans and Directors of Education
CADDE ..... Central Automatic Digital Data Encoder [*NASA*]
Cad Deb ... Cadernos de Debate [*A publication*]
CADDS...... Center Apollo Document Description Standards [*NASA*] (KSC)
CADD/TEK ... Computer-Aided Design Drafting via Tektronix (MCD)
CADDY...... Committee to Aid Democratic Dissidents in Yugoslavia (EA)
CADE .... Cade Industries, Inc. [*NASDAQ symbol*] (NQ)
CADE .... Canadian Association for Distance Education
CADE .... Caution Against Dangerous Exports [*Shipping*]
CADE .... Center for Analysis of Developing Economies [*University of Pennsylvania*] [*Research center*] (RCD)
CADE .... Coalition Against Dangerous Exports
CADE .... Combined Allied Defense Experiment [*Military*] (SDI)
CADE .... Computer-Aided Design Engineering (RDA)
CADE .... Computer-Aided Design and Evaluation (MCD)
CADE .... Controller/Attitude-Direct Electronics (NASA)
CADEC...... Christian Action for Development in the Caribbean [*Caribbean Conference of Churches*]
CADEC...... Computer-Aided Design of Electronic Circuits [*Elsevier Book Series*] [*A publication*]
CADEM .... CONUS [*Continental United States*] Air Defense Effectiveness Model (MCD)
Cadence...... Cadence Magazine [*A publication*]

CADENS... CONUS [*Continental United States*] Air Defense Engagement Simulation
CADEP...... Computer-Aided Design of Electronic Products   (IEEE)
CADES...... COMIREX [*Committee on Imagery Requirements and Exploitation*] Advanced Exploitation System   (MCD)
CADET...... Can't Add, Doesn't Even Try [*Data processing*]
CADET...... City Air Defense Evaluation Tool
CADET...... Computer-Aided Design and Electrical Test
CADET...... Computer-Aided Design and Evaluation Technology   (MCD)
CADET...... Computer-Aided Design Experiment Translator
CADET...... Computer-Associated Diagnostic and Evaluation Tests   (CAAL)
CADETRON ... Cadet Practice Squadron
CADETS ... Classroom-Aided Dynamic Educational Time-Sharing System   (IEEE)
CADF...... Cathode-Ray Tube Automatic Direction Finding   (IEEE)
CADF...... Central Air Defense Force
CADF........ Commutated Antenna Direction Finder   (IEEE)
CADF...... Computer-Aided Design and Fabrication   (MCD)
CADF...... Contract Administration Data File [*DoD*]   (AFM)
CADFISS.. Computation and Data Flow Integrated Subsystem [*Simulated flight tests*] [*NASA*]
CADI .... Central Apollo Data Index [*NASA*]   (MCD)
CADI .... Computer Access Device Input   (CET)
CADIA...... Computer-Assisted Densitometric Image Analysis [*Microbiology*]
CADIC...... Chemical Analysis Detection Instrumentation Control
CADIC...... Compagnie Africaine des Ingenieurs-Conseils
CADIC...... Computer-Aided Design of Integrated Circuits   (MCD)
CADIDW .. Cardiovascular Diseases Bulletin. Texas Heart Institute [*A publication*]
CADIN ...... Continental Air Defense Integration, North
CADISIM ... Computer-Assisted Disposal Simulation [*Game*]
CADIZ...... Canadian Air Defence Identification Zone
CADIZ...... Civil Air Defense Identification Zone   (MCD)
CADJ........ Counter Angle Deception Jammer [*Military*]   (CAAL)
CADL .... Communications and Data Link   (KSC)
CADL .... Communicative Ability in Daily Living
CADLAB... Computer Aided Design and Graphics Laboratory [*Purdue University*] [*Research center*]   (RCD)
CAD-LAB ... Computer-Aided Design Laboratory [*Pennsylvania State University*] [*Research center*]   (RCD)
CADM ...... Center Apollo Data Manager [*NASA*]   (KSC)
CADM ...... Central German Administrative Department [*Economic*] Committee [*US Military Government, Germany*]
CADM ...... Clustered Airfield Defeat Munition   (MCD)
CADM ...... Clustered Airfield Depot Munition   (MCD)
C Adm ...... Code Administratif [*France*] [*A publication*]
CADM ...... Content-Addressable Data Manager
CADM ...... CONUS [*Continental United States*] Air Defense Modernization
CADMAT ... Computer-Aided Design, Manufacture, and Test   (MCD)
Cad Med ... Cadiz Medico [*A publication*]
Cad Mens Estat Inf Inst Vinho Porto ... Cadernos Mensais de Estatistica e Informacao. Editados pelo Instituto da Vinho da Porto [*A publication*]
CADMINI ... Computer Administrative Instruction   (AABC)
Cadmium Abstr ... Cadmium Abstracts [*A publication*]
CADMP .... Computer-Aided Data Management Procedure   (MCD)
CADMS...... Costing and Data Management System
CADMSS .. Configuration and Data Management Support System
CADNET... Chemical Agent Detection Network
CADNPH... Chloroacetaldehydedinitrophenylhydrazone [*Fungicide*]
CADO........ Central Air Documents Office [*Air Force*]
CADO........ Chief, Air Doctrine and Operations   (MCD)
CADO........ Chief, Airport District Office [*FAA*]   (FAAC)
CADO........ Computer Access Device Output   (CET)
CADO........ Current Actions Duty Officer [*Air Force*]
CADOB..... Consolidate Air Defense Order of Battle   (MCD)
CADOCS... Carrier Aircraft Deck Operations Control System [*Navy*]   (NG)
CADOD..... Cahiers de l'Analyse des Donnees [*A publication*]
Cad Omega ... Caderno Omega [*A publication*]
Cad Omega Univ Fed Rural Pernambuco ... Caderno Omega. Universidade Federal Rural de Pernambuco [*A publication*]
CADOP ..... Continental Air Defense Objectives Plan   (AABC)
CADORA .. Canadian Dressage Owners and Riders Association
CADOXEN ... Cadmium Oxide - Ethylenediamine [*Cellulose solvent*]
CADP .... Central Annunciator Display Panel   (MCD)
CADPA...... Cystic Adventitial Degeneration of the Popliteal Artery [*Medicine*]
CADPIN.... Customs Automatic Data Processing Intelligence Network [*US Customs Service*]
CADPL...... Communications/Automatic Data Processing Laboratory [*Army Electronics Command*] [*Fort Monmouth, NJ*]
CADPO...... Communications and Data Processing Operation
CADR .... Clean Air Delivery Rate [*of air purifiers*]
CADR .... Computer-Aided Design Reliability
CADRBT... Coalition to Abolish the Draize Rabbit Blinding Tests   (EA)
CADRC ..... Combined Air Documents Research Center
CADRDP... Cardiovascular Drugs [*A publication*]
CADRE...... Center for Aerospace Doctrine, Research, and Education [*Air University*] [*Research center*]   (RCD)

CADRE...... Collectors, Artists, and Dealers for Responsible Equity
CADRE...... Complete ADR [*Applied Data Research, Inc.*] Environment   (EA)
CADRE...... Completed Active Duty Requirements, Enlisted [*Military*]
CADRE...... Cooperative Advanced Digital Research Experiment   (MCD)
CADRE...... Cumulative Abstracts of Defence Readings [*Department of Defence*] [*Australia*] [*Information service or system*]   (IID)
CADRE...... Current Awareness and Document Retrieval for Engineers   (DIT)
Cadres et Profes ... Cadres et Professions [*A publication*]
CADRIC .... Calculation of Drilling Coordinates   (MCD)
CADS......... Cellular Absorbed Dose Spectrometer
CADS......... Center for Assessment and Demographic Studies [*Gallaudet College*] [*Research center*]   (RCD)
CADS......... Central Air Data System [*Air Force*]
CADS......... Chemical Agent Decontamination Simulant   (MCD)
CADS......... Civil Air Defense Services
CADS......... Command and Data Simulator   (NASA)
CADS......... Commando Anticomunista del Sur [*Southern Anticommunist Commando*] [*Guatemala*]   (PD)
CADS......... Computer-Aided Design System
CADS......... Computer Aided Time Share, Inc. [*Eden Prairie, MN*] [*NASDAQ symbol*]   (NQ)
CADS......... Computer-Assisted Dispatching System [*IBM Corp.*]
CADS......... Computer-Assisted Display Systems   (MCD)
CADS......... Computerized Attack/Defense System [*Title of a science fiction novel by John Sievert*]
CADS......... Containerized Ammunition Distribution System
CADS......... Containment Atmosphere Dilution System [*Nuclear energy*]   (IEEE)
CADS......... Continental Air Defense System
CADS......... Control Air Data System   (MCD)
CADS......... Cooperative Air Defense System   (MCD)
CADS......... Crustal Accretion-Differentiation Supervent [*Geology*]
CADSAME ... Call Signs and/or Address Group Remain Same   (MUGU)
CADSAT ... Computer-Aided Design and System Analysis Tool   (MCD)
CADSI ...... Communications and Data Systems Integration   (NASA)
CADSS ...... Combined Analog-Digital Systems Simulator [*Data processing*]
CA 2d Supp ... California Appellate Reports, Second Series, Supplement [*A publication*]   (DLA)
CADSWES ... Center for Advanced Decision Support for Water and Environmental Systems [*University of Colorado at Boulder*] [*Research center*]   (RCD)
CADT .... (Carboxamidophenyl)dimethyltriazene [*Biochemistry*]
CADT .... Coalition Against Double Taxation   (EA)
CaDTe .... Cathodal Duration Tetanus [*Physiology*]
CADU ...... Control and Display Unit   (NASA)
CADUS ..... Census and Data Users Services [*Illinois State University*] [*Information service or system*]   (IID)
CADV .... Cash Advance   (DCTA)
CADW ...... Civil Air Defense Warning [*System*]
Cadwalader ... Cadwalader's Cases, United States District Court, Eastern District of Pennsylvania [*A publication*]   (DLA)
Cadw Dig ... Cadwalader's Digest of Attorney-General's Opinions [*A publication*]   (DLA)
CADX .... Cadnetix Corp. [*Boulder, CO*] [*NASDAQ symbol*]   (NQ)
CAE .... CAE Industries Ltd. [*Toronto Stock Exchange symbol*]
Cae .... Caelum [*Constellation*]
CAE .... Canadian Academy of Endodontics   (EAIO)
CAE .... Canadian Aviation Electronics
CAE .... Canadian Entomologist [*A publication*]
CAE .... CANMARC [*Canadian Machine-Readable Cataloging*] English Authority File [*Source file*] [*UTLAS symbol*]
CAE .... Caprine Arthritis-Encephalitis [*Veterinary medicine*]
CAE .... Carrier Aircraft Equipment
CAE .... Center for Academic Ethics   (EA)
CAE .... Central African Empire [*Later, CAR*]
CAE .... Central Associated Engineers, Inc. [*Versailles, KY*] [*Telecommunications service*]   (TSSD)
CAE .... Centro Anglo-Espanol   (EA)
CAE .... Cercle Archeologique d'Enghien. Annales [*A publication*]
CAE .... Certified Association Executive [*Designation awarded by American Society of Association Executives*]
CAE .... Chemical Abstracts, Even-Numbered Issue
CAE .... Chicago, Aurora & Elgin Railroad Corp. [*AAR code*]
CAE .... Chief Activation Engineer
CAE .... Chief Administrative Engineer
CAE .... Chloroacetate Esterase [*An enzyme*]
CAE .... Cholesterol Epoxide [*Biochemistry*]
CAE .... Cobrese al Entregar [*Cash on Delivery*] [*Spanish*]
CAE .... Columbia [*South Carolina*] [*Airport symbol*]
CAE .... Compagnie Europeenne d'Automatisme [*Became part of Compagnie Internationale d'Informatique*]
CAE .... Computer-Aided Education   (BUR)
CAE .... Computer-Aided Engineering
CAE .... Computer-Aided Engineering Center [*University of Wisconsin - Madison*] [*Research center*]   (RCD)
CAE .... Computer-Aided Engineering Centre [*Heriot-Watt University*] [*British*]   (CB)
CAE .... Computer-Assisted Enrollment [*IBM Corp.*]   (IEEE)

CAE .... Computer-Assisted Entry
CAE .... Computer-Assisted Estimating
CAE .... Consejo Andino de Exportadores [*Andean Council of Exporters*]
CAE .... Continental Aviation & Engineering Corp.
CAE .... Contingent Aftereffects [*Visual*]
CAE .... Corrective Action Effectiveness (MCD)
CAE .... Council of American Embroiderers (EA)
CAE .... Council on Anthropology and Education (EA)
CAEA .... California Aviation Education Association
CAEA .... Canadian Automotive Electric Association
CAEA .... Central American Economics Association
CAEAn ...... Cercle Archeologique d'Enghien. Annales [*A publication*]
CAEB......... Combat Arms Enlistment Bonus [*Military*]
CAEC......... Central American Economic Community
CAEC......... Central American Energy Commission (EAIO)
CAEC........ Committee of the Acta Endocrinologica Countries
Caecin .... Pro Caecina [*of Cicero*] [*Classical studies*] (OCD)
CAECS ...... Computer-Aided Environmental Control System (MCD)
CAEDET ... Commandable Audio Engine Detector (MCD)
CAEDETS ... Commandable Acoustic Engine Ignition Detectors (MCD)
CAEDM .... Community/Airport Economic Development Model [*FAA*]
CAED Rep Iowa State Univ Sci Tech Center Agr Econ Develop ... CAED Report. Iowa State University of Science and Technology. Center for Agricultural and Economic Development [*A publication*]
CAEDS...... Computer-Aided Engineering and Architectural Design System (RDA)
CaEDTA.... Calcium Disodium Ethylenediaminetetraacetate [*Chelating agent*]
CAEEA...... Canadian Electronics Engineering [*A publication*]
CAEF......... Cahiers. Association Internationale des Etudes Francaises [*A publication*]
CAEF......... Chinese-American Educational Foundation (EA)
CAEF......... Comite des Associations Europeennes de Fonderie [*Committee of European Foundry Associations*] (EA)
CAEF......... Computer-Aided Exercise Facility (MCD)
CAEFMS... Canadian Agricultural Economics and Farm Management Society
CAEJ .... Communaute des Associations d'Editeurs de Journaux du Marche Commun [*Common Market Newspaper Publishers' Organization - CMNPO*] [*Brussels, Belgium*] (EAIO)
CAEL......... Caelebs [*Unmarried*] [*Latin*] (ROG)
Cael........... Caelum [*Constellation*]
CAEL......... Consolidated Aerospace Equipment List (MCD)
CAEL......... Council for Adult and Experiential Learning (EA)
Cael........... De Caelo [*of Aristotle*] [*Classical studies*] (OCD)
Cael........... Pro Caelio [*of Cicero*] [*Classical studies*] (OCD)
CAE LAB .. Computer-Aided Engineering Laboratory [*Lawrence Institute of Technology*] [*Research center*] (RDA)
CAELB..... Atomic Energy Law Reports [*A publication*]
CAEM .... Association Canadienne des Educateurs de Musique [*Canadian Music Educators' Association*]
CAEM .... Canadian Association of Exposition Managers
CAEM .... Centre Africaine d'Etudes Monetaires [*African Centre for Monetary Studies*] (EAIO)
CAEM .... Certified Assistant Export Manager [*Designation awarded by American Society of International Executives*]
CAeM .... Commission for Aeronautical Meteorology [*WMO*] (MSC)
CAEM .... Conseil d'Assistance Economique Mutuelle [*Council for Mutual Economic Assistance - CMEA*] [*French*]
CAEM .... Consejo de Asistencia Economica Mutual [*Council for Mutual Economic Assistance - CMEA*] [*Spanish*]
CAEM .... Controlled Atmosphere Electron Microscopy
CAEMC.... Committee of European Associations of Catholic Doctors (EAIO)
CAE/MIS ... Computer-Assisted Estimating and Management Information Systems
CAEN .... Canadian Energy News [*A publication*]
CAENA ..... Canadian Entomologist [*A publication*]
CAENEX... Complex Atmospheric Energetics Experiment [*National Science Foundation and USSR*]
CAEO .... Coalition of Adult Education Organizations (EA)
CAEP........ Canadian Association of Emergency Physicians
CAEP........ Council of Action for Equal Pay [*Australia*]
CAEP........ Custodian of Allied and Enemy Property [*British*] [*World War II*]
CAER......... Caere Corp. [*NASDAQ symbol*] (NQ)
CAER........ Chemical Awareness and Emergency Response [*Program for handling hazards*]
CAER........ Chief Aerographer [*Navy rating*] [*Obsolete*]
CAER........ Consiliul de Ajutor Economic Reciproc [*Council for Mutual Economic Assistance*]
CAERL...... Caerulcus [*Blue*] [*Pharmacy*] (ROG)
CAERM..... Chief Aerographer's Mate [*Navy rating*] [*Obsolete*]
Caerns........ Caernarvonshire [*County in Wales*]
Caes .... Caesar [*of Plutarch*] [*Classical studies*] (OCD)
Caes .... [*Gaius Julius*] Caesar [*Roman statesman, general, and historian, 100-44BC*] (OCD)
CAES......... Canadian Agricultural Economics Society

CAES......... Canadian Ethnic Studies [*A publication*]
CAES......... Center for Action on Endangered Species (EA)
CAES......... Center for Air Environment Studies [*Pennsylvania State University*] [*Research center*] (RCD)
CAES......... Compressed Air Energy Storage (MCD)
CAES......... Connecticut Agricultural Experiment Station
Caes Contar ... Caesar Contardus [*Deceased, 1585*] [*Authority cited in pre-1607 legal work*] (DSA)
CAET......... Canadian Association of Electroencephalograph Technologists
CAETA...... Commonwealth Association for Education and Training of Adults
CAETB..... Canadian Aeronautic and Space Institute. Transactions [*A publication*]
CAET PAR ... Caeteris Paribus [*Other Things Being Equal*] [*Latin*] (ROG)
CAEU .... Casualty Air Evacuation Unit [*RAF*] [*British*]
CAEU .... Council of Arab Economic Unity (EAIO)
CAEV........ Caprine Arthritis Encephalitis Virus [*Veterinary medicine*]
CAEWW ... Carrier Airborne Early Warning Wing [*Navy*] (NVT)
CAEX........ Community Automatic Exchange [*Telephone*] (BUR)
CAF........... Caffeine
CAF........... Calcium-Activated Factor [*Meat science*]
CAF........... Calviac [*France*] [*Seismograph station code, US Geological Survey*] (SEIS)
CAF........... Canadian Advertising Foundation
CAF........... Canadian Air Force [*1920-1923*]
CAF........... Canadian Armed Forces
CAF........... Canadian Futurity Oils Ltd. [*Toronto Stock Exchange symbol*]
CAF........... CANMARC [*Canadian Machine-Readable Cataloging*] French Authority File [*Source file*] [*UTLAS symbol*]
CAF........... Captain Future [*A publication*]
CAF........... Cell Adhesion Factor [*Cytochemistry*]
CAF........... Central African Federation [*Disbanded Dec. 31, 1963*]
CAF........... Central African Republic [*ANSI three-letter standard code*] (CNC)
CAF........... Centralized Authorized File [*IRS*]
CAF........... Charities Aid Foundation [*Information service or system*] (IID)
CAF........... Charities Aid Fund [*British*]
CAF........... Chemical Analysis Facility (NRCH)
CAF........... Chief Air Fitter [*British military*] (DMA)
CAF........... Children of Alcoholics Foundation (EA)
CAF........... Children's Art Foundation (EA)
CAF........... Chinese Air Force [*Nationalist*]
CAF........... Chinese American Forum (EA)
CAF........... Citizen Action Fund (EA)
CAF........... Citric Acid Fermenter [*Microbiology*]
CAF........... Clean Assembly Facility
CAF........... Cleared as Filed (FAAC)
CAF........... Clerical, Administrative, and Fiscal [*Used with number, as, CAF-6, to indicate grade of position*] [*Civil Service*]
CAF........... Cloth Assistance Factor [*Textiles*]
CAF........... Coastal Air Force [*British*]
CAF........... Comicorum Atticorum Fragmenta [*A publication*] (OCD)
CAF........... Complete Assembly for Ferry [*Air Force*]
CAF........... Confederate Air Force (EA)
CAF........... Confederation Africaine de Football [*African Football Confederation - AFC*] (EAIO)
CAF........... Congressional Action Fund (EA)
CAF........... Conjunctive Alteration File
CAF........... Conservative Action Foundation (EA)
CAF........... Continental Air Forces
CAF........... Contraction Augmenting Factor [*Medicine*]
CAF........... Cooley's Anemia Foundation (EA)
CAF........... Cooperative Assistance Fund (EA)
CAF........... Cost Adjustment Factor
CAF........... Cost and Freight [*Shipping*]
CAF........... Council on Alternate Fuels (EA)
CAF........... Cout, Assurance, Fret [*Cost, Insurance, Freight - CIF*] [*Shipping*] [*French*]
CAF........... Critical Area Flag
CAF........... Cuban American Foundation (EA)
CAF........... Curates' Augmentation Fund [*British*]
CAF........... Currency Adjustment Factor [*Business term*]
CAF........... Customer Access Facilities [*Telecommunications*]
CAF........... Cyclophosphamide, Adriamycin, Fluorouracil [*Antineoplastic drug regimen*]
CAF........... Furr's/Bishop's LP [*NYSE symbol*] (SPSG)
CAF........... Guided Missile Heavy Cruiser (MCD)
CAFA........ Canadian Amateur Football Association
CAFA........ Canadian Arab Friendship Association
CAFA........ Chicago Academy of Fine Arts
CAFA........ Coated Abrasives Fabricators Association [*Defunct*] (EA)
CAFAC...... Commander, All Forces, Aruba-Curacao
CAFAC...... Commission Africaine de l'Aviation Civile [*African Civil Aviation Commission - AFCAC*] (EAIO)
CAFAF ..... Commander, Amphibious Force, Atlantic Fleet
CAFALSIS ... Canadian Addiction Foundation, Addictions Librarians Special Interest Section
CAFB......... Charleston Air Force Base [*South Carolina*]
CAFB......... Chemically Active Fluidized Bed [*Fuel gas*]
CAFB......... Cooke Air Force Base [*Later, VAFB*] (AAG)

CAFC......... Canadian Association of Fire Chiefs
CAFC......... Carolina First Corporation [*Greenville, SC*] [*NASDAQ symbol*]   (NQ)
CAFC......... Congressional Alcohol Fuels Caucus   (EA)
CAFCA.... Citizens Against Foreign Control of America   (EA)
CAFCA..... Conventional Armed Forces and Conventional Armaments
CAF/CANA ... Conservative Action Foundation/Coalition Against Nuclear Annihilation [*Research center*]   (RCD)
C of AFCH ... Chief of Air Force Chaplains
CAFD........ Contact Analog Flight Display
CAFDA...... Commandement Aerien des Forces de Defense Aerienne [*Air Defense Forces Air Command*]   (NATG)
Cafe........... Cafe Solo [*A publication*]
CAFE........ Canadian Association of Foundations of Education
CAFE........ Canadian Association for Free Expression
CAFE........ Computer-Aided Film Editor
CAFE........ Conventional Armed Forces in Europe   (ECON)
CAFE........ Corporate Average Fuel Economy [*Automobile industry*]
CAFE........ Magnolia Foods, Inc. [*Oklahoma City, OK*] [*NASDAQ symbol*]   (NQ)
CAFE........ Negotiations on Conventional Armed Forces in Europe
CAFEA-ICC ... Commission on Asian and Far Eastern Affairs of the International Chamber of Commerce
CAFEC..... Consumer Action for Energy Conservation [*British*]
CAFEE ..... Critical Assembly Fuel Element Exchange [*Nuclear energy*]
CAFES...... Computer-Aided Function Allocation and Evaluation System
C AFFS for COLS ... Commissioner for Affidavits for Colonies [*British*]   (ROG)
CAFG........ Commander, Air Forces, Gulf [*British military*]   (DMA)
CAFGA...... California Fish and Game [*A publication*]
CAFGA...... Computer Applications for the Graphic Arts
CAFHS...... Child and Family Health Services [*Australia*]
CAFI......... Ceramic Arts Federation International   (EA)
CAFIP ...... Canadian Association for Israel Philately
CAFIT ...... Computer-Assisted Fault Isolation Test
CAFLIS ..... Coalition for the Advancement of Foreign Languages and International Studies
CAFM....... Chief of Air Force Materiel [*Australia*]
CAFM....... Commercial Air Freight Movement
CAFM....... Computer-Aided Facility Management
CAFMC..... Combined Agricultural and Food Machinery Committee [*World War II*]
CAFMCO ... Chief, Air Force Modernization Coordination Office   (MCD)
CAFMS ..... Continental Association of Funeral and Memorial Societies   (EA)
CAFN .... Canadian Field-Naturalist [*A publication*]
CAFNA...... Canadian Field-Naturalist [*A publication*]
CAFO .... Canadian Forum [*A publication*]
CAFO .... Command Accounting and Finance Office   (AFM)
CAFO .... Confidential Admiralty Fleet Order [*British military*]   (DMA)
CAFO .... Confidential Air Force Order [*British military*]   (DMA)
CAFOB...... Combined Air Force Operating Base   (CINC)
CAFOC..... Computer-Aided Flight Operations Center
CAFOD .... Catholic Fund for Overseas Development [*British*]
CAFODQ .. Cancer Forum [*A publication*]
CAFOER .. Cancer Focus [*A publication*]
CAFOP...... Chief of Air Force Operations and Plans [*Australia*]
CAFP .... Chief of Air Force Personnel [*Australia*]
CAFP .... Cyclophosphamide, Adriamycin, Fluorouracil, Prednisone [*Antineoplastic drug regimen*]
CAFPME .. Canadian Association for Peace in the Middle East
CAfr .... Central Africa
CAfr .... Congo-Afrique [*A publication*]
CAFRAD... Centre Africain de Formation et de Recherche Administratives pour la Developpement [*African Training and Research Center in Administration for Development*]   (IID)
CAFRADES ... Centre Africain de Recherche Appliquee et de Formation en Matiere de Developpement Social [*African Center for Applied Research and Training in Social Development - ACARTSD*]   (EAIO)
C Afr Adm Publ ... Cahiers Africains d'Administration Publique [*A publication*]
CAfrRep.... Central African Republic
C Afr Secur Soc ... Cahiers Africains de la Securite Sociale [*A publication*]
CAFS......... Canadian Association for Future Studies
CAFS......... Cardinal Financial Group, Inc. [*NASDAQ symbol*]   (NQ)
CAFS......... Cartridge-Actuated Flame System [*Terminated*] [*Military*]   (MCD)
CAFS......... Center for African Family Studies   (EAIO)
CAFS........ Chinese American Food Society   (EA)
CAFS......... Content-Addressable File Store [*Data processing*]   (IEEE)
CAFSAC.... Canadian Atlantic Fisheries Scientific Advisory Committee   (ASF)
CAFSB2..... Congres. Association Francaise pour l'Avancement des Sciences [*Nancy*] [*A publication*]
CAFSC ...... Control Air Force Specialty Code
CAFSU...... Carrier and Field Service Unit   (NVT)
CAFT .... California, Arizona, Florida, and Texas
CAFT........ Combined Agencies Field Team [*US Military Government, Germany*]
CAFT........ Consolidated Advance Field Team [*Navy*]

CAFTA ...... Canadian-American Free Trade Area
CAFTA ...... Central American Free Trade Area
CAFTD..... Commercially Available/Fabricated Training Device
CAFTDR ... Commercially Available/Fabricated Training Device Requirement
CAFTR ..... Commercially Available/Fabricated Training Device Requirement
CAFTS...... Chief of Air Force Technical Services [*Australia*]
CAFU .... Civil Aviation Flying Unit [*British*]   (AIA)
CAFV......... Combined Arms Fighting Vehicle   (MCD)
CAFVP..... Cyclophosphamide, Adriamycin, Fluorouracil, Vincristine, Prednisone [*Antineoplastic drug regimen*]
CAG........... Cagliari [*Italy*] [*Airport symbol*]   (OAG)
CAG........... Caguas [*Puerto Rico*] [*Seismograph station code, US Geological Survey*]   (SEIS)
CAG........... Canadian Air Group   (MCD)
CAG........... Canadian Association of Geographers
CAG........... Canopus Acquisition Gate [*NASA*]
CAG........... Cap and Gown; a Treasury of College Verse [*A publication*]
CAG........... Carcinogen Assessment Group [*Environmental Protection Agency*]
CAG........... Carrier Air Group [*Navy*]
CAG........... Catholic Accountants Guild   (EA)
CAG........... Catholic Actors Guild of America   (EA)
CAG........... Ceratobasidium Anastomosis Group [*Phytopathology*]
CAG........... Change Analysis Group
CAG........... Chronic Atrophic Gastritis [*Medicine*]
CAG........... Citizen Action Group [*Defunct*]   (EA)
CAG........... Civic Action Group [*Military*]   (CINC)
CAG........... Civil Air Guard [*British*]
CAG........... Collective Address Group [*Navy*]   (NVT)
CAG........... Combat Analysis Group [*Joint Chiefs of Staff*]
CAG........... Combat Arms Group [*Army*]   (AABC)
CAG........... Combat Aviation Group
CAG........ Combined Action Group [*Senior command of all Combined Action Companies*] [*Military*]
CAG........... Combined Arms Group [*Army*]
CAG........... Command System Operations Analysis Group Area [*Space Flight Operations Facility, NASA*]
CAG........... Commander, Air Group [*Navy*]
CAG........... Commercial Artists' Guild
CAG........... Committee on Autonomous Groups   (EA)
CAG........... Communication Age [*A publication*]
CAG........... Competition Advocate General [*Army*]
CAG........... Composers-Authors Guild   (EA)
CAG........... Comptroller and Auditor General
CAG........... Computer-Aided Gear Changing [*Automotive engineering*]
CAG........... Computer Applications Group [*Air Force*]
CAG........... ConAgra, Inc. [*NYSE symbol*]   (SPSG)
CAG........... Concepts Analysis Group [*Army*]
CAG........... Concert Artists Guild   (EA)
CAG........... Consort Art Graphics [*British*]
CAG........... Constant Altitude Glide
CAG........... Cooperative Automation Group [*British Library*] [*Information service or system*]   (IID)
CAG........... Craig, CO [*Location identifier*] [*FAA*]   (FAAL)
CAG........... Crisis Assessment Group [*NATO*]   (NATG)
CAG........... Guided Missile Heavy Cruiser [*Navy symbol*] [*Obsolete*]
CAGA .... Catholic Actors Guild of America   (EA)
CAGA .... Church Architectural Guild of America [*Later, IFRAA*]   (EA)
CAG/ACG ... Canadian Association of Geographers/Association Canadienne des Geographes
CAGC .... Clutter Automatic Gain Control
CAGC .... Coded Automatic Gain Control
CAG/CG.... Canadian Geographer/Le Geographe Canadien. Canadian Association of Geographers [*A publication*]
CA GCL..... California General Corporation Law [*A publication*]   (DLA)
CAGD........ Computer-Aided Geometric Design   (MCD)
CAGE .... California Almond Growers Exchange [*Later, BDG*]   (EA)
CAGE .... Canadian Air-Ground Environment
CAGE .... Central Australian Gold Expedition
CAGE .... Commercial and Government Entity   (MCD)
CAGE .... Compiler and Assembler by General Electric
CAGE .... Computer-Aided Genetic Engineering
CAGE .... Computerized Aerospace Ground Equipment   (MCD)
CAGE .... Convicts' Association for a Good Environment [*Defunct*]
cage .... Courtage [*Brokerage*] [*French*]
CAGEL....... Consolidated Aerospace Ground Equipment List
CAGEL....... Consolidated AGE Ground Equipment List   (MCD)
CAGI .... Compressed Air and Gas Institute   (EA)
CAGIB....... Chemical Age International [*A publication*]
CAGIS....... Chicago Area Geographic Information Study [*University of Illinois at Chicago*] [*Also, an information service or system*]   (IID)
CAgM .... Commission for Agricultural Meteorology [*WMO*]   (MSC)
CAG(N)..... Guided Missile Heavy Cruiser (Nuclear Propulsion) [*Navy symbol*]
CAGNE ..... Commerce Action Group for the Near East [*Terminated, 1981*]
Cagno......... [*Hieronymus*] Cagnolus [*Deceased, 1551*] [*Authority cited in pre-1607 legal work*]   (DSA)

Cagnol........ [*Hieronymus*] Cagnolus [*Deceased, 1551*] [*Authority cited in pre-1607 legal work*] (DSA)
CAGNY..... Chemical Advertisers Group of New York [*Inactive*] (EA)
CAGO........ Cargo Apparent Good Order [*Shipping*]
CAGPL...... Canadian Arctic Gas Pipeline Limited
CAGQ........ Cahiers de Geographie de Quebec [*A publication*]
CAGR .... Casa Grande Ruins National Monument [*National Park Service designation*]
CAGR .... Comparison of Annual Growth Rate
CAGRA ..... California Agriculture [*A publication*]
CAGS........ Canadian Association of General Surgeons
CAGS........ Certificate of Advanced Graduate Study
CAGS........ Chet Atkins Guitar Society [*London, England*] (EAIO)
CAGW .... Citizens Against Government Waste (EA)
CAGW .... Committee Against Government Waste (EA)
CAGY .... Columbus & Greenville Railway Co. [*AAR code*]
CAGYAO .. Cardiology [*A publication*]
Ca H.......... Cahiers d'Histoire [*A publication*]
CAH........... Cambridge Ancient History [*1st edition, 1923-39*] [*A publication*] (OCD)
CAH........... Canadian Association of Hispanists [*See also ACH*]
CAH........... Canarchon Holdings Ltd. [*Toronto Stock Exchange symbol*]
CAH........... Center for Attitudinal Healing (EA)
CAH........... Chronic Active Hepatitis [*Medicine*]
CAH........... Community of All Hallows [*Anglican religious community*]
CAH........... Conference on Asian History (EA)
CAH........... Congenital Adrenal Hyperplasia [*Medicine*]
CAH........... Council of American Homeowners (EA)
CAH........... Cyanocethydrazide [*Antihelminthic*] (ADA)
CAH........... Valparaiso, FL [*Location identifier*] [*FAA*] (FAAL)
CAH² .... Cambridge Ancient History [*2nd edition*] [*A publication*] (OCD)
CAHA....... Cahiers d'Archeologie et d'Histoire d'Alsace [*A publication*]
CAHA....... Canadian Amateur Hockey Association
CAHA....... Cape Hatteras National Seashore [*National Park Service designation*]
Cah Acoust ... Cahiers d'Acoustique [*A publication*]
Cah Aerod ... Cahiers d'Aerodynamique [*A publication*]
Cah Albert Le Grand ... Cahiers Albert Le Grand [*A publication*]
Cah Albert Roussel ... Cahiers Albert Roussel [*A publication*]
Cah Alg San ... Cahiers Algeriens de la Sante [*A publication*]
Cah Als ...... Cahiers Alsaciens d'Archeologie, d'Art, et d'Histoire [*A publication*]
CAHALS... Catapult Hookup and Launch Surveillance
Cah Als Arch ... Cahiers Alsaciens d'Archeologie, d'Art, et d'Histoire [*A publication*]
Cah Am Lat ... Cahiers des Ameriques Latines [*A publication*]
Cah Am Latines Ser Sciences Homme ... Cahiers des Ameriques Latines. Serie Sciences de l'Homme [*A publication*]
Cah Anal.... Cahiers pour l'Analyse [*A publication*]
Cah Anal Text ... Cahiers d'Analyse Textuelle [*A publication*]
Cah Anesth ... Cahiers d'Anesthesiologie [*A publication*]
Cah Anesthesiol .. Cahiers d'Anesthesiologie [*A publication*]
Cah Ann..... Cahiers des Annales [*A publication*]
Cah Ann Norm ... Cahier des Annales de Normandie [*A publication*]
Cah Apic.... Cahiers Apicoles [*A publication*]
Cah A R ...... Cahiers de l'Actualite Religieuse [*A publication*]
Cah Arch.... Cahiers Archeologiques [*A publication*]
Cah Archeol Hist Berry ... Cahiers d'Archeologie et d'Histoire du Berry [*A publication*]
Cah Arch Hist Berry ... Cahiers d'Archeologie et d'Histoire du Berry [*A publication*]
Cah Arch Subaqu ... Cahiers d'Archeologie Subaquatique [*A publication*]
Cah Armee Rom ... Cahiers. Groupe de Recherches sur l'Armee Romaine et les Provinces [*A publication*]
Cah Art ...... Cahiers d'Art [*A publication*]
Cah Art Sacre ... Cahiers de l'Art Sacre [*A publication*]
Cah As Se .. Cahiers de l'Asie du Sud-Est [*A publication*]
Cah Ass Int Et Fr ... Cahiers. Association Internationale des Etudes Francaises [*A publication*]
CAHB .... Chronic Active Hepatitis Type B [*Medicine*]
Cah Berry .. Cahiers d'Archeologie et d'Histoire du Berry [*A publication*]
Cah Biloque ... Cahiers de la Biloque [*A publication*]
Cah Biol Mar ... Cahiers de Biologie Marine [*A publication*]
Cah Bio Mar ... Cahiers de Biologie Marine [*A publication*]
Cah Bleus Vet ... Cahiers Bleus Veterinaires [*A publication*]
Cah Bruges ... Cahiers de Bruges [*A publication*]
Cah Brux.... Cahiers Bruxellois [*A publication*]
Cah Byrsa .. Cahiers de Byrsa [*A publication*]
CAHC........ Center for the Advancement of Human Co-Operation (EA)
CAHC........ Compagnie d'Assurance d'Hypotheques du Canada [*Mortgage Insurance Company of Canada - MICC*]
CAHC........ Cuadernos de Arqueologia e Historia de la Ciudad [*A publication*]
Cah Canadiens M ... Cahiers Canadiens de Musique [*Canada Music Book*] [*A publication*]
Cah Cent .... Cahiers de Centreau [*A publication*]
Cah Cent Etud Rech Oper ... Cahiers. Centre d'Etudes de Recherche Operationnelle [*A publication*]
Cah Centre Tech Bois ... Cahier. Centre Technique du Bois [*A publication*]

Cah CERBOM ... Cahiers. CERBOM [*Centre d'Etudes et de Recherche de Biologie et d'Oceanographie Medicale*] [*A publication*]
CahCerclERenan ... Cahiers. Cercle Ernest Renan [*Paris*] [*A publication*]
Cah Ch Foucauld ... Cahiers Charles De Foucauld [*A publication*]
Cah Chir .... Cahiers de Chirurgie [*A publication*]
Cah Cinema ... Cahiers du Cinema [*A publication*]
Cah Civ Med ... Cahiers de Civilisation Medievale [*A publication*]
CAHCL ..... Capitol Area Health Consortium Libraries [*Library network*]
Cah Coll Med Hop Paris ... Cahiers. College de Medecine des Hopitaux de Paris [*A publication*]
Cah Communisme ... Cahiers du Communisme [*A publication*]
Cah Com Prev Batim Trav Publics ... Cahiers. Comites de Prevention du Batiment et des Travaux Publics [*France*] [*A publication*]
Cah Debussy ... Cahiers Debussy [*A publication*]
Cah Del Fr Iran ... Cahiers. Delegation Francaise en Iran [*A publication*]
Cah Docum ... Cahiers de la Documentation [*A publication*]
Cah de Droit Eur ... Cahiers de Droit Europeen [*A publication*]
Cah de Droit (Quebec) ... Cahiers de Droit (Quebec) [*Canada*] [*A publication*]
CAHDRT .. Center Ad Hoc Data Review Team [*NASA*] (KSC)
CAHE........ Canadian Heritage [*A publication*]
CAHE........ Core Auxiliary Heat Exchanger [*Nuclear energy*] (NRCH)
CAHEA ..... Committee on Allied Health Education and Accreditation (EA)
Cah Econ Br ... Cahiers Economiques de Bruxelles [*A publication*]
Cah Econ Brux ... Cahiers Economiques de Bruxelles [*A publication*]
Cah Econs Bruxelles ... Cahiers Economiques de Bruxelles [*A publication*]
Cah Econs et Monetaires ... Cahiers Economiques et Monetaires [*A publication*]
Cah Econs et Soc ... Cahiers Economiques et Sociaux [*A publication*]
Cah Elis ..... Cahiers Elisabethains [*A publication*]
Cah Enf...... Cahiers de l'Enfance [*A publication*]
Cah Et Afr ... Cahiers d'Etudes Africaines [*A publication*]
Cah d'Et Afr ... Cahiers d'Etudes Africaines. Revue Trimestrielle [*A publication*]
Cah Et Cath ... Cahiers d'Etudes Cathares [*A publication*]
Cah Etud Af ... Cahiers d'Etudes Africaines [*A publication*]
Cah Etud Anc ... Cahiers des Etudes Anciennes [*A publication*]
Cah Etud Biol ... Cahiers d'Etudes Biologiques [*A publication*]
Cah Etud Mediev ... Cahier d'Etudes Medievales [*A publication*]
Cah Expansion Reg ... Cahiers de l'Expansion Regionale [*A publication*]
Cah de la Fac de Droit Nancy ... Cahiers. Faculte de Droit et des Sciences Economiques de Nancy [*A publication*] (DLA)
Cah Fac Sci Univ Mohammed Ser Bio Anim ... Cahiers. Faculte des Sciences. Universite Mohammed 5. Serie Biologie Animale [*A publication*]
Cah Fr........ Cahiers Francais [*A publication*]
Cah Geogr Phys ... Cahiers de Geographie Physique [*A publication*]
Cah Geol.... Cahiers Geologiques [*A publication*]
Cah Geol Thoiry ... Cahiers Geologiques de Thoiry [*A publication*]
Cah Groupe Fr Rheol ... Cahiers. Groupe Francais de Rheologie [*A publication*]
Cah Haut Marnais ... Cahiers Haut-Marnais [*A publication*]
Cah Hist .... Cahiers d'Histoire [*A publication*]
Cah Hist Arch ... Cahiers d'Histoire et d'Archeologie [*A publication*]
Cah Hist Eg ... Cahiers d'Histoire Egyptienne [*A publication*]
Cah Hist M ... Cahiers d'Histoire Mondiale [*A publication*]
Cah Hist Mond ... Cahiers d'Histoire Mondiale/Journal of World History [*A publication*]
Cah Hist Soc Hist Que ... Cahiers d'Histoire. Societe Historique de Quebec [*A publication*]
CAHI .... Central Aero-Hydrodynamic Institute [*USSR*]
Cahier Dr Fiscal ... Cahiers de Droit Fiscal International [*A publication*] (DLA)
Cahiers....... Cahiers du Cinema [*A publication*]
Cahiers....... Cahiers de Droit [*A publication*]
Cahiers C ... Cahiers Cesairiens [*A publication*]
Cahiers Centre Etudes Recherche Oper ... Cahiers. Centre d'Etudes de Recherche Operationnelle [*A publication*]
Cahiers Centre Etudes Rech Oper ... Cahiers. Centre d'Etudes de Recherche Operationnelle [*Brussels*] [*A publication*]
Cahiers Cinematheque ... Cahiers de la Cinematheque [*A publication*]
Cahiers CSTB ... Cahiers. Centre Scientifique et Technique du Batiment [*A publication*]
Cahiers Droit ... Quebec [*City*]. Universite Laval. Faculte de Droit. Cahiers de Droit [*A publication*]
CahiersE.... Cahiers Elisabethains [*A publication*]
Cahiers in Eng ... Cahiers du Cinema in English [*A publication*]
CahiersF.... Cahiers Francophones [*A publication*]
Cahiers Geog Quebec ... Cahiers de Geographie de Quebec [*A publication*]
Cahiers Geol ... Cahiers Geologiques [*A publication*]
Cahiers Herne ... Cahiers de l'Herne [*A publication*]
Cahiers I ..... Cahiers Irlandais [*A publication*]
Cahiers Math Montpellier ... Cahiers Mathematiques Montpellier. Universite des Sciences et Techniques du Languedoc [*A publication*]
Cahiers ORSTOM Pedologie ... Cahiers. ORSTOM [*Office de la Recherche Scientifique et Technique d'Outre-Mer*]. Serie Pedologie [*A publication*]
Cahiers R ... Cahiers Renaniens [*A publication*]
Cahiers S ... Cahiers Staeliens [*A publication*]
Cahiers Sci ... Cahiers Scientifiques [*A publication*]
Cahiers Sci (Suppl Bois Forets Trop) ... Cahiers Scientifiques (Supplement to Bois et Forets des Tropiques) [*A publication*]

Cahiers Topologie Geom Differentielle ... Cahiers de Topologie et Geometrie Differentielle [*A publication*]

Cah I F A L ... Cahiers. Institut Francais d'Amerique Latine [*A publication*]

Cahill's Ill St ... Cahill's Illinois Statutes [*A publication*]   (DLA)

Cah Inf Stn Biol Mar Grande-Riviere ... Cahiers d'Information Station de Biologie Marine de Grande-Riviere [*A publication*]

Cah Ing Agron ... Cahiers des Ingenieurs Agronomes [*A publication*]

Cah Ingnrs Agron ... Cahiers des Ingenieurs Agronomes [*A publication*]

Cah Int....... Cahiers Internationaux [*A publication*]

Cah Internat Sociol ... Cahiers Internationaux de Sociologie [*A publication*]

Cah Int Soc ... Cahiers Internationaux de Sociologie [*A publication*]

CAHIPE.... Committee of the Associations of Honey Importers and Packers of Europe   (EAIO)

Cah Iroise .. Cahiers de l'Iroise [*A publication*]

Ca Hist....... Cahiers d'Histoire [*A publication*]

Cah Ivoiriens Rech Econ et Soc ... Cahiers Ivoiriens de Recherche Economique et Sociale [*A publication*]

CAHJ .... CAHPER [*Canadian Association for Health, Physical Education, and Recreation*] Journal [*A publication*]

CAHJP...... Central Archives for the History of the Jewish People [*Jerusalem*] [*A publication*]   (BJA)

Cah Juridiques Electr Gaz ... Cahiers Juridiques de l'Electricite et du Gaz [*A publication*]

Cah Kinesither ... Cahiers de Kinesitherapie [*A publication*]

Cah Lab Hydrobiol Montereau ... Cahiers. Laboratoire d'Hydrobiologie de Montereau [*France*] [*A publication*]

Cah Leopold Delisle ... Cahiers Leopold Delisle [*A publication*]

Cah Lex ..... Cahiers de Lexicologie [*A publication*]

Cah Lig ...... Cahiers Ligures de Prehistoire et d'Archeologie [*A publication*]

Cah Ling .... Cahiers de Linguistique Theorique et Appliquee [*A publication*]

Cah Ling As Or ... Cahiers de Linguistique Asie Orientale [*A publication*]

Cah Maboke ... Cahiers de la Maboke [*A publication*]

Cah Mariemont ... Cahiers de Mariemont [*A publication*]

CAHMB.... Cahiers de Medecine [*Paris*] [*A publication*]

Cah Med.... Cahiers de Medecine [*A publication*]

Cah Med.... Cahiers Medicaux [*A publication*]

Cah Med Assises Med ... Cahiers de Medecine. Assises de Medecine [*A publication*]

Cah Med Eur Med ... Cahiers de Medecine. Europa Medica [*A publication*]

Cah Med Interprof ... Cahiers de Medecine Interprofessionnelle [*France*] [*A publication*]

Cah Med Lyon ... Cahiers Medicaux Lyonnais [*A publication*]

Cah Med Trav ... Cahiers de Medecine du Travail [*A publication*]

Cah Med Vet ... Cahiers de Medecine Veterinaire [*A publication*]

Cah Micropaleontol ... Cahiers de Micropaleontologie [*A publication*]

Cah Monde Hisp Luso-Bresil ... Cahiers du Monde Hispanique et Luso-Bresilien [*A publication*]

Cah Mon Rus ... Cahiers du Monde Russe et Sovietique [*A publication*]

Cah Mus Forezien ... Cahiers. Musee Forezien [*A publication*]

CahN......... Cahiers Numismatiques [*A publication*]

Cah Nat...... Cahiers des Naturalistes [*A publication*]

Cah Nord Est ... Cahiers d'Archeologie du Nord-Est [*A publication*]

Cah Notes Doc ... Cahiers de Notes Documentaires [*A publication*]

Cah Notes Doc Secur Hyg Trav ... Cahiers de Notes Documentaires. Securite et Hygiene du Travail [*A publication*]

Cah Nouv Journee ... Cahiers de la Nouvelle Journee [*A publication*]

Cah Num.... Cahiers Numismatiques [*A publication*]

Cah Nurs.... Cahiers du Nursing [*Montreal*] [*A publication*]

Cah Nutr Diet ... Cahiers de Nutrition et de Dietetique [*A publication*]

CAHOA..... Canadian Hospital [*A publication*]

CAHOAX ... Canadian Hospital [*A publication*]

Cah Oceanogr ... Cahiers Oceanographiques [*A publication*]

Cah Oceanogr Suppl ... Cahiers Oceanographiques. Supplement [*A publication*]

Cah Odonto-Stomatol.... Cahiers d'Odonto-Stomatologie [*A publication*]

Cah Odontostomatol (Touraine) ... Cahiers Odontostomatologiques (Touraine) [*A publication*]

Cah Off Rech Sci Tech Outre-Mer Ser Pedol ... Cahiers. Office de la Recherche Scientifique et Technique d'Outre-Mer. Serie Pedologie [*A publication*]

Cah O-Mer ... Cahiers d'Outre-Mer [*A publication*]

Cah ORST Hy ... Cahiers. ORSTOM [*Office de la Recherche Scientifique et Technique d'Outre-Mer*]. Hydrobiologie [*A publication*]

Cah ORST Oc ... Cahiers. ORSTOM [*Office de la Recherche Scientifique et Technique d'Outre-Mer*]. Oceanographie [*A publication*]

Cah ORSTOM Physiol Plant Trop Cult ... Cahiers. ORSTOM [*Office de la Recherche Scientifique et Technique d'Outre-Mer*]. Physiologie des Plantes Tropicales Cultivees [*A publication*]

Cah ORSTOM Ser Biol ... Cahiers. ORSTOM [*Office de la Recherche Scientifique et Technique d'Outre-Mer*]. Serie Biologie [*A publication*]

Cah ORSTOM Ser Entomol Med ... Cahiers. ORSTOM [*Office de la Recherche Scientifique et Technique d'Outre-Mer*]. Serie Entomologie Medicale [*A publication*]

Cah ORSTOM Ser Entomol Med Parasitol ... Cahiers. ORSTOM [*Office de la Recherche Scientifique et Technique d'Outre-Mer*]. Serie Entomologie Medicale et Parasitologie [*A publication*]

Cah ORSTOM Ser Hydrobiol ... Cahiers. ORSTOM [*Office de la Recherche Scientifique et Technique d'Outre-Mer*]. Serie Hydrobiologie [*A publication*]

Cah ORSTOM Ser Hydrol ... Cahiers. ORSTOM [*Office de la Recherche Scientifique et Technique d'Outre-Mer*]. Serie Hydrologie [*A publication*]

Cah ORSTOM Ser Oceanogr ... Cahiers. ORSTOM [*Office de la Recherche Scientifique et Technique d'Outre-Mer*]. Serie Oceanographie [*A publication*]

Cah ORSTOM Ser Pedol ... Cahiers. ORSTOM [*Office de la Recherche Scientifique et Technique d'Outre-Mer*]. Serie Pedologie [*A publication*]

Cah ORSTOM Ser Sci Hum ... Cahiers. ORSTOM [*Office de la Recherche Scientifique et Technique d'Outre-Mer*]. Serie Sciences Humaines [*A publication*]

Cah Outre-Mer ... Cahiers d'Outre-Mer [*A publication*]

Cah Pac...... Cahiers du Pacifique [*A publication*]

Cah Pedol ORSTOM ... Cahiers de Pedologie. Office de la Recherche Scientifique et Technique d'Outre-Mer [*A publication*]

CAHPER.... Canadian Association for Health, Physical Education, and Recreation

CAHPER J ... CAHPER [*Canadian Association for Health, Physical Education, and Recreation*] Journal [*A publication*]

Cah Phys.... Cahiers de Physique [*France*] [*A publication*]

Cah P L...... Cahiers Pierre Loti [*A publication*]

Cah Presse Fr ... Cahiers de la Presse Francaise [*A publication*]

Cah Prot..... Cahiers Protestants [*A publication*]

Cah Prothese ... Cahiers de Prothese [*A publication*]

Cah Psych ... Cahiers de Psychiatrie [*A publication*]

Cah Quebecois Demographie ... Cahiers Quebecois de Demographie [*A publication*]

Cah Quentovic ... Cahiers de Quentovic [*A publication*]

CAHR........ Council for the Advancement of Hospital Recreation [*Defunct*]   (EA)

Cah Rac ..... Cahiers Raciniens [*A publication*]

Cah Rech Agron ... Cahiers de la Recherche Agronomique [*A publication*]

Cah Rech Agron Inst Rech Agron (Morocco) ... Cahiers de la Recherche Agronomique. Institut National de la Recherche Agronomique (Morocco) [*A publication*]

Cah Relig Afr ... Cahiers des Religions Africaines [*A publication*]

Cah Rene de Lucinge ... Cahiers Rene de Lucinge [*A publication*]

CAHRO...... Canadian Association of Housing and Renewal Officials

CAHS...... CAHS [*Canadian Aviation Historical Society*] Journal [*A publication*]

CAHS .... Canadian Association of Hungarian Studies [*See also ACEH*]

CAHS .... Centre for Applied Health Studies [*University of Ulster at Coleraine*] [*British*]   (CB)

CAHS .... Comprehensive Automation of the Hydrometeorological Service

Cah Sci Appl ... Cahiers de Science Appliquee [*A publication*]

Cah Sem Econ ... Cahiers du Seminaire d'Econometrie [*A publication*]

Cah Sexol Clin ... Cahiers de Sexologie Clinique [*A publication*]

CahSion..... Cahiers Sioniens [*Paris*] [*A publication*]

CAHSL...... Connecticut Association of Health Sciences Libraries [*Library network*]

CAHSLA.... Cincinnati Area Health Sciences Library Association [*Library network*]

Cah Soc Ec ... Cahiers de Sociologie Economique [*A publication*]

Cah Sociol Demogr Med ... Cahiers de Sociologie et de Demographie Medicales [*A publication*]

CAHSP...... Center for the Advancement of Human Service Practice   (EA)

Cah Sticht Bio-Wet Maatsch ... Cahiers van de Stichting Bio-Wetenschappen en Maatschappij [*A publication*]

Cah Synth Org ... Cahiers de Synthese Organique [*A publication*]

CAHT........ Cahiers de Tunisie [*A publication*]

CahTD .... Cahiers. Groupe Francois-Thureau-Dangin. I [*Paris, 1960*] [*A publication*]

Cah Tech.... Cahiers Techniques de l'Art [*A publication*]

Cah Tech Cent Nat Coord Etud Rech Nutr Aliment ... Cahiers Techniques. Centre National de Coordination des Etudes et Recherches sur la Nutrition et l'Alimentation [*A publication*]

Cah Therm ... Cahiers de la Thermique [*A publication*]

Cah Tun ..... Cahiers de Tunisie [*A publication*]

Cah Tunisie ... Cahiers de Tunisie [*A publication*]

CAHUMC ... Commission on Archives and History of the United Methodist Church   (EA)

Cah Vict Ed ... Cahiers Victoriens et Edouardiens [*A publication*]

Cah V Paret ... Cahiers Vilfredo Pareto [*A publication*]

Cah Zair Et Polit Soc ... Cahiers Zairois d'Etudes Politiques et Sociales [*A publication*]

Cah Zairois Etud Pol et Soc ... Cahiers Zairois d'Etudes Politiques et Sociales [*A publication*]

CAI .... CAIC [*Computer Assisted Instruction Center*] Technical Memo. Florida State University [*A publication*]

Cai............. Caines' New York Cases in Error [*A publication*]   (DLA)

Cai............. Caines' Reports, New York Supreme Court [*A publication*]   (DLA)

Cai............. Caines' Term Reports, New York Supreme Court [*A publication*]   (DLA)

CAI .... Cairo [*Egypt*] [*Airport symbol*]   (OAG)

CAI .... Caithness [*County in Scotland*]   (ROG)

CAI .... Calcium-Aluminum-Rich Inclusion [*Meteorite composition*]

CAI .... Canadian Aeronautical Institute

CAI .... Canadian Airlines International Ltd. [*Formed by a merger of Canadian Pacific Airlines Ltd. and Pacific Western Airlines Ltd.*]
CAI .... Canadian Arctic Island
CAI .... Canlan Investment Corp. [*Vancouver Stock Exchange symbol*]
CAI .... Canvas Awning Institute [*Later, American Canvas Institute*] (EA)
CAI .... Career Apparel Institute (EA)
CAI .... Career Assessment Inventory [*Vocational guidance test*]
CAI .... Career Awareness Inventory [*Vocational guidance test*]
CAI .... Center for Archaeological Investigations [*Southern Illinois University at Carbondale*] [*Research center*] (RCD)
CAI .... Center for Arts Information (EA)
cai............. Central American Indian [*MARC language code*] [*Library of Congress*] (LCCP)
CAI .... Chemical and Allied Industries [*Department of Employment*] [*British*]
CAI .... Children's Aid International (EA)
CAI .... Children's Authors and Illustrators [*A publication*]
CAI .... Chinese Army in India
CAI .... Civic Action Institute [*Defunct*] (EA)
CAI .... Civil Aeromedical Institute [*FAA*]
CAI .... Close Approach Indicator (IEEE)
CAI .... Clowns of America International (EA)
CAI .... Coded Acoustic Interrogator
CAI .... Codon Adaptation Index [*Genetics*]
CAI .... Comite Arctique International [*International Arctic Committee*] [*Monte Carlo, Monaco*] (EAIO)
CAI .... Commission d'Appel de l'Immigration [*Immigration Appeal Board - IAB*] [*Canada*]
CAI .... Common Air Interface [*Telecommunications*]
CAI .... Communication Advisors, Incorporated [*Southfield, MI*] [*Telecommunications*] (TSSD)
CAI .... Community Associations Institute (EA)
CAI .... Compressed Air Institute (KSC)
CAI .... Computer-Administered Instruction (RDA)
CAI .... Computer-Aided [*or -Assisted*] Instruction
CAI .... Computer Analog Input
CAI .... Computer Applications, Incorporated (MCD)
CAI .... Computer Automation, Incorporated
CAI .... Confederation of American Indians (EA)
CAI .... Conference Aeronautique Internationale [*International Aeronautical Conference*]
CAI .... Configuration Acceptance Inspection
CAI .... Configuration Audit Inspection [*Army*] (AABC)
CAI .... Configured Article Identifier
CAI .... Confused Artificial Insemination
CAI .... Conjunctive Alteration Indicator
CAI .... Connectionless Acknowledged Information
CAI .... Constructive Action, Incorporated [*Whittier, CA*] (EA)
CAI .... Control and Acquisition Interface (KSC)
CAI .... Control Alarm Indicator (MCD)
CAI .... Corporate Agents, Inc. [*Information service or system*] (IID)
CAI .... Counselor Activity Inventory [*Guidance*]
CAI .... Crochet Association International (EA)
CAIA........... California Apparel Industries Association [*Later, CFC*] (EA)
CAIA........... Clock Assemblers and Importers Association (EA)
CAIA........... Council of American Indian Artists (EA)
CAIBE........ Chemically-Assisted Ion Beam Etching (MCD)
CAIC.......... Canadian Association of Investment Clubs
CAIC.......... Caribbean Association of Industry and Commerce (EAIO)
CAIC.......... Chemical Accident/Incident Control (MCD)
CAIC.......... Civil Aviation Information Circular [*British*] (AIA)
CAIC.......... Computer-Assisted Indexing and Categorizing [*or Classification*]
CAIC.......... Computer-Assisted Instruction Center
Cai Ca .... Caines' Cases [*New York*] [*A publication*] (DLA)
Cai Cas....... Caines' New York Cases in Error [*A publication*] (DLA)
Cai Cas....... Caines' Reports, New York Supreme Court [*A publication*] (DLA)
Cai Cas....... Caines' Term Reports, New York Supreme Court [*A publication*] (DLA)
Cai Cas Err ... Caines' New York Cases in Error [*A publication*] (DLA)
CAICB....... Conseil des Associations d'Ingenieurs du Commonwealth Britannique [*Commonwealth Engineers Council*] (EAIO)
CAICO....... Chemical Accident/Incident Control Officer [*Military*] (AABC)
CAICYT .... Centro Argentino de Informacion Cientifica y Tecnologica [*Argentine Center for Scientific and Technological Information*] [*Information service or system*] (IID)
CAID .... Canadian Agency for International Development
CAID .... Civil Affairs Inland Depot [*for relief supplies to liberated territory*] [*British*] [*World War II*]
CAID .... Computer Aid
CAID .... Convention of American Instructors of the Deaf (EA)
CAIDO ...... Chief Advisor, International District Office [*FAA*] (FAAC)
CAIE........ Standing Committee on Archival Information Exchange [*Society of American Archivists*] [*Information service or system*] (IID)
CAIEF .... Cahiers. Association Internationale des Etudes Francaises [*A publication*]
CAIFI .... Committee for Artistic and Intellectual Freedom in Iran (EA)

CAIFO....... Chief Advisor, International Field Office [*FAA*] (FAAC)
Cai Forms .. Caines' Practical (New York) Forms [*A publication*] (DLA)
CAII.......... Capital Associates, Inc. [*NASDAQ symbol*] (NQ)
CAIIAK...... Centro de Investigaciones Agricolas del Noreste. Informe de Investigacion Agricola [*A publication*]
CAIL.......... Academie des Inscriptions et Belles-Lettres. Comptes Rendus des Seances [*Paris*] [*A publication*]
CAIL.......... Canadian Airlines International Limited [*Formed by a merger of Canadian Pacific Airlines Ltd. and Pacific Western Airlines Ltd.*]
Cai Lex Mer ... Caines' Lex Mercatoria Americana [*A publication*] (DLA)
CAIMAW ... Canadian Association of Industrial, Mechanical, and Allied Workers
CAIMS ...... CONUS [*Continental United States*] Army Installation Management Study
CAIMS ...... Conventional Ammunition Integrated Management System
Cain........... Caines' New York Cases in Error [*A publication*] (DLA)
Cain........... Caines' Reports, New York Supreme Court [*A publication*] (DLA)
Cain........... Caines' Term Reports, New York Supreme Court [*A publication*] (DLA)
CAIN .... Cancer Investigation [*A publication*]
CAIN .... Cataloging and Indexing Number [*Later, AGRICOLA*] [*National Agricultural Library*] [*Database*]
CAIN .... Comite Arctique International. Newsletter [*A publication*]
CAIN .... Computerized AIDS [*Acquired Immune Deficiency Syndrome*] Information Network [*Los Angeles Gay and Lesbian Community Services Center*] [*Database*]
Cain Cas in Error ... Caines' New York Cases in Error [*A publication*] (DLA)
Cain CE ..... Caines' New York Cases in Error [*A publication*] (DLA)
Cain E .... Caines' New York Cases in Error [*A publication*] (DLA)
Caine R ...... Caines' Reports [*New York*] [*A publication*] (DLA)
Caines .... Caines' New York Cases in Error [*A publication*] (DLA)
Caines .... Caines' Reports, New York Supreme Court [*A publication*] (DLA)
Caines .... Caines' Term Reports, New York Supreme Court [*A publication*] (DLA)
Caines Ca in E ... Caines' New York Cases in Error [*A publication*] (DLA)
Caines' Ca in Er ... Caines' New York Cases in Error [*A publication*] (DLA)
Caines Cas ... Caines' New York Cases in Error [*A publication*] (DLA)
Caines Cas ... Caines' Reports, New York Supreme Court [*A publication*] (DLA)
Caines Cas ... Caines' Term Reports, New York Supreme Court [*A publication*] (DLA)
Caines' Cas in Er ... Caines' New York Cases in Error [*A publication*] (DLA)
Caines (NY) ... Caines' New York Cases in Error [*A publication*] (DLA)
Caines (NY) ... Caines' Reports, New York Supreme Court [*A publication*] (DLA)
Caines (NY) ... Caines' Term Reports, New York Supreme Court [*A publication*] (DLA)
Caines' R.... Caines' Reports [*New York*] [*A publication*] (DLA)
Caines Rep ... Caines' Reports [*New York*] [*A publication*] (DLA)
Caines Term Rep (NY) ... Caines' Term Reports, New York Supreme Court [*A publication*] (DLA)
CAINS....... Carrier Aircraft [*or Alignment*] Inertial Navigation System (MCD)
Cains C ...... Caines' Cases [*New York*] [*A publication*] (DLA)
Cains R ...... Caines' Reports [*New York*] [*A publication*] (DLA)
CAINT....... Counter-Air and Interdiction
Cai (NY) .... Caines' Reports [*New York*] [*A publication*] (DLA)
CAIO .... Caribbean American Intercultural Organization (EA)
CAI/O........ Computer Analog Input/Output (DEN)
CAIO .... Corps Artillery Intelligence Officer [*British*]
CAIOGP.... Council of Active Independent Oil and Gas Producers (EA)
CAIOP....... Computer Analog Input/Output
CAIP......... Catholic Association for International Peace [*Defunct*] (EA)
CAIP......... Center for Computer Aids for Industrial Productivity [*Rutgers University*] [*Research center*] (RCD)
CAIP......... Concerned American Indian Parents (EA)
Cai Pr........ Caines' Practice [*A publication*] (DLA)
Cai R .... Caines' New York Cases in Error [*A publication*] (DLA)
Cai R .... Caines' Reports, New York Supreme Court [*A publication*] (DLA)
Cai R .... Caines' Term Reports, New York Supreme Court [*A publication*] (DLA)
CAIR......... Child Abuse Institute of Research (EA)
CAIR......... Comprehensive Assessment Information Rule [*Environmental Protection Agency*]
CAIR......... Concerned Americans for Individual Rights (EA)
CAIR......... Confidential Aviation Incident Reporting Program [*Australia*]
CAIR......... Conquest Airlines Corp. [*NASDAQ symbol*] (NQ)
CAIR......... Cost Analysis Information Report [*Air Force*] (MCD)
CAIR......... Countermeasures, Airborne Infrared
CAIRA....... Central Automated Inventory and Referral Activity [*Organization for operation of CAIRS*] [*Air Force*]
CAIRC....... Caribbean Air Command [*Air Force*]
CAIRDG.... Cardiovascular and Interventional Radiology [*A publication*]
Cairns Dec ... Cairns. Decisions in the Albert Arbitration (Reilly) [*1871-75*] [*England*] [*A publication*] (DLA)
Cairo St Engl ... Cairo Studies in English [*A publication*]

Cairo Univ Fac Sci Bull ... Cairo University. Faculty of Science. Bulletin [*A publication*]
Cairo Univ Herb Publ ... Cairo University. Herbarium. Publications [*A publication*]
CAIRS .... Central Automated Inventory and Referral System [*Air Force*]
CAIRS .... Computer-Aided Analysis and Information Recovery Systems (MCD)
CAIRS .... Computer-Assisted Information Retrieval Service [*Mississippi State University*] (OLDSS)
CAIRS .... Computer-Assisted Interactive Resources Scheduling System
CAIS .... Canadian Association for Information Science [*Ottawa, ON*]
CAIS .... Canadian Association for Irish Studies
CAIS .... Center for Applied Isotope Studies [*University of Georgia*] [*Research center*] (RCD)
CAIS .... Center for Arab-Islamic Studies (EA)
CAIS .... Central Abstracting and Indexing Service [*American Petroleum Institute*] [*Information service or system*] (IID)
CAIS .... Common APSE [*Ada Program Support Environment*] Interface Set [*Data processing*]
CAIS .... Computer-Aided Instruction (IEEE)
CAIS .... Computer-Assisted Action Information System [*NATO*]
CAIS .... Congress of Arabic and Islamic Studies [*Madrid, Spain*] (EA)
CAISA .... Campaign Against Investment in South Africa (EA)
CAIS/ACSI ... Canadian Association for Information Science/Association Canadienne des Sciences de l'Information (IID)
CaiSE .... Cairo Studies in English [*A publication*]
CAISF .... Chemical Abstracts Integrated Subject File [*Chemical Abstracts Service*] [*Database*] [*A publication*] (IID)
CAISIM .... Computer-Assisted Industrial Simulation [*Army*]
CAISMS .... Computer-Assisted Instruction Study Management System (MCD)
CAISR .... Center for Automation and Intelligent Systems Research [*Case Western Reserve University*] [*Research center*] (RCD)
CAISYS ..... Computer-Aided Instruction System [*Programming language*] [*1971*] (CSR)
Cai TR .... Caines' Term Reports, New York Supreme Court [*A publication*] (DLA)
CAITS .... Centre for Alternative Industrial and Technological Systems [*British*] (CB)
CAITS .... Chemical Agent Identification Training Set
CAITS .... Computerized Automatic Inertial Test Set (MCD)
CAIU .... Cahiers. Alliance Israelite Universelle [*A publication*]
CAIUM ..... Cahiers. Alliance Israelite Universelle [*Mahberet*] [*A publication*]
CAIV .... Computer-Assisted Interactive Video
CAIVman ... Computer Audio Interactive Video Manipulator [*Designed by Christopher Conley*]
CAIX .... Central American International [*Air carrier designation symbol*]
CAJ .... Canaima [*Venezuela*] [*Airport symbol*] (OAG)
CAJ .... Canasia Industries Corp. [*Vancouver Stock Exchange symbol*]
CAJ .... Caulked Joint
CAJ .... Center for Administrative Justice [*Later, NCAJ*] (EA)
CAJ .... Central Asiatic Journal [*A publication*]
CAJ .... College Art Journal [*A publication*]
CAJ .... Comision Andina de Juristas [*Andean Commission of Jurists - ACJ*] (EAIO)
CAJ .... Consumers' Association of Jamaica
CAJAD ...... Center po Atomn. i Jadernum Dannym [*Center for Nuclear Structure and Reaction Data*] [*USSR State Committee on the Utilization of Atomic Energy*] [*Information service or system*] (IID)
CAJC .... California Jury Instructions, Criminal [*A publication*] (DLA)
CAJE .... Coalition for the Advancement of Jewish Education (EA)
CAJE .... Coalition for Alternatives in Jewish Education (EA)
CAJE .... Comprehensive Antijam Equipment (MCD)
CAJE .... Consolidated Anti-Jam Equipment (MCD)
CAJI .... California Jury Instructions, Civil [*A publication*] (DLA)
CAJIR .... Association Canadienne d'Assistance Juridique, d'Information et de Recherche des Handicapes [*Canadian Legal Advocacy Information and Research Association of the Disabled*]
CAJL .... Central-Anzeiger fuer Juedische Litteratur [*A publication*] (BJA)
CAJM .... Council of American Jewish Museums (EA)
CAJMA3 ... Central African Journal of Medicine [*A publication*]
CAJOB ...... Canadian Journal of Ophthalmology [*A publication*]
CAJOBA ... Canadian Journal of Ophthalmology [*A publication*]
CAJOD ...... Cato Journal [*A publication*]
CAJP .... Central Archives of the Jewish People [*Jerusalem*] [*A publication*] (BJA)
CAJP .... Christian Anti-Jewish Party (BJA)
CAJR .... New York State Commission on Administration of Justice, Report [*A publication*] (DLA)
CAK .... Akron/Canton [*Ohio*] [*Airport symbol*]
CAK .... Canadian Arctic Petroleum [*Vancouver Stock Exchange symbol*]
CAK .... Command Access Keys
CAK .... Command Acknowledge (BUR)
CAK .... Concept Assessment Kit [*Child development test*]
CAK .... Conical Alignment Kit

CAK .... Cube Alignment Kit
CAKCAC ... Communications. Faculte des Sciences. Universite d'Ankara. Serie C. Sciences Naturelles [*A publication*]
CAKE .... Charlotte Charles, Inc. [*NASDAQ symbol*] (NQ)
Cal .... All India Reporter, Calcutta Series [*A publication*] (DLA)
C A L .... Cahiers. Academie Luxembourgeoise [*A publication*]
CAL .... Cahiers des Ameriques Latines [*A publication*]
Cal .... Calando [*Dying Away*] [*Music*]
Cal .... [*Laurentius*] Calcaneus [*Flourished, 15th century*] [*Authority cited in pre-1607 legal work*] (DSA)
CAL .... Calcium [*Chemical element*] [*Symbol is Ca*] (ROG)
CAL .... Calcraft [*Hangman*] [*Slang*] [*British*] (DSUE)
cAL .... Calcrete [*Geology*]
CAL .... Calculated Average Life (AAG)
CAL .... Calcutta [*Alipore*] [*India*] [*Seismograph station code, US Geological Survey*] (SEIS)
Cal .... Caldecott's English Settlement Cases [*1776-85*] [*A publication*] (DLA)
CAL .... Caldwell College for Women, Caldwell, NJ [*OCLC symbol*] (OCLC)
CAL .... Caledonia [*Scotland*] (ROG)
CAL .... Calendae [*Calends*] [*The first day of the month*] [*Latin*] (ROG)
CAL .... Calendar
Cal .... Calendars of the Proceedings in Chancery, Record Commission [*A publication*] (DLA)
CAL .... CalFed, Inc. [*NYSE symbol*] (SPSG)
CAL .... Caliber (AFM)
CAL .... Calibrate (CET)
CAL .... Calibration (MSA)
Cal .... Caliche [*A publication*]
CAL .... California
CAL .... California Law Review [*A publication*]
Cal .... California Reports [*A publication*] (DLA)
CAL .... Call Aircraft Co.
CAL .... Calomel [*Pharmacy*] (ROG)
CAL .... Calorie (MSA)
CAL .... Calspan Corp. [*Formerly, Cornell Aeronautical Laboratory*]
Cal .... Calthrop's English King's Bench Reports [*80 English Reprint*] [*A publication*] (DLA)
CAL .... Campbeltown [*Scotland*] [*Airport symbol*] (OAG)
CaL .... Campus Life [*A publication*]
CAL .... Canadian Airways Limited
CAL .... Canadian Arsenals Limited
CAL .... Capella Resources Limited [*Vancouver Stock Exchange symbol*]
CAL .... Capitol Air Lines
CAL .... Cargo Air Lines [*Israel*] (BJA)
CAL .... Caribbean Action Lobby (EA)
CAL .... Carter-Atkinson Lurmann Mechanism [*Air pollution*]
CAL .... Cavei Avir Lemitanim [*Israeli airline*] (FAAC)
CAL .... Center for Applied Linguistics (EA)
CAL .... China Airlines
CAL .... Chronic Airflow Limitation [*Medicine*]
CAL .... Colonial Air Lines
CAL .... Comandos Armados de Liberacion [*Armed Liberation Commandos*] [*Puerto Rico*] (PD)
CAL .... Command Authorization List
CAL .... Common Assembly Language (MCD)
CAL .... Component Action List [*NASA*] (KSC)
CAL .... Compressed Air Loudspeaker
CAL .... Computer-Aided [*or -Assisted*] Learning (BUR)
CAL .... Computer Animation Language
CAL .... Computer Augmented Learning (CMD)
CAL .... Confined Area Landing
CAL .... Conservation Analytical Laboratory [*Smithsonian Institution*]
CAL .... Continental Airlines, Inc. (MCD)
CAL .... Continuity Accept Limit
CAL .... Contractor Attention List
CAL .... Conversational Algebraic Language [*Adaptation of JOSS language*] [*Data processing*]
CAL .... Copy and Add Logical Word (CET)
CAL .... Copyright Agency Limited [*Australia*] (ADA)
CAL .... Cornell Aeronautical Laboratory (KSC)
CAL .... Course Author Language [*Data processing*]
CAL .... Current Antarctic Literature [*A publication*]
CAL .... Romance Writers of America. Chapter Advisory Letter [*A publication*] (EAAP)
CAla .... Alameda Free Library, Alameda, CA [*Library symbol*] [*Library of Congress*] (LCLS)
Cala .... Calcified Alluvium [*Archeology*]
CALA .... Charles A. Lindbergh Association [*Defunct*] (EA)
CALA .... Chinese-American Librarians Association (EA)
CALA .... Citizens Against Lawyer Abuse (EA)
CALA .... Civil Aviation Licensing Act (DLA)
CALA .... Combined Administrative Liquidating Agency [*Microfilmed SHAEF documents for each participating country after SHAEF was disbanded*] [*Post-World War II*]
CALA .... Community Action on Latin America (EA)
CALA .... Computer-Aided Loads Analysis (MCD)
CALAC ...... Lockheed-California Company [*Division of Lockheed Aircraft Corp.*] (MCD)

CALACS ...   Canadian Association of Latin American and Caribbean Studies
Cal Ac Sc ...   California Academy of Sciences [*A publication*]
Cal Ac Sc Mem ...   California Academy of Sciences. Memoirs [*A publication*]
Cal Ac Sc Oc P ...   California Academy of Sciences. Occasional Papers [*A publication*]
Cal Ac Sc Pr ...   California Academy of Sciences. Proceedings [*A publication*]
Cal Adm Code ...   California Administrative Code [*A publication*]   (DLA)
Cal Admin Code ...   California Administrative Code [*A publication*]   (DLA)
Cal Admin Notice Reg ...   California Administrative Notice Register [*A publication*]
Cal Admin Reg ...   California Administrative Register [*A publication*]   (DLA)
Cal Adv Legis Serv ...   California Advance Legislative Service (Deering) [*A publication*]   (DLA)
Cal Adv Leg Serv (Deering) ...   California Advance Legislative Service (Deering) [*A publication*]
Cal Ag Exp ...   University of California. College of Agriculture. Agricultural Experiment Station. Publications [*A publication*]
Cal Agr ......   California Agriculture [*A publication*]
Cal Agric Code ...   California Agriculture Code [*A publication*]   (DLA)
CALAIS .....   Council of Australian Libraries and Information Services [*Proposed*]
CALALT ...   Calculated Altitude
Cal App ...   California Appellate Reports [*A publication*]   (DLA)
Cal App 2d ...   California Appellate Reports, Second Series [*A publication*]   (DLA)
Cal App 3d ...   California Appellate Reports, Third Series [*A publication*]   (DLA)
Cal App Dec ...   California Appellate Decisions [*A publication*]   (DLA)
Cal App 2d Supp ...   California Appellate Reports, Second Series, Supplement [*A publication*]   (DLA)
Cal App 3d Supp ...   California Appellate Reports, Third Series, Supplement [*A publication*]   (DLA)
Cal App Supp ...   California Appellate Reports, Supplement [*A publication*]   (DLA)
CALAR ......   Cooperative Arid Lands Agriculture Research Program [*Established by Egypt, Israel, and the US at the University of San Diego in 1981*]
CalArts ......   California Institute of the Arts [*Valencia, CA*]
CALAS .....   Canadian Association for Laboratory Animal Science
CALAS .....   Canadian Association of Latin American Studies
CaLaSOAP ...   Calcium Lanthanum Silicate Oxyapatite   (IEEE)
CAlaUN .....   United States Naval Air Station, Alameda, CA [*Library symbol*] [*Library of Congress*]   (LCLS)
CAlb ....   Albany Free Public Library, Albany, CA [*Library symbol*] [*Library of Congress*]   (LCLS)
CALB ....   Computer-Aided Line Balance
CAlbA ....   United States Department of Agriculture, Western Regional Research Laboratory, Albany, CA [*Library symbol*] [*Library of Congress*]   (LCLS)
CAL-BIO ...   California Biotechnology, Inc.
CALBLK ...   Calibration Blank [*Spectroscopy*]
CALBR ......   Calibration   (AABC)
CAL Bull ....   Association of the Bar of the City of New York. Committee on Amendment of the Law. Bulletin [*A publication*]   (DLA)
CALC ....   Cahiers Algeriens de Litterature Comparee [*A publication*]
CALC ....   Calculated
CALC ....   Calcutta [*India*]   (ROG)
CALC ....   Cargo Allocation and Load Control [*Aviation*]
CALC ....   Chicago Academic Library Council [*Library network*]
CALC ....   Clergy and Laity Concerned   (EA)
CALC ....   Customer Access Line Charge [*Telecommunications*]
Calc ....   Indian Law Reports, Calcutta Series [*A publication*]   (DLA)
Calca ....   [*Laurentius*] Calcaneus [*Flourished, 15th century*] [*Authority cited in pre-1607 legal work*]   (DSA)
CALCAV ...   Clergy and Laymen Concerned about Vietnam [*Later, CALC*]   (EA)
CALCC ......   Charles A. Lindbergh Collectors Club   (EA)
CALCD ......   Calculated   (ADA)
Cal Ch ....   Calendar of Proceedings in Chancery Tempore Elizabeth [*1827-32*] [*A publication*]   (DLA)
Calcif Tiss ...   Calcified Tissue Research [*Later, Calcified Tissue International*] [*A publication*]
Calcif Tissue Int ...   Calcified Tissue International [*A publication*]
Calcif Tissue Res ...   Calcified Tissue Research [*Later, Calcified Tissue International*] [*A publication*]
Calcif Tissues Proc Eur Symp ...   Calcified Tissues. Proceedings of the European Symposium [*A publication*]
Calcitonin Proc Int Symp ...   Calcitonin Proceedings. International Symposium [*A publication*]
Cal Citrograph ...   California Citrograph [*A publication*]
Calc J M ....   Calcutta Journal of Medicine [*A publication*]
Calc LJ ......   Calcutta Law Journal [*A publication*]   (DLA)
Calc Med Rev ...   Calcutta Medical Review [*A publication*]
CALCO ......   Capitol Area Library Consortium, Inc. [*Library network*]
Cal Code ....   Deering's Annotated California Code [*A publication*]   (DLA)
Cal Code (Deering) ...   Deering's Annotated California Code [*A publication*]
CALCOFI ...   California Cooperative Oceanic Fishery Investigations [*Also, CCOFI*]
CALCOMP ...   California Computer Products, Inc.   (MCD)
Cal Comp Cases ...   California Compensation Cases [*A publication*]   (DLA)
CALCON ..   California Connections [*Information service or system*]   (CRD)

Cal Const ...   California Constitution [*A publication*]   (DLA)
Cal Countryman ...   California Countryman [*A publication*]
Calc Rev .....   Calcutta Review [*A publication*]
Calc Ser ......   Calcutta Series, Indian Law Reports [*A publication*]   (DLA)
Calc Tiss Res ...   Calcified Tissue Research [*Later, Calcified Tissue International*] [*A publication*]
Cal Cultivator ...   California Cultivator [*A publication*]
Calcut St ....   Calcutta Statistical Association. Bulletin [*A publication*]
Calcutta Hist J ...   Calcutta Historical Journal [*A publication*]
Calcutta LJ ...   Calcutta Law Journal [*A publication*]   (DLA)
Calcutta Med J ...   Calcutta Medical Journal [*A publication*]
Calcutta R ...   Calcutta Review [*A publication*]
Calcutta Statist Assoc Bull ...   Calcutta Statistical Association. Bulletin [*A publication*]
Calcutta WN ...   Calcutta Weekly Notes [*A publication*]   (DLA)
Calc WN ....   Calcutta Weekly Notes [*A publication*]   (DLA)
Cald ....   Caldecott's Magistrates' and Settlement Cases [*1776-85*] [*England*] [*A publication*]   (DLA)
Cald ....   [*Johannes*] Calderini [*Deceased, 1365*] [*Authority cited in pre-1607 legal work*]   (DSA)
CALD ....   Calderon [*Spanish dramatist, 1600-1682*]   (ROG)
Cald ....   Caldwell's Reports [*25-36 West Virginia*] [*A publication*]   (DLA)
CALD ....   Chronic Active Liver Disease [*Medicine*]
Cal 2d ....   California Reports, Second Series [*A publication*]   (DLA)
Cal 3d ....   California Reports, Third Series [*A publication*]   (DLA)
CALDA ......   Canadian Air Line Dispatchers' Association [*See also ACRV*]
Cal Dairym ...   California Dairyman [*A publication*]
Cald Arb ....   Caldwell. Arbitration [*2nd ed.*] [*1825*] [*A publication*]   (DLA)
Calde ....   [*Johannes*] Calderini [*Deceased, 1365*] [*Authority cited in pre-1607 legal work*]   (DSA)
Cal Dec ......   California Decisions [*A publication*]   (DLA)
CALDEF ...   Cuban American Legal Defense and Education Fund   (EA)
Cald (Eng) ...   Caldecott's Magistrates' and Settlement Cases [*1776-85*] [*England*] [*A publication*]   (DLA)
CALDEPOP ...   California Depopulation Commission   (EA)
Calder ....   [*Johannes*] Calderini [*Deceased, 1365*] [*Authority cited in pre-1607 legal work*]   (DSA)
Cald JP ......   Caldecott's Magistrates' and Settlement Cases [*1776-85*] [*England*] [*A publication*]   (DLA)
Cald Mag Cas ...   Caldecott's Magistrates' and Settlement Cases [*1776-85*] [*England*] [*A publication*]   (DLA)
Cald M Cas ...   Caldecott's Magistrates' and Settlement Cases [*1776-85*] [*England*] [*A publication*]   (DLA)
Cald Med ...   Caldas Medico [*A publication*]
CALDOC ...   Calgary Public Library Government Documents [*Information service or system*]   (IID)
Cald SC ......   Caldecott's Magistrates' and Settlement Cases [*1776-85*] [*England*] [*A publication*]   (DLA)
Cald Set Cas ...   Caldecott's Magistrates' and Settlement Cases [*1776-85*] [*England*] [*A publication*]   (DLA)
Cald Sett Cas ...   Caldecott's Magistrates' and Settlement Cases [*1776-85*] [*England*] [*A publication*]   (DLA)
CALE ....   Canadian Army Liaison Executive
CALEA ......   Canadian Air Lines Employees Association
CALEA ......   Commission on Accreditation for Law Enforcement Agencies   (EA)
CALED ......   Caledonia [*Scotland*]
Caled Med J ...   Caledonian Medical Journal [*A publication*]
CALEDQ ..   Cancer Letters [*A publication*]
CALEF ......   Calefiat [*Warm It*] [*Pharmacy*]
CALEFACT ...   Calefactus [*Made Warm*] [*Pharmacy*]   (ROG)
Cal Engl J ...   California English Journal [*A publication*]
CALEW .....   Common Assembly Language for Electronic Warfare   (MCD)
CALF ....   Combined Allied Land Forces
CALFAA ....   Canadian Air Line Flight Attendants Association
CALFAB ....   Computer-Aided Layout and Fabrication   (MCD)
CALFEX ....   Combined Arms Live Fire Exercises   (INF)
Cal Fi Ga ....   California Fish and Game [*A publication*]
CALF News Concern Am Livest Feeders ...   CALF News. Concerning America's Livestock Feeders [*A publication*]
Cal Folkl Q ...   California Folklore Quarterly [*A publication*]
Cal For For Prod ...   California Forestry and Forest Products [*A publication*]
Cal For Ital ...   Calendario Forestale Italiano [*A publication*]
CALG ....   Cal Graphite Corp. [*NASDAQ symbol*]   (NQ)
CALG ....   Calgary [*Canada*]   (ROG)
CALGB .....   Cancer and Leukemia, Group B [*Medicine*]
CALGEN ....   Courseware Authoring Language Generator [*Data processing*]   (MCD)
Cal Gen Laws Ann (Deering) ...   Deering's California General Laws, Annotated [*A publication*]   (DLA)
Cal Geogr ...   California Geography [*A publication*]
CALGIR ....   Community and Local Government Information Review [*A publication*]   (APTA)
CAlh ....   Alhambra Public Library, Alhambra, CA [*Library symbol*] [*Library of Congress*]   (LCLS)
CAlhB ....   C. F. Braun & Co., Alhambra, CA [*Library symbol*] [*Library of Congress*]   (LCLS)
Cal Hlth .....   California's Health [*A publication*]
Cali ....   California
CALI ....   Calumet Industries, Inc. [*NASDAQ symbol*]   (NQ)

Cal IAC...... Decisions of the Industrial Accident Commission of California [*A publication*]   (DLA)

Cal IACCC ... California Industrial Accident Commission. Compensation Cases [*A publication*]   (DLA)

Cal IAC Dec ... California Industrial Accident Decisions [*A publication*]   (DLA)

CALIB....... Calibrate   (AAG)

CALIBN .... Calibration   (AAG)

CALIBR .... Calibration

CALICO.... Computer Assisted Language Learning and Instruction Consortium   (EA)

CALICO.... Computer Assisted Library Instruction Company, Inc. [*Information service or system*]   (IID)

CALICO J ... CALICO [*Computer-Assisted Language Learning and Instruction Consortium*] Journal [*A publication*]

CALICON ... California Contract Show [*Western Merchandise Mart*]   (TSPED)

CALID....... Calidus [*Warm*] [*Pharmacy*]   (ROG)

CALIF .... California   (AFM)

Calif .... California Reports [*A publication*]   (DLA)

Calif Acad Sci Mem ... California Academy of Sciences. Memoirs [*A publication*]

Calif Acad Sci Occasional Paper Proc ... California Academy of Sciences. Occasional Papers and Proceedings [*A publication*]

Calif Ag Bul ... California. Department of Agriculture. Bulletin [*A publication*]

Calif Agr .... California Agriculture [*A publication*]

Calif Agric ... California Agriculture [*A publication*]

Calif Agric Calif Agric Exp Stn ... California Agriculture. California Agricultural Experiment Station [*A publication*]

Calif Agric Exp Stn Bull ... California. Agricultural Experiment Station. Bulletin [*A publication*]

Calif Agric Ext Serv Circ ... California. Agricultural Extension Service. Circular [*A publication*]

Calif Air Qual Data ... California Air Quality Data [*A publication*]

Calif Anthropol ... California Anthropologist [*A publication*]

Calif Bee Times ... California Bee Times [*A publication*]

Calif Birds ... California Birds [*A publication*]

Calif Bus .... California Business [*A publication*]

Calif Bus Ed J ... California Business Education Journal [*A publication*]

Calif Cattleman ... California Cattleman [*A publication*]

Calif Citrogr ... California Citrograph [*A publication*]

Calif Coop Oceanic Fish Invest Atlas ... California Cooperative Oceanic Fisheries Investigations. Atlas [*A publication*]

Calif Coop Oceanic Fish Invest Rep ... California Cooperative Oceanic Fisheries Investigations. Reports [*A publication*]

Calif Dep Agric Bienn Rep ... California. Department of Agriculture. Biennial Report [*A publication*]

Calif Dep Agric Bull ... California. Department of Agriculture. Bulletin [*A publication*]

Calif Dep Agric Bur Entomol Occas Pap ... California. Department of Agriculture. Bureau of Entomology. Occasional Papers [*A publication*]

Calif Dep Fish Game Fish Bull ... California. Department of Fish and Game. Fish Bulletin [*A publication*]

Calif Dep Fish Game Game Bull ... California. Department of Fish and Game. Game Bulletin [*A publication*]

Calif Dep Food Agric Lab Serv-Entomol Occas Pap ... California. Department of Food and Agriculture. Laboratory Services-Entomology. Occasional Papers [*A publication*]

Calif Dep Nat Resour Div Mines Bull ... California. Department of Natural Resources. Division of Mines. Bulletin [*A publication*]

Calif Dep Nat Resour Div Mines Spec Rep ... California. Department of Natural Resources. Division of Mines. Special Reports [*A publication*]

Calif Dep Nat Resour Div Soil Conserv Bull ... California. Department of Natural Resources. Division of Soil Conservation. Bulletin [*A publication*]

Calif Dept Agric Bur Entomol Occas Pap ... California. Department of Agriculture. Bureau of Entomology. Occasional Papers [*A publication*]

Calif Dept Nat Res Div Mines Bull ... California. Department of Natural Resources. Division of Mines. Bulletin [*A publication*]

Calif Dept Nat Res Div Mines Econ Mineral Map ... California. Department of Natural Resources. Division of Mines. Economic Mineral Map [*A publication*]

Calif Dept Nat Res Div Mines Mineral Inf Service ... California. Department of Natural Resources. Division of Mines. Mineral Information Service [*A publication*]

Calif Dept Nat Res Div Mines Rept State Mineralogist ... California. Department of Natural Resources. Division of Mines. Report of State Mineralogist [*A publication*]

Calif Dept Nat Res Div Mines Special Rept ... California. Department of Natural Resources. Division of Mines. Special Report [*A publication*]

Calif Dept Public Works Div Water Res Bull ... California. Department of Public Works. Division of Water Resources. Bulletin [*A publication*]

Calif Dept Public Works Div Water Res Water Quality Inv Rept ... California. Department of Public Works. Division of Water Resources. Water Quality Investigations Report [*A publication*]

Calif Dept Water Res Bull ... California. Department of Water Resources. Bulletin [*A publication*]

Calif Dept Water Res Div Res Plan Bull ... California. Department of Water Resources. Division of Resources. Planning Bulletin [*A publication*]

Calif Dept Water Res Rept ... California. Department of Water Resources. Report [*A publication*]

Calif Div For Fire Control Notes ... California. Division of Forestry. Fire Control Notes [*A publication*]

Calif Div Mines Geol Bull ... California. Division of Mines and Geology. Bulletin [*A publication*]

Calif Div Mines Geol Geol Data Map ... California. Division of Mines and Geology. Geologic Data Map [*A publication*]

Calif Div Mines Geol Map Sheet Ser ... California. Division of Mines and Geology. Map Sheet Series [*A publication*]

Calif Div Mines Geol Rep ... California. Division of Mines and Geology. County Report [*A publication*]

Calif Div Mines Geol Rep State Geol ... California. Division of Mines and Geology. Report of the State Geologist [*A publication*]

Calif Div Mines Geol Spec Publ ... California. Division of Mines and Geology. Special Publication [*A publication*]

Calif Div Mines Geol Spec Rep ... California. Division of Mines and Geology. Special Report [*A publication*]

Calif Div Oil Gas Annu Rep ... California. Division of Oil and Gas. Annual Report [*A publication*]

Calif Ed...... California Education [*A publication*]

Calif El Sch Adm Assn Mon ... California Elementary School Administrators Association. Monographs [*A publication*]

Calif El Sch Adm Assn Yearbook ... California Elementary School Administrators Association. Yearbook [*A publication*]

Calif Farmer ... California Farmer [*A publication*]

Calif Farmer Cent Ed ... California Farmer. Central Edition [*A publication*]

Calif Feeders Day ... California Feeders' Day [*A publication*]

Calif Fire Control Note Calif Div For ... California Fire Control Notes. California Division of Forestry [*A publication*]

Calif Fire Prev Note Calif Div For ... California Fire Prevention Notes. California Division of Forestry [*A publication*]

Calif Fish ... California Fish and Game [*A publication*]

Calif Fish Game ... California Fish and Game [*A publication*]

Calif Folklore Qu ... California Folklore Quarterly [*A publication*]

Calif For & For Prod Calif For Prod Lab ... California Forestry and Forest Products. University of California. Forest Products Laboratory [*A publication*]

Calif For Note ... California Forestry Note [*A publication*]

Calif Geol... California Geology [*A publication*]

Calif Grow Rancher Sacramento Val Ed ... California Grower and Rancher. Sacramento Valley Edition [*A publication*]

Calif Health ... California's Health [*A publication*]

Calif Hist ... California History [*A publication*]

Calif Hist Q ... California Historical Quarterly [*A publication*]

Calif Hist Soc Q ... California Historical Society. Quarterly [*San Francisco*] [*A publication*]

Calif Hist Soc Quar ... California Historical Society. Quarterly [*San Francisco*] [*A publication*]

Calif Hortic J ... California Horticultural Journal [*A publication*]

Calif Hous ... California Housing Outlook [*A publication*]

Calif Ind Accdt Com Dec ... Decisions of the Industrial Accident Commission of California [*A publication*]   (DLA)

Calif Inst Technol Earthquake Eng Res Lab (Rep) EERL ... California Institute of Technology. Earthquake Engineering Research Laboratory (Report) EERL [*A publication*]

Calif Inst Technol Jet Propul Lab Tech Memo ... California Institute of Technology. Jet Propulsion Laboratory. Technical Memorandum [*A publication*]

Calif Inst Technology Div Geol Sci Contr ... California Institute of Technology. Division of Geological Sciences. Contributions [*A publication*]

Calif J Ed Res ... California Journal of Educational Research [*A publication*]

Calif J Edu ... California Journal of Educational Research [*A publication*]

Calif J El Ed ... California Journal of Elementary Education [*A publication*]

Calif Jour Mines and Geology ... California Journal of Mines and Geology [*A publication*]

Calif J Sec Ed ... California Journal of Secondary Education [*A publication*]

Calif Libn... California Librarian [*A publication*]

Calif Librn ... California Librarian [*A publication*]

Calif L Rev ... California Law Review [*A publication*]

Calif M....... Californian Illustrated Magazine [*A publication*]

Calif Mag... California Magazine [*A publication*]

Calif Manag ... California Management Review [*A publication*]

Calif Management Rev ... California Management Review [*A publication*]

Calif Manage Rev ... California Management Review [*A publication*]

Calif Manag R ... California Management Review [*A publication*]

Calif Med... California Medicine [*A publication*]

Calif Mgt R ... California Management Review [*A publication*]

Calif Min J ... California Mining Journal [*A publication*]

Calif Mosq Control Assoc Proc Pap Annu Conf ... California Mosquito Control Association. Proceedings and Papers of the Annual Conference [*A publication*]

Calif Mosq Vector Control Assoc Proc Pap Annu Conf ... California Mosquito and Vector Control Association. Proceedings and Papers of the Annual Conference [*A publication*]

Calif Nat Hist Guides ... California Natural History Guides [*A publication*]
Calif Nurs .. California Nurse [*A publication*]
Calif Nurse ... California Nurse [*A publication*]
Calif Oil Fields ... California Oil Fields [*A publication*]
Calif Oil World ... California Oil World [*A publication*]
Calif Oil World Pet Ind ... California Oil World and Petroleum Industry [*A publication*]
California Acad Sci Proc ... California Academy of Sciences. Proceedings [*A publication*]
California Dept Water Resources Bull ... California. Department of Water Resources. Bulletin [*A publication*]
California Div Mines and Geology Bull ... California. Division of Mines and Geology. Bulletin [*A publication*]
California Div Mines and Geology Map Sheet ... California. Division of Mines and Geology. Map Sheet [*A publication*]
California Div Mines and Geology Mineral Inf Service ... California. Division of Mines and Geology. Mineral Information Service [*A publication*]
California Div Mines and Geology Spec Rept ... California. Division of Mines and Geology. Special Report [*A publication*]
California Geol ... California Geology [*A publication*]
California Med ... California Medicine [*A publication*]
California Univ Pubs Geol Sci ... California University. Publications in Geological Sciences [*A publication*]
California Univ Water Resources Center Rept ... California University. Water Resources Center. Report [*A publication*]
California West L Rev ... California Western Law Review [*A publication*]
California West Med ... California and Western Medicine [*A publication*]
Californium 252 Prog ... Californium-252 Progress [*A publication*]
Calif Pal Leg Hon Bul ... California Palace of the Legion of Honor. Museum Bulletin [*A publication*]
Calif Poult Lett Univ Calif Coop Ext ... California Poultry Letter. University of California Cooperative Extension [*A publication*]
Calif Q .... California Quarterly [*A publication*]
Calif S B ..... State Bar of California. Journal [*A publication*]
Calif SBJ ... California State Bar Journal [*A publication*] (DLA)
Calif SBJ ... State Bar of California. Journal [*A publication*]
Calif Sch .... California Schools [*A publication*]
Calif Sch Lib ... California School Libraries [*A publication*]
Calif Sch Libr ... California School Libraries [*A publication*]
Calif Sewage Works J ... California Sewage Works Journal [*A publication*]
Calif Slavic Stud ... California Slavic Studies [*A publication*]
Calif State Dep Public Health Wkly Bull ... California. State Department of Public Health. Weekly Bulletin [*A publication*]
Calif State Dept Education Bull ... California State Department of Education. Bulletin [*A publication*]
Calif State J Med ... California State Journal of Medicine [*A publication*]
Calif State Univ (Chico) Reg Programs Monogr ... California State University (Chico). Regional Programs Monograph [*A publication*]
Calif State Water Pollut Control Board Publ ... California State Water Pollution Control Board. Publication [*A publication*]
Calif State Water Pollution Control Board Pub ... California State Water Pollution Control Board. Publication [*A publication*]
Calif State Water Res Board Bull ... California State Water Resources Board. Bulletin [*A publication*]
Calif State Water Resour Control Board Publ ... California. State Water Resources Control Board. Publication [*A publication*]
Calif St Bar Jnl ... California State Bar Journal [*A publication*]
Calif St Cl Ant ... California Studies in Classical Antiquity [*A publication*]
Calif Turfgrass Cult Calif Univ Berkeley Coop Ext Serv ... California Turfgrass Culture. California University. Berkeley Cooperative Extension Service [*A publication*]
Calif Univ Agr Expt Sta Ground Water Studies ... California University. Agricultural Experiment Station. Ground Water Studies [*A publication*]
Calif Univ (Berkeley) Water Resour Cent Desalin Rep ... California University (Berkeley). Water Resources Center. Desalination Report [*A publication*]
Calif Univ Chron ... California University. Chronicle [*A publication*]
Calif Univ Inst Transp and Traffic Eng Inf Circ ... California University. Institute of Transportation and Traffic Engineering. Information Circular [*A publication*]
Calif Univ Mem ... California University. Memoirs [*A publication*]
Calif Univ Publ Geol Sci ... California University. Publications in Geological Sciences [*A publication*]
Calif Univ Pubs Astronomy ... California University. Publications in Astronomy [*A publication*]
Calif Univ Pubs Geography ... California University. Publications in Geography [*A publication*]
Calif Univ Pubs Geol Sci ... California University. Publications in Geological Sciences [*A publication*]
Calif Univ Pubs Zoology ... California University. Publications in Zoology [*A publication*]
Calif Univ (Riverside) Campus Mus Contrib ... California University (Riverside). Campus Museum. Contributions [*A publication*]
Calif Univ Scripps Inst ... California University. Scripps Institution of Oceanography. Reference Series [*A publication*]
Calif Univ Scripps Inst Oceanogr Annu Rep ... California University. Scripps Institution of Oceanography. Annual Report [*A publication*]

Calif Univ Scripps Inst Oceanography Bull ... California University. Scripps Institution of Oceanography. Bulletin [*A publication*]
Calif Univ Scripps Inst Oceanography SIO Reference ... California University. Scripps Institution of Oceanography. SIO Reference [*A publication*]
Calif Univ Scripps Inst Oceanography Submarine Geology Rept ... California University. Scripps Institution of Oceanography. Submarine Geology Report [*A publication*]
Calif Univ Scripps Inst Oceanogr Contrib ... California University. Scripps Institution of Oceanography. Contributions [*A publication*]
Calif Univ Scripps Inst Oceanogr Ref Ser ... California University. Scripps Institution of Oceanography. Reference Series [*A publication*]
Calif Univ Water Res Center Archives Archives Ser Rept Contr ... California University. Water Resources Center Archives. Archives Series Report. Contributions [*A publication*]
Calif Univ Water Resour Cent Rep ... California University. Water Resources Center. Report [*A publication*]
Calif Vector Views ... California Vector Views [*A publication*]
Calif Vet ..... California Veterinarian [*A publication*]
Calif Water Pollut Control Assoc Bull ... California Water Pollution Control Association. Bulletin [*A publication*]
Calif Western Int L J ... California Western International Law Journal [*A publication*]
Calif Western L Rev ... California Western Law Review [*A publication*]
Calif West Int'l LJ ... California Western International Law Journal [*A publication*]
Calif West L Rev ... California Western Law Review [*A publication*]
Calif West Med ... California and Western Medicine [*A publication*]
Calif West States Grape Grow ... California and Western States Grape Grower [*A publication*]
Calif W Int Law J ... California Western International Law Journal [*A publication*]
Calif W Int'l LJ ... California Western International Law Journal [*A publication*]
Calif WL Rev ... California Western Law Review [*A publication*]
Calig.......... Gaius Caligula [*of Suetonius*] [*Classical studies*] (OCD)
Cali His Nugget ... California History Nugget [*A publication*]
Cal Ind Acc Com ... Decisions of the Industrial Accident Commission of California [*A publication*] (DLA)
Cal Ind Acc Com Dec ... Decisions of the Industrial Accident Commission of California [*A publication*] (DLA)
Cal Ind Acci Dec ... California Industrial Accident Decisions [*A publication*] (DLA)
Cal Ind Com ... Decisions of the Industrial Accident Commission of California [*A publication*] (DLA)
CALINET ... California Information Network [*Library network*]
CALIP .... Campaign Against Lead in Petrol [*British*]
CALIP .... Computer Aptitude, Literacy, and Interest Profile [*Vocational guidance test*]
CALIPER ... Cost Analysis of LASER Investment, Production, Engineering, and Research Cost Mode (MCD)
CALIPS..... Calibrated Pressure Switch (KSC)
Calis.......... Callistratus [*Flourished, 3rd century*] [*Authority cited in pre-1607 legal work*] (DSA)
CALIT .... California Institute of Technology [*Also, CALT, CALTECH, CIT*] [*Pasadena*] (MCD)
Calitatea Prod & Metrol ... Calitatea Productiei si Metrologie [*A publication*]
Cal J.......... California Journal [*A publication*]
CALJ .... Canadian Alpine Journal [*A publication*]
Cal J Dev ... California Journal of Development [*A publication*]
Cal J Educ Res ... California Journal of Educational Research [*A publication*]
Cal JIC ... California Jury Instructions, Criminal [*A publication*] (DLA)
Cal J Min ... California Journal of Mines and Geology [*A publication*]
Cal J Tech ... California Journal of Technology [*A publication*]
Cal J Techn ... California Journal of Technology [*A publication*]
Cal Jur ... California Jurisprudence [*A publication*] (DLA)
Cal Jur 2d .. California Jurisprudence, Second Edition [*A publication*] (DLA)
CALL......... Callington [*England*]
Call............ Call's Virginia Reports [*5-10 Virginia*] [*1797-1825*] [*A publication*] (DLA)
CALL......... Canadian Association of Law Libraries
CALL......... Cellular Information System, Inc. [*NASDAQ symbol*] (NQ)
CALL......... Center for Army Lessons Learned (INF)
CALL......... Common Acute Lymphoblastic Leukemia [*Medicine*]
CALL......... Communications Alert and Liaison System [*Office of Fisheries*] (MSC)
CALL......... Composite Aeronautical Load List
CALL........ Computer-Aided LOFT Lines (MCD)
CALL......... Computer-Assisted Language Learning (ADA)
CALL......... Computer-Augmented Loft Lines [*Graphic arts*] (MCD)
CALL......... Conservative Alliance (EA)
CALL......... Counseling at the Local Level [*Small Business Administration*]
CALL......... Current Awareness-Library Literature [*A publication*]
CALLA ...... Common Acute Lymphoblastic Leukemia Antigen [*or Antiserum*] [*Immunochemistry*]
Cal Law...... California Lawyer [*A publication*]
Cal Law R .. California Law Review [*A publication*]
Cal Leg Adv ... Calcutta Legal Adviser [*India*] [*A publication*] (DLA)
Cal Legis Serv ... California Legislative Service (West) [*A publication*] (DLA)

Cal Legis Serv (West) ... California Legislative Service (West) [*A publication*]
Cal Leg Obs ... Calcutta Legal Observer [*A publication*] (DLA)
Cal Leg Rec ... California Legal Record [*A publication*] (DLA)
CALLG ...... Calling (ROG)
Cal Libr ...... California Librarian [*A publication*]
Callim ...... Callimachus [*Third century BC*] [*Classical studies*] (OCD)
CALLIOPE ... Computer-Assisted Legislative Liaison; On-Line Political Evaluation
Callis .... Callis on Sewers [*A publication*] (DLA)
Callis Sew .. Callis on Sewers [*A publication*] (DLA)
Cal LJ .... Calcutta Law Journal Reports [*A publication*] (DLA)
Cal LJ .... California Law Journal [*A publication*] (DLA)
Callman Unfair Comp ... Callman on Unfair Competition and Trade Marks [*A publication*] (DLA)
Call Mil L .. Callan's Military Laws of the United States [*A publication*] (DLA)
Cal LR .... Calcutta Law Reporter [*A publication*] (DLA)
Cal LR .... California Law Review [*A publication*]
Cal L Rev .. California Law Review [*A publication*]
CALLS ...... Crown and Lease Land System [*Australia*]
Call Sew ..... Callis on Sewers [*A publication*] (DLA)
Call (VA) ... Call's Virginia Reports [*5-10 Virginia*] [*1797-1825*] [*A publication*]
CALM ...... Cal-Maine Foods, Inc. [*NASDAQ symbol*] (NQ)
CALM ...... Call Monitor (NOAA)
CALM ...... Calmato [*More Calm*] [*Music*]
CalM .... Calmodulin [*Also, CaM*] [*Biochemistry*]
CALM ...... Campaign Against Lorry Menace [*British*]
CALM ...... Canadian Association of Labour Media
CALM ...... Catapult Arresting Gear and Landing Aids Maintenance [*Aviation*] (NG)
CALM ...... Catenary Anchor Leg Mooring
CALM ...... Centralized Accounting for Local Management [*Veterans Administration*]
CALM ...... Child Abuse Listening Mediation (EA)
CALM ...... Citizens Against Legalized Murder [*Opposes death penalty for criminals*] [*Defunct*]
CALM ...... Coalition Against Legalised Murder [*Australia*]
CALM ...... COBOL [*Common Business-Oriented Language*] Automatic Language Modifier [*Data processing*]
CALM ...... Cognitive and Affective Learning Model [*Psychology*]
CALM ...... Collected Algorithm for Learning Machines [*Data processing*]
CALM ...... Computer-Aided Livestock Marketing
CALM ...... Computer-Assisted Library Mechanization
CALM ...... Custody Action for Lesbian Mothers (EA)
CALMAC ... Caledonia MacBrayne [*Commercial firm*] [*British*]
Cal Man Rev ... California Management Review [*A publication*]
Cal M As ... California Miners' Association [*A publication*]
Cal Med ...... California Medicine [*A publication*]
Cal Med Bull ... California Medical Bulletin [*A publication*]
Cal Med J .. California Medical Journal [*A publication*]
Cal Med Surg Rep ... California Medical and Surgical Reporter [*A publication*]
Cal Ment Hlth Ne ... California Mental Health News [*A publication*]
Cal Mgmt Rev ... California Management Review [*A publication*]
Cal Mgt R .. California Management Review [*A publication*]
Cal Mil Laws ... Callan's Military Laws of the United States [*A publication*] (DLA)
CALMMS ... Computerized Air-Launched Missile Management System (MCD)
CALMS ..... Combined Allowance for Logistics and Maintenance Support System [*Coast Guard*] (MCD)
CALMS ..... Continuous Automatic Line Monitoring System
CALMS ..... Credit and Load Management System [*Software*] [*British*]
CalN .... Calabria Nobilissima [*A publication*]
CALN .... Calnetics Corp. [*NASDAQ symbol*] (NQ)
CALN .... Computer-Assisted Learning Network
CALNET ... California Network [*US Geological Survey*]
Cal Neva TL ... Cal-Neva Token Ledger [*A publication*]
CALO .... Cape Lookout National Seashore [*National Park Service designation*]
CALO .... Capitulo [*Chapter*] [*Latin*] (ROG)
CALO .... City Area Leases Ordinance [*Australian Capital Territory*]
CALOA ..... Calore [*A publication*]
CALOD ..... Calorie [*A publication*]
CALOGSIM ... Computer-Assisted Logistics Simulation [*Navy*]
CALOLL ..... Catholic Aviation League of Our Lady of Loreto [*Defunct*] (EA)
Calore Tecnol ... Calore e Tecnologia [*A publication*]
Calorim Therm Anal ... Calorimetry and Thermal Analysis [*A publication*]
Calp .... Calpurnius Siculus [*First century AD*] [*Classical studies*] (OCD)
CALPA ...... Canadian Airline Pilots Association
Cal P Ch ..... Calendar of Proceedings in Chancery Tempore Elizabeth [*1827-32*] [*A publication*] (DLA)
Cal Penal Code ... California Penal Code [*A publication*] (DLA)
CALPHAD Comput Coupling Phase Diagrams and Thermochem ... CALPHAD. Computer Coupling of Phase Diagrams and Thermochemistry [*A publication*]
Cal Phys Geog Club B ... California Physical Geography Club. Bulletin [*A publication*]

Cal Polyt J ... California Polytechnic Journal [*A publication*]
Cal Poult J ... California Poultry Journal [*A publication*]
Cal Poult Trib ... California Poultry Tribune [*A publication*]
Cal Prac ..... California Practice [*A publication*] (DLA)
Cal Publ Class Arch ... California Publications in Classical Archaeology [*A publication*]
Cal Public Employee Relations ... California Public Employee Relations [*A publication*]
Cal PUC ..... Decisions of the California Public Utilities Commission [*A publication*] (DLA)
Cal Q .... California Quarterly [*A publication*]
Cal Q Sec Ed ... California Quarterly of Secondary Education [*A publication*]
CalR .... Calcutta Review [*A publication*]
CA LR .... California Law Review [*A publication*]
Cal R .... California Reporter [*A publication*]
CALR .... Computer-Assisted Legal Research (DLA)
CALRAB .. California Raisin Advisory Board (EA)
Cal RC Dec ... California Railroad Commission Digest of Decisions [*A publication*] (DLA)
Cal RC Dec Dig ... California Railroad Commission Digest of Decisions [*A publication*] (DLA)
Cal R Com ... Opinions and Orders of the Railroad Commission of California [*A publication*] (DLA)
Cal Rep ...... California Reports [*A publication*] (DLA)
Cal Rep ...... Calthrop's English King's Bench Reports [*80 English Reprint*] [*A publication*] (DLA)
CALRFE .... Association for Asian Studies, Committee on American Library Resources on the Far East, Center for Research Libraries, Chicago, IL [*Library symbol*] [*Library of Congress*] (LCLS)
CALROC ... Calibration Rocket [*NASA*]
CALROSA ... Committee on American Library Resources on South Asia [*Later, CORMOSEA*] (EA)
CALROSEA ... Committee on American Library Resources on Southeast Asia [*Later, CORMOSEA*] (EA)
CAL ROT PAT ... Calendarium Rotulorum Patentium [*Calendar of the Patent Rolls*] [*Latin*]
Cal Rptr ..... California Reporter (West) [*A publication*] (DLA)
CALRS ..... Centralized Automatic Loop Reporting System [*Telecommunications*] (TEL)
CALS .... California Silver Ltd. [*NASDAQ symbol*] (NQ)
CALS .... Canadian Association of Library Schools
CALS .... Centre for Applied Language Studies [*Carleton University*] [*Canada*] [*Research center*] (RCD)
CALS .... Committee for Ammunition Logistics Support [*Army*] (MCD)
CALS .... Communications Area Local Station (NVT)
CALS .... Comprehensive Automated Learning Resources System [*Elgin Community College*] [*Information service or system*] (IID)
CALS .... Computer-Aided Acquisition and Logistics Support (MCD)
CALS .... Computer-Aided Logistics Support [*Army*]
CALS .... Computer-Assisted Logistics Simulation [*Navy*] (MCD)
CALS .... Computer-Automated Laboratory System
CALS .... Current Awareness Literature Service [*Department of Agriculture*] [*Beltsville, MD*]
Cal Saf Ne ... California Safety News [*A publication*]
Cal Savings and Loan J ... California Savings and Loan Journal [*A publication*]
Cal SBJ ...... California State Bar Journal [*A publication*] (DLA)
Cal SDA ..... Calcutta Sadr Diwani Adalat Reports [*India*] [*A publication*] (DLA)
Cal Ser .... Calcutta Series, Indian Law Reports [*A publication*] (DLA)
Cal Sew ...... Callis on Sewers [*A publication*] (DLA)
Cal Sew WJ ... California Sewage Works Journal [*A publication*]
Cal Sl St ..... California Slavic Studies [*A publication*]
CALSPHERE ... Calibration Sphere (MCD)
Cal SS .... California Slavic Studies [*A publication*]
Cal Stat ...... Statutes and Amendments to the Code of California [*A publication*] (DLA)
Cal Stat ...... Statutes of California [*A publication*]
Cal State Comm Hort B ... California State Commission of Horticulture. Monthly Bulletin [*A publication*]
Cal Stats .... Statutes of California [*A publication*] (DLA)
Cal St BJ .... California State Bar Journal [*A publication*]
Cal St Class Ant ... California Studies in Classical Antiquity [*A publication*]
Cal St J Med ... California State Journal of Medicine [*A publication*]
Cal St M Bur ... California State Mining Bureau [*A publication*]
Cal St M Bur An Rp B ... California State Mining Bureau. Annual Report. Bulletin [*A publication*]
CALSU ...... Combat Airlift Support Unit [*Air Force*]
Cal (subject) Code (Deering) ... Deering's Annotated California Code [*A publication*] (DLA)
Cal (subject) Code (West) ... West's Annotated California Codes [*A publication*] (DLA)
Cal Sup ...... California Superior Court, Reports of Cases in Appellate Departments [*A publication*] (DLA)
Cal Sup ...... California Supplement [*A publication*] (DLA)
Cal Sup (Cal) ... California Superior Court, Reports of Cases in Appellate Departments [*A publication*] (DLA)
CAlt .... Altadena Library District, Altadena, CA [*Library symbol*] [*Library of Congress*] (LCLS)

CALT........ California Institute of Technology [*Also, CALIT, CALTECH, CIT*] [*Pasadena*]

CALT........ Canadian Association of Law Teachers [*See also ACPD*]

CAltaC....... Chaffey College, Alta Loma, CA [*Library symbol*] [*Library of Congress*]   (LCLS)

CALTECH ... California Institute of Technology [*Also, CALIT, CALT, CIT*] [*Pasadena*]

CALTEX ... California Texas Oil Co.

Calth .... Calthrop's City of London Cases, King's Bench [*England*] [*A publication*]   (DLA)

Calth .... Calthrop's English King's Bench Reports [*80 English Reprint*] [*A publication*]   (DLA)

Calth Copyh ... Calthrop on Copyholds [*A publication*]   (DLA)

Calth (Eng) ... Calthrop's City of London Cases, King's Bench [*England*] [*A publication*]   (DLA)

Calth (Eng) ... Calthrop's English King's Bench Reports [*80 English Reprint*] [*A publication*]   (DLA)

Cal Th J ..... Calvin Theological Journal [*A publication*]

Calthr......... Calthrop's City of London Cases, King's Bench [*England*] [*A publication*]   (DLA)

Calthr......... Calthrop's English King's Bench Reports [*80 English Reprint*] [*A publication*]   (DLA)

CAltT......... Theosophical University, Altadena, CA [*Library symbol*] [*Library of Congress*]   (LCLS)

CAltu.......... Modoc County Free Library, Alturas, CA [*Library symbol*] [*Library of Congress*]   (LCLS)

Cal Univ Dp G B ... California University. Publications. Department of Geology. Bulletin [*A publication*]

Cal Univ Pub ... California University [*Berkeley*]. Publications in Agricultural Science [*A publication*]

Cal Univ Pub Geog ... California University. Publications in Geography [*A publication*]

Cal Univ Seism Sta B ... California University. Publications. Seismography Stations. Bulletin [*A publication*]

Cal Unrep .. California Unreported Cases [*1855-1910*] [*A publication*]   (DLA)

Cal Unrep Cas ... California Unreported Cases [*1855-1910*] [*A publication*]   (DLA)

CALUPL ... Council of Administrators of Large Urban Public Libraries [*Canada*]

CALURA... Corporations and Labor Union Returns Act

Cal Urep .... California Unreported Cases [*1855-1910*] [*A publication*]   (DLA)

CALUS...... Centre for Advanced Land Use Studies [*College of Estate Management*] [*British*]   (CB)

CALUTRON ... California University Cyclotron

CALVADA ... Carl Reiner, Sheldon Leonard, Dick Van Dyke, Danny Thomas [*Acronym is name of production company of TV series "The Dick Van Dyke Show"*]

Calvin......... Calvinus. Lexicon Juridicum [*A publication*]   (DLA)

Calvin Lex ... Calvinus. Lexicon Juridicum [*A publication*]   (DLA)

Calvin Lex Jurid ... Calvinus. Lexicon Juridicum [*A publication*]   (DLA)

Calv Lex.... Calvinus. Lexicon Juridicum [*A publication*]   (DLA)

Calv Par ..... Calvert's Parties to Suits in Equity [*A publication*]   (DLA)

Calv Parties ... Calvert's Parties to Suits in Equity [*A publication*]   (DLA)

Calv Theol J ... Calvin Theological Journal [*A publication*]

CalvTJ .... Calvin Theological Journal [*Grand Rapids, MI*] [*A publication*]

CalwerH..... Calwer Hefte zur Foerderung Biblischen Glaubens und Christlichen Lebens [*A publication*]

Cal Western Law R ... California Western Law Review [*A publication*]

Cal W Int LJ ... California Western International Law Journal [*A publication*]

Cal W Int'l LJ ... California Western International Law Journal [*A publication*]

Cal W LR.... California Western Law Review [*A publication*]

Cal WL Rev ... California Western Law Review [*A publication*]

Cal WN ..... Calcutta Weekly Notes [*A publication*]   (DLA)

Cal WR ...... Calcutta Weekly Reporter [*A publication*]   (DLA)

CAM......... Administrative Management Division [*Coast Guard*]

CAM......... CA [*Chartered Accountant*] Magazine [*A publication*]

CaM.......... Calmodulin [*Also, CalM*] [*Biochemistry*]

CAM......... CAM [*Central American Mission*] International   (EA)

CAM......... Camber [*Aerospace engineering*]

cam............ Cambodian [*MARC language code*] [*Library of Congress*]   (LCCP)

CAM......... Cambridge [*Massachusetts*] [*Seismograph station code, US Geological Survey*] [*Closed*]   (SEIS)

CAM......... Cambridge [*Municipal borough in England*]

CAM......... Cambridge, NY [*Location identifier*] [*FAA*]   (FAAL)

CAM......... Camco, Inc. [*AMEX symbol*]   (SPSG)

Cam........... Camden [*Division of Victor*] [*Record label*]

Cam........... Camelopardalis [*Constellation*]

CAM......... Camera   (KSC)

Cam........... Cameron. Reports, Upper Canada Queen's Bench [*A publication*]   (DLA)

CAM......... Cameron's Privy Council Decisions [*1832-1929*] [*Canada*] [*A publication*]   (DLA)

CAM......... Cameron's Supreme Court Cases [*Canada*] [*A publication*]   (DLA)

Cam........... Camillus [*of Plutarch*] [*Classical studies*]   (OCD)

CAM......... Camiri [*Bolivia*] [*Airport symbol*]   (OAG)

CAM......... Camisole   (DSUE)

CAM......... Camoens [*Portuguese poet, 1524-1579*]   (ROG)

CAM......... Camosun College Library [*UTLAS symbol*]

CAM......... Camouflage   (AFM)

CAM......... Campus

CAM......... Camshaft [*Automotive engineering*]

CA(M) ...... Canadian Army (Militia)

CAM......... Canam Manac Group, Inc. [*Toronto Stock Exchange symbol*]

CAM......... Cancellation of Amplitude Modulation   (MCD)

CAM......... Capsule Assembly Machine   (MCD)

Cam........... Carbamylmethyl [*Biochemistry*]

CAM......... Carboxamidomethyl [*Organic chemistry*]

CAM......... Care Aggregated Module

CAM......... Cargo Module   (MCD)

CAM......... Carrier Aircraft Modification   (NASA)

CAm.......... Casa de las Americas [*A publication*]

CAM......... Catapult Aircraft Merchantship [*Used by British RAF to catapult Hurricane fighter planes from ships to defend convoys from enemy bombers*] [*World War II*]

CAM......... Cell Adhesion Molecule [*Cytology*]

CAM......... Cell Associating Molecule [*Cytology*]

CAM......... Cellulose Acetate Methacrylate

CAM......... Center for Advanced Materials [*Berkeley, CA*] [*Lawrence Berkeley Laboratory*] [*Department of Energy*]   (GRD)

CAM......... Center for Advanced Materials [*Pennsylvania State University*] [*Research center*]   (RCD)

CAM......... Center for Applied Mathematics [*University of Georgia*] [*Research center*]   (RCD)

CAM......... Center for Applied Microbiology [*University of Texas at Austin*] [*Research center*]   (RCD)

CAM......... Central Address Memory [*Data processing*]

CAM......... Certified Administrative Manager [*Designation awarded by Administrative Management Society*]

CAM......... Championship Association of Mechanics   (EA)

CAM......... Check Authorization Method

CAM......... Checkout and Automatic Monitoring   (MSA)

CAM......... Checkout and Maintenance

CAM......... Chemical Agent Monitor [*Military*]   (RDA)

CAM......... Chief, Aircraft Maintenance

CAM......... Chloramphenicol [*Antimicrobial compound*]

CAM......... Chorioallantoic Membrane [*Embryology*] [*Assay for chemical irritability*]

CAM......... Christ in Action Ministries   (EA)

CAM......... Christian Aid Mission   (EA)

CAM......... Christian Alternative Movement [*Australia*]

CAM......... Christian Amendment Movement [*Later, CGM*]   (EA)

CAM......... Church Assembly Measure   (DLA)

CAM......... Circular Area Method

CAM......... Civil Aeronautics Manual

CAM......... Civil Air Movement

CAM......... Clean Air Movement

CAM......... Coalition for the Apostolic Ministry [*Later, ECM*]

CAM......... Cockpit Area Microphone   (MCD)

CAM......... Comite d'Action Musulman [*Mauritian political party*]

CAM......... Commercial Air Movement

CAM......... Commission for Agricultural Meteorology [*WMO*]   (ASF)

CAM......... Committee for Aquatic Microbiology [*United Nations*]   (ASF)

CAM......... Committee on Aviation Medicine [*NAS/NRC*]

CAM......... Common Access Method [*Computer programming*]   (BYTE)

CAM......... Commonwealth Association of Museums [*Calgary, AB*]   (EAIO)

CAM......... Communication, Advertising, and Marketing Education Foundation [*British*]

CAM...... Composite Army-Marine

CAM...... Computer Achievement Monitoring   (MCD)

CAM...... Computer Address Matrix

CAM...... Computer-Aided Makeup [*Graphic arts*]

CAM...... Computer-Aided Manufacturing

CAM...... Computer-Aided Mathematics

CAM...... Computer Annunciation Matrix   (MCD)

CAM...... Computer-Assisted Maintenance

CAM...... Computer-Assisted Makeup [*Graphic arts*]

CAM...... Computerized Anatomical Man [*NASA*]

CAM...... Consolidated Aircraft Maintenance

CAM...... Constant Air Monitor [*Nuclear energy*]   (NRCH)

CAM...... Containment Atmospheric Monitoring [*Nuclear energy*]   (NRCH)

CAM......... Contemporary Australian Management [*A publication*]   (APTA)

CAM......... Content-Addressable Memory [*Data processing*]

CAM......... Contingency Analysis Model   (KSC)

CAM......... Continuous Air Monitor [*Nuclear energy*]   (NRCH)

CAM......... Contract Air Mail

CAM......... Contract Audit Manual

CAM......... Contractor-Acquired Materiel   (AFM)

CAM......... Control Access Manager   (BUR)

CAM......... Cooperative Atomic Migration

CAM......... Corsica Antica e Moderna [*A publication*]

CAM......... Cost Account Manager   (MCD)

CAM......... Crane, Aircraft Maintenance   (MCD)

CAM......... Crassulacean Acid Metabolism [*Biochemistry*]

CAM......... Cruise and Maintain [*Aviation*]

CAM......... Cryogenic Acoustic Microscopy (MCD)
CAM......... Cybernetic Anthropomorphous Machine [Robot] [Army]
CAM......... Cyclophosphamide, Adriamycin, Methotrexate [Antineoplastic drug regimen]
CAM......... Cytotoxic Activated Macrophage [Biochemistry]
CAM......... Engineering Center for Automated Manufacturing Technology [Clemson University] [Research center] (RCD)
CAM......... Los Angeles County Museum of Art, Los Angeles, CA [OCLC symbol] (OCLC)
CAMA...... Centralized Automatic Message Accounting [Bell System]
CAMA...... Children's Apparel Manufacturers' Association [Canada]
CAMA...... Civil Aviation Medical Association (EA)
CAMA...... Coastal Area Management Act [1974] (MSC)
CAMA...... Computer-Assisted Method Assembly [Analytical method writing]
CAMA...... Critical Agricultural Materials Act [1984]
Cam Abs .... Cambridge Abstracts [A publication]
CAMAC...... Center for Agricultural Meteorology and Climatology [University of Nebraska - Lincoln] [Research center] (RCD)
CAMA-C ... Centralized Automatic Message Accounting - Computerized [Bell System] (TEL)
CAMAC .... Computer-Aided Measurement and Control [NASA]
CAMAC .... Computer-Automated Measurement and Control (MSA)
CaMACMH ... Altona Community Memorial Health Centre, Altona, MB, Canada [Library symbol] [Library of Congress] (LCLS)
CAMAE .... Central Air Materiel Area, Europe
CA Mag ..... CA [Chartered Accountant] Magazine [Canadian Institute of Chartered Accountants] [A publication]
CA Magazin ... CA [Chemical Abstracts] Magazine [A publication]
CA Mag J Commer Art ... CA Magazine. Journal of Commercial Art [A publication]
CAMAL..... Cambridge Algebraic System [Programming language] [1975] (CSR)
CaMAMC ... Altona Medical Centre, Altona, MB, Canada [Library symbol] [Library of Congress] (LCLS)
Cam Am LJ ... Canadian-American Law Journal [A publication] (DLA)
CAMAn..... Cercle Archeologique de Mons. Annales [A publication]
CAMA-ONI ... Centralized Automatic Message Accounting - Operator Number Identification [Telecommunications] (TEL)
CAMAR .... Common Aperture Multifunction Array RADAR
Camara Comer Bogota R ... Camara de Comercio de Bogota. Revista [A publication]
Camara Text Mex Rev Tec ... Camara Textil de Mexico. Revista Tecnica [A publication]
CAMAS..... Central Automatic Message Accounting System (CET)
CAMAS..... Commander, South Atlantic Maritime Area
CAMAS..... Computer-Assisted Manpower Analysis System (MCD)
CAMAS..... Confederation of African Medical Associations and Societies (EAIO)
CAMB .... Cambistry [Finance]
CAMB .... Camborne [Urban district in England]
CAMB .... Cambrian [Period, era, or system] [Geology]
Camb.......... Cambridge [Record label]
CAMB ...... Cambridge [Municipal borough in England]
CAMB .... [The] Cambridge Instrument Company PLC [NASDAQ symbol] (NQ)
CAMB .... Cambridge University [England]
Camb.......... Cambyses (BJA)
CAMB .... Combined Arms Maneuver Battalion [Experiment] [Army] (INF)
CAMB ...... Continued Automated Multi-Baseline (MCD)
CAMB .... Cyclophosphamide, Adriamycin, Methotrexate, Bleomycin [Antineoplastic drug regimen]
CaMBABS ... Anglican Church of Canada, Diocese of Brandon, Synod Office, Brandon, MB, Canada [Library symbol] [Library of Congress] (LCLS)
CaMBAC... Assiniboine Community College, Brandon, MB, Canada [Library symbol] [Library of Congress] (LCLS)
CaMBAg ... Canada Department of Agriculture, Research Station, Brandon, MB, Canada [Library symbol] [Library of Congress] (LCLS)
CambB .... Cambridge Bible [A publication] (BJA)
CaMBBR... Brokenhead River Regional Library, Beausejour, MB, Canada [Library symbol] [Library of Congress] (LCLS)
CaMBC...... Brandon University, Brandon, MB, Canada [Library symbol] [Library of Congress] (LCLS)
CaMBCG... Brandon University, Department of Geography, Brandon, MB, Canada [Library symbol] [Library of Congress] (LCLS)
Camb Co LJ ... Cambria County Reports [Pennsylvania] [A publication] (DLA)
CAMBDM ... Cambridge Studies in Modern Biology [A publication]
CaMBGH .. Brandon General Hospital, School of Nursing, Brandon, MB, Canada [Library symbol] [Library of Congress] (LCLS)
Camb J....... Cambridge Journal [A publication]
CAMBL..... Continuous Automatic Multi-Base Propellant Line (MCD)
Camb L J ... Cambridge Law Journal [A publication]
CaMBMH ... Brandon Mental Health Centre, Brandon, MB, Canada [Library symbol] [Library of Congress] (LCLS)
Camb Monogr Exp Biol ... Cambridge Monographs in Experimental Biology [A publication]

CaMBoM .. Boissevain and Morton Regional Library, Boissevain, MB, Canada [Library symbol] [Library of Congress] (LCLS)
CaM-BP .... Calmodulin Binding Protein [Biochemistry]
Camb Philos Soc Trans ... Cambridge Philosophical Society. Transactions [A publication]
Camb Q...... Cambridge Quarterly [A publication]
Cambr Anc Hist ... Cambridge Ancient History [A publication]
Cambr Bibl Soc Trans ... Cambridge Bibliographical Society. Transactions [A publication]
Cambr Biol Stud ... Cambridge Biological Studies [A publication]
Cambria ..... Cambria County Legal Journal [Pennsylvania] [A publication] (DLA)
Cambria Co LJ ... Cambria County Legal Journal [Pennsylvania] [A publication] (DLA)
Cambria Co (PA) ... Cambria County Legal Journal [Pennsylvania] [A publication] (DLA)
Cambrian Archaeol Ass Monogr Collect ... Cambrian Archaeological Association. Monographs and Collections [A publication]
Cambrian Law R ... Cambrian Law Review [A publication]
Cambrian LR ... Cambrian Law Review [A publication]
Cambrian L Rev ... Cambrian Law Review [A publication]
Cambridge Anthropol ... Cambridge Anthropology [A publication]
Cambridge Comput Sci Texts ... Cambridge Computer Science Texts [A publication]
Cambridge Econ Policy Rev ... Cambridge Economic Policy Review [A publication]
Cambridge Inst Ed Bulletin ... Cambridge Institute of Education. Bulletin [A publication]
Cambridge J Econ ... Cambridge Journal of Economics [A publication]
Cambridge J Economics ... Cambridge Journal of Economics [A publication]
Cambridge J Ed ... Cambridge Journal of Education [A publication]
Cambridge J Educ ... Cambridge Journal of Education [A publication]
Cambridge LJ ... Cambridge Law Journal [A publication]
Cambridge Medieval Celtic Stud ... Cambridge Medieval Celtic Studies [A publication]
Cambridge Mongraphs Math Phys ... Cambridge Monographs on Mathematical Physics [A publication]
Cambridge Monographs Mech Appl Math ... Cambridge Monographs on Mechanics and Applied Mathematics [A publication]
Cambridge Philos Soc Biol Rev ... Cambridge Philosophical Society. Biological Reviews [A publication]
Cambridge Ph Soc Pr ... Cambridge Philosophical Society. Proceedings [A publication]
Cambridge Q ... Cambridge Quarterly [A publication]
Cambridge Stud Math Biol ... Cambridge Studies in Mathematical Biology [A publication]
Cambridge Tracts in Math ... Cambridge Tracts in Mathematics [A publication]
Cambridge Univ Med Soc Mag ... Cambridge University Medical Society. Magazine [A publication]
Cam Brit .... Camden's Britannia [A publication] (DLA)
Cambr LJ... Cambridge Law Journal [A publication]
Cambr Or Ser ... Cambridge Oriental Series [A publication]
Cambr Tr Math ... Cambridge Tracts in Mathematics and Mathematical Physics [Later, Cambridge Tracts in Mathematics] [A publication]
Cambr Univ Agr Soc Mag ... Cambridge University Agricultural Society. Magazine [A publication]
Cambr Univ Eng Aeronaut ... Cambridge University Engineering and Aeronautical Societies. Journal [A publication]
Cambr Univ Eng Soc J ... Cambridge University Engineering Society. Journal [A publication]
Cambr Univ Med Soc Mag ... Cambridge University Medical Society. Magazine [A publication]
CAMBS..... Cambridgeshire [County in England]
Camb Stud Biol Anthropol ... Cambridge Studies in Biological Anthropology [A publication]
Camb Stud Biotechnol ... Cambridge Studies in Biotechnology [A publication]
Camb Stud Mod Biol ... Cambridge Studies in Modern Biology [A publication]
Camb Texts Physiol Sci ... Cambridge Texts in the Physiological Sciences [A publication]
CAMBull.... Cercle Archeologique de Malines. Bulletin [A publication]
CaMBW .... Western Manitoba Regional Library, Brandon, MB, Canada [Library symbol] [Library of Congress] (LCLS)
CAMC ...... Canadian Army Medical Corps
CAMC ...... Canadian Association of Management Consultants
CAMC .... China National Agricultural Machinery Import & Export Corporation [People's Republic of China] (IMH)
CAMCA .... CA. A Cancer Journal for Clinicians [A publication]
CAMCA .... Canadian-American Motor Carriers Association (EA)
Cam Cas..... Cameron's Supreme Court Cases [Canada] [A publication] (DLA)
CaMCB...... Boyne Regional Library, Carman, MB, Canada [Library symbol] [Library of Congress] (LCLS)
CAMCC.... Canadian Air Mail Collectors Club (EA)
CaMCh...... Churchill Public Library, Churchill, MB, Canada [Library symbol] [Library of Congress] (LCLS)
CaMChE ... Eskimo Museum, Churchill, MB, Canada [Library symbol] [Library of Congress] (LCLS)

CaMChPC ... Parks Canada, Churchill, MB, Canada [*Library symbol*] [*Library of Congress*] (LCLS)
Cam Club ... Camera Club [*A publication*]
Camcorder ... Camera and Recorder
CAMCOS ... Computer-Assisted Maintenance Planning and Control System
CAMD ...... California Micro Devices Corp. [*NASDAQ symbol*] (NQ)
CAMD ...... Center for Advanced Macrostructures and Devices [*Louisiana State University*]
CAMD ...... Computer-Aided Mechanical Drafting
CAMD ...... Computer-Assisted Molecular Design
CAMD ...... Craft and Amphibious Material Department [*British military*] (DMA)
CaMDa ...... Dauphin Public Library, Dauphin, MB, Canada [*Library symbol*] [*Library of Congress*] [*Obsolete*] (LCLS)
CaMDaP ... Parkland Regional Library, Dauphin, MB, Canada [*Library symbol*] [*Library of Congress*] (LCLS)
CaMDB ..... Bren Del Win Centennial Library, Deloraine, MB, Canada [*Library symbol*] [*Library of Congress*] (LCLS)
Camd Brit .. Camden's Britannia [*A publication*] (DLA)
CAMDEC ... Ceramics Advanced Manufacturing Development Engineering Center (EA)
Camden ...... Camden's Britannia [*A publication*] (DLA)
CAMDF ..... Canadian Agricultural Market Development Fund
CAMDG ... Civil Assistant to Medical Director-General [*Navy*] [*British*]
CAMDO ... Canadian Art Museum Directors Organization
CAMDP ... Center for Alternative Mining Development Policy (EA)
CAMDS ..... Chemical Agent Munition Disposal System [*Army*]
Cam Duc ... Camera Ducata [*Duchy Chamber*] [*Latin*] [*Legal term*] (DLA)
CaMDW ..... Delta Waterfowl Research Station, Delta, MB, Canada [*Library symbol*] [*Library of Congress*] (LCLS)
CAME .... Carme, Inc. [*NASDAQ symbol*] (NQ)
CAME .... Certification of Air Moving Equipment [*British*] (IRUK)
CAME .... Corps Airspace Management Element (MCD)
CAME .... Cost Analysis Monthly Exchange [*Army*]
CAMEA ..... California Medicine [*A publication*]
CaMeCo .... Catholic Media Council [*Aachen, Federal Republic of Germany*] (EAIO)
CAMEEW ... Cardiovascular Medicine [*A publication*]
CAMEL ..... Capital Adequacy, Asset Quality, Management, Earnings, Liquidity [*Formula used by the Federal Deposit Insurance Corp. to evaluate banks*]
CAMEL ..... Collapsible Airborne Military Equipment Lifter
CAMEL ..... Component and Material Evaluation Loop [*Nuclear energy*] (NRCH)
CAMEL ..... Critical Aeronautical Material and Equipment List
CAMELEON ... Cytarabine, Methotrexate, Leucovorin [*Folinic acid-SF*], Oncovin [*Vincristine*] [*Antineoplastic drug regimen*]
CAMELF .. Camelford [*Rural district in England*]
Camellia J ... Camellia Journal [*A publication*]
CAMELOT ... Cultural Auction of Many Extraordinary Lots of Treasure [*St. Louis, Missouri*]
CAMEO .... Capitol Area Motion Pictures Education Organization [*Washington, DC*]
CAMEO .... Chemically Active Material Ejected in Orbit (MCD)
CAMEO .... Computer-Assisted Management for Emergency Operations [*Database*]
CAMEO .... Council of Affiliated Marriage Enrichment Organizations (EA)
CAMEO .... Covert Active Modular Electro-Optical System (MCD)
CAMEO .... Creative Audio and Music Electronics Organization (EA)
CAMEO .... Cyclophosphamide, Adriamycin, Methotrexate, Etoposide, Oncovin [*Vincristine*] [*Antineoplastic drug regimen*]
Camer .... [*Bartholomaeus*] Camerarius [*Deceased, 1564*] [*Authority cited in pre-1607 legal work*] (DSA)
Camer .... Cameroon
Camera .... Camera and Cine [*A publication*] (APTA)
CAMERA ... Canadian Association of Motion Picture and Electronic Recording Artists
CAMERA ... Command Management Review and Analysis [*Army*]
CAMERA ... Committee for Accuracy in Middle East Reporting in America (EA)
CAMERA ... Computer-Aided Maneuver Evaluation, Reconstruction, and Analysis [*British*]
Camera Obsc ... Camera Obscura [*A publication*]
Camerar ..... [*Bartholomaeus*] Camerarius [*Deceased, 1564*] [*Authority cited in pre-1607 legal work*] (DSA)
C Amer Lat ... Cahiers des Ameriques Latines [*A publication*]
C Amer Lat Ser Sci Homme ... Cahiers des Ameriques Latines. Serie Sciences de l'Homme [*A publication*]
Cameron ..... Cameron's Supreme Court Cases [*Canada*] [*A publication*] (DLA)
Cameron (Can) ... Cameron's Supreme Court Cases [*Canada*] [*A publication*] (DLA)
Cameron Cas (Can) ... Cameron's Supreme Court Cases [*Canada*] [*A publication*] (DLA)
Cameron Pr ... Cameron's Practice [*Canada*] [*A publication*] (DLA)
Cameron Pr (Can) ... Cameron's Practice [*Canada*] [*A publication*] (DLA)
Cameron SC ... Cameron's Supreme Court Cases [*Canada*] [*A publication*] (DLA)
Cameron Synth Fuels Rep ... Cameron Synthetic Fuels Report [*A publication*]
Cameroon P ... Plan Quinquennal de Developpement Economique, Social, et Culturel, 1981-1986 (Cameroon) [*A publication*]

Cameroun Agric Pastor For ... Cameroun Agricole, Pastoral, et Forestier [*A publication*]
Cameroun Dir Mines Geol Act Minieres Cameroun ... Cameroun. Direction des Mines et de la Geologie. Activites Minieres au Cameroun [*A publication*]
Cameroun Territ Bull Dir Mines Geol ... Cameroun Territoire. Bulletin de la Direction des Mines et de la Geologie [*A publication*]
CAMES ..... Combined Agency for Middle East Supplies [*World War II*]
CAMESA .. Canadian Military Electronics Standards Agency (MCD)
CAMET ..... Centre for the Advancement of Mathematical Education in Technology [*Loughborough University of Technology*] [*British*] (CB)
CAMEX ..... Coastal AMOS [*Automated Meteorological Observing Station*] Experiment
CAMF .... Cyclophosphamide, Adriamycin, Methotrexate, Folinic acid-SF [*Antineoplastic drug regimen*]
CAMFET .. CAMEL [*Critical Aeronautical Material and Equipment List*] Gate Field Effect Transistors (MCD)
CaMFF ...... Flin Flon Public Library, Flin Flon, MB, Canada [*Library symbol*] [*Library of Congress*] (LCLS)
CaMFFHB ... Hudson Bay Mining & Smelting Co. Ltd., Flin Flon, MB, Canada [*Library symbol*] [*Library of Congress*] (LCLS)
CA/MG ..... Civil Affairs/Military Government
CaMGE ..... Evergreen Regional Library, Gimli, MB, Canada [*Library symbol*] [*Library of Congress*] (LCLS)
CaMGi .... Gillam Municipal Library, Gillam, MB, Canada [*Library symbol*] [*Library of Congress*] (LCLS)
CaMGPC ... Grandview Personal Care Home, Grandview, MB, Canada [*Library symbol*] [*Library of Congress*] (LCLS)
CAMHDD ... Commonwealth Association of Mental Handicap and Developmental Disabilities (EA)
CAMI .... Camisole (DSUE)
CAMI .... Canadian Mineralogist [*A publication*]
CAMI .... CareAmerica, Inc. [*NASDAQ symbol*] (NQ)
CAMI .... Citizens Against Military Injustice (EA)
CAMI .... Civil Aeromedical Institute [*FAA*]
CAMI .... Civil Aviation Medical Institute (MCD)
CAMI .... Coated Abrasives Manufacturers Institute (EA)
CAMI .... Columbia Artists Management, Incorporated
CAM-I .... Computer Aided Manufacturing International (EA)
CAMI .... Concerned Americans for Military Improvements (EA)
CAMI .... Continuing Action Maintenance Instruction
CAMIA .... Canadian Mineralogist [*A publication*]
CAMIFA ... Campaign for Independent Financial Advice [*British*] (ECON)
CAMIL .... Computer-Assisted/Managed Instructional Language (CSR)
Camil Plaut ... Camillus Plautius [*Flourished, 1533-66*] [*Authority cited in pre-1607 legal work*] (DSA)
CAMINO .. Central America Information Office (EA)
Cam Int Suc ... Cameron. Intestate Succession in Scotland [*A publication*] (DLA)
CAMIS ...... Computer-Assisted Makeup and Imaging Systems
CAMIS ...... Continental Army Management Information System (RDA)
CamJ .... Cambridge Journal [*A publication*]
CAMJ .... Canadian Mining Journal [*A publication*]
CAMJ .... Council of Arab Ministers of Justice [*See also CMAJ*] [*Rabat, Morocco*] (EAIO)
CAMJA ..... Canadian Mining Journal [*A publication*]
Cam J Educ ... Cambridge Journal of Education [*A publication*]
Cam JS Comp ... Cameron on Joint Stock Companies [*Scotland*] [*A publication*] (DLA)
CaMKL ...... Lakeland Regional Library, Killarney, MB, Canada [*Library symbol*] [*Library of Congress*] (LCLS)
CaMKTLH ... Tri-Lake Health Centre, Killarney, MB, Canada [*Library symbol*] [*Library of Congress*] (LCLS)
Caml .... Cameloypardalis [*Constellation*]
CAML .... Camelot Corp. [*NASDAQ symbol*] (NQ)
CAML .... Canadian Association of Music Libraries
CAML .... Cargo Aircraft Mine Laying (MCD)
CAML .... Coarticulation Assessment in Meaningful Language [*Speech evaluation test*]
CAMLA ..... Communications and Media Law Association [*Australia*]
CaMLdB ..... Regional Library, Lac Du Bonnet, MB, Canada [*Library symbol*] [*Library of Congress*] (LCLS)
CAMLEJ ..... Camp Lejeune [*North Carolina*] [*Marine Corps*]
CAMLR ..... Conservation of Antarctic Marine Living Resources [*International agreement signed in 1982*]
CaMLR ...... Leaf Rapids Public Library, Leaf Rapids, MB, Canada [*Library symbol*] [*Library of Congress*] (LCLS)
CAMLS ..... Cleveland Area Metropolitan Library System [*Library network*]
CAMM ...... Central Association of the Miraculous Medal (EA)
CAMM ...... Chlor-Alkali-Market Model
CAMM ...... Council of American Maritime Museums (EA)
CAMM ...... Council of American Master Mariners (EA)
CAMMAC ... Canadian Amateur Musicians (EAIO)
CAMMD ... Canadian Association of Manufacturers of Medical Devices
CaMMeS .... Southwestern Manitoba Regional Library, Melita, MB, Canada [*Library symbol*] [*Library of Congress*] (LCLS)
CaMMiR .... Minnedosa Regional Library, Minnedosa, MB, Canada [*Library symbol*] [*Library of Congress*] (LCLS)
CAMMIS .. Command Aerospace Maintenance Manpower Information System

CaMMoAg ... Canada Department of Agriculture, Research Station, Morden, MB, Canada [*Library symbol*] [*Library of Congress*] (LCLS)

CaMMoW ... Morden-Winkler Regional Library, Morden, MB, Canada [*Library symbol*] [*Library of Congress*] (LCLS)

CAMMS .... Computer-Aided Materials Management System [*Canadian provincial governments*]

CAMMS .... Computer-Assisted Map Maneuver Simulation (MCD)

CAMMS .... Computer-Assisted Map Maneuver System [*Military*] (INF)

CAMMU ... Cache/Memory Management Unit (BYTE)

Cam & N .... Cameron and Norwood's North Carolina Conference Reports [*A publication*] (DLA)

CAMN ...... Canadian Directory of Completed Master's Theses in Nursing [*University of Alberta*] [*Information service or system*] (IID)

CAMN ...... Chief Aircraft Mechanician [*British military*] (DMA)

CaMNCI .... Neepawa Collegiate Institute, Neepawa, MB, Canada [*Library symbol*] [*Library of Congress*] (LCLS)

CAMNET ... Computer Applications for Ministry Network (EA)

Cam & Nor ... Cameron and Norwood's North Carolina Conference Reports [*1800-04*] [*A publication*] (DLA)

Cam Not ..... Camera Notes [*A publication*]

CAMO .... Cam-Or, Inc. [*NASDAQ symbol*] (NQ)

CAMO .... Camouflage

CAMO .... Capulin Mountain National Monument [*National Park Service designation*]

CAMO .... Chief Administrative Medical Officer [*British*]

CAMO .... Consolidated Administrative Management Organization [*AID*]

Cam Obs .... Camera Obscura [*A publication*]

CAMOF .... Camouflage (MSA)

Cam Op ...... Cameron's Legal Opinions [*Toronto*] [*A publication*] (DLA)

CAMO-P ... Central Ammunition Management Office - Pacific [*Army*] (MCD)

CAMO-PAC ... Central Ammunition Management Office - Pacific [*Army*] (AABC)

CaMoV ...... Carnation Mottle Virus

CaMOWBC ... Winnipeg Bible College, Otterburne, MB, Canada [*Library symbol*] [*Library of Congress*] (LCLS)

CAMP .... Cabin Air Manifold Pressure [*Aviation*]

CAMP .... Calibrated Airborne Measurements Program (MCD)

CAMP .... California Amplifier, Inc. [*NASDAQ symbol*] (NQ)

CAMP .... Campaign Against Marijuana Planting

CAMP .... Campanian

Camp .... Campbell's Compendium of Roman Law [*A publication*] (DLA)

Camp .... Campbell's English Nisi Prius Reports [*A publication*] (DLA)

Camp .... Campbell's Legal Gazette Reports [*Pennsylvania*] [*A publication*] (DLA)

Camp .... Campbell's Reports [*27-58 Nebraska*] [*A publication*] (DLA)

Camp .... Campbell's Reports of Taney's United States Circuit Court Decisions [*A publication*] (DLA)

CAMP .... Campden [*England*]

Camp .... Camp's Reports [*1 North Dakota*] [*A publication*] (DLA)

CAMP .... Center for Advanced Management Programs [*University of Houston at Clear Lake*] [*Research center*] (RCD)

CAMP .... Center for Advanced Manufacturing and Production [*Southern Illinois University at Edwardsville*] [*Research center*] (RCD)

CAMP .... Center for Advanced Materials Processing [*Clarkson University*] [*Research center*] (RCD)

CAMP .... Christie, Atkins, Munch-Peterson Test [*Bacteriology*]

CAMP .... Coalition for the Abolition of Marijuana Prohibition (EA)

CAMP .... College Assistance Migrant Program

CAMP .... Command and Management Presentation [*Marine Corps*]

CAMP .... Common ADA Missile Packages (MCD)

CAMP .... Compiler for Automatic Machine Programming (BUR)

CAMP .... Comprehensive Analytical Methods of Planning

CAMP .... Computer Applications of Military Problems [*Computer users' group*]

CAMP .... Computer-Assisted Management of Portfolios

CAMP .... Computer-Assisted Match Program [*Military*]

CAMP .... Computer-Assisted Mathematics Program [*Scott, Foresman, 1968-1969*] [*Textbook series*] (BUR)

CAMP .... Computer-Assisted Menu Planning

CAMP .... Computer-Assisted Movie Production (IEEE)

CAMP .... Computerized Aircraft Maintenance Program

CAMP .... Continuous Air Monitoring Program [*or Project*] [*Environmental Protection Agency*]

CAMP .... Control and Monitor Panel

CAMP .... Control and Monitoring Processor (IEEE)

CAMP .... Council on America's Military Past (EA)

CAMP .... Cyclic Adenosine Monophosphate [*Also, cAMP*] [*Biochemistry*]

CAMP .... Cyclophosphamide, Adriamycin, Methotrexate, Procarbazine [*Antineoplastic drug regimen*]

CaMP .... Pinawa Public Library, Pinawa, MB, Canada [*Library symbol*] [*Library of Congress*] (LCLS)

Campaign ... Campaigner [*A publication*]

Campb .... Campbell's Compendium of Roman Law [*A publication*] (DLA)

Campb .... Campbell's English Nisi Prius Reports [*A publication*] (DLA)

Campb .... Campbell's Legal Gazette Reports [*Pennsylvania*] [*A publication*] (DLA)

Campb .... Campbell's Reports [*27-58 Nebraska*] [*A publication*] (DLA)

Campb .... Campbell's Reports of Taney's United States Circuit Court Decisions [*A publication*] (DLA)

CAMPB ..... Comments on Atomic and Molecular Physics [*A publication*]

Campb Dec ... Campbell's Reports of Taney's United States Circuit Court Decisions [*A publication*] (DLA)

Campbell .... Campbell's Compendium of Roman Law [*A publication*] (DLA)

Campbell .... Campbell's English Nisi Prius Reports [*A publication*] (DLA)

Campbell .... Campbell's Legal Gazette Reports [*Pennsylvania*] [*A publication*] (DLA)

Campbell .... Campbell's Lives of the Chief Justices [*A publication*] (DLA)

Campbell .... Campbell's Lives of the Lord Chancellors [*A publication*] (DLA)

Campbell .... Campbell's Reports [*27-58 Nebraska*] [*A publication*] (DLA)

Campbell .... Campbell's Reports of Taney's United States Circuit Court Decisions [*A publication*] (DLA)

Campbell L Rev ... Campbell Law Review [*A publication*]

Campbell Soup Dep Agric Res Bull ... Campbell Soup Company. Department of Agricultural Research. Bulletin [*A publication*]

Campbell Soup Dep Agric Res Res Monogr ... Campbell Soup Company. Department of Agricultural Research. Research Monograph [*A publication*]

Campb (Eng) ... Campbell's English Nisi Prius Reports [*A publication*] (DLA)

Campb (PA) ... Campbell's Legal Gazette Reports [*Pennsylvania*] [*A publication*] (DLA)

CaMPCFP ... Canadian Food Products Development Center, Portage La Prairie, MB, Canada [*Library symbol*] [*Library of Congress*] (LCLS)

Camp Ch Jus ... Campbell's Lives of the Chief Justices [*A publication*] (DLA)

Camp Cit .... Campbell on Citation and Diligence [*A publication*] (DLA)

Camp Dec .. Campbell's Reports of Taney's United States Circuit Court Decisions [*A publication*] (DLA)

Campeg ...... [*Johannes*] Campegius [*Deceased, 1511*] [*Authority cited in pre-1607 legal work*] (DSA)

CAMPEN ... Camp Pendleton [*California*] [*Marine Corps*]

Camp Ex .... Campbell on Executors and Administrators in Pennsylvania [*A publication*] (DLA)

CAMPH ..... Camphora [*Camphor*] [*Pharmacy*] (ROG)

CAM-PK ... Calmodulin-Dependent Protein Kinase [*An enzyme*]

Camp Ld Ch ... Campbell's Lives of the Lord Chancellors [*A publication*] (DLA)

Camp LG ... Campbell's Legal Gazette Reports [*Pennsylvania*] [*A publication*] (DLA)

Camp Lives Ld Ch ... Campbell's Lives of the Lord Chancellors [*A publication*] (DLA)

CaMPlp ..... Portage La Prairie Public Library, Portage La Prairie, MB, Canada [*Library symbol*] [*Library of Congress*] (LCLS)

CaMPlpM ... Manitoba School, Portage La Prairie, MB, Canada [*Library symbol*] [*Library of Congress*] (LCLS)

Camp Mag ... Camping Magazine [*A publication*]

Camp Merc L ... Campbell. Mercantile Law [*3rd ed.*] [*1904*] [*A publication*] (DLA)

Camp Neg ... Campbell. Negligence [*2nd ed.*] [*1878*] [*A publication*] (DLA)

Camp NP .. Campbell's English Nisi Prius Reports [*A publication*] (DLA)

CAMPO .... Committee to Award Miss Piggy the Oscar [*Defunct*]

Campo Suelo Argent ... Campo y Suelo Argentino [*A publication*]

CAMPP ..... Canadian Association of Motion Picture Producers

CAMPPS ... Conventional Ammunition Maintenance, Preservation, and Packaging Set (MCD)

Cam Prac ... Cameron's Supreme Court Practice [*Canada*] [*A publication*] (DLA)

Camp Rom L ... Campbell's Compendium of Roman Law [*A publication*] (DLA)

Camp Rom L Comp ... Campbell's Compendium of Roman Law [*A publication*] (DLA)

CAMP Rpt ... CAMP [*Cable Advertising, Merchandising, and Programming*] Report [*A publication*]

CAMPS ..... Centralized Automated Military Pay System

CAMPS ..... Computer-Assisted Message Processing System (MCD)

CAMPS ..... Computer-Assisted Mission Planner System (MCD)

CAMPS ..... Cooperative Area Manpower Planning System [*Environmental Protection Agency*]

CAMPS ..... Cost and Material Position System (MCD)

CAMPS ..... Cumulative Auction-Market Preferred Stock [*Investment term*]

Camp Sale ... Campbell. Sale of Goods and Commercial Agency [*2nd ed.*] [*1891*] [*A publication*] (DLA)

CAMPUS .. Coalition of American Pro-Life University Students [*Later, ACL*] (EA)

CAMPUS .. Comprehensive Analytical Method of Planning in the University Sphere [*Cost simulation technique*]

CaMPW .... Atomic Energy of Canada, Whiteshell Nuclear Research Establishment, Pinawa, MB, Canada [*Library symbol*] [*Library of Congress*] (LCLS)

CamQ .... Cambridge Quarterly [*A publication*]

CAMQA .... Canadian Metallurgical Quarterly [*A publication*]

CAM R ...... Cambrian Railway [*British*]

CamR .... Cambridge Review [*A publication*]

CAMR....... Camera (MSA)
CamR......... Campbell Reproductions Ltd., Ottawa, ON, Canada [*Library symbol*] [*Library of Congress*] (LCLS)
CAMR....... Canadian Association for the Mentally Retarded
CAMR....... Centre for Applied Microbiology and Research [*Public Health Laboratory Service*] [*British*]
CAMR....... Configuration Accounting and Management Report (MCD)
CAMRA .... Campaign for Real Ale
CAMRA .... Consolidated Air Mission Results Analysis (CINC)
CaMRa...... Rapid City Regional Library, Rapid City, MB, Canada [*Library symbol*] [*Library of Congress*] (LCLS)
CAMRAS.. Computer-Assisted Mapping and Records Activities System (IEEE)
CAMRAS.. Counter Artillery and Mortar RADAR Acquisition Simulation (MCD)
CAMRB..... Central Aircrew Medical Review Board [*Military*] (AFM)
CaMRD..... Russell and District Regional Library, Russell, MB, Canada [*Library symbol*] [*Library of Congress*] (LCLS)
CAMRDC ... Central African Mineral Resources Development Centre (EAIO)
CaMReP.... Reston and District Regional Library, Reston, MB, Canada [*Library symbol*] [*Library of Congress*] (LCLS)
CAMRF..... Camreco, Inc. [*NASDAQ symbol*] (NQ)
CaMRiP.... Prairie Crocus Regional Library, Rivers, MB, Canada [*Library symbol*] [*Library of Congress*] (LCLS)
CAMRL..... Canadian Association of Medical Record Librarians
CaMRo...... Rossburn Regional Library, Rossburn, MB, Canada [*Library symbol*] [*Library of Congress*] (LCLS)
CAMROC ... Cambridge Radio Observatory Committee
CAMRODD ... Caribbean Association on Mental Retardation and Other Development Disabilities [*Kingston, Jamaica*] (EAIO)
CaMRoH... Rossburn District Hospital, Rossburn, MB, Canada [*Library symbol*] [*Library of Congress*] (LCLS)
CAMRSS .. Center for Autonomous and Man-Controlled Robotic and Sensing Systems [*Research center*] (RCD)
CAMRT..... Canadian Association of Medical Radiation Technologists (EAIO)
CAMS........ Cabin Atmosphere Monitoring System [*NASA*]
CAMS........ Cambrian Systems, Inc. [*NASDAQ symbol*] (NQ)
CAMS........ Canadian Applied Mathematics Society (MCD)
CAMS........ Central Atmosphere Monitoring System [*Military*] (CAAL)
CAMS........ Chinese American Medical Society (EA)
CAMS........ Coastal Antimissile System (MCD)
CAMS........ COMIREX [*Committee on Imagery Requirements and Exploitation*] Automated Management System (MCD)
CAMS........ Common Aperture Multispectrum Seeker [*Army*] (MCD)
CAMS........ Communications Area Master Station (NVT)
CAMS........ Comprehensive Agrimedia Measurement Study [*Database*] [*Doane Marketing Research, Inc.*] [*Information service or system*] (CRD)
CAMS........ Computer-Aided Missile Synthesis [*Army*] (MCD)
CAMS........ Computer-Assisted Messaging Services [*Electronic mail*] [*Data processing*]
CAMS........ Computerized Automotive Maintenance System [*Buick's factory to dealership communication system*]
CAMS........ Computers for the Advancement of Medicine & Science [*Information service or system*] (IID)
CAMS........ Constant-Angle Mie Scattering [*Optics*]
CAMS........ Container Automated Marking Systems
CAMS........ Containerized Avionics Maintenance System (NG)
CAMS........ Control of Aircraft Maintenance and Servicing
CAMS........ Core Automated Maintenance System (MCD)
CAMS........ Crisis Action Management System
CAMS........ Cybernetic Anthropomorphous Machine System [*Robot*] [*Army*]
Cam Sal ..... Camillus Salernus [*Flourished, 16th century*] [*Authority cited in pre-1607 legal work*] (DSA)
Cam Salern ... Camillus Salernus [*Flourished, 16th century*] [*Authority cited in pre-1607 legal work*] (DSA)
Cam SC...... Cameron's Supreme Court Cases [*Canada*] [*A publication*] (DLA)
CaMSC...... College de St. Boniface, St. Boniface, MB, Canada [*Library symbol*] [*Library of Congress*] (LCLS)
CAM SCAC ... Camera Scaccari [*Exchequer Chamber*] [*Latin*] [*Legal term*] (DLA)
Cam Scacc ... Camera Scaccarii [*Exchequer Chamber*] [*Latin*] [*Legal term*] (DLA)
CaMSEC ... Selkirk Community Library, Selkirk, MB, Canada [*Library symbol*] [*Library of Congress*] (LCLS)
CaMSeL .... Lord Selkirk Regional School, Selkirk, MB, Canada [*Library symbol*] [*Library of Congress*] (LCLS)
CaMSeMH ... Selkirk Mental Health Centre, Selkirk, MB, Canada [*Library symbol*] [*Library of Congress*] (LCLS)
CaMSePCL ... Parks Canada, Lower Fort Garry National Historic Park, Selkirk, MB, Canada [*Library symbol*] [*Library of Congress*] (LCLS)
CaMSePN ... School of Psychiatric Nursing, Selkirk, MB, Canada [*Library symbol*] [*Library of Congress*] (LCLS)
CAMSEQ ... Conformational Analysis of Molecules in Solution by Empirical and Quantum Techniques

CaMShCFAM ... Canadian Forces Base, Royal Canadian Army Museum, Shilo, MB, Canada [*Library symbol*] [*Library of Congress*] (LCLS)
CAMSI...... Canadian-American Merchant Shipping Instructions
CAMSI...... Canadian Association of Medical Students and Interns
CAMSI...... Confidential Admiralty Merchant Shipping Instructions
CAMSIM.. Computer-Assisted Maintenance Simulation [*Army*]
CaMSL...... Snow Lake Community Library, Snow Lake, MB, Canada [*Library symbol*] [*Library of Congress*] (LCLS)
CaMSoG... Glenwood and Souris Regional Library, Souris, MB, Canada [*Library symbol*] [*Library of Congress*] (LCLS)
CAMSq...... Consolidated Aircraft Maintenance Squadron [*Air Force*]
CaMSrNW ... North-West Regional Library, Swan River, MB, Canada [*Library symbol*] [*Library of Congress*] (LCLS)
CAMSTA .. Cameron Station [*Virginia*] [*Army*] (AABC)
CaMSte...... Steinbach Public Library, Steinbach, MB, Canada [*Library symbol*] [*Library of Congress*] (LCLS)
Cam Stell ... Camera Stellate [*Star Chamber*] [*Latin*] [*Legal term*] (DLA)
CaMSteM ... Mennonite Village Museum, Steinbach, MB, Canada [*Library symbol*] [*Library of Congress*] (LCLS)
CaMStJ ..... Public Library, St. James, MB, Canada [*Library symbol*] [*Library of Congress*] (LCLS)
CaMStoS... South Interlake Regional Library, Stonewall, MB, Canada [*Library symbol*] [*Library of Congress*] (LCLS)
CaMStPJ... Jolys Regional Library, St. Pierre, MB, Canada [*Library symbol*] [*Library of Congress*] (LCLS)
CaMStR..... Sainte Rose Regional Library, Sainte Rose, MB, Canada [*Library symbol*] [*Library of Congress*] (LCLS)
CAMT .... Canada. Meteorological Translations [*A publication*]
CAMT .... Canadian Association for Music Therapy
CAMT .... Consolidated Aircraft Maintenance Training
CaMT .... Transcona Public Library, Transcona, MB, Canada [*Library symbol*] [*Library of Congress*] (LCLS)
CAMTEC .. Canadian Marine Trade Exhibition and Congress [*SHOWBEX*] (TSPED)
CaMTh ...... Thompson Public Library, Thompson, MB, Canada [*Library symbol*] [*Library of Congress*] (LCLS)
CAMTMTS ... Central Area, Military Traffic Management and Terminal Service (AABC)
CaMTp ...... The Pas Public Library, The Pas, MB, Canada [*Library symbol*] [*Library of Congress*] (LCLS)
CaMTPK... Keewatin Community College, The Pas, MB, Canada [*Library symbol*] [*Library of Congress*] (LCLS)
CAMTT..... Civil Affairs Mobile Training Team [*Military*] (CINC)
CAMUS..... Commitment Accounting and Management of Unit Supplies (MCD)
CaMV .... Cauliflower Mosaic Virus [*Also, CLMV*]
CAMV .... Cowpea Aphid-Borne Mosaic Virus
CAMVAC ... Centro de Apoyo para Mujeres Violadas [*An association*] (EAIO)
CaMVE ..... Virden-Elkhorn Regional Library, Virden, MB, Canada [*Library symbol*] [*Library of Congress*] (LCLS)
CaMW....... Winnipeg Public Library, Winnipeg, MB, Canada [*Library symbol*] [*Library of Congress*] (LCLS)
CaMWA .... Canada Department of Agriculture, Winnipeg, MB, Canada [*Library symbol*] [*Library of Congress*] (LCLS)
CaMWAG ... Canada Department of Agriculture, Research Station, Winnipeg, MB, Canada [*Library symbol*] [*Library of Congress*] (LCLS)
CaMWAMA ... Manitoba Department of Municipal Affairs, Administration Branch, Winnipeg, MB, Canada [*Library symbol*] [*Library of Congress*] (LCLS)
CaMWAMT ... Aikens, Macaulay & Thorauldson Law Firm, Winnipeg, MB, Canada [*Library symbol*] [*Library of Congress*] (LCLS)
CaMWaPCR ... Parks Canada, Riding Mountain National Park, Wasagaming, MB, Canada [*Library symbol*] [*Library of Congress*] (LCLS)
CaMWARN ... Manitoba Association of Registered Nurses, Winnipeg, MB, Canada [*Library symbol*] [*Library of Congress*] (LCLS)
CaMWAS ... Arthritis Society, Winnipeg, MB, Canada [*Library symbol*] [*Library of Congress*] (LCLS)
CaMWBM ... Bethania Mennonite Personal Care Home, Winnipeg, MB, Canada [*Library symbol*] [*Library of Congress*] (LCLS)
CaMWC .... Canadian Broadcasting Corp., Music and Record Library, Winnipeg, MB, Canada [*Library symbol*] [*Library of Congress*] (LCLS)
CaMWCA ... Cantetech, Inc., Winnipeg, MB, Canada [*Library symbol*] [*Library of Congress*] (LCLS)
CaMWCCA ... Manitoba Department of Consumer and Corporate Affairs, Winnipeg, MB, Canada [*Library symbol*] [*Library of Congress*] (LCLS)
CaMWCCH ... Health Science Centre, Children's Centre, Winnipeg, MB, Canada [*Library symbol*] [*Library of Congress*] (LCLS)
CaMWCCI ... Manitoba Department of Consumer, Corporate, and Internal Services, Consumers' Bureau, Winnipeg, MB, Canada [*Library symbol*] [*Library of Congress*] (LCLS)
CaMWCCIR ... Canada Department of Communications, Central Region Information Resources Center, Winnipeg, MB, Canada [*Library symbol*] [*Library of Congress*] (LCLS)
CaMWCH ... Concordia Hospital, Winnipeg, MB, Canada [*Library symbol*] [*Library of Congress*] (LCLS)

CaMWCHA ... Charles Howard & Associates, Winnipeg, MB, Canada [*Library symbol*] [*Library of Congress*] (LCLS)

CaMWCM ... Canadian Mennonite Bible College, Winnipeg, MB, Canada [*Library symbol*] [*Library of Congress*] (LCLS)

CaMWCT ... Manitoba Cancer Treatment and Research Foundation, Winnipeg, MB, Canada [*Library symbol*] [*Library of Congress*] (LCLS)

CaMWCU ... Credit Union Central of Manitoba, Winnipeg, MB, Canada [*Library symbol*] [*Library of Congress*] (LCLS)

CaMWCWB ... Canadian Wheat Board, Winnipeg, MB, Canada [*Library symbol*] [*Library of Congress*] (LCLS)

CaMWDL ... Deer Lodge Hospital, Winnipeg, MB, Canada [*Library symbol*] [*Library of Congress*] (LCLS)

CaMWDRR ... Manitoba Department of Renewable Resources, Winnipeg, MB, Canada [*Library symbol*] [*Library of Congress*] (LCLS)

CaMWDU ... Ducks Unlimited, Winnipeg, MB, Canada [*Library symbol*] [*Library of Congress*] (LCLS)

CaMWE .... Manitoba Department of Education, Winnipeg, MB, Canada [*Library symbol*] [*Library of Congress*] (LCLS)

CaMWECW ... Environment Canada, Canadian Wildlife Service, Winnipeg, MB, Canada [*Library symbol*] [*Library of Congress*] (LCLS)

CaMWEM ... Manitoba Environmental Management Division, Winnipeg, MB, Canada [*Library symbol*] [*Library of Congress*] (LCLS)

CaMWFD ... Fred Douglas Lodge Nursing Home, Winnipeg, MB, Canada [*Library symbol*] [*Library of Congress*] (LCLS)

CaMWFI ... Manitoba Department of Finance, Winnipeg, MB, Canada [*Library symbol*] [*Library of Congress*] (LCLS)

CaMWFP .. Winnipeg Free Press Co. Ltd., Winnipeg, MB, Canada [*Library symbol*] [*Library of Congress*] (LCLS)

CaMWFW ... Fresh Water Institute, Canada Fisheries Research Board, Winnipeg, MB, Canada [*Library symbol*] [*Library of Congress*] (LCLS)

CaMWGBP ... Guertin Brothers Paint Library, Winnipeg, MB, Canada [*Library symbol*] [*Library of Congress*] (LCLS)

CaMWGCH ... Health Sciences Centre, General Centre, Winnipeg, MB, Canada [*Library symbol*] [*Library of Congress*] (LCLS)

CaMWGH ... Grace Hospital, Winnipeg, MB, Canada [*Library symbol*] [*Library of Congress*] (LCLS)

CaMWGHA ... Gunn, Hoffer & Associates, Winnipeg, MB, Canada [*Library symbol*] [*Library of Congress*] (LCLS)

CaMWGR ... Canada Department of Agriculture, Canadian Grain Commission, Winnipeg, MB, Canada [*Library symbol*] [*Library of Congress*] (LCLS)

CaMWGW ... Great West Life Assurance Co., Winnipeg, MB, Canada [*Library symbol*] [*Library of Congress*] (LCLS)

CaMWH .... Manitoba Hydro, Winnipeg, MB, Canada [*Library symbol*] [*Library of Congress*] (LCLS)

CaMWHM ... Health Sciences Centre, Medical Library, Winnipeg, MB, Canada [*Library symbol*] [*Library of Congress*] (LCLS)

CaMWHP ... Manitoba Department of Health and Community Service, Winnipeg, MB, Canada [*Library symbol*] [*Library of Congress*] (LCLS)

CaMWHR ... Henderson Regional Library, Winnipeg, MB, Canada [*Library symbol*] [*Library of Congress*] (LCLS)

CaMWHSC ... Manitoba Health Services Commission, Winnipeg, MB, Canada [*Library symbol*] [*Library of Congress*] (LCLS)

CaMWI ..... Insurance Institute of Winnipeg, Winnipeg, MB, Canada [*Library symbol*] [*Library of Congress*] (LCLS)

CaMWIAP ... Canada Department of Indian Affairs and Northern Development, Parks Canada, Prairie Regional Office, Winnipeg, MB, Canada [*Library symbol*] [*Library of Congress*] (LCLS)

CaMWIC ... Manitoba Department of Industry and Commerce, Winnipeg, MB, Canada [*Library symbol*] [*Library of Congress*] (LCLS)

CaMWIDE ... IDE Engineering Co., Winnipeg, MB, Canada [*Library symbol*] [*Library of Congress*] (LCLS)

CaMWIE ... Indus Electronic, Winnipeg, MB, Canada [*Library symbol*] [*Library of Congress*] (LCLS)

CaMWinBH ... Bethel Hospital, Winkler, MB, Canada [*Library symbol*] [*Library of Congress*] (LCLS)

CaMWJ ..... Canada Department of Justice, Winnipeg, MB, Canada [*Library symbol*] [*Library of Congress*] (LCLS)

CaMWK .... Kelvin High School, Winnipeg, MB, Canada [*Library symbol*] [*Library of Congress*] (LCLS)

CaMWL .... Law Society of Manitoba, Winnipeg, MB, Canada [*Library symbol*] [*Library of Congress*] (LCLS)

CaMWLC ... Library Service Centre, Winnipeg School Division No. 1, Winnipeg, MB, Canada [*Library symbol*] [*Library of Congress*] (LCLS)

CaMWLCC ... Lutheran Council in Canada, Winnipeg, MB, Canada [*Library symbol*] [*Library of Congress*] (LCLS)

CaMWLR ... Manitoba Department of Labour, Labour Research Library, Winnipeg, MB, Canada [*Library symbol*] [*Library of Congress*] (LCLS)

CaMWLS .. University of Manitoba, Faculty of Law Library, Winnipeg, MB, Canada [*Library symbol*] [*Library of Congress*] (LCLS)

CaMWM ... University of Manitoba, Medical Library, Winnipeg, MB, Canada [*Library symbol*] [*Library of Congress*] (LCLS)

CaMWMBC ... Mennonite Brethren College, Winnipeg, MB, Canada [*Library symbol*] [*Library of Congress*] (LCLS)

CaMWME ... MacLaren Engineering, Winnipeg, MB, Canada [*Library symbol*] [*Library of Congress*] (LCLS)

CaMWMG ... Misericordia General Hospital, Winnipeg, MB, Canada [*Library symbol*] [*Library of Congress*] (LCLS)

CaMWMH ... Winnipeg Municipal Hospital, Winnipeg, MB, Canada [*Library symbol*] [*Library of Congress*] (LCLS)

CaMWMI ... Canada Department of Manpower and Immigration, Winnipeg, MB, Canada [*Library symbol*] [*Library of Congress*] (LCLS)

CaMWMM ... Manitoba Museum of Man and Nature, Winnipeg, MB, Canada [*Library symbol*] [*Library of Congress*] (LCLS)

CaMWMMP ... Meadowood Manor Personal Care Home, Winnipeg, MB, Canada [*Library symbol*] [*Library of Congress*] (LCLS)

CaMWMRC ... Manitoba Research Council, Winnipeg, MB, Canada [*Library symbol*] [*Library of Congress*] (LCLS)

CaMWMTC ... Manitoba Theater Center, Winnipeg, MB, Canada [*Library symbol*] [*Library of Congress*] (LCLS)

CaMWMTS ... Manitoba Teachers Society, Winnipeg, MB, Canada [*Library symbol*] [*Library of Congress*] (LCLS)

CaMWO .... Rev. Peres Oblats, Winnipeg, MB, Canada [*Library symbol*] [*Library of Congress*] (LCLS)

CaMWP .... Provincial Library of Manitoba, Winnipeg, MB, Canada [*Library symbol*] [*Library of Congress*] (LCLS)

CaMWPA ... Provincial Archives of Manitoba, Winnipeg, MB, Canada [*Library symbol*] [*Library of Congress*] (LCLS)

CaMWPCPA ... Parks Canada, Prairie Region Library, Archaeology Subsection Office, Winnipeg, MB, Canada [*Library symbol*] [*Library of Congress*] (LCLS)

CaMWPCPH ... Parks Canada, Prairie Region Library, Historic Resources Conservation Subsection Office, Winnipeg, MB, Canada [*Library symbol*] [*Library of Congress*] (LCLS)

CaMWPL ... Department of Tourism, Recreation, and Cultural Affairs, Public Library Services, Winnipeg, MB, Canada [*Library symbol*] [*Library of Congress*] (LCLS)

CaMWPNR ... Manitoba Department of Natural Resources, Park Management Library, Winnipeg, MB, Canada [*Library symbol*] [*Library of Congress*] (LCLS)

CaMWPPH ... Provincial Public Health Nursing Services, Winnipeg, MB, Canada [*Library symbol*] [*Library of Congress*] (LCLS)

CaMWPS .. Manitoba Probation Services, Winnipeg, MB, Canada [*Library symbol*] [*Library of Congress*] (LCLS)

CaMWR .... Royal Winnipeg Ballet, Winnipeg, MB, Canada [*Library symbol*] [*Library of Congress*] (LCLS)

CaMWRC ... Royal Canadian Mounted Police, Crime Laboratory, Winnipeg, MB, Canada [*Library symbol*] [*Library of Congress*] (LCLS)

CaMWRR ... Red River Community College, Learning Resources Centre, Winnipeg, MB, Canada [*Library symbol*] [*Library of Congress*] (LCLS)

CaMWRS ... Richardson Securities of Canada, Winnipeg, MB, Canada [*Library symbol*] [*Library of Congress*] (LCLS)

CaMWSA ... Saint Andrew's College, Winnipeg, MB, Canada [*Library symbol*] [*Library of Congress*] (LCLS)

CaMWSAC ... Saint Amant Center, Winnipeg, MB, Canada [*Library symbol*] [*Library of Congress*] (LCLS)

CaMWSB ... St. Boniface Public Library, Winnipeg, MB, Canada [*Library symbol*] [*Library of Congress*] (LCLS)

CaMWSBM ... St. Boniface General Hospital, Medical Library, Winnipeg, MB, Canada [*Library symbol*] [*Library of Congress*] (LCLS)

CaMWSBN ... St. Boniface General Hospital, School of Nursing, Winnipeg, MB, Canada [*Library symbol*] [*Library of Congress*] (LCLS)

CaMWSC ... Society for Crippled Children and Adults, Winnipeg, MB, Canada [*Library symbol*] [*Library of Congress*] (LCLS)

CaMWSD ... Winnipeg School Division No. 1, Teachers' Library and Resource Centre, Winnipeg, MB, Canada [*Library symbol*] [*Library of Congress*] (LCLS)

CaMWSJ .. Saint John's College, Winnipeg, MB, Canada [*Library symbol*] [*Library of Congress*] (LCLS)

CaMWSM ... Stony Mountain Institution Library, Winnipeg, MB, Canada [*Library symbol*] [*Library of Congress*] (LCLS)

CaMWSN ... Winnipeg School of Nursing, Health Science Centre, Winnipeg, MB, Canada [*Library symbol*] [*Library of Congress*] (LCLS)

CaMWSOGH ... Seven Oaks General Hospital, Education Services, Winnipeg, MB, Canada [*Library symbol*] [*Library of Congress*] (LCLS)

CaMWSP .. Saint Paul's College, Winnipeg, MB, Canada [*Library symbol*] [*Library of Congress*] (LCLS)

CaMWSPC ... Social Planning Council of Winnipeg, Winnipeg, MB, Canada [*Library symbol*] [*Library of Congress*] (LCLS)

CaMWSV ... Saint Vital Public Library, Winnipeg, MB, Canada [*Library symbol*] [*Library of Congress*] (LCLS)

CaMWT .... Winnipeg Tribune, Winnipeg, MB, Canada [*Library symbol*] [*Library of Congress*] (LCLS)

CaMWTC ... Teshmount Consultants, Winnipeg, MB, Canada [*Library symbol*] [*Library of Congress*] (LCLS)
CaMWTE ... Templeton Engineering, Winnipeg, MB, Canada [*Library symbol*] [*Library of Congress*] (LCLS)
CaMWTRC ... Manitoba. Department of Tourism, Recreation, and Cultural Affairs, Winnipeg, MB, Canada [*Library symbol*] [*Library of Congress*] (LCLS)
CaMWTS ... Manitoba Telephone System, Winnipeg, MB, Canada [*Library symbol*] [*Library of Congress*] (LCLS)
CaMWU .... University of Manitoba, Winnipeg, MB, Canada [*Library symbol*] [*Library of Congress*] (LCLS)
CaMWUAF ... University of Manitoba, Architecture and Fine Arts Library, Winnipeg, MB, Canada [*Library symbol*] [*Library of Congress*] (LCLS)
CaMWUC ... University of Winnipeg, Winnipeg, MB, Canada [*Library symbol*] [*Library of Congress*] (LCLS)
CaMWUD ... University of Manitoba, Dental Library, Winnipeg, MB, Canada [*Library symbol*] [*Library of Congress*] (LCLS)
CaMWUG ... University of Manitoba, Department of Geography, Winnipeg, MB, Canada [*Library symbol*] [*Library of Congress*] (LCLS)
CaMWUGG ... United Grain Growers, Winnipeg, MB, Canada [*Library symbol*] [*Library of Congress*] (LCLS)
CaMWUM ... University of Manitoba, Map and Atlas Collection, Winnipeg, MB, Canada [*Library symbol*] [*Library of Congress*] (LCLS)
CaMWUML ... Underwood McLellan Ltd., Winnipeg, MB, Canada [*Library symbol*] [*Library of Congress*] (LCLS)
CaMWVGH ... Victoria General Hospital, Winnipeg, MB, Canada [*Library symbol*] [*Library of Congress*] (LCLS)
CaMWVS ... Manitoba Veterinarian Services, Branch Library, Winnipeg, MB, Canada [*Library symbol*] [*Library of Congress*] (LCLS)
CaMWWA ... Winnipeg Art Gallery, Winnipeg, MB, Canada [*Library symbol*] [*Library of Congress*] (LCLS)
CaMWWC ... Winnipeg Clinic, Winnipeg, MB, Canada [*Library symbol*] [*Library of Congress*] (LCLS)
CaMWWLW ... W. L. Wardrop & Associates, Winnipeg, MB, Canada [*Library symbol*] [*Library of Congress*] (LCLS)
CAMZA .... CA Magazine. Journal of Commercial Art [*A publication*]
CAN.......... Bremerton, WA [*Location identifier*] [*FAA*] (FAAL)
CAN.......... Cahiers Francais; Revue Periodique de l'Actualite Politique, Economique, Sociale, et Culturelle de la France [*A publication*]
CAN.......... Cajun Nike [*US Navy missile*]
CaN.......... Calabria Nobilissima [*A publication*]
CAN.......... Calcium-Ammonium Nitrate [*Fertilizer*]
CAN.......... Campus Action Network [*Defunct*] (EA)
Can.......... Canaanite (BJA)
CAN.......... Canada [*ANSI three-letter standard code*] (CNC)
CAN.......... Canadian (ROG)
CAN.......... Canadian MARC [*Machine-Readable Cataloging*] [*Source file*] [*UTLAS symbol*]
Can.......... Canadiana [*A publication*]
CAN.......... Canal (ROG)
CAN.......... Canaveral [*Obsolete*] [*NASA*] (KSC)
CAN.......... Canberra [*Australia*] [*Seismograph station code, US Geological Survey*] (SEIS)
CAN.......... Cancel (AABC)
CAN.......... Cancel Character [*Keyboard*] [*Data processing*]
CAN.......... Cancrinite [*A zeolite*]
CAN.......... Canister (AAG)
CAN.......... Canon
CAN.......... Canonicorum [*England*]
Can.......... Canoniste [*A publication*]
CAN.......... Canopy (MSA)
CAN.......... Canticle [*A publication*]
CAN.......... Canto [*Melody*] [*Music*]
CAN.......... Canton [*City in China*] (ROG)
CAN.......... Cantoris [*Of the Cantor*] [*Music*]
Can.......... Canute [*King of England, Denmark, and Norway, 994-1035*] (ILCA)
CAN.......... Career Advancement Network (EA)
CAN.......... Central Autentica Nacionalista [*Nationalist Authentic Central*] [*Guatemala*] [*Political party*] (PPW)
CAN.......... Centralforbundet for Alkohol- och Narkotikaupplysning [*Swedish Council for Information on Alcohol and Other Drugs*] [*Information service or system*] (IID)
CAN.......... Ceric Ammonium Nitrate [*Inorganic chemistry*]
CAN.......... Certification Analysis Network (NASA)
CA/N .... Child Abuse and Neglect
CAN.......... Children's Action Network [*Defunct*] (EA)
CAN.......... Chlorendic Anhydride [*Also, CA*] [*Organic chemistry*]
CAN.......... Christians in the Arts Networking (EA)
CAN.......... Citizens Against Noise
CAN.......... Citizens Against Nuclear War [*Defunct*] (EA)
CAN.......... Computer Architecture News [*A publication*]
CAN.......... Configuration Accounting Number
CAN.......... Conservation Administration News [*A publication*]
CAN.......... Consumer Action Now (EA)
CAN.......... Corporate Angel Network (EA)

CAN.......... Correlation Air Navigation
CAN.......... Cost Account Number [*Accounting*] (NG)
CAN.......... Cult Awareness Network (EA)
CAN.......... Cure AIDS [*Acquired Immune Deficiency Syndrome*] Now [*An association*] (EA)
CAN.......... Customs Assigned Number [*Shipping*] [*British*]
CAN.......... Guangzhou [*China*] [*Airport symbol*] (OAG)
CAna.......... Anaheim Public Library, Anaheim, CA [*Library symbol*] [*Library of Congress*] (LCLS)
CANA .... California Association of Nurse Anesthetists [*A publication*]
CANA .... Canadian Army (NATG)
CANA .... Christian Anti-Narcotic Association [*Later, SFM*]
CANA .... Cider Association of North America (EA)
CANA .... Cremation Association of North America (EA)
CANA .... Czech American National Alliance (EA)
CANA .... FCR Automotive Group, Inc. [*NASDAQ symbol*] (NQ)
CAnaA .... North American Rockwell Corp., Autonetics Technical Library, Anaheim, CA [*Library symbol*] [*Library of Congress*] (LCLS)
CAnaA-R ... North American Rockwell Corp., A. R. Rechnitzer Oceanographic Collection, Anaheim, CA [*Library symbol*] [*Library of Congress*] (LCLS)
Can Abr...... Canadian Abridgment [*A publication*] (DLA)
Can Abr (2d) ... Canadian Abridgment [*2nd ed.*] [*A publication*] (DLA)
Can Acoust Acoust Can ... Canadian Acoustics/Acoustique Canadienne [*A publication*]
Canada Ag ... Canada. Department of Agriculture. Publication [*A publication*]
Canada Bus ... Canadian Business Magazine [*A publication*]
Canada Commerce ... Canadian Department of Industry, Trade, and Commerce (DLA)
Canada Defence Research Board Handb ... Canada Defence Research Board. Handbook [*A publication*]
Canada Dept Mines and Tech Surveys Geog Br Bibl Ser ... Canada. Department of Mines and Technical Surveys. Geographical Branch. Bibliographical Series [*A publication*]
Canada Dept Mines and Tech Surveys Geog Bull ... Canada. Department of Mines and Technical Surveys. Geographical Bulletin [*A publication*]
Canada Dept Mines and Tech Surveys Geog Paper ... Canada. Department of Mines and Technical Surveys. Geographical Paper [*A publication*]
Canada Dept Mines and Tech Surveys Mem ... Canada. Department of Mines and Technical Surveys. Memoir [*A publication*]
Canada Dept Mines and Tech Surveys Misc Paper Ser ... Canada. Department of Mines and Technical Surveys. Miscellaneous Paper Series [*A publication*]
Canada Dominion Observatory Contr Pub ... Canada Dominion Observatory Contributions. Publications [*A publication*]
Canada Geol Survey Bull ... Canada. Geological Survey. Bulletin [*A publication*]
Canada Geol Survey Econ Geology Rept ... Canada. Geological Survey. Economic Geology Report [*A publication*]
Canada Geol Survey Geophysics Paper ... Canada. Geological Survey. Geophysics Paper [*A publication*]
Canada Geol Survey Map ... Canada. Geological Survey. Map [*A publication*]
Canada Geol Survey Mem ... Canada. Geological Survey. Memoir [*A publication*]
Canada Geol Survey Paper ... Canada. Geological Survey. Paper [*A publication*]
Canada Geol Survey Prelim Ser Map ... Canada. Geological Survey. Preliminary Series. Map [*A publication*]
Canada LT ... Canadian Law Times [*A publication*] (DLA)
Canada Med J ... Canada Medical Journal and Monthly Record of Medical and Surgical Science [*A publication*]
Canad Anaesth Soc J ... Canadian Anaesthetists' Society. Journal [*A publication*]
Canada Natl Mus Bull Nat History Paper Special Contr ... Canada. National Museum Bulletin. Natural History Paper. Special Contributions [*A publication*]
Canada O & G ... Canadian Oil and Gas Handbook [*A publication*]
Canada Rpt ... Report on Canada, 1985 [*A publication*]
Canad Bar Rev ... Canadian Bar Review [*A publication*]
Canad Bookm ... Canadian Bookman [*A publication*]
Canad Chem Process ... Canadian Chemical Processing [*A publication*]
Canad Doctor ... Canadian Doctor [*A publication*]
Canad Ent ... Canadian Entomologist [*A publication*]
Canad Entom ... Canadian Entomologist [*A publication*]
Canad Fam Physician ... Canadian Family Physician [*A publication*]
Canad Fld-Nat ... Canadian Field-Naturalist [*A publication*]
Canad For Ind ... Canadian Forest Industries [*A publication*]
Canad Forum ... Canadian Forum [*A publication*]
Canad Geog J ... Canadian Geographical Journal [*Later, Canadian Geographic*] [*A publication*]
Canad Hist Assn Rep ... Canadian Historical Association. Report [*A publication*]
Canad Hist Rev ... Canadian Historical Review [*A publication*]
Canad Hosp ... Canadian Hospital [*A publication*]
Canadian Alpine Jour ... Canadian Alpine Journal [*A publication*]
Canadian Archt ... Canadian Architect [*A publication*]

Canadian Assoc Geographers Education Comm Bull ... Canadian Association of Geographers. Education Committee. Bulletin [*A publication*]
Canadian Bldg Digest ... Canadian Building Digest [*A publication*]
Canadian Ceramic Soc Jour ... Canadian Ceramic Society. Journal [*A publication*]
Canadian Geotech Jour ... Canadian Geotechnical Journal [*A publication*]
Canadian Inst Mining and Metallurgy Trans ... Canadian Institute of Mining and Metallurgy. Transactions [*A publication*]
Canadian Inst Mining Met Bulletin ... Canadian Institute of Mining and Metallurgy. Bulletin [*A publication*]
CanadianJTH ... Canadian Journal of Theology [*Toronto*] [*A publication*]
Canadian Lib Assn Bul ... Canadian Library Association. Bulletin [*A publication*]
Canadian Shipp & Mar Engng ... Canadian Shipping and Marine Engineering [*A publication*]
Canad J ...... Canadian Journal of Industry [*A publication*]
Canad J Afr Stud ... Canadian Journal of African Studies [*A publication*]
Canad J Biochem ... Canadian Journal of Biochemistry and Physiology [*A publication*]
Canad J Bot ... Canadian Journal of Botany [*A publication*]
Canad J Chem ... Canadian Journal of Chemistry [*A publication*]
Canad J Chem Engng ... Canadian Journal of Chemical Engineering [*A publication*]
Canad J Econ ... Canadian Journal of Economics [*A publication*]
Canad J Math ... Canadian Journal of Mathematics [*Ottawa, Ontario*] [*A publication*]
Canad J Med Sc ... Canadian Journal of Medical Science [*A publication*]
Canad J Med Tech ... Canadian Journal of Medical Technology [*A publication*]
Canad J Med Technol ... Canadian Journal of Medical Technology [*A publication*]
Canad J Microbiol ... Canadian Journal of Microbiology [*A publication*]
Canad Jour L ... Canadian Journal of Linguistics [*A publication*]
Canad J Phys ... Canadian Journal of Physics [*A publication*]
Canad J Pl Sci ... Canadian Journal of Plant Science [*A publication*]
Canad J Polit Sci ... Canadian Journal of Political Science [*A publication*]
Canad J Psychiatr ... Canadian Journal of Psychiatry [*A publication*]
Canad J Psychiatr Nurs ... Canadian Journal of Psychiatric Nursing [*A publication*]
Canad J Psychol ... Canadian Journal of Psychology [*A publication*]
Canad J Public Health ... Canadian Journal of Public Health [*A publication*]
Canad J Radiogr Radiother Nucl Med ... Canadian Journal of Radiography, Radiotherapy, Nuclear Medicine [*A publication*]
Canad J Soil Sci ... Canadian Journal of Soil Science [*A publication*]
Canad J Statist ... Canadian Journal of Statistics [*A publication*]
Canad J Surg ... Canadian Journal of Surgery [*A publication*]
CanadJT .... Canadian Journal of Theology [*Toronto*] [*A publication*]
Canad J Zool ... Canadian Journal of Zoology [*A publication*]
Canad J Zoology ... Canadian Journal of Zoology [*A publication*]
Canad Lib .. Canadian Library [*A publication*]
Canad Lib Assn Bul ... Canadian Library Association. Bulletin [*A publication*]
Canad Lib Assn Feliciter ... Canadian Library Association. Feliciter [*A publication*]
Canad Lib J ... Canadian Library Journal [*A publication*]
Canad M .... Canadian Magazine [*A publication*]
Canad MAJ ... Canadian Medical Association. Journal [*A publication*]
Canad Med Assoc J ... Canadian Medical Association. Journal [*A publication*]
Can Admin ... Canadian Administrator [*A publication*]
Canad Mo .. Canadian Monthly [*A publication*]
Canad Nurse ... Canadian Nurse [*A publication*]
Canad Person Industr Relat J ... Canadian Personnel and Industrial Relations Journal (Including the Canadian Training Digest) [*A publication*]
Canad Plast ... Canadian Plastics [*A publication*]
Canad Pract ... Canadian Practitioner [*A publication*]
Canad Pract and Rev ... Canadian Practitioner and Review [*A publication*]
Canad Psychiat AJ ... Canadian Psychiatric Association. Journal [*A publication*]
Canad Psychiat Ass J ... Canadian Psychiatric Association. Journal [*A publication*]
Canad Publ Adm ... Canadian Public Administration/Administration Publique du Canada [*A publication*]
Canad R Sociol Anthropol ... Canadian Review of Sociology and Anthropology [*A publication*]
Canad Slavonic Pap ... Canadian Slavonic Papers [*A publication*]
Canad Soc Lab Technol Bull ... Canadian Society of Laboratory Technologists. Bulletin [*A publication*]
Canad Vet Rec ... Canadian Veterinary Record [*A publication*]
Canad Yb Int Law ... Canadian Yearbook of International Law [*A publication*]
Can Aeronaut J ... Canadian Aeronautical Journal [*A publication*]
Can Aeronaut Space Inst Trans ... Canadian Aeronautic and Space Institute. Transactions [*A publication*]
Can Aeronaut Space J ... Canadian Aeronautics and Space Journal [*A publication*]
Can Aeronaut and Space J ... Canadian Aeronautics and Space Journal [*A publication*]
Can Aeron J ... Canadian Aeronautical Journal [*A publication*]
Can Aer Spa ... Canadian Aeronautics and Space Journal [*A publication*]

Can Agr ...... Canadian Agriculture [*A publication*]
Can Agr Eng ... Canadian Agricultural Engineering [*A publication*]
CANAGREX ... Canadian Agricultural Export Corp.
Can Agric ... Canada Agriculture [*A publication*]
Can Agric Eng ... Canadian Agricultural Engineering [*A publication*]
Can Agric Insect Pest Rev ... Canadian Agricultural Insect Pest Review [*A publication*]
CAnaGS ..... Church of Jesus Christ of Latter-Day Saints, Genealogical Society Library, Anaheim Branch, Anaheim, CA [*Library symbol*] [*Library of Congress*] (LCLS)
CAnaI .... Interstate Electronics Corp., Anaheim, CA [*Library symbol*] [*Library of Congress*] (LCLS)
CANAIR .... Air-Cushion Vehicle built by Canadian Cushion Craft [*Canada*] [*Usually used in combination with numerals*]
Can Aircr Ind ... Canadian Aircraft Industries [*A publication*]
CANAIRDEF ... Air Defense Command Headquarters, St. Hubert, Province of Quebec, Canada
CANAIRDIV ... Canadian Air Division Headquarters [*Allied Air Forces in Europe*]
CANAIRFAX ... Maritime Group Headquarters, Halifax, Nova Scotia, Canada
CANAIRHED ... Air Force Headquarters, Ottawa, Ontario, Canada
CANAIRLIFT ... Air Transport Command Headquarters, Rockcliffe, Ontario, Canada
CANAIRLON ... Air Member, Canadian Joint Staff, London, England
CANAIRMAT ... Air Material Command Headquarters, Ottawa, Ontario, Canada
CANAIRNEW ... Senior Royal Canadian Air Force Liaison Officer, St. Johns, Newfoundland, Canada
CANAIRNORWEST ... North-West Air Command Headquarters, Edmonton, Alberta, Canada
CANAIRPEG ... Canadian Fourteenth Air Training Group Headquarters, Winnipeg
CANAIRTAC ... Canadian Tactical Air Command Headquarters
CANAIRTRAIN ... Canadian Air Training Command Headquarters
CANAIRVAN ... Twelfth Air Defense Group Headquarters, Vancouver, British Columbia, Canada
CANAIRWASH ... Air Member, Canadian Joint Staff, Washington, DC
CANAL ..... Command Analysis [*Telecommunications*] (TEL)
CANAL ..... Kanizkar Le'eyl [*As Mentioned Above*] [*Hebrew*]
Can Al J ... Canadian Alpine Journal [*A publication*]
Canal Zone Sup Ct ... Canal Zone Supreme Court Reports [*A publication*] (DLA)
CAN-AM ... Canadian-American Center [*University of Maine at Orono*] [*Research center*] (RCD)
Can-Am Slav ... Canadian-American Slavic Studies [*A publication*]
Can Am Sl Stud ... Canadian-American Slavic Studies [*A publication*]
Can Anae S J ... Canadian Anaesthetists' Society. Journal [*A publication*]
Can Anaesth Soc J ... Canadian Anaesthetists' Society. Journal [*A publication*]
CAnaN-N .. Nortronics Corp., Anaheim, CA [*Library symbol*] [*Library of Congress*] (LCLS)
Can Ant Coll ... Canadian Antiques Collector [*A publication*]
Can App ..... Canadian Reports, Appeal Cases [*1828-1913*] [*A publication*] (DLA)
Can App Cas ... Canadian Appeal Cases [*A publication*] (DLA)
Can Arch .... Canadian Architect [*A publication*]
Can Arch Ybk ... Canadian Architect Yearbook [*A publication*]
Can Arct Land Use Res Prog Rep ... Canada. Arctic Land Use Research Program Report [*A publication*]
Can Art ...... Canadian Art [*A publication*]
CANAS ...... Canadian Naval Air Station
CANATA .. Canada-Australia Trade Agreement
CAnaU .... United States Borax Research Corp., Anaheim, CA [*Library symbol*] [*Library of Congress*] (LCLS)
Can Aud ..... Canadian Audubon [*A publication*]
Can Audubon ... Canadian Audubon [*A publication*]
Can Auth & Book ... Canadian Author and Bookman [*A publication*]
Can Automot Trade ... Canadian Automotive Trade [*A publication*]
Can Av .... Canadian Aviation [*A publication*]
CANAVAT ... Naval Attache [*Canadian Navy*]
CANAVBRIT ... Naval Member, Canadian Joint Staff, London, England
CANAVCHARGE ... Senior Officer [*or Officer in Charge*] at _____ [*Navy*] [*Canada*]
CANAVHED ... Naval Headquarters, Ottawa, ON, Canada
CANAVMODS ... Canadian Naval Modifications
CANAVSTORES ... Naval Stores Officer [*Canadian Navy*]
CANAVUS ... Canadian Member, Canadian Joint Staff, Washington, DC
Canb .... Canberra [*Australia*]
Can BA ...... Canadian Bar Association. Proceedings [*A publication*] (DLA)
CaNBAB .... Canada Department of the Environment, Fisheries and Marine Service, Research and Development Directorate, Biological Station, St. Andrews, NB, Canada [*Library symbol*] [*Library of Congress*] (LCLS)
CaNBACCH ... Charlotte County Historical Society, Inc., St. Andrews, NB, Canada [*Library symbol*] [*Library of Congress*] (LCLS)
Can BAJ .... Canadian Bar Association. Journal [*A publication*] (DLA)
Can Bank ... Canadian Banker [*Formerly, Canadian Banker and ICB Review*] [*A publication*]
Can Banker ... Canadian Banker [*Formerly, Canadian Banker and ICB Review*] [*A publication*]

Can Banker & ICB R ... Canadian Banker and ICB [*Institute of Canadian Bankers*] Review [*Later, Canadian Banker*] [*A publication*]
Can Banker ICB Rev ... Canadian Banker and ICB [*Institute of Canadian Bankers*] Review [*Later, Canadian Banker*] [*A publication*]
Can Bankr ... Canadian Bankruptcy Reports [*A publication*]
Can Bank R ... Canadian Bankruptcy Reports [*A publication*]
Can Bankr Ann ... Canadian Bankruptcy Reports, Annotated [*A publication*] (DLA)
Can Bankr Ann (NS) ... Canadian Bankruptcy Reports, Annotated, New Series [*A publication*] (DLA)
Can Bankr Rep ... Canadian Bankruptcy Reports [*A publication*]
Can Bar AJ ... Journal. Canadian Bar Association [*A publication*]
Can Bar J ... Canadian Bar Journal [*A publication*]
Can Bar J (NS) ... Canadian Bar Journal. New Series [*A publication*]
Can Bar R .. Canadian Bar Review [*A publication*]
Can Bar Rev ... Canadian Bar Review [*A publication*]
Can Bar Year Book ... Year Book. Canadian Bar Association [*A publication*] (DLA)
Can B Ass'n YB ... Canadian Bar Association. Year Book [*A publication*] (DLA)
CaNBBB.... Bathurst College, Bathurst, NB, Canada [*Library symbol*] [*Library of Congress*] (LCLS)
CaNBBCC ... College Communautaire du New Brunswick, Bathurst, NB, Canada [*Library symbol*] [*Library of Congress*] (LCLS)
CANBBE... Curriculum Adaptation Network for Bilingual, Bicultural Education
CaNBBN ... Nepisiguit Library Region, Bathurst, NB, Canada [*Library symbol*] [*Library of Congress*] (LCLS)
CaNBCa .... Campbellton Centennial Public Library, Campbellton, NB, Canada [*Library symbol*] [*Library of Congress*] (LCLS)
CaNBCaC ... Chaleur Library Region, Campbellton, NB, Canada [*Library symbol*] [*Library of Congress*] (LCLS)
CaNBCH ... Historical Society Nicholas Denis, Caraquet, NB, Canada [*Library symbol*] [*Library of Congress*] (LCLS)
Canb Comments ... Canberra Comments [*A publication*] (APTA)
CaNBCS.... Saint Thomas University, Fredericton, NB, Canada [*Library symbol*] [*Library of Congress*] (LCLS)
CaNBCVHA ... Le Village Historique Acadien, Caraquet, NB, Canada [*Library symbol*] [*Library of Congress*] (LCLS)
CaNBEBR ... Bibliotheque Regionale du Haut Saint-Jean, Edmundston, NB, Canada [*Library symbol*] [*Library of Congress*] (LCLS)
CaNBECC ... New Brunswick Community College, Edmundston, NB, Canada [*Library symbol*] [*Library of Congress*] (LCLS)
Can Bee J... Canadian Bee Journal [*A publication*]
Can Beekeep ... Canadian Beekeeping [*A publication*]
Canberra Anthropol ... Canberra Anthropology [*A publication*] (APTA)
Canberra Hist J ... Canberra Historical Journal [*A publication*]
CaNBESLM ... College Saint-Louis-Maillet, Edmundston, NB, Canada [*Library symbol*] [*Library of Congress*] (LCLS)
CaNBFA.... New Brunswick Provincial Archives, Fredericton, NB, Canada [*Library symbol*] [*Library of Congress*] (LCLS)
CaNBFAFA ... Anglican Church of Canada, Diocese of Fredericton, Archives, Fredericton, NB, Canada [*Library symbol*] [*Library of Congress*] (LCLS)
CaNBFAg ... Canada Department of Agriculture, Research Station, Fredericton, NB, Canada [*Library symbol*] [*Library of Congress*] (LCLS)
CaNBFB.... New Brunswick Archives, Beaverbrook Collection, Fredericton, NB, Canada [*Library symbol*] [*Library of Congress*] (LCLS)
CaNBFBS ... New Brunswick Barristers Society, Fredericton, NB, Canada [*Library symbol*] [*Library of Congress*] (LCLS)
CaNBFC.... New Brunswick Library Service, Fredericton, NB, Canada [*Library symbol*] [*Library of Congress*] (LCLS)
CaNBFE.... Canada Department of the Environment, Maritimes Forest Research Centre, Fredericton, NB, Canada [*Library symbol*] [*Library of Congress*] (LCLS)
CaNBFEn.. New Brunswick Department of the Environment, Fredericton, NB, Canada [*Library symbol*] [*Library of Congress*] (LCLS)
CaNBFHR ... New Brunswick Department of Historical Resources, Fredericton, NB, Canada [*Library symbol*] [*Library of Congress*] (LCLS)
CaNBFKL ... Kings Landing Historical Settlement, Fredericton, NB, Canada [*Library symbol*] [*Library of Congress*] (LCLS)
CaNBFL.... New Brunswick Legislative Library, Fredericton, NB, Canada [*Library symbol*] [*Library of Congress*] (LCLS)
CaNBFLM ... New Brunswick Department of Lands and Mines, Photogrammetry Branch, Fredericton, NB, Canada [*Library symbol*] [*Library of Congress*] (LCLS)
CaNBFMA ... New Brunswick Department of Municipal Affairs, Fredericton, NB, Canada [*Library symbol*] [*Library of Congress*] (LCLS)
CaNBFMM ... Medley Memorial Library, Christ Church Cathedral, Fredericton, NB, Canada [*Library symbol*] [*Library of Congress*] (LCLS)
CaNBFP.... New Brunswick Power, Fredericton, NB, Canada [*Library symbol*] [*Library of Congress*] (LCLS)
CaNBFPO ... Province of New Brunswick, Premier's Office, Fredericton, NB, Canada [*Library symbol*] [*Library of Congress*] (LCLS)

CaNBFRP ... New Brunswick Research and Productivity Council, Fredericton, NB, Canada [*Library symbol*] [*Library of Congress*] (LCLS)
CaNBFSS ... New Brunswick Department of Social Services, Fredericton, NB, Canada [*Library symbol*] [*Library of Congress*] (LCLS)
CaNBFU.... University of New Brunswick, Fredericton, NB, Canada [*Library symbol*] [*Library of Congress*] (LCLS)
CaNBFUA ... University of New Brunswick, Archives and Special Collections Department, Fredericton, NB, Canada [*Library symbol*] [*Library of Congress*] (LCLS)
CaNBFUL ... University of New Brunswick, Law Library, Fredericton, NB, Canada [*Library symbol*] [*Library of Congress*] (LCLS)
CaNBFUM ... University of New Brunswick, Government Documents Department, Map Room, Fredericton, NB, Canada [*Library symbol*] [*Library of Congress*] (LCLS)
CaNBFY.... York-Sunbury Historical Society, Fredericton, NB, Canada [*Library symbol*] [*Library of Congress*] (LCLS)
CaNBFYR ... York Regional Library, Fredericton, NB, Canada [*Library symbol*] [*Library of Congress*] (LCLS)
CaNBGACF ... Canadian Forces Base, Gagetown, NB, Canada [*Library symbol*] [*Library of Congress*] (LCLS)
CaNBGfCC ... New Brunswick Community College, Grand Falls Campus, Grand Falls, NB, Canada [*Library symbol*] [*Library of Congress*] (LCLS)
CaNBGfH ... Grand Falls Historical Society, Grand Falls, NB, Canada [*Library symbol*] [*Library of Congress*] (LCLS)
CaNBGG ... Gerrish House Society, Grand Harbour, Grand Manan Island, NB, Canada [*Library symbol*] [*Library of Congress*] (LCLS)
Canb Hist Soc Add ... Canberra and District Historical Society. Addresses [*A publication*] (APTA)
Canb Hist Soc News ... Canberra and District Historical Society. Newsletter [*A publication*] (APTA)
Can B J ...... Canadian Bar Journal [*A publication*]
Can Bkman ... Canadian Bookman [*A publication*]
Canb Letter ... Canberra Letter [*A publication*] (APTA)
CaNBMoCC ... New Brunswick Community College, Moncton, NB, Canada [*Library symbol*] [*Library of Congress*] (LCLS)
CaNBMoM ... Moncton Civic Museum, Moncton, NB, Canada [*Library symbol*] [*Library of Congress*] (LCLS)
CaNBMoRE ... Canada Department of Regional Economic Expansion, Moncton, NB, Canada [*Library symbol*] [*Library of Congress*] (LCLS)
CaNBMoU ... Universite de Moncton, Moncton, NB, Canada [*Library symbol*] [*Library of Congress*] (LCLS)
CaNBMoUA ... Universite de Moncton, Archives Acadiennes, Moncton, NB, Canada [*Library symbol*] [*Library of Congress*] (LCLS)
CaNBMOUD ... Universite de Moncton, Bibliotheque de Droit, Moncton, NB, Canada [*Library symbol*] [*Library of Congress*] (LCLS)
CaNBMoW ... Albert-Westmorland-Kent Regional Library, Moncton, NB, Canada [*Library symbol*] [*Library of Congress*] (LCLS)
CaNBN ...... Old Manse Library, Newcastle, NB, Canada [*Library symbol*] [*Library of Congress*] (LCLS)
CaNBNAM ... Miramichi Historical Society Archives, Newcastle, NB, Canada [*Library symbol*] [*Library of Congress*] (LCLS)
CaNBNdH ... New Denmark Historical Museum, New Denmark, NB, Canada [*Library symbol*] [*Library of Congress*] (LCLS)
CaNBO ...... Oromocto Public Library, Oromocto, NB, Canada [*Library symbol*] [*Library of Congress*] (LCLS)
Can Board Grain Comm Grain Res Lab Annu Rep ... Canada. Board of Grain Commissioners. Grain Research Laboratory. Annual Report [*A publication*]
Can BPI..... Canadian Business Periodicals Index [*Later, Canadian Business Index*] [*A publication*]
Can BR....... Canadian Bar Review [*A publication*]
Can B Rev.. Canadian Bar Review [*A publication*]
CaNBRN ... Nestart Library, Richibucto, NB, Canada [*Library symbol*] [*Library of Congress*] (LCLS)
CaNBS....... Saint John Regional Library, Saint John, NB, Canada [*Library symbol*] [*Library of Congress*] (LCLS)
CaNBSaB .. Fort Beausejour Museum, Sackville, NB, Canada [*Library symbol*] [*Library of Congress*] (LCLS)
CaNBSaCW ... Canada Department of the Environment, Canadian Wildlife Service, Sackville, NB, Canada [*Library symbol*] [*Library of Congress*] (LCLS)
CaNBSaM ... Mount Allison University, Sackville, NB, Canada [*Library symbol*] [*Library of Congress*] (LCLS)
CaNBSCU ... Centre Universitaire de Shippagan, Shippagan, NB, Canada [*Library symbol*] [*Library of Congress*] (LCLS)
CaNBShCM ... Centre Marin, Shippagan, NB, Canada [*Library symbol*] [*Library of Congress*] (LCLS)
CaNBSM ... New Brunswick Museum, Saint John, NB, Canada [*Library symbol*] [*Library of Congress*] (LCLS)
CaNBSU.... University of New Brunswick in Saint John, Saint John, NB, Canada [*Library symbol*] [*Library of Congress*] (LCLS)
CaNBSuH ... Kings County Historical Society, Sussex, NB, Canada [*Library symbol*] [*Library of Congress*] (LCLS)
Canb Survey ... Canberra Survey [*A publication*] (APTA)
CaNBSVS ... Saint John Vocational School, Saint John, NB, Canada [*Library symbol*] [*Library of Congress*] (LCLS)

Can Build Dig ... Canadian Building Digest [*A publication*]
Can Bull Fish Aquat Sci ... Canadian Bulletin of Fisheries and Aquatic Sciences [*A publication*]
Can Bull Nutr ... Canadian Bulletin on Nutrition [*A publication*]
Canb Univ Col Gaz ... Canberra University College. Gazette [*A publication*]   (APTA)
Canb Univ Coll Gaz ... Canberra University College. Gazette [*A publication*]   (APTA)
Can Bus...... Canadian Business [*A publication*]
Can Bus Econ ... Canadian Business Economics [*A publication*]
Can Bus Index ... Canadian Business Index [*A publication*]
Can Bus LJ ... Canadian Business Law Journal [*A publication*]
Can Bus Mag ... Canadian Business Magazine [*A publication*]
Can Bus Period Index ... Canadian Business Periodicals Index [*A publication*]
Can Bus R ... Canadian Business Review [*A publication*]
Can Bus Rev ... Canadian Business Review [*A publication*]
Canb Viewpoint ... Canberra Viewpoint [*A publication*]   (APTA)
CaNBW ..... Woodstock Public (Fisher Memorial) Library, Woodstock, NB, Canada [*Library symbol*] [*Library of Congress*]   (LCLS)
Canb Weekly ... Canberra Weekly [*A publication*]   (APTA)
CaNBWV .. Victoria-Carleton Courthouse, Woodstock, NB, Canada [*Library symbol*] [*Library of Congress*]   (LCLS)
CaNBWY .. York Regional Library Headquarters No. 2, Woodstock, NB, Canada [*Library symbol*] [*Library of Congress*]   (LCLS)
Can B Year Book ... Canadian Bar Association. Year Book [*A publication*]
CANC........ Canceled
CANC........ Cancellation
Canc .... Cancer [*Constellation*]
Can C .... Canoniste Contemporain [*A publication*]
CANC........ Cuban American National Council   (EA)
CANCAM Proc Can Congr Appl Mech ... CANCAM Proceedings. Canadian Congress of Applied Mechanics [*A publication*]
Can Cancer Conf ... Canadian Cancer Conference [*A publication*]
CANCARAIRGRP ... Carrier Air Group [*Canadian military*]
Can Cartogr ... Canadian Cartographer [*A publication*]
CANCAS Coll Acad NC Acad Sci ... CANCAS. Collegiate Academy of the North Carolina Academy of Sciences [*A publication*]
Can Cases L Torts ... Canadian Cases on the Law of Torts [*A publication*]
CAN/CAT ... Canadiana/Cataloguing Subsystem
Can Cattlemen ... Canadian Cattlemen [*A publication*]
Canc Bioc B ... Cancer Biochemistry - Biophysics [*A publication*]
Canc Bull ... Cancer Bulletin [*A publication*]
Can CC...... Canada Criminal Cases, Annotated [*A publication*]   (DLA)
Can CC...... Canadian Criminal Cases [*A publication*]
Canc Chemoth Abstr ... Cancer Chemotherapy Abstracts [*A publication*]
Canc Chemother Rep ... Cancer Chemotherapy Reports [*A publication*]
Canc Chemother Rep Suppl ... Cancer Chemotherapy Reports. Supplement [*A publication*]
Canc Ch P 1 ... Cancer Chemotherapy Reports. Part 1 [*A publication*]
Canc Ch P 2 ... Cancer Chemotherapy Reports. Part 2 [*A publication*]
Canc Ch P 3 ... Cancer Chemotherapy Reports. Part 3 [*A publication*]
Canc Curr Lit Ind ... Cancer Current Literature Index [*A publication*]
Canc Drug D ... Cancer Drug Delivery [*A publication*]
Canc Drug Del ... Cancer Drug Delivery [*A publication*]
CANCEE... Canadian National Committee for Earthquake Engineering
Can Cem Concr Rev ... Canadian Cement and Concrete Review [*A publication*]
Can Cent Miner Energy Technol Publ ... Canada. Centre for Mineral and Energy Technology. Publications [*A publication*]
Can Cent Miner Energy Technol Sci Bull ... Canada. Centre for Mineral and Energy Technology. Scientific Bulletin [*A publication*]
Can Cent Ser ... Canadian Centenary Series [*A publication*]
Can Cent Terminol Bull Terminol ... Canada. Centre de Terminologie. Bulletin de Terminologie [*A publication*]
Cancer Biochem Biophys ... Cancer Biochemistry - Biophysics [*A publication*]
Cancer Bull ... Cancer Bulletin [*A publication*]
Cancer Chemother Pharmacol ... Cancer Chemotherapy and Pharmacology [*A publication*]
Cancer Chemother Rep ... Cancer Chemotherapy Reports [*A publication*]
Cancer Chemother Rep Part 1 ... Cancer Chemotherapy Reports. Part 1 [*A publication*]
Cancer Chemother Rep Part 2 ... Cancer Chemotherapy Reports. Part 2 [*A publication*]
Cancer Chemother Rep Part 3 ... Cancer Chemotherapy Reports. Part 3 [*A publication*]
Cancer Chemother Screening Data ... Cancer Chemotherapy Screening Data [*A publication*]
Cancer Chem Rep ... Cancer Chemotherapy Reports [*A publication*]
Cancer Clin Trials ... Cancer Clinical Trials [*A publication*]
Cancer Cytol ... Cancer Cytology [*A publication*]
Cancer Detect Prev ... Cancer Detection and Prevention [*A publication*]
Cancer Drug Deliv ... Cancer Drug Delivery [*A publication*]
Cancer Genet Cytogenet ... Cancer Genetics and Cytogenetics [*A publication*]
Cancer Immunol Immunother ... Cancer Immunology and Immunotherapy [*A publication*]
Cancer Invest ... Cancer Investigation [*A publication*]
Cancer Lett ... Cancer Letters [*A publication*]
CANCERLIT ... Cancer Literature [*National Cancer Institute*] [*Information service or system*]
Cancer Metastasis Rev ... Cancer and Metastasis Reviews [*A publication*]
Cancer Nurs ... Cancer Nursing [*A publication*]

Cancer Progr ... Cancer Progress [*A publication*]
CANCERPROJ ... Cancer Research Projects [*National Cancer Intitute*] [*Information service or system*] [*Defunct*]
Cancer Rehabil ... Cancer Rehabilitation [*A publication*]
Cancer Res ... Cancer Research [*A publication*]
Cancer Res Clin Oncol ... Cancer Research and Clinical Oncology [*A publication*]
Cancer Res Inst Slovak Acad Sci Annu Rep ... Cancer Research Institute. Slovak Academy of Sciences. Annual Report [*A publication*]
Cancer Res Suppl ... Cancer Research. Supplement [*A publication*]
Cancer Semin ... Cancer Seminar [*A publication*]
Cancer Suppl ... Cancer Supplement [*A publication*]
Cancer Surv ... Cancer Surveys [*A publication*]
Cancer T R ... Cancer Treatment Reviews [*A publication*]
Cancer Treat Rep ... Cancer Treatment Reports [*A publication*]
Cancer Treat Rev ... Cancer Treatment Reviews [*A publication*]
Cancer Treat Symp ... Cancer Treatment Symposia [*A publication*]
C Anc H ..... Cambridge Ancient History [*A publication*]
CAN Charlie Chan ... Coalition of Asians to Nix Charlie Chan   (EA)
Can Chart Acc ... Canadian Chartered Accountant [*Later, CA Magazine*] [*A publication*]
Can Chart Account ... Canadian Chartered Accountant [*Later, CA Magazine*] [*A publication*]
Can Chart Acct ... Canadian Chartered Accountant [*Later, CA Magazine*] [*A publication*]
Can Chem Educ ... Canadian Chemical Education [*A publication*]
Can Chem J ... Canadian Chemical Journal [*A publication*]
Can Chem J ... Cancer Chemical Journal [*A publication*]
Can Chem Met ... Canadian Chemistry and Metallurgy [*A publication*]
Can Chem & Met ... Canadian Chemistry and Metallurgy [*A publication*]
Can Chem Metall ... Canadian Chemistry and Metallurgy [*A publication*]
Can Chem News ... Canadian Chemical News [*A publication*]
Can Chem Proc ... Canadian Chemical Processing [*A publication*]
Can Chem Process ... Canadian Chemical Processing [*A publication*]
Can Chem Process ... Canadian Chemistry and Process Industry [*A publication*]
Can Chem & Process Ind ... Canadian Chemistry and Process Industries [*A publication*]
Can Child Lit ... Canadian Children's Literature [*A publication*]
CANC INSTR ... Cancellation of Instruments [*Legal term*]   (DLA)
CANCIRCO ... Cancer International Research Cooperative
Can CL...... Canadian Current Law [*A publication*]
CANCL...... Canceling   (DCTA)
Can Clay Ceram Q ... Canadian Clay and Ceramics Quarterly [*A publication*]
CANCLG... Canceling
CANCLN .. Cancellation   (ROG)
Canc NJ ... Cancer News Journal [*A publication*]
Can Collector ... Canadian Collector [*A publication*]
Can Color Text Process ... Canadian Colorist and Textile Processor [*A publication*]
CANCOM ... Canadian Satellite Communications, Inc. [*Mississauga, ON*] [*Telecommunications*]   (TSSD)
CANCOMARLANT ... Canadian Maritime Commander, Atlantic   (NATG)
CANCOMARPAC ... Canadian Commander, Army, Pacific   (CINC)
Can Com Cas ... Canadian Commercial Law Reports [*1901-05*] [*A publication*]   (DLA)
CANCOMDESFE ... Commander, Canadian Destroyers, Far East
CANCOMDESFLOT 1 ... Commander, First Canadian Destroyer Flotilla
CANCOMDESLANT ... Commander, Canadian Destroyers, Atlantic
CANCOMDESPAC ... Commander, Canadian Destroyers, Pacific
CANCOMFLT ... Senior Officer Afloat [*Navy*] [*Canada*]
CANCOMFLTLANT ... Senior Officer Afloat Atlantic [*Navy*] [*Canada*]
CANCOMFLTPAC ... Senior Officer Afloat Pacific [*Navy*] [*Canada*]
Can Com L Guide (CCH) ... Canadian Commercial Law Guide (Commerce Clearing House) [*A publication*]   (DLA)
Can Com LJ ... Canadian Community Law Journal [*A publication*]   (DLA)
Can Com LR ... Canadian Commercial Law Reports [*1901-05*] [*A publication*]   (DLA)
Can Com L Rev ... Canadian Communications Law Review [*A publication*]   (DLA)
Can Commer ... Canada Commerce [*A publication*]
Can Commerce ... Canada Commerce [*A publication*]
Can Community LJ ... Canadian Community Law Journal [*A publication*]
Can Commun Power Conf Proc ... Canadian Communications and Power Conference. Proceedings [*A publication*]
CANCOMNEW ... Canadian Naval Commander Newfoundland
Can Comp .. Canadian Composer [*A publication*]
Can Competition Pol ... Canadian Competition Policy Record [*A publication*]
Can Composer ... Canadian Composer [*A publication*]
Can Com R ... Canadian Commercial Law Reports [*1901-05*] [*A publication*]   (DLA)
CANCON ... Canadian Control System [*For convoys in Canadian Coastal Zone*]
Can Cons Regs ... Consolidated Regulations of Canada [*A publication*]
Can Consult Eng ... Canadian Consulting Engineer [*A publication*]
Can Consum ... Canadian Consumer [*A publication*]
Can Consumer ... Canadian Consumer [*A publication*]
Can Contract Rep Hydrogr Ocean Sci ... Canadian Contractor Report of Hydrography and Ocean Sciences [*A publication*]

Can Controls & Instrum ... Canadian Controls and Instrumentation [*A publication*]
Can Controls Instrum ... Canadian Controls and Instrumentation [*A publication*]
Can Controls Instruments ... Canadian Controls and Instruments [*A publication*]
Can Copper ... Canadian Copper [*A publication*]
CanCorp..... Canadian Corporations [*Micromedia Ltd.*] [*Canada*] [*Information service or system*] (CRD)
Can Couns/Cons Can ... Canadian Counsellor/Conseiller Canadien [*A publication*]
Can Cr Acts ... Canada Criminal Acts, Taschereau's Edition [*A publication*] (DLA)
Can Crafts ... Canada Crafts [*A publication*]
Can Cr Cas ... Canadian Criminal Cases [*A publication*] (DLA)
Canc Res.... Cancer Research [*A publication*]
Canc Res Campaign Annu Rep ... Cancer Research Campaign. Annual Report [*A publication*]
Canc Res Inst Slovak Acad Annu Rep ... Cancer Research Institute. Slovak Academy of Sciences. Annual Report [*A publication*]
Canc Rev.... Cancer Review [*A publication*]
Can Crim.... Criminal Reports (Canada) [*A publication*]
Can Crim Cas ... Canadian Criminal Cases, Annotated [*A publication*] (DLA)
Can Crim Cas Ann ... Canadian Criminal Cases, Annotated [*A publication*] (DLA)
Can Crim Cas (NS) ... Canadian Criminal Cases, New Series [*A publication*] (DLA)
Can Crit Care Nurs J ... Canadian Critical Care Nursing Journal [*A publication*]
Can Cr R.... Canadian Criminal Reports [*A publication*] (DLA)
CAN/CRS ... Canadian Computer-Based Reference Service [*National Library of Canada*] [*Information service or system*] (IID)
Can CS....... Cour Supreme du Canada [*Supreme Court of Canada*] (DLA)
CAND........ Candidate (AFM)
CAND........ Cantate Domino [*Sing Unto the Lord*] [*Music*]
Can Dairy Ice Cream J ... Canadian Dairy and Ice Cream Journal [*A publication*]
Can Data.... Canadian Datasystems [*A publication*]
Can Data Rep Hydrogr Ocean Sci ... Canadian Data Report of Hydrography and Ocean Sciences [*A publication*]
Can Datasyst ... Canadian Datasystems [*A publication*]
CANDE..... Command and Edit Program [*Burroughs Corp.*] [*Data processing*] (BUR)
CANDE..... Communications and Electronics [*SHAPE*] (MCD)
Can Dent Hyg ... Canadian Dental Hygienist [*A publication*]
CANDEP... Royal Canadian Navy Depot
Can Dep Agric Annu Rep ... Canada. Department of Agriculture. Annual Report [*A publication*]
Can Dep Agric Bull ... Canada. Department of Agriculture. Bulletin [*A publication*]
Can Dep Agric Circ ... Canada. Department of Agriculture. Circular [*A publication*]
Can Dep Agric Farmers Bull ... Canada. Department of Agriculture. Farmers' Bulletin [*A publication*]
Can Dep Agric Plant Res Inst Agro-Meteorol Sect Tech Bull ... Canada. Department of Agriculture. Plant Research Institute. Agrometeorology Section. Technical Bulletin [*A publication*]
Can Dep Agric Publ ... Canada. Department of Agriculture. Publication [*A publication*]
Can Dep Agric Res Branch Monogr ... Canada. Department of Agriculture. Research Branch Monograph [*A publication*]
Can Dep Agric Res Branch Rep ... Canada. Department of Agriculture. Research Branch Report [*A publication*]
Can Dep Agric Tech Bull ... Canada. Department of Agriculture. Technical Bulletin [*A publication*]
Can Dep Energy Mines Resources Earth Phys Br Mem ... Canada. Department of Energy, Mines, and Resources. Earth Physics Branch. Memoir [*A publication*]
Can Dep Energy Mines Resources Earth Phys Br Mineral Rep ... Canada. Department of Energy, Mines, and Resources. Earth Physics Branch. Mineral Report [*A publication*]
Can Dep Energy Mines Resources Earth Sci Br Inform Circ ... Canada. Department of Energy, Mines, and Resources. Earth Science Branch. Information Circular [*A publication*]
Can Dep Energy Mines Resources Rep ... Canada. Department of Energy, Mines, and Resources. Report [*A publication*]
Can Dep Environ Can For Ser North For Res Cent Inf Rep ... Canada. Department of the Environment. Canadian Forestry Service. Northern Forest Research Centre. Information Report [*A publication*]
Can Dep Environ Mar Sci Dir Manuscr Rep Ser ... Canada. Department of the Environment. Marine Sciences Directorate. Manuscript Report Series [*A publication*]
Can Dep Fish Annu Rep ... Canada. Department of Fisheries. Annual Report [*A publication*]
Can Dep Fish For Annu Rep ... Canada. Department of Fisheries and Forestry. Annual Report [*A publication*]
Can Dep Fish For Bimon Res Notes ... Canada. Department of Fisheries and Forestry. Bimonthly Research Notes [*A publication*]

Can Dep Fish For Can For Ser Inf Rep ... Canada. Department of Fisheries and Forestry. Canadian Forestry Service. Information Report [*A publication*]
Can Dep Fish For Can For Serv Inf Rep FF-X ... Canada. Department of Fisheries and Forestry. Canadian Forestry Service. Information Report FF-X [*A publication*]
Can Dep Fish For Can For Serv Publ ... Canada. Department of Fisheries and Forestry. Canadian Forestry Service. Publication [*A publication*]
Can Dep Fish For For Branch Dep Publ ... Canada. Department of Fisheries and Forestry. Forestry Branch Departmental Publication [*A publication*]
Can Dep For For Entomol Pathol Branch Bi-Mon Prog Rep ... Canada. Department of Forestry. Forest Entomology and Pathology Branch. Bi-Monthly Progress Report [*A publication*]
Can Dep For Rural Dev Annu Rep ... Canada. Department of Forestry and Rural Development. Annual Report [*A publication*]
Can Dep For Rural Dev Annu Rep For Insect Dis Surv ... Canada. Department of Forestry and Rural Development. Annual Report. Forest Insect and Disease Survey [*A publication*]
Can Dep For Rural Dev Bi-Mon Res Notes ... Canada. Department of Forestry and Rural Development. Bi-Monthly Research Notes [*A publication*]
Can Dep For Rural Dev For Branch Dep Publ ... Canada. Department of Forestry and Rural Development. Forestry Branch. Department Publication [*A publication*]
Can Dep For Rural Dev For Branch Inf Rep FF-X ... Canada. Department of Forestry and Rural Development. Forestry Branch. Information Report FF-X [*A publication*]
Can Dep Indian North Aff Arct Land Use Res Program Rep ALUR ... Canada. Department of Indian and Northern Affairs. Arctic Land Use Research Program. Report ALUR [*A publication*]
Can Dept Forestry Bimo Res Note ... Canada. Department of Fisheries and Forestry. Bimonthly Research Notes [*A publication*]
Can Dept Forestry Disease Surv ... Canada. Department of Fisheries and Forestry. Annual Report of the Forest Insect and Disease Survey [*A publication*]
Can Dept Forestry Publ ... Canada. Department of Fisheries and Forestry. Departmental Publications [*A publication*]
Can Dept Forestry Res News ... Canada. Department of Fisheries and Forestry. Research News [*A publication*]
CANDESFE ... Canadian Destroyers Far East
CANDESFLOT 1 ... First Canadian Destroyer Flotilla
CANDESLANT ... Canadian Destroyers Atlantic
CANDESPAC ... Canadian Destroyers Pacific
CANDESRON 4 ... Fourth Canadian Destroyer Squadron [*Canadian Navy*]
Candid........ Candid Quarterly Review of Public Affairs [*A publication*]
CANDIDE ... Canadian Disaggregated Interdepartmental Economic Model
Can Dimen ... Canadian Dimension [*A publication*]
CANDIS.... Canadian Disarmament Information Service
Cand J St ... Canadian Journal of Statistics [*A publication*]
CANDLES ... Children of Auschwitz - Nazis' Deadly Lab Experiments Survivors [*Acronym is used as name of associaton*] (EA)
CANDN..... Canadian
CANDO..... Canaveral District Office [*Obsolete*] [*NASA*] (KSC)
CAN DO.... Computer Analyzed Newspaper Data On-Line [*Newspaper Advertising Bureau, Inc.*] [*Information service or system*] (IID)
CAN DO.... Consolidated Accelerated Navy Documentation Organization
Can Doct.... Canadian Doctor [*A publication*]
Cand Pharm ... Candidate of Pharmacy
Can Dp Interior Rp Chief Astronomer ... Canada. Department of the Interior. Report of the Chief Astronomer [*A publication*]
Can Dp Interior Sup Mines Rp ... Canada. Department of the Interior. Superintendent of Mines. Report [*A publication*]
Can DQ...... Canadian Defence Quarterly [*A publication*]
CANDR..... Construction and Repair [*Military*]
CANDR..... Convoy and Routing [*Section*] [*US Fleet*]
Can Drug ... Canadian Druggist [*A publication*]
Cand Techn Sci ... Candidate of Technical Science
CANDU..... Canadian Deuterium Uranium [*Family of nuclear reactors developed in Canada*]
CANDU BLW ... Canadian Deuterium Uranium Boiling Light-Water [*Nuclear reactor*]
CANDU PHW ... Canadian Natural Deuterium Uranium Pressurized Heavy-Water [*Nuclear reactor*]
CANDY..... Cigarette Advertising Normally Directed to Youth [*Student legal action organization*]
CANDY..... Continuously Advertised Nutritionally Deficient Yummies [*In cookbook title, "The Taming of the CANDY Monster"*]
Candy........ Printed Judgments of Sind, by Candy and Birdwood [*India*] [*A publication*] (DLA)
Can Dyer Color User ... Canadian Dyer and Color User [*A publication*]
Candy Ind .. Candy and Snack Industry [*A publication*]
Candy Ind Confect J ... Candy Industry and Confectioners Journal [*A publication*]
Candy MC ... Candy. Mayor's Court Practice [*1879*] [*A publication*] (DLA)
Candy Snack Ind ... Candy and Snack Industry [*A publication*]
CANE........ Cahier d'Archeologie du Nordest [*A publication*]
CANE........ Cationic Asphalt-Neoprene Emulsion [*Dust control*]
CANE........ Computer-Aided Navigation Equipment (MCD)

CANE .... Connecticut Aircraft Nuclear Experiment　(NRCH)
Can Earth Phys Branch Publ ... Canada. Earth Physics Branch. Publications [*A publication*]
CanEdI....... Canadian Education Index [*Repertoire Canadien sur l'Education*] [*A publication*]
Can Ed Res Digest ... Canadian Education and Research Digest [*A publication*]
Can Educ Index ... Canadian Education Index [*A publication*]
Can Educ Res Dig ... Canadian Education and Research Digest [*A publication*]
Cane Growers Q Bul ... Cane Growers Quarterly Bulletin [*A publication*]　(APTA)
Cane Grow Q Bull ... Cane Growers Quarterly Bulletin [*A publication*]
Cane Gr Quart Bull ... Cane Growers Quarterly Bulletin [*A publication*]　(APTA)
Cane & L .... Cane and Leigh. Crown Cases Reserved [*England*] [*A publication*]　(DLA)
CANEL...... Connecticut Advanced Nuclear Engineering Laboratory
Can Electr Assoc Trans Eng Oper Div ... Canadian Electrical Association. Transactions of the Engineering and Operating Division [*A publication*]
Can Electr Eng J ... Canadian Electrical Engineering Journal [*A publication*]
Can Electron Eng ... Canadian Electronics Engineering [*A publication*]
Can Energy News ... Canadian Energy News [*A publication*]
Can Eng ... Canadian Engineer [*A publication*]
Can Ent ...... Canadian Entomologist [*A publication*]
Can Entm ... Canadian Entomologist [*A publication*]
Can Entom ... Canadian Entomologist [*A publication*]
Can Entomol ... Canadian Entomologist [*A publication*]
Can Environ ... Canadian Environment [*A publication*]
Can Environ Law News ... Canadian Environmental Law News [*A publication*]
Can Environ LN ... Canadian Environmental Law News [*A publication*]　(DLA)
Can Environ Prot Serv Econ Tech Rev Rep ... Canada. Environmental Protection Service. Economic and Technical Review Report [*A publication*]
Can Environ Prot Serv Technol Dev Rep ... Canada. Environmental Protection Service. Technology Development Report [*A publication*]
Can Env L News ... Canadian Environmental Law News [*A publication*]　(DLA)
CANES...... Corpus of Ancient Near Eastern Seals in North American Collections [*Washington, DC*]　(BJA)
Can Essay Lit Index ... Canadian Essay and Literature Index [*A publication*]
Can Ethnic Stud ... Canadian Ethnic Studies [*A publication*]
Can Ethnic Studies ... Canadian Ethnic Studies [*A publication*]
CANEW .... Canewdon [*England*]
CANEWS ... Canadian Naval Electronic Warfare System
Can Ex ...... Canada Law Reports, Exchequer Court [*A publication*]　(DLA)
CANEX ..... Canadian Forces Exchange [*Military*]
Can Exch ... Canada Law Reports, Exchequer Court [*A publication*]　(DLA)
Can Ex CR ... Canada Law Reports, Exchequer Court [*A publication*]　(DLA)
Can Ex R.... Canada Law Reports, Exchequer Court [*A publication*]　(DLA)
Can F.......... Canadian Forum [*A publication*]
CANF .... Combined Account Number File [*IRS*]
CANF .... Combined Allied Naval Forces
CANF .... Cuban American National Foundation　(EA)
CaNfAC..... Arnolds Cove Public Library, Arnolds Cove, NF, Canada [*Library symbol*] [*Library of Congress*]　(LCLS)
Can Fam Physician ... Canadian Family Physician [*A publication*]
Can Farm Ec ... Canadian Farm Economics [*A publication*]
Can Farm Econ ... Canadian Farm Economics [*A publication*]
CaNfBI ...... Bell Island Public Library, Bell Island, NF, Canada [*Library symbol*] [*Library of Congress*]　(LCLS)
CaNfBo ...... Bonavista Public Library, Bonavista, NF, Canada [*Library symbol*] [*Library of Congress*]　(LCLS)
CaNfBot..... Botwood Public Library, Botwood, NF, Canada [*Library symbol*] [*Library of Congress*]　(LCLS)
CaNfBQ..... Rural District Memorial Library, Badgers Quay, NF, Canada [*Library symbol*] [*Library of Congress*]　(LCLS)
CaNfBR ..... Bay Roberts Public Library, Bay Roberts, NF, Canada [*Library symbol*] [*Library of Congress*]　(LCLS)
CaNfBri ..... Brigus Public Library, Brigus, NF, Canada [*Library symbol*] [*Library of Congress*]　(LCLS)
CaNfBu...... Buchans Public Library, Buchans, NF, Canada [*Library symbol*] [*Library of Congress*]　(LCLS)
CaNfBuri ... Burin Public Library, Burin, NF, Canada [*Library symbol*] [*Library of Congress*]　(LCLS)
CaNfBV ..... Baie Verte Public Library, Baie Verte, NF, Canada [*Library symbol*] [*Library of Congress*]　(LCLS)
CaNfC........ Carbonear Public Library, Carbonear, NF, Canada [*Library symbol*] [*Library of Congress*]　(LCLS)
Can FC....... Federal Court of Canada [*A publication*]　(DLA)
CaNfCa...... Carmanville Public Library, Carmanville, NF, Canada [*Library symbol*] [*Library of Congress*]　(LCLS)
CaNfCat..... Joseph E. Clouter Memorial Library, Catalina, NF, Canada [*Library symbol*] [*Library of Congress*]　(LCLS)
CaNfCB ..... Corner Brook City Library, Corner Brook, NF, Canada [*Library symbol*] [*Library of Congress*]　(LCLS)

CaNfCBM ... Memorial University Regional College at Corner Brook, Corner Brook, NF, Canada [*Library symbol*] [*Library of Congress*]　(LCLS)
CaNfCBr.... Regional Library, Corner Brook, NF, Canada [*Library symbol*] [*Library of Congress*]　(LCLS)
CaNfCBrW ... Western Memorial Hospital, Corner Brook, NF, Canada [*Library symbol*] [*Library of Congress*]　(LCLS)
CaNfCe ...... Centreville Public Library, Centreville, NF, Canada [*Library symbol*] [*Library of Congress*]　(LCLS)
CaNfCF ..... Churchill Falls Public Library, Churchill Falls, NF, Canada [*Library symbol*] [*Library of Congress*]　(LCLS)
CaNfCGH ... Carbonear General Hospital, Carbonear, NF, Canada [*Library symbol*] [*Library of Congress*]　(LCLS)
CaNfCH .... Cow Head Public Library, Cow Head, NF, Canada [*Library symbol*] [*Library of Congress*]　(LCLS)
CaNfCI ...... Changes Islands Public Library, Changes Islands, NF, Canada [*Library symbol*] [*Library of Congress*]　(LCLS)
CaNfCl....... Clarenville Public Library, Clarenville, NF, Canada [*Library symbol*] [*Library of Congress*]　(LCLS)
CaNfCo...... Cormack Public Library, Cormack, NF, Canada [*Library symbol*] [*Library of Congress*]　(LCLS)
CaNfCP ..... Channel/Port Aux Basques Public Library, Channel/Port Aux Basques, NF, Canada [*Library symbol*] [*Library of Congress*]　(LCLS)
Can FCR .... Canada Federal Court Reports [*A publication*]　(DLA)
CaNfDC..... Dark Cove Public Library, Dark Cove, NF, Canada [*Library symbol*] [*Library of Congress*]　(LCLS)
CaNfDH .... Daniels Harbour Public Library, Daniels Harbour, NF, Canada [*Library symbol*] [*Library of Congress*]　(LCLS)
Can Fd J .... Canadian Food Journal [*A publication*]
CaNfDL..... Deer Lake Public Library, Deer Lake, NF, Canada [*Library symbol*] [*Library of Congress*]　(LCLS)
Can Fed Biol Soc Proc ... Canadian Federation of Biological Societies. Proceedings [*A publication*]
Can Feed Grain J ... Canadian Feed and Grain Journal [*A publication*]
CaNfF .... Fogo Public Library, Fogo, NF, Canada [*Library symbol*] [*Library of Congress*]　(LCLS)
CaNfFH..... Fox Harbour Public Library, Fox Harbour, NF, Canada [*Library symbol*] [*Library of Congress*]　(LCLS)
CaNfFo ...... Fortune Public Library, Fortune, NF, Canada [*Library symbol*] [*Library of Congress*]　(LCLS)
CaNfFr....... Freshwater Public Library, Freshwater, NF, Canada [*Library symbol*] [*Library of Congress*]　(LCLS)
CaNfG........ Gander Public Library, Gander, NF, Canada [*Library symbol*] [*Library of Congress*]　(LCLS)
CaNfGa...... Garnish Public Library, Garnish, NF, Canada [*Library symbol*] [*Library of Congress*]　(LCLS)
CaNfGB .... Grand Bank Public Library, Grand Bank, NF, Canada [*Library symbol*] [*Library of Congress*]　(LCLS)
CaNfGfC.... Central Region Libraries, Grand Falls, NF, Canada [*Library symbol*] [*Library of Congress*]　(LCLS)
CaNfGfH ... Central Newfoundland Hospital, Grand Falls, NF, Canada [*Library symbol*] [*Library of Congress*]　(LCLS)
CaNfGfHa ... Harmsworth Public Library, Grand Falls, NF, Canada [*Library symbol*] [*Library of Congress*]　(LCLS)
CaNfGJPH ... James Paton Memorial Hospital, Gander, NF, Canada [*Library symbol*] [*Library of Congress*]　(LCLS)
CaNfGl ...... Glenwood Public Library, Glenwood, NF, Canada [*Library symbol*] [*Library of Congress*]　(LCLS)
CaNfGlo .... Glovertown Public Library, Glovertown, NF, Canada [*Library symbol*] [*Library of Congress*]　(LCLS)
CaNfGr...... Greenspond Public Library, Greenspond, NF, Canada [*Library symbol*] [*Library of Congress*]　(LCLS)
CaNfHB..... Harbour Breton Public Library, Harbour Breton, NF, Canada [*Library symbol*] [*Library of Congress*]　(LCLS)
CaNfHBa.... Hare Bay Public Library, Hare Bay, NF, Canada [*Library symbol*] [*Library of Congress*]　(LCLS)
CaNfHe ..... Hermitage Public Library, Hermitage, NF, Canada [*Library symbol*] [*Library of Congress*]　(LCLS)
CaNfHG .... Harbour Grace Public Library, Harbour Grace, NF, Canada [*Library symbol*] [*Library of Congress*]　(LCLS)
CaNfHH .... Harrys Harbour Public Library, Harrys Harbour, NF, Canada [*Library symbol*] [*Library of Congress*]　(LCLS)
CaNfHV .... Happy Valley Public Library, Happy Valley, NF, Canada [*Library symbol*] [*Library of Congress*]　(LCLS)
Can Fic Mag ... Canadian Fiction Magazine [*A publication*]
Can Fi Cu... Canadian Fish Culturist [*A publication*]
Can Field-Nat ... Canadian Field-Naturalist [*A publication*]
Can Field-Natur ... Canadian Field-Naturalist [*A publication*]
Can Fie Nat ... Canadian Field-Naturalist [*A publication*]
Can Fish Cult ... Canadian Fish Culturist [*A publication*]
Can Fisherm ... Canadian Fisherman [*A publication*]
Can Fisherman ... Canadian Fisherman [*A publication*]
Can Fish Mar Serv Data Rep Ser Cen-D ... Canada. Fisheries and Marine Service. Data Report. Series Cen-D [*A publication*]
Can Fish Mar Serv Ind Rep ... Canada. Fisheries and Marine Service. Industry Report [*A publication*]
Can Fish Mar Serv Manuscr Rep ... Canada. Fisheries and Marine Service. Manuscript Report [*A publication*]
Can Fish Mar Serv Misc Spec Publ ... Canada. Fisheries and Marine Service. Miscellaneous Special Publication [*A publication*]

Can Fish Mar Serv Resour Branch Marit Reg Inf Publ MAR-N ... Canada. Fisheries and Marine Service Resource Branch. Maritimes Region. Information Publication MAR-N [*A publication*]

Can Fish Mar Serv Resour Dev Branch Halifax Prog Rep ... Canada. Fisheries and Marine Service Resource Development Branch. Halifax Progress Report [*A publication*]

Can Fish Mar Serv Resour Dev Branch Marit Reg Rep ... Canada. Fisheries and Marine Service Resource Development Branch. Maritimes Region. Report [*A publication*]

Can Fish Mar Serv Tech Rep ... Canada. Fisheries and Marine Service. Technical Report [*A publication*]

Can Fish Mar Serv Tech Rep Ser Cen-T ... Canada. Fisheries and Marine Service. Technical Report. Series Cen-T [*A publication*]

Can Fish Rep ... Canadian Fisheries Reports [*A publication*]

Can Fish Serv Resour Dev Branch Halifax Prog Rep ... Canada. Fisheries Service. Resource Development Branch. Halifax Progress Report [*A publication*]

CaNfKP ..... Kings Point Public Library, Kings Point, NF, Canada [*Library symbol*] [*Library of Congress*]   (LCLS)

CaNfL .... Labrador City Regional Library, Labrador City, NF, Canada [*Library symbol*] [*Library of Congress*]   (LCLS)

CaNfLa ...... L'Anse Au Loup Public Library, L'Anse Au Loup, NF, Canada [*Library symbol*] [*Library of Congress*]   (LCLS)

CANFLAGLANT ... Flag Officer, Atlantic Coast [*Canada*]

CANFLAGPAC ... Flag Officer, Pacific Coast [*Canada*]

Can Fld Nat ... Canadian Field-Naturalist [*A publication*]

CaNfLe ...... Lewisporte Public Library, Lewisporte, NF, Canada [*Library symbol*] [*Library of Congress*]   (LCLS)

CaNfLHB .. Blow Me Down School/Public Library, Lark Harbour, NF, Canada [*Library symbol*] [*Library of Congress*]   (LCLS)

CaNfLIO ... Iron Ore Co. of Canada, Training Department, Labrador City, NF, Canada [*Library symbol*] [*Library of Congress*]   (LCLS)

CaNfLo ...... Lourdes Public Library, Lourdes, NF, Canada [*Library symbol*] [*Library of Congress*]   (LCLS)

CaNfLs ...... La Scie Public Library, La Scie, NF, Canada [*Library symbol*] [*Library of Congress*]   (LCLS)

CaNfLu ...... Lumsden Public Library, Lumsden, NF, Canada [*Library symbol*] [*Library of Congress*]   (LCLS)

CaNfM .... Conception Bay South Public Library, Manuels, NF, Canada [*Library symbol*] [*Library of Congress*]   (LCLS)

CaNfMa ..... Marystown Public Library, Marystown, NF, Canada [*Library symbol*] [*Library of Congress*]   (LCLS)

CaNfMG .... Memorial University of Newfoundland, Department of Geography, St. John's, NF, Canada [*Library symbol*] [*Library of Congress*]   (LCLS)

CaNfMHJ ... John B. Wheeler Memorial Library, Musgrave Harbour, NF, Canada [*Library symbol*] [*Library of Congress*]   (LCLS)

CaNfMP .... Mount Pearl Public Library, Mount Pearl, NF, Canada [*Library symbol*] [*Library of Congress*]   (LCLS)

CaNfNA ..... Norris Arm Public Library, Norris Arm, NF, Canada [*Library symbol*] [*Library of Congress*]   (LCLS)

CaNfNP ..... Norris Point Public Library, Norris Point, NF, Canada [*Library symbol*] [*Library of Congress*]   (LCLS)

Can Folk B ... Canada Folk Bulletin [*A publication*]

Can Folk Mus ... Canadian Folk Music Journal [*A publication*]

Can Food Bull ... Canadian Food Bulletin [*A publication*]

Can Food Ind ... Canadian Food Industries [*A publication*]

Can Food Pack ... Canadian Food Packer [*A publication*]

CaNfOP ..... Old Perlican Public Library, Old Perlican, NF, Canada [*Library symbol*] [*Library of Congress*]   (LCLS)

Can For Branch Dep Publ ... Canada. Forestry Branch. Departmental Publication [*A publication*]

CANFORCE ... Canadian Armed Forces   (FAAC)

CANFORCEHED ... Canadian Forces Headquarters [*NATO*]   (NATG)

Can Forces Dent Serv Q ... Canadian Forces Dental Services Quarterly [*A publication*]

Can For Entomol Pathol Branch Annu Rep ... Canada. Forest Entomology and Pathology Branch. Annual Report [*A publication*]

Can For Ind ... Canadian Forest Industries [*A publication*]

Can For J ... Canadian Forestry Journal [*A publication*]

Can For M ... Canadian Forestry Magazine [*A publication*]

Can For Prod Res Branch Annu Rep ... Canada. Forest Products Research Branch. Annual Report [*A publication*]

Can For Prod Res Branch Tech Note ... Canada. Forest Production Research Branch. Technical Note [*A publication*]

Can For Res Branch Annu Rep ... Canada. Forest Research Branch. Annual Report [*A publication*]

Can For Ser For Fire Res Inst Info Rep ... Canada. Forestry Service. Forest Fire Research Institute. Information Report [*A publication*]

Can For Serv Annu Rep For Insect Dis Surv ... Canadian Forestry Service. Annual Report of the Forest Insect and Disease Survey [*A publication*]

Can For Serv Bi-Mon Res Notes ... Canada. Forestry Service. Bi-Monthly Research Notes [*A publication*]

Can For Serv Chem Control Res Inst File Rep ... Canadian Forestry Service. Chemical Control Research Institute. File Report [*A publication*]

Can For Serv Chem Control Res Inst Rep CC-X ... Canadian Forestry Service. Chemical Control Research Institute. Report CC-X [*A publication*]

Can For Serv For Fire Res Inst Inf Rep FF-X ... Canadian Forestry Service. Forest Fire Research Institute. Information Report FF-X [*A publication*]

Can For Serv For Fire Res Inst Misc Rep FF-X ... Canadian Forestry Service. Forest Fire Research Institute. Miscellaneous Report FF-X [*A publication*]

Can For Serv For Manage Inst Inf Rep FMR-X ... Canadian Forestry Service. Forest Management Institute. Information Report FMR-X [*A publication*]

Can For Serv For Pest Manage Inst Inf Rep FPM-X ... Canadian Forestry Service. Forest Pest Management Institute. Information Report FPM-X [*A publication*]

Can For Serv For Pest Manage Inst Rep FPM-X ... Canadian Forestry Service. Forest Pest Management Institute. Report FPM-X [*A publication*]

Can For Serv For Tech Rep ... Canadian Forestry Service. Forestry Technical Report [*A publication*]

Can For Serv Gt Lakes For Cent Inf Rep O-X ... Canadian Forestry Service. Great Lakes Forestry Centre. Information Report O-X [*A publication*]

Can For Serv North For Res Cent For Rep ... Canadian Forestry Service. Northern Forest Research Centre. Forestry Report [*A publication*]

Can For Serv North For Res Cent Inf Rep NOR-X ... Canadian Forestry Service. Northern Forest Research Centre. Information Report NOR-X [*A publication*]

Can For Serv Pac For Res Cent BC-P ... Canadian Forestry Service. Pacific Forest Research Centre BC-P [*A publication*]

Can For Serv Pac For Res Cent For Pest Leafl ... Canadian Forestry Service. Pacific Forest Research Centre. Forest Pest Leaflet [*A publication*]

Can For Serv Pac For Res Cent Inf Rep BC-X ... Canadian Forestry Service. Pacific Forest Research Centre. Information Report BC-X [*A publication*]

Can For Serv Pac For Res Cent Rep BC-R ... Canadian Forestry Service. Pacific Forest Research Centre. Report BC-R [*A publication*]

Can For Serv Pac For Res Cent Rep BC-X ... Canadian Forestry Service. Pacific Forest Research Centre. Report BC-X [*A publication*]

Can For Serv Petawawa Natl For Inst Inf Rep PI-X ... Canadian Forestry Service. Petawawa National Forestry Institute. Information Report PI-X [*A publication*]

Can For Serv Publ ... Canadian Forestry Service. Publication [*A publication*]

Can Forum ... Canadian Forum [*A publication*]

Can Foundry J ... Canada's Foundry Journal [*A publication*]

Can Foundryman ... Canadian Foundryman [*A publication*]

CaNfP .... Placentia Public Library, Placentia, NF, Canada [*Library symbol*] [*Library of Congress*]   (LCLS)

CaNfPa ...... Pasadena Public Library, Pasadena, NF, Canada [*Library symbol*] [*Library of Congress*]   (LCLS)

CaNfPc ...... Pouch Cove Public Library, Pouch Cove, NF, Canada [*Library symbol*] [*Library of Congress*]   (LCLS)

CaNfPeC ... Curran Memorial Library, Port Au Port East, NF, Canada [*Library symbol*] [*Library of Congress*]   (LCLS)

CaNfPL ... Point Leamington Public Library, Point Leamington, NF, Canada [*Library symbol*] [*Library of Congress*]   (LCLS)

CaNfPS ...... Port Saunders Public Library, Port Saunders, NF, Canada [*Library symbol*] [*Library of Congress*]   (LCLS)

CaNfPw ..... Port Au Port West School/Public Library, Port Au Port West, NF, Canada [*Library symbol*] [*Library of Congress*]   (LCLS)

Can Franc .. Canada Francais [*A publication*]

CaNfRH ..... Rocky Harbour Public Library, Rocky Harbour, NF, Canada [*Library symbol*] [*Library of Congress*]   (LCLS)

CaNfRP ..... Marie S. Penney Memorial Library, Ramea, NF, Canada [*Library symbol*] [*Library of Congress*]   (LCLS)

Can Fruitgrower ... Canadian Fruitgrower [*A publication*]

CaNfSA ..... Newfoundland Archives, St. John's, NF, Canada [*Library symbol*] [*Library of Congress*]   (LCLS)

CaNfSAg ... Canada Department of Agriculture, Research Station, St. John's, NF, Canada [*Library symbol*] [*Library of Congress*]   (LCLS)

CaNfSaIC ... Charles Curtis Memorial Hospital, International Grenfell Association, St. Anthony, NF, Canada [*Library symbol*] [*Library of Congress*]   (LCLS)

CaNfSal ..... St. Albans Public Library, St. Albans, NF, Canada [*Library symbol*] [*Library of Congress*]   (LCLS)

CaNfSan .... St. Anthony Public Library, St. Anthony, NF, Canada [*Library symbol*] [*Library of Congress*]   (LCLS)

CaNfSANS ... Naskapi School/Public Library, Sops Arms, NF, Canada [*Library symbol*] [*Library of Congress*]   (LCLS)

CaNfSB ..... Spaniards Bay Public Library, Spaniards Bay, NF, Canada [*Library symbol*] [*Library of Congress*]   (LCLS)

CaNfSBC ... Boy's Club, St. John's, NF, Canada [*Library symbol*] [*Library of Congress*]   (LCLS)

CaNfSbCS ... Cape Shore Public Library, St. Brides, NF, Canada [*Library symbol*] [*Library of Congress*]   (LCLS)

CaNfSC ..... Seal Cove Public Library, Seal Cove, NF, Canada [*Library symbol*] [*Library of Congress*] (LCLS)

CaNfSCA... Children's and Adults' Library, St. John's, NF, Canada [*Library symbol*] [*Library of Congress*] (LCLS)

CaNfSCAEE ... Newfoundland Department of Consumer Affairs and Environment, Environment Division, St. John's, NF, Canada [*Library symbol*] [*Library of Congress*] (LCLS)

CaNfSCF ... College of Fisheries, St. John's, NF, Canada [*Library symbol*] [*Library of Congress*] (LCLS)

CaNfSCJ ... Charles A. Janeway Child Health Centre, St. John's, NF, Canada [*Library symbol*] [*Library of Congress*] (LCLS)

CaNfSCR... Children's Rehabilitation Centre, St. John's, NF, Canada [*Library symbol*] [*Library of Congress*] (LCLS)

CaNfSCT... College of Trades and Technology, St. John's, NF, Canada [*Library symbol*] [*Library of Congress*] (LCLS)

CaNfSCTM ... College of Trades and Technology, Medical Sciences Library, St. John's, NF, Canada [*Library symbol*] [*Library of Congress*] (LCLS)

CaNfSEC... Canada Department of Fisheries and Oceans, St. Johns, NF, Canada [*Library symbol*] [*Library of Congress*] (LCLS)

CaNfSF...... Canada Department of the Environment, Fisheries and Marine Service, Research and Development Directorate, Newfoundland Biological Station, St. John's, NF, Canada [*Library symbol*] [*Library of Congress*] (LCLS)

CaNfSFBD ... Federal Business Development Bank, St. John's, NF, Canada [*Library symbol*] [*Library of Congress*] (LCLS)

CaNfSFJG ... Saint Judes Central High School Public Library/Bay St. George South Public Library, St. Fintans, NF, Canada [*Library symbol*] [*Library of Congress*] (LCLS)

CaNfSG ..... Newfoundland Public Libraries Board, St. John's, NF, Canada [*Library symbol*] [*Library of Congress*] (LCLS)

CaNfSGe ... St. Georges Public Library, St. Georges, NF, Canada [*Library symbol*] [*Library of Congress*] (LCLS)

CaNfSGGH ... Grace General Hospital, C. A. Pippy, Jr. Medical Library, St. John's, NF, Canada [*Library symbol*] [*Library of Congress*] (LCLS)

CaNfSGGHN ... Grace General Hospital, School of Nursing, St. John's, NF, Canada [*Library symbol*] [*Library of Congress*] (LCLS)

CaNfSGH ... General Hospital, St. John's, NF, Canada [*Library symbol*] [*Library of Congress*] (LCLS)

CaNfSGHN ... General Hospital, Nursing Education, St. John's, NF, Canada [*Library symbol*] [*Library of Congress*] (LCLS)

CaNfSGo ... Gosling Library, St. John's, NF, Canada [*Library symbol*] [*Library of Congress*] (LCLS)

CaNfSHE .. Newfoundland Department of Health, Health Education Division, St. John's, NF, Canada [*Library symbol*] [*Library of Congress*] (LCLS)

CaNfSHPH ... Newfoundland Department of Health, Public Health Nursing Division, St. John's, NF, Canada [*Library symbol*] [*Library of Congress*] (LCLS)

CaNfSICA ... Institute of Chartered Accountants of Newfoundland, St. John's, NF, Canada [*Library symbol*] [*Library of Congress*] (LCLS)

CaNfSJL ... Newfoundland Department of Justice, Law Library, St. John's, NF, Canada [*Library symbol*] [*Library of Congress*] (LCLS)

CaNfSK ..... Kindale Public Library, Stephenville, NF, Canada [*Library symbol*] [*Library of Congress*] (LCLS)

CaNfSL...... Legislative Library, St. John's, NF, Canada [*Library symbol*] [*Library of Congress*] (LCLS)

CaNfSLa.... St. Lawrence Public Library, St. Lawrence, NF, Canada [*Library symbol*] [*Library of Congress*] (LCLS)

CaNfSLG... Saint Lunaire-Griquet Public Library, St. Lunaire, NF, Canada [*Library symbol*] [*Library of Congress*] (LCLS)

CaNfSLP ... Newfoundland Light & Power Co., Central Records Library, St. John's, NF, Canada [*Library symbol*] [*Library of Congress*] (LCLS)

CaNfSLS ... Law Society of Newfoundland, St. John's, NF, Canada [*Library symbol*] [*Library of Congress*] (LCLS)

CaNfSM .... Memorial University of Newfoundland, St. John's, NF, Canada [*Library symbol*] [*Library of Congress*] (LCLS)

CaNfSMA ... Newfoundland Department of Municipal Affairs, St. John's, NF, Canada [*Library symbol*] [*Library of Congress*] (LCLS)

CaNfSME ... Newfoundland Department of Mines and Energy, St. John's, NF, Canada [*Library symbol*] [*Library of Congress*] (LCLS)

CaNfSMEC ... Memorial University, Education Library, Curriculum Materials Centre, St. John's, NF, Canada [*Library symbol*] [*Library of Congress*] (LCLS)

CaNfSMEd ... Memorial University, Education Library, St. John's, NF, Canada [*Library symbol*] [*Library of Congress*] (LCLS)

CaNfSMEM ... Newfoundland Department of Mines and Energy, Mineral Development Division, St. John's, NF, Canada [*Library symbol*] [*Library of Congress*] (LCLS)

CaNfSMM ... Memorial University of Newfoundland, Faculty of Medicine Library, St. John's, NF, Canada [*Library symbol*] [*Library of Congress*] (LCLS)

CaNfSMO ... Memorial University, Ocean Engineering Centre, St. John's, NF, Canada [*Library symbol*] [*Library of Congress*] (LCLS)

CaNfSNL .. Newfoundland and Labrador Hydro, St. John's, NF, Canada [*Library symbol*] [*Library of Congress*] (LCLS)

CaNfSNLD ... Newfoundland & Labrador Development Corp., St. John's, NF, Canada [*Library symbol*] [*Library of Congress*] (LCLS)

CaNfSp ...... Springdale Public Library, Springdale, NF, Canada [*Library symbol*] [*Library of Congress*] (LCLS)

CaNfSPR... Provincial Reference Library, St. John's, NF, Canada [*Library symbol*] [*Library of Congress*] (LCLS)

CaNfSPRV ... Pictou Regional Vocational School, St. John's, NF, Canada [*Library symbol*] [*Library of Congress*] (LCLS)

CaNfSQ ..... Queen's College, St. John's, NF, Canada [*Library symbol*] [*Library of Congress*] (LCLS)

CaNfSRD .. Newfoundland Department of Rural Development, St. John's, NF, Canada [*Library symbol*] [*Library of Congress*] (LCLS)

CaNfSREx ... Canada Department of Regional Economic Expansion, St. John's, NF, Canada [*Library symbol*] [*Library of Congress*] (LCLS)

CaNfSSC ... Saint Clare's Mercy Hospital, St. John's, NF, Canada [*Library symbol*] [*Library of Congress*] (LCLS)

CaNfSSCN ... Saint Clare's Mercy Hospital, School of Nursing, St. John's, NF, Canada [*Library symbol*] [*Library of Congress*] (LCLS)

CaNfSSW ... Newfoundland Status of Women Council, St. John's, NF, Canada [*Library symbol*] [*Library of Congress*] (LCLS)

CaNfST ..... Newfoundland Department of Tourism, St. John's, NF, Canada [*Library symbol*] [*Library of Congress*] (LCLS)

CaNfSTA... Newfoundland Teachers' Association, St. John's, NF, Canada [*Library symbol*] [*Library of Congress*] (LCLS)

CaNfStC ... Stephenville Crossing Public Library, Stephenville Crossing, NF, Canada [*Library symbol*] [*Library of Congress*] (LCLS)

CaNfSu ...... Summerford Public Library, Summerford, NF, Canada [*Library symbol*] [*Library of Congress*] (LCLS)

CaNfSWH ... Waterford Hospital, Health Services, St. John's, NF, Canada [*Library symbol*] [*Library of Congress*] (LCLS)

CANFSWPA ... Combined Allied Naval Forces, Southwest Pacific Area

CANFSWPAOPPLAN ... Combined Allied Naval Forces, Southwest Pacific Ocean Area Operating Plan

CaNfTo ...... Torbay Public Library, Torbay, NF, Canada [*Library symbol*] [*Library of Congress*] (LCLS)

CaNfTr ...... Trepassey Public Library, Trepassey, NF, Canada [*Library symbol*] [*Library of Congress*] (LCLS)

CaNfTw ...... Twillingate Public Library, Twillingate, NF, Canada [*Library symbol*] [*Library of Congress*] (LCLS)

CaNfUF ..... Codroy Valley Public Library, Upper Ferry, NF, Canada [*Library symbol*] [*Library of Congress*] (LCLS)

CaNfUI ...... Upper Island Cove Public Library, Upper Island Cove, NF, Canada [*Library symbol*] [*Library of Congress*] (LCLS)

CaNfV........ Victoria Public Library, Victoria, NF, Canada [*Library symbol*] [*Library of Congress*] (LCLS)

CaNfWa..... Wabush Public Library, Wabush, NF, Canada [*Library symbol*] [*Library of Congress*] (LCLS)

CaNfWE.... Edgar L. M. Roberts Memorial Library, Woodypoint, NF, Canada [*Library symbol*] [*Library of Congress*] (LCLS)

CaNfWh .... Whitbourne Public Library, Whitbourne, NF, Canada [*Library symbol*] [*Library of Congress*] (LCLS)

CaNfWi ..... Windsor Memorial Public Library, Windsor, NF, Canada [*Library symbol*] [*Library of Congress*] (LCLS)

CaNfWin .... Winterton Public Library, Winterton, NF, Canada [*Library symbol*] [*Library of Congress*] (LCLS)

CaNfWv..... Wesleyville Public Library, Wesleyville, NF, Canada [*Library symbol*] [*Library of Congress*] (LCLS)

Can Gas J .. Canadian Gas Journal [*A publication*]

Can Gaz ..... Canada Gazette (Regulations) [*A publication*] (DLA)

Can Geog ... Canadian Geographer [*A publication*]

Can Geog J ... Canadian Geographical Journal [*Later, Canadian Geographic*] [*A publication*]

Can Geogr ... Canadian Geographer [*A publication*]

Can Geogr ... Canadian Geographic [*A publication*]

Can Geogr ... Canadian Geography [*A publication*]

Can Geographer ... Canadian Geographer [*A publication*]

Can Geographic ... Canadian Geographic [*A publication*]

Can Geogr J ... Canadian Geographical Journal [*Later, Canadian Geographic*] [*A publication*]

Can Geol Surv Bull ... Canada. Geological Survey. Bulletin [*A publication*]

Can Geol Surv Map ... Canada. Geological Survey. Map [*A publication*]

Can Geol Surv Mem ... Canada. Geological Survey. Memoir [*A publication*]

Can Geol Surv Misc Rep ... Canada. Geological Survey. Miscellaneous Report [*A publication*]

Can Geol Surv Pap ... Canada. Geological Survey. Paper [*A publication*]

Can Geoph Bull ... Canadian Geophysical Bulletin [*A publication*]

Can Geophys Bull ... Canadian Geophysical Bulletin [*A publication*]

Can Geotech J ... Canadian Geotechnical Journal [*A publication*]

Can Gov Publ Q ... Canadian Government Publications Quarterly [*A publication*]

CAngP .... Pacific Union College, Angwin, CA [*Library symbol*] [*Library of Congress*] (LCLS)

Can Grain Res Lab Annu Rep ... Canadian Grain Research Laboratory. Annual Report [*A publication*]

Can Grain Res Lab Rep ... Canadian Grain Research Laboratory. Report [*A publication*]
Can Green Bag ... Canadian Green Bag [*A publication*]   (DLA)
Can Grow Q Bull ... Cane Growers Quarterly Bulletin [*A publication*]   (APTA)
Can G S...... Canada. Geological Survey [*A publication*]
Can G S An Rp ... Canada. Geological Survey. Annual Report [*A publication*]
Can G S Mem ... Canada. Geological Survey. Memoir [*A publication*]
Can G S Mus B ... Canada. Geological Survey. Museum Bulletin [*A publication*]
Can G S Sum Rp ... Canada. Geological Survey. Summary Report [*A publication*]
Can Heritage ... Canadian Heritage [*A publication*]
Can His R .. Canadian Historical Review [*A publication*]
Can Hist Ass Ann Rep ... Canadian Historical Association. Annual Report [*A publication*]
Can Hist Assn ... Canadian Historical Association. Historical Papers [*A publication*]
Can Hist Assn Rep ... Canadian Historical Association. Report [*A publication*]
Can Hist Assoc Ann Rep ... Canadian Historical Association. Annual Report [*A publication*]
Can Hist Mag ... Canada. An Historical Magazine [*A publication*]
Can Hist R ... Canadian Historical Review [*A publication*]
Can Hist Rev ... Canadian Historical Review [*A publication*]
Can HJ ...... Canberra Historical Journal [*A publication*]
Can Home Ec J ... Canadian Home Economics Journal [*A publication*]
Can Home Econ J Rev Can Econ Familiale ... Canadian Home Economics Journal/Revue Canadienne d'Economie Familiale [*A publication*]
Can Hort.... Canadian Horticulture and Home Magazine [*A publication*]
Can Hort Beek ... Canadian Horticulturist and Beekeeper [*A publication*]
Can Hosp... Canadian Hospital [*A publication*]
CanHR...... Canadian Historical Review [*A publication*]
Can Human Rights Rep ... Canadian Human Rights Reporter [*A publication*]   (DLA)
CanI .... Canadian Periodical Index [*A publication*]
CANI .... Canaveral International Corp. [*NASDAQ symbol*]   (NQ)
Can I Food ... Canadian Institute of Food Science and Technology. Journal [*A publication*]
Can Ind ...... Canadian Periodical Index [*A publication*]
Can Ind Geosci Data ... Canadian Index to Geoscience Data [*A publication*]
Can Ind Rep Fish Aquat Sci ... Canadian Industry Report of Fisheries and Aquatic Sciences [*A publication*]
Canine Pract ... Canine Practice [*A publication*]
Can Inland Waters Branch Rep Ser ... Canada. Inland Waters Branch. Report Series [*A publication*]
Can Inland Waters Branch Sci Ser ... Canada. Inland Waters Branch. Scientific Series [*A publication*]
Can Inland Waters Dir Rep Ser ... Canada. Inland Waters Directorate. Report Series [*A publication*]
Can Inland Waters Dir Sediment Data Can Rivers ... Canada. Inland Waters Directorate. Sediment Data for Canadian Rivers [*A publication*]
Can Insect Pest Rev ... Canadian Insect Pest Review [*A publication*]
Can Inst Food Sci Technol J ... Canadian Institute of Food Science and Technology. Journal [*A publication*]
Can Inst Food Technol J ... Canadian Institute of Food Technology. Journal [*A publication*]
Can Inst Min Metall Min Soc NS Trans ... Canadian Institute of Mining and Metallurgy and the Mining Society of Nova Scotia. Transactions [*A publication*]
Can Inst Min Met Spec Vol ... Canadian Institute of Mining and Metallurgy. Special Volume [*A publication*]
Can Inst Pr ... Canadian Institute Proceedings [*A publication*]
Can Int Educ ... Canadian and International Education [*A publication*]
Can Inter Ed/Ed Can ... Canadian and International Education/Education Canadienne et Internationale [*A publication*]
Can J.......... Canadian Journal [*Toronto*] [*A publication*]
CANJA...... Canadian Anaesthetists' Society. Journal [*A publication*]
Can J Afr S ... Canadian Journal of African Studies [*A publication*]
Can J Afr Stud ... Canadian Journal of African Studies [*A publication*]
Can J Afr Studies ... Canadian Journal of African Studies [*A publication*]
Can J Ag Ec ... Canadian Journal of Agricultural Economics [*A publication*]
Can J Agr Econ ... Canadian Journal of Agricultural Economics [*A publication*]
Can J Agric Econ ... Canadian Journal of Agricultural Economics [*A publication*]
Can J Agric Econ Rev Can Econ Rurale ... Canadian Journal of Agricultural Economics/Revue Canadienne d'Economie Rurale [*A publication*]
Can J Agric Sci ... Canadian Journal of Agricultural Science [*A publication*]
Can J Agr Sci ... Canadian Journal of Agricultural Science [*A publication*]
Can J Ag Sci ... Canadian Journal of Agricultural Science [*A publication*]
Can J Anaesth ... Canadian Journal of Anaesthesia [*A publication*]
Can J Anim ... Canadian Journal of Animal Science [*A publication*]
Can J Anim Sci ... Canadian Journal of Animal Science [*A publication*]
Can J Anthropol ... Canadian Journal of Anthropology [*A publication*]
Can J Appl Sport Sci ... Canadian Journal of Applied Sport Sciences [*A publication*]
Can J Appl Sport Sciences ... Canadian Journal of Applied Sport Sciences [*A publication*]

Can J Behav Sci ... Canadian Journal of Behavioural Science [*A publication*]
Can J Beh S ... Canadian Journal of Behavioural Science [*A publication*]
Can J Beh Sc/R Can Sc Comport ... Canadian Journal of Behavioural Science/Revue Canadienne des Sciences du Comportement [*A publication*]
Can J Bioch ... Canadian Journal of Biochemistry [*A publication*]
Can J Biochem ... Canadian Journal of Biochemistry [*A publication*]
Can J Biochem Cell Biol ... Canadian Journal of Biochemistry and Cell Biology [*A publication*]
Can J Biochem Physiol ... Canadian Journal of Biochemistry and Physiology [*A publication*]
Can J Bot ... Canadian Journal of Botany [*A publication*]
Can J Cardiol ... Canadian Journal of Cardiology [*A publication*]
Can J Chem ... Canadian Journal of Chemistry [*A publication*]
Can J Chem Eng ... Canadian Journal of Chemical Engineering [*A publication*]
Can J Chem Engng ... Canadian Journal of Chemical Engineering [*A publication*]
Can J Ch En ... Canadian Journal of Chemical Engineering [*A publication*]
Can J Civ Eng ... Canadian Journal of Civil Engineering [*A publication*]
Can J Civ Engng ... Canadian Journal of Civil Engineering [*A publication*]
Can J Civ Eng/Rev Can Genie Civ ... Canadian Journal of Civil Engineering/Revue Canadienne de Genie Civil [*A publication*]
Can J Clin ... Cancer Journal for Clinicians [*A publication*]
Can J Com M ... Canadian Journal of Comparative Medicine [*A publication*]
Can J Comp Med ... Canadian Journal of Comparative Medicine [*A publication*]
Can J Comp Med Vet Sci ... Canadian Journal of Comparative Medicine and Veterinary Science [*Later, Canadian Journal of Comparative Medicine*] [*A publication*]
Can J Corr ... Canadian Journal of Corrections [*Later, Canadian Journal of Criminology*] [*A publication*]
Can J Correct ... Canadian Journal of Corrections [*A publication*]   (ILCA)
Can J Correction ... Canadian Journal of Corrections [*Later, Canadian Journal of Criminology*] [*A publication*]
Can J Crim ... Canadian Journal of Criminology and Corrections [*Later, Canadian Journal of Criminology*] [*A publication*]
Can J Crim & Correct ... Canadian Journal of Criminology and Corrections [*Later, Canadian Journal of Criminology*] [*A publication*]
Can J Criminol ... Canadian Journal of Criminology [*A publication*]   (DLA)
Can J Criminology ... Canadian Journal of Criminology [*A publication*]
Can J Criminology & Corr ... Canadian Journal of Criminology and Corrections [*Later, Canadian Journal of Criminology*] [*A publication*]
Can J Development Studies ... Canadian Journal of Development Studies [*A publication*]
Can J Development Studies (Ottawa) ... Canadian Journal of Development Studies (Ottawa) [*A publication*]
Can J Earth ... Canadian Journal of Earth Sciences [*A publication*]
Can J Earth Sci ... Canadian Journal of Earth Sciences [*A publication*]
Can J Ec..... Canadian Journal of Economics [*A publication*]
Can J Econ ... Canadian Journal of Economics [*A publication*]
Can J Econ Polit Sci ... Canadian Journal of Economics and Political Science [*Later, Canadian Journal of Economics*] [*A publication*]
Can J Econ Pol Sci ... Canadian Journal of Economics and Political Science [*Later, Canadian Journal of Economics*] [*A publication*]
Can J Econ & Pol Sci ... Canadian Journal of Economics and Political Science [*Later, Canadian Journal of Economics*] [*A publication*]
Can J Econ Rev Can Econ Univ Toronto Press Can Econ Assoc ... Canadian Journal of Economics/Revue Canadienne d'Economique. University of Toronto Press. Canadian Economics Association [*A publication*]
Can J Ed .... Canadian Journal of Education [*A publication*]
Can J Ed Comm ... Canadian Journal of Educational Communication [*A publication*]
Can J Fabr ... Canadian Journal of Fabrics [*A publication*]
Can J Family Law ... Canadian Journal of Family Law [*A publication*]
Can J Fam L ... Canadian Journal of Family Law [*A publication*]
Can J Fish Aquatic Sci ... Canadian Journal of Fisheries and Aquatic Sciences [*A publication*]
Can J Fish Aquat Sci ... Canadian Journal of Fisheries and Aquatic Sciences [*A publication*]
Can J Fish Aquat Sci J Can Sci Halieutiques Aquat [A publication] ... Canadian Journal of Fisheries and Aquatic Sciences. Journal Canadien des Sciences Halieutiques et Aquatiques [*A publication*]
Can J Forest Res ... Canadian Journal of Forest Research [*A publication*]
Can J For Res ... Canadian Journal of Forest Research [*A publication*]
Can J Gen Cyt ... Canadian Journal of Genetics and Cytology [*A publication*]
Can J Genet ... Canadian Journal of Genetics and Cytology [*A publication*]
Can J Genet Cytol ... Canadian Journal of Genetics and Cytology [*A publication*]
Can J Higher Ed ... Canadian Journal of Higher Education [*A publication*]
Can J His... Canadian Journal of History [*A publication*]
Can J Hist ... Canadian Journal of History [*A publication*]
Can J Hist Sport ... Canadian Journal of History of Sport [*A publication*]
Can J Hist Sport Phys Educ ... Canadian Journal of History of Sport and Physical Education [*Later, Canadian Journal of History of Sport*] [*A publication*]
Can J Hosp Pharm ... Canadian Journal of Hospital Pharmacy [*A publication*]

Can J Info Science ... Canadian Journal of Information Science [*A publication*]
Can J Ital ... Canadian Journal of Italian Studies [*A publication*]
Can J L ...... Canadian Journal of Linguistics [*A publication*]
Can J Ling ... Canadian Journal of Linguistics [*A publication*]
Can J Lingu ... Canadian Journal of Linguistics [*A publication*]
Can J Math ... Canadian Journal of Mathematics [*A publication*]
Can J Med Sci ... Canadian Journal of Medical Science [*A publication*]
Can J Med Surg ... Canadian Journal of Medicine and Surgery [*A publication*]
Can J Med T ... Canadian Journal of Medical Technology [*A publication*]
Can J Med Techn ... Canadian Journal of Medical Technology [*A publication*]
Can J Med Technol ... Canadian Journal of Medical Technology [*A publication*]
Can J Micro ... Canadian Journal of Microbiology [*A publication*]
Can J Microb ... Canadian Journal of Microbiology [*A publication*]
Can J Microbiol ... Canadian Journal of Microbiology [*A publication*]
Can J Nat Ed ... Canadian Journal of Native Education [*A publication*]
Can J Neurol Sci ... Canadian Journal of Neurological Science [*A publication*]
Can Jnl Nat Stud ... Canadian Journal of Native Studies [*A publication*]
Can J Occup Ther ... Canadian Journal of Occupational Therapy [*A publication*]
Can J Ophth ... Canadian Journal of Ophthalmology [*A publication*]
Can J Ophthalm ... Canadian Journal of Ophthalmology [*A publication*]
Can J Ophthalmol ... Canadian Journal of Ophthalmology [*A publication*]
Can J Optom ... Canadian Journal of Optometry [*A publication*]
Can J Otolaryngol ... Canadian Journal of Otolaryngology [*A publication*]
Can Jour Hist ... Canadian Journal of History [*A publication*]
Can J Pharm Sci ... Canadian Journal of Pharmaceutical Sciences [*A publication*]
Can J Phil ... Canadian Journal of Philosophy [*A publication*]
Can J Ph Sc ... Canadian Journal of Pharmaceutical Sciences [*A publication*]
Can J Phys ... Canadian Journal of Physics [*A publication*]
Can J Physiol Pharm ... Canadian Journal of Physiology and Pharmacology [*A publication*]
Can J Physiol Pharmacol ... Canadian Journal of Physiology and Pharmacology [*A publication*]
Can J Physl ... Canadian Journal of Physiology and Pharmacology [*A publication*]
Can J Plant ... Canadian Journal of Plant Science [*A publication*]
Can J Plant Pathol ... Canadian Journal of Plant Pathology [*A publication*]
Can J Plant Sci ... Canadian Journal of Plant Science [*A publication*]
Can J Pl Sci ... Canadian Journal of Plant Science [*A publication*]
Can J Poli ... Canadian Journal of Political Science [*A publication*]
Can J Pol Sc ... Canadian Journal of Political Science [*A publication*]
Can J Pol Sci ... Canadian Journal of Political Science [*A publication*]
Can J Pol Science ... Canadian Journal of Political Science [*A publication*]
Can J Pol Science (Ont) ... Canadian Journal of Political Science (Ontario) [*A publication*]
Can J Pol and Soc Theory ... Canadian Journal of Political and Social Theory [*A publication*]
Can J Psych ... Canadian Journal of Psychology [*A publication*]
Can J Psychiatr Nurs ... Canadian Journal of Psychiatric Nursing [*A publication*]
Can J Psychiatry ... Canadian Journal of Psychiatry [*A publication*]
Can J Psychol ... Canadian Journal of Psychology [*A publication*]
Can J Publ ... Canadian Journal of Public Health [*A publication*]
Can J Publ Hlth ... Canadian Journal of Public Health [*A publication*]
Can J Public Health ... Canadian Journal of Public Health [*A publication*]
Can J Radiogr Radiother Nucl Med ... Canadian Journal of Radiography, Radiotherapy, Nuclear Medicine [*A publication*]
Can J Radiogr Radiother Nucl Med (Engl Ed) ... Canadian Journal of Radiography, Radiotherapy, Nuclear Medicine (English Edition) [*A publication*]
Can J Rel Thought ... Canadian Journal of Religious Thought [*A publication*]
Can J Remote Sens ... Canadian Journal of Remote Sensing [*A publication*]
Can J Remote Sensing ... Canadian Journal of Remote Sensing [*A publication*]
Can J Res ... Canadian Journal of Research [*A publication*]
Can J Res Sect A ... Canadian Journal of Research. Section A. Physical Sciences [*A publication*]
Can J Res Sect B ... Canadian Journal of Research. Section B. Chemical Sciences [*A publication*]
Can J Res Sect C Bot Sci ... Canadian Journal of Research. Section C. Botanical Sciences [*A publication*]
Can J Res Sect D Zool Sci ... Canadian Journal of Research. Section D. Zoological Sciences [*A publication*]
Can J Res Sect E Med Sci ... Canadian Journal of Research. Section E. Medical Sciences [*A publication*]
Can J Res Sect F ... Canadian Journal of Research. Section F. Technology [*A publication*]
Can J Sci ... Canadian Journal of Science, Literature, and History [*A publication*]
Can J Soil ... Canadian Journal of Soil Science [*A publication*]
Can J Soil Sci ... Canadian Journal of Soil Science [*A publication*]
Can J Spect ... Canadian Journal of Spectroscopy [*A publication*]
Can J Spectrosc ... Canadian Journal of Spectroscopy [*A publication*]
Can J Spectry ... Canadian Journal of Spectroscopy [*A publication*]
Can J Statis ... Canadian Journal of Statistics [*A publication*]
Can J Surg ... Canadian Journal of Surgery [*A publication*]
Can JT ...... Canadian Journal of Theology [*A publication*]
Can J Technol ... Canadian Journal of Technology [*A publication*]

Can J Th .... Canadian Journal of Theology [*A publication*]
Can J Univ Cont Ed ... Canadian Journal of University Continuing Education [*A publication*]
Can J Vet Res ... Canadian Journal of Veterinary Research [*A publication*]
Can J Zool ... Canadian Journal of Zoology [*A publication*]
Can L .... Canadian Literature [*A publication*]
CANL .... Canal-Randolph Limited Partnership [*New York, NY*] [*NASDAQ symbol*]   (NQ)
CANLA ..... Canadian Library Association [*Also known as ACB and CLA*]
CanLA .... Canadian Library Association, Ottawa, ON, Canada [*Library symbol*] [*Library of Congress*]   (LCLS)
Can Lab ..... Canadian Labour [*A publication*]
CanLabINSPIRE ... Canadian Laboratory for Integrated Spatial Information Research and Engineering [*University of New Brunswick*] [*Research center*]   (RCD)
Can Labour ... Canadian Labour [*A publication*]
Can Lanc .... Canada Lancet and Practitioner [*A publication*]
CANLANT ... Canadian Atlantic Subarea [*Canadian Navy*]
Can Law ..... Canadian Lawyer [*A publication*]
Can Lawyer ... Canadian Lawyer [*A publication*]
Can Lbr ...... Canadian Labour [*A publication*]
Can Legal Aid Bul ... Canadian Legal Aid Bulletin [*A publication*]
Can Leg N ... Canada Legal News [*A publication*]   (DLA)
Can Leg Stud ... Canadian Legal Studies [*A publication*]   (DLA)
Can Leg Studies ... Canadian Legal Studies [*A publication*]   (DLA)
CANLF ...... United States Committee to Aid the National Liberation Front of South Vietnam
Can Lib ..... Canadian Library [*A publication*]
Can Lib Assn Bul ... Canadian Library Association. Bulletin [*A publication*]
Can Lib Bull ... Canadian Library Bulletin [*A publication*]
Can Lib J ... Canadian Library Journal [*A publication*]
Can Libr J ... Canadian Library Journal [*A publication*]
Can Lit ...... Canadian Literature [*A publication*]
Can Lit Mag ... Canadian Literary Magazine [*A publication*]
Can LJ ...... Canada Law Journal [*A publication*]   (DLA)
Can LJ NS ... Canada Law Journal, New Series [*A publication*]   (DLA)
Can LR ...... Canada Law Reports, Exchequer Court and Supreme Court [*A publication*]   (DLA)
Can LRBR ... Canadian Labour Relations Board Reports [*A publication*]   (DLA)
Can L Rev .. Canadian Law Review [*A publication*]   (DLA)
Can LS ...... Canadian Legal Studies [*A publication*]   (ILCA)
Can LT ...... Canadian Law Times [*A publication*]   (DLA)
Can L Times ... Canadian Law Times [*A publication*]   (DLA)
Can LT Occ N ... Canadian Law Times. Occasional Notes [*A publication*]   (DLA)
Can M .... Canadian Magazine [*A publication*]
CanM .... Canadian Microfilming Co., Montreal, PQ, Canada [*Library symbol*] [*Library of Congress*]   (LCLS)
Can Mach Metalwork ... Canadian Machinery and Metalworking [*A publication*]
Can MAJ ... Canadian Medical Association. Journal [*A publication*]
CANMAN ... Casopis Narodniho Muzea [*Prague*] [*A publication*]
Can Manuscr Rep Fish Aquat Sci ... Canadian Manuscript Report of Fisheries and Aquatic Sciences [*A publication*]
CANMAP ... Canada Marketing Assistance Program
CAN/MARC ... Canadian Machine-Readable Cataloguing [*National Library of Canada*] [*Information service or system*]
CANMARCOM ... Canadian Maritime Command
Can Math B ... Canadian Mathematical Bulletin [*A publication*]
Can Math Bull ... Canadian Mathematical Bulletin [*A publication*]
Can Math Teach ... Canadian Mathematics Teacher [*A publication*]
Can Med A J ... Canadian Medical Association. Journal [*A publication*]
Can Med Ass J ... Canadian Medical Association. Journal [*A publication*]
Can Med Assn J ... Canadian Medical Association. Journal [*A publication*]
Can Med Assoc J ... Canadian Medical Association. Journal [*A publication*]
Can Mental Health ... Canada's Mental Health [*A publication*]
Can Ment He ... Canada's Mental Health [*A publication*]
Can Ment Health ... Canada's Mental Health [*A publication*]
Can Ment Hlth ... Canada's Mental Health [*A publication*]
CANMET ... Canada Centre for Mineral and Energy Technology [*Department of Energy, Mines, and Resources*] [*Ottawa, ON*]
Can Metall Q ... Canadian Metallurgical Quarterly [*A publication*]
Can Metal Q ... Canadian Metallurgical Quarterly [*A publication*]
Can Metalwork/Mach Prod ... Canadian Metalworking/Machine Production [*A publication*]
Can Metalwork Prod ... Canadian Metalworking Production [*A publication*]
Can Met Quart ... Canadian Metallurgical Quarterly [*A publication*]
CANMET Rep ... CANMET [*Canada Centre for Mineral and Energy Technology*] Report [*Ottawa*] [*A publication*]
Can Milling Feed ... Canadian Milling and Feed [*A publication*]
CANMINDEX ... Canadian Mineral Occurrence Index [*Department of Energy, Mines, and Resources*] [*Information service or system*]   (IID)
Can Mineral ... Canadian Mineralogist [*A publication*]
Can Miner Ind Rev ... Canadian Mineral Industry. Review [*A publication*]
Can Miner Resour Branch Miner Bull ... Canada. Mineral Resources Branch. Mineral Bulletin [*A publication*]
Can Miner Resour Branch Miner Inf Bull ... Canada. Mineral Resources Branch. Mineral Information Bulletin [*A publication*]

Can Miner Resour Branch Miner Rep ... Canada. Mineral Resources Branch. Mineral Report [*A publication*]
Can Miner Resour Div Miner Bull ... Canada. Mineral Resources Division. Mineral Bulletin [*A publication*]
Can Miner Resour Div Oper List ... Canada. Mineral Resources Division. Operators List [*A publication*]
Can Miner Yearb ... Canadian Minerals Yearbook [*A publication*]
Can Mines Branch Inf Circ ... Canada. Mines Branch. Information Circular [*A publication*]
Can Mines Branch Invest Rep ... Canada. Mines Branch. Investigation Report [*A publication*]
Can Mines Branch Memo Ser ... Canada. Mines Branch. Memorandum Series [*A publication*]
Can Mines Branch Monogr ... Canada. Mines Branch. Monograph [*A publication*]
Can Mines Branch Radioact Div Top Rep ... Canada. Mines Branch. Radioactivity Division. Topical Report [*A publication*]
Can Mines Branch Rep ... Canada. Mines Branch. Report [*A publication*]
Can Mines Branch Res Rep ... Canada. Mines Branch. Research Report [*A publication*]
Can Mines Branch Tech Bull ... Canada. Mines Branch. Technical Bulletin [*A publication*]
Can Mines Branch Tech Pap ... Canada. Mines Branch. Technical Paper [*A publication*]
Can Mines Br Sum Rp ... Canada. Department of Mines. Mines Branch. Summary Report [*A publication*]
Can Mining J ... Canadian Mining Journal [*A publication*]
Can Mining Met Bul ... Canadian Mining and Metallurgical Bulletin [*A publication*]
Can Min J ... Canadian Mining Journal [*A publication*]
Can Min Met ... Canadian Mining and Metallurgical Bulletin [*A publication*]
Can Min Metall Bull ... Canadian Mining and Metallurgical Bulletin [*A publication*]
Can Min & Metallurg Bull ... Canadian Mining and Metallurgical Bulletin [*A publication*]
Can Min & Met Bul ... Canadian Mining and Metallurgical Bulletin [*A publication*]
Can Ml J ... Canadian Military Journal [*A publication*]
Can-Mong R ... Canada-Mongolia Review [*A publication*]
Can M Rv ... Canadian Mining Review [*A publication*]
Can Munic Util ... Canadian Municipal Utilities [*A publication*]
Can Mun J ... Canadian Municipal Journal [*A publication*]   (DLA)
Can Mus ... Canadian Musician [*A publication*]
Can Mus Bk ... Canada Music Book [*A publication*]
Can Mus Ed ... Canadian Music Educator [*A publication*]
Can Mus J ... Canadian Music Journal [*A publication*]
CANN ... Cannon [*Freight*]
CANN ... Canon, Inc. [*NASDAQ symbol*]   (NQ)
Can Nat ... Canadian Naturalist and Geologist and Proceedings of the Natural History Society of Montreal [*A publication*]
Can Native L Rep ... Canadian Native Law Reporter. Native Law Centre. University of Saskatchewan [*A publication*]   (DLA)
Can Natl Aeronaut Establ Mech Eng Rep ... Canada. National Aeronautical Establishment. Mechanical Engineering Report [*A publication*]
Can Natl Res Counc Div Mech Eng Lab Tech Rep ... Canada. National Research Council. Division of Mechanical Engineering. Laboratory Technical Report [*A publication*]
CANNB ... Canadian Nurse [*A publication*]
Can News Index ... Canadian News Index [*A publication*]
Cann Pack ... Canning and Packing [*A publication*]
Cann Trade ... Canning Trade [*A publication*]
Can Nucl ... Canada Nucleaire [*A publication*]
Can Nucl Assoc Annu Int Conf ... Canadian Nuclear Association. Annual International Conference [*A publication*]
Can Nucl Assoc Annu Int Conf (Pro) ... Canadian Nuclear Association. Annual International Conference (Proceedings) [*A publication*]
Can Nucl Assoc Report ... Canadian Nuclear Association. Report [*A publication*]
Can Nucl Soc Annu Conf Trans ... Canadian Nuclear Society. Annual Conference. Transactions [*A publication*]
Can Nucl Soc Trans ... Canadian Nuclear Society. Transactions [*A publication*]
Can Nucl Technol ... Canadian Nuclear Technology [*A publication*]
Can Nurse ... Canadian Nurse [*A publication*]
CANO ... Canoma. Canada Department of Energy, Mines, and Resources [*A publication*]
CANO ... Canonie Environmental Services Corp. [*Porter, IN*] [*NASDAQ symbol*]   (NQ)
CANO ... Catalog Number
Canoe ... Canoe Magazine [*A publication*]
Can Oil & Gas ... Canadian Oil and Gas Handbook [*A publication*]   (DLA)
Can Oil Gas Ind ... Canadian Oil and Gas Industries [*A publication*]
CAN/OLE ... Canadian Online Enquiry System [*Pronounced "can-olay"*] [*National Research Council of Canada*] [*Ottawa, ON*]
Canon Law ... Canon Law Abstracts [*A publication*]
Canon Law Abstr ... Canon Law Abstracts [*A publication*]
Can Oper Res Soc J ... Canadian Operational Research Society. Journal [*A publication*]

Can Oper Room Nurs J ... Canadian Operating Room Nursing Journal [*A publication*]
CANOT ... Canadian NOTAM [*Notice to Airmen*]   (FAAC)
CANP ... Calcium Activated Neutral Protease [*An enzyme*]
CANP ... Canadian Association of Native Peoples. Bulletin [*A publication*]
CANP ... Canister Purge Solenoid [*Automotive engineering*]
CANPAC ... Canadian National Power Alcohol Conference
Can Pac For Res Cent Rep BC X ... Canada. Pacific Forest Research Centre. Report. BC X [*A publication*]
Can/Pack ... Canner Packer World [*A publication*]
Can Paint Finish ... Canadian Paint and Finishing [*A publication*]
Can Paint Varn ... Canadian Paint and Varnish [*A publication*]
Can Pap Rural Hist ... Canadian Papers in Rural History [*A publication*]
Can Pat Office Rec ... Canadian Patent Office. Record [*A publication*]
Can Pat Office Recd ... Canadian Patent Office. Record [*A publication*]
Can Pat Off Rec ... Canadian Patent Office. Record [*A publication*]   (DLA)
Can Pat Rep ... Canadian Patent Reporter [*Information service or system*] [*A publication*]
Can Peat Soc B ... Canadian Peat Society. Bulletin [*A publication*]
Can Period Index ... Canadian Periodical Index [*A publication*]
Can Pers ... Canadian Personnel and Industrial Relations Journal (Including the Canadian Training Digest) [*A publication*]
Can Persp ... Canadian Perspectives on International Law and Organization [*A publication*]   (DLA)
Can Pet ... Canadian Petroleum [*A publication*]
Can Pet Eng ... Canadian Petroleum Engineering [*A publication*]
Can Petro Eng ... Canadian Petro Engineering [*A publication*]
Can Petrol ... Canadian Petroleum [*A publication*]
Can Pharm J ... Canadian Pharmaceutical Journal [*A publication*]
Can Phil Rev ... Canadian Philosophical Reviews [*A publication*]
Can Pkg ... Canadian Packaging [*A publication*]
Can Plant Dis Surv ... Canadian Plant Disease Survey [*A publication*]
Can Plastics ... Canadian Plastics [*A publication*]
CANPLATES ... Chrome and Nickel Plating Logistics Automated Test Electronics System   (MCD)
Can Po ... Canadian Poetry [*A publication*]
Can Poetry ... Canadian Poetry [*A publication*]
Can Poult Rev ... Canadian Poultry Review [*A publication*]
Can Poultry Rev ... Canadian Poultry Review [*A publication*]
Can Power Eng ... Canadian Power Engineering [*A publication*]
Can Power Eng Plant Maint ... Canadian Power Engineering and Plant Maintenance [*A publication*]
Can P R ... Canadian Patent Reporter [*Information service or system*] [*A publication*]
Can Printer Publ ... Canadian Printer and Publisher [*A publication*]
Can Psl & Ind Rel J ... Canadian Personnel and Industrial Relations Journal (Including the Canadian Training Digest) [*A publication*]
Can Psychi ... Canadian Psychiatric Association. Journal [*A publication*]
Can Psychiatr Assoc J ... Canadian Psychiatric Association. Journal [*A publication*]
Can Psychol ... Canadian Psychologist [*A publication*]
Can Psychology ... Canadian Psychology [*A publication*]
Can Psychol Rev ... Canadian Psychological Review [*A publication*]
Can Psych Psych Can ... Canadian Psychology/Psychologie Canadienne [*A publication*]
Can Psych R ... Canadian Psychological Review [*A publication*]
Can Pub Ad ... Canadian Public Administration [*A publication*]   (DLA)
Can Pub Admin ... Canadian Public Administration/Administration Publique du Canada [*A publication*]
Can Publ Ad ... Canadian Public Administration/Administration Publique du Canada [*A publication*]
Can Public Admin ... Canadian Public Administration [*A publication*]
Can Public Policy ... Canadian Public Policy [*A publication*]
Can Public Policy (Guelph) ... Canadian Public Policy (Guelph) [*A publication*]
Can Pub Pol ... Canadian Public Policy [*A publication*]
Can Pub Policy ... Canadian Public Policy [*A publication*]
Can Pulp Paper Ind ... Canadian Pulp and Paper Industry [*A publication*]
CANQUA ... Canadian Quaternary Association
Can Quill ... Canadian Quill [*A publication*]
CANR ... Chamber of Agriculture and Natural Resources [*Philippines*]   (DS)
CANR ... Contemporary Authors New Revision Series [*A publication*]
CANRA ... Committee on Army and Navy Religious Activities [*National Jewish Welfare Board*]
Can RAC ... Canadian Reports, Appeal Cases [*1828-1913*] [*A publication*]   (DLA)
Can R Am St ... Canadian Review of American Studies [*A publication*]
Can R App Cas ... Canadian Reports, Appeal Cases [*1828-1913*] [*A publication*]   (DLA)
Can RC ... Railway Commission of Canada   (DLA)
Can R Cas ... Canadian Railway Cases [*A publication*]   (DLA)
Can R Com L ... Canadian Review of Comparative Literature/Revue Canadienne de Litterature Comparee [*A publication*]
Can Rec N H ... Canadian Record of Natural History and Geology [*A publication*]
Can Rec Sc ... Canadian Record of Science [*A publication*]
Can Renewable Energy News ... Canadian Renewable Energy News [*A publication*]
Can Res ... Canadian Research [*A publication*]

Can Res Dev ... Canadian Research and Development [*Later, Canadian Research*] [*A publication*]
Can Res Inst Launders Clean Tech ... Canadian Research Institute of Launderers and Cleaners. Technical Report [*A publication*]
CANRESLANT ... Senior Officer Reserve Fleet East Coast [*Navy*] [*Canada*]
Can Resour Dev Branch Fish Ser Halifax Prog Rep ... Canada. Resource Development Branch. Fisheries Service. Halifax Progress Report [*A publication*]
CANRESPAC ... Senior Officer Reserve Fleet West Coast [*Navy*] [*Canada*]
Can Rev ...... Canadian Review [*A publication*]
Can Rev Am Stud ... Canadian Review of American Studies [*A publication*]
Can Rev Comp Lt ... Canadian Review of Comparative Literature/Revue Canadienne de Litterature Comparee [*A publication*]
Can Rev Sociol Anthropol ... Canadian Review of Sociology and Anthropology [*A publication*]
Can Rev Stat ... Revised Statutes of Canada [*A publication*] (DLA)
Can Rev Stud Natl ... Canadian Review of Studies in Nationalism [*A publication*]
Can R Soc .. Canadian Review of Sociology and Anthropology [*A publication*]
Can R Soc A ... Canadian Review of Sociology and Anthropology [*A publication*]
Can R Soc Anthr ... Canadian Review of Sociology and Anthropology [*A publication*]
Can R Sociol Anth ... Canadian Review of Sociology and Anthropology [*A publication*]
Can R Sociol & Anthrop ... Canadian Review of Sociology and Anthropology [*A publication*]
Can R Studies Nationalism ... Canadian Review of Studies in Nationalism [*A publication*]
Can R Stud Nat ... Canadian Review of Studies in Nationalism [*A publication*]
Can Ry Cas ... Canada Railway Cases [*A publication*] (DLA)
Can Ry & T Cas ... Canadian Railway and Transport Cases [*A publication*] (DLA)
CANS .... Canada - North of 60 [*A publication*]
CANS .... Civilian Air Navigation School
CANS .... Coastal Air Navigation Supplement (MCD)
CANS .... Computer-Assisted Network Scheduling System (IEEE)
CANSAF ... Canadian Sales Finance Long Form Report
Can Sales Tax Rep (CCH) ... Canadian Sales Tax Reporter (Commerce Clearing House) [*A publication*] (DLA)
Can Sales Tax Rep CCH ... Canadian Sales Tax Reports. Commerce Clearing House [*A publication*]
CaNSAMC ... Cumberland Regional Library, Amherst, NS, Canada [*Library symbol*] [*Library of Congress*] (LCLS)
CaNSAMRMS ... Maritime Resource Management Service, Amherst, NS, Canada [*Library symbol*] [*Library of Congress*] (LCLS)
CaNSAP ... Canadian Network for Sampling Precipitation
CaNSAR .... Annapolis Valley Regional Library, Annapolis Royal, NS, Canada [*Library symbol*] [*Library of Congress*] (LCLS)
CaNSAS .... Saint Francis Xavier University, Antigonish, NS, Canada [*Library symbol*] [*Library of Congress*] (LCLS)
CaNSASC ... Saint Francis Xavier University, Chemistry Department, Antigonish, NS, Canada [*Library symbol*] [*Library of Congress*] (LCLS)
CANSAVE ... Canadian Save the Children Fund
CaNSBS .... South Shore Regional Library, Bridgewater, NS, Canada [*Library symbol*] [*Library of Congress*] (LCLS)
Can SC .... Canada Supreme Court (DLA)
Can SC .... Canada Supreme Court Reports [*A publication*] (DLA)
CANSCAIP ... Canadian Society of Children's Authors, Illustrators, and Performers
Can Sch Exec ... Canadian School Executive [*A publication*]
Can Sci .... Canadian Scientist [*A publication*]
Can Sc Mo ... Canadian Science Monthly [*A publication*]
Can SCR .... Canada Supreme Court Reports [*A publication*] (DLA)
Can SC Rep ... Canada Supreme Court Reports [*A publication*] (DLA)
CaNSCS .... Universite Sainte Anne, Church Point, NS, Canada [*Library symbol*] [*Library of Congress*] (LCLS)
Can S Ct ..... Canada Law Reports, Supreme Court [*A publication*] (DLA)
Can S Ct ..... Canada Supreme Court Reports [*A publication*] (DLA)
CaNSD ...... Dartmouth Regional Library, Dartmouth, NS, Canada [*Library symbol*] [*Library of Congress*] (LCLS)
CaNSDB .... Canada Department of the Environment, Bedford Institute of Oceanography, Dartmouth, NS, Canada [*Library symbol*] [*Library of Congress*] (LCLS)
CaNSDE .... Environment Canada, Dartmouth, NS, Canada [*Library symbol*] [*Library of Congress*] (LCLS)
CaNSDGH ... Dartmouth General Hospital, Dartmouth, NS, Canada [*Library symbol*] [*Library of Congress*] (LCLS)
CaNSDH ... Hermes Electronics Ltd., Dartmouth, NS, Canada [*Library symbol*] [*Library of Congress*] (LCLS)
CAN/SDI .. Canadian Service for the Selective Dissemination of Information [*National Research Council of Canada*] [*Information service or system*] (IID)
CaNSDMM ... MacLaren Marex, Dartmouth, NS, Canada [*Library symbol*] [*Library of Congress*] (LCLS)
CaNSDMP ... MacLaren Plansearch Ltd., Dartmouth, NS, Canada [*Library symbol*] [*Library of Congress*] (LCLS)

CaNSDNSH ... Nova Scotia Hospital, Dartmouth, NS, Canada [*Library symbol*] [*Library of Congress*] (LCLS)
CANSERVCOL ... Canadian Services College
Can Serv Med J ... Canadian Services Medical Journal [*A publication*]
CaNSH ...... Halifax City and Regional Library, Halifax, NS, Canada [*Library symbol*] [*Library of Congress*] (LCLS)
CaNSHA ... Canada Department of the Environment, Fisheries and Marine Service, Research and Development Directorate, Halifax Laboratory, Halifax, NS, Canada [*Library symbol*] [*Library of Congress*] [*Obsolete*] (LCLS)
CaNSHAE ... Nova Scotia Department of Education, Adult Education Division, Halifax, NS, Canada [*Library symbol*] [*Library of Congress*] (LCLS)
CaNSHAG ... Art Gallery of Nova Scotia, Halifax, NS, Canada [*Library symbol*] [*Library of Congress*] (LCLS)
CaNSHAI ... Atlantic Institute of Education, Halifax, NS, Canada [*Library symbol*] [*Library of Congress*] (LCLS)
CaNSHALMH ... Abbie J. Lane Memorial Hospital, Halifax, NS, Canada [*Library symbol*] [*Library of Congress*] (LCLS)
CaNSHANSS ... Anglican Church of Canada, Diocese of Nova Scotia, Synod Office, Halifax, NS, Canada [*Library symbol*] [*Library of Congress*] (LCLS)
CaNSHAR ... Algas Resources Ltd., Halifax, NS, Canada [*Library symbol*] [*Library of Congress*] (LCLS)
CaNSHBS ... Nova Scotia Barristers Society, Halifax, NS, Canada [*Library symbol*] [*Library of Congress*] (LCLS)
CaNSHCA ... Nova Scotia College of Art, Halifax, NS, Canada [*Library symbol*] [*Library of Congress*] (LCLS)
CaNSHCB ... Canadian Broadcasting Corp., Music and Record Library, Halifax, NS, Canada [*Library symbol*] [*Library of Congress*] (LCLS)
CaNSHCBC ... Canadian British Consultants Ltd., Halifax, NS, Canada [*Library symbol*] [*Library of Congress*] (LCLS)
CaNSHCDD ... Nova Scotia Commission on Drug Dependency, Halifax, NS, Canada [*Library symbol*] [*Library of Congress*] (LCLS)
CaNSHCH ... Camp Hill Hospital, Halifax, NS, Canada [*Library symbol*] [*Library of Congress*] (LCLS)
CaNSHCIC ... Nova Scotia Communications and Information Centre, Halifax, NS, Canada [*Library symbol*] [*Library of Congress*] (LCLS)
CaNSHD ... Dalhousie University, Halifax, NS, Canada [*Library symbol*] [*Library of Congress*] (LCLS)
CaNSHDAG ... Nova Scotia Department of the Attorney-General, Halifax, NS, Canada [*Library symbol*] [*Library of Congress*] (LCLS)
CaNSHDCA ... Nova Scotia Department of Consumer Affairs, Halifax, NS, Canada [*Library symbol*] [*Library of Congress*] (LCLS)
CaNSHDD ... Nova Scotia Department of Development, Halifax, NS, Canada [*Library symbol*] [*Library of Congress*] (LCLS)
CaNSHDE ... Nova Scotia Department of the Environment, Halifax, NS, Canada [*Library symbol*] [*Library of Congress*] (LCLS)
CaNSHDF ... Nova Scotia Department of Fisheries, Halifax, NS, Canada [*Library symbol*] [*Library of Congress*] (LCLS)
CaNSHDH ... Nova Scotia Department of Highways, Halifax, NS, Canada [*Library symbol*] [*Library of Congress*] (LCLS)
CaNSHDIP ... Dalhousie University, Institute of Public Affairs, Halifax, NS, Canada [*Library symbol*] [*Library of Congress*] (LCLS)
CaNSHDL ... Dalhousie University, Law School, Halifax, NS, Canada [*Library symbol*] [*Library of Congress*] (LCLS)
CaNSHDM ... Dalhousie University, W. K. Kellog Health Sciences Library, Halifax, NS, Canada [*Library symbol*] [*Library of Congress*] (LCLS)
CaNSHDMA ... Dalhousie University, Map Library, Halifax, NS, Canada [*Library symbol*] [*Library of Congress*] (LCLS)
CaNSHDOL ... Nova Scotia Department of Labour, Halifax, NS, Canada [*Library symbol*] [*Library of Congress*] (LCLS)
CaNSHDOM ... Nova Scotia Department of Mines, Halifax, NS, Canada [*Library symbol*] [*Library of Congress*] (LCLS)
CaNSHDR ... Nova Scotia Department of Recreation, Halifax, NS, Canada [*Library symbol*] [*Library of Congress*] (LCLS)
CaNSHDT ... Nova Scotia Department of Tourism, Halifax, NS, Canada [*Library symbol*] [*Library of Congress*] (LCLS)
CaNSHE ... Nova Scotia Provincial Library, Teachers' Library, Halifax, NS, Canada [*Library symbol*] [*Library of Congress*] (LCLS)
CaNSHF .... Canada Department of the Environment, Fisheries and Marine Service, Halifax, NS, Canada [*Library symbol*] [*Library of Congress*] (LCLS)
CaNSHH .... Nova Scotia Department of Health, Halifax, NS, Canada [*Library symbol*] [*Library of Congress*] (LCLS)
CaNSHHC ... Halifax County Regional Library, Halifax, NS, Canada [*Library symbol*] [*Library of Congress*] (LCLS)
CaNSHHI ... Halifax Infirmary, Health Services Library, Halifax, NS, Canada [*Library symbol*] [*Library of Congress*] (LCLS)
CaNSHHR ... Nova Scotia Human Rights Commission, Halifax, NS, Canada [*Library symbol*] [*Library of Congress*] (LCLS)
CaNSHIAP ... Canada Department of Indian Affairs and Northern Development, Parks Canada, Atlantic Regional Office, Halifax, NS, Canada [*Library symbol*] [*Library of Congress*] (LCLS)
CaNSHJ .... Canada Department of Justice, Halifax, NS, Canada [*Library symbol*] [*Library of Congress*] (LCLS)

642   Acronyms, Initialisms & Abbreviations Dictionary • 1992

CaNSHK ... University of King's College, Halifax, NS, Canada [*Library symbol*] [*Library of Congress*] (LCLS)

CaNSHKH ... Izaak Walton Killam Hospital for Children, Halifax, NS, Canada [*Library symbol*] [*Library of Congress*] (LCLS)

CaNSHKMGM ... Kitz, Matheson, Green & MacIsaac Law Firm, Halifax, NS, Canada [*Library symbol*] [*Library of Congress*] (LCLS)

CaNSHL.... Legislative Library, Halifax, NS, Canada [*Library symbol*] [*Library of Congress*] (LCLS)

CaNSHM .. National Research Council, Halifax, NS, Canada [*Library symbol*] [*Library of Congress*] (LCLS)

CaNSHMA ... Nova Scotia Department of Municipal Affairs, Halifax, NS, Canada [*Library symbol*] [*Library of Congress*] (LCLS)

CaNSHMI ... Canada Department of Manpower and Immigration, Halifax, NS, Canada [*Library symbol*] [*Library of Congress*] [*Obsolete*] (LCLS)

CaNSHMM ... Maritime Museum of the Atlantic Library, Halifax, NS, Canada [*Library symbol*] [*Library of Congress*] (LCLS)

CaNSHMS ... Nova Scotia Museum of Science, Halifax, NS, Canada [*Library symbol*] [*Library of Congress*] (LCLS)

CaNSHMT ... Canada Ministry of Transport, Marine Library, Halifax, NS, Canada [*Library symbol*] [*Library of Congress*] (LCLS)

CaNSHMTT ... Maritime Telegraph & Telephone, Information Resource Centre, Halifax, NS, Canada [*Library symbol*] [*Library of Congress*] (LCLS)

CaNSHN ... Canada Department of National Defence Research Establishment Atlantic, Dartmouth, NS, Canada [*Library symbol*] [*Library of Congress*] (LCLS)

CaNSHN ... Defence Research Establishment, Atlantic Defence Research Board, Halifax, NS, Canada [*Library symbol*] [*Library of Congress*] (LCLS)

CaNSHND ... Canada Department of National Defence, Reference and Recreational Library [*Stadacona*], Halifax, NS, Canada [*Library symbol*] [*Library of Congress*] (LCLS)

CaNSHP.... Nova Scotia Public Archives, Halifax, NS, Canada [*Library symbol*] [*Library of Congress*] (LCLS)

CaNSHPC ... Nova Scotia Power Corporation, Halifax, NS, Canada [*Library symbol*] [*Library of Congress*] (LCLS)

CaNSHPH ... Atlantic School of Theology, Halifax, NS, Canada [*Library symbol*] [*Library of Congress*] (LCLS)

CaNSHPL ... Nova Scotia Provincial Library, Nova Scotia Union Catalogue, Halifax, NS, Canada [*Library symbol*] [*Library of Congress*] (LCLS)

CaNSHPLX ... Nova Scotia Provincial Library, Reference Services, Halifax, NS, Canada [*Library symbol*] [*Library of Congress*] (LCLS)

CaNSHPW ... Public Works Canada, Atlantic Regional Library, Halifax, NS, Canada [*Library symbol*] [*Library of Congress*] (LCLS)

CaNSHR ... Nova Scotia Research Foundation, Halifax, NS, Canada [*Library symbol*] [*Library of Congress*] (LCLS)

CaNSHRC ... Nova Scotia Rehabilitation Centre, Halifax, NS, Canada [*Library symbol*] [*Library of Congress*] (LCLS)

CaNSHRL ... Nova Scotia Regional Libraries, Halifax, NS, Canada [*Library symbol*] [*Library of Congress*] (LCLS)

CaNSHRP ... Nova Scotia Research Foundation, Photogrammetry Division, Halifax, NS, Canada [*Library symbol*] [*Library of Congress*] (LCLS)

CaNSHS.... Saint Mary's University, Halifax, NS, Canada [*Library symbol*] [*Library of Congress*] (LCLS)

CaNSHSMC ... Stewart, MacKeen & Covert, Halifax, NS, Canada [*Library symbol*] [*Library of Congress*] (LCLS)

CaNSHSS ... Nova Scotia Department of Social Services, Halifax, NS, Canada [*Library symbol*] [*Library of Congress*] (LCLS)

CaNSHSW ... Maritime School of Social Work, Halifax, NS, Canada [*Library symbol*] [*Library of Congress*] (LCLS)

CaNSHT ... Nova Scotia Technical College, Halifax, NS, Canada [*Library symbol*] [*Library of Congress*] (LCLS)

CaNSHTI ... Nova Scotia Institute of Technology, Halifax, NS, Canada [*Library symbol*] [*Library of Congress*] (LCLS)

CaNSHTU ... Nova Scotia Teachers Union, Halifax, NS, Canada [*Library symbol*] [*Library of Congress*] (LCLS)

CaNSHTU ... Tuns Library, Halifax, NS, Canada [*Library symbol*] [*Library of Congress*] (LCLS)

CaNSHV ... Mount Saint Vincent University, Halifax, NS, Canada [*Library symbol*] [*Library of Congress*] (LCLS)

CaNSHVA ... Mount Saint Vincent University, Art Gallery, Halifax, NS, Canada [*Library symbol*] [*Library of Congress*] (LCLS)

CaNSHVGH ... Victoria General Hospital, Health Sciences Library, Halifax, NS, Canada [*Library symbol*] [*Library of Congress*] (LCLS)

CaNSHVH ... Halifax Regional Vocational School, Halifax, NS, Canada [*Library symbol*] [*Library of Congress*] (LCLS)

CaNSHW .. Canada Department of the Environment, Atmospheric Environment Service, Atlantic Region, Halifax, NS, Canada [*Library symbol*] [*Library of Congress*] (LCLS)

CANSIM... Canadian Socio-Economic Information Management System [*Statistics Canada*] [*Database*] [*Ottawa, ON*] (IID)

CanSIS ...... Canadian Soil Information System [*Land Resource and Research Institute*] [*Ottawa, ON*] [*Information service or system*] (IID)

CaNSKR.... Canada Department of Agriculture, Research Station, Kentville, NS, Canada [*Library symbol*] [*Library of Congress*] (LCLS)

CaNSKS .... Nova Scotia Sanatorium, Kentville, NS, Canada [*Library symbol*] [*Library of Congress*] (LCLS)

CaNSLA .... Louisbourg Archives, Louisbourg, NS, Canada [*Library symbol*] [*Library of Congress*] (LCLS)

Can Slavonic Pa ... Canadian Slavonic Papers [*A publication*]

Can Slavonic Pap ... Canadian Slavonic Papers [*A publication*]

Can Slav P ... Canadian Slavonic Papers [*A publication*]

Can Slav Stud ... Canadian-American Slavic Studies [*A publication*]

CaNSLF .... Fortress of Louisbourg, Canada Department of Indian Affairs and Northern Development, Fortress of Louisbourg, NS, Canada [*Library symbol*] [*Library of Congress*] (LCLS)

Can Sl P ..... Canadian Slavonic Papers [*A publication*]

CaNSME... Eastern Counties Regional Library, Mulgrave, NS, Canada [*Library symbol*] [*Library of Congress*] (LCLS)

Can's Mental Health ... Canada's Mental Health [*A publication*]

CANSN ..... Canada - North of 60. Newsletter [*A publication*]

CAN/SND ... Scientific Numeric Database Service [*National Research Council of Canada*] [*Information service or system*] (IID)

CaNSNgP ... Pictou-Antigonish Regional Library, New Glasgow, NS, Canada [*Library symbol*] [*Library of Congress*] (LCLS)

Can Soc Pet Geol Mem ... Canadian Society of Petroleum Geologists. Memoir [*A publication*]

CanSP........ Canadian Slavonic Papers [*A publication*]

CANSPA ... Canadian Swimming Pool Association

Can Spec Publ Fish Aquat Sci ... Canadian Special Publication of Fisheries and Aquatic Sciences [*A publication*]

Can Spectrosc ... Canadian Spectroscopy [*A publication*]

Can Spectry ... Canadian Spectroscopy [*A publication*]

CanSS........ Canadian-American Slavic Studies [*A publication*]

CaNSSC .... Cape Breton Regional Library, Sydney, NS, Canada [*Library symbol*] [*Library of Congress*] (LCLS)

CaNSSCG ... Canada Coast Guard College, Sydney, NS, Canada [*Library symbol*] [*Library of Congress*] (LCLS)

CaNSSmM ... Memorial High School, Sidney Mines, NS, Canada [*Library symbol*] [*Library of Congress*] (LCLS)

CaNSSSRH ... Saint Rita's Hospital, Sydney, NS, Canada [*Library symbol*] [*Library of Congress*] (LCLS)

CaNSSX .... College of Cape Breton, Sydney, NS, Canada [*Library symbol*] [*Library of Congress*] (LCLS)

CaNSSXA ... College of Cape Breton, Archives and General Library, Sydney, NS, Canada [*Library symbol*] [*Library of Congress*] (LCLS)

CaNSTA.... Nova Scotia Agricultural College, Truro, NS, Canada [*Library symbol*] [*Library of Congress*] (LCLS)

CANSTAN ... Canadian Standards [*Standards Council of Canada*] [*Information service or system*] (CRD)

Can Stand Ass CSA Stand ... Canadian Standards Association. CSA Standard [*A publication*]

Can Stat ..... Statutes of Canada [*A publication*] (DLA)

Can Statis R ... Canadian Statistical Review [*A publication*]

Can Stat O & Regs ... Statutory Orders and Regulations [*Canada*] [*A publication*] (DLA)

Can Stat Rev ... Canadian Statistical Review [*A publication*]

CaNSTC.... Colchester-East Hants Regional Library, Truro, NS, Canada [*Library symbol*] [*Library of Congress*] (LCLS)

Can St Ec ... Canadian Studies in Economics [*A publication*]

Can Struct Eng Conf ... Canadian Structural Engineering Conference [*A publication*]

CaNSTT .... Nova Scotia Teachers' College, Truro, NS, Canada [*Library symbol*] [*Library of Congress*] (LCLS)

Can Studies Population ... Canadian Studies in Population [*A publication*]

Can Sulfur Symp ... Canadian Sulfur Symposium [*A publication*]

Can Sup Ct ... Canada Supreme Court Reports [*A publication*] (DLA)

Can Surv ... Canadian Surveyor [*A publication*]

Can Surveyor ... Canadian Surveyor [*A publication*]

CaNSWA.... Acadia University, Wolfville, NS, Canada [*Library symbol*] [*Library of Congress*] (LCLS)

CaNSWAG ... Acadia University, Department of Geography, Wolfville, NS, Canada [*Library symbol*] [*Library of Congress*] (LCLS)

CaNSWH .. Wolfville Historical Museum, Wolfville, NS, Canada [*Library symbol*] [*Library of Congress*] (LCLS)

CaNSY....... Western Counties Regional Library, Yarmouth, NS, Canada [*Library symbol*] [*Library of Congress*] (LCLS)

CaNSYHM ... Yarmouth County Historical Society, Yarmouth, NS, Canada [*Library symbol*] [*Library of Congress*] (LCLS)

Can Symp Remote Sensing Proc ... Canadian Symposium of Remote Sensing. Proceedings [*A publication*]

CanT .... Canadian Telefunken [*Record label*]

Can T .... Canberra Times [*A publication*]

CANT .... Cantabile [*Flowing Style*] [*Music*]

CANT .... Cantabrigiensis [*Of Cambridge University*] [*Latin*] (ROG)

Cant........... Canterbury [*Record label*]

CANT .... Canterbury [*City in England*]

CANT .... Canticle of Canticles [*Old testament book*] [*Douay version*]

Cant........... Canticles [*Song of Solomon*] [*Old Testament book*]

CANT .... Cantilever

CANT .... Canto [*Melody*] [*Music*]

CANT .... Cantor

CANT .... Chinese Atmospheric Nuclear Test (MCD)
CANT .... Coalition Against Noneffective Lightning Protection Technologies (EA)
CANTAB... Cantabile [*Flowing Style*] [*Music*]
CANTAB... Cantabrigiensis [*Of Cambridge University*] [*Latin*]
CANTASS .. Canadian Towed Array SONAR System
CANTAT... Canadian Transatlantic Telephone Cable [*Between Canada and England*]
Can Tax App Bd ... Canada Tax Appeal Board Cases [*A publication*] (DLA)
Can Taxation ... Canadian Taxation [*A publication*]
Can Tax Cas ... Canada Tax Cases [*A publication*] (DLA)
Can Tax Cas Ann ... Canada Tax Cases, Annotated [*A publication*] (DLA)
Can Tax Found ... Canadian Tax Foundation. Conference Report [*A publication*] (DLA)
Can Tax Found Rep Proc Tax Conf ... Canadian Tax Foundation. Report of Proceedings of the Tax Conference [*A publication*] (DLA)
Can Tax J .. Canadian Tax Journal [*A publication*]
Can Tax J Tax Policy ... Canadian Taxation. A Journal of Tax Policy [*A publication*]
Can Tax LJ ... Canadian Tax Law Journal [*A publication*] (DLA)
Can Tax News ... Canadian Tax News [*A publication*]
Can Tax Rep (CCH) ... Canadian Tax Reporter (Commerce Clearing House) [*A publication*] (DLA)
Can Tax Rep CCH ... Canadian Tax Reports. Commerce Clearing House [*A publication*]
CANTCO .. Cannot Comply (NVT)
Can Tech Rep Fish Aquat Sci ... Canadian Technical Report of Fisheries and Aquatic Sciences [*A publication*]
Can Tech Rep Hydrogr Ocean Sci ... Canadian Technical Report of Hydrography and Ocean Sciences [*A publication*]
Canteras Explot ... Canteras y Explotaciones [*A publication*]
CANTERB ... Canterbury [*City and county borough in England*]
Canterbury Chamber Commer Agric Bull ... Canterbury Chamber of Commerce. Agricultural Bulletin [*A publication*]
Canterbury Eng J ... Canterbury Engineering Journal [*A publication*]
Canterbury L Rev ... Canterbury Law Review [*A publication*]
Can Terr..... Territories Law Reports [*1885-1907*] [*Canada*] [*A publication*] (DLA)
Can Text J ... Canadian Textile Journal [*A publication*]
CAnth .... Current Anthropology [*A publication*]
CANTHA.. Cantharides [*Spanish Fly*] [*Pharmacy*] (ROG)
CANTHARD ... Cantharides [*Spanish Fly*] [*Pharmacy*] (ROG)
Can Theat R ... Canadian Theatre Review [*A publication*]
Can Theatre R ... Canadian Theatre Review [*A publication*]
CAnthr .... Current Anthropology [*A publication*]
C Anthropol Ecol Hum ... Cahiers d'Anthropologie et d'Ecologie Humaines [*A publication*]
CANTIL .... Cantilever (MSA)
C Antiq....... Carmarthenshire Antiquary [*A publication*]
C Antiq FPL ... Coins and Antiquities Ltd. Fixed Price List [*London*] [*A publication*]
Cant Mount ... Canterbury Mountaineer [*New Zealand*] [*A publication*]
Cant Mus Bull ... Canterbury Music Bulletin [*A publication*]
CANTO..... Cantando [*In a Singing Manner*] [*Music*] (ROG)
Can Tob Grower ... Canadian Tobacco Grower [*A publication*]
Canto Greg ... Canto Gregoriano [*A publication*]
Canto Lib ... Canto Libre [*A publication*]
CANTON ... Cantonments [*Military*] (ROG)
Cantor Med & Surg ... Cantor's Traumatic Medicine and Surgery for the Attorney [*A publication*] (DLA)
CANTRAC ... Catalog of Navy Training Courses (NVT)
CANTRAINDIV ... Canadian Training Division [*Canadian Navy*]
CANTRAINRON ... Canadian Training Squadron [*Canadian Navy*]
CANTRAN ... Canceled Transmission (CET)
Can Transp ... Canadian Transportation [*Later, Canadian Transportation and Distribution Management*] [*A publication*]
Cantrill's F ... Cantrill's Filmnotes [*A publication*]
Cantrill's Fmnts ... Cantrill's Filmnotes [*A publication*]
Can TS....... Canada Treaty Series [*A publication*] (DLA)
CANTUAR ... Cantuaria [*Canterbury*] [*Latin*]
Cantuar...... Cantuariensis [*Of Canterbury*] [*Latin*] (ILCA)
Cantwell..... Cantwell's Cases on Tolls and Customers [*Ireland*] [*A publication*] (DLA)
CANU........ Canadian Nurse [*A publication*]
CANUA..... Canadian Nurse [*A publication*]
CANUC:H ... Canadian Union Catalogue of Library Materials for the Handicapped [*National Library of Canada*] [*Information service or system*] (IID)
CANUCS... Union List of Serials in the Social Sciences and Humanities Held by Canadian Libraries
CANUDG ... Comparative Animal Nutrition [*A publication*]
CAN-UK.... Canada-United Kingdom
CAN-UK JCEC ... Canada-United Kingdom-Joint Communications Electronics Committees
CANUKUS ... Canada-United Kingdom-United States [*Agreement*]
CANUKUS JCECS ... Canada-United Kingdom-United States Joint Communications-Electronics Committees
CANUNET ... Canadian University Computer Network (MCD)
Ca Nurs..... Cancer Nursing [*A publication*]
CAN-US.... Canada-United States (AFM)
CANUSE... Canadian-United States Eastern Power Complex

Can-US Law J ... Canada-United States Law Journal [*A publication*]
Can-US LJ ... Canada-United States Law Journal [*A publication*]
CANV .... Canvas
Can Vending ... Canadian Vending [*A publication*]
Can Vet J ... Canadian Veterinary Journal [*A publication*]
Can Vet Record ... Canadian Veterinary Record [*A publication*]
Can Victoria Mem Mus B ... Canada. Victoria Memorial Museum. Bulletin [*A publication*]
Can Voc J ... Canadian Vocational Journal [*A publication*]
CANW....... Campaign Against Nuclear War (EA)
CANW....... Canada Now Social Studies Magazine for Schools [*A publication*]
Can W .... Canada Weekly [*A publication*]
CANW....... Cancer News [*A publication*]
CANWA .... Chemia Analityczna (Warszawa) [*A publication*]
Can Water Resour Branch Water Resour Pap ... Canada. Water Resources Branch. Water Resources Paper [*A publication*]
Can Water Resour Branch Water Resour Pap S ... Canada. Water Resources Branch. Water Resources Paper S. Sediment [*A publication*]
Can Water Resour J ... Canadian Water Resources Journal [*A publication*]
CANWEC ... Canadian National Committee, World Energy Conference
CANWEL ... Canadian Water Supply Energy Loop
Can Wel ..... Canadian Welfare [*A publication*]
Can Welder Fabr ... Canadian Welder and Fabricator [*A publication*]
Can Welfare ... Canadian Welfare [*A publication*]
CaNWFsPCN ... Parks Canada, Nahanni National Park, Fort Simpson, NT, Canada [*Library symbol*] [*Library of Congress*] (LCLS)
CaNWFSPCW ... Parks Canada, Wood Buffalo National Park, Fort Smith, NT, Canada [*Library symbol*] [*Library of Congress*] (LCLS)
CaNWHRN ... Northwest Territories Public Library Services, Hay River, NT, Canada [*Library symbol*] [*Library of Congress*] (LCLS)
CaNWII..... Canada Department of Indian Affairs and Northern Development, Inuvik Research Laboratory, Inuvik, NT, Canada [*Library symbol*] [*Library of Congress*] (LCLS)
Can Wildl Serv ... Canadian Wildlife Service [*A publication*]
Can Wildl Serv Occas Pap ... Canadian Wildlife Service. Occasional Papers [*A publication*]
Can Wildl Serv Prog Notes ... Canadian Wildlife Service. Progress Notes [*A publication*]
Can Wildl Serv Rep Ser ... Canadian Wildlife Service. Report Series [*A publication*]
Can in Wld Aff ... Canada in World Affairs [*A publication*] (DLA)
Can Woodl Rev ... Canadian Woodlands Review [*A publication*]
Can & World ... Canada and the World [*A publication*]
CANWP .... Canadian Network Papers. National Library of Canada [*A publication*]
CaNWPPCA ... Parks Canada, Auyuittuq National Park, Pangnirtung, NT, Canada [*Library symbol*] [*Library of Congress*] (LCLS)
CaNWYECW ... Environment Canada, Canadian Wildlife Service, Yellowknife, NT, Canada [*Library symbol*] [*Library of Congress*] (LCLS)
CaNWYGI ... Government In-Service Library, Yellowknife, NT, Canada [*Library symbol*] [*Library of Congress*] (LCLS)
CaNWYIM ... Canada Department of Indian and Northern Affairs, Yellowknife, NT, Canada [*Library symbol*] [*Library of Congress*] (LCLS)
CaNWYND ... Canada Department of National Defence, Northern Region Information System, [*NORIS*], Yellowknife, NT, Canada [*Library symbol*] [*Library of Congress*] (LCLS)
CaNWYPC ... Parks Canada, Yellowknife, NT, Canada [*Library symbol*] [*Library of Congress*] (LCLS)
CANX........ Cannon Express, Inc. [*NASDAQ symbol*] (NQ)
CANY .... Canyonlands National Park
Can YBIL .. Canadian Yearbook of International Law [*A publication*]
Can Yb of Internat ... Canadian Yearbook of International Law [*A publication*]
Can YB Int'l L ... Canadian Yearbook of International Law [*A publication*]
Cany C News ... Canyon Cinema News [*A publication*]
Can Yearb Int Law ... Canadian Yearbook of International Law [*A publication*]
Can Yearbook Int L ... Canadian Yearbook of International Law [*A publication*]
CANYPS ... Canadian National Yellow Pages Service
CANZLLI ... Current Australian and New Zealand Legal Literature Index [*A publication*] (APTA)
CAO........... Cabinet Maker and Retail Furnisher [*A publication*]
CAO........... Canadian Army Orders
CAO........... Cara Operations Ltd. [*Toronto Stock Exchange symbol*]
CAO........... Carolina Freight Corp. [*NYSE symbol*] (SPSG)
CAO........... Carotid Artery Occlusion [*Medicine*]
CAO........... Central Accounting Office [*Military*] (AFM)
CAO........... Change of Appointing Office [*Aviation*] (FAAC)
CAO........... Chemical Abstracts, Odd-Numbered Issue
CAO........... Chief Accountant Officer [*RAF*] [*British*]
CAO........... Chief Administrative Officer
CAO........... Chief Agency Officer [*Insurance*]
CAO........... Chronic Airway Obstruction [*Medicine*]
CAO........... Circuit Activation Order
CAO........... City Administrative Office

CAO.......... Civil Affairs Officer [*Navy*]
CAO.......... Clayton, NM [*Location identifier*] [*FAA*]   (FAAL)
CAO.......... Collateral Action Officer [*Army*]   (AABC)
CAO.......... Commonwealth Arts Organization   (EA)
CAO.......... Communications Allocation Order   (CINC)
CAO.......... Community Affairs Officer
CAO.......... Conception Assistee par Ordinateur [*Computer-Assisted Design - CAD*] [*French*]
CAO.......... Congress of Astrological Organizations [*Defunct*]   (EA)
CAO.......... Consumer Affairs Office [*Federal Energy Administration*]
CAO.......... Contract Administration Office [*or Officer*] [*Navy*]
CAO.......... Coordinated Atomic Operations   (CINC)
CAO.......... Cost Analysis Office [*Army*]   (RDA)
CAO.......... Cost of Analysis Organization [*Navy*]   (NG)
CAO.......... Cretans' Association "Omonoia"   (EA)
CAO.......... Crimean Astrophysical Observatory
CAO.......... Cultural Affairs Officer [*United States Information Service*]
CAO.......... Customer Assistance Office
CAO.......... Cyclophosphamide, Adriamycin, Oncovin [*Vincristine*] [*Antineoplastic drug regimen*]
CAOAA..... Civil Air Operations Officers' Association of Australia
CaOAc....... Action Public Library, Action, ON, Canada [*Library symbol*] [*Library of Congress*]   (LCLS)
CaOAcH.... Acton High School, Acton, ON, Canada [*Library symbol*] [*Library of Congress*]   (LCLS)
CaOAgG.... Gage Educational Publishing Ltd., Agincourt, ON, Canada [*Library symbol*] [*Library of Congress*]   (LCLS)
CaOAj....... Ajax Public Library, Ajax, ON, Canada [*Library symbol*] [*Library of Congress*]   (LCLS)
CaOAL...... Alliston Public Library, Alliston, ON, Canada [*Library symbol*] [*Library of Congress*]   (LCLS)
CaOAmF... Fort Malden National Historic Park, Amherstburg, ON, Canada [*Library symbol*] [*Library of Congress*]   (LCLS)
CaOArM ... Middlesex County Public Library, Arva, ON, Canada [*Library symbol*] [*Library of Congress*]   (LCLS)
CaOAtH.... Atikokan High School, Atikokan, ON, Canada [*Library symbol*] [*Library of Congress*]   (LCLS)
CaOAu....... Aurora Public Library, Aurora, ON, Canada [*Library symbol*] [*Library of Congress*]   (LCLS)
CaOAuYCE ... York County Board of Education, Aurora, ON, Canada [*Library symbol*] [*Library of Congress*]   (LCLS)
CaOB......... Brockville Public Library, Brockville, ON, Canada [*Library symbol*] [*Library of Congress*]   (LCLS)
CaOBa....... Barrie Public Library, Barrie, ON, Canada [*Library symbol*] [*Library of Congress*]   (LCLS)
CaOBaG.... Georgian Bay Regional Library, Barrie, ON, Canada [*Library symbol*] [*Library of Congress*]   (LCLS)
CaOBaGC ... Georgian College of Applied Arts and Technology, Barrie, ON, Canada [*Library symbol*] [*Library of Congress*]   (LCLS)
CaOBan..... Bancroft Public Library, Bancroft, ON, Canada [*Library symbol*] [*Library of Congress*]   (LCLS)
CaOBarF ... Frontenac County Public Library, Barriefield, ON, Canada [*Library symbol*] [*Library of Congress*]   (LCLS)
CaOBaS..... Simcoe County Co-op, Barrie, ON, Canada [*Library symbol*] [*Library of Congress*]   (LCLS)
CaOBCAB ... Town of Caledon Public Libraries, Albion-Bolton Branch, Bolton, ON, Canada [*Library symbol*] [*Library of Congress*]   (LCLS)
CaOBCCL ... Canada Cement Lafarge Ltd., Belleville, ON, Canada [*Library symbol*] [*Library of Congress*]   (LCLS)
CaOBE ...... Belleville Public Library, Belleville, ON, Canada [*Library symbol*] [*Library of Congress*]   (LCLS)
CaOBeaTE ... Thorah Eldon Historical Society, Inc., Beaverton, ON, Canada [*Library symbol*] [*Library of Congress*]   (LCLS)
CaOBeD .... Beamsville District Secondary School, Beamsville, ON, Canada [*Library symbol*] [*Library of Congress*]   (LCLS)
CaOBelL.... Loyalist College of Applied Arts and Technology, Belleville, ON, Canada [*Library symbol*] [*Library of Congress*]   (LCLS)
CaOBfNO ... Northern Ontario Public School Principals' Association, Burks Falls, ON, Canada [*Library symbol*] [*Library of Congress*]   (LCLS)
CaOBNE ... Northern Electric Co., Belleville, ON, Canada [*Library symbol*] [*Library of Congress*]   (LCLS)
CaOBolC ... Caledon Public Libraries, Bolton, ON, Canada [*Library symbol*] [*Library of Congress*]   (LCLS)
CaOBoN .... Newcastle Public Library Board, Bowmanville, ON, Canada [*Library symbol*] [*Library of Congress*]   (LCLS)
CaOBP....... Canada Department of Agriculture, Research Institute, Belleville, ON, Canada [*Library symbol*] [*Library of Congress*] [*Obsolete*]   (LCLS)
CaOBr........ Bradford Public Library, Bradford, ON, Canada [*Library symbol*] [*Library of Congress*]   (LCLS)
CaOBra...... Brampton Public Library, Brampton, ON, Canada [*Library symbol*] [*Library of Congress*]   (LCLS)
CaOBrac.... Bracebridge Public Library, Bracebridge, ON, Canada [*Library symbol*] [*Library of Congress*]   (LCLS)
CaOBram... Chinguacousy Township Public Library, Bramalea, ON, Canada [*Library symbol*] [*Library of Congress*]   (LCLS)
CaOBramB ... Bell Northern Research, Bramalea, ON, Canada [*Library symbol*] [*Library of Congress*]   (LCLS)

CaOBraNT ... Northern Telecom, Brampton, ON, Canada [*Library symbol*] [*Library of Congress*]   (LCLS)
CaOBrER .. Eldorado Resources Ltd., Blind River Refinery, Blind River, ON, Canada [*Library symbol*] [*Library of Congress*]   (LCLS)
CaOBrt ...... Brantford Public Library, Brantford, ON, Canada [*Library symbol*] [*Library of Congress*]   (LCLS)
CaOBrtBM .. Brant County Historical Museum, Brantford, ON, Canada [*Library symbol*] [*Library of Congress*]   (LCLS)
CaOBrtP.... Pauline Johnson College, Brantford, ON, Canada [*Library symbol*] [*Library of Congress*]   (LCLS)
CaOBrtWI ... Woodland Indian Cultural Educational Centre, Brantford, ON, Canada [*Library symbol*] [*Library of Congress*]   (LCLS)
CaOBSL .... Saint Lawrence College of Applied Arts and Technology, Brockville, ON, Canada [*Library symbol*] [*Library of Congress*]   (LCLS)
CaOBU ...... Burlington Public Library, Burlington, ON, Canada [*Library symbol*] [*Library of Congress*]   (LCLS)
CaOBUC ... Canada Department of Mines and Resources, Centre for Inland Waters, Burlington, ON, Canada [*Library symbol*] [*Library of Congress*]   (LCLS)
CaOBUCC ... Canadian Canners Ltd., Burlington, ON, Canada [*Library symbol*] [*Library of Congress*]   (LCLS)
CaOBUL ... Lord Elgin High School, Burlington, ON, Canada [*Library symbol*] [*Library of Congress*]   (LCLS)
CaOC........ Cathodal Opening Contraction [*Also, COC*] [*Physiology*]
CAOC........ Combat Air Operations Center   (CINC)
CAOC........ Constant Axial Offset Control   (NRCH)
CaOC .... Cornwall Public Library, Cornwall, ON, Canada [*Library symbol*] [*Library of Congress*]   (LCLS)
CaOCam .... Campbellford Public Library, Campbellford, ON, Canada [*Library symbol*] [*Library of Congress*]   (LCLS)
CaOCauHM ... Haldimand County Museum Board, Cayuga, ON, Canada [*Library symbol*] [*Library of Congress*]   (LCLS)
CaOCaW ... Waterloo Regional Library, Cambridge, ON, Canada [*Library symbol*] [*Library of Congress*]   (LCLS)
CaOCC ...... Courtaulds Ltd., Cornwall, ON, Canada [*Library symbol*] [*Library of Congress*] [*Obsolete*]   (LCLS)
CaOCGH... Cornwall General Hospital, Cornwall, ON, Canada [*Library symbol*] [*Library of Congress*]   (LCLS)
CaOCha..... Chatham Public Library, Chatham, ON, Canada [*Library symbol*] [*Library of Congress*]   (LCLS)
CaOChaH ... Chatham Public General Hospital, Chatham, ON, Canada [*Library symbol*] [*Library of Congress*]   (LCLS)
CaOChaK .. Chatham-Kent Museum, Chatham, ON, Canada [*Library symbol*] [*Library of Congress*]   (LCLS)
CaOChaKC ... Kent County Public Library, Chatham, ON, Canada [*Library symbol*] [*Library of Congress*]   (LCLS)
CaOChaT .. Thames Arts Centre, Chatham, ON, Canada [*Library symbol*] [*Library of Congress*]   (LCLS)
CaOCheRB ... Rayside-Balfour Public Library, Chelmsford, ON, Canada [*Library symbol*] [*Library of Congress*]   (LCLS)
CaOChiN... Norton Electric Co., Chippewa, ON, Canada [*Library symbol*] [*Library of Congress*]   (LCLS)
CAOCI...... Commercially Available Organic Chemicals Index [*Chemical Notation Association*] [*Databank*] [*British*]
CaOCkA .... Atomic Energy of Canada, Chalk River, ON, Canada [*Library symbol*] [*Library of Congress*]   (LCLS)
CaOCkE .... Canada Department of the Environment, Petawawa Forest Experiment Station, Chalk River, ON, Canada [*Library symbol*] [*Library of Congress*]   (LCLS)
CaOCN...... National Historic Park, Cornwall, ON, Canada [*Library symbol*] [*Library of Congress*]   (LCLS)
CaOCo .... Cobourg Public Library, Cobourg, ON, Canada [*Library symbol*] [*Library of Congress*]   (LCLS)
CaOCoA .... Art Gallery of Cobourg, Cobourg, ON, Canada [*Library symbol*] [*Library of Congress*]   (LCLS)
CaOCoc ..... Cochrane Public Library, Cochrane, ON, Canada [*Library symbol*] [*Library of Congress*]   (LCLS)
CaOCoGF ... General Foods Ltd., Cobourg, ON, Canada [*Library symbol*] [*Library of Congress*]   (LCLS)
CaOCol...... Collingwood Public Library, Collingwood, ON, Canada [*Library symbol*] [*Library of Congress*]   (LCLS)
CAOCOMNET ... Coordination of Atomic Operations Communications Net
CaOCp....... Carleton Place Public Library, Carleton Place, ON, Canada [*Library symbol*] [*Library of Congress*]   (LCLS)
CaOCpG.... Goodwood Data Systems Ltd., Carleton Place, ON, Canada [*Library symbol*] [*Library of Congress*]   (LCLS)
CaOCpL .... Leigh Instruments Ltd., Carleton Place, ON, Canada [*Library symbol*] [*Library of Congress*]   (LCLS)
CaOCpS..... I. P. Sharp Associates Ltd., Carleton Place, ON, Canada [*Library symbol*] [*Library of Congress*]   (LCLS)
CAOCS...... Carrier Aircraft Operational Compatibility System [*Navy*]
CaOCSDG ... Seaway Valley Libraries [*Formerly, Stormont, Dundas, and Glengarry Counties Public Library*], Cornwall, ON, Canada [*Library symbol*] [*Library of Congress*]   (LCLS)
CaOCSL .... Saint Lawrence College, Cornwall, ON, Canada [*Library symbol*] [*Library of Congress*]   (LCLS)
CaOCTH ... Town of Haldimand Public Libraries, Caledonia, ON, Canada [*Library symbol*] [*Library of Congress*]   (LCLS)

CaOD......... Dundas Public Library, Dundas, ON, Canada [*Library symbol*] [*Library of Congress*] (LCLS)
CAODC..... Canadian Association of Oilwell Drilling Contractors
CaODe....... Delhi Public Library, Delhi, ON, Canada [*Library symbol*] [*Library of Congress*] (LCLS)
CaODeAg.. Canada Department of Agriculture, Research Station, Delhi, ON, Canada [*Library symbol*] [*Library of Congress*] (LCLS)
CaODH..... Highland Secondary School, Dundas, ON, Canada [*Library symbol*] [*Library of Congress*] (LCLS)
CaODO..... Opeongo High School, Douglas, ON, Canada [*Library symbol*] [*Library of Congress*] (LCLS)
CaODr....... Dryden Public Library, Dryden, ON, Canada [*Library symbol*] [*Library of Congress*] (LCLS)
CaODu...... Dunnville Public Library, Dunnville, ON, Canada [*Library symbol*] [*Library of Congress*] (LCLS)
CaODur..... Durham Public Library, Durham, ON, Canada [*Library symbol*] [*Library of Congress*] (LCLS)
CAOE........ Contractor-Acquired Operational Equipment
CaOE......... Exeter Public Library, Exeter, ON, Canada [*Library symbol*] [*Library of Congress*] (LCLS)
CaOEf........ Ear Falls Public Library, Ear Falls, ON, Canada [*Library symbol*] [*Library of Congress*] (LCLS)
CaOEL....... Elliot Lake Public Library, Elliot Lake, ON, Canada [*Library symbol*] [*Library of Congress*] (LCLS)
CaOELS.... Elliot Lake Secondary School, Elliot Lake, ON, Canada [*Library symbol*] [*Library of Congress*] (LCLS)
CaOEsE..... Essex County Public Library, Essex, ON, Canada [*Library symbol*] [*Library of Congress*] (LCLS)
CAOF........ Catholic Association of Foresters (EA)
CaOFaF..... Falconbridge Nickel Mines Ltd., Metallurgical Research Library, Falconbridge, ON, Canada [*Library symbol*] [*Library of Congress*] (LCLS)
CaOFerW.. Wellington County Public Library, Fergus, ON, Canada [*Library symbol*] [*Library of Congress*] (LCLS)
CaOFF....... Fort Frances Public Library, Fort Frances, ON, Canada [*Library symbol*] [*Library of Congress*] (LCLS)
CaOFl........ Flesherton Public Library, Flesherton, ON, Canada [*Library symbol*] [*Library of Congress*] (LCLS)
CaOFWN.. Northwestern Regional Library System, Thunder Bay, ON, Canada [*Library symbol*] [*Library of Congress*] (LCLS)
CAOG........ Crown Agents for Overseas Governments [*British*]
CaOG......... Guelph Public Library, Guelph, ON, Canada [*Library symbol*] [*Library of Congress*] (LCLS)
CaOGal...... Cambridge Public Library, Cambridge, ON, Canada [*Library symbol*] [*Library of Congress*] (LCLS)
CaOGalC... Galt Collegiate Institute, Cambridge, ON, Canada [*Library symbol*] [*Library of Congress*] (LCLS)
CaOGCF.... Canada Department of Agriculture, Canadian Farm Management Data System, Guelph, ON, Canada [*Library symbol*] [*Library of Congress*] (LCLS)
CaOGDR... Uniroyal Ltd., Guelph, ON, Canada [*Library symbol*] [*Library of Congress*] (LCLS)
CaOGE....... Entomological Society of Ontario, Guelph, ON, Canada [*Library symbol*] [*Library of Congress*] (LCLS)
CaOGeG.... Georgetown District High School, Georgetown, ON, Canada [*Library symbol*] [*Library of Congress*] (LCLS)
CaOGeo..... Georgetown Public Library, Georgetown, ON, Canada [*Library symbol*] [*Library of Congress*] (LCLS)
CaOGeV.... Varian Canada, Inc., Georgetown, ON, Canada [*Library symbol*] [*Library of Congress*] (LCLS)
CaOGIAP... Canada Department of Indian Affairs and Northern Development, Parks Canada, Ontario Regional Office, Cornwall, ON, Canada [*Library symbol*] [*Library of Congress*] (LCLS)
CaOGoH.... Huron County Public Library, Goderich, ON, Canada [*Library symbol*] [*Library of Congress*] (LCLS)
CaOGra..... Gravenhurst Public Library, Gravenhurst, ON, Canada [*Library symbol*] [*Library of Congress*] (LCLS)
CaOGri...... Grimsby Public Library and Art Gallery, Grimsby, ON, Canada [*Library symbol*] [*Library of Congress*] (LCLS)
CaOGriSM... Stone Shop Museum, Grimsby, ON, Canada [*Library symbol*] [*Library of Congress*] (LCLS)
CaOGU...... University of Guelph, Guelph, ON, Canada [*Library symbol*] [*Library of Congress*] (LCLS)
CaOH........ Hamilton Public Library, Hamilton, ON, Canada [*Library symbol*] [*Library of Congress*] (LCLS)
CaOHAG... Art Gallery of Hamilton, Hamilton, ON, Canada [*Library symbol*] [*Library of Congress*] (LCLS)
CaOHaH... Haliburton County Public Library, Hastings, ON, Canada [*Library symbol*] [*Library of Congress*] (LCLS)
CaOHai..... Haileybury Public Library, Haileybury, ON, Canada [*Library symbol*] [*Library of Congress*] (LCLS)
CaOHal..... Haliburton Public Library, Haliburton, ON, Canada [*Library symbol*] [*Library of Congress*] (LCLS)
CaOHan.... Hanover Public Library, Hanover, ON, Canada [*Library symbol*] [*Library of Congress*] (LCLS)
CaOHarAg... Canada Department of Agriculture, Research Station, Harrow, ON, Canada [*Library symbol*] [*Library of Congress*] (LCLS)

CAOHC..... Council for Accreditation in Occupational Hearing Conservation (EA)
CaOHDF... Dominion Foundries & Steel Ltd., Hamilton, ON, Canada [*Library symbol*] [*Library of Congress*] (LCLS)
CaOHe....... Hearst Public Library, Hearst, ON, Canada [*Library symbol*] [*Library of Congress*] (LCLS)
CaOHEC... Hamilton Education Centre, Hamilton, ON, Canada [*Library symbol*] [*Library of Congress*] (LCLS)
CaOHk...... Hawkesbury Public Library, Hawkesbury, ON, Canada [*Library symbol*] [*Library of Congress*] (LCLS)
CaOHkC.... International Cellulose Research Ltd., Hawkesbury, ON, Canada [*Library symbol*] [*Library of Congress*] (LCLS)
CaOHIEG... East Gwillimbury Public Libraries, Holland Landing, ON, Canada [*Library symbol*] [*Library of Congress*] (LCLS)
CaOHM..... McMaster University, Hamilton, ON, Canada [*Library symbol*] [*Library of Congress*] (LCLS)
CaOHMA... McMaster University, Archives and Special Collections Division, Hamilton, ON, Canada [*Library symbol*] [*Library of Congress*] (LCLS)
CaOHMB... McMaster University, Biomedical Library, Hamilton, ON, Canada [*Library symbol*] [*Library of Congress*] (LCLS)
CaOHMC... Mohawk College of Applied Arts and Technology, Hamilton, ON, Canada [*Library symbol*] [*Library of Congress*] (LCLS)
CaOHMM... McMaster University, Map Library, Hamilton, ON, Canada [*Library symbol*] [*Library of Congress*] (LCLS)
CaOHOHS... Canadian Centre for Occupational Health and Safety, Hamilton, ON, Canada [*Library symbol*] [*Library of Congress*] (LCLS)
CaOHRB... Royal Botanical Gardens, Hamilton, ON, Canada [*Library symbol*] [*Library of Congress*] (LCLS)
CaOHS...... Hamilton Spectator, Hamilton, ON, Canada [*Library symbol*] [*Library of Congress*] (LCLS)
CaOHSC... South Central Regional Library, Hamilton, ON, Canada [*Library symbol*] [*Library of Congress*] (LCLS)
CaOHSCC... Steel Company of Canada, Hamilton, ON, Canada [*Library symbol*] [*Library of Congress*] (LCLS)
CaOHU..... Huntsville Public Library, Huntsville, ON, Canada [*Library symbol*] [*Library of Congress*] (LCLS)
CaOHW..... Canadian Westinghouse Library, Hamilton, ON, Canada [*Library symbol*] [*Library of Congress*] (LCLS)
CaOHWL... Wentworth Library, Hamilton, ON, Canada [*Library symbol*] [*Library of Congress*] (LCLS)
CaOI.......... Ingersoll Public Library, Ingersoll, ON, Canada [*Library symbol*] [*Library of Congress*] (LCLS)
CaOIf......... Iroquois Falls Public Library, Iroquois Falls, ON, Canada [*Library symbol*] [*Library of Congress*] (LCLS)
CaOIg........ Ignace Public Library, Ignace, ON, Canada [*Library symbol*] [*Library of Congress*] (LCLS)
CaOIsE...... ERCO Industries Ltd., Islington, ON, Canada [*Library symbol*] [*Library of Congress*] (LCLS)
CaOK........ Kingston Public Library, Kingston, ON, Canada [*Library symbol*] [*Library of Congress*] (LCLS)
CaOKA...... ALCAN Research & Development Ltd., Kingston, ON, Canada [*Library symbol*] [*Library of Congress*] (LCLS)
CaOKAL.... Aluminum Co. of Canada Ltd., Kingston, ON, Canada [*Library symbol*] [*Library of Congress*] (LCLS)
CaOKanA... Arctec Canada Ltd., Kanata, ON, Canada [*Library symbol*] [*Library of Congress*] (LCLS)
CaOKanMC... Miller Communications Systems Ltd., Kanata, ON, Canada [*Library symbol*] [*Library of Congress*] (LCLS)
CaOKanMD... Mitel Corp., Digital Systems, Kanata, ON, Canada [*Library symbol*] [*Library of Congress*] (LCLS)
CaOKAOS... Anglican Church of Canada, Diocese of Ontario, Synod Office, Kingston, ON, Canada [*Library symbol*] [*Library of Congress*] (LCLS)
CaOKap..... Kapuskasing Public Library, Kapuskasing, ON, Canada [*Library symbol*] [*Library of Congress*] (LCLS)
CaOKASG... Anglican Church of Canada, St. George's Cathedral, Kingston, ON, Canada [*Library symbol*] [*Library of Congress*] (LCLS)
CaOKCAA... Catholic Church, Archdiocese of Kingston, Archives, Kingston, ON, Canada [*Library symbol*] [*Library of Congress*] (LCLS)
CaOKCIL.. Millhaven Fibers Ltd., Kingston, ON, Canada [*Library symbol*] [*Library of Congress*] (LCLS)
CaOKcKT... King Township Public Library, King City, ON, Canada [*Library symbol*] [*Library of Congress*] (LCLS)
CaOKD...... Du Pont of Canada Ltd., Research Centre Library, Kingston, ON, Canada [*Library symbol*] [*Library of Congress*] (LCLS)
CaOKe....... Kenora Public Library, Kenora, ON, Canada [*Library symbol*] [*Library of Congress*] (LCLS)
CaOKeAKS... Anglican Church of Canada, Diocese of Keewatin, Synod Office, Kenora, ON, Canada [*Library symbol*] [*Library of Congress*] (LCLS)
CaOKemAF... Ontario Ministry of Agriculture and Food, Kemptville, ON, Canada [*Library symbol*] [*Library of Congress*] (LCLS)
CaOKes...... Georgina Township Public Library, Keswick, ON, Canada [*Library symbol*] [*Library of Congress*] (LCLS)

CaOKF....... Canadian Land Forces Command and Staff College, Kingston, ON, Canada [*Library symbol*] [*Library of Congress*] (LCLS)

CaOKFC.... Frontenac County Library, Kingston, ON, Canada [*Library symbol*] [*Library of Congress*] (LCLS)

CaOKit....... Kitchener Public Library, Kitchener, ON, Canada [*Library symbol*] [*Library of Congress*] (LCLS)

CaOKitM... Midwestern Regional Library, Kitchener, ON, Canada [*Library symbol*] [*Library of Congress*] (LCLS)

CaOKitW... Kitchener-Waterloo Record, Kitchener, ON, Canada [*Library symbol*] [*Library of Congress*] (LCLS)

CaOKL ...... Lake Ontario Regional Library System, Kingston, ON, Canada [*Library symbol*] [*Library of Congress*] (LCLS)

CaOKleM .. McMichael Canadian Collection, Kleinburg, ON, Canada [*Library symbol*] [*Library of Congress*] (LCLS)

CaOKlN..... Northeastern Regional Library, Kirkland Lake, ON, Canada [*Library symbol*] [*Library of Congress*] (LCLS)

CaOKlNC ... Northern College, Kirkland Lake Campus, Kirkland Lake, ON, Canada [*Library symbol*] [*Library of Congress*] (LCLS)

CaOKlT ..... Teck Centennial Public Library, Kirkland Lake, ON, Canada [*Library symbol*] [*Library of Congress*] (LCLS)

CaOKMM ... Marine Museum of the Great Lakes at Kingston, Kingston, ON, Canada [*Library symbol*] [*Library of Congress*] (LCLS)

CaOKQ...... Queen's University, Kingston, ON, Canada [*Library symbol*] [*Library of Congress*] (LCLS)

CaOKQA ... Queen's University, Agnes Ethrington Art Centre, Kingston, ON, Canada [*Library symbol*] [*Library of Congress*] (LCLS)

CaOKQAR ... Queen's University, Archives, Kingston, ON, Canada [*Library symbol*] [*Library of Congress*] (LCLS)

CaOKQG ... Queen's University, Department of Geography, Kingston, ON, Canada [*Library symbol*] [*Library of Congress*] (LCLS)

CaOKQGS ... Queen's University, Department of Geological Sciences, Kingston, ON, Canada [*Library symbol*] [*Library of Congress*] (LCLS)

CaOKQH... Queen's University, Health Sciences Library, Kingston, ON, Canada [*Library symbol*] [*Library of Congress*] (LCLS)

CaOKQL... Queen's University, Law Library, Kingston, ON, Canada [*Library symbol*] [*Library of Congress*] (LCLS)

CaOKQM... Queen's University, McArthur College of Education, Kingston, ON, Canada [*Library symbol*] [*Library of Congress*] (LCLS)

CaOKQMA ... Queen's University, Douglas Library, Map Collection, Kingston, ON, Canada [*Library symbol*] [*Library of Congress*] (LCLS)

CaOKR ...... Royal Military College, Kingston, ON, Canada [*Library symbol*] [*Library of Congress*] (LCLS)

CaOKRC ... Regiopolis College, Kingston, ON, Canada [*Library symbol*] [*Library of Congress*] (LCLS)

CaOKSL.... Saint Lawrence College of Applied Arts and Technology, Kingston, ON, Canada [*Library symbol*] [*Library of Congress*] (LCLS)

CaOKUTD ... Urban Transportation Development Corp., Kingston, ON, Canada [*Library symbol*] [*Library of Congress*] (LCLS)

CaOL .... London Public Library and Art Museum, London, ON, Canada [*Library symbol*] [*Library of Congress*] (LCLS)

CaOLAg .... Canada Department of Agriculture, Research Institute, London, ON, Canada [*Library symbol*] [*Library of Congress*] (LCLS)

CaOLaTN ... Township of Norfolk Public Library, Langston, ON, Canada [*Library symbol*] [*Library of Congress*] (LCLS)

CaOLB...... London Board of Education, London, ON, Canada [*Library symbol*] [*Library of Congress*] (LCLS)

CaOLC ...... Catholic Central High School, London, ON, Canada [*Library symbol*] [*Library of Congress*] (LCLS)

CaOLCR.... Clark Road Secondary School, London, ON, Canada [*Library symbol*] [*Library of Congress*] (LCLS)

CaOLCSSCP ... Ontario Ministry of Community and Social Services, Children's Psychiatric Research Institute, London, ON, Canada [*Library symbol*] [*Library of Congress*] (LCLS)

CaOLeI...... Canada Department of Indian Affairs and Northern Development, Point Pelee National Park, Leamington, ON, Canada [*Library symbol*] [*Library of Congress*] (LCLS)

CaOLFC .... Fanshawe College of Applied Arts and Technology, London, ON, Canada [*Library symbol*] [*Library of Congress*] (LCLS)

CaOLH...... Huron College, London, ON, Canada [*Library symbol*] [*Library of Congress*] (LCLS)

CaOLi........ Lindsay Public Library, Lindsay, ON, Canada [*Library symbol*] [*Library of Congress*] (LCLS)

CaOLiV ..... Victoria County Public Library, Lindsay, ON, Canada [*Library symbol*] [*Library of Congress*] (LCLS)

CaOLK ...... King's College, London, ON, Canada [*Library symbol*] [*Library of Congress*] (LCLS)

CaOLLCR ... Labatt's Central Research Library, London, ON, Canada [*Library symbol*] [*Library of Congress*] (LCLS)

CaOLLE.... Lake Erie Regional Library, London, ON, Canada [*Library symbol*] [*Library of Congress*] (LCLS)

CaOLOS.... Oakridge Secondary School, London, ON, Canada [*Library symbol*] [*Library of Congress*] (LCLS)

CaOLPT .... Pinchas Troester Library, Congregation B'nai Israel, London, ON, Canada [*Library symbol*] [*Library of Congress*] (LCLS)

CaOLSJ..... Saint Joseph's Hospital, London, ON, Canada [*Library symbol*] [*Library of Congress*] (LCLS)

CaOLT....... United Lodge of Theosophists, London, ON, Canada [*Library symbol*] [*Library of Congress*] (LCLS)

CaOLTMC ... Three M Canada, Inc., Technical Information Centre, London, ON, Canada [*Library symbol*] [*Library of Congress*] (LCLS)

CaOLU ...... University of Western Ontario, London, ON, Canada [*Library symbol*] [*Library of Congress*] (LCLS)

CaOLUG ... University of Western Ontario, Department of Geography, London, ON, Canada [*Library symbol*] [*Library of Congress*] (LCLS)

CaOLUH... University Hospital, London, ON, Canada [*Library symbol*] [*Library of Congress*] (LCLS)

CaOLUL.... University of Western Ontario, Law Library, London, ON, Canada [*Library symbol*] [*Library of Congress*] (LCLS)

CaOLUM .. University of Western Ontario, Health Science Centre, London, ON, Canada [*Library symbol*] [*Library of Congress*] (LCLS)

CaOLUMG ... University of Western Ontario, MacIntosh Gallery, London, ON, Canada [*Library symbol*] [*Library of Congress*] (LCLS)

CaOLURC ... London Urban Resource Centre, London, ON, Canada [*Library symbol*] [*Library of Congress*] (LCLS)

CaOLUS.... University of Western Ontario, School of Library and Information Science, London, ON, Canada [*Library symbol*] [*Library of Congress*] (LCLS)

CaOLUVA ... University of Western Ontario, Visual Arts Department, London, ON, Canada [*Library symbol*] [*Library of Congress*] (LCLS)

CaOLVH ... Victoria Hospital, London, ON, Canada [*Library symbol*] [*Library of Congress*] (LCLS)

CaOM....... Mississauga Public Library, Mississauga, ON, Canada [*Library symbol*] [*Library of Congress*] (LCLS)

CaOMa...... Markham Public Library, Markham, ON, Canada [*Library symbol*] [*Library of Congress*] (LCLS)

CaOMABP ... Abitibi-Price, Inc., Mississauga, ON, Canada [*Library symbol*] [*Library of Congress*] (LCLS)

CaOMAC .. Alkaril Chemicals Ltd., Mississauga, ON, Canada [*Library symbol*] [*Library of Congress*] (LCLS)

CaOMAECL ... AECL International, Mississauga, ON, Canada [*Library symbol*] [*Library of Congress*] (LCLS)

CAOMAF ... Command Analysis of Office of Military Assistance Funding (MCD)

CaOMaH... Markham High School, Markham, ON, Canada [*Library symbol*] [*Library of Congress*] (LCLS)

CaOMAI ... Allelix, Inc., Mississauga, ON, Canada [*Library symbol*] [*Library of Congress*] (LCLS)

CaOMap.... Vaughan Public Library, Maple, ON, Canada [*Library symbol*] [*Library of Congress*] (LCLS)

CaOMat..... Matheson Public Library, Matheson, ON, Canada [*Library symbol*] [*Library of Congress*] (LCLS)

CaOMBC .. Beak Consultants, Mississauga, ON, Canada [*Library symbol*] [*Library of Congress*] (LCLS)

CaOMCCS ... Centraide, Montreal, PQ, Canada [*Library symbol*] [*Library of Congress*] (LCLS)

CaOMCG .. Ciba/Geigy Canada Ltd., Mississauga, ON, Canada [*Library symbol*] [*Library of Congress*] (LCLS)

CaOMCSG ... Canada Systems Group, Mississauga, ON, Canada [*Library symbol*] [*Library of Congress*] (LCLS)

CaOMD..... Du Pont of Canada Ltd., Maitland, ON, Canada [*Library symbol*] [*Library of Congress*] (LCLS)

CaOMDG ... Dominion Glass Co. Ltd., Mississauga, ON, Canada [*Library symbol*] [*Library of Congress*] (LCLS)

CaOMDO ... Domglas, Inc., Corporate Library, Mississauga, ON, Canada [*Library symbol*] [*Library of Congress*] (LCLS)

CaOMDR .. Dunlop Research Centre, Sheridan Park, Mississauga, ON, Canada [*Library symbol*] [*Library of Congress*] (LCLS)

CaOMDS .. Delphax Systems, Mississauga, ON, Canada [*Library symbol*] [*Library of Congress*] (LCLS)

CaOME..... University of Toronto, Erindale College, Mississauga, ON, Canada [*Library symbol*] [*Library of Congress*] (LCLS)

CaOMGO ... Gulf Oil Canada Ltd., Mississauga, ON, Canada [*Library symbol*] [*Library of Congress*] (LCLS)

CaOMi....... Midland Public Library, Midland, ON, Canada [*Library symbol*] [*Library of Congress*] (LCLS)

CaOMiH ... Huronia Historical Park, Midland, ON, Canada [*Library symbol*] [*Library of Congress*] (LCLS)

CaOMil ..... Milton Central Library, Milton, ON, Canada [*Library symbol*] [*Library of Congress*] (LCLS)

CaOMIN ... International Nickel Co. of Canada, Mississauga, ON, Canada [*Library symbol*] [*Library of Congress*] (LCLS)

CaOMinSA ... Simcoe County Archives, Minesing, ON, Canada [*Library symbol*] [*Library of Congress*] (LCLS)

CaOMNT .. Northern Telecom, Mississauga, ON, Canada [*Library symbol*] [*Library of Congress*] (LCLS)

CaOMorUC ... Upper Canada Village, Morrisburg, ON, Canada [*Library symbol*] [*Library of Congress*] (LCLS)

CaOMPW ... Pratt & Whitney Aircraft Ltd., Mississauga, ON, Canada
[*Library symbol*] [*Library of Congress*] (LCLS)

CaOMSK ... Smith, Kline & French Canada Ltd., Niagara Falls, ON, Canada
[*Library symbol*] [*Library of Congress*] (LCLS)

CaOMSM ... Syntex, Inc., Medical Library, Mississauga, ON, Canada
[*Library symbol*] [*Library of Congress*] (LCLS)

CaONaLAC ... Lennox and Addington Counties Public Libraries, Napanee,
ON, Canada [*Library symbol*] [*Library of
Congress*] (LCLS)

CaONaLAM ... Lennox and Addington Museum, Napanee, ON, Canada
[*Library symbol*] [*Library of Congress*] (LCLS)

CaONB ...... North Bay Public Library, North Bay, ON, Canada [*Library
symbol*] [*Library of Congress*] (LCLS)

CaONbNU ... Nipissing University College, North Bay, ON, Canada [*Library
symbol*] [*Library of Congress*] (LCLS)

CaONBWF ... West Ferris Secondary School, North Bay, ON, Canada
[*Library symbol*] [*Library of Congress*] (LCLS)

CaONe .... Newmarket Public Library, Newmarket, ON, Canada [*Library
symbol*] [*Library of Congress*] (LCLS)

CaONf .... Niagara Falls Public Library, Niagara Falls, ON, Canada
[*Library symbol*] [*Library of Congress*] (LCLS)

CaONfA .... Acres Consulting Services Ltd., Niagara Falls, ON, Canada
[*Library symbol*] [*Library of Congress*] (LCLS)

CaONfCy ... Cyanamid, Niagara Falls, ON, Canada [*Library symbol*]
[*Library of Congress*] (LCLS)

CaONfLC .. Lanmer Consultants Ltd., Niagara Falls, ON, Canada [*Library
symbol*] [*Library of Congress*] (LCLS)

CaONfWPL ... W. P. London & Associates, Niagara Falls, ON, Canada
[*Library symbol*] [*Library of Congress*] (LCLS)

CaONHi .... Niagara Historical Society, Niagara-On-The-Lake, ON, Canada
[*Library symbol*] [*Library of Congress*] (LCLS)

CaONl .... New Liskeard Public Library, New Liskeard, ON, Canada
[*Library symbol*] [*Library of Congress*] (LCLS)

CaONSM .. St. Mark's Church, Niagara-On-The-Lake, ON, Canada [*Library
symbol*] [*Library of Congress*] (LCLS)

CaOOA ...... Public Archives of Canada, Ottawa, ON, Canada [*Library
symbol*] [*Library of Congress*] (LCLS)

CaOOAC ... Algonquin College, Ottawa, ON, Canada [*Library symbol*]
[*Library of Congress*] (LCLS)

CaOOACF ... Ontario Cancer Foundation, Alta Vista Branch, Ottawa, ON,
Canada [*Library symbol*] [*Library of Congress*] (LCLS)

CaOOACR ... Algonquin College, Rideau Campus, Ottawa, ON, Canada
[*Library symbol*] [*Library of Congress*] (LCLS)

CaOOAE ... Atomic Energy of Canada, Ottawa, ON, Canada [*Library
symbol*] [*Library of Congress*] (LCLS)

CaOOAEA ... Public Archives, Ethnic Archives of Canada, Ottawa, ON,
Canada [*Library symbol*] [*Library of Congress*] (LCLS)

CaOOAEC ... Atomic Energy of Canada Chemical Co., Ottawa, ON, Canada
[*Library symbol*] [*Library of Congress*] (LCLS)

CaOOAECB ... Atomic Energy Control Board, Ottawa, ON, Canada [*Library
symbol*] [*Library of Congress*] (LCLS)

CaOOAER ... Atomic Energy of Canada Ltd., Research Co., Ottawa, ON,
Canada [*Library symbol*] [*Library of Congress*] (LCLS)

CaOOAg .... Canada Department of Agriculture, Ottawa, ON, Canada
[*Library symbol*] [*Library of Congress*] (LCLS)

CaOOAgA ... Department of Agriculture, Animal Disease Research Institute,
Ottawa, ON, Canada [*Library symbol*] [*Library of
Congress*] (LCLS)

CaOOAgAR ... Department of Agriculture, Animal Research Institute,
Ottawa, ON, Canada [*Library symbol*] [*Library of
Congress*] (LCLS)

CaOOAgB ... Department of Agriculture, Plant Research Institute, Ottawa,
ON, Canada [*Library symbol*] [*Library of
Congress*] (LCLS)

CaOOAgC ... Department of Agriculture, Central Experimental Farm
Reference Library, Ottawa, ON, Canada [*Library symbol*]
[*Library of Congress*] [*Obsolete*] (LCLS)

CaOOAgCh ... Department of Agriculture, Chemistry Division, Ottawa, ON,
Canada [*Library symbol*] [*Library of Congress*]
[*Obsolete*] (LCLS)

CaOOAGCH ... Department of Agriculture, Neatby Library, Ottawa, ON,
Canada [*Library symbol*] [*Library of Congress*] (LCLS)

CaOOAgE ... Department of Agriculture, Entomology Research Institute,
Ottawa, ON, Canada [*Library symbol*] [*Library of
Congress*] (LCLS)

CaOOAgER ... Department of Agriculture, Engineering Research Service,
Ottawa, ON, Canada [*Library symbol*] [*Library of
Congress*] (LCLS)

CaOOAgFP ... Department of Agriculture, Food Production and Marketing
Branch, Laboratory Services Section, Ottawa, ON, Canada
[*Library symbol*] [*Library of Congress*] (LCLS)

CaOOAgH ... Department of Agriculture, Horticultural Division, Ottawa,
ON, Canada [*Library symbol*] [*Library of Congress*]
[*Obsolete*] (LCLS)

CaOOAgL ... Department of Agriculture, Legal Library, Ottawa, ON, Canada
[*Library symbol*] [*Library of Congress*] [*Obsolete*] (LCLS)

CaOOAgO ... Department of Agriculture, Research Station, Ottawa, ON,
Canada [*Library symbol*] [*Library of Congress*] (LCLS)

CaOOAgSR ... Department of Agriculture, Soil Research Institute, Ottawa,
ON, Canada [*Library symbol*] [*Library of
Congress*] (LCLS)

CaOOAI .... AMCA International Ltd., Ottawa, ON, Canada [*Library
symbol*] [*Library of Congress*] (LCLS)

CaOOak .... Oakville Public Library, Oakville, ON, Canada [*Library
symbol*] [*Library of Congress*] (LCLS)

CaOOakA ... Appleby College, Oakville, ON, Canada [*Library symbol*]
[*Library of Congress*] (LCLS)

CaOOakSC ... Sheridan College, Oakville, ON, Canada [*Library symbol*]
[*Library of Congress*] (LCLS)

CaOOAM ... Canada Department of National Defence, Ottawa, ON, Canada
[*Library symbol*] [*Library of Congress*] [*Obsolete*] (LCLS)

CaOOAMA ... Public Archives of Canada, National Map Collection, Ottawa,
ON, Canada [*Library symbol*] [*Library of
Congress*] (LCLS)

CaOOAMS ... Public Archives, Manuscript Division, Ottawa, ON, Canada
[*Library symbol*] [*Library of Congress*] (LCLS)

CaOOANF ... Public Archives, National Film Archives, Ottawa, ON, Canada
[*Library symbol*] [*Library of Congress*] (LCLS)

CaOOAOA ... Anglican Church of Canada, Diocese of Ottawa, Archives,
Ottawa, ON, Canada [*Library symbol*] [*Library of
Congress*] (LCLS)

CaOOAR ... Canadian Broadcasting Corp., Ottawa, ON, Canada [*Library
symbol*] [*Library of Congress*] (LCLS)

CaOOAT ... Canadian Transport Commission, Air Transport Committee,
Ottawa, ON, Canada [*Library symbol*] [*Library of
Congress*] [*Obsolete*] (LCLS)

CaOOB ...... Bank of Canada, Ottawa, ON, Canada [*Library symbol*]
[*Library of Congress*] (LCLS)

CaOOBC ... Bowmar Canada Ltd., Ottawa, ON, Canada [*Library symbol*]
[*Library of Congress*] (LCLS)

CaOOBDR ... Bell Canada Data Resource Center, Ottawa, ON, Canada
[*Library symbol*] [*Library of Congress*] (LCLS)

CaOOBE ... Ottawa Board of Education, Ottawa, ON, Canada [*Library
symbol*] [*Library of Congress*] (LCLS)

CaOOBM ... Bartonian Metaphysical Society, Ottawa, ON, Canada [*Library
symbol*] [*Library of Congress*] (LCLS)

CaOOBMC ... Canada Department of Supply and Services, Bureau of
Management and Consulting, Ottawa, ON, Canada
[*Library symbol*] [*Library of Congress*] (LCLS)

CaOOC ...... Ottawa Public Library, Ottawa, ON, Canada [*Library symbol*]
[*Library of Congress*] (LCLS)

CaOOCAC ... Canada Art Council, Ottawa, ON, Canada [*Library symbol*]
[*Library of Congress*] (LCLS)

CaOOCAP ... Canadian Periodical Reference Services, Ottawa, ON, Canada
[*Library symbol*] [*Library of Congress*] [*Obsolete*] (LCLS)

CaOOCAR ... Canadian Arctic Resources Committee, Ottawa, ON, Canada
[*Library symbol*] [*Library of Congress*] (LCLS)

CaOOCB ... Colonel By Secondary School, Ottawa, ON, Canada [*Library
symbol*] [*Library of Congress*] (LCLS)

CaOOCBC ... Conference Board in Canada, Ottawa, ON, Canada [*Library
symbol*] [*Library of Congress*] (LCLS)

CaOOCBE ... Carleton Board of Education, Ottawa, ON, Canada [*Library
symbol*] [*Library of Congress*] (LCLS)

CaOOCC ... Carleton University, Ottawa, ON, Canada [*Library symbol*]
[*Library of Congress*] (LCLS)

CaOOCCAH ... Carleton University, Department of Art History, Ottawa,
ON, Canada [*Library symbol*] [*Library of
Congress*] (LCLS)

CaOOCCFA ... Canadian Centre for Films on Art, Ottawa, ON, Canada
[*Library symbol*] [*Library of Congress*] (LCLS)

CaOOCCG ... Carleton University, Geography Department, Ottawa, ON,
Canada [*Library symbol*] [*Library of Congress*] (LCLS)

CaOOCCR ... Canada Department of Energy, Mines, and Resources, Canada
Centre for Remote Sensing, Ottawa, ON, Canada [*Library
symbol*] [*Library of Congress*] (LCLS)

CaOOCCSS ... Carleton University, Social Sciences Division, Ottawa, ON,
Canada [*Library symbol*] [*Library of Congress*]
[*Obsolete*] (LCLS)

CaOOCD ... Canadian International Development Agency, Ottawa, ON,
Canada [*Library symbol*] [*Library of Congress*] (LCLS)

CaOOCDA ... Canadian Dental Association, Ottawa, ON, Canada [*Library
symbol*] [*Library of Congress*] (LCLS)

CaOOCDC ... Computing Devices of Canada, Ottawa, ON, Canada [*Library
symbol*] [*Library of Congress*] (LCLS)

CaOOCDP ... College Dominicain de Philosophie et de Theologie, Ottawa,
ON, Canada [*Library symbol*] [*Library of
Congress*] (LCLS)

CaOOCF ... Canadian Film Institute, Ottawa, ON, Canada [*Library symbol*]
[*Library of Congress*] (LCLS)

CaOOCH ... Children's Hospital, Ottawa, ON, Canada [*Library symbol*]
[*Library of Congress*] (LCLS)

CaOOCHR ... Canadian Human Rights Commission, Ottawa, ON, Canada
[*Library symbol*] [*Library of Congress*] (LCLS)

CaOOCI .... Canada Department of Consumer and Corporate Affairs,
Ottawa, ON, Canada [*Library symbol*] [*Library of
Congress*] (LCLS)

CaOOCLC ... Canadian Labour Congress, Ottawa, ON, Canada [*Library
symbol*] [*Library of Congress*] (LCLS)

CaOOCM ... Central Mortgage & Housing Corp., Ottawa, ON, Canada
[*Library symbol*] [*Library of Congress*] (LCLS)

CaOOCMA ... Canadian Medical Association, Ottawa, ON, Canada [*Library
symbol*] [*Library of Congress*] (LCLS)

CaOOCMC ... Central Mortgage & Housing Corp., Children's Environments Advisory Service, Ottawa, ON, Canada [*Library symbol*] [*Library of Congress*] (LCLS)

CaOOCMS ... Central Mortgage & Housing Corp., Standards Information Centre, Ottawa, ON, Canada [*Library symbol*] [*Library of Congress*] (LCLS)

CaOOCN... Canadian Nurses' Association, Ottawa, ON, Canada [*Library symbol*] [*Library of Congress*] (LCLS)

CaOOCNP ... Energy, Mines, and Resources Canada, CNP Resource Centre, Ottawa, ON, Canada [*Library symbol*] [*Library of Congress*] (LCLS)

CaOOCO... Canada Department of Communications, Ottawa, ON, Canada [*Library symbol*] [*Library of Congress*] (LCLS)

CaOOCOG ... COGLA [*Canada Oil and Gas Lands Administration*] Ocean Mining Resource Centre, APGTC [*Administration du Petrole et du Gaz des Terres du Canada*], Ottawa, ON, Canada [*Library symbol*] [*Library of Congress*] (LCLS)

CaOOCOL ... Commissioner of Official Languages, Ottawa, ON, Canada [*Library symbol*] [*Library of Congress*] (LCLS)

CaOOCP ... Community Planning Association of Canada, Ottawa, ON, Canada [*Library symbol*] [*Library of Congress*] (LCLS)

CaOOCPC ... Canadian Police College, Royal Canadian Mounted Police, Ottawa, ON, Canada [*Library symbol*] [*Library of Congress*] (LCLS)

CaOOCRC ... Canadian Red Cross Society, Ottawa, ON, Canada [*Library symbol*] [*Library of Congress*] (LCLS)

CaOOCRLF ... Canadian Rights and Liberties Federation, Ottawa, ON, Canada [*Library symbol*] [*Library of Congress*] (LCLS)

CaOOCRM ... Canadian Royal Mint, Ottawa, ON, Canada [*Library symbol*] [*Library of Congress*] (LCLS)

CaOOCS ... Public Service Commission, Ottawa, ON, Canada [*Library symbol*] [*Library of Congress*] (LCLS)

CaOOCSL ... Public Service Commission, Training Centres Libraries, Ottawa, ON, Canada [*Library symbol*] [*Library of Congress*] (LCLS)

CaOOCT ... Canadian Teachers Federation, Ottawa, ON, Canada [*Library symbol*] [*Library of Congress*] (LCLS)

CaOOCU... Association of Universities and Colleges of Canada, Ottawa, ON, Canada [*Library symbol*] [*Library of Congress*] (LCLS)

CaOOCUI ... Canadian Unity Information Centre, Ottawa, ON, Canada [*Library symbol*] [*Library of Congress*] (LCLS)

CaOOCUS ... Canadian University Service Overseas, Ottawa, ON, Canada [*Library symbol*] [*Library of Congress*] (LCLS)

CaOOCW ... Canadian Council on Social Development, Ottawa, ON, Canada [*Library symbol*] [*Library of Congress*] (LCLS)

CaOOCz .... Ottawa Citizen, Ottawa, ON, Canada [*Library symbol*] [*Library of Congress*] (LCLS)

CaOODLC ... Data Logic Canada, Library Education Services, Ottawa, ON, Canada [*Library symbol*] [*Library of Congress*] (LCLS)

CaOODP... Canada Department of Supply and Services, Ottawa, ON, Canada [*Library symbol*] [*Library of Congress*] (LCLS)

CaOODPS ... Canada Department of Supply and Services, Compensation Branch, Superannuation Division, Ottawa, ON, Canada [*Library symbol*] [*Library of Congress*] (LCLS)

CaOODRC ... Canada Department of National Defence, Defence Research Establishment, Ottawa, ON, Canada [*Library symbol*] [*Library of Congress*] (LCLS)

CaOOE...... Canada Department of External Affairs, Ottawa, ON, Canada [*Library symbol*] [*Library of Congress*] (LCLS)

CaOOEAPT ... Environment Canada, Air Pollution Technology Centre, Ottawa, ON, Canada [*Library symbol*] [*Library of Congress*] (LCLS)

CaOOEAR ... Environment Canada, Archaeological Research, Ottawa, ON, Canada [*Library symbol*] [*Library of Congress*] (LCLS)

CaOOEC ... Economic Council of Canada, Ottawa, ON, Canada [*Library symbol*] [*Library of Congress*] (LCLS)

CaOOECD ... Environment Canada, Conservation Division, Ottawa, ON, Canada [*Library symbol*] [*Library of Congress*] (LCLS)

CaOOECW ... Canada Department of the Environment, Canadian Wildlife Service, Ottawa, ON, Canada [*Library symbol*] [*Library of Congress*] (LCLS)

CaOOED... Ministry of State for Economic Development, Ottawa, ON, Canada [*Library symbol*] [*Library of Congress*] (LCLS)

CaOOEDC ... Export Development Corp., Ottawa, ON, Canada [*Library symbol*] [*Library of Congress*] (LCLS)

CaOOEF.... Canada Department of the Environment, Fontaine Branch Library, Ottawa, ON, Canada [*Library symbol*] [*Library of Congress*] (LCLS)

CaOOELB ... Canada Department of External Affairs, Legal Branch, Ottawa, ON, Canada [*Library symbol*] [*Library of Congress*] (LCLS)

CaOOEME ... Canada Department of Energy, Mines, and Resources, Energy Development Sector, Ottawa, ON, Canada [*Library symbol*] [*Library of Congress*] [*Obsolete*] (LCLS)

CaOOEN... Eldorado Nuclear Ltd., Ottawa, ON, Canada [*Library symbol*] [*Library of Congress*] (LCLS)

CaOOEO... Eastern Ontario Regional Library, Ottawa, ON, Canada [*Library symbol*] [*Library of Congress*] (LCLS)

CaOOEPC ... Emergency Planning Canada, Ottawa, ON, Canada [*Library symbol*] [*Library of Congress*] (LCLS)

CaOOERE ... Canada Department of the Environment, Resource and Environmental Law Library, Ottawa, ON, Canada [*Library symbol*] [*Library of Congress*] [*Obsolete*] (LCLS)

CaOOEy .... Eyretechnics Ltd., Ottawa, ON, Canada [*Library symbol*] [*Library of Congress*] (LCLS)

CaOOF ...... Canada Department of Finance, Ottawa, ON, Canada [*Library symbol*] [*Library of Congress*] (LCLS)

CaOOFC .... Federal Court of Canada, Ottawa, ON, Canada [*Library symbol*] [*Library of Congress*] (LCLS)

CaOOFD ... Canada Department of National Health and Welfare, Food and Drug Directorate, Ottawa, ON, Canada [*Library symbol*] [*Library of Congress*] (LCLS)

CaOOFF.... Canada Department of the Environment, Ottawa, ON, Canada [*Library symbol*] [*Library of Congress*] (LCLS)

CaOOFFR ... Canada Department of the Environment, Forest Fire Research Institute, Ottawa, ON, Canada [*Library symbol*] [*Library of Congress*] (LCLS)

CaOOFP.... Canada Department of the Environment, Forest Products Laboratory, Ottawa, ON, Canada [*Library symbol*] [*Library of Congress*] (LCLS)

CaOOFS.... Canadian Documentation Centre, Fitness and Sport, Ottawa, ON, Canada [*Library symbol*] [*Library of Congress*] (LCLS)

CaOOG...... Geological Survey of Canada, Ottawa, ON, Canada [*Library symbol*] [*Library of Congress*] (LCLS)

CaOOGDC ... Gandalf Data Communications Ltd., Ottawa, ON, Canada [*Library symbol*] [*Library of Congress*] (LCLS)

CaOOGE .... Department of Supply and Services, Canadian Government Expositions Centre, Ottawa, ON, Canada [*Library symbol*] [*Library of Congress*] (LCLS)

CaOOGGH ... Grace General Hospital, Ottawa, ON, Canada [*Library symbol*] [*Library of Congress*] (LCLS)

CaOOGH .. Government House, Reference Library, Ottawa, ON, Canada [*Library symbol*] [*Library of Congress*] (LCLS)

CaOOH ..... Laboratory of Hygiene, Ottawa, ON, Canada [*Library symbol*] [*Library of Congress*] [*Obsolete*] (LCLS)

CaOOHB... National Harbours Board, Ottawa, ON, Canada [*Library symbol*] [*Library of Congress*] (LCLS)

CaOOHI.... Historical Society of Ottawa Library and the Bytown Historical Museum, Ottawa, ON, Canada [*Library symbol*] [*Library of Congress*] (LCLS)

CaOOI....... Canada Department of Industry, Ottawa, ON, Canada [*Library symbol*] [*Library of Congress*] [*Obsolete*] (LCLS)

CaOOIB .... Imperial Ballet of Canada, Ottawa, ON, Canada [*Library symbol*] [*Library of Congress*] (LCLS)

CaOOICC ... Indian Claims Commission, Ottawa, ON, Canada [*Library symbol*] [*Library of Congress*] (LCLS)

CaOOICP ... National Film Board, Phototheque, Ottawa, ON, Canada [*Library symbol*] [*Library of Congress*] (LCLS)

CaOOID .... International Development Research Centre, Ottawa, ON, Canada [*Library symbol*] [*Library of Congress*] (LCLS)

CaOOIn..... Canada Department of Insurance, Ottawa, ON, Canada [*Library symbol*] [*Library of Congress*] (LCLS)

CaOOJ ...... Canada Department of Justice, Ottawa, ON, Canada [*Library symbol*] [*Library of Congress*] (LCLS)

CaOOL...... Canada Department of Labour, Ottawa, ON, Canada [*Library symbol*] [*Library of Congress*] (LCLS)

CaOOLAP ... Canada Department of Labour, Occupational Safety and Health Branch, Ottawa, ON, Canada [*Library symbol*] [*Library of Congress*] (LCLS)

CaOOLC ... Labour College of Canada, Ottawa, ON, Canada [*Library symbol*] [*Library of Congress*] (LCLS)

CaOOLR ... Law Reform Commission, Ottawa, ON, Canada [*Library symbol*] [*Library of Congress*] (LCLS)

CaOOLRB ... Canada Labour Relations Board, Ottawa, ON, Canada [*Library symbol*] [*Library of Congress*] (LCLS)

CaOOLWB ... Department of Labour, Women's Bureau, Ottawa, ON, Canada [*Library symbol*] [*Library of Congress*] (LCLS)

CaOOM..... Department of Energy, Mines, and Resources, Canada Center for Mineral and Energy Technology, Ottawa, ON, Canada [*Library symbol*] [*Library of Congress*] (LCLS)

CaOOMC ... Metric Commission Reference Unit, Ottawa, ON, Canada [*Library symbol*] [*Library of Congress*] (LCLS)

CaOOMHS ... Merivale High School, Ottawa, ON, Canada [*Library symbol*] [*Library of Congress*] (LCLS)

CaOOMI .... Canada Employment and Immigration Department, Ottawa, ON, Canada [*Library symbol*] [*Library of Congress*] (LCLS)

CaOOML ... Metropolitan Life Insurance Co., Ottawa, ON, Canada [*Library symbol*] [*Library of Congress*] (LCLS)

CaOOMP .. Canada Department of Energy, Mines, and Resources, Physical Metallurgy Division, Ottawa, ON, Canada [*Library symbol*] [*Library of Congress*] (LCLS)

CaOOMR ... Canada Department of Energy, Mines, and Resources, Resources Economic Library, Ottawa, ON, Canada [*Library symbol*] [*Library of Congress*] (LCLS)

CaOOMSD ... Ministry of State for Social Development, Ottawa, ON, Canada [*Library symbol*] [*Library of Congress*] (LCLS)

CaOOMSS ... Canada Ministry of State for Science and Technology, Ottawa, ON, Canada [*Library symbol*] [*Library of Congress*] (LCLS)

CaOOMUA ... Canada Ministry of State for Urban Affairs, Ottawa, ON, Canada [*Library symbol*] [*Library of Congress*] (LCLS)

CaOON ..... Canada Institute for Scientific and Technical Information, National Research Council, Ottawa, ON, Canada [*Library symbol*] [*Library of Congress*] (LCLS)

CaOONAB ... Canada Institute for Scientific and Technical Information, Administration Building Library, Ottawa, ON, Canada [*Library symbol*] [*Library of Congress*] (LCLS)

CaOONAM ... Canada Institute for Scientific and Technical Information, Aeronautical and Mechanical Engineering Branch, Ottawa, ON, Canada [*Library symbol*] [*Library of Congress*] (LCLS)

CaOONBR ... Canada Institute for Scientific and Technical Information, Division of Building Research, Ottawa, ON, Canada [*Library symbol*] [*Library of Congress*] (LCLS)

CaOONC... Canada Institute for Scientific and Technical Information, Chemistry Library, Ottawa, ON, Canada [*Library symbol*] [*Library of Congress*] (LCLS)

CaOONCC ... National Capital Commission, Ottawa, ON, Canada [*Library symbol*] [*Library of Congress*] (LCLS)

CaOOND .. Department of National Defence, Ottawa, ON, Canada [*Library symbol*] [*Library of Congress*] (LCLS)

CaOONDC ... Department of National Defence, Chief Computer Services, Ottawa, ON, Canada [*Library symbol*] [*Library of Congress*] (LCLS)

CaOONDCG ... Department of National Defence, General Engineering and Maintenance, Directorate of Clothing, Ottawa, ON, Canada [*Library symbol*] [*Library of Congress*] (LCLS)

CaOONDCP ... Department of National Defence, Chief Construction and Properties, Ottawa, ON, Canada [*Library symbol*] [*Library of Congress*] (LCLS)

CaOONDEM ... Department of National Defence, Chief Engineering and Maintenance, Ottawa, ON, Canada [*Library symbol*] [*Library of Congress*] (LCLS)

CaOONDH ... Department of National Defence, Historical Section, Ottawa, ON, Canada [*Library symbol*] [*Library of Congress*] (LCLS)

CaOONDIS ... Department of National Defence, Directorate of Information Services, Ottawa, ON, Canada [*Library symbol*] [*Library of Congress*] (LCLS)

CaOONDJ ... Department of National Defence, Judge Advocate General's Library, Ottawa, ON, Canada [*Library symbol*] [*Library of Congress*] (LCLS)

CaOONDLT ... Department of National Defence, Land Technical Library, Ottawa, ON, Canada [*Library symbol*] [*Library of Congress*] (LCLS)

CaOONDM ... Department of National Defence, Medical Library, Ottawa, ON, Canada [*Library symbol*] [*Library of Congress*] (LCLS)

CaOONDMC ... Department of National Defence, Mapping and Charting Establishment, Ottawa, ON, Canada [*Library symbol*] [*Library of Congress*] (LCLS)

CaOONDMT ... Department of National Defence, Marine Technical Library, Ottawa, ON, Canada [*Library symbol*] [*Library of Congress*] (LCLS)

CaOONDORAE ... Department of National Defence, Operational Research and Analysis Establishment, Ottawa, ON, Canada [*Library symbol*] [*Library of Congress*] (LCLS)

CaOONDR ... Directorate of Scientific Information Service, Defence Research Board, Ottawa, ON, Canada [*Library symbol*] [*Library of Congress*] (LCLS)

CaOONE... National Energy Board, Ottawa, ON, Canada [*Library symbol*] [*Library of Congress*] (LCLS)

CaOONF... National Film Board, Montreal, PQ, Canada [*Library symbol*] [*Library of Congress*] (LCLS)

CaOONG .. National Gallery of Canada, Ottawa, ON, Canada [*Library symbol*] [*Library of Congress*] (LCLS)

CaOONH .. National Health and Welfare Library, Ottawa, ON, Canada [*Library symbol*] [*Library of Congress*] (LCLS)

CaOONHBR ... Department of National Health and Welfare, Banting Research Centre, Ottawa, ON, Canada [*Library symbol*] [*Library of Congress*] (LCLS)

CaOONHH ... Canada Department of National Health and Welfare, Health Protection Branch, Environmental Health Directorate, Ottawa, ON, Canada [*Library symbol*] [*Library of Congress*] (LCLS)

CaOONHHS ... Department of National Health and Welfare, Health Services and Promotion Branch, Ottawa, ON, Canada [*Library symbol*] [*Library of Congress*] (LCLS)

CaOONHL ... Canada Department of National Health and Welfare, Health Protection Branch, Laboratory Centre for Disease Control, Ottawa, ON, Canada [*Library symbol*] [*Library of Congress*] (LCLS)

CaOONL... National Library of Canada, Ottawa, ON, Canada [*Library symbol*] [*Library of Congress*] (LCLS)

CaOONLB ... National Library, Union Catalogue of Books, Ottawa, ON, Canada [*Library symbol*] [*Library of Congress*] (LCLS)

CaOONLD ... National Library, Library Systems Centre, Ottawa, ON, Canada [*Library symbol*] [*Library of Congress*] (LCLS)

CaOONLP ... National Library, Public Service Branch, Ottawa, ON, Canada [*Library symbol*] [*Library of Congress*] (LCLS)

CaOONLS ... National Library, Union Catalogue of Serials, Ottawa, ON, Canada [*Library symbol*] [*Library of Congress*] (LCLS)

CaOONM ... National Museum of Canada, Ottawa, ON, Canada [*Library symbol*] [*Library of Congress*] (LCLS)

CaOONMC ... Canadian War Museum, Ottawa, ON, Canada [*Library symbol*] [*Library of Congress*] (LCLS)

CaOONMCC ... National Museums of Canada, Canadian Conservation Institute, Ottawa, ON, Canada [*Library symbol*] [*Library of Congress*] (LCLS)

CaOONMM ... National Museums of Canada, National Museum of Man, Ottawa, ON, Canada [*Library symbol*] [*Library of Congress*] (LCLS)

CaOONMS ... National Museum of Science and Technology, Ottawa, ON, Canada [*Library symbol*] [*Library of Congress*] (LCLS)

CaOONorE ... Bell Northern Research, Ottawa, ON, Canada [*Library symbol*] [*Library of Congress*] (LCLS)

CaOONR... Canada Department of National Revenue, Customs and Excise Division, Ottawa, ON, Canada [*Library symbol*] [*Library of Congress*] (LCLS)

CaOONRE ... Canada Institute for Scientific and Technical Information, Radio and Electrical Engineering Division, Ottawa, ON, Canada [*Library symbol*] [*Library of Congress*] (LCLS)

CaOONRT ... Canada Department of National Revenue, Taxation Division, Ottawa, ON, Canada [*Library symbol*] [*Library of Congress*] (LCLS)

CaOONRTC ... Revenue Canada-Taxation, Centre for Career Development, Ottawa, ON, Canada [*Library symbol*] [*Library of Congress*] (LCLS)

CaOONS... Canada Institute for Scientific and Technical Information, Sussex Library, Ottawa, ON, Canada [*Library symbol*] [*Library of Congress*] (LCLS)

CaOONSF ... National Science Film Library, Ottawa, ON, Canada [*Library symbol*] [*Library of Congress*] (LCLS)

CaOONU .. Canada Institute for Scientific and Technical Information, Uplands Library, Ottawa, ON, Canada [*Library symbol*] [*Library of Congress*] (LCLS)

CaOONUL ... Union List of Scientific Serials in Canadian Libraries, Ottawa, ON, Canada [*Library symbol*] [*Library of Congress*] (LCLS)

CaOOO ..... Canada Department of Energy, Mines, and Resources, Earth Physics Branch, Ottawa, ON, Canada [*Library symbol*] [*Library of Congress*] (LCLS)

CaOOOA... Canada Department of Justice, Occupational Analysis Library, Ottawa, ON, Canada [*Library symbol*] [*Library of Congress*] [*Obsolete*] (LCLS)

CaOOOAG ... Office of the Auditor General, Ottawa, ON, Canada [*Library symbol*] [*Library of Congress*] (LCLS)

CaOOOCF ... Ontario Cancer Foundation, Ottawa Clinic, Ottawa, ON, Canada [*Library symbol*] [*Library of Congress*] (LCLS)

CaOOOCH ... Ottawa Civic Hospital, Ottawa, ON, Canada [*Library symbol*] [*Library of Congress*] (LCLS)

CaOOP...... Library of Parliament, Ottawa, ON, Canada [*Library symbol*] [*Library of Congress*] (LCLS)

CaOOPA ... National Arts Centre, Ottawa, ON, Canada [*Library symbol*] [*Library of Congress*] (LCLS)

CaOOPAC ... Environment Canada, Parks Canada, Ottawa, ON, Canada [*Library symbol*] [*Library of Congress*] (LCLS)

CaOOPC ... Canada Privy Council Office, Management Information, Ottawa, ON, Canada [*Library symbol*] [*Library of Congress*] (LCLS)

CaOOPH... Perley Hospital, Ottawa, ON, Canada [*Library symbol*] [*Library of Congress*] (LCLS)

CaOOPI .... Department of Energy, Mines, and Resources, Petroleum Incentives Program, Ottawa, ON, Canada [*Library symbol*] [*Library of Congress*] (LCLS)

CaOOPM .. National Postal Museum, Ottawa, ON, Canada [*Library symbol*] [*Library of Congress*] (LCLS)

CaOOPO ... Post Office Library, Ottawa, ON, Canada [*Library symbol*] [*Library of Congress*] (LCLS)

CaOOPS.... Public Service Staff Relations Board, Ottawa, ON, Canada [*Library symbol*] [*Library of Congress*] (LCLS)

CaOOPSAC ... Public Service Alliance of Canada, Ottawa, ON, Canada [*Library symbol*] [*Library of Congress*] (LCLS)

CaOOPW .. Canada Department of Public Works, Ottawa, ON, Canada [*Library symbol*] [*Library of Congress*] (LCLS)

CaOOPWC ... Canada Department of Public Works, Capital Region Library, Ottawa, ON, Canada [*Library symbol*] [*Library of Congress*] (LCLS)

CaOOPWD ... Canada Department of Public Works, Office of the Dominion Fire Commissioner, Ottawa, ON, Canada [*Library symbol*] [*Library of Congress*] [*Obsolete*] (LCLS)

CaOOPWR ... Canada Department of Public Works, Research and Development Laboratories, Ottawa, ON, Canada [*Library symbol*] [*Library of Congress*] (LCLS)

CaOOQA... Canada Department of National Defence, Quality Assurance Division, Ottawa, ON, Canada [*Library symbol*] [*Library of Congress*] (LCLS)

CaOOQP... Information Canada, Publishing Division, Ottawa, ON, Canada [*Library symbol*] [*Library of Congress*] [*Obsolete*] (LCLS)

CaOOr....... Orillia Public Library, Orillia, ON, Canada [*Library symbol*] [*Library of Congress*] (LCLS)

CaOOR...... Royal Canadian Mounted Police Headquarters Reference Library, Ottawa, ON, Canada [*Library symbol*] [*Library of Congress*] (LCLS)

CaOORD... Canada Department of Indian Affairs and Northern Development, Ottawa, ON, Canada [*Library symbol*] [*Library of Congress*] (LCLS)

CaOORE... Canadian Council for Research in Education, Ottawa, ON, Canada [*Library symbol*] [*Library of Congress*] [*Obsolete*] (LCLS)

CaOOREx ... Canada Department of Regional Economic Expansion, Ottawa, ON, Canada [*Library symbol*] [*Library of Congress*] (LCLS)

CaOOORExR ... Canada Department of Regional Economic Expansion, Reference and Enquiries Unit, Ottawa, ON, Canada [*Library symbol*] [*Library of Congress*] [*Obsolete*] (LCLS)

CaOORH... Riverside Hospital, Ottawa, ON, Canada [*Library symbol*] [*Library of Congress*] (LCLS)

CaOORM ... Regional Municipality of Ottawa-Carleton, Ottawa, ON, Canada [*Library symbol*] [*Library of Congress*] (LCLS)

CaOORO... Royal Ottawa Hospital, Ottawa, ON, Canada [*Library symbol*] [*Library of Congress*] (LCLS)

CaOORORR ... Royal Ottawa Regional Rehabilitation Centre, Royal Ottawa Hospital, Ottawa, ON, Canada [*Library symbol*] [*Library of Congress*] (LCLS)

CaOORPL ... Canada Department of Communications, Communications Research Centre, Ottawa, ON, Canada [*Library symbol*] [*Library of Congress*] (LCLS)

CaOORT ... Canadian Radio-Television and Telecommunications Commission, Ottawa, ON, Canada [*Library symbol*] [*Library of Congress*] (LCLS)

CaOORTA ... Roads and Transportation Association of Canada, Ottawa, ON, Canada [*Library symbol*] [*Library of Congress*] (LCLS)

CaOOS ...... Statistics Canada, Ottawa, ON, Canada [*Library symbol*] [*Library of Congress*] (LCLS)

CaOOSC ... Supreme Court of Canada, Ottawa, ON, Canada [*Library symbol*] [*Library of Congress*] (LCLS)

CaOOSCC ... Science Council of Canada, Ottawa, ON, Canada [*Library symbol*] [*Library of Congress*] (LCLS)

CaOOSCL ... Statistics Canada, Census Library, Ottawa, ON, Canada [*Library symbol*] [*Library of Congress*] (LCLS)

CaOOSCM ... Statistics Canada, Census Map Library, Ottawa, ON, Canada [*Library symbol*] [*Library of Congress*] (LCLS)

CaOOSG ... Canada Department of the Solicitor General, Ottawa, ON, Canada [*Library symbol*] [*Library of Congress*] (LCLS)

CaOOsh..... Oshawa Public Library, Oshawa, ON, Canada [*Library symbol*] [*Library of Congress*] (LCLS)

CaOOshD ... Durham College of Applied Arts and Technology, Oshawa, ON, Canada [*Library symbol*] [*Library of Congress*] (LCLS)

CaOOshR ... Robert McLaughlin Gallery, Oshawa, ON, Canada [*Library symbol*] [*Library of Congress*] (LCLS)

CaOOSJ .... Bibliotheque Deschatelets, Peres Oblats, Ottawa, ON, Canada [*Library symbol*] [*Library of Congress*] (LCLS)

CaOOSLM ... Saint Louis De Montfort Hospital, Ottawa, ON, Canada [*Library symbol*] [*Library of Congress*] (LCLS)

CaOOSM .. Canada Department of Energy, Mines, and Resources, Surveys and Mapping Branch, Ottawa, ON, Canada [*Library symbol*] [*Library of Congress*] (LCLS)

CaOOSMM ... Canada Department of Energy, Mines, and Resources, Map Library, Ottawa, ON, Canada [*Library symbol*] [*Library of Congress*] (LCLS)

CaOOSP.... Patent and Copyright Office, Ottawa, ON, Canada [*Library symbol*] [*Library of Congress*] (LCLS)

CaOOSS.... Canada Department of the Secretary of State, Ottawa, ON, Canada [*Library symbol*] [*Library of Congress*] (LCLS)

CaOOSST ... Canada Department of the Secretary of State, Translation Bureau, Multilingual Services Division, Ottawa, ON, Canada [*Library symbol*] [*Library of Congress*] [*Obsolete*] (LCLS)

CaOOSSTT ... Canada Department of the Secretary of State, Translation Bureau, Terminology Centre Library, Ottawa, ON, Canada [*Library symbol*] [*Library of Congress*] (LCLS)

CaOOSTI .. Canada Department of Revenue, Canada Customs and Excise, Scientific and Technical Information Centre, Laboratory and Scientific Services Division, Ottawa, ON, Canada [*Library symbol*] [*Library of Congress*] (LCLS)

CaOOSU ... Saint Paul University, Ottawa, ON, Canada [*Library symbol*] [*Library of Congress*] (LCLS)

CaOOSUA ... Saint Paul University, Oblate Fathers Archives, Ottawa, ON, Canada [*Library symbol*] [*Library of Congress*] (LCLS)

CaOOSV ... Saint Vincent Hospital, Ottawa, ON, Canada [*Library symbol*] [*Library of Congress*] (LCLS)

CaOOT...... Ministry of Transport, Ottawa, ON, Canada [*Library symbol*] [*Library of Congress*] (LCLS)

CaOOTAC ... Ministry of Transport, Airports and Construction Services, Ottawa, ON, Canada [*Library symbol*] [*Library of Congress*] (LCLS)

CaOOTAS ... Ministry of Transport, Aviation Safety Bureau, Ottawa, ON, Canada [*Library symbol*] [*Library of Congress*] (LCLS)

CaOOTB ... Canadian Government Travel Bureau, Reference Library, Ottawa, ON, Canada [*Library symbol*] [*Library of Congress*] (LCLS)

CaOOTC ... Canada Department of Industry, Trade, and Commerce, Ottawa, ON, Canada [*Library symbol*] [*Library of Congress*] (LCLS)

CaOOTCT ... TransCanada Telephone System, Ottawa, ON, Canada [*Library symbol*] [*Library of Congress*] (LCLS)

CaOOTEC ... Ottawa Teachers' College, Ottawa, ON, Canada [*Library symbol*] [*Library of Congress*] (LCLS)

CaOOTI .... Canada Ministry of Transport Training Institute, Ottawa, ON, Canada [*Library symbol*] [*Library of Congress*] (LCLS)

CaOOTR ... Tax Review Board, Ottawa, ON, Canada [*Library symbol*] [*Library of Congress*] (LCLS)

CaOOTRB ... Treasury Board, Ottawa, ON, Canada [*Library symbol*] [*Library of Congress*] (LCLS)

CaOOTRT ... Ministry of Transport, Railway Transportation Directorate, Ottawa, ON, Canada [*Library symbol*] [*Library of Congress*] (LCLS)

CaOOTT ... Canadian Transport Commission, Ottawa, ON, Canada [*Library symbol*] [*Library of Congress*] (LCLS)

CaOOTTE ... Ministry of Transport, Telecommunications and Electronics Directorate, Ottawa, ON, Canada [*Library symbol*] [*Library of Congress*] (LCLS)

CaOOU ..... University of Ottawa, Ottawa, ON, Canada [*Library symbol*] [*Library of Congress*] (LCLS)

CaOOUC... University of Ottawa, Department of Criminology, Ottawa, ON, Canada [*Library symbol*] [*Library of Congress*] (LCLS)

CaOOUD .. University of Ottawa, Faculty of Law, Ottawa, ON, Canada [*Library symbol*] [*Library of Congress*] (LCLS)

CaOOUH .. University of Ottawa, Health Sciences Library, Ottawa, ON, Canada [*Library symbol*] [*Library of Congress*] (LCLS)

CaOOUI.... Unemployment Insurance Commission, Ottawa, ON, Canada [*Library symbol*] [*Library of Congress*] [*Obsolete*] (LCLS)

CaOOUIC ... University of Ottawa, Institute of International Cooperation, Ottawa, ON, Canada [*Library symbol*] [*Library of Congress*] (LCLS)

CaOOULT ... United Lodge of Theosophists, Ottawa, ON, Canada [*Library symbol*] [*Library of Congress*] [*Obsolete*] (LCLS)

CaOOUM ... University of Ottawa, Vanier Library, Ottawa, ON, Canada [*Library symbol*] [*Library of Congress*] (LCLS)

CaOOUMA ... University of Ottawa, Map Library, Ottawa, ON, Canada [*Library symbol*] [*Library of Congress*] (LCLS)

CaOOUP... University of Ottawa, Faculty of Psychology and Education, Ottawa, ON, Canada [*Library symbol*] [*Library of Congress*] [*Obsolete*] (LCLS)

CaOOUSA ... United States Embassy, Ottawa, ON, Canada [*Library symbol*] [*Library of Congress*] (LCLS)

CaOOUSI ... United States International Communications Agency, Ottawa, ON, Canada [*Library symbol*] [*Library of Congress*] (LCLS)

CaOOV...... Canada Department of Veterans Affairs, Ottawa, ON, Canada [*Library symbol*] [*Library of Congress*] (LCLS)

CaOOVIF ... Vanier Institute of the Family, Ottawa, ON, Canada [*Library symbol*] [*Library of Congress*] (LCLS)

CaOOw...... Owen Sound Public Library, Owen Sound, ON, Canada [*Library symbol*] [*Library of Congress*] (LCLS)

CaOOwGC ... Georgian College Resource Centre, Owen Sound, ON, Canada [*Library symbol*] [*Library of Congress*] (LCLS)

CaOOwGM ... General and Marine Hospital, Health Sciences Library, Owen Sound, ON, Canada [*Library symbol*] [*Library of Congress*] (LCLS)

CaOOwT ... Tom Thomson Memorial Gallery, Owen Sound, ON, Canada [*Library symbol*] [*Library of Congress*] (LCLS)

CaOPAL... Lakehead University, Thunder Bay, ON, Canada [*Library symbol*] [*Library of Congress*] (LCLS)

CaOPALE ... Lakehead University, Faculty of Education, Thunder Bay, ON, Canada [*Library symbol*] [*Library of Congress*] (LCLS)

CaOPALG ... Lakehead University, Department of Geography, Thunder Bay, ON, Canada [*Library symbol*] [*Library of Congress*] (LCLS)

CaOPC ...... Perth Courier, Perth, ON, Canada [*Library symbol*] [*Library of Congress*] (LCLS)

CaOPd .... Port Dover Centennial Public Library, Port Dover, ON, Canada [*Library symbol*] [*Library of Congress*] (LCLS)

CaOPeEPB ... Eastern Pentecostal Bible College, Peterborough, ON, Canada [*Library symbol*] [*Library of Congress*] (LCLS)

CaOPem .... Pembroke Public Library, Pembroke, ON, Canada [*Library symbol*] [*Library of Congress*] (LCLS)

CaOPemAC ... Algonquin College, Upper Ottawa Valley Campus Resource Centre, Pembroke, ON, Canada [*Library symbol*] [*Library of Congress*] (LCLS)

CaOPenM ... Mental Health Centre, Penetanguishene, ON, Canada [*Library symbol*] [*Library of Congress*] (LCLS)

CaOPeT..... Trent University, Peterborough, ON, Canada [*Library symbol*] [*Library of Congress*] (LCLS)

CaOPeTA ... Trent University Archives, Peterborough, ON, Canada [*Library symbol*] [*Library of Congress*] (LCLS)

CaOPeTCG ... Canadian General Electric Co. Ltd., Peterborough, ON, Canada [*Library symbol*] [*Library of Congress*] (LCLS)

CaOPeTM ... Trent University, Map Library, Peterborough, ON, Canada [*Library symbol*] [*Library of Congress*] (LCLS)

CaOPeTP .. Peterborough Public Library, Peterborough, ON, Canada [*Library symbol*] [*Library of Congress*] (LCLS)

CaOPeTSF ... Sir Sandford Fleming College of Applied Arts and Technology, Peterborough, ON, Canada [*Library symbol*] [*Library of Congress*] (LCLS)

CaOPh .... Public Library, Port Hope, ON, Canada [*Library symbol*] [*Library of Congress*] (LCLS)

CaOPhE .... Eldorado Mining & Refining Co., Port Hope, ON, Canada [*Library symbol*] [*Library of Congress*] (LCLS)

CaOPhWA ... Westinghouse Canada Inc., Atomic Tower Division, Port Hope, ON, Canada [*Library symbol*] [*Library of Congress*] (LCLS)

CaOPic ...... Pickering Public Library, Pickering, ON, Canada [*Library symbol*] [*Library of Congress*] (LCLS)

CaOPiG ..... Picton Gazette, Picton, ON, Canada [*Library symbol*] [*Library of Congress*] (LCLS)

CaOPM ..... Perth Museum, Perth, ON, Canada [*Library symbol*] [*Library of Congress*] (LCLS)

CaOPmn .... Port McNicoll Public Library, Port McNicoll, ON, Canada [*Library symbol*] [*Library of Congress*] (LCLS)

CaOPoC ..... Port Colborne Public Library, Port Colborne, ON, Canada [*Library symbol*] [*Library of Congress*] (LCLS)

CaOPpP .... Port Perry High School, Port Perry, ON, Canada [*Library symbol*] [*Library of Congress*] (LCLS)

CaOPr .... Port Rowan Public Library, Port Rowan, ON, Canada [*Library symbol*] [*Library of Congress*] (LCLS)

CaOPs .... Parry Sound Public Library, Parry Sound, ON, Canada [*Library symbol*] [*Library of Congress*] (LCLS)

CaOPsA ..... Algonquin Regional Library, Parry Sound, ON, Canada [*Library symbol*] [*Library of Congress*] (LCLS)

CAOPT ...... Council of American Official Poultry Tests (EA)

CaOPteB .... Bruce County Public Library, Port Elgin, ON, Canada [*Library symbol*] [*Library of Congress*] (LCLS)

CaOQC ...... Queensway-Carleton Hospital, Ottawa, ON, Canada [*Library symbol*] [*Library of Congress*] (LCLS)

CAORC ..... Council of American Overseas Research Centers (EA)

CAORE ..... Canadian Army Operational Research Establishment

CAORF ...... Computer Aided Operations Research Facility [*Kings Point, NY*] [*National Maritime Research Center*] [*Department of Transportation*] (MCD)

CAORG ..... Canadian Army Operational Research Group (DMA)

CaORh .... Richmond Hill Public Library, Richmond Hill, ON, Canada [*Library symbol*] [*Library of Congress*] (LCLS)

CaORhCO ... Central Ontario Regional Library, Richmond Hill, ON, Canada [*Library symbol*] [*Library of Congress*] (LCLS)

CaORr .... Red Rock Public Library, Red Rock, ON, Canada [*Library symbol*] [*Library of Congress*] (LCLS)

CAOS .... Completely Automatic Operational System [*UNIVAC*]

CaOS .... Sarnia Public Library, Sarnia, ON, Canada [*Library symbol*] [*Library of Congress*] (LCLS)

CaOSAMS ... Anglican Church of Canada, Diocese of Moosonee, Synod Office, Schumacher, ON, Canada [*Library symbol*] [*Library of Congress*] (LCLS)

CaOSbM ... Morrison Library Outpost, Severn Bridge, ON, Canada [*Library symbol*] [*Library of Congress*] (LCLS)

CaOSc .... Scugog Public Library, Scugog, ON, Canada [*Library symbol*] [*Library of Congress*] (LCLS)

CaOSD ...... Dow Chemical Co., Sarnia, ON, Canada [*Library symbol*] [*Library of Congress*] (LCLS)

CaOSfAR .. Algonquin Regional Library System, Sturgeon Falls Branch, Sturgeon Falls, ON, Canada [*Library symbol*] [*Library of Congress*] (LCLS)

CaOSFC .... Fiberglass Ltd., Sarnia, ON, Canada [*Library symbol*] [*Library of Congress*] (LCLS)

CaOSI .... Imperial Oil Enterprises Ltd., Sarnia, ON, Canada [*Library symbol*] [*Library of Congress*] (LCLS)

CaOSiDM ... Eva Brook Donly Museum, Simcoe, ON, Canada [*Library symbol*] [*Library of Congress*] (LCLS)

CaOSIE ..... Imperial Oil Enterprises Ltd., Engineering Division, Sarnia, ON, Canada [*Library symbol*] [*Library of Congress*] [*Obsolete*] (LCLS)

CaOSiL ...... Lynnwood Arts Centre, Simcoe, ON, Canada [*Library symbol*] [*Library of Congress*] (LCLS)

CaOSiNH ... Norfolk Historical Society, Simcoe, ON, Canada [*Library symbol*] [*Library of Congress*] (LCLS)

CaOSiP ...... Simcoe Public Library, Simcoe, ON, Canada [*Library symbol*] [*Library of Congress*] (LCLS)

CaOSl .... Sioux Lookout Public Library, Sioux Lookout, ON, Canada [*Library symbol*] [*Library of Congress*] (LCLS)

CaOSLC .... Lambton College of Applied Arts and Technology, Sarnia, ON, Canada [*Library symbol*] [*Library of Congress*] (LCLS)

CaOSmf ..... Smith Falls Public Library, Smith Falls, ON, Canada [*Library symbol*] [*Library of Congress*] (LCLS)

CaOSML ... McNeil Laboratories (Canada) Ltd., Stouffville, ON, Canada [*Library symbol*] [*Library of Congress*] (LCLS)

CaOSNC .... Sarnia Northern Collegiate, Sarnia, ON, Canada [*Library symbol*] [*Library of Congress*] (LCLS)

CAO-SOP ... Coordination of Atomic Operations - Standard Operating Procedures

CaOSP .... Polysar Ltd., Sarnia, ON, Canada [*Library symbol*] [*Library of Congress*] (LCLS)

CaOSpNC ... Northern College of Applied Arts and Technology, Porcupine Campus, South Porcupine, ON, Canada [*Library symbol*] [*Library of Congress*] (LCLS)

CaOST .... Stratford Public Library, Stratford, ON, Canada [*Library symbol*] [*Library of Congress*] (LCLS)

CaOStC ..... St. Catharines Public Library, St. Catharines, ON, Canada [*Library symbol*] [*Library of Congress*] (LCLS)

CaOStCB ... Brock University, Saint Catharines, ON, Canada [*Library symbol*] [*Library of Congress*] (LCLS)

CaOStCBG ... Brock University, Department of Geography, Saint Catharines, ON, Canada [*Library symbol*] [*Library of Congress*] (LCLS)

CaOStCG .. Grantham High School, Saint Catharines, ON, Canada [*Library symbol*] [*Library of Congress*] (LCLS)

CaOStCGL ... Genaire Ltd., Saint Catharines, ON, Canada [*Library symbol*] [*Library of Congress*] (LCLS)

CaOStCMEC ... Montreal Engineering Company Ltd., St. Catharines, ON, Canada [*Library symbol*] [*Library of Congress*] (LCLS)

CaOStCNR ... Niagara Regional Library, Saint Catharines, ON, Canada [*Library symbol*] [*Library of Congress*] [*Obsolete*] (LCLS)

CaOStCT ... St. Catharines Teachers' College, St. Catharines, ON, Canada [*Library symbol*] [*Library of Congress*] (LCLS)

CaOStCTR ... St. Catharines Teachers' College, Reference Library, St. Catharines, ON, Canada [*Library symbol*] [*Library of Congress*] (LCLS)

CaOStJeCR ... Conseil Regional de la Sante et des Services Sociaux Laurentides Lanaudiere, Saint-Jerome, ON, Canada [*Library symbol*] [*Library of Congress*] (LCLS)

CaOStM .... Sault Ste. Marie Public Library, Sault Ste. Marie, ON, Canada [*Library symbol*] [*Library of Congress*] (LCLS)

CaOStMA ... Algoma College, Sault Ste. Marie, ON, Canada [*Library symbol*] [*Library of Congress*] (LCLS)

CaOStMAS ... Algoma Steel Corp., Quality Control and Research Department, Sault Ste. Marie, ON, Canada [*Library symbol*] [*Library of Congress*] (LCLS)

CaOStMC ... Sault College of Applied Arts and Technology, Sault Ste. Marie, ON, Canada [*Library symbol*] [*Library of Congress*] (LCLS)

CaOStMEF ... Canada Department of the Environment, Sea Lamprey Control Centre, Sault Ste. Marie, ON, Canada [*Library symbol*] [*Library of Congress*] (LCLS)

CaOStMF ... Canada Department of the Environment, Research Station, Sault Ste. Marie, ON, Canada [*Library symbol*] [*Library of Congress*] (LCLS)

CaOStMH ... Sault Ste. Marie and 49th (SSM) Field Regiment, RCA Historical Society, Sault Ste. Marie, ON, Canada [*Library symbol*] [*Library of Congress*] (LCLS)

CaOStMPH ... Plummer Public Hospital, Sault Ste. Marie, ON, Canada [*Library symbol*] [*Library of Congress*] (LCLS)

CaOStr .... Streetsville Public Library, Streetsville, ON, Canada [*Library symbol*] [*Library of Congress*] (LCLS)

CaOStrAG ... Rothmans Art Gallery, Stratford, ON, Canada [*Library symbol*] [*Library of Congress*] (LCLS)

CaOStro ..... Stround Branch Library, Stround, ON, Canada [*Library symbol*] [*Library of Congress*] (LCLS)

CaOStrP .... Strathroy Public Library, Strathroy, ON, Canada [*Library symbol*] [*Library of Congress*] (LCLS)

CaOStT ..... St. Thomas Public Library, St. Thomas, ON, Canada [*Library symbol*] [*Library of Congress*] (LCLS)

CaOStTE ... Elgin County Public Library, St. Thomas, ON, Canada [*Library symbol*] [*Library of Congress*] (LCLS)

CaOStu ...... Sturgeon Falls Public Library, Sturgeon Falls, ON, Canada [*Library symbol*] [*Library of Congress*] (LCLS)

CaOSu .... Sudbury Public Library, Sudbury, ON, Canada [*Library symbol*] [*Library of Congress*] (LCLS)

CaOSuGH ... Sudbury General Hospital, Sudbury, ON, Canada [*Library symbol*] [*Library of Congress*] (LCLS)

CaOSuL ..... Laurentian University, Sudbury, ON, Canada [*Library symbol*] [*Library of Congress*] (LCLS)

CaOSuN .... North Central Regional Library, Sudbury, ON, Canada [*Library symbol*] [*Library of Congress*] (LCLS)

CaOSunB ... Brock Township Public Library, Sunderland, ON, Canada [*Library symbol*] [*Library of Congress*] (LCLS)

CaOTA ...... Academy of Medicine, Toronto, ON, Canada [*Library symbol*] [*Library of Congress*] (LCLS)

CaOTAC .... Acres Consulting Services Ltd., Toronto, ON, Canada [*Library symbol*] [*Library of Congress*] (LCLS)

CaOTAE .... Atomic Energy of Canada, Toronto, ON, Canada [*Library symbol*] [*Library of Congress*] (LCLS)

CaOTAF .... Ontario Ministry of Agriculture and Food, Toronto, ON, Canada [*Library symbol*] [*Library of Congress*] (LCLS)

CaOTAG ... Art Gallery of Ontario, Toronto, ON, Canada [*Library symbol*] [*Library of Congress*] (LCLS)

CaOTAGAV ... Art Gallery of Ontario, Audiovisual Library, Toronto, ON, Canada [*Library symbol*] [*Library of Congress*] (LCLS)

CaOTAGC ... Attorney General of Ontario, Crown Law Office, Toronto, ON, Canada [*Library symbol*] [*Library of Congress*] (LCLS)

CaOTAH ... Ontario Ministry of Agriculture and Food, Home Economics Branch, Toronto, ON, Canada [*Closed*] [*Library symbol*] [*Library of Congress*] (LCLS)

CaOTAL.... Arts and Letters Club, Toronto, ON, Canada [*Library symbol*] [*Library of Congress*] (LCLS)

CaOTAP.... Alternative Press Centre, Toronto, ON, Canada [*Library symbol*] [*Library of Congress*] (LCLS)

CaOTAr..... Ontario Department of Public Records and Archives, Toronto, ON, Canada [*Library symbol*] [*Library of Congress*] (LCLS)

CaOTARC ... Centennial College of Applied Arts and Technology, Scarborough, ON, Canada [*Library symbol*] [*Library of Congress*] (LCLS)

CaOTB ...... Thunder Bay Public Library, Thunder Bay, ON, Canada [*Library symbol*] [*Library of Congress*] (LCLS)

CaOTbA .... Terrace Bay Public Library, Terrace Bay, ON, Canada [*Library symbol*] [*Library of Congress*] (LCLS)

CaOTBBR ... Brodie Resource Library, Thunder Bay, ON, Canada [*Library symbol*] [*Library of Congress*] (LCLS)

CaOTBC.... Canadian Broadcasting Corp., Toronto, ON, Canada [*Library symbol*] [*Library of Congress*] (LCLS)

CaOTBCC ... Confederation College, Thunder Bay, ON, Canada [*Library symbol*] [*Library of Congress*] (LCLS)

CaOTBCG .. Blake, Cassels & Graydon, Law Library, Toronto, ON, Canada [*Library symbol*] [*Library of Congress*] (LCLS)

CaOTBCIR ... Bell Canada Information Resource Centre, Toronto, ON, Canada [*Library symbol*] [*Library of Congress*] (LCLS)

CaOTBCP ... Canadian Broadcasting Corp., Program Archives, Toronto, ON, Canada [*Library symbol*] [*Library of Congress*] (LCLS)

CaOTBDHC ... Thunder Bay District Health Council, Thunder Bay, ON, Canada [*Library symbol*] [*Library of Congress*] (LCLS)

CaOTBH ... Thunder Bay Historical Society, Thunder Bay, ON, Canada [*Library symbol*] [*Library of Congress*] (LCLS)

CaOTBLP ... Lakehead Psychiatric Hospital, Staff Library, Thunder Bay, ON, Canada [*Library symbol*] [*Library of Congress*] (LCLS)

CaOTBM .. Bank of Montreal, Technical Information Centre, Willowdale, ON, Canada [*Library symbol*] [*Library of Congress*] (LCLS)

CaOTBMB ... Mary J. L. Black Library, Thunder Bay, ON, Canada [*Library symbol*] [*Library of Congress*] (LCLS)

CaOTBNS ... Bell Northern Software Research, Toronto, ON, Canada [*Library symbol*] [*Library of Congress*] (LCLS)

CaOTBOC ... Ontario Cancer Treatment and Research Foundation, Thunder Bay, ON, Canada [*Library symbol*] [*Library of Congress*] (LCLS)

CaOTBP.... Blaney, Pasternak, Smela, Eagleson & Watson, Toronto, ON, Canada [*Library symbol*] [*Library of Congress*] (LCLS)

CaOTBR.... Barringer Research Ltd., Rexdale, ON, Canada [*Library symbol*] [*Library of Congress*] (LCLS)

CaOTC ...... Ontario College of Education, Toronto, ON, Canada [*Library symbol*] [*Library of Congress*] (LCLS)

CaOTCA.... Ontario College of Art, Toronto, ON, Canada [*Library symbol*] [*Library of Congress*] (LCLS)

CaOTCAE ... Canadian Association for Adult Education, Toronto, ON, Canada [*Library symbol*] [*Library of Congress*] (LCLS)

CaOTCAG ... Canada Arctic Gas Study Ltd., Toronto, ON, Canada [*Library symbol*] [*Library of Congress*] (LCLS)

CaOTCAS ... Canadian Association in Support of the Native Peoples, Toronto, ON, Canada [*Library symbol*] [*Library of Congress*] (LCLS)

CaOTCC.... United Church of Canada Archives, Toronto, ON, Canada [*Library symbol*] [*Library of Congress*] (LCLS)

CaOTCCL ... Currie, Coopers & Lybrand Ltd., Toronto, ON, Canada [*Library symbol*] [*Library of Congress*] (LCLS)

CaOTCCP ... Canadian Centre for Philanthropy, Toronto, ON, Canada [*Library symbol*] [*Library of Congress*] (LCLS)

CaOTCCRT ... Ministry of Consumer and Commercial Relations, Technical Standards Division, Toronto, ON, Canada [*Library symbol*] [*Library of Congress*] (LCLS)

CaOTCe..... Central Library, North York, ON, Canada [*Library symbol*] [*Library of Congress*] (LCLS)

CaOTCEA ... Canadian Education Association, Toronto, ON, Canada [*Library symbol*] [*Library of Congress*] (LCLS)

CaOTCF.... Centre of Forensic Sciences, Ontario Solicitor General, Toronto, ON, Canada [*Library symbol*] [*Library of Congress*] (LCLS)

CaOTCGL ... Campbell, Godfrey & Lewtas, Toronto, ON, Canada [*Library symbol*] [*Library of Congress*] (LCLS)

CaOTCGR ... Canadian Gas Research Institute, Don Mills, ON, Canada [*Library symbol*] [*Library of Congress*] (LCLS)

CaOTCGW ... Clarkson, Gordon & Co.: Woods, Gordon & Co., Toronto, ON, Canada [*Library symbol*] [*Library of Congress*] (LCLS)

CaOTCH ... Anglican Church House, Toronto, ON, Canada [*Library symbol*] [*Library of Congress*] (LCLS)

CaOTCHA ... Canadian Hospital Association, Toronto, ON, Canada [*Library symbol*] [*Library of Congress*] (LCLS)

CaOTCHAr ... Anglican Church of Canada, Archives, Toronto, ON, Canada [*Library symbol*] [*Library of Congress*] (LCLS)

CaOTCIA ... Canadian Institute of International Affairs, Toronto, ON, Canada [*Library symbol*] [*Library of Congress*] (LCLS)

CaOTCIB .. Canadian Imperial Bank of Commerce, Toronto, ON, Canada [*Library symbol*] [*Library of Congress*] (LCLS)

CaOTCJC ... Church of Jesus Christ of Latter-Day Saints, Genealogical Society Library, Toronto Branch, Etobicoke, ON, Canada [*Library symbol*] [*Library of Congress*] (LCLS)

CaOTCL.... Connaught Medical Research Laboratories, Toronto, ON, Canada [*Library symbol*] [*Library of Congress*] (LCLS)

CaOTCLA ... Confederation Life Association, Toronto, ON, Canada [*Library symbol*] [*Library of Congress*] (LCLS)

CaOTCM .. Canadian School of Missions and Ecumenical Institute, Toronto, ON, Canada [*Library symbol*] [*Library of Congress*] (LCLS)

CaOTCMC ... Canadian Memorial Chiropractic College, Toronto, ON, Canada [*Library symbol*] [*Library of Congress*] (LCLS)

CaOTCMLA ... Canadian Music Library Association, Toronto, ON, Canada [*Library symbol*] [*Library of Congress*] (LCLS)

CaOTCom ... Cominco Ltd., Toronto, ON, Canada [*Library symbol*] [*Library of Congress*] (LCLS)

CaOTCOU ... Council of Ontario Universities, Toronto, ON, Canada [*Library symbol*] [*Library of Congress*] (LCLS)

CaOTCPB ... Toronto City Planning Board, Toronto, ON, Canada [*Library symbol*] [*Library of Congress*] (LCLS)

CaOTCR.... Ontario Ministry of Culture and Recreation, Toronto, ON, Canada [*Library symbol*] [*Library of Congress*] (LCLS)

CaOTCS.... Correctional Services of Ontario, Toronto, ON, Canada [*Library symbol*] [*Library of Congress*] (LCLS)

CaOTCSA ... Canadian Standards Association, Toronto, ON, Canada [*Library symbol*] [*Library of Congress*] (LCLS)

CaOTCSC ... Civil Service Commission of Ontario, Toronto, ON, Canada [*Library symbol*] [*Library of Congress*] (LCLS)

CaOTCT.... Canadian Tax Foundation, Toronto, ON, Canada [*Library symbol*] [*Library of Congress*] (LCLS)

CaOTCTA ... Canadian Telebook Agency, Toronto, ON, Canada [*Library symbol*] [*Library of Congress*] (LCLS)

CaOTCW .. Canada Wire & Cable Co. Ltd., Toronto, ON, Canada [*Library symbol*] [*Library of Congress*] (LCLS)

CaOTCWB ... Canadian Welding Development Institute, Toronto, ON, Canada [*Library symbol*] [*Library of Congress*] (LCLS)

CaOTDAR ... Doctors Hospital, Alexander Raxlen Memorial Library, Toronto, ON, Canada [*Library symbol*] [*Library of Congress*] (LCLS)

CaOTDE ... Ontario Department of Education, Curriculum Division, Toronto, ON, Canada [*Library symbol*] [*Library of Congress*] (LCLS)

CaOTDH... Ontario Ministry of Health, Toronto, ON, Canada [*Library symbol*] [*Library of Congress*] (LCLS)

CaOTDHA ... De Havilland Aircraft of Canada Ltd., Downsview, Toronto, ON, Canada [*Library symbol*] [*Library of Congress*] (LCLS)

CaOTDHL ... Ontario Department of Health, Laboratories Branch, Toronto, ON, Canada [*Library symbol*] [*Library of Congress*] (LCLS)

CaOTDL.... Ontario Department of Labour, Toronto, ON, Canada [*Library symbol*] [*Library of Congress*] (LCLS)

CaOTDM .. Ontario Ministry of Natural Resources, Mines Library, Toronto, ON, Canada [*Library symbol*] [*Library of Congress*] (LCLS)

CaOTDP.... Ontario Department of Public Works, Toronto, ON, Canada [*Library symbol*] [*Library of Congress*] [*Obsolete*] (LCLS)

CaOTDR ... Department of National Defence, Defence and Civil Institute of Environmental Medicine, Toronto, ON, Canada [*Library symbol*] [*Library of Congress*] (LCLS)

CaOTDRE ... Ontario Ministry of Treasury, Economics, and Inter-governmental Affairs, Toronto, ON, Canada [*Library symbol*] [*Library of Congress*] (LCLS)

CaOTDT ... Ontario Ministry of Transportation and Communications, Toronto, ON, Canada [*Library symbol*] [*Library of Congress*] (LCLS)

CaOTDU ... Ontario Ministry of Colleges and Universities, Toronto, ON, Canada [*Library symbol*] [*Library of Congress*] (LCLS)

CaOTE ...... Emmanuel College, Victoria University, Toronto, ON, Canada [*Library symbol*] [*Library of Congress*] (LCLS)

CaOTEC.... Toronto Board of Education, Education Centre, Toronto, ON, Canada [*Library symbol*] [*Library of Congress*] (LCLS)

CaOTEM .. ESSO [*Standard Oil*] Minerals of Canada, Toronto, ON, Canada [*Library symbol*] [*Library of Congress*] (LCLS)

CaOTEP.... Ontario Department of Education, Provincial Library Service, Toronto, ON, Canada [*Library symbol*] [*Library of Congress*] (LCLS)

CaOTEPS ... Environment Canada, Environmental Protection Service, Toronto, ON, Canada [*Library symbol*] [*Library of Congress*] (LCLS)

CaOTEPSE ... Environment Canada, Environmental Protection Service, Environmental Emergency Library, Toronto, ON, Canada [*Library symbol*] [*Library of Congress*] (LCLS)

CaOTER.... Ontario Institute for Studies in Education, Toronto, ON, Canada [*Library symbol*] [*Library of Congress*] (LCLS)

CaOTERM ... Ontario Department of Energy and Resources Management, Toronto, ON, Canada [*Library symbol*] [*Library of Congress*] [*Obsolete*] (LCLS)

CaOTET.... Ontario Educational Communications Authority, Toronto, ON, Canada [*Library symbol*] [*Library of Congress*] (LCLS)

CaOTEtPL ... Etobicoke Public Library, Etobicoke, ON, Canada [*Library symbol*] [*Library of Congress*] (LCLS)
CaOTEY .... East York Public Library, Toronto, ON, Canada [*Library symbol*] [*Library of Congress*] (LCLS)
CaOTF .... University of Toronto, Environmental Sciences and Engineering, Toronto, ON, Canada [*Library symbol*] [*Library of Congress*] (LCLS)
CaOTFC .... Ontario Ministry of Consumer and Commercial Relations, Toronto, ON, Canada [*Library symbol*] [*Library of Congress*] (LCLS)
CaOTFH ... Forest Hill Public Library, Toronto, ON, Canada [*Library symbol*] [*Library of Congress*] (LCLS)
CaOTFM ... Fire Marshal of Ontario, Toronto, ON, Canada [*Library symbol*] [*Library of Congress*] (LCLS)
CaOTFN .... Falconbridge Nickel Mines Ltd., Information Centre, Toronto, ON, Canada [*Library symbol*] [*Library of Congress*] (LCLS)
CaOTFT .... Financial Times, Don Mills, Toronto, ON, Canada [*Library symbol*] [*Library of Congress*] (LCLS)
CaOTGE ... Canadian General Electric Co. Ltd., Toronto, ON, Canada [*Library symbol*] [*Library of Congress*] (LCLS)
CaOTGM .. Globe and Mail, Toronto, ON, Canada [*Library symbol*] [*Library of Congress*] (LCLS)
CaOTGSB ... Ontario Ministry of Government Services, Bibliographic Centre, Toronto, ON, Canada [*Library symbol*] [*Library of Congress*] (LCLS)
CaOTH ...... Hydro-Electric Power Commission of Ontario, Toronto, ON, Canada [*Library symbol*] [*Library of Congress*] (LCLS)
CaOTHC ... Humber College of Applied Arts and Technology, Rexdale, Toronto, ON, Canada [*Library symbol*] [*Library of Congress*] (LCLS)
CaOTHMH ... Humber Memorial Hospital, Weston, ON, Canada [*Library symbol*] [*Library of Congress*] (LCLS)
CaOThoP .. Ontario Paper Co. Ltd., Thorold, ON, Canada [*Library symbol*] [*Library of Congress*] (LCLS)
CaOThor ... Thornhill Public Library, Thornhill, ON, Canada [*Library symbol*] [*Library of Congress*] (LCLS)
CaOThorF ... Falconbridge Nickel Mines Ltd., Metallurgical Laboratory, Thornhill, ON, Canada [*Library symbol*] [*Library of Congress*] (LCLS)
CaOTHP ... Ontario Department of Highways, Planning and Design Branch, Toronto, ON, Canada [*Library symbol*] [*Library of Congress*] [*Obsolete*] (LCLS)
CaOTHu .... Huntec Ltd., Toronto, ON, Canada [*Library symbol*] [*Library of Congress*] (LCLS)
CaOTi .... Timmins Public Library, Timmins, ON, Canada [*Library symbol*] [*Library of Congress*] (LCLS)
CaOTIAP ... IAPA [*Industrial Accident Prevention Association*] Library, Toronto, ON, Canada [*Library symbol*] [*Library of Congress*] (LCLS)
CaOTICA ... Institute of Chartered Accountants of Ontario, Toronto, ON, Canada [*Library symbol*] [*Library of Congress*] (LCLS)
CaOTil .... Tilbury Public Library, Tilbury, ON, Canada [*Library symbol*] [*Library of Congress*] (LCLS)
CaOTIM .... Pontifical Institute of Mediaeval Studies, University of Toronto, Toronto, ON, Canada [*Library symbol*] [*Library of Congress*] (LCLS)
CaOTIN .... International Nickel Co. of Canada, Toronto, ON, Canada [*Library symbol*] [*Library of Congress*] (LCLS)
CaOTINF .. Informart, Toronto, ON, Canada [*Library symbol*] [*Library of Congress*] (LCLS)
CaOTIO .... United Kingdom Information Office, Toronto, ON, Canada [*Library symbol*] [*Library of Congress*] (LCLS)
CaOTIOL ... Imperial Oil Ltd., Toronto, ON, Canada [*Library symbol*] [*Library of Congress*] (LCLS)
CaOTiP ..... Tillsonburg Public Library, Tillsonburg, ON, Canada [*Library symbol*] [*Library of Congress*] (LCLS)
CaOTJ .... Canada Department of Justice, Toronto, ON, Canada [*Library symbol*] [*Library of Congress*] (LCLS)
CaOTJFM ... James F. MacLaren Ltd., Willowdale, Toronto, ON, Canada [*Library symbol*] [*Library of Congress*] (LCLS)
CaOTJL .... Ontario Ministry of the Attorney General, Judges Library, Toronto, ON, Canada [*Library symbol*] [*Library of Congress*] (LCLS)
CaOTJPS .. Jerram Pharmaceuticals Ltd., Sands Pharmaceutical Division, Toronto, ON, Canada [*Library symbol*] [*Library of Congress*] (LCLS)
CaOTJS ..... Jesuit Seminary, Toronto, ON, Canada [*Library symbol*] [*Library of Congress*] (LCLS)
CaOTK ...... Knox College, University of Toronto, Toronto, ON, Canada [*Library symbol*] [*Library of Congress*] (LCLS)
CaOTL .... Ontario Legislative Library, Toronto, ON, Canada [*Library symbol*] [*Library of Congress*] (LCLS)
CaOTLC .... Ontario Ministry of Natural Resources, Information Section, Reference Library, Toronto, ON, Canada [*Library symbol*] [*Library of Congress*] (LCLS)
CaOTLCC ... Lummus Company Canada Ltd., Willowdale, ON, Canada [*Library symbol*] [*Library of Congress*] (LCLS)
CaOTLF .... Ontario Ministry of Natural Resources, Natural Resources Library, Toronto, ON, Canada [*Library symbol*] [*Library of Congress*] (LCLS)

CaOTLL .... Ontario Ministry of Natural Resources, Lands and Surveys Branch, Toronto, ON, Canada [*Library symbol*] [*Library of Congress*] (LCLS)
CaOTLP .... Ledbury Park Junior High School, Toronto, ON, Canada [*Library symbol*] [*Library of Congress*] (LCLS)
CaOTLR .... Ontario Ministry of Natural Resources, Research Branch, Toronto, ON, Canada [*Library symbol*] [*Library of Congress*] (LCLS)
CaOTLS .... Law Society of Upper Canada, Toronto, ON, Canada [*Library symbol*] [*Library of Congress*] (LCLS)
CaOTM ..... Canada Department of the Environment, Atmospheric Environment Service, Toronto, ON, Canada [*Library symbol*] [*Library of Congress*] (LCLS)
CaOTMB . McMillen Birch, Toronto, ON, Canada [*Library symbol*] [*Library of Congress*] (LCLS)
CaOTMC .. Massey College in the University of Toronto, Toronto, ON, Canada [*Library symbol*] [*Library of Congress*] (LCLS)
CaOTMCL ... Metropolitan Toronto Central Library, Toronto, ON, Canada [*Library symbol*] [*Library of Congress*] [*Obsolete*] (LCLS)
CaOTME .. Ontario Ministry of Energy, Toronto, ON, Canada [*Library symbol*] [*Library of Congress*] (LCLS)
CaOTMEN ... Ontario Ministry of the Environment, Toronto, ON, Canada [*Library symbol*] [*Library of Congress*] (LCLS)
CaOTMENL ... Ontario Ministry of the Environment, Laboratory, Toronto, ON, Canada [*Library symbol*] [*Library of Congress*] (LCLS)
CaOTMF ... McIntyre-Falconbridge Library, Toronto, ON, Canada [*Library symbol*] [*Library of Congress*] (LCLS)
CaOTMH ... MacLean-Hunter Ltd., Toronto, ON, Canada [*Library symbol*] [*Library of Congress*] (LCLS)
CaOTMI .... Royal Canadian Military Institute, Toronto, ON, Canada [*Library symbol*] [*Library of Congress*] (LCLS)
CaOTMIO ... Canada Employment and Immigration Department, Toronto, ON, Canada [*Library symbol*] [*Library of Congress*] (LCLS)
CaOTMM ... McCarthy & McCarthy, Barristers and Solicitors, Toronto, ON, Canada [*Library symbol*] [*Library of Congress*] (LCLS)
CaOTMMB ... Ontario Milks Marketing Board, Toronto, ON, Canada [*Library symbol*] [*Library of Congress*] (LCLS)
CaOTMOF ... MacDonald Ophthalmic Foundation, Toronto, ON, Canada [*Library symbol*] [*Library of Congress*] (LCLS)
CaOTMT .. Monetary Times, Toronto, ON, Canada [*Library symbol*] [*Library of Congress*] (LCLS)
CaOTMTS ... Metropolitan Toronto School Board, Toronto, ON, Canada [*Library symbol*] [*Library of Congress*] (LCLS)
CaOTN ...... Newtonbrook Secondary School, Willowdale, ON, Canada [*Library symbol*] [*Library of Congress*] (LCLS)
CaOTNA ... Ontario Ministry of Northern Affairs, Toronto, ON, Canada [*Library symbol*] [*Library of Congress*] (LCLS)
CaOTNH ... National Heritage Ltd., Toronto, ON, Canada [*Library symbol*] [*Library of Congress*] (LCLS)
CaOTNHH ... Canada Department of National Health and Welfare, Health Protection Branch, Toronto, ON, Canada [*Library symbol*] [*Library of Congress*] (LCLS)
CaOTNIMR ... National Institute on Mental Retardation, Toronto, ON, Canada [*Library symbol*] [*Library of Congress*] (LCLS)
CaOTNM .. Northern Mines, Toronto, ON, Canada [*Library symbol*] [*Library of Congress*] (LCLS)
CaOTNS .... Bank of Nova Scotia, Toronto, ON, Canada [*Library symbol*] [*Library of Congress*] (LCLS)
CaOTNY ... North York Public Library, Toronto, ON, Canada [*Library symbol*] [*Library of Congress*] (LCLS)
CaOTNYE ... North York Board of Education, F. W. Minkler Library, Willowdale, Toronto, ON, Canada [*Library symbol*] [*Library of Congress*] (LCLS)
CaOTo .... Tottenham Public Library, Tottenham, ON, Canada [*Library symbol*] [*Library of Congress*] (LCLS)
CaOTOC ... Ontario Cancer Institute, Toronto, ON, Canada [*Library symbol*] [*Library of Congress*] (LCLS)
CaOTOEC ... Ontario Economic Council, Toronto, ON, Canada [*Library symbol*] [*Library of Congress*] (LCLS)
CaOTOGR ... Ontario Geriatrics Research Society, Toronto, ON, Canada [*Library symbol*] [*Library of Congress*] (LCLS)
CaOTOH ... Ontario Housing Corp., Toronto, ON, Canada [*Library symbol*] [*Library of Congress*] (LCLS)
CaOTOHOR ... Ontario Hydro, Central Records, Toronto, ON, Canada [*Library symbol*] [*Library of Congress*] (LCLS)
CaOTOMA ... Ontario Medical Association, Toronto, ON, Canada [*Library symbol*] [*Library of Congress*] (LCLS)
CaOTOMR ... Ontario Ministry of Revenue, Toronto, ON, Canada [*Library symbol*] [*Library of Congress*] (LCLS)
CaOTOPC ... Ortho Pharmaceutical Canada Ltd., Don Mills, Toronto, ON, Canada [*Library symbol*] [*Library of Congress*] (LCLS)
CaOTP .... Toronto Public Library, Metropolitan Bibliographic Centre, Toronto, ON, Canada [*Library symbol*] [*Library of Congress*] (LCLS)
CaOTPA ... Institute of Public Administration of Canada, Toronto, ON, Canada [*Library symbol*] [*Library of Congress*] (LCLS)
CaOTPB ..... Metropolitan Toronto Central Library, Baldwin Room, Toronto, ON, Canada [*Library symbol*] [*Library of Congress*] (LCLS)

CaOTPFA ... Toronto Public Libraries, Fine Arts Libraries, Northern District, Toronto, ON, Canada [*Library symbol*] [*Library of Congress*] (LCLS)

CaOTPG .... Polar Gas Library, Toronto, ON, Canada [*Library symbol*] [*Library of Congress*] (LCLS)

CaOTPH ... Metropolitan Toronto Central Library, History Section, Toronto, ON, Canada [*Library symbol*] [*Library of Congress*] (LCLS)

CaOTPP .... Ontario Provincial Police, Toronto, ON, Canada [*Library symbol*] [*Library of Congress*] (LCLS)

CaOTPPC ... Ontario Provincial Police College, Toronto, ON, Canada [*Library symbol*] [*Library of Congress*] (LCLS)

CaOTPR .... Proctor & Redfern Group, Toronto, ON, Canada [*Library symbol*] [*Library of Congress*] (LCLS)

CaOTPW ... Ontario Ministry of Community and Social Services, Toronto, ON, Canada [*Library symbol*] [*Library of Congress*] (LCLS)

CaOTPWC ... Public Works Canada, Ontario Regional Library, Toronto, ON, Canada [*Library symbol*] [*Library of Congress*] (LCLS)

CaOTQRM ... Queen's Own Rifles of Canada Regimental Museum, Toronto, ON, Canada [*Library symbol*] [*Library of Congress*] (LCLS)

CaOTQSM ... Queen Street Mental Health Centre, Toronto, ON, Canada [*Library symbol*] [*Library of Congress*] (LCLS)

CaOTR ...... Ryerson Institute, Toronto, ON, Canada [*Library symbol*] [*Library of Congress*] (LCLS)

CaOTRA ... Royal Astronomical Society, Toronto, ON, Canada [*Library symbol*] [*Library of Congress*] (LCLS)

CaOTRC ... Canadian Forces College, Toronto, ON, Canada [*Library symbol*] [*Library of Congress*] (LCLS)

CaOTRCL ... Reichhold Chemicals Ltd., Weston, Toronto, ON, Canada [*Library symbol*] [*Library of Congress*] (LCLS)

CaOTRCS ... Canada Department of National Defence, Canadian Forces Staff School, Toronto, ON, Canada [*Library symbol*] [*Library of Congress*] (LCLS)

CaOTREC ... Regis College, Toronto, ON, Canada [*Library symbol*] [*Library of Congress*] (LCLS)

CaOTREx ... Canada Department of Regional Economic Expansion, Toronto, ON, Canada [*Library symbol*] [*Library of Congress*] (LCLS)

CaOTRF .... Ontario Research Foundation, Toronto, ON, Canada [*Library symbol*] [*Library of Congress*] (LCLS)

CaOTRIC .. Rockwell International, Collins Canada Division, Toronto, ON, Canada [*Library symbol*] [*Library of Congress*] (LCLS)

CaOTRL .... Reed Limited, Toronto, ON, Canada [*Library symbol*] [*Library of Congress*] (LCLS)

CaOTRM .. Royal Ontario Museum, Toronto, ON, Canada [*Library symbol*] [*Library of Congress*] (LCLS)

CaOTRMC ... Royal Ontario Museum, Canadiana Department, Toronto, ON, Canada [*Library symbol*] [*Library of Congress*] (LCLS)

CaOTRMF ... Royal Ontario Museum, Far Eastern Department, Toronto, ON, Canada [*Library symbol*] [*Library of Congress*] (LCLS)

CaOTS .... Statistics Canada, Toronto, ON, Canada [*Library symbol*] [*Library of Congress*] (LCLS)

CaOTSA .... Salvation Army Library, Toronto, ON, Canada [*Library symbol*] [*Library of Congress*] (LCLS)

CaOTSAP ... Spar Aerospace Products, Toronto, ON, Canada [*Library symbol*] [*Library of Congress*] (LCLS)

CaOTSC .... Seneca College, Willowdale, ON, Canada [*Library symbol*] [*Library of Congress*] (LCLS)

CaOTSCC ... Scarborough College, Scarborough, ON, Canada [*Library symbol*] [*Library of Congress*] (LCLS)

CaOTSCL ... Shell Canada Limited, Toronto, ON, Canada [*Library symbol*] [*Library of Congress*] (LCLS)

CaOTSED ... Scarborough Borough Board of Education, Toronto, ON, Canada [*Library symbol*] [*Library of Congress*] (LCLS)

CaOTSLR ... Sun Life of Canada, Reference Library, Toronto, ON, Canada [*Library symbol*] [*Library of Congress*] (LCLS)

CaOTSM ... Saint Michael's Hospital, Toronto, ON, Canada [*Library symbol*] [*Library of Congress*] (LCLS)

CaOTSMC ... Sunnybrook Medical Centre, Toronto, ON, Canada [*Library symbol*] [*Library of Congress*] (LCLS)

CaOTSP .... Scarborough Public Library, Scarborough, ON, Canada [*Library symbol*] [*Library of Congress*] (LCLS)

CaOTSPA ... Scarborough Public Library, Albert Campbell Branch, Scarborough, ON, Canada [*Library symbol*] [*Library of Congress*] (LCLS)

CaOTSPC ... Scarborough Public Library, Cedarbrae Branch, Scarborough, ON, Canada [*Library symbol*] [*Library of Congress*] (LCLS)

CaOTST .... Ontario Science Centre, Toronto, ON, Canada [*Library symbol*] [*Library of Congress*] (LCLS)

CaOTStA ... Saint Augustine's Seminary, Toronto, ON, Canada [*Library symbol*] [*Library of Congress*] (LCLS)

CaOTSTF ... Ontario Film Institute, Science Centre Library, Toronto, ON, Canada [*Library symbol*] [*Library of Congress*] (LCLS)

CaOTStM ... University of Saint Michael's College, Toronto, ON, Canada [*Library symbol*] [*Library of Congress*] (LCLS)

CaOTT ...... Toronto Transportation Commission, Toronto, ON, Canada [*Library symbol*] [*Library of Congress*] (LCLS)

CaOTTC ... University of Trinity College, Toronto, ON, Canada [*Library symbol*] [*Library of Congress*] (LCLS)

CaOTTCA ... University of Trinity College, Archives, Toronto, ON, Canada [*Library symbol*] [*Library of Congress*] (LCLS)

CaOTTDB ... Toronto Dominion Bank, Toronto, ON, Canada [*Library symbol*] [*Library of Congress*] (LCLS)

CaOTTeC .. Toronto Teachers' College, Toronto, ON, Canada [*Library symbol*] [*Library of Congress*] (LCLS)

CaOTTex ... Texaco Canada Inc., Don Mills, Toronto, ON, Canada [*Library symbol*] [*Library of Congress*] (LCLS)

CaOTTI ..... Ontario Ministry of Industry and Tourism, Toronto, ON, Canada [*Library symbol*] [*Library of Congress*] (LCLS)

CaOTTOA ... Canada Ministry of Transport, Canadian Air Transportation Administration, Ontario Region, Toronto, ON, Canada [*Library symbol*] [*Library of Congress*] (LCLS)

CaOTTR .... Thomson & Rogers, Barristers and Solicitors, Toronto, ON, Canada [*Library symbol*] [*Library of Congress*] (LCLS)

CaOTU ...... University of Toronto, Toronto, ON, Canada [*Library symbol*] [*Library of Congress*] (LCLS)

CaOTUA ... University of Toronto, Institute of Aerophysics, Toronto, ON, Canada [*Library symbol*] [*Library of Congress*] (LCLS)

CaOTUAn ... University of Toronto, Department of Anatomy, Toronto, ON, Canada [*Library symbol*] [*Library of Congress*] (LCLS)

CaOTUAP ... University of Toronto, Department of Applied Physics, Toronto, ON, Canada [*Library symbol*] [*Library of Congress*] (LCLS)

CaOTUAr ... University of Toronto, Archives, Toronto, ON, Canada [*Library symbol*] [*Library of Congress*] (LCLS)

CaOTUAV ... University of Toronto, Audiovisual Library, Toronto, ON, Canada [*Library symbol*] [*Library of Congress*] (LCLS)

CaOTUB ... University of Toronto, Department of Biochemistry, Toronto, ON, Canada [*Library symbol*] [*Library of Congress*] (LCLS)

CaOTUBP ... University of Toronto, Banting-Best Physiology Library, Toronto, ON, Canada [*Library symbol*] [*Library of Congress*] (LCLS)

CaOTUC ... University of Toronto, Department of Chemistry, Toronto, ON, Canada [*Library symbol*] [*Library of Congress*] (LCLS)

CaOTUCC ... University of Toronto, Institute of Computer Science, Toronto, ON, Canada [*Library symbol*] [*Library of Congress*] (LCLS)

CaOTUCE ... University of Toronto, Department of Chemical Engineering and Applied Chemistry, Toronto, ON, Canada [*Library symbol*] [*Library of Congress*] (LCLS)

CaOTUCi .. University of Toronto, Department of Civil Engineering, Toronto, ON, Canada [*Library symbol*] [*Library of Congress*] (LCLS)

CaOTUCr ... University of Toronto, Centre of Criminology, Toronto, ON, Canada [*Library symbol*] [*Library of Congress*] (LCLS)

CaOTUCS ... University of Toronto, Institute of Child Study, Toronto, ON, Canada [*Library symbol*] [*Library of Congress*] (LCLS)

CaOTUD ... University of Toronto, David Dunlap Observatory, Toronto, ON, Canada [*Library symbol*] [*Library of Congress*] (LCLS)

CaOTUDB ... University of Toronto, Department of Botany, Toronto, ON, Canada [*Library symbol*] [*Library of Congress*] (LCLS)

CaOTUDM ... University of Toronto, Department of Mathematics, Toronto, ON, Canada [*Library symbol*] [*Library of Congress*] (LCLS)

CaOTUDP ... University of Toronto, Clarke Institute of Psychiatry, Toronto, ON, Canada [*Library symbol*] [*Library of Congress*] (LCLS)

CaOTUEE ... University of Toronto, Department of Electrical Engineering, Toronto, ON, Canada [*Library symbol*] [*Library of Congress*] (LCLS)

CaOTUFA ... University of Toronto, Department of Fine Arts, Toronto, ON, Canada [*Library symbol*] [*Library of Congress*] (LCLS)

CaOTUFD ... University of Toronto, Faculty of Dentistry, Toronto, ON, Canada [*Library symbol*] [*Library of Congress*] (LCLS)

CaOTUFM ... University of Toronto, Faculty of Music, Toronto, ON, Canada [*Library symbol*] [*Library of Congress*] (LCLS)

CaOTUFP ... University of Toronto, Faculty of Pharmacy, Toronto, ON, Canada [*Library symbol*] [*Library of Congress*] (LCLS)

CaOTUG ... University of Toronto, Department of Geological Sciences, Toronto, ON, Canada [*Library symbol*] [*Library of Congress*] (LCLS)

CaOTUGL ... University of Toronto, Geophysics Laboratory, Toronto, ON, Canada [*Library symbol*] [*Library of Congress*] (LCLS)

CaOTUH ... University of Toronto, School of Hygiene, Toronto, ON, Canada [*Library symbol*] [*Library of Congress*] (LCLS)

CaOTUIRN ... University of Toronto, Center for Industrial Relations, the Jean and Dorothy Newman Industrial Relations Library, Toronto, ON, Canada [*Library symbol*] [*Library of Congress*] (LCLS)

CaOTUL ... University of Toronto, Faculty of Law, Toronto, ON, Canada [*Library symbol*] [*Library of Congress*] (LCLS)

CaOTULAS ... University of Toronto, Library Automation Systems, Toronto, ON, Canada [*Library symbol*] [*Library of Congress*] (LCLS)

CaOTULS ... University of Toronto, School of Library Science, Toronto, ON, Canada [*Library symbol*] [*Library of Congress*]   (LCLS)
CaOTUM .. University of Toronto, Department of Mechanical Engineering, Toronto, ON, Canada [*Library symbol*] [*Library of Congress*]   (LCLS)
CaOTUMa ... University of Toronto, Map Library, Toronto, ON, Canada [*Library symbol*] [*Library of Congress*]   (LCLS)
CaOTUME ... University of Toronto, Department of Metallurgical Engineering, Toronto, ON, Canada [*Library symbol*] [*Library of Congress*]   (LCLS)
CaOTUMi ... University of Toronto, Department of Mining Engineering, Toronto, ON, Canada [*Library symbol*] [*Library of Congress*]   (LCLS)
CaOTUN ... University of Toronto, School of Nursing, Toronto, ON, Canada [*Library symbol*] [*Library of Congress*]   (LCLS)
CaOTUP ... University of Toronto, Department of Physics, Toronto, ON, Canada [*Library symbol*] [*Library of Congress*]   (LCLS)
CaOTUPa ... University of Toronto, Department of Pathology, Banting-Best Institute, Toronto, ON, Canada [*Library symbol*] [*Library of Congress*]   (LCLS)
CaOTURS ... University of Toronto, Department of Rare Books and Special Collections, Toronto, ON, Canada [*Library symbol*] [*Library of Congress*]   (LCLS)
CaOTUSA ... University of Toronto, School of Architecture, Toronto, ON, Canada [*Library symbol*] [*Library of Congress*]   (LCLS)
CaOTUSP ... University of Toronto, School of Physical and Health Education, Toronto, ON, Canada [*Library symbol*] [*Library of Congress*]   (LCLS)
CaOTUSW ... University of Toronto, School of Social Work, Toronto, ON, Canada [*Library symbol*] [*Library of Congress*]   (LCLS)
CaOTUTD ... Urban Transportation Development Corp., Toronto, ON, Canada [*Library symbol*] [*Library of Congress*]   (LCLS)
CaOTUTF ... University of Toronto, Thomas Fisher Rare Book Library, Toronto, ON, Canada [*Library symbol*] [*Library of Congress*]   (LCLS)
CaOTUTP ... University of Toronto Press, University of Toronto, Toronto, ON, Canada [*Library symbol*] [*Library of Congress*]   (LCLS)
CaOTUZ ... University of Toronto, Department of Zoology, Toronto, ON, Canada [*Library symbol*] [*Library of Congress*]   (LCLS)
CaOTV ...... Victoria University, Toronto, ON, Canada [*Library symbol*] [*Library of Congress*]   (LCLS)
CaOTW ..... Wycliffe College, Toronto, ON, Canada [*Library symbol*] [*Library of Congress*]   (LCLS)
CaOTWC .. Workmen's Compensation Board, Toronto, ON, Canada [*Library symbol*] [*Library of Congress*]   (LCLS)
CaOTWL... William Lyon MacKenzie Collegiate Institute, Downsview, ON, Canada [*Library symbol*] [*Library of Congress*]   (LCLS)
CaOTWLC ... Warner-Lambert Canada Ltd., Sheridan Park, ON, Canada [*Library symbol*] [*Library of Congress*]   (LCLS)
CaOTWM ... William M. Mercer Ltd., Toronto, ON, Canada [*Library symbol*] [*Library of Congress*]   (LCLS)
CaOTXRA ... X-Ray Assay Laboratories Ltd., Don Mills, Toronto, ON, Canada [*Library symbol*] [*Library of Congress*]   (LCLS)
CaOTY ...... York University, Toronto, ON, Canada [*Library symbol*] [*Library of Congress*]   (LCLS)
CaOTYBE ... York Borough Board of Education, Toronto, ON, Canada [*Library symbol*] [*Library of Congress*]   (LCLS)
CaOTYCE ... York County Board of Education, Toronto, ON, Canada [*Library symbol*] [*Library of Congress*]   (LCLS)
CaOTYL.... York University, Law Library, Toronto, ON, Canada [*Library symbol*] [*Library of Congress*]   (LCLS)
CaOTYP.... York Public Library, Toronto, ON, Canada [*Library symbol*] [*Library of Congress*]   (LCLS)
Caoutch Gutta Percha ... Caoutchouc et la Gutta Percha [*A publication*]
Caoutch Latex Artif ... Caoutchoucs et Latex Artificiels [*A publication*]
Caoutch Mod ... Caoutchouc Moderne [*A publication*]
CaOVAg.... Ontario Ministry of Agriculture and Food, Horticultural Research Institute, Vineland Station, ON, Canada [*Library symbol*] [*Library of Congress*]   (LCLS)
CaOVAgR ... Canada Department of Agriculture, Research Station, Vineland Station, ON, Canada [*Library symbol*] [*Library of Congress*]   (LCLS)
CaOVan..... Vanier Public Library, Vanier, ON, Canada [*Library symbol*] [*Library of Congress*]   (LCLS)
CaOVc ...... Valley East Public Library, Val Caron, ON, Canada [*Library symbol*] [*Library of Congress*]   (LCLS)
CaOW........ Windsor Public Library, Windsor, ON, Canada [*Library symbol*] [*Library of Congress*]   (LCLS)
CaOWA ..... University of Windsor, Windsor, ON, Canada [*Library symbol*] [*Library of Congress*]   (LCLS)
CaOWAG ... Art Gallery of Windsor, Windsor, ON, Canada [*Library symbol*] [*Library of Congress*]   (LCLS)
CaOWAL .. University of Windsor, Law Library, Windsor, ON, Canada [*Library symbol*] [*Library of Congress*]   (LCLS)
CaOWall.... Wallaceburg Public Library, Wallaceburg, ON, Canada [*Library symbol*] [*Library of Congress*]   (LCLS)
CaOWaP ... Waterford Public Library, Waterford, ON, Canada [*Library symbol*] [*Library of Congress*]   (LCLS)
CaOWar .... Warkworth Public Library, Warkworth, ON, Canada [*Library symbol*] [*Library of Congress*]   (LCLS)

CaOWC ..... Centennial Secondary School, Windsor, ON, Canada [*Library symbol*] [*Library of Congress*]   (LCLS)
CaOWe ...... Welland Public Library, Welland, ON, Canada [*Library symbol*] [*Library of Congress*]   (LCLS)
CaOWeC ... Centennial Secondary School, Welland, ON, Canada [*Library symbol*] [*Library of Congress*]   (LCLS)
CaOWeN ... Niagara College of Applied Arts and Technology, Welland, ON, Canada [*Library symbol*] [*Library of Congress*]   (LCLS)
CaOWesBC ... Borden Chemical, Westhill, ON, Canada [*Library symbol*] [*Library of Congress*]   (LCLS)
CaOWH ..... Herman Collegiate Institute, Windsor, ON, Canada [*Library symbol*] [*Library of Congress*]   (LCLS)
CaOWhP ... Whitby Public Library, Whitby, ON, Canada [*Library symbol*] [*Library of Congress*]   (LCLS)
CaOWIJC ... International Joint Commission, Windsor, ON, Canada [*Library symbol*] [*Library of Congress*]   (LCLS)
CaOWL ..... Lowe Technical School, Windsor, ON, Canada [*Library symbol*] [*Library of Congress*]   (LCLS)
CaOWo ...... Woodstock Public Library, Woodstock, ON, Canada [*Library symbol*] [*Library of Congress*]   (LCLS)
CaOWoO ... Oxford County Public Library, Woodstock, ON, Canada [*Library symbol*] [*Library of Congress*]   (LCLS)
CaOWR ..... Riverside Secondary School, Windsor, ON, Canada [*Library symbol*] [*Library of Congress*]   (LCLS)
CaOWS ..... Southwestern Regional Library, Windsor, ON, Canada [*Library symbol*] [*Library of Congress*]   (LCLS)
CaOWSA... Spar Aerospace Ltd., Weston, ON, Canada [*Library symbol*] [*Library of Congress*]   (LCLS)
CaOWSC... Saint Clair College, Windsor, ON, Canada [*Library symbol*] [*Library of Congress*]   (LCLS)
CaOWt...... Waterloo Public Library, Waterloo, ON, Canada [*Library symbol*] [*Library of Congress*]   (LCLS)
CaOWtA.... Kitchener-Waterloo Academy of Medicine, Waterloo, ON, Canada [*Library symbol*] [*Library of Congress*]   (LCLS)
CaOWtG.... Kitchener-Waterloo General Hospital, Waterloo, ON, Canada [*Library symbol*] [*Library of Congress*]   (LCLS)
CaOWtL.... Wilfrid Laurier University, Waterloo, ON, Canada [*Library symbol*] [*Library of Congress*]   (LCLS)
CaOWtS.... Saint Mary's General Hospital, Waterloo, ON, Canada [*Library symbol*] [*Library of Congress*]   (LCLS)
CaOWtU ... University of Waterloo, Waterloo, ON, Canada [*Library symbol*] [*Library of Congress*]   (LCLS)
CaOWtUE ... University of Waterloo, Environmental Studies Library, Waterloo, ON, Canada [*Library symbol*] [*Library of Congress*]   (LCLS)
CaOWVM ... Vincent Massey Secondary School, Windsor, ON, Canada [*Library symbol*] [*Library of Congress*]   (LCLS)
CaOWW .... Walkerville Collegiate Institute, Windsor, ON, Canada [*Library symbol*] [*Library of Congress*]   (LCLS)
CaOWyL ... Lambton County Public Library, Wyoming, ON, Canada [*Library symbol*] [*Library of Congress*]   (LCLS)
CAP .... Azusa Pacific College, Azusa, CA [*OCLC symbol*]   (OCLC)
CAP .... Cable Access Point [*Telecommunications*]   (TSSD)
CAP .... Campaign Against Pollution
CAP .... Canada Assistance Plan
CAP .... Canadian Air Publication
CAP .... Canadian Association of Pathologists
CAP .... Canadian Association of Physicists   (MCD)
CaP .... Canadian Poetry in English [*A publication*]
CAP .... Cap Haitien [*Haiti*] [*Airport symbol*]   (OAG)
CAP .... Capacitance   (DEN)
CAP .... Capacitor   (MSA)
CAP .... Capacity   (AFM)
CAP .... Capiat [*Let the Patient Take*] [*Pharmacy*]
CAP .... Capilano College Media Centre [*UTLAS symbol*]
cap.............. Capital [*Capital*] [*Business term*] [*French*]
CAP .... Capital   (EY)
CAP .... Capital Airlines, Inc.
CAP .... Capital Dynamics [*Vancouver Stock Exchange symbol*]
CAP .... Capital Housing & Mortgage Partners LP [*AMEX symbol*]   (SPSG)
CAP .... Capitalization [*Real estate*]
Cap............. Capitol [*Record label*]
CAP .... Capitol
CAP .... Capitol International Airways   (MCD)
Cap............. Capitoli [*A publication*]
Cap............. Capitolium [*A publication*]
Cap............. Capitolo [*Chapter*] [*Italian*]   (ILCA)
CAP .... Capitulum [*Chapter*] [*Latin*]
CAP .... Capodimonte [*Italy*] [*Seismograph station code, US Geological Survey*] [*Closed*]   (SEIS)
Cap............. Capricornus [*Constellation*]
CAP .... Capsula [*Capsule*] [*Pharmacy*]
CAP .... Captain
CAP .... Capture
CAP .... Caput [*Head*] [*Latin*]
CAP .... Carbamyl Phosphate [*Also, CP*] [*Organic chemistry*]
CAP .... Card Assembly Program
CAP .... Cardioacceleratory Peptide [*Biochemistry*]
CAP .... Career Analysis Procedure [*LIMRA*]
CAP .... Career Assistance Program [*Department of Labor*]

Ca P .... Cases in Parliament [*A publication*] (DLA)
CAP .... Cash Against Policy [*Insurance*]
CAP .... Catabolite Activator Protein [*Biochemistry, genetics*]
CAP .... Catabolite Gene Activator Protein [*Biochemistry, genetics*]
CAP .... Catalog of American Portraits [*Smithsonian Institution*] [*Washington, DC*]
CAP .... Catapult and Arresting Gear Pool [*Navy*]
CAP .... CAVDA [*Citizens Alliance for Venereal Disease Awareness*]-Citizens AIDS Project (EA)
CAP .... CCMS [*Checkout, Control, and Monitor Subsystem*] Application Programs [*NASA*] (NASA)
CAP .... Cell Attachment Protein [*Cytochemistry*]
CAP .... Cellulose Acetate Propionate [*Organic chemistry*]
CAP .... Center for Academic Precocity [*Arizona State University*] [*Research center*] (RCD)
CAP .... Center for Accountability to the Public (EA)
CAP .... Central Africa Party [*Southern Rhodesia*]
CAP .... Central Africa Protectorate [*British government*]
CAP .... Central Arbitration Point [*Data processing*] (PCM)
CAP .... Central Arizona Project [*Federal water-and-power project, similar to TVA*]
CAP .... Centralized Assignment Procedures [*Military*] (INF)
CAP .... Chief Ancient Philosophies [*A publication*]
CAP .... Chief Aviation Pilot [*Navy, Coast Guard*]
CAP .... Chloramphenicol [*Antimicrobial compound*]
CAP .... Chloroacetophenone [*Also, CN*] [*Tear gas*]
CAP .... Christian Appalachian Project
CaP .... Church and Peace [*Schoeffengrund, Federal Republic of Germany*] (EAIO)
CAP .... Circuit Access Point [*Telecommunications*] (TEL)
CAP .... Citation Abstract Procurement
CAP .... Citizens Against PAC's [*Political Action Committees*] [*Commercial firm*] (EA)
CAP .... Citizens Against Pornography (EA)
CAP .... Civil Air Patrol (EA)
CAP .... Civil Air Publication [*British*] (DEN)
CAP .... Clathrin-Associated Protein [*Cytology*]
CAP .... Clean Air Package
CAP .... Clean Air Projector
CAP .... Clinical Articulation Profile [*Speech evaluation test*]
CAP .... Coalition Against Pipeline Pollution (EA)
CAP .... Code of Advertising Practices [*British*]
CAP .... Codes and Paging (NRCH)
CAP .... Collection Agency Practices
CAP .... Collection Agency Project [*Student legal action organization*] (EA)
CAP .... College of American Pathologists (EA)
CAP .... Combat Air Patrol
CAP .... Combat Aircraft Prototype (MCD)
CAP .... Combined Action Platoon
CAP .... Comite d'Action de la Pomme de Terre [*Potato Action Committee*] [*Canadian Department of Agriculture*]
CAP .... Command Action Plan (NVT)
CAP .... Command Analysis Pattern (KSC)
CAP .... Commencing at a Point
CAP .... Commission for Accountability to the Public (EA)
CAP .... Common Agricultural Policy [*Common Market*]
CAP .... Commonwealth Association of Planners [*London, England*] (EAIO)
CAP .... Communication Association of the Pacific [*Later, WCA*] (EA)
CAP .... Community Action Party [*Political party*] [*Thailand*] (FEA)
CAP .... Community Action Program [*Community Services Administration*]
CAP .... Community Alert Patrol
CAP .... Compliance Aid for Pharmaceuticals
CAP .... Composers' Autograph Publications [*Defunct*] (EA)
CAP .... Composite Aircraft Program [*Military*] (RDA)
CAP .... Compound Action Potential [*Biology*]
CAP .... Computational Arithmetic Program
CAP .... Computer Address Panel (CAAL)
CAP .... Computer-Aided Planning
CAP .... Computer-Aided [*or Assisted*] Production
CAP .... Computer-Aided Programming
CAP .... Computer-Aided Publishing
CAP .... Computer Analysts & Programmers Ltd. [*British*]
CAP .... Computer Application Program (NASA)
CAP .... Computer-Assisted Printing
CAP .... Computerized Assignment of Personnel [*Military*]
CAP .... Computerized Automated Psychophysiological Device
CAP .... Computers and People [*A publication*]
CAP .... Computing Assistance Program [*Taylor University*] [*Information service or system*] (IID)
CAP .... Concurrent Algorithmic Programming Language [*Data processing*] (CSR)
CAP .... Condenser Absolute Pressure
CAP .... Configuration Audit Plan
CAP .... Congress of African Peoples
CAP .... Console Action Processor
CAP .... Contemporary Authors: Permanent Series [*A publication*]
CAP .... Continental Africa Project [*National Academy of Sciences*]
CAP .... Contingency Amphibious Plan [*NATO*] (NATG)

CAP .... Continuous Air Patrol [*Proposed defense for missiles*] [*Military*]
CAP .... Continuous Audit Program [*Data processing*] [*Finance*] (IEEE)
CAp .... Contra Apionem [*Against Apion*] [*Josephus*] (BJA)
CAP .... Contract Administration Panel [*Military*]
CAP .... Contractor-Acquired Property (AFM)
CAP .... Control Assembly Program (BUR)
CAP .... Control and Authorization Process (KSC)
CAP .... Controlled Atmosphere Packaging
CAP .... Coriolis Acceleration Platform
CAP .... Corporate Action Project [*Defunct*] (EA)
CAP .... Cost Account Package [*Accounting*] (NASA)
CAP .... Cost Account Plan
CAP .... Cost Analysis Plan
CAP .... Council on Advanced Programming
CAP .... Council on Alcohol Policy (EA)
CAP .... Crew Activity Plan (MCD)
CAP .... Crisis Accommodation Programme [*Australia*]
CAP .... Cropland Adjustment Program
CAP .... Cryotron Associative Processor (IEEE)
CAP .... Current Assessment Plan
CAP .... Customized Assurance Plans [*Automotive engineering*]
CAP .... Cyclic-AMP [*Adenosine Monophosphate*] Receptor Protein [*Also, CRP*] [*Genetics*]
CAP .... Cyclophosphamide, Adriamycin, Platinol [*Cisplatin*] [*Antineoplastic drug regimen*]
CAP .... Cyclophosphamide, Adriamycin, Prednisone [*Antineoplastic drug regimen*]
CAP .... Cystylaminopeptidase [*An enzyme*]
CAP .... Faulty Capitalization [*Used in correcting manuscripts, etc.*]
CAP .... Foolscap [*Paper*] (ROG)
CAP .... National Cap and Patch Association (EA)
CAP .... Springfield, IL [*Location identifier*] [*FAA*] (FAAL)
CAPA........ Canada-Caribbean-Central America Policy Alternatives [*An association*]
CAPA........ Canadian Animation Producers Association
CAPA........ Canadian Association for Physical Anthropology
CAPA........ Central Airborne Performance Analyzer (MCD)
CAPA........ Central Arizona Project Association (EA)
CAPA........ Comics Amateur Press Alliance
CAPA........ Comite d'Action du Personnel Autochtone [*Native Employees Action Team*] [*Canada*]
CAPA........ Commission on Asian and Pacific Affairs [*International Chamber of Commerce*]
CAPA........ Commonwealth Association of Polytechnics in Africa [*Nairobi, Kenya*] (EAIO)
CAPA........ Corrosion and Protection Association
CAPAB..... Capability (KSC)
CAPAB..... Capetown Performing Arts Board
CAPAC..... Composers, Authors, and Publishers Association of Canada
CAPAFSA ... Child Abuse Prevention, Adoption, and Family Services Act of 1988
CAPAL...... Computer and Photographic Assisted Learning
Ca Parl...... Cases in Parliament (Shower) [*1694-99*] [*A publication*] (DLA)
CAPAV..... Committee on Atmospheric Problems of Aerospace Vehicles [*American Meteorological Society*]
CAPB........ Capitol Bancorporation [*NASDAQ symbol*] (NQ)
CAPBAY ... Catalogue of American Amphibians and Reptiles [*A publication*]
CAPBBZ ... Colorado. Agricultural Experiment Station. Bulletin [*A publication*]
CAP-BOP ... Cyclophosphamide, Adriamycin, Procarbazine, Bleomycin, Oncovin [*Vincristine*], Prednisone [*Antineoplastic drug regimen*]
CApC .... Cabrillo College, Aptos, CA [*Library symbol*] [*Library of Congress*] (LCLS)
CAPC........ California Association of Parking Controllers (EA)
CAPC........ Canadian Army Pay Corps (DMA)
CAPC........ Canadian Association of Professional Conservators
CAPC........ Central America Peace Campaign (EA)
CAPC........ Civil Aviation Planning Committee (AFM)
CaPC........ Prince Edward Island Libraries, Charlottetown, PE, Canada [*Library symbol*] [*Library of Congress*] (LCLS)
CAPCA...... Council of Australian Pest Control Associations
CaPCA...... Public Archives, Charlottetown, PE, Canada [*Library symbol*] [*Library of Congress*] (LCLS)
CaPCAg..... Canada Department of Agriculture, Research Station, Charlottetown, PE, Canada [*Library symbol*] [*Library of Congress*] (LCLS)
CAPCATS ... Capability Categories (RDA)
CaPCCA .... Confederation Art Gallery and Museum, Charlottetown, PE, Canada [*Library symbol*] [*Library of Congress*] (LCLS)
CaPCE....... Prince Edward Island Department of Education, Charlottetown, PE, Canada [*Library symbol*] [*Library of Congress*] (LCLS)
CaPCHC.... Holland College, Charlottetown, PE, Canada [*Library symbol*] [*Library of Congress*] (LCLS)
CAPCHE... Component Automatic-Program Checkout Equipment [*Aerospace*] (AAG)
Cap Chem .. Capital Chemist [*A publication*]

CaPCIMR ... Institute of Man and Resources, Charlottetown, PE, Canada [Library symbol] [Library of Congress]   (LCLS)
CaPCL .... Confederation Centre Library, Charlottetown, PE, Canada [Library symbol] [Library of Congress]   (LCLS)
CaPCLS ..... Law Society of Prince Edward Island, Charlottetown, PE, Canada [Library symbol] [Library of Congress]   (LCLS)
CaPCMA ... Prince Edward Island Department of Municipal Affairs, Charlottetown, PE, Canada [Library symbol] [Library of Congress]   (LCLS)
CAPCO ...... Capital & Counties [Property development company] [British]
CAPCO ...... China American Petrochemical Company Ltd.
CAPCOM ... Capsule Communications [or Communicator] [NASA]
CAPCON .... Capitol Consortium Network [of CUMWA] [Information service or system]
CAPCON .. Capsule Control [NASA]   (KSC)
CAPCP ...... Civil Air Patrol Coastal Patrol [Wartime]
CaPCPL ..... Planning Library, Charlottetown, PE, Canada [Library symbol] [Library of Congress]   (LCLS)
CAPCRA .... Cooperative Agricole des Producteurs de Cereales de la Region d'Arras
CaPCU ...... University of Prince Edward Island, Charlottetown, PE, Canada [Library symbol] [Library of Congress]   (LCLS)
CAP D .... Capitular Degrees [Freemasonry]   (ROG)
CAPD .... Cathodic Arc Plasma Deposition [Coating technology]
CAPD .... Chronic Ambulatory Peritoneal Dialysis [Medicine]
CAPD .... Computer-Aided Parameter Design
CAPD .... Computer-Aided Process Design   (MCD)
CAPD .... Continuous Ambulatory Peritoneal Dialysis [Medicine]
CAPDAC .... Computer-Aided Piping Design and Construction   (MCD)
CaPDi .... Calcium Pyrophosphate Dihydrate [Inorganic chemistry]
Cap Dist Bs ... Capital District Business Review [A publication]
CAPE .... Canadian Association of Professors of Education
CAPE .... Canadian Petroleum [A publication]
CAPE .... Capability and Proficiency Evaluation
CAPE .... Center for Advanced Professional Education [Canada]
CAPE .... Clifton Assessment Procedures for the Elderly [Personality development test] [Psychology]
CAPE .... Coalition of American Public Employees
CAPE .... Comite d'Appui au Peuple Espagnol [Committee of Support for Spanish People] [Canada]
CAPE .... Committee on Assessing the Progress of Education [Later, NAEP]   (EA)
CAPE .... Communication Automatic Processing Equipment
CAPE .... Computer-Aided Process Engineering
CAPE .... Computer-Assisted Policy Evaluation   (MCD)
CAPE .... Computer-Assisted Psychosocial Evaluation
CAPE .... Conduction Analysis Program Using Eigenvalues [NASA]
CAPE .... Consortium for the Advancement of Physics Education
CAPE .... Convective Available Potential Energy
CAPE .... Council for American Private Education   (EA)
Cape Good Hope Dep Nat Conserv Rep ... Cape Of Good Hope. Department of Nature Conservation. Report [A publication]
Cape Law J ... Cape Law Journal [South Africa] [A publication]   (DLA)
Cape Librn ... Cape Librarian [A publication]
Cape LJ ..... Cape Law Journal [South Africa] [A publication]   (DLA)
Cape Of Good Hope Dep Nat Conserv Invest Rep ... Cape Of Good Hope. Department of Nature Conservation. Investigational Report [A publication]
Cape Of Good Hope Dep Nat Conserv Rep ... Cape Of Good Hope. Department of Nature Conservation. Report [A publication]
Cape P Div ... Cape Provincial Division Reports [South Africa] [A publication]   (DLA)
CAPER ...... Canadian Association of Publishers' Educational Representatives
Ca Per .... Castrum Peregrini [A publication]
CAPER ...... Civilian Authority for the Protection of Everybody, Regardless [Crime-fighting unit in TV series "The Kids From C.A.P.E.R."]
CAPER ...... Combined Active/Passive Emitter Rangings
CAPER ...... Computer-Aided Pattern Evaluation and Recognition   (KSC)
CAPER ...... Computer-Aided Preparation of Electrical Routing   (MCD)
CAPER ...... Computer-Assisted Pathology Encoding and Reporting System [Medicine]   (DHSM)
CAPER ...... Configuration Analysis and Performance   (MCD)
CAPER ...... Cost of Attaining Personnel Requirement
CAPERS ..... Cost and Performance Effectiveness Ratios
CAPERTSIM ... Computer-Assisted Program Evaluation Review-Technique Simulation [Army]
Cape SA ..... Cape Of Good Hope, South Africa   (ILCA)
Cape SA ..... Cape Province, South Africa   (ILCA)
Cape SCR .. Supreme Court Reports, Cape Colony [1880-1910] [South Africa] [A publication]   (DLA)
CAPETN ... Cape Town [South Africa]   (ROG)
Cape Town Univ Dep Geol Precambrian Res Unit Annu Rep ... Cape Town. University. Department of Geology. Precambrian Research Unit. Annual Report [A publication]
Cape TR ..... Cape Times Supreme Court Reports, Cape Of Good Hope [South Africa] [A publication]   (DLA)
CAPEX ...... Capability Exercise

CAPF .... Chemical Age Project File [Pergamon ORBIT InfoLine Inc.] [Information service or system]
CAPFG ...... Capacitor Flashgun [Photography]
CAPG .... Capital Goods [Finance]
CAPG .... Civil Air Patrol Guard
CAPH .... Committee on Application of Polarized Headlights [OECD]
CAPHE ..... Consortium for the Advancement of Private Higher Education   (EA)
CAPI .... Center for the Analysis of Public Issues [Princeton, NJ]
CAPIANT ... Capiantur [Let Them Be Taken] [Pharmacy]   (ROG)
CAPIC .... Canadian Association for Production and Inventory Control
Capic .... [Antonius] Capicius [Deceased, 1545] [Authority cited in pre-1607 legal work]   (DSA)
CAPIEND ... Capiendus [To Be Taken] [Pharmacy]
CAP-II .... Cyclophosphamide, Adriamycin, High-Dose Platinol [Cisplatin] [Antineoplastic drug regimen]
CAP III ...... Centralized Assignment Procedures Computer System [Military]
CAPIL .... Capital Indexed Loan Pilot Scheme [Victoria, Australia]
CAPIO .... Commission for the Advancement of Public Interest Organizations   (EA)
CAPIR .... Computer-Assisted Photo-Interpretation Research   (MCD)
CAP/IS ...... Combined Approach Control/International Station [Aviation]   (FAAC)
CAPIS .... Customs Accelerated Passenger Inspection System [US Customs Service]
Capit .... Capital
Capit .... Capitolium [A publication]
CAPITA .... Center for Air Pollution Impact and Trend Analysis [Washington University] [Research center]   (RCD)
Capital .... Capital and Class [A publication]
Capital Goods R ... Capital Goods Review [A publication]
Capital ULR ... Capital University. Law Review [A publication]
Capital U L Rev ... Capital University. Law Review [A publication]
Capital Univ L Rev ... Capital University. Law Review [A publication]
Capita Zool ... Capita Zoologica [A publication]
Capitol Stud ... Capitol Studies [A publication]
CaPL .... Cahiers de la Pleiade [A publication]
CAPL .... Canadian Association of Public Libraries
CAPL .... Capital [Accounting; Finance; Economics]   (ROG)
CAPL .... Chronique Archeologique du Pays de Liege [A publication]
CAPL .... Coastal Anti-Pollution League [British]
CAPL .... Commission for the Accreditation of Public Libraries [Proposed]
CAPL .... Commonwealth Assistance to Public Libraries [Campaign] [Australia]
CAPL .... Continuous Annealing and Processing Line [Steel manufacture]
CAPL .... Controlled Assembly Parts List [Aerospace]   (AAG)
CAPLAR ... Computer Assisted PLA [Product License Application] Review [FDA]
CAPLD ...... Carolina Planning [A publication]
Cap Libn ...... Cape Librarian [A publication]
CAPM .... Capital-Asset Pricing Model
CAPM .... Computer-Aided Patient Management
CAPM .... Computer-Aided Plant Management
CAPMAR ... Cost Account Performance Measurement and Analysis Report   (MCD)
CAPME ..... Committee of Americans for Peace in the Middle East [Defunct]   (EA)
CAPMI ...... Computer-Assisted Post Mortem Identification   (RDA)
CAPMO .... Carrefour des Agents de Pastorale en Monde Ouvrier [Crossroads of Pastoral Agents and Workers of the World] [Canada]
CAP MOLL ... Capsula Mollis [Soft Capsule] [Pharmacy]
CAPMP ..... Committee Against the Political Misuse of Psychiatry   (EA)
CAPN .... Captain   (ROG)
CAPNA ...... Canadian Association of Practical Nursing Assistants
Cap Nurs .... Capital Nursing [A publication]
CAPO .... Canadian Army Post Office   (DMA)
CAPO .... Canadian Association of Prosthetists and Orthotists
CAPO .... Capistrano [Hazardous test facility]
CAPO .... Center Apollo Program Offices [NASA]   (KSC)
CAPO .... Civil Affairs Police Officer [British] [World War II]
CAPOSS .... Capacity Planning and Operations Sequencing System [IBM Corp.]
CAPOSS-E ... Capacity Planning and Operations Sequencing System - Extended [IBM Corp.]
Capp .... Cappadocian   (BJA)
CAPP .... Clinical Applications and Prevention Program [Bethesda, MD] [National Heart, Lung, and Blood Institute] [Department of Health and Human Services]   (GRD)
CAPP .... Computer-Aided Process Planning   (MCD)
CAPP .... Conference of Actuaries in Public Practice [Itasca, IL]   (EA)
CAPP .... Conference for the Advancement of Private Practice [in social work]
CAPP .... Content-Addressable Parallel Processor [Data processing]
C App .... Sentenza della Corte di Appello [Decision of the Court of Appeal] [Italian]   (ILCA)
CAPPA ...... Centralblatt fuer Allgemeine Pathologie und Pathologische Anatomie [A publication]
CAPPA ...... Crusher and Portable Plant Association   (EA)

CAPPI .... Constant Altitude Plan Position Indicator [*Aviation*] (FAAC)
C App R ..... Criminal Appeal Reports [*England*] [*A publication*] (DLA)
CAPPRO... Capital Property Accounting and Control (MCD)
CAPPS....... Center for Aseptic Processing and Packaging Studies [*North Carolina State University*] [*Research center*] (RCD)
CAPPS....... Centralized Army Passenger Port Call System (AABC)
CAPPS....... Chemicals and Polymers Production Statistics [*A publication*]
CAPPS....... Computer-Assisted Pricing Proposal System (MCD)
CAPPS....... Council for the Advancement of the Psychological Professions and Sciences [*Later, AAP*]
CAPPS....... Current and Past Psychopathology Scales [*Psychology*]
CAP QUANT VULT ... Capiat Quantum Vult [*Let the Patient Take as Much as He Will*] [*Pharmacy*]
Capr .... Capricornus [*Constellation*]
CAPR .... Catalog of Programs
Ca Prac CP ... Cooke's Practice Cases [*1706-47*] [*England*] [*A publication*] (DLA)
CAPRI .... Captive Reset Ignitor (NASA)
CAPRI .... Card and Printer Remote Interface
CAPRI .... Center for Applied Polymer Research [*Case Western Reserve University*] [*Research center*] (RCD)
CAPRI .... Coded Address Private Radio Intercommunication (MCD)
CAPRI .... Compact All-Purpose Range Instrument [*RADAR*] (MCD)
CAPRI .... Computer-Aided Passive Ranging Indicator [*Military*] (CAAL)
CAPRI .... Computerized Administration of Patent Documents Reclassified According to the IPC [*International Patent Classification*] [*INPADOC*] [*Information service or system*] (ADA)
CAPRI .... Computerized Advance Personnel Requirements Information [*or Inventory*] [*Navy*]
CAPRI .... Computerized Area Pricing [*Telecommunications*] (TEL)
CAPRIS..... Combat Active and Passive RADAR Identification System (MCD)
CAPS .... Caffeine, Alcohol, Pepper, Spicy Foods [*Nutrition*]
CAPS .... Call Attempts per Second [*Telecommunications*] (TEL)
CAPS .... Capitals [*Printing*]
CAPS .... Capsula [*Capsule*] [*Pharmacy*]
CAPS .... Capsule
CAPS .... Career Ability Placement Survey [*Vocational guidance test*]
CAPS .... Cashiers' Automatic Processing System (DIT)
CAPS .... Cassette Programming System [*Digital Equipment Corp.*]
CAPS .... Cavity Alternated Phase Shift (MCD)
CAPS .... Cell Atmosphere Processing System [*Nuclear energy*] (NRCH)
CAPS .... Center for Advanced Purchasing Studies [*Arizona State University*] [*Research center*] (RCD)
CAPS .... Centralized Accounting and Polling Software [*Data processing*] (PCM)
CAPS .... Child Abuse Prevention Service [*Australia*]
CAPS .... Children of Ageing Parents (EA)
CAPS .... Christian Association for Psychological Studies (EA)
CAPS .... Civil Assistant Personal Services [*Navy*] [*British*]
CAPS .... Clearinghouse on Counseling and Personnel Services [*ERIC*]
CAPS .... Coalition for Asian Peace and Security (EA)
CAPS .... Command Automated Procurement System (MCD)
CAPS .... Commitment and Payment System (MCD)
CAPS .... Common Attitude Pointing System (MCD)
CAPS .... Computer-Aided Personnel Scheduling
CAPS .... Computer-Aided Pipe Sketching [*System*] [*Du Pont*]
CAPS .... Computer-Aided Process Synthesis
CAPS .... Computer-Aided Programming System
CAPS .... Computer-Assisted Placement Service [*British*]
CAPS .... Computer-Assisted Problem Solving (IEEE)
CAPS .... Computer-Assisted Product Search [*Information service or system*] (EISS)
CAPS .... Computer-Assisted Prosthesis Selection [*Orthopedic surgery*]
CAPS .... Computerized Aircraft Performance System (MCD)
CAPS .... Computing and Data Processing Services [*University of Maine*] [*Research center*] (RCD)
CAPS .... Consolidation Aerial Port System [*or Subsystem*] [*Air Force*] (MCD)
CAPS .... Construction Advanced Planning and Sequencing [*Nuclear energy*] (NRCH)
CAPS .... Continuous Automated Placement Survey [*Department of Labor*]
CAPS .... Contracap, Inc. [*NASDAQ symbol*] (NQ)
CAPS .... Control and Auxiliary Power Supply System
CAPS .... Cooperative Agricultural Pest Survey Program [*Information service or system*] (EISS)
CAPS .... Cooperative Association of Professional Salespeople [*Willoughby Hills, OH*] (EA)
CAPS .... Cooperative Awards in Pure Science [*British*]
CAPS .... Courtauld's All-Purpose Simulator (IEEE)
CAPS .... Creative Artists Public Service Program (EA)
CAPS .... Critical Angle Prism Sensor (KSC)
CAPS .... Cyclohexylaminopropanesulfonic Acid [*A buffer*]
CAPSAH... Canadian Press [*A publication*]
CAPS AMYLAC ... Capsula Amylacea [*A Cachet*] [*Pharmacy*]
CAPSC ...... Campaign Against Public Sector Cuts [*Australia*]
CAPSCR.... Capscrew [*Technical drawings*]
CAPSE ...... Computer-Assisted Power System Engineering (MCD)
CAPSEP.... Capsule Separation [*Aerospace*] (AAG)

CAPS GELAT ... Capsula Gelatina [*A Gelatine Capsule*] [*Pharmacy*]
CAPSHIPFOR ... Capacity Ships Force
CAPSIM.... Captive Simulation (NASA)
CAPSK ...... Combined Amplitude Phase Shift Keying (MCD)
CAPSM ..... Canadian Academy of Podiatric Sports Medicine
CAPSO-N ... Capital Area, Personnel Service Office (Navy)
CAPSR ...... Cost Account Performance Status Report [*Accounting*] (MCD)
CAPSS ...... Canadian Automated Pilot Selection System
CAPST ...... Capacitor-Start [*Motor*] [*Electricity*]
CAPSTONE ... Central Automated Personnel Security Transaction or Notification Exchange [*DoD*]
Cap Stud .... Capitol Studies [*A publication*]
CAPT......... Capiat [*Let the Patient Take*] [*Pharmacy*] (ROG)
CAPT......... Captain (AAG)
CAPT......... Caption (ADA)
Capt.......... Captivi [*of Plautus*] [*Classical studies*] (OCD)
CAPT......... Center for Applications of Psychological Type (EA)
CAPT......... Conversational Parts Programming Language [*Data processing*] (IEEE)
CAPTA...... Child Abuse Prevention and Treatment Act
CAPTAIN ... Computer-Aided Processing and Terminal Access Information Network [*Rutgers University*] [*New Brunswick, NJ*] [*Library computer network*]
CAPTAIN ... Covariance Analysis Program for the Study of Augmented Inertial Navigators (MCD)
CAPTAINS ... Character and Pattern Telephone Access Information Network System [*Viewdata system*] [*Japan*]
CAPTALC ... Control and Protection of Transoceanic Air Lanes of Communication
Capt(D)...... Destroyer Captain [*Australia*]
Capt-Gen ... Captain-General [*British military*] (DMA)
CAPTIS..... Computer-Assisted Prisoner Transportation Index Service [*National Sheriffs' Association*]
Capt (N)..... Captain (Naval)
CAPTOR.... Encapsulated Torpedo [*Antisubmarine*] [*Navy*]
CAPTV ...... Computer-Animated Photographic Terrain View (MCD)
Captv Insur ... Captive Insurance Concept [*A publication*]
CAPU .... Coast African People's Union [*Kenya*]
CAPUC ...... Coordinating Area Production Urgency Committee
Cap U LR... Capital University. Law Review [*A publication*]
Cap UL Rev ... Capital University. Law Review [*A publication*]
Capv .... Capoverso [*Paragraph*] [*Italian*] (ILCA)
CAPVI ...... Catholic Association of Persons with Visual Impairment (EA)
CAPWAn... Cercle Archeologique du Pays de Waes. Annales [*A publication*]
CAPWIRE ... Capitol Wireless, Inc. [*Telecommunications service*] (TSSD)
CAPWSK .. Collision Avoidance, Proximity Warning, Station Keeping Equipment [*Military*] (NG)
CAPX......... Capitol International Airways [*Air carrier designation symbol*]
CAPY......... Capacity [*Insurance; Finance; Transportation*]
CaQ........... California Quarterly [*A publication*]
CAQ........... Caucasia [*Colombia*] [*Airport symbol*] (OAG)
CAQ........... Change Agent Questionnaire [*Interpersonal skills and attitudes test*]
CAQ........... Class Activities Questionnaire [*Teacher evaluation test*]
CAQ........... Clinical Analysis Questionnaire
CAQ........... Computer-Aided Quality
CAQ........... Constant Area Quantization (MCD)
CAQ........... Selma, AL [*Location identifier*] [*FAA*] (FAAL)
CAQA....... Computer-Aided Quality Assurance
CaQAA ...... Aluminum Co. of Canada Ltd., Arvida, PQ, Canada [*Library symbol*] [*Library of Congress*] (LCLS)
CaQALC.... College d'Alma, Lac St.-Jean, PQ, Canada [*Library symbol*] [*Library of Congress*] (LCLS)
CAQAP ..... Canadian Association of Quality Assurance Professionals
CaQArM ... Bibliotheque Municipale, Arthabaska, PQ, Canada [*Library symbol*] [*Library of Congress*] (LCLS)
CaQAsAg .. Canada Department of Agriculture, Experimental Farm, L'Assomption, PQ, Canada [*Library symbol*] [*Library of Congress*] (LCLS)
CaQAsB..... Bibliotheque Municipale, Asbestos, PQ, Canada [*Library symbol*] [*Library of Congress*] (LCLS)
CaQBE....... Beaconsfield Public Library, Beaconsfield, PQ, Canada [*Library symbol*] [*Library of Congress*] (LCLS)
CaQBEC.... Bibliotheque Municipale, Becancour, PQ, Canada [*Library symbol*] [*Library of Congress*] (LCLS)
CaQBJ .... Juniorat des Freres du Sacre-Coeur, Bromptonville, PQ, Canada [*Library symbol*] [*Library of Congress*] (LCLS)
CaQBO ...... Bibliotheque Municipale, Boucherville, PQ, Canada [*Library symbol*] [*Library of Congress*] (LCLS)
CaQBRG ... Centre Hospitalier Robert Giffard, Quebec, PQ, Canada [*Library symbol*] [*Library of Congress*] (LCLS)
CaQCB ...... Bibliotheque Municipale, Coaticook, PQ, Canada [*Library symbol*] [*Library of Congress*] (LCLS)
CaQCC ...... Bibliotheque Gaspesienne, Cap-Chat, PQ, Canada [*Library symbol*] [*Library of Congress*] (LCLS)
CaQCCRS ... Conseil Regional de la Sante et des Services Sociaux, Chicoutimi, PQ, Canada [*Library symbol*] [*Library of Congress*] (LCLS)
CaQChJC .. Jewish Convalescent Hospital, Chomedy, PQ, Canada [*Library symbol*] [*Library of Congress*] (LCLS)

CaQCmM .. Bibliotheque Municipale, Cap-De-La Madeleine, PQ, Canada [*Library symbol*] [*Library of Congress*] (LCLS)

CaQCRCN ... Campus Notre-Dame de Foy, Cap-Rouge, PQ, Canada [*Library symbol*] [*Library of Congress*] (LCLS)

CaQCRS .... Seminaire Saint Augustine, Cap Rouge, PQ, Canada [*Library symbol*] [*Library of Congress*] (LCLS)

CaQCSH ... Societe Historique du Saguenay, Chicoutimi, PQ, Canada [*Library symbol*] [*Library of Congress*] (LCLS)

CaQCU ...... Universite du Quebec, Chicoutimi, PQ, Canada [*Library symbol*] [*Library of Congress*] (LCLS)

CaQCUG ... Universite du Quebec, Departement de Geographie, Chicoutimi, PQ, Canada [*Library symbol*] [*Library of Congress*] (LCLS)

CaQCUGC ... Universite du Quebec, Cartotheque, Chicoutimi, PQ, Canada [*Library symbol*] [*Library of Congress*] (LCLS)

CAQDA ..... California Air Quality Data [*A publication*]

CaQDC ...... Canadian Celanese Ltd., Drummondville, PQ, Canada [*Library symbol*] [*Library of Congress*] (LCLS)

CaQDCE ... College Bourgchemin (CEGEP) [*College d'Enseignement General et Professionnel*], Drummondville, PQ, Canada [*Library symbol*] [*Library of Congress*] (LCLS)

CaQDM ..... Bibliotheque Municipale, Drummondville, PQ, Canada [*Library symbol*] [*Library of Congress*] (LCLS)

CaQDOPH ... Office des Personnes Handicapees du Quebec, Drummondville, PQ, Canada [*Library symbol*] [*Library of Congress*] (LCLS)

CaQGaH .... Hotel-Dieu de Gaspe, Gaspe, PQ, Canada [*Library symbol*] [*Library of Congress*] (LCLS)

CaQGC ...... College de la Gaspesie, Gaspe, PQ, Canada [*Library symbol*] [*Library of Congress*] (LCLS)

CaQGL ...... Granby Leader, Granby, PQ, Canada [*Library symbol*] [*Library of Congress*] (LCLS)

CaQGM ..... Bibliotheque Municipale, Granby, PQ, Canada [*Library symbol*] [*Library of Congress*] (LCLS)

CaQGmM ... Bibliotheque Municipale, Grand'Mere, PQ, Canada [*Library symbol*] [*Library of Congress*] (LCLS)

CaQH .... Bibliotheque Municipale, Hull, PQ, Canada [*Library symbol*] [*Library of Congress*] (LCLS)

CaQHaC .... College d'Enseignement General et Professionnel de Regional Cote Nord, Hauterive, PQ, Canada [*Library symbol*] [*Library of Congress*] (LCLS)

CaQHaCR ... Conseil Regional de la Sante et des Services Sociaux de la Region Cote-Nord, Hauterive, PQ, Canada [*Library symbol*] [*Library of Congress*] (LCLS)

CaQHC ...... College d'Enseignement General et Professionnel de l'Outaouais, Hull, PQ, Canada [*Library symbol*] [*Library of Congress*] (LCLS)

CaQHCH .. CEGEP [*College d'Enseignement General et Professionnel*] de l'Outaouais, Heritage Campus, Hull, PQ, Canada [*Library symbol*] [*Library of Congress*] (LCLS)

CaQHCRS ... Conseil Regional de la Sante et des Services Sociaux de la Region Outaouais-Hull, Hull, PQ, Canada [*Library symbol*] [*Library of Congress*] (LCLS)

CaQHE ..... E. B. Eddy Co., Research and Technical Library, Hull, PQ, Canada [*Library symbol*] [*Library of Congress*] (LCLS)

CaQHEn .... Environment Canada, Hull, PQ, Canada [*Library symbol*] [*Library of Congress*] (LCLS)

CaQHPJ .... Centre Hospitalier Pierre Janet, Hull, PQ, Canada [*Library symbol*] [*Library of Congress*] (LCLS)

CaQHSA ... Societe d'Amenagement de l'Outaouais, Hull, PQ, Canada [*Library symbol*] [*Library of Congress*] (LCLS)

CaQHSC ... Centre Hospitalier du Sacre-Coeur, Hull, PQ, Canada [*Library symbol*] [*Library of Congress*] (LCLS)

CaQHU ..... Universite du Quebec-Outaouais, Hull, PQ, Canada [*Library symbol*] [*Library of Congress*] (LCLS)

CaQJC .... College de Joliette, Joliette, PQ, Canada [*Library symbol*] [*Library of Congress*] (LCLS)

CaQJH ...... Hopital Saint-Charles, Joliette, PQ, Canada [*Library symbol*] [*Library of Congress*] (LCLS)

CaQJJ .... Seminaire de Joliette, Joliette, PQ, Canada [*Library symbol*] [*Library of Congress*] (LCLS)

CaQJMA ... Musee d'Art de Joliette, Joliette, PQ, Canada [*Library symbol*] [*Library of Congress*] (LCLS)

CaQJoC ..... College de Jonquiere, Jonquiere, PQ, Canada [*Library symbol*] [*Library of Congress*] (LCLS)

CaQKB ...... Brome County Historical Society, Knowlton, PQ, Canada [*Library symbol*] [*Library of Congress*] (LCLS)

CaQKITA ... Institut de Technologie Agricole, Kamouraska, PQ, Canada [*Library symbol*] [*Library of Congress*] (LCLS)

CaQLA ...... Bibliotheque Municipale, Laval, PQ, Canada [*Library symbol*] [*Library of Congress*] (LCLS)

CaQLAC .... CEGEP [*College d'Enseignement General et Professionnel*] Montmorency-Chomedy, Laval, PQ, Canada [*Library symbol*] [*Library of Congress*] (LCLS)

CaQLACS ... Cite de la Sante de Laval, Laval, PQ, Canada [*Library symbol*] [*Library of Congress*] (LCLS)

CaQLAIAF ... Universite du Quebec, Institut Armand-Frappier, Laval, PQ, Canada [*Library symbol*] [*Library of Congress*] (LCLS)

CaQLASC ... College de l'Assomption, L'Assomption, PQ, Canada [*Library symbol*] [*Library of Congress*] (LCLS)

CaQLASGPT ... Canada Ministry of the Solicitor General, Penitentiary, Federal Training Centre, Laval, PQ, Canada [*Library symbol*] [*Library of Congress*] (LCLS)

CaQLB ...... Bishop's University, Lennoxville, PQ, Canada [*Library symbol*] [*Library of Congress*] (LCLS)

CaQLBG .... Bishop's University, Department of Geography, Lennoxville, PQ, Canada [*Library symbol*] [*Library of Congress*] (LCLS)

CaQLe .... Bibliotheque Municipale, Levis, PQ, Canada [*Library symbol*] [*Library of Congress*] (LCLS)

CaQLeC ..... College de Levis, Levis, PQ, Canada [*Library symbol*] [*Library of Congress*] (LCLS)

CaQLo .... Bibliotheque Municipale, Longueuil, PQ, Canada [*Library symbol*] [*Library of Congress*] (LCLS)

CaQLoCE .. College Edouard-Montpetit, Longueuil, PQ, Canada [*Library symbol*] [*Library of Congress*] (LCLS)

CaQLoCRS ... Conseil Regional de la Sante et des Services Sociaux, Longueuil, PQ, Canada [*Library symbol*] [*Library of Congress*] (LCLS)

CaQLoGM ... Institut de Genie des Materiaux, Longueuil, PQ, Canada [*Library symbol*] [*Library of Congress*] (LCLS)

CaQLoU .... Pratt & Whitney Aircraft, Longueuil, PQ, Canada [*Library symbol*] [*Library of Congress*] (LCLS)

CaQLs .... Bibliotheque Municipale, La Salle, PQ, Canada [*Library symbol*] [*Library of Congress*] (LCLS)

CaQLt .... Bibliotheque Municipale, La Tuque, PQ, Canada [*Library symbol*] [*Library of Congress*] (LCLS)

CaQMA ..... Aluminum Secretariat Ltd., Montreal, PQ, Canada [*Library symbol*] [*Library of Congress*] (LCLS)

CaQMAA .. Archives de la Chancellerie, Montreal, PQ, Canada [*Library symbol*] [*Library of Congress*] (LCLS)

CaQMABB ... Asselin, Benoit, Boucher, Ducharme & Lapointe, Inc., Montreal, PQ, Canada [*Library symbol*] [*Library of Congress*] (LCLS)

CaQMaC ... McGill University, Macdonald College, Montreal, PQ, Canada [*Library symbol*] [*Library of Congress*] (LCLS)

CaQMACAR ... Carmel de Montreal, Montreal, PQ, Canada [*Library symbol*] [*Library of Congress*] (LCLS)

CaQMACL ... Quebec Association for Children with Learning Disabilities, Montreal, PQ, Canada [*Library symbol*] [*Library of Congress*] (LCLS)

CaQMACN ... Archives de la Congregation de Notre-Dame, Montreal, PQ, Canada [*Library symbol*] [*Library of Congress*] (LCLS)

CaQMADMA ... Anglican Church of Canada, Diocese of Montreal, Archives, Montreal, PQ, Canada [*Library symbol*] [*Library of Congress*] (LCLS)

CaQMAE .. Aviation Electric Ltd., Montreal, PQ, Canada [*Library symbol*] [*Library of Congress*] (LCLS)

CaQMAEC ... Atomic Energy of Canada, Montreal, PQ, Canada [*Library symbol*] [*Library of Congress*] (LCLS)

CaQMAI ... Arctic Institute of North America, Montreal, PQ, Canada [*Library symbol*] [*Library of Congress*] [*Obsolete*] (LCLS)

CaQMAL .. Air Liquide, Montreal, PQ, Canada [*Library symbol*] [*Library of Congress*] (LCLS)

CaQMALL ... Abbott Laboratories Limited, Montreal, PQ, Canada [*Library symbol*] [*Library of Congress*] (LCLS)

CaQMAM ... McGill University, Allan Memorial Institute of Psychiatry, Montreal, PQ, Canada [*Library symbol*] [*Library of Congress*] (LCLS)

CaQMAMA ... Andre Marsan & Associes, Inc., Montreal, PQ, Canada [*Library symbol*] [*Library of Congress*] (LCLS)

CaQMaPTI ... Potton Technical Industries, Mansonville, PQ, Canada [*Library symbol*] [*Library of Congress*] (LCLS)

CaQMArC ... Archives Provinciales des Capucins, Montreal, PQ, Canada [*Library symbol*] [*Library of Congress*] (LCLS)

CaQMAS ... Archives du Seminaire de Saint-Sulpice, Montreal, PQ, Canada [*Library symbol*] [*Library of Congress*] (LCLS)

CaQMASI ... Ministere des Affaires Sociales, Informatheque-Laboratoires, Ste.-Anne-De-Bellevue, PQ, Canada [*Library symbol*] [*Library of Congress*] (LCLS)

CaQMASIN ... Informatheque des Affaires Sociales du Quebec, Montreal, PQ, Canada [*Library symbol*] [*Library of Congress*] (LCLS)

CaQMaSRC ... Space Research Corp., Masonville, PQ, Canada [*Library symbol*] [*Library of Congress*] (LCLS)

CaQMASSAS ... Association pour la Sante et la Securite du Travail, Secteur Affaires Sociales, Centre de Documentation, Montreal, PQ, Canada [*Library symbol*] [*Library of Congress*] (LCLS)

CaQMAv ... Barreau de Montreal, Bibliotheque des Avocats, Montreal, PQ, Canada [*Library symbol*] [*Library of Congress*] (LCLS)

CaQMAy ... Ayerst, McKenna & Harrison Ltd., Montreal, PQ, Canada [*Library symbol*] [*Library of Congress*] (LCLS)

CaQMB ..... Bell Telephone Co. of Canada, Montreal, PQ, Canada [*Library symbol*] [*Library of Congress*] (LCLS)

CaQMBA .. Ecole des Beaux-Arts, Montreal, PQ, Canada [*Library symbol*] [*Library of Congress*] (LCLS)

CaQMBAE ... Bristol Aero Engines Ltd., Montreal, PQ, Canada [*Library symbol*] [*Library of Congress*] (LCLS)

CaQMBB ... College Bois-De-Boulogne, Montreal, PQ, Canada [*Library symbol*] [*Library of Congress*] (LCLS)

CaQMBBL ... Beauchemin, Beaton, LaPointe, Inc., Montreal, PQ, Canada [*Library symbol*] [*Library of Congress*]   (LCLS)

CaQMBD .. Canada Department of the Secretary of State, Translation Bureau, Montreal, PQ, Canada [*Library symbol*] [*Library of Congress*]   (LCLS)

CaQMBI .... Bibliotheque des Instituteurs, Montreal, PQ, Canada [*Library symbol*] [*Library of Congress*]   (LCLS)

CaQMBL ... Bell Telephone Co. of Canada, Law Department Library, Montreal, PQ, Canada [*Library symbol*] [*Library of Congress*]   (LCLS)

CaQMBM ... Bibliotheque de la Ville de Montreal, Montreal, PQ, Canada [*Library symbol*] [*Library of Congress*]   (LCLS)

CaQMBMo ... Bank of Montreal, Montreal, PQ, Canada [*Library symbol*] [*Library of Congress*]   (LCLS)

CaQMBN .. Bibliotheque Nationale du Quebec, Montreal, PQ, Canada [*Library symbol*] [*Library of Congress*]   (LCLS)

CaQMBNR ... Bell Northern Research, Montreal, PQ, Canada [*Library symbol*] [*Library of Congress*]   (LCLS)

CaQMBP ... Building Products Ltd., Montreal, PQ, Canada [*Library symbol*] [*Library of Congress*]   (LCLS)

CaQMBR . Bio-Research Laboratories Ltd., Pointe-Claire, PQ, Canada [*Library symbol*] [*Library of Congress*]   (LCLS)

CaQMBT ... Montreal Board of Trade, Montreal, PQ, Canada [*Library symbol*] [*Library of Congress*]   (LCLS)

CaQMC ..... College de Montreal, Montreal, PQ, Canada [*Library symbol*] [*Library of Congress*]   (LCLS)

CaQMCa ... Canadair Ltd., Engineering Library, Montreal, PQ, Canada [*Library symbol*] [*Library of Congress*]   (LCLS)

CaQMCAD ... Centre d'Animation, de Developpement, et de Recherche en Education, Montreal, PQ, Canada [*Library symbol*] [*Library of Congress*]   (LCLS)

CaQMCADQ ... Conservatoire d'Art Dramatique de Quebec, Montreal, PQ, Canada [*Library symbol*] [*Library of Congress*]   (LCLS)

CaQMCAE ... Canadian Aviation Electronics, Montreal, PQ, Canada [*Library symbol*] [*Library of Congress*]   (LCLS)

CaQMCAG ... College Andre Grasset, Montreal, PQ, Canada [*Library symbol*] [*Library of Congress*]   (LCLS)

CaQMCam ... Canadair Ltd., Missiles and Systems Library, Montreal, PQ, Canada [*Library symbol*] [*Library of Congress*]   (LCLS)

CaQMCAT ... Commission des Accidents du Travail, Montreal, PQ, Canada [*Library symbol*] [*Library of Congress*]   (LCLS)

CaQMCAV ... Ministere des Communications du Quebec, Direction Generale du Cinema et de l'Audiovisuel, Montreal, PQ, Canada [*Library symbol*] [*Library of Congress*]   (LCLS)

CaQMCB .. Canadian Broadcasting Corp., Montreal, PQ, Canada [*Library symbol*] [*Library of Congress*]   (LCLS)

CaQMCBE ... Canadian Broadcasting Corp., Engineering Headquarters Library, Montreal, PQ, Canada [*Library symbol*] [*Library of Congress*]   (LCLS)

CaQMCC .. Canada Cement Co. Ltd., Montreal, PQ, Canada [*Library symbol*] [*Library of Congress*]   (LCLS)

CaQMCCL ... Currie, Coopers & Lybrand Ltd., Montreal, PQ, Canada [*Library symbol*] [*Library of Congress*]   (LCLS)

CaQMCCR ... Canadian Council of Resource Ministers, Montreal, PQ, Canada [*Library symbol*] [*Library of Congress*]   (LCLS)

CaQMCD .. Centrale des Bibliotheques, Centre Documentaire, Montreal, PQ, Canada [*Library symbol*] [*Library of Congress*]   (LCLS)

CaQMCDM ... College de Maisonneuve, Montreal, PQ, Canada [*Library symbol*] [*Library of Congress*]   (LCLS)

CaQMCDP ... Caisse de Depot de Placement du Quebec, Montreal, PQ, Canada [*Library symbol*] [*Library of Congress*]   (LCLS)

CaQMCE .. Celanese Canada Ltd., Montreal, PQ, Canada [*Library symbol*] [*Library of Congress*]   (LCLS)

CaQMCEA ... Canadian Export Association, Montreal, PQ, Canada [*Library symbol*] [*Library of Congress*]   (LCLS)

CaQMCEC ... Catholic School Commission, Montreal, PQ, Canada [*Library symbol*] [*Library of Congress*]   (LCLS)

CaQMCF ... Charles E. Frosst & Co., Montreal, PQ, Canada [*Library symbol*] [*Library of Congress*]   (LCLS)

CaQMCG .. Ciba-Geigy Canada Ltd., Dorval, PQ, Canada [*Library symbol*] [*Library of Congress*]   (LCLS)

CaQMCh ... Chemcell Ltd., Montreal, PQ, Canada [*Library symbol*] [*Library of Congress*]   (LCLS)

CaQMCHC ... Montreal Chest Hospital, Montreal, PQ, Canada [*Library symbol*] [*Library of Congress*]   (LCLS)

CaQMCHL ... Centre Hospitalier de Lachine, Montreal, PQ, Canada [*Library symbol*] [*Library of Congress*]   (LCLS)

CaQMCi .... Ciba Co. Ltd., Montreal, PQ, Canada [*Library symbol*] [*Library of Congress*]   (LCLS)

CaQMCih ... Ville de Montreal, Bibliotheque de Documentation des Archives, Montreal, PQ, Canada [*Library symbol*] [*Library of Congress*]   (LCLS)

CaQMCIL ... Canadian Industries Limited, Montreal, PQ, Canada [*Library symbol*] [*Library of Congress*]   (LCLS)

CaQMCILL ... Canadian Industries Limited, Legal Department, Montreal, PQ, Canada [*Library symbol*] [*Library of Congress*]   (LCLS)

CaQMCILR ... Canadian Industries Limited, Central Research Laboratory, McMasterville, PQ, Canada [*Library symbol*] [*Library of Congress*]   (LCLS)

CaQMCIM ... Canadian Institute of Mining and Metallurgy, Montreal, PQ, Canada [*Library symbol*] [*Library of Congress*]   (LCLS)

CaQMCJ ... Canadian Jewish Congress Library, Montreal, PQ, Canada [*Library symbol*] [*Library of Congress*]   (LCLS)

CaQMCL ... CanAtom Limited, Montreal, PQ, Canada [*Library symbol*] [*Library of Congress*]   (LCLS)

CaQMCM ... Canadian Marconi Co., Montreal, PQ, Canada [*Library symbol*] [*Library of Congress*]   (LCLS)

CaQMCN .. Canadian National Railways, Montreal, PQ, Canada [*Library symbol*] [*Library of Congress*]   (LCLS)

CaQMCNC ... Canadian National Railways, Chemical Library, Montreal, PQ, Canada [*Library of Congress*]   (LCLS)

CaQMCOM ... Conservatoire de Musique de Montreal, Montreal, PQ, Canada [*Library symbol*] [*Library of Congress*]   (LCLS)

CaQMCP ... Canadian Pacific Railway Co., Montreal, PQ, Canada [*Library symbol*] [*Library of Congress*]   (LCLS)

CaQMCR .. Canadian Copper Refiners Ltd., Montreal, PQ, Canada [*Library symbol*] [*Library of Congress*]   (LCLS)

CaQMCRP ... Conference des Recteurs et des Principaux des Universites du Quebec, Montreal, PQ, Canada [*Library symbol*] [*Library of Congress*]   (LCLS)

CaQMCS ... Christian Science Reading Room, Montreal, PQ, Canada [*Library symbol*] [*Library of Congress*]   (LCLS)

CaQMCT .. Commission de Transport de la Communaute Urbaine de Montreal, Montreal, PQ, Canada [*Library symbol*] [*Library of Congress*]   (LCLS)

CaQMCTM ... Canadian Tobacco Manufacturers' Council, Montreal, PQ, Canada [*Library symbol*] [*Library of Congress*]   (LCLS)

CaQMCVM ... Commission des Valeurs Mobilieres de Quebec, Quebec, PQ, Canada [*Library symbol*] [*Library of Congress*]   (LCLS)

CaQMCW ... Canada Wire & Cable Co. Ltd., Montreal, PQ, Canada [*Library symbol*] [*Library of Congress*]   (LCLS)

CaQMD ..... Institut Genealogique Drouin, Montreal, PQ, Canada [*Library symbol*] [*Library of Congress*]   (LCLS)

CaQMDB .. College Jean-De-Brebeuf, Montreal, PQ, Canada [*Library symbol*] [*Library of Congress*]   (LCLS)

CaQMDE .. Dominion Engineering Works Ltd., Montreal, PQ, Canada [*Library symbol*] [*Library of Congress*]   (LCLS)

CaQMDH ... Douglas Hospital, Montreal, PQ, Canada [*Library symbol*] [*Library of Congress*]   (LCLS)

CaQMDL .. Domtar Limited, Montreal, PQ, Canada [*Library symbol*] [*Library of Congress*]   (LCLS)

CaQMDM ... Montreal Association for the Mentally Retarded, Montreal, PQ, Canada [*Library symbol*] [*Library of Congress*]   (LCLS)

CaQMDom ... Dominion Bridge Co. Ltd., Montreal, PQ, Canada [*Library symbol*] [*Library of Congress*]   (LCLS)

CaQMDP .. Du Pont of Canada Ltd., Economist's Office Library, Montreal, PQ, Canada [*Library symbol*] [*Library of Congress*]   (LCLS)

CaQMDPL ... Du Pont of Canada Ltd., Legal Library, Montreal, PQ, Canada [*Library symbol*] [*Library of Congress*]   (LCLS)

CaQMDT .. Dominion Textile, Montreal, PQ, Canada [*Library symbol*] [*Library of Congress*]   (LCLS)

CaQME ..... Engineering Institute of Canada, Montreal, PQ, Canada [*Library symbol*] [*Library of Congress*] [*Obsolete*]   (LCLS)

CaQMEA .. Environment Canada, Atmospheric Environment Service, Dorval, PQ, Canada [*Library symbol*] [*Library of Congress*]   (LCLS)

CaQMEC .. Montreal Engineering Co. Ltd., Montreal, PQ, Canada [*Library symbol*] [*Library of Congress*]   (LCLS)

CaQMECB ... Quebec Ministere de l'Education, Centrale des Bibliotheques, Montreal, PQ, Canada [*Library symbol*] [*Library of Congress*]   (LCLS)

CaQMEE ... Canada Department of the Environment, Environmental Protection Service, Montreal, PQ, Canada [*Library symbol*] [*Library of Congress*]   (LCLS)

CaQMEN .. Ministere de l'Environnement, Montreal, PQ, Canada [*Library symbol*] [*Library of Congress*]   (LCLS)

CaQMENT ... Ecole Nationale de Theatre, Montreal, PQ, Canada [*Library symbol*] [*Library of Congress*]   (LCLS)

CaQMEP ... Ecole Polytechnique, Montreal, PQ, Canada [*Library symbol*] [*Library of Congress*]   (LCLS)

CaQMES ... Ecole Secondaire Saint-Stanislas, Montreal, PQ, Canada [*Library symbol*] [*Library of Congress*]   (LCLS)

CaQMF ..... Fraser-Hickson Institute, Montreal, PQ, Canada [*Library symbol*] [*Library of Congress*]   (LCLS)

CaQMFA ... Montreal Museum of Fine Arts, Montreal, PQ, Canada [*Library symbol*] [*Library of Congress*]   (LCLS)

CaQMFBD ... Federal Business Development Bank, Montreal, PQ, Canada [*Library symbol*] [*Library of Congress*]   (LCLS)

CaQMFC ... First Church of Christ, Scientist, Montreal, PQ, Canada [*Library symbol*] [*Library of Congress*]   (LCLS)

CaQMFER ... Forest Engineering Research Institute of Canada, Pointe-Claire, PQ, Canada [*Library symbol*] [*Library of Congress*]   (LCLS)

CaQMFH .. Frank W. Horner Ltd., Montreal, PQ, Canada [*Library symbol*] [*Library of Congress*]   (LCLS)

CaQMFLCP ... Ministere du Loisir de la Chasse et de la Peche du Quebec, Bibliotheque de la Faune, Montreal, PQ, Canada [*Library symbol*] [*Library of Congress*]   (LCLS)

CaQMFMO ... Federation des Medecins Omnipracticiens du Quebec, Montreal, PQ, Canada [*Library symbol*] [*Library of Congress*]　(LCLS)

CaQMFMS ... Federation des Medecins Specialistes du Quebec, Montreal, PQ, Canada [*Library symbol*] [*Library of Congress*]　(LCLS)

CaQMFR ... Canada Department of the Environment, Fisheries and Marine Service, Ste.-Anne-De-Bellevue, PQ, Canada [*Library symbol*] [*Library of Congress*]　(LCLS)

CaQMFran ... Studium Franciscain de Theologie, Montreal, PQ, Canada [*Library symbol*] [*Library of Congress*]　(LCLS)

CaQMG ..... Concordia University, Sir George Williams Campus, Montreal, PQ, Canada [*Library symbol*] [*Library of Congress*]　(LCLS)

CaQMGa ... Montreal Gazette, Montreal, PQ, Canada [*Library symbol*] [*Library of Congress*]　(LCLS)

CaQMgB ... Bibliotheque Municipale, Magog, PQ, Canada [*Library symbol*] [*Library of Congress*]　(LCLS)

CaQMGB .. Grands Ballets Canadiens, Montreal, PQ, Canada [*Library symbol*] [*Library of Congress*]　(LCLS)

CaQMGG ... Concordia University, Sir George Williams Campus, Department of Geography, Montreal, PQ, Canada [*Library symbol*] [*Library of Congress*]　(LCLS)

CaQMGGM ... Concordia University, Sir George Williams Campus, Department of Geography, University Map Collection, Montreal, PQ, Canada [*Library symbol*] [*Library of Congress*]　(LCLS)

CaQMGH ... Montreal General Hospital, Montreal, PQ, Canada [*Library symbol*] [*Library of Congress*]　(LCLS)

CaQMGP .. Gerard Parizeau Ltee., Montreal, PQ, Canada [*Library symbol*] [*Library of Congress*]　(LCLS)

CaQMGS .. Grand Seminaire, Montreal, PQ, Canada [*Library symbol*] [*Library of Congress*]　(LCLS)

CaQMH .... Hydro-Quebec, Bibliotheque, Montreal, PQ, Canada [*Library symbol*] [*Library of Congress*]　(LCLS)

CaQMHD ... Hotel-Dieu Hospital, Montreal, PQ, Canada [*Library symbol*] [*Library of Congress*]　(LCLS)

CaQMHDE ... Direction de l'Environnement, Hydro-Quebec, Montreal, PQ, Canada [*Library symbol*] [*Library of Congress*]　(LCLS)

CaQMHE ... Ecole des Hautes Etudes Commerciales, Montreal, PQ, Canada [*Library symbol*] [*Library of Congress*]　(LCLS)

CaQMHGC ... Centre Hospitalier de Verdun, Montreal, PQ, Canada [*Library symbol*] [*Library of Congress*]　(LCLS)

CaQMHGF ... Hopital General Fleury, Montreal, PQ, Canada [*Library symbol*] [*Library of Congress*]　(LCLS)

CaQMHJT ... Hopital Jean Talon, Montreal, PQ, Canada [*Library symbol*] [*Library of Congress*]　(LCLS)

CaQMHM ... Centre Hospitalier Jacques Viger, Montreal, PQ, Canada [*Library symbol*] [*Library of Congress*]　(LCLS)

CaQMHME ... Hopital Marie-Enfant, Montreal, PQ, Canada [*Library symbol*] [*Library of Congress*]　(LCLS)

CaQMHMR ... Hopital Maisonneuve-Rosemont, Montreal, PQ, Canada [*Library symbol*] [*Library of Congress*]　(LCLS)

CaQMHND ... Notre Dame Hospital, Medical Library, Montreal, PQ, Canada [*Library symbol*] [*Library of Congress*]　(LCLS)

CaQMHNDI ... Hopital Notre-Dame, Bibliotheque des Services Infirmiers, Montreal, PQ, Canada [*Library symbol*] [*Library of Congress*]　(LCLS)

CaQMHRP ... Hopital Riviere-Des-Prairies, Montreal, PQ, Canada [*Library symbol*] [*Library of Congress*]　(LCLS)

CaQMHSC ... Hopital du Sacre-Coeur, Montreal, PQ, Canada [*Library symbol*] [*Library of Congress*]　(LCLS)

CaQMHSCA ... Hopital Santa Cabrini, Montreal, PQ, Canada [*Library symbol*] [*Library of Congress*]　(LCLS)

CaQMHSJ ... Hopital Louis-H.-LaFontaine, Montreal, PQ, Canada [*Library symbol*] [*Library of Congress*]　(LCLS)

CaQMHSJA ... Hopital Ste-Jeanne-D'Arc, Montreal, PQ, Canada [*Library symbol*] [*Library of Congress*]　(LCLS)

CaQMHSL ... Hopital Saint-Luc, Montreal, PQ, Canada [*Library symbol*] [*Library of Congress*]　(LCLS)

CaQMI ...... Insurance Institute of the Province of Quebec, Montreal, PQ, Canada [*Library symbol*] [*Library of Congress*]　(LCLS)

CaQMIA ... International Air Transport Association, Montreal, PQ, Canada [*Library symbol*] [*Library of Congress*]　(LCLS)

CaQMIAA ... Institut des Arts Appliques, Montreal, PQ, Canada [*Library symbol*] [*Library of Congress*]　(LCLS)

CaQMIAG ... Institut des Arts Graphiques, Montreal, PQ, Canada [*Library symbol*] [*Library of Congress*]　(LCLS)

CaQMIAP ... Institut Albert Prevost, Montreal, PQ, Canada [*Library symbol*] [*Library of Congress*]　(LCLS)

CaQMIC .... International Civil Aviation Organization, Montreal, PQ, Canada [*Library symbol*] [*Library of Congress*]　(LCLS)

CaQMICA ... Institute of Chartered Accountants of Quebec, Montreal, PQ, Canada [*Library symbol*] [*Library of Congress*]　(LCLS)

CaQMICE ... Canadian Institute of Adult Education, Montreal, PQ, Canada [*Library symbol*] [*Library of Congress*]　(LCLS)

CaQMICM ... Institut de Cardiologie de Montreal, Montreal, PQ, Canada [*Library symbol*] [*Library of Congress*]　(LCLS)

CaQMIFQ ... Informatech France-Quebec, Montreal, PQ, Canada [*Library symbol*] [*Library of Congress*]　(LCLS)

CaQMIG ... Industrial Grain Products Ltd., Montreal, PQ, Canada [*Library symbol*] [*Library of Congress*]　(LCLS)

CaQMII ..... Instituto Italiano di Cultura, Montreal, PQ, Canada [*Library symbol*] [*Library of Congress*]　(LCLS)

CaQMIIS .. McGill University, Institute of Islamic Studies, Montreal, PQ, Canada [*Library symbol*] [*Library of Congress*]　(LCLS)

CaQMILO ... International Labour Office, Montreal, PQ, Canada [*Library symbol*] [*Library of Congress*]　(LCLS)

CaQMIM .. Institut de Microbiologie et d'Hygiene de Montreal, Montreal, PQ, Canada [*Library symbol*] [*Library of Congress*]　(LCLS)

CaQMIMM ... Institut National de Productivite, Montreal, Montreal, PQ, Canada [*Library symbol*] [*Library of Congress*]　(LCLS)

CaQMIMO ... Travail-Quebec, Montreal, PQ, Canada [*Library symbol*] [*Library of Congress*]　(LCLS)

CaQMIP .... McGill University, Macdonald College, Institute of Parasitology, Montreal, PQ, Canada [*Library symbol*] [*Library of Congress*]　(LCLS)

CaQMIPP ... Institut Philippe Pinel de Montreal, Montreal, PQ, Canada [*Library symbol*] [*Library of Congress*]　(LCLS)

CaQMIRC ... Institut de Recherches Cliniques, Montreal, PQ, Canada [*Library symbol*] [*Library of Congress*]　(LCLS)

CaQMISM ... Institution des Sourds de Montreal, Centre de Ressources Multimedia, Montreal, PQ, Canada [*Library symbol*] [*Library of Congress*]　(LCLS)

CaQMIT .... Imperial Tobacco Co. of Canada Ltd., Montreal, PQ, Canada [*Library symbol*] [*Library of Congress*]　(LCLS)

CaQMITR ... Imperial Tobacco Co. of Canada Ltd., Research Library, Montreal, PQ, Canada [*Library symbol*] [*Library of Congress*]　(LCLS)

CaQMJ ...... Jewish Public Library, Montreal, PQ, Canada [*Library symbol*] [*Library of Congress*]　(LCLS)

CaQMJB ... Jardin Botanique de Montreal, Montreal, PQ, Canada [*Library symbol*] [*Library of Congress*]　(LCLS)

CaQMJES ... Joseph E. Seagram & Sons Ltd., Technical Services, Lasalle, PQ, Canada [*Library symbol*] [*Library of Congress*]　(LCLS)

CaQMJG ... Jewish General Hospital, Montreal, PQ, Canada [*Library symbol*] [*Library of Congress*]　(LCLS)

CaQMJGI ... Jewish General Hospital, Institute of Community and Family Psychiatry, Montreal, PQ, Canada [*Library symbol*] [*Library of Congress*]　(LCLS)

CaQMJGL ... Jewish General Hospital, Lady Davis Institute for Medical Research, Montreal, PQ, Canada [*Library symbol*] [*Library of Congress*]　(LCLS)

CaQMjH ... Hopital de Mont-Joli, Inc., Mont-Joli, PQ, Canada [*Library symbol*] [*Library of Congress*]　(LCLS)

CaQMJJ ... Johnson & Johnson Ltd., Montreal, PQ, Canada [*Library symbol*] [*Library of Congress*]　(LCLS)

CaQMJL ... John Lovell & Son, City Directories Ltd., Montreal, PQ, Canada [*Library symbol*] [*Library of Congress*]　(LCLS)

CaQMJM ... Canada Department of Justice, Montreal, PQ, Canada [*Library symbol*] [*Library of Congress*]　(LCLS)

CaQMJSJ ... Ministere de la Justice, Commission des Services Juridiques, Montreal, PQ, Canada [*Library symbol*] [*Library of Congress*]　(LCLS)

CaQML ..... Concordia University, Loyola Campus, Montreal, PQ, Canada [*Library symbol*] [*Library of Congress*]　(LCLS)

CaQMLCA ... Lower Canada Arms Collectors Association, Montreal, PQ, Canada [*Library symbol*] [*Library of Congress*]　(LCLS)

CaQMLCC ... Lower Canada College, Montreal, PQ, Canada [*Library symbol*] [*Library of Congress*]　(LCLS)

CaQMLG .. Lakeshore General Hospital, Pointe-Claire, PQ, Canada [*Library symbol*] [*Library of Congress*]　(LCLS)

CaQMLR ... Lethbridge Rehabilitation Centre, Montreal, PQ, Canada [*Library symbol*] [*Library of Congress*]　(LCLS)

CaQMM .... McGill University, Montreal, PQ, Canada [*Library symbol*] [*Library of Congress*]　(LCLS)

CaQMMAC ... Musee d'Art Contemporain, Montreal, PQ, Canada [*Library symbol*] [*Library of Congress*]　(LCLS)

CaQMMB ... McGill University, Blackader/Lauterman Library of Architecture and Art, Montreal, PQ, Canada [*Library symbol*] [*Library of Congress*]　(LCLS)

CaQMMBG ... McGill University, Botany-Genetics Library, Montreal, PQ, Canada [*Library symbol*] [*Library of Congress*]　(LCLS)

CaQMMBZ ... McGill University, Blacker-Wood Library, Montreal, PQ, Canada [*Library symbol*] [*Library of Congress*]　(LCLS)

CaQMMC ... Miron Co. Ltd., Montreal, PQ, Canada [*Library symbol*] [*Library of Congress*]　(LCLS)

CaQMMCH ... Montreal Children's Hospital, Montreal, PQ, Canada [*Library symbol*] [*Library of Congress*]　(LCLS)

CaQMMCR ... Musee du Chateau de Ramezay, Montreal, PQ, Canada [*Library symbol*] [*Library of Congress*]　(LCLS)

CaQMMD ... McGill University, Religious Studies Library, Montreal, PQ, Canada [*Library symbol*] [*Library of Congress*]　(LCLS)

CaQMME ... McGill University, Engineering Library, Montreal, PQ, Canada [*Library symbol*] [*Library of Congress*]　(LCLS)

CaQMMFD ... McGill University, Dentistry Library, Montreal, PQ, Canada [*Library symbol*] [*Library of Congress*]　(LCLS)

CaQMMG ... McGill University, Department of Geography, University Map Collection, Montreal, PQ, Canada [*Library symbol*] [*Library of Congress*]　(LCLS)

CaQMMGS ... McGill University, Department of Geological Sciences, Montreal, PQ, Canada [*Library symbol*] [*Library of Congress*] (LCLS)

CaQMMH ... Mental Hygiene Institute, Montreal, PQ, Canada [*Library symbol*] [*Library of Congress*] (LCLS)

CaQMMHH ... Maimonides Hospital and Home for the Aged, Montreal, PQ, Canada [*Library symbol*] [*Library of Congress*] (LCLS)

CaQMMI .. Atwater Library, Montreal, PQ, Canada [*Library symbol*] [*Library of Congress*] (LCLS)

CaQMMIQ ... Canada Employment and Immigration Department, Quebec Regional Office, Montreal, PQ, Canada [*Library symbol*] [*Library of Congress*] (LCLS)

CaQMML ... McGill University, Law Library, Montreal, PQ, Canada [*Library symbol*] [*Library of Congress*] (LCLS)

CaQMMLS ... McGill University, Graduate School of Library Science, Montreal, PQ, Canada [*Library symbol*] [*Library of Congress*] (LCLS)

CaQMMM ... McGill University, Medical Library, Montreal, PQ, Canada [*Library symbol*] [*Library of Congress*] (LCLS)

CaQMMMa ... McGill University, Map Collection, Montreal, PQ, Canada [*Library symbol*] [*Library of Congress*] (LCLS)

CaQMMMcM ... McGill University, McCord Museum, Montreal, PQ, Canada [*Library symbol*] [*Library of Congress*] (LCLS)

CaQMMN ... McGill University, Nursing Library, Montreal, PQ, Canada [*Library symbol*] [*Library of Congress*] (LCLS)

CaQMMNS ... McGill University, Northern Studies Library, Montreal, PQ, Canada [*Library symbol*] [*Library of Congress*] (LCLS)

CaQMMO ... McGill University, Osler Collection, Montreal, PQ, Canada [*Library symbol*] [*Library of Congress*] (LCLS)

CaQMMoC ... Monsanto Canada Ltd., Montreal, PQ, Canada [*Library symbol*] [*Library of Congress*] (LCLS)

CaQMMoS ... Montreal Star, Montreal, PQ, Canada [*Library symbol*] [*Library of Congress*] (LCLS)

CaQMMPS ... McGill University, Physical Sciences Centre, Montreal, PQ, Canada [*Library symbol*] [*Library of Congress*] (LCLS)

CaQMMRB ... McGill University, Department of Rare Books and Special Collections, Montreal, PQ, Canada [*Library symbol*] [*Library of Congress*] (LCLS)

CaQMMS ... McGill University, Social Work Library, Montreal, PQ, Canada [*Library symbol*] [*Library of Congress*] (LCLS)

CaQMMSC ... McGill University, Howard Ross Library of Management, Montreal, PQ, Canada [*Library symbol*] [*Library of Congress*] (LCLS)

CaQMn ...... Bibliotheque Municipale, Montreal-Nord, PQ, Canada [*Library symbol*] [*Library of Congress*] (LCLS)

CaQMNA ... Canadian Pulp and Paper Association, Montreal, PQ, Canada [*Library symbol*] [*Library of Congress*] (LCLS)

CaQMNDE ... Hopital Notre-Dame-De-L'Esperance-De-St-Laurent, Montreal, PQ, Canada [*Library symbol*] [*Library of Congress*] (LCLS)

CaQMNE .. Northern Electric Co., Montreal, PQ, Canada [*Library symbol*] [*Library of Congress*] (LCLS)

CaQMNFNI ... National Film Board, National Information and Distribution System, Montreal, PQ, Canada [*Library symbol*] [*Library of Congress*] (LCLS)

CaQMNHH ... Canada Department of National Health and Welfare, Health Protection Branch, Montreal, PQ, Canada [*Library symbol*] [*Library of Congress*] (LCLS)

CaQMNI ... National Industrial Conference Board, Montreal, PQ, Canada [*Library symbol*] [*Library of Congress*] (LCLS)

CaQMNIH ... Montreal Neurological Institute and Hospital, Montreal, PQ, Canada [*Library symbol*] [*Library of Congress*] (LCLS)

CaQMNR ... Noranda Research Centre, Montreal, PQ, Canada [*Library symbol*] [*Library of Congress*] (LCLS)

CaQMNT .. Nesbitt, Thomson & Co. Ltd., Montreal, PQ, Canada [*Library symbol*] [*Library of Congress*] (LCLS)

CaQMO ..... Oratoire Saint-Joseph du Mont-Royal, Montreal, PQ, Canada [*Library symbol*] [*Library of Congress*] (LCLS)

CaQMOB .. Ministere des Pecheries et de la Chasse, Office de Biologie, Montreal, PQ, Canada [*Library symbol*] [*Library of Congress*] (LCLS)

CaQMOCQ ... Office de la Construction du Quebec, Montreal, PQ, Canada [*Library symbol*] [*Library of Congress*] (LCLS)

CaQMOF .. Ogilvie Flour Mills Co. Ltd., Montreal, PQ, Canada [*Library symbol*] [*Library of Congress*] (LCLS)

CaQMOFJ ... Office Franco-Quebecois pour la Jeunesse, Montreal, PQ, Canada [*Library symbol*] [*Library of Congress*] (LCLS)

CaQMOI ... Ordre des Infirmieres et Infirmiers du Quebec, Montreal, PQ, Canada [*Library symbol*] [*Library of Congress*] (LCLS)

CaQMOLF ... Office de la Langue Francaise, Montreal, PQ, Canada [*Library symbol*] [*Library of Congress*] (LCLS)

CaQMPC ... Presbyterian College, Montreal, PQ, Canada [*Library symbol*] [*Library of Congress*] (LCLS)

CaQMPE ... Pezaris Electronics Co., Research Library, Montreal, PQ, Canada [*Library symbol*] [*Library of Congress*] (LCLS)

CaQMPI .... Polish Institute of Arts and Sciences in Canada, Montreal, PQ, Canada [*Library symbol*] [*Library of Congress*] (LCLS)

CaQMPM ... Peat, Marwick et Associes, Montreal, PQ, Canada [*Library symbol*] [*Library of Congress*] (LCLS)

CaQMPp ... Pulp and Paper Research Institute of Canada, Pointe Claire, PQ, Canada [*Library symbol*] [*Library of Congress*] (LCLS)

CaQMPSM ... Protestant School Board of Greater Montreal, Montreal, PQ, Canada [*Library symbol*] [*Library of Congress*] (LCLS)

CaQMPSR ... P. S. Ross & Partners, Montreal, PQ, Canada [*Library symbol*] [*Library of Congress*] (LCLS)

CaQMPW ... Price, Waterhouse & Co. Library, Vancouver, BC, Canada [*Library symbol*] [*Library of Congress*] (LCLS)

CaQMQ ..... Queen Mary Veterans Hospital, Montreal, PQ, Canada [*Library symbol*] [*Library of Congress*] (LCLS)

CaQMQAr ... Quebec Archives, Montreal, PQ, Canada [*Library symbol*] [*Library of Congress*] (LCLS)

CaQMQDP ... Quebec Commission des Droits de la Personne, Montreal, PQ, Canada [*Library symbol*] [*Library of Congress*] (LCLS)

CaQMQE .. Queen Elizabeth Hospital, Montreal, PQ, Canada [*Library symbol*] [*Library of Congress*] (LCLS)

CaQMR ..... Royal Bank of Canada, Montreal, PQ, Canada [*Library symbol*] [*Library of Congress*] (LCLS)

CaQMRA ... Railway Association of Canada, Montreal, PQ, Canada [*Library symbol*] [*Library of Congress*] (LCLS)

CaQMRAD ... Institut de Recherche Appliquee sur le Travail, Centre de Documentation, Montreal, PQ, Canada [*Library symbol*] [*Library of Congress*] (LCLS)

CaQMRC .. Royal Canadian Air Force Library, Montreal, PQ, Canada [*Library symbol*] [*Library of Congress*] (LCLS)

CaQMRD .. Reader's Digest of Canada Ltd., Montreal, PQ, Canada [*Library symbol*] [*Library of Congress*] (LCLS)

CaQMRE .. Revenue Canada, Montreal, PQ, Canada [*Library symbol*] [*Library of Congress*] (LCLS)

CaQMREG ... Regie de l'Electricite et du Gaz, Montreal, PQ, Canada [*Library symbol*] [*Library of Congress*] (LCLS)

CaQMRH ... Centre de Recherches en Relations Humaines, Montreal, PQ, Canada [*Library symbol*] [*Library of Congress*] (LCLS)

CaQMRI .... Rehabilitation Institute of Montreal, Montreal, PQ, Canada [*Library symbol*] [*Library of Congress*] (LCLS)

CaQMRL ... Centre de Documentation de la Regie du Logement, Montreal, PQ, Canada [*Library symbol*] [*Library of Congress*] (LCLS)

CaQMRM ... Reddy Memorial Hospital, Montreal, PQ, Canada [*Library symbol*] [*Library of Congress*] (LCLS)

CaQMRQ .. Radio-Quebec, Montreal, PQ, Canada [*Library symbol*] [*Library of Congress*] (LCLS)

CaQMRR .. Rolls-Royce of Canada Ltd., Montreal, PQ, Canada [*Library symbol*] [*Library of Congress*] (LCLS)

CaQMRV .. Royal Victoria Hospital Library, Montreal, PQ, Canada [*Library symbol*] [*Library of Congress*] (LCLS)

CaQMRVW ... Royal Victoria Hospital, Women's Pavillion, Montreal, PQ, Canada [*Library symbol*] [*Library of Congress*] (LCLS)

CaQMS ..... Sun Life Assurance Co. of Canada, Montreal, PQ, Canada [*Library symbol*] [*Library of Congress*] (LCLS)

CaQMSa .... Province de Quebec, Ministere des Affaires Sociales, Montreal, PQ, Canada [*Library symbol*] [*Library of Congress*] (LCLS)

CaQMSAP ... Societe des Artistes Professionels du Quebec, Montreal, PQ, Canada [*Library symbol*] [*Library of Congress*] (LCLS)

CaQMSC ... Southern Canada Power Co. Library, Montreal, PQ, Canada [*Library symbol*] [*Library of Congress*] (LCLS)

CaQMSCa ... Statistics Canada, Montreal, PQ, Canada [*Library symbol*] [*Library of Congress*] (LCLS)

CaQMSDB ... Societe de Developpement de la Baie James, Montreal, PQ, Canada [*Library symbol*] [*Library of Congress*] (LCLS)

CaQMSDL ... Sidbec-Dosco Limited, Montreal, PQ, Canada [*Library symbol*] [*Library of Congress*] (LCLS)

CaQMSEB ... Societe d'Energie de la Baie James, Montreal, PQ, Canada [*Library symbol*] [*Library of Congress*] (LCLS)

CaQMSEBJ ... Societe d'Energie de la Baie James, Centre de Documentation, Montreal, PQ, Canada [*Library symbol*] [*Library of Congress*] (LCLS)

CaQMSGE ... Office des Services de Garde a l'Enfance, Montreal, PQ, Canada [*Library symbol*] [*Library of Congress*] (LCLS)

CaQMSGME ... Gouvernement du Quebec, Ministere de l'Education, Service General des Moyens d'Enseignement, Montreal, PQ, Canada [*Library symbol*] [*Library of Congress*] (LCLS)

CaQMSH .. Societe Historique de Montreal, Montreal, PQ, Canada [*Library symbol*] [*Library of Congress*] (LCLS)

CaQMSHE ... Stadler Herter, Montreal, PQ, Canada [*Library symbol*] [*Library of Congress*] (LCLS)

CaQMSI .... Scolasticat de l'Immaculee-Conception, Montreal, PQ, Canada [*Library symbol*] [*Library of Congress*] (LCLS)

CaQMSJ ... Saint Joseph's Teachers' College, Montreal, PQ, Canada [*Library symbol*] [*Library of Congress*] (LCLS)

CaQMSK ... Smith, Kline & French Co. [*Later, SmithKline Corp.*], Montreal, PQ, Canada [*Library symbol*] [*Library of Congress*] (LCLS)

CaQMSM ... College Sainte-Marie, Montreal, PQ, Canada [*Library symbol*] [*Library of Congress*] (LCLS)

CaQMSMa ... Saint Mary's Hospital, Montreal, PQ, Canada [*Library symbol*] [*Library of Congress*] (LCLS)

CaQMSNC ... Surveyer, Nenninger & Chenevert, Inc., Montreal, PQ, Canada [*Library symbol*] [*Library of Congress*] (LCLS)

CaQMSO .. Shell Oil Co. of Canada, Montreal, PQ, Canada [*Library symbol*] [*Library of Congress*] (LCLS)

CaQMSOB ... Le Groupe SOBECO, Montreal, PQ, Canada [*Library symbol*] [*Library of Congress*] (LCLS)

CaQMStC ... College Sainte-Croix, Montreal, PQ, Canada [*Library symbol*] [*Library of Congress*] (LCLS)

CaQMSTJ ... Hopital Sainte-Justine, Centre d'Information sur la Sante de l'Enfant, Montreal, PQ, Canada [*Library symbol*] [*Library of Congress*] (LCLS)

CaQMSTJC ... Hopital Sainte-Justine, Centre d'Information sur l'Enfance et l'Adolescence Inadaptees, Montreal, PQ, Canada [*Library symbol*] [*Library of Congress*] [*Obsolete*] (LCLS)

CaQMSU .. Surete du Quebec, Montreal, PQ, Canada [*Library symbol*] [*Library of Congress*] (LCLS)

CaQMSW ... Sherwin-Williams Co. of Canada, Montreal, PQ, Canada [*Library symbol*] [*Library of Congress*] (LCLS)

CaQMSWP ... Shawinigan Engineering Co. Ltd., Montreal, PQ, Canada [*Library symbol*] [*Library of Congress*] (LCLS)

CaQMT ..... Montreal Trust Co., Montreal, PQ, Canada [*Library symbol*] [*Library of Congress*] (LCLS)

CaQMTA .. Tomenson-Aletander Ltd., Montreal, PQ, Canada [*Library symbol*] [*Library of Congress*] (LCLS)

CaQMTC .. Air Canada, Montreal, PQ, Canada [*Library symbol*] [*Library of Congress*] (LCLS)

CaQMTCP ... Quebec Ministere du Tourisme, de la Chasse, et de la Peche, Montreal, PQ, Canada [*Library symbol*] [*Library of Congress*] (LCLS)

CaQMTD .. Canada Ministry of Transport, Transportation Development Agency, Montreal, PQ, Canada [*Library symbol*] [*Library of Congress*] (LCLS)

CaQMTGC ... Teleglobe Canada, Montreal, PQ, Canada [*Library symbol*] [*Library of Congress*] (LCLS)

CaQMTH ... Institut de Tourisme et d'Hotellerie du Quebec, Montreal, PQ, Canada [*Library symbol*] [*Library of Congress*] (LCLS)

CaQMTMO ... Ministere du Travaile et de la Main-D'Oeuvre, Montreal, PQ, Canada [*Library symbol*] [*Library of Congress*] (LCLS)

CaQMTQM ... Trans-Quebec & Maritimes, Montreal, PQ, Canada [*Library symbol*] [*Library of Congress*] (LCLS)

CaQMTR .. Canada Ministry of Transport, Waterways Development, Montreal, PQ, Canada [*Library symbol*] [*Library of Congress*] (LCLS)

CaQMU ..... Universite de Montreal, Montreal, PQ, Canada [*Library symbol*] [*Library of Congress*] (LCLS)

CaQMUA ... Service des Archives de l'Universite de Montreal, Montreal, PQ, Canada [*Library symbol*] [*Library of Congress*] (LCLS)

CaQMUC .. Union Carbide Canada Ltd., Pointe-Aux-Trembles, PQ, Canada [*Library symbol*] [*Library of Congress*] (LCLS)

CaQMUDD ... Universite de Montreal, Departement de Demographie, Montreal, PQ, Canada [*Library symbol*] [*Library of Congress*] (LCLS)

CaQMUE .. Institut des Etudes Medievales, Universite de Montreal, Montreal, PQ, Canada [*Library symbol*] [*Library of Congress*] (LCLS)

CaQMUEC ... Universite de Montreal, l'Ecole de Criminologie, Montreal, PQ, Canada [*Library symbol*] [*Library of Congress*] (LCLS)

CaQMUG ... Universite de Montreal, Departement de Geographie, Montreal, PQ, Canada [*Library symbol*] [*Library of Congress*] (LCLS)

CaQMUGC ... Universite de Montreal, Departement de Geographie, Cartotheque, Montreal, PQ, Canada [*Library symbol*] [*Library of Congress*] (LCLS)

CaQMUGL ... Universite de Montreal, Cartotheque de l'Institut de Geologie, Montreal, PQ, Canada [*Library symbol*] [*Library of Congress*] (LCLS)

CaQMUM ... Universite de Montreal, Bibliotheque Medicale, Montreal, PQ, Canada [*Library symbol*] [*Library of Congress*] [*Obsolete*] (LCLS)

CaQMUO ... Universite de Montreal, Bibliotheque d'Optometrie, Montreal, PQ, Canada [*Library symbol*] [*Library of Congress*] (LCLS)

CaQMUP .. Universite de Montreal, Bibliotheque Paramedicale, Montreal, PQ, Canada [*Library symbol*] [*Library of Congress*] (LCLS)

CaQMUQ ... Universite du Quebec a Montreal, Montreal, PQ, Canada [*Library symbol*] [*Library of Congress*] (LCLS)

CaQMUQC ... Universite du Quebec a Montreal, Cartotheque, Montreal, PQ, Canada [*Library symbol*] [*Library of Congress*] (LCLS)

CaQMUQDSJ ... Universite du Quebec a Montreal, le Centre de Documentation des Sciences Juridiques, Montreal, PQ, Canada [*Library symbol*] [*Library of Congress*] (LCLS)

CaQMUQET ... Universite du Quebec, Ecole de Technologie Superieure, Montreal, PQ, Canada [*Library symbol*] [*Library of Congress*] (LCLS)

CaQMUQIC ... Universite du Quebec a Montreal, INRS-Urbanisation, Cartotheque, Montreal, PQ, Canada [*Library symbol*] [*Library of Congress*] (LCLS)

CaQMUQPA ... Universite du Quebec a Montreal, Pavillon des Arts, Montreal, PQ, Canada [*Library symbol*] [*Library of Congress*] (LCLS)

CaQMUSC ... Universite de Montreal, Bibliotheque des Sciences Sociales, Cartotheque, Montreal, PQ, Canada [*Library symbol*] [*Library of Congress*] (LCLS)

CaQMUSHS ... Universite de Montreal, Bibliotheque des Sciences Humaines et Sociales, Section de Criminologie, Montreal, PQ, Canada [*Library symbol*] [*Library of Congress*] (LCLS)

CaQMV ..... RCA Victor Co. Ltd., Montreal, PQ, Canada [*Library symbol*] [*Library of Congress*] (LCLS)

CaQMVC .. Vanier College, Media Resources Centre, Montreal, PQ, Canada [*Library symbol*] [*Library of Congress*] (LCLS)

CaQMW .... Warnock Hersey Co. Ltd., Montreal, PQ, Canada [*Library symbol*] [*Library of Congress*] (LCLS)

CaQMWM ... William M. Mercer, Montreal, PQ, Canada [*Library symbol*] [*Library of Congress*] (LCLS)

CaQMY ..... YWCA Library, Montreal, PQ, Canada [*Library symbol*] [*Library of Congress*] (LCLS)

CaQMYH ... YM-YWHA Library, Montreal, PQ, Canada [*Library symbol*] [*Library of Congress*] (LCLS)

CaQNCHRN ... Centre Hospitalier Rouyn-Noranda, Noranda, PQ, Canada [*Library symbol*] [*Library of Congress*] (LCLS)

CaQNCRS ... Conseil Regional de la Sante et des Services Sociaux Rouyn-Noranda, Noranda, PQ, Canada [*Library symbol*] [*Library of Congress*] (LCLS)

CaQNicA ... Soeurs de l'Assomption, Nicolet, PQ, Canada [*Library symbol*] [*Library of Congress*] (LCLS)

CaQNicS .... Seminaire de Nicolet, Nicolet, PQ, Canada [*Library symbol*] [*Library of Congress*] (LCLS)

CaQNIP ..... Institut de Police du Quebec, Nicolet, PQ, Canada [*Library symbol*] [*Library of Congress*] (LCLS)

CaQOTCP ... Ministere du Tourisme, de la Chasse, et de la Peche, Orsainville, PQ, Canada [*Library symbol*] [*Library of Congress*] (LCLS)

CaQPA ...... Bibliotheque Municipale, Port-Alfred, PQ, Canada [*Library symbol*] [*Library of Congress*] (LCLS)

CaQPAg .... Canada Department of Agriculture, Experimental Farm, La Pocatiere, PQ, Canada [*Library symbol*] [*Library of Congress*] (LCLS)

CaQPC .... College de Sainte-Anne, La Pocatiere, PQ, Canada [*Library symbol*] [*Library of Congress*] (LCLS)

CaQPES .... Institut de Technologie Agricole, La Pocatiere, PQ, Canada [*Library symbol*] [*Library of Congress*] (LCLS)

CaQPlM .... Bibliotheque Municipale, Plessisville, PQ, Canada [*Library symbol*] [*Library of Congress*] (LCLS)

CaQPOC ... Pointe Claire Public Library, Pointe Claire, PQ, Canada [*Library symbol*] [*Library of Congress*] (LCLS)

CaQPrM .... Bibliotheque Municipale, Princeville, PQ, Canada [*Library symbol*] [*Library of Congress*] (LCLS)

CaQQ .... Bibliotheque Municipale, Quebec, PQ, Canada [*Library symbol*] [*Library of Congress*] (LCLS)

CaQQA ...... Bibliotheque des Archives de la Province de Quebec, Quebec, PQ, Canada [*Library symbol*] [*Library of Congress*] (LCLS)

CaQQAA ... Archives de l'Archeveche de Quebec, Quebec, PQ, Canada [*Library symbol*] [*Library of Congress*] (LCLS)

CaQQAC ... Quebec Ministere des Affaires Culturelles, Quebec, PQ, Canada [*Library symbol*] [*Library of Congress*] (LCLS)

CaQQACJ ... Province du Canada-Francais, Archives de la Compagnie de Jesus, Quebec, PQ, Canada [*Library symbol*] [*Library of Congress*] (LCLS)

CaQQAg .... Ministere de l'Agriculture et de la Colonisation, Quebec, PQ, Canada [*Library symbol*] [*Library of Congress*] (LCLS)

CaQQAI .... Quebec Ministere des Affaires Intergouvernementales, Bibliotheque Administrative, Quebec, PQ, Canada [*Library symbol*] [*Library of Congress*] (LCLS)

CaQQAM ... Ministere des Affaires Municipales, Centre de Documentation, PQ, Canada [*Library symbol*] [*Library of Congress*] (LCLS)

CaQQAND ... Archives du Monastere Notre-Dame-Des-Anges, Quebec, PQ, Canada [*Library symbol*] [*Library of Congress*] (LCLS)

CaQQAPC ... Cerebral Palsy Association of Quebec, Inc., Quebec, PQ, Canada [*Library symbol*] [*Library of Congress*] (LCLS)

CaQQAQS ... Anglican Church of Canada, Diocese of Quebec, Synod Office, Quebec, PQ, Canada [*Library symbol*] [*Library of Congress*] (LCLS)

CaQQAS ... Archives du Seminaire de Quebec, Quebec, PQ, Canada [*Library symbol*] [*Library of Congress*] (LCLS)

CaQQASF ... Conseil des Affaires Sociales et de la Famille, Quebec, PQ, Canada [*Library symbol*] [*Library of Congress*] (LCLS)

CaQQBJNQ ... Bureau de la Baie James et du Nord Quebecois, Ste.-Foy, PQ, Canada [*Library symbol*] [*Library of Congress*] (LCLS)

CaQQBQ ... Ministere des Communications du Quebec, Bibliotheque Administrative, Quebec, PQ, Canada [*Library symbol*] [*Library of Congress*] (LCLS)

CaQQBS .... Bureau de la Statistique du Quebec, Quebec, PQ, Canada [*Library symbol*] [*Library of Congress*] (LCLS)

CaQQBST ... Bureau de la Science et de la Technologie, Quebec, PQ, Canada [*Library symbol*] [*Library of Congress*] (LCLS)

CaQQC ...... Defence Research Establishment, Valcartier, Canada Department of National Defence, Quebec, PQ, Canada [*Library symbol*] [*Library of Congress*] (LCLS)

CaQQCA ... Centre Antonien, Quebec, PQ, Canada [*Library symbol*] [*Library of Congress*] (LCLS)

CaQQCAD ... Conservatoire d'Art Dramatique de Quebec, Quebec, PQ, Canada [*Library symbol*] [*Library of Congress*] (LCLS)

CaQQCDP ... Quebec Commission des Droits de la Personne, Quebec, PQ, Canada [*Library symbol*] [*Library of Congress*] (LCLS)

CaQQCE ... CEGEP [*College d'Enseignement General et Professionnel*] de Limoilou, Quebec, PQ, Canada [*Library symbol*] [*Library of Congress*] (LCLS)

CaQQCH... Departement des Archives et Statistiques de la Ville de Quebec, Quebec, PQ, Canada [*Library symbol*] [*Library of Congress*] (LCLS)

CaQQCLF ... Conseil de la Langue Francaise, Quebec, PQ, Canada [*Library symbol*] [*Library of Congress*] (LCLS)

CaQQCM .. College Merici, Quebec, PQ, Canada [*Library symbol*] [*Library of Congress*] (LCLS)

CaQQCMQ ... Conservatoire de Musique du Quebec, Quebec, PQ, Canada [*Library symbol*] [*Library of Congress*] (LCLS)

CaQQCPS ... Conseil de la Politique Scientifique du Quebec, Quebec, PQ, Canada [*Library symbol*] [*Library of Congress*] (LCLS)

CaQQCRH ... Centre des Recherches Historiques, Quebec, PQ, Canada [*Library symbol*] [*Library of Congress*] [*Obsolete*] (LCLS)

CaQQCRS ... Centre de Documentation de la Regie du Logement, Montreal, PQ, Canada [*Library symbol*] [*Library of Congress*] (LCLS)

CaQQCS.... Service de Documentation et de Bibliotheque, Quebec, PQ, Canada [*Library symbol*] [*Library of Congress*] (LCLS)

CaQQCSF ... Conseil du Statut de la Femme, Quebec, PQ, Canada [*Library symbol*] [*Library of Congress*] (LCLS)

CaQQCT ... Commission de Toponymie, Quebec, PQ, Canada [*Library symbol*] [*Library of Congress*] (LCLS)

CaQQCU... Conseil des Universites du Quebec, Quebec, PQ, Canada [*Library symbol*] [*Library of Congress*] (LCLS)

CaQQDTI ... Ministere des Finances, Service du Traitement de l'Information, Duberger, PQ, Canada [*Library symbol*] [*Library of Congress*] (LCLS)

CaQQE ...... Canada Department of the Environment, Quebec Region, Ste.-Foy, Quebec, PQ, Canada [*Library symbol*] [*Library of Congress*] (LCLS)

CaQQEDOP ... Ministere de l'Education, Office des Professions du Quebec, Quebec, PQ, Canada [*Library symbol*] [*Library of Congress*] (LCLS)

CaQQEN... Quebec Ministere de l'Environnement, Quebec, PQ, Canada [*Library symbol*] [*Library of Congress*] (LCLS)

CaQQEPC ... Department of the Environment, Parks Canada, Ste.-Foy, PQ, Canada [*Library symbol*] [*Library of Congress*] (LCLS)

CaQQER ... Ministere de l'Energie et des Ressources du Quebec, Quebec, PQ, Canada [*Library symbol*] [*Library of Congress*] (LCLS)

CaQQERE ... Ministere de l'Energie et des Ressources, Secteur Energie, Centre de Documentation et de Renseignements, Quebec, PQ, Canada [*Library symbol*] [*Library of Congress*] (LCLS)

CaQQF ...... Bibliotheque Franciscaine, Quebec, PQ, Canada [*Library symbol*] [*Library of Congress*] (LCLS)

CaQQFPCE ... Ministere de la Fonction Publique, Direction de la Classification et de l'Evaluation des Emplois, Quebec, PQ, Canada [*Library symbol*] [*Library of Congress*] (LCLS)

CaQQFTI .. Ministere des Finances, Service du Traitement de l'Information, Duberger, PQ, Canada [*Library symbol*] [*Library of Congress*] (LCLS)

CaQQHD .. Hotel-Dieu de Quebec, Quebec, PQ, Canada [*Library symbol*] [*Library of Congress*] (LCLS)

CaQQHDM ... Musee des Augustines de l'Hotel-Dieu de Quebec, Quebec, PQ, Canada [*Library symbol*] [*Library of Congress*] (LCLS)

CaQQHDS ... Hotel-Dieu du Sacre-Coeur, Quebec, PQ, Canada [*Library symbol*] [*Library of Congress*] (LCLS)

CaQQHSS ... Hopital du Saint-Sacrement, Quebec, PQ, Canada [*Library symbol*] [*Library of Congress*] (LCLS)

CaQQIAP ... Canada Department of Indian Affairs and Northern Development, Parks Canada, Quebec Regional Office, Ste-Foy, Quebec, PQ, Canada [*Library symbol*] [*Library of Congress*] (LCLS)

CaQQIAS ... Informatheque des Affaires Sociales du Quebec, Quebec, PQ, Canada [*Library symbol*] [*Library of Congress*] (LCLS)

CaQQIC .... Ministere de l'Industrie et du Commerce du Quebec, Quebec, PQ, Canada [*Library symbol*] [*Library of Congress*] (LCLS)

CaQQIF..... Ministere des Institutions Financieres, Compagnies, et Cooperatives, Quebec, PQ, Canada [*Library symbol*] [*Library of Congress*] (LCLS)

CaQQIM ... Institut Maritime du Quebec, CEGEP de Rimouski, Quebec, PQ, Canada [*Library symbol*] [*Library of Congress*] (LCLS)

CaQQIQRC ... Institut Quebecois de Recherche sur la Culture, Quebec, PQ, Canada [*Library symbol*] [*Library of Congress*] (LCLS)

CaQQJ....... Ministere de la Justice du Quebec, Ste.-Foy, PQ, Canada [*Library symbol*] [*Library of Congress*] (LCLS)

CaQQL ...... Bibliotheque de la Legislature de la Province de Quebec, Quebec, PQ, Canada [*Library symbol*] [*Library of Congress*] (LCLS)

CaQQLa .... Universite Laval, Quebec, PQ, Canada [*Library symbol*] [*Library of Congress*] (LCLS)

CaQQLaA ... Universite Laval, Faculte des Sciences de l'Agriculture et de l'Alimentation, Quebec, PQ, Canada [*Library symbol*] [*Library of Congress*] (LCLS)

CaQQLaAA ... Universite Laval, Secteur Art et Architecture, Quebec, PQ, Canada [*Library symbol*] [*Library of Congress*] (LCLS)

CaQQLaAV ... Universite Laval, Ecole des Arts Visuelles, Quebec, PQ, Canada [*Library symbol*] [*Library of Congress*] (LCLS)

CaQQLaCa ... Universite Laval, Cartotheque, Quebec, PQ, Canada [*Library symbol*] [*Library of Congress*] (LCLS)

CaQQLaCI ... Universite Laval, Centre International de Recherches sur le Bilinguisme, Quebec, PQ, Canada [*Library symbol*] [*Library of Congress*] (LCLS)

CaQQLaD ... Universite Laval, Faculte de Droit, Quebec, PQ, Canada [*Library symbol*] [*Library of Congress*] (LCLS)

CaQQLaFG ... Universite Laval, Faculte de Foresterie et de Geodesie, Quebec, PQ, Canada [*Library symbol*] [*Library of Congress*] (LCLS)

CaQQLaG ... Universite Laval, Institut de Geographie, Quebec, PQ, Canada [*Library symbol*] [*Library of Congress*] (LCLS)

CaQQLaGM ... Universite Laval, Departement de Geologie et de Mineralogie, Quebec, PQ, Canada [*Library symbol*] [*Library of Congress*] (LCLS)

CaQQLaI... Universite Laval, Societe Dante Aleghieri, Quebec, PQ, Canada [*Library symbol*] [*Library of Congress*] (LCLS)

CaQQLaS ... Universite Laval, Faculte des Sciences, Quebec, PQ, Canada [*Library symbol*] [*Library of Congress*] (LCLS)

CaQQLCP ... Ministere du Loisir de la Chasse et de la Peche, Quebec, PQ, Canada [*Library symbol*] [*Library of Congress*] (LCLS)

CaQQLH ... Literary and Historical Society of Quebec, Quebec, PQ, Canada [*Library symbol*] [*Library of Congress*] (LCLS)

CaQQMC .. Ministere des Communications du Quebec, Bibliotheque Administrative, Quebec, PQ, Canada [*Library symbol*] [*Library of Congress*] (LCLS)

CaQQMF .. Canada Department of the Environment, Forest Research Laboratory, Quebec, PQ, Canada [*Library symbol*] [*Library of Congress*] (LCLS)

CaQQMQ ... Musee du Quebec, Quebec, PQ, Canada [*Library symbol*] [*Library of Congress*] (LCLS)

CaQQMR .. Musee du Royal 22e Regiment et la Regie du Royal 22e Regiment, Quebec, PQ, Canada [*Library symbol*] [*Library of Congress*] (LCLS)

CaQQOLF ... Office de la Langue Francaise, Quebec, PQ, Canada [*Library symbol*] [*Library of Congress*] (LCLS)

CaQQOP... Office de Planification et de Developpement du Quebec, Quebec, PQ, Canada [*Library symbol*] [*Library of Congress*] (LCLS)

CaQQOPC ... Office de la Protection du Consommateur, Quebec, PQ, Canada [*Library symbol*] [*Library of Congress*] (LCLS)

CaQQOPD ... Office des Promotions du Quebec, Direction de la Documentation, Quebec, PQ, Canada [*Library symbol*] [*Library of Congress*] (LCLS)

CaQQPSM ... Canada Department of Fisheries and the Environment, Fisheries and Marine Service, Quebec, PQ, Canada [*Library symbol*] [*Library of Congress*] (LCLS)

CaQQQE... Universite du Quebec, Centre Quebecois des Sciences de l'Eau, Quebec, PQ, Canada [*Library symbol*] [*Library of Congress*] (LCLS)

CaQQR ...... Reed Ltd., Technical Information Centre, Quebec, PQ, Canada [*Library symbol*] [*Library of Congress*] (LCLS)

CaQQRA ... Roche Associes Ltee., Groupe-Conseil, Ste.-Foy, PQ, Canada [*Library symbol*] [*Library of Congress*] (LCLS)

CaQQRAA ... Regie de l'Assurance Automobile du Quebec, Sillery, PQ, Canada [*Library symbol*] [*Library of Congress*] (LCLS)

CaQQRAMQ ... Regie de l'Assurance-Maladie du Quebec, Quebec, PQ, Canada [*Library symbol*] [*Library of Congress*] (LCLS)

CaQQRE ... Ministere du Revenu, Ste.-Foy, PQ, Canada [*Library symbol*] [*Library of Congress*] (LCLS)

CaQQRN... Ministere des Richesses Naturelles du Quebec, Quebec, PQ, Canada [*Library symbol*] [*Library of Congress*] (LCLS)

CaQQRNC ... Centre de Documentation de la Direction Generale de l'Energie du Ministere des Richesses Naturelles du Quebec, Quebec, PQ, Canada [*Library symbol*] [*Library of Congress*] [*Obsolete*] (LCLS)

CaQQRQ... Regie des Rentes du Quebec, Quebec, PQ, Canada [*Library symbol*] [*Library of Congress*] (LCLS)

CaQQRRQ ... Regie des Rentes du Quebec, Quebec, PQ, Canada [*Library symbol*] [*Library of Congress*] (LCLS)

CaQQRSP ... Regie des Services Publics, Ste.-Foy, PQ, Canada [*Library symbol*] [*Library of Congress*] (LCLS)

CaQQRV ... Regie des Ventes du Quebec, Quebec, PQ, Canada [*Library symbol*] [*Library of Congress*] [*Obsolete*] (LCLS)

CaQQS ...... Seminaire de Quebec, Quebec, PQ, Canada [*Library symbol*] [*Library of Congress*] (LCLS)

CaQQSIP .. Societe Quebecoise d'Initiatives Petrolieres, Ste.-Foy, PQ, Canada [*Library symbol*] [*Library of Congress*] (LCLS)

CaQQT ...... Ministere des Terres et Forets du Quebec, Quebec, PQ, Canada [*Library symbol*] [*Library of Congress*] (LCLS)

CaQQTR ... Ministere des Transports, Quebec, PQ, Canada [*Library symbol*] [*Library of Congress*] (LCLS)

CaQQU...... Couvent des Ursulines, Quebec, PQ, Canada [*Library symbol*] [*Library of Congress*] (LCLS)

CaQQUED ... Universite du Quebec, Institut National de la Recherche Scientifique (Education), Quebec, PQ, Canada [*Library symbol*] [*Library of Congress*] (LCLS)

CaQQUIE ... Universite du Quebec, Institut Nationale de la Recherche Scientifique (Eau), Quebec, PQ, Canada [*Library symbol*] [*Library of Congress*] (LCLS)

CaQQUQ ... Universite du Quebec a Quebec, Quebec, PQ, Canada [*Library symbol*] [*Library of Congress*] (LCLS)

CaQQUQEN ... Universite du Quebec, Ecole Nationale d'Administration Publique, Quebec, PQ, Canada [*Library symbol*] [*Library of Congress*] (LCLS)

CaQQUQT ... Universite du Quebec, Tele-Universite, Ste.-Foy, Quebec, PQ, Canada [*Library symbol*] [*Library of Congress*] (LCLS)

CaQQUS ... University Seminary, Quebec, PQ, Canada [*Library symbol*] [*Library of Congress*] (LCLS)

CaQQZ ...... Jardin Zoologique de Quebec, Quebec, PQ, Canada [*Library symbol*] [*Library of Congress*] (LCLS)

CaQRC ...... College de Rouyn, Rouyn, PQ, Canada [*Library symbol*] [*Library of Congress*] [*Obsolete*] (LCLS)

CaQRCB .... College Bourget, Rigaud, PQ, Canada [*Library symbol*] [*Library of Congress*] (LCLS)

CaQRCN ... College du Nord Ouest, Rouyn, PQ, Canada [*Library symbol*] [*Library of Congress*] (LCLS)

CaQRCRS ... Conseil Regional de la Sante et des Services Sociaux, Rimouski, PQ, Canada [*Library symbol*] [*Library of Congress*] (LCLS)

CaQRIB ..... Bibliotheque Municipale, Rock Island, PQ, Canada [*Library symbol*] [*Library of Congress*] (LCLS)

CaQRiC ..... College de Rimouski, Rimouski, PQ, Canada [*Library symbol*] [*Library of Congress*] (LCLS)

CaQRIM .... Institut Maritime, CEGEP de Rimouski, PQ, Canada [*Library symbol*] [*Library of Congress*] (LCLS)

CaQRo .... Sources Public Library, Roxboro, PQ, Canada [*Library symbol*] [*Library of Congress*] (LCLS)

CaQRU ...... Universite du Quebec a Rimouski, Rimouski, PQ, Canada [*Library symbol*] [*Library of Congress*] (LCLS)

CaQRUC ... Universite du Quebec a Rimouski, Cartotheque, Rimouski, PQ, Canada [*Library symbol*] [*Library of Congress*] (LCLS)

CaQRUQR ... Universite du Quebec a Rouyn, Rouyn, PQ, Canada [*Library symbol*] [*Library of Congress*] (LCLS)

CaQSeD ..... Domtar Ltd., Research Centre, Senneville, PQ, Canada [*Library symbol*] [*Library of Congress*] (LCLS)

CaQSF .... Bibliotheque Municipale, Ste.-Foy, PQ, Canada [*Library symbol*] [*Library of Congress*] (LCLS)

CaQSFAg .. Canada Department of Agriculture, Research Station, Ste.-Foy, PQ, Canada [*Library symbol*] [*Library of Congress*] (LCLS)

CaQSFC .... College d'Enseignement, Ste.-Foy, PQ, Canada [*Library symbol*] [*Library of Congress*] (LCLS)

CaQSFCAE ... Clinique d'Aide a l'Enfance, Ste.-Foy, PQ, Canada [*Library symbol*] [*Library of Congress*] (LCLS)

CaQSFCM ... College Marguerite d'Youville, Ste.-Foy, PQ, Canada [*Library symbol*] [*Library of Congress*] (LCLS)

CaQSFCP ... Commission de Police du Quebec, Ste.-Foy, PQ, Canada [*Library symbol*] [*Library of Congress*] (LCLS)

CaQSFCR ... Ministere de l'Industrie, du Commerce, et du Tourisme, Centre de Recherche Industrielle du Quebec, Complexe Scientifique, Ste.-Foy, PQ, Canada [*Library symbol*] [*Library of Congress*] (LCLS)

CaQSFS ..... SOQUEM [*Societe Quebecoise d'Exploration Miniere*], Ste.-Foy, PQ, Canada [*Library symbol*] [*Library of Congress*] (LCLS)

CaQSH ...... Stanstead Historical Society, Stanstead, PQ, Canada [*Library symbol*] [*Library of Congress*] (LCLS)

CaQSHC ... CEGEP [*College d'Enseignement General et Professionnel*] de Shawinigan, Shawinigan, PQ, Canada [*Library symbol*] [*Library of Congress*] (LCLS)

CaQSherA ... Archeveche de Sherbrooke, Sherbrooke, PQ, Canada [*Library symbol*] [*Library of Congress*] (LCLS)

CaQSherC ... Universite de Sherbrooke, Centre Hospitalier Universitaire, Sherbrooke, PQ, Canada [*Library symbol*] [*Library of Congress*] (LCLS)

CaQSherCR ... Conseil Regional de la Sante et des Services Sociaux des Cantons de l'Est, Sherbrooke, PQ, Canada [*Library symbol*] [*Library of Congress*] (LCLS)

CaQSherD ... Sherbrooke Daily Record, Sherbrooke, PQ, Canada [*Library symbol*] [*Library of Congress*] (LCLS)

CaQSherE ... College de Sherbrooke (CEGEP) [*College d'Enseignement General et Professionnel*], Sherbrooke, PQ, Canada [*Library symbol*] [*Library of Congress*] (LCLS)

CaQSherG ... Grand Seminaire des Saints-Apotres, Sherbrooke, PQ, Canada [*Library symbol*] [*Library of Congress*] (LCLS)

CaQSherH ... Huntingdon Gleaner, Sherbrooke, PQ, Canada [*Library symbol*] [*Library of Congress*] (LCLS)

CaQSherHD ... Centre Hospitalier Hotel-Dieu, Sherbrooke, PQ, Canada [*Library symbol*] [*Library of Congress*] (LCLS)

CaQSherL ... Sherbrooke Library, Sherbrooke, PQ, Canada [*Library symbol*] [*Library of Congress*] (LCLS)

CaQSherM ... Monastere de Peres Redemptoristes, Sherbrooke, PQ, Canada [*Library symbol*] [*Library of Congress*] (LCLS)

CaQSherN ... Bibliotheque Municipale de Sherbrooke, Sherbrooke, PQ, Canada [*Library symbol*] [*Library of Congress*] (LCLS)

CaQSherS ... Seminaire de Sherbrooke, Sherbrooke, PQ, Canada [*Library symbol*] [*Library of Congress*] (LCLS)

CaQSherSC ... College du Sacre-Coeur, Sherbrooke, PQ, Canada [*Library symbol*] [*Library of Congress*] (LCLS)

CaQSherSF ... Ecole Secondaire Saint-Francois, Sherbrooke, PQ, Canada [*Library symbol*] [*Library of Congress*] (LCLS)

CaQSherSH ... Societe Historique des Cantons de l'Est, Sherbrooke, PQ, Canada [*Library symbol*] [*Library of Congress*] (LCLS)

CaQSherSS ... Seminaire de Sherbrooke, Sherbrooke, PQ, Canada [*Library symbol*] [*Library of Congress*] [*Obsolete*] (LCLS)

CaQSherSV ... Centre Hospitalier St.-Vincent-De-Paul, Sherbrooke, PQ, Canada [*Library symbol*] [*Library of Congress*] (LCLS)

CaQSherU ... Universite de Sherbrooke, Sherbrooke, PQ, Canada [*Library symbol*] [*Library of Congress*] (LCLS)

CaQSherUA ... Universite de Sherbrooke, Galerie d'Art et Centre Culturel, Sherbrooke, PQ, Canada [*Library symbol*] [*Library of Congress*] (LCLS)

CaQSherUD ... Universite de Sherbrooke, Faculte de Droit, Sherbrooke, PQ, Canada [*Library symbol*] [*Library of Congress*] (LCLS)

CaQSherUG ... Universite de Sherbrooke, Departement de Geographie, Sherbrooke, PQ, Canada [*Library symbol*] [*Library of Congress*] (LCLS)

CaQSherUGC ... Universite de Sherbrooke, Departement de Geographie, Cartotheque, Sherbrooke, PQ, Canada [*Library symbol*] [*Library of Congress*] (LCLS)

CaQSHM .. Municipal Library, Shawinigan, PQ, Canada [*Library symbol*] [*Library of Congress*] (LCLS)

CaQSHS .... Seminaire Ste.-Marie, Shawinigan, PQ, Canada [*Library symbol*] [*Library of Congress*] (LCLS)

CaQSi .... Bibliotheque Municipale, Sept-Iles, PQ, Canada [*Library symbol*] [*Library of Congress*] (LCLS)

CaQSiIOM ... Iron Ore Co., Mineralogy Laboratory, Sept-Illes, PQ, Canada [*Library symbol*] [*Library of Congress*] (LCLS)

CaQSilC .... College Jesus-Marie de Sillery, Sillery, PQ, Canada [*Library symbol*] [*Library of Congress*] (LCLS)

CaQSJ .... Stanstead Journal, Stanstead, PQ, Canada [*Library symbol*] [*Library of Congress*] (LCLS)

CaQSlCR ... Champlain Regional College, Campus 1, St.-Lambert, PQ, Canada [*Library symbol*] [*Library of Congress*] (LCLS)

CaQSo .... Bibliotheque Municipale, Sorel, PQ, Canada [*Library symbol*] [*Library of Congress*] (LCLS)

CaQSoIT ... Quebec Iron & Titanium Corp., Sorel, PQ, Canada [*Library symbol*] [*Library of Congress*] (LCLS)

CaQSTAH ... Ste. Anne's Hospital, Ste.-Anne-De-Bellevue, PQ, Canada [*Library symbol*] [*Library of Congress*] (LCLS)

CaQSTAIAS ... Ministere des Affaires Sociales, Informatheque-Laboratoires, Ste.-Anne-De-Bellevue, PQ, Canada [*Library symbol*] [*Library of Congress*] (LCLS)

CaQSTAJ ... John Abbott College, Ste.-Anne-De-Bellevue, PQ, Canada [*Library symbol*] [*Library of Congress*] (LCLS)

CaQSTAS ... Spar Technology Ltd., Ste.-Anne-De-Bellevue, PQ, Canada [*Library symbol*] [*Library of Congress*] (LCLS)

CaQStBL ... Abbaye de Saint-Benoit-Du-Lac, Comte De Brome, PQ, Canada [*Library symbol*] [*Library of Congress*] (LCLS)

CaQSTFRA ... Roche Associes Ltee., Centre de Documentation, Ste.-Foy, PQ, Canada [*Library symbol*] [*Library of Congress*] (LCLS)

CaQStHHR ... Societe d'Histoire Regionale de St.-Hyacinthe, St.-Hyacinthe, PQ, Canada [*Library symbol*] [*Library of Congress*] (LCLS)

CaQStHS .. Seminaire de St.-Hyacinthe, St.-Hyacinthe, PQ, Canada [*Library symbol*] [*Library of Congress*] (LCLS)

CaQStHuM ... Canada Department of National Defence, Headquarters Mobile Command, St. Hubert, PQ, Canada [*Library symbol*] [*Library of Congress*] (LCLS)

CaQStHV .. Faculte de Medecine Veterinaire de l'Universite de Montreal, St.-Hyacinthe, PQ, Canada [*Library symbol*] [*Library of Congress*] (LCLS)

CaQStJ ...... College Militaire Royal de Saint-Jean, Saint-Jean, PQ, Canada [*Library symbol*] [*Library of Congress*] (LCLS)

CaQStJAg ... Canada Department of Agriculture, Research Station, Saint-Jean, PQ, Canada [*Library symbol*] [*Library of Congress*] (LCLS)

CaQStJB ... Bibliotheque Municipale, Saint-Jean, PQ, Canada [*Library symbol*] [*Library of Congress*] (LCLS)

CaQStJC ... College Saint-Jean-Sur-Richelieu, Saint-Jean, PQ, Canada [*Library symbol*] [*Library of Congress*] (LCLS)

CaQStJe ... Bibliotheque Municipale, Saint-Jerome, PQ, Canada [*Library symbol*] [*Library of Congress*] (LCLS)

CaQStJeJ .. Jesuites/Bibliotheque, Saint-Jerome, PQ, Canada [*Library symbol*] [*Library of Congress*] (LCLS)

CaQStJS .... Seminaire de Saint-Jean, Saint-Jean, PQ, Canada [*Library symbol*] [*Library of Congress*] [*Obsolete*] (LCLS)

CaQStL ...... Bibliotheque Municipale, Saint-Laurent, PQ, Canada [*Library symbol*] [*Library of Congress*] (LCLS)

CaQStLe .... Bibliotheque Municipale, Saint-Leonard, PQ, Canada [*Library symbol*] [*Library of Congress*] (LCLS)

CaQT .... Bibliotheque Municipale, Trois-Rivieres, PQ, Canada [*Library symbol*] [*Library of Congress*] (LCLS)

CaQTA ...... Archives Nationales du Quebec, Trois-Rivieres, PQ, Canada [*Library symbol*] [*Library of Congress*] (LCLS)

CaQTB .... Editions du Boreal Express, Montreal, PQ, Canada [*Library symbol*] [*Library of Congress*] (LCLS)

CaQTBC .... Bibliotheque Centrale de Pret de la Mauricie, Trois-Rivieres, PQ, Canada [*Library symbol*] [*Library of Congress*] (LCLS)

CaQTCE .... CEGEP [*College d'Enseignement General et Professionnel*], Trois-Rivieres, PQ, Canada [*Library symbol*] [*Library of Congress*] (LCLS)

CaQTCL .... College Lafleche, Trois-Rivieres, PQ, Canada [*Library symbol*] [*Library of Congress*] (LCLS)

CaQTCO ... Communication-Quebec, Trois-Rivieres, PQ, Canada [*Library symbol*] [*Library of Congress*] (LCLS)

CaQTCPB ... Corporation Pierre-Boucher, Trois-Rivieres, PQ, Canada [*Library symbol*] [*Library of Congress*] (LCLS)

CaQTCRD ... Conseil Regional de Developpement, Trois-Rivieres, PQ, Canada [*Library symbol*] [*Library of Congress*] (LCLS)

CaQTCRS ... Conseil Regional de la Sante et des Services Sociaux, Trois-Rivieres, PQ, Canada [*Library symbol*] [*Library of Congress*] (LCLS)

CaQTCSRV ... Commission Scolaire Regionale des Vieilles-Forges, Trois-Rivieres, PQ, Canada [*Library symbol*] [*Library of Congress*] (LCLS)

CaQTCSS ... Centre de Services Sociaux, Trois-Rivieres, PQ, Canada [*Library symbol*] [*Library of Congress*] (LCLS)

CaQTE .... Ecole Normale M. L. Duplessis, Trois-Rivieres, PQ, Canada [*Library symbol*] [*Library of Congress*] (LCLS)

CaQTHSJ ... Hopital Saint-Joseph, Trois-Rivieres, PQ, Canada [*Library symbol*] [*Library of Congress*] (LCLS)

CaQTHSM ... Hopital Sainte-Marie, Trois-Rivieres, PQ, Canada [*Library symbol*] [*Library of Congress*] (LCLS)

CaQTI .... Institut Albert Tessier, Trois-Rivieres, PQ, Canada [*Library symbol*] [*Library of Congress*] (LCLS)

CaQTO ...... Institut Agricole d'Oka, LaTrappe, PQ, Canada [*Library symbol*] [*Library of Congress*] [*Obsolete*] (LCLS)

CaQTOPDQ ... Office de Planification et de Developpement du Quebec, Trois-Rivieres, PQ, Canada [*Library symbol*] [*Library of Congress*] (LCLS)

CA Qtrly .... CA Quarterly. Facts and Figures on Austria's Economy [*A publication*]

CaQTS .... Seminaire des Trois-Rivieres, Trois-Rivieres, PQ, Canada [*Library symbol*] [*Library of Congress*] (LCLS)

CaQTT .... Trois-Rivieres High School, Trois-Rivieres, PQ, Canada [*Library symbol*] [*Library of Congress*] (LCLS)

CaQTU ...... Universite du Quebec a Trois-Rivieres, Trois-Rivieres, PQ, Canada [*Library symbol*] [*Library of Congress*] (LCLS)

CaQTUAH ... Universite du Quebec a Trois-Rivieres, Archives Historiques, Trois-Rivieres, PQ, Canada [*Library symbol*] [*Library of Congress*] (LCLS)

CaQTUGC ... Universite du Quebec a Trois-Rivieres, Departement de Geographie, Cartotheque, Trois-Rivieres, PQ, Canada [*Library symbol*] [*Library of Congress*] (LCLS)

CaQTUIH ... Universite du Quebec a Trois-Rivieres, Imprimes Historiques, Trois-Rivieres, PQ, Canada [*Library symbol*] [*Library of Congress*] (LCLS)

CaQTUrA ... Archives des Ursulines, Trois-Rivieres, PQ, Canada [*Library symbol*] [*Library of Congress*] (LCLS)

CaQTUTH ... Centre de Documentation en Theatre Quebecois, Trois-Rivieres, PQ, Canada [*Library symbol*] [*Library of Congress*] (LCLS)

CaQV .... Bibliotheque Municipale, Victoriaville, PQ, Canada [*Library symbol*] [*Library of Congress*] (LCLS)

CaQVaH .... Institut de Recherche d'Hydro-Quebec, Varennes, PQ, Canada [*Library symbol*] [*Library of Congress*] (LCLS)

CaQVauH ... Hoffman-La Roche Ltd., Vaudreuil, PQ, Canada [*Library symbol*] [*Library of Congress*] (LCLS)

CaQVC ...... College de Victoriaville, Victoriaville, PQ, Canada [*Library symbol*] [*Library of Congress*] (LCLS)

CaQVCEMBO ... College de Victoriaville, Ecole du Meuble et du Bois Ouvre, Victoriaville, PQ, Canada [*Library symbol*] [*Library of Congress*] (LCLS)

CaQVeC ..... Centre Culturel, Verdun, PQ, Canada [*Library symbol*] [*Library of Congress*] (LCLS)

CaQW .... Waterloo Public Library, Waterloo, PQ, Canada [*Library symbol*] [*Library of Congress*] (LCLS)

CaQWsmM ... Westmount Public Library, Westmount, PQ, Canada [*Library symbol*] [*Library of Congress*] (LCLS)

CAr .... Arcadia Public Library, Arcadia, CA [*Library symbol*] [*Library of Congress*] (LCLS)

CAR .... Cadena Azul de Radiodifusion [*Radio network*] [*Spain*]

CAR .... Cahiers d'Archeologie Regionale [*A publication*]

CaR .... Cakavska Ric [*A publication*]

CA R .... California Reporter [*A publication*] (DLA)

CAR .... Canadian Airborne Regiment (MCD)

CAR .... Canadian Annual Review [*A publication*]

CA(R) .... Canadian Army (Regular)

CAR .... Canadian Artists' Representation

CAR .... Canadian Association of Radiologists

CAR .... Canam Industry Corp. [*Vancouver Stock Exchange symbol*]

CAR .... Capital Authorization Request

CAR .... Caracas [*Venezuela*] [*Seismograph station code, US Geological Survey*] (SEIS)

CAR .... Carat [*Unit of measure for precious stones or gold*]

CAR .... Caravan Kampeersport. Maandblad voor Caravan/Kampeerliefhebbers [*A publication*]

Car .... Caravelle [*A publication*]

Car .... Carbohydrate [*Dietetics*]

Car .... Cardinalis [*Authority cited in pre-1607 legal work*] (DSA)

CAR .... Cargill Information Center, Wayzata, MN [*OCLC symbol*] (OCLC)

CAR .... Cargo (MSA)

car .... Carib [*MARC language code*] [*Library of Congress*] (LCCP)

CAR .... Caribbean

CAR .... Cariboo College Library [*UTLAS symbol*]

CAR .... Caribou, ME [*Location identifier*] [*FAA*] (FAAL)

Car .... Carina [*Constellation*]

CAR .... Carlow [*County in Ireland*] (ROG)

Car .... Carmelus [*A publication*]

CAR .... Carminative [*Expelling Wind*] [*Pharmacy*] (ROG)

CAR .... Carmine (ROG)

CAR .... Carolina [*United States*] [*Obsolete*] (ROG)

CAR .... Carolus [*Charles*] [*Numismatics*] (ROG)

Car .... Carovana [*A publication*]

CAR .... Carpenter [*Navy*] [*British*] (ROG)

CAR .... Carrier (CINC)

CAR .... Carronade

CAR .... Carta [*Music*]

CAR .... Carter-Wallace, Inc. [*NYSE symbol*] (SPSG)

CAR .... Caruscan Corp. [*Toronto Stock Exchange symbol*]

CAR .... Center for Aging Research

CAR .... Center for Alcohol Research [*University of Florida*] [*Research center*] (RCD)

CAR .... Center for Architectural Research [*Rensselaer Polytechnic Institute*] [*Research center*] (RCD)

CAR .... Center for Automotive Research [*Wayne State University*] [*Research center*] (RCD)

CAR .... Central African Regiment [*British military*] (DMA)

CAR .... Central African Republic

CAR .... Central Apparatus Room (DEN)

CAR .... Central Asian Review [*A publication*]

CAR .... Certification Approval Request (NASA)

CAR .... Channel Address Register [*Data processing*]

CAR .... Check Authorization Record (IBMDP)

CAR .... Chief Airship Rigger [*Navy rating*] [*Obsolete*]

CAR .... Chief, Army Reserve (AABC)

CAR .... Christian Aid for Romania (EA)

CAR .... cis-Acting REV-Responsive Sequence [*Genetics*]

CAR .... Cis Anti-Repression Sequence [*Genetics*]

CAR .... Civil Aeronautical Regulation (MCD)

CAR .... Civil Air Regulation [*FAA*]

CAR .... Civil Air Reserve (AAG)

CAR .... Cloud-Top Altitude Radiometer

CAR .... Collection Activity Reports [*IRS*]

CAR .... Command Action Report [*Army*]

CAR .... Command Assessment Review (MCD)

CAR .... Commanders Availability Report (CINC)

CAR .... Commission on Administrative Review [*House of Representatives*]

CAR .... Committee for Automobile Reform

CAR .... Commonwealth Arbitration Reports [*A publication*] (APTA)

CAR .... Community Antenna Relay [*Service*] [*FCC*]

CAR .... Computer-Assisted Research (BUR)

CAR .... Computer-Assisted Retrieval

CAR .... Concentrated Area Review [*US Postal Service*]

CAR .... Condenser Air Removal [*Nuclear energy*] (NRCH)

CAR .... Condition and Recommendation (AABC)

CAR .... Conditional Antimicrobial Reporting [*Microbiology*]

CAR .... Conditioned Avoidance Response [*Psychometrics*]

CAR .... Configuration and Acceptance Review (MCD)

CAR .... Configuration Audit Review

CAR .... Containment Air Removal [*Recirculation fan*] (IEEE)

CAR .... Contemporary Authors First Revision Series [*A publication*]

CAR .... Contract Administration Report [*DoD*]

CAR .... Contract Appraisal Report

CAR .... Contract Authorization Request (AAG)

CAR .... Contractor All Risk (AIA)

CAR .... Control of Advertisements Regulations [*Town planning*] [*British*]

CAR .... Control Advisory Release (NRCH)

CAR .... Conversion, Alteration, and Repair [*Navy*]

CAR .... Corps Automation Requirements [*Army*]

CAR .... Corrective Action Reply

CAR .... Corrective Action Report

CAR .... Corrective Action Request

CAR .... Criminal Appeal Reports [*England*] [*A publication*] (DLA)

CAR .... Customer Account Representative (AFM)

CAR .... Cytarabine [*Cytosine arabinoside*] [*Also, ara-C, CA*] [*Antineoplastic drug*]

CAR .... Cytosolic Androgen Receptor [*Endocrinology*]

CAR .... United States Army, Caribbean

CAR's .... Certificates of Automobile Receivables [*Salomon Bros.*]

CARA .... Cargo and Rescue Aircraft
CARA .... Center for Applied Research in the Apostolate (EA)
CARA .... Centers and Regional Associations (EA)
CARA .... Check Area Airports (FAAC)
CARA .... Chinese American Restaurant Association (EA)
CARA .... Citizen Alternative to Remand Accommodation [Australia]
CARA .... Civilian Appellation Review Agency [Army] (MCD)
CARA .... Classification and Rating Administration [For movies]
CARA .... Combat Aircrew Recovery [or Rescue] Aircraft [Later, ARRS, ARS]
CARA .... Combined Altitude RADAR Altimeter [Electronic defense system]
CARA .... Computer-Aided Requirements Analysis (MCD)
CARA .... Coordinated Agency-Wide Research Activities [National Science Foundation]
CARA .... Current Aerospace Research Activities (KSC)
CARAE ...... Caribbean Regional Council for Adult Education [University of the West Indies] (EAIO)
Car A and E J ... Cardozo Arts and Entertainment Journal [A publication]
CARAEWRON ... Carrier Airborne Early Warning Squadron [Navy]
CARAIRGROUP ... Carrier Air Group [Navy]
CARAL .... Canadian Abortion Rights Action League
CARALA ... Conference of American Renting and Leasing Associations (EA)
CARAS ...... Canadian Academy of Recording Arts and Sciences
CARB .... California Air Resources Board
CARB .... Carbamazepine [Also, CBZ] [An analgesic]
CARB .... Carbide
CARB .... Carbon
CARB .... Carbonate
CARB .... Carburetor (MSA)
CARB .... Center for Advanced Research in Biotechnology [Jointly sponsored by the US National Bureau of Standards and the University of Maryland]
CARB .... Current Australian Reference Books [A publication]
CARBAGAIR ... Baggage for Air Cargo
CARBASORD ... Carry Out Remainder Basic Orders
Carbide J ... Carbide Journal [A publication]
Carbide Tool J ... Carbide and Tool Journal [A publication]
CARBINE ... Computer-Automated Real-Time Betting Information Network (IEEE)
Carb Ne ...... Carbon News [A publication]
CARBO ..... Carbohydrate [Dietetics]
Carbohyd Chem ... Carbohydrate Chemistry [A publication]
Carbohyd Res ... Carbohydrate Research [A publication]
Carbohydr Metab Quant Physiol Math Model ... Carbohydrate Metabolism. Quantitative Physiology and Mathematical Modeling [A publication]
Carbohydr Res ... Carbohydrate Research [A publication]
Carbohy Res ... Carbohydrate Research [A publication]
Carbon Dio ... Carbon Dioxide and Climate. A Second Assessment [A publication]
CARBOPOL ... Carboxypolymethylene [Organic chemistry]
CArc........... Arcata Public Library, Arcata, CA [Library symbol] [Library of Congress] (LCLS)
CARC .... Canadian Agricultural Research Council
CARC .... Canadian Arctic Resources Committee [Ottawa, ON] [Research center]
CARC .... Carcano Rifle
CARC .... Censo de Archivos [Database] [Ministerio de Cultura] [Spanish] [Information service or system] (CRD)
CARC .... Central America Resource Center (EA)
CARC .... Chemical Agent Resistant Coating [A paint]
CARC .... Coalition for Auto Repair Choice (EA)
CARC .... Coast Artillery Reserve Corps
CARC .... Computer-Assisted Reference Center [Information service or system] (EISS)
CARCAE ... Caribbean Regional Council for Adult Education (EAIO)
CARCAH .. Chief, Aerial Reconnaissance Coordination, All Hurricanes [National Hurricane Center]
CARCAV ... Conceptual Armored Cavalry (MCD)
CARCBE ... Annual Report. Central and Regional Arecanut Research Stations [A publication]
CArch......... Cahiers Archeologiques [A publication]
CArcHT..... Humboldt State College, Arcata, CA [Library symbol] [Library of Congress] (LCLS)
Carcinog Abst ... Carcinogenesis Abstracts [A publication]
Carcinog Compr Surv ... Carcinogenesis: A Comprehensive Survey [A publication]
Carcinog Tech Rep Ser US Natl Cancer Inst ... Carcinogenesis Technical Report Series. United States National Cancer Institute [A publication]
CARCMYS ... Canadian Arctic Resources Committee. Monograph. Yukon Series [A publication]
Car Cr L..... Carrington. Criminal Law [3rd ed.] [1828] [A publication] (DLA)
CARCSLR ... Career Counselor [Military] (AABC)
CARD .... Campaign Against Racial Discrimination [British]
CARD .... Canadian Advertising Rates and Data
CARD .... Cardiac Resuscitator Corp. [NASDAQ symbol] (NQ)
CARD .... Cardiganshire [County in Wales] (ROG)

CARD .... Cardinal
Card .... Cardinalis [Authority cited in pre-1607 legal work] (DSA)
Card .... Cardiologia [A publication]
CARD .... Caribbean Association for the Rehabilitation of the Disabled (EAIO)
CARD .... Center for Agricultural and Rural Development [Iowa State University] [Research center] (RCD)
CARD .... Certificate for Amortizing Revolving Debts [Salomon Brothers] [Accounting]
CARD .... Channel Allocation and Routing Data (IEEE)
CARD .... Civil Aviation Research and Development [NASA]
CARD .... Coded Automatic Reading Device
CARD .... Comet and Asteroid Rendezvous Docking (MCD)
CARD .... Committee Against Registration and the Draft (EA)
CARD .... Compact Automatic Retrieval Device [Massachusetts Institute of Technology] [Data processing]
CARD .... Compact Automatic Retrieval Display [Data processing] (IID)
CARD .... Computer-Aided RADAR Design (KSC)
CARDA ..... CONUS [Continental United States] Airborne Reconnaissance for Damage Assessment (MCD)
CARDAG .. Cardiologia [A publication]
CARDAN .. Centre d'Analyse et de Recherche Documentaires pour l'Afrique Noire
CARDCODER ... Card Automatic Code System [IBM Corp.] (IEEE)
CARDDJ ... Cardiologia [Rome] [A publication]
CARDE...... Canadian Armament Research and Development Establishment
Card Flor ... Cardinalis Florentinus [Franciscus Zabarella] [Deceased, 1417] [Authority cited in pre-1607 legal work] (DSA)
CARDI....... Cardigan (DSUE)
Cardi .... Cardinalis [Authority cited in pre-1607 legal work] (DSA)
CARDIAC ... Cardboard Illustrative Aid to Computation [Bell Telephone Co.] [Data processing]
CARDIGS ... Cardiganshire [County in Wales] (ROG)
Cardil Hung ... Cardiologia Hungarica [A publication]
CARDIO ... Cardiology
cardiol .... Cardiology
Cardiol Bull ... Cardiologisches Bulletin [A publication]
Cardiol Clin ... Cardiology Clinics [A publication]
Cardiol Prat ... Cardiologia Pratica [A publication]
Cardio Res ... Cardiovascular Research [A publication]
Cardiovasc Clin ... Cardiovascular Clinics [A publication]
Cardiovasc Dis Bull Tex Heart Inst ... Cardiovascular Diseases Bulletin. Texas Heart Institute [A publication]
Cardiovasc Drugs ... Cardiovascular Drugs [A publication]
Cardiovasc Flow Dyn Meas (NATO Adv Study Inst) ... Cardiovascular Flow Dynamics and Measurements (North Atlantic Treaty Organization. Advanced Study Institute on Cardiovascular Flow Dynamics) [A publication]
Cardiovasc Interventional Radiol ... Cardiovascular and Interventional Radiology [A publication]
Cardiovasc Intervent Radiol ... Cardiovascular and Interventional Radiology [A publication]
Cardiovasc Med ... Cardiovascular Medicine [A publication]
Cardiovasc Med (NY) ... Cardiovascular Medicine (New York) [A publication]
Cardiovasc Nurs ... Cardiovascular Nursing [A publication]
Cardiovasc Radiol ... Cardiovascular Radiology [A publication]
Cardiovasc Res ... Cardiovascular Research [A publication]
Cardiovasc Res Cent Bull ... Cardiovascular Research Center. Bulletin [Houston] [A publication]
Cardiovasc Res Cent Bull (Houston) ... Cardiovascular Research Center. Bulletin (Houston) [A publication]
Cardiovas Res ... Cardiovascular Research [A publication]
Cardiovas Res Suppl ... Cardiovascular Research. Supplement [A publication]
Cardiovas Rev ... Cardiovascular Review [A publication]
CARDIS .... Cargo Data Interchange System (MCD)
CAR DI SYS ... Carbon Dioxide System [of a ship] (DS)
CARDIV.... Carrier Division [Navy]
Card Nat Hist Bull ... Cardiganshire Natural History Bulletin [A publication]
Card Ne Let ... Cardiac News Letter. Chest and Heart Association [A publication]
CARDO ..... Centre for Architectural Research and Development Overseas [University of Newcastle upon Tyne] [British] (CB)
Cardozo L Rev ... Cardozo Law Review [A publication]
CARDPAC ... Card Packet System (AABC)
CARDPLMNRY ... Cardiopulmonary
Card Prat ... Cardiologia Pratica [A publication]
Car & Dr .... Car and Driver [A publication]
CARDS...... Card-Automated Reproduction and Distribution System [Library of Congress]
CARDS...... Cardiganshire [County in Wales]
CARDS.MYS ... Catalog of Approved Requirement Documents [Army] (RDA)
CARDS...... Combat Aircraft Recording and Data System
CARDS...... Computer-Aided Reliability Data Systems [Bell System]
CARDS...... Computer-Aided Requirements Definition Software
CARDS...... Contract Award Rates Delivery Study [Army]
Card Zabarel ... Cardinalis Florentinus (Franciscus Zabarella) [Deceased, 1417] [Authority cited in pre-1607 legal work] (DSA)
CARE......... Capias ad Respondendum [That You Take to Answer] [A judicial writ] [Latin] [Legal term] (ADA)

CARE......... Capitol Reef National Monument
CARE......... [The] Care Group, Inc. [NASDAQ symbol]   (NQ)
CARE......... Center for Advanced Rehabilitation Engineering [University of Texas at Arlington] [Research center]   (RCD)
CARE......... Center for Athletes' Rights and Education   (EA)
CARE......... Centre for Applied Research in Education [University of East Anglia] [British]   (CB)
CARE......... Ceramics Applications in Reciprocating Engines [Research group] [British]
CARE......... Citizens Against Rare Earths [Australia]
CARE......... Citizens for Animals, Resources, and Environment   (EA)
CARE......... Clinical and Administrative Record [System]
CARE......... Clothing Articles Require Explanation [Student legal action organization]
CARE......... Combined Accident Reduction Effort
CARE...... Communicating Alarm Response Equipment [British Telecom]
CARE...... Computer-Aided Reliability Estimation
CARE...... Computerized Audit and Record Evaluation System [Medical records]   (DHSM)
CARE......... Consolidated Assistance and Relocation Efforts   (MCD)
CARE......... Continental Association of Resolute Employers [Washington, DC]   (EA)
CARE......... Continuous Affinity Recycle Extraction [Chemical engineering]
CARE......... Conversion and Recording Equipment   (MCD)
CARE......... Cooperative for American Remittances Everywhere [Former name]
CARE......... Coronary Artery Risk Evaluation Program [Air Force]
CAREBACO ... Caribbean Regional Badminton Confederation   (EAIO)
CAREBK... Caries Research [A publication]
CARECEN ... Central American Refugee Center   (EA)
CARED...... Centre for Applied Research and Engineering Design [McMaster University, Hamilton, ON]
Career Dev Bul ... Career Development Bulletin [A publication]
CAREERS ... Career Airmen Reenlistment Reservation System [Air Force]
Careers Bull ... Careers Bulletin [A publication]
Careers Guid Teach ... Careers and Guidance Teacher [A publication]
Careers J... Careers Journal [A publication]
CAREF...... Cooking Advancement Research and Education Foundation   (EA)
CAREIRS ... Conservation and Renewable Energy Inquiry and Referral Service [Department of Energy] [Information service or system]   (IID)
CAREL...... Cascadian Regional Library [A publication]
CAREL...... Central Atlantic Regional Educational Laboratory
CAREME ... Centre Automatique de Reception et d'Emission de Messages [French]   (MCD)
Car Eng...... Carbide Engineering [A publication]
CARES ...... Computer-Aided Railway Engineering System   (MCD)
CARESIM ... Computer-Assisted Repair Simulation [Game]
CA RESP... Capias ad Respondendum [That You Take to Answer] [A judicial writ] [Latin] [Legal term]   (ROG)
CARESS.... Center for Analytic Research in Economics and the Social Sciences [University of Pennsylvania] [Research center]   (RCD)
CARETS.... Central Atlantic Regional Ecological Test Site [Department of the Interior]
Carey......... Manitoba Reports, by Carey [1875] [A publication]   (ILCA)
Carey MR .. Manitoba Reports, by Carey [1875] [A publication]   (DLA)
Carey's Mus ... Carey's American Museum [A publication]
CARF......... Canadian Advertising Research Foundation [Founded 1949]
CARF......... Center Airman Record File [Air Force]
CARF......... Central Altitude Reservation Facility [or Function]
CARF......... Christian Amateur Radio Fellowship   (EA)
CARF......... Commission on Accreditation of Rehabilitation Facilities   (EA)
CARF......... Community Affairs and Regulatory Functions [HUD]   (OICC)
CARF......... Compartmented Consolidated Analysis Report Final   (MCD)
CARFAC... Canadian Artists' Representation/Front des Artistes Canadiens
CARG ...... Caribbean Amphibious Ready Group [Navy]   (NVT)
CARG .... Carrier Air Group
CARG .... Commander, Amphibious Ready Group [Navy]   (NVT)
CARG .... Community Action Research Group   (OICC)
CARG .... Corporate Accountability Research Group [Formed by consumer-advocate Ralph Nader]
Cargese Lect Phys ... Cargese Lectures in Physics [A publication]
Cargill Crop Bull ... Cargill Crop Bulletin [A publication]
Cargo Syst Int ... Cargo Systems International [A publication]
Car H & A ... Carrow, Hamerton, and Allen's New Sessions Cases [1844-51] [England] [A publication]   (DLA)
CARHE ..... Canadian Association for Research in Home Economics [See also ACREF]
CARHS...... Canadian-American Review of Hungarian Studies [A publication]
Cari .... Carina [Constellation]
CARI......... Civil Aeromedical Research Institute [FAA]
CARI......... Comparative Administration Research Institute [Kent State University, Ohio]
CARI......... Council of Air-Conditioning and Refrigeration Industry   (EA)
CARIAV... Caribbean Forester [A publication]
CARIB....... Caribbean   (AFM)
CARIBAIR ... Caribbean Atlantic Airlines [Puerto Rico]
CARIBANK ... Caribbean Development Bank

Caribb Agr ... Caribbean Agriculture [A publication]
Caribb Agric ... Caribbean Agriculture [A publication]
Carib Basin Econ Surv ... Caribbean Basin Economic Survey [A publication]
Caribb Bus ... Caribbean Business [A publication]
Caribbean J Math ... Caribbean Journal of Mathematics [A publication]
Caribbean Jour Sci ... Caribbean Journal of Science [A publication]
Caribbean J Sci Math ... Caribbean Journal of Science and Mathematics [A publication]
Caribbean LJ ... Caribbean Law Journal [A publication]   (DLA)
Caribbean R ... Caribbean Review [A publication]
Caribbean S ... Caribbean Studies [A publication]
Caribbean Stud ... Caribbean Studies [A publication]
Caribb For ... Caribbean Forester [A publication]
Caribb J Sci ... Caribbean Journal of Science [A publication]
Caribb Med J ... Caribbean Medical Journal [A publication]
Caribb Q .... Caribbean Quarterly [A publication]
Caribb Technol Abstr ... Caribbean Technological Abstracts [A publication]
Carib Bul... Caribbean Monthly Bulletin [A publication]
CARIBCOM ... Caribbean Command [Military]
Carib J Rel St ... Caribbean Journal of Religious Studies [A publication]
Carib LJ ... Caribbean Law Journal [A publication]   (DLA)
Carib Med J ... Caribbean Medical Journal [A publication]
CARIBNAVFACENGCOM ... Caribbean Division Naval Facilities Engineering Command
Carib Q ...... Caribbean Quarterly [A publication]
CARIBSEAFRON ... Caribbean Sea Frontier [Navy]
Carib Stud ... Caribbean Studies [A publication]
Carib Updat ... Caribbean Update [A publication]
CARIC....... Carica [A Fig] [Pharmacology]   (ROG)
caric........... Caricature [or Caricaturist]
CARIC....... Computerized Automation and Robotics Information Center [Society of Manufacturing Engineers] [Information service or system]   (IID)
CARIC....... Contractor All-Risk Incentive Contract [Air Force]
CARICARGO ... Caribbean Air Cargo Ltd. [Barbados]   (EY)
CARICOM ... Caribbean Community [or Common Market] [Barbados, Jamaica, Trinidad-Tobago, Guyana, Belize, Dominica, Grenada, St. Kitts-Nevis-Anguilla, St. Lucia, St. Vincent] [Guyana]
CARID....... Customer Acceptance Review Item Disposition   (NASA)
Caridad Cienc Arte ... Caridad Ciencia y Arte [A publication]
Caries Res ... Caries Research [A publication]
CARIFTA ... Caribbean Free Trade Association
CARIH ...... Children's Asthma Research Institute and Hospital [Denver, CO]
CARIN....... Car Information and Navigation System [Compact disc technology]
CARIN....... Central America Research Institute   (EA)
Carinthia.... Carinthia. Mitteilungen des Geschichtsverein fuer Kaernten [A publication]
Carinthia 2 Sonderh ... Carinthia 2. Sonderheft [A publication]
CARIOL..... Bishop of Carlisle [British]
CARIPLO ... Cassa di Risparmio delle Provincie Lombarde [Savings bank] [Italy]
CARIRI ..... Caribbean Industrial Research Institute
CARIS .... Computerized Agricultural Research Information System [United Nations Food and Agricultural organization information system]
CARIS .... Constant-Angle Reflection Interference Spectroscopy
CARIS .... Current Agricultural Research Information System [Food and Agriculture Organization] [United Nations] [Information service or system]   (IID)
CARISMA ... Computer-Aided Research into Stock Market Applications
CARISMA ... Corrections to Applied Research Laboratories Ion-Sputtering Mass Analyzers [Data processing]
CarJos........ Cahiers de Josephologie [Montreal, PQ] [A publication]
Car J Pharm ... Carolina Journal of Pharmacy [A publication]
Car J Sci ... Caribbean Journal of Science [A publication]
Car & K ...... Carrington and Kirwan's English Nisi Prius Reports [174, 175 English Reprint] [A publication]   (DLA)
Car & K (Eng) ... Carrington and Kirwan's English Nisi Prius Reports [174, 175 English Reprint] [A publication]   (DLA)
Car & Kir ... Carrington and Kirwan's English Nisi Prius Reports [174, 175 English Reprint] [A publication]   (DLA)
CARL......... Calibration Requirements List   (NG)
CARL......... Canadian Academic Research Libraries
CARL......... Canadian Association of Research Libraries [Also, ABRC]
CARL......... Carl Karcher Enterprises, Inc. [NASDAQ symbol]   (NQ)
Carl .... Carleton's New Brunswick Reports [A publication]   (DLA)
CARL......... Category Assignment Responsibility List   (MCD)
CARL......... Colorado Alliance of Research Libraries [Denver, CO] [Library network]
CARL......... Comparative Animal Research Laboratory [Department of Energy]   (GRD)
CARL......... Computer-Assisted Retrieval of the Law [Australia]
CARL......... Computer Audio Research Laboratory [Research center]   (RCD)
CArlA .... Arlington College, Arlington, CA [Library symbol] [Library of Congress]   (LCLS)
CARLA...... Center for Applied Research in the Language Arts [Texas Tech University] [Research center]   (RCD)

CARLA...... Code Actuated Random Load Apparatus (MCD)
Car Law Repos ... Carolina Law Repository [*North Carolina*] [*A publication*] (DLA)
Car Laws.... Caruther's History of a Lawsuit. Cases in Chancery [*A publication*] (DLA)
CARLD...... Chicorel Abstracts to Reading and Learning Disabilities [*A publication*]
Carle Sel Pap ... Carle Selected Papers [*A publication*]
Carleton Misc ... Carleton Miscellany [*A publication*]
Carleton Univ Dep Geol Geol Pap ... Carleton University. Department of Geology. Geological Paper [*A publication*]
Carleton Univ Dept Geology Geol Paper ... Carleton University. Department of Geology. Geological Paper [*A publication*]
CARLIOL ... [*Bishop of*] Carlisle [*British*]
CARLIS..... Canadian Art Libraries
Car LJ........ Carolina Law Journal [*A publication*] (DLA)
CARLJS.... Council of Archives and Research Libraries in Jewish Studies (EA)
Carl Mis..... Carleton Miscellany [*A publication*]
CarlN......... Carleton Newsletter [*A publication*]
Car LR .... Carolina Law Repository (Reprint) [*North Carolina*] [*A publication*] (DLA)
Car L Rep... Carolina Law Repository [*North Carolina*] [*A publication*] (DLA)
Car L Repos ... Carolina Law Repository (Reprint) [*North Carolina*] [*A publication*] (DLA)
CArlS......... La Sierra College, Arlington, CA [*Library symbol*] [*Library of Congress*] (LCLS)
Carlsberg Res Commun ... Carlsberg Research Communications [*A publication*]
CARM .... Carmarthen [*Welsh depot code*]
CARM .... Carmarthenshire [*County in Wales*]
CARM .... Carmelite
Carm .... Carmina [*or Odes*] [*of Horace*] [*Classical studies*] (OCD)
Carm .... Carmina [*or Odes*] [*of Sidonius Apollinaris*] [*Classical studies*] (OCD)
Car & M..... Carrington and Marshman's English Nisi Prius Reports [*1840-42*] [*A publication*] (DLA)
CARM .... Computer-Aided Reliability Model (MCD)
Car & Mar ... Carrington and Marshman's English Nisi Prius Reports [*1840-42*] [*A publication*] (DLA)
Carmarthenshire Antiq ... Carmarthenshire Antiquary [*A publication*]
CARMARTHS ... Carmarthenshire [*County in Wales*] (ROG)
Carm Arv ... Carmen Arvale [*of Calpurnius Siculus*] [*Classical studies*] (OCD)
CARMC..... Cumulative Annual Regular Military Compensation (MCD)
Car Med J ... Caribbean Medical Journal [*A publication*]
Car & M (Eng) ... Carrington and Marshman's English Nisi Prius Reports [*1840-42*] [*A publication*] (DLA)
Carm Epigr ... Carmina Epigraphica [*of Calpurnius Siculus*] [*Classical studies*] (OCD)
Carm Epigr ... Carmina Latina Epigraphica [*A publication*] (OCD)
CARMOCS ... Continental Army and Major Overseas Commands Systems [*Later, ASMIS*]
Carmody-Wait NY Prac ... Carmody-Wait. Cyclopedia of New York Practice [*A publication*] (DLA)
Carm Pop ... Carmina Popularia [*of Calpurnius Siculus*] [*Classical studies*] (OCD)
CARMS..... Carmarthenshire [*County in Wales*]
CARMS..... Computer-Aided Records Management System [*Australia*]
Carm Saec ... Carmen Saeculare [*of Horace*] [*Classical studies*] (OCD)
Carm Sal.... Carmen Saliare [*of Calpurnius Siculus*] [*Classical studies*] (OCD)
CARMSIM ... Computer-Assisted Reliability and Maintainability Simulation [*Game*]
CarMV........ Carnation Mottle Virus
CARN .... Cairn. Archives of the Canadian Rockies Newsletter [*A publication*]
CARN .... Carnarvonshire [*County in Wales*]
CARN .... Carnation (DSUE)
CARN .... Carnets de l'Enfance [*A publication*]
CARN .... Carnival
CARN .... Carrington Laboratories, Inc. [*Dallas, TX*] [*NASDAQ symbol*] (NQ)
CARNA ..... CMV [*Cucumber Mosaic Virus*] Associated Ribonucleic Acid [*Biochemistry, genetics*]
CARNARVS ... Carnarvonshire [*County in Wales*] (ROG)
Carnegie Coll Physical Ed Research Papers ... Carnegie College of Physical Education (Leeds). Research Papers in Physical Education [*A publication*]
Carnegie Inst Technol Coal Res Lab Contri ... Carnegie Institute of Technology. Coal Research Laboratory. Contribution [*A publication*]
Carnegie Inst Washington Pap Geophys Lab ... Carnegie Institution of Washington. Papers from the Geophysical Laboratory [*A publication*]
Carnegie Inst Wash Pap Geophys Lab ... Carnegie Institution of Washington. Papers from the Geophysical Laboratory [*A publication*]
Carnegie Inst Wash Publ ... Carnegie Institution of Washington. Publication [*A publication*]

Carnegie Inst Wash Year Book ... Carnegie Institution of Washington. Year Book [*A publication*]
Carnegie Mag ... Carnegie Magazine [*A publication*]
Carnegie-Mellon Univ TRI Res Rep ... Carnegie-Mellon University, Pittsburgh. Transportation Research Institute. TRI Research Report [*A publication*]
Carnegie Mus An Mem ... Carnegie Museum of Natural History. Annals. Memoirs [*A publication*]
Carnegie Mus Annals ... Carnegie Museum of Natural History. Annals [*A publication*]
Carnegie Mus Nat Hist Annu Rep ... Carnegie Museum of Natural History. Annual Report [*A publication*]
Carnegie Mus Nat Hist Spec Publ ... Carnegie Museum of Natural History. Special Publication [*A publication*]
Carnegie Res Papers ... Carnegie Research Papers [*A publication*]
Carn Enfance ... Carnets de l'Enfance [*A publication*]
Carnes Merc ... Carnes y Mercados [*A publication*]
Carnet Mus ... Carnet Musical [*A publication*]
Carnets Enfance ... Carnets de l'Enfance [*A publication*]
Carnets Enfance Assignment Child ... Carnets de l'Enfance/Assignment Children [*A publication*]
Carnets Zool ... Carnets de Zoologie [*A publication*]
CARNI....... Carnival (DSUE)
Carniv Genet Newsl ... Carnivore Genetics Newsletter [*A publication*]
Carnivore Genet Newsl ... Carnivore Genetics Newsletter [*A publication*]
CarnM .... Carnegie Magazine [*A publication*]
CARNM .... Carnmarth [*England*]
Carn Mag... Carnegie Magazine [*A publication*]
CARNS...... Carnarvonshire [*County in Wales*] (ROG)
Carn SE ..... Carnegie Series in English [*A publication*]
Carn Ser Am Educ ... Carnegie Series in American Education [*A publication*]
Carnuntum Jb ... Carnuntum-Jahrbuch [*A publication*]
CARO .... Central Army Records Office [*Australia*]
CARO .... Centre d'Analyse et de Recherche Operationnelle [*Operational Research and Analysis Establishment*] [*Canadian Department of National Defense*]
CARO .... Combined Arms Research Office
Car & O...... English Railway and Canal Cases, by Carrow, Oliver, and Others [*1835-55*] [*A publication*] (DLA)
Car O & B .. English Railway and Canal Cases, by Carrow, Oliver, Beavan, and Others [*1835-55*] [*A publication*] (DLA)
CAROEJ .... Carolinea [*A publication*]
CAROL .... Computer-Assisted Research On-Line [*Information service or system*] (EISS)
Car & Ol .... English Railway and Canal Cases, by Carrow, Oliver, and Others [*1835-55*] [*A publication*] (DLA)
Carol Biol Readers ... Carolina Biology Readers [*A publication*]
Carol Camellias ... Carolina Camellias [*A publication*]
Carolina Lecture Ser ... Carolina Lecture Series [*A publication*]
Carolina LJ ... Carolina Law Journal [*A publication*] (DLA)
Carolina L Repos ... Carolina Law Repository [*North Carolina*] [*A publication*] (DLA)
Carolina Q ... Carolina Quarterly [*A publication*]
Carol J Pharm ... Carolina Journal of Pharmacy [*A publication*]
Carol Molin ... Carolus Molinaeus [*Deceased, 1566*] [*Authority cited in pre-1607 legal work*] (DSA)
Carol Plann ... Carolina Planning [*A publication*]
Carol Q ...... Carolina Quarterly [*A publication*]
Carol Tips ... Carolina Tips [*A publication*]
CAROM ..... Career Area Rotation Model [*Air Force*]
Caro Molin ... Carolus Molinaeus [*Deceased, 1566*] [*Authority cited in pre-1607 legal work*] (DSA)
CAROSEL ... Consumable-Anode, Radial, One-Side, Electrolytic [*Automotive engineering*]
Carousel Q ... Carousel Quarterly [*A publication*]
CARP......... Call Accounting Reconciliation Process [*Telecommunications*] (TEL)
CARP......... Canadian Association of Rehabilitation Personnel
CarP.......... Carolina Playbook [*A publication*]
CARP......... Carpentaria (ROG)
CARP......... Carpenter [*or Carpentry*]
Carp .... Carpenter's Reports [*52-53 California*] [*A publication*] (DLA)
CARP......... Carpet (MSA)
Carp .... Carpmael's Patent Cases [*1602-1842*] [*England*] [*A publication*] (DLA)
Car & P ...... Carrington and Payne's English Nisi Prius Reports [*1823-41*] [*A publication*] (DLA)
CarP.......... Carrollton Press, Inc., Washington, DC [*Library symbol*] [*Library of Congress*] (LCLS)
CARP......... Center for Advanced Research in Phenomenology (EA)
CARP......... Comprehensive Agrarian Reform Program [*Philippines*] (ECON)
CARP......... Comprehensive Areal Rainfall Program [*British*]
CARP......... Computed Air-Release Point
CARP......... Computer-Aided Release Point (MCD)
CARP......... Construction of Aircraft and Related Procurement
CARP......... Cooperative Agricultural Research Program [*Tennessee State University*] [*Research center*] (RCD)
CARP......... Cooperative Auto Research Program [*Department of Transportation*]

CARP......... Council of Australian Religious Parents
CARPA....... Carhart Photo Cl A [*NASDAQ symbol*] (NQ)
CARPA...... Committee Against Repression in the Pacific and Asia (EAIO)
CARPAC ... Carriers, Pacific Fleet [*Navy*]
CARPAS ... Comision Asesora Regional de Pesca para el Atlantico Sudoccidental [*Regional Fisheries Advisory Commission for the South-West Atlantic*] [*Inactive*] (EAIO)
Car & P (Eng) ... Carrington and Payne's English Nisi Prius Reports [*1823-41*] [*A publication*] (DLA)
Carpenter... Carpenter's Reports [*52-53 California*] [*A publication*] (DLA)
CARPG...... Committee for the Advancement of Role-Playing Games (EA)
CARP M-L ... Comite de Apoio de Reconstrucao do Partido Marxista-Leninista [*Support Committee for the Reconstruction of the Marxist-Leninist Party*] [*Portugal*] [*Political party*] (PPE)
Carp Pat Cas ... Carpmael's Patent Cases [*1602-1842*] [*England*] [*A publication*] (DLA)
Carp PC ..... Carpmael's Patent Cases [*1602-1842*] [*England*] [*A publication*] (DLA)
CAR Q .... Carolina Quarterly [*A publication*]
CARQUAL ... Carrier Qualification [*Navy*] (NG)
Car Quart... Caribbean Quarterly [*A publication*]
CARR .... Cahners Advertising Research Reports [*A publication*]
CAR R........ Cardiff Railway [*Wales*]
CARR .... Carriage (ROG)
CARR .... Carried (ADA)
CARR .... Carrier [*Telecommunications*] (AFM)
CARR .... [*The*] Carrollton Railroad [*AAR code*]
CARR .... Computer-Assisted Records Retrieval (ADA)
CARR .... Conference Administrative Regionale de Radiodiffusion a Ondes Hectometriques [*Regional Administrative FM Broadcasting Conference*] [*Canada*]
CARR .... Customer Acceptance Readiness Review [*Apollo*] [*NASA*]
Carrau........ Carrau's Edition of Summary Cases [*Bengal*] [*A publication*] (DLA)
CARRC...... Central Aerospace Rescue and Recovery Center [*Air Force*]
Carr Cas..... Carran's Summary Cases [*India*] [*A publication*] (DLA)
carref......... Carrefour [*Square*] [*In addresses*] [*French*] (CED)
Carr Ham & Al ... Carrow, Hamerton, and Allen's New Sessions Cases [*1844-51*] [*England*] [*A publication*] (DLA)
Carr & M ... Carrington and Marshman's English Nisi Prius Reports [*1840-42*] [*A publication*] (DLA)
Carrobbio... Carrobbio; Rivista di Studi Bolognesi [*A publication*]
Carroll Bus Bul ... Carroll Business Bulletin [*A publication*]
CARROTC ... Chief, Army Reserve and Reserve Officers Training Corps Affairs
CARRS...... Close-In Automatic Route Restoral System [*NORAD*]
CARRS...... Coherent Anti-Stokes Resonance Raman Scattering [*Spectrometry*]
CARS........ Cable Relay Service [*or Station*] [*Television transmission*]
CARS........ Canadian Arthritis and Rheumatism Society
CARS........ Canadian Association of Rhodes Scholars
CARS........ Canadian Association of Rural Studies
CARSC....... Careers
CARS........ Center for Applications of Remote Sensing [*Oklahoma State University*] [*Research center*] (RCD)
CARS........ Center for Atomic Radiation Studies (EA)
CARS........ Centralized Automotive Reporting System [*DARCOM*] (MCD)
CARS........ Certified Automotive Repairmen's Society [*Defunct*] (EA)
CARS........ Children's Affective Reading Scale
CARS........ Classroom Adjustment Rating Scale
CARS........ Climate and Remote Sensing Group [*University of California, San Diego*] [*Research center*] (RCD)
CARS........ Coherent Anti-Stokes Raman Spectroscopy
CARS........ Collateralized Automobile Receivable Security
CARS........ Collision Avoidance RADAR Simulator [*Maritime*]
CARS........ Combat Arms Regimental System [*Army*]
CARS........ Committee Against Revising Staggers [*Group opposed to changes in the Staggers Act*]
CARS........ Common Accounting Reporting System (ADA)
CARS........ Community Antenna Relay Service [*FCC*] [*Telecommunications*]
CARS........ Comprehensive Automotive Release System [*3M Corp.*] [*Computer software*]
CARS........ Computer-Aided Reference Service [*University of Arizona Library, University of Utah*] [*Information service or system*]
CARS........ Computer-Aided Routing System
CARS........ Computer-Assisted Reference Service [*Indiana University Libraries*] (OLDSS)
CARS........ Computer-Assisted Research Services [*Brigham Young University*] [*Information service or system*] (IID)
CARS........ Computer Audit Retrieval System [*Trade name for Sage Systems, Inc., computer software product*]
CARS........ Computerized Automotive Replacement Scheduling [*Bell System*]
CARS........ Computerized Automotive Reporting Service (BUR)
CARS........ Congress for Automotive Repair and Service
CARS........ Containment Atmosphere Recirculation System [*Nuclear energy*] (NRCH)

CARS........ Continuous Alarm Reporting Service [*Telecommunications*] (TEL)
CARS........ Country and Regional Specialist [*Navy*] (MCD)
CARSCT ... Canada. Agrometeorology Research and Service. Chemistry and Biology Research Institute. Research Branch Technical Bulletin [*A publication*]
Carsh .... Carshaltown's Court Rolls [*England*] [*A publication*] (DLA)
CARSO...... Carnegie Southern Observatory [*Later, Las Campanas Observatory*]
CARSRA ... Computer-Aided Redundant System Reliability Analysis (MCD)
CARSTRIKFOR ... Carrier Striking Force [*Tactical Air Command*] (NATG)
CARSTRIKGRUONE ... Carrier Striking Group One [*NATO*] (NATG)
CARSTRIKGRUTWO ... Carrier Striking Group Two [*NATO*] (NATG)
CARSUIT ... Carrier Suitability
Carswell's Prac ... Carswell's Practice Cases [*A publication*]
Carswell's Prac Cases ... Carswell's Practice Cases [*A publication*]
CART........ Caribbean Association of Rehabilitation Therapists (EAIO)
CART........ Carta [*Music*]
CART........ Cartage [*Shipping*]
Cart .... Cartel; Review of Monopoly Development and Consumer Protections [*A publication*]
Cart .... Carter's English Common Pleas Reports [*1664-76*] [*A publication*] (DLA)
Cart .... Carter's Reports [*1, 2 Indiana*] [*A publication*] (DLA)
Cart .... Carthew's English King's Bench Reports [*1686-1701*] [*A publication*] (DLA)
CART........ Cartography
CART........ Cartridge
Cart .... Cartwright's Cases on the British North America Act [*Canada*] [*A publication*] (DLA)
CART........ Central Automated Replenishment Technique (IEEE)
CART........ Central Automatic Reliability Tester (IEEE)
CART........ Centralized Automatic Recorder and Tester
CART........ Championship Auto Racing Teams (EA)
CART........ Classification and Regression Trees
CART........ Coalition Against Regressive Taxation (EA)
CART........ Complete Automatic Reliable Testing
CART........ Completion and Ready for Test (MCD)
CART........ Computerized Automatic Rating Technique (DEN)
CART........ Conditions of Assembly and Release Transfer
CART........ Construction and Road Transport (ADA)
CART........ Cytosine Arabinoside [*ara-C*], L-Asparaginase, Rubidomycin [*Daunorubicin*], Thioguanine [*Antineoplastic drug regimen*]
CARTA...... Computer-Aided Reorder Trap Analysis [*Bell Laboratories*]
Carta Geol Chile ... Carta Geologica de Chile [*A publication*]
Carta Geol Chile Inst Invest Geol ... Carta Geologica de Chile. Instituto de Investigaciones Geologicas [*A publication*]
CARTASKFOR ... Carrier Task Force [*Navy*]
CARTB...... Canadian Association of Radio and Television Broadcasters
Cart BNA... Cartwright's Constitutional Cases [*1868-96*] [*Canada*] [*A publication*] (DLA)
CArtC .... Cerritos Junior College, Artesia, CA [*Library symbol*] [*Library of Congress*] (LCLS)
Cart Cas (Can) ... Cartwright's Cases [*Canada*] [*A publication*] (DLA)
Carte .... Carte Segrete [*A publication*]
CARTE...... Contact and Repair Test Equipment (MCD)
Cartel .... Cartel. Review of Monopoly, Developments, and Consumer Protection [*London, England*] [*A publication*] (DLA)
Carter......... Carter's English Common Pleas Reports Tempore Orlando Bridgman [*A publication*] (DLA)
Carter......... Carter's Reports [*1, 2 Indiana*] [*A publication*] (DLA)
CARTH ..... Carthage
CARTH ..... Carthaginia (ROG)
Carth .... Carthew's English King's Bench Reports [*1686-1701*] [*A publication*] (DLA)
CARTH ..... Carthusian
Carth (Eng) ... Carthew's English King's Bench Reports [*1686-1701*] [*A publication*] (DLA)
Cartm .... Cartmell's Trade Mark Cases [*1876-92*] [*England*] [*A publication*] (DLA)
CARTOG .. Cartography (MUGU)
Cartogr...... Cartography [*A publication*] (APTA)
Cartogr J.... Cartographic Journal [*A publication*]
Cart Sax...... Cartularium Saxonicum [*A publication*] (ILCA)
Cartw CC ... Cartwright's Constitutional Cases [*1868-96*] [*Canada*] [*A publication*] (DLA)
Cartwr Cas ... Cartwright's Cases [*Canada*] [*A publication*] (DLA)
CARU .... Computer Architecture Research Unit [*York University*] [*Canada*] [*Research center*] (RCD)
Carus Math Monographs ... Carus Mathematical Monographs [*A publication*]
CARV .... Campaign Alert Against Racism and Violence [*Australia*]
CARV .... Carnivore. Carnivore Research Institute [*Petersburg, IL*] [*A publication*]
Carv Carr ... Carver's Treatise on the Law Relating to the Carriage of Goods by Sea [*1885-1957*] [*A publication*] (DLA)
Carver .... Carver's Treatise on the Law Relating to the Carriage of Goods by Sea [*1885-1957*] [*A publication*] (DLA)
CARW .... Carolina Western [*AAR code*]

Cary	Cary's English Chancery Reports [1537-1604] [A publication] (DLA)
CARYAB	Caryologia [A publication]
Cary Jur	Cary on Juries [A publication] (DLA)
Cary Lit	Cary's Commentary on Littleton's Tenures [A publication] (DLA)
Cary Part	Cary. Partnership [1827] [A publication] (ILCA)
CAS	Cabin Address System [Aviation] (AIA)
CAS	Cable Activity System [Telecommunications] (TEL)
CAS	Cable Assembly Set (KSC)
CAS	Calculated Air Speed (MSA)
CAS	Calibrated Air Speed
CAS	California Academy of Sciences
CAS	California Avocado Society (EA)
CAS	Call Accounting System [or Subsystem] [Telecommunications]
CAS	Cambrian Airways Ltd.
CAS	Canadian Anaesthetists Society
CAS	Canadian Association of Slavists [See also ACS]
CAS	Canadian Astronautical Society
CAS	Canadian Astronomical Society
CAS	Canadian Business Review [A publication]
CAS	Cardiac Adjustment Scale [Psychology]
CAS	Careers and Appointments Service [University of Sydney] [Australia]
CAS	Carotid Artery System [Medicine]
CAS	Casablanca [Morocco] [Airport symbol] (OAG)
CAS	Casamari [Italy] [Seismograph station code, US Geological Survey] [Closed] (SEIS)
CAS	Cascade (MSA)
CAS	Cascades, Inc. [Toronto Stock Exchange symbol]
CAS	Casein
Cas	Casey's Reports [25-36 Pennsylvania] [A publication] (DLA)
CAS	Cashier (ROG)
Cas	Casina [of Plautus] [Classical studies] (OCD)
Cas	Cassiopeia [Constellation]
CAS	Cast Aluminum Structure
CAS	Castle (MSA)
CAS	Castle [A. M.] & Co. [AMEX symbol] (SPSG)
CAS	Casual
CAS	Casualty (AFM)
CAS	Casualty Actuarial Society (EA)
CAS	Catgut Acoustical Society (EA)
CAS	Cell Analysis System [Microscopy]
CAS	Center for Alcohol Studies (EA)
CAS	Center for Austrian Studies (EA)
CAS	Center for Auto Safety (EA)
CAS	Central Alarm Station (IEEE)
CAS	Central Alarm System (NRCH)
CAS	Central Asiatic Studies [A publication]
CAS	Centralized Attendants Service [Bell System]
CAS	Centre for Agricultural Strategy [University of Reading] [British] (CB)
CAS	Change Analysis Section
CAS	Chemical Abstracts Service [American Chemical Society] [Columbus, OH] [Database producer]
CAS	Chemical Abstracts Service, Columbus, OH [OCLC symbol] (OCLC)
CAS	Chemical Abstracts Service. Report [A publication]
CAS	Chicago Academy of Science
C of AS	Chief of Air Staff [World War II]
CAS	Chief of Air Staff [World War II]
CAS	Child Anxiety Scale [Child development test] [Psychology]
CAS	Child Attitudes Survey [Education]
CAS	Children Against Smoking [British]
CAS	China Association of Standardization [INFOTERM]
CAS	Chinese Academy of Sciences
CAS	Christian Airmen's Fellowship International [Defunct] (EA)
CAS	Christman Air System [Washington, PA] [FAA designator] (FAAC)
CAS	Church Archivists Society [Australia]
CAS	Church Army Society (EA)
CAS	Circuits and Systems [IEEE] (MCD)
CAS	Citizens Alarm System (MCD)
CAS	Civil Affairs Section
CAS	Civil Air Surgeon [of FAA]
CAS	Cleaner Air System [Automotive engineering]
CAS	Close Air Support [Military]
CAS	Cluster Activation Systems Specialist [NASA]
CAS	Coarse Alignment Servo
CAS	Coast Artillery School [British]
CAS	Coded Armaments System
CAS	Codifying Act of Sederunt (DLA)
CAS	Coherent Acquisition System (MCD)
CAS	Collected Alongside Ship [Shipping]
CAS	Collision Avoidance System [Aviation]
CAS	Column-Address Strobe (IEEE)
CAS	Combined Activities System [Vietnam] [Air Force]
CAS	Combined Antenna System (CAAL)
CAS	Command Augmentation System
CAS	Commission on American Shipbuilding
CAS	Commission for Atmospheric Sciences [WMO] (MSC)
CAS	Committee on Atlantic Studies (EA)
CAS	Communicating Applications Specifications
CAS	Communication Analysis Section
CAS	Communications Antenna Sleeve
CAS	Community Adaptation Schedule [Psychology]
CAS	Compensating Air Supply
CAS	Complete Assembly for Strike
CAS	Compressed Air Spraying
CAS	Compressed Air System (NRCH)
CAS	Computer Accounting System [Boole & Babbage, Inc.]
CAS	Computer-Aided Scheduling
CAS	Computer Arts Society (EAIO)
CAS	Computer-Assisted Search (CAAL)
CAS	Computer Audit Specialist [IRS]
CAS	Confederation of Australia Sport
CAS	Conflict Alert System [Aviation]
CAS	Connecticutensis Academiae Socius [Fellow of the Connecticut Academy of Arts and Sciences]
CAS	Consortium for Atlantic Studies [Arizona State University] [Research center] (RCD)
CAS	Consumer Aid Series [National Highway Traffic Safety Administration]
CAS	Contemporary Art Society
CAS	Continental Air Services
CAS	Contract Accounting Standard
CAS	Contract Administration Services [DoD]
CAS	Control Actuation System
CAS	Control Adjustment Strap
CAS	Control Assembly Set (MCD)
CAS	Control Augmentation System
CAS	Control Automation System [IBM Corp.]
CAS	Controlled Airspace
CAS	Controlled American Source [Military] (CINC)
CAS	Controls Assembly Set
CAS	Cooperative Applications Satellite [France] [NASA]
CAS	Coordination of Allied Supplies [World War II]
CAS	Coordinator of Army Studies (AABC)
CAS	Cost Accounting Schedule (MCD)
CAS	Cost Accounting Standards [Accounting] (MCD)
CAS	Cost Accumulation System
CAS	Council of Adult Stutterers [Later, NCS] (EA)
CAS	Council for the Advancement of Standards for Student Services/ Development Programs (EA)
CAS	Council on Atmospheric Studies
CAS	Courier Air Service
CAS	Course Alignment Servo
CAS	Court of Arbitration of Sport [See also TAS] [Lausanne, Switzerland] (EAIO)
CAS	Creativity Attitude Survey [Educational test]
CAS	Crisis Action System (MCD)
CAS	Current Australian Serials [A publication] (APTA)
CAS	Current Awareness Service [Cryogenic literature bibliography] [Cryogenic Data Center]
CA 3S	California Appellate Reports, Third Series, Supplement [A publication] (DLA)
CAS3	Combined Arms and Services Staff School [Army] (RDA)
CASA	Canadian Advertising and Sales Association
CASA	Canadian Amateur Speed Skating Association
CASA	Canadian Amputee Sports Association
CASA	Canadian Asian Studies Association [See also ACEA]
CA SA	Capias ad Satisfaciendum [A writ of execution] [Latin] [Legal term] (ROG)
CASA	Car Audio Specialists Association (EA)
CasA	Cassiopeia A [Constellation]
CASA	Castillo de San Marcos National Monument
CASA	Centre Against Sexual Assault [Australia]
CASA	Chinese Art Society of America [Later, AS] (EA)
CASA	Civil Affairs Staging Area [World War II]
CASA	Close Air Support Aircraft [Military]
CASA	Colostomy Association of South Australia
CASA	Committee for Anglophone Social Action [Canada]
CASA	Computer-Aided Systems Analysis (MCD)
CASA	Computer-Associated Self-Assessment [British]
CASA	Computer and Automated Systems Association [Later, CASA/ SME]
CASA	Confederazione Autonomi Sindacati Artigiani [Italy] (EY)
CASA	Construcciones Aeronauticas SA [Spanish] (MCD)
CASA	Consumers Association of South Australia
CASA	Court Appointed Special Advocates [In association name National CASA Association]
CA(SA)	Member of the Accountants' Society (South Africa)
CasaA	Casa de las Americas [A publication]
CASAC	Clean Air Scientific Advisory Committee [Environmental Protection Agency] [Washington, DC]
CASAE	Cahier. Supplement aux Annales du Service des Antiquites de l'Egypte [Cairo] [A publication]
CASAE	Canadian Association for the Study of Adult Education [See also ACEEA]
CASAFA	Interunion Commission on the Application of Science to Agriculture, Forestry, and Aquaculture [ICSU] [Ottawa, ON] (EAIO)

Cas App ..... Cases of Appeal to the House of Lords [*A publication*] (DLA)
CASAR ...... Communications Acquisition Status and Assessment Report (MCD)
CASARA ... Canadian Search and Rescue Association
Cas Arg & Dec ... Cases Argued and Decreed in Chancery, English [*A publication*] (DLA)
CASAS ...... Canadian Association for South Asian Studies
CASAS ...... Commonwealth Association of Scientific Agricultural Societies [*Canada*]
CASA/SME ... Computer and Automated Systems Association of Society of Manufacturing Engineers (EA)
CASAW .... Canadian Association of Smelter and Allied Workers
CASB .... Cabarrus Savings Bank, Inc. [*NASDAQ symbol*] (NQ)
CASB .... Canadian Aviation Safety Board
CAS(B) ...... Civil Affairs Service (Burma) [*British*]
CASB .... Cost Accounting Standards Board [*US*] [*Terminated*]
CaSBIN ..... Canada Department of Indian Affairs and Northern Development, Battleford National Historic Park, Battleford, SK, Canada [*Library symbol*] [*Library of Congress*] (LCLS)
CASBL ...... Continuous Automated Single Base Line [*Automated control system*]
CASBO ...... Conference of American Small Business Organizations [*Absorbed by AFSB*] (EA)
Cas BR .... Cases Banco Regis Tempore William III [*12 Modern Reports*] [*A publication*] (DLA)
Cas BR Holt ... Cases and Resolutions (of Settlements; not Holt's King's Bench Reports) [*England*] [*A publication*] (DLA)
CASBS ...... Center for Advanced Study in the Behavioral Sciences (EA)
CASBY ...... Canadian Artists Selected by You [*Music award alternative to the Canadian Juno Award*] [*Established 1985*]
CASC .... Canadian Army Service Corps [*British military*] (DMA)
CASC .... Canadian Association for Studies in Cooperation [*See also ACEC*]
CASC .... Canadian Automobile Sports Club
CASC .... Capital Area Support Center [*Military*]
CASC .... Captive Air Spacecraft (MCD)
CASC .... Cascade Corp. [*NASDAQ symbol*] (NQ)
Cas in C ...... Cases in Chancery [*England*] [*A publication*] (DLA)
CASC .... Center for Adhesives, Sealants, and Coatings [*Case Western Reserve University*] [*Research center*] (RCD)
CASC .... Certified Alfalfa Seed Council (EA)
CASC .... Ceylon Army Service Corps [*British military*] (DMA)
CASC .... Corps Area Signal Center (MCD)
CASC .... Council for the Advancement of Small Colleges [*Later, CIC*] (EA)
Cas in C ...... Select Cases in Chancery [*England*] [*A publication*] (DLA)
CaSCA .... Archibald Library, Caronport, SK, Canada [*Library symbol*] [*Library of Congress*] (LCLS)
CASCADE ... Combined Airborne Surveillance and Control for Aerospace Defense
CASCAN ... Casualty Canceled [*Navy*]
CASCC ...... Canadian Agricultural Services Coordinating Committee
CASCC ...... Current Awareness System in Coordination Chemistry
Cas Ceske Spol Ent ... Casopis Ceske Spolecnosti Entomologicke [*A publication*]
Cas Cesk Lek ... Casopis Ceskenho Lekarstnitva [*A publication*]
Cas Cesk Spolecnosti Entomol ... Casopis Ceskoslovenske. Spolecnosti Entomologicke [*A publication*]
Cas Cesk Spol Entomol ... Casopis Ceskoslovenske Spolecnosti Entomologicke [*A publication*]
Cas Ch .... Cases in Chancery [*England*] [*A publication*] (DLA)
Cas in Ch ... Cases in Chancery [*England*] [*A publication*] (DLA)
Cas Ch .... Select Cases in Chancery [*1724-33*] [*England*] [*A publication*] (DLA)
Cas Ch 1 2 3 ... Cases in Chancery Tempore Car. II [*A publication*] (DLA)
Cas CL .... Cases in Crown Law [*England*] [*A publication*] (DLA)
CASCO ...... Canada Starch Company
CASCO ...... Canadian Australian Line
Cas Com ..... Arret de la Section Commerciale de la Cour de Cassation [*Decision of the Commercial Section of the Court of Appeal*] [*French*] (ILCA)
CASCOMP ... Comprehensive Airship Sizing and Performance Computer Program
CASCON ... Close Air Support Control [*Military*] (NVT)
CASCOR ... Casualty Corrected [*Navy*]
CASCOR ... Casualty Correction Report
CASCP ...... Caribbean Area Small Craft Project
Cas CR .... Cases Tempore William III [*12 Modern Reports*] [*A publication*] (DLA)
CaSCR .... Chinook Regional Library, Swift Current, SK, Canada [*Library symbol*] [*Library of Congress*] (LCLS)
CASCU ...... Commander, Aircraft Support Control Unit [*Navy*]
CASD .... Carrier Aircraft Service Detachment [*Marine Corps*]
CASD .... Carrier Aircraft Service Division [*Navy*]
CASD .... Computer-Aided Software Development [*Data processing*]
CASD .... Computer-Aided Structural Design (MCD)
CASD .... Computer-Aided System Design [*Programming language*] (BUR)
CASDAC ... Computer-Aided Ship Design and Construction

CASDAT ... Computer-Aided System for the Development of Aircrew Training (MCD)
CASDB ...... Central African States Development Bank [*Congo*]
CASDC ...... Computer-Aided Ship Design and Construction
CASDIV ... Carrier Aircraft Service Division [*Navy*]
CASDO ..... Computer Applications Support and Development Office [*Navy*]
CASDOS ... Computer-Assisted Detailing of Ships
CASDS ...... Centre for Advanced Study in the Developmental Sciences [*British*]
CASE .... Campaign for the Advancement of State Education [*British*]
CaSE .... Carnegie Series in English [*A publication*]
CASE .... CCH [*Commerce Clearing House*] Australian Case Digest Library [*Database*]
CASE .... Center for Advanced Study in Education [*City University of New York*] [*Research center*] (RCD)
CASE .... Citizens Association for Sound Energy (EA)
CASE .... Commission on Accreditation of Service Experiences [*Later, OECC*]
CASE .... Committee for the Absorption of Soviet Emigres
CASE .... Committee on Academic Science and Engineering [*Federal Council for Science and Technology*]
CASE .... Committee on the Atlantic Salmon Emergency
CASE .... Common Access Switching Equipment (AAG)
CASE .... Commonality and Standardization Effort (MCD)
CASE .... Communications, Analysis, Simulation, and Evaluation [*Army*] (MCD)
CASE .... Computer-Aided Software Engineering
CASE .... Computer-Aided System Engineering (MCD)
CASE .... Computer-Aided System Evaluation
CASE .... Computer-Assisted Sensory Examination
CASE .... Computer-Automated Structure Evaluator [*Database*]
CASE .... Computer-Automated Support Equipment
CASE .... Confederation for the Advancement of State Education
CASE .... Conference of Association Society Executives (EA)
CASE .... Consolidated Aerospace Supplier Evaluation (NRCH)
CASE .... Council of Administrators of Special Education (EA)
CASE .... Council for Advancement of Secondary Education [*Defunct*] (EA)
CASE .... Council for Advancement and Support of Education (EA)
CASE .... Council for Alternatives to Stereotyping in Entertainment (EA)
CASE .... Counselling Assistance to Small Enterprises [*Canada*]
CASE .... New York State Center for Advanced Technology in Computer Applications and Software Engineering [*Syracuse University*] [*Research center*] (RCD)
CASEA ...... Cancer Seminar [*A publication*]
CASEA ...... Center for the Advanced Study of Educational Administration
CASEAC ... Civilian Affairs Supports for Echelon above Corps [*Military*]
CASEAREA(ONR) ... Contract Administration Southeast Area (Office of Naval Research)
Case & Com ... Case and Comment [*A publication*]
CASEE ...... Carrier Aircraft Squadron Effectiveness Evaluation
CASEE ...... Comprehensive Aircraft Support Effectiveness Evaluation (MCD)
CASEP ...... Canadian Altitude Sensing Experiment Package (MCD)
Cas Eq .... Cases in Equity, Gilbert's Reports [*A publication*] (DLA)
Cas Eq .... Cases and Opinions in Law, Equity, and Conveyancing [*A publication*] (DLA)
Cas Eq Abr ... Cases in Equity Abridged [*1667-1744*] [*England*] [*A publication*] (DLA)
Cas Err .... Caines' New York Cases in Error [*A publication*] (DLA)
Cases in Ch ... Select Cases in Chancery [*England*] [*A publication*] (DLA)
Case Stud At Phys ... Case Studies in Atomic Physics [*A publication*]
Case Stud Health Adm ... Case Studies in Health Administration [*A publication*]
Ca Sett .... Cases of Settlements and Removals [*1710-42*] [*England*] [*A publication*] (DLA)
CASEUR ... Controller Administration Service, Europe [*Air Force*]
CASEVAC ... Casualty Evacuation
Case West J Int Law ... Case Western Reserve. Journal of International Law [*A publication*]
Case West Reserve ... Case Western Reserve University. Studies in Anthropology [*A publication*]
Case West Reserve L Rev ... Case Western Reserve. Law Review [*A publication*]
Case West Res J Int'l L ... Case Western Reserve. Journal of International Law [*A publication*]
Case West Res L Rev ... Case Western Reserve. Law Review [*A publication*]
Case W Res ... Case Western Reserve. Journal of International Law [*A publication*]
Case W Reserve Law R ... Case Western Reserve. Law Review [*A publication*]
Case W Reserve L Rev ... Case Western Reserve. Law Review [*A publication*]
Case W Res J Int L ... Case Western Reserve. Journal of International Law [*A publication*]
Case W Res L Rev ... Case Western Reserve. Law Review [*A publication*]
CASEX ...... Close Air Support Exercise [*Military*] (NVT)
CASEX ...... Combined Aircraft Submarine Exercise [*NATO*] (NATG)
Casey .... Casey's Reports [*25-36 Pennsylvania*] [*A publication*] (DLA)
CASF .... Calcium-Activated Sarcoplasmic Factor [*A proteolytic enzyme*]
CASF .... Canadian Amateur Sports Federation
CASF .... Composite Air Strike Force [*Air Force*]

CASF......... Crew Augmented Stability Factor [*Boating*]
Casflow C... Cashflow Classics [*A publication*]
Cas FT .... Cases Tempore Talbot, English Chancery (Forrester) [*A publication*] (DLA)
CaSGM...... College Mathieu, Gravelbourg, SK, Canada [*Library symbol*] [*Library of Congress*] (LCLS)
CASGP...... Close Air Support Gun Program [*Military*] (MCD)
CASGS ...... Close Air Support Gun System [*Military*] (MCD)
CASH .... Cache Technologies Corp. [*NASDAQ symbol*] (NQ)
CASH .... Cashel [*City in Ireland*] (ROG)
CASH .... Cashier
CASH .... Catalog of Available and Standard Hardware [*NASA*]
CASH .... Chronic Affliction Serum Hepatitis [*Medicine*]
CASH .... Citizens Alliance for Self-Help (EA)
CASH .... Coalition Against Sexist-Racist Hiring [*Student legal action organization*]
CASH .... Committee to Abolish Sport Hunting (EA)
CASH .... Committee on Administrative Services of Hospitals
CASH .... Correct Age Stocking and Height [*Inventory*] [*Forestry*]
CASHD ...... Costing and Assessing via Substantial History
CASHD ...... Coronary Arteriosclerotic Heart Disease
Cashflow .... Cashflow Magazine [*A publication*]
Cashflow M ... Cashflow Magazine [*A publication*]
Cas HL....... Cases in the House of Lords [*England*] [*A publication*] (DLA)
CaSHPA..... Prairie Agricultural Machinery Institute, Humboldt, SK, Canada [*Library symbol*] [*Library of Congress*] (LCLS)
CASHR...... Cashier
CASI.......... Canadian Aeronautics and Space Institute
CASI.......... Chili Appreciation Society International (EA)
CASI.......... Computer Application Services, Incorporated [*Los Alamitos, CA*] [*Telecommunications*] (TSSD)
CASI.......... Conditional Amount of Sample Information [*Statistics*]
CASI.......... Convenient Automotive Services Institute (EA)
CA/SI .... Office of Consumer Affairs and Special Impact [*Federal Energy Administration*]
CASIA ...... Chemical Abstracts Subject Index Alert [*Database*] [*A publication*]
CASIB .... Center for Advanced Studies in International Business
CASID .... Center for Advanced Study of International Development [*Michigan State University*] [*Research center*] (RCD)
CASIN .... Center for Applied Studies in International Negotiations (EAIO)
CASING.... Cross Linking by Activated Species of Inert Gases (MCD)
CASI Trans ... CASI [*Canadian Aeronautics and Space Institute*] Transactions [*A publication*]
CAsJ .... Central Asiatic Journal [*A publication*]
CASK........ Canadian Associated School of Karate-Doh
Cas KB....... Cases in King's Bench [*8 Modern Reports*] [*England*] [*A publication*] (DLA)
Cas KBTH ... Cases Tempore Hardwicke (W. Kelynge's English King's Bench Reports) [*A publication*] (DLA)
Cas KBT Hard ... Cases Tempore Hardwicke (W. Kelynge's English King's Bench Reports) [*A publication*] (DLA)
CASL......... Canadian Association of Special Libraries (EAIO)
CASL......... Committee of American Steamship Lines [*Later, AIMS*] (EA)
CASL......... Computer Architecture Specification Language (CSR)
CASL......... Crosstalk Application Script Language [*Programming language*] [*1987*] [*Data processing*]
CaSL.......... Lloydminster Public Library, Lloydminster, SK, Canada [*Library symbol*] [*Library of Congress*] (LCLS)
CASL-CI ... Confederation Africaine des Syndicats Libres de Cote d'Ivoire [*African Confederation of Free Trade Unions of the Ivory Coast*]
CASLE ...... Commonwealth Association of Surveying and Land Economy [*London, England*] (EAIO)
Cas Lek Cesk ... Casopis Lekaru Ceskych [*A publication*]
Cas L & Eq ... Cases in Law and Equity [*10 Modern Reports*] [*A publication*] (DLA)
Cas L Eq .... Cases in Law and Equity [*10 Modern Reports*] [*A publication*] (DLA)
Cas L & Eq ... Gilbert's Cases in Law and Equity [*A publication*] (DLA)
CASL-FO .. Confederation Africaine des Syndicats Libres - Force Ouvriere [*African Confederation of Free Trade Unions - Workers' Force*] [*Cameroon, Chad, Gabon*]
CASL-FO-RC ... Confederation Africaine des Syndicats Libres - Force Ouvriere - Republique Centrafricaine [*African Confederation of Free Trade Unions - Workers' Force - Central African Republic*]
CASL-HV ... Confederation Africaine des Syndicats Libres de la Haute Volta [*African Confederation of Free Trade Unions of the Upper Volta*]
CASLIM.... Consortium of Academic and Special Libraries in Montana [*Library network*]
CASLP...... Conference on Alternative State and Local Policies [*Later, CPA*] (EA)
CASLPP.... Conference on Alternative State and Local Public Policies [*Later, CPA*] (EA)
CASM........ Canadian Academy of Sport Medicine [*See also CCMS*]
CAS(M)..... Civil Affairs Service (Malaya) [*British*]
CASM........ Close Air Support Missile [*Military*] (MCD)
CASM........ Combined Arms Simulation Model (MCD)

CASM........ Cyclic Air Sampling Monitor
CASMA..... Confederation des Associations et Societes Medicales d'Afrique [*Confederation of African Medical Associations and Societies - CAMAS*] (EAIO)
CaSMcPCF ... Parks Canada, Fort Walsh National Historic Park, Maple Creek, SK, Canada [*Library symbol*] [*Library of Congress*] (LCLS)
CASME ..... Commonwealth Association of Science and Mathematics Educators [*British*]
Cas Mineral Geol ... Casopis pro Mineralogii a Geologii [*A publication*]
CaSMJ ...... Moose Jaw Public Library, Moose Jaw, SK, Canada [*Library symbol*] [*Library of Congress*] (LCLS)
CaSMJP.... Palliser Regional Library, Moose Jaw, SK, Canada [*Library symbol*] [*Library of Congress*] (LCLS)
CaSMJT.... Saskatchewan Technical Institute, Moose Jaw, SK, Canada [*Library symbol*] [*Library of Congress*] (LCLS)
Cas Morav Mus (Brne) ... Casopis Moravskeho Musea (Brne) [*A publication*]
Cas Morav Mus Vedy Prir ... Casopis Moravskeho Musea. Vedy Prirodni [*A publication*]
CASMS ..... Computer-Controlled Area Sterilization Multisensor System
CASMT ..... Central Association of Science and Mathematics Teachers [*Later, SSMA*]
CaSMuSP ... Saint Peter's Abbey and College, Muenster, SK, Canada [*Library symbol*] [*Library of Congress*] (LCLS)
CASNAH .. Casopis Slezskeho Muzea. Serie A. Vedy Prirodni [*A publication*]
Cas Nar Muz Oddil Priroddoved ... Casopis Narodniho Muzea. Oddil Priroddovedny [*A publication*]
Cas Nar Muz (Prague) ... Casopis Narodniho Muzea (Prague) [*A publication*]
Cas Nar Muz Praze Rada Prirodoved ... Casopis Narodniho Muzea v Praze. Rada Prirodovedna [*A publication*]
Cas Narod Muz ... Casopis Narodniho Muzea. Historicke Muzeum Rocnik [*Prague*] [*A publication*]
CaSNB....... Lakeland Library Region, North Battleford, SK, Canada [*Library symbol*] [*Library of Congress*] (LCLS)
CASNET ... Casual-Associative Network [*for medical applications*] [*Data processing*]
CASNP...... Canadian Alliance in Solidarity with the Native People (EA)
CASO .... Canada Southern Railway [*Penn Central*] [*AAR code*]
CASO .... Cancellation Addendum Sales Order (NASA)
CASO .... Cataloging and Standardization Office [*Air Force*] (AFIT)
CASO .... Civil Affairs Staff Officer [*British*]
CASOC....... Council of American Flag-Ship Operators (EA)
CASOC...... California Arabian Standard Oil Company
CASOFF.... Control and Surveillance of Friendly Forces (MCD)
Cas Op .... Burton. Cases and Opinions [*A publication*] (DLA)
Cas w Op.... Cases with Opinions by Eminent Counsel [*1700-75*] [*A publication*] (DLA)
Cas & Op ... Cases with Opinions by Eminent Counsel [*1700-75*] [*A publication*] (DLA)
Casopis Moravskeho Musea ... Casopis Moravskeho Musea. Vedy Spolcenske [*A publication*]
Casopis Pest Mat ... Ceskoslovenska Akademie Ved. Casopis pro Pestovani Matematiky [*A publication*]
C A Source Index ... Chemical Abstracts Service. Source Index Quarterly [*A publication*]
CASP......... Canadian Atlantic Storms Program [*Meteorology*]
CASP......... Capability Support Plan
Cas P......... Cases in Parliament [*A publication*] (DLA)
CASP......... CDS Application Support Programs [*NASA*] (NASA)
CASP......... Central American Society of Pharmacology (EAIO)
CASP......... Centre for the Analysis of Social Policy [*University of Bath*] [*British*] (CB)
CASP........ Civilian Acquired Skills Program [*Military*]
CASP........ Comprehensive Area Service Plan
CASP........ Computer-Assisted Search Planning (MCD)
CASP......... Country Analysis Strategy Paper [*Bureau of Inter-American Affairs*] [*Department of State*]
CASP........ Crew Activities Scheduling Program [*NASA*] (KSC)
CASP........ Cysteamine-S-Phosphate [*Biochemical analysis*]
CASPA ...... Canadian Spectroscopy [*A publication*]
CaSPAASS ... Anglican Church of Canada, Diocese of Saskatchewan, Synod Office, Prince Albert, SK, Canada [*Library symbol*] [*Library of Congress*] (LCLS)
CaSPAF..... Saskatchewan Department of Natural Resources, Forestry Branch, Prince Albert, SK, Canada [*Library symbol*] [*Library of Congress*] (LCLS)
CaSPAIN .. Canada Department of Indian and Northern Affairs, Prince Albert, SK, Canada [*Library symbol*] [*Library of Congress*] (LCLS)
CaSPAMI ... Canada Department of Manpower and Immigration, Prince Albert, SK, Canada [*Library symbol*] [*Library of Congress*] [*Obsolete*] (LCLS)
CaSPANC ... Wapiti Regional Library, Prince Albert, SK, Canada [*Library symbol*] [*Library of Congress*] (LCLS)
CASPAR ... Cambridge Analog Simulator for Predicting Atomic Reactions [*British*] (DIT)
Cas Parl ..... Cases in Parliament [*A publication*] (DLA)
CaSPAS..... Social Service Department, Prince Albert, SK, Canada [*Library symbol*] [*Library of Congress*] (LCLS)

CASPER....   Consolidated Army System for Processing Entitlements to Reservists

CASPER....   Contact Area Summary Position Estimate Report [*Military*] (NVT)

Casp For Med ...   Casper's Forensic Medicine [*A publication*] (DLA)

CASPMT ..   Casual Payment

Cas Pr ....   Cases of Practice, English King's Bench [*A publication*] (DLA)

CASPR ....   Command Automated System for Procurement [*Army*]

CASPR ......   Computer Advanced Software Products [*Database producer*] (IID)

Cas Prac CP ...   Cases of Practice, English Common Pleas [*1702-27*] [*A publication*] (DLA)

Cas Prac KB ...   Cases of Practice, English King's Bench [*A publication*] (DLA)

Cas Pra CP ...   Cases of Practice, English Common Pleas [*1702-27*] [*A publication*] (DLA)

Cas Pra KB ...   Cases of Practice, English King's Bench [*A publication*] (DLA)

Cas Pr CP ..   Cases of Practice, English Common Pleas [*Cooke's Reports*] [*A publication*] (DLA)

Cas Pr KB ...   Cases of Practice, English King's Bench [*A publication*] (DLA)

Cas Proc .....   Cassel. Procedure in the Court of Canada [*A publication*] (DLA)

Cas Prum Chem ...   Casopis pro Prumysl Chemicky [*A publication*]

CASQ ....   Children's Attributional Style Questionnaire

Cas R ....   Casey's Reports [*25-36 Pennsylvania*] [*A publication*] (DLA)

CASR ....   Center Surveillance RADAR (FAAC)

CAsR ....   Central Asian Review [*A publication*]

CASR ....   Chemical Activity Status Report [*Chemical Information Systems, Inc.*] [*Information service or system*] (CRD)

CASR ....   Controller of American Supplies and Repair [*Ministry of Aircraft Production*] [*British*] [*World War II*]

CaSR ....   Regina Public Library, Regina, SK, Canada [*Library symbol*] [*Library of Congress*] (LCLS)

CaSRA ....   Legislative Library of Saskatchewan, Office of the Archives Division, Regina, SK, Canada [*Library symbol*] [*Library of Congress*] (LCLS)

CaSRAC ....   Alcoholism Commission of Saskatchewan, Regina, SK, Canada [*Library symbol*] [*Library of Congress*] (LCLS)

CaSRAF ....   Archibald Foundation, Regina, SK, Canada [*Library symbol*] [*Library of Congress*] (LCLS)

CaSRAg .....   Saskatchewan Department of Agriculture, Regina, SK, Canada [*Library symbol*] [*Library of Congress*] (LCLS)

CaSRAgE ..   Canada Department of Agriculture, Economics Branch, Regina, SK, Canada [*Library symbol*] [*Library of Congress*] (LCLS)

CaSRAgR ..   Canada Department of Agriculture, Research Station, Regina, SK, Canada [*Library symbol*] [*Library of Congress*] (LCLS)

CASRAT ...   Colorado State University. Annual Report [*A publication*]

CaSRBMI ...   BMI Finance, Regina, SK, Canada [*Library symbol*] [*Library of Congress*] (LCLS)

CASRBU ...   Connecticut. Storrs Agricultural Experiment Station. Research Report [*A publication*]

CaSRCA ....   Saskatchewan Department of Consumer Affairs, Regina, SK, Canada [*Library symbol*] [*Library of Congress*] (LCLS)

CaSRCB ....   Canadian Bible College, Regina, SK, Canada [*Library symbol*] [*Library of Congress*] (LCLS)

CaSRCU ....   Credit Union Central, Regina, SK, Canada [*Library symbol*] [*Library of Congress*] (LCLS)

CaSRDA ....   Dunlop Art Gallery, Regina, SK, Canada [*Library symbol*] [*Library of Congress*] (LCLS)

CaSRDL ....   Saskatchewan Department of Labour, Regina, SK, Canada [*Library symbol*] [*Library of Congress*] (LCLS)

CaSRE ....   Saskatchewan Department of the Environment, Regina, SK, Canada [*Library symbol*] [*Library of Congress*] (LCLS)

CaSREC ....   Executive Council, Regina, SK, Canada [*Library symbol*] [*Library of Congress*] (LCLS)

CaSREd .....   Saskatchewan Department of Education, Regina, SK, Canada [*Library symbol*] [*Library of Congress*] (LCLS)

CaSREIW ...   Environment Canada, Inland Waters Directorate, Regina, SK, Canada [*Library symbol*] [*Library of Congress*] (LCLS)

CASREP ....   Casualty Report [*Navy*]

CASREPT ...   Casualty Report [*Navy*]

CaSRG ....   Regina General Hospital, Regina, SK, Canada [*Library symbol*] [*Library of Congress*] (LCLS)

CaSRGE ....   Saskatchewan Government Employees Association, Regina, SK, Canada [*Library symbol*] [*Library of Congress*] (LCLS)

CaSRGH ..   Pasqua Hospital, Regina, SK, Canada [*Library symbol*] [*Library of Congress*] (LCLS)

CaSRGI .....   Saskatchewan Government Insurance, Regina, SK, Canada [*Library symbol*] [*Library of Congress*] (LCLS)

CaSRHP ....   Saskatchewan Department of Highways and Transportation, Regina, SK, Canada [*Library symbol*] [*Library of Congress*] (LCLS)

CaSRHS ....   Plains Health Centre, Health Sciences Library, Regina, SK, Canada [*Library symbol*] [*Library of Congress*] (LCLS)

CaSRIA .....   Saskatchewan Intergovernmental Affairs, Regina, SK, Canada [*Library symbol*] [*Library of Congress*] (LCLS)

CaSRISP ...   Interprovincial Steel & Pipe Corp. Ltd., Regina, SK, Canada [*Library symbol*] [*Library of Congress*] (LCLS)

CaSRL ....   Legislative Library of Saskatchewan, Regina, SK, Canada [*Library symbol*] [*Library of Congress*] (LCLS)

CaSRLC .....   Luther College, Regina, SK, Canada [*Library symbol*] [*Library of Congress*] (LCLS)

CaSRLP .....   Leader-Post, Regina, SK, Canada [*Library symbol*] [*Library of Congress*] (LCLS)

CaSRMA ....   Saskatchewan Department of Municipal Affairs, Regina, SK, Canada [*Library symbol*] [*Library of Congress*] (LCLS)

CaSRMR ...   Saskatchewan Department of Mineral Resources, Regina, SK, Canada [*Library symbol*] [*Library of Congress*] (LCLS)

CASRN ......   Chemical Abstracts Service Registry Number

CaSRN ....   Saskatchewan Registered Nurses Association, Regina, SK, Canada [*Library symbol*] [*Library of Congress*] (LCLS)

CASRO ......   Combined Arms and Support Research Office [*Fort Leavenworth, KS*]

CASRO ......   Council of American Survey Research Organizations (EA)

CaSROH ...   Occupational Health Library, Regina, SK, Canada [*Library symbol*] [*Library of Congress*] (LCLS)

CASRP .....   Close Air Support Request Processing [*Military*]

CaSRP ....   Saskatchewan Provincial Library and Union Catalogue, Regina, SK, Canada [*Library symbol*] [*Library of Congress*] (LCLS)

CaSRPC .....   Saskatchewan Power Corp., Regina, SK, Canada [*Library symbol*] [*Library of Congress*] (LCLS)

CaSRPCRD ...   Saskatchewan Power Corp., Research and Development Center, Regina, SK, Canada [*Library symbol*] [*Library of Congress*] (LCLS)

CaSRPH ....   Saskatchewan Department of Health, Regina, SK, Canada [*Library symbol*] [*Library of Congress*] (LCLS)

CaSRPS .....   Saskatchewan Public Service Commission, Regina, SK, Canada [*Library symbol*] [*Library of Congress*] (LCLS)

CaSRRC ....   Royal Canadian Mounted Police Academy, Resource Centre, Regina, SK, Canada [*Library symbol*] [*Library of Congress*] (LCLS)

CaSRREE ...   Canada Department of Regional Economic Expansion, Prairie Farm Rehabilitation Administration, Regina, SK, Canada [*Library symbol*] [*Library of Congress*] (LCLS)

CaSRRI .....   Wascana Institute of Applied Arts and Sciences, Regina, SK, Canada [*Library symbol*] [*Library of Congress*] (LCLS)

CASRS ......   Countdown and Status Receiving Station [*or System*] [*NASA*] (KSC)

CaSRS ....   Saskoil, Regina, SK, Canada [*Library symbol*] [*Library of Congress*] (LCLS)

CaSRSA .....   Saskatchewan Arts Board, Regina, SK, Canada [*Library symbol*] [*Library of Congress*] (LCLS)

CaSRSG ....   Subsurface Geological Laboratory, Regina, SK, Canada [*Library symbol*] [*Library of Congress*] (LCLS)

CaSRSH ....   Wascana Hospital, Regina, SK, Canada [*Library symbol*] [*Library of Congress*] (LCLS)

CaSRSSPT ...   Saskatchewan Department of Social Services, Personnel and Training Library, Regina, SK, Canada [*Library symbol*] [*Library of Congress*] (LCLS)

CaSRU ....   University of Regina, Regina, SK, Canada [*Library symbol*] [*Library of Congress*] (LCLS)

CaSRUC ....   University of Saskatchewan, Regina Campus, Campion College, Regina, SK, Canada [*Library symbol*] [*Library of Congress*] (LCLS)

CaSRUFA ...   University of Regina, Faculty of Fine Arts, Regina, SK, Canada [*Library symbol*] [*Library of Congress*] (LCLS)

CaSRUG ....   University of Regina, Department of Geography, Regina, SK, Canada [*Library symbol*] [*Library of Congress*] (LCLS)

CaSRUNM ...   University of Regina, Norman MacKenzie Art Gallery, Regina, SK, Canada [*Library symbol*] [*Library of Congress*] (LCLS)

CaSRW ......   Saskatchewan Wheat Pool, Research Library, Regina, SK, Canada [*Library symbol*] [*Library of Congress*] (LCLS)

CaSRWP ..   Saskatchewan Department of Social Services, Regina, SK, Canada [*Library symbol*] [*Library of Congress*] (LCLS)

CaSRWR ...   Saskatchewan Water Resources Commission, Regina, SK, Canada [*Library symbol*] [*Library of Congress*] (LCLS)

Cass ....   Arret de la Cour de Cassation [*Decision of the Court of Appeal*] [*French*] (ILCA)

CASS ....   Canadian-American Slavic Studies [*A publication*]

CASS ....   Canadian Association for Scottish Studies [*See also ACEE*]

CASS ....   Canadian Association for the Social Studies

CASS ....   Canadian Association of Sports Sciences

CASS ....   Cargo Accounts Settlement System [*IATA*] (DS)

CASS ....   Carrier Aircraft Support Study [*Navy*] (NG)

CASS ....   CAS Medical Systems, Inc. [*Branford, CT*] [*NASDAQ symbol*] (NQ)

Cass ....   Cassatie [*Appeal to High Court of Justice*] [*Netherlands*] (ILCA)

CASS ....   Cassette (MSA)

Cass ....   Cassiopeia [*Constellation*]

Cass ....   Cassite (BJA)

CASS ....   Center for Applied Social Science [*Boston University*] [*Research center*] (RCD)

CASS ....   Center for Astrophysics and Space Sciences [*University of California, San Diego*] [*Research center*] (RCD)

CASS ....   Center for Atmospheric and Space Sciences [*Utah State University*] [*Research center*] (RCD)

CASS......... Center for Auditory and Speech Sciences [*Gallaudet University*] [*Research center*] (RCD)
CASS......... CITE Augmentation Support System (MCD)
CASS......... Closed Area Security System
CASS......... Cluster Activation Systems Specialist [*NASA*] (KSC)
CASS......... Coarse Alignment Subsystem
CASS......... Collection Analysis Support Subsystem (MCD)
CASS......... Command Active Sonobuoy System [*Navy*]
CASS......... Computer Applications in Shipping and Shipbuilding [*Elsevier Book Series*] [*A publication*]
CASS......... Computer-Automated Social Simulation
CASS......... Computer Automatic Scheduling System
CASS......... Computerized Algorithmic Satellite Scheduler [*NASA*]
CASS......... Consolidated Automated Support Station (MCD)
CASS......... Contract Administration Subservice
CASS......... Coronary Artery Surgery Study [*Medicine*]
Cass........... Corte di Cassazione [*Court of Appeal*] [*Italian*] (DLA)
CASS......... Country Assistance Strategy Statement [*Military*] (CINC)
Cass........... Cour de Cassation [*Court of Appeal*] [*French*] (DLA)
CASS......... Course Alignment Subsystem
CASS......... Crab Angle Sensing System (MCD)
CaSS......... Saskatoon Public Library, Saskatoon, SK, Canada [*Library symbol*] [*Library of Congress*] (LCLS)
C Ass......... Sentenza della Corte d'Assise [*Decision of the Assize Court*] [*Italian*] (ILCA)
Cass........... Sentenza della Corte Suprema di Cassazione [*Decision or Judgment of the Supreme Court of Appeals*] [*Italian*] (ILCA)
CASSA...... Canadian Amateur Speed Skating Association
CASSA...... Canadian Amateur Synchronized Swimming Association
Cassa........ [*Guillelmus*] Cassador [*Deceased, 1528*] [*Authority cited in pre-1607 legal work*] (DSA)
CASSA...... CONARC [*Continental Army Command*] Automated System Support Agency [*Obsolete*] (AABC)
CaSSA....... University of Saskatchewan, Office of the Saskatchewan Archives, Saskatoon, SK, Canada [*Library symbol*] [*Library of Congress*] (LCLS)
CaSSAA.... Saskatchewan Institute of Applied Arts, Saskatoon, SK, Canada [*Library symbol*] [*Library of Congress*] (LCLS)
CaSSAC..... Armak Chemicals, Saskatoon, SK, Canada [*Library symbol*] [*Library of Congress*] (LCLS)
Cassad........ [*Guillelmus*] Cassador [*Deceased, 1528*] [*Authority cited in pre-1607 legal work*] (DSA)
CaSSAgR... Canada Department of Agriculture, Research Station, Saskatoon, SK, Canada [*Library symbol*] [*Library of Congress*] (LCLS)
CASSANDRA ... Chromatogram Automatic Soaking, Scanning, and Digital Recording Apparatus
CASSARS ... Computer-Assisted Simulation of Supply and Related Systems
Cass Ass Plen ... Cour de Cassation, Assemblee Pleniere [*French*] (ILCA)
CASSAW .. Cassinia [*A publication*]
CaSSC .... Cooperative College of Canada, Saskatoon, SK, Canada [*Library symbol*] [*Library of Congress*] (LCLS)
CaSSCAg... Canada Department of Agriculture, Research Station, Swift Current, SK, Canada [*Library symbol*] [*Library of Congress*] (LCLS)
Cas SC (Cape GH) ... Cases in the Supreme Court, Cape Of Good Hope [*A publication*]
CASSCF .... Complete Active Space Self Consistent Field (MCD)
Cass Ch Reun ... Cour de Cassation, Chambres Reunies [*French*] (ILCA)
CaSSCI..... Saskatoon Collegiate Institute, Saskatoon, SK, Canada [*Library symbol*] [*Library of Congress*] (LCLS)
Cass Civ ..... Arret de la Chambre Civile de la Cour de Cassation [*Decision of the Court of Appeal, Civil Division*] [*French*] (ILCA)
Cass Civ ..... Sentenza della Sezione Civile della Corte di Cassazione [*Decision of the Court of Appeal, Civil Division*] [*Italian*] (ILCA)
Cass Civ Com ... Cour de Cassation, Commerciale [*French*] (ILCA)
Cass Civ 2e ... Cour de Cassation. Deuxieme Section Civile [*France*] [*A publication*]
Cass Civ 3e ... Cour de Cassation, Troisieme Section Civile [*French*] (ILCA)
Cass Cive 2e ... Cour de Cassation, Deuxieme Section Civile [*French*] (ILCA)
Cass Civ 1re ... Cour de Cassation, Premiere Section Civile [*French*] (ILCA)
Cass Civ Soc ... Cour de Cassation, Sociale [*French*] (ILCA)
CASSCM... Close Air Support Standoff Munition (MCD)
Cass Com ... Cour de Cassation, Commerciale [*French*] (ILCA)
Cass Crim .. Arret de la Chambre Criminelle de la Cour de Cassation [*Decision of the Court of Appeal, Criminal Division*] [*French*] (ILCA)
Cass Dig..... Cassel's Digest [*Canada*] [*A publication*] (DLA)
CASSE....... Close Air Support Survivability Enhancement System [*Military*] (MCD)
CaSSECW ... Canada Department of the Environment, Canadian Wildlife Service, Prairie Migratory Bird Research Centre, Saskatoon, SK, Canada [*Library symbol*] [*Library of Congress*] (LCLS)
CaSSEDA ... SED Systems Ltd., Aerospace Products Division, Saskatoon, SK, Canada [*Library symbol*] [*Library of Congress*] (LCLS)
Cas Self Def ... Horrigan and Thompson's Cases on Self-Defense [*A publication*] (DLA)

Cassella Riedel Arch Cerebrum 1 ... Cassella Riedel Archiv Cerebrum 1 [*A publication*]
CaSSESC .. College of Emmanuel and St. Chad, Saskatoon, SK, Canada [*Library symbol*] [*Library of Congress*] (LCLS)
Cas Sett...... Cases of Settlements and Removals [*1710-42*] [*England*] [*A publication*] (DLA)
CaSSGC .... Saskatoon Gallery and Conservatory, Saskatoon, SK, Canada [*Library symbol*] [*Library of Congress*] (LCLS)
CASSI........ Chemical Abstracts Service Source Index [*American Chemical Society*] [*Information service or system*]
CaSSIC...... Saskatchewan Indian Cultural College, Saskatoon, SK, Canada [*Library symbol*] [*Library of Congress*] (LCLS)
Cassier .... Cassier's Magazine [*A publication*]
Cassingle.... Cassette Single [*Trademark of IRS Records*]
Cassinia J Ornithol East Penn South NJ Del ... Cassinia. A Journal of Ornithology of Eastern Pennsylvania, Southern New Jersey, and Delaware [*A publication*]
Cassiod ...... Cassiodorus [*Sixth century AD*] [*Classical studies*] (OCD)
Cassiod Var ... Cassiodori Variarum [*A publication*] (DLA)
CASSIS ..... Classification and Search Support Information System [*Patent and Trademark Office*] [*Information service or system*]
CASSIS ..... Communication and Social Science Information Service [*Canadian research collection network*]
CASSIT ..... Casualty Situation Report
Cas Six Cir ... Cases on the Six Circuits [*1841-43*] [*Ireland*] [*A publication*] (DLA)
Cas Slezskeho Muz Ser A Sci Nat ... Casopis Slezskeho Muzea. Serie A. Scientiae Naturales [*A publication*]
Cas Slezskeho Muz Ser A Vedy Prir ... Casopis Slezskeho Muzea. Serie A. Vedy Prirodni [*A publication*]
Cas Slezskeho Muz Vedy Prir Acta Mus Silesiae Ser A Sci Nat ... Casopis Slezskeho Muzea. Vedy Prirodni (Acta Musei Silesiae. Series A. Scientiae Naturales) [*A publication*]
Cas Slezske Muz ... Casopis Slezskeho Muzea [*A publication*]
Cass LGB... Casson's Local Government Board Decisions [*1902-16*] [*England*] [*A publication*] (DLA)
Cas Sl Muz ... Casopis Slezskeho Muzea [*A publication*]
Cas SM ...... Cases of Settlement, King's Bench [*1713-15*] [*England*] [*A publication*] (DLA)
Cass M....... Cassier's Magazine [*A publication*]
C/ASSM.... Cents per Available Seat Statute Mile [*Aviation*]
CASSM ..... Context Addressed Segment Sequential Memory [*Data processing*]
CaSSM ...... Saint Thomas More College, Saskatoon, SK, Canada [*Library symbol*] [*Library of Congress*] (LCLS)
CaSSMD ... Saskatchewan Mining Development Corp., Saskatoon, SK, Canada [*Library symbol*] [*Library of Congress*] (LCLS)
Cassoe Nesl ... Cassoe Newsletter [*A publication*]
CASSP...... Central Ammunition Supply Status Point
CaSSP........ Prairie Regional Laboratory, National Research Council, Saskatoon, SK, Canada [*Library symbol*] [*Library of Congress*] (LCLS)
Cass Pen .... Sentenza della Sezione Penale della Corte di Cassazione [*Decision of the Court of Appeal, Criminal Division*] [*Italian*] (ILCA)
CaSSPP ..... POS Pilot Plant Corp., Saskatoon, SK, Canada [*Library symbol*] [*Library of Congress*] (LCLS)
Cass Prac ... Cassel's Practice Cases [*Canada*] [*A publication*] (DLA)
Cass Prac Cas ... Cassel's Practice Cases [*Canada*] [*A publication*] (DLA)
Cass Proc ... Cassel. Procedure in the Court of Canada [*A publication*] (DLA)
CaSSR .... Saskatchewan Research Council, Saskatoon, SK, Canada [*Library symbol*] [*Library of Congress*] (LCLS)
Cass Req .... Arret de la Chambre des Requetes de la Cour de Cassation [*Decision of the Court of Appeal, Chamber of Requests*] [*French*] (ILCA)
Cass Req .... Cour de Cassation. Requetes [*France*] [*A publication*]
CaSSSA..... Saint Andrew's College, Saskatoon, SK, Canada [*Library symbol*] [*Library of Congress*] (LCLS)
Cass SC...... Cassel's Supreme Court Decisions [*A publication*] (DLA)
CaSSSI ...... Kelsey Institute of Applied Arts and Sciences, Saskatoon, SK, Canada [*Library symbol*] [*Library of Congress*] (LCLS)
Cass Soc .... Arret de la Section Sociale de la Cour de Cassation [*Decision of the Social Security and Labor Division of the Court of Appeal*] [*French*] (ILCA)
Cass Sup C Prac ... Cassel's Supreme Court Practice [*2nd ed., by Masters*] [*A publication*] (DLA)
CaSST .... Saskatchewan Teachers' Federation, Saskatoon, SK, Canada [*Library symbol*] [*Library of Congress*] (LCLS)
CaSSU ...... University of Saskatchewan, Saskatoon, SK, Canada [*Library symbol*] [*Library of Congress*] (LCLS)
CaSSUEM ... Uranerz Exploration & Mining Ltd., Saskatoon, SK, Canada [*Library symbol*] [*Library of Congress*] (LCLS)
CaSSUGP ... University of Saskatchewan, Government Publications, Saskatoon, SK, Canada [*Library symbol*] [*Library of Congress*] (LCLS)
CaSSUJD ... University of Saskatchewan, the Right Honourable John G. Diefenbaker Centre, Saskatoon, SK, Canada [*Library symbol*] [*Library of Congress*] (LCLS)
CaSSUL..... University of Saskatchewan, Law Library, Saskatoon, SK, Canada [*Library symbol*] [*Library of Congress*] (LCLS)

CaSSULS.. Lutheran Seminary, University of Saskatchewan, Saskatoon, SK, Canada [Library symbol] [Library of Congress] (LCLS)

CaSSUM ... University of Saskatchewan, Medical Library, Saskatoon, SK, Canada [Library symbol] [Library of Congress] (LCLS)

CASSW ..... Canadian Association of Schools of Social Work [See also ACESS]

CaSSW ...... Wheatland Regional Library, Saskatoon, SK, Canada [Library symbol] [Library of Congress] (LCLS)

CaSSWD ... Western Development Museum, Saskatoon, SK, Canada [Library symbol] [Library of Congress] (LCLS)

CAST......... Canadian Air/Sea Transportable Combat Group

CAST......... Capillary Action Shaping Technique (MCD)

CAST......... Cardiac Arrhythmia Suppression Trial [National Heart, Lung, and Blood Institute]

CAST......... Cast Aluminum Structure Technology

CAST......... Castile [Spain]

CAST......... Castinet

CAST......... Castle

CAST......... Castrate

CAST......... Catalogue of Approved Scientific and Technical Intelligence Tasks (MCD)

CAST......... Center for Advanced Studies in Telecommunications [Ohio State University] (TSSD)

CAST......... Center for Aerospace Technology [Weber State College] [Research center] (RCD)

CAST......... Center for Application of Sciences and Technology

CAST......... Center for Assessment and Training [Peace Corps]

CAST......... Chemical Automated Search Terminal [Computer Corp. of America] [Information service or system] (IID)

CAST......... Clearinghouse Announcements in Science and Technology [of CFSTI] [Later, WGA]

CAST......... Coatings and Surfaces Technology [National Centre for Tribology] [British]

CAST......... Color Allergy Screen Test

CAST......... Common Access Security Terminal

CAST......... Computer-Aided Software Testing (MCD)

CAST......... Computer-Aided Structural Technology (MCD)

CAST......... Computer-Assisted Scanning Techniques

CAST......... Computerized Adaptive Screening Test (MCD)

CAST......... Computerized Automatic Systems Tester (MCD)

CAST......... Consortium for an Advanced Silent Transport (MCD)

CAST......... Coordinated ASW [Antisubmarine Warfare] Services and Training [Navy] (NVT)

CAST......... Coronary Artery Surgery Trial [Medicine]

CAST......... Council for Agricultural Science and Technology (EA)

CaSTA .... Campionati Sciistici della Truppe Alpini [Alpini Ski Championships] [Italian] (INF)

CASTA ...... Candida Albicans Skin Test Antigen [Immunology]

CASTA ...... Center for Advanced Study in Theatre Arts [City University of New York] [Research center] (RCD)

CASTA ...... Colorado State University. Agricultural Experiment Station. Technical Bulletin [A publication]

CASTAFRICA ... Conference on the Application of Science and Technology to the Development of Africa

Cas Tak & Adj ... Cases Taken and Adjudged [First Edition of Reports in Chancery] [England] [A publication] (DLA)

CASTALA ... Conference on the Application of Science and Technology to the Development of Latin America

CASTASIA ... Conference on the Application of Science and Technology to the Development of Asia

Cas Tax...... Canada Tax Cases, Annotated [A publication] (DLA)

CASTAZ ... Colorado State University. Experiment Station. Technical Bulletin [A publication]

Cas T Ch II ... Cases Tempore Charles II [A publication] (DLA)

Cast Com ... Castle's Law of Commerce in Time of War [A publication] (DLA)

CASTE ...... Collision Avoidance System Technical Evaluation [Aviation] (MCD)

Cas Temp F ... Cases Tempore Finch, English Chancery [1673-81] [23 English Reprint] [A publication] (DLA)

Cas Temp H ... Cases Tempore Hardwicke, English King's Bench [95 English Reprint] [1733-38] [A publication] (DLA)

Cas Temp Hardw ... Cases Tempore Hardwicke [A publication] (DLA)

Cas Temp Lee ... Cases Tempore Lee (English Ecclesiastical) [A publication] (DLA)

Cas Temp Talb ... Cases Tempore Talbot [A publication] (DLA)

Cast Eng .... Casting Engineering [A publication]

Cast Eng/Foundry World ... Casting Engineering/Foundry World [A publication]

Cas T F ...... Cases Tempore Finch, English Chancery [1673-81] [23 English Reprint] [A publication] (DLA)

Cas T Finch (Eng) ... Cases Tempore Finch, English Chancery [1673-81] [23 English Reprint] [A publication] (DLA)

CASTFOREM ... Combined Arms and Support Task Force Evaluation Model [Army] (RDA)

Cast Forg ... Casting and Forging [Japan] [A publication]

Cast Forg Steel ... Casting and Forging of Steel [Japan] [A publication]

Cas T Geo I ... Cases Tempore George I, English Chancery [8, 9 Modern Reports] [A publication] (DLA)

Cas T H...... Cases Tempore Hardwicke, English King's Bench (Ridgway, Lee, or Annaly) [1733-38] [A publication] (DLA)

Cas T H...... Cases Tempore Holt, English King's Bench [A publication] (DLA)

Cas T H...... West's Chancery Reports Tempore Hardwicke [A publication] (DLA)

Cas T Hard by Lee ... Cases Tempore Hardwicke, by Lee [England] [A publication] (DLA)

Cas T Hardw ... Cases Tempore Hardwicke, English King's Bench (Ridgway, Lee, or Annaly) [1733-38] [A publication] (DLA)

Cas T Hardw ... West's Chancery Reports Tempore Hardwicke [England] [A publication] (DLA)

Cas T Holt ... Cases Tempore Holt, English King's Bench [A publication] (DLA)

Cas T K...... Moseley's English Chancery Reports Tempore King [A publication] (DLA)

Cas T K...... Select Cases in Chancery Tempore King, Edited by Macnaghten [1724-33] [England] [A publication] (DLA)

Cas T King ... Moseley's English Chancery Reports Tempore King [A publication] (DLA)

Cas T King ... Select Cases in Chancery Tempore King, Edited by Macnaghten [1724-33] [England] [A publication] (DLA)

CASTLE.... Computer-Assisted System for Theater Level Engineering [Army] (AABC)

Cas T Lee... Phillimore's English Ecclesiastical Cases Tempore Lee [A publication] (DLA)

Cas T Mac ... Cases Tempore Macclesfield [10 Modern Reports] [1710-25] [England] [A publication] (DLA)

Cas T Maccl ... Cases Tempore Macclesfield [10 Modern Reports] [1710-25] [England] [A publication] (DLA)

CASTME .. Commonwealth Association of Science, Technology, and Mathematics Educators [London, England] (EAIO)

Cast Met Res J ... Cast Metals Research Journal [A publication]

Cas T Nap ... Drury's Irish Chancery Reports Tempore Napier [1858-59] [A publication] (DLA)

Cas T North ... Eden's English Chancery Reports Tempore Northington [28 English Reprint] [1757-66] [A publication] (DLA)

CASTOR ... Castoreum [Castor] [Pharmacy] (ROG)

CASTOR ... College Applicant Status Report [Honeywell, Inc.] [Data processing]

CASTOR ... Corps Airborne Stand-Off RADAR (MCD)

Cas T Plunk ... Lloyd and Goold's Irish Chancery Reports Tempore Plunkett [A publication] (DLA)

Cas T QA... Cases Tempore Queen Anne [11 Modern Reports] [1702-30] [England] [A publication] (DLA)

Cas T Q Anne ... Cases Tempore Queen Anne [11 Modern Reports] [1702-30] [England] [A publication] (DLA)

Cast Rat..... Castle on Rating [4th ed.] [1903] [A publication] (DLA)

CASTS....... Canal Safe Transit System

CASTS....... Computers for Advanced Space Transportation System (MCD)

CASTS....... Countdown and Status Transmission System [NASA] (KSC)

Cas T Sugd ... Cases Tempore Sugden, Irish Chancery [A publication] (DLA)

Cas T Tal ... Cases Tempore Talbot, English Chancery [1734-38] [A publication] (DLA)

Cas T Talb ... Cases Tempore Talbot [A publication] (DLA)

Cas T Wm III ... Cases Tempore William III [12 Modern Reports] [A publication] (DLA)

CASU .... Canadian Surveyor [A publication]

CASU .... Carrier Aircraft Service Unit [Navy]

CASU .... Combat Aircraft Service Unit [Navy] (MUGU)

CASUA....... Canadian Surveyor [A publication]

CASUD7 ... Cancer Surveys [A publication]

CASUM.... Civil Affairs Summary [Navy]

CA Supp..... California Appellate Reports, Supplement [A publication] (DLA)

CASURSS ... Comptes Rendus. Academie des Sciences de l'Union des Republiques Sovietiques Socialistes [A publication]

CaSVmPCG ... Parks Canada, Grasslands National Park, Val Marie, SK, Canada [Library symbol] [Library of Congress] (LCLS)

CASW........ Canadian Association of Social Workers [See also ACTS]

CASW........ Church Association for Seamen's Work [Later, SCI] (EA)

CASW........ Close Air Support Weapon [Military] (MCD)

CASW........ Council for the Advancement of Science Writing (EA)

CaSWaPCP ... Parks Canada, Prince Albert National Park, Waskesiu Lakes, SK, Canada [Library symbol] [Library of Congress] (LCLS)

Casw Cop ... Caswall. Copyholds [3rd ed.] [1841] [A publication] (DLA)

Cas Wm I... Bigelow's Cases, William I to Richard I [A publication] (DLA)

CaSWN ..... Notre Dame College, Wilcox, SK, Canada [Library symbol] [Library of Congress] (LCLS)

CASWO .... Confidential and Secret Weekly Orders [Naval Air Stations]

Cas W Res L Rev ... Case Western Reserve. Law Review [A publication]

CASWS ..... Close Air Support Weapon System [Military] (MCD)

CaSWSE.... Southeast Regional Library, Weyburn, SK, Canada [Library symbol] [Library of Congress] (LCLS)

CASX........ Cryderman Air Service [Air carrier designation symbol]

CASY .... Casey's General Stores, Inc. [Des Moines, IA] [NASDAQ symbol] (NQ)

CaSYP .... Parkland Regional Library, Yorkton, SK, Canada [Library symbol] [Library of Congress] (LCLS)

Cat.............. Bellum Catilinae [*or De Catilinae Coniuratione*] [*of Sallust*] [*Classical studies*]   (OCD)
CAT .... Cabin Air Temperature [*Aviation*]   (NG)
CAT .... Cahiers d'Analyse Textuelle. Les Belles Lettres [*Liege*] [*A publication*]
CAT .... California Achievement Test
CAT .... California Association of Tiger-Owners   (EA)
CAT .... Camper Alert Team [*for missile sites*] [*Air Force*]
CAT .... Canadian Anti-Acoustic Torpedo Gear [*World War II*]
CAT .... Canadian Army Trophy
CAT .... Canadian Automotive Trade [*A publication*]
CAT .... Carburetor Air Temperature [*Aviation*]
CAT .... Cartridge Assembly Test   (NG)
CAT .... Cases Temporary [*Legal term*] [*British*]
CAT .... Catafalque
cat............. Catalan [*MARC language code*] [*Library of Congress*]   (LCCP)
CAT .... Catalan [*Language, etc.*]
CAT .... Catalog   (KSC)
CAT .... Catalonian [*Language, etc.*]   (ROG)
Cat.............. Catalyst [*A publication*]
cat............. Catamaran   (ADA)
CAT .... Catania [*Italy*] [*Seismograph station code, US Geological Survey*]   (SEIS)
CAT .... Cataplasma [*Poultice*] [*Pharmacy*]
CAT .... Catapult   (NG)
Cat.............. Cataract [*Ophthalmology*]
CAT .... Catechism
Cat.............. Catechistes [*Paris*] [*A publication*]
CAT .... Catecholamine [*Biochemistry*]
Cat.............. Categoriae [*of Aristotle*] [*Classical studies*]   (OCD)
CAT .... Category   (AFM)
CAT .... Caterpillar, Inc. [*NYSE symbol*] [*Wall Street slang name: "Cat"*]   (SPSG)
CAT .... Cathedral Gold Corp. [*Toronto Stock Exchange symbol*]
CAT .... Catholic   (ADA)
CAT .... Catonsville Community College, Baltimore, MD [*OCLC symbol*]   (OCLC)
CAT .... Cattle
CAT .... Caught
CAT .... Celestial Atomic Trajectile
CAT .... Central American Tropical [*In CATHOUSES, a reference to temporary US Army barracks in Honduras, 1984*]
CAT .... Centralized Automatic Testing
CAT .... Centre for Alternative Technology [*British*]   (CB)
CAT .... Certificado de Abono Tributario [*Tax Credit Certificate*] [*Spanish*]
CAT .... Chatham, NJ [*Location identifier*] [*FAA*]   (FAAL)
CAT .... Chemical Addition Tank   (NRCH)
CAT .... Children's Apperception Test [*Psychology*]
CAT .... Chloramphenicol Acetyltransferase [*An enzyme*]
CAT .... Choline Acetyl Transferase [*Also, ChA, ChAc, ChAT*] [*An enzyme*]
CAT .... Civil Action Team   (AFM)
CAT .... Civil Affairs Team
CAT .... Civil Air Transport [*Free China's international airline*]
CAT .... Civilian Actress Technician [*Term for professional actresses who worked under Army Special Services Division in soldier shows*] [*World War II*]
CAT .... Civilian Air Transport
CAT .... Classical Analytic Technique
CAT .... Classical Anaphylatoxin [*Immunology*]
CAT .... Clear Air Temperature
CAT .... Clear Air Turbulence [*Aviation*]
CAT .... Clerical Aptitude Test
CAT .... Cockpit Automation Technology [*Air Force*]
CAT .... Cognitive Abilities Test [*Education*]
CAT .... Collective Art Technology
CAT .... College Ability Test
CAT .... College Advanced Technology [*British technical colleges*]
CAT .... Color Adjusted Transmission [*Optical coating to facilitate use of binoculars in low light*] [*Steiner-Optik of West Germany*]
CAT .... Combat Aircraft Technology
CAT .... Combat Artist Team
CAT .... Combined Acceptance Trials
CAT .... Combined Arms Team   (MCD)
CAT .... Command and Triangulation
CAT .... Commander, Amphibious Troops
CAT .... Commentaire de l'Ancien Testament [*Neuchatel*] [*A publication*]
CAT .... Committee Against Torture [*See also CCT*] [*Geneva, Switzerland*]   (EAIO)
CAT .... Committee of the Associated Trades [*A union*] [*British*]
CAT .... Communications Advisory Team   (OICC)
CAT .... Communications Assist Team   (NVT)
CAT .... Communications Authority of Thailand   (DS)
CAT .... Community Action Team [*Department of Labor*]
CAT .... Commuters Air Transport, Inc.
CAT .... Compile and Test   (BUR)
CAT .... Complementary Analysis Team [*NASA*]   (KSC)
CAT .... Compressed Air Tunnel [*British*]
CAT .... Computer Adaptive Testing

CAT .... Computer-Aided Teaching
CAT .... Computer-Aided Technology   (MCD)
CAT .... Computer-Aided Test [*Telecommunications*]   (TEL)
CAT .... Computer-Aided Transcription
CAT .... Computer-Aided Translation   (IEEE)
CAT .... Computer-Assisted Testing   (BUR)
CAT .... Computer-Assisted Tomography
CAT .... Computer of Average Transients [*Spectroscopy*]
CAT .... Computerized Axial Tomography [*Also, CAAT, CT*] [*Usually used in combination, as CATscan*] [*Roentgenography*]
CaT .... Computers and Translation [*A publication*]
CAT .... Concerned about Trident [*Ecology group*]
CAT .... Conditionally Accepted Tag   (NRCH)
CAT .... Configuration Analysis Tool   (MCD)
CAT .... Configuration and Traceability   (KSC)
CAT .... Consolidated Atomic Time
CAT .... Construction Appraisal Team   (NRCH)
CAT .... Contacts, Activities, Time [*Data processing*]
CAT .... Container Anchorage Terminal   (NVT)
CAT .... Contractor Acceptance Test   (AABC)
CAT .... Control Attenuator Timer   (KSC)
CAT .... Conventional Arms Transfers
CAT .... Converted Aerial Targets   (NG)
CAT .... Cooled-Anode Transmitting   (DEN)
CAT .... Copper Alloy Tubing
CAT .... Counter-Assault Tactical [*In television movie "C.A.T. Squad"*]
CAT .... Courseware Authoring Tools [*Stanford University computer software project*]
CAT .... Crack Arrest Temperature [*Nuclear energy*]   (NRCH)
CAT .... Credit Authorization Terminal
CAT .... Crisis Action Team   (MCD)
CAT .... Cumulative Abbreviated Trouble File [*Telecommunications*]   (TEL)
CAT .... Current Adjusting Type
CAT .... Customer Activated Terminal
CAT .... Cytosine Arabinoside [*ara-C*], Adriamycin, Thioguanine [*Antineoplastic drug regimen*]
Cat.............. In Catilinam [*of Cicero*] [*Classical studies*]   (OCD)
CATA .... Canadian Advanced Technology Association [*Ottawa, ON*] [*Telecommunications service*]
CATA .... Canadian Air Transportation Administration
CATA .... Canadian Athletic Therapists Association
CATA .... Capitol Transamerica Corp. [*Madison, WI*] [*NASDAQ symbol*]   (NQ)
CATA .... Catalog
Cata........... Catalyst [*A publication*]
CATA .... Catalytic [*Automotive engineering*]
CATA .... Center for Atmospheric Theory and Analysis [*Research center*]   (RCD)
CAT-A .... Children's Apperception Test [*Child development test*] [*Psychology*]
CATA .... Commonwealth Association of Tax Administrators [*London, England*]   (EAIO)
CATA .... Community Antenna Television Association   (EA)
CATA .... Computer-Assisted Test Assembly [*Microcomputer program*]
CA/TA...... Cortical Area/Total Area (Ratio)
CATA .... Cushion Air Tread Articulate [*Vehicle*] [*Army*]
CATAB...... Centre d'Analyse et de Traitement Automatique de la Bible [*Centre of Analysis and Automatic Treatment of the Bible*] [*Canada*]
CATAC...... Commandement Aerien Tactique [*French Tactical Air Command*]
CATaH .... Atascadero State Hospital, Atascadero, CA [*Library symbol*] [*Library of Congress*]   (LCLS)
CAT-A-KIT ... Catecholamines Radioenzymic Assay Kit [*Clinical chemistry*] [*Acronym is trademark*]
Catal........... Catalepton [*of Vergil*] [*Classical studies*]   (OCD)
CATAL...... Catalog   (ROG)
Catal Chem ... Catalysts in Chemistry [*A publication*]
Catal Environ Qual ... Catalyst for Environmental Quality [*A publication*]
Catal Lett... Catalysis Letters [*A publication*]
Catal Rev ... Catalysis Reviews [*A publication*]
Catal Rev Sci Eng ... Catalysis Reviews. Science and Engineering [*A publication*]
Catalyst Envir Qual ... Catalyst for Environmental Quality [*A publication*]
Cat Am Amphib Reptiles ... Catalogue of American Amphibians and Reptiles [*A publication*]
CATAPL ... Cataplasma [*Poultice*] [*Pharmacy*]   (ROG)
Catapl ... Cataplus [*of Lucian*] [*Classical studies*]   (OCD)
CATAPLAS ... Cataplasma [*Poultice*] [*Pharmacy*]   (ROG)
CATAPLSM ... Cataplasma [*Poultice*] [*Pharmacy*]
CATAS...... Center for Accelerator Technology and Applied Sciences [*University of Texas at Arlington*] [*Research center*]   (RCD)
CATAZINE ... Catalogue Magazine
CATB........ Canadian Air Transport Board
CATB........ Coast Artillery Training Battalion
CATB........ Combined Arms Training Board [*Military*]
Cat Br Off Publications ... Catalogue of British Official Publications [*A publication*]
CATC........ Canadian Air Transport Command   (MUGU)

CATC......... Canadian Association of Token Collectors
CATC......... Carrier Air Traffic Controller   (MCD)
CATC......... Civil Affairs Training Center [*World War II*]
CATC......... Coast Artillery Training Centre [*British military*]   (DMA)
CATC......... Combined Arms Training Center [*Army*]
CATC......... Commonwealth Air Transport Commission [*or Council*] [*Australia*]   (EAIO)
CATC......... Confederation Africaine des Travailleurs Croyants [*African Confederation of Believing Workers*]
CATC......... Confederation of All Type Canaries   (EA)
CATC......... Continental Oil, Atlantic Refining, Tidewater Oil, and Cities Service [*Group of companies joined together for mutual drilling ventures*]
CATCA...... Canadian Air Traffic Control Association
Cat Calcareous Nannofossils ... Catalogue of Calcareous Nannofossils. Edizioni Tecnoscienza [*Rome*] [*A publication*]
CATCC...... Carrier Air Traffic Control Center [*Navy*]
CATCC-DAIR ... Carrier Air Traffic Control Center - Direct Altitude Identity Readout [*Navy*]   (MCD)
CATCH ..... Citizens Against the Concorde Here
CATCH ..... Community Action to Control High Blood Pressure [*HEW*]
CATCH ..... Computer Analysis of Thermochemical Data Tables [*University of Sussex*] [*Sussex, England*]
CATCH ..... Countering Attack Helicopter   (MCD)
CATCH ..... Cumberland Activity Therapy Centre Human-Potential [*Australia*]
Ca T Ch 2... Cases Tempore Charles 2 [*A publication*]   (DLA)
Cat and Classif Q ... Cataloging and Classification Quarterly [*A publication*]
CATCO ..... Carrier Air Traffic Control Officer [*Navy*]
CATCO ..... Catalytic Construction Company
CATCO ..... CSM [*Command and Service Module*] and ATM [*Apollo Telescope Mount*] Communications Specialist [*NASA*]
CATCUSAF ... Commander, Amphibious Training Command, United States Atlantic Fleet
CATD .... Cold Air Turbine Drive   (MCD)
CATD .... Combined Arms and Tactics Department [*Military*]   (INF)
CATD .... Cooperative Association of Tractor Dealers   (EA)
CATDO ...... Chief Airways Technical District Office
CATDS ...... Commission of Accredited Truck Driving Schools   (EA)
CATE......... Centre for Advanced Technology Education [*Ryerson Polytechnical Institute*] [*Canada*] [*Research center*]   (RCD)
CATE......... Citizens for Alternatives to Trident and ELF [*Extremely Low Frequency System*]   (EA)
CATE......... Commercial, Automatic Test System [*Military*]
CATE......... Computer-Aided Test Equipment   (MSA)
CATE......... Computer-Controlled Automatic Test Equipment
CATE......... Current ARDC [*Air Research and Development Command*] Technical Efforts [*DoD program*]
CATED...... Centre d'Assistance Technique et de Documentation [*Center for Technical Assistance and Documentation*] [*Technical Institute for Building and Public Works*] [*Database producer*] [*Information service or system*]   (IID)
CATEG...... Category
CATEM..... Cost Analysis Technical Manual
Ca Temp F ... Cases Tempore Finch, English Chancery [*1673-81*] [*23 English Reprint*] [*A publication*]   (DLA)
Ca Temp H ... Cases Tempore Hardwicke, English King's Bench [*95 English Reprint*] [*1733-38*] [*A publication*]   (DLA)
Ca Temp Hard ... Cases Tempore Hardwicke, English King's Bench [*95 English Reprint*] [*1733-38*] [*A publication*]   (DLA)
Ca Temp Holt ... Cases Tempore Holt, English King's Bench [*A publication*]   (DLA)
Ca Temp K ... Cases in Chancery Tempore King, King's Bench [*1724-33*] [*England*] [*A publication*]   (DLA)
Ca Temp King ... Cases in Chancery Tempore King [*25 English Reprint*] [*1724-33*] [*A publication*]   (DLA)
Ca Temp Talb ... Cases in Chancery Tempore Talbot, King's Bench [*1734-38*] [*England*] [*A publication*]   (DLA)
Ca Temp Talbot ... Cases Tempore Talbot [*A publication*]   (DLA)
Cateques Latinoamer ... Catequesis Latinoamericana [*A publication*]
Cater .... Catering [*A publication*]
Cates .... Cates' Reports [*109-127 Tennessee*] [*A publication*]   (DLA)
CATES ...... Centralized Automatic Test System [*Navy*]   (MCD)
CATES ...... Computer-Aided Training Evaluation and Scheduling   (MCD)
CATF........ Central America Task Force   (EA)
CATF........ Chinese Air Task Force
CATF........ Combined Amphibious Task Force   (NVT)
CATF........ Commander, Amphibious Task Force   (NVT)
CATF........ Cost Analysis Task Force [*NASA*]   (KSC)
Ca T F .... Finch's English Chancery Reports [*1673-81*] [*A publication*]   (DLA)
Cat Faunae Austriae ... Catalogus Faunae Austriae [*A publication*]
Cat Faunae Pol ... Catalogus Faunae Poloniae [*A publication*]
CATFO...... Chief Airways Technical Field Office
Cat Fossilium Austriae ... Catalogus Fossilium Austriae [*A publication*]
CATGD4 ... Centro Internacional de Agricultura Tropical [*CIAT*]. Series GE [*A publication*]
Ca TH .... Cases Tempore Hardwicke, English King's Bench [*95 English Reprint*] [*1733-38*] [*A publication*]   (DLA)

Ca TH .... Cases Tempore Holt [*11 Modern Reports*] [*88 English Reprint*] [*1702-10*] [*A publication*]   (DLA)
CATH .... Cathartic [*Pharmacy*]
CATH .... Cathedral
CATH .... Catheter [*Medicine*]
CATH .... Cathode   (MSA)
CATH .... Catholic
Cath .... Catholicisme. Hier, Aujourd'hui, Demain [*Paris*] [*A publication*]
CAT-H....... Children's Apperception Test - Human Figures [*Child development test*] [*Psychology*]
CATH .... Common Anti-Tank Helicopter   (MCD)
CATHA4... Carinthia 2 [*A publication*]
Ca T Hard ... Cases Tempore Hardwicke, English King's Bench [*95 English Reprint*] [*1733-38*] [*A publication*]   (DLA)
CATHART ... Cathartica [*Cathartic*] [*Pharmacy*]   (ROG)
Cath Bibl Q ... Catholic Biblical Quarterly [*A publication*]
Cath Bib Q ... Catholic Biblical Quarterly [*A publication*]
Cath Charis ... Catholic Charismatic [*A publication*]
Cath Choirmaster ... Catholic Choirmaster [*A publication*]
Cath Doc ...... Catholic Documentation [*A publication*]   (APTA)
Cath Ed R .. Catholic Educational Review [*A publication*]
CathEp....... Catholic Epistles   (BJA)
Cathet Cardiovasc Diagn ... Catheterization and Cardiovascular Diagnosis [*A publication*]
Catheterization Cardiovasc Diagn ... Catheterization and Cardiovascular Diagnosis [*A publication*]
Cath His R ... Catholic Historical Review [*A publication*]
Cath Hist R ... Catholic Historical Review [*A publication*]
Cath Hist Rev ... Catholic Historical Review [*A publication*]
Cath Hosp ... Catholic Hospital [*A publication*]
CathHR ...... Catholic Historical Review [*A publication*]
CATHL ..... Cathedral
Cathl .... Catholic Periodical and Literature Index [*A publication*]
Cath Law... Catholic Lawyer [*A publication*]
Cath Lawyer ... Catholic Lawyer [*A publication*]
Cath Libr Wld ... Catholic Library World [*A publication*]
Cath Lib W ... Catholic Library World [*A publication*]
Cath Lib World ... Catholic Library World [*A publication*]
Cath M....... Catholic Mind [*A publication*]
CathMC..... Catholic Microfilm Center, Berkeley, CA [*Library symbol*] [*Library of Congress*] [*Obsolete*]   (LCLS)
CATHOL .. Catholic
Cathol Hist Rev ... Catholic Historical Review [*A publication*]
Cathol Hosp ... Catholic Hospital [*A publication*]
Catholic Doc ... Catholic Documentation [*A publication*]   (APTA)
Catholic Law ... Catholic Lawyer [*A publication*]
Catholic Trust ... Catholic Trustee [*A publication*]
Catholic UALR ... Catholic University of America. Law Review [*A publication*]
Catholic ULR ... Catholic University. Law Review [*A publication*]
Catholic U L Rev ... Catholic University. Law Review [*A publication*]
Catholic Univ L Rev ... Catholic University. Law Review [*A publication*]
Catholic W ... Catholic Weekly [*A publication*]   (APTA)
Catholic Wkly ... Catholic Weekly [*A publication*]
Cathol Nurse (Wallsend) ... Catholic Nurse (Wallsend) [*A publication*]
Cathol Period Index ... Catholic Periodical Index [*A publication*]
Cathol Period Lit Index ... Catholic Periodical and Literature Index [*A publication*]
Ca T Holt... Cases Tempore Holt [*11 Modern Reports*] [*88 English Reprint*] [*1702-10*] [*A publication*]   (DLA)
Cath-Presb ... Catholic-Presbyterian [*A publication*]
Cath Rec Soc Pub ... Catholic Record Society. Publications [*A publication*]
Cath Sch J ... Catholic School Journal [*A publication*]
Cath UALR ... Catholic University of America. Law Review [*A publication*]
Cath U Law ... Catholic University of America. Law Review [*A publication*]
Cath ULR .. Catholic University. Law Review [*A publication*]
Cath Ul Rev ... Catholic University. Law Review [*A publication*]
Cath Univ Am Biol Stud ... Catholic University of America. Biological Studies [*A publication*]
Cath Univ Bull ... Catholic University. Bulletin [*A publication*]
Cath Univ Law Rev ... Catholic University of America. Law Review [*A publication*]
CathW .... Catholic World [*A publication*]
Cath Work ... Catholic Worker [*A publication*]
CATI......... Colorado Advanced Technology Institute
CATI......... Computer-Aided Technical Illustration   (MCD)
CATI......... Computer-Assisted Telephone Interviewing
CATIA....... Computer-Graphics Aided Three-Dimensional Interactive Application System [*IBM Corp.*]
CATIC....... China National Aero-Technology Import & Export Corporation [*People's Republic of China*]   (IMH)
CATIE .... Centro Agronomico Tropical Investigacion y Ensenanza [*Tropical Agricultural Research and Training Center*] [*Turrialba, Costa Rica*]   (EAIO)
CATIES..... Combined Arms Training Integrated Evaluation System [*Military*]
CATIES..... Common Aperture Technique for Imaging Electro-Optical Sensors   (MCD)
Cat Index ... Catalogue and Index. Library Association Cataloguing and Indexing Group [*A publication*]

Cat Invertebres Suisse Mus Hist Nat Geneve ... Catalogue des Invertebres de la Suisse. Museum d'Histoire Naturelle de Geneve [*A publication*]
CATIS .... Computer-Aided Tactical Information System   (IEEE)
CATIS .... Computer-Assisted Tactical Intelligence System   (MCD)
CATITB .... Civil Air Transport Industry Training Board   (MCD)
CATIWAR ... Combat Attrition and Intensity of War   (MCD)
Ca TK .... Cases Tempore King, Chancery [*A publication*]   (DLA)
CATK .... Counterattack   (AABC)
Ca T King ... Cases Tempore King, Chancery [*A publication*]   (DLA)
CATL .... Canadian Association of Toy Libraries and Parent Resource Centers   (EAIO)
CATL .... Cantel Inds., Inc. [*NASDAQ symbol*]   (NQ)
CATLA .... Catholic Library Association
CATLAS ..... Centralized Automatic Trouble-Locating and Analysis System [*AT & T*]   (TEL)
Ca T Lee .... Cases Tempore Lee [*1752-58*] [*A publication*]   (DLA)
CATLG ..... Catalog   (BUR)
CATLHD .. Cattle Hide
CATLINE ... Catalog On-Line [*National Library of Medicine*] [*Bibliographic database*]
Cat Lit Pap ... Catalogue of the Literary Papyri in the British Museum [*A publication*]   (OCD)
CATM .... Consolidated Air Tour Manual [*Air travel term*]
Ca T Mac ... Cases in Law and Equity [*10 Modern Reports*] [*A publication*]   (DLA)
Cat Mai ...... Cato Maior [*of Plutarch*] [*Classical studies*]   (OCD)
CATMAT ... Computer-Assisted Terrain Mobility Analysis Techniques   (MCD)
CATMDV ... Catamaran Mine Disposal System   (MCD)
Cat Min ...... Cato Minor [*of Plutarch*] [*Classical studies*]   (OCD)
CATMN ..... Consolidated Air Target Material Notices [*NOO*]
Ca T N .... Eden's English Chancery Reports Tempore Northington [*28 English Reprint*] [*1757-66*] [*A publication*]   (DLA)
Ca T Nap ... Drury's Irish Chancery Reports Tempore Napier [*1858-59*] [*A publication*]   (DLA)
CATNI .... Catchword and Trade Name Index [*A publication*]
CATNIP ..... Computer-Assisted Technique for Numerical Indexing Purposes
Ca T North ... Eden's English Chancery Reports Tempore Northington [*28 English Reprint*] [*1757-66*] [*A publication*]   (DLA)
CATNYP ... Catalog of the New York Public Library
CATO .... Canadian Association for the Treatment of Offenders
CATO .... Catapult-Assisted Takeoff
CATO .... Catoctin Mountain Park [*National Park Service designation*]
CATO .... Civil Air Traffic Operations   (AIA)
CATOC .... Compiler for Automatic Teaching Operation   (IEEE)
CATOC .... Carrier Air Traffic Control
CaTOHOR ... Ontario Hydro, Central Records, Toronto, ON, Canada [*Library symbol*] [*Library of Congress*]   (LCLS)
Cato J .... Cato Journal [*A publication*]
CATOR ..... Chemical Abuse Addiction Treatment Outcome Registry
CATOR ..... Combined Air Transport Operations Room [*Allied office, World War II*]
CAT-OX .... Catalytic Oxidation
CATP .... Classified Area Term Pass   (AAG)
CATP .... Computer-Aided Typesetting Process
CATPCE ..... Comite d'Action des Transports Publics des Communautes Europeennes [*Action Committee of Public Transport of the European Communities - ACPTEC*]   (EAIO)
Ca T Plunk ... Cases in Chancery Tempore Plunkett [*1834-39*] [*Ireland*] [*A publication*]   (DLA)
Ca T QA ..... Cases Tempore Holt [*11 Modern Reports*] [*88 English Reprint*] [*1702-10*] [*A publication*]   (DLA)
CATR .... Central Air Transport
CATRA ..... Combined Aircraft Transfer and Release Assembly   (MCD)
CATRA ...... Cutlery and Allied Trades Research Association [*British*]   (IRUK)
CATRADA ... Combined Arms Training Developments Activity [*or Agency*] [*Army*]   (RDA)
CATRADAR ... Combined Acquisition and Tracking RADAR [*NASA*]   (MCD)
CATRALA ... Car and Truck Renting and Leasing Association   (EA)
CATRAY ... Canning Trade [*A publication*]
CATRB ...... Calcified Tissue Research [*Later, Calcified Tissue International*] [*A publication*]
CATRE ...... Catholic Association of Tertiary Religious Education [*Australia*]
CATS .... Care about the Strays   (EA)
CATS .... Catalog Access System [*Project for automated library systems*]
CATS .... Center for Applied Thermodynamic Studies [*University of Idaho*] [*Research center*]   (RCD)
CATS .... Centralized Automatic Test System [*Navy*]   (MCD)
CATS .... Certificate of Accrual on Treasury Securities [*Salomon Brothers*] [*Finance*]
CATS .... Chicago Area Transportation Study
CAT-S .... Children's Apperception Test - Supplement [*Child development test*] [*Psychology*]
CATS .... Citizens Against Tobacco Smoke   (EA)
CATS .... Civil Affairs Training School [*Navy*]
CATS .... Coded-Access Teleconferencing System [*Telecommunications*]
CATS .... Coherent Acoustic Torpedo System   (MCD)

CATS .... Communications and Tracking System [*or Subsystem*]
CATS .... Comprehensive Analytical Test System
CATS .... Compute Air-Trans Systems, Inc.
CATS .... Computer-Accessed [*or-Aided*] Telemetry System
CATS .... Computer-Aided Teaching System   (IEEE)
CATS .... Computer-Aided Troubleshooting
CATS .... Computer-Assisted Test Shop
CATS .... Computer-Assisted Trading System [*American Meat Exchange, Inc.*] [*Information service or system*]
CATS .... Computer-Assisted Training System [*IRS*]
CATS .... Computer-Automated Test System [*AT & T*]
CATS .... Computer-Automated Transit Systems
CATS .... Conventional and Alternative Transportation Systems Laboratory [*University of Florida*] [*Research center*]   (RCD)
CATS .... Cost Assignment to Telecommunication Services [*Telecommunications*]
CATS .... Courier and Transport Service Ltd. [*British*]
CATscan .... Computerized Axial Tomography Scanner [*Roentgenography*]
CATSS .... Catalog Support System [*UTLAS International Canada*] [*Information service or system*]
CATSS .... Communication Analysis Tool for Space Station   (MCD)
Ca T Sugd .. Drury's Irish Chancery Reports Tempore Sugden [*A publication*]   (DLA)
CATT .... Card Agglutination Trypanosomiasis Test [*Clinical chemistry*]
CATT .... Center for Advanced Technology in Telecommunications [*Polytechnic Institute of New York*] [*Brooklyn*] [*Telecommunications service*]   (TSSD)
CATT .... Centralized Automatic Toll Ticketing [*Telecommunications*]   (TEL)
CATT .... Colorado Advanced Technology Institute
CATT .... Consumers' Association of Trinidad and Tobago
CATT .... Controlled Avalanche Transit Time [*Electronics*]
CATT .... Conveyorized Automatic Tube Tester [*Data processing*]
CATT .... Cooled-Anode Transmitting Tube
c att .... Coupon Attache [*Coupon Attached*] [*French*]
Ca T Talb ... Cases Tempore Talbot, English Chancery [*1734-38*] [*A publication*]   (DLA)
Cattlemen Beef Mag ... Cattlemen. The Beef Magazine [*A publication*]
Cat Trans C ... Catalogus Translationum et Commentariorum/Medieval and Renaissance Latin Translations and Commentaries [*A publication*]
CATTS ...... Combined Arms Tactical Training Simulator [*Army*]   (MCD)
CATTW ..... Canadian Association of Teachers of Technical Writing
C Atty .... [*The*] Complete Attorney [*A publication*]   (DLA)
Cat Type Invertebr Fossils Geol Surv Can ... Catalogue of Type Invertebrate Fossils. Geological Survey of Canada [*A publication*]
CATU .... Ceramic and Allied Trade Union [*British*]   (DCTA)
CATU .... Combat Aircrew Training Unit [*Navy*]
CATU .... Confederation of Arab Trade Unions
CATUA ...... Chimica Acta Turcica [*A publication*]
Catull .... Catullus [*First century BC*] [*Classical studies*]   (OCD)
CATV .... Cabin Air Temperature Valve [*Aviation*]
CATV .... Cable Television [*Later, CTV*]
CATV .... Cable TV Industries [*Los Angeles, CA*] [*NASDAQ symbol*]   (NQ)
CATV .... Community Antenna Television [*Later, CTV*]
CATVA ..... Computer-Assisted Total Value Assessment [*Army*]   (MCD)
Ca T Wm 3 ... Cases Tempore William 3 [*12 Modern Reports*] [*A publication*]   (DLA)
CA TX .... Civil Appeals, Texas [*A publication*]   (DLA)
CATX .... Climb and Cross [*Aviation*]   (FAAC)
cau .... California [*MARC country of publication code*] [*Library of Congress*]   (LCCP)
CA U .... California Unreported Cases [*1855-1910*] [*A publication*]   (DLA)
CAU .... Capital University, Columbus, OH [*OCLC symbol*]   (OCLC)
CAU .... Cassia Petroleum [*Vancouver Stock Exchange symbol*]
CAU .... Caucasian   (AFM)
cau .... Caucasian [*MARC language code*] [*Library of Congress*]   (LCCP)
CAU .... Civil Affairs Unit [*British*]
CAU .... Coarse Alignment Unit
CAU .... Command Acquisition Unit   (NASA)
CAU .... Command Activation Unit   (MCD)
CAU .... Command Arithmetic Unit
CAU .... Congress of American Unions
CAU .... Construccion Arquitectura Urbanismo [*A publication*]
CAU .... Converter Amplifier Unit   (MCD)
CAU .... Counter Accelerometer Unit   (MCD)
CAU .... Course Alignment Unit
CAU .... Cryptoancillary Unit   (AABC)
CAU .... Customer Acquisition Unit   (NASA)
CAUBO ..... Canadian Association of University Business Officers
CAUC .... Calculated Area under the Curve [*Statistics*]
CAUCE ...... Canadian Association for University Continuing Education
CAuD .... DeWitt State Hospital, Auburn, CA [*Library symbol*] [*Library of Congress*]   (LCLS)
CAUEOI ..... Caucasian Except as Otherwise Indicated [*Army*]
CAUFN .... Caution Advised until Further Notice [*Aviation*]   (FAAC)
CAUIS .... Computer-Automated Ultrasonic Inspecting Systems   (MCD)

CAULI....... Cauliflower (DSUE)
CAUML .... Computers and Automation Universal Mailing List (IEEE)
CAuN........ Native Sons of the Golden West, Auburn Parlor, Auburn, CA [*Library symbol*] [*Library of Congress*] (LCLS)
CAuP .... Auburn-Placer County Library, Auburn, CA [*Library symbol*] [*Library of Congress*] (LCLS)
CAUPR...... Center for Architecture and Urban Planning Research [*University of Wisconsin - Milwaukee*] [*Research center*] (RCD)
CAURA ..... Canadian Association of University Research Administrators [*See also ACARU*]
CAUS .... Causation
Caus .... Causative (BJA)
CAUS .... Citizens Against UFO [*Unidentified Flying Object*] Secrecy (EA)
CAUS .... Color Association of the United States (EA)
CAUS .... Computer-Automated Ultrasonic System (MCD)
CAUSE...... College and University Systems Exchange [*Acronym is now used as name of association*]
CAUSE...... Comprehensive Assistance to Undergraduate Science Education [*National Science Foundation*]
CAUSE...... Computer-Assisted Utility System Evaluation (MCD)
CAUSE...... Counselor Advisor University Summer Education [*Department of Labor program*]
CAUSM..... Canadian Association of University Schools of Music
CAUSN ..... Canadian Association of University Schools of Nursing [*See also ACEUN*]
Caus Pl...... De Causis Plantarum [*of Theophrastus*] [*Classical studies*] (OCD)
CAUSPS.... Canadian Association of University Student Personnel Services
CAUT .... Canadian Association of University Teachers
CAUT .... Caution (AFM)
CAUT .... Computer Automation, Inc. [*NASDAQ symbol*] (NQ)
CAUTA ..... Canadian Automotive Trade [*A publication*]
CAUT ACPU Bul ... Canadian Association of University Teachers/ Association Canadienne des Professeurs d'Universite. Bulletin [*A publication*]
CAUTG ..... Canadian Association of University Teachers of German
CAUTION ... Citizens Against Unneccessary Tax Increases and Other Nonsense [*St. Louis organization*]
CAUTRA... Coordinateur Automatique de Traffic
CAV .... Calm Air International Ltd. [*Lynn Lake, MB*] [*FAA designator*] (FAAC)
CAV .... Canine Adenovirus [*Veterinary medicine*]
CAV .... Capital University, Law Library, Columbus, OH [*OCLC symbol*] (OCLC)
CAV .... Cavalier [*Knight title*]
CAV .... Cavalry
CAV .... Cavan [*County in Ireland*] (ROG)
CAV .... Caveat [*Let Him Beware*] [*Latin*] [*A judicial writ*] [*Legal term*]
CAV .... Cavern (ROG)
CAV .... Cavitation
CAV .... Cavity (MSA)
CAV .... Chambre de Commerce et d'Industrie d'Anvers. Bulletin [*A publication*]
CAV .... Clarion, IA [*Location identifier*] [*FAA*] (FAAL)
CAV .... Composite Analog Video
CAV .... Congenital Absence of Vagina [*Medicine*]
CAV .... Congenital Adrenal Virilism [*Medicine*]
CAV .... Constant Angular Velocity [*Videodisk format*]
CAV .... Construction Assistance Vehicle [*Navy*] (MCD)
CAV .... Continuous Airworthiness Visit
CAV .... Coordinate, Anticipate, and Verify (MCD)
CAV .... Credit Account Voucher (DCTA)
CAV .... Crotalus Adamanteus Venom
CAV .... Curia Advisari Vult [*The Court Wishes to Consider*] [*Latin*] [*Legal term*]
CAV .... Cyclophosphamide, Adriamycin [*Doxorubicin*], Vincristine [*Antineoplastic drug regimen*]
CAVALCADE ... Calibrating, Amplitude-Variation, and Level-Correcting Analog-Digital Equipment (DEN)
CAVALIER ... Cooperatively Assembled Virginia Low Intensity Educational Reactor (NRCH)
CAVAMP-V ... Centralized Asset Visibility and Management Program for Vietnam [*Army*] (RDA)
CAVAT...... Carrow Auditory-Visual Abilities Test
CAVC .... Canadian Army Veterinary Corps (DMA)
CAVCTS ... Combined Acceleration Vibration Climatic Test System
CAVD........ Completion, Arithmetic, Vocabulary, Directions [*Psychology*]
CAVDA ..... Citizens Alliance for VD [*Venereal Disease*] Awareness (EA)
Cav Deb ... Cavendish's Debates, House of Commons [*A publication*] (DLA)
Cav Deb Can ... Cavender's Debates on Canada [*A publication*] (DLA)
CAVE........ Catholic Audio-Visual Educators Association (EA)
CAVe .... CCNU [*Lomustine*], Adriamycin, Vinblastine [*Antineoplastic drug regimen*]
CAVE........ Conduction Analysis via Eigenvalues [*NASA*] (MCD)
CAVE........ Consolidated Aquanauts Vital Equipment
Caveat .... Caveat Emptor [*A publication*]
CAVEAT ... Code and Visual Entry Authorization Technique [*Closed-circuit TV*] (MCD)

Cave Geol... Cave Geology [*A publication*]
Cave Res Group GB Trans ... Cave Research Group of Great Britain. Transactions [*A publication*]
Cave Res Group Great Britain Trans ... Cave Research Group of Great Britain. Transactions [*A publication*]
Cave Sci ..... Cave Science [*A publication*]
CAVF........ Coronary Arteriovenous Fistula [*Cardiology*]
CAVH........ Continuous Arteriovenous Hemofiltration [*Medicine*]
CaVIC....... Canadian Volunteers in Corrections Training Project
Cav Mon Sec ... Cavanagh's Law of Money Securities [*A publication*] (DLA)
CAVN .... CVN Companies, Inc. [*NASDAQ symbol*] (NQ)
CAVNAV .. Combat Air Vehicle Navigation and Vision
CAVNAVS ... Cavalry Navigation System (MCD)
CAVOAZ .. Contribuicoes Avulsas. Instituto Oceanografico Sao Paulo [*A publication*]
CAVOK..... Ceiling and Visibility OK [*Aviation*] (FAAC)
CAVORT... Coherent Acceleration and Velocity Observations in Real Time
CAVP........ Complex Arithmetic Vector Processor (RDA)
CAVR .... Carver Corp. [*Lynnwood, WA*] [*NASDAQ symbol*] (NQ)
CAVRA ..... Child Abuse Victims' Rights Act of 1986
CaVS .... Cahiers du Vingtieme Siecle [*A publication*]
CAVS........ Calibrated Armor Vehicle Simulator (MCD)
CAVS........ Center for Advanced Visual Studies [*Massachusetts Institute of Technology*] [*Research center*] (RCD)
CAVT........ Caveat [*Let Him Beware*] [*Latin*] [*A judicial writ*] [*Legal term*] (ROG)
CAVT........ Constant Absolute Vorticity Trajectory
CAVU .... Ceiling and Visibility Unrestricted [*or Unlimited*] [*Aviation*] (MCD)
CAW .... Caesars World, Inc. [*NYSE symbol*] (SPSG)
CAW .... Cam Action Wheel
CAW .... Campos [*Brazil*] [*Airport symbol*] (OAG)
CAW .... Canadian Auto Workers Union
CAW .... Carbon Arc Welding
CAW .... Carrier Air Wing [*Navy*]
CaW .... Catholic World [*A publication*]
CAW .... Central Aural Warning System (MCD)
CAW .... Channel Address Word [*Data processing*]
CAW .... China Aktuell [*A publication*]
CAW .... Close Assault Weapon (INF)
CAW .... Co-Ordinating Animal Welfare [*British*]
CAW .... Common Aerial Working [*Telecommunications*] (TEL)
CAW .... Computer-Aided Writing
CAWAAS ... Canadian-American Women's Association, American Section (EA)
CAWAWL ... Crusade to Abolish War and Armaments by World Law (EA)
CAWC .... Committee on Air and Water Conservation [*Later, Committee for Environmental Affairs*] [*American Petroleum Institute*]
CAWC .... Computer-Aided Written Communication
CAWCF .... Conventional Ammunition Working Capital Fund [*DoD*]
CAWE .... Canada West [*A publication*]
CAWF....... Carrier All-Weather Flying
CAWFGB .. Coopers' and Allied Workers' Federation of Great Britain [*A union*]
CAWG .... California Association of Winegrape Growers (EA)
CAWG .... Canada Asia Working Group
CAWG .... Clean Air Working Group [*An association*] (EA)
CAWG .... Coaxial Adapter Waveguide
CAWGS.... Covert All-Weather Gun System
CA WILJ... California Western International Law Journal [*A publication*]
CAWK .... Cautious Hawk [*Description of President Reagan's position on foreign affairs, used in book "Gambling with History: Reagan in the White House"*]
Cawl .... Cawley's Laws Concerning Jesuits, Etc. [*1680*] [*A publication*] (DLA)
CA WLR.... California Western Law Review [*A publication*]
CAWP .... Center for the American Woman and Politics (EA)
CAWPR..... Committee for the Aid to West Papuan Refugees [*Hague, Netherlands*] (EAIO)
CAWR .... Carrier Air Wing Reserve [*Navy*]
CAWR .... Combined Annual Wage Reporting [*IRS*]
CAWS....... Cannon Artillery Weapon Systems (MCD)
CAWS....... Central Aural Warning System (MCD)
CAWS....... Close-Assault Weapon System
CAWS....... Cockpit Alerting and Warning System (MCD)
CAWS....... Common Aviation Weather Subsystem (FAAC)
CAWS....... Computer-Aided Work Sampling
CAWSE..... Casualty Analysis for Determining Weapon System Effectiveness [*Army*] (AABC)
CAWSS ..... Crisis Action Weather Support System (MCD)
Cawthron Inst (Nelson NZ) Rep ... Cawthron Institute (Nelson, New Zealand). Report [*A publication*]
Cawthron Inst Publs ... Cawthron Institute. Publications [*A publication*]
CAWTS...... Chemical Attack Warning Transmission System (MCD)
CAWTU .... Church Action with the Unemployed [*Church of England*]
CAWU .... Clerical and Administrative Workers Union [*British*]
CAWU .... Commercial and Allied Workers' Union [*Somali Republic*]
CAX .... Capricorn Resources Ltd. [*Vancouver Stock Exchange symbol*]
CAX .... Carlisle [*England*] [*Airport symbol*] (OAG)
Cax............ Caxton Magazine [*A publication*]

CAX	Combined Arms Exercise (MCD)
CAX	Community Automatic Exchange [Telephone]
CAX	Conrac Corp. [Amherst, CT] [NYSE symbol] (SPSG)
CAXB	Composite Auxiliary Boiler [of a ship] (DS)
CAXBS	Composite Auxiliary Boiler Survey [of a ship] (DS)
CAXPAE	Connecticut. Storrs Agricultural Experiment Station. Progress Report [A publication]
CAY	Cayenne [French Guiana] [Airport symbol] (OAG)
Cay Abr	Cay's Abridgment, or the English Statutes [A publication] (DLA)
CAYAS	Children's and Young Adult Services
CAYB	Cayuga Savings Bank [Auburn, NY] [NASDAQ symbol] (NQ)
CAYBAB	Clean Air Year Book [A publication]
CAYC	Canadian Association for Young Children
CAYC	Centro de Arte y Communicacion [Center of Art and Communication] (EAIO)
CaYDaw	Dawson Public Library, Dawson, YT, Canada [Library symbol] [Library of Congress] (LCLS)
CaYDPCK	Parks Canada, Klondike Historic Site, Dawson City, YT, Canada [Library symbol] [Library of Congress] (LCLS)
CaYHjPCK	Parks Canada, Kluane National Park, Haines Junction, YT, Canada [Library symbol] [Library of Congress] (LCLS)
CAYO	Canadian Association of Youth Orchestras
CaYWA	Yukon Archives, Whitehorse, YT, Canada [Library symbol] [Library of Congress] (LCLS)
CaYWHS	Whitehorse Historical Society, Whitehorse, YT, Canada [Library symbol] [Library of Congress] (LCLS)
CaYWL	Yukon Law Library, Whitehorse, YT, Canada [Library symbol] [Library of Congress] (LCLS)
CaYWLS	Government of the Yukon, Library Services Branch, Whitehorse, YT, Canada [Library symbol] [Library of Congress] (LCLS)
CaYWPCN	Parks Canada, National Historic Sites, Whitehorse, YT, Canada [Library symbol] [Library of Congress] (LCLS)
CaYWR	Yukon Regional Library, Whitehorse, YT, Canada [Library symbol] [Library of Congress] (LCLS)
CaYWTA	Government of the Yukon, Department of Territorial Affairs, Whitehorse, YT, Canada [Library symbol] [Library of Congress] (LCLS)
CAz	Azusa Public Library, Azusa, CA [Library symbol] [Library of Congress] (LCLS)
CAZ	Can Am Gold Resources [Vancouver Stock Exchange symbol]
CAZ	Castlepoint [New Zealand] [Seismograph station code, US Geological Survey] (SEIS)
CAZ	Cazador Explorations [Vancouver Stock Exchange symbol]
CAZ	Cobar [Australia] [Airport symbol] (OAG)
CAzA	Aerojet Electrosystems Co., Azusa, CA [Library symbol] [Library of Congress] (LCLS)
CAzC	Citrus College, Azusa, CA [Library symbol] [Library of Congress] (LCLS)
CAzPC	Azusa Pacific College, Azusa, CA [Library symbol] [Library of Congress] (LCLS)
CAZS	Centre for Arid Zone Studies [University College of North Wales] [British] (CB)
CB	Allen & Hanburys [Great Britain] [Research code symbol]
CB	Battle Cruiser [Navy symbol]
CB	Belgian Congo
CB	Berkeley Public Library, Berkeley, CA [Library symbol] [Library of Congress] (LCLS)
C/B	C-Band [3900-6200 MHz]
CB	C-Battery
CB	Cadet Battalion [British military] (DMA)
CB	Cadmium Bronze
CB	Cahiers de Byrsa [A publication]
CB	Cairo Barclay's [Egypt]
CB	Call Back [Word processing]
CB	Callable Bond [Investment term]
cb	Cambodia [Democratic Kampuchea] [MARC country of publication code] [Library of Congress] (LCCP)
CB	Canadian Business [A publication]
C/B	Cancel on Back [Deltiology]
CB	Capacitor Bank
CB	Cape Breton Island
CB	Carbenicillin [Bactericide]
Cb	Carbobenzoxy [Also, CBZ] [Organic chemistry]
CB	Carbon Bond [Chemistry]
CB	Carboy (MCD)
CB	Caribair [Airlines] (OAG)
CB	Carrier-Based
CB	Carte Blanche [Credit card]
CB	Cash Book
CB	Cast Brass
CB	Casualty Branch [BUPERS]
CB	Cataclysmic Binary [Data processing]
CB	Catapult Bulletin (MCD)
CB	Catch Basin [Technical drawings]
C & B	Caught and Bowled [Cricket]
CB	Cavalry Brigade
CB	Cement Base [Technical drawings]
CB	Census Bureau [Department of Commerce]
CB	Center Back [Soccer]

CB	Center of Buoyancy
CB	Centibar
Cb	Centibels [Telecommunications]
CB	Central Bank [Philippines] (IMH)
CB	Central Battery (NATG)
CB	Central Board
CB	Century Bible [A publication]
CB	Cerebellum [Brain anatomy]
CB	Chairman of the Board
CB	Change Board (MCD)
CB	Change Bulletin
CB	Charles Bruning Reproduction Processes
CB	Chemical and Biological [Warfare] [Formerly, CBR, CEBAR] [Military]
CB	Chemically Benign [Medicine]
CB	Chest-Back [Medicine]
CB	Chester Beatty Research Institute [Great Britain] [Research code symbol]
CB	Chief Baron [British]
CB	Chief Boilermaker [Navy rating] [Obsolete]
CB	Children's Bureau [of SSA]
CB	Chinch Bug [Entomology]
CB	Chirurgiae Baccalaureus [Bachelor of Surgery]
CB	Chlorobiphenyl [Chemistry]
CB	Chlorobromomethane [Also, CBM] [Organic chemistry] (MCD)
CB	Choke Breaker [Automotive engineering]
CB	Chorale Book [Music] (ROG)
CB	Christian Businessman [Christian Business Men's Committee of United States of America] [A publication]
CB	Chronic Bronchitis [Medicine]
CB	[The] Chubb Corp. [NYSE symbol] (SPSG)
CB	Circle Bed [Medicine]
CB	Circuit Breaker
CB	Citizens Band [A radio frequency band for limited-range, two-way voice communications by persons without technical training or standard operator licenses]
CB	Classical Bulletin [A publication]
CB	Clear Back [Telecommunications] (TEL)
CB	Clin-Byla [France] [Research code symbol]
CB	Clipped and Burned [Ecology]
CB	Clydesdale Bank [British]
CB	Coach Builder (ROG)
CB	Coated on the Back Side [Carbonless paper]
CB	Cobalt Bomb [Nuclear] (AAG)
CB	Code Book (AFM)
CB	Coin Box [Telecommunications] (TEL)
CB	Col Basso [With the Bass] [Music]
C by B	Collected [or Delivered] by Barge [Shipping]
CB	Collective Bargaining (DCTA)
CB	Colombia [IYRU nationality code] (IYR)
Cb	Columbium [A chemical element; modern name is niobium, see Nb]
CB	Column Base
CB	Commander of the Most Excellent Order of the Bath [British]
CB	Commanderie de Bordeaux (EA)
CB	Commentationes Balticae [A publication]
CB	Commercial Bank
CB	Common Base [Data processing] (MSA)
CB	Common Battery [Electronics; technical drawings]
CB	Common Bench [Legal term]
CB	Common Bench Reports [A publication]
CB	Communications Buffer [Data processing]
CB	Commuter Airlines [Airline code]
CB	Companion of the [Order of the] Bath [British]
CB	Comparator Buffer [Data processing] (MUGU)
CB	Compass Bearing [Navigation]
CB	Component Board (MSA)
CB	Concrete Block
CB	Condition BIT [Binary Digit] [Data processing]
CB	Conditional Branch
CB	Conduction Band [Electronics]
CB	[The] Conference Board [Formerly, National Industrial Conference Board]
CB	Confidential Book [Navy] [British]
CB	Confidential Bulletin
CB	Configuration Baseline
CB	Confinement to Barracks [A military punishment]
C of B	Confirmation of Balance [Banking]
CB	Conjugate (Counter) Base [Chemistry]
CB	Connecting Block [Telecommunications] (TEL)
CB	Consolidated-Bathurst, Inc. [Toronto Stock Exchange symbol]
CB	Constant Bandwidth (MCD)
CB	Construction Battalion [SEABEE] [Navy]
CB	Contact Breaker
CB	Container Base (DS)
CB	Containment Building [Nuclear energy] (NRCH)
CB	Contemporary Books [Publisher's imprint]
CB	Continuous Blowdown (AAG)
CB	Contrabass [Music]
CB	Contract Brief

CB .... Control Board
CB .... Control Booth
CB .... Control Branch [*Military*]
CB .... Control Break
CB .... Control Building [*Nuclear energy*]   (NRCH)
CB .... Control Button
CB .... Conus Branch [*Anatomy*]
CB .... Coomb [*Combe*] [*British*]   (ROG)
CB .... Corned Beef [*Restaurant slang*]
CB .... Cornerback [*Football*]
CB .... Corps Brandenburgia   (EA)
C/B .... Cost/Benefit [*Accounting*]
CB .... Cottony Blight [*of turf grass*]
CB .... Coulomb [*Unit of electric charge*]
CB .... Counter Battery
CB .... Counter Bombardment [*British military*]   (DMA)
CB .... Country Bill [*Banking*]
CB .... County Borough
CB .... Coupon Bond [*Investment term*]
CB .... Crash Boat
CB .... Credit Balance
C/B .... Creosote Bushes [*Ecology*]
CB .... Crew Boat
C and B ..... Cropper and Burgess [*Bank in "He Knew He Was Right" by Anthony Trollope*]
CB .... Cuadernos Bibliograficos [*Madrid*] [*A publication*]
CB .... Cultura Biblica [*A publication*]
CB .... Cumulative Bulletin [*United States Internal Revenue Service*] [*A publication*]
CB .... Cumulonimbus [*Cloud*] [*Meteorology*]
CB .... Currency Bond
CB .... Current Background
CB .... Current Bibliography on African Affairs [*A publication*]
CB .... Current Biography [*A publication*]
CB .... Customs Bulletin [*A publication*]
CB .... Customs Bureau
CB .... Cyprair Tours Ltd. [*Cyprus*] [*ICAO designator*]   (FAAC)
CB .... Cytochalasin B [*Biochemistry*]
CB .... English Common Bench Reports [*1840-56*] [*A publication*]   (DLA)
CB .... Large Cruiser [*Navy symbol*] [*Obsolete*]
CB .... SEABEE [*Construction Battalion*] [*Navy*]   (MCD)
CB .... US Consulate [*Hong Kong*]. Current Background [*A publication*]
CB1 .... Coal Bug One [*Microbe used to remove sulfur from coal*]
CB4 .... Carbon Bond Mechanism - Version 4 [*Air pollution*]
CBA .... Association for Bright Children [*Canada*]
CBA .... C-Band Transponder Antenna [*Radio*]   (CET)
CBA .... Cake and Biscuit Alliance [*British*]
CBA .... California State College, Bakersfield, CA [*OCLC symbol*]   (OCLC)
CBA .... Cambridge Buddhist Association   (EA)
CBA .... Canadian Badminton Association
CBA .... Canadian Bankers Association
CBA .... Canadian Bar Association
CBA .... Canadian Booksellers Association
CBA .... Canadian Botanical Association
CBA .... Candy Brokers Association of America [*Later, NCBSA*]   (EA)
CBA .... Capital Builder Account [*Merrill Lynch & Co., Inc.*] [*Finance*]
CBA .... Caribbean Atlantic Airlines [*Puerto Rico*] [*ICAO designator*]
CBA .... Cast Bullet Association   (EA)
CBA .... Catholic Biblical Association of America   (EA)
CBA .... Catholic Broadcasters Association   (EA)
CBA .... Center for Book Arts   (EA)
CBA .... Central [*Common*] Battery Apparatus [*Electronics*]
CBA .... Certified Business Appraiser [*Designation awarded by Institute of Business Appraisers*]
CBA .... Chartered Bank Auditor [*Designation awarded by Bank Administration Institute*]
CBA .... Chemical Blowing Agent [*Plastics technology*]
CBA .... Chemical Bond Approach
CBA .... Chesapeake Bay Annex [*Navy*]
CBA .... Chlorobenzoic Acid [*Organic acid*]
CBA .... Christian Boaters Association   (EA)
CBA .... Christian Bodybuilding Association   (EA)
CBA .... Christian Booksellers Association   (EA)
CBA .... Christian Broadcasting Association   (EA)
CBA .... Chronic Bronchitis and Asthma [*Medicine*]
CBA .... Circuit Board Assembly   (MCD)
C/B .... Citizens for a Better America   (EA)
CBA .... Clydesdale Breeders Association of the United States [*Later, CBUS*]   (EA)
Cba .... Cobamide [*Biochemistry*]
CBA .... Cocoa Beach Apollo [*NASA*]   (MCD)
CBA .... Cold Bay [*Alaska*] [*Seismograph station code, US Geological Survey*] [*Closed*]   (SEIS)
CBA .... Collective Black Artists   (EA)
CBA .... Colliding Beam Accelerator [*High-energy physics*]
CBA .... COMLINE Business Analysis [*COMLINE International Corp.*] [*Japan*] [*Information service or system*]   (CRD)
CBA .... Commercial Bank of Australia

CBA .... Common Battery System   (MCD)
CBA .... Commonwealth Broadcasting Association [*London, England*]   (EAIO)
CBA .... Community Broadcasters of America [*Defunct*]   (EA)
CBA .... Community Broadcasters Association [*Defunct*]   (EA)
CBA .... Competitive-Binding Assay
CBA .... Component Board Assembly   (MSA)
CBA .... Computer-Based Automation
CBA .... Congressional Black Associates [*An association*]   (EA)
CBA .... Constants Board Assembly
CBA .... Consumer Bankers Association [*Arlington, VA*]   (EA)
CBA .... Continental Basketball Association   (EA)
CBA .... Cost-Benefit Analysis [*Accounting*]
CBA .... Council for British Archaeology
CBA .... Crested Butte Air Service, Inc. [*Crested Butte, CO*] [*FAA designator*]   (FAAC)
CBA .... Cronaca delle Belle Arti [*A publication*]
CBA .... Current Biotechnology Abstracts [*Royal Society of Chemistry*] [*Information service or system*]   (IID)
CBA .... Curriculum-Based Assessment [*Education*]
CBA .... Cytochemical Bioassay
CBA .... Maandstatistiek van Bevolking en Volksgezondheid [*A publication*]
CBA .... Moncton, NB [*AM radio station call letters*]
CB(AA) ...... Cavalry Brigade (Air Attack) [*Army*]
CBAA .... Cleveland Bay Association of America [*Later, Cleveland Bay Society of America*]   (EA)
CBAA .... Conservative Baptist Association of America   (EA)
CBAA .... Corset and Brassiere Association of America [*Later, AAMA*]   (EA)
CBAA .... Current Bibliography on African Affairs [*A publication*]
CBAB .... California Brandy Advisory Board [*Defunct*]   (EA)
CBABG .... CAB [*Commonwealth Agricultural Bureaux*] International Bureau of Animal Breeding and Genetics   (EAIO)
CBABS ...... [*The*] Conference Board Abstract Database [*The Conference Board, Inc.*] [*Information service or system*]   (CRD)
CBAC .... Chemical-Biological Activities [*Information service or system*] [*A publication*]
CBAC .... Combat Brigade Air Cavalry
CBAC .... Council for Business and the Arts in Canada
CBADS ...... Chemical and Biological Agent Delivery System   (MCD)
CBAE .... Commonwealth Board of Architectural Education [*London, England*]   (EAIO)
CBAE .... Competency-Based Adult Education
CBAF .... Cobalt Base Alloy Foil
CBAF .... Commercial Bank Address File [*IRS*]
CBAF .... Moncton, NB [*AM radio station call letters*]
CBAF-FM ... Moncton, NB [*FM radio station call letters*]
CBA-FM ... Moncton, NB [*FM radio station call letters*]
CBAFT ...... Moncton, NB [*Television station call letters*]
CBAG .... Children's Book Action Group [*National Book League*] [*British*]
CBAG .... Crest Corp. [*Riverton, WY*] [*NASDAQ symbol*]   (NQ)
CBaGS ...... Church of Jesus Christ of Latter-Day Saints, Genealogical Society Library, Bakersfield Branch, Bakersfield, CA [*Library symbol*] [*Library of Congress*]   (LCLS)
CBAH .... Commonwealth Bureau of Animal Health [*British*]
CBaH .... Kern Medical Center, Bakersfield, CA [*Library symbol*] [*Library of Congress*]   (LCLS)
CBA Handbook ... Commonwealth Broadcasting Association. Handbook [*A publication*]
CBAIAL .... Contributions. Arctic Institute. Catholic University of America [*A publication*]
CBAIC ...... Chemical and Biological Accident and Incident Control [*Army*]   (AABC)
CBAICP ..... Chemical and Biological Accident and Incident Control Plan [*Army*]   (AABC)
CBaK .... Kern County Library, Bakersfield, CA [*Library symbol*] [*Library of Congress*]   (LCLS)
CBaKH ...... Kern County Department of Health, Bakersfield, CA [*Library symbol*] [*Library of Congress*]   (LCLS)
CBaKM ..... Kern County Museum, Reference Library, Bakersfield, CA [*Library symbol*] [*Library of Congress*]   (LCLS)
CBAL .... Counterbalance   (KSC)
CBALS ...... Carrier-Borne Air Liaison Section [*Navy*]
CBalt .... Commentationes Balticae [*A publication*]
CBan .... Banning Union Public Library, Banning, CA [*Library symbol*] [*Library of Congress*]   (LCLS)
CBAN .... Central Bancorporation, Inc. [*Cincinnati, OH*] [*NASDAQ symbol*]   (NQ)
CBAN .... Commonwealth Bureau of Animal Nutrition [*British*]
CBAND5 ... Clinical and Biochemical Analysis [*A publication*]
CBANY ...... Covered Button Association of New York   (EA)
CBAQAB... Contribuciones Cientificas. Facultad de Ciencias Exactas y Naturales. Universidad de Buenos Aires. Serie Quimica [*A publication*]
CBAR .... Center for Bioanalytical Research [*University of Kansas*]
CBAR .... Counterbore Arbor [*Tool*]
C/BAR ...... Cross Bar [*Automotive engineering*]
CBARC ...... Columbia Basin Agricultural Research Center [*Oregon State University*] [*Research center*]   (RCD)

CBARC...... Conference Board of Associated Research Councils (EA)
CBarGS ..... Church of Jesus Christ of Latter-Day Saints, Genealogical Society Library, Barstow Branch, Barstow, CA [*Library symbol*] [*Library of Congress*] (LCLS)
CBarUSA .. United States Army, Fort Irwin Post Library, Barstow, CA [*Library symbol*] [*Library of Congress*] (LCLS)
CBaS.......... California State College, Bakersfield, CA [*Library symbol*] [*Library of Congress*] (LCLS)
CBAS........ Central [*Common*] Battery Alarm Signaling [*Electronics*]
CBAS........ Chemical Bond Approach Study
CBAS........ Combat Augmentation Subsystem (MCD)
CBASA ...... Ciba Symposia [*A publication*]
CBASF...... Current Bibliography for Aquatic Sciences and Fisheries [*A publication*]
C-BASIC ... Commercial BASIC
CBAST ...... Concentrated Boric Acid Storage Tank [*Nuclear energy*] (NRCH)
CBAT........ Central Bureau for Astronomical Telegrams (EA)
CB/ATDS ... Carrier-Based Airborne Tactical Data System (MCD)
CBb .... Burbank Public Library, Burbank, CA [*Library symbol*] [*Library of Congress*] (LCLS)
CBB.......... Cambridge Bay [*Canada*] [*Geomagnetic observatory code*]
CBB.......... Catholic Big Brothers (EA)
CBB.......... Citizens for a Balanced Budget (EA)
CBB.......... Cobra Enterprises [*Vancouver Stock Exchange symbol*]
CBB.......... Cochabamba [*Bolivia*] [*Airport symbol*] (OAG)
CBB.......... Commercial Bank of Greece. Economic Bulletin [*A publication*]
CBB.......... Commercial Blanket Bond [*Insurance*]
CBB.......... Computerized Bulletin Board
CBB.......... Contract Budget Baseline (MCD)
CBB.......... Coomassie Brilliant Blue [*A stain*]
CBBA........ Christian Brothers Boys Association (EA)
CBBAA2.... Communications in Behavioral Biology. Part A. Original Articles [*A publication*]
CBBB........ Council of Better Business Bureaus [*Arlington, VA*] (EA)
CBBC........ Council of Bible Believing Churches (EA)
CBBFC ...... Cooder Brown Band Fan Club (EA)
CBBG........ Canadian Bookbinders and Book Artists Guild
CBbH........ Hydro-Air Library, Burbank, CA [*Library symbol*] [*Library of Congress*] (LCLS)
CBBI.......... Cast Bronze Bearings Institute [*Later, NFFS*]
CBBII .... Council of the Brass and Bronze Ingot Industry (EA)
CBBK-FM ... Kingston, ON [*FM radio station call letters*]
CBbL.......... Lockheed-California Co., Burbank, CA [*Library symbol*] [*Library of Congress*] (LCLS)
CBBL-FM ... London, ON [*FM radio station call letters*]
CBBMA4... Contributions. Institut de Botanique. Universite de Montreal [*A publication*]
CBBMC.... Ciencia Biologica [*A publication*]
CBBS......... Center for Biochemical and Biophysical Studies [*Northern Illinois University*] [*Research center*] (RCD)
CBBS......... Community Bulletin Board System
CBBS......... Computer-Based Behavioral Studies (MCD)
CBBS......... Computer-Based Bibliographic Search Services
CBBS......... Computer Bulletin Board System
CBbT .... Technicolor, Inc., Burbank, CA [*Library symbol*] [*Library of Congress*] (LCLS)
CBBU .... Construction Battalion Base Unit [*Obsolete*] [*Navy*]
CB Bul....... Conference Board. Information Bulletin [*A publication*]
CBbW .... Warner Brothers, Inc., Research Library, Burbank, CA [*Library symbol*] [*Library of Congress*] (LCLS)
CBbWD .... Walt Disney Productions, Burbank, CA [*Library symbol*] [*Library of Congress*] (LCLS)
CBC .... Anahuac, TX [*Location identifier*] [*FAA*] (FAAL)
CBC .... Biola College, La Mirada, CA [*OCLC symbol*] (OCLC)
CBC .... Cadmium Bronze Connector
CBC .... Cahiers Benjamin Constant [*A publication*]
CBC .... [*The*] Cambridge Bible Commentary: New English Bible [*A publication*] (BJA)
CBC .... Cambridge Bicycle Club [*British*]
CBC .... Canadian Broadcasting Corporation [*Telecommunications*] [*Ottawa, ON*] [*Also facetiously translated as Casual Broadcasting Corporation and Communist Broadcasting Corporation*]
CBC .... Can't Be Called [*Telecommunications*] (TEL)
CBC .... Carbon County Railway Company [*AAR code*]
CBC .... Caribbean Resources Corp. [*Vancouver Stock Exchange symbol*]
CBC .... Cauchy Boundary Condition [*Mathematics*]
CBC .... Cementitious Barrier Coat [*Anticorrosive coating*]
CBC .... Central Bureau of Compensation [*See also BCC*] (EAIO)
CBC .... Centura Banks [*NYSE symbol*] (SPSG)
CBC .... Cerebro-Buccal Commissure [*Medicine*]
CBC .... Cesare Barbieri Courier [*A publication*]
CBC .... Chamberlain [*California*] [*Seismograph station code, US Geological Survey*] (SEIS)
CBC .... Chatto, Bodley Head, and Jonathan Cape Group [*Publishers*] [*British*]
CBC .... Chemically Bonded Ceramic [*Materials science*]
CBC .... Chicago Book Clinic
CBC .... Child Behavior and Characteristics

CBC .... Children's Behavior Checklist
CBC .... Children's Book Circle [*British*]
CBC .... Children's Book Council (EA)
CBC .... Christian Brothers College [*Tennessee*]
CBC .... Christian Brothers Conference (EA)
CBC .... Circuit Board Card
CBC .... Circulation Bed Combustor [*Chemical engineering*]
CBC .... Citizens for Better Care in Nursing Homes, Homes for the Aged, and Other After-Care Facilities (EA)
CBC .... Civil Budget Committee [*NATO*] (NATG)
CBC .... Closed Brayton Cycle [*Thermodynamics*]
CBC .... Collier's Bankruptcy Cases [*A publication*] (DLA)
CBC .... Columbia Bible College [*South Carolina*]
CBC .... Commercial Banking Company of Sydney [*Australia*]
CBC .... Community Based Corrections (OICC)
CBC .... Complete Blood Count [*Medicine*]
CBC .... Computer-Based Consultant (MCD)
CBC .... Conference Board of Canada
CBC .... Congressional Black Caucus (EA)
CBC .... Conservative Book Club
CBC .... Construction Battalion Center [*Navy*] (MCD)
CBC .... Continuous Boresight Correction (MCD)
CBC .... Contraband Control [*Navy*]
CBC .... Corset and Brassiere Council [*Defunct*] (EA)
CBC .... Couldn't Be Cuter [*Slang*]
CBC .... County Borough Council [*British*] (ROG)
CBC .... Large Tactical Command Ship [*Navy symbol*] [*Obsolete*]
CBCA........ Canadian Badminton Coaches Association
CBCA........ Canadian Business and Current Affairs [*Micromedia Ltd.*] [*Information service or system*] (CRD)
CBCA........ Caribbean Basin Corrections Association (EAIO)
CB Cap A ... Conference Board. Manufacturing Investment Statistics. Capital Appropriations [*A publication*]
CB Cap Inv ... Conference Board. Manufacturing Investment Statistics. Capital Investment and Supply Conditions [*A publication*]
CBCBC ...... Corn-Soybeans-Corn-Soybeans-Corn [*Crop rotation*]
CB-CC .... Centroblastic/Centrocytic [*Biochemistry*]
CBCC........ Chemical-Biological Coordination Center [*NAS/NRC*]
CBCC........ Common Bias, Common Control
CBCC........ Conviction by Civil Court
CBC (Citizens Budget Comm) Q ... CBC (Citizens Budget Commission) Quarterly [*A publication*]
CBCCUA... Central Bureau, Catholic Central Union of America (EA)
CBCD .... Citrus Bacterial Canker Disease [*Plant pathology*]
CBCE......... Comite de Bourses de la Communaute Europeenne [*Committee of Stock Exchanges in the European Community - CSEE*] (EAIO)
CBCE......... Competency-Based Career Education (OICC)
CBCES ...... Chesapeake Bay Center for Environmental Studies [*Smithsonian Institution*]
CBCF........ Carbon-Bonded Carbon Fiber
CBCF......... Citizens Banking Corporation [*Flint, MI*] [*NASDAQ symbol*] (NQ)
CBCHA ..... Clearinghouse on Business Coalitions for Health Action (EA)
CBCL........ Capitol Bancorp Ltd. [*NASDAQ symbol*] (NQ)
CBCL........ Child Behavior Checklist
CBCL........ Cutter Laboratories, Berkeley, CA [*Library symbol*] [*Library of Congress*] (LCLS)
CBCL-FM ... London, ON [*FM radio station call letters*]
CBCMA..... Carbonated Beverage Container Manufacturers Association [*Later, CMI*] (EA)
CBCMC..... Carbonated Beverage Can Makers Committee [*Division of CBCMA*] (EA)
CBCN .... Colonial Bancorp, Inc. [*Waterbury, CT*] [*NASDAQ symbol*] (NQ)
CBCNS...... CBC [*Canadian Broadcasting Corporation*] Northern Service Press Releases [*A publication*]
CBCO .... Cobanco, Inc. [*Santa Cruz, CA*] [*NASDAQ symbol*] (NQ)
CB Corp Con ... Conference Board. Report 869. Annual Survey of Corporate Contributions [*A publication*]
CBCPA ...... Comparative Biochemistry and Physiology [*A publication*]
CBCPAI...... Comparative Biochemistry and Physiology [*A publication*]
CBCP-TV-1 ... Shaunavon, SK [*Television station call letters*]
CBCP-TV-2 ... Cypress Hills, SK [*Television station call letters*]
CBCP-TV-3 ... Ponteix, SK [*Television station call letters*]
CBCS......... C-Band Checkout System (KSC)
CBCS......... Chemical-Biological Computer System
CBCS......... Chinese Banknote Collectors Society (EA)
CBCS-FM ... Sudbury, ON [*FM radio station call letters*]
CBCSM ..... Council of British Ceramic Sanitaryware Manufacturers
CBCT......... Cenvest, Inc. [*NASDAQ symbol*] (NQ)
CBCT......... Charlottetown, PE [*Television station call letters*]
CBCT......... Circuit Board Card Tester
CBCT......... Community-Based Clinical Trial [*Medicine*]
CBCT......... Customer-Bank Communication Terminal [*Computerized banking*]
CBCT-FM ... Charlottetown, PE [*FM radio station call letters*]
CBCU .... Counterbore Cutter [*Tool*] (AAG)
CBCX........ Cambridge Biotech [*NASDAQ symbol*] (NQ)
C-BD .... C-Band [*3900-6200 MHz*] (NASA)
CBD .... Call Box Discrimination [*Telecommunications*] (TEL)

CBD..........	Cannabidiol [*Organic chemistry*]
CBD..........	Carbide (MSA)
CBD..........	Cash before Delivery
CBD..........	Center for Biomedical Design [*University of Utah*] [*Research center*] (RCD)
CBD..........	Central Business District
CBD..........	Certificate of Bank Deposit
CBD..........	Chemical-Biological Defense [*Military*]
CBD..........	Chesapeake Bay Detachment [*Washington, DC*] [*Navy*] (GRD)
CBD..........	Chester, CA [*Location identifier*] [*FAA*] (FAAL)
CBD..........	Chief Benefits Director [*Department of Veterans Affairs*]
CBD..........	Children before Dogs (EA)
CBD..........	Chronic Beryllium Disease [*Medicine*] (MCD)
CBD..........	Closed Bladder Drainage [*Medicine*]
CBD..........	Coffee Berry Disease
CBD..........	Commerce Business Daily [*Department of Commerce*] [*Information service or system*] [*A publication*]
CBD..........	Common Bile Duct [*Medicine*]
CBD..........	Configuration Block Diagram [*Telecommunications*] (TEL)
CBD..........	Constant BIT [*Binary Digit*] Density [*Control feature of magnetic tape recorders*] [*Data processing*]
CBD..........	Construction Battalion Detachment [*Navy*]
CBD..........	Convergent Beam Diffraction
CBD..........	Cumberland Resources Ltd. [*Vancouver Stock Exchange symbol*]
CBD..........	Current Bibliographic Directory of the Arts and Sciences [*A publication*]
CBD..........	St. John, NB [*AM radio station call letters*]
CBDA........	Cannabidiolic Acid [*Organic chemistry*]
CBDB........	[*The*] Conference Board Data Base [*The Conference Board, Inc.*] [*Information service or system*] (CRD)
CBD-FM.....	St. John, NB [*FM radio station call letters*]
CBDI.........	Control Red Bank Demand Indicator (IEEE)
CB Dig	United States Customs Bureau, Digest of Customs and Related Laws [*A publication*] (DLA)
CBDL........	Cross Branch Data Link (MCD)
CBDNA	College Band Directors National Association (EA)
CBDQ........	Wabush, NF [*AM radio station call letters*]
CBDR	Citizens for Better Driving Records [*Later, CSD*] (EA)
CBDS........	Carcinogenesis Bioassay Data System [*National Cancer Institute*] (IID)
CBDS........	Circuit Board Design System [*IBM Corp.*]
CBDS........	Common Bile Duct Stenosis [*Medicine*]
CBDST	Commonwealth Bureau of Dairy Science and Technology [*British*]
CBDT........	Can't Break Dial Tone [*Telecommunications*] (TEL)
CBDT........	Citizenship of British Dependent Territories
CBE..........	Cabre Exploration Ltd. [*Toronto Stock Exchange symbol*]
CBE..........	Calgary Board of Education, Acquisition and Technical Services [*UTLAS symbol*]
CBE..........	Carbon Black Export (EA)
CBE..........	Central Bomber Establishment [*British military*] (DMA)
CBE..........	Centralized Branch Exchange [*Telecommunications*] (TEL)
CBE..........	Certified Bank Examiner
CBE..........	Cesium Bombardment Engine
CBE..........	Chemical Beam Epitaxy [*Solid state physics*]
CBE..........	Chemical Binding Effect
CBE..........	[*The*] Chilswell Book of English Poetry [*A publication*]
CBE..........	China Business Enterprises
CBE..........	Chlorobromoethane [*Organic chemistry*]
CBE..........	Circuit Board Extractor
CBE..........	Citizens for a Better Environment (EA)
CBE..........	Combined Book Exhibit
CBE..........	Command Budget Estimates [*Military*] (AABC)
CBE..........	Commander of the [*Order of the*] British Empire [*Facetious translation: Can't Be Everywhere*]
CBE..........	Companion of the Order of the British Empire (ADA)
CBE..........	Competency Based Education
CBE..........	Compression Bonding Encapsulation
C-BE..........	Computer-Based Education [*Project*]
CBE..........	Computer Brokers Exchange [*Information service or system*] (IID)
CBE..........	Conference of Business Economists (EA)
CBE..........	Connector Bracket Experiment (MCD)
CBE..........	Constant Blow Energy [*Teledyne Roxon 400*] [*Hydraulics*]
CBE..........	Consumer Buying Expectations Survey [*Formerly, Quarterly Survey of Intentions*] [*Bureau of the Census*]
CBE..........	Contract Budget Estimate (MCD)
CBE..........	Cooper Industries, Inc. [*Formerly, Cooper-Bessemer Corp.*] [*NYSE symbol*] (SPSG)
CBE..........	Costs, Budgeting, and Economics
CBE..........	Council for Basic Education (EA)
CBE..........	Council of Biology Editors (EA)
CBE..........	Crude Barrel Equivalent [*Oil*]
CBE..........	Cumberland [*Maryland*] [*Airport symbol*] (OAG)
CBE..........	Sociale Maandstatistiek [*A publication*]
CBE..........	Windsor, ON [*AM radio station call letters*]
CBea	Beaumont Library District Library, Beaumont, CA [*Library symbol*] [*Library of Congress*] (LCLS)
CBEA........	Catholic Business Education Association [*Later, NCBEA*] (EA)

CBEA........	Christian Brothers Education Association [*Later, RECCB*] (EA)
CBEA........	Commonwealth Banana Exporters Association (EAIO)
CBEA........	Council for a Black Economic Agenda (EA)
CBEC........	Canadian Book Exchange Centre (IID)
CB Ec 1990 ...	Conference Board. Report 864. US Economy to 1990 [*A publication*]
CBECS	Control Building Environmental Control System [*Nuclear energy*] (NRCH)
CBED........	Center for Business and Economic Development [*Auburn University at Montgomery*] [*Research center*] (RCD)
CBED........	Children with Behavioral and Emotional Difficulty
CBED........	Convergent Beam Electron Diffraction [*Analytical technique*]
CBEF	Windsor, ON [*AM radio station call letters*]
CBE-FM	Windsor, ON [*FM radio station call letters*]
CBEFT	Windsor, ON [*Television station call letters*]
CBEG-FM ...	Sarnia, ON [*FM radio station call letters*]
CBEL.........	[*The*] Cambridge Bibliography of English Literature [*A publication*]
CBelmD.....	Textron, Inc., Dalmo Victor Co., Belmont, CA [*Library symbol*] [*Library of Congress*] (LCLS)
CBelmN	College of Notre Dame, Belmont, CA [*Library symbol*] [*Library of Congress*] (LCLS)
CBelmP.....	Peninsula Library System, Belmont, CA [*Library symbol*] [*Library of Congress*] (LCLS)
CBelmS.....	San Mateo County Free Library, Belmont, CA [*Library symbol*] [*Library of Congress*] (LCLS)
CBEM........	Computer-Based Electronic Mail (MCD)
CBEMA.....	Computer and Business Equipment Manufacturers Association [*Washington, DC*] (EA)
CBEMR.....	Commercial Bank of Ethiopia. Market Report [*A publication*]
CBen	Benicia Free Public Library, Benicia, CA [*Library symbol*] [*Library of Congress*] (LCLS)
CBEN	Carolyn Bean Publishing Ltd. [*NASDAQ symbol*] (NQ)
CBEN	Commonwealth Banking Corporation. Economic Newsletter [*A publication*] (ADA)
CB (Eng)....	English Common Bench Reports (Manning, Granger, and Scott) [*135-139 English Reprint*] [*A publication*] (DLA)
CBENT......	Catholic Biblical Encyclopedia. New Testament [*A publication*] (BJA)
CBEOT......	Catholic Biblical Encyclopedia. Old Testament [*A publication*] (BJA)
CBER........	Center for Biochemical Engineering Research [*New Mexico State University*] [*Research center*] (RCD)
CBER........	Center for Biologics Evaluation and Research [*FDA*]
CBER........	Center for Business and Economic Research [*University of Alabama*] [*University, AL*] [*Information service or system*] (IID)
CBER........	Center for Business & Economics Research [*University of Nevada - Las Vegas*] [*Research center*] (RCD)
CBERA......	Caribbean Basin Economic Recovery Act
CBESD......	Caribbean Basin Economic Survey [*A publication*]
CBET........	Certified Biomedical Equipment Technician (RDA)
CBETV	Conditioned Bald Eagle Total Value
CBev..........	Beverly Hills Public Library, Beverly Hills, CA [*Library symbol*] [*Library of Congress*] (LCLS)
CBevA........	American Film Institute, Center for Advanced Film Studies, Beverly Hills, CA [*Library symbol*] [*Library of Congress*] (LCLS)
CBEVE......	Central Bureau for Educational Visits and Exchanges
CBevL........	Litton Industries, Inc., Beverly Hills, CA [*Library symbol*] [*Library of Congress*] (LCLS)
CBevT	Twentieth Century-Fox Film Corp., Beverly Hills, CA [*Library symbol*] [*Library of Congress*] (LCLS)
CB EX........	Chief Baron of the Exchequer [*British*] (ROG)
CBF...........	Canadian Bridge Federation
CBF...........	Canbra Foods Ltd. [*Toronto Stock Exchange symbol*]
CBF...........	Cancer Breaking Factor [*Antineoplastic drug*]
CBF...........	Cell Biochemistry and Function
CBF...........	Central British Fund for World Jewish Relief (EAIO)
CBF...........	Centrifugal Barrel Finishing [*of metal surfaces*]
CBF...........	Cerebral Blood Flow [*Medicine*]
CBF...........	Children's Blood Foundation (EA)
CBF...........	Colonial Bishoprics' Fund [*British*]
CBF...........	Common Beam Former
CBF...........	Coronary Blood Flow [*Medicine*]
CBF...........	Cortical Blood Flow [*Urology*]
CBF...........	Council Bluffs, IA [*Location identifier*] [*FAA*] (FAAL)
CBF...........	Montreal, PQ [*AM radio station call letters*]
CBFA........	Cerebral Blood Flow Autoregulation
CBFAP	Commander, British Forces, Arabian Peninsula [*British military*] (DMA)
CBFAS.......	Canadian Bulletin of Fisheries and Aquatic Sciences [*A publication*]
CBFC.........	Cathy Buchanan Fan Club (EA)
CBFC.........	CB Financial Corporation [*Jackson, MI*] [*NASDAQ symbol*] (NQ)
CBFC.........	Clyde Bowling Fan Club (EA)
CBFC.........	Copper and Brass Fabricators Council (EA)
CBFCA.......	Commander, British Forces, Caribbean Area [*NATO*] (NATG)
CBF-FM	Montreal, PQ [*FM radio station call letters*]

CBF-FM-1 ... Trois Rivieres, PQ [*FM radio station call letters*]
CBFFTA .... Copper and Brass Fabricators Foreign Trade Association [*Later, CBFC*] (EA)
CBFG .... Commander, British Forces, Gulf [*British military*] (DMA)
CBFMA ..... Combustion and Flame [*A publication*]
CBFMAO ... Combustion and Flame [*A publication*]
CBFMS ..... Conservative Baptist Foreign Mission Society (EA)
CBFRJ .... Carol Burnett Fund for Responsible Journalism (EA)
CBFS .... Carbon Black Feedstock
CBFSDB .... Canadian Bulletin of Fisheries and Aquatic Sciences [*A publication*]
CBFSEI ..... Clearinghouse for Community Based Free Standing Educational Institutions (EA)
CBFST-2 ... Temiscaming, PQ [*Television station call letters*]
CBFT .... Montreal, PQ [*Television station call letters*]
CBFT-2 ...... Mont-Laurier, PQ [*Television station call letters*]
CBFUDH .. Cell Biochemistry and Function [*A publication*]
CBG .... Cambridge [*England*] [*Airport symbol*] [*Obsolete*] (OAG)
CBG .... Cambridge, MN [*Location identifier*] [*FAA*] (FAAL)
CBG .... Cambridge Shopping Centres Ltd. [*Toronto Stock Exchange symbol*]
CBG .... Campus Booksellers Group [*Australia*]
CBG .... Collationes Brugenses et Gandavenses [*A publication*]
CBG .... Committee to Bridge the Gap (EA)
CBG .... Corticosteroid-Binding Globulin [*Transcortin*] [*Endocrinology*]
CBG .... Craniofacial Biology Group of the International Association for Dental Research (EA)
CBG .... Gander, NF [*AM radio station call letters*]
CBGA .... Carpathian Balkan Geological Association (EAIO)
CBGA .... Matane, PQ [*AM radio station call letters*]
CBGA-FM-8 ... Iles-de-la-Madeleine, PQ [*FM radio station call letters*]
CBGAT ...... Matane, PQ [*Television station call letters*]
CBGHN ..... Coalition on Block Grants and Human Needs (EA)
CBGLO ..... Carrier-Borne Ground Liaison Officer [*Military*] [*British*]
CBGM .... Committee of Black Gay Men (EA)
CBGN .... Ste. Anne Des Monts, PQ [*AM radio station call letters*]
CBGTU ..... Graduate Theological Union, Berkeley, CA [*Library symbol*] [*Library of Congress*] (LCLS)
CBGTU-B ... American Baptist Seminary of the West, Berkeley, CA [*Library symbol*] [*Library of Congress*] (LCLS)
CBGY .... Bonavista Bay, NF [*AM radio station call letters*]
CBH .... Bechar [*Algeria*] [*Airport symbol*] (OAG)
CBH .... Camp Beverly Hills [*California clothing store*]
CBH .... Can't Be Heard [*Telecommunications*] (TEL)
CBH .... CBI Industries, Inc. [*Formerly, Chicago Bridge & Iron Co.*] [*NYSE symbol*] (SPSG)
CBH .... Cellobiohydrolase [*An enzyme*]
CBH .... Center for Borderline History (EA)
CBH .... Childbearing Hips
CBH .... Circuit Board Holder
CBH .... Congregatie Broeders van Huybergen [*Brothers of the Immaculate Conception of the Mother of God - BICMG*] [*Huybergen, Netherlands*] (EAIO)
CB & H ...... Continent between Bordeaux and Hamburg [*Business term*]
CBH .... Cutaneous Basophil Hypersensitivity [*Immunology*]
CBH .... Hexcel Products, Technical Library, Berkeley, CA [*Library symbol*] [*Library of Congress*] (LCLS)
CBHA .... Council for Biology in Human Affairs
CBHA-FM ... Halifax, NS [*FM radio station call letters*]
CBH Byz. ... Corpus Bruxellense Historiae Byzantinae [*A publication*]
CBH-FM .... Halifax, NS [*FM radio station call letters*]
CBHFT ...... Halifax, NS [*Television station call letters*]
CBHFT-1. .. Yarmouth, NS [*Television station call letters*]
CBHFT-2. .. Mulgrave, NS [*Television station call letters*]
CBHFT-3. .. Sydney, NS [*Television station call letters*]
CBHFT-4. .. Cheticamp, NS [*Television station call letters*]
CBHHA ..... [*The*] Church of the Brethren Homes and Hospitals Association [*Later, BHOAM*] (EA)
CBHK .... Captive Boresight Harmonization Kit (MCD)
CBHL .... Council on Botanical and Horticultural Libraries (EA)
CBHM .... Coso Basin North [*California*] [*Seismograph station code, US Geological Survey*] (SEIS)
CBHMA ..... Custer Battlefield Historical and Museum Association (EA)
CBHMS ..... Conservative Baptist Home Mission Society (EA)
CBHPC ...... Commonwealth Bureau of Horticulture and Plantation Crops [*British*]
CBHSA ...... Cleveland Bay Horse Society of America (EA)
CBHSM ..... Council for Better Hearing and Speech Month (EA)
CBHT .... Cedarholm, Bland, Havens, and Townes [*Ether drift experiment*] (MUGU)
CBHT .... Halifax, NS [*Television station call letters*]
CBHT-3 .... Yarmouth, NS [*Television station call letters*]
CBHT-4 ..... Sheet Harbour, NS [*Television station call letters*]
CBHT-11 ... Mulgrave, NS [*Television station call letters*]
CBi .... Biggs Free Public Library, Biggs, CA [*Library symbol*] [*Library of Congress*] (LCLS)
CBI .... Cache Bus Interface [*Data processing*] (BYTE)
CBI .... Cahners Books International, Inc. [*Later, CBI Publishing Co., Inc.*]
CBI .... Canadian Banker [*Formerly, Canadian Banker and ICB Review*] [*A publication*]

CBI .... Canadian Business Index [*Micromedia Ltd.*] [*Database*] [*Toronto, ON*] [*A publication*]
CBI .... Canine Behavior Institute (EA)
CBI .... Carbonated Beverage Institute (EA)
CBI .... Caribbean Basin Initiative [*Financial aid package proposed by President Reagan for Central American and Caribbean countries*]
CBI .... Cast Bronze Institute [*Defunct*] (EA)
CBI .... Center for Business Information [*Information service or system*] (IID)
CBI .... Central Bible Institute [*Missouri*]
CBI .... Charles Babbage Institute for the History of Information Processing (EA)
CBI .... Chesapeake Bay Institute [*Johns Hopkins University*]
CBI .... Chesbar Resources, Inc. [*Toronto Stock Exchange symbol*]
CB & I .... Chicago Bridge & Iron Co. [*Later, CBI Industries*]
CBI .... Chichijima [*Bonin Islands*] [*Seismograph station code, US Geological Survey*] (SEIS)
CBI .... Chichijima [*Bonin Islands*] [*Geomagnetic observatory code*]
CBI .... Children's Broadcast Institute [*Canada*]
CBI .... China-Burma-India Theater [*World War II*]
CBI .... Christopher Burns, Inc. [*Also, an information service or system*] (IID)
CBI .... Close-Binding-Intimate
Cbi. .... Cobinamide [*Biochemistry*]
CBI .... Collective Bargaining Institute [*New York, NY*]
CBI .... Columbia, MO [*Location identifier*] [*FAA*] (FAAL)
CBI .... Committee on Biological Information [*British*] (DIT)
CBI .... Competency-Based Instruction
CBI .... Complete Background Investigation
CBI .... Compound Batch Identification [*Data processing*]
CBI .... Computer-Based Instruction [*Education*]
CBI .... Conditional Breakpoint Instruction
CBI .... Confederation of British Industry
CBI .... Confidential Business Information [*Environmental Protection Agency*]
CBI .... Continuous Bladder Irrigation [*Urology*]
CBI .... Cooperative Business International [*Washington, DC*] (EA)
CBI .... Council for a Beautiful Israel (EA)
CBI .... Cumulative Book Index [*Information service or system*] [*A publication*]
CBI .... Current Bibliographic Information [*A publication*]
CBI .... Curtice-Burns Foods, Incorporated [*AMEX symbol*] (SPSG)
CBI .... Information Unltd., Berkeley, CA [*Library symbol*] [*Library of Congress*] (LCLS)
CBI .... Sydney, NS [*AM radio station call letters*]
CBIAC ...... Chemical Warfare/Chemical Biological Defense Information Analysis Center [*DoD*]
CBIAC ...... Columbia Basin Inter-Agency Committee [*Department of Commerce*] (NOAA)
CBIB .... Censo de Bibliotecas [*Database*] [*Ministerio de Cultura*] [*Spanish*] [*Information service or system*] (CRD)
CBIC .... Canadian Book Information Centre
CBIC .... Caribbean Basin Business Information Center (IMH)
CBIC .... Complementary Bipolar Integrated Circuit [*Telecommunications*] (TEL)
CBIC .... Computer-Based Information Center [*Free Library of Philadelphia*] (OLDSS)
CBI (Confederation British Industry) R ... CBI (Confederation of British Industry) Review [*A publication*]
CBIE .... Canadian Bureau for International Education [*See also BCEI*]
CBI-FM ..... Sydney, NS [*FM radio station call letters*]
CBI Forsk .. CBI [*Cement-och Betonginstitutet*] Forskning [*A publication*]
CBIH .... Chemical and Biological Information Handling [*National Institutes of Health*]
CBIHPA .... China-Burma-India Hump Pilots Association (EA)
CBI Ind Trends ... CBI [*Confederation of British Industry*] Industrial Trends [*A publication*]
CBI Ind Trends Surv ... CBI [*Confederation of British Industry*] Industrial Trends Survey [*A publication*]
CBIL .... China Book Information Letter [*A publication*]
CBIL .... Common and Bulk Items List
CBIM .... Companion of the British Institute of Management (DBQ)
CBIMA .... Cahiers de Biologie Marine [*A publication*]
CBIMT ...... Iles De La Madeleine, PQ [*Television station call letters*]
CBIN .... Caribbean Basin Information Network [*Caribbean/Central American Action*] [*Information service or system*] (IID)
CBINA ...... Chemico-Biological Interactions [*A publication*]
CB Index .... Conference Board. Cumulative Index [*A publication*]
CBI News .... Confederation of British Industry. News [*A publication*]
CBIO .... California Biotechnology, Inc. [*NASDAQ symbol*] (NQ)
CBIO .... Counterbattery Intelligence Officer [*Army*] (AABC)
CBIOD .... Cell Biophysics [*A publication*]
CBIP .... Canadian Books in Print [*A publication*]
CBIS .... Campus-Based Information System [*National Science Foundation*]
CBIS .... Communist Bloc Intelligence Service (NATG)
CBIS .... Computer-Based Instruction System (IEEE)
CBisI .... Inyo County Free Library, Bishop, CA [*Library symbol*] [*Library of Congress*] (LCLS)

CBISSSH ..   Committee on Bibliography and Information Services for the Social Sciences and Humanities [*National Library of Canada*]

CBIT ....   China-Burma-India Theater [*World War II*]

CBIT ....   Contract Bulk Inclusive Tour [*Airline fare*]

CBIT ....   Sydney, NS [*Television station call letters*]

CBIT-2 ......   Cheticamp, NS [*Television station call letters*]

CBIVA ......   China-Burma-India Veterans Association   (EA)

CBJ ....   Cambior, Inc. [*Toronto Stock Exchange symbol*]

CBJ ....   Canadian Business Law Journal [*A publication*]

CBJ ....   Chicoutimi, PQ [*AM radio station call letters*]

CBJ ....   Common Bulkhead Joint

CBJ ....   Connecticut Bar Journal [*A publication*]

CBJ ....   Koopkracht. Blad voor de Konsument [*A publication*]

CBJA ....   Central Bureau for the Jewish Aged   (EA)

CBJE-FM ...   Chicoutimi, PQ [*FM radio station call letters*]

CBJET ......   Chicoutimi, PQ [*Television station call letters*]

CBJ-FM ....   Chicoutimi, PQ [*FM radio station call letters*]

CBJNA ......   Carbide Journal [*A publication*]

CBJO ....   Coordinating Board of Jewish Organizations   (EA)

CBK ....   CB Pak, Inc. [*Toronto Stock Exchange symbol*]

C Bk ....   Cheque Book [*British*]   (DAS)

CBK ....   Colby, KS [*Location identifier*] [*FAA*]   (FAAL)

CBK ....   Commercial Bank of Korea

CBK ....   Continental Bank [*NYSE symbol*]   (SPSG)

CBK ....   Economies et Societes [*A publication*]

CBK ....   Regina, SK [*AM radio station call letters*]

CBKA-FM ..   La Ronge, SK [*FM radio station call letters*]

CBKF-1 ......   Gravelbourg, SK [*AM radio station call letters*]

CBKF-2 ......   Saskatoon, SK [*AM radio station call letters*]

CBKF-FM ..   Regina, SK [*FM radio station call letters*]

CBK-FM ....   Regina, SK [*FM radio station call letters*]

CBKFT ......   Regina, SK [*Television station call letters*]

CBKFT-3 ...   Debden, SK [*Television station call letters*]

CBKFT-4 ...   St. Brieux, SK [*Television station call letters*]

CBKFT-5 ...   Zenon Park, SK [*Television station call letters*]

CBKFT-6 ...   Gravelbourg, SK [*Television station call letters*]

CBKFT-9 ...   Bellegarde, SK [*Television station call letters*]

CBKHT ......   Keno Hill, YT [*Television station call letters*]

CBKI ....   Community Banks, Inc. [*NASDAQ symbol*]   (NQ)

CBKI-TV-4 ...   Nipawin, SK [*Television station call letters*]

CBKK ....   Chuban Kenkyu [*Studies on Chinese Language and Literature*] [*A publication*]

CBKS ....   Commonwealth Bancshares Corp. [*Williamsport, PA*] [*NASDAQ symbol*]   (NQ)

CBKS-FM ...   Saskatoon, SK [*FM radio station call letters*]

CBKST ......   Saskatoon, SK [*Television station call letters*]

CBKST-1 ...   Stranraer, SK [*Television station call letters*]

CBKT ....   Regina, SK [*Television station call letters*]

CBKT-2 ......   Willow Bunch, SK [*Television station call letters*]

CBL...........   Cable   (AAG)

CBL...........   Cabline

CBL...........   Calwer Bibellexikon   (BJA)

CBL...........   Camara Brasileira do Livro [*Brazilian Chamber of Publishing*]   (EAIO)

CBL...........   Canadian Broadcasting League

CBL...........   Canadian Business Law Journal [*A publication*]

CBL...........   Carlyle Barton Laboratory   (MCD)

CBL...........   Carte Blanche [*Freedom of Action*] [*French*]

CBL...........   Caustic Boundary Layer [*Acoustics*]

CBL...........   Central Bidder's List

CBL...........   Chesapeake Biological Laboratories [*University of Maryland*]

CBL...........   Ciudad Bolivar [*Venezuela*] [*Airport symbol*]   (OAG)

CBL...........   Cleared Bidder's List

Cbl...........   Cobalamin [*Biochemistry*]

CBL...........   Collectanea Biblica Latina [*Rome*] [*A publication*]

CBL...........   Commercial Bill of Lading [*Shipping*]

CBL...........   Community Business Lothian [*British*]

CBL...........   Competency-Based Learning [*Education*]

CBL...........   Computer-Based Learning

CBL...........   Conemaugh & Black Lick Railroad Co. [*AAR code*]

CBL...........   Configuration Breakdown List

CBL...........   Cord [*Umbilical*] Blood Leukocytes [*Hematology*]

CBL...........   Corroon & Black Corp. [*NYSE symbol*]   (SPSG)

CBL...........   Crown Bute Resources Ltd. [*Vancouver Stock Exchange symbol*]

CBL...........   Cumulative Book List [*A publication*]

CBL...........   Journal of Commercial Bank Lending [*A publication*]

CBL...........   Nicholson Air Service, Inc. [*Cumberland, MD*] [*FAA designator*]   (FAAC)

CBl...........   Palo Verde Valley District Library, Blythe, CA [*Library symbol*] [*Library of Congress*]   (LCLS)

CBL...........   San Bernardino County Free Library, San Bernardino, CA [*OCLC symbol*]   (OCLC)

CBL...........   Toronto, ON [*AM radio station call letters*]

CBLA.........   Central Blood Laboratories Authority [*British*]

CBLA.........   Cibola Energy Corp. [*Albuquerque, NM*] [*NASDAQ symbol*]   (NQ)

CBLANT ...   Construction Battalions, Atlantic [*Navy*]

CBLAT ......   Geraldton, ON [*Television station call letters*]

CBLAT-1 ...   Manitouwadge, ON [*Television station call letters*]

CBLAT-3 ...   Wawa, ON [*Television station call letters*]

CBLAT-4 ...   Marathon, ON [*Television station call letters*]

CBLBA ......   Ciba Lectures in Microbial Biochemistry [*A publication*]

Cbl Brsch Not Ned ...   Correspondentieblad van de Broederschap der Notarissen in Nederland [*A publication*]

CBLC.........   Center for the Book in the Library of Congress   (EA)

CBLE ....   Cable Applications, Inc. [*NASDAQ symbol*]   (NQ)

CBLFA ......   Corn Belt Livestock Feeders Association [*Later, NCA*]

CBL-FM ....   Toronto, ON [*FM radio station call letters*]

CBLFT.......   Toronto, ON [*Television station call letters*]

CBLFT-1 ...   Sturgeon Falls, ON [*Television station call letters*]

CBLFT-2 ...   Sudbury, ON [*Television station call letters*]

CBLFT-3 ...   Timmins, ON [*Television station call letters*]

CBLFT-4 ...   Kapuskasing, ON [*Television station call letters*]

CBLFT-5 ...   Hearst, ON [*Television station call letters*]

CBLFT-6 ...   Elliot Lake, ON [*Television station call letters*]

CBLGA2....   Chronobiologia [*A publication*]

Cbl Ges Forstw ...   Centralblatt fuer das Gesamte Forstwesen [*A publication*]

CBLHI.......   California Brief Life History Inventory [*Personality development test*] [*Psychology*]

CBLJ ....   Corporate Business Law Journal [*A publication*]

CBLKAE ...   Contributions. Biological Laboratory. Kyoto University [*A publication*]

CBLLAH ...   Contributions. Bears Bluff Laboratories [*A publication*]

CBLM........   CBL Medical, Inc. [*NASDAQ symbol*]   (NQ)

CBLM........   Cluster-Bethe-Lattice Method   (MCD)

CBLO ....   Chief Bombardment Liaison Officer [*Navy*]

Cb LR........   Columbia Law Review [*A publication*]

CBLRD......   Cable Reed

CBLS ....   Carrier-Borne Air Liaison Section [*Navy*]

CBLS ....   Corn Belt Library System [*Library network*]

CBLT ....   Character Block Transfer   (BYTE)

CBLT ....   Toronto, ON [*Television station call letters*]

CBLX.........   Cable Exchange, Inc. [*NASDAQ symbol*]   (NQ)

CBM ....   Calcium-Based Minerals [*Inorganic chemistry*]

CBM ....   Cambrex Corp. [*AMEX symbol*]   (SPSG)

CBM ....   Caribou [*Maine*] [*Seismograph station code, US Geological Survey*]   (SEIS)

CBM ....   Carrierband MODEM [*Motorola, Inc.*]

CBM ....   Center for Biological Macromolecules [*State University of New York at Albany*] [*Research center*]   (RCD)

CBM ....   Central Bank Money

CBM ....   Ceramic-Based Microcircuit

CBM ....   Certified Ballast Manufacturers Association   (EA)

CBM ....   Chemical-Based Munitions   (AFM)

CBM ....   Chief Boatswain's Mate [*Navy rating*] [*Obsolete*]

CBM ....   Chlorobromomethane [*Also, CB*] [*Organic chemistry*]

CBM ....   Cigar Box Manufacturers [*Defunct*]   (EA)

CBM ....   Cognitive-Behavior Modification [*Psychology*]

CBM ....   Columbus, MS [*Location identifier*] [*FAA*]   (FAAL)

CBM ....   Common Bill of Material   (MCD)

CBM ....   Communications Buffer Memory [*Data processing*]

CBM ....   Consolidated Boulder Mountain [*Vancouver Stock Exchange symbol*]

CBM ....   Constant Boiling Mixture

CBM ....   Continental Ballistic Missile

CBM ....   Continental Baptist Mission   (EA)

CBM ....   Contour Blind & Shade (Canada) Ltd. [*Toronto Stock Exchange symbol*]

CBM ....   Conventional Buoy Mooring   (DS)

CBM ....   Corn, Beans, Miami [*Tongue-in-cheek description of a crop rotation system. Modern time-saving equipment allegedly allows farmers to rotate corn and soybeans in summer, spend winter in Miami*]

CBM ....   Cruise Ballistic Missile   (MCD)

CBM ....   Cubic Meter   (ROG)

CBM ....   Judah L. Magnes Memorial Museum, Rabbi Morris Goldstein Library, Berkeley, CA [*Library symbol*] [*Library of Congress*]   (LCLS)

CBM ....   Montreal, PQ [*AM radio station call letters*]

CBM ....   Siglum for Tablets, Etc., in the Collection of the Babylonian Section of the University Museum, Philadelphia [*Later, CBS*]   (BJA)

C³/BM ....   Command, Control, and Communications Battle Management [*Military*]

CBM's........   Confidence-Building Measures [*for European military security*]

CBMA ......   Canadian Book Manufacturing Association

CBMA ......   Canadian Business Manufacturers Association   (MCD)

CBMA ......   Certified Ballast Manufacturers Association

CBMA ......   Chief Boatswain's Mate, Acting [*Navy rating*] [*Obsolete*]

CBMAM ...   Christian Bookstall Managers Association   (EA)

CBMAM ...   Cumulonimbus Mammatus [*Cloud*] [*Meteorology*]   (FAAC)

CBMC ....   Christian Business Men of Canada

CBMC ....   Christian Business Men's Committee of USA   (EA)

CBMC ....   Communaute de Travail des Brasseurs du Marche Commun [*Working Committee of Common Market Brewers*]

CBMC ....   Corregidor-Bataan Memorial Commission [*Government agency*] [*Terminated, 1967*]

CBMCBB ..   Chief Boatswain's Mate, Construction Battalion, Boatswain [*Navy rating*] [*Obsolete*]

CBMCBS ..   Chief Boatswain's Mate, Construction Battalion, Stevedore [*Navy rating*] [*Obsolete*]
CBMCI.....   Christian Business Men's Committee International [*Later, CBMC*]   (EA)
CBMD ......   Calcified Bone Mineral Density
CBMDAW ...   Computers in Biology and Medicine [*A publication*]
CBME........   Combined Bureau, Middle East [*British military*]   (DMA)
CB Merger ...   Conference Board. Announcements of Mergers and Acquisitions [*A publication*]
CBM-FM...   Montreal, PQ [*FM radio station call letters*]
CBMI........   Christian Blind Mission International [*Bensheim, Federal Republic of Germany*]
CBMI-FM ...   Baie-Comeau, PQ [*FM radio station call letters*]
CBMKR.....   Chief Boilermaker [*Coast Guard*]
CBMM ......   Chief Boatswain's Mate, A [*Master-at-Arms*] [*Navy rating*] [*Obsolete*]
CBMMP....   Chronic Benign Mucous Membrane Pemphigoid [*Medicine*]
CBMODY ...   Cell Biology Monographs [*A publication*]
CBMP........   Conference Board of Major Printers [*Inactive*]   (EA)
CBMPE.....   Council of British Manufacturers of Petroleum Equipment
CBMPP.....   Cargo Bay Module Personnel Provisions [*NASA*]   (KSC)
CBMPTU ...   Cigar Box Makers' and Paperers' Trade Union [*British*]
CBMRB7...   Computers and Biomedical Research [*A publication*]
CBMR-FM ...   Fermont, PQ [*FM radio station call letters*]
CBMS.......   Computer-Based Message System [*Electronic mail*]
CBMS.......   Conference Board of the Mathematical Sciences   (EA)
CBMSRC ..   Chief Boatswain's Mate, Ship Repair, Crane Operator [*Navy rating*] [*Obsolete*]
CBMSRR ..   Chief Boatswain's Mate, Ship Repair, Rigger [*Navy rating*] [*Obsolete*]
CBMSRS...   Chief Boatswain's Mate, Ship Repair, Canvasman [*Navy rating*] [*Obsolete*]
CBMT........   Cross-Linked Biotinylated Microtubule [*Biochemistry*]
CBMT........   Montreal, PQ [*Television station call letters*]
CBMU ....   Construction Battalion Maintenance Unit [*Navy*]
CBMU ....   Current BIT [*Binary Digit*] Monitor Unit [*Data processing*]
CBN ....   Cabin [*Aviation*]   (FAAC)
CBN ....   Cannabinol [*A component of marijuana*]
CBN ....   Carbine   (AABC)
CBN ....   Chemical/Bacterial/Nuclear [*Military*]   (MCD)
CBN ....   Christian Broadcasting Network [*Cable-television system*]
CBN ....   Cirebon [*Indonesia*] [*Airport symbol*]   (OAG)
CBN ....   Commission on Biochemical Nomenclature [*IUPAC*]
CBN ....   Consolidated Marbenor Mines Ltd. [*Toronto Stock Exchange symbol*]
CBN ....   Construction Battalion [*Navy*]
CBN ....   Corbin [*Virginia*] [*Seismograph station code, US Geological Survey*]   (SEIS)
CBN ....   Cubic Boron Nitride [*Cutting tool edges*]
CBN ....   St. John's, NF [*AM radio station call letters*]
CBNA ....   St. Anthony, NF [*AM radio station call letters*]
CBNAT......   Grand Falls, NF [*Television station call letters*]
CBNAT-1 ..   Baie Verte, NF [*Television station call letters*]
CBNAT-4 ..   St. Anthony, NF [*Television station call letters*]
CBNAT-9 ..   Mount St. Margaret, NF [*Television station call letters*]
CBNB ....   Chemical Business NewsBase [*Royal Society of Chemistry*] [*Information service or system*]
CBNB ....   CommerceBancorp [*NASDAQ symbol*]   (NQ)
CBNC ....   Collective Bargaining Negotiations and Contracts [*Bureau of National Affairs*] [*Information service or system*]
CBNE ....   Constitution Bancorp of New England, Inc. [*NASDAQ symbol*]   (NQ)
CB NEWS ...   Community Business Scotland News [*A publication*]
CBN-FM ...   St. John's, NF [*FM radio station call letters*]
CBNH........   Community Bankshares, Inc. [*Concord, NH*] [*NASDAQ symbol*]   (NQ)
CBNJ.........   Commercial Bancshares of New Jersey [*NASDAQ symbol*]   (NQ)
CBNK ....   Centerbanc Savings Association [*St. Petersburg, FL*] [*NASDAQ symbol*]   (NQ)
CBNLT......   Labrador City, NF [*Television station call letters*]
CBNM ....   Central Bureau of Nuclear Measurements [*European Atomic Energy Community*]
CBNM ....   Marystown, NF [*AM radio station call letters*]
CBNRC.....   Communications Branch, National Research Council
CBNS.........   Center for the Biology of Natural Systems [*Washington University*]
CBNS.........   Commander, British Naval Staff
CBNS.........   Common Bench, New Series [*A publication*]
CB (NS) .....   English Common Bench Reports, New Series (Manning, Granger, and Scott) [*140-144 English Reprint*] [*A publication*]   (DLA)
CB NS (Eng) ...   English Common Bench Reports, New Series (Manning, Granger, and Scott) [*140-144 English Reprint*] [*A publication*]   (DLA)
CBNT ....   St. John's, NF [*Television station call letters*]
CBNT-1 .....   Port Rexton, NF [*Television station call letters*]
CBNT-2 .....   Placentia, NF [*Television station call letters*]
CBNT-3 .....   Marystown, NF [*Television station call letters*]
CBO ....   Canadian Continental Oil [*Vancouver Stock Exchange symbol*]
CBO ....   Cancel Back Order

CBO ....   Carrier Balloon/Omegasonde System [*National Center for Atmospheric Research*]
CBO ....   Certificate of Beneficial Ownership
CBO ....   Chesbro Reservoir [*California*] [*Seismograph station code, US Geological Survey*]   (SEIS)
CBO ....   Clarksville Branch Office [*AEC*]
CBO ....   Coding Board Officer
CBO ....   Collective Bargaining Organization
CBO ....   Combined Bomber Offensive [*World War II*]
CBO ....   Community-Based Order   (ADA)
CBO ....   Community-Based Organization [*Organization which provides employment and training services*] [*CETA*]
CBO ....   Components Business Operations [*Chrysler campaign to increase sales*]
CBO ....   Computer Burst Order   (AABC)
CBO ....   Conference of Baltic Oceanographers [*Kiel, Federal Republic of Germany*]   (EAIO)
CBO ....   Congressional Budget Office [*Washington, DC*]
CBO ....   Cotabato [*Philippines*] [*Airport symbol*]   (OAG)
CBO ....   Counter-Battery Officer
CBO ....   Cycles between Overhaul   (MCD)
CBO ....   Ottawa, ON [*AM radio station call letters*]
CBOA ....   Citizens Band Operating Area
CBOB ....   Collegiate Basketball Officials Bureau [*Later, Eastern College Basketball Association*]   (EA)
CBOC ....   Canada Business Opportunity Centre [*1986*]
CBOC ....   Commercial Bancorporation of Colorado [*Denver*] [*NASDAQ symbol*]   (NQ)
CBOC ....   Completion of Bed Occupancy Care [*Veterans Administration*]
CBOD ....   Carbonaceous Biochemical Oxygen Demand [*Environmental chemistry*]
CBO Def S ...   Defense Spending and the Economy. Congressional Budget Office Study [*A publication*]
CBOE ....   Chicago Board Options Exchange [*Chicago, IL*]   (EA)
CBOE ....   Committee of Butchery Organizations of the EEC   (EAIO)
CBOF ....   Ottawa, ON [*AM radio station call letters*]
CBOF-1 .....   Maniwaki, PQ [*AM radio station call letters*]
CBOF-FM ...   Ottawa, ON [*FM radio station call letters*]
CBO-FM ...   Ottawa, ON [*FM radio station call letters*]
CBOFT ......   Ottawa, ON [*Television station call letters*]
CBOG ....   Community Bancshares, Inc. [*NASDAQ symbol*]   (NQ)
CBOI ....   Complete Basis of Issue [*Military*]   (AABC)
CBOIP ....   Complete Basis of Issue Plan [*Military*]   (AABC)
CBOMB ....   Canadian Baptist Overseas Mission Board
CBO Med Ben ...   Changing the Structure of Medicare Benefits. Issues and Options. Congressional Budget Office [*A publication*]
CBO Nat Gas ...   Understanding Natural Gas Price Control. Congressional Budget Office Study [*A publication*]
CBON-FM ...   Sudbury, ON [*FM radio station call letters*]
CBORE......   Counterbore   (KSC)
CBOREO ..   Counterbore Other Side
CBOSS ......   Count Back Order and Sample Select [*Data processing*]
CBOT ....   Board of Trade of the City of Chicago [*Chicago, IL*]   (EAIO)
CBOT ....   Cabot Medical Corp. [*Langhorne, PA*] [*NASDAQ symbol*]   (NQ)
CBOT ....   Commissions Board of Trade
CBOT ....   Ottawa, ON [*Television station call letters*]
CBOV ....   [*The*] College Book of Verse [*A publication*]
CBp ....   Buena Park Library District Library, Buena Park, CA [*Library symbol*] [*Library of Congress*]   (LCLS)
CBP...........   Calgary Board of Education, Professional Library [*UTLAS symbol*]
CBP...........   Campbellpur [*Pakistan*] [*Seismograph station code, US Geological Survey*]   (SEIS)
CBP...........   Canadian Business Press
CBP...........   Caribe Petroleums [*Vancouver Stock Exchange symbol*]
CBP...........   Catholic Book Publishers [*Later, CBPA*]   (EA)
CBP...........   CB Review (Philippines) [*A publication*]
CBP...........   Ceramic Beam Pentode
CBP...........   Cholesterol Binding Protein [*Biochemistry*]
CBP...........   Class of Blue Copper Proteins [*Crystallography*]
CBP...........   Colchicine-Binding Protein [*Biochemistry*]
CBP...........   Columbus, OH [*Location identifier*] [*FAA*]   (FAAL)
CBP...........   Combined Black Publishers [*Defunct*]   (EA)
CBP...........   Condensate Booster Pump [*Nuclear energy*]   (NRCH)
CBP...........   Connector Bracket (Power)   (MCD)
CBP...........   Constant Boiling Point
CBP...........   County Business Patterns [*Bureau of the Census*] [*Information service or system*] [*A publication*]
CBPA.........   Catholic Book Publishers Association   (EA)
CBPA.........   Community Bancorp, Inc. [*NASDAQ symbol*]   (CTT)
CBPAB5 ....   Comparative Biochemistry and Physiology. A. Comparative Physiology [*A publication*]
CBPAC ......   Construction Battalions, Pacific [*Navy*]
CBPac ....   Pacific School of Religion, Berkeley, CA [*Library symbol*] [*Library of Congress*]   (LCLS)
CBPBB ......   Comparative Biochemistry and Physiology. B. Comparative Biochemistry [*A publication*]
CBPBB8 ....   Comparative Biochemistry and Physiology. B. Comparative Biochemistry [*A publication*]
CBPC ....   [*The*] Cambridge Book of Poetry for Children [*A publication*]

CBPC......... Canadian Book Publishers' Council
CBPCBB.... Comparative Biochemistry and Physiology. C. Comparative Pharmacology [Later, Comparative Biochemistry and Physiology. C. Comparative Pharmacology and Toxicology] [A publication]
CBPCD...... Ciments, Betons, Platres, Chaux [A publication]
CBPCEE..... Comparative Biochemistry and Physiology. C. Comparative Pharmacology and Toxicology [A publication]
CBPDC...... Canadian Book and Periodical Development Council
CBPDF...... Canadian Broadcast Program Development Fund
CBPF......... Pacific Film Archives, University Art Museum, Berkeley, CA [Library symbol] [Library of Congress] (LCLS)
CBPFC...... Commonwealth Bureau of Pastures and Field Crops [British]
CBPI......... Canadian Business Periodicals Index [Later, Canadian Business Index] [A publication]
CBPI......... Conditional Breakpoint Instruction
CBPMP..... Cold Brine Pump
CBpN......... Nutrilite Products, Inc., Technical Library, Buena Park, CA [Library symbol] [Library of Congress] (LCLS)
CBPO........ Consolidated Base Personnel Office [Air Force]
CBPOL...... Consolidated Base Personnel Office Letter [Air Force]
CBPP........ Center on Budget and Policy Priorities (EA)
CBPP........ Contagious Bovine Pleuropneumonia [Veterinary medicine]
CBPRA...... Cerebral Palsy Review [A publication]
CBPT......... CLIRA [Closed-Loop In-Reactor Assembly] Backup Plug Tool [Nuclear energy] (NRCH)
CBPTC...... Carbon Black Producers Traffic Committee
CBQ........... Calabar [Nigeria] [Airport symbol] (OAG)
CBQ........... Catholic Biblical Quarterly [A publication]
CBQ........... Chicago, Burlington & Quincy Railroad [Also known as Burlington Route] [AAR code]
CB & Q ...... Chicago, Burlington & Quincy Railroad [Also known as Burlington Route]
CBQ........... Civilian Bachelor Quarters [Air Force] (AFM)
CBQ........... Thunder Bay, ON [AM radio station call letters]
CBQ-FM ... Thunder Bay, ON [FM radio station call letters]
CBQL-FM ... Savant Lake, ON [FM radio station call letters]
CBQN-FM ... Osnaburgh, ON [FM radio station call letters]
CBQP-FM ... Pickle Lake, ON [FM radio station call letters]
CBQR-FM ... Rankin Inlet, NT [FM radio station call letters]
CBQS-FM ... Sioux Narrows, ON [FM radio station call letters]
CBQX-FM ... Kenora, ON [FM radio station call letters]
CBr............. Brawley Public Library, Brawley, CA [Library symbol] [Library of Congress] (LCLS)
CBr............. Cadernos Brasileiros [A publication]
CBR .... Calgary, AB [AM radio station call letters]
CBR .... California Bearing Ratio [Aviation]
CBR .... Canadian Bankruptcy Reports, Annotated [A publication] (DLA)
CBR .... Canadian Bar Review [A publication]
CBR .... Canadian Barranca Corp. [Vancouver Stock Exchange symbol]
CBR .... Canberra [Australia] [Airport symbol] (OAG)
CBR .... Cast Brass
CBR .... Center for Blood Research [Research center] (RCD)
CBR .... Center for Brain Research [University of Rochester] [Research center] (RCD)
CBR .... Centre for Business Research [Manchester Business School] [British] (CB)
CBR .... Change Board Register
CBR .... Charger Battery Relay (MCD)
CBR .... Chemical, Biological, and Radiological [Warfare] [Later, CB] [Military]
CBR .... China Business Report [A publication]
CBR .... China Business Review [A publication]
CBR .... Circuit Board Rack
CBR .... Colonial Bird Register [Cornell University] [Information service or system] (IID)
CBR .... Commercial Breeder Reactor
CBR .... Complete Bed Rest [Medicine]
CBR .... Comprehensive Beacon RADAR
CBR .... Computer Book Review [Comber Press] [Information service or system] (CRD)
CBR .... Computerized Bibliographic Retrieval [Hope College] (OLDSS)
CBR .... Contract Baseline Report (MCD)
CBR .... Cosmic Black-Body Radiation [Astrophysics]
C/BR......... Cost/Burden Reduction
CBR .... Cour du Banc de la Reine [Court of Queen's Bench] [Quebec] [Canada] (ILCA)
CBR .... Crude Birth Rate [Medicine]
CBR .... Crystal Brands, Inc. [NYSE symbol] (SPSG)
CBRA........ Canadian Book Review Annual [A publication]
CBRA........ Chemical, Biological, Radiological Agency [Military]
CBRA........ Copper and Brass Research Association [Later, CDA]
CBRA........ Critical Bibliography to Religion in America [A publication] (BJA)
CBRA........ Library of Congress COBRA [Source file] [UTLAS symbol]
CBRBAH... Comunicaciones. Museo Argentino de Ciencias Naturales "Bernardino Rivadavia" e Instituto Nacional de Investigacion de las Ciencias Naturales. Ciencias Botanicas [A publication]
CBRC........ Chemical, Biological, and Radiological Center [Military]

CBRC......... Current Book Review Citations [A publication]
CBRCC..... Chemical, Biological, Radiological Control Center [Military] (AABC)
CBRCF...... Canadian Barranca Corp. [NASDAQ symbol] (NQ)
C/BRD ...... Circuit Board [Automotive engineering]
CBRD .... Construction Battalion Replacement Depot [Navy]
CBRE......... Canadian Brotherhood of Railway Employees and Other Transport Workers
CBRE......... Chemical, Biological, and Radiological Element [Military] (AABC)
CBreA .... Ameron, Inc. Corrosion Control Division, Brea, CA [Library symbol] [Library of Congress] (LCLS)
CBRED...... Closed Bomb Data Reduction Program (MCD)
CBREG...... Chemical-Biological-Radiological Engineering Group [Army] (MCD)
CBreU........ Union Oil Co. of California, Brea, CA [Library symbol] [Library of Congress] (LCLS)
CB Review ... Canadian Business Review [A publication]
CBRF......... Community-Based Residential Facility
CBR-FM.... Calgary, AB [FM radio station call letters]
CBRI......... Chemistry and Biology Research Institute [Agriculture Canada Research Branch] [Research center] (RCD)
CBRI......... Children's Book Review Index [A publication]
CBri............ Mono County Free Library, Bridgeport, CA [Library symbol] [Library of Congress] (LCLS)
CBRL........ Cracker Barrel Old Country Store, Inc. [Lebanon, TN] [NASDAQ symbol] (NQ)
CBRM .... Charger-Battery-Regulator Module [NASA]
CBRN .... Chemical, Biological, Radiological, and Nuclear [Army] (AABC)
CBR (NS) .. Canadian Bankruptcy Reports, Annotated, New Series [A publication] (DLA)
CBRO .... Chemical, Biological, Radiological Officer [Army]
CBRP......... CB [Citizens Band] Radio Patrol of American Federation of Police (EA)
CBRP........ Continental Bancorp, Inc. [Philadelphia, PA] [NASDAQ symbol] (NQ)
CBRPDS.... Cell Biology International Reports [A publication]
CBRPT...... Confederation of British Road Passenger Transport (ILCA)
CB Rpt 814 ... Conference Board. Report 814. Managing the International Company. Building a Global Perspective [A publication]
CB Rpt 815 ... Conference Board. Report 815. Corporate Directorship Practices. Compensation [A publication]
CB Rpt 818 ... Conference Board. Report 818. Compensating Foreign Service Personnel [A publication]
CB Rpt 820 ... Conference Board. Report 820. Corporate Contributions Function [A publication]
CB Rpt 821 ... Conference Board. Report 821. Who Is Top Management? [A publication]
CB Rpt 823 ... Conference Board. Report 823. Impact of Social Welfare Policies in the United States [A publication]
CB Rpt 824 ... Conference Board. Report 824. Insurance Deregulation. Issues and Perspectives [A publication]
CB Rpt 825 ... Conference Board. Report 825. Regional Perspectives on Energy Issues [A publication]
CB Rpt 826 ... Conference Board. Report 826. Planning for Staff and Support Units [A publication]
CB Rpt 831 ... Conference Board. Report 831. Flexible Employee Benefit Plans. Companies' Experiences [A publication]
CB Rpt 832 ... Conference Board. Report 832. Corporate Voluntary Contributions in Europe [A publication]
CB Rpt 834 ... Conference Board. Report 834. Corporate Aid Programs in Twelve Less-Developed Countries [A publication]
CB Rpt 835 ... Conference Board. Report 835. Adapting Products for Export [A publication]
CB Rpt 837 ... Conference Board. Report 837. Organizing and Managing for Energy Efficiency [A publication]
CB Rpt 838 ... Conference Board. Report 838. Managing Business-State Government Relations [A publication]
CB Rpt 839 ... Conference Board. Report 839. New Patterns in Organizing for Financial Management [A publication]
CB Rpt 842 ... Conference Board. Report 842. Research and Development. Key Issues for Management [A publication]
CB Rpt 844 ... Conference Board. Report 844. Manufacturing. New Concepts and New Technology to Meet New Competition [A publication]
CB Rpt 845 ... Conference Board. Report 845. Organizing Corporate Marketing [A publication]
CB Rpt 846 ... Conference Board. Report 846. Economic Overview 1983. Medium-Term Corporate Forecasts [A publication]
CB Rpt 847 ... Conference Board. Report 847. Developing Strategic Leadership [A publication]
CB Rpt 849 ... Conference Board. Report 849. Innovations in Managing Human Resources [A publication]
CB Rpt 850 ... Conference Board. Report 850. Managing National Accounts [A publication]
CB Rpt 851 ... Conference Board. Report 851. From Owner to Professional Management. Problems in Transition [A publication]
CB Rpt 852 ... Conference Board. Report 852. Regulating International Data Transmission. Impact on Managing International Business [A publication]

CB Rpt 853 ... Conference Board. Report 853. International Patterns of Inflation. A Study in Contrasts [*A publication*]

CB Rpt 855 ... Conference Board. Report 855. Federal Budget Deficits and the US Economy [*A publication*]

CB Rpt 859 ... Conference Board. Report 859. Inflation Adjustment of the Individual Income Tax. Indexation or Legislation [*A publication*]

CB Rpt 860 ... Conference Board. Report 860. Managing Older Workers. Company Policies and Attitudes [*A publication*]

CB Rpt 861 ... Conference Board. Report 861. Managing International Public Affairs [*A publication*]

CB Rpt 863 ... Conference Board. Report 863. Corporate R & D Strategy. Innovation and Funding Issues [*A publication*]

CB Rpt 865 ... Conference Board. Report 865. New Look in Wage Policy and Employee Relations [*A publication*]

CB Rpt 867 ... Conference Board. Report 867. Facing Strategic Issues. New Planning Guides and Practices [*A publication*]

CB Rpt 868 ... Conference Board. Report 868. Corporations and Families. Changing Practices and Perspectives [*A publication*]

CB Rpt 870 ... Conference Board. Report 870. Trends in Corporate Education and Training [*A publication*]

CB Rpt 872 ... Conference Board. Report 872. World Economy in the 1980's [*A publication*]

CB Rpt 873 ... Conference Board. Report 873. Refocusing the Company's Business [*A publication*]

CB Rpt 874 ... Conference Board. Report 874. Developing New Leadership in a Multinational Environment [*A publication*]

CB Rpt 876 ... Conference Board. Report 876. Competitive Leverage [*A publication*]

CB Rpt 881 ... Conference Board. Report 881. Meeting Human Needs. Corporate Programs and Partnerships [*A publication*]

CB Rpt 882 ... Conference Board. Report 882. Annual Survey of Corporate Contributions. 1986 Edition [*A publication*]

CB Rpt 883 ... Conference Board. Report 883. Corporate Strategies for Controlling Substance Abuse [*A publication*]

CB Rpt 886 ... Conference Board. Report 886. Board Committees in European Companies [*A publication*]

CB Rpt 887 ... Conference Board. Report 887. Screening Requests for Corporate Contributions [*A publication*]

CBR Retail ... Current Business Reports. Annual Retail Trade [*A publication*]

CBR Retl A ... Current Business Reports. Advanced Monthly Retail Sales [*A publication*]

CBR Retl M ... Current Business Reports. Monthly Retail Trade Sales and Inventories [*A publication*]

CBR Retl S ... Current Business Reports. Revised Monthly Retail Sales and Inventories for January, 1974 - December, 1983 [*A publication*]

CBRS .... Chemical, Biological, and Radiological Section [*Military*]

CBRS .... Child Behavior Rating Scale [*Devereaux*] [*Psychology*]

CBRS .... Children's Book Review Service [*A publication*]

CBRS .... Chiropody Bibliographical Research Society

CBRS .... Computer-Based Reference Service [*Information service or system*]

CBRS .... Concepts-Based Requirements System

CBRT .... Calgary, AB [*Television station call letters*]

CBRT .... Canadian Brotherhood of Railway Transport and General Workers

CBRU .... Computer-Based Resource Units [*Education*]

CBrug......... Collationes Brugenses (BJA)

CBR Whsl S ... Current Business Reports. Revised Monthly Wholesale Trade Sales and Inventories for January, 1975 - December, 1984 [*A publication*]

CBR Whsl TM ... Current Business Reports. Monthly Wholesale Trade Sales and Inventories [*A publication*]

CBRY......... Northland Cranberries, Inc. [*NASDAQ symbol*]   (NQ)

CBS............ Caborca [*Mexico*] [*Seismograph station code, US Geological Survey*]   (SEIS)

CBS............ Call Box Station   (MSA)

CBS............ Cambodian Buddhist Society   (EA)

CBS............ Cambridge Biological Series [*A publication*]

CBS............ Cambridge BioScience Corp.

CBS............ Canadian Business Magazine [*A publication*]

CBS............ Carrier Balloon System   (MCD)

CBS............ Catalogue of the Babylonian Section [*University Museum, Philadelphia*] [*Formerly, CBM*]   (BJA)

CBS............ CBS, Inc. [*Formerly, Columbia Broadcasting System, Inc.*] [*NYSE symbol*]   (SPSG)

CBS............ Center Back Stage [*A stage direction*]

CBS............ Center for Bigfoot Studies [*An association*]   (EA)

CBS............ Central Battery Signaling   (NATG)

CBS............ Central [*Common*] Battery Supply [*Electronics*]

CBS............ Central [*Common*] Battery Switchboard [*Electronics*]

CBS............ Central [*Common*] Battery System [*Electronics*]

CBS............ Central Bibliographic System [*Library of Congress*]

CBS............ Central Bureau of Statistics [*Information service or system*]   (IID)

CBs............ Certain Boroughs [*British*]

CBS............ Channel Base Section [*World War II*]

CBS............ Christian Brothers School [*Ireland*]

CBS............ Chronic Brain Syndrome [*Medicine*]

CBS............ Chugoku No Bunka To Shakai [*Chinese Culture and Society*] [*A publication*]

CBS............ Church Building Society [*British*]

CBS............ Cinder-Block on Concrete Slab [*Construction*]

CBS............ Cinnabar Resources Ltd. [*Vancouver Stock Exchange symbol*]

CBS............ Civilian Budgeting System [*Military*]

CBS............ Clarity, Brevity, Sharpness [*Objectives of good editing, as set forth in Barry Tarshis' book "How to Write without Pain"*]

CBS............ Close Boundary Sentry [*Military*]   (AFM)

CBS............ Coarse Bearing Servo

CBS............ Coastal Base Section [*Name changed to Continental Advance Section*] [*World War II*]

CBS............ Columbia Broadcasting System [*Later, CBS, Inc.*]

CBS............ Command Battle Simulation   (MCD)

CBS............ Commission for Basic Systems [*WMO*]   (MSC)

CBS............ Committee on Boarding Schools   (EA)

CBS............ Commodity Bookform Standard   (MCD)

CBS............ Common Battery Signaling [*Telecommunications*]   (TEL)

CBS............ Common Battery System

CBS............ Commonwealth Bureau of Soils [*British*]

CBS............ Compact Buoy System

CBS............ Company Buyer Study [*Life Insurance Management and Research Association*]

CBS............ Complete Band Shape   (MCD)

CBS............ Complex Behavior Simulator

CBS............ Conference on British Studies   (EA)

CBS............ Confraternity of the Blessed Sacrament   (EA)

CBS............ Connector Backing Shell

CBS............ Connector Bracket Signal   (MCD)

CBS............ Conservative Baptist Theological Seminary, Englewood, CO [*OCLC symbol*]   (OCLC)

CBS............ Consolidated Balance Sheet [*Accounting*]

CBS............ Continental Base Section

CBS............ Continuing Balance System [*Army*]   (MCD)

CBs............ Contrabass [*Music*]

CBS............ Controlled Barrier System

CBS............ Controlled Blip Scan   (CET)

CBS............ Conventional Boom Sprayer

CBS............ Correlation Bombing System [*Air Force*]   (MCD)

CBS............ Cost Breakdown Structure   (MCD)

CBS............ Crew Ballistic Shelter   (MCD)

CBS............ Cyclohexylbenzothiazole Sulfenamide [*Organic chemistry*]

CBS............ Sisters of Bon Secours [*Roman Catholic religious order*]

CBS............ W. T. Bandy Center for Baudelaire Studies   (EA)

CBSA .... Cargo Bay Stowage Assembly (NASA)

CBSA .... Catholic Bible Society of America   (EA)

CBSA .... Centre for Business Systems Analysis [*City University*] [*British*]   (CB)

CBSA .... Cleveland Bay Society of America   (EA)

CBSA .... Copper and Brass Servicenter Association   (EA)

CBSC .... Cambridge Bible for Schools and Colleges [*A publication*]   (BJA)

CBSC .... Common Bias, Single Control

CBSD........ Cassanova Brown Streak Disease [*Plant pathology*]

CBSE .... Caboose [*Freight*]

CBSE .... Commonwealth Board of Surveying Education [*London, England*]   (EAIO)

CBSH .... Commerce Bancshares, Inc. [*Kansas City, MO*] [*NASDAQ symbol*]   (NQ)

CBSHP...... Cobbler Shop

CBSI .... Community Bank System, Incorporated [*Syracuse, NY*] [*NASDAQ symbol*]   (NQ)

CBSI .... Council on Biological Sciences Information   (DIT)

CBSI-FM... Sept-Iles, PQ [*FM radio station call letters*]

CBSISH.... Comite de la Bibliographie et des Services d'Information en Sciences Humaines [*Committee on Bibliography and Information Services for the Social Sciences and Humanities - CBISSSH*] [*National Library of Canada*]

CBSLE....... Center for Bilingual Research and Second Language Education [*Later, CLEAR*]   (GRD)

CBSM........ Comprehensive Behavioral Services Model

CBSO........ Counter Battery Staff Officer [*World War I*] [*Canada*]

CBSR .... Carcinogen Bioassay in Small Rodents

CBSR .... Chief Boilermaker, Ship Repair [*Navy*]

CBSR .... Coupled Breeding Superheating Reactor

CBSS .... Central Bancshares of the South, Inc. [*Birmingham, AL*] [*NASDAQ symbol*]   (NQ)

CBSS .... Churches at Bosra and Samaria-Sebaste [*A publication*]   (BJA)

CBSS .... Closed Breech Scavenging System

CBST .... Sept-Iles, PQ [*Television station call letters*]

CB Stat ...... Conference Board. Statistical Bulletin [*A publication*]

CBSTB........ Combustion Science and Technology [*A publication*]

CBStM....... Saint Margaret's House, Berkeley, CA [*Library symbol*] [*Library of Congress*]   (LCLS)

CBSV .... Cycles between Scheduled Visits   (MCD)

CBS-X....... Continuing Balance System - Expanded [*Army*]   (AABC)

CBT............ Cabot Corp. [*NYSE symbol*]   (SPSG)

CBT............ Cembratriene-diol [*Organic chemistry*]

CBT............ Center for Building Technology [*National Institute of Standards and Technology*] [*Gaithersburg, MD*]

CBT............ Central Battery Telephone [*Telecommunications*]

CBT........... Centre for Business Technology [*Australia*]
CBT........... Cesium Beam Tube
CBT........... Chicago Board of Trade [*A futures exchange*] [*Investment term*]
CBT........... Cincinnati Board of Trade   (EA)
CBT........... Clean Ballast Tanks [*Transportation*]
CBT........... Coin Box Telephone [*Telecommunications*]
CBT........... Combat   (AABC)
CBT........... Committee for Better Transit   (EA)
CBT........... Comprehensive Business Tax
CBT........... Computer-Based Terminal
CBT........... Computer-Based Training
CBT........... Connecticut Ballet Theatre
CBT........... Consolidated Bel-Air [*Vancouver Stock Exchange symbol*]
CBT........... Continuous Boat Track [*Navy*]   (CAAL)
CBT........... Contractor Bonding Tape [*3M Co.*]
CBT........... Cooperative Bureau for Teachers [*Superseded by IES*]   (EA)
CBT........... Grand Falls, NF [*AM radio station call letters*]
CBT........... Institute of Transportation Studies Library, University of
　　　　　　　California, Berkeley, CA [*OCLC symbol*]   (OCLC)
CBTA........ Central Battery Telephone Apparatus [*Telecommunications*]
CBTB........ CB & T Bancshares, Inc. [*Columbus, GA*] [*NASDAQ
　　　　　　　symbol*]   (NQ)
CBTDC...... China Building Technology Development Centre [*Beijing*]
　　　　　　　[*Information service or system*]   (IID)
CBTDEV ... Combat Developer
CBTE........ Advisory Committee for Chemical, Biochemical, and Thermal
　　　　　　　Engineering [*Washington, DC*] [*National Science
　　　　　　　Foundation*]   (EGAO)
CBTE........ Competency-Based Teacher Education
CBTE-FM ... Crawford Bay, BC [*FM radio station call letters*]
CBTF........ CB & T Financial Corp. [*Fairmont, WV*] [*NASDAQ
　　　　　　　symbol*]   (NQ)
CBTF........ Chlorobenzotrifluoride [*Organic chemistry*]
CBTI........ Combat Intelligence
CBTIAE ... Contributions. Boyce Thompson Institute [*A publication*]
CBTNAT... Comunicari de Botanica [*A publication*]
CBTP........ Competency-Based Teacher Preparation
CBTR........ Center for Biomedical and Toxicological Research [*Florida
　　　　　　　State University*] [*Research center*]   (RCD)
CBTR........ Clinical Behavior Therapy Review [*A publication*]
CBTRY...... Counterbattery
CBTS........ California Baptist Theological Seminary
CBTS........ Central Battery Telephone Set [*Telecommunications*]
CBTS........ Cesium Beam Time Standard
CBTS........ Computer-Based Training System   (MCD)
CBTSIG..... Child Behavior Therapy Special Interest Group   (EA)
CBTT........ Competency-Based Teacher Training
CBTTA ...... Coordinating Board of Tobacco Trade Associations [*Later,
　　　　　　　NATD*]   (EA)
CBTU .... Coalition of Black Trade Unionists   (EA)
CBTUC...... [*The*] Commonwealth of the Bahamas Trade Union
　　　　　　　Congress   (EY)
CBTV........ Coalition for Better Television
CBU.......... Bureau of the Census, Washington, DC [*OCLC
　　　　　　　symbol*]   (OCLC)
CBu.......... Burlingame Public Library, Burlingame, CA [*Library symbol*]
　　　　　　　[*Library of Congress*]   (LCLS)
CBU.......... Canadian Business Review [*A publication*]
CBU.......... Caribbean Broadcasting Union
CBU.......... CBO Resources Corp. [*Vancouver Stock Exchange symbol*]
CBU.......... Cluster Bomb Unit [*Military*]
CBU.......... Coal Age [*A publication*]
CBU.......... Collective Bargaining Unit   (MCD)
CBU.......... Commodore International Ltd. [*NYSE symbol*]   (SPSG)
CBU.......... Completely Built Up   (ADA)
CBU.......... Construction Battalion Unit [*Navy*]
CBU.......... Court of Bankruptcy, Undischarged [*British*]
CBU.......... Vancouver, BC [*AM radio station call letters*]
CBUBT-1... Canal Flats, BC [*Television station call letters*]
CBUBT-7... Cranbrook, BC [*Television station call letters*]
CBuCTA.... California Teachers Association, Burlingame, CA [*Library
　　　　　　　symbol*] [*Library of Congress*]   (LCLS)
CBUDFIN ... Chief of Budget and Finance Division [*Supreme Headquarters
　　　　　　　Allied Powers Europe*]   (NATG)
CBUF........ United States Forest Service, Pacific Southwest Forest and
　　　　　　　Range Experiment Station, Berkeley, CA [*Library symbol*]
　　　　　　　[*Library of Congress*]   (LCLS)
CBUF-FM ... Vancouver, BC [*FM radio station call letters*]
CBU-FM ... Vancouver, BC [*FM radio station call letters*]
CBUFT...... Vancouver, BC [*Television station call letters*]
CBUFT-2... Kamloops, BC [*Television station call letters*]
CBUFT-3... Terrace, BC [*Television station call letters*]
CBUIVTF ... Concerned Broadcasters Using Inter-City Video Transmission
　　　　　　　Facilities   (EA)
C Bun H ..... Chugoku Bungaku Ho [*A publication*]
CBUS........ Clydesdale Breeders of the United States   (EA)
CBUT........ Vancouver, BC [*Television station call letters*]
CBV.......... Cabin Bleed Valve [*Aviation*]   (MCD)
CBV.......... Canadian Beaver Resources [*Vancouver Stock Exchange
　　　　　　　symbol*]
CBV.......... Central Blood Volume [*Medicine*]

CBV .... Christliche Bayerische Volkspartei - Bayerische
　　　　　　　Patriotenbewegung [*Christian Bavarian People's Party -
　　　　　　　Movement of Bavarian Patriots*] [*Federal Republic of
　　　　　　　Germany*] [*Political party*]   (PPW)
CBV .... Circulating Blood Volume [*Medicine*]
CBV .... Comenius-Blaetter fuer Volkserziehung [*A publication*]
CBV .... Containment Building Ventilation [*Nuclear energy*]   (NRCH)
CBV .... Corrected Blood Volume [*Medicine*]
CBV .... Quebec, PQ [*AM radio station call letters*]
CBVD .... CCNU [*Lomustine*], Bleomycin, Vinblastine, Dexamethasone
　　　　　　　[*Antineoplastic drug regimen*]
CBVD-TV ... Malartic, PQ [*Television station call letters*]
CBVE-FM ... Quebec, PQ [*FM radio station call letters*]
CBV-FM... Quebec, PQ [*FM radio station call letters*]
CBV-FM-6 ... La Malbaie, PQ [*FM radio station call letters*]
CBVM........ Community of the Blessed Virgin Mary [*Anglican religious
　　　　　　　community*]
CBVT........ Quebec City, PQ [*Television station call letters*]
CBVT-2 ... La Tuque, PQ [*Television station call letters*]
CBVWS..... Combat Vehicle Weapons System [*Army*]   (AFIT)
CBW .... Bureau of the Census, Field Division Library, Washington, DC
　　　　　　　[*OCLC symbol*]   (OCLC)
CBW .... Canadian Broadcasting Winnipeg [*Canadian Broadcasting
　　　　　　　Company record series prefix*]
CBW .... Catholic Book Week
CBW .... Centralblatt fuer Bibliothekwesen [*A publication*]
CBW .... Chelan Butte [*Washington*] [*Seismograph station code, US
　　　　　　　Geological Survey*]   (SEIS)
CBW .... Chemical and Biological Warfare [*Military*]
CBW .... Chemical and Biological Weapons [*Military*]
CBW .... CITIBASE-Weekly [*Citicorp Database Services*] [*Information
　　　　　　　service or system*]   (IID)
CBW .... Commerical Bank of Wales [*British*]
CBW .... Congress Bi-Weekly [*A publication*]
CBW .... Consolidated Brinco Ltd. [*Toronto Stock Exchange symbol*]
CBW .... Constant Bandwidth   (MCD)
CBW .... Continuous Butt-Weld [*Metal industry*]
CBW .... Control by Wire   (MCD)
CBW .... Critical Bandwidth [*of noise*]
CBW .... [*A*] Translation in the Language of the People (1950) [*Charles B.
　　　　　　　Williams*] [*A publication*]   (BJA)
CBW .... Winnipeg, MB [*AM radio station call letters*]
CBW .... Women's History Research Center, Inc., Berkeley, CA [*Library
　　　　　　　symbol*] [*Library of Congress*]   (LCLS)
CBWA........ Central Bancorporation [*NASDAQ symbol*]   (NQ)
CBWA........ Copper and Brass Warehouse Association [*Later, CBSA*]   (EA)
CBWAT..... Kenora, ON [*Television station call letters*]
CBWBT..... Flin Flon, MB [*Television station call letters*]
CBWC........ Corset and Brassiere Women's Club [*Later, UC*]   (EA)
CBWCA...... Classic Bicycle and Whizzer Club of America   (EA)
CBWCT..... Fort Frances, ON [*Television station call letters*]
CBWDT..... Dryden, ON [*Television station call letters*]
CBW-FM.. Winnipeg, MB [*FM radio station call letters*]
CBWFT ..... Winnipeg, MB [*Television station call letters*]
CBWFT-4 ... Ste. Rose Du Lac, MB [*Television station call letters*]
CBWFT-10 ... Brandon, MB [*Television station call letters*]
CBWGT..... Fisher Branch, MB [*Television station call letters*]
CBWI........ Wright Institute, Berkeley, CA [*Library symbol*] [*Library of
　　　　　　　Congress*]   (LCLS)
CBWK-FM ... Thompson, MB [*FM radio station call letters*]
C B Worldbus ... Conference Board. Worldbusiness [*A publication*]
CBWR .... Coos Bay Wagon Road [*Lands*] [*Department of the Interior*]
CBWST..... Baldy Mountain, MB [*Television station call letters*]
CBWT........ Winnipeg, MB [*Television station call letters*]
CBWT-2 ... Lac Du Bonnet, MB [*Television station call letters*]
CBWYT..... Mafeking, MB [*Television station call letters*]
CBX .... C-Band Transponder [*Radio*]
CBX .... Cam Box
CBX .... Computer-Based Examination
CBX .... Computerized Branch Exchange [*Telecommunications*]
CBX .... Condobolin [*Australia*] [*Airport symbol*]   (OAG)
CBX .... Consolidated Boundary Explorations [*Vancouver Stock
　　　　　　　Exchange symbol*]
CBX .... Continuous Belt Xanthator [*Rayon technology*]
CBX .... Edmonton, AB [*AM radio station call letters*]
CBXAT..... Grande Prairie, AB [*Television station call letters*]
CBXAT-2... High Prairie, AB [*Television station call letters*]
CBXAT-3... Manning, AB [*Television station call letters*]
CBX-FM... Edmonton, AB [*FM radio station call letters*]
CBXFT ..... Edmonton, AB [*Television station call letters*]
CBXFT-1... Bonnyville, AB [*Television station call letters*]
CBXFT-6... Fort McMurray, AB [*Television station call letters*]
CBXFT-8... Grande Prairie, AB [*Television station call letters*]
CBXT........ Edmonton, AB [*Television station call letters*]
CBY .... Canobie [*Australia*] [*Airport symbol*] [*Obsolete*]   (OAG)
CBY .... Carboy
CBY .... Children's Book of the Year [*British*]
Cby........... Cobyric Acid [*Biochemistry*]
CBY .... Colby College, Waterville, ME [*OCLC symbol*]   (OCLC)
CBY .... Corner Brook, NF [*AM radio station call letters*]
CBYT........ Corner Brook, NF [*Television station call letters*]

CBYT-1	Stephenville, NF [*Television station call letters*]
CBYT-3	Bonne Bay, NF [*Television station call letters*]
CBZ	Campbell Island [*New Zealand*] [*Seismograph station code, US Geological Survey*] (SEIS)
CBZ	Carbamazepine [*Also, CARB*] [*An analgesic*]
CBZ	Carben Energy, Inc. [*Vancouver Stock Exchange symbol*]
CBZ	Carbobenzoxy [*Also, Cb*] [*Organic chemistry*]
CBZ	Fredericton, NB [*AM radio station call letters*]
CBZ-E	Carbamazepine-Epoxide [*An analgesic*]
CBZF-FM ...	Fredericton, NB [*FM radio station call letters*]
CBZ-FM ...	Fredericton, NB [*FM radio station call letters*]
CC	Air-Cushion Vehicle built by Cushioncraft [*England*] [*Usually used in combination with numerals*]
CC	Battle Cruiser [*Navy*]
CC	Cadet Captain
CC	Cadet Corps [*British military*] (DMA)
CC	Cadmium Council (EA)
CC	Cahiers du Cinema [*A publication*]
CC	Caius College [*Cambridge University*] (ROG)
CC	Cajal Club (EA)
cc	Calcite [*CIPW classification*] [*Geology*]
CC	Calcium Cyclamate [*Sweetener*]
CC	Calculator (MDG)
CC	Calibration Cycle (AFIT)
CC	California Compensation Cases [*A publication*] (DLA)
CC	Call Contract
CC	Calorimetry Conference (EA)
CC	[*John*] Calvin Coolidge [*US president, 1872-1933*]
CC	Camera Copy [*or Camera-Ready Copy*]
C & C	Cameron and Carroll [*A publication*] (APTA)
CC	Camouflage Critical [*Designation*] [*Army*] (RDA)
CC	Camp Century [*Greenland*] [*Seismograph station*]
CC	Camp Chair
CC	Camp Commandant
CC	Canada Council (EAIO)
CC	Canadian Club [*A whiskey*]
CC	Cancelation Clause [*Business term*]
CC	Canceled Check [*Banking*]
CC	Cancer Care (EA)
CC	Cans or Cartons [*Freight*]
C & C	Cantrell and Cochrane [*Initials used as brand name of soft drink*]
CC	Canvas Covers [*Shipping*] (DS)
CC	Capacity Coupling
CC	Cape Colony [*British Empire*]
CC	Cape Corps [*British military*] (DMA)
CC	Capita [*Chapters*] [*Latin*]
C & C	Capital & Counties [*Property development company*] [*British*]
CC	Capsule Communications [*or Communicator*] [*NASA*]
CC	Carbamylcholine [*Organic chemistry*]
CC	Carbohydrate Craver [*Nutrition*]
C-C	Carbon-Carbon (NASA)
CC	Carbon Copy
CC	Carbonaceous Chondrite
CC	Carbonate Crust [*Archeology*]
CC	Card Code
CC	Card Column
CC	Card Count [*Data processing*]
CC	Cardiac Cycle [*Medicine*]
CC	Cardinal Club (EA)
CC	Career Control (AFM)
CC	Cargo Capacity [*Shipping*] (DCTA)
CC	Cargo Control
cc-----	Caribbean Area [*MARC geographic area code*] [*Library of Congress*] (LCCP)
CC	Caribbean Commission [*Later, Caribbean Organization*]
CC	Caribbeana Council [*Defunct*] (EA)
CC	Carmel Community [*Roman Catholic women's religious order*]
CC	Carpenters' Company (EA)
C & C	Carpets and Curtains (ADA)
CC	Carriage Control
CC	Carrying Capacity (EA)
CC	Carson City [*Nevada*] [*Mint mark, when appearing on US coins*] [*Obsolete*]
Cc	Carya cardiformis [*Butternut hickory tree*]
C & C	Case and Comment [*A publication*]
CC	Cases in Chancery [*England*] [*A publication*] (DLA)
CC	Cash Commodity [*Business term*]
CC	Cash Credit [*British*]
CC	Cashier's Check
CC	Cassidy Class (EA)
CC	Cast Copper
CC	Cat Collectors [*Commercial firm*] (EA)
CC	Catalytic Cracker [*Chemical engineering*]
CC	Catecholamine Club (EA)
CC	Category Code [*Online database field identifier*]
CC	Caterpillar Club (EA)
CC	Cathodochromic [*Cathode-ray tube*]
CC	Catholic Clergyman
CC	Catholic Confraternity Version [*1941, 1952*] (BJA)
CC	Catholic Curate
CC	Cause for Concern (EA)
CC	Causes Celebres [*Quebec Provincial Reports*] [*A publication*] (DLA)
CC	Celestial Canopy [*Freemasonry*]
CC	Cell Cap [*Botany*]
CC	Cell Culture [*Cytology*]
C to C	Center to Center [*Technical drawings*]
C-C	Center to Center
CC	Center of Concern (EA)
CC	Centigrams (ROG)
CC	Central Canal [*Anatomy*]
CC	Central Coast (ADA)
CC	Central Committee
CC	Central Computer
CC	Central Console
CC	Central Control (KSC)
CC	Central Control Channel Command (MCD)
CC	Centrifugal Coating
CC	Centristas de Cataluna [*Political party*] [*Spain*] (EY)
CC	Centuries
CC	Cepi Corpus [*Latin*] [*Legal term*] (DLA)
CC	Cerebral Commissure [*Brain anatomy*]
C of C	Certificate of Competency [*Education*]
CC	Certified Check [*Banking*]
CC	Cervical Connective [*Neuroanatomy*]
C of C	Chamber of Commerce
CC	Chamber of Commerce
CC	Change for Children [*An association*] (EA)
CC	Change Code (MCD)
CC	Change Course
C/C	Change of Course [*Aviation*]
CC	Channel Command [*Refers to English Channel*] [*Military*]
CC	Channel Controller (MCD)
CC	Chapter Clerk [*Church of England in Australia*]
CC	Character Count [*Typography*]
CC	Charbonneau Connection (EA)
CC	Chargeable to Crew (MCD)
CC	Charged Current [*Physics*]
CC	Charges Collect [*Business term*]
CC	Charity Commission [*British*]
CC	Chartered Cartographer
CC	Checker Club (EA)
CC	Chemical Closet
CC	Chemical Composition [*Of precious stones*]
CC	Chemistry Consortium (EA)
CC	Chess Club
CC	Chest Complaint [*Medicine*] (ADA)
CC	Chief of Chaplains [*Later, CCH*] [*Army*]
CC	Chief Clerk
CC	Chief Complaint [*Medicine*]
CC	Chief Constable [*Scotland Yard*]
CC	Chief Controller (NATG)
CC	Chief Counsel (KSC)
CC	Chief Court [*Freemasonry*] (ROG)
CC	Child Care (ADA)
C of C	Children of the Confederacy (EA)
CC	Children's Committee 10 (EA)
CC	Chile [*Aircraft nationality and registration mark*] (FAAC)
CC	China Council [*An association*] (EA)
CC	Chocolate-Coated [*Pharmacy*]
CC	Choke Coil
CC	Choriocarcinoma [*Oncology*]
CC	Christian Century [*A publication*]
CC	Christian Coalition (EA)
CC	Christian Crusade (EA)
C & C	Christianity and Crisis [*A publication*]
CC	Christians in Crisis (EA)
CC	Christmas Club (EA)
CC	Chronometer Correction [*Navigation*]
CC	Chrysler Corporation
CC	Circuit City Stores, Inc. [*NYSE symbol*] (SPSG)
CC	Circuit Closing
C/C	Circuit Control
CC	Circuit Court
CC	Circulating Copy
CC	Circulation Council of DMA [*Direct Marketing Association*] [*New York, NY*] (EA)
CC	Circulatory Collapse [*Cardiology*]
CC	Circumnavigators Club (EA)
CC	Cirrocumulus [*Meteorology*]
CC	Citizen's Call (EA)
CC	Citizen's Choice (EA)
CC	City Corporation [*of London*]
CC	City Council [*or Councillor*]
CC	City Court (DLA)
CC	Civil Code [*A publication*] (DLA)
CC	Civil Commotion
CC	Civil Court
CC	Civilian Congress (EA)
CC	Civilta Cattolica [*A publication*]
CC	Classical Conditioning

CC .... Classification of Characteristics [*Navy*] (NG)
CC .... Classification Code [*IRS*] [*Online database field identifier*]
CC .... Clean Catch [*of urine*] [*Medicine*]
CC .... Clerk of the Crown [*British*]
CC .... Clerk of the Privy Council [*British*]
CC .... Clindamycin [*Antibacterial compound*]
CC .... Clinical Center [*National Institutes of Health*] (GRD)
CC .... Clinical Course [*Medicine*]
CC .... Clipper Club [*Pan American Airlines' club for frequent flyers*] (EA)
C/C .... Clock Coercion
CC .... Clomiphene Citrate [*Fertility drug*]
CC .... Close-Coupled [*Electricity*]
CC .... Closed Captioned [*Refers to captioning of television programs for the deaf*]
CC .... Closed Circuit [*Transmission*] (DEN)
CC .... Closed Container [*Packaging*] (DCTA)
CC .... Closing Capacity
CC .... Closing Coil
CC .... Cloud Chamber [*Physics*]
CC .... Cloud Cover (KSC)
CC .... Cluster Controller
CC .... Coaching Club (EA)
C & C .... Coal and Coke
CC .... Coal Corporation [*Philippine National Oil Co.*] (DS)
CC .... Coarse Control [*Nuclear energy*] (NRCH)
CC .... Coastal Command [*Air Force*] [*British*]
CC .... Coat Cupboard [*Classified advertising*] (ADA)
CC .... Cobra Club [*Later, SAAC*] (EA)
CC .... Cocos [*Keeling*] Islands [*ANSI two-letter standard code*] (CNC)
CC .... Code of Canon Law
CC .... Code Civil Francais (DLA)
CC .... Code Civil Suisse [*A publication*]
CC .... Code Control (AFM)
CC .... Code Converter
CC .... Codex Prophetarum Cairensis (BJA)
CC .... Codice Civile [*Civil Code*] [*Italian*] (ILCA)
CC .... Codrul Cosminului [*A publication*]
CC .... Coefficient of Contingency [*Statistics*]
CC .... Coefficient of Correlation [*Statistics*]
CC .... Coin Collect [*Telecommunications*] (TEL)
CC .... Coin Completing [*Telecommunications*] (TEL)
CC .... Cold Canvassing [*Business term*]
C & C .... Coleman and Caines' Cases [*New York*] [*A publication*] (DLA)
CC .... Coleman's Cases [*New York*] [*A publication*] (DLA)
CC .... Collect Call [*Telecommunications*] (TEL)
CC .... Collector Circle (EA)
CC .... Collector's Chronicle [*A publication*]
CC .... Collectors Club (EA)
CC .... Colon Classification [*Library science*]
CC .... Color Code [*as, for types of wire*] [*Technical drawings*]
CC .... Color Compensation [*Photography*]
CC .... Color Contrast
CC .... Color Correction [*Color printing*]
CC .... Colorado-Claro [*Medium-colored cigar*]
CC .... Column Chromatography [*Analytical chemistry*]
CC .... Combat Center [*Military*]
CC .... Combat Clothing [*NATO*]
CC .... Combat Command [*Initialism may be followed by a number as, CC2, to indicate a specific, numbered command*] [*Army*]
CC .... Combat Commandant [*Military*]
CC .... Combat Consumption [*Military*]
CC .... Combat Control [*Army*]
CC .... Combat Correspondent
CC .... Combination Companies [*Insurance*]
CC .... Combustion Chamber (KSC)
CC .... Comic Crusader [*A publication*]
C/C .... Command Center (AAG)
CC .... Command Chain [*Data processing*]
CC .... Command Code [*IRS*]
CC .... Command Computer (AAG)
CC .... Command Conference [*Viking lander mission*] [*NASA*]
C & C .... Command and Control
CC .... Command Ship [*Navy symbol*] [*Obsolete*]
C-in-C .... Commander-in-Chief (NATG)
CC .... Commercial Carrier
CC .... Commercial Consumables (CINC)
CC .... Commission Certified [*Bacteriology*]
CC .... Committee Charter (MCD)
C/C .... Committees of Correspondence [*National Center for Science Education*]
CC .... Common Carrier
CC .... Common Cause (EA)
CC .... Common Collector [*Amplifier*]
CC .... Common Control [*Telecommunications*] (TEL)
CC .... Common Council [*or Councilman*]
CC .... Common Cycle
CC .... Commonwealth Aircraft Corporation Ltd. [*Australia*] [*ICAO aircraft manufacturer identifier*] (ICAO)
CC .... Communication Center

C & C .... Communication and Cognition (EA)
CC .... Communication Commission (EA)
CC .... Communication Comptroller
CC .... Communications Central [*Military*]
CC .... Communications Control (MCD)
CC .... Communications Council (EA)
CC .... Community College
CC .... Community Communications [*Independent Local Radio*] [*British*]
CC .... Companion of the Order of Canada
CC .... Company Commander
CC .... Compass Course
CC .... Complex Conjugate (MCD)
CC .... Component Check [*Nuclear energy*] (NRCH)
CC .... Component Commander [*Military*]
CC .... Component Cooling [*Nuclear energy*] (NRCH)
CC .... Composite Cross [*Genetics*]
CC .... Compound Cathartic [*Pills*]
CC .... Compte Courant [*Current Account*] [*French*] [*Business term*]
CC .... Compulsory Censorship [*British*] [*World War II*]
CC .... Computation Center
CC .·.............. Computational Component (MCD)
CC .... Computer Calculator
CC .... Computer Center [*Telecommunications*] (TEL)
CC .... Computer Community (IEEE)
CC .... Computer Complex
C-to-C .... Computer-to-Computer (NASA)
CC .... Computer Conferencing
C & C .... Computers and Communications
CC .... Comunn na Clarsaich [*Clarsach Society*] (EAIO)
Cc .... Concave
CC .... Concentration Camp
CC .... Concept Chart (AFIT)
CC .... Concord Council (EA)
CC .... Concrete Cancer [*Refers to disintegration caused by weathering and pollutants*]
CC .... Concrete Ceiling
CC .... Concurrent Concession (MDG)
CC .... Condition Code
CC .... Conditioning Container (AAG)
CC .... Conductive Coating
CC .... Configuration Control (AAG)
CC .... Confined to Camp [*Military*]
CC .... Congressional Caucus for Women's Issues (EA)
CC .... Congressional Club (EA)
cc .... Connected Case [*Different case from case cited but arising out of same subject matter or intimately connected therewith*] [*Used in Shepard's Citations*] [*Legal term*] (DLA)
CC .... Connecting Carrier
CC .... Connector Circuit
CC .... Consolidation of [*Telecommunications*] Center (MCD)
CC .... Constant Conditions
CC .... Constitutional Commission [*An association*] (EA)
C/C .... Constraint Control
CC .... Constructing Contractor (AAG)
CC .... Construction Corps
CC .... Consular Clerk [*British*] (ROG)
CC .... Consular Corps
CC .... Consules [*Consuls*] [*Latin*]
CC .... Consumer Council [*American National Standards Institute*]
c/c .... Conta Corrente [*Current Account*] [*Business term*] [*Portuguese*]
CC .... Contact Center (EA)
CC .... Contact Closure (KSC)
CC .... Container Control (DCTA)
C/C .... Conte Corrente [*Running Account*]
CC .... Contemporary China [*A publication*]
CC .... Contemporary Civilization [*University course*]
CC .... Continuation Clause
CC .... Continuous Casting [*Metalworking*]
CC .... Continuous Current
c/c .... Conto Corrente [*Current Account*] [*Italian*]
CC .... Contra Credit [*Banking*]
CC .... Control Cabin
CC .... Control Center
CC .... Control Chamber [*Diving apparatus*]
CC .... Control Circuit
CC .... Control Computer (KSC)
CC .... Control Console
CC .... Control Converter (MCD)
CC .... Control Counter [*Data processing*]
C/C .... Controlled-Circulation [*Boiler*]
C of C .... Controller of Communications [*RAF*] [*British*]
CC .... Controllers Council (EA)
CC .... Convective Combustion (MCD)
C-C .... Convexo-Concave [*Replacement heart valves*] [*Cardiology*]
CC .... Convoy Commodore [*Navy*] (NVT)
CC .... Cooling Coil (AAG)
CC .... Coordinate Converter (AAG)
CC .... Coordinates Computed (MUGU)
CC .... Copper Chromite

CC .... Corben Club   (EA)
CC .... Cord Compression [*Medicine*]
CC .... Cornu Cervi [*Hartshorn*] [*Pharmacy*]   (ROG)
CC .... Coronary Club   (EA)
CC .... Corpora Cardiaca [*Endocrinology*]
CC .... Corporate Conversions [*Information service or system*]   (IID)
CC .... Corporation Commission
CC .... Corps Commander [*British military*]   (DMA)
CC .... Corpus Callosum [*Brain anatomy*]
CC .... Corpus Christi   (ROG)
CC .... Corpus Christianorum [*A publication*]
CC .... Correct Code   (MCD)
CC .... Correlation Coefficient   (MCD)
CC .... Correspondence Course
CC .... Correspondent Committee   (EA)
CC .... Corrosion Control [*Lloyds Register*]   (DS)
CC .... Corrugated or Cupped [*Freight*]
CC .... Cortico-Cortical Connection [*Neurology*]
CC .... Cost Center   (AFM)
CC .... Cost Code   (MCD)
CC .... Costochondral [*Anatomy*]
CC .... Council of Churches
CC .... Council on Competitiveness   (EA)
CC .... Council of Conservationists   (EA)
CC .... Counterclockwise
CC .... Countercurrent
CC .... Country Cheque [*Banking*] [*British*]
CC .... Country Clearing
CC .... Country Club
CC .... Country Code   (AFM)
CC .... Countryside Commission [*British*]
CC .... County Circuit [*As in "CC Rider," i.e., a traveling preacher*]
CC .... County Clerk [*British*]   (ROG)
CC .... County Commissioner
CC .... County Constituency [*British*]
CC .... County Council [*or Councillor*] [*British*]
CC .... County Court
CC .... Coupled Channel [*Electronics*]
CC .... Coupled Cluster [*Physical chemistry*]
CC .... Courant Continu [*Direct Current*] [*French*]
C of C .... Course of Construction
CC .... Craniocaudal [*Anatomy*]
C/C .... Crankcase [*Automotive engineering*]
CC .... Creatinine Clearance [*Clinical chemistry*]
CC .... Credentialing Commission   (EA)
CC .... Credit Card [*Business term*]   (ADA)
Cc .... Creek Chub [*Ichthyology*]
CC .... Crew Certified   (MCD)
CC .... Crew Chief   (MCD)
CC .... Crew Compartment   (MCD)
CC .... Cricket Club
CC .... Critical Care [*Medicine*]
CC .... Critical Condition [*Medicine*]
CC .... Croquet Club [*British*]
CC .... Cross Channel
CC .... Cross Correlation
CC .... Cross Couple
CC .... Cross Currents [*A publication*]
CC .... Crossword Club [*Romsey, Hampshire, England*]   (EAIO)
CC .... Crown Cases
CC .... Crown Clerk [*British*]   (ROG)
CC .... Crown Colony
CC .... Crown Court   (ILCA)
CC .... Cruisers   (NATG)
CC .... Cruising Club [*British*]
CC .... Crusaders for Christ   (EA)
CC .... Crystal Control
CC .... Crystal Current
CC .... Cubic Capacity   (DS)
cc .... Cubic Centimeter
CC .... Cubic Contents
CC .... Cucurbita Cruenta [*Cupping Glass*] [*Pharmacy*]
C/C .... Cuenta Corriente [*Current Account*] [*Business term*] [*Spanish*]
CC .... Culver Club   (EA)
cc .... Cum Correction [*With lenses*] [*Ophthalmology*]
CC .... Cumulative Changes   (NATG)
C-in-C .... Curate-in-Charge [*Church of England*]
CC .... Curling Club
CC .... Currency Collector [*A publication*]
CC .... Current Cases [*1965-71*] [*Ghana*] [*A publication*]   (DLA)
CC .... Current Challengers
CC .... Current Complaints [*Medicine*]
CC .... Current Contents [*A publication*]
CC .... Current Cost
CC .... Cursor Control [*Data processing*]   (BUR)
CC .... Cushion Craft
CC .... Custodian Contractor
CC .... Custom Chip [*Personal computers*]
CC .... Cuthbert Cudgel [*Pseudonym used by T. Houston*]
CC .... Cycle Count   (MCD)
CC .... Cyclic Code   (BUR)

CC .... Cycling Club
cc .... Cylindrical with Adaxial Channel [*Leaf characteristics*] [*Botany*]
CC .... Cypriot Classical   (BJA)
CC .... Federal Carriers Cases [*Commerce Clearing House*] [*A publication*]   (DLA)
CC .... Federal Carriers Reporter (Commerce Clearing House) [*A publication*]   (DLA)
CC .... International Air Cargo Corporation [*IACC*] [*Egypt*] [*ICAO designator*]   (FAAC)
cc .... Mainland China [*MARC country of publication code*] [*Library of Congress*]   (LCCP)
CC .... Ohio Circuit Court Reports [*A publication*]   (DLA)
CC .... R. A. Bloch Cancer Foundation [*Formerly, Cancer Connection*]   (EA)
CC .... Versatile Corporation [*Vancouver Stock Exchange symbol*]
CC³ .... Counter-C³ [*Command, Control, and Communications*] [*Pronounced "see-see-cubed"*]
CC 1992 ..... Columbus: Countdown 1992 [*An association*]   (EA)
CC (Test) ... Component Check Test [*Nuclear energy*]   (NRCH)
CCA .... Cable Commuter Airlines   (FAAC)
CCA .... California Central Airlines
CCA .... Canadian Canoe Association
CCA .... Canadian Cat Association
CCA .... Canadian Cattlemen's Association
CCA .... Canadian Centre for Architecture
CCA .... Canadian Charolais Association
CCA .... Canadian Chiropractic Association
CCA .... Canadian Colonial Airways
CCA .... Canadian Commonwealth Association
CCA .... Canadian Communication Association
CCA .... Canadian Conference of the Arts
CCA .... Canadian Construction Association
CCA .... Canadian Cowboys Association
CCA .... Canadian Cycling Association
CCA .... Cancel Corridor Assignment [*Aviation*]   (FAAC)
CCA .... Cancer Chemotherapy Abstracts [*A publication*]
CCA .... Cancer Chemotherapy Annual [*Elsevier Book Series*] [*A publication*]
CCA .... Capital Consumption Adjustment [*or Allowance*] [*Accounting*]
CCA .... Capital Cost Allowance [*Accounting*]
CCA .... Capri Class Association   (EA)
CCA .... Caribbean Conservation Association [*St. Michael, Barbados*]
CCA .... Carrier Controlled Approach [*Aircraft carrier RADAR landing system*]
CCA .... Cash Clothing Allowance
CCA .... Catholic Committee of Appalachia   (EA)
CCA .... Cattle Council of Australia
CCA .... Cecchetti Council of America   (EA)
CCA .... Cell Cycle Analyzer [*Instrumentation*]
CCA .... Cellular Cellulose Acetate [*Organic chemistry*]
CCA .... Cellular Concrete Association   (EA)
C & CA ...... Cement and Concrete Association [*British*]   (IRUK)
CCA .... Cement and Concrete Association [*British*]
CCA .... Central Computer Accounting
CCA .... Cephalin Cholesterol Antigen [*Immunochemistry*]
CCA .... Channel-to-Channel Adapter [*Data processing*]
CCA .... Chemical Coaters Association   (EA)
CCA .... Chemical Communications Association   (EA)
CCA .... Chess Collectors Association   (EA)
CCA .... Chick Cell Agglutination [*Vaccine potency test*]
CCA .... Chief of Civil Affairs [*Army*]
CCA .... Chief Clerk of the Admiralty [*British*]
C of CA ...... Chief of Coast Artillery
CCA .... Chihuahua Club of America   (EA)
CCA .... Chimpanzee Coryza Agent [*A virus*]
CCA .... Chinese Communist Army   (CINC)
CCA .... Chinese Culture Association   (EA)
CCA .... Choriocarcinoma [*Oncology*]
CCA .... Christian Chiropractors Association   (EA)
CCA .... Christian Conference of Asia   (EA)
CCA .... Christie's Contemporary Art [*Reproductions*] [*London, England*]
CCA .... Chromated Copper Arsenate [*Wood preservative*]
CCA .... Circuit Card Assembly   (MCD)
CCA .... Circuit Court of Appeals   (GPO)
CCA .... Citizens for Clean Air
CCA .... Citizens' Commission on AIDS [*Acquired Immune Deficiency Syndrome*]   (EA)
CCA .... Citizens for a Competitive America   (EA)
CCA .... Citizens' Councils of America   (EA)
CCA .... City Center Arts [*A publication*]
CCA .... Civilian Control Agency
CCa .... Civilta Cattolica [*A publication*]
CCA .... Classic Comet Club of America   (EA)
CCA .... Close Contact Annealing   (MCD)
CCA .... Cloud Chamber Analysis
CCA .... Clown Club of America [*Later, CAI*]   (EA)
CCA .... Cluster Compression Algorithm   (MCD)
CCA .... Coamo [*Puerto Rico*] [*Seismograph station code, US Geological Survey*]   (SEIS)

CCA .... Coastal Conservation Association (EA)
CCA .... Cold Cranking Ampere
CCA .... Coleman Prop Jet Sales Corp. [*Winnetka, IL*] [*FAA designator*] (FAAC)
CCA .... College Characteristics Analysis
CCA .... Collegiate Commissioners Association (EA)
CCA .... Collie Club of America (EA)
CCA .... Combat Command A
CCA .... Comics Code Authority [*Regulatory body for comic book and comic magazine publishing industry*]
CCA .... Comites Communistes pour l'Autogestion [*Communist Committees for Self-Management*] [*France*] [*Political party*] (PPW)
CCA .... Committee of Concerned Africans (EA)
CCA .... Committee for Conventional Armaments
CCA .... Common Carotid Artery [*Anatomy*]
CCA .... Common Carrier Motor Freight Association, Dallas TX [*STAC*]
CCA .... Common Communication Adapter [*Data processing*]
CCA .... Commonwealth Chess Association (EA)
CCA .... Communication Carrier Assembly [*Spaceship*]
CCA .... Company Chemists' Association [*British*]
CCA .... Company-to-Company Agreement (MCD)
CCA .... Compass Control Alarm
CCA .... Complete Cell Analysis [*Medicine*]
CCA .... Component Checkout Area (AAG)
CCA .... Computer and Control Abstracts [*IEE*] [*Information service or system*] [*A publication*]
CCA .... Computer Corp. of America
CCA .... Computer Corp. Australia
CCA .... Concerned Citizens of America [*Defunct*] (EA)
CCA .... Conference Canadienne des Arts [*Canadian Conference of the Arts - CCA*]
CCA .... Configuration Control Action (KSC)
CCA .... Congenital Contracture Arachnodactyly [*Medicine*]
CCA .... Conseil Canadien des Aveugles [*Canadian Council of the Blind*] (EAIO)
CCA .... Conseil Consultatif des Athletes [*Athletes' Advisory Council*] [*Canada*]
CCA .... Conservative Clubs of America (EA)
CCA .... Consolidated Canarctic Industries Ltd. [*Vancouver Stock Exchange symbol*]
CCA .... Consumer and Corporate Affairs Canada [*UTLAS symbol*]
CCA .... Consumers Cooperative Association [*Later, Farmland Industries*] (EA)
CCA .... Container Corporation of America [*Later, Marcor, Inc.*]
CCA .... Continental Control Area [*FAA*]
CCA .... Continuously Contemporary Accounting (ADA)
CCA .... Contract Change Authorization (KSC)
CCA .... Contribution sur les Chiffres d'Affaires [*Turnover tax*] [*Zaire*] (IMH)
CCA .... Controlled Circulation Audit [*Name changed to Business Publications Audit of Circulation*]
CCA .... Coolant Control Assembly (NASA)
CCA .... Cooperative Communicators Association (EA)
CCA .... Copper-Chrome Arsenate [*Wood preservative*] (ADA)
CCA .... Corduroy Council of America [*Defunct*] (EA)
CCA .... Corpus Christi Public Library, Corpus Christi, TX [*OCLC symbol*] (OCLC)
CCA .... Corrections Corporation of America
CCA .... Cosmopolitan Care Corp. [*AMEX symbol*] (SPSG)
CCA .... Cougar Club of America (EA)
CCA ... Council of Chemical Associations [*Defunct*] (EA)
CCA .... Council of Consumer Advisers
CCA .... County Chasers of America (EA)
CCA .... County Court Appeals [*A publication*] (DLA)
CCA .... Coupled Cluster Approach (MCD)
CCA .... Court of Criminal Appeal [*England*] [*Australia*] (DLA)
CCA .... Credit Control Act [*1969*]
CCA .... Crop Condition Assessment
CCA .... Cruising Club of America (EA)
CCA .... Current Cost Accounting
CCA .... Current Cost Accounts [*London Stock Exchange*]
CCA .... Curriculum Corp. of Australia
CCA .... Cushman Club of America (EA)
CCA .... Customs Consolidation Act [*British*]
CCA .... Fort Chaffee, AR [*Location identifier*] [*FAA*] (FAAL)
CCAA .... Canadian Colleges Athletic Association
C/CAA .... Caribbean/Central American Action (EA)
CCAA .... Chefs de Cuisine Association of America (EA)
CCAA .... Collector Car Appraisers Association (EA)
CCAAFB .... Cape Canaveral Auxiliary Air Force Base [*Obsolete*] (AAG)
CCAAP ...... Central Committee for the Architectural Advisory Panels [*British*]
CCAATF ... Close Combat Antiarmor Task Force (MCD)
CCAAWS .. Close Combat Antiarmor Weapon System (MCD)
CCAB......... Canadian Circulations Audit Board [*Founded 1937*]
CCAB......... Commandant, Civil Affairs Branch [*British*] [*World War II*]
CCAB......... Communications & Cable, Inc. [*West Palm Beach, FL*] [*NASDAQ symbol*] (NQ)

CCAB........ Consultative Committee of Accountancy Bodies [*United Kingdom and Ireland*]
CCAB........ Corsi di Cultura sull'Arte Ravennate e Bizantina [*A publication*]
CCABC...... Chris-Craft Antique Boat Club (EA)
CC/AB & ES ... Current Contents/Agriculture, Biology, and Environmental Sciences [*A publication*]
CCABF....... Common Carotid Artery Blood Flow [*Medicine*]
CCAC........ California College of Arts and Crafts [*Oakland*]
CCAC........ Canadian Casualty Assembly Centre (DMA)
CCAC........ Canadian Council on Animal Care
CCAC........ Central Computer Accounting Corporation
CCAC........ Central Council for Agricultural and Horticultural Co-Operation [*British*]
CCAC........ Child Care Action Campaign (EA)
CCAC........ Close Combat Armament Center [*Dover, NJ*] [*Army*] (GRD)
CCAC........ Combined Civil Affairs Committee [*World War II*]
CCAC........ Commonwealth Conciliation and Arbitration Commission [*Australia*]
CCAC........ Continuing Care Accreditation Commission [*American Association of Homes for Aging*]
CCACA...... Croatica Chemica Acta [*A publication*]
CCACB...... CRC [*Chemical Rubber Company*] Critical Reviews in Analytical Chemistry [*A publication*]
CCAC/L .... Combined Civil Affairs Committee, London Subcommittee [*World War II*]
CCACN ...... Command and Control Alert/Conferencing Network (CINC)
CCAC/S .... Combined Civil Affairs Committee, Supply Subcommittee [*World War II*]
CCAD .... Carnegie Council on Adolescent Development (EA)
CCAD .... Center for Computer Aided Design [*University of Iowa*] [*Research center*] (RCD)
CCAD .... Corpus Christi Army Depot (AABC)
CCAE........ Canada Committee on Agricultural Engineering
CCAE........ Council of Canning Association Executives [*Later, CFPAE*] (EA)
CCAF........ Chinese Communist Air Force
CCAF........ Community College of the Air Force (AFM)
CCAFS ..... Cape Canaveral Air Force Station (NASA)
CCAG .... Canadian Correspondence Art Gallery
CCAG .... Catalogus Codicum Astrologorum Graecorum [*A publication*] (OCD)
CCAG .... COEA [*Cost and Operational Effectiveness Analysis*] Cost Advisory Group [*Military*]
CCAG .... Conseil Canadien des Arpenteurs-Geometres [*Canadian Council of Land Surveyors - CLS*]
CCAG .... Cost Committee Advisory Group
CCAH........ Commercial & Credit America Holdings [*Arab*]
CC/A & H ... Current Contents/Arts and Humanities [*A publication*]
CCAHS...... Consumer Commission on the Accreditation of Health Services (EA)
CCAI........ Chamber of Commerce of the Apparel Industry (EA)
CC-AI .... Communication and Cognition - Artificial Intelligence (EA)
CCAI........ Continental Confederation of Adopted Indians (EA)
CCAI........ Creative Computer Applications, Incorporated [*Calabasas, CA*] [*NASDAQ symbol*] (NQ)
CCAIC...... Catholic College Admissions and Information Center (EA)
CCAIE....... Commission Canadienne de l'Annee Internationale de l'Enfant [*Canadian Commission for the International Year of the Child*]
CCAIT....... Community College Association for Instruction and Technology (EA)
CCAJAV .. Coffee and Cacao Journal [*A publication*]
CCal.......... Calexico Public Library, Calexico, CA [*Library symbol*] [*Library of Congress*] (LCLS)
CCALA...... Combined Civil Affairs Liquidating Agency [*World War II*]
CCALA...... Cry California [*A publication*]
CCali.......... Calistoga Free Public Library, Calistoga, CA [*Library symbol*] [*Library of Congress*] (LCLS)
CCALI....... Center for Computer-Assisted Legal Instruction (EA)
CCAM .... CCA Industries, Inc. [*East Rutherford, NJ*] [*NASDAQ symbol*] (NQ)
CCAM .... Certified Clinic Account Manager [*Designation awarded by American Guild of Patient Account Management*]
CCAM .... Connection Co-Processor Application Manager [*Data processing*]
CCAM .... Conversational Communication Access Method
CCAM .... Council for Complementary Alternative Medicine [*British*]
CCamarH .. Camarillo State Hospital, Camarillo, CA [*Library symbol*] [*Library of Congress*] (LCLS)
CCamarSJ ... Saint John's Seminary, Camarillo, CA [*Library symbol*] [*Library of Congress*] (LCLS)
CCAMLR .. Commission for the Conservation of the Antarctic Marine Living Resources [*Australia*] (EAIO)
C Can .... Cinema Canada [*A publication*]
CCAN........ Construction Computer Applications Newsletter [*Database*] [*Construction Industry Press*] [*Information service or system*] (CRD)
CCanC .... Cahier Canadien Claudel [*A publication*]
CCANI....... Clearinghouse on Child Abuse and Neglect Information (EA)

CCAO........ Chambre de Compensation de l'Afrique de l'Ouest [*West African Clearing House - WACH*] (EAIO)
CCAO........ Chief Civil Affairs Officer [*Navy*]
CCAO........ Contract Cost Analysis Organization [*Navy*] (AFIT)
CCAO(B)... Chief Civil Affairs Officer (Burma) [*British*]
CCAODF... INTA [*Instituto Nacional de Tecnologia Agropecuaria*] Coleccion Cientifica [*A publication*]
CCAP........ Center for Clean Air Policy (EA)
CCAP........ Citizens Crusade Against Poverty [*Absorbed by Center for Community Change*]
CCAP........ Commercial Commodity Acquisition Program [*DoD*] (RDA)
CCAP........ Committee of Concerned Artists and Professionals (EA)
CCAP........ Communications Control Applications Program
CCAP........ Community College Assessment Program [*Academic achievement and aptitude test*]
CCAP........ Crustacean Cardioactive Peptide [*Biochemistry*]
CCAP........ Culture Centre of Algae and Protozoa [*Freshwater Biological Association*] [*British*] (CB)
CCAQ........ Consultative Committee on Administrative Questions [*United Nations*]
CCAR........ CCAIR, Inc. [*NASDAQ symbol*] (NQ)
CCAR........ Central Conference of American Rabbis (EA)
CCAR........ Colorado Center for Astrodynamics Research [*University of Colorado at Boulder*] [*Research center*] (RCD)
CCarl......... Carlsbad City Library, Carlsbad, CA [*Library symbol*] [*Library of Congress*] (LCLS)
CCarm........ Harrison Memorial Library, Carmel, CA [*Library symbol*] [*Library of Congress*] (LCLS)
CCarmJ..... Robinson Jeffers Home [*Tor House*], Carmel, CA [*Library symbol*] [*Library of Congress*] (LCLS)
CCarsP....... Purex Corp., Carson, CA [*Library symbol*] [*Library of Congress*] (LCLS)
CCARY...... CCAR [*Central Conference of American Rabbis*] Yearbook [*A publication*]
CCAS........ Carrier-Controlled Approach System
CCAS........ Center for Contemporary Arab Studies [*Georgetown University*] [*Research center*] (RCD)
CCAS........ Christian Comic Arts Society (EA)
CCAS........ Citizens Council of America for Segregation (EA)
CCAS........ Comprehensive Close Air Support [*Military*]
CCAS........ Containment Cooling Actuation Signal [*Nuclear energy*] (NRCH)
CCAS........ Council of Colleges of Arts and Sciences (EA)
C de CASS ... Cour de Cassation [*Court of Appeal*] [*French*] (DLA)
CCAT........ Canadian Cognitive Abilities Test [*Academic achievement and aptitude test*]
CCAT........ Comite de Coordination de l'Assistance Technique [*ONU*]
CCAT........ Conglutinating Complement Absorption Test [*Immunochemistry*]
CCATAR... Clinica Chimica Acta [*A publication*]
CCATF...... Commander, Combined Amphibious Task Force [*Military*] (NVT)
CCATM..... Conference Canadienne des Administrateurs en Transport Motorise [*Canadian Conference of Transport Administrators*]
CCATNA... Combined Committee on Air Training in North America
CCATS...... Communications, Command, and Telemetry Systems (MCD)
CCatt......... Civilta Cattolica [*A publication*]
CCAU........ Cell Cover Arming Unit (MCD)
CCA (US).. Circuit Court of Appeals (United States) [*A publication*] (DLA)
CCA-UWM ... Center for Consumer Affairs, University of Wisconsin-Milwaukee (EA)
CCAV .... Cavanagh Communities Corp. [*NASDAQ symbol*] (NQ)
C of CAV.... Chief of Cavalry
CCAX .... Corrections Corporation of America [*Nashville, TN*] [*NASDAQ symbol*] (NQ)
CCB .... CAM Control Block [*Data processing*]
CCB .... Campbell Colpitts Bridge [*Electronics*]
CCB .... Canadian Commercial Bank
CCB .... Canadian Council of the Blind
CCB .... Canadian Custom Bonded
CCB .... Capital Cities/ABC, Inc. [*NYSE symbol*] (SPSG)
CCB .... Carroll Center for the Blind (EA)
CCB .... Cell-Cycle Box [*Genetics*]
CCB .... Center for Children's Books. Bulletin [*A publication*]
CCB .... Change Control Board [*Social Security Administration*]
CCB .... Character Control Block [*Data processing*] (IBMDP)
CCB .... Chemical Cleaning Building [*Nuclear energy*] (NRCH)
CCB .... Chicago City Ballet
CCB .... Circuit Concentration Bay (IEEE)
CCB .... Clear Creek Butte [*Alaska*] [*Seismograph station code, US Geological Survey*] [*Closed*] (SEIS)
CCB .... Close Control Bombing [*Air Force*]
CCB .... Co-Operative and Commerce Bank [*Nigeria*]
CCB .... Code de Commerce Belge (DLA)
CCB .... Coin Collecting Box [*Telecommunications*] (TEL)
CCB .... Combat Command B
CCB .... Combined Communications Board [*World War II*]
CCB .... Command Communications Boat
CCB .... Command Control Block [*Data processing*] (BUR)
CCB .... Command and Control Boat [*Navy symbol*]

CCB .... Commission Canadienne du Ble [*Canadian Wheat Board - CWB*]
CCB .... Common Carrier Bureau [*of FCC*]
CCB .... Communications Control Block [*Data processing*]
CCB .... Competence in Clearing Bacilli [*Test for leprosy bacilli*]
CCB .... Concrete Block
CCB .... Configuration Change Board [*NASA*] (MCD)
CCB .... Configuration Control Board [*DoD*]
CCB .... Console to Computer Buffer (MUGU)
CCB .... Construction Criteria Base [*Information service or system*] (EISS)
CCB .... Continuing Calibration Blank [*Laboratory analysis*]
CCB .... Contraband Control Base [*Navy*]
CCB .... Contract Change Board
CCB .... Contre Complications Bronchiques [*Vaccine for "bronchial complaints"*] [*Medicine*]
CCB .... Convertible Circuit Breaker
CCB .... Coordination Control Board (MCD)
CCB .... Cubic Capacity of Bunkers [*British*] (ADA)
CCB .... Upland, CA [*Location identifier*] [*FAA*] (FAAL)
CCBA........ Central Canada Broadcasting Association
CCBA........ Chinese Consolidated Benevolent Association (EA)
CCBA........ Christian Classic Bikers Association [*Later, ICCM*] (EA)
CCBAI...... Christian Classic Bikers Association International [*Later, ICCM*] (EA)
CCB-B....... Center for Children's Books. Bulletin [*A publication*]
CC & BB.... Cepi Corpus and Bail Bond [*Legal term*] (DLA)
CCBB........ Clinical Center Blood Bank
CCBC........ Council of Community Blood Centers (EA)
CCBCAF ... Computers in Chemical and Biochemical Research [*A publication*]
CCBD .... Change Control Board Directive [*NASA*] (MCD)
CCBD .... Configuration Control Board Data [*or Directive*] [*DoD*]
CCBD .... Council for Children with Behavioral Disorders (EA)
CCBDA...... Canadian Copper and Brass Development Association
CCBE........ Certified Credit Bureau Executive [*Designation awarded by Society of Certified Consumer Credit Executives*]
CCBE........ Conseil des Barreaux de la Communaute Europeenne [*Council of the Bars and Law Societies of the European Community*] (EAIO)
CCBE........ Consultative Committee of the Bars and Law Societies of the European Community (ILCA)
CCBEA...... Contamination Control. Biomedical Environments [*A publication*]
CCBEAL ... Contamination Control. Biomedical Environments [*A publication*]
CCBF........ CCB Financial Corp. [*Durham, NC*] [*NASDAQ symbol*] (NQ)
CCBF........ Cell-Cycle Box Factor [*Genetics*]
CCBF........ Commanderie des Cordons Bleus de France (EA)
CCBFC ...... Cole Country Band Fan Club (EA)
CCBI.......... Primo Catalogo Collettivo delle Biblioteche Italiane [*General library catalog*] [*Italy*]
CCBK........ Connecticut Community Bank [*Greenwich, CT*] [*NASDAQ symbol*] (NQ)
CCBL........ C-COR Electronics, Inc. [*State College, PA*] [*NASDAQ symbol*] (NQ)
CCBM ...... Chemically Contaminated Biological Mask (MCD)
CCBN .... Commission des Champs de Bataille Nationaux [*National Battlefields Commission - NBC*] [*Canada*]
CCBP........ Combined Communications Board Publications
CCB Rev Choc Confect Bakery ... CCB. Review for Chocolate Confectionery and Bakery [*A publication*]
CCBS .... Center for Computer-Based Behavioral Studies [*Research center*] (RCD)
CCBS .... Change Control Board Summary [*NASA*] (MCD)
CCBS .... Clear Channel Broadcasting Service (EA)
CCBS .... Commodore, Contract-Built Ships [*British military*] (DMA)
CCBS .... Country Children's Book Service [*Australia*]
CCBT........ Cape Cod Bank & Trust Co. [*NASDAQ symbol*] (NQ)
CCBUC...... Cursos e Conferencias. Biblioteca de Universidade de Coimbra [*A publication*]
CCBV........ Central Circulating Blood Volume [*Physiology*]
CCBZAG ... Contribuciones Cientificas. Facultad de Ciencias Exactas y Naturales. Universidad de Buenos Aires. Serie Zoologia [*A publication*]
CCC .... Calcium Cyanamide Citrated [*or Citrated Calcium Carbimide*] [*Pharmacology*]
CCC .... California College of Chiropody
CCC .... Calorie Control Council (EA)
CCC .... Calverton, NY [*Location identifier*] [*FAA*] (FAAL)
CCC .... Cambodia Crisis Center [*Defunct*] (EA)
CCC .... Cambodian Crisis Committee (EA)
CCC .... Cambridge Communication Corporation (MCD)
CCC .... Campus Crusade for Christ International (EA)
CCC .... Canadian Catholic Conference
CCC .... Canadian Climate Center
CCC .... Canadian Commercial Corporation [*Government-owned*] (RDA)
CCC .... Canadian Committee on Cataloguing [*Librarianship*]
CCC .... Canadian Computer Conference (MCD)
CCC .... Canadian Council of Churches (EAIO)

CCC .... Canadian Crafts Council
CCC .... Canadian Criminal Cases [*Law Book, Inc.*] [*Information service or system*]
CCC .... Cape Cod Central Railroad
CCC .... Cape Communications Control [*NASA*]
CCC .... Car Care Council   (EA)
CCC .... Care Custody and Control
CCC .... Caribbean Conference of Churches   (EAIO)
CCC .... Caribbean Conservation Corporation   (EA)
CCC .... Carpet Cushion Council   (EA)
CCC .... Carriage Control Character [*Data processing*]
CCC .... Case Collectors Club   (EA)
CCC .... Catalog Card Corporation of America [*Information service or system*]   (IID)
CCC .... Catalytic Construction Company   (MCD)
CCC .... Cathodal Closure Contraction [*Also, CaCC*] [*Physiology*]
CCC .... CCATS [*Communications, Command, and Telemetry Systems*] Command Controller [*NASA*]
CCC .... Cedar Crest College [*Pennsylvania*]
CCC .... Center for Community Change   (EA)
CCC .... Centerville Community College [*Iowa*]
CCC .... Central Citroen Club   (EA)
CCC .... Central Classification Committee [*International Federation for Documentation*]
CCC .... Central Communications Controller
CCC .... Central Computational Computer
CCC .... Central Computer Center
CCC .... Central Computer Complex
CCC .... Central Criminal Court [*Old Bailey*] [*British*]
CC & C .... Cepi Corpus and Committitur [*Legal term*]   (ILCA)
CCC .... Cercle Culturel Camerounais
CCC .... Certificate of Clinical Competence
CCC .... Challenger Communications Consultants Ltd. [*British*] [*Telecommunications service*]   (TSSD)
CCC .... Chicago Clinical Chemist [*A publication*]
CCC .... Chief Cable Censor [*Navy rating*] [*Obsolete*]
CCC .... China Christian Council
CCC .... Chinese Cooperative Catalog [*Library of Congress*] [*A publication*]
CCC .... Chlorocholine Chloride [*Organic chemistry*]
CCC .... Chow Chow Club   (EA)
CCC .... Choyce's Cases in Chancery [*1557-1606*] [*England*] [*A publication*]   (DLA)
CCC .... Christian Chamber of Commerce   (EA)
CCC .... Christian Citizens' Crusade   (EA)
CCC .... Christian College Coalition   (EA)
CCC .... Christian College Consortium   (EA)
CCC .... Christ's College (Cambridge University)   (ROG)
CCC .... Circo Craft Company, Inc. [*Toronto Stock Exchange symbol*]
CCC .... Citeaux. Commentarii Cistercienses [*A publication*]
CCC .... Citizens' Committee for Children of New York   (EA)
CCC .... Citizens for Constitutional Concerns   (EA)
CCC .... Citroen Car Club   (EA)
CCC .... City Communications Centre [*British*]   (CB)
CCC .... Civilian Conservation Centers [*Job Corps*]
CCC .... Civilian Conservation Corps [*Created, 1937; liquidated, 1943*]
CCC .... Civilta Classica e Cristiana [*A publication*]
CCC .... Claro [*Light-colored cigar*]
CCC .... Classified Control Clerk [*Army*]
CCC .... Clean Coal Coalition [*Defunct*]   (EA)
CCC .... Clear, Cancel, or Complete   (MCD)
CCC .... Cloisonne Collectors Club   (EA)
CCC .... Closed-Cycle Cooler
CCC .... Clue Computing Company [*British*]
CCC .... Coalition for Common Courtesy   (EA)
CCC .... Collection/Classification/Cannibalization [*Military*]
CCC .... College Composition and Communication [*A publication*]
CCC .... Combat Cargo Command
CCC .... Combat Command C
CCC .... Combined Case Control [*IRS*]
CCC .... Command and Control Center [*Air Force*]   (AFM)
CC & C .... Command, Control, and Communications [*Air Force*]
CCC .... Command Control Console   (KSC)
CCC .... Commercial Contract Change
CCC .... Committee on the Care of Children   (EA)
CCC .... Committee of Chinese Correspondence   (EA)
CCC .... Committee of Concerned Catholics   (EA)
CCC .... Commodity Credit Corporation [*Department of Agriculture*]
CCC .... Commonwealth Communications Council [*British*] [*World War II*]
CCC .... Communication Center Console
CCC .... Communications Center of Clarksburg [*Clarksburg, MD*] [*Telecommunications*]   (TSSD)
CCC .... Communications, Command, and Control
CCC .... Communications Control Center   (FAAC)
CCC .... Communications Control Console   (MCD)
CCC .... Comparative Capital Cost   (TEL)
CCC .... Competition and Credit Control [*British*]
CCC .... Complex Control Center   (KSC)
CCC .... Component Change Control [*Navy*]   (NG)

CCC .... Comprehensive Cancer Center [*Ohio State University*] [*Research center*]   (RCD)
CCC .... Compucats' Computer Club   (EA)
CCC .... Computer Command Control [*General Motors Corp.*]
CCC .... Computer Communications Console   (AFM)
CCC .... Computer Communications Converter   (MCD)
CCC .... Computer Composition Corp. [*Also, an information service or system*]   (IID)
CCC .... Computer Control Communication   (BUR)
CCC .... Computer Control Complex
CCC .... Computer Control Corporation
CCC .... Concerned Christian Candidates [*Australia*]
CCC .... Concrete Ceiling
CCC .... Congressional Competitiveness Caucus   (EA)
CCC .... Congressional Crime Caucus   (EA)
CCC .... Conservative Central Council [*British*]
CCC .... Conservatives for a Constitutional Convention   (EA)
CCC .... Console Control Circuit
CCC .... Consommation et Corporations Canada [*Consumer and Corporate Affairs Canada - CCA*]
CCC .... Constitutio Carolina Criminalis [*A publication*]   (DSA)
CCC .... Constitutional Consultative Committee on the Political Future of Nigeria [*Political party*]
CCC .... Consultative Committee on the Curriculum [*British*]
CCC .... Consumer Consultative Committee [*British*]
CCC .... Consumer Credit Counselors [*Banking*]
CCC .... Contaminant Control Cartridge   (MCD)
CCC .... Contract Carrier Conference [*Later, ICC*]   (EA)
CCC .... Controller Checkout Console   (NASA)
CCC .... Coordinate Conversion Computer   (MCD)
CCC .... Copyright Clearance Center   (EA)
CCC .... Corporate Capital Charge   (MCD)
CCC .... Corporate Conservation Council   (EA)
CCC .... Corpus Christi Campaign   (EA)
CCC .... Corpus Christi College [*Cambridge and Oxford*]
CCC .... Cost Category Code   (MCD)
CCC .... Council for the Care of Churches [*British*]
CCC .... Council of Community Churches [*Later, National Council of Community Churches*]   (EA)
CCC .... Council of Container Carriers
CCC .... Council for Cultural Co-Operation [*Council of Europe*]   (EY)
CCC .... Countercurrent Chromatography
CCC .... Covalently Closed Circular [*Configuration of DNA*] [*Microbiology*]
CCC .... Cox's English Criminal Cases [*A publication*]   (DLA)
CCc .... Crescent City Public Library, Crescent City, CA [*Library symbol*] [*Library of Congress*]   (LCLS)
CCC .... Critical Coagulation Concentration [*Colloidal chemistry*]
CCC .... Critical Control Circuit
CCC .... Cube-Connected Cycle   (MCD)
CCC .... Cusp Creek [*British Columbia*] [*Seismograph station code, US Geological Survey*] [*Closed*]   (SEIS)
CCC .... Customs Co-Operation Council [*See also CCD*] [*Brussels, Belgium*]   (EAIO)
CCC .... Cyclic Check Character [*Data processing*]
CCC .... Honnold Library, Claremont, CA [*Library symbol*] [*Library of Congress*]   (LCLS)
CCC .... MIT [*Massachusetts Institute of Technology*] Cell Culture Center [*Research center*]   (RCD)
CCC .... Vanguarda de Comando de Caca aos Comunistas [*Vanguard of the Commando for Hunting Communists*] [*Brazil*]   (PD)
CCCA .... Canadian Cosmetics Careers Association
CCCA .... Canadian Criminology and Corrections Association
CCCA .... Catholic Civics Clubs of America [*Defunct*]   (EA)
CCC-A .... Certificate of Clinical Competence in Audiology
CCCA .... Checker Car Club of America   (EA)
CCCA .... Classic Car Club of America   (EA)
CCCA .... Classic Comet Club of America   (EA)
CCCA .... Cocoa, Chocolate, and Confectionary Alliance [*British*]
CCCA .... Commission on Critical Choices for Americans
CCCA .... Committee of Concern for Central America   (EA)
CCCA .... Community College of Central Australia
CCCA .... Corps Commander Coast Artillery [*British*]
CCCADA ... Carolus Cordell, Catholicae Academicae Duacenae Alumnus [*Pseudonym used by Charles Cordell*]
CCCB .... Canadian Conference of Catholic Bishops
CCCB .... Component Change Control Board [*DoD*]
CCCB .... Component Configuration Control Board   (AFIT)
CCCB .... Configuration Change Control Board [*NASA*]   (KSC)
CCCBAH ... Canterbury Chamber of Commerce. Agricultural Bulletin [*A publication*]
CCCBR ...... Central Council of Church Bell Ringers [*British*]
CCC Bul ..... Canterbury Chamber of Commerce. Bulletin [*New Zealand*] [*A publication*]
CCC Bull .... Bulletin. Committee on Criminal Courts' Law and Procedure. Association of the Bar. City of New York [*A publication*]   (DLA)
CCCC .... Cape Cod Community College [*West Barnstable, MA*]
CCCC .... Cape Colony Cyclist Corps [*British military*]   (DMA)
CCCC .... Centralized COMINT Communications Center [*National Security Agency*]

CCCC........ Centrifugal Countercurrent Chromatography
CCCC........ Charles County Community College [*La Plata, MD*]
CCCC........ Chrome Card Collectors Club [*Later, D of A*] (EA)
CCCC........ Chrysler Car Club Council (EA)
CCCC........ Colonel Coon Collectors Club (EA)
CCCC........ Computerized Conferencing and Communications Center [*New Jersey Institute of Technology*] [*Research center*] (RCD)
CCCC........ Conference on College Composition and Communication (EA)
CCCC........ Consolidated Computer and Control Center
CCCC........ Cookie Cutter Collectors Club (EA)
CCCC........ Coordinating Council for Computers in Construction (EA)
CCCC........ Council of Car Care Centers (EA)
CCCC........ Countercurrent Cooling Crystallization [*Tsukishima Kikai Co., Tokyo*] [*Chemical engineering*]
CCCC........ Cover Collectors Circuit Club (EA)
CCCC........ Cross-Channel Coordination Center [*NATO*] (NATG)
CCCC........ Cut, Carat, Clarity, Color [*Factors in determining the value of a diamond*]
CCCCAK... Collection of Czechoslovak Chemical Communications [*A publication*]
CCC Cas.... Central Criminal Court Cases, Sessions Papers [*1834-1913*] [*England*] [*A publication*] (DLA)
CCCCE...... Conseil de la Cooperation Culturelle du Conseil de l'Europe [*Council for Cultural Cooperation of the Council of Europe*] (EAIO)
CCCD........ Canadian Co-Ordinating Council on Deafness
CCCD........ Citizens' Council on Civic Development [*Canada*]
CCCDA...... Conseil Canadien de Coordination de la Deficience Auditive [*Canadian Co-Ordinating Council on Deafness - CCCD*]
CCCE........ Certified Consumer Credit Executive [*Designation awarded by International Consumer Credit Association*]
CCCE........ Closed-Cycle Cryogenic Equipment
CCCE........ Consulting Chemists and Chemical Engineers
CCCEP...... Commissary Civilian Career Enhancement Program [*Air Force*]
CCCET...... Comite Canadien de la Classification Ecologique du Territoire [*Canadian Committee on Ecological (Biophysical) Land Classification - CCELC*]
CCCF........ Candlelighters Childhood Cancer Foundation (EA)
CCCF........ Central Committee on Communications Facilities
CCC Hist Bldg Ctee Min ... Cumberland County Council. Historic Buildings Committee. Minutes [*A publication*] (APTA)
CC Chr...... Chancery Cases Chronicle [*Ontario*] [*A publication*] (DLA)
CC Chron... Chancery Cases Chronicle [*Ontario*] [*A publication*] (DLA)
CCCHRON ... County Courts Chronicle [*1847-1920*] [*England*]
CCCI.......... 3CI, Inc. [*Formerly, Creative Consulting Corporation International*] [*Fort Collins, CO*] [*NASDAQ symbol*] (NQ)
CCCI.......... Campus Crusade for Christ International (EA)
CCCI.......... Candy, Chocolate and Confectionery Institute (EA)
CCCI.......... Capital Cities Communications, Incorporated
CCCI.......... Classic Chevy Club International (EA)
CCCI.......... Coca-Cola Collectors Club International (EA)
CCCI.......... Command, Control, Communications, and Intelligence [*Telecommunications*] (TEL)
CCCI.......... Conseil Canadien pour la Cooperation Internationale [*Canadian Council for International Cooperation - CCIC*]
CCCIPR..... Citizens Communication Center of the Institute for Public Representation [*Later, CCCPIPR*] (EA)
CCCist........ Citeaux. Commentarii Cistercienses [*A publication*]
CCCL........ Canadian and Catholic Confederation of Labour
CC Cl .... Cathodal Closure Clonus [*Medicine*]
CCCL........ Catholic Council on Civil Liberties [*Defunct*] (EA)
CCCL........ Citizens Committee for Constitutional Liberties [*Defunct*]
CCCL........ Cleveland, Cincinnati, Chicago & St. Louis Railway [*AAR code*]
CCCL........ Complementary Constant Current Logic [*Data processing*] (BUR)
CCCLS ...... Clackamas Cooperative County-Wide Library Services [*Library network*]
CCCM .... Canadian Consultative Council on Multiculturalism
C/CCM...... Counter/Counter-Countermeasure [*Military*]
CCCMD .... Comprehensive Cancer Center of Metropolitan Detroit [*National Cancer Institute*] [*Research center*] (RCD)
CCCMMM ... Closed Chest Cardiac Massage and Mouth-to-Mouth Resuscitation [*Medicine*] (AABC)
CCCN .... Cost Change Commitment Notice
CCCN .... Customs Co-Operation Council Nomenclature [*See also BTN*]
C in C CNA ... Commander-in-Chief, Canadian Northwest Atlantic [*World War II*]
CCCNA ..... Congregational Christian Churches National Association (EA)
CCCO .... Catalytic Construction Company (KSC)
CCCO .... CCCO [*Central Committee for Conscientious Objectors*]/An Agency for Military and Draft Counseling (EA)
CCCO .... Committee on Climatic Changes and the Ocean [*Paris, France*] (EAIO)
CC Com Proc ... Code of Civil and Commercial Procedure (DLA)
CCCP......... Carbonylcyanide-meta-chlorophenylhydrazone [*Also, CCP*] [*Organic chemistry*]
CCCP......... Combined Conversion of the Catalogues Project [*National Library of Australia*]
CC & CP .... Command Control and Communications Program [*Air Force*]

CCCP......... Comprehensive Cancer Center Program [*National Cancer Institute*]
CCCP......... Consolidated Command, Control, and Communications Program (MCD)
CCCP........ Council on Cooperative College Projects [*Later, CCP*] (EA)
CCCP......... Union of Soviet Socialist Republics [*Initialism represents Russian phrase, Soyuz Sotsialistiches Kikh Respublik*]
CCCPIPR .. Citizens Communications Center Project of the Institute for Public Representation (EA)
CCCPR ...... Client-Centered Counseling Progress Record [*Psychology*]
CCCQDV... CCQ. Critical Care Quarterly [*A publication*]
CCCQDV... Critical Care Quarterly [*A publication*]
CCCR........ CCR Video Corp. [*Los Angeles, CA*] [*NASDAQ symbol*] (NQ)
CCCR........ Citizens' Commission on Civil Rights
CCCR........ Closed Chest Cardiac Resuscitation [*Medicine*]
CCCR........ Command Classified Control Register
CCCR........ Communication and Command Control Requirements (AAG)
CCCRC...... Connecticut Chemosensory Clinical Research Center [*University of Connecticut*] [*Research center*] (RCD)
CCCS .... Canadian Cooperative Credit Society
CCCS .... Caratage, Color, Clarity, and Shape [*Factors in determining the value of a diamond*]
CCCS .... Central Control Computer System
CCCS .... Centre for Contemporary Cultural Studies [*University of Birmingham*] [*British*] (CB)
CCC-S........ Certificate of Clinical Competence in Speech
CCCS .... Colonial [*or Commonwealth*] and Continental Church Society [*British*]
CCCS .... Command, Control, and Communications System (NATG)
CCCS .... Consumer Credit Counseling Services [*Banking*]
CCCS .... Core Component Cleaning System [*Nuclear energy*] (NRCH)
CCCS .... Core Component Conditioning Station [*Nuclear energy*] (NRCH)
CC/CS ...... Current Contents/Chemical Sciences [*A publication*]
CCC Sess Pap ... Central Criminal Court Cases, Sessions Papers [*1834-1913*] [*England*] [*A publication*] (DLA)
CCC & StL ... Cleveland, Cincinnati, Chicago & St. Louis Railway
CCCT........ Cabinet Council on Commerce and Trade [*Reagan administration*]
CC Ct Cas.. Central Criminal Court Cases [*1834-1913*] [*England*] [*A publication*] (DLA)
CCCTU...... Central Council of Ceylon Trade Unions
CCCU .... Crew Compartment Cooling Unit [*NASA*] (KSC)
CCCUN ..... Communications Coordination Committee for the United Nations (EA)
CCCUNY .. City College of City University of New York
CCCV........ Coconut Cadang-Cadang Viroid [*Also, CCV*]
CCCY........ Canadian Council on Children and Youth [*Research center*] (RCD)
CCD .... Calcite Compensation Depth [*Oceanography*]
CCD .... Calibration Curve Data
CCD .... Cambridge Crystallographic Database [*England*]
CCD .... Camouflage, Concealment, and Deception (MCD)
CCD .... Canadian Car Demurrage Bureau, The, Montreal PQ CDA [*STAC*]
CCD .... Carbonate Compensation Depth [*Oceanography*]
CCD .... Cascade Airways [*Spokane, WA*] [*FAA designator*] (FAAC)
CCD .... Cash Concentration and Disbursement
CCD .... Cell Current Density
CCD .... Census County Division [*Bureau of Census*]
CCD .... Center for Community Development [*Humboldt State University*] [*Research center*] (RCD)
CCD .... Center for Curriculum Design [*Information service or system*] [*Defunct*] (IID)
CCD .... Central Command Decoder [*Spacecraft assembly*] (MCD)
CCD .... Central Commissioning Detail [*Navy*]
CCD .... Central Composite Design [*Statistical design of experiments*]
CCD .... Central Corporate Design
CCD .... Chambre de Commerce de Tunis. Bulletin [*A publication*]
CCD .... Change Control Determine (MCD)
CCD .... Charge-Coupled Device [*Data storage device*]
CCD .... Checkout Command Decoder (NASA)
CCD .... Circumscribing Circle Diameter (MCD)
CCD .... City [*or County*] Civil Defense Director
CCD .... Civil Censorship Division [*US Military Government, Germany*]
CCD .... Civil Coordination Detachment [*General Air Traffic Element at Operational Traffic and Defense Centers*] [*NATO*] (NATG)
CCD .... Coarse Control Damper [*Nuclear energy*] (NRCH)
CCD .... Cold Cathode Discharge
CCD .... Combat Center Director
CCD .... Combat Command D
CC/D .... Command Control/Destruct (MUGU)
CCD .... Command and Control Director [*Air Force*]
CCD .... Command and Control Division [*SHAPE Technical Center*] (NATG)
CCD .... Commander, Coast Defenses
CCD .... Committee for the Care of the Diabetic
CCD .... Common Core of Data [*National Center for Educational Statistics*] [*Department of Education*] (OICC)

CCD .... Commonwealth Employees Compensation Decisions [*A publication*] (APTA)
CCD .... Computer-Controlled Display
CCD .... Computing Canada [*A publication*]
CCD .... Concord Energy [*Vancouver Stock Exchange symbol*]
CCD .... Condensed Chemical Dictionary [*A publication*]
CCD .... Conference of the Committee on Disarmament [*Formerly, ENDC*] [*NATO*]
CCD .... Configuration Change Directive (KSC)
CCD .... Confraternity of Christian Doctrine
CCD .... Conseil de Cooperation Douaniere [*Customs Co-Operation Council - CCC*] (EAIO)
CCD .... Constants Change Display (MCD)
CCD .... Construction Completion Date (AFM)
CCD .... Continental Communications Division [*Military*]
CCD .... Contract Completion Date [*Telecommunications*] (TEL)
CCD .... Coordinated Cockpit Display (MCD)
CCD .... Core Current Driver
CCD .... Corona Current Detector
CCD .... Cost Center Determination (AAG)
CCD .... Countercurrent Digestion [*Ore leach process*]
CCD .... Countercurrent Distribution [*Analytical chemistry*]
CCD .... Czechoslovak Christian Democracy (EA)
CCDA .... Canberra Community Development Authority [*Australia*]
CCDA .... Charge Coupled Diode Array [*Liquid chromatography*]
CCDA .... Commercial Chemical Development Association [*Later, CDA*] (EA)
CCDA .... Committee on Cataloging: Description and Access [*Association for Library Collections and Technical Services*]
CC-DAD .... Command and Control - Division Air Defense (MCD)
CCDB .... Carbon-Carbon Data Base [*Battelle Columbus Laboratories*] [*Database*]
CCDC .... Cambridge Crystallographic Data Centre [*University of Cambridge*] [*Information service or system*] (IID)
CCDC .... Canadian Communicable Disease Center
CCDC .... Cape Cod Direction Center [*Air Force*]
CCDC .... Central Citizens' Defence Committee [*Northern Ireland*]
CCDC .... Central Control and Display Console
CCDC .... Connecticut Census Data Center [*Connecticut State Office of Policy and Management*] [*Information service or system*] (IID)
CCDD .... Coalition Concerned with Developmental Disabilities [*American Occupational Therapy Association*]
CCDD .... Command and Control Development Division [*Air Force*]
CCDD .... Controller of Chemical Defence Department [*Ministry of Supply*] [*British*]
CCDF .... Cambridge Crystallographic Data File [*Database*]
CC & DF .... Central Computer and Display Facility [*Air Force*] (CET)
CCDF .... Complementary Cumulative Distribution Function [*Mathematics*]
CCDG .... Civil Coordination Detachment General [*NATO*] (NATG)
CCDIDC ...... Catheterization and Cardiovascular Diagnosis [*A publication*]
CCDJ .... Conseil Canadien de la Documentation Juridique [*Canadian Law Information Council*]
CCDL .... CAINS [*Carrier/Aircraft Inertial Navigation System*] Covert Data Link (MCD)
CCDL .... Commander, Cruiser-Destroyer Forces, Atlantic (MCD)
CCDL .... Cross-Channel Data Link (MCD)
CCDLG ...... Coalition Canadienne pour les Droits des Lesbiennes et des Gais [*Canadian Lesbian and Gay Rights Coalition*]
CCDLNE ... Commission for Controlling the Desert Locust in the Near East [*United Nations*] (EA)
CCDLNWA ... Commission for Controlling the Desert Locust in North-West Africa [*United Nations*] (EA)
CCDM .... Consultative Committee on the Definition of the Meter [*International Bureau of Weights and Measures*]
CCDM .... Continuing Committee of Deputy Ministers [*Canada*]
CCDM .... Council on Career Development for Minorities (EA)
CCDMRB ... Command Contractor Data Management Review Board [*Air Force*] (AFIT)
CCDN .... Centre de Compilation de Donnees Neutroniques [*Neutron Data Compilation Center*] [*France*] [*Information service or system*] (IID)
CCDN .... Corporate Consolidated Data Network [*IBM Corp.*] [*Telecommunications*]
CCDO .... Canadian Classification and Dictionary of Occupations [*A publication*]
CCD(OCCE) ... Commonwealth Committee for Defence (Operational Clothing and Combat Equipment) (ADA)
CCDP .... Churchmen's Commission for Decent Publications [*Defunct*] (EA)
CCDP .... Command Control Dial Panel
CCDP .... Commission Canadienne des Droits de la Personne [*Canadian Human Rights Commission - CHRC*]
CCDP .... Computer Control and Display Panel (MCD)
CCDP .... Cooperative College Development Program
CCDR .... Contractor Cost Data Reporting (MCD)
CCDR .... Contractor Critical Design Review (MCD)
CCDR .... Cross-Cultural Dance Resources (EA)
CCDS .... Centers for the Commercial Development of Space
CCDS .... Command Control Destruct System (MUGU)

CCDS .... Command, Control, and Detection System [*Military*]
CCDS .... Commercial Computer Documentation Set (MCD)
CCDS .... Conseil Canadien de Developpement Social [*Canadian Council on Social Development*] (EAIO)
CCDS .... Consultative Committee for the Definition of the Second
CCDS .... Control Circuits Design Section
CCDS .... Control, Communication, and Display Subsystem (MCD)
CCDS .... Corpus Cultus Deae Syriae (BJA)
CCDSO ...... Command and Control Defense Systems Office
CCDU .... Coastal Command Defence Unit [*British*]
CCDU .... Coastal Command Development Unit [*British*]
CCDW .... Carrying Concealed Deadly Weapon [*Police term*]
CCE .... Caines' New York Cases in Error [*A publication*] (DLA)
CCE .... Cape Cod Experiment [*Oceanography*]
CCE .... Cases of Contested Elections [*A publication*] (DLA)
C of CE ...... Cases of Contested Elections [*United States*] [*A publication*] (DLA)
CCE .... CCC Coded Communications [*Vancouver Stock Exchange symbol*]
CCE .... Center for Conscious Evolution (EA)
CCE .... Centro de Calculo Electronico Universidad Nacional Autonoma de Mexico [*National Autonomous University of Mexico, Data Processing Center*] [*Mexico*] (CSR)
CCE .... Certified Chamber Executive [*Designation awarded by American Chamber of Commerce Executives*]
CCE .... Cesium Contact Engine
CCE .... Change Control Engineer
CCE .... Charge Composition Explorer [*Spacecraft*]
CCE .... Chief of Communications - Electronics
CCE .... Chief, Corps of Engineers [*Army*]
CCE .... Civil Communications Element [*Military*] (NATG)
CCE .... Clapeyron-Clausius Equation [*Physics*]
CCE .... Clear-Cell Carcinoma of Endometrium [*Medicine*]
CCE .... Clubbing, Cyanosis, or Edema [*Medicine*]
CCE .... Coca-Cola Enterprises, Inc. [*NYSE symbol*] (SPSG)
CCE .... College Canadien des Enseignants [*Canadian College of Teachers - CCT*]
CCE .... Combat Communications Equipment [*Military*]
CCE .... Combat Control Elements [*Army*]
CCE .... Comhaltas Ceoltoiri Eireann [*Traditional Irish Singing and Dancing Society*] (EA)
CCE .... Comite de Cooperacion Economica del Istmo Centroamericano [*Central American Economic Cooperation Committee*]
CCE .... Command Control Equipment (KSC)
CCE .... Commercial Construction Equipment [*Plan*] [*Army*]
CCE .... Commission des Communautes Europeennes [*Commission of the European Communities - CEC*] (EAIO)
CCE .... Communications Control Equipment (MCD)
CCE .... Computer Command Engineer (MCD)
CCE .... Confederation des Compagnonnages Europeens [*European Companions - EC*] (EAIO)
CCE .... Conseil Canadien des Eglises [*Canadian Council of Churches*] (EAIO)
CCE .... Conseil des Communes d'Europe [*Council of European Municipalities*]
CCE .... Console Communications Equipment (MCD)
CCE .... Consultative Committee on Electricity [*International Bureau of Weights and Measures*]
CCE .... Consulting Communications Engineers, Inc. [*Villanova, PA*] (TSSD)
CCE .... Contract Change Estimate
CCE .... Contract Closeout Extension (AFIT)
CCE .... Contractor Change Evaluation (AAG)
CCE .... Contributions to Canadian Economics [*A publication*]
CCE .... Controlled Configuration Explosive [*Military*]
CCE .... Council on Chiropractic Education (EA)
CCE .... Council for a Competitive Economy (EA)
CCE .... Council of Construction Employers [*Defunct*] (EA)
CCE .... Council for Court Excellence (EA)
CCE .... Counsel and Care for the Elderly [*British*]
CCE .... Countercurrent Electrophoresis [*Also, CE*] [*Analytical chemistry*]
CCE .... Crusade for a Cleaner Environment [*Defunct*] (EA)
CCE .... Cuadernos de Cultura Espanola [*A publication*]
CCE .... Current Cash [*or Cost*] Equivalent (ADA)
CCE .... Naples, FL [*Location identifier*] [*FAA*] (FAAL)
CCEA .... Cabinet Council on Economic Affairs [*Reagan administration*]
CCEA .... Center for Climatic and Environmental Assessment [*National Oceanic and Atmospheric Administration*] (IID)
CCEA .... Central Canada Exhibition Association
CCEA .... Central Council of Employers of Australia
CCEA .... Chief Control Electrical Artificer [*British military*] (DMA)
CCEA .... Commission de Controle de l'Energie Atomique [*Atomic Energy Control Board - AECB*]
CCEA .... Commonwealth Council for Education Administration [*Armidale, NSW, Australia*] (EAIO)
CCEAFS .... Conference of Central and East African States
CCEA Newsl ... Commonwealth Council for Educational Administration. Newsletter [*A publication*] (APTA)

CCEA SEA ... Commonwealth Council for Educational Administration. Studies in Educational Administration [*A publication*] (APTA)
CCEB......... Continuing Legal Education of the Bar, University of California Extension (DLA)
CCEBI .... Centre for Continuing Education in the Building Industry [*Polytechnic of the South Bank*] [*British*] (CB)
CCEBK...... Chronicles Concerning Early Babylonian Kings [*A publication*] (BJA)
CCEBL...... Cold Cathode Electron Beam LASER (MCD)
CCEBS ...... Committee for the Collegiate Education of Black Students
CCEC........ Chairman, Communications-Electronics Committee [*NATO*] (NATG)
CCECA...... CRC [*Chemical Rubber Company*] Critical Reviews in Environmental Control [*A publication*]
CCED .... Center for Community Economic Development
CCEDMRI ... Consultative Committee for the Standards of Measurement of Ionizing Radiations [*International Bureau of Weights and Measures*]
CCEE......... Consilium Conferentiarum Episcopalium Europae [*Council of European Bishops' Conferences*] (EAIO)
CCEEP ...... Committee for Coordination of Emergency Economic Planning [*US/Canada*]
CCEF......... Communication Countermeasures Evaluation Facility [*Air Force*] (MCD)
CCEFP...... Center for Community Education Facility Planning [*Inactive*] (EA)
CCEGR...... Coolant-Controlled Exhaust Gas Recirculation [*Automotive engineering*]
CCE & HR ... Charing Cross, Euston & Highgate (Underground) Railway [*British*] (ROG)
CCEI......... Cahiers. Centre d'Etudes Irlandaises [*A publication*]
CCEI......... Coordinating Committee for Ellis Island (EA)
CCEI......... Crown-Crisp Experimental Index [*Personality development test*] [*Psychology*]
CCEIA ...... Carnegie Council on Ethics and International Affairs (EA)
CCEJ .... Conseil Canadien d'Experimentation des Jouets [*Canadian Toy Testing Council*]
CCEL........ Chief Control Electrician [*British military*] (DMA)
CCEL........ Coolidge Center for Environmental Leadership (EA)
CCELC ...... Canada Committee on Ecological (Biophysical) Land Classification [*See also CCCET*]
CCELCN ... Canadian Committee on Ecological Land Classification. Newsletter [*A publication*]
CCELF....... Conference des Communautes Ethniques de Langue Francaise [*Standing Committee of French-Speaking Ethnical Communities - SCFSEC*] (EA)
CCEM .... CompuChem Corp. [*NASDAQ symbol*] (NQ)
CCEM .... Construction, Civil Engineering, Mining [*A publication*]
CCE/MACI ... Commercial Construction Equipment and Military Adaptation of Commercial Items (MCD)
CCEMN .... Chief Control Electrical Mechanician [*British military*] (DMA)
CCEMWD ... Close Combat, Engineering, and Mine Warfare Directorate [*Army*]
CCEN .... Care Centers, Inc. [*Dayton, OH*] [*NASDAQ symbol*] (NQ)
C Cent .... Christian Century [*A publication*]
C Centre Et Coutumes ... Cahiers. Centre d'Etudes des Coutumes [*A publication*]
CCEO .... Controller of Communications Equipment Overseas [*British*]
CCEP......... Cabinet Committee for Economic Policy [*Later, CEP*]
CCEP......... Child Care Employee Project (EA)
CCER......... Cahiers. Cercle Ernest Renan pour Libres Recherches d'Histoire du Christianisme [*Paris*] [*A publication*]
CCE/RA .... Revista de Antropologia. Casa de la Cultura Ecuatoriana, Nucleo del Azuay [*Cuenca*] [*A publication*]
CCERD...... Cabinet Committee on Economic and Regional Development [*Canada*]
CCERO...... Cahiers. Centre d'Etudes de Recherche Operationnelle [*A publication*]
CCES........ Canadian Council of Engineering Students
CCES........ Case Center for Electrochemical Sciences [*Case Western Reserve University*] [*Research center*] (RCD)
CCES........ Catholic Church Extension Society of the USA (EA)
CCES........ Catholic College of Education, Sydney [*Australia*]
CCES........ Center-Clipping Echo Suppressor (MCD)
CCES........ Center for Corporate Economics and Strategy (EA)
CCES........ Common Control Echo Suppressor [*Telecommunications*] (TEL)
CCES........ Computer Consulting and Education Services Pty. Ltd. [*Australia*]
CCESC ...... Citizens Committee on the El Salvador Crisis (EA)
CCE/SMHE ... Commercial Construction and Selected Materials Handling Equipment (RDA)
CCESO...... Committee on Contributions for Elective State Officials
CCESP...... Committee on Continuing Education for School Personnel (EA)
CCESUSA ... Catholic Church Extension Society of the United States of America (EA)
CCet........... Capitol-Cetra [*Record label*]
CCET......... Centre for Computers in Education and Training [*University of Salford*] [*British*] (CB)

CCETSW... Central Council for Education and Training in Social Work [*British*]
CCETT...... Centre Commun d'Etudes de Television et de Telecommunications [*Videotex research center*] [*France*]
CCEU .... Council on the Continuing Education Unit [*Later, IACET*] (EA)
CCEVS ...... Coolant Control Engine Vacuum Switch [*Automotive engineering*]
CCEW........ Center for Continuing Education for Women
CCEWG.... Civil Communications-Electronics Working-Group [*Military*] (NATG)
CCEWP ..... Combat Clothing and Equipment Working Party [*NATO*] (RDA)
CCEWT ..... Central Control Evaluation and Warning Team (CINC)
CCEX........ Clad Controlled Expansion
CCF........... Cahiers Economiques et Monetaires [*A publication*]
CCF........... Canadian Communications Foundation
CCF........... Cancer Cytology Foundation of America [*Later, National Cancer Cytology Center*]
CCF........... Captain, Coastal Forces [*Navy*] [*British*]
CCF........... Carbonaceous Chondrite Fission [*Geophysics*]
CCF........... Carcassonne [*France*] [*Airport symbol*] (OAG)
CCF........... Carotid Cavernous Fistula [*Medicine*]
CCF........... Central Computing Facility [*NASA*]
CCF........... Central Control Facility [*Military*] (AABC)
CCF........... Central Personnel Security Clearance Facility [*Army*] (MCD)
CCF........... Cephalin-Cholesterol Flocculation [*Clinical chemistry*]
CCF........... Cesky Casopis Filologicky [*A publication*]
CCF........... Chinese Communist Forces
CCF........... Christian Century Foundation (EA)
CCF........... Christian Children's Fund (EA)
CCF........... Cilla's Circle of Fans (EAIO)
CCF........... Cinema Center Films
CCF........... Circular Crystal Facet
CCF........... Citizens' Council Forum [*Defunct*] (EA)
CCF........... Co-Operative Commonwealth Federation [*Later, NDP*] [*Canadian*] (PPW)
CCF........... Collection Coordination Facility (MCD)
CCF........... Combined Cadet Force [*British equivalent of US ROTC*]
CCF........... Committee of Corporate Finance [*of the National Association of Securities Dealers*]
CCF........... Common Cause Failure [*Nuclear energy*] (NRCH)
CCF........... Common Cold Foundation [*Defunct*]
CCF........... Communication Central Facility [*Air Force*]
CCF........... Communications Control Field
CCF........... Compound Comminuted Fracture [*Medicine*]
CCF........... Compressed Citation File
CCF........... Concentrated Complete Fertilizer [*Imperial Chemical Industries*] [*British*]
CCF........... Concrete Floor
CCF........... Configuration Control Function [*Telecommunications*] (TEL)
CCF........... Congestive Cardiac Failure [*Medicine*]
CCF........... Congress for Cultural Freedom [*British*]
CCF........... Congressional Clearinghouse on the Future (EA)
CCF........... Consultants (Computer & Financial) [*Commercial firm*] [*British*]
CCF........... Contract Cases, Federal (AFIT)
CCF........... Converter Compressor Facility (KSC)
CCF........... Cook United, Inc. [*NYSE symbol*] (SPSG)
CCF........... Cooperative Commonwealth Federation [*Political party*] [*Later, New Democratic Party - NDP*] [*Canada*]
CCF........... Corps Contingency Force [*Army*] (AABC)
CCF........... Correctional Custody Facility [*Military*] (AABC)
CCF........... Credit Commercial de France [*Commercial Credit of France*]
CCF........... Cross-Correlation Function
CCF........... Crystal-Induced Chemotactic Factor [*Immunology*]
CCF........... Curtis Completion Form [*Psychology*]
CCFA........ Cancer Cytology Foundation of America [*Later, National Cancer Cytology Center*]
CCFA........ Caribbean Cane Farmers' Association [*Kingston, Jamaica*] [*Inactive*] (EAIO)
CCFA........ Center for Craniofacial Anomalies [*University of Illinois at Chicago*] [*Research center*] (RCD)
CCFA........ Children's Cancer Fund of America (EA)
CCFA........ Combined Cadet Force Association [*British military*] (DMA)
CCFA........ Common Cause Failure Analysis [*Nuclear energy*] (NRCH)
CCFAC...... Canadian Concerned Fathers Action Committee
CCFATU ... Coastal Command Fighter Affiliation Training Unit [*British military*] (DMA)
CCFB........ Francis Bacon Foundation, Inc., Claremont, CA [*Library symbol*] [*Library of Congress*] (LCLS)
CCFC........ Circus Clown Friends Club [*British*]
CCFC........ Citizens Committee for a Free Cuba
CCFC........ Colleen Casey Fan Club (EA)
CCFC........ Connie Causey Fan Club (EA)
CCFC........ Continental Car Ferry Centre [*British*]
CCFC........ Syndicat des Controleurs de Circulation Ferroviaire du Canada [*Union of Rail Canada Traffic Controllers - RCTC*]
CCFCSP...... Canadian Centre for Folk Culture Studies Papers. National Museum of Man Mercury Series [*A publication*]

CCFDD...... CFI. Ceramic Forum International. Berichte der Deutschen Keramischen Gesellschaft [*A publication*]
CCFDPC ... Citizens Committee on Future Directions for the Peace Corps (EA)
CCFE......... Commercial Contractor-Furnished Equipment (AAG)
CCFE......... Commercial Customer-Furnished Equipment
CCFET ...... Captain, Coastal Forces, Eastern Theater [*Navy*]
CCFF .... Canadian Cystic Fibrosis Foundation
CCFF .... Cape Canaveral Forecast Facility [*NASA*] (NASA)
CCFF .... Compensatory and Contingency Financing Facility [*International Monetary Fund*]
CCFF .... Crew Compartment Fit and Function [*NASA*]
CCFF .... Crown Cat Fanciers Federation (EA)
CCFFAA.... Contributions. Cushman Foundation for Foraminiferal Research [*A publication*]
CCFFR...... Canadian Council for Fisheries Research (ASF)
CCFHA...... Corson Family History Association (EA)
CCFHD ..... Chol Chol Foundation for Human Development (EA)
CCFIS........ Coastal Command Flying Instructors School [*British military*] (DMA)
CCFL......... Conference on Consumer Finance Law (EA)
CCFL......... Counter Current Flow Limit [*Nuclear energy*]
CCFLSA.... Citizens Committee on the Fair Labor Standards Act (EA)
CCFM....... Council of Canadian Filmmakers
CCFM....... Cryogenic Continuous Film Memory [*Data processing*] (DIT)
CCFMC..... Center for the Coordination of Foreign Manuscript Copying [*Library of Congress*]
CCFOE...... Central Committee for Forest Ownership in the EEC (EAIO)
CCFPT....... Conseil Canadien des Fabricants des Produits du Tabac [*Canadian Tobacco Manufacturers' Council*]
CCFR........ Commonwealth Committee on Fuel Research [*British*]
CCFR........ Constant Current Flux Reset
CCFRA...... Canceled Concurrent with Next Federal Register Amendment (FAAC)
CCFRU...... Comite Canadien sur le Financement de la Recherche dans les Universites [*Canadian Committee on Financing University Research - CCFUR*]
CCFSA ...... Certified Cold Fur Storage Association (EA)
CCFSF....... Chinese Culture Foundation of San Francisco (EA)
CCF-SS...... Collection Coordination Facility Support System (MCD)
CCFT......... Cold Cathode Fluorescent Technology
CCFT......... Cold Cathode Fluorescent Tube
CCFT .... Controlled Current Feedback Transformer (MSA)
CCFUR...... Canadian Committee on Financing University Research
CCFX........ ContiCurrency Foreign Exchange and Money Market Database [*No longer available online*]
CCFXe ...... Carbonaceous Chondrite Fission Xenon [*Geophysics*]
CCG......... California Carvers Guild (EA)
CCG .... Camp Century [*Greenland*] [*Seismograph station code, US Geological Survey*] [*Closed*] (SEIS)
CCG .... Canada College Library, Redwood City, CA [*OCLC symbol*] (OCLC)
CCG .... Canada-United Kingdom-United States Cryptographic Systems General Publications (MCD)
CCG .... Canadian Coast Guard
CCG .... Cargo Center of Gravity (MSA)
CCG .... Carrigan Industries Ltd. [*Vancouver Stock Exchange symbol*]
CCG .... Cartesian Coordinate Grid (NVT)
CCG .... Catalytic Coal Gasification [*Fuel technology*]
CCG .... Choral Conductors Guild (EA)
CCG .... Combat Cargo Group (CINC)
CCG .... Combat Communications Group (AFIT)
CCG .... Comite de Coordination des Experts Budgetaires Gouvernementaux [*Coordinating Committee of Government Budget Experts*] [*NATO*] (NATG)
CCG .... Commandant of the Coast Guard
CCG .... Commission Canadienne des Grains [*Canadian Grain Commission*]
CCG .... Committee for Constitutional Government (EA)
CCG .... Commodity Coordination Groups
CCG .... Computer Communications Group [*Canada*]
CCG .... Computer Control Group [*Military*] (CAAL)
CCG .... Conforms to Copyright Guidelines
CCG .... Congressional Coal Group (EA)
CCG .... Constant Current Generator
CCG .... Construction Coordination Group [*NASA*] (KSC)
CCG .... Consumer Complaint Guide
CCG .... Control Commission for Germany [*World War II*]
CCG .... Corporation Consulting Group [*British*]
CCGA .... California Cactus Growers Association (EA)
CCGA .... Communications Control Group Assembly [*Ground Communications Facility, NASA*]
CCGA .... Custom Clothing Guild of America (EA)
CCGAA ..... Canadian Certified General Accountants' Association
CCGB .... Confrerie des Chevaliers du Goute Boudin [*Brotherhood of Knights of the Black Pudding Tasters - BKBPT*] (EA)
CCGBI....... Camping Council of Great Britain and Ireland, Ltd.
CCGC........ Capillary Column Gas Chromatography
CCGCR...... Closed-Cycle Gas-Cooled Reactor (DEN)
CCGCS...... Containment Combustion Gas Control System [*Nuclear energy*] (IEEE)

CCGD........ Commander, Coast Guard District
CCGE .... Cold Cathode Gauge Experiment [*Apollo*] [*NASA*]
CCGI......... Community College Goals Inventory [*Test*]
CCGM .... Commission de la Carte Geologique du Monde [*Commission for the Geological Map of the World - GMW*] (EAIO)
CCGN........ Commanding General, Ground Forces [*World War II*]
CCGNJ....... Council on Compulsive Gambling of New Jersey (EA)
CCGS......... Canadian Coast Guard Service
CC & GTCC ... Casino Chips and Gaming Tokens Collectors Club (EA)
CCH........... California State University, Chico, Chico, CA [*OCLC symbol*] (OCLC)
CCH........... Campbell Resources, Inc. [*Formerly, Campbell Chibougamau Mines Ltd.*] [*NYSE symbol*] [*Toronto Stock Exchange symbol*] (SPSG)
CCH........... Ceskoslovensky Casopis Historicky [*A publication*]
CCH........... Channel-Check Handler [*Japan*] (MCD)
C of CH ..... Chief of Chaplains [*Later, CCH*] [*Army*]
CCH........... Chief of Chaplains [*Formerly, CC, C of CH, COFCH*] [*Army*] (AABC)
CCH........... Citizenship Clearing House
CCH........... Cochabamba [*Bolivia*] [*Seismograph station code, US Geological Survey*] (SEIS)
CCH........... Colchicine [*Biochemistry*]
CCH........... Commerce Clearing House, Inc. [*Publisher*] [*Chicago, IL*]
CCH........... Committee on Cosmic Humanism (EA)
CCH........... Computerized Criminal History [*FBI*]
CCH........... Connections per Circuit per Hour [*Telecommunications*] (TEL)
CCH........... Consumer Coalition for Health [*Inactive*] (EA)
CCH........... Cost Comparison Handbook [*A publication*] (MCD)
CCH........... Country Club Hotels [*British*]
CCH........... Creativity Checklist [*Educational test*]
CCH........... Cube Corner Holder
CCH........... Cubic Capacity of Holds [*British*] (ADA)
CCH........... Logan, UT [*Location identifier*] [*FAA*] (FAAL)
CCHA........ Canadian Catholic Historical Association [*See also SCHEC*]
CCHA........ Canadian Corps Heavy Artillery [*World War I*]
CCHA........ Central Collegiate Hockey Association (EA)
CCHA........ Community College Humanities Association (EA)
CCH Atom En L Rep ... Atomic Energy Law Reporter (Commerce Clearing House) [*A publication*] (DLA)
CCHCDE .. Chung-Hua Chieh Heh Heh Hu Hsi Hsi Chi Ping Tsa Chih [*Chinese Journal of Tuberculosis and Respiratory Diseases*] [*A publication*]
(CCH) CLC ... Company Law Cases (Commerce Clearing House) [*Australia*] [*A publication*] (APTA)
C CH COLL ... Christ Church College [*Oxford University*] (ROG)
CCH Comm Mkt Rep ... Common Market Reporter (Commerce Clearing House) [*A publication*] (DLA)
CCHCOPALLANC ... Commissioner, Chancery Court, County Palatine of Lancaster [*British*] (ROG)
CCHD........ Committee to Combat Huntington's Disease [*Later, HDFA*] (EA)
CCHE .... Carnegie Commission on Higher Education
CChE .... Certified Chemical Engineer
CCHE .... Coordinating Council for Higher Education
CChem .... Chartered Chemist [*British*]
CCHENV-LNC ... Consortium for Continuing Higher Education - Librarians' Networking Committee [*Library network*]
CCHEP...... Cement-Coated Heavy Epoxy
CCHF .... Children's Country Holiday Fund [*British*]
C-in-CHF ... Commander-in-Chief, Home Forces [*British*]
CCHFA...... Canadian Council on Health Facilities Accreditation
CCH Fed Banking L Rep ... Federal Banking Law Reports (Commerce Clearing House) [*A publication*] (DLA)
CCH Fed Sec L Rep ... Federal Securities Law Reporter (Commerce Clearing House) [*A publication*] (DLA)
CCHHAQ ... Chishitsu Chosajo Hokoku [*Geological Survey of Japan. Report*] [*A publication*]
CCHHS ..... Center for Canadian Historical Horticultural Studies [*Hamilton, ON*]
CCHI .... CCH [*Commerce Clearing House*] Tax Index [*Database*] [*Australia*] (ADA)
CChi.......... Chico Public Library, Chico, CA [*Library symbol*] [*Library of Congress*] (LCLS)
CCHI .... Crain's Chicago Business [*A publication*]
CChiGS ..... Church of Jesus Christ of Latter-Day Saints, Genealogical Society Library, Chico Branch, Stake Center, Chico, CA [*Library symbol*] [*Library of Congress*] (LCLS)
CCH Inh Est & Gift Tax Rep ... Inheritance, Estate, and Gift Tax Reports (Commerce Clearing House) [*A publication*]
CChiS .... California State University, Chico, Chico, CA [*Library symbol*] [*Library of Congress*] (LCLS)
CCHK........ Continuity Check
CCH Lab Arb Awards ... Labor Arbitration Awards (Commerce Clearing House) [*A publication*] (DLA)
CCH Lab Cas ... Labor Cases (Commerce Clearing House) [*A publication*] (DLA)
CCH Lab L Rep ... Labor Law Reporter (Commerce Clearing House) [*A publication*] (DLA)

CCH LLR .. Labor Law Reporter (Commerce Clearing House) [*A publication*] (DLA)
CCHMD.... Clinics in Chest Medicine [*A publication*]
CCHNDD ... Cell and Chromosome Newsletter [*A publication*]
CCHNEE .. Canadian Chemical News [*A publication*]
CCHP .... CCH [*Commerce Clearing House*] Publications Index (ADA)
CCHP .... Chung Chi Hsueh-Pao [*A publication*]
CCHP .... Consumer Choice Health Plan
CCHPA ...... Jianzhu Xuebao [*A publication*]
CC-HPLC ... Column Chromatography - High-Performance [*or Pressure*] Liquid Chromatography [*Analytical chemistry*]
CChR .... Calendar of Charter Rolls [*British*]
CCHR .... Chile Committee for Human Rights [*Institute for Policy Studies*] (EA)
CChr .... Corpus Christianorum [*Turnhout*] (BJA)
CCHRA ...... Church Committee for Human Rights in Asia (EA)
CCHRP...... Church Coalition for Human Rights in the Philippines (EA)
CCHS .... Conference of California Historical Societies
CCHS .... Congenital Central Hypoventilation Syndrome [*Medicine*]
CCHS .... Congregational Christian Historical Society (EA)
CCHS .... Cylinder-Cylinder-Head-Sector [*Data processing*] (IBMDP)
CCHST ...... Centre Canadien d'Hygiene et de Securite au Travail [*Canadian Centre for Occupational Health and Safety - CCOHS*]
CCH Stand Fed Tax Rep ... Standard Federal Tax Reporter (Commerce Clearing House) [*A publication*] (DLA)
CCH State Tax Cas Rep ... State Tax Cases Reports (Commerce Clearing House) [*A publication*] (DLA)
CCH State Tax Rev ... State Tax Review (Commerce Clearing House) [*A publication*] (DLA)
CCH Tax Ct Mem ... Tax Court Memorandum Decisions (Commerce Clearing House) [*A publication*] (DLA)
CCH Tax Ct Rep ... Tax Court Reporter (Commerce Clearing House) [*A publication*] (DLA)
CChu .... Chula Vista Public Library, Chula Vista, CA [*Library symbol*] [*Library of Congress*] (LCLS)
CCHW .... Citizen's Clearinghouse for Hazardous Wastes (EA)
CCHX .... Component Cooling Heat Exchanger (IEEE)
CCI............ Cache d'Or Resources [*Vancouver Stock Exchange symbol*]
CCI............ Calcium Chloride Institute [*Defunct*] (EA)
CCI............ Calculated Cetane Index [*Fuel technology*]
CCI............ Canadian Conservation Institute [*See also ICC*] [*National Museums of Canada*] [*Research center*] (RCD)
CCI............ Canadian Copyright Institute
CCI............ Canadian Credit Institute
CCI............ Canadian Crossroads International
CCI............ Cancer Care, Incorporated (EA)
CCI............ Canine Companions for Independence (EA)
CCI............ Card Computer Interface [*Data processing*] (IID)
CCI............ Cardiovascular Credentialing International (EA)
CCI............ Center for Compliance Information (EA)
CCI............ Central Control Indicator (MCD)
CCI............ Centre du Commerce International [*International Trade Center - ITC*] [*Geneva, Switzerland*] [*French*] (EAIO)
CCI............ Centre de Creation Industrielle [*Center for Industrial Creation*] [*Information service or system*] (IID)
CCI............ Centro de Comercio Internacional [*International Trade Center - ITC*] [*Spanish*]
CCI............ Certified Consultants International (EA)
CCI............ Chambers of Commerce and Industry [*ASEAN*] (DS)
CCI............ Chambers of Commerce of Ireland (EAIO)
CCI............ Chambre de Commerce Internationale [*The International Chamber of Commerce - ICC*] [*Paris, France*] (EAIO)
CCI............ Charge-Coupled Imager
CCI............ Charleston, SC [*Location identifier*] [*FAA*] (FAAL)
CCI............ Chess Collectors International (EA)
CCI............ Christian Camping International [*Later, CCI/USA*] (EA)
CCI............ Christian Communications, Incorporated (EA)
CCI............ Christians Concerned for Israel [*Superseded by NCLCI*] (EA)
CCI............ Chronic Coronary Insufficiency [*Medicine*]
CCI............ Circuit Condition Indicator
CCI............ Citicorp [*NYSE symbol*] (SPSG)
CCI............ Citrus College, Azusa, CA [*OCLC symbol*] (OCLC)
CCI............ College Characteristics Index [*A questionnaire*]
CCI............ Command Control Interface [*Army*] (AABC)
CCI............ Committee for Chilean Inquiry (EA)
CCI............ Common Carrier Interface (MCD)
CCI............ Communications Carrier, Incorporated [*Austin, TX*] [*Telecommunications*] (TSSD)
CCI............ Communications Concepts, Incorporated [*Newport Beach, CA*] [*Telecommunications*] (TSSD)
CCI............ Communications Consultants, Incorporated [*Washington, NJ*] [*Telecommunications*] (TSSD)
CCI............ Communications Control Interface (MCD)
CCI............ Community Creativity, Incorporated (EA)
CCI............ Compactor Company, Incorporated
CCI............ Component Control Index [*Navy*] (AFIT)
CCI............ Component Cost Index
CCI............ Computer Communications, Incorporated
CCI............ Computer Control Indicator (CAAL)
CCI............ Concordia [*Brazil*] [*Airport symbol*] [*Obsolete*] (OAG)
CCI............ Concordia Collegiate Institute [*New York*]

CCI............ Conseil Canadien des Ingenieurs [*Canadian Council of Engineers*]
CCI............ Consortium Communications International, Inc. [*New York, NY*] [*Telecommunications*] (TSSD)
CCI............ Construction Cost Index
CCI............ Consumer Confidence Index [*Conference Board*]
C & CI .... Contingency and Confidential Intelligence (CINC)
CCI............ Contract Change Identification (MCD)
CCI............ Control Current Impedance
CCI............ Corrected Count Increment [*Hematology*]
CCI............ Corrugated Container Institute [*Defunct*] (EA)
CCI............ Corrugated, Cupped, or Indented [*Freight*]
CCI............ Cost Control Item (MCD)
CCI............ Cotton Council International (EA)
CCI............ Council for Cable Information (EA)
CCI............ Council on Consumer Information [*Later, ACCI*] (EA)
CCI............ Cour Canadienne de l'Impot [*Tax Review Board - TRB*]
CCI............ Course Content Improvement
CcI............ Cowles Communications, Inc., New York, NY [*Library symbol*] [*Library of Congress*] (LCLS)
CCIA......... Caravan and Camping Industry Association [*Australia*]
CCIA......... Cellular Communications Industry Association [*Telecommunications*] (EA)
CCIA......... Computer and Communications Industry Association (EA)
CCIA......... Console Computer Interface Adapter
CCIA......... Consumer Credit Insurance Association [*Chicago, IL*] (EA)
CCIAESC ... Coffee Commission of the Inter-American Economic and Social Council [*United States*]
CCIAH ...... Clearinghouse Committee for Information on the Arts and Humanities
CCIA/WCC ... Commission of the Churches on International Affairs (of the World Council of Churches) (EA)
CCIB......... Central Crime Intelligence Bureau [*Australia*]
CCIBAD.... Coconut Research Institute. Bulletin [*A publication*]
CCIBP .... Canadian Committee for the International Biological Programme
CCIC......... Campus Chemical Instrument Center [*Ohio State University*] [*Research center*] (RCD)
CCIC......... Canadian Council for International Cooperation
CCIC......... Carolina Casualty Insurance Company [*Jacksonville, FL*] [*NASDAQ symbol*] (NQ)
CCIC......... Club of Channel Islands Collectors (EA)
CCIC......... Comite Catholique International de Coordination Aupres de l'UNESCO
CCIC......... Comite Consultatif International du Coton [*International Cotton Advisory Committee*]
CCIC......... Concerned Citizens Information Council [*Group opposing sex education in schools*]
CCIC......... Conference of Casualty Insurance Companies [*Indianapolis, IN*] (EA)
CCICA...... Catholic Commission on Intellectual and Cultural Affairs (EA)
CCID......... Community Colleges for International Development (EA)
CCID......... Control Channel Information Demodulator
CCID......... Countermine/Counterintrusion Department [*Army*] (RDA)
CCID......... Crew Command Input Device
CCIDA...... Canadian Centre for Information and Documentation on Archives [*National Archives of Canada*]
CCIDES..... Command Control Interactive Display Experimentation System [*Army*] (MCD)
CCIEM...... Center for Computer Integrated Engineering and Manufacturing [*University of Tennessee at Knoxville*] [*Research center*] (RCD)
CCIF .... Comite Consultatif International Telephonique des Frequences [*International Telephone Consultative Committee*] (NATG)
CCIG......... Cold Cathode Ion Gauge
CCIL .... Commander's Critical Item List [*Army*] (AABC)
CCILMB ... Interim Committee for Coordination of Investigations of the Lower Mekong Basin [*of the United Nations Economic and Social Commission for Asia and the Pacific*] (EAIO)
CCIM........ Certified Commercial Investment Member [*Designation awarded by Realtors National Marketing Institute of the National Association of Realtors*]
CCIM........ Command Computer Input Multiplexer (MCD)
CCIM........ Consolidated Cinola Mines Ltd. [*NASDAQ symbol*] (NQ)
CCIN........ Catholic Curriculum Information Network [*Australia*]
CCINC...... Cabinet Committee on International Narcotics Control [*Terminated, 1977*]
C Cinema ... Cahiers du Cinema [*A publication*]
CCIO .... Canadian Committee for Industrial Organization
CCIP.......... Canadian Cataloguing in Publication
CCIP.......... Chambre de Commerce et d'Industrie de Paris [*Paris Chamber of Commerce and Industry*] [*France*] [*Information service or system*] (IID)
CCIP.......... Commission du Commerce International des Produits de Base [*United Nations*]
CCIP.......... Continuously Computed Impact Point [*Type of bombing sighting system*] [*Air Force*]
CCIR.......... Citizens' Committee for Immigration Reform (EA)

CCIR......... Comite Consultatif International des Radiocommunications [*International Radio Consultative Committee*] [*of the International Telecommunications Union*] [*Switzerland*]
CCIR......... Committed Change Incorporation Record (KSC)
CCIRD....... Computers and Computing Information Resources Directory [*A publication*]
CCIRS .... Container and Chassis Identification and Reporting System [*Military*] (MCD)
CCIS.......... Center for Computer and Information Services [*Rutgers University, The State University of New Jersey*] [*Information service or system*] (IID)
CCIS.......... Cold Cathode Ion Source
CCIS.......... Command and Control Information System [*Hughes Aircraft Co.*]
CCIS.......... Common Channel Interoffice Signaling [*Telecommunications*]
CCIS.......... Communications and Information Systems Committee [*NATO*] (EAIO)
CCIS.......... Computer-Controlled Interconnect System (MCD)
CCIS.......... Computerized Clinical Information System [*Micromedex, Inc.*] [*Database*]
CCISA .... Canadian Controls and Instrumentation [*A publication*]
CCist......... Collectanea Cisterciensia [*A publication*]
CCIT.......... Consolidated Capital Income Trust [*Emeryville, CA*] [*NASDAQ symbol*] (NQ)
CCIT.......... Consultative Committee on International Telephony [*Later, CCITT*] [*ITU*]
CCITT .... Comite Consultatif International Telegraphique et Telephonique [*Consultative Committee on International Telegraphy and Telephony*] [*of the International Telecommunications Union*] [*Switzerland*] (CSR)
CCITU....... Coordinating Committee of Independent Trade Unions
CCIU .... Command Control Information Utility [*Military*]
CCI/USA... Christian Camping International/USA (EA)
C Civ .... Code Civil [*A publication*] (DLA)
C Civ Ann . Code Civil Annote, Dalloz [*A publication*] (ILCA)
CCIVS ...... Coordinating Committee for International Voluntary Service (EA)
CCIW........ Canada Centre for Inland Waters
CCIWD...... Canada. Centre for Inland Waters. Data Report Series [*A publication*]
CCIWF ...... Canada. Centre for Inland Waters. Field Report Series [*A publication*]
CCIWM..... Canada. Centre for Inland Waters. Manuscript Report Series [*A publication*]
CCIWT ...... Canada. Centre for Inland Waters. Technical Note Series [*A publication*]
CCIZT .... Committee of Control of the International Zone of Tangier
CCJ........... Center for Community Justice (EA)
CCJ........... Chung Chi Journal [*A publication*]
CCJ........... Coalition for Consumer Justice (EA)
CCJ........... Communicator's Journal [*A publication*]
CCJ........... Concert Resources, Inc. [*Vancouver Stock Exchange symbol*]
CCJ........... Conference of Chief Justices (EA)
CCJ........... County Court Judge (DLA)
CCJ........... Springfield, OH [*Location identifier*] [*FAA*] (FAAL)
CCJA........ Community College Journalism Association (EA)
CCJC .... Chicago City Junior College [*Illinois*]
CCJC .... Custer County Junior College [*Montana*]
CCJDA ...... Journal. Chemical Society. Section D. Chemical Communications [*A publication*]
CCJO......... Consultative Council of Jewish Organizations (EA)
CCJS......... Coalition for Constitutional Justice and Security (EA)
CCJW........ Chuck Jaws [*Tools*]
CCK .... Campbell's Creek R. R. [*AAR code*]
CCK .... Central College of Kentucky
CCK .... Chiang Ching-kuo [*Son of Nationalist Chinese leader Chiang Kai-shek*]
CCK .... Chief Cook [*Navy rating*] [*Obsolete*]
CCK .... Cholecystokinin [*Also, PZ*] [*Endocrinology*]
CCK .... Clackamas Community College Library, Oregon City, OR [*OCLC symbol*] (OCLC)
CCK .... Cocos [*Keeling*] Islands [*ANSI three-letter standard code*] (CNC)
CCK .... Cocos [*Keeling*] Islands [*Seismograph station code, US Geological Survey*] [*Closed*] (SEIS)
CCK .... Crown Cork & Seal Co., Inc. [*NYSE symbol*] (SPSG)
CCK(B)...... Chief Cook (Baker) [*Navy rating*] [*Obsolete*]
CCK-B .... Cholecystokinin-Brain Type Receptor
CCK(C)...... Chief Cook (Commissary) [*Navy rating*] [*Obsolete*]
CCK-PZ..... Cholecystokinin-Pancreozymin [*Endocrinology*]
CCL .... Cambridge Consultants Ltd. [*British*] (IRUK)
CCL .... Canadian Children's Literature [*A publication*]
CCL .... Canadian Congress of Labour
CCL........... Cancer Checking Lipid [*Oncology*]
CCL........... Carbonate Compensation Level [*Oceanography*]
CCL........... Carcinoma Cell Line [*Cytology*]
CCL........... Caribbean Congress of Labor
CCL........... Carnival Cruise Lines, Inc. [*AMEX symbol*]
CCL........... Carrier Common Line [*Telecommunications*] (IT)
CCL........... Catalytic Coal Liquefaction
CCL........... Celanese Canada, Inc. [*Toronto Stock Exchange symbol*]

CCL........... Centenary College of Louisiana [*Shreveport*]
CCL........... Center for Computer/Law (EA)
CCL........... Center for Creative Leadership (EA)
CCL........... Certified Cell Line [*ATCC*]
CCL........... Chemical and Coating Laboratory [*Army*] (MCD)
CC & L...... Chicago, Cincinnati & Louisville Railway
CCL........... Chinchilla [*Australia*] [*Airport symbol*]
CCL........... Clinical Chemistry Lookout [*Medical Information Centre*] [*Defunct*] [*Information service or system*] (CRD)
CCL........... Closed Circuit Loop (MCD)
CCl........... Cloverdale Public Library, Cloverdale, CA [*Library symbol*] [*Library of Congress*] (LCLS)
CCL........... Coal Contractors Limited [*British*]
CCL........... Coating and Chemical Laboratory [*Aberdeen Proving Ground, MD*] [*Army*]
C & CL...... Coating and Chemical Laboratory [*Aberdeen Proving Ground, MD*] [*Army*] (RDA)
CCL........... Combat Command L
CCL........... Commission Canadienne du Lait [*Canadian Dairy Commission - CDC*]
CCl........... Commission for Climatology [*WMO*]
CCL........... Commissioner of Crown Lands [*British*]
CCL........... Commodity Control List [*Office of Export Administration*]
CCL........... Common Command Language [*Data processing*] (IT)
CCL........... Commonality Candidate List [*NASA*] (NASA)
CCL........... Commonwealth Countries' League [*Middlesex, England*] (EAIO)
CCL........... Communications Circular Letter [*Navy*]
CCL........... Communications Control Language
CCL........... Composite Cell Logic
CCL........... Computer Control Loading
CCL........... Conference for Catholic Lesbians (EA)
CCL........... Conference on Christianity and Literature (EA)
CCL........... Configuration Control Logic (NASA)
CCL........... Conforms to Copyright Law
CCL........... Consultec Canada Limited [*Vancouver, BC*] [*Telecommunications*] (TSSD)
CCL........... Consumer Credit Letter [*Business Publishers, Inc.*] [*Information service or system*] (CRD)
CCL........... Control Card Listing [*Data processing*]
CCL........... Convective Condensation Level [*Meteorology*]
CCL........... Cooperative College Library Center, Atlanta, GA [*OCLC symbol*] (OCLC)
CCL........... Couple to Couple League (EA)
C Cl .... Court of Claims Reports [*United States*] [*A publication*] (DLA)
CCL........... Critical Carbohydrate Level [*Nutrition*]
CCL........... Critical Components List
CCL........... Customs Clearance (DS)
CCL........... Management Accounting [*A publication*]
CCLA........ Canadian Civil Liberties Association
CCLA........ Canadian Comparative Literature Association [*See also ACLC*]
CCLA........ Committee on Cooperation in Latin America [*of The National Council of Churches of Christ in the USA*] (EA)
CCLA........ Coos County Library Association [*Library network*]
CCLA........ Corporate Council for the Liberal Arts (EA)
CCLA........ Correspondence Chess League of America (EA)
CCLA Record ... CCLA [*Correspondence Chess League of Australia*] Record [*A publication*] (APTA)
CCLat .... Corpus Christianorum. Series Latina [*Turnhout*] [*A publication*]
C-CLAW ... Close Combat LASER Assault Weapon
CCLB........ Citrus Country Land Bureau, Inc. [*NASDAQ symbol*] (NQ)
CCLC......... Cooperative College Library Center [*Atlanta, GA*] [*Library network*]
CCLC......... Cuadernos del Congreso por la Libertad de la Cultura [*A publication*]
CCLCDY... Chinese Journal of Oncology [*A publication*]
CCLD........ Chronic Cholestatic Liver Disease [*Medicine*]
CCLDS ..... Clear of Clouds [*Aviation*] (FAAC)
CCLE......... Chronic Cutaneous (Discoid) Lupus Erythematosus [*Medicine*]
CCLE......... Crain's Cleveland Business [*A publication*]
CCLEPE.... Consultative Committee for Local Ecumenical Projects in England [*Church of England*]
CCLGF ...... Consultative Council on Local Government Finance [*British*]
CCLH ...... Committee on Canadian Labour History
CCLIB .... Cardiovascular Clinics [*A publication*]
CCLJ .... Central Committee of Lithuanian Jurists (EA)
CCLJ .... Centre County Legal Journal [*Pennsylvania*] [*A publication*] (DLA)
CCLKOB ... Counterclockwise Orbit (FAAC)
CCLKWS .. Counterclockwise (FAAC)
CCLM........ Committee on Constitutional and Legal Matters [*UN Food and Agriculture Organization*]
CCLM........ Computer Communications Line Monitor (MCD)
CCLM........ Coordinating Council of Literary Magazines [*Later, CLMP*] (EA)
CCL(ML) .. Canadian Communist League (Marxist-Leninist)
CCLN .... Consignment Note Control Label Number (DS)
CCLN .... Council for Computerized Library Networks (IID)
CCLOW .... Canadian Congress for Learning Opportunities for Women

CCLP .... Callon Consolidated Partners LP [*NASDAQ symbol*]　(NQ)
CCLP .... Contents of Current Legal Periodicals [*A publication*]
CCLP Contents Curr Leg Period ... CCLP. Contents of Current Legal Periodicals [*A publication*]
CCLR .... Commerce Clearing House, Inc. [*Riverwoods, IL*] [*NASDAQ symbol*]　(NQ)
CCLS .... Canadian Centre for Learning Systems [*Research center*]　(RCD)
CCLS .... Canadian Council of Land Surveyors [*See also CCAG*]
CCLS .... Central Colorado Regional Library Service System [*Library network*]
CCLS .... Chautauqua-Cattaraugus Library System [*Library network*]
CCLS .... Computer-Controlled Launch Set [*NASA*]　(KSC)
CCLS .... Conference on Critical Legal Studies　(EA)
CCLS .... Court of Claims
CCLSR .... Court of Claims Reports
CCLT .... Canadian Cases on the Law of Torts [*A publication*]
CCLTDH... Controlled Clinical Trials [*A publication*]
CCLU .... Canadian Civil Liberties Union
CCLV .... Council of Citizens with Low Vision　(EA)
CCLWC ..... Committee on Christian Literature for Women and Children　(EA)
CCLWCMF ... Committee on Christian Literature for Women and Children in Mission Fields [*Later, CCLWC*]　(EA)
CCM .... Augusta, ME [*Location identifier*] [*FAA*]　(FAAL)
CCM .... Cahiers de Civilisation Medievale [*A publication*]
CCM .... Canadian Committee on MARC
CCM .... Canadian Corporate Management Co. Ltd. [*Toronto Stock Exchange symbol*]
CCM .... Canarc Resources [*Vancouver Stock Exchange symbol*]
CCM .... Capel-Cure Myers [*Stockbrokers*] [*British*]
CCM .... Caribbean Common Market
CCM .... Casopis Ceskenho Musea [*A publication*]
CCM .... Center for Communications Media [*University of Massachusetts-Boston*] [*Telecommunications service*]　(TSSD)
CCM .... Center for Communications Ministry [*Formerly, NSCS*] [*Defunct*]　(EA)
CCM .... Center for Composite Materials [*University of Delaware*] [*Research center*]　(RCD)
CCM .... Central Cultural Movement [*China*]
CCM .... Centre de Controle Mixte [*Joint Control Center*] [*NATO*]　(NATG)
CCM .... Certified Cash Manager [*Designation awarded by National Corporate Cash Management Association*]
CCM .... Certified Club Manager [*Designation awarded by Club Managers Association of America*]
CCM .... Chama Cha Mapinduzi [*Revolutionary Party*] [*Tanzania*] [*Political party*]　(PPW)
CCM .... Chief of Budget and Finance Division [*Supreme Headquarters Allied Powers Europe*]　(NATG)
CCM .... Chief Carpenter's Mate [*Navy rating*] [*Obsolete*]
CCM .... Chinese Christian Mission　(EA)
CCM .... Chromatography Control Module [*Instrumentation*]
CCM .... Clays and Clay Minerals [*A publication*]
CCM .... Cloud Camera Multiplexer
CCM .... Coincident-Current Memory
CCM .... Colby College. Monographs [*A publication*]
CCM .... Combat Cargo Mission [*Air Force*]
CCM .... Combined Cipher Machine
CCM .... Combined Coding Machine
CCM .... Commodity Class Manager
CCM .... Communications Control Module [*Telecommunications*]　(TEL)
CCM .... Communications Controller Multichannel [*Data processing*]
CCM .... Community Climate Model [*Meteorology*]
CCM .... Companions of the Celtic Mission　(EAIO)
CCM .... Computer-Controlled Multiplexer　(MCD)
CC/M .... Configuration Control and Management　(MCD)
CCM .... Conseil Canadien du Multiculturalisme [*Canadian Multicultural Council*]
CCM .... Conseil Canadien de la Musique [*Canadian Music Council*]　(EAIO)
CCM .... Conseiller du Commerce Exterieur [*Paris*] [*A publication*]
CCM .... Constant Current Modulation
CCM .... Continuous Care Manikin [*Medical training*] [*Navy*]
CCM .... Continuous Casting Machine [*Metalworking*]
CCM .... Contro-Clusive Magnetism [*Pest control concept*]
CCM .... Control Civil and Military [*British*]　(AIA)
CCM .... Controlled Carrier Modulation　(KSC)
CCM .... Council of Communication Management　(EA)
CCM .... Counter-Countermeasures [*Military*]
CCM .... Crew Cargo Module [*NASA*]　(KSC)
CCM .... Crisciuma [*Brazil*] [*Airport symbol*]　(OAG)
CCM .... Critical Care Manual
CCM .... Critical Care Medicine [*A publication*]
CCM .... Cross-Country Movement [*Maps*]
CCM .... Crowell-Collier & Macmillan, Inc. [*Later, Macmillan, Inc.*] [*Publishers*]
CCM .... Cubic Centimeter　(ROG)

CCM .... Cyclophosphamide, CCNU [*Lomustine*], Methotrexate [*Antineoplastic drug regimen*]
CCM .... Engineering Research Center for Composites Manufacturing Science and Engineering [*Newark, DE*] [*Army*]　(GRD)
CCM .... Modesto Junior College, Modesto, CA [*OCLC symbol*]　(OCLC)
C³CM .... C³ [*Command, Control, and Communications*] Countermeasures [*Pronounced "see-cubed see-m"*]
C3CM .... Command, Control, and Communications Countermeasures [*Warfare*]
CCMA .... Card Clothing Manufacturers Association　(EA)
CCMA .... Catholic Campus Ministry Association　(EA)
CCMA .... Certified Color Manufacturers Association　(EA)
CCMA .... Civilian Clothing Maintenance Allowance [*Army*]　(AABC)
CCMA .... Comite de Compradores de Material Aeronautico de America Latina　(MCD)
CCMA .... Commander Corps Medium Artillery [*British*]
CCMA .... Contract Cleaning and Maintenance Association [*British*]
CCMA .... Crew Correctable Maintenance Action　(MCD)
CCMAC ..... Committee of Common Market Automobile Constructors [*EEC*]
CCMACPI ... Commission for Catholic Missions among the Colored People and the Indians　(EA)
CCMC .... Canadian Creative Music Collective [*Jazz group*]
CCMC .... Coincident-Current Magnetic Core
CCMC .... Commonwealth Mortgage Company, Inc. [*Wellesley Hills, MA*] [*NASDAQ symbol*]　(NQ)
CCMC .... Conseil des Communautes Musulmanes du Canada [*Council of Muslim Communities of Canada*]　(EAIO)
CCMCBB .. Chief Carpenter's Mate, Construction Battalion, Builder [*Navy rating*] [*Obsolete*]
CCMCBD ... Chief Carpenter's Mate, Construction Battalion, Draftsman [*Navy rating*] [*Obsolete*]
CCMCBE .. Chief Carpenter's Mate, Construction Battalion, Excavation Foreman [*Navy rating*] [*Obsolete*]
CCMCBS .. Chief Carpenter's Mate, Construction Battalion, Surveyor [*Navy rating*] [*Obsolete*]
CCMCC ..... Continuing Committee on Muslim-Christian Cooperation　(EA)
CCMD .... Chrysler Corporation Missile Division　(MCD)
C Cmd ...... Coastal Command [*Air Force*] [*British*]　(DMA)
CCMD .... Coded Command
CCMD .... Continuous Current-Monitoring Device
CCMDA ..... Cahiers. College de Medecine des Hopitaux de Paris [*A publication*]
CCMDC ..... Critical Care Medicine [*A publication*]
CCMe .... Cahiers de Civilisation Medievale [*A publication*]
CCME .... Churches' Committee on Migrants in Europe　(EAIO)
CCME .... Contract Change Mass Estimate　(NASA)
CCME .... Coordinating Council on Medical Education [*Superseded by CFMA*]　(EA)
CCMEU .... Camera de Comercio Mexico-Estados Unidos [*United States-Mexico Chamber of Commerce*]　(EAIO)
CCMF .... Calvin Coolidge Memorial Foundation　(EA)
CCMF .... [*The*] Churches' Committee for Supplementing Religious Education Among Men in HM Forces [*British military*]　(DMA)
CCMFA ..... Civilian Career Management Field Agency　(MCD)
CCMG .... Conseil Canadien de la Main-d'Oeuvre en Genie [*Canadian Engineering Manpower Council*]
CCMHF .... Coordinating Council on Manufactured Housing Finance [*Defunct*]　(EA)
CCMHRL ... Consortium of Central Massachusetts Health Related Libraries [*Library network*]
CCMIA...... Canned and Cooked Meat Importers Association　(EA)
CCMIS ..... Commodity Command Management Information System [*Army*]
CCMJ .... Contents of Contemporary Mathematical Journals [*A publication*]
CCML........ Comprehensive Core Medical Library [*Database*] [*BRS Information Technologies*] [*Information service or system*]　(IID)
CCMLO .... Chief Chemical Officer [*Army*]
CCMM ...... Computer Communications, Inc. [*Torrance, CA*] [*NASDAQ symbol*]　(NQ)
CCmO .... Orange Coast College, Costa Mesa, CA [*Library symbol*] [*Library of Congress*]　(LCLS)
CCMP........ Ceylon Corps of Military Police [*British military*]　(DMA)
CCMP........ Computer Color Match Prediction
cCMP........ Cyclic Cytidine Monophosphate [*Biochemistry*]
CCMPTC .. Central Computer Center　(AABC)
CCMR .... Central Contract Management Region [*Air Force*]
CCMR .... Conseil Canadien des Ministres des Ressources [*Canadian Council of Resource Ministers*]
CCMRD .... Coordinating Committee on Materials Research and Development [*Executive Office of the President*]
CCMRE ..... Conseil Canadien des Ministres des Ressources et de l'Environnement [*Canadian Council of Resource and Environment Ministers - CCREM*]
CCMRG .... Commonwealth Committee on Mineral Resources and Geology [*British*]
CCMS........ Central Cardiac Monitoring System

CCMS........ Central Control and Monitoring System [*for managing buildings' heating, ventilation, and security needs*]
CCMS........ Checkout Control and Monitor Subsystem [*NASA*]   (NASA)
CCMS........ Clean Catch Midstream Urine [*Medicine*]
CCMS........ CMS Advertising, Inc. [*Oklahoma City, OK*] [*NASDAQ symbol*]   (NQ)
CCMS........ Command Control and Monitor System [*NASA*]   (NASA)
CCMS........ Committee on the Challenges of Modern Society [*Brussels, Belgium*]   (EA)
CCMS........ Commodity Configuration Management System   (AFIT)
CCMS........ Community Case Management Services
CCMS........ Congress of County Medical Societies   (EA)
CCMS........ Conseil Canadien de la Medecine Sportive [*Canadian Academy of Sport Medicine - CASM*]
CCMS........ Control Commission Military Section [*British*] [*World War II*]
CCmS......... Southern California College, Costa Mesa, CA [*Library symbol*] [*Library of Congress*]   (LCLS)
CCMSC..... Caribbean Common Market Standards Council [*Georgetown, Guyana*]   (EAIO)
CCMSRB .. Chief Carpenter's Mate, Ship Repair, Boatbuilder, Wood [*Navy rating*] [*Obsolete*]
CCMSRJ... Chief Carpenter's Mate, Ship Repair, Joiner [*Navy rating*] [*Obsolete*]
CCMSS..... Computer-Controlled Microfilm Search System   (MCD)
CCMSU...... Clean Catch Midstream Urine [*Medicine*]
CCMT ...... Catechol-O-Methyltransferase [*An enzyme*]
CCMT .... Centre for Construction Market Information Ltd. [*British*]   (CB)
CCMTA..... Cape Canaveral Missile Test Annex [*Later, KSC*]
CCMTC..... Cape Canaveral Missile Test Center [*Later, KSC*]
CCMU ...... Computer Controller Multiplexer Unit
CCMU ...... Control Center Mock-Up
CCMV .... Cowpea Chloretic Mottle Virus
CCMW ...... Council for Christian Medical Work [*Later, CHH*]   (EA)
CCN .... Cachucha Ranch [*New Mexico*] [*Seismograph station code, US Geological Survey*] [*Closed*]   (SEIS)
CCN .... Campus Conference Network [*Services by Satellite, Inc.*] [*Washington, DC*] [*Telecommunications*]   (TSSD)
CCN .... Category Codes and Nomenclature   (MCD)
CCN .... Central Command Network
CCN .... Certification Control Number   (MCD)
CCN .... Chakcharan [*Afghanistan*] [*Airport symbol*] [*Obsolete*]   (OAG)
CCN .... Chinese Communist Navy   (CINC)
CCN .... Chris-Craft Industries, Inc. [*NYSE symbol*]   (SPSG)
CCN .... Christian College News [*A publication*]
CCN .... Classification Change Notice   (KSC)
CCN .... Closed Condensation Nuclei   (MCD)
CCN .... Cloud Condensation Nuclei [*Fog*]
CCN .... Command Confirmation
CCN .... Command Control Number [*Air Force*]   (AFM)
CCN .... Commonwealth Employees Compensation Notes [*A publication*]   (APTA)
CCN .... Communication Control Number   (AAG)
CCN .... Computer Call Network [*Telemarketing*]
CCN .... Configuration Control Number   (AAG)
CCN .... Consulta di i Cumitati Nationalisti [*Corsica*]   (PD)
CCN .... Contract Change Negotiation   (NASA)
CCN .... Contract Change Notice   (MCD)
CCN .... Contract Completion Notices [*DoD*]
CCN .... Cost Charge Number   (MCD)
CCN .... Cruzada Civica Nacionalista [*Nationalist Civic Crusade*] [*Venezuela*] [*Political party*]   (PPW)
CCNA .... Canadian Community Newspapers Association [*Founded 1919*]
CCNA .... Combined Committee for North Africa [*World War II*]
CCNA .... Council on Certification of Nurse Anesthetists   (EA)
CCNAA ..... Coordination Council for North American Affairs
CCNB .... Concerned Citizens for the Nuclear Breeder   (EA)
CCNB .... Counciline Newsletter. Canadian Council for Native Business [*A publication*]
CCNBC.....· Committee for the Coordination of National Bibliographic Control [*Defunct*]   (EA)
CCNC .... CCNB Corp. [*NASDAQ symbol*]   (NQ)
CCNC .... Common Channel Network Controller [*Telecommunications*]
CCNCE...... Chinese Canadian National Council for Equality
CCNCO ..... Coordinating Council of National Court Organizations   (EA)
CCND .... Children's Campaign for Nuclear Disarmament   (EA)
CCND .... Committee to Cap the National Debt   (EA)
CC-NDT .... Can't Call - No Dial Tone [*Telecommunications*]   (TEL)
CCNED ..... Chishitsu Chosasho Nenpo [*A publication*]
CC & NF ... Cell Culture and Nitrogen Fixation Laboratory [*Department of Agriculture*]
CCNF......... Committee for Consumers No-Fault   (EA)
CCNF......... Commodore Commanding Newfoundland Force [*Navy*] [*Canada*] [*World War II*]
CCNG .... Computer Communications Networks Group [*University of Waterloo*] [*Canada*] [*Information service or system*] [*Research center*]   (IID)
CCNPP...... Calvert Cliffs Nuclear Power Plant   (NRCH)
CCNR .... Canadian Coalition for Nuclear Responsibility
CCNR .... Central Commission for the Navigation of the Rhine [*Strasbourg, France*]   (EAIO)

CCNR .... Citizens Committee on Natural Resources [*Defunct*]   (EA)
CCNRA ..... Central Council of National Retail Associations   (EA)
CCNRRH .. Comite Consultatif National des Recherches sur les Ressources Hydrauliques [*National Advisory Committee on Water Resources Research*] [*Canada*]
CCNS......... Cell Cycle Nonspecific [*Antitumor agent*]
CCNS......... Christian College News Service [*A publication*]
CCNS......... Congressional Caucus on National Security   (EA)
CCNS......... Ohio Circuit Court Reports, New Series [*A publication*]   (DLA)
CCNSC...... Cancer Chemotherapy National Service Center [*National Institutes of Health*]
CCNT .... Chief Controller
CCNTB....... Current Concepts in Nutrition [*A publication*]
CCNU........ (Chloroethyl)cyclohexylnitrosourea [*Lomustine*] [*Antineoplastic drug regimen*]
CCNV .... Community for Creative Non-Violence   (EA)
CCNW .... Center on the Consequences of Nuclear War   (EA)
CCNWC .... Continuing Committee of the National Women's Conference [*Later, NW*]   (EA)
CCNY .... Canadian Club of New York   (EA)
CCNY .... Carnegie Corporation of New York   (EA)
CCNY .... Chemists' Club - of New York   (EA)
CCNY .... City College of New York [*Later, City University of New York*]
CCNYA ..... Campaign for the Creation of the National Youth Advisor   (EA)
CCO........... Calf Certifying Officer [*Ministry of Agriculture, Fisheries, and Food*] [*British*]
CCO........... Canadian College of Organists
CCO........... Carbohydrate-Craving Obesity [*Medicine*]
CCO........... Center for Contemporary Opera   (EA)
CC/O .... Certificate of Consignment/Origin [*Shipping*]   (DS)
CCO........... Chico [*California*] [*Seismograph station code, US Geological Survey*]   (SEIS)
CCO........... Chief Chemical Officer [*Army*]
CCO........... Chief of Combined Operations [*British Army*] [*World War II*]
CCO........... Chief Commanding Officer
CCO........... Circuit Control Office [*Automatic Digital Information Network*]   (CET)
CCO........... Cisco Resources [*Vancouver Stock Exchange symbol*]
CCO........... Classified Control Officer
CCO........... Clinchfield Railroad Company [*AAR code*]
CCo........... Codice di Commercio [*Commercial Code*] [*Italian*]
C Co .... Codigo Comercial [*Brazil*] [*A publication*]
CCO........... Combat Cargo Officer [*Military*]   (NVT)
CCO........... Comite Canadien d'Oceanographie [*Canadian Committee on Oceanography - CCO*]
CCO........... Command Control Order
CCO........... Commercial Contracting Officer
CCO........... Component Change Order   (MCD)
CC/O .... Composite Checkout [*Aerospace*]   (AAG)
CC-O.......... Composite Cutoff [*Aerospace*]   (AAG)
CCO........... Configuration Change Order
CCO........... Consultants and Consulting Organizations Directory [*A publication*]
CCO........... Contract Change Order
CCO........... Contracts Compliance Regional Office [*DoD*]
CCO........... Controlled Collection Objective   (MCD)
CCO........... Conversion Control Officer [*Army*]
CCO........... Convoy Control Officer [*Navy*]
CCO........... Coordinating Committee on Oceanography
CCO........... Corporate Contract Officer
CCO........... Council on Chiropractic Orthopedics   (EA)
CCO........... Council of Consulting Organizations   (EA)
CCO........... Country Clearing Office
CCO........... Credit Clearing Outward   (DCTA)
CCO........... Crystal-Controlled Oscillator
CCO........... Current-Controlled Oscillator   (IEEE)
CCO........... Newnan, GA [*Location identifier*] [*FAA*]   (FAAL)
CCO........... Occidental College, Los Angeles, CA [*OCLC symbol*]   (OCLC)
CCOA........ Cadillac Convertible Owners of America   (EA)
CCoa .... Coalinga Unified School District Library, Coalinga, CA [*Library symbol*] [*Library of Congress*]   (LCLS)
CCOA........ Comcoa, Inc. [*Wichita, KS*] [*NASDAQ symbol*]   (NQ)
CCOA........ Controller Central Operating Authority   (NATG)
CCoac........ Coachella Municipal Public Library, Coachella, CA [*Library symbol*] [*Library of Congress*]   (LCLS)
CCOAD...... Churches' Council on Alcohol and Drugs [*Church of England*]
CCoaJC ..... West Hills College, Coalinga, CA [*Library symbol*] [*Library of Congress*]   (LCLS)
CCOC .... Command Center Operations Chief   (MCD)
CCOC .... Command Control Operations Center [*Army*]   (AABC)
CCOC .... Council on Clinical Optometric Care   (EA)
CCOD........ Consultants and Consulting Organizations Directory [*Gale Research Co.*] [*Detroit, MI*] [*Information service or system*] [*A publication*]
CCOF......... California Certified Organic Farmers
CCOFI....... California Cooperative Oceanic Fisheries Investigations [*Also, CALCOFI*]   (MSC)
CCOH........ Combined Contaminants, Oxygen, and Humidity   (MCD)
CCOH........ Corrosive Contaminants, Oxygen, and Humidity   (MCD)
CCOHS ..... Canadian Centre for Occupational Health and Safety [*Ministry of Labour*]

CCol............ Chartered Colourist [*British*]   (DBQ)
CCol............ Colton Public Library, Colton, CA [*Library symbol*] [*Library of Congress*]   (LCLS)
CCOL........ Compartment Checkoff List [*Navy*]   (NVT)
CColu........ Colusa County Free Library, Colusa, CA [*Library symbol*] [*Library of Congress*]   (LCLS)
CColumC ... Columbia Junior College, Columbia, CA [*Library symbol*] [*Library of Congress*]   (LCLS)
CCOM...... Chicago College of Osteopathic Medicine
C COM....... Code de Commerce [*Commercial Code*] [*French*]   (DLA)
CCOM....... Colonial Commercial Corp. [*Valley Stream, NY*] [*NASDAQ symbol*]   (NQ)
CCOMA .... Chemical Communications [*A publication*]
C Com C .... Civil and Commercial Code [*A publication*]   (DLA)
CComC ...... Compton College, Compton, CA [*Library symbol*] [*Library of Congress*]   (LCLS)
CComD...... Dominquez Seminary, Compton, CA [*Library symbol*] [*Library of Congress*]   (LCLS)
C Comm ..... Codice Commerciale [*Commercial Code*] [*A publication*]   (ILCA)
C Comm ..... Codice di Commercio [*Italy*] [*A publication*]
CCOMM ... Corn, Corn, Oats, Meadow, Meadow [*Crop rotation*]
C Comm C ... Civil and Commercial Code [*A publication*]   (DLA)
CCOMMRGN ... Central Communications Region [*Air Force*]
C Communisme ... Cahiers du Communisme [*A publication*]
CCOMSRS ... Corps Communications Support Requirement Simulations   (MCD)
CCON........ Catalogus Codicum Orientalium [*The Netherlands*] [*A publication*]   (BJA)
CCON........ Circon Corp. [*Santa Barbara, CA*] [*NASDAQ symbol*]   (NQ)
CCONAS... Coordinating Council of National Archaeological Societies   (EA)
CConE .... Diablo Valley College, Concord, CA [*Library symbol*] [*Library of Congress*]   (LCLS)
CCOO........ Confederacion Sindical de Comisiones Obreras [*Spanish Workers' Commissions*] [*A union*]   (DCTA)
cCOP .... Calculated Colloidal Osmotic Pressure [*Clinical chemistry*]
CCOP .... Chlorine-Catalyzed Oxidative-Pyrolysis [*Chemical engineering*]
CCOP .... Constant-Control Oil Pressure   (MSA)
CCOP .... Current Cost Operating Profits [*Accounting*]
CCOPE...... Cooperative Convection Precipitation Experiment [*Meteorology*]
CCOP Newsl ... Committee for Co-Ordination of Joint Prospecting for Mineral Resources in Asian Off-Shore Areas. Newsletter [*A publication*]
CCOP/SOPAC ... Committee for Co-Ordination of Joint Prospecting for Mineral Resources in South Pacific Offshore Areas   (EAIO)
CCOR........ Centercore, Inc. [*NASDAQ symbol*]   (NQ)
CCOR .... Cubic Chain-of-Rotators [*Equation of state*]
C-CORE .... C-CORE [*Centre for Cold Ocean Resources Engineering*] Publications [*A publication*]
C-CORE .... Centre for Cold Ocean Resources Engineering [*Memorial University of Newfoundland*] [*Research center*]   (RCD)
CCorn......... Carnegie Public Library of Corning, Corning, CA [*Library symbol*] [*Library of Congress*]   (LCLS)
CCoro......... Corona Public Library, Corona, CA [*Library symbol*] [*Library of Congress*]   (LCLS)
CCoron....... Coronado Public Library, Coronado, CA [*Library symbol*] [*Library of Congress*]   (LCLS)
CCoronUN ... United States Naval Amphibious Base, Coronado, CA [*Library symbol*] [*Library of Congress*]   (LCLS)
CCOS........ Churches Commission on Overseas Students   (EAIO)
CCOS........ Combined Chiefs of Staff [*DoD*]
CCOSO ..... Coordinating Committee of Overseas Students Organization [*British*]
C Cost .... Corte Costituzionale [*Constitutional Court*] [*Italian*]   (DLA)
CC/OT....... Caudate-Caudate to Outer Table (Ratio) [*Neuroradiology*]
CCOT .... Cycling Clutch-Orifice Tube [*Automobile air-conditioning system*]
CCov .... Covina Public Library, Covina, CA [*Library symbol*] [*Library of Congress*]   (LCLS)
CCovGS ..... Church of Jesus Christ of Latter-Day Saints, Genealogical Society Library, Covina Branch, Covina, CA [*Library symbol*] [*Library of Congress*]   (LCLS)
CCOW....... Channel Control Orderwire   (CAAL)
CCP............ Cable Connector Panel
CCP............ Call Control Processing [*Telecommunications*]   (TEL)
CCP............ Canadian Children's Project, Inc.
CCP............ Canfor Capital Ltd. [*Toronto Stock Exchange symbol*]
CCP............ Carbamoylcyclopropene [*Organic chemistry*]
CCP............ Carbonylcyanide-meta-chlorophenylhydrazone [*Also, CCCP*] [*Organic chemistry*]
CCP............ Carlsbad City Library, Carlsbad, CA [*OCLC symbol*]   (OCLC)
CCP............ Casualty Collecting-Post   (NATG)
CCP............ Casualty Control Panel   (CAAL)
CCP............ Catalogue Collectif des Periodiques [*A bibliographic publication*]
CCP............ Cebu [*Philippines*] [*Later, DAV*] [*Geomagnetic observatory code*]
CCP............ Cebu City [*Philippines*] [*Seismograph station code, US Geological Survey*]   (SEIS)

CCP............ Center for Communication Programs   (EA)
CCP............ Center for Community Planning [*HEW*]
CCP............ Center Console Panel   (MCD)
CCP............ Centrifugal Charging Pump   (IEEE)
CCP............ Centro Catolico Portugues [*Portuguese Catholic Center*] [*Political party*]   (PPE)
CCP............ Certificate in Computer Programming [*Designation awarded by Institute for the Certification of Computer Professionals*]
CCP............ Certified Claims Professional
CCP............ Cesium Chloride Polymerizable [*Analytical chemistry*]
CCP............ Charge Capacitance Probe   (NASA)
CCP............ Checkout. Management im Modernen Handel [*A publication*]
CCP............ Chemical Control Procedure [*Nuclear energy*]   (NRCH)
CCP............ Chief Commissioner of Police   (DAS)
CCP............ Chilean Communist Party [*Political party*]
CCP............ China Clay Producers Trade Association   (EA)
CCP............ Chinese Communist Party [*Political party*]   (PD)
CCP............ Chronic Calcific Pancreatitis [*Medicine*]
CCP............ Cibachrome-Print [*Color photography*]
CCP............ Ciliocytophatoria [*Medicine*]
CCP............ Circulation Control Point   (AABC)
CCP............ Code of Civil Procedure [*A publication*]   (DLA)
CCP............ Collaborative Computational Projects [*Daresbury Laboratory*] [*British*]   (IRUK)
CCP............ Command Control Panel
CCP............ Command Control Post
CCP............ Commercial Casualty Products [*Insurance*]
CCP............ Commercial Change Proposal   (MCD)
CCP............ Commission Canadienne de Pedologie [*National Soil Survey Committee*] [*Canadian Department of Agriculture*]
CCP............ Commission on College Physics
CCP............ Committee on Commodity Problems [*United Nations*] [*Rome, Italy*]   (ASF)
CCP............ Communication Control Program   (BUR)
CCP............ Communications Career Program [*Military*]
CCP............ Communications Control Package
CCP............ Communications Control Panel
CCP............ Communications Control Processor
CCP............ Compendium of Copyright Office Practices [*A publication*]
CCP............ Computer Central Processing [*Telecommunications*]   (TEL)
CCP............ Computer Control Panel
CCP............ Concepcion [*Chile*] [*Airport symbol*]   (OAG)
CCP............ Conciliation Commission for Palestine [*of the UN*]
CCP............ Conference Chretienne pour la Paix [*Christian Peace Conference - CPC*] [*Prague, Czechoslovakia*]   (EAIO)
CCP............ Configuration Change Plan   (KSC)
CCP............ Configuration Change Point   (NASA)
CCP............ Configuration Change Proposal   (MCD)
CCP............ Configuration Control Panel
CCP............ Configuration Control Phase   (MCD)
CCP............ Console Command Processor [*Digital Research*]
CCP............ Console Control Package
CCP............ Consolidated Cryptologic Program [*DoD*]   (AABC)
CCP............ Consolidation/Containerization Point
CCP............ Consumer Credit Project [*Defunct*]   (EA)
CCP............ Continuous Correlation Processing
CCP............ Conto Corrente Postale [*Current Postal Account*] [*Italian*]
CCP............ Contract Configuration Process [*Telecommunications*]   (TEL)
CCP............ Contractor Change Proposal   (MCD)
CCP............ Control Configured Propulsion   (MCD)
CCP............ Coordinated Commentary Programming [*Data processing*]
CCP............ Coordinated Containerization Point
CCP............ Corcap, Inc. [*AMEX symbol*]   (SPSG)
CCP............ Core Component Pot [*Nuclear energy*]   (NRCH)
CCP............ Corporate Control Procedure   (MCD)
CCP............ Cost Control Program   (NASA)
CCP............ Council of 1890 College Presidents   (EA)
CCP............ Council for Career Planning [*Defunct*]   (EA)
CCP............ County Court Practice   (ILCA)
CCP............ Couples Communication Program [*Australia*]
CCP............ Court of Common Pleas
CCP............ Credit Card Purchase   (AFM)
CCP............ Critical Compression Pressure
CCP............ Crockett, TX [*Location identifier*] [*FAA*]   (FAAL)
CCP............ Cropland Conversion Program
CCP............ Cross-Check Procedure   (NG)
CCP............ Cross Connection Point [*Telecommunications*]   (TEL)
CCP............ Cuban Communist Party [*Political party*]
CCP............ Cubic Close Packing [*Crystallography*]
CCP............ Cultural Center of the Philippines
CCP............ Current Commonwealth Publications [*A publication*]   (APTA)
CCP............ Cytochrome-c Peroxidase [*An enzyme*]
CCpA .... Atomics International, Canoga Park, CA [*Library symbol*] [*Library of Congress*]   (LCLS)
CCPA......... California Canning Peach Association   (EA)
CCPA......... Canadian Chemical Producers Association
CCPA......... Catholics for Christian Political Action   (EA)
CCPA......... Cemented Carbide Producers Association   (EA)
CCPA......... Choline Chloride Producers Association   (EAIO)
CCPA......... Cloud Chamber Photographic Analysis
CCPA......... Committee for Congested Production Areas [*1943-1944*]

CCPA......... Communications Corporation of America [*Dallas, TX*] [*NASDAQ symbol*] (NQ)
CCPA......... Conseil Canadien de Protection des Animaux [*Canadian Council on Animal Care*]
CCPA......... Consumer Credit Protection Act [*1969*]
CCPA......... Court of Customs and Patent Appeals
CCPAB..... California Cling Peach Advisory Board
CCPAC..... Certified Claims Professional Accreditation Council (EA)
CCPBA ..... Cahiers. Comites de Prevention du Batiment et des Travaux Publics [*A publication*]
CCPBI .... Comite Canadien pour le Programme Biologique International [*Canadian Committee for the International Biological Programme - CCIBP*]
CCPC......... Canadian-Controlled Private Corporation
CCPC......... Civil Communication Planning Committee [*Military*] (NATG)
CCPC......... Comite de Coordination des Plans Civils d'Urgence [*Civil Emergency Coordinating Committee*] [*NATO*] (NATG)
CCPC......... Committee on Crime Prevention and Control [*Economic and Social Council of the UN*] [*Vienna, Austria*] (EAIO)
CCPC......... Communication Computer Programming Center (AFM)
CCPC......... Control Center Programming Center [*NASA*] (KSC)
CCPC......... Critical Collection Problems Committee [*United States Intelligence Board*] [*Obsolete*]
CCPD........ Continuous Cyclic Peritoneal Dialysis [*Medicine*]
CCPD........ Coupling Capacitor Potential Device (IEEE)
CCPDF...... Committee for the Co-Ordination of Patriotic and Democracy-Loving Forces [*Thailand*] (PD)
CCPDS...... Centralized Cancer Patient Data System
CCPDS...... Command Center Processing and Display Systems [*Air Force*] (MCD)
CCPE......... Canadian Council of Professional Engineers
CCPE......... College Certificate in Physical Education [*British*]
CCPEF....... Congres Canadien pour la Promotion des Etudes chez la Femme [*Canadian Congress for Learning Opportunities for Women*]
CCPEW ..... Combatant Craft Passive Electronic Warfare [*Navy*] (CAAL)
CCPF......... Children's Campaign for a Positive Future (EA)
CCPF......... Clergy Couples of the Presbyterian Family (EA)
CCPF......... Comite Central de la Propriete Forestiere [*Central Committee for Forest Ownership in the EEC - CCFOE*] (EAIO)
CCPF......... Commander-in-Chief, Pacific Fleet [*Navy*]
CCPG........ Chemical Corps Proving Ground [*Army*]
CCPGR...... Canada Committee on Plant Gene Resources
CCPHDZ... Cancer Chemotherapy and Pharmacology [*A publication*]
CCPI.......... Center for Corporate Public Involvement (EA)
CCPI.......... Comcast Cablevision of Philadelphia, Inc. [*NASDAQ symbol*] (NQ)
CCPI.......... Communications Control Program Initialization (MCD)
CCPI.......... Consultative Committee for Public Information [*United Nations*]
CCPIT .... China Council for the Promotion of International Trade [*People's Republic of China*] (IMH)
CCPL......... Consolidated Capital Realty Investors [*Emeryville, CA*] [*NASDAQ symbol*] (NQ)
CCPL......... Cullman County Library [*Library network*]
CCPL......... Cuyahoga County Public Library (EISS)
CCPM....... Command Career Program Management (MCD)
CCPM....... Commissioned Corps Personnel Manual
CCPM....... Constant-Choice Perceptual Maze Test
CCPMS..... Cost Center Performance Measurement System (AFM)
CCPN .... Centre de Conditionnement Pre-Natal [*Pre-Natal Conditions Centre*] [*Canada*]
CCPO .... Central Civilian Personnel Office [*Military*]
CCPO .... Conseil Canadien des Producteurs d'Oeufs [*Canadian Egg Producers Council*]
CCPO .... Consolidated Civilian Personnel Office [*Air Force*]
CCPP......... Conseil Consultatif de la Politique du Personnel [*Advisory Council on Personnel Policy*] [*Canada Public Service Commission and Treasury Board*]
CCPPD...... Canadian Communications and Power Conference. Proceedings [*A publication*]
CCPR........ Central Council of Physical Recreation [*British*]
CCPR........ Coherent Cloud Physics RADAR
CCPR........ Consultative Committee for Photometry and Radiometry [*International Committee on Weights and Measures*]
CCPR........ Crypt Cell Production Rate [*Medicine*]
CCpR .... Rockwell International, Rocketdyne Division, Technical Information Center, Canoga Park, CA [*Library symbol*] [*Library of Congress*] (LCLS)
CCPRA...... Canadian Chemical Processing [*A publication*]
CC Proc...... Code of Civil Procedure [*A publication*] (DLA)
CCPS .... Center for Chemical Process Safety
CCPS .... Center for Consumer Product Safety [*National Institute of Standards and Technology*]
CCPS .... Centre for Canadian Population Studies
CCPS .... Christopher Columbus Philatelic Society (EA)
CCPS .... Comprehensive Country Programming System [*Department of State*]
CCPS .... Consolidated Container Processing System (MCD)
CCPS .... Consultative Committee for Postal Studies [*UPU*]

CCPS .... Consultative Council for Postal Studies [*Universal Postal Union*] (EY)
CCPSHE ... Carnegie Council of Policy Studies in Higher Education [*Defunct*] (EA)
CCPT........ Center for Consumer Product Technology [*National Institute of Standards and Technology*] (GRD)
CCPT......... Comite de Coordination des Plans de Transport [*Coordinating Committee for Transport Planning*] [*NATO*] (NATG)
CCPT......... Concept, Inc. [*NASDAQ symbol*] (NQ)
CCPT......... Council on Chiropractic Physiological Therapeutics (EA)
CCpT .... Thompson-Ramo-Wooldridge, Inc., Canoga Park, CA [*Library symbol*] [*Library of Congress*] (LCLS)
CCPTAY ... Contraception [*A publication*]
CC-PU .... Conference Reguliere sur les Problemes Universitaires [*Standing Conference on University Problems*] [*Council of Europe*] [*Strasbourg, France*] (EAIO)
CCPYAF.... Comments on Contemporary Psychiatry [*A publication*]
CCQ........... Cataloguing and Classification Quarterly [*A publication*]
CCQ........... CCL Industries, Inc. [*Toronto Stock Exchange symbol*]
CCQ........... Civil Code of Quebec [*A publication*] (DLA)
CCQ........... Critical Care Quarterly [*A publication*]
CCQ Crit Care Q ... CCQ: Critical Care Quarterly [*A publication*]
CCQUA8 ... Cleveland Clinic. Quarterly [*A publication*]
CCQUD..... Cataloging and Classification Quarterly [*A publication*]
CCR .... Calendar of Close Rolls [*British*]
CCR .... Call Charge Record (ADA)
CCR .... Catholic Committee for Refugees (EA)
CCR .... Center for Cereals Research [*Pennsylvania State University*] [*Research center*] (RCD)
CCR .... Center City Report [*A publication*] (EAAP)
CCR .... Center for Climatic Research [*University of Wisconsin - Madison*] [*Research center*] (RCD)
CCR .... Center for Constitutional Rights (EA)
CCR .... Central Communications Region [*Air Force*] (MCD)
CCR .... Central Control Room (DEN)
CCR .... Centre for Catalogue Research [*University of Bath*] [*British*] (CB)
CCR .... Chacarita [*Argentina*] [*Seismograph station code, US Geological Survey*] [*Closed*] (SEIS)
CCR .... Circuit Court Reports [*A publication*] (DLA)
CCR .... Circulation Control Rotor [*Navy*]
CCR .... City Court Reports [*A publication*] (DLA)
CCR .... Claflin College. Review [*A publication*]
CCR .... Closed-Circuit Radio
CCR .... Closed-Cycle Refrigerator
CCR .... Coalition for Corporate Responsibility (EA)
CCR .... Code of Colorado Regulations [*A publication*]
CCR .... Combat Center Remoted [*Military*]
CCR .... Combat Command Reserve
CCr........... Combat Crew [*Air Force*] (AFM)
CCR .... Command Control Receiver
CCR .... Command Control Room
CCR .... Commission Centrale pour la Navigation du Rhin [*Central Commission for the Navigation of the Rhine*]
CCR .... Commission on Civil Rights
CCR .... Commodity Classification Rates [*United Kingdom*] (DS)
CCR .... Company Credit Reports [*Teikoku DataBank Ltd.*] [*Japan*] [*Information service or system*] (CRD)
CCR .... Complex Chemical Reaction
CCR .... Complex Control Room [*NASA*] (KSC)
CCR .... Component Change Request (MCD)
CCR .... Component Characteristics Record
CCR .... Computer Character Recognition
CCR .... Concord, CA [*Location identifier*] [*FAA*] (FAAL)
CCR .... Condition Code Register
CC & R....... Conditions, Covenants, and Restrictions [*On condominiums*]
CCR .... Configuration Control Room [*Social Security Administration*]
CCR .... Confrerie de la Chaine des Rotisseurs [*Paris, France*] (EAIO)
CCR .... Connectair Airlines, Inc. [*Santa Barbara, CA*] [*FAA designator*] (FAAC)
CCR .... Conradson Carbon Residue Test [*for petroleum products*]
CCR .... Consumable Case Rocket
CCR .... Contactor Control Relay (MCD)
CCR .... Continuous Catalyst Regeneration [*Chemical engineering*]
CCR .... Contract Change Release
CCR .... Contract Change Request
CCR .... Contractor Change Request (NASA)
CCR .... Contractor Cost Reduction
CCR .... Control Center Rack (MCD)
CCR .... Control Circuit Resistance
CCR .... Control Contactor (IEEE)
CCR .... Cooperative College Registry [*Defunct*]
CCR .... [*The*] Corinth & Counce Railroad Co. [*AAR code*]
CCR .... Cosumnes River College, Sacramento, CA [*OCLC symbol*] (OCLC)
CCR .... Council for Chemical Research (EA)
CCR .... Countrywide Credit Industries, Inc. [*NYSE symbol*] (SPSG)
CCR .... County Court Rules (ILCA)
CCR .... County Courts Reports [*1860-1920*] [*England*] [*A publication*] (DLA)
CCR .... Court of Crown Cases Reserved [*England*] (DLA)

CCR .... Crack Resources Ltd. [*Vancouver Stock Exchange symbol*]
CCR .... Credit Card Reader
CCR .... Creedence Clearwater Revival [*Rock music group*]
CCR .... Critical Compression Ratio
CCR .... Cross-Channel Rejection
CCR .... Crown Cases Reserved
CCR .... Crystal Can Relay
CCR .... Cube Corner Reflector
CCR .... Current Chemical Reactions [*A publication*]
CCR .... Customer Controlled Reconfiguration
              [*Telecommunications*] (TSSD)
CCR .... Rancho Santa Ana Botanic Garden, Claremont, CA [*Library
              symbol*] [*Library of Congress*] (LCLS)
CCRA .... Cape Canaveral Reference Atmosphere [*NASA*] (NASA)
CCRA .... Carotid Chemoreceptor Activation [*Medicine*]
CCRA .... Commander Corps Royal Artillery [*British*]
CCRAK ...... Combined Command for Reconnaissance Activities in Korea
CCRB .... Cahiers de la Compagnie Madeleine Renaud-Jean Louis
              Barrault [*A publication*]
CCRB .... Civilian Complaint Review Board
CCRBES .... CRC [*Chemical Rubber Company*] Critical Reviews in
              Biocompatibility [*A publication*]
CCRC .... Cataloging Code Revision Committee [*of ALA*]
CCRC .... Children's Creative Response to Conflict Program (EA)
CCRC .... Combat Crew Replacement Center [*World War II*]
CCRC .... Community Careers Resource Center (EA)
CCRC .... Complex Carbohydrate Research Center [*Athens, GA*]
CCRC .... Continuing-Care Retirement Community
CCRC .... Core Component Receiving Container [*Nuclear
              energy*] (NRCH)
CCRCA ...... Curly-Coated Retriever Club of America (EA)
CCRCAR .... Cancer Chemotherapy Screening Data [*A publication*]
CCRCDU... Contributions. Central Research Institute for Food Crops
              [*Bogor*] [*A publication*]
CCRCT ...... Commander Corps Royal Corps of Transport [*Military*]
              [*British*]
CCRD .... Controller of Chemical Research and Development [*Ministry of
              Supply*] [*British*]
CCRDC ...... Chemical Corps Research and Development Command
              [*Army*] (AAG)
CCRDES ... Concept for a Radiological Detection System (CINC)
CCRE .... Canadian Council for Research in Education
CCRE .... Commander Corps Royal Engineers [*Military*] [*British*]
CCRE .... Conseil Canadien pour la Recherche en Education [*Canadian
              Council for Research in Education*]
CCREE3 .... Cell and Chromosome Research [*A publication*]
CCREM..... Canadian Council of Resource and Environment Ministers
CC Rep....... County Courts Reporter [*in Law Journal*] [*London*] [*A
              publication*] (DLA)
CCRESPAC ... Current Cancer Research Project Analysis Center [*Database
              producer*]
C C Rev ...... Comparative Civilizations Review [*A publication*]
CCRF .... Consolidated Communications Recording Facility (MCD)
CCRG .... Canadian Classification Research Group [*International
              Federation for Documentation*]
CCRH .... Conseil Canadien pour la Readaptation des Handicapes
              [*Canadian Rehabilitation for the Disabled*] (EAIO)
CCRH .... Conseil Canadien de Recherches sur les Humanites
              [*Humanities Research Council of Canada - HRCC*]
CCRHEC... CRC [*Chemical Rubber Company*] Critical Reviews in
              Oncology/Hematology [*A publication*]
CCRHOS... Canadian Contractor Report of Hydrography and Ocean
              Sciences [*A publication*]
CCRI.......... Community College of Rhode Island [*Formerly, RIJC*]
CCRIDE.... CRC [*Chemical Rubber Company*] Critical Reviews in
              Immunology [*A publication*]
C Crim Proc ... Code of Criminal Procedure [*A publication*] (DLA)
CCRIS .... Chemical Carcinogenesis Research Information System
              [*National Library of Medicine*] [*Information service or
              system*]
C Crit .... Comparative Criticism [*A publication*]
CCRJ .... Consultative Committee on Relations with Japan [*Australia*]
CCRKBA ... Citizens Committee for the Right to Keep and Bear Arms (EA)
CCRLS ...... Chemeketa Cooperative Regional Library Service [*Library
              network*]
CCRM .... Catholic Charismatic Renewal Movement
CCRM .... Center for Chinese Research Materials (EA)
CCRM .... Comite Clandestin des Resistants Metro [*Metro Clandestine
              Committee of Resisters*] [*Guadeloupe*] (PD)
CCRMA..... Center for Computer Research in Music and Acoustics
              [*Pronounced "karma"*] [*Stanford University*]
CCR M-L... Comites Comunistas Revolucionarios, Marxistas-Leninistas
              [*Marxist-Leninist Revolutionary Communist Committees*]
              [*Portugal*] [*Political party*] (PPE)
CCRN .... Centre Commun de Recherches Nucleaires [*Joint Nuclear
              Research Center*] [*EURATOM*]
CCRN .... Critical Care Registered Nurse
CCRNEU... CRC [*Chemical Rubber Company*] Critical Reviews in Clinical
              Neurobiology [*A publication*]
CCRO .... Community Charge Registration Officer [*British*]
CCROBU .. Cancer Chemotherapy Reports. Part 1 [*A publication*]

CCROS..... Card Capacitor Read-Only Storage [*Data processing*] (IEEE)
CCRP......... Comite Consultatif de la Radioprotection [*Advisory Committee
              on Radiological Protection*] [*Canada*]
CCRP......... Continuously Computed Release Point (MCD)
C Cr Pr....... Code of Criminal Procedure [*A publication*] (DLA)
CCRR......... Conference Committee for Refugee Rabbis (EA)
CCRS......... Canadian Centre for Remote Sensing [*See also CCT*]
CCRS......... Carbonaceous Chondrite Reference Standard [*Geophysics*]
CCR(S)....... Chemical Compound Registry (System) (DIT)
CCRS......... Configuration Control Reporting System [*Navy*] (MCD)
CCRS......... Corporate Capital Resources, Inc. [*Westlake Village, CA*]
              [*NASDAQ symbol*] (NQ)
CCRS......... Cost Category Reporting System (MCD)
CCRSA ..... Confederation of the Canons Regular of Saint
              Augustine (EAIO)
CCRSEB.... Canadian Contractor Report of Hydrography and Ocean
              Sciences [*A publication*]
CCRSFF .... Commander, Central Region SEATO [*Southeast Asia Treaty
              Organization*] Field Forces (CINC)
CCRSFF(D) ... Commander, Central Region SEATO Field Forces (Designate)
CCRSS....... Conseil Canadien de Recherche en Sciences Sociales [*Social
              Sciences Research Council of Canada - SSRCC*]
CCRT......... Check Collectors Round Table [*Later, ASCC*] (EA)
CCRT......... Core Conflictional Relationships Theme [*Psychology*]
CCRTL ...... Citizens Coalition for Rational Traffic Laws [*Later,
              NMA*] (EA)
CCRU .... Common Cold Research Unit [*British Medical Council*]
CCRU .... Complete Crew
CCR (VIC) ... County Court Reports (Victoria) [*A publication*] (APTA)
CCRZ......... Climb to and Cruise [*Aviation*] (FAAC)
CCS........... CAD/CAM [*Computer-Aided Design/Computer-Aided
              Manufacturing*] Systems
CCS........... California Current System [*Oceanography*]
CCS........... Call Control Systems [*San Clemente, CA*]
              [*Telecommunications*] (TSSD)
CCS........... Calling Card Service [*Bell System*]
CCS........... Cambridge Classical Studies [*A publication*]
CCS........... Camera Control System (KSC)
CCS........... Canadian Cardiovascular Society (EAIO)
CCS........... Canadian Computer Show
CCS........... Canbec Resources [*Vancouver Stock Exchange symbol*]
CCS........... Cancer Control Society (EA)
CCS........... Cape Chelyuskin [*USSR*] [*Geomagnetic observatory code*]
CCS........... Cape Cod System [*Air Force*]
CCS........... Caracas [*Venezuela*] [*Airport symbol*] (OAG)
CCS........... Carrier Color Signal
CCS........... Cartographic Conversion Station (MCD)
CCS........... Cartoon Conservation Scales [*Educational test*]
CCS........... Cast Carbon Steel
CCS........... Casualty Clearing Station [*Military*]
CCS........... Cataloging and Classification Section [*of ALA*]
CCS........... Catholic Committee on Scouting [*Later, NCCS*]
CCS........... Cawcaw Swamp [*South Carolina*] [*Seismograph station code,
              US Geological Survey*] (SEIS)
CCS........... Cell Cycle Specific [*Antitumor agent*]
CCS........... Cent Call Seconds [*Telecommunications*]
CCS........... Center for Chinese Studies [*University of Michigan*] [*Research
              center*] (RCD)
CCS........... Center for Christian Studies (EA)
CCS........... Center for Coastal Studies [*University of California, San Diego*]
              [*Research center*] (RCD)
CCS........... Center for Community Study [*University of Rochester*]
              [*Research center*] (RCD)
CCS........... Center for Comparative Sociology
CCS........... Center for Computational Seismology [*Berkeley, CA*]
              [*Lawrence Berkeley Laboratory*] [*Department of
              Energy*] (GRD)
CCS........... Center for Cuban Studies (EA)
CCS........... Center for Cybernetic Studies [*University of Texas at Austin*]
              [*Research center*] (RCD)
CCS........... Central Certificate Service [*Stock exchange automation
              program*]
CCS........... Central Co-Operative Society Council [*Rangoon, Burma*] (EY)
CC & S .... Central Computer and Sequencer [*NASA*]
CCS........... Central Computer Station
CCS........... Central Computing System [*Data processing*]
CCS........... Central Control Section (NASA)
CCS........... Central Control Ship [*Navy*] (NVT)
CCS........... Central Control Station (MCD)
CCS........... Central Cooperative Society [*United Arab Republic*]
CCS........... Centre for Child Study [*University of Birmingham*]
              [*British*]
CCS........... Centre for Contemporary Studies [*British*] (CB)
CCS........... Centro Calculo Sabadell [*Sabadell Computing Center*]
              [*Information service or system*] (IID)
CCS........... Centum Call-Seconds [*Telecommunications*] (PCM)
CCS........... Centurion COLIDAR [*Coherent Light Detecting and Ranging*]
              System
CCS........... Certified Construction Specifier [*Construction Specifications
              Institute*] [*Automotive engineering*]
CCS........... Ceylon Civil Service [*Obsolete*]

CCS............ Change Control System
CCS............ Charge Card Service
CCS............ Chief Commissary Steward [*Navy rating*] [*Obsolete*]
CCS............ Choledocwo-Caval Shunt [*Medicine*]
CCS............ Christian Chaplain Services   (EA)
CCS............ Chronic Cerebellar Stimulation [*Medicine*]
CCS............ Church of Christ, Scientist
CCS............ Circular Cylindrical Shell
CCS............ Citizens for Common Sense   (EA)
CC/S.......... City College of San Francisco, San Francisco, CA [*OCLC symbol*]   (OCLC)
CCS............ Classification and Compensation Society   (EA)
CCS............ Clean Community System [*Waste management program*]
CCS............ Clock Coercion Signal
CCS............ Cold Cranking Simulator Test [*for petroleum products*]
CCS............ Collectanea Commissionis Synodalis [*Peking*] [*A publication*]
CCS............ Collective Call Sign [*Radio*]
CCS............ Collective Consciousness Society [*Vocal and instrumental group*]
CCS............ Combat Communications Squadron [*Air Force*]   (AFIT)
CCS............ Combat Control System [*Military*]   (CAAL)
CCS............ Combined Chiefs of Staff [*DoD*]
CCS............ Combined CUSUM [*Cumulative Sum*]/Stewart Method [*Laboratory analysis*]
CCS............ Command and Communications System [*or Subsystem*] [*NASA*]
CCS............ Command and Control Set   (MCD)
CCS............ Command and Control Subsystem   (NASA)
CCS............ Command, Control, Support [*Army*]
C & CS........ Command and Control System
CCS............ Command and Coordination Set
CCS............ Commemorative Collectors Society [*Long Eaton, Nottinghamshire, England*]   (EAIO)
CCS............ Commercial Communications Satellite [*Japan*]
CCS............ Commitment Control System   (NRCH)
CCS............ Committee on Codes and Standards [*Defunct*]   (EA)
CCS............ Committee for Collective Security [*Defunct*]   (EA)
CCS............ Committee for Common Security   (EA)
CCS............ Committee of Concerned Scientists   (EA)
CCS............ Committee on the Constitutional System   (EA)
C/CS.......... Commodities - Coal and Steel   (NATG)
CCS............ Common Channel Signaling [*Telecommunications*]   (TEL)
CCS............ Common Communications Support [*Data processing*]   (PCM)
CCS............ Communication Control System
CCS............ Compass Control System
CCS............ Complex Control Set   (NASA)
CCS............ Component Control Section
CCS............ Component Cooling System [*Nuclear energy*]   (NRCH)
CCS............ Composers Cooperative Society [*Later, Composers Theatre*]
CCS............ Computer Campaign Services [*Data processing firm in field of politics*]
CCS............ Computer Chemical System
CCS............ Computer-Chemistry-System [*Yokogawa Hewlett Packard Ltd.*] [*Japan*]
CCS............ Computer Command Subsystem [*NASA*]
CCS............ Computer Consoles, Inc. [*AMEX symbol*]   (SPSG)
CCS............ Computer Consulting Service   (BUR)
CCS............ Computer-Controlled Suspension [*Volvo*] [*Automotive engineering*]
CCS............ Computer Core Segment   (NASA)
CCS............ Concentration Camp Syndrome [*Psychiatry*]
CCS............ Condensate Cleanup System [*Nuclear energy*]   (NRCH)
CCS............ Condensate Cooling System [*Nuclear energy*]   (NRCH)
CCS............ Confidential Cover Sheet   (AAG)
CCS............ Configuration Control Secretariat   (KSC)
C2CSE........ Console Communication System   (MCD)
CCS............ Consolidate-Cargo Container Service   (DS)
CCS............ Consort Coarse Servo
CCS............ Containment Cooling System [*Nuclear energy*]   (NRCH)
CCS............ Contamination Control Station   (MCD)
CCS............ Contamination Control System   (NASA)
CCS............ CONTEL [*Continental Telecom Corporation*] Customer Support [*Telecommunications service*]   (TSSD)
CCS............ Continuous Color Sequence [*Telecommunications*]
CCS............ Continuous Commercial Service [*Equipment specifications*]
CCS............ Continuous Composite Servo [*Optical disc recording format*]   (BYTE)
CCS............ Contract Completion Studies   (MCD)
CCS............ Contrast Contour Seeker
CCS............ Control and Computation System [*or Subsystem*] [*Navy*]   (MCD)
CCS............ Controlled Combustion System [*Antipollution device for automobiles*]
CCS............ Controlled Communications Systems [*Chicago, IL*] [*Telecommunications*]   (TSSD)
CCS............ Convention on the Continental Shelf   (NOAA)
CCS............ Conversational Compiling System [*Xerox Corp.*]   (IEEE)
CCS............ Conveyor Control System
CCS............ Cooperative Computing System [*Echo detection*]
CCS............ Cornell Computer Services [*Cornell University*] [*Information service or system*]   (IID)

CCS............ Correlation Cancellation System
CCS............ Council of Communication Societies [*Defunct*]   (EA)
CCS............ Covert Camera Spy [*System*]
CCS............ Creative Computing Services [*Information service or system*]   (IID)
CCS............ Crippled Children's Services
CCS............ Custom Computer System   (IEEE)
CCS............ Custom Contract Service [*IBM Corp.*]
CCS............ Customs Clearance Status [*United Kingdom*]   (DS)
CC/S.......... Cycles per Second [*See also Hz*]
CC & S....... Nuclear Weapons Command, Control, and Security Requirements   (MCD)
CCS............ One Hundred Call-Seconds [*Also, UC*] [*Bell System*]   (TSSD)
CCS².......... Command, Control, and Subordinate Systems [*Telecommunications*]   (TEL)
CCSA........ Common Carrier Special Application
CCSA......... Common Control Switching Arrangement [*AT & T*] [*Telecommunications*]
CCSA......... Council for Christian Social Action [*Later, OCIS*] [*United Church of Christ*]
CCSAA...... Cross Country Ski Areas Association   (EA)
CCSAC...... Comite de Coordination des Services Agricoles Canadiens [*Canadian Agricultural Services Coordinating Committee*]
CCSAP...... Cancer Control Science Associates Program [*National Cancer Institute*]
CCSATU... Coordinating Council of South African Trade Unions
CCSAU...... Committee for Corporate Support of American Universities [*Later, Committee for Corporate Support of Private Universities*]   (EA)
CCSB........ Coca-Cola & Schweppes Beverages [*British*]
CCSB........ Control Commission Shipping Bureau [*Allied German Occupation Forces*]
CCSB........ Credit Card Service Bureau
CCSBA...... Credit Card Service Bureau of America [*Later, CCSB*]
CCSC........ Cardiac Control Systems, Inc. [*Palm Coast, FL*] [*NASDAQ symbol*]   (NQ)
CCSC......... Cemetery Consumer Service Council   (EA)
CCSC......... Central Connecticut State College [*Later, Central Connecticut State University*] [*New Britain*]
CCS-C........ Central Coordinating Staff, Canada   (AFM)
CCSC......... Civil Affairs Staff Center [*Wimbledon, England*]
CCSC......... Combat Cryptological Support Console   (MCD)
CCSC......... Community Concern for Senior Citizens   (EA)
CCSC......... Confederation Camerounaise des Syndicats Chretiens [*Confederation of Believing Workers of the Cameroon*]
CCSC......... Congregational Christian Service Committee [*Superseded by UCBWM*]   (EA)
CCSC......... School of Theology at Claremont, Claremont, CA [*Library symbol*] [*Library of Congress*]   (LCLS)
CCSCE...... Center for Continuing Study of the California Economy [*Information service or system*]   (IID)
CCS Cent Cienc Saude ... CCS: Centro de Ciencias da Saude [*A publication*]
CCSD........ Canadian Council on Social Development
CCSD......... Center for Computer Systems Design [*Washington University*] [*Research center*]   (RCD)
CCSD......... Chrysler Corporation Space Division   (KSC)
CCSD......... Command Communications Service Designator   (CET)
CCSD......... Complex Carbohydrate Structural Database [*University of Georgia*]
CCS/DCC ... Cataloging and Classification Section's Descriptive Cataloging Committee [*of ALA*]
CCSDS....... Closed-Circuit Saturation Diving System [*Navy*]   (CAAL)
CCSDT...... Coupled Cluster Singles Doubles and Triples [*Physical chemistry*]
CCSE......... Cognitive Capacity Screening Examination [*Psychology*]
C2CSE........ Connected Two-Color Simulated Photon Echo [*Spectroscopy*]
CCSEAS.... Canadian Council for Southeast Asian Studies [*Carleton University*] [*Research center*]   (RCD)
CCSEM..... Computer-Controlled Scanning Electron Microscope
CCSEP...... Cement-Coated Single Epoxy
CCSES....... Canada Committee on Socio-Economic Services [*See also CCSSE*]
CCSET...... Command and Control Standardization and Evaluation Team [*Military*]
CCSF......... City College of San Francisco [*California*]
CCSF......... Commander, Caribbean Sea Frontier
CCSF......... Conseil Consultatif de la Situation de la Femme [*Advisory Council on the Status of Women*] [*Canada*]
CCSFI........ Canned Chop Suey Foods Industry [*Defunct*]
CCSG......... Children's Cancer Study Group [*National Institutes of Health*]
CCSG......... Civil Censorship Study Group   (EA)
CCSG......... Computer Components and System Group [*Massachusetts Institute of Technology*]
CCSGP...... Coalition for Common Sense in Government Procurement [*Washington, DC*] [*Later, CGP*]   (EA)
CCSH .... Canadian Council on Smoking and Health
CCSI .... Custom Creamery Systems [*NASDAQ symbol*]   (NQ)
CCSIP........ Combat Control Systems Improvement Program [*Military*]   (CAAL)
C & CSIT ... Command and Control System Interface Test [*Military*]   (CAAL)

CCSJ.........	Congressional Coalition for Soviet Jews (EA)
CCSL........	Cambridge Crystallography Subroutine Library [*Database*]
CCSL........	Camp Coles Signal Laboratory [*Army*] (MCD)
CCSL........	Citizens Conference on State Legislatures [*Later, Legis 50/The Center for Legislative Improvement*]
CCSL........	Communications and Control Systems Laboratory
CCSL........	Compatible Current-Sinking Logic (MSA)
CCSL........	Confederation Congolaise des Syndicats Libres [*Congolese Confederation of Free Unions*] [*Brazzaville*]
CCSL........	Standing Lenticular Cirrocumulus [*Meteorology*] (FAAC)
CCSM........	Cambridge Conference on School Mathematics [*National Science Foundation*]
CCSN........	Comite Consultatif de la Surete Nucleaire [*Advisory Committee on Nuclear Safety*] [*Canada*]
CCSN........	Conference of Catholic Schools of Nursing (EA)
CCSP........	Canada Community Services Projects
CCSP........	Circuit Cellar Intelligent Serial EPROM Programmer [*Data processing*]
CCSP........	Communications Concentrator Software Package [*Data processing*]
CCSP........	University/Industry Cooperative Research Center for Communications and Signal Processing [*North Carolina State University*] [*Research center*] (RCD)
CCSPA......	Council of Canadian Studies Programme Administrators
CCSPP......	Clergy Counseling Service for Problem Pregnancies [*Defunct*] (EA)
CCSPSL	Centre for Criminology and the Social and Philosophical Study of Law [*University of Edinburgh*] [*United Kingdom*] (CB)
CCSPU......	Committee for Corporate Support of Private Universities
CCSQ........	Consultative Committee on Substantive Questions [*United Nations*]
CCSR........	Canadian Consortium for Social Research (IID)
CCSS........	Cali Computer Systems, Inc. [*Greenvale, NY*] [*NASDAQ symbol*] (NQ)
CCSS........	Canada Centre for Space Science [*National Research Council of Canada*] [*Research center*] (RCD)
CCSS........	Central Coolant Supply Station (MCD)
CCSS........	Centralized Command Selection System (MCD)
CCSS........	Combat and Combat Support System (MCD)
CCSS........	Command Center Support System (MCD)
CCSS........	Command and Control Simulation System (MCD)
CCSS........	Commodity Command Standard System
CCSS........	Communications Collection Standard System (MCD)
CCSS........	Cooperative College-School Science [*Program*] [*Defunct*] [*National Science Foundation*]
CCSS........	Cooperative College - School Service (OICC)
CCSS........	Coordination and Contract Summary Sheet
CCSSA......	Community College Social Science Association (EA)
CCSSA......	Control and Command Systems Support Agency [*NATO*] (NATG)
CCSSE......	Comite Canadien sur les Services Socio-Economiques [*Canada Committee on Socio-Economic Services - CCSES*]
CCSSL......	Committee for Common Sense Speed Laws [*California*] [*Defunct*] (EA)
CCSS-MOD ...	Commodity Command Standard System - Modernization
CCSSO......	Council of Chief State School Officers (EA)
CCST........	Centennial Centre of Science and Technology
CCST........	Center for Computer Sciences and Technology [*Later, ICST*] [*National Institute of Standards and Technology*]
CCST........	Consolidated Capital Special Trust [*Emeryville, CA*] [*NASDAQ symbol*] (NQ)
CCST........	CPG Cyclic Stick Trigger (MCD)
CCSTD......	Chief Commissary Steward [*Navy rating*] [*Obsolete*]
CCSTG......	Carnegie Commission on Science, Technology, and Government (EA)
CCSTP......	Cubic Centimeters at Standard Temperature and Pressure [*Also, CSTP*]
CCSU........	Captain Cook Study Unit [*American Topical Association*] (EA)
CCSU........	Computer Cross Select Unit
CCSU........	Configuration Control and Sensing Unit (CET)
CCSU........	Council of Civil Service Unions [*British*]
CCSUBJ....	Cancer Chemotherapy Reports. Part 2 [*A publication*]
CCSUDL....	Carcinogenesis: A Comprehensive Survey [*A publication*]
CC Supp.....	City Court Reports, Supplement [*New York*] [*A publication*] (DLA)
CCSVI	Comite de Coordination du Service Volontaire International [*Coordinating Committee for International Voluntary Service - CCIVS*] [*Paris, France*] (EA)
CCSW.......	Component Cooling Service Water [*Nuclear energy*] (NRCH)
CCSYS.......	CAD/CAM [*Computer-Aided Design/Computer-Aided Manufacturing*] Systems (MCD)
CCT	C-Band Communications Transponder
CCT	California Lutheran College, Thousand Oaks, CA [*OCLC symbol*] (OCLC)
CCT	Canada Cement Lafarge Ltd. [*Toronto Stock Exchange symbol*]
CCT	Canadian Centre for Toxicology [*Research center*] (RCD)
CCT	Canadian College of Teachers [*See also CCE*]
CCT	Carotid Compression Tomography [*Medicine*]
CCT	Cathodal Closure Tetanus [*Physiology*]
CCT	Cauchy Convergence Test [*Mathematics*]
CCT	Center for Children and Technology [*Bank Street College of Education*] [*Research center*] (RCD)
CCT	Center-Cracked Tension (MCD)
CCT	Central California Traction Co. [*AAR code*]
CCT	Central City, KY [*Location identifier*] [*FAA*] (FAAL)
CCT	Centre Canadien de Teledetection [*Canadian Centre for Remote Sensing - CCRS*]
CCT	Certified Corrective Therapist
CCT	Cesium Contact Thruster
CCT	Chilecito [*Argentina*] [*Seismograph station code, US Geological Survey*] [*Closed*] (SEIS)
CCT	Chocolate-Coated [*or Covered*] Tablet [*Pharmacy*]
CCT	Circle Cutting
CCT	Circuit (NATG)
CCT	Clarkson College of Technology [*Potsdam, NY*]
CCT	Coated Compressed Tablet [*Pharmacy*]
CCT	Combat Control Team (AFM)
CCT	Combat Crew Training [*Air Force*] (AFM)
CC/T.........	Combined Center/Tower [*Aviation*] (FAAC)
CCT	Comfort Cooling Tower [*Air conditioning*]
CCT	Comite Contre la Torture [*Committee Against Torture - CAT*] [*Geneva, Switzerland*] (EAIO)
CCT	Comite de Coordination des Telecommunications [*Coordinating Committee for Communications*] [*NATO*] (NATG)
CCT	Command Cadet Team [*Military*] [*British*]
CCT	Command Control Transmitter (MCD)
CCT	Common Customs Tariff [*Common Market*]
CCT	Communications Control Team [*Military*]
CCT	Comparator Chart-Tooling (MCD)
CCT	Complete Calls To [*Telecommunications*] (TEL)
CCT	Complex Coordination Test (AAG)
CCT	Compound Card Terminal (CET)
CCT	Comprehensive College Test
CCT	Computer-Compatible Tape
CCT	Computer-Compatible Terminal (MCD)
CCT	Computer-Controlled Teletext
CCT	Confederacion Centroamericana de Trabajadores [*Central American Confederation of Workers*] (EAIO)
CCT	Confrerie des Chevaliers du Tastevin (EA)
CCT	Consolidated Change Table (MCD)
CCT	Constant Current Transformer
CCT	Consultative Committee on Thermometry [*International Bureau of Weights and Measures*]
CCT	Contact Charge Transfer (MCD)
CCT	Continuous Coding Transformation (MCD)
CCT	Continuous Cooling Transformation
CCT	Contour Check Template (MCD)
CCT	Controlled Cord Traction [*Medicine*]
CCT	Coordinated Caribbean Transport [*US shipping line*] (IMH)
CCT	Coronary Care Team [*Medicine*]
CCT	Correlated Color Temperature (IEEE)
CCT	Cortical Collecting Tubule [*Anatomy*]
CCT	Council for Clinical Training [*Later, ACPE*] (EA)
CCT	Coupler Cut-Through
CCT	Covered Carriage Trucks [*British railroad term*]
CCT	Craniocerebral Trauma [*Medicine*]
CCT	Crystal-Controlled Transmitter
CCT	Cuadernos de Cultura Teatral [*A publication*]
CCT	Cuneiform Texts from Cappadocian Tablets in the British Museum (BJA)
CCT	Cyclic Control Time (MCD)
CCTA........	Canadian Cable Television Association
CCTA........	Cape Canaveral Test Annex [*Obsolete*] [*Aerospace*] (AAG)
CCTA........	Central Computer and Telecommunications Agency [*British*]
CCTA........	Centre de Controle Tactique Aerien [*Air Tactical Control Center*] [*NATO*] (NATG)
CCTA........	Coordinating Committee of Technical Assistance
CCTA........	Council of County Territorial Associations [*British military*] (DMA)
CCTB........	Consolidated Carriers Tariff Bureau
CCTC........	Canadian Communications and Transportation Commission
CCTC........	Chemical Corps Technical Command [*Army*] (MCD)
CCTC........	Command and Control Technical Center [*DoD*]
CCTC........	Computer & Commercial Technology Corporation [*NASDAQ symbol*] (NQ)
CCTCF	Communication Circuit Technical Control Facility (MCD)
CCTC-WAD ...	Command and Control Technical Center WWMCCS [*Worldwide Military Command and Control System*] ADP [*Automatic Data Processing*] Directorate [*DoD*]
CCTD........	Coordinating Committee on Toxics and Drugs (EA)
CCTDE......	Compound Cycle Turbine Diesel Engine (MCD)
CCTE........	Canadian Council of Teachers of English
CCTE........	Cathodal Closure Tetanus [*Physiology*]
CCTE........	Certified Corporate Travel Executive [*Designation awarded by National Passenger Traffic Association*]
CCTE........	Conference of College Teachers of English of Texas. Proceedings [*A publication*]
CCTE........	Council on Cooperation in Teacher Education [*Defunct*]
C/Cte	Cuenta Corriente [*Current Account*] [*Business term*] [*Spanish*]

CCTE......... Cumann Cheol Tire Eireann [*Folk Music Society of Ireland*] (EAIO)
CCTEP...... Cement-Coated Triple Epoxy
CCTF......... Combat Cargo Task Force [*British military*] (DMA)
CCTF......... Command and Control Test Facility
CCTI......... Composite Can and Tube Institute (EA)
CCTL......... Casing Cooling Tank Level (IEEE)
CCTL......... Code Clock Transfer Loop
CCTL......... Core Component Test Loop [*Nuclear energy*] (NRCH)
CCTLR...... Chief Controller [*Aviation*] (FAAC)
CCTM ...... Communications Command Technical Manual [*Army*]
CCTM ...... Council for Children's Television and Media (EA)
CCTMA..... Closed Circuit Television Manufacturers Association (EA)
CCTO .... Canadian Conference of Tourism Officials
CCT Occ Pap ... Canadian College of Teachers. Occasional Papers [*A publication*]
CCTP......... Center City Transportation Program
CCTP......... Coordination Committee for Transport Planning [*NATO*] (NATG)
CCTPP ...... Churches' Center for Theology and Public Policy (EA)
CCTR......... Centre for Cell and Tissue Research [*University of York*] [*British*] (CB)
CCTRDH .. Cancer Clinical Trials [*A publication*]
CC & T Rpt ... Corporate Controller's and Treasurer's Report [*A publication*]
CCTS......... Canaveral Council of Technical Societies
CCTS......... Carnegie Center for Transnational Studies
CCTS......... Chicago Cluster of Theological Schools [*Library network*]
CCTS......... Combat Crew Training School [*Air Force*] (AFM)
CCTS......... Combat Crew Training Squadron (MCD)
CCTS......... Command Center Terminal System (MCD)
CCTS......... Conseil Canadien sur le Tabagisme et la Sante [*Canadian Council on Smoking and Health*]
CCTS......... Contour Check Template Set (MCD)
CCTSCH ... Combat Crew Training School [*Air Force*]
C Cts Chr ... County Courts Chronicle [*1847-1920*] [*England*] [*A publication*] (DLA)
CCTSq ...... Combat Crew Training Squadron [*Air Force*]
CCTU .... Committee of Corporate Telecommunications Users [*An association*] (EA)
CCTU .... Corporate Committee of Telecommunications Users (EA)
CCTUO ..... Coordinating Committee of Trade Union Organizations [*Ceylon*]
CCTV......... Carlton Communications PLC [*NASDAQ symbol*] (NQ)
CCTV......... China Central Television [*The national Chinese network*]
CCTV......... Closed-Circuit Television
CCTV......... Command and Control Training Vehicles (MCD)
CCTWg...... Combat Crew Training Wing [*Air Force*] (AFM)
CCU .... Cabinet Casemakers' Union [*British*]
CCU .... Calcutta [*India*] [*Airport symbol*] (OAG)
CCU .... Camera Control Unit
CCU .... Canadian Commercial Bank [*Toronto Stock Exchange symbol*]
CCU .... Capillary Column Usage
CCU .... Cardiac Care Unit [*Medicine*]
CCU .... Caribbean Consumers Union (EAIO)
CCU .... Catholic Central Union [*Later, COF*]
CCU .... Cedar City [*Utah*] [*Seismograph station code, US Geological Survey*] (SEIS)
CCU .... Central Computer Unit
CCU .... Central Control Unit
CCU .... Channel Control Unit (CMD)
CCU .... Chart Comparison Unit
CCU .... Christian Computer Users (EA)
CCU .... Clear Channel Communications, Inc. [*AMEX symbol*] (SPSG)
CCU .... Cluster Control Unit
CCU .... Color Changing Unit [*Medical technology*]
CCU .... Commercial Casualty Underwriting [*Insurance*]
CCU .... Common Control Unit [*Army*] (AABC)
CCU .... Communication Control Unit
CCU .... Communication Credit Union [*Australia*]
CCU .... Communications Coupling Unit (CET)
CCU .... Community College Unit [*Office of Education*]
CCU .... Computer Control Unit
CCU .... Computer Coupling Unit (MCD)
CCU .... Confederation of Canadian Unions
CCU .... Configuration Control Unit (MCD)
CCU .... Consultative Committee for Units [*International Bureau of Weights and Measures*]
CCU .... Containment Cooling Unit [*Nuclear energy*] (NRCH)
CCU .... Conversion Computer Unit
CCU .... Convolutional Coding Unit
CCU .... Cooker Control Unit
CCU .... Cornu Cervi Ustum [*Burnt Hartshorn*] [*Pharmacy*] (ROG)
CCU .... Coronary Care Unit [*of a hospital*]
CCU .... Coronary Care Unit [*University of Southern California*] [*Research center*] (RCD)
CCU .... Correctional Custody Unit [*Navy*]
CCU .... Council on Christian Unity (EA)
CCU .... Coupling Control Unit
CCU .... Crew [*or Crewman*] Communications Umbilical [*Apollo*] [*NASA*]
CCU .... Critical Care Unit [*Medicine*]

CCU .... Croatian Catholic Union of the USA and Canada (EA)
CCU .... Cuadernos de la Catedra de Unamuno [*A publication*]
CCU .... Cycle Control Unit [*IRS*]
CCU .... Czech Catholic Union (EA)
CCUA .... Catholic Central Union of America (EA)
CCUA .... Christian Computer Users Association (EA)
CCUA .... Credit Card Users of America [*Beverly Hills, CA*] (EA)
CCUAP...... Computerized Cable Upkeep Administrative Program [*Bell System*]
C Cubano ... Cine Cubano [*A publication*]
CCUE .... Committee on Comparative Urban Economics (EA)
CCUGC ..... Central Canada University Geological Conference
CCuH......... Hughes Aircraft Co., Culver City, CA [*Library symbol*] [*Library of Congress*] (LCLS)
CCuH-C..... Hughes Aircraft Co., Communications Division Library, Airport Site, Inglewood, CA [*Library symbol*] [*Library of Congress*] (LCLS)
CCUHCL ... Cahiers. Centre Universitaire d'Histoire Contemporaine de Louvain [*A publication*]
CCuH-G..... Hughes Aircraft Co., Ground Systems Library, Fullerton, CA [*Library symbol*] [*Library of Congress*] (LCLS)
CCuH-M..... Hughes Aircraft Co., Marketing Research Library, Airport Site, Inglewood, CA [*Library symbol*] [*Library of Congress*] (LCLS)
CCuH-R..... Hughes Aircraft Co., Research Laboratories Library, Malibu, CA [*Library symbol*] [*Library of Congress*] (LCLS)
CCuH-RC.. Hughes Aircraft Co., Santa Barbara Research Center, Santa Barbara, CA [*Library symbol*] [*Library of Congress*] (LCLS)
CCuH-S ..... Hughes Aircraft Co., Semiconductor Division Library, Newport Beach, CA [*Library symbol*] [*Library of Congress*] (LCLS)
C Cul .... Chinese Culture [*A publication*]
CCult.......... Cronache Culturali [*A publication*]
CCUM .... Catholic Committee on Urban Ministry (EA)
CCuM .... Metro-Goldwyn-Mayer, Research Department, Culver City, CA [*Library symbol*] [*Library of Congress*] (LCLS)
CCUN........ Church Center for the United Nations (EA)
CCUN........ Collegiate Council for the United Nations (EA)
CCUP .... Colpocystourethropexy [*Medicine*]
CCUP .... Compucorp [*Santa Monica, CA*] [*NASDAQ symbol*] (NQ)
CCuP.......... Pacific Semiconductors, Inc., Culver City, CA [*Library symbol*] [*Library of Congress*] (LCLS)
CCUR .... Concurrent Computer Corp. [*NASDAQ symbol*] (NQ)
CCURR....... Canadian Council on Urban and Regional Research (EA)
CCUS......... Chamber of Commerce of the United States (EA)
CCUS......... Circuit Court of the United States (DLA)
CCUS......... Cleared Customs [*Aviation*] (FAAC)
CCUS......... Concerned Citizens for Universal Service (EA)
CCUSA ...... Catholic Charities USA (EA)
CCV .... Canadian Cariboo Resources Ltd. [*Vancouver Stock Exchange symbol*]
CCV .... Cape Charles, VA [*Location identifier*] [*FAA*] (FAAL)
CCV .... Centro de Cultura Valenciana [*A publication*]
CCV .... Chamber Coolant Valve (NASA)
CCV .... Channel Catfish Virus
CCV .... Chosen Coefficient of Variation [*Statistics*]
CCV .... Clark College, Library, Vancouver, WA [*OCLC symbol*] (OCLC)
CCV .... Close Combat Vehicle [*Military*]
CCV .... Coconut Cadang-Cadang Viroid [*Also, CCCV*]
CCV .... Color Contrast Value
CCV .... Combat Command V
CCV .... Conductivity Cell Volume [*Hematology*]
CCV .... Congregatio a Sacro Corde Jesu [*Congregation of the Priests of the Sacred Heart*] [*Roman Catholic religious order*]
CCV .... Continuing Calibration Verification [*Laboratory analysis*]
CCV .... Control Configured Vehicle [*Air Force*]
CCV .... Coolant Control Valve
CCV .... Coupe Concept Vehicle [*Austin Rover*]
CCV .... Craig Cove [*Vanuatu*] [*Airport symbol*] (OAG)
CCVA .... Chamber Coolant Valve Actuator (MCD)
CCVA .... Citizens Committee for Victim Assistance (EA)
CCV-AV ..... CCNU [*Lomustine*], Cyclophosphamide, Vincristine, Alternating with Adriamycin, Vincristine [*Antineoplastic drug regimen*]
CCVCS ...... Command and Control Voice Communications System [*Defense Supply Agency*]
CCVI.......... Congregatio Caritatis Verbi Incarnati [*Congregation of the Sisters of Charity of the Incarnate Word*] [*Roman Catholic religious order*]
CCVL......... Close Combat Vehicle - Light [*Army*]
CCVL......... Configuration Control Verification List (MCD)
CCVPP ...... CCNU [*Lomustine*], Cyclophosphamide, Vincristine, Procarbazine, Prednisone [*Antineoplastic drug regimen*]
CCVRE...... Churches' Committee for Voter Registration-Education (EA)
CCVS......... COBOL [*Common Business-Oriented Language*] Compiler Validation System [*Data processing*]
CCVS......... Current-Controlled Voltage Source (IEEE)
CCVT......... Coupling Capacitor Voltage Transformer
CCW .... Caldwell College for Women [*New Jersey*]

CCW	Canadian Curtiss-Wright Ltd. [*Toronto Stock Exchange symbol*]
CCW	Carrying Concealed Weapon [*Police term*]
CCW	Channel Command [*or Control*] Word [*Data processing*]
CCW	Charles City Western Railway Co. [*AAR code*]
CCW	Child Care Worker
CCW	Children's Computer Workshop
CCW	Circulation Control Wing (MCD)
CCW	Close Combat Weapon System [*Army*] (MCD)
CCW	Closed Cooling Water [*Nuclear energy*] (NRCH)
CCW	Component Cooling Water [*Nuclear energy*] (NRCH)
CCW	Condenser Circulating Water [*Nuclear energy*] (NRCH)
CCW	Condenser Cooling Water [*Nuclear energy*] (NRCH)
CCW	Cosmetic Career Women [*Later, CEW*]
CCW	Counterclockwise
CCW	International Committee on Chemical Warfare
CCW	United Church of Christ Coordinating Center for Women in Church and Society (EA)
CCWA	Catholic Construction Workers of America (EA)
C in C WA ...	Commander-in-Chief, Western Approaches [*British*] [*World War II*]
CCWAA	Collegiate Council of Women's Athletic Administrators (EA)
CCWAD	Conference of Church Workers Among the Deaf [*Later, ECD*] (EA)
CCWC	Committee of Catholics Who Care (EA)
CCW(CD) ...	International Committee on Chemical Warfare, Crop Destruction
CCWHP	Coordinating Committee on Women in the Historical Profession [*Later, CCWHP/CGWH*] (EA)
CCWHP/CGWH ...	Coordinating Committee on Women in the Historical Profession/Conference Group on Women's History (EA)
CCWL	Catholic Council on Working Life (EA)
CCWO	Command Center Watch Officer (MCD)
CCWO	Commercial Communications Work Order [*Air Force*]
CCWO	Cryptocenter Watch Officer
CCWRH	Canvas-Covered Wire-Rope Handrail [*Aerospace*] (MSA)
CC WR HDR ...	Canvas-Covered Wire-Rope Handrail [*Aerospace*] (AAG)
CCWS	Chief of the Chemical Warfare Service [*World War II*]
C of CWS ...	Chief of the Chemical Warfare Service [*World War II*]
CCWS	Closed Cooling Water System [*Nuclear energy*] (NRCH)
CCWS	Component Cooling Water System [*Nuclear energy*] (NRCH)
CCX	Caceres [*Brazil*] [*Airport symbol*] (OAG)
CCX	Cancom Industries, Inc. [*Vancouver Stock Exchange symbol*]
CCX	CCX, Inc. [*NYSE symbol*] (SPSG)
CCX	Chapman College Library, Orange, CA [*OCLC symbol*] (OCLC)
CCX	Cinquante Millions de Consommateurs [*A publication*]
CCX	Corporate Planning Office [*AFSC*]
CCX	Customer Communications Exchange [*Bell System*]
CCXD	Computer-Controlled X-Ray Diffractometer
CCXL	Contel Cellular, Inc. [*NASDAQ symbol*] (NQ)
CCY	Camping Club Youth [*British*]
CCY	Charles City, IA [*Location identifier*] [*FAA*] (FAAL)
CCY	Chief Communications Yeoman [*British military*] (DMA)
CCY	Coalition for Children and Youth [*American Occupational Therapy Association*]
CCY	Columbia College Library, Columbia, CA [*OCLC symbol*] (OCLC)
CCyC	Cypress Junior College, Cypress, CA [*Library symbol*] [*Library of Congress*] (LCLS)
CCYDA	Canadian Child and Youth Drama Association
CCYPBY ..	Cancer Chemotherapy Reports. Part 3 [*A publication*]
CCYUA	Catholic Central Youth Union of America (EA)
CCZ	Camara de Comercio de Bogota. Revista [*A publication*]
CCZ	Chub Cay [*Bahamas*] [*Airport symbol*] (OAG)
CCZ	Pittsburgh, PA [*Location identifier*] [*FAA*] (FAAL)
CCZA	Canadian Coastal Zone Atlantic
CCZP	Canadian Coastal Zone Pacific
CD	Air Commuter Ltd. [*Great Britain*] [*ICAO designator*] (FAAC)
CD	Application for Certiorari Denied [*Legal term*] (DLA)
CD	Cable Duct (MSA)
CD	Cabling Data
CD	Cadaver Donor [*Medicine*]
Cd	Cadmium [*Chemical element*]
CD	Caesarean Delivered [*Medicine*]
C de D	Cahiers de Droit [*A publication*]
CD	Cairo Document [*A publication*]
CD	Calendar Day (AFM)
CD	Calibration Device (KSC)
CD	Calling Device [*Telecommunications*]
CD	Camouflage Detection [*Often, in regard to a special photographic film, as, "CD film"*] [*Military*]
CD	Canadian Dollar [*Monetary unit*]
CD	Canadian Forces Decoration
cd	Candela [*Formerly, Candlepower*] [*Symbol*] [*SI unit of luminous intensity*]
CD	Candle [*Illumination*]
CD	Canine Distemper [*Veterinary medicine*]
CD	Canine Dose [*Veterinary medicine*]
CD	Capacitative Discharge [*Voltage source*]
CD	Capacitor Diode

CD	Capacitor Discharge [*Automotive engineering*]
CD	Captain of the Dockyard [*Obsolete*] [*British*]
CD	Car Deck
C/D	Car and Driver [*A publication*]
CD	Card (MSA)
CD	Card Distribution
CD	Cardiac Disease [*Medicine*]
CD	Cardiac Dullness [*Physiology*]
CD	Cardiovascular Disease [*Medicine*]
CD	Carrel-Dakin [*Fluid*]
CD	Carried Down [*Bookkeeping*]
CD	Carrier Detector (BUR)
C/D	Cash Against Documents [*Sales*] (ADA)
CD	Cash Discount [*Sales*]
CD	Cash Dispenser [*Banking*] (BUR)
CD	Castleman's Disease [*Oncology*]
CD	Casualty Department [*British police*]
CD	Catalogued
C-D	Catalytic-Dow (KSC)
CD	Cathedral
C & D	Cats and Dogs [*i.e., low selling items or speculative stock*] [*Slang*] [*Business term*]
CD	Caudal [*Anatomy*]
CD	Census Collection District [*Australia*]
CD	Center Director [*John F. Kennedy Space Center Directorate*] [*NASA*] (NASA)
CD	Center Distance (MSA)
CD	Central Disc [*Of flowers*] [*Botany*]
CD	Central District
CD	Centre Democratique [*Democratic Center*] [*Later, Center of Social Democrats*] [*France*] [*Political party*] (PPE)
CD	Centrum-Demokraterne [*Center Democrats*] [*Denmark*] [*Political party*] (PPE)
CD	Century Dictionary [*A publication*] (ROG)
CD	Century Edition of the American Digest System (West) [*A publication*] (DLA)
C/D	Certificate of Damage [*Tea trade*] (ROG)
C/D	Certificate of Delivery
CD	Certificate of Deposit [*Banking*]
C of D	Certificate of Deposit [*Banking*]
CD	Certificate of Destruction (AFM)
CD	Certificate of Disposal (ADA)
CD	Certification Data (AFIT)
cd	Chad [*MARC country of publication code*] [*Library of Congress*] (LCCP)
CD	Chancery Division
CD	Change Diameter (MCD)
CD	Change Directive (AAG)
CD	Change Directory [*Data processing*]
CD	Chapter Director
CD	Cheatham Dam [*TVA*]
CD	Check Digit [*IRS*]
CD	Chemically Diabetic [*Endocrinology*]
CD	Chemiluminescence Depletion [*Chemical kinetics*]
C & D	Chemist and Druggist
CD	Chief of Detectives
CD	Chief of Division
CD	Chief Draftsman (MCD)
CD	Child Development [*A publication*]
CD	Chilldown [*NASA*] (KSC)
CD	Chiroptical Discrimination [*Steroisomeric chemistry*]
CD	Chirp Duration [*Entomology*]
CD	Chlordan [*or Chlordane*] [*Insecticide*]
CD	Chlordecone (Kepone) [*Pesticide*]
CD	Chord
CD	Christian Dior [*Couturier*]
CD	Christopher Davies [*Publisher*] [*British*]
CD	Christus Dominus [*Decree on the Bishops' Pastoral Office in the Church*] [*Vatican II document*]
C/d	Cigarettes per Day [*Medicine*]
CD	Circuit Decisions [*A publication*] (DLA)
CD	Circuit Description (MSA)
CD	Circuit Diagrams
CD	Circular Dichroism [*Optics*]
CD	Circular Dispersion
CD	Citizen Diplomacy (EA)
CD	Ciudad de Dios [*A publication*]
CD	Civil Defense
CD	Claims, Defense (CAAL)
CD	Classification of Defects (AAG)
CD	Claude Dornier [*German aircraft designer, 1884-1969*]
CD	Clearance Delivery (FAAC)
CD	Clearance Diving [*Navy*] [*British*]
CD	[*The*] Clearinghouse Directory [*A publication*]
CD	Climatological Data [*A publication*]
CD	Clock Driver
CD	Closing Date
CD	Clothes Drier
CD	Club Delahaye (EA)
CD	Cluster Designation [*Immunology*]
CD	Cluster of Differentiation [*Immunology*]

CD.............. Clutch Drive [*on a ship*] (DS)
CD.............. Coalicion Democratica [*Democratic Coalition*] [*Spain*] [*Political party*] (PPE)
CD.............. Coast Defense
CD.............. Coastal Defense RADAR (MUGU)
CD.............. Code (MCD)
CD.............. Coden [*Online database field identifier*]
CD.............. Coefficient of Drag (MCD)
CD.............. Coin Dimple
CD.............. Cold-Drawn [*Metal*]
CD.............. Colla Destra [*With the Right Hand*] [*Music*]
C & D........ Collection and Delivery [*Shipping*]
C & D........ Collection and Distribution [*Transportation*]
CD.............. College Discovery [*Educational project for disadvantaged youngsters*] (EA)
CD.............. Collision Detect [*Computer science*]
CD.............. Color Developer System [*Canon, Inc.*]
CD.............. Combat Development
CD.............. Combination Die (MCD)
CD.............. Combination Drug
CD.............. Command
C & D........ Command and Decision [*Military*] (CAAL)
CD.............. Command Decoder
C/D.............. Command Destruct (AAG)
Cd.............. Command Papers [*A publication*] (DLA)
CD.............. Commander of the Order of Distinction [*Jamaica*]
CD.............. Commerce Department
CD.............. Commercial Dock [*Shipping*]
CD.............. Commission du Danube [*Danube Commission - DC*] (EAIO)
CD.............. Commissioned
CD.............. Commissioner's Decisions [*US Patent and Trademark Office*]
CD.............. Common Denominator (AAG)
CD.............. Common Digitizer [*FAA*]
CD.............. Common Duct [*Medicine*]
CD.............. Communicable Disease [*or a patient with such a disease*] [*Medicine*]
CD.............. Communicable Disease Report [*A publication*]
C & D........ Communications and Data
CD.............. Communicative Disorders
CD.............. Community Development
CD.............. Compact Design [*Automotive engineering*]
CD.............. Compact Disk [*Audio/video technology*] [*Philips*]
CD.............. Companion Dog [*Dog show term*]
CD.............. Comparative Drama [*A publication*]
CD.............. Compass Department [*British military*] (DMA)
CD.............. Competitive Design
CD.............. Complaint Docket [*Legal term*] (DLA)
CD.............. Complementary Distribution [*Linguistics*]
C/D.............. Complete Deal [*Coupon redemption*]
CD.............. Completely Denatured
CD.............. Complicated Delivery [*Obstetrics*]
CD.............. Computer-Controlled Dampers [*Automotive suspension feature*]
CD.............. Computer Design [*A publication*]
CD.............. Comyn's Digest of the Laws of England [*1762-1882*] [*A publication*] (ILCA)
CD.............. Concept Definition (MCD)
CD.............. Concept Development
CD.............. Condition of Detail
cd.............. Conductance
CD.............. Conductivity Detector
CD.............. Conference on Disarmament
CD.............. Confessor, Doctor [*Ecclesiastical*] (ROG)
CD.............. Confidential Document [*Navy*]
CD.............. Congressional District
CD.............. Conjugata Diagonalis [*Pelvic measurement*] [*Anatomy*]
CD.............. Conning Director [*Navy*]
CD.............. Consanguineous Donor [*Medicine*]
CD.............. Constrained Deconvolution Technique [*Data processing*]
CD.............. Construction Defect
C & D........ Construction and Development
CD.............. Constructive Dilemma [*Rule of inference*] [*Logic*]
CD.............. Consular Declaration
CD.............. Contact Dermatitis [*Medicine*]
CD.............. Contagious Diseases
CD.............. Continued Development
CD.............. Contract Definition [*Military*]
CD.............. Contract Demonstration [*Army*] (AFIT)
CD.............. Contract Design
CD.............. Control Diet
C/D.............. Control/Display Ratio [*Quality control*]
CD.............. Control Rod Drive [*Nuclear energy*] (IEEE)
CD.............. Controlled Dissemination (MCD)
CD.............. Controlled Drug
C-D........ CONVAIR [*Consolidated-Vultee Aircraft Corp.*] Daingerfield [*Later, General Dynamics/Daingerfield*] (AAG)
C of D........ Convention of Dublin [*Freemasonry*] (ROG)
CD.............. Conventional District [*Church of England*]
CD.............. Converging-Diverging (MCD)
CD.............. Convulsive Disorder [*Medicine*]
CD.............. Convulsive Dose [*Medicine*]

C/D.............. Cooldown [*Nuclear energy*] (NRCH)
CD.............. Coordinacion Democratica [*Democratic Coordination*] [*Spain*] [*Political party*] (PPE)
CD.............. Coordinadora Democratica [*Democratic Coordinating Board*] [*Nicaragua*] (PPW)
CD.............. Coordination Document
C & D........ Corbett and Daniell's English Election Cases [*1819*] [*A publication*] (DLA)
CD.............. Cord
CD.............. Cordoba Durchmusterung [*Star chart*]
CD.............. Corollary Discharge Neuron [*Neurophysiology*]
CD.............. Corps Diplomatique [*Diplomatic Corps*]
CD.............. Cosmo Dog
CD.............. Could
CD.............. Council of Deliberation [*Freemasonry*] (ROG)
CD.............. Council Deputies (NATG)
CD.............. Countdown [*Aerospace*] (AAG)
CD.............. Countdown [*Credit card*] [*British*]
CD.............. Counting Device
CD.............. Court Druggist [*Foresters*] [*British*] (ROG)
C & D........ Cover and Deception (CINC)
CD.............. Crash Damage (MCD)
C & D........ Crawford and Dix's Irish Circuit Court Cases [*A publication*] (DLA)
CD.............. Criminal Deportee (ADA)
CD.............. Crohn's Disease [*Medicine*]
CD.............. Cross Direction
CD.............. Crossland Industries Corp. [*Vancouver Stock Exchange symbol*]
CD.............. Crusade for Decency (EA)
CD.............. Cryogenic Distillation (MCD)
CD.............. Crystal Diode
CD.............. Crystal Driver
CD.............. Cuadernos para el Dialogo [*A publication*]
CD.............. Cultural Disadvantage
CD.............. Cum Dividendo [*With Dividend*] [*Latin*] [*Stock exchange term*]
CD.............. Curative Dose [*Medicine*]
CD.............. Current Density
CD.............. Current Digest [*A publication*]
CD.............. Current Driver
CD.............. Customs Court Decisions [*A publication*] (DLA)
CD.............. Customs Decisions [*Department of the Treasury*] [*A publication*] (DLA)
C/D.............. Customs Declaration
CD.............. Cyclodextrin [*Organic chemistry*]
CD.............. Cystic Duct [*Medicine*]
C & D........ Cystoscopy and Dilatation [*Medicine*]
CD.............. Cytochalasin D [*Biochemistry*]
CD.............. Cytotoxic Dose [*Toxicology*]
CD.............. Department of Productivity [*Government Aircraft Factory*] [*Australia*] [*ICAO aircraft manufacturer identifier*] (ICAO)
Cd.............. Drag Coefficient [*Automotive engineering*]
CD.............. Driver [*Navy rating*] (MUGU)
CD.............. Lewis D. and John J. Gilbert, Corporate Democracy (EA)
CD.............. Ohio Circuit Decisions [*A publication*] (DLA)
CD.............. RADAR Cloud Detection Report [*Meteorology*] (FAAC)
C2d.............. California Supreme Court Reports, Second Series [*A publication*] (DLA)
C3d.............. California Supreme Court Reports, Third Series [*A publication*] (DLA)
C3D.............. Cascade Charge Coupled Device [*Electronics*]
CD/50........ Median Curative Dose [*Medicine*]
CdA.............. Camp de l'Arpa [*A publication*]
CDA.............. Canada
CDA.............. Canadian Dental Association
CDA.............. Canadian Department of Agriculture
CDA.............. Canadian Diabetic Association
CDA.............. Canadian Dietetic Association
CDA.............. Canadian Transtech Industries [*Vancouver Stock Exchange symbol*]
CDA.............. Cape Douglas [*Alaska*] [*Seismograph station code, US Geological Survey*] (SEIS)
CDA.............. Casualty and Damage Assessment (MCD)
CDA.............. Catalog Data Activity [*Army*]
CDA.............. Catalog Data Agency (MCD)
CDA.............. Catholic Daughters of the Americas (EA)
CDA.............. Center for Democratic Alternatives (EA)
CDA.............. Central Design Activity (MCD)
CDA.............. Central Directed Audit [*Military*]
CDA.............. Ceramics Distributors of America (EA)
CDA.............. Certified Dental Assistant
CDA.............. Cesium Dihydrogen Arsenate
CDA.............. Chenodeoxycholic Acid [*Also, CDC, CDCA, CHENIC*] [*Biochemistry*]
CDA.............. Child Development Associate [*National certificate*] (OICC)
CDA.............. Christen Democratisch Appel [*Christian Democratic Appeal*] [*Netherlands*] [*Political party*] (PPW)
CDA.............. Circuit Distribution Assembly [*Ground Communications Facility, NASA*]

CDA........... City Demonstration Agency
CDA........... Civil Defense Agency
CDA........... Classic Desk Accessories [*Apple Computer, Inc.*] [*Utility program*] [*Data processing*]
CDA........... Coin Detection and Announcement [*Telecommunications*] (TEL)
CDA........... Colonial Dames of America (EA)
CDA........... Combined Development Agency [*Anglo-American uranium procurement*]
CDA........... Command and Data Acquisition (NASA)
CDA........... Commercial Development Association (EA)
CDA........... Common Dollar Accounting (ADA)
CDA........... Communications Distribution Amplifier (MCD)
CDA........... Community Development Administration [*HUD*]
CDA........... Compania Dominicana de Aviacion SA (MCD)
CDA........... Company Directors' Association of Australia
CDA........... Completely Denatured Alcohol
CDA........... Compound Document Architecture
CDA........... Comprehensive Dissertation Abstracts [*University Microfilms International*] [*Information service or system*]
CDA........... Computer Dealers Association [*Later, CDLA*]
CDA........... Computer Directions Advisors, Inc. [*Information service or system*] (IID)
CDA........... Concept Development Associates, Inc. [*Information service or system*] (IID)
CDA........... Configuration Design Audit (MCD)
CDA........... Congenital Dyserythropoietic Anemia [*Hematology*]
CDA........... Constant Dollar Accounting (ADA)
CDA........... Contagious Diseases Act [*British*]
CDA........... Containment Depressurization Actuation [*Nuclear energy*] (NRCH)
CDA........... Containment Depressurization Alarm [*Nuclear energy*] (IEEE)
CDA........... Control Data Corp. [*NYSE symbol*] (SPSG)
CDA........... Convolutional Decoder Assembly
CDA........... Copier Dealers Association (EA)
CDA........... Copper Development Association (EA)
CDA........... Core Disruptive Accident [*Nuclear energy*] (NRCH)
CDA........... Corporacion Dominicana de Aviacion [*Dominican Aviation Corporation*] [*Airline*] [*Dominican Republic*]
CDA........... Council for Democracy in the Americas (EA)
CDA........... Critical Design Audit (MCD)
CDA........... National Society of Colonial Dames of America (EA)
CDA........... Southwest Regional Library Service System, Durango, CO [*OCLC symbol*] (OCLC)
CDAA........ Central Data Analysis Area (KSC)
CDAA........ Chlorodiallylacetamide [*Herbicide*]
CDAA........ Circularly Disposed Antenna Array [*Radio receiver*]
CDAA........ Company Directors' Association of Australia
CDAAA...... Committee to Defend America by Aiding the Allies [*Active prior to US entry into World War II*]
CDAB........ Child Development Abstracts and Bibliography [*A publication*]
CDAB........ Crime and Delinquency Abstracts [*A publication*]
CDABO...... College of Diplomates of the American Board of Orthodontics (EA)
CDAC........ California Date Administrative Committee (EA)
CDAC........ Cetyldimethylbenzylammonium Chloride [*A surfactant*]
CDAC........ Chicago Dance Arts Coalition
CDAC........ Child Development Associate Consortium [*Superseded by CDANCP*] (EA)
CDAC........ Civil Defense Advisory Council
C & DAC.... Crawford and Dix's Irish Abridged Cases [*A publication*] (DLA)
CDAD........ Compact Digital Audio Disk (ADA)
CDAD........ Computer Dual Access Driver (MCD)
CDAE........ Civil Defense Adult Education [*Program*]
CDAEP...... Civil Defense Adult Education Program
CDAF........ Configuration Development of Advanced Fighters [*Military*] (MCD)
Cda Forest ... Canada's Domestic Consumption of Forest Products, 1960-2000 [*A publication*]
CDAI........ Crohn's Disease Activity Index [*Medicine*]
CDA J........ California Dental Association. Journal [*A publication*]
CDAL........ Cahiers des Ameriques Latines [*A publication*]
CDANC...... Committee for the Development of Art in Negro Colleges [*Later, CAA*]
CDANCP.... Child Development Associate National Credentialing Program (EA)
CDAP........ Civil Damage Assessment Program [*Army*] (AABC)
CDAP........ Climatic Data Analysis Program
CDAPAM ... Conserve e Derivati Agrumari [*A publication*]
CDAS........ Central Data Acquisition System
CDAS........ Command and Data Acquisition Station [*Aerospace*]
CDAS........ Computer Design and Architecture Series [*Elsevier Book Series*] [*A publication*]
CD/AT....... Contrast Density/Appearance Time [*of images on a film*]
CDAT........ Cordatum, Inc. [*NASDAQ symbol*] (NQ)
CDATS...... Chemical Detection and Alarm Training Simulator (MCD)
CDAW....... Controlled Data Analysis Workshops [*Magnetospheric physics*]
CDB........... California Distance Table Bureau, San Francisco CA [*STAC*]
CDB........... Caliper Disk Brake
CDB........... Capacitance Decode Box

CDB........... Cardinal Mineral Corp. Ltd. [*Vancouver Stock Exchange symbol*]
CDB........... Caribbean Development Bank [*St. Michael, Barbados*]
CDB........... Cast Double Base
CDB........... Center for Drugs and Biologics [*FDA*]
CDB........... Central Data Bank
CDB........... Central Data Buffer [*Data processing*] (MCD)
CDB........... Childhood Disability Benefits [*Social Security Administration*] (OICC)
CDB........... City Development Board (OICC)
CDB........... Cognitive Diagnostic Battery [*Test*]
CDB........... Cold Bay [*Alaska*] [*Airport symbol*] (OAG)
CDB........... Cold Bay, AK [*Location identifier*] [*FAA*] (FAAL)
CDB........... Colecao Documentos Brasileiros [*A publication*]
CDB........... Combat Development Branch
CDB........... Command Data Buffer [*Air Force*] (MCD)
CDB........... Command Database (MCD)
CdB........... Commanderie de Bordeaux (EA)
CDB........... Common Data Bus [*Data processing*]
CDB........... Common Database [*Data processing*] (CAAL)
CDB........... Community Development Bulletin [*A publication*]
CDB........... Corporate Database [*Data processing*]
C & DB...... Cough and Deep-Breathe [*Medicine*]
CDB........... Current Data BIT [*Binary Digit*] [*Data processing*]
CDB........... Cyclohexyldithiobenzothiazole [*Organic chemistry*]
CDBA........ Clearance Diver's Breathing Apparatus
CDBA........ Commonwealth Development Bank of Australia
CDBA........ Containment Design Basis Accident [*Nuclear energy*] (NRCH)
CDBAB...... California Dry Bean Advisory Board (EA)
CDBD........ Cardboard (ADA)
CDBFR...... Command Data Buffer [*Air Force*] (MCD)
CDBFR...... Common Data Buffer (NASA)
CDBG....... Community Development Block Grant [*HUD*]
CDBI........ Consultants Directory for Business and Industry [*A publication*]
CDBI........ Cost Data Bank Index
CDBK....... Candlewood Bank & Trust Co. [*NASDAQ symbol*] (NQ)
CDBN....... Column-Digit Binary Network
CdBP........ Cadmium Binding Protein
CDBP........ Chlorodihydroxybenzopyranone [*Organic chemistry*]
CDBR....... Campaign to Defend Black Rights [*Australia*]
CD/BRAC ... Carmen Division of the Brotherhood of Railway, Airline and Steamship Clerks, Freight Handlers, Express and Station Employes (EA)
CDBS........ Cost Data Bank System (AFIT)
CDC........... Cahiers de Droit Compare [*A publication*] (ILCA)
CDC........... Cairo Documents of the Damascus Covenanters [*A publication*] (BJA)
CDC........... Caisse des Depots et Consignations [*Financial institution*] [*French*]
CDC........... Calculated Date of Confinement [*Medicine*]
CDC........... California Debris Commission [*Army*]
CDC........... Call Directing Code
CDC........... Calories Don't Count [*Title of a 1961 book by Dr. Herman Taller; initialism referred to the diet and diet capsules promoted by the book*]
CDC........... Canada Development Corporation [*Toronto Stock Exchange symbol*] [*Vancouver Stock Exchange symbol*]
CDC........... Canada Road [*California*] [*Seismograph station code, US Geological Survey*] (SEIS)
CDC........... Canadian Dairy Commission
CDC........... Capsule Drive Core [*Aerospace*]
CDC........... Carbon from Dissolved Carbonates
CDC........... Career Development Center (EA)
CDC........... Career Development Course (AFM)
CDC........... Caribbean Defense Command [*or Commander*]
CDC........... Caudodorsal Cells [*Anatomy*]
CDC........... Cedar City [*Utah*] [*Airport symbol*] (OAG)
CDC........... Cedarville College, Cedarville, OH [*OCLC symbol*] (OCLC)
CDC........... Cell Division Cycle [*Cytology*]
CDC........... Center on Destructive Cultism (EA)
CDC........... Center for Developmental Change [*University of Kentucky*] [*Research center*] (RCD)
CDC........... Centers for Disease Control [*Formerly, Communicable Disease Center*] [*Department of Health and Human Services*] [*Atlanta, GA*]
CDC........... Centers for Disease Control. Publications [*A publication*]
CDC........... Central Digital Computer
CDC........... Central Document Control [*Jet Propulsion Laboratory, NASA*]
CDC........... Centre de Detection et de Control [*French air defense command and control center*]
CDC........... Ceramic Disk Capacitor
CDC........... Characteristic Distortion Compensation [*Telecommunications*] (TEL)
CDC........... Chemical Data Center, Inc. [*Information service or system*] (IID)
CDC........... Chemical Development Corporation [*Geneva, Switzerland*]
CDC........... Chenodeoxycholic Acid [*Also, CDA, CDCA, CHENIC*] [*Biochemistry*]
CDC........... Child Development Center
CDC........... Child Development Consultant

CDC .... Chinese Development Council   (EA)
CDC .... Circuit Defense Counsel
CDC .... Citizens' Defense Corps
CDC .... Civil Defense Committee   (NATG)
CDC .... Civil Defense Coordinator   (AAG)
CDC .... Clamped Dielectric Constant
CDC .... Classified Document Control
CDC .... Cleanly Designed Cigar
CDC .... Clearance Dock Club [*A union*] [*British*]
CDC .... Clearinghouse on Development Communication   (EA)
CDC .... Coaxial Directional Coupler
CDC .... Code Directing Character [*Data processing*]
CDC .... Cold-Drawn Copper   (MSA)
CDC .... Colonial Development Corporation
CDC .... Combat Development Command [*Terminated, 1973*] [*Army*]   (MCD)
CDC .... Combat Direction Center   (NVT)
CDC .... Command and Data-Handling Console
CDC .... Command Decoder Coaxial   (MCD)
CDC .... Command Destruct Control   (AAG)
CDC .... Commissioners of District of Columbia
CDC .... Committee for a Democratic Consensus   (EA)
CDC .... Commonwealth Development Corporation   (ILCA)
CDC .... Communicable Disease Center
CDC .... Communications Design Center [*Carnegie-Mellon University*] [*Research center*]   (RCD)
CDC .... Community Development Corporation [*Later, NCDC*]
CDC .... Company Data Coordinator
CDC .... Complement-Dependent Cytotoxicity [*Immunology*]
CDC .... Complete Disk Checker [*Compact disks*]
CDC .... Component Design Confirmation
CDC .... CompuDyne Corporation [*AMEX symbol*]   (SPSG)
CDC .... Computer Development Center   (KSC)
CDC .... Computer Directions Corporation
CDC .... Computer Display Channel
CDC .... Comunidad Democratica Centroamericana [*Central American Democratic Community*] [*Address unknown*]   (EAIO)
CDC .... Concert Dance Company [*Boston, MA*]
CDC .... Configuration Data Control   (AAG)
CDC .... Confined Detonating Cord   (MCD)
CDC .... Conselho de Desenvolvimento Comercial [*Government advisory body*] [*Brazil*]   (EY)
CDC .... Construction Design Criteria [*Telecommunications*]   (TEL)
CDC .... Continental Dorset Club   (EA)
CDC .... Contract Data Coordinator   (NG)
CDC .... Control Data Corporation [*Information service or system*]   (IID)
CDC .... Control Distribution Center   (AAG)
CDC .... Convergencia Democratica de Catalunya [*Democratic Convergence of Catalonia*] [*Spain*] [*Political party*]   (PPE)
CDC .... Copper Data Center [*Inactive*] [*Battelle Memorial Institute*] [*Information service or system*]
CDC .... Corporation de Developpement du Canada [*Canada Development Corporation - CDC*]
CDC .... Count - Double Count   (MUGU)
CDC .... Countdown Clock [*Aerospace*]
CDC .... Coupled Diffusion Control   (MCD)
CDC .... Course and Distance Calculator [*or Computer*]
CDC .... Criticallity Data Center
CDC .... Cryogenic Data Center [*National Institute of Standards and Technology*]
CDC .... Crystal Data Center [*National Institute of Standards and Technology*]
CDC .... Cumberland Railway & Coal Company [*AAR code*]
CDc .... Daly City Public Library, Daly City, CA [*Library symbol*] [*Library of Congress*]   (LCLS)
CDCA .... Caudodorsal Cells Autotransmitter [*Zoology*]
CDCA .... Chefs de Cuisine Association of America
CDCA .... Chenodeoxycholic Acid [*Also, CDA, CDC, CHENIC*] [*Biochemistry*]
CD Cal ...... United States District Court for the Central District of California   (DLA)
CD & CC .. Central Data and Cataloging Center   (AFM)
CDCC .... ChemDesign Corp. [*NASDAQ symbol*]   (NQ)
C & DCC .... Crawford and Dix's Irish Circuit Court Cases [*A publication*]   (DLA)
CDCCP ...... Control Data Communications Control Procedure [*Telecommunications*]   (TEL)
CDCD .... Certificate of Disposition of Classified Documents   (AAG)
CDCD .... Counter-Double-Current Distribution [*Analytical chemistry*]
CDCDA ..... Community Design Center Directors Association   (EA)
CDCDP ...... Civil Defense Career Development Program
CDCDSCA ... Children's Dress, Cotton Dress, and Sportswear Contractors Association [*Later, MAAA*]   (EA)
CDCE .... Central Data-Conversion Equipment
CDCE .... Commander, Disaster Control Element
CDCEC ...... Combat Development Command Experimentation Center [*Terminated*] [*Army*]   (MCD)
CDCF .... Commander, Disaster Control Force
CDCG .... Commander, Disaster Control Group
CDCH .... Caudodorsal Cell Hormone [*Zoology*]

CDCIA ...... Combat Development Command Infantry Agency [*Terminated*] [*Army*]
CDCIN ...... Curriculum Development Centre Information Network [*Australia*]
CDC-INTA ... Combat Development Command - Intelligence Agency [*Terminated*] [*Army*]   (MCD)
CDCK .... Craddock-Terry Shoe Corp. [*Lynchburg, VA*] [*NASDAQ symbol*]   (NQ)
CDCL........ Citizens in Defense of Civil Liberties   (EA)
CDCM ...... Carbon Dioxide Concentrating [*or Concentrator*] Module
CDCMA .... Combat Development Command Maintenance Agency [*Terminated*] [*Army*]
CDCN .... Command Document Control Number   (AFIT)
CDCN .... Contract Data Change Notice   (MCD)
CDCN .... Contract Document Change Notice   (MCD)
CDCN .... Controller Defence Communications Network [*Navy*] [*British*]
CDCNET... Control Data Corporation Distributed Communications Network [*Telecommunications*]
CDCO .... Cidco Group, Inc. [*NASDAQ symbol*]   (NQ)
CDC-OCCE ... Commonwealth Defence Conference - Operational Clothing and Combat Equipment   (EA)
CDCOM .... Coordinating Committee   (MCD)
CDCP........ Center for Disease Control and Prevention   (DHSM)
CDCP........ Command Display and Control Processor
CDCP........ Comparative Drama Conference. Papers [*A publication*]
CDCP........ Comprehensive Day Care Programs [*An association*]   (EA)
CDCP........ Construction and Development Corporation of the Philippines   (DS)
CDCP........ Milstep Central Data Collection Point [*McClellan Air Force Base*]
CDCQ .... Child Development Center Q-Sort [*Personality development test*] [*Psychology*]
CDCR .... Center for Documentation and Communication Research [*Case Western Reserve University*]
CDCR .... Children's Discovery Centers of America, Inc. [*NASDAQ symbol*]   (NQ)
CDCR .... Control Drawing Change Request   (AAG)
CDCS........ Central Data Collection System   (AFM)
CDCS........ Civil Defense Countermeasures System
CDCS........ Construction Dollar Control System [*AT & T*]
CDCS........ Customer Depot Complaint System   (MCD)
CDCT .... Centro de Documentacao Cientifica e Tecnica [*Scientific and Technical Documentation Center*] [*Portugal*] [*Information service or system*]   (IID)
CDCTA...... Combat Development Command Transportation Agency [*Terminated*] [*Army*]
CDCU .... Communications Digital Control Unit
CDCW .... Cymdeithas Diogelu Cymru Wledig [*Council for the Protection of Rural Wales*]   (EAIO)
CDD.......... Candela Resources Ltd. [*Vancouver Stock Exchange symbol*]
CDD.......... Cardiodilatin [*Biochemistry*]
CDD.......... Castilejo-Dalitz-Dyson
CDD.......... Central Data Display
CDD.......... Certificate of Disability for Discharge [*Military*]
CDD.......... Chart Distribution Data
CDD.......... Chlorinated Dibenzo-para-dioxin [*Organic chemistry*]
CDD.......... Chronic Disabling Dermatoses [*Medicine*]
CdD.......... Ciudad de Dios [*A publication*]
CDD.......... Coded Decimal Digit
CDD.......... Collateral Damage Distance   (AABC)
CDD.......... Color Data Display
CDD.......... Command Destruct Decoder
CDD.......... Common Data Dictionary   (MCD)
CDD.......... Computer-Directed Drawing
CDD.......... Conference on Dual Distribution
CDD.......... Congressional District Data [*Bureau of the Census*]
CDD.......... Cosmic Dust Detector
CDD.......... Cratering Demolition Device
CDDA .... Canadian Diamond Drilling Association
CDDA........ Compact Data Disk Association [*Defunct*]   (EA)
CD-DA...... Compact Disk Digital Audio [*Data processing*]
CDDAC ..... Cover and Deception, Direction, and Coordination   (MCD)
C & DDAC ... Cover and Deception, Direction, and Coordination
CDDC .... Center Data Descriptions Catalog   (KSC)
CD D/C...... Civil Defense Director/Coordinator
CDDD........ Comprehensive Dishonesty, Disappearance, and Destruction Policy [*Insurance*]
CDDED7 ... Cancer Drug Delivery [*A publication*]
CDDF .... Central Data Distribution Facility [*National Oceanic and Atmospheric Administration*]
CDDGP ..... Commander, Destroyer Development Group, Pacific [*Navy*]   (MCD)
CDDI .... Computer-Directed Drawing Instrument
CD-DIAL... Community Development - Data Information Analysis Laboratory   (OICC)
CDDL .... Conference of Directors of Danube Lines [*Budapest, Hungary*]   (EAIO)
CDDO....... Coalition of Digestive Disease Organizations   (EA)
CDDP .... Canadian Department of Defence Production
CDDP .... cis-Diamminadichloroplatinum [*Cisplatin*] [*Also, cis-DDP, CPDD, CPT, DDP, P*] [*Antineoplastic drug*]

CDDP .... Console Digital Display Programmer (MUGU)
CDDR .... CD [*Compact Disc*] Data Report [*Langley Publications*] [*Information service or system*] [*A publication*] (IID)
CDDR .... Coordinated Design Data Required
CDDT .... Countdown Demonstration Test [*NASA*]
CDDT .... Cyclododecatriene [*Organic chemistry*]
CDE .... Cahiers de Droit Europeen [*A publication*]
CDE .... Caledonia [*Panama*] [*Airport symbol*] (OAG)
CDE .... Canine Distemper Encephalitis [*A disease*]
CDE .... Cape Decision, AK [*Location identifier*] [*FAA*] (FAAL)
CDE .... Carbon Dioxide Economizer
c/de .... Casa De [*Care Of*] [*Spanish*]
CDE .... Center for Demography and Ecology [*University of Wisconsin - Madison*] [*Research center*] (RCD)
CDE .... Centre for the Development of Entrepreneurs [*Australia*]
CDE .... Certificate in Data Education (BUR)
CDE .... Chemical Defence Establishment [*British*]
CDE .... Chlordiazepoxide [*Librium*] [*Sedative*]
CdE .... Chronique d'Egypte [*A publication*]
CDE .... Civil Director of Economics
CDE .... Clutter Doppler Error (MCD)
CDE .... Clutter Doppler Error Gate Control (MCD)
CDE .... Code
CDE .... Coeur D'Alene Mines Corp. [*NYSE symbol*] (SPSG)
CDE .... Cognizant Development Engineer
CDE .... Combat Developments Experimentation Command [*Army*]
CDE .... Comissao Democratica Eleitoral [*Democratic Electoral Committee*] [*Portugal*] [*Political party*] (PPE)
CDE .... Command Decision Echelon (MCD)
CDE .... Command-Destruct Epoxy [*A plastic resin*]
CDE .... Condensate Demineralization Effluent [*Nuclear energy*] (NRCH)
CDE .... Conference on Confidence and Security-Building Measures and Disarmament in Europe
CDE .... Consolidated Sea Gold Corp. [*Vancouver Stock Exchange symbol*]
CDE .... Consumption Data Exchange
CDE .... Contamination-Decontamination Experiment [*Nuclear energy*]
CDE .... Continuing Dental Education
CDE .... Cooperative Defense Efforts (MCD)
CDE .... Cornell Dubilier Electronics (MUGU)
CDE .... Corporate Data Exchange (EA)
CDE .... Croix des Evades [*Belgian military decoration*]
CDE .... Current Design Expendable [*Refers to payload type*] [*NASA*]
CDEA .... Cetyl(dimethyl)ethylammonium Bromide [*A surfactant*]
CDEC .... Chloroallyl Diethyldithiocarbamate [*Herbicide*]
CDEC .... Combat Development Experimentation Center [*Fort Ord, CA*] (MCD)
CDEC .... Combat Developments Evaluation Command (MCD)
CDEC .... Combat Developments Experimentation Command [*Army*] (RDA)
CDEC .... Comprehensive Developmental Evaluation Chart [*Child development test*] [*Psychology*]
CDED .... Cleveland Diesel Engine Division [*GM Corp.*]
CDEE .... Chemical Defence Experimental Establishment [*British*]
CDEF .... Committee on the Development of Engineering Faculties
CDEGA ...... Chiba Daigaku Engeigakubu Gakujutsu Hokoko [*A publication*]
CDEI .... Control Data Education Institutes
CDEK .... Computer Data Entry Keyboard
CDEOS ...... Civil Defense Emergency Operations System
CDEP .... Central Directorate on Environmental Protection [*British*] (DCTA)
CDEP .... Civil Defense Education Program
CDER .... Center for Death Education and Research (EA)
CDES .... Chemical Defence Experimental Station [*British*] [*World War II*]
CDESDK .... Contraceptive Delivery Systems [*A publication*]
CDET .... Council for Dance Education and Training [*British*]
CDET .... Crain's Detroit Business [*A publication*]
CDEV .... Chateau De Ville [*NASDAQ symbol*] (NQ)
cdev .... Control-Device Resource [*Data processing*] (BYTE)
CDEVC ...... Computer Development Center (KSC)
CDEX .... Casual Disability Exclusion [*Insurance*]
CDEX .... Civil Defense Exercise
CDF .... Cable Distribution Frame (NASA)
CDF .... Cahiers de Droit Familial [*A publication*] (ILCA)
CDF .... Canadian Foundation Co. Ltd. [*Toronto Stock Exchange symbol*]
CDF .... Candidate Density Function (MCD)
CDF .... Canine Defense Fund (EA)
CDF .... Capital Development Fund [*United Nations*]
CDF .... Cardiff [*Welsh depot code*]
CDF .... Catholic Development Fund [*Australia*]
CDF .... Central Data Facility [*NASA*] (NASA)
CDF .... Centralni Devisni Fond [*Central Foreign Exchange Fund*]
CDF .... Champ Du Feu [*France*] [*Seismograph station code, US Geological Survey*] (SEIS)
CDF .... Champagne d'Argent Federation (EA)
CDF .... Charities Deposit Fund [*Finance*] [*British*]
CDF .... Chief of Defence Forces [*Australia*]
CDF .... Children's Defense Fund (EA)

CDF .... Chlorinated Dibenzofuran [*Organic chemistry*]
CDF .... Chlorodifluoroethylene [*Organic chemistry*]
CDF .... Chronic Disease Facility [*Medicine*]
CDF .... Circuit Design Fabrication (NASA)
CDF .... Civil Defence Force [*British military*] (DMA)
CD & F ...... Class Determination and Finding
CDF .... Class Determination and Finding
CDF .... Clutter Discriminating Fuze (MCD)
CDF .... Collider Detector at Fermilab [*Particle physics*]
CDF .... Combat Defense Force
CDF .... Combined Distribution Frame [*RADAR*]
CDF .... Combined Distribution Function (MCD)
CDF .... Command Decoder Filter
CDF .... Common Weapon Control System Development Facility (MCD)
CDF .... Communications-Data Field
CDF .... Communications Data Formatter (MCD)
CDF .... Community Development Foundation [*Absorbed by SCF*] (EA)
CDF .... Confined Detonating Fuze
CDF .... Congregation for the Doctrine of the Faith
CDF .... Conservative Democratic Forum (EA)
CDF .... Constant Current Fringes
CDF .... Control Detonating Fuses (KSC)
CDF .... Cool-Down Facility (NASA)
CDF .... Core Damage Frequency [*Nuclear energy*] (NRCH)
CDF .... Council for the Defense of Freedom (EA)
CDF .... Creative Development Fund [*Australia*]
CdF .... Cuadernos de Filologia [*A publication*]
CDF .... Cumulative Damage Function [*Nuclear energy*] (NRCH)
CDF .... Cumulative Distribution Function [*Statistics*]
CDFA .... Citizens for a Debt Free America (EA)
CDFA .... Citizens for a Drug Free America (EA)
CDFA .... Committee to Defend the First Amendment [*Later, FAR*] (EA)
CDFAB ...... California Dried Fig Advisory Board [*Later, CFAB*]
CDFB .... Contractor Design Freeze Baseline (MCD)
CDFC .... Charlie Daniels Fan Club (EA)
CDFC .... Commonwealth Development Finance Company Ltd. [*Joint government and private agency in London established to aid businesses elsewhere in British Commonwealth*]
CDFC .... Count Dracula Fan Club (EA)
CDFCHB .. Command Data Format Control Handbook [*NASA*] (KSC)
CDFCV ...... Charlie Daniels Fan Club Volunteers (EA)
CDFE .... Center for the Defense of Free Enterprise [*Bellevue, WA*] (EA)
CDFEA ...... California Dried Fruit Export Association (EA)
CDFGI ...... Charles Darwin Foundation for the Galapagos Isles (EA)
CDFHR ...... Coalition for Drug-Free Horse Racing (EA)
CDFKAW ... Annual Report. Institute of Food Microbiology. Chiba University [*A publication*]
CDFNT ...... Cold Front [*Meteorology*] (FAAC)
CDFR .... Commercial Demonstration Fast Reactor
CDFS .... Chief of Defense Force Staff (MCD)
CD/FT² ...... Candelas per Square Foot
CDF & TDS ... Circuit Design, Fabrication, and Test Data Systems (NASA)
CDG .... Canandaigua Wine Co., Inc. [*AMEX symbol*] (SPSG)
CDG .... Capacitance Diaphragm Gauge [*Instrumentation*]
CDG .... Capacitor Diode Gate
CDG .... Cardigan [*City and county in Wales*] (ROG)
CDG .... Carters Dam [*Georgia*] [*Seismograph station code, US Geological Survey*] (SEIS)
CDG .... Central Design Group
CDG .... Central Display Generator (MCD)
CDG .... Charles De Gaulle Airport [*France*]
CDG .... Check Digit Verifier
CDG .... Chloro-deoxy-glucose [*Biochemistry*]
CDG .... Circular Diffraction Grating
CDG .... Civil Disturbance Group [*Department of Justice intelligence unit*]
CDG .... Coder-Decoder Group [*Army*] (AABC)
CDG .... Coffee Development Group (EA)
CDG .... Community Design Group [*North Carolina State University*] [*Research center*] (RCD)
CDG .... Compact Disc Group (EA)
CDG .... Computer Directions Group, Inc. [*Information service or system*] (IID)
CDG .... Consumers Distributing Co. Ltd. [*Toronto Stock Exchange symbol*]
CDG .... Converter Display Group
CDG .... Costume Designers Guild (EA)
CDG .... Croix de Guerre [*French military decoration*]
CDG .... Houston, TX [*Location identifier*] [*FAA*] (FAAL)
CDG .... Paris [*France*] Charles De Gaulle Airport [*Airport symbol*] (OAG)
CDGA .... California Date Growers Association [*Defunct*] (EA)
CDGF .... Cartilage-Derived Growth Factor [*Biochemistry*]
CDGI .... Courier Dispatch Group, Incorporated [*Atlanta, GA*] [*NASDAQ symbol*] (NQ)
C Dgst .... Catholic Digest [*A publication*]
CDH .... Cable Distribution Head

CDH .... California State University, Dominguez Hills, Carson, CA [*OCLC symbol*] (OCLC)
CDH .... Camden [*Arkansas*] [*Airport symbol*] (OAG)
CDH .... Canadian Hydrocarbons Ltd. [*Toronto Stock Exchange symbol*] (SPSG)
CDH .... Centralvereinigung Deutscher Handelsvertreter- und Handelsmakler-Verbaende [*Federal Republic of Germany*] (EY)
CDH .... Centre pour les Droits de l'Homme (EAIO)
CDH .... Ceramide Dihexoside [*Biochemistry*]
C & DH...... Command and Data Handling (NASA)
CDH .... Command and Data Handling (DEN)
CDH .... Congenital Diaphragmatic Hernia [*Medicine*]
CDH .... Congenital Dislocation [*or Dysplasia*] of the Hip [*Medicine*]
CDH .... Constant Delta Height [*Aerospace*]
CDH .... Constant Differential Height [*Aerospace*] (MCD)
CDH .... Constricted Double Heterojunction (MCD)
CDHBAF... Contributions. Dudley Herbarium [*A publication*]
CDHC ...... Command and Data-Handling Console (KSC)
CDHP....... Carbamoyldihydropyridine [*Organic chemistry*]
CDHRCA .. Commission for the Defense of Human Rights in Central America (EA)
CDHRM.... Committee for Defense of Human Rights in Morocco (EA)
CDhS .... California State College, Dominguez Hills [*Later, California State University, Dominguez Hills*], Dominguez Hills, CA [*Library symbol*] [*Library of Congress*] (LCLS)
CDHS .... Canberra Historical Journal [*A publication*] (APTA)
CDHS .... CERN [*Conseil European pour la Recherche Nucleaire*]-Dortmund-Heidelberg-Saclay Collaboration
CDHS .... Comprehensive Data Handling System [*Environmental Protection Agency*]
CDHSDZ .. Canadian Data Report of Hydrography and Ocean Sciences [*A publication*]
CDHSDZ .. Rapport Statistique Canadien sur l'Hydrographie et les Sciences Oceaniques [*A publication*]
CDHW....... International Association of Cleaning and Dye House Workers
CDI .... Cambridge, OH [*Location identifier*] [*FAA*] (FAAL)
CDI .... Can Do It [*Temporary-help agency*]
CDI .... Canadian Dollar Investments (Bermuda) Ltd. [*Toronto Stock Exchange symbol*]
CDI .... Capacitor Discharge Ignition [*Automotive technology*]
CDI .... Carbodiimide [*Organic chemistry*]
CDI .... Carbonyldiimidazole [*Organic chemistry*]
CDI .... Cargo Disposition Instructions [*Shipping*]
CDI .... CDI Corp. [*NYSE symbol*] (SPSG)
CDI .... Cellular Directions, Inc. [*Telecommunications service*] (TSSD)
CDI .... Center for Defense Information (EA)
CDI .... Centre pour le Developpement Industriel [*Centre for the Development of Industry*] (EAIO)
CDI .... Chief Draftsman's Instructions (MCD)
CDI .... Children's Depression Inventory [*Personality development test*] [*Psychology*]
CDI .... Children's Diagnostic Inventory
CDI .... Christian Democrat International (EAIO)
CDI .... Church Defence Institution [*British*]
CDI .... Classified Defense Information [*Military*]
CDI .... Clearinghouse on Disability Information (EA)
CDI .... Cobalt Development Institute (EAIO)
CDI .... Collateral Duty Inspector (MCD)
CDI .... Collector Diffusion Isolation [*Electronics*]
CDI .... Command Display Indicator (MCD)
CDI .... Commander's Digest [*A publication*]
CDI .... Commission du Droit International [*United Nations*]
CDI .... Common Defense Installation (AFM)
CD-I.......... Compact Disk - Interactive
CDI .... Comprehensive Dissertation Index [*University Microfilms International*] [*Ann Arbor, MI*] [*Bibliographic database*] [*A publication*]
CDI .... Compudata, Incorporated [*Information service or system*] (IID)
CDI .... Computer-Developed Instruction
CDI .... Computer Devices, Incorporated
CDI .... Computer Direct Input [*Data processing*] (DCTA)
CDI .... Computer-Directed Instrument
CD-I.......... Computer Disk-Interactive
CDI .... Concept Development Investigation
CDI .... Consumer Demographics, Incorporated [*Information service or system*] (IID)
CDI .... Continuing Disability Investigation [*Social Security Administration*] (OICC)
CDI .... Continuous Deionization
CDI .... Contractor's Demonstration Inspection
CDI .... Control Data Institute
CDI .... Control Direction Indicator (MCD)
CDI .... Control Director Intercept (CINC)
CDI .... Controlled Direct Injection [*Automotive engineering*]
CDI .... Conventional Defense Initiative [*Military*] (SDI)
CDI .... Corollary Discharge Interneuron [*Neurology*]
CDI .... Course Deviation Indicator [*Aviation*]
CDI .... Cutting Die Institute (EA)

CDi............. Dixon Unified School District Library, Dixon, CA [*Library symbol*] [*Library of Congress*] (LCLS)
Cdia........... Concordia [*Record label*]
CDIAC....... Carbon Dioxide Information and Analysis Center [*Department of Energy*] [*Information service or system*] (IID)
CDIC......... Canada Deposit Insurance Corporation
CDIC......... Canada Development Investment Corporation [*Corporation de Developpement des Investissements du Canada*]
CDIC......... Carbon Dioxide Information Center [*Department of Energy*] [*Oak Ridge, TN*] [*Database*]
CDIC......... Cardinal Distribution, Inc. [*Dublin, OH*] [*NASDAQ symbol*] (NQ)
CDIC......... Combat Damage Information Center [*Military*]
CDIC......... Combat Data Information Center [*Army*]
CDIDC....... Committee on Data Interchange and Data Centers (MSC)
CDIF......... Component Development and Integration Facility [*Department of Energy*] [*Butte, MT*]
CDIF......... Consumer Drug Information [*American Society of Hospital Pharmacists*] [*Database*] [*Information service or system*] (IID)
CDIF......... Controller/Director Information File (AFM)
CDII.......... Concept Development, Incorporated [*NASDAQ symbol*] (NQ)
CdIL.......... Cahiers. Institut de Linguistique de Louvain [*A publication*]
CDIL......... Command Database Interface Language (MCD)
CDIN......... Coradian Corp. [*Latham, NY*] [*NASDAQ symbol*] (NQ)
CDIP......... Combined Defense Improvement Projects
CDIP......... Consolidated Defense Intelligence Program
CDIP......... Continuously Displayed Impact Point (MCD)
CDipAF..... Certified Diploma in Accounting and Finance [*British*] (DBQ)
CDIR......... Chemical Demilitarization and Installation Restoration (MCD)
CDIS......... Commodities Data Information Service [*MJK Associates*] [*Santa Clara, CA*] [*Information service or system*] (IID)
CDIS......... Curriculum Development Institute of Singapore (DS)
CDITQ....... Computer Devices, Incorporated [*Nutting Lake, MA*] [*NASDAQ symbol*] (NQ)
CDIU......... Central Import and Export Agency [*Netherlands*] (IMH)
CDIUPA.... Centre de Documentation Internationale des Industries Utilisatrices de Produits Agricoles [*International Documentation Center for Industries Using Agricultural Products*] [*Database producer*] [*Information service or system*] (IID)
CDIV .... Cum Dividendo [*With Dividend*] [*Stock exchange term*] (ADA)
CDJ........... Cash Disbursements Journal [*Accounting*]
CDJ........... Choledochoduodenal Junction [*Anatomy*]
CDJ........... Conceicao Do Araguaia [*Brazil*] [*Airport symbol*] (OAG)
CDJ........... Continental Datanet, Inc. [*Vancouver Stock Exchange symbol*]
CDJI.......... Dow Jones Index - Commodity [*Stock market*]
CDJM........ Canadian Journal of Mathematics [*A publication*]
CDK........... Cedar Key, FL [*Location identifier*] [*FAA*] (FAAL)
CDK........... Channel Data Check
CDK........... Communication Desk (BUR)
CDK........... Council for Democracy in Korea (EA)
CDKKA ..... Chiba Daigaku Kogakubu Kenkyu Hokoku [*A publication*]
CDL........... Cable Delay Line
CdL............ Cahiers de Lexicologie [*A publication*]
CDL........... Canadian Labour [*A publication*]
CDL........... Canal Defense Light
CDL........... Candle, AK [*Location identifier*] [*FAA*] (FAAL)
CDL........... Capacitor-Diode Logic (MSA)
CDL........... Carbon Dioxide LASER
CDL........... Cardinal
CDL........... Central Dental Laboratories [*Army*]
CDL........... Central Dockyard Laboratory [*British*]
CDL........... Ceramic Delay Line
CDL........... Chancellor of the Duchy of Lancaster [*British*]
CDL........... Citadel Holding Corp. [*AMEX symbol*] (SPSG)
CDL........... Citizens for Decency through Law [*Later, CLF*] (EA)
CDL........... Citizens for Decent Literature [*Later, Citizens for Decency through Law*] (EA)
CDL........... Civil Defence Legion [*British military*] (DMA)
CDL........... Clock Delay
CDL........... Coaxial Diode Limiter
CDL........... Common Bile Duct Ligation [*Medicine*]
CDL........... Common Display Logic [*Data processing*]
CDL........... Computer Description Language (BUR)
CDL........... Computer Design Language (CSR)
CDL........... Computer Development Laboratory [*Fujitsu Ltd., Hitachi Ltd., and Mitsubishi Corp.*] [*Japan*]
CDL........... Condor Data Link
CDL........... Configuration Deviation List (MCD)
CDL........... Constant Delay Line
CDL........... Contract Data List
CDL........... Contract Deficiency Listing (AFM)
CDL........... Corby Distilleries Ltd. [*Toronto Stock Exchange symbol*] [*Vancouver Stock Exchange symbol*]
CDL........... Core Diode Logic
CDL........... Cronar Dot Litho [*Du Pont*]
CDL........... Le Commerce du Levant [*Beirut*] [*A publication*]
CDL........... National Board for Certification of Dental Laboratories (EA)

CDL .... San Diego County Law Library, San Diego, CA [*OCLC symbol*] (OCLC)
CDLA .... Casa de las Americas [*A publication*]
CDLA .... Computer Dealers and Lessors Association (EA)
CDLB .... Carbon Dioxide LASER Beam (MCD)
CDLC .... Capital District Library Council for Reference and Research Resources [*Latham, NY*] [*Library network*]
CDLDM .... Comite de Defense des Libertes Democratiques au Mali [*Committee for the Defense of Democratic Liberties in Mali*] (PD)
CDLRD ...... Confirming Design Layout Report Date [*Bell System*] (TEL)
CDLS .... Commercial Driver's License Information System
CDLS .... Condor Data Link System
CdLS .... Cornelia De Lange Syndrome [*Medicine*]
CDLS .... Cost Document Library System [*Air Force*] (AFIT)
CdLSF ...... Cornelia De Lange Syndrome Foundation (EA)
CDLS(W) .. Canadian Defence Liaison Staff (Washington) (AFM)
CDM .... Cadeguomycin Deazaguanosine [*Antineoplastic drug*]
CDM .... [*Harrington-O'Shea*] Career Decision-Making System [*Vocational guidance test*]
CDM .... Cash Dispensing Machine [*Banking*]
CDM .... Center for Dance Medicine (EA)
CDM .... Central Data Management (NRCH)
CDM .... Centre de Documentation de la Mecanique [*Documentation Center for Mechanics*] [*Technical Center for Mechanical Industries*] [*Information service or system*] (IID)
CDM .... Centro Democratico de Macau [*Macao Democratic Center*] (PPW)
CDM .... Certified Decal Manufacturers (EA)
CdM .... Chant du Monde [*Record label*] [*France*]
CDM .... Chemically Defined Medium [*Microbiology*]
CDM .... Chief Decision Makers
CDM .... Chlordimeform [*Expectorant*]
CdM .... Chrysler de Mexico SA [*Chrysler Corp.*]
CDM .... Civil Defense Management
CDM .... Coalition for a Democratic Majority (EA)
CDM .... Coded Division Multiplex
CDM .... Cold Dark Matter [*Astronomy*]
CDM .... Color Difference Meter
CDM .... Communications/Data Manager (MCD)
CDM .... Companded Delta Modulation [*Telecommunications*] (TEL)
CDM .... Computer-Assisted Decision Making System
CDM .... Concept Demonstration Model
CDM .... Condemn (MSA)
CDM .... Consumer Distribution Marketing
CDM .... Contractor Developed Material
C to D of M ... Contributing to Delinquency of Minor [*FBI standardized term*]
CDM .... Curriculum Development Manager (MCD)
CDMA .... Cadema Corp. [*NASDAQ symbol*] (NQ)
CDMA ...... Canadian Direct Mail Association
CDMA ...... Canadian Direct Marketing Association
CDMA ...... Cartridge Direct Memory Access
CDMA ...... Catholic Dutch Migrant Association [*Australia*]
CDMA ...... Code Division Multiple Access
CDMBA .... California. Division of Mines and Geology. Bulletin [*A publication*]
CDMC .... Crop Dryer Manufacturers Council (EA)
CD & ME... Combat Developments and Material Evaluation [*Program*] [*Army*]
CDME .... Compagnie de Distribution de Materiel Electrique [*France*] (ECON)
CDMI .... Canadian Dun's Market Identifiers [*Dun & Bradstreet Canada Ltd.*] [*Information service or system*] (CRD)
CDMI Bul ... Centre de Documentation de Musique Internationale. Bulletin [*A publication*]
CDML ...... Crash Damage Material List (MCD)
CDMMA ... Canadian Direct Mail/Marketing Association
CDMO .... Contract Data Management Officer (MCD)
CDMP ...... Certified Direct Marketing Practitioner [*Designation awarded by Direct Marketing Association Insurance Council*]
CDMP ...... Contractor Data Management Program [*Air Force*] (AFIT)
CDMR .... Command Data Management Routine [*Data processing*]
CDMR ...... Cyclic Data Management Routine [*Data processing*]
C & DM RGA ... Cornwall and Devon Miners Royal Garrison Artillery [*British military*] (DMA)
CDMS .... Cadmus Communications Corp. [*Richmond, VA*] [*NASDAQ symbol*] (NQ)
CDMS ...... Coherent Doppler Measurement System
CDMS ...... Command Data Management System (NASA)
CDMS ...... COMRADE [*Computer-Aided Design Environment*] Data Management System
CDMS ...... Contracting Data Management System [*Military*] (MCD)
CDMS ...... Crystal Document Management System [*Printer technology*]
CDMS ...... Current Depth Measurement Subsystem [*National Ocean Survey*] (MSC)
CDMSCS .. Committee for the Development and Management of Fisheries in the South China Sea (EAIO)
CDMUAT ... Contributions. Dudley Museum [*A publication*]
CDN .... Cadence Design Systems [*NYSE symbol*] (SPSG)

CDN .... California Data Network [*Claremont McKenna College, Rose Institue of State and Local Government*] [*Information service or system*] (IID)
CDN .... Camden, SC [*Location identifier*] [*FAA*] (FAAL)
CDN .... Canadian (NATG)
CDN .... Carena-Bancorp, Inc. [*Toronto Stock Exchange symbol*]
CDN .... CDR Discrepancy Notice [*NASA*] (MCD)
CDN .... Cerro Del Durzno [*New Mexico*] [*Seismograph station code, US Geological Survey*] (SEIS)
CDN .... Chicago Daily News [*A publication*]
CDN .... Coded Decimal Notation
CDN .... Consumer Discount Network
CDN .... Convergent-Divergent Nozzle
CDN .... Coordination Message [*Aviation code*]
CDN .... To Be Continued [*Polish underground publishing house begun by author Czeslaw Bielecki*] [*Acronym represents Polish phrase*]
CDNA .... Canadian Daily Newspapers Association
cDNA .... Deoxyribonucleic Acid, Cloned [*Biochemistry, genetics*]
cDNA .... Deoxyribonucleic Acid, Complementary [*Biochemistry, genetics*]
Cdn Aviat ... Canadian Aviation [*A publication*]
Cdn Bnk Rv ... Canadian Banker and ICB [*Institute of Canadian Bankers*] Review [*Later, Canadian Banker*] [*A publication*]
CDNC .... Communications Data Network Controller (MCD)
CD/NC ...... Computer-Aided Design/Numerical Control (AABC)
Cdn Chem N ... Canadian Chemical News [*A publication*]
Cdn Chem P ... Canadian Chemical Processing [*A publication*]
Cdn Contrl ... Canadian Controls and Instrumentation [*A publication*]
Cdn Data .... Canadian Datasystems [*A publication*]
Cdn Elec E ... Canadian Electronics Engineering [*A publication*]
Cdn Elec P ... Electronics Product News. Supplement to Canadian Electronics Engineering [*A publication*]
CDNET ...... Consortium Data Network [*University of Michigan*] [*Ann Arbor*] [*Information service or system*] (IID)
Cdn Forest ... Canadian Forest Industries [*A publication*]
CDNI .... Cardinal Industries, Inc. [*NASDAQ symbol*] (NQ)
CDNI .... Committee for the Defense National Interest (CINC)
Cdn J ECE ... Canadian Journal of Early Childhood Education [*A publication*]
CDNL .... Conference of Directors of National Libraries [*Australia*]
Cdn Mach D ... Canadian Machinery and Metalworking Directory and Buying Guide [*A publication*]
Cdn Machin ... Canadian Machinery and Metalworking [*A publication*]
Cdn Mine H ... Canadian Mines Handbook [*A publication*]
CDNOPT .. Canadian Stock Options [*Toronto Stock Exchange*] [*Canada*] [*Information service or system*] (CRD)
CDNP .... Chicago Daily News. Panorama [*A publication*]
CDNPA ..... Canadian Daily Newspaper Publishers Association
Cdn Pkg ..... Canadian Packaging [*A publication*]
Cdn Pkg Mk ... Statistical Report on Canada's Packaging Market [*A publication*]
Cdn P & L .. Future Population and Labour Force of Canada. Projections to the Year 2051 [*A publication*]
Cdn Plast ... Canadian Plastics [*A publication*]
Cdn Plast D ... Canadian Plastics Directory and Buyer's Guide [*A publication*]
Cdn P & P .. Canadian Pulp and Paper Industry [*A publication*]
CDNR .... CDR Discrepancy Notice Record
CDNS .... Climatological Data, National Summary (NOAA)
CD (NS)..... Ohio Circuit Court Decisions, New Series [*A publication*] (DLA)
CDO .... Canada Orient Resources [*Vancouver Stock Exchange symbol*]
CDO .... Change Design Order [*Navy*] (NG)
CDO .... Civil Defense Organization [*United Nations*]
CDO .... Combat Development Office
CDO .... Comdisco, Inc. [*NYSE symbol*] (SPSG)
CDO .... Command Duty Officer [*Navy*]
CDO .... Commando (NATG)
CDO .... Communications Duty Officer (FAAC)
CDO .... Community Dial Office [*Small switching system*] [*Telecommunications*]
CDo .... Downey City Library, Downey, CA [*Library symbol*] [*Library of Congress*] (LCLS)
CDOA .... Car Department Officers Association (EA)
CDOA .... Christian Democratic Organisation of America (EAIO)
C Docum Ch Com Marseille ... Cahiers de Documentation de la Chambre de Commerce et d'Industrie de Marseille [*A publication*]
CDOEAP... Community Dentistry and Oral Epidemiology [*A publication*]
CdoFcsRM ... Commando Forces, Royal Marines [*British*]
CDOG........ Combat Development Objective Guide [*CDC*]
CDOH .... Coupling Display Optical Hand Controller (KSC)
CDOIPS .... Central Dispatching Organization of the Interconnected Power Systems (EAIO)
CdoLogRegtRM ... Commando Logistics Regiment, Royal Marines [*British*]
CDoN......... North American Rockwell Corp., Downey, CA [*Library symbol*] [*Library of Congress*] (LCLS)
CDOOC..... Curved Dash Olds Owners Club (EA)
CDOS .... Combat Days of Supply (MCD)
CDOS .... Controlled Date of Separation [*Military*] (AFM)
C Douanes ... Code des Douanes [*Customs Excise Code*] [*A publication*] (ILCA)

CDOVHL.. Crash Damage Overhaul   (MCD)
CDP .... Canada Permanent Mortgage Corp. [*Toronto Stock Exchange symbol*]
CDP .... Canadian Pacer Petroleum [*Vancouver Stock Exchange symbol*]
CDP .... Career Development Program   (OICC)
CDP .... Cask Decontamination Pit [*Nuclear energy*]   (NRCH)
CDP .... Center for Democratic Policy   (EA)
CDP .... Center for Design Planning   (EA)
CDP .... Center for Development Policy [*Later, ICDP*]   (EA)
CDP .... Central Distribution Panel
CDP .... Centralized Data Processing   (IEEE)
CDP .... Centre pour Democratie et Progres [*Center for Democracy and Progress*] [*Later, Center of Social Democrats*] [*France*] [*Political party*]   (PPE)
CDP .... Cerro De Punta [*Puerto Rico*] [*Seismograph station code, US Geological Survey*]   (SEIS)
CDP .... Certificate in Data Processing [*Designation awarded by Institute for Certification of Computer Professionals*]
CDP .... Checkout Data Processor [*RADAR*]
CDP .... Chemical Defense Program   (MCD)
CDP .... Chief of Defence Procurement [*British*]   (RDA)
CDP .... Child Development Programme [*British*]
CDP .... Christian Democrat Party [*Australia*] [*Political party*]
CDP .... Christian Democratic Party [*Italy*]
CDP .... Chromosome Distribution Pattern [*Genetics*]
CDP .... Coded Description Pattern   (AFIT)
CDP .... Collagenase-Digestible Protein
CDP .... Collett Dickenson Pearce [*British advertising agency*]
CDP .... Color Diaposition Plate
CDP .... Combat Developer Proponent   (MCD)
CDP .... Combat Development Phase   (MCD)
CDP .... Combat Development Plan   (MCD)
CDP .... Combat Development Process   (MCD)
CDP .... Combat Development Project [*Army*]
CDP .... Command Data Processor
CDP .... Committee of Directors of Polytechnics [*British*]
CDP .... Common Depth Point [*Seismology*]
CDP .... Communications Data Processor [*Electronics*]
CDP .... Company Distributing Point [*Army*]
CDP .... Competitive Development Phase
CDP .... Compound Diffraction Projector
CDP .... Compound Document Processor [*Data processing*]
CDP .... Comprehensive Drinker Profile [*Test*] [*Psychology*]
CDP .... Comprehensive Dwelling Policies [*Insurance*]
CDP .... Compressor Discharge Pressure
C-DP .... Comptroller-Director of Programs [*Army*]
CDP .... Concept Definition Proposal   (MCD)
CDP .... Concept Development Phase   (MCD)
CDP .... Concept Development Plan
CDP .... Concept Development Process   (MCD)
CDP .... Confidence Development Plan
CDP .... Constant Deviation Prism
CDP .... Contract Definition Phase [*DoD*]
CDP .... Contract Design Package   (MCD)
CDP .... Control Data Panel
CDP .... Control Diastolic Pressure [*Cardiology*]
CDP .... Control and Display Panel   (MCD)
CDP .... Cornu Double Prism
CDP .... Coronary Drug Project
CDP .... Correlated Data Processor
CDP .... Cost Data Plan
CDP .... Cresyl Diphenylphosphate
CDP .... Critical Decision Point
CDP .... Cross Deck Pendant   (MCD)
CDP .... Cross-Linked Dextran Polymer [*Organic chemistry*]
CDP .... Cumulative Detection Probability   (CAAL)
CDP .... Cybernetic Data Products Corporation [*Telecommunications service*]   (TSSD)
CDP .... Cytidine Diphosphate [*Biochemistry*]
CDP .... Cytosine Diphosphate [*Biochemistry*]
C3DP .... Complement 3 Degradation Product [*Immunology*]
CDPA .... Certified Data Processing Auditor [*Designation awarded by EDP Auditors Foundation*]
CDPA .... Coarse Diffraction Pattern Analysis   (MCD)
CDPA .... Command and Data Processing Area   (MCD)
CDPAbe.... Cytidine Diphosphoabequose [*Biochemistry*]
CDPAC...... Conservative Democratic Political Action Committee   (EA)
CDPC........ Central Data Processing Center
CDPC........ Central Data Processing Computer
CDPC........ Comite de Defense du Peuple Canadien (Citoyens et Residents) [*Canadian People's (Citizens and Residents) Defence Committee*]
CDPC........ Commercial Data Processing Center   (IEEE)
CDPC........ Computation and Data Processing Center   (DIT)
CDPF........ Central Data Processing Facility [*NASA*]
CDPF........ Composed Document Printing Facility [*IBM Corp.*]
CDPG .... Center for Demographic and Population Genetics [*University of Texas*] [*Research center*]   (RCD)
CDPG .... Combat Developments Planning Group   (MCD)
CDPI........ Command, Data Processing, and Instrumentation [*NASA*]
CDPIE .... Command Data Processing Interface Equipment

CDPIR....... Crash Data Position Indication Recorder   (MCD)
CDPIS .... Command, Data Processing, and Instrumentation System [*NASA*]   (NASA)
CDPL........ Cadmium Plate [*Technical drawings*]
CDPL........ Command Designated Position List   (MCD)
CDPLP ...... Committee in Defense of the Palestinian and Lebanese Peoples   (EA)
CDPO .... Director for Civil Disturbance Planning and Operations
CDPOC .... Committee for the Defense of Persecuted Orthodox Christians   (EA)
CDPPP ...... Center for Development Planning, Projections, and Policies [*United Nations*]
CDP Press Inf ... Committee of Directors of Polytechnics Press. Information [*A publication*]
CDPPV ...... Committee for the Defense of Political Prisoners in Vietnam   (EA)
CDPR........ Cathedral Priory
CDPR........ Customer Dial Pulse Receiver [*Telecommunications*]   (TEL)
CDPRD..... Cancer Detection and Prevention [*A publication*]
CDPRD4.... Cancer Detection and Prevention [*A publication*]
CD-PROM ... Compact Disk Programmable Read-Only Memory [*Data processing*]
CDPS........ Communications Data Processing System   (NVT)
CDPS........ Consolidated Decision Package Set [*Military*]
CDPV .... Council of Disabled Persons - Victoria [*Australia*]
CDPX........ Combined Displaced Persons Executive [*World War II*]
CDQ.......... Croydon [*Australia*] [*Airport symbol*] [*Obsolete*]   (OAG)
CDQD........ Collision-Dominated Quiescent Discharge
CDQR........ Critical Design and Qualification Review   (NASA)
CDR .... Cabin Discrepancy Report [*Report for airline log*]
CDR .... Cadarache [*France*] [*Seismograph station code, US Geological Survey*]   (SEIS)
CDR .... Calcium-Ion Dependent Regulator [*Biochemistry*]
CDR .... Call Detail Recording [*Telecommunications*]   (TEL)
CDR .... Call-Detail Routing [*Telecommunications*]   (TSSD)
CDR .... Carbon Dioxide Reduction [*Factor for metabolism*]
CDR .... Card Reader [*Data processing*]
CDR .... Career Development Review   (MCD)
CDR .... Cargo Delivery Receipt [*Shipping*]
CDR .... Cargo Drop Reel   (NVT)
CdR .... Cassa di Risparmio [*Savings Bank*] [*Italian*]
CDR .... CDR Resources [*Vancouver Stock Exchange symbol*]
CDR .... Center for Democratic Renewal   (EA)
CDR .... Center for Documentation on Refugees [*United Nations High Commission for Refugees*] [*Switzerland*] [*Information service or system*]   (IID)
CDR .... Central Data Recording
CDR .... Centre for Documentation on Refugees [*UNHCR*] [*Information service or system*]   (IID)
CDR .... Chadron [*Nebraska*] [*Airport symbol*]   (OAG)
CDR .... Civil Defense Receiver
CDR .... Cleaning, Decontamination Request   (MCD)
CDR .... Comitato per la Difesa della Repubblica [*Committee for the Defense of the Republic*] [*San Marino*] [*Political party*]   (PPW)
CDR .... Command Destruct Receiver   (AFM)
CDR .... Command Distribution Rack
CDR .... Commander
CDR .... Commission des Reparations [*Reparation Commission*] [*France*]
CDR .... Communicable Disease Report [*A publication*]
CDR .... Communications Desk Reference [*A publication*]   (TSSD)
CDR .... Communications and Distributed Resources Report [*International Data Corp.*] [*Defunct*] [*Information service or system*]   (CRD)
CDr .... Comparative Drama [*A publication*]
CDR .... Complementarity-Determining Region [*Immunology*]
CDR .... Complementarity-Determining Residue [*Genetics*]
CDR .... Complete Design Release [*Navy*]   (NG)
CDR .... Composite Damage Risk
CDR .... Conceptual Design Requirement   (NRCH)
CDR .... Conductor   (ADA)
CDR .... Conseil Democratique Revolutionnaire [*Democratic Revolutionary Council*] [*Chad*]   (PD)
CDR .... Constant Dose Range [*Radiation in atmosphere*]
CDR .... Construction Discrepancy Report
CDR .... Contract Data Requirement   (MCD)
CDR .... Controlled Dynamic Range
CDR .... Council on Documentation Research [*Defunct*]
CDR .... Countdown Deviation Request [*Aerospace*]   (AAG)
CDR .... Crankcase Depression Regulator [*AC Spark Plug Co.*] [*Automotive engineering*]
CDR .... Crash Damage Rate   (MCD)
CDR .... Critical Design Review   (AFM)
CDR .... Crude Death Rate [*Medicine*]
CDR .... Crystal Diffusion Reflection
CDR .... Cumulative Data Report   (MCD)
CDR .... Current Design Reusable [*Refers to payload type*] [*NASA*]
CDR .... Current Directional Relay
CDRA .... Civil Defense Research Associates

CDRA .... Committee of Directors of Research Associations and Federation of Technology Centres [*British*]
CDRA .... Corps of Drivers Royal Artillery [*British military*] (DMA)
CDRB .... Canadian Defence Research Board
CDRC .... Critical Design Review Commercial (MCD)
CDRD .... Carbon Dioxide Research Division [*Oak Ridge National Laboratory*]
Cdr(D) ...... Commander, Destroyer Flotilla
CDRD .... Computations and Data Reduction Division [*NASA*] (KSC)
CD/RDMS ... Controlled Depth/Rapid Deployment Moored Sweep [*Navy*] (CAAL)
CDRE .... Chemical Defence Research Establishment [*British*]
Cdr(E) ...... Commander, Engineering [*Australia*]
CDRE .... Commodore
C Dr Entreprise ... Cahiers de Droit de l'Entreprise [*A publication*]
CDREOR ... Canada. Defence Research Establishment. Ottawa. Reports [*A publication*]
C Dr Europ ... Cahiers de Droit Europeen [*A publication*]
CDRG .... Cedar Group, Inc. [*NASDAQ symbol*] (NQ)
CDRI .... Chihuahuan Desert Research Institute (EA)
CDRI .... Contemporary Deep Rack Interior (MCD)
CDRILL .... Counterdrill
CDRILLO ... Counterdrill Other Side
CDRL .... Canberra District Rugby League [*Australia*]
CDRL .... Cedrol
CDRL .... Contract [*or Contractor*] Data Requirements List
CDRL .... Customer Data Requirements List (MCD)
CDRM .... Chatham Division Royal Marines [*Military unit*] [*British*]
CdRMG ..... Commissioned Royal Marine Gunner [*British*]
CDRO .... Concentration - Dependent Regulation of Oxygen
CD-ROM ... Compact Disk Read-Only Memory [*Data processing*]
CDRR .... Committee to Defend Reproductive Rights (EA)
CDRR .... Contract Documentation Requirements Records [*NASA*] (NASA)
CDRS .... Charles Darwin Research Station [*Santa Cruz, Galapagos Islands*]
CDRS .... Children's Depression Rating Scale
CDRS .... Computer Data Recording System (KSC)
CDRS .... Container Design Retrieval System (MCD)
CDRS .... Control and Data Retrieval System [*Formerly, DCDRS*] [*Air Force*] (MCD)
CDR/SMDR ... Call-Detail-Recording/Station-Message-Detail-Recording [*Telecommunications*]
CDRT .... Committee on Diagnostic Reading Tests (EA)
CD-RTOS ... Compact Disk Real-Time Operating System
CDRU .... Child Development Research Unit [*Nigeria*]
CDRX .... Critical Damping Resistance External
CDS .... Campaign for Democratic Socialism [*British*]
CDS .... Canadian Depository for Securities
CDS .... Capability Design Specifications (AABC)
CDS .... Card Distribution Service [*Library of Congress*]
CDS .... Cardis Corp. [*AMEX symbol*] (SPSG)
CDS .... Cargo Delivery System [*Shipping*]
CDS .... Carl Duisberg Society [*Later, CDSI*] (EA)
CDS .... Cash on Delivery Service
CDS .... Cask Decontamination Station [*Nuclear energy*] (NRCH)
CDS .... Cataloging Distribution Service [*Library of Congress*] [*Washington, DC*]
CDS .... Cathode Dark Space
CDS .... Center for Demographic Studies [*Census*] (OICC)
CDS .... Center for Dispute Settlement (EA)
CDS .... Central Data Station
CDS .... Central Data System [*or Subsystem*] (MCD)
CDS .... Central Defence Staff [*British*]
CDS .... Central Distribution System [*Publications*] [*Navy*]
CDS .... Centre des Democrates Sociaux [*Center of Social Democrats*] [*France*] [*Political party*] (PPW)
CDS .... Centre de Documentation pour le Sport [*Sport Information Resource Centre*] [*Coaching Association of Canada*]
CDS .... Centre de Donnees Stellaires [*Stellar Data Center*] [*France*] [*Information service or system*] (IID)
CDS .... Centro Democratico y Social [*Democratic and Social Center*] [*Spain*] [*Political party*] (PPE)
CDS .... Certificate of Deposit [*Banking*]
CDS .... Certified Documentary Specialist [*Designation awarded by American Society of International Executives, Inc.*]
CDS .... Chaff Dispensing System [*or Subsystem*] (MCD)
CDS .... Chamber of Destination of Ships
CdS .... Character Disorder Sign [*Psychology*]
CDS .... Charged Droplet Scrubber
CDS .... Chemical Data System
CDS .... Chemical Discriminator System
CDS .... Chief of Defence Staff [*British*] (NATG)
CDS .... Children's Depression Scale
CDS .... Childress, TX [*Location identifier*] [*FAA*] (FAAL)
CDS .... China Defense Supplies, Inc.
CDS .... Chip Detector Sensor (MCD)
CDS .... Christian Dental Society (EA)
CDS .... Christian Doctors Sodality (EA)
CDS .... Cinema Digital Sound
CDS .... Circadian Data System (MCD)

CDS .... Circuit Data Sheet
CDS .... Circuit Design System (MCD)
CDS .... Circular Date Stamp [*Postmark of a stamp cancellation*]
CDS .... Civil Direction of Shipping (NVT)
CDS .... Cleaning and De-Icing System (MCD)
CDS .... Climatological Data Sheet [*Air Force*]
CDS(D) ...... Clonidine Displacing Substance [*Biochemistry*]
CDS .... Closeout Door System (MCD)
CDS .... Cold-Drawn Steel
CDS .... Collision Detector System (NASA)
CDS .... Color Data System
CDS .... Color Difference Signal
CDS .... Combat Direction Systems (NVT)
C & DS ...... Command and Data Simulator (NASA)
CDS .... Command and Decision System (MCD)
CDS .... Command Destruct System (MCD)
CDS .... Command Disable System [*Air Force*]
CDS .... Commander, Destroyer Squadron
CDS .... Common Doppler System (MCD)
CDS .... Communication Disorders Specialist
CDS .... Communications and Data Subsystems
CDS .... Community Development Society (EA)
CDS .... Community Dispute Services (EA)
CDS .... Compact Sounder
CDS .... Companion of the Distinguished Service Order [*British*]
CDS .... Compatible Duplex System
CDS .... Compliance Data System [*Environmental Protection Agency*] (MCD)
CDS .... Component Disassembly Station [*Nuclear energy*] (NRCH)
CDS .... Comprehensive Data Systems (OICC)
CDS .... Comprehensive Display System
CDS .... Compressed Data Storage
CDS .... Computer Data Switchboard
CDS .... Computer Data System
CDS .... Computer Duplex System (BUR)
CDS .... Computerized Dispersive Spectroscopy
CDS .... Computerized Documentation System [*UNESCO*] (IID)
CDS .... Conceptual Design Study
CDS .... Condensate Demineralization Subsystem [*Nuclear energy*] (NRCH)
CDS .... Conference of Drama Schools [*British*]
CDS .... Configuration Development System (MCD)
CDS .... Congregation of the Divine Spirit [*Roman Catholic women's religious order*]
CDS .... Congressional Data Sheet (MCD)
CDS .... Congressional Descriptive Summaries (RDA)
CDS .... Conselho de Desenvolvimento Social [*Government advisory body*] [*Brazil*] (EY)
CDS .... Consolidated Silver Standard Mines Ltd. [*Vancouver Stock Exchange symbol*]
CDS .... Construction-Differential Subsidy [*Authorized by Merchant Marine Act of 1936*]
CDS .... Construction Dollar Spreading [*System*] [*AT & T*]
CDS .... Container Delivery System [*Military*]
CDS .... Container Distribution System (MCD)
CDS .... Continuous Dynamical System
CDS .... Contractor Developed Specifications (MCD)
CDS .... Control Data System (NASA)
CDS .... Control of Destination of Ships
CDS .... Control and Display Subsystem (MCD)
CDS .... Control Distribution System
CDS .... Controlled Delivery System
C & DS ...... Controls and Displays System [*or Subsystem*] [*Aerospace*]
CDS .... Cooperative Development Services [*British*]
CDS .... Cord-Air [*Pavilion, NY*] [*FAA designator*] (FAAC)
CdS .... Corriere della Sera [*A publication*]
CDS .... Cost Data Sheet (MCD)
CDS .... Count Dracula Society (EA)
CDS .... Countermeasures Dispenser Set (MCD)
CDS .... Country Dance and Song [*A publication*]
CDS .... Crystal Diffraction Spectrometer (MCD)
CDS .... CUNY [*City University of New York*] Data Service [*Information service or system*] (IID)
CDs .... Deep Springs College, Deep Springs, CA [*Library symbol*] [*Library of Congress*] (LCLS)
CDS .... Partido do Centro Democratico Social [*Party of the Social Democratic Center*] [*Portugal*] [*Political party*] (PPE)
CDS .... San Diego State College, San Diego, CA [*OCLC symbol*] (OCLC)
CDSA .... Canadian Driver and Safety Educators Association
CDSA .... Center for Data Systems and Analysis [*Montana State University*] [*Research center*] (RCD)
CDSA .... Circuit Distribution Assembly [*Ground Communications Facility, NASA*]
CDSA .... Country Dance Society of America [*Later, CDSSA*] (EA)
CDSAC ...... Chief Defence Scientist's Advisory Committee [*Australia*]
CDSB .... Cargo Data Standards Board [*IATA*] (DS)
CdSB .... Commissioned Signals Boatswain [*British*]
CD & SC .... Central Data and Switching Center [*NASA*] (KSC)
CDSC .... Coastal District Surveillance Center [*Military*]
CDSC .... Communicable Disease Surveillance Centre [*British*]

CDSC......... Communications, Distribution, and Switching Center [*NASA*] (KSC)
CD & SC .... Communications, Distribution, and Switching Center [*NASA*] (KSC)
CDSD .... Civil Defense Support Detachments (AABC)
CDSE......... Computer-Driven Simulation Environment [*FAA*]
CDSEA...... Chuo Daigaku Rikogakubu Kiyo [*A publication*]
CDSF .... Commercially Developed Space Facility [*Proposed*]
CDSF......... COMRADE [*Computer-Aided Design Environment*] Data Storage Facility
CDSG .... Cook Data Services [*NASDAQ symbol*] (NQ)
CDSH .... Centre de Documentation Sciences Humaines [*Documentation Center for Human Sciences*] [*France*] [*Information service or system*] (IID)
CDSHA ..... Country Day School Headmasters Association of the US (EA)
CDSI .... CDS [*Carl Duisberg Society*] International (EA)
CDSI.......... Computer Data Systems, Incorporated [*Information service or system*] (IID)
CDSI.......... Computer Designed Systems, Incorporated [*Minneapolis, MN*] [*NASDAQ symbol*] (NQ)
CDSI.......... Contemporary Digital Services, Incorporated [*New Rochelle, NY*] [*Telecommunications*] (TSSD)
CDSIDS .... Command and Decision Sensor Interface Data System (MCD)
CDS/ISIS ... Computerized Documentation Service/Integrated Set of Information Systems [*UNESCO*] (IID)
CDSKAT ... Annual Report. Research Institute for Chemobiodynamics. Chiba University [*A publication*]
CDSM .... Consolidated Defense Supply Material
CdSO .... Commissioned Supply Officer [*British*]
CDSO .... Commonwealth Defence Science Organisation [*British*]
CDSO .... Companion of the Distinguished Service Order [*British*]
CDSORG.... Civil Direction of Shipping Organization (MCD)
CDSP .... Current Digest of the Soviet Press [*A publication*]
CDSPP ...... Committee for Defense of Soviet Political Prisoners (EA)
CD/SR .... Candela per Steradian
CDSR .... Consolidated Delivery Status Report (MCD)
CDSR......... Contractual Data Status Reporting System (MCD)
CDSR........ Controlled Deployment Specular Reflector [*Army*] (AABC)
CDS Rev .... Chicago Dental Society. Review [*A publication*]
CDSRS ...... Consolidated Delivery Status Report System (MCD)
CDSS........ ̦ Canadian Department of Supply and Services (MCD)
CDSS .... Command Decision Subsystem [*Military*] (CAAL)
C & DSS ... Communication and Data Subsystem
CDSS .... Compressed Data Storage System
CDSS .... Constitutionally Delayed Short Stature [*Medicine*]
CDSS .... Country Development Strategy Statement [*Agency for International Development*]
CDSSA ...... Country Dance and Song Society of America (EA)
CDSS N ..... Country Dance and Song Society. News [*A publication*]
CDST........ Central Daylight Saving Time
CDST......... Centre de Documentation Scientifique et Technique [*Scientific and Technical Documentation Center*] [*National Center for Scientific Research*] [*Information service or system*] (IID)
CDT .... Bishop, CA [*Location identifier*] [*FAA*] (FAAL)
Cdt .... Cadet [*British military*] (DMA)
CDT .... Canadian Graphite [*Vancouver Stock Exchange symbol*]
CDT .... Canyon Diablo Troilite [*Geophysics*]
CDT .... Carbon Dioxide Therapy
CDT .... Central Daylight Time
CDT .... Centre d'Excellence pour le Developpement de la Technologie Telidon [*Telidon Technology Development Center*] [*Polytechnical School of Montreal*] [*Quebec*] [*Information service or system*] (IID)
CDT .... Certified Dental Technician
CDT .... Clearance Diving Team [*Australia*]
CDT .... Clearance Diving Tender
CDT .... Command Descriptor Table (NASA)
CDT .... Command Destruct Transmitter (AFM)
CDT .... Commissioners Disability Table [*Insurance*]
CDT .... Communications Data Terminal (MCD)
CDT .... Compressed Data Tape
CDT .... Concept Developments Talks
CDT .... Concept Developments Tasks (MCD)
CDT .... Conduct (AABC)
CDT .... Conduit
CDT .... Configuration Data Table (MCD)
CDT .... Consecutive Duty Tour [*Air Force*]
CDT .... Continuous Duty Target
CDT .... Contract Definition Test
CDT .... Contractor's Development Testing (MUGU)
CDT .... Control Data Terminal
CDT .... Control Differential Transformer
CDT .... Coordinate Data Terminal (MCD)
CDT .... Coordinate Data Transmission
CDT .... Countdown Demonstration Test [*NASA*]
CDT .... Countdown Time [*Aerospace*]
CDT .... Craft Design and Technology
CDT .... Critical Dissolution Time [*Chemistry*]
CDT .... Cyclododecatriene [*Organic chemistry*]
CDTA .... Chemical Diversion and Trafficking Act [*1988*]

CDTA .... Confederation of Design and Technology Associations [*British*]
CDTA .... (Cyclohexylenedinitrilo)tetraacetic Acid [*Organic chemistry*]
C or D by T or B ... Collected or Delivered by Truck or Barge [*Shipping*]
CDTC .... Combat Development Test Center (CINC)
CDTC-V .... Combat Development Test Center - Vietnam
CDT & E.... Contractor Development Test and Evaluation
CDTE......... Council for Distributive Teacher Education
CDTEC...... Combat Development Technical Evaluation Center
CDTF .... Chemical Decontamination Training Facility [*Military*]
CDTI.......... Cockpit-Display-of-Traffic Information [*NASA*]
CDTL......... Common Data Translation Language
CDTLBS..... Computer-Directed Training Lesson Building System
CDTPM..... Campaign for the Defence of the Turkish Peace Movement [*British*]
CDTS......... Computer-Directed Training System
CDTS......... Computer-Driven Tactical System (MCD)
CDTS......... Constant-Depth Temperature Sensor [*Oceanography*]
CDTS......... Continental Divide Trail Society (EA)
CDTS......... Continuous Duty Target Source
CDTT......... Committee on Domestic Technology Transfer [*Federal Council for Science and Technology*]
CDTX .... Colonial Data Technologies Corp. [*NASDAQ symbol*] (NQ)
CDTY .... Continuous Duty (MSA)
CDU .... Cabin Display Unit [*Aviation*]
CDU .... Cable Distribution Unit [*Aerospace*] (AAG)
CDU.......... Call Director Unit
CDU.......... Central Display Unit
CDU.......... Centre de Documentation Universitaire [*A publication*]
CDU.......... Christelijk-Democratische Unie [*Christian Democratic Union*] [*Netherlands*] (PPE)
CDU.......... Christlich-Demokratische Union [*Christian Democratic Union*] [*Federal Republic of Germany*] [*Political party*] (PPW)
CDU.......... Classification Decimale Universelle [*Universal Decimal Classification*]
CDU.......... Coastal Defense RADAR for Detecting U-Boats
CDU.......... Command Destruct Unit (AABC)
CDU.......... Command Detector Unit (MCD)
CDU.......... Command Display Unit (MCD)
CDU.......... Computer Display Unit (MCD)
CDU.......... Control Data Unit
CDU.......... Control and Diagnostic Unit [*Data processing*]
CDU.......... Control and Display Unit (NASA)
CDU.......... Convergencia Democratica en Uruguay [*Democratic Convergence in Uruguay*] (PD)
CDU.......... Coolant Distribution Unit [*Data processing*]
CDU.......... Counter Display Unit (MCD)
CDU.......... Coupling Data Unit (MCD)
CDU.......... Coupling Display Unit
CDU.......... Crotonylidene Diurea [*Fertilizer*]
CDU.......... CRT [*Cathode-Ray Tube*] Display Unit (MCD)
CDU.......... Crude Distillation Unit [*Petroleum technology*]
CDU.......... University of San Diego, James S. Copley Library, San Diego, CA [*OCLC symbol*] (OCLC)
CDUCE ..... Christian Democratic Union of Central Europe (EAIO)
CDU/CSU ... Christlich Demokratische Union/Christlich Soziale Union [*Christian Democratic Union/Christian Social Union*] [*Federal Republic of Germany*] [*Political party*] (PPE)
CDUEP...... Civil Defense University Extension Program
CDuG......... Giannini Controls Corp., Duarte, CA [*Library symbol*] [*Library of Congress*] (LCLS)
CDuH .... City of Hope Medical Center, Duarte, CA [*Library symbol*] [*Library of Congress*] (LCLS)
CDuM........ Minneapolis-Honeywell Library, Duarte, CA [*Library symbol*] [*Library of Congress*] (LCLS)
CDUP .... Committee for the Defence of the Unjustly Prosecuted (EAIO)
CD-USA .... Civil Defense, United States of America [*Home study course*]
CDUSA ..... Coalition for a Decent USA [*Defunct*] (EA)
CDUSC...... Committee to Defend the US Constitution (EA)
CDV .... Canine Distemper Virus [*Veterinary medicine*]
CDV .... Capacitance Discharge Vaporization [*Nuclear energy*] (NRCH)
CDV .... Carma Developers Ltd. [*Toronto Stock Exchange symbol*]
CDV .... Carte de Visite [*Visiting Card*] [*French*]
CDV .... Chambers Development Corp. [*AMEX symbol*] (SPSG)
CDV .... Check Digit Verification (CMD)
CDV .... Commander's Distinguished Visitors [*Program*] [*Air Force*]
CDV .... Compact Disk Video [*Audio/video technology*]
CDV .... Cordova [*Alaska*] [*Airport symbol*] (OAG)
CDV .... Current Domestic Value [*of goods in the country of origin*]
CDv .... Sierra County Free Library, Downieville, CA [*Library symbol*] [*Library of Congress*] (LCLS)
CD-VI .... Compact Disk Video Interactive [*Data processing*]
CDVO........ Civilian Defense Volunteer Office
CDVU........ Composed Document Viewing Utility [*IBM Corp.*]
CDW .... Caldwell, NJ [*Location identifier*] [*FAA*] (FAAL)
CDW .... Carrying a Dangerous Weapon [*Police term*]
CDW .... Catalytic Dewaxing [*Petroleum refining*]
CDW .... Charge-Density Wave [*Physics*]
CDW .... Chilled Drinking Water [*Aerospace*] (AAG)
CDW .... Circumpolar Deep Water [*Oceanography*]
CDW .... Civil Defense Warning
CDW .... Collision Damage Waiver [*Insurance*]

CDW	Command Data Word (MCD)
CDW	Common Damage Waiver
CDW	Computer Data Word (CET)
CDWG	Countdown Working Group [*NASA*] (KSC)
CDWR	Chest of Drawers
CDWR	Chilled Drinking Water Return [*Aerospace*]
CDWS	Civil Defense Warning System
CDWT	Cord Welt
CDWU	Christian Democratic World Union (EA)
CDX	Canadex Resources Ltd. [*Toronto Stock Exchange symbol*]
CDX	Catellus Development Corp. [*NYSE symbol*] (SPSG)
CDX	Companion Dog, Excellent [*Dog show term*]
CDX	Control Differential Transmitter
CDX	Somerset, KY [*Location identifier*] [*FAA*] (FAAL)
CDX	WVC Documentatie. Systematisch Overzicht met Samenvattingen van Nieuwe Boeken, Tijdschriftartikelen, Parlementaire Stukken [*A publication*]
CDXX	CDX Corp. [*Aurora, CO*] [*NASDAQ symbol*] (NQ)
CDY	Chevy Development Corp. [*Vancouver Stock Exchange symbol*]
CDZ	Chef der Zivilverwaltung [*Chief of Civil Affairs Section*] [*German military - World War II*]
CE	Avions Mudry & Cie. [*France*] [*ICAO aircraft manufacturer identifier*] (ICAO)
CE	Beames' Costs in Equity [*A publication*] (DLA)
C & E	Cababe and Ellis' Queen's Bench Reports [*1882-85*] [*England*] [*A publication*] (DLA)
CE	Cahiers Evangiles [*A publication*]
C/E	Calculation/Experiment (NRCH)
CE	California Encephalitis [*Medicine*]
CE	California Energy Co., Inc. [*AMEX symbol*] (SPSG)
CE	Cambridge Econometrics [*British*]
C-E	Campbell-Ewald Co. [*Advertising agency*]
CE	Canada East
CE	Canadian Energy Services Ltd. [*Toronto Stock Exchange symbol*]
CE	Canadian Engineer [*A publication*]
CE	Canadian Engineers (DMA)
CE	Capillary Electrophoresis [*Physical chemistry*]
CE	Capital Equipment (AFIT)
CE	Capital Expenditure [*Accounting*]
CE	Carboxylation Efficiency [*Botany*]
CE	Carboxylesterase [*An enzyme*]
CE	Cardiac Enlargement [*Medicine*]
CE	Carotid Endarterectomy [*Medicine*]
CE	Cash Earnings [*Business term*]
CE	Cast Enamel [*Classified advertising*] (ADA)
CE	Catalog Events [*Exhibition of US company product catalogs, etc., in foreign markets*] [*Department of Commerce*]
C/E	Catch per Unit Effort [*Pisciculture*]
CE	Catholic Encyclopedia [*A publication*]
CE	Caveat Emptor [*Let the Buyer Beware*] [*Latin*]
CE	Celestial Equator
CE	Cellular Envelope [*Embryology*]
CE	Cellulose Ester [*Organic chemistry*]
Ce	Celtica [*A publication*]
C to E	Center to End
CE	Central Engine [*Galactic radio source*]
CE	Central Europe (NATG)
CE	Central Opera Service. Bulletin [*A publication*]
Ce	Cerium [*Chemical element*]
CE	Certainty Equivalent Coefficient [*Finance*]
CE	Certified Exchangor [*Designation awarded by International Exchangors Association*]
CE	Certified Exchangors [*An association*] (EA)
ce	Ceylon [*Sri Lanka*] [*MARC country of publication code*] [*Library of Congress*] (LCCP)
CE	Ceylon Economist [*A publication*]
CE	Chancellor of the Exchequer [*British*]
CE	Change Evaluation (NASA)
CE	Chartered Engineer [*British*]
CE	Chemical Energy
CE	Chemical Engineer
CE	Chemistry in Ecology [*A publication*]
C & E	Chicago & Erie Railroad Co.
CE	Chicken Embryo
CE	Chief Engineer [*Navy*]
CE	Chief of Engineers [*Later, COE*] [*Army*]
C of E	Chief of Engineers [*Later, COE*] [*Army*]
CE	Chief Executive
CE	Chief Executive [*A publication*]
CE	Childhood Education [*A publication*]
CE	Chip Enable Input [*Data processing*]
CE	Chloroform and Ether [*Mixture*]
CE	Cholesterol Esters [*Clinical chemistry*]
CE	Christian East [*A publication*]
CE	Christian Era
C and E	Christmas and Easter [*Refers to Church of England members who attend church only on those days*] (DSUE)
CE	Chronique d'Egypte [*A publication*]
CE	Chronometer Error [*Navigation*]
CE	Church of England
C of E	Church of England
CE	Cincinnati Electronics Corp. [*Information service or system*] [*Defunct*] (IID)
CE	Circles of Exchange [*Later, COE*] [*An association*] (EA)
CE	Circular Error [*Military*]
CE	Civil Engineer
CE	Civilian Enterprise
CE	Clear-Entry [*Calculators*]
CE	Clinoenstatite [*A mineral*]
CE	Close Encounter [*with a UFO*]
C & E	Clothing and Equipage
CE	Club Elite of North America (EA)
CE	Coal Equivalent
CE	Coarse Erection
CE	Cognizant Engineer
CE	College English [*A publication*]
CE	Combustion Engineering [*Navy*]
C of E	[*The*] Comedy of Errors [*Shakespearean work*]
CE	Commercial Engineer
CE	Commercial Enterprise
CE	Commodity Exchange [*Investment term*]
CE	Common Emitter
CE	Common Entrance [*Examination for entry into public school*] [*British*]
CE	Common Era
CE	Communaute EURAIL [*EURAIL Community*] [*An association*] (EAIO)
CE	Communaute Europeenne [*European Community*]
C & E	Communications and Electronics
C-E	Communications-Electronics
CE	Communications Equipment
CE	Community of the Epiphany [*Anglican religious community*]
CE	Commutator End (MSA)
Ce	Compagnie [*Company*] [*French*] (ILCA)
CE	Comparative Estimating
CE	Compass Error [*Navigation*]
C/E	Component/Equipment (MCD)
CE	Compression Engine
CE	Comptes Economiques [*Beirut*] [*A publication*]
CE	Computer Engineer
CE	Concept Exploration
CE	Conducted Emission (IEEE)
CE	Conductivity Element [*Nuclear energy*] (NRCH)
CE	Cone
C & E	Conferences and Exhibitions [*Later, Conferences and Exhibitions International*] [*A publication*]
CE	Configuration Element (AFIT)
CE	Conjugated Estrogens [*Endocrinology*]
C/E	Conseil de l'Entente [*Entente Council - EC*] (EAIO)
CE	Conseil d'Etat [*Council of State*] [*French*] (ILCA)
CE	Conseil de l'Europe [*Council of Europe*] (EAIO)
CE	Conspicuity Enhancement [*Aviation*]
CE	Constant Error [*Psychology*]
CE	Construction Electrician [*Navy rating*]
CE	Construction and Engineering [*Philippines*] [*A publication*]
C & E	Construction and Equipment
C & E	Consultation and Education
CE	Consultative Examination [*Social Security Administration*] (OICC)
CE	Consulting Engineer
CE	Consummatum Est [*It Is Finished*] [*Latin*] [*Freemasonry*] (ROG)
CE	Consumer Electronics [*A publication*]
CE	Consumption Entry [*Economics*]
CE	Continuing Education
CE	Continuous Estrus [*Endocrinology*]
CE	Continuous Evaluation [*DoD*]
CE	Contract Engineers (MCD)
CE	Contract Exploration (MCD)
CE	Contractile Element [*of skeletal muscle*]
CE	Control Electrician [*British military*] (DMA)
CE	Control Element (MCD)
C & E	Control Engineering
C & E	Control and Evaluation
C of E	Convention of Edinburgh [*Freemasonry*] (ROG)
CE	Converting Enzyme
C & E	Coordination and Equipment
CE	Corno Emplumado [*A publication*]
C of E	Corps of Engineers [*Army*]
CE	Corps of Engineers [*Army*]
CE	Correo Erudito [*A publication*]
CE	Cost Effectiveness [*Accounting*]
CE	Cost Element (MCD)
CE	Cotton Effect
CE	Council of Europe (EAIO)
CE	Countercurrent Electrophoresis [*Also, CCE*] [*Analytical chemistry*]
CE	Counterespionage
C/E	Creation/Evolution [*A publication*]
CE	Crew Evaluator [*Military*] (INF)

CE .... Critical Examination (CAAL)
CE .... Cum Entitlement [*With Entitlement*] [*Latin*] [*Legal term*] (ADA)
CE .... Current Efficiency [*Electrochemistry*]
CE .... Current Endocrinology [*Elsevier Book Series*] [*A publication*]
CE .... Current Estimate (AFIT)
CE .... Current Expendable (NASA)
CE .... Current Exploitation (MCD)
CE .... Customer Engineer [*Data processing*]
CE .... Customs and Excise
CE .... Cuvee Extra
CE .... Cytopathic Effect [*Medicine*]
CE .... Eureka City Library, Eureka, CA [*Library symbol*] [*Library of Congress*] (LCLS)
CE .... International Society of Christian Endeavor
CE .... Lease Air Ltd. [*Great Britain*] [*ICAO designator*] (FAAC)
CE .... Republic of Singapore Air Force [*ICAO designator*] (ICDA)
CE1 .... Construction Electrician, First Class [*Navy rating*]
CE2 .... Construction Electrician, Second Class [*Navy rating*]
C²E .... Continuous Comprehensive Evaluation [*Army*] (RDA)
CE3 .... Close Encounters of the Third Kind [*Movie title*]
CE3 .... Construction Electrician, Third Class [*Navy rating*]
CEA .... Cahiers d'Etudes Africaines [*A publication*]
CEA .... Cahiers des Etudes Anciennes [*A publication*]
CEA .... California Eastern Airways
CEA .... Cambridge Electron Accelerator
CEA .... Canadian Economics Association [*See also ACE*]
CEA .... Canadian Education Association
CEA .... Canadian Electrical Association
CEA .... Canadian Export Association
CEA .... Carcinoembryonic Antigen [*Immunochemistry*]
CEA .... Catholic Economic Association [*Later, ASE*] (EA)
CEA .... CEA [*College English Association*] Critic [*A publication*]
CEA .... Cement Employers Association (EA)
CEA .... Center for Early Adolescence (EA)
CEA .... Central Electricity Authority [*British*]
CEA .... Chemical Engineering Abstracts [*Royal Society of Chemistry*] [*Information service or system*]
CEA .... Chemistry Education Association [*Australia*]
CEA .... Chief Electrical Artificer [*British military*] (DMA)
CEA .... Children's Emotions Anonymous (EA)
CEA .... Chinese Exclusion Act
CEA .... Chlorendic Aldehyde [*Organic chemistry*]
CEA .... Church Evangelism Association [*Later, Masterkey Association*] (EA)
CEA .... Church Extension Association [*British*]
CEA .... Cinematograph Exhibitioners' Association of Great Britian and Ireland
CEA .... Circular Error Average [*Military*]
CEA .... Citizen Education Association (EA)
CEA .... Clearinghouse on Educational Administration [*ERIC*]
CEA .... Clearinghouse on Election Administration [*Federal Election Commission*]
CEA .... Coal Exporters Association of the United States (EA)
CEA .... College English Association (EA)
CEA .... Combustion Engineering Association [*British*]
CEA .... Comite Europeen des Assurances [*European Insurance Committee - EIC*] [*France*]
CEA .... Commissariat a l'Energie Atomique [*Atomic Energy Commission - AEC*] [*France*] [*Research center*]
CEA .... Commission Economique pour l'Afrique [*Economic Commission for Africa - ECA*] (EAIO)
CEA .... Committee for Energy Awareness [*Later, USCEA*] (EA)
CEA .... Commodity Exchange Act
CEA .... Commodity Exchange Authority [*Later, CFTC*] [*Department of Agriculture*]
CEA .... Common Error Analysis (MCD)
C-EA .... Communications-Electronics Agency [*Army*]
CEA .... Confederation des Educateurs Americains [*Confederation of American Educators*]
CEA .... Confederation Europeenne de l'Agriculture [*European Confederation of Agriculture*] (EAIO)
CEA .... Congressional Education Associates [*Private, nonpartisan consulting group*]
CEA .... Conservation Education Association (EA)
CEA .... Construction Equipment Advertisers [*Later, CEA PRC*] (EA)
CEA .... Contributions to Economic Analysis [*Elsevier Book Series*] [*A publication*]
CEA .... Control Electrical Artificer [*Navy rating*] [*British*]
CEA .... Control Electronics Assembly [*Aerospace*]
CEA .... Control Element Assembly [*Nuclear energy*] (NRCH)
CEA .... Controlled Environment Agriculture
CEA .... Cooperative Education Association (EA)
CEA .... Correctional Education Association (EA)
CEA .... Cost-Effectiveness Analysis [*Economics*]
CEA .... Council of Economic Advisers [*to the President*]
CEA .... Council for Educational Advance [*British*]
CEA .... Council on Environmental Alternatives (EA)
CEA .... Wichita, KS [*Location identifier*] [*FAA*] (FAAL)
CEAA .... Center for Editions of American Authors [*Later, CSE*]
CEAA .... Centre Europeen d'Aviation Agricole

CEAA .... Council of European-American Associations [*Later, FEAO*]
CEAAL .... Consejo de Educacion de Adultos de America Latina [*Santiago, Chile*] (EAIO)
CEAAN ...... Center for Editions of American Authors. Newsletter [*A publication*]
CEABREP ... Cost Effectiveness Analysis of Bonuses and Reenlistment Policies
CEAC .... CEA [*College English Association*] Chap Book [*A publication*]
CEAC .... Citizens Educational Advisory Committee
CEAC .... Commission Europeenne de l'Aviation Civile [*European Civil Aviation Conference - ECAC*] (EAIO)
CEAC .... Committee for European Airspace Coordination [*NATO*]
CEAC .... Control Element Assembly Calculator [*Nuclear energy*] (NRCH)
CEACO ...... Committee for Equitable Access to Crude Oil (EA)
CEACrit ...... CEA [*College English Association*] Critic [*A publication*]
CEAD .... Chief Engineer and Superintendent of Armaments Design [*British military*] (DMA)
CEADI .... Colored Electronic Attitude Director Indicator (MCD)
CEAE .... Centre d'Etudes de l'Asie de l'Est [*University of Montreal*] [*Research center*] (RCD)
CEAEA ...... Canadian Electrical Association. Transactions of the Engineering and Operating Division [*A publication*]
CEAEO ...... Commission Economique pour l'Asie et l'Extreme-Orient [*Economic Commission for Asia and the Far East - ECAFE*]
CEAF .... CEA [*College English Association*] Forum [*A publication*]
CEAfr .... Cahiers d'Etudes Africaines [*A publication*]
CEAFU ...... Concerned Educators Against Forced Unionism (EA)
CEAGD5 ... Centro Agricola [*A publication*]
C of E Agr PI ... General Agreement on Privileges and Immunities of the Council of Europe (DLA)
CEAH .... Conference on Early American History (EA)
CEAI .... Chase Econometrics Associates, Incorporated [*Information service or system*] (IID)
CEAI .... Christian Educators Association International (EAIO)
CEAIO .... Comite Europeen de l'Association Internationale de l'Ozone [*European Committee of the International Ozone Association*] (EAIO)
CEAL .... Cambridge Electron Accelerator Laboratories [*Massachusetts Institute of Technology*]
CEAL .... Centro Editor de America Latina [*A publication*]
CEAL .... Committee on East Asian Libraries
CEAM .... Center for Exposure Assessment Modeling [*Athens, GA*] [*Environmental Protection Agency*] (GRD)
CEAM .... Cost-Effectiveness Analysis Methodology [*Economics*] (MCD)
CEANAR... Commission on Education in Agriculture and Natural Resources [*National Research Council*] [*Defunct*]
CEA News ... Canadian Education Association. Newsletter [*A publication*]
CEA Notes Inf ... CEA [*Cahiers d'Etudes Anciennes*] Notes d'Information [*France*] [*A publication*]
CEAO .... Camouflage Effectiveness Assessment Office [*Army*] (RDA)
CEAO .... Commission Economique (des Nations Unies) pour l'Asie Occidentale [*United Nations Economic Commission for Western Asia - ECWA*] [*French*]
CEAPAT ... Contribuicoes para o Estudo da Antropologia Portuguesa [*A publication*]
CEAPD ...... Central Air Procurement District
CEAPE ...... Confederacion Espanola de Asociaciones Pesqueras [*Industrial association*] [*Spain*] (EY)
CEA PRC .. Construction Equipment Advertisers and Public Relations Council [*Milwaukee, WI*] (EA)
CEAR .... Center for Engineering Applications of Radioisotopes [*North Carolina State University*] [*Research center*] (RCD)
CEARC ...... Canadian Environmental Assessment Research Council
CEARC ...... Computer Education and Applied Research Center
CEARS ...... COMSEC [*Communications Security*] Equipment Asset Reporting System (MCD)
CEAS .... Center for Environmental Assessment Services [*National Oceanic and Atmospheric Administration*] [*Information service or system*] (IID)
CEAS .... Centre Ecologique Albert Schweitzer [*Albert Schweitzer Ecological Centre*] (EAIO)
CEAS .... Centre for European Agricultural Studies [*British*] (ARC)
CEASA ...... Commercial and Economic Advisory Service of Australia (ADA)
CEASC ...... Committee for European Airspace Coordination [*NATO*] (NATG)
CEASD ...... Conference of Educational Administrators Serving the Deaf (EA)
CEASD ...... Corporate Engineering and Sales Directive
CEASE ...... Citizens to End Animal Suffering and Exploitation (EA)
CEASE ...... Concerned Educators Allied for a Safe Environment (EA)
CEASPECT ... Camera Europea degli Arbitri Stragiudiziali e dei Periti Esperti Consulenti Tecnici [*European Chamber of Extra-Judicial Adjudicators and Expert Technical Advisors*] (EAIO)
CEASRS ...... Civil Engineer Automated Specification Retrieval System [*Air Force*]
CEATOS ... Cost Effectiveness Analysis of the Tactical Operations System [*Military*] (MCD)
CEAU .... Continuing Education Achievement Unit (IEEE)

CEAZD......	Centro Azucar [*A publication*]
CEB...........	Calcium Entry Blocking [*Agent*] [*Physiology*]
CEB...........	Cebu [*Philippines*] [*Airport symbol*] (OAG)
CEB...........	Central Electricity Board [*British*]
CEB...........	Cluster Effects Bomblet
CEB...........	CNO [*Chief of Naval Operations*] Executive Board
CEB...........	Combined Effects Bomb (MCD)
CEB...........	Comite Euro-International du Beton [*Euro-International Committee for Concrete*]
CEB...........	Comite Europeen du Beton [*European Committee for Concrete*]
CEB...........	Comite Europeen des Constructeurs de Broleurs [*European Committee of Manufacturers of Burners*] (EA)
CEB...........	Communications-Electronics Board (NATG)
CEB...........	Communidades Eclesiais de Base [*Brazil*]
CEB...........	Confederation Europeenne de Billard
CEB...........	Consolidated Omab Enterprises Ltd. [*Vancouver Stock Exchange symbol*]
CEB...........	Council on Employee Benefits (EA)
CEB...........	Cryogenic Expulsive Bladder
CEB...........	Edwards Air Force Base Library, Edwards AFB, CA [*OCLC symbol*] (OCLC)
CEBA........	Circuitless Electron Beam Amplifier (MCD)
CEBA........	Communications Excellence to Black Audiences [*An award*]
CEBA........	Competitive Equality Banking Act [*1987*]
CEBA........	Confederation Europeenne de Baseball Amateur [*European Amateur Baseball Confederation - EABC*] (EA)
CEBAC......	Comision Economica Brasileira-Argentina de Comercio [*Argentine-Brazilian Economic Commission on Trade*]
CEBAF	Continuous Electron Beam Accelerator Facility [*Physics*]
CEBAL	Copenhagen School of Economics and Business Administration. Language Department Publications [*A publication*]
CEBAR	Chemical, Biological, Radiological Warfare [*Later, CB*] [*Military*]
CEBEA	Centre Belge d'Etude et de Documentation des Eaux. Bulletin Mensuel [*A publication*]
CEBECOR ...	Centre Belge d'Etude de la Corrosion [*Belgium*]
CEBELCOR ...	Centre Belge d'Etude de la Corrosion [*Belgian Centre for the Study of Corrosion*] (EAIO)
CEBER	Center for Built Environment Research [*Morgan State University*] [*Research center*] (RCD)
CEBIEH	Cell Biology Monographs [*A publication*]
CEBITUR ...	Centro Brasileiro de Informacao Turistica [*Brazil*] (EY)
CEBJ	Commission of Editors of Biochemical Journals
CEBK........	Central Co-Operative Bank [*Somerville, MA*] [*NASDAQ symbol*] (NQ)
CEBLS.......	Comprehensive Evaluation of Basic Living Skills
CEBM........	Corona, Eddy Current, Beta Ray, Microwave
CEBMCA ..	Corps of Engineers Ballistic Missile Construction Agency [*Army*]
CEBMCO ...	Corps of Engineers Ballistic Missile Construction Office [*Army*]
CEBOE......	National Association of Classroom Educators in Business and Office Education (EA)
CEBR........	Cedar Breaks National Monument
CEBS	Certified Employee Benefit Specialist
CEBS(Tas) ...	Church of England Boys' Society in Tasmania [*Australia*]
CEBUD	Ceramika Budowlana [*A publication*]
CEBUS......	Confirmed Exposure but Unconscious [*Advertising*]
CEBus........	Consumer Electronics Bus [*Residential wiring standard*]
CEBV........	Chronic Epstein-Barr Virus [*Medicine*]
CEBV........	Communaute Economique du Betail et de la Viande [*Economic Community for Livestock and Meat - ECLM*] (EAIO)
CEC	Cahiers d'Etudes Cathares [*A publication*]
CEC	Cambridge Education Consultants Ltd. [*British*]
CEC	Cambridge English Classics [*A publication*]
CEC	Canada Employment Centre
CEC	Canadian Electrical Code
CEC	Capital Equipment Corporation [*Burlington, MA*]
CEC	Capsule End Cover [*Aerospace*]
CEC	Caribbean Economic Community
CEC	Caribbean Employers Confederation (EAIO)
CEC	Cation-Exchange Capacity [*Chemical technology*]
CEC	Celebrity Engineering [*Vancouver Stock Exchange symbol*]
CEC	Center for Economic Conversion (EA)
CEC	Center for Educational Change [*University of California, Berkeley*]
CEC	Central East Coast
CEC	Central Economic Committee
CEC	Centralized Electronic Control [*Navy*]
CEC	Centre Europeen de la Culture [*European Cultural Centre - ECC*] (EAIO)
CE C...........	Cepi Corpus [*I Have Taken the Body*] [*Latin*] [*Legal term*] (DLA)
CEC	Ceramic Educational Council (EA)
CEC	Cetec Corporation [*AMEX symbol*] (SPSG)
CEC	Chemical Engineering Catalog [*A publication*]
CEC	Childress [*Texas*] [*Seismograph station code, US Geological Survey*] (SEIS)
CEC	China Export Corporation
CEC	Ciliated Epithelial Cells [*Medicine*]
CEC	Citizen Exchange Council (EA)
CEC	Citizens' Electoral Council [*Australia*]

CEC	Citizens Energy Corporation [*Nonprofit*]
CEC	Citizen's Energy Council (EA)
CEC	Civil Engineer Corps [*Army*]
CEC	Clark Equipment Company (MCD)
CEC	Clothing Export Council [*United Kingdom*] (DS)
CEC	Coal Experts Committee [*Allied German Occupation Forces*]
CEC	Commission of the European Communities [*See also CCE*] (EAIO)
CEC	Commission Europeenne de la Corseterie [*European Corsetry Commission - ECC*] (EAIO)
CEC	Committee for Equitable Compensation (EA)
CEC	Commodities Exchange Center [*New York, NY*]
CEC	Commodity Exchange Commission [*Functions transferred to CFTC*]
CEC	Commons Expenditure Committee [*British*]
CEC	Commonwealth Economic Committee [*British*]
CEC	Commonwealth Education Conferences [*British*]
CEC	Commonwealth Engineering Conference (MCD)
CEC	Commonwealth Engineers Council [*See also CAICB*] [*Great Britain*] (EAIO)
CEC	Communication Effectiveness Centre [*Canada*]
CEC	Communications and Electronics Command [*Formerly, ASC*] [*Army*]
CEC	Communications-Electronics Committee (AFM)
CEC	Community Environmental Council (EA)
CEC	Complex Equipment Contract (MCD)
CEC	Compromising Emanations Control (MCD)
CEC	Conference of European Churches (EA)
CEC	Conseil Europeen de Coordination pour le Developpement des Essais de Performance des Combustibles et des Lubrifiants pour Moteurs [*Coordinating European Council for the Development of Performance Tests for Lubricants and Engine Fuels - CEC*] (EAIO)
CEC	Consejo Economico Centroamericano [*Central-American Economic Council*]
CEC	Conselho Estadual de Cultura [*A publication*]
CEC	Consolidated Electrodynamics Corporation
CEC	Consolidated Electronics Corporation
CEC	Construction Electrician, Chief [*Navy rating*]
CEC	Consulting Engineers Council [*Later, ACEC*] (EA)
CEC	Continental Entry Charts [*Air Force*]
CEC	Continuing Education Council [*Later, CNCE*] (EA)
CEC	Control Encoder Coupler (NASA)
CEC	Controlled Element Computer
CEC	Coordinating European Council for the Development of Performance Tests for Lubricants and Engine Fuels (EA)
CEC	Council for Education in the Commonwealth (EAIO)
CEC	Council of the European Communities
CEC	Council for Exceptional Children (EA)
CEC	Coupon Exchange Club [*Commercial firm*] (EA)
CEC	Crescent City [*California*] [*Airport symbol*] (OAG)
CEC	Crew Equipment Compartment (MCD)
CEC	Crown Estate Commissioner [*British*]
CEC	Cryogenic Engineering Conference (EA)
CEC	Customs Entry Charge (DCTA)
CEc	El Centro Free Public Library, El Centro, CA [*Library symbol*] [*Library of Congress*] (LCLS)
CEC	National Council on the Evaluation of Foreign Educational Credentials (EA)
CECA........	Committee of European Coffee Associations (EAIO)
CECA........	Communaute Europeenne du Charbon et de l'Acier [*European Coal and Steel Community*]
CECA........	Community Emergency Care Association (EA)
CECA........	Comunidad Europea del Carbon y del Acero [*European Coal and Steel Community - ECSC*] [*Spanish*]
CECA........	Comunita Europea del Carbone e dell'Acciaio [*European Coal and Steel Community - ECSC*] [*Italian*]
CECA........	Confederacion Espanola de Cajas de Ahorro [*Spanish Confederation of Savings Banks*] (EY)
CECA........	Constructionman Apprentice, Construction Electrician, Striker [*Navy rating*]
CECA........	Consumer Energy Council of America (EA)
CECA........	Council on Economic and Cultural Affairs [*Later, ADC*] [*Rockefeller Brothers Fund, Ford Foundation activity*]
CEcaE.......	El Camino College, Torrance, CA [*Library symbol*] [*Library of Congress*] (LCLS)
CECAF	Fishery Committee for the Eastern Central Atlantic [*See also COPACE*]
CEcajC.......	Christian Heritage Library, El Cajon, CA [*Library symbol*] [*Library of Congress*] (LCLS)
CECAL	Commission Episcopale de Cooperation Apostolique Canada-Amerique Latine
CECAPI.....	Commission Europeenne des Constructeurs d'Appareillage Electrique d'Installations [*European Commission of Manufacturers of Electrical Installation Equipment*] (EAIO)
CECA/RF ...	Consumer Energy Council of America Research Foundation (EA)

CECAVI .... Confederation Europeenne des Categories Auxiliaires des Activites Viti-Vinicole [*European Confederation of Auxiliary Occupations in the Wine Trade*] [*Common Market*]

CECB......... Conseil Europeen du Cuir Brut [*European Untanned Leather Council*]

CECC......... California Educational Computing Consortium   (EA)

CECC......... CENELEC [*Comite Europeen de Normalisation Electrotechnique*] Electronic Components Committee   (DS)

CECC......... Commonwealth Economic Consultative Council [*British*]

CECC......... Communaute Europeenne de Credit Communal [*European Municipal Credit Community*]

CECCP ...... Combustion Equilibrium Calculation Computer Program   (MCD)

CECD .... Confederation Europeenne du Commerce de Detail [*European Federation for Retail Trade*]   (EAIO)

CECDC ...... Cost Estimate Control Data Center   (AABC)

CECE......... Combined Electrolysis and Catalytic Exchange [*CANDU-reactor advantage*]

CECE......... Comision Especial para Estudiar la Formulacion de Nuevas Medidas de Cooperacion Economica [*Special Committee to Study the Formulation of New Measures of Economic Cooperation*] [*Organizacion de Estados Americanos - OEA*]

CECE......... Committee for European Construction Equipment   (EAIO)

CECEB ...... Chemical Economy and Engineering Review [*A publication*]

CECED ...... Conseil Europeen de la Construction Electrodomestique [*European Committee of Manufacturers of Electrical Domestic Equipment*]   (EA)

CECED9.... Commission des Communautes Europeennes/Commissione delle Comunita Europee/Commission of the European Communities. Eur Report [*A publication*]

CECED9.... Kommission der Europaeischen Gemeinschaften [*A publication*]

CECEEB.... Commission on English of the College Entrance Examination Board   (EA)

Ceceno-Ingus Gos Ped Inst Ucen Zap ... Ceceno-Ingusskii Gosudarstvennyi Pedagogiceskii Institut. Ucenye Zapiski [*A publication*]

CEcerB....... Western Baptist Bible College, El Cerrito, CA [*Library symbol*] [*Library of Congress*]   (LCLS)

CECF......... Children's Eye Care Foundation [*Later, NCECF*]   (EA)

CECF......... Chinese Export Commodities Fair

CECF......... Corrective Eye Care Foundation [*Later, CLMA*]   (EA)

CECH........ Comite Europeen de la Culture du Houblon [*European Hop Growers Committee*]

CECHAF... Cereal Chemistry [*A publication*]

CECI......... Centre d'Etude et de Cooperation International [*International Study and Cooperation Centre*] [*Canada*]

CEcI.......... Imperial County Free Library, El Centro, CA [*Library symbol*] [*Library of Congress*]   (LCLS)

CECIAI ..... Cecidologia Indica [*A publication*]

Cecidol Indica ... Cecidologia Indica [*A publication*]

CECIF .... Chambre Europeenne pour le Developpement du Commerce, de l'Industrie, et des Finances [*European Chamber for the Development of Trade, Industry, and Finances*] [*Brussels, Belgium*]   (EAIO)

CECIL .... Compact Electronic Components Inspection Laboratory

CECIOS .... Conseil Europeen du Comite International de l'Organisation Scientifique [*European Council of International Committee of Scientific Management*]

CECIP .... Comite Europeen des Constructeurs d'Instruments de Pesage [*European Committee of Weighing Instrument Manufacturers - ECWIM*]   (EAIO)

CECJA ...... Civil Engineering, Construction, and Public Works Journal [*India*] [*A publication*]

CECL......... Civil Engineering Computer Laboratory [*MIT*]   (MCD)

CECL......... Comite d'Etude sur les Conditions du Logement [*Study Committee Study on Housing Conditions*] [*Canada*]

CECL......... Conference of Eastern College Librarians

CECLA ...... Comision Especial de Coordinacion Latinoamericana

CECLANT ... French Commander-in-Chief, Atlantic [*NATO*]

CECLB ...... Comite Europeen de Controle Laitierbeurrier

CECM .... Composite Engineering Change Memo [*NASA*]   (KSC)

CECM .... Construction Electrician, Master Chief [*Navy rating*]

CECMED ... French Commander-in-Chief, Mediterranean [*NATO*]

CEC-MR .... Division on Mental Retardation of the Council for Exceptional Children   (EA)

CECMRL .. Communications-Electronics Consolidated Mobilization Reserve List

CECN .... Canadian Environmental Control Newsletter [*A publication*]

CECN .... CEC Industries Corp. [*NASDAQ symbol*]   (NQ)

CECN .... Constructionman, Construction Electrician, Striker [*Navy rating*]

CECO .... Center Engine Cutoff [*NASA*]   (KSC)

CECO .... Chandler Evans Corporation

CECO .... Commission d'Enquete pour le Crime Organise [*Organized Crime Investigating Commission*] [*Canada*]

CECO .... Cost Estimate Change Order   (NRCH)

CECOB...... Cement and Concrete [*A publication*]

CECODE... Centre Europeen du Commerce de Detail [*European Center of the Retail Trade*] [*Common Market*]

CECOGp ... Civil Engineer Construction Operations Group [*Air Force*]   (AFM)

CECOM .... Communications-Electronics Command [*Fort Monmouth, NJ*] [*Army*]   (GRD)

CECOMAF ... Comite Europeen des Constructeurs de Materiel Frigorifique [*European Committee of Manufacturers of Refrigeration Equipment*]   (EAIO)

C Econ Bruxelles ... Cahiers Economiques de Bruxelles [*A publication*]

C Econ Soc ... Cahiers Economiques et Sociaux [*Kinshasa*] [*A publication*]

CECOP ...... Council of Engineering Consultants of the Philippines   (DS)

CECOS...... Civil Engineers Corps Officers School [*Navy*]

CECP......... Compatibility Engineering Change Proposal [*NASA*]   (NASA)

CECPA ...... Comite Europeen du Commerce des Produits Amylaces et Derives [*European Center for Trade in Starch Products and Derivatives*] [*Common Market*]

CECR........ Central European Communication Region [*Air Force*]   (MCD)

CECR........ Century Energy Corporation [*NASDAQ symbol*]   (NQ)

CECR........ Committee for Effective Capital Recovery   (EA)

CECRA ..... CEC [*Consolidated Electrodynamics Corporation*] Recordings [*United States*] [*A publication*]

CECS......... Casualty Evacuation and Control Ship [*Navy*]   (NVT)

CECS......... Charge Exchange Cross Section

CECS......... Choices Entertainment Corp. [*NASDAQ symbol*]   (SPSG)

CECS......... Church of England Children's Society

CECS......... Closed-Loop Environmental Control System

CECS......... Communications-Electronics Coordinating Section [*NATO*]

CECS......... Construction Electrician, Senior Chief [*Navy rating*]

CECS......... Containment Environmental Control System [*Nuclear energy*]   (NRCH)

CECSD...... Citizens for Energy Conservation and Solar Development

CECSET.... Committee for Enlisted Classification Selection and Testing [*Navy*]   (NVT)

CECSR...... Contractor Employee Compensation System Review [*DoD*]

CECT........ Comite Europeen de la Chaudronnerie et de la Tolerie [*European Committee for Boilermaking and Kindred Steel Structures*]

CECTA ...... Cellulose Chemistry and Technology [*A publication*]

CECTAL ... Centre for English Cultural Tradition and Language [*University of Sheffield*] [*British*]   (CB)

CECTBI..... CEPLAC [*Comissao Executiva do Plano da Lavoura Cacaueira*] Comunicacao Tecnica [*A publication*]

CECU .... Concursos y Certamenes Culturales [*Database*] [*Ministerio de Cultura*] [*Spanish*] [*Information service or system*]   (CRD)

CECUA...... Confederation of European Computer Users Associations   (EAIO)

CECX........ Castle Energy Corporation [*NASDAQ symbol*]   (NQ)

CED .... Campaign for Economic Democracy

CED .... Canadian Encyclopedic Digest [*A publication*]   (DLA)

CED .... Capacitance Electronic Disk

CED .... Captured Enemy Documents [*Military*]   (AFM)

CED .... Cardiff East Docks [*Welsh depot code*]

CED .... Cedar Springs [*California*] [*Seismograph station code, US Geological Survey*] [*Closed*]   (SEIS)

Ced .... Cedola [*Dividend, Interest*] [*Business term*] [*Italian*]

CED .... Ceduna [*Australia*] [*Airport symbol*]   (OAG)

CED .... Center for Educational Development [*University of Illinois at Chicago*] [*Research center*]   (RCD)

CED .... Center for Entrepreneurial Development [*Carnegie-Mellon University*]

CED .... Centre for Information and Advice on Educational Disadvantage [*British*]

CED .... Centro de Esploro kaj Dokumentado pri la Monda Lingvo-Problemo [*Center for Research and Documentation on International Language Problems*]   (EAIO)

CED .... Chemical Exchange Directory SA [*Information service or system*]   (EISS)

CED .... Chief Executive Dockyard [*Navy*] [*British*]

C Ed .... Childhood Education [*A publication*]

CEd .... Classic Editions [*Record label*]

C/ED .... Clothing and Equipment Development Branch [*Army Natick Laboratories, MA*]

CED .... Cohesive Energy Density [*Solubility parameter*]

CED .... Collins English Dictionary [*A publication*] [*British*]

CED .... Committee for Economic Development   (EA)

CED .... Communaute Europeenne de Defense [*European Defense Community*]

CEd .... Communication Education [*A publication*]

CED .... Communications-Electronics Directive

CED .... Communications-Electronics Doctrine [*Series of Air Force manuals*]

CED .... Communications-Electronics Document

CED .... Community Employment Development [*Department of Labor*]

CED .... Constant Energy Differences

CED .... Cost Estimate Dispersion   (KSC)

CED .... Council on Education of the Deaf   (EA)

CED .... Critical Error Detection   (MCD)

CED .... Current Enlistment Date [*Military*]

CED .... United States Air Force, Edwards Air Force Base, AFFTC Technical Library, Edwards AFB, CA [*OCLC symbol*] (OCLC)
CEDA .... Canadian Electrical Distributors Association, Inc.
CEDA .... Central Dredging Association (EA)
CEDA .... Comite d'Etude des Droits des Autochtones [*Committee for Original Peoples' Entitlement*] [*Canada*]
CEDA .... Community Economic Development Act of 1981
CEDA .... Confederacion Espanola de Derechas Autonomas [*Spanish Confederation of Autonomous Rightist Forces*] [*Political party*] (PPE)
CEDA .... Cross-Examination Debate Association (EA)
CEdA .... United States Air Force, Flight Test Center Technical Library, Edwards AFB, CA [*Library symbol*] [*Library of Congress*] (LCLS)
CEDAC ...... Central Differential Analyzer Control
CEDAC ...... Cooling Effect Detection and Control
CEDAD2 ... Clinical and Experimental Dialysis and Apheresis [*A publication*]
CEDADE... Circulo Espanol de Amigos de Europa [*Spanish Circle of Friends of Europe*] (PD)
CEDAL...... Centro de Estudios Democraticos de America Latina
CEDAM .... Casa Editrice Dott. A. Milani [*Italian publisher*]
CEDAM .... Conservation, Exploration, Diving, Archeology, Museums [*Acronym is used as name of an international organization interested in these five subjects*] (EA)
CEDAR...... Center for Engineering Development and Research [*University of South Florida*] [*Research center*] (RCD)
CEDaR ...... Council for Educational Development and Research (EA)
CEdA-R ..... United States Air Force, Air Force Rocket Propulsion Laboratory, Edwards AFB, CA [*Library symbol*] [*Library of Congress*] (LCLS)
CEDARC... Confluent Education Development and Research Center (EA)
CEDAT...... Centre for Educational Development and Training [*Manchester Polytechnic*] [*British*] (CB)
CEDAU ..... Cruise/Entry Data Acquisition Unit [*NASA*]
CEDB......... Church Executive Development Board
CEDB......... Currency Exchange Database [*GE Information Services*] [*Information service or system*] (CRD)
CEDBR...... Center for Economic Development and Business Research [*Wichita State University*] [*Kansas*] [*Information service or system*] (IID)
CEDC .... Catalyst Energy Development Corporation [*New York, NY*] [*NASDAQ symbol*] (NQ)
CEDC .... Central European Development Corp.
CEDC .... (Chloroethyl)deoxycytidine [*Antiviral*]
CEDC .... Cost Estimating Data Center
CEDC .... Cyclic Error Detection Code (MCD)
CEDDA ..... Center for Experiment Design and Data Analysis [*National Oceanic and Atmospheric Administration*]
CEDE......... Centre d'Etudes et de Documentation Europeennes [*Montreal*]
CEDE......... Certificate Depository [*New York Stock Exchange*]
CEDEAO... Communaute Economique des Etats de l'Afrique de l'Ouest [*Economic Community of West African States - ECOWAS*] (EAIO)
CEDEC...... Centre Europeen de Documentation et de Compensation
CEDEDE... Clinical and Experimental Dermatology [*A publication*]
CEDEFOP .. Centre Europeen pour le Developpement de la Formation Professionnelle [*European Centre for the Development of Vocational Training*] (EAIO)
CEDEL...... Centrale de Livraison de Valeurs Mobilieres
CEDH........ Commission Europeenne des Droits de l'Homme [*European Commission of Human Rights - ECHR*] (EA)
CEDIM...... Comite Europeen des Federations Nationales de la Maroquinerie, Articles de Voyages, et Industries Connexes (EAIO)
CEDLA/B ... Boletin de Estudios Latinoamericanos. Centro de Estudios y Documentacion Latinoamericanos [*Amsterdam*] [*A publication*]
CEDM .... Committee on Environmental Decision Making [*National Research Council*]
CEDM .... Control Element Drive Mechanism [*Nuclear energy*] (NRCH)
CEDMB2... Clinics in Endocrinology and Metabolism [*A publication*]
CEDMCS .. Control Element Drive Mechanism Control System [*Nuclear energy*] (NRCH)
CEDN .... Classic English Detective Novel
CEDO........ Captured Enemy Documents Organization (NATG)
CEDO........ Centre for Educational Development Overseas
CEDOCAR ... Centre de Documentation de l'Armement [*Center for Documentation on Armament*] [*Ministry of Defense*] [*Information service or system*] (IID)
CEDPA...... Centre for Development and Population Activities (EA)
CEDPA...... Correction Education Demonstration Project Act of 1978
CEDPO ..... Communications-Electronics Doctrinal Projects Office [*Air Force*]
CEDPS ...... College Eye Data Processing System [*Air Force*] (MCD)
CEDR .... Cedar Income Fund Ltd. [*NASDAQ symbol*] (NQ)
CEDR .... Comite Europeen de Droit Rural (EAIO)
CEDRA ...... Community Emergency Drought Relief Act of 1977
CEDREP .. Communications - Electronics Deployment Report (MCD)
CEDRS ...... Capabilities Engineering Data Report System (MCD)

CEDS......... Center for Econometrics and Decision Sciences [*University of Florida*] [*Research center*] (RCD)
CEDS......... Continuing Education Delivery Systems
CEDS......... Control Element Drive System [*Nuclear energy*] (NRCH)
CEDS......... Council for Educational Diagnostic Services [*Council for Exceptional Children*]
CEDT......... Confederation Europeenne des Detaillants en Tabac [*European Federation of Tobacco Retail Organizations*] (EAIO)
CEDU......... (Chloroethyl)deoxyuridine [*Biochemistry*]
CEE........... Advisory Committee for Civil and Environmental Engineering [*National Science Foundation*] [*Terminated, 1985*] (EGAO)
CEE........... Cancorp Enterprises [*Vancouver Stock Exchange symbol*]
CEE........... Captured Enemy Equipment [*Military*] (AFM)
CEE........... Carbon Electrode Equipment
CEE........... Career Employment Experience [*Office of Youth Programs*] [*Department of Labor*]
CEE........... Center for Environmental Education [*Research center*] (EA)
CEE........... Chartered Electrical Engineer [*British*] (DAS)
CEE........... Chick Embryo Extract [*Culture media*]
CEE........... Clear Mines Ltd. [*Vancouver Stock Exchange symbol*]
CEE........... Cleveland, OH [*Location identifier*] [*FAA*] (FAAL)
CEE........... Combat Emplacement Excavator
CEE........... Commerce Exterieur Albanais [*A publication*]
CEE........... Commission Economique pour l'Europe [*Economic Commission for Europe - ECE*] [*French*]
CEE........... Commission Internationale de Certification de Conformite de l'Equipement Electrique [*International Commission for Conformity Certification of Electrical Equipment*] [*French*] (EA)
CEE........... Commissioner of Election Expenses [*Canada*]
CEE........... Committee on Energy and the Environment [*National Research Council*]
CEE........... Communaute Economique Europeenne [*European Economic Community*]
CEE........... Communication Electronics Element [*Army*] (AABC)
CEE........... Comunidad Economica Europea [*European Economic Community - EEC*] [*Spanish*]
CEE........... Comunita Economica Europea [*European Economic Community - EEC*] [*Italian*]
CEE........... Comunitatea Economica Europeana [*European Economic Community - EEC*]
CEE........... Conference on English Education (EA)
CEE........... Conseil d'Expansion Economique [*Economic Expansion Council*] [*Canada*]
CEE........... Controlled Experimental Ecosystem [*Study technique*]
CEE........... Cooperative Educational Enterprises
CE-E......... Corps of Engineers Guide Specifications for Emergency Type Construction [*Army*]
CEE........... Cost per Entered Employment [*Job Training and Partnership Act*] (OICC)
CEE........... Council on Electrolysis Education (EA)
CEE........... Council for Environmental Education [*British*]
CEE........... International Commission for Conformity of Certification of Electrical Equipment [*Later, IECEE*]
CEEA........ Catholic Educational Exhibitors Association [*Later, NCEE*]
CEEA........ Charging Electrical Effects Analyzer (MCD)
CEEA........ Communaute Europeenne de l'Energie Atomique
CEEAC...... Communaute Economique des Etats de l'Afrique Centrale [*Economic Community of Central African States - ECCAS*] [*Bangui, Central African Republic*] (EAIO)
CEEAS ...... Centre Europeen d'Etudes de l'Acide Sulfurique [*European Center for Studies of Sulfuric Acid*] (EAIO)
CEEB........ College Entrance Examination Board [*Known as The College Board; acronym no longer used*] (EA)
CEEC........ Comite Europeen des Economistes de la Construction [*Construction Economics European Committee*] (EA)
CEEC........ Comite Europeen pour l'Enseignement Catholique [*European Committee for Catholic Education*] (EAIO)
CEEC........ Committee for European Economic Cooperation [*Marshall Plan*] [*Post-World War II*]
CEEC........ Construction Economics European Committee (EAIO)
CEECT...... Centre for Editing Early Canadian Texts
CEED........ Center for Entrepreneurship and Economic Development [*Pan American University*] [*Research center*] (RCD)
CEED........ Centre for Economic and Environmental Development [*British*] (CB)
CEEDE...... Center for Educational Experimentation, Development, and Evaluation [*University of Iowa*] [*Research center*] (RCD)
CEEDO ..... Civil and Environmental Engineering Development Office [*Tyndall Air Force Base, FL*]
CEEF........ Clergy Economic Education Foundation [*Later, EEFC*]
CEEFA ...... Centre d'Etudes et d'Echanges Francophones en Australie [*Australia*]
CEEFAX.... See Facts [*BBC "dial-a-page" news broadcast*] [*British*]
CEEG......... Computer Electroencephalogram
CEEGAM ... Clinical Electroencephalography [*A publication*]
CEEI.......... Center for Energy and Environmental Information [*Department of Energy*] (GRD)
CEEIA .... Communications-Electronics Engineering Installation Agency [*DoD*]

CEEIA-NCC ... Communications-Electronics Engineering Installation Agency-National Communications Command [*DoD*] (RDA)

CEEMA ..... Conference Europeenne des Experts Meteorologistes de l'Aeronautique

CEEMAT .. Centre d'Etudes et d'Experimentation du Machinisme Agricole Tropical [*Center for the Study and Experimentation of Tropical Agriculture Machinery*] [*International Cooperation Center of Agricultural Research for Development*] [*Information service or system*] (IID)

CEE/ONU ... Commission Economique pour l'Europe/Organisation des Nations Unies [*Economic Commission for Europe/United Nations Organization*] (EAIO)

CEEP .... Centre Europeen de l'Entreprise Publique [*European Center of Public Enterprise - ECPE*] (EAIO)

CEEP .... Centre Europeen d'Etudes de Population [*European Center for Population Studies*]

CEEP .... Committee for Environmentally Effective Packaging (EA)

CEER .... Center for Energy and Environmental Research [*University of Puerto Rico*]

CEER .... Chemical Economy and Engineering Review [*A publication*]

CEER .... Cost Estimate Error Report

CEERA ...... Conference Europeenne des Experts Radiotelegraphistes de l'Aeronautique

CEES .... Center for Energy and Environmental Studies [*Carnegie-Mellon University*] [*Research center*] (RCD)

CEES .... Center for Environmental and Estuarine Studies [*University of Maryland*] [*Research center*]

CEES .... Comite Europeen d'Etude du Sel [*European Committee for the Study of Salt - ECSS*] (EA)

CEESAC .... Central and East European Studies Association of Canada [*See also AEECEEC*]

CEESTEM ... Centro de Estudios Economicos y Sociales del Tercer Mundo [*Center for Economic and Social Studies of the Third World*] [*Canada*]

CEESTEM/TM ... Tercer Mundo y Economia Mundial. Centro de Estudios Economicos y Sociales del Tercer Mundo [*Mexico*] [*A publication*]

CEETA ...... Communications Electronics Evaluation and Test Agency (MCD)

CEETB ...... Comite Europeen des Equipements Techniques du Batiment [*European Committee for Building Technical Equipment - ECBTE*] (EAIO)

CEEUSA ... Commission for Educational Exchange between the United States of America and Afghanistan

C of EE & W ... Council of Emperor of East and West [*Freemasonry*] (ROG)

CEF .... Canadian Expeditionary Forces

CEF .... Captain [*Commanding*] Escort Forces [*Navy*]

CEF .... Career Executive Force [*Air Force*]

CEF .... Carrier Elimination Filter

CEF .... Catalogue de l'Edition Francaise

CeF .... Ce Fastu? [*A publication*]

CEF .... Central Fund of Canada Ltd. [*AMEX symbol*] [*Toronto Stock Exchange symbol*]

CeF .... Centrala Filmarkivet Ab, Stockholm, Sweden [*Library symbol*] [*Library of Congress*] (LCLS)

CEF .... Centralized Environmental Facility

CEF .... Centre for Economic Forecasting [*London Business School*] [*British*] (CB)

CEF .... Centrifugation Extractable Fluid

CEF .... Channeling Effect Factor

CEF .... Chick Embryo Fibroblast

CEF .... Chicken Embryo Fibroblast [*Cell line*]

CEF .... Chicopee Falls, MA [*Location identifier*] [*FAA*] (FAAL)

CEF .... Chief Executives Forum [*Later, CEO*]

CEF .... Child Evangelism Fellowship (EA)

CEF .... Childbirth Education Foundation (EA)

CEF .... Children's Express Foundation (EA)

CEF .... Chinese Expeditionary Force

CEF .... Christian Educators Fellowship [*Later, CEAI*] (EA)

CEF .... Citizens for Educational Freedom (EA)

CEF .... Clearinghouse on Educational Facilities [*ERIC*]

CEF .... Closed-End Fund [*Investment term*]

CEF .... Cloth Elongation Factor [*Textiles*]

CEF .... Commission Europeenne des Forets

CEF .... Committee for Education Funding (EA)

CEF .... Complementary Emitter Follower

CEF .... Computer Execute Function (KSC)

CEF .... Contemporary Evaluation Form [*Army*]

CEF .... Controlled Environmental Forestry

CEF .... Corps Expeditionaire Francais

CEF .... Creative Education Foundation (EA)

CEF .... Cross-Range Error Function

CEF .... Cryptographic Equipment Facility (MCD)

CEFA .... Council for Educational Freedom in America (EA)

CEFAC ...... Civil Engineering Field Activities Center

CEFACD ... Comite Europeen des Fabricants d'Appareils de Chauffage et de Cuisine Domestiques [*European Committee of Manufacturers of Domestic Heating and Cooking Appliances*]

CEFC .... Country Edition Fan Club [*Inactive*] (EA)

CEFCO ...... Centre d'Etudes Franco-Canadiennes de l'Ouest [*Centre of Studies of French-Canadians of Western Canada*]

CEFCTU ... Central European Federation of Christian Trade Unions (EA)

CEFDA ...... Central European Forces Distribution Agency [*NATO*] (NATG)

CEFEPAL ... Centro de Estudos Franciscanos e Pastorais para a America Latina

CEFF .... Controlled Energy Flow Forming

CEFI .... Child Evangelism Fellowship International [*Later, CEF*] (EA)

CEFI .... Contractor Engineer - Furnish and Install (AABC)

CEFI .... Controlled Environment Farming International Ltd. [*Vancouver, BC*] [*NASDAQ symbol*] (NQ)

CEFIC .... Conseil Europeen des Federations de l'Industrie Chimique [*European Council of Chemical Manufacturers Federations - ECCMF*] [*Belgium*] (EAIO)

CEFIP .... Communications-Electronics Facility Inoperative for Parts (MCD)

C-E-F L .... Clifton-Essex-Franklin Library [*Library network*]

CEFO .... Complete Equipment Fighting Order [*British military*] (DMA)

CEFOAM ... Checkout Equipment for Onboard Automatic Maintenance

CE Focus .... Continuing Education in Nursing Focus [*A publication*]

CEFP .... Council of Educational Facility Planners (EA)

CEFPI .... Council of Educational Facility Planners, International (EA)

CEFR .... Cease Fire Corp. [*NASDAQ symbol*] (NQ)

CEFRAS .... Centre Europeen de Formation et de Recherche en Action Sociale [*European Centre for Social Welfare Training and Research - ECSWTR*] [*United Nations*] (EAIO)

CEFS .... Comite Europeen des Fabricants de Sucre [*European Committee of Sugar Manufacturers*] [*Common Market*]

CEFSR .... Committee for Evaluating the Feasibility of Space Rocketry [*Navy Bureau of Aeronautics*] [*Obsolete*]

CEFT .... Children's Embedded Figures Test [*Psychology*]

CEFT .... Concord Computing Corp. [*NASDAQ symbol*] (NQ)

CEFYM .... Central European Federal Youth Movement

CEG .... Cahners Exposition Group [*Telecommunications service*] (TSSD)

CEG .... Camel Oil & Gas Ltd. [*Toronto Stock Exchange symbol*]

CEG .... Canadian Giant Explorations [*Vancouver Stock Exchange symbol*]

CEG .... Career Employment Group [*British military*] (DMA)

CEG .... Catholic Evidence Guild (EA)

CEG .... Central Emergency Government Headquarters (MCD)

CEG .... Central Equipment Group [*Military*] (CAAL)

C Eg .... Chronique d'Egypte [*A publication*]

CEG .... Competitive Events Guidelines [*A publication*] (EAAP)

CEG .... Computer Education Group [*Australia*]

CEG .... Continuous Edge Graphics [*Edson Laboratories*] [*Data processing*]

CEG .... Council for Excellence in Government (EA)

CEG .... Cuadernos de Estudios Gallegos [*A publication*]

CEGB .... Central Electricity Generating Board [*British*]

CEGB Dig ... CEGB [*Central Electricity Generating Board*] Digest [*England*] [*A publication*]

CEGB Res ... CEGB [*Central Electricity Generating Board*] Research [*A publication*]

CEGB Tech Disclosure Bull ... CEGB [*Central Electricity Generating Board*] Technical Disclosure Bulletin [*England*] [*A publication*]

CEGE .... Combat Equipment Group, Europe (MCD)

CEGEP ...... College d'Enseignement General et Professionnel [*College of General and Professional Instruction*] [*Canada*]

CEGET ...... Centre d'Etudes en Geographie Tropicale [*Centre of Studies in Tropical Geography*] [*France*]

CEGFA ...... Centralblatt fuer das Gesamte Forstwesen [*Austria*] [*A publication*]

CEG-I .... Committee for the Economic Growth of Israel (EA)

CEGJA ...... Coalition to End Grand Jury Abuse [*Later, CPR*] (EA)

CEGJB ...... Canterbury Engineering Journal [*A publication*]

CEGL .... Cause-Effect Graph Language [*Data processing*] (IBMDP)

CEGNY ..... Catholic Evidence Guild of New York [*Defunct*] (EA)

CEGOAM ... Clinical and Experimental Obstetrics and Gynecology [*A publication*]

CEGPAP ... CEGS [*Council on Education in the Geological Sciences*] Programs Publication [*A publication*]

C E Gr .... [*C. E.*] Greene. New Jersey Equity Reports [*16-27*] [*A publication*] (DLA)

C E Greene ... [*C. E.*] Greene. New Jersey Equity Reports [*16-27*] [*A publication*] (DLA)

CEGROB ... Communaute Europeenne des Associations du Commerce de Gros de Biere des Pays Membres de la CEE [*European Community of Associations of the Wholesale Beer Trade of the EEC*]

CEGS .... Centre of European Governmental Studies [*University of Edinburgh*] [*United Kingdom*] (CB)

CEGS .... Church of Jesus Christ of Latter-Day Saints, Genealogical Society Library, Eureka Branch, Eureka, CA [*Library symbol*] [*Library of Congress*] (LCLS)

CEGS .... Committee to Establish the Gold Standard (EA)

CEGS .... Council for Economic Growth and Security [*Defunct*]

CEGS .... Council on Education in the Geological Sciences

CEGS Programs Publ ... CEGS [*Council on Education in the Geological Sciences*] Programs Publication [*A publication*]

CEGYA...... Ceskoslovenska Gynekologie [*A publication*]
CEH........... Center for Environmental Health [*Atlanta, GA*] [*Department of Health and Human Services*] (GRD)
CEH........... Central Capital Corp. [*Toronto Stock Exchange symbol*]
CEH........... Central European History [*A publication*]
CEH........... Centre on Environment for the Handicapped [*British*] (CB)
CEH........... Chapel Hill [*North Carolina*] [*Seismograph station code, US Geological Survey*] (SEIS)
CEH........... Chemical Economics Handbook [*SRI International*] [*Database*]
CEH........... Chromatography of Environmental Hazards [*Elsevier Book Series*] [*A publication*]
CEH........... Conference Europeenne des Horaires des Trains de Voyageurs [*European Passenger Timetable Conference*] [*Switzerland*]
CEH........... Humboldt County Free Library, Eureka, CA [*Library symbol*] [*Library of Congress*] (LCLS)
CEHA........ Contact Equipment Handling Area [*Nuclear energy*] (NRCH)
CEHADM ... Clinical and Experimental Hypertension. Part A. Theory and Practice [*A publication*]
CEHC........ Canever English History Club
CEHI......... Centre d'Etudis Historics Internationals [*Center for International Historical Studies*] (EA)
CEHIC....... Center for Environmental Health and Injury Control [*Atlanta, GA*] [*Centers for Disease Control*] [*Department of Health and Human Services*] (GRD)
CEHILA.... Comision de Estudios de Historia de la Iglesia en Latinoamerica [*Commission of the Studies of History of the Church in Latin America*] [*Mexico*]
C of E Hist Soc J ... Church of England Historical Society. Journal [*A publication*] (APTA)
CEHS .... Church of England Historical Society (ADA)
CEHS .... Civilian Employee Health Service
CEHSA...... Consumer and Environmental Health Services Administration [*HEW*]
CEHSJ ...... Church of England Historical Society. Journal [*A publication*] (ADA)
CEHSMO ... Historia Obrera. Centro de Estudios Historicos del Movimiento Obrero Mexicano [*A publication*]
CEHYDQ .. Clinical and Experimental Hypertension [*A publication*]
CEI............ Cambridge Electronic Industries [*British*]
CEI............ Canadian Education Index [*Repertoire Canadien sur l'Education*] [*A publication*]
CEI............ Center for Education in International Management [*Canada*]
CEI............ Center for Energy Information [*Defunct*]
CEI............ Center for Environmental Information, Inc. [*Information service or system*] (IID)
CEI............ Centre for Employment Initiatives Ltd. [*British*] (CB)
CEI............ Centre for Environmental Interpretation [*Manchester Polytechnic*] [*British*] (CB)
CEI............ Centre d'Etudes Industrielles [*Center for education in international management*] [*Switzerland*] (DCTA)
CEI............ Character Education Institute (EA)
CEI............ Chemical Engineering Index [*A publication*] (APTA)
CEI............ Chiang Rai [*Thailand*] [*Airport symbol*] (OAG)
C & EI .... Chicago & Eastern Illinois Railroad Co. [*Absorbed into Missouri Pacific System*]
CEI............ Chicago & Eastern Illinois Railroad Co. [*Absorbed into Missouri Pacific System*]
CEI............ Chicago Evangelistic Institute
CEI............ Claremont Economics Institute [*Information service or system*] (IID)
CEI............ Classroom Environment Index [*Student attitude test*]
CEI............ Co-Steel, Inc. [*Toronto Stock Exchange symbol*]
CEI............ Coated Electrodes International [*British*]
CEI............ Commission Electrotechnique Internationale [*International Electrotechnical Commission - IEC*] [*Switzerland*] (EAIO)
CEI............ Committee for Environmental Information (IID)
CEI............ Communication Electronic Instructions
CEI............ Communications Engineering and Installation Department [*Army*]
CEI............ Community Economics, Incorporated (EA)
CEI............ Comparably Efficient Interconnection [*Telecommunications*]
CEI............ Computer-Enhanced Instruction
CEI............ Computer-Extended Instruction (IEEE)
CEI............ Conferences and Exhibitions International [*A publication*]
CEI............ Configuration End Item (AFIT)
CEI............ Continuous Extravascular Infusion [*Medicine*]
CEI............ Contract End Item (MCD)
CEI............ Contractor End Item (MCD)
CEI............ Converting-Enzyme Inhibitor [*Biochemistry*]
CEI............ Correct End Item (KSC)
CEI............ Cost Effectiveness Index [*Economics*]
CEI............ Council of Engineering Institutions [*British*]
CEI............ Critical Engine Inoperative (MCD)
CEI............ Cycle Engineers' Institute
CEIA......... Communications Engineering and Installation Agency
CEIAA....... Centro di Studi per l'Ingegneria Agraria. Memorie ed Atti [*A publication*]
CEIAC....... Coastal Engineering Information Analysis Center [*Vicksburg, MS*] [*DoD*] (GRD)
CEIADR.... Commission of the European Communities. Information on Agriculture [*A publication*]

CEIB.......... Computer Equipment Information Bureau [*Information service or system*] (IID)
CEI-BOIS ... Confederation Europeenne des Industries du Bois [*European Confederation of Woodworking Industries*] (EAIO)
CEIC......... Canada Employment and Immigration Commission
CEIC......... Census and Economic Information Center [*Montana State Department of Commerce*] [*Helena*] [*Information service or system*] (IID)
CEIC......... Chemical Effects Information Center [*Department of Energy*] (IID)
CEIC......... Closed-End Investment Company [*Business term*]
CEID......... Crossed Electroimmunodiffusion [*Analytical biochemistry*]
CE/IDC ..... Chase Econometrics/Interactive Data Corporation [*Database vendor*]
CEIDD....... Committee on the Economic Impact of Defense and Disarmament (KSC)
CEIDP....... Conference on Electrical Insulation and Dielectric Phenomena [*National Academy of Sciences*]
CEIEC .... China National Electronics Import & Export Corporation [*People's Republic of China*] (IMH)
CEIED....... Chemical Engineering (International Edition) [*A publication*]
CEIF......... Council of European Industrial Federations
CEIL......... Ceiling [*Aviation*]
CEIL......... Combat Essential Items List [*Army*]
CEIL......... Consumer Education and Information Liaison [*Federal interagency group*]
CEIM......... Confederacion Empresarial Independiente de Madrid de la Pequena, Mediana, y Gran Empresa [*Employers' organization*] [*Spain*] (EY)
CEIN .... Contract End Item Number
CEIND ...... Ceramurgia International [*A publication*]
CEINEX .... Cecidologia Internationale [*A publication*]
CEIP......... Carnegie Endowment for International Peace (EA)
CEIP......... Center for Environmental Intern Programs (EA)
CEIP......... Coastal Energy Impact Program [*National Oceanic and Atmospheric Administration*]
CEIP......... Communications-Electronics Implementation Plan [*For major air command requirements within the communications-electronics area*] [*Air Force*]
CEIPA .... Communications-Electronics Implementation Plan Amendment [*See CEIP*] [*Air Force*] (AFM)
CEIPI........ Centre d'Etudes Internationales de la Propriete Industrielle
CEIR......... Civil Emergency Information Room [*NATO*] (NATG)
CEIR......... Cooperative Economic Insect Report [*Department of Agriculture*] [*A publication*]
CEIR......... Corporation for Economics and Industrial Research [*Subsidiary of Control Data Corp.*]
CEIRD...... Confirming Engineering Information Report Date [*Bell System*] (TEL)
CEIRPP..... Committee on the Exercise of the Inalienable Rights of the Palestinian People (EA)
CEIRS....... Conservation and Renewable Energy Inquiry and Referral Service [*Database*]
CEIS .... Candidate Environmental Impact Statement (MCD)
CEIS .... Central Economic Information Service [*British*]
CEIS .... Centre for European Industrial Studies [*University of Bath*] [*British*] (CB)
CEIS .... Committee on Evaluation and Information Systems (OICC)
CEIS .... Cost and Economic Information System [*DoD*] (MCD)
CEIS .... Cost Estimate Input Sheet [*Jet Propulsion Laboratory, NASA*]
CEIT .... Crew Equipment Integration [*or Interface*] Test (MCD)
CEITG ...... Chemical Effects Information Task Group [*Department of Energy*] [*Information service or system*] (IID)
CEIU .... Canada Employment and Immigration Union
CE/IWT .... Central Europe Inland Waterways Transport [*NATO*] (NATG)
CEJ........... California English Journal [*A publication*]
CEJ........... Cement-Enamel Junction [*Dentistry*]
CEJ........... Christian Educators Journal [*A publication*]
CEJ........... Compagnie Europeenne de la Jeunesse
CEJ........... Cooperative Expendable Jammer
CEJ........... Wildwood, NJ [*Location identifier*] [*FAA*] (FAAL)
CEJA .... Conseil Europeen des Jeunes Agriculteurs [*European Committee of Young Farmers*] [*Common Market*]
CEJEDP.... Central Europe Joint Emergency Defense Plan [*NATO*] (NATG)
CEJL .... Current Events in Jewish Life [*New York*] [*A publication*]
CEK .... Cahiers Economiques de Bruxelles [*A publication*]
CEK .... Cetec Engineering Co., Inc. [*Vancouver Stock Exchange symbol*]
CEK .... Computer Entry Keyboard
CEL........... Carbon Equilibrium Loop
CEL........... Celaya [*Race of maize*]
CEL........... Celebrated
CEL........... Celesta [*Music*]
CEL........... Celestial (AFM)
CEL........... Celibate
CEL........... Celico Resources [*Vancouver Stock Exchange symbol*]
CEL........... Celluloid
CEL........... Cellulose [*Botany*]
CEL........... Celsius [*Centigrade*] [*Temperature scale*]

Cel .... [*Publius Juventius*] Celsus [*Flourished, 77-129*] [*Authority cited in pre-1607 legal work*]   (DSA)
CEL .... Celtic
cel .... Celtic Group [*MARC language code*] [*Library of Congress*] [*Obsolete*]   (LCCP)
CEL .... Central European Line [*Oil pipeline*]
CEL .... Channels of English Literature [*A publication*]
CEL .... Child-Centered Experience-Based Learning [*An association*] [*Canada*]
CEL .... China Trade and Economic Newsletter [*London*] [*A publication*]
CEL .... Civil Engineering Laboratory [*Also, CIVENGRLAB*] [*Port Hueneme, CA*] [*Navy*]   (MCD)
CEL .... Coastal Ecology Laboratory [*Louisiana State University*] [*Research center*]   (RCD)
CEL .... Combat Elevation Launch
CEL .... Committee for an Extended Lifespan [*Defunct*]   (EA)
CEL .... Communications & Entertainment Ltd. [*Australia*]
CEL .... Compressor Endurance Loops   (MCD)
CEL .... Constitutional Educational League
CEL .... Contractor Experience List [*DoD*]
CEL .... Contrast Enhanced Lithography
CEL .... Contrast-Enhancement Layer [*Photoprocessing*]
CEL .... Conversational Extensible Language [*Data processing*]   (CSR)
CEL .... Cooley Electronics Laboratory [*University of Michigan*] [*Research center*]   (RCD)
CEL .... Cosine Emission Law [*Optics*]
CEL .... Council on Engineering Laws [*Defunct*]   (EA)
CEL .... Critical Experiment Laboratory
CEL .... Crop Evolution Laboratory [*University of Illinois*]
CEL .... Cryogenic Engineering Laboratory [*National Institute of Standards and Technology*]
CEL .... Customer Engineering Letter   (MCD)
CEL .... Customs and Excise Laboratory [*Canada*]
CEl .... Elsinore Free Public Library, Elsinore, CA [*Library symbol*] [*Library of Congress*]   (LCLS)
CELA .... Canadian Environmental Law Association
CEL(A) ...... Chief Electrician (Air) [*British military*]   (DMA)
CELA .... Comision Economica para America Latina [*Economic Commission for Latin America - ECLA*] [*Santiago, Chile*]
CELACS ...... Confidential Employment Listing [*American Chemical Society*]
CELADE ... Centro Latinoamericana de Demografia [*Latin American Demographic Center*] [*Economic Commission for Latin America and the Caribbean*] [*United Nations*] [*Chile*]
CELAM ..... Consejo Episcopal Latinoamericano [*Latin American Episcopal Council*]   (EAIO)
CELA Newsletter ... Canadian Environmental Law Association. Newsletter [*A publication*]   (DLA)
CELAT ...... Centre d'Etudes sur la Langue, les Arts, et les Traditions Populaires des Francophones en Amerique du Nord [*Laval University*] [*Canada*] [*Research center*]   (RCD)
CEL(AW) .. Chief Electrician (Air Weapon) [*British military*]   (DMA)
CELBA ...... Conti Elektro Berichte [*A publication*]
CELC .... CEL Communications, Inc. [*NASDAQ symbol*]   (NQ)
CELC .... Commonwealth Education Liaison Committee [*British*]
CELCA ...... Commutation et Electronique [*A publication*]
CELCAA ... Comite Europeen de Liaison des Commerces Agro-Alimentaires [*European Liaison Committee for Agricultural and Food Trades*]   (EAIO)
CELD .... Central External Liaison Department [*Chinese Secret Service*]
CELDIC .... Commission on Emotional and Learning Disorders in Children [*Canada*]
CELDS ...... Computerized Environmental Legislative Data System [*Army*]
CELESCO ... Celestial Research Corporation   (KSC)
CELESCOPE ... Celestial Telescope [*OAO*]
Celestial Mech ... Celestial Mechanics [*A publication*]
Celest Mech ... Celestial Mechanics [*A publication*]
CELEX ...... Communitatis Europae Lex [*European Community Law*] [*Commission of the European Communities*] [*Information service or system*]   (IID)
CELF .... Clinical Evaluation of Language Functions [*Speech evaluation test*]
Celfan R ..... Revue Celfan/Celfan Review [*A publication*]
CELG .... Celgene Corp. [*NASDAQ symbol*]   (NQ)
CELI .... Carrow Elicited Language Inventory [*Education*]
CELI .... Cel-Sci Corp. [*NASDAQ symbol*]   (NQ)
CELI .... Congressional Economic Leadership Institute   (EA)
CELI .... Contingent Employee Liability Insurance
CELIA ...... Continuous Electrocardiogram in Ambulatory Patients [*Medicine*]
CELIBRIDE ... Comite de Liaison International des Broderies, Rideaux, et Dentelles [*International Liaison Committee for Embroideries, Curtains, and Laces*]
CELIMAC ... Comite Europeen de Liaison des Industries de la Machine a Coudre [*European Liaison Committee for the Sewing Machine Industries - ELCSMI*]   (EAIO)
CELINTREP ... Accelerated Intelligence Report   (NATG)
CELISA ..... Competitive Enzyme-Linked Immunosorbent Assay
Celjabinsk Gos Ped Inst Trudy ... Celjabinskii Gosudarstvennyi Pedagogiceskii Institut. Trudy [*A publication*]
CELL .... Cell Technology, Inc. [*NASDAQ symbol*]   (NQ)

CELL .... Continuing Education Learning Laboratory   (EA)
CELLA4 .... Cellule [*A publication*]
Cell Biochem Funct ... Cell Biochemistry and Function [*A publication*]
Cell Biol Int Rep ... Cell Biology International Reports [*A publication*]
Cell Biol Monogr ... Cell Biology Monographs [*A publication*]
Cell Biol Ser Monogr ... Cell Biology: a Series of Monographs [*A publication*]
Cell Biol T ... Cell Biology and Toxicology [*A publication*]
Cell Biophys ... Cell Biophysics [*A publication*]
Cell Chem T ... Cellulose Chemistry and Technology [*A publication*]
Cell Chromosome Newsl ... Cell and Chromosome Newsletter [*A publication*]
Cell Chromosome Res ... Cell and Chromosome Research [*A publication*]
Cell Cult Methods Mol Cell Biol ... Cell Culture Methods for Molecular and Cell Biology [*A publication*]
Cell Differ ... Cell Differentiation [*A publication*]
Celli .... Violoncelli [*Cellos*] [*Music*]
Cell Immun ... Cellular Immunology [*A publication*]
Cell Immunol ... Cellular Immunology [*A publication*]
Cell Mol Biol ... Cellular and Molecular Biology [*A publication*]
Cell Mol Neurobiol ... Cellular and Molecular Neurobiology [*A publication*]
Cell Motil ... Cell Motility [*A publication*]
Cell Motil Cytoskeleton ... Cell Motility and the Cytoskeleton [*A publication*]
Cell Muscle Motil ... Cell and Muscle Motility [*A publication*]
CELLO ...... Violoncello [*Music*]
Cell Polym ... Cellular Polymers [*A publication*]
Cell Senescence Somatic Cell Genet ... Cellular Senescence and Somatic Cell Genetics [*A publication*]
CELLSIM ... Cell Simulation [*Programming language*] [*1973*]   (CSR)
Cell Struct Funct ... Cell Structure and Function [*A publication*]
Cell Surf Rev ... Cell Surface Reviews [*A publication*]
Cell Tis Re ... Cell and Tissue Research [*A publication*]
Cell Tiss K ... Cell and Tissue Kinetics [*A publication*]
Cell Tissue Kinet ... Cell and Tissue Kinetics [*A publication*]
Cell Tissue Res ... Cell and Tissue Research [*A publication*]
CELLUL ..... Cellular
Cellul Carta ... Cellulosa e Carta [*A publication*]
Celluloid Ind ... Celluloid Industrie [*A publication*]
Celluloid Plast Massen ... Celluloid und Plastische Massen [*A publication*]
Cellulose Chem Technol ... Cellulose Chemistry and Technology [*A publication*]
CELM .... Cellular America, Inc. [*Freehold, NJ*] [*NASDAQ symbol*]   (NQ)
CELMN ...... Chief Electrical Mechanician [*British military*]   (DMA)
CELN .... Celina Financial Corp. [*Celina, OH*] [*NASDAQ symbol*]   (NQ)
CELNAV ... Celestial Navigation   (FAAC)
CELNUCO ... Comite Europeen de Liaison des Negociants et Utilisateurs de Combustibles [*European Liaison Committee of Fuel Merchants and Users*]
CELO .... Chicken Embryo Lethal Orphan [*Virus*]
CELOGS ... Combat Effectiveness with Logistics Support   (MCD)
Celosloven Geol Konf Mater ... Celoslovenska Geologicka Konferencia. Materialy [*A publication*]
Celostatna Konf Term Anal ... Celostatna Konferencia o Termickej Analyze [*A publication*]
Celovek i Obsc ... Celovek i Obscestvo [*A publication*]
CELP .... Cellular Products, Inc. [*Buffalo, NY*] [*NASDAQ symbol*]   (NQ)
CELP .... Civilian Employment Level Plan [*DoD*]
CELPP ...... Colleges of Education Learning Programme Project [*British*]
CELR .... Canadian Environmental Law Reports [*A publication*]   (DLA)
CELRA ...... Conference of Latin Bishops of Arab Regions [*Jersalem, Israel*]   (EAIO)
CELS .... Cellular, Inc. [*Englewood, CO*] [*NASDAQ symbol*]   (NQ)
CELS .... Celsius   (ROG)
CELS .... Centre for European Legal Studies [*University of Exeter*] [*British*]   (CB)
Cel Sep ...... Cell Separation [*Cytology*]
CELSF ...... Committee to Eliminate Legal-Size Files [*Defunct*]   (EA)
CELSS ...... Closed Ecological Life Support System [*NASA*]
Celsus Med ... Celsus, De Medicina [*First century AD*] [*Classical studies*]   (OCD)
CELT .... Celltronics, Inc. [*San Diego, CA*] [*NASDAQ symbol*]   (NQ)
Celt .... Celtiberia [*A publication*]
CELT .... Celtic
CELT .... Centre for English Language Teaching [*University of Stirling*] [*British*]   (CB)
CELT .... Classified Entries in Lateral Transposition [*Indexing*]
CELT .... Coherent Emitter Location Testbed   (IEEE)
CELT .... Consolidated Entry Level Training   (MCD)
CELT .... Continuing Education for Laboratory Technicians [*Union Carbide Co.*]
CELTE ...... Constructeurs Europeens de Locomotives Thermiques et Electriques [*European Manufacturers of Thermal and Electric Locomotives*]   (EAIO)
Celtic R ...... Celtic Review [*A publication*]
Cel Tr .... Burke's Celebrated Trials [*A publication*]   (DLA)
Celul Hirtie ... Celuloza si Hirtie [*A publication*]
Celuloza Hirt ... Celuloza si Hirtie [*A publication*]
Celul Pap Grafika ... Celuloza, Papir, Grafika [*A publication*]
CELV .... Complementary Expendable Launch Vehicle [*Space technology*]
CEM .... Cahiers d'Etudes Medievales [*A publication*]
CEM .... Captured Enemy Material [*Military*]

CEM .... Cement (KSC)
CEM .... Cement Conduit [*Telecommunications*] (TEL)
CEM .... Cemetery (AABC)
CEM .... Center for Electromechnics [*University of Texas at Austin*] [*Research center*] (RCD)
CEM .... Center for Entrepreneurial Management [*New York, NY*] (EA)
CEM .... Center for the Environment and Man, Inc. [*Research center*] (RCD)
CEM .... Central [*Alaska*] [*Airport symbol*] (OAG)
CEM .... Central Error Module (CAAL)
CeM .... Central Microfilm Service Corp., St. Louis, MO [*Library symbol*] [*Library of Congress*] (LCLS)
CEM .... Certified Exposition Manager [*Designation awarded by National Association of Exposition Managers, Inc.*]
CEM .... Channel Electron Multiplier (MCD)
CEM .... Chemical Engineering Monographs [*Elsevier Book Series*] [*A publication*]
CEM .... Chief Electrician's Mate [*Navy rating*] [*Obsolete*]
CEM .... Chief Enlisted Manager
CEM .... Christian Education Movement [*British*]
CEM .... Circular Electric Mode
CEM .... Clinical and Experimental Metastasis [*A publication*]
CEM .... Combat Earthmover [*Army*]
CEM .... Combat Effectiveness Measure [*Military*] (CAAL)
CEM .... Combat Evaluation Model (MCD)
CEM .... Combination Export Management [*Small Business Administration*]
CEM .... Combined Effects Munition (MCD)
CEM .... Comissao Eleitoral Monarquica [*Monarchy Electoral Committee*] [*Portugal*] (PPE)
CEM .... Commission on Education for Mission [*National Council of Churches*] (EA)
CEM .... Communications-Electronics-Meteorological [*Equipment*]
CEM .... Compromising Emanations (AABC)
CEM .... Computer-Assisted Electron Microscope
CEM .... Computer Education for Management
CEM .... Computerized Exercise Machine
CEM .... CONAF [*Conceptual Design for the Army in the Field*] Evaluation Model
CEM .... Concepts Evaluation Model [*Military*]
CEM .... Confederacion Evangelica Mundial [*World Evangelical Fellowship*]
CEM .... Conference Europeenne des Horaires des Trains de Marchandises [*European Freight Timetable Conference*] (EAIO)
CEM .... Contagious Equine Metritis
CEM .... Contract Energy Managers [*British*]
CEM .... Contrast Enhancement Material [*Photoprocessing*]
CEM .... Control Electrical Mechanic [*British military*] (DMA)
CEM .... Conventional-Transmission Electron Microscope
CEM .... Cost Element Monitor [*Air Force*]
CEM .... Council of European Municipalities
CEM .... Counter Electromotive Cell
CEM .... Cream Silver Mines Ltd. [*Vancouver Stock Exchange symbol*]
CEM .... Cuadernos de Estudios Mancheos [*A publication*]
CEM .... Current Evangelism Ministries (EA)
CEM3 .... Combat Engineer Mission Management Module [*Software*]
CEMA .... Canadian Egg Marketing Agency
CEMA .... Canadian Electrical Manufacturers' Association
CEMA .... Channel Electron Multiplier Array (MCD)
CEMA .... Cleaning Equipment Manufacturers Association [*Later, CETA*] (EA)
CEMA .... Comite Europeen des Groupements de Constructeurs du Machinisme Agricole [*European Committee of Associations of Manufacturers of Agricultural Machinery*] (EAIO)
CEMA .... Converting Equipment Manufacturers Association (EA)
CEMA .... Conveyor Equipment Manufacturers Association (EA)
CEMA .... Council for Economic Mutual Assistance [*Also known as CMEA, COMECON*] [*Communist-bloc nations: Poland, Russia, East Germany, Czechoslovakia, Romania, Bulgaria, Hungary*]
CEMA .... Council for the Encouragement of Music and the Arts [*Later, Arts Council*]
CEMA .... Customs and Excise Management Act (DS)
CEMAD .... Coherent Echo Modulation and Detection (MCD)
CEMAFON ... Comite Europeen des Materiels et Produits pour la Fonderie [*European Committee of Foundry Materials and Products*] (EAIO)
CEMAM ... Centre d'Etudes pour le Monde Arabe Moderne [*Beirut*]
CEMAP ..... Cotton Export Market Acreage Program
CEMARS .. COMSEC [*Communications Security*] Equipment Modification Application and Reporting System [*Army*] (MCD)
CEMAS ..... Complete Element Matrix Analysis from Scatter [*Spectrometry*]
CEMATEX ... Comite Europeen des Constructeurs de Materiel Textile [*European Committee of Textile Machinery Manufacturers*] (EAIO)
CEMB .... Cembalo [*Cymbals*] [*Music*] (ROG)
CEMB .... Comite Europeen pour le Mini-Basketball [*European Committee for Mini-Basketball - ECMB*] [*Munich, Federal Republic of Germany*] (EAIO)

CEMB .... Communication-Electronic-Meteorological Board [*Air Force*]
Cem Betong ... Cement och Betong [*A publication*]
CEMBI ..... Conference to Explore Machine Readable Bibliographic Interchange
CEMBUREAU ... European Cement Association (EAIO)
CEMC .... Canadian Engineering Manpower Council
CEMC .... Centro de Estudios Mayas-Cuadernos [*A publication*]
CEMC .... Century MediCorp [*Los Angeles, CA*] [*NASDAQ symbol*] (NQ)
CEMC .... Combined Exports Market Committee [*World War II*]
CEMC .... Communications Electronics Management Center [*Air Force*] (AFIT)
CEMC .... Counter Electromotive Cell (MCD)
CEMC .... Curriculum Evaluation and Management Centre [*University of Newcastle upon Tyne*] [*British*] (CB)
CEMCBC .. Chief Electrician's Mate, Construction Battalion, Communications [*Navy rating*] [*Obsolete*]
CEMCBD ... Chief Electrician's Mate, Construction Battalion, Draftsman [*Navy rating*] [*Obsolete*]
CEMCBG ... Chief Electrician's Mate, Construction Battalion, General [*Navy rating*] [*Obsolete*]
CEMCBL .. Chief Electrician's Mate, Construction Battalion, Line and Station [*Navy rating*] [*Obsolete*]
Cem Cem Manuf ... Cement and Cement Manufacture [*A publication*]
CEMCO ..... Continental Electronics Manufacturing Company (AAG)
Cem Concr (Delhi) ... Cement and Concrete (Delhi) [*A publication*]
Cem Concrete Ass Res Rep ... Cement and Concrete Association. Research Report [*A publication*]
Cem Concr Res ... Cement and Concrete Research [*A publication*]
Cem Concr (Tokyo) ... Cement and Concrete (Tokyo) [*A publication*]
CEME .... Comite des Eglises Aupres des Migrants en Europe [*Churches' Committee on Migrants in Europe*] (EAIO)
CEMEL ..... Clothing, Equipment, and Materials Engineering Laboratory [*Army Natick Research and Development Laboratories, MA*] (RDA)
Cement Concrete Res ... Cement and Concrete Research [*A publication*]
Cem Era ..... Cement Era [*A publication*]
CEMERS .. Center for Medieval and Early Renaissance Studies (EA)
CEMET .... Cemetery (ROG)
CEMF .... Collected Essays by the Members of the Faculty [*Kyoritsu Women's Junior College*] [*A publication*]
CEMF .... Counter Electromotive Force (MCD)
CEMGC .... Comite Europeen des Materiels de Genie Civil [*Committee for European Construction Equipment - CECE*] (EAIO)
CEMI .... Commission Europeenne de Marketing Industriel [*European Commission for Industrial Marketing*] [*Brixham, Devonshire, England*] (EAIO)
CEMI .... Committee on Emergency Medical Identification (EA)
CEMICH... Michoacan Information Center on the Mexico-US Future (EA)
CEMICS.... Central Equipment Management and Inventory Control System (MCD)
Cem Ind (Tokyo) ... Cement Industry (Tokyo) [*A publication*]
CEMIRT ... Civil Engineering Maintenance, Inspection, Repair, and Training Team [*Air Force*]
CEML .... Central Electron Microscopy Laboratory [*University of Georgia*] [*Research center*] (RCD)
CEMLA ..... Centro de Estudios Monetarios Latinoamericanos [*Center for Latin American Monetary Studies*] [*Mexico City, Mexico*] (EAIO)
CEMLA/M ... Monetaria. Centro de Estudios Monetarios Latinoamericanos [*Mexico*] [*A publication*]
Cem Lime Grav ... Cement, Lime, and Gravel [*A publication*]
Cem Lime Mf ... Cement and Lime Manufacture [*A publication*]
CEMM ...... Compaq Extended Memory Manager [*Software*]
Cem Mill Quarry ... Cement Mill and Quarry [*A publication*]
CEMN .... Center for Endocrinology, Metabolism, and Nutrition [*Northwestern University*]
CEMN .... Control Electrical Mechanician [*Navy rating*] [*British*]
CEMO .... Canada Emergency Measures Organization [*Civil defense*]
CEMO .... Command Equipment Management Office [*Military*] (AFM)
CEMO .... Communications Electronics Mission Order (MCD)
CEMON .... Customer Engineering Monitor [*IBM Corp.*]
CEMPAC .. Communications-Electronics-Meteorological Program Aggregate Code [*Air Force*] (AFM)
CEMPIMS ... Communications-Electronics-Meteorological Program Implementation Management System [*Air Force*] (CET)
CEMPR ..... Command Equipment Management Program Review [*Military*] (MCD)
CEMR .... Center for Economic and Management Research [*University of Oklahoma*] [*Norman*] [*Information service or system*] (IID)
CEMR .... Center for Energy and Mineral Resources [*Texas A & M University*] [*Research center*]
CEMR ...... Contractor Estimating Methods Review [*DoD*]
CEMREL .. Central Midwest Regional Educational Laboratory
Cem Res Inst India RB ... Cement Research Institute of India. Research Bulletin [*A publication*]
CEMS .... Central Electronic Management System
CEMS .... Church of England Men's Society
CEMS .... Civil Engineer Management System (AFM)
CEMS .... Commission on Emergency Medical Services (EA)

CEMS........ Communications Electronics Management Systems
CEMS........ Comprehensive Engine Management System
CEMS........ Construction Equipment Management System
CEMS........ Conversion Electron Mossbauer Spectroscopy
CEMSq...... Communications and Electronics Maintenance Squadron (AFM)
CEMSRG .. Chief Electrician's Mate, Ship Repair, General Electrician [Navy rating] [Obsolete]
CEMSRS... Chief Electrician's Mate, Ship Repair, Shop Electrician [Navy rating] [Obsolete]
CEMSRT .. Chief Electrician's Mate, Ship Repair, IC Repairman [Navy rating] [Obsolete]
CEMT........ Cement
CEMT........ Command Equipment Management Team [Military]
CEMT........ Conference Europeenne des Ministres des Transports [European Conference of Ministers of Transport - ECMT] [Paris, France]
CEMTE..... Common Experiments Monitoring and Test Equipment (MCD)
Cem Technol ... Cement Technology [A publication]
CEMTEX .. Central Magnetic Tape Exchange [Data processing] (ADA)
Cem Vapno Azbestocem Sadra ... Cement. Vapno, Azbestocement, Sadra [A publication]
CEMW ...... Columbia Essays on Modern Writers [A publication]
Cem Wapno Gips ... Cement Wapno Gips [A publication]
CEMX .... CEM Corp. [Matthews, NC] [NASDAQ symbol] (NQ)
CEMYF.... Charles Edison Memorial Youth Fund [Later, FAS] (EA)
CEN .... Canada. Department of the Environment. Fisheries and Marine Service. Data Report Series [A publication]
CEN .... Canterra Energy Ltd. [Toronto Stock Exchange symbol]
CEN .... Captive European Nations (NATG)
CEN .... Cenozoic [Period, era, or system] [Geology]
CEN .... Centaur [Rocket] [NASA] (KSC)
Cen............. Centaurus [Constellation]
CEN .... Centenary College of Louisiana, Magale Library, Shreveport, LA [OCLC symbol] (OCLC)
CEN .... Centennial (ROG)
CEN .... Center [or Central] (AFM)
CEN .... Centigrade [Celsius] [Temperature scale] (FAAC)
CEN .... Central Airlines, Inc.
CEN .... Central Airways Corp. [Toronto, ON, Canada] [FAA designator] (FAAC)
CEN .... Central Datum
CEN .... Central Education Network [Des Plaines, IL] [Telecommunications service] (TSSD)
CEN .... Centro Nacionalista [Nationalist Center] [Bolivia] [Political party] (PPW)
CEN .... Century
CEN .... Cerro-Negro [Argentina] [Seismograph station code, US Geological Survey] (SEIS)
CEN .... Certification for Emergency Nursing
C & EN ...... Chemical and Engineering News [A publication]
CEN .... Chemische Industrie. Zeitschrift fuer die Deutsche Chemiewirtschaft [A publication]
CEN .... Church of England Newspaper
CEN .... Ciudad Obregon [Mexico] [Airport symbol] (OAG)
CEn............ Colecao Ensaio [A publication]
CEN .... Comite Europeen de Coordination des Normes [European Committee for Coordination of Standards]
CEN .... Comite Europeen de Normalisation [European Committee for Standardization] [Belgium]
CEN .... Commissariat aux Energies Nouvelles [Atomic Energy Commission] [Algeria] (EY)
CEN .... Commission pour l'Etude des Nuages [OMI]
CEN .... Computer Equipment News [A publication] (APTA)
CEN .... Construction Equipment News [A publication] (APTA)
CEN .... Copper Ethanolamine
CEN .... La Centrale des Bibliotheques [Source file] [UTLAS symbol]
CENA .... Charge Exchange Neutralo Analyzer (MCD)
CENA .... Coalition of Eastern Native Americans [Defunct] (EA)
CENADEM ... Centro Nacional de Desenvolvimento do Gerenciamento da Informacao [National Center for Information Management Development] [Brazil] [Information service or system] (IID)
CENAGRI ... Centro Nacional de Informacao Documental Agricola [National Center for Agricultural Documentary Information] [Ministry of Agriculture] [Brazil] [Information service or system] (IID)
CE/NAVFAC ... Army Corps of Engineers/Naval Facilities Engineering Command
CENB .... Centran Corp. [Cleveland, OH] [NASDAQ symbol] (NQ)
CENB .... Cercle d'Etudes Numismatiques. Bulletin [A publication]
CENC .... Convergent Exhaust Nozzle Control (MCD)
CENCATS ... Central Pacific Combat Air Transport Service
CENCBM .... Carnets de l'Enfance/Assignment Children [A publication]
CENCN .... Centre d'Etudes Nordiques. Collection Nordicana. University of Laval [A publication]
CENCOMMRGN ... Central Communications Region [Air Force] (AFM)
CENCOMS ... Center for Communications Systems [CADPL] [Army] (RDA)

CEN Constr Equip News ... CEN. Construction Equipment News [A publication] (APTA)
CEND........ Combustion Engineering Nuclear Division [AEC] (MCD)
CENDHRRA ... Center for the Development of Human Resources in Rural Asia (EAIO)
CENDI ...... Department of Commerce/National Technical Information Service, Department of Energy/Office of Scientific and Technical Information, National Aeronautics and Space Administration Scientific and Technical Information Branch, and Department of Defense/Defense Technical Information Center
CENDIS .... Centre de Documentation et d'Information Interuniversitaire en Sciences Sociales [Interuniversity Documentation and Information Center for the Social Sciences] [Information service or system] (IID)
CENDIT.... Centre for Development of Instructional Technology
CENDRAFT ... Central Drafting Officer [Navy]
CENEA...... Chemical and Engineering News [A publication]
CENECA... Centre National des Expositions et Concours Agricoles
CENEL...... Comite Europeen de Coordination des Normes Electriques [European Electrical Standards Coordinating Committee]
CENELEC ... European Committee for Electrotechnical Standardization (EAIO)
CENEUR... Central European (AFM)
Cen Eur Hist ... Central European History [A publication]
C & E News ... Chemical and Engineering News [A publication]
CENEX...... Complex Energetics Experiment
C Eng .... Chartered Engineer [British]
CEngAust .. Institution of Chartered Engineers [Australia]
CENGR ..... Civil Engineer (FAAC)
C of ENGRS ... Chief of Engineers [Later, COE] [Army]
CenHV....... [A] Century of Humorous Verse [A publication]
CENIA5..... Cenicafe [A publication]
CENID ...... Centro Nacional de Informacion y Documentacion [National Center for Information and Documentation] [Information service or system] [Chile]
CENIDS .... Centro Nacional de Informacion y Documentacion en Salud [National Center for Health Information and Documentation] [Mexico] [Information service or system] (IID)
CenL .... [A] Century of Lyrics [A publication]
CENMD .... Chemical Engineering Monographs [A publication]
CENN....... Center News [A publication]
CENO....... Central Naval Ordnance Management Information System
CENOG..... Computerized Electro Neuro-Ophthalmograph
CENPAC... Central Pacific Area [Navy]
CENPACFOR ... Central Pacific Forces
CENPAT... Central Patch and Test [Facility]
CENPRO... Census Projections [Database] (IT)
CENS......... Censor [or Censorship] (AFM)
CENS......... Council on Economics and National Security (EA)
CENSA...... Council of European and Japanese National Shipowners Associations [London, England] (EAIO)
CENSAC... Census Access System [Urban Decision Systems, Inc.] [Information service or system] [Defunct] (CRD)
CEN/SCK ... Centre d'Etude de l'Energie Nucleaire/Studiecentrum voor Kernenergie [Belgium] (EY)
CENSEI ... Center for Systems Engineering and Integration [Army] (GRD)
CENSER ... Census Servomechanism and Tape Handler
CENSHARE ... Center to Study Human-Animal Relationships and Environments [University of Minnesota] [Research center] (RCD)
CENT .... Cental [Short hundredweight] [British] (ROG)
CENT .... Centaur [Rocket] [NASA] (KSC)
Cent......... Centaurus [Constellation]
cent............. Centavo [Monetary unit] [Portugal]
CENT .... Centigrade [Celsius] [Temperature scale] (KSC)
CENT .... Centime [Monetary unit] [France]
cent............. Centimo [Centime] [Monetary unit] [Portugal]
CENT .... Central
Cent............ Central Reporter [A publication] (DLA)
CENT .... Centrifugal (KSC)
CENT .... Centum [Hundred]
CENT .... Centuri, Inc. [Binghamton, NY] [NASDAQ symbol] (NQ)
CENT .... Century
Cent............ Century Magazine [A publication]
CENTAC... Central Tactical Unit [Drug Enforcement Administration]
CENTACS ... Center for Tactical Computer Systems [CADPL] [Army] (MCD)
Cent Afr J Med ... Central African Journal of Medicine [A publication]
CENTAG... Central [European] Army Group [NATO]
Cent Agric ... Centro Agricola [A publication]
Cent Agric Publ Doc (Wageningen) Annu Rep ... Centre for Agricultural Publications and Documentation (Wageningen). Annual Report [A publication]
CENTAM ... Central America
CENTAMP ... Central Treaty Organization Allied Military Publication
Cent Arecanut Res St Tech Bull ... Central Arecanut Research Station. Technical Bulletin [A publication]
Cent Asia J ... Central Asiatic Journal [A publication]
CENTAUM ... Committee on Education Needs for Teen-Age Unwed Mothers

CentB .... Century Bible [*A publication*]   (BJA)

Cent Belge Etude Corros Rapp Tech ... Centre Belge d'Etude de la Corrosion. Rapport Technique [*A publication*]

Cent Belge Etude Doc Eaux Bull Mens ... Centre Belge d'Etude et de Documentation des Eaux. Bulletin Mensuel [*Belgium*] [*A publication*]

Centbl Ges Forstw ... Centralblatt fuer das Gesamte Forstwesen [*A publication*]

CENTCOM ... Central Pacific Communications Instructions

CENTCOM ... United States Central Command   (INF)

CENTCON ... Centralized Control Facility

Cent Crim C Cas ... Central Criminal Court Cases, Sessions Papers [*1834-1913*] [*England*] [*A publication*]   (DLA)

Cent Crim CR ... Central Criminal Court Reports [*England*] [*A publication*]   (DLA)

Cent Dict .... Century Dictionary [*A publication*]   (DLA)

Cent Dict and Cyc ... Century Dictionary and Cyclopedia [*A publication*]   (DLA)

Cent Dict & Ency ... Century Dictionary and Encyclopedia [*A publication*]   (DLA)

Cent Dig ..... Century Edition of the American Digest System (West) [*A publication*]   (DLA)

Cent Doc Sider Cir Inf Tech ... Centre de Documentation Siderurgique. Circulaire d'Information Techniques [*A publication*]

CENTED ... Center for Technology, Environment, and Development [*Clark University*]

Cent Edafol Biol Apl Salamanca Anu ... Centro de Edafologia y Biologia Aplicada de Salamanca. Anuario [*A publication*]

Centennial Mag ... Centennial Magazine [*A publication*]   (APTA)

Centen Rev ... Centennial Review [*A publication*]

Center .... Center Magazine [*A publication*]

Center Child Bk Bull ... Center for Children's Books. Bulletin [*A publication*]

Center J ..... Center Journal [*A publication*]

Center M .... Center Magazine [*A publication*]

Center Mag ... Center Magazine [*A publication*]

Cent Estud Recur Odontol Nino ... Centro de Estudios de Recursos Odontologicos para el Nino [*A publication*]

Cent Estud Zool Univ Brasil Avulso ... Centro de Estudos Zoologicos. Universidade do Brasil. Avulso [*A publication*]

Cent Etude Azote ... Centre d'Etude de l'Azote [*A publication*]

Cent Etude Rech Essais Sci Genie Univ Liege Mem ... Centre d'Etude, de Recherches, et d'Essais Scientifiques du Genie Civil. Universite de Liege. Memoires [*A publication*]

Cent Etud Rech Essais Sci Genie Civ Univ Liege Mem ... Centre d'Etudes, de Recherches, et d'Essais Scientifiques du Genie Civil. Universite de Liege. Memoires [*A publication*]

Cent Eur Fed ... Central European Federalist [*A publication*]

Cent Eur H ... Central European History [*A publication*]

Cent Eur Hist ... Central European History [*A publication*]

CENTF ...... Centrifugal

Cent Form Tech Perfect Bull ... Centre de Formation Technique et de Perfectionnement. Union des Fabricants de Biscuits, Biscottes, Aliments Dietetiques, et Divers. Bulletin [*A publication*]

Cent Geomorphol Caen Bull ... Centre de Geomorphologie de Caen. Bulletin [*A publication*]

Cent Glass Ceram Res Inst Bull ... Central Glass and Ceramic Research Institute. Bulletin [*A publication*]

Cent High-Energy Form Pro ... Center for High-Energy Forming. Proceedings. International Conference [*A publication*]

Cent High Res Res Rep Tex Austin ... Center for Highway Research. Research Report. University of Texas at Austin [*A publication*]

CENTIG .... Centigrade [*Celsius*] [*Temperature scale*]   (ROG)

Cent Inf Chrome Dur Bull Doc ... Centre d'Information du Chrome Dur. Bulletin de Documentation [*A publication*]

Cent Inf Nickel Toutes Appl Tech Ind Ser A ... Centre d'Information du Nickel pour Toutes Applications Techniques et Industrielles. Serie A. Alliages [*A publication*]

Cent Inf Nickel Toutes Appl Tech Ind Ser C ... Centre d'Information du Nickel pour Toutes Applications Techniques et Industrielles. Serie C. Fontes au Nickel [*A publication*]

Cent Inf Nickel Toutes Appl Tech Ind Ser D ... Centre d'Information du Nickel pour Toutes Applications Techniques et Industrielles. Serie D. Nickelage [*A publication*]

Cent Inf Nickel Toutes Appl Tech Ind Ser X ... Centre d'Information du Nickel pour Toutes Applications Techniques et Industrielles. Serie X. Applications du Nickel [*A publication*]

Cent Inland Fish Res Inst (Barrackpore) Annu Rep ... Central Inland Fisheries Research Institute (Barrackpore). Annual Report [*A publication*]

Cent Inland Fish Res Inst (Barrackpore) Bull ... Central Inland Fisheries Research Institute (Barrackpore). Bulletin [*A publication*]

Cent Inland Fish Res Inst (Barrackpore India) Surv Rep ... Central Inland Fisheries Research Institute (Barrackpore, India). Survey Report [*A publication*]

Cent Inland Fish Res Inst (Barrackpore) Misc Contri ... Central Inland Fisheries Research Institute (Barrackpore). Miscellaneous Contribution [*A publication*]

Cent Inland Fish Res Inst (Barrackpore) Misc Contrib ... Central Inland Fisheries Research Institute (Barrackpore). Miscellaneous Contribution [*A publication*]

Cent Inland Fish Res Inst (Barrackpore) Surv Rep ... Central Inland Fisheries Research Institute (Barrackpore). Survey Report [*A publication*]

Cent Inst Mater Onderz Afd Corr Medede ... Centraal Instituut voor Materiaal Onderzoek. Afdeling Corrosie. Mededeling [*A publication*]

Cent Inst Mater Onderz Afde Corros Circ ... Centraal Instituut voor Materiaal Onderzoek. Afdeling Corrosie. Circulaire [*A publication*]

Cent Inst Mater Onderz Afd Hout Circ ... Centraal Instituut voor Materiaal Onderzoek. Afdeling Hout. Circulaire [*A publication*]

Cent Inst Mater Onderz Afd Verf Circ ... Centraal Instituut voor Materiaal Onderzoek. Afdeling Verf. Circulaire [*A publication*]

Cent Inst Phys Inst Phys Nucl Eng Rep (Romania) ... Central Institute of Physics. Institute for Physics and Nuclear Engineering. Report (Romania) [*A publication*]

Cent Int Agric Trop Annu Rep ... Centro Internacional de Agricultura Tropical [*CIAT*]. Annual Report [*A publication*]

Cent Int Agric Trop (CIAT) Ser EE ... Centro Internacional de Agricultura Tropical (CIAT). Series EE [*A publication*]

Cent Int Agric Trop (CIAT) Ser GE ... Centro Internacional de Agricultura Tropical (CIAT). Series GE [*A publication*]

Cent Int Agric Trop Ser CE ... Centro Internacional de Agricultura Tropical [*CIAT*]. Series CE [*A publication*]

Cent Int Agric Trop Ser EE ... Centro Internacional de Agricultura Tropical [*CIAT*]. Series EE [*A publication*]

Cent Int Agric Trop Ser FE ... Centro Internacional de Agricultura Tropical [*CIAT*]. Series FE [*A publication*]

Cent Int Agric Trop Ser GE ... Centro Internacional de Agricultura Tropical [*CIAT*]. Series GE [*A publication*]

Cent Int Agric Trop Ser Semin ... Centro Internacional de Agricultura Tropical [*CIAT*]. Series Seminars [*A publication*]

Cent Int Agric Trop Tech Bull ... Centro Internacional de Agricultura Tropical [*CIAT*]. Technical Bulletin [*A publication*]

Cent Invest Agric Noreste Inf Invest Agric ... Centro de Investigaciones Agricolas del Noreste. Informe de Investigacion Agricola [*A publication*]

Cent Invest Agron Maracay Monogr ... Centro de Investigaciones Agronomicas Maracay. Monografia [*A publication*]

Cent Invest Biol Mar Contrib Tec ... Centro de Investigacion de Biologia Marina. Contribucion Tecnica [*A publication*]

Cent Invest Tecnol (Pando Urug) Inf Invest ... Centro de Investigaciones Tecnologicas (Pando, Uruguay). Informe de Investigacion [*A publication*]

Cent Jpn J Orthop Traumatic Surg ... Central Japan Journal of Orthopaedic and Traumatic Surgery [*A publication*]

Cent Lab Ochron Radiol Rap ... Centralne Laboratorium Ochrony Radiologiczncj Raport [*A publication*]

Cent Landbouwpubl Landbouwdoc Literatuuroverz ... Centrum voor Landbouwpublikaties en Landbouwdocumentatie Literatuuroverzicht [*A publication*]

CENTLANT ... Central Subarea, Atlantic [*NATO*]

Cent Law J ... Central Law Journal [*A publication*]   (DLA)

Cent LJ ...... Central Law Journal [*A publication*]   (DLA)

Cent L Mo ... Central Law Monthly [*A publication*]   (DLA)

Cent Mag ... Center Magazine [*A publication*]

Cent Mar Fish Res Inst Bull ... Central Marine Fisheries Research Institute. Bulletin [*A publication*]

Cent Med J Semin Rep (Moscow) ... Central Medical Journal. Seminar Reports (Moscow) [*A publication*]

Cent Nac Invest Cafe Bol Tec (Chinchina) ... Centro Nacional de Investigaciones de Cafe. Boletin Tecnico (Chinchina) [*A publication*]

Cent Nac Invest Cient Rev CENIC Cienc Biol ... Centro Nacional de Investigaciones Cientificas. Revista CENIC. Ciencias Biologicas [*A publication*]

Cent Nat Exploit Oceans Publ Ser Rapp Sci Tech (Fr) ... Centre National pour l'Exploitation des Oceans. Publications. Serie Rapports Scientifiques et Techniques (France) [*A publication*]

Cent Natl Doc Sci Tech Rap Act ... Centre National de Documentation Scientifique et Technique. Rapport d'Activite [*A publication*]

Cent Natl Exploit Oceans Rapp Annu ... Centre National pour l'Exploitation des Oceans. Rapport Annuel [*A publication*]

Cent Natl Rech Sci Tech Ind Cimentiere Rapp Rech ... Centre National de Recherches Scientifiques et Techniques pour l'Industrie Cimentiere. Rapport de Recherche [*A publication*]

Cent Nat Rech Sci Groupe Fr Argiles R Reun Etude ... Centre National de la Recherche Scientifique. Groupe Francais des Argiles. Compte Rendu des Reunions d'Etudes [*A publication*]

Cent Nerv Syst Pharmacol Ser ... Central Nervous System Pharmacology Series [*A publication*]

Cent Nerv Syst Trauma ... Central Nervous System Trauma [*A publication*]

Cent Nupt ... Cento Nuptialis [*of Ausonius*] [*Classical studies*]   (OCD)

CENTO ..... Central European Treaty Organization   (MCD)

CENTO ..... Central Treaty Organization [*Also, CTO*] [*Formerly, Baghdad Pact*]

CENTO Conf Ld Classif Non-Irrig Lds ... CENTO [*Central Treaty Organization*] Conference on Land Classification for Non-Irrigated Lands [*A publication*]
Cent Overseas Pest Res Misc Rep ... Centre for Overseas Pest Research. Miscellaneous Report [*A publication*]
Cent Overseas Pest Res Rep ... Centre for Overseas Pest Research. Report [*A publication*]
CENTPACBACOM ... Central Pacific Base Command [*Navy*]
Cent Pesqui Agropecu Trop Umido ... Centro de Pesquisa Agropecuaria do Tropico Umido EMBRAPA [*Empresa Brasileira de Pesquisa Agropecuaria*] [*A publication*]
Cent Pesqui Desenvolvimento Bol Tec (Estado Bahia) ... Centro de Pesquisas e Desenvolvimento. Boletim Tecnico (Estado da Bahia) [*A publication*]
Cent Phar J ... Central Pharmaceutical Journal [*A publication*]
Cent Plant Crops Res Inst (Kasaragod) Annu Rep ... Central Plantation Crops Research Institute (Kasaragod). Annual Report [*A publication*]
Cent Prov LR ... Central Provinces Law Reports [*India*] [*A publication*]   (DLA)
CentR .... Centennial Review [*A publication*]
CENTR ...... Central   (ROG)
CENTRA ... Centralized Training [*Material management subsystem*]   (MCD)
Central African J Med ... Central African Journal of Medicine [*A publication*]
Central Bank Barbados Q Rept ... Central Bank of Barbados. Quarterly Report [*A publication*]
Central Bank Ireland Q Bul ... Central Bank of Ireland. Quarterly Bulletin [*A publication*]
Central Bank Libya Econ Bul ... Central Bank of Libya. Economic Bulletin [*A publication*]
Central Bank Malta QR ... Central Bank of Malta. Quarterly Review [*A publication*]
Central Bank Nigeria Econ and Fin R ... Central Bank of Nigeria. Economic and Financial Review [*A publication*]
Central Bank Trinidad and Tobago Q Econ Bul ... Central Bank of Trinidad and Tobago. Quarterly Economic Bulletin [*A publication*]
Centralbl Allg Path u Path Anat ... Centralblatt fuer Allgemeine Pathologie und Pathologische Anatomie [*A publication*]
Centralbl Bakteriol ... Centralblatt fuer Bakteriologie und Parasitenkunde [*A publication*]
Centralbl Chir ... Centralblatt fuer Chirurgie [*A publication*]
Centralbl Gesamte Forstwes ... Centralblatt fuer das Gesamte Forstwesen [*A publication*]
Centralbl Innere Med ... Centralblatt fuer Innere Medicin [*A publication*]
Centralbl Miner ... Centralblatt fuer Mineralogie, Geologie, und Palaeontologie [*A publication*]
Central LJ ... Central Law Journal [*A publication*]   (DLA)
Central Ohio Sc As Pr ... Central Ohio Scientific Association of Urbana, Ohio. Proceedings [*A publication*]
Central Opera ... Central Opera Service. Bulletin [*A publication*]
Central Q Herald ... Central Queensland Herald [*A publication*]   (APTA)
Centr Asiat J ... Central Asiatic Journal [*A publication*]
Centr Bank Ireland Annu Rep ... Central Bank of Ireland. Annual Report [*A publication*]
Centr Bank Ireland Quart B ... Central Bank of Ireland. Quarterly Bulletin [*A publication*]
Centr Cr Ct R ... Central Criminal Court Cases, Sessions Papers [*1834-1913*] [*England*] [*A publication*]   (DLA)
Centr Cr Ct R ... Central Criminal Court Reports [*England*] [*A publication*]   (ILCA)
Cent Rech Ecol Phytosociol Gembloux Commun ... Centre de Recherches Ecologiques et Phytosociologiques de Gembloux. Communication [*A publication*]
Cent Rech Oceanogr (Abidjan) Doc Sci ... Centre de Recherches Oceanographiques (Abidjan). Documents Scientifiques [*A publication*]
Cent Rech Oceanogr (Abidjan) Doc Sci Provisoire ... Centre de Recherches Oceanographiques (Abidjan). Document Scientifique Provisoire [*A publication*]
Cent Rech Pau Bull ... Societe Nationale des Petroles d'Aquitaine. Centre de Recherches de Pau. Bulletin. [*Later, Bulletin. Centres de Recherches Exploration-Production ELF Aquitaine*] [*A publication*]
Cent Rech Sci Tech Ind Fabr Met Sect Plast Rep PL ... Centre de Recherches Scientifiques et Techniques de l'Industrie des Fabrications Metalliques. Section Plastiques. Report PL [*A publication*]
Centr Econ Plan ... Centraal Economisch Plan [*A publication*]
CENTREDOC ... Swiss Center of Documentation in Microtechnology [*Information service or system*]   (IID)
Centre Et Docum Soc (Liege) ... Centre d'Etudes et de Documentation Sociales (Liege) [*A publication*]
Centre Etud et Docum Socs Bul ... Centre d'Etudes et de Documentation Sociales. Bulletin Mensuel [*A publication*]
Centre Etud Emploi Cah ... Centre d'Etudes de l'Emploi. Cahiers [*A publication*]
Centre Info et Etud Credit Bul ... Centre d'Information et d'Etudes du Credit. Bulletin [*A publication*]
Centre Inform Chrome Dur Bull Doc ... Centre d'Information du Chrome Dur. Bulletin de Documentation [*A publication*]

Centre Nat Rech Sci Tech Ind Cimentiere Rapp Rech ... Centre National de Recherches Scientifiques et Techniques pour l'Industrie Cimentiere. Rapport de Recherche [*A publication*]
Cent Rep .... Central Reporter [*A publication*]   (DLA)
Centre Recherches Pau Bull ... Centre de Recherches de Pau. Bulletin [*A publication*]
Centre Sci & Tech Constr Note Inf Tech ... Centre Scientifique et Technique de la Construction. Note d'Information Technique [*A publication*]
CENTREX ... Central Exchange
Centr LJ ... Central Law Journal [*A publication*]   (DLA)
CENTRO ... Central New York Library Resources Council [*Syracuse, NY*] [*Library network*]
Centro Estud Demograficos R ... Centro de Estudos Demograficos. Revista [*A publication*]
Centro Estud Rurais e Urbanos Cad ... Centro de Estudos Rurais e Urbanos. Cadernos [*A publication*]
Centro Investigacion y Accion Soc R ... Centro de Investigacion y Accion Social. Revista [*A publication*]
Centro Pirenaico Biolog Exp ... Publicaciones. Centro Pirenaico de Biologia Experimental [*A publication*]
Centro pro Un Bul ... Centro pro Unione. Bulletin [*A publication*]
Cent R (PA) ... Central Reporter [*Pennsylvania*] [*A publication*]   (DLA)
Cent SS RR ... Center for Settlement Studies. University of Manitoba. Research Reports [*A publication*]
Cent St Spe ... Central States Speech Journal [*A publication*]
Cent Studi Lotta Antitermitica Pubbl ... Centro di Studi per la Lotta Antitermitica. Pubblicazione [*A publication*]
Cent Stud Ing Agrar Mem Atti ... Centro di Studi per l'Ingegneria Agraria. Memorie ed Atti [*Italy*] [*A publication*]
Cent Tech For Trop (Nogent Sur Marne Fr) Note Tech ... Centre Technique Forestier Tropical (Nogent Sur Marne, France). Note Technique [*A publication*]
Cent Tech For Trop (Nogent Sur Marne Fr) Publ ... Centre Technique Forestier Tropical (Nogent Sur Marne, France). Publication [*A publication*]
Cent Tech Union Bull ... Centre Technique de l'Union. Bulletin [*A publication*]
CENU .... Chloroethylnitrosourea [*A class of antineoplastic agents*]
CENUA ..... Courrier des Etablissements Neu [*A publication*]
CENUSA ... Centrales Nucleares Sociedad Anonima [*Nuclear energy*] [*Spain*]   (EY)
CENV .... Canadian Environment [*Database*] [*WATDOC*] [*Information service or system*]   (CRD)
CEN-VALRHO ... Centre d'Etudes Nucleaires de la Vallee du Rhone [*France*]   (EY)
C Environ LN ... Canadian Environmental Law News [*A publication*]   (DLA)
CENYC ...... Council of European National Youth Committees   (EA)
CEO .... Casualty Evacuation Officer
CEO .... Center for Electron Optics [*Michigan State University*] [*Research center*]   (RCD)
CEO .... Central Oregon Community College, Library, Bend, OR [*OCLC symbol*]   (OCLC)
CEO .... Chemical Engineering Operations [*MIT*]   (MCD)
CEO .... Chick Embryo Origin
CEO .... Chief Elected Official   (OICC)
CEO .... Chief Electoral Officer [*Canada*]
CEO .... Chief Executive Officer
CEO .... Chief Executives Organization   (EA)
CEO .... Chip Enable Output [*Data processing*]
CEO .... Comite Europeen de l'Outillage [*European Tool Committee - ETC*]   (EA)
CEO .... Command Education Officer [*Military*] [*British*]
CEO .... Command Entertainments Officer [*Military*] [*British*]
CEO .... Communications-Electronics Officer [*Air Force*]
CEO .... Community Education Officer   (ADA)
CEO .... Comprehensive Electronic Office [*Data General Corp.*]
CEO .... Courrier de l'Extreme-Orient [*A publication*]
CEO .... Cultural Exchange Officer [*United States Information Service*]
CEO .... Customs Enforcement Officer [*US Customs Service*]
CEO .... Waco Kungo [*Angola*] [*Airport symbol*]   (OAG)
CEOA .... Central Europe Operating Agency [*Versailles, France*] [*NATO*]
CEOABL ..... Centre National pour l'Exploitation des Oceans. Rapport Annuel [*A publication*]
CEOAH ..... Comite Europeen de l'Outillage Agricole et Horticole [*European Committee for Agricultural and Horticultural Tools and Implements - ECAHTI*]   (EA)
CEOAS ...... Corps of Engineers Office of Appalachian Studies [*Army*]   (AABC)
CEOC .... Confederation Europeenne d'Organismes de Controle   (EAIO)
CEOCOR .. Comite d'Etude de la Corrosion et de la Protection des Canalisations [*Committee for the Study of Pipe Corrosion and Protection*]   (EAIO)
CEOCOR ... Commission Europeenne de Corrosion des Conduites Souterraines [*Brussels, Belgium*]   (EAIO)
CEODP ..... Committee to Expose, Oppose, and Depose Patriarchy   (EA)
CEOE .... Certified Engineering Operations Executive [*Designation awarded by American Hotel and Motel Association*]
CEOE .... Confederacion Espanola de Organizaciones Empresariales [*Spanish Confederation of Employers' Organizations*] [*Spain*]   (EY)

CEOFA...... Ceskoslovenska Oftalmologie [*A publication*]
CEOI .... Communications-Electronics Operating Instruction　(CINC)
Ceol .... Ceol. Journal of Irish Music [*A publication*]
CEOP .... Communaute Europeenne des Organisations de Publicitaires [*European Community of Advertising Organizations*]
CEOR .... Certainty Equivalent of Revenues [*Business term*]
CEORS...... Center for Earth Observations and Remote Sensing [*Boulder, CO*] [*Cooperative Institute for Research in Environmental Sciences*] [*National Oceanic and Atmospheric Administration*]　(GRD)
CEOS........ Committee on Earth Observations Satellites [*NASA*]
CEOS........ County Education Officers' Society [*British*]
CEOST ...... Committee on Equal Opportunities in Science and Technology [*National Science Foundation*]
CEOTA...... Ceskoslovenska Otolaryngologie [*A publication*]
CEOYLA... Council of Eastern Orthodox Youth Leaders of the Americas　(EA)
CEP........... Calculated Error Probable
CEP........... Capability Evaluation Plan
CEP........... Capital Expenditure Proposal
CEP........... Career Exploration Profile [*Vocational guidance test*]
CEP........... CCNU [*Lomustine*], Etoposide, Prednimustine [*Antineoplastic drug regimen*]
CEP........... Central East Pacific [*Region*]
CEP........... Centralized Employment Program
CEP........... [*A*] Century of Excavation in Palestine [*A publication*]　(BJA)
Cep............ Cepheus [*Constellation*]
CEP........... Chemical Engineering Progress [*A publication*]
CEP........... Chicano Education Project　(EA)
CEP........... Chretiens pour Une Eglise Populaire [*Christians for One Common Church*] [*Canada*]
CEP........... Circle End Point
CEP........... Circle of Equal Probability
CEP........... Circular Error Probability [*Military*]
CEP........... Citizens' Energy Project　(EA)
CEP........... Civil Emergency Planning [*NATO*]　(NATG)
CEP........... Civil Engineering Package　(IEEE)
CEP........... Civilian Employment Projection　(MCD)
CEP........... Coal Employment Project　(EA)
CEP........... [*A*] Collection of English Poems [*A publication*]
CEP........... Color Evaluation Program
CEP........... Commercial Exchange of Philadelphia　(EA)
CEP........... Committee for Energy Policy [*Organization for Economic Cooperation and Development*]　(MCD)
CEP........... Common Electronic Parts
CEP........... Community Energy Program [*Office of Volunteer Liaison*] [*ACTION*]
CEP........... Community Enterprise Program [*British*]
CEP........... Compensatory Equipment Package　(MCD)
CEP........... Component Error Propagation
CEP........... Computed Ephemeris Position
CEP........... Computer Entry Punch
CEP........... Concentrated Employment Program [*Also known as CIEP*] [*Department of Labor*]
CEP........... Concepcion [*Bolivia*] [*Airport symbol*]　(OAG)
CEP........... Concept Evaluation Program [*Army*]
CEP........... Condensate Extraction Pump [*Chemical engineering*]
CEP........... Conduction Electron Polarization
CEP........... Confederation Europeenne d'Etudes Phytosanitaires [*European Confederation for Plant Protection Research*]
CEP........... Conference on Economic Progress　(EA)
CEP........... Congenital Erythropoietic Porphyria [*Medicine*]
CEP........... Consolidated Explorer Petroleum Corp. [*Vancouver Stock Exchange symbol*]
CEP........... Construction Electrician, Power [*Navy rating*]
CEP........... Contact Evaluation Plot　(NVT)
CEP........... Continuing Education Program [*State University of New York at Albany*] [*Research center*]
CEP........... Continuous Estimation Program
CEP........... Contract Estimating and Pricing　(MCD)
CEP........... Contractual Engineering Project　(AFIT)
CEP........... Coordinated Examination Program [*Internal Revenue Service*]
CEP........... Cortical Evoked Potential [*Neurophysiology*]
CEP........... Cotton Equalization Program
CEP........... Council on Economic Policy [*Inactive*]
CEP........... Council on Economic Priorities　(EA)
CEP........... Council on Energy Policy [*Proposed Presidential council*]
CEP........... Council on Environmental Pollutants
CEP........... Counterelectrophoresis [*Analytical chemistry*]
CEP........... Country Economic Profiles [*I. P. Sharp Association Pty. Ltd.*] [*Australia*] [*Information service or system*]　(CRD)
CEP........... Court Employment Project　(EA)
CEP........... Crossed Electrophoresis　(MCD)
CEP........... Current Energy Patents [*A publication*]
CEP........... Cylindrical Electrostatic Probe [*NASA*]　(MCD)
CEP........... Czechoslovak Economic Papers [*A publication*]
CEPA........ Canadian Environmental Protection Act
CEPA........ Central Europe Pipeline Agency [*Later, CEOA*] [*NATO*]　(NATG)
CEPA........ Century Pacific Corp. [*NASDAQ symbol*]　(NQ)
CEPA........ Chloroethylphosphonic Acid [*Maturation compound for fruits*]

CEPA........ Civil Engineering Program Applications　(MCD)
CEPA........ Comision Economica para Africa [*Economic Commission for Africa - ECA*] [*United Nations*] [*Spanish*]　(ASF)
CEPA........ Commission Economique pour l'Afrique [*Economic Commission for Africa - ECA*] [*United Nations*] [*French*]
CEPA........ Committee on Educational Policy in Agriculture [*National Academy of Sciences*]
CEPA........ Conseil Europeen pour la Protection des Animaux [*European Council for Animal Welfare - ECAW*]　(EA)
CEPA........ Consumers Education and Protective Association International　(EA)
CEPA........ Coupled Electron Pair Approximation [*Physics*]
CEPA........ Society for Computer Applications in Engineering, Planning, and Architecture　(EA)
CEPAC...... Confederation Europeenne de l'Industrie de Pates, Papiers, et Cartons [*European Confederation of Pulp, Paper, and Board Industries*]　(EAIO)
CEPAC...... Conferentia Episcopalis Pacifici [*Episcopal Conference of the Pacific*]　(EAIO)
CEPACC ... Chemical Education Planning and Coordinating Committee [*American Chemical Society*]
CEPAL ...... Comision Economica para America Latina y el Caribe [*Economic Commission for Latin America and the Caribbean - ECLAC*] [*United Nations*] [*Santiago, Chile*]　(EAIO)
CEPAL Rev ... CEPAL [*Comision Economica para America Latina*] Review [*A publication*]
CEPAQ...... Centre d'Etudes Politiques et Administratives du Quebec [*University of Quebec*] [*Research center*]　(RCD)
CEPB........ Civil Emergency Planning Bureau [*NATO*]　(NATG)
CEPB........ Confederacion de Empresarios Privados de Bolivia [*Employers' association*] [*Bolivia*]　(EY)
CEPBA...... Cerebral Palsy Bulletin [*A publication*]
CEPC......... Canadian Egg Producers Council
CEPC......... Chief Engineer Port Construction [*British military*]　(DMA)
CEPC......... Civil Emergency Planning Committee [*US/Canada*]
CEPC......... Comite Europeen pour les Problemes Criminels [*Conseil de l'Europe*]
CEPCAD ... Committee to Eliminate Premature Christmas Advertising and Display [*Defunct*]　(EA)
CEPCAV ... Centre de Recherches Ecologiques et Phytosociologiques de Gembloux. Communication [*A publication*]
CEPCEO ... Comite d'Etude des Producteurs de Charbon d'Europe Occidentale [*Association of the Coal Producers of the European Community*]　(EAIO)
CEPCIES .. Comision Ejecutiva Permanente del Consejo Interamericano Economico y Social [*Permanent Executive Committee of the Inter-American Economic and Social Council*]　(EA)
CEPD........ Communications-Electronics Policy Directives [*NATO*]　(NATG)
CEPE........ Central Experimental and Proving Establishment [*Canada*]　(MCD)
CEPE........ Comision Economica para Europa [*Economic Commission for Europe - ECE*] [*Spanish*]　(ASF)
CEPE........ Comite Europeen des Associations des Fabricants de Peinture, d'Encres d'Imprimerie, et de Couleurs [*European Committee of Paint, Printing Ink, and Artists' Colours Manufacturers Associations*]　(EAIO)
CEPE........ Cylindrical Electrostatic Probe Experiment [*NASA*]
CEPEA ...... Ceskoslovenska Pediatrie [*A publication*]
CEPEC Inf Tec ... CEPEC [*Centro de Pesquisas do Cacau*] Informe Tecnico [*A publication*]
CEPED ...... Civil Engineering for Practicing and Design Engineers [*A publication*]
CEPEIGE ... Centro Panamericano de Estudios e Investigaciones Geograficas [*Pan American Center for Geographical Studies and Research - PACGSR*]　(EAIO)
CEPER ...... Combined Engineering Plant Exchange Record [*Telecommunications*]　(TEL)
CEPES....... Centre Europeen pour l'Enseignement Superieur [*European Centre for Higher Education*]　(EAIO)
CEPES....... Comite Europeen pour le Progres Economique et Social [*European Committee for Economic and Social Progress*]
CEPEX ..... Centro de Exportacion de la Agrupacion de Fabricantes de Calzado [*Trade association*] [*Spain*]　(EY)
CEPEX ..... Centro de Promocion de las Exportaciones [*Paraguay*]　(IMH)
CEPEX ..... Controlled Ecosystem Pollution Experiment [*National Science Foundation project*]
CEPFAR.... Centre Europeen pour la Promotion de la Formation Milieu Agricole et Rural [*European Training and Development Centre for Farming and Rural Life - ETDCFRL*]　(EAIO)
CEPFR ...... Critical Experiment Pulsed Fast Reactor
CEPG......... Cambridge Economic Policy Group [*British*]
CEPGL...... Communaute Economique des Pays des Grands Lacs [*Economic Community of the Great Lakes Countries - ECGLC*] [*Gisenye, Rwanda*]　(EAIO)
CEPH .... Cephalic　(ROG)
Ceph........... Cepheus [*Constellation*]
CEPH .... Council on Education for Public Health　(EA)
Cephal........ [*Johannes*] Cephalus [*Deceased, 1576*] [*Authority cited in pre-1607 legal work*]　(DSA)

CEPHDF ... Cephalalgia [*A publication*]
CEPI .... Capital Expenditure Price Index
CEPI .... Circulo de Escritores y Poetas Iberoamericanos [*An association*] (EA)
CEPII .... Centre d'Etudes Prospectives et d'Informations Internationales [*Center for International Prospective Studies*] [*Database producer*] [*Paris, France*]
CEPIS .... Centro Panamericano de Ingenieria Sanitaria y Ciencias del Ambiente [*Pan American Center for Sanitary Engineering and Environmental Sciences*] [*Research center*] [*Peru*] (IRC)
CEPL .... Conference Europeenne des Pouvoirs Locaux
CEPLAC Bol Tec ... CEPLAC [*Comissao Executiva do Plano da Lavoura Cacaueira*] Boletim Tecnico [*A publication*]
CEPLAC Comun Tec ... CEPLAC [*Comissao Executiva do Plano da Lavoura Cacaueira*] Comunicacao Tecnica [*A publication*]
CEPLAO ... CEPLAC [*Comissao Executiva do Plano da Lavoura Cacaueira*] Boletim Tecnico [*A publication*]
CEPM .... Center for Educational Policy and Management [*Department of Education*] (GRD)
CEPM .... Civil Engineer Preventive Maintenance [*Air Force*]
CEPND ...... CEP [*Council on Economic Priorities*] Newsletter [*A publication*]
CEP Newsl ... CEP [*Council on Economic Priorities*] Newsletter [*A publication*]
CEPO .... Central Eastern Personnel Organization [*Computerized scouting combine for professional football teams*]
CEPO .... Central Engineering Projects Office [*NATO*] (NATG)
CEPO .... Central Europe Pipeline Office [*NATO*]
CEPO .... County Emergency Planning Officers Society [*British*]
Cepol .... [*Bartholomaeus*] Cepolla [*Deceased, 1477*] [*Authority cited in pre-1607 legal work*] (DSA)
CEPP .... Chemical Emergency Preparedness Program [*Environmental Protection Agency*]
CEPPC ...... Central Europe Pipeline Policy Committee [*NATO*]
CEPR .... Center for Energy Policy and Research (EA)
CEPR .... Centre for Economic Policy Research [*British*] (ECON)
CEPR .... College of Engineers of Puerto Rico
CEPR .... Council on Education in Professional Responsibility [*Later, CLEPR*] (EA)
CEPRA ...... Chemical Engineering Progress [*A publication*]
CEPROFI ... Certificado de Promocion Fiscal [*Mexico*] (IMH)
CEPS .... Center for Educational Policy Studies (EA)
CEPS .... Central Europe Pipeline System [*NATO*] (NATG)
CEPS .... Centre for European Policy Studies (ECON)
CEPS .... Civil Engineering Problems
CEPS .... Color Electronic Prepress Systems [*Printing technology*]
CEPS .... Combined Exercise Planning Staff [*Military*] (MCD)
CEPS .... Command Module Electrical Power System [*NASA*]
CEPS .... Components Evaluation Propulsion System (MCD)
CEPS .... Computerized Equipment Pricing System [*Council of Petroleum Accountants Societies*] [*Information service or system*] (CRD)
CEPS .... Continuous Explosion-Puffing System [*Food technology*]
CEPS .... Corporate Electronic Publishing Systems Exhibition [*or Exposition*] (ITD)
CEPS .... Council for the Education of the Partially Seeing [*Later, Division for the Visually Handicapped*] (EA)
CEPSA ...... Chemical Engineering Progress. Symposium Series [*A publication*]
CEPSB .... Ceskoslovenska Psychologie [*A publication*]
CEPT .... Conference Europeenne des Administrations des Postes et des Telecommunications [*Conference of European Postal and Telecommunications Administrations*] [*Telecommunications*] (EAIO)
CEPTIA ..... Committee to End Pay Toilets in America [*Defunct*]
CEPUP ...... Chemical Education for Public Understanding Program [*University of California, Berkley*]
CEPYA ...... Ceskoslovenska Psychiatrie [*A publication*]
CEPYME .. Confederacion Espanola de Pequena y Mediana Empresa [*Employers' organization*] [*Spain*] (EY)
CEQ .... [*The*] Centennial Group, Inc. [*AMEX symbol*] (SPSG)
CEQ .... Central Bank of Barbados. Quarterly Report [*A publication*]
CEQ .... Cinequity Corp. [*Toronto Stock Exchange symbol*]
CEQ .... Council on Environmental Quality [*of Federal Council on Science and Technology*] [*Washington, DC*]
CER .... Caesar Resources Ltd. [*Vancouver Stock Exchange symbol*]
CER .... Cahiers d'Etudes Romanes [*A publication*]
CER .... Cancer-Environment Register [*Sweden*]
CER .... Capital Expenditure Request
CER .... Capital Expenditure Review (DHSM)
CER .... Carbon Dioxide Exchange Rate [*Plant biochemistry*]
CER .... Carriage of Explosives Regulations
CER .... Catholic Educational Review [*A publication*]
CER .... Cation-Exchange Resin [*Chemical technology*]
CER .... Celanese Engineering Resins Division [*Celanese Corp.*]
CER .... Center for Economic Research [*University of Texas at Austin*] [*Research center*] (RCD)
CER .... Center for Educational Reform (EA)
CER .... Ceramic (MSA)
Cer. .... Ceramide [*Biochemistry*]

CER .... Cereal Agar
CER .... Ceres [*South Africa*] [*Seismograph station code, US Geological Survey*] (SEIS)
cer. .... Cerise [*Philately*]
CER .... Certification Evaluation Review
CER .... Cervicothoracic Orthosis [*Also, CTO*] [*Medicine*]
CER .... Cherbourg [*France*] [*Airport symbol*] (OAG)
CER .... Citicorp Economic Report [*Database*] [*Citicorp Information Services*] [*Information service or system*] (CRD)
CER .... Citizens for Eye Research (EA)
CER .... Civil Engineering Report
CER .... Climb Enroute [*Aviation*] (FAAC)
CER .... Closer Economic Relations (ADA)
CER .... Coastal and Estuarine Regimes [*Oceanography*] (MSC)
CER .... Cohesive Energy Ratio (MCD)
CER .... Colonizing Efficiency Ratio [*Forestry*]
CER .... Combat Effectiveness Report (NATG)
C & ER .... Combustion and Explosives Research (AAG)
CER .... Command and Expenditure Report
CER .... Commanders Evaluation Report [*Army*]
CER .... Committee on Educational Reconstruction
CER .... Community Educational Resources
CER .... Comparative Education Review [*A publication*]
CER .... Complete Engine Repair (NG)
CER .... Complete Engineering Release
CER .... Component Engineering Request
CER .... Conditioned Emotional Response [*Psychology*]
CER .... Contact End Resistance [*Photovoltaic energy systems*]
CER .... Controller of Research and Development Establishments and Research [*British*] (RDA)
CER .... Coordinated Experimental Research [*Program*] [*National Science Foundation*]
CER .... Coordinating Equipment Research Committee
CER .... Cost-Effective Ratio [*Economics*]
CER .... Cost Estimating Relation [*or Relationship*] (AFM)
CER .... Cost-Exchange Ratio [*DoD*]
CER .... Council of European Regions (EAIO)
CER .... Critical Experiment Reactor (NRCH)
CEr .... Eagle Rock Public Library, Eagle Rock, CA [*Library symbol*] [*Library of Congress*] (LCLS)
Cer .... Hymnus in Cererem [*of Callimachus*] [*Classical studies*] (OCD)
CERA .... Canadian Educational Researchers Association [*See also ACCE*]
CERA .... Central Electric Railfans' Association (EA)
CERA .... Chief Engine Room Artificer [*British military*] (DMA)
CERA .... Civil Engineering Research Association
CERA .... Comision Especial de Expertos para el Estudio de las Necesidades Financieras que Plantea la Ejecucion de Planes de Reforma Agraria [*Consejo Interamericano Economico y Social*] [*Washington, DC*]
CERAB ..... Ceskoslovenska Radiologie [*A publication*]
CERAM ..... British Ceramic Research Ltd. [*Research center*] (IRC)
CERAM ..... Ceramic (ROG)
Ceram Abstr ... Ceramic Abstracts [*A publication*]
Ceram Age ... Ceramic Age [*A publication*]
CERAMAL ... Ceramic and Alloy [*NASA*]
Ceram Awareness Bull ... Ceramic Awareness Bulletin [*Defense Ceramic Information Center*] [*A publication*]
CERAMBRUX ... European Centre for Medical Application and Research (EAIO)
Ceram Budow ... Ceramika Budowlana [*A publication*]
Ceram Bull ... Ceramic Bulletin [*A publication*]
Ceram Crist ... Ceramica y Cristal [*A publication*]
Ceram Eng Sci Proc ... Ceramic Engineering and Science Proceedings [*A publication*]
Ceram Forum Int ... Ceramic Forum International [*West Germany*] [*A publication*]
Ceramic Abstr ... Ceramic Abstracts [*A publication*]
Ceramic R. . Ceramic Review [*A publication*]
Ceramic S B ... American Ceramic Society. Bulletin [*A publication*]
Ceramics Int ... Ceramics International [*United Kingdom*] [*A publication*]
Ceramics Mo ... Ceramics Monthly [*A publication*]
Ceram Ind ... Ceramic Industry [*A publication*]
Ceram Ind J ... Ceramics Industries Journal [*A publication*]
Ceram Ind (Sevres Fr) ... Ceramiques Industrielles (Sevres, France) [*A publication*]
Ceram Int News ... Ceramics International News [*Italy*] [*A publication*]
Ceram Jap ... Ceramics Japan [*A publication*]
Ceram Jpn ... Ceramics Japan [*A publication*]
Ceram Laterizi ... Ceramichte e Laterizi [*A publication*]
Ceram Mo ... Ceramics Monthly [*A publication*]
Ceram Pr Kom Ceram Pol Akad Nauk Oddzial Krak ... Ceramika Prace Komisji Ceramicnyj Polska Akademie Nauk Oddzial w Krakowie [*A publication*]
Ceram Supercond Res Update ... Ceramic Superconductors. Research Update [*A publication*]
Ceram Trns ... Ceramic Transactions [*A publication*]
Ceramurgia Int ... Ceramurgia International [*A publication*]
Ceramurgia Tec Ceram ... Ceramurgia, Tecnologia Ceramica [*A publication*]
Ceramurg Int ... Ceramurgia International [*A publication*]
Ceram Verrerie ... Ceramique et Verrerie [*A publication*]

Ceram Verrerie Emaill ... Ceramique, Verrerie, Emaillerie [*A publication*]

CERAP ...... Combined Center/RAPCON [*RADAR Approach Control*] [*Aviation*] (FAAC)

CERAT ...... Ceratum [*Wax Ointment*] [*Pharmacy*]

CERATF ... Communications Era Task Force [*Defunct*] (EA)

CERB .... CERBCO, Inc. [*NASDAQ symbol*] (NQ)

CERB .... Coastal Engineering Research Board [*Vicksburg, MS*] [*Army*] (AABC)

CERBD ...... Chemical Engineering Research Bulletin (Dacca) [*A publication*]

Cerberus Elektron ... Cerberus Elektronik [*A publication*]

Cerberus R ... Cerberus Report [*A publication*]

CERBOM ... Centre d'Etudes et de Recherches de Biologie et d'Oceanographie Medicale

CERBOM Rapp Act ... CERBOM [*Centre d'Etudes et de Recherches de Biologie et d'Oceanographie Medicale*] Rapport d'Activite [*France*] [*A publication*]

CERC .... Central Engine Room Control

CERC .... Coastal Engineering Research Center [*Vicksburg, MS*] [*Army*] (AABC)

CERC .... Coastal Engineering Research Council (EA)

CERC .... Consumer Education Research Center (EA)

CERC .... Corporate Emergency Response Center [*Nuclear emergency planning*]

CERCA ...... Commonwealth and Empire Radio for Civil Aviation [*British*]

Cercet Agron Moldova ... Cercetari Agronomice in Moldova [*A publication*]

Cercetari Muzicol ... Cercetari de Muzicologie [*A publication*]

Cercet Ist ... Cercetari Istorice [*A publication*]

Cercet Metal ... Cercetari Metalurgice [*A publication*]

Cercet Metal Inst Cercet Metal (Bucharest) ... Cercetari Metalurgice. Institutul de Cercetari Metalurgice (Bucharest) [*A publication*]

Cercet Miniere Inst Cercet Miniere ... Cercetari Miniere. Institutul de Cercetari Miniere [*A publication*]

Cercet Num ... Cercetari Numismatice [*A publication*]

CERCLA ... Comprehensive Environmental Response, Compensation, and Liability Act [*1980*]

Cerc Num ... Cercetari Numismatice. Muzeul de Istorie [*A publication*]

CERCOM ... Communications and Electronics Materiel Readiness Command [*Army*]

CERD .... Center for Educational Research and Development [*University of Maryland*] [*Research center*] (RCD)

CERD .... Central Evidence of Research and Development Reports

CERD .... Chronic Endstage Renal Disease [*Nephrology*]

CERD .... Committee on the Elimination of Racial Discrimination (EAIO)

CERDA ...... Chemie der Erde [*A publication*]

CERDAC ... Centre d'Etudes et de Recherches Documentaires sur l'Afrique Centrale

CERDIC .... Centre de Recherches et de Documentation des Institutions Chretiennes [*Christian Institutions Research and Documentation Center*] [*France*] [*Information service or system*] (IID)

CER-DIP ... Ceramic Dual In-Line Package

CERDP ...... Centre Europeen de Recherche et de Documentation Parlementaires [*European Centre for Parliamentary Research and Documentation - ECPRD*] [*Luxembourg, Luxembourg*] (EAIO)

CERDS ...... Charter of Economic Rights and Duties of States [*United Nations*]

CERE .... Centre d'Essais Regional Europeen [*European Regional Test Center*] [*NATO*] (NATG)

Cer E .... Ceramic Engineer

CERE .... Comite Europeen pour les Relations Economiques

CERE .... Computer Entry and Readout Equipment (KSC)

CEREA ...... Centre de Regroupement Africain [*Center for African Regroupment*] [*Congo - Leopoldville*]

Cereal Chem ... Cereal Chemistry [*A publication*]

Cereal Chem Bull ... Cereal Chemists Bulletin [*A publication*]

Cereal Crop Ser Indian Counc Agr Res ... Cereal Crop Series. Indian Council of Agricultural Research [*A publication*]

Cereal Foods World ... Cereal Foods World [*A publication*]

Cereal F W ... Cereal Foods World [*A publication*]

Cereal Res Commun ... Cereal Research Communications [*A publication*]

Cereal Rusts Bull ... Cereal Rusts Bulletin [*A publication*]

Cereal Sci Today ... Cereal Science Today [*A publication*]

Cereb Circ Metab ... Cerebral Circulation and Metabolism [*A publication*]

Cereb Palsy J ... Cerebral Palsy Journal [*A publication*]

Cereb Palsy Rev ... Cerebral Palsy Review [*A publication*]

Cerebrovasc Brain Metab Rev ... Cerebrovascular and Brain Metabolism Reviews [*A publication*]

Cerebrovasc Dis ... Cerebrovascular Diseases [*A publication*]

Cereb Vas Dis ... Cerebral Vascular Diseases [*A publication*]

Cereb Vas Dis Int Conf ... Cerebral Vascular Diseases. International Conference [*A publication*]

CERED ...... CEGB [*Central Electricity Generating Board*] Research [*England*] [*A publication*]

CEREL ...... Civil Engineering and Evaluation Laboratory [*Navy*] (MCD)

CEREOL ... Cereolus [*An urethral bougie*] [*Pharmacy*]

CERES ...... Center for Research and Education in Sexuality [*San Francisco State University*] [*Research center*] (RCD)

CERES ...... Computer-Enhanced Radio Emission Surveillance [*British*]

CERESIS .. Centro Regional de Sismologia para America del Sur [*Regional Seismology Center for South America*] [*Research center*] [*Peru*]

Cere Vasc Dis Trans Conf ... Cerebral Vascular Diseases. Transactions of the Conference [*A publication*]

CERF .... Canine Eye Registration Foundation (EA)

CERF .... Commander, Emergency Recovery Force

CERF .... Corps of Engineers Reserve Fleet

CERF .... Council of Europe Resettlement Fund

CERFE ...... Center for Education and Research in Free Enterprise [*College Station, TX*] (EA)

CERFIRO ... Countermeasures Evaluation - Infrared and Optical

CERFS ...... Community Educational Radio Fixed Service (MSA)

CERG .... Cambridge Energy Research Group [*University of Cambridge*] [*British*] (IRUK)

CERG .... Commander, Emergency Recovery Group

CERG .... Consumer Education Research Group [*Later, CERC*] (EA)

CERH .... Comite Europeen de Rink Hockey [*European Committee for Rink Hockey*] (EAIO)

CERHU ..... Centre d'Etudes en Relations Humaines [*Centre of Studies in Human Relations*] [*Canada*]

CERI .... Canadian Energy Research Institute [*University of Calgary*] [*Research center*] (RCD)

CERI .... Center for Earthquake Research and Information [*Memphis State University*] [*Research center*] (RCD)

CERI .... Central Electrochemical Research Institute

CERI .... Centre for Educational Research and Innovation (EAIO)

CERI .... Centre Europeen de Recherches sur l'Investissement (EAIO)

CERI .... Clean Energy Research Institute [*University of Miami*] [*Research center*]

CERIC ...... Committee of Ecological Research for the Interoceanic Canal [*National Academy of Science*] (MSC)

CERILH .... Centre d'Etudes et de Recherches de l'Industrie des Liants Hydrauliques [*Center for Study and Research of the Hydraulic Binders Industry*] [*Information service or system*] (IID)

Cer Ind ...... Ceramic Industry [*A publication*]

CERIS .... Chinese Educational Resources Information System [*Database*] [*National Taiwan Normal University Library*] [*Information service or system*] (CRD)

CERL .... Cambridge Electronic Research Laboratory (KSC)

CERL .... Central Electricity Research Laboratories [*British*]

CERL .... Commercial Equipment Requirement List

CERL .... Computer-Based Education Research Laboratory [*University of Illinois*] [*Research center*]

CERL .... Construction Engineering Research Laboratory [*Champaign, IL*] [*Army*]

CERL .... Corvallis Environmental Research Laboratory [*Oregon*] [*Environmental Protection Agency*]

CERLAC ... Centre for Research on Latin America and the Caribbean [*York University*] [*Canada*] [*Research center*] (RCD)

CERLAL .... Centro Regional para el Fomento del Libro en America Latina

CERLI .... Cooperative Educational Research Laboratory, Incorporated

CERM .... Centre Europeen de Recherches Mauvernay [*France*] [*Research code symbol*]

CERMA ..... Cermica [*A publication*]

CERMB ..... Cercetari Metalurgice [*A publication*]

CERMET ... Ceramic Metal Element [*NASA*]

CERMET .. Ceramic-to-Metal Seal

CERN .... Cerner Corp. [*Kansas City, MO*] [*NASDAQ symbol*] (NQ)

CERN .... Consumer Education Resource Network

CERN .... Organisation Europeenne pour la Recherche Nucleaire [*European Organization for Nuclear Research*] [*Acronym represents previous name, Conseil Europeen pour la Recherche Nucleaire*] (EAIO)

CERNA ..... Conference des Eveques de la Region Nord de l'Afrique [*North African Episcopal Conference*] (EAIO)

CERN High Energy React Anal Group Rep ... CERN [*Conseil Europeen pour la Recherche Nucleaire*] High Energy Reaction Analysis Group Report [*A publication*]

CERN Rep ... CERN [*Conseil Europeen pour la Recherche Nucleaire*] Report [*A publication*]

CERO .... Corps Epidemiological Reference Office [*Military*]

CEROILS ... China National Cereals, Oils, and Foodstuffs Import & Export Corp. [*People's Republic of China*] (IMH)

CERP .... Civil Engineering Report of Performance (AFM)

CERP .... COCORP Extended Research Project [*Geology*]

CERP .... Confederation Europeenne des Relations Publiques [*European Confederation of Public Relations*] (EAIO)

CERP .... Continuing Education Recognition Program [*For nurses*]

CERP .... Current Economic Reporting Program [*Department of State*]

CERPB ...... Citizens for Eye Research to Prevent Blindness (EA)

CERPS ...... Centralized Expenditure/Reimbursement Processing System (NVT)

CERR .... Centre for Earth Resources Research [*Memorial University of Newfoundland*] [*Research center*] (RCD)

CERR .... Comite Europeen de Reflexion sur les Retraites [*European Pension Committee*] [*Paris, France*] (EAIO)

CERR .... Configuration Enhanced Radiation Rejection [*Space technology*]

Cerrahpasa Tip Fak Derg ... Cerrahpasa Tip Fakultesi Dergisi [*A publication*]
CERRAT ... Commonwealth Employees Redeployment and Retirement Appeals Tribunals [*Australia*]
CERRC ..... Complete Engine Repair Requirements Card [*DoD*]
CE/RRT ... Central Europe Railroad Transport [*NATO*] (NATG)
CERS .... Carrier Evaluation and Reporting System
CERS .... Commander, Emergency Recovery Section
CER-T ...... Cahiers d'Etudes de Radio-Television [*A publication*]
CE/RT ...... Central Europe Road Transport [*NATO*] (NATG)
CERT .... CERT. Civil Engineering and Road Transport [*New Zealand*] [*A publication*]
CERT .... [*A*] Certainty
CERT .... Certificate [*or Certification*] (AFM)
cert .... Certified From [*or Certified To*] [*Legal term*] (DLA)
cert .... Certify (DLA)
CERT .... Certiorari [*Legal term*] (DLA)
CERT .... Character Error Rate Test
CERT .... Combined Environmental Reliability Testing [*Air Force*] (RDA)
CERT .... Composite Electrical Readiness Test (KSC)
CERT .... Constant Extension Rate Tensile Test
CERT .... Council of Energy Resource Tribes (EA)
CertArchDraft ... Certificate in Architectural Drafting
CERTC ...... Certificate (ROG)
CERTD ...... Certified
cert den .... Certiorari Denied [*Legal term*] (DLA)
CertDesRCA ... Certificate of Designer of the Royal College of Art [*British*] (DBQ)
cert dis .... Certiorari Dismissed [*Legal term*] (DLA)
CertECTEd ... Certificate in Early Childhood Teacher Education
CertEd .... Certificate in Education [*British*] (DBQ)
CERTFD ...... Certified (ROG)
CERT GR .. Certiorari Granted [*Legal term*] (DLA)
Cert Granted ... Petition to United States Supreme Court for Writ of Certiorari Granted [*Legal term*] (DLA)
CERTICO ... Certification Committee [*American National Standards Institute*] (IEEE)
CERTIF ..... Certificate
Certifd Engr ... Certificated Engineer [*A publication*]
Certif Dent Tec ... Certified Dental Technician [*A publication*]
Certif Eng .. Certificated Engineer [*A publication*]
Certif Eng .. Certified Engineer [*A publication*]
CERTN ...... Certain (ROG)
CertNNICU ... Certificate of Neo-Natal Intensive Care Nursing
Cert RAS ... Royal Academy Schools Certificate [*British*]
CERTS ..... Certification Test System (MCD)
CERTS ...... Consolidated Eglin Real-Time System (MCD)
CERTSUB ... Certain Submarine [*Navy*] (NVT)
CERU ...... Commander, Emergency Recovery Unit
CERV .... Carnation Etched Ring Virus
CERV .... Cervix [*Anatomy*]
CERV .... Controlled Energy Relief Valve (MCD)
CERV .... Corporate Experimental Research Vehicle [*General Motors Corp.*] [*Automotive engineering*]
CERV .... Crew Emergency Vehicle (MCD)
CERVED ... Centri Elettronici Reteconnessi Valutazione Elaborazione Dati [*Central Electronic Network for Data Processing and Analysis*] [*Information service or system*] (IID)
CERVED ... Societa Nazionale di Informatica delle Camere di Commerces Italiane [*National Information Company of Italian Chambers of Commerce*] [*Information service or system*] (IID)
CES .... Cahiers Economiques et Sociaux [*Kinshasa*] [*A publication*]
CES .... Capillary Electrophoresis System [*In CES I, manufactured by Dionex Corp.*] [*Analytical biochemistry*]
CES .... Career Exploration Series [*Vocational guidance test*]
CES .... Caribbean Educational Service
CES .... Carrefour des Employees de Secretariat [*Crossroads of Secretariat Employees*] [*Canada*]
CES .... Casa El Salvador (EA)
CES .... Casualty Estimation Study [*Military*]
CES .... Cat Eye Syndrome [*Medicine*]
CES .... Center for Economic Studies [*Washington, DC*] [*Department of Commerce*] (GRD)
CES .... Center for Education Statistics [*Washington, DC*] [*Department of Education*] [*Also, an information service or system*] (IID)
CES .... Center for Energy Studies [*University of Texas at Austin*] [*Research center*] (RCD)
CES .... Center for Energy Studies [*Louisiana State University*] [*Information service or system*] (IID)
CES .... Center for Entrepreneurial Studies [*New York University*] [*Research center*] (RCD)
CES .... Center for Environmental Sciences [*University of Colorado at Denver*] [*Research center*] (RCD)
CES .... Center for Environmental Studies [*Williams College*] [*Research center*] (RCD)
CES .... Center for Environmental Studies [*Arizona State University*] [*Research center*] (RCD)
ces .... Centimes [*Monetary unit*] [*France*] (GPO)
CES .... Central Electronics System (KSC)

CES .... Central [*Nervous System*] Excitatory State
CES .... Centre for Educational Sociology [*University of Edinburgh*] [*United Kingdom*] (CB)
CES .... Centre for Educational Studies [*King's College, London*] [*British*] (CB)
CES .... Centre for Energy Studies [*Technical University of Nova Scotia*] [*Research center*] (RCD)
CES .... Centre for Environmental Studies [*British*]
CES .... Centre Europeen des Silicones [*of the European Council of Chemical Manufacturers' Federations*] (EAIO)
CES .... Cessnock [*Australia*] [*Airport symbol*] (OAG)
CES .... Chick Embryonic Skin
CES .... Chinese Economic Studies [*A publication*]
CES .... Circus Education Specialists [*In association name, CES, Inc.*] (EA)
CES .... Citicorp Economic Services [*Information service or system*] (IID)
CES .... Classroom Environment Scale [*Teacher evaluation test*]
CES .... Closed Ecological System
CES .... Coalition for Economic Survival (EA)
CES .... Coalition of Essential Schools (EA)
CES .... Coast Earth Station [*INMARSAT*]
CES .... Combined Effects Submissile (MCD)
CES .... Combined English Stores [*Commercial firm*] [*British*]
CES .... Comite Economique et Social [*Economic and Social Committee*] [*of CEE*]
CES .... Commercial Earth Station
CES .... Committee on Earth Sciences [*President's Office of Science & Technology Policy*]
CES .... Committee on Economic Security [*Terminated as formal agency, 1936, but continued informally for some time thereafter*]
CES .... Committee to Eradicate Syphilis [*Defunct*] (EA)
CES .... Committee of European Shipowners
CES .... Commonwealth Energy System [*NYSE symbol*] (SPSG)
CE and S .... Commonwealth Essays and Studies [*A publication*]
CES .... Communication Engineering Standard
CES .... Communications Errors Statistics (CMD)
CES .... Comparative Education Society [*Later, CIES*] (EA)
CES .... Comprehensive Export Schedule [*US*]
CES .... Compressor End Seal
CES .... Computer Election Systems, Inc.
CES .... Computer Engineering Service
CES .... Computer Enhanced Spectroscopy [*A publication*]
CES .... Confederation Europeenne de Scoutisme [*European Confederation of Scouts - ECS*] (EAIO)
CES .... Confederazione Europea dei Sindacati [*European Trade Union Confederation - ETUC*] [*Italian*]
CES .... Conferentia Episcopalis Scandiae [*Scandinavian Episcopal Conference - SEC*] (EAIO)
CES .... Constant Elasticity of Substitution [*Industrial production*]
CES .... Construction Electrician, Shop [*Navy rating*]
CES .... Consumer Electronics Show [*Computer industry*]
CES .... Continuous Electrical Stimulation
CES .... Control Electronics Section [*Apollo*] [*NASA*]
CES .... Control Electronics System (MCD)
CES .... Controlled Environmental System [*NASA*]
CES .... Cooperative Extension Service [*Department of Agriculture*]
CES .... Coordinated Evaluation System [*National Institute of Standards and Technology*]
CES .... Cosmos Resources, Inc. [*Vancouver Stock Exchange symbol*]
CES .... Cost Effectiveness Study [*Economics*]
CES .... Council for European Studies (EA)
CES .... Court of Exchequer [*Scotland*] (DLA)
CES .... Creative Electronic Systems
CeS .... Crew Escape System (MCD)
CeS .... Cultura e Scuola [*A publication*]
CES .... Current Employment Statistics [*Bureau of Labor Statistics*] (OICC)
CES .... Current Employment Status
CES .... Cyanoethylsucrose
CEs .... El Segundo Public Library, El Segundo, CA [*Library symbol*] [*Library of Congress*] (LCLS)
CES .... IEEE Consumer Electronics Society (EA)
CEsA .... Aerospace Corp., El Segundo, CA [*Library symbol*] [*Library of Congress*] (LCLS)
CESA .... Canadian Engineering Standards Association [*Later, Canadian Standards Association*]
CESA .... Canadian Ethnic Studies Association
CES A .... Ceskoslovenska Stomatologie [*A publication*]
CESA .... Comite Europeen des Syndicats de l'Alimentation, du Tabac, et de l'Industrie Hoteliere [*European Trade Union Committee of Food and Allied Workers*] [*Common Market*]
CESA .... Committee of EEC [*European Economic Community*] Shipbuilders' Associations (EAIO)
CESA .... Community Employment Support Agency [*Australia*]
CESA .... Consumer Electronic Suppliers Association [*Australia*]
CESA .... Cooperative Educational Service Agency [*National Science Foundation*]
CESA .... Cultural Exchange Society of America (EA)

CESAC...... Communications-Electronics Scheme Accounting and Control [*Air Force*]

CESAC...... Conference of Executives of State Associations of Counties [*Later, National Council of County Association Executives*] (EA)

CESAO...... Commission Economique et Sociale pour l'Asie Occidentale [*Economic and Social Commission for Western Asia - ESCWA*] (EAIO)

CESAR...... Canadian Expedition to Study the Alpha Ridge [*1983*]

CESAR...... Capsule Escape and Survival Applied Research [*Aerospace*]

CESAR...... Center for Engineering Systems Advanced Research [*Oak Ridge National Laboratory*] [*Department of Energy*] [*Oak Ridge, TN*]

CESARS.... Chemical Evaluation Search and Retrieval System [*Michigan Department of Natural Resources*] [*Information service or system*] (CRD)

CESB........ Center for Experimental Studies in Business [*University of Minnesota*]

CESBBA.... Connecticut. Agricultural Experiment Station. Department of Entomology. Special Bulletin [*A publication*]

CESC........ Computer Entry Systems Corporation [*Silver Spring, MD*] [*NASDAQ symbol*] (NQ)

CEsC.......... Computer Sciences Corp., Technical Library, El Segundo, CA [*Library symbol*] [*Library of Congress*] (LCLS)

CESC........ Conference on European Security and Cooperation

CEsc.......... Escondido Public Library, Escondido, CA [*Library symbol*] [*Library of Congress*] (LCLS)

CESCA....... Chemical Engineering Science [*A publication*]

CESCA...... Comunidad Economica y Social Centroamericana [*Central American Socioeconomic Community*]

CESCE ...... Comite Europeen des Services des Conseillers [*European Committee for Consultant Services - ECCS*] (EAIO)

CES (Centre Environmental Studies) R ... CES (Centre Environmental Studies) Review [*A publication*]

CESCH...... Communications Electronics School [*Air Force*]

CES Conf Paps ... Centre for Environmental Studies. Conference Papers [*A publication*]

CES-D .... Center for Epidemiologic Studies - Depression Scale [*Personality development test*] [*Psychology*]

CESD........ Centre Europeen de Formation des Statisticiens Economistes des Pays en Voie de Developpement [*European Center for Training Statisticians and Economists from Developing Countries*]

CESD........ Cholesterol Ester Storage Disease [*Medicine*]

CESD........ Composite External Symbol Dictionary (BUR)

CESDA...... Confederation of European Soft Drink Associations [*Switzerland*] (EY)

CESE .... Captured Enemy Signal Equipment [*Military*] (MCD)

CESE .... Centre Economique de Secours Europeens [*European Economic Relief Committee*] [*NATO*] (NATG)

CESE .... Civil Engineer Support Equipment [*Army*]

CESE .... Communications Equipment Support Element (MCD)

CESE .... Comparative Education Society in Europe (EAIO)

CESEMI..... Computer Evaluation of Scanning Electron Microscope Image

CESF .... College of Environmental Science and Forestry [*SUNY*]

CESF .... Commander, Eastern Sea Frontier [*Navy*]

CESG........ Cryogenic Electrically Suspended Gyroscope

CESGA....... Comments on Earth Sciences. Geophysics [*A publication*]

CESI .... Centre for Economic and Social Information [*United Nations*]

CESI .... Closed Entry Socket Insulator

CESI .... Cogenic Energy Systems, Incorporated [*New York, NY*] [*NASDAQ symbol*] (NQ)

CESI .... Communications-Electronics Standing Instruction (AABC)

CESI .... Council for Elementary Science International (EA)

CESIA .... Centre d'Etudes des Systemes d'Information des Administrations [*Center for the Study on Information Systems in Government*] [*Information service or system*] (IID)

CES Inf Paps ... Centre for Environmental Studies. Information Papers [*A publication*]

CESK........ Cable End Sealing Kit

Cesk Akad Ved Geogr Ustav Zpr ... Ceskoslovenska Akademie Ved. Geograficky Ustav Zpravy [*Brno*] [*A publication*]

Cesk Akad Ved Ved Inf CSAV ... Ceskoslovenska Akademie Ved. Vedecke Informace CSAV [*A publication*]

Ceska Mykol ... Ceska Mykologie [*A publication*]

Cesk Biol.... Ceskoslovenska Biologie [*A publication*]

Cesk Cas Fys ... Ceskoslovensky Casopis pro Fysiku. Sekce A (Prague) [*A publication*]

Cesk Cas Fys A ... Ceskoslovensky Casopis pro Fysiku. Sekce A [*A publication*]

Cesk Cas Fys Sekce A ... Ceskoslovensky Casopis pro Fysiku. Sekce A [*A publication*]

Cesk Cas Hist ... Ceskoslovensky Casopis Historicky [*A publication*]

Cesk C Fys ... Ceskoslovensky Casopis pro Fysiku. Sekce A [*A publication*]

Cesk Dermatol ... Ceskoslovenska Dermatologie [*A publication*]

Cesk Epidemiol Mikrobiol Immunol ... Ceskoslovenska Epidemiologie, Mikrobiologie, Immunologie [*A publication*]

Cesk Farm ... Ceskoslovenska Farmacie [*A publication*]

Cesk Fysiol ... Ceskoslovenska Fysiologie [*A publication*]

Cesk Gastroenterol Vyz ... Ceskoslovenska Gastroenterologie a Vyziva [*A publication*]

Cesk Gynekol ... Ceskoslovenska Gynekologie [*A publication*]

Cesk Hyg ... Ceskoslovenska Hygiena [*A publication*]

Cesk Hyg Epidemiol Mikrobiol Imunol ... Ceskoslovenska Hygiena Epidemiologie, Mikrobiologie, Imunologie [*A publication*]

Cesk Inf ..... Ceskoslovenska Informatika. Teorie a Praxe [*A publication*]

Cesk Inf Teor a Praxe ... Ceskoslovenska Informatika. Teorie a Praxe [*A publication*]

Cesk Kozarstvi ... Ceskoslovenska Kozarstvi [*A publication*]

Cesk Lit ... Ceska Literatura [*A publication*]

Cesk Mikrobiol ... Ceskoslovenska Mikrobiologie [*A publication*]

Cesk Morfol ... Ceskoslovenska Morfologie [*A publication*]

Cesk Neurol ... Ceskoslovenska Neurologie [*Later, Ceskoslovenska Neurologie a Neurochirurgie*] [*A publication*]

Cesk Neurol Neurochir ... Ceskoslovenska Neurologie a Neurochirurgie [*A publication*]

Cesk Oftalmol ... Ceskoslovenska Oftalmologie [*A publication*]

Cesk Onkol ... Ceskoslovenska Onkologie [*A publication*]

Ceskoslovensk Akad Ved Geog Ustav (Brno) Studia Geog ... Ceskoslovenska Akademie Ved. Geograficky Ustav (Brno). Studia Geographica [*A publication*]

Cesk Otolaryngol ... Ceskoslovenska Otolaryngologie [*A publication*]

Cesk Parasitol ... Ceskoslovenska Parasitologie [*A publication*]

Cesk Patol ... Ceskoslovenska Patologie [*A publication*]

Cesk Pediatr ... Ceskoslovenska Pediatrie [*A publication*]

Cesk Psychiatr ... Ceskoslovenska Psychiatrie [*A publication*]

Cesk Psycho ... Ceskoslovenska Psychologie [*A publication*]

Cesk Psychol ... Ceskoslovenska Psychologie [*A publication*]

Cesk Radiol ... Ceskoslovenska Radiologie [*A publication*]

Cesk Rentgenol ... Ceskoslovenska Rentgenologie [*A publication*]

Cesk Stand ... Ceskoslovenska Standardizace [*A publication*]

Cesk Stomatol ... Ceskoslovenska Stomatologie [*A publication*]

Cesky Vcel ... Cesky Vcelar [*A publication*]

Cesk Zdrav ... Ceskoslovenske Zdravotnictvi [*A publication*]

CESL .... Camp Evans Signal Laboratory [*Army*]

CESL .... Civil Engineering Systems Laboratory [*University of Illinois*]

CESLS........ Constant Energy Synchronous Luminescence Spectroscopy

CESMET... Civil Engineering and Services Management Evaluation Team [*Military*]

CESNEF.... Centro di Studi Nucleari Enrico Fermi [*Nuclear Engineering Institute - Enrico Fermi Nuclear Center*] [*Italy*] (NRCH)

CESO........ Canadian Executive Service Overseas

CESO........ Centrum voor de Studie van het Onderwijs in Ontwikkelingslanden [*Centre for Study of Education in Developing Countries*] (EAIO)

CESO........ Civil Engineer Support Office [*Navy*]

CESO........ Communication Electronics Staff Officer (MCD)

CESO........ Council of Engineers and Scientists Organizations

CES Occ Paps ... Centre for Environmental Studies. Occasional Papers [*A publication*]

CESOP...... Contributory Employee Stock Ownership Plan

CESP .... Centre d'Etude des Supports Publicitaires [*Center for the Study of Advertising Support*] [*Database producer*] [*Paris, France*]

CESP .... Civil Engineer Support Plan

CESP .... Confederation of European Specialists in Pediatrics (EAIO)

CESP .... Correlation Echo Sound Processor [*Oceanography*]

CESPE....... Centro Studi Politica Economica [*of the Italian Communist Party*]

CESPM ..... Commission de l'Enseignement Superieur des Provinces Maritimes [*Maritime Provinces Higher Education Commission*] [*Canada*]

CES Policy Series ... Centre for Environmental Studies. Policy Series [*A publication*]

C ESPR...... Con Espressione [*With Expression*] [*Music*] (ROG)

CESq.......... Combat Evaluation Squadron [*Air Force*]

CESR .... Canadian Electronic Sales Representatives

CESR .... Colliding Electron-Beam Storage Ring [*Nuclear energy*] (NRCH)

CESR .... Conduction Electron Spin Resonance

CESR .... Consumer Economic Study Report [*Department of Agriculture*]

CESR .... Cornell Electron Storage Ring [*Atomic physics*]

CES Res Paps ... Centre for Environmental Studies. Research Papers [*A publication*]

CES Res Series ... Centre for Environmental Studies. Research Series [*A publication*]

CES Rev..... Centre for Environmental Studies. Review [*A publication*]

CESRL Rep Univ Tex Austin Dep Civ Eng Struct Res Lab ... CESRL Report. University of Texas at Austin. Department of Civil Engineering. Structures Research Laboratory [*A publication*]

CESS .... Council of Engineering Society Secretaries [*Later, CESSE*] (EA)

CESSA...... Church of England Soldiers', Sailors', and Airmen's Club

CESSAC.... Church of England Soldiers', Sailors', and Airmen's Clubs

CESSAM.... Computer Equipment System for Surface-to-Air Missiles (MCD)

CESSAR.... Combustion Engineering Standard Safety Analysis Report [*Nuclear energy*] (NRCH)

CESSDT.... Cambridge Texts in the Physiological Sciences [*A publication*]

CESSE....... Council of Engineering and Scientific Society Executives (EA)

CESSI........ Church of England Sunday School Institute
CESSLGO ... Continuing Education Service for State and Local Government Officials
CEST .... Cost-Effective Shape Technology   (MCD)
CEST .... Cost Effective Surface Torpedo   (MCD)
Ce Sta........ Ceskoslovenska Stomatologie [*A publication*]
CESTD ...... Ceskoslovenska Standardizace [*A publication*]
CESTR ...... Cestriensis [*Signature of the Bishops of Chester*]   (ROG)
CESTR ...... Chichester [*City in England*]   (ROG)
CESTRIEN ... Cestriensis [*Signature of the Bishops of Chester*]   (ROG)
CE Studies ... Canadian Ethnic Studies/Etudes Ethniques au Canada [*A publication*]
CES Univ Wkng Paps ... Centre for Environmental Studies. University Working Papers [*A publication*]
CESUS ...... Estonian School Center in the United States   (EA)
CESV .... Combat Engineer Supply Vehicle   (MCD)
CESV .... Communications-Electronics Survivability and Vulnerability
CES Wkng Paps ... Centre for Environmental Studies. Working Papers [*A publication*]
CESX .... Contemporary Entertainment Services [*Air carrier designation symbol*]
CET........... Calibrated Engine Testing
CET........... Canadian Equestrian Team
CET........... Capsule Elapsed Time [*Aerospace*]
CET........... Casualty Evacuation Train [*British*]
CET........... Center for Educational Technology [*Florida State University*] [*Research center*]
CET........... Center for Environmental Toxicology [*Michigan State University*] [*Research center*]   (RCD)
CET........... Central European Time   (DEN)
CET........... Central Securities Corp. [*AMEX symbol*]   (SPSG)
CET........... Central Trust Co. [*Toronto Stock Exchange symbol*]
CET........... Centre Europeen de Traduction [*European Translation Center*]
Cet............ Centus [*Constellation*]
Cet............ Cetra [*Record label*] [*Italy*]
CET........... Combat Engineer Tractor [*British*]   (RDA)
CET........... Combustor Exit Temperature   (MCD)
CET........... Commission Europeenne de Tourisme [*European Travel Commission - ETC*] [*Paris, France*]
CET........... Common External Tariff [*for EEC countries*] [*Also, CXT*]
CET........... Comprehensive External Trade Policy [*Export Credits Guarantee Department*] [*British*]
CET........... Concept Evaluation Technique [*Psychometrics*]
CET........... Concept Evaluation Test   (MCD)
CET........... Consolidated Environmental Technologies [*Commercial firm*] [*British*]   (ECON)
CET........... Construction Electrician, Telephone [*Navy rating*]
CET........... Controlled Environment Testing
CET........... Cooperative English Test
CET........... Corrected Effective Temperature   (IEEE)
CET........... Council for Educational Technology [*London, England*] [*Telecommunications*] [*Information service or system*]   (TSSD)
CET........... Critical Experiment Tank
CET........... Cumulative Elapsed Time
CEt............ Etna Free Library, Etna, CA [*Library symbol*] [*Library of Congress*]   (LCLS)
CETA........ Chinese-English Translation Assistance Group   (EA)
CETA........ Civilian Electronics Technician Afloat [*Navy*]   (NVT)
CETA........ Cleaning Equipment Trade Association   (EA)
CETA........ Comprehensive Employment and Training Act [*1973*] [*Formerly, MDTA*] [*Expired, 1982*] [*Department of Labor*]
CETA........ Conference des Eglises de Toute l'Afrique [*All Africa Conference of Churches - AACC*]   (EAIO)
CETA........ Corrosion Evaluation and Test Area [*NASA*]
CETA........ Crew and Equipment Translation Aids [*NASA*]
CETAB...... Cetyltrimethylammonium Bromide [*Also, CTAB, CTBM*] [*Antiseptic*]
CETAC...... Careers, Education, and Training Advice Centre [*British*]   (CB)
C Et Afr..... Cahiers d'Etudes Africaines [*A publication*]
CETAI....... Centre d'Etudes en Administration Internationale [*Canada*]
CETAP...... Cetacean and Turtle Assessment Program [*University of Rhode Island*] [*Research center*]   (RCD)
CETAS...... Compass Equal Target Acquisition System
CETATS.... Cetyltrimethylammonium Toluenesulfonate [*Organic chemistry*]
CETC........ Centralized Electrification and Traffic Control   (MCD)
CETC........ Corps of Engineers Technical Committee [*Army*]
CETC........ Council for Export Trading Companies [*Washington, DC*]   (EA)
CETDA...... CEGB [*Central Electricity Generating Board*] Technical Disclosure Bulletin [*England*] [*A publication*]
CETDC...... China External Trade Development Council [*Taiwan*]
CETEC..... Consolidated Engineering Technology Corporation   (MCD)
CETEX...... Committee on Contamination of Extra-Terrestrial Exploration [*NASA*]
CETF........ Clothing and Equipment Test Facility [*Army*]   (RDA)
CETG........ Civil Effects Test Group [*DASA and AEC*]
CETH........ Catalyst Thermal Energy Corp. [*NASDAQ symbol*]   (NQ)

CETHEDEC ... Centre d'Etudes Theoriques de la Detection et des Communications
Ceti............ Centus [*Constellation*]
CETI......... Communication with Extraterrestrial Intelligence [*Later, SETI*] [*Radioastronomy*]
CETI......... Continuously Expecting Transfer Interface [*IBM Corp.*]
CETIA ...... Computer Electronics Telecommunications Instruments Automation   (ADA)
CETICE..... Centre d'Ecologie et de Toxicologie de l'Industrie Chimique Europeenne [*European Chemical Industry Ecology and Toxicology Center - ECETOC*]   (EAIO)
CETIE ...... Centre Technique International de l'Embouteillage [*International Technical Center of Bottling*]
CETIM...... Centre Technique des Industries Mecaniques [*Technical Center for Mechanical Industries*] [*Database producer*] [*Senlis, France*]
CETIM Informations ... CETIM Informations. Centre Technique des Industries Mechaniques [*A publication*]
CETIS....... Centre Europeen de Traitement de l'Information Scientifique [*EURATOM*]
CETIS....... Complex Effluent Toxicity Information System [*Environmental Protection Agency*]
CETO .... Centre for Educational Television Overseas [*British*]
CETO .... Civil Effects Test Operations [*DASA and AEC*]
CETP........ Cholesteryl Ester Transfer Protein [*Biochemistry*]
CETP........ Competitive Employment and Training Programs [*Australia*]
CETP........ Comprehensive Employment and Training Plan [*Department of Labor*]
CETP........ Confederation Europeenne Therapeutique Physique [*European Confederation for Physical Therapy*]   (EAIO)
CET PAR... Ceteris Paribus [*Other Things Being Equal*] [*Latin*]
CETR....... Consolidated Edison Thorium Reactor
Cetra .... China External Trade Development Council   (GEA)
CETRAMAR ... Consortium Europeen de Transports Maritimes [*Shipping company*] [*France*]   (EY)
CETRM..... Combat Effective Training Management   (MCD)
CETS .... Church of England Temperance Society
CETS .... Civilian Engineering Technical Service [*Navy*]   (NVT)
CETS .... Conference Europeenne des Telecommunications par Satellite [*European Conference on Satellite Communications*]
CETS .... Contractor Engineering and Technical Services   (AFM)
CETS .... Control Element Test Stand [*Nuclear energy*]   (NRCH)
CETSA ..... Cost Estimating Techniques for System Acquisition [*Army*]
CETSP...... Contract Engineering and Technical Services Personnel [*Air Force*]   (AFIT)
CETU .... Computer Energy Time Unit   (MCD)
CEU .... Camera Electronic Unit   (MCD)
CEU .... Centurion Gold Ltd. [*Vancouver Stock Exchange symbol*] [*Toronto Stock Exchange symbol*]
CEU .... Channel Extension Unit
CEU .... Christian Endeavor Union
CEU .... Clemson, SC [*Location identifier*] [*FAA*]   (FAAL)
CEU .... Communications Expansion Unit
CEU .... Confederation of Entertainment Unions [*British*]
CEU .... Consensus. Informatietijdschrift over Energie Mol [*A publication*]
CEU .... Constructional Engineering Union [*British*]
CEU .... Continuing Education Unit [*American Management Association*]
CEU .... Control Electronics Unit   (MCD)
CEU .... Coupler Electronics Unit
CEU .... Cyanoethylurea [*Immunochemistry*]
CEUCA..... Customs and Economic Union of Central Africa
CEUD .... Comissao Eleitoral para a Unidade Democratico [*Electoral Committee for Democratic Unity*] [*Portugal*] [*Political party*]   (PPE)
CEUF........ Cost Estimate and Updating Form   (MCD)
CEUFA..... Central European Federalist [*A publication*]
CEUM...... Centurion Gold Ltd. [*NASDAQ symbol*]   (NQ)
CEUR .... Cellular [*Freight*]
CEURBY.. Coeur [*Paris*] [*A publication*]
CEURC..... Coal Extraction and Utilization Research Center [*Southern Illinois University at Carbondale*] [*Research center*]   (RCD)
C Europ...... Cahiers Europeens [*A publication*]
CEUS........ Commission for the Exploration and Utilization of Space [*USSR*]
CEUSP ..... Consolidated Edison Uranium Solidification Program [*Oak Ridge National Laboratory*]
CEV .... Cal Denver Resources [*Vancouver Stock Exchange symbol*]
CEV .... Citrus Exocortis Viroid
CEV .... Combat Engineer Vehicle [*Army*]
CEV .... Convoy Escort Vessel [*Navy*]
CEV .... Corona Extinction Voltage   (IEEE)
CEV .... Cryogenic Explosive Valve
CEv .... Emeryville Public Library, Emeryville, CA [*Library symbol*] [*Library of Congress*]   (LCLS)
CEV .... Evergreen Valley College, San Jose, CA [*OCLC symbol*]   (OCLC)
CEVAR...... Consumable-Electrode Vacuum-Arc Remelt [*Nuclear energy*]   (NRCH)

CEVAT...... Combined Environmental, Vibration, Acceleration, Temperature [*Aerospace*]   (AAG)
CEVD .... CCNU [*Lomustine*], Etoposide, Vindesine, Dexamethasone [*Antineoplastic drug regimen*]
CEVG .... Combat Evaluation Group [*Strategic Air Command*]
CEVM .... Consumable Electrode Vacuum Melting
CEVMA..... Christian European Visual Media Association [*London, England*]   (EAIO)
CEvS.......... Shell Development Co., Emeryville, CA [*Library symbol*] [*Library of Congress*] [*Obsolete*]   (LCLS)
CEVT........ Contingency Extravehicular Transfer [*NASA*]   (KSC)
CEW .... Caravan of East and West   (EA)
CEW .... Church Employed Women   (EA)
CEW .... Circular Electric Wire
CEW .... Coextrusion Welding
CEW .... Consort Energy Corp. [*Vancouver Stock Exchange symbol*]
CEW .... Construction Electrician, Wiring [*Navy rating*]
CEW .... Continuing Education West [*University of Sydney*] [*Australia*]
CEW .... Copi-Elgot-Wright [*Electronics*]
CEW .... Cosmetic Executive Women   (EA)
CEW .... Crestview, FL [*Location identifier*] [*FAA*]   (FAAL)
CEWA ...... Combined Economic Warfare Agencies
CEWC....... Council for Education in World Citizenship [*British*]
CEWCSC .. Corps of Engineers Waterborne Commerce Statistics Center [*Army*]   (AABC)
CEWHS..... Church of England Women's Help Society [*British*]
CEWI........ Combat Electronic Warfare Intelligence
CEWISCON ... Combat Electronic Warfare and Intelligence O & S [*Operations and Support*] Concept Development
CEWLRA .. Commission on Education of the World Leisure and Recreation Association   (EAIO)
CEWMS.... Church of England Working Men's Society
CEWOA .... Chemical Engineering World [*A publication*]
CEWS .... Contractor's Early Warning System   (MCD)
CEX .... Canadian Environmental Exposition [*Heating, Refrigerating, and Air Conditioning Institute of Canada*]   (TSPED)
CEX .... Charge Exchange
CEX .... Chena Hot Springs, AK [*Location identifier*] [*FAA*]   (FAAL)
CEX .... Chief Executive [*A publication*]
CEX .... Civil Effects Exercise [*NASA*]   (KSC)
CEX .... Civil Effects Experiments [*DASA and AEC*]
CEX .... Combat Excavator [*Military*]
CEX .... Conwest Exploration Co. Ltd. [*Toronto Stock Exchange symbol*]
CEXIA ...... Clinical and Experimental Immunology [*A publication*]
CEXIAL .... Clinical and Experimental Immunology [*A publication*]
CEXMD2 .. Clinical and Experimental Metastasis [*A publication*]
CEXPB ...... Clinical and Experimental Pharmacology and Physiology [*A publication*]
CEXSBI.... Colorado State University. Experiment Station. Bulletin [*A publication*]
CEXX........ Circle Express, Inc. [*Indianapolis, IN*] [*NASDAQ symbol*]   (NQ)
CEXY........ Celerex Corp. [*NASDAQ symbol*]   (NQ)
CEY .... Cerknica [*Yugoslavia*] [*Seismograph station code, US Geological Survey*]   (SEIS)
Cey .... Ceylon
CEY .... Cuba Economic News [*A publication*]
CEY .... Murray [*Kentucky*] [*Airport symbol*]   (OAG)
Cey J Hist Soc Stud ... Ceylon Journal of Historical and Social Studies [*A publication*]
Cey Lab LJ ... Ceylon Labour Law Journal [*A publication*]   (DLA)
Ceyl Cr App R ... Ceylon Criminal Appeal Reports [*A publication*]   (DLA)
Ceyl Leg Misc ... Ceylon Legal Miscellany [*A publication*]   (DLA)
Ceyl LJ ...... Ceylon Law Journal [*A publication*]   (DLA)
Ceyl LR...... Ceylon Law Recorder [*A publication*]   (DLA)
Ceyl L Rec ... Ceylon Law Recorder [*A publication*]   (DLA)
Ceyl L Rev ... Ceylon Law Review [*A publication*]   (DLA)
Ceyl LW..... Ceylon Law Weekly [*A publication*]   (DLA)
Ceylon Assoc Adv Sci Proc Annu Sess ... Ceylon Association for the Advancement of Science. Proceedings of the Annual Session [*A publication*]
Ceylon Coconut Plant Rev ... Ceylon Coconut Planters' Review [*A publication*]
Ceylon Coconut Q ... Ceylon Coconut Quarterly [*A publication*]
Ceylon Dent J ... Ceylon Dental Journal [*A publication*]
Ceylon Fish Res St Prog Rep Biol Technol ... Ceylon. Fisheries Research Station. Progress Reports. Biological and Technological [*A publication*]
Ceylon For ... Ceylon Forester [*A publication*]
Ceylon J Med Sci ... Ceylon Journal of Medical Science [*A publication*]
Ceylon J Sci Anthropol ... Ceylon Journal of Science. Anthropology [*A publication*]
Ceylon J Sci Biol Sci ... Ceylon Journal of Science. Biological Sciences [*A publication*]
Ceylon J Sci Sect A Bot ... Ceylon Journal of Science. Section A. Botany [*A publication*]
Ceylon J Sci Sect B Zool ... Ceylon Journal of Science. Section B. Zoology [*A publication*]
Ceylon J Sci Sect C Fish ... Ceylon Journal of Science. Section C. Fisheries [*A publication*]

Ceylon J Sci Sect D Med Sci ... Ceylon Journal of Science. Section D. Medical Science [*A publication*]
Ceylon Law Rec ... Ceylon Law Recorder [*A publication*]   (DLA)
Ceylon LR ... Ceylon Law Review and Reports [*A publication*]   (DLA)
Ceylon L Soc J ... Ceylon Law Society. Journal [*A publication*]   (DLA)
Ceylon Med J ... Ceylon Medical Journal [*A publication*]
Ceylon Natl Mus Adm Rep Dir Part IV Educ Sci Art (E) ... Ceylon. National Museums Administration. Report of the Director. Part IV. Education, Science, and Art (E) [*A publication*]
Ceylon Natl Mus Ethnogr Ser ... Ceylon National Museums. Ethnographic Series [*A publication*]
Ceylon Nat Mus Adm Rep Dir Part IV Educ Sci Art ... Ceylon. National Museums Administration. Report of the Director. Part IV. Education, Science, and Art [*A publication*]
Ceylon NLR ... New Law Reports (Ceylon) [*A publication*]   (ILCA)
Ceylon Rubber Res Scheme Q Circ ... Ceylon Rubber Research Scheme. Quarterly Circular [*A publication*]
Ceylon Vet J ... Ceylon Veterinary Journal [*A publication*]
CEYMS ..... Church of England Young Men's Society
CEYPA ...... Church of England Young People's Assembly [*British*]
CEYW .... Continuing Education for Young Women
CEZ .... Cefazolin [*Antibacterial compound*]
CEZ .... Cortez [*Colorado*] [*Airport symbol*]   (OAG)
CEZA......... Comite Europeen d'Etudes de Zoologie Agricole
CEZMS ..... Church of England Zenana Missionary Society [*British*]
CEZR........ Cezar Industries Ltd. [*Sunnyvale, CA*] [*NASDAQ symbol*]   (NQ)
CF .... Cable Firing [*or Fuzing*]   (NG)
CF .... Cable, Functional
CF .... Calf
CF .... Calibration Factor
C-F............ California State Department of Fish and Game, Marine Technical Information Center, San Pedro, CA [*Library symbol*] [*Library of Congress*]   (LCLS)
Cf.............. Californium [*Chemical element*]
CF .... Call Finder [*Telecommunications*]
CF .... Came Free   (ADA)
CF .... Canada [*Aircraft nationality and registration mark*]   (FAAC)
CF .... Canada Francais [*A publication*]
CF .... Canadian Forces   (AABC)
CF .... Canadian Forum [*A publication*]
C/F............ Cancel on Face [*Deltiology*]
CF .... Cancer Free [*Medicine*]
CF .... Candlelighters Childhood Cancer Foundation   (EA)
CF .... Cannot Find
CF .... Cantus Firmus [*Plain Chant*] [*Music*]
CF .... Cape Fear Railways, Inc. [*AAR code*]
CF .... Capital Formation [*Later, NCCD*]   (EA)
CF .... Captain Future [*A publication*]
CF .... Carbolfuchsin [*A dye*]
CF .... Carbon Film
CF .... Carbon Filtered
CF .... Carbon Furnace
cf.............. Carbonate of Flake [*Archeology*]
CF .... Carboxyfluorescein [*Fluorophore*]
CF .... Cardiac Failure [*Medicine*]
CF .... Carrier-Free [*Radioisotope*]
CF .... Carrier Frequency [*Radio*]
CF .... Carry Flag [*Data processing*]   (PCM)
C/F............ Carry Forward [*Accounting*]   (MUGU)
CF .... Cash Flow
CF .... Castalia Foundation [*Defunct*]   (EA)
CF .... Cat Fund   (EA)
CF .... Cathode Follower
CF .... Ce Fastu? [*A publication*]
CF .... Cell Factor [*Biology*]
CF .... Cement Floor [*Technical drawings*]
CF .... Center Field [*or Fielder*] [*Baseball*]
CF .... Center Fire
CF .... Center of Flotation
CF .... Center Focus [*Binoculars*]
CF .... Center Forward [*Soccer*]
CF .... Center Frequency
CF .... Central African Republic [*ANSI two-letter standard code*]   (CNC)
CF .... Central Files
CF .... Centrally Funded   (AFM)
CF .... Centrifugal Force
CF .... Centripetal Force
CF .... Certificates [*in bond listings of newspapers*] [*Investment term*]
CF .... CFCF, Inc. [*Toronto Stock Exchange symbol*]
C/F............ Chaff/Flare   (MCD)
CF .... Chalcedon Foundation   (EA)
CF .... Change in Formula
CF .... Change [*or Changing*] to Frequency [*Followed by number*] [*Communications*]   (FAAC)
CF .... Chaplain of the Fleet [*Navy*] [*British*]
C of F .... Chaplain of the Fleet [*Navy*] [*British*]
CF .... Chaplain to the Forces [*British*]
CF .... Characteristic Frequency [*Acoustics*]
CF .... Chemotactic Factor [*Immunology*]

CF	Chemotherapy Foundation (EA)
CF	Chiari-Frommel (Syndrome) [*Medicine*]
CF	Chick Fibroblast [*Cytology*]
CF	Chief of Finance [*Army*]
C of F	Chief of Finance [*Army*]
CF	Child Find [*An association*] [*Later, CFA*] (EA)
CF	Chosin Few (EA)
CF	Christian Feminists (EA)
CF	Christians in Futures (EA)
CF	Christmas Factor [*Also, PTC*] [*Hematology*]
CF	Chromatic Aberration-Free [*Optics*]
CF	Chromosomal Fraction
CF	Circuit Finder
CF	Citrovorum Factor [*Biochemistry*]
CF	Clamping Fixture (MCD)
CF	Clarissima Femina [*Most Illustrious Woman*] [*Latin*]
C & F	Clark and Finnelly's English House of Lords Reports [*6-8 English Reprint*] [*A publication*] (DLA)
CF	Classical Folia [*A publication*]
CF	Clastogenic Factor [*Medicine*]
CF	Climbing Fiber [*Cytology*]
CF	Clinician Full Time [*Chiropody*] [*British*]
CF	Clothing and Footwear [*Department of Employment*] [*British*]
CF	Coastal Frontier [*Military*]
CF	Coasting Flight
CF	Coated on the Front Side [*Carbonless paper*]
CF	Code Forestier Francais [*French Forestry Code*] [*A publication*] (DLA)
CF	Coformycin [*Biochemistry*]
CF	Coil Finish (MSA)
CF	Cold-Finished [*Metal*] (MSA)
CF	Cold Front [*Meteorology*]
CF	Colicine Factor [*Immunology*]
CF	Collectanea Franciscana [*A publication*]
CF	Collins Foods International, Inc. [*NYSE symbol*] (SPSG)
CF	Colony Forming [*Cytology*]
C-F	Colored Female
CF	Column Feed [*Nuclear energy*] (NRCH)
CF	Comb Filter [*Military*] (CAAL)
C & F	Commerce and Finance
CF	Common Fund
CF	Commonwealth Foundation (EAIO)
CF	Commutation Factor
CF	Compania de Aviacion "Faucett" SA [*Peru*] [*ICAO designator*] (ICDA)
CF	Company First [*A mealtime whimsicality for use when guests are present*]
CF	Compensation Factor
CF	Compensation Fee
CF	Complement-Fixation [*Immunology*]
CF	Complete Fabrication
CF	Concept Feasibility (AABC)
CF	Concept Formulation [*DoD*]
CF	Concrete Floor [*Technical drawings*]
CF	Conditional Freedom (ADA)
CF	Confer [*Compare, Consult*] [*Latin*]
CF	Confessions
CF	Confinement Factor [*Nuclear energy*] (NRCH)
CF	Confluence [*A publication*]
cf..................	Congo [*MARC country of publication code*] [*Library of Congress*] (LCCP)
CF	Conservation Foundation (EA)
CF	Conservation Fund [*An association*] (EA)
CF	Consolidated Freightways, Inc.
CF	Constant Frequency [*Electronics*]
CF	Constant Funding (MCD)
CF	Consumption Function [*Economics*]
CF	Container Fumigated (ADA)
CF	Context Free (BUR)
CF	Continuous Flow [*Nuclear energy*] (NRCH)
CF	Contract Formulation
CF	Contract Furnished (MCD)
CF	Contractile Force [*Medicine*]
CF	Control Footing
CF	Controlled Facility [*Aerospace*] (AAG)
CF	Conversation Factor [*Data processing*]
CF	Conversion Factor (MCD)
CF	Cooling Fan (MSA)
CF	Copper Fastened
CF	Copy Furnished [*Army*] (AABC)
CF	Core Flooding System [*Nuclear energy*] (NRCH)
CF	Coro Foundation (EA)
CF	Coronary Flow [*Medicine*]
CF	Correction Factor
CF	Correction Field (MCD)
CF	Correlation Factor (AABC)
CF	Corresponding Fellow
CF	Corrugated Furnace (DS)
CF	Cosanti Foundation [*Later, Arcosanti*] (EA)
C of F	Cost of Facilities (NASA)
CF	Cost and Freight [*Shipping*]
C & F	Cost and Freight [*Shipping*]
C & F	Costo y Flete [*Cost and Freight*] [*Spanish*] [*Shipping*]
CF	Cottonseed Flour
CF	Council on Foundations (EA)
CF	Count Forward [*Data processing*]
CF	Counter Force (MCD)
CF	Counterfire [*Military*] (AFM)
CF	Counting Fingers [*Also, FC*]
CF	Coupling Factor [*Cytology*]
C & F	Cout et Fret [*Cost and Freight*] [*French*] [*Shipping*]
CF	Cover Forward
CF	Covering Force (MCD)
CF	Cross Fade
CF	Cross Front [*Photography*]
CF	Crude Fiber
CF	Cryofixation [*Electron microscopy*]
CF	Cryogenic Focusing [*Instrumentation*]
CF	Cubic Feet (AFM)
CF	Culture Filtrate [*Analytical biochemistry*]
CF	Cumulative Frequency
C of F	Custodian of Fund
CF	Customer File (MCD)
CF	Customs Form
CF	Cut Film [*Photography*]
CF	Cutting Fluid [*Metallurgy*]
CF	Cycling Fibroblast [*Cytology*]
C of F	Cyclopaedia of Freemasonry [*A publication*] (ROG)
CF	Cystic Fibrosis [*Medicine*]
CF	Cystinosis Foundation (EA)
CF	Flying-Deck Cruiser [*Navy symbol*] [*Obsolete*]
cF	Form Clearance [*Manufacturing term*]
CF	Fresno County Free Library, Fresno, CA [*Library symbol*] [*Library of Congress*] (LCLS)
CF3	Computer Form, Fit, and Function (MCD)
C2F2	Crew Compartment Fit and Function [*NASA*] (KSC)
CFA............	California Freezers Association [*Absorbed by AFFI*] (EA)
CFA............	California Gold Mines Ltd. [*Toronto Stock Exchange symbol*] [*Vancouver Stock Exchange symbol*]
CFA............	Canadian Federation of Agriculture
CFA............	Canadian Fencing Association
CFA............	Canadian Field Artillery
CFA............	Canadian Forces Attache
CFA............	Canadian Forestry Association [*See also AFC*]
CFA............	Canadian Freight Association
CFA............	Caribbean Federation of Aeroclubs (EA)
CFA............	Carrier Frequency Alarm [*Telecommunications*] (TEL)
CFA............	Cascade-Failure Analysis (IEEE)
CFA............	Cash-Flow Accounting
CFA............	Cash Free America [*An association*] (EA)
CFA............	Cat Fanciers' Association (EA)
CFA............	Catfish Farmers of America (EA)
CFA............	Center for Astrophysics [*Harvard-Smithsonian*]
CFA............	Central Bank of the Bahamas. Quarterly Review [*A publication*]
CFA............	Central Freight Association
CFA............	Centrifugal Fast Analyzer [*Analytical chemistry*]
CFA............	Certified Fitness Appraiser [*Canadian Association of Sports Sciences*]
CFA............	Chartered Financial Analyst [*Designation awarded by Institute of Chartered Financial Analysts*]
CFA............	Chartier Family Association (EA)
CFA............	Chian Federation of America (EA)
CFA............	Chief of Field Artillery
CF & A	Chief of Finance and Accounting [*Army*] (AABC)
CFA............	Child Find of America (EA)
CFA............	Chilled Foods Association (EA)
CFA............	Circus Fans Association of America (EA)
CFA............	Citizens for America [*Later, CFAEF*] (EA)
CFA............	City Facts and Abstracts [*EDIC*] [*Ringmer Near Lewes, East Sussex, England*] [*Information service or system*] (IID)
CFA............	Cleared for Approach [*Aviation*]
CFA............	Club Francais d'Amerique (EA)
CFA............	Coconut Fatty Alcohol [*Organic chemistry*]
CFA............	Cognizant Field Activity
CFA............	College Football Association (EA)
CFA............	Collocation Flutter Analysis
CFA............	Colonization Factor Antigen [*Analytical biochemistry*]
CFA............	Colony-Forming Ability [*Microbiology*]
CFA............	Color Forming Ability [*Food technology*]
CFA............	Combined Field Army (MCD)
CFA............	Commission of Fine Arts [*Independent government agency*]
CFA............	Committee for a Free Afghanistan (EA)
CFA............	Committee for the Future of America (EA)
C/FA	Commodities - Food and Agriculture (NATG)
CFA............	Commonwealth Forestry Association [*Oxford, England*] (EAIO)
CFA............	Communaute Financiere Africaine [*African Financial Community*]
CFA............	Community Facilities Administration [*of HHFA*] [*Terminated*]
CFA............	Companions of the Forest of America (EA)
CFA............	Compass Failure Annunciator
CFA............	Complement-Fixing Antibody [*Immunology*]

CFA............ Complete Freund's Adjuvant [*Immunology*]
CFA............ Computer Factory, Inc. [*NYSE symbol*]   (SPSG)
CFA............ Computer Family Architecture
CFA............ Computerized Fleet Analysis, Inc.
CFA............ Concept Feasibility Analysis
CFA............ Conformal Array   (CAAL)
CFA............ Congregatio Fratrum Cellitarum seu Alexianorum [*Alexian Brothers*] [*Roman Catholic religious order*]
CFA............ Consumer Federation of America   (EA)
CFA............ Continuous Flow Analysis
CFA............ Contractor-Furnished Accessories   (AFIT)
CFA............ Cooley Family Association of America   (EA)
CFA............ Core Flood Alarm [*Nuclear energy*]   (IEEE)
CFA............ Coronel Fontana [*Argentina*] [*Seismograph station code, US Geological Survey*]   (SEIS)
CFA............ Correctional Facilities Association   (EA)
CFA............ Correspondence Factor Analysis
CFA............ Cost, Freight, Assurance [*Shipping*]
CFA............ Council on Fertilizer Application [*Defunct*]
CFA............ Covering Force Area   (AABC)
CFA............ Covert Family Association   (EA)
CFA............ Cowl-Flap Angle [*Air Force*]
CFA............ Croquet Foundation of America   (EA)
CFA............ Cross-Functional Analysis   (ADA)
CFA............ Crossed-Field Amplifier [*Air Force*]
C & FA...... Culinary and Fine Arts Club [*Later, Culinary Arts Club*]   (EA)
CFA............ Current Files Area
CFA............ Cyclic Fatty Acid [*Organic chemistry*]
CFA............ Cyprus Federation of America
CFa .... Solano County Library, Fairfield, CA [*Library symbol*] [*Library of Congress*]   (LCLS)
CFAA......... Cooperative Finance Association of America   (EA)
CFAB........ California Fig Advisory Board   (EA)
CFAB........ Windsor, NS [*AM radio station call letters*]
CFABC...... Canadian Forestry Association of British Columbia
CFABEW .. Communications. Faculte des Sciences. Universite d'Ankara. Serie C. Biologie [*A publication*]
CFAC......... Calgary, AB [*AM radio station call letters*]
CFAC........ Citizens Foreign Aid Committee [*Defunct*]   (EA)
CFAC-TV .. Calgary, AB [*Television station call letters*]
CFAC-TV-7 ... Lethbridge, AB [*Television station call letters*]
CFAD........ Commander, Fleet Air Defense   (NATG)
CFAD........ Commander, Fleet Air Detachment
CFAD........ Composite Flight Data Processing   (FAAC)
CF & AD .... Counterfire and Air Defense   (MCD)
CFADC...... Controlled Fusion Atomic Data Center [*Department of Energy*]   (IID)
CFADD...... Canadian Foundation on Alcohol and Drug Dependencies
CFAE........ Contractor-Furnished Aircraft Equipment   (AFM)
CFAE........ Contractor-Furnished and Equipped
CFAE........ Council for Financial Aid to Education   (EA)
CFAEF ...... Citizens for America Educational Foundation   (EA)
CFAI......... Call for Action, Incorporated   (EA)
CFAI-FM .. Edmundston, NB [*FM radio station call letters*]
CFAM....... Altona, MB [*AM radio station call letters*]
CFAN .... Newcastle, NB [*AM radio station call letters*]
CFANS ...... Canadian Forces Air Navigation School
C Fantas..... Cinefantastique [*A publication*]
CFAO .... Canadian Forces Administrative Order
CFAP......... Cleared for Approach [*Aviation*]   (FAAC)
CFAP......... Committee for American Principles   (EA)
CFAP......... Constant-Adjustment Matrix, Flexible-Accelerator Path [*Economic theory*]
CFAP......... Constant False Alarm Probability [*Military*]
CFAP......... Council on Fine Art Photography   (EA)
CFAP-TV .. Quebec City, PQ [*Television station call letters*]
CfAR......... Center for Automation Research [*University of Maryland*] [*Research center*]   (RCD)
CFAR......... Citizens for Foreign Aid Reform [*Canada*]
CFAR........ Constant False Alarm Rate [*or Ratio*] [*Military*]
CFAR........ Flin Flon, MB [*AM radio station call letters*]
CFAS .... Catholic Fine Arts Society   (EA)
CFAS .... Charge-Free Anticontamination System
CFASI....... Club of the Friends of Ancient Smoothing Irons   (EA)
CFAT......... Carnegie Foundation for the Advancement of Teaching   (EA)
CFAV........ Canadian Forces Auxiliary Vessels [*Military*]
CFAW........ Canadian Food and Allied Workers
CFAW........ Commander, Fleet Air Wing
CFAW........ Committee of French American Wives [*Later, FAAC*]   (EA)
CFAWL..... Commander, Fleet Air Wing, Atlantic
CFAWP..... Commander, Fleet Air Wing, Pacific
CFAX......... Victoria, BC [*AM radio station call letters*]
CFB............ Across the Board [*A publication*]
CFB............ Camfrey Resources Ltd. [*Vancouver Stock Exchange symbol*]
CFB............ Canadian Forces Base   (NATG)
CFB............ Carey Foster Bridge [*Electronics*]
CFB............ Center for Family Business [*Cleveland, OH*]   (EA)
CFB............ Central Freight Bureau   (DS)
CFB............ Centrifugal Fluidized Bed [*Chemical engineering*]
CFB............ Cipher Feedback
CFB............ Circulating Fluid Bed [*Chemical engineering*]

CFB............ Citizens First Bancorp, Inc. [*AMEX symbol*]   (SPSG)
CFB............ Coated Front and Back [*Carbonless paper*]
CFB............ Combat Fitness Badge [*Army*]   (INF)
CFB............ Combined Food Board [*United States, United Kingdom, and Canada*] [*World War II*]
CFB............ Commonwealth Forestry Bureau [*Oxford, England*]
CFB............ Coniferous Forest Biome [*Ecological biogeographic study*]
CFB............ Continental Flood Basalt [*Geology*]
CFB............ Creep Form Block   (MCD)
CFb............ Fort Bragg Public Library, Fort Bragg, CA [*Library symbol*] [*Library of Congress*]   (LCLS)
CFBAC ...... Central Fire Brigades Advisory Council [*British*]
CFBB .... Country Fire Brigades Board [*Australia*]
CFBC .... St. John, NB [*AM radio station call letters*]
CFBE .... Certified Food and Beverage Executive [*Designation awarded by Educational Institute of the American Hotel and Motel Association*]
CFBG .... Camp Fire Boys and Girls   (EA)
CFBI .... Cullen/Frost Bankers, Incorporated [*San Antonio, TX*] [*NASDAQ symbol*]   (NQ)
CFBK .... Huntsville, ON [*AM radio station call letters*]
CFBPS....... Canada [*or Canadian*] Farm Building Plan Service
CFBPWC... Canadian Federation of Business and Professional Women's Clubs [*Established 1930*]
CFBR .... Continuously Fed Batch Reactor [*Chemical engineering*]
CFBR .... Sudbury, ON [*AM radio station call letters*]
CFBS .... Canadian Federation of Biological Societies
CFBS .... Central Fidelity Banks, Inc. [*Richmond, VA*] [*NASDAQ symbol*]   (NQ)
CFBS .... Colostrum-Free Bovine Serum
CFBT .... Creep Form Block Template   (MCD)
CFBTAJ .... Commonwealth Forestry Bureau. Technical Communication [*A publication*]
CFBUBN ... Clemson University. Department of Forestry. Forestry Bulletin [*A publication*]
CFBUS ...... Consortium of Fire Brigade Uniform Supplies [*British*]
CFBV .... Smithers, BC [*AM radio station call letters*]
CFC............ C-Band Frequency Converter
CFC............ California Fashion Creators   (EA)
CFC............ Campus-Free College
CFC............ Canadian Forestry Corps [*World War I*]
CFC............ Capillary Filtration Coefficient   (IEEE)
CFC............ Capital Formation Counselors [*Service mark of Capital Formation Counselors, Inc.*]
CFC............ Carbon Fiber Reinforced Composite
CFC............ Caribbean Food Corporation [*An association*]   (EAIO)
CFC............ Cash Flow Component
CFC............ Central Data Flow Control
CFC............ Central Fire Control [*Military*]
CFC............ Central Forms Committee [*Defunct*]   (EA)
CFC............ Centre Francais de la Couleur [*Online service*]
CFC............ CFC Financial Communications [*An association*]   (EA)
CFC............ Channel Flow Control
CFC............ Chess Federation of Canada
CFC............ Chicago Fan Club   (EA)
CFC............ Chicano Family Center   (EA)
CFC............ Chief Fire Controlman [*Navy rating*] [*Obsolete*]
CFC............ Chlorofluorocarbon [*Organic chemistry*]
CFC............ Chrysler Financial Corporation
CFC............ Cinematograph Films Council [*British*]
CFC............ Claflin College, Orangeburg, SC [*OCLC symbol*]   (OCLC)
CFC............ Coin and Fee Checking [*Telecommunications*]   (TEL)
CFC............ Colony-Forming Cell [*Cytology*]
CFC............ Combined Federal Campaign [*Federal government*]   (AABC)
CFC............ Combined Field Command   (MCD)
CFC............ Combined Forces Command [*Korea*]   (MCD)
CFC............ Commercial Finance Company [*Generic term*]
CFC............ Committee for Children   (EA)
CFC............ Committee on Foreign Correspondence [*Freemasonry*]
CFC............ Committee for a Free China   (EA)
CFC............ Company Fire Control [*Net*]   (MCD)
CFC............ Complex Facility Console [*Aerospace*]   (AAG)
CFC............ Congregation of Christian Brothers [*Formerly, Christian Brothers of Ireland*] [*Roman Catholic religious order*]
CFC............ Connecticut Film Circuit [*Library network*]
CFC............ Consolidated Freight Classification
CFC............ Construction Forecasting Committee [*Australia*]
CFC............ Contemporary French Civilization [*A publication*]
CFC............ Continuous-Flow Centrifuging [*Clinical chemistry*]
CFC............ Contract Finance Committee [*Military*]
CFC............ Contract Furnishings Council   (EA)
CFC............ Controlled Force Circulation [*Boilers*]
CFC............ Controlled Foreign Company
CFC............ Cooperative Finance Corporation [*of National Rural Utilities*]
CFC............ Council of Free Czechoslovakia   (EA)
CFC............ Cowboys for Christ   (EA)
CFC............ Crewcuts Fan Club   (EA)
CFC............ Crossed-Film Cryotron
CFC............ Cuadernos de Filologia Clasica [*A publication*]
CFC............ Fresno City College, Fresno, CA [*Library symbol*] [*Library of Congress*]   (LCLS)

CFCA......... California Fish Canners Association [*Later, TRF*] (EA)
CFCA......... Camp Fire Club of America (EA)
CFCA......... Challenge for Change. Access. National Film Board of Canada [*A publication*]
CFCA......... Christian Foundation for Children and Aging (EA)
CFCA......... Communications Fraud Control Association (EA)
CFCA......... Confederation Francaise de la Cooperation Agricole
CFCA......... Crested Fowl Club of America [*Later, CFFA*] (EA)
CFCA-FM ... Kitchener, ON [*FM radio station call letters*]
CFCB......... Computer Format Control Buffer
CFCB......... Corner Brook, NF [*AM radio station call letters*]
CFCC......... Canadian Forces Communication Command (NATG)
CFCC......... Carteret Savings & Loan Association [*NASDAQ symbol*] (NQ)
CFCCS....... Condensate and Feedwater Chemistry Control System [*Nuclear energy*] (NRCH)
CFCCT ...... Committee for Freedom of Choice in Cancer Therapy [*Later, CFCM*] (EA)
CFCD......... Canadian Federal Corporations and Directors [*Canada Systems Group*] [*Information service or system*] (IID)
CF/CD .... Concept Formulation/Contract Definition [*Procurement procedure*]
CFCE......... Conseil des Federations Commerciales d'Europe [*Council of European Commercial Federations*]
CFCF .... Camp Fire Conservation Fund (EA)
CFCF .... Central Flow Control Facility [*or Function*] (MCD)
CFCF .... Montreal, PQ [*AM radio station call letters*]
CFCF-TV ... Montreal, PQ [*Television station call letters*]
CFCH .... North Bay, ON [*AM radio station call letters*] [*Station begun by Roy Thompson in March, 1931*]
CFCL......... Timmins, ON [*AM radio station call letters*]
CFCL-TV .. Timmins, ON [*Television station call letters*]
CFCL-TV-2 ... Kearns, ON [*Television station call letters*]
CFCM........ Chief Consolidated Mining Co. [*NASDAQ symbol*] (NQ)
CFCM........ Committee for Freedom of Choice in Medicine (EA)
CFCM-TV ... Quebec City, PQ [*Television station call letters*]
CFCN......... Calgary, AB [*AM radio station call letters*]
CFCN......... Commercial Federal Corporation [*Omaha, NE*] [*NASDAQ symbol*] (NQ)
CFCN-TV ... Calgary, AB [*Television station call letters*]
CFCN-TV-1 ... Drumheller, AB [*Television station call letters*]
CFCN-TV-5 ... Lethbridge, AB [*Television station call letters*]
CFCN-TV-8 ... Medicine Hat, AB [*Television station call letters*]
CFCO......... Chatham, ON [*AM radio station call letters*]
CFCO......... Chief Fire Controlman, Operator [*Navy rating*] [*Obsolete*]
CFCP .... Courtenay, BC [*AM radio station call letters*]
CFCQ-FM ... Trois Rivieres, PQ [*FM radio station call letters*]
CFCRA ...... Coronado 15 Class Racing Association (EA)
CFCRFC.... Chewings Fescue and Creeping Red Fescue Commission (EA)
CFCS .... Canadian Force Communications System
CFCS .... Caribbean Food Crops Society [*Isabela, Puerto Rico*] (EAIO)
CFCS .... Chief Fire Controlman, Submarines [*Navy rating*] [*Obsolete*]
CFCS .... Crossed Field Closing Switch (MCD)
CFCT .... Chartered Federal Savings & Loan Association [*NASDAQ symbol*] (CTT)
CFCT .... Tuktoyaktuk, NT [*AM radio station call letters*]
CFCV-FM ... St. Andrews, NF [*FM radio station call letters*]
CFCW........ Camrose, AB [*AM radio station call letters*]
CFCW........ Canadian Federation of Communications Workers [*See also FCC*]
CFCW........ Composers' Forum for Catholic Worship [*Defunct*] (EA)
CFCY .... Charlottetown, PE [*AM radio station call letters*]
CFD .... Bryan, TX [*Location identifier*] [*FAA*] (FAAL)
CFD .... Call Forward Directive [*World War II*]
CFD .... Canadian Financial Database [*The Globe and Mail*] [*Toronto, ON*] [*Information service or system*] (IID)
CFD .... Candidate for Disposal (MCD)
CFD .... Center for Faith Development [*Later, CRFMD*] (EA)
CFD .... Clifton Star Resources, Inc. [*Vancouver Stock Exchange symbol*]
CFD .... Club Francais du Disque [*Record label*] [*France*]
CFD .... Coalition for Decency [*Later, NFF*] (EA)
CFD .... Cockfield Brown, Inc. [*Toronto Stock Exchange symbol*]
CFD .... Cold Fog Dissipation System
CFD .... Company of Fifers and Drummers (EA)
CFD .... Computation Fluid Dynamics
CFD .... Concern for Dying (EA)
CFD .... Contractor Functional Demonstration (KSC)
CFD .... Control Functional Diagram
CFD .... Converter, Frequency to DC [*Direct Current*] Voltage (MCD)
CFD .... Corporate Finance Director
CFD .... Corporate Fund for Dance
CFD .... Crawford & Co. [*NYSE symbol*] (SPSG)
CFD .... Cubic Feet per Day
CFD .... Cumulative Frequency Distribution (KSC)
CFD-5 .... Portable Compact Disc, Cassette, and Radio Machine [*Sony Corp.*]
CFDA......... Carboxyfluorescein Diacetate [*Organic chemistry*]
CFDA......... Catalog of Federal Domestic Assistance [*A publication*]
CFDA......... Cooperative Food Distributors of America [*Later, NGA*] (EA)
CFDA......... Council of Fashion Designers of America (EA)
CFDA......... Victoriaville, PQ [*AM radio station call letters*]

CFDC......... Canadian Film Development Corporation
CFDC......... Canadian Film-Makers Distribution Centre
CFDC......... Central File Document Control
CFDC......... Clean Fuels Development Coalition (EA)
CFDH .... Fresno County Department of Health, Fresno, CA [*Library symbol*] [*Library of Congress*] (LCLS)
CFDL-FM ... Deer Lake, NF [*FM radio station call letters*]
CFDMH .... Fresno County Department of Mental Health Services, Fresno, CA [*Library symbol*] [*Library of Congress*] (LCLS)
CFDMM ... Comite de Formation et de Developpement Municipaux des Maritimes [*Maritime Municipal Training and Development Board*] [*Canada*]
CFDR......... Dartmouth, NS [*AM radio station call letters*]
CFDS .... Centrifugal Fault Display System
CFDS .... Congested Freeway Driving Schedule [*For vehicle emission measurements*]
CFDTS ...... Cold Flow Development Test System [*AEC*]
CFDY......... Citizens Fidelity Corp. [*Louisville, KY*] [*NASDAQ symbol*] (NQ)
CFE .... California Fruit Exchange [*Later, BAI*] (EA)
CFE .... Canadian Forces in Europe (NATG)
CFE .... Cathode Flicker Effect
CFE .... Cell Free Extract [*Microbiology*]
CFE .... Central Fighter Establishment [*British*]
CFE .... Certified Financial Examiner [*Designation awarded by Society of Financial Examiners*]
CFE .... Characteristic Function Estimator
CFE .... Chlorotrifluoroethylene [*Organic chemistry*]
CFE .... Clandestine Fission Explosive [*Nuclear energy*] (NRCH)
CFE .... Clermont-Ferrand [*France*] [*Airport symbol*] (OAG)
CFE .... Colony-Forming Efficiency [*Cytology*]
CFE .... Committee for a Free Estonia [*Defunct*] (EA)
CFE .... Confederation Fiscale Europeenne [*European Fiscal Confederation*] (EAIO)
CFE .... Conference on Forces in Europe
CFE .... Continuous Flow Electrophoresis [*Physical chemistry*]
CFE .... Contractor-Furnished Engineers (MCD)
CFE .... Contractor-Furnished Equipment
CFE .... Controlled Flash Evaporation
CFE .... Conventional Forces in Europe [*Military*]
CFE .... Cost-Free Evaluation
CF and E.... Cost, Freight, and Exchange [*Shipping*]
CFE .... Economic Road Maps [*A publication*]
CFE .... European Fiscal Confederation (EAIO)
CFe .... Ferndale Public Library, Ferndale, CA [*Library symbol*] [*Library of Congress*] (LCLS)
CFE .... Negotiations on Conventional Armed Forces in Europe
C3FE .... Collection, Classification, Cannibalization, and Field Expedients [*Military*]
CFEA .... Collective Front-End Analysis (MCD)
CFEA .... College Fraternity Editors Association (EA)
CF(EC) ...... Chaplain to the Forces - Emergency Commission [*British*]
CFED......... Chapais, PQ [*AM radio station call letters*]
CFED......... Charter Federal Savings Bank [*NASDAQ symbol*] (NQ)
CFED........ Committee for Elimination of Death [*Later, CEL*] (EA)
CFED........ Corporation for Enterprise Development (EA)
CFEE .... Carnegie Forum on Education and the Economy (EA)
CFEG......... Canadian Film Editors Guild
CFEK........ Fernie, BC [*AM radio station call letters*]
CFEKA7 ... Chirurgisches Forum fuer Experimentelle und Klinische Forschung [*A publication*]
CFEL .... Cold Flow Electric LASER (MCD)
CFEL .... Continental Far East Lines (DS)
CFEM Ser Tec ... CFEM [*Comision Forestal del Estado de Michoacan*] Serie Tecnica [*A publication*]
CFeng......... Ching Feng [*A publication*]
CFEP .... Committee on Fair Employment Practices [*World War II*]
CFEP .... Council on Foreign Economic Policy [*Functions transferred to Secretary of State, 1961*]
CFER......... ConferTech International, Inc. [*NASDAQ symbol*] (NQ)
CFE-RISS ... Contractor-Furnished Equipment - Repairable Items Support System (MCD)
CFER-TV .. Rimouski, PQ [*Television station call letters*]
CFER-TV-2 ... Gaspe-Nord, PQ [*Television station call letters*]
CFES .... Canadian Federation of Engineers and Scientists
CFES .... Continuous Flow Electrophoresis in Space [*Physical chemistry*]
CFES .... Continuous Flow Electrophoresis System [*Chemical separation*]
CFESA........ Commercial Food Equipment Service Association (EA)
CFET .... Common Field Effect Transistor [*Data processing*] (ADA)
CFEZ......... Taber, AB [*AM radio station call letters*]
CFF .... Capuchin Franciscan Friary
CFF .... Cat Fanciers' Federation (EA)
CFF .... Christian Freedom Foundation (EA)
CFF .... Citizens Freedom Foundation (EA)
CFF .... Clermont-Ferrand [*France*] [*Seismograph station code, US Geological Survey*] (SEIS)
CFF .... Codigo Fiscal de la Federacion [*Mexico*] [*A publication*]
CFF .... Compensatory Financing Facility [*International Monetary Fund*]
CFF .... Compressible Flow Facility [*NASA*]
CFF .... Conical Flow Field

CFF........... Consolidated Callinan Flin Flon Mines Ltd. [*Vancouver Stock Exchange symbol*]
CFF........... Contract Furnishings Forum   (EA)
CFF........... Cooperative Financing Facility [*Export-Import Bank*]
CFF........... Counter Flip-Flop [*Data processing*]
CFF........... Crossflow Filtration [*Process engineering*]
CFF........... Current Fault File [*Telecommunications*]   (TEL)
CFF........... Cystic Fibrosis Foundation   (EA)
CFFA........ Chemical Fabrics and Film Association   (EA)
CFFA........ Crested Fowl Fanciers' Association   (EA)
CF-FAB..... Continuous-Flow Fast Atom Bombardment [*Spectroscopy*]
CFFAFR.... Center for Financial Freedom and Accuracy in Financial Reporting   (EA)
CFFAn...... Comite Flamand de France. Annales [*A publication*]
CFFB........ Iqaluit, NT [*AM radio station call letters*]
CFFC........ Carter Family Fan Club   (EA)
CFFC........ Catholics for a Free Choice   (EA)
CFFC........ Community Federal Savings Bank [*NASDAQ symbol*]   (NQ)
CFFC........ Connie Francis Fan Club [*Inactive*]   (EA)
CFFC........ Counterflow Film Cooling
CFFC........ Country Fire Fan Club   (EA)
CFFEP...... Committee for Full Funding of Education Programs   (EA)
CFFF........ Coal Fluid Flow Facility
CFFM-FM ... Williams Lake, BC [*FM radio station call letters*]
CFFP........ Cooperative Forest Fire Prevention [*Forest Service, Department of Agriculture*]
CFFR........ Calgary, AB [*AM radio station call letters*]
CFFR........ Cushman Foundation for Foraminiferal Research   (EA)
CFFS........ Canadian Federation of Film Societies
CFFS........ Columbia First Federal Savings & Loan Association [*NASDAQ symbol*]   (NQ)
CFFS........ Combat Field Feeding System [*Army*]   (INF)
CFFTP...... Canadian Fusion Fuels Technology Project
CFFX........ Kingston, ON [*AM radio station call letters*]
CFG.......... Camp Fire Girls [*Later, CFBG*]   (EA)
CFG.......... Canadian Film Group
CFG.......... Change for Good [*An association*]   (EA)
CFG.......... Cherry Lane Fashion [*Vancouver Stock Exchange symbol*]
CFG.......... Christian Focus on Government   (EA)
CFG.......... Cienfuegos [*Cuba*] [*Airport symbol*] [*Obsolete*]   (OAG)
CFG.......... Compact-Flake-Graphite [*Type of Iron*]
CFG.......... Copelco Financial Services [*AMEX symbol*]   (SPSG)
CFGB-FM .. Happy Valley, NF [*FM radio station call letters*]
CFGBI....... Coopers' Federation of Great Britain and Ireland [*A union*]
CFGI........ Commonwealth Savings Association [*Houston, TX*] [*NASDAQ symbol*]   (NQ)
CFGL-FM ... Laval, PQ [*FM radio station call letters*]
CFGM....... Committee for a Free Gold Market   (EA)
CFGM....... Richmond Hill, ON [*AM radio station call letters*]
CFGN....... Port-Aux-Basques, NF [*AM radio station call letters*]
CFGO....... Ottawa, ON [*AM radio station call letters*]
CFGP........ Grand Prairie, AB [*AM radio station call letters*]
CFGRS...... Commonwealth Financial Group REIT [*NASDAQ symbol*]   (NQ)
CFGS........ Church of Jesus Christ of Latter-Day Saints, Genealogical Society Library, Fresno Branch, Fresno, CA [*Library symbol*] [*Library of Congress*]   (LCLS)
CFGS-TV .. Hull, PQ [*Television station call letters*]
CFGT........ Alma, PQ [*AM radio station call letters*]
CFGX-FM ... Sarnia, ON [*FM radio station call letters*]
CFH.......... Canadian Federation for the Humanities [*See also FCEH*] [*Research center*]   (RCD)
CFH.......... Canadian Forces Hospital
CFH.......... Carmelita Petroleum [*Vancouver Stock Exchange symbol*]
CFH.......... Chloroplasts, Ferredoxin, and Hydrogenase [*Photoreactant system*]
CFH.......... Clifton Hills [*Australia*] [*Airport symbol*] [*Obsolete*]   (OAG)
CFH.......... Conference on Faith and History   (EA)
CFH.......... Council on Family Health   (EA)
CFH.......... Cubic Feet per Hour
CFH.......... Fresno Community Hospital, Fresno, CA [*Library symbol*] [*Library of Congress*]   (LCLS)
CFHA........ Canadian Field Hockey Association
CFHC........ California Financial Holding Co. [*NASDAQ symbol*]   (NQ)
CFHC........ Canadian Field Hockey Council
CFHC........ Canmore, AB [*AM radio station call letters*]
CFHC........ Cornell Feline Health Center [*Cornell University*] [*Research center*]   (RCD)
CF/HP....... Constant-Flow/High Pressure [*Oxygen system*]
CFHQ........ Canadian Forces Headquarters [*NATO*]   (NATG)
CFHRM ... Congressional Friends of Human Rights Monitors   (EA)
CFHS........ Coherent Frequency-Hopping Signal
CFHT........ Canada-France-Hawaii Telescope [*Mauna Kea, Hawaii*]
CFHT........ Continuous Flow Hypersonic Tunnel [*NASA*]
CFI........... California Fig Institute   (EA)
CFI........... California State University, Fullerton, Fullerton, CA [*OCLC symbol*]   (OCLC)
CFI........... Canadian Film Institute [*See also ICF*]
CFI........... Cancer Federation, Incorporated   (EA)
CFI........... Card Format Identifier   (NASA)
CFI........... CBI Newsbulletin [*A publication*]

CFI........... Central Fuel Injection [*Automotive engineering*]
CFI........... Centro Filatelico Internazionale
CFI........... Ceramic Foam Insulation
CFI........... Certification for Issue   (MCD)
CFI........... Certified Flight Instructor [*Aviation*]
CFI........... CF Income Partners LP [*NYSE symbol*]   (SPSG)
CFI........... Chemotactic Factor Inactivator [*Immunology*]
CFI........... Chief Flying Instructor [*RAF*] [*British*]
CFI........... Chloroform Fumigation-Incubation Technique
CFI........... Clothing and Footwear Institute [*London, England*]   (EAIO)
CFI........... Coalition for Food Irradiation   (EA)
CFI........... Coastal Fisheries Institute [*Louisiana State University*]
CFI........... College Fiord [*Alaska*] [*Seismograph station code, US Geological Survey*]   (SEIS)
CFI........... Commonwealth Forestry Institute [*British*]
CFI........... Community Fluorosis Index
CFI........... Complement Fixation Inhibition [*Test*] [*Immunology*]
CFI........... Computer Fault Isolation   (MCD)
CFI........... Continuous Fuel Injection
CFI........... Contractor Final Inspection   (MCD)
CF & I .... Contractor Furnish and Install   (MSA)
CFI........... Contractor-Furnished Information   (MCD)
CFI........... Controlled Fuel Injection [*Engineering*]
CFI........... Core Flooding System Isolation Valve Interlock [*Nuclear energy*]   (NRCH)
CFI........... Cost, Freight, and Insurance [*Shipping*]
CF & I .... Cost, Freight, and Insurance [*Shipping*]
CFI........... Credit Factoring International [*Commercial firm*] [*British*]
CFI........... Crestbrook Forest Industries Ltd. [*Toronto Stock Exchange symbol*] [*Vancouver Stock Exchange symbol*]
CFI........... Crossfire Injection [*Automotive engineering*]
CFI........... Crystal Frequency Indicator
CFI........... Cumulative Form Inception   (MCD)
CFIA......... Center for Independent Action   (EA)
CFIA......... Center for International Affairs [*Harvard University*] [*Research center*]   (RCD)
CFIA......... Component Failure Impact Analysis [*IBM Corp.*]
CFIA......... Core Flood Isolation Valve Assembly [*Nuclear energy*]   (IEEE)
CFIAAV .... Conferencia Interamericana de Agricultura [*Caracas*] [*A publication*]
CFIB .... Canadian Federation of Independent Business
CFIB .... Consolidated Fibres, Inc. [*NASDAQ symbol*]   (NQ)
CFIC .... Canned Food Information Council   (EA)
CFIC .... Central Flight Instructor Course [*Military*]
CF-ICA...... Complement-Fixing Islet Cell Antibodies [*Immunochemistry*]
CFI Ceram Forum Int Ber DKG ... CFI. Ceramic Forum International. Berichte der Deutschen Keramischen Gesellschaft [*Federal Republic of Germany*] [*A publication*]
CFI Ceram Forum Int Ber Dtsch Keram Ges ... CFI. Ceramic Forum International. Berichte der Deutschen Keramischen Gesellschaft [*A publication*]
CFI (Commonw For Inst) Occas Pap ... CFI (Commonwealth Forest Institute) Occasional Papers [*A publication*]
CFID......... Catalytic Flame Ionization Detector
CFIDS ...... Chronic Fatigue Immune Dysfunction Syndrome [*Medicine*]
CFIDSA..... Chronic Fatigue Immune Dysfunction Syndrome Association   (EA)
CFIE......... Conseil des Federations Industrielles d'Europe [*Council of European Industrial Federations*]
CFIEI........ Canadian Farm and Industrial Equipment Institute
CFIF......... Continuous Flow Isoelectric Focusing [*Materials processing*]
CFII .... Certified Flight Instructor, Instrument [*Aviation*]
CFIL-FM... Gillam, MB [*FM radio station call letters*]
CFIN......... Consumers Financial Corp. [*NASDAQ symbol*]   (NQ)
CFIN-FM .. Coaticook, PQ [*FM radio station call letters*]
CFIP .... CF & I Steel Corp. [*NASDAQ symbol*]   (NQ)
CFIQ......... Harbour Grace, NF [*AM radio station call letters*]
CFIRBF .... Colorado Fisheries Research Review [*A publication*]
CFIRS........ Central Florida Information Research Service, Inc. [*Information service or system*]   (IID)
CFIT......... Controlled Flight into Terrain
CFIUS ...... Committee on Foreign Investment in the United States
CFIX......... Chemfix Technologies, Inc. [*Metairie, LA*] [*NASDAQ symbol*]   (NQ)
CFJ........... Center for Foreign Journalists   (EA)
CF(J)......... Chaplain to the Forces (Jewish) [*British*]
CFJ........... Cobi Foods, Inc. [*Toronto Stock Exchange symbol*]
CFJ........... Control Flow Jet
CFJ........... Crawfordsville, IN [*Location identifier*] [*FAA*]   (FAAL)
CFJ........... Cross-Field Jammer
CFJB-FM ... Barrie, ON [*FM radio station call letters*]
CFJC .... Kamloops, BC [*AM radio station call letters*]
CFJC-FM ... Merritt, BC [*FM radio station call letters*]
CFJC-TV... Kamloops, BC [*Television station call letters*]
CFJD-FM ... Thetford Mines, PQ [*FM radio station call letters*]
CFJO......... Council of Federated Jewish Organizations [*Defunct*]   (EA)
CFJO-FM ... Plessisville, PQ [*FM radio station call letters*]
CFJP-TV... Montreal, PQ [*Television station call letters*]
CFJR......... Brockville, ON [*AM radio station call letters*]
CFK........... Citizens for Free Kuwait   (EA)
CFK........... Cliff Resources Corp. [*Toronto Stock Exchange symbol*]

CFK............ COMFED Bancorp, Inc. [*AMEX symbol*]   (SPSG)
CFK............ Confidence Firing Kit
CFKC.......... Creston, BC [*AM radio station call letters*]
CFKEA........ Commercial Fisheries Review [*Later, Marine Fisheries Review*] [*A publication*]
CFKM-TV ... Trois-Rivieres, PQ [*Television station call letters*]
CFKR.......... Center for Fast Kinetics Research [*University of Texas at Austin*] [*Research center*]   (RCD)
CFKS-TV.... Sherbrooke, PQ [*Television station call letters*]
CFL............. Calibrated Focal Length   (MSA)
CFL............. Call Failed [*or Failure*] [*Telecommunications*]   (TEL)
CFL............. Canadian Federation of Labour
CFL............. Canadian Football League
CFL........ Canadian Forces College Library [*UTLAS symbol*]
CFL........ Cashflow [*A publication*]
CFL............. Central Film Library [*British*]
CFL............. Ceylon Federation of Labor [*Obsolete*]
CFL............. Chinese Federation of Labor [*Nationalist China*]
CFL............. Christian Family Life   (EA)
CFL............. Citizens for Farm Labor [*Defunct*]   (EA)
CFL............. Clear Flight Level
CFL............. Close Focus Lens
CFL............. Club Francais du Livre [*French Book Club*]
CFL............. Cold Flow Laboratory [*Martin Marietta Corp.*]
CFL............. Committee on Federal Laboratories [*Federal Council for Science and Technology*] [*Terminated, 1976*]
CFL............. Committee for a Free Latvia   (EA)
CFL............. Committee for a Free Lithuania   (EA)
CFL............. Conflict   (MSA)
Cfl.............. Confluence [*A publication*]
CFL............. Constant Feed Lubricator
CFL............. Context-Free Language [*Data processing*]
CFL............. Continental Football League
CFL............. Coordinated Fire Line   (AABC)
CFL............. Corporate Foods Ltd. [*Toronto Stock Exchange symbol*]
CFL............. Corps Front Luxembourgeois [*Resistance organization in Luxembourg*] [*World War II*]
CFL............. Counterflashing [*Technical drawings*]
CFL............. Department of Conservation, Forests, and Lands [*Victoria, Australia*]
CFl............. Fullerton Public Library, Fullerton, CA [*Library symbol*] [*Library of Congress*]   (LCLS)
CFL............. Stanislaus County Free Library, Modesto, CA [*OCLC symbol*]   (OCLC)
CFLA......... Catholics for Latin America
CFLA-TV .. Goose Bay-Labrador, NF [*Television station call letters*]
CFlB........... Beckman Instruments, Inc., Fullerton, CA [*Library symbol*] [*Library of Congress*]   (LCLS)
CFLC-FM ... Churchill Falls, NF [*FM radio station call letters*]
CFlCO .... Southern California College of Optometry, Fullerton, CA [*Library symbol*] [*Library of Congress*]   (LCLS)
CFLD......... Burns Lake, BC [*AM radio station call letters*]
CFLETC.... Consolidated Federal Law Enforcement Training Center [*Later, FLETC*] [*Department of the Treasury*]
C-FLEX ..... Cobra Fleet Life Extension Program [*Military*]
CFLG......... Counterflashing   (MSA)
CFLG-FM ... Cornwall, ON [*FM radio station call letters*]
CFLH......... Hearst, ON [*AM radio station call letters*]
CFLI .... Catholic Family Life Insurance   (EA)
CFLI .... Clay Flue Lining Institute [*Defunct*]   (EA)
CFLIS .... Canadian Foresters Life Insurance Society   (EA)
CFlJ........... Fullerton Junior College, Fullerton, CA [*Library symbol*] [*Library of Congress*]   (LCLS)
CFLK......... Kapuskasing, ON [*AM radio station call letters*]
CFLLP....... Commission on Folk Law and Legal Pluralism [*of the International Union of Anthropological and Ethnological Sciences*]   (EAIO)
CFLM........ La Tuque, PQ [*AM radio station call letters*]
CFLN......... Comite Francais de Liberation Nationale [*Algeria*]
CFLN......... Goose Bay, NF [*AM radio station call letters*]
CFLOS ...... Cloud-Free Line of Sight
CFLP .... Canada Farm Labor Pool
CFLP .... Code of Fair Labor Practices   (NOAA)
CFlP.......... Pacific Christian College, Fullerton, CA [*Library symbol*] [*Library of Congress*]   (LCLS)
CFLP .... Rimouski, PQ [*AM radio station call letters*]
CFlS........... California State University, Fullerton, Fullerton, CA [*Library symbol*] [*Library of Congress*]   (LCLS)
CFLS .... Levis, PQ [*AM radio station call letters*]
C/FLT........ Captive Flight   (MUGU)
CFLT .... Courtesy Flight [*Aviation*]   (FAAC)
CFLV .... Valleyfield, PQ [*AM radio station call letters*]
CFLW........ Wabush, NF [*AM radio station call letters*]
CFLY-FM ... Kingston, ON [*FM radio station call letters*]
CFM .... Cadet Forces Medal [*British military*]   (DMA)
CFM .... Canadian Fiction Magazine [*A publication*]
CFM .... Canadian Friends of Mine   (EA)
CFM .... Captive Flight Model [*Military*]   (CAAL)
CFM .... Cassells' Family Magazine [*A publication*]   (ROG)
CFM .... Cathode Follower Mixer
CFM .... Center Frequency Modulation

CFM .... Chilldown Flow Meter
CFM .... Chlorofluoromethane [*Propellant*]
CFM .... Christian Family Movement   (EA)
CFM .... Christiane Fabre de Morlhon [*In information service name CFM Documentazione*] [*Information service or system*]   (IID)
CFM .... Cliffside [*Montana*] [*Seismograph station code, US Geological Survey*] [*Closed*]   (SEIS)
CFM .... Closed Flux Memory [*Data processing*]
CFM .... Club Francais de la Medaille [*A publication*]
CFM .... Comision Femenil Mexicana Nacional   (EA)
CFM .... Committee for a Free Mozambique [*Defunct*]   (EA)
CFM .... Companding and Frequency Modulation [*Telecommunications*]   (TEL)
CFM .... Computer Facilities Management   (MCD)
CFM .... Computer Field Maintenance [*British*]
CFM .... Confirm   (AAG)
CFM .... Consumers for the Free Market [*Pittsburgh, PA*]   (EA)
CFM .... Containment Failure Mode [*Nuclear energy*]   (NRCH)
CFM .... Contingency Financing Mechanism [*International Monetary Fund*]
CFM .... Contingency for Movement [*Army*]
CFM .... Continuous Functional Monitoring
CFM .... Contractor-Furnished Material
CFM .... Council of Foreign Ministers
CFM .... Covering Fire Mine   (MCD)
CFM .... Credit and Financial Management [*A publication*]
CFM .... Crown Life Properties, Inc. [*Toronto Stock Exchange symbol*]
CFM .... Crystal Frequency Multiplier
CFM .... Cubic Feet per Minute
CFM .... Customer-Furnished Material   (NASA)
CFM .... Roman Catholic Bishop of Fresno, Monterey-Fresno Diocesan Library, Fresno, CA [*Library symbol*] [*Library of Congress*]   (LCLS)
C3FM .... Case Center for Complex Flow Measurements [*Case Western Reserve University*] [*Research center*]   (RCD)
CFMA........ Catholic Family Missionary Alliance [*Later, MEW*]   (EA)
CFMA........ Central Financial Management Activities [*Military*]   (AABC)
CFMA........ Church Furniture Manufacturers Association   (EA)
CFMA........ Classiques Francais du Moyen Age [*A publication*]
CFMA........ Coal Fuel Mixtures Association   (EA)
CFMA........ Construction Financial Management Association   (EA)
CFMA........ Council for Medical Affairs   (EA)
CFMA........ Cutting Fluid Manufacturers Association   (EA)
CFMAS ..... Calcium, Ferrous, Magnesium, Aluminum, Silicon [*Oxide system in geology*]
CFMB........ Montreal, PQ [*AM radio station call letters*]
CFMC........ Canned Food Marketing Committee   (EA)
CFMCBO ... Central Inland Fisheries Research Institute (Barrackpore). Miscellaneous Contribution [*A publication*]
CFMC-FM ... Saskatoon, SK [*FM radio station call letters*]
CFMDC.... Canadian Film-Makers Distribution Centre
CFMen....... Mennonite Brethren Biblical Seminary, Fresno, CA [*Library symbol*] [*Library of Congress*]   (LCLS)
CFMF-FM ... Fermont, PQ [*FM radio station call letters*]
C F Mgmt .. Credit and Financial Management [*A publication*]
CFMHS....... Commission on Family Ministries and Human Sexuality   (EA)
CFMI......... Convenient Food Mart, Incorporated [*Rosemont, IL*] [*NASDAQ symbol*]   (NQ)
CFMI-FM ... New Westminster, BC [*FM radio station call letters*]
CFMJ .... Canadian Folk Music Journal [*A publication*]
CFMK-FM ... Kingston, ON [*FM radio station call letters*]
CFML........ Computational Fluid Mechanics Laboratory [*University of Arizona*] [*Research center*]   (RCD)
CFMM ...... Brothers of Our Lady of Mercy [*Roman Catholic religious order*]
CFMM ...... Canadian Federation of Mayors and Municipalities
CFMM ...... Congregatio Filiarum Minimarum Mariae [*Minim Daughters of Mary Immaculate*] [*Roman Catholic religious order*]
CFMM-FM ... Prince Albert, SK [*FM radio station call letters*]
CFMO-FM ... Ottawa, ON [*FM radio station call letters*]
CFMP-FM ... Peterborough, ON [*FM radio station call letters*]
CFMQ-FM ... Regina, SK [*FM radio station call letters*]
CFMR........ Fort Simpson, NT [*AM radio station call letters*]
CFMS........ Canadian Folk Music Society
CFMS........ Chained File Management System [*IBM Corp.*]
CFMS........ Combined Field Maintenance Shop [*Army*]   (AABC)
CFMS........ Computer-Based Financial Management System [*Harper & Shuman, Inc.*] [*Cambridge, MA*] [*Information service or system*]   (IID)
CFM/S....... Cubic Feet per Minute/Second   (DEN)
CFMSA ..... Catholic Foreign Mission Society of America   (EA)
CFMS-FM ... Victoria, BC [*FM radio station call letters*]
CFMSMSP ... Canada. Department of the Environment. Fisheries and Marine Service. Miscellaneous Special Publication [*A publication*]
CFMSTR.... Canada. Department of the Environment. Fisheries and Marine Service. Technical Report [*A publication*]
CFMTA..... Canadian Federation of Music Teachers' Associations
CFMT-TV ... Toronto, ON [*Television station call letters*]
CFMU .... Chinese Foreign Missionary Union   (EA)

CFMU-FM ... Hamilton, ON [*FM radio station call letters*]
CFMWFS ... Canadian Forces Maritime Warfare School [*Canadian Navy*]
CFMX-FM ... Cobourg, ON [*FM radio station call letters*]
CFN .... Christ for the Nations (EA)
CFN .... Church Family Newspaper [*A publication*] (ROG)
CFN .... Clifton Herbarium [*British*]
CFN .... Committee for a Free Namibia (EA)
CFN .... Confine (FAAC)
CFN .... Consolidated Fredonia Resources Ltd. [*Vancouver Stock Exchange symbol*]
CFN .... Craftsman [*Military*] [*British*]
CFN .... Los Angeles, CA [*Location identifier*] [*FAA*] (FAAL)
CFNB .... Fredericton, NB [*AM radio station call letters*]
CFND .... Communicators for Nuclear Disarmament (EA)
CFNE .... Circle Fine Art Corp. [*Chicago, IL*] [*NASDAQ symbol*] (NQ)
CFNI .... Caribbean Food and Nutrition Institute (EAIO)
CFNI .... Port Hardy, BC [*AM radio station call letters*]
CFNJ-FM ... St. Gabriel-De-Brandon, PQ [*FM radio station call letters*]
CFNL .... Fort Nelson, BC [*AM radio station call letters*]
CF/NML ... Citizens Forum on Self-Government/National Municipal League [*Information service or system*] (IID)
CFNN-FM ... St. Anthony, NF [*FM radio station call letters*]
CFNO .... Common Fund for Nonprofit Organizations [*Fairfield, CT*] (EA)
CFNO-FM ... Marathon, ON [*FM radio station call letters*]
CFNP .... Committee on Federalism and National Purpose (EA)
CFNP .... Community Food and Nutrition Programs [*Community Services Administration*]
CFNV .... Centrafarm Group NV [*Nieuwe Donk, Netherlands*] [*NASDAQ symbol*] (NQ)
CFNW .... Port-Au-Choix, NF [*AM radio station call letters*]
CFNY-FM ... Brampton, ON [*FM radio station call letters*]
CFO .... Association of Camps Farthest Out (EA)
CFO .... Calling for Orders [*Shipping*]
CFO .... Canceling Former Order
C/FO .... Cartoon/Fantasy Organization [*Defunct*] (EA)
CFO .... Ceramic Fiber Optics
CFO .... Channel for Orders [*Business term*]
CFO .... Chief Financial Officer [*Business term*]
CFO .... Chief Fire Officer [*British*] (ADA)
CFO .... Coast for Orders [*Chartering*]
CFO .... Commissioning and Fitting Out
CFO .... Complex Facility Operator [*Aerospace*] (AAG)
CFO .... Connection Fitting Out [*Navy*]
CFO .... Consolidated Function Ordinary [*IBM Corp.*]
CFO .... Consolidated Funds Ordinary [*Insurance*]
CFO .... Council of Film Organizations (EA)
CFO .... Critical Flashover [*Voltage*] (IEEE)
CFOA .... Champion Fleet Owners Association (EA)
CFoA .... United States Army, Fort Ord Library System, Fort Ord, CA [*Library symbol*] [*Library of Congress*] (LCLS)
CFoA-M .... United States Army, Presidio of Monterey Library, Monterey, CA [*Library symbol*] [*Library of Congress*] (LCLS)
CFOB .... Fort Frances, ON [*AM radio station call letters*]
CFOB-1 ..... Atikokan, ON [*AM radio station call letters*]
CFOC .... Contractor Fin Opener Crank (NG)
CFOCCRH ... Canada. Fisheries and Oceans. Canadian Contractor Report of Hydrography and Ocean Sciences [*A publication*]
CFOF .... Centre Franco-Ontarien de Folklore [*Formerly, Institut de Folklore*] [*Research center*] (RCD)
CFOI .... Canadian Forest Industries [*A publication*]
CFO J .... CFO [*Colorado Field Ornithologists*] Journal [*A publication*]
CFOK .... Westlock, AB [*AM radio station call letters*]
CFol .... Classical Folia [*A publication*]
CFOM .... Quebec, PQ [*AM radio station call letters*]
CFonK .... Kaiser Steel Corp., Fontana, CA [*Library symbol*] [*Library of Congress*] (LCLS)
CFOPB5 .... Canadian Forestry Service. Publication [*A publication*]
C For .... Code Forestier Francais [*French Forestry Code*] [*A publication*] (ILCA)
CFOR .... COMSEC [*Communications Security*] Field Office of Record [*Army*] (AABC)
CFOR .... Orillia, ON [*AM radio station call letters*]
CFORAA ... Colorado Field Ornithologist [*A publication*]
C Forum ... Cineforum [*A publication*]
CForum ...... Cultural Forum [*New Delhi*] [*A publication*]
CFOS .... CNARESTRA [*Chief of Naval Air Reserve Training*] Fleet Operating Squadrons
CFOS .... Owen Sound, ON [*AM radio station call letters*]
CFOT .... Crossed-Field Output Tube
CFOTNS ... Canada. Fisheries and Oceans. Ocean Science and Surveys. Technical Note Series [*A publication*]
CFOX-FM ... Vancouver, BC [*FM radio station call letters*]
CFOZ-FM ... Argentia, NF [*FM radio station call letters*]
CFP .... Canadian Forces Publication
CFP .... Canfor Corp. [*Toronto Stock Exchange symbol*] [*Vancouver Stock Exchange symbol*]
CFP .... Cardiac Filling Pressure [*Cardiology*]
CFP .... Carrier Frequency Pulse
CFP .... Casualty Firing Panel
CFP .... Center of Filtering and Plotting (NATG)

CFP .... Center of Fruiting Period [*Ecology*]
CFP .... Certified Financial Planner [*Designation awarded by College of Financial Planning*] [*Business term*]
CFP .... Change Flight Plan
CFP .... Chartered Financial Planner
CFP .... Chronic False Positive [*Test*] [*Medicine*]
CFP .... Cold Front [*or Frontal*] Passage [*Meteorology*] (FAAC)
CFP .... Combined Filter and Plot (NATG)
CFP .... Commission on Federal Paperwork [*Terminated, 1978*]
CFP .... Common Fisheries Policy [*EEC*]
CFP .... Community Fellows Program (EA)
CFP .... Completion Fitting-Out Period
CFP .... Computer Flight Plan
CFP .... Concentracion de Fuerzas Populares [*Concentration of Popular Forces*] [*Ecuador*] [*Political party*] (PPW)
CFP .... Concentric Flight Plan (KSC)
CFP .... Concept Formulation Package [*Military*]
CFP .... Conceptual Flight Profile (MCD)
CFP .... Congregatio Fratrum Pauperum [*Brothers of the Poor of St. Francis*] [*Roman Catholic religious order*]
CFP .... Congressional Fact Paper [*Army*]
CFP .... Contractor-Furnished Property [*Air Force*]
CFP .... Control Filter Post (NATG)
CFP .... Coordinated Financial Planning
CFP .... Corporate Finance Partner
CFP .... Covenant Fellowship of Presbyterians (EA)
CFP .... Creation Facilities Program [*Data processing*] (IBMDP)
CFP .... Cyclophosphamide, Fluorouracil, Prednisone [*Antineoplastic drug regimen*]
CFP .... Cystic Fibrosis of the Pancreas [*Medicine*]
CFP .... Pacific College, Fresno, CA [*Library symbol*] [*Library of Congress*] (LCLS)
CFPA .... Canadian Food Processors Association
CFPA .... Caribbean Family Planning Affiliation (EAIO)
CFPA .... Cationic Flocculant Producers Association (EA)
CFPAE ...... Council of Food Processors Association Executives (EA)
CFPC .... Codigo Federal de Procedimientos Civiles [*Mexico*] [*A publication*]
CFPC .... College of Family Physicians of Canada (EAIO)
CFPC .... Commission de la Fonction Publique du Canada [*Public Service Commission - PSC*] [*Canada*]
C-F/PCM .. Coarse-Fine/Pulse Code Modulator
CFPD .... Center for Foreign Policy Development (EA)
CFPDMS .... Californium-252 Plasma Desorption Mass Spectrometry
CFPF .... Central Food Preparation Facility [*Military*] (AABC)
CFPFDG ... Canadian Forestry Service. Pacific Forest Research Centre. Report BC-P [*A publication*]
CFPFT .... Committee on Free Press and Fair Trial [*of the American Newspaper Publishers Association*] (EA)
CFPG .... Coalition to Free Petkus and Gajauskas (EA)
CFPI .... Cystic Fibrosis Pancreatic Insufficiency [*Medicine*]
CFPIAM ... Canada. Department of Forestry. Forest Entomology and Pathology Branch. Annual Report. Forest Insect and Disease Survey [*A publication*]
CFPL .... London, ON [*AM radio station call letters*]
CFPL-FM ... London, ON [*FM radio station call letters*]
CFPL-TV ... London, ON [*Television station call letters*]
CFPME4 ... US Forest Service. Northern Region. Cooperative Forestry and Pest Management Report [*A publication*]
CFPNI .... Children's Friendship Project for Northern Ireland (EA)
CFPOB .... Chaud-Froid-Plomberie [*A publication*]
CFPP .... Coal-Fired Power Plant
CFPP .... Cold Filter Plugging Point
CFPPU .... Comite de Familiares de Presos Politicos Uruguayos [*Relatives' Committee for Uruguayan Political Prisoners*] [*Malmo, Sweden*] (EAIO)
CFPQAC ... Australia. Commonwealth Scientific and Industrial Research Organisation. Food Preservation Quarterly [*A publication*]
CFPR .... Center for Federal Policy Review (EA)
CFPR .... Prince Rupert, BC [*AM radio station call letters*]
CFPS .... Canadian Forces Postal System
CFPS .... Captain, Fishery Protection Squadron [*NATO*]
CFPS .... Central Food Preparation System [*Military*] (AABC)
CFPS .... Crossed-Field Plasma Sheath
CFPS .... Cystic Fibrosis Pancreatic Sufficiency [*Medicine*]
CFPS .... Port Elgin, ON [*AM radio station call letters*]
CFPSA ...... Confinia Psychiatrica [*A publication*]
CFPSAI ..... Confinia Psychiatrica/Confins de la Psychiatrie [*A publication*]
CFPSJ .... Capuchin-Franciscans (Province of St. Joseph) (EA)
CFP/TDP .. Concept Formulation Package - Technical Development Plan [*Air Force*]
CFQ .... California Folklore Quarterly [*A publication*]
CFQ .... CH Financial Co. [*Vancouver Stock Exchange symbol*]
CFQ .... Quaker Fabric Corp. [*AMEX symbol*] (SPSG)
CFQC .... Saskatoon, SK [*AM radio station call letters*]
CFQC-TV ... Saskatoon, SK [*Television station call letters*]
CFQC-TV-1 ... Stranraer, SK [*Television station call letters*]
CFQC-TV-2 ... North Battleford, SK [*Television station call letters*]
CFQM-FM ... Moncton, NB [*FM radio station call letters*]
CFQR-FM ... Montreal, PQ [*FM radio station call letters*]
CFQX-FM ... Selkirk, MB [*FM radio station call letters*]

CFR............ Caen [*France*] [*Airport symbol*] (OAG)
CFR............ Caile Ferate Romane [*Romanian Railways Board*] [*Department of Railways*]
CFR........... Carbon-Film Resistor
CFR........... Case Fatality Ratio [*Medicine*]
CFR........... Catastrophic Failure Rate
CFR........... Center for Field Research (EA)
CFR........... Central Files Repository
CFR........... Christian Family Renewal (EA)
CFR........... Citizens for Reagan (EA)
CFR........... Citrovorum-Factor Rescue [*Cancer treatment*]
CFR........... Code of Federal Regulations [*FAA*] (FAAC)
CFR........... Cold Filament Resistance
CFR........... Commander of Federal Republic of Nigeria
CFR........... Commerce Franco-Suisse [*A publication*]
CFR........... Commercial Fast Reactor [*British*]
CFR........... Commissioned from the Ranks [*Canadian Navy*]
CFR........... Committee on Foreign Resistance [*War Cabinet*] [*British*] [*World War II*]
CFR........... Committee on Friendly Relations among Foreign Students [*Later, ISS*] (EA)
CFR........... Compilation of the Federal Register
CFR........... Condensate Filter Demineralizer [*Nuclear energy*] (NRCH)
CFR........... Confirmation to Receive [*Data processing*]
CFR........... Confraternity (ROG)
CFR........... Consolidated Five Star Resources [*Vancouver Stock Exchange symbol*]
CFR........... Contact Flight Rules [*Same as VFR*] [*Meteorology*]
CFR........... Cooperative Fuels Research [*Committee*]
CFR........... Coordinating Fuel Research (MCD)
CFR........... Cost and Freight [*Business term*] ["*INCOTERM*," *International Chamber of Commerce official code*]
CFR........... Council on Foreign Relations (EA)
CFR........... Crash Fire Rescue [*Aviation*] (FAAC)
CFR........... CRI Liquidating Real Estate Investment Trust [*NYSE symbol*] (SPSG)
CFR........... Crossfire (MSA)
CFR........... Cumulative Failure Rate
CFr............ Cumulative Financial Requirements (MCD)
CFr............ Queen of the Rosary College, Fremont, CA [*Library symbol*] [*Library of Congress*] (LCLS)
CFrA.......... Alameda County Library, Fremont, CA [*Library symbol*] [*Library of Congress*] (LCLS)
CFRA......... Ottawa, ON [*AM radio station call letters*]
C Franc...... Cahiers Francais [*A publication*]
CFRB......... Toronto, ON [*AM radio station call letters*]
CFRC......... Canadian Forces Recruiting Centre
CFRC......... Community and Family Program Review Committee [*DoD*]
CFRC......... Consolidated Flight Record Custodian [*Air Force*] (AFM)
CFRC......... Kingston, ON [*AM radio station call letters*]
CFRC-FM ... Kingston, ON [*FM radio station call letters*]
CFRD......... Confidential, Formerly Restricted Data
CFRDA...... Commercial Fisheries Research and Development Act
CFRE......... Certified Fund-Raising Executive
CFRE......... Circulating Fuel Reactor Experiment [*Nuclear energy*]
CFRE........ Contract Financial Requirements Estimate [*NASA*] (KSC)
CFREAK ... Commercial Fisheries Review [*Later, Marine Fisheries Review*] [*A publication*]
CFR(EP).... Committee on Foreign Resistance, Economic Policy [*Ministry of Supply*] [*British*] [*World War II*]
CFRE-TV .. Regina, SK [*Television station call letters*]
CFRF......... Christian Forum Research Foundation [*Later, CC*] (EA)
CFR/FA..... Foreign Affairs. Council on Foreign Relations [*A publication*]
CFRG......... Canadians for Responsible Government (EAIO)
CFRJ......... Center for Russian and East European Jewry [*Later, CREEJ*] (EA)
CFRM........ Continuous Fiber Reinforcing Mat [*Fiberglass*]
CFRM........ Contract Financial Reporting Manual
CFRMB..... Chantiers de France [*A publication*]
CFRMF ..... Coupled Fast Reactivity Measurement Facility [*Idaho Falls, ID*] [*Department of Energy*] (NRCH)
CFRN......... Edmonton, AB [*AM radio station call letters*]
CFRN-TV .. Edmonton, AB [*Television station call letters*]
CFRN-TV-1 ... Grande Prairie, AB [*Television station call letters*]
CFRN-TV-2 .. Peace River, AB [*Television station call letters*]
CFRN-TV-3 ... Whitecourt, AB [*Television station call letters*]
CFRN-TV-4 .. Ashmont, AB [*Television station call letters*]
CFRN-TV-5 .. Lac La Biche, AB [*Television station call letters*]
CFRN-TV-6 .. Red Deer, AB [*Television station call letters*]
CFRN-TV-7 .. Lougheed, AB [*Television station call letters*]
CF(R of O) .. Chaplain to the Forces - Reserve of Officers [*British*]
CFRO-FM .. Vancouver, BC [*FM radio station call letters*]
CFRP......... Carbon Fiber Reinforced Plastic
CFRP......... Consolidated Fuel Reprocessing Program [*Oak Ridge National Laboratory*]
CFRP......... Forestville, PQ [*AM radio station call letters*]
CFRQAM ... Australia. Commonwealth Scientific and Industrial Research Organisation. Food Research Quarterly [*A publication*]
CFRQ-FM ... Dartmouth, NS [*FM radio station call letters*]
CFRRIIA... Council on Foreign Relations and Royal Institute of International Affairs [*British*]

CFRS-TV... Jonquiere, PQ [*Television station call letters*]
CFRT......... Cystic Fibrosis Research Trust [*British*]
CFRTBW ... Canadian Forestry Service. Northern Forest Research Centre. Forestry Report [*A publication*]
CFRU-FM ... Guelph, ON [*FM radio station call letters*]
CFRV......... Commercial Fisheries Review [*Later, Marine Fisheries Review*] [*A publication*]
CFRW......... Campaign Fund for Republican Women (EA)
CFRY......... Portage La Prairie, MB [*AM radio station call letters*]
CFS............ Cahiers Ferdinand de Saussure [*A publication*]
CFS............ California State University, Fresno, Fresno, CA [*Library symbol*] [*Library of Congress*] [*OCLC symbol*] (LCLS)
CFS............ Calls for Service Signal [*Telecommunications*] (TEL)
CFS............ Canadian Federation of Students
CFS............ Canadian Forces Station
CFS .... Canadian Forestry Service
CFS............ Canted Fuselage Station (MCD)
CFS............ Carrier Frequency Shift
CFS............ Cassegrain Feed System
CFS............ Center for Family Support (EA)
CFS............ Center Frequency Stabilization [*Radio*]
CFS............ Central Flying School [*RAF*] [*Great Britain*] [*Australia*]
CFS............ Central Frequency Synthesizer
CFS............ Centre for Fiscal Studies [*University of Bath*] [*British*] (CB)
CFS............ Cesium Feed System
CFS............ Chief of Fleet Support [*Navy*] [*British*]
CFS............ Christians for Socialism in the United States (EA)
CFS............ Chronic Fatigue Syndrome [*Medicine*]
CFS............ Civil Flying Services [*Australia*]
CFS............ Coffs Harbour [*Australia*] [*Airport symbol*] (OAG)
CFS............ Coherent Forward Scattering [*Spectrometry*]
CFS............ Coherent Frequency Synthesizer
CFS............ Cold-Finished Steel (MSA)
CFS............ Combined File Search [*IBM program*] [*Data processing*]
CFS............ Committee for Food and Shelter [*Later, NAEH*] (EA)
CFS............ Committee on World Food Security [*United Nations*] (EA)
CFS............ Common File System [*Data processing*]
CFS............ Completely Finished Sets
CFS............ Component Failure Summary (KSC)
CFS............ Composite Feed System
CFS............ Computerized Forwarding System [*US Postal Service*]
CFS............ Concept Formulation Studies
CFS............ Condensate and Feedwater System [*Nuclear energy*] (NRCH)
CFS............ Confuse (MSA)
CFS............ Container Freight Station [*Shipping*]
CFS............ Contract [*or Contractor*] Field Service (AFM)
CFS............ Contract Field Support
CFS............ Contract Financial Status (AFM)
CFS............ Controlled Foods International Ltd. [*Toronto Stock Exchange symbol*]
CFS............ Core Former Structure [*Nuclear energy*] (NRCH)
CFS............ Council of Fleet Specialists (EA)
CFS............ Counter Filling System
CFS............ Critical Field Strength (AAG)
CFS............ Cryogenic Fluid Storage
CFS............ CT Financial Services, Inc. [*Toronto Stock Exchange symbol*]
CFS............ Cubic Feet per Second
CFS............ Cystic Fibrosis Society
CFSA......... California Flyers School of Aeronautics
CFSA......... Canadian Figure Skating Association
CFSA......... College Fraternity Secretaries Association [*Later, FEA*] (EA)
CFSA......... Saint Agnes Hospital and Medical Center, Fresno, CA [*Library symbol*] [*Library of Congress*] (LCLS)
CFSAN...... Center for Food Safety and Applied Nutrition [*Washington, DC*] [*Department of Health and Human Services*] (GRD)
CFSB .... Columbia Federal Savings Bank [*Wenatchee, WA*] [*NASDAQ symbol*] (NQ)
CFSBDJ .... Communications. Faculte des Sciences. Universite d'Ankara. Serie C2. Botanique [*A publication*]
CFSBI........ Cold Finished Steel Bar Institute (EA)
CFSC .... CFS Financial Corporation [*Fairfax, VA*] [*NASDAQ symbol*] (NQ)
CFSC .... Community and Family Support Center [*Army*]
CFSC .... Cryogenic Fluid Storage Container
CF-SCAN.. Canadian Forces - Second Career Assistance Network
CFSCP...... Centrally Funded Short Course Program
CFSD........ Capitol Federal Savings & Loan Association of Denver [*Aurora, CO*] [*NASDAQ symbol*] (NQ)
CFSD........ Citizens for Space Demilitarization (EA)
CFSDT ...... Centrally Funded Second Destination Transportation [*Army*]
CFSE .... Carmelite Brothers of the Holy Eucharist [*Roman Catholic religious order*]
CFSE .... Crystal Field Stabilization Energy
CFSEA....... Canadian Food Service Executives Association
CFSEB....... Conference of Funeral Service Examining Boards of the United States (EA)
CFSF.......... Coast Federal Savings & Loan Association [*Sarasota, FL*] [*NASDAQ symbol*] (NQ)
CFSFP....... Canadian Forestry Service. Forestry Publication [*A publication*]
CFSFTR .... Canadian Forestry Service. Forestry Technical Report [*A publication*]

CFSG .... Cometary Feasibility Study Group [*European Space Research Organization*] (IEEE)
CFSGDY ... Communications. Faculte des Sciences. Universite d'Ankara. Serie C1. Geologie [*A publication*]
CFSG/NML ... Citizens Forum on Self-Government/National Municipal League [*Information service or system*] (IID)
CFSJ .... Coalition to Free Soviet Jews (EA)
CFSK .... Coherent Frequency Shift Keying
CFSK-TV... Saskatoon, SK [*Television station call letters*]
CFSL .... Century Federal Savings & Loan Association [*Santa Fe, NM*] [*NASDAQ symbol*] (NQ)
CFSL .... Weyburn, SK [*AM radio station call letters*]
CFSLP .... Center for Short-Lived Phenomena [*Cambridge, MA*]
CFSN .... Confusion (MSA)
CFSO .... Canadian Forces Supplementary Order
CFSOA ...... College Fraternity Scholarship Officers Association
CFSO-BEBO ... Crystal Field Surface Orbital-Bond Energy Bond Order [*Model for chemisorption*]
CFSOCQ ... Change Facilitator Stages of Concern Questionnaire [*Educational test*]
CFSP .... California School of Professional Psychology, Fresno, CA [*Library symbol*] [*Library of Congress*] (LCLS)
CFSR .... Canadian Forestry Service. Research News [*A publication*]
CFSR .... Commission on Financial Structure and Regulation [*White House*]
CFSR .... Contract Fund Status Report [*Army*] (AABC)
CFSR-FM ... Abbotsford, AB [*FM radio station call letters*]
CFSS .... Canadian Forces Supply System (MCD)
CFSS .... Chronic Fatigue Syndrome Society, International (EA)
CFSS .... Combined File Search Strategy [*Data processing*]
CFSS .... Committee of French Speaking Societies (EA)
CFSSA ...... Canadian Food Service Supervisors Association
CFSSB ...... Central Flight Status Selection Board [*Air Force*]
CFSSC-K... Community, Family, and Soldier Support Command - Korea [*Army*]
CFSSE .... Contractor-Furnished Special Support Equipment (AFIT)
CFST .... Context-Free Syntactical Translator
CFSTB3 ..... Canadian Institute of Food Science and Technology. Journal [*A publication*]
CFSTI .... Clearinghouse for Federal Scientific and Technical Information [*Later, NTIS*] [*National Institute of Standards and Technology*]
CFSTR ...... Continuous-Flow Stirred Tank Reactor [*Chemical engineering*]
CFSX .... Stephenville, NF [*AM radio station call letters*]
CFSXAE .... Contraception-Fertilite-Sexualite [*A publication*]
CFSZDN ... Communications. Faculte des Sciences. Universite d'Ankara. Serie C3. Zoologie [*A publication*]
CFT .... Canadian Foremost Ltd. [*Toronto Stock Exchange symbol*]
CFT .... Caster and Floor Truck Manufacturers Association [*Later, ICM*]
CFT .... Chem. Fabr. Tempelhof [*Germany*] [*Research code symbol*]
CFT .... Children's Film Theatre [*Later, Media Center for Children*]
CFT .... China's Foreign Trade [*A publication*]
CFT .... Clean Fuel Oil Tank (MSA)
CFT .... Clifton-Morenci, AZ [*Location identifier*] [*FAA*] (FAAL)
CFT .... Coated Foam Tape
CFT .... Cockpit Familiarization Trainer (MCD)
CFT .... Cold Flow Test
CFT .... Cold Fluctuating Temperature
CFT .... Common Facilities Test [*NASA*] (NASA)
CFT .... Complement-Fixation Test [*Immunology*]
CFT .... Complex Fourier Transform
CFT .... Concept Formation Test [*Psychology*]
CFT .... Conformal Fuel Tank (MCD)
CFT .... Continuous Fourier Transport
CFT .... Contract Field Technician
CFT .... Contractor Field Team (MCD)
CFT .... Contractor-Furnished Technicians (MCD)
CFT .... Core Flood Tank [*Nuclear energy*] (NRCH)
CFT .... Craft (AABC)
CFT .... Crossed-Field Tube
CFT .... Crystal Field Theory [*Chemistry*]
CFT .... Cubic Foot (DAS)
CFT .... Curd Firmness Tester [*For milk products*]
CFT .... Flight Express Cargo [*Philadelphia, PA*] [*FAA designator*] (FAAC)
CFT .... Fuller Theological Seminary, Pasadena, CA [*OCLC symbol*] (OCLC)
CFTA .... Canadian Film and Television Association
CFTA .... CECOM Flight Test Activity [*Lakehurst, NJ*] [*Army*] [*Later, AERA*] (GRD)
CF(TA) ...... Chaplain to the Forces (Territorial Army) [*British*]
CFTB .... Central Freight Tariff Bureau
CFTB .... Control Flight Test Bed
CFTB .... Cylindrical Fire Tube Boiler [*of a ship*] (DS)
CFTBS ...... Cylindrical Fire Tube Boiler Survey [*of a ship*] (DS)
CFTC .... Central Flying Training Command [*AAFCFTC*]
CFTC .... Committee on Fair Trade with China [*Medina, WA*] (EA)
CFTC .... Commodity Futures Trading Commission [*Formerly, CEA*] [*Independent government agency*]
CFTC .... Commonwealth Fund for Technical Co-Operation (EAIO)

CFTC .... Cooler Flusher Tank Cell [*Nuclear energy*] (NRCH)
CFTCA ...... Children's Film and Television Center of America (EA)
CFTD .... Confederation Francaise du Travail Democratique [*French National Trade Union Confederation*] (DCTA)
CFTE .... Cooler Flusher Tank Equipment [*Nuclear energy*] (NRCH)
CFTF .... Children's Film and Television Foundation [*British*]
CFTH .... Compagnie Francaise Thomson Houston [*French*]
CFTI .... Cape Fear Technical Institute [*Wilmington, NC*] (ASF)
CFTI-FM... Timmins, ON [*FM radio station call letters*]
CFTK .... Terrace, BC [*AM radio station call letters*]
CFTK-TV .. Terrace, BC [*Television station call letters*]
CFTM .... Captive Flight Test Missiles (MCD)
CFTM .... Conversion to Full-Time Manning
CFTMA ...... Caster and Floor Truck Manufacturers Association [*Later, ICM*] (EA)
CFTMN ..... Craftsman (MUGU)
CFTM-TV ... Montreal, PQ [*Television station call letters*]
Cftn .... Craftsman [*Military*] [*British*] (DMA)
CFTO .... Canadian Forces Technical Orders (MCD)
CFTO .... Committee for the Furtherance of Torah Observance (EA)
CFTO-TV ... Toronto, ON [*Television station call letters*]
CFTPB ...... Californium-252 Progress [*A publication*]
CFTR .... Citizens for the Republic (EA)
CFTR .... Cystic Fibrosis Transmembrane-Conductance Regulator [*Genetics*]
CFTR .... Toronto, ON [*AM radio station call letters*]
CFTRI .... Central Food Technology Research Institute [*India*]
CFTS .... Captive Firing Test Set [*Aerospace*] (AAG)
CFTTA ...... Chemiefasern und Textil-Anwendungstechnik/Textil-Industrie [*A publication*]
CFTU .... Confederation of Free Trade Unions [*India*]
CFTU-TV ... Montreal, PQ [*Television station call letters*]
CFTXA ...... Chemiefasern/Textil-Industrie [*A publication*]
CFU .... Central Firing Unit
CFU .... Chartered Financial Underwriter
CFU .... Chesterfield, VA [*Location identifier*] [*FAA*] (FAAL)
CFU .... Colony-Forming Unit [*Cytology*]
CFU .... Color Forming Units [*Food technology*]
CFU .... Control Functional Unit [*Data link*] (NG)
CFU .... Corfu [*Greece*] [*Airport symbol*] (OAG)
CFU .... Corn-Equivalent Feed Unit
CFU .... Covefort [*Utah*] [*Seismograph station code, US Geological Survey*] (SEIS)
CFU .... Croatian Fraternal Union of America (EA)
CFU .... Fullerton Junior College Library, Fullerton, CA [*OCLC symbol*] (OCLC)
CFUA .... Canadian Fire Underwriters' Association [*Later, Canadian Underwriters' Association*]
CFU-C .... Colony-Forming Unit - Culture [*Cytology*]
CFU-E .... Colony-Forming Unit/Erythroid [*Cytology*]
CFU-Eo ...... Colony-Forming Unit - Eosinophil [*Cytology*]
CFU-G .... Colony Forming Unit-Granulocyte [*Cytology*]
CFU-GEMM ... Colony-Forming Unit - Granulocyte-Erythrocyte-Monocyte-Megakaryocyte [*Cytology*]
CFU-GM ... Colony-Forming Unit/Granulocyte Macrophage [*Cytology*]
CFUJCF .... CFU [*Croatian Fraternal Union of America*] Junior Cultural Federation (EA)
CFU-L .... Colony-Forming Unit/Lymphoid [*Cytology*]
CFU-M ...... Colony-Forming Unit/Megakaryocyte [*Cytology*]
CFUN .... Vancouver, BC [*AM radio station call letters*]
CFUR .... Cochrane Furniture Co. [*Lincolnton, NC*] [*NASDAQ symbol*] (NQ)
CFU-S .... Colony-Forming Unit - Single Cell [*Cytology*]
CFUS .... Colony-Forming Unit - Spleen [*Cytology*]
CFUSAFA ... Committee to Form a US-Albania Friendship Association (EA)
CFUV-FM ... Victoria, BC [*Radio station call letters*]
CFUW .... Canadian Federation of University Women
CFV .... Cadillac Fairview Corp. Ltd. [*Toronto Stock Exchange symbol*] [*Vancouver Stock Exchange symbol*]
CFV .... Cavalry Fighting Vehicle
CFV .... Coffeyville, KS [*Location identifier*] [*FAA*] (FAAL)
CFV .... Conventional Friend Virus
CFV .... Conventionally Fueled Vehicle [*Automotive engineering*]
CFV .... Critical Flow Venturi [*Engineering*]
CFVA .... United States Veterans Administration Hospital, Fresno, CA [*Library symbol*] [*Library of Congress*] (LCLS)
CFVCO ...... Canadian Film and Videotape Certification Office
CFVD .... Constant Frequency Variable Dot
CFVD .... Ville Degelis, PQ [*AM radio station call letters*]
CFVD-FM-1 ... Cabano, PQ [*FM radio station call letters*]
CFVD-FM-2 ... Pohenegamook, PQ [*FM radio station call letters*]
CFVI .... Council of Families with Visual Impairment (EA)
CFVI .... San Joaquin Valley Information Service, Fresno, CA [*Library symbol*] [*Library of Congress*] (LCLS)
CFVM .... Amqui, PQ [*AM radio station call letters*]
CFVM .... Valley Medical Center, Fresno, CA [*Library symbol*] [*Library of Congress*] (LCLS)
CFVR .... Abbotsford-Matsqui, BC [*AM radio station call letters*]
CFVS .... Council for Fishing Vessel Safety (EA)
CFVS-TV... Val D'Or, PQ [*Television station call letters*]

CFVS-TV-1 ...	Rouyn, PQ [*Television station call letters*]
CFVU-FM ...	Victoria, BC [*FM radio station call letters*]
CFW	Calcofluor White [*A cotton whitener*]
CFW	Cereal Foods World [*A publication*]
CFW	Committee for the Free World (EA)
CFW	Condensate and Feedwater [*Nuclear energy*] (NRCH)
CFW	CONVAIR [*Consolidated-Vultee Aircraft Corp.*] Fort Worth [*Later, General Dynamics/Fort Worth*] (AAG)
CFWB........	Campbell River, BC [*AM radio station call letters*]
CFWC........	Canadian Federal Warning Center
CFWH........	Whitehorse, YT [*AM radio station call letters*]
CFWH-TV ...	White Horse, YT [*Television station call letters*]
CFWIS........	Central Fighter Weapons Instructor School (NATG)
CFWODA ...	Cereal Foods World [*A publication*]
CFWRU.....	Florida Cooperative Fish and Wildlife Research Unit [*University of Florida*] [*Research center*] (RCD)
CFWS	Condensate and Feedwater System [*Nuclear energy*] (NRCH)
CFWS	Coordinated Federal Wage System (MCD)
CFWSU	Central Flow Weather Service Unit (FAAC)
CFX...........	Cadiz, OH [*Location identifier*] [*FAA*] (FAAL)
CFX...........	Cheshire Financial Corp. [*AMEX symbol*] (SPSG)
CFX...........	Circumflex
CFX...........	Colfax Energy [*Vancouver Stock Exchange symbol*]
CFX...........	Confectie. Sociaal, Economisch, en Technisch Maandblad voor de Confectie Industrie in de Beneluxlanden [*A publication*]
CFX...........	Congregatio Fratrum Sancti Francisci Xaverii [*Brothers of St. Francis Xavier*] [*Xaverian Brothers*] [*Roman Catholic religious order*]
CFX...........	Credit for Exports [*Bank*] [*British*]
CFY...........	Clarify (FAAC)
CFY...........	Company Fiscal Year (NASA)
CFY...........	Current Fiscal Year (AFM)
CFY...........	Faraday Resources, Inc. [*Toronto Stock Exchange symbol*]
CFYK........	Yellowknife, NT [*AM radio station call letters*]
CFYK-TV ...	Yellowknife, NT [*Television station call letters*]
CFYM........	Kindersley, SK [*AM radio station call letters*]
CFYN........	Sault Ste. Marie, ON [*AM radio station call letters*]
CFYQ........	Gander, NF [*AM radio station call letters*]
CFYR........	Whitecourt, AB [*AM radio station call letters*]
CFZ...........	CFS Group, Inc. [*Toronto Stock Exchange symbol*]
CFZ...........	Chefornak, AK [*Location identifier*] [*FAA*] (FAAL)
CFZ...........	Colon Free Zone [*Free trade zone*] [*Panama*] (IMH)
CFZ...........	Contiguous Fisheries Zone [*Offshore*]
CG.............	Cage (MSA)
CG.............	Cairensis Gnosticus [*Nag Hammadi Codices*] (BJA)
CG.............	Cairo Geniza (BJA)
CG.............	Camera Gun
CG.............	Canadian Geographic [*A publication*]
CG.............	Capital Gain [*Accounting*]
CG.............	Capital Goods [*Business term*]
CG.............	Captain-General
CG.............	Captain of the Guard [*Freemasonry*]
CG.............	Captain of Gun [*British military*] (DMA)
CG.............	Carbonic Dichloride [*Phosgene*] [*Poison gas*] [*Army symbol*]
CG.............	Cardio-Green (Dye) [*Trademark*]
CG.............	Cargo Glider [*Military*]
C of G	Carriage of Goods [*by sea*] [*Shipping*]
CG.............	Cartoonists Guild (EA)
Cg.............	Carya glabra [*Pignut hickory*]
CG.............	Catalogue General des Antiquites Egyptiennes du Musee du Caire (BJA)
CG.............	Categorical Grammar
CG.............	Cement Gland [*Embryology*]
C of G	Center of Gravity
CG.............	Center of Gravity
Cg.............	Centigram
CG.............	Central of Georgia Railroad Co.
CG.............	Central Gland [*of the prostate*]
CG.............	Central Gray [*Brain anatomy*]
Cg.............	Cephalosporium gramineum [*Plant pathology*]
C & G	Ceramic and Graphite Information Center [*Air Force*] (MCD)
CG.............	Cerebral Ganglion [*Medicine*]
CG.............	Certified Genealogist
CG.............	Chain Grate (MSA)
CG.............	Change for Good (EA)
CG.............	Character Generator [*Telecommunications*]
CG.............	Chemical Gas (MCD)
CG.............	Chemie Gruenenthal GmbH [*Germany*] [*Research code symbol*]
CG.............	[*The*] Children's Garland [*A publication*]
CG.............	Choking Gas [*US Chemical Corps symbol*]
CG.............	Choreographers Guild (EA)
CG.............	Chorionic Gonadotrophin [*Endocrinology*]
CG.............	Choristers Guild (EA)
CG.............	Christians in Government (EA)
Cg.............	Chromogranin [*Biochemistry*]
CG.............	Chronic Glomerulonephritis [*Medicine*]
CG.............	Chugoku Gogaku [*A publication*]
CG.............	Ciliary Ganglion [*Neurology*]
C & G	City and Guilds of London [*British*]
CG.............	Civil Guard [*Air Force*] (MCD)

CG.............	Classiques Garnier [*A publication*]
CG.............	Clear Glass
CG.............	Clearance Group [*Customs*] (DS)
C to G	Clerk to Guardians [*British*] (ROG)
CG.............	Cloud-to-Ground Lightning [*Meteorology*]
CG.............	Clutter Gate
CG.............	Coast Guard
CG.............	Coconut Grove [*Florida*]
CG.............	Coincidence Gate
C/G...........	Coincidence Guidance
CG.............	Coldstream Guards [*British military*]
CG.............	Collagen-Glycosaminoglycan [*Physiology*]
CG.............	Colloidal Gold [*Chemistry*]
CG.............	Columbia Gas System, Inc. [*NYSE symbol*] [*Toronto Stock Exchange symbol*] (SPSG)
C & G	Columbus & Greenville Railway Co.
CG.............	Combat Group
CG.............	Command Group (MCD)
CG.............	Command Guidance [*Aerospace*] (AAG)
CG.............	Commandant General [*British military*] (DMA)
CG.............	Commanding General
CG.............	Commissary-General
CG.............	Committee for the Game (EA)
CG.............	Common Ground [*A publication*]
CG.............	Comparison Group
CG.............	Complete Games [*Baseball*]
CG.............	Comptroller General
CG.............	Computer Graphics (MCD)
CG.............	Conditional Grant
CG.............	Congo [*ANSI two-letter standard code*] (CNC)
cg.............	Congo (Kinshasa) [*Zaire*] [*MARC country of publication code*] [*Library of Congress*] (LCCP)
CG.............	Connradh na Gaedhilge [*The Gaelic League, founded in 1893*]
CG.............	Consolidated Guidance (RDA)
CG.............	Consul General
CG.............	Consultative Group [*NATO*]
CG.............	Contadora Group [*Mexico City, Mexico*] (EAIO)
CG.............	Contemporary Games [*A publication*]
CG.............	Contrast Gate (MCD)
CG.............	Control Grid
CG.............	Control Group
C & G	Control and Guidance (MCD)
C of G	Convenience of the Government
CG.............	Coral Gables [*Florida*]
CG.............	Corner Guard [*Technical drawings*]
CG.............	Courrier Graphique [*A publication*]
CG.............	Course Generator
CG.............	Covent Garden [*Royal Opera or Royal Ballet*] [*British*]
C de G	Croix de Guerre [*French military decoration*]
CG.............	Cruiser, Guided Missile [*NATO*]
CG.............	Crushed or Ground
CG.............	Cryoglobulin [*Clinical medicine*]
CG.............	Current Gain
CG.............	Cypriote Geometric (BJA)
CG.............	Glaxo Laboratories Ltd. [*Great Britain*] [*Research code symbol*]
CG.............	Guided Missile Cruiser [*Navy symbol*]
CG.............	Phosgene [*Organic chemistry*]
CG.............	Radio Frequency Component Cable Assemblies [*JETDS nomenclature*] [*Military*] (CET)
CG.............	Safair Freighters [*Pty.*] Ltd. [*ICAO designator*] (FAAC)
CG²...........	Coconut Grove and Coral Gables [*Florida*]
CGA..........	Canadian Garrison Artillery
CGA..........	Canadian Gas Association
CGA..........	Cape Garrison Artillery [*British military*] (DMA)
CGA..........	Cargo's Proportion of (General) Average [*Shipping*]
CGA..........	Caribbean Gamefishing Association
CGA..........	Carrier Group Alarm [*Telecommunications*]
CGA..........	Catholic Golden Age (EA)
CGA..........	Center for Growth Alternatives [*Defunct*] (EA)
C of GA	Central of Georgia Railroad Co.
CGA..........	Central of Georgia Railroad Co. [*AAR code*]
CGA..........	Central Grant Aid [*British*]
CGA..........	Central Guaranty Trustco Ltd. [*Toronto Stock Exchange symbol*]
CGA..........	Certified General Accountant
CGA..........	Certified Graphoanalyst
CGA..........	Chlorogenic Acid [*Organic chemistry*]
CGA..........	Chromogranin A [*Biochemistry*]
CGA..........	Citizens Global Action (EA)
CGA..........	Clutter Gate Amplifier (MCD)
CGA..........	Coast Guard Academy
CGA..........	Coast Guard Auxiliary
CGA..........	Colloidal Gas Aphron [*Physical chemistry*]
CGA..........	Color/Graphics Adapter [*Computer technology*]
CGA..........	Color Guild Associates (EA)
CGA..........	Community of the Glorious Ascension [*Anglican religious community*]
CGA..........	Compensator Group Adapter [*Military*] (CAAL)
CGA..........	Compressed Gas Association (EA)
CGA..........	Concord Grape Association (EA)

CGA.......... Contemporary Graphic Artists [*A publication*]
CGA.......... Contrast Gate Amplifier
CGA.......... Country Gentlemen's Association [*British*]
CGA.......... Craig [*Alaska*] [*Airport symbol*]   (OAG)
CGA.......... United States Coast Guard Academy, New London, CT [*OCLC symbol*]   (OCLC)
CGAA........ Copa Girls Alumnae Association   (EA)
CGAAF...... Commanding General, Army Air Forces
CGAB........ Coast Guard Air Base
CGAC........ CGA Computer Association [*NASDAQ symbol*]   (NQ)
CGACTEUR ... Coast Guard Activities Europe
CGADC...... Commanding General, Air Defense Command   (NATG)
CGAES....... Coffee Growers' Association of El Salvador [*Defunct*]   (EA)
CGAIRDET ... Coast Guard Air Detachment
CGAIRFMFPAC ... Commanding General, Aircraft Fleet Marine Force, Pacific   (MUGU)
CGAIRFMLANT ... Commanding General, Aircraft Fleet Marine Force, Atlantic   (NATG)
CGAL........ Central Georgia Associated Libraries [*Library network*]
CGAL........ Comprehensive General and Automobile Liability [*Insurance*]
CGAM....... Coast Guard Achievement Medal [*Military decoration*]
CGAMEEC ... Committee of Glutamic Acid Manufacturers of the European Economic Community   (EAIO)
CGand........ Collationes Gandavenses   (BJA)
CGARA ..... Commission Generale de l'Assurance du Risque Atomique [*Paris, France*]   (EAIO)
CGARADCOM ... Commanding General, United States Army Air Defense Command   (MUGU)
CGARP...... Committee for the Global Atmospheric Research Program
CGARY ..... Central of Georgia Railroad Co.
CGAS........ Clinton Gas Systems, Inc. [*NASDAQ symbol*]   (NQ)
CGAS........ Coast Guard Air Station
CGAS........ Cooled-Grating Array Spectrometer [*Instrumentation*]
CGAT .... Confederation Generale Africaine du Travail [*African General Confederation of Labor*]
CGAU........ Cabin Gas Analysis Unit [*Aviation*]   (NASA)
CGB.......... Central Gear Box   (MCD)
CGB.......... Ceramics and Graphite Branch [*Air Force*]
CGB.......... Christlicher Gewerkschaftsbund Deutschlands [*Confederation of German Christian Trade Unions*] [*West Germany*]
CGB.......... Coldspring Resources [*Vancouver Stock Exchange symbol*]
CGB.......... Colecao General Benicio [*A publication*]
CGB.......... Commonwealth Geographical Bureau   (EA)
CGB.......... Convert Gray to Binary
CGB.......... Corpus Glossariorum Biblicorum   (BJA)
CGB.......... Cuiaba [*Brazil*] [*Airport symbol*]   (OAG)
CGB.......... Global Church Growth Bulletin [*A publication*]
CGBASE ... Coast Guard Base
CGBCA9.... Colloquium. Gesellschaft fuer Biologische Chemie in Mosbach [*A publication*]
CGBLB...... Colorado. Geological Survey. Bulletin [*A publication*]
CGBMA .... Coal, Gold, and Base Minerals of Southern Africa [*A publication*]
CGBR .... Central Government Borrowing Requirement [*British*]
CGBUA ..... Canadian Geophysical Bulletin [*A publication*]
CGC.......... Calavo Growers of California   (EA)
CGC.......... Cape Gloucester [*Papua New Guinea*] [*Airport symbol*]   (OAG)
CGC.......... Capillary Gas Chromatograph
CGC.......... Cascade Natural Gas Corporation [*NYSE symbol*]   (SPSG)
CGC.......... Cathode-Grid Capacitance
CGC.......... Census Grievance Committee [*Vietnam*]
CGC.......... Ceramic Gold Coating
CGC.......... Church Growth Center   (EA)
CGC.......... Circuit Group Congestion [*Telecommunications*]   (TEL)
CGC.......... Clebsch-Gordan Coefficients [*Mathematics*]
CGC.......... Coast Guard Cutter
CGC.......... Combat Gap Crosser [*Army*]
CGC.......... Command Guidance Computer   (NASA)
CGC.......... Computer Guidance Corporation
CGC.......... Computerized Gas Chromatography
CGC.......... Confederation Generale des Cadres [*General Confederation of Supervisory Employees*] [*France*]
CGC.......... Consumers Packaging, Inc. [*Toronto Stock Exchange symbol*]
CGC.......... Craig [*Colorado*] [*Seismograph station code, US Geological Survey*] [*Closed*]   (SEIS)
CGC.......... Critical Grid Current
CGC.......... Cross-Guide Coupler
CGC.......... Cruise Guidance Control [*Aviation*]
CGC.......... Cruiser, Guided Missile and Command [*NATO*]
CGC.......... Cryogenic Gas Chromatography
CGCA .... Canadian Guidance and Counselling Association
CGCA .... Controller General of Civil Aviation [*British*]
CGCARC... Commanding General, Continental Army Command   (NATG)
CGCE .... Comptoir Guineen du Commerce Exterieur [*Guinean Foreign Trade Agency*]
CGCM ...... Coast Guard Commendation Medal [*Military decoration*]
CGCM ...... Coupled General Circulation Model
CGCM ...... Coupled Global Climate Model
CGCM ...... Court Martial Reports, Coast Guard Cases [*New York*] [*A publication*]   (DLA)
CGCMM ... Coast Guard Court-Martial Manual [*A publication*]   (DLA)

CGCMS..... Special Court-Martial, Coast Guard [*United States*]   (DLA)
CGCO........ Commerce Group Corp. [*NASDAQ symbol*]   (NQ)
CGCONARC ... Commanding General, Continental Army Command   (NATG)
CGCP......... Catalogue of the Greek Coins of Palestine [*A publication*]   (BJA)
CGCP......... Combined Ground Command Post   (MCD)
CGCPA....... Geological Survey of Canada. Paper [*A publication*]
CGCPAJ.... Geological Survey of Canada. Paper [*A publication*]
CGCRUITSTA ... Coast Guard Recruiting Station
CGCS......... Combustion Gas Control System [*Nuclear energy*]   (NRCH)
CGCS......... Council of the Great City Schools   (EA)
CGCT .... Confederation Generale Camerounaise du Travail [*Cameroonian General Confederation of Workers*]
CGCV .... Ceramic Gravitational Containment Vessel [*i.e., cup*] [*Slang*]
CGCYD ..... Cancer Genetics and Cytogenetics [*A publication*]
CGCYDF .... Cancer Genetics and Cytogenetics [*A publication*]
CGD.......... Canguard Health Technologies, Inc. [*Vancouver Stock Exchange symbol*]
CGD.......... Center of Genetic Diversity
CGD.......... Christliche Gewerkschaftsbewegung Deutschlands [*Christian Trade Union Movement of Germany*] [*West Germany*]
CGD.......... Chronic Granulomatous Disease [*Medicine*]
CGD.......... Coast Guard District
CGD.......... Coast Guard Docket
CGD.......... Commissural Gastric Driver [*Neurology*]
CGD.......... Commonwealth Government Directory [*Australia*] [*A publication*]
CGD.......... Comptroller General's Decision
CGDE .... Contact Glow Discharge Electrolysis
CGDIST ..... Coast Guard District
CGDK........ Coalition Government of Democratic Kampuchea
CGD-NAGC ... North American Gladiolus Council, Commercial Growers Division [*Inactive*]   (EA)
CGDO........ Coast Guard District Office
CGDS .... Computer Graphics Display System [*Army*]   (MCD)
CGE .... Cambridge, MD [*Location identifier*] [*FAA*]   (FAAL)
CGE .... Canadian General Electric Co. Ltd. [*Toronto Stock Exchange symbol*]
CGE .... Capillary Gel Electrophoresis
CGE .... Carriage
CGE .... Carriage Industries, Inc. [*NYSE symbol*]   (SPSG)
CGE .... Center for Global Education   (EA)
CGE .... Chadwick-Goldhaber Effect [*Physics*]
CGE .... Charge
CGE .... Children of the Green Earth   (EA)
CGE .... Cobalt Gray Equivalent [*Radiology*]
CGE .... Cockpit Geometry Evaluation [*Computer program*] [*Boeing Co.*]
CGE .... Compagnie Generale d'Electricite [*General Electric Company*] [*France*]
CGE .... Compagnie Generale Electrique du Canada [*Canadian General Electric Company Ltd.*]
CGE .... Controller General of Economy [*Military*] [*British*]
CGE .... Cortical Granule Exocytosis [*Cytology*]
CGE .... Cresyl Glycidyl Ether [*Organic chemistry*]
CGED .... Caribbean Group for Cooperation in Economic Development   (EA)
CGEJ .... Canadian Geographical Journal [*Later, Canadian Geographic*] [*A publication*]
CGEL........ Cover Gas Evaluation Loop [*Nuclear energy*]   (NRCH)
CGen .... Chaplain General [*British*]   (DAS)
CGEN .... Collagen Corp. [*Palo Alto, CA*] [*NASDAQ symbol*]   (NQ)
CGEN .... Consul General
C Gen Imp ... Code Generale des Impots [*General Code of Taxes*] [*A publication*]   (ILCA)
CGEOSq.... Cartographic Geodetic Squadron [*Air Force*]
CGEPAT .... Comunicacoes. Servicos Geologicos de Portugal [*A publication*]
CGER .... Caisse Generale d'Epargne et de Retraite [*State-owned bank*] [*Belgium*]   (EY)
CGES........ Colonial Gas Co. [*Lowell, MA*] [*NASDAQ symbol*]   (NQ)
CGF .... Carrier Gas Fusion [*Chemistry*]
CGF .... Central Group of Forces   (MCD)
CGF .... Chemotaxis-Generating Factor
CGF .... Chondrocyte Growth Factor [*Biochemistry*]
CGF .... City Gas Co. of Florida [*AMEX symbol*]   (SPSG)
CGF .... Cleveland, OH [*Location identifier*] [*FAA*]   (FAAL)
CGF .... Coarse Glass Frit
CGF .... College of Great Falls [*Montana*]
CGF .... Comicorum Graecorum Fragmenta [*A publication*]   (OCD)
CGF .... Commonwealth Games Federation [*London, England*]   (EAIO)
CGF .... Computer Graphics Forum [*A publication*]
CGF .... Consolidated Gold Fields [*British*]
CGFAB...... Catholic Guild for All the Blind [*Later, CCB*]   (EA)
CGFC........ Crystal Gayle Fan Club
CGFE........ Commission Geologique de Finlande. Bulletin [*A publication*]
CGFMFLANT ... Commanding General, Fleet Marine Force, Atlantic   (NATG)
CGFMFPAC ... Commanding General, Fleet Marine Force, Pacific   (MUGU)
CGFNS...... Commission on Graduates of Foreign Nursing Schools   (EA)
CGFP......... Calcined Gross Fission Product

CGFPAY ...   Colorado. Division of Game, Fish, and Parks. Special Report [*A publication*]
CGFPI ....   Consultative Group on Food Production and Investment in Developing Countries [*United Nations*]
CGFPS......   Conference Group on French Politics and Society   (EA)
CGFTD......   Cahiers. Groupe Francois-Thureau-Dangin [*A publication*]
CGG..........   Chicken Gamma-Globulin [*Immunology*]
CGG..........   Continuous Grinding Gauge
CGGA ....   China, Glass, and Giftware Association   (EA)
CGGB ....   Composers' Guild of Great Britain   (EAIO)
CGGBT.......   China, Glass, Giftware Board of Trade [*Later, CGGA*]   (EA)
CGGC ....   Constitution General Grand Chapter [*Freemasonry*]   (ROG)
CGGCM ....   Coast Guard Good Conduct Medal
CGGFA9....   Congres pour l'Avancement des Etudes de Stratigraphie et de Geologie du Carbonifere. Compte Rendu [*A publication*]
CGGP ....   Conference Group on German Politics   (EA)
C of GH......   Cape Of Good Hope
CGH...........   Cape Of Good Hope
CGH...........   Cape Of Good Hope [*South Africa*] [*Seismograph station code, US Geological Survey*] [*Closed*]   (SEIS)
CGH...........   Chorionic Gonadotrophin, Human [*Endocrinology*]
CGH...........   Computalog Gearhart Ltd. [*Toronto Stock Exchange symbol*]
CGH...........   Computer-Generated Hologram
CGH...........   Cough [*Medicine*]
CGH...........   Sao Paulo [*Brazil*] Congonhas Airport [*Airport symbol*]   (OAG)
CGHCA .....   Chongi Hakhoe Chi [*A publication*]
CGHHAK ...   Contributions. Gray Herbarium. Harvard University [*A publication*]
CGHRBH ...   Cape Of Good Hope. Department of Nature Conservation. Report [*A publication*]
CGI ....   Canadian General Investments Ltd. [*Toronto Stock Exchange symbol*]
CGI ....   Cancer Guidance Institute   (EA)
CGI ....   Cape Girardeau [*Missouri*] [*Airport symbol*]   (OAG)
CGI ....   Chief Ground Instructor [*British military*]   (DMA)
CGI ....   Chief Gunnery Instructor [*British military*]   (DMA)
CGI ....   Clinical General Impression [*Psychiatric testing*]
CGI ....   Coalition on Government Information   (EA)
CGI ....   Communications Group, Incorporated [*Concord, MA*] [*Telecommunications*]   (TSSD)
CGI ....   Computer-Generated Imagery
CGI ....   Computer Graphics Interface
CGI ....   Conseillers en Gestion et Informatique [*Montreal, PQ*] [*Telecommunications service*]   (TSSD)
CGI ....   Corrugated Galvanized Iron
CGI ....   Corticene-Grabber's Itch [*Refers to desire to "hit the deck" during bombing attacks*] [*Australian Navy slang*]   (DSUE)
CGI ....   Creative Guitar International [*A publication*]
CGI ....   Cruise Guide Indicator [*Aviation*]
CGi...........   Gilroy Free Public Library, Gilroy, CA [*Library symbol*] [*Library of Congress*]   (LCLS)
CGIA ....   City and Guilds of London Insignia Award [*British*]
CGIAR......   Consultative Group on International Agricultural Research   (EA)
CGIB..........   Comitato Glaciologico Italiano. Bollettino [*A publication*]
CGIBT ....   Commanding General, India-Burma Theater [*World War II*]
CGIC..........   Ceramics and Graphite Information Center [*Air Force*]
CGIC..........   Compressed-Gas-Insulated Cable
CGIC..........   Continental General Corporation [*NASDAQ symbol*]   (NQ)
CGIF..........   Cherry Growers and Industries Foundation   (EA)
CGII............   Collectors' Guild International, Inc. [*NASDAQ symbol*]   (NQ)
CGIIP........   Coast Guard International Ice Patrol   (NOAA)
CGIJD ....   Chinetsu Gijutsu [*A publication*]
CGIL..........   Confederazione Generale Italiana del Lavoro [*General Confederation of Labor*] [*Italian*]   (DCTA)
CGIP..........   Computer Graphics and Image Processing   (MCD)
CGIRAL ....   Cape Of Good Hope. Department of Nature Conservation. Investigational Report [*A publication*]
CGIS..........   Canada Geographic Information System [*Canada Land Data Systems Division*] [*Environment Canada*] [*Information service or system*]   (IID)
CGIT..........   Compressed-Gas-Insulated Transmission Line
CGIVS ....   Computer-Generated Image Visual System   (MCD)
CGJ............   Canadian Geographic [*A publication*]
CGJO ....   Canadian Geotechnical Journal [*A publication*]
CGJOA......   Canadian Geotechnical Journal [*A publication*]
CGKT ....   Confederation Generale Kamerounaise du Travail [*Cameroonian General Confederation of Workers*]
CGL ....   Cagle's, Inc. [*AMEX symbol*]   (SPSG)
CGL ....   Center-of-Gravity Locator
CGL ....   Children of Gays/Lesbians [*Later, CGP*]   (EA)
CGL ....   Choristers Guild. Letters [*A publication*]
CGL ....   Chronic Granulocytic Leukemia [*Medicine*]
CGL ....   Coast Guard League   (EA)
CGL ....   Coghlan Island, AK [*Location identifier*] [*FAA*]   (FAAL)
CGL ....   Command Guard List [*Navy*]   (CAAL)
CGL ....   Comprehensive General Liability [*Insurance*]
CGL ....   Computer Generated Letter
CGL ....   Conglomerate [*Lithology*]
CGL ....   Continuous Gas LASER
CGL ....   Controlled Ground Landing   (AAG)

CGL ....   Coral Energy Corp. [*Vancouver Stock Exchange symbol*]
CGL ....   Corpus Glossariorum Latinorum   (BJA)
CGL ....   Corrected Geomagnetic Latitude
CGl............   Glendale Public Library, Glendale, CA [*Library symbol*] [*Library of Congress*] [*OCLC symbol*]   (LCLS)
CGLA ....   Columbia Gay and Lesbian Alliance   (EA)
CGLAS .....   Center for Great Lakes and Aquatic Sciences [*University of Michigan*]
CGLASTA ...   Coast Guard Light Attendant Station
CGLAT......   Cassel Group Level of Aspiration Test [*Psychology*]
CGLB.........   Cheung Laboratories, Inc. [*Lanham-Seabrook, MD*] [*NASDAQ symbol*]   (NQ)
CGLBSTA ...   Coast Guard Lifeboat Station
CGL Bull.....   Coast Guard Law Bulletin [*A publication*]   (DLA)
CGlC..........   Glendale College, Glendale, CA [*Library symbol*] [*Library of Congress*]   (LCLS)
CGlCC ....   Los Angeles College of Chiropractic, Glendale, CA [*Library symbol*] [*Library of Congress*]   (LCLS)
CGLD ....   Coral Gold Corp. [*NASDAQ symbol*]   (NQ)
CGle...........   Glendora Public Library, Glendora, CA [*Library symbol*] [*Library of Congress*]   (LCLS)
CGlF ....   Forest Lawn Museum, Glendale, CA [*Library symbol*] [*Library of Congress*]   (LCLS)
CGLIA9.....   Conchiglie [*Milan*] [*A publication*]
CGLIHA....   Coastwise-Great Lakes and Inland Hull Association [*Defunct*]   (EA)
CGLKR......   Cleaning Gear Locker
CGlL ....   General Precision, Inc., Librascope Division, Glendale, CA [*Library symbol*] [*Library of Congress*]   (LCLS)
CGLM ....   Classical General Linear Model [*Statistics*]
CGLORSTA ...   Coast Guard LORAN [*Long-Range Aid to Navigation*] Transmitting Station
CGLS.........   Center for Great Lakes Studies [*University of Wisconsin - Milwaukee*] [*Research center*]   (RCD)
CGLS.........   Coast Guard LORAN [*Long-Range Aid to Navigation*] Station
CGlS ....   Glendale Sanitarium and Hospital, Glendale, CA [*Library symbol*] [*Library of Congress*]   (LCLS)
CGLSP.......   Consortium of Graduate Liberal Studies Programs   (EA)
CGLTG......   Cloud-to-Ground Lightning [*Meteorology*]   (KSC)
CGLTSTA ...   Coast Guard Light Station
CGlWD......   WED [*Walt E. Disney*] Enterprises, Inc., Research Library, Glendale, CA [*Library symbol*] [*Library of Congress*]   (LCLS)
CGM..........   Cairngorm [*Type of quartz*]   (ROG)
CGM..........   Cape Girardeau [*Missouri*] [*Seismograph station code, US Geological Survey*]   (SEIS)
CGM..........   Centigram
CGM..........   Central Gray Matter [*Physiology*]
CGM..........   Chief Gunner's Mate [*Navy rating*] [*Obsolete*]
CGM..........   Christian Government Movement [*Defunct*]   (EA)
CGM..........   Ciliated Groove to Mouth
CGM..........   Coffin Ground-Attack Missile
CGM..........   Computer Graphics Metafile
CGM..........   Conspicuous Gallantry Medal [*British*]
CGM..........   Corn Gluten Meal
CGM..........   Corrected Geomagnetic Time
CGM..........   Grant MacEwan Community College Library Technology Program, Edmonton, AB, Canada [*OCLC symbol*]   (OCLC)
CGMAG ....   Commanding General, Marine Aircraft Group
CGMAP ....   Conjugate Gradient Method of Approximate Programming
CGMARBRIG ...   Commanding General, Marine Brigade
CGMAW ...   Commanding General, Marine Aircraft Wing
CGMB ....   Commanding General, Marine Base
CGMCBG ...   Chief Gunner's Mate, Construction Battalion, Armorer [*Navy rating*] [*Obsolete*]
CGMCBP ..   Chief Gunner's Mate, Construction Battalion, Powderman [*Navy rating*] [*Obsolete*]
CGMCU ....   Council of General Motors Credit Unions [*Warren, MI*]   (EA)
CGMI ....   Church of God, Men International   (EA)
CGMIS.....   Commanding General's Management Information System [*Army*]
CGMO......   Coast and Geodetic Magnetic Observatory
CGMP ....   Controller General of Munitions Production [*Ministry of Supply*] [*British*]
CGMP ....   Current Good Manufacturing Practice [*Food and Drug Administration*]
cGMP ....   Cyclic Guanosine Monophosphate [*Biochemistry*]
CGMS ....   Coordination of Geostationary Meteorological Satellites [*National Oceanic and Atmospheric Administration*]
CGMS ....   Cover Gas Monitoring Subsystem [*Nuclear energy*]   (NRCH)
CGMT ....   Controller General of Machine Tools [*Ministry of Supply*] [*British*]
CGMTO ....   Commanding General, Mediterranean Theater of Operations [*World War II*]
CGMW ......   Commission for the Geological Map of the World   (EA)
CGN..........   Cahiers Gerard De Nerval [*A publication*]
CGN..........   Chronic Glomerulonephritis [*Medicine*]
CGN..........   Cognitronics Corp. [*AMEX symbol*]   (SPSG)
CGN..........   Cologne/Bonn [*West Germany*] [*Airport symbol*]   (OAG)

CGN.......... CTG Compression Technology Group, Inc. [*Vancouver Stock Exchange symbol*]
CGN.......... Glendale College Library, Glendale, CA [*OCLC symbol*]   (OCLC)
CGN.......... Guided Missile Cruiser (Nuclear Propulsion) [*Navy symbol*]
CGNB........ Composite Ganglioneuroblastoma [*Oncology*]
CGNE........ Calgene, Inc. [*Davis, CA*] [*NASDAQ symbol*]   (NQ)
CGNWAR ... Carnivore Genetics Newsletter [*A publication*]
CGNX........ Cognex Corp. [*NASDAQ symbol*]   (NQ)
CGO.......... Can Go Over [*Newspapers*]
CGO.......... Canadian Gold Resources [*Vancouver Stock Exchange symbol*]
CGO.......... Cargo   (AABC)
CGO.......... Chase Medical Group, Inc. [*Hialeah, FL*] [*AMEX symbol*]   (SPSG)
CGO.......... Cogeco, Inc. [*Toronto Stock Exchange symbol*]
CGO.......... Coker Gas Oil
CGO.......... Committee on Government Operations
CGO.......... Comptroller General Opinion
CGO.......... Contango [*Premium or interest paid*] [*London Stock Exchange*]
CGO.......... Contracts Group Office
CGO.......... Council of Georgist Organizations   (EA)
CGO........ Zhengzhou [*China*] [*Airport symbol*]   (OAG)
CGOB........ Coast Guard Operating Base
CGOBD6..... Contributions to Gynecology and Obstetrics [*A publication*]
CGOFE....... CONVAIR [*Consolidated-Vultee Aircraft Corp.; later, General Dynamics Corp.*] Government-Owned Facilities and Equipment   (AAG)
CGoGS....... Church of Jesus Christ of Latter-Day Saints, Genealogical Society Library, Santa Barbara Branch, Goleta, CA [*Library symbol*] [*Library of Congress*]   (LCLS)
CGOMA.... Canada. Geological Survey. Map [*A publication*]
CGOPHEOSE ... Consultative Group on Potentially Harmful Effects of Space Experiments
CGOR........ Computer Guided Optical Registration [*VISCOM Optical Products, Inc.*]
CGoR .... Raytheon Co., Goleta, CA [*Library symbol*] [*Library of Congress*]   (LCLS)
CGOS .... Combat Gunnery Officers School [*Army Air Forces*]
CGOT........ Canadian Government Office of Tourism
CGOU........ Coast Guard Oceanographic Unit
CGP.......... Cal Graphite Corp. [*Vancouver Stock Exchange symbol*]
CGP.......... Captain-General and President   (ROG)
CGP.......... Carleton Germanic Papers [*A publication*]
CGP.......... Central Grounding Point   (NASA)
CGP.......... Certified Guitar Player [*Monogram used by Chet Atkins*]
CGP.......... Chicago Public Library, Chicago, IL [*OCLC symbol*]   (OCLC)
CGP.......... Children of Gay Parentage   (EA)
CGP.......... Chittagong [*Bangladesh*] [*Airport symbol*]   (OAG)
CGP.......... Chorionic Growth Hormone - Prolactin [*Also, HCS, HPL*] [*Endocrinology*]
CGP.......... Circulating Granulocyte Pool [*Hematology*]
CGP.......... Coalition for Government Procurement   (EA)
CGP.......... Coast Guard Pension [*British*]   (ROG)
CGP.......... [*The*] Coastal Corp. [*Formerly, Coastal States Gas Producing Co.*] [*NYSE symbol*]   (SPSG)
CGP.......... Color Graphics Printer
CGP.......... Commission on Government Procurement [*Terminated, 1973*]
CGP.......... Current Geographical Publications [*A publication*]
CGPA .... Council of Governors Policy Advisors   (EA)
CGPAA...... China, Glass, and Pottery Association of America [*Later, CGGA*]   (EA)
CGPBA8.... Collection "Les Grands Problemes de la Biologie." Monographie [*A publication*]
CGPC........ Canadian Government Photo Centre
CGPC........ Cellular General Purpose Computer
CGPCAB... Colloquium. Gesellschaft fuer Physiologische Chemie [*A publication*]
CGPF........ Church of God Peace Fellowship   (EA)
CGPM .... Conseil General des Peches pour la Mediterranee [*General Fisheries Council for the Mediterranean*]
CGPP........ Comparative Guidance and Placement Program [*College Entrance Examination Board*]
CGPQA ..... Canadian Government Publications Quarterly [*A publication*]
CGPR........ Coast Guard Procurement Regulations
CGPR........ Computer-Generated Purchase Request
CGPS........ Stamford Capital Group, Inc. [*NASDAQ symbol*]   (NQ)
CGPSq...... Cartographic and Geodetic Processing Squadron [*Air Force*]   (AFM)
CGQ.......... Changchun [*China*] [*Airport symbol*]   (OAG)
CGQ.......... Consolidated Gold Standard Resources, Inc. [*Vancouver Stock Exchange symbol*]
CGQ.......... Corsicana, TX [*Location identifier*] [*FAA*]   (FAAL)
CGR........ Campo Grande [*Brazil*] [*Airport symbol*]   (OAG)
CGR........ Canadian Arrow Mines Ltd. [*Toronto Stock Exchange symbol*]
CGR........ Canadian Garrison Regiment   (DMA)
CGR........ Captured Gamma Ray
CGR........ Chariot Group, Inc. [*AMEX symbol*]   (SPSG)
CGR........ Citizens for Governmental Restraint   (EA)
CGR........ Coast Guard Regulations [*A publication*]   (DLA)
CGR........ Coast Guard Reserve
CGR........ Crime on Government Reservation

CGr .... Grass Valley Free Public Library, Grass Valley, CA [*Library symbol*] [*Library of Congress*]   (LCLS)
CGR .... United States Coast Guard Research and Development Center Library, Groton, CT [*OCLC symbol*]   (OCLC)
CGRA .... Canadian Good Roads Association
CGRADSTA ... Coast Guard Radio Station
CGRD........ Cableguard, Inc. [*Plano, TX*] [*NASDAQ symbol*]   (NQ)
CGR/DC..... Coast Guard Research and Development Center [*Groton, CT*]
CGRDO..... Coast Guard Radio   (NOAA)
CGRG .... Computer Graphics Research Group [*Ohio State University*] [*Research center*]   (RCD)
CGRI........ Center for Governmental Research Incorporated   (EA)
CGRL........ Central Gippsland Regional Library [*Australia*]
CGrl .... Gridley Public Library, Gridley, CA [*Library symbol*] [*Library of Congress*]   (LCLS)
CGrlGS...... Church of Jesus Christ of Latter-Day Saints, Genealogical Society Library, Gridley Branch, Gridley, CA [*Library symbol*] [*Library of Congress*]   (LCLS)
CGRM .... Containment Gaseous Radiation Monitor [*Nuclear energy*]   (IEEE)
CGRM .... Department of the Commandant-General, Royal Marines [*British*]
CGR & MOT for S ... Captain-General of the Religious and Military Order of the Temple for Scotland [*Freemasonry*]   (ROG)
CGRP........ Calcitonin Gene-Related Peptide [*Endocrinology*]
CGRP........ Circuit Group [*Telecommunications*]   (TEL)
CGRRAW ... Colorado Game Research Review [*A publication*]
CGRS........ Canadian Geriatrics Research Society
CGRS........ Central Gyro Reference System
CGRS........ Compact Gamma Ray Spectrometer
CGS .... Cambridge Geographical Series [*A publication*]
CGS .... Canadian Geotechnical Society
CGS .... Canadian Goat Society
CGS .... CAP-Gemini-Sogeti [*Software manufacturer*]
CGS .... Catgut Suture [*Medicine*]
CGS .... Catholic Guardian Society   (EA)
CGS .... Centimeter-Gram-Second [*System of units*]   (AAG)
CGS .... Central Gliding School [*British military*]   (DMA)
CGS .... Central Gunnery School [*British military*]   (DMA)
CGS .... Champagne Gift Service [*De Courcy Pere et Fils*] [*British*]
CGS .... Chef des Generalstabs des Heeres [*Chief of General Staff of the Army*] [*German military - World War II*]
CGS .... Chief of the General Staff [*in the field*] [*Formerly, CIGS*] [*Military*] [*British*]
CGS .... Cholesterol Gallstones [*Medicine*]
CGS .... Chromatographic Separation
CGS .... Clinical Genetical Society [*British*]
CGS .... Coast and Geodetic Survey [*Later, NOAA*] [*Rockville, MD*]   (AFM)
C & GS...... Coast and Geodetic Survey [*Later, NOAA*] [*Rockville, MD*]
CGS .... Coast Guard Specification
CGS .... College Park, MD [*Location identifier*] [*FAA*]   (FAAL)
CGS .... Colorado Genealogical Society   (EA)
C & GS...... Command and General Staff [*Military*]
CGS .... Commissary-General of Subsistence [*Army*] [*British*]
CGS .... Commission on Government Security [*Terminated, 1957*]
CGS .... Community Guidance Service   (EA)
CGS .... Concerned Guatemala Scholars   (EA)
CGr .... Confederation Generale des Syndicats [*General Confederation of Trade Unions*] [*Congo - Leopoldville*]
CGS .... Consolidated Oil & Gas, Inc. [*AMEX symbol*]   (SPSG)
CGS .... CONUS [*Continental United States*] Ground Station   (MCD)
CGS .... Council of Graduate Schools   (EA)
CGS .... Country Grammar School [*British*]
CGS .... Czechoslovak Genealogical Society   (EA)
CGSA........ Cellular Geographic Serving Area [*Telecommunications*]
CGSA........ Computer Graphics Structural Analysis
CGSA........ Connecticut General Statutes, Annotated [*A publication*]   (DLA)
CGSAC...... Commanding General, Strategic Air Command   (NATG)
CGSB........ Canadian General Standards Board [*Formerly, Canadian Government Specifications Board*]
CGSBN..... Consortium for Graduate Study in Business for Negroes [*Later, CGSM*]
CG(S)C..... Civilian Goods (Supply) Committee [*British*] [*World War II*]
CGSC........ Command and General Staff College [*Fort Leavenworth, KS*] [*Military*]
C & GSC.... Command and General Staff College [*Fort Leavenworth, KS*] [*Military*]
CGSE........ Centimeter-Gram-Second-Electrostatic
CGSE........ Common Ground Support Equipment   (MCD)
CGSEL ...... Common Ground Support Equipment List   (NVT)
CGSFAZ.... Citrus Grower and Sub-Tropical Fruit Journal [*A publication*]
CGSFU...... Ceramic [*or Clear*] Glazed Structural Facing Units [*Technical drawings*]
CGSI.......... Colorado Gold & Silver, Incorporated [*Denver, CO*] [*NASDAQ symbol*]   (NQ)
CGSI.......... Computer-Generated/Synthesized Imagery   (MCD)
CGSM .... Centimeter-Gram-Second-Electromagnetic
CGSM .... Consortium for Graduate Study in Management [*St. Louis, MO*]   (EA)

CGSMCM ... Coast Guard Supplement to Manual for Courts-Martial [*A publication*] (DLA)
CGSOC...... Command and General Staff Officer Course [*Military*] (INF)
CGSP........ Conventional Geometry Smart Projectile
CGSPBW .. Contributions to Geology. Special Paper [*A publication*]
CGSS........ Ceramics, Glass, and Solid State Science Division [*National Institute of Standards and Technology*] (GRD)
C & GSS .... Command and General Staff School [*Army*]
CGSS........ Copilot/Gunner Stabilized Sight (MCD)
CGSS........ Cryogenic Gas Storage System (MCD)
CGSSC...... Columbia Gas System Service Corporation [*of Columbia Gas System, Inc.*]
CGSTA...... Clinics in Gastroenterology [*A publication*]
CGSTA...... Coast Guard Station
CGSTA9...... Clinics in Gastroenterology [*A publication*]
CGSTB...... Cognition [*A publication*]
CGSTN...... Congestion [*Aviation*] (FAAC)
CGSU........ Centimeter-Gram-Second Unit
CGSUB...... Ceramic [*or Clear*] Glazed Structural Unit Base [*Technical drawings*]
CGSUPCEN ... Coast Guard Supply Center
CGSUS...... Council of Graduate Schools in the United States (EA)
CGT .... [*The*] Cambridge Greek Testament [*A publication*] (BJA)
CGT .... [*The*] Canada & Gulf Terminal Railway Co. [*AAR code*]
CGT .... Capital Gains Tax
CGT .... Cheguitti [*Mauritania*] [*Airport symbol*] (OAG)
CGT .... Chicago Heights, IL [*Location identifier*] [*FAA*] (FAAL)
CGT .... Chuian-Garon [*USSR*] [*Seismograph station code, US Geological Survey*] [*Closed*] (SEIS)
CGT .... Color Graphics Terminal (MCD)
CGT .... Compagnie Generale Transatlantique [*General Transatlantic Shipping Company*] [*French*]
CGT .... Compensated Gross Tons [*Measure of shipbuilding capacity*]
CGT .... Confederacion General del Trabajo [*General Confederation of Labor*] [*Argentina*] (PD)
CGT .... Confederation Generale du Travail [*General Confederation of Labor*] [*Martinique*] [*Political party*] (PPW)
CGT .... Confederation Generale du Travail [*General Confederation of Labor*] [*France*] [*Political party*] (PPE)
CGT .... Consumers' Gas Co. Ltd. [*Toronto Stock Exchange symbol*]
CGT .... Corrected Geomagnetic Time
CGT .... Current Gate Tube
CGTAC...... Commanding General, Tactical Air Command (NATG)
CGTase...... Cyclodextrin Glycosyltransferase [*An enzyme*]
CGTB........ Colombian Government Trade Bureau (EA)
CGTC .... Cambridge Greek Testament Commentary [*A publication*] (BJA)
CGTEL...... Coast Guard Teletype (NOAA)
CG & TFL ... California Grape and Tree Fruit League (EA)
CGTHIRDMAW ... Commanding General, Third Marine Air Wing (MUGU)
CGTM .... Command Guided Tactical Missile
CGTNAU .. Cognition [*A publication*]
CGTO .... Contracted Gaussian-Type Orbital [*Atomic physics*]
CGTP .... Confederacao Geral dos Trabalhadores Portugueses [*Labor union*] [*Portugal*] (EY)
CGTRASTA ... Coast Guard Training Station
CGTS......... Coast and Geodetic Tide Station
CGTS......... Coast Guard Training Station
CGTSC...... Cambridge Greek Testament for Schools and Colleges [*A publication*] (BJA)
CGTSS ..... Command Group Training Support System (MCD)
CGTT........ Cortisone Glucose Tolerance Test [*Medicine*]
CGTV .... Command Guidance Test Vehicle
CGU.......... Canadian Geophysical Union
CGU.......... Ceramic Glazed Unit [*Technical drawings*]
CGU.......... Church Guilds Union [*British*]
CGU.......... Corning Resources [*Vancouver Stock Exchange symbol*]
CGUA........ Compu/Graphics Users Association (EA)
CGUL........ Margate Ventures, Inc. [*NASDAQ symbol*] (NQ)
CGUP .... Comite Guatemalteco de Unidad Patriotica [*Guatemalan Committee of Patriotic Unity*] (PD)
CGUSA...... Common Ground - USA (EA)
CGUSACOMZEUR ... Commanding General, United States Army Communications Zone, Europe (NATG)
CGUSADC ... Commanding General, United States Army Combat Developments Command
CGUSAMC ... Commanding General, United States Army Material Command
CGUSARADCOM ... Commanding General, United States Army Air Defense Command
CGUSARAL ... Commanding General, United States Army, Alaska (MUGU)
CGUSARCDC ... Commanding General, United States Army Combat Developments Command (MUGU)
CGUSARF ... Commanding General, United States Army Forces (CINC)
CGUSARMAC ... Commanding General, United States Army Material Command (CINC)
CGUSARMC ... Commanding General, United States Army Material Command (MUGU)
CGUSARYIS ... Commanding General, United States Army, Ryukyu Islands (CINC)

CGUSCONARC ... Commanding General, United States Continental Army Command [*Obsolete*]
CGUSFET ... Commanding General, United States Forces, European Theater [*World War II*]
CGV .... Cadena Garcia Valseca [*Press agency*] [*Mexico*]
CGV .... Critical Grid Voltage
CGVHD...... Chronic Graft-Versus-Host Disease [*Medicine*]
CGVS........ Ciliated Groove to Ventral Sac
CGVT .... Commission Gastronomique, Vinicole, et Touristique (EA)
CGW .... Chattanooga, TN [*Location identifier*] [*FAA*] (FAAL)
CGW .... Citco Growth Investment [*Vancouver Stock Exchange symbol*]
CGW .... Corning Glass Works
CGW .... Golden West College Library, Huntington Beach, CA [*OCLC symbol*] (OCLC)
C & GWRY ... Chicago Great Western Railway
CGWT .... Cylindrically Guided Wave Technique [*Nuclear energy equipment*]
CGX .... Chicago [*Illinois*] Meigs Field [*Airport symbol*] (OAG)
CGX .... Guided Missile Cruiser (MCD)
CGXX .... Cattleguard, Inc. [*NASDAQ symbol*] (NQ)
CGY .... Cagayan De Oro [*Philippines*] [*Airport symbol*] (OAG)
CGY .... Calgary Centre Holdings Ltd. [*Toronto Stock Exchange symbol*]
CGYD........ Coast Guard Yard
CGZ .... Casa Grande, AZ [*Location identifier*] [*FAA*] (FAAL)
CGZ .... Casa Grande Engineering & Mines [*Vancouver Stock Exchange symbol*]
CH .... A. Nattermann & Cie [*Germany*] [*Research code symbol*]
CH .... Air-Cushion Vehicle built by Commercial Hovercraft Industries [*New Zealand*] [*Usually used in combination with numerals*]
CH .... Aviation Cruiser (MCD)
CH .... Bellanca Aircraft Corp., Champion Aircraft Corp. [*ICAO aircraft manufacturer identifier*] (ICAO)
CH .... C. Hurst & Co. [*Publisher*] [*British*]
CH .... Caeharris [*Cardiff*] [*Welsh depot code*]
CH .... Cahiers d'Histoire [*A publication*]
C & H........ Calvin and Hobbes [*Comic strip*]
CH .... Cancer Hot Line [*of Cancer Connection*] (EA)
CH .... Candle-Hour [*Illumination*]
CH .... Can't Hear [*Telecommunications*] (TEL)
CH .... Captain of Horse [*British*]
CH .... Captain of the Host [*Freemasonry*] (ROG)
CH .... Caravan House [*An association*] (EA)
C/H.......... Cards per Hour [*Data processing*]
CH .... Cargo Helicopter (AABC)
CH .... Carmarthenshire Historian [*A publication*]
CH .... Carriers Haulage [*Shipping*] (DS)
CH .... Case Harden [*Metal*] [*Technical drawings*]
CH .... Casein Hydrolyzate [*Cell growth medium*]
CH .... Cavei Avir Lemitanim [*Israel*] [*ICAO designator*] (FAAC)
CH .... Center Halfback [*Soccer*]
CH .... Central Heating
CH .... Century Hutchinson [*Publisher*] [*British*]
CH .... Certified Herbalist
CH .... Chain
CH .... Chain Home [*Aviation*]
CH .... Chair
CH .... Chairman
CH .... Chaldea (ROG)
CH .... Chaldron [*Unit of measure*] [*Obsolete*]
Ch.......... Chalmers' Colonial Opinions [*England*] [*A publication*] (DLA)
CH .... Chamber (ADA)
CH .... Champion [*Dog show term*]
CH .... Champion Products, Inc. [*AMEX symbol*] (SPSG)
CH .... Chancellor (ADA)
Ch.......... Chancellor's Court [*England*] (DLA)
CH .... Chancery [*British*]
CH .... Change (AABC)
CH .... Channel
CH .... Channel Continuity Check Transmission [*Communications*] (FAAC)
Ch.......... Channels of Communications [*A publication*]
CH .... Chaplain (AFM)
CH .... Chapter
CH .... Chapter House [*British*] (ROG)
CH .... Character [*Data processing*] (BUR)
CH .... Charcoal Hemoperfusion [*Medicine*]
CH .... Chargeable to Hardware
CH .... Chart
CH .... Charter Rolls [*British*]
CH .... Chasmogamous [*Botany*]
CH .... Chassemaree [*Ship's rigging*] (ROG)
CH .... Chatham House (DAS)
CH .... Check
CH .... Cheese (ROG)
CH .... Chemical Hazards
ch.......... Cheque [*Check*] [*Spanish*]
ch.......... Chervonets [*Monetary unit; 1922-1947*] [*Russian*]
CH .... Chest [*Medicine*]
CH .... Chestnut [*Horse racing*]
CH .... Chestnut (ADA)

CH .... Chicago [*Illinois*]   (ROG)
CH .... Chicago Helicopter Airways, Inc. [*ICAO designator*] [*Obsolete*]
CH .... Chief   (AFM)
CH .... Chiffonier
CH .... Child [*or Children*]
CH .... Children's Hospital [*Philadelphia, PA*]
CH .... Child's Fare [*Airline fare code*]
CH .... Chile Fund, Inc. [*NYSE symbol*]   (SPSG)
CH .... China [*IYRU nationality code*]   (ROG)
ch .... China, Republic of [*Taiwan*] [*MARC country of publication code*] [*Library of Congress*]   (LCCP)
CH .... Chirurgia [*Surgery*] [*Latin*]
CH .... Chlorpheniramine [*Pharmacology*]
ch .... Chocolate
Ch .... Choice [*A publication*]   (ADA)
CH .... Choice   (ADA)
CH .... Choir   (ROG)
CH .... Choir Organ
CH .... Choke   (MSA)
Ch .... Cholesterol [*Also, C, Cho, CHOL*] [*Biochemistry*]
Ch .... Choline [*Also, Cho*] [*Biochemistry*]
CH .... Christ
CH .... Christian Herald [*A publication*]
CH .... Chronic [*Medicine*]
Ch .... Chronicles [*Old Testament book*]   (BJA)
CH .... Church
CH .... Church Heritage [*A publication*]   (APTA)
CH .... Church History [*A publication*]
CH .... Church Pennant [*Navy*] [*British*]
CH .... Chute
C of H .... Circumference of Head [*Medicine*]
CH .... City of Hope   (EA)
Ch .... Cladosporium Herbarum [*A fungus*]
CH .... Clearinghouse [*Banking*]
CH .... Clock Hour   (KSC)
CH .... Clothing and Housing Research Division [*of ARS, Department of Agriculture*]
CH .... Coach House
CH .... Coastal Harbor [*Telecommunications*]   (TEL)
CH .... Coat Hook
C & H .... Cocaine and Heroin
CH .... Codex Hammurabi   (BJA)
CH .... Come Hither [*A publication*]
CH .... Community Health [*A publication*]
CH .... Companion of Honour [*British*]
CH .... Compass Heading
CH .... Competition Hot [*In "Harley-Davidson XLCH"*]
CH .... Conductor Head   (KSC)
CH .... Connchord [*A publication*]
CH .... Conquering Hero [*British, for returning soldiers*]
Ch .... Constant Human Immunoglobulin
CH .... Contact Handled
CH .... Continental Group, Inc. [*Toronto Stock Exchange symbol*]
CH .... Control Heading   (BUR)
CH .... Control Hole   (BUR)
CH .... Controlled Humidity   (MCD)
CH .... Controlled Hypertension [*Medicine*]
CH .... Corptech Industry, Inc. [*Vancouver Stock Exchange symbol*]
CH .... Country Handbooks [*A publication*]
Ch .... Court of Chancery [*New Jersey*]   (DLA)
CH .... Court House
CH .... Covenant House [*An association*]   (EA)
CH .... Critica Hispanica [*A publication*]
CH .... Critical Hours [*Broadcasting term*]
CH .... Crown-Heel [*Length of fetus*] [*Medicine*]
CH .... Cuadernos Hispanoamericanos [*Madrid*] [*A publication*]
CH .... Current History [*A publication*]
CH .... Custom House [*Business term*]
C/H .... Cycles per Hour
CH .... Cyclohexanone [*Organic chemistry*]
CH .... Cycloheximide [*Also, CHX, CXM, Cyh*] [*Fungicide*]
ch .... Cylindrical Horizontal Tank [*Liquid gas carriers*]
CH .... Cytoplasmic Hypovirulence [*Pathology*]
Ch .... English Law Reports, Chancery Appeals [*1891 onwards*] [*A publication*]   (DLA)
Ch .... English Law Reports, Chancery Division [*A publication*]   (DLA)
CH .... Hayward Public Library, Hayward, CA [*Library symbol*] [*Library of Congress*]   (LCLS)
CH .... Switzerland [*ANSI two-letter standard code*]   (CNC)
CH5 .... Clark Hill Reservoir [*Georgia*] [*Seismograph station code, US Geological Survey*]   (SEIS)
CH6 .... Clark Hill Reservoir [*Georgia*] [*Seismograph station code, US Geological Survey*]   (SEIS)
CH50 .... Complement Hemolyzing 50 [*Immunology*]
CHA .... Alameda County Public Library, Hayward, CA [*Library symbol*] [*Library of Congress*]   (LCLS)
CHA .... Cable-Harness Analyzer
CHA .... Cahiers d'Histoire et d'Archeologie [*A publication*]
CHA .... Camp Horsemanship Association   (EA)
CHA .... Canadian Health Association

CHA .... Canadian Historical Association [*See also SHC*]
CHA .... Canadian Hospital Association
CHA .... Caribbean Hotel Association   (EA)
CH & A ...... Carrow, Hamerton, and Allen's New Sessions Cases [*1844-51*] [*England*] [*A publication*]   (DLA)
CHA .... Catholic Health Association of the United States   (EA)
CHA .... Catholic Hospital Association [*Canada*]
CHA .... Center for Health Action   (EA)
CHA .... Certified Hotel Administrator [*Designation awarded by Educational Institute of the American Hotel and Motel Association*]
CHA .... Chabazite [*A zeolite*]
CHA .... Challenge. Magazine of Economic Affairs [*A publication*]
Cha .... Chamaeleon [*Constellation*]
Cha .... Chamber
CHA .... Champion International Corp. [*NYSE symbol*]   (SPSG)
CHA .... Chassis
CHA .... Chatra [*Nepal*] [*Seismograph station code, US Geological Survey*]   (SEIS)
CHA .... Chattanooga [*Tennessee*] [*Airport symbol*]
CHA .... Chauvco Resources Ltd. [*Toronto Stock Exchange symbol*]
CHA .... Chicago Helicopter Airways, Inc.
CHA .... Chickasaw Horse Association   (EA)
ChA .... Choline Acetylase [*Also, CAT, ChAc, ChAT*] [*An enzyme*]
CHA .... Christian Herald Association   (EA)
CHA .... Christian Holiness Association   (EA)
CHA .... Chronic Hemolytic Anemia [*Medicine*]
CHA .... Commerce International [*A publication*]
CHA .... Committee of Heads of Administration [*NATO*]   (NATG)
CHA .... Community Health Association
CHA .... Concise Handbooks of Art [*A publication*]
CHA .... Congenital Hypoplastic Anemia [*Hematology*]
CHA .... Crop Husbandry Adviser [*Ministry of Agriculture, Fisheries, and Food*] [*British*]
CHA .... Crosier Heritage Association   (EA)
CHA .... Cuadernos Hispanoamericanos [*Madrid*] [*A publication*]
CHA .... Cyclohexyladenosine [*Biochemistry*]
CHA .... Cyclohexylamine [*Organic chemistry*]
CHAA .... Combined Health Appeal of America   (EA)
Cha Add ..... Chapman's Addenda [*A publication*]   (DLA)
CHAALS... Communications High-Accuracy Airborne Location System [*Military*]
Cha App ..... Chancery Appeal Cases, English Law Reports [*A publication*]   (DLA)
CHAB .... Moose Jaw, SK [*AM radio station call letters*]
CHABA ..... Committee on Hearing and Bio-Acoustics
CHABAD .. Chochma, Bina, Daat [*Wisdom, Understanding, Knowledge*] [*Philosophy of the Lubavitch Movement, a Hasidic sect*]
CHAC .... Catholic Health Association of Canada
CHAC .... Catholic Hospital Association of Canada
CHAC .... Cercle Historique et Archeologique de Courtrai. Bulletin [*A publication*]
ChAc .... Choline Acetylase [*Also, CAT, ChA, ChAT*] [*An enzyme*]
Chacaras Quint ... Chacaras e Quintais [*A publication*]
CHACBull ... Cercle Historique et Archeologique de Courtrai. Bulletin [*A publication*]
Ch Acc Aust ... Chartered Accountant in Australia [*A publication*]
CHACF ...... California Hungarian American Cultural Foundation   (EA)
CHACOM ... Chain of Command
CHAC Rev ... Catholic Health Association of Canada. Review [*A publication*]
CHAD .... Amos, PQ [*AM radio station call letters*]
CHAD .... Change Display [*Utility*]
CHAD .... Charleston Army Depot [*South Carolina*] [*Closed*]   (AABC)
CHAD .... Code to Handle Angular Data   (IEEE)
CHAD .... Cyclophosphamide, Hexamethylmelamine, Adriamycin, Diammedichloroplatinum [*Cisplatin*] [*Antineoplastic drug regimen*]
ChadArch .. Chadashoth Archeologioth [*Israel*] [*A publication*]   (BJA)
ChADD ...... Children with Attention-Deficit Disorders   (EA)
CHADECJA ... Stronnictwo Chrzescijanskiej Demokracji [*Christian Democratic Party*] [*Poland*]   (PPE)
Cha Dig ...... Chaney's Digest, Michigan Reports [*A publication*]   (DLA)
CHAE .... Centre d'Histoire de l'Aeronautique et de l'Espace [*Aeronautics and Space Historical Center - ASHC*]   (EAIO)
CH AE .... Chief Artificer Engineer [*Navy*] [*British*]   (ROG)
CHAER ...... Chief Aerographer [*Navy rating*] [*Obsolete*]
CHAF .... Chafford [*England*]
CHAFAG .. Chief, Air Force Advisory Group
CHAFB ...... Chanute Air Force Base [*Illinois*]   (AAG)
CHAFFROC ... Chaff Rocket [*Military*]   (NVT)
CHAFSEC ... Chief, Air Force Section   (CINC)
CHAG .... Chain Arrester Gear   (MCD)
C-HAG ...... Community Health Awareness Group
CHAG .... Compact High-Performance Aerial Gun   (MCD)
CHAG .... Consumer Housing Assistance Grants
CHAGA ...... Chemical Age [*A publication*]
Ch Agric ...... Chambres d'Agriculture [*A publication*]
Chagyo Shikenjo Kenkyu Hokoku Bull Natl Res Inst Tea ... Chagyo Shikenjo Kenkyu Hokoku. Bulletin. National Research Institute of Tea [*A publication*]

ChaH .... Chadwyck-Healey Ltd., Bishops Stortford, Herts., United Kingdom [*Library symbol*] [*Library of Congress*]   (LCLS)
CHAI .... Concern for Helping Animals in Israel   (EA)
CHAI .... Newberry Library/D'Arcy McNickle Center for the History of the American Indian [*Research center*]   (RCD)
CHAIA ...... Chemical Age of India [*A publication*]
CHAID ...... Chi-Squared Automatic Interaction Detector
Cha Ind ..... Chaleur et Industrie [*A publication*]
Chain Drug R ... Chain Drug Review. Reporter for the Chain Drug Store Industry [*A publication*]
Chain React ... Chain Reaction [*A publication*]   (APTA)
Chain Store Age Adm Ed ... Chain Store Age. Administration Edition [*A publication*]
Chain Store Age Exec ... Chain Store Age. Executive Edition [*A publication*]
Chain Store Age Gen Merch Ed ... Chain Store Age. General Merchandise Edition [*Later, Chain Store Age. General Merchandise Trends*] [*A publication*]
Chain Store Age Supermark ... Chain Store Age Supermarkets [*A publication*]
CHAIR ...... Chairman   (EY)
CHAK .... Inuvik, NT [*AM radio station call letters*]
CHAK-TV ... Inuvik, NT [*Television station call letters*]
CHAL .... Chaldron [*Unit of measure*] [*Obsolete*]
CHAL .... Challenge   (AABC)
CHAL .... Chalmette National Historical Park
CHAL .... Chalumeau [*Reed*] [*Music*]
CHAL .... St. Pamphile, PQ [*AM radio station call letters*]
Chal Clim ... Chaleur et Climats [*A publication*]
Chal Climats ... Chaleur et Climats [*A publication*]
CHALD ..... Chaldea [*or Chaldean or Chaldaic*]
CHALICE ... Compressional Heating and Linear Injection Cusp Experiment
Chal Ind ..... Chaleur et Industrie [*France*] [*A publication*]
Challenge in Ed Admin ... Challenge in Educational Administration [*A publication*]
Challenges Mont Agr ... Challenges to Montana Agriculture [*A publication*]
Challis .... Challis on Real Property [*1885-1911*] [*A publication*]   (DLA)
CHALM .... Chalumeau [*Reed*] [*Music*]   (ROG)
Chalmers .... Chalmers on Bills of Exchange [*1878-1952*] [*A publication*]   (DLA)
Chalmers Tek Hoegsk Handl ... Chalmers Tekniska Hoegskola. Handlingar [*A publication*]
Chalmers Tek Hogsk Doktorsavh ... Chalmers Tekniska Hoegskola. Doktorsavhandlingar [*A publication*]
Chal Op ..... Chalmers' Opinions, Constitutional Law [*1669-1809*] [*England*] [*A publication*]   (DLA)
Cha L & T .. Chambers. Landlord and Tenant [*1823*] [*A publication*]   (DLA)
Cham .... Chamaeleon [*Constellation*]
Cham .... Chambers' Upper Canada Reports [*1849-82*] [*A publication*]   (DLA)
CHAM .... Chamfer [*Design engineering*]
CHAM .... Chamizal National Memorial
cham .... Chamois [*Philately*]
CHAM .... Chamomile [*Pharmacology*]   (ROG)
CHAM .... Champagne   (ROG)
CHAM .... Hamilton, ON [*AM radio station call letters*]
CHAMB .... Chamber   (MSA)
CHAMB .... Chamberlain   (ROG)
Chamb .... Chambers' Upper Canada Reports [*1849-82*] [*A publication*]   (DLA)
Chamb Dig PHC ... Chambers' Digest of Public Health Cases [*A publication*]   (DLA)
Chamb Ency ... Chambers's Encyclopaedia [*A publication*]   (ROG)
Chamber .... Chamber Reports, Upper Canada [*A publication*]   (DLA)
Chamber of Ag Vic Yrbk ... Chamber of Agriculture of Victoria. Yearbook [*A publication*]   (APTA)
Chamber Mines J ... Chamber of Mines. Journal [*A publication*]
Chamber Mines Newsl ... Chamber of Mines. Newsletter [*Johannesburg*] [*A publication*]
Chambers' Cyclopedia ... [*Ephraim*] Chambers. English Cyclopedia [*A publication*]   (DLA)
Chamb J ..... Chamber's Edinburgh Journal [*A publication*]
Chamb Mines Newsl ... Chamber of Mines. Newsletter [*A publication*]
Chamb R .... Upper Canada Chancery Chambers Reports [*1857-72*] [*Ontario*] [*A publication*]   (DLA)
Chambre de Commerce Francaise Bul ... Chambre de Commerce Francaise en Australie. Bulletin [*A publication*]   (APTA)
Chambre Commer Fr Can R ... Chambre de Commerce Francaise au Canada. Revue [*A publication*]
Chambre Commer Gabon Bul ... Bulletin. Chambre de Commerce d'Agriculture, d'Industrie, et des Mines du Gabon [*A publication*]
Chambre Commer Repub Cote D'Ivoire Bul Mensuel ... Chambre de Commerce. Republique de Cote D'Ivoire. Bulletin Mensuel [*A publication*]
Chamb Rep ... Chancery Chambers Reports, Ontario [*A publication*]   (DLA)
Chamb Rep ... Upper Canada Chambers Reports [*1846-52*] [*Ont.*] [*A publication*]   (DLA)
Cham Chy Jur ... Chambers' Chancery Jurisdiction as to Infants [*A publication*]   (DLA)
Cham Com ... Chambers. Commons and Open Spaces [*1877*] [*A publication*]   (DLA)

Cham Com Law ... Chamberlin's American Commercial Law [*A publication*]   (DLA)
Cham Est ... Chambers. Estates and Tenures [*A publication*]   (DLA)
CHAMIL .... Chameleon Micro Implementation Language [*1978*] [*Data processing*]   (CSR)
Cham Leas ... Chambers. Leases [*1819*] [*A publication*]   (DLA)
Cham L & T ... Chambers. Landlord and Tenant [*1823*] [*A publication*]   (DLA)
CHAMOMA ... Cyclophosphamide, Hydroxyurea, Dactinomycin Oncovin [*Vincristine*], Methotrexate, Adriamycin [*Antineoplastic drug regimen*]
CHAMP .... Canard Homing Antimaterial Projectile
Champ .... Champerty and Maintenance [*A publication*]   (DLA)
CHAMP .... Champion   (DSUE)
Champ .... Champion's Cases, Wine and Beer-Houses Act [*England*] [*A publication*]   (DLA)
CHAMP .... Character Manipulation Procedures
CHAMP .... Child Amputee Program [*Canada*]
CHAMP .... Comet Halley Active Monitoring Program
CHAMP .... Communications Handler for Automatic Multiple Programs
CHAMP .... Community Health Air Monitoring Program [*Environmental Protection Agency*]
CHAMP .... Competitive Health and Medical Plan [*Proposed*]
CHAMPION ... Compatible Hardware and Milestone Program for Integrating Organizational Needs [*AFSC*]
Cham Pr ..... Chambers Practice [*A publication*]   (DLA)
Cham & PRR ... Chambers and Parsons' Railroad Laws [*A publication*]   (DLA)
CHAMPUS ... Civilian Health and Medical Program of the Uniformed Services [*Military*]
CHAMPVA ... Civilian Health and Medical Program of the Veterans Administration [*Military*]
Cham Rat ... Chambers. Rates and Rating [*2nd ed.*] [*1889*] [*A publication*]   (DLA)
Cham Rep .. Chambers' Upper Canada Reports [*1849-82*] [*A publication*]   (DLA)
CHAN .... Center for the History of American Needlework   (EA)
Chan .... Chancellor   (DLA)
CHAN .... Chancery
CHAN .... Chandler Insurance Co. Ltd. [*Grand Cayman, Cayman Islands*] [*NASDAQ symbol*]   (NQ)
Chan .... Chaney's Michigan Reports [*37-58 Michigan*] [*A publication*]   (DLA)
CHAN .... Channel [*Data processing*]   (AABC)
CHAN .... Clearing House Accession Number [*Online database field identifier*]
Chan .... Gloria Chandler Recordings [*Record label*]
CHan .... Hanford Public Library, Hanford, CA [*Library symbol*] [*Library of Congress*]   (LCLS)
CHANA ..... Chemist-Analyst [*A publication*]
CHANC ..... Chancellor
CHANC ..... Chancery   (ROG)
Chan Cas ... Cases in Chancery [*England*] [*A publication*]   (DLA)
Chanc Ex ... Chancellor of the Exchequer [*British*]   (DLA)
Chan Chamb ... Chancery Chambers Reports, Upper Canada [*1857-72*] [*A publication*]   (DLA)
CHANCOM ... Channel Committee [*NATO*]   (NATG)
CHANCOMTEE ... Channel Committee [*NATO*]   (NATG)
Chanc Pow ... Chance on Powers [*1831*] [*Supplement, 1841*] [*A publication*]   (DLA)
Chan Ct ...... Chancery Court   (DLA)
Chand .... Chandler's Reports [*20, 38-44 New Hampshire*] [*A publication*]   (DLA)
Chand .... Chandler's Wisconsin Reports [*1849-52*] [*A publication*]   (DLA)
Chand Crim Tr ... Chandler's American Criminal Trials [*A publication*]   (DLA)
Chand Cr T ... Chandler's American Criminal Trials [*A publication*]   (DLA)
Chandl .... Chandler's Reports [*20, 38-44 New Hampshire*] [*A publication*]   (DLA)
Chandl .... Chandler's Wisconsin Reports [*1849-52*] [*A publication*]   (DLA)
Chandler .... Chandler's Wisconsin Reports [*1849-52*] [*A publication*]   (DLA)
Chandler Wis ... Chandler's Wisconsin Reports [*1849-52*] [*A publication*]   (DLA)
Chand (NH) ... Chandler's Reports [*20, 38-44 New Hampshire*] [*A publication*]   (DLA)
Chand R ..... Chandler's Wisconsin Reports [*1849-52*] [*A publication*]   (DLA)
Chand (Wis) ... Chandler's Wisconsin Reports [*1849-52*] [*A publication*]   (DLA)
Chaney .... Chaney's Michigan Reports [*37-58 Michigan*] [*A publication*]   (DLA)
Chaney (Mich) ... Chaney's Michigan Reports [*37-58 Michigan*] [*A publication*]   (DLA)
Chang Ed ... Changing Education [*A publication*]
Change (Par) ... Change (Paris) [*A publication*]
Changes ...... Changes Socialist Monthly [*A publication*]
Changing T ... Changing Times [*A publication*]
Chang Times ... Changing Times [*A publication*]

CHanK....... Kings County Free Library, Hanford, CA [*Library symbol*] [*Library of Congress*] (LCLS)
Channel Isles Annu Anthol ... Channel Isles Annual Anthology [*A publication*]
Chanoyu Q ... Chanoyu Quarterly [*A publication*]
CHAN PROC ... Chancery Proceedings [*British*] (ROG)
Chan Rep C ... Reports in Chancery [*21 English Reprint*] [*1615-1710*] [*A publication*] (DLA)
CHANS..... Chanson [*Song*] [*Music*]
CHANSEC ... Channel Committee Secretary [*NATO*] (NATG)
Chan Sentinel ... Chancery Sentinel [*New York*] [*A publication*] (DLA)
CHANT CERT ... Chantry Certificates [*British*] (ROG)
Chantiers Fr ... Chantiers de France [*A publication*]
Chantiers Mag ... Chantiers Magazine [*France*] [*A publication*]
Chan Toon ... Leading Cases on Buddhist Law [*A publication*] (DLA)
CHAN-TV ... Vancouver, BC [*Television station call letters*]
CHAN-TV-4 ... Courtenay, BC [*Television station call letters*]
CHAOS..... Cannon Hunters Association of Seattle (EA)
CHAOTIC ... Computer and Human-Assisted Organization of a Technical Information Center [*National Institute of Standards and Technology*]
CHAP........ Chapel
CHAP........ Chapelry [*Geographical division*] [*British*]
CHAP........ Chaplain
CHAP........ Chapman [*One who sells in a cheaping or market*] [*Said to be origin of "chap," meaning "fellow"*]
Chap........... Chappell [*Record label*] [*Great Britain*]
CHAP........ Chapter (AFM)
CHAP........ Charring Ablation Program [*NASA*]
CHAP........ Children Have a Potential [*Program for handicapped or disturbed children of Air Force personnel*] (AFM)
CHAP........ Composite HTGR [*High-Temperature Gas-Cooled Reactor*] Analysis Program [*Nuclear energy*] (NRCH)
CHAP........ Comprehensive Health Assessments and Primary Care for Children [*Proposed*]
CHAP........ Contractor-Held Air Force Property (AFM)
CHAP........ Longlac, ON [*AM radio station call letters*]
CHAPAR... Chaplain Area Representative [*Air Force*]
CHAP/FAAR ... Chaparral/Forward Area Alert RADAR [*Military*] (RDA)
CHAP-GEN ... Chaplain-General to the Forces [*British*] (ROG)
CHAPGRU ... Cargo Handling and Port Group [*Navy*] (NVT)
CHAP HO ... Chapter House [*British*] (ROG)
CHAP I of S ... Chapter Illuminators of Sweden [*Freemasonry*] (ROG)
CHAPL....... Chaplain
Ch App....... Chambre d'Appel [*French*] [*Legal term*] (DLA)
Ch App....... Court of Appeal in Chancery [*England*] (DLA)
Chapp......... Customers Having Abundant Product Possibilities [*Lifestyle classification*] [*Term coined by William F. Doescher, publisher of "D & B Reports"*]
Ch App....... Law Reports, Chancery Appeal Cases [*1865-75*] [*England*] [*A publication*] (DLA)
Ch App Cas ... Chancery Appeal Cases, English Law Reports [*A publication*] (DLA)
Cha Pr........ Chapman. Practice of the Court of King's Bench [*2nd ed.*] [*1831*] [*A publication*] (DLA)
CHAPS...... ((Cholamidopropyl)dimethylammonio)propanesulfonate [*Biochemistry*]
CHAPS...... Clearinghouse Automated Payments System [*Banking*] [*London*]
CHAPS...... Community Health Action Planning Service
Chap & Sh ... Chappell and Shoard. Copyright [*1863*] [*A publication*] (DLA)
CHAPSO.... (Cholamidopropyl)dimethylammonio(hydroxy)Propanesulfonate [*Organic chemistry*]
Chap St J ... Chaplain of the Order of St. John of Jerusalem
CHAR........ Chaparral Resources, Inc. [*Denver, CO*] [*NASDAQ symbol*] (NQ)
CHAR........ Character (KSC)
Char........... Characteres [*of Theophrastus*] [*Classical studies*] (OCD)
CHAR........ Characteristic (AABC)
CHAR........ Charcoal
CHAR........ Charcoal Accumulation Rate [*Ecology*]
Char........... Charisma [*A publication*]
Char........... Charities [*A publication*]
CHAR........ Charity
CHAR........ Charter
CHAR........ Charwoman [*Slang*] [*British*] (DSUE)
CHAR........ Committee for High Arctic Scientific Research Liaison and Information Exchange [*CHARLIE*]. News Bulletin [*A publication*]
CHAR........ Committee for Hispanic Arts and Research (EA)
CHARA..... Charabanc [*Bus used for sightseeing trips*] [*Slang*] [*British*] (DSUE)
Char Acctnt Aust ... Chartered Accountant in Australia [*A publication*]
CHARC..... Characteristic (FAAC)
Char Cham Cas ... Charley's Chamber Cases [*1875-76*] [*England*] [*A publication*] (DLA)
Chard......... Chardon du Dol et de la Fraude [*A publication*] (DLA)
CHAR-FM ... Alert, NT [*FM radio station call letters*]
CHARGE.. Coloforma, Heart Disease, Arrested Growth or Development, Genital Hypoplasia, and Ear Abnormalities [*Medicine*]
Charged React Polym ... Charged and Reactive Polymers [*A publication*]

CHARGUID ... Character Guidance [*Army*] (AABC)
CHARL ..... Charlton Kings [*Urban district in England*]
Charl Cha Cas ... Charley's Chamber Cases [*1875-76*] [*England*] [*A publication*] (DLA)
Charles Rennie Mackintosh Soc Newsletter (Glasgow) ... Charles Rennie Mackintosh Society. Newsletter (Glasgow) [*A publication*]
Charley Ch Cas ... Charley's Chamber Cases [*1875-76*] [*England*] [*A publication*] (DLA)
Charley Pr Cas ... Charley's Practice Cases [*1875-81*] [*England*] [*A publication*] (DLA)
Charlot Obs ... Charlotte Observer [*A publication*]
Charlotte Med J ... Charlotte Medical Journal [*A publication*]
Charl Pl ..... Charley's Pleading under the Judicature Acts [*A publication*] (DLA)
Charl Pr Cas ... Charley's Practice Cases [*1875-81*] [*England*] [*A publication*] (DLA)
Charl R ...... [*Robert M.*] Charlton's Georgia Reports [*1811-37*] [*A publication*] (DLA)
Charl RM .. [*Robert M.*] Charlton's Georgia Reports [*1811-37*] [*A publication*] (DLA)
Charl RP Stat ... Charley's Real Property Statutes [*A publication*] (DLA)
Charlstn G ... Charleston Gazette [*A publication*]
Charlt........ [*T. U. P.*] Charlton's Georgia Reports [*A publication*] (DLA)
Charlt........ [*Robert M.*] Charlton's Georgia Reports [*1811-37*] [*A publication*] (DLA)
Charlt (GA) ... [*Robert M.*] Charlton's Georgia Reports [*1811-37*] [*A publication*] (DLA)
Charlton's R ... [*Robert M.*] Charlton's Georgia Reports [*1811-37*] [*A publication*] (DLA)
Charlton's (Rob't M) Rep ... [*Robert M.*] Charlton's Georgia Reports [*1811-37*] [*A publication*] (DLA)
Charlt RM ... [*Robert M.*] Charlton's Georgia Reports [*1811-37*] [*A publication*] (DLA)
Charlt T U P ... [*T. U. P.*] Charlton's Georgia Reports [*A publication*] (DLA)
Charl T U P ... [*T. U. P.*] Charlton's Georgia Reports [*A publication*] (DLA)
CHARM.... CAA [*Civil Aeronautics Authority*] High-Altitude Remote Monitoring
CHARM.... Coastal Habitat Fisheries Assessment Research Mensuration [*National Oceanic and Atmospheric Administration*]
CHARM.... Complex Hazardous Air Release Model
Char Merc ... Charta Mercatoria [*Latin*] [*A publication*] (DLA)
Char Pr Cas ... Charley's Practice Cases [*1875-81*] [*England*] [*A publication*] (DLA)
Char R........ Charities Review [*A publication*]
CHART ..... Charta [*Paper*] [*Pharmacy*]
CHART ..... Clearinghouse for Augmenting Resources for Training [*DoD*]
CHART ..... Computerized Hierarchy and Relationship Table
Chart.......... Rotulus Chartarum [*Charter Roll*] [*Latin*] [*A publication*] (DLA)
CHARTAC ... Chartered Accountant
Chart Acc in Aust ... Chartered Accountant in Australia [*A publication*] (APTA)
Chart Acc Aust ... Chartered Accountant in Australia [*A publication*]
Chart Accnt in Aust ... Chartered Accountant in Australia [*A publication*] (APTA)
Chart Accountant in Aust ... Chartered Accountant in Australia [*A publication*] (APTA)
Chart Acct ... Chartered Accountant in Australia [*A publication*] (APTA)
Chart Antiq ... Chartae Antiquae [*A publication*] (DLA)
CHART BIB ... Charta Bibula [*Blotting Paper*] [*Latin*]
Chart Build ... Chartered Builder [*A publication*] (APTA)
Chart Builder ... Chartered Builder [*A publication*] (APTA)
CHART CERAT ... Charta Cerata [*Waxed Paper*] [*Pharmacy*]
Chart Eng ... Chartered Engineer [*A publication*] (APTA)
Chart Engr ... Chartered Engineer [*A publication*]
Chartered Accountant Aust ... Chartered Accountant in Australia [*A publication*] (APTA)
Chartered Inst Transport J ... Chartered Institute of Transport. Journal [*A publication*]
Chartered Surveyor Bldg & Quantity Surveying Qly ... Chartered Surveyor. Building and Quantity Surveying Quarterly [*A publication*]
Chartered Surveyor Urban Qly ... Chartered Surveyor. Urban Quarterly [*A publication*]
Chart Forest ... Charta de Foresta [*Charter of the Forest*] [*Latin*] [*A publication*] (DLA)
Chart Foresta ... Charta de Foresta [*Charter of the Forest*] [*Latin*] [*A publication*] (DLA)
Chart Inst Transp J ... Chartered Institute of Transport. Journal [*England*] [*A publication*]
Chart Land Surv Chart Miner Surv ... Chartered Land Surveyor/Chartered Minerals Surveyor [*A publication*]
Chart Mech E ... Chartered Mechanical Engineer [*A publication*]
Chart Mech Eng ... Chartered Mechanical Engineer [*A publication*]
Chart Mech Engr ... Chartered Mechanical Engineer [*A publication*]
Chart Munic Eng ... Chartered Municipal Engineer [*A publication*]
Chart Quant Surv ... Chartered Quantity Surveyor [*A publication*]
Chart Sec ... Chartered Secretary [*A publication*] (APTA)
Chart Secretary ... Chartered Secretary [*A publication*]
Chart Surv ... Chartered Surveyor [*Later, Chartered Surveyor Weekly*] [*A publication*]

Chart Surv Land Hydrogr Miner Q ... Chartered Surveyor. Land Hydrographic and Minerals Quarterly [*England*] [*A publication*]
Chart Surv Rural Q ... Chartered Surveyor. Rural Quarterly [*England*] [*A publication*]
Chart Surv Wkly ... Chartered Surveyor Weekly [*A publication*]
CHARTUL ... Chartula [*A Small Paper*] [*Pharmacy*]
CHAS .... Cambridgeshire and Huntingdonshire Archaeological Society [*A publication*]
CHAS .... Center for Health Administration Studies [*University of Chicago*] [*Research center*]   (RCD)
CHAS .... Chambers
CHAS .... Chassis   (MSA)
CHAS .... Co-Operative Housing Advice Service [*Victoria, Australia*]
Chase .... Chase's United States Circuit Court Decisions [*A publication*]   (DLA)
CHASE ...... Comet Halley American Southern-Hemisphere Expedition
CHASE ...... Cornell Hotel Administration Simulation Exercise [*Computer-programmed management game*]
CHASE ...... Cut Holes and Sink 'Em [*Navy ammunition disposal project*]
Chase Coal ... Coal Situation (Chase Bank) [*A publication*]
Chase Dec ... Chase's United States Circuit Court Decisions [*A publication*]   (DLA)
Chase Econ Bul ... Chase Economic Bulletin [*A publication*]
Chase Econ Observer ... Chase Economic Observer [*A publication*]
Chase Fin ... Chase Manhattan Bank. International Finance [*A publication*]
Chase Obsv ... Chase Economic Observer [*A publication*]
Chase's Bl ... Chase's Blackstone [*A publication*]   (DLA)
Chase's St .. Chase's Statutes at Large [*Ohio*] [*A publication*]   (DLA)
Chase Steph Dig Ev ... Chase on Stephens' Digest of Evidence [*A publication*]   (DLA)
Chase Tr .... Chase's Trial (Impeachment) by the United States Senate [*A publication*]   (DLA)
CHAS-FM ... Sault Ste. Marie, ON [*FM radio station call letters*]
CHASG ..... Advise Individual Concerned of Change of Assignment [*Military*]
CHASNAVSHIPY ... Charleston Naval Shipyard [*South Carolina*]
CHAST ...... Centre for Human Aspects of Science and Technology [*University of Sydney*] [*Australia*]
CHAT .... Chatham Manufacturing Co. [*Elkin, NC*] [*NASDAQ symbol*]   (NQ)
ChAT .... Choline Acetyl-Transferase [*Also, CAT, ChA, ChAc*] [*An enzyme*]
CHAT .... CLIRA [*Closed-Loop In-Reactor Assembly*] Holddown Assembly Tool [*Nuclear energy*]   (NRCH)
CHAT .... Coalition to Halt Auto Theft   (EA)
CHAT .... Crisis Home Alert Technique
CHAT .... Medicine Hat, AB [*AM radio station call letters*]
Cha Ti .... Changing Times [*A publication*]
CHATNE .. Chatelaine [*Jewelry*]   (ROG)
CHATT ...... Chatteris [*Urban district in England*]
CHAT-TV ... Medicine Hat, AB [*Television station call letters*]
CHAT-TV-1 ... Pivot, AB [*Television station call letters*]
CHAUC ..... Chaucer [*Fourteenth century English poet*]   (ROG)
Chaucer R .. Chaucer Review [*A publication*]
Chaucer Rev ... Chaucer Review [*A publication*]
Chaucer Soc ... Chaucer Society [*A publication*]
CHAUFF ... Chauffeur   (DSUE)
Chauf Vent Cond ... Chauffage, Ventilation, Conditionnement [*France*] [*A publication*]
ChauR .... Chaucer Review [*A publication*]
CHA-US .... Catholic Health Association of the United States   (EA)
Chaut .... Chautauquan [*A publication*]
CHAU-TV ... Carleton Place, PQ [*Television station call letters*]
CHAVB ..... Chemie-Anlagen und Verfahren [*A publication*]
CHAW .... Command Home All the Way [*Military*]   (CAAL)
CHAW .... Cuspidore Hitters Association Worldwide   (EA)
CHawN ...... National Cash Register Co., Electronics Division, Hawthorne, CA [*Library symbol*] [*Library of Congress*]   (LCLS)
CHawNo ... Northrop Corp., Aircraft Division, Hawthorne, CA [*Library symbol*] [*Library of Congress*]   (LCLS)
Chayanica Geol ... Chayanica Geologica [*A publication*]
CHAY-FM ... Barrie, ON [*FM radio station call letters*]
CHaZaL ..... Chakhamenu Zikhronam Livrakhah [*A publication*]   (BJA)
Ch B .... Bachelor of Chemistry
CHB .... Bay Area Library and Information System, Hayward, CA [*Library symbol*] [*Library of Congress*]   (LCLS)
CHB .... Cargo Handling Battalion [*Obsolete*] [*Army*]
CHB .... Center Halfback [*Soccer*]
CHB .... Chain Home Beamed [*Aviation*]
CHB .... Champion Enterprises, Inc. [*AMEX symbol*]   (SPSG)
chb .... Chibcha [*MARC language code*] [*Library of Congress*]   (LCCP)
Ch B .... Chirurgiae Baccalaureus [*Bachelor of Surgery*]
CHB .... Cholera Toxin B [*Medicine*]
CHB .... Christlicher Holz- und Bauarbeiterverband der Schweiz [*Christian Building and Woodworkers of Switzerland*]   (EY)
CHB .... Chronic Hepatitis B [*Medicine*]
CHB .... Church [*Alaska*] [*Seismograph station code, US Geological Survey*]   (SEIS)
CHB .... Commission on Highway Beautification

CHB .... Commonwealth Heraldry Board [*Papatoetoe, New Zealand*]   (EAIO)
CHB .... Complete Heart Block [*Medicine*]
CHB .... Composted Hardwood Barks
CHB .... Cooperative Housing Bulletin [*A publication*]   (EAAP)
CHBA .... Canadian Home Builders' Association
CHBA .... Congenital Heinz Body Hemolytic Anemia [*Medicine*]
CHBC .... Capitol Hill Burro Club   (EA)
CHBC .... Cleveland Hockey Booster Club   (EA)
CHBC-TV ... Kelowna, BC [*Television station call letters*]
CHBD .... Chalk Board [*Technical drawings*]
CHBEA ...... Chemische Berichte [*A publication*]
Ch B Ex ...... Chief Baron of the Exchequer [*British*]   (DLA)
CHBIE4 ...... Chronobiology International [*A publication*]
Ch Bills ..... Chitty on Bills [*A publication*]   (DLA)
CHBL .... Chesapeake Biological Laboratories, Inc. [*NASDAQ symbol*]   (NQ)
Ch Black .... Chase's Blackstone [*A publication*]   (DLA)
Ch Black .... Chitty's Edition of Blackstone's Commentaries [*A publication*]   (DLA)
CHBOSN .. Chief Boatswain [*Navy rating*] [*Obsolete*]
CHBUAER ... Chief of the Bureau of Aeronautics [*Obsolete*] [*Navy*]
CHBUDOCKS ... Chief of the Bureau of Yards and Docks [*Obsolete*] [*Navy*]
CHBUMED ... Chief of the Bureau of Medicine and Surgery [*Navy*]
CHBUORD ... Chief of the Bureau of Ordnance [*Obsolete*] [*Navy*]
CHBUPERS ... Chief of the Bureau of Naval Personnel
Ch Burn's J ... Chitty's Edition of Burn's Justice [*A publication*]   (DLA)
CHBUSANDA ... Chief of the Bureau of Supplies and Accounts [*Obsolete*] [*Navy*]
CHBUSHIPS ... Chief of the Bureau of Ships [*Obsolete*] [*Navy*]
CHBX-TV ... Sault Ste. Marie, ON [*Television station call letters*]
CHC .... Cargo Handling Charge [*Shipping*]   (DS)
CHC .... Cell Hemoglobin Concentration [*Biochemistry, medicine*]
CHC .... Centro Hispano Catolico [*Catholic Spanish Center*]   (EA)
CHC .... Chabot College, Hayward, CA [*Library symbol*] [*Library of Congress*]   (LCLS)
CHC .... Chance   (FAAC)
CHC .... Chancellor Energy Resources, Inc. [*Toronto Stock Exchange symbol*]
CHC .... Channel Control   (BUR)
CHC .... Chapel Hill [*North Carolina*] [*Seismograph station code, US Geological Survey*] [*Closed*]   (SEIS)
CH-in-C ..... Chaplain-in-Chief [*British*]
CHC .... Chaplain Corps
CHC .... Check Coil
CHC .... Chestnut Hill College [*Pennsylvania*]
CHC .... Chile Economic Report [*A publication*]
CHC .... Chiles Offshore Corp. [*AMEX symbol*]   (SPSG)
ChC .... Chinese Culture [*A publication*]
CHC .... Choke Coil   (AAG)
CHC .... Christchurch [*New Zealand*] [*Airport symbol*]   (OAG)
ChC .... Christian Century [*A publication*]
CHC .... Christian Heritage Center   (EA)
CHC .... Christian Heritage College [*El Cajon, CA*]
CHC .... Clathrin Heavy Chain [*Genetics*]
CHC .... Clean Harbors Cooperative   (EA)
CHC .... Clerk to the House of Commons   (DLA)
CHC .... Coalitions for Health Care   (EA)
CHC .... College of the Holy Cross [*Worcester, MA*]
CHC .... Committee for Handgun Control   (EA)
CHC .... Commonwealth Housing Commission [*Australia*]
CHC .... Community Health Center
CHC .... Community Health Computing
CHC .... Community Health Council [*British*]
CHC .... Community of the Holy Cross [*Anglican religious community*]
CHC .... Confederate High Command, International [*Later, AT*] [*An association*]   (EA)
CHC .... Congressional Hispanic Caucus   (EA)
CHC .... Corrected Head Count
CHC .... Crouse-Hinds Company
CHC .... Cyclohexylamine Carbonate [*Corrosion prevention*]
Ch¹c .... Christchurch Chromosome
Ch Ca .... Cases in Chancery [*England*] [*A publication*]   (DLA)
CHCA .... Chaco Canyon National Monument
Ch Ca Ch ... Choyce's Cases in Chancery [*1557-1606*] [*England*] [*A publication*]   (DLA)
CHCARP ... Chief Carpenter [*Navy rating*] [*Obsolete*]
Ch Cas .... Cases in Chancery [*England*] [*A publication*]   (DLA)
Ch Cas in Ch ... Choyce's Cases in Chancery [*1557-1606*] [*England*] [*A publication*]   (DLA)
Ch Cas Ch ... Choyce's Cases in Chancery [*1557-1606*] [*England*] [*A publication*]   (DLA)
Ch Cas (Eng) ... Cases in Chancery [*England*] [*A publication*]   (DLA)
CHCC .... Chancellor Computer Corporation [*Scotts Valley, CA*] [*NASDAQ symbol*]   (NQ)
CHCC .... Montefiore-Morrisania Comprehensive Health Care Center [*Research center*]   (RCD)
ChCen .... Christian Century [*A publication*]
CHCF .... Component Handling and Cleaning Facility [*Energy Research and Development Administration*]
CHCGA ..... Chishitsu Chosajo Geppo [*A publication*]

CHCGAX .. Chishitsu Chosajo Geppo [*A publication*]
CHCH .... Chickamauga and Chattanooga National Military Park
CHCH .... Church (ROG)
CHCH .... (Cyclohexenyl)cyclohexanone [*Organic chemistry*]
Ch Ch .... Upper Canada Chancery Chambers Reports [*A publication*] (DLA)
Ch Cham .... Upper Canada Chancery Chambers Reports [*A publication*] (DLA)
Ch Chamb ... Chancery Chambers [*Upper Canada*] (DLA)
Ch Chamb (Can) ... Chancery Chambers [*Upper Canada*] (DLA)
C & H Char Tr ... Cooke and Harwood's Charitable Trusts [*2nd ed.*] [*1867*] [*A publication*] (DLA)
CHCH-TV ... Hamilton, ON [*Television station call letters*]
ChChW ...... Chronik der Christlichen Welt [*A publication*] (BJA)
CHCIVENGS ... Chief of Civil Engineers [*Army*]
CHC J .... Children's Health Care. Journal of the Association for the Care of Children's Health [*A publication*]
CHCK .... Chief Cook [*Navy rating*] [*Obsolete*]
CHCL .... Medley, AB [*AM radio station call letters*]
Ch & Cl Cas ... Cripp's Church and Clergy Cases [*1847-50*] [*England*] [*A publication*] (DLA)
CHCLG ..... Cahiers d'Histoire Publies par les Universites de Clermont-Lyon-Grenoble [*A publication*]
CHCLS...... Canister Harpoon Control and Launch System (MCD)
CHCM....... Cell Hemoglobin Concentration Mean [*Biochemistry, medicine*]
CHCM....... Marystown, NF [*AM radio station call letters*]
ChCMV ..... Chrysanthemum Chlorotic Mottle Viroid
CHCO........ City Holding Co. [*NASDAQ symbol*] (NQ)
CHCOD..... Chemical Concepts [*A publication*]
CH COLL ... Christ's College [*Cambridge University*] (ROG)
Ch Col Op ... Chalmers' Colonial Opinions [*England*] [*A publication*] (DLA)
CHCOMNAVAIRSYS ... Chief, Command Naval Air Systems [*Later, NAVAIR*]
CHCP .... Chartercorp [*NASDAQ symbol*] (NQ)
CHCP .... Chief Justice of the Common Pleas [*British*] (DLA)
CHCP .... Correctional Health Care Program
CHCR .... Chancellor Corp. [*Boston, MA*] [*NASDAQ symbol*] (NQ)
Ch Cr L ...... Chitty's Criminal Law [*A publication*] (DLA)
CHCR-TV ... Campbellton, NB [*Television station call letters*]
CHCS .... Cabin Humidity Control Subsystem [*Aviation*] (NASA)
CHCSS ...... Chief Central Security Service
CHCT .... Caffeine Halothane Challenge Test [*Clinical chemistry*]
CHCU .... Channel Control Unit
CHCW .... Conference for Health Council Work [*Later, Conference on Community Health Planning*]
CHD .... Campaign for Human Development (EA)
C(H & D) ... Center (Hospital and Domiciliary) [*Veterans Administration*]
CHD .... Centre for Human Development [*British*] (CB)
CHD .... Chaldron [*Unit of measurement*]
CHD .... Chandler, AZ [*Location identifier*] [*FAA*] (FAAL)
CHD .... Chediak-Higashi Disease [*Medicine*]
CHD .... Chelsea Resources [*Vancouver Stock Exchange symbol*]
CHD .... Child (ROG)
CHD .... Childhood Disease [*Medicine*]
ChD........... Chile Democratico (EA)
ChD........... Chirurgiae Doctor [*Doctor of Surgery*]
CHD .... Chord (KSC)
Ch D.......... Christian Doctrine [*A publication*]
CHD .... Chronic Hemodialysis [*Nephrology*]
CHD .... Church & Dwight Co., Inc. [*NYSE symbol*] (SPSG)
CH and D... Cold, Hungry, and Dry [*Slang*]
CHD .... Committee for Handicapable Dancers (EA)
CHD .... Congenital Heart Disease [*Medicine*]
CHD .... Cordell Hull Dam [*TVA*]
CHD .... Coronary Heart Disease [*Medicine*]
CHD .... Correctional Holding Detachment [*Military*] (AABC)
CHD .... Cyclohexadiene [*Organic chemistry*]
Ch D.......... Doctor of Chemistry
Ch D.......... English Law Reports, Chancery Division [*A publication*] (DLA)
CHDB....... Compatible High-Density Bipolar Code [*Telecommunications*] (TEL)
CHDC....... Canadian Housing Design Council [*CMHC*]
CHDC....... Cyclohexenedicarboxylic Acid [*Organic chemistry*]
CHDCA..... Comptes Rendus des Seances. Academie des Sciences. Serie C. Sciences Chimiques [*A publication*]
Ch D 2d...... English Law Reports, Chancery Division, Second Series [*A publication*] (DLA)
CHDDA..... Comptes Rendus des Seances. Academie des Sciences. Serie D. Sciences Naturelles [*A publication*]
CHDEA ..... Child Development [*A publication*]
CHDEDZ.. Contributions to Human Development [*A publication*]
CHDID...... Chimica Didactica [*A publication*]
Ch Dig........ Chaney's Digest, Michigan Reports [*A publication*] (DLA)
C & H Dig ... Coventry and Hughes's Digest of the Common Law Reports [*A publication*] (DLA)
CHDIR ...... Change Directory [*Data processing*]
Ch Div........ English Law Reports, Chancery Division [*A publication*]

Ch Div (Eng) ... English Law Reports, Chancery Division [*A publication*] (DLA)
Ch Div'l Ct ... Chancery Divisional Court [*England*] (DLA)
CHDL....... Computer Hardware Description Language
CHDLG....... Chief, Defense Liaison Group (CINC)
CHDN .... Children (ROG)
CHE.......... Cahiers d'Histoire Egyptienne [*Cairo*] [*A publication*]
CHE.......... Cargo Handling Equipment [*Army*]
CHE.......... Channel End (BUR)
CHE.......... Chapel of Ease [*Church of England*]
CHE.......... Cheb [*Eger*] [*Czechoslovakia*] [*Seismograph station code, US Geological Survey*] [*Closed*] (SEIS)
che.......... Chechen [*MARC language code*] [*Library of Congress*] (LCCP)
CHE.......... Chemed Corp. [*NYSE symbol*] (SPSG)
Ch E.......... Chemical Engineer
CHE.......... Cheque [*British*] (ROG)
CHE.......... Chestnut Hill College, Philadelphia, PA [*OCLC symbol*] (OCLC)
ChE.......... Chiake Epitheoresis [*A publication*]
Ch E.......... Chief Engineer [*British military*] (DMA)
CHE.......... Chief Executive [*A publication*]
ChE.......... Cholinesterase [*An enzyme*]
CHE.......... Chronicle of Higher Education [*A publication*]
CHE.......... Coalition for Health and the Environment (EA)
CHE.......... Commonwealth Human Ecology Council [*British*]
CHE.......... Container Handling Equipment
CHE.......... Continuing Health Education (MCD)
CHE.......... Cuadernos de Historia de Espana [*A publication*]
CHE.......... Hayden, CO [*Location identifier*] [*FAA*] (FAAL)
CHe.......... Healdsburg Carnegie Public Library, Healdsburg, CA [*Library symbol*] [*Library of Congress*] (LCLS)
CHE.......... Switzerland [*ANSI three-letter standard code*] (CNC)
CHE.......... Top Flight Air Service, Inc. [*Tampa, FL*] [*FAA designator*] (FAAC)
CHEA .... Christian Home Educators Association (EA)
CHEA .... Commonwealth Hansard Editors Association (EAIO)
CHEAD .... Conference for Higher Education in Art and Design [*British*]
CHEAM .... Centre des Hautes Etudes Administratives sur l'Afrique et l'Asie Modernes [*Center for Advanced Administrative Study on Modern Africa and Asia*]
CHEAO..... Coalition of Higher Education Assistance Organizations (EA)
CHEAR ..... Council on Higher Education in the American Republics [*Later, ICHE*]
CHEAR ..... National Foundation for Children's Hearing Education and Research (EA)
CHEC........ Cascade Holistic Economic Consultants (EA)
CHEC........ Channel Evaluation and Call (IEEE)
CHEC........ Checkered [*Navigation markers*]
CHEC........ Commonwealth Human Ecology Council [*London, England*] (EAIO)
CHEC........ Community Hypertension Evaluation Clinic [*New Jersey*]
CHEC........ Comprehensive Health and Emergency Care [*Medicine*]
CHEC........ Lethbridge, AB [*AM radio station call letters*]
Check........ Checkpoint [*A publication*]
CHECKSUM ... Summation Check [*Communications transmissions*]
CHECMATE ... Compact High-Energy Capacitor Module Advanced Technology Experiment [*For development of the rail gun*]
CHECO...... Contemporary Historical Examination Current Operations [*Air Force*] (AFM)
CHED........ Children and Education Unit [*Australian Broadcasting Corp.*]
C H Ed .... Chronicle of Higher Education [*A publication*]
CHED........ Edmonton, AB [*AM radio station call letters*]
CHEDA ..... Chemical Engineering Education [*A publication*]
CHEDC ..... Chemie. Experiment und Didaktik [*A publication*]
CHEEA ..... Chemical Engineering [*New York*] [*A publication*]
Cheev Med Jur ... Cheever's Medical Jurisprudence for India [*A publication*] (DLA)
CHEF .... Chefs International, Inc. [*Point Pleasant Beach, NJ*] [*NASDAQ symbol*] (NQ)
CHEF .... Chemistry of High Elevation Fog Project [*Environment Canada*]
CHEF .... Chicken Embryo Fibroblast [*Cytology*]
CHEF .... Chinese Hamster Embryo Fibroblast [*Cytology*]
CHEF .... Citizens Honest Elections Foundation
CHEF .... Comprehensive Health Education Foundation (EA)
CHEF .... Contour-Clamped Homogeneous Electric Field [*Instrumentation*]
CHEF .... Granby, PQ [*AM radio station call letters*]
CHE INC... Center for Human Environments Associates, Incorporated [*City University of New York*] [*Research center*] (RCD)
Cheiron Tamil Nadu J Vet Sci Anim Husb ... Cheiron. The Tamil Nadu Journal of Veterinary Science and Animal Husbandry [*A publication*]
CHEJ......... Canadian Home Economics Journal [*A publication*]
Cheju Univ J ... Cheju University. Journal [*A publication*]
CHEK .... Checkpoint Systems, Inc. [*Thorofare, NJ*] [*NASDAQ symbol*] (NQ)
CHEKA ..... Chrezvychainaya Komissiya po Borbe s Kontrrevolutisiei i Sabotazhem [*Extraordinary Commission for Combating Counterrevolution and Sabotage; Soviet secret police organization, 1917-1921*]

CHEKAL...   Chung-Hua Min Kuo Hsiao Erh K'o I Hsueh Hui Tsa Chi [*A publication*]
Chekh Biol ... Chekhoslovatskaya Biologiya [*A publication*]
Chekh Fiziol ... Chekhoslovatskaya Fiziologiya [*A publication*]
Chekh Med Obozr ... Chekhoslovatskoe Meditsinskoe Obozrenie [*A publication*]
Chekhoslov Biol ... Chekhoslovatskaya Biologiya [*A publication*]
CHEK-TV ... Victoria, BC [*Television station call letters*]
CHEK-TV-5 ... Campbell River, BC [*Television station call letters*]
CHEL .... Cambridge History of English Literature
CHEL .... Chain Home Extra Low [*Aviation*]
Chel .... Chelsea [*A publication*]
Chelates Anal Chem ... Chelates in Analytical Chemistry [*A publication*]
Chel Biosfera ... Chelovek i Biosfera [*A publication*]
CHELEC ... Chief Electrician [*Navy rating*] [*Obsolete*]
C & H Elec Cas ... Clarke and Hall's Cases of Contested Elections in Congress [*1789-1834*] [*United States*] [*A publication*]   (DLA)
CHELM .... Chelmsford [*City in England*]
CHELMSF ... Chelmsford [*City in England*]   (ROG)
CHELT .... Cheltenham [*City in England*]
CHELTM .... Cheltenham [*City in England*]   (ROG)
CHEM .... Chemical [*or Chemistry*]   (AFM)
CHEM .... Chemist
CHEM .... Chempower, Inc. [*NASDAQ symbol*]   (NQ)
CHEM .... Community Health Education Monographs [*A publication*]
CHem .... Hemet Public Library, Hemet, CA [*Library symbol*] [*Library of Congress*]   (LCLS)
ChemAb ..... Chemical Abstracts [*A publication*]
Chem Abs Macromol ... Chemical Abstracts. Macromolecular Sections [*A publication*]
Chem Abstr ... Chemical Abstracts [*A publication*]
Chem Abstr Cum Subj Index ... Chemical Abstracts. Decennial Cumulative Subject Index [*A publication*]
Chem Abstr Jpn ... Chemical Abstracts of Japan [*A publication*]
Chem Abstr Serv Source Index ... Chemical Abstracts Service. Source Index [*A publication*]
Chem Abstr Subj Ind ... Chemical Abstracts. Annual Subject Index [*A publication*]
Chem Ackersmann ... Chemische Ackersmann [*A publication*]
Chem Age ..   Chemical Age [*A publication*]
Chem Age India ... Chemical Age of India [*A publication*]
Chem Age Int ... Chemical Age International [*A publication*]
Chem Age (Lond) ... Chemical Age (London) [*A publication*]
Chem Agric Int Congr ... Chemistry in Agriculture. International Congress [*A publication*]
Chem Ag Sv ... Chemical Age Survey [*A publication*]
Chem Anal (New York) ... Chemical Analysis. A Series of Monographs on Analytical Chemistry and Its Applications (New York) [*A publication*]
Chem Anal Ser Monogr Anal Chem Appl ... Chemical Analysis. A Series of Monographs on Analytical Chemistry and Its Applications [*A publication*]
Chem Anal (Warszawa) ... Chemia Analityczna (Warszawa) [*A publication*]
Chem Analyse ... Chemische Analyse [*A publication*]
Chem-Anlagen Verfahren ... Chemie-Anlagen und Verfahren [*A publication*]
CHEMAPOL ... Podnik Zahranicniho Obchodu pro Dovoz a Vyvoz Chemickych Vyrobku a Surovin [*Foreign Trade Enterprise for the Import and Export of Chemical Products and Raw Materials*]
Chem Appar ... Chemische Apparatur [*A publication*]
Chem Arb Werk Labor ... Chemie Arbeit in Werk und Labor [*A publication*]
CHEMASIA ... Asian International Chemical and Process Engineering and Contracting Show and Conference   (TSPED)
Chem Aust ... Chemistry in Australia [*A publication*]
Chem Ber ... Chemische Berichte [*A publication*]
Chem Biochem Amino Acids Pept Proteins ... Chemistry and Biochemistry of Amino Acids, Peptides, and Proteins [*A publication*]
Chem-Bio In ... Chemico-Biological Interactions [*A publication*]
Chem-Biol Interact ... Chemico-Biological Interactions [*A publication*]
Chem-Biol Interactions ... Chemico-Biological Interactions [*A publication*]
Chem Biol (Tokyo) ... Chemistry and Biology (Tokyo) [*A publication*]
Chem Biomed Environ Inst ... Chemical, Biomedical, and Environmental Instrumentation [*A publication*]
Chem & Biomed Environ Instrum ... Chemical, Biomedical, and Environmental Instrumentation [*A publication*]
Chem Biomed and Environ Instrum ... Chemical, Biomedical, and Environmental Instrumentation [*A publication*]
Chem Bk Econ ... Chemical Bank. Weekly Economic Package [*A publication*]
Chem Bk Frct ... Chemical Bank. Economic Forecast Summary [*A publication*]
Chem Br ..... Chemistry in Britain [*A publication*]
Chem in Br ... Chemistry in Britain [*A publication*]
Chem Brit ..   Chemistry in Britain [*A publication*]
Chem in Britain ... Chemistry in Britain [*A publication*]
Chem Bull ... Chemical Bulletin [*A publication*]
Chem Bus ... Chemical Business [*A publication*]
Chem Can ..   Chemistry in Canada [*A publication*]
Chem Cda ..   Chemistry in Canada [*A publication*]
Chem Chem Ind ... Chemistry and Chemical Industry [*North Korea*] [*A publication*]
Chem Chron A ... Chemika Chronika. Section A [*A publication*]

Chem Chron B ... Chemika Chronika. Section B [*A publication*]
Chem Chron Epistem Ekdosis ... Chemika Chronika. Epistemonike Ekdosis [*Greece*] [*A publication*]
Chem Chron Genike Ekdosis ... Chemika Chronika. Genike Ekdosis [*A publication*]
Chem Color Oil Daily ... Chemical, Color, and Oil Daily [*A publication*]
Chem Color Oil Rec ... Chemical, Color, and Oil Record [*A publication*]
Chem Commun ... Chemical Communications [*Journal of the Chemical Society. Section D*] [*A publication*]
Chem Communs ... Chemical Communications [*A publication*]
Chem Commun Univ Stockholm ... Chemical Communications. University of Stockholm [*A publication*]
Chem Concepts ... Chemical Concepts [*A publication*]
Chem Control Res Inst (Ottawa) Inf Rep ... Chemical Control Research Institute (Ottawa). Information Report [*A publication*]
Chem Corps J ... Chemical Corps Journal [*A publication*]
Chem Corr ... Chemical Correspondence [*A publication*]
CHEMD .... Chemsa [*A publication*]
ChemDep ... Chemical Dependency   (OICC)
Chem Depend ... Chemical Dependencies [*A publication*]
CHEMDEX ... Chemical Index [*Database*]
Chem Digest ... Chemurgic Digest [*A publication*]
Chem Div Trans Am Soc Qual Control ... Chemical Division Transactions. American Society for Quality Control [*A publication*]
Chem Drug ... Chemist and Druggist [*A publication*]
Chem E ...... Chemical Engineer
Chem Econ ... Chemical Economy and Engineering Review [*A publication*]
Chem Econ Eng Rev ... Chemical Economy and Engineering Review [*A publication*]
Chem Educ ... Chemical Education [*Japan*] [*A publication*]
Chem Eng ... Chemical Engineer
Chem Eng ..   Chemical Engineer [*A publication*]
Chem Eng ..   Chemical Engineering [*A publication*]
Chem Eng (Aust) ... Chemical Engineering (Australia) [*A publication*]
Chem Eng Comm ... Chemical Engineering Communications [*A publication*]
Chem Eng Commun ... Chemical Engineering Communications [*A publication*]
Chem Eng Costs Q ... Chemical Engineering Costs Quarterly [*A publication*]
Chem Eng Data Ser ... Chemical and Engineering Data Series [*A publication*]
Chem Eng Educ ... Chemical Engineering Education [*A publication*]
Chem Eng Fundam ... Chemical Engineering Fundamentals [*A publication*]
Chem and Engin News ... Chemical and Engineering News [*A publication*]
Chem Eng J ... Chemical Engineering Journal [*A publication*]
Chem Eng & Min R ... Chemical Engineering and Mining Review [*A publication*]   (APTA)
Chem Eng and Min Rev ... Chemical Engineering and Mining Review [*A publication*]
Chem Eng Monogr ... Chemical Engineering Monographs [*Netherlands*] [*A publication*]
Chem & Eng N ... Chemical and Engineering News [*A publication*]
Chem Eng News ... Chemical and Engineering News [*A publication*]
Chem Engng ... Chemical Engineering [*A publication*]
Chem Engng (Aust) ... Chemical Engineering (Australia) [*A publication*]
Chem Engng Commun ... Chemical Engineering Communications [*A publication*]
Chem Engng Communications ... Chemical Engineering Communications [*A publication*]
Chem Engng J ... Chemical Engineering Journal [*A publication*]
Chem Engng Journal ... Chemical Engineering Journal [*A publication*]
Chem Engng Mining Rev ... Chemical Engineering and Mining Review [*A publication*]
Chem Engng Min Rev ... Chemical Engineering and Mining Review [*A publication*]   (APTA)
Chem & Engng News ... Chemical and Engineering News [*A publication*]
Chem Engng Prog ... Chemical Engineering Progress [*A publication*]
Chem Engng Progress ... Chemical Engineering Progress [*A publication*]
Chem Engng Res Des ... Chemical Engineering Research and Design [*A publication*]
Chem Engng Sci ... Chemical Engineering Science [*A publication*]
Chem Engng Science ... Chemical Engineering Science [*A publication*]
Chem Engng World ... Chemical Engineering World [*A publication*]
Chem Engn News ... Chemical and Engineering News [*A publication*]
Chem Eng (NY) ... Chemical Engineering (New York) [*A publication*]
Chem Eng P ... Chemical Engineering Progress [*A publication*]
Chem Eng Pr ... Chemical Engineering Progress [*A publication*]
Chem Eng Process ... Chemical Engineering and Processing [*A publication*]
Chem Eng Prog ... Chemical Engineering Progress [*A publication*]
Chem Eng Prog Monogr Ser ... Chemical Engineering Progress. Monograph Series [*A publication*]
Chem Eng Progr ... Chemical Engineering Progress [*A publication*]
Chem Eng Progr Symp Ser ... Chemical Engineering Progress. Symposium Series [*A publication*]
Chem Eng Prog Symp Ser ... Chemical Engineering Progress. Symposium Series [*A publication*]
Chem Engr ... Chemical Engineer [*A publication*]
Chem Engr Diary & Process Ind News ... Chemical Engineer Diary and Process Industries News [*A publication*]
Chem Eng Res and Des ... Chemical Engineering Research and Design [*A publication*]
Chem Engrg J ... Chemical Engineering Journal [*A publication*]
Chem Engr (Lond) ... Chemical Engineer (London) [*A publication*]

Chem Eng (Rugby) ... Chemical Engineer (Rugby) [*A publication*]
Chem Eng S ... Chem Show Guide. Special Advertising Supplement from Chemical Engineering [*A publication*]
Chem Eng Sc ... Chemical Engineering Science [*A publication*]
Chem Eng Sci ... Chemical Engineering Science [*A publication*]
Chem Eng (Tokyo) ... Chemical Engineering (Tokyo) [*A publication*]
Chem Eng Works Chem ... Chemical Engineering and the Works Chemist [*A publication*]
Chem Eng World ... Chemical Engineering World [*A publication*]
Chem Equip News ... Chemical Equipment News [*A publication*]
Chem Equip Preview ... Chemical Equipment Preview [*A publication*]
Chem Era ... Chemical Era [*India*] [*A publication*]
Chem Erde ... Chemie der Erde [*A publication*]
Chem Exp Didakt ... Chemie. Experiment und Didaktik [*A publication*]
Chem Exp Technol ... Chemie. Experiment und Technologie [*A publication*]
Chem Exp + Technol ... Chemie. Experiment und Technologie [*A publication*]
Chem Fab ... Chemische Fabrik [*A publication*]
Chem Fabr ... Chemische Fabrik [*West Germany*] [*A publication*]
Chem Fact (Tokyo) ... Chemical Factory (Tokyo) [*A publication*]
Chem Farming ... Chemical Farming [*A publication*]
Chemfasern ... Chemiefasern/Textil-Industrie [*A publication*]
CHEMFET ... Chemically Sensitive Field Effect Transistor
CHEMFICO ... Chemical International Finance & Consulting [*Belgium*]
Chem Geol ... Chemical Geology [*A publication*]
Chem Geology ... Chemical Geology [*A publication*]
Chem Heterocycl Comp ... Chemistry of Heterocyclic Compounds [*A publication*]
Chem Heterocycl Comp (USSR) ... Chemistry of Heterocyclic Compounds (USSR) [*A publication*]
Chem High Polym ... Chemistry of High Polymers [*Japan*] [*A publication*]
CHEMI ..... Chemical Engineering Modular Instruction [*Project*]
Chemia Analit ... Chemia Analityczna [*Warszawa*] [*A publication*]
Chemical Engnr ... Chemical Engineer [*A publication*]
Chemica Scr ... Chemica Scripta [*A publication*]
Chemico-Biol Interactions ... Chemico-Biological Interactions [*A publication*]
ChemID ..... Chemical Identification File [*National Library of Medicine*] [*Information service or system*] (IID)
Chemiefasern Text-Anwendungstech ... Chemiefasern und Textil-Anwendungstech [*Later, Chemiefasern/Textil-Industrie*] [*A publication*]
Chemiefasern + Text-Anwendungstech Text Ind ... Chemiefasern und Textil-Anwendungstechnik/Textil-Industrie [*A publication*]
Chemiefasern/Text-Ind ... Chemiefasern/Textil-Industrie [*A publication*]
Chemie-Ingr-Tech ... Chemie-Ingenieur-Technik [*A publication*]
Chemie Tech Landw ... Chemie und Technik in der Landwirtschaft [*A publication*]
Chem Ind ... Chemical Industries [*A publication*]
Chem Ind ... Chemical Industry and Engineering [*A publication*] (APTA)
Chem Ind ... Chemistry and Industry [*A publication*]
Chem & Ind ... Chemistry and Industry [*A publication*]
Chem Ind (Berlin) ... Chemische Industrie (Berlin) [*A publication*]
Chem Ind (Berlin) Gemeinschaftsausg ... Chemische Industrie (Berlin). Gemeinschaftsausgabe [*A publication*]
Chem Ind (Berlin) Nachrichtenausg ... Chemische Industrie (Berlin). Nachrichtenausgabe [*A publication*]
Chem Ind Dev ... Chemical Industry Developments [*A publication*]
Chem Ind (Duesseldorf) ... Chemische Industrie (Duesseldorf) [*A publication*]
Chem Ind Eng ... Chemical Industry and Engineering [*A publication*] (APTA)
Chem Ind and Engng ... Chemical Industry and Engineering [*A publication*] (APTA)
Chem Ind Int ... Chemische Industrie International [*A publication*]
Chem Ind Int (Engl Transl) ... Chemische Industrie International (English Translation) [*West Germany*] [*A publication*]
Chem Ind (Jpn) ... Chemical Industry (Japan) [*A publication*]
Chem Ind (Jpn) Suppl ... Chemical Industry (Japan). Supplement [*A publication*]
Chem Ind (Lond) ... Chemistry and Industry (London) [*A publication*]
Chem Ind NZ ... Chemistry and Industry in New Zealand [*A publication*]
Chem Ind (Tenali India) ... Chemical Industry (Tenali, India) [*A publication*]
Chem Ind Week ... Chemical Industries Week [*A publication*]
Chem Infd ... Chemischer Informationsdienst [*A publication*]
Chem Inf Dienst ... Chemischer Informationsdienst [*A publication*]
Chem Info .. Chemical Information and Computer Sciences. Journal [*A publication*]
ChemInform ... Chemischer Informationsdienst [*A publication*]
Chem Informationsdienst Anorg Phys Chem ... Chemischer Informationsdienst. Anorganische und Physikalische Chemie [*A publication*]
Chem Informationsdienst Org Chem ... Chemischer Informationsdienst. Organische Chemie [*A publication*]
Chem Ing ... Chemischer Ingenieur [*Chemical Engineer*] [*German*]
Chem-Ing-T ... Chemie-Ingenieur-Technik [*A publication*]
Chem-Ing-Tech ... Chemie-Ingenieur-Technik [*A publication*]
Chem Insgt ... Chemical Insight [*A publication*]
Chem Inst Can J Conf Am Chem Soc Abstr Pap ... Chemical Institute of Canada. Joint Conference with the American Chemical Society. Abstracts of Papers [*A publication*]
Chem Instr ... Chemical Instrumentation [*A publication*]
Chem Instrum ... Chemical Instrumentation [*A publication*]
Chem Int .... Chemistry International [*A publication*]

Chemische ... Chemische Industrie [*A publication*]
Chemistry (Kyoto) Suppl ... Chemistry (Kyoto). Supplement [*Japan*] [*A publication*]
Chem J Freunde Natur ... Chemisches Journal fuer die Freunde der Naturlehre [*A publication*]
Chem Jrl .... Chemicals and Petro-Chemicals Journal [*A publication*]
Chem Kunst Aktuell ... Chemie Kunststoffe Aktuell [*A publication*]
CHEML .... Chemical (ROG)
CHEMLAB ... Chemical Modeling Laboratory [*NIH/EPA Chemical Information System*] [*Database*]
Chem Lab Betr ... Chemie fuer Labor und Betrieb [*A publication*]
Chem Lab Rep Dep Mines (NSW) ... Chemical Laboratory Report. Department of Mines (New South Wales) [*A publication*]
Chem Leafl ... Chemistry Leaflet [*A publication*]
Chem Lett .. Chemistry Letters [*A publication*]
Chem Lide ... Chemie a Lide [*A publication*]
CHEMLINE ... Chemical Dictionary On-Line [*National Library of Medicine*] [*Bethesda, MD*] [*Database*]
Chem Listy ... Chemicke Listy [*A publication*]
Chem Listy Vedu Prum ... Chemicke Listy pro Vedu a Prumysl [*A publication*]
CHEMLY ... Chemically [*Freight*]
Chem Mag ... Chemie Magazine [*Belgium*] [*A publication*]
Chem Mark ... Chemical Markets [*A publication*]
Chem Market Reptr ... Chemical Marketing Reporter [*A publication*]
Chem Mark Rep ... Chemical Marketing Reporter [*A publication*]
Chem Metall Z ... Chemisch Metallurgische Zeitschrift [*A publication*]
Chem Met Eng ... Chemical and Metallurgical Engineering [*A publication*]
Chem & Met Eng ... Chemical and Metallurgical Engineering [*A publication*]
Chem Mikrobiol Technol Lebensm ... Chemie, Mikrobiologie, Technologie der Lebensmittel [*A publication*]
Chem Mktg Rep ... Chemical Marketing Reporter [*A publication*]
Chem Mkt R ... Chemical Marketing Reporter [*A publication*]
Chem Mkt Rept ... Chemical Marketing Reporter [*A publication*]
Chem Mon ... Chemical Monthly [*A publication*]
Chem Mutagens ... Chemical Mutagens [*A publication*]
CHEMNAME ... Chemical Name Dictionary [*Dialog Information Services, Inc.*] [*Database*]
Chem Nat Compd ... Chemistry of Natural Compounds [*A publication*]
Chem Nat Compounds ... Chemistry of Natural Compounds [*A publication*]
Chem News ... Chemical News [*A publication*]
Chem News ... Chemical News and Journal of Industrial Science [*A publication*]
Chem NZ ... Chemistry in New Zealand [*A publication*]
Chem Obz .. Chemicke Obzor [*A publication*]
Chem Oil Gas Rom ... Chemistry, Oil, and Gas in Romania [*A publication*]
CHEMOLIMPEX ... CHEMOLIMPEX Magyar Vegyiaru Kulkereskedelmi Vallalat [*CHEMOLIMPEX Foreign Trade Enterprise for Hungarian Chemical Products*]
Chemothera ... Chemotherapy [*A publication*]
Chemother Fact Sheet ... Chemotherapy Fact Sheet [*A publication*]
Chemother Pro Int Congr Chemother ... Chemotherapy. Proceedings of the International Congress of Chemotherapy [*A publication*]
Chem Pap .. Chemical Papers [*A publication*]
Chem Pet Eng ... Chemical and Petroleum Engineering [*A publication*]
Chem & Pet Engng ... Chemical and Petroleum Engineering [*A publication*]
Chem Petro-Chem J ... Chemicals and Petro-Chemicals Journal [*A publication*]
Chem Pharm ... Chemical and Pharmaceutical Bulletin [*A publication*]
Chem Pharm Bull (Tokyo) ... Chemical and Pharmaceutical Bulletin (Tokyo) [*A publication*]
Chem Pharm Tech (Dordrecht Neth) ... Chemische en Pharmaceutische Technik (Dordrecht, Netherlands) [*A publication*]
Chem Phy Fract ... Chemistry and Physics of Fracture [*A publication*]
Chem Phys ... Chemical Physics [*A publication*]
Chem Phys Carbon ... Chemistry and Physics of Carbon [*A publication*]
Chem Phys L ... Chemistry and Physics of Lipids [*A publication*]
Chem Phys Lett ... Chemical Physics Letters [*A publication*]
Chem Phys Lipids ... Chemistry and Physics of Lipids [*A publication*]
Chem Phy Solid Surf ... Chemistry and Physics of Solid Surfaces [*A publication*]
Chem Phys Solids Their Surf ... Chemical Physics of Solids and Their Surfaces [*A publication*]
Chem Phys Technol Kunst Einzeldarst ... Chemie, Physik, und Technologie der Kunststoffe in Einzeldarstellungen [*A publication*]
Chem Plant Prot ... Chemistry of Plant Protection [*A publication*]
Chem Plant (Tokyo) ... Chemical Plant (Tokyo) [*A publication*]
Chem P Lett ... Chemical Physics Letters [*A publication*]
Chem Prax ... Chemische Praxis [*A publication*]
Chem Preview ... Chemical Preview [*A publication*]
Chem Process ... Chemical Processing [*A publication*]
Chem Process Eng ... Chemical and Process Engineering [*A publication*]
Chem and Process Eng ... Chemical and Process Engineering [*A publication*]
Chem Process Eng At World ... Chemical and Process Engineering and Atomic World [*A publication*]
Chem & Process Engng ... Chemical and Process Engineering [*Later, Process Engineering*] [*A publication*]
Chem Processing ... Chemical Processing [*A publication*] (APTA)
Chem Process (London) ... Chemical Processing (London) [*A publication*]
Chem Process Rev ... Chemical Processing Review [*A publication*]

Chem Proc (Sydney) ... Chemical Processing (Sydney) [*Australia*] [*A publication*]
Chem Prod ... Chemische Produktion [*A publication*]
Chem Prod Aerosol News ... Chemical Products and Aerosol News [*A publication*]
Chem Prod Chem News ... Chemical Products and the Chemical News [*England*] [*A publication*]
Chem Progr ... Chemical Progress [*A publication*]
Chem Prum ... Chemicky Prumysl [*A publication*]
Chem Purch ... Chemical Purchasing [*A publication*]
Chem Q ...... Chemists Quarterly [*A publication*]
Chem R ...... Chemical Reviews [*A publication*]
CHEMRAWN ... Chemical Research Applied to World Need [*IUPAC*]
Chem Rdsch Mitteleur ... Chemische Rundschau fuer Mitteleuropa und der Balkan [*A publication*]
Chem Rec-Age ... Chemical Record-Age [*A publication*]
Chem Reg Rep BNA ... Chemical Regulation Reporter. Bureau of National Affairs [*A publication*]
Chem Reihe ... Chemische Reihe [*A publication*]
Chem Rev ... Chemical Reviews [*A publication*]
Chem Rev Fett Harz Ind ... Chemische Revue ueber die Fett und Harz Industrie [*A publication*]
CHEMRiC ... Chemical Monograph Referral Center [*Consumer Product Safety Commission*] [*Information service or system*]   (IID)
Chem Rund ... Chemische Rundschau [*A publication*]
Chem Rundschau ... Chemische Rundschau [*A publication*]
Chem Rundsch Farbbeilage ... Chemische Rundschau. Farbbeilage [*A publication*]
Chem Rundsch Mag ... Chemische Rundschau Magazine [*A publication*]
Chem Rundsch (Solothurn) ... Chemische Rundschau (Solothurn) [*Switzerland*] [*A publication*]
Chem Saf Data Sheet ... Chemical Safety Data Sheet [*A publication*]
CHEMSAFE ... Chemical Industry Scheme for Assistance in Freight Emergencies [*A publication*]   (APTA)
Chems Brtn ... Chemistry in Britain [*A publication*]
Chem Scr ... Chemica Scripta [*A publication*]
Chem Scripta ... Chemica Scripta [*A publication*]
CHEMSEARCH ... Chemicals Selected for Equal, Analogous, or Related Character   (DIT)
Chem Sens ... Chemical Senses [*A publication*]
Chem Senses ... Chemical Senses and Flavor [*A publication*]
Chem Sep Dev Sel Pap Int Conf Sep Sci Technol ... Chemical Separations. Developed from Selected Papers Presented at the International Conference on Separations Science and Technology [*A publication*]
CHEMSIS ... CHEM Singly Indexed Substances [*DIALOG Information Services, Inc.*] [*Database*]
Chem Soc J ... Chemical Society. Journal [*London*] [*A publication*]
Chem Soc Re ... Chemical Society. Reviews [*London*] [*A publication*]
Chem Soc Rev ... Chemical Society. Reviews [*London*] [*A publication*]
Chem Soc Spec Publ ... Chemical Society. Special Publication [*London*] [*A publication*]
Chem Speciation Bioavailability ... Chemical Speciation and Bioavailability [*A publication*]
Chem Spec Manuf Assoc Proc Mid-Year Meet ... Chemical Specialties Manufacturers Association. Proceedings of the Mid-Year Meeting [*A publication*]
ChemSTAR ... Chemical Structure Analysis Routine
Chem Stosow ... Chemia Stosowana [*A publication*]
Chem Stosow Ser A ... Chemia Stosowana. Seria A [*A publication*]
Chem Stosow Ser B ... Chemia Stosowana. Seria B [*A publication*]
Chem Strojir Stavitelstvi Pristrojova Tech ... Chemicke Strojirenstvi. Stavitelstvi a Pristrojova Technika [*A publication*]
Chem Szk ... Chemia Szkole [*A publication*]
Chem Take-Off ... Chemical Take-Off [*A publication*]
ChemTeC ... Chemical Technicians Curriculum [*Project*]
Chem Tech ... Chemical Technology [*A publication*]
Chem Tech ... Chemische Technik [*A publication*]
Chem Tech (Amsterdam) ... Chemie en Techniek (Amsterdam) [*A publication*]
Chem Tech Fabr ... Chemisch Technische Fabrikant [*A publication*]
Chem Tech Fuels Oils ... Chemistry and Technology of Fuels and Oils [*A publication*]
Chem Tech Landwirt ... Chemie und Technik in der Landwirtschaft [*A publication*]
Chem Technol ... Chemical Technology [*A publication*]
Chem Technol Fuels Oils ... Chemistry and Technology of Fuels and Oils [*A publication*]
Chem Tech Rev ... Chemical Technology Review [*A publication*]
Chem Tech Rev ... Chemie und Technik Revue [*A publication*]
Chem Tech Rundsch Anz Chem Ind ... Chemisch Technische Rundschau und Anzeiger der Chemischen Industrie [*A publication*]
Chem Tech Uebers ... Chemisch Technische Uebersicht [*A publication*]
Chemtech (US) ... Chemtech (United States) [*Formerly, Chemical Technology*] [*A publication*]
Chem Thermodyn ... Chemical Thermodynamics [*A publication*]
CHEMTIC ... Chemistry Test Item Collection   (ADA)
CHEMTIPS ... Chemistry Teaching Information Processing System
Chem Titles ... Chemical Titles [*Information service or system*] [*A publication*]

Chem Titles Chicago Psychoanal Lit Index ... Chemical Titles. Chicago Psychoanalytic Literature Index [*A publication*]
Chem Trade J Chem Eng ... Chemical Trade Journal and Chemical Engineer [*A publication*]
CHEMTREC ... Chemical Transportation Emergency Center [*Chemical Manufacturers Association*]
CHEM-TV ... Trois Rivieres, PQ [*Television station call letters*]
Chem Umsch Geb Fette Oele Wachse Harze ... Chemische Umschau auf dem Gebiete der Fette, Oele, Wachse, und Harze [*A publication*]
Chem Unserer Zeit ... Chemie in Unserer Zeit [*A publication*]
Chemurg Dig ... Chemurgic Digest [*A publication*]
Chemurgic Dig ... Chemurgic Digest [*A publication*]
CHEMVVAM ... Chemical Vehicle Vulnerability Analysis Model   (MCD)
Chem W ... Chemical Week [*A publication*]
Chem Warf Bull ... Chemical Warfare Bulletin [*A publication*]
Chem Week ... Chemical Week [*A publication*]
Chem Weekbl ... Chemisch Weekblad [*Later, Chemisch Weekblad/Chemische Courant*] [*A publication*]
Chem Weekb Mag ... Chemisch Weekblad Magazine [*Later, Chemisch Magazine*] [*A publication*]
Chem Wkly ... Chemical Weekly [*A publication*]
Chem Wkr ... Chemical Worker [*A publication*]
Chemy Ind ... Chemistry and Industry [*A publication*]
Chemy Life ... Chemistry and Life [*A publication*]
Chem Zeit .. Chemiker-Zeitung [*A publication*]
Chem-Zeitun ... Chemiker-Zeitung [*A publication*]
Chem Zelle Gewebe ... Chemie der Zelle und Gewebe [*A publication*]
Chem Zent Bl ... Chemisches Zentralblatt [*A publication*]
Chem Zentr ... Chemisches Zentralblatt [*A publication*]
Chem Zentralbl ... Chemisches Zentralblatt [*A publication*]
Chem Zool ... Chemical Zoology [*A publication*]
Chem-Ztg ... Chemiker-Zeitung [*A publication*]
Chem-Ztg Chem Appar ... Chemiker-Zeitung. Chemische Apparatur [*A publication*]
Chem Zvesti ... Chemicke Zvesti [*A publication*]
CHENIC ... Chenodeoxycholic Acid [*Also, CDA, CDC, CDCA*] [*Biochemistry*]
CHEOPS.. Chemical Information Systems Operators [*Later, EUSIDIC*]
CHEOPS.. Chemical Operations System
CHEOPS.. Cyclically Harvested Earth-Orbit Production System
CHEP .... Community Health Education Project
CHEPP ...... Catastrophic Health Expense Protection Plan [*Insurance*]
CHEQ .... Cheque [*British*]   (ROG)
CHEQ-FM ... Smiths Falls, ON [*FM radio station call letters*]
CHER .... Cherry Corp. [*NASDAQ symbol*]   (NQ)
C Her .... Christian Herald [*A publication*]
Cher .... De Cherubim [*Philo*]   (BJA)
CHER .... Sydney, NS [*AM radio station call letters*]
CHERA ..... Canadian Health Economics Research Association [*See also ACRES*]
Cher Ca ...... Cherokee Case [*A publication*]   (DLA)
CHERD ..... Chemical Era [*A publication*]
CHERP ...... Central Health Education Register of Programs [*Australia*]
CHES .... Canadian Hospital Engineering Society
CHES .... Chesapeake Bay [*Virginia and Maryland*]
CHES .... Chesapeake Industries, Inc. [*Newport Beach, CA*] [*NASDAQ symbol*]   (NQ)
CHES .... Chesham [*Urban district in England*]
CHES .... Cheshire [*County in England*]
CHES .... Chestnut   (ROG)
CHES .... Cyclohexylaminoethanesulfonic Acid [*A buffer*]
Chesapeake Bay Inst Johns Hopkins Univ Tech Rep ... Chesapeake Bay Institute. Johns Hopkins University. Technical Report [*A publication*]
Chesapeake Sci ... Chesapeake Science [*A publication*]
Ches Ca ...... Report of the Chesapeake Case, New Brunswick [*A publication*]   (DLA)
Ches Co ...... Chester County Reports [*Pennsylvania*] [*A publication*]   (DLA)
Ches Co Rep ... Chester County Reports [*Pennsylvania*] [*A publication*]   (DLA)
CHESH ...... Cheshire [*County in England*]   (ROG)
Cheshire ..... Smith's New Hampshire Reports [*A publication*]   (DLA)
CHES/NAVFAC ... Chesapeake Division Naval Facilities Engineering Command [*Washington, DC*]
CHESNAVFACENGCOM ... Chesapeake Division Naval Facilities Engineering Command [*Washington, DC*]
CHESOP.. Charitable/Employee Stock Ownership Plan [*Tax plan*]
CHESS ...... Canadian Health Education Specialists Society
CHESS ...... Centers for Health, Education, and Social Systems Studies [*Formerly, Center for Health and Social Systems Research*] [*Research center*]   (RCD)
CHESS ...... Community Health and Environmental Surveillance System [*Environmental Protection Agency project*]
CHESS ...... Cornell High-Energy Synchrotron Source Laboratory [*Cornell University*] [*Research center*]
CHEST ...... Chester [*City in England*]   (ROG)
CHEST ...... Chesterton [*England*]
Chest Ca .... Case of the City of Chester on Quo Warranto [*A publication*]   (DLA)
Chest Co .... Chester County Reports [*Pennsylvania*] [*A publication*]   (DLA)

Chest Co (PA) ... Chester County Reports [*Pennsylvania*] [*A publication*] (DLA)

Chest Co Rep ... Chester County Reports [*Pennsylvania*] [*A publication*] (DLA)

Chester....... Chester County Reports [*Pennsylvania*] [*A publication*] (DLA)

Chester Co (PA) ... Chester County Reports [*Pennsylvania*] [*A publication*] (DLA)

Chester Co Rep ... Chester County Reports [*Pennsylvania*] [*A publication*] (DLA)

Chesterton Rev ... Chesterton Review [*A publication*]

Chest Heart Stroke J ... Chest, Heart, and Stroke Journal [*A publication*]

CHETA ..... Chung-Hua Erh K'o Tsa Chih [*Chinese Journal of Pediatrics*] [*A publication*]

CHETAE... Chung-Hua Erh K'o Tsa Chih [*Chinese Journal of Pediatrics*] [*A publication*]

CHETAH .. Chemical Thermodynamics and Energy Hazard Evaluation [*American Society for Testing and Materials*]

ChET Chem Exp Technol ... ChET. Chemie. Experiment und Technologie [*West Germany*] [*A publication*]

Chet Soc..... Chetham Society [*A publication*]

Chetty .... Sadr Diwani Adalat Cases, Madras [*India*] [*A publication*] (DLA)

Chetvertichn Period ... Chetvertichnyi Period [*A publication*]

CHEV .... Chevalier [*Knight title*]

CHEV .... Cheveley [*England*]

Chev .... Cheves' South Carolina Law Reports [*1839-1940*] [*A publication*] (DLA)

CHEV .... Chevrolet [*Automotive engineering*]

CHEV .... Chevron

Chev Ch ..... Cheves' South Carolina Equity Reports [*1839-1940*] [*A publication*] (DLA)

Chev Eq...... Cheves' South Carolina Equity Reports [*1839-1940*] [*A publication*] (DLA)

Cheves....... Cheves' South Carolina Law Reports [*1839-1940*] [*A publication*] (DLA)

Cheves Eq (SC) ... Cheves' South Carolina Equity Reports [*1839-1940*] [*A publication*] (DLA)

Cheves L (SC) ... Cheves' South Carolina Equity Reports [*1839-1940*] [*A publication*] (DLA)

CHEX .... Cheques [*British*] (ROG)

CHEX .... Peterborough, ON [*AM radio station call letters*]

Ch Ex Off .. Chief Executive Officer [*Also, CEO*]

CHEX-TV ... Peterborough, ON [*Television station call letters*]

CHEX-UP ... Cyclophosphamide, Hexamethylmelamine, Fluorouracil, Platinol [*Cisplatin*] [*Antineoplastic drug regimen*]

CHEY .... Cheyenne [*City in Wyoming*] (ROG)

CHEYAT... Chung-Hua Erh Pi Yen Hou K'o Tsa Chih [*A publication*]

CHEZ .... Restaurant Entertainment [*NASDAQ symbol*] (NQ)

CHEZ-FM ... Ottawa, ON [*FM radio station call letters*]

CHF .... Cahiers d'Histoire et de Folklore [*A publication*]

CHF .... Calhoun Falls [*South Carolina*] [*Seismograph station code, US Geological Survey*] (SEIS)

ch f............. Change Fixe [*Fixed Exchange*] [*French*]

CH of F ..... Chaplain of the Fleet [*Navy*] [*British*]

ChF .... Chaplain of the Fleet [*Navy*] [*British*]

CHF .... Chatham House Foundation (EA)

CHF .... Cherry Hill Free Public Library, Cherry Hill, NJ [*OCLC symbol*] (OCLC)

CHF .... Chick Heart Fibroblast [*Cytology*]

CHF .... Chief

CHF .... Chock Full O'Nuts Corp. [*NYSE symbol*] [*Wall Street slang name: "Nuts"*] (SPSG)

CHF .... Coalition for Health Funding (EA)

CHF .... Columba House Fund [*Later, CIM*] (EA)

CHF .... Community of the Holy Family [*Anglican religious community*]

CHF .... Congestive Heart Failure [*Medicine*]

CHF .... Contract History File [*Military*] (AFIT)

CHF .... Cooperative Housing Foundation (EA)

CHF .... Coupled Hartree-Fock [*Quantum mechanics*]

CHF .... Creation Health Foundation (EA)

CHF .... Critical Heat Flux [*Nuclear energy*]

CHF .... Cyclophosphamide, Hexamethylmelamine, Fluorouracil [*Antineoplastic drug regimen*]

CHF .... Czech Heritage Foundation (EA)

CHFA .... Canadian Health Food Association

CHFA .... Edmonton, AB [*AM radio station call letters*]

CHFC .... Carnegie Hero Fund Commission (EA)

ChFC .... Chartered Financial Consultant [*Designation awarded by The American College*]

CHFC .... Chemical Financial Corporation [*NASDAQ symbol*] (NQ)

CHFC .... Cheryl Hale Fan Club (EA)

CHFC .... Churchill, MB [*AM radio station call letters*]

CHFCA...... Chung-Hua Fu Ch'an K'o Tsa Chih [*Chinese Journal of Obstetrics and Gynecology*] [*A publication*]

CHFCA2.... Chung-Hua Fu Ch'an K'o Tsa Chih [*Chinese Journal of Obstetrics and Gynecology*] [*A publication*]

CHFCI....... Charlie Hodge Fan Club Internationale (EA)

CHFD .... Ceramic Hotform Die (MCD)

CHFD .... Charter Federal Savings Bank (Virginia) [*NASDAQ symbol*] (NQ)

CHFD-TV ... Thunder Bay, ON [*Television station call letters*]

CHFIE....... Cordell Hull Foundation for International Education (EA)

CHFI-FM ... Toronto, ON [*FM radio station call letters*]

CHFM-FM ... Calgary, AB [*FM radio station call letters*]

CHFR .... Critical Heat Flux Ratio [*Nuclear energy*] (NRCH)

CHFS........ Central [*Atom*] Hyperfine Structure

CHFS........ Chief Automotive Systems, Inc. [*Grand Island, NE*] [*NASDAQ symbol*] (NQ)

CHFSAG... Chung-Hua Fang She Hsueh Tsa Chih [*A publication*]

CHFT .... Canadian Home Fitness Test [*Medicine*]

CHFTN...... Chieftain (ROG)

Ch Fwd....... Charges Forward (DS)

CHFX-FM ... Halifax, NS [*FM radio station call letters*]

CHG.......... Change (AAG)

CHG.......... Charge (KSC)

CHG.......... Charge d'Affaires [*Foreign Service*]

CHG.......... Charlemagne Resources [*Vancouver Stock Exchange symbol*]

CHG.......... Chiang Mai [*Thailand*] [*Seismograph station code, US Geological Survey*] (SEIS)

CHG.......... Chicago Milwaukee Corp. [*NYSE symbol*] (SPSG)

CHG.......... Crosshatch Generator

CHG.......... Helicopter Ship, Missile-Armed [*NATO*]

CHG.......... Sisters of the Holy Ghost [*Roman Catholic religious order*]

CHGA-FM ... Maniwaki, PQ [*FM radio station call letters*]

CHGCB ..... Change Control Board [*NASA*] (KSC)

CHGD....... Center for Human Growth and Develoment [*University of Michigan*] [*Research center*] (RCD)

CHGD....... Charged (ROG)

CHGE....... Charge

CHGEA ..... Chemical Geology [*A publication*]

CHGFA ..... Costs Chargeable to Fund Authorization [*Army*]

CHGG-FM ... Limestone, MB [*FM radio station call letters*]

CHGLA ..... Chemik [*A publication*]

CHGO .... Chicago [*Illinois*]

CHGOV..... Change Over

CHGP....... Charging Pump (IEEE)

CHGPAA .. Costs Chargeable to Purchase Authorization Advice

CHGPH..... Choreography

CHGR....... Charger (MSA)

CHGS....... Charges

CHGSAL... Chromatographic Science Series [*A publication*]

CHGT....... Chargit, Inc. [*New York, NY*] [*NASDAQ symbol*] (NQ)

CHGUN .... Chief Gunner [*Navy rating*] [*Obsolete*]

CHH .... Carter Hawley Hale Stores, Inc. [*NYSE symbol*] (SPSG)

CHH .... Chain Home High [*Aviation*]

CHH .... Chatham, MA [*Location identifier*] [*FAA*] (FAAL)

CHH .... Cheswick & Harmar [*AAR code*]

CHH .... Chihuahua [*Mexico*] [*Seismograph station code, US Geological Survey*] (SEIS)

CHH .... Chronos. Vakblad voor de Uurwerkbranche [*A publication*]

ChH .... Church History [*A publication*]

Ch & H...... Church and Home [*A publication*]

CHH .... Commission on Health and Healing [*Formerly, CCMW*] (EA)

CHH .... Commission d'Histoire de l'Historiographie [*Commission of the History of Historiography*] [*Ceret, France*] (EAIO)

CHH .... Consolidated Churchill Enterprises, Inc. [*Vancouver Stock Exchange symbol*]

CHH .... Contemporary Heroes and Heroines [*A publication*]

CH & H...... Continent between Havre and Hamburg [*Business term*]

CHHA .... Canadian Hard of Hearing Association

CHHA/CHS ... Council of Home Health Agencies and Community Health Services [*Later, NAHC*]

CHHC .... Heist [*C. H.*] Corporation [*Clearwater, FL*] [*NASDAQ symbol*] (NQ)

CHHCDF .. Chung-Hua Hsin Hsuch Kuan Ping Tsa Chih [*A publication*]

CHHE........ Certified Hospitality Housekeeping Executive [*Designation awarded by Educational Institute of the American Hotel and Motel Association*]

Ch Her .... Church Herald [*A publication*]

Ch Hist ...... Church History [*A publication*]

CHHNA ... Chung-Hua Nei K'o Tsa Chih [*A publication*]

CHHNAB ... Chinese Journal of Internal Medicine [*A publication*]

CHHO .... Coalition of Holistic Health Organizations (EA)

CHHOAE ... Chronica Horticulturae [*A publication*]

CHHPA ...... Ch'ing Hua Ta Hsueh Hsueh Pao [*A publication*]

CHHR .... Committee on Health and Human Rights (EA)

CHHS........ Charles Homer Haskins Society (EA)

CHHS........ Chinese Historical Society of America (EA)

CHHSM .... Council for Health and Human Services Ministries (EA)

CHHTAT .. Chung-Hua I Hsueh Tsa Chih [*Chinese Medical Journal*] [*A publication*]

CHi .... California Historical Society, San Francisco, CA [*Library symbol*] [*Library of Congress*] (LCLS)

CHI .... Chalcone Isomerase [*An enzyme*]

CHI .... Chapleau Resources Ltd. [*Vancouver Stock Exchange symbol*]

CHI .... Chemical Hazards in Industry [*Royal Society of Chemistry*] [*Information service or system*] (IID)

CHI .... Chicago [*Illinois*]

CHI .... Chicago [*Illinois*] [*Airport symbol*] (OAG)

CHI .... Chicago - Loyola [*Illinois*] [*Seismograph station code, US Geological Survey*] (SEIS)

CHI............ Children's Hospice International (EA)
CHI............ China
CHI............ China Newsletter [*A publication*]
chi.............. Chinese [*MARC language code*] [*Library of Congress*] (LCCP)
CHI............ City Hostess International (EA)
CHI............ Clearinghouse on Health Indexes [*Public Health Service*] [*Information service or system*] (IID)
CHI............ Closed Head Injury [*Medicine*]
CHI............ Coastal, Harbor, and Inland [*Waterways*] (MCD)
CHI............ Computer-Human Interaction (BUR)
CHI............ Concordia Historical Institute (EA)
CHI............ Consortium for Health Information and Library Sciences [*Library network*]
CHI............ Cooperative High-Performance Sequential Inference Machine [*NEC Corp.*]
CHI............ Cyclohexyl Isocyanate [*Organic chemistry*]
CHIA......... Comprehensive Health Insurance Act
CHIAA ...... Crop-Hail Insurance Actuarial Association [*Later, NCIS*] (EA)
Chiang Mai Med Bull ... Chiang Mai Medical Bulletin [*A publication*]
Chiarmo..... Chiarissimo [*Form of address used when writing to distinguished persons*] [*Italian*]
Chiba Found Colloq Ageing ... Chiba Foundation. Colloquia on Ageing [*A publication*]
Chiba Med J ... Chiba Medical Journal [*A publication*]
Chi BA Rec ... Chicago Bar Association. Record [*A publication*] (DLA)
Chi Black ... Chitty's Edition of Blackstone's Commentaries [*A publication*] (DLA)
Chi B Rec... Chicago Bar Record [*A publication*]
Chi B Record ... Chicago Bar Record [*A publication*] (DLA)
CHIC......... CERMET [*Ceramic Metal Element*] Hybrid Integrated Circuit
CHIC......... Chi Chi's, Inc. [*Louisville, KY*] [*NASDAQ symbol*] (NQ)
CHIC......... Chicago [*Illinois*]
CHIC......... Commonwealth Holiday Inns of Canada
Chicag Chem Bull ... Chicago Chemical Bulletin [*A publication*]
Chicago Acad Sci Bull Nat History Misc ... Chicago Academy of Sciences. Bulletin. Natural History Miscellanea [*A publication*]
Chicago Archtl Jnl ... Chicago Architectural Journal [*A publication*]
Chicago Art Inst Bul ... Chicago Art Institute. Bulletin [*A publication*]
Chicago Art Inst Cal ... Chicago Art Institute. Calendar [*A publication*]
Chicago Art Inst Q ... Chicago Art Institute. Quarterly [*A publication*]
Chicago Bar Rec ... Chicago Bar Record [*A publication*]
Chicago Bd Options Ex Guide CCH ... Chicago Board Options Exchange Guide. Commerce Clearing House [*A publication*]
Chicago B Rec ... Chicago Bar Record [*A publication*]
Chicago Bs ... Crain's Chicago Business [*A publication*]
Chicago Dairy Prod ... Chicago Dairy Produce [*A publication*]
Chicago His ... Chicago History of Science and Medicine [*A publication*]
Chicago-Kent L Rev ... Chicago-Kent Law Review [*A publication*]
Chicago LB ... Chicago Law Bulletin [*A publication*] (DLA)
Chicago Leg News ... Chicago Legal News [*Illinois*] [*A publication*] (ILCA)
Chicago Leg News (Ill) ... Chicago Legal News [*Illinois*] [*A publication*] (DLA)
Chicago LJ ... Chicago Law Journal [*A publication*] (DLA)
Chicago L Rec ... Chicago Law Record [*Illinois*] [*A publication*] (DLA)
Chicago L Record (Ill) ... Chicago Law Record [*Illinois*] [*A publication*] (DLA)
Chicago LT ... Chicago Law Times [*A publication*] (DLA)
Chicago Med ... Chicago Medicine [*A publication*]
Chicago Med Exam ... Chicago Medical Examiner [*A publication*]
Chicago Med Rec ... Chicago Medical Record [*A publication*]
Chicago Med Recorder ... Chicago Medical Recorder [*A publication*]
Chicago Nat ... Chicago Naturalist [*A publication*]
Chicago Psychoanal Lit Ind ... Chicago Psychoanalytic Literature Index [*A publication*]
Chicago Psychoanal Lit Index ... Chicago Psychoanalytic Literature Index [*A publication*]
Chicago R .. Chicago Review [*A publication*]
Chicago Rev ... Chicago Review [*A publication*]
CHICAGORILLA ... Chicago Gorilla [*Slang for a desperado gunman*]
Chicago Sch J ... Chicago Schools Journal [*A publication*]
Chicago Stds ... Chicago Studies [*A publication*]
Chicago Studs ... Chicago Studies [*A publication*]
Chicago Trib ... Chicago Tribune [*A publication*]
Chicago Univ Dept Geography Research Paper ... Chicago. University. Department of Geography. Research Paper [*A publication*]
Chicano L Rev ... Chicano Law Review [*A publication*]
Chicg Trib ... Chicago Tribune [*A publication*]
CHICH...... Chichester [*City in England*] (ROG)
Chic LB...... Chicago Law Bulletin [*A publication*] (DLA)
Chic Leg N ... Chicago Legal News [*Illinois*] [*A publication*] (DLA)
Chic LJ ...... Chicago Law Journal [*A publication*] (DLA)
Chic LR...... Chicago Law Record [*Illinois*] [*A publication*] (DLA)
Chic LT...... Chicago Law Times [*A publication*] (DLA)
Chic Med Sch Q ... Chicago Medical School Quarterly [*A publication*]
Chic Nat Hist Mus Annu Rep ... Chicago Natural History Museum. Annual Report [*A publication*]
CHICODER ... Chinese Language Encoder
CHICOM... Chinese Communist
Chicorel Abstr Read Learn Disabil ... Chicorel Abstracts to Reading and Learning Disabilities [*A publication*]
Chic R .... Chicago Review [*A publication*]

CHICS....... Computerized Hospital Information System (MCD)
ChicSt .... Chicago Studies [*Mundelein, IL*] [*A publication*]
ChicTSemReg ... Chicago Theological Seminary. Register [*A publication*]
Chic Univ Dep Geogr Res Pap ... Chicago. University. Department of Geography. Research Paper [*A publication*]
CHID......... Combined Health Information Database [*Public Health Service*] [*Information service or system*] (IID)
CHID......... Community Human and Industrial Development, Inc. [*Office of Economic Opportunity*] [*Terminated*]
CHIDE ...... Committee to Halt Indoctrination and Demoralization in Education [*Group opposing sex education in schools*]
CHIE .... Council on Health Information and Education (EA)
CHIEF...... Combined Helmholtz Integral Equation Formulation
CHIEF...... Controlled Handling of Internal Executive Functions [*UNIVAC*]
Chief Executive Mon ... Chief Executive Monthly [*A publication*]
CHIF......... Channel Interface
CHIGW...... Chigwell [*Urban district in England*]
CHIHA...... Chi'i Hsiang Hsueh Pao [*A publication*]
Chih Wu Hsueh Pao Acta Bot Sin ... Chih Wu Hsueh Pao. Acta Botanica Sinica [*A publication*]
CHIIA........ Chemische Industrie International [*English Translation*] [*A publication*]
Chi Jrl R .... Chicago Journalism Review [*A publication*]
CHIK .... Golden Poultry Company, Inc. [*NASDAQ symbol*] (NQ)
CHIKD ...... Chi Kuang [*A publication*]
Chi-Kent LR ... Chicago-Kent Law Review [*A publication*]
Chi-Kent L Rev ... Chicago-Kent Law Review [*A publication*]
Chi-Kent Rev ... Chicago-Kent Law Review [*A publication*]
CHIK-FM ... Quebec, PQ [*FM radio station call letters*]
Chikyukagaku (Geochem) ... Chikyukagaku (Geochemistry) Nagoya [*A publication*]
CHIL .... Child (ADA)
CHIL .... Chile
CHIL .... Consolidated Hazardous Item List (MCD)
CHIL .... Current-Hogging Injection Logic [*Electronics*] (IEEE)
Chi LB .... Chicago Law Bulletin [*A publication*] (DLA)
CHILD ...... Chicago Institute for the Study of Learning Disabilities [*Research center*] (RCD)
CHILD ...... Children's Health Information about Liver Disease
CHILD ...... Children's Healthcare Is a Legal Duty (EA)
CHILD ...... Cognitive Hybrid Intelligent Learning Device
CHILD ...... Coordinated Helps in Language Development (ADA)
Child Abuse Negl ... Child Abuse and Neglect [*A publication*]
Child Care ... Child Care Quarterly [*A publication*]
Child Care Health Dev ... Child Care Health and Development [*A publication*]
Child Care Q ... Child Care Quarterly [*A publication*]
Child Contemp Soc ... Children in Contemporary Society [*A publication*]
Child Ct ... Children's Court (DLA)
Child D ... Children's Digest [*A publication*]
Child Dev... Child Development [*A publication*]
ChildDevAb ... Child Development Abstracts [*A publication*]
Child Dev Abstr Bibliogr ... Child Development Abstracts and Bibliography [*A publication*]
Child Devel ... Child Development [*A publication*]
Child Developm Absts Biblio ... Child Development Abstracts and Bibliography [*A publication*]
Child Ed..... Childhood Education [*A publication*]
CHILDHD ... Childhood
Child Health Care ... Children's Health Care [*A publication*]
Child Health Dev ... Child Health and Development [*A publication*]
Childh Educ ... Childhood Education [*A publication*]
ChildL........ Children's Literature [*A publication*]
Child Legal Rights J ... Children's Legal Rights Journal [*A publication*]
Child Legal Rts J ... Children's Legal Rights Journal [*A publication*] (DLA)
Child Lib News ... Children's Libraries Newsletter [*A publication*] (APTA)
Child Lit... Children's Literature [*A publication*]
Child Lit Abstr ... Children's Literature Abstracts [*A publication*]
Child Lit Educ ... Children's Literature in Education [*A publication*]
Child Mag Guide ... Children's Magazine Guide [*A publication*]
Child Par M ... Children. The Parents' Magazine [*A publication*]
Child Psych ... Child Psychiatry and Human Development [*A publication*]
Child Psych & Human Devel ... Child Psychiatry and Human Development [*A publication*]
Child Psychiatry Hum Dev ... Child Psychiatry and Human Development [*A publication*]
Child Psy Q ... Child Psychiatry Quarterly [*A publication*]
Childrens Lib News ... Children's Libraries Newsletter [*A publication*] (APTA)
Childs Bsn ... Children's Business [*A publication*]
Childs Nerv Syst ... Child's Nervous System [*A publication*]
Child St J.... Child Study Journal [*A publication*]
Child Stud J ... Child Study Journal [*A publication*]
Child Today ... Children Today [*A publication*]
Child Trop (Engl Ed) ... Children in the Tropics (English Edition) [*A publication*]
Child Wel... Child Welfare [*A publication*]
Child Youth Serv ... Child and Youth Services [*A publication*]
Child & Youth Serv ... Child and Youth Services [*A publication*]
Chile Econ ... Chile Economic Report [*A publication*]

Chile Econ N ... Chile Economic News [*A publication*]
Chi Leg N .. Chicago Legal News [*Illinois*] [*A publication*] (DLA)
CHILF .... Chilford [*England*]
CHILI .... [*A*] programming language [*1970*] (CSR)
Chilian .... Chilianus Koenig [*Deceased, 1526*] [*Authority cited in pre-1607 legal work*] (DSA)
Chi LJ .... Chicago Law Journal [*A publication*] (DLA)
Chil Kon ..... Chilianus Koenig [*Deceased, 1526*] [*Authority cited in pre-1607 legal work*] (DSA)
CHILL .... CCITT [*Consultative Committee on International Telegraphy and Telephony*] High-Level Language [*Telecommunications*] (TEL)
CHILL .... Chicago-University of Illinois [*RADAR system*]
Chillan Chile Estac Exp Bol Tec ... Chillan, Chile. Estacion Experimental. Boletin Tecnico [*A publication*]
Chil Nitrate Agric Serv Inf ... Chilean Nitrate Agricultural Service. Information [*A publication*]
Chi LR .... Chicago Law Record [*Illinois*] [*A publication*] (DLA)
Chil Rts Rep ... Children's Rights Report [*A publication*] (DLA)
Chi LT .... Chicago Law Times [*A publication*] (DLA)
Chilton MF ... Chilton Market Forecast [*A publication*]
CHIM .... Chief Inspector of Machinery [*Navy*] [*British*] (ROG)
Chim .... Chimica [*A publication*]
Chim Acta Turc ... Chimica Acta Turcica [*A publication*]
Chim Actual ... Chimie Actualites [*France*] [*A publication*]
Chim Agric ... Chimizarea Agriculturii [*A publication*]
Chim Anal (Bucharest) ... Chimie Analitica (Bucharest) [*Romania*] [*A publication*]
Chim Anal (Paris) ... Chimie Analytique (Paris) [*A publication*]
Chim Analyt ... Chimie Analytique [*A publication*]
Chim Chron (Athens) ... Chimika Chronika (Athens) [*A publication*]
Chim Didact ... Chimica Didactica [*A publication*]
ChIME ...... Chemical Industry for Minorities in Engineering (EA)
Chimica Ind (Milano) ... Chimica e l'Industria (Milano) [*A publication*]
Chimie Act ... Chimie Actualites [*A publication*]
Chimie & Ind ... Chimie et Industrie [*A publication*]
Chimie Mag ... Chimie Magazine [*A publication*]
Chimie Peint ... Double Liaison. Chimie des Peintures [*A publication*]
Chim Ind .... Chimica e l'Industria [*A publication*]
Chim Ind Agric Biol Realizz Corp ... Chimica nell Industria, nell Agricultura, nella Biologia e nelle Realizzazioni Corporative [*A publication*]
Chim Ind - Genie Chim ... Chimie et Industrie - Genie Chimique [*A publication*]
Chim Ind (Paris) ... Chimie et Industrie (Paris) [*A publication*]
Chim Microbiol Technol Aliment ... Chimie, Microbiologie, Technologie Alimentaire [*A publication*]
Chim Mod ... Chimie Moderne [*France*] [*A publication*]
Chim Nouv ... Chimie Nouvelle [*A publication*]
Chim Pein Encres Plast Adhes Leurs Composants ... Chimie des Peintures, des Encres, des Plastiques, des Adhesifs, et de Leurs Composants [*A publication*]
Chim Peint ... Chimie des Peintures [*A publication*]
Chim Pure Appl ... Chimie Pure et Appliquee [*A publication*]
Chim Tech ... Chimie et Technique [*A publication*]
Chim Ther ... Chimica Therapeutica [*A publication*]
Chim Ther ... Chimie Therapeutique [*A publication*]
CHIN .... Canadian Heritage Information Network [*National Museums of Canada*] [*Ottawa, ON*] [*Information service or system*] (IID)
CHIN .... [*International*] Chemical Information Network [*Information service or system*] (EISS)
CHIN .... China
CHIN .... Chinese [*Language, etc.*] (ROG)
CHIN .... Community Health Information Network [*Library network*]
CHIN .... Toronto, ON [*AM radio station call letters*]
CHINA .... Children in Need of Assistance (OICC)
CHINA .... Chronic Infectious Neuropathic Agents [*Medicine*]
China Agri ... China Agriculture to the Year 2000 [*A publication*]
China Bus R ... China Business Review [*A publication*]
China Clay Trade Rev ... China Clay Trade Review [*A publication*]
China Econ ... China Economic Model and Projections [*A publication*]
China Econ Rept ... China Economic Report [*A publication*]
China For Tr ... China's Foreign Trade [*Peking*] [*A publication*]
China Geog ... China Geographer [*Los Angeles*] [*A publication*]
Chin Agric Sci ... Chinese Agricultural Science [*People's Republic of China*] [*A publication*]
China Internat Bus ... China International Business [*A publication*]
China J ...... China Journal [*A publication*]
China J Chin Mater Med ... China. Journal of Chinese Materia Medica [*A publication*]
China Law Rev ... China Law Review [*A publication*] (DLA)
China Long ... China Long-Term Development Issues and Options [*A publication*]
China L Rep ... China Law Reporter [*A publication*]
China L Rev ... China Law Review [*A publication*] (DLA)
China Med ... China's Medicine [*A publication*]
China Med J ... China Medical Journal [*A publication*]
China Med Miss J ... China Medical Missionary Journal [*A publication*]

Chin Am J Comm Rural Reconstr Plant Ind Ser ... Chinese-American Joint Commission on Rural Reconstruction. Plant Industry Series [*A publication*]
Chin Am J Comm Rural Reconstr (Taiwan) Spec Bull ... Chinese-American Joint Commission on Rural Reconstruction (Taiwan). Special Bulletin [*A publication*]
China News Anal ... China News Analysis [*Hong Kong*] [*A publication*]
Chin Anim Husb Vet Med ... Chinese Animal Husbandry and Veterinary Medicine [*People's Republic of China*] [*A publication*]
CHINAPACK ... China National Packaging Import & Export Corp. [*People's Republic of China*] (IMH)
China Q ...... China Quarterly [*London*] [*A publication*]
China Quart ... China Quarterly [*A publication*]
China Recon ... China Reconstructs [*A publication*]
China Reconstr ... China Reconstructs [*A publication*]
China Rep .. China Report [*A publication*]
China Rep Sci Technol ... China Report. Science and Technology [*A publication*]
China's .... China's Screen [*A publication*]
China Sci Tech Abstracts Ser I Math Astronom Phys ... China Science and Technology Abstracts. Series I. Mathematics, Astronomy, Physics [*A publication*]
China Sci & Technol Abstr Ser 3 ... China Science and Technology Abstracts. Series III. Industry Technology [*A publication*]
China Sci Technol Abstr Ser II ... China Science and Technology Abstracts. Series II. Chemistry, Earth Science, Energy Sources [*A publication*]
China's Med (Peking) ... China's Medicine (Peking) [*A publication*]
Chin Astron ... Chinese Astronomy [*Later, Chinese Astronomy and Astrophysics*] [*A publication*]
CHINAT ... Chinese Nationalist
CHINATEX ... China National Textiles Import & Export Corp. [*People's Republic of China*] (IMH)
CHINATUHSU ... China National Native Produce & Animal Byproducts Import & Export Corp. [*People's Republic of China*] (IMH)
China W R ... China Weekly Review [*A publication*]
CHINB ...... Chemical Instrumentation [*New York*] [*A publication*]
Chin Bee J ... Chinese Bee Journal [*Taiwan*] [*A publication*]
Chin Cult ... Chinese Culture [*A publication*]
Chin Econ S ... Chinese Economic Studies [*A publication*]
Chin Econ Stud ... Chinese Economic Studies [*New York*] [*A publication*]
Chin Educ .. Chinese Education [*A publication*]
Chinese Ann Math ... Chinese Annals of Mathematics [*Shanghai*] [*A publication*]
Chinese Astronom ... Chinese Astronomy [*Later, Chinese Astronomy and Astrophysics*] [*A publication*]
Chinese Astronom Astrophys ... Chinese Astronomy and Astrophysics [*A publication*]
Chinese Cult ... Chinese Culture [*A publication*]
Chinese Econ Studies ... Chinese Economic Studies [*A publication*]
Chinese J Math ... Chinese Journal of Mathematics [*A publication*]
Chinese J Phys (Peking) ... Chinese Journal of Physics (Peking) [*A publication*]
Chinese Law Gvt ... Chinese Law and Government [*A publication*]
Chinese L & Govt ... Chinese Law and Government [*A publication*]
Chinese M ... Chinese Music [*A publication*]
Chinese MJ ... Chinese Medical Journal [*A publication*]
Chinese Phys ... Chinese Physics [*A publication*]
Chinese Soc'y Int'l L Annals ... Annals. Chinese Society of International Law [*Taipei, Taiwan*] [*A publication*] (DLA)
Chinese Stud Hist ... Chinese Studies in History [*A publication*]
CHIN-FM ... Toronto, ON [*FM radio station call letters*]
CHINFO ... Chief of Information [*Also, CINFO*] [*Navy*]
Chin J Antibiot ... Chinese Journal of Antibiotics [*A publication*]
Chin J Appl Chem ... Chinese Journal of Applied Chemistry [*A publication*]
Chin J Archaeol ... Chinese Journal of Archaeology [*A publication*]
Chin J Cardiol ... Chinese Journal of Cardiology [*A publication*]
Chin J Chromatogr ... Chinese Journal of Chromatography [*A publication*]
Chin J Comput ... Chinese Journal of Computers [*A publication*]
Chin J Dermatol ... Chinese Journal of Dermatology [*People's Republic of China*] [*A publication*]
Chin J Epidemiol ... Chinese Journal of Epidemiology [*A publication*]
Chin J Gynecol Obstet ... Chinese Journal of Gynecology and Obstetrics [*People's Republic of China*] [*A publication*]
Chin J Intern Med ... Chinese Journal of Internal Medicine [*People's Republic of China*] [*A publication*]
Chin J Lasers ... Chinese Journal of Lasers [*A publication*]
Chin J Mech ... Chinese Journal of Mechanics [*People's Republic of China*] [*A publication*]
Chin J Mech Eng ... Chinese Journal of Mechanical Engineering [*A publication*]
Chin J Microbiol ... Chinese Journal of Microbiology [*Later, Chinese Journal of Microbiology and Immunology*] [*A publication*]
Chin J Microbiol Immunol (Beijing) ... Chinese Journal of Microbiology and Immunology (Beijing) [*A publication*]
Chin J Microbiol Immunol (Taipei) ... Chinese Journal of Microbiology and Immunology (Taipei) [*A publication*]
Chin J Nucl Phys ... Chinese Journal of Nuclear Physics [*A publication*]
Chin J Obstet Gynecol ... Chinese Journal of Obstetrics and Gynecology [*A publication*]

Chin J Oncol ... Chinese Journal of Oncology [*A publication*]
Chin J Ophthalmology ... Chinese Journal of Ophthalmology [*People's Republic of China*] [*A publication*]
Chin J Orthop ... Chinese Journal of Orthopedics [*A publication*]
Chin J Otorhinolaryngol ... Chinese Journal of Otorhinolaryngology [*People's Republic of China*] [*A publication*]
Chin J Pediatr ... Chinese Journal of Pediatrics [*People's Republic of China*] [*A publication*]
Chin J Phys ... Chinese Journal of Physics [*A publication*]
Chin J Physiol ... Chinese Journal of Physiology [*A publication*]
Chin J Physiol Rep Ser ... Chinese Journal of Physiology. Report Series [*A publication*]
Chin J Phys (New York) ... Chinese Journal of Physics (New York) [*A publication*]
Chin J Phys (Taipei) ... Chinese Journal of Physics (Taipei) [*A publication*]
Chin J Polym Sci ... Chinese Journal of Polymer Science [*A publication*]
Chin J Prev Med ... Chinese Journal of Preventive Medicine [*A publication*]
Chin J Sci Agr ... Chinese Journal of the Science of Agriculture [*A publication*]
Chin J Semicond ... Chinese Journal of Semiconductors [*A publication*]
Chin J Surg ... Chinese Journal of Surgery [*People's Republic of China*] [*A publication*]
Chin J Tuberc Respir Dis ... Chinese Journal of Tuberculosis and Respiratory Diseases [*A publication*]
ChinL .... Chinese Literature [*A publication*]
Chin Law G ... Chinese Law and Government [*A publication*]
Chin Law Govt ... Chinese Law and Government [*New York*] [*A publication*]
Chin L and Gov ... Chinese Law and Government [*A publication*]
Chin Lit ...... Chinese Literature [*Peking*] [*A publication*]
Chin Lit Es ... Chinese Literature. Essays, Articles, Reviews [*A publication*]
Chin Med J ... Chinese Medical Journal [*A publication*]
Chin Med J (Engl Ed) ... Chinese Medical Journal (English Edition) [*A publication*]
Chin Med J (Peking) ... Chinese Medical Journal (Peking) [*A publication*]
CHINOPERL ... Conference for Chinese Oral and Performing Literature   (EA)
Chin P .... Chinese Pharmacopoeia [*A publication*]
Chin Pen .... Chinese Pen [*Taipei*] [*A publication*]
Chin Phys .. Chinese Physics [*United States*] [*A publication*]
Chin Repub Stud ... Chinese Republic Studies. Newsletter [*A publication*]
CHINS ...... Children in Need of Supervision [*Classification for delinquent children*]   (OICC)
Chin Sci ..... Chinese Science [*A publication*]
Chin Sci Tech ... Chinese Science and Technology [*A publication*]
Chin Soc A ... Chinese Sociology and Anthropology [*A publication*]
Chin Social & Pol Sci R ... Chinese Social and Political Science Review [*A publication*]
Chin Sociol Anthro ... Chinese Sociology and Anthropology [*New York*] [*A publication*]
Chin St Lit ... Chinese Studies in Literature [*A publication*]
Chin St Ph ... Chinese Studies in Philosophy [*A publication*]
Chin Stud ... Chinese Studies in History [*A publication*]
Chin Stud Hist ... Chinese Studies in History [*New York*] [*A publication*]
Chin Stud Phil ... Chinese Studies in Philosophy [*A publication*]
Chin Stud Philo ... Chinese Studies in Philosophy [*New York*] [*A publication*]
CHIP .... Allied Command Channel Intelligence Plan [*NATO*]   (NATG)
CHIP .... Canada, Hungary, Indonesia, and Poland [*Countries comprising the International Commission of Control and Supervision, charged with supervising the cease-fire in Vietnam, 1973*]
CHIP .... Canadian Home Insulation Plan
CHIP .... Center for Human Information Processing [*Research center*]   (RCD)
CHIP .... Central Hole in Pintle [*Diesel engineering*]
CHIP .... Chemical Hazard Information Profile [*Environmental Protection Agency*]
CHIP .... Chip Hermeticity in Plastic [*Electronics*]   (MDG)
Chip .... Chipman's New Brunswick Reports [*1825-35*] [*A publication*]
Chip .... [*D.*] Chipman's Vermont Reports [*1789-1824*] [*A publication*]   (DLA)
CHIP .... Chipwich, Inc. [*NASDAQ symbol*]   (NQ)
CHIP .... Comprehensive Health Insurance Plan [*or Proposal*]
Chip Cont... Chipman on the Law of Contracts [*A publication*]   (DLA)
Chip D........ [*D.*] Chipman's Vermont Reports [*1789-1824*] [*A publication*]   (DLA)
CHIP-FM ... Fort Coulonge, PQ [*FM radio station call letters*]
Chip Gov .... Chipman's Principles of Government [*A publication*]   (DLA)
CHIPITTS ... Chicago-Pittsburgh [*Proposed name for possible "super-city" formed by growth and mergers of other cities*]
Chip Ms ..... Chipman's New Brunswick Manuscript Reports [*A publication*]   (DLA)
Chip N .... [*N.*] Chipman's Vermont Reports [*1789-91*] [*A publication*]   (DLA)
CHiPS .... California Highway Patrol [*Acronym used as title of TV series*]
CHIPS .... Case Handling Information Processing System [*National Labor Relations Board*]
CHIPS .... Chemical Engineering Information Processing System
CHIPS .... Clearing House Interbank Payment System   (BUR)
CHIPS .... Consumer Health Information Program and Services [*LSCA*]
Chip Snack ... Chipper Snacker [*A publication*]
CHIPSODB ... Chipping Sodbury [*England*]

Chip (VT)... [*D.*] Chipman's Vermont Reports [*1789-1824*] [*A publication*]   (DLA)
Chip W....... Chipman's New Brunswick Reports [*1825-35*] [*A publication*]   (DLA)
CHIQ .... Concordia Historical Institute. Quarterly [*A publication*]
CHIQ-FM ... Winnipeg, MB [*FM radio station call letters*]
ChiR........... Chicago Review [*A publication*]
CHIR .... Chiricahua National Monument and Fort Bowie National Historic Site
CHIR .... Chiron Corp. [*Emeryville, CA*] [*NASDAQ symbol*]   (NQ)
Chir Aktuell ... Chirurgie Aktuell [*A publication*]
CHIRAS.... Der Chirurg [*A publication*]
Chir-Dent Fr ... Chirurgien-Dentiste de France [*A publication*]
Chir Doct ... Chirurgiae Doctor [*Doctor of Surgery*]
Chir Forum Exp Klin Forsch ... Chirurgisches Forum fuer Experimentelle und Klinische Forschung [*A publication*]
Chir Gastroenterol (Engl Ed) ... Chirurgia Gastroenterologica (English Edition) [*A publication*]
Chir Gen .... Chirurgia Generale [*A publication*]
Chir Ital ..... Chirurgia Italiana [*A publication*]
Chir Maxillofac Plast ... Chirurgia Maxillofacialis et Plastica [*A publication*]
Chir Narzadow Ruchu Ortop Pol ... Chirurgia Narzadow Ruchu i Ortopedia Polska [*A publication*]
Chiro Hist ... Chiropractic History [*A publication*]
Chir Organi Mov ... Chirurgia degli Organi di Movimento [*A publication*]
Chir Org Movimento ... Chirurgia degli Organi di Movimento [*A publication*]
CHIRP....... Chemical Engineering Investigation of Reaction Paths [*Data processing*]
Chir Patol Sper ... Chirurgia e Patologia Sperimentale [*A publication*]
Chir Pediatr ... Chirurgie Pediatrique [*A publication*]
Chir Plast... Chirurgia Plastica [*A publication*]
Chir Plast Reconstr ... Chirurgia Plastica et Reconstructiva [*A publication*]
Chir Torac ... Chirurgia Toracica [*A publication*]
CHIRURG ... Chirurgicalis [*Surgical*] [*Pharmacy*]
Chir Vet Ref Abstr ... Chirurgia Veterinaria Referate. Abstracts [*A publication*]
CHIS......... Central Health Interpreter Service [*Victoria, Australia*]
CHIS.......... Channel Islands National Monument
Chislennye Metody Din Razrezh Gazov ... Chislennye Metody v Dinamike Razrezhennykh Gazov [*A publication*]
Chislennye Metody Mekh Sploshnoi Sredy ... Chislennye Metody Mekhaniki Sploshnoi Sredy [*USSR*] [*A publication*]
Chisl Metody Mekh Sploshn Sredy ... Akademiya Nauk SSSR. Sibirskoe Otdelenie. Vychislitelnyi Tsentr. Chislennye Metody Mekhaniki Sploshnoi Sredy [*A publication*]
CHISOX.... Chicago White Sox [*Baseball team*]
Ch Is Rolls ... Rolls of the Assizes in Channel Islands [*A publication*]   (DLA)
C Hist......... Catholic Historical Review [*A publication*]
CHist .... Church History [*A publication*]
CHist .... Corse Historique [*A publication*]
C Hist Inst Maurice Thorez ... Cahiers d'Histoire. Institut Maurice Thorez [*A publication*]
Chi Sym ..... Chicago Symphony Orchestra. Program Notes [*A publication*]
CHIT .... Chitarrone [*Large Guitar*] [*Music*]
Chit .... Chitty's English Bail Court Reports [*1770-1822*] [*A publication*]   (DLA)
Chit .... Chitty's English King's Bench Practice Reports [*1819-20*] [*A publication*]   (DLA)
Chit Ap ...... Chitty's Law of Apprentices [*A publication*]   (DLA)
Chit Archb Pr ... Chitty's Edition of Archbold's Practice [*A publication*]   (DLA)
Chit Arch Pr ... Chitty's Edition of Archbold's Practice [*A publication*]   (DLA)
CHITAY.... Chirurgia Italiana [*A publication*]
Chit BC ...... Chitty's English Bail Court Reports [*1770-1822*] [*A publication*]   (DLA)
Chit Bills.... Chitty on Bills [*A publication*]   (DLA)
Chit Bl........ Chitty's Edition of Blackstone's Commentaries [*A publication*]   (DLA)
Chit Bl Comm ... Chitty's Edition of Blackstone's Commentaries [*A publication*]   (DLA)
Chit Burn's J ... Chitty's Edition of Burn's Justice [*A publication*]   (DLA)
Chit Car ..... Chitty's Treatise on Carriers [*A publication*]   (DLA)
Chit Com L ... Chitty on Commercial Law [*A publication*]   (ILCA)
Chit Com Law ... Chitty on Commercial Law [*A publication*]   (DLA)
Chit Con.... Chitty on Contracts [*A publication*]   (DLA)
Chit Cont ... Chitty on Contracts [*A publication*]   (DLA)
Chit Crim Law ... Chitty's Criminal Law [*A publication*]   (DLA)
Chit Cr L.... Chitty's Criminal Law [*A publication*]   (DLA)
Chit Cr Law ... Chitty's Criminal Law [*A publication*]   (DLA)
Chit Des ..... Chitty on the Law of Descents [*A publication*]   (DLA)
CHITEAA ... Clearing House of the Interpreters/Translators Educator Association of Australia
Chit Eq Dig ... Chitty's Equity Digest [*A publication*]   (DLA)
Chit Eq Ind ... Chitty's Equity Index [*A publication*]   (DLA)
Chit F........ Chitty's English King's Bench Forms [*A publication*]   (DLA)
Chit Gen Pr ... Chitty's General Practice [*A publication*]   (DLA)
Chit GL....... Chitty on the Game Laws [*A publication*]   (DLA)
Chit & H Bills ... Chitty and Hulme on Bills of Exchange [*A publication*]   (DLA)
Chit Jun B ... Chitty, Junior, on Bills [*A publication*]   (DLA)

Chit Lawy .. Chitty's Commercial and General Lawyer [*A publication*]   (DLA)
Chit L of N ... Chitty. Law of Nations [*1812*] [*A publication*]   (DLA)
Chi T M ..... Chicago Tribune Magazine [*A publication*]
Chit & M Dig ... Chitty and Mew's Supplement to Fisher's English Digest [*A publication*]   (DLA)
Chit Med Jur ... Chitty on Medical Jurisprudence [*A publication*]   (DLA)
Chit Nat ..... Chitty. Law of Nations [*1812*] [*A publication*]   (DLA)
CHITO ...... Container Handling in Terminal Operations [*Army study*]   (RDA)
Chit Pl .... Chitty on Pleading [*A publication*]   (DLA)
Chit Pr .... Chitty's General Practice [*A publication*]   (DLA)
Chit Prec ... Chitty's Precedents in Pleading [*A publication*]   (DLA)
Chit Prer ... Chitty's Prerogatives of the Crown [*A publication*]   (DLA)
Chit R .... Chitty's English Bail Court Reports [*1770-1822*] [*A publication*]   (DLA)
Chit St .... Chitty's Statutes of Practical Utility [*1235-1948*] [*England*] [*A publication*]   (DLA)
Chit St A .... Chitty's Stamp Act [*A publication*]   (DLA)
Chit Stat ..... Chitty's Statutes of Practical Utility [*1235-1948*] [*England*] [*A publication*]   (DLA)
Chit Sum P ... Chitty's Summary of the Practice of the Superior Courts [*A publication*]   (DLA)
Chitt .... Chitty's English Bail Court Reports [*1770-1822*] [*A publication*]   (DLA)
Chittagong Univ Stud Part II Sci ... Chittagong University. Studies. Part II. Science [*A publication*]
Chit & T Car ... Chitty and Temple on Carriers [*A publication*]   (DLA)
Chitt LJ ..... Chitty's Law Journal [*A publication*]   (DLA)
Chitt & Pat ... Chitty and Patell's Supreme Court Appeals [*India*] [*A publication*]   (DLA)
Chitty .... Chitty on Bills [*A publication*]   (DLA)
Chitty BC ... Chitty's English Bail Court Reports [*1770-1822*] [*A publication*]   (DLA)
Chitty BC (Eng) ... Chitty's English Bail Court Reports [*1770-1822*] [*A publication*]   (DLA)
Chitty Bl Comm ... Chitty's Edition of Blackstone's Commentaries [*A publication*]   (DLA)
Chitty Com Law ... Chitty on Commercial Law [*A publication*]   (DLA)
Chitty Eq Ind ... Chitty's Equity Index [*A publication*]   (DLA)
Chitty LJ ..... Chitty's Law Journal [*A publication*]
Chitty's L J ... Chitty's Law Journal [*A publication*]
CHIUA ...... Chemische Industrie [*Duesseldorf*] [*A publication*]
CHIV .... Chivalry   (ROG)
CHJ .... Cambridge Historical Journal [*A publication*]
CHJ .... Charger Resources Ltd. [*Vancouver Stock Exchange symbol*]
CHJ .... Chichibu [*Japan*] [*Seismograph station code, US Geological Survey*]   (SEIS)
CHJ .... Chief Justice [*British*]   (ROG)
CHJ .... Chino, CA [*Location identifier*] [*FAA*]   (FAAL)
CHJ .... Colel Hibath Jerusalem [*Society of the Devotees of Jerusalem*]   (EA)
CHJ .... Cooperative Housing Journal [*A publication*]   (EAAP)
CHJB .... Contribution a l'Histoire Juridique de la Ire Dynastie Babylonienne [*A publication*]   (BJA)
CHJCP ...... Chief Justice of the Common Pleas [*British*]   (ROG)
CHJIA ...... Chitaniumu Jirukoniumu [*A publication*]
CH-JM ...... Carnegie Hall - Jeunesses Musicales [*Defunct*]   (EA)
CHJPB ...... Chinese Journal of Physics [*Peking*] [*English translation*] [*A publication*]
CHJUB ...... Chief Justice of the Upper Bench [*British*]   (ROG)
CHJUSMAG ... Chief, Joint United States Military Advisory Group [*Followed by name of country*]   (CINC)
CHK .... Caterer and Hotelkeeper [*A publication*]
CHK .... Chablis Resources Ltd. [*Vancouver Stock Exchange symbol*]
CHK .... Check   (KSC)
CHK .... Check Register Against Bounds [*Data processing*]
CHK .... Chemeketa Community College, Salem, OR [*OCLC symbol*]   (OCLC)
CHK .... Chicago [*Illinois*] [*Seismograph station code, US Geological Survey*] [*Closed*]   (SEIS)
CHK .... Chickasha, OK [*Location identifier*] [*FAA*]   (FAAL)
CHK .... Christ the King
CHKAD .... Chiiki Kaihatsu [*A publication*]
CHKB .... Check Bit
CHKDSK .... Check Disk [*Data processing*]
CHKE .... Cherokee Group [*North Hollywood, CA*] [*NASDAQ symbol*]   (NQ)
CHKG .... Checking
CHKL-TV ... Kelowna, BC [*Television station call letters*]
CHKL-TV-1 ... Penticton, BC [*Television station call letters*]
CHKMAG ... Chief, Korea Military Assistance Group
CHKM-TV ... Kamloops, BC [*Television station call letters*]
CHKN .... Chicken
CHKPT .... Checkpoint [*Data processing*]   (BUR)
CHKR .... Checker   (MSA)
CHKWA .... Chijil Kwa Chiri [*A publication*]
CHKY .... Pizza Time Theatre [*NASDAQ symbol*]   (NQ)
Chl .... Biblioteca Nacional de Chile, Santiago, Chile [*Library symbol*] [*Library of Congress*]   (LCLS)
CHL .... Cambridge Higher Local Examination [*British*]   (ROG)

CHL .... Central Hockey League
CHL .... Certified Hardware List   (MCD)
CHL .... Chain Home Low [*Aviation*]
CHL .... Chaldron [*Unit of measure*] [*Obsolete*]   (ROG)
CHL .... Challenge [*A publication*]
CHL .... Chalqueno [*Race of maize*]
CHL .... Channel   (NASA)
CHL .... Charterhall Oil Canada [*Vancouver Stock Exchange symbol*]
CHL .... Chemical Banking Corp. [*NYSE symbol*]   (SPSG)
CHL .... Chicken Hepatic Lectin
CHL .... Chile [*ANSI three-letter standard code*]   (CNC)
CHL .... Chilik [*USSR*] [*Seismograph station code, US Geological Survey*] [*Closed*]   (SEIS)
CHL .... Chinese Hamster Lung [*Cell line*]
CHL .... Chlorambucil [*Antineoplastic drug*]
CHL .... Chlorite [*A mineral*]
ChL .... Chlorophyll
ChL .... Christian Liberty [*A publication*]
CHL .... Clemson Hydraulics Laboratory [*Clemson University*] [*Research center*]   (RCD)
CHL .... Cohlmia Aviation [*Dallas, TX*] [*FAA designator*]   (FAAC)
CHL .... Commentationes Humanorum Litterarum [*A publication*]   (BJA)
CHL .... Committee for Humane Legislation   (EA)
CHL .... Confinement at Hard Labor [*Army*]   (AABC)
CHL .... Cronar Halftone Litho [*Du Pont*]
ChL .... Current-Hogging Logic [*Electronics*]
Ch L .... University of Chicago. Law Review [*A publication*]
CHLA .... Canadian Health Libraries Association
CHLA .... Children's Hospital, Los Angeles, CA
ChLA .... Children's Literature Association   (EA)
CHLA .... Cyclohexyllinoleic Acid [*Organic chemistry*]
Ch L B .... Charles Lamb Bulletin [*A publication*]
CHLBA ..... Chemie fuer Labor und Betrieb [*A publication*]
CHLC .... Baie Comeau, PQ [*AM radio station call letters*]
CHLD .... Chilled   (MSA)
Chl-DNA ... Deoxyribonucleic Acid - Chloroplast [*Biochemistry, genetics*] [*Also, cpDNA, ctDNA*]
CHLGB ..... Challenge [*A publication*]
CHLG-FM-6 ... Brisay, PQ [*FM radio station call letters*]
Ch Lib Newsl ... Children's Libraries Newsletter [*A publication*]   (APTA)
ChLit .... Chinese Literature [*A publication*]
chlk .... Chalky [*Philately*]
Chllr .... Chancellor
CHLM-FM ... Rouyn, PQ [*FM radio station call letters*]
CHLN .... Chalone, Inc. [*San Francisco, CA*] [*NASDAQ symbol*]   (NQ)
CHLN .... Trois-Rivieres, PQ [*AM radio station call letters*]
CHLO .... Chloride [*Chemistry*]   (ADA)
CHLO .... Chloroform [*Organic chemistry*]   (ADA)
CHLO .... St. Thomas, ON [*AM radio station call letters*]
CHLOR ..... Chloride [*Chemistry*]   (ROG)
CHLOR ..... Chlorinated [*Freight*]
CHLOR ..... Chloroform [*Organic chemistry*]   (ROG)
CHLOREP ... Chlorine Emergency Plan [*Chlorine Institute*]
CHLP .... Montreal, PQ [*Radio station call letters*] [*1930's*]
CHLQ-FM ... Charlottetown, PE [*FM radio station call letters*]
Ch LR .... University of Chicago. Law Review [*A publication*]
Chl-rDNA ... Deoxyribonucleic Acid, Ribosomal - Chloroplast [*Biochemistry, genetics*]
CHLSA ..... Chemicke Listy [*A publication*]
CHLSSF .... Commentationes Humanarum Litterarum. Societas Scientiarum Fennica [*A publication*]
CHLT .... Charter Long Term
CHLT .... Chlorthalidone [*Diuretic*]
CHLT .... Sherbrooke, PQ [*AM radio station call letters*]
CHLT-TV ... Sherbrooke, PQ [*Television station call letters*]
ChlU .... University of Chile, Valparaiso, Chile [*Library symbol*] [*Library of Congress*]   (LCLS)
CHL VPP .. Chlorambucil, Vinblastine, Procarbazine, Prednisone [*Antineoplastic drug regimen*]
CHLW .... St. Paul, AB [*AM radio station call letters*]
CHLW-1 .... Grande Centre, AB [*AM radio station call letters*]
CHM .... Cahiers d'Histoire Mondiale/Journal of World History [*A publication*]
CHM .... Canadian Institute for Historical Microreproductions - CIHM [*Source file*] [*UTLAS symbol*]
CHM .... Chairman
CHM .... Chamber   (AAG)
CHM .... Champion Spark Plug Co. [*NYSE symbol*]   (SPSG)
CHM .... Charm [*Jewelry*]   (ROG)
CHM .... Checkmate
CHM .... Chemical [*Freight*]
CHM .... Chemisch Magazine [*A publication*]
CHM .... Chimbote [*Peru*] [*Airport symbol*] [*Obsolete*]   (OAG)
CHM .... Chimkent [*USSR*] [*Seismograph station code, US Geological Survey*] [*Closed*]   (SEIS)
Ch M .... Chirurgiae Magister [*Master of Surgery*]
CHM .... Christian Homesteading Movement   (EA)
CHM .... CHUM Ltd. [*Toronto Stock Exchange symbol*]
Chm .... Churchman [*A publication*]

CHM.......... City of Hope Medical Center, Duarte, CA [*OCLC symbol*] (OCLC)
CHM.......... Compound Handling Machine
CHM.......... Congregation of Humility of Mary [*Roman Catholic women's religious order*]
CHM.......... Diploma of Choir Master of the Royal College of Organists [*British*]
CHMA....... Canadian Holistic Medicine Association
CHMA....... Comprehensive Health Manpower Training Act [*1971*]
CHMA....... Cyclohexyl Methacrylate [*Organic chemistry*]
CHMAAG ... Chief, Military Assistance Advisory Group [*Followed by name of country*] (CINC)
CHMACH ... Chief Machinist [*Navy rating*] [*Obsolete*]
CHMAD.... Chemie Magazine [*A publication*]
CHMAN.... Chairman
CHMBR .... Chamber (MSA)
CHMC....... Children's Hospital Medical Center [*Ohio*]
CHMEB..... China's Medicine [*A publication*]
CHMEBA ... China's Medicine [*Peking*] [*A publication*]
CHMEDT ... Chief, Military Equipment Delivery Team (CINC)
CHMF .... Crazy Horse Memorial Foundation (EA)
CHMG....... [*The*] Columbia University College of Physicians and Surgeons Complete Home Medical Guide [*A publication*]
CHMG....... St. Albert, AB [*AM radio station call letters*]
CHMGA.... Chartered Mechanical Engineer [*A publication*]
CHMILTAG ... Chief, Military Technical Advisory Group (CINC)
Ch Mis I..... Church Missionary Intelligencer [*A publication*]
CHMI-TV ... Portage La Prairie, MB [*Television station call letters*]
CHMJB..... Chamber of Mines. Journal [*A publication*]
CHMK....... Chung-Hau Min Kuo [*Republic of China*]
CHML....... Hamilton, ON [*AM radio station call letters*]
CHMN ...... Chairman (AFM)
Chmn........ Churchman [*A publication*]
CHMNA.... Chantiers Magazine [*A publication*]
CHMO ...... Moosonee, ON [*AM radio station call letters*]
CHMond.... Cahiers d'Histoire Mondiale/Journal of World History [*Paris*] [*A publication*]
CHMOS.... Complementary High-Performance Metal-Oxide Semiconductor
CHMP....... Chan Hills Military Police [*British military*] (DMA)
CHMPO.... Chief, Military Planning Office (CINC)
CHMR....... Center for Hazardous Materials Research (EA)
CHMR-FM ... St. John's, NF [*FM radio station call letters*]
CHMSA .... Critical Health Manpower Shortage Areas
CHMSL..... Center High-Mounted Stop Lamp [*Pronounced "chimsel"*] [*Automotive engineering*]
CHMTB .... Chemical Technology [*A publication*]
CHMTS..... IEEE Components, Hybrids, and Manufacturing Technology Society (EA)
CHMT-TV ... Moncton, NB [*Television station call letters*]
CHMX....... Chemex Pharmaceuticals, Inc. [*Denver, CO*] [*NASDAQ symbol*] (NQ)
CHN .... Cable Health Network [*Cable-television system*] [*Viacom International, Inc.*]
CHN .... Canadian Longhorn Petroleum [*Vancouver Stock Exchange symbol*]
CHN .... Carbon, Hydrogen, Nitrogen
CHN .... Chain [*Measure*]
CHN .... Chairman (ROG)
CHN .... Change [*Telecommunications*] (TEL)
CHN .... Channel Island Aviation [*Oxnard, CA*] [*FAA designator*] (FAAC)
CHN .... Charan Industries, Inc. [*Toronto Stock Exchange symbol*]
CHN .... Child Neurology
CHN .... Children [*Genealogy*]
CHN .... China [*ANSI three-letter standard code*] (CNC)
CHN .... Chinchina [*Colombia*] [*Seismograph station code, US Geological Survey*] (SEIS)
chn.............. Chinook Jargon [*MARC language code*] [*Library of Congress*] (LCCP)
CHN .... Community Health Network (DHSM)
CHN .... Community of the Holy Name of Jesus [*Anglican religious community*]
CHN .... Fort Wayne, IN [*Location identifier*] [*FAA*] (FAAL)
CHNAVADGP ... Chief, Naval Advisory Group
CHNAVADGRU ... Chief, Naval Advisory Group [*Followed by name of country*] (CINC)
CHNAVAIRSHIPTRA ... Chief, Naval Airships Training
CHNAVGP ... Chief, Naval Advisory Group
CHNAVMAT ... Chief of Naval Material (MCD)
CHNAVMIS ... Chief, Naval Mission
CHNAVPERS ... Chief of Naval Personnel (NVT)
CHNAVSEC ... Chief, Navy Section (CINC)
CHNAVSECMAAG ... Chief, Navy Section, Military Assistance Advisory Group
CHNAVTRA ... Chief of Naval Training
CHNB-TV ... North Bay, ON [*Television station call letters*]
CHNC........ New Carlisle, PQ [*AM radio station call letters*]
ChNCAM ... Chicken Neural Cell Adhesion Molecule
CHNCDB .. Journal of Agricultural Research of China [*A publication*]
CHNE........ Cherne Enterprises, Inc. [*NASDAQ symbol*] (NQ)

CHNG .... Change (MSA)
CHNHA .... Chung-Hua Nung Hsueh Hui Pao [*A publication*]
CHNHAN ... Journal. Agricultural Association of China. New Series [*A publication*]
CHNL........ Channel [*Electrical transmission*] (AFM)
CHNL........ Kamloops, BC [*AM radio station call letters*]
CHNL-1..... Clearwater, BC [*AM radio station call letters*]
Chn Merch ... Chain Merchandiser [*A publication*]
Chn Mktg .. Chain Marketing and Management [*A publication*]
CHNN .... Channel Industries Ltd. [*Norfolk, VA*] [*NASDAQ symbol*] (NQ)
CHNO ...... Sudbury, ON [*AM radio station call letters*]
CHNOPS .. Carbon, Hydrogen, Nitrogen, Oxygen, Phosphorus, and Sulfur [*Compounds*]
CHNR........ Simcoe, ON [*AM radio station call letters*]
CHNS........ Halifax, NS [*AM radio station call letters*]
Chn Stor D ... Chain Store Age. Drug Store Edition. Annual Report of the Chain Drug Industry [*A publication*]
Chn Store... Chain Store Age [*A publication*]
Chn Str GM ... Chain Store Age. General Merchandise Trends Edition [*A publication*]
CHNSY ..... Charleston Naval Shipyard [*South Carolina*]
chnt .... Chestnut [*Philately*]
CHNYB ..... Chishitsu Nyusu [*A publication*]
C/H/O .... Cannot Hear Of [*Bookselling*]
CHO .... Carbohydrate [*Organic chemistry*]
CHO .... Charlim Explorations [*Vancouver Stock Exchange symbol*]
CHO .... Charlottesville [*Virginia*] [*Airport symbol*] (OAG)
CH/O...... Child Of [*Genealogy*]
CHO ...... Chinese Hamster Ovarian [*or Ovary*] [*Cytology*]
cho............ Choctaw [*MARC language code*] [*Library of Congress*] (LCCP)
Cho............. Choephori [*of Aeschylus*] [*Classical studies*] (OCD)
CHO .... Choice [*A publication*]
Cho............. Cholesterol [*Also, C, Ch, CHOL*] [*Biochemistry*]
Cho............. Choline [*Also, Ch*] [*Biochemistry*]
CHO ...... Choral
Cho............. Chorus [*Music*]
CHO .... Choshi [*Japan*] [*Seismograph station code, US Geological Survey*] (SEIS)
CHO .... Cyclophosphamide, Hydroxydaunomycin [*Adriamycin*], Oncovin [*Vincristine*] [*Antineoplastic drug regimen*]
CHo.......... Hollister Public Library, Hollister, CA [*Library symbol*] [*Library of Congress*] (LCLS)
CHOB....... Cannon House Office Building
CHOB....... Cyclophosphamide, Hydroxydaunomycin [*Adriamycin*], Oncovin [*Vincristine*], Bleomycin [*Antineoplastic drug regimen*]
CHOBS ..... Chief Observer [*Navy*] (NVT)
CHOC....... Center for History of Chemistry [*Later, NFHC*] (EA)
CHOC....... Chocolate
Cho Ca Ca ... Choyce's Cases in Chancery [*1557-1606*] [*England*] [*A publication*] (DLA)
Cho Ca Ch ... Choyce's Cases in Chancery [*1557-1606*] [*England*] [*A publication*] (DLA)
Choc Confiserie Fr ... Chocolaterie. Confiserie de France [*A publication*]
CHOC-FM ... Jonquiere, PQ [*FM radio station call letters*]
CHoCL ...... San Benito County Free Library, Hollister, CA [*Library symbol*] [*Library of Congress*] (LCLS)
CHOD .... Chief of Defense (NATG)
ChOd .... Chilean Odeon [*Record label*]
CHOD .... Cholesterol Oxidase [*An enzyme*]
CHOGM ... Commonwealth Heads of Government Meeting [*Canada*]
CHOH .... Chesapeake and Ohio Canal National Monument
CHOICE ... Center for Humane Options in Childbirth Experiences (EA)
CHOICE ... Concern for Health Options: Information, Care and Education [*An association*] (EA)
CHOICE ... Consumer Help on the Individual's Conservation of Energy [*Student legal action organization*]
CHOI-FM ... Quebec, PQ [*FM radio station call letters*]
Choirm .... Choirmaster [*Music*]
CHOK....... Gourmet Resources International [*NASDAQ symbol*] (NQ)
CHOK....... Sarnia, ON [*AM radio station call letters*]
CHOKE..... Care How Others Keep the Environment [*An association*]
CHOL........ Central Holding Co. [*Mount Clemens, MI*] [*NASDAQ symbol*] (NQ)
CHOL........ Cholesterol [*Also, C, Ch, Cho*] [*Biochemistry*]
CHOL........ Common High-Order Language
CHOM ..... Chomerics, Inc. [*Woburn, MA*] [*NASDAQ symbol*] (NQ)
CHOMA9 .. Chirurgia degli Organi di Movimento [*A publication*]
C Home ...... Christian Home [*A publication*]
C Home...... Clerk Home's Decisions, Scotch Court of Session [*1735-44*] [*A publication*] (DLA)
CHOM-FM ... Montreal, PQ [*FM radio station call letters*]
CHOMI..... Clearinghouse on Migration Issues [*Australia*]
CHOMPS ... Canine Home Protection System [*Acronym is title of 1979 movie*]
CHOMS ... Canadian Hydrological Operational Multipurpose Subprogramme [*Environment Canada*] [*Information service or system*] (CRD)
CHON .... Carbon, Hydrogen, Oxygen, Nitrogen [*Composition of interstellar dust*]

ChON .... Chasti Osobogo Naznacheniia [*Elements of Special Designation*] [*Political police units attached to the armed forces (1918-1924)*] [*USSR*]
CHONDF ... Contemporary Hematology/Oncology [*A publication*]
CHON-FM ... Whitehorse, YT [*FM radio station call letters*]
Chonnam Med J ... Chonnam Medical Journal [*A publication*]
CHOO .... Ajax, ON [*AM radio station call letters*]
CHOP .... Change of Operational Control [*Military*]
CHOP .... Changeover Point [*Aviation*]   (FAAC)
CHOP .... Check-Out Procedure   (CAAL)
CHOP .... Chief Operator   (NVT)
CHOP .... Cyclophosphamide, Hydroxydaunomycin [*Adriamycin*], Oncovin [*Vincristine*], Prednisone [*Antineoplastic drug regimen*]
CHOPAIR ... Change of Operational Control of Air Cover [*Military*]   (NVT)
CHOP-Bleo ... Cyclophosphamide, Hydroxydaunomycin [*Adriamycin*], Oncovin [*Vincristine*], Prednisone, Bleomycin [*Antineoplastic drug regimen*]
CHOPLN .. Change My Operation Plan [*Military*]   (AABC)
CHOPP ..... Cyclophosphamide, Hydroxydaunomycin [*Adriamycin*], Oncovin [*Vincristine*], Procarbazine, Prednisone [*Antineoplastic drug regimen*]
CHOPS ..... Chief of Operations
CHOPSUM ... Change of Operational Control Summary [*Military*]   (NVT)
CHOR .... Choir
CHOR .... Choral
CHOR .... Choreograph
CHOR .... Chorus
CHOR .... Cyclophosphamide, Hydroxydaunomycin [*Adriamycin*], Oncovin [*Vincristine*], Radiation therapy [*Antineoplastic drug regimen*]
Choral G .... Choral and Organ Guide [*A publication*]
Choral J ..... Choral Journal [*A publication*]
CHORD .... Change My Operation Order [*Military*]
CHORD CHIRURG ... Chorda Chirurgicalis [*Surgical Catgut*] [*Pharmacy*]
Choreog ...... Choreography
CHORI ...... Chief of Office of Research and Inventions [*Navy*]
CHOS-FM ... Rattling Brook, NF [*FM radio station call letters*]
CHOT-TV ... Hull, PQ [*Television station call letters*]
CHOVA2 ... Commissie voor Hydrologisch Onderzoek TNO [*Nederlandse Centrale Organisatie voor Toegepast Natuurwetenschappelijk Onderzoek*] [*A publication*]
CHO/VAC ... Cholera Vaccine [*Medicine*]
CHOVR ..... Changeover   (AAG)
CHOW .... Welland, ON [*AM radio station call letters*]
Chowder ..... Chowder Review [*A publication*]
Choyce Cas Ch ... Choyce's Cases in Chancery [*1557-1606*] [*England*] [*A publication*]   (DLA)
Choyce Cas (Eng) ... Choyce's Cases in Chancery [*1557-1606*] [*England*] [*A publication*]   (DLA)
CHOZ-FM ... St. John's, NF [*FM radio station call letters*]
CHP .... Capacitance Hole Probe
CHP .... Center on Human Policy   (EA)
CHP .... Central Heating Plant   (KSC)
CH-P .... Challenge Position [*Dancing*]
Ch & P .... Chambers and Pretty. Cases on Finance Act [*1909-10*] [*England*] [*A publication*]   (DLA)
CHP .... Champion Oil & Gas [*Vancouver Stock Exchange symbol*]
CHP .... Championship
CHP .... Channel Processor
CHP .... Chapalote [*Race of maize*]
CHP .... Charter Power Systems, Inc. [*AMEX symbol*]   (SPSG)
CHP .... Chemical Heat Pipe [*Energy storage*]
CHP .... Chicago Helicopter Airways, Inc. [*Air carrier designation symbol*]
CHP .... Child Psychiatry [*Medical specialty*]   (DHSM)
CH/P .... Chondromalacia/Patella [*Medicine*]
CHP .... Chopper   (MSA)
CHP .... Chuchupate [*California*] [*Seismograph station code, US Geological Survey*] [*Closed*]   (SEIS)
CHP .... Circle Hot Springs [*Alaska*] [*Airport symbol*] [*Obsolete*]   (OAG)
Chp .... Clinohypersthene [*Inorganic chemistry*]
CHP .... Combined-Heat-and-Power Station [*Energy production*]
CHP .... Comhuriyet Halk Partisi [*Turkey*]
CHP .... Comprehensive Health Planning [*A requirement for HEW grants to local agencies*]
CHP .... Conquest of Hunger Program [*Rockefeller Foundation*]   (EA)
CHP .... Council of Housing Producers [*Defunct*]   (EA)
CH & P .... Crew Habitability and Protection [*NASA*]   (KSC)
CHP .... Cumene Hydroperoxide [*Organic chemistry*]
CHP .... Cyril Hayes Press, Inc. [*Publisher*]
CHP .... Ferrocarril de Chihuahua al Pacifico, SA de CV [*AAR code*]
CHP .... Paymaster in Chief [*Navy*] [*British*]   (ROG)
CHPAAC ... Chirurgia e Patologia Sperimentale [*A publication*]
CHPAD ..... Journal. Korean Academy of Maxillofacial Radiology [*A publication*]
CHPAE ...... Critical Human Performance and Evaluation   (IEEE)
CHPCA ...... Chemical Processing (Chicago) [*A publication*]
CHPCLK ... Chief Pay Clerk [*Navy rating*] [*Obsolete*]

CHPE .... Center for Health Promotion and Education [*Atlanta, GA*] [*Department of Health and Human Services*]   (GRD)
CHPHAR .. Chief Pharmacist [*Navy rating*] [*Obsolete*]
CHPHD ..... Chinese Physics [*A publication*]
CHPHOT ... Chief Photographer [*Navy rating*] [*Obsolete*]
CHPI .... Characters per Inch [*Data processing*]   (CMD)
CHPI .... Christian Periodical Index [*A publication*]
CHPK .... Chesapeake Utilities Corp. [*Dover, DE*] [*NASDAQ symbol*]   (NQ)
Ch Pl .... Chitty on Pleading [*A publication*]   (DLA)
CHPLB ..... Chemical Physics Letters [*A publication*]
CHPLN ..... Chaplain
CHPN .... Chapman Energy, Inc. [*Dallas, TX*] [*NASDAQ symbol*]   (NQ)
CHPQ .... Parksville-Qualicum, BC [*AM radio station call letters*]
CHPR .... Center for Health Policy Research [*University of Florida*] [*Research center*]   (RCD)
Ch Pr .... Chancery Practice [*A publication*]   (DLA)
CHPRD ..... Center for Health Promotion Research and Development [*University of Texas*] [*Research center*]   (RCD)
CHPRD ..... Chemische Produktion [*A publication*]
Ch Pre .... Precedents in Chancery, Edited by Finch [*1689-1723*] [*England*] [*A publication*]   (DLA)
CHPR-FM ... Hawkesbury, ON [*FM radio station call letters*]
CHPROVMAAGK ... Chief, Military Assistance Advisory Group, Korea (Provisional)   (CINC)
CHPS .... Characters per Second [*Data processing*]   (CMD)
CHPS .... Chips & Technologies, Inc. [*NASDAQ symbol*]   (NQ)
CHPS .... Comprehensive Health Planning Service [*Federal government*]
CHPUA ..... Chemicky Prumysl [*A publication*]
CHPX .... Chickenpox [*Also, Cp*] [*Medicine*]
CHPXBE ... Chirurgische Praxis [*A publication*]
CHQ .... California Historical Quarterly [*San Francisco*] [*A publication*]
CHQ .... Central Headquarters   (DCTA)
CHQ .... Chania [*Greece*] [*Airport symbol*]   (OAG)
CHQ .... Charlesbourg [*Quebec*] [*Seismograph station code, US Geological Survey*]   (SEIS)
CHQ .... Charleston, MO [*Location identifier*] [*FAA*]   (FAAL)
CHQ .... Chautauqua Airlines [*Jamestown, NY*] [*FAA designator*]   (FAAC)
CHQ .... Cheque [*British*]
CHQ .... China Sea Resources Corp. [*Vancouver Stock Exchange symbol*]
Ch Q .... Church Quarterly [*A publication*]
Ch Q .... Church Quarterly Review [*A publication*]
CHQ .... Company Headquarters [*British military*]   (DMA)
CHQ .... Corps Headquarters [*Army*]
CHQB .... Chief Justice of the Queen's Bench   (DLA)
CHQB .... Powell River, BC [*AM radio station call letters*]
CHQM .... Vancouver, BC [*AM radio station call letters*]
CHQMCLK ... Chief Quartermaster Clerk [*Coast Guard*]
CHQM-FM ... Vancouver, BC [*FM radio station call letters*]
CHQR .... Calgary, AB [*AM radio station call letters*]
Ch Q R .... Church Quarterly Review [*A publication*]
CHQT .... Edmonton, AB [*AM radio station call letters*]
CHR .... Canadian Historical Review [*A publication*]
CHR .... Canadian Hotel and Restaurant [*A publication*]
C-HR .... Candle-Hour [*Illumination*]   (AAG)
CHR .... Cargo Handling Rig   (RDA)
CH & R .... Catch a Horse and Ride [*Fictitious railroad initialism used to indicate one of the most reliable modes of rural transportation*]
CHR .... Catholic Historical Review [*A publication*]
CHR .... Center for Health Research [*Wayne State University*] [*Research center*]   (RCD)
CHR .... Center for Human Radiobiology
CHR .... Center for Human Resources [*Rutgers University*] [*Research center*]   (RCD)
CHR .... Cercarienhullen Reaktion [*Medicine*]
CHR .... Character   (BUR)
CHR .... Character Register
CHR .... [*The*] Charter Co. [*NYSE symbol*]   (SPSG)
CHR .... Charter Oil Co. Ltd. [*Toronto Stock Exchange symbol*]
CHR .... Cheers International [*Vancouver Stock Exchange symbol*]
chr .... Cherokee [*MARC language code*] [*Library of Congress*]   (LCCP)
CHR .... Chestnut Ridge Railway Co. [*AAR code*]
CHR .... China Business Review [*A publication*]
Ch R .... Chitty's English King's Bench Reports [*A publication*]   (DLA)
Chr .... Chorismic Acid [*Biochemistry*]
CHR .... Christ [*or Christian*]
CHR .... Christchurch [*New Zealand*] [*Seismograph station code, US Geological Survey*]   (SEIS)
CHR .... Christchurch [*New Zealand*] [*Later, EYR*] [*Geomagnetic observatory code*]
CHR .... Christened
Chr .... Christian
CHR .... Christler Flying Service, Inc. [*Thermopolis, WY*] [*FAA designator*]   (FAAC)
Chr .... Christschall [*Record label*] [*Austria*]
CHR .... Chrome   (ROG)
CHR .... Chromium [*Chemical symbol is Cr*]   (MSA)

CHR.......... Chronic [*Medicine*]
Chr .... Chronicles [*Old Testament book*]
CHR.......... Church (MCD)
CHR.......... Commission on Human Resources [*National Research Council*]
CHR.......... Commission on Human Rights [*Geneva, Switzerland*] (EAIO)
CHR.......... Community of the Holy Rood [*Anglican religious community*]
CHR.......... Constant Hazard Ratio
CHR.......... Contemporary Hit Radio
CHR.......... Cooling Water/Hot Water Return [*Nuclear energy*] (NRCH)
CHR.......... Cooper-Harper Rating [*NASA*] (NASA)
CHR.......... Coordinated Hungarian Relief [*Defunct*] (EA)
CHR.......... Correspondentieblad van Hogere Rijksambtenaren [*A publication*]
CHR.......... Current Housing Reports [*A publication*]
Ch R .... Irish Chancery Reports [*A publication*] (DLA)
Ch-R.......... National Central Library, Rare Book Collection, Taipei, Taiwan, China [*Library symbol*] [*Library of Congress*] (LCLS)
Ch R .... Reports in Chancery [*1615-1712*] [*England*] [*A publication*] (DLA)
Ch R .... Upper Canada Chancery Chambers Reports [*A publication*] (DLA)
CHRA .... Canadian Health Record Association
CHRA .... Center Housing Rotating Assembly [*Automotive engineering*]
CHRAQ ..... Cornell Hotel and Restaurant Administration Quarterly [*A publication*]
CHRA Rec ... CHRA [*Canadian Health Record Association*] Recorder [*A publication*]
CHRB .... High River, AB [*AM radio station call letters*]
CHRBAP... Chronica Botanica [*A publication*]
CHRBRSYN ... Chronic Brain Syndrome [*Medicine*]
CHRC........ Canadian Human Rights Commission [*See also CCDP*]
Chr C.......... Christian Century [*A publication*]
CHRC .... Congressional Human Rights Caucus (EA)
CHRC .... Quebec, PQ [*AM radio station call letters*]
Chr Cent .... Christian Century [*A publication*]
Chr Ch .... Christian's Charges to Grand Juries [*A publication*] (DLA)
Chr & Cr ... Christianity and Crisis [*A publication*]
Chr Cris ..... Christianity and Crisis [*A publication*]
Chr & Crisis ... Christianity and Crisis [*A publication*]
CHRCS...... Centre for Human Relations and Community Studies [*Concordia University*] [*Canada*] [*Research center*] (RCD)
CHRD........ Drummondville, PQ [*AM radio station call letters*]
ChrDem ..... Christian Democrats (EY)
Chr Disc .... Christian Disciple [*A publication*]
CHRDS ..... Comprehensive Human Resources Data System (MCD)
CHRDT ..... Committee for Human Rights and Democracy in Turkey (EA)
ChrE .... Chronique d'Egypte [*A publication*]
CHREA ..... Chemical Reviews [*A publication*]
CH Rec ...... City Hall Recorder (Rogers) [*New York City*] [*A publication*] (DLA)
CHRE-FM ... St. Catharines, ON [*FM radio station call letters*]
Chr Eg........ Chronique d'Egypte [*A publication*]
CHRELE... Chief Radio Electrician [*Navy rating*] [*Obsolete*]
CH Rep ...... City Hall Reporter (Lomas) [*New York City*] [*A publication*] (DLA)
Ch Rep ...... Irish Chancery Reports [*A publication*] (DLA)
Ch Rep ...... Reports in Chancery [*A publication*] (DLA)
Ch Rep Ir ... Irish Chancery Reports [*A publication*] (DLA)
Ch Repts ..... Irish Chancery Reports [*A publication*] (DLA)
Ch Repts ..... Reports in Chancery [*A publication*] (DLA)
Ch Reun ..... Arret de la Cour de Cassation Toutes Chambres Reunies [*Decision of the Full Court of the Court of Appeal*] [*French*] (ILCA)
Chr Exam... Christian Examiner [*A publication*]
CHRF .... Cahiers d'Histoire de la Revolution Francaise [*A publication*]
CHRF .... Children's Hospital Research Foundation [*Research center*] (RCD)
CHRG........ Charge (AFM)
CHRGA6... Chirurgia Gastroenterologica [*English Edition*] [*A publication*]
CHRGB7 ... Chromatographia [*A publication*]
ChrGem ..... Die Christengemeinschaft [*Stuttgart*] [*A publication*]
CHRI .... Christiansted National Historic Site
CHRIE....... Council on Hotel, Restaurant, and Institutional Education (EA)
CHRIS...... Cancer Hazards Ranking and Information System
CHRIS...... Chemical Hazards Response Information System [*Coast Guard*] [*Information service or system*]
CHRIS...... Christened (ADA)
Chris Art.... Christian Art [*Boston*] [*A publication*]
Chris BL ... Christian's Bankrupt Law [*A publication*] (DLA)
Chris Q ..... Christian Quarterly Review [*A publication*]
Chris Sc Mon ... Christian Science Monitor [*A publication*]
Christ Brothers Stud ... Christian Brothers Studies [*A publication*] (APTA)
Christ Cen ... Christian Century [*A publication*]
ChristCent ... Christian Century [*Chicago*] [*A publication*]
Christiana Albertina Kiel Univ Z ... Christiana Albertina. Kieler Universitaets Zeitschrift [*A publication*]
Christian Cent ... Christian Century [*A publication*]

Christian Sci Mon ... Christian Science Monitor [*A publication*]
Christian Sci Mon Mag ... Christian Science Monitor. Magazine Section [*A publication*]
Christ Lanfran ... Christophorus Lanfranchinus [*Deceased, 1490*] [*Authority cited in pre-1607 legal work*] (DSA)
Christ Libr ... Christian Librarian [*A publication*]
Christ Lit ... Christianity and Literature [*A publication*]
Christmas Tree Grow J ... Christmas Tree Growers Journal [*A publication*]
Christ Nurse ... Christian Nurse [*A publication*]
Christ Period Index ... Christian Periodical Index [*A publication*]
Christ Sci Mon ... Christian Science Monitor [*A publication*]
ChristTod .. Christianity Today [*Washington, DC*] [*A publication*]
ChrJF .... Christlich-Juedisches Forum [*A publication*]
CHRK-FM ... Kamloops, BC [*FM radio station call letters*]
CHRL........ Roberval, PQ [*AM radio station call letters*]
Chr Lit .... Christian Literature [*A publication*]
CHRM....... Center for Holistic Resource Management (EA)
CHRM....... Chairman
Ch RM ...... [*Robert M.*] Charlton's Georgia Reports [*1811-37*] [*A publication*] (DLA)
Chrm .... Charmides [*of Plato*] [*Classical studies*] (OCD)
CHRM....... Matane, PQ [*AM radio station call letters*]
Chr Ministry ... Christian Ministry [*A publication*]
CHRMN.... Chairman
Chr Mo Spec ... Christian Monthly Spectator [*A publication*]
CHRN........ Charan Industries, Inc. [*Garden City, NY*] [*NASDAQ symbol*] (NQ)
CHRN........ Committee on Human Rights for Nicaragua [*Later, CHRPN*] (EA)
ChrNIsrael ... Christian News from Israel [*Jerusalem*] [*A publication*]
CHRO....... Chromolithograph (DSUE)
CHRO....... Pembroke, ON [*AM radio station call letters*]
CHROAU ... Chromosoma [*Berlin*] [*A publication*]
Ch Rob .... Robinson's English Admiralty Reports [*1799-1808*] [*A publication*] (DLA)
Chr Obs ..... Christian Observer [*A publication*]
CHROD..... Chronolog [*A publication*]
CHROM..... Chromium [*Chemical symbol is Cr*]
Chrom .... Chromosome [*Genetics*]
Chromatin Chromosomal Protein Res ... Chromatin and Chromosomal Protein Research [*A publication*]
Chromatogr ... Chromatographia [*A publication*]
Chromatogr Methods ... Chromatographic Methods [*A publication*]
Chromatogr Newsl ... Chromatography Newsletter [*A publication*]
Chromatogr Rev ... Chromatographic Reviews [*A publication*]
Chromatogr Sci ... Chromatographic Science [*A publication*]
Chromatogr Sci Ser ... Chromatographic Science Series [*A publication*]
Chromat Rev ... Chromatographic Reviews [*A publication*]
Chromia ..... Chromatographia [*A publication*]
CHROMO ... Chromolithograph (ROG)
Chromo Inf Serv ... Chromosome Information Service [*A publication*]
Chromos.... Chromosoma [*A publication*]
Chromos Inform Serv (Tokyo) ... Chromosome Information Service (Tokyo) [*A publication*]
Chromosome Inf Serv (Tokyo) ... Chromosome Information Service (Tokyo) [*A publication*]
Chromosome Var Hum Evol ... Chromosome Variations in Human Evolution [*A publication*]
Chron .... Chronica [*of St. Jerome*] [*Classical studies*] (OCD)
Chron .... Chronica [*of Eusebius*] [*Classical studies*] (OCD)
CHRON .... Chronicle
Chron .... Chronicles [*Old Testament book*]
CHRON .... Chronological
chron .... Chronology
CHRON .... Chronometer
Chron A Ass Cul ... Chronique Archeologique. Association Culturelle du Groupe Total [*A publication*]
Chron Actual ... Chroniques d'Actualite [*A publication*]
Chron Alum ... Chronique Aluminum [*A publication*]
Chron Aust Ed ... Chronicle of Australian Education [*A publication*] (APTA)
Chron Bot .. Chronica Botanica [*A publication*]
Chron Chim ... Chronache di Chimica [*Italy*] [*A publication*]
Chron Dermatol ... Chronica Dermatologica [*A publication*]
Chron Div Cts ... Chronicles of the Divorce Courts [*A publication*] (DLA)
Chron Egypte ... Chronique d'Egypte [*A publication*]
Chron Higher Educ ... Chronicle of Higher Education [*A publication*]
Chron Hortic ... Chronica Horticulturae [*A publication*]
Chronicles Okla ... Chronicles of Oklahoma [*A publication*]
Chron Int Com ... Chronicle of International Communication [*A publication*]
Chron Jur ... Chronica Juridicalia [*A publication*] (DLA)
Chronmy Przyr Ojczysta ... Chronmy Przyrode Ojczysta [*A publication*]
Chron Nat ... Chronica Naturae [*A publication*]
CHRONO ... Chronological (AFM)
Chronobiol Int ... Chronobiology International [*A publication*]
Chronobiologia Organ Int Soc Chronobiology ... Chronobiologia. Organ of the International Society for Chronobiology [*A publication*]
ChronOkla ... Chronicles of Oklahoma [*A publication*]
Chron OMS ... Chronique. Organisation Mondiale de la Sante [*A publication*]
Chron Pol Etrang ... Chronique de Politique Etrangere [*A publication*]
Chron Pol Etrangere ... Chronique de Politique Etrangere [*A publication*]
Chron Polit Etr ... Chronique de Politique Etrangere [*A publication*]

Chron Przyr Ojczysta ... Chronmy Przyrode Ojczysta [*A publication*]
Chron Rech Min ... Chronique de la Recherche Miniere [*Paris*] [*A publication*]
Chron Rech Miniere ... Chronique de la Recherche Miniere [*France*] [*A publication*]
Chrons Actualite ... Chroniques d'Actualite [*A publication*]
Chron Soc Fr ... Chronique Sociale de France [*A publication*]
Chron Soc France ... Chronique Sociale de France [*A publication*]
CHRONTER ... Chronometer (ROG)
ChrOost ..... Het Christelijk Oosten [*Nijmegen*] [*A publication*]
CHRO PLTD ... Chrome Plated [*Freight*]
CHRO-TV ... Pembroke, ON [*Television station call letters*]
CHRP .... Canadian Home Renovation Program
ChrPer .... Christian Perspectives [*A publication*]
Chr Per Ind ... Christian Periodical Index [*A publication*]
CHRPI .... Center for Health Resources Planning Information [*National Institutes of Health*]
CHRPN ..... Committee on Human Rights for the People of Nicaragua (EA)
CHRPRSN ... Chairperson
Chr Pr W ... Christie's Precedents of Wills [*A publication*] (DLA)
Chr Q .... Christian Quarterly [*A publication*]
Chr Q Spec ... Christian Quarterly Spectator [*A publication*]
CHRR .... Center for Human Resource Research [*Ohio State University*] [*Research center*] (RCD)
Chr R .... Christian Review [*A publication*]
CHRR .... Committee for Human Rights in Rumania (EA)
Chr Rem ..... Christian Remembrance [*A publication*]
Chr Rep ...... Chamber Reports, Upper Canada [*A publication*] (DLA)
Chr Rob ...... Christopher Robinson's English Admiralty Reports [*165 English Reprint*] [*A publication*] (DLA)
CHRS .... Canadian Heritage River System [*NPPAC*]
CHRS .... Capitol Hill Restoration Society (EA)
CHRS .... Center for Hospitality Research and Service (EA)
CHRS .... Cerebrohepatorenal Syndrome [*Medicine*]
CHRS .... Chambers (ROG)
CHRS .... Charming Shoppes, Inc. [*Bensalem, PA*] [*NASDAQ symbol*] (NQ)
CHRS .... Chrysoberyl [*Jewelry*] (ROG)
CHRS .... Committee for Human Rights in Syria (EA)
CHRS .... Containment Heat Removal System [*Nuclear energy*] (NRCH)
CHRS .... Montreal/St. Jean, PQ [*AM radio station call letters*]
Chr Sch R ... Christian Scholar's Review [*A publication*]
Chr Sci Mon ... Christian Science Monitor [*A publication*]
Chr Sci Monitor ... Christian Science Monitor [*A publication*]
ChrSoc .... Christian Socialist (EY)
CHRST ...... Characteristic (MSA)
CHRSTN ... Christian
Chr T .... Christianity Today [*A publication*]
CHRT .... St. Eleuthere, PQ [*AM radio station call letters*]
CHRTB ...... Chromosomes Today [*A publication*]
CHRTBC ... Chromosomes Today [*A publication*]
Chr Today ... Christianity Today [*A publication*]
CHRU .... Christian Union [*New York*] [*A publication*]
CHRUA ..... Chemische Rundschau [*Solothurn, Switzerland*] [*A publication*]
Chr Un .... Christian Union [*A publication*]
CHRUSNAS ... Committee on Human Rights of the US National Academy of Sciences (EA)
ChrW .... Christentum und Wissenschaft [*A publication*] (BJA)
ChrW .... Die Christliche Welt [*A publication*] (BJA)
ChrWo .... Christianskii Wostok [*A publication*] (BJA)
Chr World ... Christ to the World [*A publication*]
CHRX .... Vancouver, BC [*AM radio station call letters*]
CHRY .... Chrysler Corp.
CHRYA ..... Chemistry [*A publication*]
CHRYSANT ... Chrysanthemum [*Horticulture*] (DSUE)
CHRZ .... Computer Horizons Corp. [*NASDAQ symbol*] (NQ)
CHS .... Baghdad Chamber of Commerce. Commercial Bulletin. Bi-Weekly [*A publication*]
CHS .... California State University, Hayward, Hayward, CA [*Library symbol*] [*Library of Congress*] (LCLS)
CHS .... Cambridge Historical Series [*A publication*]
CHS .... Capitol Historical Society [*Washington, DC*]
CHS .... Catholic Homiletic Society [*Later, CPC*] (EA)
CHS .... Center for Holocaust Studies
CHS .... Center for Human Services (EA)
CHS .... Chain Store Age. Executive Edition [*A publication*]
CHS .... Chalcone Synthase [*An enzyme*]
CHS .... Charleston [*South Carolina*] [*Airport symbol*]
CHS .... Chaus [*Bernard*], Inc. [*NYSE symbol*] (SPSG)
CHS .... Chediak-Higashi Syndrome [*Medicine*]
CHS .... Chester [*British depot code*]
CHS .... Cheswick Historical Society (EA)
CHS .... Chicago Suburban Motor Carriers Association, Inc., Homewood IL [*STAC*]
CHS .... Cholinesterase [*An enzyme*]
ChS .... Christian Scholar [*A publication*]
CHS .... Church Historical Society [*Later, HSEC*] (EA)
CHS .... Chusal [*USSR*] [*Seismograph station code, US Geological Survey*] [*Closed*] (SEIS)
CHS .... Chutine Resources Ltd. [*Vancouver Stock Exchange symbol*]

CHS .... Circular Hollow Section [*Metal industry*]
CHS .... Circus Historical Society (EA)
CHS .... Citizens for Highway Safety [*Defunct*] (EA)
CHS .... Cleveland Health Sciences Library, Cleveland, OH [*OCLC symbol*] (OCLC)
CHS .... College of Health Sciences [*Iran*]
CHS .... College for Human Services [*Formerly, WTC*]
CHS .... Columbia Historical Society [*Later, HSWDC*] (EA)
CHS .... Community Health Service [*HEW*]
CHS .... Concert Hall Society [*Record label*]
CHS .... Confederate Historical Society [*British*]
CHS .... Constant Heat Summation
CHS .... Crime on High Seas
CHSA ..... Chest, Heart, and Stroke Association [*British*]
CHSA ..... Chinese Historical Society of America (EA)
CHSAA ..... Catholic High Schools Athletic Association
CHSB .... Chief Signal Boatswain [*Navy*] [*British*] (ROG)
CHSB .... Cincinnati Historical Society. Bulletin [*A publication*]
CHSB .... Connecticut Historical Society. Bulletin [*A publication*]
CHSC .... Canadian Home Shopping Club
CHSC .... St. Catharines, ON [*AM radio station call letters*]
CHSCD ..... Changing Scene [*A publication*]
CHSCLK ... Chief Ship's Clerk [*Navy rating*] [*Obsolete*]
CHSD .... Children's Health Services Division [*HEW*]
CHSD .... Council for Holocaust Survivors with Disabilities (EA)
Ch Sec .... Chartered Secretary [*A publication*]
Ch Sent ...... Chancery Sentinel [*New York*] [*A publication*] (DLA)
Ch Sent (NY) ... Chancery Sentinel [*New York*] [*A publication*] (DLA)
CHSF .... Cargo Hazardous Servicing Facility (MCD)
CHSI .... Committee on the Health Services Industry [*Cost of Living Council*] [*Abolished, 1973*]
CHSI .... Continental Health Care [*NASDAQ symbol*] (NQ)
CHSJ .... St. John, NB [*AM radio station call letters*]
CHSJ-TV .. St. John, NB [*Television station call letters*]
CHSJ-TV-1 ... Bon Accord, NB [*Television station call letters*]
CHSKED ... Change My Operation Schedule [*Military*] (MUGU)
ChSkr .... Chief Skipper [*Navy*] [*British*]
CHSM .... Centre for Health Services Management [*Leicester Polytechnic*] [*British*] (CB)
CHSM .... China Service Medal [*Military decoration*]
CHSM .... Steinbach, MB [*AM radio station call letters*]
CHSN .... Canadian Home Shopping Network [*Television*]
Ch Soc .... Church and Society [*A publication*]
C H Soc Q ... California Historical Society. Quarterly [*A publication*]
CHSOP ..... Canadian Historic Sites. Occasional Papers in Archaeology and History [*A publication*]
CHSP .... Congregate Housing Services Program [*HUD*]
CHSPR ...... Center for Health Services and Policy Research [*Northwestern University*] [*Research center*] (RCD)
CHSQ .... California Historical Society. Quarterly [*San Francisco*] [*A publication*]
CHSR .... Center for Health Services Research [*University of Iowa*] [*Research center*] (RCD)
Ch S R .... Christian Scholar's Review [*A publication*]
ChSRev ...... Christian Scholar's Review [*A publication*]
CHSR-FM ... Fredericton, NB [*FM radio station call letters*]
CHSS .... Chessco Industries, Inc. [*Westport, CT*] [*NASDAQ symbol*] (NQ)
CHSS .... Children's Hypnotic Susceptibility Scale [*Psychology*]
CHSS .... Cooperative Health Statistics System [*Medicine*]
CHSS-TV .. Wynyard, SK [*Television station call letters*]
CHST .... Canadian Historical Production/Injection File [*Petroleum Information Corp.*] [*Information service or system*] (CRD)
CHST .... Check and Store
CHSTA ...... Child Study Journal [*A publication*]
Ch St J .... Chaplain of the Order of St. John of Jerusalem
CHSTJJ ...... Chaplain of the Order of St. John of Jerusalem
CHSTNT ... Chestnut [*Horse racing*]
CHSTR ...... Characteristics of Transportation Resources File
CHSUA ...... Chartered Surveyor [*Later, Chartered Surveyor Weekly*] [*A publication*]
CHT .... Call Hold and Trace [*Telecommunications*] (TEL)
CHT .... Call Holding Time [*Telecommunications*] (TEL)
CHT .... Cathode Heating Time
CHT .... Ceiling Height [*Technical drawings*]
CHT .... Center for Human Toxicology [*University of Utah*] [*Research center*] (RCD)
CHT .... Ceramic-Heated Tunnel [*Langley Research Center*]
CHT .... Charactron Tube [*Electronics*]
CHT .... Chart House Enterprises [*NYSE symbol*] (SPSG)
CHT .... Chest [*Shipping*]
CHT .... Chillicothe, MO [*Location identifier*] [*FAA*] (FAAL)
CHT .... Chittagong [*Bangladesh*] [*Seismograph station code, US Geological Survey*] (SEIS)
CHT .... Christelijk Historisch Tijdschrift [*A publication*]
ChT .... Church Teachers [*A publication*]
CHT .... Chute (KSC)
CHT .... Collection, Holding, Transfer [*Shipboard waste disposal*] (MCD)
CHT .... Convective Heat Transfer

CHT.......... Cylinder-Head Temperature
ChTB......... Channel Terminal Bay
CHTB........ Cohasset Savings Bank [*NASDAQ symbol*]   (NQ)
CHTC........ China Technical Services Corporation [*Redditch, Worcestershire, England*] [*NASDAQ symbol*]   (NQ)
CHTCB5.... Enfant en Milieu Tropical [*A publication*]
CHTED..... Chemtech [*A publication*]
CHTG........ Charting   (AFM)
ChTg......... Chymotrypsinogen [*Biochemistry*]
CHTHA..... Chung-Shan Ta Hsueh Hsueh Pao. Tzu Jan K'o Hsueh [*A publication*]
ChTK........ Chicken Thymidine Kinase [*An enzyme*]
CHTK........ Prince Rupert, BC [*AM radio station call letters*]
CHTL........ Chantal Pharmaceutical Corp. [*Los Angeles, CA*] [*NASDAQ symbol*]   (NQ)
CHTM....... Thompson, MB [*AM radio station call letters*]
CHTN........ Charlottetown, PE [*AM radio station call letters*]
CHTN........ Cooperative Human Tissue Network
CHTO........ Chiang Mai [*Thailand*] [*Seismograph station code, US Geological Survey*]   (SEIS)
CHTORP .. Chief Torpedoman [*Navy rating*] [*Obsolete*]
CHTR........ Charter   (FAAC)
CHTRD..... Chicago Tribune [*A publication*]
CHTT........ Chattem, Inc. [*Chattanooga, TN*] [*NASDAQ symbol*]   (NQ)
CHTT........ Chicago Heights Terminal Transfer Railroad Co. [*AAR code*]
CHTTA ..... Chuko To Tanko [*A publication*]
Ch T U P... [*T. U. P.*] Charlton's Georgia Reports [*A publication*]   (DLA)
CHTW....... Canadian High Technology Week [*Trade show*]   (ITD)
CHTX........ Montreal, PQ [*AM radio station call letters*]
CHTZ........ Chlorothiazide [*Diuretic*]
CHTZA ..... Chishitsugaku Zasshi [*A publication*]
CHTZA5 ... Chishitsugaku Zasshi [*A publication*]
CHTZ-FM ... St. Catharines, ON [*FM radio station call letters*]
CHU .... Caledonia, MN [*Location identifier*] [*FAA*]   (FAAL)
CHU .... Caloric Heat Unit
CHU .... Celsius Heat Unit   (ADA)
CHU .... Centigrade Heat Unit
CHU .... Channel Resources Ltd. [*Vancouver Stock Exchange symbol*]
CHU .... Christelijk-Historische Unie [*Christian-Historical Union*] [*Netherlands*] [*Political party*]   (PPW)
CHU .... Chur [*Coire*] [*Switzerland*] [*Seismograph station code, US Geological Survey*] [*Closed*]   (SEIS)
CHU .... Church
Chu............ Church Music [*A publication*]
chu............ Church Slavic [*MARC language code*] [*Library of Congress*]   (LCCP)
CHU .... Churches Speak [*A publication*]
CHU .... Church's Fried Chicken, Inc. [*NYSE symbol*]   (SPSG)
CHU .... Humboldt State College, Arcata, CA [*OCLC symbol*]   (OCLC)
CHu .... Huntington Beach Public Library, Huntington Beach, CA [*Library symbol*] [*Library of Congress*]   (LCLS)
CHUAS ..... Cooperative Hurricane Upper Air Station [*National Weather Service*]   (NOAA)
CHUB........ Nanaimo, BC [*AM radio station call letters*]
CHUC........ Cobourg, ON [*AM radio station call letters*]
CHUCK..... Committee to Halt Useless College Killings [*Acronym is now organization's official name*]   (EA)
CHUD........ Cannibalistic Humanoid Underground Dwellers [*or Contaminated Hazard Underground Disposal*] [*Acronym used as title of movie*]
CHuG......... Golden West College, Huntington Beach, CA [*Library symbol*] [*Library of Congress*]   (LCLS)
Chugoku Agr Res ... Chugoku Agricultural Research [*A publication*]
Chugoku Shikoku Dist J Jpn Soc Obstet Gynecol ... Chugoku and Shikoku Districts Journal. Japan Society of Obstetrics and Gynecology [*A publication*]
CHUIAR ... Chung-Ang Uihak [*A publication*]
CHUM ...... Center for the Humanities [*State University of New York at Albany*] [*Research center*]   (RCD)
CHUM ...... Chart Updating Manual [*Air Force*]
CHUM ...... Chumleigh [*England*]
CHum .... Computers and the Humanities [*Database*] [*A publication*]
CHUM ...... Toronto, ON [*AM radio station call letters*]
CHuMD.... McDonnell Douglas Astronautics Co., Western Division, Huntington Beach, CA [*Library symbol*] [*Library of Congress*]   (LCLS)
CHUM-FM ... Toronto, ON [*FM radio station call letters*]
Chump .... Child of Upwardly Mobile Professionals [*Lifestyle classification*]
CHUMP.... Criminal Headquarters for Underworld Master Plan [*Organization in TV series "Lancelot Link"*]
CHUMS.... Cancer Hopefuls United for Mutual Support   (EA)
Chung-Ang J Med ... Chung-Ang Journal of Medicine [*South Korea*] [*A publication*]
Chung Hua Lin Hsueh Chi K'an Q J Chin For ... Chung-Hua Lin Hsueh Chi K'an. Quarterly Journal of Chinese Forestry [*A publication*]
Chung-Hua Nung Yeh Yen Chiu J Agric Res China ... Chung-Hua Nung Yeh Yen Chiu/Journal of Agriculture Research of China [*A publication*]

Chung-Kuo Lin Yeh K'o Hsueh Chin For Sci ... Chung-Kuo Lin Yeh K'o Hsueh/Chinese Forestry Science [*A publication*]
Chung-Kuo Nung Yeh Hua Hsueh Hui Chih J Chin Agric Chem Soc ... Chung-Kuo Nung Yeh Hua Hsueh Hui Chih/Journal of the Chinese Agriculture Chemical Society [*A publication*]
Chung-Kuo Nung Yeh K'o Hsueh Sci Agric Sin ... Chung-Kuo Nung Yeh K'o Hsueh/Scientia Agricultura Sinica [*A publication*]
Chungnam J Sci ... Chungnam Journal of Sciences [*South Korea*] [*A publication*]
Chung-Shan Univ J Nat Sci Ed ... Chung-Shan University Journal. Natural Sciences Edition [*People's Republic of China*] [*A publication*]
CHUNNEL ... Channel Tunnel [*Joint British-French project in English Channel*]
Chuppie...... Chinese Urban Professional [*Hong Kong Yuppie*] [*Lifestyle classification*]
CHUR........ Chondritic Uniform Reservoir [*Geology*]
CHUR........ Churchill Technology, Inc. [*NASDAQ symbol*]   (NQ)
CHUR........ North Bay, ON [*AM radio station call letters*]
Church & Br Sh ... Churchill and Bruce. Office and Duties of Sheriff [*2nd ed.*] [*1882*] [*A publication*]   (DLA)
Church Eng Hist Soc J ... Church of England Historical Society. Journal [*A publication*]   (APTA)
Church Hist ... Church History [*A publication*]
Church Mus (London) ... Church Music (London) [*A publication*]
Church Mus (St L) ... Church Music (St. Louis) [*A publication*]
Church Q ... Church Quarterly Review [*A publication*]
Church Q R ... Church Quarterly Review [*A publication*]
Church R.... Church Review [*A publication*]
CHUSAOSASF ... Chief, United States Army Overseas Supply Agency, San Francisco   (CINC)
CHUSMSI ... Chief, United States Military Supply Mission, India   (CINC)
CHUT........ Chutty [*Chewing gum*] [*Slang*] [*British*]   (DSUE)
CHUTE ...... Parachute   (NASA)
Chute Eq .... Chute's Equity under the Judicature Act [*A publication*]   (DLA)
CHuW........ Christentum und Wissenschaft [*A publication*]   (BJA)
CHV.......... Carl Hanser [*Publisher*]
CHV.......... Chattahoochee Valley Railway Co. [*AAR code*]
CHV.......... Check Valve   (KSC)
CH-V........ Cheval-Vapeur [*Horsepower*] [*French*]
CHV.......... Chevron Corp. [*Vancouver Stock Exchange symbol*] [*NYSE symbol*]   (SPSG)
CHV.......... Chiavari [*Italy*] [*Seismograph station code, US Geological Survey*] [*Closed*]   (SEIS)
ChV.......... Chilean Victor [*Record label*]
chv............. Chuvash [*MARC language code*] [*Library of Congress*]   (LCCP)
CHVA........ Contemporary Historical Vehicle Association   (EA)
CHVCA .... Chauffage, Ventilation, Conditionnement [*A publication*]
CHVD........ Dolbeau, PQ [*AM radio station call letters*]
CHVO........ Carbonear, NF [*AM radio station call letters*]
CHVP .... Cyclophosphamide, Hydroxydaunomycin [*Adriamycin*], VM-26 [*Teniposide*], Prednisone [*Antineoplastic drug regimen*]
CHW........ Chatwood Resources [*Vancouver Stock Exchange symbol*]
CHW........ Chemical Waste Management [*NYSE symbol*]   (SPSG)
CHW........ Chemisch Weekblad/Chemische Courant [*A publication*]
CHW........ Chesapeake Western Railway [*AAR code*]
CHW........ Chilled Water [*Aerospace*]   (AAG)
CHW........ Chowiet Island [*Alaska*] [*Seismograph station code, US Geological Survey*]   (SEIS)
CHW........ Citizens Highway Watch [*Australia*]
CHW........ Cold Heading Wire
CHW........ Cold and Hot Water
CHW........ Constant Hot Water [*British*]
CHW........ Jiuquan [*China*] [*Airport symbol*]   (OAG)
CHWCA .... Chung-Hua Wai K'o Tsa Chih [*A publication*]
CHWCAJ ... Chinese Journal of Surgery [*A publication*]
CHWDN .... Churchwarden
CHWEA .... Chemisch Weekblad [*Later, Chemisch Weekblad/Chemische Courant*] [*A publication*]
CHWHA .... Chih Wu Hsueh Pao [*A publication*]
CHWHAY ... Acta Botanica Sinica [*A publication*]
CHWK....... Chilliwack, BC [*AM radio station call letters*]
CHWKA .... Chemical Week [*A publication*]
CHWO ..... Oakville, ON [*AM radio station call letters*]
CHWOD ... Chevron World [*A publication*]
CHWPC .... Capitol Hill Women's Political Caucus   (EA)
CHWR....... Cooling Water/Hot Water Return [*Nuclear energy*]   (NRCH)
CHWS .... Council for Health and Welfare Services, United Church of Christ [*Later, CHHSM*]   (EA)
CHWTO..... Chief, Western Pacific Transportation Office   (CINC)
CHX.......... Cabin Heat Exchanger [*Aviation*]   (MCD)
CHX.......... Chaix Hill [*Alaska*] [*Seismograph station code, US Geological Survey*]   (SEIS)
CHX.......... Changuinola [*Panama*] [*Airport symbol*]   (OAG)
CHX.......... Chavin of Canada [*Vancouver Stock Exchange symbol*]
CHX.......... Chemische Rundschau. Europaeische Wochenzeitung fuer Chemie, Pharmazeutik, und die Lebensmittelindustrie [*A publication*]
CHX.......... Chiro-Xylographic [*Type of block book*]
CHX.......... Choteau, MT [*Location identifier*] [*FAA*]   (FAAL)

CH-X	Condensate Heat Exchanger (MCD)
CHX..........	Cycloheximide [Also, CH, CXM, Cyh] [Fungicide]
CHX..........	Pilgrim's Pride Corp. [NYSE symbol] (SPSG)
CHXL-FM ...	Brockville, ON [FM radio station call letters]
CHY..........	Chancery
CHY..........	Charity
chy..............	Cheyenne [MARC language code] [Library of Congress] (LCCP)
CHY..........	Chiayi [Republic of China] [Seismograph station code, US Geological Survey] (SEIS)
CHY..........	Chimney
CHY..........	Choiseul Bay [Solomon Islands] [Airport symbol] (OAG)
CHY..........	Christian Heritage Year [1984] [British]
CHY..........	Chyron Corp. [NYSE symbol] (SPSG)
CHY..........	Denver, CO [Location identifier] [FAA] (FAAL)
Chy App Rep ...	Wright's Tennessee Chancery Appeals Reports [A publication] (DLA)
CHYCDW ...	Chinese Journal of Preventive Medicine [A publication]
Chy Ch.......	Upper Canada Chancery Chambers Reports [A publication] (DLA)
Chy Chrs....	Upper Canada Chancery Chambers Reports [A publication] (DLA)
CHYD........	Churchyard
CHYM.......	Kitchener, ON [AM radio station call letters]
CHYN........	Cheyenne Resources, Inc. [Cheyenne, WY] [NASDAQ symbol] (NQ)
CHYQ........	Musgravetown, NF [AM radio station call letters]
CHYR........	Leamington, ON [AM radio station call letters]
CHYR-7.....	Leamington, ON [AM radio station call letters]
CHZ..........	Centrala Handlu Zagranicznego [Commercial Center for Foreign Trade] [Poland]
CHZ..........	Chisholm Resources [Vancouver Stock Exchange symbol]
CHZ..........	Chorzow [Poland] [Seismograph station code, US Geological Survey] (SEIS)
CHZC	Charvoz-Carsen Corp. [NASDAQ symbol] (NQ)
CHZM.......	Cheezem Development Corp. [NASDAQ symbol] (NQ)
CHZZ-FM ...	Winnipeg, MB [FM radio station call letters]
CI	C. Itoh & Co. Ltd. [Hong Kong]
CI	Call Indicator [Data processing]
CI	Cambria & Indiana Railroad Co. [AAR code]
CI	Canadian Insurance [A publication]
CI	Canadian Interiors [A publication]
CI	Cancer Investigation [A publication]
CI	Candover Investments [Finance] [British]
CI	Capability Inspection [Air Force] (AFM)
CI	Capital Intensive [Finance]
CI	Captain-Instructor [Navy] [British]
CI	Carcinogenic Index
CI	Card Input [Data processing] (BUR)
CI	Cardiac Index [Physiology]
CI	Caritas Internationalis [International Confederation of Catholic Organizations for Charitable and Social Action] [Vatican City, Vatican City State] (EAIO)
CI	Carnegie Institute [New York]
C/I..............	Carrier-to-Interference Ratio [Data processing]
CI	Cash Item [Accounting]
CI	Cast Iron
CI	Catfish Institute [An association] (EA)
CI	Cato Institute (EA)
CI	CAUSA Institute (EA)
CI	Cayman Islands
CI	Cellular, Inc. [Telecommunications service] (TSSD)
CI	Center of Impact
CI	Center Island [Nuclear energy] (NRCH)
CI	Central Interval
CI	Centrifugation Interaction
CI	Centromeric Indices [Chromosomes]
CI	Cephalic Index
CI	Cereal Institute [Defunct] (EA)
CI	Cerebral Infarction [Medicine]
C of I	Ceremony of Installation [Freemasonry] (ROG)
CI	Certificat d'Investissement [Stock exchange] [French]
C/I..............	Certificate of Indebtedness [Finance]
CI	Certificate of Insurance
CI	Certification Inspection (MCD)
CI	Cetane Index [Fuel technology]
CI	Chain Index (ADA)
CI	Channel Islands
CI	Chapters of Instruction [Freemasonry] (ROG)
CI	Characteristic Independence
CI	Chemical Injection [Nuclear energy] (NRCH)
CI	Chemical Inspectorate [British]
C + I	Chemical and Insulating
CI	Chemical Ionization [Spectrometry]
CI	Chemistry International [A publication]
CI	Chemotherapeutic Index [Medicine]
CI	Cher'd Interest [Fan club] (EA)
CI	Chest Incision [Medicine]
CI	Chief of Information [Army]
CI	Chief Inspector
CI	Chief Instructor

CI	Children, Incorporated [An association] (EA)
CI	China Institute in America (EA)
CI	Chlorine Institute (EA)
CI	Cholesteryl Iopanoate [Biochemistry]
CI	Christic Institute (EA)
CI	Chums, Inc. [An association] (EA)
C of I	Church of Ireland
CI	Ciesta Gold Exploration Ltd. [Vancouver Stock Exchange symbol]
CI	CIGNA Corp. [NYSE symbol] (SPSG)
CI	Cimetidine [Pharmacology]
Ci................	Cinus de Pistoia [Deceased, 1336] [Authority cited in pre-1607 legal work] (DSA)
CI	Circuit Interrupter (MCD)
Ci................	Cirrhosis [Medicine]
CI	Cirrus [Meteorology]
CI	City Invincible [A publication]
CI	Civil Imprisonment
CI	Civitan International (EA)
C & I	Classification and Index [Air Force] (AFM)
CI	Classification Inventory [Military]
CI	Close-In
CI	Coefficient of Intelligence
CI	Color Index
CI	Color Interior Film (MCD)
CI	Combat Indoctrination (MCD)
CI	Combat Ineffective [Military] (NVT)
CI	Combat Interviews
CI	Combination Inventory [LIMRA]
CI	Combustion Institute (EA)
CI	Comfort Index
CI	Command Information (MCD)
CI	Commander-Instructor [Navy] [British]
CI	Comment Issue
CI	Commercial Intelligencer [A publication]
CI	Communication Information
C & I	Communication and Instrumentation [NASA] (KSC)
CI	Communication and Instrumentation [NASA] (KSC)
CI	Communications Interface (MCD)
CI	Community of Interest [Telecommunications] (TEL)
CI	Compassion International (EA)
C & I	Compatibility and Interoperability (RDA)
CI	Competitive Intelligence [Corporate libraries]
CI	Complete Iridectomy [Ophthalmology]
CI	Composites Institute (EA)
CI	Compounded Interest [Business term]
CI	Compression Ignition Engine
CI	Compulsory Insurance
CI	Computer Indicator (AFM)
CI	Computer Industry
CI	Computer Inquiries
CI	Computer Intelligence Corp. [Information service or system] (IID)
CI	Computer Interrogator
CI	Computing Index [Computer analysis]
CI	Concept Identification [Psychology]
CI	Concern, Inc. [An association] (EA)
CI	Confidence Interval [Statistics]
CI	Confidential Informant [Department of Justice]
CI	Configuration Identification (MCD)
CI	Configuration Inspection (NASA)
CI	Configuration Interaction [Quantum mechanics]
CI	Configuration Item
CI	Congressional Interference
CI	Conservation International (EA)
CI	Consistency Index [Botany]
CI	Constitutional Instrument [Ghana] [A publication] (DLA)
CI	Consular Invoice
CI	Consumer Information
CI	Consumer Interpol (EA)
CI	Consuming Interest [A publication] (ADA)
CI	Containerization Institute [Later, CII]
CI	Containment Integrity [Nuclear energy] (NRCH)
CI	Containment Isolation [Nuclear energy] (NRCH)
CI	Contamination Index [Medicine]
CI	Continuous Injection [Automotive engineering]
CI	Continuous Interlock (MCD)
CI	Contract Items
CI	Contractor Inventory
C & I	Control and Indication (MCD)
CI	Control Indicator
C & I	Control and Instrumentation (NRCH)
CI	Controlled Ionization
CI	Controlled Item
CI	Conventional Instruction (RDA)
CI	Cooperating Individual [FBI]
CI	Coordinate Index
CI	Coordinating Installations (MCD)
CI	Cordage Institute (EA)
CI	Core Insulation [Nuclear energy]
CI	Cornell Index [Psychology]

CI .... Coronary Insufficiency [*Medicine*]
CI .... Corrected Count Increment [*Hematology*]
Ci .... Cosine Integral
CI .... Cosmopolitan International   (EA)
CI .... Cost Inspector
CI .... Cost and Insurance [*Shipping*]
C & I .... Cost and Insurance [*Shipping*]
CI .... Cotton Incorporated [*An association*]   (EA)
CI .... Cottonseed Protein Isolate
CI .... Counterinsurgency   (CINC)
CI .... Counterintelligence   (MCD)
CI .... Couples, Inc. [*An association*]   (EA)
CI .... Course Indicator   (IEEE)
CI .... Covert Investigation [*Police term*]
CI .... Craft Inclination [*Aerospace*]   (AAG)
CI .... Cranberry Institute   (EA)
CI .... Creative Initiative [*Later, BWF*]   (EA)
CI .... Crew Interface   (MCD)
CI .... Criminal Informant
CI .... Criminal Intelligence [*Branch of the Metropolitan Police,
                  London*]
CI .... Criminal Investigation [*or Investigator*] [*Military*]
CI .... Critical Influence
CI .... Critical Inquiry [*A publication*]
CI .... Critical Intelligence
CI .... Critical Item
CI .... Cropping Index
CI .... Crucible Institute [*Formerly, CMA*]   (EA)
CI .... Crystal Impedance
CI .... Crystalline Insulin
CI .... Cuadernos del Idioma [*A publication*]
CI .... Cubic Inch   (MCD)
CI .... Cumulative Index   (DLA)
Ci .... Curie [*Unit of radioactivity*] [*Preferred unit is Bq, Becquerel*]
CI .... Customer Item
CI .... Cut In
CI .... Cytotoxic Index [*Cytochemistry*]
CI .... Grand Cayman [*IYRU nationality code*]   (IYR)
CI .... Imperial Order of the Crown of India [*British*]
CI .... Ivory Coast [*ANSI two-letter standard code*]   (CNC)
CI .... Juedisch-Palaestinisches Corpus Inscriptionum [*A
                  publication*]   (BJA)
CI2 .... Parke, Davis & Co. [*Research code symbol*]
CI2 .... Second Computer Inquiry   (TSSD)
C³I .... Command, Control, Communications, and Intelligence
                  [*Pronounced "see-cubed eye"*]
C³I .... Computer-Controlled Coil Ignition
C³I² .... Command, Control, Communications, Intelligence, and
                  Interoperability
C⁴I²bd .... Command, Control, Communications, Computing/Information
                  and Intelligence
CI's............. Crossability Indices [*Botany*]
CIA .... California Institute of the Arts [*Valencia*] [*OCLC
                  symbol*]   (OCLC)
CIA .... Canadian Implant Association   (EAIO)
CIA .... Canadian Importers Association
CIA .... Canadian Institute of Actuaries
CIA .... Capitol Information Association   (EA)
CIA .... Captured in Action [*Military*]
CIA .... Cariana International Industries, Inc. [*Vancouver Stock
                  Exchange symbol*]
CIA .... Casein Importers Association   (EA)
CIA .... Cash in Advance
CIA .... Catholic Irish Attorneys [*Fictional organization*]
CIA .... CCNU [*Lomustine*], Ifosfamide, Adriamycin [*Antineoplastic
                  drug regimen*]
CIA .... Cement Industry Authority [*Philippines*]   (DS)
CIA .... Center for Interreligious Affairs
CIA .... Central Intelligence Agency [*Acronym has been facetiously
                  translated "Casey in Action", a reference to the agency's
                  former director*]
CIA .... Centre International des Antiparasitaires
CIA .... Ceramics International Association   (EA)
CIA .... Certified Internal Auditor [*Designation awarded by The
                  Institute of Internal Auditors, Inc.*]
CIA .... Chemical Industries Association
CIA .... Chief Inspector of Armaments
CIA .... China Institute in America   (EA)
CIA .... Chymotrypsin Inhibitor Activity
CIA .... Cigar Institute of America [*Later, CAA*]   (EA)
CIA .... Clumping Inducing Agent [*Bacteriology, genetics*]
CIA .... Collegium Internationale Allergologicum [*Berne,
                  Switzerland*]   (EA)
CIA .... Comite International d'Auschwitz [*International Auschwitz
                  Committee*]
CIA .... Commission on International Affairs   (EA)
CIA .... Commission Internationale d'Analyses
CIA .... Communications Interface Assembly [*Data processing*]
CIA .... Communications Interrupt Analysis [*Sperry UNIVAC*]   (IEEE)
Cia.............. Compagnia [*Company*] [*Italian*]
Cia.............. Companhia [*Company*] [*Portuguese*]

CIA .... Compania [*Company*] [*Spanish*]
CIA .... Computer Industry Association [*Later, CCIA*]
CIA .... Computer Interface Adapter
CIA .... Confederation Internationale des Accordeonistes [*International
                  Confederation of Accordionists*]
CIA .... Conseil International des Archives [*International Council on
                  Archives*]
CIA .... Consultant-Initiated Activity [*LIMRA*]
CIA .... Consumer Information Association
CIA .... Containment Isolation A [*Nuclear energy*]   (NRCH)
CIA .... Control Indicator Assembly   (MCD)
CIA .... Control Interface Assembly   (MCD)
CIA .... Controllers Institute of America [*Later, FEI*]
CIA .... Cooperative Immunoassay
CIA .... Cork Institute of America [*Defunct*]   (EA)
CIA .... Corpus Inscriptionum Atticarum [*A publication*]
CIA .... Correctional Industries Association   (EA)
CIA .... Cotton Importers Association   (EA)
CIA .... Cotton Insurance Association [*Defunct*]   (EA)
CIA .... Council on Islamic Affairs   (EA)
C & IA .... Counterintelligence and Investigative Activities [*Military*]
CIA .... Culinary Institute of America [*Hyde Park, NY*]
CIA .... Curtain Industry Association of Victoria [*Australia*]
CIA .... Rome [*Italy*] Ciampino Airport [*Airport symbol*]
                  [*Obsolete*]   (OAG)
CIAA......... Central Intercollegiate Athletic Association   (EA)
CIAA......... Centre International d'Aviation Agricole [*International
                  Agricultural Aviation Center*]
CIAA......... Cheese Importers Association of America   (EA)
CIAA......... College Inventory of Academic Adjustment [*Psychology*]
CIAA......... Confederation des Industries Agro-Alimentaires de la CEE
                  [*Confederation of the Food and Drink Industries of the
                  ECC*]   (EAIO)
CIAA......... Coordinator of Inter-American Affairs
CIAA de l'UNICE ... Confederation des Industries Agro-Alimentaires de
                  l'Union des Industries de la Communaute Europeenne
                  [*Commission of the Agricultural and Food Industries of the
                  Union of Industries of the European Community*]   (EAIO)
CIAB......... Coal Industry Advisory Board
CIAB......... Conseil International des Agences Benevoles [*International
                  Council of Voluntary Agencies - ICVA*]   (EA)
CIAC......... Canadian Independent Adjusters Conference
CIAC......... Canadian Indian Artcrafts. National Indian Arts and Crafts
                  Advisory Committee [*A publication*]
CIAC......... Career Information and Counseling [*Air Force*]
CIAC......... Central Industrial Applications Center [*Southeastern Oklahoma
                  State University*] [*Information service or system*]   (IID)
CIAC......... Centre d'Inter-Action Culturelle [*Center for Inter-Cultural
                  Action*]   (EAIO)
CIAC......... Contributions in Aid of Construction [*IRS*]
CIAC......... Council for Inter-American Cooperation [*Later, NFTC*]
CIACA...... International Committee for Amateur-Built Aircraft   (EA)
CIACDL.... Centro Internacional de Agricultura Tropical [*CIAT*]. Series CE
                  [*A publication*]
CIACS .... Coded Integrated Armament Control System   (MCD)
CIACT....... CNO [*Chief of Naval Operations*] Industry Advisory
                  Committee for Telecommunications [*DoD*]   (EGAO)
CIAD .... Coalition Internationale pour l'Action au Developpement
                  [*International Coalition for Development Action -
                  ICDA*]   (EAIO)
CIAD .... Counterintelligence Analysis Division [*DoD*]
CIADEC .... Confederation Internationale des Associations de Diplomes en
                  Sciences Economiques et Commerciales [*International
                  Confederation of Associations of Graduates in Economic
                  and Commercial Sciences*]
CIADFOR ... Centre Interafricain pour le Developpement de la Formation
                  Professionnelle [*Inter-African Center for the Development
                  of Professional Training*] [*Abidjan, Ivory Coast*]   (EAIO)
CIADI........ Centro Internacional de Arreglo de Diferencias Relativas a
                  Inversiones [*International Center for Settlement of
                  Investment Disputes*]
CIADI........ Clinically Important Adverse Drug Interactions [*Elsevier Book
                  Series*] [*A publication*]
CIADSR .... Comite International sur l'Alcool, les Drogues et la Securite
                  Routiere [*International Committee on Alcohol, Drugs, and
                  Traffic Safety*]   (EAIO)
CIAE......... Chicago International Art Exhibition   (ITD)
CIAE......... Crossed Immunoaffinoelectrophoresis [*Analytical
                  biochemistry*]
CIAF......... Centro Interamericano de Fotointerpretacion [*Bogota,
                  Colombia*]
CIAFMA ... Centre International de l'Actualite Fantastique et Magique
CIAGA...... Confederacion Interamericana de Ganaderos
CIAGP....... Commission Internationale des Aumoniers Generaux des
                  Prisons [*International Commission of Catholic Prison
                  Chaplains - ICPC*]   (EA)
CIAgrE ...... Companion of the Institution of Agricultural Engineers [*British*]
CIAH......... Culture, Illness, and Healing [*A publication*]
CIAI.......... Comite International d'Aide aux Intellectuels
CIAJ.......... Communications Industries Association of Japan
                  [*Telecommunications*]   (TSSD)

Cial............ Commercial [*Commercial*] [*French*]

CIAL.......... Communaute Internationale des Associations de la Librairie [*International Community of Booksellers Associations*]

CIAL.......... Corresponding Member of the International Institute of Arts and Letters

CIAL.......... Credit Industriel d'Alsace et de Lorraine [*France*]   (EY)

CIALANT ... Central Intelligence Agency, Atlantic   (MCD)

CIAM .... Caisse Industrielle d'Assurance Mutuelle [*France*]   (EY)

CIAM .... Cambridge, ON [*AM radio station call letters*]

CIAMAE.... Centro de Investigaciones Agronomicas Maracay. Monografia [*A publication*]

CIANDE.... Civil Information and Education Section of Allied Headquarters [*World War II*]

CIANS...... Collegium Internationale Activitatis Nervosae Superioris [*Milan, Italy*]   (EAIO)

CIAO .... Brampton, ON [*AM radio station call letters*]

CIAO .... Conference Internationale des Africanistes de l'Ouest

CIAO .... Congress of Italian-American Organizations

CIAP.......... Climatic Impact Assessment Program [*for high altitude aircraft*]

CIAP.......... Climatic Implications of Atmospheric Pollution

CIAP.......... Comite Interamericano de la Alianza para el Progreso [*Inter-American Committee of the Alliance for Progress*]

CIAP.......... Comprehensive Improvement Assistance Program [*HUD*]

CIAPG....... Confederation Internationale des Anciens Prisonniers de Guerre [*International Confederation of Former Prisoners of War*] [*Paris, France*]   (EAIO)

CIAPS .... Customer-Integrated Automated Procurement System   (AFM)

CIAR .... Canadian Institute for Advanced Research

CIAR.......... Center for Inter-American Relations   (EA)

CIARA....... Conference Internationale Administrative des Radiocommunications Aeronautiques

CIARA....... Conference Internationale sur l'Assistance aux Refugies en Afrique [*International Conference on Assistance for Refugees in Africa - ICARA*] [*United Nations*] [*Geneva, Switzerland*]   (EAIO)

CIARAT .... Cawthron Institute [*Nelson, New Zealand*]. Report [*A publication*]

CIAS .... California Institute of Asian Studies [*An evening graduate school*]   (EA)

CIAS .... Central Ironmoulders Association of Scotland [*A union*]

CIAS .... Chicago International Antiques Show   (ITD)

CIAS .... Conference of Independent African States   (NATG)

CIAS .... Conseil Inter-Americain de Securite [*Inter-American Safety Council*]

CIAS .... Conseil International de l'Action Sociale [*International Council on Social Welfare - ICSW*] [*Vienna, Austria*]   (EA)

CIAS .... Containment Isolation Actuation Signal [*Nuclear energy*]   (NRCH)

CIASE .... Computer Institute for Applications in Science and Engineering   (MCD)

CIAT.......... Centro Interamericano de Administracion del Trabajo [*Inter-American Center for Labor Administration*] [*Lima, Peru*]   (EAIO)

CIAT.......... Centro Interamericano de Administradores Tributarios [*Inter-American Center of Tax Administrators*]   (EAIO)

CIAT.......... Centro Internacional de Agricultura Tropical [*International Center for Tropical Agriculture*] [*Colombia*]

CIAT.......... Ciatti's, Inc. [*NASDAQ symbol*]   (NQ)

CIAT.......... Comision Interamericana del Atun Tropical [*Interamerican Tropical Tuna Commission - IATTC*]

CIAT.......... Crew-Initiated Automatic Test

CIAT Annu Rep ... CIAT [*Centro Internacional de Agricultura Tropical*] Annual Report [*A publication*]

CIATB2 ...... Centro Internacional de Agricultura Tropical [*CIAT*]. Annual Report [*A publication*]

CIATC3 ..... Centro Internacional de Agricultura Tropical [*CIAT*]. Technical Bulletin [*A publication*]

CIATF .... Comite Internacional des Associations Techniques de Fonderie [*International Committee of Foundry Technical Associations*]   (EAIO)

CIAT Ser Semin ... CIAT [*Centro Internacional de Agricultura Tropical*] Series Seminars [*A publication*]

CIAU .... Canadian Intercollegiate Athletic Union

CIB............ CALS [*Customs Acts Legislation Service*] Information Bulletin [*Australia*] [*A publication*]

CIB............ Canada Income Plus Fund Trust Units [*Toronto Stock Exchange symbol*]

CIB............ Canadian Infantry Brigade   (DMA)

CIB............ Catalina Island [*California*] Airport in the Sky [*Airport symbol*]   (OAG)

CIB............ Centra-European-International Bank Ltd. [*Hungary*]   (IMH)

CIB............ Central Intelligence Board

CIB............ Centralized Intercept Bureau [*Bell System*]

CIB............ Centrum voor Informatie Beleid [*Netherlands Center for Information Policy*] [*The Hague*] [*Information service or system*]   (IID)

CIB............ Change Impact Board   (NASA)

CIB............ Charities Information Bureaux [*British*]   (CB)

CIB............ Chartered Institute of Bankers [*London, England*]   (EAIO)

CIB............ Chartered Insurance Broker

CIB............ China, India, Burma

CIB............ Chloride Industrial Batteries [*Manufacturer*] [*British*]

CIB............ Cibus [*Meal*] [*Latin*]

CIB............ COBOL [*Common Business-Oriented Language*] Information Bulletin [*Air Force*]

CIB............ Cognac Information Bureau [*Commercial firm*]   (EA)

CIB............ Combat Infantryman's Badge [*Military decoration*]

CIB............ Command Information Bureau [*Military*]   (CINC)

CIB............ Command Input Block [*Data processing*]

CIB............ Command Input Buffer [*Data processing*]   (IBMDP)

CIB............ Commercial and Industrial Bulletin [*Ghana*] [*A publication*]   (DLA)

CIB............ Communaute Internationale Baha'ie [*Baha'i International Community*]

CIB............ Complaints Investigation Branch [*Scotland Yard*]

CIB............ Complementary Instruction Book [*Military*]

CIB............ Concrete Industry Board

CIB............ Conseil International du Batiment pour la Recherche, l'Etude, et la Documentation [*International Council for Building Research, Studies, and Documentation*]   (EAIO)

CIB............ Conseil International du Ble [*International Wheat Council - IWC*]   (EAIO)

CIB............ Containment Isolation B [*Nuclear energy*]   (NRCH)

CIB............ Cosmic Infrared Background Radiation

CIB............ Counterfeiting Intelligence Bureau [*International Chamber of Commerce*] [*British*]   (CB)

CIB............ Criminal Intelligence Bureau

CIB............ Current Intelligence Bulletin [*A publication*]

CIB............ ICC [*International Chamber of Commerce*] Counterfeiting Intelligence Bureau   (EA)

CIBA.......... Chemical Industry in Basle

Ciba.......... Ciba Symposia [*A publication*]

CIBA.......... Citizens Bank [*Murphy, NC*] [*NASDAQ symbol*]   (NQ)

Ciba Clin Symp ... Ciba Clinical Symposia [*A publication*]

Ciba Collect Med Illus ... Ciba Collection of Medical Illustrations [*A publication*]

Ciba Fdn Symp ... Ciba Foundation. Symposium [*A publication*]

Ciba Found Colloq Endocrinol ... Ciba Foundation. Colloquia on Endocrinology [*A publication*]

Ciba Found Study Group ... Ciba Foundation. Study Group [*A publication*]

Ciba Found Symp ... Ciba Foundation. Symposium [*A publication*]

Ciba Geigy J ... Ciba-Geigy Journal [*A publication*]

Ciba-Geigy Tech Notes ... Ciba-Geigy Technical Notes [*A publication*]

Ciba J......... Ciba Journal [*A publication*]

Ciba Lect Microb Biochem ... Ciba Lectures in Microbial Biochemistry [*A publication*]

Ciba R .... Ciba Review [*A publication*]

Ciba Rundsch ... Ciba Rundschau [*A publication*]

Ciba Symp ... Ciba Symposia [*A publication*]

CIBC.......... CABI [*Commonwealth Agricultural Bureaux International*] Institute of Biological Control [*United Kingdom*] [*Research center*]   (IRC)

CIBC.......... Canadian Imperial Bank of Commerce

CIBC.......... Citizens Bancorp [*NASDAQ symbol*]   (NQ)

CIBC.......... Commonwealth Institute of Biological Control [*Trinidad*]

CIBC.......... Confederation Internationale de la Boucherie et de la Charcuterie [*International Federation of Meat Traders' Associations*]

CIBC.......... Council on Interracial Books for Children   (EA)

CIBCR .... Center for International Business Cycle Research [*Columbia University*] [*New York, NY*] [*Research center*]   (RCD)

CIBE .... Confederation Internationale des Betteraviers Europeens [*International Confederation of European Sugar-Beet Growers*]   (EAIO)

CIBEP .... Commission pour le Marche Commun du Commerce International de Bulbes a Fleurs et de Plantes [*Common Market Commission for International Trade in Flower Bulbs and Plants*]

CIBER .... Cellular Intercarrier Billing Exchange Roamer Record [*A publication*]   (TSSD)

CIBG.......... Canadian Infantry Brigade Group [*British military*]   (DMA)

CIBI .... Council of Independent Black Institutions   (EA)

CIBL .... Citicorp Investment Bank Limited [*England*]

CIBL-FM .. Montreal, PQ [*FM radio station call letters*]

CIBM........ Riviere-Du-Loup, PQ [*AM radio station call letters*]

CIBMAJ.... Centro de Investigacion de Biologia Marina. Contribucion Tecnica [*A publication*]

CIBMBK ... Commonwealth Institute of Biological Control. Miscellaneous Publication [*A publication*]

CIBM-FM ... Riviere-Du-Loup, PQ [*FM radio station call letters*]

CIBO .... Council of Industrial Boiler Owners   (EA)

CIBP.......... Comite Interregional des Bibliotheques Publiques [*Interregional Committee of Public Libraries*] [*Canada*]

CIBPA .... Canadian Italian Business and Professional Men's Association

CIBQ.......... Brooks, AB [*AM radio station call letters*]

CIBR.......... California Institute of Biological Research [*La Jolla*]

CIBRASCEX ... Companhia Brasileira de Comercio Exterior [*Brazilian Foreign Trade Company*]

CIBRM...... Council for International Business Risk Management   (EA)

CIBS .... Center for Inter-American and Border Studies [*University of Texas, El Paso*] [*Research center*]   (RCD)

CIBS .... Chartered Institution of Building Service   (EAIO)

CIBS .... Chicago International Boat Show   (ITD)
CIBS .... [*Brigance Diagnostic*] Comprehensive Inventory of Basic Skills [*Academic achievement test*]
CIBS .... Conferencia Interamericana de Bienestar Social [*Interamerican Social Welfare Conference*]
CIBS .... Cosmetic Industry Buyers and Suppliers   (EA)
CIBSB......... Ciba Foundation. Symposium [*A publication*]
CIBSE...... Chartered Institution of Building Services Engineers   (EAIO)
CIBT .... Contributions of Infantry to the Battle Test [*Combat Developments Experimentation Center*] [*Army*]   (INF)
CIBV......... Consejo Internacional de Buena Vecindad, AC [*International Good Neighbor Council - IGNC*] [*Monterrey, Mexico*]   (EAIO)
CIC............ Canadian Infantry Corps
CIC............ Canadian Intelligence Corps   (DMA)
CIC............ Cancer Information Clearinghouse [*National Cancer Institute*] [*Database*]
CIC............ Capital Issues Committee [*Malaysia*]   (DS)
CIC............ Carbon-in-Column [*Gold ore processing*]
CIC............ Card Identification Code [*DoD*]   (AFIT)
CIC............ Card Inventory Control
CIC............ Cardiac Inhibition Center [*Physiology*]
CIC............ Career Information Center   (OICC)
CIC............ Catholic Interracial Council of New York   (EA)
CIC............ Cedar Rapids & Iowa City Railway Co. [*AAR code*]
CIC............ Centre for Industrial Control [*Concordia University*] [*Canada*] [*Research center*]   (RCD)
CIC............ Centre d'Informations Catholiques pour la France et l'Etranger
CIC............ Ceramic Industries Corporation [*Burma*]   (DS)
CIC............ Certified Insurance Counselor [*Designation awarded by Society of Certified Insurance Counselors*]
CIC............ Change Identification Control Number
CIC............ Chemical Industry Council
CIC............ Chemical Information Center [*Indiana University*]
CIC............ Chemical Institute of Canada
CIC............ Chico [*California*] [*Airport symbol*]   (OAG)
CIC............ Chiropractic Information Centre Ltd. [*British*]   (CB)
CIC............ Cicero [*Marcus Tullius, Roman orator and author, 106-43BC*] [*Classical studies*]
Cic............ Cicero [*of Plutarch*] [*Classical studies*]   (OCD)
CIC............ Circulating Immune Complexes [*Medicine*]
CIC............ City Investment Centres [*British*]
CIC............ Clean Intermittent Catherization [*Medicine*]
CIC............ Climatic Impact Committee [*National Academy of Sciences - National Academy of Engineering*]
CIC............ Clinical Investigation Center [*Oakland, CA*]
CIC............ Cloud in Cell
CIC............ Cobalt Information Center [*Battelle Memorial Institute*] [*Information service or system*]   (IID)
CIC............ Code d'Instruction Criminelle [*Code of Criminal Procedure*] [*A publication*]   (ILCA)
CIC............ Codex Iuris Canonici [*Code of Canon Law*] [*Latin*]
CIC............ Cogeneration Coalition [*Later, CIPCA*]   (EA)
CIC............ Cognac Information Centre [*British*]   (CB)
CIC............ Combat Information Center [*Navy*]
CIC............ Combat Intelligence Center
CIC............ Combat Intercept Control
CIC............ Combined Intelligence Committee [*World War II*]
CIC............ Comite International de la Conserve
CIC............ Comite International de Coordination pour l'Initiation a la Science et le Developpement des Activites Scientifiques Extra-Scolaires [*International Coordinating Committee for the Presentation of Science and the Development of Out-of-School Scientific Activities - ICC*]   (EAIO)
CIC............ Command Information Center [*Military*]
CIC............ Command Input Coupler   (CET)
CIC............ Command Intelligence   (MCD)
CIC............ Command Interface Control   (MCD)
CIC............ Commander-in-Chief [*Air Force*]
CIC............ Commission Internationale du Chataignier
CIC............ Committee for an Independent Canada
CIC............ Committee for Industrial Co-Operation [*European Economic Community/African, Caribbean, and Pacific States*]   (DS)
CIC............ Committee on Institutional Cooperation   (EA)
CIC............ Common-Impression Cylinder
CIC............ Communication Interface Coordinator [*NASA*]
CIC............ Communications Instructor Console   (MCD)
CIC............ Communications Intelligence Channel
CIC............ Compensated Ion Chamber
CIC............ Complex Integrated Circuit
CIC............ Comprehensive Inorganic Chemistry [*A publication*]
CIC............ Computer Industry Council   (EA)
CIC............ Computer Innovations Distribution, Inc. [*Toronto Stock Exchange symbol*]
CIC............ Computer Instruments Corporation
CIC............ Computer Intelligence Corporation [*Information service or system*]   (IID)
CIC............ Computer Interface Control [*Part of digital television computer*]
CIC............ Computers in the City Exhibition [*British*]   (ITD)

CIC............ Computing Information Center [*University of Washington*] [*Seattle*] [*Information service or system*]   (IID)
CIC............ Concrete Industries Council
CIC............ Confederation Internationale des Cadres [*International Confederation of Executive Staffs*] [*Paris. France*]   (EAIO)
CIC............ Confederation Internationale de la Coiffure [*International Conference of the Hairdressing Trade*]
CIC............ Conseil International de la Chasse et de la Conservation du Gibier [*International Council for Game and Wildlife Conservation*]   (EAIO)
CIC............ Conseil International des Compositeurs [*International Council of Composers*]
CIC............ Construction Industry Commission [*Canada*]
CIC............ Construction Industry Council [*Australia*]
CIC............ Construction Information Center Co. Ltd. [*Information service or system*]   (EISS)
CIC............ Consumer Information Center   (EA)
CIC............ Contemporary Issues Clearinghouse [*Defunct*]   (EA)
CIC............ Contemporary Issues Criticism [*A publication*]
CIC............ Content Indication Codes   (NG)
CIC............ Continental Corporation [*NYSE symbol*]   (SPSG)
CIC............ Control and Information Center   (NASA)
CIC............ Control Installation Code [*Air Force*]   (AFIT)
CIC............ Control Instrument Company   (MCD)
CIC............ Controlled Item Code [*Air Force*]   (AFIT)
CIC............ Controller-in-Charge [*Aviation*]   (FAAC)
CIC............ Coordination and Information Center [*Department of Energy*] [*Information service or system*]   (IID)
CIC............ Coordinator for Industrial Cooperation [*Functions ceased, 1937*]
CIC............ Core Image Converter [*Data processing*]
CIC............ Corporate Information Center [*Later, ICCR*]
CIC............ Cost Indicator Code [*Army*]   (AFIT)
CIC............ Council of Independent Colleges   (EA)
CIC............ Council of Intergovernmental Coordinators   (EA)
CIC............ Counter Intelligence, Combat [*World War II*]
CIC............ Counterintelligence Corps [*Military*]
CIC............ Criminal Investigation Command   (MCD)
CIC............ Critical Issues Council [*Defunct*]   (EA)
CIC............ Critical Item Code
CIC............ Cross Information Company [*Boulder, CO*] [*Telecommunications*]   (TSSD)
CIC............ Curate in Charge [*Church of England*]
CIC............ Current Indian Cases, Old Series [*India*] [*A publication*]   (DLA)
CIC............ Customer Identification Code
CIC............ Sisters of the Immaculate Conception [*Roman Catholic religious order*]
CIC............ Society of Certified Insurance Counselors [*Austin, TX*]   (EA)
CICA......... Canadian Institute of Chartered Accountants
CICA......... Captive Insurance Companies Association   (EA)
CICA......... Cogeneration Coalition of America [*Later, CIPCA*]   (EA)
CICA......... Comite International Catholique des Aveugles   (EAIO)
CICA......... Committee for International Collaborative Activities [*An association*]
CICA......... Competition in Contracting Act [*1984*]
CICA......... Confederation of International Contractors' Associations [*Paris, France*]   (EAIO)
CICA......... Confederation Internationale du Credit Agricole [*International Confederation of Agricultural Credit*] [*Zurich, Switzerland*]   (EAIO)
CICA......... Conference Internationale des Controles d'Assurances des Etats Africains [*International Conference of African States on Insurance Supervision*]   (EAIO)
CICA......... Configuration Identification Control and Accounting
CICA......... Construction Industry Computing Association   (EAIO)
CICA......... Council of International Civil Aviation
CICADA...... Central Instrumentation Control and Data   (MCD)
CICAE....... Confederation Internationale des Cinemas d'Art et d'Essai [*International Experimental and Art Film Theatres Confederation*] [*France*]
CICAR...... Cooperative Investigation of the Caribbean and Adjacent Regions [*UNESCO*]
CICARDI .. CICAR [*Cooperative Investigation of the Caribbean and Adjacent Regions*] Data Inventory [*Marine science*]   (MSC)
CICATIRS ... Comite International de Coordination et d'Action des Groupements de Techniciens des Industries de Revetements de Surface [*International Committee to Coordinate Activities of Technical Groups in Coatings Industry - ICCATCI*]   (EAIO)
CICA-TV ... Toronto, ON [*Television station call letters*]
CICB.......... Center International des Civilisations Bantu   (EAIO)
CICB.......... Criminal Injuries Compensation Board [*British*]
CICBC....... Construction Industry Collective Bargaining Commission [*Terminated, 1978*] [*Department of Labor*]   (EGAO)
CICC.......... Cargo Integration Control Center   (MCD)
CICC.......... Catholic Interracial Council of Chicago   (EA)
CICC.......... Centre International de Criminologie Comparee [*International Center for Comparative Criminology - ICCC*] [*Montreal, PQ*]   (EA)

CICC......... Conference Internationale des Charites Catholiques [*International Conference of Catholic Charities*]
CICC......... Consolidated Intelligence Communication Center　(MCD)
CICCA...... Centre International de Coordination pour la Celebration des Anniversaires
CICCE....... Comite des Industries Cinematographiques des Communautes Europeennes [*Committee of the Cinematography Industries in the European Communities*]　(EAIO)
CICC-TV ... Yorkton, SK [*Television station call letters*]
CICC-TV-1 ... Wynyard, SK [*Television station call letters*]
CICD......... Collegium Internationale Chirurgiae Digestivae [*Rome, Italy*]　(EAIO)
CICE......... Centre d'Information des Chemins de Fer Europeens [*Information Center of the European Railways*]
CICE......... Comite International des Createurs en Email [*International Committee of Enamelling Creators*]　(EAIO)
CICE......... Council for International Congresses of Entomology [*London, England*]　(EA)
CICE......... Cumann Innealtoiri Comhairle na hEirann [*Association of Consulting Engineers of Ireland*]　(EA)
CICEP....... Conseil Interamericain du Commerce et de la Production
CICERO.... Communications Integrated Control Engineering, Reporting, and Operations　(MCD)
CICESTR .. Bishop of Chichester [*British*]
CICF......... Competitive Industrial Concept Formulation
CICF......... Confederation Internationale des Corps de Fonctionnaires [*International Confederation of Public Service Officers*]
CICF......... Current Issues in Commerce and Finance [*A publication*]
CICF......... Vernon, BC [*AM radio station call letters*]
CICG......... Center for Interactive Computer Graphics [*Rensselaer Polytechnic Institute*] [*Research center*]　(RCD)
CICG......... Centre International du Commerce de Gros [*International Center for Wholesale Trade*]
CICH........ Canadian Institute of Child Health
CICH......... Centro de Informacion Cientifica y Humanistica [*Center for Scientific and Humanistic Information*] [*Mexico*] [*Information service or system*]　(IID)
CICH......... Comite International de la Culture du Houblon [*International Hop Growers Convention - IHGC*]　(EAIO)
CICh......... Corpus Inscriptionum Chaldaicarum　(BJA)
CICHE....... Consortium for International Cooperation in Higher Education　(EA)
CICHS....... Center for International Community Health Studies [*University of Connecticut*] [*Research center*]　(RCD)
CICI.......... Combined Intelligence Center, Iraq [*World War II*]
CICI.......... COMSAT [*Communications Satellite Corp.*] International Communications, Inc.　(TSSD)
CICI.......... Confederation of Information Communication Industries [*British*]
CICIAMS ... Comite International Catholique des Infirmieres et Assistantes Medico-Sociales [*International Committee of Catholic Nurses - ICCN*] [*Vatican City, Vatican City State*]　(EAIO)
CICIAMS Nouv ... CICIAMS [*Comite International Catholique des Infirmieres et Assistantes Medico-Sociales*] Nouvelles [*A publication*]
CICIBA ..... Centre International des Civilisations Bantu [*International Center for the Bantu Civilizations*] [*Research center*] [*Gabon*]　(IRC)
CICIEM .... Chambre Islamique de Commerce, d'Industrie et d'Echange des Marchandises [*Islamic Chamber of Commerce, Industry, and Commodity Exchange - ICCICE*] [*Karachi, Pakistan*]　(EAIO)
CICIH....... Confederation Internationale Catholique des Institutions Hospitalieres [*International Catholic Confederation of Hospitals*]
CICIN....... Conference on Interlibrary Communications and Information Networks [*September 28 - October 2, 1970*]
CIC Inform B Inform Gen ... CIC Informations. Bulletin d'Informations Generales [*A publication*]
CICIREPATO ... Committee for International Co-operation in Information Retrieval Among Examining Patent Offices
CICIS........ Chemicals in Commerce Information System [*Environmental Protection Agency*]
CICI-TV .... Sudbury, ON [*Television station call letters*]
CICI-TV-1 ... Elliott Lake, ON [*Television station call letters*]
CICL......... Canadian Index of Computer Literature [*A publication*]
CICM........ Commission Internationale Catholique pour les Migrations [*International Catholic Migration Commission - ICMC*] [*Geneva, Switzerland*]　(EAIO)
CICM........ Congregatio Immaculati Cordis Mariae [*Congregation of the Immaculate Heart of Mary*] [*Roman Catholic men's religious order*]
CICNEV .... Contemporary Issues in Clinical Nutrition [*A publication*]
CICNY...... Catholic Interracial Council of New York　(EA)
CICO .... Combat Information Center Office [*or Officer*] [*Navy*]　(MUGU)
CICO .... Conference of International Catholic Organizations [*Geneva, Switzerland*]　(EAIO)
CICO .... Corporate Investment Co. [*NASDAQ symbol*]　(NQ)
CICOM ..... Citizens for Informed Choices on Marijuana　(EA)
CICOP....... Catholic Inter-American Cooperation Program [*Defunct*]

CICOPA .... Comite International des Cooperatives de Production et Artisanales [*International Committee of Producers' Cooperatives*]　(EAIO)
CICO-TV-9 ... Thunder Bay, ON [*Television station call letters*]
CICO-TV-18 ... London, ON [*Television station call letters*]
CICO-TV-19 ... Sudbury, ON [*Television station call letters*]
CICO-TV-20 ... Sault Ste. Marie, ON [*Television station call letters*]
CICO-TV-24 ... Ottawa, ON [*Television station call letters*]
CICO-TV-28 ... Kitchener, ON [*Television station call letters*]
CICO-TV-32 ... Windsor, ON [*Television station call letters*]
CICO-TV-59 ... Chatham, ON [*Television station call letters*]
CICP......... Capital Investment Computer Program [*Economics*]
CICP......... Coalition for International Cooperation and Peace　(EA)
CICP......... Committee to Investigate Copyright Problems
CICP......... Communication Interrupt Control Program [*Data processing*]　(IBMDP)
CICP......... Confederation Internationale du Credit Populaire [*International Confederation of Popular Credit - ICPC*] [*Paris, France*]　(EAIO)
CICPE .... Comite d'Initiative pour le Congres du Peuple Europeen
CICPLB..... Comite International pour le Controle de la Productivite Laitiere du Betail [*International Committee for Recording the Productivity of Milk Animals - ICRPMA*]　(EAIO)
CICPR ...... Confederation Internationale pour la Chirurgie Plastique et Reconstructive [*International Confederation for Plastic and Reconstructive Surgery*]　(EAIO)
CICR........ Calcium-Induced Calcium Release [*Biochemistry*]
CICR........ Comite International Contre la Repression [*International Committee Against Repression*] [*Paris, France*]　(EAIO)
CICR........ Comite International de la Croix-Rouge [*International Committee of the Red Cross*]
CICR........ Committee on Information and Cultural Relations　(EAIO)
CICRA...... Centre International pour la Coordination des Recherches en Agriculture
CICRC....... Commission Internationale Contre le Regime Concentrationnaire
CICRD8..... Colloque Scientifique International sur le Cafe [*A publication*]
CICRED .... Comite International de Cooperation dans les Recherches Nationales en Demographie [*Committee for International Cooperation in National Research in Demography*]　(EAIO)
CICRIS...... Cooperative Industrial and Commercial Reference and Information Service
CICS......... Canadian Intergovernmental Conference Secretariat
CICS......... Central Integrated Checkout System
CICS......... Commercial or Industrial and Control Service Data System
CICS......... Customer Information Control System [*Pronounced "kicks"*] [*IBM Corp.*] [*Data processing*]
CICSA .... Change Identification Control Schedule Analysis
CICSA .... Clinical Symposia [*A publication*]
CIC-SS ...... Change Identification Control Schedule Summary
CICS/VS ... Customer Information Control System Virtual Storage [*IBM Corp.*] [*Data processing*]
CICT......... Commission on International Commodity Trade
CICT......... Conseil International du Cinema et de la Television [*International Film and Television Council*]
CICTA .... Commission Internationale pour la Conservation des Thonides de l'Atlantique [*International Commission for the Conservation of Atlantic Tunas - ICCAT*]
CICTEE..... China International Center for Technical and Economic Exchange
CICU .... Cardiovascular In-Patient Care Unit
CICU .... Central Interface Converter Unit
CICU .... Children's Intensive Care Unit　(ADA)
CICU .... Cirrocumulus [*Meteorology*]
CICU .... Commission on Independent Colleges and Universities [*Pennsylvania*]
CICU .... Computer Interface Conditioning Unit　(MCD)
CICU .... Computer Interface Control Unit　(NASA)
CICU .... Coronary Intensive Care Unit [*of a hospital*]
CICV........ Combined Intelligence Center, Vietnam
CICWO ..... Combat Information Center Watch Officer [*Navy*]
CICYP .... Consejo Interamericano de Comercio y Produccion [*Interamerican Council of Commerce and Production*]
CICYT .... Inter-American Committee on Science and Technology [*Organization of American States*]　(ASF)
CID .... Association de Consultants Internationaux en Droits de l'Homme [*Association of International Consultants on Human Rights*] [*Geneva, Switzerland*]　(EAIO)
CID .... Cable Interconnection Diagram　(KSC)
CID .... Cabling Interface Drawing　(MCD)
CID .... Capital Investment Discard
CID .... Cedar Rapids/Iowa City [*Iowa*] [*Airport symbol*]　(OAG)
CID .... CEIP [*Communications-Electronics Implementation Plan*] Implementation Directive [*Air Force*]　(CET)
CID .... Center for Industrial Development [*European Economic Community/African, Caribbean, and Pacific States*]　(DS)
CID .... Center for Infectious Diseases [*Department of Health and Human Services*]　(GRD)
CID .... Center for Innovative Diplomacy　(EA)
CID .... Center for Inquiry and Discovery [*Washington, DC, museum*]

CID .... Central Institute for the Deaf   (MCD)
CID .... Centre for Industrial Democracy [*Australia*]
CID .... Centre for Information and Documentation
     [*EURATOM*]   (MCD)
CID .... Centre for Innovation Development [*Australia*]
CID .... Centre International de Documentation [*International Center
     for Documentation*]
CID .... Centro de Informativo y Documentacion [*Press agency*]
     [*Argentina*]
CID .... Centrum voor Informatie en Documentatie [*Center for
     Information and Documentation*] [*Netherlands
     Organization for Applied Scientific Research*] [*Delft*]
     [*Information service or system*]   (IID)
CID .... Change in Design
CID .... Channel Identification   (CET)
CID .... Characteristic Item Description   (MCD)
CID .... Charge-Injection Device [*Electronics*]
CID .... Chieftain International [*AMEX symbol*] [*Toronto Stock
     Exchange symbol*]   (SPSG)
CID .... Circular Intensity Difference [*Spectrometry*]
CID .... Civil Investigative Demand [*Department of Justice*]
CID .... Cleanliness Identification [*Label*] [*Aerospace*]   (AAG)
CID .... Coalicion Institucionalista Democratica [*Democratic
     Institutional Coalition*] [*Ecuador*] [*Political party*]   (PPW)
CID .... Collision-Induced Decomposition [*or Dissociation*]
     [*Spectrometry*]
CID .... Combat Information and Detection   (NVT)
CID .... Combined Immunodeficiency Disease [*Immunology*]
CID .... Comite International de Dachau
CID .... Comite International des Derives Tensio-Actifs [*International
     Committee of Tensio-Active Derivatives*]
CID .... Command Information Division   (MCD)
CID .... Commercial Import Division [*Vietnam*]
CID .... Commercial Item Description
CID .... Commercial Item Drawing   (MCD)
CID .... Commission for International Development   (EA)
CID .... Committee for Imperial Defence [*British*]
CID .... Committee for Industrial Development [*United Nations*]
CID .... Committee on Interest and Dividends [*Terminated, 1974*]
     [*Federal Reserve Board*]
CID .... Communication Identifier [*Data processing*]   (IBMDP)
CID .... Communication Implementation Directive [*Air Force*]
CID .... Communications Identification Directory [*Air Force*]   (CET)
CID .... Compagnie Industrielle du Disque [*Record label*] [*France*]
CID .... Component Identification
CID .... Component Identification Designation   (CAAL)
CID .... Computer-Integrated Design
CID .... Computer Interface Device   (NASA)
CID .... Configuration Index Document   (MCD)
CID .... Consortium on International Development
CID .... Controlled Impact Demonstration [*FAA, NASA*]
CID .... Council for Independent Distribution [*Later, CPDA*]
CID .... Council of Industrial Design [*British*]
CID .... Creative Industries of Detroit, Inc. [*Warren, MI*]
     [*Telecommunications*]   (TSSD)
CID .... Criminal Investigation Department [*Often loosely referred to as
     Scotland Yard*] [*Facetious translation: Copper in Disguise*]
     [*British*]
CID .... Criminal Investigation Detachment
CID .... Criminal Investigation Division [*Army*]
CID .... Critical Issues Demonstration   (MCD)
CID .... Cubic Inch Displacement [*in engines*]
CID .... Curriculum and Instruction Development [*Program*] [*National
     Science Foundation*]
CID .... Customized-Information-Delivery System [*Bell
     Communications Research Laboratory*]
CID .... Cytomegalic Inclusion Disease [*Ophthalmology*]
CID .... Movement for an Independent and Democratic Cuba   (EA)
CID .... North Central Regional Library, Community Information
     Directory Project [*UTLAS symbol*]
CID$_{50}$ ...... Chimpanzee Infectious Dose for Half the Population
CIDA .... Canadian International Development Agency [*Formerly,
     External Aid Office*]
CIDA .... Centre d'Information et de Documentation Atlantique
     [*Brussels, Belgium*]
CIDA .... Centre d'Informatique et Documentation Automatique [*Center
     for Automated Information and Documentation*] [*France*]
     [*Information service or system*]   (IID)
CIDA .... Centre International de Developpement de l'Aluminium
CIDA .... Centre International de Documentation Arachnologique
     [*International Centre for Arachnological
     Documentation*]   (EAIO)
CIDA .... Change in Drawing Authorization   (MCD)
CIDA .... Channel Indirect Data Addressing   (IBMDP)
CIDA .... Christian Instrumental Directors Association   (EA)
CIDA .... Comite Interamericano de Desarrollo Agricola [*Inter-American
     Committee for Agricultural Development*]
CIDA .... Comite Intergouvernemental du Droit d'Auteur
     [*Intergovernmental Copyright Committee - IGC*]
     [*UNESCO*]   (EAIO)
CIDA .... Community Information Development Association [*Australia*]

CIDA .... Confederazione Italiana die Dirigenti di Azienda [*A union for
     executives*] [*Italy*]   (DCTA)
CIDAC ...... Cancer Information Dissemination and Analysis Center
CIDADEC ... Confederation Internationale des Associations d'Experts et de
     Conseils [*International Confederation of Associations of
     Experts and Consultants*]
CIDAL ...... Centro de Informacion, Documentacion, y Analisis
     Latinoamericano
CIDALC ..... Comite International pour la Diffusion des Arts et des Lettres
     par le Cinema [*International Committee for the Diffusion
     of Arts and Literature through the Cinema*]   (EAIO)
CIDAS .... Conversational Interactive Digital/Analog Simulator [*IBM
     Corp.*]   (IEEE)
CIDAT ...... Centre d'Informatique Appliquee au Developpement et a
     l'Agriculture Tropicale [*Center for Informatics Applied to
     Development and Tropical Agriculture*] [*Royal Museum
     of Central Africa*] [*Information service or system*]   (IID)
CIDB .... Chemie-Information und Dokumentation Berlin [*Chemical
     Information and Documentation - Berlin*] [*Information
     service or system*] [*German*]   (IID)
CIDC .... Centre Islamique pour le Developpement du Commerce
     [*Islamic Center for Development of Trade - ICDT*]
     [*Casablanca, Morocco*]   (EAIO)
CIDC .... Construction Industry Development Council [*Canada*]
CIDC-FM ... Orangeville, ON [*FM radio station call letters*]
CIDCIM .... Computer-Integrated Design - Computer-Integrated
     Manufacturing   (ADA)
CIDCOMED ... Council for Interdisciplinary Communication in Medicine
CIDCON ... Civil Disturbance Readiness Conditions [*Army*]   (AABC)
CIDD .... Conseil International de la Danse [*International Dance
     Council*]   (EAIO)
CIDE .... Caisse Israelite de Demarrage Economique [*A publication*]
CIDE .... Commission Intersyndicale des Deshydrateurs Europeens
     [*European Dehydrators Association*] [*Common Market*]
     [*Paris, France*]
CIDEC ...... Conseil International pour le Developpement du Cuivre
     [*International Copper Development Council*]
CIDECT .... Comite International pour l'Etude et le Developpement de la
     Construction Tubulaire [*International Committee for the
     Study and Development of Tubular Construction*]
     [*Canada*]
CIDEM ...... Consejo Interamericano de Musica [*Inter-American Music
     Council*]   (EA)
CIDEP .... Centre International de Documentation Concernant les
     Expressions Plastiques
CIDEP .... Chemically Induced Dynamic Electron Polarization
     [*Spectrometry*]
CIDERE ..... Civil Defense Report
CIDESA .... Centre International de Documentation Economique et Sociale
     Africaine [*International Center for African Social and
     Economic Documentation*]
CIDESCO ... Comite International d'Esthetique et de Cosmetologie
     [*International Committee for Esthetics and Cosmetology*]
CIDET .... Cooperation Internationale en Matiere de Documentation sur
     l'Economie des Transports [*International Cooperation in
     the Field of Transport Economics Documentation*]
     [*France*] [*Information service or system*]   (IID)
CIDF .... Control Interval Definition Field [*Data processing*]   (BUR)
CIDG .... Civilian Irregular Defense Group [*Military*]
CIDG .... Current Intelligence Digest [*A publication*]
CIDHAL .... Comunicacion, Intercambio, y Desarrollo Humano en America
     Latina
CIDI .... Centre International de Documentation et d'Information
CIDIA .... Centro Interamericano de Documentacion e Informacion
     Agricola [*Inter-American Center for Documentation and
     Agricultural Information*] [*Inter-American Institute for
     Cooperation on Agriculture*] [*Information service or
     system*]   (IID)
CIDIE .... Centro Internacional de Informacion Economica
CIDIN .... Common ICAO [*International Civil Aviation Organization*]
     Data Interchange Network
CIDITVA .. Centre International de Documentation de l'Inspection
     Technique des Vehicules Automobiles
CIDL .... Configuration Item Data List   (NASA)
CIDM .... Conseil International de Musique [*UNESCO*] [*Record label*]
CID-MAC ... Computer-Integrated Design - Manufacturing and Automation
     Center
CIDN .... Change in Drawing Notice
CIDN .... Computer Identics Corp. [*Canton, MA*] [*NASDAQ
     symbol*]   (NQ)
CIDNET .... CID [*Consortium on International Development*] Information
     Network
CIDNO ...... Contractor's Identification Number
CIDNP .... Chemically Induced Dynamic Nuclear Polarization
     [*Spectrometry*]
CiDOC ...... Centro Intercultural de Documentacion [*Center for
     Intercultural Documentation*] [*Cuernavaca, Mexico*]
CIDOS .... Communications Security Interservice Depot Overhaul
     Standard   (MCD)

CIDP......... Centre International de Documentation Parlementaire [*International Center for Parliamentary Documentation*]　(EAIO)

CIDP......... Confederation Internationale pour le Desarmement et la Paix [*International Confederation for Disarmament and Peace - ICDP*] [*London, England*]　(EA)

CIDPL....... Commission for International Due Process of Law　(EA)

CIDPS....... Continental Intelligence Data Processing System　(MCD)

CIDR......... Critical Intermediate Design Review　(NASA)

CIDS......... Career Information Delivery System　(OICC)

CIDS......... Cellular Immunity Deficiency Syndrome [*Medicine*]

CIDS......... Centro Intercultural de Documentacion. Sondeos [*A publication*]

CIDS......... Changi International Distribution Services Pte. Ltd. [*Singapore*]

CIDS......... Chemical Information and Data System [*Army*]

CIDS......... Concrete Island Drilling System [*Offshore oil exploration*]

CIDS......... Configuration Item Development Specifications　(MCD)

CIDS......... Coordination in Direct Support　(NVT)

CIDS......... Critical Item Development Specification　(CAAL)

CIDSE....... Cooperation Internationale pour le Developpement et la Solidarite [*International Cooperation for Development and Solidarity*] [*Formerly, Cooperation Internationale pour le Developpement Socio-Economique*]　(EAIO)

CIDSS....... Comite International pour l'Information et Documentation des Sciences Sociales [*International Committee for Social Sciences Documentation*]

CIDST....... Advisory Committee on Information Dissemination in Science and Technology

CIDSTAT ... Civil Disturbance Status Reporting [*Army*]　(AABC)

CIDT......... Cayman Islands Department of Tourism　(EA)

CIE............ CAB [*Commonwealth Agricultural Bureaux*] International Institute of Entomology [*British*]　(IRUK)

CIE............ Captain's Imperfect Entry [*Shipping*]

CIE............ Catering Industry Employee [*A publication*]

CIE............ Center for Independent Education [*Later, Cato Institute*]　(EA)

CIE............ Center for Integrated Electronics [*Rensselaer Polytechnic Institute*] [*Research center*]　(RCD)

CIE............ Central Information Exchange [*Community Service Council of Broward County, Inc.*] [*Information service or system*]　(IID)

CIE............ Centre International de l'Enfance [*International Children's Centre*] [*Paris, France*]　(EAIO)

CIE............ Centre for Internationalising the Study of English

CIE............ Certified International Executive [*Designation awarded by American Society of International Executives*]

CIE............ Cesium Ion Emission

CIE............ Citizens for Improved Education

CIE............ Cleveland Institute of Electronics [*Ohio*]

CIE............ Clothing and Individual Equipment [*Army*]　(RDA)

CIE............ Cochise, AZ [*Location identifier*] [*FAA*]　(FAAL)

CIE............ Coherent Infrared Energy　(AAG)

CIE............ Comite International des Echanges pres la Chambre de Commerce Internationale

CIE............ Commission Internationale de l'Eclairage [*International Commission on Illumination*] [*Vienna, Austria*]　(EA)

CIE............ Committee on Invisible Exports [*United Kingdom*]　(DS)

CIE............ Common Ion Effect

CIE............ Commonwealth Institute of Entomology [*British*]　(MCD)

CIE............ Communications Interface Equipment　(MCD)

Cie............ Compagnie [*Company*] [*French*]

CIE............ Companion of the [*Order of the*] Indian Empire [*British*]

CIE............ Congres International des Editeurs [*International Congress of Publishers*]　(DIT)

CIE............ Conseil International de l'Etain [*International Tin Council - ITC*]　(EAIO)

CIE............ Consejo Interamericano do Escultismo [*Inter-American Scout Committee - IASC*] [*San Jose, Costa Rica*]　(EAIO)

CIE............ Control and Indicating Equipment

CIE............ Controlled Internal Extension　(MCD)

CIE............ Coras Iompair Eireann [*Irish Transport Company*]

CIE............ Corpus Inscriptionum Elamicarum [*A publication*]　(BJA)

CIE............ Corpus Inscriptionum Etruscarum [*A publication*]

CIE............ Corrected Infection Efficiency [*of plant pathogens*]

CIE............ Corrie Resources [*Vancouver Stock Exchange symbol*]

CIE............ Council for Indian Education　(EA)

CIE............ Counterimmunoelectrophoresis [*Also, CIEP*] [*Analytical biochemistry*]

CIE............ Crossed Immunoelectrophoresis [*Analytical biochemistry*]

CIE............ Customer Initiated Entry [*Banking*]

CIE............ Customs Information Exchange [*An arm of US Customs Service*]

CIE............ Gould Laboratory Materials Research, Cleveland, OH [*OCLC symbol*]　(OCLC)

CIEA......... Centre International pour Education Artistique [*International Centre for Art Education*]　(EAIO)

CIEA......... Committee on International Environmental Affairs [*Department of State*] [*Washington, DC*]　(EGAO)

CIEA......... Conseil International d'Education des Adultes [*International Council for Adult Education*] [*Canada*]

CIE-AF...... Certified International Executive - Air Forwarding [*Designation awarded by American Society of International Executives, Inc.*]

CIEA Preclin Rep ... CIEA [*Central Institute for Experimental Animals*] Preclinical Reports [*A publication*]

CIEAS....... Committee on International Education in Agricultural Sciences [*See also SVLB*] [*Deventer, Netherlands*]　(EAIO)

CIEB......... Chilean Iodine Educational Bureau [*Defunct*]　(EA)

CIEC......... Centre International des Engrais Chimiques [*International Center of Fertilizers*]

CIEC......... Centre International pour les Etudes Chimiques [*International Center for Chemical Studies - ICCS*]　(EAIO)

CIEC......... Commission Internationale de l'Etat Civil [*International Commission on Civil Status - ICCS*]　(EAIO)

CIEC......... Confederation Interamericaine d'Education Catholique [*Inter-American Confederation of Catholic Education*]

CIEC......... Conference on International Economic Cooperation

CIEC......... Conseil International des Employeurs du Commerce [*International Council of Commerce Employers*]

CIEC......... Conseil International d'Etudes Canadiennes [*International Council for Canadian Studies - ICCS*]

CIECA....... Commission Internationale des Examens de Conduite Automobile [*International Driving Tests Committee*]　(EAIO)

CIECA....... Current Injection Equivalent Circuit Approach　(MCD)

CIECC....... Consejo Interamericano para la Educacion, la Ciencia, y la Cultura　(EA)

CIEE......... Centre Interuniversitaire d'Etudes Europeennes [*Interuniversity Centre for European Studies*] [*Canada*]

CIEE......... Companion of the Institution of Electrical Engineers [*British*]

CIEE......... Council on International Educational Exchange　(EA)

CIEEL....... Chemically Initiated Electron Exchange Luminescence

CIE-EM..... Certified International Executive - Export Management [*Designation awarded by American Society of International Executives, Inc.*]

CIEF......... Capillary Isoelectric Focusing

CIE-F........ Certified International Executive - Forwarding [*Designation awarded by American Society of International Executives, Inc.*]

CIEF......... Comite International d'Enregistrement des Frequences [*International Frequency Registration Board*]

CIEF......... Continuous Isoelectric Focusing [*Materials processing*]

Cie Fr Pet Notes Mem ... Compagnie Francaise des Petroles. Notes et Memoires [*A publication*]

CIEG......... Center for International Economic Growth [*Defunct*]　(EA)

CIEG-FM ... Egmont, BC [*FM radio station call letters*]

CIEH......... Comite Interafricain d'Etudes Hydrauliques [*Inter-African Committee for Hydraulic Studies - ICHS*] [*Ouagadougou, Burkina Faso*]　(EAIO)

CIEHV....... Conseil International pour l'Education des Handicapes de la Vue [*International Council for Education of the Visually Handicapped - ICEVH*]　(EAIO)

CIEI......... Center for International Environment Information [*Later, WEC*]　(EA)

CI/EI........ Chemical Ionization/Electron Impact [*Spectroscopy*]

CIEL......... Centre International d'Etudes du Lindane [*International Research Centre on Lindane - IRCL*]　(EAIO)

CIEL-FM .. Longueuil, PQ [*FM radio station call letters*]

CIEM......... Commission Internationale pour l'Enseignement des Mathematiques [*International Commission on Mathematical Instruction - ICMI*]　(EA)

CIEM......... Conseil International d'Education Mesologique des Pays de Langue Francaise [*Established 1977*] [*Canada*]

CIEM......... Conseil International pour l'Exploration de la Mer [*International Council for the Exploration of the Sea*]

CIEMA...... Centre International des Etudes de la Musique Ancienne [*International Center of Studies on Early Music*]

CIEMDT.... Clinical and Experimental Immunoreproduction [*A publication*]

CIEMEN ... Centre Internacional Escarre per a les Minories Etniques i Nacionalitats　(EAIO)

CIEMS...... Catalog for Information Exchange and Message Standards　(MCD)

CIEN .... Commission Interamericaine d'Energie Nucleaire [*Inter-American Nuclear Energy Commission*]

Cien Biol Ser C Biol Mol Cel ... Ciencia Biologica. Serie C. Biologia Molecular e Celular [*A publication*]

Cienc......... Ciencia [*A publication*]

Cienc Adm ... Ciencias Administrativas [*A publication*]

Cienc Agron ... Ciencia Agronomica [*A publication*]

Cienc Biol... Ciencia Biologica [*A publication*]

Cienc Biol Acad Cienc Cuba ... Ciencias Biologicas. Academia de Ciencias de Cuba [*A publication*]

Cienc Biol B ... Ciencia Biologica. B. Ecologia e Sistematica [*A publication*]

Cienc Biol Biol Mol Cel ... Ciencia Biologica. Biologia Molecular e Cellular [*A publication*]

Cienc Biol (Coimbra) ... Ciencia Biologica (Coimbra) [*Portugal*] [*A publication*]

Cienc Biol Ecol Sist ... Ciencia Biologica, Ecologia, e Sistematica [*A publication*]

Cienc Biol (Luanda) ... Ciencias Biologicas (Luanda) [*A publication*]

Cienc Biol Mol Cell Biol ... Ciencia Biologica. Molecular and Cellular Biology [*A publication*]
Cienc Cult (Maracaibo) ... Ciencia y Cultura (Maracaibo) [*A publication*]
Cienc Cult (Sao Paulo) ... Ciencia e Cultura (Sao Paulo) [*A publication*]
Cienc Cult (Sao Paulo) Supl ... Ciencia e Cultura (Sao Paulo). Suplemento [*A publication*]
Cienc Cult Saude ... Ciencia, Cultura, Saude [*A publication*]
Cienc Cult Soc Bras Progr Cienc ... Ciencia e Cultura. Sociedade Brasileira para o Progresso da Ciencia [*A publication*]
Cienc Cult (S Paulo) ... Ciencia e Cultura (Sao Paulo) [*A publication*]
Cienc For.... Ciencia Forestal [*A publication*]
Ciencia Info ... Ciencia da Informacao [*A publication*]
Ciencia y Soc ... Ciencia y Sociedad [*A publication*]
Ciencias Ser 5 ... Ciencias. Serie 5. Bioquimica Farmaceutica [*A publication*]
Ciencias Ser 1 Mat ... Ciencias. Serie 1. Matematica [*Havana*] [*A publication*]
Ciencia e Tec Fiscal ... Ciencia e Tecnica Fiscal [*A publication*]
Ciencia Tecnol ... Ciencia y Tecnologia [*A publication*]
Cienc Interam ... Ciencia Interamericana [*A publication*]
Cienc Invest ... Ciencia e Investigacion [*A publication*]
Cienc Invest Agrar ... Ciencia e Investigacion Agraria [*A publication*]
Cienc Invest (B Aires) ... Ciencia e Investigacion (Buenos Aires) [*A publication*]
Cienc Mat .. Ciencias Matematicas [*Havana*] [*A publication*]
Cienc Nat ... Ciencia y Naturaleza [*A publication*]
Cienc Neurol ... Ciencias Neurologicas [*A publication*]
Cienc Prat .. Ciencia e Pratica [*A publication*]
Cienc Ser 10 Bot (Havana) ... Ciencias. Serie 10. Botanica (Havana) [*A publication*]
Cienc Ser 4 Cienc Biol (Havana) ... Ciencias. Serie 4. Ciencias Biologicas (Havana) [*A publication*]
Cienc Ser 8 Invest Mar (Havana) ... Ciencias. Serie 8. Investigaciones Marinas (Havana) [*A publication*]
Cienc & Tec ... Ciencia y Tecnica [*A publication*]
Cienc Tec (Buenos Aires) ... Ciencia y Tecnica (Buenos Aires) [*A publication*]
Cienc Tec Fis Mat ... Ciencias Tecnicas Fisicas y Matematicas [*A publication*]
Cienc Tec Mar ... Ciencia y Tecnologia del Mar. Comite Oceanografico Nacional [*Valparaiso, Chile*] [*A publication*]
Cienc Tec Mundo ... Ciencia y Tecnica en el Mundo [*A publication*]
Cienc Tecn ... Ciencia y Tecnologia [*A publication*]
Cienc Tecnol (San Jose Costa Rica) ... Ciencia y Tecnologia (San Jose, Costa Rica) [*A publication*]
Cienc Tec Soldadura (Madrid) ... Ciencia y Tecnica de la Soldadura (Madrid) [*A publication*]
Cienc Terra ... Ciencias da Terra [*A publication*]
Cienc Vet.... Ciencias Veterinarias [*A publication*]
Cienc Vet Aliment Nutr Anim ... Ciencias Veterinarias y Alimentas y Nutricion Animal [*A publication*]
CIENES .... Centro Interamericano de Ensenanza de Estadistica
Ci Eng .... Civil Engineering [*A publication*]
Cien Tom .... Ciencia Tomista [*A publication*]
CIEO .... Catholic International Education Office [*Belgium*]
CIEO .... Centre International d'Exploitation des Oceans [*Canada*] [*See also ICOD*]
CIEP .... Commission Internationale de l'Enseignement de la Physique [*International Commission on Physics Education - ICPE*] (EAIO)
CIEP .... Committee on International Exchange of Persons
CIEP .... Concentrated Impact Employment Program [*Also known as CEP*] [*Department of Labor*]
CIEP .... Council on International Economic Policy [*Terminated, 1977*]
CIEP .... Counterimmunoelectrophoresis [*Also, CIE*] [*Analytical biochemistry*]
CIEPC .... Commission Internationale d'Etudes de la Police de Circulation [*International Study Commission for Traffic Police*]
CIEPCBC .. Committee on International Exchange of Persons Conference Board of Associated Research Councils [*Later, Council for International Exchange of Scholars*] (EA)
CIEPLAN ... Corporacion de Investigaciones Economicas para Latinoamerica
Ciep Ogrz Went ... Cieplownictwo, Ogrzewnictwo, Wentylacja [*A publication*]
CIEPP .... Comite Illusionniste d'Expertise des Phenomenes Paranormaux [*International PSI Committee of Magicians - IPSICM*] (EAIO)
CIEPRC ..... Confederation Internationale des Instituts Catholiques d'Education des Adultes Ruraux [*International Confederation of Catholic Rural People's Schools*]
CIEPS .... Conseil International de l'Education Physique et Sportive [*International Council of Sport and Physical Education*]
CIEPSS ..... Conseil International pour l'Education Physique et la Science du Sport [*International Council of Sport Science and Physical Education - ICSSPE*] (EAIO)
CIER .... Centre Interamericain d'Education Rurale
CIER .... Comision de Integracion Electrica Regional [*Commission of Regional Electrical Integration*] (EAIO)
CIER .... Commission for International Educational Reconstruction
CIER .... Conseil International des Economies Regionales [*International Council for Local Development*] (EAIO)
CIERSES .. Centre International d'Etudes et de Recherches en Socio-Economie de la Sante [*International Health Centre of Socioeconomics, Researches and Studies - IHCSERS*] [*Lailly En Val, France*] (EAIO)

CIES .... Comite International des Entreprises a Succursales [*International Association of Chain Stores*] (EAIO)
CIES .... Comparative and International Education Society (EA)
CIES .... Consejo Interamericano Economico-Social [*Inter-American Economic and Social Council*] (EA)
CIES .... Correctional Institutions Environment Scale [*Personality development test*] [*Psychology*]
CIES .... Council for International Exchange of Scholars (EA)
CIESA .... Compania Internacional Editora, Sociedad Anonima
CIESC .... Comparative and International Education Society of Canada
CIESM ...... Commission Internationale pour l'Exploration Scientifique de la Mer Mediterranee [*International Commission for the Scientific Exploration of the Mediterranean Sea - ICSEM*] [*Research center*] [*Monaco*] (IRC)
CIESPAL .. Centro Internacional de Estudios Superiores de Periodisma para America Latina [*Press agency*] [*Ecuador*]
CIESS .... Chief Inspector of Engineering and Signal Stores [*Military*] [*British*]
CIESTPM ... College International pour l'Etude Scientifique des Techniques de Production Mecanique [*International Institute for Production Engineering Research*] (EAIO)
CIET .... Chinese Institute of Engineers of Taiwan (MCD)
CIET .... Commissioners Industrial Extended Mortality Table [*Insurance*]
CIETA .... Centre International d'Etudes des Textiles Anciens [*International Center for the Study of Ancient Textiles*] [*Lyon, France*]
CIETD .... Ciencias da Terra [*A publication*]
CIE-TM..... Certified International Executive - Traffic Management [*Designation awarded by American Society of International Executives, Inc.*]
CIEURP .... Conference Internationale pour l'Enseignement Universitaire des Relations Publiques [*International Conference on University Education for Public Relations*]
CIE-USA ... Chinese Institute of Engineers - USA (EA)
CIEW-TV ... Warmley, SK [*Television station call letters*]
CIF............ Canadian Institute of Forestry
CIF............ Capacitor Input Filter
CIF............ Captive Installation Function [*Telecommunications*] (TEL)
CIF............ Carriage, Insurance, and Freight
CIF............ Cash in Fist
CIF............ Central Index File
CIF............ Central Information File
CIF............ Central Instrumentation Facility [*NASA*]
CIF............ Central Integration Facility
CIF............ Central Issue Facility [*Military*] (AABC)
CIF............ Channel Island Ferries [*British*]
CIF............ Chifeng [*China*] [*Airport symbol*] (OAG)
CIF............ Children in Families Project [*Australia*]
CIF............ China International Foundation [*Later, TIF*] (EA)
CIF............ Cloning Inhibiting Factor
CIF............ Cohesive Intermolecular Force
CIF............ Cold-Insoluble Fibrinogen [*Hematology*]
CIF............ Colonial Intermediate High Income Fund [*NYSE symbol*] (SPSG)
CIF............ Command Information Flow [*Military*] (CAAL)
CIF............ Computer-Integrated Factory
CIF............ Confederation Internationale des Fonctionnaires [*International Confederation of Public Service Officers*]
CIF............ Congressional Institute for the Future (EA)
CIF............ Conseil International des Femmes [*International Council of Women - ICW*] [*Paris, France*] (EA)
CIF............ Consolidated Indescor Corp. [*Formerly, Indescor Hydrodynamics, Inc.*] [*Vancouver Stock Exchange symbol*]
CIF............ Construction Industry Foundation [*Defunct*] (EA)
CIF............ Consumer Interests Foundation
CIF............ Corporate Income Fund
CIF............ Cost, Insurance, and Freight [*Shipping*] ["*INCOTERM,*" *International Chamber of Commerce official code*]
CIF............ Cost-Plus-Incentive Fee [*Business term*]
CIF............ Council of International Fellowship (EA)
CIF............ Critical Issues Fund [*National Trust for Historic Preservation*]
CIF............ Cultural Integration Fellowship (EA)
CIF............ Customer Information File [*Data processing*] (BUR)
CIF40........ Conseil International Formule 40 [*International F-40 Council*] [*Paris, France*] (EAIO)
CIFA .... Campaign for Independent Financial Advice [*British*]
CIFA .... Comite International de Recherche et d'Etude de Facteurs de l'Ambiance [*International Committee for Research and Study on Environmental Factors*]
CIFA .... Committee for Inland Fisheries of Africa [*UN Food and Agriculture Organization*]
CIFA .... Corporation of Insurance and Financial Advisers [*British*]
CIFA (Comm Inland Fish Afr) Tech Pap ... CIFA (Committee for Inland Fisheries of Africa) Technical Paper [*A publication*]
CIFA-FM .. Yarmouth, NS [*FM radio station call letters*]
CIFAR .... Center for International Financial Analysis and Research, Inc. [*Princeton, NJ*] [*Information service or system*] (IID)
CIFAR .... Central Institute of Foreign Affairs Research
CIFAX .... Enciphered Facsimile Communications

CIFBA6 ..... Central Inland Fisheries Research Institute (Barrackpore). Bulletin [*A publication*]
CIFC .... Centre for Interfirm Comparison [*British*]
CIF & C ... Cost, Insurance, Freight, and Commission [*Shipping*]
CIFC .... Cost, Insurance, Freight, and Commission [*Shipping*]
CIFCA .... Centro Internacional de Formacion en Ciencias Ambientales para Paises de Habla Espanol [*International Center for the Preparation of Personnel in Environmental Sciences in Spanish-Speaking Countries*] [*Spain*]
CIFCA9 ..... Communications. Instituti Forestalis Cechosloveniae [*A publication*]
CIFCE .... Cost, Insurance, Freight, Commission, and Exchange [*Shipping*]
CIFCE & I ... Cost, Insurance, Freight, Commission, Exchange, and Interest [*Shipping*]
CIFC & I .... Cost, Insurance, Freight, Commission, and Interest [*Shipping*]
CIFCI........ Cost, Insurance, Freight, Commission, and Interest [*Shipping*]
CIFCO .... Civilians in Foreign Communications Operations [*Military*]
CIFE .... Canadian International Footwear Exposition   (ITD)
CIFE .... Central Index File - Europe   (NATG)
CIFE .... Centre International de Formation Europeenne [*France*]
CiFe............ Ciencia y Fe [*A publication*]
CIFE .... Comite International du Film Ethnographique
CIFE .... Conference for Independent Further Education [*British*]
CIFE .... Conseil International du Film d'Enseignement [*International Council for Educational Films*]
CIF & E...... Cost, Insurance, Freight, and Exchange [*Shipping*]
CIFE .... Cost, Insurance, Freight, and Exchange [*Shipping*]
CIFEG .... Centre International pour la Formation et les Echanges Geologiques [*International Center for Training and Exchanges in the Geosciences*]   (EAIO)
CIFEJ .... Centre International du Film pour l'Enfance et la Jeunesse [*International Center of Films for Children and Young People*]
CIFFO .... Cost, Insurance, Freight, Free Out [*Shipping*]
CIFG-TV ... Prince George, BC [*Television station call letters*]
CIFI .... Catholic Institute of the Food Industry   (EA)
CIFI .... Cost, Insurance, Freight, and Interest [*Shipping*]
CIF & I ...... Cost, Insurance, Freight, and Interest [*Shipping*]
CIFI & E .... Cost, Insurance, Freight, Interest, and Exchange [*Shipping*]
CIFJAU ...... Canadian Institute of Food Technology. Journal [*A publication*]
CIFLT........ Cost, Insurance, Freight, London Terms [*Shipping*]
CIFM......... Contributi. Istituto di Filologia Moderna [*A publication*]
CIFM-FM ... Kamloops, BC [*FM radio station call letters*]
CIFM-FM-7 ... Pritchard, BC [*FM radio station call letters*]
CIFM-FM-8 ... Chase, BC [*FM radio station call letters*]
CIFO......... Criminal Investigation Field Office [*Military*]
CIFP .... Cancel IFR [*Instrument Flight Rules*] Flight Plan [*Aviation*]   (FAAC)
CIFP .... Comite International pour le Fair Play [*International Fair Play Committee*] [*Paris, France*]   (EAIO)
CIFP .... Committee on International Freedom to Publish   (EA)
CIFPSE ..... Catholic International Federation for Physical and Sports Education [*See also FICEP*] [*Paris, France*]   (EAIO)
CIFR .... Cancel Instrument Flight Rules Clearance Previously Given [*Aviation*]   (FAAC)
CIFR .... Cipher Data Products, Inc. [*San Diego, CA*] [*NASDAQ symbol*]   (NQ)
CIFRBL..... Central Inland Fisheries Research Institute (Barrackpore). Annual Report [*A publication*]
CIFRI (Cent Inland Fish Res Inst) Semin ... CIFRI (Central Inland Fisheries Research Institute) Seminar [*A publication*]
CIFRR .... Common Instrument Flight Rules Room [*Aviation*]   (FAAC)
CIFRS........ Common Market Group of International Rayon and Synthetic Fibres Committee   (EAIO)
CIFSBO..... Central Inland Fisheries Research Institute (Barrackpore). Survey Report [*A publication*]
CIF-SP...... Congresso Internacional de Filosofia. Anais (Sao Paulo) [*A publication*]
CIFT .... Canadian Institute of Fisheries Technology [*Technical University of Nova Scotia*] [*Research center*]   (RCD)
CIFT .... Centro Internazionale di Fisica Teorica [*International Center for Theoretical Physics - ICTP*]   (EAIO)
CIFT .... Committee on Invisibles and Financing Related to Trade [*United Nations Conference on Trade and Development*]
CIFTA .... Comite International des Federations Theatrales d'Amateurs de Langue Francaise
CIFV .... Composite Infantry Fighting Vehicle [*Army*]
CIFX .... Winnipeg, MB [*AM radio station call letters*]
CIG .... Cable Integrity Group   (NASA)
CIG .... Centre Informatique Geologique [*Geological Information Centre*] [*Canada*]
CIG .... Chemical Ion Generator   (AAG)
CIG .... Chief Intendent-General [*Freemasonry*]   (ROG)
CIG .... Cigar   (DSUE)
CIG .... Citadel Gold Mines, Inc. [*Toronto Stock Exchange symbol*]
CIg .... Cold-Insoluble globulin [*Cytochemistry*]
CIG .... Comite International de Geophysique [*International Geophysical Committee*]
CIG .... Communications and Interface Group [*NASA*]   (NASA)
CIG .... Computer Image Generator [*or Generation*]   (MCD)

CIG .... Computer-Informationsdienst Graz [*Graz Computer-Information Service*] [*Austria*]   (IID)
CIG .... Computerized Interactive Graphics   (MCD)
CIG .... Conference Internationale du Goudron [*International Tar Conference - ITC*]   (EAIO)
CIG .... Continental Graphics Corp. [*AMEX symbol*]   (SPSG)
CIG .... Coordinate Indexing Group [*ASLIB*]   (DIT)
CIG .... Corpus Inscriptionum Graecarum [*A collection of Greek inscriptions*] [*A publication*] [*Latin*]
CIG .... Counterintelligence Group [*Military*]
CIG .... Creative Industries Group, Inc. [*Auburn Hills, MI*]   (TSSD)
CIG .... Current Intelligence, Group   (NATG)
CIG .... Curriculum Interest Group [*Australia*]
C-Ig .... Cytoplasmic Immunoglobulin [*Immunology*]
CIGA .... Compagnia Italiana del Grandi Alberghi [*Italian hotel chain*]
CIGAR....... Common Interactive Graphics Application Routine [*Army*]
CIGARS .... Committee Insuring and Guaranteeing Anyone's Right to Smoke
CIGARS .... Console Internally Generated and Refreshed Symbols   (CAAL)
CIGB......... Commission Internationale des Grands Barrages [*International Commission on Large Dams - ICOLD*]   (EAIO)
CIGB-FM ... Trois Rivieres, PQ [*FM radio station call letters*]
CIGC......... Citadel Gold Mines, Inc. [*NASDAQ symbol*]   (NQ)
CIGCOREP ... Counter Infiltration - Counter Guerilla Concept and Requirement Plan   (CINC)
CIG Cryog Indus Gases ... CIG. Cryogenics and Industrial Gases [*A publication*]
CIGGA ...... Cigarette [*Australian slang*]   (DSUE)
CIGGT....... Canadian Institute of Guided Ground Transport [*Queen's University at Kingston*] [*Research center*]   (RCD)
CIGH........ Confederation Internationale de Genealogie et d'Heraldique [*International Confederation of Genealogy and Heraldry - ICGH*] [*Paris, France*]   (EAIO)
CIGI......... Canadian International Grains Institute
CIGL-FM .. Belleville, ON [*FM radio station call letters*]
CIGM-FM ... Sudbury, ON [*FM radio station call letters*]
CIGO .... Port Hawkesbury, NS [*AM radio station call letters*]
CIGP .... Capital Investment Goal Programming
CIGP .... Comite Interministeriel de la Gestion du Personnel [*Personnel Administration Interdepartmental Committee*] [*Canada*]
CIGR .... Commission Internationale du Genie Rural [*International Commission of Agricultural Engineering*] [*ICSU*]   (EAIO)
CIGRE....... Conference Internationale des Grands Reseaux Electriques a Haute Tension [*International Conference on Large High Voltage Electric Systems*]   (EAIO)
CIGS......... Centre International de Gerontologie Sociale [*International Center of Social Gerontology - ICSG*] [*Paris, France*]
CIGS......... Chief of the Imperial General Staff [*Later, CGS*] [*British*]
CIGTF .... Central Inertial Guidance Test Facility [*Air Force*]
CIGV-FM ... Penticton, BC [*FM radio station call letters*]
CIH .... Carbohydrate-Induced Hyperglyceridemia [*Medicine*]
CIH .... Central India Horse [*British military*]   (DMA)
CIH .... Certificate of Industrial Health
CIH .... Certified Industrial Hygienist
CIH .... Chain Ignition Hazard
CIH .... Changzhi [*China*] [*Airport symbol*]   (OAG)
CIH .... Children in Hospitals   (EA)
CIH .... CIS Technologies, Inc. [*Vancouver Stock Exchange symbol*]
CIH .... Colloidal Iron Hydroxide
CIH .... Committee for Italic Handwriting [*Defunct*]   (EA)
CIH .... Commonwealth Institute of Helminthology [*St. Albans, England*]
CIH .... Computers in Healthcare [*A publication*]
CIH .... Continental Illinois Holding Corp. [*NYSE symbol*]   (SPSG)
CIH .... Corpus Inscriptionum Himjariticarum   (BJA)
CIH........... Information Handling Services, Englewood, CO [*OCLC symbol*]   (OCLC)
CIHA .... Comite International d'Histoire de l'Art   (EAIO)
CIHB .... Canadian Inventory of Historic Building [*Environment Canada*] [*Information service or system*]   (IID)
CIHEAM .. Centre International de Hautes Etudes Agronomiques Mediterraneennes
CIHF-TV ... Halifax, NS [*Television station call letters*]
CIHGLF .... Comite International d'Historiens et Geographes de Langue Francaise [*International Committee of French-Speaking Historians and Geographers - ICFHG*]   (EAIO)
CIHI .... Fredericton, NB [*AM radio station call letters*]
CIHM........ Canadian Institute for Historical Microreproductions
CIHM........ Commission Internationale d'Histoire Militaire [*International Commission of Military History*]   (EAIO)
CIHMBG .. Congreso Internacional de Hematologia. Conferencias [*A publication*]
CIHO-FM ... St. Hilarion, PQ [*FM radio station call letters*]
CIHU........ Canadian Infantry Holding Unit
CIHV .... Centre International Humanae Vitae [*International Centre Humanae Vitae*] [*Paris, France*]   (EAIO)
CII............. Centre for Industrial Innovation [*British*]   (ARC)
CII............. Centro Internacional de la Infancia [*International Children's Center*]
CII............. Chartered Insurance Institute [*British*]
CII............. CII Financial, Inc. [*AMEX symbol*]   (SPSG)

CII............. Compagnie Internationale pour l'Informatique [*Formed by merger of SEA and CAE*]
CII............. Computer-Integrated Instruction (NVT)
CII............. Configuration Identification Index
CII............. Conseil International des Infirmieres [*International Council of Nurses - ICN*] [*Geneva, Switzerland*] (EA)
CII............. Containerization and Intermodal Institute (EA)
CII............. Controlled Interval Inspection (MCD)
CII............. Convention II (EA)
CII............. Council of Institutional Investors [*Washington, DC*] (EA)
CII............. Council of International Investigators (EA)
CII............. Criminal Identification and Investigation
CII............. Critical Item Inspection [*California Highway Patrol's accident inspection program*]
CII............. Crosscurrents International Institute (EA)
CII............. Current Indicator and Integrator
CII............. George M. Low Center for Industrial Innovation [*Rensselaer Polytechnic Institute*] [*Research center*] (RCD)
CIIA........... Canadian Information Industry Association [*Information service or system*] (IID)
CIIA........... Canadian Institute of International Affairs
CIIA........... Commission Internationale des Industries Agricoles et Alimentaires [*International Commission for Food Industries*] (EAIO)
CIIC........... Capital Industries, Incorporated [*Indianapolis, IN*] [*NASDAQ symbol*] (NQ)
CIIC........... Centro Internacional de Investigaciones sobre el Cancer [*International Agency for Research on Cancer*]
CIIC........... Chemical International Information Center
CIIC........... Counterintelligence Interrogation Center [*Military*]
CIIC........... Current Intelligence Indication Center (CINC)
CIICBP...... Convenio IICA-ZN-ROCAP [*Instituto Interamericano de Ciencias Agricolas-Zona Norte-Regional Organization for Central America and Panama*] Bibliografia [*A publication*]
CIIC/W ..... Canadian Industrial Innovation Centre/Waterloo [*University of Waterloo*] [*Research center*] (RCD)
CIID........... Centre de Recherches pour le Developpement International [*International Development Research Centre*] [*Canada*]
CIID........... Commission Internationale des Irrigations et du Drainage [*International Commission on Irrigation and Drainage - ICID*] (EAIO)
CIIG Bull ... CIIG [*Construction Industry Information Group*] Bulletin [*A publication*]
CIIHB........ Compagnie Internationale pour l'Informatique Honeywell-Bull [*Computer manufacturer*] [*France*]
CIII........... Centrum Industries, Incorporated [*NASDAQ symbol*] (NQ)
CI-III .... Computer Inquiry III [*FCC*]
CIII-TV ...... Paris, ON [*Television station call letters*]
CIII-TV-1 .. Windsor, ON [*Television station call letters*]
CIII-TV-2 .. Bancroft, ON [*Television station call letters*]
CIII-TV-4 .. Owen Sound, ON [*Television station call letters*]
CIII-TV-6 .. Ottawa, ON [*Television station call letters*]
CIII-TV-7 .. Midland, ON [*Television station call letters*]
CIII-TV-27 ... Peterborough, ON [*Television station call letters*]
CIII-TV-29 ... Sarnia, ON [*Television station call letters*]
CIII-TV-41 ... Toronto, ON [*Television station call letters*]
CIIM.......... Centre International d'Information de la Mutualite
CIIMDN.... Cancer Immunology and Immunotherapy [*A publication*]
CIIMS ...... Canadian Information and Image Management Society [*Information service or system*] (IID)
CIINAN..... Citrus Industry [*A publication*]
CIIP........... Clothing Initial Issue Point [*Military*] (AABC)
CIIP........... Commander, International Ice Patrol [*Coast Guard*]
CIIP........... Container Industries, Incorporated [*Somerset, NJ*] [*NASDAQ symbol*] (NQ)
CIIR.......... Catholic Institute for International Relations [*London, England*] (EAIO)
CIIR.......... Central Institute for Industrial Research (AAG)
CIIS .... Corporate Integrated Information System [*Consumer and Corporate Affairs Canada*] [*Information service or system*] (IID)
CIIT........... Chemical Industry Institute of Toxicology (EA)
CIITC .... Confederation Internationale des Industries Techniques du Cinema
CIIUAP ..... Commission on Increased Industrial Use of Agricultural Products
CIJ .... Canada Commerce [*A publication*]
CIJ .... Canadian Industrial Minerals Corp. [*Vancouver Stock Exchange symbol*]
CIJ .... Cobija [*Bolivia*] [*Airport symbol*] (OAG)
CIJ .... Commercial Investment Journal [*A publication*]
CIJ .... Commission Internationale de Juristes [*International Commission of Jurists - ICJ*] [*Switzerland*]
CIJ .... Corpus Inscriptionum Judaicarum [*A publication*] (BJA)
CIJ .... Cour Internationale de Justice [*International Court of Justice*]
CIJ .... Sisters of the Infant Jesus [*Nursing Sisters of the Sick Poor*] [*Roman Catholic religious order*]
CIJC .... Construction Industry Joint Conference (EA)
CIJE .... Current Index to Journals in Education [*United States Office of Education*] [*A publication*]

CIJED4 ..... Centro Internacional de Agricultura Tropical [*CIAT*]. Series JE [*A publication*]
CIJL........... Centre for the Independence of Judges and Lawyers [*See also CIMA*] [*Geneva, Switzerland*] (EAIO)
CIJM .... Comite International des Jeux Mediterraneens [*Athens, Greece*] (EAIO)
CIJN .... Club International des Jeunes Naturistes [*Paris, France*] (EAIO)
CIJPECEW ... Committee for International Justice and Peace of the Episcopal Conference of England and Wales (EAIO)
CIK .... Canadian Insulock [*Vancouver Stock Exchange symbol*]
CIK .... Chalkyitsik [*Alaska*] [*Airport symbol*] (OAG)
CIKI-FM ... Rimouski, PQ [*FM radio station call letters*]
CIL............ C-I-L, Inc. [*Toronto Stock Exchange symbol*]
CIL............ Canadian Industries Limited
CIL............ Central Identification Laboratory [*Hawaii*] [*Army*]
CIL............ Certificate in Lieu [*of*]
CIL............ Chicago, Indianapolis & Louisville [*Louisville & Nashville Railroad Co.*] [*AAR code*]
CIL............ Clear Indicating Light (MSA)
CIL............ Cold Intermediate Layer [*Oceanography*]
CIL............ Commercial Instrument Landing
C/I/L......... Computer/Information/Library Sciences [*Abstracts*]
CIL............ Computers in Libraries [*Australia*]
CIL............ Configuration [*or Contract*] Inspection Log
CIL............ Contemporary Indian Literature [*A publication*]
CIL............ Controlled Items List
CIL............ Cooling-Induced Luminescence [*In glass containing rare earth salts*]
CIL............ Core Image Library (CMD)
CIL............ Corpus Inscriptionum Latinarum [*A collection of Latin inscriptions*] [*A publication*] [*Latin*]
CIL............ Council, AK [*Location identifier*] [*FAA*] (FAAL)
CIL............ Council for Interinstitutional Leadership (EA)
CIL............ Crain's Illinois Business [*A publication*]
CIL............ Critical Item List (MCD)
CIL............ Current Injection Logic [*Data processing*]
CILA......... Centro Interamericano de Libros Academicos [*Inter-American Scholarly Book Center*]
CILA......... Council of International Lay Associations [*Defunct*] (EA)
CILA B ...... CILA [*Centre Internationale de Linguistique Appliquee*] Bulletin [*A publication*]
CILAD...... Colegio Ibero-Latino-Americano de Dermatologia [*Ibero Latin American College of Dermatology - ILACD*] (EA)
CILA-FM .. Lethbridge, AB [*FM radio station call letters*]
CILB......... Commission Internationale de Lutte Biologique Contre les Ennemis des Cultures
CILBA2 ..... Contributions. Institute of Low Temperature Science. Hokkaido University. Series B [*A publication*]
CILC......... California Iceberg Lettuce Commission (EA)
CILC......... Centralized Intermediate Logistics Concept (MCD)
CILC......... Commonwealth International Law Cases [*A publication*] (DLA)
CILC......... Confederation Internationale du Lin et du Chanvre [*International Linen and Hemp Confederation*] (EAIO)
CILEA ...... Consorzio Interuniversitario Lombardo per l'Elaborazione Automatica [*Lombard Interuniversity Consortium for Data Processing*] [*Information service or system*] (IID)
CILECT..... Centre International de Liaison des Ecoles de Cinema et de Television [*International Liaison Centre for Film and Television Schools*] (EAIO)
CILES........ Central Information, Library, and Editorial Section [*CSIRO*] [*Information service or system*] [*Australia*] (IID)
CILET .... Circular Letter
CILF .... Conseil International de la Langue Francaise [*International Council of the French Language - ICFL*] (EAIO)
CIL-HI...... Central Identification Laboratory - Hawaii [*Army*]
CILJDT ..... Contact and Intraocular Lens Medical Journal [*A publication*]
CILJSA ..... Comparative and International Law Journal of Southern Africa [*A publication*] (DLA)
CILK-FM .. Kelowna, BC [*FM radio station call letters*]
CILL.......... Current Inquiry into Language and Linguistics [*A publication*]
CILOP....... Conversion in Lieu of Procurement [*Military*]
CILOPGO ... Comite International de Liaison des Gynecologues et Obstetriciens
CILP .... Conferences. Institut de Linguistique de Paris [*A publication*]
CILP .... Current Index to Legal Periodicals [*University of Washington*] [*Information service or system*] (CRD)
CILPE........ Conference Internationale de Liaison entre Producteurs d'Energie Electrique [*International Conference of Producers of Electrical Energy*]
CILQ-FM ... Toronto, ON [*FM radio station call letters*]
Ci LR......... Cincinnati Law Review [*A publication*]
CILRT .... Containment Integrated Leak Rate Test [*Nuclear energy*] (NRCH)
CILS .... Carrier Instrument Landing System [*Navy*] (CAAL)
CILS .... Center for Independent Living Services
CILS .... Centralized Intermediate Logistics System (MCD)
CILS .... Compatible Instrument Landing System [*Aviation*]
CILSA .... Chief Inspector of Land Service Ammunition (NATG)
CILSIG...... Computers in Libraries Special Interest Group [*Australia*]

CILSMO ...　Command Integrated Logistics Management Office
CILSS ....　Comite Permanent Interetats de Lutte Contre la Secheresse dans le Sahel [*Permanent Interstate Committee for Drought Control in the Sahel*]　(EAIO)
CILT ....　Amsterdam Studies in the Theory and History of Linguistic Science. Series IV. Current Issues in Linguistic Theory [*A publication*]
CILT ....　Centre for Information on Language Teaching and Research [*Regent's College*] [*British*]　(CB)
CILT ....　Centre for Information on Language Training [*British*]
CILW ....　Wainwright, AB [*AM radio station call letters*]
CIM ....　Canadian Institute of Metalworking [*McMaster University*] [*Research center*]　(RCD)
CIM ....　Canadian Institute of Mining
CIM ....　Capital Investment Model [*Navy*]
CIM ....　Carina Minerals Resources Ltd. [*Vancouver Stock Exchange symbol*]
CIM ....　Cavitation Intensity Meter
CIM ....　Center for Integral Medicine [*Defunct*]　(EA)
CIM ....　Certificate in Management
CIM ....　Certified Industrial Manager
CIM ....　Charge Imaging Matrix [*Electronics*]
CIM ....　Chicago & Illinois Midland Railway Co. [*AAR code*]
C & IM ......　Chicago & Illinois Midland Railway Co.
CIM ....　Chief Industrial Magistrate [*Australia*]
CIM ....　Chief Inspector of Machinery [*Navy*] [*British*]　(ROG)
CIM ....　Children's Interaction Matrix [*Child development test*] [*Psychology*]
CIM ....　Chimachoy [*Guatemala*] [*Seismograph station code, US Geological Survey*]　(SEIS)
CIM ....　China Inland Mission
CIM ....　Christian Ireland Ministries　(EA)
CIM ....　CIM High Yield Securities [*AMEX symbol*]　(SPSG)
CIM ....　Cimarron, NM [*Location identifier*] [*FAA*]　(FAAL)
CIM ....　Cimitarra [*Colombia*] [*Airport symbol*]　(OAG)
Cim............　Cimon [*of Plutarch*] [*Classical studies*]　(OCD)
CIM ....　Cleveland Institute of Music [*Record label*]
CIM ....　Code Interface Module　(CAAL)
CIM ....　Coffin Intercept Missile
CIM ....　Colonic Intestinal Metaplasia [*Oncology*]
CIM ....　Comision Interamericana de Mujeres [*Inter-American Commission of Women*]　(EAIO)
CIM ....　Comite International du Mini-Basketball [*International Committee for Mini-Basketball*] [*Munich, Federal Republic of Germany*]　(EAIO)
CIM ....　COMLINE Industrial Monitor [*COMLINE International Corp.*] [*Japan*] [*Information service or system*]　(CRD)
CIM ....　Commission Internationale de Marketing [*International Marketing Commission - IMC*] [*Brixham, Devonshire, England*]　(EAIO)
CIM ....　Communication Interface Monitor
CIM ....　Communications Improvement Memorandum [*Military*]
CIM ....　Communications Interface Modules [*Data processing*]
CIM ....　Component Item Manager [*Air Force*]　(AFIT)
CIM ....　Compound Inserting Machine
CIM ....　Computer Input Matrix　(KSC)
CIM ....　Computer Input Microfilming　(MCD)
CIM ....　Computer Input Multiplexer　(KSC)
CIM ....　Computer-Integrated Manufacturing
CIM ....　Computer Interface Module [*Data processing*]
CIM ....　[*The*] Computers in Manufacturing Show [*British*]　(ITD)
CIM ....　Conductance Increase Mechanism
CIM ....　Congres International des Fabrications Mecaniques [*International Mechanical Engineering Congress*]
CIM ....　Congres Islamique Mondial
CIM ....　Conseil International de la Musique [*International Music Council*]
CIM ....　Consejo Internacional de Mujeres [*International Council of Women*]
CIM ....　Continuous Image Microfilm　(IEEE)
CIM ....　Continuous Imprint Marking [*of medical linen*]　(MCD)
CIM ....　Control Interface Module [*Chemistry*]
CIM ....　Convention Internationale Concernant le Transport des Marchandises par Chemins de Fer [*International Convention Concerning the Carriage of Goods by Rail*]
CIM ....　Cooperative Investigation of the Mediterranean
CIM ....　Cork Insulation Material
CIM ....　Cortically Induced Movement [*Medicine*]
CIM ....　Council of Independent Managers [*Milwaukee, WI*]　(EA)
CIM ....　Crystal Impedance Meter
CIM ....　Cumulated Index Medicus [*A publication*]
CIM ....　Curtis Institute of Music [*Pennsylvania*]
CIM ....　University of California, Irvine, Medical Sciences Library, Irvine, CA [*OCLC symbol*]　(OCLC)
CIMA ....　Centre pour l'Independance des Magistrats et des Avocats [*Centre for the Independence of Judges and Lawyers - CIJL*]　(EA)
CIMA ....　Centre for Industrial Microelectronics Applications [*Australia*]
CIMA ....　Commission Internationale de Micro Aviation　(AIA)
CIMA ....　Construction Industry Manufacturers Association　(EA)
CIMA ....　Creek Indian Memorial Association　(EA)

CIMAA......　Cellulose Insulation Manufacturers and Agents Association [*Australia*]
CIMAC......　Conseil International des Machines a Combustion [*International Council on Combustion Engines*] [*Paris, France*]　(EAIO)
CIMAe.......　Commission Internationale de Meteorologie Aeronautique [*OMI*]
CIMAGL...　Cahiers. Institut du Moyen Age Grec et Latin [*A publication*]
CIMAH .....　Control of Industrial Major Accident Hazards [*British*]
CIMA Outlk ...　Construction Industry Manufacturers Association. Outlook [*A publication*]
CIMAP......　Commission Internationale des Methodes d'Analyse des Pesticides [*Collaborative International Pesticides Analytic Council - CIPAC*]　(EAIO)
CIMAR......　Center for Intelligent Machines and Robotics [*University of Florida*] [*Research center*]　(RCD)
CIMarE......　Companion of the Institute of Marine Engineers [*British*]
CIMAS......　Conference Internationale de la Mutualite et des Assurances Sociales
CIMAS......　Cooperative Institute for Marine and Atmospheric Studies [*Coral Gables, FL*] [*NOAA, Rosenstiel School of Marine and Atmospheric Science of the University of Miami*]　(GRD)
CIMB........　CIM [*Canadian Institute of Mining and Metallurgy*] Bulletin [*A publication*]
CIMB........　Cimbalom [*Music*]
CIMB........　Construction Industry Management Board　(EA)
CIMBA......　Contractor Installation Make or Buy Authorization　(AAG)
Cimbebasia Mem ...　Cimbebasia. Memoir [*A publication*]
Cimbebasia Ser A ...　Cimbebasia. Series A [*A publication*]
Cim Beton ..　Ciment si Beton [*A publication*]
Cim Betons Platres Chaux ...　Ciments, Betons, Platres, Chaux [*France*] [*A publication*]
CIM Bull ...　CIM [*Canadian Institute of Mining and Metallurgy*] Bulletin [*A publication*]
CIM Bulletin ...　Canadian Institute of Mining and Metallurgy. Bulletin [*Montreal*] [*A publication*]
CIMC........　CIMCO, Inc. [*NASDAQ symbol*]　(NQ)
CIMC........　Commanders' Internal Management Conference [*Air Force*]
CIMC........　Committee for International Municipal Cooperation
CIMCEE ...　Comite des Industries de la Moutarde de la CEE [*EEC Committee for the Mustard Industries*]
CIMCO .....　Card Image Correction [*Data processing*]
CIMD ....　Certified Institution for the Mental Defective [*British*]
CIME........　Chartered Institute of Marine Engineers
CIME........　Comite Intergouvernemental pour les Migrations Europeennes [*Intergovernmental Committee for European Migration*]
CIME........　Confederation Internationale de Musique Electroacoustique [*International Confederation for Electroacoustic Music - ICEM*]　(EAIO)
CIMEA......　Comite International des Mouvements d'Enfants et d'Adolescents [*International Committee of Children's and Adolescents' Movements*] [*Budapest, Hungary*]　(EAIO)
CI Mech E ...　Companion of the Institution of Mechanical Engineers [*British*]
CIME-FM ...　Ste. Adele, PQ [*FM radio station call letters*]
Cimento Mustahsilleri Bul ...　Cimento Mustahsilleri Bulteni [*A publication*]
CIMEX........　Civil Military Exercise　(MCD)
CIMF-FM ...　Hull, PQ [*FM radio station call letters*]
CIMG ....　Colloque International de Marketing Gazier [*International Colloquium about Gas Marketing - ICGM*]　(EA)
CIMG ....　Consolidated Imaging Corp. [*NASDAQ symbol*]　(NQ)
CIMG-FM ...　Swift Current, SK [*FM radio station call letters*]
CIMGTechE ...　Companion of the Institution of Mechanical and General Technician Engineers [*British*]　(DBQ)
CIMH........　Comite International pour la Metrologie Historique [*International Committee for Historical Metrology*]　(EAIO)
CIMI.........　Chemical Information Management, Incorporated [*Information service or system*]　(IID)
CIMIC.......　Civilian Military Cooperation　(NATG)
CIMIDV....　Comparative Immunology, Microbiology, and Infectious Diseases [*A publication*]
CIMII ....　Continuous Intramuscular Insulin Infusion
CIMIL.......　CSIRO [*Commonwealth Scientific and Industrial Research Organisation*] Inquiry into Mechanization in Libraries [*Australia*]
CIML........　Center for Improving Mountain Living [*Western Carolina University*] [*Research center*]　(RCD)
CIML........　Contract Item Material List
CIMM ....　Canadian Institute of Mining and Metallurgy
CIMM ....　Commodity Integrated Materiel Manager
CIMM ....　Constant Impedance Mechanical Modulation　(AAG)
CIMMS.....　Civilian Information Manpower Management System [*Navy*]
CIMMS.....　Cooperative Institute for Mesoscale Meteorological Studies [*University of Oklahoma, NOAA*] [*Research center*]　(RCD)
CIMMYT ...　Centro Internacional de Mejoramiento de Maiz y Trigo [*International Maize and Wheat Improvement Center*] [*ICSU*]　(EAIO)
CIMMYT News ...　Centro Internacional de Mejoramiento de Maiz y Trigo. News [*A publication*]

CIMN .... Cimarron Corp. [*Dallas, TX*] [*NASDAQ symbol*] (NQ)
CIMNDC .. Clinical Immunology Newsletter [*A publication*]
CIMO .... Commission des Instruments et des Methodes d'Observation [*Commission for Instruments and Methods of Observation*] [*OMI*]
CIMO .... Confederation of Importers and Marketing Organizations in Europe of Fresh Fruit and Vegetables [*Brussels, Belgium*] (EA)
CIMOA ..... Chimie Moderne [*A publication*]
CIMO-FM ... Magog, PQ [*FM radio station call letters*]
CImoH .... Napa State Hospital, Imola, CA [*Library symbol*] [*Library of Congress*] (LCLS)
CIM-OMF ... China Inland Mission Overseas Missionary Fellowship [*Later, Overseas Missionary Fellowship*] (EA)
CIMP .... Conseil International de la Musique Populaire [*International Folk Music Council*]
CIMP .... Controlled Impulse (MCD)
CImp .... Imperial Public Library, Imperial, CA [*Library symbol*] [*Library of Congress*] (LCLS)
CIMPA ...... Centre International de Mathematiques Pures et Appliquees [*International Center for Pure and Applied Mathematics - ICPAM*] [*United Nations*] (EA)
CIMPM ..... Comite International de Medecine et de Pharmacie Militaires [*International Committee of Military Medicine and Pharmacy - ICMMP*] [*Liege, Belgium*] (EA)
CIMR .... Center for Interest Measurement [*University of Minnesota*] [*Research center*] (RCD)
CimR .... Cimarron Review [*A publication*]
CIMR .... Commanders' Internal Management Review [*Also known as Black Saturday*] [*Military*] (AAG)
CIMRDO .. Clinical Immunology Reviews [*A publication*]
CIMRM ..... Corpus Inscriptionum et Monumentorum Religionis Mithriacae [*A publication*] (BJA)
CIMS .... Canada. Industrial Meteorology Studies. Environment Canada. Atmospheric Environment [*A publication*]
CIMS .... Center for Innovation Management Studies [*Lehigh University*] [*Information service or system*] (IID)
CIMS .... Chemical Ionization Mass Spectrometry
CIMS .... Civilian Information Management System (AFIT)
CIMS .... Commercial Information Management System [*Department of Commerce*]
CIMS .... Communications Instructions for Merchant Ships [*Navy*]
CIMS .... Computer-Integrated Manufacturing System
CIMS .... Consociatio Internationalis Musicae Sacrae [*Rome, Italy*] (EAIO)
CIMS .... Courant Institute of Mathematical Sciences [*New York University*] [*Research center*] (RCD)
CIMSCEE ... Comite des Industries des Mayonnaises et Sauces Condimentaires de la CEE [*Committee of the Industries of Mayonnaises and Table Sauces of the European Economic Community*]
CIMT .... Centre International des Marees Terrestres [*International Centre for Earth Tides*] (EAIO)
CIMT .... Commission Internationale de la Medecine du Travail [*International Commission of Occupational Health - ICOH*] [*Information service or system*] (IID)
CIMTA ...... Cottage Industry Miniaturists Trade Association (EA)
CIMTECH ... Centre for Information Media and Technology (EAIO)
CIMTECH ... National Centre for Information Media and Technology [*British*]
CIMTP ...... Congres Internationaux de Medecine Tropicale et de Paludisme [*International Congresses on Tropical Medicine and Malaria*]
CIMT-TV ... Riviere-Du-Loup, PQ [*Television station call letters*]
CIMU .... Compatibility-Integration Mock-Up (MCD)
CIN .... Canadian Insurance [*A publication*]
CIN .... Carrier Input (MSA)
CIN .... Carroll, IA [*Location identifier*] [*FAA*] (FAAL)
CIN .... Centro de Informacoes Nucleares [*Center for Nuclear Information*] [*Brazil*] [*Information service or system*] (IID)
CIN .... Cervical Intraepithelial Neoplasia [*Medicine*]
CIN .... Change Identification Number (NASA)
CIN .... Change Incorporation Notice [*Business law*]
CIN .... Change Instrumentation Notice
CIN .... Chemical Industry Notes [*Chemical Abstracts Service*] [*Bibliographic database*] [*A publication*]
CIN .... Cincinnati [*Ohio*]
CIN .... Cincinnati Gas & Electric Co. [*NYSE symbol*] (SPSG)
CIN .... Cine [*Turkey*] [*Seismograph station code, US Geological Survey*] (SEIS)
CIN .... Code Identification Number (MSA)
CIN .... Combat Information Net
CIN .... Commission Internationale de Numismatique [*International Numismatic Commission*] [*Oslo, Norway*] (EA)
CIN .... Commodore Information Network [*Commodore Business Machines, Inc.*] [*Information service or system*] (TSSD)
CIN .... Common Interest Network (EA)
CIN .... Communication Identification Navigation
CIN .... Community Information Network [*Cable TV programming service*]

CIN .... Contract Item Number (MCD)
CIN .... Cooperative Information Network [*Library network*]
CIN .... Criminal, Immoral, and Narcotic
CIN .... United States Naval Weapons Center, China Lake, CA [*Library symbol*] [*Library of Congress*] (LCLS)
CIN .... University of Cincinnati, Cincinnati, OH [*OCLC symbol*] (OCLC)
CINA .... Canadian Intravenous Nurses Association (EAIO)
CINA .... Centralinstitut for Nordisk Asienforskning [*Scandinavian Institute of Asian Studies*] [*Later, NIAS*] (EAIO)
CINA .... Commission Internationale de la Navigation Aerienne [*International Air Navigation Commission*]
CINA .... Cook Inlet Native Association [*Defunct*] (EA)
CINAHL ... Cumulative Index to Nursing and Allied Health Literature [*Database*]
Cin Art B .... Cincinnati Art Museum. Bulletin [*A publication*]
CINAV ...... Commission Internationale de la Nomenclature Anatomique Veterinaire [*International Committee on Veterinary Anatomical Nomenclature - ICVAN*] [*Zurich, Switzerland*] (EAIO)
Cin BAJ ..... Cincinnati Bar Association. Journal [*A publication*]
Cin B Ass'n J ... Cincinnati Bar Association. Journal [*A publication*] (DLA)
CINC .... Commander-in-Chief
CINCAC ..... Commander-in-Chief, Continental Air Command (AFM)
CINCAD ..... Commander-in-Chief, Aerospace Defense (FAAC)
CINCAF .... Commander-in-Chief, Allied Forces
CINCAF .... Commander-in-Chief, [*US*] Asiatic Fleet
CINCAFE ... Commander-in-Chief, Air Forces, Europe (NATG)
CINCAFLANT ... Commander-in-Chief, Air Force Atlantic Command (AFM)
CINCAFMED ... Commander-in-Chief, Allied Forces, Mediterranean [*NATO*]
CINCAFPAC ... Commander-in-Chief, [*US*] Army Forces in the Pacific
CINCAFSTRIKE ... Commander-in-Chief, Air Force Strike Command (AFM)
CINCAIRCENT ... Commander-in-Chief, Allied Air Forces, Central Europe (MCD)
CINCAIREASTLANT ... Air Commander-in-Chief, Eastern Atlantic Area
CINCAL .... Commander-in-Chief, Alaskan Command
CINCALAIRCENEUR ... Commander-in-Chief, Allied Air Forces, Central Europe
CINCARIB ... Commander-in-Chief, Caribbean
CINCARLANT ... Commander-in-Chief, [*US*] Army Forces, Atlantic (AABC)
CINCARPAC ... Commander-in-Chief, [*US*] Army Forces, Pacific (AFM)
CINCARSTRIKE ... Commander-in-Chief, Army Strike Command (AFM)
CINCATL ... Commander-in-Chief, Atlantic
CINCAWI ... Commander-in-Chief, America West Indies Station [*British*]
CINCA & WI ... Commander-in-Chief, Atlantic and West Indies
CINCBPF ... Commander-in-Chief, British Pacific Fleet
CINCCENT ... Commander-in-Chief, Allied Forces, Central Europe [*NATO*]
CINCCHAN ... Allied Commander-in-Chief, Channel (MCD)
CINCCONAD ... Commander-in-Chief, Continental Air Defense Command (FAAC)
CINCEASTLANT ... Commander-in-Chief, Eastern Atlantic Area [*NATO*]
CINCEI ..... Commander-in-Chief, East Indies Station [*British*]
CINCENT ... Commander-in-Chief, Allied Forces, Central Europe (MCD)
CINCEUR ... Commander-in-Chief, Europe
CINCFE .... Commander-in-Chief, Far East
CINCFES .. Commander-in-Chief, Far East Station [*British*]
CINCFESTA ... Commander-in-Chief, Far East Station [*British*]
CINCFLT ... Commander-in-Chief, Fleet [*British*]
Cinch .... Cinchona [*Quinine*] [*Pharmacology*] (ROG)
CINCH ...... Computerised Information from National Criminological Holdings [*Australian Institute of Criminology Library*] [*Database*] [*Information service or system*] (IID)
CINCHAN ... Commander-in-Chief Channel and Southern North Sea
CINCHF .... Commander-in-Chief, United Kingdom Home Fleet [*Also, CINCHOMEFLT*] (NATG)
CINCHOMEFLT ... Commander-in-Chief, United Kingdom Home Fleet [*Also, CINCHF*] (NATG)
CINCIBERLANT ... Commander-in-Chief, Iberian Atlantic Area (NATG)
Cinci Dent Soc Bull ... Cincinnati Dental Society. Bulletin [*A publication*]
Cincin BJ ... Cincinnati Business Journal [*A publication*]
Cincin Bsn ... Cincinnati Business Courier [*A publication*]
Cincin Enq ... Cincinnati Enquirer [*A publication*]
Cincinnati J Med ... Cincinnati Journal of Medicine [*A publication*]
Cincinnati Med ... Cincinnati Medicine [*A publication*]
Cincinnati Mus Bul ns ... Cincinnati Art Museum. Bulletin. New Series [*A publication*]
Cincinnati Mus Bull ... Cincinnati Art Museum. Bulletin [*A publication*]
Cincinnati Mus N ... Cincinnati Art Museum. News [*A publication*]
CINCJAPA ... Commander-in-Chief, Japan Area [*World War II*]
CINCLANDCENT ... Commander-in-Chief, Allied Land Forces, Central Europe (MCD)
CINCLANT ... Commander-in-Chief, Atlantic
CINCLANTFLT ... Commander-in-Chief, Atlantic Fleet [*Navy*]
CINCLANT/PAC ... Commander-in-Chief, Atlantic and Pacific (AFIT)
Cinc L Bul ... Cincinnati Law Bulletin [*A publication*] (DLA)
CINCMAC ... Commander-in-Chief, Military Airlift Command
CINCMAIRCHAN ... Allied Maritime Air Commander-in-Chief, Channel

CINCMEAFSA ... Commander-in-Chief, Middle East/Southern Asia and Africa South of the Sahara [*Military*]
CINCMED ... Commander-in-Chief, Mediterranean
CINCMELF ... Commander-in-Chief, Middle East Land Forces (NATG)
CINCNAVEASTLANTMED ... Commander-in-Chief, Naval Forces, Eastern Atlantic and Mediterranean
CINCNE .... Commander-in-Chief, [*US*] Northeast Command
CINCNEDE ... Commander-in-Chief, Netherlands Forces in the East
CINCNELM ... Commander-in-Chief, Naval Forces, Eastern Atlantic and Mediterranean
CINCNORAD ... Commander-in-Chief, North American Air Defense
CINCNOREUR ... Commander-in-Chief, Northern Europe
CINCNORTH ... Commander-in-Chief, Allied Forces, Northern Europe [*NATO*]
Cinc (Ohio) ... Cincinnati Superior Court Reports [*Ohio*] [*A publication*] (DLA)
CINCONAD ... Commander-in-Chief, Continental Air Defense Command
CINCPAC ... Commander-in-Chief, Pacific
CINCPACAF ... Commander-in-Chief, Pacific Air Forces
CINCPAC-CINCPOA ... Commander-in-Chief, [*US*] Pacific Fleet and Pacific Ocean Areas
CINCPACFLT ... Commander-in-Chief, Pacific Fleet [*Navy*]
CINCPACHEDPEARL ... Commander-in-Chief, [*US*] Pacific Fleet Headquarters, Pearl Harbor
CINCPACREP ... Commander-in-Chief, Pacific Representative (AABC)
CINCPACREPPHIL ... Commander-in-Chief, Pacific Representative, Philippines
CINCPACSTAFFINSTR ... Commander-in-Chief, Pacific Staff Instruction (CINC)
CINCPOA ... Commander-in-Chief, Pacific Ocean Areas
CINCPOAHEDPEARL ... Commander-in-Chief, Pacific Ocean Areas Headquarters, Pearl Harbor
CINCRDAF ... Commander-in-Chief, Royal Danish Air Force (NATG)
CINCRDN ... Commander-in-Chief, Royal Danish Navy (NATG)
CINCRED ... Commander-in-Chief, Readiness Command
CINCREDCOM ... Commander-in-Chief, Readiness Command
CINCRNAF ... Commander-in-Chief, Royal Norwegian Air Force (NATG)
CINCRNORN ... Commander-in-Chief, Royal Norwegian Navy (NATG)
CINCSA .... Commander-in-Chief, South Atlantic Station [*British*]
CINCSAC ... Commander-in-Chief, Strategic Air Command
CINCSO .... Commander-in-Chief, Southern Command (AFM)
CINCSOUTH ... Commander-in-Chief, Allied Forces, Southern Europe [*NATO*]
CINCSPECOMME ... Commander-in-Chief, Specified Command, Middle East
CINCSTRIKE ... Commander-in-Chief, Strike Command
Cinc Sup Ct Rep ... Cincinnati Superior Court Reporter [*Ohio*] [*A publication*] (DLA)
Cinc Super ... Cincinnati Superior Court Reporter [*Ohio*] [*A publication*] (DLA)
CINCSWPA ... Commander-in-Chief, Southwest Pacific Area [*World War II*]
Cinc Sym Prog Notes ... Cincinnati Symphony Orchestra. Program Notes [*A publication*]
CINCTAC ... Commander-in-Chief, Tactical Air Command
CINCUKAIR ... Commander-in-Chief, United Kingdom Air Force (NATG)
CINCUNC ... Commander-in-Chief, United Nations Command
CINCUNCKOREA ... Commander-in-Chief, United Nations Command, Korea
CINCUNK ... Commander-in-Chief, United Nations Forces in Korea (MCD)
CINCUS ... Commander-in-Chief, United States Fleet [*Later, COMINCH*]
CINCUSAFE ... Commander-in-Chief, United States Air Forces in Europe
CINCUSAFLANT ... Commander-in-Chief, United States Air Force, Atlantic (AFM)
CINCUSAFNSCO ... Commander-in-Chief, United States Army Forces, Naval Supply Center, Oakland [*California*]
CINCUSAFSTRIKE ... Commander-in-Chief, United States Air Force Strike (AFM)
CINCUSAREUR ... Commander-in-Chief, United States Army, Europe
CINCUSARPAC ... Commander-in-Chief, United States Army, Pacific (AABC)
CINCUSNAVEUR ... Commander-in-Chief, United States Naval Forces, Europe
CINCUSTAF ... Commander-in-Chief, United States/Thai Forces
CINCVNN ... Commander-in-Chief, Vietnamese Navy
CINCWESPAC ... Commander-in-Chief, Western Pacific [*World War II*]
CINCWESTLANT ... Commander-in-Chief, Western Atlantic Area [*NATO*]
CIND .... Central Indiana Railway Co. [*Absorbed into Consolidated Rail Corp.*] [*AAR code*]
CIND .... Chief Intercept Director
CIND .... Computer Index of Neutron Data [*Atomic Energy Authority*] [*Databank*] [*British*]
CInd .... Indio Public Library, Indio, CA [*Library symbol*] [*Library of Congress*] (LCLS)
CINDA ...... Chrysler Improved Numerical Differencing Analyzer [*Data processing*]
CINDA ...... Computer Index of Neutron Data [*Brookhaven National Laboratory*] [*Information service or system*] (CRD)
CINDA-3G ... Chrysler Improved Numerical Differencing Analyzer for Third-Generation Computers [*Data processing*]

CINDAS .... Center for Information and Numerical Data Analysis and Synthesis [*West Lafayette, IN*] [*Department of Commerce*] (MCD)
CINDER .... Centro Interamericano para el Desarrollo Regional [*Inter-American Center for Regional Development*] (EAIO)
CINDER .... Counter Improvised Nuclear Device Emergency Response [*British*]
CINDI .... Central Information Dispatch [*Genesis Electronics Corp.*] [*Folsom, CA*] [*Telecommunications*] (TSSD)
CINE .... Cinematografia [*Ministerio de Cultura*] [*Spain*] [*Information service or system*] (CRD)
CINE .... Cinematographic (MSA)
CINE .... Council on International Nontheatrical Events (EA)
CINECA .... Cooperative Investigation of the Northern Part of the Eastern Central Atlantic
Cinegram ... Cinegram Magazine [*A publication*]
Cinema Can ... Cinema Canada [*A publication*]
Cinema J ... Cinema Journal [*A publication*]
Cinema P ... Cinema Papers [*A publication*] (APTA)
Cinemateca Rev ... Cinemateca Revista [*A publication*]
Cinematgr .. Cinematographe [*A publication*]
CINEP .... Centre d'Ingenierie Nordique [*University of Montreal*] [*Research center*] (RCD)
CINF .... Cincinnati Financial Corp. [*NASDAQ symbol*] (NQ)
CINF .... Division of Chemical Information [*American Chemical Society*] [*Information service or system*] (IID)
CINFAC .... Cultural [*formerly, Counterinsurgency*] Information Analysis Center [*Discontinued*] (MCD)
CINFO .... Chief of Information [*Also, CHINFO*] [*Navy*]
C Inform Chef Personnel ... Cahiers d'Information du Chef de Personnel [*A publication*]
CIng .... Inglewood Public Library, Inglewood, CA [*Library symbol*] [*Library of Congress*] (LCLS)
C Ingen Agron ... Cahiers des Ingenieurs Agronomes [*A publication*]
CING-FM ... Burlington, ON [*FM radio station call letters*]
CIngN .... Northrop Institute of Technology, Inglewood, CA [*Library symbol*] [*Library of Congress*] (LCLS)
CInI .... Inyo County Free Library, Independence, CA [*Library symbol*] [*Library of Congress*] (LCLS)
CINIME .... Centro de Informacion de Medicamentos [*Spanish Drug Information Center*] [*Information service or system*] (IID)
CINL .... Cumulative Index to Nursing and Allied Health Literature [*A publication*]
Cin Law Bul ... Cincinnati Law Bulletin [*A publication*] (DLA)
Cin Law Bull ... Weekly Cincinnati Law Bulletin [*Ohio*] [*A publication*] (DLA)
Cin Law Rev ... University of Cincinnati. Law Review [*A publication*]
Cin L Bull .. Cincinnati Law Bulletin [*A publication*] (DLA)
Cin L Rev ... University of Cincinnati. Law Review [*A publication*]
CINMDE ... Colloque. INSERM [*Institut National de la Sante et de la Recherche Medicale*] [*A publication*]
Cin Mun Dec ... Cincinnati Municipal Decisions [*A publication*] (DLA)
CINN .... Citizens, Inc. [*NASDAQ symbol*] (NQ)
Cinnam ...... Cinnamomum [*Cinnamon*] [*Pharmacology*] (ROG)
CINND ...... Ceramics International [*A publication*]
CINO .... Chief Inspector of Naval Ordnance [*British*]
CINOA ...... Confederation Internationale des Negociants en Oeuvres d'Art [*International Confederation of Art Dealers*] (EAIO)
CINP .... CINEP/PLUS. Bulletin du Centre d'Ingenierie Nordique de l'Ecole Polytechnique [*A publication*]
CINP .... Collegium Internationale Neuro-Psychopharmacologicum (EA)
CINP .... Comite International de Liaison pour la Navigation de Plaisance [*Pleasure Navigation International Joint Committee - PNIC*] [*The Hague, Netherlands*] (EAIO)
CINPROS ... Commission Internationale des Professionels de la Sante [*International Commission of Health Professionals for Health and Human Rights - ICHP*] (EA)
CINQ-FM ... Montreal, PQ [*FM radio station call letters*]
Cin R .... Cincinnati Superior Court Reports [*Ohio*] [*A publication*] (DLA)
Cin Rep ...... Cincinnati Superior Court Reports [*Ohio*] [*A publication*] (DLA)
CINS .... CENTO [*Central Treaty Organization*] Institute of Nuclear Science (EY)
CINS .... Children in Need of Supervision
CINS .... Circle Income Shares, Inc. [*Indianapolis, IN*] [*NASDAQ symbol*] (NQ)
CINS .... Collegium Internationale Activitatis Nervosae Superioris
CINS .... Cryogenic Inertial Navigating System
CINSA ...... Canadian Indian/Native Studies Association
Cin SCR ..... Cincinnati Superior Court Reports [*Ohio*] [*A publication*] (DLA)
Cin SC Rep ... Cincinnati Superior Court Reports [*Ohio*] [*A publication*] (DLA)
CINSGCY ... Counterinsurgency (AABC)
C Inst Amenag Urb Region Paris ... Cahiers. Institut d'Amenagement et d'Urbanisation de la Region Parisienne [*A publication*]
C Inst Crim ... Code d'Instruction Criminelle [*Code of Criminal Procedure*] [*A publication*] (ILCA)

C Instr Cr...   Code d'Instruction Criminelle [*Code of Criminal Procedure*] (DLA)
C Instr Crim ...   Code d'Instruction Criminelle [*Code of Criminal Procedure*] [*A publication*] (ILCA)
Cin Sup Ct ...   Cincinnati Superior Court Reports [*Ohio*] [*A publication*] (DLA)
Cin Sup Ct R ...   Cincinnati Superior Court Reporter [*Ohio*] [*A publication*] (DLA)
Cin Sup Ct Rep ...   Cincinnati Superior Court Reports [*Ohio*] [*A publication*] (DLA)
Cin Super Ct ...   Cincinnati Superior Court Reporter [*Ohio*] [*A publication*] (DLA)
Cin Super Ct Rep'r ...   Cincinnati Superior Court Reports [*Ohio*] [*A publication*] (DLA)
Cin Super (Ohio) ...   Cincinnati Superior Court Reports [*Ohio*] [*A publication*] (DLA)
Cin Sym .....   Cincinnati Symphony Orchestra. Program Notes [*A publication*]
CINTA......   Compania Nacional de Turismo Aereo [*Chilean airline*]
C Int C ....   Canadian Intelligence Corps
CINTC......   Chief, Intelligence Corps
CINTD ......   Communications International [*A publication*]
CINTEL ....   Computer Interface for Television (MCD)
CINTERFOR ...   Centro Interamericano de Investigacion y Documentacion sobre Formacion Profesional [*Inter-American Centre for Research and Documentation on Vocational Training - IACRDVT*] (EAIO)
CINTEX ....   CICAR [*Cooperative Investigation of the Caribbean and Adjacent Regions*] Intercalibration Experiment [*Marine science*] (MSC)
CINTEX ....   Combined In-Port Tactical Exercise [*Navy*] (NVT)
C Int Sociol ...   Cahiers Internationaux de Sociologie [*A publication*]
CINU ....   Centre d'Information des Nations Unies
CINUD .....   Computers in Industry [*A publication*]
CINV ....   Cimarron Investment Co., Inc. [*Cimarron, KS*] [*NASDAQ symbol*] (NQ)
CINVA ......   Centro Interamericano de Vivienda
CINVD7 .....   Cancer Investigation [*A publication*]
CINW ....   Committee for Immediate Nuclear War (EA)
CINWMD ...   Committee on Interpretation of the Nation-Wide Marine Definition [*Later, COI*] (EA)
CIO ....   Carrots in Oil [*Health food capsules*] [*British*]
CIO ....   Central Input-Output Multiplexer [*Data processing*]
CIO ....   Central Intelligence Organizations [*South Vietnam*]
CIO ....   Charriot Resources [*Vancouver Stock Exchange symbol*]
CIO ....   Chief Immigration Officer (DS)
CIO ....   Chief Information Officer [*Business term*]
CIO ....   Church Information Office [*British*]
CIO ....   Combat Intelligence Officer [*Navy*]
CIO ....   Comite International Olympique [*International Olympic Committee*]
CIO ....   Command Issuing Office [*or Officer*]
CIO ....   Commission Internationale d'Optique [*International Commission for Optics - ICO*] (EAIO)
CIO ....   Common Item Order (AFM)
CIO ....   Community Investment Officer [*Federal Home Loan Bank Board*]
CIO ....   Confirming Informal Order [*Telecommunications*] (TEL)
CIO ....   Congress of Industrial Organizations [*Later, AFL-CIO*] (GPO)
CIO ....   Congressus Internationalis Ornithologicus [*International Ornithological Congress - IOC*] (EA)
CIO ....   Conventional International Origin
CIO ....   Corporate Information Officer
CIOA ....   Center for Information on America (EA)
CIOA ....   Committee on International Ocean Affairs [*Department of State*] (NOAA)
CIOC ....   Combat Intelligence Operations Center (MCD)
CIOC ....   Craftsman of the Institute of Carpenters [*British*] (DBQ)
CIOC ....   Current Intelligence Operations Center (MCD)
CIOCS ......   Communications Input and Output Control System (BUR)
CIOFF ....   Comite International des Organisateurs de Festivals de Folklore [*International Committee of Folklore Festival Organizers*] [*Canada*]
CIOFF ....   Conseil International des Organisations de Festivals de Folklore et d'Arts Traditionnels [*International Council of Folklore Festival Organizations and Folk Art - ICFFO*] (EAIO)
CIOI-FM ...   Prince George, BC [*FM radio station call letters*]
CIOKKK...   Confederation of Independent Orders, Ku Klux Klan (EA)
CIOL.........   Chemical Information On-Line [*Ministry of Labour*] [*Hamilton, ON*] [*Information service or system*] (IID)
CIOM ....   Communications Input/Output Multiplexer
CIOMR .....   Comite Interallie des Officiers Medecins de Reserve [*Interallied Committee of Medical Reserve Officers*]
CIOMS......   Council for International Organizations on Medical Sciences [*Geneva, Switzerland*] (EA)
CION-FM ...   Riviere Du Loup, PQ [*FM radio station call letters*]
CIOO-FM ...   Halifax, NS [*FM radio station call letters*]
CIOP.........   CAMAC [*Computer-Aided Measurement and Control*] Input-Output Processor [*Computer*]
CIoP..........   Preston School of Industry, Ione, CA [*Library symbol*] [*Library of Congress*] (LCLS)

CIOPAC ....   Congress of Industrial Organizations, Political Action Committee [*Later, COPE*]
CIOPORA ...   Communaute Internationale des Obtenteurs de Plantes Ornementales et Fruitieres a Reproduction Asexuee [*International Community of Breeders of Asexually Reproduced Fruit Trees and Ornamental Varieties*] [*Geneva, Switzerland*] (EAIO)
CIOPW......   Charcoal, Ink, Oil, Pencil, and Watercolor [*Acronym is used as title of 1931 volume containing art works by e.e. cummings*]
CIOR ....   Confederation Interalliee des Officiers de Reserve [*Interallied Confederation of Reserve Officers*] (EAIO)
CIORF......   Charriot Resources Ltd. [*NASDAQ symbol*] (NQ)
CIOS.........   Canadian Society for the Study of Names [*See also SCEN*]
CIOS.........   Combined Intelligence Objectives Subcommittee [*World War II*]
CIOS.........   Conseil International pour l'Organization Scientifique [*World Management Council*] (EA)
CIOS-FM ..   Stephenville, NF [*FM radio station call letters*]
CIOSL ....   Confederacion Internacional de Organizaciones Sindicales Libres [*International Confederation of Free Trade Unions*]
CIOSTA .....   Commission Internationale pour l'Organisation Scientifique du Travail en Agriculture [*International Committee of Scientific Management in Agriculture*]
CIOSYS .....   Concurrent Input/Output System [*Data processing*] (PCM)
CIOT ....   Consolidated Capital Income Opportunity Trust/2 [*Emeryville, CA*] [*NASDAQ symbol*] (NQ)
CIOTF ......   Conseil International des Organismes de Travailleuses Familiales [*International Council of Home-Help Services*]
CIOU ....   Custom Input/Output Unit [*Data processing*] (IEEE)
CIOVD ....   Cistota Ovzdusia [*A publication*]
CIOZ-FM ...   Marystown, NF [*FM radio station call letters*]
CIP............   CABI [*Commonwealth Agricultural Bureaux International*] Institute of Parasitology [*United Kingdom*] [*Research center*] (IRC)
CIP............   Canadian International Paper Co.
CIP............   Canadian Premium Resources Corp. [*Vancouver Stock Exchange symbol*]
CIP............   Capital Improvements Program
CIP............   Capital Investment Program
CIP............   Capsule Internal Programmer [*Aerospace*]
CIP............   Carbon-in-Pulp [*Gold ore processing*]
CIP............   Carcinogen Information Program (EA)
CIP............   Career Intern Program (MCD)
CIP............   Cargo Investigation Panel [*IATA*] (DS)
CIP............   Carriage and Insurance Paid to Named Point [*Shipping*] (DS)
CIP............   Cascade Improvement Program [*AEC*]
CIP............   Cast-Iron Pipe [*Technical drawings*]
CIP............   Cataloging in Publication [*Pronounced "sip"*] [*Formerly, CIS*] [*Library science*]
CIP............   Catholic Institute of the Press [*Later, Catholic Alliance for Communications*] (EA)
CIP............   Catholic Intercontinental Press
CIP............   Center for Interactive Programs [*University of Wisconsin-Extension*] [*Madison*] [*Information service or system*] [*Telecommunications*] (TSSD)
CIP............   Center for International Policy (EA)
CIP............   Central Information Processor (MCD)
CIP............   Central Investment Program [*Army*] (MCD)
CIP............   Centre d'Information de Presse [*Press agency*] [*Belgium*]
CIP............   Centro Internacional de la Papa [*International Potato Center*] [*ICSU*] (EAIO)
CIP............   Certificats d'Investissement Privilegies [*French securities*]
CIP............   Chief Industrial Property
CIP............   Childhood in Poetry [*A publication*]
CIP............   Chipata [*Zambia*] [*Airport symbol*] (OAG)
CIP............   Cipolletti [*Argentina*] [*Seismograph station code, US Geological Survey*] [*Closed*] (SEIS)
CIP............   CIPSCO, Inc. [*NYSE symbol*] (SPSG)
CIP............   Citizen's Party (EA)
CIP............   Citizens in Politics (EA)
CIP............   Civilian Instruction Program (MUGU)
CIP............   Clarion, PA [*Location identifier*] [*FAA*] (FAAL)
CIP............   Clarke Institute of Psychiatry [*Research center*] (RCD)
CIP............   Class Improvement Plan [*Navy*]
CIP............   Classification of Instructional Programs [*Department of Education*] (OICC)
CIP............   Clean-in-Place [*Food processing*]
CIP............   Coast-in-Point (NVT)
CIP............   COBOL [*Common Business-Oriented Language*] Instrumentation Package [*Data processing*]
CIP............   Cold Isostatically Pressed [*Materials processing*]
CIP............   College International de Podologie [*International College of Podology*]
CIP............   Combat Intelligence Plot (NATG)
CIP............   Combined Instrument Panel
CIP............   Comite International de Photobiologie [*International Committee of Photobiology*]
CIP............   Command Information Program [*Military*] (AABC)
CIoP............   Commercial Import Program
CIP............   Commercial Instruction Processor [*Honeywell, Inc.*]

CIP	Commercially Important Person
CIP	Commission Internationale Permanente pour l'Epreuve des Armes a Feu [*Permanent International Commission for the Proof of Small-Arms - PICPSA*] (EAIO)
CIP	Commission Internationale du Peuplier [*International Poplar Commission*]
CIP	Commodities Import Program [*Military*]
CIP	Common Input Processor
CIP	Common Integrated Processor [*Hughes Air Corp.*]
CIP	Common Intersection Point [*Graphical representation*]
CIP	Communications Interface and Processing System (MCD)
CIP	Communications Interrupt Program
CIP	Community Improvement Program (EA)
CIP	Compagnie Internationale de Papier du Canada [*Canadian International Paper Co.*]
CIP	Compatible Independent Peripherals (IEEE)
CIP	Comprehensive Identification Process [*Child development test*]
CIP	Comprehensive Index to the Publications [*A bibliographic publication*]
CIP	Compressor Inlet Pressure (MSA)
CIP	Computer-Integrated Processing (ECON)
CIP	[*National Conference and Exhibition of*] Computers in Personnel [*British*] (ITD)
CIP	Consolidated Instrument Package [*Atmospheric research*]
CIP	Consolidated Intelligence Program [*Military*] (AFM)
CIP	Construction Industry Press [*Information service or system*] (ITD)
C/IP	Construction/Inspection Procedure (NRCH)
CIP	Continuation-in-Part [*Patent application*]
CIP	Continuous Inflating Pressure
CIP	Continuous Intravenous Infusion of Propranolol [*Medicine*]
CIP	Contract Implementation Plan (MCD)
CIP	Contract Information Processor
CIP	Control Inlet Panel [*Aerospace*] (AAG)
CIP	Conversion in Place [*Aerospace*] (AAG)
CIP	Cook Islands Party [*Political party*] (PPW)
CIP	Cost Improvement Program
CIP	Cost Improvement Proposal (MCD)
CIP	Council of International Programs (EA)
CIP	Counterinsurgency Plan (CINC)
CIP	Country Information Package (MCD)
CIP	Critical Intelligence Parameter (CAAL)
CIP	Current Injection Probe
CIP	Custom Interest Profile
CIP	Freight or Carriage and Insurance Paid To _____ [*"INCOTERM," International Chamber of Commerce official code*]
CIPA	Canadian Institute of Public Affairs
CIPA	Classified Information Procedures Act [*1980*]
CIPA	Comite Interamericano Permanente Antiacridiana
CIPA	Comite Interamericano de Proteccion Agricola [*Interamerican Committee for Crop Protection*]
CIPA	Comite International de Photogrammetrie Architecturale [*International Committee of Architectural Photogrammetry*] (EAIO)
CIPA	Comite International de Plastiques en Agriculture [*International Committee of Plastics in Agriculture*] (EAIO)
CIPA	Committee for Independent Political Action
CIPA	Confederazione Generale Italiana dei Professionisti e Artisti [*Artists and Professional People*] [*Italy*] (EY)
CIPA	Council on International and Public Affairs Program (EA)
CIPAC	Collaborative International Pesticides Analytical Council Ltd. [*See also CIMAP*] [*Wageningen, Netherlands*] (EAIO)
CIPA/ICPA	Comite International de Prevention des Accidents du Travail de la Navigation Interieure/International Committee for the Prevention of Work Accidents in Inland Navigation (EAIO)
CIPAP	Changes in Itinerary to Proceed to Additional Places [*Military*]
CIPAS	Center for International Programs and Studies [*University of Missouri - Rolla*] [*Research center*] (RCD)
CIPASE	Commission Internationale des Peches de l'Atlantique Sud-Est [*International Commission for the Southeast Atlantic Fisheries - ICSEAF*] [*Madrid, Spain*] (EAIO)
CIPASH	Committee for an International Program in Atmospheric Sciences and Hydrology [*United Nations*]
CIPA-TV	Prince Albert, SK [*Television station call letters*]
CIPC	Canadian Institute on Pollution Control
CIPC	Cast-in-Place Concrete [*Technical drawings*]
CIPC	Centre International de Phenomenologie Clinique (EAIO)
CIPC	Centre International Provisoire de Calcul
CIPC	Combat Intelligence Proficiency Course [*Military*] (INF)
CIPC	Combined Intelligence Priorities Committee [*Later, CIU*] [*US and British*] [*London, World War II*]
CIPC	Comite International Permanent de la Conserve [*International Permanent Committee on Canned Foods*]
CIPC	Comprehensive Industrywide Program of Communication [*Defunct*] (EA)
CIPC	Port-Cartier, PQ [*AM radio station call letters*]
CIPCA	Cogeneration and Independent Power Coalition of America (EA)

CIPCI	Conseil International des Praticiens du Plan Comptable International [*International Council of Practitioners of the International Plan of Accounts*]
CIP Circ Int Potato Cent	CIP [*Centre International de la Pomme de Terre*] Circular. International Potato Center [*A publication*]
CIPDU	Control Indicator Power Distribution Unit [*Military*] (CAAL)
CIPE	Center for International Private Enterprise [*Washington, DC*] (EA)
CIPE	Centro Interamericano de Promocion de Exportaciones [*Inter-American Export Promotion Center*]
CIPE	Conseil International de la Preparation a l'Enseignement [*International Council on Education for Teaching*]
CIPE	Consejo Internacional de la Pelicula de Ensenanza [*International Council for Educational Films*]
CIPEC	Canadian Industry Program for Energy Conservation
CIPEC	Conseil Intergouvernemental des Pays Exportateurs de Cuivre [*Intergovernmental Council of Copper Exporting Countries - ICCEC*] (EAIO)
CIPED	Carvao, Informacao, e Pesquisa [*Brazil*] [*A publication*]
CIPEM	Comite International pour les Etudes Myceniennes [*Standing International Committee for Mycenaean Studies*] (EAIO)
CIPEMAT	Centre International pour l'Etude de la Marionnette Traditionnelle [*International Center for Research on Traditional Marionettes*]
CIPER	Central Inventory of Production Equipment Records [*Army*]
CIPFA	Chartered Institute of Public Finance and Accountancy [*Formerly, IMTA*] [*British*]
CIPFS	Configuration Item Product Fabrication Specification (MCD)
CIPG	Communications and Information Processing Group [*Rensselaer Polytechnic Institute*] [*Research center*] (RCD)
CIPH	Comite International des Pharmaciens Homeopathiques [*International Committee of Homeopathic Pharmacists*] [*Karlsruhe, Federal Republic of Germany*] (EAIO)
CIPHONY	Cipher and Telephony Equipment [*Military*]
CIPIC	Center for Image Processing and Integrated Computing [*University of California at Davis*] [*Research center*] (RCD)
CIPL	Comite International Permanent des Linguistes [*Permanent International Committee of Linguists*] (EAIO)
CIPM	Comite International des Poids et Mesures [*International Committee on Weights and Measures*]
CIPM	Companion of the Institute of Personnel Management [*Formerly, FIPM*] [*British*]
CIPM	Council for International Progress in Management (EA)
CIPMAL	Clarke Institute of Psychiatry. Monograph Series [*A publication*]
CIPMP	Commission Internationale pour la Protection de la Moselle Contre la Pollution [*International Commission for the Protection of the Moselle Against Pollution - ICPMP*] (EA)
CIPN-FM	Pender Harbor, BC [*FM radio station call letters*]
CIPOM	Computers, Information Processing, and Office Machines
CIPP	Commission Indo-Pacific des Peches [*Indo-Pacific Fishery Commission - IPFC*] (EAIO)
CIPP	Context, Input, Process, Product [*Data processing*]
CIPPP	Cooperative International Pupil-to-Pupil Program (EA)
CIPPRS	Canadian Image Processing and Pattern Recognition Society
CIPR	Command Indicator Performance Review (MCD)
CIPR	Contractor Insurance and Pension Review [*DoD*]
CIPR	Corporate Industrial Preparedness Representative [*Military*]
CIPR	Cubic Inches per Revolution (MCD)
CIPRA	Cast Iron Pipe Research Association [*Later, DIPRA*] (EA)
CIPRA	Commission Internationale pour la Protection des Regions Alpines [*International Commission for the Protection of Alpine Regions*] (EAIO)
CIPRA2	Canadian Insect Pest Review [*A publication*]
CIPREC	Conversational and Interactive Project Evaluation and Control System [*IBM Corp.*]
CIPS	Canadian Information Processing Society [*Toronto, ON*]
CIPS	Cesium Ion Propulsion System
CIPS	Childhood in Poetry Supplement [*A publication*]
CIPS	Commonwealth International Philatelic Society [*Defunct*] (EA)
CIPS	Corporate Information Processing Standards (MCD)
CIPS	Counterintelligence Periodic Summary (MCD)
CIPSH	Conseil International de la Philosophie et des Sciences Humaines [*International Council for Philosophy and Humanistic Studies*] (EAIO)
CIPS Rev	CIPS [*Canadian Information Processing Society*] Review [*A publication*]
CIPTPP	Cooperative International Pupil-to-Pupil Program (EA)
CIPVDH	Comunicaciones. INIA [*Instituto Nacional de Investigaciones Agrarias*]. Serie Produccion Vegetal [*A publication*]
CIPW	Cross, Iddings, Pirsson, and Washington [*Norms*] [*Geology*]
CIQ	Confoederatio Internationalis ad Qualitates Plantarum Edulium Perquirendas [*International Association for Quality Research on Food Plants*]
CIQM-FM	London, ON [*FM radio station call letters*]
CIR	Arctic Circle Service, Inc. [*Fairbanks, AK*] [*FAA designator*] (FAAC)

CIR .... Cage Inventory Record [*Shipping*]   (DS)
CIR .... Cairo, IL [*Location identifier*] [*FAA*]   (FAAL)
CIR .... Canada-India Reactor
CIR .... Canadian Institute for Research
CIR .... Cargo Integration Review   (MCD)
CIR .... Carrier-to-Interference Ratio [*Data processing*]
CIR .... Center for Immigrants Rights   (EA)
CIR .... Center for Information Research [*Research center*]   (IID)
CIR .... Center for Inter-American Relations
CIR .... Center for International Research [*Bureau of the Census*] [*Information service or system*]   (IID)
CIR .... Center for Investigative Reporting   (EA)
CIR .... Centre International de l'Eau et l'Assainissement [*IRC International Water and Sanitation Centre*]   (EAIO)
CIR .... Change to Initial Release   (MCD)
CIR .... Change Initiation Request   (KSC)
CIR .... Chiredzi [*Rhodesia*] [*Seismograph station code, US Geological Survey*]   (SEIS)
CIR .... Cimarron Petroleum Ltd. [*Toronto Stock Exchange symbol*]
CIR .... Circa [*or Circiter or Circum*] [*About (used with dates denoting approximate time)*] [*Latin*]
Cir .... Circimus [*Constellation*]
CIR .... Circle
CIR .... Circuit   (AFM)
Cir .... Circuit Court   (DLA)
Cir .... Circuit Court of Appeals   (DLA)
CIR .... Circular   (AABC)
CIR .... Circulation   (ADA)
CIR .... Circus
CIR .... Circus Circus Enterprises, Inc. [*NYSE symbol*]   (SPSG)
CIR .... Cirrhosis [*Medicine*]
Cir .... Cirripedia [*Quality of the bottom*] [*Nautical charts*]
CIR .... Coherent Imaging RADAR
CIR .... Collection Intelligence Requirements   (NVT)
CIR .... Color Infrared [*Image*]
CIR .... Commission on Industrial Relations [*Department of Employment*] [*British*]
CIR .... Commission on Intergovernmental Relations
CIR .... Commission Internationale du Riz [*International Rice Commission - IRC*] [*United Nations*]   (EAIO)
CIR .... Commissioners of Inland Revenue [*British*]
CIR .... Committee on Changing International Realities   (EA)
CIR .... Committee of Interns and Residents   (EA)
CIR .... Common IFR [*Instrument Flight Rules*] Room [*Aviation*]   (FAAC)
CIR .... Communications Industries Report [*A publication*]   (EAAP)
CI & R .... Community Information and Referral Service [*Library science*]
CIR .... Computer-Integrated Research
CIR .... Configuration Inspection Report   (MCD)
Cir .... Connecticut Circuit Court Reports [*A publication*]   (DLA)
CIR .... Consignment Item Request   (MCD)
CIR .... Consortium for Information Resources, Framingham, MA [*OCLC symbol*]   (OCLC)
CIR .... Consumer Information Regulation [*National Highway Traffic Safety Administration*]
CIR .... Continuing Intelligence Requirement   (MCD)
CIR .... Convention des Institutions Republicaines [*Convention of Republican Institutions*] [*France*] [*Political party*]   (PPE)
CIR .... Cosmetic Ingredient Review   (EA)
CIR .... Cost Information Reports [*DoD*]
CIR .... Courant-Isaacson-Rees [*Method*]
CIR .... Court of Industrial Relations [*Philippines*]
CIR .... Crime on Indian Reservation
CIR .... Current Industrial Reports [*Census Bureau*]
CIR .... Current Instruction Register
CIR .... Customer Inspection Record
CIR .... Cycle Time and Inventory Reduction   (MCD)
CIR .... Cylindrical Internal Reflection [*Spectroscopy*]
CIRA .... Canadian Industrial Relations Association [*See also ACRI*]
CIRA .... Central Intelligence Retirees Association   (EA)
CIRA .... Centre International de Recherches sur l'Anarchisme [*International Research Center on Anarchism*] [*Geneva, Switzerland*]   (EAIO)
CIRA .... Comite International Radioaeronautique
CIRA .... Command Information Requirement Analysis   (MCD)
CIRA .... Commission Internationale pour la Reglementation des Ascenseurs et Monte-Charge [*International Committee for Lift Regulations - ICLR*]   (EAIO)
CIRA .... Committee on International Reference Atmosphere
CIRA .... Computerised Instrumented Residential Audit [*Energy auditing*]
CIRA .... Cooperative Institute for Research in the Atmosphere [*Colorado State University, NOAA*] [*Research center*]   (RCD)
CIRA .... COSPAR [*Committee on Space Research*] International Reference Atmosphere
CIRAA .... CIRP [*College International pour l'Etude Scientifique des Techniques de Production Mecanique*] Annals [*A publication*]
CIRAC .... Canadian Independent Recording Artists in Concert [*Pronounced "kerrack"*]

CIRAC ...... Canadian Institute for Research in Atmospheric Chemistry [*York University*]
CIRAD ...... Centre de Cooperation Internationale en Recherche Agronomique pour le Developpement [*International Cooperation Center of Agricultural Research for Development*] [*Information service or system*]   (IID)
CIRAD ...... Corporation for Information Systems Research and Development   (MCD)
CIRADS .... Counterinsurgency Research and Development System   (MCD)
CIRADW ... Contributions. Central Research Institute for Agriculture [*Bogor*] [*A publication*]
CIRAF ...... Conseil International pour la Recherche en Agroforesterie [*International Council for Research in Agroforestry*]   (EAIO)
CIRAG ...... Career Information Resource Advisory Group [*Canada*]
CIRAS .... Center for Industrial Research and Service
CIRAST ..... Centre d'Intervention et de Recherche pour l'Amelioration des Situations de Travail [*University of Quebec at Rimouski*] [*Research center*]   (RCD)
CIRB .... Canadian Industrial Renewal Board [*Montreal, PQ*]
CIRB .... Centre International de Recherches sur le Bilinguisme [*International Center for Research on Bilingualism*] [*Universite Laval, Quebec*] [*Canada*]
CIRB .... Corpus Inscriptionum Regni Bosporani   (BJA)
CIRB .... Crop Insurance Research Bureau [*Indianapolis, IN*]   (EA)
CIRB .... Lac Etchemin, PQ [*AM radio station call letters*]
Cir Bucal .... Cirugia Bucal [*A publication*]
CIRC .... Central Information Reference and Control   (DIT)
CIRC .... Central Intelligence Retrieval Center   (MCD)
CIRC .... Central Iowa Railway Company [*AAR code*]
CIRC .... Centralized Information Reference and Control
CIRC .... Centre International de Recherche sur le Cancer [*International Agency for Research on Cancer*]   (EAIO)
CIRC .... Chrysler Information Resources Center [*Pronounced "serk"*]
CIRC .... Circa [*or Circiter or Circum*] [*About (used with dates denoting approximate time)*] [*Latin*]
Circ .... Circimus [*Constellation*]
CIRC .... Circle
CIRC .... Circuit
CIRC .... Circular   (AFM)
CIRC .... Circularization Burn [*Orbital Maneuvering Subsystem 2*] [*NASA*]   (NASA)
CIRC .... Circulation   (EY)
CIRC .... Circulation Input Recording Center [*Data processing system*]
CIRC .... Circumcision [*Medicine*]
CIRC .... Circumference
CIRC .... Circumflex Coronary Artery [*Anatomy*]
CIRC .... Circumstance   (AABC)
CIRC .... Critical Item Review Committee [*Air Force*]   (AFIT)
CIRC .... Cross-Interleaved Reed-Solomon Code [*Data processing*]
CIRCA ...... Center for Instructional and Research Computing Activities [*University of Florida*] [*Research center*]   (RCD)
CIRCA .... Centre International de Recherche, de Creation, et d'Animation [*France*]
Circ Agric Ext Serv Univ Ark ... Circular. Agricultural Extension Service. University of Arkansas [*A publication*]
Circ Agric Ext Serv Wash St Univ ... Circular. Agricultural Extension Service. Washington State University [*A publication*]
CIRCAL .... Circuit Analysis [*Data processing*]
Circ Ala Agr Exp Sta ... Circular. Alabama Agricultural Experiment Station [*A publication*]
Circ Ala Geol Surv ... Circular. Alabama Geological Survey [*A publication*]
Circ Ala Polytech Inst Ext Serv ... Circular. Alabama Polytechnic Institute. Extension Service [*A publication*]
Circ A N Dak State Univ Agr Appl Sci Ext Serv ... Circular A. North Dakota State University of Agriculture and Applied Science. Extension Service [*A publication*]
CIRCARC ... Circular Arc
Circ Argent Odontol Bol ... Circulo Argentino de Odontologia. Boletin [*A publication*]
Circ Ariz Agric Ext Serv ... Circular. Arizona Agricultural Extension Service [*A publication*]
Circ Ark St Pl Bd ... Circular. Arkansas State Plant Board [*A publication*]
Circ Assoc Mine Managers S Afr ... Circular. Association of Mine Managers of South Africa [*A publication*]
Circ Auburn Univ Agr Ext Serv ... Circular. Auburn University. Agricultural Extension Service [*A publication*]
CIRCAZ .... Circulation [*A publication*]
Circ Bur Ent US Dep Agric ... Circular. Bureau of Entomology. United States Department of Agriculture [*A publication*]
Circ Calif Agr Ext Serv ... Circular. California Agricultural Extension Service [*A publication*]
Circ Can Beekprs Coun ... Circular. Canadian Beekeepers' Council [*A publication*]
CIRCCE .... Confederation Internationale de la Representation Commerciale de la Communaute Europeenne [*International Confederation of Commercial Representation in the European Community*]
Circ Cent Invest Agr El Bajio (CIAB) ... Circular. Centro de Investigaciones Agricolas de El Bajio (CIAB) [*A publication*]

Circ Cent Invest Agr Noroeste (CIANO) ... Circular. Centro de Investigaciones Agricolas del Noroeste (CIANO) [*A publication*]

Circ Cent Invest Agr Sudeste ... Circular. Centro de Investigaciones Agricolas del Sudeste [*A publication*]

Circ Cent Invest Basicas (CIB) ... Circular. Centro de Investigaciones del Basicas (CIB) [*A publication*]

Circ Clemson Agr Coll Ext Serv ... Circular. Clemson Agricultural College. Extension Service [*A publication*]

Circ Clemson Univ Coop Ext Serv ... Circular. Clemson University Cooperative Exension Service [*A publication*]

Circ Coll Agric Res Cent Wash State Univ ... Circular. College of Agriculture Research Center. Washington State University [*A publication*]

Circ Coll Agric Univ Ill ... Circular. College of Agriculture. University of Illinois [*A publication*]

Circ Coop Ext Serv Max C Fleischmann Coll Agric Nevada Univ ... Circular. Nevada University. Max C. Fleischmann College of Agriculture. Cooperative Extension Service [*A publication*]

Circ Coop Ext Serv N Dak St Univ ... Circular. Cooperative Extension Service. North Dakota State University [*A publication*]

Circ Coop Ext Serv Univ GA ... Circular. Cooperative Extension Service. University of Georgia [*A publication*]

Circ Coop Ext Serv Univ Hawaii ... Circular. Cooperative Extension Service. University of Hawaii [*A publication*]

Circ Coop Ext Serv Univ Ill ... Circular. Cooperative Extension Service. University of Illinois [*A publication*]

Circ Dec ..... Ohio Circuit Decisions [*A publication*] (DLA)

Circ Def Nat ... Circulaire. Ministre de la Defense Nationale [*A publication*]

Circ Div Fd Res CSIRO ... Circular. Division of Food Research. Commonwealth Scientific and Industrial Research Organisation [*A publication*] (APTA)

Circ Div Fish Oceanogr CSIRO ... Circular. Division of Fisheries and Oceanography. Commonwealth Scientific and Industrial Research Organisation [*A publication*] (APTA)

Circ Div Mech Eng CSIRO ... Circular. Division of Mechanical Engineering. Commonwealth Scientific and Industrial Research Organisation [*A publication*] (APTA)

CIRCE .... Catalogo Italiano Riviste su Calcolatore Elettronico [*Database*] [*Editrice Bibliografica*] [*Italian*] [*Information service or system*] (CRD)

CIRCE .... Circumstance

CIRCEA .... College of Investigative Remedial and Consulting Engineers of Australia

Circ Electrotech Lab (Tokyo) ... Circulars. Electrotechnical Laboratory (Tokyo, Japan) [*A publication*]

Circ Electrotech Lab (Tokyo Japan) ... Circulars. Electrotechnical Laboratory (Tokyo, Japan) [*A publication*]

Circ Eng Sec CSIRO ... Circular. Engineering Section. Commonwealth Scientific and Industrial Research Organisation [*A publication*] (APTA)

Circ Estac Exp Agric Tucuman ... Circular. Estacion Experimental Agricola de Tucuman [*A publication*]

CIRCF .... Cayman Island Reinsurance Corporation Ltd. [*NASDAQ symbol*] (NQ)

Circ Farm ... Circular Farmaceutica [*A publication*]

CIRCFCE .. Circumference (ROG)

Circ Fla Agric Exp Stn ... Circular. Florida Agricultural Experiment Station [*A publication*]

Circ Fla Agric Ext Serv ... Circular. Florida Agricultural Extension Service [*A publication*]

Circ Fla Univ Agr Ext Serv ... Circular. Florida University. Agricultural Extension Service [*A publication*]

Circ GA Agr Exp Sta ... Circular. Georgia Agricultural Experiment Stations [*A publication*]

Circ Geol Surv GA ... Circular. Geological Survey of Georgia [*A publication*]

Circ Hort Biol Serv Nova Scot Dep Agric Mktg ... Circular. Horticulture and Biology Service. Nova Scotia Department of Agriculture and Marketing [*A publication*]

Circ Ill Dep Agric ... Circular. Illinois Department of Agriculture [*A publication*]

Circ Illinois State Geol Surv ... Circular. Illinois State Geological Survey [*A publication*]

Circ Ill Nat Hist Surv ... Circular. Illinois Natural History Survey [*A publication*]

Circ Ill Natur Hist Surv ... Circular. Illinois Natural History Survey [*A publication*]

Circ Ill State Geol Surv Div ... Circular. Illinois State Geological Survey Division [*A publication*]

Circ Inf Agric Exp Stn Oreg State Univ ... Circular of Information. Agricultural Experiment Station. Oregon State University [*A publication*]

Circ Inform Oreg State Coll Agr Exp Sta ... Circular of Information. Oregon State College. Agricultural Experiment Station [*A publication*]

Circ Inst Agron ... Circular. Instituto Agronomico [*A publication*]

Circ Inst Agron Norte (Brazil) ... Circular. Instituto Agronomico do Norte (Brazil) [*A publication*]

Circ Inst Agron Sul (Pelotas) ... Circular. Instituto Agronomico do Sul (Pelotas) [*A publication*]

Circ Inst Pesq Exp Agropecuar N ... Circular. Instituto de Pesquisas e Experimentacao Agropecuarias do Norte [*A publication*]

Circ Inst Pesqui Agropecu Norte ... Circular. Instituto de Pesquisas Agropecuarias do Norte [*A publication*]

Circ Inst Pesqui Agropecu Sul ... Circular. Instituto de Pesquisas Agropecuarias do Sul [*A publication*]

Circ Int ...... Circulaire. Ministre de l'Interieur [*A publication*]

Cir Cir .... Cirugia y Cirujanos [*A publication*]

CIR/CIRD ... Circle/Dashed Circle (MCD)

Cir Cirujanos ... Cirugia y Cirujanos [*Mexico*] [*A publication*]

CIRCIT ...... Centre for International Research on Communication and Information Technology [*Australia*]

Circ Kans Agr Exp Sta ... Circular. Kansas Agricultural Experiment Station [*A publication*]

Circ Kans Agric Exp Stn ... Circular. Kansas Agricultural Experiment Station [*A publication*]

Circ Kans State Univ Agr Appl Sci Ext Serv ... Circular. Kansas State University of Agriculture and Applied Science. Extension Service [*A publication*]

Circ Kans St Ent Commn ... Circular. Kansas State Entomological Commission [*A publication*]

Circ Kans Univ Ext Serv ... Circular. Kansas University Extension Service [*A publication*]

Circ KY Agric Exp Stn ... Circular. Kentucky Agricultural Experiment Station [*A publication*]

Circ KY Univ Agr Ext Serv ... Circular. Kentucky University. Agricultural Extension Service [*A publication*]

CIRCL .... Center for Interdisciplinary Research in Computer-Based Learning [*University of Delaware*] [*Research center*] (RCD)

CIRCL .... Circular

Circ LA Agr Exp Sta ... Circular. Louisiana Agricultural Experiment Station [*A publication*]

Circ Line Elevators Farm Serv ... Circular. Line Elevators Farm Service [*A publication*]

CIRCLTR ... Circular Letter [*Military*]

CIRCM ...... Circumference

Circ Metab Cerveau ... Circulation et Metabolisme du Cerveau [*A publication*]

Circ Min .... Circulaire Ministerielle [*A publication*]

Circ Mont Agr Exp Sta ... Circular. Montana Agricultural Experiment Station [*A publication*]

Circ Mont State Coll Coop Ext Serv ... Circular. Montana State College. Cooperative Extension Service [*A publication*]

Circ MO Univ Coll Agr Ext Serv ... Circular. Missouri University. College of Agriculture. Extension Service [*A publication*]

Circ N Carol Agric Ext Serv ... Circular. North Carolina Agricultural Extension Service [*A publication*]

Circ N Dak Agr Coll Agr Ext Serv ... Circular. North Dakota Agricultural College. Agricultural Extension Service [*A publication*]

Circ New Jers Agric Exp Stn ... Circular. New Jersey Agricultural Experiment Station [*A publication*]

Circ New Jers Dep Agric ... Circular. New Jersey Department of Agriculture [*A publication*]

Circ New Mex Bur Mines Miner Resour ... Circular. New Mexico Bureau of Mines and Mineral Resources [*A publication*]

Circ New Mex St Bur Mines Miner Resour ... Circular. New Mexico State Bureau of Mines and Mineral Resources [*A publication*]

Circ NJ Agr Exp Sta ... Circular. New Jersey Agricultural Experiment Station [*A publication*]

Circ NJ Agric Exp Stn ... Circular. New Jersey Agricultural Experiment Station [*A publication*]

Circ N Mex State Univ Agr Ext Serv ... Circular. New Mexico State University. Agricultural Extension Service [*A publication*]

Circ Okla Agric Exp Stn ... Circular. Oklahoma Agricultural Experiment Station [*A publication*]

Circ Oklahoma Geol Surv ... Circular. Oklahoma Geological Survey [*A publication*]

Circ Okla State Univ Agr Appl Sci Agr Ext Serv ... Circular. Oklahoma State University of Agriculture and Applied Science. Agricultural Extension Service [*A publication*]

CIRCOL .... Central Information Reference and Control On-Line System (MCD)

CIRCOM ... Centre International de Recherches sur les Communautes Cooperatives Rurales [*International Research Center on Rural Cooperative Communities*]

CIRCOM ... Cooperative Internationale de Recherche et d'Action en Matiere de Communication (EAIO)

Circ Ont Agric Coll ... Circular. Ontario Agricultural College [*A publication*]

Circ Ont Dep Agric ... Circular. Ontario Department of Agriculture [*A publication*]

Circ Ore Agric Exp Stn ... Circular. Oregon Agricultural Experiment Station [*A publication*]

Circ Oreg State Coll Eng Exp ... Circular. Oregon State College. Engineering Experiment Station [*A publication*]

Circ Oreg State Univ Eng Exp St ... Circular. Oregon State University. Engineering Experiment Station [*A publication*]

Circ PA Agric Exp Stn ... Circular. Pennsylvania Agricultural Experiment Station [*A publication*]

Circ PA State Univ Earth Miner Sci Exp St ... Circular. Pennsylvania State University. Earth and Mineral Sciences Experiment Station [*A publication*]
Circ PA Univ Ext Serv ... Circular. Pennsylvania University Extension Service [*A publication*]
Circ Res ..... Circulation Research [*A publication*]
Circ Res Suppl ... Circulation Research. Supplement [*A publication*]
CIRCS .... Circumstances [*Slang*] (DSUE)
Circ to Sch ... Circular to Schools [*A publication*] (APTA)
Circ S Dak Agr Exp Sta ... Circular. South Dakota Agricultural Experiment Station [*A publication*]
Circ Secr Agr Secc Inform Publ Agr (Porto Alegre) ... Circular. Secretaria da Agricultura. Seccao de Informacoes e Publicidade Agricola (Porto Alegre) [*A publication*]
Circ Ser W Va Geol Econ Sur ... Circular Series. West Virginia Geological and Economic Survey [*A publication*]
Circ S Fla Agric Exp Stn ... Circular. South Florida Agricultural Experiment Station [*A publication*]
Circ S Fla Univ Agr Exp Sta ... Circular S. Florida University Agricultural Experiment Station [*A publication*]
Circ Shock ... Circulatory Shock [*A publication*]
Circ Shock (Suppl) ... Circulatory Shock (Supplement) [*A publication*]
Circ Speleol Rom Not ... Circolo Speleologico Romano. Notiziario [*A publication*]
Circ Suppl ... Circulation. Supplement [*A publication*]
Cir Ct App ... Circuit Court of Appeals (DLA)
Cir Ct Dec.. Circuit Court Decisions [*A publication*] (DLA)
Cir Ct Dec (Ohio) ... Circuit Court Decisions [*Ohio*] [*A publication*] (DLA)
Cir Ct Ohio ... Ohio Circuit Court Reports [*A publication*] (DLA)
Cir Ct R...... Circuit Court Reports [*Ohio*] [*A publication*] (DLA)
Circuits Manuf ... Circuits Manufacturing [*A publication*]
Circuits Mfg ... Circuits Manufacturing [*A publication*]
Circuits Syst ... Circuits and Systems [*A publication*]
Circular Com Parasitol Agric (Mexico) ... Circular. Comision de Parasitologia Agricola (Mexico) [*A publication*]
Circular Illinois Agric Exper Station ... Circular. Illinois Agricultural Experiment Station [*A publication*]
Circular West Virginia Agric Exper Station ... Circular. West Virginia Agricultural Experiment Station [*A publication*]
Circulation Res ... Circulation Research [*A publication*]
CIRCUM... Circumambulation [*Freemasonry*] (ROG)
CIRCUM... Circumference (KSC)
CIRCUMJAC ... Circumjacent (ROG)
Circ Univ GA Coll Agr Coop Ext Serv ... Circular. University of Georgia. College of Agriculture. Cooperative Extension Service [*A publication*]
Circ Univ Ill Coll Agr Coop Ext Serv ... Circular. University of Illinois. College of Agriculture. Cooperative Extension Service [*A publication*]
Circ Univ Ill Coop Ext Serv ... Circular. University of Illinois. Cooperative Extension Service [*A publication*]
Circ Univ KY Agr Ext Serv ... Circular. University of Kentucky. Agricultural Extension Service [*A publication*]
Circ Univ Nebr Coll Agr Home Econ Agr Exp Sta ... Circular. University of Nebraska. College of Agriculture and Home Economics. Agricultural Experiment Station [*A publication*]
Circ Univ Nev Max C Fleischmann Coll Agr Agr Ext Serv ... Circular. University of Nevada. Max C. Fleischmann College of Agriculture. Agricultural Extension Service [*A publication*]
Circ Univ Wis Coll Agr Ext Serv ... Circular. University of Wisconsin. College of Agriculture. Extension Service [*A publication*]
CIRCUS .... Calculation of Indirect Resources and Conversion to Unit Staff [*Data processing*]
Circ US Dep Agric ... Circular. United States Department of Agriculture [*A publication*]
Circ US Geol Surv ... Circular. United States Geological Survey [*A publication*]
Circ US Natn Bur Stand ... Circular. United States National Bureau of Standards [*A publication*]
Circ Utah Agric Exp Stn ... Circular. Utah Agricultural Experiment Station [*A publication*]
Circ VA Polytech Inst Agr Ext Serv ... Circular. Virginia Polytechnic Institute. Agricultural Extension Service [*A publication*]
Circ Wash Agr Exp Sta ... Circular. Washington Agriculture Experiment Station [*A publication*]
Circ Wis Univ Agric Ext Serv ... Circular. Wisconsin University of Agriculture. Extension Service [*A publication*]
Circ Wyo Agric Ext Serv ... Circular. Wyoming Agricultural Extension Service [*A publication*]
CIRDI .... Centre International pour le Reglement des Differends Relatifs aux Investissements [*International Center for Settlement of Investment Disputes*]
CIR DIB917 ... Current Industrial Reports. DIB-917. Copper-Base Mill and Foundry Products [*A publication*]
Cir Div Food Res CSIRO ... Circular. Division of Food Research. Commonwealth Scientific and Industrial Research Organisation [*A publication*] (APTA)
C of IRE ..... Church of Ireland
CIRE .... City of Refuge National Historic Park
CIRE .... Companion, Institute of Radio Engineers

CIREC .... Center for the Improvement of Reasoning in Early Childhood (EA)
CIREC .... Commercial-Investment Real Estate Council (EA)
CIREJ .... Commercial Investment Real Estate Journal [*Commercial-Investment Real Estate Council*] [*A publication*]
CI Rel .... Certificate in Industrial Relations
CIRELFA .. Conseil International pour le Recherche en Linguistique Fondamentale et Appliquee [*International Research Council on Pure and Applied Linguistics - IRCPAL*] (EA)
CIREM ...... Centre International de Recherches et d'Etudes en Management [*International Centre for Research and Studies in Management*] [*Canada*]
CIRENC .... Cirencester [*Urban district in England*]
CIRES .... Chief Inspector of Royal Engineer Stores [*British military*] (DMA)
CIRES .... Communication Instructions for Reporting Enemy Sightings [*Navy*]
CIRES .... Computerized Information Retrieval Service [*University of Houston Libraries*] (OLDSS)
CIRES .... Cooperative Institute for Research in Environmental Sciences
Cir Esp ...... Cirugia Espanola [*A publication*]
CIRF .... Centralized Intermediate Repair Facility
CIRF .... Centre International d'Information et de Recherche sur la Formation Professionnelle
CIRF .... Consolidated Intermediate Repair Facility
CIRF .... Corn Industries Research Foundation [*Later, CRA*] (EA)
CIRFAS..... Canadian Industry Report of Fisheries and Aquatic Sciences [*A publication*]
CIRFS........ Comite International de la Rayonne et des Fibres Synthetiques [*International Rayon and Synthetic Fibres Committee - IRSFC*] (EAIO)
CIRG.......... Contract Information Reporting Groups [*Navy*] (AFIT)
CIRGA....... Critical Isotope Reactor, General Atomics
Cir Ginecol Urol ... Cirurgia, Ginecologia, y Urologia [*A publication*]
CIRHS....... Critical Items and Residual Hazards List (MCD)
CIRI .... Caribbean Industrial Research Institute
CIRI.......... Ciro, Incorporated [*New York, NY*] [*NASDAQ symbol*] (NQ)
CIRIA .... Construction Industry Research and Information Association [*Research center*] [*British*] (IRC)
CIRIBK...... Congres International de Reproduction Animale et Insemination Artificielle [*A publication*]
CIRID........ Center for Interdisciplinary Research on Immunologic Diseases [*Department of Health and Human Services*] (GRD)
CIRIEC...... Centre International de Recherches et d'Information sur l'Economie Publique, Sociale, et Cooperative [*International Center of Research and Information on Public and Cooperative Economy*] [*Research center*] [*Belgium*] (IRC)
CIRIEC...... International Centre of Research and Information on Public and Co-Operative Economy (EA)
CIRIL .... College International de Recherches Implantaires et Lariboisiere [*Rouen, France*] (EAIO)
CIR-IR....... Cylindrical Internal Reflectance - Infrared Spectroscopy
CIRIS........ Central Inertial Reference Instrumentation System (MCD)
CIRIS........ Completely Integrated Range Instrumentation System [*NASA*]
CIRIS........ Consolidated Intelligence Resource Information System [*Air Force*] (MCD)
CIR ITA991 ... Current Industrial Reports. ITA-991. Titanium Mill Products, Ingots, and Castings [*A publication*]
CIRK-FM .. Edmonton, AB [*FM radio station call letters*]
Cirk Jordbrukstek Inst ... Cirkulaer. Jordbrukstekniska Institutet [*A publication*]
CIRKS .... Under the Circumstances [*Slang*] (ROG)
CIRL.......... Canadian Institute of Resources Law [*University of Calgary*] [*Research center*] (RCD)
CIRL.......... Central Investigation and Research Laboratory [*Australia*]
CIRL.......... Central Iowa Regional Library [*Library network*]
CIRL.......... Current Intelligence Requirement List (MCD)
CIRM........ Celestial Infrared Mapping [*Air Force*] (MCD)
CIRM........ Centro Internazionale Radio-Medico [*International Radio Medical Center; gives emergency medical advice to ships at sea*]
CIRM........ Comite International Radio Maritime [*International Maritime Radio Association*] (EAIO)
CIR M3-1 .. Current Industrial Reports. M3-1. Manufacturers' Shipments, Inventories, and Orders [*A publication*]
CIR M332 ... Current Industrial Reports. M33-2. Aluminum Ingot and Mill Products [*A publication*]
CIR M333 ... Current Industrial Reports. M33-3. Inventories of Steel Mill Shapes [*A publication*]
CIR M20A ... Current Industrial Reports. M20A. Flour Milling Products [*A publication*]
CIR M22A ... Current Industrial Reports. M22A. Finished Fabrics. Production, Inventories, and Unfilled Orders [*A publication*]
CIR M28A ... Current Industrial Reports. M28A. Inorganic Chemicals [*A publication*]
CIR M31A ... Current Industrial Reports. M31A. Footwear [*A publication*]
CIR M33A ... Current Industrial Reports. M33A. Iron and Steel Castings [*A publication*]

CIR MA200 ... Current Industrial Reports. MA20O. Manufacturers' Pollution Abatement Capital Expenditures and Operating Costs [*A publication*]

CIR MA350 ... Current Industrial Reports. MA-35O. Antifriction Bearings [*A publication*]

CIR MA26A ... Current Industrial Reports. MA-26A. Pulp, Paper, and Board [*A publication*]

CIR MA28A ... Current Industrial Reports. MA-28A. Inorganic Chemicals [*A publication*]

CIR MA30A ... Current Industrial Reports. MA-30A. Rubber Production Shipments and Stocks [*A publication*]

CIR MA31A ... Current Industrial Reports. MA-31A. Footwear Production by Manufacturers' Selling Price [*A publication*]

CIR MA35A ... Current Industrial Reports. MA-35A. Farm Machines and Equipment [*A publication*]

CIR MA36A ... Current Industrial Reports. MA-36A. Switchgear, Switchboard Apparatus, Relays, and Industrial Controls [*A publication*]

CIR MA39A ... Current Industrial Reports. MA-39A. Pens, Pencils, and Marking Devices [*A publication*]

CIR MA26B ... Current Industrial Reports. MA-26B. Selected Office Supplies and Accessories [*A publication*]

CIR MA28B ... Current Industrial Reports. MA-28B. Sulfuric Acid [*A publication*]

CIR MA30B ... Current Industrial Reports. MA-30B. Rubber and Plastics Hose and Belting [*A publication*]

CIR MA33B ... Current Industrial Reports. MA-33B. Steel Mill Products [*A publication*]

CIR MA38B ... Current Industrial Reports. MA-38B. Selected Instruments and Related Products [*A publication*]

CIR MA28C ... Current Industrial Reports. MA-28C. Industrial Gases [*A publication*]

CIR MA32C ... Current Industrial Reports. MA-32C. Refractories [*A publication*]

CIR MA20D ... Current Industrial Reports. MA-20D. Confectionery, Including Chocolate Products [*A publication*]

CIR MA30D ... Current Industrial Reports. MA-30D. Shipments of Selected Plastic Products [*A publication*]

CIR MA35D ... Current Industrial Reports. MA-35D. Construction Machinery [*A publication*]

CIR MA37D ... Current Industrial Reports. MA-37D. Aerospace Industry Orders, Sales, and Backlog [*A publication*]

CIR MA23E ... Current Industrial Reports. MA-23E. Men's and Boys' Outerwear [*A publication*]

CIR MA32E ... Current Industrial Reports. MA-32E. Consumer, Scientific, Technical, and Industrial Glassware [*A publication*]

CIR MA36E ... Current Industrial Reports. MA-36E. Electric Housewares and Fans [*A publication*]

CIR MA37E ... Current Industrial Reports. MA-37E. Aircraft Propellers [*A publication*]

CIR MA23F ... Current Industrial Reports. MA-23F. Women's and Children's Outerwear [*A publication*]

CIR MA24F ... Current Industrial Reports. MA-24F. Hardwood Plywood [*A publication*]

CIR MA26F ... Current Industrial Reports. MA-26F. Converted Flexible Materials for Packaging and Other Uses [*A publication*]

CIR MA28F ... Current Industrial Reports. MA-28F. Paint and Allied Products [*A publication*]

CIR MA35F ... Current Industrial Reports. MA-35F. Mining Machinery and Mineral Processing Equipment [*A publication*]

CIR MA36F ... Current Industrial Reports. MA-36F. Major Household Appliances [*A publication*]

CIR MA22F1 ... Current Industrial Reports. MA-22F1. Textured Yarn Production [*A publication*]

CIR MA22F2 ... Current Industrial Reports. MA-22F2. Spun Yarn Production [*A publication*]

CIR MA22G ... Current Industrial Reports. MA-22G. Narrow Fabrics [*A publication*]

CIR MA23G ... Current Industrial Reports. MA-23G. Underwear and Nightwear [*A publication*]

CIR MA33G ... Current Industrial Reports. MA-33G. Magnesium Mill Products [*A publication*]

CIR MA36G ... Current Industrial Reports. MA-36G. Transformers [*A publication*]

CIR MA28G84 ... Current Industrial Reports. MA-28G(84)-1. Pharmaceutical Preparations, except Biologicals [*A publication*]

CIR MA24H ... Current Industrial Reports. MA-24H. Softwood Plywood [*A publication*]

CIR MA25H ... Current Industrial Reports. MA-25H. Manufacturers' Shipments of Office Furniture [*A publication*]

CIR MA36H ... Current Industrial Reports. MA-36H. Motors and Generators [*A publication*]

CIR MA23J ... Current Industrial Reports. MA-23J. Brassieres, Corsets, and Allied Garments [*A publication*]

CIR MA32J ... Current Industrial Reports. MA-32J. Fibrous Glass [*A publication*]

CIR MA35J ... Current Industrial Reports. MA-35J. Selected Air Pollution Equipment [*A publication*]

CIR MA36K ... Current Industrial Reports. MA-36K. Wiring Devices and Supplies [*A publication*]

CIR MA33L ... Current Industrial Reports. MA-33L. Insulated Wire and Cable [*A publication*]

CIR MA35L ... Current Industrial Reports. MA-35L. Internal Combustion Engines [*A publication*]

CIR MA36L ... Current Industrial Reports. MA-36L. Electric Lighting Fixtures [*A publication*]

CIRMA/M ... Mesoamerica. Centro de Investigaciones Regionales de Mesoamerica [*A publication*]

CIR MA35M ... Current Industrial Reports. MA-35M. Air-Conditioning and Refrigeration Equipment [*A publication*]

CIR MA36M ... Current Industrial Reports. MA-36M. Home-Type Radio Receivers and TV Sets, Auto Radios, Phonos, and Record Players [*A publication*]

CIR MA34N ... Current Industrial Reports. MA-34N. Heating and Cooking Equipment [*A publication*]

CIR MA35N ... Current Industrial Reports. MA-35N. Fluid Power Products Including Aerospace [*A publication*]

CIR MA36N ... Current Industrial Reports. MA-36N. Selected Electronic and Associated Products [*A publication*]

CIR MA34P ... Current Industrial Reports. MA-34P. Aluminum Foil Converted [*A publication*]

CIR MA35P ... Current Industrial Reports. MA-35P. Pumps and Compressors [*A publication*]

CIR MA38Q ... Current Industrial Reports. MA-38Q. Selected Atomic Energy Products [*A publication*]

CIR MA35R ... Current Industrial Reports. MA-35R. Office, Computing, and Accounting Machines [*A publication*]

CIR MA22S ... Current Industrial Reports. MA-22S. Finished Broadwoven Fabric Production [*A publication*]

CIR MA35U ... Current Industrial Reports. MA-35U. Vending Machines Coin Operated [*A publication*]

CIR M28B ... Current Industrial Reports. M28B. Inorganic Fertilizer Materials and Related Products [*A publication*]

CIR M28C ... Current Industrial Reports. M28C. Industrial Gases [*A publication*]

CIR M22D ... Current Industrial Reports. M22D. Consumption on the Woolen and Worsted Systems [*A publication*]

CIR M32D ... Current Industrial Reports. M32D. Clay Construction Products [*A publication*]

CIR M36D ... Current Industrial Reports. M36D. Electric Lamps [*A publication*]

CIR M30E ... Current Industrial Reports. M30E. Plastic Bottles [*A publication*]

CIR M33E ... Current Industrial Reports. M33E. Nonferrous Castings [*A publication*]

CIR M28F ... Current Industrial Reports. M28F. Paint, Varnish, and Lacquer [*A publication*]

CIR M32G ... Current Industrial Reports. M32G. Glass Containers [*A publication*]

CIR M37G ... Current Industrial Reports. M37G. Complete Aircraft and Aircraft Engines [*A publication*]

CIR M34H ... Current Industrial Reports. M34H. Closures for Containers [*A publication*]

CIR M23I .. Current Industrial Reports. M23I. Men's, Women's, Misses', and Juniors' Selected Apparel [*A publication*]

CIR M20J ... Current Industrial Reports. M20J. Fats and Oils, Oilseed Crushings [*A publication*]

CIR M20K ... Current Industrial Reports. M20K. Fats and Oils. Production, Consumption, and Warehouse Stocks [*A publication*]

CIR M33K ... Current Industrial Reports. M33K. Inventories of Brass and Copper Wire Mill Shapes [*A publication*]

CIR M37L ... Current Industrial Reports. M37L. Truck Trailers [*A publication*]

CIR M22P ... Current Industrial Reports. M22P. Cotton, Manmade Fiber Staple, and Linters [*A publication*]

CIR MQ32A ... Current Industrial Reports. MQ-32A. Flat Glass [*A publication*]

CIR MQ36B ... Current Industrial Reports. MQ-36B. Electric Lamps [*A publication*]

CIR MQ-C1 ... Current Industrial Reports. MQ-C1. Survey of Plant Capacity [*A publication*]

CIR MQ32C ... Current Industrial Reports. MQ-32C. Refractories [*A publication*]

CIR MQ36C ... Current Industrial Reports. MQ-36C. Fluorescent Lamp Ballasts [*A publication*]

CIR MQ35D ... Current Industrial Reports. MQ-35D. Construction Machinery [*A publication*]

CIR MQ34E ... Current Industrial Reports. MQ-34E. Plumbing Fixtures [*A publication*]

CIR MQ34K ... Current Industrial Reports. MQ-34K. Steel Shipping Drums and Pails [*A publication*]

CIR MQ22Q ... Current Industrial Reports. MQ-22Q. Carpets and Rugs [*A publication*]

CIR MQ22T ... Current Industrial Reports. MQ-22T. Broadwoven Fabrics [*A publication*]

CIR MQ35W ... Current Industrial Reports. MQ-35W. Metalworking Machinery [*A publication*]

CIR MQ23X ... Current Industrial Reports. MQ-23X. Sheets, Pillowcases, and Towels [*A publication*]

CIRMS ...... Celestial Infrared Measurement System

CIR M35S ... Current Industrial Reports. M35S. Tractors, except Garden Tractors [*A publication*]

CIRNAV .... Circumnavigate (FAAC)

CIRND3 .... Comunicaciones. INIA [*Instituto Nacional de Investigaciones Agrarias*]. Serie Recursos Naturales [*A publication*]

CIRNOT .... Circuit Notice [*Aviation*] (FAAC)

CIRO .... Consolidated Industrial Relations Office (MUGU)

CIRO .... Crash Injury Research Organization [*Cornell University*]

Cir Od NWP ... Circular Orders, Northwestern Provinces [*India*] [*A publication*] (ILCA)

CIRO-FM ... St. Georges-De-Beauce, PQ [*FM radio station call letters*]

Cir Ord NWP ... Circular Orders, Northwestern Provinces [*India*] [*A publication*] (DLA)

CIRP .... Canadian Industrial Renewal Program

CIRP .... College International de Recherches pour la Production [*Later, CIESTPM*] (EAIO)

CIRP .... Conseil International des Ressources Phytogenetiques [*International Board for Plant Genetic Resources - IBPGR*] (EAIO)

CIRP .... Cooperative Institutional Research Program [*UCLA*]

CIRPA .... Canadian Independent Record Producers Association

CIRPB7 ..... Rapports et Proces-Verbaux des Reunions. Commission Internationale pour l'Exploration Scientifique de la Mer Mediterranee [*Monaco*] [*A publication*]

CIRPHO .... CIRPHO [*Cercle International de Recherches Philosophiques par Ordinateur*] Review [*A publication*]

CIRQNS .... Centre for International Relations. Queen's University. Northern Studies Series [*A publication*]

CIRQNSS ... Centre for International Relations. Queen's University. Northern Studies Series [*A publication*]

CIRR .... Center on International Race Relations [*University of Denver*]

CIRR .... Chattahoochee Industrial Railroad [*AAR code*]

CIRR .... Corporate and Industry Research Reports Index [*JA Micropublishing, Inc.*] [*Database*]

CIRS .... Chemical Information Retrieval System [*Army*] (IID)

CIRS .... Chesapeake Information Retrieval Service (IID)

CIRS .... Community Information and Referral Service [*United Way/ Crusade of Mercy*] [*Information service or system*] (IID)

CIRS .... Computerized Information Retrieval Service [*California State University, Fullerton*] (OLDSS)

CIRS .... Containment Iodine Removal System [*Nuclear energy*] (NRCH)

CIRS .... Contractor Inventory Redistribution System (MCD)

CIRSE .... Cardiovascular and Interventional Radiology Society of Europe (EA)

Cir Ser Oreg State Coll Eng Exp Stn ... Circular Series. Oregon State College. Engineering Experiment Station [*A publication*]

CIRSSE ..... NASA Center for Intelligent Robotic Systems for Space Exploration [*Rensselaer Polytechnic Institute*] [*Research center*] (RCD)

CIRSYS .... Circulation System (ADA)

CIRT .... Conference on Industrial Robot Technology

CIRTEF ..... Conseil International des Radios-Televisions d'Expression Francaise [*International Association of Broadcasting Manufacturers - IABM*] (EAIO)

CIRTS .... Centre of Information Resource & Technology, Singapore [*Information service or system*] (IID)

CIRUAL .... Circulation Research [*A publication*]

CIRUR .... Comite Intergouvernemental de Recherches Urbaines et Regionales [*Intergovernmental Committee on Urban and Regional Research*] [*Canada*]

Cir Urug ..... Cirugia del Uruguay [*A publication*]

CIRVIS ...... Communications Instructions for Reporting Vital Intelligence Sightings [*Military*]

CIRX-FM .. Prince George, BC [*FM radio station call letters*]

CIS .... Cahiers Internationaux de Sociologie [*A publication*]

CIS .... Canadian Institute for Scientific and Technical Information - CISTI [*UTLAS symbol*]

CIS .... Canadian Institute of Surveying

CIS .... Canadian Iris Society

CIS .... Cancer Information Service [*HEW*]

CIS .... Canfield Instructional Styles Inventory [*Teacher evaluation test*]

CIS .... Carcinoma In Situ [*Oncology*]

CIS .... Career Information System [*National Career Information System*] [*Eugene, OR*] [*Information service or system*] (IID)

CIS .... Cassette Information Services

CIS .... Casualty Information System (MCD)

CIS .... Catalina Island [*California*] [*Seismograph station code, US Geological Survey*] (SEIS)

CIS .... Cataloging in Source [*Later, CIP*] [*Library science*]

CIS .... Catholic Information Society [*Defunct*] (EA)

CIS .... CD-ROM [*Compact Disk Read-Only Memory*] Continuous Information Service [*International Data Group - IDG*] [*Information service or system*] (IID)

CIS .... CDIS Software, Inc. [*Vancouver Stock Exchange symbol*]

CIS .... Center-of-Inertia System

CIS .... Center for Information Sciences (KSC)

CIS .... Center for Instructional Services [*Purdue University*] [*Research center*] (RCD)

CIS .... Center for Integrated Systems [*Stanford University*] [*Research center*] (RCD)

CIS .... Center for Intelligence Studies (EA)

CIS .... Center for International Security (EA)

CIS .... Center of International Studies [*MIT*] [*Research center*] (MCD)

CIS .... Central Information Service [*University of London*] [*Information service or system*] (IID)

CIS .... Central Information Service [*The British Council*] [*Information service or system*] (IID)

CIS .... Central [*Nervous System*] Inhibitory State

CIS .... Central Installation Supply [*Air Force*]

CIS .... Central Instructor School

CIS .... Central Integration Site (NASA)

CIS .... Centralny Inspektorat Standaryzacji [*Central Inspectorate for Standardization of Imports and Exports*]

CIS .... Centre for Information Services [*Council for Scientific and Industrial Research - CSIR*] [*South Africa*] [*Information service or system*] (IID)

CIS .... Centre for Information on Standardization and Metrology [*Information service or system*] (IID)

CIS .... Centre for Information Studies [*Riverina-Murray Institute of Higher Education*] [*Australia*]

CIS .... Centre d'Informations Spectroscopiques [*Spectroscopic Information Center*] [*Group for the Advancement of Spectroscopic Methods and Physicochemical Analysis*] [*Information service or system*] (IID)

CIS .... Centre for Institutional Studies [*North East London Polytechnic*] [*British*] (CB)

CIS .... Centre International d'Informations de Securite et d'Hygiene du Travail [*International Occupational Safety and Health Information Center*] [*International Labour Office*] (IID)

CIS .... Cesium Ion Source

CIS .... Change Impact Summary (NASA)

CIS .... Channel and Isolation Supervision [*Telecommunications*] (TEL)

CIS .... Character Instruction Set (IEEE)

CIS .... Charles Ives Society (EA)

CIS .... Chemical Information Services [*Stanford Research Institute*] (IID)

CIS .... Chemical Information Systems, Inc. [*Fein-Marquart Associates*] [*Information service or system*] (IID)

CI(S) .... Chemical Injection (System) [*Nuclear energy*] (NRCH)

CIS .... Chemically-Powered Interorbital Space Shuttle (MCD)

CIS .... Chinese Industrial Standards

CIS .... Cities in Schools (EA)

CIS .... Clinical Immunology Society (EA)

CIS .... Close-In Support [*Military*] (AFM)

CIS .... College of the Siskiyous Library, Weed, CA [*OCLC symbol*] (OCLC)

CIS .... Combat Identification System

CIS .... Combat Intelligence System (MCD)

CIS .... Combined Intelligence Staff [*World War II*]

CIS .... Comitato Internazionale degli Scambi Presso la Camera Internazionale di Commercio [*International Trade Committee of the International Chamber of Commerce*] [*Italian*]

CIS .... Command Information Systems [*Army*]

CIS .... Command Instrument System

CIS .... Commercial Industrial Services Program [*Navy*]

CIS .... Commercial Instruction Set

CIS .... Communication Industrial Services

CIS .... Communication Information System (IEEE)

C & IS .... Communication and Instrumentation System [*CIS is preferred*] [*NASA*] (KSC)

CIS .... Communication and Instrumentation System [*Also, C & IS*] [*NASA*]

CIS .... Communications Interface System (MCD)

CIS .... Community Improvement Scale [*Psychology*]

CIS .... Community Industry Scheme [*Department of Employment*] [*British*]

CIS .... Community Information Section [*Public Library Association*]

CIS .... Community Information Services

CIS .... Complex Impedance Spectroscopy

CIS .... Component Identification Sheet (MCD)

CIS .... Composition Information Services [*Commercial firm*]

CIS .... CompuServe Information Service [*CompuServe, Inc.*] (IID)

CIS .... Computer-Based Information Services [*Information service or system*] (IID)

CIS .... Computer and Information Sciences Research Laboratory [*University of Alabama in Birmingham*] [*Research center*] (RCD)

CIS .... Computer Information Services [*Corporation for Public Broadcasting - CPB*] [*Information service or system*] (IID)

CIS .... Computer and Information Systems [*A publication*]

CIS .... Computer Investor Services [*Australia*]

CIS .... Computerized Information Service [*Public Library of Columbus and Franklin County*] (OLDSS)

CIS .... Computerized Information Service [*Columbus Technical Institute*] (OLDSS)

CIS............. Computing & Information Systems [*East Carolina University*] [*Research center*]   (RCD)
CIS............. Concord Fabrics, Inc. [*AMEX symbol*]   (SPSG)
CIS............. Conference of Internationally-Minded Schools
CIS............. Configuration Information System
CIS............. Configuration Item Specification
CIS............. Congressional Information Service, Inc. [*Bethesda, MD*] [*Database producer*] [*Information service or system*]
CIS............. Constant Injection System [*Automotive engineering*]
CIS............. Consumer Information Series [*National Institute of Standards and Technology*]
CIS............. Consumer Information Service [*Electronic mail*]
CIS............. Consumer Information System
CIS............. Contact Image Sensing [*Reprography*]
CIS............. Containment Isolation Signal [*Nuclear energy*]   (NRCH)
CIS............. Containment Isolation System [*Nuclear energy*]   (NRCH)
CIS............. Contractor's Information Submittal [*or Submitted*]   (MCD)
CIS............. Control Indicator Set   (MCD)
CIS............. Cooperative Insurance Society [*British*]
CIS............. Copper-Indium-Diselenide [*Inorganic chemistry*]
CIS............. Core Instrumentation Subsystem   (MCD)
CIS............. Corpus Inscriptionum Semiticarum [*A publication*]
CIS............. Corrosion Interception Sleeve
CIS............. Cost Information System
CIS............. Cost Inspection Service [*Navy*]
CIS............. Council for Inter-American Security   (EA)
CIS............. Council for Intersocietal Studies   (EA)
CIS............. Counter Information Services [*British*]
CIS............. Country Intelligence Study   (MCD)
CIS............. Coupled Impedance Synthesis
CIS............. Cryogenic Instrumentation System
CIS............. Cue Indexing System   (IEEE)
CIS............. Cultural Information Service   (EA)
CIS............. Current Index to Statistics [*MathSci database subfile*]   (IT)
CIS............. Current Information Section   (ADA)
CIS............. Current Information Selection [*IBM Technical Information Retrieval Center*] [*White Plains, NY*]
CIS............. Customer Information Squawk Sheet
CIS............. Customer Information System [*IBM Corp.*]
CIS............. NIH [*National Institutes of Health*]-EPA [*Environmental Protection Agency*] Chemical Information System [*Falls Church*] [*Information service or system*]   (IID)
CISA......... Canadian Intercollegiate Sailing Association
CISA......... Casting Industry Suppliers Association   (EA)
CISA......... Center for International and Strategic Affairs [*Research center*]   (RCD)
CISA......... Certified Information Systems Auditor [*Designation awarded by EDP Auditors Foundation*]
CISA......... Citizens Savings Bank FSB [*NASDAQ symbol*]   (NQ)
CISA......... Commission Internationale pour le Sauvetage Alpin [*International Commission for Alpine Rescue*]
CISA......... Consejo Indio de Sud America [*Indian Council of South America - ICSA*] [*Lima, Peru*]   (EAIO)
CISA......... Council for Independent School Aid   (EA)
CIS Abstr... CIS [*Congressional Information Service*] Abstracts on Cards [*A publication*]
CISAC....... Confederation Internationale des Societes d'Auteurs et Compositeurs [*International Confederation of Societies of Authors and Composers*]
CISAF....... Conseil International des Services d'Aide Familiale [*International Council of Homehelp Services - ICHS*] [*Driebergen-Rijsenburg, Netherlands*]   (EAIO)
CISAI .... Comite International de Soutien aux Antifascistes Iberiques
CISAL .... Confederazione Italiana dei Sindacati Autonomi Lavoratori [*Italian Confederation of Autonomous Labor Unions*]   (DCTA)
CISAM...... Compressed Index Sequential Access Method
CISAP .... Congres International des Sciences de l'Activite Physique [*International Congress of Physical Activity Sciences*] [*Canada*]
CISBH....... Comite International de Standardisation en Biologie Humaine [*International Committee for Standardization in Human Biology*]
CISC .... Canadian Institute of Steel Construction
CISC .... Clearinghouse for Innovation in Scientific Communication
CISC .... Comite International de Sociologie Clinique [*International Committee on Clinical Sociology - ICCS*]   (EA)
CISC .... Complex Instruction Set Computer
CISC .... Confederation Internationale des Syndicats Chretiens [*International Federation of Christian Trade Unions*]
CISC .... Conference Internationale du Scoutisme Catholique [*International Conference of Catholic Scouting*]
CISC .... Construction Industry Stabilization Committee [*Abolished, 1974*]
CISC .... Groupe International de Sociologie   (EAIO)
CISCA ...... Cast Iron Seat Collectors Association   (EA)
CISCA ...... Ceilings and Interior Systems Construction Association   (EA)
CISCA .... Cisplatin, Cyclophosphamide, Adriamycin [*Antineoplastic drug regimen*]

CISCE........ Comite International pour la Securite et la Cooperation Europeennes [*International Committee for European Security and Co-Operation - ICESC*]   (EAIO)
CISC-FM .. Gibsons, BC [*FM radio station call letters*]
CIS Chromosome Inf Serv ... CIS. Chromosome Information Service [*A publication*]
CISCO....... Civil Service Catering Organization [*British*]
CISCO....... Commodity Information Services Company   (IID)
CISCO ...... Compass Integrated System Compiler   (IEEE)
CISCO ...... Comprehensive Information System and Database
CIS & DB... Comprehensive Information System and Database
cis-DDP ..... cis-Diamminodichloroplatinum [*Cisplatin*] [*Also, CDDP, CPDD, CPT, DDP, P*] [*Antineoplastic drug*]
CISE .... Consortium for International Studies Education   (EA)
CISE-FM... Sechelt, BC [*FM radio station call letters*]
CISem........ Corpus Inscriptionum Semiticarum [*A publication*]   (OCD)
CISE Newsl ... Library Association. University and Research Section. Colleges, Institutes, and Schools of Education Subsection. Newsletter [*A publication*]
CISEP....... Cellulose Industry Standards Enforcement Program   (EA)
CISER ...... Cornell Institute for Social and Economic Research [*Cornell University*] [*Research center*]   (RCD)
CISET....... Committee on International Science, Engineering, and Technology [*US government interagency committee*] [*Washington, DC*]
CISF .... Confederation Internationale des Sages Femmes
CISGDL .... Comunicaciones. INIA [*Instituto Nacional de Investigaciones Agrarias*]. Serie General [*A publication*]
CISH......... Comite International des Sciences Historiques [*International Committee of Historical Sciences*]
CISH......... Comite International de Standardisation en Hematologie [*International Committee for Standardization in Haematology*]   (EAIO)
CISHEC .... Chemical Industries Association's Safety and Health Council [*British*]
CISI .... CIS [*Congressional Information Service*] Index [*A publication*]
CISI .... CIS Technologies, Inc. [*NASDAQ symbol*]   (NQ)
CISI .... Compagnie Internationale de Services en Informatique [*International Information Services Company*] [*Information service or system*]   (IID)
CISID .... Congressional Information Sources, Inventories, and Directories   (MCD)
CISIDR..... Comunicaciones. INIA [*Instituto Nacional de Investigaciones Agrarias*]. Serie Proteccion Vegetal [*A publication*]
CISIL........ Centralized Integrated Systems for International Logistics
CISIL........ Consolidated Interchangeable and Substitute Item List
CIS Ind ...... CIS [*Congressional Information Service*] Index [*A publication*]
CIS/Index Publ US Congr ... CIS [*Congressional Information Service*] Index to Publications of the United States Congress [*A publication*]
CISIR........ Ceylon Institute of Scientific and Industrial Research
Cisitalia...... Consorzio Industriale Sportivo Italia [*Italian sporting goods company*]
CISJA........ Comite International de Solidarite avec la Jeuness Algerienne
CISK .... Conditional Instability of the Second Kind
CISL .... Confederation Internationale des Syndicats Libres [*International Confederation of Free Trade Unions*]
CISL .... Confederazione Italiana di Sindacati Liberi [*Italian Confederation of Free Workers*]   (PPE)
CISL .... Richmond, BC [*AM radio station call letters*]
CISLANM ... Committee in Solidarity with Latin American Nonviolent Movements   (EA)
CISLB....... Comite International pour la Sauveguarde de la Langue Bretonne [*International Committee for the Defense of the Breton Language - ICDBL*]   (EAIO)
CISLE........ Centre International des Syndicalistes Libres en Exil [*International Center of Free Trade Unionists in Exile*]
Cisl Metody Meh Splosn Stredy ... Cislennye Metody Mehaniki Splosnoi Stredy [*A publication*]
CISM......... Centre International des Sciences Mecaniques
CISM......... Confederation Internationale des Societes Musicales [*International Confederation of Societies of Music - ICSM*]   (EA)
CISM......... Conseil International du Sport Militaire [*International Military Sports Council*] [*Belgium*]
CISN-FM .. Edmonton, AB [*FM radio station call letters*]
CISNU....... Confederation of Iranian Students [*Federal Republic of Germany*]   (PD)
CISO......... Comite International des Sciences Onomastiques [*International Committee of Onomastic Sciences*]
CI Soc .... Cahiers Internationaux de Sociologie [*A publication*]
CISOC .... Computerized Information System of Organic Chemistry [*Developed in China*] [*Data processing*]
CIS & P...... Canadian Institute of Surveying and Photogrammetry
CISP .... Commercial Item Support Program [*DoD*]   (RDA)
CISP .... Council for Intercultural Studies and Programs   (EA)
CISPCI ...... Commission Internationale pour la Sauvegarde du Patrimoine Culturel Islamique [*International Commission for the Preservation of Islamic Cultural Heritage - ICPICH*]   (EA)
CISPEC ..... Configuration Item Specification   (MCD)
CISPES ..... US Committee in Solidarity with the People of El Salvador   (EA)

CISPF........ Cast Iron Soil Pipe Foundation [*Defunct*]   (EA)
CISP-FM... Pemberton, BC [*FM radio station call letters*]
CISPI......... Cast Iron Soil Pipe Institute   (EA)
CISPM ...... Confederation Internationale des Societes Populaires de Musique
CISPR........ Comite International Special des Perturbations Radioelectriques [*International Special Committee on Radio Interference*]   (EAIO)
CISq.......... Communication Installation Squadron [*Air Force*]
CISQ-FM.. Squamish, BC [*FM radio station call letters*]
CISR .... Center for Information Systems Research [*Massachusetts Institute of Technology*] [*Research center*]   (RCD)
CISR .... Center for Instructional Services and Research [*Memphis State University*] [*Research center*]   (RCD)
CISR .... Center for International Systems Research
CISR .... Communication Intelligence Security Regulation   (MCD)
CISR .... Conference Internationale de Sociologie Religieuse [*International Conference of Sociology of Religion*]
CISR .... Configuration Index and Status Report   (KSC)
CISRC .... Computer and Information Science Research Center [*Ohio State University*] [*Columbus, OH*]
CISRI........ Central Iron and Steel Research Institute [*People's Republic of China*]
CISR-TV ... Santa Rosa, BC [*Television station call letters*]
CISS .... Calgary, AB [*AM radio station call letters*]
CISS .... Canadian Information Sharing Service
CISS .... Cancer Information and Support Society [*Australia*]
CISS .... Centaur Integrated Support Structure   (MCD)
CISS .... Chromosomal In Situ Suppression [*Genetics*]
CISS .... Collectif d'Informations Sexuelles et Sexologiques [*Collective of Sexual Information and Sexology*] [*Canada*]
CISS .... Comite International des Sports des Sourds [*International Committee of Sports for the Deaf*]   (EAIO)
CISS .... Communication and Instrumentation Support Services [*NASA*]   (KSC)
CISS .... Computer Industry Software, Services, and Products [*Information service or system*]   (IID)
CISS .... Conference Internationale de Service Social [*International Conference of Social Service*]
CISS .... Conferencia Interamericana de Seguridad Social [*Inter-American Conference on Social Security - IACSS*]   (EAIO)
CISS .... Conseil International des Sciences Sociales [*International Social Science Council - ISSC*]   (EAIO)
CISS .... Contract Information Subsystem   (MCD)
CISS .... Contract Items Specification and Schedule   (MCD)
CISST....... Center for Interdisciplinary Study of Science and Technology [*Northwestern University*] [*Research center*]   (RCD)
CIST .... Canadian Institute of Science and Technology Ltd.
CIST .... Centro Internazionale di Studi sui Trasporti [*International Center for Transportation Studies - ICTS*]   (EAIO)
CIST .... Chief Inspector of Supplementary Transport [*British military*]   (DMA)
Cist............ Cistellaria [*of Plautus*] [*Classical studies*]   (OCD)
CIST .... Cistron Biotechnology, Inc. [*Pine Brook, NJ*] [*NASDAQ symbol*]   (NQ)
CIST .... Coorbital Interceptor Scoring Technique
CistC.......... Cistercienserchronik [*A publication*]
CISTC....... Council on International Scientific and Technological Cooperation
CISTDQ .... Comunicaciones. INIA [*Instituto Nacional de Investigaciones Agrarias*]. Serie Tecnologia Agraria [*A publication*]
CISTI........ Canada Institute for Scientific and Technical Information [*National Research Council of Canada*]   (IID)
CISTIP...... Committee on International Scientific and Technical Information Programs [*National Academy of Sciences - National Research Council*]
CISTISER ... CISTI [*Canada Institute for Scientific and Technical Information*] Serials [*Information service or system*]   (CRD)
CISTOD.... Confederation of International Scientific and Technological Organizations for Development [*ICSU*] [*Paris, France*]   (EAIO)
Cist Stud .... Cistercian Studies [*A publication*]
CISV .... Children's International Summer Villages International Association [*Newcastle-Upon-Tyne, England*]   (EAIO)
CISW......... California Institute of Social Welfare
CISW......... Christians in Social Work/Social Welfare [*Australia*]
CISW-FM ... Whistler, BC [*FM radio station call letters*]
CISWO...... Coal Industry Social Welfare Organisation [*British*]
CISYO....... Committee for the Implementation of the Standardized Yiddish Orthography   (EA)
CIT............. Caliente Resources Ltd. [*Vancouver Stock Exchange symbol*]
CIT............. California Institute of Technology [*Pasadena*] [*OCLC symbol*]   (OCLC)
CIT............. California Institute of Technology [*Also, CALIT, CALT, CALTECH*]
CIT............. Call-In Time [*Military communications*]
CIT............. Canadian Import Tribunal [*QL Systems Ltd.*] [*Information service or system*]   (CRD)
CIT............. Career Interest Test [*Vocational guidance test*]

CIT............ Carnegie Institute of Technology [*Later, Carnegie-Mellon University*] [*Pennsylvania*]
CIT............ Case Institute of Technology [*Later, Case Western Reserve University*] [*Ohio*]
CIT............ Center for Information Technology [*Stanford University*] [*Stanford, CA*]   (CSR)
CIT............ Center for Irrigation Technology [*California State University, Fresno*] [*Research center*]   (RCD)
CIT............ Centre of Industrial Tribology [*Australia*]
CIT............ Centro de Informacion Tecnica [*Technical Information Center*] [*University of Puerto Rico*] [*Information service or system*]   (IID)
CIT............ Chartered Institute of Transport   (EAIO)
CIT............ Chita [*USSR*] [*Seismograph station code, US Geological Survey*]   (SEIS)
CiT............ Ciencia Tomista [*A publication*]
CIT............ Citadel   (ROG)
CIT............. Citation   (AFM)
CIT............ Citato [*Cited*] [*Latin*]   (ADA)
cit............. Citator [*or Cited In or Citing*] [*Legal term*]   (DLA)
Cit............. Citator and Indian Law Journal [*1908-14*] [*A publication*]   (DLA)
Cit .... Citeaux [*A publication*]
CIT............ Citizen   (AFM)
CIT............ Citrate
cit .... Citron [*Philately*]
Cit .... Citrulline [*An amino acid*]
CIT............ Cleaned in Transit
CIT............ Coal Industry Tribunal [*Australia*]
CIT............ Comite Interministeriel des Terres [*Interdepartmental Committee on Land*] [*Canada*]
CIT............ Comite International de Television [*International Television Committee*]
CIT............ Comite International des Transports Ferroviaires [*International Rail Transport Committee*]   (EAIO)
CIT............ Comite International Tzigane [*International Gypsy Committee*]
CIT............ Command Interface Test   (KSC)
CIT............ Commerce International [*A publication*]
CIT............ Commission on Instructional Technology   (EA)
CIT............ Communications and Information Technology Research [*British*]
CIT............ Communications Interface Table   (MCD)
CIT............ Compact Ignition TOKAMAK [*Toroidal Kamera Magnetic*] [*Plasma physics*]
CIT............ Compagnie Industrielle de Telecommunication [*Computer manufacturer*] [*France*]
CIT............ Compression in Transit
CIT............ Compressor Inlet Temperature   (NG)
CIT............ Computer-Integrated Telephony [*Data processing*]
CIT............ Computer Interface Technology   (IEEE)
CIT............ Computer Interface Terminal   (CET)
CIT............ Computerized Industrial Tomography [*Nondestructive testing method*]
CIT............ Computing and Information Technology [*Princeton University*] [*Research center*]   (RCD)
CIT............ Conductivity Indicator Transmitter [*Nuclear energy*]   (NRCH)
CIT............ Configuration Identification Tables   (AABC)
CIT............ Conseil International des Tanneurs [*International Council of Tanners - ICT*]   (EAIO)
CIT............ Consejo Internacional del Trigo [*International Wheat Council - IWC*]   (EAIO)
CIT............ Contact Ion Thruster
CIT............ Controlled Interceptor Trainer [*Aerospace*]   (AAG)
CIT............ Cornell Information Technologies [*Information service or system*]   (EISS)
CIT............ Corporate Income Tax [*Economics*]
CIT............ Counselor-in-Training [*for summer camps*]
CIT............ Counterintelligence Team   (NVT)
CIT............ Court of International Trade. Reports [*A publication*]   (DLA)
CIT............ Cranfield Institute of Technology [*British*]   (ARC)
CIT............ Cranfield Institute of Technology [*California*]
CIT............ Critical Item Tag   (MCD)
CIT............ Inter-American Travel Congresses   (EA)
CIT............ Near or Over Large Towns [*Aviation code*]   (FAAC)
CITA.......... Canadian Independent Telephone Association
CITA.......... Canadian Institute for Theoretical Astrophysics [*University of Toronto*] [*Research center*]   (RCD)
CITA........ Citation   (AABC)
CITA.......... Collectif d'Information et de Travail Anti-Imperialiste [*Collective of Information and Anti-Imperialist Labour*] [*Canada*]
CITA.......... Comite International de l'Inspection Technique Automobile [*International Motor Vehicle Inspection Committee*] [*Verviers, Belgium*]   (EAIO)
CITA.......... Commercial and Industrial-Type Activity   (AABC)
CITA.......... Commission Internationale de Tourisme Aerien
CITA.......... Committee for the Implementation of Textile Agreements
CITA.......... Confederation Internationale des Ingenieurs Agronomes [*International Confederation of Technical Agricultural Engineers*]

CITA......... Conference Internationale des Trains Speciaux d'Agences de Voyages [*International Conference on Special Trains for Travel Agencies*] (EAIO)

CITA......... Court Interpreters and Translators Association (EA)

CITAB...... Computer Instruction and Training Assistance for the Blind

CITAC7..... Coletanea. Instituto de Tecnologia de Alimentos [*A publication*]

CITAM...... Centre International de la Tapisserie Ancienne et Moderne [*Switzerland*]

CITARS..... Crop Identification Technology Assessment for Remote Sensing [*NASA*]

CITB......... Construction Industry Training Board (MCD)

CITBA...... Customs and International Trade Bar Association (EA)

CITC......... Canadian Institute of Travel Counsellors

CITC......... Construction Industry Training Center (MCD)

CITCA...... Committee of Inquiry into Technological Change in Australia (ADA)

CITCE...... Comite International de Thermodynamique et de Cinetique Electro-Chimiques [*International Committee of Electro-Chemical Thermodynamics and Kinetics*]

CITCM...... Canberra Income Tax Circular Memorandum [*Australia*] [*A publication*]

CiTCM...... Chinese Materials and Research Aids Service Center, Inc., Taipei, Taiwan, China [*Library symbol*] [*Library of Congress*] (LCLS)

CITD......... Center for International Trade Development [*Oklahoma State University*] [*Research center*] (RCD)

CITE......... Capsule Integrated Test Equipment [*Aerospace*]

CITE......... Cargo Integration Test Equipment (NASA)

CITE......... Certified Incentive Travel Executive [*Designation awarded by Society of Incentive Travel Executives*]

CITE......... CITES Reports. Convention on International Trade in Endangered Species of Wild Fauna and Flora [*A publication*]

CITE......... Coalition for International Trade Equity

CITE......... Compression Ignition and Turbine Engine

CITE......... Computer-Integrated Test Equipment

CITE......... Consolidated Index of Translations into English

CITE......... Contractor Independent Technical Effort [*DoD*]

CITE......... Controller Input Test Equipment

CITE......... Coordinating Information for Texas Educators [*Texas State Education Agency*] [*Information service or system*] [*No longer available*] (IID)

CITE......... Council of Institute of Telecommunication Engineers

CITE......... Current Information Tapes for Engineering

CITE......... Current Information Transfer in English

CITE......... Institute of Transportation Engineers [*District 7*] [*Canada*]

CITEA...... Chemie-Ingenieur-Technik [*A publication*]

CITEC...... Contractor Independent Technical Effort (IEEE)

CITECH... Cawkell Information & Technology Services, Ltd. [*Telecommunications*] (IID)

CITE-FM.. Montreal, PQ [*FM radio station call letters*]

CITE-FM-1... Sherbrooke, PQ [*FM radio station call letters*]

CITEJA..... Comite International Technique d'Experts Juridiques Aeriens [*International Technical Committee of Aerial Legal Experts*]

CITEL...... Conference on Inter-American Telecommunications [*Organization of American States*] [*Telecommunications*] (TSSD)

CITEM...... Center for International Trade Exhibitions and Missions [*Ministry for Trade*] [*Philippines*]

CITEN...... Comite International de la Teinture et du Nettoyage [*International Committee for Dyeing and Dry Cleaning*]

CITEP...... Community Integrated Training and Education Program

CITERAC... Chisholm Institute of Technology, Engineering Research and Advisory Centre [*Australia*]

CITERE..... Centre d'Information en Temps Reel pour l'Europe [*European Center for Information in Real Time*] [*France*] [*Information service or system*] (IID)

CITES........ Convention on International Trade in Endangered Species of Wild Fauna and Flora (EAIO)

CITF......... City Industry Task Force [*Confederation of British Industry*]

CITF......... Commercial and Industrial-Type Functions [*Army*] (MCD)

CITF......... Community Integrated Training Type Functions

CITF-FM... Quebec, PQ [*FM radio station call letters*]

CITG......... Citizens Growth Properties [*Jackson, MS*] [*NASDAQ symbol*] (NQ)

CITG......... Current Intelligence Targets Groups [*Military*]

CITGAN.... Citrograph [*A publication*]

Cit God...... City of God [*A publication*]

CITH........ Centre d'Information Textile Habillement [*Textile and Clothing Information Center*] [*Information service or system*] (IID)

CITHA...... Confederation of International Trading Houses Associations [*The Hague, Netherlands*] (EAIO)

CITI.......... Center for Information Technology Integration [*University of Michigan*] [*Research center*] (RCD)

Citi............ Citicorp

CITI.......... CitiPostal, Inc. [*NASDAQ symbol*] (NQ)

CITI.......... Confederation Internationale des Travailleurs Intellectuels [*International Confederation of Professional and Intellectual Workers*]

CITI.......... Congress of the International Theater Institute

Citibank..... Citibank. Monthly Economic Letter [*A publication*]

Citibank Mo Econ Letter ... Citibank. Monthly Economic Letter [*A publication*]

CITIBASE ... Citibank Economic Database [*Citibank, NA*] [*New York, NY*] [*Information service or system*] (IID)

CITIC........ China International Trust Investment Corporation

Cities E Rom Prov ... [*The*] Cities of the Eastern Roman Provinces [*A publication*] (OCD)

CITI-FM ... Winnipeg, MB [*FM radio station call letters*]

CITIGO..... Citizens for Good Government [*Political fund of Ling-Temco-Vought, Inc.*]

Citin Gos Ped Inst Ucen Zap ... Citinskii Gosudarstvennyi Pedagogiceskii Institut. Ucenye Zapiski [*A publication*]

CITIS........ Centralized Integrated Technical Information System (DIT)

CITIS......... Construction Industry Translation and Information Services [*Dublin, Ireland*]

CITJD ...... Chartered Institute of Transport. Journal [*A publication*]

CITL.......... Canadian Industrial Traffic League

CITL.......... Citel, Inc. [*NASDAQ symbol*] (NQ)

CITL-TV ... Lloydminster, AB [*Television station call letters*]

CITM......... Certified International Traffic Manager [*Designation awarded by American Society of International Executives, Inc.*]

CITMD...... Cahiers d'Informations Techniques/Revue de Metallurgie [*A publication*]

CITM-TV ... 100 Mile House, BC [*Television station call letters*]

CitN........... Citeaux in de Nederlande [*A publication*]

CITN .... Citizens Financial Group, Inc. [*Providence, RI*] [*NASDAQ symbol*] (NQ)

CITO DISP ... Cito Dispensetur [*Dispense Quickly*] [*Pharmacy*]

CiTom........ La Ciencia Tomista [*Salamanca*] [*A publication*]

CITO-TV... Timmins, ON [*Television station call letters*]

CITO-TV-2 ... Kearns, ON [*Television station call letters*]

CITP......... Chronic Idiopathic Thrombocytopenic Purpura [*Medicine*]

CITP......... Citizen Involvement Training Program (EA)

CITP......... Comite International des Telecommunications de Presse [*International Press Telecommunications Council - IPTC*] (EAIO)

CITP......... Contractor Input to Total Performance [*DoD*]

CITR......... Centre for Information Technology Research [*University of Queensland*] [*University of Wollongong*] [*Australia*]

CITR......... Court of International Trade. Rules [*A publication*] (DLA)

CITRE....... Cooperative Investigations of Tropical Reef Ecosystems [*Smithsonian Institution*] (MSC)

CITR-FM .. Vancouver, BC [*FM radio station call letters*]

CITRIC...... Citriculture

Citrus Grow ... Citrus Grower [*A publication*]

Citrus Grow Sub-Trop Fruit J ... Citrus Grower and Sub-Tropical Fruit Journal [*A publication*]

Citrus Ind... Citrus Industry [*A publication*]

Citrus Mag ... Citrus Magazine [*A publication*]

Citrus Subtrop Fruit J ... Citrus and Subtropical Fruit Journal [*South Africa*] [*A publication*]

Citrus Veg Mag ... Citrus and Vegetable Magazine [*A publication*]

CITS.......... Central Integrated Test System

CITS.......... Commission Internationale Technique de Sucrerie [*International Commission of Sugar Technology*] (EAIO)

CITS.......... Current Imaging Tunneling Spectroscopy

CITT.......... Canadian Institute of Traffic and Transportation

CITTA....... Confederation Internationale des Fabricants de Tapis et de Tissus d'Ameublement [*International Confederation of Manufacturers of Carpets and Furnishing Fabrics*] (EAIO)

CIT-TAFE ... Caulfield Institute of Technology, TAFE [*Technical and Further Education*] Division [*Australia*]

CITU.......... Centre of Indian Trade Unions

CITU.......... Citizens Utilities Co. [*Stamford, CT*] [*NASDAQ symbol*] (NQ)

CITV.......... Commander's Independent Thermal Viewer [*Military*] (RDA)

CITV-TV ... Edmonton, AB [*Television station call letters*]

CITW......... Canadian Institute of Treated Wood

CITY......... First City Bancorp, Inc. [*NASDAQ symbol*] (NQ)

City Adelaide Munic Yb ... Adelaide. City. Municipal Year Book [*A publication*] (APTA)

City Civ Ct Act ... New York City Civil Court Act (DLA)

City Crim Ct Act ... New York City Criminal Court Act (DLA)

City Ct........ City Court (DLA)

City Ct R ... City Court Reports [*New York*] [*A publication*] (DLA)

City Ct Rep ... City Court Reports [*New York*] [*A publication*] (DLA)

City Ct Rep Supp ... City Court Reports, Supplement [*New York*] [*A publication*] (DLA)

City Ct R Supp ... City Court Reports, Supplement [*New York*] [*A publication*] (DLA)

City Ct Supp (NY) ... City Court Reports, Supplement [*New York*] [*A publication*] (DLA)

City Hall Rec (NY) ... City Hall Recorder [*New York City*] [*A publication*] (DLA)

City Hall Rep ... City Hall Reporter (Lomas) [*New York City*] [*A publication*] (DLA)

City Hall Rep (NY) ... City Hall Reporter (Lomas) [*New York City*] [*A publication*] (DLA)
City H Rec ... New York City Hall Recorder [*A publication*] (DLA)
City H Rep ... City Hall Reporter (Lomas) [*New York City*] [*A publication*] (DLA)
City Rec ..... New York City Record [*A publication*] (DLA)
City Rec (NY) ... New York City Record [*A publication*] (DLA)
City Stoke-On-Trent Mus Archaeol Soc Rep ... City of Stoke-On-Trent Museum. Archaeological Society. Reports [*A publication*]
CITY-TV ... Toronto, ON [*Television station call letters*]
Citzn Reg ... Citizen Register [*A publication*]
CIU .... Career Information Unit (OICC)
CIU .... Central Interpretation Unit [*Military*]
CIU .... Chlorella International Union [*Later, MIU*]
CIU .... Cima Resources Ltd. [*Vancouver Stock Exchange symbol*]
CIU .... Combined Intelligence Unit [*Formerly, CIPC*] [*RAF*] [*British*]
CIU .... Command Interface Unit (KSC)
CIU .... Communications Interface Unit
CIU .... Community Information Utility (BUR)
CIU .... Computer Interface Unit
CIU .... Congress of Independent Unions (EA)
CIU .... Congress of Irish Unions
CIU .... Console Intelligence Unit (MCD)
CIU .... Controller Interface Unit (MCD)
CiU .... Convergencia i Unio [*Convergence and Union*] [*Spain*] [*Political party*] (PPE)
CIU .... Coopers' International Union of North America
CIU .... Council for International Understanding (EA)
CIU .... Sault Ste. Marie [*Michigan*] [*Airport symbol*] (OAG)
CIUC .... Chronic Idiopathic Ulcerative Colitis [*Gastroenterology*]
CIUC .... Commission of International Union of Crystallography [*British*]
CIUG .... Contractor Inventory Utilization Group (MCD)
CIUL .... Council for International Urban Liaison (EA)
CIUNA ..... Coopers' International Union of North America (EA)
CIUS .... Conseil International des Unions Scientifiques [*International Council of Scientific Unions*]
CIUS .... Corps Interim Upgrade System (MCD)
CIUS .... County Intermediate Unit Superintendents [*of NEA*] [*Later, AASA*] (EA)
CIUSS .... Catholic International Union for Social Service
CIUTI .... Conference Internationale Permanente de Direcuters d'Instituts Universitaires pour la Formation de Traducteurs et d'Interpretes [*Standing International Conference of the Directors of University Institutes for the Training of Translators and Interpreters*] (EAIO)
Civ .... Arret de la Chambre Civile de la Cour de Cassation [*Decision of the Court of Appeal, Civil Division*] [*French*] (ILCA)
CIV .... Capital Improved Value (ADA)
CIV .... Center Island Vessel [*Nuclear energy*] (NRCH)
CIV .... Central Inspectorate of Vehicles [*British military*] (DMA)
CIV .... City Imperial Volunteers [*Military unit*] [*British*]
Civ .... Civil (AFM)
Civ .... Civil Appeals [*A publication*] (DLA)
Civ .... Civile [*Civil*] [*Latin*] (DLA)
CIV .... Civilian (AFM)
CIV .... Civilisations [*A publication*]
CIV .... Civilization (ROG)
CIV .... Code Inserter Verifier [*Air Force*]
CIV .... Columbia Real Estate Investments [*AMEX symbol*] (SPSG)
CIV .... Combined Intercept Valve [*Nuclear energy*] (NRCH)
CIV .... Combined Intermediate Valve [*Nuclear energy*] (NRCH)
CIV .... Commission Internationale du Verre [*International Commission on Glass - ICG*] (EAIO)
CIV .... Containment Isolation Valve [*Nuclear energy*] (IEEE)
CIV .... Convention Internationale Concernant le Transport des Voyageurs et des Bagages par Chemins de Fer [*International Convention Concerning the Carriage of Passengers and Luggage by Rail*]
CIV .... Indian Valley Colleges Library, Novato, CA [*OCLC symbol*] (OCLC)
CIV .... Ivory Coast [*ANSI three-letter standard code*] (CNC)
Civ .... Texas Civil Appeals Reports [*A publication*] (DLA)
CIVACTGP ... Civic Action Group [*Military*] (CINC)
CIVAD .... Civil Administrator (CINC)
Civ Brux ..... Jugement du Tribunal Civil de Bruxelles [*A publication*]
CIVB-TV ... Rimouski, PQ [*Television station call letters*]
CivCatt .... La Civilta Cattolica [*Rome*] [*A publication*]
Civ Cl Crist ... Civilta Classica e Cristiana [*A publication*]
CIVCLO ..... Civilian Clothing
Civ Code Prac ... Civil Code of Practice [*A publication*] (DLA)
Civ & Cr LS ... Civil and Criminal Law Series [*India*] [*A publication*] (DLA)
Civ Ct .... Civil Court (DLA)
Civ Ct Rec ... Civil Court of Record (DLA)
CIVC-TV ... Trois-Rivieres, PQ [*Television station call letters*]
CIVD .... Cold-Induced Vasodilation
Civ D Ct ..... Civil District Court (DLA)
Civ Def Bull ... Civil Defence Bulletin [*A publication*]
Civ Develop ... Civic Development [*A publication*] (APTA)
CIVEMP ... Civilian Employee (MCD)
Civ Eng ...... Civil Engineering [*A publication*]

CIVENG .... Civil Engineering
Civ Eng Constr Public Works J ... Civil Engineering, Construction, and Public Works Journal [*India*] [*A publication*]
Civ Eng Contract ... Civil Engineering Contractor [*A publication*]
Civ Eng Jpn ... Civil Engineering in Japan [*A publication*]
Civ Eng (London) ... Civil Engineering (London) [*A publication*]
Civ Engng ... Civil Engineering [*London*] [*A publication*]
Civ Engng ASCE ... Civil Engineering. American Society of Civil Engineers [*A publication*]
Civ Engn (GB) ... Civil Engineering (Great Britain) [*A publication*]
Civ Engng (Lond) ... Civil Engineering (London) [*A publication*]
Civ Engng Pract & Des Engrs ... Civil Engineering for Practicing and Design Engineers [*A publication*]
Civ Engng Publ Wks Rev ... Civil Engineering and Public Works Review [*A publication*]
Civ Engng Trans ... Civil Engineering Transactions. Institution of Engineers of Australia [*A publication*] (APTA)
Civ Engng Trans Instn Engrs Aust ... Civil Engineering Transactions. Institution of Engineers of Australia [*A publication*] (APTA)
Civ Eng (NY) ... Civil Engineering (New York) [*A publication*]
Civ Eng Public Works Rev ... Civil Engineering and Public Works Review [*A publication*]
Civ Eng Pub Works Rev ... Civil Engineering and Public Works Review [*A publication*]
CIVENGRLAB ... Civil Engineering Laboratory [*Also, CEL*] [*Navy*] (MUGU)
Civ Eng S Afr ... Civil Engineering in South Africa [*A publication*]
CIVENGSq ... Civil Engineering Squadron [*Air Force*]
Civ Eng Trans ... Civil Engineering Transactions. Institute of Engineers [*Australia*] [*A publication*]
Civ Eng Trans Inst Eng Aust ... Civil Engineering Transactions. Institution of Engineers of Australia [*A publication*] (APTA)
CIVEX .... Civilian Extraction [*Nuclear energy*]
CIVF-TV ... Baie-Trinite, PQ [*Television station call letters*]
CIVG-TV ... Sept-Iles, PQ [*Television station call letters*]
CIVH .... Vanderhoof, BC [*AM radio station call letters*]
CIVIC .... Civic Issues Voluntary Information Council [*Michigan*]
Civic Dev ... Civic Development [*A publication*] (APTA)
CiViDiC ..... Cisplatin, Vindesine, Dacarbazine [*Antineoplastic drug regimen*]
Civil Aero J ... Civil Aeronautics Administration. Journal [*A publication*]
Civil Defence Bul ... Civil Defence Bulletin [*A publication*] (APTA)
Civil Eng ..... Civil Engineering [*A publication*]
Civil Engineering ASCE ... Civil Engineering. American Society of Civil Engineers [*A publication*]
Civil Enging ... Civil Engineering [*A publication*]
Civil Enging Practicing Des Engrs ... Civil Engineering for Practicing and Design Engineers [*A publication*]
Civil Enging Surv ... Civil Engineering Surveyor [*A publication*]
Civil Liberties R ... Civil Liberties Review [*A publication*]
Civil Liberties Rev ... Civil Liberties Review [*A publication*]
Civil Pro R ... Civil Procedure Reports [*New York*] [*A publication*] (DLA)
Civil Rights Dig ... Civil Rights Digest [*A publication*]
Civil Rights Research R ... Civil Rights Research Review [*A publication*]
Civilta Catt ... Civilta Cattolica [*A publication*]
Civilta Macch ... Civilta delle Macchine [*A publication*]
Civil War H ... Civil War History [*A publication*]
Civil War Hist ... Civil War History [*A publication*]
CIVISION ... Enciphered Television (MCD)
CIVITEX ... Civic Information & Techniques Exchange [*Citizens Forum on Self-Government/National Municipal League*] [*Information service or system*] (IID)
Civ Just Q ... Civil Justice Quarterly [*A publication*] (DLA)
CIVL .... Center International de Vol Libre [*Aguessac, France*] (EAIO)
CIV LIB ..... Civil Liberty (DLA)
Civ Lib Dock ... Civil Liberties Docket (DLA)
Civ Lib Rev ... Civil Liberties Review [*A publication*]
Civ Lib Rptr ... Civil Liberties Reporter [*A publication*]
Civ Litigation Rep ... Civil Litigation Reporter [*A publication*] (DLA)
CIVM .... Collision-Imparted Velocity Method
Civ & Military LJ ... Civil and Military Law Journal [*A publication*]
Civ and Mil LJ ... Civil and Military Law Journal [*A publication*]
CIV-M-MARP ... Civilian Mobilization Manpower Allocation/Requirements Plan
CIVM-TV ... Montreal, PQ [*Television station call letters*]
CIVO-TV ... Hull, PQ [*Television station call letters*]
CIVPERCEN ... United States Army Civilian Personnel Center (AABC)
CIVPERSINS ... Civilian Personnel Information System [*Army*]
Civ Pr .... Civil Procedure Reports [*New York*] [*A publication*] (DLA)
Civ Prac ..... Civil Practice Law and Rules [*A publication*] (DLA)
Civ Prac (NY) ... New York Civil Practice [*A publication*] (DLA)
Civ Pro .... Civil Procedure Reports [*New York*] [*A publication*] (DLA)
Civ Proc ..... Civil Procedure [*Legal term*] (DLA)
Civ Proc (NS) ... Civil Procedure Reports, New Series [*1908-13*] [*New York*] [*A publication*] (DLA)
Civ Proc (NY) ... New York Civil Procedure [*A publication*] (DLA)
Civ Proc R ... Civil Procedure Reports [*New York*] [*A publication*] (DLA)
Civ Proc Rep ... Civil Procedure Reports [*New York*] [*A publication*] (DLA)
Civ Proc Rep NS ... Civil Procedure Reports, New Series [*1908-13*] [*New York*] [*A publication*] (DLA)

Civ Proc R (NS) ... Civil Procedure Reports, New Series [1908-13] [New York] [A publication] (DLA)
Civ Pro R ... Civil Procedure Reports [New York] [A publication] (DLA)
Civ Pro Reports ... Civil Procedure Reports [New York] [A publication] (DLA)
Civ Pro R (NS) ... Civil Procedure Reports, New Series [1908-13] [New York] [A publication] (DLA)
Civ Pr Rep ... Civil Procedure Reports [New York] [A publication] (DLA)
CIVP-TV.. Chapeau, PQ [Television station call letters]
CIVQ-TV... Quebec City, PQ [Television station call letters]
CIV R........ Civil Rights (DLA)
CIVR......... Configuration Item Validation Review
CIVR......... Configuration Item Verification Review
Civ Rights Digest ... Civil Rights Digest [A publication]
Civ Rts .... Civil Rights [A publication]
Civ Rts Dig ... Civil Rights Digest [A publication]
CIV S .... Civil Service (DLA)
Civ Serv...... Civil Service (DLA)
Civ Serv J... Civil Service Journal [A publication]
CIVSITREP ... Civil Situation Reporting System (NATG)
CIVS-TV ... Sherbrooke, PQ [Television station call letters]
CIVSUB .... Civilian Substitution Program [Navy] (NVT)
CIVT......... Cargo Interface Verification Test (MCD)
CIVTA4..... Congres International de la Vigne du Vin [A publication]
CIVV......... Compressor Inlet Variable Vane (MCD)
CIVV-TV... Chicoutimi, PQ [Television station call letters]
Civ War Hist ... Civil War History [A publication]
Civ War T Illus ... Civil War Times Illustrated [A publication]
Civ War Times Illus ... Civil War Times Illustrated [A publication]
CIW .... California Institution for Women
CIW .... Cameron Iron Works, Inc. [NYSE symbol] (SPSG)
CIW .... Carnegie Institution of Washington (EA)
CIW .... Ceramic Insulated Wire
CIW .... Chicago & Illinois Western Railroad [AAR code]
CI & W...... Cincinnati, Indiana & Western Railway
CIW .... Cities of the World [A publication]
CIW .... Collingwood Energy [Vancouver Stock Exchange symbol]
CIW .... Community Information Week [Australia]
CIWA .... Condition Identification Work Authorization [Business term] (NRCH)
CIWA .... [The] Cuneiform Inscriptions of Western Asia [A publication] (BJA)
CIWDSS.... Canada. Inland Waters Directorate. Scientific Series [A publication]
CIWDSSS ... Canada. Inland Waters Directorate. Social Science Series [A publication]
CIWDTB ... Canada. Inland Waters Directorate. Technical Bulletin [A publication]
CIWF........ Clearinghouse International of the Women's Forum (EA)
CIWF........ Compassion in World Farming [British]
CIWG........ Camera Industries of West Germany [Defunct]
CIWLT ...... Cie. Internationale des Wagons-Lits et du Tourisme [International Sleeping Car Company]
CIWNP...... Clinical Information Was Not Provided [Medicine]
CIWP........ Counterintelligence Working Party [US Military Government, Germany]
CIWPAV ... Carnegie Institution of Washington. Publication [A publication]
CIWQIR.... Canada. Inland Waters Directorate. Water Quality Interpretive Reports [A publication]
CIWS........ Close-In Weapon System (NATG)
CIWS........ Concentrator Isolation Working Subsystem [Telecommunications] (TEL)
CIWW .... Ottawa, ON [AM radio station call letters]
CIWYAO... Carnegie Institution of Washington. Year Book [A publication]
CIX .... Chiclayo [Peru] [Airport symbol] (OAG)
CIX .... Consolidated BRX Mining & Petroleum Ltd. [Vancouver Stock Exchange symbol]
CIXK-FM.. Owen Sound, ON [FM radio station call letters]
CIXX-FM.. London, ON [FM radio station call letters]
CIY .... Camino Energy Corp. [Vancouver Stock Exchange symbol]
CIY .... Consolidated Cyll Industry [Vancouver Stock Exchange symbol]
CIY .... Siskiyou County Public Library, Yreka, CA [OCLC symbol] (OCLC)
CIYMS...... Church of Ireland Young Men's Society
CIYQ .... Grand Falls, NF [AM radio station call letters]
CIYR......... Hinton, AB [AM radio station call letters]
CIZ............ Central Initial Zone [in inflorescence] [Botany]
CIZ............ Chatham Islands [New Zealand] [Seismograph station code, US Geological Survey] (SEIS)
CIZ............ City Resources (Canada) Ltd. [Vancouver Stock Exchange symbol] [Toronto Stock Exchange symbol]
CIZC......... City Resources [Canada] Ltd. [NASDAQ symbol] (NQ)
CIZL-FM .. Regina, SK [FM radio station call letters]
CIZSAL..... Conseil International pour l'Exploration de la Mer. Zooplankton Sheet [A publication]
CIZZ-FM .. Red Deer, AB [FM radio station call letters]
CJ............. Amador County Free Library, Jackson, CA [Library symbol] [Library of Congress] (LCLS)
CJ............. Bay Meadows Operating Co. [AMEX symbol] (SPSG)
CJ............. Cambridge Journal [A publication]

CJ.............. Canadian Journal of Economics [A publication]
CJ.............. Caribbean Air Transport Co., Inc. [Netherlands] [ICAO designator] (FAAC)
CJ.............. Catholic Journalist [A publication] (EAAP)
cj.............. Cayman Islands [MARC country of publication code] [Library of Congress] (LCCP)
CJ.............. Ceiling Joist
CJ.............. Chamber's Journal [A publication]
CJ.............. Chapman-Jouquet [Pressures] (MCD)
CJ.............. Chelsea Journal [A publication]
CJ.............. Chief Judge [Sports]
CJ.............. Chief Justice [Various supreme courts]
CJ.............. Choral Journal [A publication]
CJ.............. Cinema Journal [A publication]
CJ.............. Circuit Judge (DLA)
CJ.............. Civilian Jeep
CJ.............. Classical Journal [A publication]
CJ.............. Cobra Jet [Automotive engineering]
CJ.............. Code of Justinian [A publication] (DSA)
CJ.............. Codex Justinianus (BJA)
CJ.............. Cold Junction
C & J......... Collection and Jamming
CJ.............. Computer Journal [British] [A publication]
CJ.............. Concordia Journal [A publication]
CJ.............. Congregatio Iosephitarum [Josephite Fathers] [Roman Catholic religious order]
CJ.............. Conjectural (ADA)
CJ.............. Conjunction
CJ.............. Conseil de la Jeunesse [Youth Council] [Senegal, Mali, Upper Volta, Niger, and Dahomey]
CJ.............. Conservative Judaism [A publication]
CJ.............. Consolidated Jalna Resources [Vancouver Stock Exchange symbol]
CJ.............. Construction Joint [Technical drawings]
CJ.............. Contemporary Japan [A publication]
CJ.............. Control Joint (MCD)
CJ.............. Corpus Juris [Body of Law] [Latin]
CJ.............. Court of Justice of the European Communities
c/j.............. Courts Jours [Short-Dated Bills] [French]
CJ.............. Coyote's Journal [A publication]
CJ.............. Creutzfeldt-Jakob Disease [Neurological disorder]
C & J......... Crime and Justice Bulletin [A publication]
C & J......... Crompton and Jervis' English Exchequer Reports [1830-32] [A publication] (DLA)
CJ.............. Curriculum Journal [Philippines] [A publication]
CJ.............. Journal of the House of Commons [A publication] (DLA)
CJ.............. Lord Chief Justice [British] [A publication] (DLA)
CJA........... Cajamarca [Peru] [Airport symbol] (OAG)
CJA........... Campbell-Johnston Associates [Commercial firm] [British]
CJA........... Canadian Journal of Archaeology [A publication]
CJA........... Chess Journalists of America (EA)
CJA........... Christlich-Juedische Arbeitsgemeinschaft [A publication]
CJa........... Cizi Jazyky ve Skole [A publication]
CJA........... Classic Jaguar Association (EA)
CJA........... Colima Resources Ltd. [Vancouver Stock Exchange symbol]
CJA........... Commonwealth Journalists Association [London, England] (EAIO)
CJA........... Conseil de la Jeunesse d'Afrique [African Youth Council] [Senegal]
CJA........... United Brotherhood of Carpenters and Joiners of America
CJAB-FM .. Chicoutimi, PQ [FM radio station call letters]
CJAC....... Central Joint Advisory Committee on Tutoral Classes [British]
CJACS...... Chemical Journals of the American Chemical Society [Information service or system] (CRD)
CJAD........ Montreal, PQ [AM radio station call letters]
CJAF .... Cabano, PQ [AM radio station call letters]
CJAfS .... Caribbean Journal of African Studies [A publication]
CJA & HSA ... Council of Justice to Animals and Humane Slaughter Association (EAIO)
CJAN........ Asbestos, PQ [AM radio station call letters]
CJ Ann...... Corpus Juris Annotations [A publication] (DLA)
CJAOAC ... Chemical Journal of the Association of Official Analytical Chemists [Association of Official Analytical Chemists] [Information service or system] (CRD)
CJap.......... Contemporary Japan [A publication]
CJAP-TV... Argentia, NF [Television station call letters]
CJAR .... The Pas, MB [AM radio station call letters]
CJAS .... Canadian Journal of African Studies [A publication]
CJaS .... Sierra Conservation Center, Jamestown, CA [Library symbol] [Library of Congress] (LCLS)
CJASB....... Country Joe and His All Star Band [Pop music group]
CJAT .... Trail, BC [AM radio station call letters]
CJAV .... Port Alberni, BC [AM radio station call letters]
CJAY-FM ... Calgary, AB [FM radio station call letters]
CJB........... Chief Judge in Bankruptcy (DLA)
CJB........... Coimbatore [India] [Airport symbol] (OAG)
CJB........... Columbia Journal of World Business [A publication]
CJBBDU ... Canadian Journal of Biochemistry and Cell Biology [A publication]
CJBC .... Cansorb Industries, Inc. [NASDAQ symbol] (NQ)
CJBC .... Toronto, ON [AM radio station call letters]

CJBC-FM-20 ... London, ON [*FM radio station call letters*]
CJBIA....... Canadian Journal of Biochemistry [*A publication*]
CJBIAE..... Canadian Journal of Biochemistry [*A publication*]
CJBK .... London, ON [*AM radio station call letters*]
CJBM .... Causapscal, PQ [*AM radio station call letters*]
CJBN-TV .. Kenora, ON [*Television station call letters*]
CJBO .... Canadian Journal of Botany [*A publication*]
CJBOA .... Canadian Journal of Botany [*A publication*]
CJBOAW .. Canadian Journal of Botany [*A publication*]
CJBPAZ.... Canadian Journal of Biochemistry and Physiology [*A publication*]
CJBQ .... Belleville, ON [*AM radio station call letters*]
CJBR .... Rimouski, PQ [*AM radio station call letters*]
CJBR-FM ... Rimouski, PQ [*FM radio station call letters*]
CJBRT....... Rimouski, PQ [*Television station call letters*]
CJBSAA ...... Canadian Journal of Behavioural Science [*A publication*]
CJBT .... Costume Jewelry Board of Trade of New York [*Inactive*]
CJBX-FM ... London, ON [*FM radio station call letters*]
CJC........... Cahiers Jean Cocteau [*A publication*]
CJC........... Calama [*Chile*] [*Airport symbol*]   (OAG)
CJC........... Cambridge Junior College [*Massachusetts*]
CJC........... Canadian Jewish Congress
CJC........... Cancapital Corp. [*Toronto Stock Exchange symbol*]
CJC........... Carver, J. C., Neptune NJ [*STAC*]
CJC........... Chipola Junior College [*Marianna, FL*]
CJC........... Cisco Junior College [*Texas*]
CJC........... Citrus Junior College [*California*]
CJC........... Coahoma Junior College [*Clarksdale, MS*]
CJC........... Colgan Airways Corp. [*Manassas, VA*] [*FAA designator*]   (FAAC)
CJC........... Community Junior College
CJC........... Compagnie des Jeunes Canadiens [*Company of Young Canadiens*] [*Federal crown corporation to employ young people, 1966-75*]
CJC........... Congress for Jewish Culture   (EA)
CJC........... Corpus Juris Civilis [*The Body of the Civil Law*] [*Latin*]   (DLA)
CJC........... Couper's Judiciary Cases [*1868-85*] [*Scotland*] [*A publication*]   (DLA)
CJC........... Poor Sisters of Jesus Crucified and the Sorrowful Mother [*Roman Catholic religious order*]
CJCA .... Edmonton, AB [*AM radio station call letters*]
CJ Can .... Corpus Juris Canonici [*The Body of the Canon Law*] [*Latin*]   (DLA)
CJCB .... Commonwealth Joint Communication Board [*British military*]   (DMA)
CJCB .... Sydney, NS [*AM radio station call letters*]
CJCB-TV... Sydney, NS [*Television station call letters*]
CJCB-TV-1 ... Inverness, NS [*Television station call letters*]
CJCB-TV-2 ... Antigonish, NS [*Television station call letters*]
CJCD......... Yellowknife, NT [*AM radio station call letters*]
CJCD-FM-1 ... Hay River, NT [*FM radio station call letters*]
CJCE .... Canadian Journal of Civil Engineering [*A publication*]
CJCEA ...... Canadian Journal of Chemical Engineering [*A publication*]
CJCH........ Halifax, NS [*AM radio station call letters*]
CJCHA....... Canadian Journal of Chemistry [*A publication*]
CJCHAG... Canadian Journal of Chemistry [*A publication*]
CJCH-TV ... Halifax, NS [*Television station call letters*]
CJCH-TV-1 ... Canning, NS [*Television station call letters*]
CJCH-TV-6 ... Caledonia, NS [*Television station call letters*]
CJCI .... Conseil de la Jeunesse de Cote d'Ivoire [*Ivory Coast Youth Council*]
CJCI .... Prince George, BC [*AM radio station call letters*]
CJ Civ .... Corpus Juris Civilis [*The Body of the Civil Law*] [*Latin*]   (DLA)
CJCJ......... Woodstock, NB [*AM radio station call letters*]
CJCL......... Toronto, ON [*AM radio station call letters*]
CJCLS...... Community and Junior College Libraries Section [*Association of College and Research Libraries*]
CJCMA...... Canadian Journal of Comparative Medicine [*A publication*]
CJCMAV .. Canadian Journal of Comparative Medicine [*A publication*]
CJCN-TV .. Grand Falls, NF [*Television station call letters*]
CJCP .... Chief Justice of the Common Pleas   (DLA)
CJCS......... Chairman, Joint Chiefs of Staff   (AFM)
CJCS......... Conference of Jewish Communal Service   (EA)
CJCS......... Stratford, ON [*AM radio station call letters*]
CJCW....... Colby Junior College for Women [*Later, CSC*] [*New Hampshire*]
CJCW .... Sussex, NB [*AM radio station call letters*]
CJCY .... Medicine Hat, AB [*AM radio station call letters*]
CJD........... Canadian Journal of Economics [*A publication*]
CJD........... Canadian Journalism Data Base [*University of Western Ontario*]   (IID)
CJD........... Candilejas [*Colombia*] [*Airport symbol*]   (OAG)
CJD........... Candol Developments Ltd. [*Toronto Stock Exchange symbol*]
CJD........... Centre des Jeunes Dirigeants d'Entreprise [*Industrial organization*] [*France*]   (EY)
CJD........... Creutzfeldt-Jakob Disease [*Neurological disorder*]
CJD........... Doctor of Criminal Jurisprudence
CJDC........ Dawson Creek, BC [*AM radio station call letters*]
CJDC-FM .. Dawson Creek, BC [*FM radio station call letters*]
CJDC-TV .. Dawson Creek, BC [*Television station call letters*]
CJDG-TV ... Lithium Mines, PQ [*Television station call letters*]

CJDM-FM ... Drummondville, PQ [*FM radio station call letters*]
CJDV......... Committee for Justice for Domingo and Viernes   (EA)
CJE............ Canadian Journal of Economics [*A publication*]
CJE............ Canadian Journal of Economics and Political Science [*Later, Canadian Journal of Economics*] [*A publication*]
CJE............ Carolina Gold [*Vancouver Stock Exchange symbol*]
CJE............ Cookeville, TN [*Location identifier*] [*FAA*]   (FAAL)
CJE............ Council for Jewish Education   (EA)
CJEC......... Court of Justice of the European Communities   (DLA)
CJECB....... Canadian Journal of Economics [*A publication*]
CJEM......... Edmundston, NB [*AM radio station call letters*]
CJEN-FM ... Jenpeg, MB [*FM radio station call letters*]
CJEPS........ Canadian Journal of Economics and Political Science [*Later, Canadian Journal of Economics*] [*A publication*]
CJER......... Central Jersey Bancorp [*Freehold, NJ*] [*NASDAQ symbol*]   (NQ)
CJES......... St. Jerome, PQ [*AM radio station call letters*]
CJES......... Canadian Journal of Earth Sciences [*A publication*]
CJESA....... Canadian Journal of Earth Sciences [*A publication*]
CJESAP .... Canadian Journal of Earth Sciences [*A publication*]
CJET......... Committee on Jobs, Environment, and Technology   (EA)
CJET......... Smiths Falls, ON [*AM radio station call letters*]
CJEZ-FM ... Toronto, ON [*FM radio station call letters*]
CJF............ Chicago Jewish Forum [*A publication*]
CJF............ Chief Justice of the Federation [*Nigeria*]   (DLA)
CJF............ Council of Jewish Federations   (EA)
CJF............ Country Joe and the Fish [*Pop music group*]
CJFA .... Canadian Journal of Fisheries and Aquatic Sciences [*A publication*]
CJFA .... Commander of Joint Forces of Australia
CJFB-TV... Swift Current, SK [*Television station call letters*]
CJFC......... Central Jersey Financial Corp. [*NASDAQ symbol*]   (NQ)
CJFC .... Chuck Jennings Fan Club   (EA)
CJFM-FM ... Montreal, PQ [*FM radio station call letters*]
CJFP.......... Riviere-Du-Loup, PQ [*AM radio station call letters*]
CJFR .... Canadian Journal of Forest Research [*A publication*]
CJFRAR.... Canadian Journal of Forest Research [*A publication*]
CJFSDX .... Canadian Journal of Fisheries and Aquatic Sciences [*A publication*]
CJFT.......... Fort Erie, ON [*AM radio station call letters*]
CJFWF...... Council of Jewish Federations and Welfare Funds [*Later, CJF*]   (EA)
CJFX .... Antigonish, NS [*AM radio station call letters*]
CJG............ Cahiers Jean Giraudoux [*A publication*]
CJG............ Canady, J. G., Charlotte NC [*STAC*]
CJG............ Chai-Na-Ta-Ginseng [*Vancouver Stock Exchange symbol*]
CJG............ Council of Jews from Germany [*London, England*]   (EAIO)
CJGC......... London, ON [*Radio station call letters*] [*1930's*]
CJGS .... Chief of the Joint General Staff [*Vietnam*]
CJGS .... Community of the Companions of Jesus the Good Shepherd [*Anglican religious community*]
CJGX......... Yorkton, SK [*AM radio station call letters*]
CJH .... Caddev Industry, Inc. [*Vancouver Stock Exchange symbol*]
CJH .... Canadian Journal of History [*A publication*]
CJH .... Muskegon, MI [*Location identifier*] [*FAA*]   (FAAL)
CJHPAV ... Canadian Journal of Hospital Pharmacy [*A publication*]
CJHS......... Canadian Jewish Historical Society [*See also SCHJ*]
CJHSJ....... Canadian Jewish Historical Society. Journal [*A publication*]
CJHSS....... Ceylon Journal of Historical and Social Studies [*A publication*]
CJI .... Canadian Jewellers Institute
CJI .... Central Juvenile Index
CJI .... Committee for the Jewish Idea   (EA)
CJI .... Concrete Joint Institute [*Defunct*]   (EA)
CJIA .... Comite Juridique International de l'Aviation
CJIB .... Vernon, BC [*AM radio station call letters*]
CJIC-TV... Sault Ste. Marie, ON [*Television station call letters*]
CJII .... CJI Industries, Inc. [*New York, NY*] [*NASDAQ symbol*]   (NQ)
CJIS.......... Canadian Journal of Irish Studies [*A publication*]
CJIS.......... Criminal Justice Information System
C J It S...... Canadian Journal of Italian Studies [*A publication*]
CJJ .... Cresco, IA [*Location identifier*] [*FAA*]   (FAAL)
CJJR-FM.. Vancouver, BC [*FM radio station call letters*]
CJK........... Chinese, Japanese, and Korean [*Library of Congress computer system*]
CJKB .... Chief Justice of the King's Bench   (DLA)
CJKL......... Kirkland Lake, ON [*AM radio station call letters*]
CJL............ Canadian Journal of Linguistics [*A publication*]
CJL............ Cesky Jazyk a Literatura [*A publication*]
CJL............ Chitral [*Pakistan*] [*Airport symbol*] [*Obsolete*]   (OAG)
CJL............ Claimer Resources [*Vancouver Stock Exchange symbol*]
CJL............ Columbia Journal of Law and Social Problems [*A publication*]
CJL............ Committee for Justice and Liberty Foundation
CJLA-FM ... Lachute, PQ [*FM radio station call letters*]
CJLB .... Thunder Bay, ON [*AM radio station call letters*]
CJLit.......... Cesky Jazyk a Literatura [*A publication*]
CJLM .... Contemporary Jewish Learning Materials [*A publication*]   (BJA)
CJLM .... Joliette, PQ [*AM radio station call letters*]
CJLMC ..... Chicago-Joliet Livestock Marketing Center   (EA)
CJLS.......... Yarmouth, NS [*AM radio station call letters*]
CJLS-FM-1 ... Shelbourne, NS [*FM radio station call letters*]

CJLS-FM-2 ... Digby, NS [*FM radio station call letters*]
CJLS/RCDS ... Canadian Journal of Law and Society/Revue Canadienne de Droit et Societe [*A publication*]
CJM............ Cell-Junctional Molecule [*Embryology*]
CJM............ Congregatio Jesu et Mariae [*Congregation of Jesus and Mary*] [*Eudist Fathers*] [*Roman Catholic religious order*]
CJM............ Congres Juif Mondial [*World Jewish Congress*]
CJM............ Johns-Manville Corp., Corporate Information Center, Denver, CO [*OCLC symbol*] (OCLC)
CJMA........ Communications Junction Module Assembly [*Ground Control Facility, NASA*]
CJMAA..... Canadian Journal of Mathematics [*A publication*]
CJ(Malta) ... Classical Journal (Malta) [*A publication*]
CJMBAE... Chinese Journal of Microbiology [*Later, Chinese Journal of Microbiology and Immunology*] [*A publication*]
CJMC........ Ste. Anne Des Monts, PQ [*AM radio station call letters*]
CJMCAG ... Conference on Jewish Material Claims Against Germany (EA)
CJMD........ Chibougamau, PQ [*AM radio station call letters*]
CJME........ Regina, SK [*AM radio station call letters*]
CJMED..... Chung-Ang Journal of Medicine [*A publication*]
CJMEDQ ... Chung-Ang Journal of Medicine [*A publication*]
CJMF-FM ... Quebec, PQ [*FM radio station call letters*]
CJMGA..... California Journal of Mines and Geology [*A publication*]
CJMG-FM ... Penticton, BC [*FM radio station call letters*]
CJMH........ Medicine Hat, AB [*AM radio station call letters*]
CJMIA ...... Canadian Journal of Microbiology [*A publication*]
CJMIAZ.... Canadian Journal of Microbiology [*A publication*]
CJMM-FM ... Rouyn-Noranda, PQ [*FM radio station call letters*]
CJMO-FM ... Moncton, NB [*FM radio station call letters*]
CJMR........ Mississauga, ON [*AM radio station call letters*]
CJMS........ Montreal, PQ [*AM radio station call letters*]
CJMSAV... Canadian Journal of Medical Science [*A publication*]
CJMT........ Chicoutimi, PQ [*AM radio station call letters*]
CJMTA ...... Canadian Journal of Medical Technology [*A publication*]
CJMTAY . Canadian Journal of Medical Technology [*A publication*]
CJMV-FM ... Val D'Or, PQ [*FM radio station call letters*]
CJMX-FM ... Sudbury, ON [*FM radio station call letters*]
CJN .... Caesars New Jersey, Inc. [*AMEX symbol*] (SPSG)
CJN .... Canadian Jewish News [*A publication*]
CJN .... Canadian Journal of Anthropology [*A publication*]
CJN .... Chelan Resources, Inc. [*Vancouver Stock Exchange symbol*]
CJN .... Chief Justice of Nigeria (DLA)
CJN .... Community of Jesus of Nazareth [*Anglican religious community*]
CJN .... Croissance de Jeunes Nations [*A publication*]
CJN .... El Cajon [*California*] [*Airport symbol*] [*Obsolete*] (OAG)
CJNB........ North Battleford, SK [*AM radio station call letters*]
CJNE........ Canadian Journal of Native Education [*A publication*]
CJNH........ Bancroft, ON [*AM radio station call letters*]
CJNL........ Merritt, BC [*AM radio station call letters*]
CJNR........ Blind River, ON [*AM radio station call letters*]
CJNS........ Canadian Journal of Native Studies [*A publication*]
CJNS........ Meadow Lake, SK [*AM radio station call letters*]
CJNSA2 .... Canadian Journal of Neurological Sciences [*A publication*]
CJO .... Chemical Journals Online [*American Chemical Society*] [*Database*]
CJO .... Communications Jamming Operator [*Military*]
CJO .... Corporate Jobs Outlook [*Information service or system*] (EISS)
CJO .... Council of Jewish Organizations in Civil Service
CJOA........ Canadian Journal on Aging [*A publication*]
CJOA........ Consortium of Jazz Organizations and Artists [*Later, AJA*] (EA)
CJOB........ Winnipeg, MB [*AM radio station call letters*]
CJOC........ Lethbridge, AB [*AM radio station call letters*]
CJOCS....... Council of Jewish Organizations in Civil Service (EA)
CJOEP...... Coordinated Joint Outline Emergency Plan [*Military*] (CINC)
CJOH-TV ... Ottawa, ON [*Television station call letters*]
CJOH-TV-6 ... Deseronto, ON [*Television station call letters*]
CJOH-TV-8 ... Cornwall, ON [*Television station call letters*]
CJOI.......... Wetaskiwin, AB [*AM radio station call letters*]
CJOK........ Fort McMurray, AB [*AM radio station call letters*]
CJOL........ Chinese Journal of Oceanology and Limnology [*A publication*]
CJOLAK ... Canadian Journal of Otolaryngology [*A publication*]
CJOM-FM ... Windsor, ON [*FM radio station call letters*]
CJON-TV ... St. John's, NF [*Television station call letters*]
CJOPA .... Chinese Journal of Physics [*Taipei*] [*A publication*]
CJORD...... Columbia Journalism Review [*A publication*]
CJOSD...... Chungnam Journal of Sciences [*A publication*]
CJOS-FM ... Gander, NF [*FM radio station call letters*]
CJOX-TV-1 ... Grand Bank, NF [*Television station call letters*]
CJOY........ Guelph, ON [*AM radio station call letters*]
CJOZ-FM ... Bonavista Bay, NF [*FM radio station call letters*]
CJP........... Canadian Journal of Psychology [*A publication*]
CJP........... Combined Jewish Philanthropies
CJP........... Communication Jamming Processor (IEEE)
CJP........... Cornu-Jellet Prism
CJPEA...... Canadian Journal of Public Health [*A publication*]
CJPEA4..... Canadian Journal of Public Health [*A publication*]
CJPF........ Corporation for Jefferson's Poplar Forest
CJPFA...... Coalition for Jobs, Peace, and Freedom in America (EA)
CJPH........ Canadian Journal of Public Health [*A publication*]

CJPHA..... Canadian Journal of Physics [*A publication*]
CJPHAD... Canadian Journal of Physics [*A publication*]
CJPhil........ Canadian Journal of Philosophy [*A publication*]
CJPI.......... Criminal Justice Periodical Index [*University Microfilms International*] [*Ann Arbor, MI*] [*Bibliographic database*] [*A publication*]
CJPM-TV ... Chicoutimi, PQ [*Television station call letters*]
CJPPA...... Canadian Journal of Physiology and Pharmacology [*A publication*]
CJPPA3..... Canadian Journal of Physiology and Pharmacology [*A publication*]
CJPR .... Blairmore, AB [*AM radio station call letters*]
CJPs .... Canadian Journal of Psychology [*A publication*]
CJPS.......... Carpenters and Joiners Protection Society [*A union*] [*British*]
CJPSA .... Canadian Journal of Psychology [*A publication*]
CJPSAC ... Canadian Journal of Psychology [*A publication*]
CJPST ...... Canadian Journal of Political and Social Theory [*A publication*]
CJPYA ...... Chinese Journal of Physiology [*A publication*]
CJQB........ Chief Justice of the Queen's Bench (DLA)
CJQM-FM ... Sault Ste. Marie, ON [*FM radio station call letters*]
CJR .... Chaurjahari [*Nepal*] [*Airport symbol*] (OAG)
CJR .... Chicago Journalism Review [*A publication*]
CJR .... Christian Jewish Relations [*A publication*]
CJR .... Colray Resources, Inc. [*Toronto Stock Exchange symbol*]
CJR .... Columbia Journalism Review [*A publication*]
CJR .... Contemporary Jewish Record [*New York*] [*A publication*]
CJR .... Secretariat for Catholic-Jewish Relations (EA)
CJR .... Study Centre for Christian-Jewish Relations [*Roman Catholic Church*] [*British*] (CB)
CJRB .... Boissevain, MB [*AM radio station call letters*]
CJRC .... Ottawa, ON [*AM radio station call letters*]
CJRE-FM ... Riviere Au Renard, PQ [*FM radio station call letters*]
CJRG-FM ... Gaspe, PQ [*FM radio station call letters*]
CJRL .... Criminal Justice Reference Library [*University of Texas*]
CJRL .... Kenora, ON [*AM radio station call letters*]
CJRMD7... Canadian Journal of Radiography, Radiotherapy, Nuclear Medicine [*English Edition*] [*A publication*]
CJRN .... Niagara Falls, ON [*AM radio station call letters*]
CJRP .... Quebec, PQ [*AM radio station call letters*]
CJRRU ...... Casey Jones Railroad Unit (EA)
CJRS .... Canadian Journal of Research in Semiotics [*A publication*]
CJRS .... Sherbrooke, PQ [*AM radio station call letters*]
CJRSC....... Chemical Journals of the Royal Society of Chemistry [*Great Britain*] [*Information service or system*] (CRD)
CJRT-FM ... Toronto, ON [*FM radio station call letters*]
CJRW........ Summerside, PE [*AM radio station call letters*]
CJS .... Canadian Jobs Strategy [*Employment and Immigration Canada program launched in 1986*]
CJS .... Canadian Joint Staff
CJS .... Center for Japanese Studies [*University of Michigan*] [*Research center*] (RCD)
CJS .... Center for Judicial Studies (EA)
CJS .... Centre for Journalism Studies [*British*] (CB)
CJS .... Ciudad Juarez [*Mexico*] [*Airport symbol*] (OAG)
CJS .... Cizi Jazyky ve Skole [*A publication*]
CJS .... Copper Jacketed Steel
CJS .... Corpus Juris Secundum [*A publication*]
CJS .... Cotton, Jute, or Sisal [*Freight*]
CJS .... Criminal Justice System
CJSA .... Costume Jewelry Salesmen's Association (EA)
CJSA .... Criminal Justice Statistics Association (EA)
CJSA .... Ste. Agathe Des Monts, PQ [*AM radio station call letters*]
CJSANS .... Committee on Joint Support of Air Navigation Services [*International Civil Aviation Organization*]
CJSB.......... Central Jersey Savings Bank SLA [*NASDAQ symbol*] (NQ)
CJSB.......... Ottawa, ON [*AM radio station call letters*]
CJSCDG.... Canadian Journal of Applied Sport Sciences [*A publication*]
CJSD-FM ... Thunder Bay, ON [*FM radio station call letters*]
CJSL.......... Estevan, SK [*AM radio station call letters*]
CJSMF....... Captain James Smith Memorial Foundation (EA)
CJSN .... Shaunavon, SK [*AM radio station call letters*]
CJSO-FM ... Sorel, PQ [*FM radio station call letters*]
CJSPA .... Conference of Jesuit Student Personnel Administrators [*Later, JASPA*] (EA)
CJSPAI ..... Canadian Journal of Spectroscopy [*A publication*]
CJSS.......... Conference on Jewish Social Studies (EA)
CJSS.......... Cornwall, ON [*AM radio station call letters*]
CJSSA .... Canadian Journal of Soil Science [*A publication*]
CJSSAR .... Canadian Journal of Soil Science [*A publication*]
CJSUA ...... Canadian Journal of Surgery [*A publication*]
CJSUAX.... Canadian Journal of Surgery [*A publication*]
CJSV-TV ... Stephenville, NF [*Television station call letters*]
CJT............ Canadian Journal of Theology [*A publication*]
CJT............ Civil Jet Transport
CJT............ Control Joint [*Technical drawings*]
CJT............ CTI Technologies Corp. [*Vancouver Stock Exchange symbol*]
CJTA .... Costume Jewelry Trade Association [*Defunct*]
CJTF.......... Commander, Joint Task Force
CJTF.......... Crossroads Joint Task Force [*Atomic weapons testing*]
CJTG.......... Commander, Joint Task Group
CJTN .... Trenton, ON [*AM radio station call letters*]

CJTR .... Trois-Rivieres, PQ [*AM radio station call letters*]
CJTT .... New Liskeard, ON [*AM radio station call letters*]
CJU............ Cheju [*South Korea*] [*Airport symbol*] (OAG)
CJU............ Chuan Hup Canada [*Vancouver Stock Exchange symbol*]
CJU............ Conjuntura Economica [*A publication*]
CJUADK... Contact. Journal of Urban and Environmental Affairs [*A publication*]
CJUB........ Chief Justice of the Common (Upper) Bench (DLA)
C Jud Proc ... Code of Judicial Procedure [*A publication*] (DLA)
C Jur Ind.... Code des Juridictions Indigenes [*A publication*]
CJV............ Charlie O Beverage [*Vancouver Stock Exchange symbol*]
CJVA .... Caraquet, NB [*AM radio station call letters*]
CJVB .... Vancouver, BC [*AM radio station call letters*]
CJVI .... Victoria, BC [*AM radio station call letters*]
CJVL .... Ste. Marie De Beauce, PQ [*AM radio station call letters*]
CJVR .... Melfort, SK [*AM radio station call letters*]
CJVS .... Cizi Jazyky ve Skole [*A publication*]
CJW........... Canyon Junction [*Wyoming*] [*Seismograph station code, US Geological Survey*] [*Closed*] (SEIS)
CJW........... Christian Jail Workers (EA)
CJW........... Columbia Journal of World Business [*A publication*]
CJWA .... Wawa, ON [*AM radio station call letters*]
CJWB .... Columbia Journal of World Business [*A publication*]
CJWB-TV ... Bonavista, NF [*Television station call letters*]
CJWILEY ... Chemical Journals of John Wiley & Sons [*John Wiley & Sons, Inc.*] [*Information service or system*] (CRD)
CJWN-TV ... Corner Brook, NF [*Television station call letters*]
CJWW........ Saskatoon, SK [*AM radio station call letters*]
CJX............ Canadian Jorex Ltd. [*Toronto Stock Exchange symbol*]
CJXX .... Grande Prairie, AB [*AM radio station call letters*]
CJY............ Utica, NY [*Location identifier*] [*FAA*] (FAAL)
CJYC-FM ... St. John, NB [*FM radio station call letters*]
CJYM........ Rosetown, SK [*AM radio station call letters*]
CJYQ......... St. John's, NF [*AM radio station call letters*]
CJYR .... Edson, AB [*AM radio station call letters*]
CJZ............ Cable Jacket Zipper
CJZ............ Canadian Journal of Zoology [*A publication*]
CJZOA .... Canadian Journal of Zoology [*A publication*]
CJZOAG.... Canadian Journal of Zoology [*A publication*]
CK .... Air Seychelles [*ICAO designator*] (FAAC)
CK .... Cake
CK .... Call Key [*Telecommunications*]
CK .... Calvin Klein [*Fashion designer, 1942-*]
CK .... Canada Packers, Inc. [*Toronto Stock Exchange symbol*]
CK .... Canine Kidney [*Physiology*]
CK .... Cape Kennedy [*NASA*] (KSC)
CK .... Carnal Knowledge [*FBI standardized term*]
C & K .... Carrington and Kirwan's English Nisi Prius Reports [*174, 175 English Reprint*] [*A publication*] (DLA)
CK .... Cask
Ck .... Chalk [*Quality of the bottom*] [*Nautical charts*]
CK .... Check (AFM)
CK .... Chesterfield Kings [*An association*] (EA)
CK .... Chicago-Kent Law Review [*A publication*]
CK .... Chicken Kidney
CK .... Choline Kinase [*An enzyme*]
CK .... Clerk (ROG)
CK .... Clock
ck .... Colombia [*ucu (United States Miscellaneous Caribbean Islands) used in records cataloged before January 1978*] [*MARC country of publication code*] [*Library of Congress*] (LCCP)
CK .... Console Keyset (MCD)
CK .... Construction Keyed Lock (ADA)
C-K............. Contact Karate
CK .... Conversion Kit (MCD)
CK .... Cook [*Navy*] [*British*]
CK .... Cook Islands [*ANSI two-letter standard code*] (CNC)
CK .... Cookery Officer [*Navy*] [*British*]
CK .... Cork (MSA)
CK .... Creatine Kinase [*Also, CPK*] [*An enzyme*]
CK .... Creek (ADA)
CK .... Crystal Kit
C to K .... Curious to Know [*An inquisitive customer*] [*Merchandising slang*]
CK .... Cyanogen Chloride [*Poison gas*] [*Army symbol*]
C the K .... Cyrus the King [*Freemasonry*] (ROG)
CK .... Cytokeratin [*Cytology*]
CK .... Cytokinin [*Biochemistry*]
CK .... King City Public Library, King City, CA [*Library symbol*] [*Library of Congress*] (LCLS)
CK .... This Is a Circuit-Continuity-Check Transmission [*Aviation code*] (FAAC)
CKA .... Catholic Knights of America (EA)
CKA .... Cherokee, OK [*Location identifier*] [*FAA*] (FAAL)
CKA .... Condaka Metals Corp. [*Vancouver Stock Exchange symbol*]
CKA .... Cook Inlet Aviation, Inc. [*Homer, AK*] [*FAA designator*] (FAAC)
CKAC .... Montreal, PQ [*AM radio station call letters*]
CKAD .... Middleton, NS [*AM radio station call letters*]
CKAFS ...... Cape Kennedy Air Force Station

CKAL-FM-1 ... Nakusp, BC [*FM radio station call letters*]
CKAL-FM-2 ... New Denver, BC [*FM radio station call letters*]
CKAL-FM-3 ... Kaslo, BC [*FM radio station call letters*]
CKAL-FM-4 ... Enderby, BC [*FM radio station call letters*]
CKAM-TV ... Upsalquitch Lake, NB [*Television station call letters*]
CKAN........ Newmarket, ON [*AM radio station call letters*]
CKAO........ Coalition to Keep Alaska Oil (EA)
CKAP58..... Kapuskasing, ON [*AM radio station call letters*]
CKAR .... Oshawa, ON [*AM radio station call letters*]
CKAT-FM ... North Bay, ON [*FM radio station call letters*]
CKAY .... Duncan, BC [*AM radio station call letters*]
CKB .... Cacquot Kite Balloon
CKB .... Carling O'Keefe Breweries of Canada Ltd. [*NYSE symbol*] [*Toronto Stock Exchange symbol*] [*Vancouver Stock Exchange symbol*] (SPSG)
CKB .... Clarksburg [*West Virginia*] [*Airport symbol*] (OAG)
CKB .... Clarksburg, WV [*Location identifier*] [*FAA*] (FAAL)
CKB .... Cork Base
CKBA........ Athabasca, AB [*AM radio station call letters*]
CKBB........ Barrie, ON [*AM radio station call letters*]
CKBC........ Bathurst, NB [*AM radio station call letters*]
CKBD .... Cork Board (AAG)
CKBG-FM ... Bracebridge, ON [*FM radio station call letters*]
CKBI......... Prince Albert, SK [*AM radio station call letters*]
CKBI-TV.... Prince Albert, SK [*Television station call letters*]
CKBI-TV-3 ... Greenwater Lake, SK [*Television station call letters*]
CKBQ-TV ... Melfort, SK [*Television station call letters*]
CKBS........ St. Hyacinthe, PQ [*AM radio station call letters*]
CKBT-1 ..... Moose Jaw, SK [*Television station call letters*]
CKBW .... Bridgewater, NS [*AM radio station call letters*]
CKBW-FM-1 ... Liverpool, NS [*FM radio station call letters*]
CKBW-FM-2 ... Shelburne, NS [*FM radio station call letters*]
CKBX........ 100 Mile House, BC [*AM radio station call letters*]
CKBY-FM ... Ottawa, ON [*FM radio station call letters*]
CKC .... California Kiwifruit Commission (EA)
CKC .... Canadian Kennel Club
CKC .... Canuck Resources Corporation [*Vancouver Stock Exchange symbol*]
CKC .... Kings County Free Library, Hanford, CA [*OCLC symbol*] (OCLC)
CKCB........ Collingwood, ON [*AM radio station call letters*]
CKCD-TV ... Campbellton, NB [*Television station call letters*]
CKCFA ...... Ceskoslovensky Casopis pro Fysiku [*A publication*]
CKCH .... Hull, PQ [*AM radio station call letters*]
CKCK........ Regina, SK [*AM radio station call letters*]
CKCKD..... Chung-Kuo Kung Ch'eng Hsueh K'an [*A publication*]
CKCK-TV ... Regina, SK [*Television station call letters*]
CKCK-TV-1 ... Colgate, SK [*Television station call letters*]
CKCK-TV-2 ... Willow Bunch, SK [*Television station call letters*]
CKCL........ Chicago-Kent College of Law
CKCL........ Truro, NS [*AM radio station call letters*]
CKCM .... Grand Falls, NF [*AM radio station call letters*]
CKCN .... Sept-Iles, PQ [*AM radio station call letters*]
CKCO-TV ... Kitchener, ON [*Television station call letters*]
CKCO-TV-2 ... Wiarton, ON [*Television station call letters*]
CKCO-TV-3 ... Sarnia, ON [*Television station call letters*]
CKCO-TV-4 ... [*The*] Muskokas, ON [*Television station call letters*]
CKCP........ CYBERTEK Corp. [*NASDAQ symbol*] (NQ)
CKCQ........ Quesnel, BC [*AM radio station call letters*]
CKCR........ Revelstoke, BC [*AM radio station call letters*]
CKCSC...... Cavalier King Charles Spaniel Club of America (EA)
CKCU-FM ... Ottawa, ON [*FM radio station call letters*]
CKCV........ Quebec, PQ [*AM radio station call letters*]
CKCW .... Moncton, NB [*AM radio station call letters*]
CKCW-TV ... Moncton, NB [*Television station call letters*]
CKCW-TV-1 ... Charlottetown, PE [*Television station call letters*]
CKCW-TV-2 ... St. Edward, PE [*Television station call letters*]
CKCY........ Sault Ste. Marie, ON [*AM radio station call letters*]
CKD .... Casopis Katolickeho Duckovenstva a Prilohou [*A publication*]
CKD .... Certified Kitchen Designer
CKD .... Chambre de Commerce et d'Industrie. Republique Populaire du Benin. Bulletin Hebdomadaire d'Information et de Documentation [*A publication*]
CKD .... Completely Knocked Down [*i.e., disassembled, as a toy or piece of furniture which must be assembled before use*] [*Freight*]
CKD .... Cooked
CKD .... Count-Key-Data Device [*Data processing*]
CKD .... Crooked Creek [*Alaska*] [*Airport symbol*] (OAG)
CKD .... Crooked Creek, AK [*Location identifier*] [*FAA*] (FAAL)
CKDA .... Victoria, BC [*AM radio station call letters*]
CKDH........ Amherst, NS [*AM radio station call letters*]
CKDK-FM ... Woodstock, ON [*FM radio station call letters*]
CKDM........ Dauphin, MB [*AM radio station call letters*]
CKDN........ Circadian, Inc. [*San Jose, CA*] [*NASDAQ symbol*] (NQ)
CKDQ........ Drumheller, AB [*AM radio station call letters*]
CKDR........ Dryden, ON [*AM radio station call letters*]
CKDS-FM ... Hamilton, ON [*FM radio station call letters*]
CKDU-FM ... Halifax, NS [*FM radio station call letters*]
CKDY........ Digby, NS [*AM radio station call letters*]
CKE .... Canalaska Resources Ltd. [*Vancouver Stock Exchange symbol*]
CKE .... Castle & Cooke, Inc. [*NYSE symbol*] (SPSG)

CKEC........ New Glasgow, NS [*AM radio station call letters*]
CKEG........ Nanaimo, BC [*AM radio station call letters*]
CKEK........ Cranbrook, BC [*AM radio station call letters*]
CKel.......... Kelseyville Free Library, Kelseyville, CA [*Library symbol*] [*Library of Congress*] (LCLS)
CKEN........ Kentville, NS [*AM radio station call letters*]
CKenM....... College of Marin, Kentfield, CA [*Library symbol*] [*Library of Congress*] (LCLS)
CKER......... Edmonton, AB [*AM radio station call letters*]
CKEY......... Toronto, ON [*AM radio station call letters*]
CKF............ Canadian Fiber Foods [*Vancouver Stock Exchange symbol*]
CKF............ Centerns Kvinnoforbund [*Women's Association of the Centre Party*] [*Sweden*] [*Political party*] (EAIO)
CKF............ Check Fixture (MCD)
CKF............ Christ the King Foundation [*Defunct*] (EA)
CKF............ Cork Floor (AAG)
CK of FC..... Carnal Knowledge of Female Child [*FBI standardized term*]
CKFC.......... Cub Koda Fan Club (EA)
CKFF.......... Cape Kennedy Forecast Facility [*NASA*] (KSC)
CKFL.......... Lac Megantic, PQ [*AM radio station call letters*]
CKFM......... Check Form [*Tool*] (AAG)
CKFM-FM ... Toronto, ON [*FM radio station call letters*]
CKG........... Chongqing [*China*] [*Airport symbol*] (OAG)
C/KG.......... Coulombs per Kilogram
CKGA......... Check Gauge [*Tool*] (AAG)
CKGA........ Gander, NF [*AM radio station call letters*]
CKGB......... Timmins, ON [*AM radio station call letters*]
CKGF.......... Grand Forks, BC [*AM radio station call letters*]
CKGL-FM ... Kitchener, ON [*FM radio station call letters*]
CKGO........ Hope, BC [*AM radio station call letters*]
CKGO-FM-1 ... Boston Bar, BC [*FM radio station call letters*]
CKGR......... Golden, BC [*AM radio station call letters*]
CKGY......... Red Deer, AB [*AM radio station call letters*]
CKH........... Koko Head, HI [*Location identifier*] [*FAA*] (FAAL)
CKHJ-FM ... Fredericton, NB [*FM radio station call letters*]
CKHMA..... Chung-Kuo Hsu Mu Shou I [*A publication*]
CKHP-TV ... Grouard Mission, AB [*Television station call letters*]
CKHP-TV-1 ... Slave Lake, AB [*Television station call letters*]
CKHR-FM ... Hay River, NT [*FM radio station call letters*]
CKI............ Central Bank of Ireland. Quarterly Bulletin [*A publication*]
CKI............ Check Issued
CKI............ Child Keyppers' International (EA)
CKI............ Circle K International (EA)
CKI............ Consolidated Stikine Silver Ltd. [*Vancouver Stock Exchange symbol*]
CKI............ Kingstree, SC [*Location identifier*] [*FAA*] (FAAL)
CKIA-FM ... Quebec, PQ [*FM radio station call letters*]
CKIC.......... Chemical Kinetics Information Center [*National Institute of Standards and Technology*]
CKIK-FM .. Calgary, AB [*FM radio station call letters*]
CKIM........ Baie Verte, NF [*AM radio station call letters*]
CKIQ......... Kelowna, BC [*AM radio station call letters*]
CKIQ-FM ... Kelowna, BC [*FM radio station call letters*]
CKIS.......... Catholic Knights Insurance Society (EA)
CKIS-FM .. Winnipeg, MB [*FM radio station call letters*]
CKIT-FM .. Regina, SK [*FM radio station call letters*]
CKIX-FM ... St. John's, NF [*FM radio station call letters*]
CKJS......... Winnipeg, MB [*AM radio station call letters*]
CKK........... Chekok [*Alaska*] [*Seismograph station code, US Geological Survey*] (SEIS)
CKK........... Miami, FL [*Location identifier*] [*FAA*] (FAAL)
CKKC........ Nelson, BC [*AM radio station call letters*]
CKKC-FM ... Nelson, BC [*FM radio station call letters*]
CKKKA...... Cho-Koon Kenkyu [*A publication*]
CKKM-TV ... Oliver/Osoyoos, BC [*Television station call letters*]
CKKQ-FM ... Victoria, BC [*FM radio station call letters*]
CKKS-FM ... Vancouver, BC [*FM radio station call letters*]
CKKW....... Kitchener, ON [*AM radio station call letters*]
CKL........... CEL Industry Ltd. [*Vancouver Stock Exchange symbol*]
CKL........... Centreville, AL [*Location identifier*] [*FAA*] (FAAL)
CKL........... Chickasaw Library System, Ardmore, OK [*OCLC symbol*] (OCLC)
CKL........... Clark Equipment Co. [*NYSE symbol*] (SPSG)
CKLA-FM ... Guelph, ON [*FM radio station call letters*]
CKLC......... Kingston, ON [*AM radio station call letters*]
CKLD......... Thetford Mines, PQ [*AM radio station call letters*]
CKLG......... Vancouver, BC [*AM radio station call letters*]
CKLH-FM ... Hamilton, ON [*FM radio station call letters*]
CKLM........ Laval, PQ [*AM radio station call letters*]
CKLP-FM ... Parry Sound, ON [*FM radio station call letters*]
CKLQ......... Brandon, MB [*AM radio station call letters*]
CKLR......... Chicago-Kent Law Review [*A publication*]
CKLR......... L'Annonciation, PQ [*AM radio station call letters*]
CKLS......... Central Kansas Library System [*Library network*]
CKLS......... La Sarre, PQ [*AM radio station call letters*]
CKLT-TV ... Saint John, NB [*Television station call letters*]
CKLW........ Windsor, ON [*AM radio station call letters*]
CKLY......... Lindsay, ON [*AM radio station call letters*]
CKLZ-FM ... Kelowna, BC [*FM radio station call letters*]
CKM........... Checkmate Resources [*Vancouver Stock Exchange symbol*]
CKM........... Clark University, Worcester, MA [*OCLC symbol*] (OCLC)

CKM.......... Clarksdale, MS [*Location identifier*] [*FAA*] (FAAL)
CKM.......... Coopers Lake [*Montana*] [*Seismograph station code, US Geological Survey*] [*Closed*] (SEIS)
CKMC-TV ... Swift Current, SK [*Television station call letters*]
CKMC-TV-1 ... Golden Prairie, SK [*Television station call letters*]
CKMF-FM ... Montreal, PQ [*FM radio station call letters*]
CKMG...... Maniwacki, PQ [*AM radio station call letters*]
CKMIC...... Class and Kind Made in Canada [*Business term*]
CKMI-TV ... Quebec City, PQ [*Television station call letters*]
CKMJ-TV ... Marquis, SK [*Television station call letters*]
CKMK........ Mackenzie, BC [*AM radio station call letters*]
CKMP......... Midland, ON [*AM radio station call letters*]
CKMR-FM ... Windsor, ON [*FM radio station call letters*]
CKMS-FM ... Waterloo, ON [*FM radio station call letters*]
CKMTA...... Cape Kennedy Missile Test Annex [*NASA*] (KSC)
CKMV........ Grand Falls, NB [*AM radio station call letters*]
CKMW...... Winkler-Morden, MB [*AM radio station call letters*]
CKN........... Chambre de Commerce, d'Agriculture, et d'Industrie du Niger. Bulletin [*A publication*]
CKN........... Consolidated Nord Resources Ltd. [*Vancouver Stock Exchange symbol*]
CKN........... Crookston, MN [*Location identifier*] [*FAA*] (FAAL)
CKNB......... Campbellton, NB [*AM radio station call letters*]
CKNC-TV ... Sudbury, ON [*Television station call letters*]
CKNC-TV-1 ... Elliot Lake, ON [*Television station call letters*]
CKND-TV ... Winnipeg, MB [*Television station call letters*]
CKND-TV-2 ... Minnedosa, MB [*Television station call letters*]
CKNG-FM ... Edmonton, AB [*FM radio station call letters*]
CKNHA..... Chung-Kuo Nung Yeh Hua Hsueh Hui Chih [*Journal of the Chinese Agriculture Chemical Society*] [*A publication*]
CKNKD..... Chikyukagaku (Nippon Chikyu Kagakkai) [*A publication*]
CKNKDM ... Geochemistry [*A publication*]
CKNL........ Fort St. John, BC [*AM radio station call letters*]
CKNM-FM ... Yellowknife, NT [*FM radio station call letters*]
CKNMIC.... Class and Kind Not Made in Canada [*Business term*]
CKNR......... Elliott Lake, ON [*AM radio station call letters*]
CKNS......... Espanola, ON [*AM radio station call letters*]
CKNSA...... Chiba-Ken Nogyo Shikenjo Kenkyu Hokoku [*A publication*]
CKNW....... New Westminster, BC [*AM radio station call letters*]
CKNX......... Wingham, ON [*AM radio station call letters*]
CKNX-FM ... Wingham, ON [*FM radio station call letters*]
CKNX-TV ... Wingham, ON [*Television station call letters*]
CKNYA...... Chung-Kuo Nung Yeh K'o Hsueh [*Scientia Agricultura Sinica*] [*A publication*]
CKNY-TV ... North Bay, ON [*Television station call letters*]
CKO........... Check Operator (DEN)
CKO........... Consolidated Knobby Lake Mines Ltd. [*Vancouver Stock Exchange symbol*]
CKO........... Cornelio Procopio [*Brazil*] [*Airport symbol*] (OAG)
CKO........... Pointe Claire, PQ [*AM radio station call letters*]
CKOA........ Arnprior, ON [*AM radio station call letters*]
CKOB......... Renfrew, ON [*AM radio station call letters*]
CKOC......... Hamilton, ON [*AM radio station call letters*]
CKO-FM-1 ... Ottawa, ON [*FM radio station call letters*]
CKO-FM-2 ... Toronto, ON [*FM radio station call letters*]
CKO-FM-3 ... London, ON [*FM radio station call letters*]
CKO-FM-4 ... Vancouver, BC [*FM radio station call letters*]
CKO-FM-5 ... Calgary, AB [*FM radio station call letters*]
CKO-FM-6 ... Edmonton, AB [*FM radio station call letters*]
CKO-FM-7 ... Winnipeg, MB [*FM radio station call letters*]
CKO-FM-9 ... Halifax, NS [*FM radio station call letters*]
CKOI-FM ... Verdun, PQ [*FM radio station call letters*]
CKOK......... Penticton, BC [*AM radio station call letters*]
CKOM........ Saskatoon, SK [*AM radio station call letters*]
CKON-FM ... Akwesasne, ON [*FM radio station call letters*]
CKOO......... Osoyoos, BC [*AM radio station call letters*]
CKOS-TV ... Yorkton, SK [*Television station call letters*]
CKOT........ Tillsonburg, ON [*AM radio station call letters*]
CKOT-FM ... Tillsonburg, ON [*FM radio station call letters*]
CKOUT ..... Checkout
CKOV........ Kelowna, BC [*AM radio station call letters*]
CKOZ-FM ... Corner Brook, NF [*FM radio station call letters*]
CKP........... Cayley-Klein Parameter [*Mathematics*]
CKP........... Central Bank of Cyprus. Bulletin [*A publication*]
CKP........... Cherokee, IA [*Location identifier*] [*FAA*] (FAAL)
CKP........... [*The*] Circle K Corp. [*NYSE symbol*] (SPSG)
CKP........... Consolidated Pace II Industries Ltd. [*Vancouver Stock Exchange symbol*]
CKPC........ Brantford, ON [*AM radio station call letters*]
CKPC-FM ... Brantford, ON [*FM radio station call letters*]
CKPE-FM ... Sydney, NS [*FM radio station call letters*]
CKPG........ Containerboard and Kraft Paper Group (EA)
CKPG........ Prince George, BC [*AM radio station call letters*]
CKPG-TV ... Prince George, BC [*Television station call letters*]
CKPR........ Thunder Bay, ON [*AM radio station call letters*]
CKPR-TV... Thunder Bay, ON [*Television station call letters*]
CKPT........ Checkpoint (MCD)
CKPT........ Cockpit
CKPT........ Peterborough, ON [*AM radio station call letters*]
CKQM-FM ... Peterborough, ON [*FM radio station call letters*]
CKQN-FM ... Baker Lake, NT [*FM radio station call letters*]

CKQR....... Castlegar, BC [*AM radio station call letters*]
CKQT-FM ... Oshawa, ON [*FM radio station call letters*]
CKR .... Check Received
CKR .... Chesapeake Computer [*Vancouver Stock Exchange symbol*]
CKR .... Cometary Kilometric Radiation [*Astrophysics*]
CKRA .... Cape Kennedy Reference Atmosphere [*Later, CCRA*] [*NASA*]   (NASA)
CKRA-FM ... Edmonton, AB [*FM radio station call letters*]
CKRB......... CheckRobot, Inc. [*Deerfield Beach, FL*] [*NASDAQ symbol*]   (NQ)
CKRB......... St. Georges De Beauce, PQ [*AM radio station call letters*]
CKRC......... Council of the Knights of the Red Cross [*Freemasonry*]   (ROG)
CKRC......... Winnipeg, MB [*AM radio station call letters*]
CKRD .... Red Deer, AB [*AM radio station call letters*]
CKRD-TV ... Red Deer, AB [*Television station call letters*]
CKRD-TV-1 ... Coronation, AB [*Television station call letters*]
CKRE .... Red Lake, ON [*AM radio station call letters*]
CKRK-FM ... Kahnawake, PQ [*FM radio station call letters*]
CKRL-FM ... Quebec, PQ [*FM radio station call letters*]
CKRM .... Regina, SK [*AM radio station call letters*]
CKRN .... Rouyn, PQ [*AM radio station call letters*]
CKRN-TV ... Rouyn, PQ [*Television station call letters*]
CKRN-TV-3 ... Bearn-Fabre, PQ [*Television station call letters*]
CKRP......... Princeton, BC [*AM radio station call letters*]
CKRS......... Jonquiere, PQ [*AM radio station call letters*]
CKRSO...... Cape Kennedy Range Safety Officer [*NASA*]   (KSC)
CKRS-TV .. Jonquiere, PQ [*Television station call letters*]
CKRT-TV ... Riviere-Du-Loup, PQ [*Television station call letters*]
CKRW .... Whitehorse, YT [*AM radio station call letters*]
CKRY-FM ... Calgary, AB [*FM radio station call letters*]
CKS........... Cell Kinetics Society   (EA)
CKS........... Centistokes [*Unit of kinematic viscosity*]
CKS........... Chiang Kai-shek
CKS........... Chicago, Kalamazoo & Saginaw Railway [*AAR code*]
CKS........... Christian Knowledge Society [*Also known as Society for Promoting Christian Knowledge*]
CKS........... Connie Kalitta Services, Inc. [*Ypsilanti, MI*] [*FAA designator*]   (FAAC)
CKS........... Coseka Resources Ltd. [*Toronto Stock Exchange symbol*]
CKSA........ Catholic Kolping Society of America   (EA)
CKSA........ Lloydminster, AB [*AM radio station call letters*]
CKSA-TV .. Lloydminster, AB [*Television station call letters*]
CKSA-TV-2 ... Bonnyville, AB [*Television station call letters*]
CKSB........ CK Federal Savings Bank [*NASDAQ symbol*]   (NQ)
CKSB........ St. Boniface, MB [*AM radio station call letters*]
CKSB-FM-6 ... Dryden, ON [*FM radio station call letters*]
CKSCDN... Journal. Chinese Society of Veterinary Science [*A publication*]
CKSG........ Catholic Knights of St. George   (EA)
CKSH-TV ... Sherbrooke, PQ [*Television station call letters*]
CKSL........ London, ON [*AM radio station call letters*]
CKSM........ Shawinigan, PQ [*AM radio station call letters*]
CKSNI....... Cape Kennedy Space Network, Incorporated [*NASA*]
CKSO .... Condon, Kinzua & Southern Railroad Co. [*AAR code*]
CKSO .... Sudbury, ON [*AM radio station call letters*]
CKSP .... Summerland, BC [*AM radio station call letters*]
CKSQ........ Stettler, AB [*AM radio station call letters*]
CKSR-FM ... Chilliwack, BC [*FM radio station call letters*]
CKSS-FM ... Red Rocks, NF [*FM radio station call letters*]
CKST .... Langley, BC [*AM radio station call letters*]
CKSW........ Swift Current, SK [*AM radio station call letters*]
CKSY-FM ... Chatham, ON [*FM radio station call letters*]
CKT .... Cape Resources, Inc. [*Vancouver Stock Exchange symbol*]
CKT .... Check Template
CKT .... Circuit   (AAG)
CKT .... Commandery of Knights Templar [*Freemasonry*]   (ROG)
CKTB........ St. Catharines, ON [*AM radio station call letters*]
CKT BKR .. Circuit Breaker   (MSA)
CKTF........ Circuit Finder   (MSA)
CKT-ID...... Circuit Identification [*Telecommunications*]   (TEL)
CKTK........ Kitimat, BC [*AM radio station call letters*]
CKTL........ Plessisville, PQ [*AM radio station call letters*]
CKTM-TV ... Trois-Rivieres, PQ [*Television station call letters*]
CKTND ..... Chayon Kwahak Taehak Nomunjip [*A publication*]
CKTNDR... Proceedings. College of Natural Sciences [*Seoul*] [*A publication*]
CKTN-TV ... Trail, BC [*Television station call letters*]
CKTO-FM ... Truro, NS [*FM radio station call letters*]
CKTS......... Sherbrooke, PQ [*AM radio station call letters*]
CKTY......... Sarnia, ON [*AM radio station call letters*]
CKU........... Cordova, AK [*Location identifier*] [*FAA*]   (FAAL)
CKUA .... Edmonton, AB [*AM radio station call letters*]
CKUA-FM ... Edmonton, AB [*FM radio station call letters*]
CKUA-FM-1 ... Calgary, AB [*FM radio station call letters*]
CKUA-FM-2 ... Lethbridge, AB [*FM radio station call letters*]
CKUA-FM-3 ... Medicine Hat, AB [*FM radio station call letters*]
CKUA-FM-4 ... Grande Prairie, AB [*FM radio station call letters*]
CKUA-FM-5 ... Peace River, AB [*FM radio station call letters*]
CKUA-FM-6 ... Red Deer, AB [*FM radio station call letters*]
CKUA-FM-13 ... Drumheller, AB [*FM radio station call letters*]
CKUT .... Wollaston Lake, SK [*AM radio station call letters*]
CKV........... Chelik Resources, Inc. [*Vancouver Stock Exchange symbol*]
CKV........... Clarksville [*Tennessee*] [*Airport symbol*]   (OAG)

CKV .... Clarksville, TN [*Location identifier*] [*FAA*]   (FAAL)
CKVD .... Val-D'Or, PQ [*AM radio station call letters*]
CKVH........ High Prairie, AB [*AM radio station call letters*]
CKVL........ Verdun, PQ [*AM radio station call letters*]
CKVM .... Ville-Marie, PQ [*AM radio station call letters*]
CKVO .... Clarenville, NF [*AM radio station call letters*]
CKVR-TV ... Barrie, ON [*Television station call letters*]
CKVT........ Temiscaming, PQ [*AM radio station call letters*]
CKVU-TV ... Vancouver, BC [*Television station call letters*]
CKW .... Cherokee, WY [*Location identifier*] [*FAA*]   (FAAL)
CKW .... Clockwise   (ADA)
CKW .... [A] New Translation in Plain English (1963) [*Charles K. Williams*] [*A publication*]   (BJA)
CKWA .... Slave Lake, AB [*AM radio station call letters*]
CKWCD9 .. Chinese Journal of Microbiology and Immunology [*Taipei*] [*A publication*]
CKWFC..... Cheryl K. Warner Fan Club   (EA)
CKWK .... Corner Brook, NF [*AM radio station call letters*]
CKWL........ Williams Lake, BC [*AM radio station call letters*]
CKWM-FM ... Kentville, NS [*FM radio station call letters*]
CKWR-FM ... Kitchener, ON [*FM radio station call letters*]
CKWS-TV ... Kingston, ON [*Television station call letters*]
CKWW ...... Windsor, ON [*AM radio station call letters*]
CKWX .... Vancouver, BC [*AM radio station call letters*]
CKX .... Brandon, MB [*AM radio station call letters*]
CKX .... Chicken, AK [*Location identifier*] [*FAA*]   (FAAL)
CKX .... Copper Lake Explorations Ltd. [*Vancouver Stock Exchange symbol*]
CKX-FM.... Brandon, MB [*FM radio station call letters*]
CKXM-FM ... Edmonton, AB [*FM radio station call letters*]
CKXR........ Salmon Arm, BC [*AM radio station call letters*]
CKX-TV..... Brandon, MB [*Television station call letters*]
CKX-TV-1 ... Foxwarren, MB [*Television station call letters*]
CKXY........ Vancouver, BC [*AM radio station call letters*]
CKY .... Conakry [*Guinea*] [*Airport symbol*]   (OAG)
CKY .... Consolidated McKinney Resources, Inc. [*Vancouver Stock Exchange symbol*]
CKY .... Winnipeg, MB [*AM radio station call letters*]
CKYB-TV ... Brandon, MB [*Television station call letters*]
CKYL........ Peace River, AB [*AM radio station call letters*]
CKYQ .... Grand Bank, NF [*AM radio station call letters*]
CKYR........ Jasper, AB [*AM radio station call letters*]
CKYR-1 ..... Grand Cache, AB [*AM radio station call letters*]
CKY-TV..... Winnipeg, MB [*Television station call letters*]
CKYW .... Chung-Kuo Yu-Wen [*A publication*]
CKYX-FM ... Fort McMurray, AB [*FM radio station call letters*]
CL .... Cabbage Looper [*Entomology*]
C & L........ Cagney and Lacey [*Television series*]
C-L .... Cain-Levine Social Competency Scale [*Psychology*]
CL .... Calamus Length
C-L .... California State Law Library, Sacramento, CA [*Library symbol*] [*Library of Congress*]   (LCLS)
CL .... Call Loan [*Banking*]
CL .... Canadair Limited [*Canada*] [*ICAO aircraft manufacturer identifier*]   (ICAO)
C and L ...... Canal and Lake
CL .... Canron, Inc. [*Toronto Stock Exchange symbol*]
CL .... Capital Loss [*Accounting*]
CL .... Capitol Air, Inc. [*ICAO designator*]   (FAAC)
CL .... Capitol International Airways [*ICAO designator*]   (FAAC)
CL .... Carapace Length [*Pisciculture*]
CL .... Cardiolipin [*Immunochemistry*]
CL .... Carload Lot [*Commerce*]
CL .... Carted Luggage   (ROG)
C/L............ Cash Letter [*Banking*]
CL .... Cathodoluminescence [*Geophysics*]
CL .... Ceiling Level
CL .... Cell Line [*Cytology*]
CL .... Celtic League [*Peel, Isle of Man, England*]   (EAIO)
CL .... Center of Lift
CL .... Center Line
CL .... Centiliter   (GPO)
CL .... Central Laboratory
CL .... Central Line
CL .... Centralis Lateralis [*Neuroanatomy*]
CL .... Centrolateral [*Nucleus of thalamus*] [*Neuroanatomy*]
CL .... Ceska Literatura [*A publication*]
CL .... Ceylon [*Sri Lanka*]
CL .... Change List
CL .... Chartered Librarian [*British*]
C/L............ Chator-Lea Sidecar [*Early motorcars*]   (ROG)
C/L............ Checklist   (KSC)
C/L............ Chemical Laboratory
CL .... Chemical LASER   (MCD)
CL .... Chemical Literature [*A publication*]
CL .... Chemiluminescence
CL .... Chest and Left Arm [*Cardiology*]
C of L .... Children of Light [*Freemasonry*]   (ROG)
CL .... Chile [*ANSI two-letter standard code*]   (CNC)
cl................ Chile [*MARC country of publication code*] [*Library of Congress*]   (LCCP)

CL..............	Chinese Literature [*A publication*]
Cl...............	Chlorine [*Chemical element*]
Cl...............	Chlorite [*A mineral*]
cl................	Chloro [*As substituent on nucleoside*] [*Biochemistry*]
CL..............	Christian Life [*A publication*]
C and L	Christianity and Literature [*A publication*]
C and L	Christianity and Literature [*A publication*]
CL..............	Christos Lavatus [*An association*] (EA)
CL..............	Churchman's Library [*A publication*]
CL..............	Chutz La'aretz (BJA)
CL..............	Cilium [*Zoology*]
CL..............	Circuit Layout [*AT & T*]
CL..............	Circular Letter
CL..............	City of London [*British*]
C of L	City of London [*British*]
CL..............	Civil Law
CL..............	Civil Liberties (ILCA)
CL..............	Clandestine Lodges [*Freemasonry*] (ROG)
CL..............	Clarendon Laboratory [*Oxford University*] (MCD)
cl................	Claret [*Philately*]
CL..............	Clarinet
CL..............	Class (AFM)
CL..............	Classical
Cl...............	Classical Strain [*Of RNA*]
CL..............	Classics (ADA)
CL..............	Classification
CL..............	Clause
CL..............	Clavicle [*Anatomy*]
Cl...............	Clavier [*A publication*]
Cl...............	Clavileno [*A publication*]
Cl...............	Clay [*Quality of the bottom*] [*Nautical charts*]
CL..............	Cleaner [*Automotive engineering*]
CL..............	Clear
CL..............	Clear Liquid [*Medicine*]
CL..............	Clearance (MSA)
CL..............	Cleistogamous [*Botany*]
CL..............	Clergy
CL..............	Clerical Aptitude Area (AABC)
CL..............	Clerk
CL..............	Cliff Leader [*British military*] (DMA)
CL..............	Climatic Laboratory [*Military*]
Cl...............	Clinic
CL..............	Clip (MSA)
Cl...............	Clone
CL..............	Close (AAG)
CL..............	Close Rolls [*British*]
CL..............	Closed Loop (KSC)
CL..............	Closet
CL..............	Closing Station (FAAC)
Cl...............	Clostridium [*Genus of microorganisms*]
CL..............	Closure [*Physiology*]
CL..............	Cloth
CL..............	Clove [*Seven pounds*] [*Unit of weight*] [*British*] (ROG)
CL..............	Cluster (NASA)
CL..............	Clutch (MSA)
CL..............	Coalition for Literacy (EA)
CL..............	Codex Leningradensis (BJA)
CL..............	Coefficient of Lift
CL..............	Coil
CL..............	Col Legno [*With the Back of the Bow*] [*Music*]
CL..............	Colgate-Palmolive Co. [*NYSE symbol*] (SPSG)
CL..............	Colistin [*Also, CO*] [*Generic form*] [*An antibiotic*]
CL..............	Collection Entry [*Banking*]
CL..............	College Letter [*British*]
CL..............	Combat and Liaison (CINC)
C/L.............	Combat Loss
C/L.............	Combined Limit [*Insurance*]
CL..............	Command Language
CL..............	Commander of the Order of Leopold
CL..............	Commercial List [*Australia*]
CL..............	Commission Leaflets, American Telephone and Telegraph Cases [*A publication*] (DLA)
CL..............	Common Law
CL..............	Common Law Reports [*1853-85*] [*A publication*] (DLA)
CL..............	Communication Lieutenant [*British military*] (DMA)
CL..............	Comparative Literature [*A publication*]
CL..............	Competency Level
CL..............	Compiled Laws [*A publication*] (DLA)
CL..............	Compiler Language [*Data processing*] (DIT)
CL..............	Component List [*DoD*]
CL..............	Computational Linguistics (IEEE)
CL..............	Concentration Length
CL..............	Conceptual Network-Based Language [*NEC Corp.*]
CL..............	Conditional Lease (ADA)
CL..............	Conference Lodges [*Freemasonry*] (ROG)
CL..............	Confidence Level [*Statistical mathematics*]
CL..............	Confidence Limits
CL..............	Congressional Liaison
CL..............	Connecting Line
C & L.........	Conner and Lawson's Irish Chancery Reports [*1841-43*] [*A publication*] (DLA)

CL..............	Conservation League (EA)
CL..............	Consolidated Listing (AFM)
CL..............	Consolidation Lodges [*Freemasonry*] (ROG)
CL..............	Contact Lens [*Ophthalmology*]
CL..............	Contact Lost [*RADAR*]
CL..............	Containment Leakage [*Nuclear energy*] (NRCH)
CL..............	Continuous Liner [*Fitting for a propeller shaft*]
CL..............	Contract Law
CL..............	Contralateral [*Anatomy*]
CL..............	Control Language [*Data processing*] (BUR)
CL..............	Control Leader [*Data processing*]
C & L.........	Control and Line (AABC)
CL..............	Control Logic
C of L	Convention of London [*Freemasonry*] (ROG)
CL..............	Conversion Loss
CL..............	Convertible Lens [*Photography*]
CL..............	Cooperative Logistics
C & L.........	Coopers & Lybrand USA [*New York, NY*] [*Telecommunications*] (TSSD)
CL..............	Coordination Line (NVT)
Cl...............	Coprinus laniger [*A fungus*]
CL..............	Corporation of Lloyds [*Also, Lloyd's of London*] [*Insurance*] (DS)
C of L	Corporation of London [*The City of London as opposed to Greater London*]
CL..............	Corpus Luteum [*Endocrinology*]
CL..............	Cost of Living [*Economics*] (AAG)
C of L	Cost of Living [*Economics*] (AAG)
CL..............	Council (ADA)
CL..............	Country Living [*A publication*]
CL..............	Course Line [*Aviation*] (FAAC)
C/L.............	Craft Loss [*Shipping*]
CL..............	Craik-Leibovich [*Physics*]
CL..............	Crane Load
CL..............	Credit Limit (DCTA)
CL..............	Critical List [*Medicine*]
CL..............	Cruiser, Light [*British military*] (DMA)
CL..............	Crystallographic Laboratory [*MIT*] (MCD)
CL..............	Cuadernos de Literatura [*A publication*]
C & L.........	Culture and Life [*A publication*]
CL..............	Cumulative List [*Internal Revenue code with names of exempt organizations*]
CL..............	Current Law Year Book [*A publication*]
CL..............	Current Liabilities [*Insurance*]
CL..............	Cut Length (ADA)
CL..............	Cutter Laboratories [*Research code symbol*]
CL..............	Cutter Location File
CL..............	Cyclotron Laboratory
CL..............	Cylinder (MCD)
CL..............	English Common Law Reports [*A publication*] (DLA)
CL..............	I Am Closing My Station [*Aviation code*] (FAAC)
CL..............	Irish Common Law Reports [*A publication*] (DLA)
cl-----	Latin America [*MARC geographic area code*] [*Library of Congress*] (LCCP)
CL..............	Lederle Laboratories [*Research code symbol*]
CL..............	Les Codes Larcier [*A publication*] (ILCA)
CL..............	Light Cruiser [*Navy symbol*]
CL..............	Los Angeles Public Library, Los Angeles, CA [*Library symbol*] [*Library of Congress*] (LCLS)
Cl...............	Rotulus Clausarum [*Close Roll*] [*England*] [*A publication*] (DLA)
C³L..............	Complementary Constant Current Logic [*Data processing*] (MCD)
CL9	Cloud Nine [*Manufacturer of remote control devices for home electronics*] [*Company founded by Stephen Wozniak*]
CLA	California State University, Los Angeles, Los Angeles, CA [*OCLC symbol*] (OCLC)
CLA	Camden Library [*A publication*]
CLA	Canadian Library Association [*Also known as ACB and CANLA*]
CLA	Canadian Linguistic Association [*See also ACL*]
CLA	Canadian Lumbermen's Association
C & LA.......	Cargo and Loading Analysis [*Shipping*]
CLA	Catholic Library Association (EA)
CLA	Center Line Average
CLA	Cervicolinguoaxial [*Dentistry*]
CLA	Chala [*Peru*] [*Seismograph station code, US Geological Survey*] [*Closed*] (SEIS)
CLA	Children's Literature Abstracts [*A publication*]
CLA	Chinese Laundry Association (EA)
CLA	Chinese Librarians Association (EA)
CLA	Christian Labor Association of the USA (EA)
CLA	Christian Law Association (EA)
CLA	Christian Literacy Associates (EA)
CLA	Church League of America (EA)
CLA	Class [*Freight*]
CLA	Clear and Add
CLA	Clear Type of Ice Formation [*Aviation code*] (FAAC)
CLA	Clearance Array (MSA)
CLA	Closed-Loop Trainer Aid (MCD)
CLA	Club de las Americas (EA)

CLA .... Coaxial Line Attenuator
CLA .... Coin Laundry Association   (EA)
CLA .... Collections Litteratures Africaines [*A publication*]
CLA .... College Language Association   (EA)
CLA .... College Language Association. Journal [*A publication*]
CLA .... Combined Language Age [*of the hearing-impaired*]
CLA .... Common Leucocyte Antigen [*Immunology*]
CLA .... Commonwealth Lawyers' Association [*London, England*]   (EAIO)
CLA .... Commonwealth Library Association
CLA .... Communication Line Adapters
CLA .... Communication Link Analyzer   (IEEE)
CLA .... Community Living Arrangement [*For the handicapped*]
CLA .... Comparative Literature Association   (EA)
CLA .... Computer Law Association   (EA)
CLA .... Computer Lessors Association [*Later, CDLA*]   (EA)
CLA .... Computers Lawyers Association   (EA)
CLA .... Conjugated Linoleic Acid [*Antineoplastic drug*]
CLA .... Conservative Library Association [*Defunct*]
CLA .... Contingency Landing Area [*NASA*]
CLA .... Control Logic Array
CLA .... Copyright Licensing Agency [*Government body*] [*British*]
CLA .... Council for Latin America [*Later, COA*]
CLA .... Country Landowners' Association [*British*]
CLA .... Cover Layer Assembly   (KSC)
CLA .... Cross Launcher Assign [*Navy*]   (CAAL)
CLA .... Cross-Linking Agent
CLA .... Crown Life Insurance Co. [*Toronto Stock Exchange symbol*]
CLA .... Cypriot Liberation Army
CLA .... San Juan, PR [*Location identifier*] [*FAA*]   (FAAL)
CLA .... University of California at Los Angeles. Law Review [*A publication*]   (DLA)
CLAA .... Antiaircraft Light Cruiser [*Navy symbol*]
CLAA .... Commercial Law Association of Australia
CLAAB ..... Commercial Law Association of Australia. Bulletin [*A publication*]
CLAA Bulletin ... Commercial Law Association of Australia. Bulletin [*A publication*]
CLAAMP .. Continuous LASER Argon-Age Microprobe
CLAB .... Celtic League, American Branch   (EA)
CLAB .... Centro Latinoamericano de Ciencias Biologicas [*Latin American Center of Biological Sciences*] [*Research center*] [*Venezuela*]   (IRC)
CLAB .... Commercial Law Association. Bulletin [*A publication*]   (APTA)
CLAB .... Custom Laboratories, Inc. [*Minneapolis, MN*] [*NASDAQ symbol*]   (NQ)
CLA Bull .... Colorado Library Association. Bulletin [*A publication*]
CLA Bulletin ... Commercial Law Association. Bulletin [*A publication*]   (APTA)
CLAc .... Academy of Motion Picture Arts and Sciences, Los Angeles, CA [*Library symbol*] [*Library of Congress*]   (LCLS)
CLAC .... Christian Labour Association of Canada
CLAC .... Closed-Loop Approach Control
CLAC .... Combined Liberated Areas Committee [*World War II*]
CLAC .... Comision Latinoamericana de Aviacion Civil [*Latin American Civil Aviation Commission - LACAC*]   (EAIO)
CLACJ ...... Confederacion Latinoamericana de Asociaciones Cristianas de Jovenes [*Latin American Confederation of YMCAs - LACYMCA*]   (EAIO)
CLACK ..... Clackmannanshire [*County in Scotland*]
CLAC(S) .... Combined Liberated Areas Committee, Supply Subcommittee [*World War II*]
CLACS ...... Latin American and Caribbean Studies Center [*University of Illinois*] [*Research center*]   (RCD)
CLACSO ... Consejo Latinoamericano de Ciencias Sociales [*Latin American Social Sciences Council - LASSC*]   (EAIO)
CLACSO/ERL ... Estudios Rurales Latinoamericanos. Consejo Latinoamericano de Ciencias Sociales. Secretaria Ejecutiva y la Comision de Estudios Rurales [*A publication*]
Cl Act Rep ... Class Action Reports [*A publication*]
CLACW ..... Conference of Liberal Arts Colleges for Women   (EA)
CLAD .... Centro Latinoamericano de Administracion para el Desarrollo [*Latin American Center for Development Administration*] [*Research center*] [*Venezuela*]   (IRC)
Clad .... Cladosporium [*A fungus*]
CLAD .... Collect Adapter
CLADA ...... Crystal Lattice Defects [*Later, Crystal Lattice Defects and Amorphous Materials*] [*A publication*]
CLADEC ... Cladistics [*A publication*]
CLADES ... Centro Latinoamericano de Documentacion Economica y Social [*Latin American Center for Economic and Social Documentation*] [*Economic Commission for Latin America and the Caribbean*] [*United Nations*] [*Information service or system*]   (IID)
CL(ADO)... Diploma in Contact Lens Fitting of the Association of Dispensing Opticians [*British*]   (DBQ)
CLAE .... Council of Library Association Executives   (EA)
CLAES .... Cryogenic Limb Array Etalon Spectrometer   (MCD)
CLAF .... Centro Latino-Americano de Fisica [*Latin American Centre for Physics*]   (EAIO)
CLAG .... Conference of Latin Americanist Geographers

CLAGB...... Clinical Allergy [*England*] [*A publication*]
CLAGBI .... Clinical Allergy [*A publication*]
CLAH .... Conference on Latin American History   (EA)
CLAH .... Container Lift Adapter for Helicopter   (MCD)
CLahF........ Foothill College, Los Altos, CA [*Library symbol*] [*Library of Congress*]   (LCLS)
CLAi .... Airsearch Manufacturing Co., Los Angeles, CA [*Library symbol*] [*Library of Congress*]   (LCLS)
CLAI .... Consejo Latinoamericano de Iglesias [*Latin American Council of Churches*]   (EAIO)
CLAIM ...... Centre for Library and Information Management [*Loughborough University of Technology*] [*British*] [*Information service or system*]   (IID)
CLAIMS/CHEM ... Class Code, Assignee, Index, Method, Search/Chemistry [*Patent database*] [*IFI/Plenum Data Co.*] [*Arlington, VA*]
CLAIMS/GEM ... Class Code, Assignee, Index, Method, Search/General, Electrical, Mechanical [*Patent database*] [*IFI/Plenum Data Co.*] [*Arlington, VA*]
CLAIR ...... Canadian Legal Advocacy Information and Research Association of the Disabled
CLAIR ...... Computerised Library of Analysed Igneous Rocks [*Australia*] [*Information service or system*]   (IID)
CLAIS ...... Center for Latin American and Iberian Studies [*Vanderbilt University*] [*Research center*]   (RCD)
CLAIS ...... Committee on Latin American and Iberian Studies [*Harvard University*] [*Research center*]   (RCD)
CLAIT .... Constitutions and Laws of the American Indian Tribes [*A publication*]   (DLA)
CLAJ .... CLA [*College Language Association*] Journal [*A publication*]
CLALS...... Centre for Latin American Linguistic Studies [*University of St. Andrews*] [*British*]   (CB)
CLAM ...... Carline Assignment Model [*General Motors Corp.*]
CLAM ...... Chemical Low-Altitude Missile [*Air Force program*]
CLAM ...... Child Language Ability Measures [*Child development test*]
CLAM ...... Clear Air Mass
CLAM .... Comite de Liaison de l'Agrumiculture Mediterraneenne [*Liaison Committee for Mediterranean Citrus Fruit Culture - LCMCFC*]   (EAIO)
CLAM .... Command Load Acceptance Message
CLamB...... Biola Library, La Mirada, CA [*Library symbol*] [*Library of Congress*]   (LCLS)
ClamB........ La Sainte Bible [*Pirot-Clamer*] [*Paris*] [*A publication*]   (BJA)
CLAMP..... Chemical Low-Altitude Missile Puny [*Air Force program*]   (MCD)
CLAMS ..... Clear Lane Marking System [*Army*]   (RDA)
CLAMS ..... Countermeasures Launcher Modular System [*Navy*]   (CAAL)
CLAMTI .... Clutter-Locked Airborne Moving Target Indicator [*Air Force*]
CLAMUC ... Consejo Latinoamericano de Mujeres Catolicas [*Latin American Council of Catholic Women*]   (EAIO)
CLAN .... Clean Air Society in the Netherlands [*See also VL*] [*Delft, Netherlands*]   (EAIO)
Clancy Husb & W ... Clancy's Treatise of the Rights, Duties, and Liabilities of Husband and Wife [*A publication*]   (DLA)
Clancy Rights ... Clancy's Treatise of the Rights, Duties, and Liabilities of Husband and Wife [*A publication*]   (DLA)
CLAND ..... Computer Languages [*A publication*]
CLANG ...... Concurrent Language [*Data processing*]
Clan Gunn Soc Mag ... Clan Gunn Society. Magazine [*A publication*]
Clan MacLeod Mag ... Clan MacLeod Magazine [*A publication*]
Clan Munro Mag ... Clan Munro Magazine [*A publication*]
CLANN ..... [*Australian*] College Libraries Activities Network [*CLANN Ltd.*] [*Information service or system*]   (CRD)
CLANN ..... Cooperating Libraries Action Network New South Wales [*Australia*]
CLANS...... Computerized Link Analysis System
CLAO .... Contact Lens Association of Ophthalmologists   (EA)
CLAO .... Contact Lens Association for Optometry   (EA)
CLAO (Contact Lens Assoc Ophthalmol) J ... CLAO (Contact Lens Association of Ophthalmologists) Journal [*A publication*]
CLAO J ..... CLAO [*Contact Lens Association of Ophthalmologists*] Journal [*A publication*]
CLAP......... Clapham [*England*]
Cl App........ Clark's Appeal Cases, House of Lords [*England*] [*A publication*]   (DLA)
CLAPTUR ... Confederacion Latinoamericana de Prensa Turistica [*Latin American Confederation of Touristic Press*] [*Medellin, Colombia*]   (EAIO)
CLAQ .... Children's Literature Association. Quarterly [*A publication*]
CLAR........ Clarendon [*Type*]   (ROG)
CLAR........ Clarification [*or Clarify*]   (AFM)
CLAR........ Clarinet
CLAR........ Clarino [*Clarion*] [*Music*]   (ROG)
Clar .... [*Julius*] Clarus [*Deceased, 1575*] [*Authority cited in pre-1607 legal work*]   (DSA)
CLar.......... Larkspur Public Library, Larkspur, CA [*Library symbol*] [*Library of Congress*]   (LCLS)
C Lar .... Les Codes Larcier [*A publication*]   (ILCA)
CLARA....... Citizens Law and Research Association [*Defunct*]   (EA)
CLARA...... Computer Load and Resource Analysis   (MCD)
CLARA...... Cornell Learning and Recognizing Automaton
CLARB...... Council of Landscape Architectural Registration Boards   (EA)

Clare Q....... Claremont Quarterly [*A publication*]
Claridad ..... Claridad Weekly [*A publication*]
Clark .... Clark's Reports [*58 Alabama*] [*A publication*]   (DLA)
CLARK....... Combat Launch and Recovery Kit   (AFM)
Clark .... English House of Lords Cases, by Clark [*A publication*]   (DLA)
Clark .... Pennsylvania Law Journal Reports, Edited by Clark [*A publication*]   (DLA)
Clark .... Supreme Court Judgments by Clark [*1917-32*] [*Jamaica*] [*A publication*]   (DLA)
Clark (Ala) ... Clark's Reports [*58 Alabama*] [*A publication*]   (DLA)
Clark App .. Clark's Appeal Cases, House of Lords [*England*] [*A publication*]   (DLA)
Clark Col Law ... Clark. Colonial Law [*1834*] [*A publication*]   (ILCA)
Clark Dig ... Clark's Digest, House of Lords Reports [*A publication*]   (DLA)
Clarke .... Clarke's Edition of 1-8 Iowa [*A publication*]   (DLA)
Clarke .... Clarke's New York Chancery Reports [*A publication*]   (DLA)
Clarke .... Clarke's Notes of Cases [*Bengal*] [*A publication*]   (DLA)
Clarke .... Clarke's Pennsylvania Reports [*5 vols.*] [*A publication*]   (DLA)
Clarke .... Clarke's Reports [*19-22 Michigan*] [*A publication*]   (DLA)
Clarke Adm Pr ... Clarke's Admiralty Practice [*A publication*]   (DLA)
Clarke B..... Clarke on Bills and Notes [*Canada*] [*A publication*]   (DLA)
Clarke Bib Leg ... Clarke's Bibliotheca Legum [*A publication*]   (DLA)
Clarke Ch... Clarke's New York Chancery Reports [*A publication*]   (DLA)
Clarke Ch (NY) ... Clarke's New York Chancery Reports [*A publication*]   (DLA)
Clarke Const ... Clarke's Constable's Manual [*Canada*] [*A publication*]   (DLA)
Clarke CR ... Clarke's New York Chancery Reports [*A publication*]   (DLA)
Clarke Cr L ... Clarke's Criminal Law [*Canada*] [*A publication*]   (DLA)
Clarke Extr ... Clarke on Extradition [*A publication*]   (DLA)
Clarke & H Elec Cas ... Clarke and Hall's Cases of Contested Elections in Congress [*1789-1834*] [*United States*] [*A publication*]   (DLA)
Clarke (IA) ... Clarke's Edition of 1-8 Iowa [*A publication*]   (DLA)
Clarke Insol ... Clarke's Insolvent Acts [*Canada*] [*A publication*]   (DLA)
Clarke Inst Psychiatry Monogr Ser ... Clarke Institute of Psychiatry. Monograph Series [*A publication*]
Clarke Insur ... Clarke's Insurance Law [*Canada*] [*A publication*]   (DLA)
Clarke (Mich) ... Clarke's Reports [*19-22 Michigan*] [*A publication*]   (DLA)
Clarke Not ... Clarke's Notes of Cases, in His "Rules and Orders" [*Bengal*] [*A publication*]   (DLA)
Clarke (PA) ... Clarke's Pennsylvania Reports [*5 vols.*] [*A publication*]   (DLA)
Clarke R & O ... Clarke's Notes of Cases, in His "Rules and Orders" [*Bengal*] [*A publication*]   (DLA)
Clarke Rom L ... Clarke's Early Roman Law [*A publication*]   (DLA)
Clarke's Chy (NY) ... Clarke's New York Chancery Reports [*A publication*]   (DLA)
Clarke & S Dr Cas ... Clarke and Scully's Drainage Cases [*Canada*] [*A publication*]   (DLA)
Clark & F ... Clark and Finnelly's English House of Lords Reports [*6-8 English Reprint*] [*A publication*]   (DLA)
Clark & F (Eng) ... Clark and Finnelly's English House of Lords Reports [*6-8 English Reprint*] [*A publication*]   (DLA)
Clark & Fin ... Clark and Finnelly's English House of Lords Cases [*1831-46*] [*A publication*]   (DLA)
Clark & Fin (NS) ... Clark and Finnelly's English House of Lords Reports, New Series [*9-11 English Reprint*] [*1847-66*] [*A publication*]   (DLA)
Clark & F (NS) ... Clark and Finnelly's English House of Lords Reports, New Series [*9-11 English Reprint*] [*1847-66*] [*A publication*]   (DLA)
Clark & F (NS) Eng ... Clark and Finnelly's English House of Lords Cases, New Series [*A publication*]   (DLA)
Clark (Jam) ... Judgments, Jamaica Supreme Court of Judicature [*A publication*]   (DLA)
Clark (PA) ... Clark's Pennsylvania Law Journal Reports [*A publication*]   (DLA)
Clarks Dig Annot ... Clark's Digest-Annotator [*A publication*]   (DLA)
Clark's Summary ... Clark's Summary of American Law [*A publication*]   (DLA)
CLARM..... International Center for Living Aquatic Resources Management   (EAIO)
CLARNICO ... Clarke, Nichols & Company [*British*]   (ROG)
CLARO..... Clarino [*Clarion*] [*Music*]
Clar Parl Chr ... Clarendon's Parliamentary Chronicle [*A publication*]   (DLA)
CLArt......... Art Center College of Design, Los Angeles, CA [*Library symbol*] [*Library of Congress*]   (LCLS)
Clart Synd ... Clartes Syndicales. Revue de Pensee et d'Action Syndicale [*A publication*]
CLARTTO ... Clarinetto [*Clarinet*] [*Music*]   (ROG)
CLAS......... Arnold Schoenberg Institute, Los Angeles, CA [*Library symbol*] [*Library of Congress*]   (LCLS)
CLAS......... Canadian Labour Arbitration Summaries [*Canada Law Book, Inc.*] [*Information service or system*]   (CRD)
CLAS......... Catholic Ladies Aid Society
CLAS......... Centre of Latin American Studies [*University of Cambridge*] [*British*]   (CB)
CLAS......... Cholesterol-Lowering Atherosclerosis Study [*National Heart, Lung, and Blood Institute - NHLBI*]
CLAS......... Chromatography Laboratory Automatic Software

CLAS......... CL Assets, Inc. [*NASDAQ symbol*]   (NQ)
CLAS......... Classify   (AFM)
CLAS......... Clinical Ligand Assay Society   (EA)
CLAS......... Communications Link Analyzer System
CLAS......... Computerized Library Acquisitions System [*Lukac Data Systems*] [*Lewis and Clark College*] [*Information service or system*] [*Discontinued*]   (IID)
CLAS......... Congress of Lung Association Staff   (EA)
CLAS......... Criminal Law Audio Series [*A publication*]
CLAS......... Cross-Lines Alternative School
CLAS......... Crowd, Lift, Actuate, Swing [*Backhoe controls for tractors*]
CLASB ...... Citizens League Against the Sonic Boom [*Defunct*]
CLASC ...... Confederacion Latinoamericana de Sindicalistas Cristianos [*Latin American Federation of Christian Trade Unionists*]
CLASIA ...... ASIA Project, Los Angeles, CA [*Library symbol*] [*Library of Congress*]   (LCLS)
CLASIX..... Computer/LASER Access Systems for Information Exchange
CLASP....... Center for Law and Social Policy   (EA)
CLASP....... Civil Liberties Action Security Project [*Canada*]
CLASP...... Claimant Advisory Service Program [*Unemployment insurance*]
CLASP...... Clients Lifetime Advisory Service Program [*Insurance*]
CLASP...... Closed Line Assembly for Single Particles   (IEEE)
CLASP...... Computer Language for Aeronautics and Space Programming [*NASA*]
CLASP...... Computer Launch and Separation Problem   (MCD)
CLASP...... Consortium of Latin American Studies Programs
CLASP...... Consortium of Local Authorities Special Programme [*British*]
CLASP...... Cylindrical LASER Plasma
CLASS...... California Library Authority for Systems and Services [*Library network*]
CLASS...... Canadian Ladies Association of Shooting Sports
CLASS...... Capacity Loading and Schedule System
CLASS...... Carrier Landing-Aid Stabilization System [*Navy*]
CLASS...... Chemical Laboratory Analysis and Scheduling System [*Data processing*]
CLASS...... Chrysler LASER Atlas Satellite System [*Automotive engineering*]
CLASS...... Class Action Study and Survey [*Student legal action organization*]
CLASS...... Classic   (ROG)
class .... Classical
CLASS...... Classification   (AFM)
CLASS...... Close Air Support System [*Military*]
CLASS...... Closed Loop Accounting for Stores Sales   (IEEE)
CLASS...... Cognitive, Linguistic, and Social-Communicative Scales [*Speech evaluation test*]
CLASS...... Computer-Based Laboratory for Automated School Systems [*System Development Corp. project*]
CLASS...... Computerized Librarian-Assisted Search Service [*Nicholls State University*]   (OLDSS)
CLASS...... Computerized Literature Access Search Service [*Colorado State University Libraries*] [*Information service or system*]
CLASS...... Cooperative Library Agency for Systems and Services [*San Jose, CA*] [*Telecommunications*]   (TSSD)
CLASS...... Crown Lands Assessment and Status System [*Australia*]
CLASS...... Current Literature Awareness Search Service [*BIOSIS*] [*Database*]
Class Act Rep ... Class Action Reports [*A publication*]   (DLA)
Class B .... Classical Bulletin [*A publication*]
ClassBull ... Classical Bulletin [*St. Louis, MO*] [*A publication*]
CLASSIC .. Circulation Library Automated System for Inventory Control [*Cincinnati Electronics Corp.*] [*Information service or system*] [*Discontinued*]   (IID)
Classic........ Classic Images [*A publication*]
Classical J ... Classical Journal [*A publication*]
Classical Philol ... Classical Philology [*A publication*]
Classical Q ... Classical Quarterly [*A publication*]
Classic F Col ... Classic Film Collector [*A publication*]
Classic Jnl ... Classical Journal [*A publication*]
CLASSICS ... Classification of Identification of Covert Satellites
Classic World ... Classical World [*A publication*]
CLASSIF... Classification
Classif........ Journal of Classification [*A publication*]
Classified Abstr Arch Alcohol Lit ... Classified Abstract Archive of the Alcohol Literature [*A publication*]
Class J .... Classical Journal [*A publication*]
Class J (C) ... Classical Journal (Chicago) [*A publication*]
Class J (L) ... Classical Journal (London) [*A publication*]
Class J SR ... Classical Journal and Scholars Review [*A publication*]
CLASSMATE ... Computer Language to Aid and Stimulate Scientific, Mathematical, and Technical Education
ClassMed... Classica et Mediaevalia [*Aarhus*] [*A publication*]
Class Mod L ... Classical and Modern Literature [*A publication*]
CLASSN.... Classification
Class Out ... Classical Outlook [*A publication*]
ClassPh...... Classical Philology [*Chicago*] [*A publication*]
Class Phil... Classical Philology [*A publication*]
Class Philol ... Classical Philology [*A publication*]
Class Q .... Classical Quarterly [*A publication*]
Class Quart ... Classical Quarterly [*A publication*]

Class R ...... Classical Review [*A publication*]
Class Rev ... Classical Review [*A publication*]
Class Rev N Ser ... Classical Review. New Series [*A publication*]
Class Soc Bull ... Classification Society. Bulletin [*A publication*]
ClassW ...... Classical Weekly [*New York*] [*A publication*]
Class W ...... Classical World [*A publication*]
Class World ... Classical World [*A publication*]
CLAST ...... College Level Academic Skills Test
CLASYC .... Chemical LASER System Code   (MCD)
CLAT .... Central Latinamericana de Trabajadores [*Latin American Central of Workers*]   (EA)
CLAT .... Communication Line Adapters for Teletype
CLAT .... Confederation of Latin-American Teachers
CLatA .... Sharpe Army Depot Library, Lathrop, CA [*Library symbol*] [*Library of Congress*]   (LCLS)
CLATDP ... Compendium de Investigaciones Clinicas Latinoamericanas [*A publication*]
CLATT ...... Comite Latinoamericano de Textos Teologicos
Clau .... Claustrum [*Neuroanatomy*]
Claud .... Claudianus [*Fourth century AD*] [*Classical studies*]   (OCD)
Claud .... Divus Claudius [*of Suetonius*] [*Classical studies*]   (OCD)
ClaudelS .... Claudel Studies [*A publication*]
Claudel St .. Claudel Studies [*A publication*]
Clausthaler Geol Abh ... Clausthaler Geologische Abhandlungen [*A publication*]
Clausthaler Hefte Lagerstaettenk Geochemie Miner Rohst ... Clausthaler Hefte zur Lagerstaettenkund und Geochemie der Mineralischen Rohstoffe [*A publication*]
CLAV .... Antelope Valley Junior College, Lancaster, CA [*Library symbol*] [*Library of Congress*]   (LCLS)
CLAV .... Clavering [*England*]
Clav .... Clavichord [*Music*]
CLAV .... Clavicle [*Anatomy*]   (DHSM)
CLAV .... Clavier [*Keyboard*] [*Music*]
Clav .... Clavileno [*A publication*]
CLavA .... Archaeological Survey Association of Southern California, La Verne, CA [*Library symbol*] [*Library of Congress*]   (LCLS)
Clava .... [*Angelus Carletus de*] Clavasio [*Deceased, 1492*] [*Authority cited in pre-1607 legal work*]   (DSA)
CLAVA .... Clavier [*A publication*]
CLavC .... La Verne College, La Verne, CA [*Library symbol*] [*Library of Congress*]   (LCLS)
Clavi .... Clavichord [*Music*]
CLavO .... Occidental Research Corp., La Verne, CA [*Library symbol*] [*Library of Congress*]   (LCLS)
Clavon .... [*James*] Clavell and Avon [*Author and publisher of the novel "Whirlwind," after whom Crown Zellerbach named the light-weight paper it developed for this book*]
CLAVR ...... Clavicular [*Medicine*]   (ROG)
CLAW .... Close Air Support Weapon [*Military*]   (MCD)
CLAW .... Clustered Atomic Warhead
CLAW .... Concept for Low-Cost Air-to-Air Weapon   (MCD)
CLAW .... Consortium of Local Authorities in Wales
CLAWA ...... Clarinet [*A publication*]
CLAWP ..... Commander, Light Attack Wing - Pacific Fleet   (MCD)
CLAWS ..... Classify, Locate, and Avoid Wind Shear [*National Center for Atmospheric Research*]
CLAWS ..... Controlled Large Aperture Wavefront Sampling   (MCD)
C Lawyer .... Catholic Lawyer [*A publication*]
CLAY .... Claydon [*England*]
CLAY .... Clayton Corp. [*St. Louis, MO*] [*NASDAQ symbol*]   (NQ)
Clay .... Clayton's English Reports, York Assizes [*A publication*]   (DLA)
Clay Clay M ... Clays and Clay Minerals [*A publication*]
Clay Conv ... Clayton on Conveyancing [*A publication*]   (DLA)
Claycraft Struct Ceram ... Claycraft and Structural Ceramics [*A publication*]
Clay L & T ... Claydon. Landlord and Tenant [*A publication*]   (DLA)
Clay Miner ... Clay Minerals [*A publication*]
Clay Miner Bull ... Clay Minerals. Bulletin [*Later, Clay Minerals*] [*A publication*]
Clay Prod J ... Clay Products Journal of Australia [*A publication*]   (APTA)
Clay Prod J Aust ... Clay Products Journal of Australia [*A publication*]   (APTA)
Clay Prod J Austr ... Clay Products Journal of Australia [*A publication*]
Clay Prod News Ceram Rec ... Clay Products News and Ceramic Record [*A publication*]
Clay Sci (Tokyo) ... Clay Science (Tokyo) [*A publication*]
Clays Clay Miner ... Clays and Clay Minerals [*A publication*]
Clay's Dig .. Clay's Digest of Laws of Alabama [*A publication*]   (DLA)
Clayt .... Clayton's English Reports, York Assizes [*A publication*]   (DLA)
Clayton .... Clayton's English Reports, York Assizes [*A publication*]   (DLA)
Clayton (Eng) ... Clayton's English Reports, York Assizes [*A publication*]   (DLA)
CLB .... Bachelor of Civil Law
CLB .... Cellular Business [*A publication*]
CLB .... Center Line Bend   (MSA)
CLB .... Center Line Block [*Philately*]
CLB .... Central Logic Bus [*Data processing*]
CLB .... Church Lads' Brigade [*Church of England*]
CLB .... Civil Liberties Bureau [*Forerunner of the American Civil Liberties Union*]

ClB .... Claiborne Industries Ltd. [*Toronto Stock Exchange symbol*]
Cl B .... Clarinette Basse [*Bass Clarinet*] [*Music*]
CLB .... Clear Both [*Data processing*]
CLB .... Climb [*Aviation*]   (FAAC)
CLB .... Club
CLB .... Combat Lessons Bulletin
CLB .... Commercial Law Bulletin [*Commercial Law League of America*] [*A publication*]
CLB .... Commonwealth Law Bulletin [*A publication*]
CLB .... Communications Law Bulletin [*A publication*]   (APTA)
ClB .... Connaitre la Bible [*Bruges*] [*A publication*]   (BJA)
CLB .... Consortia of London Boroughs [*British*]
CLB .... Constant Level Balloon
CLB .... Continuous Line Bucket [*Deep mining system*]
CLB .... Contract Labour Branch [*Admiralty*] [*British*]
CLB .... Crash Locator Beacon [*Aviation*]   (AFM)
CLB .... Curvilinear Body [*in Batten disease*]
CLB .... Long Beach Public Library, Long Beach, CA [*OCLC symbol*]   (OCLC)
CLB .... Wilmington, NC [*Location identifier*] [*FAA*]   (FAAL)
CLBANY ... Collateral Loan Brokers Association of New York   (EA)
CLBC .... Canadian Lawn Bowling Council
CLBC .... Christian Literature and Bible Center   (EA)
CLBC .... Confederacion Latinoamericana de Bioquimica Clinica [*Latin American Confederation of Clinical Biochemistry - LACCB*]   (EAIO)
CLBCBB .... Cardiologisches Bulletin [*A publication*]
CL BDS ..... Cloth Boards [*Bookbinding*]   (ROG)
CLBG .... [*The*] Colonial BancGroup, Inc. [*NASDAQ symbol*]   (NQ)
CLBI .... Climb Immediately [*Aviation*]   (FAAC)
CLBIA .... Clinical Biochemistry [*Ottawa*] [*A publication*]
CLBIAS ..... Clinical Biochemistry [*A publication*]
Cl Bills .... Clarke on Bills and Notes [*Canada*] [*A publication*]   (DLA)
CLBMF ...... Colby Resources Corp. [*Vancouver, BC*] [*NASDAQ symbol*]   (NQ)
CLBN .... Crash Locator Beacon [*Aviation*]   (FAAC)
CLBR .... Calibration
CLBR .... Calibre Corp. [*NASDAQ symbol*]   (NQ)
CLBraille ... Braille Institute of America, Los Angeles, CA [*Library symbol*] [*Library of Congress*]   (LCLS)
CLBRP .... Cannon-Launched Beam Rider Projectile   (MCD)
CLBT .... Clubmart of America [*NASDAQ symbol*]   (NQ)
CLBU .... China Law and Business Update [*A publication*]
CLBUA ...... Clinical Bulletin [*A publication*]
CLBUAU ... Clinical Bulletin [*Memorial Sloan-Kettering Cancer Center*] [*A publication*]
Cl Bull .... Classical Bulletin [*A publication*]
CLBW .... Closed-Loop Bandwidth
CLC .... Cadillac-LaSalle Club   (EA)
CLC .... Canadian Labour Congress
CLC .... Canadian League of Composers
C & LC .... Capitals and Lower Case [*Printing*]
CLC .... Carrier Liaison Committee [*An association*]   (EA)
CLC .... Catholic Ladies of Columbia
CLC .... Central Crude Ltd. [*Vancouver Stock Exchange symbol*]
CLC .... Central Labour College [*Railroad*] [*British*]   (ROG)
CLC .... Central Logic Control [*Data processing*]
CLC .... Central Logistics Command [*Republic of Vietnam Armed Forces*]
CLC .... Centrifugal Lockup Converter [*Automotive engineering*]
CLC .... Change Letter Control   (NASA)
CLC .... Cheshire Lines Committee Railway [*British*]   (ROG)
CLC .... Child Life Council   (EA)
CLC .... Children's Legal Centre   (EAIO)
CLC .... Chile Legislative Center [*An association*]   (EA)
CLC .... China Lake [*California*] [*Seismograph station code, US Geological Survey*]   (SEIS)
CLC .... Christian Literature Crusade [*British*]
CLC .... Church of the Lutheran Confession
CLC .... Civil Liability Convention [*British*]
CLC .... Clackmannan [*Town and county in Scotland*]   (ROG)
CLC .... Claritas Corporation [*Information service or system*]   (IID)
CLC .... Clark College, Atlanta, GA [*OCLC symbol*]   (OCLC)
Clc .... Classic [*Record label*] [*France*]
CLC .... Clear Carry
CLC .... Clear Lake City [*Texas*] [*Airport symbol*]   (OAG)
CLC .... Clear Lake City, TX [*Location identifier*] [*FAA*]   (FAAL)
CLC .... Closed-Loop Condensate [*Nuclear energy*]   (NRCH)
CLC .... Closed-Loop Control [*Automotive engineering*]
CLC .... Columbia & Cowlitz Railway Co. [*AAR code*]
CLC .... Columbia Library. Columns [*A publication*]
CLC .... Column Liquid Chromatography
CLC .... Command Load Controller
CLC .... Communications Line Control
CLC .... Communications Link Controller [*International Computers Ltd.*] [*Telecommunications*]
CLC .... Company Law Cases [*A publication*]   (APTA)
CLC .... Compressive Load Cell
CLC .... Computerized Lubrication Control [*Sun Oil Co.*]
CLC .... Conseil pour la Liberation du Congo-Kinshasa [*Council for the Liberation of the Congo-Kinshasa*] [*Zaire*]   (PD)

CLC............ Contact Literacy Center (EA)
CLC............ Containment Leakage Control [*Nuclear energy*] (IEEE)
CLC............ Contemporary Literary Criticism [*Reference publication; often pronounced "click"*]
CLC............ Continued Lymphocyte Culture [*Immunology*]
CLC............ Control Launch Center (MUGU)
CLC............ Convention on Civil Liability for Oil Pollution Damage (DS)
CLC............ Convention Liaison Council (EA)
CLC............ Cost of Living Council [*Also, COLC*] [*Terminated, 1974*] [*Pronounced "click"*]
CLC............ Cotton Leaf Crumple [*Plant pathology*]
CLC............ Counter-Lock-Cord [*Tennis shoe technology*] [*Autry Industries, Inc.*]
CLC............ Course-Line Computer [*Aviation*] (MCD)
CLC............ Cuadernos de Literatura Contemporanea [*A publication*]
CLC............ Current Law Consolidation [*England*] [*A publication*] (DLA)
CLC............ Tactical Command Ship [*Navy symbol*]
CLCA........ Comite de Liaison de la Construction Automobile [*Liaison Committee for the Motor Industry in the EEC Countries*] [*Brussels, Belgium*] (EAIO)
CLCAA9.... Cellulosa e Carta [*A publication*]
CLCADC... Clinical Cardiology [*A publication*]
CLCan........ Cannan Electric Co., Los Angeles, CA [*Library symbol*] [*Library of Congress*] (LCLS)
Cl Can Ins ... Clarke's Canada Insolvent Acts [*A publication*] (DLA)
CLCAPF.... Los Angeles County Air Pollution Control District Library, Los Angeles, CA [*Library symbol*] [*Library of Congress*] (LCLS)
Cl CB .... Clarinette Contre Basse [*Contrabass Clarinet*] [*Music*]
CLCB........ Committee of London Clearing Bankers [*British*]
C & LCC .... Caines and Leigh. Crown Cases [*England*] [*A publication*] (DLA)
CLCC........ Closed-Loop Continuity Check [*Aerospace*] (AAG)
CLCC........ Los Angeles Chamber of Commerce, Research Library, Los Angeles, CA [*Library symbol*] [*Library of Congress*] (LCLS)
CLCCR...... Comite de Liaison de la Construction de Carrosseries et de Remorques [*Liaison Committee of the Body- and Trailer-Building Industry*] (EAIO)
CLCCS ...... Los Angeles County Civil Service Commission, Los Angeles, CA [*Library symbol*] [*Library of Congress*] (LCLS)
CLCD........ Clearinghouse and Laboratory for Census Data [*Defunct*]
CLCE........ Communications Link Characterization Experiment [*Communications Technology Satellite*] (MCD)
CLCEA ...... Casopis Lekaru Ceskych [*A publication*]
CLCEAL.... Casopis Lekaru Ceskych [*A publication*]
CLCGH ..... Los Angeles County General Hospital, Los Angeles, CA [*Library symbol*] [*Library of Congress*] (LCLS)
CLCGM..... Closed-Loop Cover Gas Monitor [*Nuclear energy*] (NRCH)
CLCH .... Children's Hospital Society, Doctor's Library, Los Angeles, CA [*Library symbol*] [*Library of Congress*] (LCLS)
Cl Ch .... Clarke's New York Chancery Reports [*A publication*] (DLA)
CL Ch........ Common Law Chamber Reports [*Ontario*] [*A publication*] (DLA)
CLCHA ..... Clinical Chemistry [*Winston-Salem, North Carolina*] [*A publication*]
CL Chamb ... Chambers' Common Law [*Upper Canada*] [*A publication*] (DLA)
CL Chamb ... Common Law Chamber Reports [*Ontario*] [*A publication*] (DLA)
CL Chambers ... Chambers' Common Law [*Upper Canada*] [*A publication*] (DLA)
CL Chamb Rep ... Common Law Chamber Reports [*Ontario*] [*A publication*] (DLA)
CLCHAU .. Clinical Chemistry [*A publication*]
CLCHD ..... Climatic Change [*A publication*]
CLCHDX... Climatic Change [*A publication*]
CLCiC...... Los Angeles City College, Los Angeles, CA [*Library symbol*] [*Library of Congress*] (LCLS)
CLCIS........ Closed-Loop Control and Instrumentation System [*Nuclear energy*] (NRCH)
CLCL........ Computational Linguistics and Computer Languages [*A publication*]
CL & CL Comput Linguist Comput Lang ... CL & CL. Computational Linguistics and Computer Languages [*Budapest*] [*A publication*]
CLCLH...... Cedars-Sinai Medical Center, Los Angeles, CA [*Library symbol*] [*Library of Congress*] (LCLS)
CLCM........ Cellcom Corp. [*NASDAQ symbol*] (NQ)
CLCM........ Council of Lutheran Church Men [*Defunct*] (EA)
CLCM........ Los Angeles County Museum of Natural History, Los Angeles, CA [*Library symbol*] [*Library of Congress*] (LCLS)
CLCMAr ... Los Angeles County Museum of Art, Los Angeles, CA [*Library symbol*] [*Library of Congress*] (LCLS)
CLCNB...... Clinician [*Panjim-Goa, India*] [*A publication*]
CLCO .... Chalco Industries, Inc. [*Gardena, CA*] [*NASDAQ symbol*] (NQ)
CLCO .... Claremont & Concord Railway Co., Inc. [*AAR code*]
CLCO .... Los Angeles College of Optometry, Los Angeles, CA [*Library symbol*] [*Library of Congress*] (LCLS)

CLCo.......... Los Angeles County Public Library, Los Angeles, CA [*Library symbol*] [*Library of Congress*] (LCLS)
Cl Col........ Clark's Colonial Laws [*A publication*] (DLA)
CLCol........ Colorado River Board of California, Los Angeles, CA [*Library symbol*] [*Library of Congress*] (LCLS)
CLCONE... Closed Cone at Maturity [*Botany*]
CLCP........ Los Angeles County Health Department, Los Angeles, CA [*Library symbol*] [*Library of Congress*] (LCLS)
CLCR........ Celcor, Inc. [*Englewood Cliffs, NJ*] [*NASDAQ symbol*] (NQ)
CLCR........ Cheshire Lines Committee Railway [*British*] (ROG)
CLCR........ Communication Lieutenant-Commander [*British military*] (DMA)
CLCR........ Controlled Letter Contract Reduction (IEEE)
CLCS .... Chinese Language Computer Society (EA)
CLCS .... Consequence Limiting Control System [*Nuclear energy*] (NRCH)
CLCS .... Current-Logic-Current-Switching [*Electronics*]
CLCSBC.... Christian Life Commission of the Southern Baptist Convention (EA)
CLCSE...... Center for Life Cycle Software Engineering [*Communications-Electronics Command*] [*Army*]
CLCT........ Collector [*Freight*]
Cl Ct R ...... United States Claims Court Rules [*A publication*] (DLA)
CLCU........ Civil Labour Control Unit [*British*]
CLCV........ Cold Leg Check Valve [*Nuclear energy*] (NRCH)
CLCVN..... Class Convening
CLCW........ Closed-Loop Cooling Water [*Nuclear energy*] (NRCH)
CLCYAD... Clinical Cytology. A Series of Monographs [*A publication*]
CLD .... Caldera [*Chile*] [*Seismograph station code, US Geological Survey*] [*Closed*] (SEIS)
CLD .... California Library Directory [*A publication*]
CLD .... Called [*In stock listings of newspapers*] [*Business term*]
CLD .... Carlsbad [*California*] [*Airport symbol*] (OAG)
CLD .... Center for Leadership Development (EA)
CLD .... Central Bank of Malta. Quarterly Review [*A publication*]
CLD .... Central Library and Documentation Branch [*International Labor Organization*] (IEEE)
CLD .... Chemiluminescence Detector
CLD .... Children with Learning Disabilities
CLD .... Chloride Leak Detector (IEEE)
CLD .... Cholestatic Liver Disease [*Medicine*]
CLD .... Chronic Liver Disease [*Medicine*]
CLD .... Chronic Lung Disease [*Medicine*]
CLD .... Civil Liaison Division [*Army*]
CLD .... Cleared
CLD .... Cloud
CLD .... Clydesdale [*Valley in Scotland*] (ROG)
CLD .... Colored
CLD .... Comite de Liaison Commerce de Detail [*Liaison Committee of European Retail Trade Associations*] (EAIO)
CLD .... Compulaw Digest [*A publication*] (ADA)
CLD .... Computer Logic Demonstrator
CLD .... COMSAT [*Communications Satellite Corp.*], Washington, DC [*OCLC symbol*] (OCLC)
CLD .... Consolidated Airways, Inc. [*Houston, TX*] [*FAA designator*] (FAAC)
CLD .... Control Science [*Vancouver Stock Exchange symbol*]
CLD .... Cooled (MSA)
CLD .... Cost Laid Down
CLD .... Could (ADA)
CLD .... Council for Learning Disabilities (EA)
CLD .... Current-Limiting Device [*Short-circuit limiter*]
CLD .... Doctor of Civil Law
CLDA .... Clinical Data, Inc. [*Boston, MA*] [*NASDAQ symbol*] (NQ)
CLDA .... Control Logic and Drive Assembly
CLDAS...... Clinical Laboratory Data Acquisition System [*Data processing*]
CLDC........ COMSEC [*Communications Security*] Logistics Data Center (AABC)
CLDFAT ... Cell Differentiation [*A publication*]
CLDID7... Clinica Dietologica [*A publication*]
C & L Dig... Cohen and Lee's Maryland Digest [*A publication*] (DLA)
CLDL........ Canadian Labour Defence League
C/LDMO .. Chief, Logistics Data Management Office [*Army*]
CLDO .... Central Load Dispatching Office [*US Military Government, Germany*]
CLDo .... Documentation Associates, Los Angeles, CA [*Library symbol*] [*Library of Congress*] (LCLS)
CLDR........ Cliffs Drilling Co. [*NASDAQ symbol*] (NQ)
CLDS........ Canada Land Data System
CLDST ...... Closed-Loop Dynamic Stability Test (NASA)
CLDWN ... Cool Down (AAG)
CLDY........ Cloudy
CLE........... Barlow Sanatorium, Elks Tuberculosis Library, Los Angeles, CA [*Library symbol*] [*Library of Congress*] (LCLS)
CLe........... Cahiers de Lexicologie [*A publication*]
CLE........... Cahiers. Ligue Catholique de l'Evangile [*A publication*]
CLE........... Canadian Lencourt Mines Ltd. [*Toronto Stock Exchange symbol*]
CLE........... Center for Law and Education (EA)
CLE........... Centre Europeen pour les Loisirs et l'Education [*European Centre for Leisure and Education - ECLE*] (EAIO)

CLE............ Chicago Livestock Exchange
CLE............ Citizen's Library of Economics [*A publication*]
CLE............ City of London Engineers [*British military*]   (DMA)
CLE............ Claire's Stores, Inc. [*NYSE symbol*]   (SPSG)
Cle.............. Clementinae Constitutiones [*A publication*]   (DSA)
CLE............ Cleveland [*Ohio*] [*Seismograph station code, US Geological Survey*]   (SEIS)
CLE............ Cleveland [*Ohio*] [*Airport symbol*]
CLE............ Cleveland Public Library, Cleveland, OH [*OCLC symbol*]   (OCLC)
CLE............ Closed End
CLE............ Committee of Liberal Exiles [*London, England*]   (EAIO)
CLE............ Communications Line Expander [*Electrodata, Inc.*] [*Telecommunications*]
CLE............ Console Local Equipment   (MCD)
CLE............ Consumption Levels Enquiry [*British*]
CLE............ Continuing Legal Education
CLE............ Contract Lineage Equivalent [*Formula used by certain publications for calculating number of lines of advertising copy*]
CLE............ Council of Legal Education [*British*]
CLE............ Crew Loose Equipment [*Aerospace*]   (MCD)
CLE............ Key Word [*Online database field identifier*]
CLEA........ Canadian Library Exhibitors' Association
CLEA........ Chemical Leaman Corp. [*NASDAQ symbol*]   (NQ)
CLEA........ Commonwealth Legal Education Association   (EAIO)
CLEA........ Conference of LASER Engineering and Applications
CLEAA...... Comite de Liaison Entr'Aide et Action [*Help and Action Coordinating Committee*]   (EAIO)
CLEAN...... California League Enlisting Action Now [*Antiobscenity group*]
CLEAN...... Committee for Leaving the Environment of America Natural
CLEAN...... Commonwealth Law Enforcement Assistance Network [*Pennsylvania*]
Clean Air J ... Clean Air Journal [*A publication*]
Clean Air Spec Ed ... Clean Air. Special Edition [*A publication*]
Clean Fuels Biomass Wastes Symp Pap ... Clean Fuels from Biomass and Wastes. Symposium Papers [*A publication*]
Cleaning Maint Big Bldg Mgmt ... Cleaning Maintenance and Big Building Management [*A publication*]
CLEAPSE ... Consortium of Local Education Authorities for the Provision of Science Equipment [*British*]
CLEAR...... Campaign for Lead-Free Air [*British*]
CLEAR...... Center for Labor Education and Research [*University of Hawaii*] [*Research center*]   (RCD)
CLEAR...... Center for Labor Education and Research [*University of Colorado*]
CLEAR...... Center for Labor Education and Research [*University of Alabama at Birmingham*] [*Research center*]   (RCD)
CLEAR...... Center for Lake Erie Area Research [*Ohio State University*]
CLEAR...... Center for Language Education and Research [*Los Angeles, CA*] [*Department of Education*]   (GRD)
CLEAR...... Chinese Literature. Essays, Articles, Reviews [*A publication*]
CLEAR...... Closed-Loop Evaluation and Reporting System   (MCD)
CLEAR...... Compiler, Executive Program, Assembler Routines
CLEAR...... Components Life Evaluation and Reliability
CLEAR...... County Law Enforcement Applied Regionally
CLEAR...... National Clearinghouse on Licensure, Enforcement and Regulation   (EA)
Clear H ...... Clearing House [*A publication*]
Clearing H ... Clearing House [*A publication*]
Clearing House J ... Clearing House Journal [*A publication*]   (APTA)
Clearinghouse R ... Clearinghouse Review [*A publication*]
Clearinghouse Rev ... Clearinghouse Review [*A publication*]
Clearing Hse L A Soc Serv Res ... Clearing House for Local Authority Social Services Research [*A publication*]
Clear R....... Clearinghouse Review [*A publication*]
CLEARS.... Cornell Laboratory for Environmental Applications of Remote Sensing [*Cornell University*] [*Information service or system*]   (IID)
Cleary RC .. Cleary's Registration Cases [*England*] [*A publication*]   (DLA)
Cleary Reg Cas ... Cleary's Registration Cases [*Ireland*] [*A publication*]   (DLA)
Cleav Bank L ... Cleaveland's Banking Laws of New York [*A publication*]   (DLA)
CLEB........ Comunidad Latinoamericana de Escritores. Boletin [*A publication*]
C/LEC .... Citizen/Labor Energy Coalition   (EA)
CLEC........ Closed-Loop Ecological Cycle [*Aerospace*]   (AAG)
CLECA...... Clinical Endocrinology [*A publication*]
CLECAP.... Clinical Endocrinology [*A publication*]
CLECAT ... Comite de Liaison Europeen des Commissionnaires et Auxiliaires de Transport [*European Liaison Committee of Forwarders*]   (EAIO)
CLED......... Cystine-Lactose-Electrolyte Deficient [*Clinical chemistry*]
CL/EDS.... Cathodoluminescence/Energy Dispersive Spectroscopy
CLEF........ Civil Liberties Educational Foundation [*Defunct*]   (EA)
Clef Pal J .. Cleft Palate Journal [*A publication*]
CLEFT....... Cleavage of Lateral Epitaxial Film for Transfer [*Photovoltaic energy systems*]
Cleft Palate J ... Cleft Palate Journal [*A publication*]
C Leg Rec... California Legal Record [*A publication*]   (DLA)

CLEHA ..... Conference of Local Environmental Health Administrators [*Later, NCLEHA*]   (EA)
Cl Elec........ Clark's Treatise on Elections [*A publication*]   (DLA)
CLELJ .... East Los Angeles College, Los Angeles, CA [*Library symbol*] [*Library of Congress*]   (LCLS)
CLEM........ Cargo Lunar Excursion Module
CLEM........ Central Laboratory Equipment Management   (MCD)
Clem.......... Clemens' Reports [*57-59 Kansas*] [*A publication*]   (DLA)
Clem.......... Clement of Alexandria   (BJA)
Clem.......... Clementinae Constitutiones [*A publication*]   (DSA)
CleM......... [*The*] Clergy Monthly [*Ranchi, Bihar, India*] [*A publication*]
CLEM........ Closed-Loop Ex-Vessel Machine [*Formerly, EVHM*] [*Nuclear energy*]   (NRCH)
CLEM........ Composite for the Lunar Excursion Module [*NASA*]   (IEEE)
CLEM........ Contact List of Electronic Music [*Canada*] [*A publication*]
CLEM........ Continuing Legal Education, University of Montana   (DLA)
Clem.......... De Clementia [*of Seneca the Younger*] [*Classical studies*]   (OCD)
Clem Al...... Clemens Alexandrini [*First century AD*] [*Classical studies*]   (OCD)
Clem Corp Sec ... Clemens on Corporate Securities [*A publication*]   (DLA)
Clemson Univ Coll Eng Eng Exp Sta Bull ... Clemson University [*Clemson, South Carolina*]. College of Engineering. Engineering Experiment Station. Bulletin [*A publication*]
Clemson Univ Coll For Recreat Resour Dep For For Res Ser ... Clemson University. College of Forest and Recreation Resources. Department of Forestry. Forest Research Series [*A publication*]
Clemson Univ Dep For For Bull ... Clemson University. Department of Forestry. Forestry Bulletin [*A publication*]
Clemson Univ Dep For For Res Ser ... Clemson University. Department of Forestry. Forest Research Series [*A publication*]
Clemson Univ Dep For Tech Pap ... Clemson University. Department of Forestry. Technical Paper [*A publication*]
Clemson Univ Rev Ind Manage Text Sci ... Clemson University. Review of Industrial Management and Textile Science [*A publication*]
CLEN........ Monoclinic Enstatite [*Geology*]
CLENDR.... Clinical Engineering [*A publication*]
CLENE...... Continuing Library Education Network and Exchange [*American Library Association*] [*Information service or system*]   (EA)
CLENERT ... Continuing Library Education Network and Exchange Round Table   (EA)
CLENOM ... Crew Loose Equipment Nomenclature [*Aerospace*]   (MCD)
CLEO .... Clear Language for Expressing Orders [*Data processing*]   (IEEE)
CLEO .... Cleopatra Kohlique, Inc. [*NASDAQ symbol*]   (NQ)
CLEO .... Comite de Liaison Europeen des Osteopathes [*European Liaison Committee for Osteopaths - ELCO*]   (EA)
CLEO .... Commonwealth Legal Education Office [*Australia*]
CLEO .... Computer Listings of Employment Opportunities [*The Copley Press, Inc.*] [*Database*]
CLEO .... Conference on LASERs and Electro-Optics   (MCD)
CLEO .... Council on Legal Education Opportunity   (EA)
Cleom......... Cleomenes [*of Plutarch*] [*Classical studies*]   (OCD)
CLEOP...... Cleopatra [*Queen of Egypt, 69-30BC*]   (ROG)
CLEOS....... Conference on LASER and Electro-Optical Systems
CLEP........ College-Level Examination Program [*Trademark/service mark of the College Entrance Examination Board*]
CLEPA ...... Comite de Liaison de la Construction d'Equipements et de Pieces d'Automobiles [*Liaison Committee of Manufacturers of Motor Vehicle Parts and Equipment*]   (EAIO)
CLEPR ...... Council on Legal Education for Professional Responsibility   (EA)
CLER........ Classification and Labelling of Explosives Regulations
CLER........ Clergy
CLER........ Clerical
CLER........ Clerical Test [*Military*]
CLER........ Critical Laboratory Evaluation Roast [*Food technology*]
CLERG....... Clergyman
ClergyM..... [*The*] Clergy Monthly [*Ranchi, Bihar, India*] [*A publication*]
ClergyR...... [*The*] Clergy Review [*London*] [*A publication*]
Clerke Am L ... Clerke's American Law and Practice [*A publication*]   (DLA)
Clerke & Br Conv ... Clerke and Brett on Conveyancing, Etc. [*A publication*]   (DLA)
Clerke Dig ... Clerke's Digest [*New York*] [*A publication*]   (DLA)
Clerke Pr... Clerke's Praxis Curiae Admiralitatis [*A publication*]   (DLA)
Clerke Prax ... Clerke's Praxis Curiae Admiralitatis [*A publication*]   (DLA)
Clerk Home ... Clerk Home's Decisions, Scotch Court of Session [*1735-44*] [*A publication*]   (DLA)
Clermont Univ Ann Sci Geol Mineral ... Clermont. Universite. Annales Scientifiques. Geologie et Mineralogie [*A publication*]
CLER PARL ... Clericus Parliamentariorum [*Clerk of Parliaments*] [*British*]   (ROG)
CLES .... Centre for Local Economic Strategies Ltd. [*British*]   (CB)
C Let Dram ... Cineschedario-Letture Drammatiche [*A publication*]
CLETS....... California Law Enforcement Telecommunications System
CLEV........ Cleveland [*District in Yorkshire, England*]   (ROG)
CLEV......... Clevite Industries, Inc. [*Glenview, IL*] [*NASDAQ symbol*]   (NQ)
Clev B A J ... Cleveland Bar Association. Journal [*A publication*]

Clev Bar Ass'n J ... Cleveland Bar Association. Journal [*A publication*]
Clev B Assn J ... Cleveland Bar Association. Journal [*A publication*]
Clev BJ ...... Journal. Cleveland Bar Association [*A publication*] (DLA)
Cleve Bank ... Cleaveland on the Banking System [*A publication*] (DLA)
Cleve Busn ... Crain's Cleveland Business [*A publication*]
Cleve Clin J Med ... Cleveland Clinic. Journal of Medicine [*A publication*]
Cleve Clin Q ... Cleveland Clinic. Quarterly [*A publication*]
Cleveland Clin Cardiovasc Consult ... Cleveland Clinic. Cardiovascular Consultations [*A publication*]
Cleveland Clin Q ... Cleveland Clinic. Quarterly [*A publication*]
Cleveland Clin Quart ... Cleveland Clinic. Quarterly [*A publication*]
Cleveland Inst Eng Proc ... Cleveland Institution of Engineers. Proceedings [*A publication*]
Cleveland Med J ... Cleveland Medical Journal [*A publication*]
Cleveland Mus Bull ... Cleveland Museum of Art. Bulletin [*A publication*]
Cleveland Mus Nat History Mus News ... Cleveland Museum of Natural History. Museum News [*A publication*]
Cleveland Mus Nat History Sci Pubs ... Cleveland Museum of Natural History. Science Publications [*A publication*]
Cleveland SLJ ... Cleveland State Law Journal [*A publication*] (DLA)
Cleveland Symp Macromol ... Cleveland Symposium on Macromolecules [*A publication*]
Cleve Law R ... Cleveland Law Reporter [*Ohio*] [*A publication*] (DLA)
Cleve Law Rec ... Cleveland Law Record [*Ohio*] [*A publication*] (DLA)
Cleve Law Reg ... Cleveland Law Register [*Ohio*] [*A publication*] (DLA)
Cleve Law Rep ... Cleveland Law Reporter [*Ohio*] [*A publication*] (DLA)
Cleve L Rec ... Cleveland Law Record [*Ohio*] [*A publication*] (DLA)
Cleve L Rec (Ohio) ... Cleveland Law Record [*Ohio*] [*A publication*] (DLA)
Cleve L Reg ... Cleveland Law Register [*Ohio*] [*A publication*] (DLA)
Cleve L Reg (Ohio) ... Cleveland Law Register [*Ohio*] [*A publication*] (DLA)
Cleve L Rep ... Cleveland Law Reporter [*Ohio*] [*A publication*] (DLA)
Cleve LR (Ohio) ... Cleveland Law Reporter (Ohio) [*A publication*] (ILCA)
Cleve Rep ... Cleveland Law Reporter (Reprint) [*Ohio*] [*A publication*] (DLA)
Clev Insan ... Clevenger's Medical Jurisprudence of Insanity [*A publication*] (DLA)
Clev Law Rep ... Cleveland Law Reporter (Reprint) [*Ohio*] [*A publication*] (DLA)
Clev L Rec ... Cleveland Law Record [*Ohio*] [*A publication*] (DLA)
Clev L Reg ... Cleveland Law Register [*Ohio*] [*A publication*] (DLA)
Clev L Rep ... Cleveland Law Reporter [*Ohio*] [*A publication*] (DLA)
Clev-Mar L Rev ... Cleveland-Marshall Law Review [*A publication*]
Clev Orch ... Cleveland Orchestra. Program Notes [*A publication*]
Clev R ... Cleveland Law Reporter (Reprint) [*Ohio*] [*A publication*] (DLA)
Clev St L R ... Cleveland State Law Review [*A publication*]
Clev St L Rev ... Cleveland State Law Review [*A publication*]
CLEW .... Community Legal Education for Welfare Project [*Australia*]
CLEWP .... Cleared Land Explosion Widening and Proofing (MCD)
CLex .... Cahiers de Lexicologie [*A publication*]
CL EX .... Cloth Extra [*Bookbinding*] (ROG)
CLEXF .... Copper Lake Explorations Ltd. [*Vancouver, BC*] [*NASDAQ symbol*] (NQ)
Cl Extr .... Clarke on Extradition [*A publication*] (DLA)
CLEYDQ... Butterworths International Medical Reviews. Clinical Endocrinology [*A publication*]
CLF .... Calendar of Literary Facts [*A publication*]
CLF .... Capacitive Loss Factor (IEEE)
CLF .... Capital Legal Foundation (EA)
CLF .... Central Liquidity Facility [*National Credit Union Administration*]
CLF .... Chambon-La-Foret [*France*] [*Seismograph station code, US Geological Survey*] [*Closed*] (SEIS)
CLF .... Chambon-La-Foret [*France*] [*Geomagnetic observatory code*]
CLF .... Children's Legal Foundation (EA)
CLF .... Children's Liver Foundation (EA)
CLF .... Christian Librarians' Fellowship (EA)
CLF .... Chronique des Lettres Francaises [*A publication*]
CLF .... Citizens Leadership Foundation (EA)
CLF .... Civilian Labor Force [*DoD*]
Cl & F .... Clark and Finnelly's English House of Lords Cases [*1831-46*] [*A publication*] (DLA)
CLF .... Clear, AK [*Location identifier*] [*FAA*] (FAAL)
CLF .... Clear Forward [*Telecommunications*] (TEL)
CLF .... Cleveland-Cliffs, Inc. [*NYSE symbol*] (SPSG)
CLF .... Clifton Resources Ltd. [*Vancouver Stock Exchange symbol*]
CLF .... Club du Livre Francais [*A publication*]
CLF .... Colorado Union Catalog, Denver Public Library, Denver, CO [*OCLC symbol*] (OCLC)
CLF .... Commander, Landing Force [*Navy*] (NVT)
CLF .... Community Living Fund
CLF .... Comparative LOFAR Fixing [*Military*] (CAAL)
CLF .... Connecting Line Freight
CLF .... Critical Link Factor
CLF .... Current Legal Forms with Tax Analysis [*A publication*] (DLA)
CLF .... Farmer's Insurance Group, Los Angeles, CA [*Library symbol*] [*Library of Congress*] (LCLS)
CLFB .... Canadian Livestock Feed Board
CLFC .... Carol Lawrence National Fan Club (EA)
CLFC .... Closed-Loop Fire Control [*Army*] (MCD)

CLFFK ...... Company Level Field Feeding Kitchen [*Army's Combat System Test Activity*] (INF)
CLFI .... Country Lake Foods, Inc. [*NASDAQ symbol*] (NQ)
CLFIC .... Center Launch and Flight Instrumentation Center [*NASA*] (KSC)
Cl & Fin ..... Clark and Finnelly's English House of Lords Cases [*1831-46*] [*A publication*] (DLA)
CLFL .... Coastland Corp. of Florida [*NASDAQ symbol*] (NQ)
CLFMI ...... Chain Link Fence Manufacturers Institute (EA)
CLFS .... Cliffs (MCD)
CLG .... Calling (DEN)
CLG .... Ceiling [*Aviation*] (KSC)
CLG .... Center Landing Gear (MCD)
CLG .... Chalice Mining, Inc. [*Vancouver Stock Exchange symbol*]
CLG .... Change to Lower Grade [*Army*]
CLG .... Civilian Labor Group (MCD)
CLG .... Closed-Loop Gain
CLG .... Coalinga, CA [*Location identifier*] [*FAA*] (FAAL)
CLG .... College (MCD)
CLG .... Cologne [*West Germany*] [*Seismograph station code, US Geological Survey*] (SEIS)
CLG .... Combat Leader's Guide (INF)
CLG .... Compile, Load, and Go [*Data processing*] (BUR)
CLG .... Cooling (MSA)
CLG .... Cymdeithas yr Laith Gymraeg [*Welsh Language Society*] (EAIO)
CLG .... Guided Missile Light Cruiser [*Navy symbol*]
CLg .... Los Gatos Memorial Library, Los Gatos, CA [*Library symbol*] [*Library of Congress*] (LCLS)
CLGA .... Composers and Lyricists Guild of America (EA)
CLGA .... Customary Law Group of Australia
CLGAAT ... Colorado. Agricultural Experiment Station. Annual Report [*A publication*]
CLGAWD ... Cement, Lime, Gypsum, and Allied Workers Division (EA)
CLGC .... Civilian Labor Group Center [*Army*] (AABC)
CLGDC ...... Gibson, Dunn & Crutcher, Los Angeles, CA [*Library symbol*] [*Library of Congress*] (LCLS)
CLGEB8 .... Clinica Geral [*Sao Paulo*] [*A publication*]
CLGEDA ... Clinical Gerontologist [*A publication*]
CLGES ...... California Life Goals Evaluation Schedules [*Psychology*]
CLGL .... Church of Jesus Christ of Latter-Day Saints, Genealogical Society Library, Los Angeles Temple, Los Angeles, CA [*Library symbol*] [*Library of Congress*] (LCLS)
CLGLE ...... Church of Jesus Christ of Latter-Day Saints, Genealogical Society Library, Los Angeles East Branch, Los Angeles, CA [*Library symbol*] [*Library of Congress*] (LCLS)
CLGN .... Columbia General Corp. [*Dallas, TX*] [*NASDAQ symbol*] (NQ)
CLGN .... Guided Missile Light Cruiser (Nuclear Propulsion) [*Navy symbol*] [*Obsolete*]
CLgN .... Novitiate of Los Gatos, Los Gatos, CA [*Library symbol*] [*Library of Congress*] (LCLS)
CLGNA ..... Clinical Genetics [*A publication*]
CLGNAY ... Clinical Genetics [*A publication*]
CLGNM .... Citizens for a Lebanon-Grenada National Memorial (EA)
CLGO .... Getty Oil Co., Los Angeles, CA [*Library symbol*] [*Library of Congress*] (LCLS)
CLGP .... Cannon-Launched Guided Projectile
CLGP .... General Petroleum Corp., Los Angeles, CA [*Library symbol*] [*Library of Congress*] (LCLS)
CLGPC ...... George Pepperdine College, Los Angeles, CA [*Library symbol*] [*Library of Congress*] (LCLS)
CLGR .... Clinical Gerontologist [*A publication*]
CLGRC ...... Canadian Lesbian and Gay Rights Coalition
CLGS .... Cooperating Libraries of Greater Springfield [*Library network*]
CLGS .... Golden State Mutual Life Insurance Co., Los Angeles, CA [*Library symbol*] [*Library of Congress*] (LCLS)
CLGSFU .... Clear Glazed Structural Facing Units [*Technical drawings*]
CLGSO ..... Civilian Labor Group Special Orders [*Army*] (AABC)
CLGSUB ... Clear Glazed Structural Unit Base [*Technical drawings*]
CLGT .... Center for Local Government Technology [*Oklahoma State University*] [*Research center*] (RCD)
CL GT .... Cloth Gilt [*Bookbinding*] (ROG)
CLGUA ...... Colliery Guardian [*England*] [*A publication*]
CLGW .... United Cement, Lime, and Gypsum Workers International Union
CLH .... Calcutta Light Horse [*British military*] (DMA)
CLH .... Canadian Library Handbook [*A publication*]
CLH .... Cedars of Lebanon Hospital (MCD)
CLH .... Cheltenham [*United States of America*] [*Geomagnetic observatory code*]
CLH .... Cheltenham [*Maryland*] [*Seismograph station code, US Geological Survey*] [*Closed*] (SEIS)
CL H .... Clare Hall [*Cambridge University*] (ROG)
Cl & H .... Clarke and Hall's Cases of Contested Elections in Congress [*1789-1834*] [*United States*] [*A publication*] (DLA)
CLH .... Common Lodging House [*British*] (ROG)
CLH .... Coral Gold Corp. [*Vancouver Stock Exchange symbol*]
CLH .... Croix de la Legion d'Honneur [*Cross of the Legion of Honor*] [*French*]

CLH .... Hyland Laboratories, Los Angeles, CA [*Library symbol*] [*Library of Congress*] (LCLS)
CLHA .... Common Lodging Houses Act [*1851*] [*British*] (ROG)
CLHB .... Clean Harbors, Inc. [*NASDAQ symbol*] (NQ)
CLhC .... Chevron Oil Field Research Co., La Habra, CA [*Library symbol*] [*Library of Congress*] (LCLS)
CLHC .... Congregation of Our Lady, Help of the Clergy [*Roman Catholic women's religious order*]
ClHgBzO ... Chloromercuribenzoate [*Biochemistry*]
CLHi .... Historical Society of Southern California, Los Angeles, CA [*Library symbol*] [*Library of Congress*] (LCLS)
CLHJ .... Los Angeles Harbor Junior College, Wilmington, CA [*Library symbol*] [*Library of Congress*] (LCLS)
CL HL .... Clerk of the House of Lords [*British*] (ROG)
CLHMB3 .. Clinics in Haematology [*A publication*]
CLHMC .... Centennial Legion of Historic Military Commands (EA)
CLHMD .... Cahiers. Laboratoire d'Hydrobiologie de Montereau [*A publication*]
CL HO COM ... Clerk of the House of Commons [*British*] (ROG)
Cl Home ..... Clerk Home's Scotch Session Cases [*A publication*] (DLA)
CLHU .... Computer Laboratory of Harvard University
CLHU .... Hebrew Union College - Jewish Institute of Religion, Los Angeles, CA [*Library symbol*] [*Library of Congress*] (LCLS)
CLI .... Calamus Length Index
CLI .... Calling Line Identification [*or Identity*] [*Telecommunications*] (TEL)
CLI .... Canada Land Inventory
CLI .... Capacitor Leakage Indicator
CLI .... Celtic Resources Ltd. [*Vancouver Stock Exchange symbol*]
CLI .... Christian Law Institute (EA)
CLi .... Christian Librarian [*A publication*]
CLI .... Clintonville, WI [*Location identifier*] [*FAA*] (FAAL)
CLI .... Coach Lace Institute [*Defunct*] (EA)
CLI .... Coaliquid, Incorporated (MCD)
CLI .... Coefficient of Luminous Intensity
CLI .... Coherent LASER Illumination
CLI .... Coin Level Indicator [*Telephone communications*]
CLI .... Command Language Interpreter [*Data processing*]
CLI .... Command Line Interface [*For Amiga computers*]
CLI .... Command Line Interpret [*Military*] (CAAL)
CLI .... Commercial Liability Insurance [*International Risk Management Institute*] [*A publication*]
CLI .... Communication Line Interface (MCD)
CLI .... Compression Labs, Incorporated [*San Jose, CA*] [*Telecommunications*] (TSSD)
CLI .... Connaught Laboratories, Inc.
CLI .... Contractor Line Item (MCD)
CLI .... Control Level Item
CLI .... Core Logic Intervalometer
CLI .... Cornwall Light Infantry [*British military*] (DMA)
CLI .... Corticoliberin-Like Immunoreactivity
CLI .... Cost-of-Living Index [*Economics*]
CLi .... Cuadernos de Literatura [*A publication*]
CLI .... Immaculate Heart College, Los Angeles, CA [*Library symbol*] [*Library of Congress*] (LCLS)
CLI .... Immaculate Heart College, Los Angeles, CA [*OCLC symbol*] [*Inactive*] (OCLC)
CLi .... Lincoln Public Library, Lincoln, CA [*Library symbol*] [*Library of Congress*] (LCLS)
CLIA .... American Institute of Aeronautics and Astronautics, Pacific Aerospace Library, Los Angeles, CA [*Library symbol*] [*Library of Congress*] (LCLS)
CLIA .... Clinical Laboratory Improvement Act
CLIA .... Cruise Lines International Association (EA)
CLIBOC .... Chinese Linguistics Bibliography on Computer [*Cambridge University Press*] [*England*]
CLIC .... Canadian Law Information Council [*Information service or system*] (IID)
CLIC .... Center for Low-Intensity Conflict [*Army*]
CLIC .... CERN [*Conseil Europeen pour la Recherche Nucleaire*] Linear Collider [*Particle physics*]
CLIC .... Clairson International Corporation [*Ocala, FL*] [*NASDAQ symbol*] (NQ)
CLIC .... Command Language for Interrogating Computers [*Royal RADAR Establishment*] [*British*]
CLIC .... Commercial Loan Insurance Corporation
CLIC .... Communication Line Interface Computer (MCD)
CLIC .... Conversational Language for Interactive Computing
CLIC .... Cooperating Libraries in Consortium [*St. Paul, MN*] [*Library network*]
CLIC .... Council of Life Insurance Consultants (EA)
CLICC .... Cooperative Libraries in Central Connecticut [*Library network*]
CLICEC ..... Comite de Liaison International des Cooperatives d'Epargne et de Credit [*International Liaison Committee on Co-Operative Thrift and Credit - ILCCTC*] [*Paris, France*] (EA)
CLid .... Cesky Lid [*A publication*]
CLIETA ..... Comite de Liaison de l'Industrie Europeenne des Tubes d'Acier [*Liaison Committee of the EEC Steel Tube Industry*] (EAIO)

CLIF .... Cliff Engle Ltd. [*Carlstadt, NJ*] [*NASDAQ symbol*] (NQ)
Clif .... Clifford's United States Circuit Court Reports, First Circuit [*A publication*] (DLA)
CLIF .... Cliffside Railroad Co. [*AAR code*]
CLIFC .... Cecilia Lee International Fan Club (EA)
CLIFC .... Chris LeDoux International Fan Club (EA)
C Life .... Christian Life [*A publication*]
Clif El .... Clifford's English Southwick Election Cases [*1796-97*] [*A publication*] (DLA)
Clif El Cas ... Clifford's English Southwick Election Cases [*1796-97*] [*A publication*] (DLA)
Cliff .... Clifford's English Southwick Election Cases [*1796-97*] [*A publication*] (DLA)
Cliff .... Clifford's United States Circuit Court Reports, First Circuit [*A publication*] (DLA)
Cliff (CC) ... Clifford's United States Circuit Court Reports, First Circuit [*A publication*] (DLA)
Cliff El Cas ... Clifford's English Southwick Election Cases [*1796-97*] [*A publication*] (DLA)
Cliff & Rich ... Clifford and Richard's English Locus Standi Reports [*1873-84*] [*A publication*] (DLA)
Cliff & Steph ... Clifford and Stephens' English Locus Standi Reports [*1867-72*] [*A publication*] (DLA)
Clif Prob .... Clifford's Probate Guide [*A publication*] (DLA)
Clif & R ..... Clifford and Richard's English Locus Standi Reports [*1873-84*] [*A publication*] (DLA)
Clif & Rich ... Clifford and Richard's English Locus Standi Reports [*1873-84*] [*A publication*] (DLA)
CLIFS .... Cost, Life, Interchangeability, Function, and Safety [*Navy*] (NG)
Clif South El ... Clifford's English Southwick Election Cases [*1796-97*] [*A publication*] (DLA)
Clif South El Cas ... Clifford's English Southwick Election Cases [*1796-97*] [*A publication*] (DLA)
Clif & St ..... Clifford and Stephens' English Locus Standi Reports [*1867-72*] [*A publication*] (DLA)
Clif & Steph ... Clifford and Stephens' English Locus Standi Reports [*1867-72*] [*A publication*] (DLA)
Clift .... Clift's Entries [*1719*] [*England*] [*A publication*] (DLA)
C Ligures Prehist Archeol ... Cahiers Ligures de Prehistoire et d'Archeologie [*A publication*]
CLIH .... Chicago Lying-In Hospital
CLIIA .... Clinical Immunology and Immunopathology [*A publication*]
CLIIAT ...... Clinical Immunology and Immunopathology [*A publication*]
CLIM .... Climatic (AFM)
Clima Comm Internat ... Clima Commerce International [*A publication*]
CLIMAP ... Climate: Long-Range Investigation, Mapping, and Prediction [*National Science Foundation*]
Climat Data ... Climatological Data [*A publication*]
CLIMATOL ... Climatology
CLIMB8 .... Cellular Immunology [*A publication*]
Clim Change ... Climatic Change [*A publication*]
Clim Control ... Climate Control [*India*] [*A publication*]
CLIMMAR ... Centre de Liaison International des Marchands de Machines Agricoles et Reparateurs [*International Liaison Center for Agricultural Machinery Distributors and Maintenance*] [*Common Market*]
CLIMPO ... Contract Liaison and Master Planning Office [*Military*]
CLin .... Cercetari de Linguistica [*A publication*]
CLIN .... Clini-Therm Corp. [*Dallas, TX*] [*NASDAQ symbol*] (NQ)
CLIN .... Clinical
CLIN .... Contract Line Item Number [*Army*] (AABC)
CLIN .... Los Angeles Neurological Medical Group, Inc., Los Angeles, CA [*Library symbol*] [*Library of Congress*] (LCLS)
Clin Allergy ... Clinical Allergy [*A publication*]
Clin All-Round ... Clinic All-Round [*Japan*] [*A publication*]
Clin Anaesthesiol ... Clinics in Anaesthesiology [*A publication*]
Clin Androl ... Clinics in Andrology [*A publication*]
Clin Anesth ... Clinical Anesthesia [*A publication*]
Clin Approaches Probl Child ... Clinical Approaches to Problems of Childhood [*A publication*]
Clin Bacteriol (Tokyo) ... Clinical Bacteriology (Tokyo) [*A publication*]
Clin Behav Therapy Rev ... Clinical Behavior Therapy Review [*A publication*]
Clin Bioch .. Clinical Biochemistry [*A publication*]
Clin Biochem ... Clinical Biochemistry [*A publication*]
Clin Biochem Anal ... Clinical and Biochemical Analysis [*A publication*]
Clin Biofeedback Health ... Clinical Biofeedback and Health [*A publication*]
Clin Biomech ... Clinical Biomechanics [*A publication*]
Clin Bull ... Clinical Bulletin [*A publication*]
Clin Bull (Mem Sloan-Kettering Cancer Cent) ... Clinical Bulletin (Memorial Sloan-Kettering Cancer Center) [*A publication*]
Clin Cardiol ... Clinical Cardiology [*A publication*]
Clin Chem ... Clinical Chemistry [*A publication*]
Clin Chem (Winston Salem North Carolina) ... Clinical Chemistry (Winston-Salem, North Carolina) [*A publication*]
Clin Chest Med ... Clinics in Chest Medicine [*A publication*]
Clin Chim A ... Clinica Chimica Acta [*A publication*]
Clin Chim Acta ... Clinica Chimica Acta [*A publication*]
Clin Cytol Ser Monogr ... Clinical Cytology: A Series of Monographs [*A publication*]
Clin Diagn Ultrasound ... Clinics in Diagnostic Ultrasound [*A publication*]

Clin Dig...... Clinton's Digest [*New York*] [*A publication*] (DLA)
CLINE....... Carpet Information Network [*Tapistree Group, Inc.*] [*Information service or system*] (IID)
Clin EEG ... Clinical Electroencephalography [*A publication*]
Clin Electr ... Clinical Electroencephalography [*A publication*]
Clin Electroencephalogr ... Clinical Electroencephalography [*A publication*]
Clin End Me ... Clinics in Endocrinology and Metabolism [*A publication*]
Clin Endocr ... Clinical Endocrinology [*A publication*]
Clin Endocrinol ... Clinical Endocrinology [*A publication*]
Clin Endocrinol Metab ... Clinical Endocrinology and Metabolism [*A publication*]
Clin Eng..... Clinical Engineering [*A publication*]
Clin Engineer ... Clinical Engineer [*A publication*]
Clin Eng Inf Serv ... Clinical Engineering Information Service [*A publication*]
Clin Eng News ... Clinical Engineering News [*A publication*]
CLINES..... CSIRO Library Network System
Clin Eur ... Clinica Europa [*A publication*]
Clin Exp Dermatol ... Clinical and Experimental Dermatology [*A publication*]
Clin Exp Dial Apheresis ... Clinical and Experimental Dialysis and Apheresis [*A publication*]
Clin Exper Immunol ... Clinical and Experimental Immunology [*A publication*]
Clin Exp Hypertens ... Clinical and Experimental Hypertension [*A publication*]
Clin Exp Hypertens A ... Clinical and Experimental Hypertension. Part A. Theory and Practice [*A publication*]
Clin Exp Hypertens B ... Clinical and Experimental Hypertension. Part B. Hypertension in Pregnancy [*A publication*]
Clin Exp Hypertens Part A Theory Pract ... Clinical and Experimental Hypertension. Part A. Theory and Practice [*A publication*]
Clin Exp Im ... Clinical and Experimental Immunology [*A publication*]
Clin Exp Immunol ... Clinical and Experimental Immunology [*A publication*]
Clin Exp Immunoreprod ... Clinical and Experimental Immunoreproduction [*A publication*]
Clin & Exp Metastasis ... Clinical and Experimental Metastasis [*A publication*]
Clin Exp Metastasis ... Clinical and Experimental Metastasis [*A publication*]
Clin Exp Neurol ... Clinical and Experimental Neurology [*A publication*]
Clin Exp Nutr ... Clinical and Experimental Nutrition [*A publication*]
Clin Exp Obstet Gynecol ... Clinical and Experimental Obstetrics and Gynecology [*A publication*]
Clin Exp Ph ... Clinical and Experimental Pharmacology and Physiology [*A publication*]
Clin Exp Pharmacol Physiol Suppl ... Clinical and Experimental Pharmacology and Physiology. Supplement [*A publication*]
Clin Exp Pharmcol Physiol ... Clinical and Experimental Pharmacology and Physiology [*A publication*]
Clin Exp Rheumatol ... Clinical and Experimental Rheumatology [*A publication*]
C Ling .... Cercetari de Linguistica [*A publication*]
Clin Gastro ... Clinics in Gastroenterology [*A publication*]
Clin Gastroenterol ... Clinics in Gastroenterology [*A publication*]
Clin Gastroenterol Suppl ... Clinics in Gastroenterology. Supplement [*A publication*]
Clin Genet ... Clinical Genetics [*A publication*]
Clin Geral (Sao Paulo) ... Clinica Geral (Sao Paulo) [*A publication*]
Clin Geriatr Med ... Clinics in Geriatric Medicine [*A publication*]
Clin Gerontol ... Clinical Gerontologist [*A publication*]
Clin Ginecol ... Clinica Ginecologica [*A publication*]
Clin Gynecol Obstet (Tokyo) ... Clinical Gynecology and Obstetrics (Tokyo) [*A publication*]
Clin Haemat ... Clinics in Haematology [*A publication*]
Clin Haematol ... Clinics in Haematology [*A publication*]
Clin Hemorh ... Clinical Hemorheology [*A publication*]
Clin Hig Hidrol ... Clinica Higiene e Hidrologia [*A publication*]
Clinica Chim Acta ... Clinica Chimica Acta [*A publication*]
Clinica Pediat ... Clinica Pediatrica [*A publication*]
Clinica Terap ... Clinica Terapeutica [*A publication*]
Clin Imaging ... Clinical Imaging [*A publication*]
Clin Immun ... Clinical Immunology and Immunopathology [*A publication*]
Clin Immunol Immunopathol ... Clinical Immunology and Immunopathology [*A publication*]
Clin Immunol Newsl ... Clinical Immunology Newsletter [*A publication*]
Clin Immunol Rev ... Clinical Immunology Reviews [*A publication*]
Clin Invest ... Clinical and Investigative Medicine [*A publication*]
Clin Invest Med ... Clinical and Investigative Medicine [*A publication*]
CLIN JL .... Clinical Journal [*A publication*] (ROG)
Clin Lab..... Clinica y Laboratoria [*A publication*]
Clin Lab Haematol ... Clinical and Laboratory Haematology [*A publication*]
Clin Lab Med ... Clinics in Laboratory Medicine [*A publication*]
Clin Latina ... Clinica Latina [*A publication*]
Clin Libr Q ... Clinical Librarian Quarterly [*A publication*]
Clin Manage Phys Ther ... Clinical Management in Physical Therapy [*A publication*]
Clin Med..... Clinical Medicine [*A publication*]
Clin Med Ital ... Clinica Medica Italiana [*A publication*]
Clin Med Surg ... Clinical Medicine and Surgery [*A publication*]
Clin Mon Hemat ... Clinical Monographs in Hematology [*A publication*]
Clin Nephrol ... Clinical Nephrology [*A publication*]
Clin Neurol ... Clinical Neurology and Neurosurgery [*A publication*]

Clin Neurol Neurosurg ... Clinical Neurology and Neurosurgery [*A publication*]
Clin Neurol (Tokyo) ... Clinical Neurology (Tokyo) [*A publication*]
Clin Neuropathol ... Clinical Neuropathology [*A publication*]
Clin Neuropharmacol ... Clinical Neuropharmacology [*A publication*]
Clin Neuropsychol ... Clinical Neuropsychology [*A publication*]
Clin Neurosurg ... Clinical Neurosurgery [*A publication*]
Clin Notes Respir Dis ... Clinical Notes on Respiratory Diseases [*A publication*]
Clin Nucl Med ... Clinical Nuclear Medicine [*A publication*]
Clin Nutr ... Clinical Nutrition [*A publication*]
Clin Nutr (Phila) ... Clinical Nutrition (Philadelphia) [*A publication*]
Clin Obstet Gynaecol Suppl ... Clinics in Obstetrics and Gynaecology. Supplement [*A publication*]
Clin Obstet Gynecol ... Clinical Obstetrics and Gynecology [*A publication*]
Clin Obst Gynec ... Clinical Obstetrics and Gynecology [*A publication*]
Clin Oncol ... Clinical Oncology [*A publication*]
Clin Oncol (Tianjin) ... Clinical Oncology (Tianjin) [*A publication*]
Clin Ophtalmol ... Clinique Ophtalmologique [*A publication*]
Clin Orthop ... Clinical Orthopaedics [*A publication*]
Clin Orthop ... Clinical Orthopaedics and Related Research [*A publication*]
Clin Orthop Relat Res ... Clinical Orthopaedics and Related Research [*A publication*]
Clin Orthop Surg ... Clinical Orthopedic Surgery [*Japan*] [*A publication*]
Clin Ortop ... Clinica Ortopedica [*A publication*]
Clin Ostet Ginecol ... Clinica Ostetrica e Ginecologica [*A publication*]
Clin Otolaryngol ... Clinical Otolaryngology [*A publication*]
Clin Otolaryngol Allied Sci (Oxf) ... Clinical Otolaryngology and Allied Sciences (Oxford) [*A publication*]
Clin Otolaryngol (Oxf) ... Clinical Otolaryngology (Oxford) [*A publication*]
Clin Otorinolaringoiatr (Catania) ... Clinica Otorinolaringoiatrica (Catania) [*A publication*]
Clin Pediat ... Clinica Pediatrica [*A publication*]
Clin Pediat ... Clinical Pediatrics [*Philadelphia*] [*A publication*]
Clin Pediatr ... Clinical Pediatrics [*A publication*]
Clin Pediatr (Phila) ... Clinical Pediatrics (Philadelphia) [*A publication*]
Clin Pediatr (Philadelphia) ... Clinical Pediatrics (Philadelphia) [*A publication*]
Clin Perinatol ... Clinics in Perinatology [*A publication*]
Clin Pharm ... Clinical Pharmacology and Therapeutics [*A publication*]
Clin Pharmacokinet ... Clinical Pharmacokinetics [*A publication*]
Clin Pharmacol (NY) ... Clinical Pharmacology (New York) [*A publication*]
Clin Pharmacol Res ... Clinical Pharmacology Research [*A publication*]
Clin Pharmacol Ther ... Clinical Pharmacology and Therapeutics [*A publication*]
Clin Pharmacol Therap ... Clinical Pharmacology and Therapeutics [*A publication*]
Clin Pharm Symp ... Clinical Pharmacy Symposium [*A publication*]
Clin Physiol ... Clinical Physiology [*A publication*]
Clin Physiol Biochem ... Clinical Physiology and Biochemistry [*A publication*]
Clin Physiol (Oxf) ... Clinical Physiology (Oxford) [*A publication*]
Clin Phys and Physiol Meas ... Clinical Physics and Physiological Measurement [*A publication*]
Clin Plast Surg ... Clinics in Plastic Surgery [*A publication*]
Clin Podiatr Med Surg ... Clinics in Podiatric Medicine and Surgery [*A publication*]
Clin Podiatry ... Clinics in Podiatry [*A publication*]
Clin Prev Dent ... Clinical Preventive Dentistry [*A publication*]
Clin Prevent Dent ... Clinical Preventive Dentistry [*A publication*]
Clin Proc (Cape Town) ... Clinical Proceedings (Cape Town) [*A publication*]
Clin Proc Child Hosp DC ... Clinical Proceedings. Children's Hospital of the District of Columbia [*Later, Clinical Proceedings. Children's Hospital National Medical Center*] [*A publication*]
Clin Proc Child Hosp Natl Med Cent ... Clinical Proceedings. Children's Hospital National Medical Center [*A publication*]
CLINPROT ... Clinical Protocols [*National Cancer Institute*] [*Information service or system*]
Clin Psychiatr ... Clinical Psychiatry [*Japan*] [*A publication*]
Clin Radiol ... Clinical Radiology [*A publication*]
Clin Rep..... Clinical Report [*Japan*] [*A publication*]
Clin Reprod Fertil ... Clinical Reproduction and Fertility [*A publication*]
Clin Reprod Neuroendocrinol Int Semin ... Clinical Reproductive Neuroendocrinology. International Seminar on Reproductive Physiology and Sexual Endocrinology [*A publication*]
Clin Res..... Clinical Research [*A publication*]
Clin Res Cent Symp (Harrow Engl) ... Clinical Research Centre. Symposium (Harrow, England) [*A publication*]
Clin Respir Physiol ... Clinical Respiratory Physiology [*A publication*]
Clin Res Pract Drug Regul Aff ... Clinical Research Practices and Drug Regulatory Affairs [*A publication*]
Clin Res Proc ... Clinical Research Proceedings [*A publication*]
Clin Res Rev ... Clinical Research Reviews [*A publication*]
Clin Rev Allergy ... Clinical Reviews in Allergy [*A publication*]
Clin Rheumatol ... Clinical Rheumatology [*A publication*]
Clin Rheum Dis ... Clinics in Rheumatic Diseases [*A publication*]
Cl Ins .... Clarke on Law of Insurance [*Canada*] [*A publication*] (DLA)
CLINS .... Climatic Laboratory Instrumentation System (MCD)
Clin Sc........ Clinical Science [*A publication*]

Clin Sci ...... Clinical Science [*Oxford*] [*Later, Clinical Science and Molecular Medicine*] [*A publication*]
Clin Sci (Lond) ... Clinical Science (London) [*A publication*]
Clin Sci Mol Med ... Clinical Science and Molecular Medicine [*A publication*]
Clin Sci Mol Med Suppl ... Clinical Science and Molecular Medicine. Supplement [*A publication*]
Clin Sci (Oxf) ... Clinical Science (Oxford) [*Later, Clinical Science and Molecular Medicine*] [*A publication*] [*A publication*]
Clin Sci Suppl ... Clinical Science. Supplement [*A publication*]
Clin Sc Mol ... Clinical Science and Molecular Medicine [*A publication*]
Clin Sociol Rev ... Clinical Sociology Review [*A publication*]
Clin Sports Med ... Clinics in Sports Medicine [*A publication*]
Clin Superv ... Clinical Supervisor. The Journal of Supervision in Psychotherapy and Mental Health [*A publication*]
Clin Surg.... Clinical Surgery [*Japan*] [*A publication*]
Clin S Work ... Clinical Social Work Journal [*A publication*]
Clin Symp.. Clinical Symposia [*A publication*]
Clint .... Intrinsic Clearance [*Physiology*]
Clin Ter...... Clinica Terapeutica [*A publication*]
Clin Ther.... Clinical Therapeutics [*A publication*]
Clin Toxic .. Clinical Toxicology [*A publication*]
Clin Toxicol ... Clinical Toxicology [*A publication*]
Clin Toxicol Bull ... Clinical Toxicology Bulletin [*A publication*]
Clin Toxicol Consult ... Clinical Toxicology Consultant [*A publication*]
Clin Trials J ... Clinical Trials Journal [*A publication*]
Clin Vet (Milan) ... Clinica Veterinaria (Milan) [*A publication*]
Clin Virginia Mason Hosp ... Clinics of the Virginia Mason Hospital [*A publication*]
CLIO.......... Chelsea, London, Islington, Office [*Denoting a location where a manuscript was written*] [*Acronym used as pseudonym of Joseph Addison, British author, 1672-1719*]
CLIO.......... Conversational Language for Input/Output [*Data processing*]
CLIOAD.... Clinique Ophtalmologique [*A publication*]
Clio Med .... Clio Medica [*A publication*]
CLIP .... Cancel Launch in Progress [*Air Force*]
CLIP .... Cellular Logic Image Processor [*Telecommunications*] (TEL)
CLIP .... Centralized Library Information Processor [*United States Computer Corp.*] [*Information service or system*] (IID)
CLIP .... Centre for Legal Information and Publications [*College of Law, Sydney*] [*Australia*]
Clip .... Clipping [*Medicine*]
CLIP .... Close-In Improvement Program [*to increase torpedo effectiveness*] (MCD)
CLIP .... Combined LASER Instrumentation Package (NASA)
CLIP .... Compiler Language for Information Processing [*System Development Corp.*] [*Programming language*]
CLIP .... Computer Launch Interference Problems
CLIP .... Corticotrophin-Like Intermediate-Lobe Peptide [*Endocrinology*]
CLIP .... Country Logistics Improvement Program [*Air Force*]
CLIPER..... Climatology and Persistence
CLIPI......... Center for Law in the Public Interest (EA)
CLIPPR..... Consolidated Logistics Information Planning and Programming Requirements
CLIPR .... Computer Laboratory for Instruction in Psychological Research [*University of Colorado - Boulder*] [*Research center*] (RCD)
CLIPS......... Calculation Link Processing System [*Military*] (CAAL)
CLIPS........ Coincident Light Information Photographic Strips
CLIR.......... Center for Labor and Industrial Relations [*New York Institute of Technology*] [*Research center*] (RCD)
CLIRA .... Closed-Loop In-Reactor Assembly [*Nuclear energy*] (NRCH)
CLIRS........ Computerised Legal Information Retrieval System [*CLIRS Ltd.*] [*Information service or system*] (IID)
CLIRS........ Computerized Legal Information Retrieval System (ADA)
CLIS .... Clearinghouse for Library and Information Sciences
CLIS .... Contract Line Item Status (MCD)
CLIS .... Criminalistic Laboratory Information Systems [*FBI*]
CLit............ Ceska Literatura [*A publication*]
CLit............ Companion of Literature [*Royal Society of Literature award*] [*British*]
CLit............ Convorbiri Literare [*A publication*]
CLit........... Correo Literario [*A publication*]
CLITAM ... Centre de Liaison des Industries de Traitement des Algues Marines de la CEE [*Liaison Center of the Industries for the Treatment of Seaweeds in the European Economic Community*]
CLITRAVI ... Centre de Liaison des Industries Transformatrices de la CEE [*Liaison Center of the Meat Processing Industries of the EEC*] [*Belgium*]
CLIU......... Catholic Life Insurance Union (EA)
CLIV......... Cold Leg Isolation Valve [*Nuclear energy*] (NRCH)
CLIV......... Core Logic Intervalometer
CLiv .... Livermore Library, Livermore, CA [*Library symbol*] [*Library of Congress*] (LCLS)
CLivS........ Sandia Laboratories, Livermore, CA [*Library symbol*] [*Library of Congress*] (LCLS)
CLivV........ United States Veterans Administration Hospital, Livermore, CA [*Library symbol*] [*Library of Congress*] (LCLS)
CLIX.......... Compression Labs, Incorporated [*San Jose, CA*] [*NASDAQ symbol*] (NQ)

CLIXS........ Class IX Study
CLJ .... Calais Resources Ltd. [*Toronto Stock Exchange symbol*]
CLJ .... Calcutta Law Journal [*A publication*] (DLA)
CLJ .... California Law Journal [*A publication*] (DLA)
CLJ .... Cambridge Law Journal [*A publication*]
CLJ .... Canada Law Journal [*A publication*] (DLA)
CLJ .... Canadian Library Journal [*A publication*]
CLJ .... Cantrell Resources [*Vancouver Stock Exchange symbol*]
CLJ .... Cape Law Journal [*South Africa*] [*A publication*] (DLA)
CLJ .... Central Law Journal [*A publication*] (DLA)
CLJ .... Ceylon Law Journal [*A publication*] (DLA)
CLJ .... Chicago Law Journal [*A publication*] (DLA)
CLJ .... Classical Journal [*A publication*]
CLJ .... Cluj-Napoca [*Romania*] [*Airport symbol*] (OAG)
CLJ .... Colonial Law Journal Reports [*A publication*] (DLA)
CLJ .... Commander of the Order of St. Lazarus of Jerusalem
CLJ .... Commercial Law Journal [*Commercial Law League of America*] [*A publication*]
CLJ .... Control Joint (AAG)
CLJ .... Cornell Library Journal [*A publication*]
CLJ .... Criminal Law Journal [*A publication*]
CLJ .... Criminal Law Journal of India [*A publication*]
CLJ .... University of Judaism, Los Angeles, CA [*Library symbol*] [*Library of Congress*] (LCLS)
CLJA .... Closed-Loop Jumper Assembly [*Nuclear energy*] (NRCH)
CLJC .... Copiah-Lincoln Junior College [*Wesson, MS*]
CLjC .... Copley Newspapers, Inc., James S. Copley Library, La Jolla, CA [*Library symbol*] [*Library of Congress*] (LCLS)
CLjFS .... United States National Marine Fisheries Service, Southwest Fisheries Center, La Jolla, CA [*Library symbol*] [*Library of Congress*] (LCLS)
CLjL .... Library Association of La Jolla, La Jolla, CA [*Library symbol*] [*Library of Congress*] [*Obsolete*] (LCLS)
CLJ & Lit Rev ... California Law Journal and Literary Review [*A publication*] (DLA)
Cl Journ (C) ... Classical Journal (Chicago) [*A publication*]
CLK .... Cadillac & Lake City Railway Co. [*AAR code*]
CLK .... Chileka [*Malawi*] [*Seismograph station code, US Geological Survey*] (SEIS)
CLK .... Clark Aviation Corp. [*New Cumberland, PA*] [*FAA designator*] (FAAC)
CLK .... Clark Consolidated Industries, Inc. [*AMEX symbol*] (SPSG)
CLK .... Clerk (AFM)
CLK .... Clinton, OK [*Location identifier*] [*FAA*] (FAAL)
CLK .... Clock (AAG)
CLK .... Colchis Resources Ltd. [*Vancouver Stock Exchange symbol*]
CLK .... Contact-Lens-Induced Keratoconjunctivitis [*Ophthalmology*]
CLK .... Craton, Lodge and Knight [*British*]
CLK .... Hunter-Killer Ship [*Navy symbol*] [*Obsolete*]
CLK .... Kaiser Foundation Hospital, Los Angeles, CA [*Library symbol*] [*Library of Congress*] (LCLS)
CLK CT ..... Clerks of Court [*Legal term*] (DLA)
CLK-D .... Kaiser Foundation Hospital, Doctor's Library, Los Angeles, CA [*Library symbol*] [*Library of Congress*] (LCLS)
CLKG........ Caulking (MSA)
CLKH .... Comptoir du Livre [*Keren Hasefer*] [*A publication*] (BJA)
CLKJ .... Caulked Joint
CLKO .... Clerk in Orders [*Church of England*]
CLKOB ...... Clockwise Orbit [*Aviation*] (FAAC)
Clk's Mag .. Clerk's Magazine [*A publication*] (DLA)
CLKW........ Clockwise (ADA)
CLKWS...... Clockwise
CLKWZ..... Clockwise (AFM)
cll................ Calligrapher [*MARC relator code*] [*Library of Congress*] (LCCP)
CLL............ Carolin Mines Limited [*Toronto Stock Exchange symbol*] [*Vancouver Stock Exchange symbol*]
CLL............ Catholic Listener Library [*Later, Maynard Listener Library*] (EA)
CLL............ Chicken Lactose-Lectin [*Biochemistry*]
CLL............ Chief of Legislative Liaison [*Army*]
CLL............ Chippewa Library League [*Library network*]
CLL............ Cholesterol Lowering Lipid [*Biochemistry*]
CLL............ Chronic Lymphatic [*or Lymphocytic*] Leukemia [*Medicine*]
CLL............ Circulation Lift Limit
CL L............ Classical Latin [*Language, etc.*] (ROG)
CLL............ Clauses (ADA)
CLL............ Clinical Lab Letter [*A publication*]
CLL............ College Station [*Texas*] [*Airport symbol*] (OAG)
CLL............ College Station, TX [*Location identifier*] [*FAA*] (FAAL)
CLL............ Collmberg [*German Democratic Republic*] [*Seismograph station code, US Geological Survey*] (SEIS)
CLL............ Confederation of Lebanese Labor
CLL............ Contact Limit Line [*Technical drawings*]
CLL............ Contingent Liability Ledger [*DoD*]
CLL............ Council for Liberal Learning [*Defunct*] (EA)
CLL............ Creighton University, Law Library, Omaha, NE [*OCLC symbol*] (OCLC)
CLL............ Critical Labor Level (ADA)
CLL............ Critical Load Level

CLL............	Los Angeles County Law Library, Los Angeles, CA [*Library symbol*] [*Library of Congress*] (LCLS)
CLLA.........	Cahiers de Litterature et de Linguistique Appliquee [*A publication*]
CLLA.........	Commercial Law League of America [*Chicago, IL*] (EA)
CLLAAK ...	Clinica y Laboratoria [*A publication*]
CLLAN......	Collection Langues et Litteratures de l'Afrique Noire [*A publication*]
CLLBC	Canadian Ladies Lawn Bowling Council
CLLC........	Canadian Labour Law Cases [*A publication*] (DLA)
CLLDF	Civil Liberties Legal Defense Fund (EA)
CLLE.........	Center for Lifelong Education [*Ball State University*] [*Research center*] (RCD)
CLLI	Common Language location Identifier [*Telecommunications*] (TSSD)
CLLI	LIFE Bible College, Los Angeles, CA [*Library symbol*] [*Library of Congress*] (LCLS)
CLLL........	Calyx Lateral Lobe Length [*Botany*]
CLLoy........	Loyola Marymount University, Los Angeles, CA [*Library symbol*] [*Library of Congress*] (LCLS)
CL LP	Cloth Limp [*Bookbinding*] (ROG)
CLLR........	Councillor
CLLR........	Crown Lands Law Reports [*A publication*] (APTA)
CLLS	Calyx Lateral Lobe Shape [*Botany*]
CLLS	Country Life Library of Sport [*A publication*]
CLLT	Collation [*Online database field identifier*]
CLLU........	Canadian League for the Liberation of Ukraine
CLLW........	Calyx Lateral Lobe Width [*Botany*]
CLLW.......	Council for Lay Life and Work
CLM	California Air Commuter [*Novato, CA*] [*FAA designator*] (FAAC)
CLM	Care Logic Module (NASA)
CLM	Carlin Resources Corp. [*Vancouver Stock Exchange symbol*]
CLM	Certified Laundry Manager
CLM	Chinese Literature Monthly [*A publication*]
CLM	Christian Life and Ministry [*Canada*]
CLM	Christian Life Movement
CLM	Circumlunar Mission (KSC)
CLM	Claiming Race [*Horse racing*]
CLM	Clemente Global Growth Fund, Inc. [*NYSE symbol*] (SPSG)
ClM............	[*The*] Clergy Monthly [*Ranchi, Bihar, India*] [*A publication*]
CLM	Coleman [*Alberta*] [*Seismograph station code, US Geological Survey*] [*Closed*] (SEIS)
CLM	Communications Line Multiplexer
CLM	Computer Language Magazine [*Miller Freeman Publications*] [*Information service or system*] (CRD)
CLM	Contained-Liquid Membranes [*Chemical engineering*]
CLM	Continental Lithospheric Mantle [*Geology*]
CLM	Council of Logistics Management
CLM	Culham Laboratory Reports [*United Kingdom Atomic Energy Authority*]
CLM	Current Law Monthly [*A publication*] (DLA)
CLM	Los Angeles County Medical Association, Los Angeles, CA [*Library symbol*] [*Library of Congress*] (LCLS)
CLM	Port Angeles [*Washington*] [*Airport symbol*] (OAG)
CLM	Port Angeles, WA [*Location identifier*] [*FAA*] (FAAL)
CLMA	Certified Livestock Marketing Association [*Later, Livestock Marketing Association*]
CLMA	Cigarette Lighter Manufacturers Association (EA)
CLMA	Clinical Laboratory Management Association (EA)
CLMA	Clothing Monetary Allowance
CLMA	Contact Lens Manufacturers Association (EA)
CL to MAGS ...	Clerk to Magistrates [*British*] (ROG)
CLMas.......	Masonic Library of Southern California, Los Angeles, CA [*Library symbol*] [*Library of Congress*] (LCLS)
CLMBB.....	College Music Symposium [*A publication*]
CLMC........	Canadian Learning Materials Centre
CLMC........	Catholic Lay Mission Corps (EA)
CLMC........	Central Logistics Management Center (NASA)
CLMC........	Chemical LASER Mode Control
CLMDAY ...	Clio [*A publication*]
CLMEA3....	Clinical Medicine [*A publication*]
Cl Med.......	Classica et Mediaevalia [*A publication*]
Cl Mediaev ...	Classica et Mediaevalia [*A publication*]
CLMeW......	Metropolitan Water District of Southern California, Los Angeles, CA [*Library symbol*] [*Library of Congress*] (LCLS)
CLMI........	Calmar, Incorporated [*Watchung, NJ*] [*NASDAQ symbol*] (NQ)
CLMJA	California Mining Journal [*A publication*]
CLML.......	Chicago Linear Music Language
CLML.......	Clark Melvin Securities Corp. [*NASDAQ symbol*] (NQ)
CLML.......	Current List of Medical Literature
CLMNDX ...	Colemania [*A publication*]
CLMO	Chief Labour Management Officer [*Ministry of Supply*] [*British*]
CLMO	Climate Monitor. Climatic Research Unit. University of East Anglia [*A publication*]
CLMO	Coordinator and Liaison Maintenance Officer (FAAC)
CLMP........	Council of Literary Magazines and Presses (EA)
CL-MP	Los Angeles Public Library, Police Department Library, Los Angeles, CA [*Library symbol*] [*Library of Congress*] (LCLS)
CL-MR	Los Angeles Public Library, Municipal Reference Library, Los Angeles, CA [*Library symbol*] [*Library of Congress*] (LCLS)
Clms...........	Claims (DLA)
CLMS........	Clinical Laboratory Management System [*Data processing*]
CLMS........	Cluster Mission Simulator [*NASA*] (KSC)
CLMS........	Company Lightweight Mortar System [*Army*]
CLMS........	Continuous Longitudinal Manpower Survey [*Department of Labor*]
CLMSM	Mount St. Mary's College, Los Angeles, CA [*Library symbol*] [*Library of Congress*] (LCLS)
ClMthly	[*The*] Clergy Monthly [*A publication*]
Cl Mus	Classical Museum [*A publication*]
CLMV........	Cauliflower Mosaic Virus [*Also, CaMV*]
CL-MW	Los Angeles Public Library, Water and Power Department Library, Los Angeles, CA [*Library symbol*] [*Library of Congress*] (LCLS)
CLN	Caledonia Resources Ltd. [*Vancouver Stock Exchange symbol*]
CLN	Carlsbad [*New Mexico*] [*Seismograph station code, US Geological Survey*] (SEIS)
CLN	Catlin Aviation Co. [*Oklahoma City, OK*] [*FAA designator*] (FAAC)
CLN	Central Library Network [*Library network*]
CLN	Cervical Lymph Node [*Anatomy*]
CLN	Chemical and Engineering News [*A publication*]
CLN	Chicago Legal News [*Illinois*] [*A publication*] (DLA)
CLN	Children's Libraries Newsletter [*A publication*] (APTA)
CLN	Clann Ltd., Sydney, NSW, Australia [*OCLC symbol*] (OCLC)
CLN	Clean (MSA)
CLN	Clearance (KSC)
CLN	Clinica World Medical Device News [*A publication*]
CLN	Clinometer [*Engineering*]
CLN	Clipper Negative
CLN	Coleman Co., Inc. [*NYSE symbol*] (SPSG)
CLN	Colon (AABC)
CLN	Commercial Lending Newsletter [*Robert Morris Associates (National Association of Bank Loan and Credit Offices)*] [*A publication*]
C LN	Corrective Lens [*Freight*]
CLNAAU ..	Clinica [*A publication*]
CLNABV ..	Clean Air [*Parkville, Victoria*] [*A publication*]
CLNC........	Clearance (AFM)
CLND........	Clinical Diagnostics, Inc. [*Littleton, CO*] [*NASDAQ symbol*] (NQ)
CLNEA......	Clinical Neurosurgery [*A publication*]
CLNEDB...	Clinical Neuropharmacology [*A publication*]
CLNG	City of London National Guard [*British military*] (DMA)
CLNG	Cleaning
CLNh	Cumann Leabharann na hEireann [*Library Association of Ireland*] (EAIO)
CLNHBI....	Clinical Nephrology [*A publication*]
CLNL........	Comparative Literature News-Letter [*A publication*]
CLNPDA...	Clinical Neuropathology [*A publication*]
CLNR	Cleaner (NASA)
CLNSAG...	Contributions. Department of Limnology. Academy of Natural Sciences of Philadelphia [*A publication*]
CLNT........	Coolant (AAG)
CLNUEQ ..	Clinical Nutrition [*A publication*]
CLNY	Calny, Inc. [*San Mateo, CA*] [*NASDAQ symbol*] (NQ)
CLNYD3 ...	Clinical Neuropsychology [*A publication*]
CLO	Alpena, MI [*Location identifier*] [*FAA*] (FAAL)
CLO	Cahiers Linguistiques d'Ottawa [*A publication*]
CLO	Cali [*Colombia*] [*Airport symbol*] (OAG)
CLO	California State University, Long Beach, Long Beach, CA [*OCLC symbol*] (OCLC)
CLO	Chapter Liaison Officer
CLO	Civil Liaison Officer [*Army*] (AABC)
CLO	Clean Lube Oil (AAG)
CLO	Close
CLO	Closet (MSA)
CLO	Cloth [*Bookbinding*] (ROG)
CLO	Clothing (AABC)
CLO	Cod Liver Oil
CLO	Coleco Industries, Inc. [*NYSE symbol*] [*Toronto Stock Exchange symbol*] (SPSG)
CLO	Comet-Like Object
CLO	Community Law Offices
CLO	Computer Lock-On
CLO	Computerized Loan Origination [*for mortgages*]
CLO	Concentric Line Oscillator
CLO	Congressional Liaison Office
CLO	Consular Liaison Officer
CLO	Occidental College, Los Angeles, CA [*Library symbol*] [*Library of Congress*] (LCLS)
CLoaS	Southwest Regional Laboratory for Educational Research and Development, Los Alamitos, CA [*Library symbol*] [*Library of Congress*] (LCLS)
CLOAX......	Corrugated-Laminated Coaxial [*Cable*]

CLOB .... Composite [*or Consolidated*] Limit Order Book [*Stock exchange term*]
CLOB .... Core Load Overlay Builder [*General Automation, Inc.*]
CLob .... Long Beach Public Library, Long Beach, CA [*Library symbol*] [*Library of Congress*] (LCLS)
CLobB .... Bauer Hospital-Saint Mary Medical Center, Long Beach, CA [*Library symbol*] [*Library of Congress*] (LCLS)
CLobC .... Long Beach City College, Long Beach, CA [*Library symbol*] [*Library of Congress*] (LCLS)
CLobC-B .... Long Beach City College, Business and Technology Division, Long Beach, CA [*Library symbol*] [*Library of Congress*] (LCLS)
CLobD .... Douglas Aircraft Co., Technical Library, Long Beach, CA [*Library symbol*] [*Library of Congress*] (LCLS)
CLobGS ..... Church of Jesus Christ of Latter-Day Saints, Genealogical Society Library, Long Beach East Branch, Stake Center, Long Beach, CA [*Library symbol*] [*Library of Congress*] (LCLS)
CLobM ...... Long Beach Memorial Hospital, Long Beach, CA [*Library symbol*] [*Library of Congress*] (LCLS)
CLobP .... Pacific Hospital of Long Beach, Long Beach, CA [*Library symbol*] [*Library of Congress*] (LCLS)
CLobS .... California State University, Long Beach, Long Beach, CA [*Library symbol*] [*Library of Congress*] (LCLS)
CLobT .... Trustees of the California State University and Colleges, Chancellor's Office Library, Long Beach, CA [*Library symbol*] [*Library of Congress*] (LCLS)
CLobUN .... United States Naval Station Library, Long Beach, CA [*Library symbol*] [*Library of Congress*] (LCLS)
CLobVA ..... United States Veterans Administration Hospital, Long Beach, CA [*Library symbol*] [*Library of Congress*] (LCLS)
CLOC .... Clean Letter of Credit [*Banking*]
CLOC .... Commodity Letter of Credit
CLOCCI .... Comite de Liaison des Organismes Chretiens de Cooperation Internationale (EAIO)
CLOCE ...... Contingency Lines of Communication, Europe [*Military*] (AABC)
Clod .... Clodius [*of Scriptores Historiae Augustae*] [*Classical studies*] (OCD)
CLod .... Lodi Public Library, Lodi, CA [*Library symbol*] [*Library of Congress*] (LCLS)
CLODA ..... Closing Date
Clode ML ... Clode's Martial Law [*A publication*] (DLA)
CLODO ..... Comite Liquidant ou Detournant les Ordinateurs [*Committee to Liquidate or Neutralize Computers*] [*France*] (PD)
CLODS ...... Computerized Logic-Oriented Design System [*Air Force*]
CLOF .... Complete Loss of Feedwater [*Nuclear energy*] (NRCH)
CLOFNAM ... International Committee for the Check-List of the Fishes of the North-Eastern Atlantic and Mediterranean
CLOG-A ..... Chief of Logistics - Army [*Australia*]
CLOGH ...... Clogher [*Town in Northern Ireland*] (ROG)
CLOI .... Cloister (DSUE)
CLOIS .... Cornette Library Online Information Service [*West Texas State University*] (OLDSS)
CLOIS .... Council for Languages and Other International Studies [*Later, NCLIS*] (EA)
CLolC .... Loma Linda University, Loma Linda, CA [*Library symbol*] [*Library of Congress*] (LCLS)
CLom .... Lompoc Public Library, Lompoc, CA [*Library symbol*] [*Library of Congress*] (LCLS)
CLOM .... O'Melveny & Myers, Los Angeles, CA [*Library symbol*] [*Library of Congress*] (LCLS)
CLomGS .... Church of Jesus Christ of Latter-Day Saints, Genealogical Society Library, Santa Maria Branch, Lompoc, CA [*Library symbol*] [*Library of Congress*] (LCLS)
CLOND ..... Clinical Oncology [*A publication*]
CLOND9 .... Clinical Oncology [*A publication*]
CLONF ...... Clonfert [*Village in Ireland*] (ROG)
CLONG-CE ... Comite de Liaison des Organisations Non-Gouvernmentales de Developpement aupres des Communautes Europeennes [*Liaison Committee of Development Non-Governmental Organizations to the European Communities*] (EAIO)
CLOP .... CSIRO [*Commonwealth Scientific and Industrial Research Organisation*] List of Publications
CLOPP .... Continuous Level of Production Plan
CLOS .... Clear Line-of-Sight (MCD)
CLOS .... Closure (MSA)
CLOS .... Command to Line of Sight [*Military*] [*British*]
CLOS .... Common LISP Object System [*Data processing*] (BYTE)
CLOST ...... Canadian Lake & Ocean Salvage Team [*Commercial firm*]
CLOT .... Cost, Lawsuits, On-Air Requirements, and Time Available
CLOTH ..... Clothing
CLOTO ...... Close This Office (FAAC)
CLOW .... Clow Corp. [*Birmingham, AL*] [*NASDAQ symbol*] (NQ)
CLOW .... Current Literature on Water [*Database*] [*South African Water Information Centre*] [*Information service or system*] (CRD)
Clow LC on Torts ... Clow's Leading Cases on Torts [*A publication*] (DLA)
CLP .... 49-99 Cooperative Library System, Stockton, CA [*OCLC symbol*] (OCLC)
CLP .... Calpine Resources, Inc. [*Vancouver Stock Exchange symbol*]

CLP .... Campbell-Larsen Potentiometer
CLP .... Canadian Labour Party
CLP .... Center on Law and Pacifism (EA)
CLP .... City of London Police (ROG)
CLP .... Clamp (MSA)
CLP .... Clara Peak [*New Mexico*] [*Seismograph station code, US Geological Survey*] (SEIS)
CLP .... [*The*] Clarendon & Pittsford Railroad Co. [*AAR code*]
CLP .... Clarks Point [*Alaska*] [*Airport symbol*] (OAG)
CLP .... Clarks Point, AK [*Location identifier*] [*FAA*] (FAAL)
CLP .... Clasp
CLP .... Classical Philology [*A publication*]
CLP .... Cleaner/Lubricant/Preservation [*for firearms*] (MCD)
CL of P .... Clerk of the Peace [*British*] (ROG)
CLP .... Clinical Pathology
CLP .... Clipper Positive
CLP .... Combined Lease Plan
CLP .... Command Language Processor
CLP .... Common Law Procedure [*England*] [*A publication*] (DLA)
CLP .... Commonwealth Land Party [*British*] (DAS)
CLP .... Communication Line Processor
CLP .... Communist Labor Party (EA)
CLP .... Comprehensive Language Program [*Test*]
CLP .... Confederation of Labor in the Philippines
CLP .... Conference of the Labour Party [*British*]
CLP .... Congress Liberation Party [*Nyasaland*] [*Political party*]
CL & P .... Connecticut Light & Power Co.
CLP .... Constraint Logic Programming
CLP .... Continuous Line Plotter
CLP .... Contract Laboratory Program [*Environmental Protection Agency*]
CLP .... Cornell List Processor [*Data processing*]
CLP .... Council for Livestock Protection (EA)
C/LP .... Courtesy Lamp [*Automotive engineering*]
CLP .... Criminal Law and Procedure
CLP .... Cross-Linked Polyethylene [*Organic chemistry*]
CLP .... Current Laboratory Practice [*A publication*]
CLP .... Current Legal Problems [*A publication*]
CLP .... Current Line Pointer [*Data processing*] (IBMDP)
CLp .... Lakeport Carnegie Public Library, Lakeport, CA [*Library symbol*] [*Library of Congress*] (LCLS)
CLPA .... Common Law Procedure Acts (DLA)
CLPAC ..... Conservative Leadership Political Action Committee (EA)
CLP Act ..... English Common Law Procedure Act (DLA)
CL PAL ..... Cleft Palate [*Medicine*]
CLPC .... Los Angeles Pacific College, Los Angeles, CA [*Library symbol*] [*Library of Congress*] (LCLS)
CLPCA ..... Chung-Kuo K'o-Hsueh-Yuan Lan-Chou Hua-Hsueh Wu-Li Yen-Chiu-So Yen-Chiu Pao-Kao Chi-K An [*A publication*]
CLPCBD ... Clinical Approaches to Problems of Childhood [*A publication*]
CLPD .... Campaign for Labour Party Democracy [*British*]
CLPED ...... Clinics in Perinatology [*A publication*]
CLPEDL ..... Clinics in Perinatology [*A publication*]
CLPF .... Chlorine Pentafluoride [*Inorganic chemistry*] (MCD)
CLPG .... Chretiens pour la Liberation du Peuple Guadeloupeen [*Guadeloupe*] (PD)
CLPG .... Cornelia de Lange Parents Group [*Later, Cornelia de Lange Syndrome Foundation*] (EA)
CL-PGM .... Cannon-Launched Precision Guided Munition (MCD)
Cl Ph .... Classical Philology [*A publication*]
CLPHA ...... Council of Large Public Housing Authorities (EA)
CLPHDU .. Clinical Physiology [*A publication*]
CLPHEV .... Clinical Pharmacology [*A publication*]
Cl Phil .... Classical Philology [*A publication*]
CLPhil .... Philosophical Research Society, Los Angeles, CA [*Library symbol*] [*Library of Congress*] (LCLS)
CLPI .... Creative Learning Products, Inc. [*NASDAQ symbol*] (NQ)
CLPI .... Prudential Insurance Co. of America, Business, Recreation, and Field Management Libraries, Los Angeles, CA [*Library symbol*] [*Library of Congress*] (LCLS)
CLPJA .... Cleft Palate Journal [*A publication*]
CLPL .... Citizens Legal Protective League (EA)
CLPLOT .... Center-Line Plotting (MCD)
CLPM .... Canalicular Liver Plasma Membrane [*Anatomy*]
CLPNAB ... Collective Phenomena [*London*] [*A publication*]
CLPoC .... R. L. Polk & Co. of California, Los Angeles, CA [*Library symbol*] [*Library of Congress*] (LCLS)
CLPP .... Paramount Pictures Corp., Research Department, Los Angeles, CA [*Library symbol*] [*Library of Congress*] (LCLS)
CLPR .... Caliper (MSA)
CLPR .... Clapper [*Electricity*]
CLPT .... Pacific Telephone & Telegraph Co., Los Angeles, CA [*Library symbol*] [*Library of Congress*] (LCLS)
CLPTA ...... Clinical Pharmacology and Therapeutics [*A publication*]
CLPTAT .... Clinical Pharmacology and Therapeutics [*A publication*]
CLQ .... Check List Question (CAAL)
Cl Q .... Classical Quarterly [*A publication*]
Cl Q .... Colby Library. Quarterly [*A publication*]
CLQ .... Commercial Law Quarterly [*Australia*] [*A publication*]
CLQ .... Compleat Health Corp. [*Vancouver Stock Exchange symbol*]

CLQ	Cornell Law Quarterly [*A publication*]
CLQ	Crown Land Reports, Queensland [*A publication*] (DLA)
CL (Q)	Crown Lands Law Reports (Queensland) [*A publication*] (APTA)
CLQ	Queen of Angels School of Nursing, Los Angeles, CA [*Library symbol*] [*Library of Congress*] (LCLS)
Cl Qu	Classical Quarterly [*A publication*]
Cl Quart	Classical Quarterly [*A publication*]
CLR	Calcutta Law Reporter [*A publication*] (DLA)
CLR	Calendar of Liberate Rolls [*British*]
CLR	Calipatria, CA [*Location identifier*] [*FAA*] (FAAL)
CLR	Canada Law Reports [*A publication*] (DLA)
CLR	Canadian Law Review and Corporation Legal Journal [*A publication*] (DLA)
CL & R	Canal, Lake, and Rail
CLR	Cape Law Reports [*South Africa*] [*A publication*] (DLA)
CLR	Central Logic Rack [*Telecommunications*] (TEL)
CLR	Central London Underground Railway
CLR	Centurion LASER Range-Finder
CLR	Ceylon Law Reports [*A publication*] (DLA)
CLR	Children's Literature Review [*A publication*]
CLR	City of London Rifles [*British*]
Cl R	Clarke's New York Chancery Reports [*A publication*] (DLA)
Cl R	Classical Review [*A publication*]
CLR	Clean Liquid RADwater [*Nuclear energy*] (IEEE)
CLR	Clear [*Alaska*] [*BMEWS Site 1*] (MCD)
CLR	Clear (KSC)
CLR	Clear to Zero [*Data processing*]
CLR	Clearance (FAAC)
CLR	Cleared To (FAAC)
ClR	[*The*] Clergy Review [*London*] [*A publication*]
CLR	Cleveland Law Record [*Ohio*] [*A publication*] (DLA)
CLR	Collar (MSA)
CLR	Collurania [*Italy*] [*Seismograph station code, US Geological Survey*] [*Closed*] (SEIS)
CLR	Color (MSA)
CLR	Color Systems Technology, Inc. [*AMEX symbol*] (SPSG)
CLR	Colortech Corp. [*Toronto Stock Exchange symbol*]
CLR	Columbia Law Review [*A publication*]
CLR	Combined Line and Recording Trunk (IEEE)
CLR	Common Law Reports [*British*]
CLR	Commonwealth Law Reports [*A publication*] (APTA)
CLR	Computer Language Recorder
CLR	Computer Language Research (IEEE)
CLR	Control Line Register
CLR	Cooler (MSA)
CLR	Coordinating Lubricant and Equipment Research Committee [*Coordinating Research Council*]
CLR	Cornell Law Review [*A publication*] (ILCA)
CLR	Council on Library Resources (EA)
CLR	Councillor (ADA)
CLR	Crater-Lamp Recorder
CLR	Crown Lands Law Reports [*A publication*] (APTA)
CLR	Current Law Reports [*Palestine*] [*A publication*] (DLA)
CLR	Current-Limiting Resistor (MSA)
CLR	Cyprus Law Reports [*A publication*] (DLA)
CLR	New York State School of Industrial and Labor Relations, Cornell University, Ithaca, NY [*OCLC symbol*] (OCLC)
CLR	Trans American [*Englewood, CA*] [*FAA designator*] (FAAC)
CLRA	Inter-Corporate Ownership [*Canada Systems Group*] [*Information service or system*] (IID)
CLRAA	Clinical Radiology [*A publication*]
CLRAAG	Clinical Radiology [*A publication*]
CLRAP	Catholic League for Religious Assistance to Poland (EA)
CLRAP	Cleared as Planned [*Aviation*] (FAAC)
CLR (Aust)	Commonwealth Law Reports (Australia) [*A publication*]
CLRB	Canada Labour Relations Board
CLRB	Cost Limit Review Board
CLRC	Canada Law Reform Commission (DLA)
CLRC	Central Labor Relations Commission [*Japan*]
CLRC	Circuit Layout Record Card [*Telecommunications*] (TEL)
CLRC	Copyright Law Review Committee [*Australia*]
CLR (Can)	Canada Law Reports, Exchequer Court and Supreme Court [*A publication*] (DLA)
CLR (Can)	Common Law Reports [*1835-55*] [*Canada*] [*A publication*] (DLA)
CLRCR	Catholic League for Religious and Civil Rights (EA)
CLRDA	CLR [*Council on Library Resources*] Recent Developments [*A publication*]
CLRE	Contact Lens Registry Examination [*National Contact Lens Examiners*]
CLREA	Clinical Research [*A publication*]
CLREAS	Clinical Research [*A publication*]
CL Rec	Cleveland Law Record [*Ohio*] [*A publication*] (DLA)
CL Reg	Cleveland Law Register [*Ohio*] [*A publication*] (DLA)
CL Rep	Cleveland Law Reporter [*Ohio*] [*A publication*] (DLA)
CL Rev	California Law Review [*A publication*]
Cl Rev	Classical Review [*A publication*]
CLRF	Center for Law and Religious Freedom (EA)
CLRG	Clearing (MSA)
CLRG	Collector Ring [*Electricity*]
ClRh	Clara Rhodos [*A publication*]
CLRI	Central Leather Research Institute [*British*]
CLRI	Computer Language Research, Incorporated [*Carrollton, TX*] [*NASDAQ symbol*] (NQ)
CLRIT	Children's Legal Rights Information and Training [*An association*] (EA)
CLRK	CLARCOR, Inc. [*NASDAQ symbol*] (NQ)
Cl RL	Clarke's Early Roman Law [*A publication*] (DLA)
CLRM	Cool Room
CLRN	Clarion Capitol Corp. [*NASDAQ symbol*] (NQ)
CLRO	Clark Lake Radio Observatory [*University of Maryland*] [*Research center*] (RCD)
CLRO-E	Richfield Oil Corp., Economic Research Department, Los Angeles, CA [*Library symbol*] [*Library of Congress*] (LCLS)
CLRO-R	Richfield Oil Corp., Research and Development Library, Anaheim, CA [*Library symbol*] [*Library of Congress*] (LCLS)
CLRO-T	Richfield Oil Corp., Technical Library, Wilmington, CA [*Library symbol*] [*Library of Congress*] (LCLS)
CLRP	Command Logistics Review Program [*DoD*]
CLRP	Cornell Local Roads Program [*Cornell University*] [*Research center*] (RCD)
CLR Recent Devt	CLR [*Council on Library Resources*] Recent Developments [*A publication*]
CLRS	Center for Labor Research and Studies [*Florida International University*] [*Research center*] (RCD)
CLRS	Clear and Smooth [*Meteorology*] (FAAC)
CLRS	FT Industries, Inc. [*NASDAQ symbol*] (NQ)
CLRT	Command Logistics Review Team (MCD)
CLRTX	Command Logistics Review Teams Expanded (MCD)
CLRU	Cambridge Language Research Unit
CLRV	Canadian Light Rail Vehicle
CLRV	County of London Regiment (Volunteers) [*British military*] (DMA)
CLRWS	Clean Liquid Radioactive Waste System (NRCH)
CLRX	Colorocs Corp. [*Norcross, GA*] [*NASDAQ symbol*] (NQ)
CLS	Cable Laying Ship
CLS	California Library Statistics [*A publication*]
CLS	California State University, Los Angeles, Los Angeles, CA [*Library symbol*] [*Library of Congress*] (LCLS)
CLS	Calistoga [*California*] [*Seismograph station code, US Geological Survey*] [*Closed*] (SEIS)
CLS	Callex Enterprises Ltd. [*Vancouver Stock Exchange symbol*]
CLS	Cam Limit Switch
CLS	Cambridge Life Sciences [*British*]
CLS	Canada Land Surveyor
CLS	Canfield Learning Styles Inventory [*Educational test*]
CLS	Canon Law Society of America (EA)
CLS	Carleton Library System [*Carleton University*] [*Information service or system*] (IID)
CLS	Carolina Library Services, Inc. (IID)
CLS	Cask Loading Station [*Nuclear energy*] (NRCH)
CLS	Center for Libertarian Studies (EA)
CLS	Characteristic Loss Spectroscopy
CLS	Charles Lamb Society [*British*]
CLS	Charles Lamb Society. Bulletin [*A publication*]
CLS	Chehalis, WA [*Location identifier*] [*FAA*] (FAAL)
CLS	Chemical LASER Study [*or System*]
CLS	Chicago Library System [*Chicago Public Library*] [*Chicago, IL*] [*Library network*]
CLS	Christian Lawyer's Society [*Victoria, Australia*]
CLS	Christian Legal Society (EA)
CLS	Cislunar Space
CLS	Citrus Label Society (EA)
Cls	Claims (DLA)
CLS	Classify (MSA)
Cls	Clauses (DLA)
CLS	Clear Screen [*Data processing*]
CLS	Clear and Subtract (IEEE)
CLS	Clerical Support
CLS	Close [*Data processing*] (BUR)
CLS	Close Lunar Satellite
CLS	Closed-Loop Support [*Army*] (AABC)
CLS	Closed-Loop System [*Nuclear energy*] [*Chemical engineering*] (NRCH)
CLS	Closure [*Technical drawings*]
CLS	Cloud LIDAR System (MCD)
CLS	Coils [*Freight*]
CLS	Collected Least Squares [*Statistics*]
CLS	College Libraries Section [*Association of College and Research Libraries*]
CLS	Command and Launch Subsystem (MCD)
CLS	Committee on Life Sciences [*Federal interagency group*]
CLS	Common Language System [*Data processing*] (BUR)
CLS	Common Leaf Spot [*Plant pathology*]
CLS	Communications Line Switch
CLS	Comparative Literature Studies [*A publication*]
CLS	Compatible LASER System
CLS	Computer Listing Service [*Computer Listing Service, Inc.*] [*Information service or system*] (IID)

CLS............ Concept Learning System [*Data processing*]　(BUR)
CLS............ Constant Level Speech
CLS............ Consular Law Society　(EA)
CLS............ Containment Leakage System [*Nuclear energy*]　(IEEE)
CLS............ Contingency Landing Site [*NASA*]　(NASA)
CLS............ Contractor Logistics Support [*DoD*]
CLS............ Cornell Law School　(DLA)
CLS............ Creative List Services, Inc. [*Information service or system*]　(IID)
CLS............ Critical Legal Studies Philosophy
CLS............ Cross-Linked Smectites [*Inorganic chemistry*]
CLS............ Cum Laude Society　(EA)
CLS............ Harvard University, Cabot Science Library, Cambridge, MA [*OCLC symbol*]　(OCLC)
CLS............ New York Consolidated Laws Service [*A publication*]
CLSA......... Canadian Law and Society Association [*See also ACDS*]
CLSA......... Canon Law Society of America　(EA)
CLSA......... Closed-Loop Stripping Analysis [*Analytical chemistry*]
CLSA......... Conservation Law Society of America [*Defunct*]
CLSA......... Contact Lens Society of America　(EA)
CLSA......... Cooperative Logistic Support Arrangement [*Military*]　(AFM)
CLSA-DB .. California Library Services Act Statewide Data Base [*California Library Services Board*] [*Information service or system*]　(IID)
CLSAP....... Canon Law Society of America. Proceedings [*A publication*]
CLSB .... Charles Lamb Society. Bulletin [*A publication*]
CLSB .... Committee of London and Scottish Bankers [*British*]
CLSC .... Chautauqua Literary and Scientific Circle　(EA)
CLSC .... Clinical Sciences, Inc. [*Whippany, NJ*] [*NASDAQ symbol*]　(NQ)
CLSC .... Coalesce
CLSC .... COMSEC [*Communications Security*] Logistic Support Center [*Army*]　(AABC)
Cl & Sc Dr Cas ... Clarke and Scully's Drainage Cases [*Canada*] [*A publication*]　(DLA)
CLSCE....... Southern California Edison Co., Los Angeles, CA [*Library symbol*] [*Library of Congress*]　(LCLS)
CLSCS....... Cain-Levine Social Competency Scale [*Psychology*]
CLSD........ Closed　(AAG)
CLSD......... Collaborative Library System Development
C & LSE..... Clothing and Life Support Equipment [*Military*]
CLSES....... Center for Lake Superior Environmental Studies [*Universtiy of Wisconsin - Superior*] [*Research center*]　(RCD)
CLSF .... Security Pacific National Bank, Los Angeles, CA [*Library symbol*] [*Library of Congress*]　(LCLS)
CLSG........ Closing　(AAG)
CLSG......... Common Logistic Support Group [*Military*]
CLSI........ Computer Library Services, Incorporated [*Wellesley Hills, MA*]
CLSIR........ Cryogenic Limb Scanning Interferometer Radiometer　(MCD)
CLSJ.......... Company and Securities Law Journal [*A publication*]　(APTA)
CLSL .... Southwestern University, School of Law, Los Angeles, CA [*Library symbol*] [*Library of Congress*]　(LCLS)
CLSM........ Clayton Silver Mines [*NASDAQ symbol*]　(NQ)
CLSM........ Confocal LASER Scanning Microscope [*or Microscopy*]
CLSM........ Crew Life-Support Monitor [*NASA*]　(KSC)
CLSM........ Southwest Museum, Los Angeles, CA [*Library symbol*] [*Library of Congress*]　(LCLS)
CLSMDA .. Closed-Loop Systems Melt-Down Accident [*Nuclear energy*]　(NRCH)
CLSN......... College Satellite Network, Inc. [*Dallas, TX*] [*NASDAQ symbol*]　(NQ)
CLSNG...... Closing
CLSO......... Contingency Landing Support Officer　(MCD)
CLSOAT ... Contact Lens Society of America. Journal [*A publication*]
CLSP .... Composite Launch Sequence Plan　(MCD)
CLSP .... Contract Logistic Support Plan　(MCD)
CLSP .... Cooperative [*or Coordinated*] Logistics Support Program [*Air Force*]　(MCD)
CLS Q .... CLS [*Christian Legal Society*] Quarterly [*A publication*]
CLSR .... Closure　(AAG)
CLSR .... Computer Law Service Reporter
CLSR .... Control Laser International Corp. [*Orlando, FL*] [*NASDAQ symbol*]　(NQ)
CLSRC ...... Company Law and Securities Review Committee [*Australia*]
CLSS........ Classified Financial Corp. [*San Francisco, CA*] [*NASDAQ symbol*]　(NQ)
CLSS.......... Combat Logistic Support System　(AABC)
CLSS.......... Communication Link Subsystem
CLSS.......... Computerized Literature Searching Service
CLSS.......... Contractor Logistics Support Services　(MCD)
CLSSA....... Cooperative Logistic Supply Support Arrangement [*Military*]　(AFIT)
CLST .... Celestial　(FAAC)
CL Stats..... Current Law Statutes, Annotated [*A publication*]　(DLA)
CLSTBB.... Cluster Bomb [*Military*]
CLStV .... Saint Vincent College of Nursing, Los Angeles, CA [*Library symbol*] [*Library of Congress*]　(LCLS)
CLSU......... COMSEC [*Communications Security*] Logistic Support Unit [*Army*]　(AABC)
CLSU......... University of Southern California, Los Angeles, CA [*Library symbol*] [*Library of Congress*]　(LCLS)

CLSU-A..... University of Southern California, Architecture and Fine Arts Department, Los Angeles, CA [*Library symbol*] [*Library of Congress*]　(LCLS)
CLSU-B..... University of Southern California, Biochemical Library, Los Angeles, CA [*Library symbol*] [*Library of Congress*]　(LCLS)
CLSU-Bodd ... University of Southern California, H. G. Boddington Collection, Los Angeles, CA [*Library symbol*] [*Library of Congress*]　(LCLS)
CLSU-Craig ... University of Southern California, Gordon Craig Collection, Los Angeles, CA [*Library symbol*] [*Library of Congress*]　(LCLS)
CLSU-D..... University of Southern California, School of Dentistry, Los Angeles, CA [*Library symbol*] [*Library of Congress*]　(LCLS)
CLSU-Ed ... University of Southern California, Education Department, Los Angeles, CA [*Library symbol*] [*Library of Congress*]　(LCLS)
CLSU-Farm ... University of Southern California, Farmington Plan Collection, Los Angeles, CA [*Library symbol*] [*Library of Congress*]　(LCLS)
CLSU-Feucht ... University of Southern California, Feuchtwanger Memorial Collection, Los Angeles, CA [*Library symbol*] [*Library of Congress*]　(LCLS)
CLSU-H .... University of Southern California, Hancock Library of Biology and Oceanography, Los Angeles, CA [*Library symbol*] [*Library of Congress*]　(LCLS)
CLSU-Hefner ... University of Southern California, Lee Hefner Memorial Collection, Los Angeles, CA [*Library symbol*] [*Library of Congress*]　(LCLS)
CLSU-Hoose ... University of Southern California, Hoose Library of Philosophy, Los Angeles, CA [*Library symbol*] [*Library of Congress*]　(LCLS)
CLSU-L..... University of Southern California, Law Library, Los Angeles, CA [*Library symbol*] [*Library of Congress*]　(LCLS)
CLSU-Low ... University of Southern California, Kurt Lowenstein Collection, Los Angeles, CA [*Library symbol*] [*Library of Congress*]　(LCLS)
CLSU-LTorch ... University of Southern California, Gregg Lane College, Torchieu Collection, Los Angeles, CA [*Library symbol*] [*Library of Congress*]　(LCLS)
CLSU-M.... University of Southern California, School of Medicine Library, Los Angeles, CA [*Library symbol*] [*Library of Congress*]　(LCLS)
CLSU-Music ... University of Southern California, Music Library, Los Angeles, CA [*Library symbol*] [*Library of Congress*]　(LCLS)
CLSU-R..... University of Southern California, Ruther Technology Library, Los Angeles, CA [*Library symbol*] [*Library of Congress*]　(LCLS)
CLSU-Richm ... University of Southern California, Carl A. Richmond Collection, Los Angeles, CA [*Library symbol*] [*Library of Congress*]　(LCLS)
CLSU-VKSmit ... University of Southern California, Von Kleinsmit Library of World Affairs, Los Angeles, CA [*Library symbol*] [*Library of Congress*]　(LCLS)
CLSX .... Closed-Loop Support Extended [*Army*]　(AABC)
CLT............ Canadian Law Times [*A publication*]　(DLA)
CLT............ Cargo Left Trailer　(KSC)
CLT............ Center for Learning and Telecommunications [*American Association for Higher Education*] [*Information service or system*]　(IID)
CLT............ Central Limit Theorem [*Statistics*]
CLT............ Charlotte [*North Carolina*] [*Airport symbol*]　(OAG)
CLT............ Charlottesville [*Virginia*] [*Seismograph station code, US Geological Survey*] [*Closed*]　(SEIS)
CLT............ Chronic Lymphocytic Thyroiditis [*Medicine*]
CLT............ Clark Technical College, Library Resource Center, Springfield, OH [*OCLC symbol*]　(OCLC)
CLT............ Clathan Literary Institute [*British*]
CLT............ Cleat
CLT............ Clerical Technician, Medical [*Navy*]
CLT............ Client　(ROG)
CLT............ Clinical Laboratory Technician
CLT............ Closed-Loop Telemetry
CLT............ Closed-Loop Test　(NASA)
CLT............ Clot Lysis Time [*Hematology*]
CLT............ Collateral Trust [*Bond*]
CLT............ Cominco Ltd. [*AMEX symbol*] [*Toronto Stock Exchange symbol*] [*Vancouver Stock Exchange symbol*]　(SPSG)
CLT............ Communication Line Terminal [*Data processing*]
CLT............ Community Land Trust [*Agricultural economics*]
CLT............ Community Language Teaching [*Australia*]
CLT............ Compagnie Libanaise de Television [*Lebanese Television Company*]
CLT............ Compagnie Luxembourgeoise de Telediffusion [*Luxembourg broadcasting group*]
CLT............ Computer Language Translator
CLT............ Constant Load Tensile Test
CLT............ Council of the Living Theatre [*Defunct*]　(EA)
Clt .... Culture [*A publication*]

CLT........... Cuttack Law Times [*India*] [*A publication*] (ILCA)
CLT........... Los Angeles Times, Los Angeles, CA [*Library symbol*] [*Library of Congress*] (LCLS)
CLTA........ Cahiers de Linguistique Theorique et Appliquee [*A publication*]
CLTA........ Canadian Library Trustees' Association
CLTA........ Chinese Language Teachers Association (EA)
CLTAV...... Clinical Language Teachers Association of Victoria [*Australia*]
CLTB........ Commonwealth Land Transport Board [*Australia*]
CLTC........ Chief Launch Vehicle Test Conductor [*NASA*] (KSC)
CLTC........ Twentieth Century-Fox Film Corp., Research Library, Los Angeles, CA [*Library symbol*] [*Library of Congress*] (LCLS)
CLTDB..... Clinical Laboratory Test Database [*Data processing*]
CLTE........ Commissioned Loss to Enlisted Status [*Revocation of an officer's appointment*]
CLTEA4.... Clinica Terapeutica [*A publication*]
CLTG........ Collecting (MSA)
CLTGL...... Climatological (AABC)
CLTH .... C & R Clothiers, Inc. [*Culver City, CA*] [*NASDAQ symbol*] (NQ)
CLTH .... Clothes
CLTH .... Cut Length (MSA)
CLTHDG .. Clinical Therapeutics [*A publication*]
CLTHG...... Clothing (MSA)
CLTI.......... Title Insurance & Trust Co., Los Angeles, CA [*Library symbol*] [*Library of Congress*] (LCLS)
CLTL......... Continental Tyre Ltd. [*NASDAQ symbol*] (NQ)
CLT Occ N ... Canadian Law Times. Occasional Notes [*A publication*] (DLA)
CLTPD...... Chi Lin Ta Hsueh Hsueh Pao. Tzu Jan K'o Hsueh Pan [*A publication*]
CLTR........ Center for Local Tax Research (EA)
C/LTR....... Cigarette [*or Cigar*] Lighter [*Automotive engineering*]
CLTR........ Clutter (MSA)
CLTR........ Continuous Loop Tubular Reactor [*Chemical engineering*]
CLTRM..... Clutter Map (MSA)
CLT-RTL .. Compagnie Luxembourgeoise de Telediffusion - Radio Television Luxembourg
CLTS........ Chicago Lutheran Theological Seminary
CLTS........ Contributions. Institute of Low Temperature Science [*Japan*] [*A publication*]
CLTV........ Closed-Loop Television
CLTV........ Collective (MSA)
CLU.......... Canadian Labour Union
CLU.......... Capitol Line-Up [*A publication*] (EAAP)
CLU......... Celutel, Inc. [*AMEX symbol*] (SPSG)
CLU......... Central Logic Unit [*Data processing*]
CLU......... Certified Life Underwriter [*Insurance*]
CLU......... Ceylon Labor Union [*Obsolete*]
CLU......... Chartered Life Underwriter [*Designation awarded by Solomon S. Huebner School of CLU Studies, The American College*]
CLU......... Circuit Line Up
CLU......... CLU [*Chartered Life Underwriters*] Journal [*A publication*]
CLU.......... Cluj [*Kolozvar*] [*Romania*] [*Seismograph station code, US Geological Survey*] [*Closed*] (SEIS)
CLU......... Cluster [*Programming language*] [*1973*] (CSR)
CLU......... Command Launch Unit [*Military*]
CLU......... Command Logic Unit (MCD)
CLU......... Competence Level Unit [*Education*]
CLU......... Consolidated Louanna Gold Mines Ltd. [*Toronto Stock Exchange symbol*]
CLU.......... Institute of Chartered Life Underwriters of Canada
Clu............. Pro Cluentio [*of Cicero*] [*Classical studies*] (OCD)
CLU......... University of California, Los Angeles, Biomedical, Law, Physical Science, and Technology, Los Angeles, CA [*OCLC symbol*] (OCLC)
CLU.......... University of California, Los Angeles, Main Library, Los Angeles, CA [*Library symbol*] [*Library of Congress*] (LCLS)
CLU-ART ... University of California, Los Angeles, Art Library, Los Angeles, CA [*Library symbol*] [*Library of Congress*] (LCLS)
CLU-AUP ... University of California, Los Angeles, Architecture and Urban Planning Library, Los Angeles, CA [*Library symbol*] [*Library of Congress*] (LCLS)
Club Ser Univ NC State Coll Agr Eng Agr Ext Serv ... Club Series. University of North Carolina. State College of Agriculture and Engineering. Agricultural Extension Service [*A publication*]
CLUBZINE ... Club Magazine [*Generic term for a publication covering the activities of a science-fiction fan club*]
CLU-C .... University of California, Los Angeles, William Andrews Clark Memorial Library, Los Angeles, CA [*Library symbol*] [*Library of Congress*] (LCLS)
CLU-CHM ... University of California, Los Angeles, Chemistry Library, Los Angeles, CA [*Library symbol*] [*Library of Congress*] (LCLS)
CLU-COL ... University of California, Los Angeles, College Library, Los Angeles, CA [*Library symbol*] [*Library of Congress*] (LCLS)
CLUDACTDAT ... Include Accounting Data
CLUE......... Career Laboratories Utilizing Experience (OICC)

CLUE........ Clinical Literature Untoward Effects [*Service published by International Information Institute*]
CLU-EMS ... University of California, Los Angeles, Engineering and Mathematical Sciences Library, Los Angeles, CA [*Library symbol*] [*Library of Congress*] (LCLS)
CLU-E/P ... University of California, Los Angeles, Education and Psychology Library, Los Angeles, CA [*Library symbol*] [*Library of Congress*] (LCLS)
CLUG .... Community Land Use Game [*Urban-planning game*]
CLU-G/G .. University of California, Los Angeles, Geology-Geophysics Library, Los Angeles, CA [*Library symbol*] [*Library of Congress*] (LCLS)
CLU-GRS ... University of California, Los Angeles, Graduate Reserve Service, Los Angeles, CA [*Library symbol*] [*Library of Congress*] [*Obsolete*] (LCLS)
CLU J .... CLU [*Chartered Life Underwriters*] Journal [*A publication*]
Cluj Med .... Clujul Medical [*A publication*]
CLU-L .... University of California, Los Angeles, Law Library, Los Angeles, CA [*Library symbol*] [*Library of Congress*] (LCLS)
CLU-M...... University of California, Los Angeles, Biomedical Library, Los Angeles, CA [*Library symbol*] [*Library of Congress*] (LCLS)
CLU-MAP ... University of California, Los Angeles, Map Library, Los Angeles, CA [*Library symbol*] [*Library of Congress*] (LCLS)
CLU-MGT ... University of California, Los Angeles, Management Library, Los Angeles, CA [*Library symbol*] [*Library of Congress*] (LCLS)
CLUMP..... Compool Look-Up Memory Print
CLU-MUS ... University of California, Los Angeles, Music Library, Los Angeles, CA [*Library symbol*] [*Library of Congress*] (LCLS)
CLUnB ...... United California Bank, Los Angeles, CA [*Library symbol*] [*Library of Congress*] (LCLS)
CLU-N/C .. University of California, Los Angeles, Non-Circulating Reading Center, Los Angeles, CA [*Library symbol*] [*Library of Congress*] (LCLS)
CLU-O....... University of California, Los Angeles, Oriental Library, Los Angeles, CA [*Library symbol*] [*Library of Congress*] (LCLS)
CLUP........ Consolidated Labor Union of the Philippines
CLU-P .... University of California, Los Angeles, Physical Science and Technical Library, Los Angeles, CA [*Library symbol*] [*Library of Congress*] (LCLS)
CLU-PAS .. University of California, Los Angeles, Public Affairs Service, Los Angeles, CA [*Library symbol*] [*Library of Congress*] (LCLS)
CLU-PHY ... University of California, Los Angeles, Physics Library, Los Angeles, CA [*Library symbol*] [*Library of Congress*] [*Obsolete*] (LCLS)
CLUQ........ Cahiers de Linguistique. Universite du Quebec [*A publication*]
CLU-REF .. University of California, Los Angeles, URL-Reference Department, Los Angeles, CA [*Library symbol*] [*Library of Congress*] (LCLS)
CLURT...... Come, Let Us Reason Together [*Labor mediators' slogan*]
CLUS........ Cluster of Stones [*Jewelry*] (ROG)
CLUS........ Continental Limits, United States
CLUSA...... Continental Limits, United States of America [*Navy*]
CLUSA...... Cooperative League of the United States of America (EA)
CLUSAF.... United States Air Force, Technical Library, Los Angeles, CA [*Library symbol*] [*Library of Congress*] (LCLS)
CLU-S/C ... University of California, Los Angeles, Department of Special Collections, Los Angeles, CA [*Library symbol*] [*Library of Congress*] (LCLS)
Clusk Pol TB ... Cluskey's Political Text Book [*A publication*] (DLA)
Clustering Phenom Nuclei ... Clustering Phenomena in Nuclei [*Vieweg, Braunschweig*] [*A publication*]
CLUT........ Color Look-Up Table [*Computer graphics*]
CLUT........ Computer Logic Unit Tester (MCD)
CLU-T/A... University of California, Los Angeles, Theater Arts Reading Room, Los Angeles, CA [*Library symbol*] [*Library of Congress*] (LCLS)
CLUTS...... Canberra Land Use and Transportation Study [*Australia*]
CLUU .... College of Law, University of Utah (DLA)
CLU-U/A... University of California, Los Angeles, University Archives, Los Angeles, CA [*Library symbol*] [*Library of Congress*] (LCLS)
CLU-UES ... University of California, Los Angeles, University Elementary School Library, Los Angeles, CA [*Library symbol*] [*Library of Congress*] (LCLS)
CLU-URL ... University of California, Los Angeles, University Research Library, Los Angeles, CA [*Library symbol*] [*Library of Congress*] (LCLS)
CLUW ...... Coalition of Labor Union Women (EA)
CLUWCER ... Coalition of Labor Union Women Center for Education and Research (EA)
CLV .... Clarissimus Vir [*Most Illustrious Man*] [*Latin*]
CLV .... Cleve [*Australia*] [*Seismograph station code, US Geological Survey*] (SEIS)
CLV .... Clevis [*Metal shackle*] (KSC)

CLV .... Clover Aero, Inc. [*Friendswood, TX*] [*FAA designator*]   (FAAC)
CLV .... Constant Linear Velocity [*Videodisk format*]
CLV .... La Verne University, La Verne, CA [*OCLC symbol*]   (OCLC)
CLV .... Library of Vehicles, Los Angeles, CA [*Library symbol*] [*Library of Congress*]   (LCLS)
CLVA........ United States Veterans Administration Center, Medical Research Library, Los Angeles, CA [*Library symbol*] [*Library of Congress*]   (LCLS)
CLVA-B.... United States Veterans Administration Center, Brentonwood Medical Library, Los Angeles, CA [*Library symbol*] [*Library of Congress*]   (LCLS)
CLVCHD .. Clavichord [*Music*]
CLVD .... Clavichord [*Music*]
CLVEAE ... Clinica Veterinaria [*Milan*] [*A publication*]
CL to VEST ... Clerk to Vestry [*British*]   (ROG)
CLVN .... Calvin Exploration, Inc. [*Santa Fe, NM*] [*NASDAQ symbol*]   (NQ)
ClVPP........ Chlorambucil, Vinblastine, Procarbazine, Prednisone [*Antineoplastic drug regimen*]
CLW .... Capital Library Wholesale [*ACCORD*] [*UTLAS symbol*]
CLW .... Catholic Library World [*A publication*]
CLW .... Ceylon Law Weekly [*A publication*]   (ILCA)
Cl W .... Classical World [*A publication*]
CLW .... Clearwater, FL [*Location identifier*] [*FAA*]   (FAAL)
CLW .... Colville [*Washington*] [*Seismograph station code, US Geological Survey*] [*Closed*]   (SEIS)
CLW .... Commercial Laws of the World [*A publication*]   (DLA)
CLW .... Council for a Livable World   (EA)
Cl Weekly .. Classical Weekly [*A publication*]
CLWEF .... Council for a Livable World Education Fund   (EA)
CLWelf...... Welfare Planning Council, Los Angeles, CA [*Library symbol*] [*Library of Congress*]   (LCLS)
CLWestO... Western Oil and Gas Association, Los Angeles, CA [*Library symbol*] [*Library of Congress*]   (LCLS)
CLWG ...... Clear Wire Glass [*Technical drawings*]
CLWJ .... Western Jewish Institute, Los Angeles, CA [*Library symbol*] [*Library of Congress*]   (LCLS)
CLWM ...... Company Lightweight Mortar System [*Army*]   (MCD)
CLWM ...... White Memorial Medical Center, Los Angeles, CA [*Library symbol*] [*Library of Congress*]   (LCLS)
CLWP........ Committee for Liquidation of German War Potential [*Allied German Occupation Forces*]
CLWP........ Western Precipitation Corp., Los Angeles, CA [*Library symbol*] [*Library of Congress*]   (LCLS)
CLWS........ Clockwise
CLX............ Carlson Mines Ltd. [*Vancouver Stock Exchange symbol*]
CLX............ Clorox Co. [*NYSE symbol*]   (SPSG)
CLX............ Continuous Lightweight Exterior
CLY............ Calvi [*Corsica*] [*Airport symbol*]   (OAG)
C of LY...... City of London Yeomanry [*Military*] [*British*]   (ROG)
CLY............ Clay-Mill Technical Systems, Inc. [*Toronto Stock Exchange symbol*]
CLY............ Cotton Valley [*Vancouver Stock Exchange symbol*]
CLY............ Crystal Lake [*New York*] [*Seismograph station code, US Geological Survey*]   (SEIS)
CLY............ Current Law Year Book [*A publication*]   (ILCA)
CLY............ Worcester, MA [*Location identifier*] [*FAA*]   (FAAL)
CLY............ Yoshitomi Pharmaceutical Ind. Co. Ltd. [*Japan*] [*Research code symbol*]
CLYB........ Current Law Year Book [*A publication*]
CLySF........ Saint Francis Hospital, Health Science Library, Lynwood, CA [*Library symbol*] [*Library of Congress*]   (LCLS)
Clysis .... Hypodermoclysis [*Medicine*]   (DHSM)
CLY T C .... Clay or Terra Cotta [*Freight*]
CLZ............ Baton Rouge, LA [*Location identifier*] [*FAA*]   (FAAL)
CLZ............ Calabozo [*Venezuela*] [*Airport symbol*]   (OAG)
CLZ............ Canasil Resources, Inc. [*Vancouver Stock Exchange symbol*]
CLZ............ Clausthal [*Federal Republic of Germany*] [*Seismograph station code, US Geological Survey*]   (SEIS)
CLZ............ Clozapine [*A drug*]
CLZ............ Copper, Lead, or Zinc [*Freight*]
CLZR........ Candela Laser Corp. [*NASDAQ symbol*]   (NQ)
CM............ Cahiers Maynard [*A publication*]
CM............ Calibrated Magnification   (MSA)
CM............ Calibration Marker
CM............ Call Money [*Investment term*]
C/M .... Call of More [*Stock exchange term*] [*British*]   (ROG)
CM............ Camair [*Division of Cameron Iron Works, Inc.*] [*ICAO aircraft manufacturer identifier*]   (ICAO)
CM............ Cameroon [*ANSI two-letter standard code*]   (CNC)
cm.............. Cameroon [*MARC country of publication code*] [*Library of Congress*]   (LCCP)
CM............ Canada Medal
CM............ Canadian Imperial Bank of Commerce [*Toronto Stock Exchange symbol*] [*Vancouver Stock Exchange symbol*]
CM............ Canadian Materials [*A publication*]
CM............ Canadian Militia
CM............ Canadian Mining Journal [*A publication*]
CM............ Canberra Income Tax Circular Memorandum [*A publication*]
CM............ Candidate Material

CM............ Capitular Masonry [*Freemasonry*]   (ROG)
CM............ Carat, Metric
CM............ Carboxymethyl [*Also, Cm, Cme*] [*Biochemistry*]
CM............ Carcinomatous Meningitis [*Oncology*]
CM............ Cardiomyography [*Cardiology*]
CM............ Cardiomyopathy [*Medicine*]
CM............ Cards per Minute [*Data processing*]
C & M .... Care and Maintenance [*British military*]   (DMA)
CM............ Career Minister [*Department of State*]
CM............ Career Motivation   (AFM)
CM............ Cargo Management   (MCD)
CM............ Carleton Miscellany [*A publication*]
CM............ Carmelite Missionaries [*Rome, Italy*]   (EAIO)
CM............ Carnegie Museum of Natural History [*Pittsburgh, PA*]
CM............ Carpenter's Mate [*Navy*]
C & M .... Carrington and Marshman's English Nisi Prius Reports [*1840-42*] [*A publication*]   (DLA)
CM............ Cartographic Materials [*International Federation of Library Associations*]
CM............ Case Monitoring [*Air Force*]   (AFIT)
CM............ Casualty Mode [*Military*]   (CAAL)
CM............ Caudal Magnocellular [*Nuclei*] [*Neuroanatomy*]
CM............ Causa Mortis [*On Occasion of Death*] [*Latin*]
CM............ Celestial Mechanics
CM............ Cell Membrane
CM............ Center of Mass [*Atomic physics*]
C of M........ Center of Mass
CM............ Center Matched [*Technical drawings*]
cm.............. Centimeter   (GPO)
cM.............. Centimorgan [*Unit of genetic map distance*]
CM............ Central Memory [*Data processing*]   (BUR)
CM............ Century Magazine [*A publication*]
CM............ Cerebral Malaria [*Medicine*]
C of M........ Certificate of Merit
CM............ Certificated Master [*or Mistress*] [*British*]
CM............ Certified Master [*British*]
CM............ Certified Midwife
CM............ Cervical Mucus [*Obstetrics*]
CM............ Chairman's Memorandum
CM............ Chargeable to Manuals   (MCD)
C/M .... Chattel Mortgage [*Legal term*]   (DLA)
CM............ Cheap Money [*Banking*]
CM............ Chemical Corps [*Army*]   (RDA)
CM............ Chemical Manufacture [*Department of Employment*] [*British*]
CM............ Chemical Milling   (MSA)
CM............ Chemically-Induced Mutants [*Genetics*]
CM............ Chemically Malignant [*Medicine*]
CM............ Chick-Martin [*Test*] [*Microbiology*]
CM............ Chief Mechanic
CM............ Chief Metalsmith [*Navy rating*] [*Obsolete*]
CM............ Chirurgiae Magister [*Master of Surgery*]
CM............ Chloramphenicol [*Antimicrobial compound*]
CM............ Chlorinated Methane [*Organic chemistry*]
CM............ Choirmaster [*Music*]
CM............ Chopped Meat [*Medium*] [*Microbiology*]
CM............ Christian Mission   (EA)
CM............ Chrom-Moly   (MCD)
cm.............. Chromite [*CIPW classification*] [*Geology*]
CM............ Church Musician [*A publication*]
CM............ Circuit Master   (MSA)
CM............ Circular Measure
CM............ Circular Mil [*Wire measure*]
CM............ Circular Muscle [*Anatomy*]
CM............ Civilta Moderna [*A publication*]
CM............ Claims Manual [*Social Security Administration*]   (OICC)
CM............ Class Marks [*Telecommunications*]   (TEL)
CM............ Class of Material   (MCD)
CM............ Classica et Mediaevalia [*A publication*]
C & M .... Classica et Mediaevalia [*A publication*]
CM............ Classical Mechanics [*Physics*]
CM............ Classified Message
CM............ Clerical Medical [*Insurance firm*] [*British*]
CM............ Cleveland-Marshall Law Review [*A publication*]
CM............ Clinical Modification
CM............ Clio Medica [*A publication*]
CM............ Closed Mouth [*Doll collecting*]
CM............ Club Management [*Club Managers Association of America*] [*A publication*]
CM............ Club Mediterranee   (EA)
CM............ CM. Canadian Materials for Schools and Libraries [*A publication*]
C & M .... Coal and Mining
CM............ Cochlear Microphonics [*Response*] [*Auditory testing*]
CM............ Coins, Incorporating Coins and Medals [*A publication*]
CM............ Coles Myer Ltd. [*NYSE symbol*]   (CTT)
CM............ Collection Management [*A publication*]
CM............ Colloquia Mathematica. Societatis Janos Bolyai [*Elsevier Book Series*] [*A publication*]
CM............ Colorado-Maduro [*Very dark-colored cigar*]
CM............ Colorado Magazine [*A publication*]
CM............ Colorado Midland

CM.............	Columellar Muscle
CM.............	Combat Material
CM.............	Combat Mission [*Military*]
CM.............	Combustion Metamorphism [*Geology*]
CM.............	Command
CM.............	Command Module [*NASA*]
CM.............	Command Money [*British military*] (DMA)
CM.............	Commander's Manual [*Military*]
CM.............	Commentary on the Mishnah [*Maimonides*] (BJA)
CM.............	Commercial [*Rate*] [*Value of the English pound*]
CM.............	Commercial Manager (DCTA)
CM.............	Common Meter [*Music*]
CM.............	Communications Manager
CM.............	Communications Multiplexer [*Data processing*]
CM.............	Community Market Catalog
CM.............	Compania Panamena de Aviacion, SA [*Panama*] [*ICAO designator*] (FAAC)
CM.............	Comparators [*JETDS nomenclature*] [*Military*] (CET)
CM.............	Compassionate Case [*Airline notation*]
CM.............	Complementary Manual [*Military*]
CM.............	Complete Medium [*Microbiology*]
CM.............	Composite Merge
CM.............	Computer Management [*British*] [*A publication*]
CM1............	Computer Module
CM.............	Computing Media
CM.............	Concerns of Motherhood (EA)
CM.............	Conciertos Mexicanos [*Record label*] [*Mexico*]
CM.............	Condition Monitoring (DS)
CM.............	Conditioned Medium [*For growing microorganisms*]
CM.............	Confidential Memorandum
CM.............	Configuration Management
CM.............	Congenital Malformation [*Medicine*]
CM.............	Congestive Myocardiopathy [*Medicine*]
CM.............	Congregatio Mariae [*Fathers of the Company of Mary*] [*Roman Catholic religious order*]
CM.............	Congregatio Missionis Sancti Vicentii a Paulo [*Congregation of the Mission of St. Vincent de Paul*] [*Vincentians*] [*Roman Catholic men's religious order*]
CM.............	Congregation of the Mission [*Vincentians*] (DAS)
CM.............	Congregationis Missionum [*The Congregation of Lazarists*] (ROG)
CM.............	Connecticut Mutual Life Insurance Co.
CM.............	Constant Misery [*Slang*]
C & M........	Construction and Machinery
CM.............	Construction and Machinery
CM.............	Construction Management
CM.............	Construction Management [*A publication*]
CM.............	Construction Mechanic [*Navy rating*]
CM.............	Consumables Management (NASA)
CM.............	Contact Maker
CM.............	Contamination Mode [*NASA*] (KSC)
CM.............	Contemporary Musicians [*A publication*]
CM.............	Continental Marines
CM.............	Continuity Message [*Telecommunications*] (TEL)
CM.............	Continuous Monitor
CM.............	Contract Management
CM.............	Contract Modification
CM.............	Contrast Media [*Radiology*]
CM.............	Control Mark (DEN)
CM.............	Control Memory [*Telecommunications*] (TEL)
CM.............	Control Mode (MCD)
CM.............	Control Monitor (MCD)
C & M........	Control and Monitoring (NASA)
CM.............	Controlled Minefield [*Navy*]
Cm.............	Coprinus Micaceous [*A fungus*]
CM.............	Copulatory Mechanism [*Medicine*]
CM.............	Core Memory
CM.............	Cornhill Magazine [*A publication*]
CM.............	Cornmeal
CM.............	Correction Memo (MCD)
CM.............	Corrective Maintenance
CM.............	Corrective Management (MCD)
CM.............	Corresponding Member
CM.............	Costal Margin [*Medicine*]
CM.............	Cotton Mather [*Initials used as pseudonym*]
CM.............	Countermarked
CM.............	Countermeasure
CM.............	Countermortar
C/M............	Counts per Minute
c/m............	Cours Moyen [*Average Price*] [*French*]
CM.............	Court-Martial
CM.............	Court Martial Reports, Army Cases [*United States*] [*A publication*] (DLA)
CM.............	Cow's Milk
CM.............	Craft Masonry [*Freemasonry*] (ROG)
CM.............	Cras Mane [*Tomorrow Morning*] [*Pharmacy*]
CM.............	Credit Memo
CM.............	Crew Module [*NASA*] (NASA)
CM.............	Crewman (KSC)
CM.............	Criminal Matters
CM.............	CRISTA Ministries [*Later, CRISTA*] (EA)

CM.............	Critical Mass [*Later, CMEP*] [*An association*] (EA)
C & M........	Crompton and Meeson's English Exchequer Reports [*1832-34*] [*A publication*] (DLA)
CM.............	Crosier Missions (EA)
CM.............	Cruciform Monument (BJA)
CM.............	Crude Myosin [*Food technology*]
CM.............	Cruise Missile (MCD)
CM.............	Cruiser Minelayer
CM.............	Cryptic Masonry [*Freemasonry*] (ROG)
CM.............	Cub Master [*Scouting*]
CM.............	Cumulative Mortality [*Radiology*]
CM.............	Cumulonimbus Mammatus [*Cloud*] [*Meteorology*]
Cm.............	Curium [*Chemical element*]
CM.............	Current Monitor [*Instrumentation*]
C/M............	Cycles per Minute (ADA)
CM.............	Cytoplasmic Membrane [*Botany*]
CM.............	Member of the Order of Canada
CM.............	Metric Carat [*200 milligrams*] (ADA)
cm-----	Middle America [*MARC geographic area code*] [*Library of Congress*] (LCCP)
CM.............	Minelayer [*Navy symbol*] [*NATO*]
C-M............	North Atlantic Council Memorandum [*NATO*] (NATG)
CM.............	Northern Mariana Islands [*Postal code*]
CM1............	Construction Mechanic, First Class [*Navy rating*]
c/m²...........	Candles per Square Meter [*Optics*]
CM2............	Construction Mechanic, Second Class [*Navy rating*]
CM²............	Square Centimeter
CM3............	Construction Mechanic, Third Class [*Navy rating*]
C/M³...........	Coulombs per Cubic Meter
CM6............	Central Minnesota Seismic Array [*Minnesota*] [*Seismograph station code, US Geological Survey*] (SEIS)
CMA..........	Calcium Magnesium Acetate
CMA..........	Calcium Methanearsonate [*Herbicide*]
CMA..........	Calendar Marketing Agreement
CMA..........	Calendar Marketing Association (EA)
CMA..........	California Maritime Academy [*Vallejo*]
CMA..........	Campus Ministries of America (EA)
CMA..........	Canadian Manager [*A publication*]
CMA..........	Canadian Manufacturers Association
CMA..........	Canadian Marconi Co. [*Aerospace*]
CMA..........	Canadian Medical Association
CMA..........	Canadian Metric Association
CMA..........	Canadian Museums Association
CMA..........	Candle Manufacturers Association [*Later, NCA*] (EA)
CMa...........	Canis Major [*Constellation*]
CMA..........	Career Management and Assignment [*Department of State*]
CMA..........	Carmac Resources [*Vancouver Stock Exchange symbol*]
CMA..........	Cash Management Account [*Merrill Lynch*]
CMA..........	Casket Manufacturers Association of America (EA)
CMA..........	Cathodoluminescence Microscope Attachment
CMA..........	Cellulose Manufacturers Association (EA)
CMA..........	Census Metropolitan Area [*Canada*]
CMA..........	Center for Marine Affairs [*Scripps Institution of Oceanography*]
CMA..........	Centre of Management in Agriculture [*British*] (CB)
CMA..........	Certificate in Management Accounting [*Designation awarded by Institute of Management Accounting of the National Association of Accountants*]
CMA..........	Certified Medical Assistant
CMA..........	Chamber Music America (EA)
CMA..........	Channel Multiplier Array
CMA..........	Chemical Manufacturers Association (EA)
CMA..........	Childrenswear Manufacturers Association (EA)
CMA..........	Chinese Merchants Association (EA)
CMA..........	Chocolate Manufacturers Association of the USA (EA)
CMA..........	Christian Management Association (EA)
CMA..........	Christian and Missionary Alliance
CMA..........	Christian Motorcyclist Association (EA)
CMA..........	Church Music Association [*British*]
CMA..........	Cigar Manufacturers Association of America [*Later, CAA*] (EA)
CMA..........	Circular Mil Area
CMA..........	Civil-Military Affairs
CMA..........	Civilian Material Assistance (EA)
CMA..........	Classified Mail Address
CMA..........	Clear Mews [*Alaska*] [*Seismograph station code, US Geological Survey*] [*Closed*] (SEIS)
CMA..........	Closure Manufacturers Association (EA)
CMA..........	Clothespin Manufacturers of America (EA)
CMA..........	Clothing Maintenance Allowance [*Military*]
CMA..........	Clothing Manufacturers Association of the USA (EA)
CMA..........	Collection Management Authority (MCD)
CMA..........	College Media Advisers (EA)
CMA..........	Colleges of Mid-America (EA)
CMA..........	Colon Mucoprotein Antigen [*Immunochemistry*]
CMA..........	Colorado Mining Association (EA)
CMA..........	Comma (FAAC)
CMA..........	Command Modulator Assembly [*NASA*]
CMA..........	Commercial Market Appraisal
CMA..........	Commissariat for Montagnard Affairs
CMA..........	Commonwealth Magistrates' Association [*London, England*] (EAIO)

CMA .... Commonwealth Medical Association [*London, England*] (EAIO)
CMA .... Commonwealth Mortgage Partnership [*NYSE symbol*] (SPSG)
CMA .... Communications Managers Association [*Bernardsville, NJ*] [*Telecommunications service*] (TSSD)
CMA .... Communications Market Association (EA)
CMA .... Commutaire International [*Miami, FL*] [*FAA designator*] (FAAC)
CMA .... Compania Mexicana de Aviacion [*Mexican airline*]
CMA .... Competitive Market Analysis [*Real estate*]
CMA .... Complement Accumulator
CMA .... Complex Modulus Apparatus
CMA .... Computer Management Association
CMA .... Computer-Marked Assignment [*Education*] [*British*]
CMA .... Computer Monitor Adapter
CMA .... Confederate Memorial Association
CMA .... Configuration Management Accounting (NASA)
CMA .... Conical Monopole Antenna
CMA .... Construction Mechanic, Automotive [*Navy rating*]
CMA .... Contact-Making Ammeter (KSC)
CMA .... Contact Motion Analysis (CAAL)
CMA .... Contract Maintenance Activity (AFM)
CMA .... Contract Managers' Association [*A union*] [*British*]
CMA .... Contract Manufacturers Association (EA)
CMA .... Contractor's Manual Prepared after Negotiated Authorization for Contract
CMA .... Contractors Mutual Association [*Defunct*] (EA)
CMA .... Control Message Automation [*Aviation*]
CMA .... Controller Military Accounts [*British military*] (DMA)
CMA .... Convert Makers of America [*Later, CMOA*] (EA)
CMA .... Cookware Manufacturers Association (EA)
CMA .... Corn Meal Agar [*Growth medium*]
CMA .... Corps Maintenance Area
CMA .... Corps of Military Accountants [*British military*] (DMA)
CMA .... Corrective Maintenance Action [*Military*] (CAAL)
CMA .... Council for Museum Anthropology (EA)
CMA .... Countermission Analysis (MCD)
CMA .... Country Music Association (EA)
CMA .... Court of Military Appeals
CMA .... Court of Military Appeals Reports [*A publication*] (DLA)
CMA .... Crucible Manufacturers Association [*Later, CI*]
CMA .... Cunnamulla [*Australia*] [*Airport symbol*] (OAG)
CMA .... Currency Market Analysis [*MMS International*] [*Information service or system*] (CRD)
CMA .... Current Market Appraisal
CMA .... Cyclic Multilayered Alloy [*Electroplating technology*]
CMA .... Cylinder Manufacturers Association (EA)
CMA .... Cylindrical Mirror Analyzer [*Analytical instrumentation*]
CMa .... Madera County Free Public Library, Madera, CA [*Library symbol*] [*Library of Congress*] (LCLS)
CMA .... Oxnard, CA [*Location identifier*] [*FAA*] (FAAL)
CMAA .... Chief Master at Arms [*Navy rating*]
CMAA .... Church Music Association of America (EA)
CMAA .... Cigar Manufacturers Association of America [*Later, CAA*]
CMAA .... Club Managers Association of America (EA)
CMAA .... Cocoa Merchants' Association of America (EA)
CMAA .... Comics Magazine Association of America (EA)
CMAA .... Construction Management Association of America (EA)
CMAA .... Courts-Martial (Appeals) Act [*British military*] (DMA)
CMAA .... Crane Manufacturers Association of America (EA)
CMAB .... Canadian Mutual Aid Board [*World War II*]
CMAB .... Clothing Maintenance [*or Monetary*] Allowance, Basic [*Army*]
CMAB .... Combined Munitions Assignments Board [*World War II*]
CMAC .... Capital Military Assistance Command (AABC)
CMAC .... Central Management Army Commissaries (AABC)
CMAC .... Cerebellar Model Articulation Control [*System*] [*National Institute of Standards and Technology*]
CMAC .... Contingency Maintenance Allocation Chart (MCD)
CMAC .... Court-Martial Appeal Court of Canada
CMACL ..... Composite Mode Adjective Check List [*FAA*]
CMACP ..... Conseil Mondial pour l'Assemblee Constituante des Peuples [*World Council for the Peoples World Convention*]
CMACS ..... Central Monitor and Control System (MCD)
CMAD .... Computer Manufacture and Design Proprietary Ltd. [*Australia*] (ADA)
CMAEC ..... Conseil Mondial des Associations d'Education Comparee [*World Council of Comparative Education Societies - WCCES*] (EA)
CMAFP ..... Committee on Medical Aspects of Food Policy [*British*]
C Mag .... Center Magazine [*A publication*]
CMAGD .... Chemisch Magazine [*A publication*]
C Magic ..... Cinemagic [*A publication*]
CMAI .... Chemical Market Associates, Incorporated [*Information service or system*] (IID)
CMAIISS ... Clothing Monetary Allowance, Initial Issue [*Army*]
C Mail .... Courier Mail [*Brisbane*] [*A publication*]
CMAIWAC ... Clothing Monetary Allowance, Initial (Women's Army Corps)
CMAJ .... Canadian Medical Association. Journal [*A publication*]
CMaj .... Canis Major [*Constellation*]
CMAJ .... Conseil des Ministres Arabes de la Justice [*Council of Arab Ministers of Justice - CAMJ*] [*Rabat, Morocco*] (EAIO)

CMAJA ..... Canadian Medical Association. Journal [*A publication*]
CMAJAX .. Canadian Medical Association. Journal [*A publication*]
CMAK .... Conical Monopole Antenna Kit
CMAL .... Clothing Monetary Allowance List [*Military*] (AFM)
CMAL .... Controlled Multiple Address Letter (AFM)
CMalG .... J. Paul Getty Museum, Malibu, CA [*Library symbol*] [*Library of Congress*] (LCLS)
CMalH ...... Hughes Research Library, Malibu, CA [*Library symbol*] [*Library of Congress*] (LCLS)
CMalP ...... Pepperdine University, Malibu, CA [*Library symbol*] [*Library of Congress*] (LCLS)
CMAM ...... Chief Mailman [*Navy rating*] [*Obsolete*]
CMAnnual ... Coins Annual [*A publication*]
CMAO .... Consejo Mundial de Artes y Oficios [*World Crafts Council*]
CMAO .... Contract Management Assistance Officer [*NASA*] (NASA)
CMAO .... Court-Martial Appointing Order
CMAP .... Central Memory Access Priority [*Data processing*]
CMAP .... Charge Material Allocation Processor
CMAP .... Commission Mondiale d'Action Professionnelle [*World Committee for Trade Action - WCTA*] (EA)
CMAP .... Contrast Media Appearance Picture [*Also known as coronary arteriography*] [*Radiology*]
CMAPAH ... Collana di Monografie. Ateneo Parmense [*A publication*]
CMAPS ..... Council for Military Aircraft Propulsion Standards
CMAR .... Canadian Court Martial Appeal Reports [*1957-*] [*A publication*] (DLA)
CMAR .... Can't Manage a Rifle [*Formed by reversing the initials of Royal Army Medical Corps*] [*British*] [*World War I*]
C & Mar ..... Carrington and Marshman's English Nisi Prius Reports [*1840-42*] [*A publication*] (DLA)
CMAR .... Control Memory Address Register [*Data processing*]
CMAR .... Courts-Martial Appeal Rules [*British military*] (DMA)
CMar .... Mariposa County Free Library, Mariposa, CA [*Library symbol*] [*Library of Congress*] (LCLS)
C & Marsh ... Carrington and Marshman's English Nisi Prius Reports [*1840-42*] [*A publication*] (DLA)
CMartCH .. Contra Costa Historical Society, Martinez, CA [*Library symbol*] [*Library of Congress*] (LCLS)
CMartVA .. United States Veterans Administration Hospital, Martinez, CA [*Library symbol*] [*Library of Congress*] (LCLS)
CMary .... Marysville City Library, Marysville, CA [*Library symbol*] [*Library of Congress*] (LCLS)
CMaryY ..... Yuba College, Marysville, CA [*Library symbol*] [*Library of Congress*] (LCLS)
CMAS .... Calcium, Magnesium, Aluminum, Silicon [*Oxide system in geology*]
CMAS .... Clergy Mutual Assurance Society [*British*]
CMAS .... Clothing Maintenance Allowance, Standard [*Air Force*]
CMAS .... Clothing Maintenance Allowance System [*Military*]
CMAS .... Clothing Monetary Allowance, Standard [*Army*]
CMAS .... Complete Mixing Activated Sludge
CMAS .... Confederation Mondiale des Activites Subaquatiques [*World Underwater Federation - WUF*] [*ICSU*] [*Paris, France*] (EAIO)
CMAS .... Council for Military Aircraft Standards
CM-ASTT ... Certified Member, American Society of Traffic and Transportation [*Designation awarded by American Society of Transportation and Logistics*]
CMAT .... Compatible Materials List (NASA)
CMAT-A ... Chief of Materiel - Army [*Australia*]
CMAUA ... Chemoautomatyka [*A publication*]
CMAV .... Coalition Mondiale pour l'Abolition de la Vivisection [*World Coalition for the Abolition of Vivisection*]
CMAZAD ... Comunicaciones. Museo Argentino de Ciencias Naturales "Bernardino Rivadavia" e Instituto Nacional de Investigacion de las Ciencias Naturales. Zoologia [*A publication*]
CMB .... Carbolic Methylene Blue [*Clinical chemistry*]
CMB .... Cellular and Molecular Biology
CMB .... Central Midwives Board
CMB .... Central States Motor Freight Bureau, Chicago IL [*STAC*]
CMB .... [*The*] Chase Manhattan Corp. [*New York, NY*] [*NYSE symbol*] (SPSG)
CMB .... Chemical Mass Balance
CMB .... Chief Motor Boatman [*British military*] (DMA)
CMB .... Chlorambucil [*Antineoplastic drug*]
CMB .... Chloromercuribenzoic [*Organic chemistry*]
CMB .... Christian Mission to Buddhists [*See also NKB*] [*Arhus, Denmark*] (EAIO)
CMB .... Circus Model Builders, International (EA)
CMB .... CMAC Computer Systems Ltd. [*Vancouver Stock Exchange symbol*]
CMB .... Coal Mines Board (DAS)
CMB .... Coastal Motorboat [*Obsolete*] [*British*]
CMB .... Colombo [*Sri Lanka*] [*Airport symbol*] (OAG)
CMB .... Combat Maneuver Battalion [*Army*]
CMB .... Combat Medical Badge [*Military decoration*] (AABC)
CMB .... Comstock Mealybug [*Plant pest*]
CMB .... Conductivity Modulated Bipolar [*Data processing*]
CMB .... Configuration Management Branch [*NASA*] (KSC)
CMB .... Core-Mantle Boundary [*Geology*]

CMB .... Corrective Maintenance Burden
CMB .... Cosmic Microwave Background [Of radiation]
CMB .... Cuyas Manos Beso [Very Respectfully] [Spanish] [Correspondence]
CMB .... Modesto Bee, Modesto, CA [Library symbol] [Library of Congress]   (LCLS)
CMBA .... Concert Music Broadcasters Association   (EA)
CMBARMTNG ... Combined Arms Training [Military]   (NVT)
CMBBBF... Collection de Monographies de Botanique et de Biologie Vegetale [A publication]
CMBC .... Canadian Mennonite Bible College
CMBD .... Cellular and Molecular Basis of Disease [Program] [National Institutes of Health]
CMBD .... Combined
CMBES ..... Canadian Medical and Biological Engineering Society
CMBF .... Cow's Milk Base Formula
CMBG .... Canadian Mechanized Brigade Group   (MCD)
CMBHI .... Craft Member of the British Horological Institute   (DBQ)
CMBI........ Commentationes Biologicae. Societas Scientiarum Fennica [A publication]
CMBID4.... Cellular and Molecular Biology [A publication]
C & M Bills ... Collier and Miller on Bills of Sale [A publication]   (DLA)
CMBK .... [The] Cumberland Federal Bancorporation, Inc. [NASDAQ symbol]   (NQ)
CMBMC.... Conservative Mennonite Board of Missions and Charities [Later, RMM]   (EA)
CMBNY .... China Medical Board of New York   (EA)
CMBR .... Component Meantime Between Removals   (MCD)
C/MBR...... Cross Member [Automotive engineering]
CMBS........ ComSouth Bankshares, Inc. [NASDAQ symbol]   (NQ)
CMBS........ Conventional Mortgage-Backed Security
CMBSTR .. Combustor   (MSA)
CMBT........ Combat   (AFM)
CMBTSPTSq ... Combat Support Squadron [Air Force]
CMBUA .... Canadian Mathematical Bulletin [A publication]
CMBUC5 .. Australia. Commonwealth Scientific and Industrial Research Organisation. Marine Biochemistry Unit. Annual Report [A publication]
CMC .... Cable Maintenance Center [Telecommunications]   (TEL)
CmC .... California Microfilm Company, Fresno, CA [Library symbol] [Library of Congress]   (LCLS)
CMC .... Canada Manpower Centre
CMC .... Canadian Marconi Company [Toronto Stock Exchange symbol]
CMC .... Canadian Meteorological Centre [Marine science]   (MSC)
CMC .... Canadian Music Centre
CMC .... Canadian Music Council   (EAIO)
CMC .... Carboxymethylcellulose [Organic chemistry]
CMC .... Carboxymethylcysteine [Biochemistry]
CMC .... Carpometacarpal [Anatomy]
CMC .... Catholic Microfilm Center [Defunct]
CMC .... Cell-Mediated Cytolysis
CMC .... Center for Marine Conservation   (EA)
CMC .... Center for Marketing Communications [Later, Advertising Research Foundation]   (EA)
CMC .... Center for Mass Communication [Columbia University]
CMC .... Center for Medical Consumers and Health Care Information   (EA)
CM C .... Centimeter-Candle
CMC .... Central Master Control   (MCD)
CMC .... Central Military Commission [People's Republic of China]
CMC .... Certified Management Consultant [Designation awarded by Institute of Management Consultants, Inc.]
CMC .... Chemical Materials Catalog
CMC .... Cheyenne Mountain Complex [NORAD]   (MCD)
CMC .... Chopped Meat Carbohydrate [Medium] [Microbiology]
CMC .... Christian Medical Commission   (EA)
CMC .... Christian Medical Council [Defunct]   (EA)
CMC .... Chronic Mucocutaneous Candidiasis [Medicine]
CMC .... Citizen Mobilization Campaign   (EA)
CMC .... Claremont Men's College [California]
CMC .... Clark Memorial College [Mississippi]
CMC .... Clutter Mapper Card
CMC .... Co-Fired, Multilayer Ceramic [Materials science]
CMC .... Coastal Minelayer [Navy symbol]
CMC .... Code for Magnetic Characters   (IEEE)
CMC .... Coherent Multichannel Communication
CMC .... Coins, Medals, and Currency Weekly [A publication]
CMC .... Collective Measures Commission [United Nations]   (DLA)
CMC .... Color Mixture Curve
CMC .... COMARC [Cooperative Machine-Readable Cataloging Program] [Source file] [UTLAS symbol]
CMC .... Combined Meteorological Committee
CMC .... Command Management Center [Military]
CMC .... Command Module Computer [NASA]   (MCD)
CMC .... Commandant of the Marine Corps
CMC .... Commercial Metals Company [NYSE symbol]   (SPSG)
CMC .... Commission Medicale Chretienne [Christian Medical Commission] [Geneva, Switzerland]   (EA)
CMC .... Committee for Modern Courts   (EA)
CMC .... Commodity Manager Code [Military]
CMC .... Communications Mode Control

CMC .... Complement Carry
CMC .... Complete Missile Container
CMC .... Component Modification Cards [Nuclear energy]   (NRCH)
CMC .... Computer Machinery Corporation Ltd. [Subsidiary of Microdata]   (MCD)
CMC .... Computer and Management Show for Contractors   (TSPED)
CMC .... Computer-Mediated Conferencing   (IT)
CMC .... Computer Microfilm Corporation [Information service or system]   (IID)
CMC .... Computer Musician Coalition   (EA)
CMC .... Congregation de la Mere du Carmel [Congregation of Mother of Carmel] [Alwaye Kerala, India]   (EAIO)
CMC .... Conservation Monitoring Centre [World trade of endangered species products]
CMC .... Consolidated Maintenance Center   (MCD)
CMC .... Consolidated Mercantile Corp. [Toronto Stock Exchange symbol]
CMC .... Constant Mean Curvature [Mathematics]
CMC .... Construction Mechanic, Chief [Navy rating]
CMC .... Contact-Making Clock
CMC .... Continental Motosport Club   (EA)
CMC .... Continuous Membrane Column [Chemical engineering]
CMC .... Control Magnetization Curve
CMC .... Coordinated Manual Control
CMC .... Copper Mine [Northwest Territories] [Seismograph station code, US Geological Survey] [Closed]   (SEIS)
CMC .... Core Monitoring Computer [Nuclear energy]   (NRCH)
CMC .... Corporate Mountaineers Cult
CMC .... Corrective Maintenance Card   (MCD)
CMC .... Council of Mennonite Colleges   (EA)
CMC .... Crew Module Computer   (MCD)
CMC .... Critical Micelle Concentration
CMC .... Crosscurrents/Modern Critiques [A publication]
CMC .... Cruise Missile Carrier Aircraft
CMC .... Cultural Ministers Council [Australia]
C Mc .... Current Musicology [A publication]
CMC .... Curved Motion Cutter
CMC .... Cyclophosphamide, Methotrexate, CCNU [Lomustine] [Antineoplastic drug regimen]
CMC .... National Institute of Certified Moving Consultants   (EA)
CMCA .... Character Mode Communications Adapter
CMCA .... Comerica, Inc. [Detroit, MI] [NASDAQ symbol]   (NQ)
CMCA .... Cruise Missile Carrier Aircraft   (MCD)
CM/CAI .... Computer Management/Computer-Assisted Instruction   (MCD)
CMCB .... Carpenter's Mate, Construction Battalion [Navy]
CMCB .... Comments on Molecular and Cellular Biophysics [A publication]
CMCBB.... Carpenter's Mate, Construction Battalion, Builder [Navy]
CMCBD .... Carpenter's Mate, Construction Battalion, Draftsman [Navy]
CMCBE..... Carpenter's Mate, Construction Battalion, Excavation Foreman [Navy]
CMCC .... Central Magistrates' Court Committee [British]
CMCC .... Central Marine Chamber of Commerce [Defunct]   (EA)
CMCC .... Classified Matter Control Center   (AAG)
CMCC .... Computer Monitor and Control Console   (CAAL)
CMCC .... Conference of Mutual Casualty Companies [Later, CCIC]   (EA)
CMCC .... Credit de Mobilisation des Creances Commerciales [Credit secured by payments receivable] [French]   (IMH)
CMCCA..... Conference of the Methodist Church in the Caribbean and the Americas   (EAIO)
CMCCJ ..... Confederation Mondiale de Centres Communautaires Juifs [World Confederation of Jewish Community Centers]   (EAIO)
CM/CCM ... Countermeasures/Counter Countermeasures [Army]   (RDA)
CMCCS..... Configuration Management and Change Control System [Social Security Administration]
CMCD .... Chopped Meat Glucose Broth with Digoxin [Medium] [Microbiology]
CMCD .... Coins, Medals, and Currency Digest and Monthly Catalogue [A publication]
CMCEA..... Commerce [India] [A publication]
CMCH...... Company of Military Collectors and Historians [Later, CMH]   (EA)
CMCHA.... Canadian Machinery and Metalworking [A publication]
CMCHCI... Center for Medical Consumers and Health Care Information   (EA)
CMCHS .... Civilian-Military Contingency Hospital System [DoD]
CMCI........ CMC International [NASDAQ symbol]   (NQ)
CMCI........ Computed Mission Coverage Index   (MCD)
CMCL....... ChemClear, Inc. [Wayne, PA] [NASDAQ symbol]   (NQ)
CMCL....... Command Management Control List
Cmcl Law Assoc Bull ... Commercial Law Association. Bulletin [A publication]   (APTA)
Cmcl Space ... Commercial Space [A publication]
CMCM ...... Chairman, Military Committee Memorandum [NATO]
CMCM ...... Commandant of the Marine Corps Memorandum
CMCM ...... Construction Mechanic, Master Chief [Navy rating]
CMCN ...... Constructionman, Construction Mechanic, Striker [Navy rating]
CMCO .... Classified Material Control Officer   (AFIT)

CMCO .... COMB Company [*Minneapolis, MN*] [*NASDAQ symbol*] (NQ)
CMCO .... Corps Movement Control Organization [*Royal Corps of Transport*] [*British*]
CMCOLL ... Church Missionary College [*Church of England*]
CMCP .... Canadian Museum of Contemporary Photography
CMCPDU ... Comunicacoes. Museu de Ciencias. PUCRGS [*Pontificia Universidade Catolica do Rio Grande Do Sul*] [*A publication*]
CMCPPG .. Commandant, Marine Corps Program Policy and Planning Guidance
CMCR .... Centre for Mass Communication Research [*University of Leicester*] [*British*] (CB)
CMCR .... Committee for Mother and Child Rights (EA)
CMCR .... Conservative Majority for Citizen's Rights (EA)
CMCRL ..... Consolidated Master Cross-Reference List [*Defense Supply Agency*]
CMCRP ..... Center for Mass Communications Research and Policy [*University of Denver*] [*Research center*] (RCD)
CMCS .... Cam Case
CMCS .... Cambridge Medieval Celtic Studies [*A publication*]
CMCS .... Canadian Man-Computer Communications Society
CMCS .... CENTO [*Central Treaty Organization*] Military Communications System (MCD)
CMCS .... Comcast Corp. [*NASDAQ symbol*] (NQ)
CMCS .... Commandant, Marine Corps Schools [*Quantico, VA*]
CMCS .... Communications Monitoring and Control Subsystem (NVT)
CMCS .... Comprehensive Manufacturing Control System
CMCS .... COMSAT [*Communications Satellite Corp.*] Maritime Communications Satellite (MCD)
CMCS .... Construction Management Control System [*General Services Administration*]
CMCS .... Construction Mechanic, Senior Chief [*Navy rating*]
CMCSA ..... Canadian Manufacturers of Chemical Specialties Association
CMCT .... Communicate (MDG)
CMCT .... Communicating Magnetic Card Typewriter (AFIT)
CMCTL ..... Current-Mode Complementary Transistor Logic [*Data processing*] (IEEE)
CMC-VAP ... Cyclophosphamide, Methotrexate, CCNU [*Lomustine*], Vincristine, Adriamycin, Procarbazine [*Antineoplastic drug regimen*]
CMCW ...... Christian Missions to the Communist World (EA)
CMCYEO ... Cell Motility and the Cytoskeleton [*A publication*]
CMD .... California Management Review [*A publication*]
CMD .... Capital Military District [*Vietnam*]
CMD .... Carboxymethyldextran [*Organic chemistry*]
CMD .... Carboxymuconolactone Decarboxylase [*An enzyme*]
CMD .... Cataloging Management Data [*Army*]
CMD .... Center for Management Development [*American Management Association*] (EA)
CMD .... Center for Massachusetts Data [*Information service or system*] (IID)
CMD .... Central Meridian Distance [*NASA*]
CMD .... Cerebral Motor Dysfunction [*Medicine*]
CMD .... Certified Marketing Director [*Designation awarded by International Council of Shopping Centers*]
CMD .... Charter Medical Corp. [*AMEX symbol*] (SPSG)
CMD .... Chickamauga Dam [*TVA*]
CMD .... Chief Medical Director [*Department of Veterans Affairs*]
CMD .... Childhood Muscular Dystrophy
CMD .... Christian Mission for the Deaf (EA)
CMD .... Chronic Mental Defective [*British*] (ADA)
CMD .... City Merchant Developers [*British*]
CMD .... Colcemid [*Demecolcine*] [*Antineoplastic drug*]
CMD .... Colonial Medical Department [*British*]
CMD .... Color Magnitude Diagrams
CMD .... Command (EY)
CMD .... Command Airways, Inc. [*Wappingers Falls, NY*] [*FAA designator*] (FAAC)
Cmd .... Command Papers (DLA)
CMD .... Commendation (AABC)
CMD .... Common Meter Double [*Music*]
CMD .... Compression Mold Dies (MCD)
CMD .... COMSAT [*Communications Satellite Corp.*], Washington, DC [*OCLC symbol*] (OCLC)
CMD .... Congenital Myotonic Dystrophy [*Medicine*]
CMD .... Contract Management District
CMD .... Core Memory Driver
CM & D ..... Countermeasures and Deception [*RADAR*]
CMD .... Countermeasures Dispenser (MCD)
CMD/ .... Current Meter Data Base [*National Ocean Survey*] (MSC)
CM/D .... Dialogos. Colegio de Mexico [*A publication*]
CMDAC .... Current-Mode Digital-to-Analog Converter [*Data processing*]
CMDB .... Composite-Modified Double Base [*Propellants*] (KSC)
CMDC .... Central Milk Distributive Committee [*British*]
CMDC .... Compucom Development Corporation [*Indianapolis, IN*] [*NASDAQ symbol*] (NQ)
CMDCC .... Command Computer Console
CMDCDU ... Congressi Italiani di Medicina [*A publication*]
CMDD .... Commanded
CMDDC .... City Merchant Developers Development Coordination [*British*]

CMDF .... Combined Miniature Deterrent Forces [*Organization in film "Fantastic Voyage"*]
CMDG .... Commanding
CMDINSP ... Command Inspection [*Military*] (NVT)
CMD/INV ... Command Involvement Report [*Army*]
CMDJA ..... Country Music Disk Jockeys Association [*Defunct*] (EA)
CMDL .... Comdial Corp. [*Charlottesville, VA*] [*NASDAQ symbol*] (NQ)
CMDMS ... Chloromethyldimethylchlorosilane [*Organic chemistry*]
CMDMSG ... Command Message
CMDN .... Catalog Management Data Notification [*Army*] (AABC)
CMDNJ .... College of Medicine and Dentistry of New Jersey [*Newark*]
CMDO .... Commando (CINC)
CMDO .... Consolidated Material Distribution Objectives [*Air Force*]
CMDP .... Civil Member for Development and Production [*British*]
CMDP .... Cleobury, Mortimer, and Ditton Prior Light Railway [*Wales*]
CMDRL ...... Coherent Monopulse Doppler RADAR
CMDR ...... Commander (EY)
CMDR ...... Council for Microphotography and Document Reproduction [*British*] (DIT)
Cmdre .... Commodore [*British military*] (DMA)
CMdrR ...... R & D Associates, Marina Del Rey, CA [*Library symbol*] [*Library of Congress*] (LCLS)
CMDS .... Central Mine Data Systems
CMDS .... Centralized Message Data System [*Bell System*]
CMDS .... Christian Medical and Dental Society (EA)
CMDS .... Collection, Management, and Dissemination Section
CMDS .... Command Manpower Data System
CMDS .... Countermeasures Dispenser Set (MCD)
CMDSA ..... Corps Material Direct Support Activity (MCD)
CMDSW .... Command Software Subsystem [*Space Flight Operations Facility, NASA*]
CMDT .... Comdata Holdings Corp. [*NASDAQ symbol*] (NQ)
CMDT .... Commandant
CMDT .... Corrective Maintenance Downtime (MCD)
Cmdt Gen ... Commandant General [*British military*] (DMA)
CMDTY ..... Commodity (AABC)
CMDV .... Carrot Mottle Dwarf Virus
Cme .... Carboxymethyl [*Also, CM, Cm*] [*Biochemistry*]
CME .... Center for Management Effectiveness [*Pacific Palisades, CA*] (EA)
CME .... Center for Metric Education [*Western Michigan University*]
CME .... Central Mail Exchange [*British*] (ADA)
CME .... Central Memory Extension [*Data processing*]
CME .... Centre for Multicultural Education [*University of London Institute of Education*] [*British*] (CB)
CME .... Centrifuge Moisture Equivalent
CME .... Chartered Mechanical Engineer [*A publication*]
CM & E ..... Chemical Marketing and Economics
CME .... Chemically Modified Electrode [*Electrochemistry*]
CME .... Chicago Mercantile Exchange (EA)
CME .... Chief Mechanical Engineer [*Military*] [*British*]
CME .... Chloromethyl Ether [*Organic chemistry*]
CME .... Christian Methodist Episcopal Church
CME .... Ciudad Del Carmen [*Mexico*] [*Airport symbol*] (OAG)
C & ME ...... Civil and Mining Engineer
CME .... CME Capital, Inc. [*Toronto Stock Exchange symbol*]
CME .... CMS Enhancements, Inc. [*NYSE symbol*] (SPSG)
CME .... College of Medical Evangelists [*Los Angeles, CA*]
CME .... Colloid Microthruster Experiment
CME .... Commercial Multi-Engine [*Aviation*] (AIA)
CME .... Commission on Missionary Education [*Later, Department of Education for Missions*] (EA)
CME .... Committee on Militarism in Education [*Defunct*] (EA)
CME .... Common Mode Error
CME .... Computer Measurement and Evaluation
CME .... Computer Memory Element
CME .... Computerizing Medical Examination [*IBM Corp.*]
CME .... Conference of Ministers of Education [*World War II*]
CME .... Conference Mondiale de l'Energie [*World Energy Conference - WEC*] (EAIO)
CME .... Conseil Mondial d'Education [*World Council for Curriculum and Instruction*]
CME .... Continuing Medical Education
CME .... Controlled Mission Equipment (MCD)
CME .... Countermeasures Evaluation (CAAL)
CME .... Crucible Melt Extraction [*Metal fiber technology*]
CME .... Crude Marijuana Extract
CME .... Cumann Muinteoiri Eireann [*Irish National Teachers' Organization*] (EAIO)
CME .... Cystoid Macular Edema [*Ophthalmology*]
CME .... [*The*] Monthly Journal of the Institution of Mechanical Engineers [*A publication*]
CMEA ...... Canadian Music Educators' Association
CMEA ...... Central Medical Establishment, Aviation [*Air Force*]
CMEA ...... Chief Marine Engineering Artificer [*British military*] (DMA)
CMEA ...... Council for Middle East Affairs [*Defunct*] (EA)
CMEA ...... Council for Mutual Economic Assistance [*Also known as CEMA, COMECON*] [*Communist-bloc nations: Poland, Russia, East Germany, Czechoslovakia, Romania, Bulgaria, Hungary*] [*USSR*]

CMEALL ..   Cooper Monographs on English and American Language and Literature [*A publication*]

CME-AMA ...   Council on Medical Education - of the American Medical Association   (EA)

CMEAOC ...   Conference Ministerielle des Etats d'Afrique de l'Ouest et du Centre sur les Transports Maritimes [*Ministerial Conference of West and Central African States on Maritime Transportation - MCWCS*] [*Abidjan, Ivory Coast*]   (EAIO)

CMEC ....   Canadian Managing Editors' Conference

CMEC ....   Chemical Marketing and Economics

CMEC ....   Christian Methodist Episcopal Church

CMEC ....   Combined Military Exploitation Center

CMED ....   Cybermedic, Inc. [*Louisville, CO*] [*NASDAQ symbol*]   (NQ)

CMEDD4 ...   Cardiovascular Medicine [*A publication*]

C Med H ....   Cambridge Medieval History [*A publication*]

C/MEDIA ...   Corporation for Maintaining Editorial Diversity in America   (EA)

CMEDSTR ...   Canada. Marine Environmental Data Service. Technical Report [*A publication*]

CMEE ....   Chief Mechanical and Electrical Engineer [*Air Force*] [*British*]

CMEIS ......   Centre for Middle Eastern and Islamic Studies [*University of Durham*] [*British*]   (CB)

CMEM ......   Chief Marine Engineering Mechanic [*British military*]   (DMA)

CMEM ......   Complete Minimum Essential Medium

CMEMA ...   Chicago and Midwest Envelope Manufacturers Association [*Defunct*]

CMen ....   Menlo Park Public Library, Menlo Park, CA [*Library symbol*] [*Library of Congress*]   (LCLS)

CMENA ....   Chemical and Metallurgical Engineering [*A publication*]

CMenC ......   Menlo School and College, Menlo Park, CA [*Library symbol*] [*Library of Congress*]   (LCLS)

CMenS ....   Sunset Magazine Reference Library, Menlo Park, CA [*Library symbol*] [*Library of Congress*]   (LCLS)

CMenSP ....   Saint Patrick's Seminary, Menlo Park, CA [*Library symbol*] [*Library of Congress*]   (LCLS)

CMenSR....   Stanford Research Institute Library, Menlo Park, CA [*Library symbol*] [*Library of Congress*]   (LCLS)

CMenUG...   United States Geological Survey, Menlo Park, CA [*Library symbol*] [*Library of Congress*]   (LCLS)

CMEP........   Computerised Medical Systems Public Ltd. Co. [*Aylesbury, Buckinghamshire, England*] [*NASDAQ symbol*]   (NQ)

CMEP........   Critical Mass Energy Project   (EA)

CMER ......   Component and Material Engineering Request

CMER ......   Curtis, Milburn & Eastern Railroad Co. [*AAR code*]

CMERA.....   Conference Mondiale des Experts Radiotelegraphistes de l'Aeronautique

CMerC.......   Merced County Free Library, Merced, CA [*Library symbol*] [*Library of Congress*]   (LCLS)

CMerCC ....   Merced Community College, Merced, CA [*Library symbol*] [*Library of Congress*]   (LCLS)

CMerCL ....   Merced County Bar Association Law Library, Merced, CA [*Library symbol*] [*Library of Congress*]   (LCLS)

CME Reprnt ...   Chemical Marketing and Economics Reprints [*A publication*]

CMERI......   Central Mechanical Engineering Research Institute   (MCD)

CMerUSAF ...   United States Air Force, Castle Grate Air Force Base Library, Merced, CA [*Library symbol*] [*Library of Congress*]   (LCLS)

CMerUSAH ...   United States Air Force, Castle Air Force Base Hospital, Merced, CA [*Library symbol*] [*Library of Congress*]   (LCLS)

CMES........   Center for Middle Eastern Studies [*Harvard University*] [*Research center*]   (RCD)

CMES........   Center for Middle Eastern Studies [*University of California, Berkeley*] [*Research center*]   (RCD)

CMES........   Contractor Maintenance Engineering Support   (MCD)

CMET.......   Coated Metal   (AAG)

CMET........   Continental Mortgage and Equity Trust [*NASDAQ symbol*]   (NQ)

CM-ETO ...   Court-Martial, European Theater of Operations [*United States*]   (DLA)

CMEV ....   Civilian Marine Emergency Volunteers

CMEW ......   Comparative Medicine East and West [*A publication*]

CMEWDR ...   Comparative Medicine East and West [*A publication*]

CMEWS....   Concrete Missile Entry Warning System   (MCD)

CMF ....   C-Band Monopulse Feed

CMF ....   Calcium- and Magnesium-Free

CMF ....   Cannet Des Maures [*France*] [*Seismograph station code, US Geological Survey*] [*Closed*]   (SEIS)

CMF ....   Capital Maintenance Fund

CMF ....   Carbon Monofluoride [*Inorganic chemistry*]

CMF ....   Cardinal Mindszenty Foundation   (EA)

CMF ....   Career Management Field [*Military*]   (AABC)

CMF ....   Cartesian Mapping Function

CMF ....   Casopis pro Moderni Filologii [*A publication*]

CMF ....   Cast Metals Federation [*Later, NFA*]   (EA)

CMF ....   Central Maintenance Facility   (NRCH)

CMF ....   Central Mediterranean Force [*Later, AAI*] [*British*] [*World War II*]

CMF ....   Chambery [*France*] [*Airport symbol*]   (OAG)

CMF ....   Chloromethylfurfuraldehyde [*Organic chemistry*]

CMF ....   Chocolate Milk Foundation [*Defunct*]   (EA)

CMF ....   Chondromyxoid Fibroma [*Medicine*]

CMF ....   Christian Medical Foundation International   (EA)

CMF ....   Christian Military Fellowship   (EA)

CMF ....   Christian Missionary Fellowship   (EA)

CMF ....   Circular Mil Foot

CMF ....   Citizen Military Forces [*New Guinea*]

CMF ....   Coherent Memory Filter

CMF ....   Colonial Military Forces [*British*]

CMF ....   Color Mixture Function

CMF ....   Combat Mission Failure   (AABC)

CMF ....   Combat Mission Folder   (AFM)

CMF ....   Combined Master File [*Data processing*]

CMF ....   Commercial Financial Corp. Ltd. [*Toronto Stock Exchange symbol*]

CMF ....   Commercial Fishing [*Type of water project*]

CMF ....   Common Mode Failure [*Nuclear energy*]   (NRCH)

CMF ....   Commonwealth Military Forces [*British*]

CMF ....   Complex Maintenance Facility [*Deep Space Instrumentation Facility, NASA*]

CMF ....   Composite Medical Facility   (AFM)

CMF ....   Congregatio Missionariorum Filiorum Immaculati Cordis Beatae Maria Virginia [*Congregation of Missionary Sons of the Immaculate Heart of the Blessed Virgin Mary*] [*Claretians*] [*Roman Catholic religious order*]

CMF ....   Congressional Management Foundation   (EA)

CMF ....   Conventional Military Fuels   (RDA)

CMF ....   Cortical Magnification Factor

CMF ....   Countermortar Fire

CMF ....   Country Music Foundation   (EA)

CMF ....   Court-Martial Forfeiture

CMF ....   Creative Music Foundation   (EA)

CMF ....   Cross-Modulation Factor   (DEN)

CMF ....   Crosscurrents/Modern Fiction [*A publication*]

CMF ....   Customer Master File

CMF ....   Cyclophosphamide, Methotrexate, Fluorouracil [*Antineoplastic drug regimen*]

CMF ....   Cylindrical Magnetic Film

CMF ....   Cymomotive Force [*Telecommunications*]   (TEL)

CMF ....   Facilities Capital Cost of Money Factors Computation [*DoD*]

CMF ....   Sisters of the Immaculate Heart of Mary [*Roman Catholic religious order*]

CMF ....   Yugoslavia Export [*A publication*]

CMFA.......   Common Mode Failure Analysis [*Nuclear energy*]   (NRCH)

CMFAAV ...   Communications. Faculte des Sciences. Universite d'Ankara [*A publication*]

CMF/AV ...   Cyclophosphamide, Methotrexate, Fluorouracil, Adriamycin, Oncovin (Vincristine) [*Antineoplastic drug regimen*]

CMFAVP ..   Cyclophosphamide, Methotrexate, Fluorouracil, Adriamycin, Vincristine, Prednisone [*Antineoplastic drug regimen*]

CMFB.......   Chemical Fabrics Corp. [*Merrimack, NH*] [*NASDAQ symbol*]   (NQ)

CMFBD3..   CMFRI [*Central Marine Fisheries Research Institute*] Bulletin [*A publication*]

CMFC.......   China Man-Made Fiber Corporation [*Taiwan*]

CMFC.......   College des Medecins de Famille du Canada   (EAIO)

CMFC.......   Country Music Fan Club   (EA)

CMFD ......   Christian Mission for the Deaf   (EA)

CMFG ......   Coast Manufacturing Co., Inc. [*Mount Vernon, NY*] [*NASDAQ symbol*]   (NQ)

C/MFI ....   Conversion, Memory, and Fault Indication [*Telecommunications*]   (TEL)

CM/FI ....   Foro Internacional. El Colegio de Mexico [*A publication*]

CMFK.......   Camouflage Mobile Field Kitchen [*Military*]   (MCD)

CMFL.......   Casopis pro Moderni Filologii a Literaturu [*A publication*]

CMFL.......   Commission on Marriage and Family Life [*of NCC*] [*Defunct*]

CMFL.......   Compuflight, Inc. [*NASDAQ symbol*]   (NQ)

CMFLPD ..   Core Maximum Fraction of Limiting Power Density [*Nuclear energy*]   (NRCH)

CMFLR .....   Cam Follower

CMfNASA ...   National Aeronautics and Space Administration, Ames Research Center, Technical Library, Moffett Field, CA [*Library symbol*] [*Library of Congress*]   (LCLS)

CMFP.......   Cyclophosphamide, Methotrexate, Fluorouracil, Prednisone [*Antineoplastic drug regimen*]

CMFRI Bull ...   CMFRI [*Central Marine Fisheries Research Institute*] Bulletin [*A publication*]

CMFSW ....   Calcium- and Magnesium-Free Synthetic Seawater

CMFT.......   Canadian Museum of Flight and Transportation

CMFT.......   Cyclophosphamide, Methotrexate, Fluorouracil, Tamoxifen [*Antineoplastic drug regimen*]

CMFVAT ..   Cyclophosphamide, Methotrexate, Fluorouracil, Vincristine, Adriamycin, Testosterone [*Antineoplastic drug regimen*]

CMFVP ....   Cyclophosphamide, Methotrexate, Fluorouracil, Vincristine, Prednisone [*Antineoplastic drug regimen*]

CMG.........   Canada Malting Co. Ltd. [*Toronto Stock Exchange symbol*]

CMG.........   Case Mix Grouping

CMG.........   Central Machine Gun

CM & G .....   Chicago, Milwaukee & Gary Railroad [*Nickname: Cold, Miserable, and Grouchy*]

CMG.........   Chief Marine Gunner [*Navy rating*]

CMG.........   Chopped Meat Glucose [*Medium*] [*Microbiology*]

CMG .... Church of Jesus Christ of Latter-Day Saints, Genealogical Society Library, Modesto, CA [*Library symbol*] [*Library of Congress*] (LCLS)
CMG .... Color Marketing Group [*Washington, DC*] (EA)
CMG .... Commission for Marine Geology [*of the International Union of Geological Sciences*] (EAIO)
CMG .... Committee for the Monument of Garibaldi (EA)
CMG .... Companion of the Order of St. Michael and St. George [*Facetiously translated "Call Me God"*] [*British*]
CMG .... Composite Maintenance Group [*Military*] [*British*]
CMG .... Compressed Medical Gas [*Food and Drug Administration*]
CMG .... Computer Measurement Group (EA)
CMG .... Computer Modelling Group [*Research center*] (RCD)
CMG .... Consumentengids [*A publication*]
CMG .... Control Moment Gyroscope [*Aerospace*]
CMG .... Corpus Medicorum Graecorum [*A publication*] (OCD)
CMG .... Corumba Mato Grosso [*Brazil*] [*Airport symbol*] (OAG)
CMG .... Corvair Model Group (EA)
CMG .... Cystometrogram [*or Cystometrography*] [*Urology*]
CMGA ...... Control Moment Gyro Assembly [*Aerospace*]
CMGC ...... Canadian Machine Gun Corps [*World War I*]
Cm Gds ..... Coldstream Guards [*British military*] (DMA)
CMGEA .... Control Moment Gyro Electrical Assembly [*Aerospace*]
CMGEA .... Geological Survey of Canada. Bulletin [*A publication*]
CMGEAE .. Geological Survey of Canada. Bulletin [*A publication*]
CMGI .... Communications Group, Incorporated [*King Of Prussia, PA*] [*NASDAQ symbol*] (NQ)
CMGIA ...... Control Moment Gyro Inverter Assembly [*Aerospace*] (MCD)
CMGM ...... Center for Molecular and Genetic Medicine [*Stanford University*] [*Research center*]
CMGM ...... Chronic Megakaryocytic Granulocytic Myelosis [*Medicine*]
CMGPA .... Centralblatt fuer Mineralogie, Geologie, und Palaeontologie [*A publication*]
CMGS .... Control Moment Gyro System [*or Subsystem*] [*Aerospace*] (KSC)
CMGS .... Cruise Missile Guidance Set (MCD)
CMGS .... Cruise Missile Guidance System (MCD)
CMGSA ..... Congressional Monitoring Group on Southern Africa (EA)
cm-g-s-Bi... Centimeter-Gram-Second-Biot [*System of units*]
cm-g-s-Fr ... Centimeter-Gram-Second-Franklin [*System of units*]
CMGT .... Chromosome-Mediated Gene Transfer [*Biochemistry*]
CMGV .... Codling Moth Granulosis Virus
CMGW ...... E. & J. Gallo Winery, Modesto, CA [*Library symbol*] [*Library of Congress*] (LCLS)
CMH .... Cambridge Mediaeval History [*A publication*]
CMH .... Cambridge Modern History [*A publication*] (ROG)
CMH .... Campaign for the Mentally Handicapped [*British*]
CMH .... Center of Military History (AABC)
CMH .... Centimeter Height-Finder [*RADAR*]
CMH .... Ceramide Monohexoside [*Biochemistry*]
CMH .... Chemehuevi Mountains [*California*] [*Seismograph station code, US Geological Survey*] (SEIS)
CMH .... Chief of Military History [*Army*]
CMH .... Clayton Homes, Inc. [*NYSE symbol*] (SPSG)
CMH .... Collapsible Maintenance Hangar (MCD)
CMH .... Columbus [*Ohio*] [*Airport symbol*] (OAG)
CMH .... Company of Military Historians (EA)
CMH .... Congenital Malformation of Heart [*Medicine*]
CMH .... Congressional Medal of Honor
CMH .... Construction Mechanic, Construction [*Navy rating*]
CMH .... Corporal-Major of Horse [*British*]
C/MH .... Cost per Man-Hour (MCD)
CMH .... Countermeasures Homing (CET)
CM & H ..... Cox, Macrae, and Hertslet's English County Court Reports [*1847-58*] [*A publication*] (DLA)
CMH .... Modesto State Hospital, Staff Library, Modesto, CA [*Library symbol*] [*Library of Congress*] (LCLS)
CMHA .... California Mental Health Analysis [*Testing*]
CMHA .... Canadian Mental Health Association
CMHA .... Canadian Mobile Home Association
CMHA .... Community Mental Health Activities
CMHA .... Comprehensive Mental Health Assessment
C-MHA ..... Confidential - Modified Handling Authorized [*Army*] (AFM)
CMHC .... Canada Mortgage and Housing Corporation [*Government agency*]
CMHC .... Carolina Mountain Holding Company [*Highlands, NC*] [*NASDAQ symbol*] (NQ)
CMHC .... Community Mental Health Center [*or Clinic*]
CMHCA .... Community Mental Health Centers Act [*1975*]
CMHEC .... Carboxymethyl Hydroxyethyl Cellulose [*Organic chemistry*]
CMHI .... Baker-Schulberg Community Mental Health Ideology Scale [*Psychology*]
CMHIF ...... Cooperative Management Housing Insurance Fund [*Federal Housing Administration*]
CMHJAY ... Community Mental Health Journal [*A publication*]
CMHP .... Community Mental Health Program
CMHPAI... Acta Veterinaria et Zootechnica Sinica [*A publication*]
CMHQ .... Canadian Military Headquarters (DMA)
CMHS .... Congressional Medal of Honor Society (EA)
CMI .... CAB [*Commonwealth Agricultural Bureaux*] International Mycological Institute [*British*] (IRUK)

CMI .... Cambridge Memories, Incorporated
CMI .... Can Manufacturers Institute (EA)
CMI .... Canadian Magazine Index [*Micromedia Ltd.*] [*Information service or system*] (IID)
CMI .... Canadian Mediterranean Institute [*Research center*] (RCD)
CMi.......... Canis Minor [*Constellation*]
CMI .... Carbohydrate Metabolism Index [*Biochemistry*]
CMI .... Care and Maintenance Instruction [*Nuclear energy*] (NRCH)
CMI .... Career Maturity Inventory [*Vocational guidance test*]
CMI .... Caribbean Institute for Meteorology and Hydrology [*Acronym is based on former name, Caribbean Meteorological Institute*] (EAIO)
CmI .... Cascade Microfilm Systems, Inc., Portland, OR [*Library symbol*] [*Library of Congress*] (LCLS)
CMI .... Case-Mix Index [*Medicare*] (DHSM)
CMI .... Cash Management Institute (EA)
CMI .... Cell [*or Cellular*]-Mediated Immunity [*Immunochemistry*]
CMI .... Cell Multiplication Inhibition
CMI .... Center for Machine Intelligence [*Research center*] (RCD)
CMI .... Champaign [*Illinois*] [*Airport symbol*] (OAG)
CMI .... Champaign/Urbana, IL [*Location identifier*] [*FAA*] (FAAL)
CMI .... Chemical Week [*A publication*]
CMI .... Chemotactic Index [*Immunology*]
CMI .... China Market Intelligence [*National Council for US-China Trade*] [*A publication*]
CMI .... Christian Michelsen's Institute [*Norway*]
CMI .... Chronic Mesenteric Ischemia [*Medicine*]
CMI .... Chronically Mentally Ill [*Medicine*]
CMI .... Classified Military Information (MCD)
CMI .... Cleaning Management Institute (EA)
CMI .... Clerical Medical International [*British*]
CMI .... Clomipramine [*An antidepressant*] [*Medicine*]
CMI .... Club Med, Incorporated [*NYSE symbol*] (SPSG)
CMI .... Code Mark Inversion [*Telecommunications*] (TEL)
CMI .... Comite Maritime International [*International Maritime Committee - IMC*] [*Antwerp, Belgium*] (EAIO)
CMI .... Comite Meteorologique International
CMI .... Command Maintenance Inspection [*Army*]
CMI .... Commodity Microanalysis, Incorporated [*Information service or system*] (IID)
CMI .... Commonwealth Mycological Institute [*Research center*] [*British*] (IRC)
CMI .... Computer-Managed Instruction
CMI .... Conventions, Meetings, Incentive Travel [*Of CMI World, a publication aimed at those markets*]
CMI .... Coping with Medical Issues [*Elsevier Book Series*] [*A publication*]
CMI .... Core Element Assembly Motion Inhibit [*Nuclear energy*] (IEEE)
CMI .... Cornell Medical Index [*Psychology*]
CMI .... Cruise Missile Interrogation
CMI .... Cultured Marble Institute (EA)
CMI .... Cumulative Monthly Issue [*Material*] (AAG)
CMI .... Cytomegalic Inclusion Disease [*Ophthalmology*]
CMIA .... Coal Mining Institute of America [*Later, PCMIA*] (EA)
CMIA .... Command Management Inventory Accounting [*Army*]
CMIA .... Cultivated Mushroom Institute of America
CMIC........ California Microwave, Inc. [*Sunnyvale, CA*] [*NASDAQ symbol*] (NQ)
CMIC........ Catalog of Material Improvement Cards (MCD)
CMIC........ Combined Military Interrogation Center
CMIC........ Computer Microfilm International Corporation [*Information service or system*] (IID)
CMICA ...... Canada. Mines Branch. Information Circular [*A publication*]
CMICE...... Current Meter Intercomparison Experiment [*National Ocean Survey*] (MSC)
CMID .... Commodity Manager Input Data (MCD)
CM-ID .... Crew Member Identification
CMid........ Middletown Library, Middletown, CA [*Library symbol*] [*Library of Congress*] (LCLS)
CMIDB...... Chemischer Informationsdienst [*A publication*]
CMI Descr Pathog Fungi Bact ... CMI [*Commonwealth Mycological Institute*] Descriptions of Pathogenic Fungi and Bacteria [*A publication*]
CMIEB...... Centre Mondial d'Information sur l'Education Bilingue [*World Information Centre for Bilingual Education - WICBE*] (EAIO)
CMIEC...... China National Metallurgical Import & Export Corporation [*People's Republic of China*] (IMH)
CMIF........ Career Management Information File [*Military*] (AABC)
CMIFAR ... CMI [*Commonwealth Mycological Institute*] Descriptions of Pathogenic Fungi and Bacteria [*A publication*]
CMIK .... Carmike Cinemas, Inc. [*Columbus, GA*] [*NASDAQ symbol*] (NQ)
CMIL........ Camille St. Moritz, Inc. [*NASDAQ symbol*] (NQ)
CMIL........ Circular Mil [*Wire measure*] (MSA)
CMIM .... Centre for Measurement and Information in Medicine [*City University*] [*British*] (CB)
CMIMAE ... Commonwealth Mycological Institute. Mycological Papers [*A publication*]

CMIMBF .. Contributions to Microbiology and Immunology [*A publication*]
CMin......... Canis Minor [*Constellation*]
C Min......... Christian Ministry [*A publication*]
CMIN........ Computer Memories, Inc. [*NASDAQ symbol*]　(NQ)
C/MIN ...... Counts per Minute
C/MIN ...... Cycles per Minute
C Mind...... Catholic Mind [*A publication*]
CMIO .... COMSEC [*Communications Security*] Material Issuing Office [*Military*]　(NVT)
CMIP........ Cost Management Improvement Program
CMIPB...... Cahiers de Medecine Interprofessionnelle [*A publication*]
CMIR........ Common Mode Input Resistance
CMIS......... Change to Metric Information Service [*A publication*]　(APTA)
CMIS......... Command Management Information System [*Air Force*]
CMIS......... Common Military Intelligence Skills　(NVT)
CMIS......... Computerized Medical Imaging Society　(EA)
CMIS......... Contract Management Information System　(MCD)
CMIS......... Control Monitor and Isolation Subsystem　(MCD)
CMIS......... Crisis Management INTERCOM System　(MCD)
CMIT........ Canada Manpower Industrial Training
CMIT........ Current Medical Information and Terminology
CMIU of A ... Cigar Makers' International Union of America　(EA)
CMiUN...... United States Naval Shipyard, Technical Library, Mare Island, CA [*Library symbol*] [*Library of Congress*]　(LCLS)
CMIWHTE ... Companion Member of the Institution of Works and Highways Technician Engineers [*British*]　(DBQ)
CMIWSc ... Certified Member of the Institute of Wood Science [*British*]　(DBQ)
CMJ.......... Canadian Mining Journal [*A publication*]
CMJ.......... Canadian Municipal Journal [*A publication*]　(DLA)
CMJ.......... Christian Medical Society. Journal [*A publication*]
CMJ.......... Church's Ministry among Jews [*Church of England*]
CMJ.......... Code of Military Justice
CMJ.......... College of Mount St. Joseph-On-The-Ohio, Mount St. Joseph, OH [*OCLC symbol*]　(OCLC)
CMJ.......... Communicator's Journal [*A publication*]
CMJ.......... Compensation Planning Journal [*A publication*]
CMJ.......... Czechoslovak Mathematical Journal [*A publication*]
CMJ.......... Ketchikan, AK [*Location identifier*] [*FAA*]　(FAAL)
CMJ.......... Modesto Junior College, Modesto, CA [*Library symbol*] [*Library of Congress*]　(LCLS)
CM & JA ... Commonwealth Magistrates and Judges' Association　(EAIO)
CMJHL...... Canadian Major Junior Hockey League
CMJODS ... Chinese Medical Journal [*English Edition*] [*A publication*]
CMJPB .. Community and Junior College Journal [*A publication*]
CMJS........ Committee for the Maintenance of Jewish Standards　(EA)
CMJUA9... Caribbean Medical Journal [*A publication*]
CMK......... Carmel, NY [*Location identifier*] [*FAA*]　(FAAL)
CMK......... Chassis Marking Kit
CMK......... College of Marin, Kentfield, CA [*OCLC symbol*]　(OCLC)
CMK......... Colonial Intermarket, Inc. Trust I [*NYSE symbol*]　(SPSG)
CMK......... Compendium. Dagelijks Overzicht van de Buitenlandse Pers [*A publication*]
CMK......... Core-Mark International, Inc. [*Toronto Stock Exchange symbol*] [*Vancouver Stock Exchange symbol*]
CMK......... Cynomolgus Monkey Kidney [*Medicine*]
CMKA....... Christopher Morley Knothole Association　(EA)
CMKRA .... Chemical Marketing Reporter [*A publication*]
CMKZA..... Chemiker-Zeitung [*A publication*]
CML......... Canaanite Myths and Legends [*A publication*]　(BJA)
CML .... Canthomeatal Line [*Anatomy*]
CML .... Cell Management Language [*Software*]　(BYTE)
CML .... Cell-Mediated Lympholysis [*Immunology*]
CML .... Chambre de Commerce France Amerique Latine [*A publication*]
CML .... Chemical　(AABC)
CML .... Chicago Midway Laboratory [*Army*]　(MCD)
CML .... Chief Moulder [*Navy rating*] [*Obsolete*]
CML .... Choice Magazine Listening [*An "aural magazine" for the blind and visually handicapped*]
CML .... Chronic Myelocytic [*or Myeloid or Myelogenous*] Leukemia [*Oncology*]
CML .... Cincinnati Milacron, Inc., Corporate Information Center, Cincinnati, OH [*OCLC symbol*]　(OCLC)
CML .... Classical and Modern Literature: A Quarterly [*A publication*]
CML .... Clinical Medical Librarian
CML .... Clinical Microbiology Laboratory
CML .... Club du Meilleur Livre [*A publication*]
CML .... CML Group, Inc. [*NYSE symbol*]　(SPSG)
CML .... Collimated Monochromatic Light
CML .... Commercial
CML .... Commercial Law Journal [*A publication*]
CML .... Common Machine Language [*Data processing*]
CML .... Common Mode Logic
CmL .... Commonwealth Microfilm Library Ltd., Calgary, AB, Canada [*Library symbol*] [*Library of Congress*]　(LCLS)
CML .... Components and Materials Laboratory
CML .... Computer-Managed Laboratory
CML .... Computer-Managed Learning　(ADA)
CML .... Concordia Mutual Life Association　(EA)

CML .... Consolidated Material List　(MCD)
CML .... Contemporary Men of Letters [*A publication*]
CML .... Contracts Maintenance Log　(MCD)
CML .... Conversational Modeling Language [*Data processing*]
CML .... Corpus Medicorum Latinorum [*A publication*]　(OCD)
CML .... Council Moslem League [*Political party*] [*Pakistan*]
CML .... Critical Mass Laboratory
CML .... Current-Mode Logic [*Data processing*]
CMl.......... Mill Valley Public Library, Mill Valley, CA [*Library symbol*] [*Library of Congress*]　(LCLS)
CML .... Stanislaus County Law Library, Modesto, CA [*Library symbol*] [*Library of Congress*]　(LCLS)
CMLA .... Chief Martial Law Administrator [*Pakistan*] [*Facetious translation: "Cancel My Last Announcement"*]　(ECON)
CMLB....... Citrus Mealybug [*Plant pest*]
CMLC........ Camseal, Inc. [*NASDAQ symbol*]　(NQ)
CMLC........ Chemical Corps [*Army*]
CMLC........ Civilian/Military Liaison Committee
CMLCBL .. Classical and Medieval Literature Criticism [*A publication*]
CMLCBL .. Chemical Corps Biological Laboratories [*Army*]
CMLCENCOM ... Chemical Corps Engineering Command [*Army*]
CMLCMATCOM ... Chemical Corps Material Command [*Army*]
CMLCRDCOM ... Chemical Corps Research and Development Command [*Army*]
CMLCRECOM ... Chemical Corps Research and Engineering Command [*Army*]
CMLCTNGCOM ... Chemical Corps Training Command [*Army*]
CMLDEF .. Chemical Defense
CMLE........ Casual Male Corp. [*NASDAQ symbol*]　(CTT)
CMLE........ Classical Music Lovers' Exchange　(EA)
CMlG......... Golden Gate Baptist Theological Seminary, Mill Valley, CA [*Library symbol*] [*Library of Congress*]　(LCLS)
CMLHO.... Chemical Corps Historical Office [*Army*]
CMLOPS.... Chemical Operations [*Army*]　(AABC)
CM-LP ...... Comite Marxista-Leninista Portugues [*Portuguese Marxist-Leninist Committee*]　(PPE)
CMLR........ Canadian Modern Language Review [*A publication*]
CMLR........ Cleveland-Marshall Law Review [*A publication*]
CMLR........ Common Market Law Reports [*A publication*]
CMLR........ Common Market Law Review [*A publication*]　(DLA)
CML Rev .. Common Market Law Review [*A publication*]　(DLA)
CMLS........ Central Michigan Library System [*Library network*]
CMLS........ Comprehensive Mailing List System [*Library of Congress*]
CMLS........ Computer Multiple Listing Service [*Information service or system*]　(IID)
CMLS........ Confederate Memorial Literary Society　(EA)
CMLTEE .. Classified Ministry Lists of Types of Educational Establishments [*British*]
CMM .... Caldera Mines Ltd. [*Vancouver Stock Exchange symbol*]
CM & M ... Carroll, McEntee & McGinley [*Commercial firm*]
CMM .... Casopis Matice Moravske [*A publication*]
CMM .... Chemical Engineering. Chemical Technology for Profit Minded Engineers [*A publication*]
CMM .... Chemical Milling Machine
CMM .... Chief Machinist's Mate [*Navy rating*] [*Obsolete*]
CMM .... Chief Merchanist's Mate [*Navy*] [*British*]
CMM .... Chief Motor Mechanic [*British military*]　(DMA)
CMM .... Coal-Methane Mixture
CMM .... Coherent Microwave Memory
CMM .... Comma　(AABC)
CMM .... Commander of the Order of Military Merit
cmm........... Commentator [*MARC relator code*] [*Library of Congress*]　(LCCP)
Cmm........... Commission [*Business term*]
CMM .... Commission for Maritime Meteorology [*World Meteorological Organization*]
CMM .... Communications Multiplexer Module [*Data processing*]
CMM .... Component Maintenance Manual　(MCD)
CMM .... Computer Main Memory [*Telecommunications*]　(TEL)
CMM .... Concentration Module Main [*Telecommunications*]　(TEL)
CMM .... Conclave of Mystical Masons [*Freemasonry*]　(ROG)
CMM .... Condition Monitored Maintenance　(NASA)
CMM .... Congregatio Missionariorum de Mariannhill [*Congregation of Mariannhill Missionaries*] [*Mariannhill Fathers*] [*Roman Catholic religious order*] [*Italy*]
CMM .... Consistory of Masonic Magic [*Freemasonry*]　(ROG)
CMM .... Coordinate Measuring Machine
CMM .... Coordinated Management of Meaning [*Communications theory*]
CMM .... Core Mechanical Mock-Up [*Nuclear energy*]　(NRCH)
CMM .... CRI Insured Mortgage Association [*NYSE symbol*]　(SPSG)
CMM .... Cubic Millimeter
CMM .... Cutting or Molding Machine
CMM .... Mount St. Mary's College, Los Angeles, CA [*OCLC symbol*]　(OCLC)
CMM .... Technical Commission for Marine Meteorology [*WHO*] [*Geneva, Switzerland*]　(EAIO)
CMM .... US Region of Congregation of Mariannhill Missionaries　(EA)
CMMA ...... Canadian Metal Mining Association
CMMA ...... Carpet Manufacturers Marketing Association　(EA)

CMMA ...... Christian Ministries Management Association [*Later,* *CMA*] (EA)
CMMA ...... Cigar Makers' Mutual Association [*A union*] [*British*]
CMMA ...... Clock Manufacturers and Marketing Association (EA)
CMMA ...... Clothing Monetary Maintenance Allowance [*Military*] (AABC)
CMMA ...... Custom Metallized Multigate Array [*NASA*]
CMMB ...... Catholic Medical Mission Board
CMMBA ... Canadian Mining and Metallurgical Bulletin [*A publication*]
CMMBE5 ... Cell Culture Methods for Molecular and Cell Biology [*A publication*]
CMMC ...... California Marine Mammal Center [*Research center*] (RCD)
CMMC ...... Commercial International Corporation [*Los Angeles, CA*] [*NASDAQ symbol*] (NQ)
CMMC ...... COMSEC [*Communications Security*] Material Management Center (MCD)
CMMC ...... Corps Material Management Center (MCD)
CMMCA ... Cruise Missile Mission Control Aircraft (MCD)
CMMCBE ... Chief Machinist's Mate, Construction Battalion, Equipment Operator [*Navy rating*] [*Obsolete*]
CMMDA ... Command Module Multiple Docking Assembly [*NASA*] (KSC)
CMME ...... Chloromethyl Methyl Ether [*Organic chemistry*]
CMME ...... Compton's Multimedia Encyclopedia [*A publication*]
CMMF ...... Component Maintenance and Mock-Up Facility [*Nuclear energy*] (NRCH)
CMMG ...... Canadian Motor Machine Gun [*World War I*]
CMMG ...... Chief Machinist's Mate, Industrial Gas Generating Mechanic [*Navy rating*] [*Obsolete*]
CMMG ...... Civilian Manpower Management Guides [*Navy*] (NG)
CMMGB ... Canadian Motor Machine Gun Brigade (DMA)
CMMH ...... Memorial Hospital Association, Modesto, CA [*Library symbol*] [*Library of Congress*] (LCLS)
CMMI .... Civilian Manpower Management Instruction [*Navy*] (NG)
CMMI .... Command Maintenance Management Inspection [*Army*]
CMMI .... Council of Mining and Metallurgical Institutions [*London, England*] (EAIO)
CMMIO .... Communications Security Mobile Issuing Office [*Military*] (NVT)
CMML ...... Christian Missions in Many Lands (EA)
CMML ...... Chronic Myelomonocytic Leukemia [*Oncology*]
CMML ...... Civilian Manpower Management Letters [*Navy*] (NG)
CMMLIT .. Chronic Myelomonocytic Leukemia in Transition [*Oncology*]
CMMM ..... McHenry Museum, Modesto, CA [*Library symbol*] [*Library of Congress*] (LCLS)
CMMN ...... Commission
CMMN ...... Common
CMMNA ... Catholic Major Markets Newspaper Association (EA)
CMMND ... Commissioned
CMMNR ... Commissioner
CMMP ...... Canada Manpower Mobility Program
CMMP ...... Carnegie Multi-Mini Processor
CMMP ...... Commodity Management Master Plan (MCD)
CMMP ...... Convertible Money Market Preferred Stock [*Investment term*]
CMMP ...... Corps of Military Mounted Police [*British military*] (DMA)
CMMR ...... Chief Machinist's Mate, Refrigeration [*Navy rating*] [*Obsolete*]
Cmmr .... Commissioner
CMMR ...... Common Modular Multimode RADAR
CMMR ...... Confirmed and Made a Matter of Record [*Army*] (AABC)
CMMS ...... Carbon Monoxide Measuring System
CMMS ...... Center for Medical Manpower Studies [*Northeastern University*] [*Research center*] (RCD)
CMMS ...... Chief Machinist's Mate, Shop [*Navy rating*] [*Obsolete*]
CMMS ...... Columbia Mental Maturity Scale [*Psychology*]
CMMS ...... Congressionally Mandated Mobility Study [*DoD*]
CMMS ...... Corps Material Management System
CMMSC.... Chislennye Metody Mekhaniki Sploshnoi Sredy [*A publication*]
CMMSRO ... Chief Machinist's Mate, Ship Repair, Outside Machinist [*Navy rating*] [*Obsolete*]
Cmmty Serv ... Community Service Newsletter [*A publication*]
CMMU ...... Cache Memory Management Unit [*Data processing*] (BYTE)
CMMWWII ... Combat Merchant Mariners World War II (EA)
CMN .... Callahan Mining Corp. [*NYSE symbol*] (SPSG)
CMN .... Casablanca-Mohamed V [*Morocco*] [*Airport symbol*] (OAG)
CMN .... Cellular and Molecular Neurobiology [*A publication*]
CMN .... Cerium Magnesium Nitrate [*Inorganic chemistry*]
CMN .... Coleman Collieries [*Vancouver Stock Exchange symbol*]
CMN .... Common
CMN .... Common Market News [*A publication*]
CMN .... Computerized Management Network [*For Agricultural Cooperative Extension Service Education*] [*Virginia Polytechnic Institute*] [*Database*]
CMN .... Contract Management Network (MCD)
CMN .... Convention Relative au Contrat de Transport de Marchandises en Navigation Interieure [*Convention on the Carriage of Goods by Inland Waterways*]
CMN .... Corynebacteria, Mycobacteria, Nocardiae [*Trehalose containing genera*]
CMN .... Crewman (NASA)
CMN .... Crown Mine [*Nevada*] [*Seismograph station code, US Geological Survey*] [*Closed*] (SEIS)
CMN .... Cystic Medial Necrosis [*of aorta*] [*Medicine*]
CMNC .... Commence (FAAC)

CMND .... Command (IBMDP)
Cmnd .... Command Papers [*A publication*] (DLA)
CMNEDI... Cellular and Molecular Neurobiology [*A publication*]
CMNFB .... Church of Monday Night Football (EA)
CMNLD .... Chamber of Mines. Newsletter [*South Africa*] [*A publication*]
CMNPO .... Common Market Newspaper Publishers' Organization [*See also CAEJ*] [*Brussels, Belgium*] (EAIO)
CMNS ...... Committee on Mediterranean Neogene Stratigraphy
CMNT .... Comment (MSA)
CMNT .... Computer Network Technology Corp. [*NASDAQ symbol*] (NQ)
CMO .... Canonical Molecular Orbital [*Physical chemistry*]
CMO .... Capstead Mortgage [*NYSE symbol*] (SPSG)
CMO .... Cardiac Minute Output [*Physiology*]
CMO .... Caribbean Meteorological Organisation [*Formerly, Caribbean Meteorological Service*] (EA)
CMO .... Central Meteorological Observatory [*Japan*]
CMO .... Chicago, St. Paul, Minneapolis & Omaha R. R. [*AAR code*]
CMO .... Chief Maintenance Officer
CMO .... Chief Marketing Officer [*Insurance*]
CMO .... Chief Medical Officer [*Military*]
CMO .... Chief of Mission Operations [*NASA*]
CMO .... Citizen's Municipal Organisation [*Australia*]
CMO .... Civil-Military Operations (AABC)
CMO .... Clinical Medical Officer [*British*]
CMO .... Collateralized Mortgage Obligation [*Federal Home Loan Mortgage Corporation*]
CMO .... College - Fairbanks [*Alaska*] [*Seismograph station code, US Geological Survey*] [*Closed*] (SEIS)
CMO .... Commercial Oil & Gas Ltd. [*Toronto Stock Exchange symbol*]
CMO .... Common Main Objective [*Stereomicroscope optical element*]
CMO .... Common Mode Operation [*Telecommunications*] (TEL)
CMO .... Computers and Operations Research [*A publication*]
CMO .... Consolidated Management Office [*Military*]
CMO .... Contour Mapping On-Boresight (MCD)
CMO .... Contract Management Office [*Jet Propulsion Laboratory, NASA*]
CMO .... Controlled Materials Officer
CMO .... Cootamundra [*Australia*] [*Airport symbol*] (OAG)
CMO .... Corticosterone Methyl Oxidase [*An enzyme*]
CMO .... Countermeasure Office [*of Harry Diamond Laboratories*] [*Military*] (RDA)
CMO .... Court-Martial Officer
CMO .... Court-Martial Orders [*Navy*]
CMo .... Creative Moment [*A publication*]
CMO .... Crisis Management Organization [*DoD*]
CMO .... Crystal Marker Oscillator
CMO .... Ocean Minelayer [*NATO*]
CMOA ...... Continental Mark II Owner's Association (EA)
CMOA ...... Convert Movement Our Apostolate (EA)
CMOD ...... CIMM, Inc. [*NASDAQ symbol*] (NQ)
CMODE.... Collisional Mode (MCD)
CMOL .... Consumable Maintenance and Overhaul List (MCD)
C₁ Mol Chem ... C₁ Molecule Chemistry [*A publication*]
CMOML .... Consumable Maintenance and Overhaul Material List [*Navy*] (MCD)
CMOMM ... Chief Motor Machinist's Mate [*Navy rating*] [*Obsolete*]
CMOMSRD ... Chief Motor Machinist's Mate, Ship Repair, Diesel Engineering Mechanic [*Navy rating*] [*Obsolete*]
CMOMSRG ... Chief Motor Machinist's Mate, Ship Repair, Gasoline Engineering Mechanic [*Navy rating*] [*Obsolete*]
CMon .... Monrovia Public Library, Monrovia, CA [*Library symbol*] [*Library of Congress*] (LCLS)
C Monde Hisp Luso-Bresil ... Cahiers du Monde Hispanique et Luso-Bresilien [*A publication*]
C Monde Russe Sov ... Cahiers du Monde Russe et Sovietique [*A publication*]
CMONDG ... Computer Monographs [*A publication*]
CMont .... Monterey Public Library, Monterey, CA [*Library symbol*] [*Library of Congress*] (LCLS)
CMontFS... Monterey Institute of Foreign Studies, Monterey, CA [*Library symbol*] [*Library of Congress*] (LCLS)
CMonth .... Coin Monthly [*A publication*]
CMontM.... Monterey Peninsula College, Monterey, CA [*Library symbol*] [*Library of Congress*] (LCLS)
CMontNP ... United States Naval Postgraduate School, Monterey, CA [*Library symbol*] [*Library of Congress*] (LCLS)
CMontUSA ... United States Army, Army Language School Technical Library, Monterey, CA [*Library symbol*] [*Library of Congress*] (LCLS)
CMontUSN ... United States Navy, Environmental Prediction Research Facility, Monterey, CA [*Library symbol*] [*Library of Congress*] (LCLS)
CMOPAJ .. Casopis Narodniho Muzea v Praze. Rada Prirodovedna [*A publication*]
CMOPE..... Confederation Mondiale des Organisations de la Profession Enseignante [*World Confederation of Organizations of the Teaching Profession - WCOTP*] (EAIO)
C-MOPP ... Cyclophosphamide, Mechlorethamine [*Mustargen*], Oncovin [*Vincristine*], Procarbazine, Prednisone [*Antineoplastic drug regimen*]
CMORA .... Computers and Operations Research [*A publication*]

CMORAP ...	Computers and Operations Research [*A publication*]
CMOS	Canadian Meteorological and Oceanographic Society
CMOS	Capper Military Occupational Specialty [*Army*] (AABC)
CMOS	Carbon Molybdenum Steel (MSA)
CMOS	Cigarette Machine Operators' Society [*A union*] [*British*]
CMOS	Complementary Magnetic Oxide on Silicone [*Data processing*]
CMOS	Complementary Metal-Oxide Semiconductor Transistor [*Electronics*]
CMOS	Complementary Metal-Oxide Silicon (NASA)
CMOSM ...	Configuration Management Operating Systems Manual (MCD)
CMosM	Moss Landing Marine Laboratory, Moss Landing, CA [*Library symbol*] [*Library of Congress*] (LCLS)
CMOS/SOS ...	Complementary Metal-Oxide Semiconductor/Silicon-on-Sapphire [*Electronics*]
CMOST.....	Complementary Metal-Oxide Semiconductor Transistor [*Electronics*]
CMOTDY ...	Cell Motility [*A publication*]
CMP	Calcium-Binding Modulator Protein
CMP	Camp Military Police [*British military*] (DMA)
CMP	Camp-On [*Telecommunications*] (TEL)
CMP	Campeau Corp. [*Toronto Stock Exchange symbol*]
CMP	Campo Alegre [*Brazil*] [*Airport symbol*] (OAG)
CMP	Campulung [*Romania*] [*Seismograph station code, US Geological Survey*] (SEIS)
CMP	Canadian Military Pattern (DMA)
CMP	Capacitively Coupled Microwave Plasma
CMP	Cape Mounted Police [*British*] (ROG)
CMP	Cast Metal Part
CMP	Celestial Mapping Program [*Air Force*] (MCD)
CMP	Center for Manufacturing Productivity and Technology Transfer [*Rensselaer Polytechnic Institute*] [*Research center*] (RCD)
CMP	Center for Metals Production [*Carnegie Mellon University*] [*Research center*] (RCD)
CMP	Certificate in Medical Parasitology (ADA)
CMP	Chamber of Mines of the Philippines (DS)
CMP	Chloramphenicol [*Antimicrobial compound*]
CMP	Chloro(methyl)phenol [*Organic chemistry*]
CMP	Christian Movement for Peace [*See also MCP*] [*Brussels, Belgium*] (EAIO)
CMP	Civilian Marksmanship Program (MCD)
CMP	CLEM [*Closed-Loop Ex-Vessel Machine*] Maintenance Pit [*Nuclear energy*] (NRCH)
CMP	CMP Newsletter [*A publication*]
CMP	Color Mat Processor
CMP	Command Module Pilot [*Apollo*] [*NASA*]
CMP	Commercial Multi-Peril [*Insurance*]
CMP	Commodity Master Plan [*Army*]
CMP	Compare [*Data processing*]
CMP	Competitive Medical Plans
CMP	Complete Meeting Package [*Meetings industry*]
CMP	Compliance
CMP	Component Metal Parts (MSA)
cmp............	Composer [*MARC relator code*] [*Library of Congress*] (LCCP)
CMP	Compound [*Medicine*] (DHSM)
CMP	Comprehensive Care [*NYSE symbol*] (SPSG)
CMP	Comprehensive Management Plan
CMP	Comprehensive Manpower Planning (OICC)
CMP	Comprehensive Medical Plan
CMP	Comprehensive Migrant Program [*Department of Labor*]
CMP	Compression (MUGU)
CMP	Compromise (ADA)
CMP	Computational (MDG)
CMP	Computer (MUGU)
CMP	Configuration Management Plan [*or Program*]
CMP	Congruent Melting Point
CMP	Conseil Mondial de la Paix [*World Peace Council - WPC*] (EAIO)
CMP	Console Message Processor [*Data processing*]
CMP	Contemporary Music Project [*Defunct*] (EA)
CMP	Contract Monitor of Progress [*Air Force*] (AFIT)
CMP	Contract Monitoring Point (AFM)
CMP	Contractor Maintenance Personnel (MCD)
CMP	Controlled Materials Plan [*of War Production Board*] [*World War II*]
CMP	Controlled Materials Production [*Nuclear energy*]
CMP	Conversion Master Plan (CAAL)
CMP	Corps of Military Police [*British*]
CMP	Corrugated Metal Pipe [*Technical drawings*]
CMP	Council of Maritime Premiers [*See also CPMM*] [*Canada*]
CMP	Council on Municipal Performance
CMP	Countermilitary Potential
CMP	Coupled Microwave Plasma [*Spectrometry*]
CMP	Cruise Missile Planning (MCD)
CMP	Current Mathematical Publications [*A publication*]
CMP	Cytidine Monophosphate [*Biochemistry*]
CMP	Cytosine Monophosphate [*Biochemistry*]
CMPA	Campeau Corp. [*NASDAQ symbol*] (NQ)
CMPA	Canadian Medical Protective Association
CMPA	Canadian Music Publishers Association [*See also ACEM*]
CMPA	Cash Management Practitioners Association [*Later, NCCMA*] (EA)
CMPA	Center for Media and Public Affairs (EA)
CMPA	Chain Makers' Providential Association [*A union*] [*British*]
CMPA	Church Music Publishers Association (EA)
CMPAA	Certified Milk Producers Association of America (EA)
CMPBEK ..	Computer Methods and Programs in Biomedicine [*A publication*]
CMPC........	Compucare, Inc. [*Reston, VA*] [*NASDAQ symbol*] (NQ)
CMPCOM ...	Computer and Communications [*Database*] (IT)
CMPCS	Configuration Management and Project Control Staff [*Social Security Administration*]
CMPCT.....	Compact (FAAC)
CMPCTR....	Computer Center
CMPD	Compound
CMPD	Compumed, Inc. [*NASDAQ symbol*] (NQ)
CMPDA	Canadian Motion Picture Distributors Association
CMPF	Central Meat Processing Facility [*Army*] (AABC)
CMPF	Core Maximum Power Fraction [*Nuclear energy*] (IEEE)
CMPF	Cumulative Preferred [*A class of stock*] [*Investment term*]
CMPHA	Communications in Mathematical Physics [*A publication*]
CMPHE	Conference of Municipal Public Health Engineers [*Later, NCLEHA*] (EA)
CMPI	Civilian Marine Personnel Instructions [*Navy*]
CMP(I)......	Corps of Military Police (India) [*British military*] (DMA)
CMPKT.....	Cam Pocket
CMPL........	Camera Platforms International, Inc. [*Los Angeles, CA*] [*NASDAQ symbol*] (NQ)
CMPL........	Complete (MUGU)
CMPL........	Critical Materials Parts List (MCD)
CMPLDF ..	Complement [*A publication*]
CMPLM....	Complement (MSA)
CMPLT....	Complete (FAAC)
CMPLX....	Complex (FAAC)
CMPM	Catalog of Museum Publications and Media [*A publication*]
CMPM	Computer-Managed Parts Manufacture
CMPMA	Compositio Mathematica [*A publication*]
CMPN	Campaign [*A publication*]
CmpnIAP...	Companion of the Institution of Analysts and Programmers [*British*] (DBQ)
CmpnSCP ...	Companion of the Society of Certified Professionals [*British*] (DBQ)
CMPNT.....	Component (AFM)
CMPO	Chief, SEATO [*Southeast Asia Treaty Organization*] Military Planning Office (CINC)
CMPP........	((Chloro(methyl)phenoxy))propionic Acid [*Herbicide*]
CMPR........	Compare (MSA)
CMPRB.....	Coal Mining and Processing [*A publication*]
CMP Reg ...	Controlled Materials Plan Regulation (National Production) [*of War Production Board*] [*World War II*] (DLA)
CMPRT.....	Compartment (NASA)
CMPS........	Centimeters per Second
CM & PS ...	Chicago, Milwaukee & Puget Sound Railroad
CMPS........	Colosseum of Motion Picture Salesmen (EA)
CMPS........	Command Module Procedures Simulator [*NASA*]
CMPS........	Common Mode Processing System (CAAL)
CMPS........	Compass (MSA)
CMPSCTY ...	Computer Security (MSA)
CMPSD.....	Culture, Medicine, and Psychiatry [*A publication*]
CMPSN....	Composition (MSA)
CMPST.....	Composite (MSA)
CMPT........	Component (AAG)
CMPT........	Compute [*or Computer*] (AABC)
CMPT........	Contempt [*FBI standardized term*]
CMPTD.....	Computed
CMPTG.....	Computing
CMPTR.....	Computer (KSC)
CMPX........	Complex
CMPX........	Comptronix Corp. [*NASDAQ symbol*] (NQ)
CMPYAH ...	Commonwealth Mycological Institute. Phytopathological Papers [*A publication*]
CMPZBL ..	Comunicacoes. Museu de Ciencias. PUCRGS [*Pontificia Universidade Catolica do Rio Grande Do Sul*]. Serie Zoologia [*A publication*]
CMQ.........	Anchorage, AK [*Location identifier*] [*FAA*] (FAAL)
CMQ.........	Canadian Manoir Industries Ltd. [*Toronto Stock Exchange symbol*]
CMQ.........	Clermont [*Australia*] [*Airport symbol*] (OAG)
CMQ.........	Coal Mining and Quarrying
CMQ.........	Tijdschrift voor Marketing [*A publication*]
CMR	California Management Review [*A publication*]
CMR	California Manufacturers Register [*Database Publishing*] [*Information service or system*] (CRD)
CMR	Camerino [*Italy*] [*Seismograph station code, US Geological Survey*] [*Closed*] (SEIS)
CMR	Cameroon [*ANSI three-letter standard code*] (CNC)
CMR	Camreco, Inc. [*Toronto Stock Exchange symbol*]
CMR	Canadian Mounted Rifles
CMR	Cape Mounted Rifles [*British*]
CMR	Capital Markets Report [*Dow Jones & Co., Inc.*] [*Information service or system*] (CRD)

CMR .... Capital Military Region
CMR .... Carbon Magnetic Resonance [*Also, CNMR*]
CMR .... Catalytic Membrane Reactor [*Chemical engineering*]
CMR .... Center for Marine Resources [*National Oceanic and Atmospheric Administration*]
CMR .... Center for Marxist Research (EA)
CMR .... Center Materials Representative [*NASA*] (NASA)
CMR .... Center for Materials Research [*Johns Hopkins University*] [*Research center*] (RCD)
CMR .... Center for Materials Research [*Stanford University*] [*Research center*] (RCD)
CMR .... Centralized Mail Remittance [*Telecommunications*] (TEL)
CMR .... Centre for Manufacturing Renewal [*University of Warwick*] [*British*] (CB)
CMR .... Centre for Medicines Research [*British*] (CB)
CMR .... Cerebral Metabolic Rate [*Medicine*]
CMR .... Chemical Metallurgical Reporting
CMR .... Christian Management Report [*Christian Ministries Management Association*] [*A publication*]
CMR .... Classified Material Receipt
CMR .... Code of Massachusetts Regulations [*A publication*]
CMR .... College Militaire Royal [*Canada*]
CMR .... College Militaire Royal de Saint-Jean [*UTLAS symbol*]
CMR .... Colmar [*France*] [*Airport symbol*] (OAG)
CMR .... Committee on Manpower Resources for Science and Technology
CMR .... Committee on Medical Research [*Subdivision of OSRD*] [*World War II*]
CMR .... Committee on Migration and Resettlement [*Department of State*] [*World War II*]
CMR .... Common Market Reporter [*Commerce Clearing House*] [*A publication*] (DLA)
CMR .... Common Mode Rejection
CMR .... Commtron Corp. [*AMEX symbol*] (SPSG)
CMR .... Communications Monitoring Report
CMR .... Communications Moon Relay [*System*] [*NASA*]
CM & R ..... Compton, Meeson, and Roscoe's English Exchequer Reports [*1834-36*] [*A publication*] (DLA)
CMR .... Configuration Management Review (AABC)
CMR .... Consolidated Mail Room [*Air Force*] (AFM)
CMR .... Continuous Maximum Rating [*of equipment*] (DEN)
CMR .... Contract Management Region
CMR .... Contract Management Review [*DoD*]
CMR .... Contractor Management Reserve (MCD)
CMR .... Convention on the Contract for the International Carriage of Goods by Road [*Geneva*] [*19 May 1956*] (DLA)
CMR .... Countdown Modification Request [*Aerospace*] (AAG)
CMR .... Countermortar RADAR
CMR .... Court-Martial Report (AFM)
CMR .... Court of Military Review (AFM)
CMR .... Customer Material Return
CMR₂ .... Square Centimeter (ROG)
CMR₃ .... Cubic Centimeter (ROG)
CMR 17 ..... Centre Meridional de Recherche sur le Dix-Septieme Siecle [*A publication*]
CMRA .... Chemical Marketing Research Association (EA)
CMRA .... Committee on Migration and Refugee Affairs (EA)
CMRAD .... Camera [*A publication*]
CMRB .... California Melon Research Board (EA)
CMRB .... Contractor Material Review Board [*NASA*] (NASA)
CMRC .... Canadian Music Research Council
CMRC .... Coal Mining Research Centre [*Canada*]
CMRC .... Crucible Materials Research Center (MCD)
CMR Chem Bus ... Chemical Business (Supplement to Chemical Marketing Reporter) [*A publication*]
CMR Cit & Ind ... Court Martial Reports, Citators and Indexes [*A publication*] (DLA)
CMRD .... Committee on Migration, Refugees, and Demography (EA)
CMRDM ... Corpus Monumentorum Religionis Dei Menis [*A publication*]
CM & RDT ... Corris, Machynlleth & River Dovey Tramway [*Wales*]
CMRE .... California Marriage Readiness Evaluation [*Psychology*]
CMRE .... Committee for Monetary Research and Education, Inc. [*Research center*] (RCD)
CMRE .... Comstock Resources, Inc. [*NASDAQ symbol*] (NQ)
CMRED .... Council on Marine Resources and Engineering Development
CMRF .... Conditioned Medium Reconstituting Factor [*Immunochemistry*]
CMRFAS .. Canadian Manuscript Report of Fisheries and Aquatic Sciences [*A publication*]
CMRG .... Cerebral Metabolic Rate of Glucose [*Also, CMRglc*] [*Biochemistry*]
CMRG .... Core Melt Review Group [*Nuclear energy*] (NRCH)
CMRGA .... Ceylon and Mauritius Royal Garrison Artillery [*British military*] (DMA)
CMRGF .... Canadian Modern Rhythmic Gymnastics Federation
CMRglc ..... Cerebral Metabolic Rate of Glucose [*Also, CMRG*] [*Biochemistry*]
CMRI .... Certified Medical Representatives Institute (EA)
CMRI .... Children's Medical Relief International [*Defunct*]
CMRI .... Chloro(methyl)(ribityl)isoalloxazine [*Biochemistry*]
CMRI .... Combined Maintenance Removal Interval (AFIT)

CMRI .... Combined Removal Interval [*Engine*]
CMRI .... Command Maintenance Readiness Inspection [*Army*] (AABC)
CMR JAG AF ... Court Martial Reports, Judge Advocate General of the Air Force [*A publication*] (DLA)
CMR JAG & US Ct of Mil App ... Court Martial Reports, Judge Advocate General of the Armed Forces and United States Court of Military Appeals [*A publication*] (DLA)
CMRK .... Caremark, Inc. [*Newport Beach, CA*] [*NASDAQ symbol*] (NQ)
CMRL .... Consolidated Master Cross-Reference List [*Defense Supply Agency*]
CMRLR ..... Cam Roller
CMRLS ..... Central Massachusetts Regional Public Library System [*Library network*]
CMRLW .... Cape Mounted Rifles, Left Wing [*British*]
CMRN ...... Cooperative Meteorological Rocket Network [*NASA*]
CMRN ...... Military Committee for National Recovery [*Central Africa*] (PD)
CMRNG .... Chromosomally-Mediated Resistant Neisseria Gonorrhoeae [*Medicine*]
CMRO ...... COMARCO, Inc. [*NASDAQ symbol*] (NQ)
CMRO₂ ...... Cerebral Metabolic Rate for Oxygen
CMRPD3 ... Cardiovascular Medicine [*New York*] [*A publication*]
CMRR ...... Center for Magnetic Recording Research [*University of California, San Diego*] [*Research center*] (RCD)
CMRR ...... Common Mode Rejection Ratio
CMRRA ... Canadian Musical Reproduction Rights Agency
CMRRW ... Cape Mounted Rifles, Right Wing [*British*]
CMRS .... Cahiers du Monde Russe et Sovietique [*A publication*]
CMRS .... Calibration/Measurement Requirements Summary
CMRS .... Center for Medieval and Renaissance Studies (EA)
CMRS .... Countermeasures Receiving System
CMRST ..... Committee on Manpower Resources for Science and Technology [*British*]
CMRT .... Central Realty Investors, Inc. [*Formerly, Central Marketing & Realty Trust*] [*NASDAQ symbol*] (NQ)
CMRT ...... Certified Material Test Report [*Nuclear energy*] (NRCH)
CMRW ...... Coalition for the Medical Rights of Women (EA)
CMRWL.... Citizens for Media Responsibility without Law (EA)
CMS .... American Association of Councils of Medical Staffs [*Later, PDA*] (EA)
CMS .... Cabinet Makers' Society [*A union*] [*British*]
CMS .... Cable Marking System
CMS .... Calibration and Measurement Summaries [*Air Force*] (AFIT)
CMS .... California Macadamia Society (EA)
CMS .... California Medical Survey [*Psychology*]
CMS .... Cambridge Mathematical Series [*A publication*]
CMS .... Cambridge Monitor System
CMS .... Camera Model System (MCD)
CMS .... Canadian Micrographic Society
CMS .... Capital Market Statistics
cms .... Carbodiimide Residue [*As substituent on nucleoside*] [*Biochemistry*]
CMS .... Carboxymethyl Starch [*Organic chemistry*]
CMS .... Catholic Missionary Society
CMS .... Center for Management Systems (EA)
CMS .... Center for Maritime Studies [*Later, MRD*] [*Webb Institute of Naval Architecture*] [*Research center*] (EA)
CMS .... Center for Materials Science [*Los Alamos, NM*] [*Los Alamos National Laboratory*] [*Department of Energy*] (GRD)
CMS .... Center for Metropolitan Studies [*University of Missouri - Saint Louis*] [*Research center*] (RCD)
CMS .... Center for Migration Studies of New York (EA)
CMS .... Center for Multinational Studies [*Inactive*] (EA)
CMS .... Central Materiel Service Team [*Military*]
CMS .... Centralized Maintenance System [*Telecommunications*]
CMS .... Centralized Materials Section
CMS .... Centralized Munitions Systems [*USARPAC*] (MCD)
CMS .... Chicago Map Society (EA)
CMS .... Chicago Medical School
CMS .... Christian Medical Society [*Later, CMDS*] (EA)
CMS .... Chromographic Mode Sequencing [*Chromatography*]
CMS .... Church Missionary Society [*London, England*]
CMS .... Church Monuments Society (EA)
CMS .... Circuit Maintenance System [*AT & T*]
CMS .... Clarion Music Society (EA)
CMS .... Clay Minerals Society (EA)
CMS .... Cleaning Management Station
CMS .... Close Medium Shot [*A photograph or motion picture sequence taken from a relatively short distance*]
CMS .... Clyde Mood Scale [*Psychology*]
CMS .... CMS Energy Corp. [*NYSE symbol*] (SPSG)
CMS .... Cockpit Management System [*Aviation*]
CMS .... Collagen Matrix Support [*Cell culture*]
CMS .... Collapsible Maintenance Shelter (MCD)
CMS .... Collection Management System [*IRS*]
CMS .... Collectors Music Shop [*Record label*]
CMS .... College Music Society (EA)
CMS .... College Music Symposium [*A publication*]
CMS .... Combat Mission Scenario [*Army*]
CMS .... Combat Mission Simulation (MCD)

CMS	Combined Mixer Settler [Chemical engineering]
CMS	Command Module Simulator [NASA]
CMS	Common Manpower Standards (AFM)
CMS	Common Mode Signal
CMS	Communication Management System [Data processing]
CM & S	Communications Maintenance and Storage (NASA)
CMS	Compiler Monitor System (BUR)
CMS	Complete Management Systems
CMS	Complete Matched Set [Philately]
CMS	Comprehensive Medical Society [Defunct] (EA)
CMS	Computer Management System [Burroughs Corp.] (BUR)
CMS	Computer Marketing Services [Anaheim, CA] [Information service or system] (IID)
CMS	Condition Monitoring System (CAAL)
CMS	Condor Missile System
CMS	Configuration Management Staff [Social Security Administration]
CMS	Configuration Management System
CMS	Conflict Management Survey [Interpersonal skills and attitudes test]
CMS	Conservation Materials and Services
CMS	Construction Maintenance Supervisor (FAAC)
CMS	Consumer and Marketing Service [Later, AMS] [Department of Agriculture]
C & MS	Consumer and Marketing Service [Later, AMS] [Department of Agriculture]
CMS	Contemporary Music Society (EA)
CMS	Conversational Monitor System [IBM Corp.] [Data processing]
CMS	Corrective Maintenance System (NVT)
CMS	Countermeasures Set (MCD)
CMS	Cras Mane Sumendus [To Be Taken Tomorrow Morning] [Pharmacy]
CMS	Crisis Management System
CMS	Cross-Section Measurement System
CMS	Currency Market Service [Database] [Money Market Services, Inc.] [Information service or system] (CRD)
CMS	Current-Mode Switching [Data processing] (MSA)
CMS	Cytoplasmic Male Sterility [Botany]
CMS	Melodyland School of Theology, Anaheim, CA [OCLC symbol] [Inactive] (OCLC)
CMS	Senior Enlisted Advisor [AFSC]
CMS	Stanislaus County Free Library, Modesto, CA [Library symbol] [Library of Congress] (LCLS)
CMSA	Canning Machinery and Supplies Association [Later, FPM & SA] (EA)
CMSA	Chain Makers' and Strikers' Association [A union] [British]
CMSA	Consolidated Metropolitan Statistical Area [Census Bureau]
CMSAF	Chief Master Sergeant of the Air Force (AFM)
CMSC	Cape Medical Staff Corps [British military] (DMA)
CMSC	Capital Market Services Corporation [White Plains, NY] [NASDAQ symbol] (NQ)
CMSC	Catalina Marine Science Center [University of Southern California] [Research center]
CMSC	Central Missouri State College [Later, Central Missouri State University]
CMSC	Communications Mode Selection Control (MCD)
CMSCA	Contributions in Marine Science [A publication]
CMSCAY	Contributions in Marine Science [A publication]
CMSCI	Council of Mechanical Specialty Contracting Industries [Later, ASC] (EA)
CMS Cmp (Bah)	Country Market Survey. Computers and Peripheral Equipment (Bahrain) [A publication]
CMS Cmp (Cda)	Country Market Survey. Computers and Peripheral Equipment (Canada) [A publication]
CMS Cmp (Emi)	Country Market Survey. Computers and Peripheral Equipment (United Arab Emirates) [A publication]
CMS Cmp (Fra)	Country Market Survey. Computers and Peripheral Equipment (France) [A publication]
CMS Cmp (Jpn)	Country Market Survey. Computers and Peripheral Equipment (Japan) [A publication]
CMS Cmp (Kuw)	Country Market Survey. Computers and Peripheral Equipment (Kuwait) [A publication]
CMS Cmp (Sau)	Country Market Survey. Computers and Peripheral Equipment (Saudi Arabia) [A publication]
CMS Cmp (Sin)	Country Market Survey. Computers and Peripheral Equipment (Singapore) [A publication]
CMS Cmp (Swe)	Country Market Survey. Computers and Peripheral Equipment (Sweden) [A publication]
CMS Cmp (Tai)	Country Market Survey. Computers and Peripheral Equipment (Taiwan) [A publication]
CMS Cmp (UK)	Country Market Survey. Computers and Peripheral Equipment (United Kingdom) [A publication]
CMS Cmp (Yug)	Country Market Survey. Computers and Peripheral Equipment (Yugoslavia) [A publication]
CMSDMR	Canada. Marine Sciences Directorate. Department of Fisheries and Oceans. Manuscript Report [A publication]
CMSE	Center for Materials Science and Engineering [MIT] [Research center] (RCD)
CMSE	Conditional Mean Square Error [Statistics]
CM/SEC	Centimeters per Second [Telecommunications] (TEL)

CMS EIC (Aut)	Country Market Survey. Electronic Components (Austria) [A publication]
CMS EIC (Mex)	Country Market Survey. Electronic Components (Mexico) [A publication]
CMS EIC (Phl)	Country Market Survey. Electronic Components (Philippines) [A publication]
CMS EIC (Swl)	Country Market Survey. Electronic Components (Switzerland) [A publication]
CMS EIC (Tai)	Country Market Survey. Electronic Components (Taiwan) [A publication]
CMS EPS (Col)	Country Market Survey. Electric Power Systems (Colombia) [A publication]
CMS EPS (Egy)	Country Market Survey. Electric Power Systems (Egypt) [A publication]
CMS EPS (Nig)	Country Market Survey. Electric Power Systems (Nigeria) [A publication]
CMS EPS (Phi)	Country Market Survey. Electric Power Systems (Philippines) [A publication]
CMS EPS (Sau)	Country Market Survey. Electric Power Systems (Saudi Arabia) [A publication]
CMS EPS (Spa)	Country Market Survey. Electric Power Systems (Spain) [A publication]
CMS EPS (Tha)	Country Market Survey. Electric Power Systems (Thailand) [A publication]
CMS EPS (Yug)	Country Market Survey. Electric Power Systems (Yugoslavia) [A publication]
CMSER	Commission on Marine Science, Engineering, and Resources
CMS FPP (Tha)	Country Market Survey. Food Processing Packaging Equipment (Thailand) [A publication]
CMSG	"C" Message Weighting [Telecommunications] (TEL)
CMSG	Canadian Merchant Service Guild
CMS GIE (Aus)	Country Market Survey. Graphic Industries Equipment (Australia) [A publication]
CMS GIE (Jpn)	Country Market Survey. Graphic Industries Equipment (Japan) [A publication]
CMS GIE (Mex)	Country Market Survey. Graphic Industries Equipment (Mexico) [A publication]
CMS GIE (Net)	Country Market Survey. Graphic Industries Equipment (Netherlands) [A publication]
CMS GIE (Soa)	Country Market Survey. Graphic Industries Equipment (South Africa) [A publication]
CMS GIE (UK)	Country Market Survey. Graphic Industries Equipment (United Kingdom) [A publication]
CMSGT	Chief Master Sergeant
CMSh	Shell Development Co., Modesto, CA [Library symbol] [Library of Congress] (LCLS)
CMSHFT	Camshaft (MSA)
CMSI	Checkout/Control and Monitor Subsystem Interface [NASA] (NASA)
CMSI	Climatology Mission Success Indicators (MCD)
CMSI	Council of Mutual Savings Institutions [New York, NY] (EA)
CMSI	Country Music Showcase International (EA)
CMSI	Cryomedical Sciences, Inc. [NASDAQ symbol] (NQ)
CMS/IMR	International Migration Review. Center for Migration Studies [A publication]
CMSIO	Communications Security Material Sub-Issuing Office [Military] (NVT)
CMS IPC (Aus)	Country Market Survey. Industrial Process Controls (Australia) [A publication]
CMS IPC (Bra)	Country Market Survey. Industrial Process Controls (Brazil) [A publication]
CMS IPC (Fra)	Country Market Survey. Industrial Process Controls (France) [A publication]
CMS IPC (Sin)	Country Market Survey. Industrial Process Controls (Singapore) [A publication]
CMS IPC (Sok)	Country Market Survey. Industrial Process Controls (South Korea) [A publication]
CMS IPC (Spa)	Country Market Survey. Industrial Process Controls (Spain) [A publication]
CMS IPC (Tai)	Country Market Survey. Industrial Process Controls (Taiwan) [A publication]
CMSL	Cambridge Manuals of Science and Literature [A publication]
CMS Lab (Jpn)	Country Market Survey. Laboratory Instruments (Japan) [A publication]
CMS Lab (Spa)	Country Market Survey. Laboratory Instruments (Spain) [A publication]
CMS/LC	Chamber Music Society of Lincoln Center
CMSM	Chemical Material Study Model [Military] (AFIT)
CM-SM	Command Module - Service Module [Combined] [NASA] (MCD)
CMSM	Committee on a Multimedium Approach to Sludge Management [National Research Council]
CMSM	Conference of Major Superiors of Men (EA)
CMSM	Stanislaus County Medical Library, Modesto, CA [Library symbol] [Library of Congress] (LCLS)
CMS MED (Arg)	Country Market Survey. Medical Equipment (Argentina) [A publication]
CMS MED (Aus)	Country Market Survey. Medical Equipment (Australia) [A publication]
CMS MED (Bra)	Country Market Survey. Medical Equipment (Brazil) [A publication]

CMS MED (Can) ... Country Market Survey. Medical Equipment (Canada) [*A publication*]
CMS MED (Jpn) ... Country Market Survey. Medical Equipment (Japan) [*A publication*]
CMS MIE (Pak) ... Country Market Survey. Mining Industry Equipment (Pakistan) [*A publication*]
CMS MIE (Zai) ... Country Market Survey. Mining Industry Equipment (Zaire) [*A publication*]
CMS MTL (Por) ... Country Market Survey. Machine Tools (Portugal) [*A publication*]
CMSN .... Commission (FAAC)
CMSNA .... Chinese Music Society of North America   (EA)
CMSND .... Commissioned
CMSNR ..... Commissioner
CMSO .... Chief Japanese Maritime Staff Office   (CINC)
CMS PCE (Isr) ... Country Market Survey. Pollution Instrumentation and Equipment (Israel) [*A publication*]
CMS PCE (Phl) ... Country Market Survey. Pollution Instrumentation and Equipment (Philippines) [*A publication*]
CMS PCE (Tai) ... Country Market Survey. Pollution Instrumentation and Equipment (Taiwan) [*A publication*]
CMS PCE (W Ge) ... Country Market Survey. Pollution Instrumentation and Equipment (West Germany) [*A publication*]
CMSR .... Carpenter's Mate, Ship Repair [*Navy*]
CMSR .... Commercial/Military Spares Release (MCD)
CMSR .... Controller of Merchant Shipbuilding and Repairs [*Navy*] [*British*]
CMSRAB .. Communications. Research Institute of the Sumatra Planters' Association. Rubber Series [*A publication*]
CMSRB ..... Carpenter's Mate, Ship Repair, Boatbuilder-Wood [*Navy*]
CMSRB ..... Chief Metalsmith, Ship Repair, Blacksmith [*Navy rating*] [*Obsolete*]
CMSRC ..... Carpenter's Mate, Ship Repair, Carpenter [*Navy*]
CMSRC ..... Chief Metalsmith, Ship Repair, Coppersmith [*Navy rating*] [*Obsolete*]
CMSRJ ...... Carpenter's Mate, Ship Repair, Joiner [*Navy*]
CMSRK ...... Carpenter's Mate, Ship Repair, Caulker-Boat [*Navy*]
CMSRN ..... Carpenter's Mate, Ship Repair, Cement Worker-Concrete [*Navy*]
CMSRS ..... Carpenter's Mate, Ship Repair, Shipwright [*Navy*]
CMSRS ..... Chief Metalsmith, Ship Repair, Sheet Metal Worker [*Navy rating*] [*Obsolete*]
CMSS .... Circulation, Motor Ability, Sensation, and Swelling [*Medicine*]
CMSS .... Commission on Molecular Structure and Spectroscopy
CMSS .... Computerized Moment Stability System [*Navy*]
CMSS .... Council of Medical Specialty Societies   (EA)
CMS SGR (Arg) ... Country Market Survey. Sporting and Recreational Equipment (Argentina) [*A publication*]
CMS SGR (Sau) ... Country Market Survey. Sporting and Recreational Equipment (Saudi Arabia) [*A publication*]
CMS SGR (Swe) ... Country Market Survey. Sporting and Recreational Equipment (Sweden) [*A publication*]
CMS SGR (Swi) ... Country Market Survey. Sporting and Recreational Equipment (Switzerland) [*A publication*]
CMS SGR (UK) ... Country Market Survey. Sporting and Recreational Equipment (United Kingdom) [*A publication*]
C & MSSRA ... Consumer and Marketing Service, Service and Regulatory Announcements [*Later, AMS*] [*Department of Agriculture*]
CMST .... Carmelite Missionaries of St. Theresa [*Roman Catholic women's religious order*]
CMS TCE (Arg) ... Country Market Survey. Telecommunications Equipment (Argentina) [*A publication*]
CMS TCE (Chn) ... Country Market Survey. Telecommunications Equipment (China) [*A publication*]
CMS TCE (Emi) ... Country Market Survey. Telecommunications Equipment (United Arab Emirates) [*A publication*]
CMS TCE (Fra) ... Country Market Survey. Telecommunications Equipment (France) [*A publication*]
CMS TCE (Ger) ... Country Market Survey. Telecommunications Equipment (Germany) [*A publication*]
CMS TCE (Kuw) ... Country Market Survey. Telecommunications Equipment (Kuwait) [*A publication*]
CMS TCE (Pak) ... Country Market Survey. Telecommunications Equipment (Pakistan) [*A publication*]
CMS TCE (Phl) ... Country Market Survey. Telecommunications Equipment (Philippines) [*A publication*]
CMS TCE (Sau) ... Country Market Survey. Telecommunications Equipment (Saudi Arabia) [*A publication*]
CMS TCE (Spa) ... Country Market Survey. Telecommunications Equipment (Spain) [*A publication*]
CMS TCE (Tha) ... Country Market Survey. Telecommunications Equipment (Thailand) [*A publication*]
CM & StP .. Chicago, Milwaukee & St. Paul Railway
CM ST P & P ... Chicago, Milwaukee, St. Paul & Pacific Railroad Co.
CMSTRKFLT ... Commander, Striking Fleet, Atlantic   (MCD)
CMSU .... Central Missouri State University
CMSV .... Comserv Corp. [*NASDAQ symbol*]   (NQ)
CMSW .... Conference of Major Religious Superiors of Women's Institutes of the United States of America [*Later, LCWR*]
CMSWA .... Convention on the Conservation of Migratory Species of Wild Animals   (ASF)

CMT .... Cadmium Mercury Telluride [*Solid state chemistry*]
CMT .... California Mastitis Test
CMT .... Card Module Tester
CMT .... Casement Aviation [*Painesville, OH*] [*FAA designator*]   (FAAC)
CMT .... Cash Management Trust   (ADA)
CMT .... Cassette Magnetic Tape
CMT .... Cellular Mobile Telephone
CMT .... Cement [*Classified advertising*]   (ADA)
CMT .... Center for Management Technology [*Commercial firm*]   (EA)
CMT .... Center for the Ministry of Teaching   (EA)
CMT .... Centroid-Moment Tensor [*Seismology*]
CMT .... Ceramic Mosaic Tile [*Technical drawings*]
CMT .... Certified Medical Transcriptionist
CM/T .... Change Management/Tracking [*IBM Corp.*]
CMT .... Charcot-Marie-Tooth [*Atrophy*] [*Medicine*]
CMT .... Chemical Machining Template   (MCD)
CMT .... Chief Medical Technician [*British military*]   (DMA)
CMT .... Choline Magnesium Trisalicylate [*Pharmacy*]
CMT .... Code Matching Technique
CMT .... College of San Mateo Library, San Mateo, CA [*OCLC symbol*]   (OCLC)
CMT .... Combined Military Transportation [*British*]
CMT .... Comment   (AABC)
CMT .... Commissary Technician, Medical
CMT .... Commit   (MSA)
CMT .... Committee on Marine Technology [*British*]
CMT .... Common Maintenance Trainer   (MCD)
CMT .... Common Market Travel Association   (EAIO)
cmt .... Compositor [*MARC relator code*] [*Library of Congress*]   (LCCP)
CMT .... Computer Memory Tester
CMT .... Computer Micrographics Technology [*An association*]   (EA)
CMT .... Comterm, Inc. [*Toronto Stock Exchange symbol*]
CMT .... Concora Medium Test
CMT .... Confederation Mondiale du Travail [*World Confederation of Labour - WCL*] [*Brussels, Belgium*]   (EAIO)
CMT .... Contract Maintenance Team   (MCD)
CMT .... Convection Microthermal Oven
CMT .... Conversational Mode Terminal [*Friden, Inc.*]   (IEEE)
CMT .... Corporate Minimum Tax
CMT .... Corrected Mean Temperature
CMT .... Corrugating Medium Test [*For containerboard*]
CMT .... Council on Medical Television [*Later, HESCA*]   (EA)
CMT .... Craig Mountain Railway [*AAR code*]
CMT .... Crisis Management Team [*Army*]   (INF)
CMT .... Current Medical Terminology
CMTA .... Canadian Marine Transportation Administration
CMTA .... Canadian Music Therapy Association
CMTA .... Chinese Musical and Theatrical Association   (EA)
CMTBB .... Canada. Mines Branch. Technical Bulletin [*A publication*]
CMTC .... Cambridge Medical Technology Corporation [*Billerica, MA*] [*NASDAQ symbol*]   (NQ)
CMTC .... Carbondale Mining Technology Center [*Department of Energy*]   (GRD)
CMTC .... Citizens Military Training Corps   (AABC)
CMTC .... Combat Maneuver Training Complex [*Hohenfels Training Area*] [*Federal Republic of Germany*]
CMTC .... Combined Military Transportation Committee
CMTC .... Conscience and Military Tax Campaign - US   (EA)
CMT CONC ... Cement or Concrete [*Freight*]
CMTCU .... Cigarette Makers' and Tobacco Cutters' Union [*British*]
CMTCU .... Communications Message Traffic Control Unit [*Air Force*]   (AFM)
CMTD .... Center for Market and Trade Development [*People's Republic of China*]
CMTE .... Committee
CMthL .... University of California, Santa Cruz, Lick Observatory Library, Santa Cruz, CA [*Library symbol*] [*Library of Congress*]   (LCLS)
CMTI .... Celestial Moving Target Indicator
CMTI .... CMT Investment [*NASDAQ symbol*]   (NQ)
CMTK .... Cimflex Teknowledge Corp. [*NASDAQ symbol*]   (NQ)
CMTL .... Chemical Machining Template Line   (MCD)
CMTL .... Comtech Telecommunications Corp. [*NASDAQ symbol*]   (NQ)
CMTLBX .. Food Chemistry, Microbiology, Technology [*A publication*]
CMTM ...... Capsule Mechanical Training Model [*Aerospace*]   (MCD)
CMTM ...... Communications and Telemetry
CMTN .... Comten, Inc. [*NASDAQ symbol*]
CMTN .... Cytoplasmic Microtubule Network [*Cytology*]
CMTP .... Canada Manpower Training Program
CMTP .... Cometary-Mass-to-Planets [*Astronomy*]
CMTS .... Canadian Machine Tool Show   (ITD)
CMTS .... Clarendon Medieval and Tudor Series [*A publication*]
CMTS .... Computer Maintenance Test Set
CMTT .... Joint Committee on Television Transmission
CMTTEE .. Committee
CMTU .... Cartridge Magnetic Tape Unit
CMTV .... Country Music Television [*Cable-television system*]

CMTX ...... Comtex Scientific Corp. [*Stamford, CT*] [*NASDAQ symbol*]   (NQ)
CMTY ...... Community
CMU.......... Canadian Mineworkers Union
CMU.......... Carnegie-Mellon University [*Pittsburgh, PA*]
CMU.......... Central Michigan University [*Mount Pleasant*]
CMU.......... Ceylon Mercantile Union [*Obsolete*]
CMU.......... Chlorophenyldimethylurea [*Herbicide*]
CMU.......... Church Missionary Union [*British*]
C Mu .... Classical Museum [*A publication*]
CMU.......... Colliery Mazdoor Union [*India*]
CMU.......... Colonial Municipal Income Trust [*NYSE symbol*]   (SPSG)
CMU.......... Comet Industries [*Vancouver Stock Exchange symbol*]
CMU.......... Compatibility Mock-Up   (KSC)
CMU.......... Computer Memory Unit
CMU.......... Concrete Masonry Unit [*Technical drawings*]
CMU.......... Control Maintenance Unit
CMU.......... Controls Mock-Up
CMU.......... Core Memory Unit   (MCD)
CMU.......... Customer Memory Update [*Telecommunications*]
CMU.......... Kundiawa [*Papua New Guinea*] [*Airport symbol*]   (OAG)
CMUC...... Commentationes Mathematicae. Universitatis Carolinae [*A publication*]
CMUC...... Comp-U-Check, Inc. [*Southfield, MI*] [*NASDAQ symbol*]   (NQ)
CMUE B.... Council for Research in Music Education. Bulletin [*A publication*]
CMUED .... Contributions to Music Education [*A publication*]
C²MUG ..... Command and Control Micro-Computer Users Group [*Fort Leavenworth, KS*] [*Army*]   (INF)
CMUJST... CMU [*Central Mindanao University*] Journal of Science and Technology [*A publication*]
CMUMD9 ... Cell and Muscle Motility [*A publication*]
CMUS .... Censo de Museos de Espana [*Database*] [*Ministerio de Cultura*] [*Spanish*] [*Information service or system*]   (CRD)
CMUS .... Chief Musician [*Navy rating*] [*Obsolete*]
CMUS .... Council of Masajid of United States   (EA)
CMUTB .... Chemieunterricht [*A publication*]
CMU/WA ... Committee on Man's Underwater Activities   (EA)
CMUX....... Converter Multiplexer   (CAAL)
CMV .... Christlicher Metallarbeiterverband der Schweiz [*Christian Metalworkers Association of Switzerland*]   (EY)
CMV .... Commercial Motor Vehicle   (ADA)
CMV .... Common Mode Voltage
CMV .... Contact-Making Voltmeter
CMV .... Controlled Mechanical Ventilation
CMV .... Controlled Multivibrator
CMV .... Conventional Mechanical Ventilation
CMV .... Cucumber Mosaic Virus
CMV .... Current Market Value [*Business term*]   (ADA)
CMV .... Cytomegalovirus [*A virus*]
CMv .... Mountain View Public Library, Mountain View, CA [*Library symbol*] [*Library of Congress*]   (LCLS)
CMVd .... Mekhitarist Order of Vienna [*Roman Catholic men's religious order*]
CMVE .... Committee on Motor Vehicle Emissions [*National Academy of Sciences*]
CMVIG..... Cytomegalovirus Immune Globulin [*Biochemistry*]
CMVIO ..... Communications Security Material Van-Issuing Office [*Military*]   (NVT)
CMVM ...... Contact-Making Voltmeter
CMVR ...... Common Mode Voltage Range
CMVS........ Cavalry Mobile Veterinary Section [*British military*]   (DMA)
CMVS........ Contract Motor Vehicle Service
CMvS......... Sylvania Electronics Systems, Inc., Mountain View, CA [*Library symbol*] [*Library of Congress*]   (LCLS)
CMvSJ ...... Saint Joseph's College, Mountain View, CA [*Library symbol*] [*Library of Congress*]   (LCLS)
CMVT ...... Comverse Technology, Inc. [*Woodbury, NY*] [*NASDAQ symbol*]   (NQ)
CMVU....... Com Vu Corp. [*Bolinas, CA*] [*NASDAQ symbol*]   (NQ)
CMW......... Camaguey [*Cuba*] [*Airport symbol*]   (OAG)
CMW......... Campus Ministry Women   (EA)
CMW......... Canadian Marconi Co. [*AMEX symbol*] [*Toronto Stock Exchange symbol*]   (SPSG)
CMW......... Circular Magnetic Wave
CMW......... Cold Molecular Weld
CMW......... Communication World [*A publication*]
CMWB ...... Coalition of Minority Women in Business [*Washington, DC*]   (EA)
CMX.......... Canamax Resources, Inc. [*Toronto Stock Exchange symbol*]
CMX.......... Character Multiplexer [*Telecommunications*]
CMX.......... Chick Muscle Extract [*Embryology*]
CMX.......... CMI Corp. [*AMEX symbol*]   (SPSG)
CMX.......... Concentration Module Extension [*Telecommunications*]   (TEL)
CMX.......... Hancock [*Michigan*] [*Airport symbol*]   (OAG)
CMX.......... Hancock, MI [*Location identifier*] [*FAA*]   (FAAL)
CMXPAU ... Chirurgia Maxillofacialis et Plastica [*A publication*]
CMY .... Cape Mounted Yeomanry [*British military*]   (DMA)
CMY .... Civilian Man-Years [*Military*]   (AABC)

CMY .... Cockpit Motor Yacht
CMY .... Commonwealth Minerals [*Vancouver Stock Exchange symbol*]
CMY .... Community Psychiatric Centers [*NYSE symbol*]   (SPSG)
CMY .... Cyan, Magenta, and Yellow [*Color model*]   (BYTE)
CMY .... Sparta, WI [*Location identifier*] [*FAA*]   (FAAL)
CMYBA..... Canadian Minerals Yearbook [*A publication*]
CMYK ...... Cyan, Magenta, Yellow, Black [*Color model*]   (PCM)
CMZ .... Chimera Resources Ltd. [*Vancouver Stock Exchange symbol*]
CMZ .... Cincinnati Milacron, Inc. [*NYSE symbol*]   (SPSG)
CMZS....... Corresponding Member of the Zoological Society [*British*]
CN.............. Absolute Coefficient of Yawing Moments
CN.............. Atlantic Central Airlines Ltd. [*Canada*] [*ICAO designator*]   (FAAC)
CN.............. Calcineurin [*Biochemistry*]
CN.............. Calcoin News [*A publication*]
CN.............. Call Number [*Online database field identifier*]
CN.............. Calton, Inc. [*NYSE symbol*]   (SPSG)
C & N .... Cameron and Norwood's North Carolina Conference Reports [*A publication*]   (DLA)
CN.............. Can
cn.............. Canada [*MARC country of publication code*] [*Library of Congress*]   (LCCP)
CN.............. Canadian National Railways [*AAR code*]
CN.............. Canet Nordenfelt Gun
CN.............. Cannon Minerals Ltd. [*Vancouver Stock Exchange symbol*]
CN.............. Canon
C/N .... Carbon to Nitrogen Ratio
cn.............. Carbonate Nodule [*Archeology*]
CN.............. Careless and Negligent Driving [*Traffic offense charge*]
C/N .... Carrier-to-Noise [*Ratio*]
CN.............. Case of Need
CN.............. Caudate Nucleus [*Anatomy*]
CN.............. Cavity Nester [*Ornithology*]
CN.............. Cellulose Nitrate [*Organic chemistry*]
Cn.............. Center Magazine [*A publication*]
CN.............. Central Airlines, Inc.
C of N........ Certificate of Need
CN.............. Cetane Number [*Fuel technology*]
CN.............. Change Notice
CN.............. Charge Nurse [*Medicine*]
CN.............. Check Not OK [*Telecommunications*]   (TEL)
CN.............. CHExchange Network   (EA)
CN.............. Child Nutrition
CN.............. Children of the Night   (EA)
CN.............. China [*ANSI two-letter standard code*]   (CNC)
CN.............. Chinese Navy   (CINC)
CN.............. Chlorinated Naphthalene [*Organic chemistry*]
CN.............. Chloroacetophenone [*Also, CAP*] [*Tear gas*] [*Army symbol*]   (AAG)
C/N .... Chloroplasts to Nuclei per Cell [*Botany*]
Cn.............. Cinders [*Quality of the bottom*] [*Nautical charts*]
CN.............. Circular Note [*Business term*]
CN.............. Clinical Nephrology [*A publication*]
CN.............. Clinical Nursing
CN.............. Clipped and Nitrogen Added [*Ecology*]
CN.............. Clyden Airways [*Great Britain*] [*ICAO designator*]   (FAAC)
CN.............. Cochlear Nuclei [*Brain anatomy*]
CN.............. Code Napoleon [*Napoleonic Code*] [*French*] [*Legal term*]
CN.............. Coin Trunk [*Telecommunications*]   (TEL)
CN.............. Colin Energy Corp. [*Toronto Stock Exchange symbol*]
CN.............. Collective Negotiations
CN.............. Commonwealth Nation
C & N .... Communication and Navigation   (MCD)
CN.............. Communications Network
CN.............. Compass North
CN.............. Compensators [*JETDS nomenclature*] [*Military*]   (CET)
c/n .... Compte Nouveau [*New Account*] [*Business term*] [*French*]
CN.............. Condensation Nuclei
C-N .... Conico Norteno [*Race of maize*]
CN.............. Conjectanea Neotestamentica [*A publication*]   (BJA)
CN.............. Conservative Nationalist Party [*British*]
CN.............. Conservative Network   (EA)
CN.............. Consignment Note [*Shipping*]
CN.............. Consolidated [*Accounting*]
CN.............. Consols [*Consolidateds*]
CN.............. Constructionman [*Nonrated enlisted man*] [*Navy*]
CN.............. Consultants' Network   (EA)
CN.............. Consultants News [*A publication*]
CN.............. Contaminated Normal [*Statistics*]
CN.............. Contemporary Newsmakers [*Later, Newsmakers*] [*A publication*]
CN.............. Continuous Noise
CN.............. Contract Note [*Banking*]
CN.............. Contract Number [*Data processing*]
CN.............. Control Number
C of N........ Controller of the Navy [*British*]
CN.............. Convertible [*Rate*] [*Value of the English pound*]
CN.............. Coordination Number [*Chemistry*]
CN.............. Cornishman [*A publication*]
CN.............. Correction Notice   (MCD)
CN.............. Cosine

CN............. Cover Note [*Insurance*]
CN............. Cranial Nerve [*Anatomy*]
CN............. Cras Nocte [*Tomorrow Night*] [*Pharmacy*]
CN............. Credit National [*National Credit*] [*French*]
CN............. Credit Note [*Business term*]
CN............. Cuban Navy
CN............. Cultura Neolatina [*A publication*]
CN............. Cumulonimbus [*Cloud*] [*Meteorology*]
CN............. Cuneate Nucleus [*Neuroanatomy*]
CN............. Cupro Nickel
CN............. Cyanonaphthalene [*Organic chemistry*]
CN............. Morocco [*Aircraft nationality and registration mark*] (FAAC)
CN............. Napa City-County Library, Napa, CA [*Library symbol*] [*Library of Congress*] (LCLS)
CN............. Parke, Davis & Co. [*Research code symbol*]
CN............. Training and Riot Control Agent
CN4........... N4 Transportation Systems of Canada Ltd. [*Information service or system*] (IID)
CNA........... Atlantic Central Airlines Ltd. [*St. John, NB*] [*FAA designator*] (FAAC)
CNA........... Cadets Norfolk Artillery [*British military*] (DMA)
CNA........... Canadian Advertising Rates and Data [*A publication*]
CNA........... Canadian Northwest Atlantic Area
CNA........... Canadian Nuclear Association
CNA........... Canadian Nurses' Association [*See also AIC*]
CNA........... Capital Needs Analysis [*Finance*]
CNA........... Center for Natural Areas (EA)
CNA........... Center for Naval Analyses [*Navy*] [*Alexandria, VA*]
CNA........... Center for Numerical Analysis [*University of Texas at Austin*] [*Research center*] (RCD)
CNA........... Central Neuropsychiatric Association (EA)
C/NA......... Certification of Nonavailability [*DoD*]
CNA......... Certified Nurse's Aide
CNA......... Chemicals Notation Association [*British*]
CNA......... Chevrolet Nomad Association (EA)
CNA......... Chief Naval Adviser [*British*]
CNA......... Chief of Naval Air
CNA......... China News Analysis [*A publication*]
CNA......... Chlornaltrexamine [*Narcotic antagonist*] [*Pharmacochemistry*]
CNA......... Chloronitroaniline [*Organic chemistry*]
CNA......... CNA Financial Corp. [*NYSE symbol*] (SPSG)
CNA......... Code Not Allocated
CNA......... Colistin [*or Colimycin*] - Nalidixic Acid [*Antibacterial combination*] [*Clinical chemistry*]
CNA......... College of Nursing Australia
CNA......... Comite National d'Action sur la Situation de la Femme du Canada [*National Action Committee on the Status of Women*] [*Canada*]
CNA......... Commander's Narrative Analysis [*Military*]
CNA......... Common Nozzle Assembly (MCD)
CNA......... Communications Network Architects, Inc. [*Washington, DC*] [*Telecommunications service*] (TSSD)
CNA......... Communications Network Architecture
CNA......... Concerned Neighbors in Action (EA)
CNA......... Confederazione Nazionale dell'Artigianato [*Italy*] (EY)
CNA......... Consolidated Cima Resources [*Vancouver Stock Exchange symbol*]
CNA......... Continental National America [*Insurance group*]
CNA......... Copper Nickel Alloy (MSA)
CNA......... Cosmic Noise Absorption
CNA......... Council on Nutritional Anthropology (EA)
CNA......... Cyprus News Agency
CNA......... Fairbanks, AK [*Location identifier*] [*FAA*] (FAAL)
CNa......... National City Public Library, National City, CA [*Library symbol*] [*Library of Congress*] (LCLS)
CNAA........ Council for National Academic Awards [*British*]
CNAADTRA ... Chief of Naval Air Advanced Training [*Also, CNAVANTRA*] [*Formerly, CNAOPTRA, CNAOT*]
CNAAFERT ... China National Advertising Association for Foreign Economic Relations and Trade
CNAAT ..... Chief, Naval Advanced Air Training
CNAB .... Commander, Naval Air Bases
CNABAG ... Connecticut. Agricultural Experiment Station. Bulletin [*New Haven*] [*A publication*]
CNABATRA ... Chief of Naval Air Basic Training
CNABT...... Chief, Naval Air Basic Training
CNA Bull... California Nurses Association. Bulletin [*A publication*]
CNAC....... China National Aviation Corps
CNACAJ ... Connecticut. Agricultural Experiment Station. Circular [*New Haven*] [*A publication*]
CNAD....... Committee for National Arbor Day (EA)
CNAD....... Conference of National Armaments Directors [*NATO*]
CNAF....... Chinese Nationalist Air Force
CNAF .... Combined Name and Address File [*IRS*]
CNAI .... Colorado Natural Areas Inventory [*Colorado State Department of Natural Resources*] [*Denver*] [*Information service or system*] (IID)
CNAIB...... Clean Air (Brighton, England) [*A publication*]
CNAIB4.... Clean Air [*Brighton, England*] [*A publication*]
CNAIC....... China National Automotive Industry Corporation

CNAINTERMTRA ... Chief of Naval Air Intermediate Training [*Later, CNABATRA*]
CNAIP....... Council for Native American Indian Progress (EA)
CNAIT....... Chief of Naval Air Intermediate Training [*Later, CNABATRA*]
CNAL........ Chief of Naval Aviation Logistics (MCD)
CNAL........ Commander, Naval Air Force, Atlantic
CNAM...... Canadian Corporate Names [*Canada Systems Group*] [*Information service or system*] (IID)
CNAMB .... Catholic Negro-American Mission Board (EA)
CNAN........ Compagnie Nationale Algerienne de Navigation [*Algerian National Shipping Company*]
CNAOPTRA ... Chief of Naval Air Operational Training [*Later, CNAADTRA, CNAVANTRA*]
CNAOT .... Chief of Naval Air Operational Training [*Later, CNAADTRA, CNAVANTRA*]
CNAP .... Chief of Naval Air Pacific (MCD)
CNAP .... Colorado Natural Areas Program [*Colorado State Department of Natural Resources*] [*Information service or system*] (IID)
CNAPRIMTRA ... Chief of Naval Air Primary Training [*Later, CNARFSTRA*]
CNAPT...... Chief of Naval Air Primary Training [*Later, CNARFSTRA*]
CNARESTRA ... Chief of Naval Air Reserve Training
CNARFSTRA ... Chief of Naval Air Primary Training
CNAS .... Chief of Naval Air Services [*British*]
CNAS .... Civil Navigation Aids System
CNASA..... Council of North Atlantic Shipping Associations [*Also, CONASA*]
CNASAX... Chugoku Nogyo Shikenjo Hokoku. A. Sakumotsu-Bu [*A publication*]
CNat .... Cahiers des Naturalistes [*A publication*]
CNAT .... Chief of Naval Air Training
CNATE...... Chief of Naval Airships Training and Experimentation
CNATECHTRA ... Chief of Naval Air Technical Training
CNATEC (LTA) ... Commander, Naval Air Technical Training (Lighter Than Air)
CNATRA... Chief of Naval Air Training
CNATT...... Chief of Naval Air Technical Training
CNAVANTRA ... Chief of Naval Air Advanced Training [*Also, CNAADTRA*]
CNAVOP .. Chief of Naval Operations [*Also, CNO*]
CNAVRES ... Commander, Naval Reserves (NVT)
CNAVSTA ... Charleston Naval Station [*South Carolina*]
CNB .... Canadian Naval Board
CNB........... Canberra [*Australia*] (KSC)
CNB........... Centrale Nucleaire Belge [*Nuclear reactor*] [*Belgium*] (NRCH)
CNB........... Channing Aviation Ltd. [*Toronto, ON, Canada*] [*FAA designator*] (FAAC)
CNB........... Commander, Naval Base
CNB........... Community National Bancorp [*AMEX symbol*] (SPSG)
CNB........... Coonamble [*Australia*] [*Airport symbol*] (OAG)
CNB........... Coordinador Nacional de Bases [*National Coordination of Bases*] [*Colombia*] (PD)
CNB........... Cutting Needle Biopsy [*Medicine*]
CNb........... Newport Beach Public Library, Newport Beach, CA [*Library symbol*] [*Library of Congress*] (LCLS)
CNB........... Newport Beach Public Library, Newport Beach, CA [*OCLC symbol*] (OCLC)
CNBA .... County Bank FSB [*NASDAQ symbol*] (NQ)
CNbAF ...... Aeronutronic Ford Corp., Newport Beach, CA [*Library symbol*] [*Library of Congress*] (LCLS)
CNBC .... Congress of National Black Churches (EA)
CNBC .... Consumer News and Business Channel [*A cable division of NBC*]
CNBD....... Condensed Negative Binomial Distribution [*Statistics*]
CNBE .... CNB Bancshares, Inc. [*Evansville, IN*] [*NASDAQ symbol*] (NQ)
CNBK....... Century BanCorp, Inc. [*NASDAQ symbol*] (NQ)
CNBL....... Centennial Beneficial Corp. [*NASDAQ symbol*] (CTT)
CNBLA...... Commander, Naval Base, Los Angeles
CNB-TV .... Center for Non-Broadcast Television (EA)
CNB-TV .... Custom Network Broadcasting, Inc. (TSSD)
CNBUAA .. Connecticut. Storrs Agricultural Experiment Station. Bulletin [*A publication*]
CNBV .... Comissao Nacional de Bolsas de Valores [*National Stock Exchange Commission*] [*Brazil*]
Cnc........... Cancer [*Constellation*]
CNC........... Canuck Resources, Inc. [*Toronto Stock Exchange symbol*]
CNC........... Captive Nations Committee (EA)
CNC........... Carson-Newman College [*Tennessee*]
CNC........... Center for New Creation (EA)
CNC........... Center for Nonviolent Communication (EA)
CNC........... Central Navigation Computer
CNC........... Central State University, Wilberforce, OH [*OCLC symbol*] (OCLC)
CNC........... Change Notice Card (AFIT)
CNC........... Chariton, IA [*Location identifier*] [*FAA*] (FAAL)
CNC........... Chief Naval Censor [*Navy rating*] [*Obsolete*]
CNC........... Chief of Naval Communications [*Formerly, DNC*]
CNC........... Clinical Nurse Consultants [*Australia*]
CNC........... Computer Numerical Control [*Data processing*]

CNC.......... Computerized Numerical Control [*Data processing*]
CNC.......... Concord - Diablo Valley College [*California*] [*Seismograph station code, US Geological Survey*] [*Closed*]   (SEIS)
CNC.......... Concordia University Library [*UTLAS symbol*]
CNC.......... Condensation Nuclei Counter
CNC.......... Confederation Nationale de la Construction [*Civil Engineering, Road and Building Contractors, and Auxiliary Trades Confederation*] [*Brussels, Belgium*]   (EY)
CNC.......... Conseco, Inc. [*NYSE symbol*]   (SPSG)
CNC.......... Croatian National Congress   (EA)
CNC.......... Napa College, Napa, CA [*Library symbol*] [*Library of Congress*]   (LCLS)
CNc.......... Nevada City Free Public Library, Nevada City, CA [*Library symbol*] [*Library of Congress*]   (LCLS)
CNCA........ Centel Cable Television Co. [*NASDAQ symbol*]   (NQ)
CNCA........ Council for National Cooperation in Aquatics   (EA)
CNCA........ Czechoslovak National Council of America   (EA)
CNCBAQ .. Comunicaciones. Instituto Nacional de Investigacion de las Ciencias Naturales. Ciencias Botanicas [*A publication*]
CNCbl........ Cyanocobalamin [*Biochemistry*]
CNCC........ Customer Network Control Center [*Telecommunications*]   (TEL)
CNCCA ..... Canadian Cancer Conference [*A publication*]
CNCD........ Concorde Career Colleges, Inc. [*NASDAQ symbol*]   (NQ)
CNCE .... Command NODAL [*Network-Oriented Data Acquisition Language*] Control Element
CNCE .... Communications NODAL [*Network-Oriented Data Acquisition Language*] Control Element
CNCE .... Consejo Nacional de Comercio Exterior [*National Foreign Trade Council*] [*Venezuela*]
CNCE .... Council for Noncollegiate Continuing Education   (EA)
CN-CEU ..... Council for Noncollegiate Continuing Education Units
CNC/IAWPRC ... Canadian National Committee of the International Committee on Water Pollution Research and Control   (EAIO)
CNCIEC .... China National Coal Import & Export Corporation [*People's Republic of China*]   (IMH)
CNC-IPS ... Canadian National Committee - International Peat Society
CNCL .... Cancel   (FAAC)
CNCL .... Commercial National Corporation [*Shreveport, LA*] [*NASDAQ symbol*]   (NQ)
CNCL .... Concealed   (MSA)
CNCL .... Council
CNCLR...... Councillor
CNCNAS... Contamination Control [*A publication*]
CNCNT ..... Concurrently   (FAAC)
CNCO........ China Navigation Co.   (DS)
CN Conf..... Cameron and Norwood's North Carolina Conference Reports [*A publication*]   (DLA)
CNCP .... Canadian National-Canadian Pacific Railway
CNCP .... Center for New Corporate Priorities [*Defunct*]   (EA)
CNCPF ...... Concept Resources [*NASDAQ symbol*]   (NQ)
CNCR .... Cencor, Inc. [*NASDAQ symbol*]   (NQ)
CNCR .... Concurrent   (AFM)
CNCRA6 .... Cancer Chemotherapy Reports [*A publication*]
CNCRI........ Choice-in-Currency Research Institute   (EA)
CNCS........ Computer Networking and Communications Systems Program [*Georgia Institute of Technology, School of Information and Computer Science*] [*Atlanta*] [*Telecommunications service*]   (TSSD)
CNCSH ..... Comite Nordique des Commissions des Sciences Humaines [*Nordic Committee of the Research Councils for the Humanities - NCRCH*]   (EAIO)
CNCT .... Connect   (FAAC)
CNCT .... Conseil National Canadien du Travail [*National Council of Canadian Labour - NCCL*]
CNCT .... Coordenacao Nacional das Classes Trabalhadores [*Trade union*] [*Brazil*]   (EY)
CNCTRC ... Concentric   (MSA)
CNCV .... Concave   (MSA)
CND.......... Campaign for Nuclear Disarmament
CND.......... Cannot Duplicate   (MCD)
C/N)d........ Carrier-to-Noise, Downlink
CND.......... Center for a New Democracy   (EA)
CND.......... Centre National de Documentation [*National Documentation Center*] [*Morocco*] [*Information service or system*]   (IID)
CND.......... Chief of Naval Development
CND.......... Cline Development Corp. [*Vancouver Stock Exchange symbol*]
CND.......... Club National du Disque [*Record label*] [*France*]
CND.......... Code Names Dictionary [*A publication*]
CND.......... Commandant Nucleus Department [*Military*] [*British*]
CND.......... Condemned   (AABC)
CND.......... Condition   (MDG)
cnd.......... Conductor [*MARC relator code*] [*Library of Congress*]   (LCCP)
CND.......... Conduit   (KSC)
CND.......... Constanta [*Romania*] [*Airport symbol*]   (OAG)
CND.......... CONUS [*Continental United States*] Net Depot Method
CND.......... Currant [*Nevada*] [*Seismograph station code, US Geological Survey*]   (SEIS)
CND.......... Sisters of the Congregation of Notre Dame [*Roman Catholic religious order*]

CNDBA ..... Bulletin. Cincinnati Dental Society [*A publication*]
CNDCT ..... Centro Nacional de Documentacion Cientifica y Tecnologica [*National Scientific and Technological Documentation Center*] [*Information service or system*]   (IID)
CNDCT ..... Conduct   (MSA)
CNDDB..... California Natural Diversity Data Base [*California State Department of Fish and Game*] [*Information service or system*]   (IID)
CNDH .... Coalition Nationale pour les Droits des Homosexuals [*National Gay Rights Coalition*] [*Canada*]
CNDI .... Combination Die
CNDI .... Commercial Nondevelopment Items [*Military*]   (AABC)
CNDIB ...... Cahiers de Notes Documentaires [*A publication*]
CNDI-LEE ... Commercial Nondevelopment Items of Law Enforcement Equipment   (MCD)
CNDLAR... Candollea [*A publication*]
CNDM....... Composition Node Design Method [*For distillation*]
CNDN....... Canadian   (FAAC)
CNDN....... Canadian Reserve File [*Petroleum Information Corp.*] [*Information service or system*]   (CRD)
CNDN....... Chittenden Corp. [*NASDAQ symbol*]   (NQ)
CNDO....... Chief Navy Disbursing Officer
CNDO....... Complete Neglect of Differential Overlap [*Quantum mechanics*]
CNDP .... Centre National de Documentation Pedagogique [*National Center for Pedagogical Documentation*] [*Ministry of Education*] [*Information service or system*]   (IID)
CNDP .... Centre National des Documents du Personnel [*National Personnel Records Center - NPRC*]
CNDP .... Communications Network Design Program
CNDP .... Continuing Numerical Data Projects
CNDP .... Cyano(dihydroxy)pyridine [*Biochemistry*]
CNDS .... Condensate   (KSC)
CNDST...... Centre National de Documentation Scientifique et Technique [*National Scientific and Technical Documentation Center*] [*Senegal*] [*Information service or system*]   (IID)
CNDST...... Centre National de Documentation Scientifique et Technique [*National Scientific and Technical Documentation Center*] [*Royal Library of Belgium*] [*Brussels*] [*Information service or system*]   (IID)
CNDW....... Coalition for National Dance Week   (EA)
CNDY....... Cindy's, Inc. [*NASDAQ symbol*]   (NQ)
CNE .... Canadian National Exhibition [*Held annually in Toronto*]
CNE .... Childress [*Texas*] [*Seismograph station code, US Geological Survey*]   (SEIS)
CNE .... Chronic Nervous Exhaustion [*Medicine*]
CNE .... Communications Network Emulator
CNE .... Compare Numeric Equal [*Data processing*]
CNE .... Connecticut Energy Corp. [*NYSE symbol*]   (SPSG)
CNEA .... Comision Nacional de Energia Atomica [*National Atomic Energy Commission*] [*Information service or system*]   (IID)
CNEB .... Cambridge Bible Commentary: New English Bible [*A publication*]   (BJA)
CNeBC....... Los Angeles Baptist College and Theological Seminary, Newhall, CA [*Library symbol*] [*Library of Congress*]   (LCLS)
CNE Commun Navig Electron ... CNE. Communication/Navigation Electronics [*A publication*]
cnee .... Consignee [*Business term*]   (DS)
CNEEMA ... Centre National d'Etudes et d'Experimentation du Machinisme Agricole
CNEF........ Canadian National Energy Forum
CNEG .... Consolidated Equities Corp. [*NASDAQ symbol*]   (NQ)
CNEKAT... Chugoku Nogyo Shikenjo Hokoku. E. Kankyo-Bu [*A publication*]
CNEL........ Community Noise Equivalent Level
CNEN....... Comissao Nacional de Energia Nuclear [*National Commission for Nuclear Energy*] [*Brazil*] [*Information service or system*]   (IID)
CNEN....... Comitato Nazionale per l'Energia Nucleare [*Italy*]
CNENAS... Center for Near Eastern and North African Studies [*University of Michigan*] [*Research center*]   (RCD)
CNEO .... Chief Naval Engineering Officer [*British*]
CNEP........ Cable Network Engineering Program [*Bell System*]
CNEP Bol ... CNEP [*Comision Nacional para la Erradicacion del Paludismo*] Boletin [*A publication*]
CNEP (Com Nac Errad Palud) Bol ... CNEP (Comision Nacional para la Erradicacion del Paludismo) Boletin [*A publication*]
CNEPDD... Contributions to Nephrology [*A publication*]
CNES......... Centre National d'Etudes Spatiales [*National Center for Space Studies*] [*France*]
CNET .... Centre National d'Etudes des Telecommunications [*National Telecommunications Research Center*] [*Information service or system*]   (IID)
CNET .... Chief of Naval Education and Training   (MCD)
CNET .... Communication Network
CNET .... COMNET Corp. [*Formerly, Computer Network Corp.*] [*NASDAQ symbol*]   (NQ)
C-NET .... Cromemco Local Area Network [*Cromemco, Inc.*] [*Mountain View, CA*] [*Telecommunications*]   (TSSD)

CNETP...... Consolidated New Equipment Training Plan (MCD)
CNew........ Carlyle Newsletter [*A publication*]
CNEWA .... Catholic Near East Welfare Association (EA)
CNEWA .... Chemical News [*A publication*]
CNEWS..... Canadian Northeast Wideband Systems [*Air Force*] (MCD)
C News...... Cinemanews [*A publication*]
CNEWTP ... Consolidated Navy Electronic Warfare Test Plan (CAAL)
CNEXO ..... Centere National pour l'Exploitation des Oceans
CNF .... Canadian Income Plus Fund 1986 Trust Units [*Toronto Stock Exchange symbol*]
CNF .... Central NOTAM [*Notice to Airmen*] Facility [*Military*]
CNF .... Cerre Les Noroy [*France*] [*Seismograph station code, US Geological Survey*] [*Closed*] (SEIS)
CNF .... Child Nutrition Forum (EA)
CNF .... Citizens for a Nuclear Freeze (EA)
CNF .... Commander, [*US*] Naval Forces
CNF .... Commonwealth Nurses Federation (EA)
CNF .... Confine (AABC)
CNF .... Conjunctive Normal Formula
CNF .... Consolidated Freightways, Inc. [*NYSE symbol*] (SPSG)
CNF .... Consudel. Maandblad voor de Benelux, Gewijd aan de Belangen van Industrie en Handel op het Gebied van Cacao, Chocolade, Suikerwerken, Koek, Banket, Biscuit Enz [*A publication*]
CNF .... Fort Worth, TX [*Location identifier*] [*FAA*] (FAAL)
CNFA .... Citizens Network for Foreign Affairs (EA)
CNFG .... [*The*] Conifer Group, Inc. [*NASDAQ symbol*] (NQ)
CNFH....... Coalition for a Nuclear Free Harbor (EA)
CNFI........ Christian News from Israel [*A publication*]
CNFIU....... Canadian National Federation of Independent Unions [*See also FCNSI*]
CNFL......... Central Nevada Field Laboratory [*University of Nevada - Reno*] [*Research center*] (RCD)
CNFP........ Coalition for a New Foreign Policy (EA)
CNFP........ Commercial Nuclear Fuel Plant (NRCH)
CNFRA Com Nat Fr Rech Antarct ... CNFRA. Comite National Francais des Recherches Antarctiques [*A publication*]
CNFRL...... Columbia National Fisheries Research Laboratory [*Later, NFCRC*] [*Department of the Interior*] [*Columbia, MO*] (GRD)
CNFS......... California National Fuchsia Society [*Later, NFS*]
CNFS Commer News For Serv ... CNFS. Commercial News for the Foreign Service [*A publication*]
CNFSFACM ... Committee of the National Ferrous Scrap Federations and Associations of the Common Market [*See also COFENAF*] (EAIO)
CNFUN ..... Canada Income Plus Fund 1986 Trust Units [*Toronto Stock Exchange symbol*]
CNFV .... Carnation Necrotic Fleck Virus
CNG.......... Calling Tone [*Data processing*]
CNG.......... Changalane [*Mozambique*] [*Seismograph station code, US Geological Survey*] (SEIS)
CNG.......... Change [*A publication*]
CNG.......... Charge Number Grouping (MCD)
CNG.......... Christlichnationaler Gewerkschaftsbund der Schweiz [*Swiss National Trade Union Confederation*] (DCTA)
CNG.......... Coastal Airways [*Gulfport, MS*] [*FAA designator*] (FAAC)
CNG.......... Commander, Northern Group
CNG.......... Compressed Natural Gas
CNG.......... Concert Industry Ltd. [*Vancouver Stock Exchange symbol*]
CNG.......... Connecticut Natural Gas Corp.
CNG.......... Consolidated Natural Gas Co. [*NYSE symbol*] (SPSG)
CNG.......... Paducah, KY [*Location identifier*] [*FAA*] (FAAL)
CNGA........ California Natural Gas Association
CNGB........ Chief, National Guard Bureau [*Army*]
CNGGA...... Canadian Geographer [*A publication*]
CNGGAR .. Canadian Geographer [*A publication*]
CNGI........ Comite des Normes Gouvernementales en Informatique [*Government Electronic Data Processing Standards Committee*] [*Canada*]
Cngrn .... Congregation (BJA)
CNGS .... Christlich-Nationaler Gewerkschaftsbund der Schweiz [*Swiss Federation of National-Christian Trade Unions*]
CNGTA ..... Changing Times [*A publication*]
CNH.......... Canhorn Mining Corp. [*Toronto Stock Exchange symbol*]
CN(h)......... Cellulose Nitrate with Hydrophobic Edge [*Membrane filtration*]
CNH .... Central Hudson Gas & Electric Corp. [*NYSE symbol*] (SPSG)
CNH .... Central Neurogenic Hyperventilation [*Medicine*]
CNH .... Changchun [*Republic of China*] [*Seismograph station code, US Geological Survey*] (SEIS)
CNH .... Claremont, NH [*Location identifier*] [*FAA*] (FAAL)
CNH .... Community Nursing Home
CNH .... Courier. European Community, Africa, Caribbean, Pacific [*A publication*]
CNH .... Natural History Museum Foundation, Los Angeles County, Los Angeles, CA [*OCLC symbol*] (OCLC)
CNHABF .. Carnegie Museum of Natural History. Annual Report [*A publication*]
CNhB......... Bendix Aviation Corp. [*Later, Bendix Corp.*], Pacific Division, North Hollywood, CA [*Library symbol*] [*Library of Congress*] (LCLS)

CNHC...... Commonwealth National Financial [*NASDAQ symbol*] (NQ)
CNHI......... Committee for National Health Insurance (EA)
CNHM ...... Chicago Natural History Museum
CNHO .... Consortium of National Hispanic Organizations (EA)
CNHS........ Center for Neo-Hellenic Studies (EA)
CNHS........ Cherokee National Historical Society (EA)
CNHS........ Coalition for a National Health System (EA)
CNHV........ Central Neurogenic Hyperventilation [*Medicine*]
CNI .... Canadian News Index [*Micromedia Ltd.*] [*Information service or system*] [*A publication*]
CNI .... Centre National des Independants [*National Center of Independents*] [*France*] [*Political party*] (PPE)
CNI .... Centre National des Independants et des Paysans [*National Centre of Independents and Peasants*] (EAIO)
CNI .... Centro Nacional de Informaciones [*National Information Center*] [*Supersedes DINA*] [*Chile*]
CNI .... Changed Number Interception [*Telecommunications*] (TEL)
CNI .... Chief of Naval Information [*Obsolete*] [*British*]
CNI .... Chief of Naval Intelligence
CNI .... Christian News from Israel [*A publication*]
CNI .... ChurchNews International [*Database*] [*Resources for Communication*] [*Information service or system*] (CRD)
CNI .... Columbus News Index [*Public Library of Columbus and Franklin County*] [*Information service or system*] (IID)
CNI .... Committee for a New Ireland (EA)
CNI .... Committee for Nuclear Information [*Later, Committee for Environmental Information*]
CNI .... Communicating NATO Intentions (MCD)
CNI .... Communication, Navigation, and Identification
CNI .... Community Nutrition Institute (EA)
CNI .... Consolidated National Interveners [*An association*] (EA)
CNI .... Craven Resources Ltd. [*Vancouver Stock Exchange symbol*]
CNI .... Current NOTAM [*Notice to Airmen*] Indicator (FAAC)
CNIB .... Canadian National Institute for the Blind
CNIB .... Champagne News and Information Bureau (EA)
CNIC .... Centre National de l'Information Chimique [*National Center for Chemical Information*] [*Information service or system*] (IID)
CNIC .... Clinical Neurology Information Center
CNID .... Centro Nacional de Informacion y Documentacion [*National Information and Documentation Center*] [*Ministry of Labour*] [*Information service or system*] (IID)
CNIE .... Commonwealth Novel in English [*A publication*]
CNIFC....... Chuck Norris International Fan Club (EA)
CNIIIC...... China Ningxia Islamic International Investment Company
CNIL .... Conseil National de l'Industrie Laitiere du Canada [*National Dairy Council of Canada*]
C/N)im...... Carrier-to-Noise, Intermodulation
CNIMZ ..... Tsentar za Nauchna Informacija po Meditsina i Zdraveopazvane [*Center for Scientific Information in Medicine and Public Health*] [*Medical Academy*] [*Information service or system*] (IID)
CNIP......... Centre National des Independants et des Paysans [*National Center of Independents and Peasants*] [*France*] [*Political party*] (PPW)
CNIPA...... Committee of National Institutes of Patent Agents [*Winchester, Hampshire, England*] (EA)
CNIPTG.... Communications, Networks, and Information Processing Theory Group [*MIT*] (MCD)
CNIR .... Cooperative Network of In-Service Resources (OICC)
CNIRA...... Centre National d'Information et de Recherche sur l'Aide Juridique [*National Legal Aid Research Centre*] [*Canada*]
CNJ .... Canadian Numismatic Journal [*A publication*]
CNJ .... Catfish Pond [*New Jersey*] [*Seismograph station code, US Geological Survey*] [*Closed*] (SEIS)
CNJ .... Central Railroad Co. of New Jersey [*Absorbed into Consolidated Rail Corp.*] [*AAR code*]
CNJ .... Charleston Resources [*Vancouver Stock Exchange symbol*]
CNJ .... Cloncurry [*Australia*] [*Airport symbol*] (OAG)
CNJA........ Chief Naval Judge Advocate [*British*]
CNJC........ Cable Network Joint Committee
CNJFDC.... Food and Drug Administration, Notices of Judgment: Cosmetics [*A publication*] (DLA)
CNJGA..... Canadian Journal of Genetics and Cytology [*A publication*]
CNJGA8.... Canadian Journal of Genetics and Cytology [*A publication*]
CNJMAQ ... Canadian Journal of Comparative Medicine and Veterinary Science [*Later, Canadian Journal of Comparative Medicine*] [*A publication*]
CNJNA...... Canadian Journal of Animal Science [*A publication*]
CNJNAT... Canadian Journal of Animal Science [*A publication*]
Cn Jour ...... Canadian Journal of Political and Social Theory [*A publication*]
CNJPA...... Canadian Journal of Pharmaceutical Sciences [*A publication*]
CNJPAZ.... Canadian Journal of Pharmaceutical Sciences [*A publication*]
CNK.......... Concordia, KS [*Location identifier*] [*FAA*] (FAAL)
CNK.......... Confederation of Khmer Nationalists [*Kampuchea*] (PD)
CNK.......... Crompton & Knowles Corp. [*NYSE symbol*] (SPSG)
CNKP........ Committee for a New Korea Policy (EA)
CNL .... Canal [*Board on Geographic Names*]
CNL .... Cancel [*or Cancellation*] (AFM)
CNL .... Carrier Noise Level

CNL.......... Centennial Airlines, Inc. [*Laramie, WY*] [*FAA designator*] (FAAC)
CNL.......... Central Bank of Nigeria. Economic and Financial Review (Lagos) [*A publication*]
CNL.......... Central Louisiana Electric Co., Inc. [*NYSE symbol*] (SPSG)
CNL.......... Children's Nutrition Laboratory [*Baylor College of Medicine*]
CNL.......... Circuit Net Loss
CNL.......... Columbia, Newberry & Laurens Railroad Co. [*AAR code*]
CNL.......... Connel [*Washington*] [*Seismograph station code, US Geological Survey*] (SEIS)
CNL.......... Conservative and National Liberal Party [*British*]
CNL.......... Constant Net Loss [*Telecommunications*] (TEL)
CNL.......... Council on National Literatures (EA)
CNLA........ Council of National Library Associations [*Later, CNLIA*] (EA)
CNLB........ Canadian Native Law Bulletin. Native Law Centre. University of Saskatchewan [*A publication*]
CNLCI....... Comite National pour la Liberation de la Cote d'Ivoire [*National Committee for the Liberation of the Ivory Coast*]
CNLDP..... Committee for National Land Development Policy [*Defunct*]
CNLF........ CNL Financial Corp. [*NASDAQ symbol*] (NQ)
CNLFP...... Cancel Flight Plan On [*Aviation*] (FAAC)
CNLG....... Conolog Corp. [*NASDAQ symbol*] (NQ)
CNLGP..... Cannon Nonlaunched Guided Projectile
CNLI........ Irrigation Canal [*Board on Geographic Names*]
CNLIA...... Council of National Library and Information Associations (EA)
CNLMA2 .. Contact Lens Medical Bulletin [*A publication*]
CNLN....... Navigation Canal [*Board on Geographic Names*]
CNLP....... Center on National Labor Policy (EA)
CNLR....... Canadian Native Law Reporter. Native Law Centre. University of Saskatchewan [*A publication*]
CNLR....... Council on National Literatures. Quarterly World Report [*A publication*]
CNLS........ Center for Nonlinear Studies [*Los Alamos, NM*] [*Department of Energy*] (GRD)
CNLS........ Centre for Nonlinear Studies [*University of Leeds*] [*British*] (CB)
CNM........ Canadian Manager [*A publication*]
CNM........ Canfic Resources Ltd. [*Vancouver Stock Exchange symbol*]
CNM........ Carlsbad [*New Mexico*] [*Airport symbol*] (OAG)
CNM........ Carlsbad, NM [*Location identifier*] [*FAA*] (FAAL)
CNM........ Casopis Narodniho Muzea [*Prague*] [*A publication*]
CnM......... Centro Nacional de Microfilm, Madrid, Spain [*Library symbol*] [*Library of Congress*] (LCLS)
CNM........ Certified Nurse Midwife
CNM........ Chama [*New Mexico*] [*Seismograph station code, US Geological Survey*] [*Closed*] (SEIS)
CNM........ Chief of Naval Material
CNM........ Collection of the National Museum of Antiquities at Leiden (BJA)
CNM........ Contemporary Poland [*A publication*]
CNM........ Cuban Nationalist Movement
CNMAD..... Construction News Magazine [*A publication*]
CNMBB .... Canada. Mineral Resources Branch. Mineral Bulletin [*A publication*]
CNMC....... Council of Nordic Master-Craftsmen [*Oslo, Norway*] (EAIO)
CNMD...... CONMED Corp. [*NASDAQ symbol*] (NQ)
CNMEAH ... Connecticut Medicine [*A publication*]
CNMED..... Clinical Nuclear Medicine [*A publication*]
CNMEDK ... Clinical Nuclear Medicine [*A publication*]
CNMI....... Commonwealth Code, Commonwealth of the Northern Mariana Islands [*A publication*]
CNMI........ Communications Network Management Interface
CNMO...... Canadian Naval Mission Overseas
CNMR....... Carbon-13 Nuclear Magnetic Resonance [*Also, CMR*]
CNMR....... Carbon-13 Nuclear Magnetic Resonance Search System [*Netherlands Information Combine*] [*Database*]
cnmt .... Consignment [*Business term*] (DS)
CNMW...... Cincinnati Microwave, Inc. [*NASDAQ symbol*] (NQ)
CNN.......... Aviation Centers of America [*Jackson, TN*] [*FAA designator*] (FAAC)
CNN.......... Cable News Network [*Facetious translation: Chicken Noodle Network*] [*Cable-television system*]
CNN.......... Canada Trust Income Investments [*Toronto Stock Exchange symbol*]
CNN.......... Cincinnati [*Ohio*] [*Seismograph station code, US Geological Survey*] [*Closed*] (SEIS)
CNN.......... CNA Income Shares, Inc. [*NYSE symbol*] (SPSG)
CNN.......... Common Market Business Reports [*A publication*]
CNN.......... Companhia Nacional de Navegacao [*Shipping company*] [*Portugal*] (EY)
CNN.......... Condensed Nearest Neighbor [*Mathematics*]
CNN.......... Congenital Nevomelanocytic Nevi [*Medicine*]
CNNA........ Culture-Negative Neutrocytic Ascite [*Bacteriology*]
CNNS........ Canadian Native News Service [*A publication*]
CNNS........ Center for New National Security (EA)
CNNSBV... Clinical Neurology and Neurosurgery [*A publication*]
CnNT........ Coniectanea Neotestamentica [*Uppsala*] [*A publication*] (BJA)
CNNW....... Coalition for a Non-Nuclear World [*Defunct*] (EA)

CNO.......... California State University, Northridge, Northridge, CA [*OCLC symbol*] (OCLC)
CNO.......... Carbon-Nitrogen-Oxygen [*Galactic molecular formation cycle*]
C/No .... Carrier-to-Noise Density
CNO.......... Caspen Oil, Inc. [*AMEX symbol*] (SPSG)
CNO.......... Center for Nonprofit Organizations (EA)
CNO.......... Chief of Naval Operations [*Also, CNA VOP*] [*Washington, DC*]
CNO.......... Chief Nursing Officer [*British*]
CNO.......... Childress [*Texas*] [*Seismograph station code, US Geological Survey*] (SEIS)
CNO.......... Chin National Organization [*Burma*]
CNO.......... Chino, CA [*Location identifier*] [*FAA*] (FAAL)
CNO.......... CML Industries Ltd. [*Toronto Stock Exchange symbol*]
CNO-AE.... Council of National Organizations for Adult Education (EA)
CNOB....... Commander, Naval Operating Base
CNOBO..... Chief of Naval Operations Budget Office
C/NOCB.... Cincinnati/New Orleans City Ballet
CNOCC..... Chief of Naval Operations Communications Center (MCD)
CNOCOM/MIS ... Chief of Naval Operations Command/Management Information System
CNOCS ..... Captain, Naval Operations Command Systems [*British military*] (DMA)
CNOCY ..... Council of National Organizations for Children and Youth [*Later, NCOCY*] (EA)
C/No)d....... Carrier-to-Noise Density, Downlink
CNODDT ... China National Opera and Dance Drama Theater
C/No)im..... Carrier-to-Noise Density, Intermodulation
CNOL........ Clinical Notes On-Line [*IRCS Medical Science*] [*Information service or system*] [*Ceased operation*] (IID)
CNOM....... Chief of Naval Operations Memorandum
CNOM/CMCM ... Chief of Naval Operations Memorandum and Commandant of the Marine Corps Memorandum [*Joint*]
CNON .... [*The*] Cannon Group [*NASDAQ symbol*] (NQ)
CNOP....... Conditional Nonoperation [*Data processing*]
CNOR....... Canada. Northern Forest Research Centre. Information Reports [*A publication*]
CNoR........ Canadian Northern Railway
CNOR....... Cincinnati Northern [*AAR code*]
CNOR....... Command Not Operationally Ready [*Navy*] (NVT)
CNoR........ Riker Laboratories, Inc., Northridge, CA [*Library symbol*] [*Library of Congress*] (LCLS)
CNORP..... Chief of Naval Operational Requirement and Plans
CNoS .... California State University, Northridge, Northridge, CA [*Library symbol*] [*Library of Congress*] (LCLS)
C/No)t....... Carrier-to-Noise Density, Total
CNO & TP ... Cincinnati, New Orleans & Texas Pacific Railway Co.
C/No)u....... Carrier-to-Noise Density, Uplink
CNovI .... Indian Valley College, Novato, CA [*Library symbol*] [*Library of Congress*] (LCLS)
CNP.......... Canadian Northern Pacific Railway
CNP.......... Cases at Nisi Prius [*A publication*] (DLA)
CNP.......... Center for National Policy (EA)
CNP.......... Central North Pacific
CNP.......... Central North Pacific Ocean
CNP.......... Chappell, NE [*Location identifier*] [*FAA*] (FAAL)
CNP.......... Chief of Naval Personnel [*The Second Sea Lord*] [*British*]
CNP.......... Chloro(nitro)phenol [*Organic chemistry*]
CNP.......... Communications, Navigation, and Positioning [*Military*]
CNP.......... Communications Network Processor
CNP.......... Community Nurse Practitioner
CNP.......... Consecutive Number Printer
CNP.......... Continuous Negative Pressure [*Medicine*]
CNP.......... Cornucopia Resources Ltd. [*Toronto Stock Exchange symbol*] [*Vancouver Stock Exchange symbol*]
CNP.......... Council for National Parks [*British*]
CNP.......... Country Nationalist Party [*Australia*] [*Political party*]
CNP.......... Crown Central Petroleum Corp. [*AMEX symbol*] (SPSG)
CNP.......... France Pays Bas [*A publication*]
CNPA........ Cossack National Press Association (EA)
CNPB........ Continuous Negative Pressure Breathing [*Physiology*]
CNPC .... Campbell's English Nisi Prius Cases [*A publication*] (DLA)
CNPC .... Conference of National Park Concessioners (EA)
CNPC .... Cuban National Planning Council [*Later, CANC*] (EA)
CNPD........ Candidate/Nominee Protective Division [*US Secret Service*]
CNPG .... Cornucopia Resources Ltd. [*NASDAQ symbol*] (NQ)
CNPI.......... Twenty-First Century Distribution Corp. [*NASDAQ symbol*] (NQ)
CNPIA....... Canadian Pulp and Paper Industry [*A publication*]
CNPIEC.... China National Publications Import & Export Corporation
CNPL........ Confederacao Nacional das Profissoes Liberais [*Liberal Professions Confederation*] [*Brazil*] (EY)
CNPM .... Coalition of Non-Postal Media (EA)
CN/PNL.... Contractors Panel [*Aerospace*] (AAG)
CNPP........ Clinton Nuclear Power Plant (NRCH)
CNPPA...... Comments on Nuclear and Particle Physics [*A publication*]
CNPPA...... Commission on National Parks and Protected Areas [*of the International Union for Conservation of Nature and Natural Resources*] (EAIO)
CNPPSDP ... Cooperative National Plant Pest Survey and Detection Program [*Department of Agriculture*] [*Hyattsville, MD*] [*Database*]

CNPq .... Conselho Nacional de Desenvolvimento Cientifico e Tecnologico [*National Council of Scientific and Technological Development*] [*Information service or system*]   (IID)
CNPR .... Center for National Policy Review [*Defunct*]   (EA)
CNPR .... Chatterji's Non-Language Preference [*Vocational guidance test*]
CNPRA3.... Canadian Poultry Review [*A publication*]
C & NPRR ... Chicago & Northern Pacific Railroad
CNPS......... Caucus for a New Political Science   (EA)
CNPTI .... Centre National de Prevention et de Traitement des Intoxications [*National Poison Control Center*] [*Information service or system*]   (IID)
CNPY .... Canopy Cover [*Ecology*]
CNQ........... Canadian Natural Resources Ltd. [*Toronto Stock Exchange symbol*]
CNQ........... Corrientes [*Argentina*] [*Airport symbol*]   (OAG)
CNQ........... Roanoke, VA [*Location identifier*] [*FAA*]   (FAAL)
CNQBAS.... Cane Growers Quarterly Bulletin [*A publication*]
CNQX........ Cyano(nitro)quinoxalinedione [*Organic chemistry*]
CNR........... Canadian National Railways [*Facetious translation: Certainly No Rush*]
CNR........... Canadian Northern Railway   (ROG)
CNR........... Canadian Roxy Petroleum Ltd. [*Toronto Stock Exchange symbol*]
CNR........... Carboxy Nitroso Rubber [*Organic chemistry*]
CNR........... Carrier-to-Noise Ratio
CNR........... Cellular Neoprene Rubber
CNR........... Center for Nursing Research [*Ohio State University*] [*Research center*]   (RCD)
CNR........... Change to Navy Regulations
CNR........... Change Notice Request   (MCD)
CNR........... Chief Naval Representative [*British*]
CNR........... Chief of Naval Research
CNR........... Chonco [*Nicaragua*] [*Seismograph station code, US Geological Survey*]   (SEIS)
CNR........... Collection Nelson Rockefeller [*Identifying mark on art reproductions from the collection of Nelson Rockefeller*]
CNR........... Collects No Revenue [*Humorous interpretation for Canadian National Railways*]
CNR........... College of New Rochelle [*New York*]
CNR........... Combat Net Radio [*Military*]
CNR........... Commission on Natural Resources [*National Research Council*]
CNR........... Committee for Nuclear Responsibility   (EA)
CNR........... Community Noise Rating
CNR........... Composite Noise Rating [*Aviation*]
CNR........... COMSAT [*Communications Satellite Corp.*] Nonreflecting [*Solar cell*]
CNR........... Condor Aero Services, Inc. [*Cullman, AL*] [*FAA designator*]   (FAAC)
CNR........... Conner Peripherals, Inc. [*NYSE symbol*]   (SPSG)
CNR........... Consiglio Nazionale delle Ricerche [*National Research Council*] [*Italy*] [*Information service or system*]   (IID)
CNR........... Contractual Nontechnical Report   (AAG)
CNR........... Corner   (ADA)
CNR........... National Center for Atmospheric Research, Boulder, CO [*OCLC symbol*]   (OCLC)
CNR........... North Slope, AK [*Location identifier*] [*FAA*]   (FAAL)
CNRA .... Canadian National Recreation Association
CNRAG ..... Company Nuclear Review and Audit Group   (NRCH)
CNRC .... Conseil National de Recherches Canada [*National Research Council Canada*]
CNRCA2 ... Canadian Journal of Research. Section C. Botanical Sciences [*A publication*]
CNRCB...... Clinical Notes on Respiratory Diseases [*A publication*]
CNRD........ Canrad, Inc. [*NASDAQ symbol*]   (NQ)
CNRDA5 ... Canadian Journal of Research. Section D. Zoological Sciences [*A publication*]
CNRE .... Center for Nursing Research and Evaluation [*University of Wisconsin - Milwaukee*] [*Research center*]   (RCD)
CNREA8 ... Cancer Research [*A publication*]
CN Regt ..... Chota Nagpur Regiment [*British military*]   (DMA)
C N Report ... Computer Negotiations Report [*A publication*]
CNRET....... Centre for Natural Resources, Energy, and Transport [*United Nations*]
CNRF........ Chief, Naval Reserve Forces
CNRHSPP ... Council for the National Register of Health Service Providers in Psychology   (EA)
CNRI .... National Research and Investigations Center [*Zaire*]   (PD)
CNRL .... Communication and Navigation Research Laboratory   (NASA)
CNRM .... CNR [*Christian News Report*] Ministries   (EA)
CNRM .... CNRM [*Centre National de Recherches Metallurgiques*]. Metallurgical Reports [*A publication*]
CNRM .... CONRIM [*Committee on Natural Resource Information Management*] Newsletter [*Anchorage, Alaska*] [*A publication*]
CNRMAW ... Canadian Journal of Research. Section E. Medical Sciences [*A publication*]
CNRM (Cent Natl Rech Metall) Metall Rep ... CNRM (Centre National de Recherches Metallurgiques). Metallurgical Reports [*Belgium*] [*A publication*]

CNROA4... Chirurgia Narzadow Ruchu i Ortopedia Polska [*A publication*]
CNRPTF ... Canadian National Railways Pension Trust Fund [*Montreal-based pension fund*]
CNRS......... Canadian Numismatic Research Society
CNRS......... Centre National de la Recherche Scientifique [*National Center for Scientific Research*] [*Paris, France*] [*Database producer*]
CNRS......... Centre National des Republicains Sociaux [*National Center of Social Republicans*] [*France*] [*Political party*]   (PPE)
CNRS Groupe Fr Argiles Bull ... Centre National de la Recherche Scientifique. Groupe Francais des Argiles. Bulletin [*A publication*]
CNRT .... Chief, Naval Reserve Training
CNRTC ...... Naval Reserve Training Command
CNRU........ Clinical Nutrition Research Unit [*Medical College of Georgia*] [*Research center*]   (RCD)
CNRU........ Clinical Nutrition Research Unit [*Birmingham, AL*] [*Department of Health and Human Services*]   (GRD)
CNRU........ Cooperative Core Laboratories and Clinical Nutrition Research Unit [*Research center*]   (RCD)
CNRXAV... Canadian Forestry Service. Northern Forest Research Centre. Information Report NOR-X [*A publication*]
CNS .... Cairns [*Australia*] [*Airport symbol*]   (OAG)
CNS .... Camp Newspaper Service
CNS .... Canada Safeway Ltd. [*Toronto Stock Exchange symbol*]
CNS .... Canadian Naval Service
CNS .... Canadian News Service
CNS .... Catawba Nuclear Station   (NRCH)
cns .... Censor [*MARC relator code*] [*Library of Congress*]   (LCCP)
CNS .... Center for Nationalist Studies   (EA)
CNS .... Center for New Schools   (EA)
CNS .... Center for Nonviolent Studies [*An association*]   (EA)
CNS .... Center for Northern Studies [*Research center*]   (RCD)
CNS .... Center for Nuclear Studies [*Memphis State University*] [*Research center*]   (RCD)
CNS .... Central Navigation School
CNS .... Central Nervous System [*Physiology*]
CNS .... Centre for Neuroscience [*University College, London*] [*British*]   (CB)
CNS .... Cherokee Nuclear Station   (NRCH)
CNS .... Chief of the Naval Staff [*Canada*]
CNS .... Child Neurology Society   (EA)
CNS .... China News Service
CNS .... Chlorocetophenone Solution   (AAG)
CNS .... Clinical Nurse Specialist
CNS .... Co-Ordinadora Nacional Sindical [*National Trade Union Co-Ordinating Body*] [*Chile*]   (PD)
CNS .... Committee for National Security   (EA)
CNS .... Commodity News Services, Inc. [*Information service or system*]   (IID)
CNS .... Common Number System   (AAG)
CNS .... Communications, Navigation, and Surveillance
CNS .... Communications Network Service [*Satellite Business Systems*] [*McLean, VA*] [*Telecommunications*]   (TSSD)
CNS .... Communications Network Services [*Virginia Polytechnic Institute and State University*] [*Blacksburg*]   (TSSD)
CNS .... CompuServe Network Services [*CompuServe, Inc.*] [*Columbus, OH*] [*Telecommunications*]   (TSSD)
CNS .... Congress of Neurological Surgeons   (EA)
CNS .... Consolidated Heron Resources [*Vancouver Stock Exchange symbol*]
CNS .... Consolidated Stores Corp. [*NYSE symbol*]   (SPSG)
CNS .... Continuous [*Aviation code*]
CNS .... Continuous National Survey [*National Opinion Research Center*]
CNS .... Continuous Net Settlement
CNS .... Control Network System [*Chiefly British*]
CNS .... Cooper Nuclear Station   (NRCH)
CNS .... Copley News Service
CNS .... Cras Nocte Sumendus [*To Be Taken Tomorrow Night*] [*Pharmacy*]
CNS .... Crigler-Najjar Syndrome [*Medicine*]
CNS .... Naval Ocean Systems Center, San Diego, CA [*OCLC symbol*]   (OCLC)
CNSB......... Centennial Savings Bank FSB [*Durango, CO*] [*NASDAQ symbol*]   (NQ)
CNSBB5.... Chugoku Nogyo Shikenjo Hokoku. B. Chikusan-Bu [*A publication*]
CNSC......... Carrying Nuclear-Strike Cruiser
CNSC......... Conesco Industries, Ltd. [*NASDAQ symbol*]   (NQ)
CNSD......... Chronic Nonspecific Diarrhea [*Medicine*]
CNS/EBU ... Common Nacelle System/Engine Build-Up   (MCD)
CNSF......... Cornell National Supercomputer Facility [*Cornell University*] [*Research center*]   (RCD)
CNSG......... Consolidated Nuclear Steam Generator
CNSHA ..... Congenital Nonspherocytic Hemolytic Anemia [*Medicine*]
CNSIST..... Consistent
CNSISTY .. Consistency
CNSL......... Cashew Nutshell Liquid
CNSL......... Console   (KSC)
CNSL......... Consul Restaurant Corp. [*NASDAQ symbol*]   (NQ)

CNSL......... Counsel [or Counseling or Counselor] (AFM)
CNSLAY ... Consultant [Philadelphia] [A publication]
CNSLD...... Consolidate (MSA)
Cnsllr......... Counsellor
CNSM .... Cambridge Natural Science Manuals [A publication]
CNSM .... Chicago North Shore & Milwaukee R. R. [AAR code]
CNSMR..... Consumer
CNSO........ Consco Enterprises [NASDAQ symbol] (NQ)
CNSP........ Central Sprinkler Corp. [Lansdale, PA] [NASDAQ
            symbol] (NQ)
CNSP........ Conselho Nacional de Seguros Privados [Brazil] (EY)
CNSP........ Conspicuously
CNSR........ Combination Neutron Source Rod [Nuclear energy] (NRCH)
CNSR........ Consumer
CNSRG...... Canada. Northern Science Research Group. Reports [A
            publication]
CNSRGSSN ... Canada. Northern Science Research Group. Social Science
            Notes [A publication]
CNSRNN .. Center for Northern Studies and Research. McGill University.
            News Notes [A publication]
CNSS........ Canadian National Steamships [AAR code]
CNSS........ Center for National Security Studies (EA)
CNSSC...... Conference of National Social Science Councils and Analogous
            Bodies
CNSSEP.... Central Nervous System. Pharmacology Series [A publication]
CNSSO...... Chief Naval Supply and Secretariat Officer [British]
CNSTAT ... Committee on National Statistics
CNSTNT... Consistent (FAAC)
CNSVAU... Conservationist [A publication]
CNSVC...... Center for Northern Studies (Wolcott, Vermont). Contributions
            [A publication]
CNSWTG ... Commander, Naval Special Warfare Task Group (NVT)
CNSY........ Charleston Naval Shipyard [South Carolina]
CNSYD...... Charleston Naval Shipyard [South Carolina]
CNT.......... Canadian National Telecommunications
CNT.......... Canton [Kwangchow] [Republic of China] [Seismograph
            station code, US Geological Survey] (SEIS)
CNT.......... Canton [Republic of China] [Geomagnetic observatory code]
C/N)t......... Carrier-to-Noise, Total
CNT.......... Celestial Navigation Trainer
CNT.......... Centel Corp. [NYSE symbol] (SPSG)
CNT.......... Center for Neighborhood Technology (EA)
CNT.......... Chief of Naval Training
CNT.......... Coleoptile Node-Tillers of Wheat [Plant pathology]
CNT.......... Comision Nacional del Trabajo [National Commission of
            Workers] [Argentina] (PD)
CNT.......... Commentaire du Nouveau Testament [Neuchatel] [A
            publication] (BJA)
CNT.......... Commission to New Towns [British]
CNT.......... Confederacion Nacional del Trabajo [National Confederation of
            Labor] [Spain] (PPE)
CNT.......... Confederation Nationale des Travailleurs [National
            Confederation of Labor] [Burkina Faso] (EY)
CNT.......... Confraternity New Testament [A publication] (BJA)
CNT.......... Container [Shipping] (DS)
CNT.......... Count
CNT.......... Counter (MDG)
CNTA........ Contact [A publication]
CNTA........ Council of Nordic Teachers' Associations [Copenhagen,
            Denmark] (EAIO)
CNTBRD... Centerboard (MSA)
CNTC........ Contact (AABC)
CNTCCI.... Centrale Nationale des Travailleurs Croyants de Cote d'Ivoire
            [National Union of Believing Workers of the Ivory Coast]
CNTCLKWS ... Counterclockwise
CNTCLKWZ ... Counterclockwise (AFM)
CNTD........ Contained (MSA)
CNTEBJ.... Congreso Nacional de Tuberculosis y Enfermedades
            Respiratorias [A publication]
CNTF........ Chick Neurotropic Factor [Neurochemistry]
CNTF........ Ciliary Neurotrophic Factor [Biochemistry]
CNTFGL ... Centrifugal (MSA)
CNTGCY... Contingency (AABC)
CNTIB....... Constructii (Bucharest) [A publication]
CNTIC....... China National Technical Import Corporation [People's
            Republic of China]
CNTL........ Central
CNTL........ Command Nuclear Target List (MCD)
CNTL........ Control (KSC)
CNTLR...... Controller
CNTN....... Contain (AABC)
CNTNR..... Container (MSA)
CNTO....... Centocor, Inc. [NASDAQ symbol] (NQ)
CNTOR ..... Contactor (MSA)
CNTP........ Cincinnati, New Orleans & Texas Pacific Railway Co. [AAR
            code]
CNTP........ Committee for a National Trade Policy [Defunct]
CNTP........ Country and New Town Properties [British]
CNTR .... Center
CNTR .... Container (KSC)
CNTR .... Contribute (AABC)

CNTR .... Counter (MSA)
CNTR .... CPL Real Estate Investment Trust [Davenport, IA] [NASDAQ
            symbol] (NQ)
CNTRF...... Centrifugal (AABC)
CNTRFUGL ... Centrifugal [Freight]
CNTRL...... Central (FAAC)
CNTRL...... Control
CNTRL...... Controller (NASA)
CNTRLN... Centerline (FAAC)
CNTRS BB ... Containers in Barrels or Boxes [Freight]
CNTRWT ... Counterweight
Cntry Wom ... Country Women [A publication]
CNTS........ Chief of Naval Technical Services [Canada]
CNTS........ Chief of Naval Transportation Service
CNTT .... Chief of Naval Technical Training (NVT)
CNTT .... Confederacao Nacional dos Transportes Terrestres
            [Brazil] (EY)
CNTTMFA ... Confederacao Nacional dos Trabalhadores em Transportes
            Maritimos, Fluvais, e Aereos [Maritime, River, and Air
            Transport Workers Confederation] [Brazil] (EY)
CNTU .... Confederation of National Trade Unions [Canada]
CNTV .... Continental Gold Corp. [NASDAQ symbol] (NQ)
CNTW .... Committee for National Theatre Week (EA)
CNTX .... Centex Telemanagement, Inc. [NASDAQ symbol] (NQ)
CNU.......... Cameroon National Union [Political party]
CNU.......... Canadian Newspaper Unit
C/N)u....... Carrier-to-Noise, Uplink
CNU.......... Chanute, KS [Location identifier] [FAA] (FAAL)
CNU.......... Chengdu [Republic of China] [Seismograph station code, US
            Geological Survey] (SEIS)
CNU.......... Committee for Nationalist Union [British]
CNU.......... Compare Numeric Unequal [Data processing]
CNU.......... Conscot Resources Ltd. [Vancouver Stock Exchange symbol]
CNU.......... Continuum Co. [AMEX symbol] (SPSG)
CNU.......... CSM [Command and Service Module] Navigation Update
            [NASA]
CNU.......... Financial Executive [A publication]
CNU.......... National University Library Cataloging Department, San Diego,
            CA [OCLC symbol] (OCLC)
CNUCED .. Conference des Nations Unies sur le Commerce et le
            Developpement [United Nations Conference on Trade and
            Development - UNCTAD] [French]
CNUIP....... Commission des Nations Unies pour l'Inde et le Pakistan
CNUJ .... Committee for Nordic Universities of Journalism [See also
            RNJ] (EAIO)
C Nuovo ..... Cinema Nuovo [A publication]
CNUP .... Center for Neuroscience, University of Pittsburgh
CNUTA ..... Canadian Nuclear Technology [A publication]
CNUURC .. Commission des Nations Unies pour l'Unification et le
            Relevement de la Coree
CNV.......... Canavieiras [Brazil] [Airport symbol] (OAG)
CNV.......... Cannon Aviation Co., Inc. [Hickory, NC] [FAA
            designator] (FAAC)
CNV.......... Cape Canaveral [Florida] (KSC)
CNV.......... Christlijk Nationaal Vakverbond in Nederland [National
            Federation of Christian Workers] [Protestant]
            [Netherlands]
CNV.......... Colistimethate-Nystatin-Vancomycin [Antibiotic mixture]
CNV.......... Collegiate News and Views [A publication]
CNV.......... Conditioned Nausea and Vomiting [Medicine]
CNV.......... Consolidated CSA Minerals, Inc. [Vancouver Stock Exchange
            symbol]
CNV.......... Contingent Negative Variation [Electrocortical measurement]
CNV.......... Convection
CNV.......... Converse
CNV.......... Convertible Holdings [NYSE symbol] (SPSG)
CNVA........ Center for Nonviolent Alternatives (EA)
CNVA........ Committee for Nonviolent Action [Later, WRL] (EA)
CNVAA..... Combined National Veterans Association of America (EA)
CNVC........ Convenience (MSA)
CNVC........ Convoy Capital Corp. [NASDAQ symbol] (NQ)
CNVEO ..... Center for Night Vision and Electro-Optics [Fort Belvoir, VA]
            [Army] (INF)
CNVF........ Coalition for Non-Violent Food (EA)
CNVG........ Converge (FAAC)
CNVJA9 .... Canadian Veterinary Journal [A publication]
CNVL .... City Investing Co. Liquidating Trust [NASDAQ symbol] (NQ)
CNVMDL ... Clinical and Investigative Medicine [A publication]
CNVR........ Conveyor (KSC)
CNVRT...... Convert (FAAC)
CNVSN ..... Conversion (FAAC)
CNVT .... Convict (AABC)
CNVTS ..... Central Night Vision Training School [Military] [British]
CNVTV .... Convective (FAAC)
CNVYG .... Conveying
CNVYR .... Conveyor
CNW.......... Canada News-Wire [Database] [Canada News-Wire Service]
            [Information service or system] (CRD)
CNW.......... Canada Northwest Energy Ltd. [Toronto Stock Exchange
            symbol]

C & NW ..... Chicago & North Western Transportation Co. [*Also known as Northwestern Line*] [*Nicknames: Can't and Never Will, Cheap and Nothing Wasted*]
CNW .... Childress [*Texas*] [*Seismograph station code, US Geological Survey*] (SEIS)
CNW .... CNW Corp. [*NYSE symbol*] (SPSG)
CNW .... Combination Network [*Graph theory*]
CNW .... Waco, TX [*Location identifier*] [*FAA*] (FAAL)
CNWA ...... Charleston Naval Weapons Annex [*South Carolina*]
CNWDI ..... Critical Nuclear Weapons Design Information (MCD)
CNWF .... Council for a Nuclear Weapons Freeze [*Later, IFLN*] (EA)
CNWHA8 ... Contributions. New South Wales National Herbarium [*A publication*]
CNwMH .... California State Department of Mental Hygiene, Metropolitan State Hospital Professional Staff Library, Norwalk, CA [*Library symbol*] [*Library of Congress*] (LCLS)
CNWRS ..... Centre for North-West Regional Studies [*University of Lancaster*] [*British*] (CB)
CNX .... Canadian Northstar Corp. [*Toronto Stock Exchange symbol*]
CNX .... Cancel (NVT)
CNX .... Chiang Mai [*Thailand*] [*Airport symbol*] (OAG)
CNX .... Convex Computer Corp. [*NYSE symbol*] (SPSG)
CNX .... Corona, NM [*Location identifier*] [*FAA*] (FAAL)
CNXS .... CNS, Inc. [*NASDAQ symbol*] (NQ)
CNY .... City College of New York [*New York*] [*Seismograph station code, US Geological Survey*] (SEIS)
CNY .... Continental Information Systems Corp. [*NYSE symbol*] (SPSG)
CNY .... Moab [*Utah*] [*Airport symbol*] (OAG)
CNY .... Moab, UT [*Location identifier*] [*FAA*] (FAAL)
CNYB .... Crain's New York Business [*A publication*]
C NY Bs Rv ... Central New York Business Review [*A publication*]
CNYD .... Croes Newydd [*Welsh depot code*]
CNYK .... Central New York Railroad Corp. [*AAR code*]
CNZ .... Chateau [*New Zealand*] [*Seismograph station code, US Geological Survey*] (SEIS)
CNZ .... Clarendon, TX [*Location identifier*] [*FAA*] (FAAL)
CO .... Cabinet Office [*British*]
CO .... Cahiers de l'Ouest [*A publication*]
CO .... Call Option [*Investment term*]
CO .... Camouflage Officer [*British*]
CO .... Carbon Monoxide
C/O .... Carbon to Oxygen [*Ratio*]
CO .... Cardiac Output [*Cardiology*]
C/O .... Care Of [*Correspondence*]
co .... Cargo Oil (DS)
CO .... Cargo Operations [*NASA*] (MCD)
CO .... Caribbean Organization [*An international governmental body, of which the US was a member*] [*Terminated, 1965*]
CO .... Carried Over [*Accounting*]
Co .... Carya ovata [*Shagbark hickory*]
C/O .... Case Of (AAG)
C/O .... Case Oil
CO .... Cash Order [*Business term*]
CO .... Castor Oil
CO .... Casualty Officer
CO .... Cathodal Opening [*Medicine*] (ROG)
CO .... Cathode-Ray Oscillator
CO .... Cemented Only [*Of envelopes*]
CO .... Central Office
CO .... Centric Occlusion [*Dentistry*]
C/O .... Cents-Off Coupon [*Advertising*]
C/O .... Certificate of Origin [*International trade*]
CO .... Certification Office [*Trade union regulation*] [*British*]
CO .... Certified Orthotist
CO .... Cervical Orthosis [*Medicine*]
CO .... Chain Operator (AAG)
CO .... Chain Overseas [*Aviation*]
C/O .... Change Order (NG)
CO .... Change [*of*] Order
CO .... Change Over (DEN)
C/O .... Changeout [*NASA*]
C/O .... Channel Oscilloscope
CO .... Charging Order (DCTA)
CO .... Check OK [*Telecommunications*] (TEL)
CO .... Check Open [*Nuclear energy*] (NRCH)
CO .... Checkout (KSC)
C & O .... [*The*] Chesapeake & Ohio Railway Co. [*Later, Chessie System, Inc.*]
CO .... Chessie System, Inc. [*Later, CSX*] [*NYSE symbol*] [*AAR code*] (SPSG)
C/O .... Chief Officer [*Women's Royal Naval Service*] [*British*]
CO .... Chief Operator (NRCH)
CO .... Chief of Ordnance [*Army*]
CO .... Choir Organ (ROG)
CO .... Choline Oxidase [*An enzyme*]
CO .... Christian Overcomers [*An association*] (EA)
CO .... Chronicles of Oklahoma [*A publication*]
CO .... Ciclopirox Olamine [*Antifungal agent*]
CO .... Classical Outlook [*A publication*]
CO .... Cleanout (AAG)

CO .... Clergy Orphan Schools [*British*] (ROG)
CO .... Clerical Officer [*Civil Service*] [*British*]
CO .... Clock Oscillator
CO .... Close-Open
CO .... Closing Order (ROG)
CO .... Coast
Co .... Cobalt [*Chemical element*]
CO .... Code des Obligations [*Switzerland*] [*A publication*]
CO .... Coden [*Online database field identifier*]
CO .... Codice delle Obligazioni [*Switzerland*] [*A publication*]
CO .... Coefficient of Overestimation
Co .... Coenzyme [*Biochemistry*]
CO .... Coinbox Line [*Telecommunications*] (TEL)
CO .... Coinsurance
CO .... Coke Oven
Co .... Coke's English King's Bench Reports [*1572-1616*] [*A publication*] (DLA)
Co .... Coke's Institutes [*England*] [*A publication*] (DLA)
CO .... Colistin [*Also, CL*] [*Generic form*] [*An antibiotic*]
CO .... Collation [*Online database field identifier*]
CO .... Colombia [*ANSI two-letter standard code*] (CNC)
CO .... Colon [*City in Panama*] (ROG)
CO .... Colon (ADA)
CO .... Colonial Office [*British*]
CO .... Colorado [*Postal code*]
CO .... Colorado Journal of Research in Music Education [*A publication*]
CO .... Colorado Reports [*A publication*] (DLA)
Co .... Colorado State Library, Denver, CO [*Library symbol*] [*Library of Congress*] (LCLS)
Co .... [*Jacobus*] Columbi [*Flourished, 13th century*] [*Authority cited in pre-1607 legal work*] (DSA)
CO .... Combat Aptitude Area (AABC)
CO .... Combat Operation (INF)
CO .... Combined Operations
CO .... Come [*Like, As*] [*Music*] (ROG)
CO .... Command Operations [*Army*] (AABC)
CO .... Command Orders
CO .... Command Output
CO .... Commanding Officer
CO .... Commissioner for Oaths
CO .... Commissioner's Office [*Scotland Yard*]
CO .... Common Orders (DLA)
CO .... Commonwealth Office [*Formerly, CRO*] [*British*]
CO .... Communications Officer [*Navy*]
Co .... Compagnie [*Company*] [*French*]
co .... Compagno [*Partner*] [*Italian*]
Co .... Compania [*Company, Society*] [*Spanish*]
CO .... Company [*Business term*] (AAG)
C/O .... Complains Of [*Medicine*]
CO .... Compliance Officer [*Department of Labor*]
CO .... Components Only
CO .... Compositus [*Compound*] [*Pharmacy*]
c/o .... Compte Ouvert [*Open Account*] [*French*] [*Business term*]
CO .... Computing [*A publication*]
CO .... Conceptual Organization [*Psychometrics*]
CO .... Cone
Co .... Conference [*A publication*]
CO .... Congregation of the Oratory [*Oratorians*] [*Roman Catholic men's religious order*]
CO .... Coniagas Mines Ltd. [*Toronto Stock Exchange symbol*]
co .... Conical Tank [*Liquid gas carriers*]
CO .... Conjugi Optimo [*To My Most Excellent Spouse*] [*Latin*]
CO .... Conscientious Objector
C/O .... Consist Of (MSA)
CO .... Constantine Order [*Freemasonry*] (ROG)
CO .... Constantly Operating
CO .... Container
C/O .... Contamination/Overpressure (MCD)
CO .... Continental Airlines, Inc. [*CAB official abbreviation*]
CO .... Continental Airlines, Inc. [*ICAO designator*] (FAAC)
CO .... Contracting Officer [*Also, CONTRO, KO*]
C & O .... Controllability and Observability
co .... Copolymerized With [*Organic chemistry*]
CO .... Copy (ROG)
CO .... Copyright Office [*US*]
Co .... Coral [*Quality of the bottom*] [*Nautical charts*]
Co .... Corona [*A publication*]
CO .... Corporate Office (AAG)
CO .... Corps Observation
CO .... Correction
CO .... Correctional Officer
Co .... Costa [*Entomology*]
CO .... Council Officer [*British*] (ROG)
CO .... Country
CO .... County (EY)
CO .... Coupled Oscillator (DEN)
CO .... Course
CO .... Course Pennant [*Navy*] [*British*]
CO .... Covered Option [*Investment term*]
Co .... Cowling Number [*IUPAC*]

CO............. Criminal Offence [*British*]
CO............. Criminal Office
CO............. Crossover [*Genetics*]
CO............. Crown Office [*British*]
CO............. Crystal Oscillator
CO............. Cut Out
CO............. Cutoff (MSA)
CO............. Cycling Oiler [*Navy*] (MCD)
CO............. Cyclophosphamide, Oncovin [*Vincristine*] [*Antineoplastic drug regimen*]
CO............. Cytochrome Oxidase [*An enzyme*]
CO............. Oakland Public Library, Oakland, CA [*Library symbol*] [*Library of Congress*] (LCLS)
CO............. Station Open to Official Correspondence Exclusively [*ITU designation*]
C1O............. Canto Primo [*First Soprano*] [*Music*]
2 CO........... Second Corinthians [*New Testament book*]
COA......... Cal Owner's Association (EA)
COA......... California Olive Association (EA)
COA......... Camaro Owners of America [*Inactive*] (EA)
COA......... Canadian Olympic Association
COA......... Carwash Operators Association (EA)
COA......... Cathedral Organists' Association (EA)
COA........... Center on Aging [*University of Maryland*] [*Research center*] (RCD)
COA......... Center Operations Area
COA........... Central Operating Agency (NATG)
COA........... Certified Office Administrator
COA......... Change of Address
COA......... Change of Assignment
COA........... Change Order Account (AFM)
CO(A)....... Change Order (Aircraft)
COA........... Chief of Operations Analysis (MCD)
CoA........... Children of Alcoholics
COA......... Children of the Americas (EA)
COA......... Chloroxymorphamine [*Narcotic agonist*] [*Pharmacochemistry*]
COA......... Christian Outdoorsman Association (EA)
COA........... Coachella [*California*] [*Seismograph station code, US Geological Survey*] (SEIS)
COA......... Coachmen Industries, Inc. [*NYSE symbol*] (SPSG)
CoA........... Coagulation
COA........... Coal Miner [*A publication*]
CoA........... Coat of Arms [*A publication*]
CoA........... Coenzyme A [*Biochemistry*]
COA........... Cognizant Operating Authority (MUGU)
COA......... Coherent Optical Array
COA........... College of Aeronautics [*British*]
COA........... Colonial Order of the Acorn (EA)
CO A........... Colorado Court of Appeals Reports [*A publication*] (DLA)
COA........... Colorado Motor Carriers' Association, Denver CO [*STAC*]
COA........... Comanche Petroleums [*Vancouver Stock Exchange symbol*]
COA......... Commission on the Aging (OICC)
COA........... Commissioned Officers Association of the United States Public Health Service (EA)
COA......... Committee on Accreditation [*American Library Association*]
COA......... Commonwealth of Australia
COA......... Compass Operation Alarm
COA......... Comptroller of the Army
COA......... Condition on Admission [*Medicine*] (ADA)
COA......... Constant-Output Amplifier (MUGU)
COA......... Contract of Affreightment [*Shipping*]
Co A .... Cook's Lower Canada Admiralty Court Cases [*A publication*] (DLA)
COA......... Cordova Airlines, Inc.
COA......... Corporate Accounting [*A publication*]
COA......... Corporate Ombudsman Association (EA)
COA......... Corps of Ordnance Artificers [*British military*] (DMA)
COA........... Council on Accreditation of Services for Families and Children (EA)
CoA .... Council of the Americas (EA)
COA......... Cruiser Olympia Association (EA)
COA........... Current Operating Allowances
COA......... Indianapolis, IN [*Location identifier*] [*FAA*] (FAAL)
COA........... Shepard's Causes of Action [*A publication*]
COA......... Sydney Jewish Centre on Ageing [*Australia*]
COA........... University of Colorado at Denver, Auraria Libraries, Denver, CO [*OCLC symbol*] (OCLC)
COAAL ..... Coordinated Activity Allowance List [*Military*] (NVT)
COAB........ Computer Operator Aptitude Battery [*Test*]
COABER... Computer Applications in the Biosciences [*A publication*]
COAC....... Clutter-Operated Anticlutter
COAC........ College Ouest Africaine des Chirurgiens [*West African College of Surgeons - WACS*] (EAIO)
COAC........ Commanding Officer, Atlantic Coast
COAC........ Council on Adoptable Children (EA)
COACH..... Canadian Organization for Advancement of Computers in Health (EAIO)
COACH..... Computer-Aided Chartroom
Coach and Athl ... Coach and Athlete [*A publication*]
Coach Clin ... Coaching Clinic [*A publication*]
Coach Clinic ... Coaching Clinic [*A publication*]

Coaching J Bus Rev ... Coaching Journal and Bus Review [*A publication*]
Coach Rev ... Coaching Review [*A publication*]
Coach Sci Update ... Coaching Science Update [*A publication*]
Coach Women's Athl ... Coaching Women's Athletics [*A publication*]
Coach Women's Athletics ... Coaching Women's Athletics [*A publication*]
COACT ..... Combat Activity Report [*Navy*]
CO-ACTION ... UNESCO Co-Operative Action Programme (EA)
COAD........ Chronic Obstructive Airway Disease [*Medicine*]
COAD........ Coadjutor (ROG)
COAD........ Coin-Operated Amusement Device
COAD........ Columbus Army Depot [*Ohio*] (AABC)
COAD........ Company Facts and Addresses [*EDIC*] [*Ringmer Near Lewes, East Sussex, England*] [*Information service or system*] (IID)
COAD........ Continued on Active Duty (AABC)
COA(DAB) ... Comptroller of the Army (Director of the Army Budget)
COADJ...... Coadjutor (ROG)
COADJ BP ... Coadjutor Bishop (ROG)
COADS ..... Command and Administration System [*Army*]
COADS ..... Comprehensive Ocean Atmosphere Data Set
CoA/FMME ... Council of the Americas/Fund for Multinational Management Education
CoAg......... Aguilar Public Library, Aguilar, CO [*Library symbol*] [*Library of Congress*] (LCLS)
COAG....... Chronic Open Angle Glaucoma [*Ophthalmology*]
coag........... Coagulase [*An enzyme*]
COAG....... Coagulation
COAG....... Committee on Agriculture [*Food and Agricultural Organization*] [*United Nations*]
COAHR..... Committee on Appeal for Human Rights
COAIREVACRON ... Commanding Officer, Air Evacuation Squadron
CoAk......... Akron Public Library, Akron, CO [*Library symbol*] [*Library of Congress*] (LCLS)
COAL .... Alameda County Law Library, Oakland, CA [*Library symbol*] [*Library of Congress*] (LCLS)
CoAl......... City of Alamosa-Southern Peaks Library, Alamosa, CO [*Library symbol*] [*Library of Congress*] (LCLS)
COAL .... Coalition (ADA)
COAL .... Consolidated Ordnance Allowance List [*Navy*]
Co & Al ..... Cooke and Alcock's Great Britain Reports [*Ireland*] [*A publication*] (DLA)
CoAlC .... Adams State College, Alamosa, CO [*Library symbol*] [*Library of Congress*] (LCLS)
Coal Conference and Expo ... Coal Conference and Exposition [*A publication*]
COALDATA ... European Coal Data Bank [*DECHEMA*] [*Federal Republic of Germany*] [*Information service or system*] (IID)
Coal Energy Q ... Coal and Energy Quarterly [*A publication*]
Coal Geol Bul ... Coal Geology Bulletin [*A publication*]
Coal Geol Bull WV Geol Econ Surv ... Coal Geology Bulletin. West Virginia Geological and Economic Survey [*A publication*]
Coal Gold Base Miner South Afr ... Coal, Gold, and Base Minerals of Southern Africa [*A publication*]
Coal Gold Base Miner Sthn Afr ... Coal, Gold, and Base Minerals of Southern Africa [*A publication*]
Coal Ind N ... Coal Industry News [*A publication*]
Coal Manage Tech Symp ... Coal Management Techniques Symposia [*A publication*]
Coal Min (Chicago) ... Coal Mining (Chicago) [*A publication*]
Coal Mine Drain Res Symp ... Coal Mine Drainage Research Symposia [*A publication*]
Coal Min Process ... Coal Mining and Processing [*A publication*]
Coal M & P ... Coal Mining and Processing [*A publication*]
Coal Obs .... Coal Observer [*A publication*]
Coal Oper .. Coal Operator [*A publication*]
Coal Outlk ... Coal Outlook [*A publication*]
Coal Prep ... Coal Preparation [*A publication*]
Coal Prep (Gordon & Breach) ... Coal Preparation (Gordon & Breach) [*A publication*]
Coal Prep Symp ... Coal Preparation Symposia [*A publication*]
COALPRO ... Coal Research Projects [*IEA Coal Research*] [*Database*]
Coal Process Technol ... Coal Processing Technology [*A publication*]
Coal Q....... Coal Quarterly [*A publication*]
Coal Res CSIRO ... Coal Research in CSIRO [*Commonwealth Scientific and Industrial Research Organisation*] [*A publication*]
Coal Sci Technol (Peking) ... Coal Science Technology (Peking) [*A publication*]
Coal Situat ... Coal Situation [*A publication*]
Coal Technol ... Coal Technology [*A publication*]
Coal Technol (Houston) ... Coal Technology (Houston) [*A publication*]
Coal Util ... Coal Utilization [*A publication*]
Coal Util Symp ... Coal Utilization Symposia [*A publication*]
Coal Wk I .. Coal Week International [*A publication*]
COAM....... Coaming [*Naval architecture*]
COAM....... Company [*or Customer*]-Owned and Maintained (FAAC)
COAMP .... Cost Analysis of Maintenance Policy
COAMS .... Computerization of Army Movement Schedules (CINC)
COANB .... Coal News [*London*] [*A publication*]
COAP .... Combat Optimization and Analysis Program [*Air Force*]
COAP .... Cyclophosphamide, Oncovin [*Vincristine*], ara-C, Prednisone [*Antineoplastic drug regimen*]

COAP-BLEO ... Cyclophosphamide, Oncovin [*Vincristine*], ara-C [*Cytarabine*], Prednisone, Bleomycin [*Antineoplastic drug regimen*]
CoAr.......... Arvada Public Library, Arvada, CO [*Library symbol*] [*Library of Congress*] (LCLS)
COAR....... COAR [*Comunidad Oscar A. Romero*] Peace Mission (EA)
COAR....... Coherent Array RADAR (MSA)
COARC...... Coarctation [*Cardiology*]
CoArGS..... Church of Jesus Christ of Latter-Day Saints, Genealogical Society Library, Arvada Branch, Arvada, CO [*Library symbol*] [*Library of Congress*] (LCLS)
COAS .... Coarse Optical Alignment Sight (NASA)
COAS .... Council on Atmospheric Sciences
COAS .... Council of the Organization of American States [*OAS*]
COAS .... Crew [*or Crewman*] Optical Alignment Sight [*or Subsystem*] [*NASA*]
CoAs .... Pitkin County Public Library, Aspen, CO [*Library symbol*] [*Library of Congress*] (LCLS)
COASB...... Comments on Astrophysics and Space Physics [*Later, Comments on Astrophysics*] [*A publication*]
CoAsL........ Aspen Law Center, Aspen, CO [*Library symbol*] [*Library of Congress*] (LCLS)
COASP...... Coordinated Aircraft/Stores Program [*Obsolete*] [*Navy*] (NG)
COAST...... Canada. Ocean and Aquatic Sciences Central Region. Technical Notes [*A publication*]
COASTA ... Conference of Officers of Affiliated States and Territorial Associations
Coastal Bend Med ... Coastal Bend Medicine [*Texas*] [*A publication*]
Coastal Eng ... Coastal Engineering [*A publication*]
Coastal Eng Japan ... Coastal Engineering in Japan [*A publication*]
Coastal Eng Jpn ... Coastal Engineering in Japan [*A publication*]
Coastal Engng ... Coastal Engineering [*A publication*]
Coastal Engng Japan ... Coastal Engineering in Japan [*A publication*]
Coastal Res ... Journal of Coastal Research [*A publication*]
Coastal Res Notes ... Coastal Research Notes [*A publication*]
Coastal Zone Manage J ... Coastal Zone Management Journal [*A publication*]
Coastal Zone Mgt J ... Coastal Zone Management Journal [*A publication*]
Coast Zone Manage J ... Coastal Zone Management Journal [*A publication*]
COASYS ... Crude Oil Analysis System [*National Institute for Petroleum and Energy Research*] (CRD)
COAT .... Coherent Optical Adaptive Techniques
COAT .... Coherent Optical Array Techniques
COAT .... Corrected Outside Air Temperature
COATS....... Canadian Over-the-Counter Automated Trading System
COATS....... Communications-Oriented Automatic Test (MCD)
CoAul.......... Ault Public Library, Ault, CO [*Library symbol*] [*Library of Congress*] (LCLS)
CoAur.......... Aurora Public Library, Aurora, CO [*Library symbol*] [*Library of Congress*] (LCLS)
COAX .... Coaxial (AAG)
COB .... Aurora Public Library, Aurora, CO [*OCLC symbol*] (OCLC)
CoB .... Boulder Public Library, Boulder, CO [*Library symbol*] [*Library of Congress*] (LCLS)
COB .... Carry-On Box
COB .... Central Obrera Boliviana [*Bolivian Workers Confederation*]
COB .... Ceramic Oceanographic Buoy
COB .... Change Order Board (AAG)
COB .... Clear over Base [*System of paint finishing*] [*Automotive engineering*]
COB .... Clip-on-Board [*Instrumentation*]
COB .... Close of Business [*With date*]
cob.............. Cobalt [*Philately*]
COB .... Cobb [*New Zealand*] [*Seismograph station code, US Geological Survey*] (SEIS)
COB .... COBOL [*Common Business-Oriented Language*] Element Subtype [*Data processing*]
COB .... Cobouw. Dagblad voor de Bouwwereld [*A publication*]
COB .... Collocated Operating Bases (MCD)
COB .... Colorado Motor Tariff Bureau, Inc., Denver CO [*STAC*]
Co-B .... Colorado State Library for the Blind and Physically Handicapped, Denver, CO [*Library symbol*] [*Library of Congress*] (LCLS)
COB .... Columbia Laboratories, Inc. [*AMEX symbol*] (SPSG)
COB .... Command Operating Budget [*Army*]
COB .... Committee of Combined Boards
COB .... Communications Office Building (NASA)
COB .... Congregation of Oblates of Bethany [*Roman Catholic women's religious order*]
COB .... Congressional Office of the Budget
COB .... Continent-Ocean Boundary [*Geology*]
COB .... Continental-Oceanic [*Crust*] Boundary [*Geology*]
COB .... Coordination of Benefits [*Insurance*]
COB .... Cost Operating Budget (NOAA)
COB .... Cut Out Background [*Printing*]
CoBa .... Basalt Public Library, Basalt, CO [*Library symbol*] [*Library of Congress*] (LCLS)
COBA .... Commerce Bancorp, Inc. [*NASDAQ symbol*] (NQ)
COBA .... Coordinating Organization of Book Associations [*Defunct*]
CoBA .... National Center for Atmospheric Research, Boulder, CO [*Library symbol*] [*Library of Congress*] (LCLS)
COBAA ..... Cobalt [*A publication*]

COBAC ..... Compagnie Belge d'Assurance-Credit SA [*Belgium*] (EY)
COBAC ..... Computer-Based Analytical Chemistry [*Conference*] [*Munich, 1982*]
CoBA-HA ... National Center for Atmospheric Research, High Altitude Observatory, Boulder, CO [*Library symbol*] [*Library of Congress*] (LCLS)
CoBai .... Park County Public Library, Bailey, CO [*Library symbol*] [*Library of Congress*] (LCLS)
Cobalt Cobalt Abstr ... Cobalt and Cobalt Abstracts [*A publication*]
COBAS....... Council of Black Architectural Schools (EA)
COBATAME ... Committee of Black Americans for Truth about the Middle-East [*Defunct*]
CoBay .... Bayfield Public Library, Bayfield, CO [*Library symbol*] [*Library of Congress*] (LCLS)
COBB .... Cobb Resources Corp. [*NASDAQ symbol*] (NQ)
COBB .... Cobbler
Cobb........... Cobb's New Digest, Laws of Georgia [*1851*] [*A publication*] (DLA)
Cobb........... Cobb's Reports [*121 Alabama*] [*A publication*] (DLA)
Cobb........... Cobb's Reports [*4-20 Georgia*] [*A publication*] (DLA)
Cobb Dig ... Cobb's Digest of Statute Laws [*Georgia*] [*A publication*] (DLA)
Cobbey Repl ... Cobbey's Practical Treatise on the Law of Replevin [*A publication*] (DLA)
Cobbey's Ann St ... Cobbey's Annotated Statutes [*Nebraska*] [*A publication*] (DLA)
Cobble........ Cobblestone [*A publication*]
Cobb Parl Hist ... Cobbett's Parliamentary History [*A publication*] (DLA)
Cobb Pol Reg ... Cobbett's Political Register [*A publication*] (DLA)
Cobb P & Pl ... Cobbett on Pawns and Pledges [*A publication*] (DLA)
CoBBRC..... Ball Brothers Research Corporation, Boulder, CO [*Library symbol*] [*Library of Congress*] (LCLS)
COBBS...... Computer-Based Bibliographic Search Services [*Washington State University Libraries*] (OLDSS)
CoBBS ...... United States National Oceanic and Atmospheric Administration, Environmental Research Laboratories Library, Boulder, CO [*Library symbol*] [*Library of Congress*] (LCLS)
Cobb Slav... Cobb on Slavery [*A publication*] (DLA)
Cobb St Tr ... Cobbett's [*later, Howell's*] State Trials [*1163-1820*] [*England*] [*A publication*] (DLA)
COBCCEE ... Comite des Organisations de la Boucherie-Charcuterie de la CEE [*Committee of Butchery and Cooked Meats Organizations of the EEC*]
COBCRM ... Cobalt-Chrome
COBD .... Commerce Business Daily [*Department of Commerce*] [*A publication*]
COBE .... Cobe Laboratories, Inc. [*NASDAQ symbol*] (NQ)
COBE .... Command Operating Budget Estimate/Execution (MCD)
COBE .... Cosmic Background Explorer [*NASA*]
CoBen .... Adams County Public Library, Bennett, CO [*Library symbol*] [*Library of Congress*] (LCLS)
COBEO ..... National Conference of Black Elected Officials (EA)
CoBer .... Berthoud Public Library, Berthoud, CO [*Library symbol*] [*Library of Congress*] (LCLS)
COBESTCO ... Computer-Based Estimating Technique for Contractors
COBET...... Common Basic Electronics Training (MCD)
COBFE...... Council of Black Federal Employees (EA)
COBGA ..... Commentationes Biologicae. Societas Scientiarum Fennica [*A publication*]
COBGA9 ... Commentationes Biologicae. Societas Scientiarum Fennica [*A publication*]
CoBGS....... Church of Jesus Christ of Latter-Day Saints, Genealogical Society Library, Boulder Stake Branch, Boulder, CO [*Library symbol*] [*Library of Congress*] (LCLS)
COBI .... Coded Biphase
CoBIBM .... International Business Machines Corp., Systems Manufacturing Division, Boulder, CO [*Library symbol*] [*Library of Congress*] (LCLS)
COBICIL... Cooperative Bibliographic Center for Indiana Libraries
COBIDOC ... Commissie voor Bibliografie en Documentatie [*Netherlands Bibliographical and Documentary Committee*] [*Amsterdam*] [*Information service or system*] (IID)
COBIEJ..... Comunicaciones Biologicas [*A publication*]
COBIS....... Computer-Based Instruction System (IEEE)
COBK .... [*The*] Co-Operative Bank of Concord [*NASDAQ symbol*] (NQ)
Co BL.......... Coke's Bankrupt Law [*A publication*] (DLA)
COBLAO .. Coleopterists' Bulletin [*A publication*]
COBLES..... Continental Birdlife [*A publication*]
COBLIB .... COBOL [*Common Business-Oriented Language*] Library [*Data processing*] (MCD)
COBLOC... CODAP [*Control Data Assembly Program*] Language Block-Oriented Compiler (MCD)
COBLSA ... Campaign to Oppose Bank Loans to South Africa (EA)
COBOAX .. Collectanea Botanica [*Barcelona*] [*A publication*]
COBOL ..... Common Business-Oriented Language [*1959*] [*Data processing*]
COBQ........ Cum Omnibus Bonis Quiescat [*May He, or She, Repose with All Good Souls*] [*Latin*]
COBRA ..... Cabinet Office Briefing Room [*British*]
COBRA ..... Compatible On-Board Ranging
COBRA ..... Computer-Based Recruit Assignment (MCD)

COBRA ..... Computer-Based Reference Assistance [*University of Northern Colorado*]   (OLDSS)
COBRA ..... Computer Operated Branch Recording and Acquisition System   (ADA)
COBRA ..... Computerized Boolean Reliability Analysis [*Boeing*]
COBRA ..... Consolidated Omnibus Budget Reconciliation Act of 1985 [*Health insurance law*]
COBRA ..... Continent, Britain & Asia [*Commercial firm*]   (DS)
COBRA ..... Coolant Boiling and Rod Arrays [*Nuclear energy*]   (NRCH)
COBRA ..... Copenhagen, Brussels, and Amsterdam [*Refers to a group of expressionist artists based in these three cities*]
COBRA ..... Counterbattery RADAR [*Military*]
COBRAS... Comprehensive Blast and Radiation Assessment System   (MCD)
COBRD ..... Communication and Broadcasting [*A publication*]
COBRE...... Committee on Basic Research in Education
CoBri.......... Adams County Public Library, Brighton, CO [*Library symbol*] [*Library of Congress*]   (LCLS)
CoBriH-M ... Brighton Community Hospital, Medical Library, Brighton, CO [*Library symbol*] [*Library of Congress*]   (LCLS)
CoBriJ .... Adams County Juvenile Detention Center, Brighton, CO [*Library symbol*] [*Library of Congress*]   (LCLS)
CoBro......... Mamie Doud Eisenhower Public Library, Broomfield, CO [*Library symbol*] [*Library of Congress*]   (LCLS)
CoBru......... Brush Public Library, Brush, CO [*Library symbol*] [*Library of Congress*]   (LCLS)
COBS......... Caesarean-Originated, Barrier-Sustained [*Rodent breeding*]
COBS......... Chronic Organic Brain Syndrome [*Medicine*]
COBSI...... Committee on Biological Sciences Information [*NAS/NRC*]
COBSRA... Council for the British Societies for Relief Abroad   (DAS)
Cob St Tr ... Cobbett's [*later, Howell's*] State Trials [*1163-1820*] [*England*] [*A publication*]   (DLA)
COBT .... Chicago Open Board of Trade [*Later, MIDAM*]
COBT .... Chronic Obstruction of Biliary Tract [*Medicine*]
COBTU ..... Combined Over-the-Beach Terminal Unit   (NATG)
CoBue......... Buena Vista Public Library, Buena Vista, CO [*Library symbol*] [*Library of Congress*]   (LCLS)
CoBueR...... Colorado State Reformatory, Buena Vista, CO [*Library symbol*] [*Library of Congress*]   (LCLS)
CoBueRL ... Colorado State Reformatory, Law Library, Buena Vista, CO [*Library symbol*] [*Library of Congress*]   (LCLS)
CoBueRS ... Colorado State Reformatory, Staff Library, Buena Vista, CO [*Library symbol*] [*Library of Congress*]   (LCLS)
COBUILD ... Collins Birmingham University International Language Database
CoBur......... Burlington Public Library, Burlington, CO [*Library symbol*] [*Library of Congress*]   (LCLS)
CoBW .... Western Interstate Commission for Higher Education, Boulder, CO [*Library symbol*] [*Library of Congress*]   (LCLS)
COBY .... Current Operating Budget Year
COC.......... California College of Arts and Crafts, Oakland, CA [*Library symbol*] [*Library of Congress*]   (LCLS)
COC........... Camco, Inc. [*Toronto Stock Exchange symbol*]
COC........... Canadian Opera Company
COC........... Cathodal Opening Contraction [*Also, CaOC*] [*Physiology*]
COC........... Central Office Connection [*Telecommunications*]   (TSSD)
COC........... Certificate of Competency [*Small Business Administration*]
COC........... Certificate of Conformance [*DoD*]
C/OC .... Certificate of Origin and Consignment [*Shipping*]   (DS)
COC........... Certification of Completion
COC........... Chamber of Commerce
COC........... Change of Command
COC........... Change of Contract [*Business law*]   (AAG)
COC........... Change Order Conference   (AAG)
COC........... Chief of Chaplains [*Navy*]
COC........... Chlorate Oxygen Candle
COC........... CINCPAC [*Commander-in-Chief, Pacific*] Operation Center   (CINC)
COC........... Circle of Companions   (EA)
COC........... Clergy Orphan Corporation [*British*]
COC........... Cleveland Open Cup [*Flash point determination*]
COC........... Climb on Course [*Aviation*]   (FAAC)
COC........... Close-Open-Close   (NASA)
COC........... Coccygeal [*Anatomy*]
COC........... Code of Conduct [*Military*]   (AFM)
COC........... Code Operations Coordinator   (MUGU)
COC........... Coded Optical Character [*Data processing*]   (BUR)
COC........... Colloidal Organic Carbon [*Environmental chemistry*]
COC........... Colombo [*Sri Lanka*] [*Seismograph station code, US Geological Survey*]   (SEIS)
COC........... Colorado College, Colorado Springs, CO [*OCLC symbol*]   (OCLC)
COC........... Combat Operations Center [*Air Force*]
COC........... Combination Type Oral Contraceptive [*Medicine*]
COC........... Combined Operations Command [*British*]
COC........... Command Operations Center [*Military*]   (NVT)
COC........... Commandant of Cadets [*Military*]
COC........... Commissioned Officer Corps [*National Oceanic and Atmospheric Administration*]
COC........... Committee of Concern
COC........... Committees of Correspondence   (EA)

COC........... Compiler Object Code [*Telecommunications*]   (TEL)
COC........... Complete Operational Capability
COC........... Comprehensive Organic Chemistry [*A publication*]
COC........... Comptroller of the Currency
COC........... Computer Communications [*A publication*]
COC........... Computer Operators' Course
COC........... Computer Oriented Classicists   (EA)
COC........... Concordia [*Argentina*] [*Airport symbol*]   (OAG)
COC........... Contempt of Court
COC........... Control Officers' Console
COC........... Conventional Oxidation Catalysis [*of gasoline engine exhausts*]
COC......... Corps of Cadets
COC........... Council of Canadians [*An association*]
CoC .... Council on Competitiveness   (EA)
COC........... Cultuur-en Ontspanningscentrum [*Center for Culture and Recreation*] [*Netherlands*]
COC........... Customer-Originated Change   (AAG)
COc........... Oceanside Public Library, Oceanside, CA [*Library symbol*] [*Library of Congress*]   (LCLS)
CoC........... Penrose Public Library, Colorado Springs, CO [*Library symbol*] [*Library of Congress*]   (LCLS)
COCA .... Canadian Organization for Campus Activities
COCA .... Clearinghouse on Computer Accommodation [*General Services Administration*]
COCA .... CoCa Mines, Inc. [*NASDAQ symbol*]   (NQ)
COCA .... Conservation Canada [*A publication*]
COCA .... Cooperative Contracts and Agreements [*Business term*]
CoCa .... Gordon Cooper Library, Carbondale, CO [*Library symbol*] [*Library of Congress*]   (LCLS)
CoCA .... United States Air Force Academy, Colorado Springs, CO [*Library symbol*] [*Library of Congress*]   (LCLS)
COCAG ..... Commissioned Officer Corps Advisory Group [*National Oceanic and Atmospheric Administration*]   (NOAA)
CoCA-H..... United States Air Force Academy, Hospital Library, Colorado Springs, CO [*Library symbol*] [*Library of Congress*]   (LCLS)
CoCAN ...... American Numismatic Association, Colorado Springs, CO [*Library symbol*] [*Library of Congress*]   (LCLS)
COC-APHA ... College of Chaplains [*of APHA*]   (EA)
COCAST ... Council for Overseas Colleges of Arts, Sciences, and TETOC [*British*]
COCATRAM ... Comision Centroamericana de Transporte Maritimo [*Central American Commission of Maritime Transport*] [*Organization of Central American States*] [*San Salvador, El Salvador*]   (EAIO)
COCB .... Crossed Olivocochlear Bundles [*Audiology*]
COCBAX... Coconut Bulletin [*A publication*]
COCC .... California Concordia College, Oakland, CA [*Library symbol*] [*Library of Congress*]   (LCLS)
CoCc.......... Canon City Public Library, Canon City, CO [*Library symbol*] [*Library of Congress*]   (LCLS)
CoCC .... Colorado College, Colorado Springs, CO [*Library symbol*] [*Library of Congress*]   (LCLS)
COCCEE ... Comite des Organisations Commerciales des Pays de la CEE [*Committee of Commercial Organizations in the EEC Countries*]
CoCcP .... Colorado State Penitentiary, Canon City, CO [*Library symbol*] [*Library of Congress*]   (LCLS)
CoCcPL ..... Colorado State Penitentiary, Law Library, Canon City, CO [*Library symbol*] [*Library of Congress*]   (LCLS)
CoCcPM .... Colorado State Penitentiary, Medium Security Residents' Library, Canon City, CO [*Library symbol*] [*Library of Congress*]   (LCLS)
CoCcPML ... Colorado State Penitentiary, Medium Security Law Library, Canon City, CO [*Library symbol*] [*Library of Congress*]   (LCLS)
CoCcPMS ... Colorado State Penitentiary, Medium Security Staff Library, Canon City, CO [*Library symbol*] [*Library of Congress*]   (LCLS)
CoCcPS...... Colorado State Penitentiary, Staff Library, Canon City, CO [*Library symbol*] [*Library of Congress*]   (LCLS)
CoCcPW .... Colorado State Penitentiary, Colorado Women's Correctional Institution, Residents' Library, Canon City, CO [*Library symbol*] [*Library of Congress*]   (LCLS)
CoCcPWL ... Colorado State Penitentiary, Colorado Women's Correctional Institution, Law Library, Canon City, CO [*Library symbol*] [*Library of Congress*]   (LCLS)
CoCcPWS ... Colorado State Penitentiary, Colorado Women's Correctional Institution, Staff Library, Canon City, CO [*Library symbol*] [*Library of Congress*]   (LCLS)
COCD........ Canadian Ownership and Control Determination
COCD........ Center for Organizational and Community Development   (EA)
CoCD .... Colorado School for the Deaf and Blind, Colorado Springs, CO [*Library symbol*] [*Library of Congress*]   (LCLS)
COCDC ..... Career Officer Candidate Development Course [*Air Force*]
CoCe.......... Cedaredge Public Library, Cedaredge, CO [*Library symbol*] [*Library of Congress*]   (LCLS)
COCE .... Commence   (ROG)
CoCE.......... El Paso Community College, Colorado Springs, CO [*Library symbol*] [*Library of Congress*]   (LCLS)
COCEEE... Committee on Captured Enemy Electronics Equipment

COCEMA ... Comite des Constructeurs Europeens de Materiel Alimentaire [*Committee of European Plant Manufacturers for the Food Industry*] [*Common Market*]

CoCenS ...... Saguache County Library, Center Branch, Center, CO [*Library symbol*] [*Library of Congress*]   (LCLS)

COCERAL ... Comite du Commerce des Cereales et des Aliments du Betail de la Communaute Economique Europeenne [*Committee of the Cereals and Animal Feed Trade of the European Economic Community*]

COCESS .... Contractor-Operated Civil Engineer Supply Store

CoCF .... Colorado Springs Fine Arts Center, Fine Arts and Anthropology of the Southwest, Library, Colorado Springs, CO [*Library symbol*] [*Library of Congress*]   (LCLS)

CoCfC .... Crawford Community Library, Crawford, CO [*Library symbol*] [*Library of Congress*]   (LCLS)

CoCFc .... Fort Carson Library, Colorado Springs, CO [*Library symbol*] [*Library of Congress*]   (LCLS)

CoCfCE ...... Chatfield Elementary School, Clifton, CO [*Library symbol*] [*Library of Congress*]   (LCLS)

CoCfCfE .... Clifton Elementary School, Clifton, CO [*Library symbol*] [*Library of Congress*]   (LCLS)

CoCFc-M ... Fort Carson Hospital, Medical Library, Colorado Springs, CO [*Library symbol*] [*Library of Congress*]   (LCLS)

CoCGS ...... Church of Jesus Christ of Latter-Day Saints, Genealogical Society Library, Colorado Springs Branch, Colorado Springs, CO [*Library symbol*] [*Library of Congress*]   (LCLS)

COCh .... Chabot Observatory, Oakland, CA [*Library symbol*] [*Library of Congress*]   (LCLS)

COCH .... Coaches [*Freight*]

COCH .... Cochin [*Region in India*]   (ROG)

COCH .... Cochleare [*Spoonful*] [*Pharmacy*]

Coch .... Cochran's Nova Scotia Reports [*1859*] [*A publication*]   (DLA)

CO CH .... Council Chambers [*Freemasonry*]   (ROG)

COCH AMP ... Cochleare Amplum [*Tablespoonful*] [*Pharmacy*]

Coch Ch Ct ... Chief Court of Cochin, Select Decisions [*A publication*]   (DLA)

COCHDK ... Computers in Chemistry [*A publication*]

CoChey ...... American Legion Auxiliary Library, Cheyenne Wells, CO [*Library symbol*] [*Library of Congress*]   (LCLS)

Cochin .... Cochin Law Reports [*1909-48*] [*India*] [*A publication*]   (DLA)

Coch Ind ..... Cochin, India   (ILCA)

COCH INFANT ... Cochleare Infantum [*Teaspoonful*] [*Pharmacy*]

Cochin LJ .. Cochin Law Journal [*A publication*]   (DLA)

Cochin LR ..... Cochin Law Reports [*1909-48*] [*India*] [*A publication*]   (DLA)

COCHL ...... Cochleare [*Spoonful*] [*Pharmacy*]

COCHL AMPL ... Cochleare Amplum [*Tablespoonful*] [*Pharmacy*]   (ROG)

COCHLEAT ... Cochleatim [*Spoonfuls*] [*Pharmacy*]   (ROG)

COCHL INFANT ... Cochleare Infantum [*Teaspoonful*] [*Pharmacy*]

COCHL MAG ... Cochleare Magnum [*Tablespoonful*] [*Pharmacy*]   (ROG)

COCHL MED ... Cochleare Medium [*Dessertspoonful*] [*Pharmacy*]   (ROG)

COCHL MOD ... Cochleare Modicum [*Dessertspoonful*] [*Pharmacy*]   (ROG)

COCHL PARV ... Cochleare Parvum [*Teaspoonful*] [*Pharmacy*]   (ROG)

COCH MAG ... Cochleare Magnum [*Tablespoonful*] [*Pharmacy*]

COCH MAX ... Cochleare Maximum [*Tablespoonful*] [*Pharmacy*]

COCH MED ... Cochleare Medium [*Dessertspoonful*] [*Pharmacy*]

COCH MIN ... Cochleare Minimum [*Teaspoonful*] [*Pharmacy*]

COCH MOD ... Cochleare Modicum [*Dessertspoonful*] [*Pharmacy*]

Coch N Sc .. Cochran's Nova Scotia Reports [*1859*] [*A publication*]   (DLA)

COCH PARV ... Cochleare Parvum [*Teaspoonful*] [*Pharmacy*]

COCH PLEN ... Cochleare Plenum [*Tablespoonful*] [*Pharmacy*]

Cochr. .... Cochran's Nova Scotia Reports [*1859*] [*A publication*]   (DLA)

Cochr. .... Cochran's Reports [*3-10 North Dakota*] [*A publication*]   (DLA)

Cochran ...... Cochran's Reports [*3-10 North Dakota*] [*A publication*]   (DLA)

Cochr Hind L ... Cochrane's Hindu Law [*A publication*]   (DLA)

COCI .... Consortium on Chemical Information [*British*]

COCI .... Coral Companies, Inc. [*NASDAQ symbol*]   (CTT)

COCiC .... Grove Street College, Oakland, CA [*Library symbol*] [*Library of Congress*]   (LCLS)

CoCK .... Kaman Sciences Corp., Nuclear Library, Colorado Springs, CO [*Library symbol*] [*Library of Congress*]   (LCLS)

Cockb & R ... Cockburn and Rowe's English Election Cases [*1833*] [*A publication*]   (DLA)

Cockb & Rowe ... Cockburn and Rowe's English Election Cases [*1833*] [*A publication*]   (DLA)

Cocke .... Cocke. Reports [*14, 15 Florida*] [*A publication*]   (DLA)

Cocke .... Cocke. Reports [*16-18 Alabama*] [*A publication*]   (DLA)

Cocke Const Hist ... Cocke's Constitutional History of the United States [*A publication*]   (DLA)

Cockerill .... Cockerill Sambre Acier [*Belgium*] [*A publication*]

Cocke US Pr ... Cocke's Common and Civil Law Practice of the US Courts [*A publication*]   (DLA)

Cock Nat .... Cockburn on Nationality [*A publication*]   (DLA)

Cock & R .... Cockburn and Rowe's English Election Cases [*1833*] [*A publication*]   (DLA)

Cock & Rowe ... Cockburn and Rowe's English Election Cases [*1833*] [*A publication*]   (DLA)

Cock Tich Ca ... Cockburn's Charge in the Tichborne Case [*A publication*]   (DLA)

COCL .... Cathodal Opening Clonus [*Physiology*]

COCLM .... Counterclaim [*Legal term*]   (ROG)

CoClM .... Mount Garfield Junior High School Library, Clifton, CO [*Library symbol*] [*Library of Congress*]   (LCLS)

COCMIB ... Comite d'Organisation du Congres Mondial d'Implantologie des Biomateriaux [*Organizing Committee of the World Congress on Implantology and Bio-Materials - OCWCIB*] [*Rouen, France*]   (EAIO)

COCO .... Cabinet Offices Cypher Office [*British*] [*World War II*]

CO-CO ...... Central Office to Central Office [*Bell System*]

COCO .... COBOL [*Common Business-Oriented Language*] Conversion [*Data processing*]   (MCD)

COCO .... Color Computer

COCO .... Commercially Owned, Commercially Operated   (AFIT)

COCO .... Committee on Contracting Out   (EA)

COCO .... Communications. CSIRO [*A publication*]

COCO .... Community Colleges Data Base [*Information service or system*]   (EISS)

COCO .... Conference of Consumer Organizations   (EA)

COCO .... Contractor-Owned, Contractor-Operated   (AABC)

COCO .... Coordinate Conversion Routine

CoCo .... Cortez Public Library, Cortez, CO [*Library symbol*] [*Library of Congress*]   (LCLS)

CoCo .... Cover Collectors Club   (EA)

COCO .... Covert Communications

COCOA ...... Cobra Owners Club of America   (EA)

COCOA ..... Continuously Contemporary Accounting   (ADA)

COCOA ..... Council to Outlaw Contrived and Outrageous Acronyms [*Australia*]

COCOA ..... Critical Terrain; Obstacles; Cover and Concealment; Observation and Fields of Fire; Avenues of Approach [*Military*]

Cocoa Res Inst CSIR Annu Rep ... Cocoa Research Institute. Council for Scientific and Industrial Research. Annual Report [*A publication*]

Cocoa Res Inst Ghana Acad Sci Annu Rep ... Cocoa Research Institute. Ghana Academy of Sciences. Annual Report [*A publication*]

COCOAS ... CONARC [*Continental Army Command*] Class One Automated System [*Later, BASOPS*]   (MCD)

CoCOC-M ... United States Olympic Committee, Sports Medicine Division, Colorado Springs, CO [*Library symbol*] [*Library of Congress*]   (LCLS)

COCODE .. Compressed Coherency Detection [*RADAR technique*]

CoCoGS ..... Church of Jesus Christ of Latter-Day Saints, Genealogical Society Library, Durango Stake Branch, Cortez, CO [*Library symbol*] [*Library of Congress*]   (LCLS)

CoCol .... Collbran Public Library, Collbran, CO [*Library symbol*] [*Library of Congress*]   (LCLS)

COCOM .... Coordinating Committee

COCOM .... Coordinating Committee on Export Controls [*From Western to Eastern bloc nations*]

COCOMO ... Constructive Cost Model

Co-Co-Nuke ... Coal, Conservation, and Nuclear [*Energy substitutes for oil*] [*British*]

Coconut Bull ... Coconut Bulletin [*A publication*]

Coconut Res Inst Bull ... Coconut Research Institute. Bulletin [*A publication*]

Co Cop .... Coke's Compleat Copyholder [*5 eds.*] [*1630-73*] [*England*] [*A publication*]   (DLA)

COCOPEA ... Coordinating Council of Private Educational Associations

COCORP ... Consortium for Continental Reflection Profiling [*Cornell University*] [*Ithaca, NY*]

COCOS ..... Corporate Communications System [*Bell-Northern Research Ltd.*] [*Data processing*]

COCOSEERS ... Coordinating Committee for Slavic and East European Library Resources

CO COUNC ... County Council [*British*]   (ROG)

Co on Courts ... Coke on Courts [*or Fourth Institute*] [*England*] [*A publication*]   (DLA)

COCP .... Crossed Olivocochlear Potential [*Audiology*]

CoCP-M .... Penrose Hospital, Webb Memorial Library, Colorado Springs, CO [*Library symbol*] [*Library of Congress*]   (LCLS)

COCR .... Collectanea Ordinis Cisterciensium Reformatorum [*A publication*]

CoCr. .... Douglas County Public Library, Castle Rock, CO [*Library symbol*] [*Library of Congress*]   (LCLS)

Co CR .... Pennsylvania County Court Reports [*A publication*]   (DLA)

CoCra .... Craig-Moffat County Public Library, Craig, CO [*Library symbol*] [*Library of Congress*]   (LCLS)

CoCre .... Creede Public Library, Creede, CO [*Library symbol*] [*Library of Congress*]   (LCLS)

CoCri .... Cripple Creek Public Library, Cripple Creek, CO [*Library symbol*] [*Library of Congress*]   (LCLS)

CoCroo .... Crook Community Library, Crook, CO [*Library symbol*] [*Library of Congress*]   (LCLS)

COCS .... Camera Override Control System [*NASA*]   (KSC)

COCT .... Coctio [*Boiling*]

Co Ct Cas ... County Court Cases [*England*] [*A publication*]   (DLA)

Co Ct Ch .... County Courts Chronicle [*1847-1920*] [*England*] [*A publication*]   (DLA)

Co Ct Chr ... County Courts Chronicle [*1847-1920*] [*England*] [*A publication*]   (DLA)

Co Ct ILT .. Irish Law Times, County Courts [*A publication*]   (DLA)

Co Ct R ...... County Courts Reports [*1860-1920*] [*England*] [*A publication*]   (DLA)

Co Ct Rep... County Courts Reports [*1860-1920*] [*England*] [*A publication*]   (DLA)

Co Ct Rep... Pennsylvania County Court Reports [*A publication*]   (DLA)

Co Ct Rep (PA) ... County Court Reports [*Pennsylvania*] [*A publication*]   (DLA)

Co Cts .... Coke on Courts [*or Fourth Institute*] [*England*] [*A publication*]   (DLA)

COCTS ...... County Courts [*Legal*] [*British*]

COCU .... Consultation on Church Union   (EA)

COCUSA .... Chamber of Commerce of the United States   (EA)

COCWA ..... Coin-Op Car Wash Association

CoCxC .... Climax Molybdenum Company, Technical Library, Climax, CO [*Library symbol*] [*Library of Congress*]   (LCLS)

CoCZ.......... Zebulon Pike Detention Center, Colorado Springs, CO [*Library symbol*] [*Library of Congress*]   (LCLS)

COD.......... Carrier-on-Deck [*Navy carrier-based aircraft*]

COD.......... Carrier Onboard Delivery [*Naval aviation*]

COD.......... Cash [*or Collect*] on Delivery [*Business term*]

COD.......... Cause of Death [*Medicine*]

COD.......... Center Operations Directorate   (MCD)

COD.......... Certificate of Deposit [*Banking*]

COD.......... Chamber of Deputies   (DAS)

COD.......... Change Operations Directive   (MCD)

COD.......... Chemical Oxygen Demand

COD.......... Coal-Oil Dispersion [*Fuel technology*]

COD.......... Codex

COD.......... Codicil

Cod .... Codification [*Legal term*]   (ILCA)

COD.......... Coding   (MSA)

COD.......... Cody [*Wyoming*] [*Airport symbol*]   (OAG)

COD.......... Cody, WY [*Location identifier*] [*FAA*]   (FAAL)

COD.......... Coefficient of Oxygen Delivery

COD.......... Coherent Optical Device

COD.......... Communications Operating Directive   (KSC)

COD.......... Concise Oxford Dictionary [*A publication*]

COD.......... Condensed or Dried

COD.......... Constrained Optimal Design [*Data processing*]   (RDA)

COD.......... Contract Operations Data [*DoD*]

COD.......... Cordiale Resources, Inc. [*Vancouver Stock Exchange symbol*]

COD.......... Corporate Design [*A publication*]

COD.......... Correction of Deficiency   (MCD)

COD.......... Cost on Delivery   (MCD)

COD.......... Country of Destination [*International trade*]   (DCTA)

COD.......... Crack Opening Displacement

COD.......... Crane on Deck   (MCD)

COD.......... Current Operations Division [*Tactical Air Command*]

COD.......... Cyclooctadiene [*Organic chemistry*]

CoD .... Denver Public Library, Denver, CO [*Library symbol*] [*Library of Congress*]   (LCLS)

Cod .... Gibson's Codex Ecclesiastia [*1715*] [*A publication*]   (DLA)

Cod .... Gibson's Codex Juris Civilis [*A publication*]   (DLA)

COD.......... University of Colorado, Boulder, CO [*OCLC symbol*]   (OCLC)

CODA .... Cash or Deferred Arrangement

CODA .... Chemical On-Line Data Analyzer [*Interactive Elements, Inc.*]

CODA .... Children of Deaf Adults   (EA)

CoDA .... Co-Dependents Anonymous   (EA)

CODA .... Coda Energy, Inc. [*NASDAQ symbol*]   (NQ)

CODA .... Committee on Drugs and Alcohol

CODA .... Coulee Dam National Recreation Area

CODA .... Council of Dance Administrators   (EA)

CODA .... Council on Drug Abuse [*Canada*]

CoDA .... Denver Art Museum, Denver, CO [*Library symbol*] [*Library of Congress*]   (LCLS)

CODAC ..... Collateral Duty Alcoholism Counselor [*Navy*]   (NVT)

CODAC ..... Common Ownership Design and Construct [*British*]

CODAC ..... Coordination of Operating Data by Automatic Computer

CoDAD ...... United States Department of Agriculture, Agricultural Research Service, Arthropod-Borne Animal Disease Research Laboratory, Denver, CO [*Library symbol*] [*Library of Congress*]   (LCLS)

CoDAFA .... United States Air Force Accounting and Finance Center, Denver, CO [*Library symbol*] [*Library of Congress*]   (LCLS)

CODAG ..... Combined Diesel and Gas [*Turbine*]

CoDAH ...... American Humane Association, Denver, CO [*Library symbol*] [*Library of Congress*]   (LCLS)

CODAI ...... Comite pour le Developpement des Alternatives a l'Incarceration [*Committee for the Development of Alternatives to Incarceration*] [*Canada*]

CODAI ...... Committee for the Development of Alternatives to Incarceration [*Canada*]

CODAM .... Combat Damage/Assessment Model   (MCD)

CODAM .... Contractor-Oriented Data Abstract Modules [*Air Force*]

CoDAMC-M ... American Medical Center, Medical Library, Denver, CO [*Library symbol*] [*Library of Congress*]   (LCLS)

CoDAmI ..... American Institute of Islamic Studies, Denver, CO [*Library symbol*] [*Library of Congress*]   (LCLS)

CODAN ..... Carrier-Operated Device, Antinoise [*Radio*]

CODAN ..... Coded Analysis [*Navy*]

CODAP ..... Client-Oriented Data Acquisition Process [*FDA*]

CODAP ..... Comprehensive Occupational Data Analysis Program [*Military*]   (AABC)

CODAP ..... Computer Occupational Data Analysis Program

CODAP ..... Control Data Assembly Program [*Control Data Corp.*]

CoDAr .... Colorado Division of State Archives, Denver, CO [*Library symbol*] [*Library of Congress*]   (LCLS)

CODAR ..... Correlation Data Analyzer Recorder   (CAAL)

CODAR ..... Correlation Detection and Ranging   (MCD)

CODAR ..... Correlation Display Analyzing and Recording

CODAS ..... Current Operational Data System

CODAS ..... Customer-Oriented Data System   (DIT)

CODASYL ... Conference on Data Systems Languages   (EA)

CODATA .. Committee on Data for Science and Technology   (EA)

CODATA Bull ... CODATA [*Committee on Data for Science and Technology*] Bulletin [*A publication*]

CODATA Newsl ... CODATA [*Committee on Data for Science and Technology*] Newsletter [*France*] [*A publication*]

CoDAW ..... American Water Works Association, Denver, CO [*Library symbol*] [*Library of Congress*]   (LCLS)

CoDB .... Bibliographical Center for Research, Rocky Mountain Region, Denver, CO [*Library symbol*] [*Library of Congress*]   (LCLS)

CoDBB ...... Baptist Bible College, Denver, CO [*Library symbol*] [*Library of Congress*]   (LCLS)

CoDBCS .... Blue Cross & Blue Shield of Colorado, Denver, CO [*Library symbol*] [*Library of Congress*]   (LCLS)

CoDBH-M ... Bethesda Hospital, Medical Library, Denver, CO [*Library symbol*] [*Library of Congress*]   (LCLS)

CoDBI-M .. Beth Israel Hospital, Medical Library, Denver, CO [*Library symbol*] [*Library of Congress*]   (LCLS)

CoDBLM... United States Department of the Interior, Bureau of Land Management, Denver Service Center, Denver, CO [*Library symbol*] [*Library of Congress*]   (LCLS)

CoDBM ..... United States Bureau of Mines, Denver, CO [*Library symbol*] [*Library of Congress*]   (LCLS)

CoDBR....... United States Bureau of Reclamation, Denver, CO [*Library symbol*] [*Library of Congress*]   (LCLS)

CoDBW ..... United States Bureau of Sport Fisheries and Wildlife, Wildlife Research Center, Denver, CO [*Library symbol*] [*Library of Congress*]   (LCLS)

CODC........ Canadian Oceanographic Data Centre [*Later, MEDS*]

CoDC .... Clayton College, Denver, CO [*Library symbol*] [*Library of Congress*]   (LCLS)

CODC........ Combined Operations Development Centre [*British military*]   (DMA)

CoDc .... Dolores County Public Library, Dove Creek, CO [*Library symbol*] [*Library of Congress*]   (LCLS)

CODCAVE ... Committee on Decentralization of Controls after V-E Day [*War Production Board*]

CoDCB....... Conservative Baptist Theological Seminary, Denver, CO [*Library symbol*] [*Library of Congress*]   (LCLS)

CoDCC ...... Community College of Denver, Denver, CO [*Library symbol*] [*Library of Congress*]   (LCLS)

CoDCC-A .. Community College of Denver, Auraria Campus, Denver, CO [*Library symbol*] [*Library of Congress*]   (LCLS)

CoDCC-E... Community College of Denver, Aurora Educational Learning Center, North Campus, Denver, CO [*Library symbol*] [*Library of Congress*]   (LCLS)

CoDCC-N .. Community College of Denver, North Campus, Denver, CO [*Library symbol*] [*Library of Congress*]   (LCLS)

CoDCC-R .. Community College of Denver, Red Rocks Campus, Lakewood, CO [*Library symbol*] [*Library of Congress*]   (LCLS)

CoDCDH... Colorado State Department of Highways, Denver, CO [*Library symbol*] [*Library of Congress*]   (LCLS)

CoDCH-M ... Children's Hospital, Medical Library, Denver, CO [*Library symbol*] [*Library of Congress*]   (LCLS)

Cod Civ ...... Codigo Civil [*Argentina*] [*A publication*]

CoDCo .... Cobe Laboratories, Denver, CO [*Library symbol*] [*Library of Congress*]   (LCLS)

CoDCW ..... Colorado Women's College, Denver, CO [*Library symbol*] [*Library of Congress*]   (LCLS)

CODD........ Codices   (ROG)

CoDDB ...... Denver Botanic Gardens, Inc., Denver, CO [*Library symbol*] [*Library of Congress*]   (LCLS)

CoDDC ...... District Court Law Library, Second Judicial District, Denver, CO [*Library symbol*] [*Library of Congress*]   (LCLS)

Cod Dip ...... Codex Diplomaticus [*A publication*]   (ILCA)

Codd Lat Ant ... Codices Latini Antiquiores [*A publication*]   (OCD)

CoDDP ...... Denver Post, Inc., Denver, CO [*Library symbol*] [*Library of Congress*]   (LCLS)

Codd Tr M ... Coddington's Digest of the Law of Trade Marks [*A publication*]   (DLA)

CODE .... Cable On-Line Data Exchange [*Nielson Media Research*] [*Information service or system*]

CODE .... Canadian Organization for Development through Education

CODE .... Citizens Organized to Defend the Environment

CODE .... Coastal Ocean Dynamics Experiment [*National Oceanic and Atmospheric Administration*]

Code .... Code of Justinian [*A publication*]   (DLA)

Code .... Codex Justinianus [*Code of Justinian*] [*Latin*] [*A publication*]　(DLA)
CODE .... Committee on Donor Enlistment [*Later, OR*]　(EA)
CODE .... Conference of Diocesan Executives [*Episcopalian*]
CODE .... Continental Organization of Distributor Enterprises, Inc.
CODE .... Controller Decision Evaluation
CoDE .... Education Commission of the States, Denver, CO [*Library symbol*] [*Library of Congress*]　(LCLS)
Code Am .... Code Amendments [*A publication*]　(DLA)
CODEC .... Coder-Decoder　(MCD)
Code Civ .... Code Civil Francais [*A publication*]　(DLA)
Code Civ Pro ... Code of Civil Procedure [*A publication*]　(DLA)
Code of Civ Proc ... Code of Civil Procedure [*A publication*]　(DLA)
Code Civ Proc ... Code of Civil Procedure [*A publication*]　(DLA)
Code de Com ... Code de Commerce [*Commercial Code*]　(DLA)
Code Com B .. Code de Commerce Belge　(DLA)
Code Com I ... Code de Commerce Italien　(DLA)
Code Crim Proc ... Code of Criminal Procedure [*A publication*]　(DLA)
Code Cr Pro ... Code of Criminal Procedure [*A publication*]　(DLA)
Code Cr Proc ... Code of Criminal Procedure [*A publication*]　(DLA)
CODED ..... Computer-Oriented Design of Electronic Devices
CODEDG .. Contact Dermatitis [*A publication*]
Code d'Instr Crim ... Code d'Instruction Criminelle [*Code of Criminal Procedure*] [*A publication*]　(DLA)
CODEF ...... Chairman of Defense Committee　(NATG)
Code des F ... Code des Faillites et Canqueroutes [*A publication*]　(DLA)
Code Fed Reg ... Code of Federal Regulations [*A publication*]
Code For ..... Code Forestier Francais [*French Forestry Code*] [*A publication*]　(DLA)
Code Fr An ... Code Francais Annote [*A publication*]　(DLA)
Code Gen Laws ... Code of General Laws [*A publication*]　(DLA)
CODEHUCA ... Comision para la Defensa de los Derechos Humanos en Centroamerica [*Commission for the Defense of Human Rights in Central America - CDHRCA*]　(EA)
Code I .... Code d'Instruction Criminelle [*Code of Criminal Procedure*] [*A publication*]　(DLA)
CODEIN ... Computerized Drawing Electrical Information　(NG)
Code J .... Code of Justinian [*Roman law*] [*A publication*]
Code de JM ... Code de Justice Militaire [*A publication*]　(DLA)
CODEL ..... Computer Developments Limited Automatic Coding System　(IEEE)
CODEL ..... Congressional Delegate [*or Delegation*]　(CINC)
CODEL ..... Coordination in Development　(EA)
CoDel .... Delta Public Library, Delta, CO [*Library symbol*] [*Library of Congress*]　(LCLS)
Code LA ..... Civil Code of Louisiana [*A publication*]　(DLA)
CoDelC .... Delta Honor Camp, Delta, CO [*Library symbol*] [*Library of Congress*]　(LCLS)
Code M ...... Code Municipal [*Quebec*] [*A publication*]　(DLA)
CODEMAC ... Comite des Demenageurs du Marche Commun
Code N .... Code Napoleon [*Napoleonic Code*] [*French*] [*Legal term*] [*A publication*]　(DLA)
Code Nap ... Code Napoleon [*Napoleonic Code*] [*French*] [*Legal term*] [*A publication*]　(DLA)
Code NY Rep ... Code Reporter [*New York*] [*A publication*]　(DLA)
Code P .... Code Penal [*Penal Law*] [*French*] [*A publication*]　(DLA)
CODEP ...... Council for a Department of Peace　(EA)
CoDEPA .... United States Environmental Protection Agency, National Field Investigations Center Library, Denver, CO [*Library symbol*] [*Library of Congress*]　(LCLS)
Code PC ..... Code de Procedure Civile [*Code of Civil Procedure*] [*French*] [*A publication*]　(DLA)
Code Prac... Code of Practice [*Legal term*]　(DLA)
Code Pro .... Code of Procedure [*Legal term*]　(DLA)
Code Proc... Code of Procedure [*Legal term*]　(DLA)
Code Pub Gen Laws ... Code of Public General Laws [*A publication*]　(DLA)
Code Pub Loc Laws ... Code of Public Local Laws [*A publication*]　(DLA)
Code R .... Code Reporter [*New York*] [*A publication*]　(DLA)
Code Rep.... Code Reporter [*New York*] [*A publication*]　(DLA)
Code Rep NS ... New York Code Reports, New Series [*A publication*]　(DLA)
Code RNS.. Code Reports, New Series [*New York*] [*A publication*]　(DLA)
Code RNS (NY) ... Code Reports, New Series [*New York*] [*A publication*]　(DLA)
Code R (NY) ... Code Reports [*New York*] [*A publication*]　(DLA)
CO DERRY ... County Londonderry [*Northern Ireland*]
CODES ...... Collection Development and Evaluation Section [*Reference and Adult Services Division*] [*American Library Association*]
CODES ...... Commutating Detection System
CODES ...... Computer Design and Education System
CODES ...... Computer Design and Evaluation System　(IEEE)
CODES ...... Computerized Deployment Execution System
Codes Fr ..... Les Codes Francaises [*French Codes*] [*A publication*]　(DLA)
CODESH .. Council for Democratic and Secular Humanism　(EA)
CODESRIA ... Council for the Development of Economic and Social Research in Africa [*Dakar, Senegal*]　(EAIO)
Code Supp ... Supplement to the Code [*A publication*]　(DLA)
Code Th ..... Code of Theodosius [*Roman law*] [*A publication*]
Code Theod ... Code of Theodosius [*Roman law*] [*A publication*]　(DLA)
Code Theodos ... Codex Theodosianus [*Theodosian Code*] [*438AD*] [*Latin*] [*Legal term*]　(DLA)
CODEVER ... Code Verification　(IEEE)

CODEX .... Customers of Dynix Exchange [*Australia*]
CODEX ..... Exercise Code Word [*NATO*]　(NATG)
CoDEx .... Exxon Corp., Exploration Library, Denver, CO [*Library symbol*] [*Library of Congress*]　(LCLS)
CODEXAL ... Conseil Europeen du "Codex Alimentarius"
CoDF .... Fort Logan Mental Health Center, Denver, CO [*Library symbol*] [*Library of Congress*]　(LCLS)
CoDFC .... Fort Logan Mental Health Center, Children's Library, Denver, CO [*Library symbol*] [*Library of Congress*]　(LCLS)
CoDFG-M ... Fitzsimons General Hospital, Medical Technical Library, Denver, CO [*Library symbol*] [*Library of Congress*]　(LCLS)
CoDFM...... Masonic Grand Lodge, Denver, CO [*Library symbol*] [*Library of Congress*]　(LCLS)
CoDFR....... Denver Federal Records Center, Denver, CO [*Library symbol*] [*Library of Congress*]　(LCLS)
CoDFU ...... National Farmers Union Library, Denver, CO [*Library symbol*] [*Library of Congress*] [*Obsolete*]　(LCLS)
CoDGC ...... Gilliam Center, Denver, CO [*Library symbol*] [*Library of Congress*]　(LCLS)
CoDGH...... Colorado General Hospital, Residents' Library, Denver, CO [*Library symbol*] [*Library of Congress*]　(LCLS)
CoDGL ...... Church of Jesus Christ of Latter-Day Saints, Genealogical Society Library, Denver Branch, Stake Center, Denver, CO [*Library symbol*] [*Library of Congress*]　(LCLS)
CoDGR ...... Gates Rubber Co., Technical Library, Denver, CO [*Library symbol*] [*Library of Congress*]　(LCLS)
CoDGRM-M ... General Rose Memorial Hospital, Medical Library, Denver, CO [*Library symbol*] [*Library of Congress*]　(LCLS)
CoDGS....... United States Geological Survey, Denver, CO [*Library symbol*] [*Library of Congress*]　(LCLS)
CoDGS-R... United States Geological Survey, Resources/Appraisal Group, Denver, CO [*Library symbol*] [*Library of Congress*]　(LCLS)
CoDGW ..... Great Western Sugar Co., Technical Library, Denver, CO [*Library symbol*] [*Library of Congress*]　(LCLS)
CODH .... Carbon Monoxide Dehydrogenase [*An enzyme*]
CODH .... Committee for Open Debate on the Holocaust　(EA)
CoD-H .... Denver Public Library, Denver General Hospital Library, Denver, CO [*Library symbol*] [*Library of Congress*]　(LCLS)
CoDHO ...... Humble Oil & Refining Co., Mineral Department Library, Denver, CO [*Library symbol*] [*Library of Congress*]　(LCLS)
CoDHRI .... Committee for the Defense of Human Rights in India　(EA)
CODI .... Codeine Tablet [*Slang*]　(DSUE)
CODI .... Computer Dialysis Systems [*NASDAQ symbol*]　(NQ)
CoDI .... Iliff School of Theology, Denver, CO [*Library symbol*] [*Library of Congress*]　(LCLS)
CODIA ...... Customers of Dynix in Australia
CODIC ...... Color Difference Computer　(MUGU)
CODIC ...... Computer-Directed Communication
CODICOM ... Computerized Distribution and Control of Microfilm [*American Motors Corp.*]
CODIL....... Content Dependent Information Language
CODIL....... Control Diagram Language [*Data processing*]　(IEEE)
CODILS ..... Commodity-Oriented Digital Label Input System
CoDIN .... International Nuclear Corp., Denver, CO [*Library symbol*] [*Library of Congress*]　(LCLS)
CODIP....... Conference de la Haye de Droit International Prive [*Hague Conference on Private International Law*]　(EA)
CODIPHASE ... Coherent Digital Phased Array System [*ARPA*]
Co Dir .... Company Director and Professional Administrator [*New Zealand*] [*A publication*]
Co Dir Prof Adm ... Company Director and Professional Administrator [*New Zealand*] [*A publication*]
CODIS...... Completed Discharge
CODIS...... Controlled Digital Simulator
CODIT ...... Computer Direct to Telegraph
Cod Iust...... Codex Iustinianus [*Classical studies*]　(OCD)
CoDJM...... Johns-Manville Sales Corp., Corporate Information Center, Denver, CO [*Library symbol*] [*Library of Congress*]　(LCLS)
Cod Jur ...... Gibson's Codex Ecclesiastia [*1715*] [*A publication*]　(DLA)
Cod Jur Civ ... Codex Juris Civilis [*Latin*] [*A publication*]　(DLA)
CodJust...... Codex Justinianus　(BJA)
CODL .... Code-Alarm, Inc. [*NASDAQ symbol*]　(NQ)
CODL .... Codicil
CoDL .... United States Lowry Air Force Base, Denver, CO [*Library symbol*] [*Library of Congress*]　(LCLS)
CoDLC....... Legislative Council of Colorado, Denver, CO [*Library symbol*] [*Library of Congress*]　(LCLS)
CoDM........ Medical Society of the City and County of Denver, Denver, CO [*Library symbol*] [*Library of Congress*]　(LCLS)
CODMAC ... Committee on Data Management and Computation [*National Academy of Sciences*]
Cod Man.... Codices Manuscripti [*A publication*]
COD MEMB ... Codex Membranacius [*A book written on vellum or skins*] [*Latin*]　(ROG)

CoDMG ..... Medical Group Management Association, Information Reference Service, Denver, CO [*Library symbol*] [*Library of Congress*] (LCLS)

CoDMH ..... Mercy Hospital, Library and Media Resources Center, Denver, CO [*Library symbol*] [*Library of Congress*] (LCLS)

CoDMH-M ... Mercy Hospital-School of Nursing, Library, Denver, CO [*Library symbol*] [*Library of Congress*] (LCLS)

CoDMM .... Martin Marietta Corp., Research Library, Denver, CO [*Library symbol*] [*Library of Congress*] (LCLS)

CoDMNH ... Denver Museum of Natural History, Denver, CO [*Library symbol*] [*Library of Congress*] (LCLS)

CoDMO ..... Mobil Oil Corp., Exploration and Producing Division, Denver, CO [*Library symbol*] [*Library of Congress*] (LCLS)

CoDMSA ... United States Department of Labor, Mine Safety and Health Administration, Denver, CO [*Library symbol*] [*Library of Congress*] (LCLS)

CoDMSE ... Mountain States Employers Council, Information Center, Denver, CO [*Library symbol*] [*Library of Congress*] (LCLS)

CODN .... Codenoll Technology Corp. [*NASDAQ symbol*] (NQ)

CODN .... Component Operational Data Notice [*NASA*] (KSC)

CoDn .... King's Daughters Public Library, Del Norte, CO [*Library symbol*] [*Library of Congress*] (LCLS)

CoDNJ-M ... National Jewish Hospital and Research Center, Medical Library, Denver, CO [*Library symbol*] [*Library of Congress*] (LCLS)

CoDNPS .... United States National Park Service, Denver, CO [*Library symbol*] [*Library of Congress*] (LCLS)

CODOC ..... Cooperation in Documentation and Communication [*An association*]

CODOC ..... Cooperative Documents Network Project [*University of Guelph Library*] [*Information service or system*]

CODOG ..... Combined Diesel or Gas Turbine Propulsion

CoDol .... Dolores Public Library, Dolores, CO [*Library symbol*] [*Library of Congress*] (LCLS)

CODORAC ... Coded Doppler RADAR Command

CODOT ..... Classification of Occupations and Directory of Occupational Titles [*Formerly, MOLOC*] [*British*]

CoDP .... Public Service Co. of Colorado, Denver, CO [*Library symbol*] [*Library of Congress*] (LCLS)

CoDPH .... Colorado Psychiatric Hospital, Residents' Library, Denver, CO [*Library symbol*] [*Library of Congress*] (LCLS)

CoDPM-M ... Presbyterian Medical Center, Doctors' Library, Denver, CO [*Library symbol*] [*Library of Congress*] (LCLS)

CoDPo-M .. Porter Memorial Hospital, Physicians' Library, Denver, CO [*Library symbol*] [*Library of Congress*] (LCLS)

Cod Proc Pen ... Codigo Procedimiento en Materia Penal de la Nacion [*Argentina*] [*A publication*]

CoDPS .... Denver Public Schools, Professional Library, Denver, CO [*Library symbol*] [*Library of Congress*] (LCLS)

CoDR .... Regis College, Denver, CO [*Library symbol*] [*Library of Congress*] (LCLS)

CODRESS ... Coded Address [*NATO*]

CoDRT .... Regional Transportation District, Technical Library, Denver, CO [*Library symbol*] [*Library of Congress*] (LCLS)

CODS .... Canadian Ocean Data System

CODS .... Corporate Data Sciences, Inc. [*Manhattan Beach, CA*] [*NASDAQ symbol*] (NQ)

CoDS .... Sundstrand Corp., Denver Division, Engineering Department Library, Denver, CO [*Library symbol*] [*Library of Congress*] (LCLS)

CODSBM ... Centre de Recherches Oceanographiques [*Abidjan*]. Document Scientifique Provisoire [*A publication*]

CoDSC .... Shell Chemical Co., Denver, CO [*Library symbol*] [*Library of Congress*] (LCLS)

CODSIA .... Council of Defense and Space Industry Associations (EA)

CoDSM ...... United States Department of Interior, Office of Surface Mining, Denver, CO [*Library symbol*] [*Library of Congress*] (LCLS)

CoDSMC ... Swedish Medical Center, Denver, CO [*Library symbol*] [*Library of Congress*] (LCLS)

CoDSO ...... Shell Oil Co., Denver, CO [*Library symbol*] [*Library of Congress*] (LCLS)

CoDSP .... Southeast Metropolitan Board of Cooperative Services, Professional Information Center, Denver, CO [*Library symbol*] [*Library of Congress*] (LCLS)

CoDSR .... Stearns-Roger Corp., Denver, CO [*Library symbol*] [*Library of Congress*] (LCLS)

CoDSS .... Colorado State Department of Social Services, Denver, CO [*Library symbol*] [*Library of Congress*] (LCLS)

Cod St .... Codified Statutes [*A publication*] (DLA)

CoDStA-M ... Saint Anthony Hospital, Memorial Medical Library, Denver, CO [*Library symbol*] [*Library of Congress*] (LCLS)

CoDStJ-M ... Saint Joseph Hospital, Denver, CO [*Library symbol*] [*Library of Congress*] (LCLS)

CoDStL-M ... Saint Luke's Hospital, Medical-Nursing Library, Denver, CO [*Library symbol*] [*Library of Congress*] (LCLS)

CoDStT ...... Saint Thomas Seminary, Denver, CO [*Library symbol*] [*Library of Congress*] (LCLS)

CODSULI ... Conference of Directors of State University Librarians of Illinois [*Library network*]

CODT .... Crane Oral Dominance Test [*English and Spanish test*]

Cod Theod ... Codex Theodosianus [*Theodosian Code*] [*438AD*] [*Latin*] [*Legal term*] (OCD)

Cod Theodos ... Codex Theodosianus [*Theodosian Code*] [*438AD*] [*Latin*] [*Legal term*] [*A publication*] (DLA)

CoDu .... Durango Public Library, Durango, CO [*Library symbol*] [*Library of Congress*] (LCLS)

CoDU .... University of Denver, Denver, CO [*Library symbol*] [*Library of Congress*] (LCLS)

CoDUCA .... United States Circuit Court of Appeals, Tenth Circuit, Denver, CO [*Library symbol*] [*Library of Congress*] (LCLS)

CoDuF .... Fort Lewis College, Durango, CO [*Library symbol*] [*Library of Congress*] (LCLS)

CoDVA ...... United States Veterans Administration Hospital, Denver, CO [*Library symbol*] [*Library of Congress*] (LCLS)

CoDVA-M ... United States Veterans Administration Hospital, Medical Library, Denver, CO [*Library symbol*] [*Library of Congress*] (LCLS)

CODW .... Companions of Doctor Who Fan Club (EA)

CoDYC ...... Colorado Youth Center, Denver, CO [*Library symbol*] [*Library of Congress*] (LCLS)

COE .... Cab Over Engine [*Type of truck*]

COE .... Center for Optimum Environments (EA)

COE .... Central Office Equipment [*Bell System*]

COE .... Certificate of Eligibility [*Navy*]

COE .... Certification of Equivalency [*Air Force*]

COE .... Chamber Orchestra of Europe

CO(E) .... Change Order (Electronic)

COE .... Chief of Engineers [*Formerly, CE, C of E, C of ENGRS, COFENGS*] [*Army*] (AABC)

COE .... Church of England

COE .... Circles of Exchange (EA)

COE .... Coe Ranch [*California*] [*Seismograph station code, US Geological Survey*] (SEIS)

COE .... Coeur D'Alene [*Idaho*] [*Airport symbol*] (OAG)

COE .... Coeur D'Alene, ID [*Location identifier*] [*FAA*] (FAAL)

COE .... Cognizant Operations Engineer

COE .... Commission on Education [*American Occupational Therapy Association*]

COE .... Complete Operating Equipment

COE .... Conseil Oecumenique des Eglises [*World Council of Churches*]

COE .... Cooperative Energy Development Corp. [*Toronto Stock Exchange symbol*]

COE .... Corps of Engineers [*Army*] (AAG)

COE .... Cost of Electricity (MCD)

COE .... Council of Europe

COE .... Council on Optometric Education (EA)

CO & E ...... Crab Orchard & Egyptian Railroad [*American Rail Heritage Ltd.*]

COE .... Cube-On-Edge [*Metal grain structure*]

COE .... Current Operation Expenditure [*Business term*]

CoE .... Kiowa County Public Library, Eads, CO [*Library symbol*] [*Library of Congress*] (LCLS)

COE .... Pikes Peak Community College, Colorado Springs, CO [*OCLC symbol*] (OCLC)

COEA .... Chief Ordnance Electrical Artificer [*British military*] (DMA)

COEA .... Cost and Operational Effectiveness Analysis [*Military*] (AABC)

CoEa .... Eaton Public Library, Eaton, CO [*Library symbol*] [*Library of Congress*] (LCLS)

COE(ACE) ... Chief of Engineers (Assistant Chief of Engineers) [*Military*]

CoEag .... Eagle Public Library, Eagle, CO [*Library symbol*] [*Library of Congress*] (LCLS)

COEA/NPC ... Central Office Executives Association of National Panhellenic Conference (EA)

COEAO ..... Coalition of Higher Education Assistance Organizations (EA)

COEBG ..... Commission on Organization of the Executive Branch of the Government

COEBRA ... Computerized Optimization of Elastic Booster Autopilot

COEC .... CONAD [*Continental Air Defense Command*] Operational Employment Concept (AABC)

COEC .... Council Operations and Exercise Committee [*NATO*]

Coe Ch Pr .. Coe. Practice of the Judges' Chambers [*1876*] [*A publication*] (DLA)

CoEck .... Eckley Public Library, Eckley, CO [*Library symbol*] [*Library of Congress*] (LCLS)

COE(CW) ... Corps of Engineers (Civil Works) [*Army*]

COED .... Char-Oil-Energy-Development [*Process*] [*Project of Office of Coal Research*]

CO-ED .... Co-Editor

COED .... Coeducational

COED .... Composition and Editing Display [*Later, MRTT*] (MCD)

COED .... Computer-Operated [*or -Oriented*] Electronic Display

COED .... Concentration on Engineering Design (AAG)

COED .... Concise Oxford English Dictionary [*A publication*]

CoEdg .... Edgewater Public Library, Edgewater, CO [*Library symbol*] [*Library of Congress*] (LCLS)

COEES ...... Central Office Equipment Estimation System [*Bell System*]

COEF .... Coefficient (KSC)

COEFF .... Coefficient

COEI .... Component of End Items (MCD)

COEI .... Composition of Ending Inventory

COEIL....... Components of End Items List (MCD)
COEL .... Chain Overseas Extremely Low [*Aviation*]
COEL .... Chief Ordnance Electrician [*British military*] (DMA)
CoEli.......... Elizabeth Public Library, Elizabeth, CO [*Library symbol*] [*Library of Congress*] (LCLS)
COEMN.... Chief Ordnance Electrical Mechanician [*British military*] (DMA)
CoEn .... Englewood Public Library, Englewood, CO [*Library symbol*] [*Library of Congress*] (LCLS)
CoEnCA.... Colorado Academy, Englewood, CO [*Library symbol*] [*Library of Congress*] (LCLS)
CoEnCo...... Council for Environmental Conservation (EAIO)
CoEnE........ Arapahoe County Evaluation Center, Englewood, CO [*Library symbol*] [*Library of Congress*] (LCLS)
Co Engl ...... College English [*A publication*]
CoEnS-M... Swedish Hospital, Medical Staff Library, Englewood, CO [*Library symbol*] [*Library of Congress*] (LCLS)
Co Ent .... Coke's Book of Entries [*1614*] [*England*] [*A publication*] (DLA)
COEP .... Central Office for Environmental Protection [*Basle, Switzerland*]
CoEp .... Estes Park Public Library, Estes Park, CO [*Library symbol*] [*Library of Congress*] (LCLS)
COEPL...... Cognizant Operations Engineer's Parts List
COEPS....... Cortically Originating Extra-Pyramidal System [*Physiology*]
COEQD..... CoEvolution Quarterly [*A publication*]
CO-EQUAL ... Committee for Equality of Citizens Before the Courts (EA)
COER .... Crab Orchard & Egyptian Railroad [*American Rail Heritage Ltd.*] [*AAR code*]
CoEr........... Erie Public Library, Erie, CO [*Library symbol*] [*Library of Congress*] (LCLS)
COES........ Commodore Environmental Services, Inc. [*NASDAQ symbol*] (NQ)
COESA...... Committee on Extension to the Standard Atmosphere
COET .... Crude Oil Equalization Tax [*Proposed, 1978*]
COEU....... Canadian Office Employees Union [*See also SCEB*]
COEU........ Confederation of Entertainment Unions [*British*] (DCTA)
Coeur Med I ... Coeur et Medecine Interne [*A publication*]
Coeur Med Interne ... Coeur et Medecine Interne [*A publication*]
COEV .... Canadian Ocean Escort Vessel
Coevolution Qly ... Coevolution Quarterly [*A publication*]
CoEvolutn .. CoEvolution Quarterly [*A publication*]
CoEv Q....... CoEvolution Quarterly [*A publication*]
COEW .... Combined Operations Experimental Wing [*World War II*]
COF .... Canadian Order of Foresters [*Later, CFLIS*] (EA)
COF .... Canadian Orienteering Federation
COF .... Captain of the Fleet [*Navy*] [*British*]
COF .... Catholic Order of Foresters (EA)
COF .... Cause of Failure [*Telecommunications*] (TEL)
COF .... Chromatographic Optimization Function [*Analytical chemistry*]
CoF .... Cobra Factor
COF .... Cocoa, FL [*Location identifier*] [*FAA*] (FAAL)
Cof............. Coffey's California Probate Decisions [*A publication*] (DLA)
COF .... Colorado State University, Fort Collins, CO [*OCLC symbol*] (OCLC)
COF .... Columbia Leisure [*Vancouver Stock Exchange symbol*]
COF .... Computer Operations Facility
COF .... Computer Optimized Fabrication [*Sheet metal*] [*Raytheon Co.*]
COF .... Conical Fin
COF .... Construction of Facilities [*NASA*] (KSC)
COF .... Contractor Overhaul Facility
COF .... Controlled Oxygen Fugacity [*Apparatus*]
COF .... Cutoff Frequency
CoF .... Fort Collins Public Library, Fort Collins, CO [*Library symbol*] [*Library of Congress*] (LCLS)
COFA .... Central Ohio Fibrositis Association (EA)
COFA .... Collocation Flutter Analysis
COFACE ... Comite des Organisations Familiales aupres des Communautes Europeennes [*Committee of Family Organizations in the European Communities*] [*Common Market*] [*Belgium*]
COFACTS ... Cost-Factoring System for Force Readiness Projection (MCD)
COFAF...... ASEAN [*Association of South East Asian Nations*] Committee on Food, Agriculture, and Forestry [*Jakarta, Indonesia*] (EAIO)
COFAFCH ... Chief of Air Force Chaplains
COFAG ..... Comite des Fabricants d'Acide Glutamique de la CEE [*Committee of Glutamic Acid Manufacturers of the European Economic Community*] (EAIO)
COFAL...... Complement-Fixation for Avian Leucosis Virus [*Immunology*]
COFALEC ... Comite des Fabricants de Levure de Panification de la CEE [*Committee of Bread Yeast Manufacturers of the EEC*]
COFC........ Container on Flatcar [*Shipping*]
COFCAW ... Combination of Forward Combustion and Waterflooding [*Commercial oil production process*]
COFCH ..... Chief of Chaplains [*Later, CCH*] [*Army*]
COFD........ Collective Bancorp, Inc. [*NASDAQ symbol*] (NQ)
Cof Dig....... Cofer's Kentucky Digest [*A publication*] (DLA)
COFE........ Conditions of Execution (MCD)
COFEAN.... Coffee [*Turrialba*] [*A publication*]
COFEB...... Confederation of European Bath Manufacturers (EAIO)

COFENAF ... Commission des Federations et Syndicats Nationaux des Entreprises de Recuperation de Ferrailles du Marche Commun [*Committee of the National Ferrous Scrap Federations and Associations of the Common Market - CNFSFACM*] (EAIO)
COFENGRS ... Chief of Engineers (MCD)
COFENGS ... Chief of Engineers [*Later, COE*] [*Army*]
COFF........ Chief of Finance [*Army*]
COFF......... Cofferdam [*Engineering*]
COFF......... Common-Object-File Format [*Data processing*]
COFF......... Consolidation of Functions and Facilities Cutoff (MCD)
COFF......... Cut Off [*Military*] (AABC)
COFFEE.... Community Organization for Full Employment Economy
Coffee Brew Inst Publ ... Coffee Brewing Institute. Publication [*A publication*]
Coffee Cacao J ... Coffee and Cacao Journal [*A publication*]
Coffee Res Found (Kenya) Annu Rep ... Coffee Research Foundation (Kenya). Annual Report [*A publication*]
Coffee Tea Ind Flavor Field ... Coffee and Tea Industries and the Flavor Field [*A publication*]
Coffey......... Coffey's California Probate Decisions [*A publication*] (DLA)
Coffey Probate Dec ... Coffey's California Probate Decisions [*A publication*] (DLA)
Coffey Prob Dec ... Coffey's California Probate Decisions [*A publication*] (DLA)
Coffey's Prob Dec ... Coffey's California Probate Decisions [*A publication*] (DLA)
COFFI ...... Commission on Ore-Forming Fluid in Inclusions
Coff Prob... Coffey's California Probate Decisions [*A publication*] (DLA)
CoFFS....... United States Forest Service, Rocky Mountain Forest and Range Experiment Station, Fort Collins, CO [*Library symbol*] [*Library of Congress*] (LCLS)
CoFGS .... Church of Jesus Christ of Latter-Day Saints, Genealogical Society Library, Fort Collins Branch, Fort Collins, CO [*Library symbol*] [*Library of Congress*] (LCLS)
COFHE....... Consortium on Financing Higher Education (EA)
CoFHP....... Hewlett-Packard Co., Fort Collins Division, Fort Collins, CO [*Library symbol*] [*Library of Congress*] (LCLS)
COFI......... Charter One Finance, Inc. [*NASDAQ symbol*] (NQ)
COFI......... Checkout and Fault Isolation [*NASA*] (KSC)
COFI......... Committee on Fisheries [*Food and Agriculture Organization*]
COFI......... Confidential (FAAC)
COFI......... Cost of Funds Index [*Banking*]
CoFI.......... Ideal Cement Co. Research Library, Fort Collins, CO [*Library symbol*] [*Library of Congress*] (LCLS)
COFICOMEX ... Compagnie Financiere pour le Commerce Exterieur [*Financial Foreign Trade Company*] [*French*]
COFIDS .... Coherent Optical Fingerprint Identification System (MCD)
COFIL....... Core File (IEEE)
COFIMER ... Compagnie Financiere pour l'Outre-Mer [*Overseas Finance Company*] [*French*]
COFL........ Committee on Federal Laboratories [*Federal Council for Science and Technology*] [*Terminated, 1976*] (EGAO)
CoFla .... Flagler Community Library, Flagler, CO [*Library symbol*] [*Library of Congress*] (LCLS)
CoFle......... Fleming Community Library, Fleming, CO [*Library symbol*] [*Library of Congress*] (LCLS)
CoFlo .... Florence Public Library, Florence, CO [*Library symbol*] [*Library of Congress*] (LCLS)
CoFloV....... Colorado State Veterans Nursing Home, Florence, CO [*Library symbol*] [*Library of Congress*] (LCLS)
CoFlu .... Fort Lupton Public Library, Fort Lupton, CO [*Library symbol*] [*Library of Congress*] (LCLS)
COFML..... Coffee Mill
COFO .... Committee on Forestry [*Food and Agricultural Organization*] [*United Nations*]
COFO .... Council of Federated Organizations [*Also, CFO*] [*Defunct*]
COFOA ..... Companions of the Forest of America [*New York, NY*] (EA)
COFORD .. Chief of Ordnance [*Army*]
CoFow .... Fowler Public Library, Fowler, CO [*Library symbol*] [*Library of Congress*] (LCLS)
Cof Pro....... Coffey's California Probate Decisions [*A publication*] (DLA)
Cof Prob..... Coffey's California Probate Decisions [*A publication*] (DLA)
Cof Prob Dec (Cal) ... Coffey's California Probate Decisions [*A publication*] (DLA)
COFR .... Certificate of Flight Readiness [*NASA*] (NASA)
COFR .... Commercial Fisheries Review [*Later, Marine Fisheries Review*] [*A publication*]
CoFr........... Summit County Public Library, Frisco, CO [*Library symbol*] [*Library of Congress*] (LCLS)
CoFra .... Fraser Public Library, Fraser, CO [*Library symbol*] [*Library of Congress*] (LCLS)
COFRAM ... Control Fragmentation Munitions (CINC)
COFRC...... Chevron Oil Field Research Company
COFRON .. Coastal Frontier [*Coast Guard*]
COFRS...... Computerized Freight Remittance System [*Pronounced "coffers"*]
CoFru......... Fruita Public Library, Fruita, CO [*Library symbol*] [*Library of Congress*] (LCLS)
CoFruFE.... Fruita Elementary School, Fruita, CO [*Library symbol*] [*Library of Congress*] (LCLS)

CoFruFJ .... Fruita Junior High School, Fruita, CO [*Library symbol*] [*Library of Congress*] (LCLS)
CoFruFM... Fruita Monument High School, Fruita, CO [*Library symbol*] [*Library of Congress*] (LCLS)
CoFruSE.... Shelledy Elementary School, Fruita, CO [*Library symbol*] [*Library of Congress*] (LCLS)
COFS......... Chief of Staff [*Military*]
CoFS.......... Colorado State University, Fort Collins, CO [*Library symbol*] [*Library of Congress*] (LCLS)
COFSA...... Chief of Staff, United States Army [*Later, CSA*]
COFSAF.... Chief of Staff, United States Air Force (NATG)
COFSPTS ... Chief of Support Services [*Army*]
COFT........ Chief of Transportation [*Army*]
COFT........ Commander, Fleet Train
COFT........ Conduct of Fire Trainer [*Army*]
COFTI....... Conduct of Fire Trainer - Improved [*Army*] (MCD)
CoFtLVA ... United States Veterans Administration Hospital, Fort Lyon, CO [*Library symbol*] [*Library of Congress*] (LCLS)
CoFtm........ Fort Morgan Carnegie Public Library, Fort Morgan, CO [*Library symbol*] [*Library of Congress*] (LCLS)
CoFtmM .... Morgan County Community College, Fort Morgan, CO [*Library symbol*] [*Library of Congress*] (LCLS)
COFW .... Certificate of Flight Worthiness [*NASA*] (KSC)
COG.......... Cabot Oil & Gas Class A [*NYSE symbol*] (SPSG)
COG.......... Canadian Organic Growers
COG.......... Center of Gravity
COG.......... Chief of Government
CO & G...... Chocktaw, Oklahoma & Gulf Railroad
CO & G...... Clinical Obstetrics and Gynecology [*A publication*]
COG.......... Coal-Oil-Gas [*Fuel mixture*]
COG.......... Cognac (ADA)
COG.......... Cognate (ROG)
Cog............ Cognition [*The Hague*] [*A publication*]
COG.......... Cognizant (NG)
COG.......... Coke Oven Gas
CoG........... Colorado School of Mines, Golden, CO [*Library symbol*] [*Library of Congress*] (LCLS)
COG.......... Commander of the Guard [*Military*]
COG.......... Commissural Ganglion [*Neurology*]
COG.......... Compact Orbital Gears Ltd.
COG.......... Computer Operations Group
COG.......... Condoto [*Colombia*] [*Airport symbol*] (OAG)
COG.......... Congo [*ANSI three-letter standard code*] (CNC)
COG.......... Continuity of Government
COG.......... Control Orbitron Gauge
COG.......... Convenience of the Government
COG.......... Coordinator General (ADA)
COG.......... Council of Governments [*Voluntary organizations of municipalities and counties*]
COG.......... Course Made Good over the Ground [*Military*] (NVT)
COG.......... Covenant of the Goddess (EA)
COG.......... Credit Officers Group (EA)
COG.......... Current Operational Group [*NATO*] (NATG)
COG.......... Customer-Owned Goods
COG.......... Garfield County System, New Castle, CO [*OCLC symbol*] (OCLC)
Co G .... Reports and Cases of Practice in Common Pleas Tempore Anne, George I, and George II, by Sir G. Coke [*Same as Cooke's Practice Reports*] [*1706-47*] [*England*] [*A publication*] (DLA)
CoGA .... AMAX, Inc., Golden, CO [*Library symbol*] [*Library of Congress*] (LCLS)
COGAP ..... Combustion Gas Analyzer Program [*Nuclear energy*] (NRCH)
COGARD .. Coast Guard
COGAS ...... Coal [*into*] Gas [*Process*]
COGAT ..... Cognitive Abilities Test [*Academic achievement and aptitude test*]
COGB .... Certified Official Government Business
COGCA ..... Century Oil/Gas Cl A [*NASDAQ symbol*] (NQ)
COGCA ..... Chemistry, Oil, and Gas in Romania [*A publication*]
COGD........ Cogdean [*England*]
CoGD......... Dow Chemical Co., Rocky Flats Division, Golden, CO [*Library symbol*] [*Library of Congress*] (LCLS)
COGECA .. Comite General de la Cooperation Agricole de la CE [*General Committee of Agricultural Cooperation in the EC*] (EAIO)
COGEL...... Council on Governmental Ethics Laws (EA)
COGENE .. Committee on Genetic Experimentation [*ICSU*]
COGENT .. Compiler and Generalized Translator [*Argonne National Laboratory*] [*List processor*] (IEEE)
COGENT .. Cooperative Generic Technology [*Centers for cooperative government and industry work*]
CoGeo .... John Tomay Memorial Public Library, Georgetown, CO [*Library symbol*] [*Library of Congress*] (LCLS)
COGEODATA ... Commission on Storage, Automatic Processing, and Retrieval of Geological Data (EAIO)
COGG........ Coggeshall [*England*]
CoGG .... Golden Gate Youth Camp, Residents' Library, Golden, CO [*Library symbol*] [*Library of Congress*] (LCLS)
Cogh Epit... Coghlan's Epitome of Hindu Law Cases [*A publication*] (DLA)
COGI .... Children's Own Garden International [*See also BjBI*] (EAIO)

CoGJ.......... Jefferson County Library, Golden, CO [*Library symbol*] [*Library of Congress*] (LCLS)
CoGj.......... Mesa County Public Library, Grand Junction, CO [*Library symbol*] [*Library of Congress*] (LCLS)
CoGjAE ..... Appleton Elementary School, Grand Junction, CO [*Library symbol*] [*Library of Congress*] (LCLS)
CoGjBoJ .... Bookcliff Junior High School, Grand Junction, CO [*Library symbol*] [*Library of Congress*] (LCLS)
CoGjBrE .... Broadway Elementary School, Grand Junction, CO [*Library symbol*] [*Library of Congress*] (LCLS)
CoGjCeH ... Central High School, Grand Junction, CO [*Library symbol*] [*Library of Congress*] (LCLS)
CoGjCoE.... Columbine Elementary School, Grand Junction, CO [*Library symbol*] [*Library of Congress*] (LCLS)
CoGjCsE .... Columbus Elementary School, Grand Junction, CO [*Library symbol*] [*Library of Congress*] (LCLS)
CoGjEJ ...... East Junior High School, Grand Junction, CO [*Library symbol*] [*Library of Congress*] (LCLS)
CoGjFE...... Fruitvale Elementary School, Grand Junction, CO [*Library symbol*] [*Library of Congress*] (LCLS)
CoGJ-G ..... Golden Regional Library (J. Lester Trezise Regional Library), Golden, CO [*Library symbol*] [*Library of Congress*] (LCLS)
CoGjGH.... Grand Junction High School, Grand Junction, CO [*Library symbol*] [*Library of Congress*] (LCLS)
CoGjGS ..... Church of Jesus Christ of Latter-Day Saints, Genealogical Society Library, Grand Junction Branch, Stake Center, Grand Junction, CO [*Library symbol*] [*Library of Congress*] (LCLS)
CoGjLOE... Lincoln Orchard Mesa Elementary School, Grand Junction, CO [*Library symbol*] [*Library of Congress*] (LCLS)
CoGjLPE ... Lincoln Park Elementary School, Grand Junction, CO [*Library symbol*] [*Library of Congress*] (LCLS)
CoGjM .... Mesa College, Grand Junction, CO [*Library symbol*] [*Library of Congress*] (LCLS)
CoGjME .... Mesa View Elementary School Library, Grand Junction, CO [*Library symbol*] [*Library of Congress*] (LCLS)
CoGjNE ..... Nisley Elementary School, Grand Junction, CO [*Library symbol*] [*Library of Congress*] (LCLS)
CoGjOAE .. Orchard Avenue Elementary School, Grand Junction, CO [*Library symbol*] [*Library of Congress*] (LCLS)
CoGjOMJ ... Orchard Mesa Junior High School, Grand Junction, CO [*Library symbol*] [*Library of Congress*] (LCLS)
CoGjPE...... Pomona Elementary School, Grand Junction, CO [*Library symbol*] [*Library of Congress*] (LCLS)
CoGjRE ..... Riverside Elementary School, Grand Junction, CO [*Library symbol*] [*Library of Congress*] (LCLS)
CoGjSD ..... School District No. 51, Special Services Media Materials, Grand Junction, CO [*Library symbol*] [*Library of Congress*] (LCLS)
CoGjSD-P ... School District No. 51, Professional Library, Grand Junction, CO [*Library symbol*] [*Library of Congress*] (LCLS)
CoGjSD-V .. School District No. 51, Vocational Department, Grand Junction, CO [*Library symbol*] [*Library of Congress*] (LCLS)
CoGjSE...... Scenic Elementary School, Grand Junction, CO [*Library symbol*] [*Library of Congress*] (LCLS)
CoGjT .... Colorado State Home and Training School, Grand Junction, CO [*Library symbol*] [*Library of Congress*] (LCLS)
CoGjTE...... Tope Elementary School, Grand Junction, CO [*Library symbol*] [*Library of Congress*] (LCLS)
CoGjThE ... Thunder Mountain Elementary School Library, Grand Junction, CO [*Library symbol*] [*Library of Congress*] (LCLS)
CoGjTS...... Colorado State Home and Training School, Staff Library, Grand Junction, CO [*Library symbol*] [*Library of Congress*] (LCLS)
CoGjUC ..... Union Carbide Corp., Grand Junction, CO [*Library symbol*] [*Library of Congress*] (LCLS)
CoGjW .... Colorado State Library, Western Slope Clearinghouse, Grand Junction, CO [*Library symbol*] [*Library of Congress*] (LCLS)
CoGjWE .... Wingate Elementary School Library, Grand Junction, CO [*Library symbol*] [*Library of Congress*] (LCLS)
CoGjWJ..... West Junior High School, Grand Junction, CO [*Library symbol*] [*Library of Congress*] (LCLS)
CoGJY .... Jefferson County Youth Center, Golden, CO [*Library symbol*] [*Library of Congress*] (LCLS)
CoGl.......... Grand Lake Public Library, Grand Lake, CO [*Library symbol*] [*Library of Congress*] (LCLS)
COGLA ..... Canada Oil and Gas Lands Administration
COGLAC Newsl ... COGLAC [*Coal Gasification, Liquefaction, and Conversion to Electricity*] Newsletter [*A publication*]
CoGLM ..... Lookout Mountain School for Boys, Golden, CO [*Library symbol*] [*Library of Congress*] (LCLS)
COGME .... Council for Opportunity in Graduate Management Education [*Cambridge, MA*] (EA)
COGN........ Cognos, Inc. [*NASDAQ symbol*] (NQ)
Cognitive Psychol ... Cognitive Psychology [*A publication*]
Cognit Rehabil ... Cognitive Rehabilitation [*A publication*]
Cognit Sci... Cognitive Science [*A publication*]

Cognit Ther Res ... Cognitive Therapy and Research [*A publication*]
COGNOSYS ... Cognitive Operating System [*NASA*]
COGN W... Cognate With (ROG)
COGO....... Commercially Owned, Government-Operated (AFIT)
COGO....... Coordinated Geometry [*Programming language*] [*1957*] (CSR)
CoGO......... Oil Shale Corp., Research Center Library, Golden, CO [*Library symbol*] [*Library of Congress*] (LCLS)
COGOG..... Combined Gas Turbine or Gas Turbine Propulsion
COGP........ Commission on Government Procurement [*Terminated, 1973*]
Cog Psyc .... Cognitive Psychology [*A publication*]
Cog Psychol ... Cognitive Psychology [*A publication*]
COGR .... [*The*] Colonial Group, Inc. [*Boston, MA*] [*NASDAQ symbol*] (NQ)
COGR........ Council on Governmental Relations (EA)
CoGr .... Greeley Public Library, Greeley, CO [*Library symbol*] [*Library of Congress*] (LCLS)
CoGR .... Rockwell International Corp., Atomics International Division, Rocky Flats Plant, Golden, CO [*Library symbol*] [*Library of Congress*] (LCLS)
CoGrA........ Aims College, Greeley, CO [*Library symbol*] [*Library of Congress*] (LCLS)
CoGra .... Granada Public Library, Granada, CO [*Library symbol*] [*Library of Congress*] (LCLS)
CoGranG ... Grand County Public Library, Granby Branch, Granby, CO [*Library symbol*] [*Library of Congress*] (LCLS)
CoGrR........ Rocky Mountain Special Education Instructional Materials Center, Greeley, CO [*Library symbol*] [*Library of Congress*] (LCLS)
CoGrU .... University of Northern Colorado, Greeley, CO [*Library symbol*] [*Library of Congress*] (LCLS)
CoGrW ...... Weld County Library, Greeley, CO [*Library symbol*] [*Library of Congress*] (LCLS)
COGS .... Church of Jesus Christ of Latter-Day Saints, Genealogical Society Library, Oakland Branch, Oakland, CA [*Library symbol*] [*Library of Congress*] (LCLS)
COGS .... Combat-Oriented General Support [*Army*]
COGS .... Committee on General Staffing [*Australia*]
COGS .... Commodity Oriented General Support
COGS .... Computer Oriented Geological Society [*Database producer*] (IID)
COGS .... Consumer Goods System [*Data processing*]
COGS .... Continuous Orbital Guidance System
COGS .... Cost of Goods Sold
COGS .... Council of Graphological Societies (EA)
CoGs .... Glenwood Springs Public Library, Glenwood Springs, CO [*Library symbol*] [*Library of Congress*] (LCLS)
COGSA ..... Carriage of Goods by Sea Act [*Shipping*]
CoGsC........ Colorado Mountain College, Western Campus, Glenwood Springs, CO [*Library symbol*] [*Library of Congress*] (LCLS)
COGSC..... Combat-Oriented General Support Center (MCD)
CoGSE .... Solar Energy Research Institute, Golden, CO [*Library symbol*] [*Library of Congress*] (LCLS)
COGSO ..... Northern Territory Council of Government School Organisations [*Australia*]
CoGT .... Tosco Corp., Technical Information Center, Golden, CO [*Library symbol*] [*Library of Congress*] (LCLS)
COGTT ...... Cortisone [*Primed*] Oral Glucose Tolerance Test [*Medicine*]
CoGu.......... Gunnison County Public Library, Gunnison, CO [*Library symbol*] [*Library of Congress*] (LCLS)
CoGuW ...... Western State College of Colorado, Gunnison, CO [*Library symbol*] [*Library of Congress*] (LCLS)
CoGwGS .... Gateway School, Gateway, CO [*Library symbol*] [*Library of Congress*] (LCLS)
CoGy .... Gypsum Community Library, Gypsum, CO [*Library symbol*] [*Library of Congress*] (LCLS)
COGYA ..... Clinical Obstetrics and Gynecology [*A publication*]
COGYAK .. Clinical Obstetrics and Gynecology [*A publication*]
CoGyS........ Sweetwater Library, Gypsum, CO [*Library symbol*] [*Library of Congress*] (LCLS)
COH .... Alameda County Health Department, Oakland, CA [*Library symbol*] [*Library of Congress*] (LCLS)
COH .... Carbohydrate
COH .... Carrier Overhaul (MCD)
COH .... Center for Occupational Hazards (EA)
COH .... Christelijk Oosten en Hereniging [*A publication*]
COH .... Cochiti [*New Mexico*] [*Seismograph station code, US Geological Survey*] (SEIS)
COH .... Coefficient of Haze [*Environment*]
COH .... Coheir [*Joint heir*] [*Genealogy*]
COH .... Coherence [*Statistics*]
COH .... Coho Resources Ltd. [*Toronto Stock Exchange symbol*]
COH .... Cohu, Inc. [*AMEX symbol*] (SPSG)
COH .... Commercial Helicopters, Inc. [*New Iberia, LA*] [*FAA designator*]
COH .... Compensatory Ovarian Hypertrophy [*Endocrinology*]
COH .... Complex Overhaul (NVT)
COH .... Computer Operator Handbook
COH .... Control of Official Histories [*British*]
COH .... Corporal of Horse [*British military*] (DMA)

COH .... United States Air Force Academy, USAF Academy, CO [*OCLC symbol*] (OCLC)
COHA ...... Canadian Oldtimers Hockey Association
COHA ...... Canadian Oral History Association [*See also SCHO*]
COHA ...... Council on Hemispheric Affairs (EA)
CoHa .... Haxtun Public Library, Haxtun, CO [*Library symbol*] [*Library of Congress*] (LCLS)
COHAJ .... Canadian Oral History Association. Journal/Societe Canadienne d'Histoire Orale. Journal [*A publication*]
CoHay........ Hayden Public Library, Hayden, CO [*Library symbol*] [*Library of Congress*] (LCLS)
COHB........ Carboxyhemoglobin [*Biochemistry*]
COHbA ..... Carboxyhemoglobin A [*Biochemistry*]
Co Hd......... Coral Head [*Quality of the bottom*] [*Nautical charts*]
COHE........ College of Osteopathic Healthcare Executives (EA)
COHEB .... Community Health (Bristol) [*A publication*]
COHEBY .. Community Health [*Bristol*] [*A publication*]
Cohen Adm Law ... Cohen's Admiralty Jurisdiction, Law, and Practice [*A publication*] (DLA)
COHETA .. Conseil pour l'Homologation des Etablissements Theologiques en Afrique [*Accrediting Council for Theological Education in Africa - ACTEA*] (EAIO)
CoHi .... Colorado State Historical Society, Denver, CO [*Library symbol*] [*Library of Congress*] (LCLS)
COHI .... Consumers Organization for the Hearing Impaired [*Defunct*] (EA)
COHI......... Crippled and Other Health Impaired [*Obsolete*]
CoHlV........ Colorado State Veterans Center, Homelake, CO [*Library symbol*] [*Library of Congress*] (LCLS)
COHMAP ... Cooperative Holocene Mapping Project [*Geology*]
CO HO ...... Coffee House (ROG)
COHO........ Coherent Oscillator [*RADAR*]
CO HO ...... Copyhold [*British*] [*Legal term*] (ROG)
COHO........ Council of Health Organizations
CO HO ...... Court House [*British*] (ROG)
CoHo.......... Holyoke Public Library, Holyoke, CO [*Library symbol*] [*Library of Congress*] (LCLS)
CoHol........ Women's Civic Club Library, Holly, CO [*Library symbol*] [*Library of Congress*] (LCLS)
COHORT ... Cohesion, Operational Readiness, and Training [*Army*]
CoHotch..... Hotchkiss Public Library, Hotchkiss, CO [*Library symbol*] [*Library of Congress*] (LCLS)
COHQ .... Combined Operations Headquarters [*World War II*]
COHR........ Center for Oral Health Research [*University of Pennsylvania*] [*Research center*] (RCD)
COHR........ Coherent, Inc. [*NASDAQ symbol*] (NQ)
COHRIMS ... Committee on Human Rights in Malaysia and Singapore (EA)
COHS........ Center for Occupational Health and Safety [*University of Waterloo*] [*Research center*] (RCD)
COHS........ Chesapeake and Ohio Historical Society (EA)
COHSE ..... Confederation of Health Service Employees [*Pronounced "cozy"*] [*A union*] [*British*] (DCTA)
CoHsp........ Grand County Public Library, Hot Sulphur Springs, CO [*Library symbol*] [*Library of Congress*] (LCLS)
CoHu.......... Hugo Public Library, Hugo, CO [*Library symbol*] [*Library of Congress*] (LCLS)
CoHud........ Hudson Public Library, Hudson, CO [*Library symbol*] [*Library of Congress*] (LCLS)
COHVENT ... Coherent Event [*Trademark*]
COHY........ Consolidated Hydro, Inc. [*Greenwich, CT*] [*NASDAQ symbol*] (NQ)
COI .... Advisory Committee on the NAIC [*National Astronomy and Ionosphere Center*] Nation-Wide Marine Definition (EA)
COI .... Called Output Image
COI .... Camp of Israel [*Freemasonry*] (ROG)
COI .... Center of Influence [*Military*]
COI .... Central Office of Information [*London, England*]
COI .... Certificate of Incorporation [*Business law*]
COI .... Certificate of Indebtedness [*Finance*]
COI .... Coast Orbital Insertion (MCD)
COI .... Cocoa, FL [*Location identifier*] [*FAA*] (FAAL)
COI .... Coimbra [*Portugal*] [*Geomagnetic observatory code*]
COI .... Coimbra [*Portugal*] [*Seismograph station code, US Geological Survey*] (SEIS)
COI .... Coin Lake Gold Mines Ltd. [*Toronto Stock Exchange symbol*]
COI .... Coin Slot Location [*A publication*]
Co-I .... Coinvestigator
COI .... Commission Oceanographique Intergouvernementale [*Intergovernmental Oceanographic Commission - IOC*] (EAIO)
COI .... Communications Operations Instructions [*Air Force*]
COI .... Community of Interest [*DoD*]
COI .... Conflict of Interest [*Legal term*]
COI .... Conjugi [*To My Spouse*] [*Latin*]
COI .... Conseil Oleicole International [*International Olive Oil Council - IOOC*] (EAIO)
COI .... Contingency Orbit Insertion [*NASA*] (KSC)
COI .... Coordinator of Information
COI .... Course of Instruction [*Military*]
COI .... Cube Order Index Rule
COI .... Iliff School of Theology, Denver, CO [*OCLC symbol*] (OCLC)

COIA .... Conservative Orthopedics International Association (EA)
COIB .... Correctional Officers' Interest Blank [*Screening and placement test*]
COIC .... Careers and Occupational Information Centre (IID)
COIC .... Combat Operations Intelligence Center (MCD)
COIC .... Combined Operational Intelligence Center [*Navy*]
COID .... Council of Industrial Design [*British*]
COIDIEA .. Conseil des Organisations Internationales Directement Interessees a l'Enfance et a l'Adolescence [*Council of International Organizations Directly Interested in Children and Youth*] [*Geneva, Switzerland*] (EAIO)
COIE .... Committee on Invisible Exports [*United Kingdom*] (DS)
COIF .... Charities Official Investment Fund [*Finance*] [*British*]
COIF .... Control of Intensive Farming [*British*]
COlg .... Ignacio Public Library, Ignacio, CO [*Library symbol*] [*Library of Congress*] (LCLS)
COII .... Canadian Occupational Interest Inventory [*Vocational test*]
COIK .... Clear Only if Known [*Buzz words, acronyms, etc., that are clear in context only if already known to the reader*]
COIL .... Central Oil Identification Laboratory [*Coast Guard*] [*Groton, CT*] (MSC)
COIL .... Chemical Oxygen Iodine LASER (MCD)
COIL .... Coast Guard Oil Identification Laboratory [*Groton, CT*]
COIL .... Coiled [*Freight*]
COIL .... Combat Illumination (MCD)
COIL .... Conference of Insurance Legislators [*Later, NCOIL*] (EA)
COIL .... Crude Oil Analyses File [*Petroleum Information Corp.*] [*Information service or system*] (CRD)
COILS ...... CONUS [*Continental United States*] Installation Logistics Support (MCD)
Coil Winding Int ... Coil Winding International [*A publication*]
COIM .... Checkout Interpreter Module (MCD)
COIMAS ... Coimbra Medica [*A publication*]
Coimbra Med ... Coimbra Medica [*A publication*]
Coimbra Med Rev Mens Med Cir ... Coimbra Medica. Revista Mensal de Medicina e Cirurgia [*A publication*]
Coimbra Univ Mus Lab Mineral Geol Mem Not ... Coimbra. Universidade. Museu e Laboratorio Mineralogico e Geologico. Memorias e Noticias. [*Coimbra, Portugal*] [*A publication*]
COIMDV .. Comprehensive Immunology [*A publication*]
COIMEW ... Concepts in Immunopathology [*A publication*]
Co Imo .... Come Primo [*As at First*] [*Music*]
COIMS ...... CONUS [*Continental United States*] Installation Maintenance Support (MCD)
COIN .... California Olive Industry News
COIN .... Central Ohio Interlibrary Network [*Library network*]
COIN .... Coin Phone Operational and Information Network System [*Telecommunications*] (TEL)
COIN .... Committee on Information Needs
COIN .... Community Outreach Information Network
COIN .... Complete Operating Information [*Data processing*]
COIN .... Consumers Opposed to Inflation in the Necessities (EA)
COIN .... Continuation Incentive Pay [*Proposed*] [*Army*]
COIN .... Coordinated Occupational Information Network [*COIN Educational Products*] [*Information service or system*] (IID)
COIN .... Council of Oil-Importing Nations
COIN .... Counterinsurgency
COIN .... First Coinvestors, Inc. [*NASDAQ symbol*] (NQ)
COINAV ... Colloques Internationaux. Centre National de la Recherche Scientifique [*A publication*]
CO IN HES ... Communications and Information Handling Equipment and Services
Coin Medal Bull ... Seaby's Coin and Medal Bulletin [*A publication*]
COINOPS ... Counterinsurgency Operations
Coin Rev ..... Coin Review [*A publication*]
COINS .... Calspan On-Line Information Service [*Calspan Corp.*] [*Information service or system*] (IID)
COINS .... Coinsurance
COINS .... Committee on Improvement of National Statistics [*Inter-American*]
COINS .... Community On-Line Intelligence Network System [*Computer network*] [*National Science Administration and Central Intelligence Agency*]
COINS .... Computer and Information Sciences
COINS .... Control in Information Systems
COINS .... Cooperative Intelligence Network System [*Proposed*] [*Navy*]
Co Inst .... Coke's Institutes [*England*] [*A publication*] (DLA)
Co Inst (Eng) ... Coke's Institutes [*England*] [*A publication*] (DLA)
COINTELPRO ... Counterintelligence Program [*FBI program carried out against political activists from 1956 to 1971*]
COIP .... Current Oil in Place [*Petroleum technology*]
COIR .... Commanders Operational Intelligence Requirements (MCD)
COIs .... Idaho Springs Public Library, Idaho Springs, CO [*Library symbol*] [*Library of Congress*] (LCLS)
COISS ...... CONUS [*Continental United States*] Installation Supply Support (MCD)
COIT .... Central Office of the Industrial Tribunal [*Department of Employment*] [*British*]
COITS ...... CONUS [*Continental United States*] Installation Transportation System (MCD)

COITU ...... Confederation of Insurance Trade Unions [*British*] (DCTA)
COIU .... Congress of Independent Unions
COJ .... Cogesco Mining Resources [*Toronto Stock Exchange symbol*]
COJ .... Commodity Journal [*A publication*]
COJ .... Continental Jet, Inc. [*Palm Springs, CA*] [*FAA designator*] (FAAC)
COJ .... Coonabarabran [*Australia*] [*Airport symbol*] (OAG)
COJ .... Court of Justice
COJAC ...... Committee on Justice and the Constitution (EA)
COJAC ...... Congress of Joke-Abused Cities
COJE .... Central Organization for Jewish Education (EA)
COJM .... Concentrated Orange Juice for Manufacturing
COJO .... Comite Organisateur de Jeux Olympiques [*Organizing Committee of the Olympic Games (1976)*] [*Canada*]
CoJo .... Glenn A. Jones, MD, Memorial Library, Johnstown, CO [*Library symbol*] [*Library of Congress*] (LCLS)
COJOA ..... Colloid Journal of the USSR [*English Translation*] [*A publication*]
COJPA8 ... Colorado Journal of Pharmacy [*A publication*]
CoJu .... Julesburg Public Library, Julesburg, CO [*Library symbol*] [*Library of Congress*] (LCLS)
Co Jurid .... Collectanea Juridica [*England*] [*A publication*] (DLA)
COK .... Cochin [*India*] [*Airport symbol*] (OAG)
COK .... Cook Islands [*ANSI three-letter standard code*] (CNC)
CoK .... Cost of Knowing
COK .... Cous Creek Copper Mines [*Vancouver Stock Exchange symbol*]
CoK .... Elbert County Public Library, Kiowa, CO [*Library symbol*] [*Library of Congress*] (LCLS)
COKCA ..... Coke and Chemistry USSR [*English Translation*] [*A publication*]
COKE .... Coca-Cola Bottling Co. Consolidated [*NASDAQ symbol*] (NQ)
COKE .... Cocaine [*Slang*] (DSUE)
Coke .... Coke's English King's Bench Reports [*1572-1616*] [*A publication*] (DLA)
Coke Chem R ... Coke and Chemistry USSR [*A publication*]
Coke Chem USSR ... Coke and Chemistry USSR [*A publication*]
Coke (Eng) ... Coke's English King's Bench Reports [*1572-1616*] [*A publication*] (DLA)
Coke Ent .... Coke's Book of Entries [*1614*] [*England*] [*A publication*] (DLA)
Coke Inst .... Coke's Institutes [*England*] [*A publication*] (DLA)
Coke Lit ..... Coke on Littleton [*England*] [*A publication*] (DLA)
Coke Res Rep ... Coke Research Report [*England*] [*A publication*]
COKR .... Cooker Restaurant Corp. [*NASDAQ symbol*] (NQ)
CoKr .... Kremmling Public Library, Kremmling, CO [*Library symbol*] [*Library of Congress*] (LCLS)
COKRA ..... Coke Research Report [*A publication*]
COL .... Capsule-Orbiting Bus Link [*NASA*]
COL .... Carry-On Laboratory [*NASA*]
COL .... Chain Overseas Low [*Aviation*]
COL .... Checkout Language [*NASA*] (NASA)
COL .... CircOlectric Bed [*A trademark*] [*Medicine*]
COL .... Citizens for Ocean Law (EA)
COL .... Coherent Optical LASER
COL .... Cola [*or Colatus*] [*Strain*] [*See also COLAT*] [*Pharmacy*]
CO-L .... Colatitude [*Navigation*]
Col .... Coldwell's Reports [*41-47 Tennessee*] [*A publication*] (DLA)
Col .... Coleman's Reports [*99, 101-106, 110-129 Alabama*] [*A publication*] (DLA)
Col .... Coleoptera [*Entomology*]
COL .... Collagen [*Biochemistry*]
COL .... Collar
COL .... Collate
COL .... Collect
COL .... College
COL .... College [*Alaska*] [*Geomagnetic observatory code*]
COL .... College Outpost [*Alaska*] [*Seismograph station code, US Geological Survey*] (SEIS)
COL .... Collegium (ROG)
Col .... Collision (DS)
COL .... Colloidal
Col .... Colloquium. Freien Universitaet [*A publication*]
COL .... Colombia
COL .... Colombia [*ANSI three-letter standard code*] (CNC)
COL .... Colonel [*Military*] (AABC)
COL .... Colonial (ROG)
Col .... Colonist
COL .... Colony
COL .... Color
COL .... Colorado
COL .... Colorado Music Educator [*A publication*]
Col .... Colorado Reports [*A publication*] (DLA)
COL .... Colored
Col .... Colossians [*New Testament book*]
COL .... Colts Neck, NJ [*Location identifier*] [*FAA*] (FAAL)
Col .... Columba [*Constellation*]
COL .... Columbus (ROG)
COL .... Column (AAG)
COL .... Commissioner of Official Languages [*Canada*]
COL .... Communications-Oriented Language

COL .... Computer-Oriented Language [*Programming language*] [*Data processing*]
COL .... Construction and Operating License
COL .... Cornell Linguistic Contributions [*A publication*]
COL .... Corrida Oils Limited [*Toronto Stock Exchange symbol*]
COL .... Cost of Living [*Economics*]
COL .... Council on Occupational Licensing [*Later, NCOL*]   (EA)
COL .... Council on Ocean Law   (EA)
COL .... Counsel
COL .... Crisis on Location [*Psychological test*]
Col .... De Coloribus [*of Aristotle*] [*Classical studies*]   (OCD)
COL .... Lansing Library Service, Oakland, CA [*Library symbol*] [*Library of Congress*]   (LCLS)
COL .... Loretto Heights College, Denver, CO [*OCLC symbol*]   (OCLC)
ColA .... Coloquio Artes [*A publication*]
COLA .... Committee on Library Automation [*American Library Association*]
COLA .... Constant-Output Level Adapter
COLA .... Cost of Living Adjustment
COLA .... Cost of Living Allowance [*Economics*]
COLAA ...... Coal Age [*A publication*]
COLAC ...... Central Organization of Liaison for Allocation of Circuit   (NATG)
COLAC ...... Confederacion Latinoamericana de Cooperativas de Ahorro y Credito [*Latin American Confederation of Savings and Loan Cooperatives*]   (EAIO)
CoLaf .... Lafayette Public Library, Lafayette, CO [*Library symbol*] [*Library of Congress*]   (LCLS)
CoLak .... Lakewood Regional Library, Lakewood, CO [*Library symbol*] [*Library of Congress*]   (LCLS)
CoLakJ ...... Jefferson County School District R-1, Library Media Processing, Lakewood, CO [*Library symbol*] [*Library of Congress*]   (LCLS)
CoLam .... Lamar Carnegie Public Library, Lamar, CO [*Library symbol*] [*Library of Congress*]   (LCLS)
CoLamC ..... Lamar Community College, Lamar, CO [*Library symbol*] [*Library of Congress*]   (LCLS)
COL-AMCHAM ... Colombian-American Chamber of Commerce   (EA)
COLANFORASCU ... Commanding Officer, Landing Force Air Support Control Unit
Col App ...... Colorado Appeals Reports [*A publication*]   (DLA)
CoLas .... Las Animas Public Library, Las Animas, CO [*Library symbol*] [*Library of Congress*]   (LCLS)
CoLasA ...... Lower Arkansas Valley Regional Library, Las Animas, CO [*Library symbol*] [*Library of Congress*]   (LCLS)
COLASL ... Compiler, Los Alamos Scientific Laboratories
COLAT ...... Colatus [*Strained*] [*See also COL*] [*Pharmacy*]
CoLav .... LaVeta Public Library, LaVeta, CO [*Library symbol*] [*Library of Congress*]   (LCLS)
ColBG .... Collationes Brugenses et Gandavenses [*Brugge*] [*A publication*]
ColBiQ .... College of the Bible. Quarterly [*Lexington, KY*] [*A publication*]
Colb Pr ...... Colby's Practice [*A publication*]   (DLA)
Colburn ...... Colburn's New Monthly Magazine [*A publication*]
Col Bus Rev ... Colorado Business Review [*A publication*]
Colby Libr ... Colby Library. Quarterly [*A publication*]
COL C .... Col Canto [*With the Melody*] [*Music*]
COLC .... Colorado National Bankshares, Inc. [*NASDAQ symbol*]   (NQ)
COLC .... Cost of Living Council [*Also, CLC*] [*Terminated, 1974*]
CoLc .... Lake City Public Library, Lake City, CO [*Library symbol*] [*Library of Congress*]   (LCLS)
COLC .... Laney College, Oakland, CA [*Library symbol*] [*Library of Congress*]   (LCLS)
Col & Cai ... Coleman and Caines' Cases [*New York*] [*A publication*]   (DLA)
Col & Cai Cas ... Coleman and Caines' Cases [*New York*] [*A publication*]   (DLA)
Col & Caines Cas (NY) ... Coleman and Caines' Cases [*New York*] [*A publication*]   (DLA)
Col Cas ...... Coleman's Cases of Practice [*New York*] [*A publication*]   (DLA)
Col Cas (NY) ... Coleman's Cases of Practice [*New York*] [*A publication*]   (DLA)
COLCAT ... College Cataloguing   (ADA)
Col CC .... Collyer's English Chancery Cases [*1845-47*] [*A publication*]   (DLA)
Col & C Cas ... Coleman and Caines' Cases [*New York*] [*A publication*]   (DLA)
COLCEL ... Columbia Cellulose [*Company*] [*Canada*]
ColcFranc ... Collectanea Franciscana [*Rome*] [*A publication*]
COLCH ... Colchester [*Municipal borough in England*]
Colchester Archaeol Group Annu Bull ... Colchester Archaeological Group. Annual Bulletin [*A publication*]
COLCIENCIAS ... Fondo Colombiano de Investigaciones Cientificas y Proyectos Especiales [*Colombian Fund for Scientific Research and Special Projects*] [*Bogota*] [*Information service or system*]   (IID)
ColCM .... Colby College. Monographs [*A publication*]
Col Comp & Comm ... College Composition and Communication [*A publication*]
Col Crim Law ... Colby's Criminal Law and Practice [*New York*] [*A publication*]   (DLA)
ColctCist .... Collectanea Cisterciensa [*Forges, Belgium*] [*A publication*]

ColcTFujen ... Collectanea Theologica Universitatis Fujen [*Taipei, Taiwan*] [*A publication*]
ColctMech ... Collectanea Mechlinensia [*Mechelen, Belgium*] [*A publication*]
ColctT .... Collectanea Theologica [*Warsaw*] [*A publication*]
COLD .... Chronic Obstructive Lung Disease [*Medicine*]
COLD .... Coherent Light Detector
Cold .... Coldwell's Tennessee Supreme Court Reports [*1860-70*] [*A publication*]   (DLA)
COLD .... Collated   (ROG)
COLD .... Colored   (ROG)
Cold Reg Sci Technol ... Cold Regions Science and Technology [*Netherlands*] [*A publication*]
Cold S Harb ... Cold Spring Harbor Symposia on Quantitative Biology [*A publication*]
Colds Pr ..... Coldstream's Scotch Court of Session Procedure [*A publication*]   (DLA)
Cold Spr Harb Symp ... Cold Spring Harbor Symposia on Quantitative Biology [*A publication*]
Cold Spring Harbor Conf Cell Proliferation ... Cold Spring Harbor Conference on Cell Proliferation [*A publication*]
Cold Spring Harbor Monogr Ser ... Cold Spring Harbor Monograph Series [*A publication*]
Cold Spring Harbor Rep Neurosci ... Cold Spring Harbor Reports in the Neurosciences [*A publication*]
Cold Spring Harbor Symp Quant Biol ... Cold Spring Harbor Symposia on Quantitative Biology [*A publication*]
Cold Spring Harbor Symp Quantit Biol ... Cold Spring Harbor Symposia on Quantitative Biology [*A publication*]
Cold Spring Harb Symp Quant Biol ... Cold Spring Harbor Symposia on Quantitative Biology [*A publication*]
Cold Storage Prod Rev ... Cold Storage and Produce Review [*A publication*]
Cold (Tenn) ... Coldwell's Reports [*41-47 Tennessee*] [*A publication*]   (DLA)
Coldw .... Coldwell's Reports [*41-47 Tennessee*] [*A publication*]   (DLA)
Coldwell ..... Coldwell's Reports [*41-47 Tennessee*] [*A publication*]   (DLA)
Coldw (Tenn) ... Coldwell's Reports [*41-47 Tennessee*] [*A publication*]   (DLA)
COLE .... Coefficient of Linear Extensibility
Cole .... Coleman's Reports [*99, 101-106, 110-129 Alabama*] [*A publication*]   (DLA)
Cole .... Cole's Edition of Iowa Reports [*A publication*]   (DLA)
COLE .... College of Our Lady of the Elms [*Chicopee, MA*]
CoLe .... Lake County Public Library, Leadville, CO [*Library symbol*] [*Library of Congress*]   (LCLS)
CoLeC .... Colorado Mountain College, Eastern Campus, Leadville, CO [*Library symbol*] [*Library of Congress*]   (LCLS)
Colec Agropec Inst Nac Tec Agropec (Argentina) ... Coleccion Agropecuaria. Instituto Nacional de Tecnologia Agropecuaria (Argentina) [*A publication*]
Cole & Cai Cas ... Coleman and Caines' Cases [*New York*] [*A publication*]   (DLA)
Colecao....... Colecao das Leis [*Brazil*] [*A publication*]
Cole Cas...... Coleman's Cases [*New York*] [*A publication*]   (DLA)
Cole Cases ... Coleman's Cases [*New York*] [*A publication*]   (DLA)
Cole Cas Pr ... Coleman's Cases [*New York*] [*A publication*]   (DLA)
Coleccion Estud CIEPLAN ... Coleccion Estudios CIEPLAN [*Corporacion de Investigaciones Economicas para Latinoamerica*] [*A publication*]
Colec Monograf Mem Mat ... Coleccion de Monografias y Memorias de Matematicas [*A publication*]
COLECO... Connecticut Leather Company [*Original name of Coleco Industries*]
Cole Cond .. Cole. Particulars and Conditions of Sale [*1879*] [*A publication*]   (DLA)
Cole Cr Inf ... Cole. Criminal Informations [*1843*] [*A publication*]   (DLA)
Colect Monogr Bot Biol Veg ... Collection de Monographies de Botanique et de Biologie Vegetale [*A publication*]
COLED ..... Combat Loss and Expenditure Data   (MCD)
Cole Dig ..... Colebrooke's Digest of Hindu Law [*A publication*]   (DLA)
COLED-V ... Combat Loss and Expenditure Data - Vietnam
Cole Ejec .... Cole. Ejectment [*1857*] [*A publication*]   (DLA)
Cole Eject... Cole. Ejectment [*1857*] [*A publication*]   (DLA)
ColeFranc .. Collectanea Franciscana [*Rome*] [*A publication*]
Colem .... Coleman's Cases [*New York*] [*A publication*]   (DLA)
Coleman..... Coleman's Cases [*New York*] [*A publication*]   (DLA)
Colem Cas ... Coleman's Cases [*New York*] [*A publication*]   (DLA)
Colem & C Cas ... Coleman and Caines' Cases [*New York*] [*A publication*]   (DLA)
ColEng .... College English [*A publication*]
COLENT..... Colentur [*Let Them Be Strained*] [*Pharmacy*]   (ROG)
Coleopt Bull ... Coleopterists' Bulletin [*A publication*]
Coleopts Bull ... Coleopterists' Bulletin [*A publication*]
COLEPAC ... Continuing Library Education Planning and Advisory Project
COLER........ Coleridge [*England*]
Coler .... [*Matthias*] Colerus [*Deceased, 1587*] [*Authority cited in pre-1607 legal work*]   (DSA)
COLET........ Coletur [*Let It Be Strained*] [*Pharmacy*]
ColeT .... Collectanea Theologica [*Warsaw*] [*A publication*]
Coletanea Inst Tecnol Aliment ... Coletanea. Instituto de Tecnologia de Alimentos [*A publication*]
Colet Inst Tecnol Aliment ... Coletanea. Instituto de Tecnologia de Alimentos [*A publication*]
ColetMech ... Collectanea Mechlinensia [*Mechelen, Belgium*] [*A publication*]

COLEX...... CIRC [*Central Information Reference and Control*] Online Experiment
COLEX...... Control of Logistics Expense [*USAREUR*] (MCD)
ColF.......... Columbia Forum [*A publication*]
Col Farm.... Colegio Farmaceutico [*A publication*]
COLG........ Cold Leg [*Nuclear energy*]
ColG.......... Collationes Gandavenses [*A publication*]
ColGer....... Colloquia Germanica [*A publication*]
COLGTH .. Cone Length [*Botany*]
CoLH......... Loretto Heights College, Denver, CO [*Library symbol*] [*Library of Congress*] (LCLS)
Col Hist Soc Rec ... Columbia Historical Society. Records [*A publication*]
Col Hum RL Rev ... Columbia Human Rights Law Review [*A publication*]
Col Hu Ri LR ... Columbia Human Rights Law Review [*A publication*]
COLI.......... Colloredo [*Italy*] [*Seismograph station code, US Geological Survey*] (SEIS)
COLI......... Colonel's Island [*AAR code*]
CoLi.......... Comparative Literature [*A publication*]
COLI......... Cost-of-Living Index [*Economics*]
CoLi.......... Edwin A. Bemis Public Library, Littleton, CO [*Library symbol*] [*Library of Congress*] (LCLS)
CoLiA .... Arapahoe Regional Library District, Littleton, CO [*Library symbol*] [*Library of Congress*] (LCLS)
CoLiAJ ...... Arapahoe Community College, Littleton, CO [*Library symbol*] [*Library of Congress*] (LCLS)
COLIBI ..... Comite de Liaison des Fabricants de Bicyclettes (EA)
COLIDAR ... Coherent Light Detecting and Ranging [*RADAR*] [*Hughes Aircraft*]
COLIDS .... Coherent Light Detector System (MCD)
CoLiGS...... Church of Jesus Christ of Latter-Day Saints, Genealogical Society Library, Littleton Branch, Littleton, CO [*Library symbol*] [*Library of Congress*] (LCLS)
COLIM...... Collimator (MSA)
CoLim .... Limon Memorial Public Library, Limon, CO [*Library symbol*] [*Library of Congress*] (LCLS)
CoLiM .... Marathon Oil Co., Technical Information Section, Littleton, CO [*Library symbol*] [*Library of Congress*] (LCLS)
COLIME... Comite de Liaison des Industries Metalliques Europeennes
CoLimP...... Plains and Peaks Public Library System, Limon, CO [*Library symbol*] [*Library of Congress*] (LCLS)
COLINGO ... Compile Online and Go [*Data processing*]
Col Interam Defensa R ... Colegio Interamericano de Defensa Revista [*A publication*]
Col Int'l Dr Comp ... Colloque International de Droit Compare [*A publication*] (DLA)
COLIPA .... Comite de Liaison des Associations Europeennes de l'Industrie de la Parfumerie, des Produits Cosmetiques, et de Toilette [*European Federation of the Perfume, Cosmetics, and Toiletries Industry*] (EAIO)
COLIPED ... Comite de Liaison des Fabricants de Pieces et Equipements de Deux Roues des Pays de la CEE [*Liaison Committee of Manufacturers of Parts and Equipment for Two-Wheeled Vehicles*] (EAIO)
CoLiSD...... Arapahoe County School District 6, Littleton, CO [*Library symbol*] [*Library of Congress*] (LCLS)
Co Lit .... Coke on Littleton [*England*] [*A publication*] (DLA)
Co Litt........ Coke on Littleton [*England*] [*A publication*] (DLA)
Co Litt........ Commentaries upon Littleton, by Sir Edward Coke [*A publication*] (DLA)
Co Litt (Eng) ... Coke on Littleton [*England*] [*A publication*] (DLA)
Co LJ .... Cochin Law Journal [*A publication*] (DLA)
Co LJ .... Colonial Law Journal [*A publication*] (DLA)
CoLj.......... Woodruff Memorial Library, La Junta, CO [*Library symbol*] [*Library of Congress*] (LCLS)
CoLjaGS.... Church of Jesus Christ of Latter-Day Saints, Genealogical Society Library, LaJara Branch, Stake Center, LaJara, CO [*Library symbol*] [*Library of Congress*] (LCLS)
Col J Environ L ... Columbia Journal of Environmental Law [*A publication*]
Col J Env L ... Columbia Journal of Environmental Law [*A publication*]
Col J L and Soc Prob ... Columbia Journal of Law and Social Problems [*A publication*]
Col JL & Soc Probl ... Columbia Journal of Law and Social Problems [*A publication*]
CoLjO .... Otero Junior College, La Junta, CO [*Library symbol*] [*Library of Congress*] (LCLS)
Col Jour Rev ... Columbia Journalism Review [*A publication*]
ColJR......... Columbia Journalism Review [*A publication*]
Col J Transnat'l L ... Columbia Journal of Transnational Law [*A publication*]
Col J Tr L ... Columbia Journal of Transnational Law [*A publication*]
Col J World Bus ... Columbia Journal of World Business [*A publication*]
COLL......... Collagen [*Biochemistry*]
Coll............ Collarette [*Horticulture*]
COLL......... Collateral
Coll............ Collatio [*Novels of Justinian*] [*A publication*] (DSA)
COLL......... Collato [*Collated*] [*Latin*]
COLL......... Collator
COLL......... Colleague
COLL......... Collect [*or Collection*] (AFM)
Coll............ Collector (DLA)
COLL......... College [*or Collegiate*]

Coll............. Colles' English Parliamentary Cases [*1697-1714*] [*A publication*] (DLA)
COLL......... Colliery
COLL......... Collision [*Insurance*]
COLL......... Colloid
COLL......... Colloquial
Coll............ Colloquium: The Australian and New Zealand Theological Review [*A publication*] (APTA)
Coll........... Collyer's English Chancery Cases [*1845-47*] [*A publication*] (DLA)
COLL......... Collyrium [*Eye Wash*] [*Pharmacy*] (ROG)
Col(L)........ Coloquio (Lisbon) [*A publication*]
COLLAB .. Collaborate (ROG)
COLLAB .. Collaboration (MSA)
Collab Proc Ser Int Inst Appl Syst Anal ... Collaborative Proceedings Series. International Institute for Applied Systems Analysis [*A publication*]
Collagen Relat Res ... Collagen and Related Research [*A publication*]
Coll Agric (Nagpur) Mag ... College of Agriculture (Nagpur). Magazine [*A publication*]
Coll Agric Nat Taiwan Univ Spec Publ ... College of Agriculture. National Taiwan University. Special Publication [*A publication*]
Coll Agric Univ Tehran Bull ... College of Agriculture. University of Tehran. Bulletin [*A publication*]
Coll Alex.... Collectanea Alexandrina [*A publication*] (OCD)
Coll Amis Hist ... Collection. Amis de l'Histoire [*A publication*]
Coll Am Statis Assn ... Collections. American Statistical Association [*A publication*]
Collana Accad Accad Patav Sci Lett Arti ... Collana Accademica. Accademia Patavina di Scienze, Lettere, ed Arti [*A publication*]
Collana Monogr Ateneo Parmense ... Collana di Monografie. Ateneo Parmense [*A publication*]
Collana Monogr Oli Essenz Sui Deri Agrum ... Collana di Monografie sugli Oli Essenziali e Sui Derivati Agrumari [*A publication*]
Collana Monogr Rass Med Sarda ... Collana di Monografie di Rassegna Medica Sarda [*A publication*]
Collana Verde Minist Agric For (Roma) ... Collana Verde. Ministero dell'Agricoltura e della Foreste (Roma) [*A publication*]
Coll Antropol ... Collegium Antropologicum [*A publication*]
Coll Art J ... College Art Journal [*A publication*]
COLLAT ... Collateral [*Finance*]
ColLat........ Collection Latomus [*A publication*]
Col Law Rep ... Colorado Law Reporter [*A publication*] (DLA)
Col Law Rev ... Columbia Law Review [*A publication*] (ILCA)
Col Law Review ... Columbia Law Review [*A publication*]
Coll Bank ... Collier's Law of Bankruptcy [*A publication*] (DLA)
Coll Bd R ... College Board Review [*A publication*]
CollBrugGand ... Collationes Brugenses et Gandavenses [*Gent, Belgium*] [*A publication*]
Coll Caus Cel ... Collection des Causes Celebres [*French*] [*A publication*] (DLA)
Coll CC ...... Collyer's Chancery Cases Tempore Bruce, V-C [*63 English Reprint*] [*1844-45*] [*A publication*] (ILCA)
Coll Cist ..... Collectanea Cisterciensia [*A publication*]
Coll Comp & Comm ... College Composition and Communication [*A publication*]
Coll Composition & Commun ... College Composition and Communication [*A publication*]
Coll Contr .. Collier's Law of Contribution [*1875*] [*A publication*] (DLA)
Coll Courant ... College Courant [*A publication*]
Coll CR ...... Collyer's English Chancery Reports [*A publication*] (DLA)
COLL & CR A ... Collection and Credit Agency (DLA)
Coll Czech ... Collection of Czechoslovak Chemical Communications [*A publication*]
Coll Czech Chem Communications ... Collection of Czechoslovak Chemical Communications [*A publication*]
COLLD...... Collated (ROG)
COLLD...... Collected (ROG)
ColldeClercq ... Collection De Clercq. Catalogue Methodique et Raisonne: Antiquites Assyriens [*A publication*] (BJA)
Coll Dir Etudes Rech Elec France ... Collection. Direction des Etudes et Recherches d'Electricite de France [*A publication*]
CollE.......... College English [*A publication*]
Coll & E Bank ... Collier and Eaton's American Bankruptcy Reports [*A publication*] (DLA)
Collec Czechosl Chem Commun ... Collection of Czechoslovak Chemical Communications [*A publication*]
Coll Ecole Norm Sup Jeunes Filles ... Collection. Ecole Normale Superieure de Jeunes Filles [*A publication*]
Coll d'Ecologie ... Collection d'Ecologie [*A publication*]
COLLECT ... Collectively (ROG)
COLLECT ... Connecticut On-Line Law-Enforcement Communications and Teleprocessing [*Computer law-enforcement system*]
Collect Biol Evol ... Collection de Biologie Evolutive [*A publication*]
Collect Bot (Barc) ... Collectanea Botanica (Barcelona) [*A publication*]
Collect Breed ... Collecting and Breeding [*A publication*]
Collect Colloq Semin Inst Fr Pet ... Collection. Colloques et Seminaires. Institut Francais du Petrole [*A publication*]
Collect Czech Chem Commun ... Collection of Czechoslovak Chemical Communications [*A publication*]

Collect Czechoslovak Chem Commun ... Collection of Czechoslovak Chemical Communications [*A publication*]
Collect Dir Etudes Rech Elec France ... Collection. Direction des Etudes et Recherches d'Electricite de France [*A publication*]
Collect Ec Fr Rome ... Collection. Ecole Francaise de Rome [*A publication*]
Collect Ecole Norm Sup Jeunes Filles ... Collection. Ecole Normale Superieure de Jeunes Filles [*A publication*]
Collect Ecologie ... Collection d'Ecologie [*A publication*]
Collected Studies Ser ... Collected Studies Series [*London*] [*A publication*]
Collect Enseignement Sci ... Collection Enseignement des Sciences [*A publication*]
Collect Grands Probl Biol Monogr ... Collection "Les Grands Problemes de la Biologie." Monographie [*A publication*]
Collective Bargaining Negot & Cont BNA ... Collective Bargaining, Negotiations, and Contracts. Bureau of National Affairs [*A publication*]
Collect Math ... Collectanea Mathematica [*A publication*]
Collect Monogr Bot Biol Veg ... Collection de Monographies de Botanique et de Biologie Vegetale [*A publication*]
Collect Pap Annu Symp Fundam Cancer Res ... Collection of Papers Presented at the Annual Symposium on Fundamental Cancer Research [*A publication*]
Collect Pap Changchun Inst Appl Chem Acad Sin ... Collected Papers. Changchun Institute of Applied Chemistry. Academia Sinica [*A publication*]
Collect Pap Earth Sci Nagoya Univ Dep Earth Sci ... Collected Papers on Earth Sciences. Nagoya University. Department of Earth Sciences [*A publication*]
Collect Papers Lister Inst Prevent Med ... Collected Papers. Lister Institute of Preventive Medicine [*A publication*]
Collect Papers Math Soc Wakayama Univ ... Collected Papers. Mathematical Society. Wakayama University [*A publication*]
Collect Papers School Hyg and Pub Health Johns Hopkins Univ ... Collected Papers. School of Hygiene and Public Health. Johns Hopkins University [*A publication*]
Collect Pap Fac Sci Osaka Imp Univ Ser A ... Collected Papers. Faculty of Science. Osaka Imperial University. Series A. Mathematics [*A publication*]
Collect Pap Fac Sci Osaka Imp Univ Ser B ... Collected Papers. Faculty of Science. Osaka Imperial University. Series B. Physics [*A publication*]
Collect Pap Fac Sci Osaka Imp Univ Ser C ... Collected Papers. Faculty of Science. Osaka Imperial University. Series C. Chemistry [*A publication*]
Collect Pap Fac Sci Osaka Univ Ser B ... Collected Papers. Faculty of Science. Osaka University. Series B. Physics [*A publication*]
Collect Pap Fac Sci Osaka Univ Ser C ... Collected Papers. Faculty of Science. Osaka University. Series C. Chemistry [*A publication*]
Collect Pap Inst Appl Chem Acad Sin ... Collected Papers. Institute of Applied Chemistry. Academia Sinica [*A publication*]
Collect Pap Inst Appl Chem Chin Acad Sci ... Collected Papers. Institute of Applied Chemistry. Chinese Academy of Sciences [*A publication*]
Collect Pap Jpn Soc Civ Eng ... Collected Papers. Japan Society of Civil Engineers [*A publication*]
Collect Pap Mayo Clin Mayo Found ... Collected Papers. Mayo Clinic and Mayo Foundation [*A publication*]
Collect Pap Med Mayo Clin Mayo Found ... Collected Papers in Medicine. Mayo Clinic and Mayo Foundation [*A publication*]
Collect Pap Med Sci Fukuoka Univ ... Collected Papers on Medical Science. Fukuoka University [*A publication*]
Collect Pap Res Lab Parke Davis Co ... Collected Papers. Research Laboratory of Parke, Davis & Company [*A publication*]
Collect Pap Surg Mayo Clin Mayo Found ... Collected Papers in Surgery. Mayo Clinic and Mayo Foundation [*A publication*]
Collect Pap Technol Sci Fukuoka Univ ... Collected Papers on Technological Sciences. Fukuoka University [*A publication*]
Collect Pharm Suec ... Collectanea Pharmaceutica Suecica [*A publication*]
Collect Phenom ... Collective Phenomena [*A publication*]
Collect Rep Nat Sci Fac Palacky Univ (Olomouc) ... Collected Reports. Natural Science Faculty. Palacky University (Olomouc) [*A publication*]
Collect Sci Pap Econ Agric Univ (Ceske Budejovice) Biol Part ... Collection of Scientific Papers. Economic Agricultural University (Ceske Budejovice). Biological Part [*A publication*]
Collect Sci Works Fac Med Charles Univ (Hradec Kralove) ... Collection of Scientific Works. Faculty of Medicine. Charles University (Hadec Kralove) [*A publication*]
Collect Studies Ser ... Collected Studies Series [*A publication*]
Collect Tech Pap AIAA/ASME/SAE Struct Dyn Mater Conf ... Collection of Technical Papers. AIAA/ASME/SAE Structural Dynamics and Materials Conference [*A publication*]
Collect Theses Kwang Woon Inst Technol ... Collection of Theses. Kwang Woon Institute of Technology [*Republic of Korea*] [*A publication*]
Collect Trav Acad Int Hist Sci ... Collection des Travaux. Academie Internationale d'Histoire des Sciences [*A publication*]
Collect Travaux Acad Internat Hist Sci ... Collection des Travaux. Academie Internationale d'Histoire des Sciences [*A publication*]
Collect Trav Univ Brazzaville ... Collection des Travaux. Universite de Brazzaville [*A publication*]

Collect Treatises Fac Hum Univ Fukuoka ... Collection of Treatises Published by the Faculty of Humanity. University of Fukuoka [*Japan*] [*A publication*]
Collect Works Cardio-Pulm Dis ... Collected Works on Cardio-Pulmonary Disease [*A publication*]
COLLEG ... Collegiate (ROG)
College L Dig Natl Assn College & Univ Attys ... College Law Digest. National Association of College and University Attorneys [*A publication*]
College M Symposium ... College Music Symposium [*A publication*]
College Mus ... College Music Symposium [*A publication*]
College & Research Lib ... College and Research Libraries [*A publication*]
Coll Eng ..... College English [*A publication*]
Coll Engl ..... College English [*A publication*]
Coll Enseignement Sci ... Collection Enseignement des Sciences [*Paris*] [*A publication*]
Colles .... Colles' English Parliamentary Cases [*1697-1714*] [*A publication*] (DLA)
Colles (Eng) ... Colles' English Parliamentary Cases [*1697-1714*] [*A publication*] (DLA)
Colles PC ... Colles' English Parliamentary Cases [*1697-1714*] [*A publication*] (DLA)
Coll Fr .... Collectionneur Francais [*A publication*]
Coll Fran ..... Collectanea Franciscana [*A publication*]
Coll G .... Colloquia Germanica [*A publication*]
Coll Hist Sci ... Collection d'Histoire des Sciences [*Paris*] [*A publication*]
Coll Id .... Collinson on the Law of Idiots and Lunatics [*A publication*] (DLA)
Coll I Dr Comp ... Colloque International de Droit Compare [*International Symposium on Comparative Law*] (DLA)
Collier Bank ... Collier and Eaton's American Bankruptcy Reports [*A publication*] (DLA)
Collier Bankr ... Collier's Law of Bankruptcy [*A publication*]
Collier Bankr Cas ... Collier's Bankruptcy Cases [*A publication*] (DLA)
Collier Bankr Cas 2d MB ... Collier Bankruptcy Cases. Second Series. Matthew Bender [*A publication*]
Collier & E Am Bankr ... Collier and Eaton's American Bankruptcy Reports [*A publication*] (DLA)
Collier's ...... Collier's National Weekly [*A publication*]
Collier's Yrbk ... Collier's Encyclopedia Yearbook [*A publication*]
Colliery Eng ... Colliery Engineering [*A publication*]
Colliery Eng (London) ... Colliery Engineering (London) [*A publication*]
Colliery Eng (Scranton PA) ... Colliery Engineer (Scranton, Pennsylvania) [*A publication*]
Colliery Guard ... Colliery Guardian [*A publication*]
Colliery Guardian J Coal Iron Trades ... Colliery Guardian and Journal of the Coal and Iron Trades [*A publication*]
Col Lit .... College Literature [*A publication*]
Col LJ .... Colonial Law Journal [*A publication*] (DLA)
Col LJNZ .. Colonial Law Journal (New Zealand) [*A publication*] (DLA)
Coll Jurid ..... Collectanea Juridica [*England*] [*A publication*] (DLA)
Coll L .... College Literature [*A publication*]
Coll Latomus ... Collection Latomus [*A publication*]
Coll L Bull ..... College Law Bulletin [*A publication*] (DLA)
Coll L Dig .. College Law Digest [*A publication*] (DLA)
Coll L D et O ... Collection des Lois, Decrets, et Ordonnances [*French*] [*A publication*] (DLA)
Coll Lit .... College Literature [*A publication*]
Coll Lun ..... Collinson on the Law of Idiots and Lunatics [*A publication*] (DLA)
Coll Manage ... Collection Management [*A publication*]
Coll Mass Hist Soc ... Collections. Massachusetts Historical Society [*A publication*]
Coll Math .. Colloquium Mathematicum [*A publication*]
CollMech ... Collectanea Mechlinensia [*Mechelen, Belgium*] [*A publication*]
Coll Med Ann (Mosul) ... College of Medicine. Annals (Mosul) [*A publication*]
Coll Mgt ..... College Management [*A publication*]
Coll & Mil BS ... Collier and Miller on Bills of Sale [*A publication*] (DLA)
Coll Min ..... Collier's Law of Mines [*A publication*] (DLA)
Coll Music ... College Music Symposium [*A publication*]
COLLN ... Collection
Coll NC ...... Collyer's Chancery Cases Tempore Bruce, V-C [*63 English Reprint*] [*1844-45*] [*A publication*] (DLA)
Colln Czech Chem Commun ... Collection of Czechoslovak Chemical Communications [*A publication*]
Colln Etud Mus Vie Wallonne ... Collection d'Etudes Publiee par le Musee de la Vie Wallonne [*A publication*]
Coll News ... College News [*A publication*] (APTA)
Collns INSEE Ser C ... Collections. Institut National de la Statistique et des Etudes Economiques. Serie C. Comptes et Planification [*A publication*]
Collns INSEE Ser D ... Collections. Institut National de la Statistique et des Etudes Economiques. Serie D. Demographie et Emploi [*A publication*]
Collns INSEE Ser E ... Collections. Institut National de la Statistique et des Etudes Economiques. Serie E. Entreprises [*A publication*]
Collns INSEE Ser M ... Collections. Institut National de la Statistique et des Etudes Economiques. Serie M. Menages [*A publication*]
Collns INSEE Ser R ... Collections. Institut National de la Statistique et des Etudes Economiques. Serie R. Regions [*A publication*]

Coll N & V ... Collegiate News and Views [*A publication*]
Colloid Chem ... Colloid Chemistry [*A publication*]
Colloides Biol Clin Ther ... Colloides en Biologie. Clinique et Therapeutique [*A publication*]
Colloid Interface Sci Pro Int Conf ... Colloid and Interface Science. Proceedings of the International Conference on Colloids and Surfaces [*A publication*]
Colloid J ..... Colloid Journal of the USSR [*A publication*]
Colloid J USSR ... Colloid Journal of the USSR [*A publication*]
Colloid Polymer Sci ... Colloid and Polymer Science [*A publication*]
Colloid Polym Sci ... Colloid and Polymer Science [*A publication*]
Colloid P S ... Colloid and Polymer Science [*A publication*]
Colloid Sci ... Colloid Science [*A publication*]
Colloids Surf ... Colloids and Surfaces [*A publication*]
Colloids and Surf ... Colloids and Surfaces [*A publication*]
Colloid Surf Sci Symp ... Colloid Surface Science Symposium [*A publication*]
Colloid Symp Monogr ... Colloid Symposium Monograph [*A publication*]
COLLOQ .. Colloquial
Colloq Art .. Colloquies on Art and Archaeology in Asia [*A publication*]
Colloq Club Jules Gonin ... Colloque. Club Jules Gonin [*A publication*]
Colloq Ger ... Colloquia Germanica [*A publication*]
Colloq Ges Biol Chem Mosbach ... Colloquium. Gesellschaft fuer Biologische Chemie in Mosbach [*A publication*]
Colloq Ges Physiol Chem ... Colloquium. Gesellschaft fuer Physiologische Chemie [*A publication*]
Colloq INSERM (Inst Natl Sante Rech Med) ... Colloque. INSERM (Institut National de la Sante et de la Recherche Medicale) [*A publication*]
Colloq Inst Natl Sante Rech Med ... Colloque. Institut National de la Sante et de la Recherche Medicale [*France*] [*A publication*]
Colloq Int Blennorragie ... Colloque International sur la Blennorragie. Comptes Rendus [*A publication*]
Colloq Int Cent Natl Rech Sci ... Colloques Internationaux. Centre National de la Recherche Scientifique [*A publication*]
Colloq Int Chim Cafes C R ... Colloque International sur la Chimie des Cafes. Comptes Rendus [*A publication*]
Colloq Int CNRS ... Colloques Internationaux. Centre National de la Recherche Scientifique [*A publication*]
Colloq Int Electr Sol ... Colloque International sur l'Electricite Solaire. Comptes Rendus [*A publication*]
Colloq Internat CNRS ... Colloques Internationaux. Centre National de la Recherche Scientifique [*A publication*]
Colloq Int Potash Inst ... Colloquium. International Potash Institute [*A publication*]
Colloq Math ... Colloquium Mathematicum [*Warsaw*] [*A publication*]
Colloq Math Soc Janos Bolyai ... Colloquia Mathematica. Societatis Janos Bolyai [*A publication*]
Colloq Metall ... Colloque de Metallurgie [*A publication*]
Colloq Pflanzenphysiol Humboldt Univ Berlin ... Colloquia Pflanzenphysiologie. Humboldt-Universitaet zu Berlin [*A publication*]
Colloq Phytosociol ... Colloques Phytosociologiques [*A publication*]
Colloq Spectro Int Pro ... Colloquium Spectroscopicum Internationale. Proceedings [*A publication*]
Colloq Spectrosc Int Acta ... Colloquium Spectroscopicum Internationale. Acta [*A publication*]
Colloques Int Cent Natn Rech Scient ... Colloques Internationaux. Centre National de la Recherche Scientifique [*A publication*]
Colloques Internat CNRS ... Colloques Internationaux. Centre National de la Recherche Scientifique [*A publication*]
Colloques Int Path Insectes ... Colloques Internationaux de la Pathologie des Insectes [*A publication*]
Colloques Nat CNRS ... Colloques Nationaux. Centre National de la Recherche Scientifique [*A publication*]
Colloqui Sod ... Colloqui del Sodalizio [*A publication*]
Colloquiumsber Inst Gerbereichem Tech Hochsch (Darmstadt) ... Colloquiumsberichte. Instituts fuer Gerbereichemie. Technischen Hochschule (Darmstadt) [*A publication*]
Coll'Ott ...... Coll'Ottava [*With the Octave*] [*Music*]
COLL'OTTA ... Coll'Ottava [*With the Octave*] [*Music*]
Coll Part ..... Collyer's Law of Partnership [*A publication*]   (DLA)
Coll Pat ...... Collier on Patents [*A publication*]   (DLA)
Coll PC .... Colles' English Parliamentary Cases [*1697-1714*] [*A publication*]   (DLA)
Coll Phil ..... Collection Philosophica [*A publication*]
Coll Polym Sci ... Colloid and Polymer Science [*A publication*]
Coll Press ... College Press Service [*A publication*]
Coll Programmation Rech Oper Appl ... Collection. Programmation Recherche Operationnelle Appliquee [*A publication*]
COLLR ...... Collector [*Business term*]
Col LR .... Columbia Law Review [*A publication*]
Coll Relat Res ... Collagen and Related Research [*A publication*]
Col L Rep ..... Colorado Law Reporter [*A publication*]   (DLA)
Coll Res Li ... College and Research Libraries [*A publication*]
Coll & Res Lib ... College and Research Libraries [*A publication*]
Coll & Res Lib N ... College and Research Libraries News [*A publication*]
Coll Res Libr ... College and Research Libraries [*A publication*]
Col L Rev ..... Columbia Law Review [*A publication*]
COLLS ...... Collateral Branches [*Genealogy*]   (ROG)
Coll Sci Mat ... Collana di Scienze Matematiche [*A publication*]

Coll Statist Agric Et ... Collections de Statistique Agricole. Etudes [*A publication*]
Coll St L ..... Collinson on the Stamp Laws [*A publication*]   (DLA)
Coll Stud J ... College Student Journal [*A publication*]
Coll Stud Pers Abstr ... College Student Personnel Abstracts [*A publication*]
Coll Surfaces ... Colloids and Surfaces [*A publication*]
Coll Tor ...... Collet on Torts and Measure of Damages [*A publication*]   (DLA)
Coll Tr .... Collateral Trust   (DLA)
Coll Travaux Acad Internat Hist Sci ... Collection des Travaux. Academie Internationale d'Histoire des Sciences [*A publication*]
Coll & U ..... College and University [*A publication*]   (DLA)
COLLUN .. Collunarium [*Nose Wash*] [*Pharmacy*]
Coll & Univ ... College and University [*A publication*]
Coll & Univ Bus ... College and University Business [*A publication*]
Coll & Univ J ... College and University Journal [*A publication*]
COLLUT ... Collutorium [*Mouthwash*] [*Pharmacy*]
Coll Works Cardio-Pulm Dis ... Collected Works on Cardio-Pulmonary Disease [*A publication*]
COLLY ...... Colliery   (ROG)
Colly .... Collyer's English Vice Chancellors' Reports [*1845-47*] [*A publication*]   (DLA)
Colly Ch Cas (Eng) ... Collyer's English Chancery Cases [*1845-47*] [*A publication*]   (DLA)
Colly Part ... Collyer's Law of Partnership [*A publication*]   (DLA)
COLLYR ... Collyrium [*Eye Wash*] [*Pharmacy*]
ColM .... Colorado Magazine [*A publication*]
COLM .... Colorado National Monument
Colm .... Columba [*Constellation*]
COLM .... Columbus Mills, Inc. [*NASDAQ symbol*]   (NQ)
COLM .... Column   (AFM)
COLMA9 .. Colorado Medicine [*A publication*]
Col Mass Pr ... Colby's Massachusetts Practice [*A publication*]   (DLA)
COLM/ATC ... Continental Land Masses Air Traffic Control [*NASA*]   (MCD)
CoLmE .... Loma Elementary, Loma, CO [*Library symbol*] [*Library of Congress*]   (LCLS)
ColMech ... Collectanea Mechlinensia [*Mechelen, Belgium*] [*A publication*]
Col Med ..... Colegio Medico [*A publication*]
Col Med Vida Med ... Colegio Medico Vida Medica [*A publication*]
Colmen Esp ... Colmenero Espanol [*A publication*]
COLMGP ... Column Gap [*Army*]   (AABC)
Col Mgt ...... College Management [*A publication*]
Col Mines .. Collier's Law of Mines [*A publication*]   (DLA)
Col Mon ...... Colonial Monthly [*A publication*]
Col Monograf Mem Mat ... Coleccion de Monografias y Memorias de Matematicas [*Madrid*] [*A publication*]
Col Mort ...... Colby on Mortgage Foreclosures [*A publication*]   (DLA)
Col Mun B ... Coler's Law of Municipal Bonds [*A publication*]   (DLA)
ColN .... Colonial Newsletter [*A publication*]
COLN .... Column
Col Nac Mem ... Memoria. El Colegio Nacional [*A publication*]
Col NP .... Colorado Nisi Prius Decisions [*A publication*]   (DLA)
COLO .... Colonial National Historic Park
COLO .... Colorado   (AFM)
Colo .... Colorado Reports [*A publication*]   (DLA)
CoLo .... Longmont Public Library, Longmont, CO [*Library symbol*] [*Library of Congress*]   (LCLS)
Colo Admin Code ... Code of Colorado Regulations [*A publication*]   (DLA)
Colo Ag Exp ... Colorado. Agricultural Experiment Station. Publications [*A publication*]
Colo Agric Exp Stn Annu Rep ... Colorado. Agricultural Experiment Station. Annual Report [*A publication*]
Colo Agric Exp Stn Bull ... Colorado. Agricultural Experiment Station. Bulletin [*A publication*]
Colo Agric Exp Stn Tech Bull ... Colorado. Agricultural Experiment Station. Technical Bulletin [*A publication*]
Colo App .... Colorado Court of Appeals Reports [*A publication*]   (DLA)
COLOB ..... Colourage [*A publication*]
Colo Bur Mines Ann Rept ... Colorado. Bureau of Mines. Annual Report [*A publication*]
Colo Bus ..... Colorado Business [*A publication*]
Colo Bus R ... Colorado Business Review [*A publication*]
Colo Code Regs ... Code of Colorado Regulations [*A publication*]
Colo Const ... Colorado Constitution [*A publication*]   (DLA)
Colo Country Life ... Colorado Country Life [*A publication*]
COLOCYNTH ... Colocynthus [*Bitter Apples*] [*Pharmacy*]   (ROG)
COLOD ..... Completed Loading [*Navy*]
Colo Dec ..... Colorado Decisions [*A publication*]   (DLA)
Colo Dec Fed ... Colorado Decisions, Federal [*A publication*]   (DLA)
Colo Dec Supp ... Colorado Decisions Supplement [*A publication*]   (DLA)
Colo Dep Game Fish Parks Spec Rep ... Colorado. Department of Game, Fish, and Parks. Special Report [*A publication*]
Colo Div Game Fish Parks Fish Res Rev ... Colorado. Division of Game, Fish, and Parks. Fisheries Research Review [*A publication*]
Colo Div Game Fish Parks Game Res Rev ... Colorado Division of Game, Fish, and Parks. Game Research Review [*A publication*]
Colo Div Game Fish Parks Spec Rep ... Colorado. Division of Game, Fish, and Parks. Special Report [*A publication*]
Colo Div Game Parks Game Res Rev ... Colorado. Division of Game, Fish, and Parks. Game Research Review [*A publication*]

Colo Div Wildl Div Rep ... Colorado. Division of Wildlife. Division Report [*A publication*]
Colo Div Wildl Spec Rep ... Colorado. Division of Wildlife. Special Report [*A publication*]
Colo Div Wildl Tech Publ ... Colorado. Division of Wildlife. Technical Publication [*A publication*]
Colo Energy Factbook ... Colorado Energy Factbook [*A publication*]
Colo Engineer ... Colorado Engineer [*A publication*]
Colo Farm & Home Res ... Colorado Farm and Home Research [*A publication*]
Colo Field Ornithol ... Colorado Field Ornithologist [*A publication*]
Colo Fish Res Rev ... Colorado Fisheries Research Review [*A publication*]
COLOG ..... Cologarithm [*Mathematics*]
Colo Game Fish Parks Dep Spec Rep ... Colorado. Game, Fish, and Parks Department. Special Report [*A publication*]
Colo Game Res Rev ... Colorado Game Research Review [*A publication*]
Colo Geol Surv Bull ... Colorado. Geological Survey. Bulletin [*A publication*]
Colo Geol Surv Map Ser ... Colorado. Geological Survey. Map Series [*A publication*]
Colo Geol Surv Spec Publ ... Colorado. Geological Survey. Special Publication [*A publication*]
Colo Ground Water Basic Data Rep ... Colorado Ground Water Basic Data Report [*A publication*]
Colo IC .... Colorado Industrial Commission Report [*A publication*] (DLA)
Colo J Pharm ... Colorado Journal of Pharmacy [*A publication*]
Colo J Res Mus Ed ... Colorado Journal of Research in Music Education [*A publication*]
Colo Law .... Colorado Lawyer [*A publication*]
Colo Lib Assn Bul ... Colorado Library Association. Bulletin [*A publication*]
Colo LR ...... Colorado Law Reporter [*A publication*] (DLA)
Colo L Rep ... Colorado Law Reporter [*A publication*] (DLA)
Colom .... Colombia
ColoM .... Colorado Magazine [*A publication*]
Colo Mag ... Colorado Magazine [*A publication*]
Colomb Inst Geogr Agustin Codazzi Dep Agrol Publ ... Colombia. Instituto Geografico "Agustin Codazzi." Departamento Agrologico. Publicaciones [*A publication*]
Colomb Inst Geogr Agustin Codazzi Dir Agrol Publ ... Colombia. Instituto Geografico "Agustin Codazzi." Direccion Agrologica. Publicaciones [*A publication*]
Colomb Inst Geol Nac Compil Estud Geol Of Colomb ... Colombia. Instituto Geologica Nacional. Compilacion de los Estudios Geologicos Oficiales en Colombia [*A publication*]
Colomb Minist Agric Div Invest Inf Tec ... Colombia. Ministerio de Agricultura. Division de Investigacion. Informacion Tecnica [*A publication*]
Colomb Minist Minas Energ Mem ... Colombia. Ministerio de Minas y Energia. Memoria [*A publication*]
Colombo LJ ... Colombo Law Journal [*A publication*] (DLA)
Colombo L Rev ... Colombo Law Review [*A publication*]
Colomb Repub Minist Minas Pet Bol Minas ... Republica de Colombia. Ministerio de Minas y Petroleos. Boletin de Minas [*A publication*]
Colomb Repub Minist Minas Pet Bol Nac Minas ... Republica de Colombia. Ministerio de Minas y Petroleos. Boletin Nacional de Minas [*A publication*]
Colo Med ... Colorado Medicine [*A publication*]
COLON ..... Colonial
CoLoN .... Northern Colorado Educational Board of Cooperative Services, Longmont, CO [*Library symbol*] [*Library of Congress*] (LCLS)
Colon Auton ... Colonies Autonomes [*A publication*]
COLONET ... Colorado Library Network [*Colorado State Library*] [*Denver, CO*] [*Library network*]
Colon Geol Miner Resour Suppl Bull Suppl ... Colonial Geology and Mineral Resources. Supplement Series. Bulletin Supplement [*A publication*]
Colonial Geology and Mineral Res ... Colonial Geology and Mineral Resources [*A publication*]
Colonial Research Pub ... Colonial Research Publications [*A publication*]
Colo NP Dec ... Colorado Nisi Prius Decisions [*A publication*] (DLA)
Colon Pl Anim Prod ... Colonial Plant and Animal Products [*A publication*]
Colon Plant Anim Prod ... Colonial Plant and Animal Products [*A publication*]
Colo Nurse ... Colorado Nurse [*A publication*]
Colo Nurse Update ... Colorado Nurse Update [*A publication*]
Colon Waterbirds ... Colonial Waterbirds [*A publication*]
Colo Outdoors ... Colorado Outdoors [*A publication*]
COLOP ..... Collection Opportunity (MCD)
Colo PUC ... Colorado Public Utilities Commission Decisions [*A publication*] (DLA)
Colo PUC Rep ... Colorado Public Utilities Commission Report [*A publication*] (DLA)
ColoQ .... Colorado Quarterly [*A publication*]
Coloquio ..... Coloquio Letras [*A publication*]
COLOR ..... Coloretur [*Let It Be Colored*] [*Pharmacy*] (ROG)
Colorado Med ... Colorado Medicine [*A publication*]
Colorado School Mines Prof Contr ... Colorado School of Mines. Professional Contributions [*A publication*]

Colorado-Wyoming Acad Sci Jour ... Colorado-Wyoming Academy of Science. Journal [*A publication*]
Colo Rancher Farmer ... Colorado Rancher and Farmer [*A publication*] (APTA)
Colo Reg ..... Colorado Register [*A publication*]
Color Eng ... Color Engineering [*A publication*]
Colo Rev Stat ... Colorado Revised Statutes [*A publication*]
Color Mater ... Color Materials [*Japan*] [*A publication*]
Color Res Appl ... Color Research and Application [*A publication*]
Color Res and Appl ... Color Research and Application [*A publication*]
Color Sch Mines Q Bull ... Colorado School of Mines. Quarterly Bulletin [*A publication*]
Color Tr J .. Color Trade Journal and Textile Chemist [*A publication*]
COLOS..... Command Off the Line of Sight [*Military*] [*British*]
Colo Sch Mines Mag ... Colorado School of Mines. Magazine [*A publication*]
Colo Sch Mines Mineral Energy Resources Bul ... Colorado School of Mines. Mineral and Energy Resources Bulletin [*A publication*]
Colo Sch Mines Miner Ind Bull ... Colorado School of Mines. Mineral Industries Bulletin [*A publication*]
Colo Sch Mines Q ... Colorado School of Mines. Quarterly [*A publication*]
Colo Sch Mines Quart ... Colorado School of Mines. Quarterly [*A publication*]
Colo Sci Soc Proc ... Colorado Scientific Society. Proceedings [*A publication*]
Colo Sess Laws ... Session Laws of Colorado [*A publication*] (DLA)
COLOSS ... Colossians [*New Testament book*] (ROG)
Colo State Univ Annu Rep ... Colorado State University. Annual Report [*A publication*]
Colo State Univ Exp Stn Bull ... Colorado State University. Experiment Station. Bulletin [*A publication*]
Colo State Univ Exp Stn Tech Bull ... Colorado State University. Experiment Station. Technical Bulletin [*A publication*]
Colo State Univ Expt Sta Bull ... Colorado State University. Experiment Station. Bulletin [*A publication*]
Colo State Univ (Fort Collins) Hydrol Pap ... Colorado State University (Fort Collins). Hydrology Papers [*A publication*]
Colo State Univ (Fort Collins) Proj Themis Tech Rep ... Colorado State University (Fort Collins). Project Themis Technical Reports [*A publication*]
Colo State Univ News ... Colorado State University News [*A publication*]
Colo State Univ Range Sci Dep Range Sci Ser ... Colorado State University. Range Science Department. Range Science Series [*A publication*]
Colo State Univ Range Sci Dep Sci Ser ... Colorado State University. Range Science Department. Range Science Series [*A publication*]
Colo St BA ... Colorado State Bar Association Report [*A publication*] (DLA)
COL OTTA ... Coll'Ottava [*With the Octave*] [*Music*] (ROG)
CoLou .... Louisville Public Library, Louisville, CO [*Library symbol*] [*Library of Congress*] (LCLS)
Colo Univ Eng Expt Sta Circ Highway Ser Studies Gen Ser ... Colorado University. Engineering Experiment Station Circular. Highway Series. Studies. General Series [*A publication*]
Co Louth Archaeol Hist J ... County Louth Archaeological and Historical Journal [*A publication*]
CoLov .... Loveland Public Library, Loveland, CO [*Library symbol*] [*Library of Congress*] (LCLS)
Colo Water Conserv Board Ground-Water Ser Bull Circ ... Colorado Water Conservation Board. Ground-Water Series Bulletin. Circular [*A publication*]
Colo Water Conserv Board Ground Water Ser Circ ... Colorado. Water Conservation Board. Ground Water Series. Circular [*A publication*]
Colo-Wyo Acad Sci Jour ... Colorado-Wyoming Academy of Science. Journal [*A publication*]
COLP......... Center for Oceans Law and Policy (EA)
COL P........ Colla Parte [*With the Solo Part*] [*Music*] (ROG)
COLP......... Columbian Energy Company Limited Partnership [*Topeka, KS*] [*NASDAQ symbol*] (NQ)
COLPA...... Commission on Law and Public Affairs
COLPA...... National Jewish Commission on Law and Public Affairs
Col Part...... Collyer's Law of Partnership [*A publication*] (DLA)
Col Phys Ed Assn Proc ... College Physical Education Association. Proceedings [*A publication*]
Col Press.... College Press Service [*A publication*]
COLPS ...... Center for Oceans Law and Policy. University of Virginia. Oceans Policy Studies [*A publication*]
COLPS ...... Collapse
ColQ........... Colorado Quarterly [*A publication*]
Colq............ Colquit's Reports [*1 Modern*] [*England*] [*A publication*] (DLA)
Colq Civ Law ... Colquhoun on Roman Civil Law [*A publication*] (DLA)
Colq CL...... Colquhoun on Roman Civil Law [*A publication*] (DLA)
Colq Jud A ... Colquhoun on the Judicature Acts [*A publication*] (DLA)
Colq Rom Civ Law ... Colquhoun on Roman Civil Law [*A publication*] (DLA)
Colq Rom Law ... Colquhoun on Roman Civil Law [*A publication*] (DLA)
COLQUAP ... Consumer Level Quality Audit Program [*Military*]
Col Quim-Farm ... Colegio Quimico-Farmaceutico [*A publication*]
Col Quim Ing Quim Costa Rica Rev ... Colegio de Quimicos e Ingenieros Quimicos de Costa Rica. Revista [*A publication*]
Colquit .... Colquit's Reports [*1 Modern*] [*England*] [*A publication*] (DLA)
COLR .... Circuit Order Layout Record [*Telecommunications*] (TEL)

COLREGS ... International Regulations for Preventing Collisions at Sea [*1972*]

Col Rep ...... Colorado Reports [*A publication*]   (DLA)

Col and Research Libs ... College and Research Libraries [*A publication*]

Col and Research Libs News ... College and Research Libraries News [*A publication*]

Col & Res Lib ... College and Research Libraries [*A publication*]

Col Rev Stat ... Colorado Revised Statutes [*A publication*]   (DLA)

COLS......... Columns   (ROG)

COLSEC ... Collective Security [*Army*]   (MCD)

COLSED ... Collection Statute Expiration Date [*IRS*]

COL-SERGT ... Colour-Sergeant [*Army*] [*British*]

Col-Sgt ... Colour-Sergeant [*Army*] [*British*]   (DMA)

Col Soc Mass Publ ... Colonial Society of Massachusetts. Publications [*A publication*]

Col Soc Mass Trans ... Colonial Society of Massachusetts. Transactions [*A publication*]

COLSS ...... Core Operating Limit Supervisory System [*Nuclear energy*]   (NRCH)

COLSS ...... Core Operating Limit Support System [*Nuclear energy*]   (NRCH)

Colston Pap ... Colston Papers [*A publication*]

Colston Res Soc Proc Symp ... Colston Research Society. Proceedings of the Symposium [*A publication*]

ColStuAb ... College Student Personnel Abstracts [*A publication*]

COLT .... CO_2 LASER Technology [*Military*]

Colt .... Coltman's Registration Appeal Cases [*1879-85*] [*England*] [*A publication*]   (ILCA)

COLT .... Combat Observation and Lasing Teams [*Army*]   (INF)

COLT .... Combined Operations Lasing Team [*Army*]   (INF)

COLT .... Communication Line Terminator [*IBM Corp.*]

COLT .... Computer-Oriented Language Translator   (IEEE)

COLT .... Computerized Online Testing

COLT .... Control Language Translator [*Data processing*]   (IEEE)

COLT .... Council on Library-Media Technical-Assistants   (EA)

Colt G Vinic Ital ... Coltivatore e Giornale Vinicolo Italiano [*A publication*]

Coltiv G Vinic Ital ... Coltivatore e Giornale Vinicolo Italiano [*A publication*]

Coltm .... Coltman's Registration Appeal Cases [*1879-85*] [*England*] [*A publication*]   (DLA)

Colt News... Colt Newsletter [*A publication*]

Colt Prot .... Colture Protette [*A publication*]

Colt Protette ... Colture Protette [*A publication*]

Colt (Reg Ca) ... Coltman's Registration Appeal Cases [*1879-85*] [*England*] [*A publication*]   (DLA)

Colt Reg Cas ... Coltman's Registration Appeal Cases [*1879-85*] [*England*] [*A publication*]   (DLA)

COLTS ...... Continuously Offered Long-Term Securities [*Merrill Lynch & Co.*] [*Finance*]

COLTS ...... Contrast Optical LASER Tracking Subsystem [*Missile guidance*]

COLTS ...... Count on Losing this Sunday [*Humorous interpretation of NFL team name*]

COLUDE .. Committee for the Democratic Struggle [*Mexico*]

COLUM .... Columbia   (ROG)

COLUMB ... Columbia   (ROG)

Columb Bsn ... Columbus Business Journal [*A publication*]

Columbia Hist Soc Rec ... Columbia Historical Society. Records [*A publication*]

Columbia J-Ism R ... Columbia Journalism Review [*A publication*]

Columbia J Law and Social Problems ... Columbia Journal of Law and Social Problems [*A publication*]

Columbia J of L and Soc Probl ... Columbia Journal of Law and Social Problems [*A publication*]

Columbia Journalism Rev ... Columbia Journalism Review [*A publication*]

Columbia J Transnat Law ... Columbia Journal of Transnational Law [*A publication*]

Columbia J Wld Busin ... Columbia Journal of World Business [*A publication*]

Columbia J World Bus ... Columbia Journal of World Business [*A publication*]

Columbia Law R ... Columbia Law Review [*A publication*]

Columbia Law Rev ... Columbia Law Review [*A publication*]

Columbia Lib C ... Columbia Library. Columns [*A publication*]

Columbia Libr Col ... Columbia Library. Columns [*A publication*]

Columbia Libr Columns ... Columbia Library. Columns [*A publication*]

Columbia U Q ... Columbia University. Quarterly [*A publication*]

Columb J L ... Columbia Journal of Law and Social Problems [*A publication*]

Columb Jrl ... Columbia Journal of World Business [*A publication*]

Columb J Tr ... Columbia Journal of Transnational Law [*A publication*]

Columb J W ... Columbia Journal of World Business [*A publication*]

Columb Law ... Columbia Law Review [*A publication*]

Columbus Dent Soc Bull ... Columbus [*Ohio*] Dental Society. Bulletin [*A publication*]

Columbus Gal Bul ... Columbus, Ohio. Columbus Gallery of Fine Arts. Bulletin [*A publication*]

Colum Disp ... Columbus Dispatch [*A publication*]

Colum Forum ... Columbia Forum [*A publication*]

Colum His S ... Columbia Historical Society. Records [*A publication*]

Colum Human Rights L Rev ... Columbia Human Rights Law Review [*A publication*]

Colum Hum Rts L Rev ... Columbia Human Rights Law Review [*A publication*]

Colum J Environ L ... Columbia Journal of Environmental Law [*A publication*]

Colum J Envtl L ... Columbia Journal of Environmental Law [*A publication*]

Colum J Int'l Aff ... Columbia Journal of International Affairs [*A publication*]   (DLA)

Colum J Law & Soc Prob ... Columbia Journal of Law and Social Problems [*A publication*]

Colum J L & Soc Prob ... Columbia Journal of Law and Social Problems [*A publication*]

Colum Journalism R ... Columbia Journalism Review [*A publication*]

Colum Jr .... Columbia Jurist [*A publication*]   (DLA)

Colum J Transnat L ... Columbia Journal of Transnational Law [*A publication*]

Colum J Transnat'l Law ... Columbia Journal of Transnational Law [*A publication*]

Colum Jur .. Columbia Jurist [*A publication*]   (DLA)

Colum J World Bus ... Columbia Journal of World Business [*A publication*]

Colum L Rev ... Columbia Law Review [*A publication*]

Colum LT... Columbia Law Times [*A publication*]   (DLA)

Colum Soc'y Int'l L Bull ... Columbia Society of International Law. Bulletin [*A publication*]   (DLA)

Colum Survey Human Rights L ... Columbia Survey of Human Rights Law [*A publication*]   (DLA)

Colum Surv Hum Rts L ... Columbia Survey of Human Rights Law [*A publication*]   (DLA)

Colum Univ Q ... Columbia University. Quarterly [*A publication*]

Col & Univ ... College and University [*A publication*]

Col Univ ... College and University [*A publication*]

Col & Univ Bsns ... College and University Business [*A publication*]

Col Univ Gerona Secc Cien An ... Colegio Universitario de Gerona. Seccion de Ciencias. Anales [*A publication*]

Col & Univ J ... College and University Journal [*A publication*]

Colvil......... Colvil's Manuscript Decisions, Scotch Court of Session [*A publication*]   (DLA)

CoLvM...... Molybdenum Corp. of America, Louviers, CO [*Library symbol*] [*Library of Congress*]   (LCLS)

COL VO ...... Colla Voce [*With the Voice*] [*Music*]

COL VOCE ... Colla Voce [*With the Voice*] [*Music*]   (ROG)

CoLw.......... Villa Regional Library, Lakewood, CO [*Library symbol*] [*Library of Congress*]   (LCLS)

COLX .... Columbine Explorations Corp. [*NASDAQ symbol*]   (NQ)

COLYAHAR ... Columbia, Yale, Harvard [*Used to refer to a project involving the medical libraries of these universities*]

Coly Guar (De) ... Colyar on Guarantees [*A publication*]   (DLA)

Com............ Blackstone's Commentaries on the Laws of England [*A publication*]   (DLA)

COM.......... Cahiers d'Outre-Mer [*A publication*]

COM.......... Candorado Mines Ltd. [*Vancouver Stock Exchange symbol*]

COM.......... Cassette Operating Monitor

COM.......... Center of Mass [*Coordinate system*]   (MCD)

COM.......... Change Order Modification   (KSC)

COM.......... Character-Oriented Message   (RDA)

COM.......... Checkout Operations Manual   (AAG)

COM.......... Choice Old Marsala

COM.......... Chronic Otitis Media [*Medicine*]

C & OM ..... Clothing and Organic Materials [*Army*]   (MCD)

C/OM .... Clothing and Organic Materials Laboratory [*Army Natick Laboratories, MA*]

COM.......... Coal-Oil Mixture

CoM.......... Coenzyme M

COM.......... Coleman, TX [*Location identifier*] [*FAA*]   (FAAL)

COM.......... Comair, Inc. [*Cincinnati, OH*] [*FAA designator*]   (FAAC)

Com............ Comberbach's English King's Bench Reports [*1685-99*] [*A publication*]   (DLA)

COM.......... Comedian [*or Comedy*]   (ROG)

COM.......... Comedy

COM.......... Comet Stories [*A publication*]

COM.......... Comic

COM.......... Comitan [*Mexico*] [*Seismograph station code, US Geological Survey*]   (SEIS)

COM.......... Comitatus [*County*] [*Latin*]   (ROG)

COM.......... Comiteco [*Race of maize*]

COM.......... Comma   (ROG)

COM.......... Command   (AAG)

COM.......... Commandant [*Military*]

COM.......... Commander

COM.......... Commemoration   (ADA)

Com............ Comment [*Legal term*]   (DLA)

Com............ Commentari [*A publication*]

COM.......... Commentary [*A publication*]

COM.......... Commentary

COM.......... Commerce

COM.......... Commercial   (ROG)

COM.......... Commissary

COM.......... Commissary Operating Manual   (AABC)

COM.......... Commission [*or Commissioner*]   (AABC)

COM.......... Commissioned Officers Mess [*Navy*]

COM.......... Committee   (AABC)

COM.......... Commode [*Medicine*]

COM.......... Commodo [*In an Easy Style*] [*Music*]
COM.......... Commodore
COM.......... Common
COM.......... Commonwealth
COM.......... Commune
COM.......... Communicant [*Religion*]   (ROG)
COM.......... Communicate [*or Communications*]
COM.......... Communications Processor
COM.......... Communist
COM.......... Community   (AABC)
COM.......... Commuter
COM.......... Comoros [*ANSI three-letter standard code*]   (CNC)
COM.......... Companions
Com.......... Compass: Theology Review [*A publication*]   (APTA)
COM.......... Complement   (MUGU)
COM.......... Completions
COM.......... Composer [*A publication*]
COM.......... Compromise   (ROG)
COM.......... Computer
COM.......... Computer Output Microfilm [*or Microfiche or Microform*]   (BUR)
Com.......... Comstock's Reports [*1-4 New York Court of Appeals*] [*A publication*]   (DLA)
Com.......... Comyn's English King's Bench Reports [*1695-1741*] [*A publication*]   (DLA)
COM.......... Condition Monitoring   (MCD)
COM.......... Copper Oxide Modulator
COM.......... Cost and Management [*A publication*]
COM.......... Cost of Money [*DoD*]
COM.......... Council of Ministers [*European Economic Commission*]   (DLA)
COM.......... County Office Manager
COM.......... Crowley, Milner & Co. [*AMEX symbol*]   (SPSG)
COM.......... Cyclophosphamide, Oncovin [*Vincristine*], MeCCNU [*Semustine*] [*Antineoplastic drug regimen*]
COM.......... Cyclophosphamide, Oncovin [*Vincristine*], Methotrexate [*Antineoplastic drug regimen*]
COM.......... Merritt College, Oakland, CA [*Library symbol*] [*Library of Congress*]   (LCLS)
COM.......... Mesa College, Grand Junction, CO [*OCLC symbol*]   (OCLC)
Com.......... Plowden's English King's Bench Commentaries [*or Reports*] [*A publication*]   (DSA)
Com.......... United States Commerce Court Opinions [*A publication*]   (DLA)
3COM.......... Number 3 Common [*Lumber*]
COMA....... Committee on Medical Aspects of Food Policy [*British*]
COMA....... Computer Operations Management Association
COMA....... Council on Mind Abuse [*Canada*]
COMA....... Court of Military Appeals
COMA....... Cyclophosphamide, Oncovin [*Vincristine*], Methotrexate, ara-C [*Antineoplastic drug regimen*]
CoMa.......... Mancos Public Library, Mancos, CO [*Library symbol*] [*Library of Congress*]   (LCLS)
COMA-A... Cyclophosphamide, Oncovin [*Vincristine*], Methotrexate/citrovorum factor, Adriamycin, ara-C [*Cytarabine*] [*Antineoplastic drug regimen*]
COMAAC ... Commander, Alaskan Air Command   (MCD)
COMAAFV ... Commander, Australian Army Forces, Vietnam
ComAb....... Computer Abstracts [*A publication*]
COMAC.... Commander, Military Airlift Command [*Formerly, COMATS*]   (AFM)
COMAC.... Continuous Multiple Access Collator [*Proposed by Mortimer Taube, 1957*] [*Data processing*]
COMACA ... Committee for Medical Aid to Central America   (EA)
Com Act ..... Commonwealth Act   (DLA)
COMACT ... Commonwealth Acts [*Database*] [*Australia*]
COMADC ... Commander, Air Defense Command
COMAEGEANBASE ... Commander, Aegean Defense Sector   (NATG)
COMAF .... Comite des Constructeurs de Materiel Frigorifique de la CEE [*Committee of Manufacturers of Refrigeration Equipment of the EEC*]
COMAF .... Commodore, Amphibious Forces [*British military*]   (DMA)
COMAFFOR ... Commander, Air Force Forces   (AABC)
Com Affrs .. Community Affairs   (DLA)
COMAFV .. Commander, Australian Forces, Vietnam
COMAINT ... Command Maintenance [*Military*]   (AABC)
COMAIR... Commander, Air Forces [*Navy*]
COMAIR... Commercial Air   (NOAA)
COMAIRBALTAP ... Commander, Allied Air Forces, Baltic Approaches   (AABC)
COMAIRCANLANT ... Air Commander, Canadian Atlantic Subarea
COMAIRCENT ... Commander, Allied Air Forces, Central Europe
COMAIRCENTLANT ... Air Commander, Central Atlantic Subarea
COMAIRLANT ... Commander, Air Force, Atlantic Fleet
COMAIRNON ... Commander, Allied Air Forces, North Norway   (NATG)
COMAIRNORECHAN ... Air Commander, Northeast Subarea Channel
COMAIRNORLANT ... Air Commander, Northern Atlantic Subarea
COMAIRNORTH ... Commander, Allied Air Forces, Northern Europe
COMAIRPAC ... Commander, Air Force, Pacific Fleet
COMAIRPLYMCHAN ... Air Commander, Plymouth Subarea Channel
COMAIRSHIPGR ... Commander, Airship Group

COMAIRSOLS ... Commander, Air Forces, Solomons
COMAIRSONOR ... Commander, Allied Air Forces, South Norway   (NATG)
COMAIRSOPAC ... Commander, Air Forces, South Pacific Force
COMAIRSOUTH ... Commander, Allied Air Forces, Southern Europe
COMAIRTRANS ... Commander, Air Transport
COMAIRTRANSRON ... Commander, Air Transport Squadron
COMALAMGRU ... Commander, Alameda Group
COMALNAVNOREUR ... Commander, Allied Naval Forces, Northern Europe
COMALSEAFRON ... Commander, Alaskan Sea Frontier   (MUGU)
COMALSEC ... Commander, Alaskan Sector
COMAM... Continuous Motion Assembly Machine
Com Amer ... Commerce America [*A publication*]
COMANBAT ... Combat Maneuver Battalion [*Army*]
COMANEX ... Combat Analysis Extended
COMANTARCTICSUPPACT ... Commander, Antarctic Support Activities
COMANTDEFCOM ... Commander, Antilles Defense Command   (AABC)
CoManz ..... Manzanola Public Library, Manzanola, CO [*Library symbol*] [*Library of Congress*]   (LCLS)
COMAP .... Committee for the Alliance for Progress [*Department of Commerce*]
COM APP ... Commissioner of Appeals   (DLA)
COMAR.... Code of Maryland Regulations [*A publication*]
COMAR.... Computer, Aerial Reconnaissance
COMAR.... Contour Mapping RADAR System   (MCD)
COMARC ... Cooperative Machine-Readable Cataloging Program [*Library of Congress*]
COMARCARAREA ... Commander, Marshalls-Carolines Area
COMARE ... Committee on Medical Aspects of Radiation in the Environment [*British*]
COMAREGRU ... Commander, Mare Island Group
COMARFOR ... Commander, Army Forces
COMARRHIN ... Commander, Maritime Rhine   (NATG)
COMART ... Commander, Marine Air Reserve Training
COMAS .... Combined Orbital Maneuvering and Abort System [*NASA*]   (NASA)
COMAS .... Concentration-Modulated Absorption Spectrometry
COMASIII ... Computerized Maintenance and Administration Support III [*Telecommunications*]   (TEL)
Co Mass Pr ... Colby's Massachusetts Practice [*A publication*]   (DLA)
COMASWFOR ... Commander, Antisubmarine Warfare Force
COMASWFORLANT ... Commander, Antisubmarine Warfare Forces, Atlantic   (MUGU)
COMASWFORPAC ... Commander, Antisubmarine Warfare Forces, Pacific   (CINC)
COMASWGRU ... Commander, Antisubmarine Warfare Group
COMAT .... Characteristics of Materials   (KSC)
COMAT .... Committee on Materials [*Federal Council for Science and Technology*]
COMAT .... Commodore Air Train [*Navy*]
COMAT .... Compatibility of Materials   (MCD)
COMAT .... Computer-Assisted Training   (IEEE)
COMATAFSONOR ... Commander, Allied Tactical Air Forces, Southern Norway
COMATF ... Commander, Amphibious Task Force   (AABC)
COMATKCARAIRWING ... Commander, Attack Carrier Air Wing
COMATKCARSTRIKEFOR ... Commander, Attack Carrier Striking Force
COMATS ... Commander, Military Air Transport Service [*Later, COMAC*]
Com Att...... Complete Attorney [*A publication*]   (DLA)
COMAX.... Cotton Management Expert [*Computer program to improve crop production*]
CoMay .... Maybell Public Library, Maybell, CO [*Library symbol*] [*Library of Congress*]   (LCLS)
COMB....... Canadian Outdoor Measurement Bureau
COMb........ Carboxymyoglobin [*Biochemistry*]
COMB....... Center of Marine Biology [*University of Maryland*]
Comb........ Comberbach's English King's Bench Reports [*1685-99*] [*A publication*]   (DLA)
COMB....... Combination [*or Combine*]   (AFM)
COMB....... Combined Cos. [*NASDAQ symbol*]   (NQ)
COMB....... Combustion   (AAG)
COMB....... Command Confirmation Buffer
Com B .... Common Bench Reports (Manning, Granger, and Scott) [*1846-65*] [*England*] [*A publication*]   (DLA)
COMB....... Console-Oriented Model Building [*Data processing*]
COMB....... Cyclophosphamide, Oncovin [*Vincristine*], MeCCNU [*Semustine*], Bleomycin [*Antineoplastic drug regimen*]
COMB....... Cyclophosphamide, Oncovin [*Vincristine*], Methotrexate, Bleomycin [*Antineoplastic drug regimen*]
COMBA .... Combustion [*A publication*]
COMBALTAP ... Allied Command Baltic Approaches [*NATO*]
COMBARFORCLANT ... Commander, Barrier Forces, Atlantic   (NATG)
COMBARPAC ... Commander, Barrier Pacific   (CINC)
COMBASE ... Communications Data Base [*Canada*] [*Information service or system*]   (IID)
COMBASFRANCE ... Commander, [*US*] Ports and Bases, France
COMBAT ... Coalition of Municipalities to Ban Animal Trafficking   (EA)
COMBAT ... Cost-Oriented Models Built to Analyze Tradeoffs   (MCD)
COMBATCRULANT ... Commander, Battleships-Cruisers, Atlantic Fleet   (MUGU)
COMBATDIV ... Commander, Battleship Division

COMBATEX ... Combat Exercises [*Canadian Navy*]
COMBATLANT ... Commander, Battleships, Atlantic Fleet
COMBATPAC ... Commander, Battleships, Pacific Fleet
COMBAX ... Compact Blazing Combustion Axiom [*Auto engineering*]
Comb Cumul Index Pediatr ... Combined Cumulative Index to Pediatrics [*A publication*]
COMB EFF ... Combustion Efficiency
COMBENECHAN ... Commander, BENELUX Subarea Channel
Comb Eng .. Combustion Engineering [*A publication*]
COMBEX ... Combined Exercise [*Military*] (NVT)
Comb Expl (R) ... Combustion, Explosion, and Shock Waves (USSR) [*A publication*]
Comb Flame ... Combustion and Flame [*A publication*]
ComBibSJeron ... Commentario Biblico "San Jeronimo" [*A publication*] (BJA)
COMBIMAN ... Computerized Biomechanical Man-Model [*Air Force*]
Combined Pension Ass Vic News ... Combined Pensioners' Association of Victoria. News [*A publication*]
COMBISCLANT ... Commander, Bay Of Biscay Atlantic Subarea [*NATO*]
COMBISLANT ... Commander, Bay of Biscay Atlantic Subarea [*NATO*]
COMBL..... Combustible (MSA)
Com Black ... A'Beckett's Comic Blackstone [*A publication*] (DLA)
COMBLACKBASE ... Commander, Black Sea Defense Sector (NATG)
COMBLUE ... Commander Blue (Friendly) Force [*Navy*] (CAAL)
COMBN.... Combustion
comb nov .... Combinatio Nova [*New Combination*] [*Biology, taxonomy*]
Com BNS... English Common Bench Reports, New Series [*A publication*] (DLA)
COMBO.... Computation of Miss Between Orbits [*Air Force*] (MCD)
COMBOIS ... Internationale Gemeinschaft fuer Holz-technologie-Transfer [*International Community for Wood-Technology Transfer*] (EAIO)
COMBOMRON ... Commander, Bombing Squadron
COMBOSFORT ... Commander, Bosphorus Fortifications (NATG)
Comb Proc Int Plant Propagators Soc ... Combined Proceedings. International Plant Propagators' Society [*A publication*]
COMBQUARFOR ... Combined Quarantine Force [*US/Venezuela/Dominican Republic/Argentina*]
COMBRAX ... Commodore, Royal Canadian Navy Barracks at [*Place*]
COMBREMGRU ... Commander, Bremerton Group
COMBRESTCHAN ... Commander, Brest Subarea Channel
COMBRITELBE ... Commander, British Naval Elbe Squadron (NATG)
COMBRITRHIN ... Commander, British Naval Rhine Squadron (NATG)
COMBS..... Contractor-Managed Base Supply [*Facility*] (MCD)
Comb Sci T ... Combustion Science and Technology [*A publication*]
COMBSNGRU ... Commander, Boston Group
COMBT .... Combat (CINC)
Combust Combust ... Combustione e Combustibile [*A publication*]
Combust Eng Assoc Doc ... Combustion Engineering Association. Document [*England*] [*A publication*]
Combust Explos and Shock Waves ... Combustion, Explosion, and Shock Waves [*A publication*]
Combust Explos Shock Waves ... Combustion, Explosion, and Shock Waves [*USSR*] [*A publication*]
Combust and Flame ... Combustion and Flame [*A publication*]
Combust Flame ... Combustion and Flame [*A publication*]
Combustion Sci Tech ... Combustion Science and Technology [*A publication*]
Combust Sci Technol ... Combustion Science and Technology [*A publication*]
Combust Sci Technol Book Ser ... Combustion Science and Technology. Book Series [*A publication*]
COMC....... Chicago Osteopathic Medical Center
Co MC .... Coke's Magna Charta [*or Second Institute*] [*A publication*] (DLA)
Com C .... Commercial Code (DLA)
COMC....... Communications Controller (MCD)
COMC....... Mills College, Oakland, CA [*Library symbol*] [*Library of Congress*] (LCLS)
COMCABCO ... Commercial Cable Company
COMCAM ... Compressible Cell and Maker
Com Canada ... Commerce Canada [*A publication*]
COMCANLANT ... Commander, Canadian Atlantic Subarea [*NATO*]
COMCAP ... Combat Capabilities (MCD)
COMCARANTISUBAIRGRU ... Carrier Antisubmarine Air Group [*Navy*]
COMCARASWAIRGRU ... Commander, Carrier Antisubmarine Air Group
COMCARDIV ... Commander, Carrier Division
COMCARE ... Commission for the Safety, Rehabilitation, and Compensation of Commonwealth Employees [*Australia*]
COMCARIBSEAFRON ... Commander, Caribbean Sea Frontier (NATG)
COMCARSTRIKFOR ... Commander, Carrier Striking Force (AFM)
COMCARSTRIKGRU ... Commander, Carrier Striking Group
COMCARSTRIKGRUONE ... Commander, Carrier Striking Group One (AFM)
COMCARSTRIKGRUTWO ... Commander, Carrier Striking Group Two (AFM)
Com Cas..... Commercial Cases [*1896-1941*] [*England*] [*A publication*] (DLA)
Com Cas..... Company Cases [*India*] [*A publication*] (DLA)
COMCAS ... Computer-Oriented Modal Control and Appraisal System
Com Cas SCC ... Commercial Cases, Small Cause Court [*1851-60*] [*Bengal, India*] [*A publication*] (DLA)
COMCASU ... Commander, Carrier Aircraft Service Unit

COMCAT ... Computer Output Microform Catalog
COMCBLANT ... Commander, Naval Construction Battalions, Atlantic Fleet
COMCBPAC ... Commander, Naval Construction Battalions, Pacific Fleet
COMCEN ... Communications Center [*NATO*] (NATG)
COMCENPAC ... Commander, Central Pacific
COMCENTAG ... Commander, Central Army Group, Central Europe
COMCENTLANT ... Commander, Central Atlantic Subarea [*NATO*]
COMCERTS ... Combat Systems Certification Site [*Navy*]
Com Challenges of Mod Soc Air Pollution ... Committee on the Challenges of Modern Society. Air Pollution [*A publication*]
COMCHASNGRU ... Commander, Charleston Group
COMCHERCHAN ... Commander, Cherbourg Subarea Channel
COMCM ... Communication Countermeasures
COMCOGARD ... Commander, Coast Guard District
Com Col Can ... Community Colleges of Canada [*A publication*]
Com Coll Front ... Community College Frontiers [*A publication*]
Com Coll R ... Community College Review [*A publication*]
COMCOLUMGRU ... Commander, Columbia River Group
Com Com ... Journal of Community Communications [*A publication*]
COMCOMRON ... Commander, Composite Squadron
COMCON ... Combat Control [*Army*]
Com Con .... Comyn's Law of Contracts [*A publication*] (DLA)
Com on Con .... Comyn's Law of Contracts [*A publication*] (DLA)
Com Con Psy ... Comments on Contemporary Psychiatry [*A publication*]
COMCONSUP ... Combat, Control, Support [*Army*]
Com Crew ... Combat Crew [*A publication*]
COMCRUDES ... Commander, Cruiser-Destroyer Force
COMCRUDESFLOT ... Commander, Cruiser-Destroyer Flotilla [*Acronym always followed by a number*] [*Navy*]
COMCRUDESLANT ... Commander, Cruiser-Destroyer Forces, Atlantic [*Navy*]
COMCRUDESPAC ... Commander, Cruiser-Destroyer Forces, Pacific [*Navy*] (MCD)
COMCRUDIV ... Commander, Cruiser Division
COMCRULANT ... Commander, Cruiser Forces, Atlantic Fleet (MCD)
COMCRUPAC ... Commander, Cruiser Forces, Pacific Fleet
COMCRUSCORON ... Commander, Cruiser Scouting Squadron
COMCVW ... Commander, Carrier Air Wing [*Navy*] (NVT)
COMD....... Command (AFM)
COMD....... Command Airways, Inc. [*NASDAQ symbol*] (NQ)
Com D........ Commercial Division [*New South Wales Supreme Court*] [*Australia*]
COMD....... Countermedia. Alaska Journalism Review and Supplement [*A publication*]
COMDAC ... Comite d'Action en France
COMDARFORT ... Commander, Dardanelles Fortifications (NATG)
COMDC... Catalogue of Oriental Manuscripts in Danish Collections (BJA)
COMD DSR ... Command Dental Service Report [*Air Force*]
COMDEC ... Command Decision and Movement Control Charts
Com Dec..... Commissioners' Decisions [*US Patent and Trademark Office*] [*A publication*]
COMDES ... Commander, Destroyers
COMDESDEVGRU ... Commander, Destroyer Development Group [*Navy*]
COMDESDIV ... Commander, Destroyer Division
COMDESFLOT ... Commander, Destroyer Flotilla
COMDESGRU ... Commander, Destroyer Group
COMDESLANT ... Commander, Destroyers, Atlantic Fleet
COMDESPAC ... Commander, Destroyers, Pacific Fleet
COMDESRON ... Commander, Destroyer Squadron
Com Develop J ... Community Development Journal [*A publication*]
Com Dev J ... Community Development Journal [*A publication*]
Com Dev Pancha Raj D ... Community Development and Panchayati Raj Digest [*A publication*]
COMDEX ... Computer Dealer's Exposition
COMDG.... Commanding (AFM)
COMDG.... Commanding Officer [*Military*] [*British*] (ROG)
COMDGEN ... Commanding General
COMDG OF ... Commanding Officer
COMDIEGOGRU ... Commander, San Diego Group
Com Dig..... Comyn's Digest of the Laws of England [*1762-1882*] [*A publication*] (DLA)
COMDO.... Commando (AFM)
COMDOC ... Combat Documentation (AFM)
Com Dow ... Comstock's Digest of the Law of Dower [*A publication*] (DLA)
COMDR.... Commander (AFM)
COMDRE ... Commodore (ADA)
COMDSGTMAJ ... Command Sergeant Major [*Army*] (AABC)
COMDT.... Commandant [*Air Force*] (AFM)
COMDTCOGARD ... Coast Guard Commandant
COMDTINST ... Commandant's Instruction
COMDTMARCORPS ... Commandant of the Marine Corps
COMDTNOB ... Commandant, Naval Operating Base
COMDTNY ... Commandant, Navy Yard
COMDTUSCG ... Commandant, United States Coast Guard
COMDTUSMC ... Commandant, United States Marine Corps
COM(D) WA ... Commodore, (Destroyers) Western Approaches [*British*]
COME....... Chief Ordnance Mechanical Engineer [*British*] (ADA)
COME....... Commentary (ROG)
COME....... Commercial Decal, Inc. [*NASDAQ symbol*] (NQ)
COME....... Committee (ROG)
COME....... Committee on the Ministry of Elders [*Australia*]

COME ...... Committee on Missionary Evangelism (EA)
COME ...... Computer Output Microfilm Equipment
COMe .... Cyclophosphamide, Oncovin [*Vincristine*], Methotrexate [*Antineoplastic drug regimen*]
CoMe .... Meeker Public Library, Meeker, CO [*Library symbol*] [*Library of Congress*] (LCLS)
COMEAO ... Concours Medical [*A publication*]
COMEASTFRON ... Commander, Eastern Sea Frontier [*Navy*] (MUGU)
COMEASTLANT ... Commander, Eastern Atlantic Forces
COMEASTSEAFRON ... Commander, Eastern Sea Frontier [*Navy*]
COMECE ... Commission des Episcopats de la Communaute Europeenne [*Association of Episcopacies of the European Community*] (EA)
COMECON ... Council for Mutual Economic Assistance [*Also known as CEMA, CMEA*] [*Communist-bloc nations: Poland, Russia, East Germany, Czechoslovakia, Romania, Bulgaria, Hungary*]
COMED .... Combined Map and Electronic Display (MCD)
COMED .... Communications Editing Unit (NOAA)
COMEDBASE ... Commander, Mediterranean Defense Sector (NATG)
COMEDCENT ... Commander, Central Mediterranean
COMEDEAST ... Commander, Eastern Mediterranean (AFM)
COMEDNOREAST ... Commander, Northeast Mediterranean (AABC)
COMEDOC ... Commander, Mediterranean Operations Center
COMEDS ... CONUS [*Continental United States*] Meteorological Data [*or Distribution*] System (MCD)
COMEDSOUEAST ... Commander, Southeast Mediterranean (AFM)
COMEINDORS ... Composite Mechanized Information and Document Retrieval System
COMEL ..... Comite de Coordination des Constructeurs des Machines Tournantes Electriques du Marche Commun [*Coordinating Committee for Common Market Associations of Manufacturers of Rotating Electric Machinery*] (EAIO)
COMEL ..... Coordinating Committee for Common Market Associations of Manufacturers of Rotating Electrical Machinery [*London, England*] (EAIO)
COMELEC ... Commission on Elections [*Philippines*]
Com & Electronics ... Communication and Electronics [*A publication*]
COMELEVEN ... Commandant, Eleventh Naval District (MUGU)
COMENER ... Comision Centroamericana de Energia [*Central American Energy Commission*] (EAIO)
COMEPP .. Cornell Manufacturing Engineering and Productivity Program [*Cornell University*] [*Research center*] (RCD)
C O-Mer .... Cahiers d'Outre-Mer [*A publication*]
CoMeR ...... Rio Blanco County Traveling Library, Meeker, CO [*Library symbol*] [*Library of Congress*] [*Obsolete*] (LCLS)
Comercio Exterior de Mexico ... Comercio Exterior de Mexico [*A publication*]
Comercio Prod ... Comercio y Produccion [*A publication*]
Comer Exterior Mexico ... Comercio Exterior de Mexico [*A publication*]
ComErm ..... Communications. Musee National de l'Ermitage [*A publication*]
Comer e Mercados ... Comercio e Mercados [*A publication*]
Comer y Produccion ... Comercio y Produccion [*A publication*]
CoMes .... Mesa Verde Community Library, Mesa Verde National Park, CO [*Library symbol*] [*Library of Congress*] (LCLS)
COMESA ... Committee on the Meteorological Effects of Stratospheric Aircraft
COMET .... Child-Operated Mobile Electric Transport
COMET .... Coherent Electromagnetic Energy Transmission
COMET .... Collegium Medicorum Theatri (EA)
COMET .... Combined Organic Movement for Education and Training [*British*]
COMET .... Command Evaluation Teams (MCD)
COMET .... Committee of Middle East Trade [*British Overseas Trade Board*] (DS)
COMET .... Computer Message Transmission
COMET .... Computer-Operated Machine Evaluation Technique [*Air Force*] (MCD)
COMET .... Computer-Operated Management Evaluation Technique [*AEC-Army*]
COMET .... Computerized Muscle Exerciser and Trainer [*Bodylog, Inc.*]
COMET .... Consent to Medical Treatment [*British Medical Association computer program*]
COMET .... Continental [*United States*] Meteorological Teletype System [*Navy*]
COMET .... Cost Measurement Technique (AAG)
COMET .... Meteorological Office Computer [*British*] (DEN)
COMETS .. Community Electronic Teller System
COMETS .. Computer-Operated Multifunction Electronic Test System (MCD)
COMEX .... Commence Exercise [*Military*] (NVT)
COMEX .... Commodity Exchange (EA)
COMEX .... Commonwealth Expedition [*British*]
COMEX .... Communications Exhibition [*Trade fair*] [*British*]
COMEXAZ ... Comite de Mexico y Aztlan (EA)
COMEXDIV ... Commander, Experimental Division [*Navy*]
Com Ext Mexico ... Comercio Exterior de Mexico [*A publication*]
Com Ext Tchecosl ... Commerce Exterieur Tchecoslovaque [*A publication*]
COMF .... Cyclophosphamide, Oncovin [*Vincristine*], Methotrexate, Fluorouracil [*Antineoplastic drug regimen*]

CoMFA ...... Comparative Molecular Field Analysis [*Software*]
Com Fac Sci Univ Ankara Ser A3 Astronom ... Universite d'Ankara. Faculte des Sciences. Communications. Serie A3. Astronomie [*A publication*]
COMFAIR ... Commander, Fleet Air
COMFAIRADAK ... Commander, Fleet Air, Adak, Alaska
COMFAIRALAMEDA ... Commander, Fleet Air, Alameda
COMFAIRBERMUDA ... Commander, Fleet Air, Bermuda
COMFAIRBRUNSWICK ... Commander, Fleet Air, Brunswick
COMFAIRELM ... Commander, Fleet Air, Eastern Atlantic and Mediterranean (NATG)
COMFAIRHAWAII ... Commander, Fleet Air, Hawaii (MUGU)
COMFAIRJAPAN ... Commander, Fleet Air, Japan
COMFAIRJAX ... Commander, Fleet Air, Jacksonville, Florida
COMFAIRKEFLAVIK ... Commander, Fleet Air, Keflavik, Iceland
COMFAIRMED ... Commander, Fleet Air, Mediterranean
COMFAIRNORFOLK ... Commander, Fleet Air, Norfolk, Virginia
COMFAIRQUONSET ... Commander, Fleet Air, Quonset Point, Rhode Island
COMFAIRSANDIEGO ... Commander, Fleet Air, San Diego, California
COMFAIRSOWESTPAC ... Commander, Fleet Air, Southwest Pacific (MUGU)
COMFAIRWESTPAC ... Commander, Fleet Air, Western Pacific
COMFAIRWING ... Commander, Fleet Air Wing
COMFAIRWINGLANT ... Commander, Fleet Air Wing, Atlantic (NATG)
COMFAIRWINGNORLANT ... Commander, Fleet Air Wing, Northern Atlantic (AABC)
COMFAX ... Chip Operational Multifunction Auxiliary Computer (MCD)
COMFAX ... Communications Facility [*Control and Processing Company*]
COMFIGHTRON ... Commander, Fighting Squadron
Com and Fin Chr ... Commercial and Financial Chronicle. Statistical Section [*A publication*]
COMFIRSTFLEET ... Commander, [*US*] First Fleet
COMFIRSTFLT ... Commander, [*US*] First Fleet (MUGU)
Com Fish .... Commercial Fishing [*A publication*]
COMFITWING ... Commander Fighter Wing (MCD)
COMFIVE ... Commandant, Fifth Naval District (MUGU)
COMFIVEATAF ... Commander, Fifth Allied Tactical Air Force (AFM)
COMFLAGRU ... Commander, Florida Group
COMFLDCOMDASA ... Commander, Field Command, Defense Atomic Support Agency (AABC)
COMFLETRAGRU ... Commander, Fleet Training Group
COMFLETRAGRUWATE ... Commander, Fleet Training Group and Underway Training Element (MUGU)
COMFLOGWING ... Commander, Fleet Logistic Air Wing
COMFLTBASTILLES ... Commander, Atlantic Fleet Bases, Antilles
COMFOR ... Commercial Wire Center Forecast Program [*Telecommunications*] (TEL)
Com Forms ... Comer's Forms of Writs [*A publication*] (DLA)
Com For Rev ... Commonwealth Forestry Review [*A publication*]
COMFOURATAF ... Commander, Fourth Allied Tactical Air Force, Central Europe
COMG .... Comgen Technology [*NASDAQ symbol*] (NQ)
COM'G ...... Commencing
COMGAR ... Comando Geral do Ar [*Brazilian Air Force*]
COMGEN ... Command Generation Program [*Mariner*] [*NASA*]
COMGEN ... Commanding General
Com-Gen .... Commissary-General [*British military*] (DMA)
COMGEN ... Common Specifications Statements Generator (KSC)
COMGENAFMIDPAC ... Commanding General, Army Forces, Mid-Pacific [*World War II*]
COMGENEUCOM ... Commanding General, European Command (NATG)
COMGENMED ... Commanding General, Mediterranean Theater of Operations [*World War II*]
COMGENPOA ... Commanding General, Pacific Ocean Areas [*World War II*]
COMGENSOPAC ... Commanding General, South Pacific Area [*World War II*]
COMGENTEN ... Commanding General, Tenth Army
COMGENTHIRDAIR ... Commanding General, Third Air Division (NATG)
COMGENUSAFE ... Commanding General, United States Air Forces, Europe (NATG)
COMGENUSAREUR ... Commanding General, United States Army, Europe (NATG)
COM-GEOM ... Combinatorial Geometry
COMGERNORSEA ... Commander, German North Sea Subarea (NATG)
COMGIB ... Commander, Gibraltar [*Navy*] (AABC)
COMGIBLANT ... Commander, Atlantic Approaches Gibraltar (NATG)
COMGIBMED ... Commander, Gibraltar-Mediterranean Command (AFM)
Com Glaciol Ital Boll Ser 2 ... Comitato Glaciologico Italiano. Bollettino. Serie Seconda [*A publication*]
COMGREPAT ... Commander, Greenland Patrol
COMGRU ... Commander of a Numbered Group
COMGS ... Commissioner of the Great Seal [*British*] (ROG)
Com G & W ... Comstock on Guardian and Ward [*A publication*] (DLA)
COMH ...... Committee of the House [*British*] (ROG)
COMHA ... Committee on Mental Health Advocacy [*Australia*]
COMHAWSEAFRON ... Commander, Hawaiian Sea Frontier [*Navy*]
COMHEDRON ... Commander, Headquarters Squadron
Com Hlth Serv Bul ... Community Health Services Bulletin [*A publication*]

Com Hort ... Commercial Horticulture [*A publication*]

COMHUKFORLAN ... Commander, Hunter-Killer Force, Atlantic Fleet

Com/I........ Commercial Invoice (DS)

COMI........ Computer Microfilm Corp. [*NASDAQ symbol*] (NQ)

COMIBERLANT ... Commander, Iberian Atlantic Area (NATG)

COMIC ... Colorant Mixture Computer [*Du Pont trademark*]

COMICEASWGRU ... Commander, Iceland Antisubmarine Warfare Group

COMICEDEFOR ... Commander, Iceland Defense Force

COMIDEASTFOR ... Commander, Middle East Force (AABC)

COMIFA... Commission Internationale pour l'Etude Scientifique de la Famille [*International Scientific Commission on the Family*]

COM III .... Communications III, Inc. [*Columbus, OH*] (TSSD)

COMIL...... Chairman of Military Committee (NATG)

COMIN..... Commander, Minecraft [*Navy*]

COMINCH ... Commander-in-Chief [*US fleet*]

COMINDIV ... Commander, Minecraft Division [*Navy*]

COMINELANT ... Commander, Mine Force, Atlantic Fleet [*Navy*]

COMINEPAC ... Commander, Mine Force, Pacific Fleet [*Navy*]

COMINEWARFOR ... Commander Mine Warfare Forces

COMINFIL ... Communist Infiltration [*Name of 1960's FBI campaign against infiltrators*]

COMINFLOT ... Commander, Mine Flotilla

COMINFORM ... Communist Information

COMINGRP ... Commander, Mine Group

COMINGRPOK ... Commander, Mine Group, Okinawa

COMINLANT ... Commander, Mine Force, Atlantic Fleet [*Navy*]

COMINPAC ... Commander, Minecraft, Pacific Fleet [*Navy*]

COMINRON ... Commander, Mine Squadron

COMINST ... Communications Instructions [*Navy*]

Com Inst Agron Sul ... Comunicado. Instituto Agronomico do Sul [*A publication*]

COMINT .. Communications Intelligence [*Military*]

Com Interam Atun Trop Bol ... Comision Interamericana del Atun Tropical. Boletin [*A publication*]

Comintern.. Communist International (PPE)

Com Internaz ... Communita Internazionale [*A publication*]

Com Int Etude Bauxites Alumine Alum Trav ... Comite International pour l'Etude des Bauxites, de l'Alumine, et d'Aluminium. Travaux [*A publication*]

Com Int Etude Bauxites Oxydes Hydroxydes Alum Trav ... Comite International pour l'Etude des Bauxites, des Oxydes, et des Hydroxydes d'Aluminium. Travaux [*A publication*]

Com Int Poids Mes Com Consult Def Metre Trav ... Comite International des Poids et Mesures. Comite Consultatif pour la Definition du Metre. Travaux [*A publication*]

Com Int Poids Mes Com Consult Electr Trav ... Comite International des Poids et Mesures. Comite Consultatif d'Electricite. Travaux [*A publication*]

Com Int Poids Mes Com Consult Etalons Mes Radiat Ionis Trav ... Comite International des Poids et Mesures. Comite Consultatif pour les Etalons de Mesure des Radiations Ionisantes. Travaux [*A publication*]

Com Int Poids Mes Com Consult Photom Trav ... Comite International des Poids et Mesures. Comite Consultatif de Photometrie. Travaux [*A publication*]

Com Int Poids Mes Com Consult Thermom Trav ... Comite International des Poids et Mesures. Comite Consultatif de Thermometrie. Travaux [*A publication*]

Com Invest Cient Prov Buenos Aires Inf ... Comision de Investigaciones Cientificas de la Provincia de Buenos Aires. Informes [*A publication*]

COMIREX ... Committee on Imagery Requirements and Exploitation [*United States Intelligence Board*]

COMIS...... Collection Management Information System (MCD)

COMIS...... Command Management Information System [*Air Force*]

COMIS...... Committee Meeting Information System (MCD)

COMISH-US ... Congo Military Mission - United States

Comision Nac Valores Bol ... Comision Nacional de Valores. Boletin [*A publication*]

COMISS ... Commission on Ministries in Specialized Settings [*Federal government*]

COMISS ... Commission on Pastoral Research (EA)

COMISS ... Computerized Medical Information Support System [*Veterans Administration*]

COMIT ..... Compiler/Massachusetts Institute of Technology (IEEE)

COMITA... Income Tax Assessment Act [*Database*] [*Australia*]

Comitato Naz Energia Nucleare Notiz ... Comitato Nazionale per l'Energia Nucleare. Notiziario [*A publication*]

COMIT CAUS ... Comitatis Causa [*For the County's Sake*] [*Latin*] (ROG)

COMITEXTIL ... Comite de Coordination des Industries Textiles de la Communaute Economique Europeenne [*Coordination Committee for the Textile Industries in the European Economic Community*] [*Brussels, Belgium*] (EAIO)

COMJAM ... Communications Jamming [*Military*]

COMJD .... Commodity Journal [*A publication*]

COMJEF .. Commander, Joint Expeditionary Force

Com Jour ... Journals of the House of Commons [*A publication*] (DLA)

Com & Jr Coll ... Community and Junior College Journal [*A publication*]

Com & Jr Coll J ... Community and Junior College Journal [*A publication*]

COMJTF .. Commander, Joint Task Force (AABC)

COMJUWATF ... Commander, Joint Unconventional Warfare Task Force (AABC)

COMKD.... Completely Knocked Down [*i.e., disassembled, as a toy or piece of furniture which must be assembled before use*] [*Freight*]

COML....... Columbia & Millstadt R. R. [*AAR code*]

COML...... Commercial (AFM)

Com L....... Commercial Law [*Canada*] (DLA)

COML....... Committal (ROG)

Com and L ... Communications and the Law [*A publication*]

Com LA..... Commercial Law Annual [*A publication*] (DLA)

COMLA ..... Commonwealth Library Association (EAIO)

COMLA .... Cyclophosphamide, Oncovin [*Vincristine*], Methotrexate with Leucovorin, ara C [*Antineoplastic drug regimen*]

COMLAB ... Commerce Laboratory [*NASA*]

COMLAIRDIR ... Travel via Commercial Aircraft Is Directed [*Where Government Aircraft Is Not Available*] (MCD)

COMLANDCENT ... Commander, Allied Land Forces, Central Europe

COMLANDENMARK ... Commander, Allied Land Forces, Denmark (NATG)

COMLANDFOR ... Commander, Land Forces [*Army*] (AABC)

COMLANDJUT ... Commander, Allied Land Forces, Schleswig-Holstein and Jutland (AABC)

COMLANDMARK ... Commander, Allied Land Forces, Denmark (AFM)

COMLANDNON ... Commander, Land Forces, North Norway (NATG)

COMLANDNORWAY ... Commander, Allied Land Forces, Norway

COMLANDSCHLESWIG ... Commander, Allied Land Forces, Schleswig-Holstein

COMLANDSOUTH ... Commander, Allied Land Forces, Southern Europe

COMLANDSOUTHEAST ... Commander, Allied Land Forces, Southeastern Europe

COMLANDZEALAND ... Commander, Allied Land Forces, Zealand (AABC)

COMLANTFLTWPNRNGE ... Commander, Atlantic Fleet Weapons Range

Com L Assoc Bull ... Commercial Law Association. Bulletin [*A publication*] (APTA)

Com Law.... Commercial Law (DLA)

Com Law.... Communications and the Law [*A publication*]

Com & Law ... Communications and the Law [*A publication*]

Com Law Ann ... Commercial Law Annual [*A publication*] (DLA)

Com Law Jnl ... Commercial Law Journal [*A publication*]

Com Law R ... English Common Law Reports [*A publication*] (DLA)

Com Law Rep ... English Common Law Reports [*A publication*] (DLA)

COMLBEACHGRU ... Commander, Long Beach Group

Com & Leg Rep ... Commercial and Legal Reporter [*A publication*] (DLA)

Com L J ... Commercial Law Journal [*A publication*]

Com L League J ... Commercial Law League. Journal [*A publication*] (DLA)

COMLO.... Combined Operations Material Liaison Officer

COMLO.... Compass Locator

COMLOG ... Communications Equipment Logistics (MCD)

COMLOGNET ... Combat Logistics Network [*DoD*]

COMLOGNET ... Communications Logistics Network (IEEE)

Com LQ ..... Commercial Law Quarterly [*A publication*]

Com LR...... Commonwealth Law Review [*A publication*]

Com LR...... English Common Law Reports [*A publication*] (DLA)

Com L Rep ... Common Law Reports [*1853-85*] [*A publication*] (DLA)

Com L & T ... Comyn on Landlord and Tenant [*A publication*] (DLA)

COMLTRANSAUTH ... Travel via Commercial Transportation Authorized [*Military*]

Comm......... Blackstone's Commentaries on the Laws of England [*A publication*] (DLA)

COMM...... Cellular Communications, Inc. [*New York, NY*] [*NASDAQ symbol*] (NQ)

COMM...... Commander

COMM...... Commencement (ROG)

COMM...... Commentary

COMM...... Commerce [*or Commercial*]

COMM...... Commercial Mission [*NASA*]

COMM...... Commissary (ADA)

COMM...... Commission (KSC)

COMM...... Commitment (MCD)

COMM...... Committee

COMM...... Commodore

Comm......... Commodus [*of Scriptores Historiae Augustae*] [*Classical studies*] (OCD)

COMM...... Common

Comm........ Commonweal [*A publication*]

COMM..... Commonwealth

Comm........ Communal

COMM..... Communication (AFM)

Comm........ Communication. Kodak Research Laboratories [*A publication*]

Com M....... Communication Monographs [*A publication*]

COMM..... Communion [*Service*] (ROG)

COMM..... Communist Party [*Political party*]

COMM..... Commutator

COMM..... Department of Commerce

COMMA... Composite Maneuver Augmentation (MCD)

Comm ACM ... Communications. ACM [*Association for Computing Machinery*] [*A publication*]

COMM/ADP ... Communications/Automatic Data Processing Center [*Fort Monmouth, NJ*] [*Army*] (GRD)

COMMAGROCV ... Commander, Military Assistance Group, Republic of China, Vietnam
COMMAIRCENTLANT ... Commander, Maritime Air Central Subarea [*NATO*]
COMMAIRCHAN ... Commander, Allied Maritime Air Force Channel [*NATO*]
COMMAIREASTLANT ... Commander, Maritime Air Eastern Atlantic Area [*NATO*]
COMMAIRGIBLANT ... Commander, Maritime Air Gibraltar Subarea [*NATO*] (NATG)
COMMAIRNORECHAN ... Commander, Maritime Air Northeast Subarea Channel [*NATO*] (AABC)
COMMAIRNORLANT ... Commander, Maritime Air Northern Subarea [*NATO*]
COMMAIRPLYMCHAN ... Commander, Maritime Air Plymouth Subarea Channel [*NATO*] (AABC)
Comm Algeb ... Communications in Algebra [*A publication*]
Comm Algebra ... Communications in Algebra [*A publication*]
Comm Alkali React Concr Nat Prog Rep H ... Committee on Alkali Reactions in Concrete. Danish National Institute of Building Research and the Academy of Technical Sciences. Progress Report. Series H. Methods of Evaluation of Alkali Reactions [*A publication*]
Comm Alkali React Concr Prog Rep A ... Committee on Alkali Reactions in Concrete. Danish National Institute of Building Research and the Academy of Technical Sciences. Progress Report. Series A. Alkali Reactions in Concrete. General [*A publication*]
Comm Alkali React Concr Prog Rep D ... Committee on Alkali Reactions in Concrete. Danish National Institute of Building Research and the Academy of Technical Sciences. Progress Report. Series D. Aggregate Types of Denmark [*A publication*]
Comm Alkali React Concr Prog Rep F ... Committee on Alkali Reactions in Concrete. Danish National Institute of Building Research and the Academy of Technical Sciences. Progress Report. Series F. Alkali Contents of Concrete Components [*A publication*]
Comm Alkali React Concr Prog Rep I ... Committee on Alkali Reactions in Concrete. Danish National Institute of Building Research and the Academy of Technical Sciences. Progress Report. Series I. Inhibition of Alkali Reactions by Admixtures [*A publication*]
Comm Alkali React Concr Prog Rep N ... Committee on Alkali Reactions in Concrete. Danish National Institute of Building Research and the Academy of Technical Sciences. Progress Report. Series N. Observed Symptoms of Deterioration [*A publication*]
COMMAND ... Command Model for Analysis and Design (MCD)
Comman Dig ... Commander's Digest [*A publication*]
Comm AR .. Commonwealth Arbitration Reports [*A publication*] (APTA)
Comm Archives Centrales Orgue ... Communications. Archives Centrales de l'Orgue/Mededelingen. Centraal Orgelarchief [*A publication*]
COMMARFOR ... Commander, Marine Forces
COMMARIANAS ... Commander, Marianas
Comm B ..... Common Bench Reports (Manning, Granger, and Scott) [*1846-65*] [*England*] [*A publication*] (DLA)
COMMBCA ... Department of Commerce Board of Contract Appeals
Comm Bibl Hist Med Hungar ... Communicationes. Bibliotheca Historiae Medicae Hungarica [*A publication*]
COMMBOND ... Commonwealth Bank Bond Index [*Database*] [*Australia*]
Comm Broadc ... Communication and Broadcasting [*A publication*]
Comm Bul .. Commercial Bulletin for Teachers in Secondary Schools [*A publication*] (APTA)
Comm C ..... Commercial Code (DLA)
COMMCE ... Commence (ROG)
COMMCE ... Commerce (ROG)
COMMCEN ... Communications Center
COMMCM ... Communications Countermeasures [*Military*] (NVT)
Comm Communautes Eur ... Commission des Communautes Europeennes [*A publication*]
Comm Ct .... Commerce Court (DLA)
Commctn Age ... Communication Age [*A publication*]
commd .... Commissioned (DLA)
COMMDAC ... Communications Direction and Coordination
Comm Data Sci Technol Spec Rep (ICSU) ... Committee on Data for Science and Technology. Special Report (International Council of Scientific Unions) [*A publication*]
COMM DECK ... Common Decking [*Lumber*]
Comm Del Order ... Commissioner's Delegation Order (DLA)
Comm Den Or ... Community Dentistry and Oral Epidemiology [*A publication*]
COMMDET ... Commissioning Detail
COMMDET ... Communications Detachment (MCD)
Comm Dev J ... Community Development Journal [*A publication*]
COMMDG ... Commanding
Comm and Dist Res ... Communications and Distributed Resources Report [*A publication*]
COMMDR ... Commander
COMMDT ... Commandant

Comm Dublin Inst Adv Studies Ser A ... Communications. Dublin Institute for Advanced Studies. Series A [*A publication*]
Comm Ed ... Commercial Education [*A publication*]
Comm Educ ... Communication Education [*A publication*]
COMMEL ... Communications-Electronics
COMMEM ... Commemorate
COMMEM ... Commemoration (DSUE)
COMMEMG ... Commemorating
Commen ..... Commentary [*A publication*]
COMMEN ... Compiler Oriented for Multiprogramming and Multiprocessing Environments (IEEE)
COMMEND ... Computer-Oriented Mechanical Design (MCD)
Comm Energie At (Fr) Serv Doc Ser Bibliogr ... Commissariat a l'Energie Atomique (France). Service de Documentation. Serie Bibliographie [*A publication*]
Com Men Health J ... Community Mental Health Journal [*A publication*]
Commentat Biol ... Commentationes Biologicae [*A publication*]
Commentat Biol Soc Sci Fenn ... Commentationes Biologicae. Societas Scientiarum Fennica [*A publication*]
Commentat Phys-Math ... Commentationes Physico-Mathematicae [*A publication*]
Commentat Phys-Math Suppl ... Commentationes Physico-Mathematicae. Supplement [*A publication*]
Commentat Pontif Acad Sci ... Commentationes Pontificiae. Academiae Scientiarum [*A publication*]
Comment on Ed ... Comment on Education [*A publication*]
Com Ment Health J ... Community Mental Health Journal [*A publication*]
Comment Math Helv ... Commentarii Mathematici Helvetici [*A publication*]
Comment Math Prace Mat ... Roczniki Polskiego Towarzystwa Matematycznego. Seria I. Commentationes Mathematicae Prace Matematyczne [*A publication*]
Comment Math Special Issue ... Commentationes Mathematicae. Special Issue [*A publication*]
Comment Math Univ Carolin ... Commentationes Mathematicae. Universitatis Carolinae [*A publication*]
Comment Math Univ Carolinae ... Commentationes Mathematicae. Universitatis Carolinae [*A publication*]
Comment Math Univ St Paul ... Commentarii Mathematici. Universitatis Sancti Pauli [*A publication*]
Comment Phys Math Soc Sci Fenn ... Commentationes Physico-Mathematicae. Societas Scientiarum Fennica [*A publication*]
Comment Plant Sci ... Commentaries in Plant Science [*A publication*]
Comment Pontif Acad Sci ... Commentario. Pontificia Academia Scientiarum [*A publication*]
Comment Res Breast Dis ... Commentaries on Research in Breast Disease [*A publication*]
Comments Astrophys ... Comments on Astrophysics [*United States, England*] [*A publication*]
Comments Astrophys Comments Mod Phys Part C ... Comments on Astrophysics. Comments on Modern Physics. Part C [*A publication*]
Comments Astrophys Space Phys ... Comments on Astrophysics and Space Physics [*Later, Comments on Astrophysics*] [*A publication*]
Comments At Mol Phys ... Comments on Atomic and Molecular Physics [*A publication*]
Comments Contemp Psychiatry ... Comments on Contemporary Psychiatry [*A publication*]
Comments Earth Sci Geophys ... Comments on Earth Sciences. Geophysics [*A publication*]
Comments Mol and Cell Biophys Comments Mod Biol Part A ... Comments on Molecular and Cellular Biophysics. Comments on Modern Biology. Part A [*A publication*]
Comments Nucl & Part Phys ... Comments on Nuclear and Particle Physics [*A publication*]
Comments Nucl Part Phys ... Comments on Nuclear and Particle Physics [*A publication*]
Comments Nucl Part Phys Suppl ... Comments on Nuclear and Particle Physics. Supplement [*A publication*]
Comments Plasma Phys Controlled Fusion ... Comments on Plasma Physics and Controlled Fusion [*England*] [*A publication*]
Comments Plasma Phys & Controlled Fusion ... Comments on Plasma Physics and Controlled Fusion [*A publication*]
Comments Plasma Phys Controll Fus ... Comments on Plasma Physics and Controlled Fusion [*A publication*]
Comments Solid State Phys ... Comments on Solid State Physics [*A publication*]
Commer Am ... Commerce America [*A publication*]
Commer Bank Australia Econ R ... Commercial Bank of Australia. Economic Review [*A publication*]
Commerce et Coop ... Commerce et Cooperation [*A publication*]
Commerce Ind & Min R ... Commerce, Industrial, and Mining Review [*A publication*] (APTA)
Commerce Int ... Commerce International [*A publication*]
Commercial ... Commercial Appeal [*A publication*]
Commercium Lit Rei Med et Sc Nat ... Commercium Litterarium ad Rei Medicae et Scientiae Naturali Incrementum Institutum [*A publication*]
Commer Fert Plant Food Ind ... Commercial Fertilizer and Plant Food Industry [*A publication*]

Commer Fert Yearb ... Commercial Fertilizer Yearbook [*A publication*]
Commer Fin J ... Commercial Finance Journal [*A publication*]
Commer Fish Abstr ... Commercial Fisheries Abstracts [*A publication*]
Commer Fish Rev ... Commercial Fisheries Review [*Later, Marine Fisheries Review*] [*A publication*]
Commer Ind ... Commercial Index [*A publication*]
Commer Ind & Min Rev ... Commerce, Industrial, and Mining Review [*A publication*] (APTA)
Commer Letter Can Imperial Bank Commer ... Commercial Letter. Canadian Imperial Bank of Commerce [*A publication*]
Commer Levant ... Commerce du Levant [*A publication*]
Commer Motor ... Commercial Motor [*A publication*]
Commer News USA ... Commercial News USA [*A publication*]
Commer Rabbit ... Commercial Rabbit [*A publication*]
Commer Stand Mon ... Commercial Standards Monthly [*A publication*]
Commer W ... Commercial West [*A publication*]
Comm Eur Communities Eur Rep ... Commission of the European Communities. Eur Report [*A publication*]
Comm Eur Communities Inf Agric ... Commission of the European Communities. Information on Agriculture [*A publication*]
COMMEX ... Communications Exploitation (MCD)
COMMFACMEDME ... Communication Facilities Mediterranean and Middle East
Comm Fac Sci Univ Ankara Ser A ... Communications. Faculte des Sciences. Universite d'Ankara. Serie A. Mathematiques-Physique-Astronomie [*A publication*]
Comm Fert ... Commercial Fertilizer [*A publication*]
COMMFEX ... Communications Field Exercise [*Military*] (NVT)
Comm & Fin ... Commerce and Finance [*A publication*]
Comm & Fin Chr ... Commercial and Financial Chronicle [*A publication*]
Comm & Fin Chron ... Commercial and Financial Chronicle [*A publication*]
Comm Fut L Rep ... Commodity Futures Law Reporter [*Commerce Clearing House*] [*A publication*] (DLA)
Comm Fut L Rep CCH ... Commodity Futures Law Reports. Commerce Clearing House [*A publication*]
Comm Gouv ... Commissaire du Gouvernement [*French*] (ILCA)
Comm Heal S ... Community Health Studies [*A publication*] (APTA)
Comm Health ... Community Health [*A publication*]
Comm Hist Art Med ... Communicationes de Historia Artis Medicinae [*A publication*]
Comm Hydrol Onderz TNO Versl Meded ... Commissie voor Hydrologisch Onderzoek TNO [*Nederlandse Centrale Organisatie voor Toegepast Natuurwetenschappelijk Onderzoek*]. Verslagen en Mededelingen [*A publication*]
Comm Hydrol Onderz TNO Versl Tech Bijeenkomst ... Commissie voor Hydrologisch Onderzoek TNO [*Nederlandse Centrale Organisatie voor Toegepast Natuurwetenschappelijk Onderzoek*]. Verslag van de Technische Bijeenkomst [*A publication*]
Comm Hydrol Res TNO (Cent Organ Appl Sci Res Neth) Proc Inf ... Committee for Hydrological Research TNO (Central Organization for Applied Scientific Research in the Netherlands). Proceedings and Informations [*A publication*]
commie....... Communist [*Slang*]
Comm (India) ... Commerce (India) [*A publication*]
Comm Intnl ... Communications International [*A publication*]
Comm Int Prot Acque Italo-Svizz Rapp ... Commissione Internazionale per la Protezione delle Acque. Italo-Svizzere Rapporti [*A publication*]
Commis Energ At (Fr) Rapp ... Commissariat a l'Energie Atomique (France). Rapport [*A publication*]
COMMISR ... Commissioner (ROG)
Commiss .... Commission (DLA)
Comm Ital Com Int Geofis Pubbl ... Commissione Italiana del Comitato Internazionale di Geofisica. Pubblicazioni [*A publication*]
COMMITS ... Communications Integration Test Site [*Military*] (CAAL)
Comm Journ ... House of Commons Journals [*England*] [*A publication*] (DLA)
Comm Jud J ... Commonwealth Judicial Journal [*A publication*] (DLA)
COMML ... Commercial (ROG)
Comm L Assoc Bull ... Commercial Law Association. Bulletin [*A publication*] (APTA)
Comm LB.. ... Commonwealth Law Bulletin [*A publication*]
Comml Grow ... Commercial Grower [*A publication*]
Comm L Law ... Common Law Lawyer [*A publication*]
COMMLOADEX ... Communications Load Exercise [*Military*] (CAAL)
Comm LQ .. Commercial Law Quarterly [*Australia*] [*A publication*]
Comm LR... Commercial Law Reports [*Canada*] [*A publication*] (DLA)
Comm LR... Commonwealth Law Reports [*A publication*] (APTA)
Comm M... Commerce Monthly [*A publication*]
Comm Market L Rev ... Common Market Law Review [*A publication*] (DLA)
Comm Math H ... Commentarii Mathematici Helvetici [*A publication*]
Comm Math P ... Communications in Mathematical Physics [*A publication*]
Comm Math Phys ... Communications in Mathematical Physics [*A publication*]
Comm Ment H ... Community Mental Health Journal [*A publication*]
Comm Mkt ... Common Market (DLA)
Comm Mkt LR ... Common Market Law Reports [*A publication*]
Comm Mkt L Rep ... Common Market Law Reports [*A publication*]

Comm Mkt L Rev ... Common Market Law Review [*A publication*]
Comm Mkt Rep ... Common Market Reporter [*Commerce Clearing House*] [*A publication*] (DLA)
Comm Monogr ... Communication Monographs [*A publication*]
Comm Mot ... Commercial Motor [*A publication*]
COMMN... Commission
COMMND ... Commissioned
Comm News ... Communications News [*A publication*]
COMMO... Commodore
COMMO... Communications Officer
Com Mod ... Commerce Moderne [*A publication*]
COMMOD ... Commodity
Commod Bul Dep Agric NSW Div Mark Econ ... Commodity Bulletin. Department of Agriculture of New South Wales. Division of Marketing and Economics [*A publication*]
Commodities M ... Commodities Magazine [*A publication*]
Commodity Futures L Rep ... Commodity Futures Law Reporter [*Commerce Clearing House*] [*A publication*] (DLA)
Commod J ... Commodity Journal [*A publication*]
Commod Jrl ... Commodity Journal [*A publication*]
Commod Mag ... Commodities Magazine [*A publication*]
Common..... Common Sense [*A publication*]
Common Agric ... Commonwealth Agriculturist [*A publication*] (APTA)
Common Cause M ... Common Cause Membership [*A publication*]
Common Exp Build Stn NSB ... Australia. Commonwealth Experimental Building Station. Notes on the Science of Building [*A publication*] (APTA)
Common Mkt L Rev ... Common Market Law Review [*A publication*] (DLA)
Common Mkt Rep CCH ... Common Market Reports. Commerce Clearing House [*A publication*]
Commonw .. Commonwealth (DLA)
Commonw Act ... Commonwealth Act (DLA)
Commonw Agric ... Commonwealth Agriculturist [*A publication*] (APTA)
Commonw Bur Anim Breed Genet Tech Commun ... Commonwealth Bureau of Animal Breeding and Genetics. Technical Communication [*A publication*]
Commonw Bur Anim Health Rev Ser ... Commonwealth Bureau of Animal Health. Review Series [*A publication*]
Commonw Bur Anim Nutr Tech Commun ... Commonwealth Bureau of Animal Nutrition. Technical Communication [*A publication*]
Commonw Bur Hortic Plant Crops (GB) Tech Commun ... Commonwealth Bureau of Horticulture and Plantation Crops (Great Britain). Technical Communication [*A publication*]
Commonw Bur Nutr Tech Commun ... Commonwealth Bureau of Nutrition. Technical Communication [*A publication*]
Commonw Bur Pastures Field Crops Bull ... Commonwealth Bureau of Pastures and Field Crops. Bulletin [*A publication*]
Commonw Bur Pastures Field Crops (GB) Rev Ser ... Commonwealth Bureau of Pastures and Field Crops (Great Britain). Review Series [*A publication*]
Commonw Bur Pastures Field Crops Hurley Berkshire Bull ... Commonwealth Bureau of Pastures and Field Crops. Hurley Berkshire Bulletin [*A publication*]
Commonw Bur Plant Breed Genet Tech Commun ... Commonwealth Bureau of Plant Breeding and Genetics. Technical Communication [*A publication*]
Commonw Bur Soils Spec Publ ... Commonwealth Bureau of Soils. Special Publication [*A publication*]
Commonw Bur Soils Tech Commun ... Commonwealth Bureau of Soils. Technical Communication [*A publication*]
Commonwealth Club Cal Transactions ... Commonwealth Club of California. Transactions [*A publication*]
Commonwealth J ... Commonwealth Journal [*A publication*]
Commonwealth Phytopathol ... Commonwealth Phytopathological News [*A publication*]
Commonwealth Road Trans Index ... Commonwealth Road Transport Index [*A publication*] (APTA)
Commonw Eng ... Commonwealth Engineer [*A publication*]
Commonw Engr ... Commonwealth Engineer [*A publication*] (APTA)
Commonw Exp Build Stat Bull ... Australia. Commonwealth Experimental Building Station. Bulletin [*A publication*] (APTA)
Commonw Exp Build Stat RF ... Australia. Commonwealth Experimental Building Station. CEBS Researchers and Facilities [*A publication*] (APTA)
Commonw Exp Build Stat SR ... Australia. Commonwealth Experimental Building Station. Special Report [*A publication*] (APTA)
Commonw Exp Build Stat TS ... Australia. Commonwealth Experimental Building Station. Technical Study [*A publication*] (APTA)
Commonw Fert ... Commonwealth Fertilizer [*A publication*] (APTA)
Commonw For Bur Tech Commun ... Commonwealth Forestry Bureau. Technical Communication [*A publication*]
Commonw For Rev ... Commonwealth Forestry Review [*A publication*]
Commonw Geol Liaison Off Liaison Rep ... Commonwealth Geological Liaison Office. Liaison Report [*A publication*]
Commonw Geol Liaison Off Spec Liaison Rep ... Commonwealth Geological Liaison Office. Special Liaison Report [*London*] [*A publication*]
Commonw Inst Biol Control Misc Publ ... Commonwealth Institute of Biological Control. Miscellaneous Publication [*A publication*]

Commonw Inst Helminthol (Albans) Tech Commun ... Commonwealth Institute of Helminthology (Saint Albans). Technical Communication [*A publication*]

Commonw L Rep ... Commonwealth Law Reports [*A publication*]

Commonw L Rev ... Commonwealth Law Review [*A publication*]   (DLA)

Commonw Min Metall Congr Proc ... Commonwealth Mining and Metallurgical Congress. Proceedings [*A publication*]

Commonw Mycol Inst Descr Pathog Fungi Bact ... Commonwealth Mycological Institute. Descriptions of Pathogenic Fungi and Bacteria [*A publication*]

Commonw Mycol Inst Mycol Pap ... Commonwealth Mycological Institute. Mycological Papers [*A publication*]

Commonw Mycol Inst Phytopathol Pap ... Commonwealth Mycological Institute. Phytopathological Papers [*A publication*]

Commonw Phytopath News ... Commonwealth Phytopathological News [*A publication*]

Commonw Rec ... Commonwealth Record [*A publication*]

COMMOPNSO ... Communications Operations Officer [*Air Force*]

COMMOSCH ... Communications Officer School [*Air Force*]

Comm Part D ... Communications in Partial Differential Equations [*A publication*]

Comm Partial Differential Equations ... Communications in Partial Differential Equations [*A publication*]

Comm Phys-M ... Commentationes Physico-Mathematicae [*A publication*]

Comm Phytopathol News ... Commonwealth Phytopathological News [*A publication*]

Comm Print ... Congressional Committee Prints [*A publication*]   (DLA)

Comm Probl Drug Depend Proc Annu Sci Meet US Nat Res Counc ... Committee on Problems of Drug Dependence. Proceedings of the Annual Scientific Meeting. United States National Research Council [*A publication*]

Comm Prop J ... Community Property Journal [*A publication*]

Comm Pure Appl Math ... Communications on Pure and Applied Mathematics [*A publication*]

Comm Q ..... Communication Quarterly [*A publication*]

COMMR ... Commissioner   (EY)

Comm Rec ... Commonwealth Record [*A publication*]

Comm Rep ... Commerce Reports [*A publication*]

Comm Res ... Communication Research [*A publication*]

Comm Res Trends ... Communication Research Trends [*A publication*]

Comm Roy Soc Edinburgh Phys Sci ... Communications. Royal Society of Edinburgh. Physical Sciences [*A publication*]

COMMS ... Central Office Maintenance Management System [*Telecommunications*]   (TEL)

COMMS ... Communications

COMMS ... Communications Management Subsystem

COMMSC ... Commander, Military Sealift Command

Comm Sec .. Commonwealth Secretariat   (DLA)

COMMSECACT ... Communication Security Activity

Comms N ... Communications News [*A publication*]

Comm Soil S ... Communications in Soil Science and Plant Analysis [*A publication*]

COMMS-PM ... Central Office Maintenance Management System - Preventive Maintenance [*Telecommunications*]   (TEL)

COMMSq ... Communications Squadron [*Air Force*]

COMMSR ... Commissioner   (ROG)

COMMSTA ... Communications Station   (MCD)

Comm St A ... Communications in Statistics. Part A. Theory and Methods [*A publication*]

Comm Statis ... Communications in Statistics [*A publication*]

Comm Statist A Theory Methods ... Communications in Statistics. Part A. Theory and Methods [*A publication*]

Comm Statist B Simulation Comput ... Communications in Statistics. Part B. Simulation and Computation [*A publication*]

Comm Statist Econometric Rev ... Communications in Statistics. Econometric Reviews [*A publication*]

Comm Statist Sequential Anal ... Communications in Statistics. Part C. Sequential Analysis [*A publication*]

Comm Statist Simulation Comput ... Communications in Statistics. Part B. Simulation and Computation [*A publication*]

Comm Statist Theory Methods ... Communications in Statistics. Part A. Theory and Methods [*A publication*]

Comm St B ... Communications in Statistics. Part B. Simulation and Computation [*A publication*]

COMM-STOR ... Communications Storage Unit

COMMSUPACT ... Communication Supplementary Activity

COMMSUPDET ... Communication Supplementary Detachment

COMMSWITCH ... Communications-Failure Detecting and Switching Equipment   (MDG)

COMMT ... Commencement   (ROG)

Comm Tel Cas ... Commission Telephone Cases Leaflets [*New York*] [*A publication*]   (DLA)

Comm Th Phy ... Communications in Theoretical Physics [*A publication*]

Comm Today ... Commerce Today [*A publication*]

Commu LB ... Communications Law Bulletin [*Australia*] [*A publication*]

commun ..... Communicable [*Medicine*]

COMMUN ... Communications

Commun ..... Communio. International Catholic Review [*A publication*]

Commun ..... Communion [*A publication*]

COMMUN ... Community

Commun Abstr ... Communication Abstracts [*A publication*]

Commun ACM ... Communications. ACM [*Association for Computing Machinery*] [*A publication*]

Commun Action ... Community Action [*A publication*]

Commun Algebra ... Communications in Algebra [*A publication*]

Commun Arts Mag ... Communication Arts Magazine [*A publication*]

Commun Aust ... Communications Australia [*A publication*]

Commun Balai Penjelidikan Pemakaian Karet ... Communication. Balai Penjelidikan dan Pemakaian Karet [*A publication*]

Commun Behav Biol Part A Orig Artic ... Communications in Behavioral Biology. Part A. Original Articles [*A publication*]

Commun Biohist ... Occasional Communications. Utrecht University. Biohistorical Institute [*A publication*]

Commun Broadc ... Communication and Broadcasting [*A publication*]

Commun Broadcast ... Communication and Broadcasting [*England*] [*A publication*]

Commun Care ... Community Care [*A publication*]

Commun Cent Rech Zootech Univ Louv ... Communication. Centre de Recherches Zootechniques. Universite de Louvain [*A publication*]

Commun Cybern ... Communication and Cybernetics [*A publication*]

Commun and Cybernet ... Communication and Cybernetics [*A publication*]

Commun Dep Agric Res R Trop Inst (Amst) ... Communication. Department of Agricultural Research. Royal Tropical Institute (Amsterdam) [*A publication*]

Commun Dep Anat Univ Lund (Swed) ... Communication. Department of Anatomy. University of Lund (Sweden) [*A publication*]

Commun Dev J ... Community Development Journal [*A publication*]

Commun Dublin Inst Adv Stud A ... Communications. Dublin Institute for Advanced Studies. Series A [*A publication*]

Commun Dublin Inst Adv Stud Ser A ... Communications. Dublin Institute for Advanced Studies. Series A [*A publication*]

Commun Dublin Inst Adv Stud Ser D ... Communications. Dublin Institute for Advanced Studies. Series D. Geophysical Bulletin [*A publication*]

Commun Electron ... Communications and Electronics [*England*] [*A publication*]

Commun Eng ... Communication Engineering [*A publication*]

Commun Eng Int ... Communications Engineering International [*A publication*]

Commun Equip & Syst Des ... Communications Equipment and Systems Design [*A publication*]

Commun Fac Med Vet Univ Etat Gand ... Communications. Faculte de Medecine Veterinaire. Universite de l'Etat Gand [*A publication*]

Commun Fac Sci Univ Ankara ... Communications. Faculte des Sciences. Universite d'Ankara [*A publication*]

Commun Fac Sci Univ Ankara Ser A2 ... Communications. Faculte des Sciences. Universite d'Ankara. Serie A2. Physique [*A publication*]

Commun Fac Sci Univ Ankara Ser B ... Communications. Faculte des Sciences. Universite d'Ankara. Serie B. Chimie [*A publication*]

Commun Fac Sci Univ Ankara Ser B Chem Chem Eng ... Communications. Faculte des Sciences. Universite d'Ankara. Series B. Chemistry and Chemical Engineering [*A publication*]

Commun Fac Sci Univ Ankara Ser C ... Communications. Faculte des Sciences. Universite d'Ankara. Serie C. Sciences Naturelles [*A publication*]

Commun Fac Sci Univ Ankara Ser C Biol ... Communications. Faculte des Sciences. Universite d'Ankara. Serie C. Biologie [*A publication*]

Commun Fac Sci Univ Ankara Ser C II Bot ... Communications. Faculte des Sciences. Universite d'Ankara. Serie C-II. Botanique [*A publication*]

Commun Fac Sci Univ Ankara Ser C Sci Nat ... Communications. Faculte des Sciences. Universite d'Ankara. Serie C. Sciences Naturelles [*A publication*]

Commun Fac Vet Med State Univ (Ghent) ... Communications. Faculty of Veterinary Medicine. State University (Ghent) [*A publication*]

Communicable Disease Rep ... Communicable Disease Report [*A publication*]

Communic Afr ... Communications Africa [*A publication*]

COMMUNICAT ... Communications Satellite   (MUGU)

Communication Studies Bull ... Communication Studies Bulletin [*United Kingdom*] [*A publication*]

Communication Tech Impact ... Communications Technology Impact [*A publication*]

Communic et Lang ... Communication et Langages [*A publication*]

Communic Rei Cret Rom Faut ... Communicationes Rei Cretariae Romanae Fautores [*A publication*]

Commun Inst For Cech ... Communicationes. Instituti Forestalis Cechosloveniae [*A publication*]

Commun Inst For Csl ... Communicationes. Instituti Forestalis Cechosloveniae [*A publication*]

Commun Inst For Fenn ... Communicationes. Instituti Forestalis Fenniae [*A publication*]

Commun Inst For Res Agric Univ (Wageningen) ... Communication. Institute of Forestry Research. Agricultural University (Wageningen) [*Netherlands*] [*A publication*]

Commun Inst Therm Appl Ec Polytech Fed Lausanne ... Communication. Institut de Thermique Appliquee. Ecole Polytechnique Federale de Lausanne [*Switzerland*] [*A publication*]

Commun Int ... Communications International [*A publication*]

Commun Int Assoc Theor Appl Limnol ... Communications. International Association of Theoretical and Applied Limnology [*A publication*]

Communist China Dig ... Communist China Digest [*A publication*]

Communist Chin Sci Abstr ... Communist Chinese Scientific Abstracts [*A publication*]

Communist R ... Communist Review [*A publication*]   (APTA)

Communist Rev ... Communist Review [*A publication*]   (APTA)

Communit .. ... Communities [*A publication*]

Communit Health S Afr ... Community Health in South Africa [*A publication*]

Community Dent Health ... Community Dental Health [*London*] [*A publication*]

Community Dent Oral Epidemiol ... Community Dentistry and Oral Epidemiology [*A publication*]

Community Dev Abstr ... Community Development Abstracts [*A publication*]

Community Devel J ... Community Development Journal [*A publication*]

Community Develop J ... Community Development Journal [*A publication*]

Community Development J ... Community Development Journal [*A publication*]

Community Dev J ... Community Development Journal [*A publication*]

Community Econ Univ Wis Dep Agric Econ Coop Ext Serv ... Community Economics. University of Wisconsin. Department of Agricultural Economics. Cooperative Extension Service [*A publication*]

Community Health Stud ... Community Health Studies [*Australia*] [*A publication*]

Community Hlth Stud ... Community Health Studies [*A publication*]

Community Jr Coll J ... Community and Junior College Journal [*A publication*]

Community and Junior Coll Libr ... Community and Junior College Libraries [*A publication*]

Community Med ... Community Medicine [*A publication*]

Community Ment Health J ... Community Mental Health Journal [*A publication*]

Community Ment Health Rev ... Community Mental Health Review [*Later, Prevention in Human Services*] [*A publication*]

Community Ment Hlth J ... Community Mental Health Journal [*A publication*]

Community Nurs ... Community Nursing [*US*] [*A publication*]

Community Nutr ... Community Nutritionist [*A publication*]

Community Prop J ... Community Property Journal [*A publication*]

Commun Jajasan Penjelidikan Pemakain Karet ... Communications. Jajasan Penjelidikan dan Pemakain Karet [*A publication*]

Commun J Inst Nucl Res (Dubna) ... Communications. Joint Institute for Nuclear Research (Dubna) [*A publication*]

Commun Kamerlingh Onnes Lab Univ Leiden ... Communications. Kamerlingh Onnes Laboratory. University of Leiden [*A publication*]

Commun Kamerlingh Onnes Lab Univ Leiden Suppl ... Communications. Kamerlingh Onnes Laboratory. University of Leiden. Supplement [*A publication*]

Commun & Law ... Communications and the Law [*A publication*]

Com & Mun L Rep ... Commercial and Municipal Law Reporter [*A publication*]   (DLA)

Commun Lunar & Planet Lab ... Communications. Lunar and Planetary Laboratory [*A publication*]

Commun Math Inst Rijksuniv Utrecht ... Communications. Mathematical Institute. Rijksuniversiteit Utrecht [*A publication*]

Commun Math Phys ... Communications in Mathematical Physics [*A publication*]

Commun News ... Communications News [*A publication*]

Commun Newsl ... Communique Newsletter [*Milwaukee, Wisconsin*] [*A publication*]

Commun Nurs Res ... Communicating Nursing Research [*A publication*]

Commun NV K Ned Springstoffenfabr ... Communication. NV [*Naamloze Vennootschap*] Koninklijke Nederlandsche Springstoffenfabrieken [*A publication*]

Commun Part Differ Equ ... Communications in Partial Differential Equations [*A publication*]

Commun Phys ... Communications on Physics [*A publication*]

Commun Phys Lab Univ Leiden ... Communications. Physical Laboratory. University of Leiden [*A publication*]

Commun Psychopharmacol ... Communications in Psychopharmacology [*A publication*]

Commun Pure Appl Math ... Communications on Pure and Applied Mathematics [*A publication*]

Commun Quart ... Communication Quarterly [*A publication*]

Commun Res Inst Sumatra Plant Assoc Rubber Ser ... Communications. Research Institute of the Sumatra Planters' Association. Rubber Series [*A publication*]

Commun R Soc Edinburgh ... Communications. Royal Society of Edinburgh [*A publication*]

Commun R Soc Edinburgh Phys Sci ... Communications. Royal Society of Edinburgh. Physical Sciences [*A publication*]

Commun Sci & Tech Inf ... Communicator of Scientific and Technical Information [*Later, Communicator*] [*A publication*]

Communs Electron (Lond) ... Communications and Electronics (London)

Communs Fac Sci Univ Ankara ... Communications. Faculte des Sciences. Universite d'Ankara. Serie C [*A publication*]

Commun Soil Sci Plant Anal ... Communications in Soil Science and Plant Analysis [*A publication*]

Commun Stat ... Communications in Statistics [*A publication*]

Commun Stat A ... Communications in Statistics. Part A. Theory and Methods [*A publication*]

Commun Stat B ... Communications in Statistics. Part B. Simulation and Computation [*A publication*]

Commun Stat Part A Theory Methods ... Communications in Statistics. Part A. Theory and Methods [*A publication*]

Commun Stat Part B ... Communications in Statistics. Part B. Simulation and Computation [*A publication*]

Commun Stat Simulation and Comput ... Communications in Statistics. Part B. Simulation and Computation [*A publication*]

Commun Stat Theory and Methods ... Communications in Statistics. Part A. Theory and Methods [*A publication*]

Commun Sugar Milling Res Inst ... Communications. Sugar Milling Research Institute [*A publication*]

Commun Swed Sugar Corp ... Communications. Swedish Sugar Corporation [*A publication*]

Commun Syst and Manage ... Communications Systems and Management [*A publication*]

Commun Tech Inf ... Communicator of Technical Information [*Later, Communicator*] [*A publication*]

Commun Theor Phys ... Communications in Theoretical Physics [*A publication*]

Commun Transport Q ... Community Transport Quarterly [*A publication*]

COMMUNV ... Communicative

Commun Vet ... Communicationes Veterinariae [*A publication*]

Commutat & Electron ... Commutation et Electronique [*A publication*]

Commutation Electron ... Commutation et Electronique [*A publication*]

Commutat and Transm ... Commutation and Transmission [*A publication*]

Commuter W ... Commuter World [*A publication*]

Comm Veh ... Commercial Vehicles [*A publication*]

CommViat ... Communio Viatorum. A Theological Quarterly [*Prague*] [*A publication*]

Commw ...... Commonwealth   (DLA)

Commw Arb ... Commonwealth Arbitration Reports [*A publication*]

Commw Art ... Commonwealth Arbitration Reports [*A publication*]

Commw Ct ... Commonwealth Court   (DLA)

Commw Exp Build Stat NSB ... Commonwealth Experimental Building Station. Notes on the Science of Building [*A publication*]   (APTA)

Commw Jud J ... Commonwealth Judicial Journal [*A publication*]   (DLA)

Commw LB ... Commonwealth Law Bulletin [*A publication*]

Commw LR ... Commonwealth Law Reports [*A publication*]

Commw Sec ... Commonwealth Secretariat   (DLA)

Commwth Eng ... Commonwealth Engineer [*A publication*]   (APTA)

COMMY ... Commissary

COMMZ ... Communications Zone   (MUGU)

COMN ...... Commission

COMN ...... Common

COMN ...... Communication

COMNAB ... Commander, Naval Air Bases

Com Nac Energ Nucl (Braz) Bol ... Comissao Nacional de Energia Nuclear (Brazil). Boletim [*A publication*]

Com Nac Energ Nucl (Mex) Publ ... Comision Nacional de Energia Nuclear (Mexico). Publicacion [*A publication*]

COMNADEFLANT ... Commander, North American Defense Force, Atlantic [*NATO*]   (NATG)

COMNAS(EA) ... Commodore, Naval Air Stations, East Africa [*British*]

COMNAV ... Navy Command [*Part of North American Air Defense Command*]

COMNAVACTS ... Naval Activity

COMNAVAIR ... Commander, Naval Air Force

COMNAVAIRLANT ... Commander, Naval Air Force, Atlantic Fleet   (MCD)

COMNAVAIRPAC ... Commander, Naval Air Force, Pacific Fleet   (MCD)

COMNAVBALTAP ... Commander, Allied Naval Forces, Baltic Approaches   (AABC)

COMNAVBASE ... Commander, Naval Base

COMNAVBASEDIEGO ... Commandant, Naval Base, San Diego

COMNAVBREM ... Commander, Bremerhaven Naval Group   (NATG)

COMNAVCAG ... Commander, Naval Forces, Central Army Group Area and Bremerhaven   (NATG)

COMNAVCENT ... Commander, Allied Naval Forces, Central Europe

COMNAVCOMM ... Commander, Naval Communications   (NVT)

COMNAVCRUITCOMINST ... Navy Recruiting Command Instructions

COMNAVDEFOREEASTPAC ... Commander, Naval Defense Forces, Eastern Pacific   (MUGU)

COMNAVDIST WASHDC ... Commandant, Naval District, Washington, DC

COMNAVEASTLANTMED ... Commander, [*US*] Naval Forces, Eastern Atlantic and Mediterranean

COMNAVEU ... Commander, [*US*] Naval Forces, Europe

COMNAVFE ... Commander, [*US*] Naval Forces, Far East

COMNAVFMARIANAS ... Commander, [*US*] Naval Forces, Marianas

COMNAVFOR ... Commander, [*US*] Naval Forces

COMNAVFORCONAD ... Commander, [*US*] Naval Forces, Continental Air Defense Command   (MUGU)

COMNAVFORGER ... Commander, [*US*] Naval Forces, Germany   (MCD)
COMNAVFORICE ... Commander, [*US*] Naval Forces, Iceland
COMNAVFORJAPAN ... Commander, [*US*] Naval Forces, Japan   (AFM)
COMNAVFORKOREA ... Commander, [*US*] Naval Forces, Korea
COMNAVFORPHIL ... Commander, [*US*] Naval Forces, Philippines
COMNAVFORV ... Commander, [*US*] Naval Forces, Vietnam
COMNAVGER ... Commander, [*US*] Naval Forces, Germany
COMNAVGERBALT ... Commander, German Naval Forces, Baltic   (NATG)
COMNAVICE ... Commander, [*US*] Naval Forces, Iceland
COMNAVINSWARLANT ... Commander, Naval Inshore Warfare Command, Atlantic
COMNAVJAP ... Commander, Naval Activities, Japan
COMNAVMARIANAS ... Commander, [*US*] Naval Forces, Marianas   (CINC)
COMNAVMILPERSCOM ... Commander, Navy Military Personnel Command   (NVT)
COMNAVNAW ... Commander, [*US*] Naval Forces, Northwest African Waters
COMNAVNON ... Commander, Allied Naval Forces, North Norway   (AABC)
COMNAVNORCENT ... Commander, Northern Area Forces, Central Europe   (NATG)
COMNAVNORTH ... Commander, Allied Naval Forces, Northern Europe   (NATG)
COMNAVSCAP ... Commander, Allied Naval Forces, Scandinavian Approaches   (AABC)
COMNAVSONOR ... Commander, Allied Naval Forces, South Norway   (NATG)
COMNAVSOUTH ... Commander, Naval Forces, Southern Europe   (NATG)
COMNAVSUPPACT ... Commander, Naval Support Activity   (AFM)
COMNAVSUPPFOR ... Commander, Naval Support Force
COMNAVSUPPFORANTARCTIC ... Commander, Naval Support Force, Antarctic
COMNAVSURFLA ... Commander, Naval Surface Forces, Atlantic
COMNAVTELCOM ... Commander, Naval Telecommunications Command   (NVT)
COMNAVZOR ... Commander, [*US*] Naval Forces, Azores
Com Naz Energ Nucl Not ... Comitato Nazionale per l'Energia Nucleare. Notiziario [*A publication*]
Com Naz Energ Nucl Repr ... Comitato Nazionale per l'Energia Nucleare. Reprints [*A publication*]
Com Naz Ric Nucl (Italy) Not ... Comitato Nazionale per le Ricerche Nucleari (Italy). Notiziario [*A publication*]
COMNB.... Commentary [*A publication*]
COMND.... Commissioned
COMNDW ... Commandant, Naval District, Washington, DC
COMNEATLANT ... Commander, Northeast Atlantic   (NATG)
COMNEED ... Communications Need
COMNET ... Communications Network   (AFM)
COMNET ... Computer Network Corp. [*Information service or system*]   (IID)
COMNET ... International Network of Centres for Documentation and Communication Research and Policies   (EAIO)
COMNEWLONGRU ... Commander, New London Group
COMNEWZEDV ... Commander, New Zealand Assistance Detachment, Vietnam
COMNINE ... Commandant, Ninth Naval District   (MUGU)
COMNMC ... Commander, Naval Missile Center   (MUGU)
COMNO ... Combined Officer of Merchant Navy Operations [*British*]
COMNON ... Commander, Allied Forces, North Norway   (NATG)
COMNORASDEFLANT ... Commander, North American Antisubmarine Defense Force, Atlantic [*NATO*]
COMNORECHAN ... Commander, Northeast Subarea Channel
COMNORLANT ... Commander, Northern Atlantic Subarea [*NATO*]
COMNORPAC ... Commander, North Pacific Force
COMNORSEACENT ... Commander, North Sea Subarea, Central Europe   (NATG)
COMNORTHAG ... Commander, Northern Army Group, Central Europe
COMNORVAGRU ... Commander, Norfolk Group
Comnty....... Community Newspapers [*A publication*]
COMNYKGRU ... Commander, New York Group
COMNZAFFE ... Commander, New Zealand Army Forces, Far East
COMO....... Coherent Master Oscillator   (NG)
COMO....... Comanche Oil Explorations [*NASDAQ symbol*]   (NQ)
COMO....... Commodo [*In an Easy Style*] [*Music*]   (ROG)
COMO....... Commodore
COMO....... Communications Officer
COMO....... Comprehensive Model
COMO....... Computer Model   (MCD)
COMO....... Council of Military Organization
CoMo......... Montrose County Regional District Library, Montrose, CO [*Library symbol*] [*Library of Congress*]   (LCLS)
CO 1MO.... Canto Primo [*First Soprano*] [*Music*]   (ROG)
COMOCEANLANT ... Commander, Ocean Atlantic Subarea [*NATO*]
COMOCEANSUBAREA ... Commander, Ocean Subarea
COMOCEANSYSLANT ... Commander, Oceanographic Surveillance Systems, Atlantic   (MUGU)
COMOCEANSYSPAC ... Commander, Oceanographic Surveillance Systems, Pacific
COMOFORM ... Cold Molded Thermoforming [*Fiberglass production*]
COMOI..... Committee on Manpower Opportunities in Israel [*Later, IAC*]

COMONE ... Commandant, First Naval District   (MUGU)
COMOPCONCEN ... Commander, Operational Control Center
COMOPDEVFOR ... Commander, Operational Development Force [*Navy*]
COMOPT ... Combined Optical [*Photography*]
COMOPTEVFOR ... Commander, Operational Test and Evaluation Force [*Navy*]
COMOPTIONS ... Commodity Options [*I. P. Sharp Associates*] [*Database*]
COMOR.... Committee on Overhead Reconnaissance [*Later, COMIREX*]
COMORANGE ... Commander Orange (Aggressor) Force [*Navy*]   (CAAL)
CoMorM.... Mount View School for Girls, Morrison, CO [*Library symbol*] [*Library of Congress*]   (LCLS)
COMOROCLANT ... Commander, Maritime Forces, Morocco
COMORSEAFRON ... Commander, Moroccan Sea Frontier Forces
COMORTEXGRU ... Commander, Orange, Texas, Group; Inactive Reserve Fleet, Atlantic
CoMos .... Mosca Public Library, Mosca, CO [*Library symbol*] [*Library of Congress*]   (LCLS)
ComOT ...... Commentaar op het Oude Testament [*Kampen*] [*A publication*]   (BJA)
COMP .... CCNU [*Lomustine*], Oncovin [*Vincristine*], Methotrexate, Procarbazine [*Antineoplastic drug regimen*]
COMP .... Charlotte Ordnance Missile Plant
COMP .... Companion   (MSA)
COMP .... Company
COMP .... Comparative
COMP .... Comparator   (CET)
COMP .... Compare
COMP .... Comparison
COMP .... Compartment   (MCD)
Comp.......... Compass [*A publication*]
COMP .... Compass
COMP .... Compatible
COMP .... Compensate [*or Compensating*]   (KSC)
Comp.......... Competition
COMP .... Competitor   (ADA)
COMP .... Compilation   (ROG)
COMP .... Compiler
COMP .... Complaint
COMP .... Complement   (AFM)
COMP .... Complete   (ROG)
comp.......... Complication [*Medicine*]
COMP .... Compliment   (ROG)
COMP .... Complimentary Copy
COMP ...... Component   (AFM)
COMP ...... Composer   (ROG)
COMP ...... Composite   (AFM)
COMP ...... Composite Operational Mission Profiles   (MCD)
COMP ...... Composition
COMP .... Compositor [*Printers' term*]   (DSUE)
COMP .... Compositus [*Compound*] [*Pharmacy*]
COMP ...... Compound
COMP .... Comprehensive
COMP .... Compressed
COMP .... Compressor [*Automotive engineering*]
COMP .... Comptroller
COMP ...... Computation   (AFM)
COMP .... Computation Subsystem [*Space Flight Operations Facility, NASA*]
COMP ...... Computer   (AFM)
COMP ...... Council on Municipal Performance   (EA)
COMP .... Cyclophosphamide, Oncovin [*Vincristine*], Methotrexate, Prednisone [*Antineoplastic drug regimen*]
Comp.......... De Compositione Verborum [*of Dionysius Halicarnassensis*] [*Classical studies*]   (OCD)
compa........ Companhia [*Company, Society*] [*Spanish*]
COMPA .... Compost Science [*Later, Bio Cycle*] [*A publication*]
COMPA .... Compressed Air
COMPA .... Conference of Minority Public Administrators   (EA)
COMPAC ... Commonwealth Transpacific [*Submarine cable in Pacific*]
COMPAC ... Computer Output Microfilm Package
COMPAC ... Computer Packages   (MCD)
COMPAC ... Computer Program for Automatic Control
COMPACMISRAN ... Commander, Pacific Missile Range   (MUGU)
COMPACS ... Computer Outputer Microforms Program and Concept Study   (MCD)
COMPACT ... Combined Passive Active Detection [*RADAR*]
COMPACT ... Commercial Product Acquisition Team   (EA)
COMPACT ... Committee to Preserve American Color Television   (EA)
COMPACT ... Committee to Promote Action [*Poverty program*]
COMPACT ... Commodity Put and Call Trading Data [*Database*] [*Chronometrics*] [*Information service or system*]   (CRD)
COMPACT ... Compatible Algebraic Compiler and Translator
COMPACT ... Computer Planning and Control Technique   (BUR)
COMPACT ... Computer-Programmed Automatic Checkout and Test System
COMPACT ... Computerization of World Facts [*Stanford Research Institute*] [*Databank*]
COMPACT ... Consolidation of Military Personnel Activities at Fixed Installations   (AABC)
COMPAD ... Combined Office Material Procurement and Distribution
Comp Admin Sci Q ... Comparative Administrative Science Quarterly [*A publication*]   (DLA)

Comp Ad New ... Computer Advertising News, Incorporated into Adweek's Computer and Electronics Marketing [*A publication*]
COMPAF ... Commander, Pacific Air Fleet
Compagn Franc Petrol Notes Mem ... Compagnie Francaise des Petroles. Notes et Memoires [*A publication*]
COMPAID ... Control of Materials Planning and Isometric Drawings
Comp Air ... Compressed Air [*A publication*]
Comp Air Mag ... Compressed Air Magazine [*A publication*]
Com P A Math ... Communications on Pure and Applied Mathematics [*A publication*]
COMPAN ... Compost Science [*Later, Bio Cycle*] [*A publication*]
COMPANDER ... Compressor Expander [*Telecommunications*]   (IEEE)
Comp Anim Nutr ... Comparative Animal Nutrition [*A publication*]
Companion IGasE ... Companion of the Institution of Gas Engineers [*British*]   (DBQ)
Company Law ... Company Lawyer [*A publication*]
COMPAR ... Comparative
Comparative Ed ... Comparative Education [*A publication*]
Comparative Educ R ... Comparative Education Review [*A publication*]
Comparative Pol Studies ... Comparative Political Studies [*A publication*]
COMPARE ... Computerized Performance and Analysis Response Evaluator   (IEEE)
COMPARE ... Console for Optical Measurement and Precise Analysis of Radiation from Electronics
Compare..... Journal. Comparative Education Society in Europe (British Section) [*A publication*]
Compar Educ ... Comparative Education [*A publication*]
Compar Educ Rev ... Comparative Education Review [*A publication*]
Comparisons in L & Monet Com ... Comparisons in Law and Monetary Comments [*A publication*]   (DLA)
Comp Armed Forces ... Compendium of Laws of Armed Forces [*United States*] [*A publication*]   (DLA)
Comp Ar et Men ... Comparatio Aristophanis et Menandri [*of Plutarch*] [*Classical studies*]   (OCD)
Compar Pol Stud ... Comparative Political Studies [*A publication*]
COMPAS ... Committee on Physics and Society [*of American Institute of Physics*]
COMPASEAFRON ... Commander, Panama Sea Frontier
COMPASS ... Automotive Competitive Assessment Data Bank [*Ward's Research*] [*Database*]
COMPASS ... Competitive Aircraft Data Summary Sheets   (MCD)
COMPASS ... Compiler-Assembler
COMPASS ... Comprehensive Assembler System [*Programming language*] [*1964*] [*Control Data Corp.*]
COMPASS ... Computer-Adjusted Spectrometry System
COMPASS ... Computer-Assisted Classification and Assignment System   (IEEE)
COMPASS ... Computer-Assisted Surveillance Subsystem   (MCD)
COMPASS ... Computer Assisted Yeast Identification System [*AFRC Institute of Food Research*] [*Information service or system*]   (IID)
COMPASS ... Computerized Movement Planning and Status System [*Military*]   (AABC)
COMPASS ... Controlled Overhead Management Performance and Standard System
COMPASU ... Commander, Patrol Aircraft Service Unit
COM PAT ... Commissioner of Patents [*Legal term*]   (DLA)
COMPAT ... Compatibility   (KSC)
COMPAT ... Computer-Aided Trade   (DS)
COMPATE ... Compassionate [*Army*]   (AABC)
COMPATENFC ... Compassionate Reassignment Not Favorably Considered [*Army*]   (AABC)
COMPATFOR ... Commander, Patrol Forces   (NATG)
COMPATFORNORLANT ... Commander, Patrol Forces, Northern Subarea, Atlantic   (NATG)
COMPATPLANEREPRONSPAC ... Command Patrol Plane Replacement Squadrons Pacific
COMPATRON ... Commander, Patrol Squadron
Comp & Automation ... Computers and Automation [*Later, Computers and People*] [*A publication*]
COMPAY ... Computer Payroll   (BUR)
COMPBAL ... Compensation Balance [*Watchmaking*]   (ROG)
Comp Bioc A ... Comparative Biochemistry and Physiology. A [*A publication*]
Comp Bioc B ... Comparative Biochemistry and Physiology. B [*A publication*]
Comp Bioc C ... Comparative Biochemistry and Physiology. C [*A publication*]
Comp Biochem Physiol ... Comparative Biochemistry and Physiology [*A publication*]
Comp Biochem Physiol A Comp Physiol ... Comparative Biochemistry and Physiology. A. Comparative Physiology [*A publication*]
Comp Biochem Physiol B ... Comparative Biochemistry and Physiology. B. Comparative Biochemistry [*A publication*]
Comp Biochem Physiol B Comp Biochem ... Comparative Biochemistry and Physiology. B. Comparative Biochemistry [*A publication*]
Comp Biochem Physiol C ... Comparative Biochemistry and Physiology. C. Comparative Pharmacology [*Later, Comparative Biochemistry and Physiology. C. Comparative Pharmacology and Toxicology*] [*A publication*]

Comp Biochem Physiol C Comp Pharmacol ... Comparative Biochemistry and Physiology. C. Comparative Pharmacology [*Later, Comparative Biochemistry and Physiology. C. Comparative Pharmacology and Toxicology*] [*A publication*]
Comp Biochem Physiol C Comp Pharmacol Toxicol ... Comparative Biochemistry and Physiology. C. Comparative Pharmacology and Toxicology [*A publication*]
Comp Bul ... Computer Bulletin [*A publication*]
Comp Cas... Company Cases [*India*] [*A publication*]   (DLA)
Comp Cda .. Computing Canada [*A publication*]
Comp Cda F ... Computing Canada Focus [*A publication*]
Comp Chem ... Computers and Chemistry [*A publication*]
Comp Civ R ... Comparative Civilizations Review [*A publication*]
Comp Comm ... Computer Communications [*A publication*]
Comp Compacts ... Computer Compacts [*A publication*]
COMPCON ... Computer Conference
COMPCOURDET ... Upon Completion of Course of Instruction, Detach [*Navy*]
Comp Cred ... Composition with Creditors [*A publication*]   (DLA)
CompD....... Comparative Drama [*A publication*]
COMPD.... Compound
Comp Data ... Computer Data [*A publication*]
Comp Dec .. Computer Decisions [*A publication*]
Comp Dec .. Decisions of the Comptroller of the United States Treasury [*A publication*]   (DLA)
Comp Decisions ... Computer Decisions [*A publication*]
COMPDES ... Compensator Design [*Data processing*]
Comp Des ... Computer Design [*A publication*]
COMPDESFLTSURG ... Upon Completion of Duty, Hereby Designated Flight Surgeon [*Navy*]
Com P Div ... Common Pleas Division, English Law Reports [*1875-80*] [*A publication*]   (DLA)
CompDr ..... Comparative Drama [*A publication*]
Comp Drama ... Comparative Drama [*A publication*]
Comp Ed .... Comparative Education [*A publication*]
Comp in Ed ... Computers in Education [*A publication*]
Comp Ed R ... Comparative Education Review [*A publication*]
Comp Ed Rev ... Comparative Education Review [*A publication*]
Comp Educ ... Comparative Education [*A publication*]
Comp & Educ ... Computers and Education [*A publication*]
Comp Educ R ... Comparative Education Review [*A publication*]
Comp Edu Re ... Comparative Education Review [*A publication*]
COMPEL.. Compute Parallel   (IEEE)
COMPELS ... Computerized Evaluation of the Logistics System [*Army*]
COMPEN ... Compensate [*or Compensator*]   (AABC)
Compend Contin Educ Dent ... Compendium of Continuing Education in Dentistry [*A publication*]
Compend Dtsch Ges Mineraloelwiss Kohlechem ... Compendium. Deutsche Gesellschaft fuer Mineraloelwissenschaft und Kohlechemie [*East Germany*] [*A publication*]
COMPENDEX ... Computerized Engineering Index [*Engineering Index, Inc.*] [*New York, NY*] [*Bibliographic database*]
Compend Invest Clin Latinoam ... Compendium de Investigaciones Clinicas Latinoamericanas [*A publication*]
Compend Tech Pap Annu Meet Inst Transp Eng ... Compendium of Technical Papers. Annual Meeting. Institute of Transportation Engineers [*A publication*]
Compens Benefits Rev ... Compensation and Benefits Review [*A publication*]
Compens Med ... Compensation Medicine [*A publication*]
COMPENSON ... Compensation   (ROG)
Compens R ... Compensation Review [*A publication*]
Compens Rev ... Compensation Review [*A publication*]
COMPES.. Contingency Operation Mobility Planning and Execution System [*Military*]
COMPET ... Competitive
COMPEX ... Competition Evaluation Exercise
Comp Ex..... Comstock on Executors [*A publication*]   (DLA)
COMPF.... Composition Floor
Comp Fluids ... Computers and Fluids [*A publication*]
Comp Focus ... Computerworld Focus [*A publication*]
COMPG ... Comprehending   (ROG)
COMPGEN ... Comptroller General
Comp Gen .. Decisions of the Comptroller General [*A publication*]   (DLA)
COMPGENDEC ... Comptroller General Decisions [*Navy*]
Comp Gen Op ... Comptroller General Opinion [*A publication*]   (DLA)
Comp Gen Pharmacol ... Comparative and General Pharmacology [*A publication*]
Comp Gra Forum ... Computer Graphics Forum [*A publication*]
Comp Graphics ... Computer Graphics [*A publication*]
Comp Graph Wrld ... Computer Graphics World [*A publication*]
Comp G Wld ... Computer Graphics World [*A publication*]
COMPHIB ... Commander, Amphibious Force
COMPHIBEU ... Commander, Amphibious Force, Europe
COMPHIBFOR ... Commander, Amphibious Force
COMPHIBFORPAC ... Commander, Amphibious Force, Pacific Fleet   (MUGU)
COMPHIBGRU ... Commander, Amphibious Group   (CINC)
COMPHIBLANT ... Commander, Amphibious Force, Atlantic Fleet
COMPHIBNAW ... Commander, Amphibious Force, Northwest African Waters

COMPHIBPAC ... Commander, Amphibious Force, Pacific Fleet
COMPHIBRON ... Commander, Amphibious Squadron
COMPHIBTRALANT ... Commander, Amphibious Training Command, Atlantic
COMPHIBTRAPAC ... Commander, Amphibious Training Command, Pacific
COMPHILAGRU ... Commander, Philadelphia Group
COMPHILMAGV ... Commander, Philippine Military Assistance Group, Vietnam
CompIEE ... Companion of the Institution of Electrical Engineers [*British*]   (EY)
CompIERE ... Companion of the Institution of Electronic and Radio Engineers [*British*]
COMPILE ... Customs On-Line Method of Preparing from Invoices Lodgeable Entries [*Australia*]
Compil Res Work Accomplished Weld Res Inst (Bratislava) ... Compilation of Research Work Accomplished in the Welding Research Institute (Bratislava) [*A publication*]
Comp Immunol Microbiol Infect Dis ... Comparative Immunology, Microbiology, and Infectious Diseases [*A publication*]
Comp Ind Rpt ... Computer Industry Report [*A publication*]
Comp Indus ... Computers in Industry [*A publication*]
Comp Int Law J South Afr ... Comparative and International Law Journal of Southern Africa [*A publication*]
Comp & Int LJ South Africa ... Comparative and International Law Journal of Southern Africa [*A publication*]
Comp & Int'l LJS Afr ... Comparative and International Law Journal of Southern Africa [*A publication*]
CompIP ...... Companion of the Institute of Plumbing [*British*]   (DBQ)
COMPIS ... Comprehensive Information Service
Comp J .... Computer Journal [*A publication*]
Comp Jurid Rev ... Comparative Juridical Review [*A publication*]
Comp Jur Rev ... Comparative Juridical Review [*A publication*]
Com Pl .... Common Pleas [*Legal term*]   (DAS)
Com Pl .... Common Pleas Division, English Law Reports [*1875-80*] [*A publication*]   (DLA)
Comp L ...... Comparative Literature [*A publication*]
COMPL ..... Complement
COMPL ..... Complete   (AAG)
COMPL ..... Compliance
COMPL ..... Complication [*Medicine*]
COMPL ..... Compliment
CompL .... Computational Linguistics [*A publication*]
Comp & L ... Computers and Law [*Australia*] [*A publication*]
Comp Lab Law ... Comparative Labor Law [*A publication*]
COMPLAINT ... Complainant   (ROG)
COMPLAN ... Communications Plan
Com Plan R ... Community Planning Review [*A publication*]
Comp Law ... Computer Law and Tax Report [*A publication*]
Comp & Law ... Computers and Law [*A publication*]   (DLA)
Comp Law J ... Computer/Law Journal [*A publication*]
Comp Laws ... Compiled Laws [*A publication*]   (DLA)
Comp Lawy ... Company Lawyer [*A publication*]
Com Pl Div ... Common Pleas Division, English Law Reports [*1875-80*] [*A publication*]   (DLA)
COMPLEX ... Committee on Planetary and Lunar Exploration [*National Research Council*]
COMPLI ... Compliance   (KSC)
COMPLIP ... Computation of Manpower Programs Using Linear Programming   (MCD)
Comp Lit ... Comparative Literature [*A publication*]
Comp Lit Index ... Computer Literature Index [*A publication*]
Comp Lit St ... Comparative Literature Studies [*A publication*]
Comp Lit Stud ... Comparative Literature Studies [*A publication*]
Comp LJ .... Company Law Journal [*A publication*]   (DLA)
Comp LJ .... Computer/Law Journal [*A publication*]
COMPLON ... Completion   (ROG)
Com Pl Reptr ... Common Pleas Reporter [*Scranton, PA*] [*A publication*]   (DLA)
Comp L Rev ... Comparative Law Review [*A publication*]
Comp L Rev Japan Inst ... Comparative Law Review. Japan Institute of Comparative Law [*A publication*]
Com Pl R (PA) ... Common Pleas Reporter [*Scranton, PA*] [*A publication*]   (DLA)
Comp LS .... Comparative Law Series. United States Bureau of Foreign and Domestic Commerce. General Legal Bulletin [*A publication*]   (DLA)
Comp L Ser ... Comparative Law Series. United States Bureau of Foreign and Domestic Commerce. General Legal Bulletin [*A publication*]
COMPLT .. Complainant
COMPLT .. Complaint   (ROG)
Comp L Yb ... Comparative Law Yearbook [*A publication*]   (DLA)
COMPLYMCHAN ... Commander, Plymouth Subarea Channel
COMPMARK ... Computer Marketing [*Standard & Poor's*]
Comp Master Marin Aust J ... Company of Master Mariners of Australia. Journal [*A publication*]   (APTA)
Comp Math ... Compositio Mathematica [*A publication*]
Comp and Maths with Appls ... Computers and Mathematics with Applications [*A publication*]
Comp & Med ... Computers and Medicine [*A publication*]

Comp Med East West ... Comparative Medicine East and West [*A publication*]
Comp Methods Appl Mech Eng ... Computer Methods in Applied Mechanics and Engineering [*A publication*]
Comp Mgmt ... Computer Management [*A publication*]
COMPMR ... Commander, Pacific Missile Range   (AAG)
COMPMRINST ... Commander, Pacific Missile Range Instruction   (MUGU)
COMPMRNOTE ... Commander, Pacific Missile Range Notice   (MUGU)
COMPN .... Compensation   (ADA)
COMPN .... Composition
COMPN .... Compression [*Automotive engineering*]
Comp Net ... Computer Networks [*A publication*]
Comp News-Rec ... Composers News-Record [*A publication*]
COMPO ..... Compensation [*Australian slang*]   (DSUE)
COMPO ..... Composition   (ROG)
COMPO .... Council of Motion Picture Organizations [*Defunct*]   (EA)
Components Rep ... Components Report [*A publication*]
Component Technol ... Component Technology [*A publication*]
COMPOOL ... Common Data Pool   (MCD)
COMPOOL ... Communications Tag Pool
Comp Oper Res ... Computers and Operations Research [*A publication*]
COMPORON ... Composite Squadron
COMPOS ... Composition
Compos ...... [*Bernardus*] Compostellanus [*Authority cited in pre-1607 legal work*]   (DSA)
Composites Technol Rev ... Composites Technology Review [*A publication*]
Compositio Math ... Compositio Mathematica [*A publication*]
Compos Mater ... Composite Materials [*A publication*]
Compos Polym ... Composite Polymers [*A publication*]
Compost ..... [*Bernardus*] Compostellanus [*Authority cited in pre-1607 legal work*]   (DSA)
COMPOST ... Computerized Principles of Structures   (ADA)
Compos Technol Rev ... Composites Technology Review [*A publication*]
Compostell ... [*Bernardus*] Compostellanus [*Authority cited in pre-1607 legal work*]   (DSA)
Compost Sci ... Compost Science [*Later, Bio Cycle*] [*A publication*]
Compost Sci Land Util ... Compost Science/Land Utilization [*Later, Bio Cycle*] [*A publication*]
Compos Wood ... Composite Wood [*A publication*]
Comp Pathol Bull ... Comparative Pathology Bulletin [*A publication*]
Comp & People ... Computers and People [*A publication*]
Comp Perf ... Computer Performance [*A publication*]
Comp Pers ... Computer Personnel [*A publication*]
Comp Phys Comm ... Computer Physics Communications [*A publication*]
Comp Physiol Ecol ... Comparative Physiology and Ecology [*A publication*]
Comp Pol ... Comparative Politics [*A publication*]
Comp Poli S ... Comparative Political Studies [*A publication*]
Comp Polit ... Comparative Politics [*A publication*]
Comp Polit Stud ... Comparative Political Studies [*A publication*]
Comp Pol Stud ... Comparative Political Studies [*A publication*]
Comp Psychi ... Comprehensive Psychiatry [*A publication*]
COMPR .... Commerce Department Procurement Regulations
COMPR .... Compare   (FAAC)
Comp R ...... Compensation Review [*A publication*]
COMPR .... Composition Roof
COMPR .... Compression   (KSC)
COMPR .... Compressor   (MSA)
Compr Anal Chem ... Comprehensive Analytical Chemistry [*A publication*]
COMPRD ... Comprised   (ROG)
Comprehensive Ed ... Comprehensive Education [*A publication*]
Comprehensive Nurs Mon (Tokyo) ... Comprehensive Nursing Monthly (Tokyo) [*A publication*]
Comprehensive Psychiat ... Comprehensive Psychiatry [*A publication*]
COMPREP ... Composite Reporting System   (MCD)
Com P Reptr ... Common Pleas Reporter [*Scranton, PA*] [*A publication*]   (DLA)
Compres Air ... Compressed Air [*A publication*]
Comp Resell ... Computer Reseller News [*A publication*]
COMPRESS ... Commercial Production of Electronic Solid State Systems   (MCD)
COMPRESS ... Computer Research, Systems, and Software   (IEEE)
Compress Air ... Compressed Air [*A publication*]
Compressed Gas Assoc Tech Suppl Annu Rep ... Compressed Gas Association. Technical Supplement to the Annual Report [*A publication*]
COMPRET ... Upon Completion Return Duty Station and Resume Duties [*Navy*]
Comp Rev ... Compensation Review [*A publication*]
Comp Rev ... Computing Reviews [*A publication*]
Compr Immunol ... Comprehensive Immunology [*A publication*]
Compr Nurs Q ... Comprehensive Nursing Quarterly [*A publication*]
COMPROC ... Command Processor [*Data processing*]
Com Prof ... Commonwealth Professional [*A publication*]
COMPROG ... Computer Program   (IEEE)
Compr Pediatr Nurs ... Comprehensive Pediatric Nursing [*A publication*]
Compr Psychiatry ... Comprehensive Psychiatry [*A publication*]
COMPRT ... Compartment   (FAAC)
Compr Ther ... Comprehensive Therapy [*A publication*]
Comp Rtl .... Computer Retail News. The Newspaper for Systems and Software Retailing [*A publication*]
Compr Virol ... Comprehensive Virology [*A publication*]

COMPS..... Consolidation of Military Pay Services [*Strategic Air Command proposal*]

COMPS..... Contracted Out Money-Purchase Schemes [*Pension plan*] [*British*]

COMPS..... Council on Multiemployer Pension Security   (EA)

COMPSAC ... Computer Software and Applications Conference

Comp Sci T ... Composites Science and Technology [*A publication*]

Comp and Sec ... Computers and Security [*A publication*]

COMPSERSq ... Computer Service Squadron [*Air Force*]

COMPSG ... Compensating   (MSA)

CompSLEAT ... Companion of the Society of Licensed Aircraft Engineers and Technologists [*British*]   (DBQ)

COMPSN ... Composition

COMPSO ... Computer Software and Peripheral Show   (IEEE)

Comp Sol ... Complete Solicitor [*A publication*]   (DLA)

Comp St ..... Compiled Statutes [*A publication*]   (DLA)

Comp Stan ... Computers and Standards [*A publication*]

Comp Stand ... Computers and Standards [*A publication*]

Comp Stat .. Compiled Statutes [*A publication*]   (DLA)

Comp Strat ... Comparative Strategy [*A publication*]

Comp Stud S ... Comparative Studies in Society and History [*A publication*]

Comp Stud Soc Hist ... Comparative Studies in Society and History [*A publication*]

Comp Stud Soc & Hist ... Comparative Studies in Society and History [*A publication*]

Comp Surv ... Computing Surveys [*A publication*]

COMPSY.. Computer Support in Military Psychiatry [*Project*]   (RDA)

COMPSYSANLSTPGMR ... Computer Systems Analyst and Programmer [*Air Force*]

COMPT..... Compartment   (KSC)

COMPT..... Complainant   (ROG)

COMPT..... Compliment   (ROG)

compt......... Comptant [*Cash*] [*French*] [*Business term*]

COMPT..... Comptroller

COMPT..... Comptroller of the Navy

Comp Talk ... Computer Talk [*A publication*]

Comp Tech Rev ... Composites Technology Review [*A publication*]

COMPTEL ... Competitive Telecommunications Association   (EA)

Comptes Rend ... Comptes Rendus. Academie des Sciences [*A publication*]

Comptes Rendus ... Comptes Rendus Hebdomadaires des Seances. Academie des Sciences [*A publication*]

CompTI...... Companion of the Textile Institute [*British*]

COMPTR ... Comparator [*Data processing*]

Compt Rend Acad ... Comptes Rendus des Seances. Academie des Inscriptions et Belles-Lettres [*A publication*]

Compt Rend Acad Agr France ... Comptes Rendus. Academie d'Agriculture de France [*A publication*]

Compt Rend Acad Bulg Sci ... Comptes Rendus. Academie Bulgare des Sciences [*A publication*]

Compt Rend Acad Sci ... Comptes Rendus. Academie des Sciences [*A publication*]

Compt Rend Acad Sci Outre-Mer ... Comptes Rendus Trimestriels des Seances. Academie des Sciences d'Outre-Mer [*A publication*]

Compt Rend Acad Sc (Paris) ... Comptes Rendus Hebdomadaires des Seances. Academie des Sciences (Paris) [*A publication*]

Compt Rend Cong Internat Med Trop et Hyg ... Comptes Rendus. Congres International de Medecine Tropicale et d'Hygiene [*A publication*]

Compt Rend Soc Biol (Paris) ... Comptes Rendus des Seances. Societe de Biologie et de Ses Filiales et Associees (Paris) [*A publication*]

Comptr Treas Dec ... Comptroller Treasury Decisions [*A publication*]   (DLA)

COMPTS.. Compliments   (ROG)

COMPTU ... Composite Training Unit [*Military*]   (NVT)

COMPTU ... New York Council of Motion Picture and Television Unions   (EA)

COMPTUEX ... Composite Training Unit Exercise [*Military*]   (NVT)

COMPUL ... Compulsory   (DSUE)

COMPUNET ... Computer Networking Stand Alone Program

COMPUNICATIONS ... Computers and Communications

Comp Urb Res ... Comparative Urban Research [*A publication*]

Comput ...... Computer [*A publication*]

Comput Abstr ... Computer Abstracts [*A publication*]

Comput Acquis Syst Ser ... Computerized Acquisitions Systems Series [*A publication*]

Comput Age ... Computer Age [*A publication*]

Comput Aided Des ... Computer-Aided Design [*A publication*]

Comput Appl ... Computer Applications [*A publication*]

Comput Appl ... Computers and Their Applications [*A publication*]

Comput Appl Archaeol ... Computer Applications in Archaeology [*A publication*]

Comput Appl Biosci ... Computer Applications in the Biosciences [*A publication*]

Comput Appl Chem (China) ... Computers and Applied Chemistry (China) [*A publication*]

Comput Appl Nat and Soc Sci ... Computer Applications in the Natural and Social Sciences [*A publication*]

Comput Appl New Ser ... Computer Applications. New Series [*A publication*]

Comput Appl Serv ... Computer Applications Service [*A publication*]

Comput Arch Elektron Rechn ... Computing. Archiv fuer Elektronisches Rechnen [*A publication*]

Comput Arch Inf Num ... Computing. Archiv fuer Informatik und Numerik [*A publication*]

Comput Archit News ... Computer Architecture News [*A publication*]

Comput Autom ... Computers and Automation [*Later, Computers and People*] [*A publication*]

Comput and Autom and People ... Computers and Automation and People [*A publication*]

Comput Biol Med ... Computers in Biology and Medicine [*A publication*]

Comput Biol and Med ... Computers in Biology and Medicine [*A publication*]

Comput Biom ... Computers and Biomedical Research [*A publication*]

Comput Biomed Res ... Computers and Biomedical Research [*A publication*]

Comput and Biomed Res ... Computers and Biomedical Research [*A publication*]

Comput Bull ... Computer Bulletin [*A publication*]

Comput Busn ... Computer Business News [*A publication*]

Comput Bus News ... Computer Business News [*A publication*]

Comput Cardiol ... Computers in Cardiology [*A publication*]

Comput Cat Syst Ser ... Computerized Cataloging Systems Series [*A publication*]

Comput Chem ... Computers and Chemistry [*A publication*]

Comput Chem Biochem Res ... Computers in Chemical and Biochemical Research [*A publication*]

Comput Chem Eng ... Computers and Chemical Engineering [*A publication*]

Comput & Chem Eng ... Computers and Chemical Engineering [*A publication*]

Comput Chem Instrum ... Computers in Chemistry and Instrumentation [*A publication*]

Comput Circ Syst Ser ... Computerized Circulation Systems Series [*A publication*]

Comput Commun ... Computer Communications [*A publication*]

Comput Commun Rev ... Computer Communication Review [*A publication*]

Comput & Contr Abstr ... Computer and Control Abstracts [*IEE*] [*Information service or system*] [*A publication*]

Comput Contrib ... Computer Contributions [*A publication*]

Comput Control Abstr ... Computer and Control Abstracts [*IEE*] [*Information service or system*] [*A publication*]

Comput Control Abstracts ... Computer and Control Abstracts [*IEE*] [*Information service or system*] [*A publication*]

Comput Control Inf Theory ... Computers, Control, and Information Theory [*A publication*]

Comput Data ... Computer Data [*A publication*]

Comput and Data Process Technol ... Computer and Data Processor Technology [*A publication*]

Comput Decis ... Computer Decisions [*A publication*]

Comput Des ... Computer Design [*A publication*]

Comput Educ ... Computer Education [*A publication*]

Comput and Educ ... Computers and Education [*A publication*]

Comput & Electr Eng ... Computers and Electrical Engineering [*A publication*]

Comput Electr Eng ... Computers and Electrical Engineering [*A publication*]

Comput Electr Engrg ... Computers and Electrical Engineering [*A publication*]

Comput Elem Syst ... Computer Elements and Systems [*A publication*]

Comput Engrg Ser ... Computer Engineering Series [*A publication*]

Comput Enhanc Spectrosc ... Computer Enhanced Spectroscopy [*A publication*]

Comput Environ Urban Syst ... Computers, Environment, and Urban Systems [*England*] [*A publication*]

Comput Equip Rev ... Computer Equipment Review [*A publication*]

Computer Aided Des ... Computer-Aided Design [*A publication*]

Computer D ... Computer Digest [*A publication*]

Computer Educ ... Computer Education [*A publication*]

Computer Engrg Ser ... Computer Engineering Series [*A publication*]

Computer Hu ... Computers and the Humanities [*Database*] [*A publication*]

Computer J ... Computer Journal [*A publication*]

Computer LJ ... Computer Law Journal [*A publication*]

Computer L Serv Rep ... Computer Law Service Reporter [*A publication*]   (DLA)

Computer L & Tax ... Computer Law and Tax Report [*A publication*]   (DLA)

Computer L & T Rep ... Computer Law and Tax Report [*A publication*]   (DLA)

Computer Mus J ... Computer Music Journal [*A publication*]

Computer Pe ... Computers and People [*A publication*]

Computer Ph ... Computer Physics Communications [*A publication*]

Computer Pr ... Computer Programs in Biomedicine [*A publication*]

Computers & Chem Engng ... Computers and Chemical Engineering [*A publication*]

Computers and Ed ... Computers and Education [*A publication*]

Computers and Educ ... Computers and Education [*A publication*]

Computers Geosci ... Computers and Geosciences [*A publication*]

Computers and L ... Computers and Law [*A publication*]

Computer Wkly ... Computer Weekly [*A publication*]

COMPUTEX ... Irish Computer Exhibition [*SDL Exhibitions Ltd.*]   (TSPED)

Comput and Fluids ... Computers and Fluids [*A publication*]

Comput Fraud and Secur Bull ... Computer Fraud and Security Bulletin [*A publication*]

Comput & Geosci ... Computers and Geosciences [*A publication*]

Comput Geosci ... Computers and Geosciences [*A publication*]

Comput & Graphics ... Computers and Graphics [*A publication*]

Comput Graphics ... Computers and Graphics [*A publication*]

Comput Graphics and Art ... Computer Graphics and Art [*A publication*]

Comput Graphics and Image Process ... Computer Graphics and Image Processing [*A publication*]
Comput Graphics Image Process ... Computer Graphics and Image Processing [*A publication*]
Comput Graphics World ... Computer Graphics World [*A publication*]
Comput Healthc ... Computers in Healthcare [*A publication*]
Comput Hosp ... Computers in Hospitals [*A publication*]
Comput Hum ... Computers and the Humanities [*Database*] [*A publication*]
Comput & Human ... Computers and the Humanities [*Database*] [*A publication*]
Comput & Humanities ... Computers and the Humanities [*Database*] [*A publication*]
Comput Ind ... Computers in Industry [*Netherlands*] [*A publication*]
Comput and Ind Eng ... Computers and Industrial Engineering [*A publication*]
Comput Ind Eng ... Computers and Industrial Engineering [*A publication*]
Comput Inf ... Computer Information [*A publication*]
Comput & Info Sys ... Computer and Information Systems [*A publication*]
Comput Inf Syst ... Computer and Information Systems [*A publication*]
Comput Inf Syst Abstr J ... Computer and Information Systems Abstracts Journal [*A publication*]
Computing J Abs ... Computing Journal Abstracts [*A publication*]
Computing Suppl ... Computing. Supplementum [*A publication*]
Comput J ... Computer Journal [*A publication*]
Comput L ... Computational Linguistics [*A publication*]
Comput Lang ... Computer Languages [*A publication*]
Comput & Law ... Computers and Law [*A publication*]   (DLA)
Comput/Law J ... Computer/Law Journal [*A publication*]
Comput Linguist and Comput Lang ... Computational Linguistics and Computer Languages [*A publication*]
Comput Mach Fi ... Computing Machinery Field [*A publication*]
Comput Manage ... Computer Management [*A publication*]
Comput Marketplace ... Computer Marketplace [*A publication*]
Comput & Math with Appl ... Computers and Mathematics with Applications [*A publication*]
Comput Math Appl ... Computers and Mathematics with Applications [*A publication*]
Comput Med ... Computers and Medicine [*A publication*]
Comput and Medieval Data Process ... Computers and Medieval Data Processing [*A publication*]
Comput Med Imaging Graphics ... Computerized Medical Imaging and Graphics [*A publication*]
Comput Method Program Biomed ... Computer Methods and Programs in Biomedicine [*A publication*]
Comput Methods Appl Mech & Eng ... Computer Methods in Applied Mechanics and Engineering [*A publication*]
Comput Methods Appl Mech Eng ... Computer Methods in Applied Mechanics and Engineering [*A publication*]
Comput Methods Appl Mech & Engng ... Computer Methods in Applied Mechanics and Engineering [*A publication*]
Comput Methods Appl Mech Engrg ... Computer Methods in Applied Mechanics and Engineering [*A publication*]
Comput Methods Programs Biomed ... Computer Methods and Programs in Biomedicine [*A publication*]
Comput Mgmt ... Computer Management [*A publication*]
Comput Monogr ... Computer Monographs [*A publication*]
Comput Mus ... Computer Music Journal [*A publication*]
Comput Music J ... Computer Music Journal [*A publication*]
Comput Networks ... Computer Networks [*A publication*]
Comput News ... Computer News [*A publication*]
Comput Newsl Schools Bus ... Computing Newsletter for Schools of Business [*A publication*]
Comput Nurs ... Computers in Nursing [*A publication*]
Comput OA ... Computerworld Office Automation [*A publication*]
Comput OC ... Computerworld on Communications [*A publication*]
Comput & Oper Res ... Computers and Operations Research [*A publication*]
Comput and Oper Res ... Computers and Operations Research [*A publication*]
Comput and People ... Computers and People [*A publication*]
Comput Performance ... Computer Performance [*A publication*]
Comput Peripherals Rev ... Computer Peripherals Review [*A publication*]
Comput Pers ... Computer Personnel [*A publication*]
Comput Phys Comm ... Computer Physics Communications [*A publication*]
Comput Phys Commun ... Computer Physics Communications [*A publication*]
Comput Phys Rep ... Computer Physics Reports [*A publication*]
Comput Prax ... Computer Praxis [*A publication*]
Comput Program Abstr ... Computer Program Abstracts [*A publication*]
Comput Programs Biomed ... Computer Programs in Biomedicine [*A publication*]
Comput Programs Chem ... Computer Programs for Chemistry [*A publication*]
Comput Psychiatry/Psychol ... Computers in Psychiatry/Psychology [*A publication*]
Comput Radiol ... Computerized Radiology [*A publication*]
Comput Rep Dep Archit Sci Syd Univ ... Computer Report. Department of Architectural Science. University of Sydney [*A publication*]   (APTA)
Comput Rev ... Computing Reviews [*A publication*]
Comput Rev Bibliogr Subj Index Curr Comput Lit ... Computing Reviews. Bibliography and Subject Index of Current Computing Literature [*A publication*]
Computrwld ... Computerworld [*A publication*]
Computrwl X ... Computerworld Extra [*A publication*]

Computrwoc ... Computerwoche [*A publication*]
Comput S Afr ... Computing South Africa [*A publication*]
Comput Sch ... Computers in Schools [*A publication*]
Comput Sci Appl Math ... Computer Science and Applied Mathematics [*A publication*]
Comput Sci and Inf ... Computer Science and Informatics [*A publication*]
Comput Sci Monographs (Tokyo) ... Computer Science Monographs (Tokyo) [*A publication*]
Comput and Secur ... Computers and Security [*A publication*]
Comput Ser Syst Ser ... Computerized Serials Systems Series [*A publication*]
Comput and Soc ... Computers and Society [*A publication*]
Comput Stat and Data Anal ... Computational Statistics and Data Analysis [*A publication*]
Comput and Struct ... Computers and Structures [*A publication*]
Comput Struct ... Computers and Structures [*A publication*]
Comput and Structures ... Computers and Structures [*A publication*]
Comput Stud Hum & Verbal Behav ... Computer Studies in the Humanities and Verbal Behavior [*A publication*]
Comput Suppl ... Computing. Supplementum [*Vienna*] [*A publication*]
Comput Surv ... Computer Survey [*A publication*]
Comput Surv ... Computing Surveys [*A publication*]
Comput Survey ... Computing Surveys [*A publication*]
Comput Surveys ... Computing Surveys [*A publication*]
Comput Syst ... Computer Systems [*A publication*]
Comput Syst Sthn Afr ... Computer Systems in Southern Africa [*A publication*]
Comput Talk ... Computer Talk [*A publication*]
Comput Terminals Rev ... Computer Terminals Review [*A publication*]
Comput Times with Computacards ... Computer Times with Computacards [*A publication*]
Comput Today ... Computing Today [*A publication*]
Comput Tomogr ... Computerized Tomography [*A publication*]
Comput Vision Graphics and Image Process ... Computer Vision. Graphics and Image Processing [*A publication*]
Comput Week ... Computer Week [*A publication*]
Comput Wkly ... Computer Weekly [*A publication*]
Comput Wkly Int ... Computer Weekly International [*A publication*]
Comput World ... Computer World [*A publication*]
Computwrld ... Computerworld [*A publication*]
COMPW ... Composite Wing   (MCD)
Comp Wkly ... Computer Weekly [*A publication*]
Comp Wld BG ... Computerworld Buyer's Guide [*A publication*]
Compwrld on Comm ... Computerworld on Communications [*A publication*]
Compwrld OA ... Computerworld Office Automation [*A publication*]
COMPY ..... Company   (ROG)
ComQ .... Commonwealth Quarterly [*A publication*]
COMR ...... Comair Holdings, Inc. [*NASDAQ symbol*]   (NQ)
COMR ...... Commissar
COMR ...... Commissioner
COMR ...... Court of Military Review   (AFM)
COMRAC ... Combat Radius Capability [*Military*]
COMRADE ... Computer-Aided Design Environment [*Software system*]   (IEEE)
COMRADEX ... Containment and Meteorology for Radiation Exposure [*Nuclear energy*]   (NRCH)
COMRAT ... Commuted Rations [*Acronym refers to married Marine living off base and receiving these special pay dispensations*]
COMRATE ... Committee on Mineral Resources and the Environment [*National Research Council*]
COMRAZ ... Communication, Range, and Azimuth Unit [*Data processing*]
Comrc Intl ... Commerce International [*A publication*]
COMR & DSAT ... Communication Research and Development Satellite [*NASA*]   (NASA)
COMRDW ... Computerized Radiology [*A publication*]
COMREC ... Care-Oriented Medical Record [*University of Alabama*]
COMREC ... Component Reclamation   (AFIT)
COMRECONATKRON ... Reconnaissance Attack Squadron [*Navy*]
COMRECONATKWING ... Reconnaissance Attack Wing [*Navy*]
COMREG ... Commonwealth Statutory Rules [*Database*] [*Australia*]
COMREL ... Community Relations [*Military*]   (NVT)
ComRelMiss ... Commentarium pro Religionis et Missionariis [*Rome*] [*A publication*]   (BJA)
Com Rep .... Commerce Reporter [*A publication*]
COMREP ... Commonwealth Acts: Pamphlet Reprints [*Database*] [*Australia*]
Com Rep .... Comyn's English King's Bench Reports [*1695-1741*] [*A publication*]   (DLA)
COMRESDESRON ... Commander, Reserve Destroyer Squadron
ComRev ... Computing Reviews [*A publication*]
COMRI ..... Communications Routing Indicator
COMRIVDIV ... Commander, River Division
COMRIVFLOT ... Commander, River Flotilla
COMRIVFLOTONE ... Commander, River Flotilla One
COMRIVPATFOR ... Commander, River Patrol Force
COMRIVSUPPRON ... Commander, River Support Squadron
COMRL ... Major Commands Material Readiness List   (AFIT)
COMRNDN ... Commander, Riverine Division [*Navy*]
COMRNFLOT ... Commander, Riverine Flotilla [*Navy*]
COMRNRON ... Commander, Riverine Squadron [*Navy*]
COMROKFV ... Commander, Republic of Korea Forces, Vietnam
COMROKMAGV ... Commander, Republic of Korea Military Assistance Group, Vietnam

COMROUTE ... Commander-in-Chief, [*US Fleet*], Convoy and Routing Section
COMRT .... Commissariat
COMRTMAGV ... Commander, Royal Thai Military Assistance Group, Vietnam
COMS .... 3Com Corp. [*NASDAQ symbol*]   (NQ)
COMS .... College of Osteopathic Medicine and Surgery   (OICC)
COMS .... Commissioner
COMS .... Communication Subsystem   (MCD)
COMS .... Communications   (ROG)
COMS .... Communications Support
Coms .... Comstock's Reports [*1-4 New York Court of Appeals*] [*A publication*]   (DLA)
CoMs .... Manitou Springs Public Library, Manitou Springs, CO [*Library symbol*] [*Library of Congress*]   (LCLS)
COMSAMAR ... Commander, Straits and Marmara Defense Sector   (NATG)
COMSANFRANGRU ... Commander, San Francisco Group
COMSAT ... Communications Satellite Corp. [*Assignee of operational and developmental responsibilities for Telstar and other international communications space devices*]
COMSATCOM ... Commercial Satellite Communications System
COMSATCORP ... Communications Satellite Corporation [*See also COMSAT*]
COMSAT Tech Rev ... COMSAT [*Communications Satellite Corp.*] Technical Review [*A publication*]
COMSC..... Commander, Military Sealift Command
COMSCELM ... Commander, Military Sealift Command, Eastern Atlantic and Mediterranean
COMSCFE ... Commander, Military Sealift Command, Far East
COMSCGULF ... Commander, Military Sealift Command, Gulf Subarea
COMSCLANT ... Commander, Military Sealift Command, Atlantic
COMSCMED ... Commander, Military Sealift Command, Mediterranean
COMSCOR ... Consolidation and Management of Supply Consumption Rates   (MCD)
COMSCORON ... Commander, Scouting Squadron
COMSCPAC ... Commander, Military Sealift Command, Pacific
COMSE..... Committee on Marine Science and Engineering [*Federal Council for Science and Technology*]   (NOAA)
COMSEAFRON ... Commander, Sea Frontier
COMSEC ... Communications Security [*Military*]
COMSEC ... Communications Security Association   (EA)
COMSEC ... Community Security   (NVT)
COMSECFLTHQ ... Commander, Second Fleet, Headquarters   (MCD)
COMSECLOG ... Communications Security Logistics   (MCD)
COMSECONDFLT ... Commander, Second Fleet   (MUGU)
COMSED ... Continental Margin Sedimentology [*Oceanography*]   (MSC)
COMSENEX ... Combined Sensor Tracking Exercise [*Military*]   (NVT)
COMSERFORSOPACSUBCOM ... Commander, Service Force, South Pacific Subordinate Command
Com Serj .... Common Serjeant [*British*]   (ILCA)
COMSERPAC ... Command Service Force, Pacific   (MCD)
COMSERV ... Commander, Service Force
COMSERVLANT ... Commander, Service Force, Atlantic Fleet
COMSERVPAC ... Commander, Service Force, Pacific Fleet
COMSERVRON ... Commander, Service Squadron
COMSERVSOWESPAC ... Commander, Service Force, Southwest Pacific
COMSEVENTHFLT ... Commander, Seventh Fleet   (MUGU)
COMSFOR ... Combined Surveillance and Foliage Penetration RADAR   (MCD)
COMSICL ... Common/See Individual Components List   (MCD)
COMSIXATAF ... Commander, Sixth Allied Tactical Air Force   (AFM)
COMSIXFLT ... Commander, Sixth Fleet   (NATG)
COMSIXTHFLT ... Commander, Sixth Fleet   (NATG)
COMSL..... Communication System Simulation Language [*Data processing*]   (IEEE)
COMSN .... Commission   (AFM)
COMSNR ... Commissioner
COMSOAL ... Computer Method of Sequencing Operations for Assembly Lines   (MCD)
COMSOC ... Communications Spacecraft Operation Center [*NASA*]
COMSOEASTPAC ... Commander, Southeast Pacific Force
COMSOLANT ... Commander, South Atlantic Force
COMSOPAC ... Commander, South Pacific
COMSOS ... Common Supply Support Overseas [*Military*]
COMSOSECWESTSEAFRON ... Commander, Southern Sector, Western Sea Frontier   (MUGU)
COMSOTFE ... Commander, Support Operations Task Force, Europe   (AFM)
COMSOWESPAC ... Commander, Southwest Pacific Force
Com Spec Katanga Ann Ser Mines Ser Geogr Geol ... Comite Special du Katanga. Annales du Service des Mines et du Service Geographique et Geologique [*A publication*]
ComSpirAT/NT ... Commenti Spirituali dell'Antico Testamento/del Nuovo Testamento [*Rome*] [*A publication*]   (BJA)
COMSPK ... Communications Speaker
COMSQN ... Communications Squadron [*Marine Corps*]
COMSR..... Communications Support Requirements   (MCD)
COMSRY ... Commissary
COMSSIC ... Combat System Ship Interface Criteria [*Navy*]   (CAAL)
Comst .... Comstock's Reports [*1-4 New York Court of Appeals*] [*A publication*]   (DLA)

COMSTA ... Communication Station [*Military*]   (CAAL)
COMSTAC ... Commercial Space Transportation Advisory Committee [*Department of Transportation*] [*Washington, DC*]   (EGAO)
COMSTAC ... Commission on Standards and Accreditation of Services for the Blind [*Superseded by NAC*]
COMSTAT ... Communications Status Report   (MCD)
COM-STAT ... Computer Stock Timing and Analysis Technique
Com Stat Energ Nucl Inst Fiz At Rep (Rom) ... Comitetul de Stat pentru Energia Nucleara. Institutul de Fizica Atomica. Report (Romania) [*A publication*]
COMSTATRPT ... Communications Status Report [*Military*]   (NVT)
COM-STEP ... Computerized Spot Television Evaluation and Processing [*Advertising*]
COMSTOCKGRU ... Commander, Stockton Group
COMSTRATRESCENT ... Commander, Strategic Reserve, Allied Land Forces, Central Europe   (NATG)
COMSTRIKFLANT ... Commander, Striking Fleet, Atlantic   (AABC)
COMSTRIKFLANTREPEUR ... Commander, Striking Fleet, Atlantic Representative in Europe   (NATG)
COMSTRIKFLTLANT ... Commander, Striking Fleet, Atlantic   (AFM)
COMSTRIKFORSOUTH ... Commander, Striking and Support Forces, Southern Europe
COMSTS .. Commander, Military Sea Transportation Service [*Obsolete*]
COMSTSELMAREA ... Commander, Military Sea Transportation Service, Eastern Atlantic and Mediterranean Area
COMSTSFE ... Commander, Military Sea Transportation Service, Far East   (CINC)
COMSTSGULFSUBAREA ... Commander, Military Sea Transportation Service, Gulf Subarea
COMSTSLANTAREA ... Commander, Military Sea Transportation Service, Atlantic Area
COMSTSMIDPACSUBAREA ... Commander, Military Sea Transportation Service, Mid-Pacific Subarea
COMSTS/MIS ... Commander, Military Sea Transportation Service, Management Information System
COMSTSNORPACSUBAREA ... Commander, Military Sea Transportation Service, Northern Pacific Subarea
COMSTSPACAREA ... Commander, Military Sea Transportation Service, Pacific Area
COMSTSSEA ... Commander, Military Sea Transportation Service, Southeast Asia   (CINC)
COMSTSWESTPACAREA ... Commander, Military Sea Transportation Service, West Pacific Area
COMSUBACLANT ... Commander, Submarine Allied Command, Atlantic   (AABC)
COMSUBASE ... Commander, Submarine Base
COMSUBCOMNELMCOMHEDSUPPACT ... Commander, Subordinate Command, [*US*] Naval Forces Eastern Atlantic and Mediterranean, Commander Headquarters Support Activities [*Said to be the longest English-language acronym*]
COMSUBDEVGRU ... Commander, Submarine Development Group
COMSUBDIV ... Commander, Submarine Division
COMSUBEASTLANT ... Commander, Submarine Force, Eastern Atlantic
COMSUBFLO ... Commander, Submarine Flotilla
COMSUBFLOT ... Commander, Submarine Flotilla   (MUGU)
COMSUBGRU 8 ... Commander Submarine Group 8
COMSUBLANT ... Commander, Submarine Force, Atlantic
COMSUBLEDNOREAST ... Commander, Submarines, Northeast Mediterranean   (NATG)
COMSUBMED ... Commander, Submarine Force, Mediterranean   (AABC)
COMSUBMEDNOREAST ... Commander, Submarine Force, Northeast Mediterranean   (AABC)
COMSUBPAC ... Commander, Submarine Force, Pacific
COMSUBRON ... Commander, Submarine Squadron
COMSUBS ... Commander, Submarines
COMSUBSSOWESPAC ... Commander, Submarines, Southwest Pacific Force
COMSUBTRAFAC ... Commander, Submarine Training Facilities
COMSUBWESTLANT ... Commander, Submarine Force, Western Atlantic Area   (AABC)
COMSUCOMLANTFLT ... Commander, Subordinate Command, [*US*] Atlantic Fleet   (NATG)
COMSUFRHIN ... Commander, French Rhine River Squadron [*NATO*]   (NATG)
COMSUP ... Combat Support Units [*Army*]
COMSY..... Commissary [*Air Force*]   (AFM)
COMSYMP ... Communist Sympathizer
COMSYS .. Communication Systems Ltd. [*London, England*] [*Telecommunications*]   (TSSD)
COMSYSTR ... Commissary Store [*Army*]   (AABC)
COMT .... Catechol-O-Methyltransferase [*An enzyme*]
COMT .... Comet Entertainment, Inc. [*NASDAQ symbol*]   (NQ)
COMT .... Commandant
Comt.......... Commentary [*A publication*]
COMT .... Commit   (AAG)
COMT .... Communications Technician   (MCD)
COMTAC ... Command Tactical [*Navy*]   (NVT)
COMTAC ... Commander, Tactical Air Command   (AFM)
COMTAC ... Communications and Tactical [*Publications*] [*Navy*]   (NVT)

COMTACGRU ... Commander, Tactical Air Control Group
COMTACRON ... Commander, Tactical Air Control Squadron
COMTAFDEN ... Commander, Tactical Air Force, Denmark (NATG)
COMTAFNORNOR ... Commander, Allied Tactical Air Force, North Norway (AABC)
COMTAFSONOR ... Commander, Allied Tactical Air Force, South Norway (AABC)
COMTAIWANDEFCOMD ... Commander, Taiwan Defense Command (MUGU)
COMTAIWANPATFOR ... Commander, Taiwan Patrol Force (CINC)
COMTASKFORNON ... Commander, Allied Task Forces, North Norway (AFM)
COMTBFLOT ... Commander, Motor Torpedo Boat Flotilla
COMTBRON ... Commander, Motor Torpedo Boat Squadron
COMTBRONTRACENT ... Commander, Motor Torpedo Boat Squadron Training Center
COMTE .... Committee
COMtec ..... Computer Micrographics Technology (EA)
COMTECHREP ... Complementary Technical Report [*Military*] (AFM)
COMTEL ... International Computer and Telecommunications Conference [*International Conference Management, Inc.*] [*Dallas, TX*] [*Telecommunications*] (TSSD)
COMTEMDET ... Upon Completion of Temporary Duty, Detach [*Navy*]
COMTEMDIRDET ... Upon Completion of Temporary Duty and When Directed, Detach [*Navy*]
COMTEMINS ... Upon Completion of Temporary Duty under Instruction [*Navy*]
COMTEXGRU ... Commander, Texas Group
COMTHIRTEEN ... Commandant, Thirteenth Naval District (MUGU)
COMTHREE ... Commandant, Third Naval District (MUGU)
Com Today ... Commerce Today [*A publication*]
COMTONGRU ... Commander, Tongue Point Group, Inactive Reserve Fleet, Pacific
COMTORPRON ... Commander, Torpedo Squadron
COMTR .... Commutator [*Automotive engineering*]
COMTRAC ... Computer-Based Case Tracing [*Medicine*]
COMTRAINCARRONPAC ... Commander, Carrier Training Squadron, Pacific Fleet
COMTRALANT ... Commander, Training Command, Atlantic
COMTRAN ... [*A*] programming language (CSR)
COMTRAN ... Commercial Translator
COMTRANSDIV ... Commander, Transport Division
COMTRANSGR ... Commander, Transport Group
COMTRANSGRSOPAC ... Commander, Transport Group, South Pacific Force
COMTRANSPHIB ... Commander, Transports, Amphibious Force
COMTRANSPHIBLANT ... Commander, Transports, Amphibious Force, Atlantic Fleet
COMTRANSPHIBPAC ... Commander, Transports, Amphibious Force, Pacific Fleet
COMTRAPAC ... Commander, Training Command, Pacific
COMTWELVE ... Commandant, Twelfth Naval District (MUGU)
COMTWOATAF ... Commander, Second Allied Tactical Air Force
COMU .... Commerce Union Corp. [*NASDAQ symbol*] (NQ)
COMUKADR ... Commander, United Kingdom Air Defense Region (AFM)
COMUL .... Complement-Fixation for Murine Leukemia [*Test*] [*Immunology*]
Comun Acad Rep Pop Romine ... Comunicarile. Academiei Republicii Populare Romine [*A publication*]
Comun Acad Repub Pop Rom ... Comunicarile. Academiei Republicii Populare Romine [*A publication*]
Comun Bot ... Comunicari de Botanica [*A publication*]
Comun Bot Mus Hist Nat Montev ... Comunicaciones Botanicas. Museo de Historia Natural de Montevideo [*A publication*]
Comun Coloq Invest Agua ... Comunicaciones Presentadas al Coloquio de Investigaciones sobre el Agua [*A publication*]
Comun y Cult ... Comunicacion y Cultura [*A publication*]
Comunicacao e Soc ... Comunicacao e Sociedade [*A publication*]
Comunicari Bot ... Comunicari de Botanica [*A publication*]
Comun INIA (Inst Nac Invest Agrar) Ser Gen ... Comunicaciones. INIA (Instituto Nacional de Investigaciones Agrarias). Serie General [*A publication*]
Comun INIA (Inst Nac Invest Agrar) Ser Tecnol ... Comunicaciones. INIA (Instituto Nacional de Investigaciones Agrarias). Serie Tecnologia [*A publication*]
Comun INIA (Inst Nac Invest Agrar) Ser Tecnol Agrar ... Comunicaciones. INIA (Instituto Nacional de Investigaciones Agrarias). Serie Tecnologia Agraria [*A publication*]
Comun INIA Prot Veg ... Comunicaciones. INIA [*Instituto Nacional de Investigaciones Agrarias*]. Serie Proteccion Vegetal [*A publication*]
Comun INIA Ser Prod Veg ... Comunicaciones. INIA [*Instituto Nacional de Investigaciones Agrarias*]. Serie Produccion Vegetal [*A publication*]
Comun INIA Ser Prod Veg Inst Nac Invest Agrar ... Comunicaciones. INIA [*Instituto Nacional de Investigaciones Agrarias*]. Serie Production Vegetal [*A publication*]
Comun INIA Ser Prot Veg ... Comunicaciones. INIA [*Instituto Nacional de Investigaciones Agrarias*]. Serie Proteccion Vegetal [*A publication*]

Comun INIA Ser Pro Veg (Spain) ... Comunicaciones. INIA [*Instituto Nacional de Investigaciones Agrarias*]. Serie Proteccion Vegetal (Spain) [*A publication*]
Comun INIA Ser Recur Nat ... Comunicaciones. INIA [*Instituto Nacional de Investigaciones Agrarias*]. Serie Recursos Naturales [*A publication*]
Comun Inst Cienc Nat Mat Univ El Salvador ... Comunicaciones. Instituto de Ciencias Naturales y Matematicas. Universidad de El Salvador [*A publication*]
Comun Inst For Invest Exp (Madrid) ... Comunicacion. Instituto Forestal de Investigaciones y Experiencias (Madrid) [*A publication*]
Comun Inst Nac Invest Cienc Nat Cienc Bot ... Comunicaciones. Instituto Nacional de Investigacion de las Ciencias Naturales. Ciencias Botanicas [*A publication*]
Comun Inst Trop Invest Cient ... Comunicaciones. Instituto Tropical de Investigaciones Cientificas [*A publication*]
Comun Intern ... Comunita Internazionale [*A publication*]
Comunita Int ... Comunita Internazionale [*A publication*]
Comunita Internaz ... Comunita Internazionale [*A publication*]
ComUnMil ... Committee on the Unisex Military (EA)
Comun Missao Estud Agron Ultramar (Lisb) ... Comunicacao-Missao de Estudos Agronomicos do Ultramar (Lisbon) [*A publication*]
Comun Mus Cienc PUCRGS (Pontif Univ Catol Rio Grande Do Sul) ... Comunicacoes. Museu de Ciencias. PUCRGS (Pontificia Universidade Catolica do Rio Grande Do Sul) [*A publication*]
Comun Paleontol Mus Hist Nat Montev ... Comunicaciones Paleontologicas. Museo de Historia Natural de Montevideo [*A publication*]
Comun Serv Geol Port ... Comunicacoes. Servicos Geologicos de Portugal [*A publication*]
Comun Soc Malacol Urug ... Comunicaciones. Sociedad Malacologica del Uruguay [*A publication*]
Comun Stiint Simp Biodeterior Clim ... Comunicari Stiintifice. Simpozion de Biodeteriorare si Climatizare [*A publication*]
Comun Tec Empresa Pesqui Agropecu Bahia ... Comunicado Tecnico. Empresa de Pesquisa Agropecuaria da Bahia [*A publication*]
Comun Tec Empresa Pesqui Agropecu Estado Rio De J ... Comunicado Tecnico. Empresa de Pesquisa Agropecuaria do Estado do Rio De Janeiro [*A publication*]
Comun Tec Inst Ecol Exp Agric ... Comunicados Tecnicos. Instituto de Ecologia e Experimentacao Agricolas [*A publication*]
Comun Univ El Salvador Inst Cienc Nat Mat ... Comunicaciones. Universidad de El Salvador. Instituto de Ciencias Naturales y Matematicas [*A publication*]
Comun Zool ... Comunicari de Zoologie [*A publication*]
Comun Zool Mus Hist Nat Montev ... Comunicaciones Zoologicas. Museo de Historia Natural de Montevideo [*A publication*]
COMUS .... Commander, United States Forces (CINC)
Com Us ... Comyn on the Law of Usury [*A publication*] (DLA)
COMus ...... Oakland Museum, Oakland, CA [*Library symbol*] [*Library of Congress*] (LCLS)
COMUSAFFOR ... Commander, United States Air Force Forces
COMUSAFSO ... Commander, United States Air Force Southern Command (AFM)
COMUSAFTF ... Commander, United States Air Force Task Force (AABC)
COMUSARFOR ... Commander, United States Army Forces
COMUSARJAPAN ... Commander, United States Army, Japan (CINC)
COMUSARSO ... Commander, United States Army Forces Southern Command (AABC)
COMUSARTF ... Commander, United States Army Task Force
COMUSBASFRANCE ... Commander, United States Ports and Bases, France
COMUSE ... Conference on Computers in Undergraduate Science Education
COMUSFAIRWINGMED ... Commander, United States Fleet Air Wing, Mediterranean (AABC)
COMUSFORAZ ... Commander, United States Forces, Azores (AFM)
COMUSJ .. Commander, United States Forces, Japan (MCD)
COMUSJAPAN ... Commander, United States Forces, Japan (AFM)
COMUSJTF ... Commander, United States Joint Task Force (AABC)
COMUSJUWTF ... Commander, United States Joint Unconventional Warfare Task Force
COMUSK ... Commander, United States Forces, Korea (MCD)
COMUSKOREA ... Commander, United States Forces, Korea (AFM)
COMUSLANDFOR ... Commander, United States Land Forces
COMUSLANT ... Commander, United States Atlantic Subarea
COMUSMACTHAI ... Commander, United States Military Assistance Command, Thailand (AFM)
COMUSMACV ... Commander, United States Military Assistance Command, Vietnam
COMUSMARFOR ... Commander, United States Marine Forces (AABC)
COMUSMARIANAS ... Commander, United States Forces, Marianas
COMUSMARTF ... Commander, United States Marine Task Force (AABC)
COMUSMILGP ... Commander, United States Military Group (AFM)
COMUSNAVFOR ... Commander, United States Naval Forces (AABC)
COMUSNAVSO ... Commander, United States Naval Forces, Southern Command (MUGU)
COMUSNAVTF ... Commander, United States Naval Task Force (AABC)
COMUSRHIN ... Commander, United States Rhine River Patrol (NATG)
COMUSSAG ... Commander, United States Special Advisory Group (AFM)

COMUSSEASIA ... Commander, United States Forces, Southeast Asia (CINC)
COMUSTDC ... Commander, United States Taiwan Defense Command (AFM)
COMUT.... CONUS [*Continental United States*] and Overseas Microfilm User Tests
COMUTRON ... Commander, Utility Squadron
COMUTWING ... Commander, Utility Wing
COMUTWINGSERVLANT ... Commander, Utility Wing, Service Force, Atlantic
COMUTWINGSERVPAC ... Commander, Utility Wing, Service Force, Pacific
CoMv .... Monte Vista Public Library, Monte Vista, CO [*Library symbol*] [*Library of Congress*] (LCLS)
Com Via ..... Communio Viatorum [*A publication*]
ComViat.... Communio Viatorum [*Prague*] [*A publication*] (BJA)
Comw .... Commonweal [*A publication*]
COMW...... Commonwealth Savings & Loan Association FA [*NASDAQ symbol*] (NQ)
COMWESTAF ... Commander, Western Transport Air Force [*Travis AFB*] (CINC)
COMWESTSEAFRON ... Commander, Western Sea Frontier (MUGU)
Com'w'th... Commonwealth (DLA)
COMX...... Comtrex Systems Corp. [*Mount Laurel, NJ*] [*NASDAQ symbol*] (NQ)
COMYARD ... Commander of the Dockyard at [*place*]
Comyn........ Comyn's English King's Bench Reports [*1695-1741*] [*A publication*] (DLA)
Comyns ...... Comyn's English King's Bench Reports [*1695-1741*] [*A publication*] (DLA)
Comyn's Dig ... Comyn's Digest of the Laws of England [*1762-1882*] [*A publication*] (DLA)
COMZ....... Communications Zone
COMZONE ... Communication Zone [*British military*] (DMA)
CON.......... Cast-Out-Nines
CON........ Certificate of Need
CON.......... Commander of the Order of the Niger [*Nigeria*]
Con.......... Commission [*Commission*] [*French*] [*Business term*]
CON.......... Commission on the Nomenclature of Organic Chemistry [*IUPAC*]
CON.......... Concanavalin [*Biochemistry*]
CON.......... Concentration
CON.......... Concepcion [*Chile*] [*Seismograph station code, US Geological Survey*] (SEIS)
CON.......... Concerning (ADA)
CON....... Concerto [*Music*]
CON....... Concession (MSA)
CON.......... Concisus [*Cut*] [*Medicine*] (ROG)
CON.......... Conclusion
CON.......... Concord [*City in California, Massachusetts, New Hampshire, and North Carolina*] (ROG)
CON.......... Concord, NH [*Location identifier*] [*FAA*] (FAAL)
CON.......... Concrete
CON.......... Confidence (ADA)
CON.......... Confluence (ROG)
CON.......... Congress [*or Congressman*]
CON........ Conic (ADA)
CON.......... Conico [*Race of maize*]
CON.......... Conjunction [*Grammar*] (ROG)
CON.......... Conjux [*Consort, Spouse*] [*Genealogy*]
CON.......... Connecticut (ROG)
CON.......... Connection
CON.......... Connelly Containers, Inc. [*AMEX symbol*] (SPSG)
Con............ Connoly's New York Surrogate Reports [*A publication*] (DLA)
Con .... Conover's Reports [*Wisconsin*] [*A publication*] (DLA)
CON.......... Conrotatory [*Chemistry*]
CON.......... Conscientious Objectors' News [*British*]
CON.......... Consciousness
CON.......... Consecrated (ROG)
Con v .... Consensus
CON.......... Conservation (AABC)
CON.......... Conservator. Vaktijdschrift voor de Iisfrica Branche [*A publication*]
CON.......... Conservatorium (ADA)
CON.......... Consideration
CON.......... Consol [*Navigation*] (AIA)
CON.......... Consolidated
CON.......... Consolidated Andex Resources Ltd. [*Vancouver Stock Exchange symbol*]
CON.......... Constantinople [*Later, Istanbul*] [*Turkey*] (ROG)
CON.......... Constructor (ADA)
CON.......... Consul [*or Consulate*] (AABC)
CON.......... Consultation (DSUE)
Con .... Contact [*A publication*]
CON.......... Continental (AFM)
CON.......... Continental Oil Co. [*Ponca City, OK*] [*FAA designator*] (FAAC)
CON.......... Contingency [*Type classification*] (MCD)
Con .... Continuation of Rolle's Reports [*2 Rolle*] [*A publication*] (DLA)
CON.......... Continued

Con............ Contour [*A publication*]
CON.......... Contra [*Against*] [*Latin*]
CON.......... Contract (ROG)
CON.......... Contralto [*Music*]
CON.......... Control (AFM)
CON.......... Controller (AFM)
CON.......... Convenience (ADA)
CON.......... Conversation (AABC)
CON.......... Convict (ADA)
Con.......... Convivium [*A publication*]
CON.......... Cross of the Order of the Niger
CON.......... National Oceanic and Atmospheric Administration, Boulder, CO [*OCLC symbol*] (OCLC)
COn........... Ontario Public Library, Ontario, CA [*Library symbol*] [*Library of Congress*] (LCLS)
CONA........ Canadian Orthopaedic Nurses' Association
Con A .... Concanavalin A [*Biochemistry*]
CONA........ Conna Corp. [*NASDAQ symbol*] (NQ)
CoNa.......... Naturita Public Library, Naturita, CO [*Library symbol*] [*Library of Congress*] (LCLS)
CONAB..... Commanding Officer, Naval Advanced Base
CONAB..... Commanding Officer, Naval Air Base
CONAC..... [*El*] Congreso Nacional de Asuntos Colegiales (EA)
CONAC..... Continental Air Command
CONACYT ... Consejo Nacional de Ciencia y Tecnologia [*National Council of Science and Technology*] [*Information service or system*] (IID)
CONAD..... Continental Advance Section [*Originally called Coastal Base Section*] [*World War II*]
CONAD..... Continental Air Defense Command [*Discontinued, 1975*]
CONAEL... Contaminacion Ambiental [*A publication*]
CONAES... Committee on Nuclear and Alternative Energy Systems [*National Research Council*] [*Defunct*]
CONAF ..... Conceptual Design for the Army in the Field
CON/AGG ... International Concrete and Aggregates Show (ITD)
CONAIR ... Commanding Officer, Naval Air Wing
CONA J..... CONA [*Canadian Orthopaedic Nurses Association*] Journal [*A publication*]
CONALOG ... Contact Analog [*Submarine instrumentation*] (MCD)
CONALOG ... Continuity and Logic Unit
CONALT... CONARC [*Continental Army Command*] Alternate Headquarters Plan [*Obsolete*]
CONALT... Construction and Repair, Alteration [*Coast Guard*]
CONAME ... Committee on New Alternatives in the Middle East [*Later, FOR*] (EA)
CONAN..... Companhia de Navegacao do Norte [*Shipping company*] [*Brazil*] (EY)
CON AN..... Con Anima [*With a Soulful Feeling*] [*Music*] (ROG)
CONAP..... Controlled Atmosphere Protected [*Army*] (MCD)
CONAR ..... Commanding Officer's Narrative Report
CONAR ..... Continental Army
CONARC .. Continental Air Command (MCD)
CONARC .. Continental Army Command [*Responsible for induction, processing, training of active duty personnel*] [*Superseded by FORSCOM*]
CONARESTRAPROG ... Connection Naval Air Reserve Training Program
CONAS ..... Commanding Officer, Naval Air Station
CONASA .. Council of North Atlantic Shipping Associations [*Also, CNASA*]
ConBib....... Coniectanea Biblica [*Lund*] [*A publication*] (BJA)
Con BJ .... Connecticut Bar Journal [*A publication*]
CONC....... Australian Conferences: Complete [*Database*]
CONC....... Concentrate [*or Concentration*] (AFM)
CONC....... Concentratus [*Concentrated*] [*Pharmacy*] (ROG)
CONC....... Concentric
CONC....... Concerning (ROG)
CONC....... Concerto [*Music*]
Conc .... Concilium. Internationale Zeitschrift fuer Theologie [*Einsiedeln/Zurich/Mainz*] [*A publication*]
CONC....... Concise (ROG)
conc .... Conclusion
CONC....... Concordance (ROG)
CONC....... Concrete
CONC....... Continuing Care Associates, Inc. [*Canton, MA*] [*NASDAQ symbol*] (NQ)
CoNc.......... Garfield County Public Library, New Castle, CO [*Library symbol*] [*Library of Congress*] (LCLS)
CONCA..... Continue Calling Until (FAAC)
CONCACAF ... Confederacion Norte, Centroamericana, y del Caribe de Futbol [*North and Central American and Caribbean Football Confederation*] (EAIO)
Concast Technol News ... Concast Technology News [*Switzerland*] [*A publication*]
CONCAWE ... Oil Companies' European Organization for Environmental and Health Protection (EA)
CONCD..... Concentrated
Concept Immunopathol ... Concepts in Immunopathology [*A publication*]
Concepts Pediatr Neurosurg ... Concepts in Pediatric Neurosurgery [*A publication*]
Concepts Toxicol ... Concepts in Toxicology [*A publication*]
CONCG..... Concerning [*Legal term*] (ROG)

CONCH..... Conchology
CONCIL.... Conciliation (ROG)
Conciliation Courts R ... Conciliation Courts Review [*A publication*]
Concimi Concimaz ... Concimi e Concimazione [*A publication*]
CONCIS.... Concisus [*Cut*] [*Medicine*]
CONCISE ... Computer-Oriented Notation Concerning Infrared Spectral Evaluation [*Programming language*] [*Analytical chemistry*]
CONCL..... Conclusion (MSA)
Concl.......... Conclusions du Ministere Public [*A publication*]
CONCLON ... Conclusion (ROG)
Conc Milk Ind ... Concentrated Milk Industries [*A publication*]
CONCN..... Concentration
CONCOM ... Council of Nature Conservation Ministers [*Australia*]
CONCOMO ... Convoy Commodore [*Navy*]
CONCON ... Constellate Consultants (P) Ltd. [*Information service or system*] (IID)
CON-CON ... Constitutional Convention
Concor........ Concordia Theological Monthly [*A publication*]
CONCOR ... Construction Corps of the Philippines [*World War II*]
Concord Theol Mthl ... Concordia Theological Monthly [*A publication*]
Concor H Inst Q ... Concordia Historical Institute. Quarterly [*A publication*]
Concor J..... Concordia Journal [*A publication*]
CONCORP ... Construction Corporation [*Burma*] (DS)
Concor Th Q ... Concordia Theological Quarterly [*A publication*]
Concours Med ... Concours Medical [*A publication*]
ConcPo....... Concerning Poetry [*A publication*]
Conc Poet... Concerning Poetry [*A publication*]
CONCR..... Concrete
Concr Abstr ... Concrete Abstracts [*A publication*]
Concr Cem Age ... Concrete Cement Age [*A publication*]
Concr Constr ... Concrete Construction [*A publication*]
Concr Constr Eng ... Concrete and Constructional Engineering [*A publication*]
Concr Constru Eng ... Concrete and Constructional Engineering [*A publication*]
Concr Eng .. Concrete Engineering [*A publication*]
Concrete P ... Concrete Products [*A publication*]
Concrete Q ... Concrete Quarterly [*A publication*]
Concrete Qly ... Concrete Quarterly [*A publication*]
Concrete Wks ... Concrete Works [*A publication*]
Concr Inst Aust News ... Concrete Institute of Australia. News [*A publication*] (APTA)
Concr J....... Concrete Journal [*Japan*] [*A publication*]
Concr Quart ... Concrete Quarterly [*A publication*]
Concr Soc Tech Rep ... Concrete Society. Technical Report [*A publication*]
CONCTD .. Concentrated
CONCTG .. Concentrating
Conc Theol Mthly ... Concordia Theological Monthly [*A publication*]
ConcTM ... Concordia Theological Monthly [*St. Louis, MO*] [*A publication*]
Conc Trid ... Concilium Tridentinum [*A publication*]
Con Cus... Conroy's Custodian Reports [*1652-1788*] [*Ireland*] [*A publication*] (DLA)
CONCUSS ... Concussion (DSUE)
COND........ Commanding Officer, Naval Divisions [*Canada*]
COND........ Condensed
COND........ Condenser [*Automotive engineering*]
COND........ Condition (AFM)
COND........ Conditional (Tense) [*Linguistics*]
COND....... Condor Services, Inc. [*NASDAQ symbol*] (NQ)
COND....... Conduct [*or Conductivity*] (ROG)
Cond.......... Conductometric
COND........ Conductor (KSC)
Cond Ch R ... Condensed English Chancery Reports [*A publication*] (DLA)
CONDEC .. Consolidated Diesel Electric Company
CONDECA ... Consejo de Defensa Centroamericana [*Central American Defense Council*] [*Guatemala, Guatemala*] (EAIO)
Cond Eccl... Condensed Ecclesiastical Reports [*A publication*] (DLA)
Cond Ecc R ... Condensed Ecclesiastical Reports [*A publication*] (DLA)
CONDEEP ... Concrete Deep Water Structure [*Oil platform*]
CONDEF .. Contract Definition
Condem...... Condemnation [*Legal term*] (DLA)
Cond Eng Ch ... Condensed English Chancery Reports [*A publication*] (DLA)
Condensed Rep ... Louisiana Supreme Court Condensed Reports [*A publication*] (DLA)
Condensed Rep ... Peters' Condensed United States Reports [*A publication*] (DLA)
CONDEPE ... Conselho Nacional de Desenvolvimento Pecuario [*Government advisory body*] [*Brazil*] (EY)
CON DEVE ... Con Devotione [*With Devotion*] [*Music*] (ROG)
Cond Exch R ... Condensed Exchequer Reports [*A publication*] (DLA)
Cond Ex R ... Condensed Exchequer Reports [*A publication*] (DLA)
CONDG..... Condensing
COND GEN ... Conductor Generalis (DLA)
Cond HC...... Conders. Highway Cases [*A publication*] (DLA)
Con Dig...... Connor's Irish Digest [*A publication*] (DLA)
Con Dig Ind ... Conover's Digested Index [*Ohio, Indiana, and Illinois*] [*A publication*] (DLA)
Condition ... Conditions [*A publication*]
Condit Sale - Chat Mort Rep ... Conditional Sale - Chattel Mortgage Reporter [*Commerce Clearing House*] [*A publication*] (DLA)
Condiz dell'Aria ... Condizionamneto dell'Aria [*A publication*]

CONDL..... Conditional (ROG)
Cond Lou'a Reps ... Louisiana Supreme Court Condensed Reports [*A publication*] (DLA)
Cond Marsh ... Condy's Edition of Marshall on Insurance [*A publication*] (DLA)
CON DOL ... Con Dolore [*With Sadness*] [*Music*] (ROG)
CONDOMIN ... Condominium [*Real estate*] (DLA)
CONDON ... Condition [*Legal term*] (ROG)
CONDOP ... Condominium/Cooperative [*Real estate*]
Condotta Med ... Condotta Medica [*A publication*]
CONDR..... Condenser
CONDR..... Conditioner (NASA)
CONDR..... Conductor (AAG)
Cond R .... Peters' Condensed United States Reports [*A publication*] (DLA)
Cond Refl ... Conditional Reflex [*A publication*]
Cond Reflex ... Conditional Reflex [*A publication*]
Cond Rep ... Peters' Condensed United States Reports [*A publication*] (DLA)
Cond Rep US ... Peters' Condensed United States Reports [*A publication*] (DLA)
CONDT..... Conduit [*Automotive engineering*]
CONDTG ... Conditioning [*Automotive engineering*]
CONDTN ... Condition (MSA)
CONDTR .. Conditioner
CONDUIT ... Computers at Oregon State University, North Carolina Educational Computing Service, Dartmouth College, and the Universities of Iowa and Texas at Austin [*An educational consortium*]
CONE........ Collectors of Numismatic Errors
CONE........ Controller Error (AFM)
CONEA ..... Confederation of National Educational Associations
CONEAT ... Confinia Neurologica [*A publication*]
CONEC ..... Connection (AABC)
CONECA .. Combined Organizations of Numismatic Error Collectors of America (EA)
CONECS... Connectorized Exchange Cable Splicing [*Telecommunications*] (TEL)
CONEDS... CONARC [*Continental Army Command*] Education Data System [*Obsolete*] (AABC)
CONEFO .. Conference of New Emerging Forces [*Indonesia*] (CINC)
CONEG..... Coalition of Northeastern Governors
CONELA... Confraternidad Evangelica Latinoamericana [*Confraternity of Evangelicals in Latin America*] [*Guatemala, Guatemala*] (EAIO)
CONELL... Conference of New Law Librarians
CONELRAD ... Control of Electromagnetic Radiations [*Purpose is to deny the enemy aircraft the use of electromagnetic radiations for navigation, while still providing essential services*]
ConEMA ... Conveyor Equipment Manufacturers Association
CON ESP .. Con Espressione [*With Expression*] [*Music*]
CON ESPR ... Con Espressione [*With Expression*] [*Music*]
CONESTAB ... Connection Establishment (MCD)
CONEX..... Connecticut Construction Exposition [*Key Productions, Inc.*] (TSPED)
CONEX..... Container for Export (NATG)
CONEX..... Container Express [*Army*] (AABC)
CONEX..... Continental Exercise [*Military*]
Con Ex .... Controversiarum Excerpta [*of Seneca the Elder*] [*Classical studies*] (OCD)
CONEXION ... Contract Design Exposition [*Atlanta Market Center*] (TSPED)
CONF .... Australian Conferences: Current [*Database*]
CONF .... Confectio [*Confection*] [*Pharmacy*]
CONF .... Confer [*Compare*] [*Latin*]
CONF .... Conference (AFM)
Conf........... Conference Reports, by Cameron and Norwood [*North Carolina*] [*A publication*] (DLA)
CONF .... Conferences in Energy, Physics, and Mathematics [*Fachinformationszentrum Karlsruhe GmbH*] [*Federal Republic of Germany*] [*Information service or system*] (CRD)
Conf........... Conferencia [*A publication*]
CONF .... Confessor (ROG)
CONF .... Confidential (AFM)
CONF .... Configuration
CONF .... Confine [*or Confinement*] (AFM)
CONF .... Confirmation [*Purchasing*]
Conf........... Conflict. An International Journal [*A publication*]
Conf........... Confluence [*A publication*]
CONF .... Conformance
CONF .... Continental Federal Savings & Loan Association [*NASDAQ symbol*] (NQ)
Conf........... De Confusione Linguarum [*Philo*] (BJA)
CONFA ... Confructa [*A publication*]
CONFAC... Consolidated Facilities Corp. [*Railroads*]
CONFAD ... Concept of a Family of Army Divisions (AABC)
Conf Adrenal Cortex Trans ... Conference on Adrenal Cortex. Transactions [*A publication*]
Conf Adv Magn Mater Their Appl ... Conference on Advances in Magnetic Materials and Their Applications [*A publication*]

Conf Appl Sci Technol Benefit Less Devel Areas UN ... Conference on Application of Science and Technology for the Benefit of Less Developed Areas. United Nations [*A publication*]

Conf Aust Fract Group (Proc) ... Australian Fracture Group Conference (Proceedings) [*A publication*]   (APTA)

CONFAW ... Confructa [*A publication*]

Conf Bd Bsns Mgt Rec ... Conference Board. Business Management Record [*A publication*]

Conf Bd Bsns Rec ... Conference Board. Business Record [*A publication*]

Conf Bd Rec ... Conference Board. Record [*A publication*]

Conf Biol Antioxid Trans ... Conference on Biological Antioxidants. Transactions [*A publication*]

Conf Blood Clotting Allied Probl Trans ... Conference on Blood Clotting and Allied Problems. Transactions [*A publication*]

Conf Board Rec ... Conference Board. Record [*A publication*]

Conf Brd ..... Across the Board [*A publication*]

CONFBUL ... Confidential Bulletin [*Navy*]

Conf Capturing Sun Bioconver Pro ... Conference on Capturing the Sun through Bioconversion. Proceedings [*A publication*]

CONFCE ... Conference   (ROG)

Conf Char and Correc ... National Conference of Charities and Correction. Proceedings [*A publication*]

Conf on Char Found NYU Proc ... Conference on Charitable Foundations. New York University. Proceedings [*A publication*]

Conf on Char Found NYU Proc ... Conference on Charitable Foundations. Proceedings. New York University [*A publication*]   (DLA)

Conf Chart ... Confirmatio Chartarum [*Confirmation of the Charters*] [*Latin*] [*Legal term*]   (DLA)

Conf Circompolaire Ecol Nord R ... Conference Circompolaire sur l'Ecologie du Nord. Compte Rendu [*A publication*]

Conf City Govt ... National Conference for Good City Government. Proceedings [*A publication*]

Conf City Planning ... National Conference on City Planning. Proceedings [*A publication*]

Conf Comm Uniformity Legis ... Conference of Commissioners on Uniformity of Legislation in Canada   (DLA)

Conf Compat Propellants Explos Pyrotech Plast Addit ... Conference on Compatibility of Propellants, Explosives, and Pyrotechnics with Plastics and Additives [*A publication*]

Conf Connect Tissues Trans ... Conference on Connective Tissues. Transactions [*A publication*]

Conf Control Gaseous Sulphur Nitrogen Comp Emiss ... Conference on the Control of Gaseous Sulphur and Nitrogen Compound Emission [*A publication*]

CONFCOOPERATIVE ... Confederazione Cooperative Italiane [*Cooperative Confederation of Italy*]   (EY)

CONFCTY ... Confectionary

Conf Cult Mar Invertebr Anim Proc ... Conference on Culture of Marine Invertebrate Animals. Proceedings [*A publication*]

CONFD ..... Confederation   (ADA)

CONFD ..... Conferred   (ROG)

CONFD ..... Confidential [*Security classification*] [*Military*]

CONFDC .. Confidence   (FAAC)

Conf Dig Int Electr Electron Conf Expo ... Conference Digest. International Electrical, Electronics Conference Exposition [*A publication*]

CONFEC ... Confectioner   (ROG)

Confect Manuf ... Confectionery Manufacture [*A publication*]

Confect Prod ... Confectionery Production [*A publication*]

CONFED .. Confederation   (EY)

CONFEDEM ... Confederacion Nacional de Empresarios de la Mineria y de la Metalurgia [*Industrial association*] [*Spain*]   (EY)

Confederazione Gen Ind Ital Notiz ... Confederazione Generale dell'Industria Italiana Notiziario [*A publication*]

Confed Nac Com ... Confederacao Nacional do Comercio [*A publication*]

Confed Nat Mutualite Coop Cred Agric Congres ... Confederation Nationale de la Mutualite de la Cooperation et du Credit Agricoles Congres [*A publication*]

CONFEMEN ... Conference des Ministres de l'Education des Pays d'Expression Francaise

CONFEMETAL ... Confederacion Espanola de Organizaciones Empresariales del Metal [*Spain*]   (EY)

Conf Environ Chem Hum Anim Health Proc ... Conference on Environmental Chemicals. Human and Animal Health. Proceedings [*A publication*]

Conference Bd Rec ... Conference Board. Record [*A publication*]

Conference (NC) ... Conference Reports [*North Carolina*] [*A publication*]   (DLA)

Confer Sem Mat Univ Bari ... Conferenze. Seminario di Matematica. Universita di Bari [*A publication*]

Conf Eur Microcirc ... Conference Europeenne sur la Microcirculation [*A publication*]

Conf Exhib Int ... Conferences and Exhibitions International [*A publication*]

CONFG ..... Conferring   (ROG)

CONFG ..... Configuration Process [*Telecommunications*]   (TEL)

Conf Great Lakes Res Proc ... Conference on Great Lakes Research. Proceedings [*A publication*]

CONFI ...... Confidential   (DSUE)

CONFICS ... Cobra Night Fire Control System [*Military*]

CONFID .... Confidential   (ADA)

CONFIDAL ... Conjugate Filter Data Link

CONFIG .... Configuration   (KSC)

CONFIGN ... Configuration   (FAAC)

Confinia Neurol ... Confinia Neurologica [*A publication*]

Confin Neurol ... Confinia Neurologica [*A publication*]

Confin Psychiat ... Confinia Psychiatrica [*A publication*]

Confin Psychiatr ... Confinia Psychiatrica [*A publication*]

Conf Inst Nac Invest Agron Min Agr (Spain) ... Conferencias. Instituto Nacional de Investigaciones Agronomicas. Ministerio Agricultura (Spain) [*A publication*]

Conf Inst Nac Invest Agron (Spain) ... Conferencias. Instituto Nacional de Investigaciones Agronomicas (Spain)

Conf Interam Agric (Caracas) ... Conferencia Interamericana de Agricultura (Caracas) [*A publication*]

CONFIRM ... Conversational File Information Retrieval and Management System [*Data processing*]   (MCD)

CONF L ..... Conflict of Laws [*Legal term*]   (DLA)

Confl .... Confluences. Revue des Lettres et des Arts [*A publication*]

CONFLEX ... Conditioned Reflex [*Machine*]   (IEEE)

Conflict Mgt and Peace Science ... Conflict Management and Peace Science [*A publication*]

Conflict Q .. Conflict Quarterly [*A publication*]

Conf Liver Inj Trans ... Conference on Liver Injury. Transactions [*A publication*]

Conf Metab Interrelat Trans ... Conference on Metabolic Interrelations. Transactions [*A publication*]

CONF-MH ... Confidential - Modified Handling [*Army*]

CONFMOD ... Confidential - Modified Handling Authorized [*Army*]

CONFORM ... Contract Formulation

Conform Anal Pap Int Symp ... Conformational Analysis. Scope and Present Limitations Papers Presented at the International Symposium [*A publication*]

Conf Palais Decouverte Ser A ... Conferences. Palais de la Decouverte. Serie A [*A publication*]

Conf Pap Inst Metall Tech (London) ... Conference Papers. Institute of Metallurgical Technicians (London) [*A publication*]

Conf Pap Int Cosmic Ray Conf ... Conference Papers. International Cosmic Ray Conference [*A publication*]

Conf Pers Fin LQR ... Conference on Personal Finance Law. Quarterly Report [*A publication*]

Conf Pers Fin L Q Rep ... Conference on Personal Finance Law. Quarterly Report [*A publication*]

CONFPONT ... Confessor Pontifex [*Confessor and Bishop*] [*Latin*]   (ADA)

Conf Probl Aging Trans ... Conference on Problems of Aging. Transactions [*A publication*]

Conf Probl Conscious Trans ... Conference on Problems of Consciousness. Transactions [*A publication*]

Conf Probl Early Infancy Trans ... Conference on Problems of Early Infancy. Transactions [*A publication*]

Conf Probl Infancy Child Trans ... Conference on Problems of Infancy and Childhood. Transactions [*A publication*]

Conf Proc Annu Symp Comput Archit ... Conference Proceedings. Annual Symposium on Computer Architecture [*A publication*]

Conf Proc Int Conf Fire Saf ... Conference Proceedings. International Conference on Fire Safety [*A publication*]

Conf Proc Inter-Amer Bar Assoc ... Conference Proceedings. Inter-American Bar Association [*A publication*]   (DLA)

Conf Proc Intersoc Energy Convers Eng Conf ... Conference Proceedings. Intersociety Energy Conversion Engineering Conference [*A publication*]

Conf Proc Recycl World Congr ... Conference Proceedings. Recycling World Congress [*A publication*]

Conf Prod Prop Test Aggregates Pap ... Conference on the Production, Properties, and Testing of Aggregates. Papers [*A publication*]

Conf Psych ... Confinia Psychiatrica [*A publication*]

Conf Publ Inst Mech Eng ... Conference Publications. Institution of Mechanical Engineers [*A publication*]

Conf Publiques Univ Damas ... Conferences Publiques. Universite de Damas [*A publication*]

CONF R ..... Confirmation Rolls   (ROG)

Confr .... Confrontation [*A publication*]

Conf Read (Univ Chicago) ... Conference on Reading (University of Chicago). Proceedings [*A publication*]

Conf on Read (Univ Pittsburgh) Rep ... Conference on Reading (University of Pittsburgh). Report [*A publication*]

Conf Rec Annu Pulp Pap Ind Tech Conf ... Conference Record. Annual Pulp and Paper Industry Technical Conference [*A publication*]

Conf Rec Asilomar Conf Circuits Syst Comput ... Conference Record. Asilomar Conference on Circuits Systems and Computers [*A publication*]

Conf Rec IAS Annu Meet ... Conference Record. IAS [*IEEE Industry Applications Society*] Annual Meeting [*A publication*]

Conf Rec IEEE Photovoltaic Spec Conf ... Conference Record. IEEE [*Institute of Electrical and Electronics Engineers*] Photovoltaic Specialists Conference [*A publication*]

Conf Renal Funct Trans ... Conference on Renal Function. Transactions [*A publication*]

Conf Rep R Aust Inst Parks Rec ... Conference Report. Australian Institute of Parks and Recreation [*A publication*]   (APTA)

Conf Rept ... Conference Report   (DLA)

Confrontat ... Confrontation [*A publication*]

Confront Radio-Anatomo-Clin ... Confrontations Radio-Anatomo-Cliniques [*France*] [*A publication*]
Conf Solid State Devices Mater ... Conference on Solid State Devices and Materials [*A publication*]
Conf Solid State Devices Proc ... Conference on Solid State Devices. Proceedings [*A publication*]
Conf e Studi Accad Polacca Sci Bibl Centro Studi Roma ... Conferenze e Studi. Accademia Polacca delle Scienze. Biblioteca e Centro di Studi a Roma [*A publication*]
Conf Superionic Conduct Chem Phys Appl Pro ... Conference on Superionic Conductors. Chemistry, Physics, and Applications. Proceedings [*A publication*]
CON FUO ... Con Fuoco [*With Force*] [*Music*] (ROG)
CON FUR ... Con Furia [*With Fury*] [*Music*] (ROG)
CONG........ Congestion [*Telecommunications*] (TEL)
CONG........ Congius [*Gallon*] [*Pharmacy*]
Cong........... Congolese
Cong........... Congregation (BJA)
CONG........ Congregational
Cong........... Congregationalist [*A publication*]
CONG........ Congress (AFM)
CONG........ Congressional (ROG)
Cong........... Congressman
CoNgA ... Adams County Public Library, Northglenn, CO [*Library symbol*] [*Library of Congress*] (LCLS)
CONGA.... Combat Operations, Naval Gunfire Activity
CONGA.... Concept Game [*A war game*]
Cong Cient Mexicano Mem Cienc Fisicas y Matematicas ... Congreso Cientifico Mexicano. Memoria. Ciencias Fisicas y Matematicas [*A publication*]
Cong Deb ... Congressional Debates [*United States*] [*A publication*] (DLA)
Cong Dig.... Congdon's Digest [*Canada*] [*A publication*] (DLA)
Cong Dig.... Congressional Digest [*A publication*]
Cong Digest ... Congressional Digest [*A publication*]
Cong El Cas ... Congressional Election Cases [*United States*] [*A publication*] (DLA)
CONGEN ... Congenital [*Medicine*]
CONGEN ... Constrained Structure Generation
CONGEN ... Consul General
Congenital Anom ... Congenital Anomalies [*A publication*]
Cong Gl...... Congressional Globe [*A publication*] (DLA)
Cong Globe ... Congressional Globe [*A publication*] (DLA)
CoNgGS..... Church of Jesus Christ of Latter-Day Saints, Genealogical Society Library, Denver North Branch, Northglenn, CO [*Library symbol*] [*Library of Congress*] (LCLS)
Cong Index (CCH) ... Congressional Index (Commerce Clearing House) [*A publication*] (DLA)
CONGINT ... Interest by Member of Congress
Cong Internat Med C R ... Congres International de Medecine. Comptes Rendus [*A publication*]
Congiunt Econ Lombarda ... Congiuntura Economica Lombarda [*A publication*]
Congiuntura Econ Laziale ... Congiuntura Economica Laziale [*A publication*]
Congiuntura Ital ... Congiuntura Italiana [*A publication*]
CONGL..... Conglomerate
CONGL..... Congregational
CONGL..... Congressional
CONG LIB ... Congressional Library (ROG)
Cong M...... Congregational Magazine [*A publication*]
Cong Min L ... Congdon's Mining Laws of California [*A publication*] (DLA)
Cong Mo.... Congregationalist Monthly Review [*A publication*]
CONGN.... Congregation (ROG)
CONGO .... Conference on Non-Governmental Organizations in Consultative Status with the United Nations Economic and Social Council (EAIO)
CONGO ..... Congregationalist [*Slang*] (DSUE)
CongOrat ... Congregation of the Oratory [*Oratorians*] [*Roman Catholic men's religious order*]
Cong and Presidency ... Congress and the Presidency [*A publication*]
Cong Q........ Congressional Quarterly [*A publication*]
Cong of Q Coop ... Congress of Queensland Cooperatives. Papers and Proceedings [*A publication*] (APTA)
Cong Q W Rept ... Congressional Quarterly. Weekly Report [*A publication*]
CONGR..... Congregational
Cong R .... Congregational Review [*A publication*]
CONGR..... Congruent (MSA)
CON GRA ... Con Grazia [*With Grace*] [*Music*] (ROG)
Congr A Fr ... Congres Archeologique de France [*A publication*]
Congr Assoc Fr Av Sci (Nancy) ... Congres. Association Francaise pour l'Avancement des Sciences (Nancy) [*A publication*]
Congr Assoc Geol Carpatho-Balkan Bull ... Congres. Association Geologique Carpatho-Balkanique. Bulletin [*A publication*]
CONGRATS ... Congratulations (DSUE)
CONGRATS ... Continuous Gradient Ray Tracing System
Congr Av Etud Stratigr Geol Carbonif CR ... Congres pour l'Avancement des Etudes de Stratigraphie et de Geologie du Carbonifere. Compte Rendu [*A publication*]
Congr Av Etud Stratigr Geol Carbonifere C R ... Congres pour l'Avancement des Etudes de Stratigraphie et de Geologie du Carbonifere. Compte Rendu [*A publication*]
Congr Bras Apic ... Congresso Brasileiro de Apicultura [*A publication*]

Congr Conv Simp Sci CNR ... Congressi. Convegni e Simposi Scientifici. Consiglio Nazionale delle Richerche [*A publication*]
Congr Dig .. Congressional Digest [*A publication*]
Congre........ Congregationalist [*A publication*]
Cong Rec ... Congressional Record [*A publication*]
Congres Archeol ... Congres Archeologique de France [*A publication*]
Congres Archeol de France ... Congres Archeologique de France [*A publication*]
Congresb Wereldcongr Oppervlaktebehandel Met ... Congresboek. Wereldcongres voor Oppervlaktebehandeling van Metalen [*A publication*]
Congres Pomol ... Congres Pomologique [*A publication*]
Congres des Rel Ind ... Congres des Relations Industrielles. Universite Laval. Rapport [*A publication*]
CONGRESS ... Contiguous Node Group Restoral Supervision and Switching
Congress Numer ... Congressus Numerantium [*A publication*]
Congress St ... Congressional Studies [*A publication*]
Congr Eur Soc Exp Surg Abst ... Congress. European Society for Experimental Surgery. Abstracts [*A publication*]
Congr Geol Argent Relat ... Congreso Geologico Argentino. Relatorio [*A publication*]
Congr Group Av Methodes Anal Spectrogr Prod Metall ... Congres du Groupement pour l'Avancement des Methodes d'Analyse Spectrographique des Produits Metallurgiques [*A publication*]
Congr Hung Pharmacol Soc Pro ... Congress. Hungarian Pharmacological Society. Proceedings [*A publication*]
Congr Ibero-Am Geol Econ ... Congreso Ibero-Americano de Geologia Economica [*A publication*]
Congr Industr Chem ... Compte Rendu. Congres International de Chemie Industrielle [*A publication*]
Congr Int Annu Assoc Nucl Can ... Congres International Annuel. Association Nucleaire Canadienne [*A publication*]
Congr Int Ass Seed Crushers ... Congress. International Association of Seed Crushers [*A publication*]
Congr Int Bot Rapp Commun ... Congres International de Botanique. Rapports et Communications [*A publication*]
Congr Int Chim Cim Proc ... Congres International de la Chimie des Ciments. Procedes [*A publication*]
Congr Int Cybern Actes ... Congres International de Cybernetique. Actes [*A publication*]
Congr Int Estud Pirenaicos Resumen Comun ... Congreso Internacional de Estudios Pirenaicos. Resumen de las Comunicaciones [*A publication*]
Congr Int Fed Soc Cosmet Chem Prepr Sci Pap ... Congress of International Federation of Societies of Cosmetic Chemists. Preprint of Scientific Papers [*A publication*]
Congr Int Hematol Conf ... Congreso Internacional de Hematologia. Conferencias [*A publication*]
Congr Int Jus Fruits ... Congres International des Jus de Fruits [*A publication*]
Congr Int Mineralurgie CR ... Congres International de Mineralurgie. Compte Rendu [*A publication*]
Congr Int Potash Inst ... Congress. International Potash Institute [*A publication*]
Congr Int Reprod Anim Insemin Artif ... Congres International de Reproduction Animale et Insemination Artificielle [*A publication*]
Congr Int Reprod Anim Insemination Artif ... Congres International de Reproduction Animale et Insemination Artificielle [*A publication*]
Congr Int Stratigr Geol Carbonifere C R ... Congres International de Stratigraphie et de Geologie du Carbonifere. Compte Rendu [*A publication*]
Congr Int Vigne Vin ... Congres International de la Vigne du Vin [*A publication*]
CONGRIPS ... Conference Group on Italian Politics and Society (EA)
Congr Ital Med ... Congressi Italiani di Medicina [*A publication*]
Congr Mond Recyclage Textes Conf ... Congres Mondial du Recyclage. Textes de la Conference [*A publication*]
Congr Nac Tuberc Enferm Respir ... Congreso Nacional de Tuberculosis y Enfermedades Respiratorias [*A publication*]
Congr Natl Soc Savantes Sect Sci C R ... Congres National. Societes Savantes. Section des Sciences. Comptes Rendus [*A publication*]
Congr Numer ... Congressus Numerantium [*A publication*]
Congr Print ... Congress in Print [*A publication*]
Congr Proc Recycl World Congr ... Congress Proceedings. Recycling World Congress [*A publication*]
Congr Rec Dly ... Congressional Record. Daily Edition [*US*] [*A publication*]
Congr Venez Cir ... Congreso Venezolano de Cirugia [*A publication*]
Congr Yellow Book ... Congressional Yellow Book [*A publication*]
CoNgSD .... Adams County School District No. 12, Northglenn, CO [*Library symbol*] [*Library of Congress*] (LCLS)
CON GUST ... Con Gustoso [*With Taste*] [*Music*] (ROG)
CONH....... Continental Homes Holding Corp. [*NASDAQ symbol*] (NQ)
CONH....... United States Naval Hospital, Oakland, CA [*Library symbol*] [*Library of Congress*] (LCLS)
CONHYDROLANT ... Confidential Hydrographic Office [*later, Naval Oceanographic Office*] Reports - Atlantic [*Navy*]
CONICET ... Consejo Nacional de Investigaciones Cientificas y Tecnicas [*National Council for Scientific and Technical Research*] [*Information service or system*] (IID)

CONICYT ... Comision Nacional de Investigacion Cientifica y Tecnologica [*National Commission for Scientific and Technological Research*] [*Information service or system*]   (IID)

ConiNT ...... Coniectanea Neotestamentica [*Uppsala*] [*A publication*]   (BJA)

Con Int Explor Mer Bull Stat Peches Marit ... Conseil International pour l'Exploration de la Mer. Bulletin Statistique des Peches Maritimes [*A publication*]

CONIO ...... Console Input/Output

CONIRIS .. Calibrated Optical and Near Infrared Imaging System   (MCD)

CONIT ...... Connector for Networked Information Transfer [*Massachusetts Institute of Technology*] [*Information service or system*]   (IID)

CONJ .... Conjugation

CONJ .... Conjunction

CONJ .... Conjunctivitis [*Medicine*]

CONJ .... In Conjunction With   (ADA)

Conjonct Econ Lorr ... Conjoncture Economique Lorraine [*A publication*]

Conjonct Econ Maroc ... Conjoncture Economique Marocaine [*A publication*]

Conjoncture Econ Maroc ... Conjoncture Economique au Maroc [*A publication*]

CONJUG .. Conjugation   (ADA)

Conjuntura Econ ... Conjuntura Economica [*A publication*]

Conk Adm ... Conkling's Admiralty [*A publication*]   (DLA)

Conk Ex Pow ... Conkling's Executive Powers [*A publication*]   (DLA)

Conk JP ..... Conkling's Iowa Justice of the Peace [*A publication*]   (DLA)

Conk Treat ... Conkling's Treatise on Jurisdiction and Practice of the United States Courts [*A publication*]   (DLA)

Conk US Pr ... Conkling's Treatise on Jurisdiction and Practice of the United States Courts [*A publication*]   (DLA)

CONL .... Conical   (MSA)

Con & L ...... Connor and Lawson's Irish Chancery Reports [*1841-43*] [*A publication*]   (DLA)

ConL .... Contemporary Literature [*A publication*]

CONL .... Control

Con & Law ... Connor and Lawson's Irish Chancery Reports [*1841-43*] [*A publication*]   (DLA)

Con Life ..... Consecrated Life [*A publication*]

CONLIS .... Committee on National Library Information Systems

ConLit .... Contemporary Literature [*A publication*]

ConLit .... Convorbiri Literare [*A publication*]

CONLOS .. CONARC [*Continental Army Command*] Logistics Operations - Streamline [*Obsolete*]

Con LR .... Connecticut Law Review [*A publication*]

Con L Rev ... Connecticut Law Review [*A publication*]

CONMET ... Combined Operations Nuclear Medical Evaluation Team   (MCD)

CON MO ... Con Moto [*With the Movement*] [*Music*]   (ROG)

Con Mus Ed ... Contribution to Music Education [*A publication*]

CONN .... Connected   (ROG)

CONN .... Connecticut

Conn. .... Connecticut Reports [*A publication*]   (DLA)

CONN .... Connector   (KSC)

CONN .... Connellan Airways Ltd.

Conn. .... Connexions [*A publication*]

Conn. .... Connoisseur [*A publication*]

Conn. .... Connolly's New York Surrogate Reports [*A publication*]   (DLA)

Conn. ...., Connotation [*A publication*]

CONN .... Connotation

Conna .... [*Franciscus*] Connanus [*Deceased, 1551*] [*Authority cited in pre-1607 legal work*]   (DSA)

Conn Acad Arts & Sci Mem (New Haven) ... Connecticut Academy of Arts and Sciences. Memoirs (New Haven) [*A publication*]

Conn Acad Arts & Sci Trans ... Connecticut Academy of Arts and Sciences. Transactions [*A publication*]

Conn Acts .. Connecticut Public and Special Acts   (DLA)

Conn Agencies Reg ... Regulations of Connecticut State Agencies [*A publication*]   (DLA)

Conn Agencies Regs ... Regulations of Connecticut State Agencies [*A publication*]

Conn Agr Expt Sta Bull ... Connecticut. Agricultural Experiment Station. Bulletin [*New Haven*] [*A publication*]

Conn Agric Exp Stn Bull (New Haven) ... Connecticut. Agricultural Experiment Station. Bulletin (New Haven) [*A publication*]

Conn Agric Exp Stn Dep Entomol Spec Bull ... Connecticut. Agricultural Experiment Station. Department of Entomology. Special Bulletin [*A publication*]

Conn Agric Exp Stn (New Haven) Circ ... Connecticut. Agricultural Experiment Station. Circular (New Haven) [*A publication*]

Conn Agric Exp Stn (Storrs) Misc Publ ... Connecticut. Agricultural Experiment Station (Storrs). Miscellaneous Publication [*A publication*]

Conn Agric Exp Stn (Storrs) Res Rep ... Connecticut. Agricultural Experiment Station (Storrs). Research Report [*A publication*]

Connais Art ... Connaissance des Arts [*A publication*]

Connaiss Arts ... Connaissance des Arts [*A publication*]

Connaiss Loire ... Connaissance de la Loire [*A publication*]

Connaiss Plast ... Connaissance des Plastiques [*A publication*]

Conn App ... Connecticut Appellate Reports [*A publication*]

Conn App Proc ... Maltbie's Appellate Procedure [*A publication*]   (DLA)

Conn Arbor Bull ... Connecticut Arboretum Bulletin [*A publication*]

Conn Bar J ... Connecticut Bar Journal [*A publication*]

Conn B J ..... Connecticut Bar Journal [*A publication*]

Conn Busn ... Connecticut Business [*A publication*]

Conn Cir. ..... Connecticut Circuit Court Reports [*A publication*]   (DLA)

Conn Cir Ct ... Connecticut Circuit Court Reports [*A publication*]   (DLA)

Conn Comp Com ... Connecticut Compensation Commissioners, Compendium of Awards [*A publication*]   (DLA)

Conn Comp Dec ... Connecticut Workmen's Compensation Decisions [*A publication*]   (DLA)

Conn Const ... Connecticut Constitution [*A publication*]   (DLA)

Conn Dec ..... Connecticut Decisions [*A publication*]   (DLA)

Connecticut L Rev ... Connecticut Law Review [*A publication*]

Connecticut Med ... Connecticut Medicine [*A publication*]

Connecticut R ... Connecticut Reports [*A publication*]   (DLA)

Connecticut Rep ... Connecticut Reports [*A publication*]   (DLA)

Connecticut Water Resources Bull ... Connecticut Water Resources Bulletin [*A publication*]

Connections J ... Connections Journal [*A publication*]

Connector Symp Proc ... Connector Symposium. Proceedings [*A publication*]

Connect Rep ... Connecticut Reports [*A publication*]   (DLA)

Connect Tis ... Connective Tissue Research [*A publication*]

Connect Tissue Res ... Connective Tissue Research [*A publication*]

ConNeot ..... Coniectanea Neotestamentica [*Uppsala*] [*A publication*]   (BJA)

Conn Gen Stat ... General Statutes of Connecticut [*A publication*]   (DLA)

Conn Gen Stat Ann ... Connecticut General Statutes, Annotated [*A publication*]   (DLA)

Conn Gen Stat Ann (West) ... Connecticut General Statutes, Annotated (West) [*A publication*]

Conn Geol Natur Hist Surv Bull ... Connecticut. Geological and Natural History Survey. Bulletin [*A publication*]

Conn Govt ... Connecticut Government [*A publication*]

Conn Greenhouse Newsl Univ Conn Coop Ext Ser ... Connecticut Greenhouse Newsletter. University of Connecticut. Cooperative Extension Service [*A publication*]

Conn Health Bull ... Connecticut Health Bulletin [*A publication*]

Conn His S ... Connecticut Historical Society. Collections [*A publication*]

Conn Hist Soc ... Connecticut Historical Society [*A publication*]

Conn Hist Soc Bull ... Connecticut Historical Society. Bulletin [*A publication*]

Conn Hist Soc Coll ... Connecticut Historical Society. Collections [*A publication*]

Conn Hlth Bull ... Connecticut Health Bulletin [*A publication*]

ConnHSB ... Connecticut Historical Society. Bulletin [*A publication*]

Conn Ind .... Connecticut Industry [*A publication*]

CONNIVER ... [*A*] programming language [*1973*]   (CSR)

Conn Legis Serv ... Connecticut Legislative Service (West) [*A publication*]   (DLA)

Conn Lib .... Connecticut Libraries [*A publication*]

Conn Lib Assn Bul ... Connecticut Library Association. Bulletin [*A publication*]

Conn LJ ..... Connecticut Law Journal [*A publication*]

Conn LR ..... Connecticut Law Review [*A publication*]

Conn L Rev ... Connecticut Law Review [*A publication*]

Conn M ...... Connecticut Magazine [*New Haven*] [*A publication*]

Conn Med .. Connecticut Medicine [*A publication*]

Conn Med J ... Connecticut Medicine Journal [*A publication*]

Conn Mineral Folio ... Connecticut. Mineral Folios [*A publication*]

Conn Nurs News ... Connecticut Nursing News [*A publication*]

Connoly ...... Connolly's New York Surrogate Reports [*A publication*]   (DLA)

Connoly Sur Rep ... Connolly's New York Surrogate Reports [*A publication*]   (DLA)

Connoly Surr Rep ... Connolly's New York Surrogate Reports [*A publication*]   (DLA)

Connor & L ... Connor and Lawson's Irish Chancery Reports [*1841-43*] [*A publication*]   (DLA)

Conn Pub Acts ... Connecticut Public Acts [*A publication*]   (DLA)

Conn R .... Connaught Rangers [*Military*] [*British*]   (DAS)

Conn R .... Connecticut Reports [*A publication*]   (DLA)

Conn R .... Connecticut Review [*A publication*]

CONN RANG ... Connaught Rangers [*Military*] [*British*]   (ROG)

Conn Rep ... Connecticut Reports [*A publication*]   (DLA)

Conn Reports ... Connecticut Reports [*A publication*]   (DLA)

Conn Rev .... Connecticut Review [*A publication*]

CONNROD ... Connecting-Rod

Conn S .... Connecticut Supplement [*A publication*]   (DLA)

Con(NS) ..... Convivium (New Series) [*A publication*]

Conn Spec Acts ... Connecticut Special Acts [*A publication*]   (DLA)

Conn State Ag Exp ... Connecticut. State Agricultural Experiment Station. Publications [*A publication*]

Conn State Geol Nat Hist Surv Bull ... Connecticut. State Geological and Natural History Survey. Bulletin [*A publication*]

Conn State Geol Nat Hist Surv Misc Ser ... Connecticut. State Geological and Natural History Survey. Miscellaneous Series [*A publication*]

Conn State Geol Nat Hist Surv Quadrangle Rep ... Connecticut. State Geological and Natural History Survey. Quadrangle Report [*A publication*]

Conn State Geol Nat Hist Surv Rep Invest ... Connecticut. State Geological and Natural History Survey. Report of Investigations [*A publication*]

Conn State Med J ... Connecticut State Medical Journal [*A publication*]

Conn Storrs Agric Exp Stn Bull ... Connecticut. Storrs Agricultural Experiment Station. Bulletin [*A publication*]

Conn Storrs Agric Exp Stn Prog Rep ... Connecticut. Storrs Agricultural Experiment Station. Progress Report [*A publication*]
Conn Storrs Agric Exp Stn Res Rep ... Connecticut. Storrs Agricultural Experiment Station. Research Report [*A publication*]
Conn Sup ... Connecticut Supplement [*A publication*]　(DLA)
Conn Supp ... Connecticut Supplement [*A publication*]　(DLA)
Conn Surr .. Connolly's New York Surrogate Reports [*A publication*]　(DLA)
Conn Surr Rep ... Connolly's New York Surrogate Reports [*A publication*]　(DLA)
ConNSW ... Conservatorium of Music, New South Wales [*Australia*]
ConNT .... Coniectanea Neotestamentica [*Uppsala*] [*A publication*]　(BJA)
CONNT..... Connaissement [*Bill of Lading*] [*Legal term*] [*French*]
Conn Tiss ... Connective Tissues [*A publication*]
Conn Tiss Res ... Connective Tissue Research [*A publication*]
Conn Univ Eng Exp Stn Bull ... Connecticut. University Engineering Experiment Station. Bulletin [*A publication*]
Conn Veg Grow Assoc Proc Annual Meet ... Connecticut Vegetable Growers' Association. Proceedings. Annual Meeting [*A publication*]
Conn Water Res Comm Conn Water Res Bull ... Connecticut Water Resources Commission. Connecticut Water Resources Bulletin [*A publication*]
Conn Water Resour Bull ... Connecticut Water Resources Bulletin [*A publication*]
Conn Woodl ... Connecticut Woodlands [*A publication*]
Conn Woodlands ... Connecticut Woodlands [*A publication*]
CONO .... Congou [*Tea trade*]　(ROG)
CO/NO .... Current Operator - Next Operator [*Data processing*]　(MDG)
CoNo .... Norwood Public Library, Norwood, CO [*Library symbol*] [*Library of Congress*]　(LCLS)
CONOBJTR ... Conscientious Objector
Con Occup Ther Bull ... Connecticut Occupational Therapy Bulletin [*A publication*]
CONOCO ... Continental Oil Company
CON OF .... Consisting Of [*Freight*]
CONOPPR ... CONARC [*Continental Army Command*] Operating Program [*Obsolete*]　(AABC)
CONOPS ... Continental United States Operations [*Army*]
CONOPS .. Continuity of Operations　(MCD)
Conover...... Conover's Reports [*Wisconsin*] [*A publication*]　(DLA)
ConP .... Concerning Poetry [*A publication*]
Con P .... Contemporary Poetry [*A publication*]
CONPADRI ... Cyclophosphamide, Oncovin [*Vincristine*], L-PAM [*Melphalan*], Adriamycin [*Antineoplastic drug regimen*]
Con Par ...... Connell on Parishes [*A publication*]　(DLA)
CONPASP ... Construction Project Alternative Selection Program [*Bell System*]
CONPASS ... Consortium of Professional Associations to Supervise Studies of Special Programs for the Improvement of Instruction in American Education
CONPLAN ... Concept Plan　(NVT)
CONPLAN ... Contingency Plan [*Military*]
CONPOR .. Conference of Private Organizations　(EA)
CONPRESDU ... Continue Present Duty [*Military*]
CONPY ..... Contact Party [*Army*]
CONQ .... Conquest　(ROG)
CONQAV ... Conquest [*A publication*]
Conqu......... Conquest [*A publication*]
Conquest J Res Def Soc ... Conquest. Journal of the Research Defence Society [*A publication*]
Conr .... Conroy's Custodian Reports [*1652-1788*] [*Ireland*] [*A publication*]　(DLA)
ConR .... Contemporary Review [*A publication*]
CONRAD ... Computerized National Range Documentation
Conrad ...... Conradiana [*A publication*]
CONRAD ... Contraceptive Research and Development Program [*Research center*]　(RCD)
CONRAIL ... Consolidated Rail Corp. [*Also, CR, CRC*]
CONREC ... Conference for Reconciliation, Restitution Fund　(EA)
CONREP... CONARC [*Continental Army Command*] Emergency Relocation Plan [*Obsolete*]
CONREP... Connected Replenishment [*Military*]　(NVT)
Con Res Mag ... Consumers' Research Magazine [*A publication*]
CONROD ... Connecting-Rod
CONROUTE ... Convoy and Routing [*Section*] [*US Fleet*]
CONS .... Carrier-Operated Noise Suppression
CONS .... Consecrated
Cons .... Consecratione [*Decretum Gratiani*] [*A publication*]　(DSA)
CONS .... Consecutive　(ADA)
Cons .... Conseil [*Council*] [*French*]　(DLA)
Cons .... Conseiller [*Councillor, Judge*] [*French*]　(ILCA)
CONS .... Consequence
CONS .... Conserva [*Conserve*] [*Pharmacy*]
CONS .... Conservation News. National Wildlife Federation [*A publication*]
CONS .... Conservative
CONS .... Conservative Savings Bank [*Omaha, NE*] [*NASDAQ symbol*]　(NQ)
Cons .... Conservatoire [*Conservatory*] [*French*]
Cons .... Conservator　(DLA)
CONS .... Consider　(AABC)
Cons .... Considerant [*Whereas, In View*] [*French*]　(ILCA)

CONS........ Consign
Cons .... Consigna [*A publication*]
CONS........ Consignment [*Business term*]
CONS........ Consist　(AABC)
CONS........ Console [*Data processing*]
CONS........ Consolidate
CONS........ Consonant
CONS........ Constable
CONS........ Constitution
CONS........ Construction
CONS........ Consul
CONSA...... Consult [*Medicine*]
CONSA...... Consular Shipping Adviser
CONSAL.... Congress of Southeast Asian Librarians　(EAIO)
CONSCAN ... Conical Scan　(NG)
CONSCE... Consequence　(ROG)
CONSCIENCE ... Committee on National Student Citizenship in Every National Case of Emergency
CONSCO .. Committee of National Security Companies [*Memphis, TN*]　(EA)
Cons & Com Cred (P-H) ... Consumer and Commercial Credit (Prentice-Hall) [*A publication*]　(DLA)
Cons Com Ext ... Conseiller du Commerce Exterieur [*A publication*]
Cons Const ... Conseil Constitutionnel [*Constitutional Council*] [*French*]　(DLA)
Cons Cred Guide ... Consumer Credit Guide [*Commerce Clearing House*] [*A publication*]　(DLA)
CONSD..... Commanding Officer, Naval Supply Depot　(MCD)
CONSD..... Considered [*Legal*] [*British*]　(ROG)
CONSEC... Consecutive　(MSA)
Cons Econ Wallon R ... Conseil Economique Wallon. Revue [*A publication*]
CONSED... Continental Shelf Sedimentology [*Oceanography*]　(MSC)
Consejo Sup Invest Cient Bibl Bol ... Consejo Superior de Investigaciones Cientificas. Biblioteca General. Boletin [*Madrid*] [*A publication*]
Consensus Dev Conf Summ Natl Inst Health ... Consensus Development Conference Summaries. National Institutes of Health [*A publication*]
CONSEQCE ... Consequence [*Legal*] [*British*]　(ROG)
CONSEQT ... Consequent [*Legal*] [*British*]　(ROG)
CONSER... Cooperative Online Serials [*Library of Congress*]
Conser Ser Dep Cap T ... Conservation Series. Department of the Capital Territory [*A publication*]　(APTA)
CONSERV ... Conservation
Conserv...... Conservationist [*A publication*]
CONSERV ... Conservatory
Conservation Found Letter ... Conservation Foundation Letter [*A publication*]
Conserve Deriv Agrum ... Conserve e Derivati Agrumari [*A publication*]
Conserver Soc Notes ... Conserver Society Notes [*Canada*] [*A publication*]
Conserv Found Lett ... Conservation Foundation. Letter [*A publication*]
Conserv Nat ... Conservation of Nature [*Japan*] [*A publication*]
Conserv News ... Conservation News [*A publication*]
Conserv R... Conservative Review [*A publication*]
Conserv Recycl ... Conservation and Recycling [*A publication*]
Conserv & Recycling ... Conservation and Recycling [*A publication*]
Conserv Recycling ... Conservation and Recycling [*England*] [*A publication*]
Conserv Res Rep US Agr Res Serv ... Conservation Research Report. US Agricultural Research Service [*A publication*]
Conserv Res Rep US Dep Agric Agric Res Serv ... Conservation Research Report. United States Department of Agriculture. Agricultural Research Service [*A publication*]
Conserv Ser Dep Cap T ... Conservation Series. Department of the Capital Territory [*A publication*]　(APTA)
Conserv Volunteer ... Conservation Volunteer [*A publication*]
CONSGEE ... Consignee [*Business term*]　(ROG)
CONSGEN ... Consul General　(EY)
CONSGOLD ... Consolidated Gold Fields [*British*]
CONSGT... Consignment [*Business term*]
Cons Hawai ... Construction in Hawaii [*A publication*]
CONSHELF ... Continental Shelf
CONSHIP ... Control by Ship　(NATG)
Cons Hon ... De Consulatu Honorii [*of Claudianus*] [*Classical studies*]　(OCD)
CONSHORE ... Control from Shore　(NATG)
CONSID.... Consider　(ROG)
CONSIDO ... Consolidated Special Information Dissemination Office [*Proposed for military intelligence gathering, late 1940's, but never activated*]
Con & Sim ... Connor and Simonton's South Carolina Equity Digest [*A publication*]　(DLA)
CONSIM... Console Simulator [*Data processing*]
Cons Int Explor Mer Bull Stat Peches Marit ... Conseil International pour l'Exploration de la Mer. Bulletin Statistique des Peches Maritimes [*A publication*]
Cons Int Explor Mer Zooplankton Sheet ... Conseil International pour l'Exploration de la Mer. Zooplankton Sheet [*A publication*]
Consist .... English Consistorial Reports, by Haggard [*1788-1821*] [*A publication*]　(DLA)
Consist Rep ... English Consistorial Reports, by Haggard [*1788-1821*] [*A publication*]　(DLA)
Cons Jud .... Conservative Judaism [*A publication*]

CONSLTNT ... Consultant (AABC)
Cons L Today ... Consumer Law Today [*A publication*]
Cons del M ... Il Consolato del Mare [*A publication*] (DLA)
Consmr BG ... Consumer Reports Buying Guide [*A publication*]
Consmr Elc ... Consumer Electronics Annual Review [*A publication*]
Consmr Rpt ... Consumer Reports [*A publication*]
CONSN ..... Consultation [*Legal*] [*British*] (ROG)
Cons N ...... Consumer News [*A publication*]
Cons Natl Rech Can Bull ... Conseil National de Recherches du Canada. Bulletin [*A publication*]
Cons Natl Rech Can Div Genie Mec Rapp Tech Lab ... Conseil National de Recherches du Canada. Division de Genie Mecanique. Rapport Technique de Laboratoire [*A publication*]
ConsNP ...... Conservative Nationalist Party [*Australia*] [*Political party*]
CONSO ..... Consolan Facility [*Aviation*]
CONSOB .. Commissione Nazionale per le Societa e la Borsa [*National Commission for Companies and the Stock Exchange*] [*Italian counterpart of the American Securities and Exchange Commission*] [*Milan*]
CONSOL .. Consolidate (AFM)
CONSOL-BNR ... Consolidation Coal - Bethlehem Steel - National Steel - Republic Steel [*Coke pellet process developed by four-company group of steel and coke producers*]
CONSOLEX ... Consolidation Exercise [*Military*] (NVT)
Consol Frt Classif ... Consolidated Freight Classification [*A publication*]
Consolid Ord ... Consolidated General Orders in Chancery [*A publication*]
Consol del Mare ... Il Consolato del Mare [*A publication*] (DLA)
CONSOLS ... Consolidated Annuities [*Insurance*] (DSUE)
CONSOLTD ... Consolidated (ADA)
CONSON ... Consideration
Cons Ord in Ch ... Consolidated General Orders in Chancery [*A publication*] (DLA)
CONSORT ... Conversational System with On-Line Remote Terminals [*Data processing*] (IEEE)
Consortium Q ... Consortium Quarterly [*A publication*]
Consort Newsl ... Consortium Newsletter [*A publication*]
Consp .... Conspiracy (ILCA)
CONSPERG ... Conspergere [*Dust or Sprinkle*] [*Pharmacy*]
conspic .... Conspicuous
CONS et PRUD ... Consilio et Prudentia [*By Counsel and Prudence*] [*Latin*] (ADA)
Cons Rech Dev For Que Etude ... Conseil de la Recherche et du Developpement Forestiers du Quebec. Etude [*A publication*]
Cons Recur Nat No Renov Publ (Mex) ... Consejo de Recursos Naturales No Renovables. Publicacion (Mexico) [*A publication*]
Cons Rep .... Consumer Reports [*A publication*]
Cons Res Mag ... Consumers' Research Magazine [*A publication*]
Cons Sci Int Rech Trypanosomiases ... Conseil Scientifique International de Recherches sur les Trypanosomiases [*A publication*]
Cons Stil .... De Consulatu Stilichonis [*of Claudianus*] [*Classical studies*] (OCD)
CONSSTOCS ... Contingency Support Stocks [*Military*] (AABC)
Const .... Bott's Poor Laws, by Const [*1560-1833*] [*A publication*] (DLA)
CONST ...... Consent (ROG)
CONST ...... Consignment [*Business term*] (ROG)
Con St .... Consolidated Statutes [*A publication*] (DLA)
CONST ...... Constable
CONST ...... Constant
CONST ...... Constantine [*Roman emperor, 272-337AD*] (ROG)
CONST ...... Constantinople [*Later, Istanbul*] [*Turkey*] (ROG)
CONST ...... Constituency
CONST ...... Constitutio [*Point at Issue, Regulation, Settlement*] [*Latin*] (OCD)
CONST ...... Constitution [*or Constitutional*]
Const .... Constitutional Reports, Printed by Harper [*1 South Carolina*] [*A publication*] (DLA)
Const .... Constitutional Reports, Printed by Mills [*South Carolina*] [*A publication*] (DLA)
Const .... Constitutional Reports, Printed by Treadway [*South Carolina*] [*A publication*] (DLA)
CONST ...... Construct (AFM)
Const .... Const's Edition of Bott's Poor Law Cases [*A publication*] (DSA)
CONSTAB ... Constabulary (AABC)
Const Afr States ... Constitutions of African States [*A publication*] (DLA)
Const Amend ... Amendment to the Constitution (DLA)
Constan Copti ... Constantinus Coptius [*Flourished, 16th century*] [*Authority cited in pre-1607 legal work*] (DSA)
Constan Roger ... Constantius Rogerius [*Flourished, 16th century*] [*Authority cited in pre-1607 legal work*] (DSA)
CONSTANT ... Constantinople [*Later, Istanbul*] [*Turkey*] (DSUE)
Constant ..... De Constantia Sapientis [*of Seneca the Younger*] [*Classical studies*] (OCD)
Con Stat ..... Consolidated Statutes [*A publication*] (DLA)
Const Bott ... Const's Edition of Bott's Poor Law Cases [*A publication*] (DLA)
Const Commentary ... Constitutional Commentary [*A publication*] (DLA)
Const Dep & Sp Sov ... Constitutions of Dependencies and Special Sovereignties [*A publication*] (DLA)

Const Endocr Metab ... Constituicao, Endocrinologie, e Metabolismo [*A publication*]
CONSTENGR ... Construction Engineer
Const Hist ... Hallam's Constitutional History of England [*A publication*] (DLA)
CONSTI .... Constipated (DSUE)
CONSTIT ... Constituency
Constitutional and Parliamentary Info ... Constitutional and Parliamentary Information [*A publication*]
CONSTL ... Constitutional
CONSTN .. Constitution
Const Nations ... Constitutions of Nations [*A publication*] (DLA)
Const NS .... Constitutional Reports, New Series, Printed by Mills [*South Carolina*] [*A publication*] (DLA)
CONSTOCS ... Contingency Support Stocks [*Military*] (NVT)
CONSTON ... Constitution (ROG)
Const Oth .. Constitutiones Othoni [*At the end of Lyndewood's Provinciale*] [*A publication*] (DLA)
Const & Parliam Inf ... Constitutional and Parliamentary Information [*A publication*] (DLA)
CONSTR ... Constraint (KSC)
Constr .... Construct State (BJA)
Constr .... Construction [*A publication*]
CONSTR ... Construction
CONSTR ... Construe (ROG)
Constr Contracting ... Construction Contracting [*A publication*]
Constr Eng Res Lab Tech Rep ... Construction Engineering Research Laboratory. Technical Report [*A publication*]
Const Rep .. Constitutional Reports [*South Carolina*] [*A publication*] (DLA)
Const Rev ... Constitutional Review [*A publication*] (DLA)
Const Rev ... Construction Review [*A publication*]
Constr Frct ... Construction Industry Forecast [*A publication*]
Constrl Rev ... Constructional Review [*A publication*] (APTA)
Constrl Rev Tech Suppl ... Constructional Review. Technical Supplement [*A publication*] (APTA)
Constr Mach ... Construction Machinery [*Japan*] [*A publication*]
Constr Mach Equip ... Construction Machinery and Equipment [*A publication*]
Constr Mech (Tokyo) ... Construction Mechanization (Tokyo) [*A publication*]
Constr Met ... Construction Metallique [*A publication*]
Constr Metal ... Construction Metallique [*A publication*]
Constr Meth ... Construction Methods [*A publication*]
Constr Methods Equip ... Construction Methods and Equipment [*A publication*]
CONSTRN ... Construction
Constr News ... Construction News [*A publication*]
Constr News (London) ... Construction News (London) [*A publication*]
Constr News Mag ... Construction News Magazine [*England*] [*A publication*]
Constr News Magazine ... Construction News Magazine [*A publication*]
CONSTRON ... Construction (ROG)
Constr Paps ... Construction Papers [*A publication*]
Constr Plant & Equip ... Construction Plant and Equipment [*A publication*]
Constr Plant Equip ... Construction Plant and Equipment [*A publication*]
Constr Q .... Constructive Quarterly [*A publication*]
Constr R ..... Construction Review [*A publication*]
Constr Ref ... Construction References [*A publication*]
Constr Rev ... Construction Review [*A publication*]
Constr Rev ... Constructional Review [*A publication*]
Constr Road Trans ... Construction and Road Transport [*A publication*] (APTA)
Constr S Afr ... Construction in Southern Africa [*A publication*]
Const RSC ... Constitutional Reports, Printed by Treadway [*South Carolina*] [*A publication*] (DLA)
Constr South Afr ... Construction in Southern Africa [*A publication*]
Constr Specifier ... Construction Specifier [*A publication*]
Constr Sthn Afr ... Construction in Southern Africa [*A publication*]
Constr Tech Bull ... Construction Technical Bulletin [*A publication*] (APTA)
Construct-Amenag ... Construction-Amenagement [*A publication*]
Constructional R ... Constructional Review [*A publication*] (APTA)
Construction Law ... Construction Lawyer [*A publication*]
Construction R ... Construction Review [*A publication*]
Constru Masini ... Constructia de Masini [*A publication*]
Const SC .... Constitutional Reports, Printed by Treadway [*South Carolina*] [*A publication*] (DLA)
Const SCNS ... Constitutional Reports, New Series, Printed by Mills [*South Carolina*] [*A publication*] (DLA)
Const US .... Constitution of the United States [*A publication*] (DLA)
Const US Amend ... Amendment to the Constitution of the United States (DLA)
CONSUB .. Continental Shelf Submersible [*Undersea exploration vehicle*] (MCD)
Consuet Feud ... Consuetudines Feudorum [*The Book of Feuds*] [*Latin*] [*A publication*] (DLA)
CONSUL .... Consular Corps College and International Consular Academy (EA)
CONSUL ... Control Subroutine Language [*Data processing*] (IEEE)
CONSULT ... Consultant
Consult En ... Consulting Engineer [*A publication*]
Consult Eng ... Consulting Engineer [*A publication*]

Consult Eng (Barrington, Illinois) ... Consulting Engineer (Barrington, Illinois) [*A publication*]
Consult Eng (London) ... Consulting Engineer (London) [*A publication*]
Consult Engr ... Consulting Engineer [*A publication*]
Consult Eng (St Joseph Mich) ... Consulting Engineer (St. Joseph, Michigan) [*A publication*]
CONSULTN ... Consultation
CONSUM ... Consumer
Consum Brief Summ ... Consumer Briefing Summary [*A publication*]
Consumer Buying Prosp ... Consumer Buying Prospects [*A publication*]
Consumer Cred Guide (CCH) ... Consumer Credit Guide (Commerce Clearing House) [*A publication*]   (DLA)
Consumer N ... Consumer News [*A publication*]
Consumer Prod Safety Guide (CCH) ... Consumer Product Safety Guide (Commerce Clearing House) [*A publication*]   (DLA)
Consumer Rep ... Consumer Reports [*A publication*]
Consumers Res Mag ... Consumers' Research Magazine [*A publication*]
Consum Health Perspect ... Consumer Health Perspectives [*A publication*]
Consum Ind ... Consumer's Index [*A publication*]
Consum Index Prod Eval Inf Source ... Consumers Index to Product Evaluations and Information Sources [*A publication*]
CONSUMP ... Consumption   (ROG)
Consum Rep ... Consumer Reports [*A publication*]
Consum Rep (Consum Union US) ... Consumer Reports (Consumers Union of United States, Inc.) [*A publication*]
Consum Res Mag ... Consumers' Research Magazine [*A publication*]
Con Sur ... Connoly's New York Surrogate Reports [*A publication*]   (DLA)
Consv ... Conservatorship   (DLA)
CONSV ... Conservatory
CONSV ... Conserve   (AABC)
Cont ... Contact [*Canadian Studies Foundation*] [*A publication*]
CONT ... Contact   (KSC)
CONT ... Contact. Journal of Urban and Environmental Affairs [*A publication*]
CONT ... Container   (MCD)
CONT ... Containing
CONT ... Contano [*Parts so marked to rest*] [*Music*]
CONT ... Contemporary   (ADA)
CONT ... Contents
CONT ... Contested
CONT ... Continent
Cont ... Continental
CONT ... Continental Medical Systems, Inc. [*Mechanicsburg, PA*] [*NASDAQ symbol*]   (NQ)
CONT ... Contingency   (MCD)
CONT ... Continue   (AFM)
CONT ... Continuentur [*Continue*] [*Pharmacy*]   (ROG)
CONT ... Continuo [*Thorough Bass*] [*Music*]
Cont ... Continuum [*A publication*]
CONT ... Contra [*Against*] [*Latin*]
CONT ... Contract
CONT ... Control   (MSA)
CONT ... Controller   (KSC)
CONT ... Contusus [*Bruised*] [*Medicine*]
Cont ... De Vita Contemplativa [*Philo*]   (BJA)
CONTA ... Conference on Conceptual and Terminological Analysis in the Social Sciences [*1981*]
CONTA ... Control Assembly
Contabilidad Admin ... Contabilidad. Administracion [*A publication*]
CONTAC ... Conference on the Atlantic Community   (EA)
CONTAC ... Continuous Action [*Acronym is brand of decongestant capsule*]
CONTAC ... Coordinated Navy Total Acquisition Control [*System*]
CONTACA ... Conventional Tactical Air Model   (MCD)
Contact ... 3-2-1 Contact [*A publication*]
CONTACT ... Conformal Tactical Array   (MCD)
Contact Intraocul Lens Med J ... Contact and Intraocular Lens Medical Journal [*A publication*]
Contact J Urban Environ Aff ... Contact. Journal of Urban and Environmental Affairs [*A publication*]
Contact Lens Med Bull ... Contact Lens Medical Bulletin [*A publication*]
Contact Lens Soc Am J ... Contact Lens Society of America. Journal [*A publication*]
CONTAD ... Concealed Target Detection   (MCD)
CONTAG ... Contagious
CONT (AH) ... Continent, Antwerp-Hamburg Range [*Shipping*]   (DS)
Containerisation Int ... Containerisation International [*A publication*]
CONTAM ... Committee on Nationwide Television Audience Measurement
CONTAM ... Contaminated   (KSC)
Contam Control ... Contamination Control [*A publication*]
Contam Control Biomed Environ ... Contamination Control. Biomedical Environments [*A publication*]
Cont App Dec (CCH) ... Contract Appeals Decisions (Commerce Clearing House) [*A publication*]   (DLA)
Cont Appl St ... Contributions to Applied Statistics [*A publication*]
CONTAX ... Consumers and Taxpayers
Cont of Banking (P-H) ... Control of Banking (Prentice-Hall) [*A publication*]   (DLA)
CONTBD ... Contraband
CONTBG ... Contributing   (ADA)
CONT (BH) ... Continent, Bordeaux-Hamburg Range [*Shipping*]   (DS)
Cont Birdlife ... Continental Birdlife [*A publication*]

CONT BON MOR ... Contra Bonos Mores [*Contrary to Good Manners*] [*Latin*]
Cont Cas Fed ... Contract Cases, Federal [*A publication*]   (DLA)
Cont Cas Fed CCH ... Contracts Cases, Federal. Commerce Clearing House [*A publication*]
CONTCE ... Continuance
CONTCOP ... Confederacao Nacional dos Trabalhadores em Comunicacoes e Publicidade [*Communications and Advertising Workers Confederation*] [*Brazil*]   (EY)
Cont Crises ... Contemporary Crises [*A publication*]
CONTD ... Contained
CONTD ... Continued
Cont Drug P ... Contemporary Drug Problems [*A publication*]
CONTDVD ... Continental Divide [*FAA*]   (FAAC)
Cont Ed ... Contemporary Education [*A publication*]
Cont Educ ... Contemporary Education [*A publication*]
Cont El ... Controverted Elections Judges [*England*]   (DLA)
Cont Elect Case ... Contested Election Cases [*United States*] [*A publication*]   (DLA)
CONTEM ... Contemplate   (AABC)
Contemp ... Contemporaneo [*A publication*]
CONTEMP ... Contemporary
Contemp ... Contemporary Review [*A publication*]
Contemp Adm ... Contemporary Administrator [*A publication*]
Contemp Adm Long Term Care ... Contemporary Administrator for Long-Term Care [*A publication*]
Contemp Agric ... Contemporary Agriculture [*A publication*]
Contemp Anesth Pract ... Contemporary Anesthesia Practice [*A publication*]
Contemp As R ... Contemporary Asia Review [*A publication*]
Contemp China ... Contemporary China [*A publication*]
Contemp Concepts Phys ... Contemporary Concepts in Physics [*A publication*]
Contemp Crises ... Contemporary Crises [*A publication*]
Contemp Drug ... Contemporary Drug Problems [*A publication*]
Contemp Drug Prob ... Contemporary Drug Problems [*A publication*]
Contemp Drug Problems ... Contemporary Drug Problems [*A publication*]
Contemp Ed ... Contemporary Education [*A publication*]
Contemp Educ ... Contemporary Education [*A publication*]
Contemp Educ Psychol ... Contemporary Educational Psychology [*A publication*]
Contemp Hematol Oncol ... Contemporary Hematology/Oncology [*A publication*]
Contemp Issues Clin Biochem ... Contemporary Issues in Clinical Biochemistry [*A publication*]
Contemp Issues Clin Nutr ... Contemporary Issues in Clinical Nutrition [*A publication*]
Contemp Issues Infect Dis ... Contemporary Issues in Infectious Diseases [*A publication*]
Contemp Jewish Rec ... Contemporary Jewish Record [*A publication*]
Contemp Lit ... Contemporary Literature [*A publication*]
Contemp Longterm Care ... Contemporary Longterm Care [*A publication*]
Contemp M ... Contemporary Marxism [*A publication*]
Contemp Neurol Ser ... Contemporary Neurology Series [*A publication*]
Contemp Nutr ... Contemporary Nutrition [*A publication*]
Contemp Ob Gyn ... Contemporary Ob/Gyn [*A publication*]
Contemp Orthop ... Contemporary Orthopaedics [*A publication*]
Contemp Pharm Pract ... Contemporary Pharmacy Practice [*A publication*]
Contemp Phys ... Contemporary Physics [*A publication*]
Contemp Poland ... Contemporary Poland [*A publication*]
Contemp Polit ... Contemporary Politics [*A publication*]
Contemp Probl Cardiol ... Contemporary Problems in Cardiology [*A publication*]
Contemp Psychoanal ... Contemporary Psychoanalysis [*A publication*]
Contemp Psychol ... Contemporary Psychology [*A publication*]
Contemp R ... Contemporary Review [*A publication*]
Contemp Rev ... Contemplative Review [*A publication*]
Contemp Rev ... Contemporary Review [*A publication*]
Contemp Sociol ... Contemporary Sociology [*A publication*]
Contemp Sociology ... Contemporary Sociology [*A publication*]
Contemp Surg ... Contemporary Surgery [*A publication*]
Contemp Top Anal Clin Chem ... Contemporary Topics in Analytical and Clinical Chemistry [*A publication*]
Contemp Top Immunobiol ... Contemporary Topics in Immunobiology [*A publication*]
Contemp Top Immunochem ... Contemporary Topics in Immunochemistry [*A publication*]
Contemp Top Mol Immunol ... Contemporary Topics in Molecular Immunology [*A publication*]
CON TENA ... Con Tenerezza [*With Tenderness*] [*Music*]   (ROG)
Contents Contemp Math J ... Contents of Contemporary Mathematical Journals [*A publication*]
Contents Contemp Math J New Publ ... Contents of Contemporary Mathematical Journals and New Publications [*A publication*]
Contents Curr Leg Period ... Contents of Current Legal Periodicals [*A publication*]
Contents Pages Manage ... Contents Pages in Management [*A publication*]
Contents Recent Econ J ... Contents of Recent Economics Journals [*A publication*]
CONTER ... Contere [*Rub Together*] [*Pharmacy*]
Cont Fr Civ ... Contemporary French Civilization [*A publication*]

CONTG..... Containing
CONTG..... Contingency (KSC)
CONTH..... Continue to Hold [*Aviation*] (FAAC)
CONT (HH) ... Continent, Havre-Hamburg Range [*Shipping*] (DS)
Cont Hum De ... Contributions to Human Development [*A publication*]
CONTIC.... CONARC [*Continental Army Command*] Intelligence Center [*Obsolete*] (AABC)
Conti Elektro Ber ... Conti Elektro Berichte [*West Germany*] [*A publication*]
CONTIG ... Contiguous (NASA)
CONTIN ... Continental (ROG)
CONTIN ... Continuance [*Legal term*] (DLA)
CONTIN ... Continuetur [*Let It Be Continued*] [*Pharmacy*]
CONTIND ... Continued (ROG)
Contin Educ ... Continuing Education in New Zealand [*A publication*]
Contin Edu Lect (Soc Nucl Med Southeast Chapter) ... Continuing Education Lectures (Society of Nuclear Medicine. Southeastern Chapter) [*A publication*]
Continentl.. Continental Comment [*A publication*]
Contin Mo ... Continental Monthly [*A publication*]
CONTIN REM ... Continuetur Remedium [*Let the Medicine Be Continued*] [*Pharmacy*] (ROG)
Continuing Ed Fam Physician ... Continuing Education for the Family Physician [*A publication*]
Continuing Educ for the Fam Physician ... Continuing Education for the Family Physician [*A publication*]
Continuing Med Educ Newsletter ... Continuing Medical Education Newsletter [*A publication*]
Cont Jew Rec ... Contemporary Jewish Record [*A publication*]
Cont Keybd ... Contemporary Keyboard [*A publication*]
CONTL ..... Continental (AABC)
CONTL ...... Control
Cont Learning ... Continuous Learning [*A publication*]
Contl Eng S ... Control Products Specifier. Special Issue of Control Engineering [*A publication*]
Contl & I .... Control and Instrumentation [*A publication*]
Cont Lit...... Contemporary Literature [*A publication*]
Cont L Rev ... Contemporary Law Review [*India*] [*A publication*] (DLA)
ConTM ...... Concordia Theological Monthly [*A publication*]
Cont Marx ... Contemporary Marxism [*A publication*]
Cont Metall Chem Eng ... Continental Metallurgical and Chemical Engineering [*A publication*]
CONTN..... Contain (ROG)
CONTN..... Continuation
CONTNR.. Container (KSC)
Cont P .... Contemporary Poetry [*A publication*]
Cont & Packag ... Containers and Packaging [*A publication*]
Cont Paint Resin News ... Continental Paint and Resin News [*England*] [*A publication*]
Cont Philos ... Contemporary Philosophy [*A publication*]
Cont Phys .. Contemporary Physics [*A publication*]
Cont Psycha ... Contemporary Psychoanalysis [*A publication*]
Cont Psycho ... Contemporary Psychology [*A publication*]
CONTR..... Container (KSC)
Cont R........ Contemporary Review [*A publication*]
CONTR..... Contra [*Against*] [*Latin*] (ROG)
CONTR..... Contract [*or Contractor*] (AFM)
CONTR..... Contradiction (ADA)
CONTR..... Contralto [*Music*]
CONTR..... Contrary
CONTR..... Contrast
CONTR..... Contribution
CONTR..... Control
CONTRA .. Contraindicated [*Medicine*]
CONTRA .. Contrario [*Opponent or Enemy*] [*Spanish*]
Contracept ... Contraception [*A publication*]
Contracept Delivery Syst ... Contraceptive Delivery Systems [*A publication*]
Contracept-Fertil-Sex ... Contraception-Fertilite-Sexualite [*A publication*]
Contra Costa Dent Bull ... Contra Costa Dental Bulletin [*US*] [*A publication*]
Contract ...... Contractor [*A publication*]
Contract & Constr Eng ... Contracting and Construction Engineer [*A publication*] (APTA)
Contracting ... Contracting and Construction Equipment [*A publication*] (APTA)
Contracting ... Contracting and Public Works [*A publication*] (APTA)
Contract Int ... Contract Interiors [*A publication*]
Contract Inter ... Contract Interiors [*A publication*]
Contract J .. Contract Journal [*England*] [*A publication*]
Contract Jnl ... Contract Journal [*A publication*]
Contract Rec Eng Rev ... Contract Record and Engineering Review [*Canada*] [*A publication*]
Contract Rep Eur Space Res Organ ... Contractor Report. European Space Research Organization [*A publication*]
Contract Rep US Army Eng Waterw Exp Stn ... Contract Report. US Army Engineer Waterways Experiment Station [*A publication*]
CONTRAIL ... Condensation Trail [*in the air*]
CONTRAN ... Control Translator [*Honeywell, Inc.*] [*Data processing*]
CONTRANS ... Conceptual Thought, Random Net Simulation (MUGU)
CONTRAST ... Condensed Strike Data Transmission System (MCD)
CONTR BON MOR ... Contra Bonos Mores [*Contrary to Good Manners*] [*Latin*] (ROG)

Contr Boyce Thompson Inst Pl Res ... Contributions. Boyce Thompson Institute for Plant Research [*A publication*]
Contr Canada Dep For Forest Res Brch ... Contribution. Canada Department of Forestry. Forest Research Branch [*A publication*]
Contr Dep Hort Univ Ill ... Contributions. Department of Horticulture. University of Illinois [*A publication*]
Contr Drama ... Contributions in Drama and Theatre Studies [*A publication*]
CONTREAT ... Continue Treatment at Naval Hospital or Medical Facility Indicated
CONT REM ... Continuentur Remedia [*Continue the Medicines*] [*Pharmacy*]
Contr Eng... Control Engineering [*A publication*]
Contr Fonds Rech For Univ Laval ... Contribution. Fonds de Recherches Forestieres. Universite Laval [*A publication*]
Contr Herb Aust ... Contributions. Herbarium Australiense [*A publication*] (APTA)
CONTRIB ... Contribution (MSA)
Contrib Am Entomol Inst (Ann Arbor) ... Contributions. American Entomological Institute (Ann Arbor) [*A publication*]
Contrib Arct Inst Cathol Univ Am ... Contributions. Arctic Institute. Catholic University of America [*A publication*]
Contrib Asian St ... Contributions to Asian Studies [*A publication*]
Contrib As Stud ... Contributions to Asian Studies [*A publication*]
Contrib Atmos Phys ... Contributions to Atmospheric Physics [*A publication*]
Contrib Avulsas Inst Oceanogr Sao Paulo ... Contribuicoes Avulsas. Instituto Oceanografico Sao Paulo [*A publication*]
Contrib Bears Bluff Lab ... Contributions. Bears Bluff Laboratories [*A publication*]
Contrib Biol Lab Kyoto Univ ... Contributions. Biological Laboratory. Kyoto University [*A publication*]
Contrib Biol Lab Sci Soc China Bot Ser ... Contributions. Biological Laboratory. Science Society of China. Botanical Series [*A publication*]
Contrib Biol Lab Sci Soc China Zool Ser ... Contributions. Biological Laboratory. Science Society of China. Zoological Series [*A publication*]
Contrib Bot ... Contributii Botanice [*A publication*]
Contrib Boyce Thompson Inst ... Contributions. Boyce Thompson Institute for Plant Research [*A publication*]
Contrib Can Biol Fish ... Contributions to Canadian Biology and Fisheries [*A publication*]
Contrib Cent Res Inst Agric (Bogor) ... Contributions. Central Research Institute for Agriculture (Bogor) [*A publication*]
Contrib Cent Res Inst Food Crops ... Contributions. Central Research Institute for Food Crops [*A publication*]
Contrib Centro Linceo Interdisc Sci Mat Appl ... Contributi. Centro Lindeo Interdisciplinare di Scienze Matematiche e loro Applicazioni [*Rome*] [*A publication*]
Contrib Cient Fac Cienc Exactas Nat Univ B Aires Ser Bot ... Contribuciones Cientificas. Facultad de Ciencias Exactas y Naturales. Universidad de Buenos Aires. Serie Botanica [*A publication*]
Contrib Cient Fac Cienc Exactas Nat Univ B Aires Ser Geol ... Contribuciones Cientificas. Facultad de Ciencias Exactas y Naturales. Universidad de Buenos Aires. Serie Geologia [*A publication*]
Contrib Cient Fac Cienc Exactas Nat Univ B Aires Ser Quim ... Contribuciones Cientificas. Facultad de Ciencias Exactas y Naturales. Universidad de Buenos Aires. Serie Quimica [*A publication*]
Contrib Cient Fac Cienc Exactas Nat Univ B Aires Ser Zool ... Contribuciones Cientificas. Facultad de Ciencias Exactas y Naturales. Universidad de Buenos Aires. Serie Zoologia [*A publication*]
Contrib Cient Univ Buenos Aires Fac Cienc Exactas Nat Ser C ... Contribuciones Cientificas. Facultad de Ciencias Exactas y Naturales. Universidad de Buenos Aires. Serie C. Quimica [*A publication*]
Contrib Curr Res Geophys ... Contributions to Current Research in Geophysics [*A publication*]
Contrib Cushman Found Foraminiferal Res ... Contributions. Cushman Foundation for Foraminiferal Research [*A publication*]
Contrib Dan Pharmacopoeia Comm ... Contributions. Danish Pharmacopoeia Commission [*A publication*]
Contrib Dep Biol Univ Laval (Que) ... Contributions. Departement de Biologie. Universite Laval (Quebec) [*A publication*]
Contrib Dep Geol Mineral Niigata Univ ... Contributions. Department of Geology and Mineralogy. Niigata University [*A publication*]
Contrib Dep Limnol Acad Nat Sci Phila ... Contributions. Department of Limnology. Academy of Natural Sciences of Philadelphia [*A publication*]
Contrib Dudley Herb ... Contributions. Dudley Herbarium [*A publication*]
Contrib Dudley Mus ... Contributions. Dudley Museum [*A publication*]
Contrib Econom Anal ... Contributions to Economic Analysis [*Amsterdam*] [*A publication*]
Contrib Epidemiol Biostat ... Contributions to Epidemiology and Biostatistics [*A publication*]
Contrib Estud Cienc Fis Mat Ser Mat Fis ... Contribucion al Estudio de las Ciencias Fisicas y Matematicas. Serie Matematico Fisica [*A publication*]

Contrib Estud Cienc Fis Mat Ser Tec ... Contribucion al Estudio de las Ciencias Fisicas y Matematicas. Serie Tecnica [*A publication*]

Contrib Estudo Antropol Port ... Contribuicoes para o Estudo da Antropologia Portuguesa [*A publication*]

Contrib Fac Sci Haile Selassie I Univ Ser C Zool ... Contributions. Faculty of Science. Haile Selassie I University. Series C. Zoology [*A publication*]

Contrib Fac Sci Univ Coll Addis Ababa (Ethiop) Ser C (Zool) ... Contributions. Faculty of Science. University College of Addis Ababa (Ethiopia). Series C (Zoology) [*A publication*]

Contrib Gen Agric Res Stn (Bogor) ... Contributions. General Agricultural Research Station (Bogor) [*A publication*]

Contrib Geol ... Contributions to Geology [*A publication*]

Contrib Geol Spec Pap ... Contributions to Geology. Special Paper [*A publication*]

Contrib Geol Univ Wyo ... Contributions to Geology. University of Wyoming [*A publication*]

Contrib Geophys Inst Kyoto Univ ... Contributions. Geophysical Institute. Kyoto University [*A publication*]

Contrib Geophys Inst Slovak Acad Sci ... Contributions. Geophysical Institute. Slovak Academy of Sciences [*A publication*]

Contrib Geophys Inst Slovak Acad Sci Ser Meteorol ... Contributions. Geophysical Institute. Slovak Academy of Sciences. Series of Meteorology [*A publication*]

Contrib Geophys Obs Haile Sellassie I Univer Ser A ... Contributions. Geophysical Observatory. Haile Sellassie I University. Series A [*A publication*]

Contrib Gray Herb Harv Univ ... Contributions. Gray Herbarium. Harvard University [*A publication*]

Contrib Gynecol Obstet ... Contributions to Gynecology and Obstetrics [*A publication*]

Contrib Herb Aust ... Contributions. Herbarium Australiense [*A publication*]

Contrib Hum Dev ... Contributions to Human Development [*A publication*]

Contrib Ind Sociol ... Contributions to Indian Sociology [*A publication*]

Contrib Inst Antart Argent ... Contribuciones. Instituto Antartico Argentino [*A publication*]

Contrib Inst Bot Univ Montreal ... Contributions. Institut de Botanique. Universite de Montreal [*A publication*]

Contrib Inst Chem Nat Acad Peiping ... Contributions. Institute of Chemistry. National Academy of Peiping [*A publication*]

Contrib Inst Geol Paleontol Tohoku Univ ... Contributions. Institute of Geology and Paleontology. Tohoku University [*A publication*]

Contrib Inst Low Temp Sci A ... Contributions. Institute of Low Temperature Science. Series A [*A publication*]

Contrib Inst Low Temp Sci Hokkaido Univ ... Contributions. Institute of Low Temperature Science. Hokkaido University [*A publication*]

Contrib Inst Low Temp Sci Hokkaido Univ B ... Contributions. Institute of Low Temperature Science. Hokkaido University. Series B [*A publication*]

Contrib Inst Low Temp Sci Hokkaido Univ Ser A ... Contributions. Institute of Low Temperature Science. Hokkaido University. Series A [*A publication*]

Contrib Inst Low Temp Sci Hokkaido Univ Ser B ... Contributions. Institute of Low Temperature Science. Hokkaido University. Series B [*A publication*]

Contrib Inst Low Temp Sci Ser A ... Contributions. Institute of Low Temperature Science. Series A [*A publication*]

Contrib Inst Phys Nat Acad Peiping ... Contributions. Institute of Physics. Natural Academy of Peiping [*A publication*]

Contrib Iowa Corn Res Inst ... Contributions. Iowa Corn Research Institute [*A publication*]

Contrib Istanbul Sci Clin ... Contributions d'Istanbul a la Science Clinique [*A publication*]

Contrib Ist Ric Agrar Milano ... Contributi. Istituto di Ricerche Agrarie Milano [*A publication*]

Contrib Lab Vertebr Biol Univ Mich ... Contributions. Laboratory of Vertebrate Biology. University of Michigan [*A publication*]

Contrib Lunar Sci Inst ... Contributions. Lunar Science Institute [*A publication*]

Contrib Mar Sci ... Contributions in Marine Science [*A publication*]

Contrib Med Hist ... Contributions in Medical History [*A publication*]

Contrib Med Psychol ... Contributions to Medical Psychology [*A publication*]

Contrib Meteorit Soc ... Contributions. Meteoritical Society [*A publication*]

Contrib Microbiol Immunol ... Contributions to Microbiology and Immunology [*A publication*]

Contrib Mineral Petrol ... Contributions to Mineralogy and Petrology [*A publication*]

Contrib Mineral & Petrol ... Contributions to Mineralogy and Petrology [*A publication*]

Contrib Mineral Petrol Beitr Mineral Petrol ... Contributions to Mineralogy and Petrology/Beitraege zur Mineralogie und Petrologie [*Berlin-Heidelberg-New York*] [*A publication*]

Contrib Mineral Petrology ... Contributions to Mineralogy and Petrology [*A publication*]

Contrib Mus Paleontol Univ Mich ... Contributions. Museum of Paleontology. University of Michigan [*A publication*]

Contrib Nat Res Inst Geol Acad Sin ... Contributions. National Research Institute of Geology. Academia Sinica [*A publication*]

Contrib Nepal Stud ... Contributions to Nepalese Studies [*A publication*]

Contrib Nephrol ... Contributions to Nephrology [*A publication*]

Contrib NSW Herb ... Contributions. New South Wales National Herbarium [*A publication*] (APTA)

Contrib NSW Natl Herb ... Contributions. New South Wales National Herbarium [*A publication*]

Contrib NSW Natl Herb Flora Ser ... Contributions. New South Wales National Herbarium. Flora Series [*A publication*]

Contrib Oncol ... Contributions to Oncology [*A publication*]

CONTRIBOR ... Contributor (ROG)

Contrib Paleolimnol Lake Biwa Jpn Pleistocene ... Contribution on the Paleolimnology of Lake Biwa and the Japanese Pleistocene [*A publication*]

Contrib Perkins Obs ... Contributions. Perkins Observatory [*A publication*]

Contrib Perkins Obs Ser 1 ... Contributions. Perkins Observatory. Series 1 [*A publication*]

Contrib Perkins Obs Ser 2 ... Contributions. Perkins Observatory. Series 2 [*A publication*]

Contrib Primatol ... Contributions to Primatology [*A publication*]

Contrib Qd Herb ... Contributions. Queensland Herbarium [*A publication*] (APTA)

Contrib Queensl Herb ... Contributions. Queensland Herbarium [*A publication*] (APTA)

Contrib Sci (Los Ang) ... Contributions in Science (Los Angeles) [*A publication*]

Contrib Sedimentology ... Contributions to Sedimentology [*A publication*]

Contrib Sens Physiol ... Contributions to Sensory Physiology [*A publication*]

Contrib Shanghai Inst Entomol ... Contributions. Shanghai Institute of Entomology [*A publication*]

Contrib Soc Res Meteorites ... Contributions. Society for Research on Meteorites [*A publication*]

Contrib Symp Immunol Ges Allerg Immunitaetsforsch ... Contributions. Symposium on Immunology. Gesellschaft fuer Allergie und Immunitaetsforschung [*A publication*]

Contrib Univ Mich Herb ... Contributions. University of Michigan Herbarium [*A publication*]

Contrib US Natl Herb ... Contributions. United States National Herbarium [*A publication*]

Contrib Vertebr Evol ... Contributions to Vertebrate Evolution [*A publication*]

Contrib Welder Wildl Found ... Contribution. Welder Wildlife Foundation [*A publication*]

Contrib Zool ... Contributions to Zoology [*A publication*]

Contr Inst Bot Univ Montreal ... Contributions. Institut de Botanique. Universite de Montreal [*A publication*]

Contr Inst For Prod Univ Wash ... Contribution. Institute of Forest Products. University of Washington. College of Forest Resources [*A publication*]

Contr Inst Met Belg ... Contributions. Institut Royal de Meteorologie de Belgique [*A publication*]

Contr Instr ... Control and Instrumentation [*A publication*]

Contr Instrum ... Control and Instrumentation [*A publication*]

Contr Jard Bot Rio J ... Contributions. Jardin Botanique de Rio De Janeiro [*A publication*]

Contr Jeff Phys Lab Harv ... Contributions. Jefferson Physical Laboratory of Harvard University [*A publication*]

CONTRL ... Control (KSC)

Contr Lab Vertebr Biol ... Contributions. Laboratory of Vertebrate Biology. University of Michigan [*A publication*]

Contr Lab Vertebr Genet Univ Mich ... Contributions. Laboratory of Vertebrate Genetics. University of Michigan [*A publication*]

Contrl Eng ... Control Engineering [*A publication*]

Contr Marine Sci ... Contributions in Marine Science [*A publication*]

Contr Mar S ... Contributions in Marine Science [*A publication*]

Contr Min P ... Contributions to Mineralogy and Petrology [*A publication*]

Contr Mus Geol ... Contributions. Museum of Geology. University of Michigan [*A publication*]

Contr Mus Paleont ... Contributions. Museum of Paleontology. University of Michigan [*A publication*]

Contr NSW Natn Herb ... Contributions. New South Wales National Herbarium [*A publication*] (APTA)

CONTRO .. Contracting Officer [*Also, CO, KO*] (KSC)

Control Abstr ... Control Abstracts [*A publication*]

Control Automat Process ... Control and Automation Process [*England*] [*A publication*]

Control Cibern & Autom ... Control Cibernetica y Automatizacion [*A publication*]

Control and Comput ... Control and Computers [*A publication*]

Control & Cybern ... Control and Cybernetics [*A publication*]

Control Cybern ... Control and Cybernetics [*A publication*]

Control Cybernet ... Control and Cybernetics [*Polish Academy of Sciences. Institute of Applied Cybernetics*] [*A publication*]

Control Eng ... Control Engineering [*A publication*]

Control Engng ... Control Engineering [*A publication*]

Control Feed Behav Biol Brain Protein-Calorie Malnutr ... Control of Feeding Behavior and Biology of the Brain in Protein-Calorie Malnutrition [*A publication*]

Control Instrum ... Control and Instrumentation [*A publication*]

Control and Instrum ... Control and Instrumentation [*A publication*]

Controlled Clin Trials ... Controlled Clinical Trials [*A publication*]

Control Power Syst Conf Expo Conf Rec ... Control of Power Systems Conference and Exposition. Conference Record [*A publication*]
Control Rev ... Control Review [*A publication*]
Control Ser VA Polytech Inst State Univ Coop Ext Serv ... Control Series. Virginia Polytechnic Institute and State University Cooperative Extension Service [*A publication*]
Control Sys ... Control Systems [*A publication*]
CONTROR ... Contractor (ROG)
Controv ... Controversiae [*of Seneca the Elder*] [*Classical studies*] (OCD)
CONTROV ... Controversy (ROG)
Contr Palaeont ... Contributions to Palaeontology [*A publication*]
Contr Prim ... Contributions to Primatology [*A publication*]
Contr Qd Herb ... Contributions. Queensland Herbarium [*A publication*] (APTA)
Contr Sc ... Contributions in Science [*A publication*]
Contr Sci ... Contributions in Science [*A publication*]
Contr Sci Prat Migl Conosc Util Legno ... Contributi Scientifico. Pratici per una Migliore Conoscenza ed Utilizzazione del Legno [*A publication*]
Contr Ser Bull Mass Agr Exp Sta ... Control Series Bulletin. Massachusetts Agricultural Experiment Station [*A publication*]
Contr Soc ... Contrat Social. Revue Historique et Critique des Faits et des Idees [*A publication*]
CONTRTN ... Concentration
Contr US Nat Herb ... Contributions. United States National Herbarium [*A publication*]
CONTRY .. Contrary (ROG)
CONTS ...... Contains (ROG)
Cont Shelf Res ... Continental Shelf Research [*A publication*]
Cont Sociol ... Contemporary Sociology [*A publication*]
CONTT ..... Contract [*Legal term*]
CONTU ..... National Commission on New Technological Uses of Copyrighted Works [*Terminated, 1978*] [*Library of Congress*]
CONTUND ... Contundere [*To Be Bruised, Pounded*] [*Pharmacy*] (ROG)
CONTUS ... Contusus [*Bruised*] [*Medicine*]
CONTW ... Continuous Window
CONTWR ... Conning Tower [*Naval architecture*]
CoNu .... Nucla Public Library, Nucla, CO [*Library symbol*] [*Library of Congress*] (LCLS)
CONUBS .. Compact Nuclear Brayton System
CONUS ..... Contiguous United States
CONUS ..... Continental United States
CONUSA .. CONUS [*Continental United States*] Army (MCD)
CONUSAMDW ... Continental United States and the Military District of Washington [*Refers to the numbered armies in that area*] (AABC)
CONUS INTEL ... Continental United States Intelligence [*Domestic intelligence project*] [*Army*]
CONUS OTH ... Continental United States Over-the-Horizon [*RADAR system*]
CONUS OTH-B ... Continental United States Over-the-Horizon-Backscatter [*RADAR system*]
CONV .... Convalescent [*Medicine*] (AFM)
CONV .... Convenient
CONV .... Convent
CONV .... Convention [*or Conventional*]
CONV .... Conversation
CONV .... Conversion
CONV .... Converted (DCTA)
CONV .... Converter (KSC)
CONV .... Convertible
CONV .... Conveyance [*Transportation*] (DCTA)
Conv .... Conveyancer [*or Conveyancing*] [*Legal term*] (DLA)
conv .... Conveyancer and Property Lawyer [*A publication*]
CONV .... Convict
Conv .... Convivium [*A publication*]
CONV .... Convocation
CONV .... Convoy (NVT)
CON 8VA ... Con Ottava [*With the Octave*] [*Music*] (ROG)
CONVAIR ... Consolidated-Vultee Aircraft Corp. [*Later, General Dynamics Corp.*]
CONVAL .. Convalescent [*Medicine*] (ROG)
CONVALESC ... Convalescent [*Medicine*] (ROG)
CONVATE ... Connection Reactivation
CONVCE .. Conveyance
CONVD ..... Conveyed (ROG)
CONVDD ... Converted Destroyer
CONVDF .. Convergence [*A publication*]
CONVEN .. Convenience
Conven Proc Agric Vet Chem Assoc Aust ... Convention Proceedings. Agricultural and Veterinary Chemicals Association of Australia [*A publication*] (APTA)
CONVERS ... Connection Conversion
CONVERS ... Conversation (ROG)
CONVERS ... Conversazione [*Conversation*] [*Italian*] (ROG)
CONVERSIONEX ... Contact Conversion Exercise [*Military*] (NVT)
CONVERSN ... Conversion (ROG)
CONVERT ... [*A*] programming language [*1965*] (CSR)
Conv Est ..... Convention of the Estates of Scotland [*A publication*] (DLA)

CONVEX .. Convoy Exercise [*Navy*] (NVT)
Convey .... Conveyancer [*Legal term*] (DLA)
Convey .... Conveyancer and Property Lawyer [*A publication*]
Convey NS ... Conveyancer and Property Lawyer. New Series [*A publication*]
Conv FJ ...... European Community Convention on the Jurisdiction of the Courts and Enforcement of Judgments in Civil and Commercial Matters [*27 Sept. 1968*] (DLA)
CONVG ..... Convergence (MSA)
CON-VID ... Concerned Broadcasters Using Inter-City Video Transmission Facilities (EA)
Conv IICA-ZN-ROCAP Bibliogr ... Convenio IICA-ZN-ROCAP [*Instituto Interamericano de Ciencias Agricolas-Zona Norte-Regional Organization for Central America and Panama*] Bibliografia [*A publication*]
Conv IICA-ZN-ROCAP Publ Misc ... Convenio IICA-ZN-ROCAP [*Instituto Interamericano de Ciencias Agricolas-Zona Norte-Regional Organization for Central America and Panama*] Publicacion Miscelanea [*A publication*]
Conv Int Acque Sotterranee Atti ... Convegno Internazionale sulle Acque Sotterranee. Atti. Ente Sviluppo Agricolo in Sicilia [*Palermo*] [*A publication*]
Conv Int Geom Diff ... Convegno Internazionale di Geometria Differenziale [*A publication*]
Conv Int Idrocarb ... Convegno Internazionale sugli Idrocarburi [*A publication*]
Conv Ital Sci Macromol Atti ... Convegno Italiano di Scienza delle Macromolecole. Atti [*A publication*]
CONVL ..... Conventional (AFM)
ConvLit ...... Convorbiri Literare [*A publication*]
CONVN ..... Convection (MSA)
CONVN ..... Convection (AABC)
Conv (NS) .. Conveyancer and Property Lawyer. New Series [*A publication*]
CONVOC ... Convocation
CONVOLV JAP ... Convolvulus Jalapa [*Jalap Plant*] [*Pharmacology*] (ROG)
Conv and Prop Law ... Conveyancer and Property Lawyer [*A publication*]
CONVR ..... Convector (MSA)
Conv Rev .... Conveyancing Review [*1957-63*] [*Scotland*] [*A publication*] (DLA)
Conv Sept Sap ... Convivium Septem Sapientium [*of Plutarch*] [*Classical studies*] (OCD)
CONVT ..... Convenient (ROG)
CONVT ..... Convert (AABC)
Convulsive Ther ... Convulsive Therapy [*A publication*]
Conv YB .... Conveyancers' Year Book [*1940-51*] [*A publication*] (DLA)
Con W .... Congress Weekly [*A publication*]
CONW .... Consumers Water Co. [*NASDAQ symbol*] (NQ)
CONZINE ... Convention Magazine [*Generic term for a publication covering science-fiction fans' conventions*]
COO .... Cessna Owners Organization (EA)
COO .... Chicago Operations Office [*Energy Research and Development Administration*]
COO .... Chief Operating Officer
COO .... Chief Ordnance Officer
COO .... Chief of Outpost [*CIA officer in charge of a field office*]
COO .... Chronicles of Oklahoma [*A publication*]
COO .... College of Optometry of Ontario
COO .... Colonial Oil & Gas Ltd. [*Toronto Stock Exchange symbol*]
COO .... Committee on Organization [*American Library Association*]
COO .... Concept of Operations (MCD)
COO .... Contract on Order (AFIT)
COO .... Cooney Tunnel [*Armidale*] [*Australia*] [*Seismograph station code, US Geological Survey*] (SEIS)
COO .... [*The*] Cooper Companies, Inc. [*NYSE symbol*] (SPSG)
COO .... Cornell University, Ithaca, NY [*OCLC symbol*] (OCLC)
COO .... Cost-of-Ownership
COO .... Cotonou [*Benin*] [*Airport symbol*] (OAG)
COO .... Council of Oriental Organizations
COO .... Country of Origin [*International trade*] (DCTA)
COO .... Covington, TN [*Location identifier*] [*FAA*] (FAAL)
CO1O .... Canto Primo [*First Soprano*] [*Music*]
Coo Agr T .. Cooke. Agricultural Tenancies [*3rd ed.*] [*1882*] [*A publication*] (DLA)
Coo & Al .... Cooke and Alcock's Irish King's Bench Reports [*1833-34*] [*A publication*] (DLA)
COOAL ..... Coordinated Activity List [*Navy*] (NVT)
COOBA ..... Chief Operating Officer of Business Affairs [*Proposed alternative to the hiring of a baseball commissioner*]
Coo Bankr ... Cooke's Bankrupt Laws [*A publication*] (DLA)
COOBSRON ... Commanding Officer, Observation Squadron
COOC .... Calgary Olympic Organizing Committee [*Calgary, AB*] (EAIO)
CoOc .... Oak Creek Public Library, Oak Creek, CO [*Library symbol*] [*Library of Congress*] (LCLS)
Coo Cop ..... Cooke's Enfranchisement of Copyholds [*2nd ed.*] [*1853*] [*A publication*] (DLA)
COOD .... Chronic Obstructive Outflow Disease [*Medicine*]
Coo Def ...... Cooke's Law of Defamation [*A publication*] (DLA)
Coode Leg Exp ... Coode's Legislative Expression [*A publication*] (DLA)
Coode Wr L ... Coode on the Written Law [*A publication*] (DLA)
COOFA ..... Cahiers Oceanographiques (France) [*A publication*]

Coo & H Tr ... Cooke and Harwood's Charitable Trusts Acts [*A publication*] (DLA)
Coo IA .... Cooke's Inclosure Acts [*A publication*] (DLA)
COOK .... Cook Transit R. R. [*AAR code*]
COOK .... Cookham [*England*]
Cook Adm ... Cooke's Admiralty Cases [*Quebec*] [*A publication*] (DLA)
Cook Adm ... Cook's Vice-Admiralty Reports [*Canada*] [*A publication*] (DLA)
Cook Corp ... Cook on Corporations [*A publication*] (DLA)
Cooke .... Cases under Sugden's Act [*1838*] [*England*] [*A publication*] (DLA)
Cooke .... Cooke. Act Book of the Ecclesiastical Court of Whalley [*A publication*] (DLA)
Cooke .... Cooke's Cases of Practice, English Common Pleas [*A publication*] (DLA)
Cooke .... Cooke's Tennessee Reports [*A publication*] (DLA)
Cooke & A ... Cooke and Alcock's Reports [*Ireland*] [*A publication*] (DLA)
Cooke Agr Hold ... Cooke on the Agricultural Holdings Act [*A publication*] (DLA)
Cooke Agr T ... Cooke. Agricultural Tenancies [*3rd ed.*] [*A publication*] (DLA)
Cooke & Al ... Cooke and Alcock's Reports [*Ireland*] [*A publication*] (DLA)
Cooke & Alc ... Cooke and Alcock's Reports [*Ireland*] [*A publication*] (DLA)
Cooke & Al (Ir) ... Cooke and Alcock's Irish King's Bench Reports [*1833-34*] [*A publication*] (DLA)
Cooke BL ... Cooke's Bankrupt Laws [*A publication*] (DLA)
Cooke Cop ... Cooke's Enfranchisement of Copyholds [*2nd ed.*] [*1853*] [*A publication*] (DLA)
Cooke CP ... Cooke's English Common Pleas Reports [*1706-47*] [*A publication*] (DLA)
Cooke Def .. Cooke's Law of Defamation [*A publication*] (DLA)
Cooke (Eng) ... Cooke's Cases of Practice [*125 English Reprint*] [*A publication*] (DLA)
Cooke & H Ch Tr ... Cooke and Harwood's Charitable Trusts Acts [*A publication*] (DLA)
Cooke High ... Cooke's New York Highway Laws [*A publication*] (DLA)
Cooke & IA .... Cooke's Inclosure Acts [*A publication*] (DLA)
Cooke Incl Acts ... Cooke's Inclosure Acts [*A publication*] (DLA)
Cooke Ins ... Cooke on Life Insurance [*A publication*] (DLA)
Cooke Pr Cas ... Cooke's Practice Reports, English Common Pleas [*A publication*] (DLA)
Cooke Pr Reg ... Cooke's Practical Register of the Common Pleas [*A publication*] (DLA)
Cooke's Rep ... Cooke's Tennessee Reports [*A publication*] (DLA)
Cooke (Tenn) ... Cooke's Tennessee Reports [*A publication*] (DLA)
COOKI ...... Coordinated Keysort Index (ADA)
Cook's Pen Code ... Cook's Penal Code [*New York*] [*A publication*] (DLA)
Cook Stock Stockh & Corp Law ... Cook on Stock, Stockholders, and General Corporation Law [*A publication*] (DLA)
Cook V Adm ... Cook's Vice-Admiralty Reports [*Canada*] [*A publication*] (DLA)
Cook Vice-Adm ... Cook's Vice-Admiralty Reports [*Canada*] [*A publication*] (DLA)
COOL .... Campus Outreach Opportunity League (EA)
COOL .... Checkout-Oriented Language [*Data processing*] (IEEE)
COOL .... Control-Oriented Language [*Data processing*] (IEEE)
COOL .... Coolant (MSA)
COOL .... Cooper Development Co. [*NASDAQ symbol*] (NQ)
Cool Black ... Cooley's Edition of Blackstone's Commentaries [*A publication*] (DLA)
COOLBM ... Coolia [*A publication*]
Cool Con Law ... Cooley's Constitutional Law [*A publication*] (DLA)
Cool Con Lim ... Cooley's Constitutional Limitations [*A publication*] (DLA)
Cooley .... Cooley's Reports [*5-12 Michigan*] [*A publication*] (DLA)
Cooley Bl Comm ... Cooley's Edition of Blackstone's Commentaries [*A publication*] (DLA)
Cooley Const Law ... Cooley's Constitutional Law [*A publication*] (DLA)
Cooley Const Lim ... Cooley on Constitutional Limitations [*A publication*] (DLA)
Cooley Const Limit ... Cooley on Constitutional Limitations [*A publication*] (DLA)
Cooley L Rev ... Cooley Law Review [*A publication*] (DLA)
Cooley Tax ... Cooley on Taxation [*A publication*] (DLA)
Cooley Tax'n ... Cooley on Taxation [*A publication*] (DLA)
COOLG ..... Cooling
Cool Mich Dig ... Cooley's Michigan Digest [*A publication*] (DLA)
Cool Tax .... Cooley on Taxation [*A publication*] (DLA)
Cool Torts .. Cooley on Torts [*A publication*] (DLA)
Coombe Lodge Rep ... Coombe Lodge Reports [*A publication*]
Coombe Lodge Repts ... Coombe Lodge Reports [*A publication*]
Coo Mort .... Coote on Mortgages [*A publication*] (DLA)
COOP .... Co-Op North [*A publication*]
COOP .... Communities Organization of People
COOP .... Contingency of Operations Planning (MCD)
COOP .... Continuity of Operations Plan [*Army*]
COOP .... Conventional Old Oil Prices
Coop .... Cooperation [*A publication*]
COOP .... Cooperative (AABC)
COOP .... Cooperative Degree Program [*Army*] (INF)
Coop .... [*Charles Purton*] Cooper's English Chancery Cases Tempore Brougham [*A publication*] (DLA)

Coop .... [*Charles Purton*] Cooper's English Chancery Cases Tempore Cottenham [*A publication*] (DLA)
Coop .... [*Charles Purton*] Cooper's English Chancery Practice Cases [*A publication*] (DLA)
Coop .... [*George*] Cooper's English Chancery Reports Tempore Eldon [*A publication*] (DLA)
Coop .... Cooper's Reports [*21-24 Florida*] [*A publication*] (DLA)
Coop .... Cooper's Tennessee Chancery Reports [*A publication*] (DLA)
COOP .... Customer On-Line Order Processing System
Coop Agr ...... Cooperation Agricole [*A publication*]
Coop Agric ... Cooperation Agricole [*A publication*]
Coop Agric Coop Fed Que ... Cooperateur Agricole la Cooperative Federee de Quebec [*A publication*]
Co-Op Bull Taiwan For Res Inst ... Co-Operative Bulletin. Taiwan Forestry Research Institute [*A publication*]
Coop Can ... Cooperation Canada [*A publication*]
Coop CC ..... [*Charles Purton*] Cooper's English Chancery Cases Tempore Cottenham [*A publication*] (DLA)
Coop Ch ..... Cooper's Tennessee Chancery Reports [*A publication*] (DLA)
Coop Ch (Eng) ... [*George*] Cooper's English Chancery Reports [*A publication*] (DLA)
Coop Chy ... Tennessee Chancery Reports (Cooper) [*A publication*] (DLA)
COOPCOMM ... Communications Facilities in Support of DA [*Department of the Army*] Continuity of Operations Plan (AABC)
Coop and Conflict ... Cooperation and Conflict [*A publication*]
Coop Consum ... Cooperative Consumer [*A publication*]
Coop Corp ... Cooperative Corporations (DLA)
Coop C P .... [*Charles Purton*] Cooper's Cases Tempore Cottenham [*1846-48*] [*47 English Reprint*] [*A publication*] (DLA)
Coop C & PR ... Cooper's Chancery and Practice Reporter [*Upper Canada*] [*A publication*] (DLA)
Coop y Desarrollo ... Cooperativesmo y Desarrollo [*A publication*]
Coop et Development ... Cooperation et Developpement [*A publication*]
Co-Op Dig ... Co-Operative Digest, United States Reports [*A publication*] (DLA)
Coop-Distrib-Consom ... Cooperation-Distribution-Consommation [*A publication*]
Co-Op Econ Insect Rep ... Cooperative Economic Insect Report [*Department of Agriculture*] [*A publication*]
Co-Op Electr Res ... Co-Operative Electrical Research [*A publication*]
Coop Eq Dig ... Cooper's Equity Digest [*A publication*] (DLA)
Coop Eq Pl ... Cooper's Equity Pleading [*A publication*] (DLA)
Cooper .... [*Charles Purton*] Cooper's English Chancery Cases Tempore Brougham [*A publication*] (DLA)
Cooper .... [*Charles Purton*] Cooper's English Chancery Cases Tempore Cottenham [*A publication*] (DLA)
Cooper .... [*Charles Purton*] Cooper's English Chancery Practice Cases [*A publication*] (DLA)
Cooper .... [*George*] Cooper's English Chancery Reports Tempore Eldon [*A publication*] (DLA)
Cooper .... Cooper's Florida Reports [*21-24 Florida*] [*A publication*] (DLA)
Cooper .... Cooper's Tennessee Chancery Reports [*A publication*] (DLA)
Cooper .... Upper Canada Chancery Chambers Reports [*1857-72*] [*A publication*] (DLA)
Cooper Ch ... Cooper's Tennessee Chancery Reports [*A publication*] (DLA)
Cooper Just Inst ... Cooper's Institutes of Justinian [*A publication*] (DLA)
Cooper Pr Cas (Eng) ... [*Charles Purton*] Cooper's English Chancery Practice Cases [*A publication*] (DLA)
Cooper T Brougham ... [*Charles Purton*] Cooper Tempore Brougham [*A publication*] (DLA)
Cooper T Cott ... [*Charles Purton*] Cooper Tempore Cottenham [*1846-48*] [*A publication*] (DLA)
Cooper T Eldon ... [*George*] Cooper's English Chancery Reports Tempore Eldon [*A publication*] (DLA)
Cooper Un Bull ... Cooper Union Bulletin. Engineering and Science Series [*A publication*]
Cooper Union Chron ... Cooper Union Museum Chronicle [*A publication*]
Coop Fr ...... Cooperateur de France [*A publication*]
COOPG ..... Cooperage [*Freight*]
Coop G .... [*George*] Cooper's English Chancery Reports [*A publication*] (DLA)
Coop Grain Quart ... Coop Grain Quarterly [*A publication*]
Coop Inf ..... Cooperation Information [*A publication*]
Coop Inf Int Labor Off ... Co-Operative Information. International Labor Office [*A publication*]
Coop Inst .... Cooper's Institutes of Justinian [*A publication*] (DLA)
Coop Internat ... Cooperation Internationale. Culturelle, Scientifique, Technique [*A publication*]
COOP-JCS ... Continuity of Operations Plan of the Joint Chiefs of Staff
Coop Judg ... Cooper's Judgment [*A publication*] (DLA)
COOPLAN ... Continuity of Operations Plan [*Navy*]
Coop Lib ..... Cooper's Law of Libel [*A publication*] (DLA)
Coop Manager & F ... Cooperative Manager and Farmer [*A publication*]
Coop Meat Trade D ... Cooperatives Meat Trade Digest [*A publication*] (APTA)
Coop Mediterr Energ Sol Rev Int Heliotech ... Cooperation Mediterraneenne pour l'Energie Solaire. Revue Internationale d'Heliotechnique [*France*] [*A publication*]
Coop Med Jur ... Cooper's Medical Jurisprudence [*A publication*] (DLA)
Co-Op News ... Co-Operative News [*A publication*]

Coop News ... Co-Operative News Digest [*A publication*]   (APTA)

Coop PC..... [*Charles Purton*] Cooper's English Chancery Practice Cases [*A publication*]   (DLA)

Coop Pr C .. [*Charles Purton*] Cooper's English Chancery Practice Cases [*A publication*]   (DLA)

Coop Pr Cas ... [*Charles Purton*] Cooper's English Chancery Practice Cases [*A publication*]   (DLA)

Coop Rec.... Cooper's Public Records of Great Britain [*A publication*]   (DLA)

Coop Resour Rep Ill State Water Survey Ill State Geol Surv ... Cooperative Resources Report. Illinois State Water Survey and Illinois State Geological Survey [*A publication*]

Coop Res Rep Int Counc Explor Sea Ser A ... Cooperative Research Report. International Council for the Exploration of the Sea. Series A [*A publication*]

Coop Res Rep Int Council Explor Sea ... Cooperative Research Report. International Council for the Exploration of the Sea [*A publication*]

CO-OPS .... Carbon Dioxide Observational Platform System [*NASA*]

Coop Sel Ca ... [*George*] Cooper's Select Cases Tempore Eldon, English Chancery [*A publication*]   (DLA)

Coop Sel EC ... Cooper's Select Early Cases [*Scotland*] [*A publication*]   (DLA)

Coop T Br .. [*Charles Purton*] Cooper's English Chancery Cases Tempore Brougham [*A publication*]   (DLA)

Coop T Brough ... [*Charles Purton*] Cooper's English Chancery Cases Tempore Brougham [*A publication*]   (DLA)

Coop T Brougham ... [*Charles Purton*] Cooper's English Chancery Cases Tempore Brougham [*A publication*]   (DLA)

Coop T Brougham (Eng) ... [*Charles Purton*] Cooper Tempore Brougham [*A publication*]   (DLA)

Coop T Cott ... [*Charles Purton*] Cooper's English Chancery Cases Tempore Cottenham [*A publication*]   (DLA)

Coop T Cott (Eng) ... [*Charles Purton*] Cooper Tempore Cottenham [*1846-48*] [*A publication*]   (DLA)

Coop Tech ... Cooperation Technique [*A publication*]   (APTA)

Coop T Eld ... [*George*] Cooper's English Chancery Reports Tempore Eldon [*A publication*]   (DLA)

Coop T Eld (Eng) ... [*George*] Cooper's English Chancery Reports Tempore Eldon [*A publication*]   (DLA)

Coop T Eldon ... [*George*] Cooper's Select Cases Tempore Eldon, English Chancery [*A publication*]   (DLA)

Coop Temp Brougham ... [*Charles Purton*] Cooper Tempore Brougham [*A publication*]   (DLA)

Coop Temp Cottenham ... [*Charles Purton*] Cooper Tempore Cottenham [*1846-48*] [*A publication*]   (DLA)

Coop Temp Eldon ... [*George*] Cooper's English Chancery Reports Tempore Eldon [*A publication*]   (DLA)

Coop Ten Chy ... Cooper's Tennessee Chancery Reports [*A publication*]   (DLA)

Coop Tenn Ch ... Cooper's Tennessee Chancery Reports [*A publication*]   (DLA)

COOR........ Coordinate

COORAUTH ... Coordinating Authority   (NATG)

COORD..... Coordinate [*or Coordination*]   (AFM)

CoOrd .... Ordway Public Library, Ordway, CO [*Library symbol*] [*Library of Congress*]   (LCLS)

Coord Ch Re ... Coordination Chemistry Reviews [*A publication*]

Coord Guidel Wildl Habitats US For Serv Calif Reg ... Coordination Guidelines for Wildlife Habitats. United States Forest Service. California Region [*A publication*]

COORDN ... Coordination

Coord Res Counc CRC Rep ... Coordinating Research Council. CRC Report [*A publication*]

COORS ..... Communications Outage Reporting System

COORS ...... Communications Outage Restoral Section [*ADC*]

COOS .... Chemical Orbit-to-Orbit Shuttle [*NASA*]

CoOs .... Olney Springs Public Library, Olney Springs, CO [*Library symbol*] [*Library of Congress*]   (LCLS)

COOT........ Oakland Tribune, Oakland, CA [*Library symbol*] [*Library of Congress*]   (LCLS)

CoOt .... Otis Public Library, Otis, CO [*Library symbol*] [*Library of Congress*]   (LCLS)

Coote .... Coote on Mortgages [*A publication*]   (DLA)

Coote Adm ... Coote's Admiralty Practice [*A publication*]   (DLA)

Coote Ecc Pr ... Coote's Ecclesiastical Court Practice [*A publication*]   (DLA)

Coote L & T ... Coote's Law of Landlord and Tenant [*A publication*]   (DLA)

Coote Mor ... Coote on Mortgages [*A publication*]   (DLA)

Coote Pro Pr ... Coote. Practice of the Court of Probate [*9th ed.*] [*1883*] [*A publication*]   (DLA)

Coote & Tr Pr Pr ... Coote. Practice of the Court of Probate, Edited by Tristram [*A publication*]   (DLA)

CoOu......... Ouray Public Library, Ouray, CO [*Library symbol*] [*Library of Congress*]   (LCLS)

COOUA..... Colorado Outdoors [*A publication*]

CoOv......... Ovid Public Library, Ovid, CO [*Library symbol*] [*Library of Congress*]   (LCLS)

COP .... Cam-Operated Plunger

COP .... Canada Olympic Park [*Calgary, AB*]

COP .... Canceled or Postponed

COP .... Capability Objective Package   (MCD)

COP .... Capillary Osmotic Pressure [*Physiology*]

COP .... Capsule Observation Panel [*Aerospace*]

COP .... Career Opportunities Program [*Office of Education*]   (EA)

COP .... Career Orientation Program [*LIMRA*]

COP .... Catalyst Oriented Packing [*Chemical engineering*]

COP .... Celescope Optical Package   (KSC)

COP .... Certificate of Posting [*Post Office receipt*] [*British*]

COP .... Change of Plaster [*Medicine*]

COP .... Changeover Panel   (NATG)

COP .... Changeover Point [*Aviation*]   (FAAC)

COP .... Chief of Police

COP .... City of Prineville Railway [*AAR code*]

COP .... Coast-Out Point   (NVT)

COP .... Code of Practice [*Telecommunications*]   (TEL)

COP .... Coefficient of Performance

COP .... Coherent Optical Processor

COP .... Colloidal Osmotic Pressure [*Analytical biochemistry*]

COP .... Colorado School of Mines, Golden, CO [*OCLC symbol*]   (OCLC)

COP .... Combat Organization Potential [*DoD*]

COP .... Combat Outpost

COP .... Combined Operations Personnel [*Navy*] [*British*]

COP .... Combined Opposition Parties [*Politics*]

COP .... Combined Opposition Party [*Pakistan*] [*Political party*]   (FEA)

COP .... Command Objective Plan [*Air Force*]

COP .... Command Observation Post   (AABC)

COP .... Command Operating Program [*Army*]   (AABC)

COP .... Commissary Operating Program [*Air Force*]   (AFM)

COP .... Commission on Practice [*American Occupational Therapy Association*]

COP .... Common On-Line Package [*Fujitsu Ltd.*] [*Japan*]

COP .... Communication Output Printer

COP .... Community-Oriented Police

COP .... Compact Periscope   (MCD)

COP .... Computer Optimization Package [*or Program*] [*General Electric Co.*]

COP .... Computerization of PAYE [*Pay as You Earn*] Taxation [*Inland Revenue*] [*British*]

COP .... Computermarkt [*A publication*]

COP .... Conjugable Oxidation Product [*Fuel technology*]

COP .... Consolidated Rio Plata Resources [*Vancouver Stock Exchange symbol*]

COP .... Constable on Patrol

COP .... Constant Offset Profile [*Seismology*]

COP .... Contingency Operations Plan   (MCD)

COP .... Continuity of Operations Plan [*Military*]

COP .... Continuous Operation Program [*Data processing*]   (MDG)

COP .... Control of Operation Programs

Cop............ Copacabana [*Record label*] [*Brazil*]

Cop............ Copeia [*A publication*]

COP .... Copenhagen [*Denmark*] [*Later, RSV*] [*Geomagnetic observatory code*]

COP .... Copenhagen [*Denmark*] [*Seismograph station code, US Geological Survey*]   (SEIS)

COP .... Copernicus   (ROG)

COP .... Copley Properties, Inc. [*AMEX symbol*]   (SPSG)

COP .... Copper [*Chemical symbol is Cu*]   (MSA)

cop............. Coptic [*MARC language code*] [*Library of Congress*]   (LCCP)

COP .... Coptic

COP .... Copulative

COP .... Copying of Parts   (ADA)

COP .... Copyrighted

COP .... Cost Operating Profits [*Accounting*]

COP .... Crisis-Oriented Program

COP .... Crude Oil Production [*Database*] [*Petroleum Intelligence Weekly*] [*Information service or system*]   (CRD)

COP .... Current Operating Procedure   (MCD)

COP .... Custom of the Port [*Shipping*]

COP .... Customer Order Processing   (BUR)

COP .... Customer-Orienting Program [*Data processing*]

COP .... Customer-Owned Property

COP .... Cyclophosphamide, Oncovin [*Vincristine*], Prednisone [*Also, CVP*] [*Antineoplastic drug regimen*]

CoP .... Pueblo Regional Library, Pueblo, CO [*Library symbol*] [*Library of Congress*]   (LCLS)

COPA .... Canadian Office Products Association

COPA .... Canadian Owners and Pilots Association

COPA .... Center Overage Pending Assignment   (MCD)

COPA .... Center for Overseas Program Analysis [*Department of State*]

COPA .... Comite des Organisations Professionnelles Agricoles de la CEE [*Committee of Professional Agricultural Organizations in the EEC*]

COPA .... Compania Panamena de Aviacion, SA [*Panamanian airline*]

COPA .... Control of Pollution Act [*1974*] [*British*]   (DCTA)

Copa......... Copacabana [*Record label*] [*Brazil*]

COPA .... Corporate Purchasing Agreements   (MCD)

COPA .... Council on Postsecondary Accreditation   (EA)

COPA .... Cyclophosphamide, Oncovin [*Vincristine*], Prednisone, Adriamycin [*Antineoplastic drug regimen*]

COPAAC... Continuity of Operations, Alaskan Air Command

COPAAR... Copeia [*A publication*]

COPA-BLEO ... Cyclophosphamide, Oncovin [*Vincristine*], Prednisone, Adriamycin, Bleomycin [*Antineoplastic drug regimen*]

COPAC ...... CCNU [*Lomustine*], Oncovin [*Vincristine*], Prednisone, Adriamycin, Cyclophosphamide [*Antineoplastic drug regimen*]

COPAC ...... Comite Commun pour la Promotion de l'Aide aux Cooperatives [*Joint Committee for the Promotion of Aid to Cooperatives*] [*UN Food and Agriculture Organization*]

COPAC ...... Continuous Operation Production Allocation and Control [*Data processing*]

COPACE ... Comite des Peches pour l'Atlantique Centre-Est [*Fishery Committee for Eastern Central Atlantic*] (EAIO)

COPAD ..... Cyclophosphamide, Oncovin [*Vincristine*], Prednisone, Doxorubicin [*Adriamycin*] [*Antineoplastic drug regimen*]

COPAFS ... Council of Professional Associations on Federal Statistics (EA)

COPAG ..... Collision Prevention Advisory Group [*US*]

COPAL ...... Cocoa Producers' Alliance

CO PAL ..... Counts Palatine [*Rulers of historical region now part of Germany*] (DLA)

CoPal .... Palisade Public Library, Palisade, CO [*Library symbol*] [*Library of Congress*] (LCLS)

CoPalJS ..... Palisade Junior-Senior High School, Palisade, CO [*Library symbol*] [*Library of Congress*] (LCLS)

CoPalTE .... Taylor Elementary School, Palisade, CO [*Library symbol*] [*Library of Congress*] (LCLS)

COPAN ..... Command Post Alerting Network [*Military*]

COPANT ... Comision Panamericana de Normas Tecnicas [*Pan American Standards Commission - PASC*] (EAIO)

CoPao .... Paonia Public Library, Paonia, CO [*Library symbol*] [*Library of Congress*] (LCLS)

COPAR ..... Computerized Operational Audit Routine

COPAR ...... Cooperative Preservation of Architectural Records (EA)

CoParD ..... Douglas County Public Library, Parker Branch, Parker, CO [*Library symbol*] [*Library of Congress*] (LCLS)

COPARS ... Contractor-Operated Parts Stores [*Military*]

COPART ... Counterpart

COPB .... Children's Organization for Peace and Brotherhood [*Defunct*] (EA)

COP/B .... Command Operating Program/Budget [*DoD*] (MCD)

COPB .... Cyclophosphamide, Oncovin [*Vincristine*], Prednisone, Bleomycin [*Antineoplastic drug regimen*]

COP-BLAM ... Cyclophosphamide, Oncovin [*Vincristine*], Prednisone, Bleomycin, Adriamycin, Matulane [*Procarbazine*] [*Antineoplastic drug regimen*]

COP-BLEO ... Cyclophosphamide [*or Chlorambucil*], Oncovin [*Vincristine*], Prednisone, Bleomycin [*Antineoplastic drug regimen*]

Co PC .... Coke's Pleas of the Crown [*or Third Institute*] [*A publication*] (DLA)

CoPC .... Colorado Fuel & Iron Co., Pueblo, CO [*Library symbol*] [*Library of Congress*] (LCLS)

COPC .... Combined Operational Planning Committee [*Royal Air Force and US 8th Air Force*] [*World War II*]

COPC .... Commanding Officer, Pacific Coast [*Navy*] [*Canada*]

COPC .... Community-Oriented Primary Care [*Medicine*]

COPCOM ... Controllers' Operations/Procedures Committee [*FAA*] (FAAC)

COPCON .. Comando de Operacoes do Continente [*Continental Operations Command*] [*Portugal*]

Cop Cop ..... Copinger. Copyright [*11th ed.*] [*1971*] [*A publication*] (DLA)

CoPCS .... Colorado State Hospital, Hospital Community Library, Pueblo, CO [*Library symbol*] [*Library of Congress*] (LCLS)

CoPCS-C ... Colorado State Hospital, Children's Center, Pueblo, CO [*Library symbol*] [*Library of Congress*] (LCLS)

CoPCS-M .. Colorado State Hospital, Professional Library, Pueblo, CO [*Library symbol*] [*Library of Congress*] (LCLS)

COPD .... Chronic Obstructive Pulmonary Disease [*Medicine*]

COPD .... Coppered

COPDAB ... Conflict and Peace Data Bank

COPDAF ... Continuity of Operations Plan, Department of the Air Force (AFM)

COPE .... Campership Outdoor Program of Education [*Federal antipoverty program*]

COPE .... Carbon Monoxide Pollution Experiment [*NASA/General Electric*]

COPE .... Career-Oriented Preparation for Employment [*Federal antipoverty program*]

COPE .... Chronic Obstructive Pulmonary Emphysema [*Medicine*]

COPE .... Claus Oxygen-Based Process Expansion [*Petroleum technology*]

COPE .... Committee for Original People's Entitlement [*Eskimo claim to Canadian land*]

COPE .... Committee on Parenthood Education [*Defunct*] (EA)

COPE .... Committee on Political Education [*AFL-CIO*] (EA)

COPE .... Communications-Oriented Peripheral [*or Processing*] Equipment

COPE .... Community-Oriented Police Enforcement

COPE .... Comprehensive Offender Program Effort [*Department of Labor*]

COPE .... Concepts of Postal Economics [*A series of newsletters of Mail Advertising Corp.*]

COPE .... Conference of Podiatry Executives (EA)

Cope .... Congress of the People [*South Africa*] [*Political party*] (PPW)

COPE .... Console Operator Proficiency Examination [*Computer Usage Co.*]

COPE .... Consortium of Publishers for Employment

Cope .... Cope's Reports [*63-72 California*] [*A publication*] (DLA)

COPE .... Coping Operations Preference Enquiry [*Personality development test*] [*Psychology*]

COPE .... Copolyester Elastomer [*Plastics technology*]

COPE .... Cost Progress Evaluation (MCD)

COPE .... Council on Population and Environment (EA)

COPE .... Council of Protocol Executives (EA)

COPE .... Currency Overprinting and Processing Equipment [*Bureau of Printing and Engraving*]

COPE .... Custodian of Postal Effects [*Military*] (AFM)

COPECIAL ... Comite Permanent des Congres Internationaux pour l'Apostolat des Laics [*Permanent Committee of International Congresses for the Lay Apostolate*] [*Italy*]

COPED ..... Cooperative Project for Educational Development [*Office of Education*]

COPEL ...... Spanish Prisoners' Trade Union (PD)

COPEMCI ... Conference Permanente Mediterraneenne pour la Cooperation Internationale [*Standing Mediterranean Conference for International Cooperation*] (EA)

Copenhagen Univ Mineralog Geol Mus Contr Mineralogy ... Copenhagen University. Mineralogical and Geological Museum. Contributions to Mineralogy [*A publication*]

COPEP ...... Committee on Public Engineering Policy [*National Academy of Engineering*]

COPER ...... Agencia Noticiosa Corporacion de Periodistas [*Press agency*] [*Chile*]

COPER ...... Conference on Psychoanalytic Education and Research

COPERS ... Commission Preparatoire Europeenne de Recherches Spatiales [*European Preparatory Commission for Space Research*]

COPES ...... Career Orientation Placement and Evaluation Survey [*Vocational guidance test*]

COPES ...... Committee on Program Evaluation and Support [*American Library Association*]

COPES ...... Community-Oriented Programs Environment Scale [*Psychosocial assessment test*]

COPES ...... Cost Planning and Evaluations System

COPESCAL ... Comision de Pesca Continental para America Latina [*Commission for Inland Fisheries of Latin America*] (EAIO)

CoPfAF ...... United States Air Force, Base Library, Peterson Field, CO [*Library symbol*] [*Library of Congress*] (LCLS)

COPH .... Congress of Organizations of the Physically Handicapped (EA)

COPHL ...... Conference of Public Health Laboratorians (EA)

COPHT ..... Canadian Organization of Public Housing Tenants

COPI .... Committee on Policy Implementation [*American Library Association*]

COPI .... Computer-Oriented Programmed Instruction (IEEE)

COPI .... Consolidated Products, Incorporated [*Indianapolis, IN*] [*NASDAQ symbol*] (NQ)

COPI .... Cooperative Projects with Industry [*National Research Council, Canada*]

COPIC ...... Computer Program Information Center (MCD)

COPICS .... Communications-Oriented Production Information and Control System [*IBM Corp.*]

COPICS .... Copyright Office Publication and Interactive Cataloging System [*Library of Congress*] [*Washington, DC*]

COPICS EDL ... Communications-Oriented Production Information and Control System Executive Data Link [*IBM Corp.*]

Cop Ind Pr ... Copinger's Index to Precedents [*A publication*] (DLA)

Co Pl .... Coke's Pleadings [*Sometimes published separately*] [*A publication*] (DLA)

COPL .... Combat Outpost Line

COPL .... Committee for Oil Pipe Lines [*Later, AOPL*]

CoPl .... Platteville Public Library, Platteville, CO [*Library symbol*] [*Library of Congress*] (LCLS)

CO PLAC .. County Placita [*British*] (ROG)

COPM .... Computer Operations Procedures Manual

COPMBU ... Computer Programs in Biomedicine [*A publication*]

COPNDZ .. Concepts in Pediatric Neurosurgery [*A publication*]

COPO .... Catholic One Parent Organization (EA)

COPO .... Chief, Office of Personnel Operations [*Army*]

COPO .... Council of Philatelic Organizations (EA)

COPOC ..... Committee of Publicly Owned Companies (EA)

COPOE ..... Commanding Officer, Port of Embarkation

COPOLCO ... Committee on Consumer Policy [*ISO*] (DS)

COPP .... CCNU [*Lomustine*], Oncovin [*Vincristine*], Procarbazine, Prednisone [*Antineoplastic drug regimen*]

COPP .... Change of Personal Particulars (ADA)

COPP .... Cobaltiprotoporphyrin [*Medicine*]

COPP .... Combined Operations Pilotage Party

COPP .... COSAL [*Coordinated Shipboard Allowance List*] Processing Point

COPP .... Crude Oil Processing Plant

COPP .... Cyclophosphamide, Oncovin [*Vincristine*], Procarbazine, Prednisone [*Antineoplastic drug regimen*]

COPPA ...... Coordinated Procurement Program Appraisal [*DoD*]

Copp All Bull ... Copper Alloy Bulletin [*A publication*]

Copp Ct Mar ... Copp's Manual for Courts-Martial [*A publication*] (DLA)

COPPE...... Council on Plastics and Packaging in the Environment (EA)

CoPPE....... Parkview Episcopal Hospital, Pueblo, CO [*Library symbol*] [*Library of Congress*] (LCLS)

COPPER ... Consolidation of Pay and Personnel Functions [*Military*]

Copper Abstr ... Copper Abstracts [*A publication*]

Copper Dev Assoc Tech Rep ... Copper Development Association. Technical Report [*A publication*]

Copper Dev Assoc Tech Sur ... Copper Development Association. Technical Survey [*A publication*]

Copper Development Assocn Information Sheet ... Copper Development Association. Information Sheet [*A publication*]

Copper Stud ... Copper Studies [*A publication*]

Copp Land ... Copp's Land Office Decisions [*A publication*] (DLA)

Copp LL...... Copp's Public Land Laws [*A publication*] (DLA)

Copp Min Dec ... Copp's United States Mining Decision [*A publication*] (DLA)

Copp Pub Land Laws ... Copp's Public Land Laws [*A publication*] (DLA)

Copp Pub LL ... Copp's Public Land Laws [*A publication*] (DLA)

COPPS...... Committee on Power Plant Siting [*National Academy of Engineering*]

CO-PPT..... Coprecipitation

COPR .... Centre for Overseas Pest Research [*England*]

COPR .... Computerized Outside Plant Records [*Telecommunications*] (TEL)

COPR .... Copper [*Chemical symbol is Cu*]

COPR .... Copper Range R. R. [*AAR code*]

COPR .... Copyright (TEL)

COPR .... Critical Officer Personnel Requirement [*Air Force*]

COPRA...... Comparative Postwar Recovery Analysis (MCD)

COPRAQ .. Cooperative Program of Research on Aquaculture [*UN Food and Agriculture Organization*]

COPREC ... Command Post Record Capability [*Military*]

COPRED... Consortium on Peace Research, Education, and Development (EA)

COPRED-SPN ... COPRED Students Peace Network [*Later, COPRED-SPWG*] (EA)

COPRED-SPWG ... COPRED [*Consortium on Peace Research, Education, and Development*] Students Peace Working Group (EA)

COPREX... Coprecipitation X-Ray Fluorescence Spectroscopy

COPRL...... Command Operations Priority Requirements List [*Air Force*] (AFM)

COPRO ..... Co-Production

COPRO ..... Coproporphyrin [*Also, CP*] [*Clinical chemistry*]

CoPs........... Archuleta County Public Library, Pagosa Springs, CO [*Library symbol*] [*Library of Congress*] (LCLS)

COPS........ California Occupational Preference Survey

COPS........ Canadian Operating Statistics [*Database*] [*Statistics Canada*] [*Information service or system*] (CRD)

COPS........ Catalytic Optimum Profit-Sharing

COPS........ Centre of Policy Studies [*Australia*]

COPS........ Chrysler Optical Processing Scanner

COPS........ Circuit Order Preparation [*or Processing*] System [*AT & T*]

COPS........ Coherent Optical Processing System

COPS........ College of Osteopathic Physicians and Surgeons

COPS........ Computer-Oriented Partial Sum (NVT)

COPS........ Computerized Officer Planning System [*Navy*] (NVT)

COPS........ Contingency Operations Plans Report (NVT)

COPS........ Conversion of Production System [*Engineering Index, Inc.*]

COPS........ Council on Postal Suppression

COPS........ Council on Professional Standards in Speech-Language Pathology and Audiology (EA)

COPS........ Current Operations

COPS........ Customer Order Processing System

CoPS.......... Southern Colorado State College, Pueblo, CO [*Library symbol*] [*Library of Congress*] (LCLS)

COPS-A..... Chief of Operations - Army [*Australia*]

COPSCAULD ... Council of Pennsylvania State College and University Library Directors [*Library network*]

COPSI....... Council of Profit Sharing Industries [*Later, PSCA*] (EA)

COPSS...... Committee of Presidents of Statistical Societies (EA)

CoPStMH ... Saint Mary Corwin Hospital, Pueblo, CO [*Library symbol*] [*Library of Congress*] (LCLS)

CoPT.......... Colorado State Home and Training School, Residents' Library, Pueblo, CO [*Library symbol*] [*Library of Congress*] (LCLS)

COPT .... Completed Procedure Turn [*Aviation*] (FAAC)

COPT .... Coptic

COPT .... Copyright

COPT .... Counterpart (ROG)

COPT .... Counterpoint [*Music*] (ROG)

Coptic Ch R ... Coptic Church Review [*A publication*]

Coptic Stu .. Coptic Studies [*A publication*]

Cop Tit D .. Copinger on Title Deeds [*A publication*] (DLA)

CoPTP .... Coalition of Publicly Traded Partnerships (EA)

CO-PTR ... Co-Partner (ROG)

COPTRAN ... Communication Optimization Program Translator [*NASA*]

CoPTS .... Colorado State Home and Training School, Staff Library, Pueblo, CO [*Library symbol*] [*Library of Congress*] (LCLS)

COPUL...... Copulative (ROG)

COPUOS... United Nations Committee on the Peaceful Uses of Outer Space (EA)

COPUS...... National Coalition of Independent College and University Students [*Acronym represents organization's former name*] (EA)

COPWE..... Commission for Organizing the Party of the Working People of Ethiopia (PD)

COPY .... Copyright (DLA)

COPY .... Copytele, Inc. [*NASDAQ symbol*] (NQ)

COPYA...... Comprehensive Psychiatry [*A publication*]

COPYAV... Comprehensive Psychiatry [*A publication*]

Copy Bull ... Copyright Bulletin [*A publication*] (DLA)

Copy Dec... Copyright Decisions [*A publication*] (DLA)

COPYLIB ... Copy Libraries

COPY & LIT P ... Copyright and Literary Property [*Legal term*] (DLA)

Copy Rep ... Copyright Reporter [*A publication*] (APTA)

Copyright Bul ... Copyright Bulletin [*A publication*]

Copyright Bull ... UNESCO Copyright Bulletin [*A publication*] (DLA)

Copyright L Dec CCH ... Copyright Law Decisions. Commerce Clearing House [*A publication*]

Copyright L Rep (CCH) ... Copyright Law Reporter (Commerce Clearing House) [*A publication*] (DLA)

Copyright L Sym (ASCAP) ... Copyright Law Symposium. American Society of Composers, Authors, and Publishers [*A publication*]

Copyright L Symp(ASCAP) ... Copyright Law Symposium. American Society of Composers, Authors, and Publishers [*A publication*] (DLA)

COPYS...... Collection Operation Potential Yield System [*IRS*]

Copy Soc Aust News ... Copyright Society of Australia. Newsletter [*A publication*] (APTA)

Copy Soc Bull ... Bulletin. Copyright Society of the USA [*A publication*]

COQ.......... Certificate of Qualification (KSC)

COQ.......... Cloquet, MN [*Location identifier*] [*FAA*] (FAAL)

COQ.......... Coastoro Resources [*Vancouver Stock Exchange symbol*]

CoQ........... Coenzyme Q [*Ubiquinone*] [*Also, Q, U, UQ*] [*Biochemistry*]

COQ.......... Conquista [*Brazil*] [*Airport symbol*] (OAG)

COQ.......... Coque [*Boil*] [*Pharmacy*]

COQ.......... Southeast Metropolitan Board of Cooperative Services, Processing Center, Littleton, CO [*OCLC symbol*] (OCLC)

COQ ad MED CONSUMPT ... Coque ad Medietatis Consumptionem [*Boil to the Consumption of Half*] [*Pharmacy*] (ROG)

Coq SA....... Coque Secundum Artem [*Boil According to Rule*] [*Pharmacy*]

COQ in SA ... Coque in Sufficiente Aquae [*Boil in Sufficient Water*] [*Pharmacy*] (ROG)

COR .... Business America [*A publication*]

COR .... Cardiac Output Recorder [*Physiology*]

COR .... Cargo Outturn Report (AABC)

COR .... Carrier-Operated Relay

COR .... Cash on Receipt

COR .... Center for Operations Research [*MIT*] (MCD)

COR .... Center of Rotation

COR .... Central Office of Record [*DoD*]

COR .... Ceska Odborova Rada [*Czech Trade Union Council*] (EY)

COR .... Chopper Mines Ltd. [*Vancouver Stock Exchange symbol*]

COR .... Circular of Requirements

CoR .... Club of Rome (EA)

Co R .... Code Reporter [*New York*] [*A publication*] (DLA)

COR .... Coherent Optical Receiver

COR .... Combat Operations Report

COR .... Cominco Resources International Ltd. [*Toronto Stock Exchange symbol*] [*Vancouver Stock Exchange symbol*]

COR .... Command Operationally Ready [*Navy*] (NVT)

COR .... Committee of Responsibility

COR .... Communications Operations Report [*Air Force*]

COR .... Concentric-Orbit Rendezvous [*NASA*]

COR .... Conditioned Orientation Reflex

COR .... Confederation of Regions [*Canada*] [*Political party*]

CoR .... Congo Red [*A dye*]

COR .... Contactor, Running

CoR .... Contemporary Review [*A publication*]

COR .... Continental Operations Range (MCD)

COR .... Contracting Officer's Representative (TEL)

COR .... Contractor

COR .... Contractors' Operational Representative

COR .... Cooperative Research [*in agriculture*]

COR .... Copper Oxide Rectifier

COR .... Coral (ROG)

COR .... Coram [*Before*] [*Latin*] (ROG)

COR .... Corcoran, CA [*Location identifier*] [*FAA*] (FAAL)

COR .... Cordoba [*Argentina*] [*Airport symbol*] (OAG)

Cor .... Corinthians [*New Testament book*]

Cor .... Coriolanus [*Shakespearean work*]

Cor .... Cornell Law Review [*A publication*]

COR .... Corner (KSC)

COR .... Cornet

cor .... Cornish [*MARC language code*] [*Library of Congress*] (LCCP)

COR .... Corno [*Cornet or Horn*] [*Music*] (ROG)

COR .... Corona [*A publication*]

COR .... Coroner (ROG)

COR .... Coroners' Rolls [*British*]

COR .... Coronet (ADA)

COR.......... Corporate Source [*Online database field identifier*]
COR.......... Corporation Law Review [*A publication*]
COR.......... Corpus [*Body*] [*Latin*]
COR.......... Correct　(ROG)
COR.......... Correction
COR.......... Correlative
COR.......... Correspond　(ROG)
COR.......... Correspondence
Cor .... Correspondent [*A publication*]
COR.......... Corridor　(AABC)
COR.......... Corrosive
COR.......... Corrupt
COR.......... Corsica　(ROG)
COR.......... Cortisone [*Endocrinology*]
COR.......... Corvallis [*Oregon*] [*Seismograph station code, US Geological Survey*]　(SEIS)
Cor .... Coryton's Reports [*Bengal*] [*A publication*]　(DLA)
COR.......... Councillor　(ROG)
COR.......... Crown Office Rules [*A publication*]　(DLA)
COR.......... Crystal Oil Corp. [*AMEX symbol*]　(SPSG)
COr .... Orange Free Public Library, Orange, CA [*Library symbol*] [*Library of Congress*]　(LCLS)
COR.......... Regis College, Denver, CO [*OCLC symbol*]　(OCLC)
CORA .... Coherent RADAR Array
CORA .... Commission on Religion in Appalachia　(EA)
CORA .... Conditional Response Analog Machine
CORA .... Conditioned Reflex Analog　(IEEE)
CorA .... Corona Australis [*Constellation*]
CoRa .... Rangely Public Library, Rangely, CO [*Library symbol*] [*Library of Congress*]　(LCLS)
CoRaC........ Colorado Northwestern Community College, Rangely, CO [*Library symbol*] [*Library of Congress*]　(LCLS)
CORAD ...... Correlation RADAR
CORAD6 .. Corax [*A publication*]
CORADCOM ... Communications Research and Development Command [*Fort Monmouth, NJ*] [*Army*]
CORAL...... Class-Oriented Ring-Associative Language [*Data processing*]
CORAL...... Coherent Optical RADAR Laboratory
CORAL...... Command Radio Link
CORAL...... Comparison of Recognition Algorithms [*US Postal Service*]
CORAL...... Computer On-Line Real-Time Applications Language [*Data processing*]　(IEEE)
CORAL...... Coordinated Regional Allowance List　(AFIT)
CORAL...... Correlation Radio Link　(MUGU)
CORAL...... Council on Religion and Law　(EA)
CORAL...... Council of Research and Academic Libraries [*Library network*]
Coran N ..... Coran Nobis and Allied Statutory Remedies [*A publication*]　(DLA)
CORAP...... Configuration Report and Accounting Program [*Military*]
CORAPRAN ... Cobelda RADAR Automatic Preflight Analyzer　(IEEE)
Coras.......... [*Johannes*] Corasius [*Deceased, 1572*] [*Authority cited in pre-1607 legal work*]　(DSA)
CORAS...... Corridor Assignment [*Aviation*]　(FAAC)
Corasi........ [*Johannes*] Corasi [*Deceased, 1572*] [*Authority cited in pre-1607 legal work*]　(DSA)
CORAT ..... Christian Organisations Research and Advisory Trust [*Church of England*]
CorB.......... Corona Borealis [*Constellation*]
Corb & D.... Corbett and Daniell's English Election Cases [*1819*] [*A publication*]　(DLA)
Corb & Dan ... Corbett and Daniell's English Election Cases [*1819*] [*A publication*]　(DLA)
CORBFUS ... Copy of Reply Be Furnished This Office [*Army*]　(AABC)
Cor-Bl Naturf-Ver Riga ... Correspondenzblatt. Naturforscher-Verein zu Riga [*A publication*]
Corbul .... [*Aurelius*] Corbulus [*Flourished, 16th century*] [*Authority cited in pre-1607 legal work*]　(DSA)
COrC .... Chapman College, Orange, CA [*Library symbol*] [*Library of Congress*]　(LCLS)
CORC .... Chief, Office of Reserve Components [*Army*]　(AABC)
CORC .... Control-Oriented Computer　(MCD)
CORC .... Conventional Ordnance Release Computer　(NG)
CORC .... Corcom, Inc. [*NASDAQ symbol*]　(NQ)
CORC .... Cornell Computing Language [*Data processing*]
CORCAPS ... Consolidated Reserve Components Reporting System　(MCD)
Cor Cas ...... American and English Corporation Cases [*A publication*]　(DLA)
C & OR Cas ... Carrow and Oliver's English Railway and Canal Cases [*A publication*]　(DLA)
CORCC ..... Canadian Overseas Military Railway Construction Corps [*World War I*]
COrCL........ Orange County Public Library, Orange, CA [*Library symbol*] [*Library of Congress*]　(LCLS)
CORCN ..... Coercion　(MSA)
CORCN ..... Correction Control Number [*Army*]
CORCO ..... Commonwealth Refining Company [*Puerto Rico*]
CORCOM ... Corps Communications　(MCD)
CORCOM ... Correcting Command　(MCD)
CORCOM ... Corrupt Commissioners [*Federal operation investigating illegal practices by Oklahoma's county commissioners*]
CORD........ Canadian On-Line Record Database

CORD........ Cascade Orificial Restrictive Device　(MCD)
CORD........ Chief of Ordnance [*Army*]
C of ORD .. Chief of Ordnance [*Army*]
CORD........ Chronic Obstructive Respiratory Disease [*Medicine*]
CORD........ Commanding Officer Reserve Divisions [*World War II*] [*Canada*]
CORD........ Commissioned Officer Residency Deferment [*Program of Public Health Service*]
CORD........ Computer with On-Line Remote Devices [*National Institute of Standards and Technology*]
CORD........ Congress on Research in Dance　(EA)
CORD........ Consortium Research Development [*Office of Education*]
CORD........ Coordinating of Research and Development [*Navy*]
CORD........ Cordis Corp. [*NASDAQ symbol*]　(NQ)
Cord .... Corduroy [*A publication*]
CORDASF ... Commissary Resale Division of the Army Stock Fund　(AABC)
CORDAT ... Coordinate Data Set
CORDIC.... Coordinate Rotation Digital Computer
CORDIVEM ... Corps Division Evaluation Model [*Army*]　(RDA)
Cord Mar Wom ... Cord on Legal and Equitable Rights of Married Women [*A publication*]　(DLA)
Cord Med... Cordoba Medica [*A publication*]
CORDO...... Chief Ordnance Officer
CORDPO...... Correlated RADAR Data Printout [*Electronics*]
CORDPO-SORD ... Correlated RADAR Data Printout - Separation of RADAR Data [*Electronics*]
CORDS...... Civil Operations Revolutionary Development Support [*Army*]　(AABC)
CORDS...... Civil Operations for Rural Development Support [*Army*]
CORDS...... Coherent-on-Receive Doppler System [*RADAR*]
CORDS...... Coordination of Record and Data Base System [*Telecommunications*]　(TEL)
CORDS...... Corduroy Trousers [*Slang*]　(DSUE)
Cord Sol ..... Cordery. Solicitors [*6th ed.*] [*1968*] [*A publication*]　(DLA)
CORE .... Canadian Offshore Resources Exposition　(ITD)
CO-RE .... Co-Respondent　(DSUE)
CORE .... Coherent-on-Receive
CORE .... Commission on Rehabilitation Education [*American Occupational Therapy Association*]
CORE .... Committee on Research Evaluation [*US*]
CORE .... Common Operational Research Equipment　(NASA)
CORE .... Common Register of Development Projects [*United Nations*]
CORE .... Competitive Operational Readiness Evaluation [*Air Force*]
CORE .... Computer-Oriented Reporting Efficiency　(AFM)
CORE .... Computer Research, Inc. [*NASDAQ symbol*]　(NQ)
CORE .... Congress of Racial Equality　(EA)
CORE .... Construction Review [*A publication*]
CORE .... Contingency Response Program [*DoD*]
CORE .... Cooperative Research Institute [*Defunct*]　(EA)
CORE .... Council of Reprographics Executives [*Inactive*]　(EA)
CoRe .... Redcliff Public Library, Redcliff, CO [*Library symbol*] [*Library of Congress*]　(LCLS)
COREBG..... Conditional Reflex [*A publication*]
CORECT... Citizens Organized to Restore an Effective Corporate Tax　(EA)
COREDITOR ... Computer Retrieval Editor [*Used to manage CORKIPER file family*]
Core J Obst/Gyn ... Core Journals in Obstetrics/Gynecology [*A publication*]
Core J Pediatr ... Core Journals in Pediatrics [*A publication*]
CORELAP ... Computerized Relationship Layout Planning
COREN ...... Corps of Engineers [*Army*]　(MUGU)
Co Rep .... Code Reporter [*New York*] [*A publication*]　(DLA)
Co Rep .... Coke's English King's Bench Reports [*1572-1616*] [*A publication*]　(DLA)
COREP...... Combined Operations Repair Organization [*For invasion of France*] [*World War II*]
COREP...... Combined Overload Repair Control　(MCD)
COREPER ... Commission de Representants Permanents [*Committee of Permanent Representatives*] [*EEC*]
COREPER ... European Communities Committee of Permanent Representatives　(DLA)
COREQ..... Confirming Requisition Follows [*Aviation*]　(FAAC)
CORESCEL ... Communications Requirements Systems Configuration and Equipment List　(NVT)
CORESTA ... Centre de Cooperation pour les Recherches Scientifiques Relatives au Tabac [*Cooperation Center for Scientific Research Relative to Tobacco*] [*Paris, France*]　(EA)
CORETECH ... Council on Research and Technology　(EA)
COREX...... Coordinated Electronic Countermeasures Exercise [*Military*]　(NVT)
CORF .... Committee on Radio Frequencies [*National Academy of Sciences*]
CORF .... Comprehensive Outpatient Rehabilitation Facility [*American Occupational Therapy Association*]
CoRf........... Rocky Ford Public Library, Rocky Ford, CO [*Library symbol*] [*Library of Congress*]　(LCLS)
CORFDL... Coral Reefs [*A publication*]
CORG......... Combat Operational Reserve Group　(AAG)
COrGH....... Orange County General Hospital, Orange, CA [*Library symbol*] [*Library of Congress*]　(LCLS)

CORgS....... Orange County California Genealogical Society, Orange, CA [Library symbol] [Library of Congress] (LCLS)

CORI......... Community and Organization Research Institute [Research center] (RCD)

CoRi.......... Rifle Public Library, Rifle, CO [Library symbol] [Library of Congress] (LCLS)

CoRicD...... Dolores County School District, Rico, CO [Library symbol] [Library of Congress] (LCLS)

COriK........ John F. Kennedy University, Orinda, CA [Library symbol] [Library of Congress] (LCLS)

Cor Int LJ .. Cornell International Law Journal [A publication]

CORIS........ Computerized Operating Room Information System

Cor Jud ...... Correspondances Judiciaires [Canada] [A publication] (DLA)

CORK....... Canadian Olympic Regatta at Kingston

CORK....... Corken International Corp. [NASDAQ symbol] (NQ)

CORKIPER ... Computer Retrieval of Kinetic Parameters of Electrode Reactions

CORL........ Collection Opportunity Requirements List (MCD)

CorL.......... Correo Literario [A publication]

COrL.......... Loyola Marymount University, Orange Campus, Orange, CA [Library symbol] [Library of Congress] (LCLS)

COrl.......... Orland Free Library, Orland, CA [Library symbol] [Library of Congress] (LCLS)

Cor LQ....... Cornell Law Quarterly [A publication]

Cor LR .... Cornell Law Review [A publication]

CORM....... Council on Optical Radiation Measurement

CORMES ... Communication Oriented Message System [IBM Corp.]

CORMOSEA ... Committee on Research Materials on Southeast Asia (EA)

Cormosea Newsl ... Cormosea Newsletter [A publication]

CORN........ Canadian Clearinghouse for Ongoing Research in Nursing [University of Alberta] (IID)

CORN....... Controlled Range Network (MCD)

CORN....... Cornell (ROG)

Corn .... Cornell University [Record label]

Corn .... [Petrus Philippus de] Cornia [Deceased, 1492] [Authority cited in pre-1607 legal work] (DSA)

CORN....... Cornish (ROG)

CORN....... Cornwall [County in England]

Corn .... Pro Cornelio de Maiestate [of Cicero] [Classical studies] (OCD)

Corn A....... Cornish Archaeology [A publication]

Corn Ann ... Corn Annual [A publication]

Corn Deeds ... Cornish on Purchase Deeds [A publication] (DLA)

Corn Dig ... Cornwell's Digest [A publication] (DLA)

CORNEA .. Consortium of Registered Nurses for Eye Acquisition [Later, ANET] (EA)

Cornell Ag Exp ... Cornell University. Agricultural Experiment Station. Publications [A publication]

Cornell Agric Waste Manage Conf Proc ... Cornell Agricultural Waste Management Conference. Proceedings [A publication]

Cornell Eng ... Cornell Engineer [A publication]

Cornell Ext Bull ... Cornell Extension Bulletin [A publication]

Cornell Ext Bull NY State Coll Agr Ext Serv ... Cornell Extension Bulletin. New York State College of Agriculture. Extension Service [A publication]

Cornell Feed Serv NY State Coll Agr Ext Serv ... Cornell Feed Service. New York State College of Agriculture. Extension Service [Cornell University] [A publication]

Cornell Hotel & Rest Adm Q ... Cornell Hotel and Restaurant Administration Quarterly [A publication]

Cornell Hotel & Restau Adm Q ... Cornell Hotel and Restaurant Administration Quarterly [A publication]

Cornell Hotel Restaur Adm Q ... Cornell Hotel and Restaurant Administration Quarterly [A publication]

Cornell Hotel and Restaurant Admin Q ... Cornell Hotel and Restaurant Administration Quarterly [A publication]

Cornell Hotel Restaurant Adm Q ... Cornell Hotel and Restaurant Administration Quarterly [A publication]

Cornell I J ... Cornell International Law Journal [A publication]

Cornell Internat Law J ... Cornell International Law Journal [A publication]

Cornell Internat LJ ... Cornell International Law Journal [A publication]

Cornell Int L J ... Cornell International Law Journal [A publication]

Cornell Intl LJ ... Cornell International Law Journal [A publication]

Cornell Int Symp Workshop Hydrogen Econ ... Cornell International Symposium and Workshop on the Hydrogen Economy [A publication]

Cornell J S ... Cornell Journal of Social Relations [A publication]

Cornell J Soc Rel ... Cornell Journal of Social Relations [A publication]

Cornell J Soc Relat ... Cornell Journal of Social Relations [A publication]

Cornell Law Q ... Cornell Law Quarterly [A publication]

Cornell Law R ... Cornell Law Review [A publication]

Cornell Law Rev ... Cornell Law Review [A publication]

Cornell LF ... Cornell Law Forum [A publication]

Cornell Lib J ... Cornell Library Journal [A publication]

Cornell LJ ... Cornell Law Journal [A publication] (DLA)

Cornell L Q ... Cornell Law Quarterly [A publication]

Cornell L R ... Cornell Law Review [A publication]

Cornell L Rev ... Cornell Law Review [A publication]

Cornell Med J ... Cornell Medical Journal [A publication]

Cornell Plant ... Cornell Plantations [A publication]

Cornell Plantat ... Cornell Plantations [A publication]

Cornell R.... Cornell Review [A publication]

Cornell Univ Dep Struc Eng Rep ... Cornell University. Department of Structural Engineering. Report [A publication]

Cornell Univ Lib Bull ... Cornell University Libraries. Bulletin [A publication]

Cornell Vet ... Cornell Veterinarian [A publication]

Cornell Vet Suppl ... Cornell Veterinarian. Supplement [A publication]

CORNET... Construction Information Online Retrieval Network [Information service or system] (EISS)

CORNET... Corporation Network [Telephone communications]

Cornh .... Cornhill Magazine [A publication]

CORNI ...... Columbus, Ohio Regional News Index [Grandview Heights Public Library] [Information service or system] (IID)

Corning Res ... Corning Research [A publication]

Corn Inst Eng Trans ... Cornish Institute of Engineers. Transactions [A publication]

Cornish Arch ... Cornish Archaeology [A publication]

Cornish Archaeol ... Cornish Archaeology [A publication]

Cornish Purch Deeds ... Cornish on Purchase Deeds [A publication] (DLA)

Corn J Soc Rel ... Cornell Journal of Social Relations [A publication]

Corn Mimeogr Tex Res Found ... Corn Mimeograph. Texas Research Foundation [A publication]

CORN NEP ... Cornelius Nepos [Historian, 31-14BC] (ROG)

Corn Pr ...... Corner's Queen's Bench Practice [A publication] (DLA)

Corn Pur D ... Cornish on Purchase Deeds [A publication] (DLA)

Corn Rem ... Cornish on Remainders [A publication] (DLA)

Co R NS..... Code Reports, New Series [New York] [A publication] (DLA)

Corn Us...... Cornish on Uses [A publication] (DLA)

CORNW.... Cornwall [County in England] (ROG)

Corn Wr ..... Corner's Forms of Writs on the Crown Side [A publication] (DLA)

Cornw Tab ... Cornwall's Table of Precedents [A publication] (DLA)

Co R (NY) ... Code Reporter [New York] [A publication] (DLA)

CORO........ Chicago Operations and Regional Office [Department of Energy] (GRD)

CORO........ Coronado National Memorial

COro .... Oroville Public Library, Oroville, CA [Library symbol] [Library of Congress] (LCLS)

COroB........ Butte County Library, Oroville, CA [Library symbol] [Library of Congress] (LCLS)

CORODIM ... Correlation of the Recognition of Degradation with Intelligibility Measurements [Telecommunications] (TEL)

COROIPAS ... Conferences on Research on International Peace and Security [Founded International Peace Research Association]

COROL ..... Corollary

COROLL... Corollary (ADA)

CORON..... Coroner (DLA)

CORONA ... Control Rod Analysis [Nuclear energy]

COROS ..... Collectors of Religion on Stamps (EA)

CORP .... Corporal

CORP .... Corporate (ROG)

CORP .... Corporation (AFM)

CORP .... Corpori [To the Body] [Pharmacy]

CORP .... Corpse (DSUE)

Corp .... Pennsylvania Corporation Reporter [A publication] (DLA)

CORPA...... Clinical Orthopaedics [A publication]

CORPAL.... Control Room Patching and Labeling

Corp & Ass'ns ... Corporations and Associations [A publication] (DLA)

Cor Pat....... Coryton on Patents [A publication] (DLA)

Corp Bulletin ... Bureau of Corporate Affairs. Bulletin [A publication]

Corp C........ Corporations Code [A publication] (DLA)

Corp Comment ... Corporate Commentary [A publication]

Corp Counsel Rev ... Corporate Counsel Review [A publication] (DLA)

Corp Counsel Rev J Corp Counsel Section St B Tex ... Corporate Counsel Review. Journal of the Corporate Counsel Section. State Bar of Texas [A publication]

Corp Dep.... Corporate Depositary (DLA)

Corp Fit and R ... Corporate Fitness and Recreation [A publication]

Corp Forms (P-H) ... Corporation Forms (Prentice-Hall, Inc.) [A publication]

Corp Guide ... Corporation Guide [Prentice-Hall, Inc.] [A publication] (DLA)

Corp Guide P-H ... Corporation Guide. Prentice-Hall [A publication]

Corp J .... Corporation Journal [A publication]

CORP JUR ... Corpus Juris [Body of Law] [Latin] (ROG)

Corp Jur Can ... Corpus Juris Canonici [The Body of the Canon Law] [Latin] [A publication] (DLA)

Corp Jur Civ ... Corpus Juris Civilis [The Body of the Civil Law] [Latin] [A publication] (DLA)

Corp Jur Germ ... Corpus Juris Germaniel [A publication] (DLA)

Corp Jus Canon ... Corpus Juris Canonici [The Body of the Canon Law] [Latin] [A publication] (DLA)

CORPL...... Corporal

Corp Law ... Journal of Comparative Corporate Law and Securities Regulation [A publication] (ILCA)

Cor-PLD.... Corynebacterium Pseudotuberculosis Phospholipase D [An enzyme]

Corp L Guide ... Corporation Law Guide [Commerce Clearing House] [A publication]

Corp LR ..... Corporation Law Review [A publication]

Corp L Rev ... Corporation Law Review [A publication]

Corp-Mgmt Ed (P-H) ... Corporation-Management Edition (Prentice-Hall, Inc.) [A publication] (DLA)

Corp Mgt Tax Conf ... Corporate Management Tax Conference [*A publication*]
Corp Month ... Corporate Monthly [*A publication*]
CORPN ..... Corporation
Corporate Rept ... Corporate Report [*A publication*]
CORPPIN ... Corporeal Pin [*Method of tuberculin and histoplasmin testing*] [*Medicine*]
Corp Prac Com ... Corporate Practice Commentator [*A publication*]
Corp Prac Comm ... Corporate Practice Commentator [*A publication*]
Corp Prac Comment ... Corporate Practice Commentator [*A publication*]
Corp Prac Rev ... Corporate Practice Review [*A publication*]   (DLA)
Corp Prac Ser (BNA) ... Corporate Practice Series (Bureau of National Affairs) [*A publication*]
Corp Pract Comment ... Corporate Practice Commentator [*A publication*]
Corp Pract Rev ... Corporate Practice Review [*A publication*]   (DLA)
Corp Reorg ... Corporate Reorganizations [*A publication*]   (DLA)
Corp Reorg & Am Bank Rev ... Corporate Reorganization and American Bankruptcy Review [*A publication*]   (DLA)
Corp Rep.... Pennsylvania Corporation Reporter [*A publication*]   (DLA)
Corp Rep (PA) ... Pennsylvania Corporation Reporter [*A publication*]   (DLA)
CORPS ...... Comprehensive Radiance Profile Synthesizer
CORPS ...... Customs Optical Reader Passport Systems [*A scanning device capable of reading the latest US passports*]
CORPSE ... Coordination of Recent and Projected System Efforts [*DoD*]
CORPSMAN ... Children's Organ Replacement Program Special Medical Alert Network
CorpTann... Corpus Tannaiticum   (BJA)
CorpTech... Corporate Technology Information Services, Inc. [*Information service or system*]   (IID)
Corp Tr ...... Corporate Trustee   (DLA)
CORPUS... CORPUS [*Corps of Reserve Priests United for Service*] - National Association Resigned/Married Priests   (EA)
Corpus Christi Geol Soc Bull ... Corpus Christi Geological Society. Bulletin [*A publication*]
CORR .... Chemicals on Reporting Rules Database [*Environmental Protection Agency*]
CORR .... Correct [*or Corrected or Correction*]   (AFM)
CORR .... Correlation   (KSC)
CORR .... Correlative
corr .... Correspond   (DLA)
CORR .... Correspondence   (AFM)
corr .... Correspondent   (DLA)
CORR .... Corresponding
corr .... Corrigenda   (BJA)
COR R ..... Corris Railway [*Wales*]
CORR .... Corrosion   (KSC)
CORR ..... Corrugated
CORR .... Corrupt
CORR .... Corruption   (ROG)
Corr .... Tribunal Correctionnel [*Court of First Instance in Penal Matters*] [*Belgium*]   (ILCA)
CORRAL... Computer-Oriented Retrieval of Auto Larcenists
Corr Blad ... Correspondentieblad van de Broederschap der Notarissen in Nederland [*A publication*]
Corr Brux... Jugement du Tribunal Correctionnel de Bruxelles [*A publication*]
CORRC ..... Coordinating Office for Regional Resource Centers
CORRE...... Coalition on Resource Recovery and the Environment   (EA)
CORRE...... Correlate   (MSA)
CORREC... Corrective
Correct Mag ... Corrections Magazine [*A publication*]
Correct Today ... Corrections Today [*A publication*]
CORREGATE ... Correctable Gate [*Data processing*]   (MDG)
Correio Agric ... Correio Agricola [*A publication*]
Correio Med Lisb ... O Correio Medico de Lisboa [*A publication*]
CORREL... Correlative
Corr Eng ... Corrosion Engineer [*A publication*]
CORRES.. Correspond   (MSA)
CORRESP ... Correspondence [*or Corresponding*]
Corresp Bl Schweiz Aerzte ... Correspondenz Blatt fuer Schweizer Aerzte [*A publication*]
Correspondance Munic ... Correspondance Municipale [*A publication*]
Correspondances Jud ... Correspondances Judiciaires [*Canada*] [*A publication*]   (DLA)
Corresp Orient Et ... Correspondance d'Orient. Etudes [*A publication*]
CORRF...... Coralta Resources Ltd. [*NASDAQ symbol*]   (NQ)
Corr Farm.. Corriere del Farmacista [*A publication*]
Corr Farmac ... Corriere del Farmacista [*A publication*]
Corr Fotogr ... Corriere Fotografico [*A publication*]
Corr Fotogr Sudam ... Correo Fotografico Sudamericano [*A publication*]
Corrie Herring Hooks Ser ... Corrie Herring Hooks Series [*A publication*]
Corr Mater Prot ... Corrosion and Material Protection [*A publication*]
Corr Met Finish (S Afr) ... Corrosion and Metal Finishing (South Africa) [*A publication*]
CORRO ..... Central Overseas Recruiting and Rotation Office [*Military*]
Corros Abstr ... Corrosion Abstracts [*A publication*]
Corros Anti-Corros ... Corrosion et Anti-Corrosion [*France*] [*A publication*]
Corros Australas ... Corrosion Australasia [*A publication*]   (APTA)
Corros Bull ... Corrosion Bulletin [*A publication*]
Corros Coat S Afr ... Corrosion and Coatings South Africa [*A publication*]
Corros Eng (Tokyo) ... Corrosion Engineering (Tokyo) [*A publication*]

Corrosion Prev Contr ... Corrosion Prevention and Control [*A publication*]
Corrosion Prev Control ... Corrosion Prevention and Control [*A publication*]
Corrosion Prevention ... Corrosion Prevention and Control [*A publication*]
Corrosion Sci ... Corrosion Science [*A publication*]
Corros Maint ... Corrosion and Maintenance [*India*] [*A publication*]
Corros Mar Environ ... Corrosion in Marine Environment [*A publication*]
Corros Mar Environ Int Sourceb ... Corrosion in Marine Environment. International Sourcebook [*A publication*]
Corros Pre Contr ... Corrosion Prevention and Control [*A publication*]
Corros Prev Control ... Corrosion Prevention and Control [*A publication*]
Corros Prot ... Corrosion y Proteccion [*A publication*]
Corros Prot Mater ... Corrosao e Proteccao de Materiais [*A publication*]
Corros Sci .. Corrosion Science [*A publication*]
Corros Technol ... Corrosion Technology [*England*] [*A publication*]
Corros Trait Prot Finition ... Corrosion, Traitements, Protection, Finition [*A publication*]
Corr Rom ... Correctio Romana [*Edition of the Decretals*] [*A publication*]   (DSA)
Corr Soc Ps ... Corrective and Social Psychiatry [*A publication*]
corrte.......... Corriente [*Current*] [*Spanish*]
CORRTEX ... Continuous Reflectometry for Radius Versus Time Experiment [*Nuclear testing verification*]
Corrugated Newsl ... Corrugated Newsletter [*A publication*]
CORRUP... Corrupted [*or Corruption*]
CORS........ Canadian Operational Research Society
CORS........ Cargo Outturn Reporting System
CORS........ Composite Operational Reporting System   (CAAL)
CORS........ Corsica
CORS........ Cronholm-Ottosson Rating Scale [*Psychopathology*]
COrS.......... Santiago Library System, Orange, CA [*Library symbol*] [*Library of Congress*]   (LCLS)
CORSA...... Corvair Society of America   (EA)
CORSA...... Cosmic Ray Satellite [*Japan*]
CORSAC... Council of Regional School Accrediting Commissions   (EA)
CORSAIR ... Computer-Oriented Reference System for Automatic Information Retrieval [*Forsvarets Forskningsamsalt*] [*Sweden*]
Corse .... [*Antonius*] Corsettus [*Flourished, 15th century*] [*Authority cited in pre-1607 legal work*]   (DSA)
Corse Hist ... Corse Historique. Etudes et Documents [*A publication*]
Corse Med ... Corse Medicale [*A publication*]
Corse Mediterr Med ... Corse Mediterranee Medicale [*A publication*]
Corsi Semin Chim ... Corsi e Seminari di Chimica. Consiglio Nazionale delle Ricerche e Fondazione "F. Giordani" [*A publication*]
CORS J ..... CORS [*Canadian Operational Research Society*] Journal [*A publication*]
COrSJH ..... Saint Joseph Hospital, Orange, CA [*Library symbol*] [*Library of Congress*]   (LCLS)
Cor Soc Cas ... Coroner's Society Cases [*England*] [*A publication*]   (DLA)
CORSPERS ... Committee on Remote Sensing Programs for Earth Resource Survey [*Formerly, COSPEAR*] [*National Academy of Sciences*]
CORST...... Council of Resident Summer Theatres   (EA)
C ORSTOM Ser Sci Hum ... Cahiers. ORSTOM [*Office de la Recherche Scientifique et Technique d'Outre-Mer*]. Serie Sciences Humaines [*A publication*]
CORT .... Certified Operating Room Technician
CORT .... Coratomic, Inc. [*NASDAQ symbol*]   (NQ)
CORT .... Cornet
CORT .... Cortex [*Bark*] [*Pharmacy*]
cort .... Cortical
CORT .... Corticosterone [*A hormone*]
cort .... Cortisone [*Endocrinology*]
CORT .... Council of Repertory Theatres [*British*]
CORTB...... Clinical Orthopaedics and Related Research [*A publication*]
CORTBR... Clinical Orthopaedics and Related Research [*A publication*]
CORT CINCHON ... Cortex Cinchonae [*Bark of Cinchona or Peruvian Bark*] [*Pharmacy*]   (ROG)
CORTDIV ... Escort Division
CORTDT... Contemporary Orthopaedics [*A publication*]
CORTEX... Communications-Oriented Real-Time Executive
CORTEX... Computer-Based Optimization Routines and Techniques for Effective X   (DIT)
Cortisone Invest ... Cortisone Investigator [*A publication*]
CORTRAIN ... Corps and Division Training Coordination Program [*DoD*]
CORTRON ... Escort Squadron
CORTS...... Canada-Ontario Rideau-Trent-Severn Study Committee
CORTS...... Conversion of Range Telemetry Systems   (MCD)
CORU........ Corrugated
Corv............ Corvus [*Constellation*]
Corvin El... Corvinus. Elementa Juris Civilis [*A publication*]   (DLA)
Corv Jus ..... Corvinus' Jus Feodale [*A publication*]   (DLA)
COR/WR... Corner Wear [*Deltiology*]
CORX .... Cortex Pharmaceuticals, Inc. [*NASDAQ symbol*]   (NQ)
Cory .... Coryton's Reports [*Calcutta*] [*A publication*]   (DLA)
Cory Acc .... Cory on Accounts [*A publication*]   (DLA)
Cory Cop .... Coryton on Copyrights [*A publication*]   (DLA)
Cory Pat..... Coryton on Patents [*A publication*]   (DLA)
Cory St R ... Coryton on Stage Rights [*A publication*]   (DLA)
Coryton ...... Coryton's Reports, Calcutta High Court [*A publication*]   (DLA)
COS .... Carry-On Oxygen System   (MCD)

COS .... Cash-on-Shipment
COS .... Cassette-Operated System (MSA)
COS .... Central Opera Service (EA)
COS .... Chamber of Shipping (DAS)
COS .... Change of Subscribers (TEL)
COS .... Changeover Switch (NATG)
COS .... Charity Organization Society [British]
COS .... Chief of Section
COS .... Chief of Staff [Military]
COS .... Chief of State
COS .... Chief of Station [CIA country team]
COS .... Cinema Organ Society [British]
COS .... Civilian Occupational Specialty
COS .... Class of Service [Telecommunications] (TEL)
COS .... Clinical Orthopedic Society (EA)
COS .... Colorado Springs [Colorado] [Airport symbol] (OAG)
COS .... Colorado Springs, CO [Location identifier] [FAA] (FAAL)
COS .... Commercial Office of Spain (EA)
COS .... Communication Operation Station
COS .... Communications Operating System
COS .... Communications Oriented Software
COS .... Companies (ROG)
COS .... Compatibility Operating System [Data processing]
COS .... Complete Operational System (MCD)
COS .... Conceptual Operational System
COS .... Concurrent Operating System [Sperry UNIVAC] [Data processing] (IEEE)
COS .... Condemned or Suppressed
COS .... Conservative Opportunity Society (EA)
COS .... Console Operating System (NASA)
COS .... Consul [Latin] (OCD)
COS .... Contactor, Starting
COS .... CONUS, Inc. [Jonesboro, AR] [FAA designator] (FAAC)
COS .... Cooper Ornithological Society (EA)
COS .... Copperweld Corp. [Formerly, Copperweld Steel Co.] [NYSE symbol] (SPSG)
COS .... Corporation for Open Systems (EA)
COS .... Cosiguina [Nicaragua] [Seismograph station code, US Geological Survey] (SEIS)
COS .... Cosine [Mathematics] (MCD)
Cos .... Cosmic Stories [A publication]
COS .... Cosmopolitan [A publication]
Cos .... Cosmos Science Fiction and Fantasy Magazine [A publication]
COS .... Cray Operating System [Data processing]
COS .... Customer's Other Service [Telecommunications] (TEL)
COS .... Cutoff Signal (KSC)
COS .... University of Southern Colorado, Pueblo, CO [OCLC symbol] (OCLC)
COSA .... Car Wash Owners and Suppliers Association (EA)
COSA .... Chairman of the Office of Savings Accounts
COSA .... Co-Dependents of Sexual Addicts [Acronym is now organization's official name] (EA)
COSA .... Combat Operational Support Aircraft (NVT)
CO SA ...... Come Sopra [As Above] [Music] (ROG)
COSA .... Corps Service Area [Army] (AABC)
COSA .... Cost of Sales Adjustment [Economics] (DCTA)
CoSa .... Salida Public Library, Salida, CO [Library symbol] [Library of Congress] (LCLS)
COSADL... Configuration Status Accounting Data List (MCD)
COSAG ..... Combined Steam and Gas [Propulsion] (MCD)
CoSag.......... Saguache County Public Library, Saguache, CO [Library symbol] [Library of Congress] (LCLS)
COSAGE... Combat Sample Generator [Military]
COSAL...... Consolidated Ships Allowance List
COSAL...... Coordinated Shipboard [or Shorebased] Allowance List [Navy]
COSAL...... Council of Spokane Area Libraries [Library network]
COSALFA ... Centro Panamericano de Fiebre Aftosa [South American Commission for the Control of Foot-and-Mouth Disease] (EAIO)
COSAM .... COBOL [Common Business-Oriented Language] Shared Access Method [Pertec]
COSAM .... Cosite Analysis Model [Data processing]
COSAMREG ... Consolidation of Supply and Maintenance Regulations [Military] (AABC)
COSAN .... Conversational Statistical Analysis (MCD)
COSAR...... Compression Scanning Array RADAR [Raytheon]
COSAT...... Committee to Support the Antitrust Laws (EA)
COSATI ... Committee on Scientific and Technical Information [Defunct] [Federal Council for Science and Technology]
COSAWR ... Committee on South African War Resistance (EAIO)
COSBA...... Computer Service and Bureaux Association [British]
COSBAL..... Coordinated Shipboard [or Shorebased] Allowance List [Navy]
COSBE...... Committee for Small Business Exports (EA)
COSC........ Canadian Chiefs of Staff Committee
Co-SC....... Colorado Supreme Court, Denver, CO [Library symbol] [Library of Congress] (LCLS)
COSC........ Combat Operations Specialist Course [Air Force] (AFM)
COSC........ Combined Operational Service Command
COSCA ..... Conference of State Court Administrators (EA)
COSCA...... Council of Senior Citizens Associations [Australia]
COSCAA... Council of State Community Affairs Agencies (EA)

Cos Chem... Cosmetic Chemists. Journal of the Society [A publication]
COSCL...... Common Operating System Control Language
COSCO ..... China Ocean Shipping Company
COSCOM ... Corps Support Command [Army] (AABC)
COSCTRACEN ... Commanding Officer, Submarine Chaser Training Center
COSD .... Combined Operations Supply Depot
COSD .... Command Supply Depot [British military] (DMA)
COSD .... Council of Organizations Serving the Deaf [Defunct] (EA)
COSDIF .... Cost Differential (MCD)
COSE........ Common Sense. Journal of Information for Environmentally Concerned Citizens. Kootenay Environmental Institute [Galena Bay, British Columbia] [A publication]
CoSe .... Security Public Library, Security, CO [Library symbol] [Library of Congress] (LCLS)
COSEC...... Coordinating Secretariat of National Unions of Students [in Africa]
COSEC...... Cosecant
COSECH... Cosecant, Hyperbolic [Mathematics] (ROG)
Co & Sec Law Journal ... Company and Securities Law Journal [Australia] [A publication]
COSECTBASE ... Commanding Officer, Section Base [Navy]
CoSed........ Sedgwick Public Library, Sedgwick, CO [Library symbol] [Library of Congress] (LCLS)
COSEMCO ... Comite des Semences du Marche Commun [Seed Committee of the Common Market]
COSEP ...... Committee on Special Educational Projects [Cornell University]
COSEPP.... Committee for Science, Engineering, and Public Policy
COSEPUP ... Committee for Science, Engineering, and Public Policy [Formerly, COSPUP] [National Academy of Sciences] [Washington, DC]
COSERV ... National Council for Community Services to International Visitors [Later, NCIV]
COSF........ Cosmetic & Fragrance Concepts, Inc. [Beltsville, MD] [NASDAQ symbol] (NQ)
COSH .... Committee on Shipping Hydrography [General Council of British Shipping] (DS)
COSH .... Cosine, Hyperbolic [Mathematics]
COSHB ..... Cahiers. ORSTOM [Office de la Recherche Scientifique et Technique d'Outre-Mer]. Hydrologie [A publication]
COSHD..... Committee for Oil Shale Development [Defunct] (EA)
CO/SHFT ... Countershaft [Automotive engineering]
COSHH..... Control of Substances Hazardous to Health [British]
COSHI ...... Clearinghouse for Occupational Safety and Health Information [HEW] (IID)
COSI......... Closeout System Installation (NASA)
COSI......... Committee on Scientific Information [Federal Council for Science and Technology]
COSI......... Cost of Service Indexing
CoSi .... Silverton Public Library, Silverton, CO [Library symbol] [Library of Congress] (LCLS)
CoSIDA ..... College Sports Information Directors of America (EA)
COSIE....... Commission on Software Issues in the 80s (EA)
COSIGN.... Coordination of Systems, Integrated Goals, and Networks [DoD]
COSI-KON ... Crimp-On Snap-In Contacts (MUGU)
COSIN....... Control Staff Instructions [Army] (MCD)
COSINE..... Committee on Computer Science in Electrical Engineering Education [Military]
Cos Intnl .... Cosmetics International [A publication]
COSIP .... College Science Improvement Program [National Science Foundation] [Defunct]
COSIRA .... Council for Small Industries in Rural Areas [British]
COSIRS..... Case-Oriented Studies Information Retrieval System [Later, TISCA] [Navy]
COSIS .... Care of Supplies in Storage [Military] (AABC)
CoSl .... Costilla County Library, San Luis, CO [Library symbol] [Library of Congress] (LCLS)
COSLA...... Chief Officers of State Library Agencies (EA)
COSLA...... Convention of Scottish Local Authorities (EAIO)
Cosm......... Cosmic Science Fiction [A publication]
COSMAL ... Coordinated Shore Maintenance Allowance List [Navy] (CAAL)
COSMAL ... Coordinated Shorebased Material Allowance List [Air Force] (AFIT)
COSMAT ... Committee on the Survey of Materials Science and Engineering [Obsolete] [National Academy of Sciences]
COSMD ... Combined Operations Signal Maintenance Depot
COSMED ... Chiefs of Staff, Mediterranean [Military]
COSMEP .. Combined Stratospheric Measuring Program [Army]
COSMEP .. Committee of Small Magazine Editors and Publishers [In association name COSMEP, The International Association of Independent Publishers] (EA)
Cosmet J .... Cosmetic Journal [A publication]
Cosmet News ... Cosmetic News [A publication]
Cosmet Perfum ... Cosmetics and Perfumery [A publication]
Cosmet Technol ... Cosmetic Technology [A publication]
Cosmet & Toiletries ... Cosmetics and Toiletries [A publication]
Cosmet Toiletry Fragrance Assoc Cosmet J ... Cosmetic, Toiletry, and Fragrance Association. Cosmetic Journal [A publication]
COSMIC... Chief of Staff, Military Intelligence Committee (NATG)

COSMIC ... Coherent Optical System of Modular Imaging Collectors
COSMIC ... Coherent Space Mirror Complex
COSMIC ... Common Systems Main Interconnecting [*Frame system*] [*Bell System*]
COSMIC ... Computer Software Management and Information Center [*University of Georgia*] [*NASA*] [*Research center*] (RCD)
Cosmic Electrodyn ... Cosmic Electrodynamics [*A publication*]
Cosmic Res ... Cosmic Research [*A publication*]
COSMIS ... Computer System for Medical Information Services (DIT)
COSMMOS ... Countersurge Missile Mortar System (MCD)
COSMO ... Combined Operations Signal Maintenance Officer
Cosmoceutical ... Cosmetic Pharmaceutical
COSMOG ... Cosmography
COSMON ... Component Open/Short Monitor
Cosmop ...... Cosmopolitan [*A publication*]
Cosmopol ... Cosmopolitan [*A publication*]
COSMOS ... Centralization of Supply Management Operations [*DoD*]
COSMOS ... Coast Survey Marine Observation System
COSMOS ... Colorado Springs Maintenance and Operations System [*Space Defense Center*]
COSMOS ... Committee on SONAR Model Standards [*Navy*]
COS/MOS ... Complementary Symmetry/Metal Oxide Semiconductor
COSMOS ... Computer-Oriented System for Management Order Synthesis [*IBM Corp.*] (BUR)
COSMOS ... Computer System for Main Frame Operations [*Bell System*]
COSMOS ... Console-Oriented Statistical Matrix Operator System [*Data processing*]
COSMOS ... Countersurge Mortar System (MCD)
COSNOSTRA ... Computer-Oriented System - Newly Organized Storage-to-Retrieval Apparatus (KSC)
COSO .... Combined Operations Signal Officer
CO SO ...... Come Sopra [*As Above*] [*Music*]
COSOD ..... Conference on Scientific Ocean Drilling [*JOIDES*]
COSOS ...... Conference on Self-Operating Systems [*Data processing*]
CoSp .... Baca County Public Library, Springfield, CO [*Library symbol*] [*Library of Congress*] (LCLS)
COSP........ Canada Oil Substitution Program
COSP........ Central Office Signaling Panel [*Telecommunications*] (TEL)
COSP........ Cosponsor
COSPA ...... Council of Student Personnel Associations in Higher Education [*Defunct*]
COSPAR ... Committee on Space Research [*of the International Council of Scientific Unions*] [*French*]
COSPAR Inf Bull ... COSPAR [*Committee on Space Research*] Information Bulletin [*Netherlands*] [*A publication*]
COSPAS.... Cooperation in Space [*USSR*]
COSPB ...... Comments on Solid State Physics [*A publication*]
COSPEAR ... Committee on Space Programs for Earth Observations (EGAO)
COSPEC ... Correlation Spectrometer
COSPLUM ... Crystalline Overthrust Structures on the Platform Localizing Unconventional Methane
COSPOIR ... Conhairle Natsiunta Spoirt [*National Sports Council*] (EAIO)
COSPUP ... Committee on Science and Public Policy [*Later, COSEPUP*] [*National Academy of Sciences*]
COSR........ Coastal Ocean Surface RADAR
COSR........ Cutoff Shear [*Tool*] (AAG)
COSRIMS ... Committee on Support of Research in the Mathematical Sciences [*National Academy of Sciences*]
COSRIVRON ... Coastal River Squadron [*Navy*] (NVT)
COSRO ..... Conical Scan-on-Receive Only (NG)
COSRRIB ... Combat Support Rearm and Refuel in Battalions [*Study*] [*Army Logistics Center*]
COSS........ Commander's Operations Security Support System (MCD)
COSS........ Consules [*Consuls*] [*Latin*]
COSS........ Contractor-Operated Storage Site (MCD)
COSS........ Conventional Ordnance Status System (MCD)
COSS........ Cosmetic Sciences [*NASDAQ symbol*] (NQ)
CoSs .... Werner Memorial Public Library, Steamboat Springs, CO [*Library symbol*] [*Library of Congress*] (LCLS)
COSSA ...... Consortium of Social Science Associations (EA)
COSSA ...... Containerized Shipment and Storage of Ammunition (MCD)
COSSA ...... CSIRO [*Commonwealth Scientific and Industrial Research Organisation*] Office for Space Science and Applications [*Australia*]
COSSAC ... Chief of Staff to Supreme Allied Commander [*Europe*] [*World War II*]
COSSACT ... Command Systems Support Activity
COSSMHO ... Coalition of Spanish Speaking Mental Health Organizations [*Later, NCHHHSO*] (EA)
COSSTA ... Computer for Special Small Tactical Application
COSSU ...... Coins on Stamps Unit [*American Topical Association*] (EA)
CoSsU........ United States International University, Colorado Alpine Campus, Steamboat Springs, CO [*Library symbol*] [*Library of Congress*] (LCLS)
COS SUFF ... Consul Suffectus [*Latin*] (OCD)
COST........ Coalition Opposed to Signal Theft (EA)
COST........ Coalition on Sensible Transport
COST........ Command Standard [*Program, Commissary*] (MCD)
COST........ Committee on Office Systems and Technology [*Stanford University*] [*Stanford, CA*] (CSR)

COST........ Committee of Singled-Out Taxpayers [*Later, American Council of Taxpayers*] (EA)
COST........ Computer Optimized Sheetmetal Technology [*Raytheon Co.*]
COST........ Congressional Office of Science and Technology
COST........ Contaminated Oil Settling Tank (AAG)
COST........ Continental Offshore Stratigraphic Test [*Offshore oil technology*]
COST........ Contingency Operations Selection Techniques (MCD)
COST........ Cost-Oriented Systems Technique
COST........ Costco Wholesale Corp. [*NASDAQ symbol*] (NQ)
COST........ Costume (ROG)
COST........ Council of Stock Theatres
CoSt .... Sterling Public Library, Sterling, CO [*Library symbol*] [*Library of Congress*] (LCLS)
COSTA ...... Cost Accounting Code [*NASA*] (NASA)
Cost Acc'g Stand Guide ... Cost Accounting Standards Guide [*Commerce Clearing House*] [*A publication*] (DLA)
Cost Accounting Stand Guide CCH ... Cost Accounting Standards Guide. Commerce Clearing House [*A publication*]
COSTALD ... Corresponding States Liquid Density [*Chemical engineering*]
CO-STAR ... Combat-Service to the Army (KSC)
COSTAR ... Combat Support of the Army (AFIT)
COSTAR ... Computer-Stored Ambulatory Record (MCD)
CO-STAR ... Covert Submarine Transmitter and Receiver (MCD)
Costa Rica B Fomento ... Costa Rica. Boletin de Fomento [*A publication*]
Costa Rica Centro de Estudios Sismologicos An ... Costa Rica. Centro de Estudios Sismologicos. Anales [*A publication*]
Costa Rica Inst Geog Informe Semestral Informe Trimestral ... Costa Rica. Instituto Geografico. Informe Semestral. Informe Trimestral [*A publication*]
Costa Rica Minist Agric Ganad Bol Misc ... Costa Rica. Ministerio de Agricultura y Ganaderia. Boletin Miscelaneo [*A publication*]
Costa Rica Minist Agric Ganad Bol Tec ... Costa Rica. Ministerio de Agricultura y Ganaderia. Boletin Tecnico [*A publication*]
Cost Bul ..... Cost Bulletin [*A publication*] (APTA)
Cost Bull .... Cost Bulletin [*A publication*]
COSTED ... Comite de la Science et de la Technologie dans les Pays en Voie de Developpement [*Committee on Science and Technology in Developing Countries*]
Cost Eng .... Cost Engineering [*A publication*]
COSTEP ... Commissioned Officer Student Training and Extern Program [*Public Health Service*]
COSTER ... Costermonger [*Fruit or vegetable seller*] [*British*] (DSUE)
Costerus Es ... Costerus. Essays in English and American Language and Literature. New Series [*A publication*]
COSTHA .. Conference on Safe Transportation of Hazardous Articles (EA)
COSTI ...... National Center of Scientific and Technological Information [*National Council for Research and Development*] [*Israel*] [*Also, CSTI*] (IID)
Cost and Man ... Cost and Management [*A publication*]
Cost Manage ... Cost and Management [*A publication*]
Cost & Mgt ... Cost and Management [*A publication*]
CoStN .... Northeastern Junior College of Colorado, Sterling, CO [*Library symbol*] [*Library of Congress*] (LCLS)
Cos & Toil ... Cosmetics and Toiletries [*A publication*]
COSTPRO ... Canadian Organization for the Simplification of Trade Procedures
CoStr.......... Stratton Public Library, Stratton, CO [*Library symbol*] [*Library of Congress*] (LCLS)
Costr Met... Costruzioni Metalliche [*A publication*]
COSTS ...... Committee on Sane Telephone Service
COSU .... Combined Operations Scout Unit
COSUD .... Colloids and Surfaces [*A publication*]
COSUD3 ... Colloids and Surfaces [*A publication*]
COSUR ..... Cooperative de Surveillance des Produits Exportes [*Export Products Supervisory Cooperative*] [*Cambodian*]
COSVN ..... Central Office of South Vietnam [*North Vietnamese high command in the South*]
COS(W)..... Chiefs of Staff, Washington [*Military*]
CoSw .... Swink Public Library, Swink, CO [*Library symbol*] [*Library of Congress*] (LCLS)
COSWA .... Committee on the Status of Women in Anthropology (EA)
COSWA .... Conference on Science and World Affairs
COSWAP ... Coaxial Switch and Alternator Panel
COSWL..... Committee on the Status of Women in Librarianship [*American Library Association*]
Cos Wld N ... Cosmetic World News [*A publication*]
COSY........ Checkout Operating System
COSY........ Compiler System
COSY........ Compressed Symbolic [*Programming language*] [*Control Data Corp.*]
COSY........ Correction System
COSY........ Correlated Spectroscopy
COT .... At the Coast [*Aviation code*] (FAAC)
COT .... Cathodal Opening Tetanus [*Physiology*]
COT .... Center for Office Technology (EA)
COT .... Central Office Terminal [*Telecommunications*] (TEL)
COT .... Checkout Time
COT .... Cholesteryl Oleate-Triglyceride [*Biochemistry*]
COT .... Clutter on Target (MCD)

COT .... Cockpit Orientation Trainer [*Aviation*]   (MCD)
COT .... Colombia Today [*A publication*]
COT .... Colony Overlay Test [*Microbiology*]
COT .... Colt Industries, Inc. [*NYSE symbol*]   (SPSG)
COT .... Combined Oil and Tanker Group   (NATG)
COT .... Commander of Troops [*for a parade or review*] [*Military*]
COT .... Commentaar op het Oude Testament [*A publication*]   (BJA)
COT .... Committee on Toxicity [*British*]
COT .... Conciliation Officer (Tribunal) [*British*]
COT .... Consecutive Oversea Tour [*Military*]   (AFM)
COT .... Consolidated Operability Test [*or Trial*]   (NG)
COT .... Consort Observation Time
COT .... Construction and Overhaul Testing
COT .... Continuity [*Telecommunications*]   (TEL)
COT .... Contralateral Optic Tectum [*Medicine*]
COT .... Coordinated Operability Test
COT .... Coscan Development Corp. [*Toronto Stock Exchange symbol*]
COT .... Cotangent [*Mathematics*]
COT .... Cotquean   (DSUE)
COT .... Cotter
COT .... Cotton   (MSA)
COT .... Cotulla, TX [*Location identifier*] [*FAA*]   (FAAL)
COT .... Counter-Obstacle Team [*Army*]   (INF)
COT .... Course Ordered Transmitter
COT .... Court   (DLA)
COT .... Cuneiform Inscriptions and the Old Testament   (BJA)
COT .... Current Operating Time
COT .... Customer-Operated Terminal [*Data processing*]
COT .... Customer-Oriented Terminal [*Data processing*]
COT .... Customers Own Transport   (DCTA)
COT .... Cyclooctatetraene [*or Cyclooctatetraenyl*] [*Organic chemistry*]
COT .... National Center for State Courts, Williamsburg, VA [*OCLC symbol*]   (OCLC)
CoT .... Trinidad Carnegie Public Library, Trinidad, CO [*Library symbol*] [*Library of Congress*]   (LCLS)
COTA .... Caribbean Organization of Tax Administrators   (EAIO)
COTA .... Certified Occupational Therapy Assistant
COTA .... Cinetheodolite Orientation Target Array
CoTA .... Colorado State Home for the Aged, Trinidad, CO [*Library symbol*] [*Library of Congress*]   (LCLS)
COTA .... Confirming Telephone [*or message*] Authority Of
COTA .... Cost and Training Effectiveness Analysis
Cot Abr ...... Cotton's Abridgment of the Records [*A publication*]   (DLA)
COTAC ..... Conference on Training Architects in Conservation [*London, England*]
Co-T/Agt ... Co-Transfer Agent   (DLA)
COTAL...... Confederacion de Organizaciones Turisticas de la America Latina [*Confederation of Tourist Organizations of Latin America*]
COTANCE ... Confederation of Tanners' Associations in the European Community [*Brussels, Belgium*]   (EAIO)
COTAR ..... Correction Tracking and Ranging Station
COTAR ..... Correlated Orientation Tracking and Ranging   (MSA)
COTAR ..... Correlation Tracking and Ranging [*System*] [*Satellite and missile tracking term*] [*RADAR*]
COTAR-AME ... Correlation Tracking and Ranging Angle Measuring Equipment [*RADAR*]
COTAR-DAS ... Correlation Tracking and Ranging Data Acquisition System [*RADAR*]
COTAR-DME ... Correlation Tracking and Ranging Data Measuring Equipment [*RADAR*]
COTAT...... Correlation Tracking and Triangulation
COTAWS ... Collision and Obstacle/Terrain Avoidance Warning System
COTC .... Canadian Officers Training Corps
COTC .... Canadian Overseas Telecommunications Corporation
COTC .... Commander, Fleet Operational Training Command
COTCLANT ... Commander, Fleet Operational Training Command, Atlantic Fleet
COTCO ..... Consolidation of Telecommunications Center on Oahu   (MCD)
COTCPAC ... Commander, Fleet Operational Training Command, Pacific Fleet
COTCPACSUBCOM ... Commander, Fleet Operational Training Command, Pacific Subordinate Command
COTDS...... Commanding Officer's Tactical Display System [*Navy*]   (MCD)
COTe .... Cathodal Opening Tetanus [*Physiology*]
COTE .... Comprehensive Occupational Therapy Evaluation [*Scale*]
COTED ..... Coal Technology [*A publication*]
COTEN & JT O ... Cotenancy and Joint Ownership [*Legal term*]   (DLA)
COTF........ Commander Operational Test and Evaluation Force [*Navy*]   (CAAL)
Cotg........... Cotgrave's Dictionary [*A publication*]   (ROG)
COTG........ Cottage Savings Association FA [*NASDAQ symbol*]   (NQ)
COTH........ Cotangent, Hyperbolic [*Mathematics*]
COTH........ Council of Teaching Hospitals   (EA)
COTHD3.... Comprehensive Therapy [*A publication*]
COTH Rep ... COTH [*Council of Teaching Hospitals*] Report [*A publication*]
Coth Stat.... Cothran's Annotated Statutes of Illinois [*A publication*]   (DLA)
CO-TIE...... Cooperation via Televised Instruction in Education [*Colorado State University*]
CoTJ .... Trinidad State Junior College, Trinidad, CO [*Library symbol*] [*Library of Congress*]   (LCLS)

COTM ...... Committee of Ten Million   (EA)
COTM .... Customer Owned and Telephone Company Maintained [*Telecommunications*]   (TEL)
COTNSD... Cottonseed [*Freight*]
COTOEP... Concepts in Toxicology [*A publication*]
Coton Fibres Trop ... Coton et Fibres Tropicales [*A publication*]
Coton Fibres Trop Bull Anal ... Coton et Fibres Tropicales. Bulletin Analytique [*A publication*]
Coton Fibres Trop Engl Ed ... Coton et Fibres Tropicales. English Edition [*A publication*]
Coton Fibr Trop ... Coton et Fibres Tropicales [*A publication*]
COTP .... Captain of the Port [*Coast Guard*]
COTP .... Commanding Officer's Tactical Plan [*or Plot*] [*Navy*]   (NG)
Co-Tr .... Co-Trustee   (DLA)
COTR .... Cockpit Orientation Trainer [*Aviation*]   (NG)
COTR .... Contracting Officers' Technical Representative [*Army*]
Cotr .... Cotgrave's Dictionary [*A publication*]   (ROG)
COTRAN .. COBOL [*Common Business-Oriented Language*]-to-COBOL Translator   (IEEE)
COTRAN .. Conversational Traffic Analysis   (MCD)
COTRANS ... Coordinated Transfer Application System [*For medical students*]
COTS......... Central Officers' Training School
COTS......... Checkout Test Set   (AAG)
COTS......... Commercial Off-the-Shelf [*Software*]
COTS......... Container Offloading and Transfer System   (MCD)
COTS......... Container Over-the-Shore
COTS......... Council on Thai Studies
COTSD2.... Clinical Otolaryngology and Allied Sciences [*A publication*]
COTSW..... Cotswold [*England*]
COTT .... Cottage   (ADA)
Cott .... Cottenham. Reports, Chancery [*1846-48*] [*England*] [*A publication*]   (DLA)
COTT .... Cottesloe [*England*]
COTT .... Cotton   (ROG)
Cott Impr Conf ... Cotton Improvement Conference [*A publication*]
Cott Mss .... Cottonian Manuscripts [*British Museum*] [*A publication*]   (DLA)
Cotton Cts ... Cotton Counts Its Customers. Quantity of Cotton Consumed in Final Uses in the United States [*A publication*]
Cotton Dev ... Cotton Development [*A publication*]
Cotton Dig ... Cotton Digest [*A publication*]
Cotton Grow Rev ... Cotton Growing Review [*A publication*]
Cotton Int Ed ... Cotton International Edition [*A publication*]
Cotton Res Corp Cotton Res Rep ... Cotton Research Corporation. Cotton Research Reports [*A publication*]
Cotton Res Corp Prog Rep Exp Stn ... Cotton Research Corporation. Progress Reports from Experiment Stations [*A publication*]
Cotton Res Inst Sindos Sci Bull New Ser ... Cotton Research Institute. Sindos Science Bulletin. New Series [*A publication*]
Cotton Rev ... Cotton. Monthly Review of the World Situation [*A publication*]
Cotton Wool Situat CWS US Dep Agric Econ Stat Serv ... Cotton and Wool Situation. CWS. United States Department of Agriculture. Economics and Statistics Service [*A publication*]
Cotton WS ... Cotton. World Statistics [*A publication*]
COTTS...... Cottages
COTU........ Central Organization of Trade Unions
COTUC ..... University of Toronto, Department of Chemistry, Toronto, ON, Canada [*Library symbol*] [*Library of Congress*]   (LCLS)
COTUG..... Combined Operations Tug Organization [*For invasion of France*] [*World War II*]
COTUNE .. COBOL [*Common Business-Oriented Language*] Tuner
COTY .... Car of the Year
COU.......... Cable Orderwire Unit   (MCD)
COU.......... Clip-On Unit   (DCTA)
CoU.......... Coalition Unity Party [*British*]
cou............. Colorado [*MARC country of publication code*] [*Library of Congress*]   (LCCP)
COU.......... Columbia [*Missouri*] [*Airport symbol*]   (OAG)
COU.......... Columbia, MO [*Location identifier*] [*FAA*]   (FAAL)
COU.......... Coralta Resources [*Vancouver Stock Exchange symbol*]
COU.......... Couch
COU.......... Country   (ROG)
Cou............. Couper's Justiciary Reports [*1868-85*] [*Scotland*] [*A publication*]   (DLA)
COU.......... Courrier des Pays de l'Est. Mensuel d'Informations Economiques [*A publication*]
COU.......... Courtaulds Ltd. [*AMEX symbol*]   (SPSG)
CoU.......... University of Colorado, Boulder, CO [*Library symbol*] [*Library of Congress*]   (LCLS)
COU.......... University of Colorado, Medical Center, Denver, CO [*OCLC symbol*]   (OCLC)
COUCH..... Couchant [*Heraldry*]   (ADA)
CoU-CS ..... University of Colorado at Colorado Springs, Colorado Springs, CO [*Library symbol*] [*Library of Congress*]   (LCLS)
CoU-DA..... University of Colorado at Denver, Auraria Libraries, Denver, CO [*Library symbol*] [*Library of Congress*]   (LCLS)
COUD-I..... Collectors of Unusual Data - International   (EA)
COUGH..... Congregation Organized by United Genial Hackers
CoU-GH .... University of Colorado, Colorado General Hospital, Denver, CO [*Library symbol*] [*Library of Congress*]   (LCLS)

CoU-IA ...... University of Colorado, Institute of Arctic and Alpine Research, World Data Center A for Glaciology, Boulder, CO [*Library symbol*] [*Library of Congress*]   (LCLS)
COUL .... Coulomb [*Unit of electric charge*]
Coul .... Coulometric
Coul & F Wat ... Coulston and Forbes on Waters [*6th ed.*] [*1952*] [*A publication*]   (DLA)
CoU-M .... University of Colorado, Medical Center, Denver, CO [*Library symbol*] [*Library of Congress*]   (LCLS)
COUN .... Council
COUN .... Counsel
COUNC ..... Council   (ROG)
Counc Agric Sci Technol Rep ... Council for Agricultural Science and Technology. Report [*A publication*]
Counc Brit Archaeol Annu Rep ... Council for British Archaeology. Annual Report [*A publication*]
Counc Brit Archaeol Res Rep ... Council for British Archaeology. Research Reports [*A publication*]
Counc Econ Prior Newsl ... Council on Economic Priorities. Newsletter [*A publication*]
Council Anthropol Educ Qu ... Council on Anthropology and Education. Quarterly [*A publication*]
Council Eur Inf Bull ... Council of Europe. Information Bulletin [*A publication*]
Council Legal Educ Prof Resp Newsl ... Council on Legal Education for Professional Responsibility. Newsletter [*A publication*]
Council Research M Education Bul ... Council for Research in Music Education. Bulletin [*A publication*]
Counc Notes ... Council Notes [*A publication*]
Counc Sci Indones Publ ... Council for Sciences of Indonesia. Publication [*A publication*]
COUNS ..... Counselor
Couns Ed Su ... Counselor Education and Supervision [*A publication*]
Counsel Ed & Sup ... Counselor Education and Supervision [*A publication*]
Counsel Educ & Superv ... Counselor Education and Supervision [*A publication*]
Counsel Val ... Counseling and Values [*A publication*]
Counsel & Values ... Counseling and Values [*A publication*]
Couns For .. Counsellor's Forum [*A publication*]
Couns Mag ... Counsellors' Magazine [*1796-98*] [*A publication*]   (DLA)
Couns Psych ... Counseling Psychologist [*A publication*]
COUNT .... Computer-Operated Universal Test
COUNTCL ... Counterclaim [*Legal term*]   (DLA)
Count Cts Ch ... County Courts Chronicle [*1847-1920*] [*England*] [*A publication*]   (DLA)
Count Cts Chron ... County Courts Chronicle [*1847-1920*] [*England*] [*A publication*]   (DLA)
COUNTERF ... Counterfeiting   (DLA)
Counterpt ... Counterpoint [*A publication*]
Countrmsrs ... Electronic, Electro-Optic, and Infrared Countermeasures [*A publication*]
Country ...... Country Kids [*A publication*]
Country Cal ... Country Calendar [*A publication*]
Country Gent ... Country Gentleman [*A publication*]
Country Hour J ... Country Hour Journal [*A publication*]   (APTA)
Countryman's Mag ... (Western Mail) Countryman's Magazine [*A publication*]   (APTA)
Countryside Comm J ... Countryside Commission. Journal [*A publication*]
Countryside M ... Countryside Magazine [*A publication*]
Countryside M ... Countryside Magazine and Suburban Life [*A publication*]
Country Traders R ... Country Traders' Review [*A publication*]   (APTA)
County Cc Cas ... County Council Cases [*Scotland*] [*A publication*]   (DLA)
County Co Cas ... County Council Cases [*Scotland*] [*A publication*]   (DLA)
County Court ... Pennsylvania County Court Reports [*A publication*]   (DLA)
County Court R ... Pennsylvania County Court Reports [*A publication*]   (DLA)
County Court Rep ... Pennsylvania County Court Reports [*A publication*]   (DLA)
County Cts & Bankr Cas ... County Courts and Bankruptcy Cases [*A publication*]   (DLA)
County Cts Chron ... County Courts Chronicle [*1847-1920*] [*England*] [*A publication*]   (DLA)
County Cts Rep ... County Courts Reports [*1860-1920*] [*England*] [*A publication*]   (DLA)
County Newsl ... County Newsletter [*A publication*]
County R .... County Reports [*A publication*]   (DLA)
COUP .... Chicken Ovalbumin Upstream Promoter [*Genetics*]
COUP .... Congress of Unrepresented People
Coup .... Couper's Justiciary Reports [*1868-85*] [*Scotland*] [*A publication*]   (DLA)
COUP .... Coupon   (ROG)
coup .... Coupon [*Coupon*] [*French*]
coup .... Coupure [*Denomination*] [*French*] [*Business term*]
Couper .... Couper's Justiciary Reports [*1868-85*] [*Scotland*] [*A publication*]   (DLA)
Coup Just ... Couper's Justiciary Reports [*1868-85*] [*Scotland*] [*A publication*]   (DLA)
COUPLE ... Communications-Oriented User Programming Language
COUP-TF ... Chicken Ovalbumin Upstream Promoter Transcription Factor [*Genetics*]
COUR .... Courant [*Of the Current Month*] [*French*]

COUR .... Courier
COUR .... Courier-Journal [*A publication*]
CoUr .... Uravan Public Library, Uravan, CO [*Library symbol*] [*Library of Congress*]   (LCLS)
COURA ..... Clinica Otorinolaringoiatrica [*A publication*]
COURAZ .. Clinica Otorinolaringoiatrica [*Catania*] [*A publication*]
Cour Forschungsinst Senckenb ... Courier Forschungsinstitut Senckenberg [*A publication*]
Courier Jl ... Courier-Journal [*A publication*]
Cour & Macl ... Courtnay and Maclean's Scotch Appeals [*6, 7 Wilson and Shaw*] [*A publication*]   (DLA)
Cour Mus France ... Courrier Musical de France [*A publication*]
Courr Apic ... Courrier Apicole [*A publication*]
Courr Centre Int Enfance ... Courrier. Centre International pour l'Enfance [*A publication*]
Courr Etabl Neu ... Courrier des Etablissements Neu [*France*] [*A publication*]
Courr Extr-Orient ... Courrier de l'Extreme-Orient [*A publication*]
Courrier ..... Courrier Revue Medico-Sociale de l'Enfance [*A publication*]
Courrier du CNRS ... Courrier du Centre National de la Recherche Scientifique [*A publication*]
Courrier M France ... Courrier Musical de France [*A publication*]
Courrier Pays Est ... Courrier des Pays de l'Est [*A publication*]
Courr Nat ... Courrier de la Nature [*A publication*]
Courr Norm ... Courrier de la Normalisation [*A publication*]
Courr Pays Est ... Courrier des Pays de l'Est [*A publication*]
Courr UNESCO ... Courrier. UNESCO [*A publication*]
Cours Doc Bil ... Cours et Documents de Biologie [*A publication*]
COURSEWRITER ... [*A*] programming language [*1965*]   (CSR)
Cours Perfect Pediatr Prat ... Cours de Perfectionnement en Pediatrie pour le Practicien [*A publication*]
Cours Perfect Soc Suisse Psychiatr ... Cours de Perfectionnement. Societe Suisse de Psychiatrie [*A publication*]
Court .... Bott's Poor Laws, by Court [*A publication*]   (DLA)
court .... Courtage [*Brokerage*] [*French*] [*Business term*]
Court Appeals ... Texas Court of Appeals Reports [*A publication*]   (DLA)
Court Cl ..... United States Court of Claims Reports [*A publication*]   (DLA)
Court J & Dist Ct Rec ... Court Journal and District Court Record [*A publication*]   (DLA)
Court & Macl ... Courtnay and Maclean's Scotch Appeals [*6, 7 Wilson and Shaw*] [*A publication*]   (DLA)
Court Man Jnl ... Court Management Journal [*A publication*]
Court Mgt J ... Court Management Journal [*A publication*]
Court Sess Ca ... Court of Session Cases [*Scotland*] [*A publication*]   (DLA)
COUS .... Charitable Organizations of the US [*A publication*]
COUS .... Cousin
COUS .... Cousins Properties, Inc. [*NASDAQ symbol*]   (NQ)
COUSNAB ... Commander, United States Naval Advanced Base [*Weser River, West Germany*]
COUSS ...... Commanding Officer, United States Ship
COUSSF(P) ... Commanding Officer, United States Special Forces (Provisional)   (CINC)
COuT .... Commentaar op het Oude Testament [*Kampen*] [*A publication*]   (BJA)
Cout .... Coutlee's Unreported Cases [*1875-1907*] [*Canada*] [*A publication*]   (DLA)
COUTA ..... Coal Utilization [*A publication*]
Cout Dig ..... Coutlee's Digest, Canada Supreme Court [*A publication*]   (DLA)
Coutlee .... Coutlee's Unreported Cases [*1875-1907*] [*Canada*] [*A publication*]   (DLA)
Coutlee Unrep (Can) ... Coutlee's Unreported Cases [*1875-1907*] [*Canada*] [*A publication*]   (DLA)
Cout de N ... Coutumes de Normandie [*A publication*]   (DLA)
Cout de P ... Coutumes de Paris [*A publication*]   (DLA)
Cout SC ...... Notes of Unreported Cases, Supreme Court of Canada (Coutlee) [*A publication*]   (DLA)
COV .... Calculus of Variation [*NASA*]
COV .... Checkout Valve
COV .... Coefficient of Variation [*Mathematics*]
COV .... Colchester [*Vermont*] [*Seismograph station code, US Geological Survey*]   (SEIS)
COV .... Concentrated Oil of Vitriol
COV .... Connellsville, PA [*Location identifier*] [*FAA*]   (FAAL)
COV .... ConVest Energy Corp. [*AMEX symbol*]   (SPSG)
COV .... Corona Onset Voltage
COV .... Counter-Obstacle Vehicle [*Military*]   (RDA)
COV .... Counter-Operating Voltage
COV .... Cove Resources [*Vancouver Stock Exchange symbol*]
COV .... Covenant
COV .... Coventry [*City in England*]
COV .... Cover   (MSA)
COV .... Crossover Value [*Genetics*]
COV .... Cutoff Valve
COV .... Cutoff Voltage
COV .... Cutout Valve
COV .... University of Northern Colorado, Greeley, CO [*OCLC symbol*]   (OCLC)
CoV .... Victor Public Library, Victor, CO [*Library symbol*] [*Library of Congress*]   (LCLS)
Cova .... [*Didacus*] Covarruvias [*Deceased, 1577*] [*Authority cited in pre-1607 legal work*]   (DSA)

CoVa .... Vail Public Library, Vail, CO [*Library symbol*] [*Library of Congress*] (LCLS)
COVAAN .. Cor et Vasa [*A publication*]
COVAM .... Capture Orbit Vehicle Assembly Mode
COVAR ..... Consumption Variation (MCD)
Covar .... [*Didacus*] Covarruvias [*Deceased, 1577*] [*Authority cited in pre-1607 legal work*] (DSA)
Covarru ...... [*Didacus*] Covarruvias [*Deceased, 1577*] [*Authority cited in pre-1607 legal work*] (DSA)
COVART ... Computation of Vulnerable Area and Repair Time (MCD)
COVC .... Colorado Venture Capital Corp. [*NASDAQ symbol*] (NQ)
Cov Conv Ev ... Coventry. Conveyancers' Evidence [*1832*] [*A publication*] (DLA)
COVD .... College of Optometrists in Vision Development (EA)
COVD .... Covered
Coventry Eng Soc J ... Coventry Engineering Society. Journal [*A publication*]
COVER ...... Cutoff Velocity and Range
COVERS ... Combat Vehicle Ram Simulation (MCD)
COVEX ..... Coverage Exercise (MUGU)
CoVF .... Cobra Venom Factor [*Immunochemistry*]
COVFF ...... Coverings, Facing, or Floor [*Freight*]
Cov & H Dig ... Coventry and Hughes' Digest of the Common Law Reports [*A publication*] (DLA)
COVI .... Continental Ventures, Inc. [*NASDAQ symbol*] (NQ)
Cov Mort .... Coventry. Mortgage Precedents [*1827*] [*A publication*] (DLA)
COVPAY .... Centre for Overseas Pest Research. Report [*A publication*]
COV PT ..... Cover Point [*Cricket*] (ROG)
Cov Q .... Covenant Quarterly [*A publication*]
Cov Rec ...... Coventry. Common Recoveries [*1820*] [*A publication*] (DLA)
Covrt Act .... Covert Action [*A publication*]
COVT .... Covenant (ROG)
COVT .... Covington Development Group, Inc. [*NASDAQ symbol*] (NQ)
COVTD ..... Covenanted [*Legal term*] (ROG)
COVTEE .... Covenantee [*Legal term*] (ROG)
COVTOR .. Covenantor [*Legal term*] (ROG)
COW .... Canal Capital Corp. [*Formerly, United Stockyards Corp.*] [*NYSE symbol*] (SPSG)
COW .... Chlorinated Organics in Wastewater
COW .... Coal-Oil-Water [*Fuel mixture*]
COW .... Collection on Wheels [*Shipping*] (DS)
COW .... Committee on Water [*National Academy of Science*] (MSC)
COW .... Committee of the Whole [*United Nations*]
COW .... Cooperative Observational Week (MUGU)
COW .... Cornwall Petroleum [*Vancouver Stock Exchange symbol*]
COW .... Countries of the World and Their Leaders Yearbook [*A publication*]
COW .... Coventry Ordnance Works [*British military*] (DMA)
COW .... Cow Castle Creek [*South Carolina*] [*Seismograph station code, US Geological Survey*] (SEIS)
Cow .... Cowen's New York Reports [*A publication*] (DLA)
Cow .... Cowper's English King's Bench Reports [*1774-78*] [*A publication*] (DLA)
COW .... Crude Oil Washing [*of cargo tank*]
CoW .... Jackson County Public Library, Walden, CO [*Library symbol*] [*Library of Congress*] (LCLS)
COW .... Western State College of Colorado, Gunnison, CO [*OCLC symbol*] (OCLC)
COWA .... Council for Old World Archaeology [*Defunct*] (EA)
CoWa .... Huerfano County Public Library, Walsenburg, CO [*Library symbol*] [*Library of Congress*] (LCLS)
COWA .... Surveys and Bibliographies. Council for Old World Archaeology. Department of Sociology and Anthropology. Boston University [*A publication*]
COWAC ..... Council on Women and the Church [*Later, JFW*] (EA)
COWAEW ... Colonial Waterbirds [*A publication*]
CoWaL .... Lathrop Park Youth Camp, Walsenburg, CO [*Library symbol*] [*Library of Congress*] (LCLS)
CoWals ...... Walsh Public Library, Walsh, CO [*Library symbol*] [*Library of Congress*] (LCLS)
COWAR .... Joint ICSU-UATI Coordinating Committee on Water Research (EAIO)
Cow Att ...... Cowen on Warrants of Attachment [*A publication*] (DLA)
CoWc .... Custer County Public Library, Westcliffe, CO [*Library symbol*] [*Library of Congress*] (LCLS)
Cow Cr .... Cowen's Criminal Reports [*New York*] [*A publication*] (DLA)
Cow Cr Dig ... Cowen's Criminal Digest [*A publication*] (DLA)
Cow Crim (NY) ... Cowen's Criminal Reports [*New York*] [*A publication*] (DLA)
Cow Cr L ..... Cowen's Criminal Law [*New York*] [*A publication*] (DLA)
Cow Cr R ..... Cowen's Criminal Reports [*New York*] [*A publication*] (DLA)
Cow Cr Rep ... Cowen's Criminal Reports [*New York*] [*A publication*] (DLA)
Cow Dic ...... Cowell's Law Dictionary [*A publication*] (DLA)
Cow Dict .... Cowell's Law Dictionary [*A publication*] (DLA)
Cow Dig ...... Cowell's East India Digest [*A publication*] (DLA)
Cow Dig ..... Digest to Cowen's New York Reports [*A publication*] (DLA)
Cowd L Enc ... Cowdery's Law Encyclopaedia [*California*] [*A publication*] (DLA)
COWEAEX ... Cold Weather Exercise [*Military*] (NVT)
Cowell .... Cowell's Interpreter [*A publication*] (DLA)
Cowell .... Cowell's Law Dictionary [*A publication*] (DLA)

CoWeT .... Colorado State Home and Training School, Wheatridge, CO [*Library symbol*] [*Library of Congress*] (LCLS)
CoWeT-M ... Colorado State Home and Training School, Medical Library, Wheatridge, CO [*Library symbol*] [*Library of Congress*] (LCLS)
CoWi .... Windsor Public Library, Windsor, CO [*Library symbol*] [*Library of Congress*] (LCLS)
Cow Inst ..... Cowell's Institutiones Juris Anglicani [*A publication*] (DLA)
Cow Int .... Cowell's Interpreter [*A publication*] (DLA)
Cow JP .... Cowen's New York Treatise on Justices of the Peace [*A publication*] (DLA)
Cow Just .... Cowen's New York Treatise on Justices of the Peace [*A publication*] (DLA)
COWL .... Council of Wisconsin Libraries [*Information service or system*] (IID)
COWLEX ... Cold Weather Landing Exercise [*Military*] (NVT)
COWLR .... Conference on Oriental-Western Literary Relations [*Later, ALD*] (EA)
Cow LR ..... Cowan. Land Rights in Scotland [*A publication*] (ILCA)
COWM .... Coal-Oil-Water Mixture [*Fuel*]
CoWm .... Westminster Public Library, Westminster, CO [*Library symbol*] [*Library of Congress*] (LCLS)
Cow NY ..... Cowen's New York Reports [*A publication*] (DLA)
COWP .... Cowpens National Battlefield Site
Cowp .... Cowper's English King's Bench Reports [*1774-78*] [*A publication*] (DLA)
CoWp .... Woodland Park Public Library, Woodland Park, CO [*Library symbol*] [*Library of Congress*] (LCLS)
COWPA .... California Oil World and Petroleum Industry [*A publication*]
Cowp Cas ... Cowper's Cases [*Third volume of Reports in Chancery*] [*A publication*] (DLA)
Cowp (Eng) ... Cowper's English King's Bench Reports [*1774-78*] [*A publication*] (DLA)
COWPS ..... Council on Wage and Price Stability [*Also, CWPS*] [*Abolished, 1981*]
Cow R .... Cowen's New York Reports [*A publication*] (DLA)
CoWr .... Wray Public Library, Wray, CO [*Library symbol*] [*Library of Congress*] (LCLS)
CoWrN ...... Northeast Colorado Regional Library, Wray, CO [*Library symbol*] [*Library of Congress*] (LCLS)
COWRR .... Committee on Water Resources Research [*US*]
COWS .... Classification Order Watch Service [*Research Publications, Inc.*]
COWS .... Cold to the Opposite and Warm to the Same Side [*Audiometry*]
CO/WT ..... Counterweight [*Automotive engineering*]
Cow Tr .... Cowen's New York Treatise on Justices of the Peace [*A publication*] (DLA)
COX .... Calcium Oxalate [*Organic chemistry*]
Cox .... Cox's English Chancery Reports [*1783-96*] [*A publication*] (DLA)
Cox .... Cox's English Criminal Cases [*A publication*] (DLA)
Cox .... Cox's Reports [*25-27 Arkansas*] [*A publication*] (DLA)
COX .... Coxswain
COx .... Oxnard Public Library, Oxnard, CA [*Library symbol*] [*Library of Congress*] (LCLS)
COX .... University of Colorado at Colorado Springs, Colorado Springs, CO [*OCLC symbol*] (OCLC)
Cox Adv ..... Cox. Advocate [*1852*] [*A publication*] (DLA)
Cox Am T Cas ... Cox's American Trade-Mark Cases [*A publication*] (DLA)
Cox Am TM Cas ... Cox's American Trade-Mark Cases [*A publication*] (DLA)
Cox Anc L ... Cox. Law and Science of Ancient Lights [*1871*] [*A publication*] (ILCA)
Cox & Atk ... Cox and Atkinson's Registration Appeal Cases [*1843-46*] [*England*] [*A publication*] (DLA)
COXCBS ... Coxswain, Construction Battalion, Stevedore
Cox CC .... Cox's County Court Cases [*1860-1919*] [*England*] [*A publication*] (DLA)
Cox CC .... Cox's Crown Cases [*A publication*] (DLA)
Cox CC .... Cox's English Criminal Cases [*A publication*] (DLA)
Cox Ch .... Cox's English Chancery Cases [*A publication*] (DLA)
Cox Ch Cas (Eng) ... Cox's English Chancery Cases [*A publication*] (DLA)
Cox Ch Pr .. Cox's Chancery Practice [*A publication*] (DLA)
Cox CL Pr ... Cox's Common Law Practice [*A publication*] (DLA)
Cox Cr Ca .. Cox's English Criminal Cases [*A publication*] (DLA)
Cox Cr Cas ... Cox's English Criminal Cases [*A publication*] (DLA)
Cox Cr Dig ... Cox's Criminal Law Digest [*A publication*] (DLA)
Cox Crim Cas ... Cox's English Criminal Cases [*A publication*] (DLA)
Cox Cty Ct Ca ... Cox's County Court Cases [*1860-1919*] [*England*] [*A publication*] (DLA)
Cox Cty Ct Cas ... Cox's County Court Cases [*1860-1919*] [*England*] [*A publication*] (DLA)
Coxe .... Coxe's Reports [*1 New Jersey Law*] [*A publication*] (DLA)
Coxe Bract ... Coxe's Translation of Guterbach's Bracton [*A publication*] (DLA)
Cox Elect .... Cox's Registration and Elections [*14th ed.*] [*1885*] [*A publication*] (DLA)
Cox Eq .... Cox's Equity Cases [*England*] [*A publication*] (DLA)
Cox Eq Cas ... Cox's Equity Cases [*England*] [*A publication*] (DLA)
Cox Gov ..... Cox's Institutions of the English Government [*A publication*] (DLA)

COXI .... Cytochrome Oxidase [*An enzyme*]
Cox Inst ..... Cox's Institutions of the English Government [*A publication*] (DLA)
Cox JS Cas ... Cox's Joint Stock Company Cases [*1864-72*] [*England*] [*A publication*] (DLA)
Cox JS Comp ... Cox's Joint Stock Company Cases [*1864-72*] [*England*] [*A publication*] (DLA)
Cox Jt Stk ... Cox's Joint Stock Company Cases [*1864-72*] [*England*] [*A publication*] (DLA)
Cox Mag Ca ... Cox's Magistrates' Cases [*1859-1919*] [*England*] [*A publication*] (DLA)
Cox Mag Cas ... Cox's Magistrates' Cases [*1859-1919*] [*England*] [*A publication*] (ILCA)
Cox Man Tr M ... Cox's Manual of Trade-Mark Cases [*A publication*] (DLA)
Cox & M'C ... Cox, Macrae, and Hertslet's English County Court Cases [*1847-58*] [*A publication*] (DLA)
Cox MC ..... Cox's Magistrates' Cases [*1859-1919*] [*England*] [*A publication*] (DLA)
Cox Mc & H ... Cox, Macrae, and Hertslet's English County Court Reports [*1847-58*] [*A publication*] (DLA)
Cox M & H ... Cox, Macrae, and Hertslet's English County Court Reports [*1847-58*] [*A publication*] (DLA)
Coxn.......... Coxswain [*British military*] (DMA)
Cox Pun ..... Cox's Principles of Punishment [*1877*] [*A publication*] (DLA)
Cox PW ...... Cox's Edition of Peere Williams' Reports [*England*] [*A publication*] (DLA)
Cox Ques ... Cox's Questions for the Use of Students [*A publication*] (DLA)
COXRALM ... Composite Optical/X-Ray LASER Microscope
Cox Reg...... Cox's Registration and Elections [*14th ed.*] [*1885*] [*A publication*] (DLA)
Cox & S Cr L ... Cox and Saunders' Criminal Law Consolidation Acts [*3rd ed.*] [*1870*] [*A publication*] (DLA)
COXSRR ... Coxswain, Ship Repair, Rigger
COXSRS ... Coxswain, Ship Repair, Canvasman
Cox Tr M ... Cox's Manual of Trade-Mark Cases [*A publication*] (DLA)
Cox Tr M Ca ... Cox's American Trade-Mark Cases [*A publication*] (DLA)
Cox Tr M Cas ... Cox's American Trade-Mark Cases [*A publication*] (DLA)
COY........... Car of the Year
COY.......... Colossal Energy, Inc. [*Vancouver Stock Exchange symbol*]
COY.......... Company
COY.......... Denver Law Librarians Group, Denver, CO [*OCLC symbol*] (OCLC)
COY.......... St. Croix, VI [*Location identifier*] [*FAA*] (FAAL)
CoY.......... Yuma Public Library, Yuma, CO [*Library symbol*] [*Library of Congress*] (LCLS)
CoYa .... Yampa Women's Club Library, Yampa, CO [*Library symbol*] [*Library of Congress*] (LCLS)
COYOTE .. Come Off Your Old Tired Ethics [*Prostitutes' lobbying group*]
Coyuntura Econ ... Coyuntura Economica [*A publication*]
COZ.......... Calpetro Resources, Inc. [*Vancouver Stock Exchange symbol*]
COZ.......... Colorado State Library, Denver, CO [*OCLC symbol*] (OCLC)
COZ.......... Cousin (ROG)
COZA .... Combined Operations Headquarters, Zara [*Yugoslavia*] [*World War II*]
COZE .... Coastal Zone. Informal Newsletter of the Resources of the Pacific and Western Arctic Coasts of Canada [*A publication*]
COZI .... Communications Zone Indicator [*Air Force*]
COZID ...... Cable Operated Zero Impedence Decoupler (MCD)
COZOAH ... Comunicari de Zoologie [*A publication*]
COZY .... Cortez International Ltd. [*Vancouver, BC*] [*NASDAQ symbol*] (NQ)
CP .... Avions Mudry & Cie. [*France*], Lockheed Aircraft Corp. [*ICAO aircraft manufacturer identifier*] (ICAO)
CP .... Bolivia [*Aircraft nationality and registration mark*] (FAAC)
CP .... Caixa Postal [*Post Office Box*] [*Portuguese*] [*Correspondence*]
CP .... Caja Postale [*Post Office Box*] [*Spanish*] [*Correspondence*]
CP .... Calendar Process [*Telecommunications*] (TEL)
CP .... Calibration Procedure
CP .... Call Paid [*Telecommunications*] (ADA)
CP .... Call Processor [*Data processing*]
CP .... Callaway Plant (NRCH)
CP .... Callose Platelets [*Botany*]
CP .... Caminhos de Ferro Portugueses [*Railway*] [*Portugal*] (EY)
CP .... Camp
CP .... Campaign for Prosperity (EA)
CP .... Canadian Pacific Airlines Ltd. [*ICAO designator*] (FAAC)
CP .... Canadian Pacific Ltd. [*NYSE symbol*] [*Toronto Stock Exchange symbol*] [*Vancouver Stock Exchange symbol*] (SPSG)
CP .... Canadian Press
CP .... Candlepower [*Physics*]
cp.............. Canton and Enderbury Islands [*MARC country of publication code*] [*Library of Congress*] (LCCP)
C & P......... Capabilities and Procedures
CP .... Cape Province [*of South Africa*]
CP .... Capillary Pressure [*Physiology*]
CP .... Captain of the Parish [*British*] (ROG)
CP .... Car Park (ADA)
CP .... Car Pricing
CP .... Carbamyl Phosphate [*Also, CAP*] [*Organic chemistry*]
CP .... Carbon Paste

CP .... Carbonate Platform [*Archaeology*]
CP .... Card Punch [*Data processing*] (BUR)
CP .... Cardinal Point (ROG)
CP .... Cardiopulmonary [*Medicine*]
C & P......... Care and Preservation [*Army*] (AABC)
CP .... Cargo Program [*or Projects*] Office [*NASA*] (MCD)
C & P......... Carriage and Packing [*Shipping*] (ADA)
CP .... Carriage Paid
C & P......... Carrington and Payne's English Nisi Prius Reports [*1823-41*] [*A publication*] (DLA)
CP .... Cars of the Past [*An association*] (EA)
C-P............. Cartesian to Polar
CP .... Carto-Philatelists (EA)
Cp.............. Carya pecan [*Pecan tree*]
CP .... Case Postale [*Post Office Box*] [*French*] [*Correspondence*]
CP .... Case Preparation
C/P............. Case Project [*IRS*]
CP .... Casetta Postale [*Post Office Box*] [*Italian*] [*Correspondence*]
Cp.............. Cassiopeium [*An early name for the chemical element lutetium*]
CP .... Castrum Peregrini [*A publication*]
CP .... Cat Pack [*"Women's Wear Daily" slang for jetsetters*]
CP .... Catch Phrase
CP .... Cathodic Protection [*Metallurgy*]
CP .... Cattle-Plague (ROG)
CP .... Caudate Putamen [*Neuroanatomy*]
CP .... Cell Pack [*Horticulture*]
CP .... Cellulose Paper
CP .... Center of Pressure
CP .... Center Punch (MSA)
CP .... Centerpartiet [*Center Party*] [*Finland*] [*Political party*] (PPE)
CP .... Centerpartiet [*Center Party*] [*Sweden*] [*Political party*] (PPE)
CP .... Centipoise [*Unit of viscosity*]
C/P............. Central to Peripheral Ratio [*Anatomy*]
CP .... Central Point
CP .... Central Press
CP .... Central Problem [*Psychometrics*]
CP .... Central Processor [*Data processing*]
CP .... Central Procurement [*or Centrally Procured*] (AFM)
CP .... Central Provinces [*Later, Madhya Pradesh, India*]
CP .... Centrifugal Photosedimentation
CP .... Centrum Partii [*Center Party*] [*Netherlands*] [*Political party*] (EY)
CP .... Cerebral Palsy [*Medicine*]
CP .... Cerebral Peduncle [*Brain anatomy*]
CP .... Certification of Purchase
CP .... Certified Patient [*British*]
CP .... Certified Prosthetist
Cp.............. Ceruloplasmin [*Biochemistry*]
CP .... Cesspits (ROG)
CP .... Cesspool (AAG)
CP .... Chamber Pressure
CP .... Change Package (AAG)
CP .... Change Pages (MCD)
CP .... Change Point [*Surveying*]
CP .... Change Proposal (KSC)
CP .... Chappel-Perry Medium [*Microbiology*]
CP .... Chapter
CP .... Character Printer [*Data processing*]
CP .... Charge Parity [*Atomic physics*]
CP .... Charging Pump (NRCH)
CP .... Charles Pfizer & Co. [*Research code symbol*]
CP .... Charter Party [*Transportation*]
CP .... Checkpoint
CP .... Chemical Polish
CP .... Chemical Practitioner (DAS)
CP .... Chemical Propulsion
CP .... Chemical Pulp
CP .... Chemically Pure [*Chemistry*]
C & P......... Chemicals and Polymers Group [*British*]
CP .... Chicago Pile [*Nuclear reactor*]
Cp.............. Chickenpox [*Also, CHPX*] [*Medicine*]
CP .... Chief Patriarch
CP .... Chief Pilot
CP .... Chief of Police
CP .... Child Psychiatry
CP .... Child Psychology
CP .... Childsave Project (EA)
CP .... China Pictorial [*A publication*]
CP .... Chirp Period [*Entomology*]
CP .... Chlorinated Paraffin [*Organic chemistry*]
CP .... Chloroprocaine [*A local anesthetic*]
C/P............. Cholesterol/Phospholipid Ratio [*Clinical chemistry*]
CP .... Chondritic Porous [*Aggregate*] [*Inorganic chemistry*]
CP .... Chromatin Protein [*Biochemistry*]
CP .... Chrome Plated
CP .... Chronic Progressive [*Medicine*]
CP .... Chronic Pyelonephritis [*Urology*]
CP .... Churchman Publishing [*British*]
CP .... Cicatricial Pemphigoid [*Medicine*]
CP .... Circadian Pacemaker [*Neurophysiology*]

CP	Circuit Package (MSA)
CP	Circular Pitch [*Technical drawings*]
CP	Circular Polarization [*Optics*]
CP	Circulation Pump
CP	Citizen's Party (EA)
CP	Civil Parish [*British*]
CP	Civil Power
CP	Civil Procedure [*Legal term*]
CP	Civil Procedure Reports [*New York*] [*A publication*] (DLA)
CP	Civilian Population (MCD)
CP	Clarenden Press (DAS)
CP	Clarissima Puella [*Most Illustrious Maiden*] [*Latin*]
CP	Classical Philology [*A publication*]
CP	Classical Philosophy
CP	Claw Plate [*Technical drawings*]
CP	Clay Pipe [*Technical drawings*]
CP	Cleft Palate [*Medicine*]
CP	Clerk of the Peace [*British*]
CP	Climate Pay [*British military*] (DMA)
CP	Clinical Pathology
CP	Clinical Physiology [*A publication*]
CP	Clock Phase
CP	Clock Pulse
CP	Close Packed (MSA)
CP	Closed Position [*Dancing*]
CP	Closing Pressure [*Medicine*]
CP	Closing Price [*Business term*]
CP	Closing Purchase [*Business term*]
CP	Coalicion Popular [*Popular Coalition*] [*Spain*] [*Political party*] (PPW)
CP	Coat [*or Capsid*] Protein [*Cytology*]
CP	Cochlear Potential [*Otolaryngology*]
CP	Code Penal [*Penal Law*] [*French*] [*A publication*] (DLA)
CP	Code of Practice [*Legal term*]
CP	Code of Procedure [*Legal term*]
CP	Code Proficiency [*Amateur radio*]
CP	Codex Petropolitanus (BJA)
Cp	Codice Penale [*Criminal Code*] [*A publication*] (ILCA)
CP	Codice Penale Svizzero [*A publication*]
CP	Codigo Penal [*Brazil*] [*A publication*]
CP	Coefficient of Performance (IEEE)
CP	Coefficient of Protection [*Against insects*]
CP	Cold Pack [*Medicine*]
CP	Cold Pipe [*Nuclear energy*] (NRCH)
CP	Cold-Punched [*Metal*]
CP	Coldplate (KSC)
CP	Colla Parte [*With the Solo Part*] [*Music*]
CP	Collar Pricing [*Investment term*]
C & P	Collated and Perfect (ADA)
CP	College of Preceptors [*British*]
CP	Color Perception [*Medicine*]
CP	Color Printing [*Filter*] [*Photography*]
CP	Column Product [*Nuclear energy*] (NRCH)
CP	Combat Power [*DoD*]
CP	Combining Power
CP	Comedy Prescription [*An association*] (EA)
CP	Command Paymaster [*British military*] (DMA)
CP	Command Pilot (AFM)
CP	Command Point (AFIT)
CP	Command Post [*Military*]
CP	Command Pouch [*Air Force*] (AFM)
CP	Command Processor [*Data processing*] (BUR)
CP	Command Pulse (MSA)
CP	Commercial Paper [*Banking*]
CP	Commission de Paris [*Paris Commission - PARCOM*] (EAIO)
CP	Committee on Propagation [*National Defense Research Committee*]
CP	Commodity Prices [*A publication*]
CP	Common Pleas [*Legal term*]
CP	Common Prayer
CP	Common Process [*Telecommunications*] (TEL)
CP	Commonwealth Party [*Gibraltar*] [*Political party*] (PPE)
CP	Communication Personnel [*Marine Corps*]
CP	Communications Processor
CP	Communications Programs [*NASA*]
CP	Communications Project (EA)
CP	Communist Party [*Political party*]
CP	Community Placement
CP	Community of the Presentation [*Anglican religious community*]
CP	Company Policy (MCD)
CP	Compare
C & P	Compensation and Pension
CP	Compline
CP	Component Parts (MCD)
CP	Compound [*Medicine*]
CP	Compressed Tablet [*Pharmacy*]
CP	Computed Point [*Navigation*]
CP	Computer Paragraph
CP	Computer Program (MCD)
CP	Computers [*JETDS nomenclature*] [*Military*] (CET)
CP	Concerning Poetry [*A publication*]
CP	Concrete Piercing
CP	Concurrent Planometric [*A discrimination task*]
CP	Condition Precedent [*Legal term*]
CP	Conditional Pardon (ADA)
CP	Conditional Proof [*Method in logic*]
CP	Conditional Purchase [*Business term*] (ADA)
CP	Conductive Plastic
CP	Cone Point (MSA)
CP	Conference Paper
CP	Conference Proceedings (ADA)
C to P	Confined to Post
CP	Congregatio Passionis [*Congregation of the Passion*] [*Passionists*] [*Roman Catholic religious order*]
CP	Congregazione della Passione [*Congregation of the Passion*] (EAIO)
CP	Congress Party [*India*] [*Political party*]
CP	Conjugation-Parity [*Physics*]
CP	Connection Pending [*Telecommunications*] (TEL)
CP	Connection Point [*Data processing*] (IBMDP)
CP	Connector Panel
CP	Conservative Party [*Uganda*] [*Political party*] (PPW)
CP	Conservative Party [*An association*] (EA)
CP	Console Processor (NASA)
CP	Constant Parity [*Physics*]
CP	Constant Potential (DEN)
CP	Constant Pressure (MSA)
CP	Constant Property
CP	Constantinople Pentateuch (BJA)
CP	Constitutionalist Party [*Malta*] [*Political party*] (PPE)
CP	Constrained Procedure (AAG)
CP	Construction Apprentice (MUGU)
CP	Construction Permit [*FCC*]
CP	Construction Procedures [*Nuclear energy*] (NRCH)
CP	Constructive Placement [*Railcar*]
C/P	Consultation Paper (DCTA)
CP	Consulting Physician (ROG)
CP	Contact Party [*Army*]
CP	Containment Purge [*Nuclear energy*] (NRCH)
CP	Contemporary Psychology [*A publication*]
CP	Contestacion Pagada [*Reply Paid*] [*Spanish*] [*Correspondence*]
CP	Continental Pharma [*Belgium*] [*Research code symbol*]
CP	Continental Plan [*Hotel rate*]
CP	Continental Polar Air Mass
CP	Contingency Planning (MCD)
CP	Continuous Path [*Robotics*]
C/P	Contract Price
CP	Contrappunto [*Counterpoint*] [*Music*] (ROG)
CP	Contributory Place (ROG)
CP	Control Panel
CP	Control Pascal [*Compiler*] [*Data processing*]
CP	Control Point
CP	Control Post [*RADAR*]
CP	Control Procedures (MCD)
C & P	Control and Processing [*Company*] [*INSCOM*]
CP	Control Processor (IEEE)
CP	Control Program [*Data processing*]
C/P	Converter/Programmer (MCD)
CP	Convicted Poacher [*Legal*] [*British*] (ROG)
CP	Coolant Pump [*Nuclear energy*] (NRCH)
CP	Cooperative Power [*Later, SPG*] (EA)
CP	Coordinating Panel [*NATO*] (RDA)
CP	Coordination Processor [*Telecommunications*]
CP	Copilot
CP	Copper Pair [*Telecommunications*]
CP	Coproporphyrin [*Also, COPRO*] [*Clinical chemistry*]
CP	Copula Pyramidna [*Neuroanatomy*]
CP	Copy (MCD)
CP	Cor Pulmonale [*Medicine*]
CP	Coracoid Process [*Anatomy*]
CP	Coronagraph Polarimeter
CP	Corrosion Protection [*Telecommunications*] (TEL)
CP	Cortical Plate [*Neuroanatomy*]
CP	Cost and Performance
CP	Cost Plus [*Insurance*]
CP	Cost Price [*Business term*] (ADA)
CP	Cost Proposal
CP	Couch Potatoes (EA)
CP	Council of Presidents (EA)
CP	Council for the Principality [*British*]
CP	Counterpoint [*Music*]
CP	Countries and Peoples [*A publication*]
CP	Country Profile (ADA)
CP	Coupling
CP	Coupon
CP	Court of Common Pleas (DLA)
CP	Court Physician (ROG)
CP	Court of Probate
CP	Couterpoise Procedure [*Physical chemistry*]
CP	Cover Point [*Lacrosse position*]
CP	Cowpea

CP	Coyoti Prints. Caribou Tribal Council Newsletter [*A publication*]
CP	Crack Propagation (AAG)
C & P..........	Craig and Phillips' English Chancery Reports [*1840-41*] [*A publication*] (DLA)
CP	Creatine Phosphate [*Phosphocreatine; see PC*] [*Biochemistry*]
CP	Critical Path
CP	Critical Period
CP	Critical Power [*Nuclear energy*] (NRCH)
CP	Crop Protection [*A publication*]
CP	Cross Polarization [*Atomic physics*]
CP	Cross Pollinated [*Genetics*]
CP	Cross Products [*Statistics*]
CP	Crown Pleas [*Legal term*] (DLA)
CP	Crude Protein
CP	Crystal Palace, Sydenham [*British*]
CP	Crystalline or Powdered
CP	Cuadernos Politicos [*Ediciones Era*] [*A publication*]
CP	Cultura Politica [*Rio De Janeiro*] [*A publication*]
CP	Current Paper
CP	Current Period
C/P.............	Current/Pneumatic [*Nuclear energy*] (NRCH)
CP	Current Practices
CP	Cushioning Pads
C/P.............	Custom and Port [*International trade*]
CP	Customer Proven [*GMC truck marketing*]
CP	Customized Processor [*IBM Corp.*] (IEEE)
C & P..........	Cut and Paste
CP	Cuticular Plate [*Biology*]
CP	Cyclic Permuted
Cp..............	Cyclopentadienyl [*Also, cp*] [*Organic radical*]
CP	Cyclophosphamide [*Cytoxan*] [*Antineoplastic drug*]
CP	Cyclophosphamide, Prednisone [*Antineoplastic drug regimen*]
CP	Cylindrical Perforated
CP	Cyprus [*IYRU nationality code*] (IYR)
C & P..........	Cystoscopy and Panendoscopy [*Medicine*]
C & P..........	Cystoscopy and Pyelogram [*Medicine*]
CP	General Call to Two or More Specified Stations [*Telecommunications*] (FAAC)
CP	Law Reports, Common Pleas [*England*] [*A publication*] (DLA)
CP	Pasadena Public Library, Pasadena, CA [*Library symbol*] [*Library of Congress*] (LCLS)
Cp..............	Prismatic Coefficient [*Boat design*]
CP	Sisters of the Cross and Passion [*Roman Catholic women's religious order*]
CP	Station Open to Public Correspondence [*ITU designation*]
CP	Upper Canada Common Pleas [*Legal term*] (DLA)
CP3	MIT [*Massachusetts Institute of Technology*]-Industry Composites and Polymer Processing Program [*Research center*] (RCD)
CP-5............	Chicago Pile-5 [*Nuclear heavy-water-research reactor*]
CPA	Ambassador College, Pasadena, CA [*Library symbol*] [*Library of Congress*] (LCLS)
CPA	Australian Commercial Parachute Association
CPA	Cadmium Pigments Association (EAIO)
CPA	Calcium-Binding Para-Albumin [*Biochemistry*]
CPA	California Pistachio Association (EA)
CPA	Campaign Poster Award [*British*]
CPA	Canadian Pacific Airlines Ltd. [*Facetious translations: Can't Possibly Arrive, Come Push Along*]
CPA	Canadian Payments Association
CPA	Canadian Petroleum Association
CPA	Canadian Pharmaceutical Association (MCD)
CPA	Canadian Philosophical Association
CPA	Canadian Physiotherapy Association
CPA	Canadian Police Association
CPA	Canadian Postmaster's Association
CPA	Canadian Psychiatric Association
CPA	Canadian Psychological Association (MCD)
CPA	Cape Palmas [*Liberia*] [*Airport symbol*] (OAG)
CPA	Capitol Air Service, Inc. [*Manhattan, KS*] [*FAA designator*] (FAAC)
CPA	Carboxypeptidase A [*An enzyme*]
CPA	Carotid Phonoangiography [*Medicine*]
CPA	Carry Propagate Adder [*Computer*]
CPA	Cash Purchasing Agent (AFM)
CPA	Catholic Press Association (EA)
CPA	Center for Policy Alternatives (EA)
CPA	Center for Public Affairs [*Arizona State University*] [*Research center*] (RCD)
CPA	Central Pacific Area [*Hawaiian area*] [*World War II*]
CPA	Central Processing Area (ADA)
CPA	Central Pulse Amplifier (MCD)
CPA	Central Purchasing Authority [*Military*] (NVT)
CPA	Centre for Policy on Ageing
CPA	Cerebellopontine Angle [*Brain anatomy*]
CPA	Certified Public Accountant
CPA	Cessna Pilots Association (EA)
CPA	Cha-Pa [*Vietnam*] [*Geomagnetic observatory code*]
CPA	Charged Particle Activation
CPA	Chartered Patent Agent
CPA	Chartered Public Accountant
CPA	Chemical Propulsion Abstracts [*Database*] [*Chemical Propulsion Information Agency*] [*Information service or system*] (CRD)
CPA	Cherokee Pilots Association [*Commercial firm*] (EA)
CPA	Chicago Pacific Corp. [*NYSE symbol*] (SPSG)
CPA	Chicano Press Association (EA)
CPA	Chief of Public Affairs (AABC)
CPA	Chlorobenzine Producers Association (EA)
CPA	Chlorophenoxyacetic Acid [*Plant growth hormone*]
CPA	Chlorophenylalanine [*Biochemistry*]
CPA	Chloropicolinic Acid [*Organic chemistry*]
CPA	Christian Palestinian Aramaic (BJA)
CPA	Christian Patriot Association (EA)
CPA	Christian Pilots Association (EA)
CPA	Church Penitentiary Association [*British*]
CPA	Circularly Polarized Antenna [*or Array*]
CPA	Circulating Platelet Aggregate [*Hematology*]
CPA	City Parks Administration [*Australia*]
CPA	Civil Practice Act [*New York*] (DLA)
CPA	Civilian Personnel Advisor [*Military*]
CPA	Civilian Production Administration [*Became part of Office of Temporary Controls, 1946*]
CPA	Civilian Property Agent
CPA	Classroom Publishers Association (EA)
CPA	Clay Products Association (EA)
CPA	Closest Point of Approach [*Navigation*]
CPA	Coast Protection Act [*Town planning*] [*British*]
CPA	Cocoa Producers' Alliance (EAIO)
CPA	Coherent Potential Approximation [*Physics*]
CPA	Color Phase Alternation
CPA	Combination Publication Authority
CPA	Comite des Paysans Africains [*African Farmers Committee - AFC*] (EAIO)
CPA	Commonwealth Parliamentary Association [*London, England*] (EAIO)
CPA	Commonwealth Pharmaceutical Association [*London, England*] (EAIO)
CPA	Commonwealth Preference Area
CPA	Communist Party of Arakan [*Burma*] [*Political party*]
CPA	Communist Party of Argentina [*Political party*]
CPA	Communist Party of Australia [*Political party*] (PPW)
CPA	Community Pride Association (EA)
CPA	Commutative Principle for Addition [*Mathematics*]
CPA	Compressed Pulse Altimeter
CPA	Compulsory Purchase Act [*Town planning*] [*British*]
CPA	Computer Performance Analysis [*Boole & Babbage, Inc.*]
CPA	Computer Press Association (EA)
CPA	Computer Program Abstracts [*NASA*] [*A publication*]
CPA	Concrete Pipe Associations (EA)
CPA	Concurrent Photographic Amplification
CPA	Concurrent Photon Amplification [*Air Force*]
CPA	Conjugation-Parity Asymmetry [*Physics*]
CPA	Conservative Party of Australia [*Political party*] (ADA)
CPA	Consolidated Property Account (MCD)
CPA	Constant Potential Accelerator
CPA	Constantinopolitana (ROG)
CPA	Consumer Protection Act
CPA	Consumer Protection Agency
CPA	Contingency Planning Aid (NASA)
CPA	Continuous Patrol Aircraft
CPA	Control of Pollution Act [*1974*] [*British*]
CPA	Control Program Assist [*IBM Corp.*]
CPA	Control Purchasing Authority (NVT)
CPA	Controlled Products Area
CPA	Cooperative Power Association [*Nuclear energy*] (NRCH)
CPA	Cooperative Publication Association (EA)
CPA	Copolar Attenuation [*Telecommunications*] (TEL)
CPA	Corporate Oil & Gas [*Vancouver Stock Exchange symbol*]
CPA	Cost and Performance Analysis [*Air Force*] (AFIT)
CPA	Cost Planning and Appraisal [*Air Force Systems Command, Aeronautical Systems Division*]
CPA	Cost Plus Award [*Military*]
CPA	Cotswold Personality Assessment [*Psychology*]
CPA	Coudersport & Port Allegany [*AAR code*]
CPA	Cour Permanente d'Arbitrage [*Permanent Court of Arbitration - PCA*] [*Hague, Netherlands*] (EAIO)
CPA	CPA [*American Institute of Certified Public Accountants*] Journal [*A publication*]
CPA	Crash Phone Activated [*Aviation*] (FAAC)
CPA	Creative Printers of America
CPA	Criminology and Penology Abstracts [*A publication*]
CPA	Critical Path Analysis
CPA	Cross Program Auditor [*Applied Data Research, Inc.*]
CPA	Cycle Parts and Accessories Association (EA)
CPA	Cyclophosphamide [*Cytoxan*] [*Antineoplastic drug*]
CPA	Cyproterone Acetate [*Endocrinology*]
CPa	Palo Alto City Library, Palo Alto, CA [*Library symbol*] [*Library of Congress*] (LCLS)
CPA	Pasadena City College, Pasadena, CA [*OCLC symbol*] (OCLC)
CPAA.........	Canadian Postmasters and Assistants Association

CPAA........ Charged Particle Activation Analysis [*Analytical chemistry*]

CPAA........ Colloquia for Presidents and Academic Administrators [*Formerly, ICUA*]   (EA)

CPAA........ CPA [*Certified Public Accountant*] Associates   (EA)

CPAA........ Cultured Pearl Association of America   (EA)

CPAA........ Current Physics Advance Abstracts [*A publication*]

CPAA........ Cycle Parts and Accessories Association   (EA)

CPaB........ Beckman Instruments, Inc., Technical Library, Palo Alto, CA [*Library symbol*] [*Library of Congress*]   (LCLS)

CPAB........ California Cling Peach Advisory Board

CPAB........ California Prune Advisory Board [*Later, CPB*]

CPAB........ Computer Programmer Aptitude Battery [*Test*]

CPAC........ Center for Process Analytical Chemistry [*University of Washington*] [*Research center*]   (RCD)

CPAC........ Chicago Pacific Corporation [*Chicago, IL*] [*NASDAQ symbol*]   (NQ)

C-PAC ...... Clinical Probes of Articulation Consistency [*Speech evaluation test*]

CPAC........ Coalition to Preserve the American Copyright   (EA)

CPAC........ Color Photographic Association of Canada

CPAC........ Community Planning Association of Canada

CPAC........ Computer Program Associated Contractor

CPAC........ Concurrent Processor Architecture Control   (MCD)

CPAC........ Conservative Political Action Conference

CPACS ...... Coded Pulse Anticlutter System   (CET)

CPAD .... Central Pay Accounts Division [*Navy*]

CP Adm .... Certificate in Public Administration

CPADN ..... Career Planning and Adult Development Network   (EA)

CPAE........ Coalition to Protect Animals in Entertainment   (EA)

CPAE........ Commission of Professors of Adult Education   (EA)

CPaE........ Electric Power Research Institute, Palo Alto, CA [*Library symbol*] [*Library of Congress*]   (LCLS)

CPAF........ Chlorpropamide-Alcohol Flushing [*Medicine*]

CPAF........ Cost Plus Award Fee [*Business term*]

CPAGA ..... California Prune and Apricot Growers Association [*Later, Sunsweet Growers*]

CPaGE...... General Electric Co., Traveling Wave Tube Production Section, Palo Alto, CA [*Library symbol*] [*Library of Congress*]   (LCLS)

CPaHP...... Hewlett-Packard Co., Corporate Library, Palo Alto, CA [*Library symbol*] [*Library of Congress*]   (LCLS)

CPAI......... Canvas Products Association International [*Later, IFAI*]   (EA)

CPA-IGWAP ... Canadian Psychological Association - Interest Group on Women and Psychology

CPAir....... Canadian Pacific Airlines Ltd.

CPAJ .... CPA [*American Institute of Certified Public Accountants*] Journal [*A publication*]

CPAJA ...... Canadian Psychiatric Association. Journal [*A publication*]

CPAK........ CPAC, Inc. [*NASDAQ symbol*]   (NQ)

CPAL........ Canadian Pacific Airlines Limited

CPal .... Codices Palatini   (BJA)

CPAL........ Containment Person Air Lock [*Nuclear energy*]   (IEEE)

CPaL......... Lockheed Missiles & Space Corp., Palo Alto, CA [*Library symbol*] [*Library of Congress*]   (LCLS)

CPAM ...... Caisse Primaire d'Assurance Maladie [*French*]   (DLA)

CPAM ...... Certified Patient Account Manager [*Designation awarded by American Guild of Patient Account Management*]

CPAM ...... CNO [*Chief of Naval Operations*] Program Analysis Memorandum

CPAM ...... Continental Polar Air Mass   (MSA)

CPAM ...... Countermeasures Penetrating Antiarmor Munitions   (MCD)

CPAMA..... Communications on Pure and Applied Mathematics [*A publication*]

CPAO .... Canoga Park Area Office [*AEC*]   (MCD)

CPAOD ..... Chongqing Daxue Xuebao [*A publication*]

CPAP........ Center for Public Administration and Policy [*Virginia Polytechnic Institute and State University*] [*Research center*]   (RCD)

CPAP........ Century Papers, Inc. [*NASDAQ symbol*]   (NQ)

CPAP........ Constant Positive Airway Pressure [*Medicine*]

CPAP........ Continuous Positive Airway Pressure [*Resuscitation system*] [*Medicine*]

CPAP........ Control Parameter Assembly Program

CPAP........ Cyclopenta(alpha)phenanthrene [*Organic chemistry*]

CPaP......... Philco-Ford Corp., Western Development Laboratories, Palo Alto, CA [*Library symbol*] [*Library of Congress*]   (LCLS)

CPAPA4.... Colonial Plant and Animal Products [*A publication*]

CPA-PE ..... Carbazopropionyl - Phosphatidyl Ethanolamine [*Organic chemistry*]

C Papers .... Cinema Papers [*A publication*]

CPAPR ..... Coalition to Protect Animals in Parks and Refuges   (EA)

CPARD...... Cerpadla Potrubi Armatury [*A publication*]

CPAS........ Church Pastoral Aid Society [*British*]

CPAS........ Civilian Personnel Accounting System [*Military*]   (MCD)

CPAS........ Construction Program Administration System [*Telecommunications*]   (TEL)

CPaS.......... Syntex Corp., Research Library, Palo Alto, CA [*Library symbol*] [*Library of Congress*]   (LCLS)

CPASAD ... Commentationes Pontificiae. Academiae Scientiarum [*A publication*]

CPASC ...... Canadian Permanent Army Service Corps   (DMA)

CPASTATS ... Canadian Petroleum Association Statistics [*Information service or system*]   (CRD)

CPaSy .... SYVA Co., Palo Alto, CA [*Library symbol*] [*Library of Congress*]   (LCLS)

CPAT........ Coalition to Promote America's Trade [*Washington, DC*]   (EA)

CPAT........ Commercial Product Acquisition Team [*Later, COMPACT*] [*An association*]   (EA)

CPATBH ... Canada. Department of Agriculture. Plant Research Institute. Agrometeorology Section. Technical Bulletin [*A publication*]

CPAV........ Cinque Ports Artillery Volunteers [*British military*]   (DMA)

CPaVA....... United States Veterans Administration Hospital, Palo Alto, CA [*Library symbol*] [*Library of Congress*]   (LCLS)

CPAWS ..... Computer-Planning and Aircraft-Weighing Scales

CPaX........ Xerox Corp., Research Center, Palo Alto, CA [*Library symbol*] [*Library of Congress*]   (LCLS)

CPB........... California Prune Board   (EA)

CPB........... Campbell Soup Co. [*NYSE symbol*]   (SPSG)

CPB........... Caneco Audio-Publishers, Inc. [*Vancouver Stock Exchange symbol*]

CPB........... Carboxypeptidase B [*An enzyme*]

CPB........... Cardiopulmonary Bypass [*Medicine*]

CPB........... Career Planning Board [*Navy*]   (NVT)

CPB........... Casual Payments Book [*British*]   (ADA)

CPB........... Censorship Policy Board [*World War II*]

CPB........... Censorship of Publications Board [*Ireland*]

CPB........... Center of Pressure Back

CPB........... Channel Program Block [*Data processing*]

CPB........... Charged Particle Beam [*Weapon*] [*DoD*]

CPB........... China Phone Book and Business Directory [*A publication*]

CPB........... Civilian Personnel Branch [*BUPERS*]

CPB........... Clinical Physiology and Biochemistry [*A publication*]

CPB........... Colombo Plan Bureau   (EAIO)

CPB........... Colorado Potato Beetle

CPB........... Communist Party of Belgium [*Political party*]

CP (b)........ Communist Party (Bolsheviks) [*Political party*]

CPB........... Companion to the Authorized Daily Prayer Book [*A publication*]   (BJA)

CPB........... Competitive Protein Binding [*Clinical chemistry*]

CPB........... Computer Program Book

CPB........... Confederacion Panamericana de Badminton [*Panamerican Badminton Conferation - PBC*]   (EAIO)

CPB........... Confederacion Panamericana de Basketball [*Pan American Basketball Confederation - PABC*]   (EAIO)

CPB........... Contractors Pump Bureau   (EA)

CPB........... Corporation for Public Broadcasting   (EA)

CPB........... Culver, IN [*Location identifier*] [*FAA*]   (FAAL)

CPB........... Current Physics Bibliographies [*A publication*]   (MCD)

CPB........... Cuyos Pies Beso [*Very Respectfully*] [*Formal correspondence*] [*Spanish*]

CPB........... Cypher Policy Board [*British*] [*World War II*]

CPB........... Cyprus Popular Bank Newsletter [*A publication*]

CPBA........ Chloroperbenzoic Acid [*Organic acid*]

CPBA........ (Chlorophenoxy)butanoic Acid [*Biochemistry*]

CPBA........ Competitive Protein-Binding Analysis

CPBC......... Central Pacific Base Command [*Hawaiian Islands*] [*World War II*]

CPB-E........ Burroughs Corp., Western Region Central Technical Library, Pasadena, CA [*Library symbol*] [*Library of Congress*]   (LCLS)

CPBE......... Certified Professional Bureau Executive [*Designation awarded by Medical-Dental-Hospital Bureaus of America*]

CPBH .... Bell & Howell Co., Research Laboratories, Pasadena, CA [*Library symbol*] [*Library of Congress*]   (LCLS)

CPBI .... CPB, Inc. [*NASDAQ symbol*]   (NQ)

CPBIDP..... Clinical Physiology and Biochemistry [*A publication*]

CPBL .... Capable [*or Capability*]   (AFM)

CPBLAV .. Comparative Pathology Bulletin [*A publication*]

CPBP .... Cancer Prevention Benefit Program [*National Cancer Institute*]

CPBS .... Colorado Potato Beetle Spiroplasma [*Insect pathogen*]

CPBTA ...... Chemical and Pharmaceutical Bulletin (Tokyo) [*A publication*]

CPBX .... Computerized Private Branch Exchange [*Telecommunications*]

CPC........... Cabin Pressure Controller [*Aviation*]   (MCD)

CPC........... Calibration Procedure

CPC........... California Pistachio Commission   (EA)

CPC........... Calling Party's Category [*Telecommunications*]   (TEL)

CPC........... Cameroon Protestant College

CPC........... Canada Post Corporation Library [*UTLAS symbol*]

CPC........... Canadian Packaging [*A publication*]

CPC........... Canadian Pension Commission

CPC........... Canadian Postal Corps [*Later, RCPC*]

CPC........... Canadian Public Administration [*A publication*]

CPC........... Capital Press Club   (EA)

CPC........... Card Programmed Calculator [*IBM Corp. - late 1940's*] [*Data processing*]

CPC........... Cargo Processing Contract   (MCD)

CPC........... Carolina Population Center [*University of North Carolina*] [*Research center*]   (RCD)

CPC........... Carroll Publishing Co. [*Information service or system*]   (IID)

CPC........... Carswell's Practice Cases [*A publication*]

CPC........... Cells per Colony [*Microbiology*]

CPC............ Cement-Plaster Ceiling [*Technical drawings*]
CPC............ Center for Plant Conservation (EA)
CPC............ Central Planning Center (NASA)
CPC............ Central Posterior Curve [*Ophthalmology*]
CPC............ Central Processing Console [*NBDS*]
CPC............ Central Property Control
CPC............ Centrifugal Partition Chromatography
CPC............ Century Publishing Company
CPC............ Ceramic-Wafer Printed Circuit
CPC............ Cerebral Palsy Clinic
CPC............ Cerebral Performance Category
CPC............ Cerebro-Pedal Commissure [*Medicine*]
CPC............ Certified Personnel Consultant [*Designation awarded by National Association of Personnel Consultants*]
CPC............ Certified Professional Chemist
CPC............ Cetylpyridinium Chloride [*Organic chemistry*]
CPC............ Channel Program Commands
CPC............ Chapelco [*Argentina*] [*Airport symbol*] (OAG)
CPC............ Characteristics Properties Code [*NASA*] (NASA)
CPC............ Characters per Column [*Typesetting*]
CPC............ Cherry Point [*North Carolina*] [*Seismograph station code, US Geological Survey*] [*Closed*] (SEIS)
CPC............ Chevrolet-Pontiac-Canada Group [*General Motors Corp.*]
CPC............ Chief Pay Clerk [*Navy rating*] [*Obsolete*]
CPC............ Chief Planning and Control Staff [*Coast Guard*]
CPC............ Christian Peace Conference [*See also CCP*] [*Prague, Czechoslovakia*] (EAIO)
CPC............ Christian Preaching Conference [*Defunct*] (EA)
CPC............ Christmas Philatelic Club (EA)
CPC............ Chronic Passive Congestion [*Medicine*]
CPC............ Church Pensions Conference (EA)
CPC............ Church Periodical Club (EA)
CPC............ Circumferential Pneumatic Compression [*Medicine*]
CPC............ City Police Commissioner (DAS)
CPC............ City Police Court [*British*] (DAS)
CPC............ Civilian Personnel Circular [*Army*]
CPC............ Clerk of the Privy Council [*British*]
CPC............ Clinical Pathology Conference
CPC............ Clock Pulsed Control
CPC............ Coastal Patrol Boat [*Navy symbol*]
CPC............ Coated Paper Copier [*Reprography*]
CPC............ Coated Powder Cathode
CPC............ Code of Civil Procedure [*Quebec*] [*A publication*] (DLA)
CPC............ Code de Procedure Civile [*Code of Civil Procedure*] [*French*] [*A publication*] (DLA)
CPC............ Codice di Procedura Civile [*Code of Civil Procedure*] [*A publication*] (ILCA)
CPC............ Codigo de Processo Civil [*Brazil*] [*A publication*]
CPC............ Coldplate Clamp
CPC............ College Placement Council (EA)
CPC............ Color Pack Camera
CPC............ Columbia Pacific Airlines [*Richland, WA*] [*FAA designator*] (FAAC)
CPC............ Column Position Counter
CPC............ Combat Psychiatric Casualty [*Military*] (INF)
CPC............ Combined Policy Committee [*NATO*] (NATG)
CPC............ Command Point of Contact [*Navy*] (AFIT)
CPC............ Commerce Productivity Center
CPC............ Commercial Property Coverage [*Insurance*]
CPC............ Committee for Program and Coordination [*Economic and Social Council*] [*United Nations*]
CPC............ Committee for a Progressive Congress (EA)
CPC............ Communication Planning Corporation [*Jacksonville, FL*] [*Telecommunications*] (TSSD)
CPC............ Communications Processing Center (CET)
CPC............ Communist Party of Canada [*Political party*]
CPC............ Communist Party of China [*Chung-Kuo Kung-Ch'an Tang*] [*Taiwan*] [*Political party*] (PPW)
CPC............ Communist Party of Colombia [*Political party*] (PPW)
CPC............ Community Patent Convention [*European Common Market*]
CPC............ Component Parts Clause (AIA)
CPC............ Compound Parabolic Concentrator [*Solar energy research*]
CPC............ Computer Petroleum Corporation [*Information service or system*] (IID)
CPC............ Computer Power Center
CPC............ Computer Print Console
CPC............ Computer Process Control
CPC............ Computer Program Components (MCD)
CPC............ Computer Programming Concepts (BUR)
CPC............ Computing Centre [*University of East Anglia*] [*British*] (IRUK)
CPC............ Conservative Political Centre [*British*]
CPC............ Consortium for Peaceful Coexistence (EA)
CPC............ Consortium Perfectae Caritatis [*Association of Perfect Love*] (EA)
CPC............ Constant Product Curve [*Economics*]
CPC............ Consultative Political Council [*Laos*]
CPC............ Consumer Protection Center (EA)
CPC............ Contract Progress Control (MCD)
CPC............ Control Point Custodian [*Military*] (AFIT)
CPC............ Control and Processing Center (MCD)

CPC............ Controlled-Pore Ceramic [*Organic chemistry*]
CPC............ Controlled-Potential Coulometer [*Nuclear energy*] (NRCH)
CPC............ Cooper Canada Ltd. [*Toronto Stock Exchange symbol*]
CPC............ [*Charles Purton*] Cooper's English Chancery Practice Cases [*A publication*] (DLA)
CPC............ Copper Phthalocyanine [*Colored pigment*]
CPC............ Copy Payments Center [*for copyrighted material*]
CPC............ Core Protection Calculator [*or Computer*] [*Nuclear energy*] (NRCH)
CPC............ Council on Professional Certification (EA)
CPC............ CPC International, Inc. [*Formerly, Corn Products Company*] [*NYSE symbol*] (SPSG)
C-P-C......... Craven-Pamlico-Carteret Regional Library [*Library network*]
CPC............ Cresolphthalein Complexone [*Analytical chemistry*]
CPC............ Current Papers on Computers and Control [*A publication*]
CPC............ Custodial, Protective, and Crafts [*US government workers*]
CPC............ Cycle Program Control (MCD)
CPC............ Cycle Program Counter (IEEE)
CPC............ Cyclic Permutation Code
CPC............ Pacific Christian College, Fullerton, CA [*OCLC symbol*] (OCLC)
CPC............ Whiteville, NC [*Location identifier*] [*FAA*] (FAAL)
CPCA......... Cigarette Pack Collectors Association (EA)
CPCA......... Cyclopropanecarboxylic Acid [*Organic chemistry*]
CPCA......... University of California. Publications in Classical Archaeology [*A publication*]
CPCB......... Crew Procedures Control Board [*NASA*] (NASA)
.CPCC........ Chicago Playing Card Collectors (EA)
CPCC........ Communications Processor Conversion Center
CPCEAF.... Canine Practice [*A publication*]
CPCEAISD ... Comite Permanent du CE de l'Association Internationale de la Savonnerie et de la Detergence [*Standing EEC Committee of the International Association of the Soap and Detergent Industry - SEECCIASDI*] [*Brussels, Belgium*] (EAIO)
CPCEI .... Computer Program Contract End Item
CPCEMR .. Circum-Pacific Council for Energy and Mineral Resources (EA)
CPCFA ...... Council of Pollution Control Financing Agencies [*Defunct*] (EA)
CPCGN ..... Canadian Permanent Committee on Geographical Names
CPCH .... Calling Party Cannot Hear [*Telecommunications*] (TEL)
CPCH .... Collier de Perles, Carre de Hermes [*Pearl Necklace, Silk Scarf from the boutique Hermes*] [*French Yuppie garb*]
CPCHAO .. Clinical Proceedings. Children's Hospital of the District of Columbia [*Later, Clinical Proceedings. Children's Hospital National Medical Center*] [*A publication*]
CPCI .... Canadian Prestressed Concrete Institute [*See also ICBP*]
CPCI .... Ciprico, Incorporated [*NASDAQ symbol*] (NQ)
CPCI .... Computer Program Change Instruction (NASA)
CPCI .... Computer Program Configuration Identification
CPCI .... Computer Program Configured Item (MCD)
CPCI .... CPU Power Calibration Instrument
CPCI .... Cross-Pointer Course Indicator (MCD)
CPCI .... Cruise Passengers Club International (EA)
CPCIAR .... CEPEC [*Centro de Pesquisas do Cacau*] Informe Tecnico [*A publication*]
CPCiC........ Pasadena City College, Pasadena, CA [*Library symbol*] [*Library of Congress*] (LCLS)
CPCIP .... Commission Permanente de la Convention Internationale des Peches [*Permanent Commission of the International Fisheries Convention*] [*Political party*] (MSC)
CPCIZ .... Comite Permanent des Congres Internationaux de Zoologie [*Permanent Committee of International Zoological Congresses*] [*France*]
CPCJD ...... Chemicals and Petro-Chemicals Journal [*A publication*]
CPcK......... Kaiser Permanente Medical Center, Health Science Library, Panorama City, CA [*Library symbol*] [*Library of Congress*] (LCLS)
CPCL .... Combined Passenger Check List (ADA)
CPCL .... Computer Program Change Library (NASA)
CPCL .... Computer Program Control Library (MCD)
CPCL .... Congenital Pulmonary Cystic Lymphangiectasis [*Medicine*]
CPCM........ Certification as Professional Contract Manager (RDA)
CPC(M-L) ... Communist Party of Canada (Marxist-Leninist) [*Political party*]
CPC & N..... Certificate of Public Convenience and Necessity
CPCN .... Civilian Position Control Number
CPCNG ..... Comite Permanent Canadien des Noms Geographiques [*Canadian Permanent Committee on Geographical Names - CPCGN*]
CPCO .... Central Port Call Office [*Army*] (AABC)
CpCo.......... Clearwater Publishing Co., Inc., New York, NY [*Library symbol*] [*Library of Congress*] (LCLS)
C P Coop .... [*Charles Purton*] Cooper's English Chancery Practice Cases [*A publication*] (DLA)
CP Cooper ... [*Charles Purton*] Cooper's English Chancery Practice Cases [*A publication*] (DLA)
CPCP........ Chronic Progressive Coccidioidal Pneumonitis [*Medicine*]
CPCP........ Civilian Personnel Career Plan [*Air Force*]
CPCP........ University of California. Publications in Classical Philology [*A publication*]
CPCR........ Computer Program Change Request (NASA)

CPCR........ Contractor Packaging Capability Review [*DoD*]
CPCR........ Crew Procedures Change Request   (MCD)
CPCR........ Crop Protection Chemicals Reference
CPCS........ Cabin Pressure Control System [*Aviation*]
CPCS......... Caithness Paperweight Collectors Society [*Perth, Scotland*]   (EAIO)
CPCS........ Central Property Control System   (MCD)
CPCS........ Check Processing Control System [*IBM Corp.*]   (BUR)
CPCS........ Coast Phase Control System [*Army*]   (AABC)
CPCS........ Common Program Control Station [*Emergency Broadcast System*]
C-PCS....... Congenital Portocaval Shunt [*Medicine*]
CPCS........ Conversion Process Controller System
CPCS........ Cost Planning and Control System   (MCD)
CPCS........ Cyclic Pitch Control Stick
CPCSF....... Construction Permit Containment Support Fixture   (NRCH)
CPCT........ Committee to Protect Our Children's Teeth [*Defunct*]   (EA)
CPC T Br... [*Charles Purton*] Cooper's English Chancery Cases Tempore Brougham [*A publication*]   (DLA)
CPC T Cott ... [*Charles Purton*] Cooper's English Chancery Cases Tempore Cottenham [*A publication*]   (DLA)
CPCU .... Chartered Property and Casualty Underwriter [*Designation awarded by American Institute for Property and Liability Underwriters*]
CPCU .... Council of Protestant Colleges and Universities [*Defunct*]   (EA)
CPCU .... Custody Pending Completion of Use
CPCU .... Society of Chartered Property and Casualty Underwriters [*Malvern, PA*]   (EA)
CPCUG..... Capital PC [*Personal Computer*] User Group   (EA)
CPD .... Camping Products Division [*of Industrial Fabrics Association International*]   (EA)
CPD .... Canadian Performance Distributors
CPD .... Cape Provincial Division Reports [*South Africa*] [*A publication*]   (DLA)
CPD .... Cards per Day [*Data processing*]   (BUR)
CPD .... Catalog of the Public Documents [*A bibliographic publication*]
CPD .... Center for Professional Development [*University of Kentucky*] [*Research center*]   (RCD)
CPD .... Center Program Director [*NASA*]   (KSC)
CPD .... Central Personnel Directorate [*British*]
CPD .... Central Postal Directory [*Army*]   (AABC)
CPD .... Central Procurement Division [*Marine Corps*]
CPD .... Central Pulse Distributor [*Telecommunications*]   (TEL)
CPD .... Cephalopelvic Disproportion [*Gynecology*]
CPD .... Cerro La Pandura [*Puerto Rico*] [*Seismograph station code, US Geological Survey*]   (SEIS)
CPD .... Charge Priming Device [*Video technology*]
CPD .... Chemical Propulsion Division [*NASA*]   (KSC)
CPD .... Chorioretinopathy and Pituitary Dysfunction [*Medicine*]
CPD .... Circuit Protection Device
CPD .... Citrate-Phosphate-Dextrose [*Anticoagulant*] [*Hematology*]
CPD .... Clips per Day [*Photocopying, microfilming*]
CPD .... Coaxial Power Divider
CPD .... Combat Potential Display [*SAGE*] [*Air Force*]
CPD .... Commercial Product Development
CPD .... Commercial Program Development
CPD .... Commission on Presidential Debates   (EA)
CPD .... Commissioner of Public Debt
CPD .... Committee on the Present Danger   (EA)
CPD .... Committee on Public Doublespeak   (EA)
CPD .... Common Pleas Division [*Legal term*]
CPD .... Commonwealth Parliamentary Debates [*A publication*]   (APTA)
CPD .... Communications Planning and Development
CPD .... Communist Party of Denmark [*Political party*]
CPD .... Community Planning and Development [*HUD*]   (OICC)
CPD .... Compound
CPD .... Comptroller General's Procurement Decisions [*A publication*]
CPD .... Computer Products Directory [*Information service or system*]   (EISS)
CPD .... Congressional Presentation Document
CPD .... Consolidated Programming Document
CPD .... Constituency Proportion Distribution
CPD .... Contact Potential Difference
CPD .... Contagious Pustular Dermatitis [*Dermatology*]
CPD .... Contract Potential Difference   (MCD)
CPD .... Contract and Purchase Department [*British military*]   (DMA)
CPD .... Controller of Projectile Development [*Ministry of Supply*] [*British*] [*World War II*]
CPD .... Convention a Paiement Differe [*Deferred Payment Agreement*] [*French*] [*Business term*]
CPD .... Converter, Pulse to DC [*Direct Current*] Voltage   (NASA)
CPD .... Coober Pedy [*Australia*] [*Airport symbol*]   (OAG)
CPD .... Counter-Propaganda Directorate [*British*]
CPD .... Coupled   (FAAC)
CPD .... Courier and Periodicals Division [*Later, UNESCO Publications and Periodicals*]
CPD .... Crew Passive Dosimeter [*NASA*]   (KSC)
CPD .... Crew Procedures Division [*NASA*]   (NASA)
CPD .... Crossing Protective Device
CPD .... Cumulative Population Doubling

CPD .... Cumulative Probability Distribution   (IEEE)
CPD .... Cupboard
CPD .... Cycles per Day
CPD .... Cyclopentadiene [*Organic chemistry*]
Cp D.......... Doctor of Chiropody
CPD .... Falmouth, MA [*Location identifier*] [*FAA*]   (FAAL)
CPD .... Law Reports, Common Pleas Division [*England*] [*A publication*]   (DLA)
CPD .... Palomar College, San Marcos, CA [*OCLC symbol*]   (OCLC)
CPD .... Popular Democratic Coalition [*Ecuador*] [*Political party*]   (PPW)
CPD .... South African Law Reports, Cape Provincial Division [*South Africa*] [*A publication*]   (DLA)
CPDA .... Chloramphenicol-Amended Potato Dextrose Agar [*Microbiology*]
CPDA .... Citrate-Phosphate-Dextrose-Adenine [*Anticoagulant*] [*Hematology*]
CPDA .... Copper Products Development Association [*Later, INCRA*]
CPDA .... Council for Periodical Distributors Associations   (EA)
CPDAMS.. Computer Program Development and Management System
CPDC........ Canadian People's [*Citizens and Residents*] Defence Committee
CPDC........ Command Processor Distributor Control   (MCD)
CPDC........ Community Planning and Design Center [*Information service or system*]   (EISS)
CPDC........ Computer Program Development Center [*Air Force*]   (MCD)
CPDC........ Conservative Party's Defense Committee [*British*]
cPDD .... cis-Platinum Diammine Dichloride [*Cisplatin*] [*Also, CDDP, cis-DDP, CPT, DDP, P*] [*Antineoplastic drug*]
CPDD .... Command Post Digital Display [*SAGE*] [*Air Force*]
CPDD .... Conceptual Project Design Description   (NRCH)
CPDDS...... Computer Program Detail Design Specification   (MCD)
CPDE........ Clinical Pharmacology and Drug Epidemiology [*Elsevier Book Series*] [*A publication*]
CPD/EW ... Campaign for Peace and Democracy/East and West   (EA)
CPDF........ Central Personnel Data File [*Office of Personnel Management*] [*Washington, DC*]
CPDF........ Centrifuge Plant Demonstration Facility [*Department of Energy*]
CPD (HR) ... Commonwealth Parliamentary Debates (House of Representatives) [*A publication*]   (APTA)
CP Div....... Common Pleas Division, English Law Reports [*1875-80*] [*A publication*]   (DLA)
CP Div (Eng) ... Common Pleas Division, English Law Reports [*1875-80*] [*A publication*]   (DLA)
CPDL........ Canadian Patents and Developments Limited
CPDL........ Cumulative Population Doubling Level
CPDLC...... Bellefonte District Library Center [*Library network*]
cpDNA....... Deoxyribonucleic Acid, Chloroplast [*Biochemistry, genetics*] [*Also, Chl-DNA, ctDNA*]
CPDP........ Computer Program Development Plan
CPD (R) ..... Commonwealth Parliamentary Debates (House of Representatives) [*A publication*]   (APTA)
CPDR........ Computer Program Deviation Request   (MCD)
CPDR........ Contractor's Preliminary Design Review   (MCD)
CPDRD..... Current Problems in Diagnostic Radiology [*A publication*]
CPDS........ Carboxypyridine Disulfide [*Biochemistry*]
CPD (S) ..... Commonwealth Parliamentary Debates (Senate) [*A publication*]   (APTA)
CPDS........ Computer Program Design [*or Development*] Specification [*NASA*]   (NASA)
CPDS........ Crew Procedures Documentation System   (MCD)
CPDSAS.... Canadian Plant Disease Survey [*A publication*]
CPDT........ Centre de Preparation Documentaire a la Traduction [*Center for Translation Documentation*] [*Information service or system*]   (IID)
CPDU .... (Chloropropyl)deoxyuridine [*Antiviral*]
CPDYCONTR ... Command Post Duty Controller [*Air Force*]
CPE............ Cable Pressurization Equipment
CPE............ Camp Elliot [*California*] [*Seismograph station code, US Geological Survey*]   (SEIS)
CPE............ Campeche [*Mexico*] [*Airport symbol*]   (OAG)
CPE............ Cape
CPE............ Carbon Paste Electrode [*Electrochemistry*]
CPE............ Carboxypeptidase E [*An enzyme*]
CPe............ Castrum Peregrini [*A publication*]
CPE............ Cathodic Protection Equipment
CPE............ Cellulose Polyethylene [*Organic chemistry*]
CPE............ Center for Packaging Education   (EA)
CPE............ Center for Popular Economics   (EA)
CPE............ Central Processing Element [*Data processing*]
CPE............ Central Programmer and Evaluator
CPE............ Centrally Planned Economy
CPE............ Centrum voor Postoraal in Europa [*Centre for Pastoral Work in Europe*]
CPE............ Cercle Populaire Europeen [*European Popular Circle - EPC*]   (EAIO)
CPE............ Certificate for Physical Education [*British*]   (ROG)
CPE............ Charged Particle Equilibrium   (DEN)
CPE............ Chief Polaris Executive [*Missiles*]
CPE............ Chief Program Engineer [*NASA*]   (NASA)

CPE........... Chlorinated Polyethylene [*Organic chemistry*]
CPE........... Chronic Pulmonary Emphysema [*Medicine*]
CPE........... Chronique de Politique Etrangere [*A publication*]
CPE........... Circadian Periodicity Experiment [*Skylab*] [*NASA*]
CPE........... Circular Probable Error
CPE........... Cloud Processing Equipment (AABC)
CPE........... Collective Protection Equipment
CPE........... Colorado Prime [*AMEX symbol*] (SPSG)
CPE........... Committee for Positive Education (EA)
CPE........... Common Professional Examination (DLA)
CPE........... Communist Party of Ecuador [*Political party*]
CPE........... Comparing Political Experiences [*National Science Foundation project*]
CPE........... Compass Resources Ltd. [*Vancouver Stock Exchange symbol*]
CPE........... Computer Performance Evaluation
CPE........... Computer Peripheral Equipment (KSC)
CPE........... Congres du Peuple Europeen
CPE........... Continuous Particle Electrophoresis
CPE........... Contractor Performance Evaluation
CPE........... Controlled-Potential Electrolysis
CPE........... Conventional Polyethylene
CPE........... Council on Podiatry Education [*Later, CPME*] (EA)
CPE........... Crew Personal Equipment
CPE........... Cryptopathic Effect
CPE........... Current Papers in Electrical and Electronics Engineering [*A publication*]
CPE........... Current Product Engineering
CPE........... Customer Premises Equipment [*Telecommunications*]
CPE........... Customer Provided Equipment [*Telecommunications*]
CPE........... Cytopathogenic [*or Cytopathic*] Effect [*Microbiology*]
CPE........... Pepperdine University, Malibu, CA [*OCLC symbol*] (OCLC)
CPe........... Petaluma Free Public Library, Petaluma, CA [*Library symbol*] [*Library of Congress*] (LCLS)
CPEA........ College Physical Education Association [*Later, NAPEHE*]
CPEA........ Concentrated Phosphate Export Association
CPEA........ Cooperative Program in Educational Administration
CPEB........ Central Physical Evaluation Board [*Navy*] (NVT)
CPEB........ Council for Professional Education for Business [*Later, AACSB*]
CPEB........ Cryogenic Positive Expulsion Bladder
CPEC........ Cranfield Product Engineering Centre [*Cranfield Institute of Technology*] [*British*] (CB)
CPEC........ Cyclopentenylcytosine [*Biochemistry*]
CPECD...... Comparative Physiology and Ecology [*A publication*]
CPECDM ... Comparative Physiology and Ecology [*A publication*]
CPed .... Certified Pedorthist
CPEDA...... Clinical Pediatrics [*Philadelphia*] [*A publication*]
C Pedag.... Cahiers Pedagogiques [*A publication*]
C Pedag Inst Et Occitanes ... Cahiers Pedagogiques. Institut d'Etudes Occitanes [*A publication*]
CPEDAM ... Clinical Pediatrics [*A publication*]
CPEDDP... Chirurgie Pediatrique [*A publication*]
CPEFIBA .. Conference Permanente de l'Europe de la Federation Internationale de Basketball [*Standing Conference for Europe of the International Basketball Federation*] (EAIO)
CPEG........ Contractor Performance Evaluation Group
CPEGA...... Canadian Petro Engineering [*A publication*]
CPEHS...... Consumer Protection and Environmental Health Service [*Later, Environmental Health Service*] [*US government*]
CPEI .... Centro de Promocion de Exportaciones e Inversiones [*Export and Investment Promotion Center*] [*Costa Rica*] (GEA)
CPEI .... Columbia Pictures Entertainment, Inc. [*NASDAQ symbol*] (NQ)
CPEI .... Computer Program End Item (NASA)
CPEI .... Electro-Optical Systems, Inc., Pasadena, CA [*Library symbol*] [*Library of Congress*] (LCLS)
CPEIP....... Center for Training, Experimentation, and Research on Education (IID)
CPEM....... Conference on Precision Electromagnetic Measurements (EA)
CPEMRC .. Circum-Pacific Energy and Mineral Resources Conference
C Pen......... Code Penal [*Penal Law*] (ILCA)
CPEN........ Cooper Resources & Energy [*NASDAQ symbol*] (NQ)
CPENA...... Chemical and Process Engineering [*London*] [*A publication*]
CPENB...... Chemical Processing and Engineering [*A publication*]
CPENC...... Canadian PEN Center (EAIO)
CP-ENDOR ... Circularly Polarized-Electron Nuclear Double Resonance [*Spectroscopy*]
CP (Eng) .... Common Pleas Division, English Law Reports [*1875-80*] [*A publication*] (DLA)
CPEO .... Chronic Progressive External Ophthalmoplegia [*Ophthalmology*]
CPEO .... Coalition of Public Employee Organizations (EA)
CPEO .... Cooperative Program for Educational Opportunity (EA)
CPEP .... Committee on Public Engineering Policy [*National Academy of Engineering*]
CPEP .... Contractor Performance Evaluation Plan [*or Program*] [*Military*] (AABC)
C-PER....... Calculated Protein Efficiency Ration [*Nutrition*]
CPER........ Consolidated Papers, Inc. [*NASDAQ symbol*] (NQ)
CPER........ Contractor Personnel Employment Report (NG)

CPer .... Perris Public Library, Perris, CA [*Library symbol*] [*Library of Congress*] (LCLS)
CPERF ...... Committee on Professional Ethics, Rights, and Freedom (EA)
CPermK ..... Kaiser Aluminum & Chemical Corp., Permanente, CA [*Library symbol*] [*Library of Congress*] (LCLS)
CPERS-A .. Chief of Personnel - Army [*Australia*]
CPES .... Contractor Performance Evaluation System
CPES .... Crew Procedures Evaluation Simulator (MCD)
CPES/RPS ... Revista Paraguaya de Sociologia. Centro Paraguayo de Estudios Sociologicos [*A publication*]
CPET .... Canadian Pacific Express and Transport
CPET .... Centennial Petroleum, Inc. [*NASDAQ symbol*] (NQ)
CPET .... Charged Particle Electrostatic Thruster
CPET .... Crystallized Polyethylene Terephthalate [*Plastics technology*]
CPETA ...... Canadian Petroleum [*A publication*]
CPEUG...... Computer Performance Evaluation Users Group (EA)
CPEx......... Command Post Exercise [*Military*]
CPF .... Canadian Patrol Frigate [*Canadian Navy*]
CPF .... Cargo Processing Facility [*Shipping*] (NASA)
CPF .... Catholic Peace Fellowship (EA)
CPF .... Catholic Press Features
CPF .... Central Post Fund [*Army*]
CPF .... Central Processing Facility (MCD)
CPF .... Chlorine Pentafluoride [*Inorganic chemistry*]
CPF .... Church Pension Fund (EA)
CPF .... Communist Party of Finland [*Political party*]
CPF .... Community Projects Foundation [*British*]
CPF .... Complete Power Failure [*Aviation*]
CPF .... Compromised Pulmonary Functions [*Medicine*]
CPF .... Comstock Partners Strategy Fund, Inc. [*NYSE symbol*] (SPSG)
CPF .... Conditional Peak Flow [*Biology*]
CPF .... Consolidated Professor Mines Ltd. [*Toronto Stock Exchange symbol*]
CPF .... Control Program Facility (MCD)
CPF .... Cost per Flight [*NASA*]
CPF .... Cotton Plant - Fargo Railway Co. [*AAR code*]
CPF .... Creative Playthings Foundation [*Defunct*]
CPF .... Cumulative Percentage Frequency
CPF .... Pepperdine University, Law Library, Malibu, CA [*OCLC symbol*] (OCLC)
CPFA .... Concerned Persons for Adoption (EA)
CPFA .... Cyclopropenoid Fatty Acid [*Biochemistry*]
CPFC .... Carl Perkins Fan Club (EA)
CPFC .... Charley Pride Fan Club (EA)
CPFC .... Comision de Proteccion Fitosanitaria para el Caribe [*Caribbean Plant Protection Commission - CPPC*] (EAIO)
CPFE .... COMSEC [*Communications Security*] Priorities Field Evaluation (MCD)
CPFF .... Christian Pro-Family Forum [*Australia*]
CPFF .... Cost Plus Fixed Fee [*Business term*]
CPFG........ CNO [*Chief of Naval Operations*] Program Fiscal Guidance [*Navy*] (CAAL)
CPFH .... Center for Population and Family Health [*Columbia University*] [*Research center*] (RCD)
CPFI .... Christian Pharmacists Fellowship International (EA)
CPFIA8 ..... Canadian Forestry Service. Pacific Forest Research Centre. Information Report BC-X [*A publication*]
CPFL .... Conference on Personal Finance Law [*Later, CCFL*] (EA)
CPFL .... Contingency Planning Facilities Lists (CINC)
CPFLBI ..... Computers and Fluids [*A publication*]
CPFMS...... COMRADE [*Computer-Aided Design Environment*] Permanent File Management System
CPFP .... Canadian Patrol Frigates Program [*Canadian Navy*]
CPFP .... Cancer Prevention Fellowship Program [*NCI*]
CPFR .... Calling Party Forced Release [*Telecommunications*] (TEL)
CPFR .... Continuous Page Facsimile Recorder
CPFRC ...... Central Pacific Fisheries Research Center [*National Oceanic and Atmospheric Administration*]
CPFSK...... Continuous Phase Frequency Shift Keying
CPFT .... Consolidated Professor Mines Ltd. [*NASDAQ symbol*] (NQ)
CPFT .... Contact Personality Factor Test [*Psychology*]
CPFT .... Customer-Premises Facility Terminal [*Telecommunications*] (TEL)
CPFT .... Fuller Theological Seminary, Pasadena, CA [*Library symbol*] [*Library of Congress*] (LCLS)
CPFV .... Commercial Passenger Fishing Vessel
CPFV .... Cucumber Pale Fruit Viroid
cpg............. Calcified Pea Gravel [*Archeology*]
CPG .... Canadian Plastics [*A publication*]
CPG .... Candidate Pass Generator [*NASA*]
CPG .... Capitol Publishing Group [*Information service or system*] (EISS)
CPG .... Central Pattern Generator [*Neurochemistry*]
CPG .... Champagne Resources Ltd. [*Vancouver Stock Exchange symbol*]
CPG .... Change Planning Group (NASA)
CPG .... Chromatopyrography [*for polymer characterization*]
CPG .... Civil Preparedness Guide [*Civil Defense*]
CPG .... Clavis Patrum Graecorum (BJA)
CPG .... Clock Pulse Generator
CPG .... Club for Philately in Gerontology (EA)

CPG .... Collector Platemakers Guild   (EA)
CPG .... College Publishers Group   (EA)
CPG .... Communications Publishing Group, Inc. [*Boston, MA*]
       [*Information service or system*]
       [*Telecommunications*]   (TSSD)
CPG .... Computer Power Group [*Australia*]
CPG .... Constant Pattern Generator
CPG .... Control Pattern Generator
CPG .... Controlled-Pore Glass [*Corning*]
CPG .... Conversion Programmer's Guide
CPG .... Coronary Prevention Group [*British*]
CPG .... Cotton Piece Goods
CPg .... Pacific Grove Public Library, Pacific Grove, CA [*Library
       symbol*] [*Library of Congress*]   (LCLS)
CPG .... Palm Springs Public Library, Palm Springs, CA [*OCLC
       symbol*]   (OCLC)
CPGA .... California Persimmon Growers Association   (EA)
CPGA .... China Pottery and Glassware Association   (EA)
CPGAF ...... Commission on Population Growth and the American Future
       [*Presidential commission*]
CPGB....... Communist Party of Great Britain [*Political party*]   (DCTA)
CPGC....... Course per Gyro Compass [*Navigation*]
CPgH .... Hopkins Marine Station, Pacific Grove, CA [*Library symbol*]
       [*Library of Congress*]   (LCLS)
CPGPAY ... Comparative and General Pharmacology [*A publication*]
CPH .... Capital Holding Corp. [*NYSE symbol*]   (SPSG)
CPH .... Captain Cook [*Hawaii*] [*Seismograph station code, US
       Geological Survey*]   (SEIS)
CPH .... Cards per Hour [*Data processing*]
CPH .... Catch per Hour [*Pisciculture*]
CPH .... Central Powerhouse
CPH .... Certificate in Public Health [*British*]
CPH .... Characters per Hour [*Data processing*]
CPH .... Chronic Persistent Hepatitis [*Medicine*]
CPh .... Classical Philology [*A publication*]
CPH .... Clay Products Haulers Bureau, Inc., Worthington OH [*STAC*]
CPH .... Close-Packed Hexagonal [*Metallography*]
CPH .... Colecao Poetas de Hoje [*A publication*]
CPH .... Communistische Partij Holland [*Communist Party of Holland*]
       [*Netherlands*]   (PPE)
CPH .... Compu-Home Systems International, Inc. [*Toronto Stock
       Exchange symbol*]
CPH .... Copenhagen [*Denmark*] [*Airport symbol*]   (OAG)
cph............. Copyright Holder [*MARC relator code*] [*Library of
       Congress*]   (LCCP)
CPH .... Counts per Hour
CPH .... Huntington Memorial Hospital, Pasadena, CA [*Library symbol*]
       [*Library of Congress*]   (LCLS)
CPhA .... Canadian Pharmaceutical Association   (EAIO)
CPHA .... Canadian Public Health Association
CPHA .... Commission on Professional and Hospital Activities   (EA)
CPHADV .. Clinical Pharmacy [*A publication*]
CPHC .... Central Pacific Hurricane Center [*Honolulu*] [*National Weather
       Service*]   (NOAA)
CPHCA ...... Chemistry and Physics of Carbon [*A publication*]
CPHCC...... Computers and the Humanities [*Database*] [*A publication*]
CPhCE....... United States Naval Civil Engineering Laboratory, Port
       Hueneme, CA [*Library symbol*] [*Library of
       Congress*]   (LCLS)
CPHE .... Common Personal Hygiene Equipment   (KSC)
CPHE .... Crew Personal Hygiene Equipment
CPHGM ..... Conference of Prince Hall Grand Masters   (EA)
CPHHC..... Card Programmable Hand-Held Calculator/Computer   (MCD)
CPhil.......... Classical Philology [*A publication*]   (OCD)
CPHJ........ Committee for Prisoner Humanity and Justice   (EA)
CPHL .... Central Professional Hockey League
CPHL .... Central Public Health Laboratory [*British*]   (IRUK)
CPHLD ..... Conference of Public Health Laboratory Directors [*Later,
       COPHL*]   (EA)
CPHM ...... Chief Pharmacist's Mate [*Navy rating*] [*Obsolete*]
CPHMA .... Commentationes Physico-Mathematicae [*A publication*]
CPHMDP ... Chief Pharmacist's Mate, Dental Prosthetic Technician [*Navy
       rating*] [*Obsolete*]
CPHM(RPA) ... Chief Pharmacist's Mate (Radium Plaque Adaptometer
       Operator) [*Navy rating*] [*Obsolete*]
CPHO .... Chief Photographer [*Navy rating*] [*Obsolete*]
CPHOM.... Chief Photographer's Mate [*Navy rating*] [*Obsolete*]
CPHPA...... Chieh P'ou Hsueh Pao [*A publication*]
CPHPA5.... Acta Anatomica Sinica [*A publication*]
CPHRDE... Clinical Pharmacology Research [*A publication*]
CPHRDE... International Journal of Clinical Pharmacology Research [*A
       publication*]
CPHS......... Center for Public Health Studies [*Portland State University*]
       [*Research center*]   (RCD)
CPHS......... Containment Pressure High Signal [*Nuclear energy*]   (IEEE)
CPHS......... Cost per Hand Stitch [*Tailoring*]
CPHSLA .... Central Pennsylvania Medical Librarians [*Library network*]
CPHV .... Center to Prevent Handgun Violence   (EA)
CPHV .... Conference of Public Health Veterinarians   (EA)
CPHYDZ... Colloques Phytosociologiques [*A publication*]
CPI............ Cable Pair Identification [*Telecommunications*]   (TEL)

CPI............ California Personality [*or Psychological*] Inventory
CPI............ Call Progress Indicator [*Telecommunications*]   (TEL)
CPI............ Caltex Pacific Indonesia
CPI............ Canadian Periodical Index [*The Globe and Mail*] [*Information
       service or system*]   (CRD)
CPI............ Cancer Potential Index
CPI............ Capital Planning Information Ltd. [*Information service or
       system*]   (IID)
CPI............ Capitol Publications, Inc. [*Information service or
       system*]   (EISS)
CPI............ Capri [*Italy*] [*Geomagnetic observatory code*]
CPI............ Capri Resources Ltd. [*Vancouver Stock Exchange symbol*]
CPI............ Carbon Preference Index [*Organic geochemistry*]
CPI............ Carboxypeptidase Inhibitor [*in potatoes*]
CPI............ Carded Packaging Institute   (EA)
CPI............ Cathedral Peace Institute   (EA)
CPI............ Center Pressure Index
CPI............ Center of Programmed Instruction   (DIT)
CPI............ Central Patents Index [*A publication*]
CPI............ Centrally Procured Items   (MCD)
CPI............ Change Package Identification
CPI............ Channel Port Index
CPI............ Characters per Inch [*Typesetting*]
CPI............ Chemical Process Industry
CPI............ Chief Patrol Inspector [*Immigration and Naturalization
       Service*]
CPI............ Chief Postal Inspector [*US Postal Service*]
CPI............ Chief of Public Information [*Army*]
CPI............ Chip Performance Index [*Data processing*]
CPI............ Chronic Pancreatic Insufficiency [*Medicine*]
CPI............ Church Planting International   (EA)
CPI............ Clay Pipe Institute   (EA)
CPI............ Clergy Pensions Institution [*Church of England*]
CPI............ Clock Pulse Interval
CPI............ Closed Pore Insulation
CPI............ Coherent Processing Interval [*Data processing*]
CPI............ Cohort Production Intervals
CPI............ Command Performance Indicator   (MCD)
CPI............ Commission Permanente Internationale de l'Acetylene, de la
       Soudure Autogene, et des Industries qui S'y Rattachent
       [*Permanent International Committee on Acetylene, Oxy-
       Acetylene Welding, and Allied Industries*]
CPI............ Commission Permanente Internationale Europeenne des Gaz
       Industriels et du Carbure de Calcium [*Permanent
       International European Commission on Industrial Gases
       and Calcium Carbide*]   (EAIO)
CPI............ Commission on Personnel Interchange [*Presidential*]
CPI............ Commission Phytosanitaire Interafricaine
CPI............ Common Program Interface [*Data processing*]
CPI............ Communist Party of India [*Political party*]   (PPW)
CPI............ Communist Party of Indonesia [*Political party*]   (PD)
CPI............ Communist Party of Ireland [*Political party*]   (PPW)
CPI............ Community Products, Incorporated
CPI............ Computer-Prescribed Instruction   (IEEE)
CPI............ Computer Projects, Incorporated [*Greensboro, NC*]
       [*Telecommunications*]   (TSSD)
CPI............ Concert Productions International [*Canada*]
CPI............ Conference Papers Index [*Cambridge Scientific Abstracts*]
       [*Bethesda, MD*] [*Information service or system*] [*A
       publication*]
CPI............ Conference Proceedings Index [*Database*] [*British Library*]
       [*Information service or system*]   (CRD)
CPI............ Constituent Particulars Index [*Australia*]
CPI............ Constitutional Psychopathic Inferior [*or Inferiority*]
CPI............ Consumer Price Index [*Department of Labor*] [*Database*]
CPI............ Contractor Preliminary Inspection
CPI............ Corps of Permanent Instructors [*British military*]   (DMA)
CPI............ Cost per Inquiry
CPI............ Cost per Instruction [*Data processing*]
CPI............ Cost Performance Index   (MCD)
CPI............ Cost Plus Incentive [*Business term*]   (MSA)
CPI............ Cottage Program International   (EA)
CPI............ Crash Position Indicator [*Aviation*]   (AFM)
CPI............ Crating, Packaging Instructions
CPI............ Credit Professionals International   (EA)
CPI............ Crop Protection Institute   (EA)
CPI............ Cross Pointer Indicator   (MCD)
CPI............ Cultural Pollution Index
CPI............ Cumulative Paperback Index 1939-1959 [*A publication*]
CPI............ Current Physics Index [*A publication*]
CPI............ Current Physics Information [*American Institute of Physics*]
       [*New York, NY*] [*Information service or system*]
CPI............ Current Priority Indicator
CPI............ Customs Port Investigator [*US Customs Service*]
CPI............ Cysteine Proteinase Inhibitor [*Biochemistry*]
CPI............ Public Health Division [*Coast Guard symbol*]
CPIA .... Cathodic Protection Industry Association   (EA)
CPIA .... Chemical Propulsion Information Agency [*Laurel, MD*] [*DoD*]
CPIA .... Chlorinated Paraffins Industry Association   (EA)
CPIA .... Close-Pair Interstitial Atom

CPIAAX .... Central Plantation Crops Research Institute [*Kasaragod*]. Annual Report [*A publication*]
CPIAF .... Cost-Plus-Incentive-Award Fee [*Business term*] (MCD)
CPIB .... Chlorophenoxyisobutyrate [*Pharmacology*]
CPIC .... Canadian Police Information Centre
CPIC .... Charged Particles Information Center [*ORNL*]
CPIC .... Coastal Patrol and Interdiction Craft [*Navy symbol*]
CPIC .... Combined Photographic Interpretation Center
CPIC .... Communist Party of Indo-China [*Political party*] (PPW)
CPIC .... Company Pensions Information Centre [*British*] (CB)
CPIC .... Computer Program Integration Contractor
CPIC .... Consumer Product Information Center
CPIC .... Cost Price of the Items Canceled [*Business term*]
CPIF .... Character Position in Frame
CPIF .... Cost-Plus-Incentive Fee [*Business term*] (AFM)
CPI/FDR ... Crash Position Indicator/Flight Data Recorder [*Aviation*] (MCD)
CPII .... Consumer Products Information Index [*National Institute of Standards and Technology*]
CP-ILS...... Correlation-Protected Instrument Landing System
CPI(M)...... Communist Party of India (Marxist) [*Political party*] (PPW)
CPI Mgmt ... CPI [*Current Physics Index*] Management Service [*A publication*]
CPI(ML).... Communist Party of India (Marxist-Leninist) [*Political party*] (PD)
CPI M-L .... Communist Party of Ireland (Marxist-Leninist) [*Political party*] (PPW)
CPIN......... Canadian Press Information Network (IID)
CPIN......... Change Package Identification Number
CPIN......... Computer Program Identification Numbers (MCD)
CPIN......... Crankpin (MSA)
CP Ind....... Central Provinces, India (DLA)
CPIP .... Computer Pneumatic Input Panel
CPIP .... Computer Program Implementation Process
CPI/PPI .... Consumer and Producer Price Indexes [*Department of Labor*] [*Database*]
CPIR......... Command Performance Indicator Review (MCD)
CPIRA .... Carbon Paper and Inked Ribbon Association [*Defunct*] (EA)
CPIRA .... Copying Products and Inked Ribbon Association (EA)
CPIS .... Center Pivot Irrigation System
CPIS .... Computerised Personnel Information System [*British*]
CPIS .... Consumer Price Index for Services
CPISRA ..... Cerebral Palsy International Sports and Recreation Association [*Arnhem, Netherlands*] (EAIO)
CPIT .... Contract Price of Items Terminated [*Business term*]
CPITUS..... Comite Permanent International des Techniques et de l'Urbanisme Souterrains [*Permanent and International Committee of Underground Town Planning and Construction*]
CPI-U .... Consumer Price Index for All Urban Consumers (OICC)
CPIUS .... Comite Permanent International d'Urbanisme Souterrain
CPIV......... Comite Permanent des Industries du Verre de la CEE [*Brussels, Belgium*] (EAIO)
CPIV......... Comite Permanent International du Vinaigre [*Permanent International Committee on Vinegar*] [*Common Market*]
CPIW........ Certified Professional Insurance Woman [*Designation awarded by National Association of Insurance Women*]
CPI-W ...... Consumer Price Index for Urban Wage Earners and Clerical Workers (OICC)
CPJ .... Canadian Pharmaceutical Journal [*A publication*]
CPJ .... Care Point Medical Centres Ltd. [*Vancouver Stock Exchange symbol*]
CPJ .... Center for Public Justice (EA)
CPJ .... Chambre de Commerce et d'Industrie de Nouvelle Caledonie. Bulletin [*A publication*]
CPJ .... Collision Parts Journal [*A publication*] (EAAP)
CPJ .... Committee to Protect Journalists (EA)
CPJ .... Committee for Public Justice (EA)
CPJ .... Conoseal Pipe Joint
CPJ .... Corpus Papyrorum Judaicarum (BJA)
CPJI.......... Cour Permanente de Justice Internationale [*Permanent Court of International Justice*] [*Later, CIJ*]
CPJI-A/B .. Cour Permanente de Justice Internationale. Serie A/B. Recueil des Arrets. Avis Consultatifs et Ordonnances [*A publication*]
CPJI-B....... Cour Permanente de Justice Internationale. Serie B. Recueil des Avis Consultatifs [*A publication*]
CPJO .... Circumpolar Journal [*A publication*]
CPJOAC ... Canadian Pharmaceutical Journal [*A publication*]
CPJP......... Jet Propulsion Laboratory, Pasadena, CA [*Library symbol*] [*Library of Congress*] (LCLS)
CPK .... Cabbage Patch Kids
CPK .... Central Pastry Kitchen [*Army*] (AABC)
CPK .... Cents per Kilometer (ADA)
CPK .... Communist Party of Kampuchea [*Political party*] (PD)
CPK .... Communist Party of Kazakhstan [*Soviet Union*] [*Political party*]
CPK .... Cone Peak [*Hawaii*] [*Seismograph station code, US Geological Survey*] (SEIS)
CPK .... Corey-Pauling-Koltun [*Molecular models*]
CPK .... Creatine Phosphokinase [*Preferred form is CK*] [*An enzyme*]

CPKD .... Creatine Phosphokinase Depleted [*Medicine*]
CPKNDH .. Clinical Pharmacokinetics [*A publication*]
CPL .... Calgary Public Library [*UTLAS symbol*]
CPL............ Capability Password Level [*Telecommunications*] (TEL)
CPL............ Carnegie Library of Pittsburgh, Pittsburgh, PA [*OCLC symbol*] (OCLC)
CPL............ Carolina Power & Light Co. [*NYSE symbol*] (SPSG)
CPL............ CAST [*Computerized Automatic System Tester*] Programming Language
CPL............ Cement Plaster (AAG)
CPL............ Certified Professional Logistician (MCD)
CPL............ Chaparral Airlines [*Abilene, TX*] [*FAA designator*] (FAAC)
CPL............ Chapel Resources, Inc. [*Vancouver Stock Exchange symbol*]
CPL............ Chaplin [*Connecticut*] [*Seismograph station code, US Geological Survey*] [*Closed*] (SEIS)
CPL............ Characters per Line [*Typesetting*]
CPL............ Chief of Personnel and Logistics [*Navy*] [*British*]
CPL............ Chord Plane Line (MCD)
CPL............ Circularly Polarized Luminescence [*Spectroscopy*]
CPL............ Civilian Personnel Letter
CPL............ Clavis Patrum Latinorum (BJA)
CPL............ Collective Pitch Lever
CPL............ Combined Programming Language [*Data processing*]
CPL............ Command Programming Language
CPL............ Commercial Pilot's Licence [*British*] (DBQ)
CPL............ Commercial Products List (AFIT)
CPL............ Common Program Language [*Data processing*] (AABC)
CPL............ Common Pulse Line
CPL............ Communist Party of Lesotho [*Political party*] (PD)
CPL............ Communist Party of Luxembourg [*Political party*]
CPL............ Complement
CPL............ Complete
CPL............ Component Preparation Laboratory [*Oak Ridge*] [*Energy Research and Development Administration*]
CPL............ Comprehensive Personal Liability [*Insurance*]
CPL............ Computer Program Library (BUR)
CPL............ Computer Projects Limited
CPL............ Contractor Procurement List (NATG)
CPL............ Conversational Programming Language [*High-level language*] [*Digital Equipment Corp.*] [*Data processing*]
CPL............ Converted Prelease (ADA)
CPL............ Conveyancer and Property Lawyer. New Series [*A publication*]
CPL............ Core Performance Log [*Nuclear energy*] (IEEE)
CPL............ Corporal [*Military*] (AABC)
CPL............ Corps Phase Line
CPL............ Corpus Poetarum Latinorum [*A publication*] (OCD)
CPL............ Council of Planning Librarians (EA)
CPL............ Couple (KSC)
CPL............ Criminal Procedure Law [*New York, NY*] [*A publication*]
CPL............ Critical Path Length
CPL............ Current Flight Plan Message [*Aviation code*]
CPL............ Current Privilege Level [*Computer programs*] (BYTE)
CPL............ Current Property Law [*British*]
CPL............ Current Property Lawyer [*1852-53*] [*England*] [*A publication*] (DLA)
CPL............ Cycle Proof Listing [*IRS*]
CPl .... Placentia District Library, Placentia, CA [*Library symbol*] [*Library of Congress*] (LCLS)
CPLA .... Conference for Progressive Labor Action
CPla .... El Dorado County Free Library, Placerville, CA [*Library symbol*] [*Library of Congress*] (LCLS)
CPLC .... Center for Philosophy, Law, Citizenship (EA)
CPL & D..... Civilian Personnel Letters and Dispatches
CPLD........ Coupled (MSA)
CPLE .... Center for Policy and Law in Education [*University of Miami*] [*Research center*] (RCD)
CPLE .... Constantinople [*Later, Istanbul*] [*Province in Turkey*]
CPLEE ...... Charged Particle Lunar Environment Experiment [*NASA*]
CPLF .... Congres des Psychanalystes de Langue Francaise [*Congress of Romance Language Psychoanalysts*] (EAIO)
CPLG........ Coupling (KSC)
CPlhC .... Contra Costa County Library, Pleasant Hill, CA [*Library symbol*] [*Library of Congress*] (LCLS)
CPLI .... Catholic Periodical and Literature Index [*A publication*]
CPLIA .... Contracting Plasterers' and Lathers' International Association [*Later, IAWCC*] (EA)
CPLJ......... Camp Lejeune Railroad Co. [*AAR code*]
CPLK........ Comite Permanent de Liaison des Kinesitherapeutes de la CEE [*Standing Liaison Committee of Physiotherapists within the EEC - SLCP*] [*Copenhagen, Denmark*] (EAIO)
CPLMB ..... Chief Plumber [*British military*] (DMA)
CPLMT ..... Complement
CPLN........ California Palace of the Legion of Honor [*San Francisco*]
C Pl Phys C Fus ... Comments on Plasma Physics and Controlled Fusion [*A publication*]
CPLR......... Center of Pillar
CPLR......... Central Provinces Law Reports [*India*] [*A publication*] (DLA)
CPLR......... Civil Practice Law and Rules [*New York, NY*]
CPLR........ Coupler (AAG)
CPLRBW .. Chirurgia Plastica et Reconstructiva [*A publication*]
CPLRY ...... Capillary (MSA)

CPLS .... Care Plus, Inc. [*NASDAQ symbol*]   (NQ)
CPLSA .... Canadian Journal of Plant Science [*A publication*]
CPLSAY ..... Canadian Journal of Plant Science [*A publication*]
C/PLSEL ... Clothing and Personal Life Support Equipment Laboratory
　　　　　　　　[*Army Natick Laboratories, MA*]
CPLT .... Camino, Placerville & Lake Tahoe Railroad Co. [*AAR code*]
CPLT .... Complete   (ROG)
CPLT .... Copilot
CPLX .... Complex
CPM .... Call Protocol Message [*Telecommunications*]   (TEL)
CPM .... Capsule Positioning Mechanism [*Aerospace*]
CPM .... Cards per Minute [*Data processing*]
CPM .... Cargo Propulsion Module [*NASA*]   (KSC)
CPM .... Cathode Pulse Modulation
CPM .... CCNU [*Lomustine*], Procarbazine, Methotrexate
　　　　　　　　[*Antineoplastic drug regimen*]
CPM .... Center Program Manager [*NASA*]   (KSC)
CPM .... Central Path Method [*Data processing*]
CPM .... Central Pontine Myelinolysis [*Medicine*]
CPM .... Central Processing Modules [*Data processing*]   (MCD)
CPM .... Centre for Pest Management [*Simon Fraser University*]
　　　　　　　　[*Canada*] [*Research center*]   (RCD)
CPM .... Certified Property Manager [*Designation awarded by Institute
　　　　　　　　of Real Estate Management*]
CPM .... Certified Purchasing Manager [*Designation awarded by
　　　　　　　　National Association of Purchasing Management, Inc.*]
CPM .... Cesarean Prevention Movement   (EA)
CPM .... Characters per Minute [*Data processing*]
CPM .... Chief Patternmaker [*Navy rating*] [*Obsolete*]
CPM .... Chlorpheniramine Maleate [*Antihistamine*]
CPM .... Chosen People Ministries   (EA)
CPM .... Coarse Particulate Matter [*Pisciculture*]
CPM .... College of Petroleum and Minerals [*Dhahran, Saudi Arabia*]
CPM .... Colliding-Pulse-Mode [*LASER*]
CPM .... Colonial Police Medal [*British*]
CPM .... Coloured Progressive Matrices
CPM .... Combat Air Patrol Mission [*Air Force*]
CPM .... Comite pro Maria [*An association*]   (EAIO)
CPM .... Comite du Patrimoine Mondial [*World Heritage Committee -
　　　　　　　　WHC*]   (EAIO)
CPM .... Command Processor Module
CPM .... Common Particular Meter [*Music*]
CPM .... Communist Party of India - Marxist [*Political party*]   (FEA)
CPM .... Communist Party of Malaya [*Malaysia*] [*Political party*]   (PD)
CPM .... Communist Party of Malta [*Political party*]
CPM .... Communist Party Marxist
CPM .... Community Planning and Management [*HUD*]
CPM .... Commutative Principle for Multiplication [*Mathematics*]
CPM .... Compton, CA [*Location identifier*] [*FAA*]   (FAAL)
CPM .... Computer Performance Management
CPM .... Computer Program Module   (NASA)
CPM .... Computer Programmer's Manual   (MCD)
CPM .... Conference Permanente d'Etudes sur les Civilisations du
　　　　　　　　Monde Mediterraneen [*Standing Conference of Studies on
　　　　　　　　the Civilisations of the Mediterranean World*]   (EAIO)
CPM .... Conference Permanente Mediterraneenne pour la Cooperation
　　　　　　　　Internationale [*Standing Mediterranean Conference for
　　　　　　　　International Cooperation - COPEMCI*]   (EAIO)
CPM .... Conference Preparatory Meeting [*ITU/WARC*]
CPM .... Congregation of Priests of Mercy [*Fathers of Mercy*] [*Roman
　　　　　　　　Catholic religious order*]
CPM .... Continental Pharma Cryosan, Inc. [*Toronto Stock Exchange
　　　　　　　　symbol*]
CPM .... Continuous Passive Motion [*Medicine*]
CPM .... Contract Program Manager   (MCD)
CPM .... Contractor Performance Measurement   (MCD)
CP/M .... Control Program for Microcomputers [*Operating system*]
CP/M .... Control Program/Monitor [*Data processing*]
CPM .... Conversational Program Module [*Fujitsu Ltd.*] [*Japan*]
CPM .... Cost per Thousand [*Advertising*]
CPM .... Counts per Minute
CPM .... Critical-Path Management
CPM .... Critical Path Method [*Graph theory*]
　　　　　　　　[*Telecommunications*]   (TEL)
CPM .... Current Physics Microform [*A publication*]
CPM .... Current Processor Mode
CPM .... Cycles per Minute
CPM .... Cyclophosphamide [*Cytoxan*] [*Antineoplastic drug*]
CPMA .... Central Processor Memory Address [*Data processing*]
CPMA .... Common Price and Marketing Arrangement [*British*]
CPMA .... Computer Peripheral Manufacturers Association
CPMAA ..... Cuoio, Pelli, Materie Concianti [*A publication*]
CPMAJO .. Conference of Presidents of Major American Jewish
　　　　　　　　Organizations   (EA)
CPMAS ..... Communications Performance Monitoring and Assessment
　　　　　　　　[*Military*]
CPMAS ..... Cross-Polarization Magic Angle Spinning [*Spectroscopy*]
CPMB .... Concrete Plant Manufacturers Bureau   (EA)
CPMC .... (Chlorophenyl)methylcarbamate [*Organic chemistry*]
CPMC .... Construction Products Manufacturers Council   (EA)

CPmD .... Defense Language Institute, West Coast Branch, Presidio of
　　　　　　　　Monterey, CA [*Library symbol*] [*Library of
　　　　　　　　Congress*]   (LCLS)
CPME .... Conseil Parlementaire du Mouvement Europeen
CPME .... Council on Podiatric Medical Education   (EA)
CPMF .... Case Project Master File [*IRS*]
CpMF .... Casopis pro Moderni Filologii [*A publication*]
CPMG .... Carr-Purcell-Meiboom-Gill [*Radiologic instrumentation*]
CPMHA6 .. Comunicaciones Paleontologicas. Museo de Historia Natural de
　　　　　　　　Montevideo [*A publication*]
CPMI .... Command Personnel Management Inspections   (AABC)
CPMIS ...... Civilian Personnel Management Information System   (MCD)
CPMJ .... Canadian Paper Money Journal [*A publication*]
CPMLS ..... Centre for Petroleum and Mineral Law Studies [*University of
　　　　　　　　Dundee*] [*United Kingdom*]   (CB)
CPMM ...... Conseil des Premiers Ministres des Maritimes [*Council of
　　　　　　　　Maritime Premiers - CMP*] [*Canada*]
CPMMAL ... Collected Papers in Medicine. Mayo Clinic and Mayo
　　　　　　　　Foundation [*A publication*]
CPM-ML ... Communist Party of Malaya - Marxist-Leninist [*Malaysia*]
　　　　　　　　[*Political party*]   (PD)
CPMN ...... Central Pacific Minerals NL [*NASDAQ symbol*]   (NQ)
CPMO .... Compendium of Plausible Materiel Options [*Army*]
CPMO .... Contract Parts Material Order
CPMO .... Control Processes in Multicellular Organisms
CPMOS ..... Career Progression Military Occupational Specialty   (MCD)
CPMP .... Civilian Personnel Modernization Project [*Military*]
CPMP .... Crew Procedures Management Plan [*NASA*]   (NASA)
CPMR .... Conference of Peripheral Maritime Regions of the EEC   (EAIO)
CPMR .... Conference des Regions Peripheriques Maritimes de la CEE
　　　　　　　　[*Conference of Peripheral Maritime Regions of the
　　　　　　　　EEC*]   (EAIO)
CPM-RF .... Communist Party of Malaya - Revolutionary Faction
　　　　　　　　[*Malaysia*] [*Political party*]   (PD)
CPMS .... Cable Pressure Monitoring System [*Bell System*]
CPMS .... Canadian Paper Money Society
CPMS .... Check Plus Minus Subroutine
CPMS .... Communications Procedures Management System   (MCD)
CPMS .... Comprehensive Power Management System [*Military*]   (CAAL)
CPMS .... Contractor Property Management System
CPMSB6 .... Colloid and Polymer Science [*A publication*]
CPMSR ...... Canada. Fisheries and Marine Service. Pacific Marine Science
　　　　　　　　Report [*A publication*]
CPmuN ...... United States Navy, Naval Missile Center, Point Mugu, CA
　　　　　　　　[*Library symbol*] [*Library of Congress*]   (LCLS)
CPMV .... Cowpea Mosaic Virus
CPMYAN ... Contributions to Primatology [*A publication*]
CPN .... Air Transportable Pulse RADAR Navigation Aid
　　　　　　　　[*Aviation*]   (FAAC)
CPN .... Butte, MT [*Location identifier*] [*FAA*]   (FAAL)
CPN .... Canadian Press Newstex [*The Canadian Press*] [*Information
　　　　　　　　service or system*]   (IID)
CPN .... Cape Rodney [*Papua New Guinea*] [*Airport symbol*]   (OAG)
CPN .... Chronic Pyelonephritis [*Urology*]
CPN .... Commercial Paper Note [*Banking*]
CPN .... Communist Party of Nepal [*Political party*]   (FEA)
CPN .... Communist Party of Norway [*Political party*]
CPN .... Communistische Partij van Nederland [*Communist Party of the
　　　　　　　　Netherlands*]   (PPE)
CPN .... Comp-Data International, Inc. [*Vancouver Stock Exchange
　　　　　　　　symbol*]
CPN .... Contractor Profit News [*A publication*] [*Also, an information
　　　　　　　　service or system*]   (IID)
CPN .... Corporation   (ROG)
CPN .... Country Progressive National [*Australia*] [*Political party*]
CPN .... Coupon   (ADA)
CP du N .... Cours de Perfectionnement du Notariat [*A publication*]
CPN .... CP-17 [*Nevada*] [*Seismograph station code, US Geological
　　　　　　　　Survey*] [*Closed*]   (SEIS)
CPN .... CP National Corp. [*NYSE symbol*]   (SPSG)
CPN .... Crime Prevention News [*A publication*]
CPN .... Critical Path Network
CPN .... Personal Names from Cuneiform Inscriptions of the Cassite
　　　　　　　　Period   (BJA)
CPNA .... Community Psychiatric Nursing Association [*British*]
CPNC .... Cameroon People's National Congress
CPNC .... Cherry Point, North Carolina [*Marine Corps Air Station*]
CPNF .... Cost Plus No Fee [*Business term*]   (MCD)
CPNMAQ ... Clinical Proceedings. Children's Hospital National Medical
　　　　　　　　Center [*A publication*]
CPNMR .... Cross-Polarization Nuclear Magnetic Resonance [*Physics*]
CPNS .... CP National Network Services [*Concord, CA*]
　　　　　　　　[*Telecommunications*]   (TSSD)
CPNSC ...... Crystal Palace National Sports Centre [*British*]
CPNTR ...... Carpenter   (MSA)
CPNZ .... Communist Party of New Zealand [*Political party*]
CPO .... California Polytechnic State University, Pomona, CA [*OCLC
　　　　　　　　symbol*]   (OCLC)
CPO .... Cases per Officer [*Term used by crime laboratories*]
CPO .... Catholic Press Office [*British*]
CPO .... Center for Population Options   (EA)

CPO .... Central Planning Office [*NASA*] (KSC)
CPO .... Central Procurement Office (AABC)
CPO .... Central Project Office [*of ARS, Department of Agriculture*]
CPO .... Central Provision Office [*World War II*]
CPO .... Certified Prosthetist and Orthotist
CPO .... Changing Path of Operation
CPO .... Chief Petty Officer [*Navy*]
CPO .... Chief Political Officer [*British Military Administration*]
CPO .... Chief Post Office [*British*] (ADA)
CPO .... Chief Preventive Officer [*Customs*] [*British*] (ROG)
CPO .... Christian Publicity Organisation [*British*]
CPO .... Circular Parking Orbit [*Aerospace*] (AAG)
CPO .... Civil Post Office (AFM)
CPO .... Civilian Personnel Office [*or Officer*]
CPO .... Cloud Physics Observatory [*University of Hawaii*]
CPO .... Code Practice Oscillator
CPO .... Command Post Officer [*Military*]
CPO .... Command Pulse Output
CPO .... Committee on Period One [*US committee concerned with the period between the end of the German War and the end of the Japanese War*] [*World War II*]
CPO .... Commodity Pool Operator
CPO .... Community Post Office
CPo .... Comparative Politics [*A publication*]
CPO .... Complete Provisions Only
CPO .... Component Pilot Overhaul [*Navy*] (NG)
CPO .... Compulsory Purchase Order [*British*]
CPO .... Computer Printout (ADA)
CPO .... Concurrent Peripheral Operations (BUR)
CPO .... Conference of Private Organizations (EA)
CPO .... Controlled Precision Oscillator
CPO .... Corporate Aircraft Co. [*Gardner, KS*] [*FAA designator*] (FAAC)
CPO .... Cost Proposal Outline (AAG)
CPO .... Cumberland Plateau [*Tennessee*] [*Seismograph station code, US Geological Survey*] (SEIS)
CPO .... Custom Patrol Officer [*British*]
CPO .... Mount Wilson Observatory, Pasadena, CA [*Library symbol*] [*Library of Congress*] (LCLS)
CPOA .... Concerned Pet Owners' Association (EA)
CPOA .... United States Coast Guard Chief Petty Officer Association (EA)
CPOACMN ... Chief Petty Officer, Aircrewman [*British military*] (DMA)
CPOB .... Cyclophosphamide, Prednisone, Oncovin [*Vincristine*], Bleomycin [*Antineoplastic drug regimen*]
CPOC .... Calculated Particulate Organic Carbon [*Oceanography*]
CPOC .... Chrysler Product Owners Club (EA)
CPOC .... Clay Pigmented Organic Coating
CPOCA ..... Chief Petty Officer, Caterer [*British military*] (DMA)
CPOCK ..... Chief Petty Officer, Cook [*British military*] (DMA)
CPODA ..... Contention Priority-Oriented Demand Assignment [*Protocol*] [*Data processing*]
CPOEA ...... Canadian Power Engineer [*A publication*]
CPOEB ...... Canadian Power Engineering and Plant Maintenance [*A publication*]
CPOL .... Communications Procedure-Oriented Language [*Data processing*]
CPOM .... Coarse Particulate Organic Matter
CPom .... Pomona Public Library, Pomona, CA [*Library symbol*] [*Library of Congress*] (LCLS)
CPOMA ..... Chief Petty Officer, Medical Assistant [*British military*] (DMA)
CPomCP .... California Polytechnic State University, Pomona, CA [*Library symbol*] [*Library of Congress*] (LCLS)
CPomG ...... General Dynamics Corp., Pomona Division Library, Pomona, CA [*Library symbol*] [*Library of Congress*] (LCLS)
CPOMP ..... Center for Population Options' Media Project (EA)
CPomP ...... Pacific State Hospital, Pomona, CA [*Library symbol*] [*Library of Congress*] (LCLS)
CPOP .... Certified Park Operators Program (EA)
CPOPT ..... Chief Petty Officer, Physical Trainer [*British military*] (DMA)
CPor .... Porterville Public Library, Porterville, CA [*Library symbol*] [*Library of Congress*] (LCLS)
CPorH .... Porterville State Hospital, Porterville, CA [*Library symbol*] [*Library of Congress*] (LCLS)
C-PORT .... Committee for Private Offshore Rescue and Towing (EA)
CPOS .... Civilian Personnel Occupational Standards [*Military*] (AABC)
CPOS .... Continuous Production Operation Sheet
CPOS .... Cursor Position (MCD)
CPOSA ...... Chief Petty Officer, Stores Accountant [*British military*] (DMA)
CPOSMA ... Conference of Presidents and Officers of State Medical Associations [*Later, FMA*] (EA)
CPOSTD ... Chief Petty Officer, Steward [*British military*] (DMA)
CPOW .... Chief Petty Officer of the Watch [*Navy*]
CPOWTR ... Chief Petty Officer, Writer [*British military*] (DMA)
CPOX .... CP Overseas, Inc. [*NASDAQ symbol*] (NQ)
CPP .... Calprop Corp. [*AMEX symbol*] (SPSG)
CPP .... Caltech Population Program [*Agency for International Development*] (IID)
CPP .... Canada Pension Plan
CPP .... Capital Punishment Project (EA)

CPP .... Card Punching Printer [*Computer output device*] [*Data processing*] (BUR)
CPP .... Career Planning Program [*Vocational guidance test*]
CPP .... Center for Plutonium Production [*France*] (NRCH)
CPP .... Center for Policy Process [*Defunct*]
CPP .... Center for the Progress of Peoples (EAIO)
CPP .... Central Perfusion Pressure [*Medicine*]
CPP .... Central Processing Point [*Data processing*]
CPP .... Cerebral Perfusion Pressure [*Medicine*]
CPP .... Certified Protection Professional [*Designation awarded by American Society for Industrial Security*]
CPP .... Children's Plea for Peace [*Later, World Pen Pals*]
CPP .... Chondrosoma Permeation Pattern [*Oncology*]
CPP .... Choroid Plexus Papilloma [*Medicine*]
CPP .... Civilian Personnel Pamphlet [*Military*]
CPP .... Coal and Petroleum Products [*Department of Employment*] [*British*]
CPP .... Coalition for Prompt Pay (EA)
CPP .... Codice di Procedura Penale [*Code of Criminal Procedure*] [*A publication*] (ILCA)
CPP .... Coil Power Programmer [*Nuclear energy*] (NRCH)
CPP .... Collaborative Perinatal Project
CPP .... Commercial Practices Program [*Air Force*]
CPP .... Commercial Property Products
CPP .... Committee on Persistent Pesticides (EA)
CPP .... Committee on Political Parties
CPP .... Commonwealth Parliamentary Papers [*A publication*] (APTA)
CPP .... Communist Party of the Philippines [*Political party*]
CPP .... Competitive Prototype Phase (MCD)
CPP .... Computer Program Package (CAAL)
CPP .... Conductive Plastic Potentiometer
CPP .... Conference of Actuaries in Public Practice. Proceedings [*A publication*]
CPP .... Consolidated Pipe Lines Co. [*Toronto Stock Exchange symbol*]
CPP .... Constant Purchasing Power
CPP .... Consumer Pesticide Project (EA)
CPP .... Containment Pressure Protection [*Nuclear energy*] (IEEE)
CPP .... Contract Pricing Proposal (MCD)
CPP .... Control and Protection Panel
CPP .... Controllable Pitch Propeller [*For ships*] (MCD)
CPP .... Convention People's Party [*1949-1966*] [*Ghana*]
CPP .... Copiapo [*Chile*] [*Seismograph station code, US Geological Survey*] (SEIS)
CPP .... Coronary Perfusion Pressure [*Cardiology*]
CPP .... Corpus of Dated Palestinian Pottery (BJA)
CPP .... Corpus of Palestinian Pottery (BJA)
CPP .... Corrosion Prevention Panel
CPP .... Council of Psychoanalytic Psychotherapists (EA)
CPP .... Country Policy Programme [*Foreign trade*] [*British*]
CPP .... Critical Path Planning
CPP .... Croatian Peasant Party (EA)
CPP .... Cullman, AL [*Location identifier*] [*FAA*] (FAAL)
CPP .... Current Papers in Physics [*A publication*]
CPP .... Current Purchasing Power
CPP .... Cyclopyrophosphoglycerate [*Biochemistry*]
CPP .... Pasadena Public Library, Pasadena, CA [*OCLC symbol*] (OCLC)
CPPA .... Canadian Periodical Publishers Association
CPPA .... Canadian Potash Producers Association
CPPA .... Canadian Pulp and Paper Association [*See also ACPPP*]
CPPA .... Center for Prevention of Premature Arterial Sclerosis
CPPA .... (Chlorophenoxy)propionic Acid [*Biochemistry*]
CPPA .... Chrysler Performance Parts Association (EA)
CPPA .... Classroom Periodical Publishers Association [*Later, CPA*] (EA)
CPPA .... Coated and Processed Paper Association [*Defunct*]
CPPA .... Conference for Progressive Political Action
CPPA .... Crusher and Portable Plant Association
CPPA Newsprint Data ... CPPA [*Canadian Pulp and Paper Association*] Newsprint Data [*A publication*]
CPPA Newsprint Rept ... CPPA [*Canadian Pulp and Paper Association*] Monthly Newsprint Report [*A publication*]
CPPA Press Dig ... CPPA [*Canadian Pulp and Paper Association*] Press Digest [*A publication*]
CPPA Ref Tables ... CPPA [*Canadian Pulp and Paper Association*] Reference Tables [*A publication*]
CPPA Tech Sect Proc ... CPPA [*Canadian Pulp and Paper Association*] Technical Section. Proceedings [*A publication*]
CPPB .... Continuous Positive Pressure Breathing [*Physiology*]
CPPC .... Caribbean Plant Protection Commission [*See also CPFC*] [*Port Of Spain, Trinidad*] (EAIO)
CPPC .... Century Park Pictures Corporation [*Minneapolis, MN*] [*NASDAQ symbol*] (NQ)
CPPC .... Collatis Pecuniis Poni Curaverunt [*They Collected the Money and Had Put in Position*] [*Latin*]
CPPC .... Cost Plus a Percentage of Cost
CPPCA ...... California Probation, Parole, and Correctional Association
CPPCA ...... Colour Printed Pottery Collectors Association (EA)
CPPCC ...... Chinese People's Political Consultative Conference
CP-PCO .... Cargo Projects - Program Control Office [*NASA*] (NASA)
CPPD .... Calcium Pyrophosphate Deposition [*Medicine*]

CPPD........	Calcium Pyrophosphate Dihydrate [*Inorganic chemistry*]
CPPD........	Capped (MSA)
CPPD........	Chest Physiotherapy and Physical Drainage [*Medicine*]
CPPD........	Consumers Public Power District
CPPG........	CNO [*Chief of Naval Operations*] Policy and Planning Guidance
CPPI........	Competitive Pipeline Price Index
CPPI........	Computer Peripheral Products [*NASDAQ symbol*] (NQ)
CPPI........	Consultative Panel on Public Information [*United Nations*] [*Telecommunications*] (TEL)
CPPI........	Coolant Pump Power Inverters (MCD)
CPPL........	Civilian Personnel and Payroll Letter [*Military*]
CPPM........	Civilian Personnel Procedures Manual [*Military*]
CPPM........	Clinical Physics and Physiological Measurement [*A publication*]
CPPM........	Communication Prediction Program [*NASA*] (KSC)
CPPMA....	Canadian Public Personnel Management Association
CPPMD5...	Clinical Physics and Physiological Measurement [*A publication*]
CPP/ML....	Communist Party of the Philippines/Marxist-Leninist [*Political party*]
CPPN........	Children's Public Policy Network [*Later, CAN*] (EA)
CPPO........	Certified Public Purchasing Officer [*Canadian*]
CPPO........	Claimant Procurement Planning Officer
CPPO........	Controlled Production Planning Officer
CPPP........	Center for Philosophy and Public Policy [*Later, IPPP*] (EA)
CPPPN......	Commission on Private Philanthropy and Public Needs [*Defunct*] (EA)
CPPR........	Cassel Psychotherapy Progress Record [*Psychology*]
CPPR........	Construction Permit Power Reactor (NRCH)
CPpR........	Will Rogers State Historic Park, Pacific Palisades, CA [*Library symbol*] [*Library of Congress*] (LCLS)
CPPS........	Combined Procurement Processing Series (MCD)
CPPS........	Comision Permanente del Pacifico Sur [*Permanent Commission for the South Pacific - PCSP*] (EAIO)
CPPS........	Commission Permanente du Pacifique Sud [*Permanent Commission for the South Pacific*]
CPPS........	Composite Professional Performance Score
CPPS........	Computer Programming Performance Specification (MCD)
CPPS........	Congregatio Pretiosissimi Sanguinis [*Society of the Most Precious Blood*] [*Roman Catholic religious order*]
CPPS........	Critical Path Planning and Scheduling
CPPS........	Cyclohexylphenyl(piperidinylethyl)silanol [*Organic chemistry*]
CPPSBL....	Contemporary Psychoanalysis [*A publication*]
CPPSBOSH ...	Committee for Purchase of Products and Services of the Blind and Other Severely Handicapped [*Later, Committee for Purchase from the Blind and Other Severely Handicapped*]
CPPT........	Cooperative Program Planning and Teaching [*Australia*]
CPPT........	Coronary Primary Prevention Trial [*National Heart, Lung, and Blood Institute*]
CPPT........	Cost per Positive Termination [*Job Training and Partnership Act*] (OICC)
CPP/TMH ...	Citizens Participation Project/the Missing Half [*Defunct*] (EA)
CPPUI......	Center for Public Policy, Union Institute (EA)
CPPV........	Continuous Positive Pressure Ventilation [*Medicine*]
CPQ........	Campinas [*Brazil*] [*Airport symbol*] (OAG)
CPQ........	Children's Personality Questionnaire [*Psychology*]
CPQ........	Civil Procedures, Quebec
CPQ........	Compaq Computer Corp. [*NYSE symbol*] (SPSG)
CPQ........	Conpac Resources Ltd. [*Vancouver Stock Exchange symbol*]
CPQ........	Conpak Seafoods, Inc. [*Toronto Stock Exchange symbol*]
CPQ........	Lansing, MI [*Location identifier*] [*FAA*] (FAAL)
CPR........	Calendar of Patent Rolls [*British*]
CPR........	Cam Plate Readout
CPR........	Campaign for Political Rights [*Defunct*] (EA)
CPR........	Canadian Pacific Railway [*Facetious translations: Can't Pay Rent, Can't Promise Returns*]
CPR........	Canadian Patent Reporter [*Information service or system*] [*A publication*]
CPR........	Cape Peninsular Rifles [*British military*] (DMA)
CPR........	Cape Romanzof [*Alaska*] [*Seismograph station code, US Geological Survey*] [*Closed*] (SEIS)
CP/R........	Card Punch and Reader [*Data processing*]
CPR........	Cardiac Pulmonary Reserve [*Physiology*]
CPR........	Cardiopulmonary Resuscitation [*Medicine*]
CPR........	Career Placement Registry, Inc. [*Database producer*] [*Information service or system*] (IID)
CPR........	Carrier Performance Rating (AABC)
CPR........	Casper [*Wyoming*] [*Airport symbol*] (OAG)
CPR........	Casper, WY [*Location identifier*] [*FAA*] (FAAL)
CPR........	Ceiling Price Regulation (DLA)
CPR........	Center for Parapsychological Research [*Defunct*] (EA)
CPR........	Center for Policy Research (EA)
CPR........	Center for Political Research [*Later, Government Research Corporation*]
CPR........	Center for Public Representation (EA)
CPR........	Center for Public Resources (EA)
CPR........	Central Premonitions Registry (EA)
CPR........	Centripetal Rub [*Medicine*]
CPR........	Cerebral-Pedal Regulator [*Neurobiology*]

CPR...........	Chemicals, Plastic Research
CPR...........	Child Protection Report [*A publication*]
CPR...........	Chinese People's Republic
CPR...........	Chlorophenyl Red [*A dye*]
CPR...........	Civilian Personnel Records [*Military*]
CPR...........	Civilian Personnel Regulation [*Military*]
CPR...........	Clearport Petroleum Ltd. [*Vancouver Stock Exchange symbol*]
CPR...........	Clerk (Pay and Records) [*British military*] (DMA)
CPR...........	Clock Pulse Repeater
CPR...........	Clothing Pattern Repository [*DoD*]
CPR...........	Cloud Physics Radiometer
C Pr...........	Code of Procedure [*Legal term*] (DLA)
C Pr...........	Code de Procedure Civile [*Code of Civil Procedure*] [*French*] [*A publication*] (DLA)
CPR...........	Code of Professional Responsibility [*American Bar Association*]
CPR...........	Cold Pressor Response Test [*Medicine*]
CPR...........	Cold Protective Response [*Physiology*]
CPR...........	Committee on Polar Research [*Later, PRB*] [*US*]
CPR...........	Commodity Policy and Relief [*British*]
CPR...........	Company Persistency Rater [*LIMRA*]
CPR...........	Component to Part Record
CPR...........	Component Pilot Rework [*Navy*] (NG)
CPR...........	Computerized Performance Rating [*of a horse*]
CPR...........	Conditional Prepayment Rate [*for mortgages*]
CPR...........	Consolidated Progress Report
CPR...........	Consumer Product and Manufacturer Ratings [*A publication*]
CPR...........	Consumer Product Safety Commission, Washington, DC [*OCLC symbol*] (OCLC)
CPR...........	Continuing Property Records
CPR...........	Continuous Plankton Recorder [*Oceanography*] (MSC)
CPR...........	Continuous Progress Indicator [*Telecommunications*] (TEL)
CPR...........	Contract Pricing Report
CPR...........	Contract Procurement Request (MUGU)
CPR...........	Contractor Performance Record [*DoD*]
CPR...........	Contractor Performance Report
CP-R...........	Control Program - Real-Time [*Xerox Corp.*]
CPR...........	Copper [*Chemical symbol is Cu*]
CPR...........	Copper. Quarterly Report [*A publication*]
CPR...........	Corporate Air, Inc. [*Hartford, CT*] [*FAA designator*] (FAAC)
CPR...........	Cost Performance Report (MCD)
CPR...........	Cost Proposal Requirement (MCD)
CPR...........	Crater Production Rate [*Geology*]
CPR...........	Crew Provisioning Report
CPR...........	Critical Power Ratio [*Nuclear energy*] (NRCH)
CPR...........	Critical Problem Report [*NASA*] (NASA)
CPR...........	Cumberland Poetry Review [*British*]
CPR...........	Current Population Reports [*A publication*]
CPR...........	Cut Paraboloidal Reflector
CPr...........	Cycle Pressure Ratio (MCD)
CPr...........	Paso Robles Public Library, Paso Robles, CA [*Library symbol*] [*Library of Congress*] (LCLS)
CPR 20.......	Current Population Reports. Population Characteristics. Series P-20 [*A publication*]
CPR 23.......	Current Population Reports. Special Studies. Series P-23 [*A publication*]
CPR 25.......	Current Population Reports. Population Estimates and Projections. Series P-25 [*A publication*]
CPR 26.......	Current Population Reports. Federal-State Cooperative Program for Population Estimates. Series P-26 [*A publication*]
CPR 27.......	Current Population Reports. Farm Population. Series P-27 [*A publication*]
CPR 28.......	Current Population Reports. Special Censuses. Series P-28 [*A publication*]
CPR 60.......	Current Population Reports. Consumer Income. Series P-60 [*A publication*]
CPR 65.......	Current Population Reports. Consumer Buying Indicators. Series P-65 [*A publication*]
CPR 20-398 ...	Current Population Reports. Household and Family Characteristics. Series P20-398 [*A publication*]
CPR 25-986 ...	Current Population Reports. Population Estimates and Projections. Households and Families, 1986-2000. Series P-25. No.986 [*A publication*]
CPR 27-57 ...	Current Population Reports. Farm Population of the US. Series P-27-57 [*A publication*]
CPR 60-148 ...	Current Population Reports. Characteristics of Households and Persons Receiving Selected Noncash Benefits. Series P-60-148 [*A publication*]
CPR 60-147 ...	Current Population Reports. Characteristics of the Population below the Poverty Level. Series P-60-147 [*A publication*]
CPR 60-146 ...	Current Population Reports. Money Income of Households, Families, and Persons in the US. Series P-60-146 [*A publication*]
CPR 60-149 ...	Current Population Reports. Money, Income, Poverty Status of Families and Persons in the US. Series P-60-149 [*A publication*]
CPRA.........	Chemical Public Relations Association [*Later, CCA*] (EA)
CPRA.........	Communications Processor Assembly [*Ground Control Facility, NASA*]
CPRA.........	Compressed Pulse RADAR Altimeter
CPRA.........	Congo Protestant Relief Agency [*Defunct*]

C Pratiq...... Cinema Pratique [*A publication*]
CPRB........ Combined Production and Resources Board [*World War II*]
CPRC......... California Primate Research Center [*Research center*] (RCD)
CPRC......... Canadian Plains Research Center [*University of Regina*] [*Information service or system*] (IID)
CPRC......... Caribbean Primate Research Center [*University of Puerto Rico*] [*Research center*] (RCD)
CPRC......... Center for Population Research and Census [*Portland State University*] [*Oregon*] [*Information service or system*] (IID)
CPRC......... Chrysler Products Restorers Club [*Later, CRC*] (EA)
CPRC......... Civilian Payroll Circular
CPRC......... Coastal Plains Regional Commission [*FAA*] (FAAC)
CPRC......... Coloured Persons' Representative Council [*South Africa*] (PPW)
CPRC......... Combined Personnel Recovery Center (CINC)
CPRC......... Computer Components Corp. [*Morrisville, NC*] [*NASDAQ symbol*] (NQ)
CPRC......... Corporate Plan and Review Committee [*Library Association of Australia*]
C Pr Civ ..... Code de Procedure Civile [*Code of Civil Procedure*] [*A publication*] (ILCA)
CPRC (NS) ... Civil Procedure Reports, New Series [*1908-13*] [*New York*] [*A publication*] (DLA)
CPRD........ Cable Programming Resource Directory [*A publication*] (TSSD)
CPRD........ Committee on Prosthetics Research and Development [*National Research Council*]
CPRD........ Computer Products, Inc. [*NASDAQ symbol*] (NQ)
CPRD........ Consumer and Professional Relations Division [*of HIAA*] [*Washington, DC*] (EA)
CPR (2d).... Canadian Patent Report, Second Series [*A publication*] (DLA)
CPRDDM ... Clinical Preventive Dentistry [*A publication*]
CPRDM........ Committee on the Acquisition and Use of Scientific and Technical Information in Pesticide Regulatory Decision Making at the Federal and State Levels [*National Research Council*]
CPRE........ Center for Policy Research in Education [*New Brunswick, NJ*] [*Department of Education*] (GRD)
CPRE........ Council for the Protection of Rural England (EAIO)
CPREA...... Canadian Peace Research and Education Association [*See also ACREP*]
CPREDP ... Canadian Psychological Review [*A publication*]
CPREF ...... Candelabra Prefocused
CP Rep....... Common Pleas Reporter [*Scranton, PA*] [*A publication*] (DLA)
CP Rept...... Common Pleas Reporter [*Scranton, PA*] [*A publication*] (DLA)
CPRESS .... Compound Pressure
CPRF .... Confinement Physics Research Facility
CPRG......... Computer Personnel Research Group [*Later, Special Interest Group for Computer Personnel Research*]
CPRH .... Council on Peace Research in History (EA)
CPRI......... Canadian Peace Research Institute
CPRI......... Central Psi Research Institute (EA)
C Priv .... Committee for Privileges, House of Commons/Lords (DLA)
CPRK........ Caprock Corp. [*NASDAQ symbol*] (NQ)
CPRM........ Companhia Portuguesa Radio Marconi [*Portuguese Radio Marconi Company*] [*Lisbon*] [*Information service or system*] (IID)
CPRMBD ... Centre for Overseas Pest Research. Miscellaneous Report [*A publication*]
CPR-NICHD ... Center for Population Research - National Institute of Child Health and Human Development [*Bethesda, MD*] [*Department of Health and Human Services*] (GRD)
CPR (NS)... Civil Procedure Reports, New Series [*1908-13*] [*New York*] [*A publication*] (DLA)
CPROA...... Chemical Processing [*London*] [*A publication*]
C Proc Civ ... Code de Procedure Civile [*Code of Civil Procedure*] [*French*] [*A publication*] (DLA)
CPRP......... Ciskei People's Rights Protection Party [*Political party*] [*South Africa*] (EY)
CPRP......... Civilian Personnel Reduction Plan (MCD)
cPRP......... Platelet-Rich Plasma, citrated [*Hematology*]
CPRP......... Ralph M. Parsons, Electronics Division, Pasadena, CA [*Library symbol*] [*Library of Congress*] (LCLS)
C Pr Pen..... Code de Procedure Penale [*Code of Criminal Procedure*] [*A publication*] (ILCA)
CPR Proc ... Computer Personnel Research Proceedings [*A publication*]
CPRQC...... Castle Entertainment [*NASDAQ symbol*] (NQ)
CPRR........ Civil Pilots for Regulatory Reform (EA)
CPR/R....... Component Pilot Rework/Repair [*Navy*] (MCD)
CPRR........ Construction Permit Research Reactor (NRCH)
CPRR-NEA ... Commission on Professional Rights and Responsibilities of the NEA [*Defunct*] (EA)
CPRS........ Canadian Public Relations Society
CPRS .... Central Policy Review Staff [*British*]
CPRS .... Centralized Personnel Record System [*Telecommunications*] (TEL)
CPRS .... CINCPAC [*Commander-in-Chief, Pacific*] Route Slip (CINC)
CPRS .... Comprehensive Psychopathological Rating Scale

CPRS......... Compress (MSA)
CPRSD...... Controller of Physical Research and Signals Development [*Ministry of Supply*] [*British*]
CPRSN...... Compression (MSA)
CPRSR...... Compressor (MSA)
CPRT........ Cold Pressor Response Test [*Medicine*]
CPRTR.... Chief Printer [*Navy rating*] [*Obsolete*]
CPRTRL.... Chief Printer, Lithographer [*Navy rating*] [*Obsolete*]
CPRTRM .. Chief Printer, Offset Process [*Navy rating*] [*Obsolete*]
CPRV......... Cabin Pressure Relief Valve [*Aviation*] (KSC)
CPRV......... Canister Purge Regulator Valve [*Automotive engineering*]
CPRV......... Cinque Ports Rifle Volunteers [*British military*] (DMA)
CPRW........ Council for the Protection of Rural Wales (EAIO)
CPS............ Air Transportable Pulse RADAR Search [*Aviation*] (FAAC)
CPS............ C-Polysaccharide [*Clinical chemistry*]
CPS............ Cabinet Pressurization System
CPS............ California Polytechnic State University, San Luis Obispo, CA [*OCLC symbol*] (OCLC)
CPS............ Calling Processing Subsystem [*Telecommunications*] (TEL)
CPS............ Cambridge Physical Series [*A publication*]
CPS............ Canada Plan Service
CPS............ Canadian Institute for International Peace and Security [*UTLAS symbol*]
CPS............ Canadian Paediatric Society (EAIO)
CPS............ Canadian Penitentiary Service
CPS............ Canadian Population Society [*See also SCP*]
CPS............ Canadian Power Squadrons [*Boating*]
CPS............ Carbamyl-Phosphate Synthetase [*An enzyme*]
CPS............ Card Programming System [*Data processing*] (CMD)
CPS............ Cards per Second [*Data processing*]
CPS............ Carlson Psychological Survey [*Test*]
CPS............ Cataloging and Provisioning System (MCD)
CPS............ Cathode Potential Stabilized
CPS............ Catholic Pamphlet Society of the United States (EA)
CPS............ Cell Processor System (MCD)
CPS............ Center for Peace Studies (EA)
CPS............ Center for Philosophy of Science [*University of Pittsburgh*] [*Research center*] (RCD)
CPS............ Center for Process Studies (EA)
CPS............ Centipoise [*Unit of viscosity*]
CPS............ Central Power Supply
CPS............ Central Power System
CPS............ Central Processing System [*Data processing*]
CPS............ Centralized Payroll System (ADA)
CPS............ Centre for Policy Studies [*British*]
CPS............ Cephalo Pedal Sinus
CPS............ Certificate of Prior Submission [*Navy*]
CPS............ Certified Professional Secretary [*Designation awarded by Institute for Certifying Secretaries*]
CPS............ Certified Public Secretary
CPS............ Chairmakers' Protection Society [*A union*] [*British*]
CPS............ Change Processing Station (AAG)
CPS............ Characters per Second [*Data processing*]
CPS............ Charles S. Peirce Society (EA)
CPS............ Chemical Process Synthesis [*Chemical engineering*]
CPS............ Circuit Package Schematic (MSA)
CPS............ Circuit Provision System [*AT & T*]
CPS............ Citizens Protection Society [*British*]
CPS............ Civilian Public Service
CPS............ Clerk of Petty Sessions [*British*] (ADA)
CPS............ Close-Packed Structure
CPS............ Cloth Pressers' Society [*A union*] [*British*] (DCTA)
CPS............ Coastal Plains Sands
CPS............ Coils per Slot [*Technical drawings*]
CPS............ Collective Protective System [*Navy*]
CPS............ College Placement Services [*Later, CCDM*] (EA)
CPS............ College Press Service (EA)
CPS............ College of Psychic Studies [*London*]
CPS............ Collimated Photon Scattering (MCD)
CPS............ Color Picture Signal
CPS............ Combined Planning Staff [*Military*] [*British*]
CPS............ Combined Principles Simulator [*Nuclear engine*]
CPS............ Command Personnel Summary (AABC)
CPS............ Commission du Pacifique Sud [*South Pacific Commission - SPC*] (EAIO)
CPS............ Commission on the Patent System
CPS............ Committee for Production Sharing (EA)
CPS............ Communications Processing System
CPS............ Company [*or Corporate*] Policy Statement
CPS............ Comparative Political Studies [*A publication*]
CPS............ Compendium of Pharmaceuticals and Specialities [*A publication*]
CPS............ Compensation and Pension Service [*Veterans Administration*]
CPS............ Composite Primary Structures (MCD)
CPS............ Computer Power Supply
CPS............ Computer Program Specification (AFM)
CPS............ Computer Program System [*Boeing Co.*]
CPS............ Computer Programming Service
CPS............ Comrey Personality Scale
CPS............ Condensate Polishing System [*Nuclear energy*] (NRCH)
CPS............ Condensation Pressure Spread

CPS............	Conference of Philosophical Societies (EA)
CPS............	Conference on the Public Service
CPS............	Congregational Publishing Society
CPS............	Consolidated Energy Partners [*AMEX symbol*] (SPSG)
CPS............	Constitutional Psychopathic State
CPS............	Consumer Purchasing Service
CPS............	Containment Purge System [*Nuclear energy*] (NRCH)
CPS............	Contract Pilot School
CPS............	Contract [*or Contractor*] Plant Services (NG)
CPS............	Control Panel Subassembly
CPS............	Control Power Supply
CPS............	Control Pressure System (AAG)
CPS............	Control Programs Support (IEEE)
CPS............	Controlled Path System [*Data processing*]
CPS............	Controller Processor Signal (CAAL)
CPS............	Conversational Programming System [*Data processing*]
CPS............	Conversion Program System (NRCH)
CPS............	Convertible Preferred Stock [*Investment term*]
CPS............	Copy Processing System [*Photocomposition*]
CPS............	Council for Philosophical Studies (EA)
CPS............	Counts per Second (DEN)
CPS............	Covered Pedestrian Space
CPS............	Crew Procedures Simulator
CPS............	Critical Path Scheduling [*or System*]
CPS............	Croatian Philatelic Society (EA)
CPS............	Crown Prosecution Service [*British*] (ECON)
CPS............	Cumulative Preferred Stock [*Investment term*]
CPS............	Current Population Survey [*Census Bureau*]
CPS............	Customer Premises System [*Bell System*]
CPS............	Custos Privati Sigilli [*Keeper of the Privy Seal*] [*Latin*]
CPS............	Cycles per Second [*See also Hz*]
CPS............	East St. Louis, IL [*Location identifier*] [*FAA*] (FAAL)
CPS............	Missionary Sisters of the Precious Blood [*Italy*]
CPs............	Palm Springs Public Library, Palm Springs, CA [*Library symbol*] [*Library of Congress*] (LCLS)
CPS............	Stuart Co., Pasadena, CA [*Library symbol*] [*Library of Congress*] (LCLS)
CPSA........	Canadian Political Science Association
CPSA........	Canine Pulmonary Surfactant
CPSA........	Catholic Poetry Society of America [*Defunct*] (EA)
CPSA........	Central Pennsylvania Financial Corp. [*Shamokin, PA*] [*NASDAQ symbol*] (NQ)
CPSA........	Chronopotentiometric Stripping Analysis [*Analytical electrochemistry*]
CPSA........	Civil and Public Services Association [*British*]
CPSA........	Clay Pigeon Shooting Association [*British*]
CPSA........	Communist Party of South Africa [*Political party*] (PD)
CPSA........	Conservative Party of South Africa [*Konserwatiewe Party van Suid-Afrika*] [*Political party*] (PPW)
CPSA........	Consumer Product Safety Act [*1972*]
CPSA........	Cuban Philatelic Society of America (EA)
CPSA........	Current Physics Selected Articles [*A publication*] (MCD)
CPSAC......	Cycles per Second Alternating Current (AAG)
CPS Act	Consumer Product Safety Act [*1972*] (DLA)
CPSAH......	Committee to Promote the Study of Austrian History (EA)
CPSAR	Commonwealth Public Service Arbitration Reports [*A publication*] (APTA)
CPSC	Canadian Permanent Signal Corps [*British military*] (DMA)
CPSC	Canadian Posture and Seating Centre [*Research center*] (RCD)
CPSC	Consumer Product Safety Commission [*Federal agency*]
CPSC	Contingency Planning Support Capability (AFM)
CPSC	CPS Chemical Co., Inc. [*NASDAQ symbol*] (NQ)
CPSCI.......	Central Personnel Security Clearance Index [*Nuclear energy*] (NRCH)
CPSCS.......	Children's Perceived Self-Control Scale
CPSCS-UTM ...	Children's Perceived Self-Control Scale - Usually That's Me
CPSD........	Cross-Power Spectral Density
CPSDF	Catch per Standard Day of Fishing [*Fishery management*] (MSC)
CPSE	Carr-Purcell Spin-Echo
CPSE	Common Payload Support Equipment [*NASA*] (NASA)
CPSE	Complementary Pair Switch Element
CPSE	Counterpoise (MSA)
CPSE	Crew and Passenger Support Equipment [*Military*] (AFIT)
CPSES.......	Commanche Peak Steam Electric Station (NRCH)
CPSF	Candle Power/Square Foot (KSC)
CPSG........	China Philatelic Study Group (EA)
CPSG........	China Policy Study Group [*British*]
CPSG........	Common Power Supply Group
CPSGD2...	Canadian Psychology [*A publication*]
CPSI	CPS - Corporate Planning Services, Inc. [*NASDAQ symbol*] (NQ)
CPSK	Cathodic Protection Survey Kit
CPSK	Coherent Phase Shift Keyed [*System*] [*Data processing*]
CPSL	Canadian Professional Soccer League
CPSL	Capsule (MSA)
CPSL	Communist Party of Sri Lanka [*Political party*] (FEA)
CPSL	Communist Party of Syria and the Lebanon [*Political party*] (BJA)
CPSL	CSC Industries, Inc. [*NASDAQ symbol*] (NQ)

CPSM........	Comite Permanent des Sous-Ministres [*Continuing Committee of Deputy Ministers - CCDM*] [*Canada*]
CPSM........	Computer Program Submodule (MCD)
CPSM........	Critical Path Scheduling Method [*Management*]
CPSMA	Canadian Podiatric Sports Medicine Academy
CPSMBI...	Collected Papers in Surgery. Mayo Clinic and Mayo Foundation [*A publication*]
CPSN........	Capstan
CPSO........	Cumberland Plateau Seismological Observatory
CPSOA......	Composites [*A publication*]
CPSPA......	Common Pleas Subpoena [*Legal*] [*British*] (ROG)
CPSR	Calibration Procedure Status Report [*Polaris missile*]
CPSR	Commonwealth Public Service Arbitration Reports [*A publication*] (APTA)
CPSR	Computer Professionals for Social Responsibility (EA)
CPSR	Contractor Procurement System Review [*DoD*]
CPSR	Controlled Process Serum Replacements [*Cell culture*]
CPSR	Cost and Performance Summary Report [*Army*]
CPSS.........	Central Processing Subsystem [*Data processing*]
CPSS.........	Chemist's Personal Software Series
CPSS.........	Cold Plate Support Structure (MCD)
CPSS.........	Committee of Presidents of Statistical Societies (EA)
CPSS.........	Common Program Support System
CPSS.........	Compagnie des Pretres de St. Sulpice [*Society of the Priests of St. Sulpice - SPSS*] [*Paris, France*] (EAIO)
CPSS.........	Component Percentage Shipment Schedule (NG)
CPSS.........	Computer Power Support System
CPSS.........	Computerized Parcel Shipping System
CPSS.........	Critical Phase System Software [*NASA*] (NASA)
CPST	Commission on Professionals in Science and Technology (EA)
CPST	Committee to Promote Science and Technology
CPST	CPC-Rexcel, Inc. [*NASDAQ symbol*] (NQ)
CPSTB......	Current Psychiatric Therapies [*A publication*]
CPSU........	Calcutta Port Shramik Union [*India*]
CPSU........	Central Processor Subunit [*Data processing*]
CPSU........	Chemistry and Physics Study Unit (EA)
CPSU........	Communist Party of the Soviet Union [*Kommunisticheskaya Partiya Sovetskovo Soyuza*] [*Political party*] (PPW)
CPSU........	Cooperative National Park Resources Studies Unit [*Research center*] (RCD)
CPSUA......	Current Problems in Surgery [*A publication*]
CPSUG......	CPS [*Itek Copy Processing System*] User Group (EA)
CPSU/UH ...	Cooperative National Park Resource Studies Unit, University of Hawaii [*Research center*] (RCD)
CPSVN......	Comprehensive Plan, South Vietnam (CINC)
CPSX	Ceramics Process Systems Corp. [*NASDAQ symbol*] (NQ)
CPsy.........	Cognitive Psychology [*A publication*]
CPSZDP...	Communications in Psychopharmacology [*A publication*]
CPT...........	California Institute of Technology, Pasadena, CA [*Library symbol*] [*Library of Congress*] (LCLS)
CPT...........	Camp Pendleton [*California*] [*Seismograph station code, US Geological Survey*] (SEIS)
CPT...........	Canstat Petroleum Corp. [*Vancouver Stock Exchange symbol*]
CPT...........	Cape Town [*South Africa*] [*Airport symbol*] (OAG)
CPT...........	Capiat [*Let the Patient Take*] [*Pharmacy*] (ROG)
CPT...........	Captain [*Military*]
CPT...........	Captopril [*Antihypertensive drug*]
CPT...........	Cargo Processing Technician (NASA)
CPT...........	Caribou Performance Test
CPT...........	Carpet [*Classified advertising*] (ADA)
CPT...........	Casement Projected Transom [*Technical drawings*]
CPT...........	Center for Particle Theory [*University of Texas at Austin*] [*Research center*] (RCD)
CPT...........	Central Planning Team (NATG)
CPT...........	Ceramic Planar Tube
CPT...........	Charge Conjugation - Parity - Time-Reversal [*Theorem*] [*Atomic physics*]
CPT...........	Charge, Parity, and Time Coordinates [*Physics*]
CPT...........	Chest Physiotherapy [*Medicine*]
CPT...........	Chicago Produce Terminal Co. [*Later, CPTC*] [*AAR code*]
CPT...........	Chief Programmer Team [*Data processing*]
CPT...........	Cisplatin [*Also, cis-DDP, CDDP, CPDD, DDP, P*] [*Antineoplastic drug*]
CPT...........	Civilian Pilot Training [*Became War Training Service*] [*World War II*]
CPT...........	Clock, Programming, and Timing [*NASA*] (KSC)
CPT...........	Cockpit Procedures Trainer [*Air Force*] (AFM)
CPT...........	Color Pyramid Test [*Psychology*]
CPT...........	Colored People's Time [*Slang*]
CPT...........	Committee for Pedestrian Tolls (EA)
CPT...........	Communist Party of Thailand [*Political party*] (PD)
CPT...........	Communist Party of Turkey [*Political party*] (PD)
CPT...........	Comparison Test (MCD)
CPT...........	Compatibility
cpt	Comptant [*Cash*] [*French*] [*Business term*]
CPT...........	Compumat, Inc. [*AMEX symbol*] (CTT)
CPT...........	Computer Program Tapes (MCD)
CPT...........	Consolidated Pilot Training Program [*Air Force*]
CPT...........	Continuous Performance Test [*Psychology*]
Cpt	Contrepoint [*Record label*] [*France*]
CPT...........	Control Power Transformer (MSA)

CPT............ Corporate Air [*Billings, MT*] [*FAA designator*] (FAAC)
CPT............ Counterpoint [*Music*]
CPT............ Crew Procedures Trainer
CPT............ Critical Path Technique
CPT............ Cryogenic Pressure Transducer
CPT............ Crystal Pressure Transducer
CPT............ Current Physics Titles [*A publication*]
CPT............ Current Procedural Terminology [*American Medical Association*]
CPT............ Point Loma College, San Diego, CA [*OCLC symbol*] (OCLC)
CPTA......... Ciliary Particle Transport Activity
CPTA......... Computer Programming and Testing Activity (IEEE)
CPTB .... Clay Products Technical Bureau [*British*]
CPTC......... Canadian Passenger Transportation Corporation [*Proposed*]
CPTC......... Central Processor Test Console [*Data processing*]
CPTC......... Chicago Produce Terminal Company [*Formerly, CPT*] [*AAR code*]
CPTC......... CPT Corporation [*NASDAQ symbol*] (NQ)
CPTD........ Computer Data Systems, Inc. [*NASDAQ symbol*] (NQ)
CPTD........ Cumulative Pulmonary Toxicity Dose [*Deep-sea diving*]
CPTE......... Committee for the Preservation of the Tule Elk (EA)
cpte............ Compte [*Account*] [*French*] [*Business term*]
CPT & E .... Computer Program Test and Evaluation
CPTEA ...... Chemical and Petroleum Engineering [*English Translation*] [*A publication*]
cpte ct........ Compte Courant [*Current Account*] [*French*] [*Business term*]
CPTF......... Central Plains Turfgrass Foundation [*Later, KTF*] (EA)
CPTHA ...... Component Technology [*A publication*]
CPTHDA .. Butterworths International Medical Reviews. Clinical Pharmacology and Therapeutics [*A publication*]
CpTI.......... Cowpea Trypsin Inhibitor [*Biochemistry*]
CPTL......... Computer Telephone Corp. [*NASDAQ symbol*] (NQ)
CPTLP....... Coalition of Publicly Traded Limited Partnerships [*Later, CoPTP*] (EA)
CPTNG MATS RGS ... Carpeting Mats or Rugs [*Freight*]
CPTPL....... Computer Program Test Plan (CAAL)
CPTPR....... Computer Program Test Procedures (CAAL)
CPTR......... Capture (AABC)
CPTR......... Carpenter (AABC)
CPTR......... Chemical Propulsion Technology Reviews [*Chemical Propulsion Information Agency*] (MCD)
CPTR......... Chief Painter [*Navy rating*] [*Obsolete*]
CPTRV ...... Chief Painter, Aircraft [*Navy rating*] [*Obsolete*]
CPTS......... Coalition for Peace through Strength [*Later, CCNS*] (EA)
CPtSH....... Patton State Hospital, Patton, CA [*Library symbol*] [*Library of Congress*] (LCLS)
CPTSq ...... Comptroller Service Squadron [*Air Force*]
CPTST....... Contrapuntist [*Music*]
CPTY......... Capacity (FAAC)
CPU .... Canadian Paperworkers Union
CPU .... Card Pick Up (DCTA)
CPU .... Caudate-Putamen Complex [*Anatomy*]
CPU .... Central Processing Unit [*Data processing*]
CPU .... Children's Peace Union [*Defunct*] (EA)
CPU .... Church Peace Union [*Later, CRIA*]
CPU .... Collective Protection Unit (IEEE)
CPU .... Commercial Property Underwriting [*Insurance*]
CPU .... Commonwealth Press Union [*London, England*] (EAIO)
CPU .... Communications Processing Unit (CET)
CPU .... Communications Processor Utility [*Telecommunications*] (TEL)
CPU .... Compugraphic Corp. [*NYSE symbol*] (SPSG)
CPU .... Computer Peripheral Unit (IEEE)
CPU .... Computer Printer Unit (MCD)
CPU .... Computer Processor Unit
CPU .... Computer Program Update
CPU .... Control Phasing Unit [*for aircraft*] (RDA)
CPU .... Control Processing Unit (MCD)
CPU .... Controlled Production Unit [*Project sponsored by the Elder Craftsmen*]
CPU .... Coon Peak [*Utah*] [*Seismograph station code, US Geological Survey*] (SEIS)
CPU .... Cost per Unit
CPU .... Crime Prevention Unit [*British*]
CPU .... ME Compu Software, Inc. [*Vancouver Stock Exchange symbol*]
CPU .... Pacific Union College, Angwin, CA [*OCLC symbol*] (OCLC)
CPUBINFO ... Chief of Public Information Division [*NATO*] (NATG)
CPUC .... Common Pleas Reports [*Upper Canada*] [*A publication*] (DLA)
CPUE........ Catch per Unit Effort [*Pisciculture*] (MSC)
CPUE........ Chest Pain of Unknown Etiology [*Medicine*]
CPUG .... Cuadernos de Prehistoria. Universidad de Granada [*A publication*]
CPUI.......... Commercial Programming Unlimited, Incorporated [*New York, NY*] [*NASDAQ symbol*] (NQ)
CPUID...... Central Processing Unit Identification Number [*Data processing*]
CPUN .... United States Naval Ordnance Test Station, Pasadena, CA [*Library symbol*] [*Library of Congress*] (LCLS)
CPUNCH .. Counterpunch (KSC)

CPUP......... Catalogo Colectivo de Publicaciones Periodicas [*Database*] [*Ministerio de Cultura*] [*Spanish*] [*Information service or system*] (CRD)
CPURMC ... Committee to Promote Uniformity in the Regulation of Motor Carriers
CPUS........ Coalition for the Peaceful Uses of Space (EA)
CPUS........ Constitution Parties of the United States [*An association*] (EA)
CPUSA...... Communist Party of the United States of America [*Political party*] (EA)
CPUSAC ... Crafted with Pride in USA Council (EA)
CPUSA/ML ... Communist Party of the USA/Marxist Leninist [*Political party*] (EA)
CPUSOFBLNJ ... Committee on Peaceful Uses of the Sea-Bed and Ocean Floor Beyond Limits of National Jurisdiction [*United Nations*] (EA)
CPUSTAL ... Congreso Permanente de Unidad Sindical de los Trabajadores de America Latina [*Permanent Congress of Trade Union Unity of Latin American Workers - PCTUULAW*] [*Mexico City, Mexico*] (EAIO)
CPV .... Campina Grande [*Brazil*] [*Airport symbol*] (OAG)
CPV .... Canine Parovirus
CPV .... Canopus Probe near Limb of Venus Angle [*NASA*]
CPV .... Cape Verde [*ANSI three-letter standard code*] (CNC)
CPV .... Chinese Communist People's Volunteers (MCD)
CPV .... Circulating Plasma Volume [*Hematology*]
CPV .... Coated Polycarbonate Visor
CPV .... Command Post Vehicle [*British military*] (DMA)
CPV .... Communist Party of Venezuela [*Political party*]
CPV .... Compania Peruana de Vapores [*Peruvian airline*]
CP-V .... Control Program-Five [*Operating system*] [*Xerox Corp.*]
CPv .... Palos Verdes Library District, Palos Verdes Estates, CA [*Library symbol*] [*Library of Congress*] (LCLS)
CPVC........ Chlorinated Poly(vinyl Chloride) [*Organic chemistry*]
CPVC........ Critical Pigment Volume Concentration [*Paint technology*]
CPVE........ Certificate of Professional and Vocational Education [*British*]
CPVEA...... Carl Perkins Vocational Education Act [*1984*] (OICC)
CPvMC...... Marymount College, Palos Verdes Estates, CA [*Library symbol*] [*Library of Congress*] [*Obsolete*] (LCLS)
CPVR........ Committee on Procedure and Valuation of Reparations [*Allied German Occupation Forces*]
CPW .... Canadian Pawnee Oil [*Vancouver Stock Exchange symbol*]
CPW .... Capitol Peak [*Washington*] [*Seismograph station code, US Geological Survey*] (SEIS)
CPW .... Chippewa Air Commuter, Inc. [*Manistee, MI*] [*FAA designator*] (FAAC)
CPW .... Circumpolar Water [*Oceanography*]
CPW .... Club of Printing Women of New York (EA)
CPW .... Commercial Projected Window [*Technical drawings*]
CPW .... Confectionery Production [*A publication*]
CPW .... Coplanar Waveguide
CPW .... Western Personnel Institute, Pasadena, CA [*Library symbol*] [*Library of Congress*] (LCLS)
CPWD ...... Caucus for Producers, Writers, and Directors (EA)
CPWDA .... Canadian Paint and Wallpaper Dealers' Association
CPWE .... Centre for Pastoral Work in Europe [*See also CPE*] (EAIO)
CPWi........ Wuanco Engineering Technical Library, Pasadena, CA [*Library symbol*] [*Library of Congress*] (LCLS)
CPWR .... Computer Power, Inc. [*High Bridge, NJ*] [*NASDAQ symbol*] (NQ)
CPWU .... Ceylon Plantation Workers' Union [*Obsolete*]
CPX........... Charged Pigment Xerography (IEEE)
CPX........... Cineplex Odeon Corp. [*NYSE symbol*]-[*Toronto Stock Exchange symbol*]
CPX........... Clinopyroxene [*A mineral*]
CPX........... Command Post Exercise [*Military*]
CPX........... Command Post Experience [*Army*] [*British*]
CPX........... CP1 [*Nevada*] [*Seismograph station code, US Geological Survey*] (SEIS)
CPX........... Culebra [*Puerto Rico*] [*Airport symbol*] (OAG)
CPX........... Isla De Culebra, PR [*Location identifier*] [*FAA*] (FAAL)
CPY........... Carboxypeptidase Y [*An enzyme*]
CPY........... Clips per Year [*Photocopying, microfilming*]
CPY........... Consolidated Paymaster [*Vancouver Stock Exchange symbol*]
CPY........... Copy (BUR)
CPY........... Copyright [*Deltiology*]
CPY........... CPI Corp. [*NYSE symbol*] (SPSG)
CPZ........... Chlorpromazine [*Sedative*]
CPZ........... La Pryor, TX [*Location identifier*] [*FAA*] (FAAL)
CPZOAO .. Chronmy Przyrode Ojczysta [*A publication*]
CQ............. Call to Quarters [*General call preceding transmission of radio signals*]
CQ............. Cambridge Quarterly [*A publication*]
CQ............. Camera Quality (MUGU)
CQ............. Canine Quarterly: a Parody of the World's Most Elegant Magazine for Men [*A publication*]
CQ............. Carbazilquinone [*Antineoplastic drug*]
CQ............. Caribbean Quarterly [*A publication*]
CQ............. Carolina Quarterly [*A publication*]
CQ............. Carrier Qualification [*Navy*] (CAAL)
CQ............. Central Queensland [*Australia*]
C/Q........... Certificate of Assignment of Quarters [*Navy*]

CQ	Charge of Quarters [Army]
CQ	Checklist Question (CAAL)
CQ	China Quarterly [A publication]
CQ	Chloroquine [Antimalarial drug]
CQ	Classical Quarterly [A publication]
CQ	Commercial Quality
CQ	Communications Satellite Corp. [See also COMSAT] [NYSE symbol] (SPSG)
cq	Comoro Islands [MARC country of publication code] [Library of Congress] (LCCP)
CQ	Conceptual Quotient [Psychology]
CQ	Conditionally Qualified (AFM)
CQ	Congressional Quarterly, Inc. [Washington, DC]
CQ	Correct
CQ	Creativity Quotient [Testing term]
CQ	Cree Questionnaire [Psychology]
CQ	Crew Quarters (KSC)
CQ	Critical Quarterly [A publication]
CQA	Celina, OH [Location identifier] [FAA] (FAAL)
CQA	Component Quality Assurance
CQAR	Corporate Quality Assurance Regulations (MCD)
CQB	Chandler, OK [Location identifier] [FAA] (FAAL)
CQB	Chiquita Brands International [NYSE symbol] (SPSG)
CQB	Close-Quarter Battle [British military] (DMA)
CQB	Cornell Hotel and Restaurant Administration Quarterly [A publication]
CQC	Citizens for a Quieter City [New York City] (EA)
CQC	Continental Quilting Congress (EA)
CQC	Crop Quality Council (EA)
CQC	Cusac Industries Ltd. [Toronto Stock Exchange symbol] [Vancouver Stock Exchange symbol]
CQCC	Citroen Quarterly Car Club (EA)
CQCL	Plumas County Free Library, Quincy, CA [Library symbol] [Library of Congress] (LCLS)
CQCM	Cryogenic Quartz Crystal Microbalance
CQCP	Correspondence Quality Control Program (MCD)
CQCQA	CQ [Call to Quarters]. Radio Amateur's Journal [A publication]
CQD	Canacord Resources, Inc. [Toronto Stock Exchange symbol]
CQD	Come Quick - Danger [International distress signal, used before SOS]
CQD	Customary Quick Dispatch
CQD	Erie, PA [Location identifier] [FAA] (FAAL)
CQDR	Critical Qualification Design Review (NASA)
CQE	Cognizant Quality Engineer (NRCH)
CQE	Command Qualification Examination (MCD)
CQE	Critical Quality Element (NRCH)
CQF	Canada Lease Financing Ltd. [Toronto Stock Exchange symbol]
CQFMAR	Colegio Quimico-Farmaceutico [A publication]
CQG	Carson Gold Corp. [Vancouver Stock Exchange symbol]
CQG	Chain Store Age [A publication]
CQH	Philadelphia, PA [Location identifier] [FAA] (FAAL)
CQI	Commodity Quotations, Inc. (EISS)
CQI	Continuous Quality Improvement [Quality control]
CQI	Council, ID [Location identifier] [FAA] (FAAL)
CQJ	Asheboro, NC [Location identifier] [FAA] (FAAL)
CQK	Conjunctuur [A publication]
CQL	Carbondale, CO [Location identifier] [FAA] (FAAL)
CQL	Consolidated Lone Star Resource Corp. [Vancouver Stock Exchange symbol]
CQM	Chief Quartermaster [Navy rating] [Obsolete]
CQM	Constructing Quartermaster [Army]
CQM	Control Quality Monitor
CQM	Crystal Quartz Modern
CQMC	Chief Quartermaster Clerk [Navy rating] [Obsolete]
CQMS	Camp Quartermasters Store [British military] (DMA)
CQMS	Circuit Quality Monitoring System
CQMS	Company Quartermaster-Sergeant
CQMS	Cost Quality Management System [for hospitals]
CQMTA	Colloque de Metallurgie [A publication]
CQN	Chattanooga, TN [Location identifier] [FAA] (FAAL)
CQO	Canadian Microcool Corp. [Vancouver Stock Exchange symbol]
CQO	China Quarterly [A publication]
CQPR	Cumulative Quality Point Ratio
CQR	Chandalar Lake, AK [Location identifier] [FAA] (FAAL)
CQR	Chloroquine Resistance [Chemoprophylaxis]
CQR	Church Quarterly Review [A publication]
CQR	Classical Quarterly Review [A publication]
CQR	Complete Controlled Quick Release
CQR	Controlled Quick Release
CQR	Cost Quote Request
CQR	Crest Resources Ltd. [Vancouver Stock Exchange symbol]
CQ Radio Amat J	CQ [Call to Quarters]. Radio Amateur's Journal [A publication]
CQS	California Q-Set [Psychology]
CQS	Chase Resources [Vancouver Stock Exchange symbol]
CQS	Chloroquinoxaline Sulfonamide [Antineoplastic drug]
CQS	Court of Quarter Sessions [Legal] [British] (ROG)
CQS	Custom Quality Studio [Photography]
CQSW	Certificate as a Qualified Social Worker [British]
CQT	Capacitor Qualification Test
CQT	Caquetania [Colombia] [Airport symbol] (OAG)
CQT	Control Question Test [For lie detectors]
CQT	Correct [Data processing] [British]
CQTU	Carrier Qualification Training Unit
C Qu	Classical Quarterly [A publication]
CQU	College Qualification Test
C-Quam	Compatible Quadrature Amplitude Modulation [Radio design] [Motorola, Inc.]
C Quebec	Cinema Quebec [A publication]
CQV	Consolidated Suntec Ventures [Vancouver Stock Exchange symbol]
CQW	Cheraw, SC [Location identifier] [FAA] (FAAL)
CQX	Conquest Exploration Co. [AMEX symbol] [Vancouver Stock Exchange symbol] (SPSG)
CR	Aerocaribbean SA [Cuba] [ICAO designator] (FAAC)
CR	Air Traffic Control Requests [Aviation] (FAAC)
C & R	Bureau of Construction and Repair [Until 1940] [Navy]
CR	Cable Rack (KSC)
CR	Calcutta Review [A publication]
CR	Caledonian Railway [Scotland]
CR	Calendrier Republicain [Republican Calendar] [French]
CR	Call Request [Telecommunications]
CR	Cambrian Railway [British] (ROG)
CR	Camera Rehearsal
CR	Camera Repairman [Navy rating]
CR	Canadian Reports, Appeal Cases [1828-1913] [A publication] (DLA)
CR	Canadian Restricted [Broadcasting term]
C & R	Canal and Rail [Transportation]
CR	Cancellation Ratio [Aviation] (FAAC)
CR	Card Reader [Data processing] (NVT)
CR	Cardiorespiratory [Medicine]
CR	Carnegie-Rochester Conference Series on Public Policy [Elsevier Book Series] [A publication]
CR	Carolina Regina [Queen Caroline] [Latin]
CR	Carolus Rex [King Charles] [Latin]
CR	Carriage Return
CR	Carrier's Risk [Shipping]
CR	Cartercar Registry (EA)
CR	Cash Reserve [Business term]
CR	Cathode Ray
CR	Cathode Reaction
CR	Cellular Radio
CR	Cement Render
CR	Centennial Review [A publication]
CR	Center (DS)
CR	Center of Resistance
CR	Central Railway [British] (ROG)
CR	Central Recorder Subsystem [NASA]
CR	Central Registry [of the Ordnance Survey] [British]
CR	Central Reporter [A publication] (DLA)
CR	Centric Relation [Dentistry]
CR	Cerebral Ridge [Medicine]
C of R	Certificate of Registration (ADA)
C/R	Certificate of Retirement (MUGU)
CR	Certification Requirement (MCD)
CR	Certified Remodeller
CR	Chancery Reports Tempore Car. I to Queen Anne [A publication] (DLA)
C/R	Change of Rating
CR	Change Recommendation (AFM)
CR	Change Release [Military]
CR	Change Request
CR	Channels Ratio
CR	Characteristic Relief
CR	Chemical Report
CR	Chest and Right Arm [Cardiology]
CR	Chest Roentgenogram [Radiology]
CR	Chicago Reactor (NRCH)
CR	Chief Ranger
CR	Child Resistant
CR	Chimeric Receptor
CR	China Corporation Register (Taiwan) [Chinese ship classification society] (DS)
CR	China Reconstructs [A publication]
CR	Chloroprene Rubber
CR	Christian Research (EA)
CR	Christiana [City in South Africa] (ROG)
Cr	Chromium [Chemical element]
CR	Chronic Rejection [Medicine]
CR	Church Record [Genealogy]
CR	Chylomicron Remnant [Physiology]
CR	Circle (ROG)
cr-----	Circumcaribbean [MARC geographic area code] [Library of Congress] (LCCP)
CR	Cited Reference [Online database field identifier]
CR	Civil Rights
CR	Civis Romanus [Roman Citizen] [Latin]
CR	Class Rate [Business term]
CR	Classical Review [A publication]
CR	Classification Research
CR	Classified Register (AAG)

CR .... Clear Record [*Telecommunications*]   (TEL)
CR .... Clear Round [*Show jumping*]   (ADA)
CR .... Clearance Required [*Civil Service*]
C & R .... Clifford and Richard's English Locus Standi Reports [*1873-84*] [*A publication*]   (DLA)
CR .... Clinical Record [*Medicine*]
CR .... Clot Retraction [*Medicine*]
CR .... Co-Responsibility Levy [*Cereal production tax*] [*British*]
C & R .... Cockburn and Rowe's English Election Cases [*1833*] [*A publication*]   (DLA)
CR .... Cockroach Antigen [*Immunology*]
C-R .... Codd-Rennie [*Boundary condition*] [*Nuclear energy*]   (NRCH)
CR .... Code Reporter [*New York*] [*A publication*]   (DLA)
CR .... Codex Reuchlinianus   (BJA)
CR .... Coefficient of Retraction
CR .... Cold-Rolled [*Metal*]
CR .... Collaborative Research, Inc.
C/R .... Collection/Requirements
CR .... Collins Resources Ltd. [*Vancouver Stock Exchange symbol*]
CR .... Colon Resection [*Medicine*]
CR .... Columbia Law Review [*A publication*]
CR .... Combat Reaction
CR .... Combat Ready   (AFM)
CR .... Combat Reserve [*Military*]
C/R .... Command Receiver   (KSC)
CR .... Command Register
CR .... Command Representative   (CINC)
Cr .... Commander [*Navy*] [*British*]
CR .... Commencement of Rifling   (NATG)
CR .... Commendation Ribbon [*Military decoration*]
CR .... Commercial Radio
CR .... Commodity Rate
CR .... Commonwealth Record [*A publication*]
CR .... Communication Representative
CR .... Communication Resources [*Haddonfield, NJ*] [*Telecommunications*]   (TSSD)
CR .... Communications Register
CR .... Community Regeneration   (EA)
CR .... Community Relations   (AABC)
CR .... Community of the Resurrection [*Anglican religious community*]
C/R .... Commutation Rate   (MCD)
CR .... Company's Risk [*Insurance*]
CR .... Competing Risks
CR .... Complement Receptor [*Immunology*]
CR .... Complete Remission [*Medicine*]
CR .... Complete Response [*Medicine*]
CR .... Complete Round [*Technical drawings*]
CR .... Component Repair   (MSA)
CR .... Compression Ratio
CR .... Computing Reviews [*A publication*]
CR .... Concentric Rings [*Botany*]
CR .... Conditional Release [*Nuclear energy*]   (NRCH)
C/R .... Conditioned Reflex [*or Response*] [*Psychometrics*]
CR .... Conference Report
CR .... Configuration Review   (MCD)
CR .... Congregatio Resurrectionis [*Congregation of the Resurrection*] [*Roman Catholic religious order*]
CR .... Congregation of Clerics Regular [*Theatine Fathers*] [*Roman Catholic religious order*]
CR .... Congressional Record [*United States*] [*A publication*]
CR .... Connaught Rangers [*Military*] [*British*]
CR .... Connector Replacement   (MCD)
CR .... Consciousness-Raising
CR .... Conseiller de la Reine [*Queen's Counsel*] [*Canada*]
C-R .... Conservatism-Radicalism Opinionaire [*Student attitude test*]
CR .... Consolidated Rail Corp. [*AAR code*] [*Also, CONRAIL, CRC*]
CR .... Consolidated Report
CR .... Constant Routine
CR .... Constitutional Revival   (EA)
CR .... Construction Recruit [*Navy*]
C and R ..... Construction and Repair [*Coast Guard*]
CR .... Constructionman Recruit [*Navy*]
CR .... Consultant Report   (NATG)
CR .... Consumer Reports [*A publication*]
CR .... Consumer Research Bulletin [*A publication*]
CR .... Consumers' Research   (EA)
CR .... Containment Rupture [*Nuclear energy*]   (NRCH)
CR .... Contemporary Review [*A publication*]
CR .... Continence Restored   (EA)
CR .... Contingency Reserve   (MCD)
CR .... Continuing Resolution
CR .... Continuing Revolution
CR .... Continuous-Release [*Pharmacy*]
CR .... Continuous Rod   (NG)
CR .... Contract-Relax Method [*Medicine*]
CR .... Contract [*or Contractor*] Report
C/R .... Contract Requirement
CR .... Control Rating [*British military*]   (DMA)
CR .... Control Relay
C and R ..... Control and Reporting   (NATG)

CR .... Control Rod [*Nuclear energy*]   (NRCH)
CR .... Control Room   (MSA)
CR .... Control Routine
CR .... Controlled Rectifier
CR .... Controlled Release [*Chemical technology*]
CR .... Controlled Rheology [*Plastics technology*]
C & R .... Convalescent and Rehabilitation [*Military*]
CR .... Conveyancing Review [*1957-63*] [*Scotland*] [*A publication*]   (DLA)
C & R .... Convoy and Routing [*Section*] [*US Fleet*]
CR .... Corbin Research [*An association*]   (EA)
CR .... Core
CR .... Coronation   (ROG)
CR .... Corpus Reformatorum   (BJA)
CR .... Corrosion Resistant [*Material*] [*Manufacturing*]   (DCTA)
CR .... Cosmic Ray
CR .... Cost per Region [*Agricultural economics*]
CR .... Cost Reimbursement
cr .... Costa Rica [*MARC country of publication code*] [*Library of Congress*]   (LCCP)
CR .... Costa Rica [*ANSI two-letter standard code*]   (CNC)
CR .... Councillor   (ADA)
CR .... Count Reverse [*Data processing*]
CR .... Coupled Range-Finders
CR .... Court Reporting Program [*Association of Independent Colleges and Schools specialization code*]
Cr .... [*Sir T.*] Craig. Jus Feudale [*A publication*]   (DLA)
Cr .... Cranch. Circuit Court Reports [*United States*] [*A publication*]   (DLA)
Cr .... [*William*] Cranch. Supreme Court Reports [*United States*] [*A publication*]   (DLA)
CR .... Crane [*Shipping*]   (DS)
CR .... Crane Co. [*NYSE symbol*]   (SPSG)
CR .... Cranial [*Anatomy*]
CR .... Cras [*Tomorrow*] [*Pharmacy*]
CR .... Crate
cr .... Cream [*Philately*]
CR .... Crease [*Deltiology*]
CR .... Created [*or Creation*]
Cr .... Creatinine [*Biochemistry*]
CR .... Creation Research
CR .... Credit   (AFM)
CR .... Credit Rating [*Business term*]   (ADA)
CR .... Credit Report [*Business term*]
CR .... Credit Requisition   (MCD)
CR .... Creditable Record
CR .... Creditor   (ROG)
CR .... Credo [*Creed*] [*Latin*]
CR .... Creek [*Maps and charts*]
CR .... Creeping [*Horticulture*]
CR .... Crescendo [*Music*]   (ROG)
CR .... Crescentic
CR .... Crew   (MSA)
CR .... Crew Rest [*Military*]   (AFM)
Cr .... Criminal   (DLA)
CR .... Criminal Reports [*A publication*]
CR .... Crimson   (ROG)
CR .... Crisis Relocation   (MCD)
CR .... Cristobalite [*A mineral*]
Cr .... Criterion [*A publication*]
CR .... Critical Ratio
CR .... Critical Review [*A publication*]
CR .... Crochet
CR .... Crop Research [*A publication*]
CR .... Crops Research Division [*of ARS, Department of Agriculture*]
CR .... Crossroads [*Maps and charts*]
CR .... Crown [*Paper size*]
CR .... Crown
CR .... Crown-Rump Length [*of fetus*] [*Medicine*]
CR .... Cruiser
CR .... Cruiser Flag [*Navy*] [*British*]
Cr .... Crux [*A publication*]
CR .... Cryptographer [*Navy rating*]
CR .... Crystal Rectifier   (AAG)
CR .... Crystals [*JETDS nomenclature*] [*Military*]   (CET)
C/R .... Cuenta y Riesgo [*For Account and Risk Of*] [*Spanish*] [*Business term*]
CR .... Cum Rights [*With Rights*]   (ADA)
CR .... Curia Regis [*King's Court*] [*Latin*] [*Legal term*]   (DLA)
CR .... Currency Regulation
CR .... Current Rate [*Business term*]
CR .... Current Relay   (MSA)
C & R .... Curriculum and Research   (ADA)
CR .... Customer's Report [*Telecommunications*]   (TEL)
CR .... Custos Rotulorum [*Keeper of the Rolls*] [*Latin*]
CR .... Cutter [*Ship*]   (ROG)
CR .... Cylinder Rate   (NVT)
Cr .... La Sainte Bible (1923) [*A. Crampon*] [*A publication*]   (BJA)
CR .... Portugal [*Aircraft nationality and registration mark*]   (FAAC)
CR .... Station Open to Limited Public Correspondence [*ITU designation*]

Cr	Texas Court of Appeals Reports (Criminal Cases) [*A publication*] (DLA)
Cr	Texas Criminal Reports [*A publication*] (DLA)
CR's	Complete Responders [*to medication*]
CRa	Cahiers Raciniens [*A publication*]
CRA	California Redwood Association (EA)
CRA	Camera-Ready Art [*Publishing*]
CRA	Canadian Racquetball Association
CRA	Canadian Restaurant Association
CRA	Canonesses Regular of St. Augustine [*Roman Catholic women's religious order*]
CRA	Carbon Rod Atomizer [*Spectroscopy*]
CRA	Cargo Reinsurance Association [*New York, NY*] (EA)
CRA	Cassegrain Reflector Antenna
CRA	Catalog Recovery Area [*Data processing*]
CRA	Cave Research Associates (EA)
CRA	Center for Rural Affairs
CRA	Central Research Agency [*Cuc Nghien-Chu Trung-Uong*] [*North Vietnamese intelligence agency*]
CRA	Central Retinal Artery [*Ophthalmology*]
CRA	Centralized Referral Activity [*Military*] (AFM)
CRA	Centralized Repair Activity [*Air Force*] (AFIT)
CRA	Certified Retinal Angiographer
CRA	Charles River Associates Library, Boston, MA [*OCLC symbol*] (OCLC)
CRA	Chernovtsy [*USSR*] [*Seismograph station code, US Geological Survey*] [*Closed*] (SEIS)
CRA	Children's Rights of America (EA)
CRA	China Research Associates
CRA	Chinese Restaurant Asthma [*Medicine*]
CRA	Christian Restoration Association (EA)
CRA	Chromium Release Assay [*Clinical chemistry*]
CRA	Civil Rights Act [*1957, 1964, 1968*]
CRA	Clydesdale Runner's Association (EA)
CRA	Colorado River Association (EA)
CRA	Coma Recovery Association (EA)
CRA	Command Relationship Agreements [*Army*] (AABC)
CRA	Commander, Royal Artillery [*Division level*] [*British*]
CRA	Committee for Real Ale (EA)
CRA	Committee to Resist Abortion (EA)
CRA	Commons Registration Act [*Town planning*] [*British*]
CRA	Community Radio Association [*British*]
CRA	Community Redevelopment Agency
CRA	Community Reinvestment Act [*1977*] [*Requires banks to list credit facilities available to the communities they serve*]
CRA	Community Research Associates (EA)
CRA	Commuter Airlines [*Binghamton, NY*] [*FAA designator*] (FAAC)
CRA	Component Reword Analyst (MCD)
CRA	Composite Research Aircraft
CRA	Compte-Rendu Analytique des Travaux du Conseil Colonial. Puis Conseil de Legislation [*A publication*]
CRA	Congress of Russian Americans (EA)
CRA	Contemporaneous Reserve Accounting [*Banking*]
CRA	Continuing Resolution Authority [*Military*] (AFM)
CRA	Control Relay Automatic
CRA	Control Repeater Amplifier
CRA	Control Rod Assembly [*Nuclear energy*] (NRCH)
CRA	Controlled Rupture Accuracy (MUGU)
CRA	Cooperative Research Act
CRA	Corn Refiners Association (EA)
CRA	Corolla Resources Ltd. [*Vancouver Stock Exchange symbol*]
CrA	Corona Australis [*Constellation*]
CRA	Cosmic Ray Altimeter
CRA	Craddock [*City in South Africa*] (ROG)
CRA	Craig Corp. [*NYSE symbol*] (SPSG)
CRA	Craiova [*Romania*] [*Airport symbol*] (OAG)
Cra	Cranch. Circuit Court Reports [*United States*] [*A publication*] (DLA)
CRA	Crater (ROG)
Cra	Cratylus [*of Plato*] [*Classical studies*] (OCD)
CRA	Crease Recovery Angle [*Textile technology*]
CRA	Crew Reception Area [*Apollo*] [*NASA*]
Cr d'A	Critica d'Arte [*A publication*]
CRA	Sandoz Pharmaceuticals [*Research code symbol*]
CrAA	Commander at Arms [*Navy*] [*British*]
CRAA	Committee of Religion and Art of America [*Later, FAAR*] (EA)
CRAABull ...	Commissions Royales d'Art et d'Archeologie. Bulletin [*A publication*]
CRAB	Caging Retainer and Boresight [*Air Force*]
CRAB	California Raisin Advisory Board (EA)
CRAB	Captain Crab, Inc. [*NASDAQ symbol*] (NQ)
CRAB	Cement Riverine Assault Boat [*Navy*] (MCD)
CRAB	Centralized Requisitioning Accounting and Billing
CRAB	Coastal Research Amphibious Buggy [*Army*] (MSC)
CRAB	Combined Resources Allocation Board [*World War II*]
CRAB	Communications Research Advisory Board [*Canada*]
CRAB	Controlled Range Air Burst Fuze (RDA)
Crab	Crabbe's United States District Court Reports [*A publication*] (DLA)

CRABB	Cellular Remote Access Bulletin Board [*Cellular Communications Industry Association*] [*Information service or system*] (IID)
CRABB	Current Affairs Bulletin [*A publication*]
Crabb CL ...	Crabb on the Common Law [*A publication*] (DLA)
Crabb Com Law ...	Crabb on the Common Law [*A publication*] (DLA)
Crabb Conv ...	Crabb's Treatise on Conveyancing [*A publication*] (DLA)
Crabb Dig Stat ...	Crabb's Digest of Statutes [*A publication*] (DLA)
Crabbe	Crabbe's United States District Court Reports [*A publication*] (DLA)
Crabb Eng ...	Crabb's English Synonyms [*A publication*] (DLA)
Crabb Eng L ...	Crabb's History of the English Law [*A publication*] (DLA)
Crabb Eng Law ...	Crabb's History of the English Law [*A publication*] (ILCA)
Crabb Hist Eng Law ...	Crabb's History of the English Law [*A publication*] (DLA)
Crabb Prec ...	Crabb's Precedents in Conveyancing [*A publication*] (DLA)
Crabb Real Prop ...	Crabb on the Law of Real Property [*A publication*] (DLA)
Crabb RP ...	Crabb on the Law of Real Property [*A publication*] (DLA)
Crabb Technol Dict ...	Crabb's Technological Dictionary [*A publication*] (DLA)
CRABP	Cellular Retinoic Acid-Binding Protein [*Biochemistry*]
CRABS	Computerized Reference and Bibliographic Services [*University of Maryland at Baltimore*] (OLDSS)
CRAC	Calculations of Reactor Accident Consequences (NRCH)
CRAC	Canadian Reports, Appeal Cases [*1828-1913*] [*A publication*] (DLA)
CRAC	Careers Research and Advisory Centre [*British*]
CRAC	Central Religious Advisory Committee [*British*]
CRAC	Club Royale d'Automobile du Canada [*Royal Automobile Club of Canada*]
CRAC	Commander, Royal Armoured Corps [*British military*] (DMA)
CRAC	Community Relations Advisory Council [*Military*]
CRAC	Conseil de Recherche Agricole du Canada [*Canadian Agricultural Research Council*]
CRAC	Contract-Relax, Antagonistic-Contract Method [*Medicine*]
CRACA	Council on Roentgenology of the American Chiropractic Association (EA)
CR Acad Agric France ...	Comptes Rendus Hebdomadaires des Seances. Academie d'Agriculture de France [*A publication*]
CR Acad Agric Georgi Dimitrov ...	Comptes Rendus. Academie Agricole Georgi Dimitrov [*A publication*]
CR Acad Bulgare Sci ...	Comptes Rendus. Academie Bulgare des Sciences [*A publication*]
CR Acad Bulg Sci ...	Comptes Rendus. Academie Bulgare des Sciences [*A publication*]
CRAcad Inscr ...	Comptes Rendus. Academie des Inscriptions et Belles-Lettres [*A publication*] (OCD)
CR Acad Sci ...	Comptes Rendus. Academie des Sciences [*A publication*]
CR Acad Sci ...	Comptes Rendus Hebdomadaires des Seances. Academie des Sciences [*A publication*]
CR Acad Sci Agric Bulg ...	Comptes Rendus. Academie des Sciences Agricoles en Bulgarie [*A publication*]
CR Acad Sci (Paris) ...	Comptes Rendus. Academie des Sciences (Paris) [*A publication*]
CR Acad Sci (Paris) Ser A-B ...	Comptes Rendus Hebdomadaires des Seances. Academie des Sciences (Paris). Serie A et B [*A publication*]
CR Acad Sci (Paris) Ser III Sci Vie ...	Comptes Rendus des Seances. Academie des Sciences (Paris). Serie III. Sciences de la Vie [*A publication*]
CR Acad Sci (Paris) Ser II Mec Phys Chim Sci ...	Comptes Rendus des Seances. Academie des Sciences (Paris). Serie II. Mecanique, Physique, Chimie, Sciences de la Terre, Sciences de l'Univers [*A publication*]
CR Acad Sci (Paris) Ser I Math ...	Comptes Rendus des Seances. Academie des Sciences (Paris). Serie I. Mathematique [*A publication*]
CR Acad Sci (Paris) Vie Academique ...	Comptes Rendus Hebdomadaires des Seances. Academie des Sciences. Vie Academique (Paris) [*Later, Comptes Rendus des Seances. Academie des Sciences. Vie Academique*] [*A publication*]
CR Acad Sci Ser 2 ...	Comptes Rendus. Academie des Sciences. Serie 2. Mecanique, Physique, Chimie, Sciences de l'Univers, Sciences de la Terre [*A publication*]
CR Acad Sci Ser 3 ...	Comptes Rendus. Academie des Sciences. Serie 3. Sciences de la Vie [*A publication*]
CR Acad Sci Ser Gen Vie Sci ...	Comptes Rendus. Academie des Sciences. Serie Generale. La Vie des Sciences [*A publication*]
CR Acad Sci Ser II Mec Phys ...	Comptes Rendus des Seances. Academie des Sciences. Serie II. Mecanique, Physique, Chimie, Sciences de la Terre, Sciences de l'Univers [*A publication*]
CRACC	Communication and RADAR Assignment Coordinating Committee
Cra CC	Cranch. Circuit Court Reports [*United States*] [*A publication*] (DLA)
CRACCUS ...	Comite Regional d'Afrique Centrale pour la Conservation et l'Utilisation du Sol
CRACH	Central Register and Clearing House [*British*]
CR Ac Inscr ...	Comptes Rendus des Seances. Academie des Inscriptions et Belles Lettres [*A publication*]
CRAC-KIT ...	Croft Readiness Assessment in Comprehension Kit [*Child development test*]

CRACL...... Civil Rights Act Compliance Log   (OICC)
CRACS...... Control Room Air Conditioning System [*Nuclear energy*]   (NRCH)
CR Ac Sci A ... Comptes Rendus Hebdomadaires des Seances. Academie des Sciences. Serie A [*A publication*]
CR Ac Sci B ... Comptes Rendus Hebdomadaires des Seances. Academie des Sciences. Serie B [*A publication*]
CR Ac Sci C ... Comptes Rendus Hebdomadaires des Seances. Academie des Sciences. Serie C [*A publication*]
CR Ac Sci D ... Comptes Rendus Hebdomadaires des Seances. Academie des Sciences. Serie D [*A publication*]
Cr Act........ Criminal Act   (DLA)
CRAD .... Centre de Recherches en Amenagement et en Developpement [*Laval University*] [*Canada*] [*Research center*]   (RCD)
CRAD .... Chief, Research and Development [*Department of National Defence*] [*Canada*]
CRAD .... Composite RADAR Data Processing   (FAAC)
CRAD .... Contract Research and Development
CRADS...... Contraves/Raytheon Air Defense System
CRAE......... Combat Readiness Assessment Exercise [*Obsolete*] [*Navy*]   (NG)
CRAE......... Combined Readiness Air Exercise   (MCD)
CRAE......... Committee for the Reform of Animal Experimentation [*British*]
CRAF........ Central Reserve Air Fleet
CRAF........ Civil Reserve Air Fleet [*Department of Commerce*]
CRAF........ Comet Rendezvous and Asteroid Flyby [*Proposed NASA mission*]
CRAFREP ... Civil Reserve Air Fleet Summary Report [*Department of Commerce*]
CRAFT ...... Centre Regional Africain de Conception et de Fabrication Techniques [*African Regional Centre for Engineering Design and Manufacturing - ARCEDEM*]   (EAIO)
CRAFT ...... Changing Radio Automatic Frequency Transmission
CRAFT ...... Combat Reserve Air Fleet [*Military*]
CRAFT ...... Comparing Reading Approaches in First Grade Teaching
CRAFT ...... Computerized Relative Allocation of Facilities Technique [*IBM Corp.*]
CRAFT ...... Continuous Random Analog to Frequency Transmission
Craft A .... Craft Australia [*A publication*]   (APTA)
Craft Aust .. Craft Australia [*A publication*]
Craft Horiz ... Craft Horizons [*A publication*]
CRAFTS.... Central Regional Automated Funds Transfer System
CRAFTS.... Credit Card Authorisation and Fund Transfer System [*British*]
CRAG .... Carrier Replacement Air Group [*Navy*]
CRAG .... Cranfield Robotics and Automation Group [*British*]
CRAGAP... Caribbean Agriculture [*A publication*]
CRAGS...... Chemistry Records and Grading System [*Data processing*]
CRAHCA .. Center for Research in Ambulatory Health Care Administration   (EA)
CRAI......... Comptes Rendus. Academie des Inscriptions et Belles Lettres [*A publication*]
CRAIBL .... Comptes Rendus. Academie des Inscriptions et Belles Lettres [*A publication*]
Craig Dict .. Craig's Etymological, Technological, and Pronouncing Dictionary [*A publication*]   (DLA)
Craigius Jus Feud ... Craigius Jus Feudale [*A publication*]   (DLA)
Craig Jus Feud ... Craigius Jus Feudale [*A publication*]   (DLA)
Craig & P ... Craig and Phillips' English Chancery Reports [*1840-41*] [*A publication*]   (DLA)
Craig & Ph ... Craig and Phillips' English Chancery Reports [*1840-41*] [*A publication*]   (DLA)
Craig & Ph (Eng) ... Craig and Phillips' English Chancery Reports [*1840-41*] [*A publication*]   (DLA)
Craig Pr ..... Craig's Practice [*A publication*]   (DLA)
Craig S & P ... Craigie, Stewart, and Paton's Scotch Appeal Cases [*1726-1821*] [*A publication*]   (DLA)
Craig & St .. Craigie, Stewart, and Paton's Scotch Appeal Cases [*1726-1821*] [*A publication*]   (DLA)
Craig St & Pat ... Craigie, Stewart, and Paton's Scotch Appeal Cases [*1726-1821*] [*A publication*]   (DLA)
Craik CC.... Craik's English Causes Celebres [*A publication*]   (DLA)
Crain Detro ... Crain's Detroit Business [*A publication*]
Crain Illin .. Crain's Illinois Business [*A publication*]
Crains NY ... Crain's New York Business [*A publication*]
CRAL......... Compte Rendu. Association Lyonnaise de Recherches Archeologiques [*A publication*]
CRALC...... Cedar Rapids Area Library Consortium [*Library network*]
CRALOG... Council of Relief Agencies Licensed for Operation in Germany [*Post-World War II*]
CRAM .... Card Random-Access Memory [*NCR Corp.*] [*Data processing*]
CRAM .... Centre de Recherches sur l'Afrique Mediterraneenne
CRAM .... Centre for Research on Atoms and Molecules [*Laval University*] [*Canada*] [*Research center*]   (RCD)
CRAM .... Collapsible Rollup Antenna Mast
CRAM .... Combat Resource Allocation Model   (MCD)
CRAM .... Computerized Reliability Analysis Method
CRAM .... Conditional Relaxation Analysis Method
CRAM .... CONRAIL [*Consolidated Rail Corp.*] Analysis Model [*Data processing*]
CRAM .... Contractual Requirements, Recording, Analysis, and Management [*Air Force*]

CRAM .... Core and Random Access Manager [*General Automation, Inc.*]
CRAMMM ... Chain Store Renovation and Maintenance, Materials, Modernization
Cramp Mag ... Crampton's Magazine [*A publication*]
CRAMPS .. Combined Rotation and Multiple-Pulse Spectroscopy [*Physics*]
CRAMRA ... Convention on the Regulation of Antarctic Mineral Resource Activities [*Australia*]
CRAMSHIP ... Complete Round Ammunition Shipment
Cran .... [*William*] Cranch. Supreme Court Reports [*United States*] [*A publication*]   (DLA)
cran .... Cranial [*Anatomy*]
CRAN .... Craniology
CRAN .... Cross-Scan Terrain-Avoidance Displays
CRAN .... Crown Andersen, Inc. [*Peachtree City, GA*] [*NASDAQ symbol*]   (NQ)
CRANB ..... Cranborne [*England*]
Cranbrook Inst Sci Bull ... Cranbrook Institute of Science. Bulletin [*A publication*]
Cranbrook Inst Sci Bull News Letter ... Cranbrook Institute of Science. Bulletin. News Letter [*A publication*]
Cran CCR .. [*William*] Cranch. Circuit Court Reports [*District of Columbia*] [*A publication*]   (DLA)
Cranch ...... [*William*] Cranch. Supreme Court Reports [*United States*] [*A publication*]   (DLA)
Cranch ...... Cranch's District of Columbia Reports [*1-5 District of Columbia*] [*1801-40*] [*A publication*]   (DLA)
Cranch CC ... Cranch. Circuit Court Reports [*United States*] [*A publication*]   (DLA)
Cranch CC ... District of Columbia Appeals Cases Reports [*1-5 United States*] [*A publication*]   (DLA)
Cranch CC ... District of Columbia Supreme Court Reports [*1-5 District of Columbia*] [*1801-40*] [*A publication*]   (DLA)
Cranch CC Rep ... [*William*] Cranch. Circuit Court Reports [*District of Columbia*] [*A publication*]   (DLA)
Cranch (C Ct) ... [*William*] Cranch. Circuit Court Reports [*District of Columbia*] [*A publication*]   (DLA)
Cranch DC ... [*William*] Cranch. Circuit Court Reports [*District of Columbia*] [*A publication*]   (DLA)
Cranch Pat Dec ... Cranch's Patent Decisions [*United States*] [*A publication*]   (DLA)
Cranch R.... [*William*] Cranch. Supreme Court Reports [*United States*] [*A publication*]   (DLA)
Cranch Rep ... [*William*] Cranch. Supreme Court Reports [*United States*] [*A publication*]   (DLA)
Cranch (US) ... [*William*] Cranch. Supreme Court Reports [*United States*] [*A publication*]   (DLA)
CRAND ..... Cosmic Ray Albedo Neutron Decay [*Geophysics*]
CRANE ...... Cosmic Ray Nuclear Experiment   (MCD)
Crane........ Crane's Reports [*22-29 Montana*] [*A publication*]   (DLA)
Crane CC ... Cranenburgh's Criminal Cases [*India*] [*A publication*]   (DLA)
CraneR....... Crane Review [*A publication*]
CRANIOL ... Craniology   (ROG)
CRANIOM ... Craniometry   (ROG)
CRANIOT ... Craniotomy   (ROG)
Cran Rep.... [*William*] Cranch. Supreme Court Reports [*United States*] [*A publication*]   (DLA)
Cra NY Pr ... Crary's New York Practice, Special Pleading [*A publication*]   (DLA)
CRAO .... Central Retinal Artery Occlusion [*Ophthalmology*]
CRAOC ...... Commander, Royal Army Ordnance Corps [*Military*] [*British*]
CRAP........ Canfield, Rodeman, Adams, and Preller [*Philadelphia law firm in Spiro Agnew's book, "The Canfield Decision"*]
CRAP........ Committee to Resist Acronym Proliferation
CRAP........ Committee on Rhetoric, Administration, and Perspicacity [*Satirical bureaucracy term*]
CRAP........ Comptes Rendus. Academie Polonaise des Sciences et des Lettres [*A publication*]
CRAP........ Constructive Republican Alternative Programs [*Position papers on legislative issues prepared for Republican House leaders during Lyndon Johnson administration*]
Cr App .... Criminal Appeals   (DLA)
Cr App R.... Criminal Appeal Reports [*England*] [*A publication*]   (DLA)
Cr App Rep ... Criminal Appeal Reports [*England*] [*A publication*]   (DLA)
Cr App R(S) ... Criminal Appeal Reports (Sentencing) [*England*] [*A publication*]   (DLA)
CRAR .... Center for Research Animal Resources [*Cornell University*] [*Research center*]   (RCD)
CRAR .... Committee for the Recovery of Archaeological Remains
CRAR .... Control ROM [*Read-Only Memory*] Address Register [*Data processing*]
CRAR .... Critical Reliability Action Report   (AAG)
CRARA...... Canadian Rock Art Research Associates
Crar Pr .... Crary's New York Practice, Special Pleading [*A publication*]   (DLA)
CRAS........ Canadian Review of American Studies [*A publication*]
CRAS........ Centennial Review of Arts and Sciences [*Later, Centennial Review*] [*A publication*]
CRAS........ Coder and Random Access Switch   (AAG)
CRAS........ Cost Reduction Alternative Study [*Economics*]   (NASA)
CRASC...... Commander, Royal Army Service Corps [*British*]
CRASH...... Center for Reproductive and Sexual Health   (EA)

CRASH...... Citizens to Reduce Airline Smoking Hazards [*Student legal action organization*]
CRASH...... Citizens Responsible Action for Safety on the Highways
CRASH...... Creep in Axisymmetric Shells
CRASR...... Comptes Rendus. Academie des Sciences de Russie [*A publication*]
CRASS ...... Convoy, Routing, and Scheduling System [*USAREUR*]
Crass.......... Crassus [*of Plutarch*] [*Classical studies*]   (OCD)
CR Assoc Anat ... Comptes Rendus. Association des Anatomistes [*A publication*]
CR Assoc Int Essais Semences ... Comptes Rendus. Association Internationale d'Essais de Semences [*A publication*]
CRAST ...... Crastinus [*Of Tomorrow*] [*Pharmacy*]
CRASTE.... Committee to Review Australian Studies in Tertiary Education
CRAT......... Centre Regional Africain de Technologie [*African Regional Centre for Technology - ARCT*]   (EA)
CRAT......... Colonel, Royal Artillery Training [*British*]
Crat .... Crater [*Constellation*]
CRATT...... Covered Radio Teletype   (NVT)
CRATTZ ... Communication Radio and Teletype (Secure) System
Crav........... [*Aymo*] Cravetta [*Deceased, 1569*] [*Authority cited in pre-1607 legal work*]   (DSA)
CRAVS...... Control Room Area Ventilation System [*Nuclear energy*]   (NRCH)
CR/AVTC ... Conflict Resolution/Alternatives to Violence Training Center   (EA)
CRAW ...... Carrier Replacement Air Wing [*Navy*]
CRAW ...... Combat Readiness Air Wing
Craw.......... Crawford's Reports [*53-69, 72-101 Arkansas*] [*A publication*]   (DLA)
Craw (Ark) ... Crawford's Reports [*53-69, 72-101 Arkansas*] [*A publication*]   (DLA)
Craw Co Leg J (PA) ... Crawford County Legal Journal [*Pennsylvania*] [*A publication*]   (DLA)
Craw & D ... Crawford and Dix's Irish Circuit Court Cases [*A publication*]   (DLA)
Craw & D Ab Cas ... Crawford and Dix's Irish Abridged Cases [*A publication*]   (DLA)
Craw & D Abr Cas ... Crawford and Dix's Irish Abridged Cases [*A publication*]   (DLA)
Craw & DCC (Ir) ... Crawford and Dix's Irish Circuit Court Cases [*A publication*]   (DLA)
Craw & D (Ir) ... Crawford and Dix's Irish Abridged Cases [*A publication*]   (DLA)
Craw & Dix ... Crawford and Dix's Irish Circuit Court Cases [*A publication*]   (DLA)
Crawf & D ... Crawford and Dix's Irish Circuit Court Cases [*A publication*]   (DLA)
Crawf & D Abr Cas ... Crawford and Dix's Irish Abridged Cases [*A publication*]   (DLA)
Crawf & Dix ... Crawford and Dix's Irish Circuit Court Cases [*A publication*]   (DLA)
Crawf & Dix ... Crawford and Dix's Irish Criminal Cases [*A publication*]   (DLA)
Crawford Co Leg Jour ... Crawford County Legal Journal [*Pennsylvania*] [*A publication*]   (DLA)
CRAY .... Cray Computer Corp. [*NASDAQ symbol*]   (NQ)
CRAY .... Crayfish   (DSUE)
CRAZI...... Count Routine Applied to Zero Input [*Computer program*]
CRB .... Cab Research Bureau [*Later, ITA*]   (EA)
CRB .... Cahiers de la Compagnie Madeleine Renaud-Jean Louis Barrault [*A publication*]
CRB .... Cahiers de la Revue Biblique [*Paris*] [*A publication*]
CRB .... Cam Ranh Bay [*Vietnam*]
CRB .... Cambridge Research Biochemicals [*British*]
CRB .... Certified Residential Broker [*Designation awarded by Realtors National Marketing Institute of the National Association of Realtors*]
CRB .... Change Review Board [*NASA*]   (KSC)
CRB .... Chemical, Radiological, Biological Warfare [*NATO*]   (NATG)
CRB .... Chernovtsy [*USSR*] [*Seismograph station code, US Geological Survey*] [*Closed*]   (SEIS)
CRB .... China Report [*A publication*]
CRB .... Clemency Review Board [*for Vietnam War draft dodgers and defectors*]
CRB .... Clutch Release Bearing
CRB .... Clutter Reject Band   (MCD)
CRB .... Columbia River Basalts [*Geology*]
CRB .... Command Review Board [*Aerospace*]
CRB .... Commodity Research Bureau
CRB .... Composite Razor Blade   (MCD)
CRB .... Container Repair Building
CRB .... Contingency Reference Book   (MCD)
CRB .... Corbit-Calloway Memorial Library, Odessa, DE [*OCLC symbol*]   (OCLC)
CrB............. Corona Borealis [*Constellation*]
CRB .... Council on Research in Bibliography, Inc.   (DIT)
CRB .... Council of Review Board [*Army*]
CRB .... Country Radio Broadcasters   (EA)
CRB .... Courier de la Bourse et de la Banque [*A publication*]
CrB............. Critisch Bulletin [*A publication*]

CRB .... Crop Reporting Board
CRB .... Current Research in Britain [*A publication*]
CRB .... Customer Records and Billing [*Bell System*]
CRBA........ Christian Record Benevolent Association [*Later, CRBF*]
CRBA........ Cinnamon Rabbit Breeders Association   (EA)
CRBAL...... Carpatho-Russian Benevolent Association Liberty   (EA)
CRBBB .... Complete Right Bundle Branch Block [*Cardiology*]
CRBC........ Canadian Radio Broadcasting Commission [*Later, Canadian Broadcasting Corporation*]
CRBC........ Chick Red Blood Cells
CRbCL....... Tehama County Free Library, Red Bluff, CA [*Library symbol*] [*Library of Congress*]   (LCLS)
CRBDDO .. Commentaries on Research in Breast Disease [*A publication*]
CRBE........ Conversational Remote Batch Entry [*Data processing*]
CRBEDR ... CRC [*Chemical Rubber Company*] Reviews in Biomedical Engineering [*A publication*]
CRBF........ Christian Record Braille Foundation [*Later, CRS*]   (EA)
CRBI........ Cal Rep Bancorp, Inc. [*NASDAQ symbol*]   (NQ)
CRBIF ...... Crisis Basic Imagery File   (MCD)
CRBL........ Charles River Breeding Laboratories
CRBL-A..... Carre Bleu [*A publication*]
CRBM .... Centre de Recherche en Biologie Marine [*Marine Biology Research Center*] [*Research center*]   (RCD)
CRBN .... Calgon Carbon Corp. [*NASDAQ symbol*]   (NQ)
CRBNATD ... Carbonated
CRBNT...... Carbonate   (MSA)
CRBO .... Centralized Records Business Office [*Telecommunications*]   (TEL)
CRBP........ Carboxyribitol Bisphosphate [*Biochemistry*]
CRBP........ Cellular Retinol-Binding Protein [*Biochemistry*]
CRBP........ Colorado River Basin Project
CRBP........ Construction Report, Building Permits [*A publication*]
CRBR........ Cerberonics, Inc. [*NASDAQ symbol*]   (NQ)
CRBR........ Clinch River Breeder Reactor
CRBR........ Controlled Recirculation Boiling Water Reactor
CRBRAT ... Carbohydrate Research [*A publication*]
CRBRP ..... Clinch River Breeder Reactor Plant [*Department of Energy*]
CRBSD ...... Curbside   (MSA)
CRBT........ Columbia River Basin Treaty   (NOAA)
CRBTE5 .... CRC [*Chemical Rubber Company*] Critical Reviews in Biotechnology [*A publication*]
CRBW ...... Carson's Rule Bandwidth
CRC .... Cable Communications Resource Center   (EA)
CRC .... Calibration and Repair Center
CRC .... California Railroad Commission Digest of Decisions [*A publication*]   (DLA)
CRC .... Calomel, Rhubarb, Colocynth [*Medicine*]
CRC .... Cambridge Research Center [*Air Force*]
CRC .... Camera-Ready Copy [*Publishing*]
CRC .... Canadian Railway Cases [*A publication*]   (DLA)
CRC .... Canadian Railway Commission
CRC .... Canadian Religious Conference
CRC .... Canadian Reprography Collective
CRC .... Cancer Research Campaign [*British*]
CRC .... Cardiovascular Reflex Conditioning [*Medicine*]
CRC .... Carlow College, Pittsburgh, PA [*OCLC symbol*]   (OCLC)
CRC .... Carolco Pictures, Inc. [*NYSE symbol*] [*Toronto Stock Exchange symbol*]   (SPSG)
CRC .... Carriage Return Contact
CRC .... Carrier Return Character [*Data processing*]
CRC .... Cartago [*Columbia*] [*Airport symbol*]   (OAG)
CRC .... Castle Rock [*California*] [*Seismograph station code, US Geological Survey*]   (SEIS)
CRC .... Cataloging Responsibility Code
CRC .... Cavity Rim Cup [*A contraceptive device*]
CRC .... Central Registry of Charities [*British*]
CRC .... Central Requirements Committee
CRC .... Central Rhine Commission [*Post-World War II*]
CRC .... Century Research Center Corp. [*Information service or system*]   (EISS)
CRC .... Ceramic Refraction Coating
CRC .... Certified Rehabilitation Counselor
CRC .... Chemical Referral Center   (EA)
CRC .... Chemical Research Consultants, Inc.
CRC .... Chemical Resistant Coating
CRC .... Chemical Rubber Company
CRC .... Chesapeake Research Consortium
CRC .... Chief of Reserve Components [*Army*]
CRC .... Child-Resistant Closure [*Medicine containers, etc.*]
CRC .... Christian Reformed Church
CRC .... Chrysler Restorers Club [*Formerly, CPRC*]   (EA)
CRC .... Circle   (FAAC)
CRC .... Circle, AK [*Location identifier*] [*FAA*]   (FAAL)
CRC .... Civil Rights Commission [*Federal government*]
CRC .... Clinical Research Center [*Case Western Reserve University*] [*Research center*]   (RCD)
CRC .... Clinical Research Center [*Massachusetts Institute of Technology*] [*Research center*]   (RCD)
CRC .... Clinical Research Center [*University of Rochester*] [*Research center*]   (RCD)

CRC .... Clinical Research Center [*University of Tennessee*] [*Research center*] (RCD)
CRC .... Clinical Research Center [*University of Utah*] [*Research center*] (RCD)
CRC .... Clinical Research Center [*UCLA*] [*Research center*]
CRC .... Clinical Research Center [*Medical Research Institute of Delaware*] [*Research center*]
CRC .... Clinical Research Centre [*British*] (CB)
CRC .... Collectors Record Club (EA)
CRC .... Collins Radio Company (KSC)
CRC .... Colorado Research Corporation (AAG)
CRC .... Colorectal Carcinoma [*Oncology*]
CRC .... Column Research Council [*Later, SSRC*] (EA)
CRC .... Combat Reporting Center (AFM)
CRC .... Command Reporting Center
CRC .... Committee to Restore the Constitution (EA)
CRC .... Communication Research Center [*Boston University*] [*Research center*] (RCD)
CRC .... Communication Research Center [*University of Florida*] [*Research center*] (RCD)
CRC .... Communication Research Center [*Florida State University*] [*Research center*] (RCD)
CRC .... Communications Regulatory Commission
CRC .... Communications Relay Center [*Air Force*]
CRC .... Communications Research Center [*University of Tennessee at Knoxville*] [*Research center*] (RCD)
CRC .... Communications Research Centre [*Defunct*] [*Canada*]
CRC .... Community Relations Commission [*British*]
CRC .... Community Research Center [*University of Illinois*] [*Research center*] (RCD)
CRC .... Complete Round Chart
CRC .... Computer Response Corporation
CRC .... Computer Results Corporation [*Information service or system*] (IID)
CRC .... COMSEC [*Communications Security*] Repair Center [*Army*] (NG)
CRC .... Condition Reservation Code [*Army*] (AABC)
CRC .... Conflict Resolution Center (EA)
CRC .... Congressional Report on Communications [*Arlington, VA*] [*A publication*] (TSSD)
CRC .... Congressional Rural Caucus (EA)
CRC .... Consistency Recording Controller
CRC .... Consolidated Rail Corporation [*Also, CR, CONRAIL*]
CRC .... Consolidated Reactor Uranium [*Vancouver Stock Exchange symbol*]
CRC .... Constitutional Reform Centre [*British*] (CB)
CRC .... Contract Requirement Card
CRC .... Contractor-Recommended Coding (MCD)
CRC .... Contre-Reforme Catholique [*In association name CRC Canada*] [*Catholic Counter-Reform Canada*]
CRC .... Control and Reporting Center [*Air Force*]
CRC .... Cooperative Research Council
CRC .... Coordinating Research Council (EA)
CRC .... Copper Recovery Corporation
CRC .... Copy Research Council (EA)
CRC .... Corrosion of Reinforcing Steel in Concrete [*Rilem Technical Committee*] [*British*]
CRC .... Corrosion-Resistant Cladding [*Nuclear energy equipment*]
CRC .... Cost Reduction Curve [*Economics*] (NASA)
CRC .... Cost Reimbursement Contract [*Government contracting*]
CRC .... Cotton Research Corporation
CRC .... CRC Press [*Boca Raton, FL*]
CRC .... Credit Research Center [*Purdue University*] [*Research center*] (RCD)
CRC .... Crew Chief
CRC .... Critical Reactor Component (NRCH)
CRC .... Critical Rule Curve (NOAA)
CRC .... Cuba Resource Center (EA)
CRC .... Cumulative Results Criterion (IEEE)
CRC .... Current Replacement Cost [*Accounting*]
CRC .... Cyclic Redundancy Check [*Data processing*]
CRC .... Czechoslovak Red Cross
CRC .... General Clinical Research Center [*University of Vermont*] [*Research center*] (RCD)
CRc .... Redwood City Public Library, Redwood City, CA [*Library symbol*] [*Library of Congress*] (LCLS)
CRC .... World Development [*A publication*]
CRCA .... Canadian Recreational Canoeing Association
CRCA .... Canadian Roofing Contractors' Association
CRCA .... Cellular Radio Communications Association [*Later, CCIA*] (EA)
CRCA .... Cold-Rolled Close-Annealed [*Metal*]
CRCA .... Construction Report, Construction Activity [*A publication*]
CRCA .... Crown Circuit Assistant [*Legal term*] (DLA)
CRcAm ...... Ampex Corp., Redwood City, CA [*Library symbol*] [*Library of Congress*] (LCLS)
CRC/AODA ... Certification Reciprocity Consortium/Alcoholism and Other Drug Abuse [*LA NCRC/AODA*] (EA)
Cr Cas Res ... Crown Cases Reserved (DLA)
CRCAT ...... Combat Readiness Categories [*Navy*] (NG)

CRCBAK ... Cardiovascular Research Center. Bulletin [*Houston*] [*A publication*]
CRCC......... Central Rural Construction Command [*Military*] (CINC)
CRCC......... Clarence River County Council [*Australia*]
CRCC......... Commission on Rehabilitation Counselor Certification (EA)
CRCC......... Communist Rebel Combat Captives (CINC)
CRCC......... Consolidated Record Communications Center [*Army*] (AABC)
CRCC......... Craftmatic/Contour Industries, Inc. [*Trevose, PA*] [*NASDAQ symbol*] (NQ)
Cr CC .... Cranch. Circuit Court Reports [*United States*] [*A publication*] (DLA)
CRCC......... Cyclic Redundancy Check Character [*Data processing*] (IEEE)
CRCCC...... Canton Island Range Communications Control Center [*Military*] (MCD)
CRCCF ...... Centre de Recherche en Civilisation Canadienne-Francaise [*Center for Research in French Canadian Civilisation*]
CRCCH ..... Chile Resource Center and Clearinghouse (EA)
Cr CC Rep ... [*William*] Cranch. Circuit Court Reports [*District of Columbia*] [*A publication*] (DLA)
CRC Critical Reviews in Environmental Control ... Chemical Rubber Company. Critical Reviews in Environmental Control [*A publication*]
CRC Crit Rev Anal Chem ... CRC [*Chemical Rubber Company*] Critical Reviews in Analytical Chemistry [*A publication*]
CRC Crit Rev Biochem ... CRC [*Chemical Rubber Company*] Critical Reviews in Biochemistry [*A publication*]
CRC Crit Rev Biocompat ... CRC [*Chemical Rubber Company*] Critical Reviews in Biocompatibility [*A publication*]
CRC Crit Rev Bioeng ... CRC [*Chemical Rubber Company*] Critical Reviews in Bioengineering [*A publication*]
CRC Crit Rev Biomed Eng ... CRC [*Chemical Rubber Company*] Critical Reviews in Biomedical Engineering [*A publication*]
CRC Crit Rev Biotechnol ... CRC [*Chemical Rubber Company*] Critical Reviews in Biotechnology [*A publication*]
CRC Crit Rev Clin Lab Sci ... CRC [*Chemical Rubber Company*] Critical Reviews in Clinical Laboratory Sciences [*A publication*]
CRC Crit Rev Clin Neurobiol ... CRC [*Chemical Rubber Company*] Critical Reviews in Clinical Neurobiology [*A publication*]
CRC Crit Rev Clin Radiol Nucl Med ... CRC [*Chemical Rubber Company*] Critical Reviews in Clinical Radiology and Nuclear Medicine [*A publication*]
CRC Crit Rev Diagn Imaging ... CRC [*Chemical Rubber Company*] Critical Reviews in Diagnostic Imaging [*A publication*]
CRC Crit Rev Environ Control ... CRC [*Chemical Rubber Company*] Critical Reviews in Environmental Control [*A publication*]
CRC Crit Rev Food Sci Nutr ... CRC [*Chemical Rubber Company*] Critical Reviews in Food Science and Nutrition [*A publication*]
CRC Crit Rev Food Technol ... CRC [*Chemical Rubber Company*] Critical Reviews in Food Technology [*A publication*]
CRC Crit Rev Immunol ... CRC [*Chemical Rubber Company*] Critical Reviews in Immunology [*A publication*]
CRC Crit Rev Microbiol ... CRC [*Chemical Rubber Company*] Critical Reviews in Microbiology [*A publication*]
CRC Crit Rev Oncol/Hematol ... CRC [*Chemical Rubber Company*] Critical Reviews in Oncology/Hematology [*A publication*]
CRC Crit Rev Plant Sci ... CRC [*Chemical Rubber Company*] Critical Reviews in Plant Sciences [*A publication*]
CRC Crit Rev Radiol Sci ... CRC [*Chemical Rubber Company*] Critical Reviews in Radiological Sciences [*A publication*]
CRC Crit Rev Solid Sci ... CRC [*Chemical Rubber Company*] Critical Reviews in Solid State Sciences [*A publication*]
CRC Crit Rev Solid State Mater Sci ... CRC [*Chemical Rubber Company*] Critical Reviews in Solid State and Materials Sciences [*A publication*]
CRC Crit Rev Ther Drug Carrier Syst ... CRC [*Chemical Rubber Company*] Critical Reviews in Therapeutic Drug Carrier Systems [*A publication*]
CRC Crit Rev Toxicol ... CRC [*Chemical Rubber Company*] Critical Reviews in Toxicology [*A publication*]
CRC Crit R Microbiol ... CRC [*Chemical Rubber Company*] Critical Reviews in Microbiology [*A publication*]
CRC C R NEU ... CRC [*Chemical Rubber Company*] Critical Reviews in Clinical Neurobiology [*A publication*]
CRCD .... Canadian Rehabilitation Council for the Disabled
CRCD .... Codercard, Inc. [*Irvine, CA*] [*NASDAQ symbol*] (NQ)
CRCE......... Centre for Research into Communist Economies [*United Kingdom*] [*Research center*] (IRC)
CRCE......... Chicago Rice and Cotton Exchange (EA)
CRCE......... Chief Railway Construction Engineer [*British military*] (DMA)
CRCFA ...... Crescendo International [*A publication*]
CRCFBSR ... Community Research Center. Fairbanks North Star Borough. Special Report [*A publication*]
CRCH .... Centre de Recherche sur la Croissance Humaine [*University of Montreal*] [*Research center*] (RCD)
CRCH .... Crew Chief
CRC Handb Exp Aspects Oral Biochem ... CRC [*Chemical Rubber Company*] Handbook of Experimental Aspects of Oral Biochemistry [*A publication*]
CRC Handb Nat Occurring Food Toxicants ... CRC [*Chemical Rubber Company*] Handbook of Naturally Occurring Food Toxicants [*A publication*]

CRC Handb Nutr Suppl ... CRC [*Chemical Rubber Company*] Handbook of Nutritional Supplements [*A publication*]
CRC Handb Stereoisomers Drugs Psychopharmacol ... CRC [*Chemical Rubber Company*] Handbook of Stereoisomers. Drugs in Psychopharmacology [*A publication*]
CRCHF ...... Crew Chief (FAAC)
CRCIDA .... CRIEPI [*Central Research Institute of Electric Power Industry*] Report [*A publication*]
Cr Cir Comp ... Crown Circuit Companion [*Ireland*] [*A publication*] (DLA)
CRCJ .... Center for the Rights of Campus Journalists (EA)
CRcK .... Kaiser-Permanente Medical Center, Medical Library, Redwood City, CA [*Library symbol*] [*Library of Congress*] (LCLS)
CRCL .... Canadian Review of Comparative Literature/Revue Canadienne de Litterature Comparee [*A publication*]
CR-CL .... Civil Rights-Civil Liberties (DLA)
CRCL .... Clearinghouse for Research in Child Life [*Federal Security Administration*]
CRCL .... Columbia River Conservation League (EA)
CRCL .... Contractor-Recommended Change List
CRCLT ..... Circulate (MSA)
CRCM .... Commission on Recent Crustal Movements [*Oceanography*] (MSC)
CRCMC ..... Creem Magazine [*A publication*]
CRCMCL ... Cereal Research Communications [*A publication*]
CRCMF .... Circumference (MSA)
CRCO .... Capital Reserve Corp. [*NASDAQ symbol*] (NQ)
Cr Code ...... Criminal Code [*A publication*] (DLA)
Cr Code Prac ... Criminal Code of Practice [*A publication*] (DLA)
CRCODS .... Carlsberg Research Communications [*A publication*]
CRCOM .... Change Review Committee [*Military*] (AABC)
CR Congr Ind Gaz ... Compte Rendu. Congres de l'Industrie du Gaz [*France*] [*A publication*]
CR Congr Int Chim Ind ... Comptes Rendus. Congres Internationaux de Chimie Industrielle [*A publication*]
CR Congr Int Phenom Contact Electr ... Comptes Rendus. Congres International sur les Phenomenes de Contact Electrique [*A publication*]
CR Congr Int Psychother ... Comptes Rendus. Congres International de Psychotherapie [*A publication*]
CR Congr Union Phytopathol Mediterr ... Comptes Rendus. Congres de l'Union Phytopathologique Mediterraneenne [*A publication*]
CRCP .... Certificate of the Royal College of Physicians [*British*]
CRCP .... Committee of Religious Concern for Peace (EA)
CRCPD ...... Clinical Research Center for Periodontal Disease [*University of Minnesota*]
CRCPD ...... Conference of Radiation Control Program Directors (EA)
CRCPI .... Coordinating Research Council of the Petroleum Industry
CRCR .... Center for Rate Controlled Recordings [*Defunct*] (EA)
Cr Crafts .... Creative Crafts [*A publication*]
CRCS .... Cardiovascular Reflex Conditioning System [*Medicine*]
CRCS .... Center Range Control Station [*NASA*] (KSC)
CRCS .... Centre de Recherches sur les Communications [*Sherbrooke University*] [*Canada*] [*Research center*] (RCD)
CRCS .... Certificate of the Royal College of Surgeons [*British*]
CRCS .... Clerici Regulares Congregationis Somaschae [*Somaschi Fathers*] [*Roman Catholic religious order*]
CRCS .... Clinical Record Cover Sheet [*Army medical*]
CRCS .... CR [*Christian Rovsing*] Computer Systems, Inc. [*Los Angeles, CA*] [*Telecommunications*] (TSSD)
CRCSU ...... Ceylon Railway Clerical Service Union [*Obsolete*]
CRCT .... Center for Research in Computing Technology [*Harvard University*] [*Research center*] (RCD)
CRCT .... Circuit (KSC)
CRCT .... Commander, Royal Corps of Transport [*Military*] [*British*]
CRCT .... Crescott, Inc. [*NASDAQ symbol*] (NQ)
CRCTA ...... Composite Reactor Components Test Activity (NRCH)
CRCTD ..... Corrected (MSA)
Cr Cu .... Cross Currents [*A publication*]
CRCWLM ... Christian Reformed Church World Literature Ministries (EA)
CRD .... Capacitor-Resistor Diode
CRD .... Card Reader [*Data processing*]
CRD .... Cavedale Road [*California*] [*Seismograph station code, US Geological Survey*] (SEIS)
CRD .... Center for Resource Development in Adult Education [*University of Missouri - Kansas City*] [*Research center*] (RCD)
CRD .... Center for Responsive Design [*Inactive*] (EA)
CRD .... Central Recruiting Division [*Military*]
CRD .... Central Registration Depository [*Investment term*]
CRD .... Central Repair Depot (NATG)
CRD .... Change Request Disposition (MCD)
CRD .... Chief of Research and Development [*Army*]
CR & D ...... Chief of Research and Development [*Army*]
CRD .... Chronic Renal Disease [*Medicine*]
CRD .... Chronic Respiratory Disease [*Medicine*]
CRD .... Civil Rights Division [*Department of Justice*]
CRD .... College Recruitment Database [*Executive Telecom System, Inc.*] [*Information service or system*] (CRD)
CRD .... Columbia River Datum

CRD .... Committee on Reciprocal Deliveries [*Allied German Occupation Forces*]
CRD .... Community Relations Director
CRD .... Comodoro Rivadavia [*Argentina*] [*Airport symbol*] (OAG)
CRD .... Complete Reaction of Degeneration [*Physiology*]
CRD .... Complex Repetitive Discharge [*Neurophysiology*]
CRD .... Computer-Readable Databases [*A publication*]
CRD .... Confidential Restricted Data
CRD .... Conrad, MT [*Location identifier*] [*FAA*] (FAAL)
CRD .... Constant Ringing Drop [*Alarm system*]
CRD .... Continuous Ream Discharge [*Papermaking*]
CRD .... Control Rod Drive [*or Driveline*] [*Nuclear energy*] (NRCH)
CRD .... Controlled Release Device (KSC)
CRD .... Controller of Research and Development [*Ministry of Aircraft Production*] [*British*]
Crd .... Cordierite [*A mineral*]
CRD .... Coronado Resources, Inc. [*Vancouver Stock Exchange symbol*]
CRD .... Corporate Director [*A publication*]
CRD .... Corporate Research and Development
CRD .... Cosmic Ray Detector [*NASA*]
CRD .... Critical Ratio of the Difference
CRD .... Cross-Reacting Determinant [*Immunochemistry*]
CRD .... Customs Rules Decisions [*A publication*] (DLA)
CRD .... Monsanto Chemical Co. [*Research code symbol*]
CRD .... Southern California Rapid Transit District, Los Angeles, CA [*OCLC symbol*] (OCLC)
CRD .... Tanabe Seiyaku Co. Ltd. [*Japan*] [*Research code symbol*]
CR 3d .... Criminal Reports. Third Series . Annotated [*A publication*]
CRDA .... Candidates Reply Date Agreement [*Education*]
CRDA .... Chief of Research, Development, and Acquisition [*Army*] (RDA)
CRDA .... Control Rod Drive Assembly [*Nuclear energy*] (IEEE)
CRDA .... Cooperative Research and Development Agreement [*Construction Engineering Research Laboratory and private industry*]
CRDB .... Computer-Readable Databases: a Directory and Data Sourcebook [*A publication*]
CRdb .... Redondo Beach Public Library, Redondo Beach, CA [*Library symbol*] [*Library of Congress*] (LCLS)
CRdbT .... TRW Systems Group, Redondo Beach, CA [*Library symbol*] [*Library of Congress*] (LCLS)
CRDC .... Centre de Reperage des Debouches du Canada [*Canada Business Opportunity Centre - CBOC*]
CRDC .... Chemical Research and Development Center [*Aberdeen Proving Ground, MD*] [*Army*] (RDA)
CRDC .... Columbia Research and Development Corporation (MCD)
CRDCS ...... Contingency Rerouting of Communications [*NATO*] (NATG)
CRDCS ...... Control Rod Drive Control System [*Nuclear energy*] (NRCH)
CRDD .... Control Rod Disconnect Driveline [*Nuclear energy*] (NRCH)
CRDE .... Certified Rooms Division Executive [*Designation awarded by Educational Institute of the American Hotel and Motel Association*]
CRDEC ...... Center for Research and Documentation on the European Community [*American University*] [*Research center*] (RCD)
CRDEC ...... Chemical Research, Development, and Engineering Center [*Aberdeen Proving Ground, MD*] [*Army*] (RDA)
CRDF .... Canadian Radio-Direction Finder (MCD)
CRDF .... Cardiff Commercial, Inc. [*NASDAQ symbol*] (NQ)
CRDF .... Cathode-Ray Direction Finder [*RADAR*]
CRDG .... Curriculum Research and Development Group [*University of Hawaii*] [*Research center*] (RCD)
CRdGLECS ... Comptes Rendus. Groupe Linguistique d'Etudes Chamito-Semitiques [*Paris*] [*A publication*]
CRDH .... Centre de Recherche en Developpement Humain [*Centre for Research in Human Development*] [*Concordia University*] [*Canada*] [*Research center*] (RCD)
CRDHS ..... Control Rod Drive Hydraulic System [*Nuclear energy*] (NRCH)
CRDIDF .... CRC [*Chemical Rubber Company*] Critical Reviews in Diagnostic Imaging [*A publication*]
Cr & Dix .... Crawford and Dix's Irish Circuit Court Cases [*A publication*] (DLA)
Cr & Dix Ab Ca ... Crawford and Dix's Irish Abridged Cases [*A publication*] (DLA)
Cr & Dix Ab Cas ... Crawford and Dix's Irish Abridged Cases [*A publication*] (DLA)
Cr & Dix CC ... Crawford and Dix's Irish Circuit Court Cases [*A publication*] (DLA)
CRDL .... Chemical Research and Development Laboratories [*Edgewood Arsenal, MD*] [*Army*]
CRDL .... Contract Required Detection Limits
CRDL .... Cradle (MSA)
CRDM .... Chief RADARman [*Navy rating*] [*Obsolete*]
CRDM ...... Control Rod Drive Motor [*Nuclear energy*] (IEEE)
CRDMBP ... Chronica Dermatologica [*A publication*]
CRDMS ..... Control Rod Drive Mechanism Shroud [*Nuclear energy*] (NRCH)
CRDN .... Ceradyne, Inc. [*Costa Mesa, CA*] [*NASDAQ symbol*] (NQ)

CRD Newsl US Dep Agric Ext Community Rural Dev ... CRD Newsletter. United States Department of Agriculture. Science and Education Administration. Extension, Community, and Rural Development [*A publication*]

CRDO........ Colorado Energy Corp. [*NASDAQ symbol*]   (NQ)

CR & DO ... Commanders Research and Development Objective

CR (Dokl) Acad Sci URSS ... Comptes Rendus (Doklady). Academie des Sciences de l'Union des Republiques Sovietiques Socialistes [*A publication*]

CRDP........ Computer Resources Development Plan [*NASA*]   (NASA)

CRDR........ Corridor [*Board on Geographic Names*]

CRDR/A.... Control Room Design Review/Audit [*Nuclear energy*]   (NRCH)

CRDS........ Chemical Reactions Documentation Service [*Derwent Publications Ltd.*] [*Bibliographic database*]   (IID)

CRDS........ Colgate-Rochester Divinity School [*Rochester, NY*]

CRDS........ Component Repair Data Sheets   (NG)

CRDS........ Control Rod Drive System [*Nuclear energy*]   (NRCH)

CRDSD...... Current Research and Development in Scientific Documentation [*A publication*]

CRDU........ Command Relay Driver Unit   (MCD)

CRDVA ..... Canadian Research and Development [*Later, Canadian Research*] [*A publication*]

CRDVF...... Control Rod Drive Ventilating Fan [*Nuclear energy*]   (NRCH)

CRDWA .... Canal, River, and Dock Watchmen's Association [*A union*] [*British*]

CRE........... Care Enterprises [*AMEX symbol*]   (SPSG)

CRE .... Cation-Responsive Electrode

CRE .... Cauchy-Riemann Equation [*Mathematics*]

CRE .... Central Reconnaissance Establishment [*British military*]   (DMA)

CRE .... Central Research Establishment [*Home Office Forensic Science Service*] [*Great Britain*] [*Information service or system*]   (IID)

CRE .... Chemical Reaction Engineering

CRE .... Chief Radio Electrician [*Navy rating*] [*Obsolete*]

CRE .... Coal Research Establishment [*British*]   (IRUK)

CRE .... Collection, Repair, Evacuation   (MCD)

CRE .... Combat Readiness Evaluation [*Army*]

CRE .... Command Receiver Equipment   (KSC)

CRE .... Commander, Royal Engineers [*British*]

CRE .... Commercial Relations and Exports   (DS)

CRE .... Commission for Racial Equality [*British*]

CRE .... Communications Research Establishment   (NATG)

CRE .... Compensation Review [*A publication*]

CRE .... Compton Recoil Electron

CRE .... Conference Permanente des Recteurs, Presidents, et Vice Chanceliers des Universites Europeennes   (EAIO)

CRE .... Conseil des Regions d'Europe [*Council of European Regions - CER*]   (EAIO)

CRE .... Conservation and Renewable Energy

C & RE....... Conservation and Renewable Energy Program [*Department of Energy*]

CRE .... Console Remote Equipment   (MCD)

CRE .... Consolidated Rail Corp. (Eastern District) [*AAR code*]

CRE .... Controlled Residual Element [*Nuclear energy*]

CRE .... Corrosion Resistant   (AAG)

CRE .... Credit [*A publication*]

cre.............. Cree [*MARC language code*] [*Library of Congress*]   (LCCP)

CRE .... Creosote

CRE .... Cross-Range Error

CRE .... Cumulative Radiation Effect

CRE .... Cyclic-AMP [*Adenosine Monophosphate*]-Responsive Transcriptional Enhancer [*Genetics*]

CRE .... North Myrtle Beach, SC [*Location identifier*] [*FAA*]   (FAAL)

CREA........ Canadian Real Estate Association

CREA........ Certified Real Estate Appraiser [*Designation awarded by National Association of Real Estate Appraisers*]

CREA........ Chief Radio Electrical Artificer [*British military*]   (DMA)

CREA........ Congressional Reports Elimination Act

C Read .... Christian Reader [*A publication*]

Creamery J ... Creamery Journal [*A publication*]

Creamery Milk Plant Mon ... Creamery and Milk Plant Monthly [*A publication*]

CREAMS .. Chemicals, Runoff, and Erosion from Agricultural Management Systems [*Agricultural Research Service*]

Creas Col Const ... Creasy's Colonial Constitutions [*A publication*]   (DLA)

Creas Eng Cons ... Creasy's Rise and Progress of the English Constitution [*A publication*]   (DLA)

Creas Int L ... Creasy on International Law [*A publication*]   (DLA)

Creasy........ Creasy's Ceylon Reports [*A publication*]   (DLA)

creat .... Creatine [*Biochemistry*]

creat .... Creatinine [*Biochemistry*]

Creat Crafts ... Creative Crafts [*A publication*]

Creat Detect Excited State ... Creation and Detection of the Excited State [*A publication*]

CREATE ... Center for Research and Evaluation in Applications of Technology in Education [*Palo Alto, CA*]

CREATE ... Computational Requirements for Engineering and Simulation, Training and Education [*Time-sharing computer complex*] [*Air Force*]

CREATION ... Cultural and Recreational Education Achieved through Investigations Ordinarily Neglected [*University course*]

Creation Res Soc Q ... Creation Research Society. Quarterly [*A publication*]

Creative Comput ... Creative Computing [*A publication*]

Creative Photogr ... Creative Photography [*A publication*]

Creat Photogr ... Creative Photography [*A publication*]

Creat Res Soc Q ... Creation Research Society. Quarterly [*A publication*]

Creatv Comp ... Creative Computing [*A publication*]

CREB......... Champion Parts, Inc. [*NASDAQ symbol*]   (NQ)

CREC......... Combat Readiness Evaluation Criteria [*Navy*]   (NG)

CREC......... COMSEC [*Communications Security*] Research and Engineering Coordinating Group [*Army*]   (AABC)

CRECD...... Conservation and Recycling [*A publication*]

CRECD2..... Conservation and Recycling [*A publication*]

CRECON .. Counterreconnaissance [*Army*]

CRECORD ... Congressional Record On-Line [*Capitol Services, Inc.*] [*Washington, DC*] [*Bibliographic database*]

CRED .... Center for Research on Economic Development [*University of Michigan*] [*Research center*]   (RCD)

CRED .... Credit   (AABC)

CRED .... Crediton [*England*]

CRED .... Credo Petroleum Corp. [*NASDAQ symbol*]   (NQ)

CREDATA ... Communications Resources Data System [*Defense Communications Agency*]   (MCD)

CRED B ..... Creditors' Bill [*Legal term*]   (DLA)

CRedCL..... Shasta County Free Library, Redding, CA [*Library symbol*] [*Library of Congress*]   (LCLS)

CRedGS..... Church of Jesus Christ of Latter-Day Saints, Genealogical Society Library, Redding Branch, Redding, CA [*Library symbol*] [*Library of Congress*]   (LCLS)

CREDIF .... Bulletin Bibliographique de CREDIF [*Centre de Recherche et d'Etude pour la Diffusion du Francais*] Service de Documentation [*A publication*]

CREDIOP ... Consorzio di Credito per le Opere Pubbliche [*Financial institution*] [*Rome, Italy*]   (EY)

CREDIT .... Cost Reduction Early Decision Information Techniques [*Hughes Aircraft Co.*]

Creditanst-Bankverein Wirtschaftsber ... Creditanstalt-Bankverein. Wirtschaftsberichte [*A publication*]

Credit Communal Belgique Bul Trim ... Credit Communal de Belgique. Bulletin Trimestriel [*A publication*]

CREDITEL ... Canadian Credit Management Association [*Formerly, Creditel of Canada Ltd.*]

Credit Financ Manage ... Credit and Financial Management [*A publication*]

Credit & Fin Mgt ... Credit and Financial Management [*A publication*]

Credit M .... Credit Monthly [*A publication*]

Credit Suisse Bul ... Credit Suisse. Bulletin [*A publication*]

Credit Suisse Bul (Zurich) ... Credit Suisse. Bulletin (Zurich) [*A publication*]

Credit Union M ... Credit Union Magazine [*A publication*]

Credit Wld ... Credit World [*A publication*]

CRedl .... A. K. Smiley Public Library, Redlands, CA [*Library symbol*] [*Library of Congress*]   (LCLS)

CRedlG...... Grand Central Rocket Co., Redlands, CA [*Library symbol*] [*Library of Congress*]   (LCLS)

CRedlI........ Inland Library System, Redlands, CA [*Library symbol*] [*Library of Congress*]   (LCLS)

CRedlU...... University of Redlands, Redlands, CA [*Library symbol*] [*Library of Congress*]   (LCLS)

CREDO ..... Centre for Curriculum Renewal and Educational Development Overseas

CREDO ..... Chaplains' Relevance to the Emerging Drug Order [*Navy*]

CREDOC... Centre de Recherche Documentaire [*Documentary Research Center*] [*Information service or system*]   (IID)

Cred Rur ..... Credito Rural [*A publication*]

Cred Suisse B ... Credit Suisse. Bulletin [*A publication*]

CREE .... Conseil des Relations Economiques Exterieures [*Council of Foreign Economic Relations*] [*Lebanon*]   (GEA)

CREEC...... Consortium of Regional Environmental Education Councils

CREED...... Christian Rescue Effort for the Emancipation of Dissidents [*Acronym now used as organization name*]   (EA)

CREEJ....... Center for Russian and East European Jewry   (EA)

CReeK........ Kings View Hospital, Reedley, CA [*Library symbol*] [*Library of Congress*]   (LCLS)

Creem M .... Creem Magazine [*A publication*]

CREEP ...... Committee to Re-Elect the President [*Also, CRP*] [*1972*]

CREEP ...... Committee to Resist the Efforts of the Ex-President [*Opposed Richard Nixon's visit to Oxford University, 1978*]

CREES ...... Center for Russian and East European Studies [*University of Michigan*] [*Research center*]   (RCD)

CREES ...... Centre for Russian and East European Studies [*University of Birmingham*] [*British*]   (CB)

CREET ...... Campaign to Re-Elect Mrs. [*Margaret*] Thatcher [*British*] [*Obsolete*]

CREF .... Cardiothoracic Research and Education Foundation   (EA)

CREF .... Centre de Recherche sur l'Enseignement du Francais [*St. Anne University*] [*Canada*] [*Research center*]   (RCD)

CREF .... College Retirement Equities Fund [*New York, NY*]   (EA)

CREF .... Cross Reference   (AFM)

CREFAL.... Centro Regional de Educacion de Adultos y Alfabetizacion Funcional para America Latina [*Regional Center for Adult Education and Functional Literacy for Latin America*] [*Patzcuaro Michoacan, Mexico*]   (EAIO)

CREG .... Cancer Research Emphasis Grants

CREG .... Concentrated Range Extension with Gain [*Telecommunications*]   (TEL)

CREGO ..... Chief Regulating Officer [*Southwest Pacific Area, World War II*] [*Army*]

CREI......... Capitol Radio Engineering Institute [*Now known only by initialism*]

Creighton L Rev ... Creighton Law Review [*A publication*]

CREIPAC ... Centre de Rencontres et d'Echanges Internationaux du Pacifique [*Center of International Cultural and Linguistic Exchanges in the Pacific*] [*Noumea, New Caledonia*]   (EAIO)

CREJ .... Contents of Recent Economics Journals [*A publication*]

CREL......... Cahiers Roumains d'Etudes Litteraires [*A publication*]

CREL......... Chief Radio Electrician [*British military*]   (DMA)

CREL........ Cold Regions Engineering Laboratory

CRELIQ .... Centre de Recherche en Litterature Quebecoise [*Universite Laval, Quebec*] [*Canada*]

Cre LR ...... Creighton Law Review [*A publication*]

CREM ...... Cremate [*or Crematorium*]   (DSUE)

CREM .... La Delite Ltd. [*Long Island City, NY*] [*NASDAQ symbol*]   (NQ)

CREME..... Commander, Royal Electrical and Mechanical Engineers [*Military*] [*British*]

CREMN .... Chief Radio Electrical Mechanician [*British military*]   (DMA)

CREN .... Crendon [*England*]

CRENGR... Construction Engineer   (FAAC)

CREO .... Career Reenlistment Objectives [*Navy*]

CREO .... Central Real Estate Office [*Military*]

CREO .... Conservation and Renewable Energy Office [*Canada*]

CREO .... Counter-Racism, Equal Opportunity [*Military*]   (NVT)

CREOG ..... Council on Resident Education in Obstetrics and Gynecology   (EA)

CREOL...... Center for Research in Electro-Optics and Lasers [*University of Central Florida*] [*Research center*]   (RCD)

CREP......... Crepitus [*Crepitation*] [*Medicine*]

CREPE...... Cosmic Ray Emulsion Plastic Equipment [*NASA*]   (MCD)

CRER .... Centre for Research in Ethnic Relations [*University of Warwick*] [*British*]   (CB)

CRES .... Center for Research in Engineering Science [*University of Kansas*]

CRES .... Chief of Army Reserves [*Australia*]

CRES .... Condominium Research and Education Society

CRES .... Conservation Reporting and Evaluation System [*Department of Agriculture*]

CRES .... Corrosion-Resistant Steel [*Manufacturing*]

CRES .... Crescendo [*Music*]

CRES .... Crescent   (MCD)

Cres........... Cresset [*A publication*]

CRES .... Crestmont Federal Savings and Loan Association [*NASDAQ symbol*]   (NQ)

CRESC ...... Crescendo [*Music*]

Cresc .... [*Marcus*] Crescentius [*Authority cited in pre-1607 legal work*]   (DSA)

Crescendo Int ... Crescendo International [*A publication*]

CRESH...... Constant Ratios of Elasticities of Substitution-Homothetic [*Statistics*]

CRESM ..... Centre de Recherche et d'Etudes sur les Societes Mediterraneennes [*Center for Research and Studies on Mediterranean Societies*] [*Information service or system*]   (IID)

CRESO...... Crescendo [*Music*]

CRESP....... Center for Religion, Ethics, and Social Policy [*Cornell University*] [*Research center*]   (RCD)

CRESS...... Central Regulatory Electronic Stenographic System   (NRCH)

CRESS....... Centre for Research in Experimental Space Science [*York University*] [*Canada*] [*Research center*]   (RCD)

CRESS....... Claims Representative Exam for Social Security [*Federal job exam*]

CRESS....... Clearinghouse on Rural Education and Small Schools [*ERIC*]

CRESS....... Combined Reentry Effort in Small Systems

CRESS....... Computerized Reader Enquiry Service System   (IEEE)

Cress .... Cresswell's Insolvency Cases [*1827-29*] [*England*] [*A publication*]   (DLA)

CRESS/AU ... Center for Research in Social Systems of the American University   (IEEE)

Cress Ins Ca ... Cresswell's Insolvency Cases [*1827-29*] [*England*] [*A publication*]   (ILCA)

Cress Ins Cas ... Cresswell's Insolvency Cases [*1827-29*] [*England*] [*A publication*]   (DLA)

Cress Insolv Cas ... Cresswell's Insolvency Cases [*1827-29*] [*England*] [*A publication*]   (DLA)

CRESST .... Center for Research on Evaluation, Standards, and Student Testing [*Los Angeles, CA*] [*Department of Education*]   (GRD)

CREST ...... Calcinosis, Raynaud's Phenomenon, Esophageal Dysfunction, Sclerodactyly, and Telangiectasia [*A medical syndrome*]

CREST ...... Center for Cold Regions Engineering, Science, and Technology [*State University of New York at Buffalo*] [*Research center*]   (RCD)

CREST ...... Combat Readiness by Electronic Service Testing [*Army*]   (AABC)

CREST ...... Combat Reporting System [*Air Force*]   (MCD)

CREST ...... Committee on Reactor Safety Technology

CREST ...... Committee on Rural Economic and Social Trends

CREST ...... Consolidated Reporting and Evaluating System, Tactical [*Computer program*] [*Air Force*]

CREST ...... Crew Escape Technologies [*Air Force*]

CREST ...... Crewstation Evaluation Facility [*Warminster, PA*] [*Naval Air Development Center*]   (GRD)

CREST ...... Crown Estate Commissioner [*British*]

Crest Colect ... Cresterea Colectiilor. Caiet Selectiv de Informare Bibliotecii Academii Republicii Socialiste Romania [*A publication*]

Crest Patr Muz Bul ... Cresterea Patrimoniului Muzeal Buletin [*A publication*]

CRESTS .... Courtauld's Rapid Extract, Sort, and Tabulate System   (IEEE)

CRET........ Cathode-Ray Electron Tube

CRET......... Commission Regionale Europeenne du Tourisme

CRET......... Cretaceous [*Geology*]

Cretaceous Res ... Cretaceous Research [*A publication*]

CRETB...... Current [*New York*] [*A publication*]

CRETE...... Common Radio and Electronic Test Equipment [*Navy*] [*British*]   (DEN)

CRET PP... Creta Praeparata [*Prepared Chalk*] [*Pharmacy*]   (ROG)

C Rev .... Chesterton Review [*A publication*]

C Rev AS... Canadian Review of American Studies [*A publication*]

C Rev B ..... Conch Review of Books [*A publication*]

CREVO ..... Creation-Evolution

CREVS ..... Control Room Emergency Ventilation System   (IEEE)

C Revue...... Cine Revue [*A publication*]

CREWTAF ... Crew Training Air Force

CRF........... Calendar Reform Foundation   (EA)

CRF........... Capacitor Resonance Frequency

CRF........... Capital Recovery Factor

CRF........... Carrier Frequency Telephone Repeater [*Telecommunications*]

CRF........... Cathode-Ray Furnace

CRF........... Cave Research Foundation   (EA)

CRF........... Central Repair Facility   (MCD)

CRF........... Change Request Forms

CRF........... Christian Rural Fellowship [*Defunct*]   (EA)

CRF........... Chromatofocusing [*Analytical biochemistry*]

CRF........... Chromatographic Response Factor

CRF........... Chronic Renal Failure [*Medicine*]

CRF........... Citizens' Research Foundation   (EA)

CRF........... Clean Report of Findings [*Societe Generale de Surveillance SA*]   (DS)

CRF........... Coalition for Religious Freedom   (EA)

CRF........... Combustion Research Facility [*Department of Energy*] [*Livermore, CA*]

CRF........... Comicorum Romanum Fragmenta [*A publication*]   (OCD)

CRF........... Committee for Religious Freedom   (EA)

CRF........... Community Residential Facility [*For the handicapped*]

CRF........... Composite Rear Fuselage

CRF........... Computer Dealers Forum [*Acronym represents organization's former name*] [*Later, NCDF*]   (EA)

CRF........... Connection-Related Function [*Telecommunications*]

CRF........... Conservation and Research Foundation   (EA)

CRF........... Constitutional Rights Foundation   (EA)

CRF........... Consumer Reports [*A publication*]

CRF........... Contingency Relief Force [*Military*]

CRF........... Continuous Reinforcement [*Psychometrics*]

CRF........... Control Relay Forward

CRF........... Corfu [*Washington*] [*Seismograph station code, US Geological Survey*]   (SEIS)

CRF........... Correspondence Routing Form   (NRCH)

CRF........... Corticotrophin-Releasing Factor [*Also, CRH*] [*Endocrinology*]

CRF........... Cosmic Ray Flux

CRF........... Credit Research Foundation [*Lake Success, NY*]   (EA)

CRF........... Cross-Reference File

CRF........... Crown Forest Industries Ltd. [*Toronto Stock Exchange symbol*] [*Vancouver Stock Exchange symbol*]

CRF........... Cryptographic Repair Facilities

CRF........... Current Requisition File [*DoD*]

CRF........... Current Research File [*NIOSH*] [*Database*]

CR & FA ... Canadian Restaurant and Foodservices Association

CRFA........ Czechoslovak Rationalist Federation of America   (EA)

CRFABX ... Coffee Research Foundation [*Kenya*]. Annual Report [*A publication*]

CRFB......... Committee for a Responsible Federal Budget   (EA)

CRFC........ Charlie Rich Fan Club   (EA)

CRFC........ Crestar Financial Corporation [*NASDAQ symbol*]   (NQ)

CRFCA...... Cliff Richard Fan Club of America   (EA)

CRFDP...... Columbia River Fisheries Development Program

CRFEDD... Clinical Reproduction and Fertility [*A publication*]

CRFG........ California Rare Fruit Growers   (EA)

CRFH........ Craft House Corp. [*NASDAQ symbol*]   (NQ)

CRFI......... Custom Roll Forming Institute   (EA)

CRFK........ Crandell Feline Kidney [*Cytology*]

CRFL......... Centre de Recherches Forestieres des Laurentides [*Laurentian Forest Research Center*] [*Canada*] (ARC)
CRF-LI ...... Corticotropin-Releasing Factor-Like Immunoreactivity [*Medicine*]
CRFMD..... Center for Research in Faith and Moral Development (EA)
CRFNN ..... Cassandra: Radical Feminist Nurses Network (EA)
CRFS .... Combined Reference Frequency System
CRFS .... Crash-Resistant Fuel System (RDA)
CRFSDL.... Rapport a l'Industrie Canadien sur les Sciences Halieutiques et Aquatiques [*A publication*]
CRFT .... Computer Craft, Inc. [*NASDAQ symbol*] (NQ)
CRFT .... Crowfoot (MSA)
CRFTLA.... Centre Regional de Formation aux Techniques des Leves Aeriens [*Regional Center for Training in Aerial Surveys - RECTAS*] (EAIO)
CRFUSAIC ... Central Records Facility, United States Army Intelligence Center
CRG .... Carriage (MSA)
CRG .... Catalytic Rich Gas
CRG .... Cenergy Corp. [*NYSE symbol*] (SPSG)
CRG .... Center for Responsive Governance (EA)
CRG .... Chessminster Group Ltd. [*Vancouver Stock Exchange symbol*]
CRG .... Children's Record Guild [*Record label*]
CRG .... Children's Rights Group (EA)
CRG .... Classification Research Group [*British*]
CRG .... Coast Community College District, Orange Coast College, Costa Mesa, CA [*OCLC symbol*] (OCLC)
CRG .... Communications Relay Group (MCD)
CRG .... Computer Research Group, Inc. [*Information service or system*] (IID)
CRG .... Control Rate Gyro [*Aerospace*] (KSC)
CRG .... Correspondence Review Group [*NASA*] (NASA)
CRG .... Cosmic Ray Gas
CRG .... Council of Regional Groups [*Association for Library Collections and Technical Services*]
CRG .... Council for Responsible Genetics (EA)
CRG .... Counterfire Reference Grid (AABC)
CRG .... Cross Grain [*Technical drawings*]
CRG .... Jacksonville, FL [*Location identifier*] [*FAA*] (FAAL)
CRGAA3 .. Chirurgia [*Bucharest*] [*A publication*]
CRGAB4.... Cocoa Research Institute. Ghana Academy of Sciences. Annual Report [*A publication*]
CRGIA....... Ceramurgia, Tecnologia Ceramica [*A publication*]
CRGO........ Competitive Research Grants Office [*for federal research in agriculture*]
CRGP........ Caseless Round Gun Program [*Military*] (MCD)
CRGR .... Committee to Review Generic Requirements [*Nuclear Regulatory Commission*]
CRGS........ Chemical Regulations and Guidelines System [*CRC Systems, Inc.*] [*Information service or system*] (IID)
CRGT .... Control Rod Guide Tube [*Nuclear energy*] (NRCH)
CRH.......... Calibre-Radius Head [*of projectile*] [*British*]
CRH.......... Carson Hill [*California*] [*Seismograph station code, US Geological Survey*] (SEIS)
CRH.......... Casualty Receiving Hospital [*British*]
CRH.......... Constant Rate of Heating
CRH.......... Control Relay Hand
CRH.......... Corticotrophin-Releasing Hormone [*Also, CRF*] [*Endocrinology*]
CRH.......... Council on Religion and the Homosexual [*Defunct*] (EA)
Cr H .... Craft Horizons [*A publication*]
CRH.......... Critical Relative Humidity
CRH.......... Rio Hondo Junior College Library, Whittier, CA [*OCLC symbol*] (OCLC)
CRHA .... Canadian Railroad Historical Association
CRHA .... Colorado Ranger Horse Association (EA)
CRH Acad Sci Ser A Sci Math ... Comptes Rendus Hebdomadaires des Seances. Academie des Sciences. Serie A. Sciences Mathematiques [*A publication*]
CRH Acad Sci Ser B Sci Phys ... Comptes Rendus Hebdomadaires des Seances. Academie des Sciences. Serie B. Sciences Physiques [*A publication*]
CRH Acad Sci Ser C Sci Chim ... Comptes Rendus Hebdomadaires des Seances. Academie des Sciences. Serie C. Sciences Chimiques [*A publication*]
CRH Acad Sci Ser D Sci Natur ... Comptes Rendus Hebdomadaires des Seances. Academie des Sciences. Serie D. Sciences Naturelles [*A publication*]
CRHB .... CP Rehabilitation Corp. [*NASDAQ symbol*] (NQ)
CRHBull.... Commission Royale d'Histoire. Bulletin [*A publication*]
CRHC........ Controlled-Release Hydrocodone [*An analgesic*] [*Pennwalt Corp.*]
CRHC........ CRH, PLC [*NASDAQ symbol*] (NQ)
CRHD........ Council for Rural Housing and Development (EA)
CRHDDK ... Clinics in Rheumatic Diseases [*A publication*]
CR Hebd Acad Sci Ser 2 ... Comptes Rendus Hebdomadaires des Seances. Academie des Sciences. Serie 2 [*A publication*]
CR Hebd Acad Sci Ser D ... Academie des Sciences. Comptes Rendus Hebdomadaires des Seances. Serie D. Sciences Naturelles [*Paris*] [*A publication*]

CR Hebd Seanc Acad Sci ... Comptes Rendus Hebdomadaires des Seances. Academie des Sciences [*A publication*]
CR Hebd Seanc Acad Sci Jekaterinoslaw ... Compte Rendu Hebdomadaire des Seances. Academie des Sciences de Jekaterinoslaw [*A publication*]
CR Hebd Seanc Acad Sci (Paris) D ... Comptes Rendus Hebdomadaires des Seances. Academie des Sciences (Paris). Serie D. Sciences Naturelles [*A publication*]
CR Hebd Seances Acad Agric Fr ... Comptes Rendus Hebdomadaires des Seances. Academie d'Agriculture de France [*A publication*]
CR Hebd Seances Acad Sci ... Comptes Rendus Hebdomadaires des Seances. Academie des Sciences [*A publication*]
CR Hebd Seances Acad Sci Ser 2 ... Comptes Rendus Hebdomadaires des Seances. Academie des Sciences. Serie 2. Mecanique-Physique, Chimie, Sciences de l'Univers, Sciences de la Terre [*A publication*]
CR Hebd Seances Acad Sci Ser 3 ... Comptes Rendus Hebdomadaires des Seances. Academie des Sciences. Serie 3. Sciences de la Vie [*A publication*]
CR Hebd Seances Acad Sci Ser A ... Comptes Rendus Hebdomadaires des Seances. Academie des Sciences. Serie A [*A publication*]
CR Hebd Seances Acad Sci Ser A Sci Math ... Comptes Rendus Hebdomadaires des Seances. Academie des Sciences. Serie A. Sciences Mathematiques [*A publication*]
CR Hebd Seances Acad Sci Ser B ... Comptes Rendus Hebdomadaires des Seances. Academie des Sciences. Serie B [*A publication*]
CR Hebd Seances Acad Sci Ser C ... Comptes Rendus Hebdomadaires des Seances. Academie des Sciences. Serie C. Sciences Chimiques [*A publication*]
CR Hebd Seances Acad Sci Ser D ... Comptes Rendus Hebdomadaires des Seances. Academie des Sciences. Serie D. Sciences Naturelles [*A publication*]
CR Hebd Seances Acad Sci Ser D Sci Nat ... Comptes Rendus Hebdomadaires des Seances. Academie des Sciences. Serie D. Sciences Naturelles [*A publication*]
CR Hebd Seances Acad Sci Ser II ... Comptes Rendus Hebdomadaires des Seances. Academie des Sciences. Serie II [*A publication*]
CRHH .... Cold-Rolled Half Hard [*Metal*]
CRHIFC .... Carla Riggs-Hall International Fan Club (EA)
CRHL .... Collaborative Radiological Health Laboratory [*Colorado State University*] [*Department of Health and Human Services*] [*Research center*] (RCD)
CRHO........ [*The*] Crab House, Inc. [*NASDAQ symbol*] (NQ)
CRHPR ..... Cahiers de la Revue d'Histoire et de Philosophie Religieuses [*A publication*]
CRHS .... Commonwealth Regional Health Secretariat (EA)
CRHS .... Competent Reliability History Survey [*Navy*]
CRHS .... Construction Report, Housing Starts [*A publication*]
CRHSI....... Center for Research in the Hospitality Service Industries (EA)
CRI .... Cambridge Reports, Inc. [*Database producer*] (IID)
CRI .... Canarsie, NY [*Location identifier*] [*FAA*] (FAAL)
CRI .... Carbohydrate Research Institute [*Queen's University at Kingston*] [*Canada*] [*Research center*] (RCD)
CRI .... Career Resources Information [*JA Micropublishing, Inc.*] [*Information service or system*] (IID)
CRI .... Caribbean Research Institute [*College of the Virgin Islands*]
CRI .... Caring Relationship Inventory [*Psychology*]
CRI .... Carpet and Rug Institute (EA)
CRI .... Catheter-Related Infection [*Medicine*]
CRI .... Cell Research Institute [*University of Texas at Austin*] [*Research center*] (RCD)
CRI .... Cellulose Research Institute [*Syracuse University*]
CRI .... Ceramic Industry [*A publication*]
CRI .... Change Routing Indicator (MCD)
CRI .... Chemical Rust-Inhibiting
CR & I........ [*The*] Chicago River & Indiana Railway Co. [*Absorbed into Consolidated Rail Corp.*]
CRI .... [*The*] Chicago River & Indiana Railway Co. [*Absorbed into Consolidated Rail Corp.*] [*AAR code*]
CRI .... Children's Rights, Incorporated [*Superseded by CFC*] (EA)
CRI .... Christian Research Institute (EA)
CRI .... Christian Response International (EA)
CRI .... Circuit Reliability Improvement
CRI .... Code Relations Index
CRI .... Color Rendition Index [*Measure of color distortion*]
CRI .... Committee for Reciprocity Information [*A federal government body*]
CRI .... Communications Research Institute (MCD)
CRI .... Complex Refraction Index
CRI .... Composer Recordings, Incorporated [*Recording label*]
CRI .... Concentrated Rust-Inhibiting
CRI .... Conflict Resolution Inventory [*Psychology*]
CRI .... Conservation Resources International [*Australia*]
CRI .... Constant Rate Injector [*Instrumentation*]
CRI .... Control Room Isolation [*Nuclear energy*] (NRCH)
CRI .... Core Industries, Inc. [*NYSE symbol*] (SPSG)
CRI .... Costa Rica [*ANSI three-letter standard code*] (CNC)
CRI .... Craigmont Mines [*Toronto Stock Exchange symbol*] [*Vancouver Stock Exchange symbol*]
CRI .... Cray Research, Incorporated
CRI .... Credit [*A publication*]

CRI .... Crikey [*An exclamation*] [*British*]   (DSUE)
CRI .... Crime
CRI .... Crimean
Cri .... Criterion [*A publication*]
CRI .... Criterion [*Theatre and restaurant at Piccadilly Circus*] [*London*]   (DSUE)
CRI .... Criterion-Referenced Instruction
Cri .... Crito [*of Plato*] [*Classical studies*]   (OCD)
CRI .... Croce Rossa Italiana [*Italian Red Cross*]
CRI .... Crooked Island [*Bahamas*] [*Airport symbol*]   (OAG)
CRI .... Cross-Reactive Idiotype [*Genetics*]
CRI .... Cure Rate Index [*Rubber technology*]
CRI .... Cybernetics Research Institute
CRIA......... Canadian Recording Industry Association
CRIA......... Committee to Rescue Italian Art
CRIA......... Communication Research Institute of Australia
CRIA......... Council on Religion and International Affairs [*Later, CCEIA*]   (EA)
CRI Abstr .. Cement Research Institute of India. Abstracts [*A publication*]
CRIAC....... Centre de Recherches Industrielles en Afrique Centrale
CRIARL .... Consortium of Rhode Island Academic and Research Libraries [*Library network*]
CRIAW...... Canadian Research Institute for the Advancement of Women [*Research center*]   (RCD)
CRIA/W .... Worldview. Council on Religion and International Affairs [*A publication*]
CRIB........ Chemotherapy Research Bulletin
CRIB........ Computerized Resources Information Bank [*United States Geological Survey*] [*Later, MRDS*]   (IID)
CRIC......... Canonici Regulares Immaculate Conceptionis [*Canons Regular of the Immaculate Conception*] [*Roman Catholic men's religious order*]
CRIC......... Citizens Research and Investigative Committee [*California*]
CRIC......... Collaborative Research, Incorporated [*NASDAQ symbol*]   (NQ)
CRIC......... Components Response Information Center   (MCD)
CRIC......... Cost Reimbursement Incentive Contracting [*Government contracting*]
CRic .... Richmond Public Library, Richmond, CA [*Library symbol*] [*Library of Congress*]   (LCLS)
CRICAP .... Carpet and Rug Industry Consumer Action Panel [*Defunct*]
CRicC......... Chevron Research Co., Technical Information Center, Richmond, CA [*Library symbol*] [*Library of Congress*]   (LCLS)
CRicCR...... California Research Corp., Richmond, CA [*Library symbol*] [*Library of Congress*]   (LCLS)
CRICISAM ... Center for Research in College Instruction of Science and Mathematics   (EA)
CRICKET ... Cold Rocket Instrument Carrying Kit
CRICO....... Committee for the Revision of the Criminal Code [*Allied German Occupation Forces*]
CRICON.... Crisis Confrontation
CRicS......... Stauffer Chemical Co., Richmond, CA [*Library symbol*] [*Library of Congress*]   (LCLS)
CRID .... Capital ROK [*Republic of Korea*] Infantry Division
CRID .... Centro di Riferimento Italiano DIANE [*Italian Reference Center for EURONET DIANE*] [*National Research Council*] [*Information service or system*]   (IID)
CRIDP....... Centre for Research in Industrial Democracy and Participation [*University of Glasgow*] [*United Kingdom*]   (CB)
CRIE........ Cosmic Ray Isotope Experiment   (MCD)
CRIE........ Crossed Radioimmunoelectrophoresis [*Analytical biochemistry*]
CRIEH....... Centre de Recherches. Institut d'Etudes Hispaniques [*A publication*]
CRIEPI (Cent Res Inst Electr Power Ind) Rep ... CRIEPI (Central Research Institute of Electric Power Industry) Report [*A publication*]
CRIF .... Centre de Recherches Scientifiques et Techniques de l'Industrie des Fabrications Metalliques [*Center for Scientific and Technical Research for the Metal Manufacturing Industry*] [*Information service or system*]   (IID)
CRIF .... Centre for Research in Finance [*University of New South Wales*] [*Information service or system*]   (IID)
CRIFC....... Cheryl Roth International Fan Club   (EA)
CRIFO....... Civilian Research, Interplanetary Flying Objects
CRIG......... Capacitor Rate-Integrating Gyroscope
CRIG......... Cumberland Gold Group, Inc. [*NASDAQ symbol*]   (NQ)
CRIGB....... Cryogenic and Industrial Gases [*A publication*]
CRII.......... Computer Resources, Incorporated [*NASDAQ symbol*]   (NQ)
CRIJA .... Ceramic Industries Journal [*A publication*]
CRIK......... Compliance Recycling Industries, Inc. [*NASDAQ symbol*]   (NQ)
CRIL......... Colorado Research in Linguistics [*A publication*]
CRIL......... Consolidated Repairable Item List
Crim .... Arret de la Chambre Criminelle de la Cour de Cassation [*Decision of the Court of Appeal, Criminal Division*] [*French*]   (ILCA)
CRIM........ Center for Research in Integrated Manufacturing [*University of Michigan*] [*Research center*]   (RCD)
CRIM........ Clinical Research Institute of Montreal [*University of Montreal*] [*Research center*]   (RCD)

CRIM......... Comite Regional Intersyndical de Montreal [*Montreal Regional Inter-Trade Union Committee*] [*Canada*]
CRIM........ Component Record Intensive Management
CRIM........ Crime Control, Inc. [*NASDAQ symbol*]   (NQ)
CRIM........ Criminal   (AFM)
Crim .... Criminology [*A publication*]
CRIM........ Crimson   (ROG)
CrimAb ...... Abstracts on Criminology and Penology [*A publication*]
Crim App ... Court of Criminal Appeals [*England*]   (DLA)
Crim App ... Criminal Appeal Reports [*England*] [*A publication*]   (DLA)
Crim App ... Law Reports. Criminal Appeal Reports [*United Kingdom*] [*A publication*]
Crim App (Eng) ... Criminal Appeal Reports [*England*] [*A publication*]   (DLA)
Crim App R ... Criminal Appeal Reports [*England*] [*A publication*]   (DLA)
Crim App Rep ... Cohen's Criminal Appeals Reports [*England*] [*A publication*]   (DLA)
Crim Case & Com ... Criminal Case and Comment [*A publication*]   (DLA)
Crim Code ... Criminal Code [*A publication*]   (DLA)
CRIM CON ... Criminal Conversation [*Adultery*] [*Slang*]   (DSUE)
Crim Def ... Criminal Defense [*A publication*]
Crim & Delin ... Crime and Delinquency [*A publication*]
CRIME...... Censorship Records and Information Middle East [*Military*]
Crime .... Crime in the United States [*A publication*]
Crime & Del ... Crime and Delinquency [*A publication*]   (DLA)
Crime Delin ... Crime and Delinquency [*A publication*]
Crime & Delin ... Crime and Delinquency [*A publication*]
Crime & Delin'cy ... Crime and Delinquency [*A publication*]
Crime & Delin'cy Abst ... Crime and Delinquency Abstracts [*A publication*]   (DLA)
Crime & Delin'cy Lit ... Crime and Delinquency Literature [*A publication*]   (DLA)
Crime & Delinq ... Crime and Delinquency [*A publication*]
Crime Delinq Abstr ... Crime and Delinquency Abstracts [*A publication*]
Crime Delinq Lit ... Crime and Delinquency Literature [*A publication*]
Crime and Just ... Crime and Justice [*A publication*]
Crime Prev News ... Crime Prevention News [*A publication*]
Crime & Soc Just ... Crime and Social Justice [*A publication*]
Crimin........ Criminology [*A publication*]
Criminal Justice Q ... Criminal Justice Quarterly [*A publication*]
Criminal Justice R ... Criminal Justice Review [*A publication*]
Criminal Law Bul ... Criminal Law Bulletin [*A publication*]
Criminal L Mag & Rep ... Criminal Law Magazine and Reporter [*A publication*]
Criminal LQ ... Criminal Law Quarterly [*A publication*]
Crim Inj Comp Bd ... Criminal Injuries Compensation Board [*British*]   (DLA)
Criminol..... Criminologica [*A publication*]   (DLA)
Criminol..... Criminologie [*Criminology*] [*French*]   (DLA)
Criminol..... Criminologist   (DLA)
CRIMINOL ... Criminology   (ADA)
Crim J and Beh ... Criminal Justice and Behavior [*A publication*]
Crim JJ...... Criminal Justice Journal [*A publication*]   (DLA)
Crim Just ... Crime and Social Justice [*A publication*]
Crim Just B ... Criminal Justice and Behavior [*A publication*]
Crim Just & Behav ... Criminal Justice and Behavior [*A publication*]
Crim Just Ethics ... Criminal Justice Ethics [*A publication*]
Crim Justice Abstr ... Criminal Justice Abstracts [*A publication*]
Crim Justice Period Index ... Criminal Justice Periodical Index [*A publication*]
Crim Just J ... Criminal Justice Journal [*A publication*]
Crim Just Newsl ... Criminal Justice Newsletter [*A publication*]
Crim Just Q ... Criminal Justice Quarterly [*A publication*]   (DLA)
Crim Just Rev ... Criminal Justice Review [*A publication*]   (DLA)
CRIML....... Criminal   (ROG)
Crim Law ... Criminal Law   (DLA)
Crim Law Bul ... Criminal Law Bulletin [*A publication*]
Crim Law J ... Criminal Law Journal [*A publication*]
Crim Law Q ... Criminal Law Quarterly [*A publication*]
Crim Law R ... Criminal Law Review [*A publication*]
Crim Law Reps (Green) ... Criminal Law Reports, by Green [*United States*] [*A publication*]   (DLA)
Crim L Bul ... Criminal Law Bulletin [*A publication*]
Crim L Bull ... Criminal Law Bulletin [*A publication*]
Crim LJ...... Criminal Law Journal [*A publication*]   (APTA)
Crim LJI ... Criminal Law Journal of India [*A publication*]
Crim LJ Ind ... Criminal Law Journal of India [*A publication*]
Crim LJ (Sydney) ... Criminal Law Journal (Sydney) [*Australia*] [*A publication*]
Crim L Mag ... Criminal Law Magazine [*A publication*]   (DLA)
Crim L Q.... Criminal Law Quarterly [*A publication*]
CRIM LR .. Criminal Law Reports [*A publication*]
Crim L R ... Criminal Law Review [*A publication*]
Crim L Rec ... Criminal Law Recorder [*A publication*]   (DLA)
Crim L Rep ... Criminal Law Reporter [*A publication*]
Crim L Rep BNA ... Criminal Law Reporter. Bureau of National Affairs [*A publication*]
Crim L Rev ... Criminal Law Review [*A publication*]
Crim L Rev (England) ... Criminal Law Review (England) [*A publication*]
Crim L Rptr ... Criminal Law Reporter [*A publication*]
CRIMP...... Consolidated RVNAF [*Republic of Vietnam Armed Forces*] Improvement and Modernization Program   (AABC)

CRIMP...... Crisis Management Plan   (MCD)
Crim Penol Abstr ... Criminology and Penology Abstracts [*A publication*]
Crim Pro .... Criminal Procedure [*Legal term*]   (DLA)
Crim Proc... Criminal Procedure [*Legal term*]   (DLA)
Crim R (Can) ... Criminal Reports (Canada) [*A publication*]
Crim Rec .... Criminal Recorder [*A publication*]   (DLA)
Crim Rep... Criminal Reports [*Carswell Company*] [*A publication*]
CRIMREP ... Crisis Management Information Report
Crim Rep NS ... Criminal Reports. New Series [*A publication*]
CRINBJ..... Annual Report. Nigeria Cocoa Research Institute [*A publication*]
CRINC....... University of Kansas Center for Research, Incorporated [*Research center*]   (RCD)
CRIO .... COMSEC [*Communications Security*] Regional Issuing Office [*or Officer*] [*Army*]   (AABC)
CRIP......... Australian Computing Research in Progress [*Information service or system*]   (ADA)
CRI & P ..... Chicago, Rock Island & Pacific Railroad Co. [*Nickname: The Baby Road*]
CRIP......... Controlled Retracting Injection Port [*System for underground coal burning*]
CRIPEL..... Cahiers de Recherches. Institut de Papyrologie et d'Egyptologie de Lille [*A publication*]
Cripp Ch Cas ... Cripp's Church and Clergy Cases [*1847-50*] [*England*] [*A publication*]   (DLA)
Cripp Ch L ... Cripp's Law Relating to Church and Clergy [*8th ed.*] [*1937*] [*A publication*]   (DLA)
Cripp Comp ... Cripp's Compulsory Acquisition of Land [*11th ed.*] [*1962*] [*A publication*]   (DLA)
Cripps .... Cripp's Church and Clergy Cases [*1847-50*] [*England*] [*A publication*]   (DLA)
Cripps Cas ... Cripp's Church and Clergy Cases [*1847-50*] [*England*] [*A publication*]   (DLA)
Cripp's Ch Cas ... Cripp's Church and Clergy Cases [*1847-50*] [*England*] [*A publication*]   (DLA)
Cripps Church Cas ... Cripp's Church and Clergy Cases [*1847-50*] [*England*] [*A publication*]   (DLA)
CRIPS........ Church Research and Information Projects
CRIQ .... Centre de Recherche Industrielle du Quebec [*Industrial Research Center of Quebec*] [*Information service or system*]   (IID)
CRIS .... Calibration Recall Information Systems   (KSC)
CRIS .... Centre for Research on Intelligent Systems [*Australia*]
CRIS .... Coalition for Retirement Income Security   (EA)
CRIS .... Collectif de Recherche et d'Information Sociales [*Collective of Research and Social Information*] [*Canada*]
CRIS .... Combined Retrospective Index Sets [*Information service or system*]   (IID)
CRIS .... Command Retrieval Information System
CRIS .... Community Resources Information Service, Inc. [*Information service or system*]   (IID)
CRIS .... Computerized Recall Identification System [*Automobile industry*]
CRIS .... Computerized Research Information Service [*Colorado School of Mines*]   (OLDSS)
CRIS .... Control Risks Information Services [*London, England*] [*Information service or system*]   (IID)
CRIS .... Corporate Research Information Service [*Frederick Research*]
CRIS .... Council for Religion in Independent Schools   (EA)
CRIS .... Counterintelligence Records Information System [*Army*]
CRIS .... Crime Report Information System [*Metropolitan Police database*] [*British*]
CRIS .... Current Research Information System [*Department of Agriculture*] [*Information service or system*]
CRISCI...... Center for Research in Innovative Services for the Communicatively Impaired [*Memphis State University*] [*Research center*]   (RCD)
CRISCO .... Cream Received in Separating Cottonseed Oil
CRISCON ... Crisis Condition   (MCD)
Crisia .... Crisia Culegere de Materiale si Studii [*A publication*]
CRISL........ Contract Repair Initial Support List   (AFIT)
CRISP........ Center for Research on Industrial Strategy and Policy [*Illinois Institute of Technology*] [*Research center*]   (RCD)
CRISP........ Centre for Information Studies Publications [*Kuring-Gai College of Education*] [*Australia*]
CRISP........ Computer Resources Integrated Support Plan [*Military*]   (AFIT)
CRISP........ Computer Retrieval of Information on Scientific Projects [*National Institutes of Health*] [*Information service or system*]   (IID)
CRISP........ Cosmic Ray Ionization Program [*NASA*]
CRISP........ Creep Isostatic Pressing
CRISS........ Center for Research in Surface Science and Submicron Analysis [*Montana State University*] [*Research center*]   (RCD)
Criss-Cross ... Criss-Cross Art Communications [*A publication*]
CRISTAL.. Contract Regarding an Interim Supplement to Tanker Liability for Oil Pollution [*Oil industry*]
Cristianismo Soc ... Cristianismo y Sociedad [*A publication*]
Crist y Soc ... Cristianismo y Sociedad [*A publication*]
Crit............ Criterio [*A publication*]
CRIT......... Criterion   (AABC)

Crit............ Criterion [*A publication*]
CRIT......... Criterion Group, Inc. [*Houston, TX*] [*NASDAQ symbol*]   (NQ)
Crit............ Criterium. Letterkundig Maandblad [*A publication*]
Crit............ Critic [*A publication*]
Crit............ Critica [*A publication*]
CRIT......... Critical [*Telecommunications*]   (TEL)
CRIT......... Critical   (KSC)
CRIT......... Criticism
Crit............ Criticism. A Quarterly for Literature and the Arts [*A publication*]
Crit............ Critique. A Review of Contemporary Art [*A publication*]
Crit............ Critique: Studies in Modern Fiction [*A publication*]
Crit d A ..... Critica d'Arte [*A publication*]
Crit Arte..... Critica d'Arte [*A publication*]
Crit Arts..... Critical Arts [*A publication*]
Crit Care Med ... Critical Care Medicine [*A publication*]
Crit Care Nurse ... Critical Care Nurse [*A publication*]
Crit Care Q ... Critical Care Quarterly [*A publication*]
Crit Care Update ... Critical Care Update [*A publication*]
Critch........ Critchfield's Reports [*5-21 Ohio State*] [*A publication*]   (DLA)
Critch (Ohio St) ... Critchfield's Reports [*5-21 Ohio State*] [*A publication*]   (DLA)
Crit C Nurse ... Critical Care Nurse [*A publication*]
CRITCOM ... Critical Communications System [*Military*]   (AABC)
Crit CQ ...... Critical Care Quarterly [*A publication*]
Crit Econ Polit ... Critiques de l'Economie Politique [*A publication*]
Criterio Econ ... Criterio Economico [*A publication*]
Crit Eval Some Equil Constants Involv Alkylammonium Extr ... Critical Evaluation of Some Equilibrium Constants Involving Alkylammonium Extractants [*A publication*]
CRITF .... Critical Frequency   (MSA)
CRITHOUS ... Critical Housing Shortage At [*named place*] [*Army*]
Criti............ Critias [*of Plato*] [*Classical studies*]   (OCD)
Crit I .... Critical Inquiry [*A publication*]
CRITIC...... Critical Intelligence Report   (CINC)
Critical Soc Policy ... Critical Social Policy [*A publication*]
CRITICOM ... Critical Intelligence Communications System [*DIN/DSSCS*]
CRITICOMM ... Critical Intelligence Communication
Crit Inq ...... Critical Inquiry [*A publication*]
Critiq.......... Critique [*A publication*]
Critique of Anthropol ... Critique of Anthropology [*A publication*]
Critique Reg ... Critique Regionale [*A publication*]
Critique S... Critique: Studies in Modern Fiction [*A publication*]
Critiques Econ Pol ... Critiques de l'Economie Politique [*A publication*]
Crit List ..... Critical List [*A publication*]
Critm.......... Criticism [*A publication*]
Crit Marx... Critica Marxista [*A publication*]
Crit Mass J ... Critical Mass Journal [*A publication*]
Crit Pen...... Critica Penale [*A publication*]
Crit Perspe ... Critical Perspectives [*A publication*]
Crit Pol ...... Critica Politica [*A publication*]
Crit Q......... Critical Quarterly [*A publication*]
Critq.......... Critique [*A publication*]
Crit Quart .. Critical Quarterly [*A publication*]
Crit R .... Critical Review [*A publication*]
Crit Rev...... Critical Review [*A publication*]   (APTA)
Crit Rev Anal Chem ... Critical Reviews in Analytical Chemistry [*A publication*]
Crit Rev Biochem ... Critical Reviews in Biochemistry [*A publication*]
Crit Rev Biochem Mol Biol ... Critical Reviews in Biochemistry and Molecular Biology [*A publication*]
Crit Rev Biocompat ... Critical Reviews in Biocompatibility [*A publication*]
Crit Rev Bioeng ... Critical Reviews in Bioengineering [*A publication*]
Crit Rev Biomed Eng ... Critical Reviews in Biomedical Engineering [*A publication*]
Crit Rev Biotechnol ... Critical Reviews in Biotechnology [*A publication*]
Crit Rev Clin Lab Sci ... Critical Reviews in Clinical Laboratory Sciences [*A publication*]
Crit Rev Clin Neurobiol ... Critical Reviews in Clinical Neurobiology [*A publication*]
Crit Rev Clin Radiol Nucl Med ... Critical Reviews in Clinical Radiology and Nuclear Medicine [*A publication*]
Crit Rev Diagn Imaging ... Critical Reviews in Diagnostic Imaging [*A publication*]
Crit Rev Environ Control ... Critical Reviews in Environmental Control [*A publication*]
Crit Rev Food Sci Nutr ... Critical Reviews in Food Science and Nutrition [*A publication*]
Crit Rev Food Technol ... Critical Reviews in Food Technology [*A publication*]
Crit Rev Immunol ... Critical Reviews in Immunology [*A publication*]
Crit Rev Microbiol ... Critical Reviews in Microbiology [*A publication*]
Crit Rev Oncol/Hematol ... Critical Reviews in Oncology/Hematology [*A publication*]
Crit Rev Plant Sci ... Critical Reviews in Plant Sciences [*A publication*]
Crit Rev Solid State Mater Sci ... Critical Reviews in Solid State and Materials Sciences [*A publication*]
Crit Rev Solid State Sci ... Critical Reviews in Solid State Sciences [*A publication*]

Crit Rev Ther Drug Carrier Syst ... Critical Reviews in Therapeutic Drug Carrier Systems [*A publication*]
Crit Rev Toxicol ... Critical Reviews in Toxicology [*A publication*]
CritS............. Critical Survey [*A publication*]
Crit Soc...... Critica Sociale [*A publication*]
Crit Social (Paris) ... Critique Socialiste (Paris) [*A publication*]
Crit Sociol (Roma) ... Critica Sociologica (Roma) [*A publication*]
Crit Stor..... Critica Storica [*A publication*]
CRIV.......... Charles River Breeding Laboratories [*NASDAQ symbol*]   (NQ)
CRiv........... Riverside Public Library and Riverside County Free Library, Riverside, CA [*Library symbol*] [*Library of Congress*]   (LCLS)
CRivGS...... Church of Jesus Christ of Latter-Day Saints, Genealogical Society Library, Riverside Branch, Riverside, CA [*Library symbol*] [*Library of Congress*]   (LCLS)
CRivGS-W ... Church of Jesus Christ of Latter-Day Saints, Genealogical Society Library, Riverside West Branch, Riverside, CA [*Library symbol*] [*Library of Congress*]   (LCLS)
CRivL......... Loma Linda University, Riverside Campus, Riverside, CA [*Library symbol*] [*Library of Congress*]   (LCLS)
CRIWG...... Central Region Interface Working Group [*NATO*]   (NATG)
CRIX.......... Control Resource Industries, Inc. [*Michigan City, IN*] [*NASDAQ symbol*]   (NQ)
CRJ............ Cash Receipts Journal [*Accounting*]
CRJ............ Claude Resources, Inc. [*Toronto Stock Exchange symbol*]
CRJ............ Commission for Racial Justice   (EA)
CRJ............ Contemporary Religions in Japan [*A publication*]
CRJBS....... Community of Reparation to Jesus in the Blessed Sacrament [*Anglican religious community*]
CRJE.......... Conversational Remote Job Entry [*Data processing*]
Cr JF.......... [*Sir T.*] Craig. Jus Feudale [*A publication*]   (DLA)
CRJO.......... Commission on Reform Jewish Outreach   (EA)
CRJO......... Cost Reduction Journal
CR Journ Natl Compos ... Comptes Rendus des Journees Nationales sur les Composites [*A publication*]
CRJP......... Center for Research on Judgment and Policy [*University of Colorado - Boulder*] [*Research center*]   (RCD)
CRJSA4..... Caribbean Journal of Science [*A publication*]
Cr Just....... Criminal Justice [*A publication*]
CRJWA ..... Council of Religious Jewish Workers of America [*Defunct*]   (EA)
CRK .... Campbell Red Lake Mines Ltd. [*NYSE symbol*] [*Toronto Stock Exchange symbol*]   (SPSG)
CRK .... Clean Room Kit
CRK .... Cork
CRK .... Crank   (KSC)
CRK .... Crankcase
CRK .... Creek   (MCD)
CRKC........ Crankcase   (KSC)
CRKSFT... Crankshaft
CRKSHV.. Cranksheave   (MSA)
CRL............ Cadmium Red Line
CRL............ Calibration Requirements List   (MCD)
CRL............ Cambridge Research Laboratory
CRL............ Canonici Regulares Lateranenses [*Canons Regular of the Lateran*]
CRL............ Carleton, MI [*Location identifier*] [*FAA*]   (FAAL)
CRL............ Carloforte [*Sardinia*] [*Seismograph station code, US Geological Survey*] [*Closed*]   (SEIS)
CRL............ Cathode-Ray Lamp
CRL............ Center for Research Libraries [*Library network*]   (EA)
CRL............ Center for Research Libraries, Chicago, IL [*OCLC symbol*] [*Inactive*]   (OCLC)
CRL............ Central Reference Library [*British*]   (DIT)
CRL............ Centre for Research in Librarianship [*University of Toronto*] [*Research center*]   (RCD)
CRL............ Cereal Rust Laboratory [*Department of Agriculture*]   (GRD)
CRL............ Certified Record Librarian
CRL............ Choctawhatchee Regional Library [*Library network*]
CRL............ Cholera Research Laboratory [*Bangladesh*]
CRL............ Classical Roman Law [*A publication*]
CRL............ Clonal Apple Rootstock Liner
CRL............ College and Research Libraries [*A publication*]
C & RL....... College and Research Libraries [*A publication*]
CRL............ Communications Research Laboratories [*Information service or system*]   (IID)
CRL............ Communications Research Laboratory [*McMaster University*] [*Canada*] [*Research center*]   (RCD)
CRL............ Complement Receptor Lymphocyte [*Immunology*]
CRL............ Computing Research Laboratory [*New Mexico State University*] [*Research center*]   (RCD)
CRL............ Control Record Listing [*IRS*]
CRL............ Control Relay Latch
Crl.............. Coral [*Record label*] [*USA, Europe*]
CRL............ Cornell University Research Laboratory
CRL............ Crain, Inc. [*Toronto Stock Exchange symbol*]
CRL............ Crew Research Laboratory [*Randolph Air Force Base, TX*]
Cr L............ Criminal Lawyer [*India*] [*A publication*]   (DLA)
CRL............ Critical Review of Theological and Philosophical Literature [*A publication*]
CRL............ Crossland Savings FSB [*NYSE symbol*]   (SPSG)

CRL............ Crown-Rump Length [*of fetus*] [*Medicine*]
CRL............ Customer Requirements List   (MCD)
CRLA........ Canadian Railway Labour Association
CRLA........ Crater Lake National Park
Cr Law Mag ... Criminal Law Magazine [*A publication*]   (DLA)
Cr Law Rec ... Criminal Law Recorder [*A publication*]   (DLA)
Cr Law Rep ... Criminal Law Reporter [*A publication*]
CRLC......... Capitol Region Library Council [*Library network*]
CRLC......... Central Reserve Life Corporation [*NASDAQ symbol*]   (NQ)
CRLC......... Chicana Research and Learning Center   (EA)
CRLC......... Circulate   (FAAC)
CRLDD...... Cornell University Research Laboratory for Diseases of Dogs
CRLEA....... Canadian Railway Labour Executives' Association
CR/LF .... Carriage Return/Line Feed [*Data processing*]
CRLI.......... Circuit Research Laboratories, Inc. [*NASDAQ symbol*]   (NQ)
Cr LJ.......... Criminal Law Journal of India [*A publication*]
CRLL......... Conclusions, Recommendations, and Lessons Learned
CRLLB ..... Center for Research on Language and Language Behavior [*University of Michigan*]
CRLM....... CRREL [*Cold Regions Research and Engineering Laboratory*] Monograph Series [*United States*] [*A publication*]
Cr L Mag ... Criminal Law Magazine [*A publication*]   (DLA)
CRLN .... Carolin Mines Ltd. [*NASDAQ symbol*]   (NQ)
CRLN .... Comparative Romance Linguistics Newsletter [*A publication*]
CRLR......... Chemical and Radiological Laboratories [*Army*]
Cr LR .... Criminal Law Reporter [*A publication*]
CRLS .... Carlsberg Corp. [*NASDAQ symbol*]   (NQ)
CRLS .... Chronic Reactive Lymphadenopathy Syndrome [*Medicine*]
CRLT......... Center for Research on Learning and Teaching [*University of Michigan*] [*Research center*]   (RCD)
CRLT......... Central Research Laboratory of Tashiba
CRLY......... Crowley Financial Services, Inc. [*Fort Lauderdale, FL*] [*NASDAQ symbol*]   (NQ)
CRM .... Camera-Ready Mechanical
CRM .... Cash by Return Mail [*Business term*]
CRM .... Catarman [*Philippines*] [*Airport symbol*]   (OAG)
CRM .... Centre de Reflexion sur le Monde Non Occidental [*Center for the Study of the Non-Occidental World*]   (EA)
CRM .... Certified Records Manager [*Designation awarded by Institute of Certified Records Managers*]   (MCD)
CRM .... Certified Reference Materials
CRM .... Change Request Material   (AAG)
CRM .... Charles Rennie Mackintosh Society   (EAIO)
CRM .... Chemical Release Module   (MCD)
CRM .... Chemical Remanent Magnetization [*Geophysics*]
CRM .... Chief Radioman [*Navy rating*] [*Obsolete*]
CRM .... Christian Renewal Ministry   (EA)
CRM .... Chrome   (MSA)
CRM .... Citizens' Rights Movement [*Israel*] [*Political party*]   (ECON)
CRM .... Clerici Regulares Minores [*Clerics Regular Minor*] [*Adorno Fathers*] [*Roman Catholic religious order*]
CRM .... Clinch River Mile [*Energy Research and Development Administration*]
CRM .... Cloud-Croft Radiation Measurement
CRM .... Combat Readiness Medal [*Military decoration*]   (AFM)
CRM .... Comet Rendezvous Mission
CRM .... Command Receiver Monitor   (AAG)
CRM .... Communications/Research/Machines, Inc. [*Publisher*]
CRM .... Conceptual Reference Mission [*NASA*]
CRM .... Confusion Reflector Material
CRM .... Conseil de Recherches Medicales [*Medical Research Council*] [*Canada*]
CRM .... Consolidated Rexspar Minerals & Chemicals Ltd. [*Toronto Stock Exchange symbol*]
CRM .... Construction Risk Management [*International Risk Management Institute*] [*A publication*]
CRM .... Containment Radiation Monitor [*Nuclear energy*]   (IEEE)
CRM .... Control Relay Master
CRM .... Control and Reproducibility Monitor   (IEEE)
CRM .... Coordinacion Revolucionaria de las Masas [*Revolutionary Coordination of the Masses*] [*El Salvador*]   (PD)
CRM .... Core Restraint Mechanism [*Nuclear energy*]   (NRCH)
CRM .... Count Rate Meter
CRM .... CounterRADAR Measures
CRM .... CounterRADAR Missile
CRM .... Cream   (ADA)
CRM .... Credit Management [*A publication*]
CR/M .... Crew Member
CRM .... Criterion-Referenced Measurement [*Education*]
Cr & M....... Crompton and Meeson's English Exchequer Reports [*1832-34*] [*A publication*]   (DLA)
CRM .... Cross-Reacting Material [*Immunology*]
CRM .... Curriculum Resource Materials
CRM .... Customer Relations Manager   (DCTA)
CRM .... Cyber Record Manager [*Data processing*]
CRMA .... Centre de Recherche de Mathematiques Appliquees [*University of Montreal*] [*Research center*]   (RCD)
CRMA .... City and Regional Magazine Association   (EA)
CRMA .... Commercial Refrigerator Manufacturers Association   (EA)
CR Mag ..... CR [*Chemische Rundschau*] Magazin [*A publication*]

CRMB ...... Combined Raw Materials Board [*US and Britain*] [*World War II*]
CRM Boletin de Informacion ... Consejo de Recursos Minerales. Boletin de Informacion [*A publication*]
CRMC .... Center for Research for Mothers and Children [*National Institutes of Health*] (GRD)
CRMC .... Classic Racing Motorcycle Club (EA)
CRMD ...... Class for Retarded in Mental Development
CRMD .... Clerici Regulares Matris Dei [*Clerics Regular of the Mother of God*] [*Roman Catholic religious order*]
CRMD ...... Computer Resources Management Data (MCD)
CRMD ...... Creative Medical Systems, Inc. [*NASDAQ symbol*] (NQ)
CRME .... Council for Research in Music Education (EA)
CRME .... Council for Research in Music Education. Bulletin [*A publication*]
CRMF .... Congo-Red Millipore Filter
CRMI .... Clerici Regulares Ministrantes Infirmis [*Clerics Regular Attendant on the Sick, Camillini, Camilliani*] [*Roman Catholic religious order*]
CRMK .... Cermetek Microelectronics, Inc. [*NASDAQ symbol*] (NQ)
CRML .... Coalition for Responsible Mining Law (EA)
CRMN .... Crewman (AABC)
CRMO .... Craters of the Moon National Monument
CRMP .... Computer Resource Management Plan [*Army*] (RDA)
CRMP .... Crump [*E. H.*] Cos. [*NASDAQ symbol*] (NQ)
CRMPT ..... Commendation Ribbon with Metal Pendant [*Military decoration*]
CRMR .... Continuous-Reading Meter Relay
CRMR .... Cramer, Inc. [*NASDAQ symbol*] (NQ)
Cr M & R ... Crompton, Meeson, and Roscoe's English Exchequer Reports [*1834-36*] [*A publication*] (DLA)
CRMS .... Center for Research in Management Science [*University of California*] (MCD)
CRMS .... Clerks Regular, Ministers of the Sick [*Rome, Italy*] (EAIO)
CRMSS ..... Central Registry of Magazine Subscription Solicitors [*Defunct*] (EA)
CRMT .... Chromate (MSA)
CRM-USA ... Cliff Richard Movement - USA [*Later, CRFCA*] (EA)
CRMWD ... Colorado River Municipal Water District
CRN .... Carolina & Northwestern Railway Co. [*AAR code*]
CRN .... Carrigan Industries Ltd. [*Vancouver Stock Exchange symbol*]
CRN .... Carson Pirie Scott & Co. [*NYSE symbol*] (SPSG)
CRN .... CERMET [*Ceramic Metal Element*] Resistor Network
CRN .... Complement Requiring Neutralizing
CRN .... Continuous-Random-Network [*Noncrystalline structure*]
CRN .... Contract Revision Number (NASA)
CRN .... Corinaldo [*Italy*] [*Seismograph station code, US Geological Survey*] (SEIS)
Crn .... Corrin [*Biochemistry*]
CRN .... Corrosion-Resistant Nebulizer
CRN .... Council for Responsible Nutrition (EA)
CRN .... Crane (MSA)
CRN .... Cross Lake Minerals [*Vancouver Stock Exchange symbol*]
CRN .... Crown (MSA)
CRN .... Customs Registered Number [*United Kingdom*] (DS)
CRN .... Sparrevohn, AK [*Location identifier*] [*FAA*] (FAAL)
CRN .... United States Commission on Civil Rights, Washington, DC [*OCLC symbol*] (OCLC)
CRNA .... Certified Registered Nurse Anesthetist
CRNA .... CrownAmerica, Inc. [*NASDAQ symbol*] (NQ)
cRNA .... Ribonucleic Acid, Chromosomal [*Biochemistry, genetics*]
cRNA .... Ribonucleic Acid, Complementary [*Biochemistry, genetics*]
CRNC .... College Republican National Committee (EA)
CRNGDP .. Carcinogenesis [*London*] [*A publication*]
CRNHP ...... Concerned Relatives of Nursing Home Patients (EA)
CRNI .... Crown Auto, Incorporated [*Eden Prairie, MN*] [*NASDAQ symbol*] (NQ)
CRNIA .... Current Notes on International Affairs [*Australia*] [*A publication*]
CRNL .... Chalk River Nuclear Laboratories [*Atomic Energy of Canada Ltd.*] [*Information service or system*] [*Research center*] (IID)
CRNMTC ... Chronometric
CRNMTR ... Chronometer
CRNPR ...... Corrected Relative Net Protein Ratio [*Nutrition*]
CRNR .... Chronar Corp. [*NASDAQ symbol*] (NQ)
CRNS .... Code Reports, New Series [*New York*] [*A publication*] (DLA)
CRNS .... Criminal Reports. New Series [*A publication*]
CRNSBP ... Chironomus [*A publication*]
CRNVD2 ... Carnivore [*Seattle*] [*A publication*]
CRNWL .... Cornwall [*County in England*]
CRO .... Carded for Record Only
CRO .... Carnarvon Tracking Station [*NASA*]
CRO .... Carnasaw Mountain - Lookout Tower [*Oklahoma*] [*Seismograph station code, US Geological Survey*] (SEIS)
CRO .... Cathode-Ray Oscilloscope [*or Oscilloscope*]
CRO .... Central Radio Office [*Telecommunications*] (TEL)
CRO .... Central Records Office
CRO .... Central Research Organization [*Burma*] (DS)
CRO .... Centric Relation Occlusion [*Dentistry*]
CRO .... Chief Recruiting Officer [*British military*] (DMA)

CRO .... Civil Readjustment Officer [*Military*]
CRO .... Civilian Repair Organization [*Aircraft*]
CRO .... Commonwealth Relations Office [*Later, CO*] [*British*]
CRO .... Companies Registration Office [*British*] (DS)
CRO .... Complete with Related Order [*Telecommunications*] (TEL)
CRO .... Computer Readable Output [*Data processing*] (PCM)
CRO .... Continuous Receiver On [*Electronic device*]
CRO .... Contractor Resident Office (AAG)
CRO .... Control Room Operator [*Nuclear energy*] (NRCH)
CRO .... Corcoran, CA [*Location identifier*] [*FAA*] (FAAL)
CRO .... Cosmic Ray Observatory
CRO .... Criminal Record Office [*Scotland Yard*]
Cro .... Croke's English King's Bench Reports [*1582-1641*] [*A publication*] (DLA)
CRO .... Crown Airways, Inc. [*DuBois, PA*] [*FAA designator*] (FAAC)
Cro .... Keilway's English King's Bench Reports [*72 English Reprint*] [*A publication*] (DLA)
CRo .... Roseville Public Library, Roseville, CA [*Library symbol*] [*Library of Congress*] (LCLS)
CROACUS ... Comite Regional Ouest-Africain pour la Conservation et l'Utilisation du Sol
Croat .... Croatia
Croat Chem ... Croatica Chemica Acta [*A publication*]
Croat Chem A ... Croatica Chemica Acta [*A publication*]
Croat Chem Acta ... Croatica Chemica Acta [*A publication*]
Croatia Pr ... Croatia Press [*A publication*]
CROB .... Center for Research in Oral Biology [*University of Washington*] [*Research center*] (RCD)
C Rob .... Christopher Robinson's English Admiralty Reports [*165 English Reprint*] [*A publication*] (DLA)
C Rob Adm ... Christopher Robinson's English Admiralty Reports [*165 English Reprint*] [*A publication*] (DLA)
C Rob (Eng) ... Christopher Robinson's English Admiralty Reports [*165 English Reprint*] [*A publication*] (DLA)
CROC .... Combat Required Operational Capability (AFIT)
CROC .... Committee for Rejection of Obnoxious Commercials
CROC .... Computer Review and Orientation Course
CROC .... Crocodile (DSUE)
CROC .... Crocus Saffron [*Pharmacy*] (ROG)
Cro Car ...... Croke's English King's Bench Reports Tempore Charles I [*1625-41*] [*A publication*] (DLA)
Cro Car (Eng) ... Croke's English King's Bench Reports Tempore Charles I [*1625-41*] [*A publication*] (DLA)
Cro Cas ...... Croke's English King's Bench Reports Tempore Charles I [*1625-41*] [*A publication*] (DLA)
CROCB ...... Chronache di Chimica [*A publication*]
Crock Cor ... Crocker on the Duties of Coroners in New York [*A publication*] (DLA)
Crockford ... English Maritime Law Reports, Published by Crockford [*1860-71*] [*A publication*] (DLA)
Crock Forms ... Crocker's Notes on Common Forms [*Massachusetts*] [*A publication*] (DLA)
Crock Notes ... Crocker's Notes on the Public Statutes of Massachusetts [*A publication*] (DLA)
Crock Sh .... Crocker on Sheriffs and Constables [*A publication*] (DLA)
CROCP ...... Committee for Review of Our China Policy [*Defunct*]
CRocS .... Sierra College, Rocklin, CA [*Library symbol*] [*Library of Congress*] (LCLS)
CRODAI ... Centre de Recherches Oceanographiques [*Abidjan*]. Documents Scientifiques [*A publication*]
CRodSpol ... Casopis Rodopisne Spolecnosti Ceskoslovenske [*A publication*]
CROEA ..... Cronache Economiche [*A publication*]
CROED ...... Civil Rights Office, Education Department (OICC)
Cro Eliz ...... Croke's English King's Bench Reports Tempore Elizabeth [*1582-1603*] [*A publication*] (DLA)
Cro Eliz (Eng) ... Croke's English King's Bench Reports Tempore Elizabeth [*1582-1603*] [*A publication*] (DLA)
CROFC ...... Clint Ritchie Official Fan Club (EA)
CROG .... Croghan [*New York*] [*Seismograph station code, US Geological Survey*] (SEIS)
C(RO & H) ... Center (Regional Office and Hospital) [*Veterans Administration*]
CROHMS ... Columbia River Operational Hydromet Management System (NOAA)
C(RO & INS) ... Center (Regional Office and Insurance) [*Veterans Administration*]
Cro Jac .... Croke's English King's Bench Reports Tempore James (Jacobus) I [*A publication*] (DLA)
Cro Jac (Eng) ... Croke's English King's Bench Reports Tempore James (Jacobus) I [*A publication*] (DLA)
Croke .... Croke's English King's Bench Reports [*1582-1641*] [*A publication*] (DLA)
Croke .... Keilway's English King's Bench Reports [*72 English Reprint*] [*A publication*] (DLA)
CROM ...... Capacitive Read-Only Memory [*Data processing*] (IEEE)
CROM ...... Control Read-Only Memory [*Data processing*]
Crom .... Crompton's Office of a Justice of the Peace [*1637*] [*A publication*] (DLA)
CROM .... [*Oliver*] Cromwell [*British general and statesman, 1599-1658*] (ROG)

CRom......... Cuget Romanesc [*A publication*]
C (Romania) ... Cinema (Romania) [*A publication*]
Cromp........ Star Chamber Cases, by Crompton [*A publication*] (DLA)
Cromp Cts ... Crompton's Jurisdiction of Courts [*A publication*] (DLA)
Cromp Exch R ... Crompton's English Exchequer Reports [*A publication*] (DLA)
Cromp Ex R ... Crompton's English Exchequer Reports [*A publication*] (DLA)
Cromp & F ... Fitzherbert's Justice, Enlarged by Crompton [*A publication*] (DLA)
Cromp & J ... Crompton and Jervis' English Exchequer Reports [*1830-32*] [*A publication*] (DLA)
Cromp JC .. Crompton's Jurisdiction of Courts [*A publication*] (DLA)
Cromp & J (Eng) ... Crompton and Jervis' English Exchequer Reports [*1830-32*] [*A publication*] (DLA)
Cromp & Jer ... Crompton and Jervis' English Exchequer Reports [*1830-32*] [*A publication*] (DLA)
Cromp & Jerv ... Crompton and Jervis' English Exchequer Reports [*1830-32*] [*A publication*] (DLA)
Cromp Jur ... Crompton's Jurisdiction of Courts [*A publication*] (DLA)
Cromp Just ... Crompton's Office of a Justice of the Peace [*1637*] [*A publication*] (DLA)
Cromp & M ... Crompton and Meeson's English Exchequer Reports [*1832-34*] [*A publication*] (DLA)
Cromp & Mees ... Crompton and Meeson's English Exchequer Reports [*1832-34*] [*A publication*] (DLA)
Cromp & M (Eng) ... Crompton and Meeson's English Exchequer Reports [*1832-34*] [*A publication*] (DLA)
Cromp M & R ... Crompton, Meeson, and Roscoe's English Exchequer Reports [*1834-36*] [*A publication*] (DLA)
Cromp M & R (Eng) ... Crompton, Meeson, and Roscoe's English Exchequer Reports [*1834-36*] [*A publication*] (DLA)
Cromp R & C Pr ... Crompton's Rules and Cases of Practice [*A publication*] (DLA)
Crompt....... Star Chamber Cases, by Crompton [*A publication*] (DLA)
CRomR ...... Rosemead Graduate School of Psychology, Rosemead, CA [*Library symbol*] [*Library of Congress*] (LCLS)
Cron .... Cronos [*A publication*]
CRON........ Crown Brands, Inc. [*NASDAQ symbol*] (NQ)
Cronache Econ ... Cronache Economiche [*A publication*]
Cron Agric ... Cronica Agricola [*A publication*]
Cron A Stor Art ... Cronache di Archeologia e di Storia dell'Arte [*A publication*]
Cron Catania ... Cronache di Archeologia e di Storia dell'Arte. Universita de Catania [*A publication*]
Cron Chim ... Cronache de Chimica [*A publication*]
Cron Dent .. Cronica Dental [*A publication*]
Cron Econ .. Cronache Economiche [*A publication*]
Cron Erc..... Cronache Ercolanesi [*A publication*]
Cron Ercol ... Cronache Ercolanesi [*A publication*]
Croner's ...... Croner's Export Digest [*A publication*]
Croner's Ref Book Employ ... Croner's Reference Book for Employers [*A publication*]
Croner's Ref Book Export ... Croner's Reference Book for Exporters [*A publication*]
Cron Farm ... Cronache Farmaceutiche [*A publication*]
Cron Med (Lima) ... Cronica Medica (Lima) [*A publication*]
Cron Med Mex ... Cronica Medica Mexicana [*A publication*]
Cron Med Mexicana ... Cronica Medica Mexicana [*A publication*]
Cron Med-Quir Habana ... Cronica Medico-Quirurgica de La Habana [*A publication*]
Cron Pomp ... Cronache Pompeiane [*A publication*]
Cron Vin Cer ... Cronica de Vinos y Cereales [*A publication*]
CROP .... Centre de Recherches sur l'Opinion Publique [*Research Centre on Public Opinion*] [*Canada*]
CROP .... Christian Rural Overseas Program [*Acronym is now the official name of organization*] (EA)
CROP .... Crop Genetics International Corp. [*NASDAQ symbol*] (NQ)
CROP .... Cyclophosphamide, Rubidazone [*Zorubicin*], Oncovin [*Vincristine*], Prednisone [*Antineoplastic drug regimen*]
Crop Bull Can Board Grain Comm ... Crop Bulletin. Canada Board of Grain Commissioners [*A publication*]
Crop Bull Grain Res Lab (Can) ... Crop Bulletin. Grain Research Laboratory (Canada) [*A publication*]
Crop Improv ... Crop Improvement [*A publication*]
Crop Prod .. Crop Production [*A publication*]
Crop Prod Conf Rep Crop Qual Counc ... Crop Production Conference Report. Crop Quality Council [*A publication*]
Crop Prod Sci ... Crop Production Science [*A publication*]
Crop Prot ... Crop Protection [*A publication*]
Crop Res .... Crop Research [*A publication*]
Crop Res ARS ... Crops Research ARS [*Agricultural Research Service*] [*A publication*]
Crop Res News Dep Sci Ind Res (NZ) ... Crop Research News. New Zealand Department of Scientific and Industrial Research [*A publication*]
Crop Res News NZ Dep Sci Ind Res ... Crop Research News. New Zealand Department of Scientific and Industrial Research [*A publication*]
CROPS...... Concerned Residents Opposing the Pulp Siting [*Australia*]
Crop Sci ..... Crop Science [*A publication*]

Crop Soil NC State Univ ... Crop Soils. North Carolina State University [*A publication*]
Crops Soils Mag ... Crops and Soils Magazine [*A publication*]
CROS........ Capacitor Read-Only Storage [*Data processing*]
CROS........ Committee on Radiation Oncology Studies [*National Cancer Institute*]
CROS........ Common Real-Time Operating System (CAAL)
CROS........ Computerized Reliability Organization System
CROS........ Contralateral Routing of Signal [*Audiometry*]
CROS........ Crossland Industries Corp. [*New York, NY*] [*NASDAQ symbol*] (NQ)
CROSS...... Committee to Retain Our Segregated Schools [*Group in Arkansas, organized to oppose STOP*]
CROSS...... Computerized Rearrangements of Special Subjects [*or Subject Specialties*]
CROSSBOW ... Computer Retrieval of Organic Structures Based on Wiswesser
Cross C ...... Cross Currents [*A publication*]
Cross & Cr ... Cross and Crown [*A publication*]
Cross Cur ... Cross Currents [*A publication*]
Cross Curr ... Cross Currents [*A publication*]
Cross Lien ... Cross. Lien and Stoppage in Transitu [*1840*] [*A publication*] (DLA)
CROSSPATE ... Coordinative Retrieval of Selectively Sorted Permuted Analogue-Title Entries [*Data processing*]
Crossref Hum Resour Manage ... Cross-Reference on Human Resources Management [*A publication*]
CROSSTABS ... [*A*] programming language (CSR)
Cros Wills ... Crosley on Wills [*1828*] [*A publication*] (DLA)
Crosw Pat Ca ... Croswell's Collection of Patent Cases [*United States*] [*A publication*] (DLA)
Crosw Pat Cas ... Croswell's Collection of Patent Cases [*United States*] [*A publication*] (DLA)
Crot .... [*Johannes*] Crotus [*Flourished, 16th century*] [*Authority cited in pre-1607 legal work*] (DSA)
CROTCE... Crotonyloxymethyl(trihydroxy)cyclohexene [*Antineoplastic drug*]
Crounse...... Crounse's Reports [*3 Nebraska*] [*A publication*] (DLA)
CROVL...... C-Rating Overall [*Military*] (CAAL)
CROW ...... Center for Research on Women [*Stanford University*] [*Research center*] (RCD)
CROW ...... Center for Research on Women [*Duke University, University of North Carolina*] [*Research center*] (RCD)
CROW ...... Combined Rocket Warhead (KSC)
CROW ...... Counter-Rotating Optical Wedge
Crow.......... Crowther's Ceylon Reports [*A publication*] (DLA)
CROWCASS ... Central Registry of War Criminals and Security Suspects [*World War II*]
CROWD.... Central Registry of World Dancers (EA)
Crown Agents QR ... Crown Agents Quarterly Review [*A publication*]
Crown Ag R ... Crown Agents Review [*A publication*]
Crown Col .. Crown Colonist [*A publication*]
Crown C Rev ... Crown Counsel's Review [*A publication*]
Crown LC... Crown Land Cases [*Australia*] [*A publication*] (DLA)
Crowth ...... Crowther's Ceylon Reports [*A publication*] (DLA)
Crowther .... Crowther's Ceylon Reports [*A publication*] (DLA)
Crowther FPL ... D. J. Crowther Ltd. Fixed Price List [*A publication*]
CROWT & MIN ... Crowthorne and Minety [*England*]
CROYD..... Croydon [*Borough of London*]
CRP........... C-Reactive Protein [*Clinical chemistry*]
CRP........... Calendarium Rotulorum Patentum [*Calendar of the Patent Rolls*] [*Latin*]
CRP........... CAPE [*Capability and Proficiency Evaluation*] Review Period
CRP........... Carbinol Reduction Potential [*Chemistry*]
CRP........... Card Reader/Punch [*Data processing*]
CRP........... Center for Responsive Politics (EA)
CRP........... Center for Responsive Psychology (EA)
CRP........... Centers for Radiological Physics
CRP........... Central R. R. of Pennsylvania [*AAR code*]
CRP........... Centralized Receiving Point
CRP........... Chemical Research Project [*Military*]
CRP........... Chicago Review Press [*Publisher*]
CRP........... Chicana Rights Project (EA)
CRP........... Chopp Computer Corp. [*Vancouver Stock Exchange symbol*]
CRP........... Civil Rights Party [*Republic of Korea*] [*Political party*] (PPW)
CRP........... Clauson Rolling Platform
CRP........... Climate Research Project [*Boulder, CO*] [*Department of Commerce*] (GRD)
CRP........... Comando de Resistencia Popular Javier Carrera [*Javier Carrera Popular Resistance Commando*] [*Chile*] (PD)
CRP........... Combat Reconnaissance Platoon
CRP........... Combat Reporting Post
CRP........... Command Read Pulse (KSC)
CRP........... Committee to Re-Elect the President [*Also, CREEP*] [*1972*]
CRP........... Community Renewal Program
CRP........... Complement Regulatory Protein [*Genetics*]
CRP........... Component Reliability Prediction
CRP........... Composition Reduction Printing
CRP........... Compton Recoil Particle
CRP........... Computer Reset Pulse (KSC)
CRP........... Computer Resident Planning (MCD)

CRP............ COMSEC [*Communications Security*] Resources Program [*Army*] (AABC)
CRP............ Configuration Requirements Processing (MCD)
CRP............ Congregatio Reformatorium Praemonstratensium [*Premonstratensians*] [*Roman Catholic men's religious order*]
CRP............ Continuous Record of Personnel (ADA)
CRP............ Control and Reporting Post [*RADAR*] [*Air Force*]
CRP............ Controllable and Reversible Pitch Propeller [*For ships*] (MCD)
CRP............ Controlled Referral Plan
CRP............ Cooperative Research Program [*Military and Office of Education*]
CRP............ Coordinated Reconnaissance Plan (CINC)
CRP............ Coordinated Resources Plan
CRP............ Corporate Air Travel, Inc. [*Tallahassee, FL*] [*FAA designator*] (FAAC)
CRP............ Corpus Christi [*Texas*] [*Airport symbol*] (OAG)
CRP............ Cosmic Ray Particle
CRP............ Cost Reduction Program [*Economics*] (AFM)
crp .... Creoles and Pidgins [*MARC language code*] [*Library of Congress*] (LCCP)
Cr P............ Criminal Procedure [*Legal term*] (DLA)
CRP............ Crimp [*Engineering*]
CRP............ Crisis Relocation Plans [*Federal Emergency Management Agency*]
CRP............ Cross-Reference Project
CRP............ Crystal River Plant (NRCH)
CRP............ Cuban Refugee Program [*HEW*]
CRP............ Cyclic-AMP [*Adenosine Monophosphate*] Receptor Protein [*Also, CAP*] [*Genetics*]
CRP............ Riverside City and County Public Library, Riverside, CA [*OCLC symbol*] (OCLC)
CRPA........ C-Reactive Protein Antiserum [*Clinical chemistry*]
CRPA........ Controlled Radiation [*or Reception*] Pattern Antenna
CRPADH .. Clinical Research Practices and Drug Regulatory Affairs [*A publication*]
CRPAG...... Calendar Reform Political Action Group (EA)
Cr Pat Dec ... Cranch's Decisions on Patent Appeals [*A publication*] (DLA)
CRPB........ Cerprobe Corp. [*NASDAQ symbol*] (NQ)
CRPC........ Centre for Research on Perception and Cognition [*University of Sussex*] [*British*] (CB)
CRPD........ Clinical Research Practices and Drug Regulatory Affairs [*A publication*]
CR (Petersb) ... Compte Rendu. Commission Imperiale Archeologique (St. Petersbourg) [*A publication*]
CRPF .... Chloroquine-Resistant Plasmodium Falciparum [*Chemoprophylaxis*]
CRPG........ Centre de Recherches Petrographiques et Geochimiques [*Center for Petrographic and Geochemical Research*] [*Information service or system*] (IID)
CRPG........ CR/PL, Inc. [*Evanston, IL*] [*NASDAQ symbol*] (NQ)
CRPH .... Conference on Research in Peace History (EA)
Cr & Ph ...... Craig and Phillips' English Chancery Reports [*1840-41*] [*A publication*] (DLA)
CRPI .... Control Rod Position Indication [*Nuclear energy*] (NRCH)
CRPL........ Central Radio Propagation Laboratory [*Later, ITS*]
CRPL........ Centre for Research in Philosophy and Literature [*University of Warwick*] [*British*] (CB)
CRPL........ Chromium Plate [*Metallurgy*]
CRPL........ Consolidated Repair Parts List (MCD)
CRPL........ Cosmic Rays Physics Laboratory (NASA)
CRPLF....... Communaute des Radios Publiques de Langue Francaise (EAIO)
CRPM....... Combined Registered Publication Memorandum
CRPM....... Communication Registered Publication Memoranda
CRPO .... Consolidated Reserve Personnel Office [*Air Force*] (AFM)
CRPO .... Continuous Rating Permitting Over-Load
CRPOCS ... Cultural Resources Protection on the Outer Continental Shelf [*Oceanography*] (MSC)
Crp Rpt KC ... Corporate Report Kansas City [*A publication*]
Crp Rpt MN ... Corporate Report Minnesota [*A publication*]
CRpS.......... California State College, Sonoma, Rohnert Park, CA [*Library symbol*] [*Library of Congress*] (LCLS)
CRPS .... Cuban Refugee Program Staff [*HEW*]
CRPSA ...... Crop Science [*A publication*]
CRPSD3 ... CRC [*Chemical Rubber Company*] Reviews in Plant Sciences [*A publication*]
CRPT .... Carpet [*Classified advertising*] (ADA)
CRPV........ Canister Return Purge Valve [*Automotive engineering*]
CRPV........ Cottontail Rabbit Papillomavirus
CR PV Mem Ass Breton ... Compte Rendu. Proces-Verbaux et Memoires. Association Bretonne [*A publication*]
CRQ........... Air Creebec [*Val D'Or, PQ, Canada*] [*FAA designator*] (FAAC)
CRQ........... Call Request [*Telecommunications*] (TEL)
CRQ........... Carlsbad, CA [*Location identifier*] [*FAA*] (FAAL)
CRQ........... Commutation of Rations and Quarters [*Military*]
CRQ........... Console Reply Queuing
CrQ............ Critical Quarterly [*A publication*]
CRQ........... Current Requirements
CR & R....... Calibration, Repair, and Return

CRR .... Canadian Regulatory Reporter [*Database*] [*Canadian Law Information Council*] [*Information service or system*] (CRD)
CRR .... Carrizo [*California*] [*Seismograph station code, US Geological Survey*] (SEIS)
CRR .... Center for Radiation Research [*National Institute of Standards and Technology*]
CRR .... Center for Reformation Research (EA)
CRR .... Center for Renewable Resources (EA)
CRR .... Chandler Flyers [*Chandler, AZ*] [*ICAO designator*] (FAAC)
CRR .... Chief Registrar's Reports [*England*] [*A publication*] (DLA)
CRR .... Chinese Refugee Relief [*Defunct*] (EA)
CRR .... Churchill Research Range [*Air Force*]
CRR .... Circle, MT [*Location identifier*] [*FAA*] (FAAL)
CRR .... Clutter Rejection RADAR
CRR .... [*The*] Coinage of the Roman Republic [*A publication*] (OCD)
CRR .... Combat Readiness Requirements [*Canadian Navy*]
CRR .... Combat Ready Rate (MCD)
CRR .... Committee for the Restoration of the Republic (EA)
CRR .... Complete Remission Rate [*Oncology*]
CRR .... Compte Rendu. Rencontre Assyriologique Internationale [*A publication*]
CRR .... Computer Run Report (NASA)
CRR .... Conservation Research Report [*A publication*]
CRR .... Consolidated Rail Corp. [*NYSE symbol*] (SPSG)
CRR .... Consolidated Rambler Mines Ltd. [*Toronto Stock Exchange symbol*]
CRR .... Constant Ringing Relay [*Alarm system*]
CRR .... Consumer's Reliability Risk
CRR .... Contemporaneous Reserve Requirements [*Banking*]
CRR .... Contractor Reports Register
crr.............. Corrector [*MARC relator code*] [*Library of Congress*] (LCCP)
CRR .... Cost Reduction Report [*Economics*]
CRR .... Cost Reporting Requirements
Cr R .... Criminal Reports [*A publication*]
CRR .... Critical Requirements Review (NASA)
Cr R .... Curia Regis Rolls [*British*] [*Legal term*] (DLA)
CRRA .... Compte Rendu. Rencontre Assyriologique Internationale [*A publication*]
CRRAG ..... Countryside Recreation Research Advisory Group [*British*]
CRRC........ Cold Regions Research Company (MCD)
CRRC........ Community Resource and Research Center [*University of Nebraska - Lincoln*] [*Research center*] (RCD)
CRRC........ Construction Requirements Review Committee [*Military*] (AABC)
CRRC......... Courier Corporation [*NASDAQ symbol*] (NQ)
CRRC......... Cream Ridge Fruit Research Center [*Rutgers University*] [*Research center*] (RCD)
CRRDB...... CRC [*Chemical Rubber Company*] Critical Reviews in Radiological Sciences [*A publication*]
CRRE........ Community for Religious Research and Education (EA)
CRRE........ Cross-Leveling, Redistribution, Replenishment, and Excessing (MCD)
CR Rech Bibl Immigr ... Comptes Rendus de Recherches et Bibliographie sur l'Immigration [*A publication*]
CR Rech Inst Encour Rech Sci Ind Agric ... Comptes Rendus de Recherches. Institut pour l'Encouragement de la Recherche Scientifique dans l'Industrie et l'Agriculture [*Belgium*] [*A publication*]
CRRED...... Carbonization Research Report [*A publication*]
CRREF ...... Cross Reference
CRREL...... Cold Regions Research and Engineering Laboratory [*Hanover, NH*] [*Army*] [*Also, an information service or system*] (IID)
CRREL...... CRREL [*Cold Regions Research and Engineering Laboratory*] Report [*United States*] [*A publication*]
CRRELDT ... CRREL [*Cold Regions Research and Engineering Laboratory*] Draft Translation [*United States*] [*A publication*]
CRREL Monograph ... Cold Regions Research and Engineering Laboratory. Monograph [*A publication*]
CRRELR ... CRREL [*Cold Regions Research and Engineering Laboratory*] Report [*United States*] [*A publication*]
CRREL Rep ... CRREL [*Cold Regions Research and Engineering Laboratory*] Report [*A publication*]
CRREL Report ... Cold Regions Research and Engineering Laboratory. Report [*A publication*]
CRRELRR ... CRREL [*Cold Regions Research and Engineering Laboratory*] Research Reports [*United States*] [*A publication*]
CRRELSR ... CRREL [*Cold Regions Research and Engineering Laboratory*] Special Report [*United States*] [*A publication*]
CRRELTR ... CRREL [*Cold Regions Research and Engineering Laboratory*] Technical Reports [*United States*] [*A publication*]
CR Rencontre Moriond ... Compte Rendu de la Rencontre de Moriond [*A publication*]
Cr Rep........ Criminal Reports [*A publication*]
CRRERI .... Commonwealth Regional Renewable Energy Resources Index [*A publication*] (APTA)
CRRERIS.. Commonwealth Regional Renewable Energy Resources Information Service (IID)
CRRES .... Chemical Release and Radiation Effects Satellite [*NASA*]
Cr Rg......... Criminal Rulings [*Bombay, India*] [*A publication*] (DLA)
CRRL......... Contour Rolls (AAG)

CRRN .... Certified Rehabilitation Registered Nurse
CRR of NJ ... Central Railroad Co. of New Jersey [*Absorbed into Consolidated Rail Corp.*]
CRRS .... Combat Readiness Rating System [*Air Force*]
CRRS .... Crown Resources Corp. [*NASDAQ symbol*] (NQ)
CRRSDD... Cretaceous Research [*A publication*]
CRRT .... Children's Reading Round Table
CRRVAJ ... Chromatographic Reviews [*A publication*]
CRS .... Cable Reinforcement Set (MCD)
CRS .... Cable Running Sheets
CRS .... Calibration Recall System [*Army*]
CRS .... Calibration Requirements Summary
CRS .... Camp Reception Station [*A kind of field hospital*] [*British*]
CRS .... Camp Sentinel RADAR [*Military*] (RDA)
CRS .... Canada Remote System
CRS .... Canada Remote Systems Ltd. [*Information service or system*] (EISS)
CRS .... Canopy Removal System [*for helicopters*] (RDA)
CRS .... Capital Recovery Schedule
CRS .... Carbon Dioxide Reduction Subsystem (NASA)
CRS .... Career Reserve Status [*Air Force*]
CRS .... Carolina Southern Railway Co. [*AAR code*]
CRS .... Carpenter Technology Corp. [*Formerly, Carpenter Steel Co.*] [*NYSE symbol*] (SPSG)
CRS .... Case Review Section [*Social Security Administration*] (OICC)
CRS .... Cash by Return Steamer [*Business term*]
CRS .... Catholic Record Society (EA)
CRS .... Catholic Relief Services [*Later, CRS-USCC*]
CRS .... Catholic Renascence Society [*Defunct*] (EA)
CRS .... Caudill, Rowlett & Scott [*Architectural firm*]
CRS .... Center on Religion and Society (EA)
CRS .... Center for Rural Studies [*University of Vermont*] [*Research center*] (RCD)
CRS .... Central Recorder Subsystem [*NASA*]
CRS .... Central Reference Supply
CRS .... Central Repeater System (MCD)
CRS .... Centralized Referral System [*Military*] (AFM)
CRS .... Centralized Results System [*Telecommunications*] (TEL)
CRS .... Centre for Remote Sensing [*Imperial College of Science and Technology*] [*British*]
CRS .... Centre for Resource Studies [*Queen's University at Kingston*] [*Canada*] [*Research center*] (RCD)
CRS .... Certified Residential Specialist [*Designation awarded by Realtors National Marketing Institute of the National Association of Realtors*]
CRS .... Chain RADAR System
CRS .... Charismatic Renewal Services (EA)
CRS .... Check Reporting Service
CRS .... Chief Radio Supervisor [*Australia*]
CRS .... Chinese Restaurant Syndrome [*Monosodium glutamate sensitivity*] [*Medicine*]
CRS .... Christian Record Services (EA)
CRS .... Cis Repressor Sequence [*Genetics*]
CRS .... Clericorum Regularium Somaschensium [*Clerics Regular of Somasca*] [*Somascan Fathers*] [*Roman Catholic religious order*]
CRS .... Co-Operative Retail Services [*British*]
CRS .... Coarse (AAG)
CRS .... Coelliptic Rendezvous Sequence [*Aerospace*]
CRS .... Cold-Rolled Steel
CRS .... Collectors Record Society [*Record label*]
CRS .... Colon and Rectal Surgery [*Medicine*]
CRS .... Command Readout Station [*Military*]
CRS .... Command Relationship Study
CRS .... Command Retrieval System (DEN)
CRS .... Commonwealth Record Series [*Australia*]
CRS .... Communications Relay Set (MCD)
CRS .... Community Relations Service [*Terminated*] [*Department of Justice*]
CRS .... Community Research Services [*Illinois State University*] [*Normal*] [*Information service or system*] (IID)
CRS .... Component Repair Squadron (MCD)
CRS .... Computer Reservation System
CRS .... Computerized Radiology Society [*Later, CMIS*] (EA)
CRS .... Computerized Reference Service [*William Paterson College of New Jersey*] (OLDSS)
CRS .... Computerized Retrieval Service
CRS .... Conductivity Recording Switch [*Nuclear energy*] (NRCH)
CRS .... Congenital Rubella Syndrome [*Medicine*]
CRS .... Congressional Research Service [*Formerly, Legislative Reference Service*] [*Library of Congress*] [*Washington, DC*] [*OCLC symbol*]
CRS .... Containment Recirculation Spray System [*Nuclear energy*] (NRCH)
CRS .... Containment Rupture Signal [*Nuclear energy*] (IEEE)
CRS .... Contingency Retention Stock [*Military*] (AFIT)
CRS .... Contract Repair Service (MCD)
CRS .... Contractor Relations Specialist [*DoD*]
CRS .... Control and Reporting System (NATG)
CRS .... Controlled Release Society (EA)

CRS .... Cooperative Recreation Service [*Later, World Around Songs*] (EA)
CRS .... Cooperative Research Service [*Kentucky State University*] [*Research center*] (RCD)
CRS .... Correctional Reporting System [*Army*]
CRS .... Corsicana, TX [*Location identifier*] [*FAA*] (FAAL)
CRS .... Cosmic Ray Shower
CRS .... Cosmic-Ray Subsystem [*Astrophysics*]
CRS .... Council of Rehabilitation Specialists (EA)
CRS .... Countermeasures Receiving Set
CRS .... Course (AABC)
CRS .... Creation Research Society (EA)
CRS .... Creative Research Systems [*Information service or system*] (IID)
CRS .... Crescent (ADA)
CRS .... Crescent Airways, Inc. [*Hollywood, FL*] [*FAA designator*] (FAAC)
CRS .... Crescent Mines Ltd. [*Vancouver Stock Exchange symbol*]
CRS .... Crew Reserve Status [*Military*] (AFM)
CrS .... Cristianesimo nella Storia [*A publication*]
CrS .... Critica Storica [*A publication*]
CRS .... Cross (ADA)
CRS .... Cross-Section
CRS .... Crypto Radio Service
CRS .... Cubic Spline Regression [*Statistics*]
CRS .... Customer Reaction Survey
CRSA .... Administration Sciences Research Centre [*University of Moncton*] [*Canada*] [*Research center*] (RCD)
CRSA .... Canadian Regional Science Association [*See also ACSR*]
CRSA .... Canadian Review of Sociology and Anthropology [*A publication*]
CRSA .... Centralized Repair Service Attendants [*Telecommunications*] (TEL)
CRSA .... Control Rod Scram Accumulator [*Nuclear energy*] (IEEE)
CRSAIBL.. Comptes Rendus des Seances. Academie des Inscriptions et Belles-Lettres [*A publication*]
CRSAS ...... Centro Regional de Sismologia para America del Sur [*Regional Center for Seismology for South America - RCSSA*] (EAIO)
CRSB .... Center for Research in Social Behavior [*University of Missouri - Columbia*] [*Research center*] (RCD)
CRSBA ...... Comptes Rendus des Seances. Societe de Biologie et de Ses Filiales [*A publication*]
CRSC .... Californian Rabbit Specialty Club (EA)
CRSC .... Center for Remote Sensing and Cartography [*University of Utah Research Institute*] [*Research center*] (RCD)
CRSC .... Center for Research in Scientific Communication [*Johns Hopkins University*] (IID)
CRSC .... Center for Research in Social Change [*Emory University, Atlanta, GA*] (IID)
CRSC .... Chemicals Review Sub-Committee [*Australia*]
CRSC .... Contract Review and Selection Criteria [*DoD*]
CRSCT ...... Crescent (ROG)
CRSD .... Contractor Required Shipment Date
CRSDA ...... Community Recreation and Skill Development Activities (AABC)
CRSE .... Central Research and Support Establishment [*Information service or system*] (EISS)
CRSE .... Course
CR Seance Publ Ann Acad Pharm ... Comptes Rendus de la Seance Publique Annuelle. Academie de la Pharmacie [*A publication*]
CR Seances Acad Agric Fr ... Comptes Rendus des Seances. Academie d'Agriculture de France [*A publication*]
CR Seances Acad Sci Roum ... Comptes Rendus des Seances. Academie des Sciences de Roumanie [*A publication*]
CR Seances Acad Sci Ser A ... Comptes Rendus des Seances. Academie des Sciences. Serie A. Sciences Mathematiques [*France*] [*A publication*]
CR Seances Acad Sci Ser B ... Comptes Rendus des Seances. Academie des Sciences. Serie B. Sciences Physiques [*France*] [*A publication*]
CR Seances Acad Sci Ser C ... Comptes Rendus des Seances. Academie des Sciences. Serie C. Sciences Chimiques [*France*] [*A publication*]
CR Seances Acad Sci Ser D ... Comptes Rendus des Seances. Academie des Sciences. Serie D. Sciences Naturelles [*France*] [*A publication*]
CR Seances Acad Sci Ser I ... Comptes Rendus de Seances. Academie des Sciences. Serie I. Mathematique [*A publication*]
CR Seances Acad Sci Ser II ... Comptes Rendus des Seances. Academie des Sciences. Serie II. Mecanique, Physique, Chimie, Sciences de la Terre, Sciences de l'Univers [*A publication*]
CR Seances Acad Sci Ser III ... Comptes Rendus des Seances. Academie des Sciences. Serie III. Sciences de la Vie [*A publication*]
CR Seances Acad Sci Ser III Sci Vie ... Comptes Rendus de Seances. Academie des Sciences. Serie III. Sciences de la Vie [*A publication*]
CR Seances Acad Sci Vie Acad ... Comptes Rendus des Seances. Academie des Sciences. Vie Academique [*A publication*]
CR Seances Inst Geol Roum ... Comptes Rendus des Seances. Institut Geologique de Roumanie [*A publication*]

CR Seances Mens Soc Sci Nat Phys Maroc ... Comptes Rendus des Seances Mensuelles. Societe des Sciences Naturelles et Physiques du Maroc [*A publication*]
CR Seances Soc Biogeogr ... Compte Rendu des Seances. Societe de Biogeographie [*A publication*]
CR Seances Soc Biol Fil ... Comptes Rendus des Seances. Societe de Biologie et de Ses Filiales [*A publication*]
CR Seances Soc Biol (Paris) ... Comptes Rendus des Seances. Societe de Biologie (Paris) [*A publication*]
CR Seances Soc Phys Hist Nat Geneve ... Compte Rendu des Seances. Societe de Physique et d'Histoire Naturelle de Geneve [*A publication*]
CR Seanc Mens Soc Sci Nat Phys Maroc ... Comptes Rendus des Seances Mensuelles. Societe des Sciences Naturelles et Physiques du Maroc [*A publication*]
CR Seanc Soc Biol ... Comptes Rendus des Seances. Societe de Biologie [*A publication*]
CR Seanc Soc Biol Fil ... Comptes Rendus des Seances. Societe de Biologie et de Ses Filiales [*A publication*]
CR Sem Geol Com Nat Malgache Geol ... Comptes Rendus de la Semaine Geologique. Comite National Malgache de Geologie [*A publication*]
CRSF .... CUNA [*Credit Union National Association*] Retirement Savings Fund
CRSFF .... Central Region SEATO [*Southeast Asia Treaty Organization*] Field Forces   (CINC)
CRSHA ...... Circulatory Shock [*A publication*]
CRSHAG .... Circulatory Shock [*A publication*]
CRSHC ...... Conseil de Recherches en Sciences Humaines du Canada [*Social Sciences and Humanities Research Council of Canada - SSHRCC*]
CRSHD ..... Crosshead   (MSA)
CRSI .... Ceramic Reusable Surface Insulation   (NASA)
CRSI .... Concrete Reinforcing Steel Institute   (EA)
CRSIGR .... Comptes Rendus des Seances. Institut de Geologie Roumaine [*A publication*]
CRSL .... Comptes Rendus. Societe des Sciences et des Lettres de Lodz [*A publication*]
CRSL .... Computer Recognition Systems Ltd. [*British*]
CRSLub ..... Comptes Rendus. Societe des Sciences et des Lettres. Universite Catholique de Lublin [*A publication*]
CRSM .... Calcium-Reduced Skim Milk
CRSM .... Center for Robotic Systems in Microelectronics [*Research center*]   (RCD)
CRSM .... Certified Real Estate Securities Member [*Designation awarded by Real Estate Securities and Syndication Institute of the National Association of Realtors*]   (MSA)
CRSN .... Corrosion
CRS-NCWC ... Catholic Relief Services - National Catholic Welfare Conference [*Later, CRS-USCC*]   (EA)
CRSO .... Cellular Radio Switching Office [*Telecommunications*]
CRSO .... Center for Research on Social Organization [*University of Michigan*] [*Research center*]   (RCD)
CRSOA ...... Crops and Soils [*A publication*]
CR Soc Biol ... Comptes Rendus des Seances. Societe de Biologie et de Ses Filiales [*A publication*]
CR Soc Biol (Paris) ... Comptes Rendus des Seances. Societe de Biologie (Paris) [*A publication*]
CR Soc Franc Gynec ... Comptes Rendus. Societe Francaise de Gynecologie [*A publication*]
CR Soc Fr Gynecol ... Comptes Rendus. Societe Francaise de Gynecologie [*A publication*]
CR Soc Geol Fr ... Comptes Rendus Sommaire des Seances. Societe Geologique de France [*A publication*]
CR Soc Roy Econ Pol ... Comptes Rendus des Travaux. Societe Royale d'Economie Politique de Belgique [*A publication*]
CR Soc Sci Nat Phys Maroc ... Comptes Rendus des Seances Mensuelles. Societe des Sciences Naturelles et Physiques du Maroc [*A publication*]
CR Somm Seances Soc Geol Fr ... Compte Rendu Sommaire des Seances. Societe Geologique de France [*A publication*]
CR Somm Seanc Soc Biogeogr ... Compte Rendu Sommaire des Seances. Societe de Biogeographie [*A publication*]
CR Som Seances Soc Geol Fr ... Comptes Rendus Sommaire des Seances. Societe Geologique de France [*A publication*]
CRSP .... Center for Research in Security Prices [*University of Chicago*] [*Chicago, IL*] [*Information service or system*]   (IID)
CRSP .... Clerici Regulares Pauperum Matris Dei Scholarum Piarum [*Clerics Regular of the Poor Men of the Mother of God for Pious Schools*] [*Piarists*] [*Roman Catholic religious order*]
CRSP .... Clerici Regulares Sancti Pauli [*Clerics Regular of St. Paul*] [*Barnabites*] [*Also, Barn*] [*Roman Catholic men's religious order*]
CRSP .... Collaborative Research Support Program [*Agency for International Development*]
CRSP .... Colorado River Storage Project [*Department of the Interior*]
CRSP .... Comptes Rendus. Societe des Sciences et des Lettres de Poznan [*A publication*]
Cr S & P ..... Craigie, Stewart, and Paton's Scotch Appeal Cases [*1726-1821*] [*A publication*]   (DLA)
CRSP .... Criminally Receiving Stolen Property

CRSPPA .... International Pen-Pals Association [*Acronym is based on former name, Cross River State Pen-Pals Association*]   (EAIO)
CRSQ .... Creation Research Society. Quarterly [*A publication*]
CRSR .... Center for Radiophysics and Space Research [*Cornell University*] [*Research center*]
CRSS .... California Rug Study Society   (EA)
CRSS .... Canadian Remote Sensing Society   (EAIO)
CRSS .... Certified Real Estate Securities Sponsor [*Designation awarded by Real Estate Securities and Syndication Institute of the National Association of Realtors*]
CRSS .... Chemically Rigidized Space Structure
CRS(S) ...... Chief Radio Supervisor (Special) [*British military*]   (DMA)
CRSS .... Children's Reinforcement Survey Schedule
CRSS .... Critical Resolved Shear Stress
CRST .... Calcinosis, Raynaud's Phenomenon, Sclerodactyly, and Telangiectasia [*A medical syndrome*]
CRST .... [*The*] Claremont Ras Shamra Tablets [*A publication*]   (BJA)
CRST .... Cold Regions Science and Technology [*A publication*]
Cr & St ...... Craigie, Stewart, and Paton's Scotch Appeal Cases [*1726-1821*] [*A publication*]   (DLA)
CRST .... Crestek, Inc. [*Trenton, NJ*] [*NASDAQ symbol*]   (NQ)
CRST .... Crystallographic [*Origin*] [*Of precious stones*]
CRSTB ..... Proceedings. Conference on Remote Systems Technology [*A publication*]
CRSTD ...... Cold Regions Science and Technology [*A publication*]
CRSTIAC ... Cold Regions Science and Technology Information Analysis Center [*DoD*]   (MSC)
CRSTPA .... Columbia River Salmon and Tuna Packers Association   (EA)
CRSUPT ... Construction Superintendent   (FAAC)
CRSUPVR ... Construction Supervisor   (FAAC)
CRS-USCC ... Catholic Relief Services - US Catholic Conference   (EA)
CRSV .... Carnation Ringspot Virus
CRSV .... Corrosive   (MSA)
CRSVa .... Comptes Rendus. Societe des Sciences et des Lettres de Varsovie [*A publication*]
CRSVI .... Conference Regionale du Service Volontaire International [*Regional Conference on International Voluntary Service*]   (EAIO)
CRSVR ...... Crossover [*Technical drawings*]   (MSA)
CRS(W) ...... Chief Radio Supervisor (Warfare) [*British military*]   (DMA)
CRSW .... Comptes Rendus. Societe des Sciences et des Lettres de Wroclaw [*A publication*]
CR Symp Int Jets Mol ... Comptes Rendus. Symposium International sur les Jets Moleculaires [*A publication*]
CRT .... C-Band RADAR Transponder
CRT .... Canadian Railway Troops [*World War I*]
CRT .... Cardiac Resuscitation Team [*Medicine*]
CRT .... Cartuja [*Granada*] [*Spain*] [*Seismograph station code, US Geological Survey*]   (SEIS)
CRT .... Cash Register Tape
CRT .... Cathode-Ray Terminal
CRT .... Cathode-Ray Tube
CRT .... Cathode-Ray Typesetting
CRT .... Center for Rehabilitation Technology [*Georgia Institute of Technology*] [*Research center*]   (RCD)
CRT .... Centre de Recherche sur les Transports [*Center for Transport Research*] [*University of Montreal*] [*Research center*]   (RCD)
CRT .... Centre for Rural Transport [*St. David's University College*] [*British*]   (CB)
CRT .... Certainteed Corp. [*NYSE symbol*]   (SPSG)
CRT .... Charactron Tube [*Electronics*]
CRT .... Chief Radio Technician [*Navy rating*] [*Obsolete*]
CRT .... Circuit Requirement Table   (MSA)
CRT .... Classroom Trainer   (MCD)
CRT .... Clerici Regulares Theatini [*Theatines*] [*Roman Catholic religious order*]
CRT .... Cold-Rolled and Tempered [*Metal*]
CR & T ...... Columbia River and Tributaries Study   (NOAA)
CRT .... Combat Rated Thrust [*Navy*]   (NG)
CRT .... Combat Reaction Time
CRT .... Combat Readiness Trainer [*or Training*]
CRT .... Combined Radiation Test
CRT .... Combined Radiation Treatment [*Oncology*]
CRT .... Composite-Rate Tax [*British*]
CRT .... Composite Readiness Test
CRT .... Computer Remote Terminal   (MCD)
CRT .... Continuous Ring Tone [*Telecommunications*]   (TEL)
CRT .... Control of Radio Transmission [*British*] [*World War II*]
CRT .... Control Route Tag   (MCD)
CRT .... Copyright Royalty Tribunal [*Library of Congress*]
CRT .... Correct   (MUGU)
CRT .... CorRecTerm [*Mergenthaler typesetting*]
CRT .... Cortisone-Resistant Thymocyte [*Biochemistry*]
CRT .... Cosmic Ray Telescope
CRT .... Count Reduction Technique [*Food bacteriology*]
CRT .... Counter Recovery Time
CRT .... Court
CRT .... Crate
Crt .... Crater [*Constellation*]

CRT .... Criterion-Referenced Test [*or Testing*] [*Education*]
CRT .... Crossett, AR [*Location identifier*] [*FAA*]   (FAAL)
CRT .... Crown Trust Co. [*Toronto Stock Exchange symbol*]
CRT .... Current Transformer
Crt .... With Certificate [*Philately*]
8CRT .... Eight Card Redrawing Test [*Psychology*]
CRTA .... Chief of Rocket Troops and Artillery   (MCD)
CRTB .... Critical Reasoning Test Battery
CRTC .... Canadian Radio-Television and Telecommunications
              Commission [*Conseil de la Radiodiffusion et des
              Telecommunications Canadiennes*] [*Ottawa, ON*]
              [*Telecommunications*]
CRTC .... Canadian Railway and Transport Cases [*A publication*]   (DLA)
CRTC .... Cathode-Ray Tube Controller
CRTC .... Cavalry Replacement Training Center
CRTC .... Circle Repertory Theater Company
CRTC .... Cold Regions Test Center [*Army*] [*Seattle, WA*]   (RDA)
CRTD .... Cold Regions Technical Digest [*A publication*]
CRTED .... Crystal Research and Technology [*A publication*]
CRTF .... Central Receiver Test Facility [*Department of Energy*]
CRTF .... Core Restraint Test Facility [*Nuclear energy*]   (NRCH)
CRTF .... Corporate Responsibility Task Force of the Business
              Roundtable   (EA)
CRTFCA .... Chicago Religious Task Force on Central America   (EA)
CRTFP ...... Commission des Relations de Travail dans la Fonction
              Publique [*Public Service Staff Relations Board - PSSRB*]
              [*Canada*]
CRTFY ...... Certify   (FAAC)
CRTG .... Cartridge   (MSA)
CRTH .... Council for Research on Turkish History [*Defunct*]   (EA)
CRTI .... Center for the Rights of the Terminally Ill   (EA)
CRTIS .... Chicago Railroad Terminal Information System [*Pronounced
              "Curtis"*]
CRTK .... Cardinal Technologies, Inc. [*NASDAQ symbol*]   (NQ)
CRTL .... Criticality
CRTN .... Carton [*Packaging*]
CRTN .... Certron Corp. [*NASDAQ symbol*]   (NQ)
CRTN .... Correction   (MUGU)
CRTO .... Cathode-Ray Tube Oscillograph
CRTOG ...... Cartographer [*or Cartography*]   (AFM)
CRTP .... Consciousness Research and Training Project   (EA)
CRTR .... Charter-Crellin, Inc. [*New York, NY*] [*NASDAQ
              symbol*]   (NQ)
CRTR .... Courtier
CRTR .... Current Retail Trade Reports [*A publication*]
CR Trav Carlsb ... Comptes Rendus des Travaux. Laboratoire Carlsberg [*A
              publication*]
CR Trav Fac Sci Univ Aix Marseille ... Comptes Rendus des Travaux. Faculte
              des Sciences. Universite de l'Aix Marseille [*A publication*]
CR Trav Lab Carlsberg ... Comptes Rendus des Travaux. Laboratoire
              Carlsberg [*A publication*]
CR Trav Lab Carlsberg Ser Chim ... Comptes Rendus des Travaux.
              Laboratoire Carlsberg. Serie Chimique [*A publication*]
CR Trav Lab Carlsberg Ser Physiol ... Comptes Rendus des Travaux.
              Laboratoire Carlsberg. Serie Physiologique [*A publication*]
CR Trim Acad Sci O-Mer ... Comptes Rendus Trimestriels. Academie des
              Sciences d'Outre-Mer [*A publication*]
CR Tr Lab C ... Comptes Rendus des Travaux. Laboratoire Carlsberg [*A
              publication*]
CRTS .... Cathode-Ray Tube Shield
CRTS .... COMINT [*Communications Intelligence*] Receiver Test
              System   (MCD)
CRTS .... Constant Returns to Scale [*Econometrics*]
CRTS .... Controllable RADAR Target Simulator
CRTSEO .... CRC [*Chemical Rubber Company*] Critical Reviews in
              Therapeutic Drug Carrier Systems [*A publication*]
CRTT .... Cathode-Ray Tube Tester
CRTT .... Certified Respiratory Therapy Technician
CRTU .... Combined Receiving and Transmitting Unit
CRTV .... Composite Reentry Test Vehicle   (MCD)
CRTV .... Creative Technologies Corp. [*NASDAQ symbol*]   (NQ)
CRTXA ...... Cortex [*A publication*]
CRTY .... Commonwealth Realty Trust [*NASDAQ symbol*]   (NQ)
CRU .... Card Reader Unit [*Data processing*]
CRU .... Carriacou [*Windward Islands*] [*Airport symbol*]   (OAG)
CRU .... Catalytic Reforming Unit [*Petroleum refining*]
CRu .... Ceskoslovenska Rusistika [*A publication*]
CRU .... Children's Research Unit [*Market research company*] [*British*]
CRU .... Civil Resettlement Unit [*British*]   (DAS)
CRU .... Civilian Repair Unit [*British military*]   (DMA)
CRU .... Clinical Research Unit
CRU .... Collective Reserve Unit [*International finance*]
CRU .... Combined Rotating Unit [*Nuclear energy*]
CRU .... Command and Response Unit
CRU .... Commodities Research Unit Ltd. [*Originator and Databank*]
              [*Information service or system*]   (IID)
CRU .... Compliance Review Unit   (OICC)
CRU .... Computer Resource Unit
CRU .... Constitutional Repeating Unit [*Organic chemistry*]
CRU .... Control Relay Unlatch
CRU .... Control and Reporting Unit

CRU .... Converter Regulator Unit   (MCD)
CRU .... Cooperatives Research Unit [*British*]
CRU .... Corps Reinforcement Unit [*British military*]   (DMA)
CRU .... Credit Union
CRU .... Crisan Resources Ltd. [*Vancouver Stock Exchange symbol*]
Cru .... Cruise's Digest of the Law of Real Property [*1804-35*] [*England*]
              [*A publication*]   (DLA)
CRU .... Crutchfield [*Kentucky*] [*Seismograph station code, US
              Geological Survey*]   (SEIS)
Cru .... Crux [*Constellation*]
CrU .... Universidad de Costa Rica, San Jose, Costa Rica [*Library
              symbol*] [*Library of Congress*]   (LCLS)
CRU .... University of California, Riverside, Riverside, CA [*OCLC
              symbol*]   (OCLC)
CRUBATFOR ... Cruisers, Battle Force [*Navy*]
CRUDE ..... Committee to Remove Unnatural Deposits from the
              Environment [*Student legal action organization*]
CRUDESFLOT ... Cruiser-Destroyer Flotilla [*Navy symbol*]
CRUDESLANT ... Cruiser-Destroyer Force, Atlantic Fleet [*Navy symbol*]
CRUDESPAC ... Cruiser-Destroyer Force, Pacific Fleet [*Navy symbol*]
Cru Dig ...... Cruise's Digest of the Law of Real Property [*1804-35*] [*England*]
              [*A publication*]   (DLA)
Cru Dign ..... Cruise on Dignities [*A publication*]   (DLA)
CRUDIV.... Cruiser Division [*Navy*]
CRUDZINE ... Crude Magazine [*Generic term for a one-person science-
              fiction fan magazine, produced by an inexperienced
              publisher*]
CRUEL...... Commission on Reform of Undergraduate Education and
              Living [*University of Illinois*]
Cru Fin....... Cruise's Fines and Recoveries [*A publication*]   (DLA)
CRUFON .. Citizens Radio UFO [*Unidentified Flying Object*] Network
CRUIK...... [*George*] Cruikshank [*English artist, 1792-1878*]   (ROG)
CRUIS....... Cruising   (KSC)
Cruise Dig ... Cruise's Digest of the Law of Real Property [*1804-35*] [*England*]
              [*A publication*]   (DLA)
Cruise Rep Geol Surv Jap ... Cruise Report. Geological Survey of Japan [*A
              publication*]
Cruise's Dig ... Cruise's Digest of the Law of Real Property [*1804-35*]
              [*England*] [*A publication*]   (DLA)
CRUITNOP ... Recruiting Station and Office of Naval Officer Procurement
CRUITSTA ... Recruiting Station
CRULANT ... Cruisers, Atlantic Fleet [*Navy*]
CRULANTFLT ... Cruisers, Atlantic Fleet [*Navy*]
CRUMA .... Council of Retired Union Members Associations [*Australia*]
CRUMBS.. Continuous, Remote, Unobstructive Monitoring of
              Biobehavioral Systems
Crump Ins ... Crump on Marine Insurance [*A publication*]   (DLA)
Crump Jud Pr ... Crump. Practice under the Judicature Acts [*A
              publication*]   (DLA)
Crump Mar Ins ... Crump on Marine Insurance [*A publication*]   (DLA)
Crump S & Pl ... Crump. Sale and Pledge [*A publication*]   (DLA)
Crumrine.... Crumrine's Reports [*116-146 Pennsylvania*] [*A
              publication*]   (DLA)
Crumrine.... Pittsburgh Reports, Edited by Crumrine [*A publication*]   (DLA)
CRUNCH ... Consolidated Record of Uncontrolled Naval Calamitious
              Happenings
CRUPAC... Cruisers, Pacific Fleet [*Navy*]
CRUPACFLT ... Cruisers, Pacific Fleet [*Navy*]
CRUS........ Centre for Research on User Studies [*University of Sheffield*]
              [*England*] [*Information service or system*]   (IID)
CRus .... Ceskoslovenska Rusistika [*A publication*]
CRUS........ Cirrus Logic, Inc. [*NASDAQ symbol*]   (NQ)
CRUS........ [*The*] Consultancy and Research Unit, University of Sheffield
              [*England*] [*Information service or system*]   (IID)
CRUS........ Customs Regulations of the United States
CRUSA...... Crustaceana [*Leiden*] [*A publication*]
CRUSBP ... Campaign to Remove US Bases from the Philippines [*Later,
              CAB*]   (EA)
CRUSCOFOR ... Cruiser-Scouting Force [*Navy*]
CRUSCORON ... Cruiser-Scouting Squadron [*Navy*]
Crush Grind Min Quarr J ... Crushing, Grinding, Mining, and Quarrying
              Journal [*A publication*]
Crushing Grinding Min Quarrying J ... Crushing, Grinding, Mining, and
              Quarrying Journal [*A publication*]
CRUSK...... Center for Research on Utilization of Scientific Knowledge
              [*University of Michigan*]
Crustaceana Suppl (Leiden) ... Crustaceana. Supplement (Leiden) [*A
              publication*]
CRUTEPO ... Commission Regionale de l'Utilisation des Terres et des Eaux
              au Proche-Orient [*Regional Commission on Land and
              Water Use in the Near East - RCLWUNE*]   (EAIO)
Cru Titl ...... Cruise on Titles of Honor [*A publication*]   (DLA)
Cru Us........ Cruise on Uses [*A publication*]   (DLA)
CRUZEIRO ... Servicos Aereos Cruzeiro do Sul SA [*Brazilian airline*]
CRV .... Caraveli [*Peru*] [*Seismograph station code, US Geological
              Survey*] [*Closed*]   (SEIS)
CRV .... Central Retinal Vein [*Ophthalmology*]
CRV .... Certificate of Reasonable Value [*Veterans Administration*]
CRV .... Chrome Vanadium
CRV .... Cloth, Rollers, and Varnished [*Maps*]   (ROG)
CRV .... Coast Distribution Systems [*AMEX symbol*]   (SPSG)

CRV .... Comment Recevez-Vous? [*French*]
CRV .... Committee of Returned Volunteers [*Defunct*] (EA)
CRV .... Conditional Release Violator [*FBI standardized term*]
CRV .... Contact Resistance Variation [*Telecommunications*] (TEL)
CRV .... Corvette Petroleum Corp. [*Vancouver Stock Exchange symbol*]
Crv .... Corvus [*Constellation*]
CRV .... Creditanstalt-Bankverein. Wirtschaftsberichte [*A publication*]
CRV .... Curve (MSA)
CRVAN ..... Chrome Vanadium
CRVC........ Cambridgeshire Rifle Volunteer Corps [*British military*] (DMA)
CRVC........ Cross-Range Velocity Correlator (MUGU)
CR VESP... Cras Vespere [*Tomorrow Evening*] [*Pharmacy*]
CRVI.......... Coast [*R. V.*] Incorporated [*NASDAQ symbol*] (NQ)
CRVICS..... Containment and Reactor Vessel Isolation Control System (NRCH)
CRVMAC ... CRC [*Chemical Rubber Company*] Critical Reviews in Microbiology [*A publication*]
CRVO .... Central Retinal Vein Occlusion [*Ophthalmology*]
Cr 8vo........ Crown Octavo [*Book size*]
CRVR........ Computerized Register of Voice Research [*No longer maintained*] [*Southern Illinois University at Carbondale*] [*Information service or system*] (IID)
CRVS........ California Relative Value Studies [*Medicine*] (DHSM)
CRVS........ Corvus Systems, Inc. [*NASDAQ symbol*] (NQ)
CRW .... Carrier Wave [*A form of radio transmission in code*] (KSC)
CRW .... Charleston [*West Virginia*] [*Airport symbol*] (OAG)
CRW .... Charleston, WV [*Location identifier*] [*FAA*] (FAAL)
CRW .... Cinram Ltd. [*Toronto Stock Exchange symbol*]
CRW .... Clean RADWASTE [*Radioactive waste*] [*Nuclear energy*] (NRCH)
CRW .... Commission on Rural Water [*Defunct*] (EA)
CRW .... Community Radio Watch
CRW .... Conceptual Recoilless Weapons (MCD)
CRW .... Continuous Rod Warhead (MCD)
CRW .... Control Read/Write (MCD)
CRW .... Counter-Revolutionary Warfare [*British military*] (DMA)
CRW .... Counter-Revolutionary Wing [*Special Air Service*] [*Military*] [*British*]
CRW .... Crown Crafts, Inc. [*AMEX symbol*] (SPSG)
CRWA .... Community Resources Workshop Association [*Later, NAIEC*] (EA)
CRWAD .... Conference of Research Workers in Animal Diseases (EA)
CRWC .... Connecticut River Watershed Council (EA)
CRWF........ Catalyst Resource on the Work Force and Women [*Catalyst Information Center*] [*Information service or system*] (IID)
CRWG .... Computer Resources Working Group [*Military*] (AFIT)
CRWI........ Coalition for Responsible Waste Incineration (EA)
CRWLRA .. Commission on Research of the World Leisure and Recreation Association (EA)
CRWM ...... Committee on Radioactive Waste Management [*Later, BRWM*] (EA)
CRWMP.... Commendation Ribbon with Medal Pendant [*Military decoration*]
CRWN .... Crown Books Corp. [*NASDAQ symbol*] (NQ)
CRWO .... Coding Room Watch Officer [*Navy*]
CRWP........ Census Registration Working Party [*US Military Government, Germany*]
CRWR .... Center for Research in Water Resources [*University of Texas at Austin*] [*Research center*] (RCD)
CRWR .... Centre for Rural Welfare Research [*Riverina-Murray Institute of Higher Education*] [*Australia*]
CRWRC..... Christian Reformed World Relief Committee (EA)
CRWSD4... West Virginia University. Agricultural and Forestry Experiment Station. Current Report [*A publication*]
CRWSS ..... Condensate and Refueling Water Storage System [*Nuclear energy*] (NRCH)
Cr Wtg ...... Creative Writing [*A publication*]
CRX .... Corinth, MS [*Location identifier*] [*FAA*] (FAAL)
CRX .... Crownx, Inc. [*Toronto Stock Exchange symbol*]
CRX .... CRSS, Inc. [*NYSE symbol*] (SPSG)
CRY .... Chrysolite [*Jewelry*] (ROG)
CRY .... Clovis, NM [*Location identifier*] [*FAA*] (FAAL)
CRY .... Crystal [*or Crystallography*]
CRYBA...... Cryobiology [*A publication*]
Crybiol .... Cryobiology [*A publication*]
Cry Calif .... Cry California [*A publication*]
CRYD .... Cryodynamics, Inc. [*Mountainside, NJ*] [*NASDAQ symbol*] (NQ)
CRYG .... Carrying (MSA)
CRYNG ..... Carrying [*Freight*]
CRYO .... Cryogenic
CRYO .... Cryotech Industries, Inc. [*Tallahassee, FL*] [*NASDAQ symbol*] (NQ)
CRYOA ...... Cryogenics [*England*] [*A publication*]
CRYOG ..... Cryogenic (KSC)
Cryog......... Cryogenics [*A publication*]
Cryog Eng .. Cryogenic Engineering [*Japan*] [*A publication*]
Cryog Eng News ... Cryogenic Engineering News [*A publication*]
Cryog & Ind Gases ... Cryogenic and Industrial Gases [*A publication*]

Cryog Suppl ... Cryogenics. Supplement [*A publication*]
Cryog Technol ... Cryogenic Technology [*A publication*]
Cryo Lett ... Cryo Letters [*A publication*]
CRYOSAR ... Cryostatic Switching-Avalanche and Recombination (MCD)
CRYPTA ... Cryptanalysis [*Air Force*] (AFM)
CRYPTO ... Cryptographic [*or Cryptography*] (AFM)
Cryptogam Bryol Lichenol ... Cryptogamie: Bryologie et Lichenologie [*A publication*]
Cryptogamica Helv ... Cryptogamica Helvetica [*A publication*]
CRYPTONET ... Crypto-Communication Network (MDG)
CRYS ... Crystal
Crys Lattice Defects ... Crystal Lattice Defects [*Later, Crystal Lattice Defects and Amorphous Materials*] [*A publication*]
CRYSNET ... Crystallographic Computing Network [*AEC*] (IID)
CRYST ...... Crystal [*or Crystalline or Crystallize or Crystallography*]
CRYSTAL ... Crystallography (ROG)
CRYSTALLOG ... Crystallography (ROG)
Crystallogr Comput Tech Proc Int Summer Sch ... Crystallographic Computing Techniques. Proceedings of an International Summer School [*A publication*]
Crystallogr (Sov Phys) ... Crystallography (Soviet Physics) [*A publication*]
Cryst Chem Non-Met Mater ... Crystal Chemistry of Non-Metallic Materials [*A publication*]
CRYSTD ... Crystallized
Cryst Field Eff Met Alloys (Proc Int Conf) ... Crystal Field Effects in Metals and Alloys (Proceedings of the International Conference on Crystal Field Effects in Metals and Alloys) [*A publication*]
Cryst Latt... Crystal Lattice Defects [*Later, Crystal Lattice Defects and Amorphous Materials*] [*A publication*]
Cryst Lattice Defects ... Crystal Lattice Defects [*Later, Crystal Lattice Defects and Amorphous Materials*] [*A publication*]
Cryst Lattice Defects Amorphous Mater ... Crystal Lattice Defects and Amorphous Materials [*A publication*]
Cryst Lattice Defects and Amorphous Mater ... Crystal Lattice Defects and Amorphous Materials [*A publication*]
CRYSTMET ... Metals Crystallographic Data File [*Canada Institute for Scientific and Technical Information*] [*Information service or system*] (CRD)
CRYSTN ... Crystallization
Cryst Res and Technol ... Crystal Research and Technology [*A publication*]
Cryst Res Technol ... Crystal Research and Technology [*A publication*]
Cryst Struct Commun ... Crystal Structure Communications [*Italy*] [*A publication*]
CRZ .... Cape Reinga [*New Zealand*] [*Seismograph station code, US Geological Survey*] (SEIS)
CRZ .... Close Reconnaissance Zone [*Army*] (AABC)
CRZ .... Corning, IA [*Location identifier*] [*FAA*] (FAAL)
CRZ .... Cruise (FAAC)
CRZLAT ... Communication. Centre de Recherches Zootechniques. Universite de Louvain [*A publication*]
CRZWTR .. Cruise Well to Right [*Aviation*] (FAAC)
CRZY........ Crazy Eddie, Inc. [*Edison, NJ*] [*NASDAQ symbol*] (NQ)
CS .... Adventist Community Services (EA)
CS .... British Airways [*formerly, British European Airways and British Overseas Airways Corp.*] Regional Division (Cambrian Section) [*ICAO designator*] [*Obsolete*] (FAAC)
CS .... Cable Ship [*Followed by name of cable-laying ship*]
CS .... Cabletron Systems, Inc. [*NYSE symbol*] (SPSG)
CS .... Caesarean Section [*Medicine*]
CS .... Cahiers Sioniens [*Paris*] [*A publication*]
CS .... Cahiers du Sud [*A publication*]
CS .... Calcium Intake Score [*Medicine*]
C-S............. California State Library, Sutro Branch, San Francisco, CA [*Library symbol*] [*Library of Congress*] (LCLS)
CS .... Calix Society (EA)
CS .... Call Sign [*or Signal*] [*Radio*]
CS .... Call Store [*Telecommunications*] (TEL)
CS .... Calls per Second [*Telecommunications*] (TEL)
CS .... Camden Society. Publications [*A publication*]
CS .... Camera Site [*NASA*] (KSC)
CS .... Camillus Salernus [*Flourished, 16th century*] [*Authority cited in pre-1607 legal work*] (DSA)
CS .... Camouflage-Sensitive [*Designation*] [*Army*] (RDA)
CS .... CanSurmount (EA)
CS .... Canvasback Society (EA)
CS .... Capital Ship [*Bomb*]
CS .... Capital Stock
CS .... Car Service [*Railroads*]
CS .... Carbon Steel
CS .... Card Station [*Data processing*] (BUR)
CS .... Cardiogenic Shock
CS .... Careers Services [*Navy*] [*British*]
CS .... Carrier Stability
CS .... Carrier Supply (MSA)
C to S.......... Carting to Shipside [*Shipping*]
CS .... Case
CS .... Case Supervisor [*Red Cross*] [*Services to the Armed Forces; Disaster Services*]
C/S............. Cash Sale [*Business term*] (ADA)
CS .... Cassenne [*France*] [*Research code symbol*]
CS .... Cast Steel

CS	Cast Stone (AAG)
CS	Category Stimulus [*To light*]
CS	Cathedral Series [*A publication*]
CS	Caught Stealing [*Baseball*]
CS	Cechoslovakische Statistik [*Czechoslovakia*]
CS	Cedars-Sinai Medical Center [*Los Angeles, CA*]
CS	Census
CS	Center Section
CS	Center Stage [*A stage direction*]
CS	Center for Statistics [*Later, CES*] [*Department of Education*] (IID)
CS	Centistere [*Metric*]
cs	Centistoke [*Also, cSt*] [*Unit of kinematic viscosity*]
CS	Central School (ADA)
CS	Central Service [*Medicine*] (DHSM)
C/S..............	Central Site
CS	Central States [*An association*] (EA)
C/S..............	Central Station [*NASA*]
CS	Central Supply (KSC)
CS	Centrifugal Spraying
CS	Cephalic Sinus
Cs	Cephalosporium Stripe [*of wheat*] [*Plant pathology*]
CS	Cerebrospinal [*Medicine*]
CS	Certificate of Service [*Military*] (MCD)
CS	Cerulein and Secretin (Test) [*Clinical chemistry*]
Cs	Cesium [*Chemical element*]
CS	Champlain Society (EA)
CS	Change Sheet [*Marine Corps*]
CS	Change of Status (NASA)
C & S..........	Changes and Specifications
CS	Channel Status
CS	Characteristic Slope
CS	Charge for Service
CS	Check Sorter
CS	Checkout Station (MCD)
CS	Checksum Error (MCD)
CS	Chemical Society [*Later, RSC*] [*British*]
CS	Chest Strap [*Medicine*]
CS	Chi Square
CS	Chief Secretary (ADA)
C of S..........	Chief of Section
C of S..........	Chief of Section
C of S..........	Chief of Staff [*Military*]
CS	Chief of Staff [*Military*]
CS	Chief Superintendent (ADA)
CS	Child Support Rulings [*Australian Taxation Office*] [*A publication*]
CS	China Spring (EA)
CS	Chinese Alliance for Democracy (EA)
CS	Chip Select Input [*Data processing*]
CS	Chlorobenzalmalononitrile [*Tear gas*] [*Army symbol*]
CS	Chondroitin Sulfate [*Biochemistry*]
CS	Chorionic Somatomammotrophin [*Endocrinology*]
CS	Christian Scholar [*A publication*]
CS	Christian Science
CS	Christopher Street [*A publication*]
CS	Chromate Sensitivity [*Immunology*]
CS	Chrysoberyl [*Jewelry*] (ROG)
CS	Church Scene [*A publication*] (APTA)
C of S..........	Church of Scotland
CS	Churches Speak [*A publication*]
CS	Cincinnatus Society (EA)
CS	Cinemascope
CS	Circuit Switching [*Telecommunications*]
CS	Circumsporozoite [*Protozoology*]
CS	Cirrostratus [*Meteorology*]
CS	Cities in Schools [*An association*] (EA)
CS	Citizen Soldier (EA)
C & S..........	Citizens & Southern Corp.
CS	Citrate Synthase [*An enzyme*]
CS	Civil Servant (DLA)
CS	Civil Service
CS	Civil Society (EA)
CS	Civil Surgeon (DAS)
C & S..........	Clarke and Scully's Drainage Cases [*Canada*] [*A publication*] (DLA)
CS	Clarsach Society (EAIO)
CS	Class of Service [*Telecommunications*] (TEL)
CS	Class of Supply [*Military*]
C and S.......	Clean and Sober [*Slang*]
CS	Clear and Subtract
CS	Clerk of Sessions [*British*] (ROG)
CS	Clerk to the Signet [*British*]
C & S..........	Clerk and Steward [*British*]
C & S..........	Clifford and Stephens' English Locus Standi Reports [*1867-72*] [*A publication*] (DLA)
C of S..........	Climates of the States [*A publication*]
CS	Clinical Staging [*Oncology*]
CS	Clinical State
CS	Clinical Studies [*Elsevier Book Series*] [*A publication*]
CS	Clock Synchronization
CS	Close Shot [*Photography*]
CS	Close Support [*Army*]
CS	Closed Shell
CS	Closing Sale [*Business term*]
CS	Cloth Sides [*Bookbinding*]
CS	Clymer System
CS	Coal and Steel (NATG)
CS	Coaling Station [*As part of a symbol*]
CS	[*The*] Coastal Society (EA)
CS	Coblentz Society (EA)
CS	Coco Solo, Canal Zone
CS	Code Segment [*Data processing*]
CS	Coding Specification
CS	Cognitive Stimulation [*Experimental psychology*]
CS	Cognizance Symbol
CS	Coil Sketch (MSA)
CS	COINTELPRO [*FBI Counterintelligence Program*] Survivors (EA)
CS	Cold Storage
CS	Coleopterists' Society (EA)
C/S..............	Colla Sinistra [*With the Left Hand*] [*Music*]
CS	Colliery Screened (ROG)
CS	Colonial Secretary [*British*] (ADA)
CS	Color Specification
CS	Color Strength [*Dye technology*]
C & S..........	[*The*] Colorado & Southern Railway Co.
CS	[*The*] Colorado & Southern Railway Co. [*AAR code*]
CS	Colorimetric Solution
CS	Columbian Squires (EA)
CS	Combat Support
CS	Combat System [*Military*] (CAAL)
CS	Come Sopra [*As Above*] [*Music*]
CS	Comedy Store [*Nightclub in which inexperienced comedians appear free in return for exposure to an audience*]
CS	Command Selector
C & S..........	Command and Staff
CS	Command System (NATG)
CS	Commercial Standard [*A publication*]
CS	Commercial System [*Data General Corp.*]
C/S..............	Commercial Vehicle Substitute
CS	Commissary Store [*Navy*]
CS	Commissary of Subsistence [*Military*] [*British*] (ROG)
CS	Commissaryman [*Navy rating*]
CS	Commissioners of Sewers [*British*] (ROG)
CS	Commit Stop (AAG)
CS	Common Serjeant [*British*] (ROG)
CS	Common Set (MCD)
CS	Common Slavic [*Language, etc.*]
CS	Common and Standard [*Items*] (AAG)
CS	Common Steel [*Projectile*]
CS	Common Stock [*Investment term*]
CS	Commonwealth Secretariat [*London, England*] (EAIO)
CS	Communication Segment (MCD)
CS	Communication Station
CS	Communications Satellite [*Japan*]
CS	Communications Simulator [*Sperry UNIVAC*]
CS	Communications Switcher
CS	Communications System
CS	Communis [*Common*] [*Latin*]
CS	Community Service [*An association*] (EA)
CS	Company of the Savior [*Roman Catholic women's religious order*]
CS	Company Secretary
CS	Competitive Sensitive (MCD)
CS	Competitive Strategies [*NATO*]
CS	Compiled Statutes [*A publication*] (DLA)
CS	Complex Spikes
CS	Component Specification (AAG)
CS	Component Supports (NRCH)
CS	Composite Service [*Army*] (AABC)
CS	Comptroller and Surveyor [*British*] (ROG)
C/S..............	COMPUSTAT Services, Inc. [*Information service or system*] (IID)
CS	Computer Science (BUR)
CS	Computer Simulation (RDA)
CS	Computers and Standards [*A publication*]
CS	Computers and Systems (MCD)
C & S..........	Computers and Systems (IEEE)
CS	Con Sordino [*With Mute*] [*Music*]
CS	Concentrated Strength [*of solutions*] [*Pharmacy*]
CS	Concrete Society [*London, England*] (EAIO)
CS	Concurrent Stereometric [*A discrimination task*]
CS	Condition Status [*Data processing*]
CS	Condition Subsequent [*Legal term*]
CS	Conditioned Stimulus [*Psychometrics*]
CS	Conducted Susceptibility (IEEE)
CS	Conestoga Society (EA)
CS	Congenital Syphilis [*Medicine*]
CS	Congregatio Missionariorum a Sancto Carlo [*Congregation of the Missionary Fathers of St. Charles*] [*Formerly, PSSC*] [*Roman Catholic religious order*]

CS .... Congressional Session [*Online database field identifier*]
C & S......... Conjunctiva and Sclera [*Ophthalmology*]
CS .... Connecticut Supplement [*A publication*]   (DLA)
CS .... Consciousness
CS .... Conservation Society [*British*]   (DCTA)
CS .... Consolidated Statutes [*A publication*]   (DLA)
CS .... Constantian Society   (EA)
CS .... Construcciones Aeronauticas SA [*Spain*] [*ICAO aircraft manufacturer identifier*]   (ICAO)
CS .... Consul
CS .... Consulting Surgeon [*British*]   (ROG)
CS .... Consumables Status   (MCD)
CS .... Consumer Sourcebook [*A publication*]
CS .... Containment Safety [*Nuclear energy*]   (NRCH)
CS .... Containment Spray [*Nuclear energy*]   (NRCH)
CS .... Contemporary Sociology [*A publication*]
CS .... Contingency Sample [*NASA*]   (KSC)
CS .... Continue-Specific [*Mode*] [*Data processing*]   (IBMDP)
CS .... Continuous Service [*British military*]   (DMA)
CS .... Continuous Stationery [*Commercial firm*] [*British*]
CS .... Continuous Survey   (DS)
CS .... Contract Surgeon [*Military*]
CS .... Contracts Station   (AAG)
CS .... Control Scanner
CS .... Control Segment   (MCD)
CS .... Control Set
CS .... Control Signal
CS .... Control Slip   (CINC)
CS .... Control Station   (MCD)
CS .... Control Store
CS .... Control Switch   (MSA)
CS .... Control Systems   (MCD)
CS .... Controlled Stress [*Physiology*]
CS .... Convalescent Status [*Medicine*]
CS .... Convergent Stereoscopic [*Photography*]
CS .... Conveyor Section of the Material Handling Institute   (EA)
CS .... Cooperative Society
CS .... Copper or Steel [*Freight*]
CS .... Coppersmith [*British*]
CS .... Coppersmiths Society [*A union*] [*British*]
C & S......... Cordon and Search [*Military*]
CS .... Core Segment   (NASA)
CS .... Core Shift
CS .... Core Spray [*Nuclear energy*]   (NRCH)
CS .... Corn Stunt [*Plant pathology*]
CS .... Cornish Studies [*A publication*]
CS .... Coronary Sclerosis [*Medicine*]
CS .... Coronary Sinus [*Cardiology*]
CS .... Coronary Status [*Cardiology*]
CS .... Corporate Source [*Online database field identifier*]
CS .... Corps of Signals [*British*]   (DAS)
CS .... Correct Selection [*Statistics*]
CS .... Corriere della Sera [*A publication*]
CS .... Corse Air International [*France*] [*ICAO designator*]   (ICDA)
CS .... Corticosteroid [*Endocrinology*]
CS .... Cosmetology Program [*Association of Independent Colleges and Schools specialization code*]
C/S............. Cost of Sale [*Accounting*]
CS .... Cost Sharing
CS .... Cotton Seed
CS .... Counselor Structured
CS .... Counter-Sabotage   (AABC)
CS .... Countershocks
CS .... Countersink [*Technical drawings*]
CS .... Counterstamped [*Numismatics*]
CS .... Counting Switch
C/S............. Counts per Second   (NASA)
CS .... Coupled States [*Physics*]
cs .... Cours [*Quotation, Price*] [*French*] [*Business term*]
CS .... Court of Session [*Scotland*]
C/S............. Crankshaft [*Automotive engineering*]
CS .... Cream Shade [*Paper*]
CS .... Credit Suisse [*Bank*]
CS .... Creo Society   (EA)
C/S............. Crew-Served Weapon
CS .... Crew Station [*NASA*]   (KSC)
CS .... Crew Systems
CS .... Crime Stoppers USA [*Later, CSI*]   (EA)
CS .... Critica Storica [*A publication*]
CS .... Critical Sensitive
CS .... Croatia Sacra [*A publication*]
CS .... Cromolyn Sodium [*Pharmacology*]
CS .... Cross Section
CS .... Crown Side [*Records*] [*British*]   (ROG)
CS .... Cruiser, Scout
CS .... Cruiser Squadron [*Navy*]
CS .... Crustacean Society   (EA)
CS .... Crystallographic Shear [*Crystallography*]
CS .... Ctenidial Sinus [*Biology*]
C & S......... Cultura e Scuola [*A publication*]
CS .... Cultura e Scuola [*A publication*]

CS .... Cultural Survival   (EA)
C & S......... Culture and Sensitivity
CS .... Currency Sign [*Telecommunications*]   (TEL)
CS .... Current Scene [*Hong Kong*] [*A publication*]
CS .... Current Series [*Army*]
CS .... Current Source
CS .... Current Strength
CS .... Curtain Sided Trailer [*Shipping*]   (DCTA)
CS .... Customer Service   (BUR)
CS .... Customer Support   (BUR)
CS .... Custos Sigilli [*Keeper of the Seal*] [*Latin*]
CS .... Cutting Specification   (AAG)
CS .... Cycad Society   (EA)
CS .... Cycle Shift
C/S............. Cycles per Second [*See also Hz*]
cs .... Czechoslovakia [*MARC country of publication code*] [*Library of Congress*]
CS .... Czechoslovakia [*ANSI two-letter standard code*]   (CNC)
CS .... IEEE Communications Society   (EA)
CS .... IEEE Computer Society   (EA)
CS .... Portugal [*Aircraft nationality and registration mark*]   (FAAC)
CS .... Quebec Supreme Court Reports [*A publication*]   (DLA)
CS .... Recueil de Jurisprudence. Cour Superieure [*Quebec, Canada*] [*A publication*]
CS .... Sacramento City-County Library System, Sacramento, CA [*Library symbol*] [*Library of Congress*]   (LCLS)
CS .... St. Clair Resources Ltd. [*Vancouver Stock Exchange symbol*]
CS .... Scout Cruiser [*Navy symbol*] [*Obsolete*]
CS .... Southern International Air Transport Ltd. [*Great Britain*] [*ICAO designator*]   (FAAC)
CS .... STS [*Space Transportation System*] Cargo Operations [*Kennedy Space Center Directorate*] [*NASA*]   (NASA)
CS .... Sumitomo Chemical Co. [*Japan*] [*Research code symbol*]
CS .... Tear Gas [*US Chemical Corps symbol*]
C1S .... Coated One Size [*Paper*]
CS1 .... Commissaryman, First Class [*Navy rating*]
CS² .... Combat Service Support Level [*Military*]   (INF)
CS2 .... Commissaryman, Second Class [*Navy rating*]
CS2 .... Cost Schedule Control System   (MCD)
C3S .... College Chemistry Consultants Service
CS3 .... Combat Service Support System [*Army*]
CS3 .... Commissaryman, Third Class [*Navy rating*]
CS³ .... Conceptual Satellite Surveillance System
CS3 .... Critically Sensitive Level 3 [*Information*]
CS4 .... Critically Sensitive Level 4 [*Information*]
C⁴S² .... Command, Control, Communications, and Combat Service Support [*Military*]   (INF)
CSA........... Assistant Chief of Staff for Studies and Analysis [*Air Force*]
CSA........... Cahiers. Societe Asiatique [*A publication*]
CSA........... California State University, Sacramento, Sacramento, CA [*OCLC symbol*]   (OCLC)
CSA........... Called Subscriber Answer [*Telecommunications*]   (TEL)
CSA........... Cambridge Scientific Abstracts [*Information service or system*]   (IID)
CSA........... Camphorsulfonic Acid [*Organic chemistry*]
CSA........... Campus Safety Association [*of the National Safety Council*]   (EA)
CSA........... Canadian Semiotic Association [*See also ACS*]
CSA........... Canadian Shipping Act [*1970*]   (MSC)
CSA........... Canadian Ski Association
CSA........... Canadian Soccer Association
CSA........... Canadian Society of Agronomy
CSA........... Canadian Space Agency
CSA........... Canadian Speech Association
CSA........... Canadian Standards Approval
CSA........... Canadian Standards Association
CSA........... Cancer Support Association [*Australia*]
CSA........... Cape Sarichef [*Alaska*] [*Seismograph station code, US Geological Survey*] [*Closed*]   (SEIS)
CSA........... Caravan Sites Act [*Town planning*] [*British*]
CSA........... Caribbean Studies Association   (EA)
CSA........... Caricaturists Society of America   (EA)
CSA........... Casualty Surgeons Association [*British*]
CSA........... Catalog Services Association [*Defunct*]   (EA)
CSA........... Catch Society of America [*Defunct*]   (EA)
CSA........... Cebu Stevedores Association [*Philippines*]
CSA........... Cell Surface Antigens [*Immunology*]
CSA........... Cellulose Synthase Activator [*Biochemistry*]
CSA........... Cemetery Supply Association [*Later, ICSA*]   (EA)
CSA........... Center for Social Analysis [*State University of New York at Binghamton*] [*Research center*]   (RCD)
CSA........... Center for the Study of Aging   (EA)
CSA........... Center for Sustainable Agriculture   (EA)
CSA........... Central Bank of Trinidad and Tobago. Quarterly Economic Report [*A publication*]
CSA........... Central South Africa Railway   (ROG)
CSA........... Central South Australia   (ADA)
CSA........... Central & Southern Motor Freight Tariff Association, Inc., Louisville KY [*STAC*]
CSA........... Central Supplies Agency   (NATG)
CSA........... Central Supply Association [*Later, ASA*]   (EA)

CSA...........	Ceskoslovenske Aerolinie [Czechoslovak Airlines] [Prague]
CSA...........	Channel Swimming Association [Foldestone, Kent, England] (EAIO)
CSA...........	Character Scan or Alternate [Data processing]
CSA...........	Chemical Shift Anisotropy [Physical chemistry]
CSA...........	Chemical Sources Association (EA)
CSA...........	Chemical Storage Area (NRCH)
CSA...........	Chemical Structure Association (EAIO)
CSA...........	Chief Scientific Adviser [British] (RDA)
CSA...........	Chief Special Artificer [Navy rating] [Obsolete]
C of SA.......	Chief of Staff, United States Army [Later, CSA]
CSA...........	Chief of Staff, United States Army [Formerly, COFSA, C of SA]
CSA...........	China Society of America (EA)
CSA...........	Chios Societies of America (EA)
CSA...........	Chondroitin Sulfate A [Biochemistry]
CSA...........	Chopper Stabilized Amplifier
CSA...........	Christliche-Sozialistische Arbeitsgemeinschaft [Christian Social-Workers' Community] [Lithuania] [Political party] (PPE)
CSA...........	Chromogenic Systems Analyzer
CSA...........	Cigar Smokers of America [Defunct] (EA)
CSA...........	Clinical Sociology Association [Later, SPA] (EA)
CSA...........	Close Support Area [Military] (CAAL)
CSA...........	Coalition on Southern Africa (EA)
CSA...........	Coast Savings Financial, Inc. [NYSE symbol] (SPSG)
CSA...........	College Stores Association
CSA...........	Collegiate Soaring Association (EA)
CSA...........	Colony-Stimulating Activity [Genetics]
CSA...........	Combat Surveillance Agency [Signal Corps]
CSA...........	Combat System Architecture [Military]
CSA...........	Commercial Service Area [Military] (AFM)
CSA...........	Commercial Service Authorization [Military]
CSA...........	Committee for Sustainable Agriculture (EA)
CSA...........	Common Service Area [Data processing] (BUR)
CSA...........	Commonwealth Sugar Agreement
CSA...........	Communal Studies Association (EA)
CSA...........	Communications Service Authorization [Obsolete]
CSA...........	Communications Support Area
CSA...........	Communications Systems Agency [Fort Monmouth, NJ] [Army] (RDA)
CSA...........	Community Service Activities [AFL-CIO]
CSA...........	Community Services Administration [Superseded Office of Economic Opportunity] [HEW]
CSA...........	Compensation System Analyst
CSA...........	Compound Spectral Array
CSA...........	Computer Sciences of Australia Pty. Ltd. [Information service or system] (IID)
CSA...........	Computer Security Act [1987]
CSA...........	Computer Services Association [British]
CSA...........	Computer System Analyst (BUR)
CSA...........	Computer Systems Association
CSA...........	Computing Services Association [British]
CSA...........	Concerned Senators for the Arts (EA)
CSA...........	Confederacion Sudamericana de Atletismo [South American Athletic Confederation - SAAC] (EAIO)
CSA...........	Confederate Stamp Alliance (EA)
CSA...........	Confederate States of America
CSA...........	Confederate States Army
CSA...........	Confederation Syndicale Africaine [African Trade Union Confederation]
CSA...........	Configuration Status Accounting
CSA...........	Conical Scan Antenna
CSA...........	Conseil Scientifique pour l'Afrique au Sud de Sahara [Scientific Council for Africa South of the Sahara]
CSA...........	Conservative Society of America
CSA...........	Consular Shipping Adviser
CSA...........	Contract Services Association of America (EA)
CSA...........	Contractor Support Area (KSC)
CSA...........	Control Switching Assembly
CSA...........	Core Special Assembly [Nuclear energy] (NRCH)
CSA...........	Core Structure Accident [Nuclear energy] (NRCH)
CSA...........	Corps Service Area
CSA...........	Corps Storage Area [Military] (AABC)
CSA...........	Correctional Service Associates
CSA...........	Costume Society of America (EA)
CSA...........	Council for a Secure America (EA)
CSA...........	Council on Southern Africa (EA)
CSA...........	Countermeasures Set, Acoustic (NVT)
CSA...........	Criminology Series [A publication]
CSA...........	Cross-Service Agreement [Obsolete] [Military]
CSA...........	Cryogenic Society of America (EA)
CSA...........	CSA Fraternal Life [Acronym represents organization's former name] (EA)
CSA...........	CSA Management Ltd. [Toronto Stock Exchange symbol]
CSA...........	Current Source Amplifier
CSA...........	Customer Supply Assistance [Military]
CSA...........	Cyclic Strain Attenuator (NASA)
CSA...........	Cyclosporin A [See CYA] [An immunosuppressant drug]
CSA...........	Cymbidium Society of America (EA)
CSA...........	Czechoslovak Society of America [Later, CSA Fraternal Life]
CSa	San Anselmo Public Library, San Anselmo, CA [Library symbol] [Library of Congress] (LCLS)
CSA...........	Sisters of Charity (of St. Augustine) [Roman Catholic religious order]
CSA...........	Sisters of the Congregation of St. Agnes [Roman Catholic religious order]
CSAA........	Canadian Sociology and Anthropology Association [See also ACSA]
CSAA........	Central Station Alarm Association (EA)
CSAA........	Child Study Association of America [Defunct] (EA)
CSAA........	Civil Service Arbitration Awards (DLA)
CSAA........	Composite Structures for Advanced Aircraft (MCD)
CSAA........	Council of Specialized Accrediting Agencies [Defunct] (EA)
CSAAA......	Annual Reports on the Progress of Chemistry. Section A. General, Physical, and Inorganic Chemistry [A publication]
CSA-AZA-P ...	Cyclosporin A, Azathioprine, Prednisone [Antineoplastic drug regimen]
CSAB........	California Strawberry Advisory Board (EA)
CSAB........	Civil Service Arbitration Awards (DLA)
CSAB........	Combat Support Aviation Battalion [Army]
CSAB........	Combined Shipping Adjustment Board [World War II]
CSAB........	Contract Settlement Appeal Board [United States] (DLA)
CSAB........	Counseling Services Assessment Blank [Test for counseling centers]
2CSAB......	Two Complete Science Adventure Books [A publication]
CSABGC ...	Cymdeithas Swyddogion Addysg Bellach a Gwasanaeth Leuctid Cymru [Welsh Association of Further Education and Youth Service Offices]
CSA Bull....	CSA [Canadian Standards Association] Bulletin [A publication]
CSAC........	Cameron State Agricultural College [Oklahoma]
CSAC........	Canadian Society for Aesthetics
CSAC........	Central Ships Alignment Console [Navy] (NG)
CSAC........	Citizens' Stamp Advisory Committee [US Postal Service] (EA)
CSAC........	Civil Service Association of Canada
CSAC........	Coalition for Safety of Abortion Clinics [Defunct] (EA)
CSAC........	Combat Support Aviation Company [Army]
CSAC........	Command Study Advisory Committee [TRADOC] (MCD)
CSAC........	Congregatio Sororum Apostolatus Catholici [Pallottine Sisters of the Catholic Apostolate] [Roman Catholic religious order]
CSAC........	Connors State Agricultural College [Oklahoma]
CSACCS...	Customer Service Administration Control Center System [Telecommunications] (TEL)
CSACIS....	Centre for the Study of Arms Control and International Security [University of Lancaster, Fylde College] [British] (CB)
CSACJ.......	CSAC [Civil Service Association of Canada] Journal [A publication]
CSACS	Centralized Status, Alarm, and Control System [Bell System]
CSACSO ...	Council of South Australia College Students Organisations
CSAD........	Capsule Systems Advanced Development [Aerospace] (MCD)
CSAD........	Center for Soviet-American Dialogue (EA)
CSAD........	Chief Special Artificer, Synthetic Training Devices [Navy rating] [Obsolete]
CSAD........	Combat System Alignment Document (NVT)
CSAD........	Configuration Status Accounting Document (MCD)
CSadC........	Calaveras County Free Library, San Andreas, CA [Library symbol] [Library of Congress] (LCLS)
CSADR......	Configuration Status Accounting Data Requirements (MCD)
CSAE........	Canadian Society of Agricultural Engineering
CSAE........	Committee for the Study of the American Electorate (EA)
CSAF........	Chief of Staff, United States Air Force
CSAFF......	Center for the Study of the American Family Farm (EA)
CSAFM......	Chief of Staff Air Force Memorandum (AFM)
CSAG........	Philips Roxane Laboratories [Research code symbol]
CSAGI.......	Comite Special de l'Annee Geophysique Internationale [Special Committee for the International Geophysical Year] [Superseded by CIG]
CSAGM.....	Committee for the Suit Against Government Misconduct (EA)
CSah	St. Helena Public Library, St. Helena, CA [Library symbol] [Library of Congress] (LCLS)
CSAI..........	Chief Special Artificer, Instruments [Navy rating] [Obsolete]
CSAI..........	Cognitive Systems, Inc. [New Haven, CT] [NASDAQ symbol] (NQ)
CSAITR......	Chief Special Artificer, Instruments, Typewriter and Office Equipment Repairman [Navy rating] [Obsolete]
CSAIWR ...	Chief Special Artificer, Instruments, Watch Repairman [Navy rating] [Obsolete]
CSAKA......	Chemia Stosowana. Seria A. Kwartalnik Poswiecony Zagadnieniom Technologii Chemicznej [A publication]
CSAL........	Cadbury Schweppes Australia Ltd.
CSal	Salinas Public Library, Salinas, CA [Library symbol] [Library of Congress] (LCLS)
CSalCL......	Monterey County Library, Salinas, CA [Library symbol] [Library of Congress] (LCLS)
CSalH	Hartnell College, Salinas, CA [Library symbol] [Library of Congress] (LCLS)
CSalJS.......	John Steinbeck House, Salinas, CA [Library symbol] [Library of Congress] (LCLS)
CSalM	Monterey Bay Area Cooperative System, Salinas, CA [Library symbol] [Library of Congress] (LCLS)
CSAM........	Chief of Staff, Army Memorandum [Air Force]
CSAM........	Circular Sequential Access Memory

CSAM........ Coalition to Save America's Music (EA)
CSAM........ Computer Support Applications Manager [*Computer Support Corp.*] [*Data processing*]
C-SAM ...... Contingency Special Airlift Mission [*Air Force*]
CSAM........ Crinkled Single Aluminized Mylar (NASA)
CSAN .... Coin, Stamp, and Antique News [*A publication*]
CSA Neurosci Abstr ... CSA [*Cambridge Scientific Abstracts*] Neurosciences Abstracts [*A publication*]
CSANSC ... Campus Safety Association of the National Safety Council (EA)
CSAO .... Chief Special Artificer, Optical [*Navy rating*] [*Obsolete*]
CSAO .... Customer Supply Assistance Office [*Military*]
CSAP........ Comedian Society for Amateurs and Professionals [*Defunct*] (EA)
CSAP........ Committee for Single Adoptive Parents (EA)
CSAPC ...... Case Studies in Atomic Physics [*A publication*]
C & S App ... Clifford and Stephens' English Locus Standi Reports, Appendix [*A publication*] (ILCA)
CSAR........ American River College, Sacramento, CA [*Library symbol*] [*Library of Congress*] (LCLS)
CSAR........ Calstar, Inc. [*Edina, MN*] [*NASDAQ symbol*] (NQ)
CSAR........ Combat Search and Rescue [*Aviation*]
CSAR........ Communications Satellite Advanced Research [*AFSC*]
CSAR........ Configuration Status Accounting Report (KSC)
CSAR........ Control Store Address Register
CSARCX ... Cancer Research Institute. Slovak Academy of Sciences. Annual Report [*A publication*]
CSARJ....... Commission on Social Action of Reform Judaism (EA)
CSARS ...... Close Support Artillery Rocket System (MCD)
CSAS .... Canadian Society of Animal Science
CSAS .... Canadian Society for Asian Studies
CSAS .... Cargo Security Advisory Standards [*Department of Transportation*]
CSAS .... Central States Anthropological Society (EA)
CSAS .... Centre for Southern African Studies [*University of York*] [*British*] (CB)
CSAS .... Configuration Status Accounting System
CSAS .... Containment Spray Actuating Signal [*Nuclear energy*] (NRCH)
CSAS .... Czechoslovak Society of Arts and Sciences (EA)
CSASA ...... Czechoslovak Society of Arts and Sciences in America [*Later, CSAS*] (EA)
CSASP....... Classical Scattering Aerosol Spectrometer [*Aerosol measurement device*]
CSAT .... Cell-Substrate Attachment [*Immunology*]
CSAT .... Center Science Assessment Team [*NASA*]
CSAT .... Civil Service Arbitration Tribunal [*British*]
CSAT .... CME-SAT, Inc. [*NASDAQ symbol*] (NQ)
CSAT .... Combat System Alignment Test
CSAT .... Combined Systems Acceptance Test (MCD)
CSaT......... San Francisco Theological Seminary, San Anselmo, CA [*Library symbol*] [*Library of Congress*] (LCLS)
CSATC ...... Climb so as to Cross [*Aviation*] (FAAC)
CSATD6.... Department of the Capital Territory. Conservation Series [*Canberra*] [*A publication*]
Csatornamue Inf ... Csatornamue Informacio [*A publication*]
CSATR ...... Climb so as to Reach [*Aviation*] (FAAC)
CSau .... Sausalito Free Public Library, Sausalito, CA [*Library symbol*] [*Library of Congress*] (LCLS)
CSA/USA ... Celiac Sprue Association/United States of America (EA)
CSAUSA ... Clan Sinclair Association (USA) (EA)
CSAV........ Ceskoslovenska Akademie Ved [*A publication*]
CSAV........ Compania Sud America de Vapores [*Chilean airline*]
CSAV........ Continental Savings of America [*NASDAQ symbol*] (CTT)
CSAVR...... Council of State Administrators of Vocational Rehabilitation (EA)
CSAW....... Close Support Assault Weapon [*Obsolete*] [*Navy*] (MCD)
CSAWS ..... Close Support Artillery Weapon System (MCD)
CSB........... Bachelor of Christian Science
CSB........... California State College, San Bernardino, San Bernardino, CA [*OCLC symbol*] (OCLC)
CSB........... Cambridge, NE [*Location identifier*] [*FAA*] (FAAL)
CSB........... Canada Savings Bond [*Investment term*]
CSB........... Cataloging Service Bulletin [*A publication*]
CSB........... Cathedral Service Book [*A publication*]
CSB........... Catholic Slovak Brotherhood
CSB........... Center Stage Back [*A stage direction*]
CSB........... Central Statistical Board [*Functions taken over by Bureau of the Budget, 1940*]
CSB........... Central Statistics Bureau [*British Columbia Ministry of Industry and Small Business Development*] [*Information service or system*] (IID)
CSB........... Centralized Support Base [*Military*]
CSB........... Christian Service Brigade (EA)
CSB........... Civil Service Board (AAG)
CSB........... Civilian Supply Branch [*Army Service Forces*] [*World War II*]
CSB........... Closely Spaced Basing [*Proposed plan for protecting MX missiles from enemy attack*]
CSB........... Coalition for Scenic Beauty [*Later, SA*] (EA)
CSB........... Collectors Service Bureau (EA)
CSB........... College of St. Benedict [*St. Joseph, MN*]
CSB........... College Service Bureau (EA)

CSB........... Colonia Sabana [*Puerto Rico*] [*Seismograph station code, US Geological Survey*] (SEIS)
CSB........... Combined S-Band
CSB........... Combined Signal Board [*North Africa*] [*World War II*]
CSB........... Combustible Storage Building (AAG)
CSB........... Committee for Safe Bicycling [*Defunct*] (EA)
CSB........... Common Market Business Reports (Spain) [*A publication*]
CSB........... Common Schools Board [*Australia*]
CSB........... Communication Scanner Base (IBMDP)
CSB........... Community Services Board [*Australia*]
CSB........... Companies and Securities Bulletin [*A publication*] (APTA)
CSB........... Computer Support Base (AFIT)
CSB........... Concrete Splash Block [*Technical drawings*]
CSB........... Congregatio Sancti Basilii [*Congregation of the Priests of St. Basil*] [*Basilians*] [*Roman Catholic men's religious order*]
CSB........... Congregation of St. Brigid [*Roman Catholic women's religious order*]
CSB........... Consolidated Silver Butte Mines [*Vancouver Stock Exchange symbol*]
CSB........... Consolidated Spot Buying [*Radio and TV advertising*]
CSB........... Consumer Sounding-Board (IEEE)
CSB........... Consumer Sourcebook [*A publication*]
CSB........... Continuous Subcarrier Barrage (MCD)
CSB........... Copper Shielding Braid
CSB........... Core Support Barrel [*Nuclear energy*] (NRCH)
CSB........... Corps Support Brigade
CSB........... Corpus Scriptorum Historiae Byzantinae [*A publication*]
C & SB ...... Correspondence and Service Branch [*BUPERS*]
CSB........... Customer Support Branch (AFIT)
CSb .... San Bernardino Public Library, San Bernardino, CA [*Library symbol*] [*Library of Congress*] (LCLS)
CSBA .... Char-Swiss Breeders Association (EA)
CSBA .... Chief Sick Berth Attendant [*British military*] (DMA)
CSBA .... Columbia Sheep Breeders Association of America (EA)
CSBA .... Community and Special Broadcasting Agency [*British*]
CSBA .... Cookie and Snack Bakers Association (EA)
CSBA .... County Savings Bank [*Santa Barbara, CA*] [*NASDAQ symbol*] (NQ)
CSbC......... California State College, San Bernardino, San Bernardino, CA [*Library symbol*] [*Library of Congress*] (LCLS)
CSBC .... Central & Southern Holding Co. [*NASDAQ symbol*] (NQ)
CSBC .... China Shipbuilding Corporation
CSBC .... Comite des Services Bibliographiques pour le Canada [*Committee on Bibliographical Services for Canada*]
CSBC .... Consolidated Statutes of British Columbia [*A publication*] (DLA)
CSbCL....... San Bernardino County Free Library, San Bernardino, CA [*Library symbol*] [*Library of Congress*] (LCLS)
CSBE .... Committee for Small Business Exports (EA)
CSBF .... Citizens Savings Bank FSB [*Silver Spring, MD*] [*NASDAQ symbol*] (NQ)
CSBF .... Civil Service Benevolent Fund [*British*]
CSBF .... Coronary Sinus Blood Flow [*Cardiology*]
CSBG........ Community Services Block Grant
CSBG........ Concerned Seniors for Better Government (EA)
CSbGS ...... Church of Jesus Christ of Latter-Day Saints, Genealogical Society Library, San Bernardino Branch, San Bernardino, CA [*Library symbol*] [*Library of Congress*] (LCLS)
CSBIED..... Cambridge Studies in Biotechnology [*A publication*]
CSBISSS ... Commission on Soil Biology of the International Society of Soil Science (EAIO)
CSBK .... Carolina Southern Bank [*NASDAQ symbol*] (NQ)
CSBKA ...... Chemia Stosowana. Seria B. Kwartalnik Poswiecony Zagadnieniom Inzynierii i Aparatury Chemicznej [*A publication*]
CSBL .... Consolidated Site Base Loading
CSBL-A ..... Casabella [*A publication*]
CSBM........ City Savings Bank of Meriden [*Meriden, CT*] [*NASDAQ symbol*] (NQ)
CSBN .... Captured Steam Bubble Nuclear
CSBN......... Community Savings Bank [*Holyoke, MA*] [*NASDAQ symbol*] (NQ)
CSBP .... Committee for Solidarity with the Bolivian People (EA)
CSBPC....... Control Stick Boost and Pitch Compensator (MCD)
CSBPD ..... CINCPAC [*Commander-in-Chief, Pacific*] Supplement to DoD [*Department of Defense*] Basic Planning (CINC)
CSBR .... Champions Sports, Inc. [*NASDAQ symbol*] (NQ)
CSbr........... San Bruno Free Public Library, San Bruno, CA [*Library symbol*] [*Library of Congress*] (LCLS)
CSBR .... United States Bureau of Reclamation, Sacramento, CA [*Library symbol*] [*Library of Congress*] (LCLS)
CSbrS .... Skyline College, San Bruno, CA [*Library symbol*] [*Library of Congress*] (LCLS)
CSBS .... Canadian Society of Biblical Studies [*See also SCEB*]
CSBS .... Civil Service Building Society [*British*]
CSBS .... Combat to Support Balance Study
CSBS .... Commander's Statement and Budget Summary (AFIT)
CSBS .... Conference of State Bank Supervisors [*Washington, DC*] (EA)
CSBS .... Course Setting Bombsight
CSBSR....... Center for Social and Behavior Science Research [*Research center*] (RCD)

CSbUSAF ... United States Air Force, Norton Air Force Base, San Bernardino, CA [Library symbol] [Library of Congress] (LCLS)
CSBV .... Cucumber Soilborne Virus
CSBW .... Chicago Sun Book Week [A publication]
CSC............ Cadmium-Sulfide Cell
CSC............ California State College, California, PA [OCLC symbol] (OCLC)
C-SC .... California Supreme Court, San Francisco, CA [Library symbol] [Library of Congress] (LCLS)
CSC............ Campbell Soup Co. Ltd. [Toronto Stock Exchange symbol]
CSC............ Canada Supreme Court (DLA)
CSC............ Canadian Society of Cinematographers
CSC............ Canadian Society of Cytology
CSc............ Candidate of Historical Sciences
C Sc............ Candidate of Science
CSC............ Cape Support Coordinator [NASA] (KSC)
CSC............ Capital Speakers Club (EA)
C & SC .... Capitals and Small Capitals [Printing]
CSC............ Cardinal Stritch College [Wisconsin]
CSC............ Cargo Services Conference [IATA] (DS)
CSC............ Cartridge Storage Case
CSC............ Central Security Control [Military] (AFM)
CSC............ Central Serous Chorioretinopathy [Medicine]
CSC............ Central State College [Ohio, Oklahoma]
CSC............ Central Switching Center [Telecommunications] (TEL)
CSC............ Central Switching Concept (KSC)
CSC............ Centralized Supervisory and Control (BUR)
CSC............ Certificate of Security Clearance (NATG)
CSC............ Change Schedule Chart
CSC............ Charles Stuart Calverley [19th-century British parodist]
C & SC .... Chicago and South Consortium [Library network]
CSC............ Chief Commissaryman [Later, MSC] [Navy rating]
CSC............ Child Safety Council [Later, NCSC] (EA)
CSC............ Child Study Center [Brown University] [Research center] (RCD)
CSC............ Childhood Sensuality Circle (EA)
CSC............ Children's Self-Conceptions Test
CSC............ Chile Solidarity Campaign (EAIO)
CSC............ China Solidarity Committee [An association] (EA)
CSC............ Christian Service Club (EA)
CSC............ Christian Service Corps [Inactive] (EA)
CSC............ Church of Scientology of California (EA)
CSC............ Cigarette Smoke Condensate
CSC............ Cincinnati Service Center [IRS]
CSC............ Circuit Switching Center [Telecommunications] (TEL)
CSC............ Citizens' Service Corps
CSC............ Civil Service Club [British]
CSC............ Civil Service College [British]
CSC............ Civil Service Commission [Later, MSPB]
CSC............ Civilian Screening Center
CSC............ Civilian Skill Code (MCD)
CSC............ Classic Stage Company
CSC............ Clock Start Command
CSC............ Clothing and Survival Equipment Change [Naval Air Systems Command] (NG)
CSc............ Coastal Surveillance Center
C Sc............ Cognitive Science [A publication]
CSC............ Coil Stock Cradle
CSC............ Coins, Stamps, and Collecting [A publication]
CSC............ Colby-Sawyer College [Formerly, CJCW] [New London, NH]
CSC............ Collagen Sponge Contraceptive
CSC............ College of St. Catherine [St. Paul, MN]
CSC............ Colorado State College [Later, University of Northern Colorado]
CSC............ Columbia [South Carolina] [Seismograph station code, US Geological Survey] [Closed] (SEIS)
CSC............ Combat Support Company [Army]
CSC............ Combat System Coordinator [Military] (CAAL)
CSC............ Combined Shipbuilding Committee [World War II]
CS/C .... Combined Station/Center [Aviation] (FAAC)
CSC............ Command Selector Control
CSC............ Command and Staff College [Air Force]
CSC............ Command Support Center (MCD)
CSC............ Commander of Service Cross [British] (ROG)
CSC............ Commemorative Stamp Club [US Postal Service]
CSC............ Commercial Solvents Corporation
CSC............ Commercial Steamship Company
CSC............ Commissariat Staff Corps [British military] (DMA)
CSC............ Committed Stem Cell [Hematology]
CSC............ Committee of Southern Churchmen (EA)
CSC............ Committee for the Survey of Chemistry [National Academy of Sciences]
CSC............ Common Signaling Channel (IEEE)
CSC............ Commonwealth Science Council [London, England] (EAIO)
CSC............ Commonwealth Scientific Committee [British]
CSC............ Commonwealth Service Corps [British]
CSC............ Commonwealth Supply Council [British] [World War II]
CSC............ Communication Skills Corporation [British]
CSC............ Communications Satellite Corporation [See also COMSAT]

CSC............ Communications Subcommittee [Allied German Occupation Forces]
CSC............ Communications Switchboard Console
CSC............ Communications Systems Center
CSC............ Community of the Servants of the Cross [Anglican religious community]
CSC............ Community Service Council of Central Indiana [United Way of Central Indiana] [Also, an information service or system] (IID)
CSC............ Community of the Sisters of the Church [Anglican religious community]
CSC............ Commuter Services Corporation [Formerly, ACSC]
CSC............ Compass System Controller (MCD)
CSC............ Complex Support Controller [NASA] (KSC)
CSC............ Comprehensive Self-Check [Computer]
CSC............ Computer Science Center [North Carolina A & T State University] [Research center] (RCD)
CSC............ Computer Science Center [University of Maryland] [Research center] (RCD)
CSC............ Computer Sciences Corporation [El Segunda, CA] [Database originator] [NYSE symbol] (SPSG)
CSC............ Computer Search Center [Illinois Institute of Technology Research Center] [Chicago, IL] [Defunct]
CSC............ Computer Service Center
CSC............ Computer Set Control (CAAL)
CSC............ Computer Society of Canada
CSC............ Computer Subsystem Controller
CSC............ Computer Systems Command [Also, ACSC] [Army]
CSC............ Computing Services Center [Texas A & M University] [Research center] (RCD)
CSC............ Confederation des Syndicats Canadiens [Confederation of Canadian Unions - CCU]
CSC............ Confederation des Syndicats Chretiens [Trade union] [Belgium] (DCTA)
CSC............ Configuration Switch Controller (CET)
CSC............ Congregatio a Sancta Cruce [Congregation of Holy Cross] [Roman Catholic religious order]
CSC............ Congressional Space Caucus (EA)
CSC............ Congressional Staff Club (EA)
CSC............ Congressional Steel Caucus (EA)
CSC............ Conical Shaped Charge (NASA)
CSC............ Consolidated Statutes of Canada [A publication] (DLA)
CSC............ Conspicuous Service Cross [Later, DSC] [British]
CSC............ Construction Scheduling and Coordination [AT & T]
CSC............ Construction Specifications Canada [Toronto, ON]
CSC............ Container Safety Convention [ISO] (DS)
CSC............ Containment Spray Cooling [Nuclear energy] (NRCH)
CSC............ Continental Service Corps (EA)
CSC............ Continental Shelf Crawler
CSC............ Contingency Support Center (MCD)
CSC............ Continuous Service Certificate [Navy]
CSC............ Convention-Seminar Cassettes [Commercial firm]
CSC............ Cooking for Survival Consciousness (EA)
CSC............ Core Standby Cooling [Nuclear energy] (IEEE)
CSC............ Core Support Cylinder [Nuclear energy] (NRCH)
CSC............ Corresponding Studies Course [DoD]
CSC............ Corsica/Sardinia/Calabria Microplate [Geology]
CSC............ Cosecant [Mathematics] (GPO)
C/SC .... Cost/Schedule Control (MCD)
CSC............ Course and Speed Calculator [or Computer]
CSC............ Court of Session Cases [Scotland] [A publication] (DLA)
CSC............ Criminal Sexual Conduct
CSC............ Crown and Sleeve Coping Prosthesis [Dentistry]
CSC............ Cryogenic Storage Container
CSC............ Cued Speech Center (EA)
CSC............ Culver-Stockton College [Canton, MO]
CSC............ Cyclosporin C [An immunosuppressant drug]
CSC............ Cylinder Stroke Control
CSC............ Cypher Security Committee [British] [World War II]
CSC............ International Convention for Safe Containers
C2SC.......... Command and Control Steering Committee
CSCA .... California Studies in Classical Antiquity [A publication]
CSCA .... Central States College Association [Defunct]
CSCA .... Clumber Spaniel Club of America (EA)
CSCA .... Combined Setter Clubs of America (EA)
CSCA .... Committee to Stop Chemical Atrocities (EA)
CSCA .... Conference of State Cable Agencies (EA)
CSCA .... Council of Scottish Clan Associations [Later, COSCA] (EA)
CSCA .... Country Shire Councils' Association [Australia]
C of S Ca .... Court of Session Cases [Scotland] [A publication] (DLA)
CSCAA ...... College Swimming Coaches Association of America (EA)
C of S Ca 2d Series ... Court of Session Cases, Second Series, by Dunlop, Bell, and Murray [Scotland] [A publication] (DLA)
C-SCAN .... Carrier System for Control Approach of Naval Aircraft
CSCAR ...... Citizens for Sensible Control of Acid Rain (EA)
C of S Ca 3rd Series ... Court of Session Cases, Third Series, by Macpherson, Lee, and Bell [Scotland] [A publication] (DLA)
CSCAS ...... Conference of State Cemetery Association Secretaries (EA)
C of S Ca 1st Series ... Court of Session Cases, First Series, by Shaw, Dunlop, and Bell [Scotland] [A publication] (DLA)

C of S Ca 4th Series ... Court of Session Cases, Fourth Series, by Rettie, Crawford, and Melville [*Scotland*] [*A publication*]   (DLA)
C of S Ca 5th Series ... Court of Session Cases, Fifth Series [*Scotland*] [*A publication*]   (DLA)
CSCB......... Civil Service Cadet Battalion [*British military*]   (DMA)
CSCB......... Command Scheduling Control Block [*Data processing*]   (BUR)
CSCB......... Contractor's Summary Cost Breakdown   (MCD)
CSCBS....... Commodore Superintendent Contract Built Ships [*Navy*] [*British*]
CSCC......... Canadian Steel Construction Council
CSCC......... Centre for the Study of Communication and Culture [*British*]   (CB)
CSCC......... Combat Support Coordination Center
CSCC......... Command Support Control Console
CSCC......... Commonwealth-State Consultative Committee on Nuclear Codes [*Australia*]
CSCC......... Communications System Category Code [*Air Force*]   (AFIT)
CSCC......... Communications System Control Console
CSCC......... Comprehensive Sickle Cell Center [*Terminated, 1977*] [*HEW*]
CSCC......... Council of State Chambers of Commerce   (EA)
CSCC......... Cumulative Sum Control Charts [*Statistics*]
CSCCC...... CSC Clearing Corporation   (EA)
CSCCL...... Center for Studies in Criminology and Criminal Law [*Later, SCSCCL*]   (EA)
CSCCU...... Computer Select and Cross Connect Unit   (MCD)
CSCD........ Center for Sickle Cell Disease   (EA)
CSCD........ Character Set Computer Development
CSCD........ Coalition to Support Cuban Detainees   (EA)
CSCD........ Committee on Sugar Cane Diseases   (EA)
CSCE......... Canadian Society for Civil Engineering
CSCE......... Centre Senegalais du Commerce Exterieur [*Senegalese Centre for External Trade*]   (GEA)
CSCE......... Coffee, Sugar, and Cocoa Exchange   (EA)
CSCE......... Commission on Security and Cooperation in Europe [*Washington, DC*]   (EGAO)
CSCE......... Communication System Control Element [*of TCCF*]   (MCD)
CSCE......... Communications Support Control Element   (MCD)
CSCE......... Communications System Control Equipment
CSCE......... Conference on Security and Cooperation in Europe   (PD)
CSCF......... California State College at Fresno
CSCF......... Center for the Study of the College Fraternity   (EA)
CSCFE....... Civil Service Council for Further Education [*British*]
CSCG........ Communications Security Control Group [*Navy*]   (MCD)
CSCh.......... Cahier Special des Charges [*A publication*]
CSCH........ Canadian Society of Church History [*See also SCHE*]
CSCH........ Cardio Search, Inc. [*NASDAQ symbol*]   (NQ)
CSCH........ Ceskoslovensky Casopis Historicky [*A publication*]
C of S Ch.... Church of Scotland Chaplain [*British military*]   (DMA)
CSCH........ Cosecant, Hyperbolic [*Mathematics*]   (GPO)
CSChE....... Canadian Society for Chemical Engineering
CsChrO...... Corpus Scriptorum Christianorum Orientalium [*Louvain*]   (BJA)
CSC-I......... Civil Service Commission - Investigations
CSCI......... Computer Software Configuration Item [*Data processing*]
CSCIH....... Canadian Society for Cultural and Intellectual History
CSCJ......... Center for Studies in Criminal Justice   (EA)
CSCL........ Close Surveillance Contractor List [*DoD*]
CSCl......... Community of St. Clare [*Anglican religious community*]
CScL.......... Lenkurt Electric Co., San Carlos, CA [*Library symbol*] [*Library of Congress*]   (LCLS)
CSCLK...... Chief Ship's Clerk [*Navy rating*] [*Obsolete*]
CSCM........ Combat System Configuration Matrix [*Military*]   (CAAL)
CSCM........ Commissaryman, Master Chief [*Navy rating*]
CSCM........ Committee to Stop Children's Murder [*Defunct*]   (EA)
CSCN........ Character Scan Command [*Data processing*]
CSCN......... Compuscan, Inc. [*NASDAQ symbol*]   (NQ)
CSCN/CHSA ... Commander, Subordinate Command, [*US*] Naval Forces Eastern Atlantic and Mediterranean, Commander Headquarters Support Activities
CScO......... Chief Scientific Officer [*Also, CSO*] [*Ministry of Agriculture, Fisheries, and Food*] [*British*]
CSCO......... Comparator Systems [*NASDAQ symbol*]   (NQ)
CSCO........ Corpus Scriptorum Christianorum Orientalium [*A publication*]
C-SCOPE.. Cathode-Ray Screen [*Air Force*]
C of SCOT ... Church of Scotland
CSCPAC.... Commonwealth-State Consumer Products Advisory Committee [*Australia*]
CSCPC3 .... Australia. Commonwealth Scientific and Industrial Research Organisation. Division of Chemical Physics. Annual Report [*A publication*]
CSCPCA.... Comite Scientifique Consultatif des Peches Canadiennes dans l'Atlantique [*Canadian Atlantic Fisheries Scientific Advisory Committee - CAFSAC*]   (ASF)
CSCPRC.... Committee on Scholarly Communications with the People's Republic of China
CSCR........ Center for Surface Coatings Research [*Lehigh University*]
CSCR........ Central Society for Clinical Research   (EA)
CSCR........ Cincinnati Superior Court Reporter [*Ohio*] [*A publication*]   (DLA)
CSCR........ Complementary Semiconductor
CSCR......... Complementary Semiconductor Controlled Rectifier   (MSA)

CSCR......... Consumnes River College, Sacramento, CA [*Library symbol*] [*Library of Congress*]   (LCLS)
CSCRR...... Centre for the Study of Community and Race Relations [*Brunel University*] [*British*]   (CB)
CSCRS....... Calcutta Sanskrit College Research Series [*A publication*]
CSCS......... Centre for the Study of Comprehensive Schools [*Wentworth College, University of York*] [*British*]   (CB)
CSCS......... [*Piers-Harris*] Children's Self-Concept Scale
CSCS......... Civil Service Cooperative Society [*British*]
CSCS......... Continental Steel Corporation [*NASDAQ symbol*]   (NQ)
CSCS......... Core Standby Cooling System [*Nuclear energy*]   (NRCH)
CSCS......... Cost/Schedule Control System   (MCD)
CSCS......... Crusader Swire Container Service   (DS)
CSCS......... Senior Chief Commissaryman [*Navy rating*] [*Later, MSCS*]
CSCSAT.... Commercial Synchronous Communication Satellite   (NASA)
CSCSC....... Canadian Society for the Comparative Study of Civilizations [*See also SCECC*]
C/SCSC.... Cost/Schedule Control System Criteria
CSCSGL... Computer Systems Command Support Group, Fort Lee   (MCD)
CSCSI........ Canadian Society of Computational Studies of Intelligence
CS & CSS .. Christmas Seal and Charity Stamp Society   (EA)
CSCT........ Columbia Studies in the Classical Tradition [*A publication*]
CSCT........ Communications Security Control Terminal   (MCD)
CSCU......... Countersink Cutter
CSCUC...... Community Service Credit Union Council   (EA)
CSCW........ Church Society for College Work   (EA)
CSCW........ Computer-Supported Cooperative Work [*Data processing*]
CSCWO...... Command Support Center Watch Officer   (MCD)
CSD........... C. S. Draper Laboratory, Inc. Cambridge, MA [*OCLC symbol*]   (OCLC)
CSD........... Calibrated Sweep Delay
CSD........... Canberra Skydivers [*Australia*]
CSD........... Car Service Department
CSD........... Cat Scratch Disease [*Medicine*]
CSD........... Central Supplies Department [*Singapore*]   (DS)
CSD........... Centrale des Syndicats Democratiques [*Congress of Democratic Unions*]
CSD........... Centrifugal Spray Deposition [*Steelmaking*]
CSD........... Character Sequence Detector   (MCD)
CSD........... Chemical Systems Division [*NASA*]   (NASA)
CSD........... Chief Scientist's Directorate [*Nature Conservancy Council*] [*British*]
CSD........... Children's Services Division [*American Library Association*] [*Later, ALSC*]   (EA)
CSD........... (Chlorosulfonyl)dicyclohexylamine [*Antineoplastic drug*]
CSD........... Church of Spiritual Discovery   (EA)
CSD........... Circuit Switched Data [*Telecommunications*]
CSD........... Circular Standard Deviation [*Statistics*]
CSD........... Citizens for Safe Drivers [*Formerly, CBDR*]   (EA)
CSD........... Civil Service Department [*British*]
CSD........... Civilian Supply Division [*Allied Military Government*] [*World War II*]
CSD........... Closed Shelter Deck [*Shipping*]   (DS)
CSD........... Coalition on Sexuality and Disability   (EA)
CSD........... Cold Shutdown [*Nuclear energy*]   (NRCH)
CSD........... Cold Side
CSD........... Combat System Detection [*Military*]   (CAAL)
CSD........... Combined Support Division [*Canadian Navy*]
CSD........... Command Signal Decoder
CSD........... Commissioner of Stamp Duties [*Australia*]
CSD........... Committee for Stable Deterrence   (EA)
CSD........... Committee on Statistics of Drilling [*American Association of Petroleum Geologists*]   (IID)
CSD........... Common Strategic Doppler   (MCD)
CSD........... Commonwealth Society for the Deaf   (EAIO)
CSD........... Community of St. Denys [*Anglican religious community*]
CSD........... Computer Science Division
CSD........... Computer Services Division [*University of South Carolina at Columbia*] [*Research center*]   (RCD)
CSD........... Computer Systems Director   (KSC)
CSD........... Computing Services Division [*Seton Hall University*] [*Research center*]   (RCD)
CSD........... Concise Scots Dictionary [*Aberdeen University Press*] [*A publication*]
CSD........ Configuration Standardization Document [*Deep Space Instrumentation Facility, NASA*]
CSD........... Constant-Speed Drive
CSD........... Constant Stimulus Difference [*Pair comparison*] [*Aircraft noise*]
CSD........... Construction Statistics Division [*Washington, DC*] [*Department of Commerce*]   (OICC)
CSD........... Continental Shelf Discus [*Buoy system*]   (MSC)
CSD........... Contract Support Detachment
CSD........... Control System Development   (MCD)
CSD........... Controlled-Slip Differentials   (IEEE)
CSD........... Convection Suppression Device [*for energy collectors*]
CSD........... Convective Storms Division [*National Center for Atmospheric Research*]
CSD........... Convex Set Stochastic Dominance [*Statistics*]
CSD........... Core Shift Driver   (CET)
CSD........... Cortical Spreading Depression [*Medicine*]

CSD .... Crew Systems Division [*NASA*]
CSD .... Critical Solvent De-Ashing [*Coal processing*]
CSD .... Critical Subsystems Development (MCD)
CSD .... Cross-Strike Discontinuity [*Tectonics*]
CSD .... Crystal Size Distribution
CSD .... Crystallographic Structural Database [*University of Cambridge*] [*Great Britain*] [*Information service or system*] (CRD)
CSD .... Cumulative Sum Diagram [*Statistics*]
CSD .... Current Source-Density [*Neuroelectricity*]
CSD .... Cyclosporin D [*An immunosuppressant drug*]
CSD .... Doctor of Christian Science [*Used by teachers who received instruction directly from Mary Baker Eddy*]
CSd .... San Diego Public Library, San Diego, CA [*Library symbol*] [*Library of Congress*] (LCLS)
CSDA .... Canadian Stamp Dealers' Association
CSDA .... Center for the Study of Development and Aging [*University of Detroit*] [*Research center*] (RCD)
CSDA .... Central Systems Design Agency
CSDA .... Concrete Sawing and Drilling Association (EA)
CSdA .... Fine Arts Gallery of San Diego, San Diego, CA [*Library symbol*] [*Library of Congress*] (LCLS)
CSDB .... Continuous Seam Diffusion Bonding
CSDC .... Circuit Switched Digital Capability [*AT & T*]
CSDC .... Continental Scientific Drilling Committee [*National Academy of Science*]
CSdCiC ...... San Diego City College, San Diego, CA [*Library symbol*] [*Library of Congress*] (LCLS)
CSdCL .... San Diego County Library, San Diego, CA [*Library symbol*] [*Library of Congress*] (LCLS)
CSdCu .... Cubic Corp., San Diego, CA [*Library symbol*] [*Library of Congress*] (LCLS)
CSDD .... Center for the Study of Drug Development [*Tufts University*] [*Research center*] (RCD)
CSDD ...... Cluster Systems Description Document (KSC)
CSDD ...... Conceptual System Design Description
CSDD ...... Control Systems Development Division [*NASA*] (NASA)
CSDE .... Center for Studies in Demography and Ecology [*University of Washington*] [*Research center*] (RCD)
CSDE .... Central Servicing Development Establishment (MCD)
CSDE .... Ceskoslovenska Socialni Demokracie v Exilu [*Czechoslovak Social Democratic Party*] (EAIO)
CSDF .... Canadian Student Debating Federation
CSDF .... Central Source Data File (MCD)
CSDF .... Core Segment Development Facility [*Nuclear energy*] (NRCH)
CSdG .... General Dynamics/Convair Aerospace Division, San Diego, CA [*Library symbol*] [*Library of Congress*] (LCLS)
CSdGA ...... General Atomic Co., San Diego, CA [*Library symbol*] [*Library of Congress*] (LCLS)
CSdGS .... Church of Jesus Christ of Latter-Day Saints, Genealogical Society Library, San Diego Branch, San Diego, CA [*Library symbol*] [*Library of Congress*] (LCLS)
CSDH .... Coalition to Save Our Documentary Heritage (EA)
CSDH .... Council of Societies in Dental Hypnosis (EA)
CSDHA ..... Centre for Social Development and Humanitarian Affairs [*United Nations*] [*Vienna, Austria*] (EAIO)
CSdHi .... San Diego Historical Society, Junipero Serra Museum Library, San Diego, CA [*Library symbol*] [*Library of Congress*] (LCLS)
CSDI .... Center for the Study of Democratic Institutions [*Later, Robert Maynard Hutchins Center for the Study of Democratic Institutions*] (EA)
CSDI .... Coalition for the Strategic Defense Initiative (EA)
CSdI .... United States International University, San Diego, CA [*Library symbol*] [*Library of Congress*] (LCLS)
CSDIC .... Combined Services Detailed Interrogation Center [*World War II*]
CSDICNOI ... Combined Services Detailed Interrogation Center - Nonoperational Intelligence [*World War II*]
C & S Dig ... Connor and Simonton's South Carolina Digest [*A publication*] (DLA)
C & S DIP ... City and State Directories in Print [*A publication*]
CSDIP .... City and State Directories in Print [*A publication*]
CSDIR .... Centro Studi e Documentazione sull'Italia Romana [*A publication*]
CSdJ .... Jewish Community Center, Samuel and Rebecca Astor Judaica Library, San Diego, CA [*Library symbol*] [*Library of Congress*] (LCLS)
CSDL .... Charles Stark Draper Laboratory, Inc. [*MIT*] [*Research center*] (NASA)
CSDL .... Confederazione Sammarinese del Lavoro [*Trade union*] [*San Marino*] (EY)
CSDM .... Continuous Slope Delta Modulation [*Telecommunications*]
CSdN .... San Diego Society of Natural History, Natural History Museum, Balboa Park, San Diego, CA [*Library symbol*] [*Library of Congress*] (LCLS)
CSdNEL .... United States Navy, Electronics Laboratory, San Diego, CA [*Library symbol*] [*Library of Congress*] (LCLS)
CSdNH ...... United States Naval Hospital, San Diego, CA [*Library symbol*] [*Library of Congress*] (LCLS)

CSdNPS .... United States National Park Service, Cabrillo National Monument, San Diego, CA [*Library symbol*] [*Library of Congress*] (LCLS)
CSdNUC ... United States Navy, Naval Undersea Center, San Diego, CA [*Library symbol*] [*Library of Congress*] (LCLS)
CSDP .... Center for the Study of Data Processing [*Washington University*] [*Research center*] (RCD)
CSDP .... Center for the Study of Drug Policy [*Absorbed by NORML*] (EA)
CSDP .... Command Supply Discipline Program [*Army*]
CSDP .... Coordinated Ship Development Plan [*Navy*]
CSDP .... Customer Service Department Procedure
CSdP .... Point Loma College, San Diego, CA [*Library symbol*] [*Library of Congress*] (LCLS)
CSDR .... Combat System Design Requirement [*Military*] (CAAL)
CSDR .... Computed Slant Detection Range
CSDR .... Consider (FAAC)
CSDR .... Control Store Data Register
CSDR .... Cross-Section Data Reduction
CSdRA .... Ryan Aeronautical Co., Lindbergh Field, San Diego, CA [*Library symbol*] [*Library of Congress*] (LCLS)
CSDRBL ... Considerable (FAAC)
CSDRBT ... Coalition to Stop Draize Rabbit Blinding Tests [*Later, CADRBT*] (EA)
CSdRS .... Rees-Stealy Medical Clinic, San Diego, CA [*Library symbol*] [*Library of Congress*] (LCLS)
CSDS .... Center for Control Science and Dynamical Systems [*University of Minnesota*] [*Research center*] (RCD)
CSDS .... Center for the Study of Democratic Societies (EA)
CSDS .... Centre for the Study of Developing Societies [*Information service or system*] (IID)
CSDS .... Command Ship Data System [*Navy*] (MUGU)
CSDS .... Communication Signal Distribution System
CSDS .... Constant-Speed Drive/Starter (NG)
CSdSC .... Stromberg-Datagraphix, San Diego, CA [*Library symbol*] [*Library of Congress*] (LCLS)
CSdSer .... Serra Cooperative Library System, San Diego, CA [*Library symbol*] [*Library of Congress*] (LCLS)
CSdS-IV ... San Diego State University, Imperial Valley Campus, Imperial, CA [*Library symbol*] [*Library of Congress*] (LCLS)
CSDT .... Computer Software Data Tapes (MCD)
CSdU .... University of San Diego, San Diego, CA [*Library symbol*] [*Library of Congress*] (LCLS)
CSdU-L ..... University of San Diego Law School, San Diego, CA [*Library symbol*] [*Library of Congress*] (LCLS)
CSdUT .... San Diego Union-Tribune Publishing Co., San Diego, CA [*Library symbol*] [*Library of Congress*] (LCLS)
CSdV .... United States Veterans Administration Hospital, San Diego, CA [*Library symbol*] [*Library of Congress*] (LCLS)
CSDWPUSCC ... Committee on Social Development and World Peace of the US Catholic Conference (EA)
CSE .... Canadian Society of Extension
CSE .... Carnegie Series in English [*A publication*]
CSE .... Center for Scholarly Editions [*Formerly, CEAA*] (EA)
CSE .... Center for the Study of Economics [*Columbia, MD*] (EA)
CSE .... Center for the Study of Evaluation [*Department of Education*] (GRD)
CSE .... Central Signals Establishment [*Military*] [*British*]
CSE .... Centre for Software Engineering Ltd. [*British*] (CB)
CSE .... Certificate of Secondary Education [*British*]
CSE .... Chargeable to Support Equipment (MCD)
CSE .... Child Support Enforcement [*Department of Health and Human Services*]
CSE .... Childress [*Texas*] [*Seismograph station code, US Geological Survey*] (SEIS)
CSE .... Chip Select
CSE .... Cincinnati Stock Exchange [*Ohio*]
CSE .... Citizens for a Sound Economy [*Washington, DC*] (EA)
CSE .... Civil and Sanitary Engineering (MCD)
CSE .... Cognizant Sustaining Engineer
CSE .... Cold Start Entry [*Data processing*]
CSE .... College of Saint Elizabeth [*Convent Station, NJ*]
CSE .... College of Saint Elizabeth, Convent Station, NJ [*OCLC symbol*] (OCLC)
CSE .... Combat System Engineer [*Military*] (CAAL)
CSE .... Combined Services Entertainment [*British military*] (DMA)
CSE .... Commission on Science Education
CSE .... Commission Seismologique Europeenne [*European Seismological Commission - ESC*] (EAIO)
CSE .... Committee on Scholarly Editions (EA)
CSE .... Committee of Security Experts [*Military*] (CINC)
CSE .... Common Support Equipment (NASA)
CSE .... Communications Satellite for Experimental Purposes [*Japan*] [*Telecommunications*] (TEL)
CSE .... Communications Support Element [*Military*] (AFM)
CSE .... Communications Systems Engineer (KSC)
CSE .... Competitive Study Engineer
CSE .... Computer Science and Engineering
CSE .... Computer Support Equipment (MCD)
CSE .... Conference sur la Securite Europeenne [*Conference on Security in Europe*] (NATG)

CSE........... Conference Spatiale Europeenne [*European Space Conference*]
CSE........... Configuration Switching Equipment (MCD)
CSE........... Connaught Biosciences, Inc. [*Toronto Stock Exchange symbol*]
CSE........... Containment Steam Explosion [*Nuclear energy*] (IEEE)
CSE........... Containment Systems Experiment [*Nuclear energy*]
CSE........... Control and Switching Equipment [*RADAR*]
CSE........... Control Systems Engineering
CSE........... Copenhagen Stock Exchange [*Denmark*]
CSE........... Core Storage Element
CSE........... Cornell Studies in English [*A publication*]
CSE........... Corresponding States Equation [*Physics*]
CSE........... Cosmetics International [*A publication*]
CSE........... Cost Engineering [*A publication*]
CSE........... Costs of the Soviet Empire [*International economics*]
CSE........... Course
CSE........... Cruise
CSE........... Steam Explosion in Containment [*Nuclear energy*] (NRCH)
CSEA..... Civil Service Employees Association (EA)
CSEA........ Combat System Engineering Authorization
CSeaGS ..... Church of Jesus Christ of Latter-Day Saints, Genealogical Society Library, Monterey Branch, Seaside, CA [*Library symbol*] [*Library of Congress*] (LCLS)
CSEB........ Canadian Society of Environmental Biologists. Newsletter/ Bulletin [*A publication*]
CSEB........ Clothing and Survival Equipment Bulletin (MCD)
CSeb........... Sebastopol Public Library, Sebastopol, CA [*Library symbol*] [*Library of Congress*] (LCLS)
C/SEC .... Cesareans/Support, Education, and Concern [*An association*] (EA)
CSEC......... Clothing and Survival Equipment Change [*Naval Air Systems Command*]
CSEC......... Commercial Security Bancorporation [*Salt Lake City, UT*] [*NASDAQ symbol*] (NQ)
CSEC......... Computer Security Evaluation Center
CSECT ..... Control Section (MCD)
CSED......... Collection Statute Expiration Date [*IRS*]
CSED......... Combat System Engineering Development [*Military*] (CAAL)
CSED......... Consolidated Ships Electronic Design [*Navy*] (NG)
CSED......... Coordinated Ship Electronics Device [*Navy*]
CSEDC...... Centre for Study of Education in Developing Countries (EAIO)
CSEDS ...... Combat System Engineering Development Site
CSEE ...... Canadian Society for Electrical Engineers (MCD)
CSEE......... Committee of Stock Exchanges in the European Community [*See also CBCE*] (EAIO)
CSEEB....... Communications Security Equipment Engineering Bulletin (MCD)
CSEES....... Center for Slavic and East European Studies [*University of Connecticut*] [*Research center*] (RCD)
CSEES....... Center for Soviet and East European Studies [*University of Connecticut*] [*Research center*] (RCD)
CSEF........ Canadian Siberian Expeditionary Force
CSEHD ..... Center for Studies in Education and Human Development [*Gallaudet College*] [*Research center*] (RCD)
CSEI .... Coopersmith Self-Esteem Inventories [*Personality development test*] [*Psychology*]
CSEI .... Coopersmith Self-Esteem Inventory [*Psychometrics*]
CSEIP....... Center for the Study of the Evaluation of Instructional Programs
CSEL .... Caribbean Select, Inc. [*NASDAQ symbol*] (NQ)
CSEL .... Communication Systems Engineering Laboratory [*NASA*] (MCD)
CSEL .... Corpus Scriptorum Ecclesiasticorum Latinorum [*A publication*]
CSELT Rappo Tec ... CSELT [*Centro Studi e Laboratori Telecomunicazioni*] Rapporti Tecnici [*A publication*]
CSELT Rapp Tec ... CSELT [*Centro Studi e Laboratori Telecomunicazioni*] Rapporti Tecnici [*A publication*]
CSEM........ Committee for the Study of Environmental Manpower [*National Research Council*]
CS En .... Certificate in Sales Engineering
CSEOL...... Center for the Study of Evolution and the Origin of Life [*University of California at Los Angeles*] [*Research center*]
CSEP .... Center for the Study of Ethics in the Professions [*Illinois Institute of Technology*] [*Research center*] (RCD)
CSEP .... College Senior Engineering Program [*Air Force*]
CSEP .... Communications Systems Engineering Program [*Army*] (RDA)
CSEP .... Corticosomatosensory Evoked Potential [*Electrophysiology*]
CSEPA ...... Central Station Electrical Protection Association [*Later, CSAA*] (EA)
CSEPA ...... Comite de Surveillance Ecologique des Pulverisations Seriennes [*Canada*]
Cs Epidem ... Ceskoslovenska Epidemiologie, Mikrobiologie, Immunologie [*A publication*]
CSepVA..... United States Veterans Administration Hospital, Sepulveda, CA [*Library symbol*] [*Library of Congress*] (LCLS)
CSERA ...... Center for Studies of Ethnicity and Race in America [*University of Colorado at Boulder*] [*Research center*] (RCD)
CSERB ...... Computer Systems and Electronics Requirements Board [*British*]
CSES .... Center for the Study of Earth from Space [*University of Colorado*] [*National Oceanic and Atmospheric Administration*] [*Research center*] (GRD)

CSES .... College Self-Expression Scale
CSES .... Connaught Biosciences, Inc. [*NASDAQ symbol*] (NQ)
CSES .... Council for Social and Economic Studies (EA)
CSESAS .... Center for State Employment Security Automated Systems
CSESD .... Communications Security Equipment Systems Document [*National Security Agency*] (MCD)
C Sess .... Court of Session [*Scotland*] [*A publication*] (DLA)
CSEU........ Combined Services Entertainment Unit [*British military*] (DMA)
CSEU......... Confederation of Shipbuilding and Engineering Unions [*British*]
CSEV .... Climatological Studies. Environment Canada. Atmospheric Environment [*A publication*]
CSF .... Cambridge Studies in French [*A publication*]
CSF .... Canada Studies Foundation [*See also FEC*]
CSF .... Canadian Schizophrenia Foundation (EA)
CSF .... Canadian Spooner Resources, Inc. [*Toronto Stock Exchange symbol*]
CSF .... Canadian Standard Freeness [*Drainage rate of synthetic pulps*]
CSF .... Canadian Sugar Factories Ltd.
CSF .... Caribbean Sea Frontier [*Navy*]
CSF .... Carrier Striking Force [*Tactical Air Command*]
CSF .... Casualty Staging Facility [*Military*] (AFM)
CSF .... Center for Southern Folklore (EA)
CSF .... Center Stage Front [*A stage direction*]
CSF .... Center for Study of Federalism [*Temple University*] [*Research center*] (RCD)
CSF .... Center for the Study of the Future (EA)
CSF .... Central Service Facility (NRCH)
CSF .... Central Supply Facility (MCD)
CSF .... Central Switching Facility
CSF .... Centrifugation-Sugar Flotation [*Soil testing*]
CSF .... Cerebrospinal Fluid [*Medicine*]
CSF .... Character Scan or Fail [*Data processing*]
CSF .... Chi-Squared Function
CSF .... Chief Shipfitter [*Navy rating*] [*Obsolete*]
CSF .... Civil Service Forum (EA)
CSF .... Coalition for Safe Food [*Defunct*] (EA)
CSF .... College of Saint Francis [*Joliet, IL*]
CSF .... Colony-Stimulating Factor [*Hematology*]
CSF .... Combat Support Force
CSF .... Commentationes Humanarum Litterarum. Societas Scientiarum Fennica [*A publication*]
CSF .... Community of St. Francis [*Anglican religious community*]
CSF .... Community Systems Foundation (EA)
CSF .... Condensate Storage Facility [*Nuclear energy*] (NRCH)
CSF .... Congregation of the Sacerdotal Fraternity [*Montreal, PQ*] (EAIO)
CSF .... Consol Synthetic Fuel [*Coal liquefaction process*]
CSF .... Containment Support Fixture [*Nuclear energy*] (NRCH)
CSF .... Contract Stationers Forum (EA)
CSF .... Contract Status File [*Military*] (AFIT)
CSF .... Contract Supply Facility
CSF .... Contractor Support Facility (MCD)
CSF .... Contrast Sensitivity Function [*of the retina*]
CSF .... Control and Simulation Facility (MCD)
CSF .... Cost Sensitivity Factor (NASA)
csf.............. Costo, Seguro, Fiete [*Cost, Insurance, Freight*] [*Spanish*] [*Business term*]
CSF .... Council on Synthetic Fuels (EA)
CSF .... Creation Science Foundation [*Australia*]
CSF .... Critical Success Factor [*Management tool*]
CSF .... Cylindrically Symmetrical Field
CSF .... Cytostatic Factor [*Cytology*]
CSf............. San Francisco Public Library, San Francisco, CA [*Library symbol*] [*Library of Congress*] (LCLS)
CSF .... San Francisco State University, San Francisco, CA [*OCLC symbol*] (OCLC)
CSfA .... California Academy of Sciences, San Francisco, CA [*Library symbol*] [*Library of Congress*] (LCLS)
CSFA .... California School of Fine Arts
CSFA .... Canadian Science Film Association
CSFA .... Center for the Study of Foreign Affairs (EA)
CSFA .... Citizens Savings & Loan FA [*NASDAQ symbol*] (NQ)
CSFA .... Citizens' Scholarship Foundation of America (EA)
CSfAR...... American Russian Institute, San Francisco, CA [*Library symbol*] [*Library of Congress*] (LCLS)
CS Faraday Transactions 1 ... Chemical Society. Faraday Transactions 1 [*A publication*]
Cs Farm ..... Ceskoslovenska Farmacie [*A publication*]
CSfB........... Bank of California, San Francisco, CA [*Library symbol*] [*Library of Congress*] (LCLS)
CSFB .... Credit Suisse First Boston [*Bank*]
CSfBe......... Bechtel Group, Inc., San Francisco, CA [*Library symbol*] [*Library of Congress*] (LCLS)
CSfBk .... Book Club of California, San Francisco, CA [*Library symbol*] [*Library of Congress*] (LCLS)
CSfBo......... Bohemian Club, San Francisco, CA [*Library symbol*] [*Library of Congress*] (LCLS)
CSfBPH..... Brobeck, Phleger, and Harrison, San Francisco, CA [*Library symbol*] [*Library of Congress*] (LCLS)

CSFC .... Canadian Sailfish Corporation [*See also OCPS*]
CSFC .... Chicago Standbys Fan Club   (EA)
CSFC .... Church of Scotland and Free Churches [*British military*]   (DMA)
CSFC .... Citizens Savings Financial Corporation [*NASDAQ symbol*]   (NQ)
CSFC .... Committee for the Survival of a Free Congress
CSFC .... Connie Stevens Fan Club   (EA)
CSfCAB ..... Crocker National Bank, San Francisco, CA [*Library symbol*] [*Library of Congress*]   (LCLS)
CSFCBM ... Chief Shipfitter, Construction Battalion, Mechanical Draftsman [*Navy rating*] [*Obsolete*]
CSFCBP .... Chief Shipfitter, Construction Battalion, Pipe Fitter and Plumber [*Navy rating*] [*Obsolete*]
CSFCBR .... Chief Shipfitter, Construction Battalion, Rigger [*Navy rating*] [*Obsolete*]
CSFCBS .... Chief Shipfitter, Construction Battalion, Steel Worker [*Navy rating*] [*Obsolete*]
CSFCBW ... Chief Shipfitter, Construction Battalion, Welder [*Navy rating*] [*Obsolete*]
CSfCC .... San Francisco Chamber of Commerce, Research Department Library, San Francisco, CA [*Library symbol*] [*Library of Congress*]   (LCLS)
CSfCCL ..... Commonwealth Club of California, San Francisco, CA [*Library symbol*] [*Library of Congress*]   (LCLS)
CSFCh .... Church of Scotland and Free Churches Chaplain [*Navy*] [*British*]
CSfCI .... California Institute of Asian Studies, San Francisco, CA [*Library symbol*] [*Library of Congress*]   (LCLS)
CSfCiC ...... City College of San Francisco, San Francisco, CA [*Library symbol*] [*Library of Congress*]   (LCLS)
CSfCP .... Society of California Pioneers, San Francisco, CA [*Library symbol*] [*Library of Congress*]   (LCLS)
CSfCPS ..... College of Physicians and Surgeons, and School of Dentistry, San Francisco, CA [*Library symbol*] [*Library of Congress*]   (LCLS)
CSfCR .... Catholic Russian Center, San Francisco, CA [*Library symbol*] [*Library of Congress*]   (LCLS)
CSfCSM .... California State Division of Mines, San Francisco, CA [*Library symbol*] [*Library of Congress*]   (LCLS)
CSfCW ...... San Francisco College for Women, San Francisco, CA [*Library symbol*] [*Library of Congress*]   (LCLS)
CSfCWL .... Chinese World, San Francisco, CA [*Library symbol*] [*Library of Congress*]   (LCLS)
CSfCZ .... Crown Zellerbach Corp., San Francisco, CA [*Library symbol*] [*Library of Congress*]   (LCLS)
CSfD .... Donahue Library [*Catholic Library of San Francisco*], San Francisco, CA [*Library symbol*] [*Library of Congress*]   (LCLS)
CSfDeY ..... M. H. de Young Memorial Museum, San Francisco, CA [*Library symbol*] [*Library of Congress*]   (LCLS)
CSfeQ .... Queen of the Angels Seminary, San Fernando, CA [*Library symbol*] [*Library of Congress*]   (LCLS)
CSfeVA ..... United States Veterans Administration Hospital, San Fernando, CA [*Library symbol*] [*Library of Congress*]   (LCLS)
CSFF .... Commander, SEATO [*Southeast Asia Treaty Organization*] Field Forces   (CINC)
CSfFB .... Federal Reserve Bank of San Francisco, San Francisco, CA [*Library symbol*] [*Library of Congress*]   (LCLS)
CSfFD .... Foremost Dairies, Inc., San Francisco, CA [*Library symbol*] [*Library of Congress*]   (LCLS)
CSfFL .... French Library [*L'Alliance Francaise*], San Francisco, CA [*Library symbol*] [*Library of Congress*]   (LCLS)
CSfFRC ..... Federal Records Center, San Francisco, CA [*Library symbol*] [*Library of Congress*]   (LCLS)
CSfFU .... Insurance Underwriters Association of the Pacific, San Francisco, CA [*Library symbol*] [*Library of Congress*]   (LCLS)
CSfGB .... Grizzly Bear Club, San Francisco, CA [*Library symbol*] [*Library of Congress*]   (LCLS)
CSfGG ...... Golden Gate College, San Francisco, CA [*Library symbol*] [*Library of Congress*]   (LCLS)
CSfGG-L ... Golden Gate University, School of Law, San Francisco, CA [*Library symbol*] [*Library of Congress*]   (LCLS)
CSfH .... University of California, San Francisco, Hastings College of the Law, San Francisco, CA [*Library symbol*] [*Library of Congress*]   (LCLS)
CSfHP .... Howard, Prim, Rice, Nemerovski, Canady & Pollak, San Francisco, CA [*Library symbol*] [*Library of Congress*]   (LCLS)
CSFI .... Coalition to Stop Food Irradiation [*Later, NCSFWI*]   (EA)
CSFI .... Company Standard Form Instruction
CSfII .... Industrial Indemnity Co., San Francisco, CA [*Library symbol*] [*Library of Congress*]   (LCLS)
CSfIL .... International Longshoremen's and Warehousemen's Union, San Francisco, CA [*Library symbol*] [*Library of Congress*]   (LCLS)
CSFJA .... Citrus and Subtropical Fruit Journal [*A publication*]
CSFJAW ... Citrus and Subtropical Fruit Journal [*A publication*]
CSfK .... Kaiser-Permanente Medical Center, San Francisco, CA [*Library symbol*] [*Library of Congress*]   (LCLS)

CSFL .... Central States Football League
CSfL .... San Francisco Law Library, San Francisco, CA [*Library symbol*] [*Library of Congress*]   (LCLS)
CSfLH .... California Palace of the Legion of Honor, San Francisco, CA [*Library symbol*] [*Library of Congress*]   (LCLS)
CSfLM ...... Lone Mountain College, San Francisco, CA [*Library symbol*] [*Library of Congress*]   (LCLS)
CSfLP .... Langley-Porter Neuropsychiatric Institute, San Francisco, CA [*Library symbol*] [*Library of Congress*]   (LCLS)
CSFLpc ..... Cerebrospinal Fluid Leukocyte Particle Counter [*Instrumentation*]
CSfMetL .... Metropolitan Life Insurance Co., San Francisco, CA [*Library symbol*] [*Library of Congress*]   (LCLS)
CSfMI .... Mechanics Institute, San Francisco, CA [*Library symbol*] [*Library of Congress*]   (LCLS)
CSfMM ..... San Francisco Maritime Museum, San Francisco, CA [*Library symbol*] [*Library of Congress*]   (LCLS)
CSFMS ...... Centralized Ships Force Management System
CSfMus ...... San Francisco Museum of Art, San Francisco, CA [*Library symbol*] [*Library of Congress*]   (LCLS)
CSFN .... Cell Surface Fibronectin [*Biochemistry*]
CSFN .... Congregatio Sororum Sacrae Familiae de Nazareth [*Sisters of the Holy Family of Nazareth*] [*Roman Catholic religious order*]
CSFN .... Corestates Financial Corp. [*NASDAQ symbol*]   (NQ)
CSFO .... Copeland/Sewell Family Organization   (EA)
CSFOD ...... Combined Special Forces Operational Detachment   (CINC)
CSFP .... Commodity Supplemental Food Program [*Food and Nutrition Service*]
CSFP .... Credit Suisse Financial Products [*British*]   (ECON)
CSfPaul ...... Paulist Library, San Francisco, CA [*Library symbol*] [*Library of Congress*]   (LCLS)
CSFPCPM ... Chambre Syndicale des Fabricants de Papiers a Cigarettes et Autres Papiers Minces   (EAIO)
CSfPG .... Pacific Gas & Electric Co., San Francisco, CA [*Library symbol*] [*Library of Congress*]   (LCLS)
CSFPN ...... Commission on Soil Fertility and Plant Nutrition [*of the International Society of Soil Science*]   (EA)
CSfPP .... Planned Parenthood of Alameda, San Francisco, San Francisco, CA [*Library symbol*] [*Library of Congress*]   (LCLS)
CSfPr .... Press and Union League Club of San Francisco, San Francisco, CA [*Library symbol*] [*Library of Congress*]   (LCLS)
CSFPSC .... Commander, Subordinate Command, Service Force Pacific Fleet [*Navy*]
CSfPUC ..... Pacific Union Club, San Francisco, CA [*Library symbol*] [*Library of Congress*]   (LCLS)
CSFRD ...... Cameron Synthetic Fuels Report [*A publication*]
CSFS .... Cal-Star Financial Services, Inc. [*NASDAQ symbol*]   (NQ)
CSfSA .... Strybing Arboretum Society of Golden Gate Park, San Francisco, CA [*Library symbol*] [*Library of Congress*]   (LCLS)
CSFSAC .... Civil Service Foreign Service Allowances Committee [*British*]
CSfSC .... Sierra Club, San Francisco, CA [*Library symbol*] [*Library of Congress*]   (LCLS)
CSFSD ...... Ciencias Forestales [*A publication*]
CSfSFL ...... California Labor Federation AFL-CIO Library, San Francisco, CA [*Library symbol*] [*Library of Congress*]   (LCLS)
CSfSM ...... Saint Mary's Hospital, San Francisco, CA [*Library symbol*] [*Library of Congress*]   (LCLS)
CSfSO .... Standard Oil Co. of California, San Francisco, CA [*Library symbol*] [*Library of Congress*]   (LCLS)
CSfSP .... Southern Pacific Co., San Francisco, CA [*Library symbol*] [*Library of Congress*]   (LCLS)
CSfSPA ..... Saint Peter's Academy, San Francisco, CA [*Library symbol*] [*Library of Congress*]   (LCLS)
CSFSR ...... Chief Shipfitter, Ship Repair [*Navy rating*] [*Obsolete*]
CSfSRA ..... Saint Rose Academy, San Francisco, CA [*Library symbol*] [*Library of Congress*]   (LCLS)
CSFSRP .... Chief Shipfitter, Ship Repair, Pipe Fitter and Plumber [*Navy rating*] [*Obsolete*]
CSFSRW ... Chief Shipfitter, Ship Repair, Welder [*Navy rating*] [*Obsolete*]
CSfSt .... San Francisco State University, San Francisco, CA [*Library symbol*] [*Library of Congress*]   (LCLS)
CSfTheo ..... Theosophical Society, San Francisco, CA [*Library symbol*] [*Library of Congress*]   (LCLS)
CSfU .... University of San Francisco, San Francisco, CA [*Library symbol*] [*Library of Congress*]   (LCLS)
CSFUDY ... Cell Structure and Function [*A publication*]
CSfUM ...... United States Bureau of Mines, Fuels Technology Library, San Francisco, CA [*Library symbol*] [*Library of Congress*]   (LCLS)
CSF/USA .. Correctional Service Federation - USA   (EA)
CSfUSA ..... United States Army, Sixth Army Command, Reference Center Library and Library Depot, San Francisco, CA [*Library symbol*] [*Library of Congress*]   (LCLS)
CSfUSA-L ... United States Army, Sixth Army Command, Letterman General Hospital Libraries, San Francisco, CA [*Library symbol*] [*Library of Congress*]   (LCLS)
CSfV .... United States Veterans Administration Hospital, San Francisco, CA [*Library symbol*] [*Library of Congress*]   (LCLS)

CSfW .... Wine Institute, San Francisco, CA [*Library symbol*] [*Library of Congress*] (LCLS)
CSfWA ...... World Affairs Council of Northern California, San Francisco, CA [*Library symbol*] [*Library of Congress*] (LCLS)
CSfWF ...... Wells Fargo Bank, San Francisco, CA [*Library symbol*] [*Library of Congress*] (LCLS)
CSfWF-H .. Wells Fargo Bank, History Room Library, San Francisco, CA [*Library symbol*] [*Library of Congress*] (LCLS)
CSfWT ...... World Trade Center Libraries, San Francisco, CA [*Library symbol*] [*Library of Congress*] (LCLS)
Cs Fysiol .... Ceskoslovenska Fysiologie [*A publication*]
CSG .... Calibration Signal Generator
CSG .... Canada Systems Group [*Database producer*] [*Ottawa, ON*] [*Information service or system*]
CSG .... Can't Say Good-By
CSG .... Capital Systems Group, Inc. [*Information service or system*] (IID)
CSG .... Career-Shortening Gesture
CSG .... Casing (KSC)
CSG .... Chimney Sweep Guild [*Later, NCSG*] (EA)
CSG .... Clean Sweep Generator (NVT)
CSG .... Coast Range Resources Ltd. [*Vancouver Stock Exchange symbol*]
CSG .... Columbus [*Georgia*] [*Airport symbol*] (OAG)
CSG .... Combat Service Group [*Army*]
CSG .... Combat Support Group [*Army*]
CSG .... Combined Studies Group [*Central Intelligence Agency operation in Southeast Asia*]
CSG .... Comite Permanent des Secretaires Generaux [*Standing Committee of Secretaries General*] [*NATO*] (NATG)
CSG .... Command Signal Generator
CSG .... Command Subsystem Group (MCD)
CSG .... Community Service Grant [*Corporation for Public Broadcasting*]
CSG .... Console Set Group
CSG .... Constructive Solid Geometry
CSG .... Control Synthetic Gas [*Process*]
CSG .... Council of State Governments (EA)
CSG .... Course and Speed Made Good over the Ground [*Military*] (NATG)
CSG .... Cryptologic Support Group [*Military*] (NVT)
CSG .... Guided Missile Strike Cruiser [*Navy symbol*] (NVT)
CSG .... Sacramento City College Library, Sacramento, CA [*OCLC symbol*] (OCLC)
CSG2 .... Commander, Service Group Two [*Navy*]
CSGA .... Citizens & Southern Georgia Corp. [*NASDAQ symbol*] (NQ)
Cs Gastrent Vyz ... Ceskoslovenska Gastroenterologie a Vyziva [*A publication*]
CSGB .... Cartophilic Society of Great Britain
CSGB .... Cremation Society of Great Britain
CSGC .... Consumer Safety Glazing Committee
CSGCAG ... Congres International de Stratigraphie et de Geologie du Carbonifere. Compte Rendu [*A publication*]
CSGCC ...... Commission on Soil Genesis, Classification, and Cartography [*of the International Society of Soil Science*] (EA)
CSGEA ...... Compass. Sigma Gamma Epsilon [*A publication*]
CSGH .... Chosen Gakuno [*A publication*]
CSGI .... Citizens Security Group, Incorporated [*Red Wing, MN*] [*NASDAQ symbol*] (NQ)
CSGLL ...... Canadian Studies in German Language and Literature [*A publication*]
CSGN .... Nuclear-Powered Strike Cruiser
CSGp .... Combat Support Group [*Air Force*] (AFM)
CSGS .... Campaign to Stop Government Spying [*Later, CPR*] (EA)
CSGS .... Church of Jesus Christ of Latter-Day Saints, Genealogical Society Library, Sacramento Branch, Sacramento, CA [*Library symbol*] [*Library of Congress*] (LCLS)
C/Sgt .... Colour-Sergeant [*Army*] [*British*] (DMA)
CSGUS ...... Clinical Society of Genito-Urinary Surgeons (EA)
CSGV .... Coalition to Stop Gun Violence (EA)
CSGW .... Coalition to Stop Government Waste (EA)
CSGYAF ... Contemporary Surgery [*A publication*]
Cs Gynek ... Ceskoslovenska Gynekologie [*A publication*]
CSH .... Cableshare, Inc. [*Toronto Stock Exchange symbol*]
CSH .... Calcium Silicate Hydrate [*Inorganic chemistry*]
CSH .... California State [*University*], Hayward [*California*] [*Seismograph station code, US Geological Survey*] (SEIS)
CSH .... California State University, Hayward, Hayward, CA [*OCLC symbol*] (OCLC)
CSH .... Called Subscriber Held [*Telecommunications*] (TEL)
CSH .... Cash (DCTA)
CsH .... Celuloza si Hirtie [*A publication*]
CSH .... Center for Socialist History (EA)
CSH .... Chronic Subdural Hematoma [*Medicine*]
CSH .... Coalition on Smoking or Health (EA)
CSH .... College of the Sacred Heart [*Puerto Rico*]
CSH .... Combat Support Hospital (AABC)
CSH .... Communications Soft Hat [*NASA*] (KSC)
CSh .... Signal Hill Public Library, Signal Hill, CA [*Library symbol*] [*Library of Congress*] (LCLS)
CSHA .... Civil Service Housing Association [*British*]

CSHA .... Council of State Housing Agencies (EA)
CSHAFT ... Crankshaft
CSHB .... Corpus Scriptorum Historiae Byzantinae [*A publication*]
CSHCAL ... Cold Spring Harbor Conferences on Cell Proliferation [*A publication*]
CSHEP ...... Constriction, Sclerosis, Hemorrhage, Exudate, Papilledema [*Ophthalmology*]
C/SHFT .... Cross Shaft [*Automotive engineering*]
CSHG .... Committee on the Standardization of Hospital Graphics [*Defunct*]
CSHL.......... Centre for the Study of Human Learning [*Brunel University*] [*British*] (CB)
CSHM ...... Canadian Society for the History of Medicine [*See also SCHM*]
CSHM ...... Committee for the Study of Handgun Misuse (EA)
CSHN .... Cushion
CSHO .... Compliance Safety and Health Officer [*Occupational Safety and Health Administration*]
CSHP.......... Canadian Society of Hospital Pharmacists
CSHP.......... CompuShop, Inc. [*NASDAQ symbol*] (NQ)
CSHP.......... Conference of Societies for the History of Pharmacy [*Madrid, Spain*] (EAIO)
CSHPE ...... Center for Study of Higher and Postsecondary Education [*University of Michigan*] [*Research center*] (RCD)
CSHPM .... Canadian Society for the History and Philosophy of Mathematics [*See also SCHPM*]
CSHPS ...... Canadian Society for the History and Philosophy of Science [*See also SCHPS*]
CSHR .... Canadian Society for the History of Rhetoric [*See also SCHR*]
CSHR .... Center for the Study of Human Rights (EA)
CSHR .... Commercial Shearing, Inc. [*NASDAQ symbol*] (NQ)
CSHS .... Chief Superintendent of Hydrographic Supplies
CSHSA ...... Cold Spring Harbor Symposia on Quantitative Biology [*A publication*]
CSHSAZ ... Cold Spring Harbor Symposia on Quantitative Biology [*A publication*]
CSHVB ...... Computer Studies in the Humanities and Verbal Behavior [*A publication*]
CSHX .... Containment Spray Heat Exchange [*Nuclear energy*] (NRCH)
CSI .... C-Band Sensitivity Improvement [*Navy*] (MCD)
CSI .... Campus Studies Institute (EA)
CSI .... Cancer Serum Index
CSI .... Canned Salmon Institute [*Later, SI*] (EA)
CSI .... Cannon Street Investments [*Finance*] [*British*]
CSI .... Capitol Services, Incorporated [*Database producer*] [*Information service or system*] (IID)
CSI .... Casino [*Australia*] [*Airport symbol*] (OAG)
CSI .... Cellulose Sponge Institute [*Defunct*] (EA)
CSI .... Center Point, TX [*Location identifier*] [*FAA*] (FAAL)
CSI .... Center for the Study of Instruction [*of NEA*]
CSI .... Cesium Iodide
CSI .... Cetacean Society International (EA)
CSI .... Change Seeker Index
CSI .... Chartered Surveyors' Institution [*British*] (DAS)
CSI .... Chemical Substructure Index [*Trademark*]
CSI .... Chlorosulfonyl Isocyanate [*Organic chemistry*]
CSI .... Cholesterol Saturation Index [*Clinical chemistry*]
CSI .... Christian Schools International (EA)
CSI .... Christian Solidarity International [*Zurich, Switzerland*] (EAIO)
CSI .... Chromatography Signal Interface
CSI .... Church of South India
CSI .... Cinematheque Scientifique Internationale [*International Scientific Film Library*]
CSI .... Clarion State College, School of Library Media, Clarion, PA [*OCLC symbol*] (OCLC)
CSI .... Clean Sites, Inc. (EA)
CSI .... Coalition of Service Industries [*Washington, DC*] (EA)
CSI .... Coastal Studies Institute [*Louisiana State University*] [*Research center*]
CSI .... Coelliptic Sequence Initiation [*Aerospace*]
CSI .... College of Staten Island [*New York*]
CSI .... Colloquium Spectroscopicum Internationale
CSI .... Combat Studies Institute [*Command and General Staff College, Fort Leavenworth*] [*Army*] (INF)
CSI .... Combat System Integration (MCD)
CSI .... Command String Interpreter [*Digital Equipment Corp.*]
CSI .... Commission Sericicole Internationale [*International Sericultural Commission - ISC*] (EAIO)
CSI .... Commission Sportive Internationale [*Auto racing*]
CSI .... Commissioners Standard Industrial Mortality Table [*Insurance*]
CSI .... Commodity Systems, Incorporated [*Information service or system*] (IID)
CSI .... Communications Services, Incorporated [*Junction City, KS*]
CSI .... Communications Solutions, Incorporated [*San Jose, CA*] [*Information service or system*] [*Telecommunications*] (TSSD)
CSI .... Communications Systems, Incorporated
CSI .... Companion of the [*Order of the*] Star of India [*British*]
CSI .... Company Source Inspection
CSI .... Computer Search International Corp. [*Database producer*]
CSI .... Computer Security Institute (EA)

CSI............ Computer Synthesized Imagery (MCD)
CSI............ Computer Systems International
CSI............ Computerized Stress Inventory [*Personality development test*] [*Psychology*]
CSI............ Concentric Sequence Initiation [*Aerospace*]
CSI............ [*United States*] Conference of Secular Institutes (EA)
CSI............ Consortium for the Study of Intelligence (EA)
CSI............ Consorzio per il Sistema Informativo Piemonte [*Piedmont Consortium for Information Systems*] [*Information service or system*] (IID)
CSI............ Construction Specifications Institute (EA)
CSI............ Construction Surveyors Institute [*Later, Architects and Surveyors Institute*] (EA)
CSI............ Consumer Satisfaction Index
CSI............ Contractor Standard Item (AAG)
CSI............ Control Servo Input (NASA)
CSI............ Control Software, Incorporated
CSI............ CONUS [*Continental United States*] Sustaining Increment [*Army*] (AABC)
CSI............ Correct Seating Institute
CSI............ Cost System Indicator (AFIT)
CSI............ Council for the Securities Industry [*Stock exchange*] [*London, England*]
CSI............ Counseling Satisfaction Inventory [*Education*]
CSI............ Credit Systems Incorporated
CSI............ Crew Software Interface (MCD)
CSI............ Crime Stoppers International (EA)
CSI............ CSIRO [*Commonwealth Scientific and Industrial Research Organisation*] Index [*A publication*] (APTA)
CSI............ Culture Shock Inventory [*Interpersonal skills and attitudes test*]
CSI............ Customer Satisfaction Index [*Automotive retailing*]
CSI............ Cycle-Significant Items (MCD)
CSI............ Decisions of the Commissioners under the National Insurance (Industrial Injuries) Acts Relating to Scotland [*A publication*] (DLA)
CSIA.......... Canadian Ski Instructors' Alliance
CSIA.......... Canadian Solar Industries Association
CSIA.......... Center for Science and International Affairs [*Harvard University*] [*Research center*]
CSIA.......... Chimney Safety Institute of America (EA)
CSIC.......... Computer Stock Inventory Control (MCD)
CSIC.......... Computer System Interface Circuits (IEEE)
CSIC.......... Consejo Superior de Investigaciones Cientificas [*Council for Scientific Research*] [*Information service or system*] (EISS)
CSIC Cent Edafol Biol Apl Anu ... Consejo Superior de Investigaciones Cientificas. Centro de Edafologia y Biologia Aplicada. Anuario [*A publication*]
CSIC Estud Geol ... Consejo Superior de Investigaciones Cientificas. Estudios Geologicos [*Madrid*] [*A publication*]
CSICOP .... Committee for the Scientific Investigation of Claims of the Paranormal (EA)
CSIC Patronato Juan De La Cierva Invest Tec Cuad ... Consejo Superior de Investigaciones Cientificas. Patronato Juan De La Cierva de Investigaciones Tecnicas. Cuaderno [*A publication*]
CSICU .... Cardiac Surgical Intensive Care Unit [*Medicine*]
CSID .... Convergence Source-Image Distortion [*Crystal*]
CSIE .... Center for the Study of Information and Education [*Syracuse University*] (IID)
CSIE .... Centre for Studies on Integration in Education [*British*] (CB)
CSIE .... Council for Sex Information and Education (EA)
CSie............ Sierra Madre Free Public Library, Sierra Madre, CA [*Library symbol*] [*Library of Congress*] (LCLS)
CSIET....... Council on Standards for International Educational Travel (EA)
CSIF .... Collagen Synthesis Inhibitory Factor [*Biochemistry*]
CSIF .... Communications Systems Industrial Funds (MCD)
CSIGC .... Chief, Signal Corps [*Army*]
CSIGO....... Chief Signal Officer [*Army*]
CSII .... Communications Systems, Incorporated [*NASDAQ symbol*] (NQ)
CSII .... Continuous Subcutaneous Insulin Infusion [*Medicine*]
CSIICG...... Combat System Integration and Interface Control Group [*Military*] (CAAL)
CSIM........ Combat System Integration Manager [*Military*] (CAAL)
CSIM........ Consilium, Inc. [*NASDAQ symbol*] (NQ)
CSIM........ Consortium for Sharing Instructional Materials [*Library network*]
CSIN.......... Chemical Substances Information Network [*No longer exists*] [*Environmental Protection Agency*] [*Information service or system*]
CSIO Commun ... CSIO [*Central Scientific Instruments Organisation*] Communications [*India*] [*A publication*]
CSion .... Cahiers Sioniens [*Paris*] [*A publication*]
CS:IP .... Code Segment:Instruction Pointer [*Data processing*]
CSIP .... Combat System Initialization Procedure [*Military*] (CAAL)
CSIPP....... Committee to Support Irish Political Prisoners (EA)
CSISR .... Computer Systems Integration Review (NASA)
CSIR .... Council of Scientific and Industrial Research [*Information service or system*] (IID)
CSIRA .... Canadian Steel Industry Research Association

CSIR Air Pollut Res Group Rep APRG (S Afr) ... Council for Scientific and Industrial Research. Air Pollution Research Group. Report APRG (South Africa) [*A publication*]
CSIRB4 ..... Suid-Afrikaanse Wetenskaplike en Nywerheidnavorskingsraad Navorsingsverslag [*A publication*]
CSIR (Counc Sci Ind Res S Afr) Ann Rep ... CSIR (Council for Scientific and Industrial Research, South Africa) Annual Report [*A publication*]
CSIR Dep Mines Asbestos Min Ind Asbestosis Res Proj Annu Rep ... Council for Scientific and Industrial Research and Department of Mines and the Asbestos Mining Industry. Asbestosis Research Project. Annual Report [*A publication*]
CSIR News (India) ... CSIR [*Council for Scientific and Industrial Research*] News (India) [*A publication*]
CSIRO .... Commonwealth Scientific and Industrial Research Organisation [*Australia*]
CSIRO Abstr ... CSIRO [*Commonwealth Scientific and Industrial Research Organisation*] Abstracts [*A publication*]
CSIRO An Health Div TP ... CSIRO [*Commonwealth Scientific and Industrial Research Organisation*] Division of Animal Health and Production. Technical Paper [*A publication*] (APTA)
CSIRO Annu Rep ... CSIRO [*Commonwealth Scientific and Industrial Research Organisation*] Annual Report [*A publication*] (APTA)
CSIRO An Res Labs TP ... CSIRO [*Commonwealth Scientific and Industrial Research Organisation*] Animal Research Laboratories. Technical Paper [*A publication*] (APTA)
CSIRO Aust Div Trop Crops Pastures Tech Pap ... CSIRO [*Commonwealth Scientific and Industrial Research Organisation*] Australia. Division of Tropical Crops and Pastures. Technical Paper [*A publication*]
CSIRO Bio Mem News ... Bio Membrane News CSIRO [*Commonwealth Scientific and Industrial Research Organisation*] Biomembrane Committee [*A publication*] (APTA)
CSIRO Build Res Div Building Study ... CSIRO [*Commonwealth Scientific and Industrial Research Organisation*] Division of Building Research. Building Study [*A publication*] (APTA)
CSIRO Build Res Div Rep ... CSIRO [*Commonwealth Scientific and Industrial Research Organisation*] Division of Building Research. Report [*A publication*] (APTA)
CSIRO Build Res Div Tech Pap ... CSIRO [*Commonwealth Scientific and Industrial Research Organisation*] Division of Building Research. Technical Paper [*A publication*] (APTA)
CSIRO Build Res Div TP ... CSIRO [*Commonwealth Scientific and Industrial Research Organisation*] Division of Building Research. Technical Paper [*A publication*] (APTA)
CSIRO Bull ... CSIRO [*Commonwealth Scientific and Industrial Research Organisation*] Bulletin [*Australia*] [*A publication*]
CSIRO Chem Res Labs TP ... CSIRO [*Commonwealth Scientific and Industrial Research Organisation*] Chemical Research Laboratories. Technical Paper [*A publication*] (APTA)
CSIRO Chem Res Lab Tech Pap ... CSIRO [*Commonwealth Scientific and Industrial Research Organisation*] Chemical Research Laboratories. Technical Paper [*A publication*] (APTA)
CSIRO Coal Res Div Ref TC ... CSIRO [*Commonwealth Scientific and Industrial Research Organisation*] Division of Coal Research. Reference TC [*Technical Communication*] [*A publication*] (APTA)
CSIRO Coal Res Div Tech Commun ... CSIRO [*Commonwealth Scientific and Industrial Research Organisation*] Division of Coal Research. Technical Communication [*A publication*] (APTA)
CSIRO Coal Res Lab Invest Rep ... CSIRO [*Commonwealth Scientific and Industrial Research Organisation*] Coal Research Laboratory. Division of Mineral Chemistry. Investigation Report [*A publication*] (APTA)
CSIRO Coal Res Lab Tech Commun ... CSIRO [*Commonwealth Scientific and Industrial Research Organisation*] Coal Research Laboratory. Division of Mineral Chemistry. Technical Communication [*A publication*] (APTA)
CSIRO Computing Res Sect Memo ... CSIRO [*Commonwealth Scientific and Industrial Research Organisation*] Computing Research Section. Memorandum [*A publication*] (APTA)
CSIRO Consumer Liaison Ser Leaflet ... Consumer Liaison Service Leaflet CSIRO [*Commonwealth Scientific and Industrial Research Organisation*]. Division of Food Research [*A publication*] (APTA)
CSIRO Dig of Curr Act ... CSIRO [*Commonwealth Scientific and Industrial Research Organisation*] Digest of Current Activities [*A publication*] (APTA)
CSIRO Div Anim Genet Ann Rep ... CSIRO [*Commonwealth Scientific and Industrial Research Organisation*] Division of Animal Genetics. Annual Report [*A publication*]
CSIRO Div Appl Geomech Prog Circ ... Computer Program Users Manual CSIRO [*Commonwealth Scientific and Industrial Research Organisation. Division of Applied Geomechanics*] [*A publication*] (APTA)
CSIRO Div Appl Organic Chem Res Rep ... CSIRO [*Commonwealth Scientific and Industrial Research Organisation*] Division of Applied Organic Chemistry. Research Report [*A publication*] (APTA)

CSIRO Div Atmos Phys Tech Pap ... CSIRO [*Commonwealth Scientific and Industrial Research Organisation*] Division of Atmospheric Physics. Technical Paper [*Australia*] [*A publication*]

CSIRO Div Build Res Publ ... CSIRO [*Commonwealth Scientific and Industrial Research Organisation*] Division of Building Research. Publications [*A publication*] (APTA)

CSIRO Div Chem Phys Ann Rep ... CSIRO [*Commonwealth Scientific and Industrial Research Organisation*] Division of Chemical Physics. Annual Report [*A publication*] (APTA)

CSIRO Div Chem Phys Annu Rep ... CSIRO [*Commonwealth Scientific and Industrial Research Organisation*] Division of Chemical Physics. Annual Report [*A publication*]

CSIRO Div Chem Technol Tech Pap ... CSIRO [*Commonwealth Scientific and Industrial Research Organisation*] Division of Chemical Technology. Technical Paper [*A publication*] (APTA)

CSIRO Div Entomol Annu Rep ... CSIRO [*Commonwealth Scientific and Industrial Research Organisation*] Division of Entomology. Annual Report [*A publication*]

CSIRO Div Fish Oceanogr Rep ... CSIRO [*Commonwealth Scientific and Industrial Research Organisation*] Division of Fisheries and Oceanography. Report [*A publication*] (APTA)

CSIRO Div Fish Oceanogr Rep (Aust) ... CSIRO [*Commonwealth Scientific and Industrial Research Organisation*] Division of Fisheries and Oceanography. Report (Australia) [*A publication*]

CSIRO Div Food Res Rep Res ... CSIRO [*Commonwealth Scientific and Industrial Research Organisation*] Division of Food Research. Report of Research [*A publication*] (APTA)

CSIRO Div Forest Prod Technol Paper ... CSIRO [*Commonwealth Scientific and Industrial Research Organisation*] Division of Forest Products. Technological Paper [*A publication*]

CSIRO Div For Res Ann Rep ... CSIRO [*Commonwealth Scientific and Industrial Research Organisation*] Division of Forest Research. Annual Report [*A publication*] (APTA)

CSIRO Div Land Use Res Publ ... CSIRO [*Commonwealth Scientific and Industrial Research Organisation*] Division of Land Use Research. Publications [*A publication*] (APTA)

CSIRO Div Mech Eng Info Serv Leafl ... CSIRO [*Commonwealth Scientific and Industrial Research Organisation*] Division of Mechanical Engineering. Information Service Leaflet [*A publication*] (APTA)

CSIRO Div Mineral Invest Rep ... CSIRO [*Commonwealth Scientific and Industrial Research Organisation*] Division of Mineralogy. Investigation Report [*A publication*] (APTA)

CSIRO Div Mineral Tech Commun ... CSIRO [*Commonwealth Scientific and Industrial Research Organisation*] Division of Mineralogy. Technical Communication [*A publication*] (APTA)

CSIRO Div Miner Chem Invest Rep ... CSIRO [*Commonwealth Scientific and Industrial Research Organisation*] Division of Mineral Chemistry. Investigation Report [*A publication*] (APTA)

CSIRO Div Miner Phys Invest Rep ... CSIRO [*Commonwealth Scientific and Industrial Research Organisation*] Division of Mineral Physics. Investigation Report [*A publication*] (APTA)

CSIRO Div Plant Ind Field Stn Rec Aust ... Australia. Commonwealth Scientific and Industrial Research Organisation. Division of Plant Industry. Field Station Record [*A publication*] (APTA)

CSIRO Div Text Phys Ann Rep ... CSIRO [*Commonwealth Scientific and Industrial Research Organisation*] Division of Textile Physics. Annual Report [*A publication*] (APTA)

CSIRO Div Trop Agron Annu Rep ... CSIRO [*Commonwealth Scientific and Industrial Research Organisation*] Division of Tropical Agronomy. Annual Report [*A publication*]

CSIRO Div Trop Crops Pastures Trop Agron Tech Memo ... CSIRO [*Commonwealth Scientific and Industrial Research Organisation*] Division of Tropical Crops and Pastures. Tropical Agronomy Technical Memorandum [*A publication*] (APTA)

CSIRO Engng Sect C ... CSIRO [*Commonwealth Scientific and Industrial Research Organisation*] Engineering Section. Circular [*A publication*] (APTA)

CSIRO Engng Sect Int Rept ... CSIRO [*Commonwealth Scientific and Industrial Research Organisation*] Engineering Section. Internal Report [*A publication*] (APTA)

CSIRO Entomol Div Tech Pap ... CSIRO [*Commonwealth Scientific and Industrial Research Organisation*] Division of Entomology. Technical Paper [*A publication*] (APTA)

CSIRO Entomol Div TP ... CSIRO [*Commonwealth Scientific and Industrial Research Organisation*] Division of Entomology. Technical Paper [*A publication*] (APTA)

CSIRO Fd Pres Div Circ ... CSIRO [*Commonwealth Scientific and Industrial Research Organisation*] Division of Food Preservation. Circular [*A publication*] (APTA)

CSIRO Fd Preserv Div Tech Pap ... CSIRO [*Commonwealth Scientific and Industrial Research Organisation*] Division of Food Preservation. Technical Paper [*A publication*] (APTA)

CSIRO Fd Preserv Q ... CSIRO [*Commonwealth Scientific and Industrial Research Organisation*] Food Preservation Quarterly [*A publication*] (APTA)

CSIRO Fd Res Q ... CSIRO [*Commonwealth Scientific and Industrial Research Organisation*] Food Research Quarterly [*A publication*] (APTA)

CSIRO Fish Div C ... CSIRO [*Commonwealth Scientific and Industrial Research Organisation*] Division of Fisheries and Oceanography. Circular [*A publication*] (APTA)

CSIRO Fish Div Fish Synopsis ... CSIRO [*Commonwealth Scientific and Industrial Research Organisation*] Division of Fisheries and Oceanography. Fisheries Synopsis [*A publication*] (APTA)

CSIRO Fish Div Oceanogrl Cruise Rep ... CSIRO [*Commonwealth Scientific and Industrial Research Organisation*] Division of Fisheries and Oceanography. Oceanographical Cruise Report [*A publication*] (APTA)

CSIRO Fish Div Oceanogrl Stn List ... CSIRO [*Commonwealth Scientific and Industrial Research Organisation*] Division of Fisheries and Oceanography. Oceanographical Station List [*A publication*] (APTA)

CSIRO Fish Div Oceanogr Station List ... CSIRO [*Commonwealth Scientific and Industrial Research Organisation*] Division of Fisheries and Oceanography. Oceanographical Station List [*A publication*] (APTA)

CSIRO Fish Div Rep ... CSIRO [*Commonwealth Scientific and Industrial Research Organisation*] Division of Fisheries and Oceanography. Report [*A publication*] (APTA)

CSIRO Fish Div Tech Pap ... CSIRO [*Commonwealth Scientific and Industrial Research Organisation*] Division of Fisheries and Oceanography. Technical Paper [*A publication*] (APTA)

CSIRO Fish Div TP ... CSIRO [*Commonwealth Scientific and Industrial Research Organisation*] Division of Fisheries and Oceanography. Technical Paper [*A publication*] (APTA)

CSIRO Food Pres Div C ... CSIRO [*Commonwealth Scientific and Industrial Research Organisation*] Division of Food Preservation. Circular [*A publication*] (APTA)

CSIRO Food Pres Div TP ... CSIRO [*Commonwealth Scientific and Industrial Research Organisation*] Division of Food Preservation. Technical Paper [*A publication*] (APTA)

CSIRO Food Preserv Q ... CSIRO [*Commonwealth Scientific and Industrial Research Organisation*] Food Preservation Quarterly [*A publication*]

CSIRO Food Res Q ... CSIRO [*Commonwealth Scientific and Industrial Research Organisation*] Division of Food Research. Food Research Quarterly [*A publication*] (APTA)

CSIRO Food Res Q Suppl Ser ... CSIRO [*Commonwealth Scientific and Industrial Research Organisation*] Division of Food Research. Food Research Quarterly. Supplementary Series [*A publication*] (APTA)

CSIRO Forest Prod Newsl ... CSIRO [*Commonwealth Scientific and Industrial Research Organisation*] Forest Products Newsletter [*A publication*]

CSIRO For Prod Div Technol P ... CSIRO [*Commonwealth Scientific and Industrial Research Organisation*] Division of Forest Products. Technological Paper [*A publication*] (APTA)

CSIRO For Prod Div Technol Pap ... CSIRO [*Commonwealth Scientific and Industrial Research Organisation*] Division of Forest Products. Technological Paper [*A publication*] (APTA)

CSIRO For Prod Newsl ... CSIRO [*Commonwealth Scientific and Industrial Research Organisation*] Division of Forest Products. Forest Products Newsletter [*A publication*] (APTA)

CSIRO For Prod Newslett ... CSIRO [*Commonwealth Scientific and Industrial Research Organisation*] Forest Products Newsletter [*A publication*] (APTA)

CSIRO For Prod Newsletter ... CSIRO [*Commonwealth Scientific and Industrial Research Organisation*] Forest Products Newsletter [*A publication*] (APTA)

CSIRO For Prod Tech Notes ... CSIRO [*Commonwealth Scientific and Industrial Research Organisation*] Division of Forest Products. CSIRO Forest Products Technical Notes [*A publication*] (APTA)

CSIRO Ind Res News ... CSIRO [*Commonwealth Scientific and Industrial Research Organisation*] Industrial Research News [*A publication*] (APTA)

CSIRO Inst Earth Resour Invest Rep ... CSIRO [*Commonwealth Scientific and Industrial Research Organisation*] Institute of Earth Resources. Investigation Report [*A publication*] (APTA)

CSIRO Inst Earth Resour Tech Commun ... CSIRO [*Commonwealth Scientific and Industrial Research Organisation*] Institute of Earth Resources. Technical Communication [*A publication*] (APTA)

CSIRO Irrig Res Stat TP ... CSIRO [*Commonwealth Scientific and Industrial Research Organisation*] Irrigation Research Stations. Technical Paper [*A publication*] (APTA)

CSIRO Land Res Regional Surv Div Tech Pap ... CSIRO [*Commonwealth Scientific and Industrial Research Organisation*] Division of Land Research and Regional Survey. Technical Paper [*A publication*] (APTA)

CSIRO Land Res Regional Surv Div TP ... CSIRO [*Commonwealth Scientific and Industrial Research Organisation*] Division of Land Research and Regional Survey. Technical Paper [*A publication*] (APTA)

CSIRO Land Res Ser ... CSIRO [*Commonwealth Scientific and Industrial Research Organisation*] Land Research Series [*A publication*] (APTA)

CSIRO Leaflet Ser ... CSIRO [*Commonwealth Scientific and Industrial Research Organisation*] Leaflet Series [*A publication*] (APTA)

CSIRO Mar Biochem Unit Annu Rep ... CSIRO [*Commonwealth Scientific and Industrial Research Organisation*] Marine Biochemistry Unit. Annual Report [*A publication*]

CSIRO Marine Biochem Unit Ann Rep ... CSIRO [*Commonwealth Scientific and Industrial Research Organisation*] Marine Biochemistry Unit. Annual Report [*A publication*] (APTA)

CSIRO Math Statist Div Tech Pap ... CSIRO [*Commonwealth Scientific and Industrial Research Organisation*] Division of Mathematical Statistics. Technical Paper [*A publication*] (APTA)

CSIRO Math Statist Div TP ... CSIRO [*Commonwealth Scientific and Industrial Research Organisation*] Division of Mathematical Statistics. Technical Paper [*A publication*] (APTA)

CSIRO Mech Engng Div Circ ... CSIRO [*Commonwealth Scientific and Industrial Research Organisation*] Division of Mechanical Engineering. Circular [*A publication*] (APTA)

CSIRO Mech Engng Div Rep ... CSIRO [*Commonwealth Scientific and Industrial Research Organisation*] Division of Mechanical Engineering. Report [*A publication*] (APTA)

CSIRO Met Phys Div Tech Pap ... CSIRO [*Commonwealth Scientific and Industrial Research Organisation*] Division of Meteorological Physics. Technical Paper [*A publication*] (APTA)

CSIRO Minerag Investig TP ... CSIRO [*Commonwealth Scientific and Industrial Research Organisation*] Mineragraphic Investigations. Technical Paper [*A publication*] (APTA)

CSIRO Minerag Invest Tech Pap ... CSIRO [*Commonwealth Scientific and Industrial Research Organisation*] Mineragraphic Investigations. Technical Paper [*A publication*] (APTA)

CSIRO Miner Phys Sect Invest Rep ... CSIRO [*Commonwealth Scientific and Industrial Research Organisation*] Mineral Physics Section. Investigation Report [*A publication*] (APTA)

CSIRO Miner Res Lab Ann Rep ... CSIRO [*Commonwealth Scientific and Industrial Research Organisation*] Minerals Research Laboratories. Annual Report [*A publication*] (APTA)

CSIRO Miner Res Lab Annu Rep ... CSIRO [*Commonwealth Scientific and Industrial Research Organisation*] Minerals Research Laboratories. Annual Report [*A publication*]

CSIRO Miner Res Lab Div Mineral Tech Commun ... CSIRO [*Commonwealth Scientific and Industrial Research Organisation*] Minerals Research Laboratories. Division of Mineralogy. Technical Communication [*A publication*] (APTA)

CSIRO Miner Res Lab Invest Rep ... CSIRO [*Commonwealth Scientific and Industrial Research Organisation*] Minerals Research Laboratories. Investigation Report [*A publication*]

CSIRO Miner Res Lab Res Rev ... CSIRO [*Commonwealth Scientific and Industrial Research Organisation*] Minerals Research Laboratories. Research Review [*A publication*] (APTA)

CSIRO Miner Res Lab Tech Commun ... CSIRO [*Commonwealth Scientific and Industrial Research Organisation*] Minerals Research Laboratories. Technical Communication [*A publication*] (APTA)

CSIRO Natl Meas Lab Bienn Rep ... CSIRO [*Commonwealth Scientific and Industrial Research Organisation*] National Measurement Laboratory. Biennial Report [*A publication*]

CSIRO Natl Meas Lab Tech Pap ... CSIRO [*Commonwealth Scientific and Industrial Research Organisation*] National Measurement Laboratory. Technical Paper [*A publication*]

CSIRO Natl Measure Lab Biennial Rep ... CSIRO [*Commonwealth Scientific and Industrial Research Organisation*] National Measurement Laboratory. Biennial Report [*A publication*] (APTA)

CSIRO Natl Stand Lab Bienn Rep ... CSIRO [*Commonwealth Scientific and Industrial Research Organisation*] National Standards Laboratory. Biennial Report [*A publication*]

CSIRO Nat Stand Lab Div Appl Phys Test Pamph ... CSIRO [*Commonwealth Scientific and Industrial Research Organisation*] National Standards Laboratory. Division of Applied Physics. Test Pamphlet [*A publication*] (APTA)

CSIRO Nat Stands Lab Circ ... CSIRO [*Commonwealth Scientific and Industrial Research Organisation*] National Standards Laboratory. Circular [*A publication*] (APTA)

CSIRO Nat Stands Lab Tech Pap ... CSIRO [*Commonwealth Scientific and Industrial Research Organisation*] National Standards Laboratory. Technical Paper [*A publication*] (APTA)

CSIRO Nat Stands Lab Test Pamphl ... CSIRO [*Commonwealth Scientific and Industrial Research Organisation*] National Standards Laboratory. Test Pamphlet [*A publication*] (APTA)

CSIRO Nat Stands Lab TP ... CSIRO [*Commonwealth Scientific and Industrial Research Organisation*] National Standards Laboratory. Technical Paper [*A publication*] (APTA)

CSIROOA Bul ... CSIROOA Bulletin. Journal of the Association of Officers of the Commonwealth Scientific and Industrial Research Organisation [*A publication*] (APTA)

CSIRO Phys Met Sec Tech Pap ... CSIRO [*Commonwealth Scientific and Industrial Research Organisation*] Physical Metallurgy Section. Technical Paper [*A publication*] (APTA)

CSIRO Plant Ind Div Field Sta Rec ... CSIRO [*Commonwealth Scientific and Industrial Research Organisation*] Division of Plant Industry. Field Station Record [*A publication*] (APTA)

CSIRO Plant Ind Div Field Stn Rec ... CSIRO [*Commonwealth Scientific and Industrial Research Organisation*] Division of Plant Industry. Field Station Record [*A publication*] (APTA)

CSIRO Plant Ind Div Tech Pap ... CSIRO [*Commonwealth Scientific and Industrial Research Organisation*] Division of Plant Industry. Technical Paper [*A publication*] (APTA)

CSIRO Plant Ind Div TP ... CSIRO [*Commonwealth Scientific and Industrial Research Organisation*] Division of Plant Industry. Technical Paper [*A publication*] (APTA)

CSIRO Plant Ind TP ... CSIRO [*Commonwealth Scientific and Industrial Research Organisation*] Division of Plant Industry. Technical Paper [*A publication*] (APTA)

CSIRO Radiophys Div Rept ... CSIRO [*Commonwealth Scientific and Industrial Research Organisation*] Division of Radiophysics. Report [*A publication*] (APTA)

CSIRO Sci Index ... CSIRO [*Commonwealth Scientific and Industrial Research Organisation*] Science Index [*A publication*] (APTA)

CSIRO Soil Mechanics Sect Geotech Rep ... CSIRO [*Commonwealth Scientific and Industrial Research Organisation*] Soil Mechanics Section. Geotechnical Report [*A publication*] (APTA)

CSIRO Soil Mechanics Sect Tech Rep ... CSIRO [*Commonwealth Scientific and Industrial Research Organisation*] Soil Mechanics Section. Technical Report [*A publication*] (APTA)

CSIRO Soil Mech Div Tech Pap ... CSIRO [*Commonwealth Scientific and Industrial Research Organisation*] Division of Soil Mechanics. Technical Paper [*A publication*] (APTA)

CSIRO Soil Mech Div Tech Rep ... CSIRO [*Commonwealth Scientific and Industrial Research Organisation*] Division of Soil Mechanics. Technical Report [*A publication*] (APTA)

CSIRO Soil Mech Sect Tech Rep ... CSIRO [*Commonwealth Scientific and Industrial Research Organisation*] Soil Mechanics Section. Technical Report [*A publication*] (APTA)

CSIRO Soil Pub ... CSIRO [*Commonwealth Scientific and Industrial Research Organisation*] Soil Publications [*A publication*] (APTA)

CSIRO Soils Div SLU ... CSIRO [*Commonwealth Scientific and Industrial Research Organisation*] Division of Soils. Soils and Land Use Series [*A publication*] (APTA)

CSIRO Text Ind Div Rep ... CSIRO [*Commonwealth Scientific and Industrial Research Organisation*] Division of Textile Industry. Report [*A publication*] (APTA)

CSIRO Text News ... CSIRO [*Commonwealth Scientific and Industrial Research Organisation*] Wood Research Laboratory. Textile News [*A publication*] (APTA)

CSIRO Text Phys Div Rep ... CSIRO [*Commonwealth Scientific and Industrial Research Organisation*] Division of Textile Physics. Report [*A publication*] (APTA)

CSIRO Trop Pastures Div TP ... CSIRO [*Commonwealth Scientific and Industrial Research Organisation*] Division of Tropical Pastures. Technical Paper [*A publication*] (APTA)

CSIRO Wheat Res Unit Annu Rep ... CSIRO [*Commonwealth Scientific and Industrial Research Organisation*] Wheat Research Unit. Annual Report [*A publication*]

CSIRO Wildl Res ... CSIRO [*Commonwealth Scientific and Industrial Research Organisation*] Wildlife Research [*A publication*]

CSIRO Wildl Res Div Tech Pap ... CSIRO [*Commonwealth Scientific and Industrial Research Organisation*] Division of Wildlife Research. Technical Paper [*A publication*] (APTA)

CSIRO Wildl Res Div TP ... CSIRO [*Commonwealth Scientific and Industrial Research Organisation*] Division of Wildlife Research. Technical Paper [*A publication*] (APTA)

CSIRO Wildl Surv Sect TP ... CSIRO [*Commonwealth Scientific and Industrial Research Organisation*] Wildlife Survey Section. Technical Paper [*A publication*] (APTA)

CSIRO Wool Text News ... CSIRO [*Commonwealth Scientific and Industrial Research Organisation*] Division of Textile Industry. Wool Textile News [*A publication*] (APTA)

CSIRO Wool Text Res Labs Rep ... CSIRO [*Commonwealth Scientific and Industrial Research Organisation*] Wool Textile Research Laboratories. Report [*A publication*] (APTA)

CSIRO Wool Text Res Labs TC ... CSIRO [*Commonwealth Scientific and Industrial Research Organisation*] Wool Textile Research Laboratories. Trade Circular [*A publication*] (APTA)

CSIRO Wool Text Res Labs TP ... CSIRO [*Commonwealth Scientific and Industrial Research Organisation*] Wool Textile Research Laboratories. Technical Paper [*A publication*] (APTA)

CSIR Res Rep ... CSIR [*Council for Scientific and Industrial Research*] Research Report [*A publication*]

CSIR Res Rev ... CSIR [*Council for Scientific and Industrial Research*] Research Review [*A publication*]

CSIR Spec Rep FIS ... CSIR [*Council for Scientific and Industrial Research*] Special Report FIS [*A publication*]
CSIRT ...... Comite Scientifique International de Recherches sur les Trypanosomiases
CSIR Zool Monogr ... CSIR [*Council for Scientific and Industrial Research*] Zoological Monograph [*A publication*]
CSIS .... Canadian Security and Intelligence Service
CSIS .... Canadian Society for Industrial Security
CSIS .... Canadian Society for Italian Studies
CSIS .... Center for Strategic and International Studies [*Georgetown University*]
CSIS .... Central Secondary Item Stratification [*Military*]   (AFIT)
CSIS .... Civil Service Insurance Society [*British*]
CSIS .... Comtrol Systems [*NASDAQ symbol*]   (NQ)
CSIS .... Containment Spray Injection System [*Nuclear energy*]   (NRCH)
CSIS (Cent Strategic Int Stud) Energy Policy Ser ... CSIS (Center for Strategic and International Studies) Energy Policy Series [*A publication*]
CSISM...... Cryptographic Supplement to the Industrial Security Manual [*DoD*]
CSISRS ..... Cross-Section Information Storage and Retrieval System [*Brookhaven National Laboratory*] [*Information service or system*]
CSIT .... Chapin Social Insight Test [*Psychology*]
CSIT .... Combat System Integration Test [*Military*]   (CAAL)
CSIT .... Combat System Interface Test [*Military*]   (CAAL)
CSIT .... Comite Sportif International du Travail [*International Workers Sport Committee*] [*Brussels, Belgium*]   (EAIO)
CSITSL ..... Comite Syndical International du Tourisme Social et des Loisirs [*International Trade Unions Committee of Social Tourism and Leisure - ITUCSTL*]   (EA)
CSITT....... Combat System Interface Test Tool   (NVT)
CSIU.......... Core Segment Interface Unit   (NASA)
CSJ .... Cape San Juan [*Puerto Rico*] [*Seismograph station code, US Geological Survey*]   (SEIS)
CSJ .... Carolian Systems International, Inc. [*Toronto Stock Exchange symbol*]
CSJ .... Casopis pro Slovanske Jazyky, Literaturu, a Dejiny SSSR [*A publication*]
CSJ .... Christian Science Journal [*A publication*]
CSJ .... Citizens for Social Justice   (EA)
CSJ .... Civil Service Journal [*A publication*]
CSJ .... Commission for Social Justice   (EA)
CSJ .... Computer Security Journal [*A publication*]
CSJ .... Congregatio Sancti Joseph [*Congregation of St. Joseph*] [*Roman Catholic religious order*]
CSJ .... Control System Jet
CSJ .... Court of Summary Jurisdiction [*British*]   (ROG)
CSJ .... Crime and Social Justice [*Australia*] [*A publication*]
CS & J........ Cushing, Storey, and Joselyn's Election Cases [*Massachusetts*] [*A publication*]   (DLA)
CSj .... San Jose Public Library, San Jose, CA [*Library symbol*] [*Library of Congress*]   (LCLS)
CSJ .... San Jose State University, San Jose, CA [*OCLC symbol*]   (OCLC)
CSJjac.......... San Jacinto Public Library, San Jacinto, CA [*Library symbol*] [*Library of Congress*]   (LCLS)
CSJAGA.... Military Affairs Division, Office of Judge Advocate General, United States Army   (DLA)
CSJjB.......... Berliner, Cohen & Biogini, Law Library, San Jose, CA [*Library symbol*] [*Library of Congress*]   (LCLS)
CSJB......... Community of St. John the Baptist [*Anglican religious community*]
CSJjb .... San Juan Bautista City Library, San Juan Bautista, CA [*Library symbol*] [*Library of Congress*]   (LCLS)
CSJCA....... Central Sephardic Jewish Community of America   (EA)
CSJjCiC....... San Jose City College, San Jose, CA [*Library symbol*] [*Library of Congress*]   (LCLS)
CSJjCL .... Santa Clara County Free Library, San Jose, CA [*Library symbol*] [*Library of Congress*]   (LCLS)
CSJjCLA ..... Cooperative Library Agency for Systems and Services, San Jose, CA [*Library symbol*] [*Library of Congress*]   (LCLS)
CSJE.......... Community of St. John the Evangelist [*Anglican religious community*]
CSJjE.......... Evergreen Valley College, San Jose, CA [*Library symbol*] [*Library of Congress*]   (LCLS)
CSJF......... Case Study and Justification Folder
CSJjGS .... Church of Jesus Christ of Latter-Day Saints, Genealogical Society Library, San Jose Branch, San Jose, CA [*Library symbol*] [*Library of Congress*]   (LCLS)
CSJjIBM ..... International Business Machines Corp., San Jose, CA [*Library symbol*] [*Library of Congress*]   (LCLS)
CSJMENA ... Community for Social Justice in the Middle East and North Africa   (EA)
CSJP.......... Cahiers Saint-John Perse [*A publication*]
CS of JT..... Chief Superintendent of Juvenile Templars [*Order of Good Templars*] [*Freemasonry*]   (ROG)
CSJjU .... San Jose State University, San Jose, CA [*Library symbol*] [*Library of Congress*]   (LCLS)
CSJWOE... Commission on the Status of Jewish War Orphans in Europe, American Section [*Inactive*]   (EA)

CSK............ Cable Splicing Kit
CSK............ Cap Skirring [*Senegal*] [*Airport symbol*]   (OAG)
CSK............ Carnes Creek Explorations [*Vancouver Stock Exchange symbol*]
CSK............ Cask
CSK............ Cathodic Survey Kit
CSK............ Catskill Airways [*Oneonta, NY*] [*FAA designator*]   (FAAC)
CSK............ Chesapeake Corp. [*NYSE symbol*]   (SPSG)
CSK............ Chief Storekeeper [*Navy rating*] [*Obsolete*]
CSK............ Community of St. Katharine of Egypt [*Anglican religious community*]
CSK............ Consumer Survival Kit [*Program on public TV*]
CSK............ Cooperative Study of the Kuroshio [*UNESCO*]
CSK............ Countersink   (KSC)
CSK............ Czechoslovakia [*ANSI three-letter standard code*]   (CNC)
CSKCB ...... Chief Storekeeper, Construction Battalion, Stevedore [*Navy rating*] [*Obsolete*]
CSKD........ Chief Storekeeper, Disbursing [*Navy rating*] [*Obsolete*]
CSKH........ Countersunk Head
CSKK........ CSK Corp. [*NASDAQ symbol*]   (NQ)
CSKKA ...... Chikusan Shikenjo Kenkyu [*A publication*]
CSKNA...... Ceskoslovenska Neurologie [*Later, Ceskoslovenska Neurologie a Neurochirurgie*] [*A publication*]
CSKO .... Countersink Other Side
CSKS .... Casks
CSKT .... Chief Storekeeper, Technical [*Navy rating*] [*Obsolete*]
CSKV .... Chief Storekeeper, Aviation [*Navy rating*] [*Obsolete*]
CSL............ Cambridge Studies in Linguistics [*A publication*]
CSL............ Canada Steamship Lines
CSL............ Canadian Slovak League
CSL............ Canreos Minerals [*Vancouver Stock Exchange symbol*]
CSL............ Carlisle Companies [*NYSE symbol*]   (SPSG)
CSL............ Center for the Study of Learning [*Pittsburgh, PA*] [*Department of Education*]   (GRD)
CSL............ Ceskoslovenska Strana Lidova [*Czechoslovak People's Party*]   (PPE)
CSL............ Chemical Systems Laboratory [*Later, CRDC*] [*Army*]   (RDA)
CSL............ Chicago Short Line Railway Co. [*AAR code*]
CSL............ Cinderella Softball Leagues   (EA)
CSL............ Circle of State Librarians [*British*]
CSL............ Circuit Switched Line [*Telecommunications*]   (MCD)
CSL............ Coaxial Slotted Line
CSL............ Code Selection Language [*Data processing*]   (BUR)
CSL............ Coles Signal Laboratory [*Army*]   (MCD)
CSL............ Combat Support Liaison   (CINC)
CSL............ Combat Surveillance Laboratory
CSL............ Combined Single Limit [*Insurance*]
CSL............ Command Signal Limiter   (MCD)
CSL............ Commander Service Force, Atlantic   (MCD)
CSL............ Common Specification Language   (NATG)
CSL............ Commonwealth Serum Laboratories [*Australia*]
CSL............ Communication Sciences Laboratory [*University of Florida*]
CSl............ Communication Services Limited [*Hong Kong*] [*Telecommunications*]   (TSSD)
CSL............ Community of St. Laurence [*Anglican religious community*]
CSL............ Comparative Systems Laboratory
CSL............ Complete Service Life
CSL............ Component Save List [*Military*]   (AFIT)
CSL............ Computer Sensitive Language [*Programming language*]
CSL............ Computer Simulation Language   (BUR)
CSL............ Computer Status Lights   (MCD)
CSL............ Computer Structure Language [*1974*] [*Data processing*]   (CSR)
CSL............ Computer System Language
CSL............ Computer Systems Laboratory [*Bethesda, MD*] [*Department of Health and Human Services*]   (GRD)
CSL............ Confederation des Syndicats Libres [*Formerly, Confederation Francaise du Travail*] [*France*]   (EY)
CSL............ Conseil Superieur de Livre [*Canada*]
CSL............ Console   (AAG)
CSL............ Control and Simulation Language [*Data processing*]
CSL............ Control and Status Logic   (KSC)
CSL............ Control Systems Laboratory [*University of Illinois*]   (MCD)
CSL............ Coordinated Science Laboratory [*University of Illinois*] [*Research center*]
CSL............ Corpus Scriptorum Ecclesiasticorum Latinorum [*A publication*]
CSL............ Cosmopolitan Soccer League   (EA)
CSL............ Counsel   (ROG)
CSL............ Crew Systems Laboratory [*NASA*]   (NASA)
CSL............ Current Switch Logic   (IEEE)
CSl .... San Leandro Community Library Center, San Leandro, CA [*Library symbol*] [*Library of Congress*]   (LCLS)
CSL............ San Luis Obispo, CA [*Location identifier*] [*FAA*]   (FAAL)
CSL............ Scanshore [*A publication*]
CSL............ University of Southern California, Los Angeles, CA [*OCLC symbol*]   (OCLC)
CSLA .... Canadian School Library Association
CSLA .... Canadian Society of Landscape Architects
CSLA .... Church and Synagogue Library Association   (EA)
CSLA .... Communications Security Logistics Agency   (MCD)
CSLA .... Computer Science Lecturers' Association [*British*]
CSLB .... Computer Services - Long Beach   (MCD)
CSLBTS .... Combat System Land-Based Test Site   (CAAL)

CSLBull..... C. S. Lewis Society. Bulletin [*New York*] [*A publication*]
CSLC......... Center for Studies in Language and Communication [*Gallaudet College*] [*Research center*]　(RCD)
CSLC......... Coherent Side-Lobe Cancellation
CSLC......... Confederation des Syndicats Libres du Congo [*Congolese Free Trade Union Federation*]
CSLC......... Consolidated Statutes of Lower Canada [*A publication*]　(DLA)
CSLDB...... California Spanish Language Data Base [*Information service or system*]　(IID)
CSLDF...... Creation Science Legal Defense Fund　(EA)
CSLDT...... Consolidate [*Accounting*]　(FAAC)
CSLEA...... Center for the Study of Liberal Education for Adults　(EA)
CSLES...... Children's Stressful Life Events Scale
CSLFC...... Council of Savings and Loan Financial Corporations　(EA)
CSLGC...... Committee on State and Local Government Cooperation
CSLH......... Cotton States Life & Health Insurance Co. [*NASDAQ symbol*]　(NQ)
CSLHA...... Chartered Surveyor. Land Hydrographic and Minerals Quarterly [*A publication*]
CSLI......... Center for the Study of Language and Information [*Stanford University*] [*Research center*]　(RCD)
C & SLib... Church and Synagogue Libraries [*A publication*]
CSLIN...... Contract Subline Item Number　(MCD)
C & SLJ..... Company and Securities Law Journal [*Australia*] [*A publication*]
CSLJa........ Casopis pro Slovanske Jazyky, Literaturu, a Dejiny SSSR [*A publication*]
Cslka Derm ... Ceskoslovenska Dermatologie [*A publication*]
Cslka Farm ... Ceskoslovenska Farmacie [*A publication*]
Cslka Fysiol ... Ceskoslovenska Fysiologie [*A publication*]
Cslka Stomat ... Ceskoslovenska Stomatologie [*A publication*]
CSLL......... Sacramento County Law Library, Sacramento, CA [*Library symbol*] [*Library of Congress*]　(LCLS)
CSLM....... Consolidated Mercantile Corp. [*NASDAQ symbol*]　(NQ)
CSLMR.... Chief Sailmaker [*British military*]　(DMA)
CSLN......... California State Library Newsletter [*A publication*]
CSLP......... Canada Student Loans Program
CSLP......... Canadian Slavonic Papers [*A publication*]
CSLP......... Center for Short-Lived Phenomena　(EA)
CSLP......... Center for the Study of Law and Politics　(EA)
CSLR......... City and South London Railway ["*The Tube*"]　(ROG)
C & SLR... City and South London Railway ["*The Tube*"]　(ROG)
CSLR......... Cleveland State Law Review [*A publication*]
CSLR......... Consulier Industries, Inc. [*NASDAQ symbol*]　(NQ)
CSLS......... Center for the Study of Law and Society [*University of California, Berkeley*] [*Research center*]　(RCD)
CSLS......... Centre for Socio-Legal Studies [*British*]　(CB)
CSLS......... Civil Service Legal Society [*British*]
CSLS......... Cost Schedule, Logistics, and NATO Standardization　(MCD)
CSLT......... Canadian Society of Laboratory Technologists　(EAIO)
CSLT......... Community Shares Limited [*Fond Du Lac, WI*] [*NASDAQ symbol*]　(NQ)
CSlu.......... San Luis Obispo Public Library, San Luis Obispo, CA [*Library symbol*] [*Library of Congress*]　(LCLS)
CSluCL...... San Luis Obispo County Free Library, San Luis Obispo, CA [*Library symbol*] [*Library of Congress*]　(LCLS)
CSluCu....... Cuesta College, San Luis Obispo, CA [*Library symbol*] [*Library of Congress*]　(LCLS)
CSluGS...... Church of Jesus Christ of Latter-Day Saints, Genealogical Society Library, San Luis Obispo Branch, San Luis Obispo, CA [*Library symbol*] [*Library of Congress*]　(LCLS)
CSluSP...... California Polytechnic State University, San Luis Obispo, CA [*Library symbol*] [*Library of Congress*]　(LCLS)
CSM......... Call Supervision Module [*Telecommunications*]　(TEL)
CSM......... Camborne School of Mines [*British*]　(IRUK)
CSM......... Camouflage Signature Measurement [*Army*]　(RDA)
CSM......... Carotid Sinus Massage [*Cardiology*]
CSM......... Casamicciolo [*Isola D'Ischia*] [*Italy*] [*Seismograph station code, US Geological Survey*] [*Closed*]　(SEIS)
CS & M...... Cellular Sales & Marketing [*Creative Communications*] [*Information service or system*]　(IID)
CSM......... Cellular Slime Mold [*Biology*]
CSM......... Cerebrospinal Meningitis [*Medicine*]
CSM......... Certified Shopping Center Manager [*Designation awarded by International Council of Shopping Centers*]
CSM......... Chaparral Steel Co. [*NYSE symbol*]　(SPSG)
CSM......... Chemical Surety Material　(MCD)
CSM......... Chief Signalman [*Navy rating*] [*Obsolete*]
CSM......... Chief of Staff Memorandum [*Military*]　(AABC)
CSM......... Christian Science Monitor [*A publication*]
CSM......... Circumstellar Matter [*Astrophysics*]
CSM......... Clinton, OK [*Location identifier*] [*FAA*]　(FAAL)
CSM......... Close Support Missile [*Air Force*]　(MCD)
CSM......... Coalition for Sound Money　(EA)
CSM......... Coaxial Switching Matrix
CSM......... Coffin Strategic Missile
CSM......... College of Saint Mary [*Omaha, NE*]
CSM......... College of San Mateo [*California*]
CSM......... Colonial Society of Massachusetts　(EA)
CSM......... Colorado School of Mines [*Golden, CO*]
Csm.......... Colosseum [*Record label*]

CSM......... Combat System Manager [*Military*]　(CAAL)
CSM......... Combustion Stability Monitor
CSM......... Command Sergeant Major [*Army*]
CSM......... Command and Service Module [*NASA*]　(MCD)
CSM......... Commission on Soil Mineralogy　(EA)
CSM......... Commission for Synoptic Meteorology
CSM......... Committee on the Safety of Machines [*British*]
CSM......... Committee on Safety of Medicines [*British*]
CSM......... Committee of Special Means [*British military*]　(DMA)
CSM......... Common Support Module [*NASA*]　(NASA)
CSM......... Company Sergeant-Major [*Army*] [*British*]
CSM......... Composite Signal Mixer
CSM......... Computer Status Matrix　(MCD)
CSM......... Computer System Manual
CSM......... Confessing Synod Ministries　(EA)
CSM......... Consolidated Manitou Resources [*Vancouver Stock Exchange symbol*]
CSM......... Consolidated Statutes of Manitoba [*A publication*]　(DLA)
CSM......... Continental Shelf Mining
CSM......... Continuous Sampler Monitor [*Radioactivity*]
CSM......... Continuous Sheet Memory [*Data processing*]　(BUR)
CSM......... Continuous Sheet Music　(MCD)
CSM......... Continuous Slowing Down Models [*Physics*]
CSM......... Continuous Survey of Machinery
CSM......... Control Stick Maneuver　(MCD)
CSM......... Convention Services Manager
CSM......... Convexity, Symmetry, Maximum [*Statistics*]
CSM......... Corn, Soybean, and Milk Products [*Main ingredients of a formulated food*]
CSM......... Cottonseed Meal
CSM......... Council of the Southern Mountains　(EA)
CSM......... Council for the Study of Mankind [*Defunct*]　(EA)
CSM......... Creation Science Movement [*British*]
CSM......... Master of Christian Science
CSM......... McGeorge School of Law, University of the Pacific, Sacramento, CA [*Library symbol*] [*Library of Congress*]　(LCLS)
CSm.......... San Marino Public Library, San Marino, CA [*Library symbol*] [*Library of Congress*]　(LCLS)
CSM......... Sisters of St. Martha of Prince Edward Island [*Roman Catholic religious order*]
CSM......... Southern California College, Costa Mesa, CA [*OCLC symbol*]　(OCLC)
CSMA....... Canadian Society of Marine Artists
CSMA....... Carrier Sense Multiple Access [*Telecommunications*]
CSMA....... Celiac, Superior Mesenteric Artery [*Anatomy*]
CSMA....... Chain Saw Manufacturers Association [*Later, PPEMA*]　(EA)
CSMA....... Chemical Specialties Manufacturers Association　(EA)
CSMA....... Communications Systems Management Association　(MCD)
CSM and AA ... Community of St. Michael and All Angels [*Anglican religious community*]
CSMA/CA ... Carrier Sense Multiple Access with Collision Avoidance [*Networking technique*]
CSMA/CD ... Carrier Sense Multiple Access with Collision Detection [*Networking technique*]
CSMAM.... CINCPAC [*Commander-in-Chief, Pacific*] Supplement to the Military Assistance Manual　(CINC)
CSmarP..... Palomar College, San Marcos, CA [*Library symbol*] [*Library of Congress*]　(LCLS)
CSmat........ San Mateo Public Library, San Mateo, CA [*Library symbol*] [*Library of Congress*]　(LCLS)
CSmatC...... College of San Mateo, San Mateo, CA [*Library symbol*] [*Library of Congress*]　(LCLS)
CSmatHi..... San Mateo County Historical Association, San Mateo, CA [*Library symbol*] [*Library of Congress*]　(LCLS)
CSmatT...... San Mateo Times, San Mateo, CA [*Library symbol*] [*Library of Congress*]　(LCLS)
CSMB........ Center for Study of Multiple Birth　(EA)
CSMBDC.. Cambridge Studies in Mathematical Biology [*A publication*]
CSMC........ Catholic Students' Mission Crusade [*Defunct*]
CSMCC..... Charles Stewart Mott Community College [*Formerly, Genesee Community College*] [*Flint, MI*]
CSMD........ Combat System Mission Demonstration [*Military*]　(CAAL)
CSMDA..... Canadian Services Medical Journal [*A publication*]
CSMDAF.. Canadian Services Medical Journal [*A publication*]
CSME........ Canadian Society for Mechanical Engineering
CSME........ Catholic Society for Marriage Education [*Australia*]
CSME........ Confederation Syndicale Mondiale des Enseignants [*World Confederation of Teachers - WCT*] [*Brussels, Belgium*]　(EAIO)
CSMed....... Sacramento County Medical Society, Sacramento, CA [*Library symbol*] [*Library of Congress*]　(LCLS)
CSMF........ Carl Schurz Memorial Foundation [*Later, NCSA*]　(EA)
CSMFB..... Central States Motor Freight Bureau
CSMFTA... Central & Southern Motor Freight Tariff Association, Inc.
CSMG........ Castable Smoke Mix Grenade　(MCD)
CSMG........ Center for the Study of Multiple Gestation [*Later, CSMB*]　(EA)
CSmH........ Henry E. Huntington Library, San Marino, CA [*Library symbol*] [*Library of Congress*]　(LCLS)
CSMHA.... Center for Studies of Mental Health of the Aging [*National Institute of Mental Health*]　(GRD)

CSMI......... Company Sergeant-Major Instructor [Army] [British]
CSmi .... Smith River Library, Smith River, CA [Library symbol] [Library of Congress] (LCLS)
CSMIA ...... Mineral Industries Bulletin. Colorado School of Mines [A publication]
CSMITH... Coppersmith (KSC)
CSMJAX... Connecticut State Medical Journal [A publication]
CSML....... Contractor Support Material List (MCD)
CSMLA5.... Comunicaciones. Sociedad Malacologica del Uruguay [A publication]
CSMLT ..... Cambridge Studies in Medieval Life and Thought [A publication]
CSMM ...... Camborne School of Metalliferous Mining [British]
CSMM ...... Crew Station Maintenance Manual [Navy] (CAAL)
CSMMCA ... Clinical Science and Molecular Medicine [A publication]
CSMMG.... Conjoint Society of Massage and Medical Gymnastics [British]
CSMMI.... Canadian Society of Military Medals and Insignia
CSMMS.... Christian Science Monitor. Magazine Section [A publication]
CSMO .... Close Station March Order (MCD)
CSMO .... Cosmo Communications Corp. [NASDAQ symbol] (NQ)
CSMOL..... Control Station Manual Operating Level (AAG)
C S Mon Mag ... Christian Science Monitor. Magazine Section [A publication]
CSMP........ Combat System Management Plan [Military] (CAAL)
CSMP........ Continuous System Modeling Program [Data processing]
CSMP........ Current Ship's Maintenance Project
CSMPS..... Computerized Scientific Management Planning System (AAG)
CSMQD .... Colorado School of Mines. Quarterly [A publication]
CSMR....... Centre for the Study of Mental Retardation [Canada]
CSMRCP .. Australia. Commonwealth Scientific and Industrial Research Organisation. Minerals Research Laboratories. Annual Report [A publication]
CSMS .... Central System Maintenance Support (NATG)
CSMS .... College of Saint Mary of the Springs [Ohio]
CSMS .... Combined Support Maintenance Shop [USNG] (MCD)
CSMS .... Communications Security Material System (MCD)
CSMS .... Consolidated State Maintenance Shop [USNB] (MCD)
CSMS .... Corps Support Missile System (MCD)
CSMS .... CSM Systems, Inc. [NASDAQ symbol] (NQ)
CSMT........ Casement [Technical drawings]
CSMT........ Circuit Switching Magnetic Tape [Telecommunications] (AFM)
CSMTS ..... Card Setting Machine Tenters' Society [A union] [British] (DCTA)
CSMV........ Celiac, Superior Mesenteric Vein [Anatomy]
CSMV........ Community of St. Mary the Virgin [Anglican religious community]
CSMV........ Mountain Valley Library System, Sacramento, CA [Library symbol] [Library of Congress] (LCLS)
CSmyS .... St. Mary's College of California, St. Mary's College, CA [Library symbol] [Library of Congress] (LCLS)
CSN .... Campana de Solidaridad con Nicaragua [Nicaragua Solidarity Campaign] (EAIO)
CSN .... Canadian Saturday Night [A publication]
CSN .... Card Security Number [Banking]
CSN .... Casanova, VA [Location identifier] [FAA] (FAAL)
CSN .... Catholic Scholarships for Negroes (EA)
CSN .... Century Sports Network
CSN .... Child Support Network [Defunct] (EA)
CSN .... Cincinnati Bell, Inc. [NYSE symbol] (SPSG)
CSN .... Circuit Switching Network [Telecommunications]
CSN .... Cognos, Inc. [Toronto Stock Exchange symbol]
CSN .... Committee to Support Nicaragua (EA)
CSN .... Common Services Network [Telecommunications] (TEL)
CSN .... Community Support Network [Australia]
CSN .... Computer Sequence Number
CSN .... Concession
CSN .... Confederate States Navy
CSN .... Confederation des Syndicats Nationaux [Confederation of National Trade Unions - CNTU] [Canada]
CSN .... Contract Serial Number (AFM)
CSN .... Contract Surgeon [Military] (AABC)
CSN .... Control Symbol Number (AFM)
CSN .... Cousin [Genealogy]
CSN .... Crosby, Stills, Nash [Rock music group] [Later, CSN & Y]
CSNA .... Classification Society of North America (EA)
CSNB........ Consolidated Statutes of New Brunswick [A publication] (DLA)
CSNC........ Chemical Societies of the Nordic Countries (EAIO)
CSND .... Center for Studies of Nonlinear Dynamics [Research center] (RCD)
CSNET ...... Computer Science Network [University Corporation for Atmospheric Research]
Cs Neur...... Ceskoslovenska Neurologie [Later, Ceskoslovenska Neurologie a Neurochirurgie] [A publication]
CSNF........ Campaign to Save Native Forests [Australia]
CSNF........ Common Source Noise Figure
CSNI......... Committee on the Safety of Nuclear Installation [Nuclear Regulatory Commission] (NRCH)
CSNM .... Chief Superintendent of Naval Meteorology [British]

CSNMDU ... Center for the Study of Non-Medical Drug Use [Later, CSDP] (EA)
CSNRT...... Corrected Sinus Node Recovery Time [Medicine]
CSNS........ Chemical Structure and Nomenclature System [Environmental Protection Agency]
CSNSAV ... Australia. Commonwealth Scientific and Industrial Research Organisation. National Standards Laboratory. Biennial Report [A publication]
CSNVTAL ... Combat Surveillance Night Vision and Target Acquisition Laboratories [Army] (RDA)
CSNWC.... Civil Service National Whitley Council [British]
CSNY........ Canadian Society of New York (EA)
CSN & Y ... Crosby, Stills, Nash, and Young [Rock music group] [Formerly, CSN]
CSNYS ..... Canal Society of New York State (EA)
CSO .... Car Service Order
CSO .... Catholics Speak Out [Quixote Center] (EA)
CSO .... Center Standards Officer [Job Corps]
CSO .... Central Selling Organization [London diamond exchange]
CSO .... Central Services Organization
CSO .... Central Sign Off (AAG)
CSO .... Central Standards Office (OICC)
CSO .... Central Statistical Office [British] [Information service or system] (IID)
CSO .... Centralized Service Observation [Telecommunications] (TEL)
CSO .... Chained Sequential Operation
CSO .... Chemically Stable Oxide
CSO .... Chicago Symphony Orchestra
CSO .... Chief Scientific Officer [Also, CScO] [Ministry of Agriculture, Fisheries, and Food] [British]
CSO .... Chief Signal Officer [Army]
CSO .... Chief Staff Officer
CSO .... Clothing Supply Office [Military]
CSO .... Coastal States Organization (EA)
CSO .... Cognizant Security Office [Controls industrial security at government facilities] [Military]
CSO .... Combined Sewer Overflow
CSO .... Commissioners Standard Ordinary Table [Insurance]
CSO .... Communication Standing Order
CSO .... Complex Safety Officer [Air Force] (AFM)
CSO .... Complex Support Office [NASA] (KSC)
CSO .... Computer Systems Officer (ADA)
CSO .... Consular Security Officer
CSO .... Consumer Services Organization (EA)
CSO .... Corn Stunt Organism [Plant pathology]
CSO .... Correspondence Survey Officer (MCD)
CSO .... Cross-Service Order [Military] (AFM)
CSO .... Crown Solicitor's Office [British] (ADA)
CSO .... Customer Support Operation
CSO .... Maandstatistiek Financiewezen [A publication]
CSO .... Sonoma State College, Rohnert Park, CA [OCLC symbol] (OCLC)
CSo............ Sonora Public Library, Sonora, CA [Library symbol] [Library of Congress] (LCLS)
CSOA .... CS Owner's Association (EA)
CSOB........ Clothing Store Operating Budgets [Air Force] (AFIT)
CSOC........ Communist Suppression Operations Command [Thailand]
CSOC........ Consolidated Security Operations Center [Military]
CSOC........ Consolidated Space Operations Center [Colorado Springs, CO] [Military]
CSOC........ Construction Special Operations Center
CSOC........ Current SIGINT [Signal Intelligence] Operations Center [National Security Agency] (MCD)
C Soc .... Current Sociology [A publication]
C Soc Dem Med ... Cahiers de Sociologie et de Demographie Medicales [A publication]
C Soc Econ ... Cahiers de Sociologie Economique [A publication]
C Societa .... Cinema Societa [A publication]
C Sociol Demogr Medic ... Cahiers de Sociologie et de Demographie Medicales [A publication]
CSoCL .... Tuoloumne County Free Public Library, Sonora, CA [Library symbol] [Library of Congress] (LCLS)
CSOD .... Combat System Operational Design [Military] (CAAL)
CSOF........ Chief Superintendent of Ordnance Factories [British] [World War II]
CSOF........ Corporate Software, Inc. [NASDAQ symbol] (NQ)
Cs Oft........ Ceskoslovenska Oftalmologie [A publication]
CSOG........ Circle Seven Oil [NASDAQ symbol] (NQ)
CSO-HNS ... Canadian Society of Otolaryngology - Head and Neck Surgery (EAIO)
C Sol........... Complete Solicitor [A publication] (DLA)
CSOL......... Convergent Solutions, Inc. [NASDAQ symbol] (NQ)
C Sol St Phys ... Comments on Solid State Physics [A publication]
CSOM .... Chief SONARman [Navy rating] [Obsolete]
CSOM .... Chronic Suppurative Otitis Media [Otolaryngology]
CSOM .... Combat System Operability Monitor [Military] (CAAL)
CSOM .... Conical Scanning Optical Microscope
CSom .... Sonoma Public Library, Sonoma, CA [Library symbol] [Library of Congress] (LCLS)
CSOMH .... Chief SONARman, Harbor Defense [Navy rating] [Obsolete]
Cs Onkol.... Ceskoslovenska Onkologie [A publication]

CSOP.........	Clothing Store Operating Programs [*Air Force*] (AFIT)
CSOP........	Coastal Shelf Oceanography Program [*Marine science*] (MSC)
CSOP.........	Commission to Study the Organization of Peace (EA)
CSOP.........	Crew Systems Operating Procedures (MCD)
CSOPAR ...	Casopis Ceskoslovenske. Spolecnosti Entomologicke [*A publication*]
CSORO	Conical Scan-on-Receive Only (CET)
CSOS.........	Center for Social Organization of Schools [*Department of Education*] [*Research center*] (GRD)
CSOS.........	Center for Social Organization Studies [*University of Chicago*] [*Research center*] (RCD)
Csos............	[*John*] Chrysostom [*Deceased, 407*] [*Authority cited in pre-1607 legal work*] (DSA)
CSOS.........	Communications Switch Operating System (MCD)
CSOSA	Communications in Soil Science and Plant Analysis [*A publication*]
CSOSA2	Communications in Soil Science and Plant Analysis [*A publication*]
CSOST	Canadian Service for Overseas Students and Trainees
CSOT.........	Canadian Society of Orthopaedic Technologists (EAIO)
CSOT.........	Combat Systems Operability Test (NVT)
CSP............	Cahiers du Seminaire Ch. Gide [*A publication*]
CSP............	Cahiers Sextil Puscariu [*A publication*]
CSP............	Calendar of State Papers [*British*] (ROG)
CSP............	California State Publications [*A publication*]
CSP............	Camas Prairie Railroad Co. [*AAR code*]
CSP............	Canadian Slavonic Papers [*A publication*]
CSP............	Canadian Student Pugwash
CSP............	Cape Spencer, AK [*Location identifier*] [*FAA*] (FAAL)
CSP............	Casper Air Service [*Casper, WY*] [*FAA designator*] (FAAC)
CSP............	Catholic School Paper [*A publication*] (APTA)
CSP............	Cedar Springs [*California*] [*Seismograph station code, US Geological Survey*] (SEIS)
CSP............	Cell Surface Protein [*Also known as LETS protein*] [*Cytochemistry*]
CSP............	Cellulose Sodium Phosphate [*Organic chemistry*]
CSP............	Center for Security Policy (EA)
CSP............	Center for Space Policy, Inc. [*Cambridge, MA*] [*Telecommunications*] (TSSD)
CSP............	Center for the Study of Power [*Later, SPI*] (EA)
CSP............	Center for the Study of the Presidency (EA)
CSP............	Center for Surrogate Parenting (EA)
CSP............	Central Service Point [*DoD*] (AFIT)
CSP............	Central Signal Processor
CSP............	Certified Safety Professional [*Designation awarded by Board of Certified Safety Professionals*]
CSP............	Certified Speaking Professional
CSP............	Certified Systems Professional [*Designation awarded by Institute for Certification of Computer Professionals*]
CSp	Ceskoslovensky Spisovatel [*A publication*]
CSP............	Chaplain Service Personnel [*Air Force*]
CSP............	Chartered Society of Physiotherapy [*British*]
CSP............	Chief Specialist [*Navy rating*] [*Obsolete*]
CSP............	Chiral Stationary Phase [*Chemical separation technique*]
CSP............	Christlich Soziale Partei [*Christian Social Party*] [*Liechtenstein*] [*Political party*] (PPW)
CSP............	Circumsporozoite Precipitation [*Clinical chemistry*]
CSP............	Clerk of State Papers [*British*] (ROG)
CSP............	Coder Sequential Pulse
CSP............	Coherent Signal Processor
CSP............	Colonial Society of Pennsylvania (EA)
CSP............	Column Shock Protection [*Chromatography*]
CSP............	Combined Staff Planners
CSP............	Combustion Engineering, Inc. [*NYSE symbol*] (SPSG)
CSP............	Commander Service Force, Pacific (MCD)
CSP............	Commemorative Stamp Posters
CSP............	Commercial Subroutine Package [*IBM Corp.*] (BUR)
CSP............	Commission on the Study of Peace (EA)
CSP............	Committed to Scheduled Programs [*Military*] (CINC)
CSP............	Communications Satellite Program [*NASA*]
CSP............	Communications Security Publication
C/SP..........	Communications/Symbiont Processor [*Sperry UNIVAC*]
CSP............	Community of St. Peter [*Anglican religious community*]
CSP............	Community Services Program [*Canada*]
CSP............	Community Shelter Plan [*Civil Defense*]
CSP............	Community Support Program [*National Institute of Mental Health*]
CSP............	Company of Saint Paul (EA)
CSP............	Company Standard Practice
CSP............	Computer Simulation Program
CSP............	Computer Support Program [*NASA*] (NASA)
CSP............	Concurrent Spare Parts (AFM)
CSP............	Congregatio Sancti Pauli [*Paulists*] [*Roman Catholic men's religious order*]
CSP............	Conseil du Salut du Peuple [*People's Salvation Council*] [*Upper Volta*] (PD)
CSP............	Consolidated Ascot Petroleum [*Toronto Stock Exchange symbol*] [*Vancouver Stock Exchange symbol*]
CSP............	Containment Spray Pump [*Nuclear energy*] (NRCH)
CSP............	Contents of Selected Periodicals [*A publication*]
CSP............	Continuous Sampling Plan (IEEE)

CSP............	Continuous Stratification Profiler
CSP............	Contract Strategy Paper
CSP............	Contractor Standard Parts
CSP............	Contractor Support Plan
CSP............	Control Signal Processor [*for spacecraft*]
CSP............	Control Switching Point (BUR)
CSP............	Controlled Surface Porosity
CSP............	Controlled Surface Process
CSP............	Cooperative School Program [*US Employment Service*] [*Department of Labor*]
CSP............	Cooperative Statistical Program [*For IUD data*]
CSP............	Coproduction for Security Program [*US and Italy*]
CSP............	Corporation Standard Practice (AAG)
CSP............	Council to Save the Postcard (EA)
CSP............	Council for Scientific Policy
CS & P	Craigie, Stewart, and Paton's Scotch Appeal Cases [*1726-1821*] [*A publication*] (DLA)
CSP............	Criminal Sexual Psychopath
CSP............	Crisis Staffing Procedures (MCD)
CSP............	Crystallographic Shear Plane
CSP............	Cumulative Sporulation [*of fungal colonies*]
CSp	South Pasadena Public Library, South Pasadena, CA [*Library symbol*] [*Library of Congress*] (LCLS)
CSP............	Stockton and San Joaquin County Public Library, Stockton, CA [*OCLC symbol*] (OCLC)
CSPA	California State Psychological Association
CSPA	Canadian Sport Parachuting Association (EA)
CSPA	Catholic School Press Association [*Defunct*] (EA)
CSPA	Chesapeake Seafood Packers Association (EA)
CSPA	Chief Specialist, Physical Training Instructor [*Navy rating*] [*Obsolete*]
CSPA	Civil Service Pensioners Alliance [*British*]
CSPA	Clay Sewer Pipe Association (EA)
CSPA	Columbia Scholastic Press Association (EA)
CSPA	Committee for a Strong Peaceful America (EA)
CSPA	Council of Sales Promotion Agencies [*New York, NY*] (EA)
CSPA	Council of State Policy and Planning Agencies [*Later, CGPA*] (EA)
CSPAA	Columbia Scholastic Press Advisers Association (EA)
CSPAA	Conference de Solidarite des Pays Afro-Asiatiques
CSPAC	Campaign for Space Political Action Committee (EA)
CSPADO ...	Comunicaciones. INIA [*Instituto Nacional de Investigaciones Agrarias*]. Serie Produccion Animal [*A publication*]
C-SPAN.....	Cable Satellite Public Affairs Network [*Cable-television system*]
CSPAR	Center for the Study of Parental Acceptance and Rejection , [*University of Connecticut*] [*Research center*] (RCD)
Cs Parasit ..	Ceskoslovenska Parasitologie [*A publication*]
CSpaW	Contra Costa College, San Pablo, CA [*Library symbol*] [*Library of Congress*] (LCLS)
CSPBI........	Comite Special du Programme Biologique International [*Special Committee for the International Biological Program*]
CSPC	California State Polytechnic College [*Later, California Polytechnic State University*]
CSPC	Cargo Systems and Procedures Committee [*IATA*] (DS)
CSPC	Coal and Steel Planning Committee [*NATO*] (NATG)
CSPC	Communication Satellite Planning Center [*Stanford University*] [*Research center*] (RCD)
CSPC	Conference of Small Private Colleges [*Defunct*] (EA)
CSPC	Cost and Schedule Planning and Control
CSPCA	Chinese Shar-Pei Club·of America (EA)
CSPCC	Canadian Society for the Prevention of Cruelty to Children
C/SPCS	Cost/Schedule Planning and Control Specification [*Air Force*]
CSPD.........	Comprehensive System of Personnel Development [*Education*]
CSPD.........	Cruising Speed
CSPDT	Crawford Small Parts Dexterity Test [*Education*]
CSPE	Chlorosulphonated Polyethylene
CSPE	Communications System Planning Element
CSPEC.......	Confederation of Socialist Parties of the European Community [*Political party*] [*Brussels, Belgium*] (EAIO)
Cs Pediat....	Ceskoslovenska Pediatrie [*A publication*]
CSPF	Central States Pension Fund
CSPG.........	Chrondroitin Sulfate Proteoglycans [*Biochemistry*]
CSPG.........	Committee in Solidarity with the People of Guatemala (EA)
CSPG........	Common Source Power Gain
CSPG Mem ...	CSPG [*Canadian Society of Petroleum Geologists*] Memoir [*A publication*]
CSPG Reservoir ...	Canadian Society of Petroleum Geologists. Reservoir [*A publication*]
CSPh..........	Cornell Studies in Classical Philology [*A publication*]
CSPHA......	Conference of State and Provincial Health Authorities of North America [*Defunct*] (EA)
CSPHA......	Contributions to Sensory Physiology [*A publication*]
CSPHA8.....	Contributions to Sensory Physiology [*A publication*]
CSPI	Center for Science in the Public Interest (EA)
CSPI	Center for the Study of Parent Involvement (EA)
CSPI	College Student Personnel Institute [*Defunct*]
CSPI	Committee in Solidarity with the People of Iran (EA)
CSPI	CSP Incorporated [*NASDAQ symbol*] (NQ)
CSPJA........	Canadian Aeronautics and Space Journal [*A publication*]
CSPM........	Code Ship Parametric Model (MCD)
CSPM........	Communication Security Publication Memorandum [*Army*]

CSPM........ Computer Services Procedures Manual
CSPMBO .. Conseil International pour l'Exploration de la Mer. Bulletin Statistique des Peches Maritimes [*A publication*]
CSPMP ..... Chief Specialist, Motion Picture Production [*Navy rating*] [*Obsolete*]
CSPO........ Chief Specialist, Petroleum Inspector [*Navy rating*] [*Obsolete*]
CSPO........ Communications Satellite Project Office
CSPOCP.... Conference of Speakers and Presiding Officers of Commonwealth Parliaments [*Ottawa, ON*] (EAIO)
CSPOS ...... Community Shelter Planning Officer, State [*Civil Defense*]
CSPP .... California School of Professional Psychology
CSPP .... Campaign to Save the People of Palestine (EA)
CSPP .... Centre for the Study of Public Policy [*University of Strathclyde*] [*United Kingdom*] (CB)
CSPP .... Coalition for State Prompt Pay (EA)
CSPPA....... Comite de Solidarite avec les Prisonniers Politiques Arabes et du Proche Orient [*Solidarity Committee for Arab and Near-Eastern Political Prisoners*]
CSPPHLD ... Conference of State and Provincial Public Health Laboratory Directors (EA)
CSPPLB .... Chief Specialist, Laboratory [*Navy rating*] [*Obsolete*]
CSPPPG.... Chief Specialist, Photogrammetry [*Navy rating*] [*Obsolete*]
CSPPVM... Chief Specialist, V-Mail [*Navy rating*] [*Obsolete*]
CSPR........ California Department of Parks and Recreation, Sacramento Area State Parks, Sacramento, CA [*Library symbol*] [*Library of Congress*] (LCLS)
CSPR........ Chief Specialist, Identification [*Navy rating*] [*Obsolete*]
CSPR........ Chief Specialist, Recruiter [*Navy rating*] [*Obsolete*]
CSPR........ Conference on Science, Philosophy, and Religion (EA)
CSPRU ...... Civil Service Pay Research Unit (DLA)
CSPS......... C. S. [*Charles Sanders*] Peirce Society (EA)
CSPS......... Canadian Society of Patristic Studies [*See also ACEP*]
CSPS......... Chief Specialist, Personnel Supervisor [*Navy rating*] [*Obsolete*]
CSPS......... Chief Specialist, Shore Patrol and Security [*Navy rating*] [*Obsolete*]
CSPS......... Christian Science Publishing Society (EA)
CSPS......... Coherent Signal Processing System [*Army*] (AABC)
CSPS......... Committee to Save the Peace Symbol [*Student legal action organization*]
CSPS......... Continued Skin Peeling Syndrome [*Dermatology*]
CSPSD....... Canadian Special Publication of Fisheries and Aquatic Sciences [*A publication*]
CSPSDA.... Canadian Special Publication of Fisheries and Aquatic Sciences [*A publication*]
CSPSR....... Chinese Social and Political Science Review [*Peking*] [*A publication*]
CSpSR .... Stanford Research Institute, South Pasadena, CA [*Library symbol*] [*Library of Congress*] (LCLS)
Cs Psych .... Ceskoslovenska Psychiatrie [*A publication*]
Cs Psych .... Ceskoslovenska Psychologie [*A publication*]
CSPT .... Chief Specialist, Teacher [*Navy rating*] [*Obsolete*]
CSPT .... Conference for the Study of Political Thought (EA)
CSP-T........ Contents of Selected Periodicals - Technical [*A publication*]
CSPTE....... Center for the Study of Pharmacy and Therapeutics for the Elderly (EA)
CSPTLT .... Chief Specialist, Link Trainer Instructor [*Navy rating*] [*Obsolete*]
C of SptS.... Chief of Support Services [*Army*] (AABC)
CSPU......... Core Segment Processing Unit (NASA)
CSPUP ...... California State Polytechnic University of Pomona (MCD)
CSPV .... Chief Specialist, Transport Airman [*Navy rating*] [*Obsolete*]
CSPW .... Chief Specialist, Chaplain's Assistant [*Navy rating*] [*Obsolete*]
CSPX .... Brothers of St. Pius X [*Roman Catholic religious order*]
CSPX .... Chief Specialist, All Designators [*Navy rating*] [*Obsolete*]
CSPY .... Chief Specialist, Control Tower Operator [*Navy rating*] [*Obsolete*]
CSQ .... Cassiar Mining Corp. [*Toronto Stock Exchange symbol*]
CSQ .... Christian Science Quarterly [*A publication*]
CSQ .... Coastal Sentry Quebec
CSQ .... College Student Questionnaires [*Psychology*]
CSQ .... Creston, IA [*Location identifier*] [*FAA*] (FAAL)
CSQ .... Cryptofacility Security Questionnaire [*Army*]
CSQ .... Genus Equity Corp. [*Toronto Stock Exchange symbol*]
CSR........... Anchorage/Ft. Richardson, AK [*Location identifier*] [*FAA*] (FAAL)
CSR........... Cable Spreading Room [*Nuclear energy*] (NRCH)
CSR........... Campaign for Surplus Rosaries (EA)
CSR........... Cell Surface Reviews [*Elsevier Book Series*] [*A publication*]
CSR........... Center for Seafarers' Rights (EA)
CSR........... Center for Social Research [*City University of New York*] [*Research center*] (RCD)
CSR........... Center for Social Research [*Stanford University*] [*Research center*] (RCD)
CSR........... Center for Space Research [*Massachusetts Institute of Technology*] [*Research center*] (RCD)
CSR........... Center for Space Research and Applications [*University of Texas at Austin*] [*Research center*] (RCD)
CSR........... Center for Strategy Research, Inc. [*Information service or system*] (IID)
CSR........... Center for the Study of Reading [*Later, RREC*] [*Department of Education*] (GRD)

CSR.......... Center for Survey Research [*University of Massachusetts*] [*Research center*] (RCD)
CSR.......... Central & South West Corp. [*NYSE symbol*] (SPSG)
CSR.......... Central Supply Room
CSR.......... Centre for Software Reliability [*City University*] [*British*] (IRUK)
CSR.......... Certification Status Report (NASA)
CSR.......... Certified Shorthand Reporter
CsR.......... Ceskoslovenska Rusistika [*A publication*]
CSR.......... Change Status Report (MCD)
CSR.......... Chartered Stenographic Reporter
CSR.......... Chase Ranch [*California*] [*Seismograph station code, US Geological Survey*] (SEIS)
CSR.......... Check Signal Return (NASA)
CSR.......... Check Status Reply (KSC)
CSR.......... Cheyne-Stokes Respiration [*Medicine*]
CSR.......... Chief of Staff Regulations
CSR.......... Chlorinated Synthetic Rubber
CSR.......... Christian Scholar's Review [*A publication*]
CSR.......... Civil Service Reserve [*British*] (ROG)
CSR.......... Civil Service Retirement
CSR.......... Civil Service Rule
CSR.......... Clamped Speed Regulator
CSR.......... Clock-Sync Receiver Assembly [*Deep Space Instrumentation Facility, NASA*]
CSR.......... Coastal Surveillance RADAR (MCD)
CSR.......... Coaxial Single-Pole Relay
CSR.......... College of Saint Rose [*Albany, NY*]
CSR.......... Combat Search and Rescue [*Aviation*] (MCD)
CSR.......... Combat Surveillance RADAR
CSR.......... Commando Shackle Relay [*Intelligence gathering*] [*Vietnam*] (MCD)
CSR.......... Commercial Spares Release
CSR.......... Common Services Rack [*Telecommunications*] (TEL)
CSR.......... Commonwealth Strategic Reserve [*Australia*]
CSR.......... Communication Service Request
CSR.......... Communication Systems Research Ltd. [*Ilkley, W. Yorkshire, England*] (TSSD)
CSR.......... Communications Satellite Relay (NG)
CSR.......... Compensation System Review
CSR.......... Component Selection Record
CSR.......... Composite Station Rate
CSR.......... Comstate Resources Ltd. [*Toronto Stock Exchange symbol*]
CSR.......... Conference on Science and Religion [*Later, UDC*] (EA)
CSR.......... Configuration Selection Register
CSR.......... Connected Speech Recognition (MCD)
CSR.......... Continental Shelf Research [*A publication*]
CSR.......... Continuous Service Rating [*Engine technology*]
CSR.......... Contract Status Report
CSR.......... Control Section Report [*NATO*] (NATG)
CSR.......... Control Shift Register (CET)
CSR.......... Control Status Register
CSR.......... Controlled Supply Rate (AABC)
CSR.......... Copper Sulfide Rectifier
CSR.......... Corps Specifications Revision (AAG)
CSR.......... Corrected Sedimentation Rate [*Medicine*]
CSR.......... Council Situation Room [*NATO*] (NATG)
CSR.......... Council on the Study of Religion (EA)
CSR.......... Course Status Report
CSR.......... Crankshaft Rate (NVT)
CSR.......... Crew Station Review [*NASA*] (NASA)
CSR.......... Critical Shortage Report (AAG)
CSR.......... Culture Supply Room [*Microbiology*]
CSR.......... Current Situation Room (MCD)
CSR.......... Custom Spherical Resins
CSR.......... Customer Service Representative
CSR.......... Customer Signature Required (MSA)
CSr........... San Rafael Public Library, San Rafael, CA [*Library symbol*] [*Library of Congress*] (LCLS)
CSRA........ Canadian Street Rod Association
CSRA........ Civil Service Reform Act [*1978*] (RDA)
CSRA........ Comite Scientifique pour les Recherches Antarctiques [*Scientific Committee on Antarctic Research*] (MSC)
CSRA........ Corporate Security Regulation Appendices
CS(RAF).... Chief Scientist (Royal Air Force) [*British*]
CSR Agric Circ ... CSR [*Colonial Sugar Refining Company Limited*] Agricultural Circular [*A publication*] (APTA)
CSraS........ Shell Chemical Co., Information Services Library, San Ramon, CA [*Library symbol*] [*Library of Congress*] (LCLS)
C S R Bul ... Council on the Study of Religion. Bulletin [*A publication*]
CSRC......... Chicano Studies Research Center [*University of California, Los Angeles*] [*Research center*] (RCD)
CSRC......... Communication Science Research Center [*Battelle Memorial Institute*] (MCD)
CSRC......... Complex Systems Research Center [*University of New Hampshire*] [*Research center*] (RCD)
CSRCBA .... Central States Roller Canary Breeders Association (EA)
CSrCL........ Marin County Free Library, San Rafael, CA [*Library symbol*] [*Library of Congress*] (LCLS)
CSRCO...... Communications Status and Restoration Coordination Office

CSRCSP .... Center for the Study of Race, Crime, and Social Policy [*Cornell University*] [*Research center*] (RCD)

CSRD .... Center for Supercomputing Research and Development [*University of Illinois*] [*Urbana*] [*Information service or system*] (IID)

CSRD .... Chief Superintendent, Research Department [*British military*] (DMA)

CSrD .... Dominican College of San Rafael, San Rafael, CA [*Library symbol*] [*Library of Congress*] (LCLS)

CSRDF ...... Civil Service Retirement and Disability Fund

CSRDF ...... Crew Station Research and Development Facility [*Ames Research Center*]

CSRE .... Canadian Society of Rural Extension

CSRE .... Center for Social Research and Education (EA)

CSRE .... Closed System Respirator Evaluator (KSC)

CSRE .... Comshare, Inc. [*NASDAQ symbol*] (NQ)

CSREDC ... Cell Surface Reviews [*A publication*]

Cs Rentgen ... Ceskoslovenska Rentgenologie [*A publication*]

CSRes .... California Resources Agency, Sacramento, CA [*Library symbol*] [*Library of Congress*] (LCLS)

CSRF .... Civil Service Retirement Fellowship [*British*]

CSRG .... Commission for Scientific Research in Greenland. Newsletter [*A publication*]

CSRG .... Commonwealth Special Research Grant Scheme [*Australia*]

CSRHFA ... Charles Simkins and Rachel Hawthorne Family Association (EA)

CSRI .... Centre for the Study of Regulated Industries [*McGill University*] [*Canada*] [*Research center*] (RCD)

CSRI .... Computer Systems Research Institute [*University of Toronto*] [*Research center*] (RCD)

CSRI .... Creative Strategies Research International [*Information service or system*] (IID)

CSRI .... Customer Satisfaction Research Institute [*Lenexa, KS*] [*Telecommunications*] (TSSD)

CSRL .... Cambridge Studies in Russian Literature [*A publication*]

CSRL .... Cascade Steel Rolling Mills, Inc. [*NASDAQ symbol*] (NQ)

CSRL .... Center for Study of Responsive Law (EA)

CSRL .... Common Strategic Rotary Launcher

CSRL .... Communications Strategic Rotary Launcher [*Military*]

CSRM .... Controlled Solid Rocket Motors (KSC)

CSRO .... Chief, Superintendent Range Operations [*NASA*] (KSC)

CSRO .... Comite Scientifique pour les Recherches Oceaniques [*Scientific Committee on Oceanic Research - SCOR*] [*French*] (MSC)

CSRO .... Consolidated Standing Route Order [*Army*] (AABC)

CSRO .... Contract Service Rework Orders (NG)

CSRP .... Computers and Software Review Panel [*NASA*] (NASA)

CSRPB ...... Chemica Scripta [*A publication*]

CSRQA ...... Chartered Surveyor. Rural Quarterly [*A publication*]

CSRR .... Combat Systems Readiness Review [*Navy*] (MCD)

CSRS .... Canadian Society for Renaissance Studies [*See also SCER*]

CSRS .... Civil Service Retirement System (MCD)

CSRS .... Coherent Stokes Raman Spectroscopy

CSRS .... Composite Standard Reference Section

CSRS .... Containment Spray Recirculation System [*Nuclear energy*] (NRCH)

CSRS .... Cooperative State Research Service [*Department of Agriculture*] [*Washington, DC*]

CSRSAH ... Colorado State University. Range Science Department. Range Science Series [*A publication*]

CSRT .... Canadian Society of Radiological Technicians

CSRT .... Combat Systems Readiness Test (NVT)

CSRT .... Comprehensive System Readiness Tests (MCD)

CSRUIDR ... Chemical Society Research Unit in Information Dissemination and Retrieval [*British*] (DIT)

CSRV .... Civil Service Rifle Volunteers [*British*]

CSRVB ...... Chemical Society. Reviews [*A publication*]

CSRW .... Commission of the Status and Role of Women (EA)

CSS .... California Slavic Studies [*A publication*]

CSS .... California State University, Sacramento, Sacramento, CA [*Library symbol*] [*Library of Congress*] (LCLS)

CSS .... Canadian Slavic Studies [*A publication*]

CSS .... Canadian Statistical Society

CSS .... Car Service Section [*Railroads*]

CSS .... Caribbean Super Station [*Satellite television system*]

CSS .... Carotid Sinus Stimulation [*Cardiology*]

CSS .... Cask Support Structure [*Nuclear energy*] (NRCH)

CSS .... Cassilandia [*Brazil*] [*Airport symbol*] (OAG)

CSS .... CBPO [*Consolidated Base Personnel Office*] Strength Summary Card (AFM)

CSS .... Centaur Standard Shroud [*NASA*]

CSS .... Center for Self-Sufficiency (EA)

CSS .... Center for Separation Science [*University of Arizona*]

CSS .... Center for the Social Sciences [*Columbia University*] [*Research center*] (RCD)

CSS .... Center for Sports Sponsorship (EA)

CSS .... Central Security Service [*Obsolete*] [*National Security Agency*] (AABC)

CSS .... Central Structure Storage [*Data processing*] (BYTE)

CSS .... Certificate of Sanitary Science [*British*]

CSS .... Certificate in Social Service [*British*] (DBQ)

CSS .... Ceskoslovenska Strana Socialisticka [*Czechoslovak Socialist Party*] (PPE)

CSS .... Character Start-Stop

CSS .... Character String Scanner [*Computer program*]

CSS .... Chewing, Sucking, Swallowing [*Medicine*]

CSS .... Chicago South Shore & South Bend Railroad [*AAR code*]

CSS .... Chief of Support Services [*Army*]

CSS .... China Stamp Society (EA)

CSS .... Chronic Subclinical Scurvy [*Medicine*]

CSS .... Cinegraphic Scoring System (MCD)

CSS .... Circuit Switching Station [*Telecommunications*] (CET)

CSS .... Clock Subsystem (CET)

CSS .... Clothing Sales Store (AABC)

CSS .... Coastal Survey Ship [*Marine science*] (MSC)

CSS .... Coded Switch System [*To permit or deny the ability to arm nuclear weapons in strategic aircraft*]

CSS .... Cognitive Science Society (EA)

Cs .... College of Saint Scholastica [*Duluth, MN*]

CSS .... College Scholarship Service [*Service mark of the College Entrance Examination Board*]

CSS .... College Selection Service [*Peterson's Guides*] [*Information service or system*] (IID)

CSS .... Color Sync Signal

CSS .... Columbus City School, Columbus, OH [*OCLC symbol*] (OCLC)

CSS .... Combat Service Support [*DoD*] (AABC)

CSS .... Command Security Service (MCD)

CSS .... Command Supply Support (MCD)

CSS .... Command Synchronizer Slave (MCD)

CSS .... Commercial Satellite Systems [*Berkeley, CA*] [*Telecommunications*] (TSSD)

CSS .... Commit Sequence Summary (AAG)

CSS .... Committee on State Sovereignty [*Defunct*] (EA)

CSS .... Committee in Support of Solidarity (EA)

CSS .... Commodity Stabilization Service [*Name changed to Agricultural Stabilization and Conservation Service, 1961*]

CSS .... Common Services Subsystem [*Telecommunications*] (TEL)

CSS .... Communication Support System (MCD)

CSS .... Communications Security System (MCD)

CSS .... Communications Subsystem

CSS .... Complete Statistical System

CSS .... Computer Search Services

CSS .... Computer Sharing Services, Inc. [*Information service or system*] (IID)

CSS .... Computer Subsystem (NASA)

CSS .... Computer System Simulator [*Programming language*] [*1969*]

CSS .... Computing Support Services [*California Institute of Technology*] [*Research center*] (RCD)

CSS .... Condensate Storage System [*Nuclear energy*] (NRCH)

CSS .... Confederate States Ship

CSS .... Confederated Spanish Societies [*Defunct*] (EA)

CSS .... Conference of State Societies [*Later, National Conference of State Societies*] (EA)

CSS .... Congregation of the Sacred Stigmata [*Stigmatine Fathers and Brothers*] [*Roman Catholic religious order*]

CSS .... Consolidated Supply Support Activity (MCD)

CSS .... Consolidated Support System

CSS .... Consort Speed Servo

CSS .... Constant Security Surveillance [*Shipping*]

CSS .... Constituted Soil Columns [*Agronomy*]

CSS .... Containment Spray System [*Nuclear energy*] (NRCH)

CSS .... Contemporary Science Series [*A publication*]

CSS .... Contemporary Specialty Services [*Merchandiser*] [*Chicago, IL*]

CSS .... Contingency Support Staff (MCD)

CSS .... Continuity of Service Set (MCD)

CSS .... Continuous Surveillance Service (MCD)

CSS .... Contractor Storage Site (AFM)

CSS .... Contrans Corp. [*Toronto Stock Exchange symbol*]

CSS .... Control Signaling Subsystem [*Telecommunications*] (TEL)

CSS .... Control and Status System [*NASCOM*] (MCD)

CSS .... Control Stick Steering [*Aviation*] (NG)

CSS .... Control Subsystem

CSS .... Control Systems Society (EA)

CSS .... Conversational Software System [*National CSS, Inc.*]

CSS .... Coordinated Situation System

CSS .... Core Segment Simulator (NASA)

CSS .... Core Support Structure [*Nuclear energy*] (NRCH)

CSS .... Corn Stunt Spiroplasma [*Plant pathology*]

CSS .... Corn Syrup Solids

CSS .... Council for Science and Society [*British*]

CSS .... Council of Social Service [*British*]

CSS .... County Surveyors Society [*British*] (DCTA)

CSS .... Crew Safety System

CSS .... Critical Shear Stress

CSS .... Cross-Sectional Sensitivity [*Aviation*] (FAAC)

CSS .... Cryogenic Storage System [*Apollo project*] [*NASA*]

CSS .... CSS Industries, Inc. [*AMEX symbol*] (SPSG)

CSS .... Current Steering Switch (KSC)

CSS .... Cursus Sacrae Scripturae [*Paris*] (BJA)

CSS .... Customer Service System [*Computer surveillance*] [*British*]

CSS .... Customer Switching System [*Telecommunications*] (TEL)

CSS............ IEEE Circuits and Systems Society   (EA)
CSS............ IEEE Control Systems Society   (EA)
CSS............ Ontario Ministry of Community and Social Services Library [*UTLAS symbol*]
CSS............ Washington Court House, OH [*Location identifier*] [*FAA*]   (FAAL)
CSSA......... Cactus and Succulent Society of America   (EA)
CSSA......... Canadian Sanitation Standards Association
CSSA......... Central Supply Support Activity
CSSA......... Civil Service Supply Association [*British*]
CSSA......... Civilian Science Systems Administration [*Proposed for National Science Foundation*]
CSSA......... Clothing and Small Stores Account [*Military*]
CSSA......... Combat Service Support Area [*Army*]
CSSA......... Communications Supply Service Association   (EA)
CSSA......... Concrete Society of Southern Africa   (EAIO)
CSSA......... Conseil Superieur du Sport en Afrique [*Supreme Council for Sport in Africa - SCSA*] [*Yaounde, Cameroon*]   (EAIO)
CSSA......... Control Stick Sensor Assembly   (MCD)
CSSA......... Crop Science Society of America   (EA)
CSSA......... Seaman Apprentice, Commissaryman, Striker [*Navy rating*]
CSSAA...... Computer Systems Selection and Acquisition Agency [*Army*]   (MCD)
CSSAD...... Committee for the Scientific Survey of Air Defence [*British*] [*World War II*]
CSSAO...... Committee for the Scientific Survey of Air Offence [*British*] [*World War II*]
CSSA Spec Publ ... CSSA [*Crop Science Society of America*] Special Publication [*A publication*]
CSSAW..... Committee for the Scientific Survey of Air Warfare [*British*] [*World War II*]
CSSB......... Cedar Shake and Shingle Bureau   (EA)
CSSB......... Civil Service Selection Board [*Pronounced "sissby"*] [*British*]
CSSB......... Civilian Supervisory Selection Battery [*Military*]   (AFM)
CSSB......... Compatible Single Sideband
CSSC......... CBPO [*Consolidated Base Personnel Office*] Strength Summary Card   (AFM)
CSSC......... Center for Space Structures and Controls [*University of Colorado at Boulder*] [*Research center*]   (RCD)
CSSC......... Center Special Slotted Container [*Packaging*]
CSSC......... Clans and Scottish Societies of Canada
CSSCA...... Circus Saints and Sinners Club of America   (EA)
CSSCC....... Congregatio Sacratissimorum Cordium [*Missionaries of the Sacred Hearts of Jesus and Mary*] [*Roman Catholic religious order*]
CSSCD...... Communications in Statistics. Part B. Simulation and Computation [*A publication*]
CSS/CG..... Container Systems Standardization/Coordination Group
CSSCiC...... Sacramento City College, Sacramento, CA [*Library symbol*] [*Library of Congress*]   (LCLS)
CSSCO...... Staff Communications Office, Office of the Chief of Staff [*Army*]
CSSCS...... Combat Service Support Control System [*Army*]
CSSD......... Ceskoslovenska Socialnedemokraticka Strana Delnicka [*Czechoslovak Social Democratic Workers' Party*]   (PPE)
CSSD......... Chemically Sensitive Semiconductor Devices
CSSD......... Coated Solid-State Device [*Sensor*]
CSSD......... Communications System Status Display   (KSC)
CSSD......... Contact Soil Sampling Device [*Aerospace*]
CSSDA...... Council of Social Science Data Archives [*Defunct*]
CSSE......... Canadian Society of Safety Engineering
CSSE......... Canadian Society for the Study of Education [*See also SCEE*] [*University of Ottawa*] [*Research center*]   (RCD)
CSSE......... Center for Social Studies Education   (EA)
CSSE......... Combat System Support Equipment [*Military*]   (CAAL)
CSSE......... Conference of State Health and Environmental Managers [*Acronym is based on former name, Conference of State Sanitary Engineers*]   (EA)
CSSE......... Control System Simulation Equipment   (MCD)
CSSEA...... Computer Services Support and Evaluation Agency
CSSEAS.... Center for South and Southeast Asian Studies [*University of Michigan*] [*Research center*]   (RCD)
CSSEC...... Computer Systems Support and Evaluation Command
CSSEDC.... Conference for Secondary School English Department Chairpersons   (EA)
CSSER....... Center for Solid State Electronics [*Arizona State University*] [*Research center*]   (RCD)
CSSF......... Clothing and Small Stores Fund [*Military*]
CSSF......... Congregation of the Sisters of St. Felix [*Felician Sisters*] [*Roman Catholic religious order*]
CSsf .... South San Francisco Free Public Library, South San Francisco, CA [*Library symbol*] [*Library of Congress*]   (LCLS)
CSSF......... Sutter's Fort State Monument, Sacramento, CA [*Library symbol*] [*Library of Congress*]   (LCLS)
CSSG......... Chairman, Special Studies Group [*Joint Chiefs of Staff*]
CSSG......... Combat Service Support Group [*Army*]
CSSG......... Combat System Steering Group [*Military*]   (CAAL)
CSSGS....... Croatian Serbian Slovene Genealogical Society   (EA)
CSSH......... Chief of Staff Supreme Headquarters [*British*]
CSSH......... Comparative Studies in Society and History [*A publication*]
CSSH......... Society for the Comparative Study of Society and History   (EA)

CSSHE...... Canadian Society for the Study of Higher Education [*See also SCEES*]
CSSHS...... Creation Social Science and Humanities Society   (EA)
CSSI.......... Coriolis Sickness Susceptibility Index [*Orientation*]
CSSID....... Center for the Study of Sensory Integrative Dysfunction [*American Occupational Therapy Association*]
CSSJ......... Central States Speech Journal [*A publication*]
CSSL.......... Canada Steamship Lines [*AAR code*]
CSSL.......... Central Sierra Snow Laboratory [*Norden, CA*]
CSSL.......... Continuous Systems Simulation Language [*Data processing*]
CSSM .... Chief Ship's Service Man [*Navy rating*] [*Obsolete*]
CSSM .... Children's Special Service Mission [*British*]
CSSM .... Coso Springs South [*California*] [*Seismograph station code, US Geological Survey*]   (SEIS)
CSSMB ...... Chief Ship's Service Man, Barber [*Navy rating*] [*Obsolete*]
CSSMC ...... Chief Ship's Service Man, Cobbler [*Navy rating*] [*Obsolete*]
CSSME ..... Centre for Studies in Science and Mathematical Education [*University of Leeds*] [*British*]   (CB)
CSSME ..... Coalition for Strategic Stability in the Middle East   (EA)
CSSML...... Chief Ship's Service Man, Laundryman [*Navy rating*] [*Obsolete*]
CSSMMP ... Congregation des Soeurs de Sainte Marie-Madeleine Postel [*Saint Sauveur-Le-Vicomte, France*]   (EAIO)
CSSMT ...... Chief Ship's Service Man, Tailor [*Navy rating*] [*Obsolete*]
CSSN......... Canadian Society for the Study of Names [*See also SCEN*]
CSSN......... Common Source Spot Noise
CSSN......... Seaman, Commissaryman, Striker [*Navy rating*]
CSSNF....... Common Source Spot Noise Figure
CSSO......... Consolidated Surplus Sales Office [*Military - Merged with Defense Supply Agency*]
CSSOP ...... Center for Settlement Studies. University of Manitoba. Series 5. Occasional Papers [*A publication*]
CSSP.......... Center for Studies of Suicide Prevention [*National Institute of Mental Health*]
CSSP.......... Center for the Study of Social Policy   (EA)
CSSP.......... Circuits, Systems, and Signal Processing [*A publication*]
CSSP.......... Classical Scattering Spectrometer Probe [*Aerosol measurement device*]
CSSP.......... Combined Services Support Program [*Navy*]   (NG)
CSSP.......... Congregatio Sancti Spiritus [*Congregation of the Holy Ghost*] [*Holy Ghost Fathers*] [*Roman Catholic religious order*]
CSSP.......... Council of Scientific Society Presidents   (EA)
CSS PCC ... Combat Service Support Precommand Course
CSSPT....... Common Supply Support [*Military*]   (AABC)
CSSQT ...... Combat System Ship Qualification Trial [*Military*]   (CAAL)
CSSR .... Canadian Society for the Study of Religion [*See also SCER*]
CSSR .... Communication Systems Sector [*or Segment*] Replacement [*Military*]
CSSR .... Congregatio Sanctissimi Redemptoris [*Congregation of the Most Holy Redeemer*] [*Redemptionists*] [*Roman Catholic men's religious order*]
CSSR .... Consolidated Stock Status Report
CSSR .... Cost Schedule Status Report [*Military*]
CSSR .... Council of Societies for the Study of Religion   (EA)
CSSR .... Czechoslovak Socialist Republic
CSSRA ...... Canadian Shipbuilding and Ship Repairing Association
CSSRNA ... Center for Supplying Services by Redemptorists for North America
CSSRR....... Center for Settlement Studies. University of Manitoba. Series 2. Research Reports [*A publication*]
CSSS.......... Canadian Soil Science Society   (MCD)
CSSS.......... Combat Service Support System [*Army*]
CSSS.......... Conceptual Satellite Surveillance System
CSSS.......... Council of State Science Supervisors   (EA)
CSSS.......... Cross-Spin Stabilization Systems
CSST .... Commission de la Sante et de la Securite du Travail du Quebec [*Quebec Workers Health and Security Commission*] [*Montreal*] [*Information service or system*]   (IID)
CSST .... Compatible Sidelobe Suppression Technique   (AAG)
CSST .... Computer System Science Training [*IBM Corp.*]
CSSTC....... Cambridge Series for Schools and Training Colleges [*A publication*]
CSSTPB .... Cap Screw and Special Threaded Products Bureau [*Defunct*]   (EA)
CSSU......... Cats on Stamps Study Unit [*American Topical Association*]   (EA)
CSSU......... Church Sunday School Union [*British*]
CSSU......... Converter Simulator Signal Unit   (MCD)
CS Supp .... Supplement to the Compiled Statutes [*A publication*]   (DLA)
CSSV......... Combat Support Smoke Vehicle [*Army*]
CSS-X-4.... China Surface-to-Surface Experimental Number 4 [*Rocket*]
CSSYPT.... Committee for Single Six-Year Presidential Term   (EA)
cs sz........... Csekk-Szamla [*Bank Account, Checking Account*] [*Hungarian*]
CST............ Capital Stock Tax Ruling, Internal Revenue Bureau [*United States*] [*A publication*]   (DLA)
CST............ Capsule Systems Test [*NASA*]
CST............ Carmelite Sisters of St. Therese of the Infant Jesus [*Roman Catholic religious order*]
CST............ Carrier Power Supply, Transistorized [*Telecommunications*]   (TEL)
CST............ Cast Stone [*Technical drawings*]

CST............ Castaway [*Fiji*] [*Airport symbol*]   (OAG)
CST............ Castrovirreyna [*Peru*] [*Seismograph station code, US Geological Survey*]   (SEIS)
CST............ Cavernous Sinus Thrombosis [*Medicine*]
CST............ Celeste Resources [*Vancouver Stock Exchange symbol*]
CST............ Center for Sustainable Transportation   (EA)
cSt............ Centistoke [*Also, cs*] [*Unit of kinematic viscosity*]
CST............ Central Standard Time
CST............ Channel Status Indicator [*Data processing*]   (MDG)
CST............ Chicago Sunday Tribune [*A publication*]
CST............ Chief Steward [*Later, MSC*] [*Navy rating*]
CST............ Chief of Supplies and Transport [*Navy*] [*British*]
CST............ Child Study Team [*Education*]
CST............ [*The*] Christiana Companies, Inc. [*NYSE symbol*]   (SPSG)
CST............ Classification on Science and Technology
CST............ Clerical Selection Test [*Australia*]
CST............ Coal Science and Technology [*Elsevier Book Series*] [*A publication*]
CST............ Coast [*Board on Geographic Names*]
CST............ Code Segment Table [*Data processing*]
CSt............ Colecao Studium [*A publication*]
CST............ College of Saint Teresa [*Winona, MN*]
CST............ College of St. Thomas [*St. Paul, MN*]
CST............ College of Speech Therapists [*British*]
CST............ Colloidal System Test
CST............ Combat Support Training [*Military*]   (AABC)
CST............ Combat Systems Training   (NVT)
CST............ Combined Service Territory [*Red Cross*]
CS/T............ Combined Station/Tower [*Aviation*]
CST............ Combined Systems Test
CST............ Commander Sea Training [*Canadian Navy*]
CST............ Commerce, Science, and Transportation   (DLA)
CST............ Commit Start   (AAG)
CST............ Common Specialist Training
CST............ Communications Surveillance Transistor
CST............ Communications Systems Technician   (MCD)
CST............ Complex Safety Technician [*Air Force*]   (AFM)
CST............ Compound Series Test [*Intelligence test*]
CST............ Comprehensive Screening Tool for Determining Optimal Communication Mode [*Speech evaluation test*]
C St............ Comunicazioni i Studi [*A publication*]
CST............ Concentration Stress Test [*Psychical stress*]
CST............ Conceptual Systems Test
CST............ Condensate Storage Tank [*Nuclear energy*]   (NRCH)
CST............ Conical Shock Tube
CST............ Consortium on Soils of the Tropics
CST............ Constitution Federale [*Switzerland*] [*A publication*]
CST............ Container Service Tariff [*Shipping*]   (DS)
CST............ Contemporary Studies in Theology [*London*] [*A publication*]
CST............ Continuously Stirred Tank
CST............ Contract Supplemental Tooling   (NASA)
CST............ Contraction Stress Test [*Obstetrics*]
CST............ Control System Test   (AAG)
CST............ Conventional Stability Talks [*Arms control*]
CST............ Convulsive Shock Therapy [*Medicine*]
CST............ Cortico-Spinal Tract [*Anatomy*]
CST............ Cost and Management [*A publication*]
CST............ Council on Student Travel [*Later, CIEE*]   (EA)
CST............ Crew Station Trainer [*NASA*]
CST............ Crew Systems Trainer [*NASA*]   (NASA)
CST............ Critical Solution Temperature
CST............ Critical Surface Tension [*Physical chemistry*]
CSt............ Crystalline Style
CST............ Current Summary of Threat   (MCD)
CSt............ Cycling Strength Test
CST............ School of Theology at Claremont Library, Claremont, CA [*OCLC symbol*]   (OCLC)
CSt............ Stanford University, Stanford, CA [*Library symbol*] [*Library of Congress*]   (LCLS)
CSTA........ Canadian String Teachers' Association
CSTA........ Civil Service Typists' Association [*A union*] [*British*]
CSTA........ Cloak and Suit Trucking Association   (EA)
CSTA........ Combat Surveillance and Target Acquisition [*Army*]
CSTA........ Combat Systems Test Activity [*Army*] [*Aberdeen Proving Ground, MD*]   (RDA)
CSTA........ Consolidating Station
CSTA........ Crew Software Training Aid   (MCD)
CSta........... Santa Ana Public Library, Santa Ana, CA [*Library symbol*] [*Library of Congress*]   (LCLS)
CStaB-E..... Borg-Warner Corp., B-J Electronics Division, Santa Ana, CA [*Library symbol*] [*Library of Congress*]   (LCLS)
CStaC........ Santa Ana College, Santa Ana, CA [*Library symbol*] [*Library of Congress*]   (LCLS)
CS & TAE ... Combat Surveillance and Target Acquisition Equipment [*Army*]
CStaE........ Electron Engineering Co. of California, Santa Ana, CA [*Library symbol*] [*Library of Congress*]   (LCLS)
CSTAIN .... Commander's Surveillance and Target Acquisition Information Needs   (MCD)
CSTAL ...... Combat Surveillance and Target Acquisition Laboratory [*Army*]   (RDA)
C Stand ...... Christian Standard [*A publication*]

CStaOL...... Orange County Law Library, Santa Ana, CA [*Library symbol*] [*Library of Congress*]   (LCLS)
CSTAR ...... Classified Scientific and Technical Aerospace Reports [*NASA*]
CSTAR ...... Combat Surveillance Target Acquisition RADAR
CSTA R ..... CSTA [*Canadian Society of Technical Agriculturists*] Review [*A publication*]
CSTA Rev ... CSTA [*Canadian Society of Technical Agriculturists*] Review [*A publication*]
CSTATC.... Combat Surveillance and Target Acquisition Training Command [*Army*]
CSTB........ Cahiers. Centre Scientifique et Technique du Batiment [*A publication*]
CSTB........ California State Bank [*NASDAQ symbol*]   (NQ)
CStb........... Santa Barbara Public Library, Santa Barbara, CA [*Library symbol*] [*Library of Congress*]   (LCLS)
CSt-B........ Stanford University, Graduate School of Business, Stanford, CA [*Library symbol*] [*Library of Congress*]   (LCLS)
CStbCiC.... Santa Barbara City College, Santa Barbara, CA [*Library symbol*] [*Library of Congress*]   (LCLS)
CStbF........ Fielding Institute, Santa Barbara, CA [*Library symbol*] [*Library of Congress*]   (LCLS)
CStbGE...... General Electric Co., Santa Barbara, CA [*Library symbol*] [*Library of Congress*]   (LCLS)
CStbGR ..... General Research Corp., Effects Technology, Inc., Santa Barbara, CA [*Library symbol*] [*Library of Congress*]   (LCLS)
CStbM .... Santa Barbara Museum of Natural History, Santa Barbara, CA [*Library symbol*] [*Library of Congress*]   (LCLS)
CStbOL .... Our Lady of Light Catholic Library, Santa Barbara, CA [*Library symbol*] [*Library of Congress*]   (LCLS)
CStbOM .... Old Mission Santa Barbara Seminary, Santa Barbara, CA [*Library symbol*] [*Library of Congress*]   (LCLS)
CSTBR ...... Continuous Stirred Tank Biological Reactor [*Chemical engineering*]
CStC .... Center for Advanced Study in the Behavioral Sciences, Stanford, CA [*Library symbol*] [*Library of Congress*]   (LCLS)
CSTC .... Ceskoslovensky Terminologicky Casopis [*A publication*]
CSTC .... Charleston Submarine Training Center [*South Carolina*]
CSTC .... Combined Strategic Targets Committee [*World War II*]
CStcl .... Santa Clara Public Library, Santa Clara, CA [*Library symbol*] [*Library of Congress*]   (LCLS)
CStclF........ FMC Corp., Santa Clara, CA [*Library symbol*] [*Library of Congress*]   (LCLS)
CStclGS..... Church of Jesus Christ of Latter-Day Saints, Genealogical Society Library, Santa Clara Branch, Santa Clara, CA [*Library symbol*] [*Library of Congress*]   (LCLS)
CStclI........ Intel Corp., Santa Clara, CA [*Library symbol*] [*Library of Congress*]   (LCLS)
CStclM ...... Memorex Corp., Santa Clara, CA [*Library symbol*] [*Library of Congress*]   (LCLS)
CStclR........ Rolm Corp. Library, Santa Clara, CA [*Library symbol*] [*Library of Congress*]   (LCLS)
CStclU .... University of Santa Clara, Santa Clara, CA [*Library symbol*] [*Library of Congress*]   (LCLS)
CStclU-L ... University of Santa Clara, Law Library, Santa Clara, CA [*Library symbol*] [*Library of Congress*]   (LCLS)
CStcrCL..... Santa Cruz Public Library [*Santa Cruz City and County Library*], Santa Cruz, CA [*Library symbol*] [*Library of Congress*]   (LCLS)
CSTC Rev ... CSTC [*Centre Scientifique et Technique de la Construction*] Revue [*A publication*]
CStcrF........ Forest History Society, Santa Cruz, CA [*Library symbol*] [*Library of Congress*]   (LCLS)
CSTCS...... Combat Systems Technical School Command
CSTCS...... Cost Schedule Technical Control System
CSTC Trim ... Revue Trimestrielle. Centre Scientifique et Technique de la Construction [*Belgium*] [*A publication*]
CSTD........ United Nations Center for Science and Technology for Development   (EA)
CSTDPHE ... Conference of State and Territorial Directors of Public Health Education   (EA)
CSTE........ Council of State and Territorial Epidemiologists   (EA)
CSTES....... Center for Student Testing, Evaluation, and Standards [*Later, CRESST*] [*Department of Education*]   (GRD)
CSTF .... Canadian Standardized Test of Fitness
CsTFA .... Cesium Trifluoroacetate [*Reagent*]
CSTG........ Casting   (KSC)
CSt-H........ Stanford University, Hoover Institution on War, Revolution, and Peace, Stanford, CA [*Library symbol*] [*Library of Congress*]   (LCLS)
CSTHBT ... Special Report. National Institute of Animal Industry [*A publication*]
CSTHOPHS ... Conference of State and Territorial Health Officers with Public Health Service   (EA)
CSTI .... Centre for Scientific and Technological Information [*Council for Scientific and Industrial Research*] [*Pretoria, South Africa*]
CSTI .... Challenger International Ltd. [*NASDAQ symbol*]   (NQ)
CSTI .... Chattanooga State Technical Institute [*Tennessee*]

CSTI — Clearinghouse for Scientific and Technical Information [*Later, NTIS*] [*National Institute of Standards and Technology*]

CSTI — Committee on Scientific and Technical Information [*Defunct*] [*Federal Council for Science and Technology*] (IEEE)

CSTI — Control Stick Tie-In [*Aviation*] (MUGU)

CSTIP — Combat System Test Implementation Plan [*Military*] (CAAL)

CStJ — Commander, Order of St. John of Jerusalem [*British*]

CSTK — Comstock Group, Inc. [*NASDAQ symbol*] (NQ)

CSTL — Castellate

CSTL — Coastal

CSTL — Constellation Bancorp [*Elizabeth, NJ*] [*NASDAQ symbol*] (NQ)

CSt-L — Stanford University, Lane Medical Library, Stanford, CA [*Library symbol*] [*Library of Congress*] (LCLS)

CSt-Law — Stanford University, Law Library, Stanford, CA [*Library symbol*] [*Library of Congress*] (LCLS)

CStma — Santa Maria Public Library, Santa Maria, CA [*Library symbol*] [*Library of Congress*] (LCLS)

CStmaAH — Allan Hancock College, Santa Maria, CA [*Library symbol*] [*Library of Congress*] (LCLS)

CStmo — Santa Monica Public Library, Santa Monica, CA [*Library symbol*] [*Library of Congress*] (LCLS)

CStmoCiC — Santa Monica City College, Santa Monica, CA [*Library symbol*] [*Library of Congress*] (LCLS)

CStmoD — Douglas Aircraft Co., Santa Monica Division, Santa Monica, CA [*Library symbol*] [*Library of Congress*] (LCLS)

CStmoI — INTREC, Inc., Santa Monica, CA [*Library symbol*] [*Library of Congress*] (LCLS)

CStmoR — Rand Corp., Santa Monica, CA [*Library symbol*] [*Library of Congress*] (LCLS)

CStmoR-W — Rand Corp., Washington, DC [*Library symbol*] [*Library of Congress*] (LCLS)

CStmoS — System Development Corp., Technical Information Center Library, Santa Monica, CA [*Library symbol*] [*Library of Congress*] (LCLS)

CSTMR — Continuous Stirred Tank Membrane Reactor [*Chemical engineering*]

CSTMS — Customs

CSt-Mus — Stanford University, Music Library, Stanford, CA [*Library symbol*] [*Library of Congress*] (LCLS)

CSTN — Cokesbury Satellite Television Network [*United Methodist Publishing House*] [*Telecommunications service*] (TSSD)

CSTN — Cornerstone Financial Corp. [*Derry, NH*] [*NASDAQ symbol*] (NQ)

CSTNAC — Castanea [*A publication*]

CSTO — Country Standard Technical Order (MCD)

CSto — Stockton and San Joaquin County Public Library, Stockton, CA [*Library symbol*] [*Library of Congress*] (LCLS)

CStoC — University of the Pacific, Stockton, CA [*Library symbol*] [*Library of Congress*] (LCLS)

CStoC-PM — University of the Pacific, Pacific Marine Station, Dillon Beach, CA [*Library symbol*] [*Library of Congress*] (LCLS)

CStoC-S — University of the Pacific, Science Library, Stockton, CA [*Library symbol*] [*Library of Congress*] (LCLS)

CStoF — [*The*] 49-99 Cooperative Library System, Stockton, CA [*Library symbol*] [*Library of Congress*] (LCLS)

CStoGH — San Joaquin County General Hospital, Stockton, CA [*Library symbol*] [*Library of Congress*] (LCLS)

CStoGS — Church of Jesus Christ of Latter-Day Saints, Genealogical Society Library, Stockton Branch, Stockton, CA [*Library symbol*] [*Library of Congress*] (LCLS)

CStoH — Humphreys College, Stockton, CA [*Library symbol*] [*Library of Congress*] (LCLS)

CStoHD — San Joaquin County Local Health District, Stockton, CA [*Library symbol*] [*Library of Congress*] (LCLS)

C-STOL — Controlled Short Takeoff and Landing [*Acronym used for a type of aircraft*]

CSTOM — Combat System Tactical Operation Manual [*Navy*] (NVT)

CStoPM — San Joaquin Pioneer Museum and Haggin Art Galleries Library, Stockton, CA [*Library symbol*] [*Library of Congress*] (LCLS)

C-STORE — Convenience Store

CStoSC — San Joaquin Delta College, Stockton, CA [*Library symbol*] [*Library of Congress*] (LCLS)

CStoSH — Stockton State Hospital, Stockton, CA [*Library symbol*] [*Library of Congress*] (LCLS)

CStoSJ — Saint Joseph Hospital, Stockton, CA [*Library symbol*] [*Library of Congress*] (LCLS)

CStoSL — San Joaquin County Law Library, Stockton, CA [*Library symbol*] [*Library of Congress*] (LCLS)

CSTOT — Combat System Team Operational Trainer [*Military*] (CAAL)

CStoTP — San Joaquin County Teachers' Professional Library, Stockton, CA [*Library symbol*] [*Library of Congress*] (LCLS)

CStp — Blanchard Community Library, Santa Paula, CA [*Library symbol*] [*Library of Congress*] (LCLS)

CSTP — Congress Street Properties, Inc. [*Jackson, MS*] [*NASDAQ symbol*] (NQ)

CSTP — Crew Scheduling and Training Plan (NVT)

CSTP — Cubic Centimeters at Standard Temperature and Pressure [*Also, CCSTP*]

CSTPA — Council on Soil Testing and Plant Analysis (EA)

CStP & KC — Chicago, St. Paul & Kansas City Railway

CStPM & O — Chicago, St. Paul, Minneapolis & Omaha Railway

CSTR — Canister (KSC)

CSTR — Centre for Speech Technology Research [*British*] (CB)

CSTR — Committee on Solar-Terrestrial Research [*National Academy of Sciences*]

CSTR — Computer Software Trouble Report (MCD)

CSTR — Continuous Stirred Tank Reactor [*Chemical engineering*]

CSTR — Continuously Stirred Tank Reactor [*Chemical engineering*]

CSTR — Costar Corp. [*Cambridge, MA*] [*NASDAQ symbol*] (NQ)

CStr — Santa Rosa-Sonoma County Free Public Library, Santa Rosa, CA [*Library symbol*] [*Library of Congress*] (LCLS)

CSTRC — COMSAT [*Communications Satellite Corp.*] Technical Review [*A publication*]

CStrJC — Santa Rosa Junior College, Santa Rosa, CA [*Library symbol*] [*Library of Congress*] (LCLS)

CStRLIN — Research Libraries Information Network, Stanford, CA [*Library symbol*] [*Library of Congress*] (LCLS)

CSTR/UF — Continuous Stirred Tank Reactor with an Ultrafiltration Membrane [*Chemical en gineering*]

CSTS — Combined System Test Stand (IEEE)

CSTS — Condensate Storage and Transfer System [*Nuclear energy*] (NRCH)

CSTS — Construction and Startup/Turnover Surveillance Group [*Nuclear energy*] (NRCH)

CSTS — Copper Sulfate Treated Sorbeads

CSTS — Cryogenic Storage and Transfer System (MCD)

CSTS — CS Television, Inc. [*New York, NY*] [*NASDAQ symbol*] (NQ)

CSTSF — Combat Systems Test and Support Facility [*Canadian Navy*]

CSTT — Catastrophic Sexual Transmutation Theory [*Plant genetics*]

CSTT — Core Storage Terminal Table [*Data processing*]

CSTU — Combat System Training Unit (NVT)

CSTU — Combined Systems Test Unit (MCD)

CSTU — Composite Standard Time Units

CSt-V — Stanford University, Nathan Van Patten Library, Stanford, CA [*Library symbol*] [*Library of Congress*] (LCLS)

CSTWA — Chemia Stosowana [*A publication*]

CSU — California State University [*Formerly, San Francisco State College*]

CSU — Canadian Seamen's Union

CSU — Canadian Shopcraft Union

CSU — Casualty Staging Unit [*Military*] (AFM)

CSU — Catheter Specimen of Urine [*Medicine*]

CSU — Central Services Unit for University Careers and Appointments Services [*British*]

CSU — Central State University [*Wilberforce, OH*]

CSU — Central Statistical Unit [*of VLRL*]

CSU — Central Switching Unit

CSU — Channel Service Unit [*Telecommunications*] (TEL)

CSU — Channel Synchronizer Unit [*Data processing*]

CSU — Check Signal Unit [*Telecommunications*] (TEL)

CSU — Chemistry Study Unit [*Later, CPSU*] (EA)

CSU — Chess on Stamps Unit (EA)

CSU — Christian Social Union [*Federal Republic of Germany*]

CSU — Christlich-Soziale Union [*Political party in Bavaria connected with the CDU*] [*West Germany*]

CSU — Christmas Study Unit [*American Topical Association*] (EA)

CSU — Circuit Switching Unit [*Telecommunications*] (CET)

CSU — Civil Service Union [*British*]

CSU — Civilian Service Unit (AFM)

CSU — Cleveland State University, Cleveland, OH [*OCLC symbol*] (OCLC)

CSU — Colorado State University [*Fort Collins*]

CSU — Combat Support Units [*Army*]

CSU — Combined Shaft Unit

CSU — Common Services Unit [*Telecommunications*] (TEL)

CSU — Communications Switching Unit (CAAL)

CSU — Consolidated Cisco Resources [*Vancouver Stock Exchange symbol*]

CSU — Constant Speed Unit [*Aviation*] (ADA)

CSU — Consumers' Research Magazine [*A publication*]

CSU — Crystalline Sucrose Unit [*i.e., sugar cube*] [*Slang*]

CSU — Current Sensor Unit [*American Solenoid Co.*] [*Somerset, NJ*]

CSU — Customer Set-Up [*Data processing*]

CSU — Customer Support Unit (AFIT)

CSUC — California State University, Chico

CSUC — California State University and Colleges [*System*]

CSUC — Consolidated Statutes of Upper Canada [*A publication*] (DLA)

CSuc — Sun City Branch Library, Sun City, CA [*Library symbol*] [*Library of Congress*] (LCLS)

CSUCA — Confederacion Universitaria Centroamericana [*Confederation of Central American Universities*] (EAIO)

CSUCA/ESC — Estudios Sociales Centroamericanos. Consejo Superior de Universidades Centroamericanas, Confederacion Universitaria Centroamericana, Programa Centroamericano de Ciencias Sociales [*A publication*]

CSUCE — Conference of State Utility Commission Engineers [*Later, NCRUCE*] (EA)

Csud — Cinemasud [*A publication*]

CSuLas — Lassen County Free Library, Susanville, CA [*Library symbol*] [*Library of Congress*] (LCLS)

CSULB ...... California State University, Long Beach
CSUN .... California State University, Northridge
CSUPS ...... Combat Supplies [British]
CSURF ...... Colorado State University Research Foundation [Research center] (RCD)
CSUS .... California State University, Sacramento
CSUSA ...... Copyright Society of the USA (EA)
CSUTCB ... Confederacion Sindical Unica de los Trabajadores Campesinos de Bolivia [Trade union] [Bolivia] (EY)
CSV............ Cammed-Gear Speed Variator
Csv .... Cash Surrender Value [Insurance]
CSV............ Casino Silver Mines [Vancouver Stock Exchange symbol]
CSV............ Cathodic Stripping Voltammetry [Analytical chemistry]
CSV............ Cellular Size Volume
CSV............ Characteristic Statistical Value
CSV............ Chreschtlech-Sozial Vollekspartei [Christian Social Party] [Luxembourg] [Political party] (PPW)
CSV............ Chrysanthemum Stunt Viroid
CSV............ Circuit Switched Voice [Telecommunications]
CSV............ Citicorp Scrimgeour Vickers [Commercial firm] [British] (ECON)
CSV............ Clerici Sancti Viatoris [Clerics of St. Viator] [Viatorian Fathers] [Roman Catholic religious order]
CSV............ Columbia Savings & Loan Association [NYSE symbol] (SPSG)
CSV............ Combat Support Vehicle (MCD)
CSV............ Comma Separated Values File [Data processing]
CSVI.......... Community Service Volunteers [British]
CSV............ Community Services Victoria [Australia]
CSV............ Conical Shell Vibration
CSV............ Corona Starting Voltage
CSV............ Crossville, TN [Location identifier] [FAA] (FAAL)
CSv............ Sunnyvale Public Library, Sunnyvale, CA [Library symbol] [Library of Congress] (LCLS)
CSVAH ..... Chronique. Societe Vervietoise d'Archeologie et d'Histoire [A publication]
CSVC........ Core Sample Vacuum Container [NASA]
CSvE........ ESL, Inc., Sunnyvale, CA [Library symbol] [Library of Congress] (LCLS)
CSVLI....... Cash Surrender Value of Life Insurance
CSVP .... Sisters of Charity of St. Vincent de Paul [Roman Catholic religious order]
CSVT .... Close Space Vapor Transport [Photovoltaic energy systems]
CSvUT....... United Technology Center, Sunnyvale, CA [Library symbol] [Library of Congress] (LCLS)
CSW .... Cahiers Simone Weil [A publication]
CSW .... Canada Southern Petroleum Ltd. [Toronto Stock Exchange symbol]
CSW .... Center for Signals Warfare [Warrenton, VA] [Army] (GRD)
CSW .... Center for the Study of Writing [Berkeley, CA] [Department of Education] (GRD)
CSW .... Certified Social Worker
CSW .... Channel Status Word [Data processing] (BUR)
CSW .... Chartered Surveyor Weekly [A publication]
CSW .... Childress [Texas] [Seismograph station code, US Geological Survey] (SEIS)
CSW .... Chilled Sea Water [Pisciculture]
CSW .... Command Surveillance and Weather
CSW .... Commission on the Status of Women [Economic and Social Council of the UN] [Vienna, Austria] (EAIO)
CSW .... Community of St. Wilfrid [Anglican religious community]
CSW .... Computer Sports World [Information service or system] (IID)
CSW .... Continental Shelf Wave
CSW .... Control Switch (MSA)
CSW .... Conventional Standoff Weapon
CSW .... Course and Speed Made Good through the Water [Military] (NATG)
CSWA........ Captain, Surface Weapons Acceptance [British military] (DMA)
CSWAE ..... Commission on the Status of Women in Adult Education [Later, WISE] (EA)
CSWAP ..... Committee on the Status of Women in the Archival Profession (EA)
CSWC........ Capital Southwest Corporation [NASDAQ symbol] (NQ)
CSWC........ Crew-Served Weapons Captured
CSWD .... Center for the Survival of Western Democracies (EA)
CSWE .... Council on Social Work Education (EA)
CSWEP ..... Committee on the Status of Women in the Economics Profession (EA)
CSWFB ..... Canadian Society of Wildlife and Fishery Biologists
CSWG........ Chemical Selection Working Group [National Cancer Institute]
CSWG........ Combat System Working Group [Military] (CAAL)
CSWG........ COMSEC [Communications Security] Wargaming [Simulation] (MCD)
CSWG........ CROSSBOW [Computer Retrieval of Organic Structures Based on Wiswesser] Subcommittee Working Group
CSWL........ Committee on the Status of Women in Linguistics (EA)
CSWM....... Committee on the Status of Women in Microbiology (EA)
CSWP........ Civil Service Working Party [US Military Government, Germany]
CSWP........ Committee for the Status of Women in Philosophy (EA)
CSWPA ..... Chung-Kuo Shui Sheng Wu Hui Pao [A publication]

CSWPL ..... Center on Social Welfare Policy and Law (EA)
CSWS .... Committee on the Status of Women in Sociology (EA)
CSWS .... Corps Support Weapon System
CSWS .... Crew-Served Weapon Sight
CSWTS ...... Crew-Served Weapon Thermal Sight [Army] (INF)
CSWU .... Christlich-Soziale Waehler Union im Saarland [Christian Social Voters' Union in Saarland] [Federal Republic of Germany] [Political party] (PPW)
CSWY........ Causeway (KSC)
CSX............ Changsha [China] [Airport symbol] (OAG)
CSX............ Conventional Solvent Extraction [Separation science and technology]
CSX............ CSIRO [Commonwealth Scientific and Industrial Research Organisation] Index [Information service or system] (ADA)
CSX............ CSX Corp. [Formed by merger of Chessie System, Inc. and Seaboard Coast Line Railroad] [Formerly, CO] [NYSE symbol] (SPSG)
CSY............ Casey [Australia] [Geomagnetic observatory code]
CSY............ Coastline Resources [Vancouver Stock Exchange symbol]
CSY............ CSCE [Centre Senegalais du Commerce Exterieur] Informations [A publication]
CSY............ San Francisco, CA [Location identifier] [FAA] (FAAL)
CSY............ Skyline College Library, San Bruno, CA [OCLC symbol] (OCLC)
CSY............ Sulphocynogen [Pharmacy] (ROG)
CSYI.......... Circuit Systems, Inc. [NASDAQ symbol] (NQ)
CSYIB .... Cargo Systems International [A publication]
CSYS .... Central Banking System, Inc. [NASDAQ symbol] (NQ)
CSYS .... Certificate of Sixth Year Studies [Scotland] (DBQ)
CSZ............ Athens, TX [Location identifier] [FAA] (FAAL)
CSZ............ Coastal Security Zone (MCD)
CSZ............ Copper, Steel, or Zinc [Freight]
CSZ............ Cubic Stabilized Zirconia
CSZ............ University of Southern California, Norris Medical Library, Los Angeles, CA [OCLC symbol] (OCLC)
Cs Zdrav .... Ceskoslovenske Zdravotnictvi [A publication]
CT .... Cable, Test
C/T .... Cable Transfer [of funds]
C/T .... Cable Tray (KSC)
CT .... Cable Twist
CT .... Cahiers Thomistes [A publication]
CT .... Cahiers de Tunisie [A publication]
CT .... Calcitonin [Also, TCA, TCT] [Endocrinology]
CT .... Calibration Technician (KSC)
CT .... California Real Estate Investment Trust SBI [NYSE symbol] (SPSG)
CT .... California Terms [Grain shipping]
CT .... California Tomorrow [An association] (EA)
CT .... Cameroon Tribune [A publication]
CT .... Canada Trustco Mortgage Co. [Toronto Stock Exchange symbol]
CT .... Canadian Token [A publication]
CT .... Canberra Times [A publication] (APTA)
Ct............. Canticles [Song of Solomon] [Old Testament book] (BJA)
CT .... Canton and Enderbury Islands [ANSI two-letter standard code] (CNC)
CT .... Cape Times [A publication] (DLA)
CT .... Captive Test
CT .... Carat [Unit of measure for precious stones or gold]
CT .... Carbon Tetrachloride [Also, CTC] [Organic chemistry]
CT .... Cardiac Type
CT .... Cardiothoracic Ratio [Medicine]
CT .... Cargo Tank [Shipping] (DS)
CT .... Carotid Tracing [Medicine]
CT .... Carpal Tunnel [Medicine]
CT .... Carrier Telephone Channel
CT .... Carrier's Tax (DLA)
CT .... Carrier's Tax Ruling [IR Bulletin] [A publication] (DLA)
CT .... Cartographer [Navy rating]
CT .... Carton (MCD)
CT .... Cash Trade [Investment term]
CT .... Cassette Tape
CT .... Casters and Towbar
Ct............. Cataphyll [Botany]
CT .... Catering Times [A publication]
CT .... Cattle Containers (DCTA)
CT .... Caught
CT .... Cellular Therapy [Medicine]
CT .... Cement Tile [Classified advertising] (ADA)
C/T .... Cenomanian/Turonian [Geological boundary zone]
CT .... Cent [Monetary unit]
CT .... Cental [Short hundredweight] [British] (ROG)
CT .... Center Tap [Technical drawings]
CT .... Central Time (GPO)
C/T .... Centrifugal Throwout [Automotive engineering]
CT .... Centum [Hundred]
CT .... Ceramic Tile [Technical drawings]
CT .... Cerebral Thrombosis [Medicine]
CT .... Cerebral Tumor [Medicine]
CT .... Certificate [Stock exchange term] (SPSG)

CT	Certificate of Title
CT	Certificated Teacher [*British*]
CT	Charcoal Treated
CT	Charge-Transfer [*Intermolecular electron transfer*]
CT	Chart
CT	Check Template (MCD)
CT	Check Test (MCD)
CT	Chemical Test (MCD)
CT	Chemical Titles [*Information service or system*] [*A publication*]
CT	Chemical Transfer (MCD)
CT	Chemotherapy [*Medicine*]
CT	Chest, Training [*Parachute*]
CT	Chest Tube [*Medicine*]
CT	Chicago Tribune [*A publication*]
C of T	Chief of the Tabernacle [*Freemasonry*] (ROG)
CT	Chief Telegrapher [*Navy rating*] [*Obsolete*]
C of T	Chief of Transportation [*Army*]
CT	Chief of Transportation [*Army*]
CT	Child Trends (EA)
CT	Children Today [*A publication*]
CT	China Theater [*World War II*]
CT	China To-Day [*A publication*]
CT	Chlorothiazide [*Diuretic*]
CT	Cholera Toxin [*Medicine*]
CT	Choreographers Theatre (EA)
CT	Christianity Today [*A publication*]
CT	Chymotrypsin [*An enzyme*]
CT	Ciencia Tomista [*A publication*]
CT	Ciguatoxin
CT	Cipher Text [*Telecommunications*] (MCD)
CT	Circadian Time [*Physiology*]
CT	Circle Card Test [*For syphilis*]
CT	Circuit
CT	Circuit Theory [*Electricity*] (MCD)
CT	Circular Tank System [*Pisciculture*]
CT	Circulation Time [*Cardiology*]
CT	Civic Trust (DCTA)
C & T	Classification and Testing [*Air Force*] (AFM)
C/T	Classroom Teaching (OICC)
CT	Classroom Trainer (MCD)
C/T	Clean and Tight [*Publishing*]
CT	CLEM [*Closed-Loop Ex-Vessel Machine*] Transporter [*Nuclear energy*] (NRCH)
CT	Clipped, Torched [*Ecology*]
CT	Clock Time
CT	Close Tolerance
C & T	Clothing and Textiles
CT	Clotrimazole [*Antifungal agent*]
CT	Clotting [*or Coagulation*] Time [*Hematology*]
C-T	Cloudiness-Temperature [*Hypothesis*] [*Meteorology*]
CT	Coastal Telegraph Station [*ITU designation*] (CET)
CT	Coated Tablet [*Pharmacy*]
CT	Code des Droits de Timbre [*A publication*]
CT	Code Telegram
CT	Codex Theodosianus [*Theodosian Code*] [*438AD*] [*Latin*] [*Legal term*] (BJA)
CT	Coffin Texts (BJA)
CT	Collar Tie
CT	Collateral Trust [*Bond*]
CT	Collectanea Theologica [*A publication*]
C by T	Collected [*or Delivered*] by Truck [*Shipping*]
CT	Collective Training [*Army*]
CT	Combat Team
CT	Combined Transport [*Shipping*]
CT	Combined Trials [*Shipbuilding*]
C/T	Command Transmitter (KSC)
C and T	Commencement and Termination [*British railroad term*]
CT	Commercial Translator (IEEE)
CT	Commercial Traveler
C of T	Commissioner of Taxation (ADA)
CT	Committee of Transylvania (EA)
C & T	Communication and Tracking [*NASA*] (NASA)
CT	Communication Trench [*Military*]
CT	Communications Technician [*Navy rating*]
CT	Communications Terminal [*Data processing*]
CT	Communist Terrorist
CT	Community Transit [*System*] [*Shipping*] [*EEC*] (DS)
CT	Compact Toroid (MCD)
CT	Company Team [*Combat Electronic Warfare Intelligence*] [*Army*]
CT	Comparative Testing
CT	Compatibility Test (MCD)
CT	Complete Translation [*Telecommunications*] (TEL)
CT	Component Test (KSC)
CT	Composers Theatre (EA)
CT	Compressed Tablet [*Pharmacy*]
CT	Computed Tomography [*Also, CAAT, CAT*] [*Roentgenography*]
CT	Computer Technology (IEEE)
CT	Computer Transformer
CT	Computer Transponder (MCD)

CT	Condensed Tannin [*Botany*]
CT	Conference Terms (DS)
CT	Confirmatory Test [*Army*] (AABC)
CT	Connecticut [*Postal code*]
CT	Connecticut Reports [*A publication*] (DLA)
Ct.	Connecticut State Library, Hartford, CT [*Library symbol*] [*Library of Congress*] (LCLS)
CT	Connective Tissue
CT	Connectivity Table [*Data processing*]
CT	Constitutiones Tiberii [*A publication*] (DLA)
CT	Constitutive Transcript [*Genetics*]
CT	Consulting Teacher
CT	Contact Approach [*Aviation*] (FAAC)
CT	Contact Tension
CT	Container Tariff
CT	Container Terminal [*Shipping*]
CT	Contemporary Theatre [*A publication*]
C & T	Contingency and Training [*Army*] (AABC)
CT	Continue Treatment [*Medicine*]
CT	Continuity Transceiver [*Telecommunications*] (TEL)
CT	Continuous-Flow Tub
CT	Continuous Tone [*Color printing*]
CT	Contour Template
CT	Contraceptive Technique [*Gynecology*]
CT	Contractor's Training (MCD)
CT	Contrast
CT	Control Tag (MCD)
CT	Control Tower [*For chart use only*] [*Aviation*]
CT	Control Transformer
CT	Controlled Temperature
CT	Controlled Term [*Online database field identifier*]
CT	Conventional Therapy [*Medicine*]
CT	Conventional Tillage [*Agroecosystem*]
CT	Convergent Technologies Expo [*Publications and Communications, Inc.*] (TSPED)
CT	Cooling Tower [*Nuclear energy*] (NRCH)
CT	Coombs' Test [*for the presence of globulin on the surface of red cells*] [*Hematology*]
CT	Cordless Telephone
CT	Corneal Transplant [*Medicine*]
CT	Coronary Thrombosis [*Medicine*]
CT	Corporation Tax [*British*]
CT	Corps of Transportation [*Army*]
CT	Corrective Therapist [*or Therapy*]
CT	Cortical Plate Thickness [*Anatomy*]
CT	Corticosterone [*A hormone*]
Ct.	Cotyledon [*Botany*]
CT	Count
CT	Counter
CT	Counter Timer
CT	Countertenor [*Music*]
CT	Counterterrorist (ADA)
CT	Countertrade [*Economics*] (IMH)
CT	Country Team [*Military*] (CINC)
CT	County
CT	Courant [*Of the Current Month*] [*French*]
CT	Court
CT	Court Rolls [*British*]
CT	Court Trust [*Includes executor, administrator, guardian*] [*Legal term*] (DLA)
CT	Cover Test [*Ophthalmology*]
C/T	Crawler/Transporter [*Aerospace*] (KSC)
CT	Creative Time (EA)
CT	Creativity Tests for Children [*Child development test series*]
CT	Credit [*or Creditor*] (ROG)
CT	Credit Transfer
C-T	Cretaceous and Tertiary [*Geology*]
CT	Crista Terminalis [*Cardiology*]
CT	Cristobalite-Tridymite [*A form of silica*]
CT	Critical Temperature
CT	Crossmatch: Transfusion
CT	Crosstrail [*Military*]
CT	CT Financial Services [*Formerly, Canada Trustco Mortgage Co.*] [*Vancouver Stock Exchange symbol*]
CT	Cubic Tonnage [*Shipping*]
C & T	Culture and Tradition [*A publication*]
CT	Cuneiform Texts from Babylonian Tablets in the British Museum (BJA)
CT	Current
CT	Current Transactions (NATG)
CT	Current Transformer
CT	Cycle Time (NVT)
CT	Cystine-Tellurite [*Medium*] [*Microbiology*]
CT	Cytotechnologist
CT	Journal of Computed Tomography [*A publication*]
CT	Torrance Public Library, Torrance, CA [*Library symbol*] [*Library of Congress*] (LCLS)
CT	Training Cruiser (MCD)
CT	Transit Switching Center [*Telecommunications*] (TEL)
CT1	Communications Technician, First Class [*Navy rating*]
CT2	Communications Technician, Second Class [*Navy rating*]

CT3 .... Communications Technician, Third Class [*Navy rating*]
CTA .... Association of Civilian Technicians
CTA .... Cable Twist Angle
CTA .... Call to Australia [*Political party*] (ADA)
CTA .... Call Time Adjustor [*Military communications*]
CTA .... Canadian Telebook Agency [*ACCORD*] [*Source file*] [*UTLAS symbol*]
CTA .... Canadian Testing Association
CTA .... Canadian Trotting Association
CTA .... Cargo Traffic Analysis (MCD)
CTA .... Caribbean Tourism Association [*Later, Caribbean Tourism Organization*] (EA)
CTA .... Carpenter Lake Resources [*Vancouver Stock Exchange symbol*]
CTA .... Catania [*Italy*] [*Airport symbol*] (OAG)
CTA .... Catering Teachers Association [*British*]
CTA .... Cellulose Triacetate [*Organic chemistry*]
CTA .... Center for Technology and Administration [*American University*] [*Research center*] (RCD)
CTA .... Center for Tropical Agriculture [*University of Florida*] [*Research center*] (RCD)
CTA .... Central TMDE [*Test, Measuring, and Diagnostic Equipment*] Activity [*Army*] (MCD)
CTA .... Central Transport Authority (ADA)
CTA .... Centre Technique de Cooperation Agricole et Rural [*Technical Centre for Agricultural and Rural Cooperation*] (EAIO)
CTA .... Cetyltrimethylammonium [*Organic chemistry*]
CTA .... [*The*] Channel Tunnel Association [*British*]
CTA .... Chaplain of the Territorial Army [*British*]
CTA .... Charters Towers [*Australia*] [*Seismograph station code, US Geological Survey*] (SEIS)
CTA .... Chemical Toilet Association (EA)
CTA .... Chicago Transit Authority
CTA .... Children's Theatre Association of America [*Formerly, CTC*] (EA)
CTA .... Children's Transplant Association (EA)
CTA .... Cinema Theatre Association [*British*]
CTA .... Circuit Terminating Arrangement
CTA .... Classic Thunderbird Association (EA)
Cta .... Comandita [*Conditional Partnership*] [*Portuguese*] [*Business term*]
CTA .... Combined Target Area
CTA .... Commercial Trailer Association [*British*]
CTA .... Committee on Thrombolytic Agents
CTA .... Commodity Trading Advisor
CTA .... Common Table of Allowances [*Army*] (AABC)
CTA .... Communiquer a Toutes Adresses [*To Be Circulated to All Addresses*] [*Telecommunications*] [*French*]
CTA .... Compagnie de Transports Aeriens [*Airline*] [*Switzerland*]
CTA .... Companion Trainer Aircraft
CTA .... Compatibility Test Area [*NASA*] (KSC)
CTA .... Component Test Area
CTA .... Computer Technology Associates [*Goddard Spaceflight Center - Greenbelt, MD*] [*NASA*] (NASA)
CTA .... Computer and Telecommunications Acronyms [*A publication*]
CTA .... Computerized Travel Aid [*Mobility device for the blind*]
CTA .... Comut Aire of Michigan, Inc. [*Pontiac, MI*] [*FAA designator*] (FAAC)
CTA .... Consolidated Tape Association (EA)
CTA .... Continental Airlines, Inc. Holding [*AMEX symbol*] (SPSG)
CTA .... Continental Transportation Association [*Inactive*] (EA)
CTA .... Contractor Technical Assistance (MCD)
CTA .... Control Area [*Aviation*] (FAAC)
CTA .... Controlled Thrust Assembly (NASA)
CTA .... Copper Trade Association
CTA .... Corpus des Tablettes en Cuneiformes Alphabetiques Decouvertes a Ras Shamra-Ugarit de 1929 a 1939 (BJA)
CTA .... Council for Technological Advancement (EA)
CTA .... Counter-Target-Acquisition (MCD)
CTA .... Covered Threads Association [*Defunct*] (EA)
CTA .... Cum Testamento Annexo [*With the Will Annexed*] [*Latin*]
CTA .... Customs Tariff Act [*Canada*]
CTA .... Cystine Trypticase Agar [*Microbiology*]
CTAA .... Children's Theatre Association of America [*Formerly, CTC*] (EA)
CTAA .... Corporate Transfer Agents Association [*New York, NY*] (EA)
CTAB .... Cetyltrimethylammonium Bromide [*Also, CETAB, CTBM*] [*Antiseptic*]
CTAB .... Commerce Technical Advisory Board [*Terminated, 1981*] [*Department of Commerce*] (EGAO)
CTAB .... Cross Tabulation of Frequencies
CTAC .... Cancer Treatment Advisory Committee [*HEW*] (EGAO)
CTAC .... Center for Teaching about China (EA)
CTAC .... International Conference on Computational Techniques and Applications [*Australia*]
CTAC .... Portable Word Processor
CTACl .... Cetyltrimethylammonium Chloride [*Organic chemistry*]
cta cte .... Cuenta Corriente [*Current Account*] [*Spanish*] [*Business term*]
CTA-DLP ... Call to Australia - Democratic Labor Party Coalition [*Political party*] (ADA)
CTAF .... Committee to Abolish the Fed (EA)

CTAF .... Common Traffic Advisory Frequency (FAAC)
CTAF .... Crew Training Air Force
CTaf .... Taft College, Taft, CA [*Library symbol*] [*Library of Congress*] (LCLS)
CTAH .... Center for Tropical Animal Health [*Texas A & M University*] [*Research center*] (RCD)
CTAI .... Clinical Technologies Associates, Inc. [*NASDAQ symbol*] (NQ)
CTAIR .... Code des Taxes Assimilees aux Impots sur les Revenus [*A publication*]
CTA J .... CTA [*Cine Technicians' Association*] Journal [*India*] [*A publication*]
CTAK .... Cipher Text Auto Key [*Data processing*]
CTAL .... Confederacion de Trabajadores de America Latina [*Confederation of Latin-American Workers*]
CTAL .... Crystal
CTAM .... Cable Television Administration and Marketing Society (EA)
CTAM .... Climb to and Maintain [*Aviation*] (FAAC)
CTAM .... Continental Tropical Air Mass (MSA)
CTAN .... CINCPAC [*Commander-in-Chief, Pacific*] Teletype Automated Net (NVT)
C TANT.... Cum Tanto [*With the Same Amount Of*] [*Pharmacy*]
CTAO .... Charters Towers [*Australia*] [*Seismograph station code, US Geological Survey*] (SEIS)
CTAPCJS ... Commodore Thomas ap Catesby Jones Society [*Defunct*] (EA)
C-TAPE ..... Committee for Thorough Agricultural Political Education [*Associated Milk Producers, Inc.*]
Ct App CC ... Texas Civil Cases [*A publication*] (DLA)
Ct App CC ... Texas Court of Appeals Reports [*A publication*] (DLA)
Ct App NZ ... Court of Appeals Reports [*New Zealand*] [*A publication*] (DLA)
Ct Apps ...... Texas Court of Appeals Reports [*A publication*] (DLA)
CTAQ .... Cooperating Teachers' Attitude Questionnaire
CTAR .... Centaur Sciences, Inc. [*NASDAQ symbol*] (NQ)
CTarA .... American Astronomical Society, Tarzana, CA [*Library symbol*] [*Library of Congress*] (LCLS)
CTarB .... Edgar Rice Burroughs, Inc., Tarzana, CA [*Library symbol*] [*Library of Congress*] (LCLS)
Ctary .... Commentary [*A publication*]
CTAS .... Centralized Transient Accounting System (MCD)
CTAS .... Cintas Corp. [*NASDAQ symbol*] (NQ)
CTAS .... Cobalt Thiocyanate Active Substance [*Organic analysis*]
CTAS .... Commonwealth Trans-Antarctic Expedition [*1955-58*]
CTAS .... Constant Temperature Anemometer System
CTASC ...... Corps/Theater Automatic Data Processing Service Center [*Military*]
CTASD...... China Science and Technology Abstracts [*A publication*]
CTAT........ Cetyl Trimethylammonium Tosylate [*Organic chemistry*]
CTAT......... Colloque sur le Traitement Automatique des Textes [*Colloquium on the Computer Processing of Textual Data - CCPTD*]
CTAT......... Computerized Transaxial Tomography
CTAU .... Catholic Total Abstinence Union
CTAUA ...... Catholic Total Abstinence Union of America (EA)
CTAX........ Climb to and Cross [*Aviation*] (FAAC)
C Tax C...... Canadian Tax Cases [*A publication*] (DLA)
CtB............. Bridgeport Public Library, Bridgeport, CT [*Library symbol*] [*Library of Congress*] (LCLS)
CTB........... Calibration Test Box
CTB........... California Test Bureau [*Psychology*] [*McGraw Hill, Inc.*]
CTB........... Canberra Tourist Bureau [*Australia*]
CTB........... Ceased to Breathe [*Medicine*]
CTB........... Central Tracing Bureau [*Post-World War II*]
CTB........... Ceramic-Tile Base [*Technical drawings*]
CTB........... Ceylon Tourist Board (EAIO)
CTB........... Chief of Tariff Bureau
CTB........... Cholera Toxin B [*Medicine*]
CTB........... Classification Test Battery [*Aptitude and skills test*]
CTB........... Coast Torpedo Boat [*Navy symbol*] [*Obsolete*]
CTB........... Code Table Buffer
CTB........... Coffee Table Book [*Large, extensively illustrated book designed for display and browsing*]
CTB........... Collateral Trust Bond [*Investment term*]
CTB........... Combined Travel Board [*Allied German Occupation Forces*]
CTB........... Command Telemetry Buoy
CTB........... Commercial Text-Books [*A publication*]
CTB........... Commercial Traffic Bulletin
CTB........... Commonwealth Telecommunications Board [*Later, CTO*] [*British*] (DEN)
CTB........... Companies and Their Brands [*Formerly, TND:CI*] [*A publication*]
CTB........... Comprehensive Test Ban [*Nuclear weapons*]
CTB........... Computer Time Bookers
CTB........... Concentrator Terminal Buffer [*Data processing*] (IBMDP)
CTB........... Consulting Traffic Bureau
CTB........... Control Test Bed
CTB........... Controlled Temperature Bath
CTB........... Cooper Tire & Rubber Co. [*NYSE symbol*] (SPSG)
CTB........... Curacao Tourist Board (EA)
CTB........... Cut Bank, MT [*Location identifier*] [*FAA*] (FAAL)
CTBA......... Commonwealth Trading Bank of Australia

CTBC.........	Centerre Bancorporation [*NASDAQ symbol*] (NQ)
CTBF........	Cinema and Television Benevolent Fund [*British*]
CtBFAST...	Fannie Smith School, Bridgeport, CT [*Library symbol*] [*Library of Congress*] (LCLS)
CTBL.........	Calyx Tube Length [*Botany*]
CtBl...........	Prosser Public Library, Bloomfield, CT [*Library symbol*] [*Library of Congress*] (LCLS)
CtBlE	Emhart Manufacturing Co. [*Later, Emhart Corp.*], Bloomfield, CT [*Library symbol*] [*Library of Congress*] (LCLS)
CtBlST.......	Saint Thomas Seminary, Bloomfield, CT [*Library symbol*] [*Library of Congress*] (LCLS)
CTBM........	Chief Testboard Man [*Telecommunications*] (TEL)
CtBN..........	Bridgeport City Normal School, Bridgeport, CT [*Library symbol*] [*Library of Congress*] [*Obsolete*] (LCLS)
CTBN	Carboxyl-Terminated Butadiene-Acrylonitrile [*Organic chemistry*]
CTBP.........	Cytotactin-Binding Proteoglycan
Ct-BPH......	Regional Library for the Blind and Physically Handicapped, Hartford, CT [*Library symbol*] [*Library of Congress*] (LCLS)
CTBR........	Committee to Defend Black Rights [*Australia*]
CTBR.........	Commonwealth Taxation Board of Review Decisions [*A publication*] (APTA)
CTBR NS ..	Commonwealth Taxation Board of Review Decisions. New Series [*A publication*] (APTA)
CTBROS ...	Commonwealth Taxation Board of Review Decisions. Old Series [*A publication*] (ADA)
CTBS.........	California Test of Basic Skills [*Education*]
CTBS.........	Canadian Test of Basic Skills [*Education*]
CTBS.........	Comprehensive Tests of Basic Skills [*Education*]
CtBSH	Sacred Heart University, Bridgeport, CT [*Library symbol*] [*Library of Congress*] (LCLS)
CTBT........	Citizens Trust Co. [*NASDAQ symbol*] (NQ)
CTBT.........	Comprehensive Test Ban Treaty
CtBU..........	University of Bridgeport, Bridgeport, CT [*Library symbol*] [*Library of Congress*] (LCLS)
CTBUH	Council on Tall Buildings and Urban Habitat (EA)
CTBX........	Centerbank [*NASDAQ symbol*] (NQ)
CTC	Cab Trade Council [*A union*] [*British*]
CTC	Cam Timing Contact
CTC	Camera, Timing, and Control (NASA)
CTC	Canada Tax Cases [*A publication*] (DLA)
CTC	Canadian Theological College
CTC	Canadian Transport Commission
CTC	Cape Town Cavalry [*British military*] (DMA)
CTC	Capsule Test Conductor [*NASA*] (KSC)
CTC	Captain Consolidated Resources [*Vancouver Stock Exchange symbol*]
CTC	Carbon Tetrachloride [*Also, CT*] [*Organic chemistry*]
CTC	Career Technologies Corp. [*Database producer*] (IID)
CTC	Cargo Tank Center (DS)
CTC	Catamarca [*Argentina*] [*Airport symbol*] (OAG)
CTC	Catholic Teachers College [*Rhode Island*]
CTC	CCATS [*Communications, Command, and Telemetry Systems*] Telemetry Controller [*NASA*]
CTC	Center for Trace Characterization [*Texas A & M University*] [*Research center*] (RCD)
CTC	Center on Transnational Corporations [*United Nations*]
CTC	Central Trading Committee [*Ministry of Finance and Petroleum*] [*Qatar*] (IMH)
CTC	Central Traffic Control
CTC	Central Training Council [*Department of Employment*] [*British*]
CTC	Certified Travel Counselor [*Designation awarded by Institute of Certified Travel Agents*]
CTC	Ceskoslovensky Terminologicky Casopis [*A publication*]
CTC	Channel-to-Channel (MCD)
CTC	Charleston Training Center [*South Carolina*]
CTC	Chetwynd [*British Columbia*] [*Seismograph station code, US Geological Survey*] [*Closed*] (SEIS)
CTC	Chicago Teachers College [*Later, Chicago State University*]
CTC	Chicago Technical College
CTC	Chicano Training Center (EA)
CTC	Chief Test Conductor (NASA)
CTC	Chief Turret Captain [*Obsolete*] [*Navy*]
CTC	Children's Theatre Conference (EA)
CTC	Chlortetracycline [*Antibiotic*]
CTC	Circuit Trial Counsel
CTC	Citizens' Training Corps
CTC	City Tattersall's Club [*Australia*]
CTC	City Technology Colleges [*British*]
CTC	Cleveland Trust Company
CTC	Climate Test Chamber
CTC	Cold Type Composition [*Selection of Printing Industries of America*]
CTC	Combat Training Center [*Army*] (INF)
CTC	Combined Training Center
CTC	Commando Training Centre [*British*]
CTC	Commissariat and Transport Corps [*British military*] (DMA)
CTC	Commission on Transnational Corporations [*United Nations*]

CTC	Communication Training Consultants, Inc. [*New York, NY*] [*Telecommunications*] (TSSD)
CTC	Communications Technician, Chief [*Navy rating*]
CTC	Compact Transpiration Cooling
CTC	Compania de Telefonos de Chile SA [*Santiago*] [*Telecommunications service*] (TSSD)
CTC	Compaq Telecommunications Corporation [*Dallas, TX*]
CTC	Compatibility Test Capsule
CTC	Computer Technology Center
CTC	Computer Telecommunications Corp. [*Australia*]
CTC	Concordia Teachers College [*Illinois, Nebraska*]
CTC	Conditional Transfer of Control
CTC	Congres du Travail du Canada [*Canadian Labour Congress - CLC*]
CTC	Congressional Textile Caucus (EA)
CTC	Constant Temperature Circulator [*Instrumentation*]
CTC	Constant Torque Compensation
CTC	Contact
CTC	Contel Corporation [*NYSE symbol*] (SPSG)
CTC	Continuity Test Current
CTC	Continuous Thymus-Cell [*Cell line*]
CTC	Contract Journal [*A publication*]
CTC	Contract Target Cost (MCD)
CTC	Contract Technical Compliance (MUGU)
CTC	Contract Termination and Completion (MCD)
CTC	Corn Trade Clauses [*Shipping*]
CTC	Counter/Timer Circuit [*Data processing*]
CTC	Counter-Timer Control
CTC	Cross-Track Contiguous
CTC	Crush, Tear, Curl [*Tea processing*]
CTC	Customs Transaction Code (DS)
CTC	Cut, Tear, and Curl [*Tea*]
CTC	Cyclists' Touring Club
CTC	Manual Communications Unit
CTC	Treasury Department, Comptroller of the Currency, Washington, DC [*OCLC symbol*] (OCLC)
CTCA........	Cairn Terrier Club of America (EA)
CTCA........	Canadian Telecommunications Carriers Association
CTCA........	Channel-to-Channel Adapter [*Data processing*] (IBMDP)
CTCA........	Channel and Traffic Control Agency [*of AACS*]
CTCA........	Commission for Technical Cooperation for Africa
CTCA........	Corpus des Tablettes en Cuneiformes Alphabetiques Decouvertes a Ras Shamra-Ugarit de 1929 a 1939 (BJA)
CTCC........	Central Transport Consultative Committee [*British*]
CTCC........	Change [*or Changing*] to Center Control [*Aviation*] (FAAC)
CTCC........	Confederation des Travailleurs Catholiques du Canada [*Catholic Federation of Labour, 1922-1960*]
CTCC........	Contact Center Control [*Aviation*] (FAAC)
CTCC........	Continental Division, Transport Control Center [*Military*]
CTCCC......	Close Type Control Circuit Contact (MSA)
CTCEA......	Current Therapeutic Research. Clinical and Experimental [*A publication*]
CTCEN......	Contact Center [*Aviation*] (FAAC)
CTCF.........	Channel and Technical Control Facility [*In a tape-relay station in the AIRCOMNET*]
CTCI.........	China Technical Consultants, Incorporated
CTCI..........	Classic Thunderbird Club International (EA)
CTCI..........	Contract Technical Compliance Inspection
CTCL........	Community and Technical College Libraries
CTCL........	Count Clock [*NASA*] (KSC)
CTCL........	Cutaneous T-Cell Lymphoma [*Medicine*]
Ct Cl........	United States Court of Claims Reports [*A publication*] (DLA)
Ct Cl Act	Court of Claims Act (DLA)
Ct Cl Act	New York Court of Claims Act [*A publication*]
Ct Cl NY	Court of Claims Reports [*New York*] [*A publication*] (DLA)
CTCLR	Cape Times Common Law Reports [*South Africa*] [*A publication*] (DLA)
Ct Cl R	Court of Claims Rules [*A publication*] (DLA)
CTCLS.......	Court of Claims
Ct Cls	United States Court of Claims (DLA)
Ct of Cls	United States Court of Claims (DLA)
CTCM........	Communications Technician, Master Chief [*Navy rating*]
CTCNC......	Christian Temperance Council for the Nordic Countries (EA)
CTCO	Cross & Trecker Corporation [*NASDAQ symbol*] (NQ)
Ct Com Pl ..	Court of Common Pleas (DLA)
CTCOR......	Chrysler Town and Country Owners Registry (EA)
CTCP.........	Clinical Toxicology of Commercial Products [*Dartmouth Medical School; University of Rochester*] [*Database - inactive*] [*A publication*]
CTCP.........	Combat Theater Communications Program [*Air Force*] (MCD)
CTCP.........	Contract Task Change Proposal (AAG)
CTCPD......	Changchun Dizhi Xueyuan Xuebao [*A publication*]
CTCQ	Check Technology Corp. [*NASDAQ symbol*] (NQ)
CTCR.........	Chrysler Town and Country Owners Registry (EA)
CTCRA......	Current Topics in Cellular Regulation [*A publication*]
CTCRDH ..	Australia Commonwealth Scientific and Industrial Research Organisation. Tropical Crops and Pastures. Divisional Report [*A publication*]
CTCRI.......	Central Tuber Crops Research Institute
CTCRM.....	Commando Training Centre, Royal Marines [*British military*] (DMA)

CTCS......... Cabin/Cockpit Temperature Control Systems [*Aviation*]
CTCS......... Communications Technician, Senior Chief [*Navy rating*]
CTCS......... Consolidated Telemetry Checkout System [*Air Force*]
CTCTSC.... China Trade Consultation and Technical Service Corporation [*Ministry of Foreign Economic Relations and Trade*] [*People's Republic of China*]   (IMH)
CTCU .... Canadian Textile and Chemical Union
CTCU .... Channel and Traffic Control Unit [*Subordinate unit of the Channel and Traffic Control Agency*]
Ct Cust App ... Court of Customs Appeals   (DLA)
Ct Cust App ... Court of Customs Appeals Reports [*1919-29*] [*A publication*]   (DLA)
Ct Cust & Pat App ... Court of Customs and Patent Appeals   (DLA)
CTCZ......... Carrier Tactical Control Zone [*Military*]   (NVT)
CTD .... Cahiers. Groupe Francois-Thureau-Dangin [*Paris*] [*A publication*]
CTD .... Canadian Transportation and Distribution Management [*A publication*]
CTD .... Carboxyl-Terminal Domain [*Genetics*]
CTD .... Carpal Tunnel Decompression [*Medicine*]
C/T)d .... Carrier-to-Noise Temperature, Downlink
CTD .... Catalogue des Theses de Doctorat [*A bibliographic publication*] [*France*]
CTD .... Celestial Training Device   (MCD)
CTD .... Central Target Director [*Military*]   (CAAL)
CTD .... Certificate of Tax Deposit [*British*]
CTD .... Certificate for Teachers of the Deaf [*Australia*]
CTD .... Certified Test Data
C Td .... Ceylon Today [*A publication*]
CTD .... Charge-Transfer Device [*Electronics*]
CTD .... Charged Tape Detection [*Fuel-failure monitor*] [*Nuclear energy*]   (NRCH)
CTD .... Circulation Time Distribution [*Chemical engineering*]
CTD .... Clutter Threshold Detector   (CET)
CTD .... Coated   (KSC)
CTD .... College Training Detachment
CTD .... Combined Transport Document [*Shipping*]
CTD .... Commander, Transportation Division
CTD .... Commission de Toponymie et Dialectologie [*A publication*]
CTD .... Communications Trade Division   (EA)
CTD .... Community Training and Development [*An association*]   (EA)
CTD .... Completion Tour of Duty
CTD .... Conductivity, Temperature, and Depth [*Oceanography*]
CTD .... Connective-Tissue Disease [*Medicine*]
CTD .... Continuity Tone Detector [*Telecommunications*]   (TEL)
CTD .... Control Data Corp. [*Toronto Stock Exchange symbol*]
CTD .... Controlled Thermolytic Dissociation
CTD .... Convalescent Training Depot   (NATG)
CTD .... Corporate Technology Database [*Corporate Technology Information Services, Inc.*]   (CRD)
CTD .... Council for Television Development [*Defunct*]
Ct D .... Court Decisions, National Labor Relations Act [*A publication*]   (DLA)
CTD .... Crew Task Demand
CTD .... Crew Task Detail
CTD .... Cross-Track Distance [*Aerospace*]
CTD .... Cultuurtechnische Dienst [*A publication*]
CTD .... Current, Temperature, Density
CtD............. Darien Library, Darien, CT [*Library symbol*] [*Library of Congress*]   (LCLS)
CTD .... Western Connecticut State College, Haas Library, Danbury, CT [*OCLC symbol*]   (OCLC)
CTDA .... Ceramic Tile Distributors Association   (EA)
CTDA .... Custom Tailors and Designers Association of America   (EA)
CtDab......... Danbury Public Library, Danbury, CT [*Library symbol*] [*Library of Congress*]   (LCLS)
CtDabN ..... Western Connecticut State College, Danbury, CT [*Library symbol*] [*Library of Congress*]   (LCLS)
CT & DB ..... Cough, Turn, and Deep Breathe [*Medicine*]
CTDBA...... Current Topics in Developmental Biology [*A publication*]
CTDC .... Chemical Thermodynamics Data Center [*National Institute of Standards and Technology*]
CTDC .... Company Technical Document Center
CTDC .... Control Track Direction Computer   (AABC)
CTDCS...... Common Test Data Collection System   (MCD)
CtDe.......... Derby Public Library, Derby, CT [*Library symbol*] [*Library of Congress*]   (LCLS)
Ct Dec NLRA ... Court Decisions, National Labor Relations Act [*A publication*]   (DLA)
CTDF......... Community Telecommunications Development Foundation [*Washington, DC*]   (TSSD)
CTDH........ Command and Telemetry Data Handling   (IEEE)
CTDMIS ... Combat and Training Development Management Information System
CTDN........ Countdown [*NASA*]   (KSC)
ctDNA........ Deoxyribonucleic Acid, Chloroplast [*Biochemistry, genetics*] [*Also, Chl-DNA, cpDNA*]
CTDO .... Central Technical Documents Office [*Naval Ordnance Systems Command*] [*Information service or system*]   (IID)
CTDR .... Commercial Training Device Requirement

CTDS......... Canadian Transportation Documentation System [*Database*] [*Transport Canada Library and Information Center*] [*Information service or system*]   (CRD)
CTDS......... Code Translation Data System [*Air Force*]
C/TDS .... Count/Time Data System   (IEEE)
CTE........... Cable Termination Equipment   (CET)
CTE........... Canton and Enderbury Islands [*ANSI three-letter standard code*]   (CNC)
CTE........... Car-Tours in Europe, Inc.
CTE........... Carti [*Panama*] [*Airport symbol*]   (OAG)
CTE........... Cartier Resources, Inc. [*Toronto Stock Exchange symbol*]
CTE........... Center for Teaching Effectiveness [*University of Texas at Austin*] [*Research center*]   (RCD)
CTE........... Central Telegraph Exchange [*British*]
CTE........... Central Timing Equipment
CTE........... Central Translation Evidence
CTE........... Channel Translating Equipment [*Telecommunications*]   (TEL)
CTE........... Charge Transfer Efficiency [*In photodetectors*]
CTE........... Coefficient of Thermal Expansion
CTE........... Commander, Task Element
CTE........... Commercial Test Equipment   (MCD)
CTE........... Component Test Equipment   (KSC)
CTE........... Compte [*Account*] [*French*] [*Business term*]   (ROG)
CTE........... Computer TELEX Exchange [*RCA Corp.*]
CTE........... Conditioning Thio Emulsion [*Roux Laboratories, Inc.*]
CTE........... Contractor Technical Evaluation   (CAAL)
CTE........... Contractor Test and Evaluation   (MCD)
Cte.............. Corriente [*Current*] [*Spanish*] [*Business term*]
CTE........... Cross-Track Error
CTE........... Cultured Thymic Epithelium [*Immunochemistry*]
CTE........... Customer's Terminal Equipment [*Telecommunications*] [*British*]
CTEA........ Canadian Telephone Employees' Association [*See also ACET*]
CTEA........ Channel Transmission and Engineering Activation
CTEA........ Cost and Training Effectiveness Analysis
CTEA........ Council for Technology Education Associations   (EA)
CTEAA7.... Comunicados Tecnicos. Instituto de Ecologia e Experimentacao Agricolas [*A publication*]
CtEahav .... Hagaman Memorial Library, East Haven, CT [*Library symbol*] [*Library of Congress*]   (LCLS)
CTEB........ Council of Technical Examining Bodies [*British*]
CTEC........ City Training and Education Centre [*Sydney, Australia*]
CTEC........ Combined Transportation Equipment Committee [*Combined Production and Resources Board*] [*World War II*]
CTEC........ Commonwealth Tertiary Education Commission [*Australia*]
CTEC........ Communication Technical Evaluation Console   (KSC)
CTEC........ Component Technology Corporation [*NASDAQ symbol*]   (NQ)
CTED........ Civilian Training, Education, and Development   (MCD)
CTEE........ Committee
CTEEA ...... Current Topics in Experimental Endocrinology [*A publication*]
CTEGA ...... Cutting Tool Engineering [*A publication*]
CtEh.......... East Hartford Public Library, East Hartford, CT [*Library symbol*] [*Library of Congress*]   (LCLS)
CtEhad...... Rathbun Memorial Library, East Haddam, CT [*Library symbol*] [*Library of Congress*]   (LCLS)
CtEhUA..... United Aircraft Corp., East Hartford, CT [*Library symbol*] [*Library of Congress*]   (LCLS)
CTEK........ Commercial Intertech Corp. [*NASDAQ symbol*]   (NQ)
CTELP ...... Central Telephone Pfd [*NASDAQ symbol*]   (NQ)
CTEM........ Conventional-Transmission Electron Microscope
CTEN........ Counter Tenor [*Music*]
CtEnA .... Asnuntuck Community College, Learning Resources Center, Enfield, CT [*Library symbol*] [*Library of Congress*]   (LCLS)
CTEOC...... Caterpillar Truck Engine Owners Club
CTEP .... Cancer Therapy Evaluation Program [*Bethesda, MD*] [*National Cancer Institute*] [*Department of Health and Human Services*]   (GRD)
CTEP .... Centre for Transport Engineering Practice [*Loughborough University of Technology*] [*British*]   (CB)
Ct of Er and Appeals ... Court of Errors and Appeals [*New Jersey*]   (DLA)
CT ERR .... Court of Error [*Legal term*]   (DLA)
Ct Err & App ... Court of Errors and Appeals [*New Jersey*]   (DLA)
Ct Errors and App ... Court of Errors and Appeals [*New Jersey*]   (DLA)
CTETF .... Cargo Technical Evaluation Task Force [*IATA*]   (DS)
CTEX......... C-TEC Corp. [*Formerly, Context Industries, Inc.*] [*NASDAQ symbol*]   (NQ)
CTF........... C-Band Temperature
CTF........... Canadian Teachers Federation
CTF........... Cancer Therapy Facility
CTF........... Career Training Foundation   (EA)
CTF........... Cask Tilting Fixture [*Nuclear energy*]   (NRCH)
CTF........... Cavity Turnable Filter
CTF........... Central Task Force
CTF........... Central Training Facility   (MCD)
CTF........... Ceramic-Tile Floor [*Technical drawings*]
CTF........... Ceramic Tube Fabrication
CTF........... Certificate
CTF........... Change [*or Changing*] to Tower Frequency [*Aviation*]   (FAAC)
CTF........... Chaplain to the Territorial Forces [*British*]

CTF........... Chesterfield, SC [*Location identifier*] [*FAA*]   (FAAL)
CTF........... Chlorine Trifluoride [*Inorganic chemistry*]
CTF........... Chlorotriflurorethane [*Organic chemistry*]
CTF........... Clinical Treatment Failure
CTF........... Collective Training Facility [*Army*]   (INF)
CTF........... Combat Training Facilities [*DoD*]
CTF........... Combined Task Force [*NATO*]   (NATG)
CTF........... Combined Test Force [*Military*]
CTF........... Commander, Task Force
CTF........... Common Test Facility
CTF........... Communications Test Facility [*Fort Huachuca, AZ*] [*United States Army Electronic Proving Ground*]   (GRD)
CTF........... Community Task Force [*British*]
CTF........... Congress Task Force   (EA)
CTF........... Consolidated Training Facility [*Army*]
CTF........... Continentaler Stahlmarkt (Frankfurt Am Main) [*A publication*]
CTF........... Contrast Transfer Function [*Video technology*]
CTF........... Controlled Temperature Furnace
CTF........... Controlled Thermonuclear Fusion
CTF........... Core Test Facility
CTF........... Correction to Follow
CTF........... Correctional Training Facility [*Army*]   (AABC)
CTF........... Counsellors Tandem [*NYSE symbol*]   (SPSG)
CTF........... Credit Transfer Fee [*Business term*]
CTF........... Crisis Task Force   (MCD)
CTF........... Cytotoxic Factor
CtF........... Farmington Village Library, Farmington, CT [*Library symbol*] [*Library of Congress*]   (LCLS)
CTF........... [*The*] Following groups have been referred back to the originator for confirmation or correction [*Communications*]   (FAAC)
CTFA........ Cosmetic, Toiletry, and Fragrance Association   (EA)
CtFa.......... Fairfield Public Library, Fairfield, CT [*Library symbol*] [*Library of Congress*]   (LCLS)
CTFA Cosmet J ... CTFA [*Cosmetic, Toiletry, and Fragrance Association*] Cosmetic Journal [*A publication*]
CTFA Sci Monogr Ser ... CTFA (Cosmetic, Toiletry, and Fragrance Association) Scientific Monograph Series [*A publication*]
CtFaU........ Fairfield University, Fairfield, CT [*Library symbol*] [*Library of Congress*]   (LCLS)
CTFC........ Central Time and Frequency Control
CTFC........ Conway Twitty Fan Club   (EA)
CTFE........ Chlorotrifluoroethylene [*Organic chemistry*]
CTFG........ Counterfeiting [*FBI standardized term*]
CTFJC....... Centre Terry Fox de la Jeunesse Canadienne [*Terry Fox Canadian Youth Centre*]
CTFM........ Continuous-Transmission Frequency-Modulated [*SONAR*]
CTFMD....... Ciencias Tecnicas Fisicas y Matematicas [*A publication*]
CTFO........ Controlled Tuning Fork Oscillator
CTFPHE ... Canadian Task Force on the Periodic Health Examination
CTFT .... Contemporary Theatre, Film, and Television [*A publication*]
CTFT .... Counterfeit [*FBI standardized term*]
CTG .... Canadian Coast Guard [*Ottawa, ON, Canada*] [*FAA designator*]   (FAAC)
CTG .... Cardiotocography [*Gynecology*]
CTG .... Cartage
CTG .... Cartagena [*Colombia*] [*Airport symbol*]   (OAG)
ctg.............. Cartographer [*MARC relator code*] [*Library of Congress*]   (LCCP)
CTG .... Cartridge   (AABC)
CTG .... Channel Tunnel Group [*British*]
CTG .... Coating   (MSA)
CTG .... Combined Task Group [*NATO*]   (NATG)
CTG .... Commander, Task Group
CTG .... Communications Task Group [*CODASYL*]
CTG .... Comtech Group International Ltd. [*Toronto Stock Exchange symbol*]
CTG .... Connecticut Natural Gas Corp. [*NYSE symbol*]   (SPSG)
CTG .... Containing
CTG .... Contributing   (ADA)
CTG .... Control Techniques Guidelines [*Environmental Protection Agency*]
CTG .... Corporate Technology Group [*British*]
CTG .... Counting   (KSC)
CTG .... Crating   (MSA)
CTG .... Cutting   (MSA)
CTG .... Cyclodextrin Transglycosylase [*An enzyme*]
CTGAAH .. Citrus Grower [*A publication*]
CTGC........ California Table Grape Commission   (EA)
CTGE........ Cartage [*Shipping*]
CTGE........ Cottage   (ADA)
CTGF........ Clean Tanks, Gas Free   (NVT)
CTGH........ Cotangent, Hyperbolic [*Mathematics*]
CTGH........ Cryptograph   (MSA)
CtGr........... Groton Public Library, Groton, CT [*Library symbol*] [*Library of Congress*]   (LCLS)
CtGre .... Greenwich Library, Greenwich, CT [*Library symbol*] [*Library of Congress*]   (LCLS)
CtGreN ...... News Bank, Inc., Greenwich, CT [*Library symbol*] [*Library of Congress*]   (LCLS)

CtGrN-M... United States Navy Submarine Base, Naval Submarine Medical Research Laboratory, Groton, CT [*Library symbol*] [*Library of Congress*]   (LCLS)
CtGroN-M ... United States Navy Submarine Base, Naval Submarine Medical Research Laboratory, Groton, CT [*Library symbol*] [*Library of Congress*] [*Obsolete*]   (LCLS)
CtGrU........ University of Connecticut, Southeastern Branch, Groton, CT [*Library symbol*] [*Library of Congress*]   (LCLS)
CTGUF...... CTG Inc. Uts [*NASDAQ symbol*]   (NQ)
CTGY .... Category   (FAAC)
C Th .... Candidate of Theology
CTH........... Catalogue des Textes Hittites [*Paris*]   (BJA)
CTH........... Catalytic Transfer Hydrogenation
CTH........... Ceramide Trihexosides [*Biochemistry*]
C Th .... Code of Theodosius [*Roman law*] [*A publication*]   (DSA)
CTH........... Committee on Tidal Hydraulics [*Army*]
CTH........... Commonwealth   (ADA)
Ct-H........... Connecticut State Department of Health, Hartford, CT [*Library symbol*] [*Library of Congress*]   (LCLS)
CTH........... Contractions Handbook
CTH........... Corinth Resources Ltd. [*Vancouver Stock Exchange symbol*]
CTH........... Craftech Manufacturing, Inc. [*Toronto Stock Exchange symbol*]
CTH........... Cycle Test Hours
CtH .... Hartford Public Library, Hartford, CT [*Library symbol*] [*Library of Congress*]   (LCLS)
CTh............ Theodosian Code   (BJA)
CtHa .... Theodore A. Hungerford Memorial Library, Harwinton, CT [*Library symbol*] [*Library of Congress*]   (LCLS)
CTHAAM ... Contributions. Herbarium Australiense [*A publication*]
CtHamQ .... Quinnipiac College, Hamden, CT [*Library symbol*] [*Library of Congress*]   (LCLS)
CtHB.......... Hartford Bar Library Association, Hartford, CT [*Library symbol*] [*Library of Congress*]   (LCLS)
CTHBAr...... Comite des Travaux Historiques et Scientifiques. Bulletin Archeologique [*A publication*]
CTHBP...... Citizens for the Treatment of High Blood Pressure   (EA)
CTHBull.... Comite des Travaux Historiques et Scientifiques. Bulletin Archeologique [*A publication*]
CTHBullH ... Comite des Travaux Historiques et Scientifiques. Bulletin Historique et Philologique [*A publication*]
CTHC........ Certificate in the Teaching of Handicapped Children   (ADA)
CtHC.......... Hartford Seminary Foundation, Hartford, CT [*Library symbol*] [*Library of Congress*]   (LCLS)
CTHDL ..... Cathedral
C Theod ..... Codex Theodosianus [*Theodosian Code*] [*438AD*] [*Latin*] [*A publication*]   (DLA)
CTHF .... Canadian Team Handball Federation
CtHHC...... Hartford Conservatory, Hartford, CT [*Library symbol*] [*Library of Congress*]   (LCLS)
CtHHy....... Hillyer College, Hartford, CT [*Library symbol*] [*Library of Congress*]   (LCLS)
CTHI .... Cancer Treatment Holdings, Incorporated [*NASDAQ symbol*]   (NQ)
CtHi .... Connecticut Historical Society, Hartford, CT [*Library symbol*] [*Library of Congress*]   (LCLS)
CtHJH....... Julius Hartt Musical Foundation, Hartford, CT [*Library symbol*] [*Library of Congress*]   (LCLS)
CTHL .... Continental Health Affiliates, Inc. [*NASDAQ symbol*]   (NQ)
CThM........ Concordia Theological Monthly [*A publication*]
CtHM .... Hartford Medical Society, Hartford, CT [*Library symbol*] [*Library of Congress*]   (LCLS)
CtHMTH .. Mark Twain Memorial, Hartford, CT [*Library symbol*] [*Library of Congress*]   (LCLS)
Ct Ho .... Courthouse
CTHP .... C3, Inc. [*NASDAQ symbol*]   (NQ)
CTHS .... Comite des Travaux Historiques et Scientifiques [*Ministere de l'Education Nationale*] [*Database*]
CtHSD....... Stowe-Day Memorial Library and Historical Foundation, Hartford, CT [*Library symbol*] [*Library of Congress*]   (LCLS)
CtHT......... Trinity College, Hartford, CT [*Library symbol*] [*Library of Congress*]   (LCLS)
CtHT-W .... Trinity College, Watkinson Library, Hartford, CT [*Library symbol*] [*Library of Congress*]   (LCLS)
CtHU .... University of Connecticut, MBA Library, Hartford, CT [*Library symbol*] [*Library of Congress*]   (LCLS)
CtHWa ...... Wadsworth Atheneum, Hartford, CT [*Library symbol*] [*Library of Congress*]   (LCLS)
CTI............ Cambridge Technology, Incorporated
CTI............ Camera Timing Indicator
CTI............ CCD [*Charge-Coupled Device*] Transit Instrument [*Telescope*]
CTI............ Center for Telephone Information [*Laguna Hills, CA*] [*Telecommunications*]   (TSSD)
CTI............ Central Technical Institute [*Netherlands*]
CTI............ Centralized Ticket Investigation [*Telecommunications*]
CTI............ Centre de Traitement de l'Information [*Data Processing Center*] [*Ministry of Economic Affairs*] [*Belgium*] [*Information service or system*]   (IID)
CTI............ Centre de Traitement de l'Information [*Universite Laval*] [*Canada*] [*Research center*]
CTI............ Cheap Trick International   (EA)

CTI............	Citicorp [*Toronto Stock Exchange symbol*]
CTI............	Columbus Technical Institute, Columbus, OH [*OCLC symbol*] (OCLC)
CTI............	Command Technical Inspection [*Army*] (AABC)
CTI............	Communication Technology Impact [*A publication*]
CTI............	Competent to Instruct [*British military*] (DMA)
CTI............	Complaint Type Investigation [*Army*] (AABC)
CTI............	Composition Technology, Incorporated
CTI............	Computer Translation, Incorporated [*Information service or system*] (IID)
CTI............	Contract Technical Instructor [*Army*] (AABC)
CTI............	Contract Termination Inventory [*DoD*]
CTI............	Cooling Tower Institute (EA)
CTI............	Corporate Travel Index [*A publication*]
CTI............	Creed Taylor, Incorporated [*Recording label*]
CTI............	Critical Transportation Item (MCD)
CTI............	Crossroads Technical Instrumentation [*Atomic weapons testing*]
CTI............	Current Technology Index [*Library Association Publishing Ltd.*] [*London, England*] [*Information service or system*] [*A publication*]
CTI............	Documentatieblad van het Centraal Orgaan van de Landelijke Opleidingsorganen van het Bedrijfsleven [*A publication*]
CTIA........	Cellular Telecommunications Industry Association (EA)
CTIA........	Committee to Investigate Assassinations
CTIA........	Communications Transmission, Inc. [*NASDAQ symbol*] (NQ)
CTIA........	Counter Technical Intelligence Activities (MCD)
CTIAC.......	Chemical Transportation Industry Advisory Committee
CTIAC.......	Concrete Technology Information Analysis Center [*Army Corps of Engineers*] [*Vicksburg, MS*] (IID)
CTIBBV.....	Contemporary Topics in Immunobiology [*A publication*]
CTibF........	United States National Marine Fisheries Service, Southwest Fisheries Center, Tiburon Laboratory, Tiburon, CA [*Library symbol*] [*Library of Congress*] (LCLS)
CTIC	Cable Television Information Center (EA)
CTIC.........	Coal Technology Information Centre [*Alberta Research Council*] [*Information service or system*] (IID)
CTIC	Corporate Technical Information Center (DIT)
CTICD2.....	Catalogue of Type Invertebrate Fossils. Geological Survey of Canada [*A publication*]
CTI Commun Technol Impact ...	CTI. Communication Technology Impact [*A publication*]
CTICU.......	Cardiothoracic Intensive Care Unit
CTIF	Centre Technique des Industries de la Fonderie [*Database producer*]
CTIF	Comite Technique International de Prevention et d'Extinction du Feu [*International Technical Committee for the Prevention and Extinction of Fire*] (EAIO)
CTIF	Commercial Travelers Insurance Federation [*Defunct*]
CTII	Computrac Instruments [*NASDAQ symbol*] (NQ)
CTIL.........	Capsule Technology International Limited
C/T)im......	Carrier-to-Noise Temperature, Intermodulation
CTIO	Cerro-Tololo Inter-American Observatory [*Chile*] [*National Science Foundation*]
CTIOA......	Ceramic Tile Institute of America (EA)
CTIP.........	Committee for Truth in Psychiatry (EA)
CTIPB5	Carolina Tips [*A publication*]
CTIR	Center for Teaching International Relations
CTIS	Crawler/Transporter Intercom System [*Aerospace*] (KSC)
CTIX.........	Canadian Trade Index [*Canada Systems Group*] [*Information service or system*] (IID)
CTJ	Calvin Theological Journal [*A publication*]
CTJ	Canadian Tax Journal [*A publication*]
CTJ	Canadian Textile Journal [*A publication*]
CTJ	Canadian Trace Minerals Ltd. [*Vancouver Stock Exchange symbol*]
CTJ	Carrollton, GA [*Location identifier*] [*FAA*] (FAAL)
CTJ	Cato Journal [*A publication*]
CTJ	Citizens for Tax Justice (EA)
CTJ	Concerned Theater of Japan [*A publication*]
CTJ	Concerned Theatre Japan [*A publication*]
CTJC.........	Centralia Township Junior College [*Illinois*]
CT J Comput Tomogr ...	CT. Journal of Computed Tomography [*A publication*]
CT J Comput Tomography ...	CT. Journal of Computed Tomography [*A publication*]
CTJOA......	Canadian Textile Journal [*A publication*]
CTJTF.......	Counterterrorist Joint Task Force [*Military*]
Ct Just......	Court of Justiciary (DLA)
CTK	Canton, IL [*Location identifier*] [*FAA*] (FAAL)
CTK	Cases Tempore King, Chancery [*A publication*] (DLA)
CTK	Ceskoslovenska Tiskova Kancelar [*Czechoslovak News Agency*]
CTK	Composite Tool Kit [*Military*] (AFIT)
CTK	Comptek Research, Inc. [*AMEX symbol*] (SPSG)
CTK	Copper Stack Resources Ltd. [*Vancouver Stock Exchange symbol*]
CTK	Crimping Tool Kit
CTKIAR.....	Cell and Tissue Kinetics [*A publication*]
CTKR........	COM-TEK Resources, Inc. [*Denver, CO*] [*NASDAQ symbol*] (NQ)

CTL............	CAGE [*Computerized Aerospace Ground Equipment*] Test Language [*Data processing*] (KSC)
CTL............	Cahiers - Theatre Louvain [*A publication*]
CTL............	Canadian Talent Library
CTL............	Canoga Test Laboratory [*NASA*] (NASA)
CTL............	Carrier Tracking Loop
CTL............	Cassette Tape Loader
CTL............	Cattle
CTL............	Cental [*Short hundredweight*] [*British*] (ROG)
CTL............	Central (MSA)
CTL............	Central Airlines, Inc. [*Kansas City, KS*] [*FAA designator*] (FAAC)
CTL............	Century Telephone Enterprises, Inc. [*NYSE symbol*] (SPSG)
CTL............	Certified Tool List (AAG)
CTL............	Charleville [*Australia*] [*Airport symbol*] (OAG)
CTL............	Checkout Test Language [*Data processing*]
CTL............	Chilworth Technology Ltd. [*British*] (IRUK)
CTL............	Combat Training Launch (AFM)
CTL............	Complementary Transistor Logic [*Data processing*]
CTL............	Component Test Laboratory (KSC)
CTL............	Composite Tape Lay-Up [*Engineering*]
CTL............	Condensed Tannin Leucoanthocyanin
CTL............	Confidence Training Launch
CTL............	Connecticut College, New London, CT [*OCLC symbol*] (OCLC)
CTL............	Consolidated Tenants League (EA)
CTL............	Constructive Total Loss [*Insurance*]
CTL............	Continental Bank of Canada [*Toronto Stock Exchange symbol*]
CTL............	Control (AAG)
CTL............	Core Transistor Logic [*Data processing*]
CTL............	Crown Theological Library [*A publication*]
CTL............	Cytolytic Thymus-Dependent Lymphocyte [*Cell biology*]
CTL............	Cytotoxic T Lymphocyte [*Hematology*]
CTL............	Other Air Traffic Services Messages [*Aviation code*] (FAAC)
CTLA........	Control Area [*Aviation*] (FAAC)
CTLA........	Council of Tree and Landscape Appraisers (EA)
CTLB........	Control Boundary [*Aviation*] (FAAC)
CTLC........	Consolidated-Tomoka Land Co. [*NASDAQ symbol*] (NQ)
CTLF........	Cuttlefish. Unalaska City School. Unalaska [*A publication*]
CtLHi........	Litchfield Historical Society, Litchfield, CT [*Library symbol*] [*Library of Congress*] (LCLS)
CTLI.........	Combat Training Launch Instrumentation [*Minuteman*]
CTLJ.........	California Trial Lawyers Journal [*A publication*] (DLA)
CTLL........	Cytolytic T-Lymphocyte Line [*Cell line*]
CTLMAA ...	Cattleman [*A publication*]
CTLO	Cervicothoracolumbar Orthosis [*Medicine*]
CTLO	Constructive Total Loss Only [*Insurance*]
CTLP.........	Cytolytic T-Lymphocyte Precursor [*Immunochemistry*]
CTLR........	Controller [*Aviation*] (FAAC)
CTLRY......	Cutlery (MSA)
CTLS	Central Texas Library System [*Library network*]
CTLS	Centre for Teaching and Learning Services [*McGill University*] [*Canada*] [*Research center*] (RCD)
CTLSF.......	Cumberland Trail Library System [*Library network*]
CTLSF.......	Continental Silver Corp. [*NASDAQ symbol*] (NQ)
CTLSO......	Cervicothoracolumbosacral Orthosis [*Medicine*]
CTLST.......	Catalyst (MSA)
CTLT	Cadet Troop Leader Training (MCD)
CTLZ........	Control Zone [*Aviation*]
CTM	Cable Testing Meter
CTM	Cable Transfer Machine [*Nuclear energy*] (NRCH)
CTM	Canada Tungsten Mining Corp. Ltd. [*Toronto Stock Exchange symbol*]
CTM	Cardiotachometer [*Medicine*]
CTM	Castle Mountain [*California*] [*Seismograph station code, US Geological Survey*] (SEIS)
CTM	Catholic Traditionalist Movement (EA)
CTM	Cavity Transfer Mixer [*Chemical engineering*]
CTM	Center for Telecommunications Management [*UCLA*] (TSSD)
CTM	Certified Traffic Manager
CTM	Chetumal [*Mexico*] [*Airport symbol*] (OAG)
CTM	Chief Torpedoman's Mate [*Navy rating*] [*Obsolete*]
CTM	Christ Truth Ministries (EA)
CTM	Christian Television Mission (EA)
CTM	Close Talking Microphone
C & TM.....	Clothing and Textile Materiel [*Army*] (AABC)
CTM	Coal Traffic Manager
CTM	Cognizant Technical Manager
CTM	Collective Trademark (MCD)
CTM	Com Systems [*AMEX symbol*] (SPSG)
CTM	Communications Technology Management, Inc. [*McLean, VA*] [*Telecommunications*] (TSSD)
CTM	Communications Terminal Module [*Data processing*]
CTM	Complete Treatment Module [*Telecommunications*] (TEL)
CTM	Complimentary Technical Manual
CTM	Concordia Theological Monthly [*A publication*]
CTM	Concordia Tract Mission (EA)
CTM	Configuration and Tuning Module [*Data processing*]
CTM	Connective Tissue Massage [*Medicine*]
CTM	Consulting Traffic Manager
CTM	Continuity Transceiver Module [*Telecommunications*] (TEL)

CTM .... Contract Management [*A publication*]
CTM .... Contract Technical Manager
CTM .... Contract Termination Manual   (AAG)
CTM .... Contractor Technical Meeting   (AAG)
CTM .... Coolimation Test Module [*Nuclear energy*]   (NRCH)
CT/M .... Count per Minute   (MSA)
CTM .... Critical Thermal Maximum
CTM .... Crystalline Transitional Material   (NASA)
CTM .... Cutaneous Trunci Muscle [*Anatomy*]
CtM .... Russell Public Library, Middletown, CT [*Library symbol*] [*Library of Congress*]   (LCLS)
CTMA .... Camping Trailer Manufacturers Association [*Later, RVIA*]
CTMA .... Cutting Tool Manufacturers of America   (EA)
CTMA .... Cutting Tool Manufacturers Association [*Later, Cutting Tool Manufacturers of America*]   (EA)
CtMaHi ..... Mansfield Historical Society, Mansfield Center, CT [*Library symbol*] [*Library of Congress*]   (LCLS)
CtMan........ Mary Cheney Library, Manchester, CT [*Library symbol*] [*Library of Congress*]   (LCLS)
CtManC..... Manchester Community College, Manchester, CT [*Library symbol*] [*Library of Congress*]   (LCLS)
CtManGS .. Church of Jesus Christ of Latter-Day Saints, Genealogical Society Library, Hartford Branch, Manchester, CT [*Library symbol*] [*Library of Congress*]   (LCLS)
CTMC .... Canadian Tobacco Manufacturers' Council
CTMC .... Centurion Mines Corporation [*NASDAQ symbol*]   (NQ)
CTMC .... Communications Terminal Module Controller [*Data processing*]
CTMC .... Confederation des Travailleurs des Madagascar et Comores [*Confederation of Workers of Madagascar and the Comores*]
CTMC .... Connective-Tissue-Type Mast Cell [*Cytology*]
CTME........ Chief Torpedoman's Mate, Electrical [*Navy rating*] [*Obsolete*]
CTME........ Clothestime, Inc. [*NASDAQ symbol*]   (NQ)
CtMer .... Curtis Memorial Public Library, Meriden, CT [*Library symbol*] [*Library of Congress*]   (LCLS)
CTMF........ Ceramic Tile Marketing Federation   (EA)
CtMG......... Godfrey Memorial Library, Middletown, CT [*Library symbol*] [*Library of Congress*]   (LCLS)
Ct Mgmt J ... Court Management Journal [*A publication*]   (DLA)
CTMGSA.. Commercial Trailer-Mounted Generator Set Assembly
CTMIA...... Current Topics in Microbiology and Immunology [*A publication*]
CTMIA3.... Ergebnisse der Mikrobiologie und Immunitaetsforschung [*A publication*]
CTMIB4.... Contemporary Topics in Molecular Immunology [*A publication*]
CTML........ Computer Terminal Systems [*NASDAQ symbol*]   (NQ)
CTMM ...... California Test of Mental Maturity
CTMM ...... Computed Tomographic Metrizamide Myelography
CTMMA ... Central Technical Manual Management Activity [*Navy*]   (NVT)
CTMMEJ ... Current Topics in Medical Mycology [*A publication*]
CtMor .... Morris Public Library, Morris, CT [*Library symbol*] [*Library of Congress*]   (LCLS)
CTMP........ Chemithermomechanical Pulp [*Papermaking*]
CTMP........ Contractor Technical Manual Plan [*DoD*]
CTMPP..... Committee of Tin Mill Products Producers   (EA)
CTMS........ Carrier Transmission Maintenance System [*Bell System*]
CTMS........ Ceramic-to-Metal Seal
CTMS........ Clinical Trials Monitoring System
CTMS........ Commanders Training Management System [*DoD*]
CTMS........ Countermeasures   (AABC)
CTMS........ Current Topics in Materials Science [*Elsevier Book Series*] [*A publication*]
CTMSOA ... Central Telegraph Male Superintending Officers' Association [*A union*] [*British*]
CT/MSS.... Crawler/Transporter/Mobile Service Structure [*Aerospace*]   (KSC)
CTMT........ Combined Thermomechanical Treatment
CTMT........ Containment   (IEEE)
CTMTA2.... Current Topics in Membranes and Transport [*A publication*]
CTMV .... Chief Torpedoman's Mate, Aviation [*Navy rating*] [*Obsolete*]
CtMyMHi ... Mystic Seaport, Inc., Mystic, CT [*Library symbol*] [*Library of Congress*]   (LCLS)
CTN .... Cable Termination Network
CTN .... CANCOM [*Canadian Satellite Communications, Inc.*] Teleconference Network, Inc. [*Telecommunications service*]   (TSSD)
CTN .... Canton Railroad Co. [*AAR code*]
CTN .... Carleton University Library [*UTLAS symbol*]
CTN .... Carton
CTN .... Cases Tempore Northington [*Eden's English Chancery Reports*] [*A publication*]   (DLA)
CTN .... Catholic Television Network [*Cable-television system*]
CTN .... Caution
CTN .... Centennial Minerals [*Toronto Stock Exchange symbol*] [*Vancouver Stock Exchange symbol*]
CTN .... Centre d'Etudes des Consequences Generales des Grands Techniques Nouvelles [*Center for the Study of the General Results of New Technologies*]   (EA)

CTN .... Certification Test Network [*NASA*]   (KSC)
CTN .... China Trade Report [*A publication*]
CTN .... Codigo Tributario Nacional [*Brazil*] [*A publication*]
CTN .... Confectionery, Tobacco, and Newsagent [*British*]
CTN .... Cooktown [*Australia*] [*Airport symbol*]   (OAG)
CTN .... Cotangent [*Mathematics*]
CTN .... Cotton
CT/N .... Counter, n Stages [*Electronics*]   (DEN)
CTN .... Cowboy Television Network
CTN .... Ctenidial Nerve [*Biology*]
CTNA .... Catalina 25 National Association   (EA)
CTNA .... Catholic Telecommunications Network of America [*Staten Island, NY*]   (TSSD)
CTNA .... Committee on Societal Consequences of Transportation Noise Abatement [*National Research Council*]
CtNaUSR .. Uniroyal, Inc., Chemical Division, Information Center Library, Naugatuck, CT [*Library symbol*] [*Library of Congress*]   (LCLS)
CtNb .... New Britain Public Library, New Britain, CT [*Library symbol*] [*Library of Congress*]   (LCLS)
CtNbT........ Central Connecticut State College, New Britain, CT [*Library symbol*] [*Library of Congress*]   (LCLS)
CTnC .... Cardiac Troponin C [*Biochemistry*]
CTNC .... Commission on Transnational Corporations [*United Nations*]
CTNC .... Cross-Track Noncontiguous
CtNc .... New Canaan Library, New Canaan, CT [*Library symbol*] [*Library of Congress*]   (LCLS)
CtNcHi ...... New Canaan Historical Society, New Canaan, CT [*Library symbol*] [*Library of Congress*]   (LCLS)
CTNDS...... Commercial Transport Navigation Display System
CTNE .... Compania Telefonica Nacional de Espana [*National Telephone Company of Spain*] [*Telecommunications*]   (TSSD)
CTNEEY ... Current Topics in Neuroendocrinology [*A publication*]
CtNeV........ United States Veterans Administration Hospital, Newington, CT [*Library symbol*] [*Library of Congress*]   (LCLS)
CTNF........ Computerized Telephone Number File [*FBI listing, begun in 1970, of political activists' telephone numbers*] [*Obsolete*]
CTNF........ Controlled Thermonuclear Fusion
CtNh .... New Haven Free Public Library, New Haven, CT [*Library symbol*] [*Library of Congress*]   (LCLS)
CtNhA .... Albertus Magnus College, New Haven, CT [*Library symbol*] [*Library of Congress*]   (LCLS)
CtNhAS.... Connecticut Agricultural Experiment Station, New Haven, CT [*Library symbol*] [*Library of Congress*]   (LCLS)
CtNhH .... Human Relations Area Files, New Haven, CT [*Library symbol*] [*Library of Congress*]   (LCLS)
CtNhHi...... New Haven Colony Historical Society, New Haven, CT [*Library symbol*] [*Library of Congress*]   (LCLS)
CtNhMH ... Connecticut Mental Health Center, New Haven, CT [*Library symbol*] [*Library of Congress*]   (LCLS)
CtNhN .... Southern Connecticut State College, New Haven, CT [*Library symbol*] [*Library of Congress*]   (LCLS)
CtNhO .... Olin Corp., New Haven, CT [*Library symbol*] [*Library of Congress*]   (LCLS)
CtNhU .... University of New Haven, New Haven, CT [*Library symbol*] [*Library of Congress*]   (LCLS)
CtNhW ...... Winchester-Western Co., New Haven, CT [*Library symbol*] [*Library of Congress*]   (LCLS)
CTNL......... Center for the New Leadership   (EA)
CtNl .... New London Public Library, New London, CT [*Library symbol*] [*Library of Congress*]   (LCLS)
CtNlC......... Connecticut College, New London, CT [*Library symbol*] [*Library of Congress*]   (LCLS)
CtNlCG...... United States Coast Guard Academy, New London, CT [*Library symbol*] [*Library of Congress*]   (LCLS)
CtNlHi....... New London County Historical Society, New London, CT [*Library symbol*] [*Library of Congress*]   (LCLS)
CTNOR ..... Canada. Task Force on Northern Oil Development. Report [*A publication*]
CtNowa ...... Norwalk Public Library, Norwalk, CT [*Library symbol*] [*Library of Congress*]   (LCLS)
CtNowaB ... Burndy Corp., Technical Library, Norwalk, CT [*Library symbol*] [*Library of Congress*]   (LCLS)
CtNowaS... Saint Mary's Seminary, Ferndale, Norwalk, CT [*Library symbol*] [*Library of Congress*]   (LCLS)
CtNowaT ... Technoserve, Norwalk, CT [*Library symbol*] [*Library of Congress*]   (LCLS)
CTNSA...... Catalina 22 National Sailing Association   (EA)
CtNwchA ... Norwich Free Academy, Norwich, CT [*Library symbol*] [*Library of Congress*]   (LCLS)
CTO .... Calverton, NY [*Location identifier*] [*FAA*]   (FAAL)
CTO .... Canceled to Order [*Philately*]
CTO .... Cape Town [*South Africa*] [*Later, HER*] [*Geomagnetic observatory code*]
CTO .... Cape Town [*South Africa*] [*Seismograph station code, US Geological Survey*] [*Closed*]   (SEIS)
CTO .... Caribbean Tourism Organization   (EAIO)
CTO .... Carmelite Third Order [*Rome, Italy*]   (EAIO)
CT O .... Catering Officer [*British military*]   (DMA)
CTO .... Cavity Tuned Oscillator
CTO .... Central Telegraph Office [*British*]   (ROG)

CTO.......... Central Telephone Operator [*British*]   (ROG)
CTO.......... Central Torpedo Office
CTO.......... Central Treaty Organization [*Also, CENTO*] [*Formerly, Baghdad Pact*]
CTO.......... Cervicothoracic Orthosis [*Also, CER*] [*Medicine*]
CTO.......... Charge Transforming Operator   (IEEE)
CTO.......... Chest Tube Out [*Medicine*]
CTO.......... Chief Technical Officer [*British*]   (ADA)
CTO.......... China Theater of Operations [*World War II*]
CTO.......... Circular Terminal Orbit [*Aerospace*]   (AAG)
CTO.......... Cognizant Transportation Office [*or Officer*] [*Air Force*]   (AFM)
CTO.......... Combined Transport Operator [*Shipping*]
CTO.......... Commercial Transportation Officer
CTO.......... Commonwealth Telecommunications Organization [*England*]
CTO.......... Concerto [*Music*]
CTO.......... Container Terminal Operator [*Shipping*]   (DS)
CTO.......... Control Tower Operator [*Army*]   (AABC)
CTO.......... Conventional Takeoff [*Aviation*]   (NATG)
CTO.......... Coolant Temperature Override [*Automotive engineering*]
CTO.......... Courier Transfer Office [*or Officer*]
Ct/O......... Court Order   (DLA)
CTO.......... Crude Tall Oil [*Industrial chemistry*]
CTO.......... Cutoff [*Telecommunications*]   (TEL)
CTO.......... Cyprus Tourism Organization   (EA)
CTO.......... San Joaquin Delta College, Stockton, CA [*OCLC symbol*]   (OCLC)
CTOA....... Cable and Telegraph Operators' Association [*A union*] [*British*]
CTO/A...... Chief Technical Officer/Airworthiness [*Australia*]
CTOA....... Creative Tour Operators Association
CTOC....... Central Technical Order Coordination Unit
CTOC....... Communications Technical Operations Center [*Air Force*]
CTOC....... Corps Tactical Operations Center
CTOCU..... Central Technical Order Control [*or Coordination*] Unit   (MCD)
C Today...... Christianity Today [*A publication*]
CtOg......... Perrot Memorial Library, Old Greenwich, CT [*Library symbol*] [*Library of Congress*]   (LCLS)
CToL........ California Lutheran College, Thousand Oaks, CA [*Library symbol*] [*Library of Congress*]   (LCLS)
CTOL........ Conventional Takeoff and Landing [*Aviation*]
C Tom....... Ciencia Tomista [*A publication*]
CTOMD.... Computerized Tomography [*A publication*]
CTOMDS... Computerized Tomography [*A publication*]
CTON....... Compútone Systems, Inc. [*NASDAQ symbol*]   (NQ)
CToR........ Rockwell International, Science Center, Thousand Oaks, CA [*Library symbol*] [*Library of Congress*]   (LCLS)
CTORP...... Chief Torpedoman [*Navy rating*] [*Obsolete*]
CTOS........ Cassette Tape Operating System   (IEEE)
CTOS........ Corps Tactical Operations System   (MCD)
CTOS........ Council of the Thirteen Original States   (EA)
CTOXA..... Clinical Toxicology [*A publication*]
CTOXAO... Clinical Toxicology [*A publication*]
CTP.......... California Test of Personality [*Psychology*]
CTP.......... Capacitor Test Program
CTP.......... Catapilco [*Chile*] [*Seismograph station code, US Geological Survey*]   (SEIS)
CTP.......... Central Maine Power Co. [*NYSE symbol*]   (SPSG)
CTP.......... Central Training Program
CTP.......... Central Transfer Point
CTP.......... Challenge Test Plan
CTP.......... Charge-Transfer Photography
CTP.......... Charge Transforming Parameter   (IEEE)
CTP.......... Chemical Treatment Pond   (IEEE)
CTP.......... Children as the Peacemakers   (EA)
CTP.......... Christmas Tree Pattern
CTP.......... Coded Telemetry Processor
CTP.......... Collective Training Plan [*Army*]
CTP.......... Command Translator and Programmer
CTP.......... Commercial Type Property
CTP.......... Communications Timing Procedure   (NASA)
CTP.......... Community Telephone Plan   (ADA)
CTP.......... Comprehensive Testing Program [*Academic achievement and aptitude test*]
CTP.......... Compulsory Third Party [*Australia*]
CTP.......... Condensed Tannin Proanthocyanidin
CTP.......... Confidence Test Program [*NASA*]   (KSC)
CTP.......... Conservez Taxe Payee [*Retain Charge Paid*] [*French*] [*Business term*]
CTP.......... Construction Test Procedure   (NRCH)
CTP.......... Contractor Transition Plan
CTP.......... Controlled Temperature Profile [*Vapor trap*] [*Nuclear energy*]   (NRCH)
CTP.......... Coordinated Test Plan [*Obsolete*]
CTP.......... Coordinated Test Program [*Military*]   (AABC)
CTP.......... Corporate Trade Payment [*Automated Clearing House*]
CTP.......... Creative Times Project [*Later, CT*]   (EA)
CTP.......... Cumhuriyetci Turk Partisi [*Republican Turkish Party*] [*Turkish Cyprus*] [*Political party*]   (PPE)
CTP.......... Customs Tariff Proposals [*A publication*]   (APTA)
CTP.......... Cyclic Time Processor   (MCD)

CTP.......... Cyclohexylthiophthalimide [*Organic chemistry*]
CTP.......... Cytidine Triphosphate [*Biochemistry*]
CTP.......... Cytosine Triphosphate [*Biochemistry*]
CTPB....... Carboxyl-Terminated Polybutadiene Binder [*Organic chemistry*]
CTPB....... Central Tracing Policy Board [*Post-World War II*]
CTPC....... Cargo Traffic Procedures Committee [*IATA*]   (DS)
CTPD....... Crew Training and Procedures Division [*Johnson Space Center*] [*NASA*]   (NASA)
CTPDA...... Canadian Television Producers and Directors Association
CTPEC...... Coal Tar Pitch Emulsion Council [*Defunct*]   (EA)
CTPHBG... Ergebnisse der Pathologie [*A publication*]
CTPI........ Canadian Textbook Publishers' Institute
CTPI........ Conventional Weapon Technical Proficiency Inspection [*Military*]   (CAAL)
CTPL........ Commission for Teacher Preparation and Licensing
CT-PS...... Changeable Type-Plate Style
CTPV....... Coal Tar Pitch Volatile [*Organic chemistry*]
CTQ........ Computable. Automatiseringsvakblad voor de Benelux [*A publication*]
CTQ......... Consolidated PCR Industries Ltd. [*Vancouver Stock Exchange symbol*]
CTQ......... Contemporary Thought Quarterly [*A publication*]
CTR......... C-Band Tracking RADAR
CTR......... California Tumor Registry
CTR......... Canadian Theatre Review [*A publication*]
CTR......... Canadian Tire Corp. Ltd. [*Toronto Stock Exchange symbol*]
CTR......... Canaveral Test Report
CTR......... Cape Times Supreme Court Reports, Cape Of Good Hope [*South Africa*] [*A publication*]   (DLA)
CTR......... Cardiothoracic Ratio [*Medicine*]
CTR......... Carrier Telegraph Receiver
CTR......... Castle Rock [*New York*] [*Seismograph station code, US Geological Survey*]   (SEIS)
CTR......... Caterpillar Tractor Co. [*NYSE symbol; later, CAT*] [*Wall Street slang name: "Cat"*]   (SPSG)
CTR......... Cavitation Tendency Ratio
CTR......... Center   (AAG)
CTR......... Center for Telecommunications Research [*Columbia University*] [*New York, NY*] [*Telecommunications service*]   (TSSD)
CTR......... Center for Transportation Research [*University of Texas at Austin*] [*Research center*]   (RCD)
Ctr.......... Centner [*100 kilograms*] [*German*] [*Business term*]
CTR......... Central Territory Railroad Tariff Bureau
CTR......... Central Tool Room
CTR......... Certification Test Requirement [*NASA*]
CTR......... Certified Test Results   (NRCH)
CTR......... Chemical Temperature Resistant [*Automotive engineering*]
CTR......... Chester, MA [*Location identifier*] [*FAA*]   (FAAL)
CTr.......... Code du Travail [*A publication*]
CTR......... Collective Training Range   (MCD)
CTR......... Composite Teacher Rating
CTR......... Computer Tape Recorder
CTR......... COMSAT [*Communications Satellite Corp.*] Technical Review [*A publication*]
CTR......... Consolidate Time Rate
CTR......... Consolidated Training Request [*Military*]
CTR......... Constar International, Inc. [*NYSE symbol*]   (SPSG)
CTR......... Continuous-Flow Tank Reactor [*Chemical engineering*]
CTR......... Continuous Tubular Reactor [*Chemical engineering*]
CTR......... Contour   (MSA)
CTR......... Contract Technical Representative   (NASA)
CTR......... Contractual Technical Report   (AAG)
CTR......... Contributor
CTR......... Control Zone [*Aviation*]
CTR......... Controllable Twist Rotor [*Aviation*]
CTR......... Controlled Thermonuclear Reaction [*or Reactor*] [*National Institute of Standards and Technology*]
CTR......... Controlled Thermonuclear Research
CTR......... Controlled Tornado Research   (MCD)
CTR......... Core Transistor Register
C Tr......... Corporate Trust [*Legal term*]   (DLA)
CTR......... Council for Tobacco Research
CTR......... Counter   (KSC)
CT R........ Court Rolls [*British*]   (ROG)
CTR......... Currency Transaction Report [*IRS*]
CTR......... Current Transfer Ratio [*Bell System*]
CTR......... Cutter   (MSA)
CTR......... Standing Committee for Controlled Thermonuclear Research [*AEC*]
CTR......... Transaction Technology, Inc., Technical Library, Los Angeles, CA [*OCLC symbol*]   (OCLC)
CTRA........ Cash Transaction Reports Agency [*Australia*]
CTRAC..... Common Terminal RADAR Approach Control [*Aviation*]   (FAAC)
C Tracts... Cine Tracts [*A publication*]
CTRAP..... Customer Trouble Report Analysis Plan [*Telecommunications*]   (TEL)
C Trav...... Code du Travail [*Labor Code*] [*A publication*]   (ILCA)
CTRB........ Chymotrypsinogen B [*Biochemistry*]

CTRC......... Caribbean Tourism Research and Development Centre [*Later, Caribbean Tourism Organization*]   (EAIO)
CTRC......... Colorado Technical Reference Center [*University of Colorado - Boulder*] [*Information service or system*]   (IID)
CTRC......... Computer Transceiver [*NASDAQ symbol*]   (NQ)
CTRCLM .. Counterclaim [*Legal term*]   (ROG)
CTRDA...... Canadian Tuberculosis and Respiratory Disease Association
CTRED...... Cancer Treatment Reviews [*A publication*]
CTREDJ.... Cancer Treatment Reviews [*A publication*]
Ct Rep NZ ... Court of Appeals Reports [*New Zealand*] [*A publication*]   (DLA)
CTREPTR ... Court Reporter   (AABC)
CTRF......... Canadian Transportation Research Forum
CTRF......... Center Frequency   (MSA)
CTRFAS.... Canadian Technical Report of Fisheries and Aquatic Sciences [*A publication*]
CTRG .... Centering
CTRHOS... Canadian Technical Report of Hydrography and Ocean Sciences [*A publication*]
CTRI......... Catholic Tape Recorders, International   (EA)
CTRI......... CleveTrust Realty Investors [*NASDAQ symbol*]   (NQ)
CTRIPS..... Concepts, Trends, Relationships, Issues, Problems, Solutions
CTRIS .... Canadian Transportation Research Information Service
CTRL........ Central
CTRL........ Central Corp. [*NASDAQ symbol*]   (NQ)
CTRL........ Control Character [*Keyboard*]   (CINC)
CTRM ...... Control Room [*Nuclear energy*]   (NRCH)
CTRMA6.. Citrus Magazine [*A publication*]
CTRN ...... Cortronic Corp. [*Ronkonkoma, NY*] [*NASDAQ symbol*]   (NQ)
CtRogR ...... Rogers Corp., Lurie Research and Development Center, Rogers, CT [*Library symbol*] [*Library of Congress*]   (LCLS)
CTRPT ...... Counterpart [*Legal term*]   (ROG)
CTRQA ..... Current Topics in Radiation Research. Quarterly [*A publication*]
CTRR......... Current Topics in Radiation Research [*Elsevier Book Series*] [*A publication*]
CTRRA..... Current Topics in Radiation Research [*A publication*]
CTRRD...... Cancer Treatment Reports [*A publication*]
CTRRDO... Cancer Treatment Reports [*A publication*]
CTRS......... Component Test Requirements Specifications   (MCD)
CTRS......... Conners Teaching Rating Scale
CTRS......... Contrast   (MSA)
CTRSDR ... Rapport Technique Canadien des Sciences Halieutiques et Aquatiques [*A publication*]
CTRSES.... Current Topics in Research on Synapses [*A publication*]
CTR-USA ... Council for Tobacco Research - USA   (EA)
Ctry Demogr Profiles ... Country Demographic Profiles [*A publication*]
Ctry Gentleman ... Country Gentleman [*A publication*]
Ctry J .... Country Journal [*A publication*]
Ctry Landowner ... Country Landowner [*A publication*]
Ctry Life.... Country Life [*A publication*]
Ctry Life Am ... Country Life in America [*A publication*]
Ctry Profiles ... Country Profiles [*A publication*]
Ctry Women ... Country Women [*A publication*]
CTS........... Cable Telemetry System
CTS........... Cable Terminal Section [*Telecommunications*]   (TEL)
CTS........... Cable Test Set   (MCD)
CTS........... Cable Turning Section [*Telecommunications*]   (TEL)
CTS........... Canadian Technology Satellite   (MCD)
CTS........... Canadian Theological Seminary
CTS........... Canadian Theological Society [*See also SCT*]
CTS........... Capistrano Test Site
CTS........... Captive Trajectory System [*Air Force*]
CTS........... Card-to-Magnetic Tape Conversion System [*Data processing*]   (DIT)
CTS........... Carpal Tunnel Syndrome [*Medicine*]
CTS........... Carrier Test Switch   (IEEE)
CTS........... Carrier Transfer Station
CTS........... Cartographic Test Standard [*Air Force*]
CTS........... Cassette Transport System
CTS........... Castel Tesino [*Italy*] [*Geomagnetic observatory code*]
CTS........... Catalase [*An enzyme*]
CTS........... Center on Technology and Society, Inc. [*Research center*]   (RCD)
CTS........... Center for Telecommunications Studies [*Formerly, Broadcast Research Center*] [*Ohio University*] [*Research center*]   (RCD)
CTS........... Center for Theoretical Studies [*University of Miami*] [*Research center*]   (RCD)
CTS........... Center for Transportation Studies [*Morgan State University*] [*Research center*]   (RCD)
cts.............. Centimes [*Monetary unit*] [*France*]
CTS........... Central Tactical System [*RAF*]   (MCD)
CTS........... Central Target Simulator [*Navy*]   (MCD)
CTS........... Central Timing System
CTS........... Central Training Section [*Air Force*]   (AFM)
CTS........... Centralized Title Service [*A publication*]
CTS........... Centralized Translation System [*Communications*]
CTS........... Certification Test Specification [*NASA*]   (KSC)
CTS........... Cesium Time Standard
CTS........... Charge-Transfer Spectrum

CTS........... Chicago Theological Seminary
CTS........... Chief, Technical Services
CTS........... Children's Television Standards [*Australia*] [*A publication*]
CTS........... Circuit Test Set [*Electricity*]
CTS........... Clear to Send
CTS........... Close to Shoulder   (MSA)
CTS........... Cloud Top Scanner   (MCD)
CTS........... College Theology Society   (EA)
CTS........... Command and Telemetry System   (AAG)
CTS........... Commandant's Training Strategy [*Military*]
CTS........... Committee on the Teaching of Science [*ICSU*]   (IRUK)
CTS........... Commodity Transportation Survey [*Census Bureau*]
CTS........... Common Test Subroutine [*Data processing*]
CTS........... Communications Technology Satellite
CTS........... Communications Technology Specialist [*Designation awarded by International Communications Industries Association*]   (TSSD)
CTS........... Communications Terminal, Synchronous [*Data processing*]
CTS........... Communications Test Station [*NASA*]
CTS........... Communications and Tracking System [*or Subsystem*]
CTS........... Community Tenant Scheme [*Australia*]
CTS........... Compass Tilt Signal
CTS........... Component Test Set   (MCD)
CTS........... Composite Training School [*British military*]   (DMA)
CTS........... Computed Thermography System [*Data processing*]
CTS........... Computer Telewriter Systems   (MCD)
CTS........... Computer Test Set
CTS........... Computer Training System
CTS........... Computer Typing System
CTS........... Computerized Tomography Society [*Later, Computerized Radiology Society - CRS*]   (EA)
CTS........... Computerized Topographic Scanner [*Medicine*]
CTS........... Computerized Training System [*Army Signal Center and School*] [*Fort Monmouth, NJ*]   (RDA)
CTS........... Concentrate Transfer System [*Nuclear energy*]   (NRCH)
CTS........... Concise Tax Service [*Australia*] [*A publication*]
CTS........... Concordia Theological Seminary [*Later, Concordia Seminary*] [*Missouri*]
CTS........... Condensate Transfer and Storage [*Nuclear energy*]   (NRCH)
CTS........... Consolidated Tape System [*Preferred name is Consolidated Transaction Reporting System*] [*Investment term*]
CTS........... Consolidated Translation Survey [*CIA*]
CTS........... Consolidated Treaty Series [*A publication*]   (DLA)
CTS........... Contact Test Set [*Military*]
CTS........... Contingency Transfer System [*Aerospace*]
CTS........... ContiTire System [*German*]
CTS........... Contract [*or Contractor*] Technical Services [*Air Force*]
CTS........... Contract Termination Settlement
CTS........... Contractor Technical Support   (MCD)
CTS........... Conversational Terminal System [*Data processing*]   (BUR)
CTS........... Conversational Time-Sharing [*Data processing*]   (IEEE)
CTS........... Coolant Temperature Sensor [*Automotive engineering*]
CTS........... Coordinate Transformation System   (MCD)
CTS........... Cosmic Top Secret   (NATG)
CTS........... Counseling and Testing Site
CT/S .... Count per Second   (MSA)
CTS........... Countess
CTS........... Country Television Services [*Australia*]
CTS........... Courier Transfer Station
CTS........... Course Training Standard [*Air Force*]   (AFM)
CTS........... Crates
CTS........... Cream of Tartar Substitute
CTS........... Crescomm Transmission Services, Inc. [*Fairfield, NJ*] [*Telecommunications*]   (TSSD)
CTS........... Critical Tool Service
CTS........... Crosier Theological Seminary [*Onamia, MN*]
CTS........... Cryogenic Temperature Sensor [*or Source*]
CTS........... CTS Corp. [*NYSE symbol*]   (SPSG)
CTS........... Current Time Sensing   (CAAL)
CTS........... Sapporo/Chitose [*Japan*] [*Airport symbol*]   (OAG)
CTS........... Shell Chemical Co., Torrance, CA [*Library symbol*] [*Library of Congress*] [*Obsolete*]   (LCLS)
CtS .... Stamford Public Library, Stamford, CT [*Library symbol*] [*Library of Congress*]   (LCLS)
CTSA .... Advanced Composite Wing Cover-to-Substructure Attachment   (MCD)
CtSA .... American Cyanamid Co., Stamford, CT [*Library symbol*] [*Library of Congress*]   (LCLS)
CTSA .... Catholic Theological Society of America   (EA)
CTSA .... Counted Thread Society of America   (EA)
CTSA .... Seaman Apprentice, Communications Technician, Striker [*Navy rating*]
CTSAP ...... Catholic Theological Society of America. Proceedings [*A publication*]
CTSB .... Combined Travel Security Board [*Allied German Occupation Forces*]
CTSC .... Centre for Technology and Social Change [*Australia*]
CTSC .... Citisource, Inc. [*New York, NY*] [*NASDAQ symbol*]   (NQ)
CTSD........ Computer Test Sequences Document   (MCD)
CTSDB ...... Centralized Theater Surveillance Database   (MCD)
CTSE .... Chicago, Terre Haute & Southeastern R. R. [*AAR code*]

CTSE......... Common Test/Support Equipment (MCD)
Ct Sess Cas ... Court of Session Cases [Scotland] [A publication] (DLA)
Ct Sess Ist Ser ... Scotch Court of Session Cases, First Series [A publication] (DLA)
CTSF......... California Traffic Safety Foundation [Defunct] (EA)
CTSF......... Conservation Treaty Support Fund [An association] (EA)
CTSG......... Central Timing Signal Generator [Air Force] (MCD)
CTSHFT ... Countershaft (MSA)
CTSI......... Capital Tel Systems, Incorporated [Fairfield, NJ] [NASDAQ symbol] (NQ)
CTSI......... Central Terminal Signaling Interface [Telecommunications] (TEL)
CTSI......... Common Track Stores Indicator (CAAL)
CTSI......... Computer Transceiver Systems, Incorporated
CTSK......... Countersunk
CTSKLS.... Catskills [FAA] (FAAC)
CTSL......... Central Track Store Locator (MCD)
CTSN......... Seaman, Communications Technician, Striker [Navy rating]
CTSOA...... Central Telegraph Superintending Officers' Association [A union] [British]
CtSoP........ Pequot Library Association, Southport, CT [Library symbol] [Library of Congress] (LCLS)
CTSP......... Contract Technical Services Personnel (AFM)
CT SPEC SESS ... Court of Special Sessions [Legal term] (DLA)
CTSRC....... Cell and Tissue Research [A publication]
CTSRCS..... Cell and Tissue Research [A publication]
CTS Reg..... Chicago Theological Seminary. Register [A publication]
CTSRTS..... Clear to Send/Request to Send
CTSS......... Communication and Tracking Subsystem (MCD)
CTSS......... Compatible Time-Sharing System [Massachusetts Institute of Technology] [Data processing]
CTSS......... Countess
CTST......... Coaxial Triple-Stud Tuner
CtStr.......... Stratford Library Association, Stratford, CT [Library symbol] [Library of Congress] (LCLS)
CtSU......... University of Connecticut, Stamford Branch, Stamford, CT [Library symbol] [Library of Congress] (LCLS)
CTSWG..... Consolidated Training Support Work Group [DoD]
CTSX......... Central Track Stores Index (MCD)
CTSYEH ... Cancer Treatment Symposia [A publication]
CTT.......... Cable Trouble Ticket [Telecommunications] (TEL)
CTT.......... Capital Transfer Tax [British]
CTT.......... Card-to-Tape Tape [Data processing]
CTT.......... Carousel Transfer Tube
C/T)t......... Carrier-to-Noise Temperature, Total
C T T......... Cases Tempore Talbot, English Chancery [1734-38] [A publication] (DLA)
CTT.......... Cask Transfer Tunnels [Nuclear energy] (NRCH)
CTT.......... Central Trunk Terminal
CTT.......... Centre for Technology Transfer [Australia]
CTT.......... Challenger International Ltd. [Formerly, Coastal International Ltd.] [Toronto Stock Exchange symbol]
CTT.......... College of Trades and Technology [St. John's, NF]
CTT.......... Combat Targeting Team [Military]
CTT.......... Combat Tracking Team
CTT.......... Combat Training Theater
CTT.......... Combined Test Team (MCD)
CTT.......... Common Task Test [Army] (INF)
CTT.......... Compressed Tablet Triturate [Pharmacology]
CTT.......... Computed Transaxial Tomography [Later, CT]
CTT.......... Coras Trachtala [Irish Export Board]
CTT.......... Corrugated TEFLON Tubing
CTT.......... Crew Transfer Tunnel [NASA]
CTT.......... Critical Temperature Threshold [Chemical technology]
CTT.......... Critical Tracking Task [System for preventing drunken driver from starting car]
CTTB......... Central Trade Test Board [British]
CTTB......... Checkout Techniques Test Bed (NASA)
CTTBA...... Canadian Transport Tariff Bureau Association
CTTC........ Canadian Toy Testing Council
CTTC........ Canadian Trade and Tariffs Committee
CTTC........ Chanute Technical Training Center [Air Force]
CTTC........ Congressional Travel and Tourism Caucus (EA)
CTTCO...... Central Test Technology Coordinating Office [Army] (RDA)
CTTE........ Council on Technology Teacher Education (EA)
CTTEE....... Committee (EY)
CTTL........ Complementary Transistor-Transistor Logic
CTTM....... Cok Tarafli Ticaret Muzekereleri [Multilateral Trade Negotiations] [Turkish]
CTTR......... Center for Transportation Training and Research [Texas Southern University] [Research center] (RCD)
CTTRE...... Center for Tissue Trauma Research and Education (EA)
CTU.......... California State College, Stanislaus, Turlock, CA [OCLC symbol] (OCLC)
CTU.......... Capsule Test Unit [Aerospace]
CTU.......... Captive Test Unit (MCD)
CTU.......... Cardiac/Thoracic Unit [Medicine]
CTU.......... Cardiology Transcription Unit [Medicine]
C/T)u......... Carrier-to-Noise Temperature, Uplink
CTU.......... Cartridge Tape Unit [Telecommunications] (TEL)
CTU.......... Centigrade Thermal Unit

CTU.......... Central Terminal Unit [Telecommunications]
CTU.......... Central Timing Unit (KSC)
CTU.......... Central Trades' Union [British]
CTU.......... Chateau Stores of Canada Ltd. [Toronto Stock Exchange symbol]
CTU.......... Chengdu [China] [Airport symbol] (OAG)
CTU.......... Circuit Terminal Unit [Mercury Communications Ltd.] [British]
CTU.......... Combat Training Unit
CTU.......... Commander, Task Unit
CTU.......... Commercial Telegraphers' Union [Later, C/UBC] (EA)
CTU.......... Committee for Time Uniformity [Defunct]
CTU.......... Compatibility Test Unit
CTU.......... Components Test Unit (AAG)
CTU.......... Conference on Transportation Unity [Defunct] (EA)
ctu.......... Connecticut [MARC country of publication code] [Library of Congress] (LCCP)
CTU.......... Conservative Trade Unionists [British]
CTU.......... Consolidated TOE Update [DoD]
CTU.......... Constitutive Transcription Unit [Genetics]
CTU.......... Construction Training Unit
CTU.......... Control and Timing Unit [Data processing]
CTU.......... Custom, Tradition, and Usage (MCD)
CtU.......... University of Connecticut, Storrs, CT [Library symbol] [Library of Congress] (LCLS)
CTUBDP... Collection des Travaux. Universite de Brazzaville [A publication]
CTUC....... Central Trade Union Council [Czechoslovakia]
CTUC....... Committee on Tunneling and Underground Construction (EA)
CTUC....... Commonwealth Trade Union Council [London, England] (EAIO)
CTUC....... [The] Continuum Company, Inc. [NASDAQ symbol] (NQ)
CTUF....... Ceylon Trade Union Federation [Obsolete]
CtU-H....... University of Connecticut, Health Center Library, Hartford, CT [Library symbol] [Library of Congress] (LCLS)
CTul........ Tulare Free Public Library, Tulare, CA [Library symbol] [Library of Congress] (LCLS)
CtU-L....... University of Connecticut, School of Law, West Hartford, CT [Library symbol] [Library of Congress] (LCLS)
C Tunisie.... Cahiers de Tunisie [A publication]
CTUP........ Com Tel, Inc. [Salt Lake City, UT] [NASDAQ symbol] (NQ)
CTur........ Turlock City Library, Turlock, CA [Library symbol] [Library of Congress] (LCLS)
CTurS........ California State College, Stanislaus, Turlock, CA [Library symbol] [Library of Congress] (LCLS)
CTUS........ Cetus Corp. [NASDAQ symbol] (NQ)
CTUSA...... ComputerTown, United States of America (EA)
CTUSA...... Contact Teleministries USA (EA)
CTUSA5.... Comunicaciones. Instituto Tropical de Investigaciones Cientificas [A publication]
CtU-SW..... University of Connecticut, School of Social Work, West Hartford, CT [Library symbol] [Library of Congress] (LCLS)
CTV.......... Cable Television [Formerly, CATV]
CTV.......... Canadian Television Network
CTV.......... Canarctic Ventures [Vancouver Stock Exchange symbol]
CTV.......... Captive Test Vehicle
CTV.......... Centro Televisivo Vaticano [Vatican Television Center] [1984]
CTV.......... Channel Television [Channel Islands network]
CTV.......... Charlottesville [Virginia] [Seismograph station code, US Geological Survey] [Closed] (SEIS)
CTV.......... Citrus Tristeza Virus
CTV.......... Coaxial Thermal Voltmeter
CTV.......... Cockpit Television Sensor (MCD)
CTV.......... Color Television (DEN)
CTV.......... Comedy Television [Cable-television system]
CTV.......... Commercial Television
CTV.......... Constant Tangential Velocity
CTV.......... Control Test Vehicles
CTV.......... Cotton. Monthly Review of the World Situation [A publication]
CTV.......... Crown Television Productions [Commercial firm] [British]
CTV.......... Curly Top Virus
CTVC........ Cable Trays Vertical Chase [Nuclear energy] (NRCH)
CTVD........ Cinema Television Digest
CTVM .... Centre for Tropical Veterinary Medicine [Overseas Development Administration] [British] (DS)
CTVMDT ... Current Topics in Veterinary Medicine [A publication]
CTVS........ Calibration and Tracking Visible Sensor (MCD)
CTVS........ Centrevest Corp. [Southfield, MI] [NASDAQ symbol] (NQ)
CTVS........ Cockpit Television Sensor
CTVWA..... Charitable Trust for Vietnam War Art (EA)
CTW.......... Can't Tell What [Accounting slang]
CTW.......... Cargo Tank Wing [of a ship] (DS)
CTW.......... Catlow Resources Ltd. [Vancouver Stock Exchange symbol]
CTW.......... Children's Television Workshop (EA)
CT & W...... Commercial Travellers' and Warehousemen's Association [Australia]
CTW.......... Cottonwood Mountains [California] [Seismograph station code, US Geological Survey] (SEIS)
CTW.......... Counterweight (AAG)
CTW.......... Course Made Good through the Water [Military] (NATG)

CTW	Eastern Connecticut State College, J. Eugene Smith Library, Willimantic, CT [*OCLC symbol*] (OCLC)
CTW	Newcomerstown, OH [*Location identifier*] [*FAA*] (FAAL)
CtW	Wesleyan University, Middletown, CT [*Library symbol*] [*Library of Congress*] (LCLS)
CtWAB	Anaconda American Brass Co., Waterbury, CT [*Library symbol*] [*Library of Congress*] (LCLS)
CTWALK..	Catwalk
CtWat	Watertown Library, Watertown, CT [*Library symbol*] [*Library of Congress*] (LCLS)
CtWatU	University of Connecticut, Waterbury Branch, Waterbury, CT [*Library symbol*] [*Library of Congress*] (LCLS)
CtWB	Silas Bronson Public Library, Waterbury, CT [*Library symbol*] [*Library of Congress*] (LCLS)
CtWehar	West Hartford Public Library, West Hartford, CT [*Library symbol*] [*Library of Congress*] (LCLS)
CtWeharS ...	Saint Joseph College, West Hartford, CT [*Library symbol*] [*Library of Congress*] (LCLS)
CtWeharU ...	University of Hartford, West Hartford, CT [*Library symbol*] [*Library of Congress*] (LCLS)
CtWehavM ...	Miles Laboratories, Inc., Miles Pharmaceutical, West Haven, CT [*Library symbol*] [*Library of Congress*] (LCLS)
CtWehavV ...	United States Veterans Administration Hospital, West Haven, CT [*Library symbol*] [*Library of Congress*] (LCLS)
CtWep	Westport Public Library, Westport, CT [*Library symbol*] [*Library of Congress*] (LCLS)
CtWepSC...	Save the Children, Westport, CT [*Library symbol*] [*Library of Congress*] (LCLS)
CtWetHi	Wethersfield Historical Society, Wethersfield, CT [*Library symbol*] [*Library of Congress*] (LCLS)
CtWillN	Eastern Connecticut State College, Willimantic, CT [*Library symbol*] [*Library of Congress*] (LCLS)
CTWL........	Chartwell Group Ltd. [*NASDAQ symbol*] (NQ)
CTWO	Center for Third World Organizing (EA)
CTWS........	Connecticut Water Service, Inc. [*NASDAQ symbol*] (NQ)
CTWT	Counterweight (KSC)
CTX	Cargo Tank Common [*of a ship*] (DS)
CTX	Cefotaxime [*An antibiotic*]
CTX	Center of Technical Excellence [*Army*] (RDA)
CTX	Centex Corp. [*NYSE symbol*] (SPSG)
CTX	Centrex System Number [*Bell System*] [*Telecommunications*] (TEL)
CTX	Cerebrotendinous Xanthomatosis [*Medicine*]
CTX	Charybdotoxin [*Biochemistry*]
ctx	Cholera Toxin [*Medicine*]
CTX	Clear-Type Exterior Trim [*Weyerhaeuser Co.*]
CTX	Cobra Toxin
CTX	Consoltex Canada, Inc. [*Toronto Stock Exchange symbol*]
CTX	Continuously Variable Transaxle [*Automotive engineering*]
CTX	Corporate Trade Exchange [*Automated Clearing House*]
CTX	Corrosion Center of Excellence [*US Army Materials Technology Laboratory*]
CTX	Cytoxan [*Cyclophosphamide*] [*Also, C, CP, CPA, CPM, CY, CYC, CYP, CYT*] [*Antineoplastic drug*]
CTXBA3....	Clinical Toxicology Bulletin [*A publication*]
CTXCO......	Centrex Central Office [*Telecommunications*] (TEL)
CTXCU......	Centrex Customer [*Telecommunications*] (TEL)
CTX-PLAT ...	Cyclophosphamide, Platinol [*Cisplatin*] [*Antineoplastic drug regimen*]
CTY	Century Communications Corp. Class A [*AMEX symbol*] (SPSG)
CTY	City
CTY	Community
Cty............	Contemporary Records [*Los Angeles*] [*Record label*]
CTY	Control Energy [*Vancouver Stock Exchange symbol*]
CTY	County [*Board on Geographic Names*]
CTY	Cross City, FL [*Location identifier*] [*FAA*] (FAAL)
CTY	Cryderman Air Service [*Drayton Plains, MI*] [*FAA designator*] (FAAC)
CtY............	Yale University, New Haven, CT [*Library symbol*] [*Library of Congress*] (LCLS)
CtY-A........	Yale University, School of Fine Arts, New Haven, CT [*Library symbol*] [*Library of Congress*] (LCLS)
CtY-B........	Yale University, Osborn Memorial Laboratories of Biological Sciences, New Haven, CT [*Library symbol*] [*Library of Congress*] (LCLS)
CtY-BA	Yale University, Yale Center for British Art, New Haven, CT [*Library symbol*] [*Library of Congress*] (LCLS)
CtY-BR	Yale University, Beinecke Rare Book and Manuscript Library, New Haven, CT [*Library symbol*] [*Library of Congress*] (LCLS)
CtY-BS	Yale University, Babylonian Seminary, New Haven, CT [*Library symbol*] [*Library of Congress*] (LCLS)
CtY-C........	Yale University, Sterling Chemistry Laboratories, New Haven, CT [*Library symbol*] [*Library of Congress*] (LCLS)
Cty Ct Chron ...	County Courts Chronicle [*1847-1920*] [*England*] [*A publication*] (DLA)
Cty Ct R	County Courts Reports [*1860-1920*] [*England*] [*A publication*] (DLA)
CtY-D	Yale University, Divinity School, New Haven, CT [*Library symbol*] [*Library of Congress*] (LCLS)
CtY-E........	Yale University, Department of Economics, Economic Growth Center, New Haven, CT [*Library symbol*] [*Library of Congress*] (LCLS)
CtY-EC	Yale University, Elizabethan Club, New Haven, CT [*Library symbol*] [*Library of Congress*] (LCLS)
CtY-EP	Yale University, Department of Epidemiology and Public Health, New Haven, CT [*Library symbol*] [*Library of Congress*] (LCLS)
CTYF	CityFed Financial Corp. [*NASDAQ symbol*] (NQ)
CtY-FE	Yale University, Far Eastern Library, New Haven, CT [*Library symbol*] [*Library of Congress*] (LCLS)
CtY-FS.......	Yale University, School of Forestry, New Haven, CT [*Library symbol*] [*Library of Congress*] (LCLS)
CtY-H	Yale University, Hammond Metallurgical Laboratories, New Haven, CT [*Library symbol*] [*Library of Congress*] (LCLS)
CtY-K........	Yale University, Kirkland Hall, New Haven, CT [*Library symbol*] [*Library of Congress*] (LCLS)
CTYKA.....	Ch'uan-Kuo Ti-I-Chieh Yeh-Chin Kuo-Ch Eng Wu-Li Hua-Hsueh Hsueh-Shu Pao-Kao-Hui Lun-Wen Chi [*A publication*]
CtY-KS	Yale University, Kline Science Library, New Haven, CT [*Library symbol*] [*Library of Congress*] (LCLS)
CtY-L........	Yale University, Law Library, New Haven, CT [*Library symbol*] [*Library of Congress*] (LCLS)
CtY-M........	Yale University, Medical School, New Haven, CT [*Library symbol*] [*Library of Congress*] (LCLS)
CtY-Mus....	Yale University, School of Music, New Haven, CT [*Library symbol*] [*Library of Congress*] (LCLS)
CtyNY.......	Contemporary Records (New York) [*Record label*]
CtY-P........	Yale University, Peabody Museum of Natural History, New Haven, CT [*Library symbol*] [*Library of Congress*] (LCLS)
CtY-SSE	Yale University, Social Sciences and Economic Growth Center, New Haven, CT [*Library symbol*] [*Library of Congress*] (LCLS)
CtY-T........	Yale University, Transportation Library, New Haven, CT [*Library symbol*] [*Library of Congress*] (LCLS)
CTZ	Capital. Das Deutsche Wirtschaftsmagazin [*A publication*]
CTZ	Chemoreceptor Trigger Zone
CTZ	Citizens & Southern Corp. [*NYSE symbol*] (SPSG)
CTZ	Clinton, NC [*Location identifier*] [*FAA*] (FAAL)
CTZ	Control Zone [*Aviation*]
CTZ	Corps Tactical Zone [*Military*]
CTZN	Citizens Financial Corp. [*NASDAQ symbol*] (NQ)
CU.............	Cable Untwist
CU.............	California Unreported Cases [*1855-1910*] [*A publication*] (DLA)
CU.............	Call-Us, Inc.
CU.............	Cambridge University [*England*]
CU.............	Camouflage Unit [*Military*]
CU.............	Canadian Underwriter [*A publication*]
CU.............	Canadian Utilities Ltd. [*Toronto Stock Exchange symbol*]
CU.............	Casualties Union (EA)
CU.............	Catholic University
CU.............	Cattlemen's Union of Australia
CU.............	Certification Unit
CU.............	Children of the Universe [*Defunct*] (EA)
CU.............	Christian Union [*University student group*] [*British*]
CU.............	Chronic Urticaria [*Immunology*]
CU.............	Church Union [*British*] (DAS)
CU.............	Chymotrypsin Unit
CU.............	Clavieruebung [*Music*]
CU.............	Clinical Unit
CU.............	Close-Up [*A photograph or motion picture sequence taken from a short distance*]
CU.............	Coefficient of Utilization
C & U	College and University [*A publication*]
CU.............	Columbia University [*New York, NY*]
C/U............	Come-Up
CU.............	Commercial Union Assurance Co. PLC [*British*] (ECON)
CU.............	Common Use (ROG)
CU.............	Communications Unlimited [*Charlotte, NC*] [*Telecommunications*] (TSSD)
CU.............	Composite Utility
CU.............	Computer Unit (EA)
CU.............	Congregational Union
CU.............	Congressional Union (EA)
CU.............	Construction Unit [*Data processing*]
C & U	Construction and Use (DCTA)
CU.............	Consumers Union of United States (EA)
CU.............	Control Unit [*Data processing*]
CU.............	Convalescent Unit [*of a hospital*]
CU.............	Conversion Unit [*British military*] (DMA)
CU.............	Cornell University [*Ithaca, NY*]
CU.............	Corrected Unpostable [*IRS*]
CU.............	Couplers [*JETDS nomenclature*] [*Military*] (CET)
cu.............	Cours Unique [*Sole Quotation*] [*Stock exchange*] [*French*] [*Business term*]
CU.............	Credit Union
CU.............	Cross-Talk Unit

CU .... Crystal Unit [*Piezoelectricity*]
cu .... Cuba [*MARC country of publication code*] [*Library of Congress*] (LCCP)
CU .... Cuba [*ANSI two-letter standard code*] (CNC)
CU .... Cuba [*Aircraft nationality and registration mark*] (FAAC)
CU .... Cubana Airways (DS)
CU .... Cube
CU .... Cubic (EY)
CU .... Cubitainer (MCD)
CU .... CUC International, Inc. [*Formerly, Comp-U-Card International*] [*NYSE symbol*] (SPSG)
CU .... Cucumber [*Slang*] (DSUE)
CU .... Culinary Arts Program [*Association of Independent Colleges and Schools specialization code*]
CU .... Cumulative List Indicator [*IRS*]
CU .... Cumulus [*Cloud*] [*Meteorology*]
Cu .... Cuprum [*Copper*] [*Chemical element*]
CU .... Curacao [*Netherlands Antilles*]
CU .... Customer Premise (NRCH)
CU .... Customs Union [*British*] (DAS)
CU .... Empresa Consolidada Cubana de Aviacion [*Cuba*] [*ICAO designator*] (FAAC)
CU .... Piezoelectric-Crystal Unit (IEEE)
CU .... University of California, Berkeley, Main Library, Berkeley, CA [*Library symbol*] [*Library of Congress*] (LCLS)
CUA .... Catholic University of America [*Washington, DC*]
CUA .... Catholic University of America, Washington, DC [*OCLC symbol*] (OCLC)
CUA .... Cattlemen's Union of Australia
CUA .... Circuit Unit Assembly
CUA .... Committee for University Assistance [*Military*] [*British*]
CUA .... Common User Access [*Data processing*] (BYTE)
CUA .... Commonly Used Acronym
CUA .... Communication International [*Vancouver Stock Exchange symbol*]
CUA .... Compugraphics Users Association [*Bend, OR*] (EA)
CUA .... Computer Users Association
CUA .... Confederated Unions of America [*Later, NFIU*]
CUA .... Cooperative Upper-Air Unit [*National Weather Service*]
CUA .... Council for Urban Affairs [*Terminated, 1970*]
Cu A .... Cuadernos Americanos [*A publication*]
CUA .... Cuajimalpa [*Mexico*] [*Later, TEO*] [*Geomagnetic observatory code*]
CU-A .... University of California, Davis, Main Library, Davis, CA [*Library symbol*] [*Library of Congress*] (LCLS)
CUA/AQ ... Anthropological Quarterly. Catholic University of America. Catholic Anthropological Conference [*A publication*]
CUAB .... Catholic University of America. Bulletin [*A publication*]
CUACS ...... Center for Urban Affairs and Community Services [*North Carolina State University*] [*Research center*] (RCD)
Cuad A (Barcel) ... Cuadernos de Arqueologia e Historia de la Ciudad (Barcelona) [*A publication*]
Cuad Actual Tec Asoc Argent Consorcios Reg Exp Agric ... Cuaderno de Actualizacion Tecnica. Asociacion Argentina de Consorcios Regionales de Experimentacion Agricola [*A publication*]
Cuad Amer ... Cuadernos Americanos [*A publication*]
Cuad Arquit Urban ... Cuadernos de Arquitectura y Urbanismo [*A publication*]
Cuad Cienc Biol Univ Granada ... Cuadernos de Ciencias Biologicas. Universidad de Granada [*A publication*]
Cuad Cirug ... Cuadernos de Cirugia [*A publication*]
Cuad CVF .. Cuadernos de la Corporacion Venezolana de Fomento [*A publication*]
Cuad de Derecho Angloamer ... Cuadernos de Derecho Angloamericano [*Barcelona, Spain*] [*A publication*] (DLA)
Cuad de Derecho Franc ... Cuadernos de Derecho Frances [*Barcelona, Spain*] [*A publication*] (DLA)
Cuad Econ (Barcelona) ... Cuadernos de Economia (Barcelona) [*A publication*]
Cuad Econ (Santiago) ... Cuadernos de Economia (Santiago) [*A publication*]
Cuadern Inst Mat Beppo Levi ... Cuadernos. Instituto de Matematica Beppo Levi [*A publication*]
Cuadernos H ... Cuadernos Hispanoamericanos [*A publication*]
Cuadern Teorema ... Cuadernos Teorema [*A publication*]
Cuad Fil ..... Cuadernos de Filosofia [*A publication*]
Cuad Fil Cl .. Cuadernos de Filologia Clasica [*A publication*]
Cuad Filo Clas ... Cuadernos de Filologia Clasica [*A publication*]
Cuad Filol Cl ... Cuadernos de Filologia Clasica [*A publication*]
Cuad Filosof ... Cuadernos de Filosofia [*A publication*]
Cuad Gall... Cuadernos de Estudios Gallegos [*A publication*]
Cuad Gallegos ... Cuadernos de Estudios Gallegos [*A publication*]
Cuad Geogr Colom ... Cuadernos de Geografia de Colombia [*A publication*]
Cuad Geol Iber ... Cuadernos de Geologia Iberica [*A publication*]
Cuad Geol Univ Granada ... Cuadernos de Geologia. Universidad de Granada [*A publication*]
Cuad (Granada) ... Cuadernos de Prehistoria (Universidad de Granada) [*A publication*]
Cuad Hisp ... Cuadernos Hispanoamericanos [*A publication*]
Cuad Hist Econ Cataluna ... Cuadernos de Historia de la Economia Catuluna [*A publication*]
Cuad Hist Esp ... Cuadernos de Historia de Espana [*A publication*]

Cuad Hist Espan ... Cuadernos de Historia de Espana [*A publication*]
Cuad Hist Med Esp ... Cuadernos de Historia de la Medicina Espanola [*A publication*]
Cuad Hist Primit ... Cuadernos de Historia Primitiva [*A publication*]
Cuad Hist Salud Publica ... Cuadernos de Historia de la Salud Publica [*A publication*]
Cuad Hist Sanit ... Cuadernos de Historia Sanitaria [*A publication*]
Cuad Inform Econ Sociol ... Cuadernos de Informacion Economica y Sociologica [*A publication*]
Cuad Inst Hist (Mex) ... Cuadernos. Instituto de Historia (Mexico) [*A publication*]
Cuad Inst Hist Ser Antr ... Cuadernos. Instituto de Historia. Seria Antropologica [*Mexico*] [*A publication*]
Cuad Inst Nac Antropol ... Cuadernos. Instituto Nacional de Antropologia [*A publication*]
Cuad Laborales ... Cuadernos Laborales [*A publication*]
Cuad Manch ... Cuadernos de Estudios Manchegos [*A publication*]
Cuad Med .. Cuadernos Medicos [*A publication*]
Cuad Med Divulg Cient ... Cuadernos Medicos y de Divulgacion Cientifico [*A publication*]
Cuad Min Geol Univ Tuc ... Cuadernos de Mineralogia y Geologia. Universidad de Tucuman [*A publication*]
Cuad Num ... Cuadernos de Numismatica [*A publication*]
Cuad Oceanogr Univ Oriente (Cumana) ... Cuadernos Oceanograficos. Universidad de Oriente (Cumana) [*A publication*]
Cuad P Arq Cast ... Cuadernos de Prehistoria y Arqueologia Castellonense [*A publication*]
Cuad Pol .... Cuadernos Politicos [*Ediciones Era*] [*A publication*]
Cuad Pr Hist A ... Cuadernos de Prehistoria y Arqueologia [*A publication*]
Cuad Realidades Socs ... Cuadernos de Realidades Sociales [*A publication*]
Cuad Rom .. Cuadernos de Trabajos. Escuela Espanola de Historia y Arqueologia en Roma [*A publication*]
Cuad Ruedo Iber ... Cuadernos de Ruedo Iberico [*A publication*]
Cuad Sind .. Cuadernos. Centro de Estudios Sindicales [*A publication*]
Cuad Teol .. Cuadernos Teologicos [*A publication*]
CU-AGRI .. University of California, Berkeley, Agriculture Library, Berkeley, CA [*Library symbol*] [*Library of Congress*] (LCLS)
CU-AL ...... University of California, Davis, Law Library, Davis, CA [*Library symbol*] [*Library of Congress*] (LCLS)
CUALR ...... Catholic University of America. Law Review [*A publication*]
CUALS ...... Catholic University of America Law School (DLA)
CU-AM ...... University of California, Davis, Health Sciences Library, Davis, CA [*Library symbol*] [*Library of Congress*] (LCLS)
CUAN .... Current Anthropology [*A publication*]
CU-ANTH ... University of California, Berkeley, Anthropology Library, Berkeley, CA [*Library symbol*] [*Library of Congress*] (LCLS)
CUAP .... Active Pass, BC [*ICAO location identifier*] (ICLI)
CUAPS ...... Catholic University of America. Patristic Studies [*A publication*]
CUAS .... Computer Utilization Accounting System (IEEE)
CUAS .... Cooperative Upper-Air Station [*National Weather Service*] (NOAA)
CUASRL ... Catholic University of America. Studies in Romance Languages and Literatures [*A publication*]
CUASRLL ... Catholic University of America. Studies in Romance Languages and Literatures [*A publication*]
CU-ASTR ... University of California, Berkeley, Astronomy Library, Berkeley, CA [*Library symbol*] [*Library of Congress*] (LCLS)
CUB .... Carlton United Breweries [*Australia*]
CUB .... Catholic University. Bulletin [*A publication*]
CUB .... Clean Up Buck (MCD)
CUB .... Columbia, SC [*Location identifier*] [*FAA*] (FAAL)
CUB .... Commonality Usage Board (NASA)
CUB .... Companies Update Bulletin [*National Companies and Securities Commission*] [*A publication*]
CUB .... Concerned United Birthparents (EA)
CUB .... Control Unit Busy (CMD)
CuB .... Copper Band [*Dentistry*]
CUB .... Council for UHF Broadcasting (EA)
CUB .... Cuba [*ANSI three-letter standard code*] (CNC)
CUB .... Cube Resources [*Vancouver Stock Exchange symbol*]
CUB .... Cubic
CUB .... Cubic Corp. [*AMEX symbol*] (SPSG)
CUB .... Cubicle (MSA)
CUB .... Customary Behavior [*Psychology*]
CUBA .... College and University Business Administration, Administrative Service [*National Association of College and University Business Officers*] [*A publication*]
Cuba .... Cubatimes [*A publication*]
Cuba Bibl ... Cuba Bibliotecologica [*A publication*]
Cuba Dir Montes B Minas ... Cuba. Direccion de Montes y Minas. Boletin de Minas [*A publication*]
CUBAEXPORT ... Empresa Cubana Exportadora de Alimentos y Productos Varios [*Cuban Enterprise for the Export of Foodstuffs and Various Products*]
CUBAFRUTAS ... Empresa Cubana Exportadora de Frutas Tropicales [*Cuban Tropical Fruit Exporting Enterprise*]

CUBAINDUSTRIA ... Empresa Exportadora de Productos Industriales [*Industrial Products Exporting Enterprise*] [*Cuba*]
CUBAINDUSTRIAL ... Empresa Cubana Importadora de Plantas Completas [*Cuban Complete Plant Importing Enterprise*]
CUBAMETALES ... Empresa Importadora de Metales [*Cuban Enterprise for the Import of Metals*]
CU-BANC ... University of California, Berkeley, Bancroft Library, Berkeley, CA [*Library symbol*] [*Library of Congress*] (LCLS)
CUBANIQUEL ... Empresa Cubana Exportadora de Minerales y Metales [*Cuban Enterprise for the Export of Minerals and Metals*]
Cuban J Agric Sci ... Cuban Journal of Agricultural Science [*A publication*]
CUBAPESCA ... Empresa Importadora de Buques y Equipos de Pesca [*Cuban Enterprise for the Import of Fishing Ships and Fishing Equipment*]
Cuba Revw ... Cuba Review [*A publication*]
CUBARTIMPEX ... Empresa Cubana Exportadora e Importadora de Articulos de Arte y Cultura [*Cuban Enterprise for Export and Import of Items of Art and Culture*]
Cuba Soc .... Cuba Socialista [*A publication*]
CUBATABACO ... Empresa Cubana de Tabaco [*Cuban Tobacco Enterprise*]
CUBATEX ... Empresa Cubana Importadora de Fibras, Tejidos, Cueros, y Sus Productos [*Cuban Enterprise for the Import of Fibers, Fabrics, Leathers, and Their By-Products*]
CUBAZUCAR ... Empresa Cubana Exportadora de Azucar y Sus Derivados [*Cuban Enterprise for Export of Sugar and Sugar By-Products*]
CUBBA2 .... Contribuciones Cientificas. Facultad de Ciencias Exactas y Naturales. Universidad de Buenos Aires. Serie Botanica [*A publication*]
CUBC .... Citizen Utility Board Campaign (EA)
C/UBC .... CWA/UTW Bargaining Council (EA)
CUBE .... Conceptual Understanding through Blind Evaluation [*Educational test*]
CUBE .... Concertation Unit for Biotechnology in Europe
CUBE .... Cooperating Users of Burroughs Equipment (EA)
CUBE .... Cubicle
CUBG .... College and University Booksellers' Group [*British*]
Cu Bi .... Cultura Biblica [*A publication*]
CuBib .... Cultura Biblica [*Segovia, Spain*] [*A publication*]
CUBIC .... Common User Baseline for the Intelligence Community (MCD)
CU-BIOC .. University of California, Berkeley, Biochemistry Library, Berkeley, CA [*Library symbol*] [*Library of Congress*] (LCLS)
CU-BIOL ... University of California, Berkeley, Biology Library, Berkeley, CA [*Library symbol*] [*Library of Congress*] (LCLS)
CUBMW ... Canadian Union of Base Metal Workers
CUBN .... CU Bancorp [*NASDAQ symbol*] (SPSG)
CUBOL ..... Computer Usage's Business-Oriented Language [*Data processing*]
CUBS .... Center for Urban Black Studies (EA)
CUBS .... City University Business School [*London, England*]
CUBS .... Congress for the Unity of Black Students
CubV .... Cuban Victor [*Record label*]
CUC .... Cahiers Universitaires Catholiques [*A publication*]
CUC .... Cameroon United Congress [*Political party*]
CUC .... Canadian Union College
CUC .... Canadian Unitarian Council
CUC .... Cask Unloading Cell [*Nuclear energy*] (NRCH)
CUC .... Chronic Ulcerative Colitis [*Medicine*]
CUC .... Clinical Unit Coordinator
CUC .... Coal Utilisation Council [*British*]
CUC .... Columbia Union College, Takoma Park, MD [*OCLC symbol*] (OCLC)
CUC .... Comite de Unidad Campesina [*Committee of Peasant Unity*] [*Guatemala*] [*Political party*] (PD)
CUC .... Communications Union Canada
CUC .... Computer Usage Control (NASA)
CUC .... Computers Users' Committee [*United Nations Development Program*]
CUC .... Continuous until Cancelled [*Insurance*]
CUC .... Cooperative Union of Canada
CUC .... Crystal Unit Cell
CUC .... Cucuta [*Colombia*] [*Airport symbol*] (OAG)
CUC .... Culbro Corporation [*NYSE symbol*] (SPSG)
CUC .... Cultura Universitaria (Caracas) [*A publication*]
CUC .... Cutlass Industries Corporation [*Vancouver Stock Exchange symbol*]
CUC .... Cyrillic Union Catalog [*Library of Congress*]
CUCA .... Carpet and Upholstery Cleaners Association of Australia
CUCA .... Columbia University. Contributions to Anthropology [*A publication*]
CuCanI .... Cuadernos Canarios de Investigacion [*A publication*]
CUCB .... Cumulus and Cumulonimbus [*Clouds*] [*Meteorology*]
CUC Gaz .... Canberra University College. Gazette [*A publication*] (APTA)
CU-CHEM ... University of California, Berkeley, Chemistry Library, Berkeley, CA [*Library symbol*] [*Library of Congress*] (LCLS)
CUCM .... Cubic Centimeter
CUCM .... Master Chief Constructionman [*Navy rating*]

CUCND ..... Combined Universities Campaign for Nuclear Disarmament [*Canada*]
CUCO .... Conservative and Unionist Central Office [*British*] (DAS)
CUCO .... Cucos, Inc. [*NASDAQ symbol*] (NQ)
CuCo .... Cursos y Conferencias [*A publication*]
CUCOSS ... California Universities Council on Space Sciences
CUCR .... Complementary Under-Color Removal [*Printing technology*]
CUCS .... Centre for Urban and Community Studies [*University of Toronto*] [*Research center*] (RCD)
CU-CS .... University of California, Berkeley, Center for Chinese Studies, Berkeley, CA [*Library symbol*] [*Library of Congress*] (LCLS)
Cu Ct .... Customs Court Reports [*A publication*] (DLA)
CUCUC ..... College and University Computer Users Conference (EA)
CUCURB CRUENT ... Cucurbitula Cruenta [*Cupping Glass with Scarificator*] [*Pharmacy*] (ROG)
CUCV .... Commercial Utility Cargo Vehicle [*Army*] (RDA)
CUD .... Caloundra [*Australia*] [*Airport symbol*] (OAG)
CUD .... Craft Union Department [*AFL-CIO*]
CUDAT ..... Common User Data [*Telecommunications*] (TEL)
CUDAT ..... Common User Data Terminal [*Military*] (AABC)
CUDD .... Cuddesdon Theological College [*Later, Rippon College, Cuddesdon*] [*Oxford*] [*British*] (ROG)
Cudd Copyh ... Cuddon. Copyhold Acts [*1865*] [*A publication*] (ILCA)
CUDIX ...... Common User Digital Information Exchange [*Satellite communication*] (NVT)
CUDIXS .... Common User Digital Information Exchange System [*or Subsystem*] [*Satellite communication*] (MCD)
CUDN .... Common User Data Network (ADA)
CU-DOCU ... University of California, Berkeley, Documents Department, Berkeley, CA [*Library symbol*] [*Library of Congress*] (LCLS)
CUDOS ..... Continuously Updated Dynamic Optimizing Systems (IEEE)
CUDPB ...... Chile. Universidad. Departamento de Astronomia. Publicaciones [*A publication*]
CUDS .... Cumulative Data Statistics (NASA)
CUDWR ..... Columbia University, Division of War Research
CUE .... Catch per Unit Effort [*Pisciculture*]
CUE .... Center for Urban Education [*Research center*] (RCD)
CUE .... Coastal Upwelling Experiment [*Marine science*] (MSC)
CUE .... Cognizant User Engineer [*Deep Space Network, NASA*]
CUE .... Common Usage Equipment (NASA)
CUE .... Communications Unit Executor
CUE .... Computer Update Equipment
CUE .... Computer User Education [*An association*]
CUE .... Concentrated Urban Enforcement [*Bureau of Alcohol, Tobacco, and Firearms*]
CUE .... Configuration Utilization Efficiency (BUR)
CUE .... Control Unit End (CMD)
CUE .... Cooperating Users' Exchange
CUE .... Credit Union Executive [*A publication*]
CUE .... Cruiser Minerals [*Vancouver Stock Exchange symbol*]
CUE .... Cucumber [*Slang*] (DSUE)
CUE .... Cuenca [*Ecuador*] [*Airport symbol*] (OAG)
CUE .... IUME/ERIC [*Institute for Urban and Minority Education/ Educational Resources Information Center*] Clearinghouse on Urban Education [*Columbia University*] [*Research center*] (RCD)
CUE .... Quantum Chemical Corp. [*NYSE symbol*] (SPSG)
CUEA .... Coastal Upwelling Ecosystems Analysis [*Marine science*] (MSC)
CUEA .... Conseil de l'Unite Economique Arabe [*Council of Arab Economic Unity - CAEU*] [*French*]
CUEA .... Consejo de la Unidad Economica Arabe [*Council of Arab Economic Unity - CAEU*] [*Spanish*]
CU-EART ... University of California, Berkeley, Earth Sciences Library, Berkeley, CA [*Library symbol*] [*Library of Congress*] (LCLS)
CU-EAST ... University of California, Berkeley, East Asiatic Library, Berkeley, CA [*Library symbol*] [*Library of Congress*] (LCLS)
CUEBS ...... Commission on Undergraduate Education in the Biological Sciences
CUEC .... Congressional Underwater Explorers Club (EA)
CUEC .... Quantum Chemical Corp. [*NASDAQ symbol*] (NQ)
CUECOS ... University College Cardiff English Centre for Overseas Students [*British*] (CB)
CUED .... Center for Urban Economics Development [*University of Illinois at Chicago*] [*Research center*] (RCD)
CUED .... National Council for Urban Economic Development (EA)
CU-EDUC ... University of California, Berkeley, Education-Psychology Library, Berkeley, CA [*Library symbol*] [*Library of Congress*] (LCLS)
CUEFS ...... Cooperative Users of Equimatics Financial Systems (CSR)
Cu EG .... Cuadernos de Estudios Gallegos [*A publication*]
CUEI .... Cue Industries [*Antonia, MO*] [*NASDAQ symbol*] (NQ)
CUE J .... Computer Using Educators of BC [*British Columbia*] Journal [*Canada*] [*A publication*]
Cu EM .... Cuadernos de Estudios Manchegos [*A publication*]

CU-ENGI .. University of California, Berkeley, Engineering Library, Berkeley, CA [*Library symbol*] [*Library of Congress*]   (LCLS)
CU-ENTO ... University of California, Berkeley, Entomology Library, Berkeley, CA [*Library symbol*] [*Library of Congress*]   (LCLS)
CU-ENVI .. University of California, Berkeley, Environmental Design Library, Berkeley, CA [*Library symbol*] [*Library of Congress*]   (LCLS)
CUEP........ Central Unit on Environmental Pollution [*British*]
CUEPACS ... Congress of Unions of Employees in the Public and Civil Services [*Malaya*]
CUES........ Center for Urban Environmental Studies   (EA)
CUES........ College and University Environment Scales [*Psychology*]
CUES........ Computer Utility Educational System   (MCD)
CUES........ Credit Union Executives Society
CUEW....... Canadian Union of Educational Workers
CUF .... Canada Income Plus Fund 1987 Trust Units [*Toronto Stock Exchange symbol*]
CUF .... Catholicarum Universitatum Federatio [*Federation of Catholic Universities*]
CUF .... Catholics United for the Faith   (EA)
CUF .... Columbia, CA [*Location identifier*] [*FAA*]   (FAAL)
CUF .... Columbia University. Forum [*A publication*]
CUF .... Common University Fund [*British*]
CUF .... Cross Utilization File   (MCD)
CUF .... Cumuliform [*Cloud*] [*Meteorology*]   (FAAC)
CUF .... University of San Francisco, Gleeson Library, San Francisco, CA [*OCLC symbol*]   (OCLC)
CUFAM .... Cooperative Users of FICS and MARS [*Atlanta, GA*]   (CSR)
CUFC........ Consortium of University Film Centers [*Library network*]   (EA)
CU-FORE ... University of California, Berkeley, Forestry Library, Berkeley, CA [*Library symbol*] [*Library of Congress*]   (LCLS)
CUFOS...... Center for UFO [*Unidentified Flying Object*] Studies [*Information service or system*]   (IID)
CU-FPRO ... University of California, Berkeley, Forest Products Laboratory, Berkeley, CA [*Library symbol*] [*Library of Congress*]   (LCLS)
CUFR........ Cumulus Fractus [*Cloud*] [*Meteorology*]   (FAAC)
CUFRA...... Cumulus Fractus [*Cloud*] [*Meteorology*]   (FAAC)
CUFRB3.... Clemson University. Department of Forestry. Forest Research Series [*A publication*]
CUFT........ Center for the Utilization of Federal Technology [*National Technical Information Service*] [*Springfield, VA*]
CUFT........ Cubic Feet [*or Foot*]   (MSA)
CUFTA8.... Clemson University. Department of Forestry. Technical Paper [*A publication*]
CUG.......... Census User Guide
CUG.......... Closed User Group [*Communications*]
CUG.......... Common User Group [*SAGE*]
CUG.......... Concurrency Update Group
CUG.......... Continental Gold Corp. [*Vancouver Stock Exchange symbol*]
CUG.......... Credit Union Magazine [*A publication*]
CUG.......... Crosfield Users Group   (EA)
CUG.......... Cuglieri [*Italy*] [*Seismograph station code, US Geological Survey*]   (SEIS)
CUG.......... Cystourethrogram [*Medicine*]
CUG.......... Orange-Cudal [*Australia*] [*Airport symbol*]   (OAG)
CUG.......... University of California, Los Angeles, Graduate School of Library and Information Science, Los Angeles, CA [*OCLC symbol*]   (OCLC)
CUGA........ Cumberland Gap National Historical Park [*National Park Service designation*]
CUGS .... Columbia University. Germanic Studies [*A publication*]
CUGS .... Community United Group Services [*British*]
CUH .... Control Users Handbook
CuH .... Cuadernos Hispanoamericanos [*Madrid*] [*A publication*]
CUH .... Cumulus Technology Ltd. [*Vancouver Stock Exchange symbol*] [*Toronto Stock Exchange symbol*]
Cu H.......... Current History [*A publication*]
CUH .... Cushing, OK [*Location identifier*] [*FAA*]   (FAAL)
CUH .... University of California, San Francisco, Hastings College of the Law, Library, San Francisco, CA [*OCLC symbol*]   (OCLC)
CUHA........ Quaqtaq, PQ [*ICAO location identifier*]   (ICLI)
CUHL........ Columbia University Hudson Laboratory
CUHP........ Council of Urban Health Providers [*Defunct*]   (EA)
CUHS........ Computer Use in the Health Service [*British*]
CU-HUMA ... University of California, Berkeley, Humanities Graduate Service, Berkeley, CA [*Library symbol*] [*Library of Congress*]   (LCLS)
CUI .... Character-Based User Interface [*Data processing*]
CUI .... Childhelp USA, Incorporated   (EA)
CUI .... Chymotrypsin Units Inhibited
CUI .... Cincinnati Uplink, Incorporated [*Cincinnati, OH*] [*Telecommunications*]   (TSSD)
CUI .... Common User Interface [*Data processing*]
CUI .... Currie Rose Resources, Inc. [*Vancouver Stock Exchange symbol*]
CU-I.......... University of California, Irvine, General Library, Irvine, CA [*Library symbol*] [*Library of Congress*]   (LCLS)

CUI .... University of California, Irvine, Irvine, CA [*OCLC symbol*]   (OCLC)
Cuia........... [*Jacobus*] Cuiacius [*Deceased, 1590*] [*Authority cited in pre-1607 legal work*]   (DSA)
Cuiac......... [*Jacobus*] Cuiacius [*Deceased, 1590*] [*Authority cited in pre-1607 legal work*]   (DSA)
CUIC .... Cardiff University Industry Centre [*United Kingdom*]   (IRUK)
CUIC .... Computer Instruments Corporation [*Hempstead, NY*] [*NASDAQ symbol*]   (NQ)
CUIDES ..... Consejo Universitario Inter-Americana para el Desarrollo Economico y Social [*Inter-American University Council for Economic and Social Development - IUCESD*]   (EA)
CU-IG .... University of California, Berkeley, Institute of Governmental Studies, Berkeley, CA [*Library symbol*] [*Library of Congress*]   (LCLS)
CUIL......... Common Usage Item List   (NASA)
CU-I-M...... University of California, Irvine, College of Medicine, Irvine, CA [*Library symbol*] [*Library of Congress*]   (LCLS)
CUIN .... Cubic Inch
CUIR .... Cuirassed [*Numismatics*]
CUIRL....... Committee of University Industrial Relations Librarians
CU-IS .... University of California, Berkeley, Institute of International Studies, Berkeley, CA [*Library symbol*] [*Library of Congress*]   (LCLS)
CU-IT .... University of California, Berkeley, Institute of Transportation Studies, Berkeley, CA [*Library symbol*] [*Library of Congress*]   (LCLS)
CUIUA ...... Council of University Institutes for Urban Affairs [*Later, UAA*]   (EA)
CUIVA...... Cuivre, Laitons, Alliages [*A publication*]
CUJ........... CPCU [*Chartered Property and Casualty Underwriters*] Journal [*A publication*]
CUJ........... Cujus [*Of Which*] [*Latin*]
CU/JIA ...... Journal of International Affairs. Columbia University. School of International Affairs [*A publication*]
CUJ LIB .... Cujus Libet [*Of Any You Please*] [*Pharmacy*]
CUJS......... Canadian Union of Jewish Students
CUJSD ...... Cheju University. Journal (South Korea) [*A publication*]
CUJT........ Complementary Unijunction Transistor   (IEEE)
CUJUSL.... Cujus Libet [*Of Any You Please*] [*Pharmacy*]   (ROG)
CUK .... Cuir. Journal Trihebdomadaire d'Informations du Cuir et de la Chaussure [*A publication*]
CUk........... Ukiah Public Library, Ukiah, CA [*Library symbol*] [*Library of Congress*]   (LCLS)
CUKC .... Citizens of the United Kingdom and Commonwealth
CUKCC...... Canada-United Kingdom Chamber of Commerce   (DS)
CUKE .... Cucumber [*Slang*]   (DSUE)
CUKOA ..... Cukoripar [*A publication*]
CUL .... Cambridge University Library [*Great Britain*]   (DLA)
CUL .... Canonical Unit of Length
CUL .... Carmi, IL [*Location identifier*] [*FAA*]   (FAAL)
CUL .... Catholics United for Life   (EA)
CUL .... Chukyo University [*UTLAS symbol*]
CUL .... Command Uplink [*NASA*]   (KSC)
Cul............. Culex [*Classical studies*]   (OCD)
CUL .... Culiacan [*Mexico*] [*Seismograph station code, US Geological Survey*] [*Closed*]   (SEIS)
CUL .... Culiacan [*Mexico*] [*Airport symbol*]   (OAG)
CUL .... Culinary   (ADA)
CUL .... Cullinet Software, Inc. [*NYSE symbol*]   (SPSG)
CUL .... Cuyahoga Community College, Learning Resource Center, Cleveland, OH [*OCLC symbol*]   (OCLC)
CUL .... See You Later [*Telegrapher's slang*]
CU-L.......... University of California, Berkeley, Law Library, Berkeley, CA [*Library symbol*] [*Library of Congress*]   (LCLS)
CU-Lbl...... University of California, Lawrence Berkeley Laboratory, Berkeley, CA [*Library symbol*] [*Library of Congress*]   (LCLS)
Cul Dair Prod J ... Cultured Dairy Products Journal [*A publication*]
CulEA .... Cultural Events in Africa [*A publication*]
CULER...... Cryogenic Upper Atmosphere Limb Emission Radiometer   (MCD)
CU-LIBR ... University of California, Berkeley, Library School Library, Berkeley, CA [*Library symbol*] [*Library of Congress*]   (LCLS)
CULL........ Corning Uniformity Limit Level
CULL........ Cross-Reference Utility [*Data processing*]
CULL........ Cullompton [*England*]
CULL........ Cullum Companies, Inc. [*NASDAQ symbol*]   (NQ)
Cull BL .... Cullen's Bankrupt Law [*A publication*]   (DLA)
CULO .... Cornell University Laboratory of Ornithology   (EA)
CULP........ California Union List of Periodicals [*Cooperative Library Agency for Systems and Services*] [*Database*]
CULP........ Computer Usage List Processor   (IEEE)
CULP........ Culp, Inc. [*NASDAQ symbol*]   (NQ)
CULR .... Catholic University. Law Review [*A publication*]
CU-Lrl .... University of California, Lawrence Livermore Laboratory, Livermore, CA [*Library symbol*] [*Library of Congress*]   (LCLS)
CULS........ Convertible Unsecured Loan Stock [*Finance*]

Cul Stud Cerc (Brasov) ... Culegere de Studii si Cercetari (Brasov) [*A publication*]
CULT........ Central Off-Equatorial Pacific Upper Layer Temperature [*Oceanography*]
CULT........ Common User Land Transportation [*Military*] (NVT)
cult .... Cultivated [*Botany*]
Cult .... Cultura [*A publication*]
CULT........ Cultural
CULT........ Culture [*Microbiology*]
Cult .... Culture [*A publication*]
Cult Atesina ... Cultura Atesina [*A publication*]
Cult B.......... Cultura Biblica [*A publication*]
CultBib...... Cultura Biblica [*Segovia, Spain*] [*A publication*]
CultBibl...... Cultura Biblica [*Segovia, Spain*] [*A publication*]
Cult Corr.... Cultural Correspondence [*A publication*]
Cult Dairy Prod J ... Cultured Dairy Products Journal [*A publication*]
Cult et Devel ... Cultures et Developpement [*A publication*]
CULTER ... University of Colorado at Boulder Long-Term Ecological Research Project [*Research center*] (RCD)
Cult Esp ..... Cultura Espanola [*A publication*]
Cult Fr........ Culture Francaise [*A publication*]
Cult Franc ... Culture Francaise [*A publication*]
Cult Hermen ... Cultural Hermeneutics [*A publication*]
CULTIVON ... Cultivation (ROG)
Cult Med.... Cultura Medica [*A publication*]
Cult Med Mod ... Cultura Medica Moderna [*A publication*]
Cult Med Psych ... Culture, Medicine, and Psychiatry [*A publication*]
Cult Med Psychiatry ... Culture, Medicine, and Psychiatry [*A publication*]
Cult Mod.... Cultivador Moderno [*A publication*]
Cult Neol.... Cultura Neolatina [*A publication*]
Cult Neolat ... Cultura Neolatina [*A publication*]
Cult Resour Rep US For Serv Southwest Reg ... Cultural Resource Report. United States Forest Service. Southwestern Region [*A publication*]
Cult Sc .... Cultura e Scuola [*A publication*]
Cult Scuol .. Cultura e Scuola [*A publication*]
Cult Stomat ... Cultura Stomatologica [*A publication*]
Cult Stud.... Cultural Studies [*A publication*]
Cult Surv.... Cultural Survival Newsletter [*A publication*]
Cult Univ ... Cultura Universitaria [*A publication*]
Cultural Cor ... Cultural Correspondence [*A publication*]
Cultura Med Mod ... Cultura Medica Moderna [*A publication*]
CULTURE ... Creative Use of Leisure Time under Restrictive Environments [*Federally funded prison program*]
CULTUREX ... Association for Cultural Exchange (EA)
CULTVR... Cultivator
CULV .... Culvert
CUM.......... Cambridge University Mission
CUM.......... Casualty Underwriting Manual [*Insurance*]
CUM.......... Central Unit-Memory (MCD)
CUM.......... Committee on the Unisex Military (EA)
Cum........... Concerteum [*Record label*] [*France*]
CUM.......... Credit Union Management [*A publication*]
CUM.......... Cubic Meter
CUM.......... Cumana [*Venezuela*] [*Seismograph station code, US Geological Survey*] (SEIS)
CUM.......... Cumana [*Venezuela*] [*Airport symbol*] (OAG)
CUM.......... Cummins Engine Co., Inc. [*NYSE symbol*] (SPSG)
CUM.......... Cumulative (KSC)
CUM.......... Curry College, Milton, MA [*OCLC symbol*] (OCLC)
CU-M .... University of California, San Francisco, Medical Center, San Francisco, CA [*Library symbol*] [*Library of Congress*] (LCLS)
Cuma.......... [*Raphael*] Cumanus [*Deceased, 1427*] [*Authority cited in pre-1607 legal work*] (DSA)
Cumana Univ Oriente Inst Oceanogr Bol ... Cumana. Universidad de Oriente. Instituto Oceanografico. Boletin [*A publication*]
CU-MAPS ... University of California, Berkeley, Maps Collection, Berkeley, CA [*Library symbol*] [*Library of Congress*] (LCLS)
CU-MARK ... University of California, Berkeley, Mark Twain Collection, Berkeley, CA [*Library symbol*] [*Library of Congress*] (LCLS)
CU-MATH ... University of California, Berkeley, Mathematics/Statistics Library, Berkeley, CA [*Library symbol*] [*Library of Congress*] (LCLS)
CUMB .... Cumberland [*County in England*]
Cumb.......... Cumberland College of Health Sciences [*Australia*]
Cumb.......... Cumberland Law Journal [*Pennsylvania*] [*A publication*]
CUMBB .... Currents in Modern Biology [*The Netherlands*] [*A publication*]
Cumberland LJ (PA) ... Cumberland Law Journal [*Pennsylvania*] [*A publication*] (DLA)
Cumberland L Rev ... Cumberland Law Review [*A publication*]
Cumberland-Samford ... Cumberland-Samford Law Review [*A publication*]
Cumberland-Samford L Rev ... Cumberland-Samford Law Review [*A publication*]
Cumberland Sem ... Cumberland Seminarian [*A publication*]
Cumber-Sam L Rev ... Cumberland-Samford Law Review [*A publication*]
Cum B Ind ... Cumulative Book Index [*A publication*]
Cumb Law Jrnl ... Cumberland Law Journal [*Pennsylvania*] [*A publication*] (DLA)

Cumb L Rev ... Cumberland Law Review [*A publication*]
Cumb Nat... Cumberland's Law of Nature [*A publication*] (DLA)
Cum Book .. Cumulative Book Index [*A publication*]
Cumb Q..... Cumberland Presbyterian Quarterly Review [*A publication*]
Cumb-Sam L Rev ... Cumberland-Samford Law Review [*A publication*] (DLA)
Cum Bull.... Cumulative Bulletin [*United States Internal Revenue Service*] [*A publication*]
Cum Civ L ... Cummins' Manual of Civil Law [*A publication*] (DLA)
Cum Comput Abstr ... Cumulative Computer Abstracts [*A publication*]
CUMD...... Continuous Update Memory Display
Cum Div..... Cum Dividend [*With Dividend*] [*Latin*] [*Stock exchange term*]
Cum & Dun Rem Tr ... Cummins and Dunphy's Remarkable Trials [*A publication*] (DLA)
CUME...... Cumulative Audience [*Telecommunications*]
CUMECS.. Cubic Meters per Second
CUMFU .... Complete Utter Monumental Foul-Up [*Military slang*] [*Bowdlerized version*]
CUMHDA ... Contributions. University of Michigan Herbarium [*A publication*]
CUMI .... Council for Understanding Mental Illness [*Defunct*] (EA)
CUMIA ..... Coeur et Medecine Interne [*A publication*]
CUMIAA .. Coeur et Medecine Interne [*A publication*]
Cumidava... Cumidava Culegere de Studii si Cercetari [*A publication*]
Cum LR..... Cumberland Law Review [*A publication*]
Cum L Rev ... Cumberland Law Review [*A publication*]
CUMM....... Council of Underground Machinery Manufacturers [*British*]
CUMM....... Cubic Millimeter
CUMMFU ... Complete Utter Monumental Military Foul-Up [*Slang*] [*Bowdlerized version*]
Cummins.... Cummins' Reports [*1866-67*] [*Idaho*] [*A publication*] (DLA)
CUMO....... Cumo Resources Ltd. [*NASDAQ symbol*] (NQ)
CUMOA.... Cultivador Moderno [*A publication*]
CU-MODE ... University of California, Berkeley, Modern Authors Collection, Berkeley, CA [*Library symbol*] [*Library of Congress*] (LCLS)
CU-MORR ... University of California, Berkeley, Morrison Collection, Berkeley, CA [*Library symbol*] [*Library of Congress*] (LCLS)
CUMP .... Central Unit-Memory Programmer (MCD)
Cum PP...... Cumulative Pocket Parts (DLA)
cumpto....... Cumprimento [*Salutation*] [*Portuguese*] [*Correspondence*]
CUMREC ... College and University Machine Records Conference [*Later, CUCUC*] (EA)
CUMS .... Canadian University Music Society [*See also SMUC*]
CUMS .... Cumulated Summaries
Cum-Sam ... Cumberland-Samford Law Review [*A publication*]
Cum Sam L Rev ... Cumberland-Samford Law Review [*A publication*] (DLA)
Cum Supp ... Cumulative Supplement (DLA)
CUMU....... Cubic Micron
Cumul Index Med ... Cumulated Index Medicus [*A publication*]
Cumul Index Nurs Allied Health Lit ... Cumulative Index to Nursing and Allied Health Literature [*A publication*]
Cumul Index Nurs Lit ... Cumulative Index to Nursing Literature [*A publication*]
CU-MUSI ... University of California, Berkeley, Music Library, Berkeley, CA [*Library symbol*] [*Library of Congress*] (LCLS)
CUMWA... Consortium of Universities of the Metropolitan Washington Area
CUN.......... Canadian United Minerals [*Vancouver Stock Exchange symbol*]
CUN.......... Cancun [*Mexico*] [*Airport symbol*] (OAG)
Cu N.......... Cultura Neolatina [*A publication*]
CUN.......... Cumulonimbus [*Cloud*] [*Meteorology*]
Cun............. Cunningham's English King's Bench Reports [*A publication*] (DLA)
CUN.......... Fairbanks, AK [*Location identifier*] [*FAA*] (FAAL)
CUN.......... Nanzan University Library [*UTLAS symbol*]
CUN.......... University of California, San Francisco, CA [*OCLC symbol*] (OCLC)
CUNA....... Credit Union National Association (EA)
CUNB....... Cupertino National Bancorp [*NASDAQ symbol*] (NQ)
Cun Bill Exch ... Cunningham's Law of Notes and Bills of Exchange [*A publication*] (DLA)
Cun Bills .... Cunningham's Bills, Notes, and Insurances [*A publication*] (DLA)
Cun Dict..... Cunningham's Dictionary [*A publication*] (DLA)
CUNE........ Clandestine Underwater Nuclear Explosion
CU-NEWS ... University of California, Berkeley, Newspaper and Microcopy Division, Berkeley, CA [*Library symbol*] [*Library of Congress*] (LCLS)
Cun Hind L ... Cunningham on Hindu Law [*A publication*] (DLA)
Cu Nim....... Cumulonimbus [*Cloud*] [*Meteorology*] (AIA)
Cun LD ...... Cunningham's Law Dictionary [*A publication*] (DLA)
Cunn........... Cunningham's English King's Bench Reports [*A publication*] (DLA)
Cunningham ... Cunningham's English King's Bench Reports [*A publication*] (DLA)
Cunningham (Eng) ... Cunningham's English King's Bench Reports [*A publication*] (DLA)
Cunobelin... Cunobelin Yearbook. British Association of Numismatic Societies [*A publication*]

Cun Pl .... Cunningham's Maxims and Rules of Pleading [*A publication*] (DLA)
CUNR .... Campaign for UN Reform (EA)
CUNR .... Conference of UN Representatives, UNA [*United Nations Association*]-USA (EA)
CUNRE .... Center for UN Reform Education (EA)
CUNS .... Center for UN Studies (EAIO)
Cun Sim ..... Cunningham on Simony [*A publication*] (DLA)
CUNY/CP ... Comparative Politics. City University of New York, Political Science Program [*A publication*]
CUNZA ..... Chemie in Unserer Zeit [*A publication*]
CUO .... Continental Materials Corp. [*AMEX symbol*] (SPSG)
CUO .... Copper Oxide (KSC)
CUO .... Current Sociology [*A publication*]
CUOE .... Canadian Union of Operating Engineers and General Workers
CU-OPTO ... University of California, Berkeley, Optometry Library, Berkeley, CA [*Library symbol*] [*Library of Congress*] (LCLS)
Cuore Circ ... Cuore e Circolazione [*A publication*]
Cuore Circol ... Cuore e Circolazione [*A publication*]
CUOTC .... Cambridge University Officer Training Corps [*British military*] (DMA)
CUP .... Cambridge University Press
CUP .... Carupano [*Venezuela*] [*Airport symbol*] (OAG)
CUP .... Cascade Uprating Program [*AEC*]
CUP .... Cask Unloading Pool [*Nuclear energy*] (NRCH)
CUP .... Center for Urban Policy [*Loyola University of Chicago*] [*Research center*] (RCD)
CUP .... Center for Urban Programs [*St. Louis University*] [*Research center*] (RCD)
CUP .... Central Utah Project [*Federal aqueduct-and-reservoir plan*]
CUP .... Code Universel de Produit [*Universal Product Code*] [*French*]
CUP .... Cohesive Unit Program [*Army*]
CUP .... Columbia Computing Services Ltd. [*Toronto Stock Exchange symbol*]
CUP .... Columbia University Press
CUP .... Commonality Usage Proposal (NASA)
CUP .... Communications User Program [*Sperry UNIVAC*]
CUP .... Culebra [*Puerto Rico*] [*Seismograph station code, US Geological Survey*] (SEIS)
CUP .... Cupboard
Cup .... Cupol [*Record label*] [*Sweden*]
CUP .... Cupola
CUPA .... College and University Personnel Association (EA)
CUPAD ..... Current Energy Patents [*A publication*]
CUPE .... Canadian Union of Public Employees
CUPE .... Cranfield Unit for Precision Engineering [*British*]
CU & PFC ... Criminally Uttering and Publishing False [*or Forged*] Check [*Legal term*]
CU-PHIL ... University of California, Berkeley, Philosophy Library, Berkeley, CA [*Library symbol*] [*Library of Congress*] (LCLS)
CU-PHYS ... University of California, Berkeley, Physics Library, Berkeley, CA [*Library symbol*] [*Library of Congress*] (LCLS)
CUPID ...... Combat Using Price Incentives Doctrine
CUPID ...... Completely Universal Processor and I/O [*Input/Output*] Design [*Data processing*]
CUPID ...... Computer for Uprange Point-of-Impact Determination [*NASA*] (KSC)
CUpl .... Upland Public Library, Upland, CA [*Library symbol*] [*Library of Congress*] (LCLS)
CUPLE ...... Cambridge University Press Limited Editions
CUPLL ...... Coalition for Uniform Product Liability Law (EA)
CUPM .... Clinically Undetectable Primary Malignancy [*Oncology*]
CUpp .... Upper Lake Library District, Upper Lake, CA [*Library symbol*] [*Library of Congress*] (LCLS)
CUPPI .... Circumstances Undetermined Pending Police Investigation
CUPR .... Catholic University of Puerto Rico
CUPS .... Concentrated Urban Placement Service [*Department of Labor*]
CUPS .... Consolidated Unit Personnel Section
CUPTE .... Canadian Union of Professional and Technical Employees
CUPU .... Committee of Urban Program Universities
CU-PUBL ... University of California, Berkeley, Public Health Library, Berkeley, CA [*Library symbol*] [*Library of Congress*] (LCLS)
CU-PU-FU ... National Clean Up - Paint Up - Fix Up Bureau [*Defunct*] (EA)
CUPW .... Canadian Union of Postal Workers
CUQ .... Coen [*Australia*] [*Airport symbol*] (OAG)
CUQ. .... Columbia University. Quarterly [*A publication*]
CUQC .... Stirling, ON [*ICAO location identifier*] (ICLI)
CUR .... Cambridge University Rifles [*British military*] (DMA)
CUR .... Chagan-Uzun [*USSR*] [*Seismograph station code, US Geological Survey*] (SEIS)
CUR .... Command Uplink Request [*NASA*] (KSC)
CUR .... Complex Utility Routine
CUR .... Council on Undergraduate Research (EA)
CUR .... Curacao [*Netherlands Antilles*] [*Airport symbol*] (OAG)
CUR .... Curate (ROG)
CUR .... Curative [*Medicine*]
CUR .... Curator Resources [*Vancouver Stock Exchange symbol*]
CUR .... Curia [*Court*] [*Latin*] (DLA)

CUR .... Curia Regis Rolls [*British*]
CUR .... Curious (ROG)
CUR .... Currency
CUR .... Current (AAG)
CUR .... Current Income Shares, Inc. [*NYSE symbol*] (SPSG)
CUR .... Currentis [*Of the Current Month or Year*] [*Latin*]
Cur .... Curtis' United States Circuit Court Reports [*A publication*] (DLA)
CUR .... University of Colorado. Law Review [*A publication*]
CUR .... University of Redlands, Redlands, CA [*OCLC symbol*] (OCLC)
CURA .... Center for Urban and Regional Affairs [*University of Minnesota*] [*Research center*] (RCD)
CURABA ..... Current Archives Bibliography Australia [*A publication*] (APTA)
Cur Ab Tit ... Curwen's Abstract of Titles [*A publication*] (DLA)
Cur Accts ... Current Accounts [*A publication*] (APTA)
CUR ADV VULT ... Curia Advisari Vult [*The Court Wishes to Consider*] [*Latin*] [*Legal term*] (ROG)
CURAGI .... Comite pour l'Utilisation des Resultats de l'Annee Geophysique Internationale [*IGY completion committee*]
Cur Anthro ... Current Anthropology [*A publication*]
Cur Anthrop ... Current Anthropology [*A publication*]
Cur Anthropol ... Current Anthropology [*A publication*]
CU-RARE ... University of California, Berkeley, Rare Books and Special Collections Department, Berkeley, CA [*Library symbol*] [*Library of Congress*] (LCLS)
CURAT ..... Curatio [*A Dressing*] [*Pharmacy*]
CURB .... Curtis Bay Railroad Co. [*AAR code*]
Cur Backg .. Current Background [*A publication*]
Cur Bibliog African Affairs ... Current Bibliography on African Affairs [*A publication*]
Cur Biog ..... Current Biography [*A publication*]
Cur Biog Yrbk ... Current Biography Yearbook [*A publication*]
Cur Bl .... Curry's Abridgment of Blackstone [*A publication*] (DLA)
Cur Brit For Pol ... Current British Foreign Policy [*A publication*]
Curc. .... Curculio [*of Plautus*] [*Classical studies*] (OCD)
CUR-in-CH ... Curate-in-Charge [*Church of England*] (ROG)
Cur Com ..... Current Comment and Legal Miscellany [*A publication*] (DLA)
Cur Cr Proc ... Indian Code of Criminal Procedure, Curries' Edition [*A publication*] (DLA)
Cur Dec ...... Curtis' Decisions of the United States Supreme Court [*A publication*] (DLA)
CURDS ...... Centre for Urban and Regional Development Studies [*University of Newcastle upon Tyne*] [*British*] (CB)
CURE .... Center for Ulcer Research and Education [*University of California, Los Angeles*] [*Research center*] (RCD)
CURE .... Center for UN Reform Education (EA)
CURE .... Christians United for Responsible Entertainment (EA)
CURE .... Citizens United for Racial Equality
CURE .... Citizens United for Rehabilitation of Errants (EA)
CURE .... Citizens United for Research and Education (EA)
CURE .... Citizens United for Responsible Energy (EA)
CURE .... Clean Urban River Environments [*Project*]
CURE .... Color Uniformity Recognition Equipment [*Quality control*]
CURE .... Conference for Universal Reason and Ethics [*Founded by motion picture actor Lew Ayres*]
CURE .... Conference Upon Research and Education in World Government (EA)
CURE .... Consumers United for Rail Equity (EA)
CURE .... Council for Unified Research and Education (EA)
CURE .... Council of Urban Rebuilding Enterprises
CURE .... CURE [*Citizens United to Reduce Emmissions*] Formaldehyde Poisoning Association (EA)
CURE .... Curecanti Recreation Area [*National Park Service designation*]
CURE .... Smith Collins Pharmaceutical, Inc. [*Chevy Chase, MD*] [*NASDAQ symbol*] (NQ)
CU-REFE .. University of California, Berkeley, Reference and Bibliography Collection, Berkeley, CA [*Library symbol*] [*Library of Congress*] (LCLS)
CURES ...... Computer Utilization Reporting System (IEEE)
Cur Ev .... Current Events [*A publication*]
CURFCOE ... Common Usage Radio Frequency Checkout Equipment (KSC)
Cur Health ... Current Health [*A publication*]
Cur Hist ..... Current History [*A publication*]
Cur Hist M NY Times ... Current History Magazine of the New York Times [*A publication*]
CURI .... College University Resource Institute (EA)
Cur IC .... Current Indian Cases [*1912-15*] [*A publication*] (DLA)
CURIE .... Canadian Universities' Reciprocal Insurance Exchange
Cur Ind Cas ... Current Indian Cases [*1912-15*] [*A publication*] (DLA)
CURIO .... Curiosity (DSUE)
Cur Issues Higher Ed ... Current Issues in Higher Education [*A publication*]
Cur Issues Higher Educ Ann Ser ... Current Issues in Higher Education. Annual Series [*A publication*]
CU-Riv .... University of California, Riverside, Main Library, Riverside, CA [*Library symbol*] [*Library of Congress*] (LCLS)
CU-RivA .... University of California, Riverside, Bioagriculture Library, Riverside, CA [*Library symbol*] [*Library of Congress*] (LCLS)

CU-RivP .... University of California, Riverside, Physical Sciences Library, Riverside, CA [*Library symbol*] [*Library of Congress*] (LCLS)
CURL .... Children's Understanding of Reading Language [*A publication*] (APTA)
CURL .... Compartment of Uncoupling Receptor and Ligand [*Cytology*]
CURL .... Consortium of University Research Libraries [*British*] (IID)
Cur Lab Dev ... Current Labour Developments [*A publication*]
Cur Lit....... Current Literature [*A publication*]
Cur LR ..... Current Law Reports [*Ceylon*] [*A publication*] (DLA)
CURMCO ... City Urban Renewal Management Corporation [*New York City*]
Cur Muni Prob ... Current Municipal Problems [*A publication*]
CURN........ Conduct and Utilization of Research in Nursing
Cur Opinion ... Current Opinion [*A publication*]
Cur Ov Ca ... Curwen's Overruled Cases [*Ohio*] [*A publication*] (DLA)
CUR PHIL ... Curia Phillippica [*Latin*] (DLA)
Cur Prop L ... Current Property Law [*British*] [*A publication*] (DLA)
Cur Psychol Rev ... Current Psychological Reviews [*A publication*]
CURR .... Currency (AFM)
CURR .... Current (EY)
CURR .... Curriculum
Cur R.......... Curriculum Review [*A publication*]
Curr Abstr Chem Index Chem ... Current Abstracts of Chemistry and Index Chemicus [*A publication*]
Curr Adv Genet ... Current Advances in Genetics [*A publication*]
Curr Adv Plant Sci ... Current Advances in Plant Science [*A publication*]
Curr Affairs Bull ... Current Affairs Bulletin [*A publication*] (APTA)
Curr Aff B ... Current Affairs Bulletin [*A publication*]
Curr Aff Bull ... Current Affairs Bulletin [*A publication*]
Curr Agric ... Current Agriculture [*A publication*]
Curr Alcohol ... Currents in Alcoholism [*A publication*]
Curr Anthr ... Current Anthropology [*A publication*]
Curr Anthrop ... Current Anthropology [*A publication*]
Curr Anthropol ... Current Anthropology [*A publication*]
Curr Archaeol ... Current Archaeology [*A publication*]
Curr Aus NZ Leg Lit Ind ... Current Australian and New Zealand Legal Literature Index [*A publication*]
Curr Aust New Z Leg Lit Index ... Current Australian and New Zealand Legal Literature Index [*A publication*]
Curr Aware Biol Sci CABS ... Current Awareness in Biological Sciences. CABS [*A publication*]
Curr Awareness Bull ... Current Awareness Bulletin [*A publication*]
Curr Awareness Libr Lit CALL ... Current Awareness - Library Literature. CALL [*A publication*]
Curr Bibl Aquatic Sci & Fish ... Current Bibliography for Aquatic Sciences and Fisheries [*A publication*]
Curr Bibliogr Middle East Geol ... Current Bibliography of Middle East Geology [*A publication*]
Curr Book Rev Citations ... Current Book Review Citations [*A publication*]
Curr Bus..... Survey of Current Business [*United States*] [*A publication*]
Curr Chem Pap ... Current Chemical Papers [*A publication*]
Curr Concepts Cerebrovasc Dis Stroke ... Current Concepts of Cerebrovascular Disease: Stroke [*A publication*]
Curr Concepts Emerg Med ... Current Concepts in Emergency Medicine [*A publication*]
Curr Concepts Hosp Pharm Manage ... Current Concepts in Hospital Pharmacy Management [*A publication*]
Curr Concepts Nutr ... Current Concepts in Nutrition [*A publication*]
CurrCont.... Current Contents [*A publication*]
Curr Contents ... Current Contents [*A publication*]
Curr Contents Agric Biol Environ Sci ... Current Contents. Agriculture, Biology, and Environmental Sciences [*A publication*]
Curr Contents Behav Soc Educ Sci ... Current Contents/Behavioral, Social, and Educational Sciences [*A publication*]
Curr Contents Behav Soc Manage Sci ... Current Contents/Behavioral, Social, and Management Sciences [*A publication*]
Curr Contents Clin Med ... Current Contents/Clinical Medicine [*A publication*]
Curr Contents Clin Pract ... Current Contents/Clinical Practices [*A publication*]
Curr Contents Educ ... Current Contents/Education [*A publication*]
Curr Contents Eng Tech Appl Sci ... Current Contents/Engineering, Technology, and Applied Sciences [*A publication*]
Curr Contents Eng Technol ... Current Contents/Engineering and Technology [*A publication*]
Curr Contents Life Sci ... Current Contents/Life Sciences [*A publication*]
Curr Contents Pharm Publ ... Current Contents of Pharmaceutical Publications [*A publication*]
Curr Contents Phys Chem Earth Sci ... Current Contents/Physical, Chemical, and Earth Sciences [*A publication*]
Curr Contents Soc Behav Sci ... Current Contents/Social and Behavioral Sciences [*A publication*]
CURRD ..... Current [*A publication*]
Curr Dev Psychopharmacol ... Current Developments in Psychopharmacology [*A publication*]
Curr Dig Sov Press ... Current Digest of the Soviet Press [*A publication*]
Curr Econ Bus Aspects Wine Ind Symp ... Current Economics and Business Aspects of the Wine Industry. Symposium [*A publication*]
Curr Econ Comm ... Current Economic Comment [*A publication*]
CUR REG ... Curia Regis [*King's Court*] [*Latin*] [*Legal term*] (ROG)

Cur Reg R .. Curia Regis Rolls [*British*] [*Legal term*] (DLA)
Curr Energy Pat ... Current Energy Patents [*A publication*]
Curr Eng Pract ... Current Engineering Practice [*A publication*]
Current....... Against the Current [*A publication*]
CURRENT ... Committee Urging Regulatory Reform for Efficient National Trucking [*Later, BCIPT*] (EA)
Current Accts ... Current Accounts [*A publication*] (APTA)
Current Adv Plant Sci ... Current Advances in Plant Science [*A publication*]
Current Affairs Bul ... Current Affairs Bulletin [*A publication*] (APTA)
Current Chem Transl ... Current Chemical Translations [*A publication*]
Current Com & Leg Mis ... Current Comment and Legal Miscellany [*A publication*] (DLA)
Current Dig Soviet Pr ... Current Digest of the Soviet Press [*A publication*]
Current Hist ... Current History [*A publication*]
Current Index Statist Appl Methods Theory ... Current Index to Statistics; Applications-Methods-Theory [*A publication*]
Current Ind Rept ... Current Industrial Reports [*Census Bureau*] [*A publication*]
Current Inf Constr Ind ... Current Information in the Construction Industry [*A publication*]
Current L ... Current Law [*A publication*]
Current Law ... Current Law and Social Problems [*A publication*]
Current Legal Prob ... Current Legal Problems [*A publication*]
Current Lit Traff Transp ... Current Literature in Traffic and Transportation [*A publication*]
Current L & Soc Probl ... Current Law and Social Problems [*A publication*]
Current LY ... Current Law Year Book [*A publication*] (DLA)
Current LYB ... Current Law Year Book [*A publication*]
Current Math Publ ... Current Mathematical Publications [*A publication*]
Current Med ... Current Medicine for Attorneys [*A publication*]
Current Med for Att'ys ... Current Medicine for Attorneys [*A publication*] (DLA)
Current Mun Prob ... Current Municipal Problems [*A publication*]
Current Mus ... Current Musicology [*A publication*]
Current Musicol ... Current Musicology [*A publication*]
Current Notes ... Current Notes on International Affairs [*A publication*] (APTA)
Current Prop L ... Current Property Law [*British*] [*A publication*] (DLA)
Current Sociol (Sage) ... Current Sociology (Sage Publications Ltd.) [*A publication*]
Current Tech Index ... Current Technology Index [*A publication*]
Curr Eye Res ... Current Eye Research [*A publication*]
Curr Farm Econ ... Current Farm Economics [*A publication*]
Curr Genet ... Current Genetics [*A publication*]
Curr Hepatol ... Current Hepatology [*A publication*]
Curr Hist.... Current History [*A publication*]
CURRIC.... Curriculum
Curric Inq .. Curriculum Inquiry [*A publication*]
Curric Inquiry ... Curriculum Inquiry [*A publication*]
Curric News ... Curriculum News [*A publication*] (APTA)
Curric P..... Curriculum Perspective [*A publication*]
Curric R ..... Curriculum Review [*A publication*]
Curric & Research Bul ... Curriculum and Research Bulletin [*A publication*] (APTA)
Curric Stud and Ed Res B ... Curriculum Study and Educational Research Bulletin [*A publication*]
Curric Theo ... Curriculum Theory Network [*A publication*]
Curriculum Perspect ... Curriculum Perspective [*A publication*] (APTA)
Curriculum Res Bull ... Curriculum and Research Bulletin [*A publication*] (APTA)
Curr Ind Commonw Leg Per ... Current Index to Commonwealth Legal Periodicals [*A publication*]
Curr Index Commonw Leg Period ... Current Index to Commonwealth Legal Periodicals [*A publication*]
Curr Index J Educ ... Current Index to Journals in Education. CIJE [*A publication*]
Curr Index Stat ... Current Index to Statistics [*A publication*]
Curr Index Stat Appl Methods Theory ... Current Index to Statistics; Applications-Methods-Theory [*A publication*]
Curr Indian Stat ... Current Indian Statutes [*A publication*]
Curr Ind Rept Footwear ... Current Industrial Reports. M31A. Footwear [*A publication*]
Curr Ind Rept Plast Bottles ... Current Industrial Reports. M30E. Plastic Bottles [*A publication*]
Curr Induced React Int Summer Inst Theor Part Phys ... Current Induced Reactions. International Summer Institute on Theoretical Particle Physics [*A publication*]
Curr Inform Ser Univ Idaho Coll Agr Ext Serv ... Current Information Series. University of Idaho. College of Agriculture. Agricultural Extension Service [*A publication*]
Curr Inf Ser Idaho Agric Exp Stn ... Idaho. Agricultural Experiment Station. Current Information Series [*A publication*]
Curr Issues Psychoanal Pract ... Current Issues in Psychoanalytic Practice [*A publication*]
Curr Issues Stud US Nat Res Counc ... Current Issues and Studies. United States National Research Council [*A publication*]
Curr Jod Lit ... Current Jodine Literature [*A publication*]
Curr Lab Pract ... Current Laboratory Practice [*A publication*]
Curr Law Case Cit ... Current Law Case Citator [*A publication*]
Curr Law Cit ... Current Law Citator [*A publication*]
Curr Law Index ... Current Law Index [*A publication*]

Curr Law Soc Probl ... Current Law and Social Problems [*A publication*]
Curr Law Statut Cit Index ... Current Law Statute Citator and Index [*A publication*]
Curr Leather Lit ... Current Leather Literature [*A publication*]
Curr Legal Prob ... Current Legal Problems [*A publication*]   (DLA)
Curr Leg Probl ... Current Legal Problems [*A publication*]
Curr Lit Aging ... Current Literature on Aging [*A publication*]
Curr Lit Blood ... Current Literature of Blood [*A publication*]
Curr Lit Vener Dis ... Current Literature on Venereal Disease [*A publication*]
Curr LSP ... Current Law and Social Problems [*A publication*]
Curr LYB ... Current Law Year Book [*A publication*]
Curr Math Publ ... Current Mathematical Publications [*A publication*]
Curr Med ... Current Medicine [*A publication*]
Curr Med Abstr Practit ... Current Medical Abstracts for Practitioners [*A publication*]
Curr Med Dig ... Current Medical Digest [*A publication*]
Curr Med Drugs ... Current Medicine and Drugs [*A publication*]
Curr Med Pract ... Current Medical Practice [*A publication*]
Curr Med Pract (India) ... Current Medical Practice (India) [*A publication*]
Curr Med Res ... Current Medical Research [*A publication*]
Curr Med Res Opin ... Current Medical Research and Opinion [*A publication*]
Curr Microbiol ... Current Microbiology [*A publication*]
Curr Mod Biol ... Currents in Modern Biology [*A publication*]
Curr Mod Biol Biosyst ... Currents in Modern Biology. Biosystems [*A publication*]
Curr Mun Pr ... Current Municipal Problems [*A publication*]
Curr Music ... Current Musicology [*A publication*]
Curr Nephrol ... Current Nephrology [*A publication*]
Curr Neurosurg Pract ... Current Neurosurgical Practice [*A publication*]
Curr No Int Aff ... Current Notes on International Affairs [*A publication*]
Curr Notes ... Current Notes on International Affairs [*A publication*]   (APTA)
Curr Notes Int Aff ... Current Notes on International Affairs [*A publication*]
Curr Notes Int Affairs ... Current Notes on International Affairs [*A publication*]   (APTA)
Curr Opin .. Current Opinion [*A publication*]
Curr Opin G ... Current Opinion in Gastroenterology [*A publication*]
Curr Pap Aeronaut Res Counc (UK) ... Current Papers. Aeronautical Research Council (United Kingdom) [*A publication*]
Curr Pap Build Res Establ ... Current Paper. Building Research Establishment [*A publication*]
Curr Papers Phys ... Current Papers in Physics [*A publication*]
Curr Pap Phys ... Current Papers in Physics [*A publication*]
Curr P Card ... Current Problems in Cardiology [*A publication*]
Curr Phys Index ... Current Physics Index [*A publication*]
Curr Pop Rep ... Current Population Reports [*A publication*]
Curr Pop Rep Special Studies ... Current Population Reports. Special Studies. Series P-23 [*A publication*]
Curr Popul Rep Consum Income ... Current Population Reports. Consumer Income. Series P-60 [*United States*] [*A publication*]
Curr Popul Rep P-26 ... Current Population Reports. Series P-26. Federal-State Cooperative Program for Population Estimates [*A publication*]
Curr Popul Rep Popul Charact ... Current Population Reports. Population Characteristics. Series P-20 [*United States*] [*A publication*]
Curr Popul Rep Popul Estim Proj ... Current Population Reports. Population Estimates and Projections. Series P-25 [*United States*] [*A publication*]
Curr Popul Rep Spec Censuses ... Current Population Reports. Special Censuses. Series P-28 [*United States*] [*A publication*]
Curr Popul Rep Spec Stud ... Current Population Reports. Special Studies. Series P-23 [*United States*] [*A publication*]
Curr Pract Environ Eng ... Current Practices in Environmental Engineering [*A publication*]
Curr Pract Gerontol Nurs ... Current Practice in Gerontological Nursing [*A publication*]
Curr Pract Obstet Gynecol Nurs ... Current Practice in Obstetric and Gynecologic Nursing [*A publication*]
Curr Pract Orthop Surg ... Current Practice in Orthopaedic Surgery [*A publication*]
Curr Pract Pediatr Nurs ... Current Practice in Pediatric Nursing [*A publication*]
Curr Prob Dermatol ... Current Problems in Dermatology [*A publication*]
Curr Probl ... Current Problems [*A publication*]
Curr Probl Cancer ... Current Problems in Cancer [*A publication*]
Curr Probl Cardiol ... Current Problems in Cardiology [*A publication*]
Curr Probl Clin Biochem ... Current Problems in Clinical Biochemistry [*A publication*]
Curr Probl Derm ... Current Problems in Dermatology [*A publication*]
Curr Probl Dermatol ... Current Problems in Dermatology [*A publication*]
Curr Probl Diagn Radiol ... Current Problems in Diagnostic Radiology [*A publication*]
Curr Probl Epilepsy ... Current Problems in Epilepsy [*A publication*]
Curr Probl Ped ... Current Problems in Pediatry [*A publication*]
Curr Probl Pediatr ... Current Problems in Pediatrics [*A publication*]
Curr Probl Rad ... Current Problems in Radiology [*A publication*]
Curr Probl Surg ... Current Problems in Surgery [*A publication*]
Curr P Surg ... Current Problems in Surgery [*A publication*]
Curr Psychiatr Ther ... Current Psychiatric Therapies [*A publication*]
Curr Psychol ... Current Psychology [*A publication*]
Curr Psychol Res ... Current Psychological Research [*A publication*]

Curr Psychol Res & Rev ... Current Psychological Research and Reviews [*A publication*]
Curr Psychol Res Rev ... Current Psychological Research and Reviews [*A publication*]
Curr Psychol Rev ... Current Psychological Reviews [*A publication*]
Curr Pulmonol ... Current Pulmonology [*A publication*]
Curr Radiol ... Current Radiology [*A publication*]
Curr Rep W Va Univ Agr Exp Sta ... Current Report. West Virginia University. Agricultural Experiment Station [*A publication*]
Curr Res ..... Current Research [*A publication*]
Curr Res Anesth Analg ... Current Researches in Anesthesia and Analgesia [*A publication*]
Curr Res Canc Chemoth ... Current Research in Cancer Chemotherapy [*A publication*]
Curr Res Geol Surv Isr ... Current Research. Geological Survey of Israel [*A publication*]
Curr Res Neth Biol ... Current Research in the Netherlands. Biology [*A publication*]
Curr Rev Agr Cond Can ... Current Review of Agricultural Conditions in Canada [*A publication*]
Curr Rev Nurse Anesth ... Current Reviews for Nurse Anesthetists [*A publication*]
Curr Rev Recov Room Nurses ... Current Reviews for Recovery Room Nurses [*A publication*]
Curr Rev Respir Ther ... Current Reviews in Respiratory Therapy [*A publication*]
Curr Sc .... Current Science [*A publication*]
Curr Sci ...... Current Science [*India*] [*A publication*]
Curr Sociol ... Current Sociology [*A publication*]
Curr Stud Hematol Blood Transfus ... Current Studies in Hematology and Blood Transfusion [*A publication*]
Curr Surg ... Current Surgery [*A publication*]
Curr Swed .. Current Sweden [*A publication*]
CURRT ...... Current (ROG)
Curr Theory Res Motiv Nebr Symp Motiv ... Current Theory and Research in Motivation. Nebraska Symposium on Motivation [*A publication*]
Curr Ther ... Current Therapy [*A publication*]
Curr Ther (Phila) ... Current Therapy (Philadelphia) [*A publication*]
Curr Ther R ... Current Therapeutic Research. Clinical and Experimental [*A publication*]
Curr Ther Res ... Current Therapeutic Research [*A publication*]
Curr Ther Res Clin Exp ... Current Therapeutic Research. Clinical and Experimental [*A publication*]
Curr Tit Electrochem ... Current Titles in Electrochemistry [*A publication*]
Curr Titles Electrochem ... Current Titles in Electrochemistry [*A publication*]
Curr Titles Turk Sci ... Current Titles in Turkish Science [*A publication*]
Curr T M ... Currents in Theology and Mission [*A publication*]
Curr Top Bioenerg ... Current Topics in Bioenergetics [*A publication*]
Curr Top Cell Regul ... Current Topics in Cellular Regulation [*A publication*]
Curr Top Chin Sci Sect D Biol ... Current Topics in Chinese Science. Section D. Biology [*A publication*]
Curr Top Chin Sci Sect G Med Sci ... Current Topics in Chinese Science. Section G. Medical Science [*A publication*]
Curr Top Clin Chem ... Current Topics in Clinical Chemistry [*A publication*]
Curr Top Comp Pathobiol ... Current Topics in Comparative Pathobiology [*A publication*]
Curr Top Crit Care Med ... Current Topics in Critical Care Medicine [*A publication*]
Curr Top Dev Biol ... Current Topics in Developmental Biology [*A publication*]
Curr Top Devel Biol ... Current Topics in Developmental Biology [*A publication*]
Curr Top Exp Endocrinol ... Current Topics in Experimental Endocrinology [*A publication*]
Curr Top Eye Res ... Current Topics in Eye Research [*A publication*]
Curr Top Hematol ... Current Topics in Hematology [*A publication*]
Curr Top Immunol Ser ... Current Topics in Immunology Series [*A publication*]
Curr Top Med Mycol ... Current Topics in Medical Mycology [*A publication*]
Curr Top Membranes Transp ... Current Topics in Membranes and Transport [*A publication*]
Curr Top Membr Transp ... Current Topics in Membranes and Transport [*A publication*]
Curr Top Microbiol Immunol ... Current Topics in Microbiology and Immunology [*A publication*]
Curr Top Mol Endocrinol ... Current Topics in Molecular Endocrinology [*A publication*]
Curr Top Neurobiol ... Current Topics in Neurobiology [*A publication*]
Curr Top Neuroendocrinol ... Current Topics in Neuroendocrinology [*A publication*]
Curr Top Nutr Dis ... Current Topics in Nutrition and Disease [*A publication*]
Curr Top Pathol ... Current Topics in Pathology [*A publication*]
Curr Top Radiat Res ... Current Topics in Radiation Research [*A publication*]
Curr Top Radiat Res Q ... Current Topics in Radiation Research. Quarterly [*A publication*]
Curr Top Reprod Endocrinol ... Current Topics in Reproductive Endocrinology [*A publication*]
Curr Top Res Synapses ... Current Topics in Research on Synapses [*A publication*]

Curr Top Surg Res ... Current Topics in Surgical Research [*A publication*]
Curr Top Thyroid Res Proc Int Thyroid Conf ... Current Topics in Thyroid Research. Proceedings of the International Thyroid Conference [*A publication*]
Curr Top Vet Med ... Current Topics in Veterinary Medicine [*A publication*]
Curr Top Vet Med Anim Sci ... Current Topics in Veterinary Medicine and Animal Science [*A publication*]
Curr US Gov Per Mfiche ... Current US Government Periodicals on Microfiche [*A publication*]
Curr Work Hist Med ... Current Work in the History of Medicine [*A publication*]
Curry .... Curry's Reports [*6-19 Louisiana*] [*A publication*]   (DLA)
CURS .... Center for Urban and Regional Studies   (EA)
curs. .... Cursive   (BJA)
CURS BE .. Cursitor Baron of the Exchequer [*British*]   (ROG)
CUR SCACC ... Cursus Scaccarii [*Latin*]   (DLA)
CURS CAN ... Cursus Cancellariae [*Latin*]   (DLA)
Cur Scene ... Current Scene [*A publication*]
Cur Sci .... Current Science [*A publication*]
Cur Seni ..... [*Franciscus*] Curtius, Senior [*Deceased, 1495*] [*Authority cited in pre-1607 legal work*]   (DSA)
Cursos Congr Univ Santiago De Compostela ... Cursos y Congresos. Universidad de Santiago De Compostela [*A publication*]
Cur Stat ...... Curwen's Statutes of Ohio [*A publication*]   (DLA)
CURT .... Current
CURT .... Curtain   (MSA)
Curt .... Curteis' English Ecclesiastical Reports [*A publication*]   (DLA)
Curt .... Curtis' Circuit Court Reports [*United States*] [*A publication*]   (DLA)
Curt .... Curtis' Edition, United States Supreme Court Reports [*A publication*]   (DLA)
Curt Adm Dig ... Curtis' Admiralty Digest [*A publication*]   (DLA)
CURTAGE ... Current or Voltage
Curt CC ...... Curtis' United States Circuit Court Decisions [*A publication*]   (DLA)
Curt Cond .. Curtis' Edition, United States Supreme Court Reports [*A publication*]   (DLA)
Curt Cond Rep ... Curtis' Decisions of the United States Supreme Court [*A publication*]   (DLA)
Curt Conv .... Curtis' American Conveyancer [*A publication*]   (DLA)
Curt Cop ..... Curtis' Copyright [*1847*] [*A publication*]   (DLA)
Curt Dec ..... Curtis' Decisions of the United States Supreme Court [*A publication*]   (DLA)
Curt Dig ..... Curtis' Digest [*United States*] [*A publication*]   (DLA)
Curt Ecc ..... Curteis' English Ecclesiastical Reports [*A publication*]   (DLA)
Curt Eccl .... Curteis' English Ecclesiastical Reports [*A publication*]   (DLA)
Curt Eccl (Eng) ... Curteis' English Ecclesiastical Reports [*A publication*]   (DLA)
Curt Eq Pr ... Curtis' Equity Precedents [*A publication*]   (DLA)
Curtis .... Curtis' Circuit Court Reports [*United States*] [*A publication*]   (DLA)
Curtis .... Curtis' Edition, United States Supreme Court Reports [*A publication*]   (DLA)
Curtis CC ... Curtis' United States Circuit Court Reports [*A publication*]   (DLA)
Curtis's Bot Mag New Ser ... Curtis's Botanical Magazine. New Series [*A publication*]
Curtis SC Reports ... Curtis' Decisions of the United States Supreme Court [*A publication*]   (DLA)
Curtis US Sup Ct R ... Curtis' Decisions of the United States Supreme Court [*A publication*]   (DLA)
Curt Jur ..... Curtis on the Jurisdiction of United States Courts [*A publication*]   (DLA)
Curt Pat ..... Curtis on Patents [*A publication*]   (DLA)
CURTS ...... Communications User Radio Transmission Sounding [*Navy*]
Curt US Const ... Curtis' History of the Constitution of the United States Courts [*A publication*]   (DLA)
Curt US Courts ... Curtis' Commentaries on the United States Courts [*A publication*]   (DLA)
CURV .... Cable-Controlled Underwater Research Vehicle
Curw .... Curwen's Overruled Cases [*Ohio*] [*A publication*]   (DLA)
Curw .... Curwen's Statutes of Ohio [*A publication*]   (DLA)
Curw LO .... Curwen's Laws of Ohio [*1 vol.*] [*1854*] [*A publication*]   (DLA)
Curw Ov Cas ... Curwen's Overruled Cases [*Ohio*] [*A publication*]   (DLA)
Curw RS ..... Curwen's Revised Statutes of Ohio [*A publication*]   (DLA)
CURY .... Bombay Palace Restaurants, Inc. [*New York, NY*] [*NASDAQ symbol*]   (NQ)
CUS .... Canadian Union of Students
Cus .... Cantus [*Record label*] [*Sweden*]
CUS .... Center for Urban Studies [*University of Chicago*] [*Research center*]   (RCD)
CUS .... Center for Urban Studies [*Wayne State University*] [*Research center*]   (RCD)
C (US) .... Cinema (United States) [*A publication*]
CUS .... Cities of the United States [*A publication*]
CUS .... Clean-Up System   (IEEE)
CUS .... Columbus, NM [*Location identifier*] [*FAA*]   (FAAL)
CUS .... Common User System [*Telecommunications*]   (TEL)
CUS .... Continental United States
CUS .... Course [*Ships*]   (CINC)

CUS .... Cusco [*Peru*] [*Seismograph station code, US Geological Survey*]   (SEIS)
cus .... Cushitic [*MARC language code*] [*Library of Congress*]   (LCCP)
CUS .... Customedix Corp. [*AMEX symbol*]   (SPSG)
CUS .... Customer Code [*Telecommunications*]   (TEL)
CUS .... University of California, San Diego, La Jolla, CA [*OCLC symbol*]   (OCLC)
CU-S .... University of California, San Diego, Main Library, La Jolla, CA [*Library symbol*] [*Library of Congress*]   (LCLS)
CUSA .... Catholics United for Spiritual Action   (EA)
CUSA .... Cavitron Ultrasonic Aspirator [*Medicine*]
CUSA .... Centrifugal Urine Separator Assembly [*Aerospace*]   (MCD)
CUSA .... Congress of Unions of South Africa
CUSAR ...... Commission on US-African Relations   (EA)
CUSARROTC ... Chief, United States Army Reserve and Reserve Officers Training Corps Affairs
CUSAT .... Customer Satisfaction
CU-SB .... University of California, Santa Barbara, Main Library, Santa Barbara, CA [*Library symbol*] [*Library of Congress*]   (LCLS)
CU-SC .... University of California, Santa Cruz, Main Library, Santa Cruz, CA [*Library symbol*] [*Library of Congress*]   (LCLS)
CUSCA .... Current Science [*India*] [*A publication*]
CUSCDP .... Chittagong University. Studies. Part II. Science [*A publication*]
CUSCLN .... Committee of United States Citizens Living in Nicaragua   (EA)
CUSCM ...... Center for US Capital Markets   (EA)
CUSE .... Computer Usage Co. [*NASDAQ symbol*]   (NQ)
CUSEC ...... Canada-United States Environmental Council   (EA)
CUSEC ...... Cubic Feet per Second
CUSEC ...... Czechoslovak-US Economic Council   (EA)
CUSEM ...... Computer Users Survival Electronic Magazine [*Information service or system*]   (IID)
CUSH .... Computer Users in Speech and Hearing   (EA)
Cush .... Cushing's Massachusetts Supreme Judicial Court Reports [*1848-53*] [*A publication*]   (DLA)
CUSH .... Cushion   (MSA)
CUSH .... Cushman Electronics, Inc. [*NASDAQ symbol*]   (NQ)
Cush .... Cushman's Reports [*23-29 Mississippi*] [*A publication*]   (DLA)
Cush Elec Cas ... Cushing's Election Cases in Massachusetts [*A publication*]   (DLA)
Cushing ...... Cushing's Reports [*1848-53*] [*A publication*]   (DLA)
Cush Law & Prac Leg Assem ... Cushing's Law and Practice of Legislative Assemblies [*A publication*]   (DLA)
Cush Leg Ass ... Cushing's Law and Practice of Legislative Assemblies [*A publication*]   (DLA)
Cushm .... Cushman's Reports [*23-29 Mississippi*] [*A publication*]   (DLA)
Cush Man .. Cushing's Manual of Parliamentary Law [*A publication*]   (DLA)
Cushman Found Foraminiferal Res Spec Publ ... Cushman Foundation for Foraminiferal Research. Special Publication [*A publication*]
Cushman Found Foram Research Contr ... Cushman Foundation for Foraminiferal Research. Contributions [*A publication*]
Cushman Found Foram Research Contr Special Pub ... Cushman Foundation for Foraminiferal Research. Contributions. Special Publication [*A publication*]
Cush (Mass) ... Cushing's Reports [*1848-53*] [*A publication*]   (DLA)
Cus Ho .... Customhouse
Cush Parl Law ... Cushing's Law and Practice of Legislative Assemblies [*A publication*]   (DLA)
Cush Rom Law ... Cushing's Study of the Roman Law [*A publication*]   (DLA)
Cush Trust Pr ... Cushing on Trustee Process [*A publication*]   (DLA)
CUSI .... Cusac Industries Ltd. [*NASDAQ symbol*]   (NQ)
CUSJ .... Citizens United for Safety and Justice [*Canada*]
CUSLAR ... Commission of United States Latin American Relations   (EA)
CusM .... Custom Microfilm Systems, Inc., Riverside, CA [*Library symbol*] [*Library of Congress*]   (LCLS)
CU-SM ...... University of California, San Diego, Biomedical Library, San Diego, CA [*Library symbol*] [*Library of Congress*]   (LCLS)
CUSMAP .. Conterminous United States Mineral Resource Assessment Program [*Department of the Interior*]
CUSNO ...... Customs Has Been Notified [*Aviation*]   (FAAC)
CUSO .... Canadian University Service Overseas
CU-SOCS ... University of California, Berkeley, Graduate Social Science Library, Berkeley, CA [*Library symbol*] [*Library of Congress*]   (LCLS)
CU-SOCW ... University of California, Berkeley, Social Welfare Library, Berkeley, CA [*Library symbol*] [*Library of Congress*]   (LCLS)
CUSP .... Central Unit for Scientific Photography [*Royal Aircraft Establishment*] [*British*]
CUSP .... Commonly Used System Programs [*Digital Equipment Corp.*]
CUSPAR ... Cusparia [*Angustura Bark*] [*Pharmacology*]   (ROG)
CUSQ .... Cultural Survival Quarterly [*A publication*]
CUSR .... Canada/United States Region   (NATG)
CUSR .... Central United States Registry [*Army*]
CUSRPG ... Canada-United States Regional Planning Group [*NATO*]
CUSS .... Centre for Urban and Social Studies [*Australia*]
CUSS .... Continental, Union, Shell, and Superior [*In CUSS I, ocean drilling barge named after oil companies that financed its development*]

CUSS......... Cooperative Union Serials System
CU-SSe...... University of California, San Diego, Science and Engineering Library, San Diego, CA [*Library symbol*] [*Library of Congress*] (LCLS)
CU-SSh ..... University of California, San Diego, Society-University Hospital, San Diego, CA [*Library symbol*] [*Library of Congress*] (LCLS)
CU-SSi....... University of California, San Diego, Scripps Institute of Oceanography, San Diego, CA [*Library symbol*] [*Library of Congress*] (LCLS)
CUSSN...... Computer Use in Social Services Network (EA)
CUSSR...... Commission on US-Soviet Relations (EA)
CUST........ Chicago Union Station Co. [*AAR code*]
CUST........ Custer Battlefield National Monument [*National Park Service designation*]
CUST........ Custodian [*Banking*] (AFM)
CUST........ Custody (AFM)
CUST........ Custom [*Automotive engineering*]
CUST........ Customer (MSA)
CUST........ Customs
Cust A .... United States Customs Appeals (DLA)
Cust App.... United States Customs Appeals (DLA)
Cust B & Dec ... Customs Bulletin and Decisions [*A publication*] (DLA)
Cust Bull ... Customs Bulletin [*A publication*] (DLA)
CUSTCT ... Customs Court
Cust Ct ...... Customs Court Reports [*United States*] [*A publication*] (DLA)
Cust Ct R ... Customs Court Rules [*A publication*] (DLA)
Cust D .... Customs Duties and Import Regulations [*A publication*] (DLA)
CUSTMY.. Customary (ROG)
CUSTOD... Custodian (ADA)
Customs ..... United States Customs Service [*A publication*] (DLA)
Custom Tar J ... Customs Tariff Schedule for Japan, 1986 [*A publication*]
Cust & Pat App (Cust) (F) ... Customs and Patent Appeals Reports (Customs) [*A publication*] (DLA)
Cust & Pat App (Pat) (F) ... Customs and Patent Appeals Reports (Patents) [*A publication*] (DLA)
Cust Pen Dec ... Customs Penalty Decisions [*A publication*] (DLA)
CUSTR...... Customer
Cust Rep .... Custer's Ecclesiastical Reports [*A publication*] (DLA)
CUSUM ... Cumulative Sum
CUSURDI ... Council of United States Universities for Rural Development in India
CUS & US ... Customs and Usages (DLA)
CUSUSSRI ... Center for US-USSR Initiatives (EA)
CUSUSWASH ... Council of United States Universities for Soil and Water Development in Arid and Sub-Humid Areas
CUT .... Canonical Unit of Time
CUT .... Church Universal and Triumphant (EA)
CUT .... Circuit under Test [*Electricity*] (IEEE)
CUT .... Come-Up Time [*Time required for a retort to reach operating conditions*]
CUT .... Control Unit Terminal [*Data processing*]
CUT .... Control Unit Tester [*Sperry UNIVAC*] (BUR)
CUT .... Coordinated Universal Time (NASA)
CUT .... Cross Utilization Training
CUT .... Curtin University of Technology [*Australia*]
CUT .... Custom Petroleum [*Vancouver Stock Exchange symbol*]
CUT .... Cutral-Co [*Argentina*] [*Airport symbol*] (OAG)
CUT .... Cutter [*Ship*]
CUT .... Hancock, MI [*Location identifier*] [*FAA*] (FAAL)
Cut............. Indian Law Reports, Orissa Series [*A publication*] (DLA)
CUT .... University of California, Santa Barbara, Santa Barbara, CA [*OCLC symbol*] (OCLC)
CUTA .... Canadian Urban Transit Association
CUTA .... Conduccion Unica de los Trabajadores Argentinos [*United Leadership of Argentinian Workers*] (PD)
CUTAS...... Committee on Uniform Traffic Accident Statistics [*Later, Traffic Records Committee*] (EA)
CUTBA..... Current Topics in Bioenergetics [*A publication*]
CUTC .... China United Trading Corporation [*Ministry of Foreign Economic Relations and Trade*] [*People's Republic of China*] (IMH)
CUTC .... Combat Unit Training Center [*Army*] (MCD)
CUTC .... Cutco Industries, Inc. [*NASDAQ symbol*] (NQ)
CUTE .... Canadian Union of Transportation Employees
CUTE .... Common Use Terminal Equipment [*Travel industry*]
CUTG .... Cutting
CUTH........ Council of University Teaching Hospitals [*Defunct*] (EA)
CUTHB .... Cuthbert College (ROG)
CUTHE ..... Canadian University Teachers of Home Economics [*See also PEDUC*]
CUTIE....... Coolest Ultra Tiny Individuals on Earth [*Toy figures*] [*Mattel, Inc.*]
Cut Ins L .... Cutler's Insolvent Laws of Massachusetts [*A publication*] (DLA)
Cut Leg Sys ... Cutler's Legal System of the English, the Hindoos, Etc. [*A publication*] (DLA)
Cutler......... Reports of English Patent Cases [*1884*] [*A publication*] (DLA)
Cut LT........ Cuttack Law Times [*India*] [*A publication*] (DLA)
CuTM .... Currents in Theology and Mission [*A publication*]

Cut Nat ...... Cutler on Naturalization Laws [*A publication*] (DLA)
Cut Pat Cas ... Cutler's Trademark and Patent Cases [*A publication*] (DLA)
CUTS........ Cassette User Tape System
CUTS........ Computer Utilized Turning System [*Warner & Swasey*]
CUTS........ Cut Stone
Cuttington Res J ... Cuttington Research Journal [*A publication*]
Cutting Tool Eng ... Cutting Tool Engineering [*A publication*]
Cutt LT ...... Cuttack Law Times [*India*] [*A publication*] (DLA)
Cut Tool En ... Cutting Tool Engineering [*A publication*]
CUTVC...... Clean Up TV Campaign (EA)
CUU.......... Calnor Resources Ltd. [*Vancouver Stock Exchange symbol*]
CUU.......... Chihuahua [*Mexico*] [*Airport symbol*] (OAG)
CU-UARC ... University of California, Berkeley, Archives Collection, Berkeley, CA [*Library symbol*] [*Library of Congress*] (LCLS)
CU-UC...... University of California, Union Catalog, Berkeley, CA [*Library symbol*] (LCLS)
CUUCV ...... Cultura Universitaria. Universidad Central de Venezuela [*A publication*]
CU-UNDE ... University of California, Berkeley, Moffitt Undergraduate Library, Berkeley, CA [*Library symbol*] [*Library of Congress*] (LCLS)
CUUP .... Ottawa/Uplands, Canadian Forces Base ON [*ICAO location identifier*] (ICLI)
CUV.......... Commercial Utility Vehicle
CUV.......... Construction Unit Value (DCTA)
CUV.......... Cuvier Mines, Inc. [*Toronto Stock Exchange symbol*]
CUV.......... University of California, Davis, Shields Library, Davis, CA [*OCLC symbol*] (OCLC)
CUVA .... [*The*] Cuyahoga Valley Railway Co. [*AAR code*]
Cuvas Gos Ped Inst Ucen Zap ... Cuvasskii Gosudarstvennyi Pedagogiceskii Institut Imeni I. Ja. Jakovleva Ucenye Zapiski [*Cheboksary*] [*A publication*]
Cuvas Gos Univ I Cuvas Gos Ped Inst Ucen Zap ... Cuvasskii Gosudarstvennyi Universitet Imeni I. N. Ul'janova Cuvasskii Gosudarstvennyi Pedagogiceskii Institut Imeni I. Ja. Jakovleva Ucenyi Zapiski [*A publication*]
CuW .... Christentum und Wissenschaft [*Leipzig*] [*A publication*]
CUW.......... CNI-Computer Networks International Ltd. [*Vancouver Stock Exchange symbol*]
CUW.......... Colorado-Utah-Wyoming Committee, Chicago IL [*STAC*]
CUW.......... Committee on Undersea Warfare
CUWPL..... Columbia University. Working Papers in Linguistics [*A publication*]
CU-WR...... University of California, Berkeley, Water Resources Center Archives, Berkeley, CA [*Library symbol*] [*Library of Congress*] (LCLS)
CUWS .... Cask Unloading Warm Shop [*Nuclear energy*] (NRCH)
CUWTF..... Combined Unconventional Warfare Task Force (CINC)
CUX.......... Casau Explorations Ltd. [*Vancouver Stock Exchange symbol*]
CUX.......... Corpus Christi, TX [*Location identifier*] [*FAA*] (FAAL)
CUX.......... University of California, Davis, Health Sciences Library, Davis, CA [*OCLC symbol*] (OCLC)
CUY.......... Cutty Resources, Inc. [*Vancouver Stock Exchange symbol*]
CUY.......... University of California, Berkeley, Berkeley, CA [*OCLC symbol*] (OCLC)
CUYD........ Cubic Yard
CUZ........... Broken Bow, NE [*Location identifier*] [*FAA*] (FAAL)
CUZ........... Capilano Resources, Inc. [*Vancouver Stock Exchange symbol*]
CUZ........... Cuzco [*Peru*] [*Airport symbol*] (OAG)
CUZ........... University of California, Santa Cruz, Santa Cruz, CA [*OCLC symbol*] (OCLC)
CUZZ .... Cousins Home Furnishings, Inc. [*NASDAQ symbol*] (NQ)
CV .... Aircraft Carrier [*Navy symbol*]
CV .... Calorific Value [*of a fuel*]
C(V) .... Capacitance as a Function of Voltage (IEEE)
cv .... Cape Verde [*Islands*] [*MARC country of publication code*] [*Library of Congress*] (LCCP)
CV .... Cape Verde [*ANSI two-letter standard code*] (CNC)
CV .... Cardiff Valleys [*Welsh depot code*]
CV .... Cardinal Virtues [*Freemasonry*] (ROG)
CV .... Cardiovascular [*Medicine*]
CV .... Career Vitae [*Job applications*] (DCTA)
CV .... Cargolux Airlines International [*Luxembourg*] [*ICAO designator*] (FAAC)
CV .... Caritas. Zeitschrift des Schweizerischen Caritasverbandes [*A publication*]
C de V .... Carte de Visite [*Visiting Card*] [*French*]
CV .... Cataclysmic Variable [*Astronomy, physics*]
cv .... Cavalo-Vapor [*Horsepower*] [*Portuguese*]
CV .... Cave (ROG)
CV .... Cell Volume [*Hematology*]
CV .... Cellular Ventures, Inc. [*Atlanta, GA*] [*Telecommunications*] (TSSD)
CV .... Central Vein [*or Venous*] [*Anatomy*]
CV .... Central Vermont Public Service Corp. [*NYSE symbol*] (SPSG)
CV .... Central Vermont Railway, Inc. [*AAR code*]
CV .... Cerebrovascular [*Medicine*]
CV .... Cerf-Volant [*A publication*]
C/V .... Certificate of Value (DS)
CV .... Cervical Vertebra [*Medicine*]

CV .... Cervico [*Vertical*] [*Medicine*]   (ROG)
CV .... Chairman of Volunteers [*Red Cross*]
CV .... Check Valve
CV .... Cheval-Vapeur [*Horsepower*] [*French*]
CV .... Chief Value
CV .... Chikungunya Virus
CV .... Christian Voice   (EA)
CV .... Circular Vection [*Optics*]
CV .... Citta di Vita [*A publication*]
CV .... Civilta Fascista [*A publication*]
CV .... Classical Views [*A publication*]
CV .... Closing Volume [*Physiology*]
CV .... Code Variante [*Codification*]   (NATG)
CV .... Coefficient of Variation [*Mathematics*]
CV .... Colla Voce [*With the Voice*] [*Music*]
CV .... Collection Voucher
CV .... Color Vision [*Ophthalmology*]
CV .... Combat Vehicle [*Army*]
CV .... Command Vehicle
CV .... Command Verification [*NASA*]
CV .... Commanditaire Vennootschap [*Limited Partnership*] [*Dutch*] [*Business term*]
CV .... Commentationes Vindobonenses [*A publication*]
CV .... Commercial Value
CV .... Common Version [*Bible*]
CV .... Communio Viatorum [*Prague*] [*A publication*]
CV .... Compact Video
cv .... Compte Vieux [*Old Account*] [*French*] [*Business term*]
CV .... Computer Vision
CV .... Computervision [*Commercial firm*] [*British*]
CV .... Conduction Velocity [*Neurology*]
CV .... Confraternity Version   (BJA)
CV .... Conjugata Vera [*Conjugate diameter of pelvic inlet*] [*Anatomy*]
CV .... Connersville, IN [*Location identifier*] [*FAA*]   (FAAL)
CV .... Consonant-Vowel
CV .... Constant Value
CV .... Constant Velocity
CV .... Constant-Viscosity [*Rubber*]
CV .... Constant Volume
CV .... Constitution of Virginia [*A publication*]   (DLA)
CV .... Continuous Vulcanization
CV .... Continuously Variable
CV .... Contrast Value
CV .... Contributing Value [*Shipping*]
CV .... Control Valve
CV .... Control Van [*Diving apparatus*]
CV .... Conventional
CV .... Conventional Ventilation [*Medicine*]
CV .... Conversational Voice [*Medicine*]
CV .... Converters [*Electronic*] [*JETDS nomenclature*] [*Military*]   (CET)
CV .... Convertible [*Stock exchange term*]   (SPSG)
CV .... Convertible [*Automotive engineering*]
CV .... Coronavirus
CV .... Corpuscular Volume [*Hematology*]
CV/ .... Cost Variance   (MCD)
C/V .... Coulombs per Volt
C and V ...... Counseling and Values [*A publication*]
CV .... Counter Voltage
CV .... Cove
CV .... Cras Vespere [*Tomorrow Evening*] [*Pharmacy*]
CV .... Cresyl Violet [*Biological stain*]
CV .... Crkoven Vestnik [*A publication*]
CV .... Cross of Valour [*Military award*] [*Canada*]
CV .... Cruise Vehicle [*Military*]   (AFM)
CV .... Crystal Violet [*An indicator*] [*Chemistry*]
CV .... Cult of the Virgin   (EA)
cv .... Cultivar [*Cultural Variety*] [*Biology*]
CV .... Curriculum Vitae [*Job applications*]
CV .... Cyclic Voltammetry [*Analytical electrochemistry*]
cv .... Cylindrical Vertical Tank [*Liquid gas carriers*]
CV .... General Dynamics Corp. [*ICAO aircraft manufacturer identifier*]   (ICAO)
CV .... Luttenberg's Chronologische Verzameling [*A publication*]
CV .... Single Cotton Varnish [*Wire insulation*]   (AAG)
CV .... Station Open Exclusively to the Correspondence of a Private Agency [*ITU designation*]   (CET)
CV .... Vallejo Public Library, Vallejo, CA [*Library symbol*] [*Library of Congress*]   (LCLS)
CVA .... Attack Aircraft Carrier [*Navy symbol*]
CVA .... Cardiovascular Accident [*Medicine*]   (DHSM)
CVA .... Cerebrovascular Accident [*Medicine*]
CVA .... Chance Vought Aircraft, Inc. [*Obsolete*]
CVA .... Columbia Valley Authority
CVA .... Committee for the Visual Arts [*Later, CVAAS*]   (EA)
CVA .... Commonwealth Veterinary Association
CVA .... Consecutive-Valve Actuation [*Nuclear energy*]   (NRCH)
CVA .... Constant Velocity Alignment [*Drive system coupling*]
CVA .... CONVAIR [*Consolidated-Vultee Aircraft Corp.*] Astronautics Corp. [*Later, General Dynamics Corp.*]   (AAG)

CVA .... Cordova [*Alaska*] [*Seismograph station code, US Geological Survey*]   (SEIS)
CVA .... Corporate Value Associates [*Commercial firm*] [*British*]
CVA .... Corpus Vasorum Antiquorum [*A publication*]
CVA .... Costovertebral Angle [*Medicine*]
CVA .... Crown Victoria Association   (EA)
CVA .... Current Value Accounting
CVA .... Current Variable Attenuator
CVA .... Cyclophosphamide, Vincristine, Adriamycin [*Antineoplastic drug regimen*]
CVA .... Davenport, IA [*Location identifier*] [*FAA*]   (FAAL)
CVa .... Vacaville District Library, Vacaville, CA [*Library symbol*] [*Library of Congress*]   (LCLS)
CV-8A .... Cleared V-8 Juice Agar [*Microbiology*]
C 8VA .... Coll'Ottava [*With the Octave*] [*Music*]   (ROG)
CVAA .... Cold Vapor Atomic Absorption Spectrometry [*Also, CVAAS*]
CVAAS ...... Cold Vapor Atomic Absorption Spectrometry [*Also, CVAA*]
CVAAS ...... Committee for the Visual Arts/Artists Space   (EA)
CVA-BMP ... Cyclophosphamide, Vincristine, Adriamycin, BCNU [*Carmustine*], Methotrexate, Procarbazine [*Antineoplastic drug regimen*]
CVAC .... Consolidated-Vultee Aircraft Corporation [*Later, General Dynamics Corp.*]
CVAD .... Converter, Voltage, AC [*Alternating Current*] to DC [*Direct Current*]   (MCD)
CVAE........ Coordinated Vocational-Academic Education
CVAG .... Chelmsford Victims Action Trust [*Australia*]
C/VAL....... Control Valve [*Automotive engineering*]
CValA .... California Institute of the Arts, Valencia, CA [*Library symbol*] [*Library of Congress*]   (LCLS)
CVAN .... Attack Aircraft Carrier (Nuclear Propulsion) [*Navy symbol*]
CVAN .... CINCPAC [*Commander-in-Chief, Pacific*] Voice Automated Net   (NVT)
CVanA .... United States Air Force, Base Library, Vandenberg Air Force Base, CA [*Library symbol*] [*Library of Congress*]   (LCLS)
CVAS........ Configuration Verification and Accounting System
CVAST ...... Combat Vehicle Armament System Technology [*Army*]
CV-ASWM ... Carrier-Based Antisubmarine Warfare Module [*Navy*]   (CAAL)
CVB .... Canadian Vent Corp. [*Vancouver Stock Exchange symbol*]
CVB .... Castroville, TX [*Location identifier*] [*FAA*]   (FAAL)
CVB .... CCNU [*Lomustine*], Vinblastine, Bleomycin [*Antineoplastic drug regimen*]
CVB .... Chorionic Villi Biopsy [*Medicine*]
CVB .... Combined VHF [*Very-High-Frequency*]-Band
C & VB...... Convention and Visitors Bureau
CVB .... CVB Financial Corp. [*AMEX symbol*]   (SPSG)
CVB .... Large Aircraft Carrier [*Navy symbol*] [*Obsolete*]
CV-8B .... Cleared V-8 Juice Broth [*Microbiology*]
CVBC........ Cape Volunteer Bearer Corps [*British military*]   (DMA)
CVBC........ Chatto & Windus, Virago, Bodley Head, and Jonathan Cape Group [*Publishers*] [*British*]
CVBG .... Carrier Battle Group [*Navy*]
CVC .... Cablevision Systems Corporation [*AMEX symbol*]   (SPSG)
CVC .... Canadian Overseas Exploration [*Vancouver Stock Exchange symbol*]
CVC .... Carrier Virtual Circuit [*Telecommunications*]
CVC .... Central Venous Catheter [*Medicine*]
CVC .... Cesium Vapor Cathode
CVC .... Chemical and Volume Control [*Nuclear energy*]   (NRCH)
CVC .... Cholame Valley [*California*] [*Seismograph station code, US Geological Survey*]   (SEIS)
CVC .... Clovis-Carver Public Library, Clovis, NM [*OCLC symbol*]   (OCLC)
CVC .... Combat Vehicle Crewmen   (MCD)
CVC .... Committee for a Voluntary Census   (EA)
CVC .... Compact Video Cassette Recorder
CVC .... Conservative Victory Committee [*An association*]   (EA)
CVC .... Conserved Vector Current
CVC .... Consonant-Vowel-Consonant [*Cuneiform sign*]   (BJA)
CVC .... Contactless Vacuum Controller
CVC .... Convalescent Camp [*Military*]
CVC .... Cryogenic Vacuum Calorimeter
CVCC........ Compound Vortex Combustion Chamber [*Auto engine*]
CV/CC........ Constant Voltage/Constant Current [*IEEE*]
CVCF........ Citicorp Venture Capital Fund [*Investment term*]
CVCF........ Constant Voltage and Constant Frequency   (BUR)
CVCHD...... Chonnam Medical Journal [*A publication*]
CVCO........ Cavco Industries, Inc. [*NASDAQ symbol*]   (NQ)
CVCP........ Committee of Vice-Chancellors and Principals of the Universities of the United Kingdom [*British*]
CVCR........ Control Van Connecting Room   (NATG)
CVCS........ Cardiovascular Conditioning Suit [*Medicine*]
CVCS........ Chemical and Volume Control System [*Nuclear energy*]   (NRCH)
CVCUS...... Combat Vehicle Crewman Uniform System [*Army*]   (INF)
CVD........... Canova Resources Ltd. [*Vancouver Stock Exchange symbol*]
CVD........... Cardiovascular Disease [*Medicine*]
CVD........... Cash Versus Documents
CVD........... Chemical Vapor Deposition [*Coating technology*]
CVD........... Collagen Vascular Disease [*Medicine*]

CVD...........	Color Vision Deviate [*Ophthalmology*]
CVD...........	Column Valve Diaphragm
CVD...........	Communication Valve Development [*British*]
CVD...........	Conversion Industries, Inc. [*AMEX symbol*] (SPSG)
CVD...........	Countervailing Duty [*Customs*] (FEA)
CVD...........	Coupled Vibration Dissociation (IEEE)
CVD...........	Current-Voltage Diagram
cvd.............	Curved
CVD...........	Sisters of Bethany [*Roman Catholic religious order*]
CVDA.........	Converter, Voltage Discrete, AC [*Alternating Current*] (NASA)
CVDE........	CVD Equipment Corp. [*Deer Park, NY*] [*NASDAQ symbol*] (NQ)
CVDP.........	Coupled Vibration Dissociation Process
CVDS........	Cardiovascular Disease Study [*British*]
CVDV........	Coupled Vibration Dissociation Vibration (IEEE)
CVE...........	Cahiers Victoriens et Edouardiens [*A publication*]
CVE...........	Calibration Vibration Exciter
CVE...........	Central Pulmonary Vessels Enlargement [*Medicine*]
CVE...........	Coatesville, PA [*Location identifier*] [*FAA*] (FAAL)
CVE...........	Complete Verification Record (MCD)
CVE...........	Complex Vehicle Erector (KSC)
CVE...........	COMSAT [*Communications Satellite Corp.*] Video Enterprises [*Washington, DC*] (TSSD)
CVE...........	Continuously Variable, for Emergency
CVE...........	Conversion Industries, Inc. [*Vancouver Stock Exchange symbol*]
CVE...........	Customer-Vended Equipment (AAG)
CVE...........	Escort Aircraft Carrier [*Navy symbol*]
CVEGA......	Civil Engineering [*A publication*]
CVEH........	Combat Vehicle [*Army*] (AABC)
CVen.........	Canes Venatici [*Constellation*]
CVer..........	Vernon Public Library, Vernon, CA [*Library symbol*] [*Library of Congress*] (LCLS)
C Verd Isls ...	Cape Verde Islands
CVETAA...	Communicationes Veterinariae [*A publication*]
CVETB......	Civil Engineering Transactions. Institution of Engineers of Australia [*A publication*]
CVEVDJ ...	Contributions to Vertebrate Evolution [*A publication*]
CVF...........	Calvi [*Corsica*] [*Seismograph station code, US Geological Survey*] (SEIS)
CVF...........	Castle Convertible Fund, Inc. [*AMEX symbol*] (SPSG)
CVF...........	Central Visual Field [*Optics*]
CVF...........	Circular Variable Filter [*Instrumentation*]
CVF...........	Cobra Venom Factor [*Immunochemistry*]
CVF...........	Continuously Variable Filter [*Spectrometry*]
CVF...........	Controlled Visual Flight
CvF............	Conversion Factor
CVF...........	Correspondent Validity File [*IRS*]
CVF...........	Courchevel [*France*] [*Airport symbol*] (OAG)
CVFC.........	Concord Video and Film Council (EAIO)
CV/FES.....	Children's Version/Family Environment Scale [*Child development test*] [*Psychology*]
CVFM........	Cyclophosphamide, Vincristine, Fluorouracil, Methotrexate [*Antineoplastic drug regimen*]
CVFR.........	Cancel Visual Flight Rules Flight Plan [*Aviation*] (FAAC)
CVFR.........	Controlled Visual Flight Rules [*Military*]
CVFS.........	Cesium Vapor Feed System
CVFS.........	Circular Variable Filter Spectrometer
CVG...........	Carrier Air Group [*Navy*] (MUGU)
CVG...........	Cincinnati [*Ohio*] [*Airport symbol*] (OAG)
CVG...........	Cincinnati [*Ohio*] - Covington [*Kentucky*] [*Airport symbol*]
CVG...........	Constructive Variational Geometry [*Data processing*]
CVG...........	Coronary Vein Graft [*Medicine*]
CVG...........	Covington, KY/Cincinnati, OH [*Location identifier*] [*FAA*] (FAAL)
CVGE........	Coverage
CVGI.........	[*The*] Congress Video Group, Incorporated [*New York, NY*] [*NASDAQ symbol*] (NQ)
CVGK........	Customs Value per Gross Kilogram (DS)
CVGMAX ...	Citrus and Vegetable Magazine [*A publication*]
CVGP.........	Customs Value per Gross Pound (DS)
CVGT........	Convergent, Inc. [*NASDAQ symbol*] (NQ)
CVH...........	Aircraft Carrier, Helicopter [*NATO*]
CVH...........	Calvada Resources [*Vancouver Stock Exchange symbol*]
CVH...........	Compound Valve Hemispherical Head [*Engine*]
CVH...........	Containment Vent Header [*Nuclear energy*] (NRCH)
CVHA........	Assault Helicopter Aircraft Carrier [*Navy symbol*] [*Obsolete*]
CVHC.........	Coastal Helicopter Aircraft Carrier [*Ship symbol*] (NATG)
CVHE.........	Escort Helicopter Aircraft Carrier [*Navy symbol*]
CVHEE	Coalition for Vocational Home Economics Education (EA)
CVHQ.........	Central Volunteer Headquarters [*Military*] [*British*]
CV-HRU.....	Combat Vehicle - Heading Reference Unit
CVHT........	Continuously Variable Hydromechanical Transmission [*Engineering*]
CVI...........	Cape Verde Islands
CVI...........	Cardiovascular Institute [*Boston University*] [*Research center*] (RCD)
CVI...........	Central Vehicle Index [*Record of cars lost or stolen in London*]
CVI...........	Cerebrovascular Insufficiency [*Medicine*]
CVI...........	Certified Vendor Information (NRCH)
CVI...........	Chemical Vapor Infiltration [*Materials science*]
CVI...........	Cholera Vaccine Immunization [*Medicine*]
CVI...........	Cofield, NC [*Location identifier*] [*FAA*] (FAAL)
CVI...........	College of the Virgin Islands
CVI...........	Colorado Video, Incorporated
CVI...........	Common Variable Immunodeficiency [*Medicine*]
CVI...........	Competitive Voluntary Indefinite [*Status*] [*Army*] (INF)
CVI...........	Conditional Voluntary Indefinite [*Status*] [*Army*] (INF)
CVI...........	Configuration Verification Index
CVI...........	Containment Ventilation Isolation [*Nuclear energy*] (NRCH)
CVI...........	Current Variable Inductor
CVI...........	CV REIT, Inc. [*NYSE symbol*] (SPSG)
CVI...........	Printing World [*A publication*]
CVi...........	Visalia Public Library, Visalia, CA [*Library symbol*] [*Library of Congress*] (LCLS)
CVIA.........	Computer Virus Industry Association (EA)
CVIC.........	Aircraft Carrier Intelligence Center (NVT)
CVIC.........	Conditional Variable Incremental Computer (IEEE)
CViCL........	Tulare County Free Library, Visalia, CA [*Library symbol*] [*Library of Congress*] (LCLS)
CViCS........	College of the Sequoias, Visalia, CA [*Library symbol*] [*Library of Congress*] (LCLS)
C Vict	Dominion of Canada Statutes in the Reign of Victoria [*A publication*] (DLA)
CViKD	Kaweah Delta District Hospital, Visalia, CA [*Library symbol*] [*Library of Congress*] (LCLS)
C VINAR...	Cyathus Vinarius [*Wineglassful*] [*Pharmacy*] (ROG)
C Vind	Commentationes Vindobonenses [*A publication*]
CVIS.........	Computerized Vocational Information System [*Guidance program*]
cVit............	Chicken Vitellogenin
CVIU.........	Computer Vision and Understanding
CViVC	Visalia Community Counseling Center, Visalia, CA [*Library symbol*] [*Library of Congress*] (LCLS)
CVJ...........	Continuous Velocity Joint [*Automotive engineering*]
CVK...........	Centerline Vertical Keel
CVK...........	Cherokee Village, AR [*Location identifier*] [*FAA*] (FAAL)
CVK...........	Consolidated Amhawk Enterprise [*Vancouver Stock Exchange symbol*]
CVKI.........	Combat Vehicle Kill Indicator (MCD)
CVKI-PD...	Combat Vehicle Kill Indicator Pyrotechnic Device (MCD)
CVL...........	Calcutta Volunteer Lancers [*British military*] (DMA)
CVL...........	Cape Vogel [*Papua New Guinea*] [*Airport symbol*] (OAG)
CVL...........	Central Veterinary Laboratory [*Research center*] [*British*] (IRC)
CVL...........	Cenvill Development Corp. A [*AMEX symbol*] (SPSG)
CVL...........	Civil (MSA)
CVL...........	Colville River, AK [*Location identifier*] [*FAA*] (FAAL)
CVL...........	Computer Vision Laboratory [*University of Maryland*] [*Research center*] (RCD)
CVL...........	Configuration Verification List (MCD)
CVL...........	Crystal Violet Lactone [*Organic chemistry*]
CVL...........	Small Aircraft Carrier [*Navy symbol*]
CVLA........	Coosa Valley Librarians Association [*Library network*]
CVL/CVE ...	Light/Escort Carrier [*Ship symbol*] (NATG)
CVLD........	Combat Vehicle LASER Detector Assembly (MCD)
CVLG........	Guided Missile Light Aircraft Carrier (MCD)
CVLGN	Nuclear-Powered Guided Missile Light Aircraft Carrier (MCD)
CVLI.........	Cash Value Life Insurance
CVLN........	Nuclear-Powered Light Aircraft Carrier (MCD)
CVLS.........	Central Vacuum Loading System
CVM...........	Alton, IL [*Location identifier*] [*FAA*] (FAAL)
CVM...........	California Maritime Academy, Vallejo, CA [*Library symbol*] [*Library of Congress*] (LCLS)
CVM...........	Capacitance Voltage Measurements (MCD)
CVM...........	Cardiovascular Monitor [*Medicine*]
CVM...........	Central Vehicle Monitoring [*Automotive engineering*]
CVM...........	Ciudad Victoria [*Mexico*] [*Airport symbol*] (OAG)
CVM...........	Cluster Variation Method [*Physics*]
CVM...........	COBOL [*Common Business-Oriented Language*] Virtual Machine
CVM...........	College of Veterinary Medicine [*University of Florida*] [*Research center*] (RCD)
CVM...........	Comissao de Valores Mobiliarios [*Equity Shares Commission*] [*Portuguese*]
CVM...........	Consumable Vacuum Melt [*Steel*]
CVM...........	Contingent Value Method [*Pisciculture*]
CVM...........	Control Valve Module (NASA)
CVM...........	Council for a Volunteer Military [*Defunct*] (EA)
CVM...........	Cramer - von Mises Test [*Statistics*]
CVM...........	Cyclophosphamide, Vincristine, Methotrexate [*Antineoplastic drug regimen*]
CVM...........	Cylindrical Vibration Mount
CVMA	Canadian Veterinary Medical Association (EAIO)
CVMAS.....	Continuously Variable Mechanical Advantage Shifter
CVMI........	Commercial Vehicle Maintenance Implications (MCD)
CVMO........	Commercial Value Movement Order (DCTA)
CVMP........	Combat Vehicle Maintenance Policy Study
CVMP........	Committee on Veterans Medical Problems [*US*]
CVN...........	Aircraft Carrier, Nuclear Propulsion [*Navy symbol*] (NVT)
CVN...........	C & S Sovran Corp. [*NYSE symbol*] (SPSG)
CVN...........	Cable Value Network [*Television*]

CVn .... Canes Venatici [*Constellation*]
CVN .... Carl Vinson Nuclear Powered Carrier [*DoD*]
CVN .... Casualty Vulnerability Number
CVN .... Change Verification Notice
CVN .... Charpy V-Notch [*Nuclear energy*]   (NRCH)
CVN .... CINCPAC Voice Alert Net   (MCD)
CVN .... Clovis [*New Mexico*] [*Airport symbol*]   (OAG)
CVN .... Clovis, NM [*Location identifier*] [*FAA*]   (FAAL)
CVN .... Construction Verification Notification [*Nuclear energy*]   (NRCH)
CVN .... Convene   (AABC)
CVN .... Courvan Mining Company Ltd. [*Toronto Stock Exchange symbol*]
CVnCR ...... Carnation Research Laboratories, Van Nuys, CA [*Library symbol*] [*Library of Congress*]   (LCLS)
CVnITT ..... International Telephone & Telegraph Corp., Gilfillan Division, Engineering Library, Van Nuys, CA [*Library symbol*] [*Library of Congress*]   (LCLS)
CVnL .... Los Angeles Valley College, Van Nuys, CA [*Library symbol*] [*Library of Congress*]   (LCLS)
CVNPA ...... Carolinas-Virginia Nuclear Power Associates, Inc.
CVnRCAM ... Radio Corp. of America, West Coast Missile & Surface RADAR Division, Van Nuys, CA [*Library symbol*] [*Library of Congress*]   (LCLS)
CVNS .... Conveyance News [*A publication*]
CVNTL .... Conventional   (MSA)
CVO .... Cascades Volcano Observatory [*US Geological Survey*]
CVO .... Certificate of Value and Origin   (DS)
CVO .... Chevy Oil Corp. [*Vancouver Stock Exchange symbol*]
CVO .... Chief Veterinary Officer [*Ministry of Agriculture, Fisheries, and Food*] [*British*]
CVO .... Commander of the Royal Victorian Order [*British*]
CVO .... Communications Validating Office   (CET)
CVO .... Conjugata Vera Obstetrica [*Conjugate diameter of pelvic inlet*] [*Anatomy*]
CVO .... Corvallis, OR [*Location identifier*] [*FAA*]   (FAAL)
CVOA .... Cosworth Vega Owner's Association   (EA)
C VOC ...... Colla Voce [*With the Voice*] [*Music*]
CVP .... Callao Caves [*Philippines*] [*Seismograph station code, US Geological Survey*]   (SEIS)
CVP .... Cardiovascular and Pulmonary Technology. Journal [*A publication*]
CVP .... Carma Ltd. [*Toronto Stock Exchange symbol*]
CVP .... Cell Volume Profile [*Hematology*]
CVP .... Central Valley Project [*California*]   (ECON)
CVP .... Central Venous Pressure [*Medicine*]
CVP .... Chemical Vapor Plating
CVP .... Christelijke Volkspartij [*Christian Social Party*] [*Also, PSC*] [*Belgium*] [*Political party*]   (PPW)
CVP .... Christlichdemokratische Volkspartei der Schweiz [*Christian Democratic Party of Switzerland*] [*Political party*]   (PPE)
CVP .... Christliche Volkspartei [*Christian People's Party*] [*Pre-1945 Germany*] [*Political party*]   (PPE)
CVP .... Climate, Vegetation, Productivity
CVP .... Consolidated Carma Corp. [*Toronto Stock Exchange symbol*]
CVP .... Containment Vacuum Pump [*Nuclear energy*]   (IEEE)
CVP .... Cost-Volume-Profit [*Analysis*]   (MCD)
CVP .... Covina Public Library, Covina, CA [*OCLC symbol*]   (OCLC)
CVP .... Crystal Violet-Pectate [*Microbiological medium*]
CVP .... Cyclophosphamide, Vincristine, Prednisone [*Also, COP*] [*Antineoplastic drug regimen*]
CVPC .... Control Valve Primary Coolant   (MCD)
CVPETS ..... Condenser Vacuum Pump Effluent Treatment System [*Nuclear energy*]   (NRCH)
CVP J Cardiovasc Pulm Technol ... CVP. Journal of Cardiovascular and Pulmonary Technology [*A publication*]
CVPP .... CCNU [*Lomustine*], Vinblastine, Prednisone, Procarbazine [*Antineoplastic drug regimen*]
CVPP .... Cyclophosphamide, Vinblastine, Procarbazine, Prednisone [*Antineoplastic drug regimen*]
CVPP-CCNU ... Cyclophosphamide, Vinblastine, Procarbazine, Prednisone, CCNU [*Lomustine*] [*Antineoplastic drug regimen*]
CVPR .... Combat Vehicle Program Review
CVPV .... Containment Vacuum Pump Valve [*Nuclear energy*]   (NRCH)
CVQ .... Carnarvon [*Australia*] [*Airport symbol*]   (OAG)
CVQ .... Coventry Ventures [*Vancouver Stock Exchange symbol*]
CVR .... Calaveras Reservoir [*California*] [*Seismograph station code, US Geological Survey*]   (SEIS)
CVR .... Cardiovascular-Renal [*Medicine*]
CVR .... Cardiovascular Respiratory System [*Medicine*]
CVR .... Carrier Vessel Reactor
CVR .... Ceramic Vacuum Relay
CVR .... Cerebrovascular Resistance [*Medicine*]
CVR .... Change Verification Record
CVR .... Chicago Rivet & Machine Co. [*AMEX symbol*]   (SPSG)
CVR .... Cockpit Voice Recorder
CVR .... Command Verification
CVR .... Command Voltage Regulator
CVR .... Computer Voice Response
CVR .... Configuration Verification Review   (MCD)
CVR .... Conservation Voltage Reduction [*Public Utilities Commission*]

CVR .... Constant Velocity Recording
CVR .... Constant Voltage Reference
CVR .... Continental Silver [*Vancouver Stock Exchange symbol*]
CVR .... Continuous Vertical Retort [*Metallurgy*] [*Fuel technology*]
CVR .... Contraceptive Vaginal Ring [*Gynecology*]
CVR .... Controlled Visual Rules [*FAA*]
CVR .... Coronary Vascular Resistance [*Medicine*]
CVR .... Cover
CVR .... Crystal Video Receiver
CVR .... Culver City, CA [*Location identifier*] [*FAA*]   (FAAL)
CVR .... Current Viewing Resistor
CVRC .... Consensus Voluntary Reference Compound [*Environmental science*]
CVRD .... Cardiovascular Renal Disease [*Medicine*]
CVRD .... Cardiovascular Respiratory Disease [*Medicine*]
CVR/D .... Command Verification/Drop
CVRD .... Converter, Variable Resistance, to DC [*Direct Current*] Voltage [*NASA*]
CVRD HPR ... Covered Hopper [*Freight*]
CVREAU ... Cardiovascular Research [*A publication*]
CVRI .... Cardiovascular Research Institute [*University of California, San Francisco*] [*Research center*]   (RCD)
CVRM .... Chemico-Viscous Remanent Magnetization [*Geophysics*]
CVRP .... Commercial Vehicle Repair Parts   (MCD)
CVRS .... Converse, Inc. [*NASDAQ symbol*]   (NQ)
CVRSN .... Conversion   (MSA)
CVR(T) ...... Combat Vehicle, Reconnaissance (Tracked) [*British military*]   (MCD)
CVRTC ...... Cardiovascular Research and Training Center [*University of Alabama in Birmingham*] [*Research center*]   (RCD)
CVRTC ...... Nora Eccles Harrison Cardiovascular Research and Training Center [*University of Utah*] [*Research center*]   (RCD)
CVR(W) ..... Combat Vehicle, Reconnaissance (Wheeled) [*British military*]   (DMA)
CVS .... ASW [*Antisubmarine Warfare*] Support Aircraft Carrier [*Navy symbol*]
CVS .... Calibration Verification Sample [*Spectroscopy*]
CVS .... Cardiovascular Surgery [*Medicine*]
CVS .... Cardiovascular System [*Medicine*]
CVS .... Center for Vietnamese Studies [*Southern Illinois University at Carbondale*] [*Research center*]   (RCD)
CVS .... Center for Visual Science [*University of Rochester*] [*Research center*]   (RCD)
CVS .... Center for a Voluntary Society [*Defunct*]   (EA)
CVS .... Challenge Virus Strain
CVS .... Chorionic Villi Sampling [*Medicine*]
CVS .... Classiques du XXe Siecle [*A publication*]
CVS .... Clean Voided Specimen [*Medicine*]
CVS .... Clovis, NM [*Location identifier*] [*FAA*]   (FAAL)
CVS .... Combat Vehicle Simulator   (MCD)
CVS .... Committee on Valuation of Securities
CVS .... Common Video System
CVS .... Community Volunteer Services Commission of B'nai B'rith International   (EAIO)
CVS .... Constant Voltage Source
CVS .... Constant Volume Sampling [*ACF Industries*]
CVS .... Consumer Value Stores
CVS .... Continuous Vent System   (KSC)
CVS .... Continuously Variable Stroke [*Automotive engineering*]
CVS .... Covert Viewing System
CVS .... Current Vital Signs [*Medicine*]
CVS .... Seaplane Carrier [*Navy symbol*] [*Obsolete*]
CVSA .... Commission on Voluntary Service and Action   (EA)
CVSC .... Community Volunteer Services Commission of B'nai B'rith International   (EA)
CVSC .... Control Valve Secondary Coolant   (MCD)
CVSCC ...... Coolant Vacuum Switch Cold Closed [*Automotive engineering*]
CVSD .... Continuously Variable Slope Delta Modulation [*Telecommunications*]
CVSDM ..... Continuously Variable Slope Delta Modulation [*Telecommunications*]   (TEL)
CVSG .... Carrier Antisubmarine Air Group [*Navy*]   (NVT)
CVSG .... Channel Verification Signal Generator
CVSI .... Conditional Value of Sample Information [*Statistics*]
CVSMO ..... Casopis Vlasteneckeho Spolku Musejniho v Olomouci [*A publication*]
CVSMOL .. Casopis Vlasteneckeho Spolku Musejniho v Olomouci [*A publication*]
CVSSUS ... Central Verband der Siebenburger Sachsen of the United States [*Later, Alliance of Transylvanian Saxons*]   (EA)
CVSU .... Cardiovascular Studies Unit [*University of Pennsylvania*] [*Research center*]   (RCD)
CVT .... Calvert Gas & Oils Ltd. [*Toronto Stock Exchange symbol*]
CVT .... Cavernous Sinus Thrombosis [*Medicine*]
CVT .... Center for Vocational and Technical Education, Ohio State University, Columbus, OH [*OCLC symbol*] [*Inactive*]   (OCLC)
CVT .... Central Vermont Railway, Inc.
CVT .... Chemical Vapor Transport
CVT .... Color Video Tape   (MCD)
CVT .... Command Verify/Transmit

CVT .... Communication Vector Table   (BUR)
CVT .... Concept Verification Test   (NASA)
CVT .... Configuration Verification Test
CVT .... Constant Velocity Transmission
CVT .... Constant Voltage Transformer
CVT .... Continuously Variable Transmission [*Of engines*]
CVT .... Controlled Variable Time [*Fuze*]   (NVT)
CVT .... Convert
CVT .... Convertible [*Stock exchange term*]
CVT .... Coventry [*England*] [*Airport symbol*]   (OAG)
CVT .... TCW Convertible Security Fund [*NYSE symbol*]   (SPSG)
CVT .... Training Aircraft Carrier [*Navy symbol*]
CVt .... Ventura County-City Free Library, Ventura, CA [*Library symbol*] [*Library of Congress*]   (LCLS)
c/vta .... Cuenta de Venta [*Sales Account*] [*Spanish*] [*Business term*]
CVTAE ...... Center for Vocational, Technical, and Adult Education [*University of Wisconsin - Stout*] [*Research center*]   (RCD)
CVtB .... Black Gold Cooperative Library System, Ventura, CA [*Library symbol*] [*Library of Congress*]   (LCLS)
CVtGS .... Church of Jesus Christ of Latter-Day Saints, Genealogical Society Library, Ventura Branch, Ventura, CA [*Library symbol*] [*Library of Congress*]   (LCLS)
CVTJA ...... Ceylon Veterinary Journal [*A publication*]
CVTR .... Carolinas-Virginia Tube Reactor
CVTR .... Charcoal Viral Transport [*Medium*] [*Microbiology*]
CVTRBC ... Connective Tissue Research [*A publication*]
CVTSC ...... Carrier-Based Tactical Support Center [*Navy*]   (NVT)
CVtV .... Ventura College, Ventura, CA [*Library symbol*] [*Library of Congress*]   (LCLS)
CVU .... Constant Voltage Unit
CVU .... Contact Ventures [*Vancouver Stock Exchange symbol*]
CVU .... Utility Aircraft Carrier [*Navy symbol*] [*Obsolete*]
CVUSA ...... Children's Village, USA [*of International Orphans Inc.*] [*Later, CVC*]   (EA)
CVV .... Aircraft Carrier, Medium Sized [*Navy symbol*]   (MCD)
CVV .... Charlottesville [*Virginia*] [*Seismograph station code, US Geological Survey*]   (SEIS)
CVV .... Control Variable Valve
CVVIDV .... Connaissance de la Vigne et du Vin [*A publication*]
CVW .... Attack Carrier Air Wing [*Navy symbol*]
CVW .... Consolidated General Western Industries Ltd. [*Vancouver Stock Exchange symbol*] [*Toronto Stock Exchange symbol*]
CVWA ...... Canadian Vintage Wireless Association [*Defunct*]   (EA)
CVWM ...... Combined Volume-Weighted Mean [*Statistics*]
CVWS .... Combat Vehicle Weapons System [*Army*]
CVWS(LR) ... Combat Vehicle Weapons System (Long-Range) [*Army*]
CVX .... Charlevoix, MI [*Location identifier*] [*FAA*]   (FAAL)
CVX .... Cleveland Electric Illuminating Co. [*NYSE symbol*]   (SPSG)
CVX .... Consolidated TVX Mining Corp. [*Toronto Stock Exchange symbol*]
CVX .... Convex   (MSA)
CVY .... Charlie/Victor/Yankee [*Military*]   (CAAL)
CVY .... Conventures Ltd. [*Toronto Stock Exchange symbol*]
CVY .... Fort Riley, KS [*Location identifier*] [*FAA*]   (FAAL)
CVZ .... Caara Ventures, Inc. [*Vancouver Stock Exchange symbol*]
CVZ .... Centralverein-Zeitung [*A publication*]   (BJA)
CVZOAW ... Congreso Venezolano de Cirugia [*A publication*]
CW .... Air Continental Ltd. [*Great Britain*] [*ICAO designator*]   (FAAC)
C & W .... Cable and Wireless Ltd. [*Telecommunications*]   (TEL)
CW .... Call Waiting [*Telephone communication*]
CW .... Camping Women   (EA)
CW .... Canada West
CW .... Canadian Welfare [*A publication*]
CW .... Carapace Width
CW .... Carcass Weight [*Animal husbandry*]
CW .... Cardiac Work [*Physiology*]
C and W ..... Carriage and Wagon Work [*British railroad term*]
CW .... Carrier Wave [*A form of radio transmission in code*]
C/W .... Carter-Wallace, Inc.
CW .... Casework [*or Caseworker*]
CW .... Catholic Workman   (EA)
CW .... Catholic World [*A publication*]
C & W .... Caution and Warning [*Aerospace*]   (KSC)
CW .... Cavity Wall
CW .... Cedar Waxwing [*Ornithology*]
CW .... Cell Wall
CW .... Chemical Warfare
CW .... Chemical Weapons
CW .... Chest Wall [*Medicine*]
CW .... Child Welfare
CW .... Children's Ward [*of a hospital*]
CW .... China Weekly [*A publication*]
CW .... Christ und Welt [*A publication*]
C & W .... Christentum und Wissenschaft [*A publication*]
CW .... Christliche Welt [*A publication*]
C-W .... Chronometer Time Minus Watch Time [*Navigation*]
CW .... Churchwarden
CW .... Circulating Water [*Nuclear energy*]   (NRCH)

CW .... Cities of the World [*A publication*]
CW .... Civil Works [*Assistant Secretary of the Army*]
CW .... Classical Weekly [*A publication*]
CW .... Classical World [*A publication*]
CW .... Classical Writers [*A publication*]
CW .... Clean Water   (IEEE)
CW .... Clifford & Wills [*Commercial firm*]
CW .... Clockwise
CW .... Clothes Washer
CW .... Coal-Water [*Fuel mixture*]
CW .... Coast Waiter [*Coast Guard*] [*British*]   (ROG)
CW .... Coin World [*A publication*]
CW .... Cold War   (CINC)
CW .... Cold Water [*Technical drawings*]
CW .... Cold Welding
CW .... Cold-Worked [*Nuclear energy*]   (NRCH)
CW .... [*The*] Colorado & Wyoming Railway Co. [*AAR code*]
CW .... Column Waste [*Nuclear energy*]   (NRCH)
CW .... Comfortably Weird [*In the record business, refers to a successful performer who has retained his individuality*]
CW .... Command Word [*Data processing*]   (MCD)
CW .... Commander's Office Writer [*British military*]   (DMA)
CW .... Commercial Weight
CW .... Commission and Warrant [*British military*]   (DMA)
Cw .... Commonwealth
C/W .... Complete With   (MSA)
CW .... Complied With   (AFIT)
CW .... Composite Wave   (IEEE)
CW .... Composite Wood [*A publication*]
CW .... Computer Wizard [*Information service or system*]   (IID)
CW .... Computerworld [*A publication*]
CW .... Concealed Weapons
CW .... Congress Watch   (EA)
CW .... Constant Wear   (KSC)
CW .... Continuous Wave [*A form of radio transmission*]
CW .... Continuous-Wound   (DEN)
CW .... Control Word   (MCD)
CW .... Conventional Wisdom [*Professional political opinion*]
cw .... Cook Islands [*MARC country of publication code*] [*Library of Congress*]   (LCCP)
CW .... Cooling Water [*Nuclear energy*]   (NRCH)
CW .... Copper Weld
CW .... Copywriting
CW .... Cotton or Wool [*Freight*]
C/W .... Counterweight   (AAG)
CW .... Counties (Wales)
CW .... Countries of the World [*A publication*]
C & W .... Country and Western [*Music*]
CW .... Coursewriter [*IBM Corp. programming language*]
CW .... Covers [*JETDS nomenclature*] [*Military*]   (CET)
CW .... Crawlerway [*NASA*]   (KSC)
CW .... Crutch Walking [*Medicine*]
CW .... Cubic Weight
C & W .... Cunningham & Walsh [*Advertising agency*]
CW .... Curtiss-Wright Corp. [*NYSE symbol*]   (SPSG)
CW .... Curtiss-Wright Corp. [*ICAO aircraft manufacturer identifier*]   (ICAO)
CW .... Cypher Writing [*Freemasonry*]   (ROG)
C & W .... Transactions. Cumberland and Westmorland Antiquarian and Archaeological Society [*A publication*]
CW2 .... Chief Warrant Officer 2 [*Army*]
CW3 .... Chief Warrant Officer 3 [*Army*]
CW4 .... Chief Warrant Officer 4 [*Army*]
CWA .... C. W. - Tariff Agency, Inc., Lansing MI [*STAC*]
CWA .... California Wheelchair Aviators   (EA)
CWA .... Canadian Western Approaches
CWA .... Caution and Warning Annunciator   (MCD)
CWA .... Central Wholesalers Association   (EA)
CWA .... Children's Wear Association   (EA)
CWA .... Chinese Women's Association   (EA)
CWA .... Civil Works Administration [*1933-1934*]
CWA .... Clean Water Act [*Environmental Protection Agency*]
CWA .... Clean Water Action [*An association*]   (EA)
CWA .... Clean Work Area [*NASA*]   (NASA)
CWA .... Coalition for Women's Appointments   (EA)
CWA .... Cockcroft-Walton Accelerator [*Physics*]
CWA .... Comedy Writers Association   (EA)
CWA .... Communication Workers Alliance [*Philippines*]
CWA .... Communications Workers of America   (EA)
CWA .... Concerned Women for America   (EA)
CWA .... Construction Writers Association   (EA)
CWA .... Container News [*A publication*]
CWA .... Contractor Work Authorization   (KSC)
CWA .... Control Word Address
CWA .... Controlled Work Area   (MCD)
CWA .... Country Women's Association
CWA .... Crime Writers' Association   (EAIO)
CWA .... Curtiss-Wright of Canada [*Toronto Stock Exchange symbol*]
CWA .... Customer Work Authorization   (AAG)
CWA .... Mosinee, WI [*Location identifier*] [*FAA*]   (FAAL)

CWA .... Wausau [*Wisconsin*] Central Wisconsin [*Airport symbol*] (OAG)
CWAA ...... Cotton Warehouse Association of America (EA)
CWAA ...... Country Women's Association of Australia
CWAA ...... Croatian Workers Association of America (EA)
CWABBA ... Canadian Western Amateur Bodybuilding Association
CWAC ...... Canadian Women's Army Corps
CWAD ...... Concurrent with Aircraft Delivery (MCD)
CWAF .... Combined Welfare Administration Fund
CWAG ...... Cold War Activities Group [*Military*] (CINC)
CWAHAT ... Commonwealth Bureau of Animal Health. Review Series [*A publication*]
Cwal .... Cwaliton [*Qualiton*], Swansea [*Record label*] [*Wales*]
CWAO ...... Coalition of Women's Art Organizations
CWAO ...... Montreal, PQ [*ICAO location identifier*] (ICLI)
CWAP .... Clean Water Action Project [*Later, CWA*] (EA)
CWAPAJ .. Commonwealth Bureau of Horticulture and Plantation Crops. Technical Communication [*A publication*]
CWAR ...... Continuous Wave Acquisition RADAR [*Military*]
CWAS .... Centre of West African Studies [*University of Birmingham*] [*British*] (CB)
CWAS .... Committee on Women in Asian Studies (EA)
CWAS .... Contractor's Weighted Average Share in Cost Risk [*Accounting*]
CWasB ...... Bioferm Corp., Research Library, Wasco, CA [*Library symbol*] [*Library of Congress*] (LCLS)
CWASP ..... Catholic White Anglo-Saxon Protestant
CWAT .... Continuous Wave Acquisition and Track (MCD)
CWats .... Watsonville Public Library, Watsonville, CA [*Library symbol*] [*Library of Congress*] (LCLS)
CWB .... Canadian Weekly Bulletin [*A publication*]
CWB .... Canadian Western Bank [*Toronto Stock Exchange symbol*]
CWB .... Canadian Wheat Board
CWB .... Canadian Wheat Board Library [*UTLAS symbol*]
CWB .... Center for Wooden Boats (EA)
CWB .... Central Welsh Board
CW & B ..... Cincinnati, Washington & Baltimore Railroad
CWB .... Coalition on Women and the Budget (EA)
CWB .... Curitiba [*Brazil*] [*Airport symbol*] (OAG)
CWB .... Czernowitzer Wochenblatt [*A publication*]
CWBA .... Chinese Women's Benevolent Association (EA)
CWBCNA ... Credit Women's Breakfast Clubs of North America [*Later, CPI*] (EA)
CWBF .... Battle Harbour, NF [*ICAO location identifier*] (ICLI)
CWBH .... Continuous Wage and Benefit History [*Unemployment insurance*]
CWBHP .... Center for the Well-Being of Health Professionals (EA)
CWBL .... Catholic Women's Benevolent Legion (EA)
CWBS .... Contract Work Breakdown Structure
CWBSAX .. Commonwealth Bureau of Soils. Technical Communication [*A publication*]
CWbT .... Chaldaeisches Woerterbuch ueber die Targumim [*A publication*] (BJA)
CWBW ...... Chemical Warfare - Bacteriological Warfare
CWC .... Calibrating Work Center (AFIT)
CWC .... Cam Wedge Clamp
CWC .... Canadian Wood Council
CWC .... Carpet Wool Council [*Defunct*]
CWC .... Catering Wages Commission [*British*] (DAS)
CWC .... Center on War and the Child (EA)
CWC .... Ceylon Workers' Congress (EAIO)
C & WC ..... Charleston & Western Carolina Railway Co. [*Seaboard Coast Line Railroad*]
CWC .... Charleston & Western Carolina Railway Co. [*Seaboard Coast Line Railroad*] [*AAR code*]
CWC .... Chemical Weapons Convention [*Proposed treaty*]
CWC .... Child Welfare Center [*British*] (DAS)
CWC .... Clear Write Condition
CWC .... Cold War Council
CWC .... Colorado Women's College [*Formerly, Temple Buell College*]
CWC .... Combined Wage Claim [*Unemployment insurance*]
CWC .... Comenius World Council (EA)
CWC .... Committee for Western Civilization (EA)
CWC .... Commonwealth Gold [*Vancouver Stock Exchange symbol*]
CWC .... Commonwealth of World Citizens
CWC .... Communication Workers of Canada
CWC .... Communications, Electronic, Technical, and Salaried Workers of Canada
CWC .... Competition with Confidence (AFIT)
CWC .... Composite Warfare Commander [*Military*] (NVT)
CWC .... Conventional [*Non-Nuclear*] War Capability (AAG)
CWC .... Cottonwood [*California*] [*Seismograph station code, US Geological Survey*] (SEIS)
CWC .... Council of Women Chiropractors (EA)
CWC .... Council of Women Citizens
CWC .... Country Whence Consigned [*Shipping*] (DS)
CWC .... Country Women's Council USA (EA)
CWC .... Curtiss-Wright Corporation
CWC .... National Committee for a Confrontation with Congress (EA)
CWC .... Whittier College, Whittier, CA [*OCLC symbol*] (OCLC)
CWCA .... Civil War Centennial Association
CW-Can Welf ... CW-Canadian Welfare [*A publication*]

CWCB .... Central Wisconsin Bankshares, Inc. [*NASDAQ symbol*] (NQ)
CWCBAL .. Connecticut Water Resources Bulletin [*A publication*]
CW/CBD ... Chemical Warfare/Chemical Biological Defense (RDA)
CWCC .... Capital Wire & Cable Corporation [*Plano, TX*] [*NASDAQ symbol*] (NQ)
CWCC .... Civil War Centennial Commission [*Terminated, 1966*]
CWCCA ..... Cardigan Welsh Corgi Club of America (EA)
CWCCI ..... Crayon, Water Color, and Craft Institute (EA)
CWcD .... Dow Chemical USA, Western Division Library, Walnut Creek, CA [*Library symbol*] [*Library of Congress*] (LCLS)
CWCDA ... Collected Works on Cardio-Pulmonary Disease [*A publication*]
CWCDAR ... Collected Works on Cardio-Pulmonary Disease [*A publication*]
CWCE .... Cold Weather Clothing and Individual Equipment [*Military*]
CWCG .... Cool Water Coal Gasification [*Fuel technology*]
CWCI .... Center for World Christian Interaction (EA)
CWCI .... CW Communications, Incorporated [*Publisher*]
CWCL .... Conspectus of Workers' Compensation Legislation [*Australia*] [*A publication*]
CWCMF .... Professor Chen Wen-Chen Memorial Foundation (EA)
CW/CMG ... CW Conference Management Group [*Framingham, MA*] [*Telecommunications service*] (TSSD)
CWCP .... Combat Wing Command Post
CWCP .... Contemporary Writers in Christian Perspective [*A publication*]
CWCS .... Combined Wheat Control Section [*Allied German Occupation Forces*]
CWCS .... Common Weapon Control System [*Military*]
CWCT .... [*A*] Child's Wish Come True (EA)
CWD .... Casualty Weapon Director
CWD .... Catchword
Cwd .... Catholic World [*A publication*]
CWD .... Cell Wall Defective [*Microbiology*]
CWD .... Civilian War Dead
CWD .... Cold-Water Detergent
CWD .... Concealed Weapon Detector
CWD .... Credit World [*A publication*]
CWD .... Creosoted Wood Duct [*Telecommunications*] (TEL)
CWD .... Crowder Communications Corp. [*Vancouver Stock Exchange symbol*]
CWD .... Current Wage Developments [*A publication*]
CWD .... Cyclotron Wave Device
CWDD .... Chemical Warfare Directional Detector [*Military*] (CAAL)
CWDE .... Centre for World Development Education [*Regent's College*] [*British*] (CB)
CWDE .... Chemical Warfare Defense Equipment
CWDF .... Central Waste Disposal Facility [*Oak Ridge National Laboratory*]
CWDI .... Craft World International, Inc. [*NASDAQ symbol*] (NQ)
CWDIC ..... Cooperative Weapons Data Indexing Committee [*AEC and DoD*]
CWDMA ... Canadian Window and Door Manufacturers Association
CWDP .... Casualty Weapon Director Panel
CWDR ...... Concurrent with Design Release (MCD)
C W Dud .... [*C. W.*] Dudley's Law [*or Equity*] Reports [*South Carolina*] [*A publication*] (DLA)
C W Dud Eq ... [*C. W.*] Dudley's South Carolina Equity Reports [*A publication*] (DLA)
C W Dudl Eq ... [*C. W.*] Dudley's South Carolina Equity Reports [*A publication*] (DLA)
CWDWD... Committee for World Development and World Disarmament [*Defunct*] (EA)
CWE .... Cactus West Explorations Ltd. [*Vancouver Stock Exchange symbol*]
CWE .... California Western School of Law Library, San Diego, CA [*OCLC symbol*] (OCLC)
CWE .... Caution and Warning Electronics (NASA)
CWE .... Caution and Warning Equipment [*NASA*] (KSC)
CWE .... Center for Water and Environment [*University of Minnesota*]
CWE .... Chemical Week [*A publication*]
CWE .... Cleared without Examination [*Business term*]
CWE .... Clerical Work Evaluation [*British*]
CWE .... Coated Wire Electrode [*Sensor*]
CWE .... Cockcroft-Walton Experiment [*Physics*]
CWE .... Coil Winding Equipment
CWE .... Commonwealth Edison Co. [*NYSE symbol*] (SPSG)
CWE .... Contractor's Work Estimate [*Military*]
CWE .... Current Working Estimate [*Military*]
CWE .... National Commission for Women's Equality (EA)
CWE .... Welen [*USSR*] [*Geomagnetic observatory code*]
CWEA .... Canadian Wind Engineering Association
CWEA .... Caution and Warning Electronics Assembly [*Apollo*] [*NASA*]
Cweal .... Commonweal [*A publication*]
Cwealth ...... Commonwealth [*A publication*]
Cwealth Agriculturist ... Commonwealth Agriculturist [*A publication*] (APTA)
Cwealth Eng ... Commonwealth Engineer [*A publication*] (APTA)
Cwealth Jeweller ... Commonwealth Jeweller and Watchmaker [*A publication*] (APTA)
Cwealth Jeweller and Watchmaker ... Commonwealth Jeweller and Watchmaker [*A publication*] (APTA)
Cwealth Pub Serv Board Bul ... Commonwealth Public Service Board. Bulletin [*A publication*] (APTA)

CWED ...... Conwed Corp. [*NASDAQ symbol*] (NQ)
CWEEA..... Cooperative Work Experience Education Association (EA)
CWeeC....... College of the Siskoyous, Weed, CA [*Library symbol*] [*Library of Congress*] (LCLS)
CWEG .... Edmonton, AB [*ICAO location identifier*] (ICLI)
CWEI........ Canadian Wood Energy Institute
CWEPT..... Cockpit Weapons Emergency Procedural Trainer [*Military*]
CWERA ..... Catholic Women for the ERA (EA)
CWERSI.... Committee on Women's Employment and Related Social Issues (EA)
CWeT .... Trinity County Free Library, Weaverville, CA [*Library symbol*] [*Library of Congress*] (LCLS)
CWEU .... Caution and Warning Electronics Unit (MCD)
CWF .... Career Women's Forum (EAIO)
CWF .... Charnwood Forest [*England*] [*Seismograph station code, US Geological Survey*] (SEIS)
CWF .... China First Capital [*Vancouver Stock Exchange symbol*]
CWF .... Christian Women's Fellowship (EA)
CWF .... Civilian Welfare Fund (AABC)
CWF .... Clean Water Fund [*An association*] (EA)
CWF .... Coal-Water Mixture Fuel
CWF .... Commonwealth Weightlifting Federation [*Ammanford, Dyfed, Wales*] (EAIO)
CWF .... Composite Wave Filter
CWF .... Consolidated Working Fund (OICC)
CWF .... Cornwell-Weisskopf Formula
CWF .... Crosswind Force
CWF2 .... Cornell Word Form 2 [*Psychology*]
CWFF .... Closed, Well-Formed Formula [*Logic*]
CWFHC ... Canadian Weightlifting Federation/Halterophile Canadienne
CWFI........ Children's Wish Foundation International (EA)
CWFM ..... Continuous Wave Frequency-Modulated (MSA)
CWFN ...... Canadian Wildlife and Fisheries Newsletter [*A publication*]
CWFO .... Catlow/Whitney Family Organization (EA)
CWFO .... Commercial Warehouse Field Officer [*Military*]
CWFRA ..... Commonwealth Forestry Review [*A publication*]
CWFRAG ... Commonwealth Forestry Review [*A publication*]
CWFS .... Crashworthy Fuel Systems [*Aviation*]
CWFSP....... Caution and Warning/Fire Suppression Panel (MCD)
CWG .... Campaign for World Government (EA)
CWG......... Caro-Wings Flight Service, Inc. [*Rock Hill, SC*] [*FAA designator*] (FAAC)
CWG......... Clayton, W. G., III, Buffalo NY [*STAC*]
CWG......... Closed Waveguide
CWG......... Colonial Waterbird Group [*Later, CWS*] (EA)
CWG......... Colostomy Welfare Group [*British*]
CWG......... Committee for Women in Geophysics [*Defunct*] (EA)
CWG......... Community of the Will of God [*Anglican religious community*]
CWG......... Conformal Wire Grating
CWG......... Consolidated Wellington Resources [*Vancouver Stock Exchange symbol*]
CWG......... Constant-Wear Garment [*Apollo*] [*NASA*]
CWG......... Continuous Wave Gas
CWG......... Corrugated Wire Glass [*Technical drawings*]
CWGA ...... Catholic Writers Guild of America (EA)
CWGC .... Commonwealth War Graves Commission [*Maidenhead, Berkshire, England*] (EAIO)
CWGEA .... Cooperative Whole Grain Education Association (EA)
CWGV ...... Chronik. Wiener Goetheverein [*A publication*]
CWH......... Canadian Warplane Heritage, Inc.
CWH......... Civil War History [*A publication*]
CWH......... Clarke, W. H., New York NY [*STAC*]
CWH......... Committee of the Whole House, House of Lords [*British*] (DLA)
CWH......... Huntsville, AL [*Location identifier*] [*FAA*] (FAAL)
CWh.......... Whittier Public Library, Whittier, CA [*Library symbol*] [*Library of Congress*] (LCLS)
CWhA .... American Potash & Chemical Corp., Whittier, CA [*Library symbol*] [*Library of Congress*] (LCLS)
CWhC .... Whittier College, Whittier, CA [*Library symbol*] [*Library of Congress*] (LCLS)
CWhC-L .... Whittier College, School of Law, Whittier, CA [*Library symbol*] [*Library of Congress*] (LCLS)
CWHFAO ... Contributions. New South Wales National Herbarium. Flora Series [*A publication*]
CWHJ .... Holberg, BC [*ICAO location identifier*] (ICLI)
CWHM...... Current Work in the History of Medicine [*A publication*]
CWHN ...... Church of What's Happening Now (EA)
CWhR .... Rio Hondo Junior College, Whittier, CA [*Library symbol*] [*Library of Congress*] (LCLS)
CWHS .... Continuous Work History Sample [*Department of Labor*]
CWHSS..... Coalition for Women in the Humanities and Social Sciences [*Defunct*] (EA)
CWHSSA ... Contract Work Hours and Safety Standards Act
CWHX ...... Bedford, NS [*ICAO location identifier*] (ICLI)
CWI .... Call Waiting Indication [*Telecommunications*] (TEL)
CWI .... Cardiac Work Index [*Physiology*]
CWI .... CCW System Ltd. [*Vancouver Stock Exchange symbol*]
CWI .... Chicago & Western Indiana Railroad Co. [*AAR code*]
CWI .... Child Welfare Institute (EA)
CWI .... Christian Witness International [*British*]

CWI .... Clean World International [*Brighton, East Sussex, England*] (EAIO)
CWI .... Clearinghouse on Women's Issues (EA)
CWI .... Clinton [*Iowa*] [*Airport symbol*] (OAG)
CWI .... Clinton, IA [*Location identifier*] [*FAA*] (FAAL)
CWI .... Coil Winding International Exhibition [*Great Britain*] (ITD)
CWI .... Commerce [*A publication*]
CWI .... Continuous Wave Illuminator (NG)
CWI .... Conventional Weapon Index (MCD)
CWI .... Country Workshops, Incorporated [*An association*] (EA)
CW-I .... Credit Women - International [*Later, CPI*] (EA)
CWI .... Cultural Work, Incorporated [*An association*] (EA)
CWI .... Decisions of the Commissioners under the National Insurance (Industrial Injuries) Acts Relating to Wales [*A publication*] (DLA)
CWIAU ..... Canadian Women's Intercollegiate Athletic Union
CWIC........ Chase World Information Corporation [*Information service or system*] (IID)
CWIC........ Clearinghouse on Women's Issues in Congress [*Later, CWI*] (EA)
CWIC........ Competition with Industrial Cooperation
CWID .... Coalition for Women in International Development (EA)
CWIF........ Continuous Wave Intermediate Frequency
CWII......... Communications World International, Inc. [*NASDAQ symbol*] (NQ)
CWIK........ Chemical World Index Key
CWIK........ Cutting with Intent to Kill
CWiN........ North State Cooperative Library System, Willows, CA [*Library symbol*] [*Library of Congress*] (LCLS)
CWINJ ...... Cold Weather Injury [*Military*]
CWIP........ Clerical Work Improvement Program [*British*]
CWIP........ Construction Work in Progress
CWIR .... Continuous Wave Illuminator RADAR [*Military*]
CWIR .... Victoria Marine Radio, BC [*ICAO location identifier*] (ICLI)
CWIS........ Cotton Warehouse Inspection Service [*Defunct*] (EA)
CWIS........ Council for Women in Independent Schools (EA)
CWIS/NPC ... Child Welfare Information Services/Non-Profit Computer Services [*Information service or system*] (IID)
CWIT........ Concordance Words in Titles [*Indexing*]
CWit .... Willits Public Library, Willits, CA [*Library symbol*] [*Library of Congress*] (LCLS)
CWiW........ Willows Public Library, Willows, CA [*Library symbol*] [*Library of Congress*] (LCLS)
CWiWCL... Glen County Library, Willows, CA [*Library symbol*] [*Library of Congress*] (LCLS)
CWJ.......... Comparative Wage Justice (ADA)
CWJ.......... Continuous Wave Jammer (MCD)
CWK .... Cam-Net Communications Network, Inc. [*Vancouver Stock Exchange symbol*]
CWKT .... Cam-Net Communications Network, Inc. [*Vancouver, BC*] [*NASDAQ symbol*] (NQ)
CWL .... Calm Water Line
CWL .... Cancer Patients, Weight Losing
CWL .... Cardiff [*Wales*] [*Airport symbol*] (OAG)
CWL .... Carney, William L., Bresman IN [*STAC*]
CWL .... Case Western Reserve. Law Review [*A publication*]
CWL .... Case Western Reserve University Law Library, Cleveland, OH [*OCLC symbol*] (OCLC)
CWL .... Chemical Warfare Laboratories [*Army Chemical Center, MD*] (MCD)
Cwl............ Commonwealth [*A publication*]
CWL .... Continuous Wave LASER
CWL .... Cornwall R. R. [*AAR code*]
CWL .... Cutaneous Water Loss
CWLA .... Child Welfare League of America (EA)
CWLD .... Child World, Inc. [*Avon, MA*] [*NASDAQ symbol*] (NQ)
CWLM ...... Caution and Warning Limit Module [*NASA*] (NASA)
CWLM ...... Chung-Wai Literary Monthly [*A publication*]
CWLR .... California Western Law Review [*A publication*]
CWLS .... Canadian Well Logging Society
CWLS .... Conventional Weighted Least Square
CWLSBG .. Canadian Wildlife Service [*A publication*]
CWLTH .... Commonwealth
Cwlth Record ... Commonwealth Record [*A publication*] (DLA)
CWlvC .... Canyon Research Group, Inc., Westlake Village, CA [*Library symbol*] [*Library of Congress*] (LCLS)
CWM........ Camino Resources Ltd. [*Vancouver Stock Exchange symbol*]
CWM........ Cashflow Magazine [*A publication*]
CWM........ Catholic Worker Movement (EA)
CWM........ Cell Wall Material [*Biochemistry*]
CWM........ Change Weight Manifest [*Aviation*] (FAAC)
C & WM .... Chicago & West Michigan Railroad
CWM........ Coal-Water Mixture Fuel
CWM........ Coil Winding Machine
CWM........ Commercial Water Movement Number
CWM........ Communist Workers' Movement [*British*] (PPW)
CWM........ Conference for World Mission [*British Council of Churches*]
CWM........ Convertible Wraparound Mortgage [*Banking*]
CWM........ Council for World Mission [*Australia*]
CWM........ Countrywide Mortgage Investments [*NYSE symbol*] (SPSG)
CWM........ Cruciform Wing Module (MCD)

CWMA ...... Church Women's Missionary Association [*Episcopalian*]
CWMAA ... Clock and Watch Manufacturers Association of America [*Defunct*]
CWME ...... Commission on World Mission and Evangelism (EAIO)
CWMEWCC ... Commission on World Mission and Evangelism of the World Council of Churches [*Later, CWME*] (EA)
CWMK ...... Simcoe, ON [*ICAO location identifier*] (ICLI)
CWML ...... Colorado Weights and Measures Laboratory [*National Institute of Standards and Technology*]
CWMN ...... Mount Forest, ON [*ICAO location identifier*] (ICLI)
CWMTU ... Cold Weather Materiel Test Unit [*Military*]
CWN .... Calcutta Weekly Notes [*A publication*] (DLA)
CWN .... Canadian Western Natural Gas Co. Ltd. [*Toronto Stock Exchange symbol*]
CWN .... Certificate of War Necessity [*World War II*]
CWN .... CircuitWriter Network [*Information service or system*] (IID)
CWN .... Commodity World News Network [*Later, Futures World News*] [*Information service or system*] (IID)
CWN .... Contract Work Notification (KSC)
CWN .... Cosmetic World News [*A publication*]
CWN .... North Conway, NH [*Location identifier*] [*FAA*] (FAAL)
CWNC .... Christian Women's National Concerns (EA)
CWNIB ...... Coalition of Women in National and International Business [*Boston, MA*] (EA)
CWNMR ..... Continuous Wave Nuclear Magnetic Resonance
CWNS .... C & W [*Cable & Wireless North America, Inc.*] Network Services [*Dallas, TX*] [*Telecommunications*] (TSSD)
CWNS .... Canadian War Narrative Section [*World War I*]
CWO .... Canadian War Office (DMA)
CWO .... Capital Work Order (NRCH)
CWO .... Cash with Order [*Business term*]
CWO .... Chief Warrant Officer [*Army*] (GPO)
CWO .... Chief Watch Officer [*Navy*]
CWO .... Command Works Office [*British military*] (DMA)
CWO .... Commissioned Warrant Officer
CWO .... Communication Watch Officer
CWO .... Continuous Wave Oscillator
CWO .... Council of Writers Organizations (EA)
CWO .... Custom Work Order [*Telecommunications*] (TEL)
CWo .... Woodland Free Public Library, Woodland, CA [*Library symbol*] [*Library of Congress*] (LCLS)
CWO-2 ...... Chief Warrant Officer, W-2 [*Army*] (AABC)
CWO-3 ...... Chief Warrant Officer, W-3 [*Army*] (AABC)
CWO-4 ...... Chief Warrant Officer, W-4 [*Army*] (AABC)
CWODAJ ... Connecticut Woodlands [*A publication*]
CWOH .... Ste. Agathe Des Monts, PQ [*ICAO location identifier*] (ICLI)
CWOHC ..... Commissioned Warrant Officer Hospital Corps
CWohL ...... Litton Industries, Inc., Guidance and Central Systems Division, Engineering Library, Woodland Hills, CA [*Library symbol*] [*Library of Congress*] (LCLS)
CWOIH ..... Council of World Organizations Interested in the Handicapped [*Later, ICOD*] (EA)
CWON .... Canadian Women of Note [*Database*] [*York University*] [*Defunct*] [*Information service or system*] (CRD)
CWON .... Center for a Woman's Own Name [*An association*] [*Defunct*] (EA)
CWOP .... Childbirth without Pain
CWOP .... Cold Weather Operations [*Military*]
CWOPAL ... Canadian Wildlife Service. Occasional Papers [*A publication*]
CWORF ..... Customer Work Order File (MCD)
CWoY .... Yolo County Free Library, Woodland, CA [*Library symbol*] [*Library of Congress*] (LCLS)
CWP .... Cable & Wireless Ltd. ADS [*NYSE symbol*] (SPSG)
CWP .... Cheese Whey Powder
CWP .... Chicago, West Pullman & Southern Railroad Co. [*AAR code*]
CWP .... Christian Workers Party [*Malta*] [*Political party*] (PPE)
CWP .... Circulating Water Pump
CWP .... Civil Works Program
CWP .... Cloud Water Project [*A cooperative ecosystem study*]
CWP .... Coal Workers' Pneumoconiosis [*Black lung*] [*Medicine*]
CWP .... Communicating Word Processor
CWP .... Communist Workers Party [*Political party*]
CWP .... Community of the Whole Person (EA)
CWP .... Comparable Worth Project (EA)
CWP .... Consolidated WWMCCS [*Worldwide Military Command and Control System*] Program [*DoD*]
CWP .... Contractor Work Plan (NRCH)
CWP .... Control Withdrawal Prohibit [*Nuclear energy*] (NRCH)
CWP .... Coordinating Working Party on Atlantic Fishery Statistics
CWP .... Council of the World Poultry [*British*]
CWP .... Cumulative Weight Percent
CWP .... Current Word Pointer
CWP .... Cutting and Welding Permit
CWPA .... Committee for Women in Public Administration (EA)
CWPBA ..... California Water Pollution Control Association. Bulletin [*A publication*]
CWPC .... Calcined Waste Packaging Cell [*Nuclear energy*] (NRCH)
CWPC .... Cam Wedge Power Clamp
CWPC .... Canadian Women's Press Club [*Later, Media Club of Canada*]
CWPC .... Civil War Press Corps (EA)
CWPC .... Pincher Creek, AB [*ICAO location identifier*] (ICLI)

CWPD .... Class Work Planning Document [*Navy ship overhauls*]
CWPEA ..... Childbirth without Pain Education Association [*Also known as Lamaze Birth without Pain Education Association*] (EA)
CWPH .... Circulating Water Pumphouse [*Nuclear energy*] (NRCH)
CWPI .... Configuration Work Package Item [*Army*] (AABC)
CWPL .... Cornell Working Papers in Linguistics [*A publication*]
CWPM .... Correct Words per Minute [*Typewriting, etc.*]
CWPNBL ... Canadian Wildlife Service. Progress Notes [*A publication*]
CWPNM ..... Center for War, Peace, and the News Media (EA)
CWPO .... Pilot Mount, MB [*ICAO location identifier*] (ICLI)
CWPOS ..... Cane, Wicker, and Perambucot Operatives' Society [*A union*] [*British*]
CW/PS ...... Center for War/Peace Studies (EA)
CWPS .... Center for Women Policy Studies (EA)
CWPS .... Civil War Philatelic Society [*Later, AHPS*] (EA)
CWPS .... Communicating Word Processing System
CWPS .... Council on Wage and Price Stability [*Also, COWPS*] [*Abolished, 1981*]
CWQ .... Curlew Lake [*Vancouver Stock Exchange symbol*]
CWR .... Cabinet War Room
CWR .... Calculated Weight Report
CWR .... California Western Railroad [*AAR code*]
CWR .... Case Western Reserve University, Cleveland, OH [*OCLC symbol*] (OCLC)
CWR .... Center for Welding Research [*Ohio State University*] [*Research center*] (RCD)
CWR .... Central Western Region
CWR .... Ceylon Weekly Reporter [*A publication*] (ILCA)
CWR .... Coalition on Women and Religion (EA)
CWR .... Coastal Watching RADAR (NATG)
CWR .... Compliance with Requirements (MCD)
CWR .... Continuously Welded Rail (ADA)
CWR .... Cooling Water Return [*Nuclear energy*] (NRCH)
CWRA .... Conditioned Wrinkle Recovery Angle [*Textile technology*]
CWRC .... Civilian Welfare and Recreation Committee (MUGU)
CWRC .... Climb Well to Right of Course [*Aviation*] (FAAC)
CWRENAF ... Chief WREN [*Women's Royal Naval Service*] Air Fitter [*British military*] (DMA)
CWRENCINE ... Chief WREN [*Women's Royal Naval Service*] Cinema Operator [*British military*] (DMA)
CWRENCK ... Chief WREN [*Women's Royal Naval Service*] Cook [*British military*] (DMA)
CWRENDHYG ... Chief WREN [*Women's Royal Naval Service*] Dental Hygienist [*British military*] (DMA)
CWRENDSA ... Chief WREN [*Women's Royal Naval Service*] Dental Surgery Assistant [*British military*] (DMA)
CWRENEDUC ... Chief WREN [*Women's Royal Naval Service*] Education Assistant [*British military*] (DMA)
CWRENMET ... Chief WREN [*Women's Royal Naval Service*] Meteorological Observer [*British military*] (DMA)
CWRENPHOT ... Chief WREN [*Women's Royal Naval Service*] Photographer [*British military*] (DMA)
CWRENQA ... Chief WREN [*Women's Royal Naval Service*] Quarters Assistant [*British military*] (DMA)
CWREN(R) ... Chief WREN [*Women's Royal Naval Service*] (RADAR) [*British military*] (DMA)
CWRENREG ... Chief WREN [*Women's Royal Naval Service*] Regulating [*British military*] (DMA)
CWRENREL ... Chief WREN [*Women's Royal Naval Service*] Radio Electrician [*British military*] (DMA)
CWRENRS(M) ... Chief WREN [*Women's Royal Naval Service*] Radio Supervisor (Morse) [*British military*] (DMA)
CWRENSA ... Chief WREN [*Women's Royal Naval Service*] Stores Accountant [*British military*] (DMA)
CWRENS(C) ... Chief WREN [*Women's Royal Naval Service*] Stores Assistant (Clothes) [*British military*] (DMA)
CWRENSTD ... Chief WREN [*Women's Royal Naval Service*] Steward [*British military*] (DMA)
CWRENS(V) ... Chief WREN [*Women's Royal Naval Service*] Stores Assistant (Victualling) [*British military*] (DMA)
CWRENTEL ... Chief WREN [*Women's Royal Naval Service*] Telephonist [*British military*] (DMA)
CWRENTSA ... Chief WREN [*Women's Royal Naval Service*] Training Support Assistant [*British military*] (DMA)
CWRENWA ... Chief WREN [*Women's Royal Naval Service*] Weapon Analyst [*British military*] (DMA)
CWRENWTR(G) ... Chief WREN [*Women's Royal Naval Service*] Writer (General) [*British military*] (DMA)
CWRENWTR(P) ... Chief WREN [*Women's Royal Naval Service*] Writer (Pay) [*British military*] (DMA)
CWRENWW ... Chief WREN [*Women's Royal Naval Service*] Welfare Worker [*British military*] (DMA)
CWRJ .... Canadian Water Resources Journal [*A publication*]
CWR J Int L ... Case Western Reserve. Journal of International Law [*A publication*]
CWRL .... Cooperative Wildlife Research Laboratory [*Southern Illinois University at Carbondale*] [*Research center*] (RCD)
CWR LR .... Case Western Reserve. Law Review [*A publication*]
CWRM .... Cell Water Removal Mechanism
CWRO .... Canadian War Records Office [*World War I*]
CWRR .... Center for Water Resources Research [*University of Nevada*]

CWRR .... Curtiss-Wright Research Reactor
CWRSBC .. Canadian Wildlife Service. Report Series [*A publication*]
CWRTA .... Civil War Round Table Associates (EA)
CWRU ...... Case Western Reserve University [*Cleveland, OH*]
CWRUAH ... Australia Commonwealth Scientific and Industrial Research Organisation. Wheat Research Unit. Annual Report [*A publication*]
CWS .... Canadian Home Shopping Network Ltd. [*Toronto Stock Exchange symbol*]
CWS .... Canadian Wildlife Service, Quebec Region [*Environment Canada*] [*Research center*]
CWS .... Cancer Patients, Weight Stable
CWS .... Caribbean Writers Series [*Heinemann Educational Books Ltd.*] [*British*]
CWS .... Casework Supervisor [*Red Cross*]
CWS .... Catalog Typing Worksheet [*for MT/ST typist*]
CWS .... Caucus for Women in Statistics (EA)
CWS .... Caution and Warning Status (MCD)
C & WS ...... Caution and Warning System [*NASA*] (KSC)
CWS .... Cell Wall Skeleton [*Cytology*]
CWS .... Center for Women and Sport (EA)
CWS .... Center Work System [*NASA*] (KSC)
CWS .... Central Wireless Station [*Air Force*] [*British*]
CWS .... Centre for Women's Studies [*Australia*]
CWS .... Charles Williams Society [*London, England*] (EAIO)
CWS .... Chemical Warfare Service [*Army*]
CWS .... Chest Wall Stimulation [*Medicine*]
CWS .... Child Welfare Service
CWS .... Chilled Water Supply [*Aerospace*] (AAG)
CWS .... Church World Service [*Later, CWSW*] (EA)
CWS .... Circulating Water System [*Nuclear energy*] (NRCH)
CWS .... Civil War Society (EA)
CWS .... Clearinghouse on Women's Studies (EA)
CWS .... Clockwise (AAG)
CWS .... Co-Operative Wholesale Society [*British*]
CWS .... Coal-Water Slurry [*Fuel*]
CWS .... Cold-Water Soluble
CW-S .... College Work-Study [*Program*]
CWS .... Collision Warning System (MCD)
CWS .... Colonial Waterbird Society (EA)
CWS .... Commander's Weapons Station (MCD)
CWS .... Community War Services [*of FSA*] [*World War II*]
CWS .... Complex Wiring System
CWS .... Consolidated Western Steel (AAG)
CWS .... Continental Wage Schedule [*Military*] (AABC)
CWS .... Contract War Service
CWS .... Contract Work Statement (MCD)
CWS .... Control Wheel Steering (NG)
CWS .... Conway, AR [*Location identifier*] [*FAA*] (FAAL)
CWS .... Cooling Water System [*Nuclear energy*] (NRCH)
CWS .... Cooperative Wholesale Society [*British*]
CWS .... Copper Weld Steel [*Telecommunications*] (TEL)
CWS .... Crew Weapons Sight
CWS .... Metropolitan Chamber of Commerce and Industry. Chamber News [*A publication*]
CWS .... Westmont College, Santa Barbara, CA [*OCLC symbol*] (OCLC)
CWSA .... Canadian Water Ski Association
CWSA .... Canadian Wheelchair Sports Association
CWSA .... Canadian Women's Studies Association [*See also ACEF*]
CWSAB ..... Canadian War Supplies Assignment Board [*World War II*]
CWSAHA ... Church World Service Aids for the Horn of Africa (EA)
CWSAM .... Continuous Wave Surface-to-Air Missile (MCD)
CWSD .... Continuous Wave Space Duplexed
CWSF .... Catholic Women's Seminary Fund [*Defunct*] (EA)
CWSF .... Coal-Water Slurry Fuel
CWSF .... Commander, Western Sea Frontier
CWSIRP .... Church World Service, Immigration and Refugee Program (EA)
CWSJ .... Congressional Wives for Soviet Jewry (EA)
CWSL .... California Wilderness Survival League (EA)
CWSO ...... Chemical Warfare Service Officer [*Army*]
CWSOP ..... Canadian Wildlife Service. Occasional Papers [*A publication*]
CWSP .... College Work-Study Program
CWSP .... Communications with and Service to the Public [*Army*] (AABC)
CWSPA7 ... Colorado. Division of Wildlife. Special Report [*A publication*]
CWSPN ..... Canadian Wildlife Service. Progress Notes [*A publication*]
CWSRA ..... Canadian Women's Sailboat Racing Association
CWSRA ..... Chester White Swine Record Association
CWSRS ..... Canadian Wildlife Service. Report Series [*A publication*]
CWSS .... Center for Women's Studies and Services (EA)
CWST .... Combat Water Survival Test [*Army*] (INF)
CWSU .... Caution and Warning Status Unit [*NASA*] (NASA)
CWSU ...... Center Weather Service Unit (FAAC)
CWSU .... Condensate Water Servicing Unit
CWSW .... Church World Service and Witness (EA)
CWT .... Cadre Weather Team (MCD)
CWT .... Center for World Thanksgiving (EA)
CWT .... Chemical Warfare Specialist, Medical [*Navy rating*]
CWT .... Chief Water Tender [*Navy rating*] [*Obsolete*]

CWT .... Childress [*Texas*] [*Seismograph station code, US Geological Survey*] (SEIS)
CWT .... Coalition for Workplace Technology (EA)
CWT .... Coded Wire Tagging [*Pisciculture*]
CWT .... Cold Water Tank
CWT .... Cold Water Temperature
CWT .... Cold Water Treatment [*Medicine*]
CWT .... Color Word Test
CWT .... Compensated Work Therapy
CWT .... Constant Wall Temperature [*Engineering*]
CWT .... Consumers for World Trade (EA)
CWT .... Conventional Weapons Technology (MCD)
CWT .... Cooperative Wind Tunnel
CWT .... Council on World Tensions [*Later, Institute on Man and Science*] (EA)
C/WT .... Counterweight [*Automotive engineering*]
CWT .... Cowra [*Australia*] [*Airport symbol*] (OAG)
CWT .... Crew Natural Resources [*Vancouver Stock Exchange symbol*]
CWT .... Hundredweight (AFM)
CWTA ...... Cold Water Reactor Test Assembly
CWTB .... Cylindrical Water Tube Boiler [*of a ship*] (DS)
CWTBS ..... Cylindrical Water Tube Boiler Survey [*of a ship*] (DS)
CWTC .... Chemical Warfare Technical Committee
CWTC .... Chemical Waste Transportation Council [*Washington, DC*] (EA)
CWTC .... Community Welfare Training Council [*Australia*]
CWTD .... Continuous Wave Target Detection (NATG)
CWTDC ..... Continuous Wave Tactical Detection Console (NATG)
CWTE .... Commonwealth Telephone Enterprises, Inc. [*NASDAQ symbol*] (NQ)
CWTG .... Computer World Trade Group [*British*]
Cwth .... Commonwealth
CWTI .... Civil War Times Illustrated [*A publication*]
CWTI .... Civilian Wartime Injuries
CWTO .... Toronto, ON [*ICAO location identifier*] (ICLI)
CWTP .... Community Work and Training Program [*Department of Labor*]
CWTP .... Comprehensive Work Training Program [*Employment and Training Administration*] [*Department of Labor*]
CWTR ...... California Water Service Co. [*NASDAQ symbol*] (NQ)
CWTR ...... Climb Well to Right [*Aviation*] (FAAC)
CWTS .... Civil War Token Society (EA)
CWTS .... Country Wide Transport Services, Inc. [*NASDAQ symbol*] (NQ)
CWTV ...... Cable West Corp. [*NASDAQ symbol*] (NQ)
CWTWT .... Continuous Wave Traveling Wave Tube (MCD)
CWU .... Camp Williams [*Utah*] [*Seismograph station code, US Geological Survey*] (SEIS)
CWU .... Caution and Warning Unit (MCD)
CWU .... Chemical Workers' Union
CWU .... Christliche Waehlerunion Bayern [*Christian Voters' Union of Bavaria*] [*Federal Republic of Germany*] [*Political party*] (PPW)
CWU .... Church Women United (EA)
CWU .... Colonial Warriors United (EA)
CWU .... Composite Weighted Work Unit (AFM)
CWU .... Congress of World Unity (EA)
CWU .... Czech World Union (EA)
CWUL .... Montreal, PQ [*ICAO location identifier*] (ICLI)
CWV .... Catholic War Veterans of the USA (EA)
CWV .... Continuous Wave Video
CWV .... Croesus Resources, Inc. [*Vancouver Stock Exchange symbol*]
CWVA ...... Bonavista, NF [*ICAO location identifier*] (ICLI)
CWVA ...... Catholic War Veterans of the USA Ladies Auxiliary [*Later, CWVUSAA*] (EA)
CWVR ...... Vancouver, BC [*ICAO location identifier*] (ICLI)
CWVS .... College Women's Volunteer Service [*World War II*]
CWVUSAA ... Catholic War Veterans of the USA Auxiliary (EA)
CWW .... California's Wine Wonderland [*A publication*] (EAAP)
CWW .... Canadian Woodmen of the World (EA)
CWW .... Canadian Worldwide Energy Ltd. [*Toronto Stock Exchange symbol*]
CWW .... Cruciform Wing Weapon (MCD)
CWWF .... Churches Committee for Work Among Women Serving with HM Forces [*British military*] (DMA)
CWWFAV ... Contribution. Welder Wildlife Foundation [*A publication*]
CWWG ...... Winnipeg, MB [*ICAO location identifier*] (ICLI)
CW & WOA ... Chief Warrant and Warrant Officers Association, United States Coast Guard (EA)
CWX .... Canwest Trustco [*Vancouver Stock Exchange symbol*]
CWX .... Continuous Wave Transmitter (CAAL)
CWY .... Clackamas, OR [*Location identifier*] [*FAA*] (FAAL)
CWY .... Clearway [*Aviation code*]
CX .... Blister Gas [*US Chemical Corps symbol*]
CX .... Canceled (CINC)
CX .... Cargo/Transport Aircraft - Experimental
CX .... Carrier [*Telecommunications*] (CET)
CX .... Cathay Pacific Airways Ltd. [*ICAO designator*] (FAAC)
CX .... Centerior Energy Corp. [*NYSE symbol*] (SPSG)
cx .... Central African Republic [*MARC country of publication code*] [*Library of Congress*] (LCCP)

CX	Central Exchange
CX	Cervix [*Anatomy*]
CX	Charing Cross Station [*England*] (ROG)
CX	Chest X-Ray [*Medicine*]
CX	Christmas Island [*ANSI two-letter standard code*] (CNC)
Cx	Clearance [*Physiology*]
CX	Coin Collecting Box, Pay Station [*Telecommunications*] (TEL)
CX	Coinbox Set [*Telecommunications*] (TEL)
CX	Color Exterior Film (MCD)
CX	Column Extractant [*Nuclear energy*] (NRCH)
CX	Compatible Expansion [*Noise-reduction system for manufacturing phonograph records*] [*CBS*]
CX	Complex (KSC)
CX	Composite
CX	Composite Signaling [*Telecommunications*] (TEL)
CX	Connection [*Technical drawings*]
CX	Control Transmitter (MUGU)
CX	Convex
CX	Correct Copy [*A printing direction*]
CX	Count Register [*Data processing*]
CX	Criticality Experiment [*Nuclear energy*] (NRCH)
CX	Cylinder Axis [*Optometry*]
CX	Nonradio Frequency Cable Assemblies [*JETDS nomenclature*] [*Military*]
CX	Uruguay [*Aircraft nationality and registration mark*] (FAAC)
C2X	Command and Control Exercise
CXA	Caicara [*Venezuela*] [*Airport symbol*] (OAG)
CXA	Cancel Approved Arrival [*Aviation*] (FAAC)
CXA	Chambre de Commerce, d'Agriculture, et d'Industrie de la Republique Togolaise. Bulletin Mensuel [*A publication*]
CXA	Consolidated HCI Holdings Corp. [*Toronto Stock Exchange symbol*]
CXB	Can-Mac Exploration Ltd. [*Vancouver Stock Exchange symbol*]
CXB	Cosmic X-Ray Background
CXB	Cox's Bazar [*Bangladesh*] [*Airport symbol*] (OAG)
CXBG	Comprehensive Extended Term Banker's Guarantee (DS)
CXC	Caribbean Examinations Council [*St. Michael, Barbados*] (EAIO)
CXC	Chitina, AK [*Location identifier*] [*FAA*] (FAAL)
Cxc	Clavibacter Xyli Cynodontis [*Microbiology*]
CXC	CMX Corporation [*AMEX symbol*] (SPSG)
CXC	Computrex Centres [*Vancouver Stock Exchange symbol*]
CXCS	Center for Cross-Cultural Studies [*University of Alaska, Fairbanks*] [*Research center*] (RCD)
cxCu	Cold-Extractable Copper
CXD	Cancel Approved Departure [*Aviation*] (FAAC)
CXE	Chase City, VA [*Location identifier*] [*FAA*] (FAAL)
CXE	China Informatie [*A publication*]
CXE	Colonial High Income Municipal Trust [*NYSE symbol*] (SPSG)
CXE	Xerox Corp., El Segundo, CA [*OCLC symbol*] (OCLC)
CXF	Coldfoot, AK [*Location identifier*] [*FAA*] (FAAL)
CXF	Continental Pacific [*Vancouver Stock Exchange symbol*]
CXG	Commerce in Belgium [*A publication*]
CXG	Coxheath Gold Holdings Ltd. [*Toronto Stock Exchange symbol*]
CXGLN	Glands on Calyx Margin [*Botany*]
CXH	Colonial Investment Grade Municipal [*NYSE symbol*] (SPSG)
CXH	Vancouver-Harbour Seaport [*Canada*] [*Airport symbol*] (OAG)
CX-HLS	Cargo/Transport Aircraft Experimental - Heavy Logistics System (KSC)
cxHM	Citrate-Extractable Heavy Metal
CXI	Caulfield Resources Ltd. [*Vancouver Stock Exchange symbol*]
CXI	Christmas Island [*Kiribati*] [*Airport symbol*] (OAG)
CXI	Common X Interface [*Data processing*]
CXI	Crosstell Input
CXIM	Criticare Systems, Inc. [*NASDAQ symbol*] (NQ)
CXK	Bellaire, MI [*Location identifier*] [*FAA*] (FAAL)
CXK	Consolidated Norex Resources Corp. [*Toronto Stock Exchange symbol*] [*Vancouver Stock Exchange symbol*]
CXL	Calexico, CA [*Location identifier*] [*FAA*] (FAAL)
CXM	Camindex Mines Ltd. [*Toronto Stock Exchange symbol*]
CXM	Cefuroxime [*Antibacterial drug*]
CXM	Cycloheximide [*Also, CH, CHX, Cyh*] [*Fungicide*]
CXM	Traverse City, MI [*Location identifier*] [*FAA*] (FAAL)
CXMD	Canine X-Linked Muscular Dystrophy
CXN	Chromex Nickel Mines Ltd. [*Vancouver Stock Exchange symbol*]
CXNHAX	Contributions. United States National Herbarium [*A publication*]
CXO	Comox Resources Ltd. [*Vancouver Stock Exchange symbol*]
CXO	Conroe, TX [*Location identifier*] [*FAA*] (FAAL)
CXO	Crosstell Output
CxP	Celery and Parsley Cross [*Genetics*]
CXP	Cilicap [*Indonesia*] [*Airport symbol*] (OAG)
CXP	Cuyahoga County Public Library, Cleveland, OH [*OCLC symbol*] (OCLC)
CXPVF	CT Exploranda Ltd. [*NASDAQ symbol*] (NQ)
CXR	Carrier [*Telecommunications*]
CXR	Chardon, OH [*Location identifier*] [*FAA*] (FAAL)

CXR	Chest X-Ray [*Medicine*]
CXR	Christmas Island [*ANSI three-letter standard code*] (CNC)
CXR	Comaplex Resources International Ltd. [*Toronto Stock Exchange symbol*]
CXR	CXR Corp. [*AMEX symbol*] (CTT)
CXRC	Cox Resources Corporation [*NASDAQ symbol*] (NQ)
CXRL	CXR Telcom Corp. [*NASDAQ symbol*] (NQ)
CXS	Consort Parallax Servo
CXS	Counsel Corp. [*Toronto Stock Exchange symbol*]
CXT	Banco Nacional de Comercio Exterior. Comercio de Exterior [*A publication*]
CXT	Canamera Explorations, Inc. [*Vancouver Stock Exchange symbol*]
CXT	Charters Towers [*Australia*] [*Airport symbol*] (OAG)
CXT	Common External Tariff [*EEC*] [*Also, CET*]
CXU	Camilla, GA [*Location identifier*] [*FAA*] (FAAL)
CXU	Charge Spotting Bomb Unit
CXV	Cavalier Homes, Inc. [*AMEX symbol*] (SPSG)
CXX	Callex Mineral Exploration [*Vancouver Stock Exchange symbol*]
CXY	Canadian Occidental Petroleum Ltd. [*AMEX symbol*] [*Toronto Stock Exchange symbol*] (SPSG)
CXY	Cat Cay [*Bahamas*] [*Airport symbol*] (OAG)
CXY	Harrisburg, PA [*Location identifier*] [*FAA*] (FAAL)
CXZ	Can-Ex Resources Ltd. [*Vancouver Stock Exchange symbol*]
CY	Calendar Year (TEL)
CY	Capacity (ADA)
CY	Carry
CY	Case Copy [*Data processing*]
CY	Cases and Cabinets [*JETDS nomenclature*] [*Military*] (CET)
CY	Central Yiddish (BJA)
CY	Ceylon [*Sri Lanka*] (ROG)
CY	Chief Yeoman [*Navy rating*] [*Obsolete*]
C & Y	Children and Youth
CY	Choay [*France*] [*Research code symbol*]
CY	Chun-ying [*Leung*] [*Hong Kong politician*]
CY	City (MCD)
CY	Colby Resources Corp. [*Vancouver Stock Exchange symbol*]
CY	Communication Yeoman [*Navy rating*] [*British*]
Cy	Connolly's New York Surrogate Reports [*A publication*] (DLA)
CY	Container Yard [*Shipping*] (DCTA)
CY	Convention of York [*Freemasonry*] (ROG)
CY	Copy (AABC)
CY	Country [*Online database field identifier*]
CY	County
Cy	Crawdaddy [*A publication*]
Cy	Csakeyhtioe [*Joint-Stock Company*] [*Finland*] (CED)
CY	Cubic Yard (KSC)
CY	Currency
CY	Current Yield [*Banking*]
CY	Cyanogen [*Toxic compound*]
CY	Cycle (AAG)
CY	Cyclophosphamide [*Cytoxan*] [*Antineoplastic drug*]
CY	Cyclosporine [*An immunosuppressant drug*]
CY	Cylinder
CY	Cypress Semiconductor Corp. [*NYSE symbol*] (SPSG)
Cy	Cyprianus Florentinus [*Flourished, 12th century*] [*Authority cited in pre-1607 legal work*] (DSA)
Cy	Cypriote (BJA)
CY	Cyprus [*ANSI two-letter standard code*] (CNC)
cy	Cyprus [*MARC country of publication code*] [*Library of Congress*] (LCCP)
CY	Cyprus Airways Ltd. [*ICAO designator*] (FAAC)
CY	People's Republic of China [*License plate code assigned to foreign diplomats in the US*]
CY	Sri Lanka [*IYRU nationality code*] (IYR)
CYA	Canadian Yachting Association
CYA	Carded Yarn Association [*Later, AYSA*] (EA)
CYA	Catholic Youth Adoration Society [*Defunct*] (EA)
CYA	Cheyenne Airways, Inc. [*Cheyenne, WY*] [*FAA designator*] (FAAC)
CYA	Choya [*Argentina*] [*Seismograph station code, US Geological Survey*] (SEIS)
CYA	Classic Yacht Association (EA)
CYA	Claymore Resources [*Vancouver Stock Exchange symbol*]
CYA	Covenant Young Adults [*Defunct*] (EA)
CYA	Cover Your Anatomy [*Military, government slang*] [*Bowdlerized version*]
CYA	Cyclosporin A [*See CSA*] [*An immunosuppressant drug*]
Cya	Cysteic Acid [*An amino acid*]
CYAA	Ottawa, ON [*ICAO location identifier*] (ICLI)
CYAB	Arctic Bay, NT [*ICAO location identifier*] (ICLI)
CYAD	Cytoplasm Average Optical Density [*Microscopy*]
CyADIC	Cyclophosphamide, Adriamycin, DIC [*Dacarbazine*] [*Antineoplastic drug regimen*]
CYAJ	Komakuk, YT [*ICAO location identifier*] (ICLI)
CYAL	Alert Bay, BC [*ICAO location identifier*] (ICLI)
CYAM	Sault Ste. Marie, ON [*ICAO location identifier*] (ICLI)
CYAMEX	Cyana-Mexique (MSC)
CYAN	Cyanosis [*Medicine*]
CYAN	Cyanotech Corp. [*Woodinville, WA*] [*NASDAQ symbol*] (NQ)

Cyanamid Int Mitt ... Cyanamid International. Mitteilungen [*A publication*]

Cyanamid Int Vet Bull ... Cyanamid International. Veterinary Bulletin [*A publication*]

Cyanamid Mag ... Cyanamid Magazine [*A publication*]

Cyanam New Prod Bull ... Cyanamid New Product Bulletin [*A publication*]

CYAP......... Constrained Youth Allowances Package [*Australia*]

CYATH ..... Cyathus [*Glassful*] [*Pharmacy*]

CYATH AMP ... Cyathus Amplus [*Tumblerful*] [*Pharmacy*]

CYATH THEAE ... Cyatho Theae [*In a Cup of Tea*] [*Pharmacy*]   (ROG)

CYATH VIN ... Cyathus Vinosus [*Wineglassful*] [*Pharmacy*]

CYATH VINOS ... Cyathus Vinosus [*Wineglassful*] [*Pharmacy*]   (ROG)

CYAV .... Winnipeg/St. Andrews, MB [*ICAO location identifier*]   (ICLI)

CYAW .... Halifax/Shearwater Canadian Forces Base, NS [*ICAO location identifier*]   (ICLI)

CYAWP..... Cover Your Anatomy with Paper [*Military, government slang*] [*Bowdlerized version*]

CYAY .... St. Anthony, NF [*ICAO location identifier*]   (ICLI)

CYAZ........ Tofino, BC [*ICAO location identifier*]   (ICLI)

CYB .... Cayman Brac [*West Indies*] [*Airport symbol*]   (OAG)

CYB .... Commodity Year Book [*A publication*]

CYB .... Cybermedix, Inc. [*Toronto Stock Exchange symbol*]

Cyb............ Cybernetica [*A publication*]

Cyb............ Cybernetics [*A publication*]

Cyb............ Cybium. Bulletin de l'Association des Amis du Laboratoire des Peches Coloniales [*A publication*]

CYBA........ Banff, AB [*ICAO location identifier*]   (ICLI)

CYBB........ Pelly Bay, NT [*ICAO location identifier*]   (ICLI)

CYBC........ Baie Comeau, PQ [*ICAO location identifier*]   (ICLI)

CyBC........ Cyprus Broadcasting Corporation

CYBE........ CyberOptics Corp. [*NASDAQ symbol*]   (NQ)

CYBER...... Cybernetics   (ADA)

CYBERLOG ... Cybernetic Logistics Planning, Control, and Management Information System [*Military*]   (AABC)

Cybernet Systems ... Cybernetics and Systems [*A publication*]

Cybern and Syst ... Cybernetics and Systems [*A publication*]

Cybern Syst ... Cybernetics and Systems [*A publication*]

CYBG .... Bagotville Canadian Forces Base, PQ [*ICAO location identifier*]   (ICLI)

CYBK........ Baker Lake, NT [*ICAO location identifier*]   (ICLI)

CYBL........ Campbell River, BC [*ICAO location identifier*]   (ICLI)

CYBNA ..... Cybernetics [*English Translation*] [*A publication*]

CYBORG... Cybernetic Organism [*Concept of machine to alter man's bodily functions for space environment*]

CYBR........ Brandon, MB [*ICAO location identifier*]   (ICLI)

CYBR........ Cybermatics, Inc. [*NASDAQ symbol*]   (NQ)

CYBT........ Brochet, MB [*ICAO location identifier*]   (ICLI)

CYC .... Canterbury Yeomanry Cavalry [*British military*]   (DMA)

CYC .... Chinese Youth Council [*Later, CDC*]   (EA)

CYC .... Colby Junior College for Women [*Later, CSC*], New London, NH [*OCLC symbol*] [*Inactive*]   (OCLC)

CYC .... Company of Young Canadians [*Federal crown corporation to employ young people, 1966-75*]

CYC .... Crow Canyon [*California*] [*Seismograph station code, US Geological Survey*]   (SEIS)

CyC .... Cursos y Conferencias [*A publication*]

Cyc .... Cyclazocine [*Morphine antagonist*]

CYC .... Cycle

CYC .... Cyclone

CYC .... Cyclopedia

CYC .... Cyclopedia of Law and Procedure [*New York*] [*A publication*]   (DLA)

CYC .... Cyclophosphamide [*Cytoxan*] [*Antineoplastic drug*]

Cyc .... Cyclops [*of Euripides*] [*Classical studies*]   (OCD)

CYC .... Cyclops Industries [*NYSE symbol*]   (SPSG)

CYC .... Cyclorama [*Staging and scenery*]

CYCA .... Cartwright, NF [*ICAO location identifier*]   (ICLI)

CYCA .... Craft Yarn Council of America   (EA)

Cyc Ann ..... Cyclopedia of Law and Procedure Annotations [*A publication*]

CYCB........ Cambridge Bay, NT [*ICAO location identifier*]   (ICLI)

CYcCL....... Sutter County Free Library, Yuba City, CA [*Library symbol*] [*Library of Congress*]   (LCLS)

Cyc Corp .... Fletcher's Cyclopedia of Corporations [*A publication*]   (DLA)

CYCD .... Nanaimo, BC [*ICAO location identifier*]   (ICLI)

Cyc Dict ..... Cyclopedia Law Dictionary [*A publication*]   (DLA)

CYCG .... Castlegar, BC [*ICAO location identifier*]   (ICLI)

CYCH .... Chatham Canadian Forces Base, NB [*ICAO location identifier*]   (ICLI)

CYCIS .... Child and Youth Centered Information Systems

CYCL .... Charlo, NB [*ICAO location identifier*]   (ICLI)

CYCL........ Cycle

CYCL........ Cyclopedia

CYCLA ...... Cycles [*A publication*]

Cycl Anat and Physiol ... Cyclopaedia of Anatomy and Physiology [*A publication*]

Cyc Law & Proc ... Cyclopedia of Law and Procedure [*A publication*]   (DLA)

CYCLD...... Cycloidal Propeller [*on a ship*]   (DS)

Cycle Aust ... Cycle Australia [*A publication*]   (APTA)

CYCLES.... Cyclonic Extratropical Storms [*National Oceanic and Atmospheric Administration*]

CYCLGN... Cyclogenesis [*Meteorology*]   (FAAC)

CYCLO...... Cyclopedia

cyclo .... Cyclopropane (Anesthetic) [*Organic chemistry*]

Cyclop Dict ... Shumaker and Longsdorf's Cyclopedic Dictionary [*A publication*]   (DLA)

CYCO .... Central Yiddish Culture Organization   (EA)

CYCO .... Coppermine, NT [*ICAO location identifier*]   (ICLI)

CYCS......... Chesterfield Inlet, NT [*ICAO location identifier*]   (ICLI)

CYCT .... Coronation, AB [*ICAO location identifier*]   (ICLI)

CYCV .... Montreal/Cartierville, PQ [*ICAO location identifier*]   (ICLI)

CYCW .... Chilliwack, BC [*ICAO location identifier*]   (ICLI)

CYCX........ Camp Gagetown Canadian Forces Base, NB [*ICAO location identifier*]   (ICLI)

CYCY .... Clyde River, NT [*ICAO location identifier*]   (ICLI)

CYD .... Carlyle Energy Ltd. [*Toronto Stock Exchange symbol*]

CYD .... College Young Democrats of America   (EA)

CYD .... Cubic Yard   (ADA)

Cyd............ Cytidine [*Also, C*] [*A nucleoside*]

CYDA .... Dawson, YT [*ICAO location identifier*]   (ICLI)

CYDAC ..... Cytophotometric Data Converter [*Instrumentation*]

CYDB .... Burwash, YT [*ICAO location identifier*]   (ICLI)

CYDC .... Princeton, BC [*ICAO location identifier*]   (ICLI)

CYDEF ...... Cyrenaica Defence Force [*British military*]   (DMA)

CYDF .... Deer Lake, NF [*ICAO location identifier*]   (ICLI)

CYDL......... Dease Lake, BC [*ICAO location identifier*]   (ICLI)

CYDN .... Dauphin, MB [*ICAO location identifier*]   (ICLI)

CYDQ .... Dawson Creek, BC [*ICAO location identifier*]   (ICLI)

CYDR .... Broadview, SK [*ICAO location identifier*]   (ICLI)

CYE .... Cal Dynamics Corp. [*Vancouver Stock Exchange symbol*]

CYE .... Charcoal Yeast Extract [*Agar medium*] [*Microbiology*]

CYE .... Cheyenne Software, Inc. [*AMEX symbol*]   (SPSG)

CYE .... Wilkes-Barre, PA [*Location identifier*] [*FAA*]   (FAAL)

CYEC........ Commonwealth Youth Exchange Council [*British*]

CYECF ...... Cal Dynamics Corp. [*NASDAQ symbol*]   (NQ)

CYED .... Edmonton/Namao Canadian Forces Base, AB [*ICAO location identifier*]   (ICLI)

CYEE......... Central Youth Employment Executive [*Department of Employment*] [*British*]

CYEG .... Edmonton International, AB [*ICAO location identifier*]   (ICLI)

CYEK........ Eskimo Point, NT [*ICAO location identifier*]   (ICLI)

CYEN .... Estevan, SK [*ICAO location identifier*]   (ICLI)

CYENA ..... Cryogenic Engineering News [*A publication*]

CYEP .... Estevan Point, BC [*ICAO location identifier*]   (ICLI)

CYET .... Edson, AB [*ICAO location identifier*]   (ICLI)

CYEU .... Eureka, NT [*ICAO location identifier*]   (ICLI)

CYEV .... Inuvik, NT [*ICAO location identifier*]   (ICLI)

CYF............ Chefornak [*Alaska*] [*Airport symbol*]   (OAG)

CYF............ Chefornak, AK [*Location identifier*] [*FAA*]   (FAAL)

CYF............ Conservative Youth Federation   (EA)

CYFB .... Frobisher, NT [*ICAO location identifier*]   (ICLI)

CYFC........ Fredericton, NB [*ICAO location identifier*]   (ICLI)

CYFE......... Forestville, PQ [*ICAO location identifier*]   (ICLI)

CYFL......... Fort Reliance, NT [*ICAO location identifier*]   (ICLI)

CYFO .... Flin Flon, MB [*ICAO location identifier*]   (ICLI)

CYFR......... Fort Resolution, NT [*ICAO location identifier*]   (ICLI)

CYFS......... Fort Simpson, NT [*ICAO location identifier*]   (ICLI)

CYG .... Caprock Energy Ltd. [*Vancouver Stock Exchange symbol*]

CYG .... Captain of the Yeoman of the Guard [*British*]   (ROG)

Cyg............ Cygnus [*Constellation*]

CYGA .... Gagnon, PQ [*ICAO location identifier*]   (ICLI)

CYGK .... Kingston, ON [*ICAO location identifier*]   (ICLI)

CYGL........ La Grande Riviere, PQ [*ICAO location identifier*]   (ICLI)

CYGM .... Gimli, MB [*ICAO location identifier*]   (ICLI)

Cygn.......... Cygnus [*Constellation*]

CYGP .... Gaspe, PQ [*ICAO location identifier*]   (ICLI)

CYGQ .... Geraldton (North), ON [*ICAO location identifier*]   (ICLI)

CYGR .... Iles De La Madeleine, PQ [*ICAO location identifier*]   (ICLI)

CYGT .... Igloolik, NT [*ICAO location identifier*]   (ICLI)

CYGW .... Kuujjuarapik, PQ [*ICAO location identifier*]   (ICLI)

CYGX........ Gillam, MB [*ICAO location identifier*]   (ICLI)

CYGY .... Deception, PQ [*ICAO location identifier*]   (ICLI)

CYGZ .... Grise Fiord, NT [*ICAO location identifier*]   (ICLI)

CYH .... Continental Tyre Ltd. [*Vancouver Stock Exchange symbol*]

CYH .... Coyote Hills [*California*] [*Seismograph station code, US Geological Survey*]   (SEIS)

Cyh............ Cycloheximide [*Also, CH, CHX, CXM*] [*Fungicide*]

CYH........... Springerville, AZ [*Location identifier*] [*FAA*]   (FAAL)

CYHA .... Canadian Youth Hostels Association

CYHB .... Hudson Bay, SK [*ICAO location identifier*]   (ICLI)

CYHD .... Dryden, ON [*ICAO location identifier*]   (ICLI)

CYHE .... Hope, BC [*ICAO location identifier*]   (ICLI)

CYHI .... Holman/Holman Island, NT [*ICAO location identifier*]   (ICLI)

CYHK .... Gjoa Haven, NT [*ICAO location identifier*]   (ICLI)

CYHM .... Hamilton, ON [*ICAO location identifier*]   (ICLI)

CYHO .... Hopedale, NF [*ICAO location identifier*]   (ICLI)

CYHONC ... Committee of Youth Hostel Organizations in the Nordic Countries   (EA)

CYHQ .... Ottawa, ON [*ICAO location identifier*]   (ICLI)

CYHU........ Montreal/St. Hubert, PQ [*ICAO location identifier*]   (ICLI)

CYHY .... Hay River, NT [*ICAO location identifier*]   (ICLI)

CYHZ........ Halifax/International, NS [*ICAO location identifier*]   (ICLI)

CYI .... Canary Islands   (KSC)

CYI .... Chiayi [*Taiwan*] [*Airport symbol*]   (OAG)
CYI .... Cooperative Youth Initiative [*British*]
CYI .... Cymric Resources Ltd. [*Toronto Stock Exchange symbol*]
CYIB .... Atikokan, ON [*ICAO location identifier*]   (ICLI)
CYIO .... Pond Inlet, NT [*ICAO location identifier*]   (ICLI)
CYIR .... Council of Young Israel Rabbis   (EA)
CYIV .... Island Lake/Garden Hill, MB [*ICAO location identifier*]   (ICLI)
CYJ .... Chandeleur Bay [*Vancouver Stock Exchange symbol*]
CYJA .... Jasper, AB [*ICAO location identifier*]   (ICLI)
CYJN .... Saint-Jean, PQ [*ICAO location identifier*]   (ICLI)
CYJT .... Stephenville, NF [*ICAO location identifier*]   (ICLI)
CYK .... Consider Yourself Kissed [*Correspondence*]
CYK .... Copconda-York [*Vancouver Stock Exchange symbol*]
CYKA .... Kamloops, BC [*ICAO location identifier*]   (ICLI)
CYKF .... Waterloo-Wellington/Kitchener, ON [*ICAO location identifier*]   (ICLI)
CYKL .... Schefferville, PQ [*ICAO location identifier*]   (ICLI)
CYKY .... Kindersley, SK [*ICAO location identifier*]   (ICLI)
CYKZ .... Toronto/Buttonville, ON [*ICAO location identifier*]   (ICLI)
CYL .... Cassidy's Limited [*Toronto Stock Exchange symbol*]
CYL .... Communist Youth League
CYL .... Controlled Yeast Lysate
CYL .... Cylinder   (AAG)
CYL .... Cylindrical Lens [*Ophthalmology*]
CYl .... Yorba Linda District Library, Yorba Linda, CA [*Library symbol*] [*Library of Congress*]   (LCLS)
CYLA .... Langara, BC [*ICAO location identifier*]   (ICLI)
CYLC .... Lake Harbour, NT [*ICAO location identifier*]   (ICLI)
CYLD .... Chapleau, ON [*ICAO location identifier*]   (ICLI)
CYLDET... Cylinder-Pressure Monitoring and Conditioning Detection System
CYL DRM ... Cylinder or Drum [*Freight*]
CYLH .... Lansdowne House, ON [*ICAO location identifier*]   (ICLI)
CYLJ .... Meadow Lake, SK [*ICAO location identifier*]   (ICLI)
CYLL .... Cylinder Lock
CYLL .... Cylindric Lens   (ROG)
CYLL .... Cylindrical   (ROG)
CYLL .... Lloydminster, AB [*ICAO location identifier*]   (ICLI)
CYLNDL... Cylindrical
CYLO .... Shilo Canadian Forces Base, MB [*ICAO location identifier*]   (ICLI)
CYLPDN... Acta Pharmacologica Sinica [*A publication*]
CYLS .... Cylindrical Surface   (MSA)
CYLT .... Alert, NT [*ICAO location identifier*]   (ICLI)
CYLW .... Kelowna, BC [*ICAO location identifier*]   (ICLI)
CYLY .... Lytton, BC [*ICAO location identifier*]   (ICLI)
CYM .... Cayman Islands [*ANSI three-letter standard code*]   (CNC)
CYM .... Chatham, AK [*Location identifier*] [*FAA*]   (FAAL)
CYM .... Crystal Mountain [*Vancouver Stock Exchange symbol*]
Cym........... Cymbeline [*Shakespearean work*]
CYM .... Cymric [*Language, etc.*]   (ROG)
CYM .... Cyprus Minerals Co. [*NYSE symbol*]   (CTT)
CYMA .... Mayo, YT [*ICAO location identifier*]   (ICLI)
CYMD....... Mould Bay, NT [*ICAO location identifier*]   (ICLI)
CYMJ........ Moose Jaw Canadian Forces Base, SK [*ICAO location identifier*]   (ICLI)
CYMK .... Canadian Ukrainian Youth Association
CYMK .... Cyan, Yellow, Magenta, Black [*Color model*]   (PCM)
CYMM .... Fort McMurray, AB [*ICAO location identifier*]   (ICLI)
CYMO....... Moosonee, ON [*ICAO location identifier*]   (ICLI)
CYMR .... Merry Island, BC [*ICAO location identifier*]   (ICLI)
Cym Trans ... Honourable Society of Cymmrodorion. Transactions [*A publication*]
CYMV .... Clover Yellow Mosaic Virus
CYMW .... Maniwaki, PQ [*ICAO location identifier*]   (ICLI)
CYMX .... Montreal/Mirabel International, PQ [*ICAO location identifier*]   (ICLI)
CYN .... Canyon
CYN .... City National Corp. [*NYSE symbol*]   (SPSG)
CYN .... Communications Yeoman [*Navy rating*]
CYN .... Consolidated Ramrod Gold Corp. [*Vancouver Stock Exchange symbol*]
CYN .... Coyle, NJ [*Location identifier*] [*FAA*]   (FAAL)
CYN .... Coyotepe [*Nicaragua*] [*Seismograph station code, US Geological Survey*]   (SEIS)
CYN .... Cyanide   (KSC)
Cyn........... Cynegeticus [*of Xenophon*] [*Classical studies*]   (OCD)
Cyn........... Cynipidae [*Entomology*]
CYNA .... Natashquan, PQ [*ICAO location identifier*]   (ICLI)
CYNAP.... Cytotoxicity Negative - Absorption Positive [*Immunology*]
CYND....... Gatineau, PQ [*ICAO location identifier*]   (ICLI)
CYNI .... Nitchequon, PQ [*ICAO location identifier*]   (ICLI)
CYNM .... Matagami, PQ [*ICAO location identifier*]   (ICLI)
CYNR .... Canyon Resources Corp. [*Golden, CO*] [*NASDAQ symbol*]   (NQ)
CYNY .... Enderby, BC [*ICAO location identifier*]   (ICLI)
CYO .... Catholic Youth Organization
CYO .... Circleville, OH [*Location identifier*] [*FAA*]   (FAAL)
CYO .... Council on Youth Opportunity [*Disbanded 1971; functions taken over by Domestic Council and OMB*]
CYO .... Cyrano Resources, Inc. [*Vancouver Stock Exchange symbol*]

CYOC .... Old Crow, YT [*ICAO location identifier*]   (ICLI)
CYOD....... Cold Lake Canadian Forces Base, AB [*ICAO location identifier*]   (ICLI)
CYOJ .... High Level, AB [*ICAO location identifier*]   (ICLI)
CYoM .... Yosemite Museum, Nature Library, Yosemite, CA [*Library symbol*] [*Library of Congress*]   (LCLS)
CYOW .... Ottawa/International, ON [*ICAO location identifier*]   (ICLI)
CYP .... Calbayog [*Philippines*] [*Airport symbol*]   (OAG)
CYP .... Canadian Youth for Peace
CYP .... Cheyenne Petroleums [*Vancouver Stock Exchange symbol*]
CYP .... Christian Yellow Pages [*A publication*]
CYP .... Commonwealth Youth Programme   (EAIO)
CyP .... Contaminacion y Prevencion [*A publication*]
CYP .... Cyanopindolol [*Organic chemistry*]
CYP .... Cyclopedia of Portraits
CYP .... Cyclophosphamide [*Cytoxan*] [*Antineoplastic drug*]
Cyp........... Cypher [*A publication*]
CYP .... Cypress [*Botany*]   (ROG)
Cyp........... Cyprianus Florentinus [*Flourished, 12th century*] [*Authority cited in pre-1607 legal work*]   (DSA)
CYP .... Cyprus [*ANSI three-letter standard code*]   (CNC)
CYP .... Cyprus Airways Ltd.
CYP .... Cytoproct [*Protozoology*]
CYPA .... Children and Young Persons Act [*British*]
CYPA .... Prince Albert, SK [*ICAO location identifier*]   (ICLI)
CYPE .... Peace River, AB [*ICAO location identifier*]   (ICLI)
CYPF .... Esquimalt, BC [*ICAO location identifier*]   (ICLI)
Cypfruvex .. Kibris Sebze, Meyve Isletmeleri Ltd. [*Cyprus Vegetable and Fruit Processing and Exporting Corp. Ltd.*]
CYPG........ Portage La Prairie, MB [*ICAO location identifier*]   (ICLI)
CYPH .... Inukjuak, PQ [*ICAO location identifier*]   (ICLI)
CYPHERTEXT ... Cyphernetics Text Processing Language [*1970*] [*Data processing*]   (CSR)
CYPK........ Pitt Meadows, BC [*ICAO location identifier*]   (ICLI)
CYPL .... Pickle Lake, ON [*ICAO location identifier*]   (ICLI)
CYPN .... Port Menier, PQ [*ICAO location identifier*]   (ICLI)
CYPR........ Cyprus
CYPR........ Prince Rupert, BC [*ICAO location identifier*]   (ICLI)
Cypr Agric J ... Cyprus Agricultural Journal [*A publication*]
Cypr Med J ... Cyprus Medical Journal [*A publication*]
Cypr Orn Soc Bull ... Cyprus Ornithological Society. Bulletin [*A publication*]
Cypr Publ Hlth ... Cyprus Public Health [*A publication*]
Cyprus Agric J ... Cyprus Agricultural Journal [*A publication*]
Cyprus Agric Res Inst Annu Rep ... Cyprus Agricultural Research Institute. Annual Report [*A publication*]
Cyprus Agric Res Inst Misc Publ ... Cyprus Agricultural Research Institute. Miscellaneous Publications [*A publication*]
Cyprus Agric Res Inst Prog Rep ... Cyprus Agricultural Research Institute. Progress Report [*A publication*]
Cyprus Agric Res Inst Tech Bull ... Cyprus Agricultural Research Institute. Technical Bulletin [*A publication*]
Cyprus Agric Res Inst Tech Pap ... Cyprus Agricultural Research Institute. Technical Paper [*A publication*]
Cyprus Dep Agric Annu Rep ... Cyprus Department of Agriculture. Annual Report [*A publication*]
Cyprus Geol Surv Dep Bull ... Cyprus. Geological Survey Department. Bulletin [*A publication*]
Cyprus Geol Surv Dep Mem ... Cyprus. Geological Survey Department. Memoir [*A publication*]
Cyprus Ind ... Cyprus Industrial Journal [*A publication*]
Cyprus LR ... Cyprus Law Reports [*A publication*]   (DLA)
CYPS......... Cypress Savings Association [*NASDAQ symbol*]   (NQ)
CYPY .... Fort Chipewyan, AB [*ICAO location identifier*]   (ICLI)
CYQA .... Muskoka, ON [*ICAO location identifier*]   (ICLI)
CYQB .... Quebec, PQ [*ICAO location identifier*]   (ICLI)
CYQD .... The Pas, MB [*ICAO location identifier*]   (ICLI)
CYQF........ Red Deer Industrial, AB [*ICAO location identifier*]   (ICLI)
CYQG........ Windsor, ON [*ICAO location identifier*]   (ICLI)
CYQH........ Watson Lake, YT [*ICAO location identifier*]   (ICLI)
CYQI .... Yarmouth, NS [*ICAO location identifier*]   (ICLI)
CYQK .... Kenora, ON [*ICAO location identifier*]   (ICLI)
CYQL .... Lethbridge, AB [*ICAO location identifier*]   (ICLI)
CYQM .... Moncton, NB [*ICAO location identifier*]   (ICLI)
CYQN........ Nakina, ON [*ICAO location identifier*]   (ICLI)
CYQQ........ Comox Canadian Forces Base, BC [*ICAO location identifier*]   (ICLI)
CYQR .... Regina, SK [*ICAO location identifier*]   (ICLI)
CYQT .... Thunder Bay, ON [*ICAO location identifier*]   (ICLI)
CYQU........ Grande Prairie, AB [*ICAO location identifier*]   (ICLI)
CYQV........ Yorkton, SK [*ICAO location identifier*]   (ICLI)
CYQW....... North Battleford, SK [*ICAO location identifier*]   (ICLI)
CYQX .... Gander/International, NF [*ICAO location identifier*]   (ICLI)
CYQY .... Sydney, NS [*ICAO location identifier*]   (ICLI)
CYQZ........ Quesnel, BC [*ICAO location identifier*]   (ICLI)
CYR .... Cairo, GA [*Location identifier*] [*FAA*]   (FAAL)
CYR .... Carleton and Regiment [*British military*]   (DMA)
CYR .... Colonia [*Uruguay*] [*Airport symbol*]
CYR .... Core Ventures [*Vancouver Stock Exchange symbol*]
CYR .... Cray Research, Inc. [*NYSE symbol*]   (SPSG)
CyR .... Cruz y Raya [*A publication*]
Cyr .... Cyropaedia [*of Xenophon*] [*Classical studies*]   (OCD)

CYR .... Cyrus [*Persian emperor, d. 529BC*] (ROG)
Cyr .... Die Inschriften von Cyros, Koenig von Babylon [*A publication*] (BJA)
CYRA .... Commission's Yellowfin Regulatory Area [*Inter-American Tropical Tuna Commission*] (MSC)
CYRB......... Resolute, NT [*ICAO location identifier*] (ICLI)
CYRI .... Riviere Du Loup, PQ [*ICAO location identifier*] (ICLI)
CYRJ .... Roberval, PQ [*ICAO location identifier*] (ICLI)
CYRM .... Rocky Mountain House, AB [*ICAO location identifier*] (ICLI)
CYRQ .... Trois-Rivieres, PQ [*ICAO location identifier*] (ICLI)
CYrS .... Siskiyou County Public Library, Yreka, CA [*Library symbol*] [*Library of Congress*] (LCLS)
CYRT......... Rankin Inlet, NT [*ICAO location identifier*] (ICLI)
CYS............. Board of Education for the City of York Library [*UTLAS symbol*]
CYS............. Calypso Development Ltd. [*Vancouver Stock Exchange symbol*]
CYS............. Cathays [*Cardiff*] [*Welsh depot code*]
CYS............. Cheyenne [*Wyoming*] [*Airport symbol*] (OAG)
CYS............. Cheyenne, WY [*Location identifier*] [*FAA*] (FAAL)
CYS............. Chief Yeoman of Signals [*Australia*]
CYS............. CyCare Systems, Inc. [*NYSE symbol*] (SPSG)
Cys .... Cysteine [*Also, C, CySH*] [*An amino acid*]
Cys .... Cystine [*Also, CyS*] [*An amino acid*]
CYS............. Cystoscopy [*Medicine*]
CYSA .... Cape York Space Agency [*Australia*]
CYSA .... Combed Yarn Spinners Association [*Later, AYSA*] (EA)
CYSA .... Sable Island, NS [*ICAO location identifier*] (ICLI)
CYSB......... Sudbury, ON [*ICAO location identifier*] (ICLI)
CYSC......... Sherbrooke, PQ [*ICAO location identifier*] (ICLI)
CYSD......... Cytoplasm Sum Optical Density [*Microscopy*]
CYSD......... Suffield, AB [*ICAO location identifier*] (ICLI)
CY/SEC..... Cycles per Second [*See also Hz*]
CYSF......... Stony Rapids, SK [*ICAO location identifier*] (ICLI)
CySH .... Cysteine [*Also, C, Cys*] [*An amino acid*]
CYSH .... Cytoplasmic Shape [*Microscopy*]
CYSJ .... Saint John, NB [*ICAO location identifier*] (ICLI)
CYSK .... Sanikiluaq/Belcher Island, NT [*ICAO location identifier*] (ICLI)
CYSM........ Fort Smith, NT [*ICAO location identifier*] (ICLI)
CYSP .... Community Youth Special Projects [*Australia*]
CYSR .... Nanisivik/Strathcona Sound, NT [*ICAO location identifier*] (ICLI)
CYSS .... Children's and Youth Services Section [*Australian Library*]
CYSS .... Slate Island, ON [*ICAO location identifier*] (ICLI)
CYSTEX.... Combat System Exercise (MCD)
Cysto .... Cystoscopy [*Medicine*]
CYSU......... Summerside Canadian Forces Base, PE [*ICAO location identifier*] (ICLI)
CYSV......... Concordia - Youth Service Volunteers (EAIO)
CYSY .... Sachs Harbour, NT [*ICAO location identifier*] (ICLI)
CYSYDH... Cybernetics and Systems [*A publication*]
CYSYS...... Center for Cybernetics Systems Synergism
CYSZ......... Cytoplasmic Size [*Microscopy*]
CYT .... Cassidy Resources Ltd. [*Vancouver Stock Exchange symbol*]
CYT .... City Trust Bancorp [*NYSE symbol*] (SPSG)
CYT .... Crystal Shamrock [*Minneapolis, MN*] [*FAA designator*] (FAAC)
Cyt.............. Cytochrome [*Biochemistry*]
CYT .... Cytology
Cyt.............. Cytosine [*Also, C*] [*Biochemistry*]
CYT .... Cytoxan [*Cyclophosphamide*] [*Antineoplastic drug*]
CYT .... Yakataga, AK [*Location identifier*] [*FAA*] (FAAL)
CYTA........ California Yoga Teachers Association (EA)
CYTA........ Cyprus Telecommunications Authority [*Nicosia, Cyprus*] [*Telecommunications service*] (TSSD)
CytaBOM ... Cytarabine [*ara C*], Bleomycin, Oncovin [*Vincristine*], Methotrexate with Leucovorin [*Antineoplastic drug regimen*]
CYTB......... CytRx Biopool Ltd. [*NASDAQ symbol*] (NQ)
CYTBA...... Cytobios [*A publication*]
CYTC......... County Tower Corporation [*NASDAQ symbol*] (NQ)
CYTC......... Ethelda Bay, BC [*ICAO location identifier*] (ICLI)
CYTD......... Cytochalasin D [*Biochemistry*]
CYTE......... Cape Dorset, NT [*Canada*] [*ICAO location identifier*] (ICLI)
CYTEA...... Cryogenic Technology [*A publication*]
CYTECH... Cytotechnology
CYTGA...... Cytogenetics [*Switzerland*] [*A publication*]
CYTH........ Thompson, MB [*ICAO location identifier*] (ICLI)
CYTI......... Cytocare, Inc. [*NASDAQ symbol*] (SPSG)
CYTL......... Big Trout Lake, ON [*ICAO location identifier*] (ICLI)
CYTO........ Cytogen Corp. [*Princeton, NJ*] [*NASDAQ symbol*] (NQ)
CYTOA ..... Cytologia [*A publication*]
Cytobiologie Z Exp Zellforsch ... Cytobiologie; Zeitschrift fuer Experimentelle Zellforschung [*A publication*]
Cytog C Gen ... Cytogenetics and Cell Genetics [*A publication*]
Cytogen...... Cytogenetics [*A publication*]
CYTOGENET ... Cytogenetics
Cytogenet Cell Genet ... Cytogenetics and Cell Genetics [*A publication*]
Cytol........... Cytologia [*A publication*]
CYTOL...... Cytology

Cytol Genet ... Cytology and Genetics [*English Translation of Tsitologiya i Genetika*] [*A publication*]
Cytol Genet (Engl Transl Tsitol Genet) ... Cytology and Genetics (English Translation of Tsitologiya i Genetika) [*A publication*]
Cytol Neurol Stud Fac Med Univ Kanazawa ... Cytological and Neurological Studies. Faculty of Medicine. University of Kanazawa [*A publication*]
Cytol Stud Kanaz ... Cytological Studies. Faculty of Medicine. University of Kanazawa [*A publication*]
CYTR......... CytRx Corp. [*Atlanta, GA*] [*NASDAQ symbol*] (NQ)
CYTR......... Trenton Canadian Forces Base, ON [*ICAO location identifier*] (ICLI)
CYTS......... Timmins, ON [*ICAO location identifier*] (ICLI)
CYTX......... Cytox Corp. [*NASDAQ symbol*] (NQ)
CYTZ......... Toronto Island, ON [*ICAO location identifier*] (ICLI)
CYTZA...... Cytobiologie [*A publication*]
CYU .... Cheryl Resources, Inc. [*Vancouver Stock Exchange symbol*]
CYUA .... Shingle Point, YT [*ICAO location identifier*] (ICLI)
CYUB .... Tuktoyaktuk, NT [*ICAO location identifier*] (ICLI)
CYUC .... Nicholson Peninsula, NT [*ICAO location identifier*] (ICLI)
CYUC (M-L) ... Communist Youth Union of Canada (Marxist-Leninist)
CYUF .... Pelly Bay, NT [*ICAO location identifier*] (ICLI)
CYUH........ Clinton Point, NT [*ICAO location identifier*] (ICLI)
CYUI .... Cape Young, NT [*ICAO location identifier*] (ICLI)
CYUJ .... Lady Franklin Point, NT [*ICAO location identifier*] (ICLI)
CYUK .... Byron Bay, NT [*ICAO location identifier*] (ICLI)
CYUL .... Montreal/Dorval International, PQ [*ICAO location identifier*] (ICLI)
CYUQ........ Jenny Lind Island, NT [*ICAO location identifier*] (ICLI)
CYUR .... Gladman Point, NT [*ICAO location identifier*] (ICLI)
CYUS .... Shepherd Bay, NT [*ICAO location identifier*] (ICLI)
CYUT .... Repulse Bay, NT [*ICAO location identifier*] (ICLI)
CYUV .... Longstaff Bluff, NT [*ICAO location identifier*] (ICLI)
CYUX .... Hall Beach, NT [*ICAO location identifier*] (ICLI)
CYUY .... Rouyn, PQ [*ICAO location identifier*] (ICLI)
CYVADACT ... Cyclophosphamide, Vincristine, Adriamycin, Dactinomycin [*Actinomycin D*] [*Antineoplastic drug regimen*]
CYVADIC ... Cyclophosphamide, Vincristine, Adriamycin, Dacarbazine [*Antineoplastic drug regimen*]
CYVC......... La Ronge, SK [*ICAO location identifier*] (ICLI)
CYVG .... Vermilion, AB [*ICAO location identifier*] (ICLI)
CYVM .... Broughton Island, NT [*ICAO location identifier*] (ICLI)
CYVMAD ... Cyclophosphamide, Vincristine, Methotrexate, Adriamycin, Dacarbazine [*Antineoplastic drug regimen*]
CYVN .... Cape Dyer, NT [*ICAO location identifier*] (ICLI)
CYVO .... Val D'Or, PQ [*ICAO location identifier*] (ICLI)
CYVP .... Quujjuaq, PQ [*ICAO location identifier*] (ICLI)
CYVQ .... Norman Wells, NT [*ICAO location identifier*] (ICLI)
CYVR......... Vancouver/International, BC [*ICAO location identifier*] (ICLI)
CYVT......... Buffalo Narrows, SK [*ICAO location identifier*] (ICLI)
CYVV .... Clover Yellow Vein Virus
CYVV .... Wiarton, ON [*ICAO location identifier*] (ICLI)
CYW .... Clay Center, KS [*Location identifier*] [*FAA*] (FAAL)
CYW .... Color Your World, Inc. [*Toronto Stock Exchange symbol*]
CYWA .... Petawawa Canadian Forces Base, ON [*ICAO location identifier*] (ICLI)
CYWG .... Winnipeg/International, MB [*ICAO location identifier*] (ICLI)
CYWK .... Wabush, NF [*ICAO location identifier*] (ICLI)
CYWL .... Williams Lake, BC [*ICAO location identifier*] (ICLI)
CYWO....... Lupin, NT [*ICAO location identifier*] (ICLI)
CYWR .... White River, ON [*ICAO location identifier*] (ICLI)
CYWY .... Wrigley, NT [*ICAO location identifier*] (ICLI)
CYX .... Colony Pacific Explorations Ltd. [*Toronto Stock Exchange symbol*] [*Vancouver Stock Exchange symbol*]
CYXC........ Cranbrook, BC [*ICAO location identifier*] (ICLI)
CYXD .... Edmonton/Municipal, AB [*ICAO location identifier*] (ICLI)
CYXE .... Saskatoon, SK [*ICAO location identifier*] (ICLI)
CYXH........ Medicine Hat, AB [*ICAO location identifier*] (ICLI)
CYXI .... Killaloe/Bonnechere, ON [*ICAO location identifier*] (ICLI)
CYXJ .... Fort St. John, BC [*ICAO location identifier*] (ICLI)
CYXL .... Sioux Lookout, ON [*ICAO location identifier*] (ICLI)
CYXN .... Whale Cove, NT [*ICAO location identifier*] (ICLI)
CYXP .... Pangnirtung, NT [*ICAO location identifier*] (ICLI)
CYXR .... Earlton, ON [*ICAO location identifier*] (ICLI)
CYXS .... Prince George, BC [*ICAO location identifier*] (ICLI)
CYXT .... Terrace, BC [*ICAO location identifier*] (ICLI)
CYXU .... London, ON [*ICAO location identifier*] (ICLI)
CYXX .... Abbotsford, BC [*ICAO location identifier*] (ICLI)
CYXY .... Whitehorse, YT [*ICAO location identifier*] (ICLI)
CYY .... Carpita Corp. [*Toronto Stock Exchange symbol*]
CYYB .... North Bay, ON [*ICAO location identifier*] (ICLI)
CYYC......... Calgary/International, AB [*ICAO location identifier*] (ICLI)
CYYD .... Smithers, BC [*ICAO location identifier*] (ICLI)
CYYE .... Fort Nelson, BC [*ICAO location identifier*] (ICLI)
CYYF .... Penticton, BC [*ICAO location identifier*] (ICLI)
CYYG .... Charlottetown, PE [*ICAO location identifier*] (ICLI)
CYYH .... Spence Bay, NT [*ICAO location identifier*] (ICLI)
CYYJ .... Victoria/International, BC [*ICAO location identifier*] (ICLI)
CYYL .... Lynn Lake, MB [*ICAO location identifier*] (ICLI)
CYYN .... Swift Current, SK [*ICAO location identifier*] (ICLI)
CYYO........ Wynyard, SK [*ICAO location identifier*] (ICLI)

CYYQ........ Churchill, MB [*ICAO location identifier*] (ICLI)
CYYR........ Goose Bay, NF [*ICAO location identifier*] (ICLI)
CYYT........ St. John's, NF [*ICAO location identifier*] (ICLI)
CYYU........ Kapuskasing, ON [*ICAO location identifier*] (ICLI)
CYYW........ Armstrong, ON [*ICAO location identifier*] (ICLI)
CYYY........ Mont-Joli, PQ [*ICAO location identifier*] (ICLI)
CYYZ........ Toronto/International, ON [*ICAO location identifier*] (ICLI)
CYZ.......... Canterbury Resources, Inc. [*Vancouver Stock Exchange symbol*]
CYZ.......... Cauayan [*Philippines*] [*Airport symbol*] (OAG)
CYZ.......... Grand Rapids, MI [*Location identifier*] [*FAA*] (FAAL)
CYZA........ Ashcroft, BC [*ICAO location identifier*] (ICLI)
CYZD........ Toronto/Downsview, ON [*ICAO location identifier*] (ICLI)
CYZE........ Gore Bay, ON [*ICAO location identifier*] (ICLI)
CYZF........ Yellowknife, NT [*ICAO location identifier*] (ICLI)
CYZH........ Slave Lake, AB [*ICAO location identifier*] (ICLI)
CYZP........ Sandspit, BC [*ICAO location identifier*] (ICLI)
CYZR........ Sarnia, ON [*ICAO location identifier*] (ICLI)
CYZS........ Coral Harbour, NT [*ICAO location identifier*] (ICLI)
CYZT........ Port Hardy, BC [*ICAO location identifier*] (ICLI)
CYZU........ Whitecourt, AB [*ICAO location identifier*] (ICLI)
CYZV........ Sept-Iles, PQ [*ICAO location identifier*] (ICLI)
CYZW....... Teslin, YT [*ICAO location identifier*] (ICLI)
CYZX........ Greenwood Canadian Forces Base, NS [*ICAO location identifier*] (ICLI)
CZ............ Business Flight Ltd. [*Canada*] [*ICAO designator*] (FAAC)
CZ............ Cambata Aviation Ltd. [*India*] [*ICAO designator*] [*Obsolete*] (FAAC)
cz.............. Canal Zone [*MARC country of publication code*] [*Library of Congress*] (LCCP)
CZ............ Canal Zone [*Postal code*] (AFM)
CZ............ Cefazolin [*An antibiotic*]
CZ............ Cela Zimes [*A publication*]
CZ............ Coahuila & Zacatecas Railway [*AAR code*]
CZ............ Combat Zone
CZ............ Communications Zone (MCD)
CZ............ Control Zone [*For chart use only*] [*Aviation*]
CZ............ Convergence Zone [*Military*] (NVT)
CZ............ Coryza [*Medicine*]
CZ............ Crown Zellerbach Corp.
CZ............ Cubic Zirconia [*Simulated diamonds*]
CZ............ Czechoslovakia [*IYRU nationality code*]
CZ............ Czochralski Crystal Growth [*Crystallization process*]
Cz.............. Czytelnik [*A publication*]
CZA.......... Chichen Itza [*Mexico*] [*Airport symbol*] (OAG)
CZA.......... San Mateo County Free Library, Belmont, CA [*OCLC symbol*] (OCLC)
CZAG........ Committee for Zero Automobile Growth (EA)
C Zair Et Polit Soc ... Cahiers Zairois d'Etudes Politiques et Sociales [*A publication*]
C Zair Rech Develop ... Cahiers Zairois de la Recherche et du Developpement [*A publication*]
CZARTAC ... CZ [*Convergence Zone*] Area Reduction Tactic [*Military*] (CAAL)
Czas Geogr ... Czasopismo Geograficzne [*Geographical Journal*] [*A publication*]
Czas Praw Hist ... Czasopismo Prawno-Historyczne [*A publication*]
Czas Roln... Czasopismo Rolnicze [*A publication*]
Czas Stomat ... Czasopismo Stomatologiczne [*A publication*]
Czas Stomatol ... Czasopismo Stomatologiczne [*A publication*]
Czas Tech (Krakow) ... Czasopismo Techniczne (Krakow) [*A publication*]
Czas Tech M ... Czasopismo Techniczne. M. Mechanika [*A publication*]
Czas Tow Aptek (L) ... Czasopismo Towarzystwa Aptekarskiego (Lwow) [*A publication*]
CZB.......... Carbon Zinc Battery
CZB.......... Casey, IL [*Location identifier*] [*FAA*] (FAAL)
CZB.......... Cruz Alta [*Brazil*] [*Airport symbol*] (OAG)
CZBA........ Canal Zone Biological Area [*A preserve administered by the Smithsonian Institution*] [*Later, Smithsonian Tropical Research Institute*]
CZBN........ Citizens Bancorp of Wisconsin [*NASDAQ symbol*] (NQ)
CzBrS........ Statni Vedecka Knihova [*State Scientific Library*], Brno, Czechoslovakia [*Library symbol*] [*Library of Congress*] (LCLS)
CzBrU....... Universita J. E. Purkyne [*Purkyne University*], Brno, Czechoslovakia [*Library symbol*] [*Library of Congress*] (LCLS)
CzBU......... Univerzita Komenskeho Bratislava [*Comenius University of Bratislava*], Bratislava, Czechoslovakia [*Library symbol*] [*Library of Congress*] (LCLS)
CzBUK...... Ustredna Kniznica Slovenskej Akademie Vied [*Central Library of the Slovak Academy of Science*], Bratislava, Czechoslovakia [*Library symbol*] [*Library of Congress*] (LCLS)
CZC.......... Canal Zone Code [*A publication*] (DLA)
CZC.......... Chromated Zinc Chloride [*Wood preservative*]
CZC.......... Copper Center, AK [*Location identifier*] [*FAA*] (FAAL)
CZCAA...... Chemiker-Zeitung. Chemische Apparatur [*A publication*]
CZ Chem-Tech ... CZ Chemie-Technik [*A publication*]
CZ Code..... Canal Zone Code [*A publication*] (DLA)

CZCP......... CZ [*Convergence Zone*] Confirmation Pattern [*Military*] (CAAL)
CZCS......... Coastal Zone Color Scanner
CZD.......... Calculated Zenith Distance
CZD.......... Cozad, NE [*Location identifier*] [*FAA*] (FAAL)
CZE........... Capillary Zone Electrophoresis [*Physical chemistry*]
CZE........... Clarksville, AR [*Location identifier*] [*FAA*] (FAAL)
CZE........... Compare Zone Equal [*Data processing*]
CZE........... Coro [*Venezuela*] [*Airport symbol*] (OAG)
CZE........... Czech [*Language, etc.*]
cze............. Czech [*MARC language code*] [*Library of Congress*] (LCCP)
CZE........... Czechoslovak Foreign Trade [*A publication*]
CZECH ..... Czechoslovakia
Czech Acad Sci Bot Inst Hydrobiol Lab Annu Rep ... Czechoslovak Academy of Sciences. Botanical Institute. Hydrobiological Laboratory. Annual Report [*A publication*]
Czech Acad Sci Inst Landscape Ecol Hydrobiol Lab Annu Rep ... Czechoslovak Academy of Sciences. Institute of Landscape Ecology. Hydrobiological Laboratory. Annual Report [*A publication*]
Czech Acad Sci Inst Landscape Ecol Sect Hydrobiol Annu Rep ... Czechoslovak Academy of Sciences. Institute of Landscape Ecology. Section of Hydrobiology. Annual Report [*A publication*]
Czech Bibliogr Ind Hyg Occup Dis ... Czechoslovak Bibliography on Industrial Hygiene and Occupational Diseases [*A publication*]
Czech Congr Gastroenterol ... Czechoslovak Congress of Gastroenterology [*A publication*]
Czech F ...... Czechoslovak Film [*A publication*]
Czech Fg T ... Czechoslovak Foreign Trade [*A publication*]
Czech Heavy Ind ... Czechoslovak Heavy Industry [*A publication*]
Czech J Int'l L ... Czechoslovak Journal of International Law [*A publication*] (DLA)
Czech J Phys ... Czechoslovak Journal of Physics [*A publication*]
Czech J Phys Sect B ... Czechoslovak Journal of Physics. Section B [*A publication*]
Czech Math J ... Czechoslovak Mathematical Journal [*A publication*]
Czech Med ... Czechoslovak Medicine [*A publication*]
Czechosl Econ Pap ... Czechoslovak Economic Papers [*A publication*]
Czechoslovak Econ Dig ... Czechoslovak Economic Digest [*A publication*]
Czechoslovak J Phys ... Czechoslovak Journal of Physics [*A publication*]
Czechoslovak J Phys B ... Czechoslovak Journal of Physics. Section B [*A publication*]
Czechoslovak Math J ... Czechoslovak Mathematical Journal [*A publication*]
Czech Res Inst Crop Prod Annu Rep ... Czechoslovakia. Research Institutes for Crop Production. Annual Report [*A publication*]
Czech Res W ... Czechoslovak Research Work [*A publication*]
Czech Tr J ... Czechoslovak Trade Journal [*A publication*]
Czech Urad Vynalezy Objevy Vestn ... Czechoslovakia. Urad pro Vynalezy a Objevy. Vestnik [*A publication*]
Czech YB Int'l L ... Czechoslovak Yearbook of International Law [*A publication*] (DLA)
Czec J Phys ... Czechoslovak Journal of Physics. Section B [*A publication*]
Czec Math J ... Czechoslovak Mathematical Journal [*A publication*]
CZEG......... Edmonton, AB [*ICAO location identifier*] (ICLI)
CZE-MS.... Capillary Zone Electrophoresis - Mass Spectrometry [*Analytical chemistry*]
CZF........... Canusa Financial Corp. [*Vancouver Stock Exchange symbol*]
CZF........... Cape Romanzof [*Alaska*] [*Airport symbol*] (OAG)
CZF........... Cape Romanzof, AK [*Location identifier*] [*FAA*] (FAAL)
CZFA........ Faro, YT [*ICAO location identifier*] (ICLI)
CZFM........ Fort McPherson, NT [*ICAO location identifier*] (ICLI)
CZG.......... Canal Zone Government [*Superseded by Panama Canal Commission*]
CZG.......... Casa Grande, AZ [*Location identifier*] [*FAA*] (FAAL)
CZG.......... Cheni Gold Mines, Inc. [*Toronto Stock Exchange symbol*] [*Vancouver Stock Exchange symbol*]
CZH.......... Castello Resources Ltd. [*Vancouver Stock Exchange symbol*]
CZH.......... Corozal [*Belize*] [*Airport symbol*] (OAG)
CZH.......... Jacksonville, FL [*Location identifier*] [*FAA*] (FAAL)
CZHIA ..... Czechoslovak Heavy Industry [*A publication*]
CZI............ Chemiker-Zeitung. Chemie, Technische Chemie, Chemiewirtschaft; mit Chemie-Borse und Bezugsquellen fuer die Chemische Industrie [*A publication*]
CZI............ Crazy Woman, WY [*Location identifier*] [*FAA*] (FAAL)
CZI............ Crystalline Zinc Insulin [*Medicine*]
CZINVEST ... CZ [*Convergence Zone*] Investigation [*Military*] (CAAL)
CZIP.......... CZ [*Convergence Zone*] Investigation Pattern [*Military*] (CAAL)
CZJ........... Center, TX [*Location identifier*] [*FAA*] (FAAL)
CZJ........... Citadel Capital Corp. [*Toronto Stock Exchange symbol*]
CZJ........... Corazon De Jesus [*Panama*] [*Airport symbol*] (OAG)
CZJC......... Canal Zone Junior College
CZK.......... Cascade Locks, OR [*Location identifier*] [*FAA*] (FAAL)
CZK.......... Colossus Resources [*Vancouver Stock Exchange symbol*]
CZKR........ Czechoslovakian Kronen [*Monetary unit*]
CZL........... Calhoun, GA [*Location identifier*] [*FAA*] (FAAL)
CZL........... Canus Laboratories Ltd. [*Vancouver Stock Exchange symbol*]
CZL........... Connecticut State Library, Hartford, CT [*OCLC symbol*] (OCLC)

CZL............ Constantine [*Algeria*] [*Airport symbol*] (OAG)
CZM .... CalMat Co. [*NYSE symbol*] (SPSG)
CZM .... Coastal Zone Management
CZM .... Cozumel [*Mexico*] [*Airport symbol*] (OAG)
CZMA .... Coastal Zone Management Act [*1972*]
CZMAC..... Coastal Zone Management Advisory Committee [*Department of Commerce*] (MSC)
CZMJA ..... Czechoslovak Mathematical Journal [*A publication*]
CZMJB ..... Coastal Zone Management Journal [*A publication*]
CZMMAN ... Comunicaciones Zoologicas. Museo de Historia Natural de Montevideo [*A publication*]
CZN........... Casopis za Zgodovino in Narodpisje [*A publication*]
CZN........... Chisana [*Alaska*] [*Airport symbol*] (OAG)
CZN........... Chisana, AK [*Location identifier*] [*FAA*] (FAAL)
CZNB .... North Bay Canadian Forces Base, ON [*ICAO location identifier*] (ICLI)
CznBh .... Panama Canal Zone Library-Museum, Balboa Heights, CZ [*Library symbol*] [*Library of Congress*] (LCLS)
CZO .... Chistochina, AK [*Location identifier*] [*FAA*] (FAAL)
CZON....... Cefuzonam [*Antibacterial*]
CZOOA5... Carnets de Zoologie [*A publication*]
CZP........... Convergence Zone Propagation [*Military*]
CZP........... Curragh Resources, Inc. [*NYSE symbol*] (SPSG)
CZP........... Peninsula Library System, Belmont, CA [*OCLC symbol*] (OCLC)
Cz PH .... Czasopismo Prawno-Historyczne [*A publication*]
CZPS .... Czechoslovak Philatelic Society [*Later, SCP*]
CzPS .... Statni Technicka Knihova, Ustredi Vedeckych, Technickych a Ekonomickych Informaci, Prague, Czechoslovakia [*Library symbol*] [*Library of Congress*] (LCLS)
CZQM .... Moncton, NB [*ICAO location identifier*] (ICLI)
CZQX .... Gander, NF [*ICAO location identifier*] (ICLI)
CZR .... Center for Zoroastrian Research (EA)
CZR .... Convergence Zone Range [*Military*] (CAAL)
CZR .... Czar Resources Ltd. [*Toronto Stock Exchange symbol*]
CZ Rep....... Canal Zone Reports, Supreme and District Courts [*A publication*] (DLA)
CZRP......... Convergence Zone Resolution Pattern [*Military*] (CAAL)
CZ-RSV ..... Rous Sarcoma Virus, Carr-Zilber Strain
CZS........... Cruzeiro Do Sul [*Brazil*] [*Airport symbol*] (OAG)
CZS........... Czechoslovakia
CZSG........ Canal Zone Study Group (EA)
CZ-SLOV .. Czechoslovakia
CZSTA ...... Czasopismo Stomatologiczne [*A publication*]
CZT .... Carrizo Springs, TX [*Location identifier*] [*FAA*] (FAAL)
CZT .... Chlorozotocin [*Antineoplastic drug*]
CZT .... Combustion Zone Temperature [*Fuel technology*]
CZT .... Port Alfred [*Formerly, Crozet*] [*South Africa*] [*Geomagnetic observatory code*]
CZU .... Compare Zone Unequal [*Data processing*]
CZU .... South Portland, ME [*Location identifier*] [*FAA*] (FAAL)
CZUE .... Cape Parry, NT [*ICAO location identifier*] (ICLI)
CZUL........ Montreal, PQ [*ICAO location identifier*] (ICLI)
C (Zurich) .. Cinema (Zurich) [*A publication*]
CZVR......... Vancouver, BC [*ICAO location identifier*] (ICLI)
CZW .... Convergence Zone Width [*Military*] (CAAL)
CZWG .... Winnipeg, MB [*ICAO location identifier*] (ICLI)
CZX .... Canaustra Gold Explorations [*Vancouver Stock Exchange symbol*]
CZX .... Crosyton, TX [*Location identifier*] [*FAA*] (FAAL)
CZY .... Canadian Estate Land Corp. [*Vancouver Stock Exchange symbol*]
CZYPA ...... Czechoslovak Journal of Physics [*A publication*]
CZYZ........ Toronto, ON [*ICAO location identifier*] (ICLI)
CZZ .... Campo, CA [*Location identifier*] [*FAA*] (FAAL)
CZZ .... Consolidated Talcorp Ltd. [*Toronto Stock Exchange symbol*]

D

D .... Air-Cushion Vehicle built by Denny Brothers [*England*] [*Usually used in combination with numerals*]
D .... Air Force Training Category [*Inactive duty training periods and 15 days active duty training per year*]
D .... Application for Writ of Error Dismissed for Want of Jurisdiction [*Legal term*]   (DLA)
D .... Arithmetic Factor Register [*Data processing*]
D .... Aspartic Acid [*One-letter symbol; see Asp*]
d .... British Penny [*Derived from Latin "denarius"*]
D .... Chemiewerke Homburg [*Germany*] [*Research code symbol*]
D .... Cleared to Depart from the Fix [*Aviation*]   (FAAC)
D .... Codex Bezae   (BJA)
d .... Collision Diameter of a Molecule [*Symbol*] [*IUPAC*]
D .... Combustible Metals [*Fire classification*]
D .... Court of Divorce and Matrimonial Causes [*England*]   (DLA)
D .... Da [*Give*] [*Pharmacy*]
D .... Dacoromania [*A publication*]
D .... Dahlonega [*Georgia*] [*Mint mark, when appearing on US coins*]
D .... Daily
D .... Daler [*Numismatics*]
D .... Dallas' Pennsylvania and United States Reports [*A publication*]   (DLA)
D .... Dallas' United States Supreme Court Reports [*A publication*]   (DLA)
D .... Dam
D .... Damasus [*Flourished, 13th century*] [*Authority cited in pre-1607 legal work*]   (DSA)
D .... Dame
D .... Damn
D .... Dance [*A publication*]
D .... Dance Halls (Commercial) [*Public-performance tariff class*] [*British*]
D .... Danger Area [*Aviation*]   (FAAC)
d .... Dangling, at Bedside [*Medicine*]
D .... Darcy [*Physics*]
D .... Darkness [*or Darktime*] [*Endocrinology*]
D .... Data
D .... Date
D .... Dative   (ROG)
D .... Datum
D .... Daughter
D .... Daunorubicin [*Daunomycin, Rubidomycin*] [*Also, DNR, DRB, R*] [*Antineoplastic drug*]
D .... Day [*Broadcasting term*]
d .... Day [*SI symbol*]
D .... Day [*Approach and landing charts*] [*Aviation*]
D .... Day Return [*Round trip fare within one calendar day*] [*British*]
d .... De [*Of*] [*Spanish*]
D .... Deacon
D .... Dead [*or Deceased*]
D .... Dead Air Space
D .... Dean
D .... Dear   (ROG)
D .... Death
D .... Debe [*Debit*] [*Spanish*] [*Business term*]
D .... Debenture [*Type of bond*] [*Investment term*]
D .... Debit [*Debit*] [*French*] [*Business term*]
D .... Debye [*Unit of electric moment*]
D .... Decalin [*A trademark*]
D .... Decca [*Record label*] [*Great Britain, Europe, Australia, etc.*]
D .... Deceased
D .... December
D .... December [*A publication*]
D .... Decessit [*Died*] [*Latin*]
d .... Deci [*A prefix meaning divided by ten*] [*SI symbol*]
D .... Deciduous
D .... Decimal   (BUR)
D .... Decision   (ADA)
D .... Deck   (NASA)
D .... Declination
D .... Decoy [*Missile mission symbol*]

D .... Decree   (ADA)
D .... Decret [*Decree*] [*French*]   (ILCA)
D .... Decreto [*Decree*] [*Italian*]   (ILCA)
D .... Decretum [*Decree*] [*Latin*]
D .... Deed   (ROG)
D .... Deep   (MSA)
d .... Deepwell Pump [*Liquid gas carriers*]
D .... [*In*] Default [*Standard & Poor's bond rating*] [*Investment term*]
D .... Defeated
D .... Defense [*Basketball; lacrosse*]
D .... Defense Department [*US government*]
D .... Defense Notice [*Classification given to British news items which are considered harmful to national security and which are voluntarily censored by the press*]
D .... Deferred [*Finance*]
D .... Degree
d .... Deictic [*Linguistics*]
D .... Delaware Reports [*A publication*]   (DLA)
D .... Delay [*Electronics*]
D .... Deleted
D .... Delivery [*or Delivered*]
D .... Delta [*Phonetic alphabet*] [*International*]   (DSUE)
D .... Demain [*A publication*]
D .... Demand Curve [*Economics*]
d .... Demande [*Request, Claim*] [*French*]
D .... Democrat [*or Democratic*]
D .... Demy [*Half*] [*Size of paper*]   (ADA)
D .... Denarii [*Pence*] [*Monetary unit*] [*Great Britain*]
D .... Denarius [*or Denarii*] [*Silver coin in Ancient Rome; gold coin in Roman Empire*]
D .... Denied [*Legal term*]   (DLA)
D .... Denio's New York Reports [*A publication*]   (DLA)
D .... Denison's English Crown Cases [*1844-52*] [*A publication*]   (DLA)
D .... Denmark [*IYRU nationality code*]
D .... Denominator [*In formulas for life annuities and life insurance premiums*]
D .... Density
D .... Dental
D .... Dental Surgery Attendant [*Ranking title*] [*British Royal Navy*]
D .... Dentes [*Applied to Teeth*]   (ROG)
D .... Dentur [*Give*] [*Pharmacy*]
D .... Denver [*Colorado*] [*Mint mark, when appearing on US coins*]
d .... Deoxy [*or Desoxy*] [*Biochemistry*]
D .... Depart
D .... Department
D .... Depositus [*Laid to Rest*] [*Latin*]
D .... Depreciation
D .... Depression
D .... Depth
D .... Depth of Ship
D .... Deputy
D .... Dermatologist [*or Dermatology*]
D .... Descend [*Aviation*]   (FAAC)
D .... Deserter [*Military*]
D .... Design   (AAG)
D .... Destination
D .... Destra [*Right*] [*Italian*]
D .... Destroyed
D .... Destroyer [*Navy*] [*British*]
D .... Detail   (AAG)
D .... Detective
D .... Deus [*God*] [*Latin*]   (GPO)
D .... Deuterium [*Also, H² Radioisotope of hydrogen*]
D .... Deuteronomist Source of the Pentateuch   (BJA)
D .... [*Otto Erich*] Deutsch [*When used in identifying Schubert's compositions, refers to cataloging of his works by musicologist Deutsch*]
D .... Deutschland [*Germany*] [*German*]
D .... Deve [*Debit*] [*Portuguese*] [*Business term*]
D .... Development

D	Deviation
D	Devonian Period [Geology]
d	Devteron [A nuclear particle]
D	Dewoitine [French aircraft type] [World War II]
D	Dexamethasone [Also, DEX, DXM] [Antineoplastic drug]
D	Dexter [Right] [Latin]
D	Dextro [Configuration in chemical structure]
d	Dextro(rotatory) [Chemistry]
D	Diagnosis
D	Diagonal Engines (DS)
D	Diagonal Polarization [Physics] (ECON)
D	Diagram
D	Dialectica [A publication]
D	Diameter
d	Diameter [Symbol] [IUPAC]
D	Diamond (ADA)
D	Diaphragm
d	Dias [Day] [Spanish]
D	Diathermy [Medicine]
D	Diazepam [Also, DAP, DZ] [A sedative]
D	Dickensian [A publication]
D	Dicta (DLA)
D	Dictum (DLA)
D	Didymium [Mixture of rare-earth elements] [Chemistry] (ROG)
D	Died
D	Dielectric
D	Dies [Day] [Latin]
D	Diesel [British Waterways Board sign]
D	Diesel Oil
D	Dietitian
D	Difference
D	Differential Coefficient
D	Differential (of)
D	Differentiation
D	Diffuse [Immunology]
D	Diffusing Capacity
D	Diffusion Coefficient [Symbol] [IUPAC]
D	Digest of Justinian [A publication] (DLA)
D	Digest of Public General Bills [Library of Congress] [A publication]
D	Digit [or Digital] (MDG)
D	Digno [Worthy, Deserving] [Portuguese] [Correspondence]
D	Dihydrotestosterone [Also, DHT] [Endocrinology]
D	Dihydrouridine [One-letter symbol; see H₂Urd]
D	Dime [Monetry unit]
D	Dimensional
D	Dinar [Monetary unit] [Tunisia]
D	Diode (MDG)
D	Diopter [Also, DIOPT] [Optics]
D	Dip
D	Diplomat [License plate code assigned to foreign diplomats in the US]
D	Direction [Data processing]
D	Director aircraft capable of controlling drones or missiles [Designation for all US military aircraft]
D	Director [Films, television, etc.]
D	Director [A publication]
D	Dirt [Gossip] [Slang]
D	Disc Issuer and Assistant [Sports]
D	Discharged
D	Discount
D	Disease
D	Dismissed [Legal term] (DLA)
D	Disney's Ohio Superior Court Reports [A publication] (DLA)
D	Dispenser (MCD)
D	Displacement
D	Display (MDG)
D	Dispose [or Destroy] [Routing slip]
D	Disqualified [Horse racing]
D	Dissertation (BJA)
D	Dissonances. Revue Musicale Independante [A publication]
D	Distal [Medicine]
D	Distance
D	Distance Winner [Horse racing]
D	Distinctio [Decretum Gratiani] [A publication] (DSA)
D	Distinguished (ADA)
d	Distinguished [Case at bar different either in law or fact from case cited for reasons given] [Used in Shepard's Citations] [Legal term] (DLA)
D	District Court [Federal] (DLA)
D	Diver [British military] (DMA)
D	Diversity [Genetics]
D	Dividend [Investment term]
D	Division
D	Divorced
D	Divus [The Late] [Latin]
D	Doctor
D	Document
D	Dog [Phonetic alphabet] [World War II] (DSUE)
D	Doit [Debit] [French] [Business term]

D	Doivent [Owing, Due] [French] [Business term]
D	Dollar [Monetary unit]
D	Dom [Port] [Latin] (ROG)
D	Domain [Telecommunications]
D	Dome
D	Dominant [Applied to a species]
D	Dominion Resources, Inc. [NYSE symbol] (SPSG)
D	Dominion Rubber Co. [Canada] [Research code symbol]
D	Dominus [The Lord] [Latin] (GPO)
D	Don [Sir (title)] [Spanish]
D	Don [Phonetic alphabet] [Pre-World War II] (DSUE)
D	Donative (ROG)
D	Donor
D	Doriden [Glutethimide] [Sedative]
D	Dorsal
D	Dosis [Dose] [Pharmacy]
D	Douane [Customs] [French]
D	Double
D	Doublet
D	Doubtful
D	Dowager
d	Down (Quark) [Atomic physics]
D	Downrange Distance during Launch [NASA]
D	Doxorubicin [Also, DOX, DXR] [Formerly, ADR, Adriamycin] [Antineoplastic drug]
D	Drachma [Monetary unit in Greece]
D	Draft (ROG)
D	Drafting Program [Association of Independent Colleges and Schools specialization code]
D	Drag (MCD)
D	Dragoons [Military unit] [British]
D	Drain [Electron device] (MSA)
D	Drama
D	Drammaturgia [A publication]
D	Draw
D	Dressing [Medicine]
D	Drive [State] [Psychology]
D	Driver [British military] (DMA)
D	Driving
D	Drizzling [Meteorology]
D	Droit [Right] [French]
D	Drone Plane [Navy symbol]
D	Drop
D	Droppable Fuel Tank [Suffix to plane designation]
D	Drug
D	Druids [Freemasonry]
D	Drum (MDG)
D	Dry-Bulk Container [Packaging] (DCTA)
D	Dual Capacity [London Stock Exchange]
D	Duchess
D	Duchy
D	Dues
D	Duff [Phonetic alphabet] [Royal Navy] [World War I] (DSUE)
D	Duke
D	Dulcis [Dear One] [Latin]
D	Dull
D	Dummy [in game of bridge]
D	Dump
D	Dun [Thoroughbred racing]
D	Dunlop, Bell, and Murray's Scotch Court of Session Cases, Second Series [1838-62] [A publication] (DLA)
D	Duodecimo [Book up to 20 centimeters in height]
D	Duodenum [Anatomy]
D	Duplex
D	Duration
D	Dusio [In Cisitalia car model "D46"]
D	Dust [Meteorology]
D	Dutch
D	Duty [Navy]
D	Duxbury's High Court Reports [South African Republic] [A publication] (DLA)
D	Dwarf
D	Dye [Classification key in textile printing]
D	Dyer's Edition of Valiant's English King's Bench Reports [1513-82] [A publication] (DLA)
D	Dynamic Capital Corp. [Toronto Stock Exchange symbol]
D	Dyne [Unit of force] [Also, Dy, dyn] [Preferred unit is N, Newton]
D	Electric Displacement [Symbol]
D	Faulty Diction [Used in correcting manuscripts, etc.]
D	Five Hundred [Roman numeral]
D	Germany [Aircraft nationality and registration mark] (FAAC)
D	Intermediate Dialing Center on a Toll Ticket [Telecommunications] (TEL)
D	Knoll AG [Germany] [Research code symbol]
D	Labs. Dr. J. Auclair [France] [Research code symbol]
D	Medium [Men's shoe width]
D	Morison's Dictionary of Scotch Session Cases [A publication] (DLA)
D	Naturally Aspirated [Automotive engineering]
D	Penny [Nail size]

D	Recueil Dalloz [*French*] [*A publication*] (DLA)
d	Relative Density [*Symbol*] [*IUPAC*]
D	Response to Detail [*Rorschach*] [*Psychology*]
d	Response to Small Detail [*Rorschach*] [*Psychology*]
D	Siegfried AG [*Switzerland*] [*Research code symbol*]
D	Troponwerke Dinklage & Co. [*Germany*] [*Research code symbol*]
D	Usually Reliable Source of Intelligence [*Military*]
D	Wide [*Women's shoe width*]
D1	Double First Class
D_1	First Dorsal Vertebra [*Second dorsal vertebra is D_2, etc.*] [*Medicine*]
1-D	Selective Service Class [*for Qualified Member of Reserve Component, or Student Taking Military Training, Including ROTC and Accepted Aviation Cadet Applicant*]
2-D	Selective Service Class [*for Registrant Deferred Because of Study for the Ministry*]
2-D	Two-Dimensional
3-D	Decapitation, Disembowelment, and Dismemberment [*Types of movies*]
D^3	Detection, Discrimination, and Designation
3-D	Selective Service Class [*for Man Deferred from Military Service Because Induction Would Cause Extreme Hardship and Privation to a Wife, Child, or Parent*] [*Obsolete*]
3-D	Three-Dimensional [*Pictures or films*]
3-D	Triple-Diffusion Process (MDG)
4-D	Dead, Dying, Diseased, Disabled [*Food processors' classification of animals unfit for use*]
4-D	Four-Dimensional (MSA)
4-D	Selective Service Class [*for a Minister of Religion*]
D-66	Democraten '66 [*Democrats '66*] [*Netherlands*] (PPW)
3D's	Denazification, Demilitarization, Deindustrialization [*Allied policy for Germany after World War II*]
4D's	Drugs, Debt, Deforestation, and Democracy [*US foreign policy concerns in Latin America*]
D (Bank)	Data Bank
D (Day)	Decimalisation Day [*February 15, 1971, day English money was decimalized*]
D (Day)	General military term designating the day on which a specific action is planned to commence; by extension, the beginning of any activity of importance [*Precise meaning of "D" is uncertain. Theories include "Departure," cited by Brig. Gen. Robert Shulz, Gen. Dwight D. Eisenhower's executive assistant; "Disembarkation" or "Debarkation"; and "Decision." Another theory holds that the term is simply alliterative, as in "H-Hour."*]
D (Layer)	Lowest layer of the ionosphere (AAG)
DA	CRS/Sirrine, Inc. [*Later, CRX*] [*AMEX symbol*] (SPSG)
DA	Daily (AFIT)
DA	Daily Abstract [*Tea trade*] (ROG)
Da	Dakota Territory Reports [*A publication*] (DLA)
DA	Damaged (CINC)
Da	Damasus [*Flourished, 13th century*] [*Authority cited in pre-1607 legal work*] (DSA)
DA	Dan-Air Services Ltd. [*Great Britain*] [*ICAO designator*] (FAAC)
DA	Danish
DA	Danish Army (NATG)
DA	Dansylaspartate [*Biochemistry*]
DA	Dark Agouti [*Rat strain*]
DA	Dassault-Breguet [*Avions Marcel Dassault*] [*France*] [*ICAO aircraft manufacturer identifier*] (ICAO)
DA	Data Acquisition (MDG)
DA	Data Adapter (MCD)
DA	Data Administrator
DA	Data Analysis (AFM)
DA	Data Assembler
DA	Data Automation (AFM)
DA	Data Available
DA	Date [*Online database field identifier*]
DA	Daughter
DA	Daunorubicin, ara-C [*Cytarabine*] [*Antineoplastic drug regimen*]
DA	Day
DA	Days after Acceptance [*Business term*]
DA	Deaerator (NRCH)
DA	Dealers Alliance (EA)
D & A	Dear and Anderson's Scotch Session Cases [*1829-32*] [*A publication*] (DLA)
D/A	Debt to Asset Ratio [*Economics*]
DA	Debtors Anonymous (EA)
da	Deca [*A prefix meaning multiplied by 10*] [*SI symbol*]
DA	Decimal Add
DA	Decimal-to-Analog (CET)
DA	Decision Area (MCD)
D/A	Deductible Average [*Business term*]
DA	Defence Act (DLA)
DA	Defence Adviser [*British*]
DA	Defence of Airfields [*British*] [*World War II*]
DA	Defence Attache [*British*] (DS)
DA	Defense Aid [*Lend-Lease*] [*World War II*]
D & A	Defense & Armament Magazine [*A publication*]
DA	Deferred Annuity [*Insurance*] (ADA)
DA	Define Area
DA	Degenerative Arthritis
DA	Delayed Action [*Pharmacy*]
DA	Delayed Arming [*of explosive device*]
DA	Delta Air Lines, Inc. (AAG)
DA	Delta Amplitude (AAG)
D of A	Deltiologists of America (EA)
DA	Deluxe Paint Animation [*Electronic art*]
DA	Demand Assignment [*Telecommunications*] (TEL)
DA	Democratic Agenda (EA)
DA	Democratic Alliance [*Political party*] [*Philippines*] (FEA)
DA	Democrats Abroad (EA)
DA	Density Altitude [*Navigation*]
DA	Dental Anesthetic [*Medicine*]
DA	Dental Apprentice
DA	Dental Assistant
DA	Department of Agriculture
D of A	Department of Agriculture
DA	Department of the Army
D of A	Department of Aviation [*Australia*]
DA	Departure Approved [*Aviation*] (FAAC)
DA	Depletion Allowance [*Business term*]
DA	Deployment Assembly [*Skylab*] [*NASA*]
DA	Deposit Account [*Banking*]
DA	Deposit Administration
DA	Deputy Administrator (FAAC)
DA	Deputy Advocate [*Legal term*] (DLA)
DA	Deputy Assistant (DAS)
DA	Descending Aorta [*Anatomy*]
DA	Design Agent (CAAL)
DA	Design Authorization
DA	Design Automation (BUR)
DA	Designated Adult [*Most serious person in a group of flippant people*]
DA	Desk Accessory [*Data processing*] (BYTE)
DA	Destination Address
DA	Detector Assembly
DA	Detergent Aid
DA	Detroit Arsenal [*Michigan*] [*Army*] (MCD)
DA	Deutsche Aussenpolitik [*A publication*]
DA	Deutsches Archiv [*A publication*]
DA	Deutschtum und Ausland [*A publication*]
DA	Developing Agency (CAAL)
DA	Development Assistance
DA	Developmental Age
DA	Deviation Authorization
DA	Devil's Advocate
DA	Dextrose Agar [*Microbiology*]
DA	Diagnostic Analyzer
DA	Dicti Anni [*Of the Said Year*] [*Latin*]
DA	Dictionary of Americanisms [*A publication*]
DA	Differential Amplifier
DA	Differential Analyzer (IEEE)
DA	Digestive Anlage
DA	Digital Alternator
D-to-A	Digital-to-Analog [*Converter*] [*Data processing*]
D-A	Digital-to-Analog [*Converter*] [*Data processing*]
DA	Dinar [*Monetary unit*] [*Algeria*]
DA	Dinner Ale [*British*] (ADA)
DA	Diphenylchloroarsine [*Tear gas*] [*Army symbol*]
DA	Diploma in Anesthetics [*British*]
DA	Diploma in Art
DA	Direct Access (BUR)
DA	Direct Action [*A publication*] (APTA)
DA	Direct Action [*Bomb or shell fuze*]
d/a	Direct Advertising [*Later, Printing Paper Quarterly*] [*A publication*]
DA	Direct Agglutination [*Clinical chemistry*]
DA	Direct Ascent (AAG)
DA	Direction Action [*Bomb fuze*]
DA	Directional Antenna
DA	Director of Aircraft (MUGU)
D of A	Director of Artillery [*British*]
DA	Directory Assistance [*Telecommunications*] (TEL)
DA	Disability Assistance
DA	Disassemble
D/A	Discharge and Advise [*Medicine*]
DA	Discharge Afloat
DA	Discrete Address
DA	Discretionary Account [*Investment term*]
DA	Discrimination Acuity
DA	Discrimination Analysis [*Agronomy*]
DA	Dislocation Allowance [*Military*] (AFM)
DA	Dispensing Allowance [*British military*] (DMA)
DA	Display Adapter
D/A	Dissemin/Action (EA)
DA	Dissertation Abstracts [*Later, Dissertation Abstracts International*] [*A publication*]
DA	Dissolved Acetylene

DA.............. Distribution Amplifier
DA.............. Distribution Assembly [*Ground Communications Facility, NASA*]
DA.............. District Administrator
DA.............. District Agent [*Insurance*]
DA.............. District Assembly [*British*]
DA.............. District Attorney
DA.............. District Authorities [*British*]
DA.............. Division Artillery [*Army*]
DA.............. Divorce Anonymous   (EA)
DA.............. Do Not Answer
DA.............. Docking Adapter [*Aerospace*]   (MCD)
DA.............. Doctor of Archaeology
DA.............. Doctor of Arts
DA.............. Documentary Bill for Acceptance
DA.............. Documentation Abstracts [*A publication*]
DA.............. Documentation Associates Information Services, Inc.   (IID)
D/A............ Documenti Contro Accettazione [*Documents Against Acceptance*] [*Italian*] [*Business term*]
D/A............ Documentos Contra Aceptacion [*Documents Against Acceptance*] [*Spanish*] [*Business term*]
D/A............ Documents for Acceptance [*Banking*]   (ROG)
D/A............ Documents Against Acceptance [*Banking*]
DA.............. Documents Attached
D/A............ Documents Contre Acceptation [*Documents Against Acceptance*] [*French*] [*Banking*]
DA.............. Doesn't Answer   (ADA)
D/A............ Dokumente Gegen Akzept [*Documents Against Acceptance*] [*German*] [*Banking*]
D/A............ Dokumente Teen Akseptasie [*Documents Against Acceptance*] [*Afrikaans*] [*Business term*]
DA.............. Dollar Averaging Cost [*Investment term*]
DA.............. Domestic Android [*Quasar Industries*]
DA.............. Dominion Arsenal [*World War I*] [*Canada*]
DA.............. Dominion Atlantic Railway Co. [*Absorbed into CP Rail*] [*AAR code*]
DA.............. Donor-Acceptor
DA.............. Dopamine [*Biochemistry*]
DA.............. Dormant Account [*Banking*]
DA.............. Dorsal Aorta [*Anatomy*]
DA.............. Dorsal Area [*Anatomy*]
DA.............. Dose Assessment [*Nuclear energy*]   (NRCH)
DA.............. Double-Acting
DA.............. Double Aged [*Metals*]
DA.............. Double Amplitude   (KSC)
DA.............. Double Armor [*Telecommunications*]   (TEL)
DA.............. Draft Action   (EA)
DA.............. Dragon Airways Ltd.
DA.............. Drift Angle [*Navigation*]
D d A.......... Droit d'Auteur [*A publication*]
DA.............. Drug Addict
DA.............. Drugs Anonymous   (EA)
DA.............. Dual Action
DA.............. Ducktail [*Hair style*] [*Bowdlerized version*]
DA.............. Ductus Arteriosus [*Anatomy*]
DA.............. Dummy Antenna
DA.............. Dummy Load [*JETDS nomenclature*] [*Military*]   (CET)
DA.............. Dunlap & Associates, Inc.   (MCD)
DA.............. DUSTOFF [*Dedicated Unhesitating Service to Our Fighting Forces*] Association   (EA)
DA.............. Dynamic Analysis Branch [*Redstone Arsenal*]
Da.............. [*The*] "Holy Scriptures" (1881) [*J. N. Darby*] [*A publication*]   (BJA)
D & A........ International Defense and Aid Fund for Southern Africa, US Committee   (EA)
DA.............. Istituto de Angeli [*Italy*] [*Research code symbol*]
DA.............. National Council, Daughters of America [*Harrisburg, OH*]   (EA)
D of A........ National Council, Daughters of America
DA.............. Recueil Analytique Dalloz [*French*] [*A publication*]   (DLA)
D1A........... Dickey [*Maine*] [*Seismograph station code, US Geological Survey*]   (SEIS)
DA-1 .... Directional Antenna Day and Night [*Broadcasting term*]
D2A........... Dickey [*Maine*] [*Seismograph station code, US Geological Survey*]   (SEIS)
DA-2 .... Directional Antenna with Changing Patterns, Day and Night [*Broadcasting term*]
D3A........... Dickey [*Maine*] [*Seismograph station code, US Geological Survey*]   (SEIS)
DA-3 .... Directional Antenna with Changing Patterns, Day and Night with Additional Pattern Change [*Broadcasting term*]
DA's.......... Domestic Afflictions [*Menstruation*] [*Slang*]   (DSUE)
DAA.......... Data Access Arrangement [*Telecommunications*] [*Obsolete*]
DAA.......... Data Automation Activity   (AFM)
DAA.......... Days after Anthesis [*Botany*]
DAA.......... Deaf Artists of America   (EA)
DAA.......... Decimal Adjust Accumulator
DAA.......... Dehydroascorbic Acid [*Also, DHA*] [*Oxidized form of Vitamin C*] [*Biochemistry*]
DAA.......... Department of Aeronautics and Astronautics [*MIT*]   (MCD)
DAA.......... Dependents Assistance Act

DAA.......... Deputy Assistant Adjutant [*Military*] [*British*]   (ROG)
DAA.......... Derivative Activation Analysis [*Analytical chemistry*]
DAA.......... Desaparagine Insulin [*Pharmacology*]
DAA.......... Designated Approval Authority   (MCD)
DAA.......... Diacetone Acrylamide [*Organic chemistry*]
DAA.......... Diaminoacetanilide [*Organic chemistry*]
DAA.......... Diaminoanisole [*A dye*] [*Organic chemistry*]
DAA.......... Diesel Automobile Association   (EA)
DAA.......... Digital Automatic Acquisition   (MCD)
DAA.......... Direct Access Arrangement [*Telecommunications*]
DAA.......... Director of Army Automation
DAA.......... Division Administrative Assistant
DAA.......... Divisional Administrative Area [*Military*] [*British*]
DAA.......... Doctor of Applied Arts
DAA.......... Documents Against Acceptance [*Banking*]
DA & A ...... Drug Addiction and Alcoholism [*Title XVI*] [*Social Security Administration*]   (OICC)
DAA.......... Drug and Alcohol Abuse   (OICC)
DAA.......... Drugs Available Abroad [*A publication*]
DAA.......... Durene Association of America   (EA)
DAA.......... Fort Belvoir, VA [*Location identifier*] [*FAA*]   (FAAL)
DAAA........ Alger [*Algeria*] [*ICAO location identifier*]   (ICLI)
DAAA........ Department of the Army Administrative Area
DAA & AM ... Defense Aid [*Lend-Lease*] Aircraft and Aeronautical Material [*World War II*]
DAAB........ Blida [*Algeria*] [*ICAO location identifier*]   (ICLI)
DAAC........ Digital Adaptive Area Correlation
DAAC........ Director of Allied Air Cooperation [*World War II*]
DAACA ..... Delegation for Afro-American and Caribbean Cultural Affairs
DAACA ..... Department of the Army Allocation Committee, Ammunition   (AABC)
DAACCE... Department of the Army Alternate Command and Control Element   (AABC)
DAAD........ Bou Saada [*Algeria*] [*ICAO location identifier*]   (ICLI)
DAAD........ Deutscher Akademischer Austauschdienst [*German Academic Exchange Service*]   (EA)
DAADB ..... Department of the Army Active Duty Board
DAAE........ Bejaia/Soummam [*Algeria*] [*ICAO location identifier*]   (ICLI)
DAAE........ Defense Aid [*Lend-Lease*] Administration Expenses [*World War II*]
DAAE........ Diethylamine Analog of Ethmozine [*Biochemistry*]
DAAF .... Aoulef [*Algeria*] [*ICAO location identifier*]   (ICLI)
DAAG........ Alger/Houari Boumediene [*Algeria*] [*ICAO location identifier*]   (ICLI)
DAAG........ Deputy Assistant Adjutant-General [*British*]
DAAG........ Dose Assessment Advisory Group [*Department of Energy*] [*Las Vegas, NV*]   (EGAO)
DA-AHEW ... Department of the Army Plan for Assistance in Department of Health, Education, and Welfare   (AABC)
DAAI & OC ... Defense Aid [*Lend-Lease*] Agricultural, Industrial, and Other Commodities [*World War II*]
DAAIUGM ... Disaster Aid Association of the International Union of Gospel Missions   (EA)
DAAJ........ Djanet [*Algeria*] [*ICAO location identifier*]   (ICLI)
DAAK .... Boufarik [*Algeria*] [*ICAO location identifier*]   (ICLI)
DAAL........ Alger [*Algeria*] [*ICAO location identifier*]   (ICLI)
DAAL .... Directory of Australian Academic Libraries [*A publication*]   (APTA)
DAALPS ... Detachement d'Armee des Alpes [*French*]
DAAM....... Telergma [*Algeria*] [*ICAO location identifier*]   (ICLI)
DAAMP .... Department of the Army Avionics Master Plan   (AABC)
DAAMRA ... Department of the Army Acquisition Management Review Agency   (MCD)
DAAN........ Doklady Azerbajdzanskogo Filiala. Akademii Nauk SSSR [*A publication*]
DAAN........ Reggan [*Algeria*] [*ICAO location identifier*]   (ICLI)
DAAO........ D-Amino Acid Oxidase [*An enzyme*]
DAA w/o OP ... Driving Away Auto without Owner's Permission [*FBI standardized term*]
DAAP .... Department of the Army Audiovisual Program
DAAP .... Illizi [*Algeria*] [*ICAO location identifier*]   (ICLI)
DAAPP...... Department of the Army Audiovisual Production Program   (MCD)
DAAPPP ... Data Archive on Adolescent Pregnancy and Pregnancy Prevention [*Sociometrics Corp.*] [*Information service or system*]   (IID)
DAAPS...... Division of Advanced Automotive Power Systems [*Energy Research and Development Administration*]
DAAQ........ Ain Oussera [*Algeria*] [*ICAO location identifier*]   (ICLI)
DAA & QMG ... Deputy Assistant-Adjutant and Quartermaster-General [*British*]
DAAR .... Daily Air Activity Report   (CINC)
DAAR .... Department of the Army, Office of the Chief, Army Reserve
DAARL...... Directory of Australian Academic and Research Libraries [*Australia*] [*A publication*]
DAAS .... Defense Activity Address System   (MCD)
DAAS .... Defense Automatic Addressing System   (AFIT)
DAAS .... Diamineanisole Sulfate [*Organic chemistry*]
DAAS .... Discrete Automatic Address System
DAAS .... DoD [*Department of Defense*] Automatic Addressing System   (NG)

DAAS .... Setif/Ain-Arnat [*Algeria*] [*ICAO location identifier*] (ICLI)
DAASM .... Doppler Arrival Angle Spectral Measurement System [*Geophysics*]
DAASO ..... Defense Automatic Addressing System Office (NATG)
DAAT .... Tamanrasset [*Algeria*] [*ICAO location identifier*] (ICLI)
DAATCO .. Department of the Army Air Traffic Coordinating Officer
DAATL ...... Detachement d'Armee de l'Atlantique [*French*]
DAAUW .... American Association of University Women Educational Foundation, Washington, DC [*Library symbol*] [*Library of Congress*] (LCLS)
DAAV .... Jijell/Taher [*Algeria*] [*ICAO location identifier*] (ICLI)
DAAVMPP ... Department of the Army Audiovisual Media Production Program
DAAW .... Bordj Omar Driss [*Algeria*] [*ICAO location identifier*] (ICLI)
DAAX .... Cheragas [*Algeria*] [*ICAO location identifier*] (ICLI)
DAAY .... Mecheria [*Algeria*] [*ICAO location identifier*] (ICLI)
DAAZ .... Relizane [*Algeria*] [*ICAO location identifier*] (ICLI)
DAB .... Daily Audience Barometer [*British*] (ADA)
DAB .... Data Acquisition Bus (NASA)
DAB .... Daytona Beach [*Florida*] [*Airport symbol*] (OAG)
DAB .... Deacon Air Ballistic (MUGU)
DAB .... Defense Acquisition Board [*DoD*]
DAB .... Delayed Action Bomb
DAB .... Design Arts Board [*Australia*]
DAB .... Destroyer Advisory Board [*Navy*]
DAB .... Deutsches Arzneibuch [*German Medical Book*] [*Medicine*]
DAB .... Devereux Adolescent Behavior [*Rating scale*] [*Also, ABRS*] [*Psychology*]
DAB .... Diabrasive International Ltd. [*Toronto Stock Exchange symbol*]
DAB .... Diagnostic Achievement Battery
DAB .... Diaminobenzene [*Organic chemistry*]
DAB .... Diaminobenzidine [*Organic chemistry*]
DAB .... Diaminobutanoic Acid [*An amino acid*]
DAB .... Diazabutadiene [*Organic chemistry*]
DAB .... Dictionary of American Biography [*A publication*]
DAB .... Dictionary of Assyrian Botany [*A publication*] (BJA)
DAB .... Dictionnaire d'Archeologie Biblique [*A publication*]
DAB .... Dimethylaminoazobenzene [*Organic chemistry*]
DAB .... Directly Authorised Body [*Securities and Investments Board*] [*British*]
DAB .... Director of the Army Budget
DAB .... Disciplinary Appeal Board [*Australia*]
DAB .... Display Assignment BITS [*Binary Digits*]
DAB .... Display Attention BITS [*Binary Digits*] [*Data processing*]
DAb .... Dissertation Abstracts [*Later, Dissertation Abstracts International*] [*A publication*]
DAB .... Dun and Bradstreet Reports [*A publication*]
DAB .... Dysrhythmic Aggressive Behavior
DABA .... Deutsche Aussenhandelsbank [*German Foreign Trade Bank*]
DABA .... Diaminobenzanilide [*Organic chemistry*]
DABA .... Diaminobenzoic Acid [*Organic chemistry*]
DABAA ..... Dissertation Abstracts International. Section A [*A publication*]
DABAWAS ... Datenbank fuer Wassergefahrdende Stoffe [*Data Bank on Substances Harmful to Water*] [*Information service or system*] [*Federal Republic of Germany*] (IID)
DABB .... Annaba/El Mellah [*Algeria*] [*ICAO location identifier*] (ICLI)
DABBB ..... Dissertation Abstracts International. Section B [*A publication*]
DABC .... African Bibliographic Center, Washington, DC [*Library symbol*] [*Library of Congress*] (LCLS)
DABC .... Constantine/Ain El Bey [*Algeria*] [*ICAO location identifier*] (ICLI)
DABCO ..... Diazabicyclooctane [*Organic chemistry*]
DABI .... DAB Industries, Inc. [*NASDAQ symbol*] (NQ)
DABIA ...... (Dimethylaminoazobenzene)iodoacetamide [*Organic chemistry*]
DABITC .... (Dimethylaminoazobenzene)isothiocyanate [*Organic chemistry*]
DABLC ..... Director, Advanced Base Logistics Control [*Navy*]
DABOA ..... Director, Advanced Base Office, Atlantic [*Navy*]
DABOP ..... Director, Advanced Base Office, Pacific [*Navy*]
Da & Bos .... Darby and Bosanquet's Statutes of Limitation [*2nd ed.*] [*1893*] [*A publication*] (DLA)
DABP .... Skikda [*Algeria*] [*ICAO location identifier*] (ICLI)
D Abr .... D'Anvers' General Abridgment of the Common Law [*A publication*] (DLA)
DABRK ..... Daybreak
DABS .... Desert Arabian Bloodstock [*NASDAQ symbol*] (NQ)
DABS .... Direct Access Beacon System (MCD)
DABS .... Discrete Address Beacon System
DABS .... Dynamic Air Blast Simulator (MCD)
DABS .... Tebessa [*Algeria*] [*ICAO location identifier*] (ICLI)
DABSAQ ... Dissertation Abstracts International. Section B. Sciences and Engineering [*A publication*]
DABT .... Batna [*Algeria*] [*ICAO location identifier*] (ICLI)
DABT .... Diamino(tribromopropyl)triazine [*Flame retardant*] [*Organic chemistry*]
DABW .... Directory of American Book Workers [*A publication*]
DAC .... Dacca [*Bangladesh*] [*Airport symbol*]
DAC .... Dachiardite [*A zeolite*]
Dac .... Dacia [*A publication*]
Dac .... Dacoromania [*A publication*]

DAC .... Darwin [*California*] [*Seismograph station code, US Geological Survey*] (SEIS)
DAC .... Data Acquisition Camera
DAC .... Data Acquisition Chassis (AAG)
DAC .... Data Acquisition Computer
DAC .... Data Acquisition and Control (NASA)
DAC .... Data Acquisition Controller
DAC .... Data Analysis Computer
DAC .... Data Analysis Console (AFM)
DAC .... Data Analysis Control (MCD)
DAC .... Day Activity Center
DAC .... Days after Contact
DAC .... Days after Contract [*Business term*] (MCD)
DAC .... Decrement Accumulator
DAC .... Deductible Average Clause [*Insurance*]
DAC .... Defect Action Sheet [*A publication*]
DAC .... Defenders of the American Constitution (EA)
DAC .... Defense Acquisition Circular [*DoD*] (RDA)
DAC .... Delayed Atomization Cuvette [*Laboratory analysis*]
DAC .... Delivery Against Cost [*Business term*]
DAC .... Demand Assignment Controller
DAC .... Democratic Action Committee [*Political party*] [*Pakistan*]
DAC .... Democratic Action Congress [*Trinidad and Tobago*] [*Political party*] (PPW)
DAC .... Department of the Army Civilian
DAC .... Design Augmented by Computer [*General Motors Corp.*]
DAC .... Development Assistance Committee [*Organization for Economic Cooperation and Development*] [*Paris, France*] (EAIO)
DAC .... Developmental Activity Center
DAC .... Dhaka [*Bangladesh*] [*Airport symbol*] (OAG)
DAC .... Diallyl Chlorendate [*Fire retardant*]
DAC .... Diamond Anvil Cell [*Spectrometry*]
DAC .... Dictionary of the Apostolic Church [*A publication*] (BJA)
DAC .... Dictionnaire d'Archeologie Chretienne et de Liturgie [*A publication*]
DAC .... Digital-to-Analog Converter [*Data processing*]
DAC .... Digital Arithmetic Center
DAC .... Diocesan Advisory Committee [*Church of England*]
DAC .... Direct Access Capability (MCD)
DAC .... Direct Access Communications (MCD)
DAC .... Direct Access Computing (MCD)
DAC .... Direct Access Control (MCD)
DAC .... Direct Air Cycle
DAC .... Director Assignment Console (NVT)
DAC .... Directors Advisory Committee [*National Institutes of Health*]
DAC .... Directory of Associations in Canada [*Micromedia, Ltd.*] [*Information service or system*] [*A publication*] (IID)
DAC .... Disabled Adult Child [*Social Security Administration*] (OICC)
DAC .... Disablement Advisory Committee [*Department of Employment*] [*British*]
DAC .... Disaster Assistance Centers [*Federal Emergency Management Agency*]
DAC .... Display Analysis Console
DAC .... Distribution Advisory Committee [*Australia*]
DAC .... Distribution Automation and Control (MCD)
DAC .... Division of Adult Corrections (OICC)
DAC .... Division of Ambulatory Care [*Later, DACHP*] (EA)
DAC .... Divisional Ammunition Column (ADA)
D Ac .... Doctor of Accounts
DAC .... Document Availability Code (MCD)
DAC .... Domestic Affairs Council [*Replaced Urban Affairs Council, Rural Affairs Council, and Cabinet Committee on Environment*] [*White House*]
DAC .... Domestic Annual Fishing Capacity [*Fishery management*] (MSC)
DAC .... Double-Action Cylinder
DAC .... Douglas Aircraft Company [*of McDonnell Douglas Corp.*]
DAC .... Downed Aircraft (NVT)
DAC .... Drug Abuse Council [*Defunct*]
DAC .... Duplicate Aperture Card
DAC .... Durex Abrasives Corporation [*Defunct*] (EA)
DAC .... Dynamic Accelerated Cooling [*Sumitomo Metals*]
DAC .... McDonnell Douglas Corp. [*Santa Monica, CA*] [*FAA designator*] (FAAC)
DAC .... National Society, Daughters of the American Colonists (EA)
DAC .... Yuma, AZ [*Location identifier*] [*FAA*] (FAAL)
DACA .... Days after Contract Award [*Business term*] (MCD)
DACA .... Department of the Army Certificate of Achievement
DACA .... Disability Advisory Council of Australia
DACAD ..... Dansylcadaverine [*Biochemistry*]
DACAN ..... Data Acquisition and Analysis (NOAA)
DACAN ..... Douglas Aircraft Co. of Canada [*of McDonnell Douglas Corp.*] (MCD)
DACAN ..... Military Committee Standing Group Distribution and Accounting Agency, NATO
DACAR ..... Damage Assessment and Casualty Report [*Military*]
DACAS ..... Damage Assessment and Casualty Report [*Military*] (AFM)
DACAS ..... Drug Abuse Current Awareness System [*A publication*]
DACB .... Data Acquisition and Control Buffer (MCD)
DACBU ..... Data Acquisition and Control Buffer Unit (NASA)

DACC .... Danish American Chamber of Commerce (EA)
DACC .... De Havilland Aircraft Company, Canada
DACC .... Department of the Army Communications Center (AABC)
DACC .... Direct Access Communications Channels
D Acc .... Doctor of Accountancy [*or Accounting*]
Dacca .... All India Reporter, Dacca Series [*1949-50*] [*A publication*] (DLA)
Dacca .... Pakistan Law Reports, Dacca Series [*A publication*] (DLA)
Dacca Univ Bull ... Dacca University. Bulletin [*A publication*]
Dacca Univ J ... Dacca University. Journal [*A publication*]
Dacca Univ Or Publ Ser ... Dacca University. Oriental Publications Series [*A publication*]
Dacca Univ St ... Dacca University. Studies [*A publication*]
Dacca Univ Stud Part A ... Dacca University. Studies. Part A [*A publication*]
Dacca Univ Stud Part B ... Dacca University. Studies. Part B [*A publication*]
Dacca U Stud ... Dacca University. Studies [*A publication*]
DACCC ...... Defense Area Communications Control Center
DACCC ...... Detroit Area Consortium of Catholic Colleges [*Library network*]
DACCC-AL ... Defense Area Communications Control Center, Alaska
DACCC-CON ... Defense Area Communications Control Center, CONUS
DACCEUR ... Defense Area Communications Control Center, Europe (NATG)
DACCP ...... Diaminocyclohexane(carboxyphthalato)platinum [*Antineoplastic drug*]
DACCS ...... Department of the Army Command and Control System (AABC)
DACE .... Data Acquisition and Control Executive [*Hewlett-Packard Co.*]
DACE .... Data Administration Center Equipment [*Telecommunications*] (TEL)
DACE .... Department of the Army Alternate Command and Control Element (AABC)
DACE .... Design and Computational Experiments
DACE .... Doctor of Air Conditioning Engineering
DACE .... United States Army, Corps of Engineers, Office of the Chief of Engineers Library, Washington, DC [*Library symbol*] [*Library of Congress*] (LCLS)
DACEMS ... Data Communications Equipment Monitoring and Switching (MCD)
DAC Eng ... Doctor of Air Conditioning Engineering
DACFC ...... David Allan Coe Fan Club (EA)
DACG .... Departure Airfield Control Group [*Military*] (AABC)
DACG .... Deputy Assistant Chaplain-General [*British*]
DACG .... Deputy Assistant Commissary-General [*Military*] [*British*] (ROG)
DA Chem ... Doctor of Applied Chemistry
DACHP ..... Division of Ambulatory Care and Health Promotion [*of the American Hospital Association*] (EA)
DACI .... Direct Adjacent Channel Interference
DACI .... Dual Audio Cassette Interface
Dacia .... Dacia. Revue d'Archeologie et d'Histoire Ancienne [*A publication*]
DACIL ...... Department of the Army Critical Items List
DACL .... Depression Adjective Check Lists [*Psychology*]
DACL .... Dictionnaire d'Archeologie Chretienne et de Liturgie [*A publication*]
DACL .... Dynamic Analysis and Control Laboratory [*MIT*] (MCD)
DACM .... Defensive Air Combat Maneuvering [*Military*]
DACM .... (Dimethylamino(methyl)coumarinyl)maleimide [*Organic chemistry*]
DACM .... Dissimilar Air Combat Maneuvers
DACMIS ... Development and Configuration Management Information System (MCD)
DACO .... Data Consistency Orbit
DACO .... Divisional Administrative Contracting Officer [*Military*]
DACO .... Douglas Aircraft Company Overseas [*Obsolete*]
DACO .... Dynamic American Corporation [*NASDAQ symbol*] (NQ)
DACOM .... Data Communications Corporation of Korea [*Seoul, South Korea*] [*Telecommunications service*] (TSSD)
Da-Com ...... Data Communications, Inc. [*Information service or system*] (IID)
DACOM .... Datascope Computer Output Microfilmer [*Eastman Kodak Co.*]
DACOMP ... Damage Assessment Computer Program [*Military*]
DACON ..... Data Controller
DACON ..... Digital-to-Analog Converter [*Data processing*]
Dacor .... Dacoromania [*A publication*]
DACOR ..... Data Correction [*IBM Corp.*]
DACOR ..... Data Correlator
DACOR ..... Diplomatic and Consular Officers, Retired (EA)
DACOS ..... Data Communication Operating System
DACOS ..... Deputy Assistant Chief of Staff (NATG)
DACOWITS ... Defense Advisory Committee on Women in the Services [*DoD*] [*Washington, DC*]
DACP .... Deserving Airman Commissioning Program [*Military*]
DACPO ..... Data Count Printout [*Data processing*]
DACR .... Director of Airfield and Carrier Requirements [*British*]
DACRB ...... Department of the Army Compassionate Review Board
DACRP ...... Department of the Army Communication Resources Plan (AABC)

DACRS ...... Department of the Army Classification Review Committee (MCD)
DACRYLON ... Dacron and Nylon
DACS .... American Chemical Society, Washington, DC [*Library symbol*] [*Library of Congress*] (LCLS)
DACS .... Data Acquisition, Control, and Simulation Centre [*University of Alberta*] [*Research center*] (RCD)
DACS .... Data Acquisition Control System (IEEE)
DACS .... Data and Analysis Center for Software [*Air Force*] [*Information service or system*] (IID)
DACS .... DCSOPS [*Deputy Chief of Staff for Operations and Plans*]/ ACSI [*Assistant Chief of Staff for Intelligence*] Computer System [*Army*]
DACS .... De La Rue Automatic Cash System [*Banknote-disbursing equipment*] [*British*]
DACS .... Design and Artists Copyright Society Ltd. [*British*]
DACS .... Digital Access and Crossconnect System [*Telecommunications*] (TEL)
DACS .... Digital Acquisition and Control System (MCD)
DACS .... Digital Animated Control System
DACS .... Discrete Address Communications System
DACT .... Dactinomycin (Actinomycin-D) [*Also, act-D, AMD*] [*Antineoplastic drug*]
DACT .... Deactivate (KSC)
DACT .... Direct Acting
DACT .... Disposable Absorption Collection Trunk (MCD)
DACT .... Dissimilar Air Combat Tactics [*Navy*] (MCD)
DACT .... Dissimilar Air Combat Training (MCD)
DACT .... United States ACTION Library, Washington, DC [*Library symbol*] [*Library of Congress*] (LCLS)
Dac Terr ..... Dacotah Territory [*A publication*]
DACTS ...... Dispersion Against Concealed Targets [*Experiment*] [*Army*] (RDA)
Dactyl .... Dactylography [*A publication*]
DACU .... Data Acquisition and Control Unit
DACU .... Device Attachment Control Unit [*IBM Corp.*]
DACU .... Digital-to-Analog Converter Unit [*Data processing*]
DACU .... Digitizing and Control Unit
DAD .... Danang [*North Vietnam*] [*Airport symbol*] (OAG)
DA & D ...... Data Acquisition and Distribution
DAD ...... Data Automation Digest [*A publication*]
DAD ...... Data Description Language [*Data processing*]
DAD ...... Davis Distributing Ltd. [*Toronto Stock Exchange symbol*]
DAD ...... Depression after Delivery (EA)
DAD ...... Deputy Assistant Director
DAD ...... Design Approval Data
DAD ...... Design and Development (ADA)
DAD ...... Designated Alert Detachment [*Military*] (MCD)
DAD ...... Diffuse Alveolar Damage [*Medicine*]
DAD ...... Digital Angle Data
DAD ...... Digital Audio Disc [*Audio/video technology*]
DAD ...... Dignity after Death (EA)
DAD ...... Directional Aerial Disposal [*Insecticide spray*]
DA-D .... Directional Antenna Daytime Only [*Broadcasting term*]
DAD ...... Directory of Australian Directories [*A publication*]
DAD ...... Dispense as Directed [*Pharmacy*]
DAD ...... Documents Against Discretion [*Banking*]
DAD ...... Donor-Acceptor-Donor [*Physiology*]
DAD ...... Double-Acting Door [*Technical drawings*]
DAD ...... Double-Amplitude Displacement (MCD)
DAD .... Douglas County Public Library, Castle Rock, CO [*OCLC symbol*] (OCLC)
DAD .... Drum and Display [*Data processing*] (ADA)
DAD .... Dual Air Density [*Explorer satellite*] [*NASA*]
Dada .... Dada/Surrealism [*A publication*]
DADA .... Deputy Assistant Director of Artillery [*British*]
DADA .... Diisopropylamine [*or Diisopropylammonium*] Dichloroacetate [*Pharmacology*]
DADAC ..... Department of the Army Distribution/Allocation Committee (AABC)
DADAC ..... Digital-to-Analog Deck Angle Converter [*Data processing*] [*Navy*]
DADADS .. Deputy Assistant Director of Army Dental Services [*British*]
DADAG ..... Diacetyldianhydrogalacitol [*Antineoplastic drug*]
DADAH .... Deputy Assistant Director of Army Health [*British*]
DADAVS ... Deputy Assistant Director, Army Veterinary Services
DADB .... Data Analysis Database
DADB .... Directory of Australian Data Collections [*Database*]
DADC .... Digital Air Data Computer
DADC .... Digital Audio Disc Corporation [*Sony Corp.*]
DAD-C2 ..... Division Air Defense Command and Control (MCD)
DAD-C3 ..... Division Air Defense Command, Control, and Communications [*Study*] (MCD)
DADCAP ... Dawn and Dusk Combat Air Patrol
DADCMI .. Department of the Army Policy for Disclosure of Classified Military Information [*to foreign government*] (AABC)
DADCOK .. Digital Air Data Computer Status
DADCSLOG ... Department of the Army, Deputy Chief of Staff for Logistics
DADCTS ... Digital Air Data Computer Test Set
DADDS ..... Diacetyldiaminodiphenylsulfone [*Antibacterial compound*]

DADDTC .. Diethylammonium Diethyldithiocarbamate [*Organic chemistry*]
DADE .... Data Acquisition and Decommutation Equipment
DADE .... Digital Acquisition and Documentation Equipment (KSC)
DADE .... Drugs and Drug Abuse Education [*A publication*]
DADE .... Dual Air Density Explorer [*Satellite*] [*NASA*]
DADEE ...... Dynamic Analog Differential Equation Equalizer
DADEMS ... Department of the Army Data Elements Management System (MCD)
DADF .... Diacetyldihydrofluorescein [*Organic chemistry*]
DADG .... Danish Arctic Station of Disko Island, Greenland. Publications [*A publication*]
DADGMS ... Deputy Assistant Director-General of Medical Services [*British*] (ADA)
DADHT ..... Diacetyldioxohexahydrotriazine [*Laundry bleach activator*]
DAdI .... Adas Israel Congregation, Washington, DC [*Library symbol*] [*Library of Congress*] (LCLS)
DADIC ...... Data Dictionary [*Data processing*]
DADiSP ..... Data Acquisition and Digital Signal Processing
DADISP ..... Data Analysis and Display [*Data processing*]
DADIT ...... Daystrom Analog-to-Digital Integrating Translator
DADIWT ... Deputy Assistant Director of Inland Water Transport [*British military*] (DMA)
DADL .... (D-Ala, D-Leu) Enkephalin [*Biochemistry*]
DADL .... Deputy Assistant Director of Labor [*Allied Control Commission*] [*World War II*]
DADLE ..... (D-Ala, D-Leu) Enkephalin [*Biochemistry*]
DADM .... Decision Authority, Decision Memorandum [*Military*] (MCD)
D Adm .... Doctor of Administration
DADMC .... Defense Advanced Disposal Management Course [*Army*]
DADMCS ... Department of the Army Decoration for Meritorious Civilian Service
DADME .... Deputy Assistant Director of Mechanical Engineering [*British military*] (DMA)
D Adm Eng ... Doctor of Administrative Engineering
DADMS .... Defense Automated Document Management System (MCD)
DADMS .... Deputy Assistant Director of Medical Services
DAD/MSD ... Deputy Assistant Director for Management Support Division [*Vietnam*]
DADO .... Data Automation Design Office [*Air Force*] (AFM)
DADOS ..... Deputy Assistant Director of Ordnance Services [*Australia*]
DADOS ..... Deputy Assistant Director of Ordnance Stores [*Military*]
DADOS(E) ... Deputy Assistant Director of Ordnance Services (Engineering) [*British*]
DADOTA .. Drug and Alcohol Dependent Offenders' Treatment Act of 1986
dADP .... Deoxyadenosine Diphosphate [*Biochemistry*]
DAD/PE ..... Deputy Assistant Director for Plans and Evaluation [*Vietnam*]
DADPE ..... Diaminodiphenyl Ether [*Organic chemistry*]
DADPM ..... Diaminodiphenyl Methane [*Organic chemistry*]
DAD/POD ... Deputy Assistant Director for the Psychological Operations Division [*Vietnam*]
DADPR ..... Deputy Assistant Director of Public Relations [*British military*] (DMA)
DADPS ...... Diaminodiphenyl Sulfone [*Also, DAPSONE, DDS*] [*Pharmacology*]
DADPTC ... Defence Automatic Data Processing Training Centre [*British military*] (DMA)
DADQ .... Deputy Assistant Director of Quartering [*British*]
DADR .... Deputy Assistant Director of Remounts [*British*]
DADR .... Digital Angle Data Recorder
DADRT ..... Deputy Assistant Director of Railway Transport [*British military*] (DMA)
DADS .... DARCOM [*Development and Readiness Command, Army*] Announcement Distribution System (RDA)
DADS .... Data Acquisition and Display System [*or Subsystem*]
DADS .... Defense Audiovisual Depository System
DADS .... Defense Automated Depot System (MCD)
DADS .... Digital Air Data System
DADS .... Digital Analog Data System (CAAL)
DADS .... Digital Audio Distribution System
DADS .... Director of Army Dental Services [*British*]
DADS .... Dittler Airline Data Systems [*Information service or system*] (EISS)
DADS .... Dosimetry Acquisition and Display System
DADS .... Dual Air Density Satellite [*NASA*] (NASA)
DADS .... Dynamic Analysis and Design Software
DADSM ..... Dynamic Analysis and Design of Systems (RDA)
DADSM ..... Direct Access Device Space Management (MCD)
DADSOT .. Digital/Analog Daily System Operability Tests (MCD)
DADST ..... Deputy Assistant Director of Supplies and Transport [*British*]
DADT .... Deputy Assistant Director of Transportation [*British*]
DADTA ..... Durability and Damage Tolerance Analysis [*Air Force*]
DADU .... Data Accumulation and Distribution Units [*Navy*] (MCD)
DADVRS ... Deputy Assistant Director of Veterinary and Remount Services [*British military*] (DMA)
DADVS ..... Deputy Assistant Director of Veterinary Services (DMA)
Dady .... Dadyburjar. Small Court Appeals [*India*] [*A publication*] (DLA)
DAE .... Data Acquisition Equipment (KSC)
DAE .... Data Automation Equipment
DAE .... Days after Emergence [*Botany*]

DAE .... Dealers Art Exchange (EA)
DAE .... Defense Acquisition Executive (MCD)
DAE .... Developments in Agricultural Engineering [*Elsevier Book Series*] [*A publication*]
DAE .... Dictionary of American English [*A publication*]
DAE .... Differential-Algebraic Equations [*Mathematics*]
DAE .... Diphenylanthracene Endoperoxide [*Organic chemistry*]
DAE .... Diploma in Advanced Education (ADA)
DAE .... Diploma in Advanced Engineering [*British*]
DAE .... Director of Aircraft Equipment [*Ministry of Aircraft Production*] [*British*]
DAE .... Director of Army Education [*British*]
DAE .... District Airport Engineer
DAE .... Division of Adult Education [*Office of Education*]
D Ae .... Doctor of Aeronautics
DAE .... Doctor of Art Education
DAE .... DSA [*Defense Supply Agency*] Augmentation Element
DAEA .... Dimethyl Aminoethyl Acetate [*Organic chemistry*]
DAEA .... Drug Abuse Education Act (OICC)
DAEC .... Danish Atomic Energy Commission
DAEC .... Deutscher Aero Club [*German*]
DAEC .... Duane Arnold Energy Center (NRCH)
DAE Circ LA Agr Exp Sta Dept Agr Econ ... DAE Circular. Louisiana Agricultural Experiment Station. Department of Agricultural Economics [*A publication*]
Daed .... Daedalus [*A publication*]
DAEDA ..... Daedalus [*A publication*]
DAEDAC .. Drug Abuse Epidemiology Data Center [*Ceased operation*] [*Texas Christian University*] (IID)
DAEDARC ... Department of the Army Equipment Data Review Committee (AABC)
D Ae E .... Doctor of Aeronautical Engineering
D Ae Eng .... Doctor of Aeronautical Engineering
DAEEP ...... Division of Applied Experimental and Engineering Psychologists (EA)
DAEM .... Deutsches Archiv fuer Erforschung des Mittelalters [*A publication*]
DAEM .... Directorate of Aircraft Engineering and Maintenance (MCD)
DAEMON ... Data Adaptive Evaluator and Monitor
DAENDT .. Developments in Agricultural Engineering [*A publication*]
DAEP .... Department of the Army Equipment Publication
DAEP .... Diamino(adamantyl)ethylpyrimidine [*Biochemistry*]
DAERA ..... Disability Alliance Educational and Research Association [*British*]
DAE Res Rep Dep Agric Econ Agribusiness LA State Univ ... DAE Research Report. Department of Agricultural Economics and Agribusiness. Louisiana State University [*A publication*]
D Aero E ..... Doctor of Aeronautical Engineering
DAES .... Diploma in Advanced Educational Studies, University of Newcastle [*British*] (DBQ)
DAES .... Division of Adult Education Service [*of NEA*]
D Ae S .... Doctor of Aeronautical Science
DAES .... Proceedings. Devon Archaeological Exploration Society [*A publication*]
D Ae Sc ...... Doctor of Aeronautical Science
DAF .... Dafare [*Djibouti*] [*Seismograph station code, US Geological Survey*] (SEIS)
DAF .... Data Acquisition Facility [*of STADAN*]
DAF .... Data Analysis Facility
DAF .... Days after Flowering [*Botany*]
DAF .... Decay-Accelerating Factor [*Biochemistry*]
DAF .... Dedicated Access Facility [*Library science*]
DAF .... Deferred Annuity Fund
DAF .... Delayed Action Fuse
DAF .... Delayed Auditory Feedback [*Audiology*]
DAF .... Delivered at Frontier [*Seller's responsibility is fulfilled when goods have arrived at frontier, but before "customs border," of country named*] [*"INCOTERM," International Chamber of Commerce official code*]
DAF .... Demonstration Air Force
DAF .... Denmark-America Foundation (EA)
DAF .... Department of Agriculture and Fisheries [*Scotland*]
DAF .... Department of the Air Force
DAF .... Departure Airfield (AABC)
DAF .... Desalkylflurazepam [*Sedative*]
DAF .... Desert Air Force [*British*]
DAF .... Design Action to Follow
DAF .... Destination Address Field [*Data processing*] (IBMDP)
DaF .... Deutsch als Fremdsprache [*A publication*]
DAF .... Deutsche Arbeitsfront [*German Workers Front*] [*Post-World War II*]
DAF .... Diacetylferrocene [*Organic chemistry*]
DAF .... Diacetylfluorescein [*Organic chemistry*]
DAF .... Discard at Failure (MCD)
DAF .... Dissolved Air Flotation
DAF .... Dressing after Finish [*Manufacturing term*]
DAF .... Dry and Ash-Free [*Coal*]
DAF .... Due and Ancient Form [*Freemasonry*]
DAF .... Van Doorn's Automobile Fabrieken [*Dutch automobile manufacturer; acronym used as name of its cars*]

DAFA .... American Forestry Association, Washington, DC [*Library symbol*] [*Library of Congress*]   (LCLS)
DAFB .... Dyess Air Force Base [*Texas*]   (AAG)
DAFC .... Departure Airfield Control   (AABC)
DAFC .... Dictionnaire Apologetique de la Foi Catholique [*A publication*]   (BJA)
DAFC .... Digital Automatic Frequency Control
DAFCCS ... Department of the Air Force Command and Control System
DAFCG ..... Departure Airfield Control Group [*Military*]   (AABC)
DAFCS ...... Digital Automatic Flight Control System
DAFD .... Dayton Air Force Depot
DAFD .... Department of the Army Forward Depot   (AABC)
DAFDS ..... Digital Autopilot Flight Director System   (MCD)
DAF & E .... Defense Aid [*Lend-Lease*] Facilities and Equipment [*World War II*]
DAFF .... Daffodil   (DSUE)
DAFFD ..... Department of the Army Forward-Floating Depot   (AABC)
Daffod Tul Yb ... Daffodil and Tulip Year Book [*A publication*]
Daffod Yb .. Daffodil Yearbook [*A publication*]
DAFFS ...... Design of Advanced Fossil Fuel System
DAFFY ...... Direct Aid for Full Yaw
DAFH .... Tilrempt/Hassi R'Mel [*Algeria*] [*ICAO location identifier*]   (ICLI)
DAFI .... Directorate of Air Force Intelligence [*Australia*]
DAFI .... Djelfa/Tletsi [*Algeria*] [*ICAO location identifier*]   (ICLI)
DAFICCS ... Department of the Air Force Integrated Command and Control Systems   (MCD)
DAFIE .... Directorate for Armed Forces Information and Education [*Military*]
DAFL .... American Federation of Labor and Congress of Industrial Organizations Library, Washington, DC [*Library symbol*] [*Library of Congress*]   (LCLS)
DAFM .... Department of the Army Field Manuals
DAFM .... Direct Access File Manager
DAFM .... Discard-at-Failure Maintenance   (IEEE)
DAFM .... Distal Accessory Flexor Muscle [*of a lobster*]
DAFO .... Division Accounting and Finance Office [*Air Force*]   (AFIT)
DAFOSR ... United States Air Force, Office of Scientific Research, Washington, DC [*Library symbol*] [*Library of Congress*]   (LCLS)
DAFR .... Documents on American Foreign Relations [*A publication*]
DAFS .... Damage Analysis and Fundamental Studies   (MCD)
DAFS .... Department of Agriculture and Fisheries for Scotland
DAFS .... Direct Aerial Fire Support [*Military*]   (AABC)
DAFS .... Director of Army Fire Services [*British*]
DAFS .... Duty Air Force Specialty
DAFSC ...... Duty Air Force Specialty Code
DAFSO ...... Department of the Air Force Special Order   (AFM)
DAFT .... Dansk Ornithologisk Forenings Tidsskrift [*A publication*]
DAFT .... Data Acquisition Frequency Table   (MCD)
DAFT .... Digital-to-Analog Function Table [*Packard Bell Computer Corp.*]
DAFW .... Directorate of Air Force Welfare [*British*]
DAG .... Agriculture Canada Library [*UTLAS symbol*]
DAG .... Daggett, CA [*Location identifier*] [*FAA*]   (FAAL)
DAG .... Danmarkshavn [*Greenland*] [*Seismograph station code, US Geological Survey*]   (SEIS)
DAG .... Defense Aerial Gunner
DAG .... Defense Special Security Communications System Address Group   (MCD)
DAG .... Dekagram [*Unit of measure*]
DAG .... Deputy Adjutant-General [*Military*]
DAG .... Deputy Advocate-General [*Military*] [*British*]   (ROG)
DAG .... Development Assistance Group
DAG .... Diacylglycerol [*Organic chemistry*]
DAG .... Dianilinogossypol [*Organic chemistry*]
DAG .... Division Advisory Group   (MCD)
DAG .... Division Artillery Group [*Military*]   (AABC)
D Ag .... Doctor of Agriculture
DAG .... Doll Artisan Guild   (EA)
DAGC .... Delayed Automatic Gain Control   (MSA)
DAGC .... Digital Automatic Gain Control   (MCD)
Dag Cr L .... Dagge's Criminal Law [*A publication*]   (DLA)
Dag Ct M ... D'Aguilar on Courts-Martial [*A publication*]   (DLA)
DAGDL ...... Diacetyl(glucarodilactone) [*Biochemistry*]
Dagestan Gos Univ Ucen Zap ... Dagestanskii Gosudarstvennyi Universitet Imeni V. I. Lenina Ucenyi Zapiski [*Makhachkala*] [*A publication*]
DAGM .... Deutsches Archiv fuer Geschichte des Mittelalters [*A publication*]
DAGMAR ... Defining Advertising Goals for Measured Advertising Results [*Title of book written by Russell Colley and published by the Association of National Advertisers*]
DAGMAR ... Drift and Ground-Speed Measuring Airborne RADAR
DAGN .... Diaminoguanidine Nitrate [*Organic chemistry*]
DAGNA ..... Association of the German Nobility in North America   (EA)
DAGNA ..... Deutsche Adels-Gesellschaft in Nord Amerika [*Association of the German Nobility in North America*]   (EA)
DAGO .... District Aviation Gas Office [*Navy*]
DAGR .... Dictionnaire des Antiquites Grecques et Romaines [*A publication*]

DAGR .... Dictionnaire des Antiquites Grecques et Romaines d'Appres les Textes et les Monuments [*A publication*]   (BJA)
D Agr .... Doctor of Agriculture
DAGR .... Green [*Daniel*] Co. [*NASDAQ symbol*]   (NQ)
DAGRA ..... Deputy Adjutant-General, Royal Artillery [*British military*]   (DMA)
D Agr E ...... Doctor of Agricultural Engineering
D Agr Eng ... Doctor of Agricultural Engineering
D Agric .... Doctor of Agriculture
D Agr S ...... Doctor of Agricultural Science
D Agr Sc .... Doctor of Agricultural Science
DAgSc .... Doctor of Agricultural Science   (ADA)
DAGUERR ... Daguerrotype [*Photography*]   (ROG)
D'Agu Oeuv ... D'Aguesseau. Oeuvres [*A publication*]   (DLA)
DAH .... Dahomey   (ROG)
DAH .... Dictionary of American History [*A publication*]
DAH .... Dictionary of American Hymnology [*Database*] [*Hymn Society of America, Inc.*] [*Information service or system*]   (IID)
DAH .... Disordered Action of the Heart [*Medicine*]
DAH .... Domestic Annual Harvest
DAH .... National Society Women Descendants of the Ancient and Honorable Artillery Company   (EA)
DAHAC ..... Department of the Army Historical Advisory Committee [*Washington, DC*]   (EGAO)
DAHC .... Dutch-American Historical Commission   (EA)
DAHE .... Department of Allied Health Evaluation [*AMA*]
DAHL .... Dahlberg, Inc. [*Minneapolis, MN*] [*NASDAQ symbol*]   (NQ)
DAHL .... Dahlen [*Saxony*]   (ROG)
Dahl Mar Int L ... Dahlgren's Maritime International Law [*A publication*]   (DLA)
Dahl Yb ...... Dahlia Year Book [*A publication*]
DAHM ...... Division of Allied Health Manpower [*Bureau of Health Professions Education and Manpower Training, HEW*]
DAHP .... Division of Associated Health Professions [*DHHS*]
DAHQ .... Di-tert-amylhydroquinone [*Organic chemistry*]
DAHS .... Danish American Heritage Society   (EA)
DAI .... Dairen [*Republic of China*] [*Seismograph station code, US Geological Survey*] [*Closed*]   (SEIS)
DAI .... Dairy Industries International [*A publication*]
DAI .... Data Architects, Incorporated [*AMEX symbol*]   (SPSG)
DAI .... Death from Accidental Injuries [*Military*]
DAI .... Death Attitude Indicator
DAI .... Demonstrators Association of Illinois   (EA)
DAI .... Detroit Adjustment Inventory [*Psychology*]
DAI .... Diamidinoindole [*Organic chemistry*]
D-AI .... Diplomate, American Board of Allergy and Immunology   (DHSM)
DAI .... Director of Aeronautical Inspection [*British*]
DAI .... Director of Army Instruction
DAI .... Discrete Activity Indicator [*NASA*]   (KSC)
DAI .... Disease Activity Index [*Medicine*]
DAI .... Dissertation Abstracts International [*A publication*]
DAI .... Distributed Artificial Intelligence [*Data processing*]
DAI .... Dittberner Associates, Incorporated [*Bethesda, MD*] [*Information service or system*] [*Telecommunications*]   (TSSD)
DAI .... Drift Angle Indicator [*Navigation*]
DAIA .... American Institute of Architects, Washington, DC [*Library symbol*] [*Library of Congress*]   (LCLS)
DAI Athens ... Mitteilungen. Deutsches Archaeologische Institut. Athenische Abteilung [*A publication*]
DAIC .... United States Industrial College of the Armed Forces [*Fort McNair*], Washington, DC [*Library symbol*] [*Library of Congress*]   (LCLS)
DAICS ...... Data Inventory Control System   (MCD)
DAID .... United States Agency for International Development, Office of Population, Washington, DC [*Library symbol*] [*Library of Congress*]   (LCLS)
DAIE .... Dai'ei, Inc. [*NASDAQ symbol*]   (NQ)
DAIG .... Department of the Army Inspector General
Dail Deb ..... Dail Debates [*Ireland*] [*A publication*]
Daily Leg News (PA) ... Daily Legal News (Pennsylvania) [*A publication*]   (DLA)
Daily Leg (PA) ... Daily Legal Record [*Pennsylvania*] [*A publication*]   (DLA)
Daily L N ... Daily Legal News [*Pennsylvania*] [*A publication*]   (DLA)
Daily L R ... Daily Legal Record [*Pennsylvania*] [*A publication*]   (DLA)
Daily News ... Daily News Record [*A publication*]
Daily Oil Bull ... Daily Oil Bulletin [*A publication*]
Daily Oklah ... Daily Oklahoman [*A publication*]
Daily Trans ... New York Daily Transcript, Old and New Series [*A publication*]   (DLA)
Daily Transc ... New York Daily Transcript [*A publication*]   (DLA)
DAIM .... Data Analysis Information Memorandum
DAIM .... Dynamic Active Index Matrix   (BUR)
DAIMC ...... Defense Advanced Inventory Management Course [*Army*]
DAIMS ...... Department of the Army Integrated Materiel Support
Dainichi-Nippon Cables Rev ... Dainichi-Nippon Cables Review [*Japan*] [*A publication*]
DAIO .... Data I/O Corp. [*NASDAQ symbol*]   (NQ)
DAIO .... Divisional Artillery Intelligence Officer [*British*]
DAIP .... Defense Acquisition Improvement Program [*DoD*]

DAIP......... Deliquency Account Inventory Profile [*IRS*]
DAIP......... Department of the Army Intelligence Plan
DAIP......... Diallyl Isophthalate [*Organic chemistry*]
DAIPR...... Department of the Army in Process Review (MCD)
DAIR........ Debit Accounting Information Retrieval
DAIR........ Direct Altitude and Identification Readout [*Aviation*] (MCD)
DAIR........ Driver Aid, Information, and Routing [*Data processing*]
DAIR........ Dynamic Allocation Interface Routine [*Data processing*] (BUR)
DAIRE........ Direct Altitude and Identification Readout Equipment [*Aviation*] (FAAC)
Dai Reg...... New York Daily Register [*A publication*] (DLA)
DAIRI....... Dissertation Abstracts International. Retrospective Index [*A publication*]
DAIRO...... Department of the Army International Rationalization Office (RDA)
DAIRS....... Dial Access Information Retrieval System [*Shippensburg State College, Shippensburg, PA*]
Dairy Annu ... Dairy Farming Annual [*A publication*]
Dairy Counc Dig ... Dairy Council Digest [*A publication*]
Dairy Eng ... Dairy Engineering [*A publication*]
Dairy F....... Dairy Farmer [*A publication*]
Dairy Farm ... Dairy Farmer [*A publication*]
Dairyfarm Annu ... Dairyfarming Annual [*A publication*]
Dairy Farmer Dairy Beef Prod ... Dairy Farmer and Dairy Beef-Producer [*A publication*]
Dairyfarming Dig ... Dairyfarming Digest [*A publication*]
Dairyfmg Dig ... Dairyfarming Digest [*A publication*] (APTA)
Dairy Goat J ... Dairy Goat Journal [*A publication*]
Dairy Herd Manage ... Dairy Herd Management [*A publication*]
Dairy Herd Mgt ... Dairy Herd Management [*A publication*]
Dairy and Ice Cream Fld ... Dairy and Ice Cream Field [*A publication*]
Dairy Ind ... Dairy Industries [*Later, Dairy Industries International*] [*A publication*]
Dairy Ind ... Dairy Industries International [*A publication*]
Dairy Ind Int ... Dairy Industries International [*A publication*]
Dairy Inds ... Dairy Industries International [*A publication*]
Dairy Indus ... Dairy Industries [*Later, Dairy Industries International*] [*A publication*]
Dairymen's Digest South Reg Ed ... Dairymen's Digest. Southern Region Edition [*A publication*]
Dairymen's Dig North Cent Reg Ed ... Dairymen's Digest. North Central Region Edition [*A publication*]
Dairy Prod ... Dairy Produce [*A publication*]
Dairy Res Rep ... Dairy Research Report [*A publication*] (APTA)
Dairy Res Rep Dep Agric Fish ... Dairy Research Report. South Australia Department of Agriculture and Fisheries [*A publication*] (APTA)
Dairy Sci Abstr ... Dairy Science Abstracts [*A publication*]
Dairy Sci Handb ... Dairy Science Handbook [*A publication*]
Dairy Tales Calif Univ Berkeley Coop Ext Serv ... Dairy Tales. California University, Berkeley. Cooperative Extension Service [*A publication*]
DAIS.......... Data Avionics Information System (MCD)
DAIS.......... Dealer Association Information Service [*Association of Free Newspapers*] [*British*]
DAIS.......... Defense Automatic Integrated Switching [*Army communications system*]
DAIS.......... Digital Avionics Information System [*Air Force*]
DAIS.......... Digital Avionics Integration System
DAIS.......... Directorate of Aeronautical Inspection Services [*British*]
DAIS.......... Directory of Automated Information Systems (MCD)
DAISY...... Daily Summary (MCD)
DAISY...... Data Acquisition and Interpretation System
DAISY...... Decision Aiding Information System
DAISY...... Double-Precision Automatic Interpretive System
DAITA...... Database of Antiviral and Immunomodulatory Therapies for AIDS [*Acquired Immune Deficiency Syndrome*]
DAITDM .. Department of the Army Integrated Technical Document Manual (MCD)
DAIU......... Digital-to-Analog Interface Unit [*Data processing*]
DAIV......... Data Area Initializer and Verifier [*Telecommunications*] (TEL)
Daiwa......... Daiwa Investment Monthly [*A publication*]
DAJ.......... Derbyshire Archaeological Journal [*A publication*]
DAJAG...... Deputy Assistant Judge Advocate General [*Legal term*] (DLA)
DAJO........ Danish Journal [*A publication*]
DAJS......... Distributed Area Jamming System [*Air Force*]
DA Jur ...... (Dalloz) Analytique. Jurisprudence [*France*] [*A publication*]
DAK.......... Dakar [*Senegal*] [*Seismograph station code, US Geological Survey*] [*Closed*] (SEIS)
dak............ Dakota [*MARC language code*] [*Library of Congress*] (LCCP)
Dak........... Dakota Territory Reports [*A publication*] (DLA)
DAK.......... Decision Acknowledge (BUR)
DAK.......... Deny All Knowledge [*Telecommunications*] (TEL)
DAK.......... Deutsches Afrika Korps [*World War II*]
DAK.......... Fayetteville, AR [*Location identifier*] [*FAA*] (FAAL)
Dakar Med ... Dakar Medical [*A publication*]
DAKEA...... Dansk Kemi [*A publication*]
Dak Law Rev ... Dakota Law Review [*A publication*]
Dak L Rev ... Dakota Law Review [*A publication*]

DAKMAJ ... Deutsches Archiv fuer Klinische Medizin [*A publication*]
Dakota .... Dakota Reports [*A publication*] (DLA)
Dakota F .... Dakota Farmer [*A publication*]
Dakota Law Rev ... Dakota Law Review [*A publication*]
Dal .... Benloe and Dalison's English Common Pleas Reports [*A publication*] (DLA)
DAL .... Dalhousie University Library [*UTLAS symbol*]
Dal .... Dalison's English Common Pleas Reports [*A publication*] (DLA)
DAL .... Dallas [*Texas*] [*Seismograph station code, US Geological Survey*] (SEIS)
DAL .... Dallas/Fort Worth [*Texas*] Love [*Airport symbol*] (OAG)
DAL .... Dallas [*Texas*] Love Field [*Airport symbol*]
Dal .... Dallas' Pennsylvania Reports [*A publication*] (DLA)
Dal .... Dallas' United States Reports [*A publication*] (DLA)
Dal .... Dalrymple. Scotch Court of Session Cases [*A publication*] (DLA)
Dal .... Daly's New York Common Pleas Reports [*A publication*] (DLA)
DAL .... Dash Lake Resources [*Vancouver Stock Exchange symbol*]
DAL .... Data Access Line
DAL .... Data Accession List (NASA)
DAL .... Data Acquisition Language [*Data processing*] (CSR)
DAL .... Data Acquisition List (MCD)
DAL .... Data Address Line
DAL .... Data-Aided Loop [*NASA*]
DAL .... Data Analysis Laboratory [*Temple University*] [*Research center*]
DAL .... Defect Action Level [*FDA*]
DAL .... Defence Analysts Ltd. [*British*]
DAL .... Dekaliter [*Unit of measure*]
DAL .... Delta Air Lines, Inc. [*NYSE symbol*] [*Air carrier designation symbol*] (SPSG)
DAL .... Design Analysis Language [*Programming language*]
DAL .... Dictionnaire d'Archeologie Chretienne et de Liturgie [*A publication*]
DAL .... Directional Arm Lock
DAL .... Distribution Authority List (MCD)
DAL .... Dog at Large [*Humorous notation put on letters that cannot be delivered*] [*British postmen's slang*]
DAL .... Drawing Assembly List (MCD)
DAL .... United States Army Library, Pentagon Building, Arlington, VA [*Library symbol*] [*Library of Congress*] (LCLS)
DALA .... (D-Ala²)-Met-enkephalinamide [*Analgesic peptide*]
DALA .... Delta-Aminolevulinic Acid [*Biochemistry*]
D Alaska .... United States District Court for the District of Alaska (DLA)
DALATS ..... Data Logging and Transmission System (MCD)
DALB .... Dictionary of American Library Biography [*A publication*]
DALB .... Dictionary of American Literary Biography [*A publication*]
DALC .... Danquah. Akan Laws and Customs [*Ghana*] [*A publication*] (DLA)
DALC .... Deployment Area Location Code [*Army*] (AABC)
DALC .... Divided Access Line Circuit
DALC .... Dubuque Area Library Consortium [*Library network*]
DALC .... Dynamic Asynchronous Logic Circuit
Dal Coop .... Dallas' Report of Cooper's Opinion on the Sentence of a Foreign Court of Admiralty [*A publication*] (DLA)
Dal C P ...... Dalison's English Common Pleas Reports [*A publication*] (DLA)
DALDO ..... Disposite d'Aide a la Designation d'Objectif [*Target Designation Aid System*] [*French*]
Dale .... Dale's Judgments [*1868-71*] [*England*] [*A publication*] (DLA)
Dale .... Dale's Reports [*2-4 Oklahoma*] [*A publication*] (DLA)
DALE .... Developmental Assessment of Life Experiences [*Test*]
DALE .... Drug Abuse Law Enforcement [*Department of Justice*]
Dale Cl HB ... Dale's Clergyman's Legal Handbook [*A publication*] (DLA)
Dale Ecc..... Dale's Ecclesiastical Reports [*England*] [*A publication*] (DLA)
Dale Eccl..... Dale's Ecclesiastical Reports [*England*] [*A publication*] (DLA)
Dale Leg Rit ... Dale's Legal Ritual [*Ecclesiastical Reports*] [*1868-71*] [*England*] [*A publication*] (DLA)
Dale Par Ch ... Dale's Law of the Parish Church [*5th ed.*] [*1975*] [*A publication*] (DLA)
Dalgetys Annual Wool D ... Dalgetys Annual Wool Digest [*A publication*] (APTA)
Dalgetys Annual Wool R ... Dalgetys Annual Wool Review [*A publication*] (APTA)
DALGT...... Daylight (FAAC)
Dalhousie Dent J ... Dalhousie Dental Journal [*A publication*]
Dalhousie L J ... Dalhousie Law Journal [*A publication*]
Dalhousie R ... Dalhousie Review [*A publication*]
Dalhousie Rev ... Dalhousie Review [*A publication*]
Dalhous Rev ... Dalhousie Review [*A publication*]
Dalh Rev .... Dalhousie Review [*A publication*]
DALIS .... Directory of Automated Library and Information Systems in Australia [*A publication*] (APTA)
Dalison ...... Dalison's English Common Pleas Reports [*Bound with Benloe*] [*123 English Reprint*] [*A publication*] (DLA)
Dal in Keil ... Dalison's Reports in Keilway [*1533-64*] [*England*] [*A publication*] (DLA)
Dall .... Dallam's Texas Supreme Court Decisions [*A publication*] (DLA)

Dall .... Dallas' Laws of Pennsylvania [*A publication*]   (DLA)
Dall .... Dallas' Pennsylvania and United States Reports [*A publication*]   (DLA)
Dall .... Dallas' Styles of Writs [*Scotland*] [*A publication*]   (DLA)
Dallam Dig (Tex) ... Dallam's Digest [*Texas*] [*A publication*]   (DLA)
Dallas......... Dallas' Pennsylvania and United States Reports [*A publication*]   (DLA)
Dallas Med J ... Dallas Medical Journal [*A publication*]
Dallas New ... Dallas Morning News [*A publication*]
Dallas Sym ... Dallas Symphony Orchestra. Program Notes [*A publication*]
Dall Coop... Dallas' Report of Cooper's Opinion on the Sentence of a Foreign Court of Admiralty [*A publication*]   (DLA)
Dall Dec..... Dallam's Texas Decisions, from Dallam's Digest [*A publication*]   (DLA)
Dall Dig ..... Dallam's Digest and Opinions [*Texas*] [*A publication*]   (DLA)
Dal LJ........ Dalhousie Law Journal [*A publication*]
Dall in Keil ... Dallison [*or Dalison*] in Keilway's Reports, English King's Bench [*A publication*]   (DLA)
Dall L......... Dallas' Laws of Pennsylvania [*A publication*]   (DLA)
Dall Laws... Dallas' Laws of Pennsylvania [*A publication*]   (DLA)
Dall Med J ... Dallas Medical Journal [*A publication*]
Dalloz......... Recueil Dalloz/Sirey [*French*] [*A publication*]   (DLA)
Dalloz Dic .. Dalloz. Dictionnaire de Droit [*French*] [*A publication*]   (DLA)
Dalloz Enc ... Dalloz. Encyclopedie Juridique [*French*] [*A publication*]   (DLA)
Dall (PA) ... Dallas' Pennsylvania Reports [4] [*A publication*]   (DLA)
Dall R......... Dallas Reports [*A publication*]
Dall S C ..... Dallas' United States Supreme Court Reports [*A publication*]   (DLA)
Dalls FW B ... Dallas/Fort Worth Business Journal [*A publication*]
Dall Sty...... Dallas' Styles of Writs [*Scotland*] [*A publication*]   (DLA)
Dall Tex ..... Dallas' Supreme Court Decisions [*Texas*] [*A publication*]   (DLA)
DALM .... Dysplasia-Associated Lesion or Mass [*Medicine*]
DALMACIJACEMENT ... Dalmatian Cement Export-Import Establishment
Dal'nevost Fiz Sb ... Dal'nevostochnyi Fizicheskii Sbornik [*A publication*]
Dal'nevost Nauchno Issled Inst Stroit Sb Nauchn Rab ... Dal'nevostochnyi Nauchno-Issledovatel'skii Institut po Stroitel'stvu Sbornik Nauchnykh Rabot [*A publication*]
Dal Nevostocn Gos Univ Ucen Zap ... Dal'nevostocnyi Gosudarstvennyi Universitet Ucenyi Zapiski Serija Fiziko-Matematiceskih Nauk [*A publication*]
Dal'nevostocn Mat Sb ... Dal'nevostochnyi Matematiceskii Sbornik [*A publication*]
DALO........ Defense Attache Liaison Officer   (AFM)
DALO........ Disconnect at Lift-Off [*NASA*]   (KSC)
Dal R.......... Dalhousie Review [*A publication*]
Dalr............ Dalrymple. Decisions of the Scotch Court of Session [*A publication*]   (DLA)
Dalr............ (Dalrymple of) Stair's Decisions of the Scotch Court of Session [*A publication*]   (DLA)
DALR .... Dry Adiabatic Lapse Rate [*Heat transfer*]
Dalr Dec..... Dalrymple. Decisions of the Scotch Court of Session [*A publication*]   (DLA)
Dalr Ent ..... Dalrymple on the Polity of Entails [*A publication*]   (DLA)
Dal Rev ..... Dalhousie Review [*A publication*]
Dalr Feud Prop ... Dalrymple on Feudal Property [*A publication*]   (DLA)
Dalr Feu Pr ... Dalrymple on Feudal Property [*A publication*]   (DLA)
DALRLV ... Department of the Army Logistics Readiness Liaison Visits   (AABC)
Dalr Ten..... Dalrymple on Tenures [*A publication*]   (DLA)
DALRTF ... Department of the Army Long-Range Technological Forecast
Dalrymple ... [*Sir David*] (Dalrymple of) Hailes' Scotch Session Cases [*A publication*]   (DLA)
Dalrymple ... [*Sir James*] (Dalrymple of) Stair's Scotch Session Cases [*A publication*]   (DLA)
Dalrymple ... [*Sir Hew*] Dalrymple's Scotch Session Cases [*A publication*]   (DLA)
DAL S........ Dal Segno [*Repeat from the Sign*] [*Music*]
DALS......... Data Acquisition Logging System
DALS........ Director [*or Directorate*] of Army Legal Services [*British*]
DALS........ Distress Alerting and Locating System
DALS........ Dive Auditory Location System   (MCD)
DALS........ Double-Acting Limit Switch
DALSCOM ... DoD [*Department of Defense*] ATE Language Standardization Committee
DAL SEG .. Dal Segno [*Repeat from the Sign*] [*Music*]
Dal Sh........ Dalton on Sheriffs [*A publication*]   (DLA)
DALSO...... Department of Army Logistics Support Officer
DALT .... Dalton Communications, Inc. [*New York, NY*] [*NASDAQ symbol*]   (NQ)
Dalt .... Dalton's Justices of the Peace [*Many eds.*] [*1618-1746*] [*A publication*]   (DLA)
DALT .... Department of the Army Liaison Team   (AABC)
DALT .... Drop Altitude
Dalt Just .... Dalton's Justices of the Peace [*Many eds.*] [*1618-1746*] [*A publication*]   (DLA)
DALTS ...... Data Link Test Set
Dalt Sh....... Dalton's Sheriff [*A publication*]   (DLA)
DALV .... Deutsches Archiv fuer Landes und Volksforschung [*A publication*]

DALVP...... Delay Enroute Authorized as Ordinary Leave Provided It Does Not Interfere with Reporting Date [*Military*]
Daly .... Daly's New York Common Pleas Reports [*A publication*]   (DLA)
Daly May Ct ... Daly's Hand-Book on Practice in the Lord Mayor's Court [*A publication*]   (DLA)
Daly's R ..... Daly's New York Common Pleas Reports [*A publication*]   (DLA)
Daly Sur..... Daly's Nature of Surrogate's Courts [*New York*] [*A publication*]   (DLA)
DAM.......... Damage   (AABC)
DAM.......... Damascus [*Syria*] [*Airport symbol*]   (OAG)
DAM.......... Damocles [*Greek courtier, c.300BC*]   (ROG)
DAM.......... Damson Oil Corp. [*AMEX symbol*]   (SPSG)
DAM.......... Data Addressed Memory [*Data processing*]
DAM.......... Data Association Message
DAM.......... Defended Area Model [*Army*]   (AABC)
DAM.......... Definition, Analysis, and Mechanization
DAM.......... Degraded Amyloid [*Medicine*]
DAM.......... Dekameter
DAM.......... Descriptor Attribute Matrix
DAM.......... Detection and Mapping [*Package*] [*NASA*]
DAM.......... Diacetyl Monooxime [*Organic chemistry*]
DAM.......... Diacetylmorphine [*Pharmacology*]
DAM.......... Diagnostic Abilities in Math [*Educational test*]
DAM.......... Diallyl Maleate [*Organic chemistry*]
DAM.......... Diallylmelamine [*Organic chemistry*]
DAM.......... Diamond Asset Management [*Subsidiary of Mitsubishi Bank*] [*Japan*]
DAM.......... Dictionary of Abbreviations in Medicine [*A publication*]
DAM.......... Digital-to-Analog Multiplier   (IEEE)
DAM.......... Direct Access Memory [*Data processing*]   (BUR)
DAM.......... Direct Access Method [*Sperry UNIVAC*] [*Data processing*]
DAM.......... Director of Air Material [*Navy*] [*British*]
DAM.......... Director Attack Mine [*Air Force*]   (MCD)
DAM.......... Double Aluminized Mylar   (NASA)
DAM.......... Downrange Antimissile Program [*Army*]
DAM.......... Driver Amplifier Module   (NASA)
DAM.......... United States Army Topographic Command, Washington, DC [*Library symbol*] [*Library of Congress*]   (LCLS)
DAM² .... Square Dekameter
DAM³ .... Cubic Dekameter
DAMA .... American Medical Association, Washington Office, Washington, DC [*Library symbol*] [*Library of Congress*]   (LCLS)
Dama.......... [*Pope*] Damasus [*Deceased, 384*] [*Authority cited in pre-1607 legal work*]   (DSA)
DAMA .... Data Administration Management Association International   (EA)
DAMA .... Demand-Assignment Multiple Access [*Telecommunications*]
DAMA ...... Department of the Army Materiel Annex   (AABC)
Damas........ Damasus [*Flourished, 13th century*] [*Authority cited in pre-1607 legal work*]   (DSA)
DAMC .... Dimethylaminomethylcoumarin [*Organic chemistry*]
DAM³/D.... Cubic Decameters per Day
DAMDD5 ... Dakar Medical [*A publication*]
DAME........ Data Acquisition and Monitoring Equipment [*Electronics*]
DAME........ Defense Against Methods of Entry [*Military intelligence*]
DAME........ Determination of Air-Launched Missile Environment   (MCD)
DAME........ Developments in Agricultural and Managed-Forest Ecology [*Elsevier Book Series*] [*A publication*]
DAME........ Dictionary of American English [*A publication*]
DAME........ Distance and Angularity Measurement Equipment [*Navy*]   (MCD)
DAME........ Distance Azimuth Measuring Equipment [*Navy*]   (MCD)
DAME........ Division Airspace Management Element [*Military*]   (INF)
DAMF .... Director of Air Ministry Factories [*British*] [*World War II*]
DAMG....... Damages [*Legal term*]   (DLA)
DAM-Geog ... United States Army Topographic Command, Office of Geography, Washington, DC [*Library symbol*] [*Library of Congress*]   (LCLS)
DAMGO.... Deputy Assistant Master-General of Ordnance [*British*]
DAMI......... Designated Aircraft Maintenance Inspector
DAMIF...... David Minerals Ltd. [*NASDAQ symbol*]   (NQ)
DAM II-EE ... Defended Area Model II Engagement Evaluation [*Army*]   (AABC)
DAM II-EP ... Defended Area Model II Engagement Planning [*Army*]   (AABC)
DAMIS...... Department of the Army Management Information System   (AABC)
DAMIT ..... Data Analysis [*Program*] of Massachusetts Institute of Technology
DAMJA..... Dallas Medical Journal [*A publication*]
DAmL........ AMTRAK Library, Washington, DC [*Library symbol*] [*Library of Congress*]   (LCLS)
DAML .... Directorate, Army MAP [*Military Assistance Program*] Logistics
DAMLG .... Dental Amalgamator
DAMM....... Alger [*Algeria*] [*ICAO location identifier*]   (ICLI)
DAMM....... Drinkers Against Mad Mothers   (EA)
DAMMO... Directorate of Ammunition [*Military*] [*Canada*]

DAMMS ... Department of the Army Movements Management System (MCD)

DAMN ...... Diaminomaleonitrile [*Organic chemistry*]

DA MOB C2S ... Department of the Army Mobilization Command and Control System (MCD)

DAMOS ...... Disposal Area Monitoring System

DAMP ...... Dallas Area Media Project [*Library network*]

dAMP .... Deoxyadenosine Monophosphate [*Biochemistry*]

DAMP ...... Department of the Air Member for Personnel [*British*]

DAMP ...... Department of the Army Materiel Program

DAMP ...... Diacetoxydiphenylmethylpyridine [*Pharmacology*]

DAMP ...... Dibutyryl CAMP [*Cyclic Adenosine Monophosphate*] [*Biochemistry*]

DAMP ...... Dinitroanilino Amino-Methylpropylamine

DAMP ...... Distribution Amplifier (MSA)

DAMP ...... Downrange Antimissile Measurement Program [*RADAR*]

Dampier MSS ... Dampier's Paper Book, Lincoln's Inn Library [*A publication*] (DLA)

DAMPL ..... Department of the Army Master Priority List (AABC)

DAMPL ..... Department of the Army Material Priority List

DAMPMT ... Department of the Army Military Personnel Management Team (AABC)

DAMPR .... Digital Automatic Multiple Pressure Recorder [*Lewis Research Center*]

DAMPRE ... Drill Attendance Monitoring Procedure and Report [*National Guard*]

DAMPS ..... Data Acquisition Multiprogramming System [*IBM Corp.*] [*Data processing*]

DAMP/TVPB ... Department of the Army Motion Picture/Television Production Board (AABC)

DAMP/TVPP ... Department of the Army Motion Picture/Television Production Program

DAMQAM ... Dynamically Adaptive Multicarrier Quadrative Amplitude Modulation [*Data processing*]

DAMR ...... Director of Aircraft Maintenance and Repair [*Navy*] [*British*]

DAMRC .... Department of the Army Material Readiness Command (MCD)

DAMRIP ... Department of the Army Management Review and Improvement Program (AABC)

DAMR(N) ... Director of Aircraft Maintenance and Repair (Naval) [*British*]

DAMR(W) ... Director of Aircraft Maintenance and Repair (Washington) [*Navy*]

DAMS ...... Deductive Analysis of Missile Systems (MCD)

DAMS ...... Defencively Armed Merchant Ship [*British*] [*World War I*]

DAMS ...... Defense Against Missiles Systems

DAMS ...... Deputy Assistant Military Secretary [*British*]

DAMS ...... Direct Access Management System

DAMS ...... Disposal Accounting Management System [*DoD*]

DAMSEL .. Directory of Australian Manufactured Scientific Equipment and Laboratoryware [*A publication*] (APTA)

DAMSO .... Department of the Air Member for Supply and Organization [*British*]

DAMSO .... Deputy of the Air Member for Supply and Organization [*British*]

DAMSU .... Digital Automanual Switching Unit [*Telecommunications*] (TEL)

DAMT ...... Department of the Air Member for Training [*British*]

DAMV ...... Destruction of Aircraft or Motor Vehicles

DAMV ...... Double-Air Movement Valve

DAMWO ... Department of the Army Modification Work Order

DAN .... Army and Navy Club, Washington, DC [*Library symbol*] [*Library of Congress*] (LCLS)

DAN .... Dana College, C. A. Dana-Life Library, Blair, NE [*OCLC symbol*] (OCLC)

Dan .... Dana's Reports [*31-39 Kentucky*] [*A publication*] (DLA)

DAN .... Dane [*Ontario*] [*Seismograph station code, US Geological Survey*] [*Closed*] (SEIS)

Dan .... Daniel [*Old Testament book*]

DAN .... Daniel Industries, Inc. [*NYSE symbol*] (SPSG)

Dan .... Daniell's Exchequer and Equity Reports [*159 English Reprint*] [*1817-23*] [*A publication*] (DLA)

Dan .... Daniels' Compendium Compensation Cases [*England*] [*A publication*] (DLA)

dan .... Danish [*MARC language code*] [*Library of Congress*] (LCCP)

DAN .... Danish

Dan .... Danner's Reports [*42 Alabama*] [*A publication*] (DLA)

DAN .... Danube [*River in central Europe*]

D'An .... D'Anvers' General Abridgment of the Common Law [*A publication*] (DLA)

DAN .... Danville [*Virginia*] [*Airport symbol*] (OAG)

DAN .... Danville, VA [*Location identifier*] [*FAA*] (FAAL)

DAN .... Deacon and Nike [*Research rocket*]

DAN .... Defense Activity North Carolina (MCD)

daN .... Dekanewton [*Unit of force*]

DAN .... Deployment Adjustment Notification [*Military*] (CINC)

DAN .... Deposit Account Number (NG)

D-AN .... Diplomate, American Board of Anesthesiology (DHSM)

DA-N .... Directional Antenna Nighttime Only [*Broadcasting term*]

DAN .... Distributed Audio Network [*Sound Apprentice*]

DAN .... Doklady Akademii Nauk SSSR [*A publication*]

DAN .... Dual Area Nozzle (KSC)

DAN .... Duration Mines Ltd. [*Toronto Stock Exchange symbol*] [*Vancouver Stock Exchange symbol*]

Dana .... Dana's Kentucky Supreme Court Reports [*1833-40*] [*A publication*] (DLA)

DANA .... Deutsche Allgemeine Nachrichten Agentur [*German general news agency, sponsored by US newspapermen as a successor to the NAZI-controlled DNB*] [*Post-World War II*]

DANA .... Drug and Alcohol Nursing Association (EA)

Dan Abr ..... Dane's Abridgment of American Law [*A publication*] (DLA)

Dan AEC Res Establ Riso Rep ... Danish Atomic Energy Commission. Research Establishment. Risoe Report [*A publication*]

Dana (KY) ... Dana's Reports [*31-39 Kentucky*] [*A publication*] (DLA)

Dan Arct Res ... Danish Arctic Research [*A publication*]

Dana-Rep ..... Dana-Report. Carlsberg Foundation [*A publication*]

Dana-Rep Carlsberg Found ... Dana-Report. Carlsberg Foundation [*A publication*]

Dan Atomenergikomm Forsoegsanlaeg Risoe Rep ... Dansk Atomenergikommissionens Forsoegsanlaeg Risoe. Report [*A publication*]

Dan Att ...... Daniel's Law of Attachment [*A publication*] (DLA)

Dana Wh .... Dana's Edition of Wheaton's International Law [*A publication*] (DLA)

DANB .... Danbury [*England*]

DANB .... Dental Assisting National Board (EA)

DAN Bolg .. Doklady Bolgarskoi Akademii Nauk [*A publication*]

Dan Bot Ark ... Dansk Botanisk Arkiv [*A publication*]

Dan Brygg Tid ... Dansk Bryggeritidende [*A publication*]

DANC .... Decontaminating Agent, Noncorrosive

DANCA ..... Dimethylamino(naphthoyl)cyclohexanoic Acid [*Organic chemistry*]

Dance .... Dance Magazine [*A publication*]

Dance in Can ... Dance in Canada [*A publication*]

Dance Chron ... Dance Chronicle [*A publication*]

Dance Mag ... Dance Magazine [*A publication*]

Dance N ..... Dance News [*A publication*]

Dance Per .. Dance Perspectives [*A publication*]

Dance Res A ... Dance Research Annual [*A publication*]

Dance Res An ... Dance Research Annual [*A publication*]

Dance Res J ... Dance Research Journal [*A publication*]

Dance Sco ... Dance Scope [*A publication*]

Dan Ch ...... Daniell's Chancery Practice [*A publication*] (DLA)

Dan Ch Pr ... Daniell's Chancery Practice [*A publication*] (DLA)

Dancing Tim ... Dancing Times [*A publication*]

DAND .... Dandus [*To Be Given*] [*Pharmacy*]

Dan Dendrol Arsskr ... Dansk Dendrologisk Arsskrift [*A publication*]

DANDOK ... Danish Committee for Scientific and Technical Information and Documentation [*Information service or system*] (IID)

DANE .... Defense Activity for Nontraditional Education Support [*Military*] (MCD)

Dane Abr .... Dane's Abridgment of American Law [*A publication*] (DLA)

Dan Erhvervsfjerkrae ... Dansk Erhvervsfjerkrae [*A publication*]

Dane's Abr ... Dane's Abridgment of American Law [*A publication*] (DLA)

Dan Exch ... Daniell's Exchequer and Equity Reports [*159 English Reprint*] [*1817-23*] [*A publication*] (DLA)

Dan Exch (Eng) ... Daniell's Exchequer and Equity Reports [*159 English Reprint*] [*1817-23*] [*A publication*] (DLA)

DanF .... Danske Folkemaal [*A publication*]

Dan Farm Aarb ... Dansk Farmaceutisk Aarbog [*A publication*]

DANFIP .... Danish Federation for Information Processing and Management (CSR)

Dan Fisk Tid ... Dansk Fiskeritidende [*A publication*]

Dan Forms ... Daniell. Forms and Precedents in Chancery [*7th ed.*] [*1932*] [*A publication*] (DLA)

Danfoss J ... Danfoss Journal [*A publication*]

DANFS ...... Dictionary of American Naval Fighting Ships [*A publication*]

DANG .... Dangerous [*FBI standardized term*]

DANG .... Director of the Army National Guard

Dan Geol Unders Arbog ... Danmarks Geologiske Undersoegelse. Arbog [*A publication*]

Dan Geol Unders III Raekke ... Danmarks Geologiske Undersoegelse. III Raekke [*A publication*]

Dan Geol Unders II Raekke ... Danmarks Geologiske Undersoegelse. II Raekke [*A publication*]

Dan Geol Unders IV Raekke ... Danmarks Geologiske Undersoegelse. IV Raekke [*A publication*]

Dan Geol Unders Rapp ... Danmarks Geologiske Undersoegelse. Rapport [*A publication*]

Dan Geol Unders Ser A ... Danmarks Geologiske Undersoegelse. Serie A [*A publication*]

Dan Geol Unders Ser B ... Danmarks Geologiske Undersoegelse. Serie B [*A publication*]

Dan Haveb ... Dansk Havebrug [*A publication*]

Dan Havetid ... Dansk Havetidende [*A publication*]

Dani .... Daniel [*Old Testament book*] (DSA)

DANI .... Department of Agriculture for Northern Ireland [*United Kingdom*] (IRUK)

DANIDA ... Danish International Development Agency

Daniell Ch Pl & Prac ... Daniell's Chancery Pleading and Practice [*A publication*] (DLA)

Daniell Ch Pr ... Daniell's Chancery Pleading and Practice [*A publication*] (DLA)
Daniell Ch Prac ... Daniell's Chancery Pleading and Practice [*A publication*] (DLA)
Daniel Neg Inst ... Daniel's Negotiable Instruments [*A publication*] (DLA)
Dan Ingeniorforen Spildevandskom Skr ... Dansk Ingeniorforening Spildevandskomiteen Skrift [*A publication*]
DANIS....... Datennachweis Informationssystem [*Arbeitsgemeinschaft Sozialwissenschaftlicher Institut*] [*Federal Republic of Germany*] [*Information service or system*] [*Defunct*] (CRD)
Danish M Bull ... Danish Medical Bulletin [*A publication*]
DANK....... Danker Laboratories, Inc. [*NASDAQ symbol*] (NQ)
DANK....... Deutsch-Amerikanischer National-Kongress [*German-American National Congress*] (EA)
DANKA..... Doklady Akademii Nauk SSR [*A publication*]
Dan Kemi... Dansk Kemi [*A publication*]
Danl........ Daniel [*Old Testament book*]
Dan & L..... Danson and Lloyd's English Mercantile Cases [*A publication*] (DLA)
Dan Landbr ... Dansk Landbrug [*A publication*]
Dan & Ll.... Danson and Lloyd's English Mercantile Cases [*A publication*] (DLA)
Dan & Lld.. Danson and Lloyd's English Mercantile Cases [*A publication*] (DLA)
Danmarks Geol Undersoegelse ... Danmarks Geologiske Undersoegelse [*A publication*]
Dan Med B ... Danish Medical Bulletin [*A publication*]
Dan Med Bull ... Danish Medical Bulletin [*A publication*]
Dan Med Bull Suppl ... Danish Medical Bulletin. Supplement [*A publication*]
Dan Medicinhist Arbog ... Dansk Medicinhistorisk Arbog [*A publication*]
Dan Moll ... Daniel Moller [*Deceased, 1600*] [*Authority cited in pre-1607 legal work*] (DSA)
Dann .... Danner's Reports [*42 Alabama*] [*A publication*] (DLA)
DANN .... Danning Medical Technology, Inc. [*NASDAQ symbol*] (NQ)
Dann .... Dann's Reports [*22 California*] [*2nd ed.*] [*1871*] [*A publication*] (DLA)
Dann .... Dann's Reports [*1 Arizona*] [*A publication*] (DLA)
Dan Naturfr ... Dansk Naturfredning [*A publication*]
Dan Naturfredning ... Dansk Naturfredning [*A publication*]
Dan Naturfredningsforen Arsskr ... Danmarks Naturfredningsforenings Arsskrift [*A publication*]
Dan Neg Ins ... Daniel's Negotiable Instruments [*A publication*] (DLA)
Danner .... Danner's Reports [*42 Alabama*] [*A publication*] (DLA)
Dan Ord..... Danish Ordinances [*A publication*] (DLA)
Dan Ornithol Foren Feltornithol ... Dansk Ornithologisk Forening. Feltornithologen [*A publication*]
Dan Ornithol Foren Fuglevaern ... Dansk Ornithologisk Forening. Fuglevaern [*A publication*]
Dan Ornithol Foren Tidsskr ... Dansk Ornithologisk Forenings Tidsskrift [*A publication*]
Dan Pelsdyravl ... Dansk Pelsdyravl [*A publication*]
Dan Pest Infest Lab Annu Rep ... Danish Pest Infestation Laboratory. Annual Report [*A publication*]
Danquah .... Cases in Gold Coast Law [*A publication*] (DLA)
Dan Rev Game Biol ... Danish Review of Game Biology [*A publication*]
DANS .... Dimethylaminonaphthalenesulfonyl Chloride [*Also, DNSC*] [*Fluorescent reagent*]
DANS .... Director of Army Nursing Services [*British military*] (DMA)
DANSE...... Dance Artists' Nationwide Space Emergency [*In association name, DANSE Coalition*] (EA)
Dan Selsk Bygningsstatik Bygningsstatiske Medd ... Dansk Selskab foer Bygningsstatik, Bygningsstatiske Meddelelser [*A publication*]
DaNSHC... Cambridge Military Library, Halifax, NS, Canada [*Library symbol*] [*Library of Congress*] (LCLS)
Dansk Aarbog Mf ... Dansk Aarbog for Musikforskning [*A publication*]
Dansk Audiol ... Dansk Audiologopaedi [*A publication*]
Dansk Bog ... Dansk Bogfortegnelse [*A publication*]
Dansk Botan ... Dansk Botanisk Arkiv [*A publication*]
Dansk Dendrol Arsskr ... Dansk Dendrologisk Arsskrift [*A publication*]
Danske Bnk ... Bank Letter den Danske Landsmandsbank [*A publication*]
Danske Vid Selsk Mat-Fys Medd ... Det Kongelige Danske Videnskabernes Selskab. Matematisk-Fysiske Meddelelser [*A publication*]
Dansk Geol Foren Medd ... Dansk Geologisk Forening Meddelelser [*A publication*]
Dansk Geol Foren Meddel ... Dansk Geologisk Forening Meddelelser [*A publication*]
Dansk Mt... Dansk Musiktidsskrift [*A publication*]
Dansk Mus ... Dansk Musiktidsskrift [*A publication*]
Dan Skovforen Tidsskr ... Dansk Skovforenings Tidsskrift [*A publication*]
Dansk Rad Ind ... Dansk Radio Industri [*A publication*]
Dansk Tekn Tidsskr ... Dansk Teknisk Tidsskrift [*A publication*]
Dansk T Farm ... Dansk Tidsskrift foer Farmaci [*A publication*]
Dansk Tidssk Farm ... Dansk Tidsskrift foer Farmaci [*A publication*]
Dans & L.... Danson and Lloyd's English Mercantile Cases [*A publication*] (DLA)
Dans & LL ... Danson and Lloyd's English Mercantile Cases [*A publication*] (DLA)
DAN SSSR ... Doklady Akademii Nauk SSSR [*A publication*]

Dansyl........ Dimethylaminonaphthalenesulfonyl [*Also, Dns, DNS*] [*Biochemical analysis*]
Dan Tdsskr Farm ... Dansk Tidsskrift foer Farmaci [*A publication*]
Dan Tek Tidsskr ... Dansk Teknisk Tidsskrift [*Denmark*] [*A publication*]
DANTES... Defense Activity for Nontraditional Education Support [*Military*]
Dan Tidsskr Farm Supple ... Dansk Tidsskrift foer Farmaci. Supplementum [*A publication*]
DANTISC ... Dantiscum [*Dantzig*] (ROG)
Dan T M ... Daniel. Trade Marks [*1876*] [*A publication*] (DLA)
DANTS....... Day and Night Television System [*Army*] (MCD)
DanTTs...... Dansk Teologisk Tidsskrift [*Copenhagen*] [*A publication*]
DanU .... Dansk Udsyn [*A publication*]
Danv........... D'Anvers' General Abridgment of the Common Law [*A publication*] (DLA)
Danv Abr ... D'Anvers' General Abridgment of the Common Law [*A publication*] (DLA)
Dan Veterinaertidsskr ... Dansk Veterinaertidsskrift [*A publication*]
Danv Q....... Danville Quarterly Review [*A publication*]
DANY........ Dandees Enterprises, Inc. [*NASDAQ symbol*] (NQ)
DANY........ Dannemora [*New York*] [*Seismograph station code, US Geological Survey*] (SEIS)
Dan Yrbk Phil ... Danish Yearbook of Philosophy [*A publication*]
Danzig Uniw Wydz Biol Nauk Ziemi Zesz Nauk Geogr ... Danzig. Uniwersytet. Wydzial Biologii i Nauk o Ziemi. Zeszyty Naukowe. Geografia [*A publication*]
DAO .... Data Automation Officer [*Air Force*]
DAO .... Dayton Area Office [*Energy Research and Development Administration*]
DAO .... Deasphalted Oil [*Petroleum refining*]
DAO .... Defense Attache Office (AFM)
DAO .... Department Administrative Order [*Department of Commerce*] (NOAA)
DAO .... Dial Assist Operator (CET)
DAO .... Diamine Oxidase [*Also, DO*] [*An enzyme*]
DAO .... District Accounting Office [*or Officer*] [*Navy*]
DAO .... District Aviation Office [*or Officer*] [*Navy*]
DAO .... Division Air Officer
DAO .... Division Ammunition Office [*or Officer*] [*Army*]
DAO .... Divisional Agricultural Officer [*Ministry of Agriculture, Fisheries, and Food*] [*British*]
DAO .... Doctor of Art of Oratory
DAO .... Dorsal Accessory Olive [*Neuroanatomy*]
DAO .... Duly Authorized Officer
DAO .... Fort Huachuca, AZ [*Location identifier*] [*FAA*] (FAAL)
DAOB........ Tiaret [*Algeria*] [*ICAO location identifier*] (ICLI)
DAOC........ Bechar/Ouakda [*Algeria*] [*ICAO location identifier*] (ICLI)
DAOC........ Deputy Air Officer Commanding [*British military*] (DMA)
DAOC-in-C ... Deputy Air Officer Commanding-in-Chief [*British military*] (DMA)
DAOD........ Defending All Outdoors. Alberta Fish and Game Association [*A publication*]
DAOE........ Bou Sfer [*Algeria*] [*ICAO location identifier*] (ICLI)
DAOF........ Tindouf [*Algeria*] [*ICAO location identifier*] (ICLI)
DAOI........ Ech-Cheliff [*Algeria*] [*ICAO location identifier*] (ICLI)
DAOL........ Oran/Tafaroui [*Algeria*] [*ICAO location identifier*] (ICLI)
DAON........ Tlemcen/Zenata [*Algeria*] [*ICAO location identifier*] (ICLI)
DAOO........ Oran/Es Senia [*Algeria*] [*ICAO location identifier*] (ICLI)
DAO & OS ... Defense Aid [*Lend-Lease*] Ordnance and Ordnance Stores [*World War II*]
DA-OPRR ... Department of the Army Plan for [*Possession, Control, and*] Operation of Railroads (AABC)
DAOR........ Bechar/Ouakda [*Algeria*] [*ICAO location identifier*] (ICLI)
DAOREO.... Diseases of Aquatic Organisms [*A publication*]
DAOS........ Sidi Bel Abbes [*Algeria*] [*ICAO location identifier*] (ICLI)
DAOT........ Director of Air Organisation and Training [*British military*] (DMA)
DAOV........ Ghriss [*Algeria*] [*ICAO location identifier*] (ICLI)
DAP.......... Application for Writ of Error Dismissed by Agreement of Parties [*Legal term*] (DLA)
DAP.......... Data Access Protocol [*Digital Equipment Corp.*]
DAP.......... Data Acquisition Plan (MCD)
DA & P....... Data Acquisition and Processing
DAP.......... Data Analysis Program
DAP.......... Data Automation Panel (MCD)
DAP.......... Data Automation Proposal (AFM)
DAP.......... Days after Pollination [*Botany*]
DAP.......... Declines Appointment (NOAA)
DAP.......... Decontamination Apparatus, Portable
DAP.......... Deformation of Aligned Phase (MCD)
DAP.......... Delayed Alpha Particle
DAP.......... Democratic Action Party [*Malaysia*] [*Political party*] (PPW)
DAP.......... Democratic Action Party [*Malta*] [*Political party*] (PPE)
DAP.......... Department of the Army Pamphlet
DAP.......... Depolarizing After-Potential [*Neurochemistry*]
DAP.......... Depot Acceptance Procedures
DAP.......... Derived Attainable Performance [*Industrial engineering*]
DAP.......... Designated Acquisition Program
DAP.......... Detail Assembly Panel
DAP.......... Deutsche Aussenpolitik [*A publication*]
DAP.......... Developmental Articulation Profile [*Speech evaluation test*]

DAP	Diabetes-Associated Peptide [*Biochemistry*]
DAP	Diallyl Phthalate [*Organic chemistry*]
DAP	Diaminopimelic Acid [*Also, DAPA, DPM*] [*An amino acid*]
DAP	Diaminopurine [*Biochemistry*]
DAP	Diaminopyridine [*Organic chemistry*]
DAP	Diammonium Phosphate [*Inorganic chemistry*]
DAP	Diazepam [*Also, D, DZ*] [*A sedative*]
DAP	Diffused Alloy Power
DAP	Digital Assembly Program (MCD)
DAP	Digital Autopilot (MCD)
DAP	Dihydroxyacetone Phosphate [*Also, DHAP*] [*Organic chemistry*]
DAP	Dipeptidyl Aminopeptidase [*An enzyme*]
DAP	Direct Latex Agglutination Pregnancy [*Test*] [*Medicine*]
DAP	Directed Audit Program (AFM)
DAP	Director of Aeroplane Production [*Air Ministry*] [*British*] [*World War II*]
DAP	Director of Air Personnel [*Air Force*] [*British*]
DAP	Director of Ammunition Production [*Ministry of Supply*] [*British*] [*World War II*]
DAP	Director of Army Programs (AABC)
DAP	Director of Army Psychiatry [*British*]
DAP	Director Assign Panel (MCD)
DAP	Directorate of Accident Prevention [*RAF*] [*British*]
DAP	Distant Aiming Point
DAP	Distributed Array Processor [*Sperry UNIVAC*] [*Telecommunications*]
DAP	Division of Air Pollution [*Obsolete*] [*Public Health Service*]
DAP	Do All Possible
DAP	Documents Against Payment [*Banking*] (ADA)
DAP	Domestic Action Program [*Army*] (INF)
DAP	Domestic Annual Processing
DAP	Double-Amplitude Peak (DEN)
DAP	Double Antiparallel [*Molecular biology*]
D-A-P.	Draw-a-Person [*Psychology*]
DAP	Dynamic Assertion Processor [*Data processing*]
DAP	Quarterly. Department of Antiquities in Palestine [*A publication*]
DAPA	Diaminopimelic Acid [*Also, DAP, DPM*] [*An amino acid*]
DAPA	Drug and Alcohol Abuse Program Advisor [*Navy*] (NVT)
DAPAC	Danger Areas in the Pacific
DA PAM	Department of the Army Pamphlet
DAPATF	Department of the Army Property Accountability Task Force (MCD)
DAPB	Diallylpentobarbital [*Sedative*]
DAPBAB	Data Acquisition and Processing in Biology and Medicine [*A publication*]
DAPC	Diarachidoylphosphatidylcholine [*Biochemistry*]
DAPD	Directorate of Aircraft Production Development [*British*] (DEN)
DAP & E	Diploma in Applied Parasitology and Entomology [*British*]
DAPEP	Department of the Army Panel on Environmental Physiology
DAPF	Data Analysis and Processing Facility
DAPFS	Direct-Ascent Powered-Flight Simulation [*NASA*]
DAPG	Deutsch-Amerikanische Petroleum Gesellschaft [*German-American Petroleum Society*]
DAPG	Drug and Allied Products Guild [*Later, NAPM*]
DAPh	American Pharmaceutical Association, Washington, DC [*Library symbol*] [*Library of Congress*] (LCLS)
Daphn	Daphnis. Zeitschrift fuer Mittlere Deutsche Literatur [*A publication*]
DAPHNE	Dido and Pluto Handmaiden for Nuclear Experiments [*Nuclear reactor at Harwell, England*]
DAPI	American Petroleum Institute, Washington, DC [*Library symbol*] [*Library of Congress*] (LCLS)
DAPI	Diamidinophenylindole [*A dye*] [*Organic chemistry*]
DAP-II	Dianhydrogalactitol, Adriamycin, Platinol [*Cisplatin*] [*Antineoplastic drug regimen*]
DAPJD4	Date Palm Journal [*A publication*]
DAPL	Directory of Australian Public Libraries [*Australia*] [*A publication*]
DAPM	Deputy Assistant Provost-Marshall [*British*]
DAPM	Diaminodiphenylmethane [*Also, DDM, MDA*] [*Organic chemistry*]
DAPMC	Defense Advanced Procurement Management Course [*Army*]
DAPN	Dauphin Deposit Corp. [*NASDAQ symbol*] (NQ)
DAPN	Directional Antenna Phasing Network
DAPNA	Doklady Akademii Pedagogicheskikh Nauk RSFSR [*A publication*]
DAPO	Deep Attack Programs Office [*Army*]
DAPO	Digital Advance Production Order [*Telecommunications*] (TEL)
DAPOAG	Deutsche Apotheker [*A publication*]
D Apoth Ztg	Deutsche Apotheker-Zeitung [*A publication*]
DAPP	Daily Patient Photophase [*Biochronometry*]
DAPP	Data Acquisition and Processing Program [*Later, DMSP*] [*Air Force*]
DAPP	Design Aid for Post-Processors [*IBM Corp.*]
DAPP	Development Aid from People to People (EAIO)
DAPPER	Distribution Analysis for Power Planning, Evaluation, and Reporting [*Data processing*]

DAPPL	Department of the Army Programming Priority List
DAppSc	Doctor of Applied Science (ADA)
DAPR	Department of the Army Program Report
DAPR	Department of the Army Program Review (RDA)
DAPR	Digital Automatic Pattern Recognition (IEEE)
DAPRE	Daily Adjustable Progressive Resistance Exercise
DAPRU	Drug Abuse Prevention Resource Unit [*National Institute on Drug Abuse*] [*Databank*]
DAPS	Data Acquisition and Processing System
DAPS	Data Processing Automatic Publication Service
DAPS	Direct Access Programming System [*Data processing*]
DAPS	Director of Army Postal Services [*British*]
DAPS	Distributed Application Processing System
DAPS	Double Absorption Photofragment Spectroscopy
DAPS	Downed Airman Power Source [*Navy*]
DAPSAS	Developments in Applied Spectroscopy [*A publication*]
DAPSONE	Diaminodiphenyl Sulfone [*Also, DADPS, DDS*] [*Pharmacology*]
DAPSRB	Department of the Army Physical Security Review Board (MCD)
DAPT	Diamino(diethoxyphosphinyl)triazine [*Organic chemistry*]
DAPT	Diaminophenylthiazole [*Pharmacology*]
DAPT	Direct Agglutination Pregnancy Test [*Clinical chemistry*]
DAPTRA	Drug Abuse Prevention, Treatment, and Rehabilitation Act [*1972*]
DAPU	Data Acquisition and Processing Unit [*Viking orbiter system*] [*NASA*]
D-APV	D-Amino Phosphonovaleric Acid
DAQ	Develop and Qualify
DAQC	Data Acquisition Center (KSC)
DA & QMG	Deputy Adjutant and Quartermaster General [*British*]
DAQMG	Deputy Assistant Quartermaster General
DAR	Daily Activity Report [*Military*]
Da R	Dalhousie Review [*A publication*]
DAR	Damage Assessment Routines (MDG)
DAR	Damned Average Raiser [*A diligent student*] [*Slang*]
DAR	Dar Es Salaam [*Tanzania*] [*Airport symbol*] (OAG)
DAR	Darien Library [*UTLAS symbol*]
DAR	Darwin [*Australia*] [*Seismograph station code, US Geological Survey*] [*Closed*] (SEIS)
DAR	Data Access Register [*Data processing*] (MDG)
DAR	Data Acquisition Recorder
DAR	Data-Aided Receiver [*NASA*]
DAR	Data Article Requirements (AAG)
DAR	Data Automation Requirement
DAR	[*National Society*] Daughters of the American Revolution (EA)
DAR	Day-After Recall [*Advertising*]
DAR	Debrett Ancestry Research [*British*]
DAR	Defense Acquisition RADAR
DAR	Defense Acquisition Regulation [*or Requirement*]
DAR	Deficiency Action Report (NATG)
DAR	Delinquent Accounts and Returns [*IRS*]
DAR	Deployment Adjustment Request [*Military*] (CINC)
DAR	Design Action Request (MCD)
DAR	Design Assessment Report [*Nuclear energy*] (NRCH)
DAR	Detroit Arsenal [*Michigan*] [*Army*] (NATG)
DAR	Deviation Approval Request [*NASA*] (KSC)
DAR	Differentiation with Asymmetrical Reinforcement
DAR	Digital Angle Recorder
DAR	Digital Autopilot Requirements (NASA)
DAR	Director of Army Requirements [*British*]
DAR	Directorate of Armament Requirements [*RAF*] [*British*]
DAR	Directorate of Army Research (GRD)
DAR	Distributed Array RADAR (MCD)
DAR	Drawing Analysis Record (MCD)
DAR	Driver Augmented Readout [*Data processing*]
DARA	Deputy Associate Regional Administrator
DARA	Deutsche Arbeitsgemeinschaft fuer Rechen-Anlagen [*German Working Committee for Computing Machines*]
DARAC	Damped Aerodynamic Righting Attitude Control
DARACS	Damped Aerodynamic Righting Attitude Control System
DARAS	Direction and Range Acquisition System (MCD)
Darbai Liet Vet Akad	Darbai. Lietuvos Veterinarijos Akademijos [*A publication*]
Darb & B Lim	Darby and Bosanquet's Statutes of Limitations [*2nd ed.*] [*1893*] [*A publication*] (DLA)
DARC	American National Red Cross, Washington, DC [*Library symbol*] [*Library of Congress*] (LCLS)
DARC	Data Acquisition and Reports Control [*Army*] (AABC)
DARC	Defense Acquisition Regulatory Council (MCD)
DARC	Direct-Access RADAR Channel [*System*] [*Aviation*]
DARC	Documentation and Automatization of Researches for Correlations [*For molecular structure*] [*Chemical physics*]
DARCEE	Demonstration and Research Center for Early Education [*George Peabody College, Nashville*]
D Arch	Dialoghi di Archeologia [*A publication*]
D Arch	Diploma in Architecture [*British*]
D Arch	Doctor of Architecture
D Arch	Dodekanesiakon Archeion [*A publication*]
D Arch Des	Doctor of Architectural Design
D Arch E	Doctor of Architectural Engineering

D Arch Eng ... Doctor of Architectural Engineering

D Arch Klin Med ... Deutsches Archiv fuer Klinische Medizin [*A publication*]

DArChr...... Dictionnaire d'Archeologie Chretienne et de Liturgie [*A publication*]

DArChrL ... Dictionnaire d'Archeologie Chretienne et de Liturgie [*A publication*]

DARCIMC ... Development and Readiness Command Installation Management Course [*Military*]

DARCOM ... Development and Readiness Command [*Formerly, AMC*] [*See also MDRC*] [*Alexandria, VA*] [*Army*]

DARCOMALMSA ... Development and Readiness Command Automated Logistics Management Systems Agency [*Army*] (AABC)

DARCOMFASC ... Development and Readiness Command Facilities and Services Center [*Army*] (AABC)

DARCOMFSA ... Development and Readiness Command Field Safety Agency [*Army*] (AABC)

DARCOMI & SA ... Development and Readiness Command Installations and Service Agency [*Army*] (AABC)

DARCOMLDC ... Development and Readiness Command Logistics Data Center [*Army*] (AABC)

DARCOMLSSA ... Development and Readiness Command Logistics Systems Support Agency [*Army*] (AABC)

DARCOMPI ... Development and Readiness Command Procurement Instruction [*Army*] (MCD)

DARD........ Data Acquisition Requirements Document (KSC)

DARD........ Depressives Anonymous: Recovery from Depression (EA)

DARDC........ Device for Automatic Remote Data Collection [*National Weather Service*]

DARDO..... Direct Access to Remote Data Bases Overseas [*Italy*] [*Telecommunications*] (TSSD)

DARE .... Data Automatic Reduction Equipment (CET)

DARE .... Data Automation Research and Experimentation (CET)

DARE .... Data Retrieval Area (MCD)

DARE .... Decision Aids for Resource Expenditure (MCD)

DARE .... Diagnostic Analysis of Reading Errors [*Educational test*]

DARE .... Dictionary of American Regional English [*A publication*]

DARE .... Dictionary of American Regional English Project [*University of Wisconsin - Madison*] [*Research center*] (RCD)

DARE .... Differential Analyzer Replacement [*Programming language*] [*1967*] (CSR)

DARE .... Director Action for Rehabilitation and Employment [*Ex-offenders*] (OICC)

DARE .... Document Abstract Retrieval Equipment (IEEE)

DARE .... Documentation Automated Retrieval Equipment [*System*] [*Army*]

DARE .... Doppler and Range Evaluation

DARE .... DOVAP [*Doppler Velocity and Position*] Automatic Reduction Equipment (AAG)

DARE .... Drug Abuse Resistance Education

DARE .... Drug Addiction Rehabilitation Enterprise (EA)

DARES...... Data Analysis and Reduction System

Daresbury Lab Prepr DL/P ... Daresbury Laboratory. Preprint DL/P [*A publication*]

Daresbury Lab Prepr DL/SRF/P ... Daresbury Laboratory. Preprint DL/SRF/P [*A publication*]

Daresbury Lab Rep ... Daresbury Laboratory. Report [*A publication*]

Daresbury Lab Tech Memo ... Daresbury Laboratory. Technical Memorandum [*A publication*]

Daresbury Nucl Phys Lab Rep ... Daresbury Nuclear Physics Laboratory. Report [*A publication*]

Daresbury Nucl Phys Lab Tech Memo ... Daresbury Nuclear Physics Laboratory. Technical Memorandum [*A publication*]

Daresbury Synchrotron Radia Lect Note Ser ... Daresbury Synchrotron Radiation Lecture Note Series [*A publication*]

Dar Es Salaam Med J ... Dar Es Salaam Medical Journal [*A publication*]

DARF .... Defense Atomic Research Facility (MCD)

DARFAX... Department of the Army Secure Facsimile (AABC)

DARFD ..... Depressives Anonymous: Recovery from Depression (EA)

DARG........ Discourse Analysis Research Group [*University of Calgary*] [*Research center*] (RCD)

DARI .... Center for Applied Research in the Apostolate [*CARA*], African Research and Information Center, Washington, DC [*Library symbol*] [*Library of Congress*] (LCLS)

DARI .... Digital Angular Readout by LASER Interferometry (MCD)

DARIS....... Detroit Art Registration Information System [*Detroit Institute of Arts*] [*Information service or system*] (IID)

Dari Seama Sedintelor Com Stat Geol (Rom) ... Dari de Seama ale Sedintelor. Comitetul de Stat al Geologiei (Romania) [*A publication*]

Dari Seama Sedintelor Inst Geol (Rom) ... Dari de Seama ale Sedintelor. Institutul Geologie (Romania) [*A publication*]

Dari Seama Sedint RPR Com Geol ... Dari de Seama ale Sedintelor. Republica Populara Romana Comitetul Geologic [*A publication*]

D Ariz .... United States District Court for the District of Arizona (DLA)

DARK .... Discrimination Analysis Technique Adapted and Refined at Kwajalein [*Army*] (AABC)

D Ark .... Doctor of Archaeology

Darkroom Photogr ... Darkroom Photography [*A publication*]

DARL .... Darling [*Correspondence*] (DSUE)

DARL .... Douglas Advanced Research Laboratories [*Obsolete*] (KSC)

DARLI....... Digital Angular Readout by LASER Interferometry (MCD)

Darl Pr Ct Sess ... Darling. Practice of the Scotch Court of Session [*A publication*] (DLA)

DARMA .... Discrete Autoregressive-Moving Average Model [*Statistics*]

DAR Mag .. Daughters of the American Revolution. Magazine [*A publication*]

DArmD...... Directorate of Armament Development [*Ministry of Aircraft Production*] [*British*] [*World War II*]

DARME .... Director, Armament Engineering [*Military*] [*Canada*]

DARMS.... Digital Alternate Representation of Musical Symbols

DARMS.... Drifting Automatic Radiometeorological Station

Darmstaedter Beitr Neuen M ... Darmstaedter Beitraege zur Neuen Musik [*A publication*]

DARNG...... Director of the Army National Guard

DARO........ Days after Receipt of Order (MCD)

DARO........ Defense ADPE [*Automatic Data Processing Equipment*] Reutilization Office

DARPA...... Defense Advanced Research Projects Agency [*DoD*] [*Arlington, VA*]

DARPP...... Dopamine- and Cyclic AMP-Regulated Phosphoprotein [*Biochemistry*]

DARR .... Department of the Army Regional Representative (AABC)

DARR .... Drawing and Assembly Release Record (AAG)

DARRIS.... Department of the Army Requisitioning, Receipt, and Issue System

DARS........ Data Accumulating and Reporting Sheet

DARS........ Data Acquisition Recording System

DARS........ Data Acquisition and Reduction System

DARS........ Decommutation and Readout System [*Data processing*]

DARS........ Defense Acquisition Regulatory System [*DoD*] (RDA)

DARS........ Department of the Army Relocation Sites (AABC)

DARS........ Differential-Absorption Remote Sensing [*LASER*]

DARS........ Digital Adaptive Recording System

DARS........ Digital Attitude and Rate System (IEEE)

DARS........ Digital Attitude Reference System

Dar Sag...... Dictionnaire des Antiquites Grecques et Romaines (Daremberg and Saglio) [*A publication*]

D Ar Sc ...... Doctor of Arts and Sciences

Darshana Int ... Darshana International [*A publication*]

DARSS...... Diode Array Rapid Scan Spectrometer

DART .... Daily Automatic Rescheduling Technique [*Data processing*]

DART .... Dart Group Corp. [*Landover, MD*] [*NASDAQ symbol*] (NQ)

Dart............ Dart on Vendors and Purchasers [*A publication*] (DLA)

DART .... Data Analysis Real-Time [*Southwest Research Institute*]

DART .... Data Analysis Recording Tape

DART .... Data Reduction Translator

DART .... Decentralized Advanced Replenishment Technique (AFIT)

DART .... Decomposed Ammonia Radioisotope Thruster [*Aerospace*]

DART .... Delay and Retransmit

DART .... Deployable Automatic Relay Terminal [*Air Force*]

DART .... Depot Automatic Rescheduling Technique

DART .... Depression: Awareness, Recognition, and Treatment [*National Institute of Mental Health program*]

DART .... Detection, Action, and Response Technique

DART .... Development of Advanced Rate Techniques

DART .... Diagnostic-Assistance Reference Tool

DART .... Dial-a-Ride Transportation

DART .... Direct Advisory of Recorded Transactions (AABC)

DART .... Directional Automatic Realignment of Trajectory (NG)

DART .... Director of Army Research and Technology [*Washington, DC*] (GRD)

DART .... Director and Response Tester (KSC)

DART .... Directory of American Research and Technology [*R. R. Bowker Co.*] [*Information service or system*] [*A publication*]

DART .... Disappearing Automatic Retaliatory Target [*Military*] (RDA)

DART .... Disaster Assistance Recovery Teams [*Military*]

DART .... Distant Area Reduced Toll [*Telecommunications*] (TSSD)

DART .... Drill Attendance Reporting Test [*National Guard*]

DART .... Dual Axis Rate Transducer [*A gyroscope*]

DART .... Dublin Area Rapid Transit [*Ireland*]

DART .... Dynamic Acoustic Response Trigger (IEEE)

DART .... Dynamic Simulation of Auto and Passenger Rail Transports

DART .... Dynamically Adaptive Receiver Transmitter (CAAL)

Dart Bi-Mo ... Dartmouth Bi-Monthly [*A publication*]

Dart Col Ca ... Dartmouth College Case [*A publication*] (DLA)

DARTM .... Dartmouth [*Municipal borough in England*]

DARTM .... Defeat Armor Road Target Mine

Dartm Coll Bull ... Dartmouth College. Bulletin [*A publication*]

Dartmouth Alumni Mag ... Dartmouth Alumni Magazine [*A publication*]

DARTS...... Deployable Acoustic Readiness Training System (MCD)

DARTS...... Digital Antijam Radio Teletype System (MCD)

DARTS...... Digital Automated RADAR Tracking System (MCD)

DARTS...... Digital Azimuth Range Tracking System

DARTS...... Drug and Alcohol Rehabilitation Testing System [*Navy*] (NVT)

DARTS...... Dutch-Auction-Rate Transferable Securities [*Investment term*]

Dart Vend .. Dart on Vendors and Purchasers [*A publication*] (DLA)

DARWAG ... Darwiniana [*Buenos Aires*] [*A publication*]

Darw Cr L ... Darwin's Criminal Law [*A publication*] (DLA)

Darwin .... Darwiniana. Revista del Instituto de Botanica Darwinion [*A publication*]

DARYL......	Data Analysing Robot Youth Lifeform [From the movie entitled "D.A.R.Y.L."]
Das............	Common Law Reports, Volume 3 [England] [A publication] (DLA)
DAS	Daisetta, TX [Location identifier] [FAA] (FAAL)
Das.............	Dasent's Bankruptcy and Insolvency Reports [1853-55] [England] [A publication] (DLA)
DAS	Dassen Gold Resources Ltd. [Vancouver Stock Exchange symbol]
DAS	Data Access Security
DAS	Data Accountability System
DAS	Data Acquisition Station
DAS	Data Acquisition System
DAS	Data Administration Section (MCD)
DAS	Data Amplification Sheet (KSC)
DAS	Data Analysis Software [Telecommunications] (TEL)
DAS	Data Analysis Station (NASA)
DAS	Data Automation System [or Subsystem] [NASA]
DAS	Data Auxiliary Set [Telecommunications] (TEL)
DAS	Datatron Assembly System [Burroughs Corp.]
DAS	Date Arrived Station [Military] (AFM)
DAS	Death Anxiety Scale
DAS	Defense Against Self-Defense [Suggested program against falling missiles]
DAS	Defense Analysis Seminar [Military]
DAS	Defense Attache System [Department of State]
DAS	Defense Audit Service [Abolished 1982, functions transferred to Office of the Inspector General (DoD)]
DAS	Deficiency Analysis Summary
DAS	Delivered Alongside Ship
DAS	Demand-Assignment Signaling (MCD)
DAS	Dendrite Arm Spacing (RDA)
DAS	Developments in Atmosphere Science [Elsevier Book Series] [A publication]
DAS	Dextroamphetamine Sulfate [CNS stimulant]
DAS	Diacetoxyscirpenol [Fungal toxin]
DAS	Dial Assistance Switchboard (CET)
DAS	Dialdehyde Starch [Wet-strength agent]
DAS	Diaminostilbenedisulfonic Acid [Also, DASD, DASDS] [Organic chemistry]
DAS	Dictionary of American Slang [A publication]
DAS	Differential-Absorption and Scattering [Remote sensing technique]
DAS	Digital Address System (MCD)
DAS	Digital Aircraft Simulator (MCD)
DAS	Digital Altimeter Scanner
DAS	Digital Analog Simulator [Data processing]
DAS	Digital Attenuator System
DAS	Digital Avionics System (MCD)
DAS	Dimethoxyanthracene Sulfonate [Organic chemistry]
DAS	Dipole Antenna System
DAS	Direct Acting Steam (MSA)
DAS	Direct Air Support [Military] (AFM)
DAS	Direct Automotive Support
DAS	Director of Administrative Services [US Military Government, Germany]
DAS	Director of Armament Supplies [British] [World War II]
DAS	Director of the Army Staff
DAS	Directorate for Advanced Systems [Army] (RDA)
DAS	Directorate of Aerospace Studies [Kirtland Air Force Base, NM]
DAS	Directory Assistance System [Telecommunications] (TEL)
DAS	Disturbance Analysis System [Nuclear energy] (NRCH)
DAS	Division of Applied Sciences [Harvard University] [Research center] (RCD)
DAS	Division of Assistance to States [Department of Education]
DAS	Division of Atmospheric Surveillance [Environmental Protection Agency]
DAS	Doctor of Applied Science
D As	Doctor of Astronomy
DAS	Document Analysis Sheet (MCD)
DAS	Documentation Accountability Sheet (MCD)
DAS	Doyle's Australian Scouts (DMA)
DAS	Dramatic Authors' Society [British]
DAS	Dynamic Angle Spinning [Spectroscopy]
DAS	Dynamo Alert System (AAG)
DAS	United States Department of Commerce, National Oceanic and Atmospheric Administration, Atmospheric Sciences Library, Silver Spring, MD [Library symbol] [Library of Congress] (LCLS)
DAS3	Decentralized Automated Service Support System [Army] (RDA)
DASA	DASA Corp. [Stoneham, MA] [NASDAQ symbol] (NQ)
DASA	Defense Atomic Support Agency [Later, DNA]
DASA	Department of the Army Security Agency (MCD)
DASA	Dual Aerospace Servo Amplifier (NASA)
DASA-DC ...	Defense Atomic Support Agency Data Center
DASAT	Data Selector and Tagger (MUGU)
DASA-TP ...	Defense Atomic Support Agency Technical Publications
DASC	Defence Aid Supply Committee [Later, ISC] [World War II]
DASC........	Defense Automotive Supply Center
DASC........	Department of the Army System Coordinator (RDA)

DASC........	Direct Air Support Center [Later, ASOC]
DASc........	Doctor in Agricultural Sciences
DA Sc........	Doctor of Applied Science
DASCH	Disk Automation Storage Control Hardware [Macintosh computer]
DASCOTAR ...	Data Acquisition System, Correlation Tracking and Ranging [Air Force]
DASD	Data Acquisition Support Document (KSC)
DASD	Department of the Army Shipping Document
DASD	Deputy Assistant Secretary of Defense
DASD	Deutsche Akademie fuer Sprache und Dichtung (Darmstadt). Jahrbuch [A publication]
DASD	Diaminostilbenedisulfonic Acid [Also, DAS, DASDS] [Organic chemistry]
DASD	Direct Access Storage Device [Pronounced "daz-dee"] [Data processing]
DASD	Director, Anti-Submarine Division [British military] (DMA)
DASD	Director of Army Staff Duties [British] (RDA)
DASDJ	Deutsche Akademie fuer Sprache und Dichtung (Darmstadt). Jahrbuch [A publication]
DASDL......	Data and Structure Definition Language [Data processing] (BUR)
DASDR......	Direct Access Storage Dump Restore
DASDS......	Diaminostilbenedisulfonic Acid [Also, DAS, DASD] [Organic chemistry]
DASE........	Defense Against Sound Equipment [Military intelligence]
DAS & E	Defense Aid [Lend-Lease] Services and Expenses [World War II]
DASE........	Denver Articulation Screening Exam [Speech evaluation test]
DASE........	Digital Automatic Stabilization Equipment (MCD)
DASEB......	Department of the Army Suitability Evaluation Board (AABC)
DASEC......	Digital Automatic Stabilization Equipment Computer (MCD)
Dasent.......	Acts of the Privy Council (Dasent) [England] [A publication] (DLA)
Dasent........	Dasent's Bankruptcy and Insolvency Reports [1853-55] [England] [A publication] (DLA)
DASET	Deputy Assistant Secretary for Employment and Training [Department of Labor]
DASF........	Defense Aid [Lend-Lease] Special Fund [World War II]
DASF........	Direct Access Storage Facility [Data processing]
DASF........	Direct Air Support Flight [Military] (AFM)
DASH.......	Dash Industries, Inc. [NASDAQ symbol] (NQ)
DASH.......	Database Acquisition for Student Health
DASH.......	Destroyer, Antisubmarine Helicopter
DASH........	Developmental Assessment for the Severely Handicapped [Test]
DASH........	Direct Access Storage Handler [Telecommunications] (TEL)
DASH........	Distress Alarm for Severely Handicapped [British]
DASH........	Downtown Area Short Hops [Battery-powered bus service in Long Beach, California]
DASH........	Drishat Shalom [Best Regards] [Hebrew]
DASH........	Drone Antisubmarine Helicopter [Air Force, Navy]
DASH........	Dual Access Storage Handling
DASHAA ..	Symposium for the Salivary Gland [A publication]
DASI........	Developmental Activities Screening Inventory [Psychology]
DASI........	Digital Altimeter Setting Indicators [Aviation] (FAAC)
DASIAC.....	DoD [Department of Defense] Nuclear Information and Analysis Center [Acronym is based on former name, Defense Atomic Support Agency Information and Analysis Center] [Kaman Tempo] [Information service or system] (IID)
Dasika Hron ...	Dasika Hronika [A publication]
DASJA	Journal. Dental Association of South Africa [A publication]
DASL........	Data Access System Language
DASL........	Department of the Army Strategic Logistics [Study]
DASL........	Directory of Special Libraries in Australia [A publication]
DASM.......	Direct Access Storage Media [Data processing]
DASM.......	Director of Advanced Systems Management
DA/SM......	Director of Antisubmarine Material [British]
DAS/M......	Directory Assistance System/Microfilm [Bell System]
DASO	Demonstration and Shakedown Operations [Military] (AFM)
DASO	Department of the Army Special Order
DASO	District Armament Supply Officer [British]
DASOC	Disturbance Accommodation Standard-Deviation Optimal Controller [Space telescope] [NASA]
DASOP......	Demonstration and Shakedown Operation Piggyback [Kit] [Military]
DASP........	Director of Advanced Systems Planning
DASP........	Double Antibody Solid-Phase Radioimmunoassay [Clinical chemistry]
DASP........	Double Arm Magnetic Spectrometer
DASPA......	Defense Attache System Property Accounting (MCD)
DASPO......	Department of the Army Special Photographic Office (AABC)
DASPS......	Department of the Army Standard Port System
DASPS-E....	Department of the Army Standard Port System - Enhanced (MCD)
DASPS-E-SDG ...	Department of the Army Standard Port System - Enhanced - System Development Group (MCD)
DASq........	Direct Air Support Squadron [Military] (AFM)
DASR........	Data Acquisition Statistical Recorder
DASR........	Defense Analysis Special Report (MCD)

DASS......... Demand-Assignment Signaling and Switching Unit
DASS......... Diesel Air Start System (IEEE)
DASS......... Digital Acoustic Simulation System (MCD)
DASS......... Disturbance Analysis and Surveillance System [*NRC*]
D As S........ Doctor of Association Science
DASSC....... Dante Alighieri Society of Southern California (EA)
D As Sc....... Doctor of Association Science
Dass Dig.... Dassler's Kansas Digest [*A publication*] (DLA)
Dass Ed...... Dassler's Edition, Kansas Reports [*A publication*] (DLA)
Dass Ed (Kan) ... Dassler's Edition, Kansas Reports [*A publication*] (DLA)
DASSO...... Data Systems Support Office (MCD)
DASSO...... Department of the Army Systems Staff Officer (AABC)
DASSq....... Direct Air Support Squadron [*Air Force*]
Dass Stat.... Dassler's Kansas Statutes [*A publication*] (DLA)
DaSt........... Dante Studies [*A publication*]
DAST......... Denver Audiometric Screening Test
DAST......... Design, Architecture, Software, and Testing (MCD)
DAST......... Detective - Agents - Science Fiction - Thriller [*Acronym used as title of magazine*]
DAST......... Device Assignment Table
DAST......... Diethylaminosulfur Trifluoride [*Organic chemistry*]
DAST......... Direct Air Support Team [*Military*] (CINC)
DAST......... Directorate of Advanced Systems Technology
DASTARD ... Destroyer Antisubmarine Transportable Array Detector
DASTL...... Defense Atomic Support Agency Technical Letters
DASTM...... Double-Acting Steam
DASV........ Differential Anodic Stripping Voltammetry [*Electronics*]
DASVA...... Defense Attache System Vehicle Accounting (MCD)
DASW........ Data Switch Corp. [*NASDAQ symbol*] (NQ)
DA/SW....... Director of Antisubmarine Warfare [*British*]
DASWE..... Director, Admiralty Surface Weapons Establishment [*Navy*] [*British*]
DASY........ Data Analysis System
DAT........... Dangerous Articles Tariff
DAT........... Data Acceptance Tests
DAT........... Data Acquisition Test [*Later, DST*]
DAT........... Data File [*Data processing*]
DAT........... Data General Corp., Westboro, MA [*OCLC symbol*] (OCLC)
DAT........... Datamation [*A publication*]
DAT........... Dative
DAT........... Datum (MSA)
DAT........... Datumone Petroleum [*Vancouver Stock Exchange symbol*]
DAT........... Daunomycin, ara-C [*Cytarabine*], Thioguanine [*Antineoplastic drug regimen*]
DAT........... Days after Treatment [*Agriculture*]
DAT........... Decorative Arts Trust (EA)
DAT........... Defense Attache
DAT........... Delayed Action Tablet [*Pharmacy*]
DAT........... Dementia Alzheimer Type [*Medicine*]
DAT........... Den, Aoyama, and Takemake [*Early investors in automobile manufacturer Nissan*] [*Initials used in creating automobile name DATSUN*] [*Japan*]
DAT........... Dental Admission Test [*Education*]
DAT........... Deoxyaconitine [*Biochemistry*]
DAT........... Department Approved Training (OICC)
DAT........... Depot a Terme [*Time Deposit*] [*French*] [*Business term*]
DAT........... Design Acceptance [*or Approval*] Test
DAT........... Desktop Analysis Tool [*A publication*]
DAT........... Detail Assembly Template
DAT........... Deutsch-Atlantische Telegraphengesellschaft [*German-Atlantic Telegraph Company*] [*Federal Republic of Germany*]
DAT........... Development Acceptance Test [*Army*]
DAT........... Development Assist Test
DAT........... Device Assignment Table (MCD)
DAT........... Diaminotropolone [*Biochemistry*]
DAT........... Diet as Tolerated [*Medicine*]
DAT........... Differential Agglutination Titer [*Hematology*]
DAT........... Differential Aptitude Test [*Psychology*]
DAT........... Digital Acoustic Target
DAT........... Digital Audio Tape [*Also facetiously translated as Damn the Artist and Talent*]
DAT........... Di(isoamyloxy)thiocarbanilide [*Pharmacology*]
DAT........... Diphtheria Antitoxin [*Immunology*]
DAT........... Direct Action Team (MCD)
DAT........... Direct Amylase Test [*Clinical chemistry*]
DAT........... Direct Antiglobulin Test [*Clinical chemistry*]
DAT........... Director [*or Directorate*] of Advanced Technology [*Air Force*]
DAT........... Director of Army Training [*British*]
DAT........... Director of Army Transportation
DAT........... Disaster Action Team [*Red Cross*]
DAT........... Disconnect Actuating Tools [*Nuclear energy*] (NRCH)
DAT........... Disk Allocation Table [*Data processing*] (IBMDP)
DAT........... Division of Applied Technology [*Coast Guard*]
DAT........... Docking Alignment Target [*NASA*] (MCD)
DAT........... Drone Assisted Torpedo
DAT........... Duration Adjusting Type
DAT........... Dynamic Address Translation [*Data processing*]
DATA........ DataImage, Inc. [*NASDAQ symbol*] (NQ)
DATA........ Defense Air Transportation Administration [*Abolished 1962, functions transferred to Office of the Under Secretary of Commerce for Transportation*]

DATA........ Derivation & Tabulation Associates, Inc. [*Information service or system*] (IID)
DATA........ Development and Technical Assistance
DATA........ Dial a Teacher Assistance [*Telephone service*]
DATA........ Direct Access Terminal Application [*Data processing*] (BUR)
DATA........ Display Automated Telemetry Analyzer (MCD)
DATA........ Drawing for Army Training Aids
Data Acquis Process Biol Med ... Data Acquisition and Processing in Biology and Medicine [*A publication*]
Data Acquis Process Biol Med Proc Rochester Conf ... Data Acquisition and Processing in Biology and Medicine. Proceedings of the Rochester Conference [*A publication*]
Data At Power ... Data of Atomic Power [*Japan*] [*A publication*]
Database J ... Database Journal [*A publication*]
Database Jrnl ... Database Journal [*A publication*]
Data Base News ... Data Base Newsletter [*A publication*]
Database Sys ... ACM [*Association for Computing Machinery*] Transactions on Database Systems [*A publication*]
Data Bus ... Data Business [*A publication*]
DATAC ..... Data Acquisition Division [*National Weather Service*]
DATAC ..... Data Analog Computer
Data C .... Data Communications [*A publication*]
DATAC ..... Defense and Tactical Armament Control
DATAC ..... Digital Automatic Tester and Classifier
Data Chan ... Data Channels [*A publication*]
D Atache .... Defence Attache [*A publication*]
DATACOL ... Data Collection
DATACOM ... Data Communications
Data Comm ... Data Communications [*A publication*]
Data Commun ... Data Communications [*A publication*]
DATACORTS ... Data Correlation and Transfer System
Data C Xtra ... Data Communications Extra [*A publication*]
Data Dyn.... Data Dynamics [*A publication*]
Data Ed.... Data Education [*A publication*]
DATAFIT ... [*A*] programming language [*1973*] (CSR)
DATAGEN ... Data File Generator (MCD)
Data Hand Sci Technol ... Data Handling in Science and Technology [*A publication*]
DATAMAN ... Data Management System [*Data processing*] (MCD)
Data Manage ... Data Management [*A publication*]
DATAMAP ... Data from Aeromechanics' Test and Analytics-Management and Analysis Package (RDA)
Data Mgmt ... Data Management [*A publication*]
Data Mgt ... Data Management [*A publication*]
Datam NR ... Datamation News Release [*A publication*]
DATAN ..... Data Analysis (IEEE)
DATANET ... Data Network (CET)
DATAP...... Data Transmission and Processing (NATG)
Data Proc ... Data Processing [*A publication*]
Data Proc Dig ... Data Processing Digest [*A publication*]
Data Proces ... Data Processing [*A publication*]
Data Process ... Data Processing [*A publication*]
Data Process ... Data Processing Digest [*A publication*]
Data Process Dig ... Data Processing Digest [*A publication*]
Data Process Educ ... Data Processing for Education [*North American Publishing Co.*] [*A publication*]
Data Process Mag ... Data Processing Magazine [*A publication*]
Data Process Med ... Data Processing in Medicine [*A publication*]
Data Process Pract ... Data Processing Practitioner [*A publication*]
Datapro Rep Data Commun ... Datapro Reports on Data Communications [*A publication*]
Datapro Rep Minicomput ... Datapro Reports on Minicomputers [*A publication*]
Datapro Rep Office Syst ... Datapro Reports on Office Systems [*A publication*]
DATAR ..... Digital Automatic Tracking and Ranging [*or Remoting*] [*Air Force*]
DATAR ..... Digital Autotransducer and Recorder (IEEE)
Data Rec Oceanogr Obs Explor Fish (Hokkaido) ... Data Record of Oceanographic Observations and Exploratory Fishing (Hokkaido) [*A publication*]
Data Rep.... Data Report [*A publication*]
Data Sys..... Data Systems [*A publication*]
Data Syst ... Data Systems [*A publication*]
Data Systems N ... Data Systems News [*A publication*]
DATA-TEXT ... [*A*] programming language (CSR)
Data Trng.. Data Training [*A publication*]
Data User Ns ... Data Users News [*A publication*]
DATB .... Department of the Army Technical Bulletin (MCD)
DATB .... Diaminotrinitrobenzene [*An explosive*]
DATBP...... Diallyl Tetrabromophthalate [*Organic chemistry*]
DATC .... Data Card Corp. [*NASDAQ symbol*] (NQ)
DATC .... Development and Training Center [*Navy*] (NVT)
DATC .... Dichloroallyl Diisopropylthiocarbamate [*Di-allate*] [*Herbicide*]
DATC .... Direct Assistance and Training Command [*Navy*] (NVT)
DATC .... Director of Air Training Corps [*British*]
DATCIG.... Deferred Adverse Tax Consequences Implementation Group [*IRS*]
DATCOM ... Data Compendium (MCD)
DATCOM ... Data Support Command [*Army*]
DATD .... Diallyltartardiamide [*Also, DATDA*] [*Organic chemistry*]

DATDA..... Diallyltartardiamide [*Also, DATD*] [*Organic chemistry*]
DATDC..... Data Analysis and Technique Development Center
DA/TDMA ... Demand Assigned/Time Division Multiple Access
DATE .... Dash Automatic Test Equipment
DATE .... Data for Allotments Transmitted Electronically (MCD)
DATE .... DATICO [*Digital Automatic Tape Intelligence Checkout*] Acceptance Test Evaluation (MCD)
DATE .... Designation Accuracy Test Equipment
DATE .... Digital Angular Torquing Equipment
DATE .... Digital Audio for Television [*System to improve sound*] [*Public Broadcasting Service*]
DATE .... Directory of Australian Tertiary Education [*A publication*] (APTA)
DATE .... Dynamics, Acoustics, and Thermal Environment (NASA)
DATEC...... Data Technical Support Group [*Telecommunications*] (TEL)
DATEC...... Data and Telecommunications
DATEC...... Digital Adaptive Technique for Efficient Communications
Date Grow Inst Rep ... Date Growers' Institute. Report [*A publication*]
DATEL...... Data Telecommunications [*RCA Global Communications Data Transmission Service over Telephone Circuits*] [*Telecommunications*] (TEL)
Datenverarb Med ... Datenverarbeitung in der Medizin [*A publication*]
Datenverarb Recht ... Datenverarbeitung im Recht [*A publication*]
DATEP...... Department of the Army Telecommunications Plan (MCD)
Date Palm J ... Date Palm Journal [*A publication*]
DATHF..... Dideazatetrahydrofolic Acid [*Antineoplastic drug*]
DATI .... Director of Army Technical Information (AABC)
DATICO.... Data Analysis and Technique Development Center [*Alexandria, VA*]
DATICO.... Digital Automatic Tape Intelligence Checkout
DATICS .... Data Inventory Control System
DATIMTEX ... Data, Images, and Text [*European Patent Office*]
DATIN ...... Data Inserter
DATJBM .. Datenjournal [*A publication*]
DATM....... Bordj Mokhtar [*Algeria*] [*ICAO location identifier*] (ICLI)
DATM....... Datum, Inc. [*NASDAQ symbol*] (NQ)
DATM....... Department of the Army Technical Manual (NATG)
DATMOBAS ... David W. Taylor Model Basin [*Also, DTMB, TMB*] [*Later, DTNSRDC, NSRDC*] (MUGU)
DATMRPSTL ... Department of the Army Technical Manual Repair Parts Special Tool List
DATN....... Datricon Corp. [*NASDAQ symbol*] (NQ)
DATO........ Disbursing and Transportation Office
DATO........ Discover America Travel Organizations, Inc. [*Later, TIA*]
DATOC..... Division Artillery Tactical Operations Center (MCD)
DATOM.... Data Aids for Training, Operations, and Maintenance
DATOM.... Direct Access to Members [*Trade union membership database*] [*British*]
DATOR..... Data Operational Requirements Board [*NATO Military Committee*] (NATG)
DATOR..... Digital Data, Auxiliary Storage, Track Display, Outputs, and RADAR Display
DATOS ..... Detection and Tracking of Satellites (CINC)
DAT & OV ... Defense Aid [*Lend-Lease*] Tanks and Other Vehicles [*World War II*]
dATP .... Deoxyadenosine Triphosphate [*Biochemistry*]
DATP .... Detailed Acceptance Test Procedure (KSC)
DATP .... Detroit Arsenal Tank Plant [*Army*]
DATP .... Dissolved Adenosine Triphosphate [*Oceanography*]
DATPR...... Domestic Air Transport Policy Review [*A publication*] (APTA)
DATR .... Datron Corp. [*NASDAQ symbol*] (NQ)
DATR .... Design Acceptance [*or Approval*] Test Report
DATRDA .. Defense Aid [*Lend-Lease*] Testing, Reconditioning, etc., of Defense Articles [*World War II*]
DATREC... Data Recording (CET)
DATRIX.... Direct Access to Reference Information [*Xerox Corp.*]
DAtS.......... Atonement Seminary of the Holy Ghost, Washington, DC [*Library symbol*] [*Library of Congress*] (LCLS)
DATS........ Data Accumulation and Transfer Sheet
DATS........ Data Acquisition and Transmission System (MCD)
DA/TS....... Data Acquisition/Transmittal Sheet
DATS........ Data Transmission System
DATS........ Despun Antenna Test Satellite [*Air Force*]
DATS........ Detailed Acceptance Test Specification (KSC)
DATS........ Director, Auxiliary Territorial Service [*British military*] (DMA)
DATS........ Drill and Transfer System
DATS........ Dynamic Accuracy Test Set [*or System*]
DATSC...... Department of the Army Training and Support Committee (AABC)
DATST...... Datura stramonium [*Jimsonweed*]
DATT .... Defense Attache (AFM)
DATTA...... Diagnostic and Therapeutic Technology Assessment [*Medicine*]
DATUM..... Dokumentations- und Ausbildungszentrum fuer Theorie und Methode der Regionalforschung [*Documentation and Training Center for Theory and Methods of Regional Research*] [*Germany*]
Datum Collect Tokai Reg Fish Res Lab ... Datum Collection. Tokai Regional Fisheries Research Laboratory [*A publication*]
DATX .... Data Translation, Inc. [*Marlborough, MA*] [*NASDAQ symbol*] (NQ)

DAU.......... American University, Washington, DC [*Library symbol*] [*Library of Congress*] (LCLS)
DAU.......... Daniels Canyon [*Utah*] [*Seismograph station code, US Geological Survey*] (SEIS)
DAU.......... Daru [*Papua New Guinea*] [*Airport symbol*] (OAG)
DAU.......... Data Acquisition Unit
DAU.......... Data Adapter Unit
DAU.......... Data Arithmetic Unit [*Data processing*]
DAU.......... Datamation [*A publication*]
DAU.......... Daughter
DAU.......... Declaration of Atlantic Unity [*Defunct*]
DAU.......... Dental Auxiliary Utilization
DAU.......... Digital Adapter Unit (MCD)
DAU.......... Digital Applique Unit (MCD)
DAU.......... Display Assembly Unit (MCD)
DAU.......... Drugs of Abuse in Urine [*Toxicology*]
DAUA........ Adrar/Touat [*Algeria*] [*ICAO location identifier*] (ICLI)
DAUB........ Biskra [*Algeria*] [*ICAO location identifier*] (ICLI)
DAU & COH ... Daughter and Co-Heir [*Genealogy*] (ROG)
Dau Co Rep ... Dauphin County Reports [*Pennsylvania*] [*A publication*] (DLA)
DAUD........ Director of Anti-U-Boat Division [*British*] [*World War II*]
D Au E ...... Diploma in Automobile Engineering [*British*]
D Au E ...... Doctor of Automobile Engineering
DAUE........ El Golea [*Algeria*] [*ICAO location identifier*] (ICLI)
D Au Eng ... Doctor of Automobile Engineering
DAUG........ Ghardaia/Noumerate [*Algeria*] [*ICAO location identifier*] (ICLI)
DAUGR..... Daughter
DAU & H... Daughter and Heir [*Genealogy*] (ROG)
DAUH .... Hassi-Messaoud/Oued Irara [*Algeria*] [*ICAO location identifier*] (ICLI)
DAUHS..... Daughters (ROG)
DAUI......... In Salah [*Algeria*] [*ICAO location identifier*] (ICLI)
DAUK........ Deutsche Arbeiten der Universitaet Koeln [*A publication*]
DAUK........ Touggourt/Sidi Mahdi [*Algeria*] [*ICAO location identifier*] (ICLI)
DAU-L....... American University, Washington College of Law, Washington, DC [*Library symbol*] [*Library of Congress*] (LCLS)
DAUL........ Laghouat [*Algeria*] [*ICAO location identifier*] (ICLI)
DAUO........ El Oued/Guemar [*Algeria*] [*ICAO location identifier*] (ICLI)
Dauph .... Dauphin County Reporter [*Pennsylvania*] [*A publication*] (DLA)
Dauph Co Rep ... Dauphin County Reporter [*Pennsylvania*] [*A publication*] (DLA)
Dauph Med ... Dauphine Medical [*A publication*]
DAUS........ Defense Against Underwater Swimmers [*Military*] (MCD)
DAusE .... Australian Embassy, Washington, DC [*Library symbol*] [*Library of Congress*] (LCLS)
DAUT........ Timimoun [*Algeria*] [*ICAO location identifier*] (ICLI)
DAUU........ Ouargla [*Algeria*] [*ICAO location identifier*] (ICLI)
DAUWE.... Director, Admiralty Underwater Weapons Establishment [*Navy*] [*British*]
DAUZ........ Zarzaitine/In Amenas [*Algeria*] [*ICAO location identifier*] (ICLI)
DAV.......... Data Available (MCD)
DAV.......... Data Valid (IEEE)
DAV.......... Data above Voice [*Telecommunications*] (TEL)
DAV.......... Davao [*Philippines*] [*Seismograph station code, US Geological Survey*] (SEIS)
DAV.......... Davao [*Philippines*] [*Geomagnetic observatory code*]
Dav.......... Davar. Revista Literaria [*A publication*]
DAV.......... David [*Panama*] [*Airport symbol*] (OAG)
DAV.......... David Minerals Ltd. [*Vancouver Stock Exchange symbol*]
Dav.......... Davies' English Patent Cases [*1785-1816*] [*A publication*] (DLA)
Dav.......... Davies' Irish King's Bench and Exchequer Reports [*1604-12*] [*A publication*] (DLA)
Dav............ Davies' United States District Court Reports [*Republished as 2 Ware*] [*A publication*] (DLA)
Dav............ Davis' Hawaiian Reports [*A publication*] (DLA)
Dav............ Davis' Reports [*Abridgment of Sir Edward Coke's Reports*] [*A publication*] (DLA)
Dav............ Davis' United States Supreme Court Reports [*A publication*] (DLA)
DAV.......... Delta-Aminovaleric Acid [*Organic chemistry*]
DAV.......... Diaminovaleric Acid [*Biochemistry*]
DAV.......... Disabled American Veterans (EA)
Dav.......... Reports of Irish Cases, by Sir John Davis [*1604-11*] [*A publication*] (DLA)
DAVA........ Defense Audiovisual Agency [*DoD*]
DAVA........ Director [*or Directorate*] of Audiovisual Activities [*Army*]
DAVA........ Disabled American Veterans Auxiliary (EA)
Dav Ann ..... Davies on Annuities [*A publication*] (DLA)
DAVBADS ... Defense Audiovisual Booking and Distribution System
Dav B & B .. Davidson on Banks and Banking [*Canada*] [*A publication*] (DLA)
Dav Bdg Soc ... David on Building Societies [*A publication*] (DLA)
DAVC........ Delayed Automatic Volume Control
Dav Can ..... Davis' English Church Canons [*A publication*] (DLA)
Dav Coke ... Davis' Abridgment of Coke's Reports [*A publication*] (DLA)

Dav Conv ... Davidson's Conveyancing [*A publication*]   (DLA)
Dav Cr Cons ... Davis' Criminal Law Consolidation Acts [*A publication*]   (DLA)
Dav Cr Law ... Davis' Criminal Law [*A publication*]   (DLA)
Dav & Dic Pr ... Davidson and Dicey's Concise Precedents in Conveyancing [*A publication*]   (DLA)
Dav Dig...... Davis' Indiana Digest [*A publication*]   (DLA)
DAVDS ..... Data Acquisition and Visual Display System   (NRCH)
DAVE .... Data Addition, Verification, and Editing [*Lotus 1-2-3*]
DAVEDJ ... Dansk Veterinaertidsskrift [*A publication*]
Dav Elec..... Davis' Law of Registration and Election [*A publication*]   (DLA)
Dav Eng Ch Can ... Davis' English Church Canons [*A publication*]   (DLA)
Dav Fr Merc Law ... Davies on French Mercantile Law [*A publication*]   (DLA)
Dav Fr Soc ... Davis on Friendly Societies and Trade Unions [*A publication*]   (DLA)
DAVH........ Dibromodulcitol, Adriamycin, Vincristine, Halotestin [*Fluoxymesterone*] [*Antineoplastic drug regimen*]
DAVI .... Department of Audiovisual Instruction [*of NEA*] [*Later, AECT*]   (EA)
DAVI .... Dynamic Antiresonant Vibration Isolator
DAVID ...... Defense of Airborne Vehicles in Depth
DAVID ...... Dynamic Audio Video Interactive Device [*Hearing aid*]
Davidson .... Davidson's Reports [*92-111 North Carolina*] [*A publication*]   (DLA)
DAVIE....... Department of the Army Vocabulary of Information Elements   (AABC)
Davies .... [*Sir John*] Davies' Irish King's Bench Reports [*A publication*]   (DLA)
Davies .... Davies' Patent Cases [*1785-1816*] [*A publication*]   (DLA)
Davies .... Davies' United States District Court Reports [*Republished as 2 Ware*] [*A publication*]   (DLA)
Davies (Eng) ... Davies' English Patent Cases [*1785-1816*] [*A publication*]   (DLA)
Davies (Ir) ... [*Sir John*] Davies' Irish King's Bench Reports [*A publication*]   (DLA)
Davies (US) ... Davies' District Court Reports [*2 Ware*] [*United States*] [*A publication*]   (DLA)
Dav Ind Dig ... Davis' Indiana Digest [*A publication*]   (DLA)
Dav Ind Soc ... Davis on Industrial and Provident Societies [*A publication*]   (DLA)
DAVIPP .... Department of the Army Visual Information Production Program
Dav Ir......... [*Sir John*] Davies' Irish King's Bench Reports [*A publication*]   (DLA)
Dav Ir K B ... [*Sir John*] Davies' Irish King's Bench Reports [*A publication*]   (DLA)
Davis.......... [*Sir John*] Davies' Irish King's Bench Reports [*A publication*]   (DLA)
Davis .... Davis' Hawaiian Reports [*A publication*]   (DLA)
Davis .... Davis' United States Supreme Court Reports [*A publication*]   (DLA)
DAVIS...... Defense Audiovisual Information System [*DoD*]
DAVIS...... Defense Automated Visual Information System [*Database*]   (EISS)
Davis Admin Law ... Davis' Administrative Law Treatise [*A publication*]   (DLA)
Davis Bdg... Davis' Law of Building Societies [*A publication*]   (DLA)
Davis Bldg Soc ... Davis' Law of Building Societies [*A publication*]   (DLA)
Davis Cr Law ... Davis' Criminal Law [*A publication*]   (DLA)
Davis (JCB) ... Davis' United States Supreme Court Reports [*A publication*]   (DLA)
Davis Land Ct Dec (Mass) ... Davis' Land Court Decisions (Massachusetts) [*1898-1908*] [*A publication*]   (ILCA)
Davis L Ct Cas ... Davis' Land Court Decisions [*1898-1908*] [*A publication*]   (DLA)
Davis Mass Convey Hdbk ... Davis' Massachusetts Conveyancer's Handbook [*A publication*]   (DLA)
Davis Rep... Davis' Hawaiian Reports [*A publication*]   (DLA)
Dav Jus...... Davis' Justice of the Peace [*A publication*]   (DLA)
Dav & Kim IRL ... Davidge and Kimball's Internal Revenue Laws [*A publication*]   (DLA)
DAVL .... Data Available - Low   (MCD)
Dav Lab L.. Davis on the Labor Laws [*A publication*]   (DLA)
Dav Land Ct Cas ... Davis' Land Court Decisions [*1898-1908*] [*A publication*]   (DLA)
DAVLB..... Desacetylvincaleukoblastine
Dav & M ... Davison and Merivale's English Queen's Bench Reports [*A publication*]   (DLA)
D Av Med .. Diploma in Aviation Medicine [*British*]
Dav & M (Eng) ... Davison and Merivale's English Queen's Bench Reports [*A publication*]   (DLA)
Dav & Mer ... Davison and Merivale's English Queen's Bench Reports [*A publication*]   (DLA)
Dav M & S ... Davis' Law of Master and Servant [*A publication*]   (DLA)
DAVNO..... Division Aviation Officer
DAVO........ Daylight Visual Observation   (MCD)
DAVO........ Dynamic Analog of Vocal Tract
DAVOR..... Datenbank fuer Forderungsvorhaben [*Ongoing Research Project Data Bank*] [*Ministry for Research and Technology*] [*Information service or system*]   (IID)

DAV & OW ... Defense Aid [*Lend-Lease*] Vessels and Other Watercraft [*World War II*]
Dav Pat Cas ... Davies' English Patent Cases [*1785-1816*] [*A publication*]   (DLA)
Dav P C...... Davies' English Patent Cases [*1785-1816*] [*A publication*]   (DLA)
Dav Prec Conv ... Davidson's Precedents in Conveyancing [*A publication*]   (DLA)
Dav Prec Ind ... Davis' Precedents of Indictment [*A publication*]   (DLA)
DAVR .... Division of Adult and Vocational Research [*Office of Education*]
Dav Reg..... Davison on Registration and Elections [*A publication*]   (DLA)
Dav Rep ..... [*Sir John*] Davies' Irish King's Bench Reports [*A publication*]   (DLA)
DAVRS...... Director of Army Veterinary and Remount Services [*British*]
DAVS .... Developments in Animal and Veterinary Sciences [*Elsevier Book Series*] [*A publication*]
DAVSA...... Defense Audiovisual Support Activity
DAVSDR... Developments in Animal and Veterinary Sciences [*A publication*]
DAVSS ...... Doppler Acoustic Vortec Sensing System [*FAA*]   (MCD)
Dav Tr Un ... Davis' Trade Unions [*A publication*]   (DLA)
Dav (US).... Davies' District Court Reports [*2 Ware*] [*United States*] [*A publication*]   (DLA)
DAVX .... Davox Corp. [*NASDAQ symbol*]   (NQ)
Davy........... [*Sir John*] Davies' Irish King's Bench Reports [*A publication*]   (DLA)
Davys .... Davys' English King's Bench Reports [*A publication*]   (DLA)
Davys (Eng) ... Davys' English King's Bench Reports [*A publication*]   (DLA)
DAW .... Daw [*New Britain*] [*Seismograph station code, US Geological Survey*] [*Closed*]   (SEIS)
DAW.......... Dawson College Library [*UTLAS symbol*]
DAW.......... Days a Week [*Classified advertising*]
DAW.......... Denkschriften der Akademie der Wissenschaften in Wien [*A publication*]
DAW......... Dienstanweisung [*Service regulations*] [*German military - World War II*]
DAW.......... Director of Naval Air Warfare [*British military*]   (DMA)
DAW.......... Directorate of Atomic Warfare
DAW.......... Dispense as Written [*Prescription cannot be filled using a generic equivalent*] [*Pharmacy*]
DAWA....... Danish American Women's Association [*Defunct*]   (EA)
DAWA....... Divinatory Arts World Association [*See also AMAD*] [*Rillieux-La-Pape, France*]   (EAIO)
Daw Ar....... Dawe on Arrest in Civil Cases [*A publication*]   (DLA)
Daw Att...... Dawson's Attorney's [*A publication*]   (DLA)
DAWB .... Deutsche Akademie der Wissenschaften zu Berlin [*A publication*]
DAWBIDSL ... Deutsche Akademie der Wissenschaften zu Berlin. Institut fuer Deutsche Sprache und Literatur [*A publication*]
Daw Cr & Pun ... Dawe on Crimes and Punishments [*A publication*]   (DLA)
Dawe Dig ... Dawe Digest [*A publication*]
DAWG....... Dynamic Air War Game [*Military*]
DAWID ..... Device for Automatic Word Identification and Discrimination [*Data processing*]
DAWK .... Dove and Hawk [*One who took a moderate position on the Vietnam War*]
Daw Land Pr ... Dawe's Epitome of the Law of Landed Property [*A publication*]   (DLA)
DAWN....... Development Alternatives with Women for a New Era [*See also MUDAR*] [*Rio De Janeiro, Brazil*]   (EAIO)
DAWN....... Digital Automatic Weather Network
DAWN....... Drug Abuse Warning Network [*Public Health Service*] [*Rockville, MD*]
DAWNS .... Design of Aircraft Wing Structures [*Computer program*]
Daw Or Leg ... Dawson's Origo Legum [*A publication*]   (DLA)
Daw Real Pr ... Dawe's Real Estate Law [*A publication*]   (DLA)
DAWS .... Director of Army Welfare Services [*British*]
DAWS .... Diver Alternative Work System
Dawson's Code ... Dawson's Code of Civil Procedure [*Colorado*] [*A publication*]   (DLA)
DAWT .... Director of Naval Air Warfare and Flying Training [*British*]
DAWW...... Denkschriften der Akademie der Wissenschaften in Wien [*A publication*]
DAX.......... Data Acquisition and Control
DAX.......... Data Exchange
DAXBT...... Deep Airborne Expendable Bathythermograph [*Naval Oceanographic Office*]
Dax Exch Pr ... Dax's Exchequer Precedents [*A publication*]   (DLA)
DAXI .... Digital Auxiliary Information Code [*Data processing*]
Dax Mast Pr ... Dax's Practice in the Offices of the Masters [*A publication*]   (DLA)
DAXREP... Department of the Army Command and Control Reporting System   (AABC)
DAY.......... Day International [*NYSE symbol*]   (SPSG)
Day............ Day's Connecticut Reports [*A publication*]   (DLA)
Day............ Day's Election Cases [*1892-93*] [*England*] [*A publication*]   (DLA)
DAY.......... Dayton [*Ohio*] [*Airport symbol*]   (OAG)
DAY.......... Dayton, OH [*Location identifier*] [*FAA*]   (FAAL)
DAY.......... Dialysis and You [*of the DAY Association*] [*Defunct*]   (EA)

DAY	Dwarf Aster Yellows [*Plant pathology*]
DAY	University of Dayton, Dayton, OH [*OCLC symbol*] (OCLC)
Day Care & Early Educ	Day Care and Early Education [*A publication*]
Day(Conn)	Connecticut Reports, by Day [*1802-13*] [*A publication*] (DLA)
Day Elect Cas	Day's Election Cases [*1892-93*] [*England*] [*A publication*] (DLA)
DAyM	Doctor of Ayurvedic Medicine
DAYS	Days Inns Corp. [*Atlanta, GA*] [*NASDAQ symbol*] (NQ)
Day's Ca	Day's Connecticut Reports [*A publication*] (DLA)
Day's Ca Er	Day's Connecticut Reports [*A publication*] (DLA)
Day's Cases	Day's Connecticut Reports [*A publication*] (DLA)
Day's Conn Rep	Day's Connecticut Reports [*A publication*] (DLA)
Day Sur	Dayton's Law of Surrogates [*A publication*] (DLA)
Dayton	Dayton Superior and Common Pleas Reports [*Ohio*] [*A publication*] (DLA)
Dayton	University of Dayton. Intramural Law Review [*A publication*] (DLA)
Dayton Med	Dayton Medicine [*A publication*]
Dayton (Ohio)	Dayton Reports [*Ohio*] [*A publication*] (DLA)
Dayton Rep	Dayton Reports [*Ohio*] [*A publication*] (DLA)
DAYTOP	Drug Addicts Yield to Persuasion [*of Daytop Village, Inc., a narcotics-addiction rehabilitation facility*]
Dayt Sur	Dayton's Law of Surrogates [*A publication*] (DLA)
Dayt Term Rep	Dayton Term Reports [*Ohio*] [*A publication*] (DLA)
DAZ	Deutsche Allgemeine Zeitung [*A publication*]
DAZ	Deutsche Angler-Zeitung [*A publication*]
DAZ	Deutsche Apotheker-Zeitung [*A publication*]
DAZD	Double Anode Zener Diode
DAZEA2	Deutsche Apotheker-Zeitung [*A publication*]
DAZX	Daisy System Corp. [*NASDAQ symbol*] (NQ)
DAZZ	Danceable Jazz [*In music group name Dazz Band*]
DB	Bachelor of Divinity
Db	Base Diameter [*Manufacturing term*]
DB	Bomber [*Russian aircraft symbol*]
DB	Daily Bulletin [*Military*] (AABC)
DB	Daimler-Benz [*Name of German engine factory*] [*World War II*]
DB	Damned Bad
DB	Data Bank
DB	Data Bus [*Data processing*] (MCD)
DB	Database [*Data processing*]
DB	Date of Birth
DB	Day Book [*Accounting*]
DB	Dead Band
DB	Deaf/Blind
DB	Deals and Battens [*Business term*]
D & B	Deals and Boards [*Business term*] (ROG)
D & B	Dearsley and Bell's English Crown Cases [*1856-58*] [*A publication*] (DLA)
DB	Debenture [*Type of bond*] [*Investment term*]
D/b	Debetbrief [*Debit Note*] [*Afrikaans*] [*Business term*]
DB	Debit
dB	Decibel [*Symbol*] [*SI unit of sound level*]
D/B	Decimal to Binary [*Data processing*] (KSC)
DB	Deep Basing [*Underground placement of missiles*]
DB	Deep Breathe [*Medicine*]
DB	Defensive Back [*Football*]
DB	Deficit Budget
DB	Delayed Broadcast [*Television*]
DB	Dental Branch [*British military*] (DMA)
DB	Departmentalized Billing
D/B	Deposit Book
DB	Depth Bomb [*Military*]
DB	Der Betrieb [*Information service or system*] [*A publication*]
DB	Der Betrieb-Data Bank [*Handelsblatt GmbH*] [*Federal Republic of Germany*] [*Information service or system*] (IID)
DB	Describe (FAAC)
DB	Desert Biome [*Ecological biogeographic study*]
DB	Design Baseline (NASA)
DB	Design Burst (KSC)
DB	[*Charles*] Deutsch and [*Rene*] Bonnet [*In association name DB - Panhard Registry*]
DB	Deutsche Bibliographie [*A publication*]
DB	Deutsche Bibliothek [*Database producer*]
DB	Deutsche Bundesbahn [*German Federal Railway*] [*Since 1949*] [*Federal Republic of Germany*]
DB	Developmental Bulletin (MCD)
DB	Developments in Biochemistry [*Elsevier Book Series*] [*A publication*]
D & B	Devereux and Battle's North Carolina Equity Reports [*A publication*] (DLA)
D & B	Devereux and Battle's North Carolina Law Reports [*A publication*] (DLA)
DB	DFD Fluggesellschaft mbH & Co. KG, Gelsenkirchen [*West Germany*] [*ICAO designator*] (FAAC)
DB	Dialektolohicnyi Bjuleten [*A publication*]
DB	Dibromodifluoromethane [*Organic chemistry*] [*Fire extinguishing agent*] (ADA)
DB	Diconjugate Bilirubin [*Biochemistry*]
DB	Dictionary of the Bible [*A publication*] (BJA)
DB	Dictionnaire de la Bible [*A publication*] (BJA)
DB	Die Bahn [*Tourist card for rail travel*] [*Federal Republic of Germany*]
DB	Diet Beverage
DB	Diffused Base
DB	Digital Block [*Data processing*]
DB	Dip Brazing
DB	Direct Billing
DB	Director Bomber [*Air Force*]
DB	Dirty Book
DB	Disciplinary Barracks
DB	Dispersal Base [*Military*] (AFM)
DB	Display Buffer [*Data processing*]
DB	Distobuccal [*Dentistry*]
DB	Distribution Box [*Technical drawings*]
DB	Dive Bank
DB	Dive Bomb
DB	Dive Bomber Aircraft
DB	Division Base [*Army*]
DB	Dock Brief [*British*] (ADA)
D/B	Documentary Bill (ADA)
DB	Doitsu Bungaku [*A publication*]
D/B	Dokumente Teen Betaling [*Documents Against Payment*] [*Afrikaans*] [*Business term*]
DB	Dolly Back [*Films, television, etc.*]
DB	Domesday Book [*Census-like record of the lands of England, 1085-86*]
DB	Double-Barreled (ADA)
DB	Double Bass [*Music*]
DB	Double Biased (CET)
DB	Double Bottom (MSA)
DB	Double Braid (AAG)
DB	Double Break
DB	Double Breasted [*Clothing industry*]
DB	Double-Ended Boiler [*Shipping*] (DS)
db	Drab [*Philately*]
DB	Draw Bar (ADA)
DB	Drop-By [*Brief social appearance*]
DB	Dry Basis
DB	Dry Bath [*Instrumentation*]
DB	Dry Bulb [*Thermometer, of a psychrometer*] [*Meteorology*]
DB	Duke of Buccleuch [*British*] (ROG)
D & B	Dun & Bradstreet, Inc.
DB	Dunnage Board
DB	Dunya Bankasi [*World Bank*] [*Turkish*]
DB	Durch Boten [*By Messenger*] [*German*]
DB	Dutch Belted [*Rabbits*]
DB	Dynamic Braking
DB	Execaire Aviation Ltd. [*Canada*] [*ICAO designator*] (FAAC)
DBA	Bar Association of the District of Columbia, Washington, DC [*Library symbol*] [*Library of Congress*] (LCLS)
DBA	Baumarkt. Zeitschrift fuer Wirtschaftliche Unternehmensfuehrung [*A publication*]
DBA	Danish Brotherhood in America (EA)
DBA	Dansk Botanisk Arkiv [*A publication*]
DBA	Database Administration [*or Administrator*] [*Data processing*] (BUR)
DBA	Davis-Bacon Act [*1921*]
DBA	Days before Anthesis [*Botany*]
DBA	Daytime Broadcasters Association [*Defunct*] (EA)
DBA	De Bonis Asportatis [*Trespass to Personalty*] [*Latin*] [*Legal term*] (DLA)
DBA	Dead before Arrival [*Term used by some members of Congress to describe 1986 federal budget proposals*]
DBA	Dealer Bank Association [*Washington, DC*] (EA)
dB(A)	Decibel A-Weighted
dba	Decibels on the A Scale
dBA	Decibels, Adjusted
DBA	Deep Battle Area (INF)
DBA	Defense Base Act
DBA	Dense Blasting Agent (MCD)
DBA	Design Basis Accident [*Nuclear energy*]
DBA	Dibasic Acid [*Waste from adipic acid production*]
DBA	Dibenzanthracene [*Carcinogen*]
DBA	Dibenzoylacetylene [*Organic chemistry*]
DBA	Dibenzylamine [*Organic chemistry*]
DBA	Dihydro-Dimethyl-Benzopyranbutyric Acid
DBA	Directory of British Associations [*A publication*]
DBA	Doctor of Business Administration
DBA	Doing Business As [*Followed by company name*]
DBA	Dolichos biflorus Agglutinin [*Immunology*]
DBA	Duct Burner Augmentation
DBAAM	Disk Buffer Area Access Method
DBACS	Database Administrator Control System
DB Ad	Doctor of Business Administration
DB Adm	Doctor of Business Administration
DBAE	Dihydroxyborylaminoethyl [*Organic chemistry*]
DBAF	Database Access Facility
DBAH	Diisobutylaluminum Hydride [*Also, DIBAH*] [*Organic chemistry*]
DBAM	Database Access Method

DBAO........ Digital Block And-Or Gate [Data processing] (IEEE)
DBAS......... DBA Systems, Inc. [NASDAQ symbol] (NQ)
DBATS...... Dynamic Balancing and Tracking System (MCD)
DBAWG ... Database Administration Working Group [CODASYL]
DBB .... Bethune-Cookman College, Daytona Beach, FL [OCLC symbol] (OCLC)
DBB .... Deals, Battens, and Boards [Business term]
DBB .... Detector Back Bias
DBB .... Detector Balanced Bias
DBB .... Deutsche Bibliographie. Das Deutsche Buch. Auswahl Wichtiger Neuerscheinungen [A publication]
DBB .... Deutsche Bundesbahn [German Federal Railway] [Since 1949] [Federal Republic of Germany]
DBB .... Developments in Bioenergetics and Biomembranes [Elsevier Book Series] [A publication]
DBB .... Dibenzoylbenzene [Organic chemistry]
DBB .... United States Office of Management and Budget, Washington, DC [Library symbol] [Library of Congress] (LCLS)
DBBA .... Danny Boy Breeders Association (EA)
DBBB........ Cotonou/Cadjehoun [Benin] [ICAO location identifier] (ICLI)
DBBC........ Cana/Bohicon [Benin] [ICAO location identifier] (ICLI)
DBBD........ Djougou [Benin] [ICAO location identifier] (ICLI)
DBBK .... Kandi [Benin] [ICAO location identifier] (ICLI)
DBBN........ Natitingou [Benin] [ICAO location identifier] (ICLI)
DBBO........ Porga [Benin] [ICAO location identifier] (ICLI)
DBBP........ Dibutyl Butylphosphonate [Organic chemistry]
DBBP........ Parakou [Benin] [ICAO location identifier] (ICLI)
DBBR .... Bimbereke [Benin] [ICAO location identifier] (ICLI)
DBBS .... Save [Benin] [ICAO location identifier] (ICLI)
DBBV .... Cotonou [Benin] [ICAO location identifier] (ICLI)
DBC .... D. B. Communications, Inc. [Bethesda, MD] [Telecommunications service] (TSSD)
DBC .... Data Bibliography Card
DBC .... Data Bus Control [Data processing] (MCD)
DBC .... Data Bus Coupler [Data processing] (MCD)
DBC .... Database Computer (MCD)
DBC .... Deaf Broadcasting Campaign [British]
DBC .... Decatur Baptist College [Iowa]
dBc .... Decibels above One Carrier
DBC .... Delamination, Bond, Crack [Plastics technology]
DBC .... Democratic Business Council (EA)
DBC .... Denied-Boarding Compensation [Airlines]
DBC .... Deputy Brigade Commander [Army]
DBC .... Desert Bighorn Council (EA)
DBC .... Developmental Biology Center [Case Western Reserve University] [Research center] (RCD)
DBC .... Diameter Bolt Circle [Technical drawings]
DBC .... Dictionnaire Biographique du Canada [A publication]
DBC .... Digital-to-Binary Converter [Data processing]
DBC .... Dimethylbenzimidazolylcobamide [Biochemistry]
DBC .... Director of Barrack Construction [British military] (DMA)
DBC .... Doctor of Beauty Culture
DBC .... Dodge Brothers Club (EA)
DBC .... Don Bosco College [Newton, NJ]
DBC .... Double Bottom Center [of a ship] (DS)
DBC .... Duck Book Communications Ltd. [Vancouver Stock Exchange symbol]
DBC .... Dye-Binding Capacity
DBC .... United States Bureau of the Census, Suitland, MD [Library symbol] [Library of Congress] (LCLS)
DBCAA ..... Dutch Belted Cattle Association of America (EA)
DBCATA... Disposable Barrel Cartridge Area Target Ammunition [Weapon launcher]
DBCB........ Database Control Block
D & B CC... Dearsley and Bell's English Crown Cases [1856-58] [A publication] (DLA)
DBCC .... Decrement, Test, Branch if Condition True [Data processing]
DBCC .... District Business Conduct Committee [of the National Association of Securities Dealers]
DBCD .... Differential Base Current Drift
DBCE........ Division of Building Construction and Engineering [Australia]
DBCI......... Dartmouth Bancorp, Inc. [NASDAQ symbol] (SPSG)
DBCL........ Database Command Language
DBCO .... Digital Block Clock Oscillator [Data processing]
DBCP........ Dibromochloropropane [Pesticide]
DBCP........ Double Bounce, Circularly Polarized
DBCRB2.... Diabetologia Croatica [A publication]
D & BCS .... D & B Computing Services [Information service or system] (IID)
DBCS........ Database Control System
DBCS........ Double-Byte Character Set [Data processing] (PCM)
DBCU .... Data Bus Control Unit [Data processing] (KSC)
DBD.......... Air Niagara [1978] Ltd. [Toronto, ON, Canada] [FAA designator] (FAAC)
DBD.......... Dashboard
DBD.......... Database Definition (BYTE)
DBD.......... Database Description [Data processing] (BUR)
DBD.......... Database Design Document
DBD.......... Demokratische Bauernpartei Deutschlands [Democratic Farmers' Party of Germany] [German Democratic Republic] (PPW)

DBD........... Detailed Budget Decision (AFM)
DBD........... Dibromodulcitol [Mitolactol] [Antineoplastic drug]
DBD........... Diebold, Inc. [NYSE symbol] (SPSG)
DBD........... Diesel Belt Drive (MSA)
DBD........... Digital Bargraph Display
DBD........... Digoxigenin Bisdigitoxoside [Biochemistry]
DBD........... Double-Base Diode
DBD........... Double Beta Decay
DBDA .... Database Design Aid [Data processing] (BUR)
DBDA .... Design Basis Depressurization Accident [Nuclear energy] (NRCH)
DB/DC ...... Database/Data Communications [IBM Corp.]
DBDC........ Dennis Brutus Defense Committee (EA)
DBDD .... Database Design Document (MCD)
DBDK........ Daito Bunka Daigaku Kiyo [A publication]
DBDKK .... Daito Bunka Daigaku Kangakkaishi [A publication]
DBDL........ Database Definition Language
DBDPO ..... Decabromodiphenyl Oxide [Flame retardant] [Organic chemistry]
DBDS .... Data Base Directory Service [Formerly, Data Base User Service] [Knowledge Industry Publications, Inc.] [Database]
DBDU........ Digital Bargraph Display Unit
DBE .... British Embassy, Washington, DC [Library symbol] [Library of Congress] (LCLS)
DBE .... Dame Commander of the [Order of the] British Empire
DBE .... Data Bus Element [Data processing]
DBE .... Data Bus Enable [Data processing]
DBE .... De Bene Esse [Conditionally] [Latin] [Legal term] (DLA)
DBE .... Design Basis Earthquake [Nuclear energy] (NRCH)
DBE .... Design Basis Event [Nuclear energy] (NRCH)
DBE .... Dibasic Ester [DuPont organic solvent]
DBE .... Dibenzyl Ether [Organic chemistry]
DBE .... Dibromoethane [Same as EB, EDB] [Organic chemistry]
DBE .... Disadvantaged Business Enterprise [Business term]
DBE .... Dispatch Payable Both Ends [Shipping] (DS)
DBE .... Division of Biological Effects [Bureau of Radiological Effects]
DBE .... Double Bond Equivalent [Analytical chemistry]
DBE .... Dynamic Balancing Equipment
DBE .... National Society, Daughters of the British Empire in the United States of America (EA)
DBEATS ... Dispatch Payable Both Ends All Time Saved [Shipping] (DS)
DBED .... Diabetes Educator [A publication]
DBED .... Dibenzylethylenediamine [Organic chemistry]
DB Ed .... Doctor of Business Education
D Bei .... Deutsche Beitraege [A publication]
DBELTS.... Dispatch Payable Both Ends on Laytime Saved [Shipping] (DS)
DBER .... Division of Biomedical and Environmental Research [Later, Office of Health and Environmental Research] [Department of Energy]
DBF .... Dansk Databehandlinsforening [Danish Data Processing Association] (CSR)
DBF .... Data Base File [Military] (AABC)
DBF .... Demodulator Band Filter (MSA)
DBF .... Design Basis Fault [Nuclear energy] (NRCH)
DBF .... Dictionnaire de Biographie Francaise [A publication]
DBF .... Distributie Vandaag. Maandblad over Verkooppromotie en Moderne Handelstechniek [A publication]
DBF .... Dominant Bubble Frequency [Nuclear energy] (NRCH)
DBF .... Double Book Form [Photography] (ROG)
DBF .... Dressing before Finish [Manufacturing term]
DBF .... Drexel Bond-Debenture Trading Fund [NYSE symbol] (SPSG)
DBF .... Dual Bowl Feeder
DBFB .... Deep-Bed Filter and Blower Building [Nuclear energy] (NRCH)
DBFC........ David Birney Fan Club (EA)
DBFC........ Debby Boone Fan Club (EA)
DBFF .... Digital Block Flip-Flop [Data processing]
DBFL........ Design Basis Flooding Level [Nuclear energy] (NRCH)
DBFM ...... Dun & Bradstreet France Marketing [Dun & Bradstreet France] [Database]
DBFN .... Data Bus File Number (NASA)
DBFN .... Database File Numbers (MCD)
DBFR .... Domestic Base Factor Report [Army]
DBFS .... Deep Bed Farming Society (EA)
DBFS .... Dull Black Finish Slate (KSC)
DBG.......... Data Bus Group [Data processing] (MCD)
DBG.......... Database Generator
DBG.......... David Ben-Gurion (BJA)
DBG.......... Desert Botanical Garden [An association] (EA)
DBG.......... Division of Basic Grants [Office of Education]
DBGCM ... Dun & Bradstreet Guide to Canadian Manufacturers [Information service or system] (EISS)
DBGEN .... Database Generation [Data processing]
DBGGA .... Dopovidi Akademii Nauk Ukrains'koi RSR. Seriya B. Geologiya, Geofizika, Khimiya, ta Biologiya [A publication]
DBGLS...... Development Bank of the Great Lake States (EAIO)
DBGMP .... Data Bus Generation and Maintenance Package [Data processing] (MCD)
DBGS........ Database Generation System (MCD)

DBGU........ Deutsche Beitraege zur Geistigen Ueberlieferung [*A publication*]
DBH.......... Development Big Hydrofoil [*Also, DEH*] (MCD)
DBH.......... Diameter at Breast Height [*Of trees*]
DBH.......... Diamond-Bathurst, Inc. [*NYSE symbol*] (SPSG)
DBH.......... Diazabicycloheptene [*Organic chemistry*]
DBH.......... Division Beachhead [*Army*]
DBH.......... Dopamine Beta-Hydroxylase [*An enzyme*]
DBHI........ DBH [*Dopamine Beta-Hydroxylase*] Index
DBHI........ Dow B. Hickam, Incorporated [*Sugar Land, TX*] [*NASDAQ symbol*] (NQ)
DBHN....... Dibutyl Hyponitrite [*Organic chemistry*]
DBHP....... Drawbar Horsepower
DBHR....... Debrett's Business History Research [*British*]
DBHS....... Database Handling System
DBHVA.... Deutsche Bibliographie. Halbjahres-Verzeichnis [*A publication*]
DBI .... Brookings Institution, Washington, DC [*Library symbol*] [*Library of Congress*] (LCLS)
DBI .... Data Base Index [*SDC Information Services*]
DBI .... Data Bus Interface Unit-Launch [*Data processing*] (MCD)
DBI .... Decibels (Isotropic) (MCD)
DBI .... Defense Budget Intelligence [*A publication*]
DBI .... Design Basis Incident [*Nuclear energy*] (NRCH)
DBI .... Deutsches Bibliotheksinstitut [*German Library Institute*] [*Information service or system*] (IID)
DBI .... Development at Birth Index [*Medicine*]
DBI .... Diazepam Binding Inhibitor [*Biochemistry*]
DBI .... Dibi Resources, Incorporated [*Vancouver Stock Exchange symbol*]
DBI .... Dictionary of the Bible [*A publication*] (BJA)
DBI .... Differential Bearing Indicator
DBI .... Diver Biographical Inventory [*Navy*]
DBI .... Double Byte Interleaved
DBIA .... Danish Brotherhood in America (EA)
DBIA .... Data Bus Interface Adapter [*Data processing*] (MCD)
DBIA .... Data Bus Isolation Amplifier [*Data processing*] (MCD)
DBIA .... Digital Block Inverter Amplifier [*Data processing*]
D Bib........ Douay Bible
D Bi Ch ..... Doctor of Biochemistry
D Bi Chem ... Doctor of Biochemistry
DBIDI....... Database Imagery Derived Information (MCD)
D Bi E .... Doctor of Biological Engineering
D Bi Eng ... Doctor of Biological Engineering
D Bien Zt ... Deutsche Bienenzeitung [*A publication*]
DBII.......... Dunserve II [*Canada Systems Group*] [*Information service or system*] (IID)
DBIL........ Database Input Languages [*Data processing*]
DBIL........ Direct Bilirubin [*Also, DBili*] [*Clinical chemistry*]
DBili .... Direct Bilirubin [*Also, DBIL*] [*Clinical chemistry*]
DBIN........ Data Bus In [*Data processing*]
DBIO........ Damon Biotech, Inc. [*NASDAQ symbol*] (NQ)
DBIOA ..... Doklady Biochemistry [*English Translation*] [*A publication*]
DBIOC ..... Database Input/Output Control
D Bi Phy ... Doctor of Biological Physics
DBIR........ Directory of Biotechnology Information/Resources [*American Type Culture Collection*] [*Information service or system*] (CRD)
D Bi S....... Doctor of Biological Sciences
DBIS......... Document-Based Indexing System (ADA)
D Bi Sc..... Doctor of Biological Sciences
DBIU........ Data Bus Interface Unit [*Data processing*] (MCD)
DBJ........... Duke Bar Journal [*A publication*]
DBJb......... Deutsches Biographisches Jahrbuch [*A publication*]
DBK.......... Data Bank (AABC)
dBK.......... Decibels above One Kilowatt (DEN)
DBK.......... Drawback [*Business term*]
DBL.......... Damage before Launch (CINC)
DBL.......... Dantrolene Blood Level [*Clinical chemistry*]
DBL.......... Database List (CINC)
DBL.......... Database Load [*Data processing*]
DBL.......... Debarred Bidder's List
DBL.......... Desbromoleptophos [*Insecticide*]
DBL.......... Deutsche Biologische Literatur [*German Biological Literature*] [*Also, DT BIOL*] [*Database*] [*Forschungsinstitut Senckenberg*] [*Information service or system*] (CRD)
DBL.......... Direct Broadcasting Limited [*British*]
DBL.......... Direct Business Lines [*Telecom Canada*] [*Telecommunications service*] (TSSD)
DBL.......... Disability Benefit Law [*Insurance*]
DBL.......... Displaced Business Loan [*Small Business Administration*]
DBL.......... Double (AAG)
DBL.......... Drawing Breakdown List
DBLE........ Double (ROG)
DBLE........ Double Eagle Petroleum & Mining Co. [*NASDAQ symbol*] (NQ)
Dble Dealer ... Double Dealer [*A publication*]
DBLF........ Double Face
DBLO........ Diablo Oil Co. [*NASDAQ symbol*] (NQ)
DBLR........ Doubler (KSC)
DBLRA..... Doklady Akademii Nauk BSSR [*A publication*]
DBLTG...... Database Language Task Group [*CODASYL*]

DBLW .... Double Wall
DBM.......... Data Buffer Module (IEEE)
DBM.......... Data Bus Monitor [*Data processing*]
DBM.......... Database Management [*or Manager*] [*Data processing*] (NVT)
DBM.......... Decarboxylase Base Moeller [*Medium*] [*Microbiology*]
DBM.......... Decibel Meter (KSC)
dBM.......... Decibels above One Milliwatt
DBM.......... Demineralized Bone Matrix [*Substance which, when surgically implanted, stimulates development of new bone*]
DBM.......... Dense-Branching Morphology [*Physical chemistry*]
DBM.......... Deputy Base Manager (MUGU)
DBM.......... Diabetic Management [*Medicine*]
DBM.......... Diazobenzyloxymethol [*Organic chemistry*]
DBM.......... Dibromomannitol [*Mitobronitol*] [*Antineoplastic drug*]
DBM.......... Dibutyl Maleate [*Organic chemistry*]
DBM.......... Dibutylmagnesium [*Organic chemistry*]
DBM.......... Dielectric Breakdown Model [*Physics*]
DBM.......... Direct Branch Mode
D/BM .... Directorate of Ballistic Missiles
DBM.......... Division Battle Model (MCD)
DBM.......... Doctor of Business Management
DBM.......... Double Balanced Mixer
DBM.......... Drake Beam Morin, Inc.
DBM.......... Dry Bulk Material
DB & M ..... Dunlop, Bell, and Murray's Scotch Court of Session Cases, Second Series [*1838-62*] [*A publication*] (DLA)
DBM.......... Dun's Business Month [*A publication*]
DB/M² ...... Decibels above Milliwatt per Square Meter (MCD)
DBMA...... Dibenzylmethylamine [*Organic chemistry*]
DBMA...... Distillate Burner Manufacturers Association (EA)
DBMAD .... Auerbach Data Base Management [*A publication*]
DBMC...... Di-tert-butyl-m-cresol [*Organic chemistry*]
DBMCS..... Database Management and Control System (MCD)
DBMIB...... Dibromomethyl(isopropyl)benzoquinone [*Organic chemistry*]
dBm0p........ Decibels above One Milliwatt, Referred to or Measured at a Point of Zero Transmission Level, Psophometrically Weighted
DBMS....... Database Management Software [*Data processing*]
DBMS....... Database Management System [*or Subsystem*] [*Data processing*] (BUR)
DBMS....... Director of Base Medical Services
DBMSPSM ... Database Management System Problem Specification Model
DBMV...... Digital Block Multivibrator [*Data processing*]
DBN.......... Data Bus Network [*Data processing*]
DBN.......... De Bilt [*Netherlands*] [*Later, WIT*] [*Geomagnetic observatory code*]
DBN.......... De Bilt [*Netherlands*] [*Seismograph station code, US Geological Survey*] (SEIS)
DBN.......... De Bonis Non [*Of the Goods Not Yet Administered*]
DBN.......... Diazobicyclononene [*Organic chemistry*]
DBN.......... Dibutylnitrosamine [*Also, DBNA*] [*Organic chemistry*]
DBN.......... Double Bassoon [*Music*]
DBN.......... Dublin, GA [*Location identifier*] [*FAA*] (FAAL)
Dbn .... Durban [*South Africa*] (ILCA)
DBNA....... Dibutylnitrosamine [*Also, DBN*] [*Organic chemistry*]
DBNA....... Digital Block Noninverting Amplifier [*Data processing*]
DBNK....... Data Bank
DBNM...... Darmstaedter Beitraege zur Neuen Musik [*A publication*]
DBNPA ..... Dibromonitrilopropionamide [*Organic chemistry*]
DBNPG ..... Dibromoneopentyl Glycol [*Flame retardant*] [*Organic chemistry*]
DBNPS...... Davis-Besse Nuclear Power Station (NRCH)
DBNS .... Digital Bombing-Navigation System
DBO.......... Dawn Battle Order [*British military*] (DMA)
DBO.......... Diploma of British Orthoptics
DBO.......... Directorate of Biological Operations [*Pine Bluff Arsenal, AR*]
DBO.......... Directors and Boards [*A publication*]
DBO.......... Distobucco-Occlusal [*Dentistry*]
DBO.......... District Barrack Officer [*British military*] (DMA)
DBO.......... Drop Build-Out Capacitor [*Telecommunications*] (TEL)
DBO.......... Dual Beam Oscilloscope
DBO.......... Dubbo [*Australia*] [*Airport symbol*] (OAG)
DBOA....... Delayed Breeder or Alternative [*Nuclear energy*] (NRCH)
DBOEP...... Di(butoxyethyl) Phthalate [*Organic chemistry*]
DBOI........ Developmental Basis of Issue [*Military*] (AABC)
DBOMP .... Database Organization and Maintenance [*or Management*] Processor
DBOps....... Director of Bombing Operations [*Air Ministry*] [*British*] [*World War II*]
DBOS .... Disk-Based Operating System [*Data processing*] (IEEE)
D Bot Ms ... Deutsche Botanische Monatsschrift [*A publication*]
DBP .... Darband [*Pakistan*] [*Seismograph station code, US Geological Survey*] (SEIS)
DBP .... Database Processor
dBP .... Decibels above One Picowatt (DEN)
DBP .... Defense Budget Project (EA)
DBP .... Demineralized Bone Powder [*Medicine*]
DBP .... Descent Battery Pack (KSC)
DBP .... Design Baseline Program (MCD)
DBP .... Deutsche Bundespost [*West Germany*] [*Telecommunications service*] (TSSD)

DbP............ Dewan Bahasa Dan Pustaka, Kuala Lumpur, Malaysia [*Library symbol*] [*Library of Congress*]   (LCLS)

DBP........... Diastolic Blood Pressure [*Medicine*]

DBP........... Dibromophenol [*Organic chemistry*]

DBP........... Dibutyl Phthalate [*Also, DBPh*] [*Organic chemistry*]

DBP........... Dibutylphosphoric Acid [*Organic chemistry*]

DBP........... Dichlorobenzophenone [*Also, DCBP*] [*Organic chemistry*]

DBP........... Dicionario Bibliografico Portugues [*A bibliographic publication*] [*Portugal*]

DBP........... Distobuccopulpal [*Dentistry*]

DBP........... DNA [*Deoxyribonucleic Acid*]-Binding Protein [*Genetics*]

DBP........... Double-Base Propellant   (AAG)

DBP........... Drawbar Pull

DBP........... Dried Bakery Products [*An animal feed*]

DBPB......... Design Basis Pipe Break [*Nuclear energy*]   (NRCH)

DBPC........ Di-tert-butyl-p-cresol [*Also, BHT*] [*Antioxidant*]

DBPCl........ Dibenzylphosphoryl Chloride [*Organic chemistry*]

DBPh.......... Dibutyl Phthalate [*Also, DBP*] [*Organic chemistry*]

DBPH.......... Division for the Blind and Physically Handicapped [*Later, NLS*] [*Library of Congress*]

DBPO........ Data Buoy Project Office [*Later, NDBC*] [*National Oceanic and Atmospheric Administration*]

DBPR......... DB - Panhard Registry   (EA)

D & B Pr Pr ... Dodd and Brook. Probate Practice [*A publication*]   (ILCA)

DBQ........... Database Query   (MCD)

DBQ........... [*The*] Dictionary of Biographical Quotation [*A publication*]

DBQ........... Dubuque [*Iowa*] [*Seismograph station code, US Geological Survey*]   (SEIS)

DBQ........... Dubuque [*Iowa*] [*Airport symbol*]   (OAG)

DBR........... Database Retrieval

DBR........... Dialectes Belgo-Romans [*A publication*]

DBR........... Director of Biological Research [*Military*] [*British*]

DBR........... Disk, Balls, and Roller

DBR........... Distributed Bragg Reflector [*LASER*]

DBR........... Doppler Beam Rider   (MCD)

DBR........... Doubly Buffered Ringer [*Physiology*]

DBR........... Dubrovnik [*Yugoslavia*] [*Seismograph station code, US Geological Survey*] [*Closed*]   (SEIS)

DBR........... National Society, Daughters of the Barons of Runnemede   (EA)

dBRAP....... Decibels above Reference Acoustic Power   (DEN)

DBRC........ Dairy Breeding Research Center [*Pennsylvania State University*] [*Research center*]   (RCD)

DBRE........ Association of American Railroads, Economics and Finance Department Library, Washington, DC [*Library symbol*] [*Library of Congress*]   (LCLS)

DBRF......... Dog Bite-Related Fatality

DBRI.......... Danish Building Research Institute

DBRL......... Dibrell Brothers, Inc. [*NASDAQ symbol*]   (NQ)

DBRN........ Data Bank Release Notice   (NASA)

dBRN........ Decibels above Reference Noise

DBRN........ [*The*] Dress Barn, Inc. [*NASDAQ symbol*]   (NQ)

dBRNC....... Decibels above Reference Noise, C-Message Weighted   (IEEE)

D & B Rpts ... D and B [*Dun and Bradstreet*] Reports [*A publication*]

DBRS......... De Beers Consolidated Mines [*NASDAQ symbol*]   (NQ)

DBS........... Danbus Resources, Inc. [*Vancouver Stock Exchange symbol*]

DBS........... Darwin Omnibus Service [*Australia*]

DBS........... Database Access Service [*Eastern Telecommunications Philippines, Inc.*] [*Information service or system*]   (IID)

DBS........... Database System   (MCD)

DBS........... Demodulator BIT [*Binary Digit*] Synchronizer   (MCD)

DBS........... Despeciated Bovine Serum

DBS........... Dibromosalicil [*Germicide*]

DBS........... Dibutyl Sebacate [*Organic chemistry*]

DBS........... Dibutyl Sulfate [*Organic chemistry*]

DBS........... Dictionnaire de la Bible. Supplement [*A publication*]   (BJA)

DBS........... Digital Beacon Simulator   (MCD)

DBS........... Direct Broadcast Satellite [*Television transmission system in which signals are transmitted by satellite directly to individual locations*]   (MCD)

DBS........... Direct Broadcast System

DBS........... Distressed British Seaman [*Granted a free passage home*]

DBS........... Division of Biologics Standards [*FDA*]

DBS........... Doctor of Business Science

DBS........... Dodecyl Benzenesulfonate [*Organic chemistry*]

DBS........... Dominion Bureau of Statistics [*Canada*]

DBS........... Doppler Beam Sampling [*Air navigation*]

DBS........... Doppler Beam Sharpener

DBS........... Double Bass [*Music*]

DBS........... Double Beam Spectrophotometer

DBS........... Double Blind Study

DBS........... Drama Book Specialists

DBS........... Drinking Behavior Scale [*Test*]

DBS........... Dual-Beam-Sputtering [*Coating technology*]

DBS........... Dubois, ID [*Location identifier*] [*FAA*]   (FAAL)

DBS........... United States National Bureau of Standards, Gaithersburg, MD [*Library symbol*] [*Library of Congress*]   (LCLS)

DBSA......... Dawn Bible Students Association   (EA)

DBSA......... Direct Broadcast Satellite Association [*Later, SBCA*]   (EA)

DBSC......... (Dibutylaminosulfenyl)methylcarbamate [*Insecticide*]

DBSC......... Digital Block Slave Clock [*Data processing*]

DBSC......... Direct Broadcast Satellite Corporation [*Bethesda, MD*] [*Telecommunications*]   (TSSD)

DB Sc......... Doctor of Business Science

DBSE......... Distance between Shaft Ends [*Mechanical engineering*]

DBSM....... Decibels per Square Meter

DBSO......... District Base Service Office

DB Sound Eng Mag ... DB. The Sound Engineering Magazine [*A publication*]

DBSP......... Double-Base Solid Propellant   (MSA)

DBSR/SQL ... Database System Relational/Structured Query Language [*NCR Corp.*]

DBSSS....... Double Bowl Stainless Steel Sink [*Classified advertising*]   (ADA)

DBST......... Digital Block Schmitt Trigger [*Data processing*]

DBST......... Double Bituminous Surface Treatment

DBST......... Double British Summer Time

DBT........... Deballasted Test Vehicle

DBT........... Debit   (ROG)

DBT........... Deck Board Tie Connector [*Simpson Strong-Tie*] [*Construction*]

DBT........... Design Basis Tornado [*Nuclear energy*]   (NRCH)

DBT........... Dibenzothiophene [*Organic chemistry*]

DBT........... Dictionary of Biblical Theology [*A publication*]   (BJA)

DBT........... (Dodecylbenzyl)trimethylammonium Chloride [*Organic chemistry*]

DBT........... Doppler Bearing Tracker [*Military*]   (CAAL)

DBT........... Double-Base Transistor

Dbt............ Downbeat [*A publication*]

DBT........... Dry Bed Training [*Medicine*]

DBT........... Dry Bulb Temperature

DBTEAD..... Diabete [*Later, Diabete et Metabolisme*] [*A publication*]

DBTF......... Doubtful   (FAAC)

DBTG........ Database Task Group [*CODASYL*]

DBTGAJ..... Diabetologia [*A publication*]

DBTL......... Dibutyltin Dilaurate [*Organic chemistry*]

DBTO......... Di(benzotriazolyl)oxalate [*Organic chemistry*]

DBTT......... Ductile to Brittle Transition Temperature

dBU............ Decibel Unit

DBU........... Diazabicycloundecene [*Biochemistry*]

DBU........... Diazobicycloundecane [*Organic chemistry*]

DBU........... Digital Buffer Unit

DBU........... Disadvantaged Business Utilization   (MCD)

DBUR......... Databank Update Request   (NASA)

DBus......... Doctor of Business   (ADA)

DBUS........ Dun & Bradstreet United States [*STM Systems Corp.*] [*Canada*] [*Information service or system*]   (CRD)

DBUT........ Database Update Time

DBV........... De Badande Vannerna [*Sweden*]

dBV............ Decibels above One Volt

DBV........... Deutsches Bucherverzeichnis [*A bibliographic publication*] [*German*]

DBV........... Diagonal Braked Vehicle [*FAA*]

DBV........... Distributed Budget Variance   (MCD)

DBV........... Dubrovnik [*Yugoslavia*] [*Airport symbol*]   (OAG)

DBVF......... Dual Bowl Vibratory Feeder

DBW......... Data Bus Wire [*Data processing*]   (MCD)

dBW........... Decibels above One Watt

DBW......... Design Bandwidth

DBW......... Desirable Body Weight [*Medicine*]

DBW......... Differential Ballistic Wind

DBW......... Dresdner Bank Wirtschaftsbericht [*A publication*]

DBWBD .... Deutsche Bibliographie. Woechentliches Verzeichnis. Reihe B [*A publication*]

DBWC....... Differential Ballistic Wind Computer

DBWCD .... Deutsche Bibliographie. Woechentliches Verzeichnis. Reihe C [*A publication*]

DBWO...... Differential Ballistic Wind Offset

DBWVA .... Deutsche Bibliographie. Woechentliches Verzeichnis. Reihe A [*A publication*]

DBX........... Decibel Above the Reference Coupling   (MCD)

dbx............ Decibels Expanded [*Initialism is name of electronics company and brand name of its products*]

DBY........... Dalby [*Australia*] [*Airport symbol*]   (OAG)

DBZ........... Deutsche Bauzeitung [*A publication*]

DBZT-A .... Deutsche Bauzeitung [*A publication*]

DC............. Caribbean Air Cargo Ltd. [*Barbados*] [*ICAO designator*]   (FAAC)

DC............. Complete Depolarization

DC............. Cuba [*License plate code assigned to foreign diplomats in the US*]

DC............. Da Capo [*Return to Beginning*] [*Music*]

DC............. Daily Census [*Medicine*]

DC............. [*The*] Daily Chronicle [*A publication*]

DC............. Dairylea Cooperative   (EA)

DC............. Daisy Chains [*Oil industry term*]

DC............. "Daisy Cutter" [*A type of World War II bomb*]

DC............. Dalloz. Recueil Critique de Jurisprudence et de Legislation [*French*] [*A publication*]   (DLA)

DC............. Damage Control [*or Controlman*] [*Navy*]

DC............. DANSE Coalition   (EA)

DC............. Danube Commission   (EA)

DC............. Data Call

DC.............	Data Camera
DC.............	Data Cartridge
DC.............	Data Cell [*Data processing*]
DC.............	Data Center (EA)
DC.............	Data Channel [*Data processing*]
DC.............	Data Check (BUR)
DC.............	Data Classifier (IEEE)
DC.............	Data Code
DC.............	Data Collection
DC.............	Data Communication [*Data processing*] (BUR)
DC.............	Data Concentrator [*Data processing*] (BUR)
DC.............	Data Control (AFM)
D/C.............	Data Conversion [*Data processing*] (KSC)
DC.............	Data Coordinator (MCD)
DC.............	Datametrics Corp. [*AMEX symbol*] (SPSG)
DC.............	Daughters of Charity of St. Vincent de Paul [*Roman Catholic religious order*]
DC.............	Daughters of the Cincinnati (EA)
D of C........	Daughters of the Confederacy
DC.............	Daughters of the Cross [*Roman Catholic religious order*]
D & C........	David & Charles [*Commercial firm*] [*British*]
DC.............	Davy Crockett [*A tactical atomic weapon*] [*Army*]
DC.............	De Candolle [*Botanist, 1778-1841*] (ROG)
D & C........	Deacon and Chitty's English Bankruptcy Reports [*1832-35*] [*A publication*] (DLA)
DC.............	Dead Center
D & C........	Dean and Chapter [*Anglican Church*]
DC.............	Death Certificate
DC.............	Debit Collection
DC.............	Decade Counter
DC.............	Decertify
DC.............	Decimal Classification
DC.............	Deck Cargo
DC.............	Deck Court
DC.............	Decoder Connector
DC.............	Decontamination
DC.............	Decorators Club (EA)
DC.............	Deep Discount Issue [*In bond listings of newspapers*] [*Investment term*]
DC.............	Defense Committee (NATG)
DC.............	Defense Counsel
DC.............	Define Constant (MDG)
DC.............	Definitive Contract
DC.............	Degree of Conjugation [*Analytical biochemistry*]
DC.............	Degrees Celsius (KSC)
DC.............	Deiters' Cell [*Anatomy*]
DC.............	Delay Code
DC.............	Delayed Coker [*Chemical engineering*]
DC.............	Deleted Unpostable from Cards [*IRS*]
DC.............	Delray Connecting Railroad Co. [*AAR code*]
DC.............	Democracia Cristiana [*Christian Democratic Party*] [*Colombia*] [*Political party*] (PPW)
DC.............	Democracia Cristiana [*Christian Democratic Party*] [*Paraguay*] [*Political party*] (PD)
DC.............	Dendritic Cell [*Cytology*]
DC.............	Density Controller
DC.............	Dental Corps [*Navy*]
dC.............	Deoxycytidylate [*Biochemistry*]
DC.............	Department of Commerce
D of C........	Department of Commerce
DC.............	Departmental Circulars
DC.............	Departmental Computing
DC.............	Deposited Carbon
DC.............	Depth Charge [*Aerial*] [*Navy*]
DC.............	Deputy Captain [*Military*] [*British*] (ROG)
DC.............	Deputy Chief
DC.............	Deputy Commandant
DC.............	Deputy Commissioner [*British*] (ADA)
DC.............	Deputy Consul
DC.............	Deputy Counsel [*British*] (ADA)
DC.............	Design Change (AAG)
DC.............	Design Contractor (NRCH)
DC.............	Design Cooperative [*British*]
DC.............	Designs for Change [*An association*] (EA)
DC.............	Destruct Charge
DC.............	Detail Condition (MDG)
DC.............	Detection Coil [*Magneto-encephalography*]
DC.............	Detective Constable [*Scotland Yard*]
D/C.............	Detention Clause [*Insurance*]
DC.............	Deterioration Control
DC.............	Developed Country
DC.............	Development Center (MCD)
DC.............	Development Characteristic
DC.............	Development Commission [*British*]
DC.............	Development Committee
DC.............	Development Costs
DC.............	Developments in Crop Science [*Elsevier Book Series*] [*A publication*]
DC.............	Deviation Clause [*Business term*]
DC.............	Device Control
DC.............	Device Coordinate
DC.............	Dewey Decimal Classification [*Also, DDC*]
DC.............	Diagnostic Center
DC.............	Diagnostic Code [*Medicine*]
DC.............	Diagonal Conjugate [*Medicine*]
DC.............	Dielectric Constant
DC.............	Difference, Center
DC.............	Different Coupling [*Music*]
DC.............	Differential Calculus (AAG)
DC.............	Differential Correction
DC.............	Difficult Communication
DC.............	Digit Copying [*Psychiatry*]
DC.............	Digital Clock
DC.............	Digital Code (AAG)
DC.............	Digital Comparator
DC.............	Digital Computer
DC.............	Dihydrocodeine [*An analgesic*]
DC.............	Dilated Cardiomyopathy [*Cardiology*]
D & C........	Dilation and Curettage [*of the uterus*] [*Obstetrics*]
DC.............	Dinero Contante [*Cash*] [*Spanish*] [*Business term*]
DC.............	Diners Club, Inc. (ADA)
DC.............	Dip Coating
DC.............	Diphenylcyanoarsine [*A war gas*]
DC.............	Diplomatic Corps
DC.............	Direct Command
DC.............	Direct Coupled
DC.............	Direct Current
DC.............	Direct Cycle
DC.............	Directed Change (MCD)
DC.............	Direction Center [*SAGE*] [*RADAR*]
DC.............	Direction Cosine (KSC)
DC.............	Direction Cycle (MDG)
DC.............	Directional Control [*Rocket*] (RDA)
DC.............	Directional Coupler
DC.............	Directives Control [*Employment and Training Administration*] [*Department of Labor*]
DC.............	Director of Ceremonies [*Freemasonry*] (ROG)
DC.............	Director Deputy of Communications-Electronics (AFIT)
DC.............	Directory Clearinghouse (EA)
DC.............	Dirt [*or Dust*] Collector (AAG)
DC.............	Disabled Child [*Title XVI*] [*Social Security Administration*] (OICC)
DC.............	Disarmament Commission [*Also, DC (UN), UNDC*]
DC.............	Disaster Control (AAG)
DC.............	Discharge [*or Discharged*]
DC.............	Disciples of Christ
DC.............	Discommensurate Model [*Physics*]
DC.............	Discontinue
DC.............	Discrepancy Check (KSC)
DC.............	Discrete Command
DC.............	Dishonored Check [*IRS*]
DC.............	Disk Controller [*Data processing*] (IEEE)
DC.............	Disorderly Conduct
DC.............	Dispersion Coefficient
DC.............	Display Code
DC.............	Display Compartments [*Freight*]
DC.............	Display Computer
DC.............	Display Console (KSC)
D & C........	Display and Control (KSC)
DC.............	Display Coupler (MCD)
DC.............	Dissimilarity Coefficient [*Numerical taxonomy*]
DC.............	Distocervical [*Dentistry*]
DC.............	Distribution Code
DC.............	Distribution Coefficient
D of C........	District of Columbia
DC.............	District of Columbia [*Postal code*]
DC.............	District of Columbia Reports [*A publication*] (DLA)
DC.............	District Commissioner [*British government*]
DC.............	District Council [*British*]
D & C........	District and County Reports [*Pennsylvania*] [*A publication*] (DLA)
DC.............	District Court
DC.............	Division of Classification [*Energy Research and Development Administration*]
DC.............	Division of Contracts
DC.............	Divisional Court [*Legal term*] (DLA)
DC.............	Doctor of Chiropractic
DC.............	Doctor of Chiropraxis
DC.............	Document Code [*Data processing*]
DC.............	Document Control
DC.............	Documentation Catholique [*A publication*]
DC.............	Domestic Council [*Executive Office of the President*] [*Abolished 1978, functions transferred to the President*]
DC.............	Donor's Cells [*Medicine*]
DC.............	Door Closer (AAG)
DC.............	Dopo Cristo [*After Christ*] [*Italian*]
DC.............	Dorsal Cortex [*Neuroanatomy*]
DC.............	Double Cap [*or Crown*] [*Paper size*]
DC.............	Double Column
DC.............	Double-Concentric
DC.............	Double Conductor
DC.............	Double Contact [*Switch*]

DC............ Double Cotton [*Wire insulation*]   (AAG)
DC............. Double Crochet
DC............. Double Cropped [*Agriculture*]
DC............. Double Crown [*Monetary unit*] [*Great Britain*]
dc............. Double-Cylinder Tank [*Liquid gas carriers*]
D & C......... Dow and Clark's English House of Lords Cases [*A publication*]   (DLA)
DC............. Downconverter [*Satellite communications*]
DC............. Downtime Costs [*Quality control*]
DC............. Dracula and Company [*An association*]   (EA)
DC............. Drag Coefficient
DC............. Drain Channel   (NRCH)
DC............. Drama Criticism [*A publication*]
DC............. Drawing Center   (EA)
DC............. Drawing Change   (AAG)
D/C............ Drift Chamber   (MCD)
D/C............ Drift Correction
D & C......... Drug and Cosmetic Colors
DC............. Dual Capable   (NATG)
DC............. Dual Channel
DC............. Dublin Castle
DC............. Duchy of Cornwall [*British*]   (ROG)
DC............. Duct Carcinoma [*Oncology*]
DC............. Duplicate Copy
DC............. Duty Controller [*Tactical Air Command*]
DC............. I/S Datacentralen [*Information service or system*]   (IID)
DC............. [*The*] Item Previously Reported as DO [*Due Out*] Has Been Cancelled Because It Is Obsolete, Rescinded, Superseded, or Has Been Due Out for More Than 270 Days. If Still Required, Please Submit a New Request [*Advice of supply action code*] [*Army*]
DC............. McDonnell-Douglas Aircraft Co., Inc. [*ICAO aircraft manufacturer identifier*]   (ICAO)
DC............. Partito della Democrazia Cristiana [*Christian Democratic Party*] [*Italy*] [*Political party*]   (PPW)
DC............. Pennsylvania District and County Reports [*A publication*]   (DLA)
DC............. Treasury Department Circular [*United States*] [*A publication*]   (DLA)
DC............. United States Department of Commerce, Washington, DC [*Library symbol*] [*Library of Congress*]   (LCLS)
DC............. United States District Court   (DLA)
DC³........... Distributed Command, Control, and Communications [*Army*]
DC24......... Drug Crisis 24 Hours [*Television program*] [*Australia*]
DCA.......... Corcoran Art Gallery, Washington, DC [*Library symbol*] [*Library of Congress*]   (LCLS)
DCA.......... Dachshund Club of America   (EA)
DCA.......... Dalmatian Club of America   (EA)
DCA.......... Damage Control Assessment   (MCD)
DCA.......... Damage Control Assistant [*Military*]   (NVT)
DCA.......... Dance Critics Association   (EA)
DCA.......... Data Communications Administrator
DCA.......... Data Correction Amplifier
DCA.......... Debt Collection Agency   (DCTA)
DCA.......... Decade Counting Assembly   (IEEE)
DCA.......... Defense Communications Agency [*DoD*] [*Arlington, VA*]
DCA.......... Defense Contract Administrator   (MCD)
DCA.......... Defense Contre Aeronefs [*Antiaircraft Defense*] [*French*]
DCA.......... Defense Control Administration
DCA.......... Defense Cooperation Agreement   (MCD)
DCA.......... Deferred Commercial Annuity [*Insurance*]
DCA.......... Deflection Coil Amplifier
DCA.......... Democratic Congress Alliance [*Gambia*]
DCA.......... Demolition Contractors Association [*Australia*]
DCA.......... Denmark Cheese Association   (EA)
DCA.......... Deoxycholate-Citrate Agar [*Microbiology*]
DCA.......... Deoxycholic Acid [*Biochemistry*]
DCA.......... Deoxycorticosterone [*or Desoxycorticosterone*] Acetate [*Also, DOCA*] [*Endocrinology*]
DCA.......... Department of Civil Aviation [*Australia*]
DCA.......... Deputy Chief Architect [*British*]
DCA.......... Deputy Chief of Staff for Administration
DCA.......... Deputy County Architect [*British*]
DCA.......... Design Change Authorization   (KSC)
D/CA......... DeSoto Club of America   (EA)
DCA.......... Detachable Container Association [*Inactive*]   (EA)
DCA.......... Devon Cattle Association   (EA)
DCA.......... Diagnostic Connector Assembly   (RDA)
DCA.......... Diamond Council of America   (EA)
DCA.......... Diastematic Club of America [*Later, IDC*]   (EA)
DCA.......... Dicarboxylic Aciduria [*Medicine*]
DCA.......... Dichloroacetate [*Organic chemistry*]
DCA.......... Dichloroaniline [*Dye intermediate*]
DCA.......... Dictionary of Christian Antiquities [*A publication*]   (BJA)
DCA.......... Dicyanoanthracene [*Organic chemistry*]
DCA.......... Digital Command Assembly [*NASA*]   (KSC)
DCA.......... Digital Communications Associates, Inc. [*NYSE symbol*]   (SPSG)
DCA.......... Digital Computer Association   (MUGU)
DCA.......... DiLucia Chinese Alphabet [*57-character Chinese type font created for typewriter keyboards*]

DCA.......... Direct-Current Amplifier
DCA.......... Direct-Current Arc
DCA.......... Direction Center Active [*SAGE*] [*RADAR*]
DCA.......... Director of Civil Affairs [*Military*] [*British*]
DCA.......... Directorate of Civil Aviation
DCA.......... Distributed Communications Architecture   (BUR)
DCA.......... Distribution Contractors Association [*Tulsa, OK*]   (EA)
DCA.......... Distribution Control Assembly   (MCD)
DCA.......... Divisional Court of Appeal [*Legal term*]   (ILCA)
DCA.......... Doctor of Commercial Arts
DCA.......... Document Content Architecture [*IBM Corp.*]
DCA.......... Doll Collectors of America   (EA)
DCA.......... Dorion's Queen's Bench Reports [*Canada*] [*A publication*]   (DLA)
DCA.......... Dosimeter Corporation of America [*Nuclear energy*]   (NRCH)
DCA.......... Double Conversion Adapter
DCA.......... Downlink Channel Assignment   (CAAL)
DCA.......... Drift Correction Angle
DCA.......... Driver Control Area [*Data processing*]   (BUR)
DCA.......... Dual-Capable Aircraft   (MCD)
DCA.......... Washington [*DC*] National Airport [*Airport symbol*]
DCAA........ Defense Contract Audit Agency [*DoD*]
DCAA...... Dichloroacetic Acid [*Organic chemistry*]
DCAAP...... Defense Contract Audit Agency Pamphlets [*DoD*]
DCAB .... United States Civil Aeronautics Board, Washington, DC [*Library symbol*] [*Library of Congress*]   (LCLS)
DCABG .... Double Coronary Artery Bypass Graft [*Medicine*]
DCAC...... Defense Communications Agency Circular
DCACA .... Data Collection, Analysis, and Corrective Action   (CAAL)
DCaE........ Canadian Embassy, Washington, DC [*Library symbol*] [*Library of Congress*]   (LCLS)
DCAe........ Diploma of the College of Aeronautics [*British*]
DCAEUR .. Defense Communications Agency, Europe   (NATG)
DCAF........ Design Corrective Action Form
DCAI........ Defense Communications Agency Instruction
DCAI........ Digital Consulting Associates, Incorporated [*Andover, MA*] [*Telecommunications*] [*Later, DCI*]   (TSSD)
DCAI........ Direct-Current Analog Input   (MCD)
DCAJ........ Dixie Council of Authors and Journalists   (EA)
DCAL .... Center for Applied Linguistics, Washington, DC [*Library symbol*] [*Library of Congress*]   (LCLS)
DCAL .... Danquah. Cases in Akan Law [*Ghana*] [*A publication*]   (DLA)
DCAM....... Data Collection Access Method
DCAM....... Director of Craft and Amphibious Material [*British military*]   (DMA)
DCAMIP... Data Center for Atomic and Molecular Ionization Processes
DCA/MSO ... Defense Communications Agency/MILSATCOM [*Military Satellite Communications*] Systems Office [*Arlington, VA*]
DCAN....... Defense Communications Agency Note [*or Notice*]
D Can L..... Doctor of Canon Law
DCAO........ Digital Card And-Or Gate [*Data processing*]
DCAOC...... Defense Communications Agency Operations Center
DCap......... Capitol [*Record label*] [*Great Britain*]
DCAP .... Deficiency Corrective Action Program [*Surface missile systems*]
DCAP .... Dihydrocapaicin [*Biochemistry*]
DCAP .... Double Foolscap [*Paper*]   (ADA)
DC App...... District of Columbia Appeals Reports [*A publication*]   (DLA)
DCAR .... Design Corrective Action Report   (NASA)
DCAR .... Discrepancy and Corrective Action Report
DCAR .... Dreamcar Holdings, Inc. [*NASDAQ symbol*]   (NQ)
DCARE...... Driver Control Area Region Extension [*Data processing*]   (BUR)
DCAS........ Corcoran School of Art, Washington, DC [*Library symbol*] [*Library of Congress*]   (LCLS)
DCAS........ Data Collection and Analysis System [*NASA*]
DCAS........ Deca Energy Corp. [*NASDAQ symbol*]   (NQ)
DCAS........ Defense Contract Administration Services [*DoD*]
DCAS........ Deputy Chief of the Air Staff [*British*]
DCAS........ Deputy Commander of Aerospace Systems [*Inglewood, CA*] [*Air Force*]
DCAS........ Distribution Cost Analysis System   (MCD)
DCASD...... Defense Contract Administration Services District [*DoD*]   (AABC)
DCASEF.... Defense Communications Agency Systems Engineering Facility [*Reston, VA*]
DCASMA ... Defense Contract Administration Services Management Area [*DoD*]   (MCD)
DCASO ..... Defense Contract Administration Services Office [*DoD*]   (AABC)
DCASPRO ... Defense Contract Administration Services Plant Representative Office [*DoD*]   (AABC)
DCASR...... Defense Contract Administration Services Region [*DoD*]
DCAT .... Developing Cognitive Abilities Test [*Canadian Comprehensive Assessment Program*]
DCAT .... Directional Control Antitank [*Missile*]
DCAT .... Drug, Chemical, and Allied Trades Association   (EA)
DCB .... Dame Commander of the Order of the Bath [*British*]   (ADA)
DCB .... Data Control Block [*Data processing*]
D & CB....... Debt and Correspondence Branch [*BUPERS*]
DCB .... Decimal Code Binaire [*Binary Coded Decimal*] [*French*] [*Data processing*]

DCB	Defense Communications Board
DCB	Design Certificate Board
DCB	Destination Code Base
DCB	Developments in Cell Biology [*Elsevier Book Series*] [*A publication*]
DCB	Devereux Child Behavior [*Rating scale*] [*Psychology*]
DCB	Dichlorobenzidine [*Organic chemistry*]
DCB	Dichlorobenzoate [*Organic chemistry*]
DCB	Dichlorobiphenyl [*Organic chemistry*]
DCB	Dictionary of Canadian Biography [*A publication*]
DCB	Dictionary of Christian Biography [*London*] [*A publication*]
DCB	Dictionary of Christian Biography and Literature [*A publication*]　(OCD)
DCB	Dicyanobenzene [*Also, DCNB*] [*Organic chemistry*]
DCB	Disciplinary Control Board [*Air Force*]
DCB	Distant-Control Boat
DCB	Dithionite-Citrate-Bicarbonate [*Extractive chemistry*]
DCB	Division Crime Buffer
DCB	Document Control Book　(MCD)
DCB	Double Cantilever Beam [*Stress condition of aluminum alloy*]
DCB	United States Bureau of Customs, Washington, DC [*Library symbol*] [*Library of Congress*]　(LCLS)
DCBD	Division of Cancer Biology and Diagnosis [*National Cancer Institute*]
DCBD	Division for Children with Behavioral Disorders [*of Council for Exceptional Children*]　(EA)
DCB J	DC Bar Journal [*A publication*]
DCBP.........	Dichlorobenzophenone [*Also, DBP*] [*Organic chemistry*]
DCBRE......	Defence Chemical, Biological, and Radiation Establishment [*Canada*]
DCBRL......	Defence Chemical, Biological, and Radiation Laboratories [*Canada*]
DCBTF	Dichlorobenzotrifluoride [*Organic chemistry*]
DCC	Chamber of Commerce of the United States, Washington, DC [*Library symbol*] [*Library of Congress*]　(LCLS)
DCC	Chief Damage Controlman [*Navy*]
DCC	Dale Carnegie Course
DCC	Dallas Cowboys Cheerleaders
DCC	Damage Control Center　(NATG)
DCC	Data Circuit Concentration
DCC	Data Collection Center [*Army Infantry Board*]　(RDA)
DCC	Data Communications Channel
DCC	Data Communications Controller [*Data processing*]
DCC	Data Communications Corporation [*Information service or system*]　(IID)
DCC	Data Computation Complex [*NASA*]　(NASA)
DCC	Data Condition Code
DCC	Data Control Characters　(CMD)
DCC	Day Care Center
DCC	Dean and Chapter of Canterbury [*Anglican Church*]　(ROG)
DCC	Debarkation Control Center [*Navy*]　(CAAL)
DCC	Defence Construction Canada
DCC	Defense Concessions Committee
DCC	Defense Control Center　(AABC)
DCC	Delayed Contact Closure
DCC	Delcommune [*Zaire*] [*Seismograph station code, US Geological Survey*]　(SEIS)
DCC	Delegation Catholique pour la Cooperation　(EA)
DCC	Deleted in Colorectal Carcinomas [*A gene*]
DCC	Deputy Chief Constable
DCC	Design Change Control
DCC	Design Concept Change　(AAG)
DCC	Development Capital Corporation [*British*]
DCC	Development Control Center
DCC	Device Cluster Controller
DCC	Device Control Character [*Data processing*]　(IEEE)
DCC	Devis de Construction Canada [*Construction Specifications Canada*] [*Formerly, Association des Redacteurs de Devis du Canada - ARDC*]
DCC	Dextran-Coated Charcoal
DC & C	Diabetes Control and Complications [*Medicine*]
DCC	Dick Clark Companies
DCC	Dicyclohexylcarbodiimide [*Also, DCCD, DCCI*] [*Organic chemistry*]
DCC	Dielectric Constant Change [*Analytical chemistry*]
DCC	Digital Control Computer
DCC	Digital Cross Current
DCC	Diocesan Consistory Court [*Legal term*]　(DLA)
DCC	Direct Computer Control
DCC	Direct Control Channel
DCC	Disaster Control Center　(AAG)
DCC	Discrimination and Control Computer　(MUGU)
DCC	Display Channel Complex　(FAAC)
DCC	Display Control Console　(KSC)
DCC	Distribution Control Center　(AAG)
DCC	District Communications Center [*Navy*]
DCC	Division of Cataloging and Classification [*Later, CCS, RTSD*] [*American Library Association*]
DCC	Division of Consumer Credit [*Federal Trade Commission*]
DCC	Document Control Center
DCC	Document Control Chief [*NASA*]

DCC	Dodge City College [*Kansas*]
DCc	Double Concave [*Medicine*]
DCC	Double Cotton Covered [*Wire insulation*]
DCC	Dow Chemical Company
DCC	Downtown Copy Center [*Washington, DC*] [*Telecommunications*]　(TSSD)
DCC	Drone Control Center [*Military*]　(MCD)
DCC	Dry-Column Chromatography
DCC	Dual Cam Clutch
D & CC	Pennsylvania District and County Reports [*A publication*]　(DLA)
DCCA	Dextran-Coated Charcoal Analysis [*Analytical biochemistry*]
DCCA	Dichloroisocyanuric Acid [*Organic chemistry*]
DCCA	District of Columbia Compensation Act　(DLA)
DCCA	Drying Control Chemical Additive [*Ceramic technology*]
DCCAO	Deputy Chief Civil Affairs Officer [*US and Britain*]
DCCB	Defense Center Control Building [*Army*]　(AABC)
DCCC	Data Communication Control Character　(IEEE)
DCCC	Defense Communications Control Center
DCCC	Democratic Congressional Campaign Committee　(EA)
DCCC	Double Current Cable Code [*Telecommunications*]
DCCC	Droplet Countercurrent Chromatography
DCCD	Dicyclohexylcarbodiimide [*Also, DCC, DCCI*] [*Organic chemistry*]
DCCD	Division for Children with Communication Disorders [*Council for Exceptional Children*]
DCCE	District of Columbia Code Encyclopedia [*A publication*]　(DLA)
DCCH.......	Commerce Clearing House, Washington, DC [*Library symbol*] [*Library of Congress*]　(LCLS)
DCCI........	Dicyclohexylcarbodiimide [*Also, DCC, DCCD*] [*Organic chemistry*]
DC Cir.......	District of Columbia Court of Appeals Cases [*A publication*]　(DLA)
DC Cir R	District of Columbia Circuit Court Rules [*A publication*]　(DLA)
DCCM	Master Chief Damage Controlman [*Navy rating*]
DCCMP.....	Daunorubicin, Cyclocytidine [*Ancitabine*], Mercaptopurine, Prednisone [*Antineoplastic drug regimen*]
DCCN.......	Dimensions of Critical Care Nursing [*A publication*]
DCCO........	Digital Card Clock Oscillator [*Data processing*]
DC Code.....	District of Columbia Code [*A publication*]　(DLA)
DC Code Ann ...	District of Columbia Code, Annotated [*A publication*]　(DLA)
DC Code Encycl ...	District of Columbia Code Encyclopedia [*A publication*]　(DLA)
DC Code Legis & Admin Serv ...	District of Columbia Code Legislative and Administrative Service (West) [*A publication*]　(DLA)
DCCP........	Design Change Control Program
DCCP........	Digital Computer Control Panel
DCCRM	Center for Chinese Research Materials, Washington, DC [*Library symbol*] [*Library of Congress*]　(LCLS)
DCCS........	Defense Communications Control System [*Air Force*]
DCCS........	Design Change Clearance Sheet　(MCD)
DCCS........	Digital Camera Control System
DCCS........	Digital Command Communications System　(MCD)
DCCS........	Senior Chief Damage Controlman [*Navy rating*]
DCCSA	Dictionary of Computer and Control Systems Abbreviations, Signs, and Symbols [*New York: Odyssey Press, 1965*] [*A publication*]
DCCT	Diabetes Control and Complications Trial
DCCTC......	United States Department of Defense, Command and Control Technical Center, the Pentagon, Washington, DC [*Library symbol*] [*Library of Congress*]　(LCLS)
DCCU	Data Communications Control Unit　(DEN)
DCCU	Data Correlation Control Unit
DCCU	Decommutator Conditioning Unit　(KSC)
DCCU	Digital Command and Control Unit　(NASA)
DCCU	Digital Communications and Control Unit　(MCD)
DCCU	Display Computer Control Unit　(MCD)
DCCVS......	Domestic Council Committee on Veterans Services [*Veterans Administration*]
DCCWS.....	Deputy Chief, Chemical Warfare Service [*Army*]
DCD..........	Congressional Digest, Washington, DC [*Library symbol*] [*Library of Congress*]　(LCLS)
DCD..........	Damage Control Diagrams [*Naval Ship Systems Command*]
DCD..........	Data Carrier Detect [*or Detector*] [*Data communication signal*] [*Telecommunications*]　(TEL)
DCD..........	Deceased　(ADA)
DCD..........	Decennial Census Division [*Census*]　(OICC)
DCD..........	Decode　(MSA)
DCD..........	Decomposition Diagramer [*Data processing*]
DCD..........	Defecation-Collection Device [*Apollo*] [*NASA*]
DCD..........	Deflection Coil Drive
DCD..........	Department of Community Development [*Proposed government department*]
DCD..........	Design Change Document
DCD..........	Design Control Drawing
DCD..........	Dicyandiamide [*or Dicyanodiamide*] [*Also, DICY*] [*Organic chemistry*]
DCD..........	Differential Current Density

DCD.......... Digital Compact Disk
DCD.......... Digital Countdown Display [*Data processing*]
DCD.......... Dimensional Control Drawing
DCD.......... Diode-Capacitor-Diode
DCD.......... Diploma in Chest Diseases [*British*]
DCD.......... Direct Contact Desulfation
DCD.......... Direct-Current Dump
DCD.......... Director of Combat Development [*British*]   (RDA)
DCD.......... Director of Communications Development [*Ministry of Aircraft Production*] [*British*]
DCD.......... Director of Compass Department [*British military*]   (DMA)
DCD.......... Directorate of Combat Developments [*Army*]
DCD.......... Don't-Care-a-Damn [*British naval slang term for torpedo-boat destroyer*] [*World War I*]
DCD.......... Double Channel Duplex
DCD.......... Dynamic Computer Display   (IEEE)
DCD.......... Kredietwaardigheden [*A publication*]
DCD.......... NAVSHIPS [*Naval Ship Systems Command*] Damage Control Diagrams
D & C2d ..... District and County, Second Series [*A publication*]   (DLA)
DC 2d......... Pennsylvania District and County Reports, Second Series [*A publication*]   (DLA)
DCDA........ Data Communication Dealers Association   (EA)
DCDA........ Delyn Cooperative Development Agency [*British*]
DC/DC ...... Data Communication to Disk Control
DC/DC ...... Direct Current to Direct Current [*Telecommunications*]
DCDCEC... Division on Career Development of the Council for Exceptional Children   (EA)
DCDD....... Dichlorodibenzodioxin [*Also, DDD*] [*Organic chemistry*]
DCDFL...... Defense Civil Disturbance Facility List
DCDG....... Diode-Capacitor-Diode Gate
DCDH ...... Diploma in Child Dental Health [*British*]   (DBQ)
DCDI .... Dairy Council Digest [*A publication*]
DC Dist Col ... United States District Court for the District of Columbia   (DLA)
DCDL .... Digital Control Design Language [*1968*] [*Data processing*]   (CSR)
DCDL .... Double Cylinder Deadlock
DCDM....... Digitally Controlled Delta Modulator   (MCD)
DCDMA.... Diamond Core Drill Manufacturers Association   (EA)
DCDP .... Defense Center Data Processing [*Army*]   (AABC)
dCDP .... Deoxycytidine Diphosphate [*Biochemistry*]
DCDPO..... Directorate for Civil Disturbance Planning and Operations [*Army*]   (AABC)
DCDPS...... Dichlorodiphenylsulfone [*Organic chemistry*]
DCDR....... Data Collection and Data Relay [*Telecommunications*]   (TEL)
DCDR........ Decoder   (AAG)
DCDR........ Direct Cycle Diphenyl Reactor
DCDRS...... Drone Control and Data Retrieval System [*Later, CDRS*] [*Air Force*]   (MCD)
DCDS .... Deputy Chief of Defence Staff [*British*]
DCDS .... Digital Control Design System   (IEEE)
DCDS .... Digital Countdown Display System [*Data processing*]
DCDS .... Distributed Computer Design System   (SDI)
DCDS .... Double Cotton Double Silk [*Wire insulation*]
DCDS .... Dual Channel Dual Speed
DCDS(OR) ... Deputy Chief of Defence Staff (Operational Requirements) [*British*]
DCDT....... Direct-Current Differential Transformer
DCDU........ Data Collection and Distribution Units [*Military*]   (AABC)
DCE .... Dallas Cotton Exchange   (EA)
DCE .... Data Circuit-Terminating Equipment [*Data processing*]   (BUR)
DCE .... Data Communication Equipment
DCE .... Data Conversion Equipment [*Data processing*]
DCE .... Defense Combat Evaluation   (AABC)
DCE .... Department of Conservation and Environment [*Proposed name for US Department of the Interior*]
DCE .... Despin Control Electronics [*Aerospace*]
DCE .... Developments in Civil Engineering [*Elsevier Book Series*] [*A publication*]
DCE .... Device Control Entry [*Data processing*]
DCE .... Dichloroethane [*Organic chemistry*]
DCE .... Dicyanoethylene [*Organic chemistry*]
DCE .... Diploma of Curative Education [*British*]
DCE .... Direct Contact Evaporator [*Chemical engineering*]
DCE .... Director [*or Directorate*] of Civil Engineering [*Air Force*]
DCE .... Director [*or Directorate*] of Communications - Electronics [*ADC*]
DCE .... Discounted Cash Equivalent   (ADA)
DCE .... Division of Career Education [*Office of Education*]
DCE .... Doctor of Civil Engineering
DCE .... Domestic Credit Expansion
DCE .... Drive Control Equipment
DCEA .... Democratic Council on Ethnic Americans   (EA)
DCEC .... Defense Communications Engineering Center [*Reston, VA*] [*DoD*]   (GRD)
DC Ed .... Doctor of Commercial Education
DCEE......... Defence Components and Equipment Exhibition [*British*]   (ITD)
DCEE......... Dichloroethyl Ether [*Organic chemistry*]
D Ce Eng.... Doctor of Cement Engineering

DCEF........ Discounted Cash Equivalent Flow   (ADA)
DCEL........ Direct-Current Electroluminescence
DCEO .... Defense Communications Engineering Office [*Army*]
DCEO .... Division Communications-Electronics Officer [*Military*]   (AABC)
DCEP........ Diploma of Child and Educational Psychology   (ADA)
DCER .... United States Army, Corps of Engineers, Coastal Engineering Research Center, Fort Belvoir, VA [*Library symbol*] [*Library of Congress*]   (LCLS)
D Cer E ..... Doctor of Ceramic Engineering
D Cer Eng .. Doctor of Ceramic Engineering
DCERR.... Depot Component/Equipment Rework Report [*Navy*]   (NG)
DCES........ Data Collection and Evaluation System   (NVT)
DCES........ Discretionary Capital Expenditure System [*Bell System*]
DCES........ DSS [*Deep Space Station*] Communications Equipment Subsystem
DCET........ Dicarbethoxythiamine [*Pharmacology*]
DCEU ...... Dictionary of Carribean English Usage [*A publication*]
DCEV .... Diabetes Center of Eastern Virginia [*Eastern Virginia Medical School*]
DCF .... Claretian Fathers Library, Washington, DC [*Library symbol*] [*Library of Congress*]   (LCLS)
DCF .... Daniell. Forms and Precedents in Chancery [*7th ed.*] [*1932*] [*A publication*]   (ILCA)
DCF .... Data Channel Filter [*Data processing*]
DCF .... Data Collection Form [*Civil Defense*]
DCF .... Data Control Facility   (MCD)
DCF .... Data Correlation Facility
DCF .... Deal-Cased Frame [*Carpentry*]
DCF .... Defenders of the Christian Faith [*Later, CCI*]   (EA)
DCF .... Democratic Candidate Fund   (EA)
DCF .... Democratie Chretienne Francaise [*French Christian Democracy*] [*Political party*]   (PPE)
DCF .... Deoxycoformycin [*Also, dCF*] [*Antileukemia drug*]
DCF .... Dependency Certificate Filed
DCF .... Deputy Chief   (FAAC)
DCF .... Deputy for Contract Financing [*Air Force*]
DCF .... Dicarboxyfluorescein [*A biological stain*]
DCF .... Die Casting Federation   (EA)
DCF .... Direct Centrifugal Flotation [*Parasitology*]
DCF .... Direct Control Feature [*CMD*]
DCF .... Direction Commerciale Francaise [*A publication*]
DCF .... Disaster Control Force
DCF .... Discounted Cash Flow
DCF .... Dishonored Check File [*IRS*]
DCF .... Disk Controller/Formatter [*Data processing*]
DCF .... Dispersion Coated Fabric [*Plastics technology*]
DCF .... Distribution Chart File
DCF .... Doctor of City Forestry
DCF .... Document Composition Facility [*IBM Corp.*]
DCF .... Dominica-Cane [*West Indies*] [*Airport symbol*]   (OAG)
DCF .... Dose Commitment Factor [*Radioactivity calculations*]
DCF .... Dose Conversion Factor [*Radioactivity calculations*]   (NRCH)
DCF .... Droplet Combustion Facility
DCF .... Dynamic Coercive Force
DCFA........ Damage Controlman, Fireman Apprentice [*Navy*]
DCFC....... Dale Chapp Fan Club   (EA)
DCFC....... Danny Cooksey Fan Club   (EA)
DCFC....... David Copperfield Fan Club   (EA)
DCFC....... Dehydrated and Convenience Foods Council [*Defunct*]   (EA)
DCFC....... Desiree Coleman Fan Club   (EA)
DCFC....... Dick Curless Fan Club   (EA)
DCFEM..... Dynamic Crossed-Field Electron Multiplication
DCFF .... Digital Card Flip-Flop [*Data processing*]
DCFG .... Direct-Current Free Gyro
DCFL......... Direct-Coupled FET [*Field Effect Transistor*] Logic [*Integrated circuitry*]
DCFLOS ... Dynamic Cloud Free Line of Sight   (MCD)
DCFM ...... Discounted Cash Flow Method
DCFMD .... Director of Coastal Forces Material Department [*British*]
DCFN .... Damage Controlman, Fireman [*Navy*]
DCFP........ Dynamic Crossed-Field Photomultiplier
DCFRN...... Developing Countries Farm Radio Network   (EAIO)
DCFRR...... Discounted Cash Flow Rate of Return [*Business term*]
DCFT......... Commodity Futures Trading Commission, Washington, DC [*Library symbol*] [*Library of Congress*]   (LCLS)
DCFT......... Double-Coated Foam Tape
DCG.......... Dancing   (ADA)
DCG.......... Data Control Group   (MCD)
DCG.......... Decigram [*Unit of measure*]
DCG.......... Decisions of the Comptroller General
DCG.......... Definite Clause Grammar [*Computer programming*]   (BYTE)
DCG.......... Deoxycorticosterone Glucoside [*Also, DOCG*] [*Endocrinology*]
DCG.......... Dependent Charge Group [*Telecommunications*]   (TEL)
DCG.......... Deputy Chaplain-General [*British*]
DCG.......... Deputy Commanding General
DCG.......... Deputy Commissary-General
DCG.......... Designs Coordination Group [*Telecommunications*]   (TEL)
DCG.......... Dichromated Gelatin
DCG.......... Dictionary of Christ and the Gospels [*A publication*]   (BJA)
DCG.......... Diode-Capacitor Gate

DCG.......... Direct-Current Generator
DCG.......... Disaster Control Group
DCG.......... Displacement Cardiograph [*Medicine*]
DCG.......... Double Current Generator
DCG.......... Dynamic Cardiogram
DCG.......... Hereditary Order of the Descendants of Colonial Governors (EA)
DCG.......... San Diego, CA [*Location identifier*] [*FAA*] (FAAL)
DC/GCI..... Direction Center - Ground Controlled Intercept [*SAGE*] [*RADAR*] (CINC)
DCG/CONARC ... Deputy Commanding General, Continental Army Command [*Later, DCG/T*] [*Army*]
DCGICP.... Deputy Commanding General for International Cooperative Programs [*Army*]
DCGO........ District Coast Guard Officer
DCGRDA .. Deputy Commanding General for Research, Development, and Acquisition [*Army*]
DCGS .... Deputy Chief of the General Staff in the Field [*Military*] [*British*]
DCG/T....... Deputy Commanding General, Training [*Formerly, DCG/CONARC*] [*Army*]
D Ch.......... Chirurgiae Doctor [*Doctor of Surgery*]
DCH .... Data Channel [*Data processing*]
DCH .... Data Chief
D & Ch ...... Deacon and Chitty's English Bankruptcy Reports [*1832-35*] [*A publication*] (DLA)
DCH .... Deep Case Hardened
D Ch.......... Delaware Chancery Reports [*A publication*] (DLA)
DCH .... Denote Chassis
D Ch.......... Deutsche Chirurgie [*A publication*]
DCH .... Dicyclohexyl [*Organic chemistry*]
DCH .... Diploma in Child Health [*British*]
DCH .... District Chaplain [*Navy*]
DCH .... Drain Collection Header [*Nuclear energy*] (NRCH)
DCH .... Reports of the United States District Court of Hawaii [*A publication*] (DLA)
DCHAN.... Difference Channel (MSA)
DCHC........ Dunbarton College of Holy Cross [*Closed, 1973*] [*Washington, DC*]
DChD........ Doctor Chirurgiae Dentalis [*Doctor of Dental Surgery*] [*British*]
D Ch E ...... Doctor of Chemical Engineering
D Che E ..... Doctor of Chemical Engineering
DCHEM.... Dry Chemical
D Chem E .. Doctor of Chemical Engineering
D Ch Eng .. Doctor of Chemical Engineering
DCHi .... Columbia Historical Society, Washington, DC [*Library symbol*] [*Library of Congress*] (LCLS)
D Chip........ [*D.*] Chipman's Vermont Supreme Court Reports [*1789-1824*] [*A publication*] (DLA)
D Chipm .... [*D.*] Chipman's Vermont Reports [*1789-1824*] [*A publication*] (DLA)
D Chip (VT) ... [*D.*] Chipman's Vermont Reports [*1789-1824*] [*A publication*] (DLA)
D & Chit..... Deacon and Chitty's English Bankruptcy Reports [*1832-35*] [*A publication*] (DLA)
D Ch O ...... Diploma in Opthalmic Surgery [*British*]
DCHP........ Dicyclohexyl Phthalate [*Organic chemistry*]
DCHQ....... Damage Control Headquarters [*Military*] [*British*]
D Chr Ed.... Doctor of Christian Education
DCHS .... Center for Hellenic Studies, Harvard University, Washington, DC [*Library symbol*] [*Library of Congress*] (LCLS)
DCHS .... Disciples of Christ Historical Society (EA)
DCHT........ Diploma in Community Health in Tropical Countries [*British*] (DBQ)
DCHT........ Direct-Contact Heat Transfer [*Chemical engineering*]
DCHTA ..... Doklady Chemical Technology [*English Translation*] [*A publication*]
DCHV........ Domiciliary Care for Homeless Veterans [*Department of Veterans Affairs*]
DCI .... Carnegie Institution of Washington, Washington, DC [*Library symbol*] [*Library of Congress*] (LCLS)
DCI .... DARCOM [*Development and Readiness Command, Army*] Career/Control Inventory (MCD)
DCI .... Data Communications, Incorporated
DCI .... Data Composition, Incorporated [*Information service or system*] (IID)
DCI .... Data Courier, Inc. (IID)
DCI .... Deaf Communications Institute (EA)
DCI .... Defence for Children International Movement [*See also DEI*] [*Database producer*] (EAIO)
DCI .... Defence Council Instructions [*Military*] [*British*]
DCI .... Defense Computer Institute
DCI .... Deliverable Contract Item (KSC)
DCI .... DeLorean Club International (EA)
DCI .... Department of Central Index [*Computer center*] [*Department of Health and Social Security*] [*British*]
DCI .... Department of Central Intelligence [*Thailand*] (CINC)
DCI .... Deputy Chief for Intelligence
DCI .... Des Moines & Central Iowa Railway Co. [*AAR code*]
DCI .... Desorption Chemical Ionization
DCI .... Developpement et Civilisation [*A publication*]

DCI .... Dialing Code Information [*Telecommunications*] [*British*]
DCI .... Dichloroisoprenaline
DCI .... Dichloroisoproterenol [*Pharmacology*]
DCI .... Dielectric Constant Indicator
DCI .... Digital Clock Indicator
DCI .... Digital Consulting, Incorporated [*Andover, MA*] (TSSD)
DCI .... Direct Carrier Injection
DCI .... Direct Channel Interface
DCI .... Direct Computer Input (MCD)
DCI .... Director of Central Intelligence
DCI .... Director of Corporate Information
DCI .... Disk Core Image (CMD)
DCI .... Distribution Codes Institute [*Defunct*] (EA)
DCI .... Division of Chemical Information [*American Chemical Society*] [*Information service or system*] (IID)
DCI .... Documentation Change Instruction (KSC)
DCI .... Donaldson Company, Incorporated [*NYSE symbol*] (SPSG)
DCI .... Dramatic Criticism Index [*A publication*]
DCI .... Driving Car Intoxicated
DCI .... Driving Control Indicator
DCI .... Drum Corps International (EA)
DCI .... Dry Creek [*Idaho*] [*Seismograph station code, US Geological Survey*] (SEIS)
DCI .... Ductile Cast Iron
DC³I .... Distributed Command, Control, Communications, and Intelligence [*Army*] (RDA)
DCIA .... Digital Card Inverting Amplifier [*Data processing*]
DCIB.......... Data Communication Input Buffer
DCIB.......... Defense Counterintelligence Board (MCD)
DCIC.......... Defense Ceramic Information Center [*Later, MCIC*] [*Battelle Memorial Institute*] (MCD)
DCIC.......... Double Column Ion Chromotography
DCID .... Director of Central Intelligence Directive
DCID .... Director of Central Intelligence Document
D & Cie ..... Darier & Compagnie [*Bank*] [*Switzerland*]
DCIEM...... Defence and Civil Institute of Environmental Medicine [*Canada*]
DCI-G .... Carnegie Institution of Washington, Geophysical Laboratory, Washington, DC [*Library symbol*] [*Library of Congress*] (LCLS)
DCIGS....... Deputy Chief of the Imperial General Staff [*Military*] [*British*]
DCII.......... Defense Central Index of Investigations (AFM)
DCII.......... Douglas Computer International [*NASDAQ symbol*] (NQ)
DCILM...... Direct Computer Input Load Module (MCD)
DCIM .... Display System Computer Input Multiplexer (MCD)
DCIMDQ .. Developmental and Comparative Immunology [*A publication*]
DCINA ...... Drug and Cosmetic Industry [*A publication*]
D & C Ind.... Drug and Cosmetic Industry [*A publication*]
DCIO .... Direct Channel Interface Option
DCIP.......... Data Correction Indicator Panel (MUGU)
DCIP.......... Dichlorophenolindophenol [*Also, DCPI, DCPIP, DPIP*] [*Analytical reagent*]
DCIP.......... Disk Cartridge Initialization Program (CMD)
DCIPT .... Damage Control In-Port Training (NVT)
DCIR .... Daily Cadweld Inspection Report [*Nuclear energy*] (NRCH)
DCIS .... Dartmouth College Information System [*Library network*] (IT)
DCIS .... Defense Criminal Investigation Service
DCIS .... Delta Computec, Inc. [*NASDAQ symbol*] (NQ)
DCIS .... Distribution Construction Information System [*IBM Corp.*]
DCIS .... Downrange Computer Input System (MUGU)
DCIS .... Duct Carcinoma In Situ [*Oncology*]
DCIST .... Directory of Computerized Information in Science and Technology [*Leonard Cohen, ed., New York: Science Associates International, 1968*] [*A publication*]
DCI-T .... Carnegie Institution of Washington, Department of Terrestrial Magnetism, Washington, DC [*Library symbol*] [*Library of Congress*] (LCLS)
DCIU .... Digital Control and Interface Unit (MCD)
DCI-USA... Defense for Children International - United States of America (EA)
DCJ........... Carmelitae Divini Cordis Jesu [*Carmelite Sisters of the Divine Heart of Jesus*] [*Roman Catholic religious order*]
DCJ........... District Court Judge
DCJ........... Doctor of Criminal Jurisprudence
DCJC......... Dawson County Junior College [*Montana*]
DC Jur....... (Dalloz) Critique. Jurisprudence [*France*] [*A publication*]
DCK .... Dahl Creek, AK [*Location identifier*] [*FAA*] (FAAL)
DCKG......... Docking (MSA)
DCKHDL .. Denryoku Chuo Kenkyusho Hokoku [*A publication*]
DCKNG..... Docking [*Aerospace*] (NASA)
DCKP........ Direct-Current Key Pulsing (IEEE)
DCL .... Data Checklist
DCL .... Data Control Language [*NCR Corp.*]
DCL .... Decalitre
DCL .... Declaration (ADA)
DCL .... Defence Construction [*1951*] Limited [*Canada*]
DCL .... Delayed Call Limited [*Telecommunications*] (TEL)
DCL .... Demountable Cathode Lamp
DCL .... Deputy Commander for Logistics (MCD)
DCL .... Design Capability Line [*Army*] (AABC)
DCL .... Design Change Listing

DCL .... Designate Command Line [*Data processing*]
DCL .... Designer Choice Logic
DCL .... Detailed Checklist
DCL .... Detailed Configuration List   (MCD)
DCL .... Detroit College of Law [*Michigan*]
DCL .... Diagnostic Chemicals Ltd.
DCL .... Digital Channel Link
DCL .... Digital Computer Laboratory [*Massachusetts Institute of Technology*]   (MCD)
DCL .... Digital Control Loading [*System*]   (MCD)
DCL .... Direct Coal Liquefaction [*Fuel science*]
DCL .... Direct Communications Link [*US/USSR*]
DCL .... Direct-Coupled Logic
DCL .... Director of Contract Labour [*Admiralty*] [*British*]
DCL .... Division of Chemical Literature [*ACS*]
DCL .... Doctor of Canon Law
DCL .... Doctor of Civil Law
DCL .... Doctor of Classical Literature
DCL .... Doctor of Commercial Law
DCL .... Doctor of Comparative Law   (DLA)
DCL .... Document Change List   (MCD)
DCL .... Door Closer
D & Cl .... Dow and Clark's Reports [*A publication*]   (DLA)
DCL .... Drawing Change List
DCL .... Dynamic Characteristic Load
DCL .... United States Department of Commerce, Washington, DC [*OCLC symbol*]   (OCLC)
DCLA .... Deputy Chief of Staff, Logistics and Administration [*NATO*]   (NATG)
DC Lab S ... Dominion of Canada Labour Service [*Commerce Clearing House*] [*A publication*]   (DLA)
DCLC .... Drift Cyclotron Loss Cone [*Plasma physics*]
DCLF .... Diploma in Contact Lens Fitting [*British*]   (DBQ)
DCLI .... Duke of Cornwall's Light Infantry [*Military unit*] [*British*]
DC Lib ...... District of Columbia Libraries [*A publication*]
D Clin North America ... Dental Clinics of North America [*A publication*]
DCLIR ...... Dead Cat Lying in the Road [*Traffic report*]
DCLM .... Department of Command, Leadership, and Management [*DoD*]
DCLN .... Direct Coupled Loop Network [*Data processing*]
DCLOG-A ... Deputy Chief of Logistics - Army [*Australia*]
DCLP .... Diploma in Contact Lens Practice [*British*]   (DBQ)
DCLPT ...... In-Port Damage Control Training [*Navy*]   (NVT)
DCLR .... Decelerate   (MSA)
DCLR .... District Court Law Reports [*Hong Kong*] [*A publication*]   (ILCA)
DCLR(Can) ... Dominion Companies Law Reports [*Canada*] [*A publication*]   (DLA)
DCLRT ...... Decelerate   (FAAC)
DCLS .... Data Collection and Location System [*Telecommunications*]
DCLS .... Deoxycholate-Citrate-Lactose-Sucrose [*Agar*] [*Microbiology*]
DClSc .... Doctor of Clinical Science   (ADA)
DCLTC ...... Dry Cargo Loading Technical Committee [*NATO*]   (NATG)
DCLTR ...... Decline Transfer   (NOAA)
DCLU .... Declutch
DCM .... Chester, SC [*Location identifier*] [*FAA*]   (FAAL)
DCM .... Data Channel Module [*Data processing*]   (NOAA)
DCM .... Data Communications Multiplexer
DCM .... Data Conversion Machine   (MCD)
DCM .... Day Care Mother   (ADA)
DCM .... Decameter
DCM .... Decommutator Control Memory   (MCD)
DCM .... Deep Chlorophyll Maximum [*Oceanography*]
DCM .... Defense Combat Maneuvers   (FAAC)
DCM .... Defense Common Market   (MCD)
DCM .... Defensive Countermaneuvering
DCM .... Defined Culture Medium [*For blastoderms*]
DCM .... Deputy Chief of Maintenance
DCM .... Deputy Chief of Mission [*Diplomatic corps*]
DCM .... Diagnostic Controlled MODEM [*Data processing*]   (BUR)
DCM .... Dichloromaleic Acid [*Organic chemistry*]
DCM .... Dichloromethane [*Anesthetic*] [*Organic chemistry*]
DCM .... Dichloromethotrexate [*Also, DCMTX*] [*Antineoplastic drug*]
DCM .... Die Casting Mold   (MCD)
DCM .... Digital Circuit Module [*Data processing*]
DCM .... Dilated Cardiomyopathy [*Cardiology*]
DCM .... Direct Connection Module [*Data processing*]
DCM .... Direction Cosine Matrix   (MCD)
DCM .... Director of Civilian Marksmanship [*Army*]
DCM .... Directorate for Classification Management [*DoD*]
DCM .... Display and Control Module   (MCD)
DCM .... Distinguished Conduct Medal [*British*]
DCM .... District Court-Martial [*Facetious translation: "Don't Come Monday," in reference to a one-day suspension*] [*British*]
DCM .... District Cub Master [*Scouting*]
DCM .... Division of Civilian Marksmanship [*Army*]
DCM .... Doctor of Comparative Medicine
DCM .... Dominican Campaign Medal
DCM .... Double Common Meter [*Music*]
DCM .... Double Common Multiple [*Mathematics*]   (ROG)

DCM .... Dovize Cevrilebilir Mevduat [*Convertible Lira Account*] [*Turkish*] [*Business term*]
DCM .... Drawing Control Manual   (MCD)
DCM .... Dreyfus California Municipal Income, Inc. [*AMEX symbol*]   (CTT)
DCMA .... Defense Contract Management Agency
DCMA .... District of Columbia Manpower Administration
DCMA .... Dry Color Manufacturers Association   (EA)
DCMA .... Duty Cycle Modulation Alternator
DCMB .... Development Configuration Management Board   (MCD)
DCMD .... District of Columbia Military District   (AABC)
DCMDA .... Demonstration Cities and Metropolitan Development Act
DCME .... Dichloromethyl Methyl Ether [*Organic chemistry*]
DCME .... Digital Circuit Multiplication Equipment [*Telecommunications*]
DCMG .... Dame Commander of the Order of St. Michael and St. George [*British*]
DCM & G .. Direct Current Motor and Generator Facility [*General Electric Co.*]
DCMH .... Data Collection Module, High Speed
DCMI .... Disclosure of Classified Military Information [*to foreign governments*]   (AFM)
DCML .... Data Collection Module, Low Speed
DCML .... Diplomatic Conference of International Maritime Law
DCMO ...... Dairy, Cowshed, and Milk Shop Order [*1885-1886*] [*Legal*] [*British*]   (ROG)
DCMP .... Daunorubicin, Cytarabine, Mercaptopurine, Prednisone [*Antineoplastic drug regimen*]
dCMP .... Deoxycytidine Monophosphate [*Biochemistry*]
DCMPO ..... Deputy Chief of the Military Planning Office
DCMPS ..... Degaussing Compass
DCMPTR ... Degaussing Computer
DCMR .... District Of Columbia Municipal Regulations [*A publication*]
DCMS .... Data Control Multiplex System
DCMS .... Deccan College. Monograph Series [*A publication*]
DCMS .... Dedicated Computer Message Switching
DCMS .... Depot Command Management System
DCMS .... Deputy Commissioner Medical Services [*British*]   (DAS)
DCMS .... Digital Capacitance Measuring System   (MCD)
DCMS .... Director Communications Material Security   (MCD)
DCMSN ..... Decommission   (FAAC)
DCMSND ... Decommissioned
DCMT .... Diploma in Clinical Medicine of the Tropics [*British*]
DCMT .... Document   (FAAC)
DCMTX ..... Dichloromethotrexate [*Also, DCM*] [*Antineoplastic drug*]
DCMU .... (Dichlorophenyl)dimethylurea [*Herbicide*]
DC Mun App ... Municipal Court of Appeals for the District of Columbia   (DLA)
DC Mun Regs ... DC [*District of Columbia*] Municipal Regulations [*A publication*]
DCMV .... Digital Card Multivibrator [*Data processing*]
DCMX .... Dichloro-meta-Xylenol [*Organic chemistry*]
DCN .... Daily Commercial News and Shipping List [*A publication*]   (APTA)
DCN .... Daily Consumer News [*Consumers' Association*] [*Information service or system*]   (IID)
DCN .... Dana Corporation [*NYSE symbol*]   (SPSG)
DCN .... Data Change Notice   (KSC)
DCN .... Debt Crisis Network   (EA)
DCN .... Deep Cerebellar Nuclei [*Brain anatomy*]
DCN .... Defence Communication Network [*British*]   (NATG)
DCN .... Dental Care Network [*Blue Cross and Blue Shield*] [*Insurance*]
DCN .... Depot Control Number
DCN .... Design Change Notice
DCN .... Development Change Notice [*Aerospace*]
DCN .... Dichloronitrosalicylanilide [*Economic poison*] [*Organic chemistry*]
DCN .... Dicyanonaphthalene [*Organic chemistry*]
DCN .... Discalced Carmelite Nuns [*Rome, Italy*]   (EAIO)
DCN .... Disconnect
DCN .... Distributed Computer Network
DCN .... Document Change Notice
DCN .... Document Control Number   (AFM)
DCN .... Dorsal Cardiac Nerve [*Anatomy*]
DCN .... Dorsal Cutaneous Nerve
DCN .... Double Crown [*Monetary unit*] [*Great Britain*]   (ADA)
DCN .... Draft Change Notice   (MCD)
DCN .... Drawing Change Notice
DCNA .... Data Communication Network Architecture   (BUR)
DCNA .... Deputy Chief Naval Adviser [*British*]
DCNA .... Dichloronitroaniline [*Also, DICHLORAN*] [*Fungicide*]
DCNA .... Digital Card Noninverting Amplifier [*Data processing*]
DCNAA ..... Dental Clinics of North America [*A publication*]
DCNAAC .. Dental Clinics of North America [*A publication*]
DCNB .... Dicyanobenzene [*Also, DCB*] [*Organic chemistry*]
DCNEO ..... Deputy Chief Naval Engineering Officer [*British*]
DCNET ..... Direct Current Network [*Solutions for resistive components and voltage sources*]
DCNF .... Dishonored Check Name File [*IRS*]
DCNG .... District of Columbia National Guard   (AABC)

DCNI......... Department of the Chief of Naval Information [*British military*] (DMA)
D Cn L .... Doctor of Canon Law
DCNM...... Deputy Chief of Naval Material
DCNM(D) ... Deputy Chief of Naval Material, Development
DCNM(M & F) ... Deputy Chief of Naval Material, Material and Facilities
DCNM(M & O) ... Deputy Chief of Naval Material, Management and Organization
DCNM(P & FM) ... Deputy Chief of Naval Material, Programs and Financial Management
DCNNAH ... Decheniana [*A publication*]
DCNO....... Deputy Chief of Naval Operations
DCNOA..... Deputy Chief of Naval Operations, Administration
DCNO(AIR) ... Deputy Chief of Naval Operations (Air)
DCNO(D) ... Deputy Chief of Naval Operations (Development)
DCNOFOR ... Deputy Chief of Naval Operations, Fleet Operations and Readiness
DCNO(L) .. Deputy Chief of Naval Operations (Logistics)
DCNO(M & NR) ... Deputy Chief of Naval Operations (Manpower and Naval Reserve)
DCNO(P & P) ... Deputy Chief of Naval Operations (Plans and Policies)
DCNO(P & R) ... Deputy Chief of Naval Operations (Personnel and Naval Reserve)
DCNO(R).. Deputy Chief of Naval Operations (Readiness) [*British*]
DCNP....... Document Change Notice Proposal (MCD)
DCNP....... Donald C. Cook Nuclear Power Plant (NRCH)
DCNPP..... Diablo Canyon Nuclear Power Plant (NRCH)
DCNQ....... Devon and Cornwall. Notes and Queries [*A publication*]
DCNS .... Deputy Chief of Naval Staff [*Marine Corps; also, British Navy*]
DCNS .... Deputy Commander of Naval Services [*Australia*]
DC Nurs Action ... District of Columbia Nursing Action [*A publication*]
DCO........... Covington & Burling, Washington, DC [*OCLC symbol*] (OCLC)
DCO........... Data Center Operations [*Social Security Administration*]
DCO........... Data Collection Order (MCD)
DCO........... Data Control Office (AAG)
DCO........... Debt Collection Order (DCTA)
DCO........... Deco Plantminder [*Vancouver Stock Exchange symbol*]
DCO........... Dehydrated Castor Oil [*Organic chemistry*]
DCO........... Depth Cut Out [*Navy*] (NG)
DCO........... Deputy Censorship Office [*London*] [*World War II*]
DCO........... Deputy Chief Officer [*Australia*]
DCO........... Deputy Chief of Staff, Operations [*NATO*] (NATG)
DCO........... Deputy Commanding Officer
DCO........... Detailed Checkout
DCO........... Development Contract Officer (MUGU)
DCO........... Dial Central Office (MCD)
DCO........... Digital Central Office [*Trademark of the Stromberg-Carlson Corp.*] [*Telecommunications*]
DCO........... Diploma of the College of Optics [*British*] (EY)
DCO........... Direct Clinical Observation [*Psychology*]
DCO........... Director of Combat Operations
DCO........... Director of Combined Operations [*British Army*] [*World War II*]
DCO........... Disaster Control Officer (AAG)
DCO........... District Camouflage Office [*or Officer*]
DCO........... District Clothing Office [*or Officer*]
DCO........... District Communication Officer
DCO........... District Council Office [*British*] (ROG)
DCO........... Division Classification Officer
DCO........... DnC Monthly Survey of Norwegian Trade, Industry, and Finance [*A publication*]
D Co .... Doctor of Cosmology
DCO........... Draft Collection Only [*Business term*]
DCO........... Drawing Change Order (MUGU)
DCO........... Ducommun, Inc. [*AMEX symbol*] (SPSG)
DCO........... Duke of Cambridge's Own [*Military unit*] [*British*]
DCO........... Duke of Connaught's Own [*Military unit*] [*British*]
DCO........... Duty Cypher Officer [*Military*] [*British*]
DCOC....... Drain Cutoff Current
DCOFS..... Deputy Chief of Staff
DCOG....... Diploma of College of Obstetricians and Gynecologists
D & COH... Daughter and Co-Heiress [*Genealogy*]
DCO(I)...... Director of Combined Operations (India)
D-COL...... Double Column (ADA)
D Colo....... United States District Court for the District of Colorado (DLA)
DColU....... Columbia Union College, Takoma Park, MD [*Library symbol*] [*Library of Congress*] (LCLS)
DCOM...... Departmental Coordinating Committee on Ocean Minings [*Canada*]
DCOM...... Dicomed Corp. [*NASDAQ symbol*] (NQ)
DCOM...... Disk Communications Area (CMD)
D Com .... Doctor of Commerce
D Com Adm ... Doctor of Commercial Administration
DCO(ME) ... Director of Combined Operations (Middle East)
DComL...... Doctor of Commercial Law (ADA)
DComm...... Doctor of Commerce
DCOMP.... Data Center Operations Management Plan [*Social Security Administration*]
D Comp L .. Doctor of Comparative Law
D Com Sc... Doctor of Commercial Science

D Conn ...... United States District Court for the District of Connecticut (DLA)
DCOP........ Detailed Checkout Procedures (MCD)
DCOP........ Displays, Controls, and Operation Procedures (NASA)
DCOPA ..... Dichloropropyl Acrylate [*Organic chemistry*]
DCOPO..... Deputy Chief of Personnel Operations (AABC)
DCOPS-A ... Deputy Chief of Operations - Army [*Australia*]
DCOR....... Decor Corp. [*NASDAQ symbol*] (NQ)
DCOR....... Defense Committee on Research [*Air Force*]
D of CORN LI ... Duke of Cornwall's Light Infantry [*Military unit*] [*British*] (ROG)
DCos .... Cosmos Club, Washington, DC [*Library symbol*] [*Library of Congress*] (LCLS)
DCOS .... Data Collection Operating System
DCOS .... Data Communication Output Selector (KSC)
DCOS .... Deputy Chief of Staff (NATG)
DCOS .... Direct Couple Operating System
DCOS .... Downrange Computer Output System (MUGU)
DCOT........ Distant Central Office Transceivers
DCOTFP.... Deputy Commander, Operational Test and Evaluation Force, Pacific [*Navy*]
DCov .... Covington & Burling, Washington, DC [*Library symbol*] [*Library of Congress*] (LCLS)
DCP .... Daily Cumulative Persistence [*Environmental science*]
DCP .... Daniell's Chancery Practice [*A publication*] (DLA)
DCP .... Data Change Proposal
DCP .... Data Collection Plan (MCD)
DCP .... Data Collection Platform [*National Weather Service*] [*Weather satellite system*]
DCP .... Data Communication Processor [*Data processing*] (BUR)
DCP .... Dean and Chapter of St. Paul's [*Anglican Church*] (ROG)
DCP .... Decision Coordinating Paper
DCP .... Defense Concept Paper [*Military*] (RDA)
DCP .... Degree Completion Program [*Army*] (INF)
DCP .... Dental Continuation Pay [*Military*] (AABC)
DCP .... Depot Condemnation Percent (NASA)
DCP .... Depth-Charge Projector
DC(P)........ Deputy Controller (Polaris) [*Navy*] [*British*]
DCP .... Deputy Controller of Property [*World War II*]
DCP .... Desen Computer Industries, Inc. [*Vancouver Stock Exchange symbol*]
DCP .... Design Change Package (IEEE)
DCP .... Design Change Proposal
DCP .... Design Criteria Plan (IEEE)
DCP .... DEU [*Display Electronics Unit*] Control Program [*NASA*] (NASA)
DCP .... Development Concept Paper (MCD)
DCP .... Development Cost Plan (NASA)
DCP .... Dicalcium Phosphate [*Inorganic chemistry*]
DCP .... Dicapryl Phthalate [*Organic chemistry*]
DCP .... Dicetyl Phosphate [*Organic chemistry*]
DCP .... Dichlorophenol [*Organic chemistry*]
DCP .... Dichloropropane [*Pesticide*]
DCP .... Dicumyl Peroxide [*Organic chemistry*]
DCP .... Dicyclopentadiene [*Also, DCPD*] [*Organic chemistry*]
DCP .... Differential Computing Potentiometer
DCP .... Digital Clock Pulse
DCP .... Digital Computer Processor (IEEE)
DCP .... Digital Computer Programming [*Data processing*] (BUR)
DCP .... Dipeptidyl Carboxypeptidase [*An enzyme*]
DCP .... Diploma in Clinical Pathology [*British*]
DCP .... Diploma in Clinical Psychology [*British*]
DCP .... Direct Current Panel
DCP .... Direct-Current Plasma [*Spectrometry*]
DCP .... Director of Civilian Personnel [*Navy*]
DCP .... Disaster Control Plan (AFM)
DCP .... Discrete Component Part
DCP .... Display Control Panel
DCP .... Distributed Communications Processor [*Sperry UNIVAC*]
DCP .... Distribution Common Point [*Telecommunications*] (TEL)
DCP .... District Community Physician
DCP .... Division de Chimie Physique [*Division of Physical Chemistry - DPC*] (EAIO)
DCP .... Doctor of City Planning
DCP .... Doctor in Clinical Pathology
DCP .... Donald C. Cook Plant [*Nuclear energy*] (NRCH)
DCP .... Drill Cluster Plate (MCD)
DCP .... Dynamic Compression-Plate
DCP .... Freight or Carriage Paid To _____ [*"INCOTERM," International Chamber of Commerce official code*]
DCP .... United States Patent Office, Washington, DC [*OCLC symbol*] (OCLC)
DCPA .... Defense Civil Preparedness Agency [*FEMA*] [*Washington, DC*]
DCPA .... Dichloropropionanilide [*Also, DPA*] [*Herbicide*]
DCPA .... Dimethyl Tetrachloroterephthalate [*Herbicide*]
DCPANDP .. Deputy Chief of Staff, Plans and Policy [*NATO*] (NATG)
DC Path ..... Diploma of the College of Pathologists [*British*]
DCPB........ Departmental Civilian Personnel Branch
DC-PBH ... Double-Channel Planar Buried Heterostructure
DCPC........ Dichlorodiphenylmethylcarbinol [*Also, DMC*] [*Insecticide*]

DCPC........ Division of Cancer Prevention and Control [*National Cancer Institute*]
DCPCM..... Differentially Coherent Pulse Code Modulation
DCPD........ Dicalcium Phosphate Dihydrate [*Inorganic chemistry*]
DCPD........ Dicyclopentadiene [*Also, DCP*] [*Organic chemistry*]
DCPE........ Documentacion y Comunicacion Publicitaria Espanola [*Database*] [*Universidad Complutense de Madrid*] [*Spanish*] [*Information service or system*] (CRD)
DCPEI....... DEU [*Display Electronics Unit*] Control Program End Item [*NASA*] (NASA)
DCPERS-A ... Deputy Chief of Personnel - Army [*Australia*]
DCPG........ Defense Communications Planning Group (KSC)
DCPG........ Digital Clock Pulse Generator
DCPI........ Deputy Chief Patrol Inspector [*Immigration and Naturalization Service*]
DCPI........ Dichlorophenolindophenol [*Also, DCIP, DCPIP, DPIP*] [*Analytical reagent*]
DCPI........ Dick Clark Productions, Inc. [*NASDAQ symbol*] (NQ)
DCPIP....... Dichlorophenolindophenol [*Also, DCIP, DCPI, DPIP*] [*Analytical reagent*]
DCPL........ Distributed Control Programming Language [*Data processing*] (CSR)
DCPL........ District of Columbia Public Library
DCP-LA..... Direct-Current Plasma-LASER Ablation
DCPLS...... Data Collection and Platform Location System [*National Weather Service*] [*Weather satellite system*] (NOAA)
DCPMAS.. Double Cross-Polarization, Magic Angle Spinning [*Spectroscopy*]
DCPMU.... (Dichlorophenyl)methylurea [*Organic chemistry*]
DCPO........ Deputy Chief Political Officer [*British Military Administration*]
DCPO........ Deputy Chief of Staff, Personnel and Organization [*NATO*] (NATG)
DCPO........ Deputy Chief of Staff, Plans and Operations (MCD)
DCPO........ District Civilian Personnel Office [*or Officer*]
DCPO........ DSA [*Defense Supply Agency*] Civil Preparedness Office
DCPolaris.. Deputy Controller (Polaris) [*Navy*] [*British*]
DCPP........ Data Communication Preprocessor
DCPR........ Defense Contractor Planning Report
DCPR........ Deputy Chief of Staff for Plans and Research
DCPRS...... Data Collection Platform Radio Sets [*National Weather Service*] [*Weather satellite system*] (NOAA)
DCPS........ Data Communication Processing System
DCPS........ Data Control Panel Submodule
DCPS........ Digitally Controlled Power Source (IEEE)
DCPS........ Dynamic Crew Procedures Simulator
DCPSK...... Differential Coherent Phase Shift Keyed [*System*] [*Data processing*]
DCPSP...... Direct-Current Power Supply Panel (AAG)
DCPT........ Direct-Current Plasma Torch
DCPT........ Doctor of Chiropractic and Physiological Therapeutics
DCPTA...... (Dichlorophenoxy)triethylamine [*Herbicide*]
DCPY........ Datacopy Corp. [*NASDAQ symbol*] (NQ)
DCQM...... Deputy Chief Quartermaster
DCQM...... Digital Circuit Quality Monitor [*Data processing*]
DCR........ Dacro-Cysto-Rhinostomy [*Medicine*]
DCR........ Daily Communication Report
DC/R........ Data Collection/Relay (MCD)
DCR........ Data Conversion Receiver [*Data processing*]
DCR........ Data Coordinator and Retriever [*Data processing*]
DCR........ Decatur, IN [*Location identifier*] [*FAA*] (FAAL)
DCR........ Decision Circuit Reception
DCR........ Decoration (AABC)
DCR........ Decrease (KSC)
DCR........ Degree of Cell Rupture
DCR........ Dental Corps, General Service [*USNR officer designation*]
DCR........ Design Certification Review [*NASA*] (KSC)
DCR........ Design Change Recommendation [*or Request*]
DCR........ Design Characteristic Review (AAG)
DCR........ Design Concern Report (NASA)
DCR........ Destruct Command Receiver (KSC)
DCR........ Detail Condition Register
DCR........ Development Council for Research (MUGU)
DCR........ Developments in Cancer Research [*Elsevier Book Series*] [*A publication*]
DCR........ Dewar Cryogenic Refrigerator
DCR........ Differential Correlation Radiometer (MCD)
DCR........ Digital Cassette Recorder
DCR........ Digital Coded RADAR
DCR........ Digital Concentration Readout [*Data processing*]
DCR........ Digital Conversion Receiver
DCR........ Direct Conversion Reactor
DCR........ Direct Cortical Response
DCR........ Direct-Current Restorer
DCR........ District Chief Ranger [*Ancient Order of Foresters*]
DCR........ District Chief Ruler [*Australia*]
DCR........ District Court Reports [*A publication*] (APTA)
DCR........ Division of Computer Research [*Formerly, OCA*] [*National Science Foundation*]
DCR........ Doctor of Comparative Religion
D Cr........ Doctor of Criminology
DCR........ Document Change Record (NASA)

DCR........ Dominant Control Region [*Genetics*]
DCR........ Drawing Change Request
DCR........ Drawing Copy Request (MCD)
DCR........ Drayage Carriers Inc., Fort Wayne IN [*STAC*]
DCR........ Dual Channel Radiometer
DCR........ Dual Channel Receiver (MCD)
DCR........ Dual Cycle Rifle
DCR........ Plane Things, Inc. [*Tampa, FL*] [*FAA designator*] (FAAC)
DCRA...... DCASR [*Defense Contract Administration Services Region*], Atlanta
DCRA...... Dominion of Canada Rifle Association
DCRA........ Dry Crease Recovery Angle [*Textile technology*]
DCRABS.. Disk Copy Restore and Backup System
DCRB...... DCASR [*Defense Contract Administration Services Region*], Boston
DCRB...... Design Change Review Board
DCRB...... Drawn Cup Roller Bearing
DCRC...... DCASR [*Defense Contract Administration Services Region*], San Francisco
DCRCH..... Duke of Connaught's Royal Canadian Hussars [*British military*] (DMA)
DCRD........ DCASR [*Defense Contract Administration Services Region*], Detroit
DCRDR.... Detailed Control Room Design Review [*Nuclear energy*] (NRCH)
DCRE........ Deputy Commandant Royal Engineers [*British*]
DC Reg...... District of Columbia Register [*A publication*]
DCREO..... Design Change Request Engineering Order
DCRF........ Die Casting Research Foundation (EA)
DCRI........ DCASR [*Defense Contract Administration Services Region*], Chicago
DCRK........ Democratic Confederate Republic of Koryo [*Reunified Korean state*] [*Proposed*]
DCRL........ DCASR [*Defense Contract Administration Services Region*], Los Angeles
DCR MU ... Diploma of the College of Radiographers in Medical Ultra Sound [*British*] (DBQ)
DCRN........ Dashpot Cup Retention Nut [*Nuclear energy*] (NRCH)
DCRN........ DCASR [*Defense Contract Administration Services Region*], New York
DCR (NSW) ... District Court Reports (New South Wales) [*A publication*] (APTA)
DCRO........ DCASR [*Defense Contract Administration Services Region*], Cleveland
DCRO........ District Civil Readjustment Office [*or Officer*]
DCRP........ DCASR [*Defense Contract Administration Services Region*], Philadelphia
DCRP........ Department of City and Regional Planning [*MIT*] (MCD)
DCRP........ Design Controlled Repair Parts (MCD)
DCRP........ Developmental Cycle Research Plan
DCRP........ Disaster Control Recovery Plan
DCR & Regs ... District of Columbia Rules and Regulations [*A publication*] (DLA)
DCR RNI... Diploma of the College of Radiographers in Radionuclide Imaging [*British*] (DBQ)
DCRS........ Data Collection and Reduction System
DCRS........ DCASR [*Defense Contract Administration Services Region*], St. Louis
D-CRS....... Diplomate, American Board of Colon and Rectal Surgery (DHSM)
DCRS........ Document Control Remote Station
DCRSEO... Design Change Request Serial Engineering Order (MCD)
DCRT........ DCASR [*Defense Contract Administration Services Region*], Dallas
DCRT........ Division of Computer Research and Technology [*National Institutes of Health*] [*Bethesda, MD*]
DCRTO..... DSA [*Defense Supply Agency*] Central Regional Telecommunications Office
DCRZ........ Descend to and Cruise [*Aviation*] (FAAC)
DCS........ Dalton Computer Services, Inc. [*Information service or system*] (IID)
DCS........ Damage Control School [*Navy*]
DCS........ Damage Control Suit [*Navy*]
DCS........ Damage Control System (KSC)
DCS........ Data Capture Subsystem (MCD)
DCS........ Data Carrier System [*Teltone Corp.*] [*Kirkland, WA*] (TSSD)
DCS........ Data Collection System [*or Subsystem*] [*Data processing*]
DCS........ Data Communication Services [*Regie des Telegraphes et des Telephones*] [*Brussels, Belgium*] (TSSD)
DCS........ Data Communication System [*or Subsystem*]
DCS........ Data Conditioning System [*NASA*]
DCS........ Data Control Services (BUR)
DCS........ Data Control System [*Burroughs Corp.*] (AAG)
DCS........ Data Conversion System [*Data processing*]
DCS........ Davis Computer Systems, Inc.
DCS........ Deck Cooling System (MCD)
DCS........ Decompression Sickness [*Deep-sea diving*]
DCS........ Defects in Crystalline Solids [*Later, Defects in Solids*] [*Elsevier Book Series*] [*A publication*]
DCS........ Defense Communications System [*DoD*]
DCS........ Defense Construction Service (NATG)

DCS	Deflection Coil Set
DCS	Delayed Coincidence Spectroscopy
DCS	Department of Computer Science [*University of Illinois*] [*Research center*] (RCD)
DCS	Department of Computing Service [*University of Waterloo*] [*Research center*] (RCD)
DCS	Department of Correctional Services (OICC)
DCS	Departure Control System [*IATA*] (DS)
DCS	Deputy Chief of Staff
DC of S......	Deputy Chief of Staff
DCS	Deputy Clerk of Session [*British*]
DCS	Deputy Crown Solicitor (ADA)
DCS	Design Change Schedule
DCS	Design Change Summary (AAG)
DCS	Design Communication System (MCD)
DCS	Design Control Specification (KSC)
DCSN	Design Criteria Specification (NASA)
DCS	Despin Control Subsystem [*Aerospace*]
DCS	Destruct Command System (MUGU)
DCS	Detail Checkout Specifications (MCD)
DCS	Diagnostic Control Store
DCS	Dichlorosilane [*Photovoltaic energy systems*]
DCS	Digital Command System [*or Subsystem*]
DCS	Digital Communication System [*Data processing*]
DCS	Digital Computer System [*Vancouver Stock Exchange symbol*]
DCS	Digital Control Station [*Data processing*]
DCS	Digital Control System
DCS	Digital Countdown System [*Data processing*]
DCS	Digital Cross-Connect System [*Telecommunications*]
DCS	Dimensional Control Standard (MCD)
DCS	Direct Couple System
DCS	Direct-Current Sensor
DCS	Direction Center Standby [*SAGE*] [*RADAR*]
DCS	Director of Clothing and Stores [*Military*] [*British*]
DCS	Director Comptroller Systems (AABC)
DCS	Disadvantaged Children Series [*A publication*]
DCS	Discount Communications Services [*Telecommunications service*] (TSSD)
DCS	Dispatch Critical System (MCD)
DCS	Display and Control Station
D & CS.......	Display and Control Subsystem (NASA)
DCS	Distributed Computer Systems (MDG)
DCS	Distributed Control System [*Engineering*]
DCS	Diversity Combiner System
DCS	Divisional Chief Superintendent [*British police*]
DCS	Doctor of Christian Science
DCS	Doctor of Christian Service
DCS	Doctor of Commercial Science
DCS	Doctrine and Command Systems [*Army*] (RDA)
DCS	Document Control System [*Data processing*]
DCS	Dorsal Column Stimulator [*Pain killer*]
DCS	Double Channel Simplex
DCS	Double Compton Scattering
DCS	Double Cotton Single Silk [*Wire insulation*] (AAG)
DCS	Drawing Change Summary
DCS	Drone Control System [*Military*]
DCS	Dual Checkout Station (MCD)
DCS	United States Civil Service Commission, Washington, DC [*Library symbol*] [*Library of Congress*] (LCLS)
DCS	University of South Carolina, College of Librarianship, Columbia, SC [*OCLC symbol*] (OCLC)
DC of SA....	Deputy Chief of Staff, Army
DCSA.........	Direct-Current Servo Amplifier
DCSADN ..	Defense Communications System Automatic Digital Network [*DoD*]
DC/SAF	Deputy Chief of Staff, Air Force
DCSAIROPNET ...	Defense Communications System Air Operational Network (AFM)
DCSAO	Defense Customer Supply Assistance Office [*DoD*]
DCSAR......	Defense Contract Services Administration Region
DCS/AUTODIN ...	Defense Communications System Automatic Digital Information Network [*DoD*]
DCSC.........	Defense Construction Supply Center [*Defense Supply Agency*]
DCS/C.......	Deputy Chief of Staff, Comptroller
DCSC.........	Digital Card Slave Clock [*Data processing*]
DC Sc.........	Doctor of Commercial Science
DCSCD......	Deputy Chief of Staff for Combat Developments (AABC)
DCSCDC	Developments in Crop Science [*A publication*]
DCSC-E......	Deputy Chief of Staff, Communications-Electronics [*Army*] (AABC)
DCSCI.......	Defense Communications Systems Configuration Items (MCD)
DCSCOMPT ...	Deputy Chief of Staff, Comptroller (AABC)
DCS/D.......	Deputy Chief of Staff, Development
DCSD	Doctrine and Command Systems Directorate [*Army*] (RDA)
DCSDATANET ...	Defense Communications System Data Network (NG)
DCSDOC.....	Deputy Chief of Staff for Doctrine
DC Se.........	Doctor of Commercial Service
DCSFOR....	Deputy Chief of Staff, Force Development (AABC)
DCSG	Data Computation Subsystem Group
DCSG	David Cassidy Support Group (EA)
DCSH	Department of Community Services and Health [*Australia*]

DCS & H....	Department of Community Services and Health [*Australia*]
DCSHJ......	Daughters of Charity of the Sacred Heart of Jesus [*See also FCSCJ*] [*Vihiers, France*] (EAIO)
DCSI.........	Data and Control Signal Interface (NASA)
DCSI.........	Deputy Chief of Staff for Intelligence [*Army*] (AABC)
DCSI.........	Distributed Computer Systems [*NASDAQ symbol*] (NQ)
DCSIM......	Deputy Chief of Staff for Information Management [*Army*]
DCS/INT ..	Deputy Chief of Staff, Intelligence [*Air Force*] (MCD)
DCSL	Deputy Chief of Staff, Logistics [*Army*] (KSC)
DCSLAM..	Development of a Corps Logistics Analysis Methodology
DCSLOG...	Deputy Chief of Staff, Logistics [*Army*]
DCSM	Deputy Chief of Staff, Materiel
DCSMG	Deputy Chief of Staff for Military Government [*World War II*]
DCSMIS...	Deputy Chief of Staff, Management Information Systems (AABC)
DC/SMO...	Deputy Chief of Staff, Military Operations [*Army*]
DCSN	Decision Systems, Inc. [*NASDAQ symbol*] (NQ)
DCSO	Defense Communications System Organization
DCSO	Deputy Chief Scientific Officer [*British*]
DCSO	Deputy Chief Signal Officer [*British military*] (DMA)
DCSO	Deputy Chief of Staff, Operations
DCSO	DSA [*Defense Supply Agency*] Command Security Support Office
DCSOA	Deputy Chief of Staff, Operations and Administration
DCSOC.....	Defense Communications System Operations Center (RDA)
DCSOI.......	Deputy Chief of Staff for Operations and Intelligence (AABC)
DCSOPS ..	Deputy Chief of Staff for Operations [*Army*]
DCSOPS ..	Deputy Chief of Staff for Operations and Plans [*Army*]
DCSO & T ..	Deputy Chief of Staff, Operations and Training (AABC)
DCSP........	Defense Communications Satellite Project [*or Program*]
DCS/P.......	Deputy Chief of Staff, Personnel
DCSP........	Digital Control Signal Processor (NASA)
DCSPA	Deputy Chief of Staff, Personnel and Administration (AABC)
DCSPAL....	Deputy Chief of Staff for Personnel, Administration, and Logistics
DCS/PEAB ...	Defense Communications System - Personnel Emergency Actions Book
DCSPER....	Deputy Chief of Staff, Personnel [*Army*]
DCS/P & O ...	Deputy Chief of Staff for Plans and Operations (AFM)
DCS/P & P ...	Deputy Chief of Staff for Plans and Programs
DCSPR......	Deputy Chief of Staff for Plans and Research [*Army*]
DCS/P & R ...	Deputy Chief of Staff for Programs and Resources (AFM)
DCSR........	Da Capo Senza Replica [*From the Beginning, Playing Only Once the Parts Marked with Repeats*] [*Music*]
DC/SR......	Display and Control/Storage and Retrieval
DCSR........	Dominican College of San Rafael [*California*]
DCS/RC.....	Deputy Chief of Staff, Reserve Components [*Army*]
DCSR & D ..	Deputy Chief of Staff, Research and Development [*Army*]
DCSRDA...	Deputy Chief of Staff for Research, Development, and Acquisition [*Army*]
DCSRM.....	Deputy Chief of Staff for Resource Management (AABC)
DCSROTC ..	Deputy Chief of Staff for Reserve Officers' Training Corps (AABC)
DCS/R & T ...	Deputy Chief of Staff, Research and Technology
DCSS	Damage Control Suit System [*Navy*]
DCSS.........	Defense Communications Satellite System [*Telecommunications*] (TEL)
DCSS.........	Digital Communications Satellite Subsystem (MCD)
DCS/S & L ...	Deputy Chief of Staff, Systems and Logistics
DCST........	Deputy Chief of Staff for Training [*Army*]
DCST........	Digital Card Schmitt Trigger [*Data processing*]
DCST........	Dynamic Combat System Test [*Military*] (CAAL)
DC Stat	District of Columbia Statutes at Large [*A publication*]
DCSTS	Deputy Chief of Staff for Training and Schools (AABC)
DCSTTYNET ...	Defense Communications System Teletype Network (AFM)
DCSU	Differential Corrected Spectral Unit [*Spectrometry*]
DCSU	Digital Computer Switching Unit (MCD)
DCT	Damage Control Texts [*Naval Ship Systems Command*]
DCT	Data Communications Terminal
DCT	Data Conversion Transmitter [*Data processing*]
DCT	Deaf Communicating Terminal [*Telephone for the deaf*]
DCT	Decimal Code Translator
DCT	Department of Classroom Teachers [*of NEA*] (EA)
DCT	Depth-Charge Thrower
DCT	Depth-Charges Track
DCT	Depth Control Tank
DCT	Deputy Commissioner of Taxation [*Australia*]
DC & T.......	Detection, Classification, and Targeting
DCT	Detection, Classification, and Targeting [*or Tracking*] (MCD)
DCT	Device Characteristics Table [*Data processing*] (IBMDP)
DCT	Digital Communications Terminal (MCD)
DCT	Dihydrotestosterone, Corticosterone, and Thyroxine [*Endocrinology*]
DCT	Diode Curve Tracer
DCT	Direct [*In relation to flight plan clearances and type of approach*] [*Aviation*]
DCT	Direct Carbon Transfer
DCT	Direct Coombs' Test [*Medicine*]
DCT	Director, Control Tower [*British military*] (DMA)
DCT	Disaster Control Team (AFM)

DCT	Discrete Cosine Transform [*Telecommunications*]
DCT	Dissector Camera Tube
DCT	Distal Convoluted Tubule [*Nephrology*]
D Ct	District Court [*Usually federal*] (DLA)
DCT	Diversified Computer Technology, Inc. (MCD)
DCT	Docked Configuration Transfer (MCD)
D & CT	Docking and Crew Transfer [*Aerospace*]
DCT	Doctor of Christian Theology
DCT	Doctor of Christian Training
DCT	Document (ADA)
DCT	Dodrill, Charles T., Hurricane WV [*STAC*]
DCT	Doklady Chemical Technology
DCT	DSS [*Deep Space Station*] Communications Terminal Subsystem
DCT	NAVSHIPS [*Naval Ship Systems Command*] Damage Control Texts
D Ct	Selected Judgments of the Divisional Courts [*Ghana*] [*A publication*] (DLA)
DCTA	Diaminocyclohexanetetraacetic Acid [*Also, OCTA*] [*Organic chemistry*]
DCTAF	(Dichlorotriazinyl)aminofluorescein [*Also, DTAF*] [*Analytical biochemistry*]
DCTB	Data Communications Testing Branch [*Social Security Administration*]
DCTC	Dependent Care Tax Credit
DCTC	Digital Centroid Terminal Correlation
DCTC	District of Columbia Teachers College [*Later, University of the District of Columbia*]
DCTG	Dihydrotestosterone, Corticosterone, Thyroxine, and Growth Hormone [*Endocrinology*]
DCTL	Direct-Coupled Transistor Logic
DCTL	Docutel/Olivetti Corp. [*NASDAQ symbol*] (NQ)
DCTLC	Direct-Coupling Transistor Logic Circuit
DCTM	Direct-Current Torque Motor
DCTMA	Desoxycorticosterone Trimethylacetate [*Endocrinology*]
DCTP	Deoxycytidinetriphosphate [*Organic chemistry*]
DCTP	Duct Type
dCTPase	Deoxycytidinetriphosphatase [*An enzyme*]
DCTR	DC Trading & Development [*NASDAQ symbol*] (NQ)
DCTR	Division of Controlled Thermonuclear Research [*Energy Research and Development Administration*]
DCTS	Digital Coordinate Transformation System
DC & TSC	Defense Clothing and Textile Supply Center [*Later, Defense Personnel Support Center*] [*DoD*]
DCTSC	Defense Clothing and Textile Supply Center [*Later, Defense Personnel Support Center*] [*DoD*]
DCTT	Division Contract Termination Team (AAG)
DCTV	Digital Color Television
DCU	Catholic University of America, Washington, DC [*Library symbol*] [*Library of Congress*] (LCLS)
DCU	Data Collection Unit
DCU	Data Command Unit (MCD)
DCU	Data Communications Unit
DCU	Data Communications Utility [*Social Security Administration*]
DCU	Data Control Unit
DCU	Decade Counting Unit
DCU	Decatur, AL [*Location identifier*] [*FAA*] (FAAL)
DCU	Decimal Counting Unit
DCU	Deer Creek Reservoir [*Utah*] [*Seismograph station code, US Geological Survey*] (SEIS)
DCU	Detection and Control Unit (MCD)
DCU	Device Control Unit
DCU	Digital Coefficient Unit [*Data processing*] (RDA)
DCU	Digital Computer Unit (MCD)
DCU	Digital Control Unit (KSC)
DCU	Digital Counting Unit
DCU	Disbandment Control Unit [*Allied Military Government of Occupied Territory*] [*Post-World War II*]
DCU	Discrete Control Unit [*American Solenoid Co.*] [*Somerset, NJ*]
DCU	Dispenser Control Unit (RDA)
DCU	Display and Control Unit (CET)
DCU	Distribution Control Unit
dcu	District of Columbia [*MARC country of publication code*] [*Library of Congress*] (LCCP)
DCU	Drum Control Unit (AABC)
DCU	Dynamic Checkout Unit [*Aerospace*] (AAG)
DCUA	Division of College and University Assistance [*HEW*]
DCU-C	Catholic University of America, Clementine Library, Washington, DC [*Library symbol*] [*Library of Congress*] (LCLS)
DCUC	Defense Credit Union Council (EA)
DCU-H	Catholic University of America, Hyvernat Collection, Washington, DC [*Library symbol*] [*Library of Congress*] (LCLS)
DCU-IA	Catholic University of America, Ibero-American Collection, Washington, DC [*Library symbol*] [*Library of Congress*] (LCLS)
DC (UN)	Disarmament Commission of the United Nations [*Also, DC, UNDC*]
DCU-R	Data Control Unit-Receiver (MCD)
DCUTL	Direct-Coupled Unipolar Transistor Logic

DCV	Dacarbazine, CCNU [*Lomustine*], Vincristine [*Antineoplastic drug regimen*]
DCV	Dense-Cored Vesicles [*Anatomy*]
DCV	Derivative Cyclic Voltammetry [*Analytical electrochemistry*]
DCV	Design Change Verification
DCV	Direct-Current Volts
DCV	Directional Control Valve
DCV	Double-Check Valve
DCV	Double Cotton Varnish [*Wire insulation*] (AAG)
DCVC	Dichlorovinylcysteine [*Biochemistry*]
DCVG	Dichlorovinylglutathione [*Biochemistry*]
DCVG	Digital Control and Vector Generator
DCVO	Dame Commander of the Royal Victorian Order [*British*]
DCVR	Direct-Current Voltage Reference
DCVR	Direct-Current Voltage Regulator
D/CVR	Dust Cover [*Automotive engineering*]
DCW	Data Control Word (CMD)
DCW	Dean and Chapter of Westminster [*Anglican Church*] (ROG)
DCW	Define Constant with Wordmark
DCW	Digital Chart of the World [*Database*] [*Army*]
DCW	National Society, Daughters of Colonial Wars
DCWO	Design Change Work Order
DCWOS	Deaerating Cold Weather Oil System
DCWS	Division of Church World Service [*Later, CWSW*] (EA)
DCWV	Direct-Current Working Volts
DCX	Device Control Character [*Data processing*] (CMD)
DCX	Digital Equipment Corp., Colorado Springs, Colorado Springs, CO [*OCLC symbol*] (OCLC)
DCX	Direct-Current Experiments [*Nuclear energy*] (NRCH)
DCX	Double-Charge Exchange
DCx	Double Convex
DCX	Miami, FL [*Location identifier*] [*FAA*] (FAAL)
DCXI	DCX, Inc. [*NASDAQ symbol*] (NQ)
DCY	Dicon Systems Ltd. [*Toronto Stock Exchange symbol*]
DCY	Discount Corp. of New York [*NYSE symbol*] (SPSG)
DCY	Washington, IN [*Location identifier*] [*FAA*] (FAAL)
DCYRA	Duster Class Yacht Racing Association (EA)
DCZ	Dichloro Analog of Zomepirac [*Biochemistry*]
DCZ	Die Cast Zinc
DD	Associate Directorate for Design [*Kennedy Space Center*] [*NASA*] (NASA)
DD	Association Internationale: Donnees pour le Developpement [*Data for Development International Association - DFD*] (EA)
DD	Bayu Indonesia Air Pt. [*Indonesia*] [*ICAO designator*] (FAAC)
DD	Daily Double [*Horse racing*]
DD	Dance and Dancers [*A publication*]
DD	Dangerous Defective [*British*]
DD	Dangerous Drugs [*British*]
DD	Data Definition [*Data processing*] (BUR)
DD	Data Demand
DD	Data Depository (MCD)
DD	Data Description (MCD)
DD	Data Dictionary [*Data processing*]
DD	Data Display (NASA)
DD	Data Division [*Data processing*]
D/D	Date of Draft [*Business term*]
D/D	Dated
DD	Days after Date [*Business term*]
DD	Day's Date
DD	Days after Delivery
DD	Dayton Development Corp. [*Vancouver Stock Exchange symbol*]
DD	De Dato [*Of Today's Date*] [*Latin*]
DD	De Die [*Daily*] [*Pharmacy*]
DD	Deadline Date
DD	Death from Disease [*Military*]
D & D	Death and Dying [*Medical course*]
DD	Decimal Display
DD	Decimal Divide
DD	Declaration Date [*of dividend payment*] [*Investment term*]
DD	Decoder Driver (MCD)
D & D	Decontaminate and Decommission [*Nuclear energy*]
D & D	Decoration and Design [*Building*] [*New York City*]
DD	Dederunt [*They Gave*] [*Latin*]
DD	Dedicated Displays (MCD)
DD	Dedit [*or Dedicavit*] [*Gave, Dedicated*] [*Latin*]
DD	Deep-Drawn [*Metals*]
DD	Defense Department [*US government*] (MCD)
DD	Defense Depot [*DoD*]
DD	Deferred Delivery [*Especially, of securities*]
DD	Definitely Dull [*Medicine*]
D & D	Degaussing and Deperming [*Navy*]
DD	Degree Days
DD	Degree of Difficulty [*Diving*]
DD	Delay Driver (MCD)
DD	Delayed Delivery [*Especially, of Securities*]
D/D	Deletions/Deferments [*Military*]
DD	Delivered
DD	Delivered at Docks
DD	Demand Draft [*Business term*]

DD .... Deo Dedit [*He Gave to God*] [*Latin*]
DD .... Department of Defense
DD .... Departure Date
DD .... Dependent Drainage [*Medicine*]
D & D....... Deposit and Difference [*Tea trade*]   (ROG)
DD .... Deputy Director
DD .... Design Deviation [*Aerospace*]   (AAG)
DD .... Designator Detector   (MCD)
D & D....... Desk and Derrick [*Oil industry*]
DD .... Desmethyldiazepam [*Biochemistry*]
DD .... Destination/Destination [*Inspection/Acceptance point*]   (MCD)
DD .... Destroyer [*Navy symbol*]
DD .... Destructive Dilemma [*Rule of inference*] [*Logic*]
DD .... Determination of Dependency
DD .... Detur Ad [*Let It Be Given To*] [*Pharmacy*]
D-D .... Deuterium-Deuterium Reaction [*Nuclear energy*]   (NRCH)
DD .... Deutsche Dialektgeographie [*A publication*]
DD .... Developer Demonstrator
DD .... Developer's Digest [*Australia*] [*A publication*]
DD .... Development Digest [*A publication*]
DD .... Development Directive
DD .... Developmental Disability [*Medicine*]
DD .... Deviation Difficulty [*Aerospace*]   (AAG)
D & D....... Devonshire and Dorset Regiment [*British military*]   (DMA)
DD .... Dewey Decimal Number [*Online database field identifier*]
DD .... Dichloropropene-Dichloropropane [*Pesticide*]
DD .... Diesel Direct   (MSA)
DD .... Differential Diagnosis [*Medicine*]
DD .... Differential Doppler
DD .... Diffusion Destainer [*Electrophoresis*]
DD .... Digital Data   (CET)
D-to-D ..... Digital-to-Digital
DD .... Digital Display
DD .... Dignissimo [*Most Dignified*] [*Portuguese*] [*Correspondence*]
DD .... Dionicko Drustvo [*Joint-Stock Company*] [*Yugoslavian*]
D-D .... Diplomate, American Board of Dermatology   (DHSM)
DD .... Direct Debit [*Banking*]
DD .... Direct Development [*Phylogeny*]
DD .... Direct Dialing [*or Dialed*] [*Telecommunications*]   (TEL)
D & D....... Direct and Distribution [*Postal Service*]
DD .... Direct Drive
DD .... Directives Documentation [*NASA*]   (NASA)
D of D...... Director of Dockyards [*Admiralty*] [*British*]
DD .... Disability Determination [*Social Security Administration*]   (OICC)
DD .... Discharged Dead [*On a serviceman's papers*]
DD .... Disconnecting Device   (MSA)
DD .... Discriminating Digit [*Telecommunications*]   (TEL)
DD .... Discrimination Difficulty [*Psychometrics*]
DD .... Dishonorable Discharge
dd .... Disk Diameter [*Ophthalmology*]
DD .... Diskussion Deutsch [*A publication*]
DD .... Display Driver
DD .... District Director
DD .... Divinitatis Doctor [*Doctor of Divinity*] [*Latin*]
DD .... Dockyard Department [*Navy*] [*British*]
D en D...... Docteur en Droit [*Doctor of Law*] [*French*]
DD .... Doctor Divinitatis [*Doctor of Divinity*] [*Latin*]
DD .... Doctor of Divinity in Metaphysics
D/D........... Documentary Draft   (ADA)
DD .... Dogs for the Deaf   (EA)
DD .... Domestic Duties   (ADA)
D/D........... Donation on Discharge
DD .... Donum Dedit [*Gave, Dedicated*] [*Latin*]
DD .... Double Dacron Braid Lacquered   (MDG)
DD .... Double Dark [*Photography*]   (ROG)
DD .... Double Deck
DD .... Double Density
DD .... Double Diamond   (MSA)
DD .... Double Diffusion [*Test*]
DD .... Double Diode
DD .... Double-Dipper [*Retired military-government employee*]
DD .... Double Dominance [*Ethology*]
DD .... Double Draft [*Banking*]   (ROG)
DD .... Double Drift [*As used in a navigator's log*]
DD .... Doubled
DD .... Drama Desk   (EA)
DD .... Drawing Deviation   (MCD)
DD .... Drop Dead
DD .... Drug Discrimination [*Psychopharmacology*]
DD .... Drum Demand
D & D....... Drunk and Dirty [*Military*]
D & D....... Drunk and Disorderly
DD .... Dry Days [*Ecology*]
DD .... Dry Dressing [*Medicine*]
DD .... Drydock
DD .... Du Pont [*E. I.*] De Nemours & Co., Inc. [*NYSE symbol*]   (SPSG)
DD .... Due Date
D & D....... Dungeons and Dragons [*Game*]

DD .... Duplex-Drive [*Amphibious tank*]
DD .... Dutch Door [*Technical drawings*]
DD .... Duty Driver [*Military*]
DD .... Dynein Defective Cilia [*Medicine*]
DD .... German Democratic Republic [*ANSI two-letter standard code*]   (CNC)
Dd .... Response to Very Small Detail [*Rorschach*] [*Also written dd*] [*Psychology*]
DD1 .... First Development Decade [*Ten-year plan designed to bring about self-sufficiency in developing countries*] [*United Nations*]
DD2 .... Second Development Decade [*Ten-year plan designed to bring about self-sufficiency in developing countries*] [*United Nations*]
DDA.......... Dallas, TX [*Location identifier*] [*FAA*]   (FAAL)
DDA.......... Dangerous Drugs Act [*British*]
DDA.......... Demand Deposit Accounting [*Banking*]   (MDG)
DDA.......... Dental Dealers of America   (EA)
DD & A...... Depreciation, Depletion, and Amortization
DDA.......... Depth-Duration-Area
DDA.......... Deputy Director for Administration [*National Security Agency*]
DDA.......... Deputy Director of Armaments [*British*]
DDA.......... Designated Deployment Area
DDA.......... Designated Development Agency   (MCD)
DDA.......... Detroit Diesel Allison Division [*of General Motors Corp.*]
DDA.......... Development Display Assembly
ddA............ Dideoxyadenosine [*Biochemistry*] [*Medicine*]
DDA.......... Diemakers and Diecutters Association [*Later, NADD*]   (EA)
DDA.......... Digital Dealers Association   (EA)
DDA.......... Digital Differential Analyzer [*Algorithm*] [*Data processing*]
DDA.......... Digital Directory Assistance, Inc. [*Information service or system*]   (EISS)
DDA.......... Digital Display Alarm
DDA.......... Digital Drive Amplifier   (AABC)
DDA.......... Digitally Directed Analog   (MSA)
DDA.......... Direct Data Attachment
DDA.......... Direct Disk Attachment
DDA.......... Directed Duty Assignment [*Military*]   (AFM)
DDA.......... Disabled Drivers' Association [*British*]
DDA.......... Discrete Dipole Approximation [*Physics*]
DDA.......... Display and Decision Area
DDA.......... Dividend Disbursing Agent   (DLA)
DDA.......... Division of Drug Advertising [*FDA*]
DDA.......... Doctor of Dramatic Art
DDA.......... Dr. Dvorkovitz & Associates [*Information service or system*]   (IID)
DDA.......... Dodecenyl Acetate [*Pheromone*] [*Organic chemistry*]
DDA.......... Dodecyldimethylamine [*or Dimethyldodecylamine*] [*Organic chemistry*]
DDA.......... Dominica Democratic Alliance [*Political party*]   (PPW)
DDA.......... Drawing Departure Authorization   (KSC)
DDA.......... Duty Deferment Account [*Customs*]   (DS)
DDA.......... Duty Deposit Account [*Customs*]   (DS)
DDA.......... Dynamic Demand Assignment [*Army*]   (MCD)
DDA.......... Dynamics Differential Analyzer   (IEEE)
DDA.......... ICD [*Interface Control Document*] Departure Authorization [*NASA*]   (NASA)
DDAD........ Detroit Diesel Allison Division [*of General Motors Corp.*]
DDAFP..... Diesel-Driven Auxiliary Feed Water Pump   (IEEE)
DDALV..... Days Delay Enroute Authorized Chargeable as Leave [*Military*]
DDALVAHP ... Days Delay at Address within CONUS [*Continental United States*] Authorized Chargeable as Leave [*Military*]
DDAM....... Dynamic Design Analysis Method [*Navy*]
DDANS ..... Deputy Director of Army Nursing Services [*British military*]   (DMA)
DDAP........ Deutsche Demokratische Arbeiterpartei [*German Democratic Workers' Party*] [*Federal Republic of Germany*] [*Political party*]   (PPW)
DDAPS..... Digital Data Acquisition and Processing System
DDAR....... Division of Defense Aid Reports [*Abolished, 1941*] [*Military*]
DDAS........ Dedicated Demand Assignment Signaling   (MCD)
DDAS .... Design of Data Acquisition Subsystem   (NOAA)
DDAS .... Digital Data Acquisition System
DDAS .... Digital Data Archives System
DDAS (ET) ... Deputy Director of Armament Supply (Eastern Theater)
DDAT........ Diagonal Data Corp. [*NASDAQ symbol*]   (NQ)
DDATS...... Deputy Director, Auxiliary Territorial Service [*British military*]   (DMA)
DDAU........ Doctoral Dissertations Accepted by American Universities [*A bibliographic publication*]
DDAVP..... Deamino-D-arginine Vasopressin [*Antidiuretic*]
DDB.......... Colorado State Publications Depository and Distribution Center, Denver, CO [*OCLC symbol*]   (OCLC)
DDB.......... Data Display Board
DDB.......... Data Display Buffer
DDB.......... Der Deutsche Beamte [*A publication*]
DDB.......... Design Data Book
DDB.......... Dial Drive Belt
DDB.......... Digital Data Buffer
DDB.......... Digital Database   (MCD)
DDB.......... Distributed Database

DdB............ Distrito de Braga [*A publication*]
DDB........... Division of Drug Biology [*Department of Health and Human Services*] (GRD)
DDB........... Dodecylbenzene [*Organic chemistry*]
DDB........... Don't Ditch a Buddy [*Promise made by members of the Junior Woodchucks, organization to which comic strip character Donald Duck's nephews belonged*]
DDB........... Dortmund Data Bank [*University of Dortmund*] [*Federal Republic of Germany*] [*Information service or system*] (IID)
DDB........... Double Declining Balance [*Depreciation method*] [*Accounting*]
DDB........... Doyle Dane Bernbach, Inc. [*Advertising agency*]
DDBA......... Dutch Dairy Bureau (EA)
DDBA......... Digioxigenin(dibromoacetate) [*Biochemistry*]
DDBDBFC ... Dave Durham and the Bull Durham Band Fan Club (EA)
DDBF........ Damaged DNA [*Deoxyribonucleic Acid*] Binding Factor [*Biochemistry*]
DDBJ......... DNA [*Deoxyribonucleic Acid*] Data Bank of Japan
DDBMS..... Distributed Database Management System [*Data processing*]
DDBOps.... Deputy Director of Bomber Operations [*Air Ministry*] [*British*] [*World War II*]
DDBP........ Dance Data Bank Project [*University of California*] [*Los Angeles*] [*Information service or system*] (IID)
DDBS........ Descriptor Database System
DDBS........ Dodecyl Benzenesulfonate [*Organic chemistry*]
DDBSA...... Dodecylbenzenesulfonic Acid [*Organic chemistry*]
DDBTP...... Digital Database Transformation Program (MCD)
DDC........... Corvette [*Navy symbol*] [*Obsolete*]
DDC........... Dangerous Drug Cabinet [*Lockable auxiliary to bathroom medicine chest*]
DDC........... Data Display Central
DDC........... Data Display Controller
DDC........... Data Distribution Center
DDC........... Data Documentation Costs
DDC........... Date Due Calibration [*Military*] (AFIT)
DDC........... Decision, Design, and the Computer [*Symposium*]
DDC........... Deck Decompression Chamber [*Undersea technology*]
DDC........... Defense Documentation Center [*for Scientific and Technical Information*] [*Later, DTIC*] [*Alexandria, VA*]
DDC........... Defensive Driving Course [*National Safety Council*]
DDC........... Departmental Data Coordinator (MCD)
DDC........... Designed Data [*Vancouver Stock Exchange symbol*]
DDC........... Detroit Data Center [*IRS*]
DDC........... Developmental Disability Center [*Columbia University*] [*Research center*] (RCD)
DDC........... Dewey Decimal Classification [*Also, DC*]
DDC........... Diamond Dealers Club (EA)
DDC........... Dicarbethoxydihydrocollidine [*Biochemistry*]
DDC........... Dideoxycytidine [*Biochemistry*]
DDC........... Diethyldithiocarbamate [*Also, DDTC, DEDC*] [*Organic chemistry*]
DDC........... Digital Data Cell (NASA)
DDC........... Digital Data Converter
DDC........... Digital Display Converter (BUR)
DDC........... Digitally Directed Control (MSA)
DDC........... Direct Data Channel
DDC........... Direct Digital Control
DDC........... Direct Drawing Change (AAG)
DDC........... Distributed Digital Control [*Data processing*]
DDC........... District Court, District of Columbia (DLA)
DDC........... Division Data Center [*Army*] (RDA)
DDC........... Division of Drug Chemistry [*Department of Health and Human Services*] (GRD)
DDC........... Docteur en Droit Canonique [*Doctor of Canon Law*] [*French*] (ILCA)
DDC........... Dodge City [*Kansas*] [*Airport symbol*] (OAG)
DDC........... Dominican House of Studies, Immaculate Conception Convent Library, Washington, DC [*Library symbol*] [*Library of Congress*] [*OCLC symbol*] (LCLS)
DDC........... Dopa Decarboxylase [*An enzyme*]
DDC........... Doris Day Collectors (EA)
DDC........... Double-Doped Crystal
D & DC...... Drunk and Disorderly Conduct
DDC........... Dual Diversity Comparator
DDC........... Duration of Disease Control
DDCA........ Defense Communications Agency, Technical Library, Washington, DC [*Library symbol*] [*Library of Congress*] (LCLS)
DDCA........ Deputy Director of Civil Affairs [*War Office*] [*British*] [*World War II*]
DDCA........ Director, Defense Communications Agency (CINC)
DDCAS...... Deputy Director, Contract Administration Services [*DoD*]
DDCASM ... Deputy Director, Contract Administration Services Memorandum [*DoD*]
DDCC........ Decision Data Computer Corporation [*Horsham, PA*] [*NASDAQ symbol*] (NQ)
DDCC........ Developmental Disability Center for Children [*Louisiana State University*] [*Research center*] (RCD)
DDCDM..... Didemethylchlordimeform [*A pesticide*]
DDCE........ Digital Data Conversion Equipment
DDCI......... Douglas Development Company - Irvine [*California*]

DDCMP .... Digital Data Communications Message Protocol [*Digital Equipment Corp.*]
DDCO (I).... Deputy Director of Combined Operations (India)
DDCONUS ... Date Departed Continental United States [*Military*] (AFM)
DDCP........ Department of Defense Claimant Program
DDCP........ Draft Development Concept Paper (RDA)
DDCS........ Data Definition Control System
DD & CS.... Dedicated Display and Control Subsystem (NASA)
DDCS........ Digital Data Calibration System (KSC)
DDCS........ Digital Display and Control Set (MCD)
DDCS........ Direct Digital Control System
DDCS........ Double Differential Cross Section
DDD.......... Comprehensive Dishonesty, Disappearance, and Destruction Policy [*Insurance*]
DDD.......... Dat, Dicat, Dedicat [*He Gives, Devotes, and Dedicates*] [*Latin*]
DD/D......... Data Dictionary/Directory [*Data processing*]
DDD.......... Date Deficiency [*or Discrepancy*] Discovered (MCD)
DD in D...... De Die in Diem [*From Day to Day*] [*Latin*]
DDD.......... Deadline Delivery Date
DDD.......... Debility, Dependency, and Dread [*Factors producing compliance in hostages, prisoners, etc.*]
DDD.......... Degenerative Disc Disease [*Medicine*]
DDD.......... Deputy Director of Design [*British*]
DDD.......... Design Definition Document [*NASA*] (NASA)
DDD.......... Design Disclosure Data
DDD.......... Desired Delivery Date (AFM)
DDD.......... Detailed Data Display
DDD.......... Deutscher Depeschen-Dienst [*Press agency*] [*Federal Republic of Germany*]
DDD.......... Dichlorodibenzodioxin [*Also, DCDD*] [*Organic chemistry*]
DDD.......... Dichlorodiphenyldichloroethane [*Also, TDE*] [*Insecticide*]
DDD.......... Diesel Direct Drive
DDD.......... Digital Data Distributor (CET)
DDD.......... Digital Display Driver (KSC)
DDD.......... Dihydroxydinaphthyl Disulfide [*Analytical chemistry*]
DDD.......... Direct Deposit of Dividends
DDD.......... Direct Distance Dialing [*of telephone numbers for toll calls*]
DDD.......... Display Decoder Drive (MCD)
DDD.......... Domestic Door-to-Door [*Personal property*]
DDD.......... Dono Dedit Dedicavit [*He Gave and Dedicated as a Gift*] [*Latin*]
DDD.......... Duplexed Display Distributor
DDD.......... Dynamic Dummy Director
DDDA........ Decimal Digital Differential Analyzer
DDDA........ Dodecadienyl Acetate [*Pheromone*] [*Organic chemistry*]
DDDA........ Dodecanedioic Acid [*Organic chemistry*]
DDDC........ Didehydrodideoxycytidine [*Antiviral*]
DDDD........ Dignum Deo Donum Dedit [*Latin*] (DLA)
DDDEP...... Defense Development Data Exchange Program (MCD)
DDDI......... Downey Designs International, Inc. [*NASDAQ symbol*] (NQ)
DDDL........ Digital Data Down Link [*Data processing*] (MCD)
DDDM....... Dihydroxydichlorodiphenylmethane [*Fungicide*]
DDDOL..... Dodecandienol [*Pheromone*] [*Organic chemistry*]
DDDP........ Discrete Differential Dynamic Programming [*Data processing*]
DDDRE...... Deputy Director, Defense Research and Engineering [*Army*]
DD/DS....... Data Dictionary/Directory System [*Data processing*]
DDDS........ Deputy Director of Dental Services [*Military*] [*British*]
DDDS........ Dichlorodiphenyl Disulfide [*Insecticide*]
DDDS........ Digital Data Display System
DDDS........ Directorate of Documentation and Drawing Services (MCD)
DDDT........ Didehydrodideoxythymidine [*Antiviral*]
DDDU........ Digital Decoder Driver Unit (MCD)
DDE........... Decentralized Data Entry (IEEE)
DDE........... Deputy Director of Equipment [*Air Force*] [*British*]
DDE........... Dichlorodiphenyldichloroethylene [*Pesticide residue*]
DDE........... Diospyrin Dimethyl Ether [*Biochemistry*]
DDE........... Direct Data Entry [*Data processing*] (BUR)
DDE........... Direct Digital Encoder
DDE........... Director Design Engineering (KSC)
DDE........... Distributed Data Entry
DDE........... Diversified Entertainment [*Vancouver Stock Exchange symbol*]
DDE........... Dual Displacement Engine
DDE........... Dwight David Eisenhower [*US general and president, 1890-1969*]
DDE........... Dynamic Data Exchange [*Message protocol*] [*Data processing*] (BYTE)
DDE........... Escort Destroyer [*Navy symbol*]
DDEC........ Detroit Diesel Electronic [*or Engine*] Control [*Automotive engineering*]
D Dec......... Dix's School Law Decisions [*New York*] [*A publication*] (DLA)
DDEDS..... Defense Disposal Executive Development Seminar [*DoD*]
d de JC...... Despues de Jesucristo [*After Jesus Christ*] [*Spanish*] (GPO)
DDEL........ Defense Development and Engineering Laboratories [*Military*]
DDEL........ Dwight D. Eisenhower Library
D Del......... United States District Court for the District of Delaware (DLA)
DDEOC..... Destroyer Engineered Operating Cycle (MCD)
DDEP........ Defense Development Exchange Program (AFM)
DDEP........ Dicarbethoxy(dimethyl)(ethyl)dihydropyridine [*Biochemistry*]
DDEP........ Double Diffusion Epitaxial Plane
DDEPHS... Dwight D. Eisenhower Philatelic and Historical Society (EA)

DDERS......	Direct Data Entry Replacement System
DDES	Data-Design Laboratories [*NASDAQ symbol*] (NQ)
DDES	Direct Data Entry System
D Des	Doctor of Design
DDESB......	Department of Defense Explosives Safety Board [*Alexandria, VA*]
D Dev Rd ...	Deutsche Devisen-Rundschau [*A publication*]
DDF...........	Defense Department Form (AAG)
DDF...........	Dental Documentary Foundation
DDF...........	Deputy Director for Field Management and Evaluation [*National Security Agency*]
DDF...........	Design Discharge Format
DDF...........	Design Disclosure Formats [*Naval Applied Science Laboratory*]
DDF...........	Dielectric Dissipation Factor
DDF...........	Digital Distribution Frame [*Telecommunications*] (TEL)
DDF...........	Diocesan Development Fund [*Australia*]
DDF...........	Director's Discretionary Fund
DDF...........	Discontinued Depreciation Function
DDF...........	Dominion Drama Festival [*Canada*]
DDF...........	Double Defruit [*Aviation*] (FAAC)
DDF...........	Downtown Development Foundation [*Washington, DC*] (EA)
DDF...........	Dual Doctor Families (EA)
DDF...........	Due-In - Due-Out File [*AFIT*]
DDF...........	Food and Drug Administration Medical Library, Rockville, MD [*OCLC symbol*] (OCLC)
DDF...........	Military Order, Devil Dog Fleas (EA)
DDFC........	Deoxydifluorocytidine [*Antineoplastic drug*]
DDFT	Design, Development, Fabrication, Testing
DDG...........	Data Display Generator
DDG...........	Decoy Discrimination Group (AAG)
DDG...........	Deer Lodge, MT [*Location identifier*] [*FAA*] (FAAL)
DDG...........	Deoxy-D-glucose [*Also, DG, DOG*] [*Biochemistry*]
DDG...........	Deputy Director-General [*British*]
DDG...........	Deutsche Dermatologische Gesellschaft [*German Dermatological Society*] (EAIO)
DDG...........	Deutsche Dialektgeographie [*A publication*]
DDG...........	Dial Depth Gauge
DDG...........	Didecyl Glutarate [*Organic chemistry*]
DDG...........	Digital Data Generator (IEEE)
DDG...........	Digital Data Group
DDG...........	Digital Display Generator
DDG...........	Distillers Dried Grain
DDG...........	Double Derivatized Guar [*Chemical technology*]
DDG...........	Guided Missile Destroyer [*Navy symbol*]
DDGC........	Dishonorable Discharge, General Court-Martial, after Confinement in Prison [*Navy*]
DDGE........	Digital Display Generator Element
DDGI.........	Dishonorable Discharge, General Court-Martial, Immediate [*Navy*]
DDGM.......	District Deputy Grand Master [*Freemasonry*] (ROG)
DDGMR....	Deputy Director-General of Military Railways [*British military*] (DMA)
DDGOF.....	Deputy Director-General of Ordnance Factories [*Ministry of Supply*] [*British*] [*World War II*]
DDGOF(E) ...	Deputy Director-General of Ordnance Factories, Engineering Factories [*Ministry of Supply*] [*British*] [*World War II*]
DDGOF(F) ...	Deputy Director-General of Ordnance Factories, Filling Factories [*Ministry of Supply*] [*British*] [*World War II*]
DDGP........	Deputy Director-General of Production [*Ministry of Aircraft Production*] [*British*] [*World War II*]
DDGP........	Dishonorable Discharge, General Court-Martial, after Violation of Probation [*Navy*]
DDGS........	Distillers' Dried Grain with Solubles [*Feedstuff*]
DDGT........	Deputy Director-General of Transportation [*British military*] (DMA)
DDGX.......	Guided Missile Destroyer
DDH	Destroyer, Antisubmarine Helicopter [*NATO*]
DDH	Dialogo Dor Haemshej [*A publication*]
DDH	Dichlorodimethylhydantoin [*Organic chemistry*]
DDH	Digital Data Handling
DDH	Diploma in Dental Health [*British*]
DDH	Director, Division of Health [*New Zealand*]
DDH	Dissociated Double Hypertropia [*Ophthalmology*]
DDH	Division of Dental Health [*Bureau of Health Professions Education and Manpower Training, HEW*]
DDH	Dodecahedron [*Golf ball design*]
DDH & DS ...	Digital Data Handling and Display System (NRCH)
DDHG.......	Deputy Director, Home Guard [*British military*] (DMA)
DD/HH:MM:SS ...	Day/Hour:Minute:Second (NASA)
DDHO.......	Deputy Director of Home Operations [*Air Ministry*] [*British*] [*World War II*]
DDHP........	Deputy Director of Hygiene and Pathology [*Military*] [*British*]
DDHP........	Deringer Duell Head Process
DDHS........	Digital Data Handling System (NOAA)
DDI............	Data Development, Inc. [*Database producer*] (IID)
DDI............	Data Display Indicator
DDI............	Daydream Island [*Australia*] [*Airport symbol*] (OAG)
DDI............	Dedicated Display Indicator (NASA)
DDI............	Dehra Dun [*India*] [*Seismograph station code, US Geological Survey*] (SEIS)

DDI............	Dehra Dun [*India*] [*Later, SAB*] [*Geomagnetic observatory code*]
DDI............	Delivery Distribution Indicator (MCD)
DDI............	Density Dependent Inhibition [*of cell growth*]
DDI............	Depression Deviation Indicator
DDI............	Depth Deviation Indicator
DDI............	Deputy Director of Intelligence [*Air Ministry*] [*British*] [*World War II*]
DDI............	Diazodicyanoimidazole [*Organic chemistry*]
ddI............	Dideoxyinosine [*Medicine*]
DDI............	Diethyl Dicarbocyanine Iodide [*Organic chemistry*]
DDI............	Digital Display Indicator (MCD)
DDI............	Direct Dial In (BUR)
DDI............	Direct Digital Interface
DDI............	Directed Drawing Instrument
DDI............	Discrete Data Input (MCD)
DDI............	Discrete Digital Input (NASA)
DDI............	Divisional Detective Inspector [*British police*]
DDI............	Document Disposal Indicator
DDI............	Documenti Diplomatici Italiani [*A publication*]
DDI............	Dodecylimidazole [*Antifungal*]
DDI............	Drug Dynamics Institute [*University of Texas at Austin*] [*Research center*] (RCD)
DDIAEW...	Dialogue on Diarrhoea [*A publication*]
D Did	Doctor of Didactics
DDIE	Direct Digital Interface Equipment [*Telecommunications*] (TEL)
D Di E	Doctor of Diesel Engineering
D Di Eng....	Doctor of Diesel Engineering
DDIFC......	Dick Damron International Fan Club (EA)
DDII	Disease Detection International, Inc. [*NASDAQ symbol*] (NQ)
D Dipl	Doctor of Diplomacy
DDIR........	District Directors of Internal Revenue [*IRS*]
DDIR........	Division of Drug Information Resources [*Public Health Service*] [*Information service or system*] (IID)
D/DIRNSA ...	Deputy Director, National Security Agency
DDIS..........	Data Display
DDIS..........	Document Data Indexing Set
DDIS..........	Document Depository Index System (MCD)
DDIWT	Deputy Director of Inland Water Transport [*British military*] (DMA)
DDIX.........	DDI Pharmaceuticals, Inc. [*Mountain View, CA*] [*NASDAQ symbol*] (NQ)
DDJ	Deutsches Dante Jahrbuch [*A publication*]
DDJ	Digital Differencing Junction
DDJ	Dr. Dobb's Journal [*M & T Publishing, Inc.*] [*Information service or system*] (CRD)
DDK..........	Daini Denden Kikaku
DDK..........	Dunsink Observatory [*Ireland*] [*Seismograph station code, US Geological Survey*] (SEIS)
DDK..........	Hunter-Killer Destroyer [*Navy ship symbol*] [*Navy*] [*Obsolete*]
DDL...........	Data Definition Language [*NCR Corp.*]
DDL...........	Data Description Language [*Data processing*]
DDL...........	Data-Design Laboratories [*NYSE symbol*] (SPSG)
DDL...........	Data Dialog
DDL...........	Data Distribution List
DDL...........	Data Down Link [*Data processing*] (MCD)
DDL...........	Data Drawing List
DDL...........	DDL Foodshow [*Food emporium which derives its name from its creator, movie producer Dino DeLaurentiis*]
DDL...........	Delegation of Disclosure Authority Letters [*Military*] (AFIT)
DDL...........	Deputy Director of Labour [*British*]
DDL...........	Det Danske Luftfartselskab A/S [*Airline*] [*Denmark*]
DDL...........	Detailed Data List (MCD)
DDL...........	Differential Distribution Law [*Meteorology*]
DDL...........	Digital Data Link
DDL...........	Digital Data Logger
DDL...........	Digital Delay Line [*Electronic musical instruments*]
DDL...........	Digital Design Language [*Air Force*] [*Data processing*]
DDL...........	Diode-Diode Logic [*Physics*]
DDL...........	Dispersive Delay Line
DDL...........	Doctor of Divine Literature
DDL...........	Document Description Language [*Data processing*]
DDL...........	Documentation Distribution List (KSC)
DDL...........	Light Destroyer (ADA)
DDLC	Data Description Language Committee [*CODASYL*]
DDLDS......	Date Departed Last Duty Station [*Military*] (AFM)
DDLP........	Database Definition Language Processor (BYTE)
DDLS........	Dump Data Line Switch (MCD)
DDLT........	Diagnostic Decision Logic Table [*Data processing*]
DDM..........	Data Demand Module (IEEE)
DDM..........	Data Display Module (MCD)
DDM..........	Data Display Monitoring (MCD)
DDM..........	Defense Disposal Manual [*DoD*] (AFIT)
DDM..........	Department of Data Management [*Veterans Administration*]
DDM..........	Derived Delta Modulation
DDM..........	Design Decision Memo (MCD)
DDM..........	Diaminodiphenylmethane [*Also, DAPM, MDA*] [*Organic chemistry*]
DDM..........	Dichlorodiphenylmethane [*Organic chemistry*]
DDM..........	Difference in Depth of Modulation (IEEE)

DDM......... Digital Database Maps (MCD)
DDM......... Digital Display Machine
DDM......... Digital Display Makeup
DDM......... Diploma in Dermatological Medicine [British]
DDM......... Discrete Data Management (MCD)
DDM......... Distributed Data Manager
DDM......... Doctor of Dental Medicine
DDM......... Dodecylmorpholine [Antifungal]
DDM......... Donnely Dome [Alaska] [Seismograph station code, US Geological Survey] (SEIS)
DDM......... Double Diffused Mesa
DDM......... Master of Dental Medicine
DDMA....... Disk Direct Memory Access
DDMC...... Design and Drafting Management Council [Defunct] (EA)
DDMC...... Disabled Drivers' Motor Club [British]
DDME....... Deputy Director of Mechanical Engineering [British]
DDMI....... Deputy Director of Military Intelligence [British]
DDMIIS.... David Davies Memorial Institute of International Studies (MSC)
DDMOI..... Deputy Director of Military Operations and Intelligence [British]
DDMOW .. Deputy Director of Medical Organization for War [Military] [British]
DDMP...... Deep-Drawn Metal Part
DDMP...... Defense Depot - Mechanicsburg, Pennsylvania [DoD]
DDMP...... Deputy Director of Manpower Planning [Military] [British]
DDMQ ...... Deputy Director of Movements and Quartering [Military] [British]
DDMS....... Department of Defense Manned Space Flight
DDMS....... Deputy Director of Medical Services [British]
DDMS....... Digital Data Measuring System
DDMS....... DoD [Department of Defense] Manager for Space Shuttle Support (MCD)
DDMT...... Defense Depot - Memphis, Tennessee [DoD]
DDMT...... Deputy Director of Military Training [British]
DDMTMA ... Department of Defense Military Traffic Management Agency (AAG)
DDN .... Deep Draft Navigation [Type of water project]
DDN .... Defense Data Network
DDN .... Delta Downs [Australia] [Airport symbol] [Obsolete] (OAG)
DDN .... Digital Data Network
D Dn.......... Doctor of Design
DDN .... Documentation Development Notification (KSC)
DDN .... Documented Discount Notes [Banking]
DDNC....... Deputy Director of Naval Construction [British]
DDNC...... Digestive Disease National Coalition (EA)
DDNC....... Direct Digital Numerical Controller
DDNI........ Deputy Director of Naval Intelligence [British]
DDNJ FDC ... Food and Drug Administration, Notices of Judgment [A publication] (DLA)
DDNN .... Dominis Nostris [To Our Lords] [Latin]
DDNO .... Dodecyldimethylamine [or Dimethyldodecylamine] N-Oxide [Organic chemistry]
DDNP........ Diazodinitrophenol [Organic chemistry]
ddNTP .... Dideoxyribonucleotide Triphosphate [Organic chemistry]
DDNTP ..... Didicyclohexylammonium Naphthylthiolphosphate [Organic chemistry]
DDO .... Dansyl Derivative of Oligothymidilate [Biochemistry]
DDO .... Deputy Director of Operations [Air Force]
DDO .... Deputy Director of Organisation [Air Ministry] [British]
DDO .... Der Deutsche Oekonomist [A publication]
DDO .... Destroyers, Disbursing Office [Navy]
DDO .... Developmental Disabilities Office [Department of Health and Human Services]
DDO .... Diocesan Director of Ordinands [Church of England]
DDO .... Diploma in Dental Orthopaedics [British]
DDO .... Director, Development and Operations (MUGU)
DDO .... Discrete Data Output (MCD)
DDO .... Discrete Digital Output (MCD)
DDO .... Dispatch Discharging Only [Shipping] (DS)
DDO .... District Dental Office [or Officer] [Navy]
DDO .... Double Draw-Off [Crystallizer] [Chemical engineering]
DDO .... Dumbarton Oaks Research Library of Harvard University, Washington, DC [Library symbol] [Library of Congress] [OCLC symbol] (LCLS)
DDOATS .. Deputy Director of Organisation, Auxiliary Territorial Service [British military] (DMA)
DDOCE..... Digital Data Output Conversion Element [or Equipment]
DDOD .... Deputy Director of Operations Division [Air Ministry] [British]
DDOE........ United States Department of Energy, Washington, DC [Library symbol] [Library of Congress] (LCLS)
DDOF(X)... Deputy Director of Ordnance Factories, Explosives Factories [Ministry of Supply] [British] [World War II]
DDOI......... Deputy Director of Operations and Intelligence [Air Ministry] [British]
DDOMC.... Defense Depot Operations Management Course [DoD]
DDOP........ DSA [Defense Supply Agency] Disposal Operating Procedures
DDORCPS Glas ... Diplomate in Dental Orthoptics of the Royal College of Physicians and Surgeons of Glasgow [British]
DDOS........ Deputy Director of Ordnance Services [British]

DDOT........ United States Department of Transportation, Washington, DC [Library symbol] [Library of Congress] (LCLS)
DDOU .... Defense Depot - Ogden, Utah [DoD]
DDP .... Daily Delinquency Penalty [IRS]
DDP .... Data Distribution Panel (KSC)
DDP .... Data Distribution Point [NATO] (NATG)
DDP .... Datagram Delivery Protocol
DDP .... Declaration of Design Performance [British]
DDP .... Defense Dissemination Program (MCD)
DDP .... Delivered Duty Paid ["INCOTERM," International Chamber of Commerce official code]
DDP .... Delivery Distribution Point (MCD)
DDP .... Delta Dental Plan
DDP .... Demand Development Period (MCD)
DDP .... Department of Defense Production
DDP .... Deputy Director of Plans [CIA]
DDP .... Derecha Democratica Espanola [Spanish Right-Wing Democratic Party] (PPW)
DDP .... Design Data Package
DDP .... Design Development Plan (NASA)
DDP .... Deutsche Demokratische Partei [German Democratic Party] [Political party] (PPE)
DDP .... Diamminodichloroplatinum [Cisplatin] [Also, CDDP, cis-DDP, CPDD, CPT, P] [Antineoplastic drug]
DDP .... Didecyl Phthalate [Organic chemistry]
DDP .... Die Deutsche Post [A publication]
DDP .... Digital Data Processor
DDP .... Digital Display Processor (CMD)
DDP .... Direct Deposit of Payroll
DDP .... Director [or Directorate] of Development Planning [Air Force]
DDP .... Distributed Data Processing
DDP .... Distribution Drop Point (AABC)
DDP .... Doctors for Disaster Preparedness (EA)
DDP .... Dodecylpyrene [Organic chemistry]
DDP .... Dorado [Puerto Rico] [Airport symbol] (OAG)
DDP .... Double Diode-Pentode
DDP .... Dry Discharge Pump
DDP .... Erato (Discophiles de Paris Series) [Record label] [France]
DDP .... San Juan, PR [Location identifier] [FAA] (FAAL)
DDPA .... Delta Dental Plans Association (EA)
DDPC .... DCSLOG [Deputy Chief of Staff for Logistics] Data Processing Center [Military] (AABC)
DDPC .... Departmental Data Processing Center [Department of Labor]
DDPC .... Digital Data Processing Center [or Complex] (MCD)
DDPE .... Digital Data Processing Equipment
DDPF........ Dedicated Display Processing Function (NASA)
DDPH........ Diploma in Dental Public Health [British]
DDPHP..... Deputy Director of Post-Hostilities Plans [Military] [British]
DDPHRCS Eng ... Diploma in Dental Public Health, Royal College of Surgeons of England
DDPL .... Data Drawing and Parts List
DDPOW.... Deputy Director of Prisoners of War [British]
DDPP .... Deputy Director for Plans and Policy [National Security Agency]
DDPR .... Deputy Director for Programs and Resources [National Security Agency]
DDPR .... Deputy Director of Public Relations [Military] [British]
DDPS........ Data Directed Programming System [British] (DIT)
DDPS........ Department of Defense Project Specification (MCD)
DDPS........ Deputy Director of Personal Services [Navy] [British]
DDPS........ Digital Data Processing System
DDPS........ Discrete Depth Plankton Sampler
DDPS........ Discrimination Data Processing System (AABC)
DDPU........ Digital Data Processing Unit (IEEE)
DDQ .... Deputy Director of Quartering [Military] [British]
DDQ .... Dichlorodicyanobenzoquinone [Organic chemistry]
DDQ .... Dimensions Description Questionnaire
DDQ .... Minot, ND [Location identifier] [FAA] (FAAL)
DDR.......... Daily Demand Rate
DDR.......... DASD [Direct Access Storage Device] Dump Restore [Data processing] (IBMDP)
DDR........... Data Direction Register [Microcomputer]
DDR........... Data Discrepancy Report (MCD)
DDR........... Daughters of the Defenders of the Republic, USA (EA)
DDR........... Daughters of the Divine Redeemer [Roman Catholic religious order]
DDR........... Decoy Discrimination RADAR
DDR........... Deficiency and Disposition Report [Nuclear energy] (NRCH)
DDR........... Delinquency Delivery Report (MCD)
DDR........... Density Dependent Recruitment [Pisciculture]
DDR........... Design Development Record (MCD)
DDR........... Detail Design Review (MCD)
DDR........... Detector Dependent Response [Measurement]
DDR........... Deutsche Demokratische Republik [German Democratic Republic (East Germany)]
D Dr .... Deutsche Drama [A publication]
DDR........... Development Discrepancy Report
DDR........... Developments in Diabetes Research [Elsevier Book Series] [A publication]
DDR........... Device Dependent Routine
DDR........... Dialed Digit Receiver [Telecommunications] (TEL)

DDR.........	Digital Data Receiver
DDR.........	Diploma in Diagnostic Radiology [*British*]
DDR.........	Direct Debit [*Banking*] (DCTA)
DDR.........	Direct Drive
DDr..........	District Deputy Ruler [*Australia*]
DDr..........	Doctor of Divinity (EY)
DDR.........	Dodaira [*Japan*] [*Seismograph station code, US Geological Survey*] (SEIS)
DDR.........	Double Drift Region (IEEE)
DDR.........	Downrange Data Report
DDR.........	Dynamic Device Reconfiguration [*IBM Corp.*] [*Data processing*] (MDG)
DDR.........	German Democratic Republic [*IYRU nationality code*] [*ANSI three-letter standard code*] [*Aircraft nationality and registration mark*] (CNC)
DDR.........	RADAR Picket Destroyer [*Navy symbol*] [*Navy*]
DDRA.......	Deputy Director of Royal Artillery [*Military*] [*British*]
DDRB.......	Danish Defense Research Board
DD & RB...	Document Distribution and Reproduction Branch [*NTIS*]
DDRC.......	Drawing Data Required for Change (KSC)
DDRD.......	Deputy Director of Recruiting and Demobilization [*Military*] [*British*]
DDRE.......	Danish Defense Research Establishment (NATG)
DDR & E...	Defense Development Research and Engineering (MCD)
DDR & E...	Detailed Design Review and Evaluation (MCD)
DDRE.......	Director [*or Directorate*] of Defense Research and Engineering [*DoD*]
DDR & E...	Director [*or Directorate*] of Defense Research and Engineering [*DoD*]
DDREDK ..	Drug Development Research [*A publication*]
DDRF.......	Degenerative Diseases Research Foundation (EA)
DDRG.......	Dart Drug Stores, Inc. [*NASDAQ symbol*] (NQ)
DDRH	Digital Data Recording Head
DDRI	Design Drafting Reference Information
DDRI	Diversified Data Resources, Incorporated [*Information service or system*] (IID)
DDRKA	Doshisha Daigaku Rikogaku Kenkyu Hokoku [*A publication*]
DDRM.......	Direct Dial Response Marketing, Inc. [*Information service or system*] (EISS)
DDR-Med-Rep ...	DDR-Medizin-Report [*A publication*]
DDRR	Directional Discontinuity Ring Radiator
DDRS	Declassified Documents Reference System [*Research Publications, Inc.*] [*Woodbridge, CT*]
DDRS	Demographic Data Retrieval System [*Census Bureau*] [*Information service or system*] (IID)
DDRS	Digital Data Recording System
DDS	Damien Dutton Society for Leprosy Aid (EA)
DDS	Data Dialog System (MCD)
DDS	Data Dictionary System [*Data processing*]
DDS	Data Display Set (MCD)
DDS	Data Display System [*or Subsystem*]
DDS	Data Dissemination System [*European Space Agency - Information Retrieval Service*] [*Rome, Italy*] (TSSD)
DDS	Data Distribution System [*or Subsystem*]
DDS	Data-Phone Digital Service [*Trademark of the American Telephone & Telegraph Co.*]
DDS	Decoy Dispensing Set (MCD)
DDS	Deep-Diving System
DDS	Defense Dissemination System (MCD)
DD/S	Delivered Sound [*Shipping*]
DDS	Demos D Scale [*Psychology*]
DDS	Deployable Defense System (IEEE)
DDS	Deputy Director of Science [*Military*] [*British*]
DDS	Design Data Sheet [*Naval Ship Engineering Center*]
DDS	Design Disclosure Standard
DDS	Designator Detection System (MCD)
DDS	Detailed Design Specification (MCD)
DDS	Development Data Sheet (MCD)
DDS	Developmental Disabilities Service
DDS	Dialysis Disequilibrium Syndrome
DDS	Diaminodiphenyl Sulfone [*Also, DADPS, DAPSONE*] [*Pharmacology*]
D & DS.......	Dictatorships and Double Standards [*Title of an article written by Jeane Kirkpatrick in 1979 that differentiates between authoritarian and totalitarian regimes and was adopted by certain conservatives as a basis for foreign policy*]
DDS	Digest of Dental Science [*A publication*]
DDS	Digital Data Service (ADA)
DDS	Digital Data Servo
DDS	Digital Data Storage [*Data processing*]
DDS	Digital Data System
DDS	Digital Design [*A publication*]
DDS	Digital Display Scope
DDS	Digital Drafting System
DDS	Digital Dynamics Simulator (IEEE)
DDS	Dillard Department Stores, Inc. Class A [*NYSE symbol*] (SPSG)
DDS	Direct Distance Service
DDS	Director of Dental Services [*British*]
DDS	Director of Dental Surgery [*Australia*]
DDS	Directory Development Study
DDS	Display and Debriefing Subsystem (MCD)
DDS	Distillation Desalination System
DDS	Diving Dentists Society (EA)
DDS	Doctor of Dental Science
DDS	Doctor of Dental Surgery
DDS	Documentation Distribution System (NASA)
DDS	Doppler Detection Station [*Detection station on the Mid-Canada Line*]
DDS	Doppler Detection System
DDS	Dose Detector System
DDS	Drug Delivery System [*Pharmacy*]
DDS	Drug Development (Scotland) Ltd. [*United Kingdom*] (IRUK)
DDS	Dummy Director Set
DDS	Dynamic Diagnostic System (MCD)
DDSB	Duke Divinity School. Bulletin [*Later, Duke Divinity School. Review*] [*A publication*]
DDSC	Delta Data Systems Corporation [*NASDAQ symbol*] (NQ)
DD Sc.........	Doctor of Dental Science
DDSCD	Digestive Diseases and Sciences [*A publication*]
DDSCDJ ...	Digestive Diseases and Sciences [*A publication*]
DDSD	Deputy Director of Staff Duties [*Military*] [*British*]
DDSE	Design Disclosure for Systems and Equipment
DDSG	Digital Data Switching Group (CAAL)
DD & Shpg ...	Dock Dues and Shipping (DLA)
DDSLA.......	Damien Dutton Society for Leprosy Aid (EA)
DDSM	Decontrolled Defense Supply Material
DDSM	Defense Distinguished Service Medal [*Military decoration*]
DDSM	Digital Data Switching Matrix
DDSN........	Parkfield Downhole Digital Seismic Network [*Seismology*]
DDSOT	Digital Daily System Operability Test
DDSP.........	Defense Development Sharing Program [*US and Canada*] (RDA)
DDSP.........	Deputy Director of Selection of Personnel [*Military*] [*British*]
DDSS	Developmental Disabilities Special Interest Section [*American Occupational Therapy Association*]
DDSSJ.......	Drone Deceptive Self-Screening Jammer [*Military*] (MCD)
DDST	Denver Developmental Screening Test [*For mental development of infants*]
DDST	Deputy Director of Supply and Transport [*British*]
DDSU	Digital Data Storage Unit
DD Sur.......	Doctor of Dental Surgery
DDT...........	Darling Downs Times [*A publication*] (APTA)
DDT...........	Data Debugging Tool
DDT...........	Data Description Table (BUR)
DDT...........	Davidson Tisdale Mines Ltd. [*Toronto Stock Exchange symbol*]
DDT...........	Death Defying Theatre [*Australia*]
DDT...........	Debye Dipole Theory [*Physics*]
DDT...........	Deduct
DDT...........	Define Device Table (MCD)
DDT...........	Deflagration to Detonation Transition (IEEE)
DDT...........	Delayed Dialing Tone [*Telecommunications*] (TEL)
DDT...........	Design Data Transmittal (NRCH)
DDT...........	Design Development Test
DDT...........	Design and Drafting Techniques
DDT...........	Diagnostic Decision Table [*Data processing*]
DDT...........	DIBOL Debugging Technique [*Digital Equipment Corp.*]
DDT...........	Dichlorodiphenyltrichloroethane [*Insecticide*]
DDT...........	Digital Data Terminal (MCD)
DDT...........	Digital Data Transceiver
DDT...........	Digital Data Transmitter
DDT...........	Digital Debugging Tape
DDT...........	Digital Demodulation Technique
DDT...........	Digital Diagnostic Tool [*Automotive engineering*]
DD of T......	Director, Division of Traffic
DDT...........	Doctor of Drugless Therapy
DDT...........	Doppler Data Translator
DDT...........	Double Deflection Tube (BUR)
DDT...........	Double Diode-Triode
DDT...........	Ductus Deferens Tumor [*Type of cell line*]
DDT...........	Duplex-Drive Tank
DDT...........	Dynamic Debugging Technique (DEN)
DDT...........	Dynamic Display Tester
DDT...........	Dyslexia Determination Test [*Educational test*]
DDTA	Deputy Director of Technical Administration [*Ministry of Supply*] [*British*]
D/DTA	Durability/Damage Tolerance Analysis [*Air Force*]
DDTC	Defense Depot - Tracy, California [*DoD*]
DDTC	Diethyldithiocarbamate [*Also, DDC, DEDC*] [*Organic chemistry*]
DDTCA	Dandie Dinmont Terrier Club of America (EA)
DD-T & E ..	Deputy Director for Test and Evaluation [*NASA*]
DDT & E ...	Design, Development, Test, and Evaluation
DDTE	Digital Data Terminal Equipment
DDTE	Director, Defense Test and Evaluation [*Army*] (RDA)
DDTE	OSD [*Office of the Secretary of Defense*] Developmental Test and Evaluation (RDA)
DDTESM ...	Digital Data Terminal Equipment Service Module
DDTF	Dynamic Docking Test Facility [*NASA*]
DDTI	Deputy Director of Tactical Investigation [*Military*] [*British*]
DDTO........	Demonstration Detail Test Objectives (AAG)
DDTO........	District Domestic Transportation Office [*or Officer*]

DDTS .... Digital Data Transmission System   (KSC)
DDTS .... Direct Dial Telephone System
DDTS .... Dynamic Docking Test System [*NASA*]   (NASA)
DDTT .... Davidson Tisdale Mines Ltd. [*NASDAQ symbol*]   (NQ)
ddTTP...... Dideoxythymidine Triphosphate [*Biochemistry*]
DDTV .... Darling Downs Television Ltd. [*Australia*]
DDTV .... Dry Diver Transport Vehicle [*Navy*]
DDU .... Data Display Unit   (NASA)
DDU .... Decommutator Distribution Unit   (MCD)
DDU .... Diagnostic Display Unit   (MCD)
DDU .... Digital Data Unit   (MUGU)
DDU .... Digital Display Unit
DDU .... Digital Distributing Unit
DDU .... Diploma in Diagnostic Ultrasound
DDU .... Disk Data Unit
DDU .... Display and Debug Unit [*Data processing*]   (MDG)
DDU .... Display Driver Unit   (NASA)
DDU .... Dual Diversity Unit
DDU .... University of District of Columbia, Van Ness Campus, Washington, DC [*OCLC symbol*]   (OCLC)
D in DUP ... Detur in Duplo [*Let Twice as Much Be Given*] [*Pharmacy*]
DDUS .... Date Departed United States [*Military*]
DDV .... Columbus, OH [*Location identifier*] [*FAA*]   (FAAL)
DDV .... Deck Drain Valve
DDV .... Deep-Diving Vehicle [*Navy*]
DDVP .... Dimethyl Dichlorovinyl Phosphate [*Insecticide*]
DDVRS...... Deputy Director, Veterinary Remount Service [*British military*]   (DMA)
DDVS .... Deputy Director of Veterinary Services [*British military*]   (DMA)
DDW.......... Deionized-Distilled Water
DDW.......... Direct Digital Writer
DDWE & M ... Deputy Director of Works, Electrical and Mechanical [*British*]
DDWP .... Deputy Directorate of Weapons, Polaris [*Navy*] [*British*]
DDX.......... Digital Data Exchange [*Telecommunications*]   (TEL)
DDX.......... Goldsboro, NC [*Location identifier*] [*FAA*]   (FAAL)
DDX-P...... Digital Data Exchange-Packet [*Telecommunications*]   (TSSD)
DDY.......... Dynayoke Deflection Yoke
DDZ.......... Dokumentation der Zeit [*A publication*]
DDZZA ..... DDZ. Das Deutsche Zahnaerzteblatt [*A publication*]
DE.............. Assistant Vice Director for Estimates   (MCD)
DE.............. Dail Eireann [*House of Representatives*] [*Ireland*]   (ILCA)
DE.............. Daily Express [*United Kingdom*] [*A publication*]
DE.............. Damage Expectancy   (NATG)
DE.............. Data Element [*Data processing*]
DE.............. Data Encoder
DE.............. Data Entry
DE.............. Date of Entry [*Military*]
DE.............. Date of Extension [*Military*]
DE.............. Daughters of Evrytania   (EA)
DE.............. DE. Journal of Dental Engineering [*A publication*]
DE.............. December   (ADA)
DE.............. Decimeter [*Unit of measure*]
DE.............. Decision Element
DE.............. Decision Error
DE.............. Deck and Engineering Duties, General Service [*USNR officer designation*]
DE.............. Deckle-Edged [*Paper*]
DE.............. Declared Excess [*Military*]
DE.............. Deemphasis
DE.............. Deep Etch [*Lithography term*]
DE.............. Deere & Co. [*NYSE symbol*]   (SPSG)
DE.............. Defense Emergency   (AABC)
DE.............. Defensive End [*Football*]
DE.............. Deflection Error [*Military*]
DE.............. Delaware [*Postal code*]
De.............. Delaware. Department of Community Affairs and Economic Development, Division of Libraries, Dover, DE [*Library symbol*] [*Library of Congress*]   (LCLS)
DE.............. Delivered Energy
DE.............. Delta Air Transport [*ICAO designator*]   (FAAC)
DE.............. Demokratiki Enosis [*Democratic Union*] [*Greek*]   (PPE)
DE.............. Dene Express. Fort Good Hope [*A publication*]
DE.............. Denmark   (NATG)
DE.............. Department of Education [*Generic*]
DE.............. Department of Employment [*Formerly, DEP, MOL*] [*British*]
DE.............. Department of Energy   (ILCA)
DE.............. Departmental Estimate   (AAG)
D/E.............. Depression/Elevation   (CAAL)
DE.............. Deprived Eye [*Optics*]
DE.............. Descent Engine [*NASA*]   (KSC)
DE.............. Descriptor [*Online database field identifier*]
DE.............. Design Engineering   (KSC)
DE.............. Design Evaluation
DE.............. Designation Equipment
DE.............. Destroyer Escort
DE.............. Deutsche Erde [*A publication*]
de.............. Deve [*Debit*] [*Portuguese*] [*Business term*]
DE.............. Developing Economies [*A publication*]
DE.............. Development Engineering
DE.............. Development Ephemeris

DE.............. Development Estimate
DE.............. Device End
DE.............. Dextrose Equivalent [*Food technology*]
DE.............. Dictation Equipment
DE.............. Die Deborah   (BJA)
DE.............. Diesel Electric
DE.............. Differential Equation
DE.............. Digital Element   (IEEE)
DE.............. Digital Encoder   (MSA)
D & E.......... Dilatation and Evacuation [*Medicine*]
DE.............. Direct Encounter   (KSC)
DE.............. Directed Energy [*Weaponry*]   (INF)
DE.............. Director of Engineering [*Navy*] [*British*]
DE.............. Director Error [*Military*]   (AFM)
DE.............. Directorate of Design Engineering [*NASA*]   (KSC)
DE.............. Diritto Ecclesiastico [*A publication*]
DE.............. Disk Electrophoresis
DE.............. Display Electronics   (KSC)
DE.............. Display Element
DE.............. Display Equipment
DE.............. Distant Element   (MDG)
DE.............. Distributive Education
DE.............. District Engineer [*Army*]
DE.............. Division Entry   (BUR)
DE.............. Division Equivalent   (MCD)
DE.............. Doctor of Engineering
DE.............. Doctor of Entomology
DE.............. Doppler Extractor   (MCD)
DE.............. Dose Equivalent [*Radioactivity calculations*]
DE.............. Double Elephant [*Paper*]   (ADA)
DE.............. Double Enamel [*Insulation*]   (MSA)
DE.............. Double End [*Technical drawings*]
DE.............. Double Entry [*Bookkeeping*]
DE.............. Double Extension [*Camera stand*]   (ROG)
DE.............. Drive End   (MSA)
DE.............. Drug Evaluation
DE.............. Dual Camshafts and Electronic Management [*Automotive engineering*]
DE.............. Duke of Edinburgh's Wiltshire Regiment [*Military unit*] [*British*]   (ROG)
D & E........ Durnford and East's (Term) Reports, English King's Bench [*1785-1800*] [*A publication*]   (DLA)
DE.............. Dynamic Economics [*Elsevier Book Series*] [*A publication*]
DE.............. Dynamic Energy [*Foglight*] [*Hella, Inc.*] [*Automotive engineering*]
DE.............. Dynamic Engineer
DE.............. Dynamics Explorer [*NASA*]
DE.............. Escort Ship [*Destroyer Escort*] [*Navy symbol*]
DE.............. Federal Republic of Germany [*ANSI two-letter standard code*]   (CNC)
DE.............. From [*Use to precede the call sign of the calling station*] [*Aviation code*]   (FAAC)
DE.............. Journal of Dental Engineering [*A publication*]
DE.............. Journal of Drug Education [*A publication*]
DEA........... ANSA [*Agenzia Nazionale Stampa Associata*]'s Electronic Documentation Service [*ANSA Agency*]   (IID)
DEA .... Daily Engineering Articles [*A publication*]   (APTA)
DEA .... Dance Educators of America   (EA)
DEA .... Data Encryption Algorithm
DEA .... Data Exchange Agreement
DEA .... Data Exchange Annex   (AABC)
DEA .... Davis Escape Apparatus [*British military*]   (DMA)
DEA .... Deacon
Dea........... Deady's United States Circuit and District Court Reports [*A publication*]   (DLA)
DEA .... Deak International Resources Corp. [*Toronto Stock Exchange symbol*]
DEA .... Dean   (ROG)
DEA .... Defense Exchange Agreement   (MCD)
DEA .... Deflection Error Average [*Military*]   (MUGU)
DEA .... Department of Economic Affairs [*Department of Agriculture*]
DEA .... Deployed Electronics Assembly   (MCD)
DEA .... Desethylamiodarone [*Biochemistry*]
DEA .... Design Engineering Analysis [*Army*]
DEA .... Development, Engineering, and Acquisition [*Directorate*] [*Army*]   (RDA)
DEA .... Dictionary of Electronics Abbreviations, Signs, and Symbols [*A publication*]
DEA .... Dielectric Analyzer
DEA .... Diethanolamine [*Also, DIOLAMINE*] [*Organic chemistry*]
DEA .... Diethoxyanthracene [*Organic chemistry*]
DEA .... Diethylamine [*Organic chemistry*]
DEA .... Dimethylaniline [*Organic chemistry*]
DEA .... Directory of European Associations [*A publication*]
DEA .... Display Electronics Assemblies   (KSC)
DEA .... Division of Ecumenical Affairs [*Church of England*]
DEA .... Dominican Educational Association   (EA)
DEA .... Driver Evaluation Assembly [*Nuclear energy*]   (NRCH)
DEA .... Drug Enforcement Administration [*Formerly, Bureau of Narcotics and Dangerous Drugs*]
DEA .... Drug Enforcement Agency [*New South Wales, Australia*]

DEA .... Dynamo Electric Amplifier
DEAC .... Data Exchange Auxiliary Console (CAAL)
DEAC .... Deacon
Deac .... Deacon's English Bankruptcy Reports [1835-40] [A publication] (DLA)
DEAC .... Dealer Election Action Committee [Campaign funding]
DEAC .... Defense Economic Analysis Council (MCD)
DEAC .... Diethylaluminum Chloride [Organic chemistry]
DEAC .... Disability Employment Action Centre [Melbourne, Australia]
Deac Bank Pr ... Deacon's Bankruptcy Law and Practice [3rd ed.] [1864] [A publication] (DLA)
Deac & C .... Deacon and Chitty's English Bankruptcy Reports [1832-35] [A publication] (DLA)
Deac & Ch ... Deacon and Chitty's English Bankruptcy Reports [1832-35] [A publication] (DLA)
Deac & Chit ... Deacon and Chitty's English Bankruptcy Reports [1832-35] [A publication] (DLA)
Deac Cr Law ... Deacon on Criminal Law of England [A publication] (DLA)
Deac Dig .... Deacon's Digest of the Criminal Law [A publication] (DLA)
Dea & Ch ... Deacon and Chitty's English Bankruptcy Reports [1832-35] [A publication] (DLA)
Dea & Chit ... Deacon and Chitty's English Bankruptcy Reports [1832-35] [A publication] (DLA)
DEACON .. Defense Estimates Analytical Computer On-Line Network (MCD)
DEACON .. Direct English Access and Control [Data processing]
Deacon Bankr Cas ... Deacon's English Bankruptcy Cases [A publication] (DLA)
Deacon Bankr (Eng) ... Deacon's English Bankruptcy Cases [A publication] (DLA)
Deacon & C ... Deacon and Chitty's English Bankruptcy Reports [1832-35] [A publication] (DLA)
Deacon & C Bankr Cas ... Deacon and Chitty's English Bankruptcy Records [1832-35] [A publication] (DLA)
Deacon & C Bankr Cas (Eng) ... Deacon and Chitty's English Bankruptcy Cases [A publication] (DLA)
Deaconess Hosp Med Bull ... Deaconess Hospital. Medical Bulletin [A publication]
DEACT ...... Deactivation (KSC)
DEAD .... Dallas Encephalopathic and Abortifactive Disease [Acronym used as title of novel]
DEAD .... Dedicated to Eliminating Acronymic Designations [An association]
DEAD .... Diethyl Azodicarboxylate [Organic chemistry]
DEAD .... Doppler Evaluated Attack Depth [Navy] (CAAL)
Dead Or Laws ... Deady and Lane's Oregon General Laws [A publication] (DLA)
DEADS ..... Detroit Air Defense Sector [ADS]
Deady .... Deady's United States Circuit and District Court Reports [A publication] (DLA)
DEAE .... Diethylaminoethanol [Organic chemistry]
DEAE .... Diethylaminoethyl [Organic radical]
DEAE .... Division of Eligibility and Agency Evaluation [OE]
DEAE-D .... Diethylaminoethyl Dextran [Organic chemistry]
DEAEM .... Diethylaminoethyl Mercaptan [Organic chemistry]
Deafness Res & Train Cent ... Deafness Research and Training Center [A publication]
DEAFWATCH ... Demanding Equal Access to Facts and Warnings Aired on TV for Citizens Who are Hearing-Impaired [Student legal action organization] (EA)
DEAL .... Data Entry Application Language
DEAL .... Decision Evaluation and Logic
DEAL .... Detachment Equipment Authorization List [Military]
DEAL .... Dignity, Education, and Language Commmunication Centre [Melbourne, Australia]
Dealerscop ... Dealerscope Merchandising [A publication]
De Alex Fort ... De Fortuna Alexandri [of Plutarch] [Classical studies] (OCD)
DEALS .... Demountable Externally Anchored Low-Stress Magnet (MCD)
De An .... De Anima [of Aristotle] [Classical studies] (OCD)
DEAN .... Deputy Educators Against Narcotics [Defunct]
Deane .... Deane and Swabey's English Ecclesiastical Reports [A publication] (DLA)
Deane .... Deane and Swabey's English Probate and Divorce Reports [A publication] (DLA)
Deane .... Deane's English Blockade Cases [A publication] (DLA)
Deane .... Deane's Reports [24-26 Vermont] [A publication] (DLA)
Deane Bl ..... Deane's English Blockade Cases [A publication] (DLA)
Deane Ecc .. Deane and Swabey's English Ecclesiastical Reports [A publication] (DLA)
Deane Ecc Rep ... Deane and Swabey's English Ecclesiastical Reports [A publication] (DLA)
Deane Ecc Rep B ... Deane and Swabey's English Ecclesiastical Reports [A publication] (DLA)
Deane Neut ... Deane on the Effect of War as to Neutrals [A publication] (DLA)
Deane & S Eccl ... Deane and Swabey's English Ecclesiastical Reports [A publication] (DLA)
Deane & S Eccl (Eng) ... Deane and Swabey's English Ecclesiastical Reports [A publication] (DLA)
Deane & S Eccl Rep ... Deane and Swabey's English Ecclesiastical Reports [A publication] (DLA)

Deane & Sw ... Deane and Swabey's English Ecclesiastical Reports [A publication] (DLA)
De Anim ..... De Testimonio Animae [of Tertullian] [Classical studies] (OCD)
Dean Med Jur ... Dean's Medical Jurisprudence [A publication] (DLA)
De Antr Nymph ... De Antro Nympharum [of Porphyry] [Classical studies] (OCD)
DEAP .... Diffused Eutectic Aluminum Process (IEEE)
DEAP .... Division of Engineering and Applied Physics [Harvard University] (MCD)
DEAPA ...... Diethylaminopropylamine [Organic chemistry]
De-Ar .... Delaware Department of State, Division of Historical and Cultural Affairs, Hall of Records, Dover, DE [Library symbol] [Library of Congress] (LCLS)
DEAR .... Diamonds, Emeralds, Amethysts, and Rubies
De Arch ...... De Architectura [of Vitruvius] [Classical studies] (OCD)
DEARG PIL ... Deargentur Pilulae [Let The Pills Be Silverized] [Pharmacy]
Dears .... Dearsley's English Crown Cases Reserved [169 English Reprint] [1852-56] [A publication] (DLA)
Dears & B .. Dearsley and Bell's English Crown Cases [1856-58] [A publication] (DLA)
Dears & BCC ... Dearsley and Bell's English Crown Cases [1856-58] [A publication] (DLA)
Dears & B Crown Cas ... Dearsley and Bell's English Crown Cases [1856-58] [A publication] (DLA)
Dears C C .. Dearsley's English Crown Cases [1852-56] [A publication] (DLA)
Dears Cr Pr ... Dearsley's Criminal Process [1853] [A publication] (DLA)
Dearsl Cr Pr ... Dearsley's Criminal Process [1853] [A publication] (ILCA)
DEARTG ... Deaerating
DEAS .... Data Entry Aboard Ship [Navy] (NVT)
Deas & A .... Deas and Anderson's Decisions [1829-33] [Scotland] [A publication] (DLA)
DEASA ...... Dental Assistant [A publication]
Deas & And ... Deas and Anderson's Decisions [1829-33] [Scotland] [A publication] (DLA)
DEA-SOG ... Drug Enforcement Administration - Special Operations Group
Deas Ry ...... Deas on the Law of Railways in Scotland [A publication] (DLA)
Dea & Sw ... Deane and Swabey's English Ecclesiastical Reports [A publication] (DLA)
Death Educ ... Death Education [A publication]
Death Pen Rep ... Death Penalty Reporter [A publication]
Death Stud ... Death Studies [A publication]
DEAUR ..... Deauretur [Let It Be Gilded] [Pharmacy]
DEAUR PIL ... Deaurentur Pilulae [Let The Pills Be Gilded] [Pharmacy]
DEB .... Data Extent Block (MCD)
DEB .... De Baca Resources, Inc. [Vancouver Stock Exchange symbol]
DEB .... Debenture [Type of bond] [Investment term]
deb .... Debit [Debit] [French] [Business term]
DEB .... Debit
DEB .... Debrecen [Hungary] [Seismograph station code, US Geological Survey] [Closed] (SEIS)
DEB .... Debutante
DEB .... Decaying Extrastellar Body [Astronomy]
DEB .... Defense Estimative Brief (MCD)
DEB .... Dental Examining Board
DEB .... Department of State. Bulletin [A publication]
DEB .... Dictionnaire Encyclopedique de la Bible [A publication]
DEB .... Digital European Backbone [System] (MCD)
DEB .... Division of Environmental Biology [National Science Foundation]
DEB .... Downward Ejection Bomblet (MCD)
DEB .... Dynamic Ephemeral Bodies [Planetary science]
DEB .... Dystrophic Epidermolysis Bullosa [Medicine]
De Bapt ...... De Baptismo [of Tertullian] [Classical studies] (OCD)
DEBE .... Does Everything but Eat [Superseded by DITTO] [Data processing]
DEBEAC ... Decheniana Beihefte [A publication]
DEBEDF ... Deviant Behavior [A publication]
DEBFDI .... Developments in Environmental Biology of Fishes [A publication]
DEBHS ...... Dr. Edward Bach Healing Society (EA)
DEBIAO .... Developmental Biology [A publication]
DEBIDR .... Developments in Biochemistry [A publication]
Deb Jud ...... Debates on the Judiciary [A publication] (DLA)
DEBK .... Debark (AABC)
DEBl .... Deutsch-Evangelische Blaetter [A publication]
DeB Mar Int L ... DeBurgh's Maritime International Laws [A publication] (DLA)
De Bow .... De Bow's Commercial Review [A publication]
DEBR .... Division of Economic and Business Research [University of Arizona] [Tucson] [Information service or system] (IID)
DEBRA ...... Dystrophic Epidermolysis Bullosa Research Association of America (EA)
DEBRE ...... Debenture [Investment term] (ROG)
Debrecceni Mezogazd Akad Tud Evk ... Debrecceni Mezogazdasagi Akademia Tudomanyos Evkonyve [A publication]
Debrecceni Sz ... Debrecceni Szemle [A publication]
Debrec Muz Evk ... Debreceni Deri Muzeum Evokoenyve [A publication]
DEBS .... Deb Shops, Inc. [NASDAQ symbol] (NQ)

DEBS......... Digital Electron Beam Scanner
DEBSAK ... Developmental Biology. Supplement [*A publication*]
DEB SPISS ... Debita Spissitudo [*Proper Consistence*] [*Pharmacy*]
Debt & Cred ... Debtor and Creditor   (DLA)
DEBUT...... Daughters of the Elderly Bridging the Unknown Together   (EA)
DEBZA...... Deutsche Bauzeitschrift. Fachblatt fuer Entwurf und Ausfuehrung [*A publication*]
DeC........... Claymont Public Library, Claymont, DE [*Library symbol*] [*Library of Congress*]   (LCLS)
DEC.......... Control Escort Vessel [*Navy symbol*]
DEC.......... Davis and Elkins College [*West Virginia*]
DEC.......... Deaf Broadcasting Campaign [*England*]
Dec............ Decade of Short Stories [*A publication*]
DEC.......... Decani [*Of the Dean*] [*Music*]
DEC.......... Decanta [*Pour Off*] [*Pharmacy*]
Dec............ Decanus [*Dean*] [*Latin*]   (ILCA)
DEC.......... Decatur [*Illinois*] [*Airport symbol*]   (OAG)
dec............ Decayed [*Quality of the bottom*] [*Nautical charts*]
DEC.......... Decca
DEC.......... Deceased
Dec............ Decede [*Deceased*] [*French*]   (ILCA)
DEC.......... December   (EY)
DEC.......... Deception Island [*Antarctica*] [*Seismograph station code, US Geological Survey*] [*Closed*]   (SEIS)
Dec............ [*Tiberius*] Decianus [*Deceased, 1581*] [*Authority cited in pre-1607 legal work*]   (DSA)
DEC.......... Decimal   (KSC)
DEC.......... Decimal Equivalent Chart
DEC.......... Decimate   (ROG)
DEC.......... Decimeter [*Unit of measure*]   (ROG)
DEC.......... Decision
DEC.......... Decision Sciences [*A publication*]
DEC.......... Declaration
DEC.......... Declared [*Cricket*]   (ROG)
DEC.......... Declension   (ROG)
DEC.......... Declination
DEC.......... Decoder
DEC.......... Decompose
DEC.......... Decorated [*or Decoration*]   (ROG)
DEC.......... Decorative
Dec............ Decort [*Deduct*] [*German*] [*Business term*]
DEC.......... Decrease   (AAG)
DEC.......... Decrement
DEC.......... Decrescendo [*Decreasing in Loudness*] [*Music*]   (ROG)
DEC.......... Deductible Employee Contribution [*IRS*]
DEC.......... Deltec Resources Ltd. [*Vancouver Stock Exchange symbol*]
DEC.......... Dendritic Epidermal Cell [*Cytology*]
DEC.......... Deutscher Baustellen Informationsdienst [*A publication*]
DEC.......... Developing Economies [*A publication*]
DEC.......... Development and Education Command
DEC.......... Diecast Exchange Club   (EA)
DEC.......... Diethylaminoethyl Chloride [*Organic chemistry*]
DEC.......... Diethylcarbamazine [*Anthelmintic drug*]
DEC.......... Digital Equipment Corporation [*Maynard, MA*] [*NYSE symbol*]   (SPSG)
DEC.......... Digital Equipment Corporation, Corporate Library, Maynard, MA [*OCLC symbol*]   (OCLC)
DEC.......... Digital Evaluation Computer
DEC.......... Diplome d'Etudes Collegiales [*Canada*]
DEC.......... Direct Energy Conversion
DEC.......... Disposable Extraction Column
DEC.......... Distributor Electronic Control
DEC.......... Division for Early Childhood   (EA)
D Ec........... Doctor of Economics
DEC.......... Drug Evaluation Center
DEC.......... Dry Electrolytic Capacitor
DEC.......... Dynamic Energy Conversion
DECA......... Decathalon Association [*Acronym is used as name of association*]   (EA)
DECA .... Descent Engine Control Assembly [*Apollo*] [*NASA*]
DECA .... Digital Electronic Countermeasures Analyzer   (MCD)
DE(CA)...... Director of Economics, Civil Affairs [*War Office*] [*British*] [*World War II*]
DECA .... Display/AGAP [*Attitude Gyro Accelerometer Package*] Electronic Control Assembly   (KSC)
DECA .... Distributive Education Clubs of America   (EA)
DECAA ..... Dental Cadmos [*A publication*]
DECAF...... Distribution Control Analysis File [*NASA*]   (MCD)
Decal........ De Decalogo [*Philo*]   (BJA)
DECAL...... Decalcomania
DECAL...... Detailed Experimental Computer-Assisted Language
DECAL...... Digital Equipment Corporation Author Language [*Data processing*]   (CSR)
Decalogue J ... Decalogue Journal [*A publication*]
DECAN ..... Distance Measuring Equipment Command and Navigation
DE C Ann .. Delaware Code, Annotated [*A publication*]   (DLA)
DECAP-CHUTE ... Decontamination Capabilities - Chemical Units and Teams   (MCD)
DECARB... Decarburization   (MSA)
DECAT...... Driver Energy Conservation Awareness Training [*US government program*]

DECB......... Data Event Control Block [*Data processing*]   (BUR)
DECC .... Diethylcarbamazine Citrate [*Biochemistry*]
DECC .... Diethylcarbamoyl Chloride [*Organic chemistry*]
DECC .... Disciples Ecumenical Consultative Council   (EA)
DECCA...... Defense Commercial Communications Activity [*Military*]
DECCC...... Defense Commercial Communications Center [*Military*]
Decc Geogr ... Deccan Geographer [*A publication*]
Dec Ch .... Decisions from the Chair (Parliamentary) [*England*] [*A publication*]   (DLA)
DECCO ..... Defense Commercial Communications Office [*Military*]
Dec Col ...... Coleccion de los Decretos [*A publication*]   (DLA)
Dec Comm'r Pat ... Patents, Decisions of the Commissioner and of United States Courts [*A publication*]   (DLA)
Dec Com Pat ... Decisions of the Commissioner of Patents [*A publication*]   (DLA)
DECD........ Deceased   (AFM)
DECD........ Declared
DECD........ Decreased   (MUGU)
Dec Dig ...... American Digest System, Decennial Digests [*A publication*]   (DLA)
DECE........ Decease   (ROG)
DECE......... Denominational Executives of Christian Education   (EA)
DECEA ...... Defense Communication Engineering Agency   (AABC)
DECED ...... Deceased   (ROG)
DECEL...... Deceleration   (NVT)
DECELERON ... Decelerator and Aileron [*NASA*]
Decen Dig .. American Digest (Decennial Edition) [*A publication*]   (ILCA)
DECENT... Distribution of Exact Classical Energy Transfer [*Physics*]
DECEO ..... Defense Communications Engineering Office [*Army*]   (AABC)
Dec-FB....... Decrease Feedback
Dec Fed Mar Comm'n ... Decisions of the Federal Maritime Commission [*United States*] [*A publication*]   (DLA)
Dec Fern .... Decretos del Fernando [*Mexico*] [*A publication*]   (DLA)
DE CH...... Delaware Chancery Reports [*A publication*]   (DLA)
DECH........ Diethylcyclohexane [*Organic chemistry*]
DE Ch E...... Doctor of Electro-Chemical Engineering
DECHEMA ... Deutsche Gesellschaft fuer Chemisches Apparatewesen, Chemische Technik, und Biotechnologie eV [*Database producer*]   (IID)
DECHEMA Monogr ... DECHEMA [*Deutsche Gesellschaft fuer Chemisches Apparatewesen, Chemische Technik, und Biotechnologie eV*] Monographien [*A publication*]
DE Ch Eng ... Doctor of Electro-Chemical Engineering
Decheniana Beih ... Decheniana Beihefte [*A publication*]
Deci............ [*Tiberius*] Decianus [*Deceased, 1581*] [*Authority cited in pre-1607 legal work*]   (DSA)
Decian........ [*Tiberius*] Decianus [*Deceased, 1581*] [*Authority cited in pre-1607 legal work*]   (DSA)
DECID....... Deciduous
Decid Fruit Grow ... Deciduous Fruit Grower [*A publication*]
Decid Fruit Grow Sagtevrugteboer ... Deciduous Fruit Grower. Die Sagtevrugteboer [*A publication*]
Deciduous Fruit Grow ... Deciduous Fruit Grower [*A publication*]
DECIM...... Decimeter [*Unit of measure*]
Decimal Research Bul ... Decimal Research Bulletin [*A publication*]   (APTA)
Dec of Ind Acc Com ... Decisions of the Industrial Accident Commission of California [*A publication*]   (DLA)
Decis Geogr Bd Can ... Decisions. Geographic Board of Canada [*A publication*]
Decis Sci .... Decision Sciences [*A publication*]
Decis US Geogr Bd ... Decisions. United States Geographic Board [*A publication*]
DECIT....... Decimal Digit   (DIT)
De Civ D ... De Civitate Dei [*of Augustine*] [*Classical studies*]   (OCD)
Dec Jt Com ... Decisions of Joint Commission [*A publication*]   (DLA)
DECL........ Declaration   (ROG)
DECL........ Declare
DECL........ Declassify [*Military*]   (NVT)
DECL........ Declension
DECL........ Decline
DECL........ Direct Energy Conversion Laboratory [*Johnson Space Center*] [*NASA*]   (NASA)
DECLAB ... Digital Equipment Corp. Laboratory
DECLAN... Declaration   (ROG)
DECLG...... Double-Ended Cold Leg Guillotine [*Nuclear energy*]   (NRCH)
Decl J......... Declaratory Judgements [*A publication*]   (DLA)
DECLON .. Declaration   (ROG)
DECM ...... Deceptive Electronic Countermeasure [*Military*]   (CAAL)
DECM ...... Defense Electronic Countermeasure
DECN .... Decision   (AFM)
DECN .... Declaration   (ADA)
DECN .... Declension
DECN........ Decontamination
DECNET... Digital Equipment Corporation Telecommunications Network
DECO .... Decreasing Consumption of Oxygen [*Endocrinology*]
DECO .... Direct Energy Conversion Operation
DECO........ Document Engineering Company, Inc. [*Information service or system*]   (IID)
Dec O .... Ohio Decisions [*A publication*]   (DLA)
DECOCT... Decoctum [*Decoction*] [*Pharmacy*]

De Col .... De Colyar's English County Court Cases [*1867-82*] [*A publication*] (DLA)
De Col Guar ... De Colyar's Law of Guaranty [*A publication*] (DLA)
De Coly ...... De Colyar's English County Court Cases [*1867-82*] [*A publication*] (DLA)
DECOM .... Decommissioned (AFM)
DECOM .... Decommutator
DECOM .... Delay Cost Model
DECOM .... Low-Rate Engineering Decommutator Executive [*Computer program*] [*NASA Viking Mission*]
DECOMG ... Decommissioning [*Date*] [*Navy*] (NVT)
DECOMM ... Decommissioning [*Date*] [*Navy*] (NVT)
DECOMM ... Decommutation
DECOMNET ... Dedicated Communications Network (MCD)
decomp .... Decompensation [*Cardiology*]
DECOMP ..... Decomposition
DECOMP ... Decomposition Mathematical Programming System
DECOMPN ... Decompression (MSA)
DECOMPR ... Decompression
DECON ..... Decontaminate (AABC)
DECON ..... Decontamination
D Econ ...... Doctor of Economics (EY)
D Econ Sc .. Doctor of Economic Science
DECONTN ... Decontamination (KSC)
De Cor .... De Corona [*of Demosthenes*] [*Classical studies*] (OCD)
DECOR ...... DECHEMA [*Deutsche Gesellschaft fuer Chemisches Apparatewesen, Chemische Technik, und Biotechnologie eV*] Corrosion Data Base [*Federal Republic of Germany*] [*Information service or system*] (CRD)
DECOR ..... Decorative (ROG)
DECOR ..... Digital Electronic Continuous Ranging
Decorative Arts Soc Jnl ... Decorative Arts Society. Journal [*A publication*]
Decorator ... Decorator and Painter for Australia and New Zealand [*A publication*] (APTA)
DECPSK ... Differentially Encoded Coherent Phase Shift Keying [*Telecommunications*] (TEL)
DECR .... December (ROG)
DECR .... Decrease [*or Decrement*] (MSA)
Dec R .... Ohio Decisions Reprint [*A publication*] (DLA)
DECRDP... Drugs under Experimental and Clinical Research [*A publication*]
Dec Re .... Ohio Decisions Reprint [*A publication*] (DLA)
Dec Rep ..... Ohio Decisions Reprint [*A publication*] (DLA)
Dec Repr .... Ohio Decisions Reprint [*A publication*] (DLA)
DECRES ... Decrescendo [*Decreasing in Loudness*] [*Music*]
DECRESC ... Decrescendo [*Decreasing in Loudness*] [*Music*]
Decretal ...... Decretalia of the Canon Law [*A publication*] (DLA)
Decret Childeb ad L Salic ... Decreta Childeberti ad Legem Salicam [*A publication*] (DLA)
Decret Greg IX ... Decretales Gregorii IX [*A publication*] (DSA)
DECRT...... Decrement (MSA)
DECRTN... Decoration
DECS........ Data Entry Control System
Decs .... Decision [*A publication*]
DECS........ Decoration for Exceptional Civilian Service [*Army civilian employee award*]
Dec SDA .... Bengal Sadr Diwani Adalat Decisions [*A publication*] (DLA)
DECT........ Digital European Cordless Telecommunications
Dec T H & M ... Admiralty Decisions Tempore Hay and Marriott [*England*] [*A publication*] (DLA)
DECTP...... Diethylchlorothiophosphate [*Ethyl Chemical Co.*] [*Organic chemistry*]
DECTRA... Decca Tracking and Ranging (MCD)
DECU .... Data Exchange Control Unit (NASA)
DECUB ..... Decubitus [*Lying Down*] [*By extension, the medical term for bedsores*]
DECUK .... Duane Eddy Circle, United Kingdom (EAIO)
DECUS...... Digital Equipment Computer Users Society (EA)
DECUS...... Duane Eddy Circle, USA (EA)
Dec US Comp Gen ... Decisions of the Comptroller General of the United States [*A publication*] (DLA)
Dec US Compt Gen ... Decisions of the United States Comptroller General [*A publication*] (DLA)
Dec US Mar Comm'n ... Decisions of the United States Maritime Commission [*A publication*] (DLA)
DED.......... Data Element Dictionary [*A publication*] [*Army*]
DED.......... Date Expected Delivery [*Medicine*]
DED.......... Declared Dead [*Military*]
Ded............ Dedalo [*A publication*]
DED.......... Dedendum [*Design engineering*]
DED.......... Dedicated [*or Dedication*] (ROG)
DED.......... Deduct (AABC)
DED.......... Deland, FL [*Location identifier*] [*FAA*] (FAAL)
DED.......... Design Engineering Directorate (KSC)
DED.......... Diesel Engine Driven (NATG)
DED.......... Director of the Education Department [*Navy*] [*British*]
DED.......... Director of Engine Development [*Ministry of Aircraft Production*] [*British*]
DED.......... Distant End Disconnect [*Telecommunications*] (TEL)
D Ed .... Doctor of Education
DED.......... Doctor of English Divinity

DED.......... Double Error Detection
DED.......... Dutch Elm Disease
DEDA....... Data Entry and Display Assembly [*Apollo*] [*NASA*]
DEDAAS... Digital Electrophysiological Data Acquisition and Analysis System [*Neurometrics*]
D Ed AS..... Diploma in Education Administration and Supervision
DEDB....... Digital Elevation Database (RDA)
DEDC....... Diethyl Dicarbonate [*Fungistatic agent*]
DEDC....... Diethyldithiocarbamate [*Also, DDC, DDTC*] [*Organic chemistry*]
DED/D...... Data Element Dictionary/Directory [*A publication*]
DE D in D... De Die in Diem [*From Day to Day*] [*Latin*]
DEDD....... Diesel-Electric Direct Drive
De De .... [*Bertrandus*] De Deucio [*Deceased, 1355*] [*Authority cited in pre-1607 legal work*] (DSA)
DEDE....... Density-Depth
DEDEC..... Detroit Deere Corporation [*Proposed trademark*]
De Def Or .. De Defectu Oraculorum [*of Plutarch*] [*Classical studies*] (OCD)
De Deo .... [*Bertrandus*] De Deucio [*Deceased, 1355*] [*Authority cited in pre-1607 legal work*] (DSA)
De Deo Soc ... De Deo Socratico [*of Apuleius*] [*Classical studies*] (OCD)
DEDIA ..... Dental Digest [*A publication*]
DEDIC...... Dedication
DEDIP....... Department of Environmental and Drug-Induced Pathology [*Later, DETP*] (EA)
DEDL .... Data Element Description List [*Data processing*]
DEDO....... Defense Engineering Data Office
De Dog Plat ... De Dogmate Platonis [*of Apuleius*] [*Classical studies*] (OCD)
DE Dom Eng ... DE. Domestic Engineering [*Formerly, DE Journal*] [*A publication*]
DEDP .... Data Entry and Display Panel (MCD)
DEDS .... Data Entry and Display Subsystem
DeDS .... Delaware State College, Dover, DE [*Library symbol*] [*Library of Congress*] (LCLS)
DEDS .... Digital Error Detection Subsystem [*Data processing*] (AABC)
DEDS .... Directory of Engineering Document Services [*A publication*]
DeDT .... Delaware Technical and Community College, Dover, DE [*Library symbol*] [*Library of Congress*] (LCLS)
DEduc .... Doctor of Education (ADA)
DEDUCOM ... Deductive Communicator (IEEE)
DEE .... Dee Corp. ADR [*NYSE symbol*] (SPSG)
DEE .... Del Norte Chrome [*Vancouver Stock Exchange symbol*]
DEE .... Diethoxyethylene [*Organic chemistry*]
DEE .... Digital Evaluation Equipment
DEE .... Digital Events Evaluator (MCD)
DEE .... Dioikisis Exoterikou Emboriou [*Foreign Trade Administration*] [*Greek*]
DEE .... Diploma in Electrical Engineering (ADA)
DEE .... Direct Engineering Estimate (MCD)
DEE .... Discrete Event Evaluator (KSC)
DEE .... Dixie Airways [*Nashville, TN*] [*FAA designator*] (FAAC)
DEE .... Doctor of Electrical Engineering
DeEc .... De Economist [*A publication*]
DEEC........ Digital Electronic Engine Control (MCD)
DEECAL ... Dental Echo [*A publication*]
DEED .... Death Education. Pedagogy, Counseling, Care [*A publication*]
DE Eng ...... Doctor of Electrical Engineering
DEEO .... Director of Equal Employment Opportunity [*Department of Labor*]
DEEP........ Data Exception Error Protection
DEEP........ Developmental Economic Education Program
Deep Sea Drill Proj Initial Rep ... Deep Sea Drilling Project. Initial Reports [*A publication*]
Deep-Sea Oceanogr Abstr ... Deep-Sea Research and Oceanographic Abstracts [*A publication*]
Deep Sea Re ... Deep-Sea Research [*Later, Deep-Sea Research with Oceanographic Literature Review*] [*A publication*]
Deep Sea Res ... Deep-Sea Research [*Later, Deep-Sea Research with Oceanographic Literature Review*] [*A publication*]
Deep Sea Res & Oceanogr Abstr ... Deep Sea Research and Oceanographic Abstracts [*A publication*]
Deep Sea Res Oceanogr Abstr ... Deep Sea Research and Oceanographic Abstracts [*A publication*]
Deep-Sea Res Part A ... Deep-Sea Research. Part A. Oceanographic Research Papers [*Later, Deep-Sea Research with Oceanographic Literature Review*] [*A publication*]
Deep-Sea Res Part A Oceanogr Res Pap ... Deep-Sea Research. Part A. Oceanographic Research Papers [*Later, Deep-Sea Research with Oceanographic Literature Review*] [*A publication*]
Deep Sea Res Part B Oceanogr Lit Rev ... Deep Sea Research. Part B. Oceanographic Literature Review [*A publication*]
Deep-Sea Res Pt A Oceanogr Res Pap ... Deep-Sea Research. Part A. Oceanographic Research Papers [*Later, Deep-Sea Research with Oceanographic Literature Review*] [*A publication*]
Deep-Sea Res Pt B Oceanogr Lit Rev ... Deep-Sea Research. Part B. Oceanographic Literature Review [*A publication*]
DEEPSEAT ... Deep-Sea System for Evaluating Acoustic Transducers [*Navy*] (MCD)
DEEPSUBSYS ... Deep Submergence Systems [*Navy*]
DEEPSUBSYSPROJO ... Deep Submergence Systems Project Office [*Navy*]

DEER .... Deer Environment Ecology and Resources [*An association*]
DEER .... Deerfield Federal Savings & Loan Association [*NASDAQ symbol*] (NQ)
DEER .... Directional Explosive Echo Ranging
Deer Farm ... Deer Farmer [*A publication*]
Deering's Cal Adv Legis Serv ... Deering's California Advance Legislative Service [*A publication*] (DLA)
Deering's Cal Code Ann ... Deering's Annotated California Code [*A publication*] (DLA)
Deering's Cal Gen Laws Ann ... Deering's California General Laws, Annotated [*A publication*] (DLA)
DEERS ...... Defense Enrollment Eligibility Reporting System [*DoD*]
DEES .... Dynamic Electromagnetic Environment Simulator
Dees Ins ... Dees on the Law of Insolvent Debtors [*A publication*] (DLA)
DEET .... Diethyl-m-toluamide [*Insect repellent*]
DEEVAL... Detailed European Evaluation (MCD)
De Exil ...... De Exilio [*of Plutarch*] [*Classical studies*] (OCD)
DEF .... Dansk Eksportfinancieringfond [*Export credit agency*] [*Denmark*]
DEF .... Data Entry Facility
DEF .... Decayed, Extracted, or Filled [*Dentistry*]
DEF .... Default [*Business term*]
DEF .... Defeated
DEF .... Defecation
DEF .... Defective (MSA)
DEF .... Defendant
DEF .... Defense (AFM)
DEF .... Defensor [*Defender*] [*Coin inscription*] [*Latin*] (ROG)
DEF .... Deferred
DEF .... Defiance College, Defiance, OH [*OCLC symbol*] (OCLC)
def .... Deficiency [*or Deficient*]
DEF .... Deficit
DEF .... Define [*or Definite*] (KSC)
DEF .... Definition
DEF .... Definitive (ROG)
DEF .... Defoliation
DEF .... Defruiter [*Aviation*] (FAAC)
DEF .... Defunctus [*Deceased*] [*Latin*] (ADA)
DEF .... Disarm Education Fund (EA)
DEFA .... Daily Express Film Award [*British*]
De Fac ...... De Facie in Orbe Lunae [*of Plutarch*] [*Classical studies*] (OCD)
Def Aer ...... Defence Aerienne [*A publication*]
Defarmhera ... Defense and Armament Heracles International [*A publication*]
DEFAZET Dtsche Farben Z ... DEFAZET. Deutsche Farben Zeitschrift [*A publication*]
DEFBA ...... Domestic European Ferret Breeders Association (EA)
DEFCE ...... Defence (ROG)
DEFCLOTH & TEXSUPCEN ... Defense Clothing and Textile Supply Center [*Later, Defense Personnel Support Center*] [*DoD*]
DEFCOM ... Defense Command
DEFCON ... Defense Readiness Condition [*Army*]
DEFCON .. Defensive Concentration
DEFCONTRSUPCEN ... Defense Construction Supply Center [*Defense Supply Agency*]
DEFCS ...... Digital Electronic Flight Control System (MCD)
Def Daily.... Defense Daily [*A publication*]
DEFECT ... Defective Verb [*Grammar*] (ROG)
DEFEDZ ... Defenders [*A publication*]
Defektol ..... Defektologija [*A publication*]
Defektosk... Defektoskopiya [*A publication*]
DEFEL ...... Deferred Delivery
DEFELECSUPCEN ... Defense Electric Supply Center
Def Elect .... Defense Electronics [*A publication*]
Def Electron ... Defense Electronics [*A publication*]
Defence Sci J ... Defence Science Journal [*Delhi*] [*A publication*]
Defenders Wildl ... Defenders of Wildlife Magazine [*Later, Defenders*] [*A publication*]
Defenders Wildl Int ... Defenders of Wildlife International [*A publication*]
Defenders Wildl News ... Defenders of Wildlife News [*A publication*]
Defense A... Defense Africa and the Middle East [*A publication*]
Defense Jpn ... Defense of Japan, 1984 [*A publication*]
Defense L J ... Defense Law Journal [*A publication*]
Defense Mgt J ... Defense Management Journal [*A publication*]
Defense Nat ... Defense Nationale [*A publication*]
Defense Ns ... Defense News [*A publication*]
Defense Sci J ... Defense Science Journal [*A publication*]
Defense Veg ... Defense des Vegetaux [*A publication*]
Defens R & D ... Defense R and D Update. Space, Aeronautics, and Electronic Systems [*A publication*]
DEFEWS... Design Engineers Field Experience with Soldiers [*Army*] (RDA)
DEFGA ...... Deciduous Fruit Grower [*South Africa*] [*A publication*]
DEFGENSUPCEN ... Defense General Supply Center
DEFGR ...... Defogger [*Automotive engineering*]
Def Heli W ... Defense Helicopter World [*A publication*]
DEFI .... Defiance, Inc. [*NASDAQ symbol*] (NQ)
DEFI .... Digital Electronic Fuel Injection [*Automotive engineering*]
DEFIB .... Defibrillate [*Cardiology*]
DEFIC .... Deficiency (ROG)
DEFINDPLANTEQUIPCEN ... Defense Industrial Plant Equipment Center [*DoD*]

DEFINDSUPCEN ... Defense Industrial Supply Center
DEFINDSUPDEP ... Defense Industrial Supply Depot
DEFINTELAGCY ... Defense Intelligence Agency [*Formerly, JJ-2*]
Def J .... Defence Journal [*A publication*]
DEFL........ Deflect [*or Deflection*] (MSA)
DEFL........ Deflector [*Automotive engineering*]
DEFL........ Diode Emitter Follower Logic
3DEFL........ Triple Diffused Emitter-Follower Logic (MDG)
Def Latin A ... Defensa Latino Americana [*A publication*]
Def Law J... Defense Law Journal [*A publication*]
Def L J ...... Defense Law Journal [*A publication*]
DEFLOWH ... Defense Liaison Officer to the White House (AABC)
DEFLT ...... Deflect (AAG)
DEFLTN .... Deflection (AAG)
DEFLTR.... Deflector (AAG)
Def Man J ... Defense Management Journal [*A publication*]
Def Mark Technol ... Defense Markets and Technology [*A publication*]
Def Med Soc ... Defensa Medico Social [*A publication*]
Def Ment.... Deficience Mentale [*A publication*]
DeF Min .... De Fooz on Mines [*A publication*] (DLA)
Def Mntr.... Defense Monitor [*A publication*]
DEFN........ Deficiency (AABC)
Def Nat ...... Defense Nationale [*A publication*]
Def Natl ..... Defense Nationale [*A publication*]
Def Occident ... Defense de l'Occident [*A publication*]
DEFOL...... Defoliation (CINC)
De For Af... Defense and Foreign Affairs [*A publication*]
deform........ Deformity
Deform Met ... Deformacion Metalica [*A publication*]
Deform Razrushenie Neravnomernykh Temp Polyakh ... Deformatsiya i Razrushenie v Neravnomernykh Temperaturnykh Polyakh [*A publication*]
De Fort Rom ... De Fortuna Romanorum [*of Plutarch*] [*Classical studies*] (OCD)
DEFPERSUPPCEN ... Defense Personnel Support Center
DEFR........ Defrauding [*FBI standardized term*]
DEFR........ Defroster [*Automotive engineering*]
DEFRA .... Deficit Reduction Act [*1984*]
De Frat Amor ... De Fraterno Amore [*of Plutarch*] [*Classical studies*] (OCD)
DEFREP.... Defense Readiness Posture [*Army*] (AABC)
DEFREPNAMA ... Defense Representative, North Atlantic and Mediterranean Area
Def Res Abs Contractors Edn ... Defence Research Abstracts. Contractors Edition [*England*] [*A publication*]
DEFSATCOM ... Defense Satellite Communications System [*Military*]
DEFSCAP ... Defense Standard Contract Administration Procedure
DEFSCE.... Defeasance (ROG)
Def Sci .... Defense Science 2001 [*A publication*]
Def Sci J .... Defence Science Journal [*A publication*]
DEFSEC.... Defense Sector [*Navy*]
DEFSIP..... Defense Scientists Immigration Program (AFM)
DEFSMAC ... Defense Special Missile and Astronautics Center [*Pronounced "deff-smack"*] [*National Security Agency*]
Def Stand Lab DSL Rep ... Australia. Defence Standards Laboratories. DSL Report [*A publication*] (APTA)
Def Stand Lab Rep ... Australia. Defence Standards Laboratories. Report [*A publication*] (APTA)
Def Stand Lab Tech Memo ... Australia. Defence Standards Laboratories. Technical Memorandum [*A publication*] (APTA)
Def Stand Lab Tech Note ... Australia. Defence Standards Laboratories. Technical Note [*A publication*] (APTA)
DEFSUBSUPCEN ... Defense Subsistence Supply Center [*Later, Defense Personnel Support Center*]
Def Sys Rv ... Defense Systems Review and Military Communications [*A publication*]
Def Syst Man Rev ... Defense Systems Management Review [*A publication*]
DEFT........ Defendant
DEFT........ Definite-Time [*Relay*]
DEFT........ Deflection (ADA)
DEFT........ Design Effect [*Ratio used in statistics*]
DEFT........ Development and Evaluation of a Firearms Training Facility
DEFT........ Diagnostic Expert-Final Test [*IBM Corp.*]
DEFT........ Direct Electronic Fourier Transform [*Camera*]
DEFT........ Direct Epifluorescence Filter Technique [*Microbiology*]
DEFT........ Display Evaluation Flight Testing (MCD)
DEFT........ Driven Equilibrium Fourier Transform [*Mathematics*]
DEFT........ Dynamic Error-Free Transmission
Def Tech Inf Cent Dig ... Defense Technical Information Center. Digest [*A publication*]
Def Today .. Defense Today [*A publication*]
Def Transp J ... Defense Transportation Journal [*A publication*]
Def Veg ...... Defense des Vegetaux [*A publication*]
DEFWEAPSYSMGTCEN ... Defense Weapons System Management Center
Def Wildl ... Defenders of Wildlife [*A publication*]
Def Wildl Int ... Defenders of Wildlife International [*A publication*]
Def Wildl News ... Defenders of Wildlife News [*A publication*]
DEG.......... Dawson Eldorado Gold [*Vancouver Stock Exchange symbol*]
De G .... De Gex's English Bankruptcy Reports [*A publication*] (DLA)
DEG.......... De Laurentiis Entertainment Group, Inc. [*AMEX symbol*] (SPSG)
DEG.......... Degaussing Calibration (NVT)

DEG........... Degenerate Electron Gas
DEG........... Degeneration
DEG........... Degrade
DEG........... Degree (AFM)
Deg............. DeGroot, Dr. A. T., Texas Christian University, Fort Worth, TX [*Library symbol*] [*Library of Congress*] (LCLS)
DEG........... Design [*London*] [*A publication*]
DEG........... Destroyer Escort, Guided Missile [*British military*] (DMA)
DEG........... Development Economics Group
DEG........... Developments in Economic Geology [*Elsevier Book Series*] [*A publication*]
DEG........... Diagnostic Educational Grouping
DEG........... Diethylene Glycol [*Organic chemistry*]
DEG........... Diethylglycine [*Biochemistry*]
DEG........... Double-Ended Guillotine [*Nuclear energy*] (NRCH)
DEG........... Guided Missile Escort Ship [*Navy symbol*]
DEGA........ Depth Gauge
DEGA........ Diethylene Glycol Adipate [*Organic chemistry*]
De Garr...... De Garrulitate [*of Plutarch*] [*Classical studies*] (OCD)
DEGB........ Double-Ended Guillotine Break [*Nuclear energy*] (NRCH)
De G Bankr ... De Gex's English Bankruptcy Reports [*A publication*] (DLA)
De G Bankr (Eng) ... De Gex's English Bankruptcy Reports [*A publication*] (DLA)
degC........... Degree Celsius [*British Standards Institution*]
DEGCALB ... Degaussing Calibration (NVT)
DEG & DEP ... Degaussing and Deperming [*Navy*]
DeGE......... Eleutherian Mills Historical Library, Greenville, DE [*Library symbol*] [*Library of Congress*] (LCLS)
DEGEA3 ... Deutsche Gesundheitswesen [*A publication*]
De Gen....... De Genio Socratis [*of Plutarch*] [*Classical studies*] (OCD)
degen........ Degeneration
DeGeT .... Delaware Technical and Community College, Southern Campus, Georgetown, DE [*Library symbol*] [*Library of Congress*] (LCLS)
De Gex .... De Gex's English Bankruptcy Reports [*A publication*] (DLA)
De Gex F & J ... De Gex, Fisher, and Jones' English Chancery Reports [*A publication*] (DLA)
De Gex J & S ... De Gex, Jones, and Smith's English Chancery Reports [*A publication*] (DLA)
De Gex M & G ... De Gex, Macnaghten, and Gordon's English Reports [*A publication*] (DLA)
De Gex M & GB ... De Gex, Macnaghten, and Gordon's English Bankruptcy Reports [*A publication*] (DLA)
degF .... Degree Fahrenheit [*British Standards Institution*]
De G F & J ... De Gex, Fisher, and Jones' English Chancery Reports [*A publication*] (DLA)
Degge .... Degge's Parson's Counsellor and Law of Tithes [*A publication*] (DLA)
De Gids ...... De Gids op Maatschappelijk Gebied [*A publication*]
De G & J .... De Gex and Jones' English Chancery Reports [*A publication*] (ILCA)
De G & JB ... De Gex and Jones' English Bankruptcy Appeals [*1857-59*] [*A publication*] (DLA)
De G & J By ... De Gex and Jones' English Bankruptcy Appeals [*1857-59*] [*A publication*] (ILCA)
De G J & S ... De Gex, Jones, and Smith's English Chancery Reports [*A publication*] (DLA)
De G J & S By ... De Gex, Jones, and Smith's English Bankruptcy Appeals [*1862-65*] [*A publication*] (DLA)
De G J & S (Eng) ... De Gex, Jones, and Smith's English Chancery Reports [*A publication*] (DLA)
De G J & Sm ... De Gex, Jones, and Smith's English Chancery Reports [*A publication*] (DLA)
degK .... Degree Kelvin [*British Standards Institution*]
De Glor Ath ... De Gloria Atheniensium [*of Plutarch*] [*Classical studies*] (OCD)
DEGLUT... Deglutiatur [*Swallow*] [*Pharmacy*]
DEGLUTIEND ... Deglutiendus [*To be Taken or Swallowed*] [*Pharmacy*] (ROG)
De G M & G ... De Gex, Macnaghten, and Gordon's English Bankruptcy Reports [*A publication*] (DLA)
De G M & G ... De Gex, Macnaghten, and Gordon's English Chancery Reports [*A publication*] (DLA)
De G M & G By ... De Gex, Macnaghten, and Gordon's English Bankruptcy Appeals [*1837-55*] [*A publication*] (DLA)
DEGN........ Diethylene Glycol Dinitrate [*Explosive*]
degR .... Degree Rankine [*British Standards Institution*]
DEGRA ..... Degradation (DSUE)
De G & S.... De Gex and Smale's English Chancery Reports [*63-64 English Reprint*] [*1846-52*] [*A publication*] (DLA)
DEGS........ Diethylene Glycol Succinate [*Organic chemistry*]
DEG/SEC ... Degrees per Second
De G & Sm ... De Gex and Smale's English Chancery Reports [*63-64 English Reprint*] [*1846-52*] [*A publication*] (ILCA)
DEGSVC ... Degaussing Services [*Navy*] (NVT)
DEGUSG .. Degaussing
DEH........... Dallas Enviro-Health Systems Ltd. [*Vancouver Stock Exchange symbol*]
DeH .... De Homine [*A publication*]
DEH........... Decorah, IA [*Location identifier*] [*FAA*] (FAAL)
DEH........... Deepwater Escort Hydrofoil [*Also, DBH*] (MCD)

DEH........... Diethylhydroxylamine [*Also, DEHA*] [*Organic chemistry*]
DEH........... Digital Electrohydraulic (NRCH)
DEH........... Digital Encoder Handbook
DEH........... Direct Engineering Hours (MCD)
DEH........... Directorate of Engineering and Housing [*Army*] (RDA)
DEHA........ Di(ethylhexyl) Adipate [*Also, DOA*] [*Organic chemistry*]
DEHA........ Diethylhydroxylamine [*Also, DEH*] [*Organic chemistry*]
De Hart Mil Law ... DeHart on Military Law [*A publication*] (DLA)
DEHB........ Digital Encoder Handbook
DEHB........ Double Extra Hard Black [*Pencil leads*] (ROG)
DEHEA8... Dental Health [*London*] [*A publication*]
DEHFT..... Developmental Hand Function Test
DeHi .... Historical Society of Delaware, Wilmington, DE [*Library symbol*] [*Library of Congress*] (LCLS)
DeH ML .... DeHart on Military Law [*A publication*] (DLA)
DEHP........ Diethyl Hydrogen Phosphite [*Organic chemistry*]
DEHP........ Di(ethylhexyl)phthalate [*Also, DOP, DHP*] [*Organic chemistry*]
DEHPA ..... Di(ethylhexyl)phosphoric Acid [*Organic chemistry*]
DEHYD.... Dehydrated
DEHYD3... Developments in Hydrobiology [*A publication*]
DEI........... Defense Electronics, Incorporated
DEI........... Defense des Enfants - International [*Defence for Children International Movement - DCI*] (EAIO)
DEI........... Denis Island [*Seychelles Islands*] [*Airport symbol*] (OAG)
DEI........... Dent [*Idaho*] [*Seismograph station code, US Geological Survey*] [*Closed*] (SEIS)
DEI........... Design Engine Inspection (AFM)
DEI........... Design Engineering Identification (NASA)
DEI........... Development Engineering Inspection (MCD)
DEI........... Display Evaluation Index
DEI........... Diversified Energies, Incorporated [*NYSE symbol*] (SPSG)
DEI........... Dose Equivalent Iodine [*Nuclear energy*] (NRCH)
DEI........... Dutch East Indies
DEI........... Export-Import Bank of the United States, Washington, DC [*Library symbol*] [*Library of Congress*] (LCLS)
DEIB........ Developmental Engineering Inspection Board (AAG)
DEIC......... Diver Equipment Information Center [*Battelle Memorial Institute*] [*Information service or system*] (IID)
DEIMD6 ... Developments in Immunology [*A publication*]
De Imit....... De Imitatione [*of Dionysius Halicarnassensis*] [*Classical studies*] (OCD)
DEIMOS... Development Investigations in Military Orbiting Systems
DEIMS...... Defense Economic Impact Modeling System
Deiot......... Pro Rege Deiotaro [*of Cicero*] [*Classical studies*] (OCD)
DEIS......... Defense Energy Information System [*DoD*] [*Washington, DC*] (AFM)
DEIS......... Design Engineering Inspection Simulation (NASA)
DEIS......... Design Evaluation Inspection Simulator (NASA)
DEIS......... Director of Engineering and Industrial Services [*Edgewood Arsenal, MD*]
DEIS......... DoD [*Department of Defense*] Worldwide Energy Information System (MCD)
DEIS......... Draft Environmental Impact Statement [*NRC*] (MSC)
DEIS......... IEEE Dielectrics and Electrical Insulation Society (EA)
De Is et Os ... De Iside et Osiride [*of Plutarch*] [*Classical studies*] (OCD)
DEJ........... Albany, NY [*Location identifier*] [*FAA*] (FAAL)
DEJ........... David Ezekiel Joshua [*Shanghai*] (BJA)
DE/J.......... DE Journal [*Later, DE. Domestic Engineering*] [*A publication*]
DEJ........... Dejour Mines Ltd. [*Toronto Stock Exchange symbol*]
DEJ........... Dento-Enamel Junction [*Dentistry*]
DEJ........... Dermoepidermal Junction [*Anatomy*]
DEJ ALVI ... Dejectiones Alvi [*Discharge from the Bowels*] [*Pharmacy*] (ROG)
DE J Dent Eng ... DE. Journal of Dental Engineering [*A publication*]
Dejiny Ved Tech ... Dejiny Ved a Techniky [*A publication*]
De Jure Mar ... Hale's De Jure Maris, Appendix to Hall on the Sea Shore [*A publication*] (DLA)
DEK........... Data Entry Keyboard [*Data processing*] (MCD)
DEK........... Dekeleia [*Greece*] [*Later, PEN*] [*Geomagnetic observatory code*]
DEK........... Demokratiki Enosis Kyprou [*Democratic Union of Cyprus*] [*Greek Cyprus*] [*Political party*] (PPE)
DEK........... Devtek Corp. [*Toronto Stock Exchange symbol*]
DEK........... Diethyl Ketone [*Organic chemistry*]
DEKAG .... Dekagram [*Unit of measure*]
DEKAL...... Dekaliter [*Unit of measure*] (ROG)
DeKalb ...... DeKalb Literary Arts Journal [*A publication*]
DeKalb Lit ... DeKalb Literary Arts Journal [*A publication*]
DEKAM ..... Dekameter [*Unit of measure*] (ROG)
DEKE .... Doppler Ekelund Ranging [*Navy*] (CAAL)
Dek Iskusstvo ... Dekorativnoe Iskusstvo SSSR [*A publication*]
DEKO........ Demokratiko Komma [*Democratic Party*] [*Greek Cyprus*] [*Political party*] (PPE)
Dekor Isk SSSR ... Dekorativnoe Iskusstvo SSSR [*A publication*]
De Krets..... DeKretser's Matara Appeals [*Ceylon*] [*A publication*] (DLA)
DEL........... Data Entry Language
DEL........... Defence Electric Light [*British military*] (DMA)
DEL........... Del Electronics Corp. [*AMEX symbol*] (SPSG)
Del............. Delane's English Revision Cases [*1832-35*] [*A publication*] (DLA)

DEL .... Delary [*Sweden*] [*Seismograph station code, US Geological Survey*] (SEIS)
DEL .... Delaware (AFM)
del.............. Delaware [*MARC language code*] [*Library of Congress*] (LCCP)
Del.............. Delaware County Reports [*Pennsylvania*] [*A publication*] (DLA)
Del.............. Delaware Reports [*A publication*] (DLA)
Del.............. Delaware Supreme Court Reports [*1832-*] [*A publication*] (ILCA)
DEL .... Delay
DEL .... Delay Message [*Aviation code*] (FAAC)
DEL .... Delegacy (ROG)
DEL .... Delegate [*or Delegation*] (ADA)
DEL .... Delete Character [*Keyboard*] (CMD)
DEL .... Delhi [*India*] [*Airport symbol*] (OAG)
DEL .... Delineation (MSA)
DEL .... Delineavit [*He (or She) Drew It*] [*Latin*] (ROG)
DEL .... Delinquent
Del.............. Delitzsch (BJA)
DEL .... Deliver [*or Delivery*] (KSC)
DEL .... Dellaterra Resources Ltd. [*Vancouver Stock Exchange symbol*]
Del.............. Delphinus [*Constellation*]
DEL .... Delusion
DEL .... Deorbit, Entry, and Landing [*Aerospace*] (MCD)
DEL .... Direct Electrical Linkage
DEL .... Direct Exchange Line [*Telecommunications*]
DEL .... Directly Employed Labour [*British*]
D El............ Doctor of Elements
DEL .... Doctor of English Literature
DEL .... Donor Energy Level
Del.............. Hymnus in Delum [*of Callimachus*] [*Classical studies*] (OCD)
DELA .... Del Paint Corp. [*Oklahoma City, OK*] [*NASDAQ symbol*] (NQ)
DELA .... Delactonized Ascorbate [*Biochemistry*]
DElA .... Dictionary of Electrical Abbreviations, Signs, and Symbols [*A publication*]
DELACCT ... Delinquent Account
Del Ag Exp ... Delaware. Agricultural Experiment Station. Publications [*A publication*]
Del Agric Exp Stn Bull ... Delaware. Agricultural Experiment Station. Bulletin [*A publication*]
Del Agric Exp Stn Circ ... Delaware. Agricultural Experiment Station. Circular [*A publication*]
Delane........ Delane's Revision Courts Decisions [*England*] [*A publication*] (DLA)
DELASEM ... Delegation for Assistance to Jewish Emigrants [*World War II organization*]
De Lat Viv ... De Latenter Vivendo [*of Plutarch*] [*Classical studies*] (OCD)
Delaware Co Inst Sc Pr ... Delaware County Institute of Science. Proceedings [*A publication*]
Delaware Co Reps ... Delaware County Reports [*Pennsylvania*] [*A publication*] (DLA)
Delaware Hist Soc Papers ... Delaware Historical Society. Papers [*A publication*]
Delaware J Corp L ... Delaware Journal of Corporate Law [*A publication*] (DLA)
Del C Ann .. Delaware Code, Annotated [*A publication*] (ILCA)
DELCAP ... Delay/Capacity [*Airport terminal*] [*FAA*]
Del Cas ...... Delaware Cases [*1792-1830*] [*A publication*] (DLA)
DELCD....... Declared (ROG)
Del Ch........ Delaware Chancery Reports [*A publication*] (DLA)
Del-Chem Bull ... Del-Chem Bulletin [*A publication*]
Del Civ Dec ... Delaware Chancery Reports [*A publication*] (DLA)
Del Civ Dec ... Delhi Civil Decisions [*India*] [*A publication*] (DLA)
DELCO ..... Dayton Engineering Laboratories Company
Del Co .... Delaware County Reports [*Pennsylvania*] [*A publication*] (DLA)
Del Code .... Delaware Code (DLA)
Del Code Ann ... Delaware Code, Annotated [*A publication*] (DLA)
Del Co L J (PA) ... Delaware County Law Journal [*Pennsylvania*] [*A publication*] (DLA)
Del Const ... Delaware Constitution [*A publication*] (DLA)
Del Co (PA) ... Delaware County Reports [*Pennsylvania*] [*A publication*] (DLA)
Del Co R..... Delaware County Reports [*Pennsylvania*] [*A publication*] (DLA)
Del Co Reps ... Delaware County Reports [*Pennsylvania*] [*A publication*] (DLA)
Del County ... Delaware County Reports [*Pennsylvania*] [*A publication*] (DLA)
Del County Rep ... Delaware County Reports [*Pennsylvania*] [*A publication*] (DLA)
Del Cr Cas ... Delaware Criminal Cases [*A publication*] (DLA)
Del Ct M.... Delafon on Naval Courts Martial [*A publication*] (DLA)
Del Cty Farm Home News ... Delaware County Farm and Home News [*A publication*]
DELD .... Delivered
Dele........... Deleatur [*Delete*] [*Latin*] (DLA)
D El Ed ...... Diploma in Elementary Education
DELEG...... Delegate

DELEG...... Delegation (ROG)
Delehanty .. New York Miscellaneous Reports [*A publication*] (DLA)
Del El Cas ... Delane's Election Revision Cases [*England*] [*A publication*] (DLA)
DELENT... Delete in Its Entirety (AAG)
DELEX...... Destroyer Life Extension [*Canadian Navy program*]
DELFIA..... Dissociation Enhanced Lanthanide Fluoroimmunoassay [*Clinical chemistry*]
DELFIC..... Defense Land Fallout Interpretive Code (MCD)
Delft Prog Rep ... Delft Progress Report [*A publication*]
Delft Prog Report ... Delft Progress Report [*A publication*]
Delft Prog Rep Ser A ... Delft Progress Report. Series A. Chemistry and Physics, Chemical and Physical Engineering [*A publication*]
Delft Prog Rep Ser B ... Delft Progress Report. Series B. Electrical, Electronic, and Information Engineering [*A publication*]
Delft Prog Rep Ser C ... Delft Progress Report. Series C. Mechanical and Aeronautical Engineering and Shipbuilding [*A publication*]
Delft Prog Rep Ser D ... Delft Progress Report. Series D. Architecture, Industrial Design, Social Sciences [*A publication*]
Delft Prog Rep Ser E ... Delft Progress Report. Series E. Geosciences [*A publication*]
Delft Prog Rep Ser F ... Delft Progress Report. Series F. Mathematical Engineering, Mathematics, and Information Engineering [*A publication*]
Delft Progress Rep Ser F ... Delft Progress Report. Series F [*A publication*]
Del GCL.... Delaware General Corporation Law [*A publication*] (DLA)
Del Geol Surv Bull ... Delaware. Geological Survey. Bulletin [*A publication*]
Del Geol Survey Ann Rept Bull Rept Inv ... Delaware. Geological Survey. Annual Report. Bulletin. Report of Investigations [*A publication*]
Del Geol Surv Rep Invest ... Delaware. Geological Survey. Report of Investigations [*A publication*]
Delgn.......... Delegation
DelH .... Delaware History [*A publication*]
Delhi Alum Patrika ... Delhi Aluminium Patrika [*A publication*]
Delhi L R ... Delhi Law Review [*A publication*]
Delhi L Rev ... Delhi Law Review [*A publication*]
Delhi L Times ... Delhi Law Times [*A publication*]
Del Hist ..... Delaware History [*A publication*]
Del Hlth News ... Delaware Health News [*A publication*]
DELI.......... Delicatessen
DELIB....... Deliberation (ROG)
DELIC....... Delicatamente [*Delicately*] [*Music*]
DELICAT ... Delicatamente [*Delicately*] [*Music*] (ROG)
DELICATISS ... Delicatissimo [*Very Delicately*] [*Music*] (ROG)
Delin .... Delineator [*A publication*]
DELIND.... Delineated (ROG)
DELINQ.... Delinquent (MUGU)
DELINUS ... Authorized to Delay [*Number of Days*], Any Portion of Which May Be Taken in CONUS [*Navy*]
DELIQ....... Deliquescent
Delius......... Delius Society. Journal [*A publication*]
Del J Corp L ... Delaware Journal of Corporate Law [*A publication*]
Delkeletdunantuli Mezogazd Kiserl Intez Kozl ... Delkeletdunantuli Mezogazdasagi Kiserleti Intezet Kozlemenye [*A publication*]
DELL......... Dell Computer Corp. [*NASDAQ symbol*] (NQ)
Del Law...... Delaware Lawyer [*A publication*] (DLA)
Del Laws .... Laws of Delaware [*A publication*] (DLA)
Del L R...... Delhi Law Review [*A publication*]
DELMAR ... Data Element Management Accounting and Reporting
DELMARVA ... Delaware, Maryland, Virginia [*Peninsula*]
Del Med J ... Delaware Medical Journal [*A publication*]
DelN .... Delaware Notes [*A publication*]
Del Note...... Delaware Notes [*A publication*]
Del Notes ... Delaware Notes [*A publication*]
DELNQY .. Delinquency
Del Nurs .... Delaware Nurse [*A publication*]
DELO .... Delicato [*Delicately*] [*Music*] (ROG)
D Elo .... Doctor of Elocution
De Lolme Eng Const ... De Lolme on the English Constitution [*A publication*] (DLA)
Del Order... Delegation Order
Delos.......... Explorations Archeologiques de Delos [*A publication*]
DELPARTURE ... Authorized to Delay [*Number of Days*], Any Portion of Which May Be Taken Prior to or after Departure [*Navy*]
Delph .... Delphinus [*Constellation*]
DELPHO .. Deliver by Telephone [*Message handling*]
Del PM Ex ... Delafield on Post Mortem Examinations [*A publication*] (DLA)
DELPRO... Delegated Procurement System [*Science*]
DELQ .... Delinquent
DELR........ Deliver (ROG)
DELRAC... DECCA Long-Range Area Coverage (MCD)
Del Reg of Regs ... Delaware Register of Regulations [*A publication*] (DLA)
DELREP... Authorized to Delay [*Number of Days*], in Reporting [*Navy*]
DELREPANY ... Authorized to Delay [*Number of Days*], in Reporting, Any Portion of Which May Be Taken Prior to or after Reporting at Temporary Duty Station [*Navy*]

DELREPARUS ... Authorized to Delay [*Number of Days*], Any Portion of Which May Be Taken Prior to or after Arrival in United States [*Navy*]

DELREPGRAD ... Authorized to Delay [*Number of Days*], in Reporting, to Count as Graduation Leave [*Navy*]

DELREPVAN ... Authorized to Delay [*Number of Days*], in Reporting, Keep New Station Advised Address [*Navy*]

DELRIBACO ... Delaware River Basin Commission [*Successor to INCODEL*]

DELRIVEPOE ... Delay in Arriving at Port of Embarkation [*Navy*]

DELSA ...... Doppler Electrophoretic Light Scanning Analyzer

Del Sea Grant Tech Rep DEL-SG ... Delaware Sea Grant Technical Report. DEL-SG [*A publication*]

Del State Med J ... Delaware State Medical Journal [*A publication*]

Del St Med J ... Delaware State Medical Journal [*A publication*]

DELT .... Deck Edge Light   (AAG)

DELT .... Delete   (AAG)

DELT .... Delineavit [*He (or She) Drew It*] [*Latin*]

DELT .... Dynamic Environmental Laboratory Test

DELTA ...... Detailed Labor and Time Analysis [*PERT*]

DELTA ...... Determination Effective Levels of Task Automation [*Data processing*]

DELTA ...... Differential Electronically-Locking Test Accessory

DELTA ...... Distributed Electronic Test and Analysis

DELTABANK ... Drug Effects on Laboratory Tests: Attention [*Worldwide Medical Information Ltd.*] [*Database*]

Delta ES ..... Delta. Revue du Centre d'Etudes et de Recherche sur les Ecrivains du Sud aux Etats-Unis [*A publication*]

Delt Agrotikes Trapezes ... Deltion Agrotikes Trapezes [*A publication*]

Delta Kappa Gamma Bull ... Delta Kappa Gamma Bulletin [*A publication*]

Delta Pi Epsilon J ... Delta Pi Epsilon Journal [*A publication*]

Delt Arch ... Deltion Archaiologikon [*A publication*]

Delt Bibl Melet ... Deltion Biblikon Meleton [*A publication*]

Del Term R ... Delaware Term Reports [*A publication*]   (DLA)

Delt Hellen Mikrobiol Hyg Hetair ... Deltion Hellenikes Mikrobiologikes kai Hygieinologikes Hetaireias [*Greece*] [*A publication*]

Delt Hell Geogr Het ... Deltion Hellenikes Geografikes Hetaireias [*A publication*]

Delt Hell Geol Hetair ... Deltion tes Hellenikes Geolokne Hetaireias [*A publication*]

Delt Hell Kteniatr Hetair ... Deltion tes Hellenikes Kteniatrikes Hetaireias [*A publication*]

Delt Hell Mikr Hyg Het ... Deltion Hellenikes Mikrobiologikes kai Hygieinologikes Hetaireias [*A publication*]

Delt Hell Mikrobiol Hygieinol Hetair ... Deltion Hellenikes Mikrobiologikes kai Hygieinologikes Hetaireias [*A publication*]

DELTIC .... Delay Line Time Compression

Delt IKA .... Deltion Hidrymatos Koinonikon Asphaliseon [*A publication*]

Delt Inst Technol Phytikon Proionton ... Deltion tou Institoutou Technologias Phytikon Proionton [*A publication*]

Deltion .... Archaiologikon Deltion [*A publication*]

Del Univ Sea Grant Program Annu Rep ... Delaware University. Sea Grant Program. Annual Report [*A publication*]

Del Univ Water Resour Semin Proc ... Delaware University. Water Resources Seminars. Proceedings [*A publication*]

DELV .... Deliver   (ADA)

Delv .... Delivered   (DLA)

Del Val Bus D ... Delaware Valley Business Digest [*A publication*]

DELV'D ..... Delivered

DELWU .... Delegate [*or Delegation*] to Western Union [*NATO*]   (NATG)

DELY .... Delivery

Dely .... Delyse [*Record label*] [*Great Britain*]

DEM .... Data Entry Mode   (MCD)

Dem .... De Demosthene [*of Dionysius Halicarnassensis*] [*Classical studies*]   (OCD)

De M .... De Mello's Extradition Cases [*1877-1913*] [*Malaya*] [*A publication*]   (DLA)

DEM .... Decoy Ejection Mechanism

DEM .... Delta Modulation [*Telecommunications*]   (TEL)

DEM .... Demagogue   (ROG)

Dem .... Dema'i   (BJA)

DEM .... Demand

Dem .... Demarest's New York Surrogate's Court Reports [*A publication*]   (DLA)

DEM .... Dembidollo [*Ethiopia*] [*Airport symbol*]   (OAG)

Dem .... Demerol [*Meperidine hydrochloride*] [*Analgesic compound*] [*Trademark*]

DEM .... Demijohn [*Freight*]

DEM .... Democrat [*or Democratic*]   (EY)

DEM .... Demodulator [*Telecommunications*]   (KSC)

Dem .... Demografia [*A publication*]

DEM .... Demolish [*Technical drawings*]

DEM .... Demonstration

DEM .... Demonstration Account [*For messages to and from UTLAS*]

Dem .... Demonstrative   (BJA)

DeM .... DeMorgans Theorems [*Rules of replacement*] [*Logic*]

Dem .... Demosthenes [*Greek orator, 384-322BC*] [*Classical studies*]

Dem .... Demosthenes [*of Plutarch*] [*Classical studies*]   (OCD)

DEM .... Demote   (AABC)

DEM .... Demulcent [*Softening, Lubricating*] [*Pharmacy*]   (ROG)

DEM .... Demurrage [*Shipping*]

DEM .... Demy [*Half*] [*Size of paper*]

DEM .... Detective, Enigma, and Mystery [*Publisher*] [*USSR*]   (ECON)

DeM .... Deus Misereatur [*67th Psalm*] [*Music*]

DEM .... Developments in Environmental Modelling [*Elsevier Book Series*] [*A publication*]

DEM .... Diethyl Maleate [*Biochemistry*]

DEM .... Directional Emittance Measurement

DEM .... Distribution, Excretion, and Metabolism [*Environmental chemistry*]

DEMA .... Data Entry Management Association   (EA)

DEMA .... Diesel Engine Manufacturers Association   (EA)

DEMA .... Distributed Emission Magnetron Amplifier   (MSA)

DEMA .... Diving Equipment Manufacturers Association   (EA)

DEMAB .... Dental Management [*A publication*]

DEMAEP ... Dental Materials [*A publication*]

Demag Nachr ... Demag Nachrichten [*A publication*]

DEMAND ... Digitalized Electronics MARC [*Machine-Readable Cataloging*] and Non-MARC [*Machine-Readable Cataloging*] Display [*Library of Congress*]

DEMAR ..... Data Element Management Accounting and Reporting   (MCD)

Demarest .... Demarest's New York Surrogate's Court Reports [*A publication*]   (DLA)

DEMATRON ... Distributed Emission Magnetron Amplifier

DEMBOMB ... Demolition Bomb

Dem Cond Etran ... Demangeat's Condition Civile, Etrangers en France [*A publication*]   (DLA)

DEMD .... Demised   (ROG)

Dem Dir ..... Democrazia e Diritto [*A publication*]

DEME .... Director of Electrical and Mechanical Engineering [*Military*] [*British*]

DE-ME-DRIVE ... Decoding Memory Drive [*Data processing*]   (MDG)

Demetr .... Demetrius [*of Plutarch*] [*Classical studies*]   (OCD)

DEMIL ...... Demilitarize   (AABC)

DEMIZ ...... DEW [*Distant Early Warning*] East Military Identification Zone

DEML .... Detached Enlisted Men's List [*Army*]

DEM/LAB ... Demographics Laboratory [*Information service or system*]   (IID)

DEML(CIC) ... Enlisted Men on Duty with the Counter Intelligence Corps [*Army*]

DEML(NG) ... Enlisted Men on Duty with the National Guard [*Army*]

DEML(OR) ... Enlisted Men on Duty with the Organized Reserves [*Army*]

DEML(ROTC) ... Enlisted Men on Duty with the Reserve Officers' Training Corps [*Army*]

DemNPN ... Democratic Non-Party Nationalist Party [*British*]

Dem (NY) .. Demarest's New York Surrogate's Court Reports [*A publication*]   (DLA)

Demo .... Democracy [*A publication*]

DEMO ...... Demography [*A publication*]

DEMO ...... Demolition

DEMO ...... Demonstrator   (KSC)

DEMOB .... Demobilize   (AABC)

Demo & Chr ... Democrat and Chronicle [*A publication*]

Democr .... Democritus [*Fifth century BC*] [*Classical studies*]   (OCD)

Democratic R ... Democratic Review [*A publication*]

Democr e Dir ... Democrazia e Diritto [*A publication*]

DEMOD .... Demodulator [*Telecommunications*]   (AAG)

DEMOD .... Deployment Model [*Army*]   (AABC)

DEMOG .... Demography

Demogr .... Demografia [*A publication*]

Demogr .... Demography [*A publication*]

Demografia y Econ ... Demografia y Economia [*A publication*]

Demogr Bull ... Demographic Bulletin [*New Zealand*] [*A publication*]

Demogr y Econ ... Demografia y Economia [*A publication*]

Demokr Recht ... Demokratie und Recht [*A publication*]

DEMOL .... Demolition

Demol .... Demolombe's Code Napoleon [*A publication*]   (DLA)

Demol C N ... Demolombe's Code Napoleon [*A publication*]   (DLA)

Demo Left .. Democratic Left [*A publication*]

Demo Left .. Newsletter of the Democratic Left [*A publication*]

DEMON .... Decision Mapping via Optimum Go-No Networks

DEMON .... Demodulated Noise   (CAAL)

Demon .... Demonax [*of Lucian*] [*Classical studies*]   (OCD)

DEMON .... Demonstrative

DEMON .... Digital Electric Monitor

DEMON .... Diminishing Error Method of Optimization for Networks [*Data processing*]   (RDA)

De Monog .. De Monogamia [*of Tertullian*] [*Classical studies*]   (OCD)

DEMONS ... Demonstrative   (ROG)

DEMONST ... Demonstrator

DEMONSTR ... Demonstrative (Pronoun) [*Linguistics*]

Demonstratio Math ... Demonstratio Mathematica [*A publication*]

DEMP .... Democratic Party [*Slang*]

DEMP .... Drug Emporium, Inc. [*NASDAQ symbol*]   (NQ)

Dempa Dig ... Dempa Digest [*A publication*]

Dem R ...... Democratic Review [*A publication*]

DEMR .... Department of Energy, Mines, and Resources [*Canada*]

DEMS .... Defensively-Equipped Merchant Ship

DEMS .... Development Engineering Management System [*Air Force*]

DEMS .... Differential Electrochemistry/Mass Spectrometry

DEMS .... Digital Electronic Message Systems

DEMS........ Digital Error Monitoring System   (MCD)
DEMS........ Diver Equivalent Manipulator System [*General Electric*]
DEMS........ Dormant Equipping of Merchant Ships [*Organization*]   (MCD)
DEMSS ...... Defensively-Equipped Merchant Ship School
DemStud .... Demotische Studien [*Leipzig*] [*A publication*]
Dem Surr ... Demarest's New York Surrogate's Court Reports [*A publication*]   (DLA)
DEMU....... Diesel Electric Multiple Unit   (ADA)
De Mul Vir ... De Mulierum Virtutibus [*of Plutarch*] [*Classical studies*]   (OCD)
DEMUR....... Demurrer   (ROG)
De Mus ...... De Musica [*of Plutarch*] [*Classical studies*]   (OCD)
DEMUX.... Demultiplexer [*Data processing*]
DEM/VAL ... Demonstration/Validation   (MCD)
DEMYC .... Democrat Youth Community of Europe [*Formerly, Conservative and Christian Democrat Youth Community of Europe*]   (EA)
DEN.......... Data Element Number   (MCD)
DEn.......... Delavska Enotnost [*A publication*]
DEN.......... Denbighshire [*County in Wales*]   (ROG)
Den............ Denied [*Legal term*]   (DLA)
den............ Denier [*Later, tex*]
Den............ Denio's New York Reports [*A publication*]   (DLA)
Den............ Denis' Reports [*32-46 Louisiana*] [*A publication*]   (DLA)
DEN.......... Denison Mines Ltd. [*Toronto Stock Exchange symbol*] [*Vancouver Stock Exchange symbol*]
Den............ Denison and Pearce's English Crown Cases Reserved [*169 English Reprint*] [*1844-52*] [*A publication*]   (DLA)
DEN.......... Denmark
DEN.......... Denote   (MSA)
DEN.......... Denouement   (ROG)
DEN.......... Density
DEN.......... Dental   (AABC)
DEN.......... Denver [*Colorado*] [*Seismograph station code, US Geological Survey*]   (SEIS)
DEN.......... Denver [*Colorado*] [*Airport symbol*]
DEn.......... Department of Energy [*British*]
DEN.......... Device Evaluation Network [*FDA*] [*Information service or system*]
DEN.......... Diethylnitrosamine [*Also, DENA*] [*Carcinogen*]
DE(N)........ Director of Engineering (Naval) [*British military*]   (DMA)
DEN.......... District Enrolled Nurse [*British*]
D En.......... Doctor of English
DEN.......... Dow Epoxy Novolac
DeN........... Newark Free Library, Newark, DE [*Library symbol*] [*Library of Congress*]   (LCLS)
DENA........ Diethylnitrosamine [*Also, DEN*] [*Carcinogen*]
DENALT... Density Altitude [*Computer*]
Den App..... Denying Appeal   (DLA)
DENAS...... Daily European Naval Activity Summary   (MCD)
DENAT ..... Denatured
DENB .... Denbighshire [*County in Wales*]
Den BA Rec ... Denver Bar Association. Record [*A publication*]   (DLA)
DENBIGHS ... Denbighshire [*County in Wales*]
DENBS...... Denbighshire [*County in Wales*]
DENC .... Dencor Energy Cost Controls, Inc. [*NASDAQ symbol*]   (NQ)
DENC .... Divergent Exhaust Nozzle Control   (MCD)
Den C C...... Denison's English Crown Cases [*1844-52*] [*A publication*]   (DLA)
DeNcD....... Delaware State Hospital, New Castle, DE [*Library symbol*] [*Library of Congress*]   (LCLS)
DENCO..... Dental Company [*Marine Corps*]
DeND....... E. I. Du Pont de Nemours & Co., Stine Laboratory, Newark, DE [*Library symbol*] [*Library of Congress*]   (LCLS)
DENDRAL ... Dendritic Algorithm [*Organic molecules*]
DENEB ..... Fog Dispersal Operations [*Aviation code*]   (FAAC)
DENED7 ... Developmental Neuroscience [*A publication*]
DENFA7 ... Dendroflora [*A publication*]
D Eng .... Doctor of Engineering
DEngg........ Doctor of Engineering
Den'gi i Kred ... Den'gi i Kredit [*A publication*]
D Eng P...... Doctor of Engineering Physics
D Eng Sc..... Doctor of Engineering Science
DENI .... Department of Education of Northern Ireland [*British*]
DENIF....... Denison Mines Ltd. [*NASDAQ symbol*]   (NQ)
Deniliquin Hist Soc News ... Deniliquin Historical Society. Newsletter [*A publication*]   (APTA)
DENIM ..... Fabric name derived from "serge de Nimes," a sturdy textile made in Nimes, France, during the Middle Ages
Denio.......... Denio's New York Supreme Court Reports [*1845-48*] [*A publication*]   (DLA)
Denio R ...... Denio's New York Reports [*A publication*]   (DLA)
Denis.......... Denis' Reports [*32-46 Louisiana*] [*A publication*]   (DLA)
Denison Cr Cas ... Denison's English Crown Cases [*1844-52*] [*A publication*]   (DLA)
Denison Univ Sci Lab Jour ... Denison University. Scientific Laboratories. Journal [*A publication*]
Denison Univ Sc Lab B ... Denison University. Scientific Laboratories. Bulletin [*A publication*]
Den JILP ... Denver Journal of International Law and Policy [*A publication*]

Den J Int'l L & Pol'y ... Denver Journal of International Law and Policy [*A publication*]
Den J Int L and Pol ... Denver Journal of International Law and Policy [*A publication*]
DENK........ Dual Employed, No Kids [*Lifestyle classification*]
Denki Kag ... Denki Kagaku [*A publication*]
Denkm Pfl Bad Wuert ... Denkmalpflege in Baden-Wuerttemberg [*A publication*]
Denk Pfl Rhein Pfalz ... Denkmalpflege in Rheinland-Pfalz [*A publication*]
Denkschriften (Wien) ... Oesterreichische Akademie der Wissenschaften. Philosophisch-Historische Klasse. Denkschriften (Wien) [*A publication*]
Denkschr Schweiz Naturforsch Ges ... Denkschriften. Schweizerische Naturforschende Gesellschaft [*A publication*]
DENL .... Denelcor, Inc. [*NASDAQ symbol*]   (NQ)
Den LCJ ... Denver Law Center. Journal [*A publication*]
Den L J ..... Denver Law Journal [*A publication*]
Den L N ..... Denver Legal News [*A publication*]   (DLA)
DENM...... Denmark
Denmark Gronlands Geol Undersogelse Rapp ... Denmark. Groenlands Geologiske Undersoegelse Rapport [*A publication*]
DENN....... Dene Nation Newsletter [*A publication*]
DENN....... Denomination   (ROG)
DENOM... Denomination
denom....... Denominative [*or Denominator*]   (BJA)
Den & P...... Denison and Pearce's English Crown Cases [*1844-52*] [*A publication*]   (DLA)
DENPA ..... Density Phenomena [*Japan*]
DENPA3 ... Dental Progress [*A publication*]
DENPAY... Dental Pay
Den & PCC ... Denison and Pearce's English Crown Cases [*1844-52*] [*A publication*]   (DLA)
DENPRE... Density Probe   (MUGU)
Den Q........ Denver Quarterly [*A publication*]
DENR....... Denominator   (ROG)
DENR....... Department of Energy and Natural Resources
Den Rearg ... Denying Reargument [*Legal term*]   (DLA)
Den Reh ..... Denying Rehearing [*Legal term*]   (DLA)
Den Res Establ Risoe Rep ... Denmark. Research Establishment Risoe. Report [*A publication*]
Den Res Establ Risoe Rep ... Denmark. Research Establishment Risoe. Risoe Report [*A publication*]
DENS .... Denosa. Department of Northern Saskatchewan [*A publication*]
DENS .... Density   (AFM)
Dens .... Denslow's Notes to Second Edition [*1-3 Michigan*] [*A publication*]   (DLA)
Den & Sc Pr ... Denison and Scott's House of Lords Appeal Practice [*A publication*]   (DLA)
DENT .... Dental   (ROG)
DENT .... Dentistry
DENT .... Dentition [*Medicine*]
DENT .... Dentur [*Give*] [*Pharmacy*]
DENT .... Directions for Education in Nursing via Technology
D Ent......... Doctor of Entomology
Dent Abstr ... Dental Abstracts [*A publication*]
DENTAC... Dental Activity   (AABC)
Dent Anaesth Sedat ... Dental Anaesthesia and Sedation [*A publication*]
Dent Angles ... Dental Angles [*A publication*]
Dent Assist ... Dental Assistant [*A publication*]
Dent Bull.... Dental Bulletin [*A publication*]
Dent Cadm ... Dental Cadmos [*A publication*]
Dent Cadmos ... Dental Cadmos [*A publication*]
DENTCAP ... Dental Civic Action Program [*Vietnam*]
Dent Clin N Am ... Dental Clinics of North America [*A publication*]
Dent Clin N Am ... Dental Clinics of North America [*A publication*]
Dent Clin North Am ... Dental Clinics of North America [*A publication*]
Dent Conc .. Dental Concepts [*A publication*]
Dent Concepts ... Dental Concepts [*A publication*]
DENTCORPS ... Dental Corps [*Air Force*]
Dent Cosm ... Dental Cosmos [*A publication*]
Dent Delin ... Dental Delineator [*A publication*]
Dent Dialogue ... Dental Dialogue [*A publication*]
Dent Dig..... Dental Digest [*A publication*]
Dent Dimens ... Dental Dimensions [*A publication*]
Dent Discourse ... Dental Discourse [*A publication*]
Dent Echo .. Dental Echo [*A publication*]
Den Tech Univ Struct Res Lab Rep ... Denmark. Technical University. Structural Research Laboratory. Report [*A publication*]
Dent Econ .. Dental Economics [*A publication*]
Dent Fabr .. Dental Fabrikant [*A publication*]
Dent Fr....... Dentiste de France [*A publication*]
Dent Health (Lond) ... Dental Health (London) [*A publication*]
Dent Hyg ... Dental Hygiene [*A publication*]
Dent Images ... Dental Images [*A publication*]
Dent Ind..... Dental Literature Index [*A publication*]
Dent Items Interest ... Dental Items of Interest [*A publication*]
Dent J .... Dental Journal [*A publication*]
Dent J Aust ... Dental Journal of Australia [*A publication*]
Dent J Austr ... Dental Journal of Australia [*A publication*]
Dent J Malaysia Singapore ... Dental Journal of Malaysia and Singapore [*A publication*]

Dent Jpn (Tokyo) ... Dentistry in Japan (Tokyo) [*A publication*]
DENTL...... Dental
Dent Lab Bl ... Dental Laboratorie Bladet [*A publication*]
Dent Labor (Munch) ... Dental Labor (Munich) [*A publication*]
Dent Lab Rev ... Dental Laboratory Review [*A publication*]
Dent Mag... Dental Magazine [*A publication*]
Dent Mag... Dental Magazine and Oral Topics [*A publication*]
Dent Mag... Dentists' Magazine [*A publication*]
Dent Mag Oral Top ... Dental Magazine and Oral Topics [*A publication*]
Dent Manage ... Dental Management [*A publication*]
Dent Mater ... Dental Materials [*A publication*]
Dent Mater J ... Dental Materials Journal [*A publication*]
Dent Mirror (Atlanta) ... Dental Mirror (Atlanta) [*A publication*]
Dent Mirror (Quezon City) ... Dental Mirror (Quezon City) [*A publication*]
Dent Obs.... Dental Observer [*A publication*]
Dento Maxillo Fac Radiol ... Dento Maxillo Facial Radiology [*A publication*]
Dent Outlook ... Dental Outlook [*Japan*] [*A publication*]
Dent Pract ... Dental Practitioner [*A publication*]
Dent Pract (Cincinnati) ... Dental Practice (Cincinnati) [*A publication*]
Dent Pract Dent Rec ... Dental Practitioner and Dental Record [*England*] [*A publication*]
Dent Pract (Ewell) ... DP. Dental Practice (Ewell) [*England*] [*A publication*]
Dent Pract Manage ... Dental Practice Management [*A publication*]
Dent Press ... Dental Press [*A publication*]
Dent Prog... Dental Progress [*A publication*]
Dent Qu ... Dental Quarterly [*A publication*]
Dent Radiogr Photogr ... Dental Radiography and Photography [*A publication*]
Dent Rec .... Dental Record [*A publication*]
Dent Refl.... Dental Reflector [*A publication*]
Dent Res Grad Study Q ... Dental Research and Graduate Study Quarterly. Northwestern University [*A publication*]
Dent Rev .... Dental Revue [*A publication*]
DENTS...... Director of Naval Education and Training Support
Dent Sci J Austr ... Dental Science Journal of Australia [*A publication*]
Dent Stud... Dental Student [*A publication*]
Dent Surg ... Dental Surgeon [*A publication*]
Dent Surv ... Dental Survey [*A publication*]
DENT TAL DOS ... Dentur Tales Doses [*Give in Such Doses*] [*Pharmacy*]
Dent Tech .. Dental Technician [*A publication*]
Dent Ther Newsl ... Dental Therapeutics Newsletter [*A publication*]
Dent Update ... Dental Update [*A publication*]
Dent Wld ... Dental World [*A publication*]
DE-NUM .. Data Element Dictionary Number
DENV........ Denver [*Colorado*] (ROG)
Denver Bus ... Denver Business [*A publication*]
Denver J Internat Law and Policy ... Denver Journal of International Law and Policy [*A publication*]
Denver J Int Law Policy ... Denver Journal of International Law and Policy [*A publication*]
Denver J Int'l L ... Denver Journal of International Law [*A publication*] (DLA)
Denver J Int L & Pol ... Denver Journal of International Law and Policy [*A publication*]
Denver J Int L & Policy ... Denver Journal of International Law and Policy [*A publication*] (DLA)
Denver Law ... Denver Law Journal [*A publication*]
Denver LCJ ... Denver Law Center. Journal [*A publication*]
Denver L J ... Denver Law Journal [*A publication*]
Denver L N ... Denver Legal News [*A publication*] (DLA)
Denver Med Bull ... Denver Medical Bulletin [*A publication*]
Denver Med Times ... Denver Medical Times [*A publication*]
Denver Mus Nat History Mus Pictorial Pop Ser Proc ... Denver Museum of Natural History. Museum Pictorial Popular Series. Proceedings [*A publication*]
DenverQ..... Denver Quarterly [*A publication*]
Denver West Roundup ... Denver Western Roundup [*A publication*]
Denv Med Tim ... Denver Medical Times [*A publication*]
Denvr Post ... Denver Post [*A publication*]
DENW........ Denver Western Petroleum [*NASDAQ symbol*] (NQ)
DENYG..... Denying
DENZAX .. Deutsche Entomologische Zeitschrift [*A publication*]
Deo............ De Deo [*Philo*] (BJA)
DEO.......... Deck Edge Outlet [*Navy*]
DEO.......... Deobstruent [*Removing Obstructions*] [*Pharmacy*] (ROG)
DEO.......... Department of Executive Officer
Deo........... [*Bertrandus de*] Deucio [*Deceased, 1355*] [*Authority cited in pre-1607 legal work*] (DSA)
DEO.......... Digital End Office [*Telecommunications*]
DEO.......... District Engineer Officer [*Army*]
DEO.......... Divisional Education Officer [*British*]
DEO.......... Divisional Entertainments Officer [*British*]
DEO.......... Divisional Executive Officer [*British*]
DEO.......... Doped Erbium Oxide
DEO.......... Duke of Edinburgh's Own [*Military unit*] [*British*]
DEOPDB... Developments in Ophthalmology [*A publication*]
De Or ...... De Oratore [*of Cicero*] [*Classical studies*] (OCD)
De Orat ...... Cicero's De Oratore [*A publication*] (DLA)
DEORB ..... Deorbit (NASA)
DEOS .... Data Exchange Optimization Study [*DoD*] (MCD)

DEOS .... Director of Equipment and Ordnance Stores [*British military*] (DMA)
DEOT .... Disconnect, End of Transmission
DEOVR ..... Duke of Edinburgh's Own Volunteer Rifles [*Military unit*] [*British*]
DEOWRB ... Dictionaries, Encyclopedias, and Other Word-Related Books [*A publication*]
DEP .... Damson Energy Co. [*AMEX symbol*] (SPSG)
DEP .... Data Entry Panel (MCD)
DEP .... Data Exchange Program
DEP .... Decorated End-Papers [*Publishing*]
DEP .... Dedicated Experiment Processor [*Spacelab mission*]
DEP .... Deep External Pudendal Artery [*Anatomy*]
DEP .... Defense Electronic Products
DEP .... Defense Estimate for Production (MCD)
DEP .... Deflection Error Probable [*Military*] (AFM)
DEP .... Degraduation Effects Program
DEP .... Delayed Enlistment [*or Entry*] Program [*Military*] (AFM)
DEP .... Dense Electronic Population
Dep .... Density Dependent [*Biology*]
DEP .... Depart (AFM)
dep............ Departement [*Department*] [*French*] [*Correspondence*]
DEP .... Department
DEP .... Department of Employment and Productivity [*Later, DE*] [*British*]
DEP .... Departure Message [*Aviation code*]
DeP .... DePaul Law Review [*A publication*]
DEP .... Dependencies (ROG)
DEP .... Dependent
DEP .... Deployment
DEP .... Deponent
DEP .... Deport (ROG)
DEP .... Deportation [*FBI standardized term*]
DEP .... Deposed
DEP .... Deposit (EY)
DEP .... Depositary [*Banking*]
DEP .... Deposition (ADA)
DEP .... Depot (AFM)
DEP .... Depressed [*Technical drawings*]
DEP .... Depth
DEP .... Deputatus [*Purified*] [*Pharmacy*]
DEP .... Deputy (AFM)
DEP .... Design External Pressure (NRCH)
DEP .... Design Eye Point [*Cockpit visibility*]
DEP .... Detailed Experiment Plan (MCD)
DEP .... Diagnostic Execution Program (NOAA)
DEP .... Dielectrophoresis
DEP .... Diethyl Pyrocarbonate [*Chemical preservative*] [*Also, DEPC*] [*Organic chemistry*]
DEP .... Diethylpropanediol [*Biochemistry*]
DEP .... Displaced Employee Program [*Department of Labor*]
DEP .... Division of Electronic Products [*Series*] [*A publication*]
DEP .... Domestic Emergency Plan (AAG)
DEP .... Double-Ended Pivot
DEP .... Draft Experiment Publication (MCD)
DEP .... Dual Element Pump
DEPA ...... Defense Electric Power Administration [*Terminated, 1977*] [*Department of the Interior*]
DEPA ...... Defense Entry and Departure Act [*1918*]
DEPA ...... Diversified Economic and Planning Associates
DEPA .... United States Environmental Protection Agency, Headquarters Library, Washington, DC [*Library symbol*] [*Library of Congress*] (LCLS)
DEPACTV ... Depot Activity
Dep Agric Straits Settlements Fed Malay States Econ Ser ... Department of Agriculture. Straits Settlements and Federated Malay States. Economic Series [*A publication*]
Dep Agric Straits Settlements Fed Malay States Gen Ser ... Department of Agriculture. Straits Settlements and Federated Malay States. General Series [*A publication*]
Dep Agric Straits Settlements Fed Malay States Sci Ser ... Department of Agriculture. Straits Settlements and Federated Malay States. Scientific Series [*A publication*]
Dep Agric (Victoria Aust) Tech Bull ... Department of Agriculture (Victoria, Australia). Technical Bulletin [*A publication*]
DEPAIR .... Air Deputy [*NATO*] (NATG)
DEPA-NA ... United States Environmental Protection Agency, Office of Noise Abatement and Control, Washington, DC [*Library symbol*] [*Library of Congress*] (LCLS)
DEPART ... Department
De Paul L Rev ... De Paul Law Review [*A publication*]
DEPBA...... Developmental Psychobiology [*A publication*]
DEPBA5...... Developmental Psychobiology [*A publication*]
Dep Biol Coll Bourget Rigaud Bull ... Departement de Biologie. College Bourget Rigaud. Bulletin. [*A publication*]
Dep Bull US Dep Agric ... Department Bulletin. United States Department of Agriculture [*A publication*]
DEPC .... Defence Equipment Policy Committee [*British*] (RDA)
DEPC......... DEP Corporation [*NASDAQ symbol*] (NQ)
DEPC......... Diethyl Pyrocarbonate [*Chemical preservative*] [*Also, DEP*] [*Organic chemistry*]

DEPCA ...... Digital Ethernet Personal Computer Adapter
Dep Cap Territ Conserv Ser (Canberra) ... Department of the Capital Territory. Conservation Series (Canberra) [*A publication*]
DEPCDR(R & D) ... Deputy Commander for Research and Development [*Navy*]
DEPCDR(SA) ... Deputy Commander for Ship Acquisitions [*Navy*]
DEPCH ..... Deputy Chief (CINC)
Dep Circ US Dep Agric ... Department Circular. United States Department of Agriculture [*A publication*]
DEPCOMOPTEVFORPAC ... Deputy Commander, Operational Test and Evaluation Force, Pacific [*Navy*]
DEPCOMSTRIKFORSOUTH ... Deputy Commander, Naval Striking and Support Forces, Southern Europe (NATG)
DEPCOMSTS ... Deputy Commander, Military Sea Transport Service [*Obsolete*] [*Navy*]
DEPCOMUSMACTHAI ... Deputy Commander, United States Military Assistance Command, Thailand
DEPCOMUSMACV ... Deputy Commander, United States Military Assistance Command, Vietnam
DEPCON .. Departure Control
DEPCOS ... Deputy Chief of Staff [*Military*] (CAAL)
DEPCRU ... Dependents' Daylight Cruise [*Navy*] (NVT)
DEP in CT ... Deposits in Court [*Legal term*] (DLA)
DEPD .... Division Engineering Planning Document
DEPDA ..... Deployment Data File
Dep Def Aeronaut Res Lab Mech Eng Rep (Aust) ... Department of Defence. Aeronautical Research Laboratories. Mechanical Engineering Report (Australia) [*A publication*]
DEPDIR .... Deputy Director
DEPDIRPACDOCKS ... Deputy Director Pacific Division, Bureau of Yards and Docks [*Later, NFEC*] [*Navy*]
Dep Environ Fire Res St Fire Res Tech Pap (UK) ... Department of the Environment. Fire Research Station. Fire Research Technical Paper (United Kingdom) [*A publication*]
DEPERMSTA ... Deperming and Flashing Station [*Navy*]
DEPEVACPAY ... Dependents' Evacuation Pay [*Military*]
DEPEX ...... Deployment on NIKE/X Study [*Military*]
Dep For (Queensl) Res Note ... Department of Forestry (Queensland). Research Note [*A publication*]
Dep For (Queensl) Res Pap ... Department of Forestry (Queensland). Research Paper [*A publication*]
Dep Harb Mar (Queensl) Fish Notes ... Department of Harbours and Marine (Queensland). Fisheries Notes [*A publication*]
Dep Harbours Mar Queensl Fish Notes ... Queensland Department of Harbours and Marine. Fisheries Notes [*A publication*]
Dep Health Educ Welfare Natl Inst Health Publ ... Department of Health, Education, and Welfare. National Institutes of Health. Publication [*A publication*]
Dep Health Educ Welfare Natl Inst Occup Saf Health Publ (US) ... Department of Health, Education, and Welfare. National Institute for Occupational Safety and Health. Publication (United States) [*A publication*]
Dep Health Educ Welfare Publ (Health Serv Adm) (US) ... Department of Health, Education, and Welfare. Publication (Health Services Administration) (United States) [*A publication*]
De Phil .... De Philosophia [*A publication*]
DE Phy ...... Doctor of Engineering Physics
DEPI .... Differential Equations Pseudocode Interpreter [*Jet Propulsion Laboratory, NASA*]
DEPIC .... Dual-Expanded Plastic-Insulated Conductor [*Telecommunications*] (TEL)
DEPID ...... Deployment Indicator Code
DEPILAT ... Depilatorium [*Depilatory*] [*Pharmacy*]
Dep Ind (Bombay) Bull ... Department of Industries (Bombay). Bulletin [*A publication*]
DEPL .... Depletion (KSC)
DEPL .... Deploy (KSC)
DEPL .... Deprenyl Research Ltd. [*NASDAQ symbol*] (NQ)
DEPL-MAN ... Deployment Manifest [*Army*]
DEPLOC ... Daily Estimated Position Location [*Navy*] (NVT)
DeP LR ...... DePaul Law Review [*A publication*]
DEPMED ... Deployable Medical [*Equipment*] [*Military*]
DEPMEDS ... Deployable Medical System [*Military*]
DEPMIS .... Depot Management Information System [*Army*]
DEPN .... Dependent (AFM)
Dep Nac Agric (Costa Rica) Bol Tec ... Departamento Nacional de Agricultura (Costa Rica). Boletin Tecnica [*A publication*]
DEPNAV ... Naval Deputy [*NATO*] (NATG)
DEPNOTAUTH ... Dependents Not Authorized Overseas Duty Station [*Military*]
depo .... Deposit
DEPO .... Devils Postpile National Monument
DEPOL ...... Depolarization
DEPOPSDEP ... Deputy Operations Deputy [*In JCS system*] [*Military*]
DEPOS .... Depositary [*Banking*] (EY)
DEPOS & D ... Deposition and Discovery [*Legal term*] (DLA)
DEPOSN .... Deposition
DEPOT ...... Desktop and Electronic Publishing Online Terminal
DEPP .... Daily Encephalic Photophase [*Biochronometry*]
DEPP .... Deep Earth Penetrating Projectile (MCD)
DEPPC ...... Declared Excess Personal Property Catalog [*Military*]

Dep Primary Ind Brisbane Fish Branch Fish Notes (New Ser) ... Department of Primary Industries. Brisbane Fisheries Branch. Fisheries Notes (New Series) [*A publication*]
Dep Primary Ind Fish Res Annu Rep (Port Moresby) ... Department of Primary Industries. Fisheries Research Annual Report (Port Moresby) [*A publication*]
DEPR .... Depreciation [*Accounting, Economics*]
DEPR .... Depression [*Board on Geographic Names*] (MSA)
DEPRA ..... Defense European and Pacific Redistribution Activity [*DoD*] (AFIT)
De Praescr Haeret ... De Praescriptione Haereticorum [*of Tertullian*] [*Classical studies*] (OCD)
DEPREC ... Depreciation
DEPREP ... Deployment Reporting System
DEPRESS ... Depressurize (NASA)
Depressive Illness Ser ... Depressive Illness Series [*A publication*]
De Prof Virt ... De Profectu in Virtute [*of Plutarch*] [*Classical studies*] (OCD)
DEPS .... Departmental Entry Processing Systems [*Customs processing for sea and airports*] [*October, 1981*] [*British*] (DCTA)
DEPS .... Deposit Guaranty Corp. [*NASDAQ symbol*] (NQ)
DEPS .... Double-Ended Pump Suction [*Nuclear energy*] (NRCH)
DEPSACLANT ... Deputy Supreme Allied Commander, Atlantic (NATG)
DEPSEC .... Deputy Secretary (ADA)
DEPSECDEF ... Deputy Secretary of Defense (AABC)
DEPSK ...... Differential Encoding Phase Shift Keying (MCD)
DEPSO ...... Department Standardization Office [*Navy*]
DEPSTAR ... Deployment Status of Army Units (AABC)
Dep St Bull ... US Department of State. Bulletin [*A publication*]
DEPSUM ... Daily Estimated Position Summary [*Navy*]
DEPSUM ... Deployment Summary Report [*Air Force*]
DEPT .... Depart
DEPT .... Department (EY)
DEPT .... Deponent [*Legal term*] (ROG)
DEPT .... Deposit (ROG)
DEPT .... Deputy
DEPT .... Distortionless Enhancement by Polarization Transfer [*Spectroscopy*]
DEPTAR ... Department of the Army
DEPTAR/MAIN ... Department of the Army/Main (AABC)
Dept Bull US Dept Agric ... Department Bulletin. United States Department of Agriculture [*A publication*]
DEPTD ...... Division of Electric Power Transmission and Distribution [*Energy Research and Development Administration*]
Dep Tech Rep Tex Agric Exp Stn ... Departmental Technical Report. Texas Agricultural Experiment Station [*A publication*]
Dept Econ et Sociol Rurales Bul Info ... Departement d'Economie et de Sociologie Rurales. Bulletin d'Information [*A publication*]
Dept of Ed and Science Repts ... Department of Education and Science: Reports on Education [*London*] [*A publication*]
DEPTEL .... State Department Telegram (NATG)
Dept El Sch Prin B ... Department of Elementary School Principals. Bulletin [*A publication*]
Dept Employment Gaz (Gt Britain) ... Department of Employment. Gazette (Great Britain) [*A publication*]
DEPTM ..... Draft Equipment Publication Technical Manual (MCD)
Dept R .... Department Reports, State Department [*New York*] [*A publication*] (DLA)
Dept R Un ... New York State Department Reports, Unofficial [*A publication*] (DLA)
DEPTS ...... Commonwealth Government Departments [*Database*] [*Australia*]
Dept Sec Sch Prin B ... Department of Secondary School Principals. Bulletin [*A publication*]
Dept S Fct ... Department Store Sales Fact File [*A publication*]
Dept Sta Bul ... Department of State. Bulletin [*A publication*]
Dept Sta Nl ... Department of State. Newsletter [*A publication*]
Dept State Bul ... Department of State. Bulletin [*A publication*]
Dept State Bull ... Department of State. Bulletin [*A publication*]
Dept State Newsletter ... Department of State. Newsletter [*A publication*]
Dept St Bull ... Department of State. Bulletin [*A publication*]
DEPU .... De Paul University [*Chicago, IL*]
DEPUTN ... Deputation
DEPV .... Air-Cushion Vehicle built by Research Vehicle Department [*Brazil*] [*Usually used in combination with numerals*]
DEPY .... Deputy
De Pyth Or ... De Pythiae Oraculis [*of Plutarch*] [*Classical studies*] (OCD)
DEQ .... DeQueen, AR [*Location identifier*] [*FAA*] (FAAL)
DEQ .... Dequeue [*Data processing*]
DE/Q .... Design Evaluation/Qualification (KSC)
DEQ .... Dose Equivalent [*Radioactivity calculations*] (IEEE)
DEQUIP ... DECHEMA [*Deutsche Gesellschaft fuer Chemisches Apparatewesen, Chemische Technik, und Biotechnologie eV*] Equipment Suppliers Databank [*Database*]
DEQUISA ... Desarrollo Quimico Industrial, SA [*Spain*]
DER .... Declining Error Rate
DER .... Defective Equipment Review (MCD)
DER .... Delegated Engineering Representative
DER .... Demonstration and Evaluation Report (MCD)
DER .... Denar Mines Ltd. [*Vancouver Stock Exchange symbol*]
DER .... Derby [*Colorado*] [*Seismograph station code, US Geological Survey*] [*Closed*] (SEIS)

DER	Derekh Erets Rabbah [or Derek Erez Rabbah] (BJA)
DER	Derim [Papua New Guinea] [Airport symbol] (OAG)
DER	Derivation [or Derivative]
DER	Derived (ROG)
DER	Dermatine
DER	Derricks (DS)
DER	Design Electrical Rating [Nuclear energy] (NRCH)
DER	Designated Engineer Representative [FAA title] (AFM)
DER	Development Engineering Review (AAG)
DER	Diesel Engine, Reduction Drive
DER	Directly Executable Representation
DER	Distributed Energy Release [Computer program]
DER	Division of Economic Research [Washington, DC] [Social Security Administration] (GRD)
DER	Division of Engineering Research [Michigan State University] [Research center] (RCD)
DER	Division of Evaluation and Research [Department of Labor] (GRD)
DER	Document Error Report
DER	Double Edge Receiver (MCD)
DER	Double-Ended Rupture [Nuclear energy] (NRCH)
DER	Drawing Error Report (NASA)
DER	RADAR Picket Escort Ship [Navy symbol]
DeR	Reaction of Degeneration [Physiology]
DER	United States Army Engineer Research and Development Laboratory, Technical Documents Center, Fort Belvoir, VA [Library symbol] [Library of Congress] (LCLS)
DERA	Defense Eastern Regional Audit Office [DoD]
DERA	Defense Environmental Restoration Account [DoD]
DERA	Defense European Redistribution Activity [DoD] (MCD)
DERA	Direction de l'Analyse Economique et Regionale [Economic and Regional Analysis Branch] [Transport Canada]
DERA	Directory of Education Research and Researchers in Australia [Commonwealth Department of Education Research and Youth Affairs] [Information service or system] (IID)
DERAAC...	Dermatologica [Basel] [A publication]
DERAX.....	Detection and Range [Early name for RADAR]
DERB	Derby (ROG)
DERB	Derbyshire [County in England]
Derbs.........	Derbyshire [County in England] (DAS)
DERBSH...	Derbyshire [County in England] (ROG)
DERBY.....	Derbyshire [County in England]
DERBYS ...	Derbyshire [County in England]
Derbyshire Archaeol J ...	Derbyshire Archaeological Journal [A publication]
Derbyshire Arch J ...	Derbyshire Archaeological Journal [A publication]
DERC	Development Economics Research Centre [University of Warwick] [British] (CB)
DERC	Directory of Executive Recruitment Consultants [A publication]
DERCCA...	Derbyshire England Red Cap Club of America (EA)
DERD.......	Diesel Electric Reduction Drive
DERDA	United States Energy Research and Development Administration, Washington, DC [Library symbol] [Library of Congress] (LCLS)
DERE	Dounreay Experimental Reactor Establishment [British]
Derecho Reforma Agrar Rev ...	Derecho y Reforma Agraria Revista [A publication]
Derecho Vivo ...	Actas Procesales del Derecho Vivo [A publication]
DEREES ...	Developmental Review [A publication]
DERES......	DECHEMA [Deutsche Gesellschaft fuer Chemisches Apparatewesen, Chemische Technik, und Biotechnologie e V] Research and Education Databank [Frankfurt Am Main, Federal Republic of Germany] [Information service or system] (IID)
Derevoobrab Prom-St ...	Derevoobrabatyvaiushchaia Promyshlennost [A publication]
Derevopererab Lesokhim Promst ...	Derevopererabatyvayushchaya i Lesokhimicheskaya Promyshlennost [A publication]
Derev Prom ...	Derevoobrabatyvaiushchaia Promyshlennost [A publication]
DERF........	Division of Educational and Research Facilities [Bureau of Health Professions Education and Manpower Training, HEW]
DERF........	Dynamical Extended Range Forecasting [Meteorology]
Derg Rev Fac For Univ Istanbul Ser A ...	Dergisi. Review of the Faculty of Forestry. University of Istanbul. Series A [A publication]
DERI.........	Deep Electric Research Investigation [Navy]
DERI.........	Diethyl(ribityl)isoalloxazine [Biochemistry]
DERIA......	Dermatologia Internationalis [A publication]
DERIA2.....	Dermatologia Internationalis [A publication]
DERIC.......	De Ea Re Ita Censuere [Concerning That Matter Have So Decreed] [Latin] [Legal term] (DLA)
DERIGID..	Derigidize (NASA)
Deri Muz Ev ...	Deri Muzeum Evkoenyve [A publication]
Der Integr ..	Derecho de la Integracion [A publication]
DERIV......	Derivation [or Derivative]
DERIV......	Derived (ROG)
DERL........	Derived Emergency Reference Level [of radiation]
DERM......	Delayed Echo RADAR Marker
DERM	Derma [Skin] [Medicine] (ROG)
DERM	Derma-Lock Medical Corp. [Norway] (NQ)
DERM	Dermatitis [Medicine]

Derm	Dermatologia [A publication]
DERM	Dermatology [or Dermatologist]
DERMAE ...	Dermatologia [Mexico] [A publication]
DERMATOL ...	Dermatology
Dermatol Clin ...	Dermatologic Clinics [A publication]
Dermatol Int ...	Dermatologia Internationalis [A publication]
Dermatol Monatsschr ...	Dermatologische Monatsschrift [A publication]
Dermatolog ...	Dermatologica [A publication]
Dermatologica Suppl ...	Dermatologica Supplementum [A publication]
Dermatol Trop Ecol Geogr ...	Dermatologia Tropica et Ecologia Geographica [A publication]
Dermatol Update ...	Dermatology Update [A publication]
Dermatol Venerol ...	Dermatologiya i Venerologiya [A publication]
Dermatol Wochenschr ...	Dermatologische Wochenschrift [A publication]
Dermatoses Prof ...	Dermatoses Professionnelles [A publication]
Dermato-Vener ...	Dermato-Venerologie [A publication]
Dermat Wochnschr ...	Dermatologische Wochenschrift [A publication]
Derm Beruf Umwelt ...	Dermatosen in Beruf und Umwelt [A publication]
Derm Ib Lat Amer ...	Dermatologia Ibero Latino-Americana [A publication]
Dermos	Dermosifilografo [A publication]
Derm Vener ...	Dermato-Venerologia [A publication]
Derm Venerol ...	Dermato-Venerologie [A publication]
DEROG.....	Derogatory (DCTA)
DEROS......	Date Eligible for Return from Overseas [Military]
DEROS......	Date of Estimated Return from Overseas [Military]
DERP.......	Defective Equipment Repair Program [Telephone company]
DERP.......	Deficient Equippage Reporting Procedures
DERR.......	Daily Effective Repair Rate (MCD)
DERR.......	Duke of Edinburgh's Royal Regiment [Military unit] [British]
DERRY.....	Londonderry [County in Ireland] (ROG)
DERS........	Data Entry Reporting System
DERS........	Division of Educational Research Services [University of Alberta] [Research center] (RCD)
DERTO	DSA [Defense Supply Agency] Eastern Regional Telecommunications Office
DERV	Diesel Engined Road Vehicle
DERVA7 ...	Dermato-Venerologie [Bucharest] [A publication]
Derwent Archaeol Soc Res Rep ...	Derwent Archaeological Society. Research Reports [A publication]
DES	Custom Aviation, Inc. D/B/A Desert Sun Airlines [Long Beach, CA] [FAA designator] (FAAC)
DES	Data Elements Standardization Requirements (MCD)
DES	Data Encryption Standard [National Institute of Standards and Technology]
DES	Data Engineering Section
DE/S.........	Data Entry/Separation (MCD)
DES	Data Entry System
DES	Data Exchange System (NASA)
DES	Department of Education and Science [British]
Des	Desaussure. South Carolina Equity Reports [1784-1816] [A publication] (DLA)
DES	Descend To [Aviation]
DES	Descent (KSC)
DES	Desert [Hawaii] [Seismograph station code, US Geological Survey] (SEIS)
DES	Desert Botanical Garden [An association] (EA)
DES	Desertion
DES	Desferrioxamine [Also, Deferoxamine] [A chelating agent]
DES	Design (NASA)
DES	Design Engineering Show and Conference (ITD)
DES	Design Expansion System
DES	Designator (KSC)
DES	Designatus [Named] [Latin]
DES	Designavit [He, or She, Drew It] [Latin] (ROG)
DES	Desire (AABC)
DES	Destroyer [Navy]
DES	Diesel Electronic Submarine (MCD)
DES	Diethyl Succinate [Organic chemistry]
DES	Diethyl Sulfate [Organic chemistry]
DES	Diethylstilbestrol [Endocrinology]
DES	Differential Energy Spectrum
DES	Differential Equation Solver
DES	Diffuse Esophageal Spasm [Medicine]
DES	Digital Expansion System
DES	Director of Educational Services [Air Force] [British]
DES	Director of Engineer Stores Service [British]
DES	Discrete Elastic System
DES	Dispersed Emergency Station (NATG)
DES	Division of Educational Services [Department of Education]
DES	Division of Energy Storage [Energy Research and Development Administration]
DES	Doctor of Engineering Science
DES	Doctors Emergency Service [New York City]
DES	Dow Education Systems [Dow Chemical Corp.]
DES	Draft Environmental Statement [Bureau of Outdoor Recreation]
DES	Drug Education Specialist [Military] (AABC)
DES	Dual Exciter System
DES	Ducosyn Excitation Switch
DES	Dynamic Electrospeaker
DES	Dynamic Environment Simulator [Air Force]

DES .... Office of Economic Security, Department of Economic Security, St. Paul, MN [*OCLC symbol*] (OCLC)
DESAC...... Destroyer SONAR Analysis Center [*Navy*] (NVT)
DESAD...... Diethylstilbestrol Adenosis [*Oncology*]
DESAF...... Destroyers, Asiatic Fleet [*Navy*]
Desai.......... Handbook of Criminal Cases [*India*] [*A publication*] (DLA)
Desalinatn ... Desalination [*A publication*]
De Sanctis Stor Rom ... De Sanctis, Storia dei Romani [*1907-1966*] [*A publication*] (OCD)
Desarr Econ ... Desarrollo Economico [*A publication*]
Desarr Indoamer ... Desarrollo Indoamericano [*A publication*]
Desarrollo Econ ... Desarrollo Economico [*A publication*]
Desarrollo Indoam ... Desarrollo Indoamericano [*A publication*]
Desarrollo y Soc ... Desarrollo y Sociedad [*A publication*]
Desarr Rural Am ... Desarrollo Rural en las Americas [*A publication*]
Desarr Rur Amer ... Desarrollo Rural en las Americas [*A publication*]
Des Arts Educ ... Design for Arts in Education [*A publication*]
DESAT...... Defense Small Business Advanced Technology Program
DESAT...... Desaturated (NASA)
Desaus ...... Desaussure. South Carolina Equity Reports [*A publication*] (DLA)
Desaus Eq ... Desaussure. South Carolina Equity Reports [*A publication*] (DLA)
DESB........ Delaware Savings Bank FSB [*NASDAQ symbol*] (NQ)
DESB........ Delta Epsilon Sigma Bulletin [*A publication*]
DESB........ Desborough [*England*]
DESB........ Devereux Elementary School Behavior [*Rating scale*] [*Psychology*]
DESBATFOR ... Destroyer Battle Force [*Navy*]
DESC........ Data Entry System Controller
DESC........ Defense Electronics Supply [*or Support*] Center [*DSA*]
DESC........ Descend
DESC........ Descent (NASA)
desc .... Desconto [*Deduction, Discount*] [*Portuguese*] [*Business term*]
DESC........ Description (MCD)
DESC........ Digital Equation-Solving Computer (IEEE)
De Sc........ Doctor of Engineering Science
DESC & D ... Descent and Distribution [*Legal term*] (DLA)
DESCDT ... Descendant
DESCHA... Destination Change [*Military*] (NVT)
DESCNET ... Data Network on Environmentally Significant Chemicals (DCTA)
DESCOFOR ... Destroyer Scouting Force [*Navy*]
DESCOM ... Depot Systems Command [*Army*] (RDA)
Des Compon Engn ... Design and Components in Engineering [*A publication*]
DESCP...... Description (MSA)
DESCR...... Describe (KSC)
DESCRD... Described (ROG)
Descrip Appl Ling ... Descriptive and Applied Linguistics [*A publication*]
De Script Eccles Proleg ... De Scriptoribus Ecclesiasticis Prolegomena [*of St. Jerome*] [*Classical studies*] (OCD)
DESCRON ... Description
DESCRUPAC ... Destroyers/Cruisers, Pacific Fleet [*Navy*]
descto .... Descuento [*Discount*] [*Spanish*]
DESDEVGRU ... Destroyer Development Group [*Navy*]
DESDIV.... Destroyer Division [*Navy*]
Des Econ ...... Desarrollo Economico [*A publication*]
DESEFF...... Deserter's Effects [*Military*]
Des Electron ... Design Electronics [*A publication*]
Des Eng...... Design Engineering [*A publication*]
Des Engng (GB) ... Design Engineering (Great Britain) [*A publication*]
Des Engng (USA) ... Design Engineering (United States of America) [*A publication*]
Des Eng (Toronto) ... Design Engineering (Toronto) [*A publication*]
De Sera ...... De Sera Numinis Vindicta [*of Plutarch*] [*Classical studies*] (OCD)
Desert Bot Gard (Phoenix) Sci Bull ... Desert Botanical Garden (Phoenix). Science Bulletin [*A publication*]
Desert Inst Bull ... Desert Institute. Bulletin [*A publication*]
Desert Inst Bull ARE ... Desert Institute. Bulletin ARE [*A publication*]
Desert Locust Control Organ E Afr Tech Rep ... Desert Locust Control Organization for Eastern Africa. Technical Report [*A publication*]
Desert Mag ... Desert Magazine [*A publication*]
DESEX...... Deployment Staff Exercise (MCD)
DESFEX.... Desert Field Exercise [*Military*] (NVT)
DESFIREX ... Desert Firing Exercise [*Military*] (NVT)
DESFLOT ... Destroyer Flotilla [*Navy*]
DESFTD ... Department of Employment, Small Firms and Tourism Division [*British*]
DESG........ Designate (AFM)
DESI......... Designated Hitter [*Formerly, DPH*] [*Also, DH*] [*Baseball*]
DESI......... Designs, Inc. [*NASDAQ symbol*] (NQ)
DESI......... Drug Efficacy Study Implementation Notice [*Food and Drug Administration*]
DESID....... Desideratum [*Wanted*] [*Latin*] (ADA)
DESIG....... Designate [*or Designation*] (KSC)
DESIGDISBAGENT ... Designated Special Disbursing Agent
Design........ Design Magazine [*A publication*]
DESIGNAP ... Designated as Naval Aviation Pilot [*Marine Corps*]
Design for Ind ... Design for Industry [*A publication*]

Design Ind ... Design for Industry [*A publication*]
Design & Manage Resour Recovery ... Design and Management for Resource Recovery [*A publication*]
Design Q ... Design Quarterly [*A publication*]
Design Qly ... Design Quarterly [*A publication*]
Design Qly (Heery) ... Design Quarterly (Heery) [*A publication*]
DESILU ... Desi-Lucille Arnaz Co.
Desinfekt Gesundheitswes ... Desinfektion und Gesundheitswesen [*A publication*]
Desinfekt Schaedlingsbekaempf ... Desinfektion Schaedlingsbekaempfung [*A publication*]
DESIR .... Direct English Statement Information Retrieval [*Military*]
DESK......... Desk Top Financial Solutions, Inc. [*NASDAQ symbol*] (NQ)
Desk Comp ... Desktop Computing [*A publication*]
DESL......... Double-Ended Suction Leg Slot [*Nuclear energy*] (NRCH)
DESLANT ... Destroyer Force, Atlantic Fleet [*Navy symbol*]
Des Manage Resour Recovery ... Design and Management for Resource Recovery [*A publication*]
DESMC..... Department of Defense Systems Management Center (MCD)
DESMO .... DoD [*Department of Defense*] Logistics Data Element Standardization and Management Office
DESNAVAV ... Designated Student Naval Aviator
Des News ... Design News [*A publication*]
DESO .... De Soto National Memorial
DESO .... District Educational Services Officer [*Navy*]
DESOIL...... Diesel Oil
De Soll An ... De Sollertia Animalium [*of Plutarch*] [*Classical studies*] (OCD)
DESOMS.. Deaf Sons of Master Masons
DESP........ Department of Elementary School Principals [*of NEA*] (EA)
DESP........ Despatch
desp .... Despesa [*Cost*] [*Portuguese*] [*Business term*]
DESP......... Primeros Puestos del Deporte Espanol [*Ministerio de Cultura*] [*Spain*] [*Information service or system*] (CRD)
DESPAC ... Destroyer Force, Pacific Fleet [*Navy symbol*]
De Spect..... De Spectaculis [*of Tertullian*] [*Classical studies*] (OCD)
DESPORT ... Daily Equipment Status Report [*Army*] (AABC)
DESPOT ... Design Performance Optimization (NASA)
Des Prod Appln ... Design Products and Applications [*A publication*]
DESR......... Daily Effective Supply Rate (MCD)
DESRAD... Desiccant-Enhanced Radiative Cooling [*Solar-cooling concept*]
DESRAY ... Deep-Sea Research [*Later, Deep-Sea Research with Oceanographic Literature Review*] [*A publication*]
Des RCA ... Diploma of Designer, Royal College of Art [*British*]
DESREP..... Destroyer Repair [*Navy*]
DESREP..... Destroyer Representative [*Navy*]
DESROC... Destroyer Rocket
DESRON .. Destroyer Squadron [*Navy*]
DESS........ Department of Economics and Social Science [*MIT*] (MCD)
Dess .... Dessaussure's Equity [*South Carolina*] [*A publication*] (DLA)
DESS........ Destroyer Schoolship [*Navy*] (NVT)
Dessaus...... Dessaussure's Equity [*South Carolina*] [*A publication*] (DLA)
DESSIM.... Defense System Simulator
DESSIM.... Design Simulator
D Es S LJ... Dar Es Salaam Law Journal [*A publication*] (DLA)
DESSOWESPAC ... Destroyers, Southwest Pacific Fleet [*Navy*]
Des Special Needs ... Design for Special Needs [*A publication*]
Des in Steel ... Design in Steel [*A publication*] (APTA)
D Es S ULJ ... Dar Es Salaam University. Law Journal [*A publication*] (DLA)
DeST.......... Delaware Technical and Community College, Stanton Campus, Newark, DE [*Library symbol*] [*Library of Congress*] (LCLS)
DEST........ Denver Eye Screening Test
DEST........ DEST Corp. [*Milpitas, CA*] [*NASDAQ symbol*] (NQ)
DEST........ Destillata [*Distilled*] [*Pharmacy*]
DEST........ Destination (AABC)
DEST........ Destra [*Right*] [*Italian*]
DEST........ Destroy (AABC)
DEST........ Destroyer [*Navy*] [*British*]
DEST........ Destruct (KSC)
DESTA...... Deutsche Stomatologie [*A publication*]
DESTA6.... Deutsche Stomatologie [*A publication*]
Dest Cal Dig ... Desty's California Digest [*A publication*] (DLA)
Dest Com & Nav ... Desty on Commerce and Navigation [*A publication*] (DLA)
DEST-DIST ... Destructively Distilled
Dest Fed Cit ... Desty's Federal Citations [*A publication*] (DLA)
Dest Fed Cons ... Desty on the Federal Constitution [*A publication*] (DLA)
Dest Fed Proc ... Desty's Federal Procedure [*A publication*] (DLA)
DESTIL..... Destilla [*Distill*] [*Pharmacy*] (ROG)
Destill Lehrling ... Destillateur Lehrling [*A publication*]
Destill Likoerfabr ... Destillateur Likoerfabrikant [*A publication*]
DESTN...... Destination
DESTR...... Desires to Transfer (NOAA)
DESTR...... Destroyed [*or Destructor*] (AAG)
Dest Sh & Adm ... Desty on Shipping and Admiralty [*A publication*] (DLA)
Desty Tax'n ... Desty on Taxation [*A publication*] (DLA)
DESUA9.... Dental Survey [*A publication*]
DESUBEX ... Destroyer/Submarine Antisubmarine Warfare Exercise [*Military*] (NVT)
De Superst ... De Superstitione [*of Plutarch*] [*Classical studies*] (OCD)

DESY......... Deutsches Elektronen-Synchrotron [*A publication*] [*Also, an information service or system*]
DET .... Design Evaluation Test
DET .... Detach
Det .... Detachable (DLA)
DET .... Detachment
DET .... Detail
DET .... Detainee
DET .... Detection [*or Detector*] (AFM)
DET .... Detective
DET .... Detent [*Mechanical Engineering*] (NASA)
DET .... Detergent (ROG)
DET .... Determination [*or Determine*] (KSC)
DET .... Determinative (ROG)
DET .... Determiner [*Linguistics*]
DET .... Detonator (MSA)
DET .... Detroit [*City in Michigan*] (ROG)
DET .... Detroit [*Michigan*] City Airport [*Airport symbol*] (OAG)
DET .... Detur [*Give*] [*Pharmacy*]
DET .... Diesel Electric Tandem Motor Drive
DET .... Diethyltartarate [*Organic chemistry*]
DET .... Diethyltoluamide [*Also, DETA*] [*Insect repellant*] [*Organic chemistry*]
DET .... Diethyltryptamine [*Hallucinogenic drug*]
DET .... Digital Event Timer (KSC)
DET .... Direct Energy Transfer
DET .... Displaced Equipment Training [*DoD*]
DET .... Domestic Escorted Tour [*Travel*]
DET .... Double Eagle Energy [*Vancouver Stock Exchange symbol*]
Det .... Quod Deterius Potiori Insidiari Soleat [*Philo*] (BJA)
DETA .... Del Taco Restaurants, Inc. [*NASDAQ symbol*] (NQ)
DETA .... Dielectric Thermal Analysis
DETA .... Diethylenetriamine [*Also, DTA*] [*Organic chemistry*]
DETA .... Diethyltoluamide [*Also, DET*] [*Insect repellant*] [*Organic chemistry*]
DETA .... Divisao de Exploracao dos Transportes Aereos [*Angolan airline*]
DETAB...... Decision Table [*Data processing*]
DETAB-X ... Decision Table, Experimental [*Data processing*]
DETAC...... Digital Equipment Technology Analysis Center (MCD)
Detali Mash Podemno Transp Mash ... Detali Mashin i Pod'emno Transportnye Mashiny [*A publication*]
DETALL ... Detached from Duty Indicated and from All Other Duty Assigned
DETAP...... Decision Table Processor [*IBM Corp.*]
Det BJ .... Detroit Bar Journal [*A publication*] (DLA)
DETC......... Detection Systems, Inc. [*NASDAQ symbol*] (NQ)
DETC......... Diethylthiacarbocyanine [*Organic chemistry*]
DETC......... Digital Element Tester Console (MCD)
Det CLR...... Detroit College of Law. Review [*A publication*]
Det CL Rev ... Detroit College of Law. Review [*A publication*]
Det Coll LR ... Detroit College of Law. Review [*A publication*]
Det Coll L Rev ... Detroit College of Law. Review [*A publication*]
DET CON ... Detective Constable [*Scotland Yard*] [*British*] (ADA)
DETD .... Determined
DET in DUP ... Detur in Duplo [*Let Twice as Much Be Given*] [*Pharmacy*]
DETe .... Diethyltelluride
DETEC...... Detection (KSC)
DETED...... Determined (ROG)
DETEN ..... Detention (DSUE)
DETEQ...... DECHEMA [*Deutsche Gesellschaft fuer Chemisches Apparatewesen, Chemische Technik, und Biotechnologie e V*] Environmental Technology Equipment Databank [*Information service or system*] [*Federal Republic of Germany*] (IID)
DETER...... Determination (KSC)
DETERMD ... Determined (ROG)
DETERME ... Determine (ROG)
determin..... Determination
DETERMN ... Determination [*Legal term*] (ROG)
Determ Org Struct Phys Methods ... Determination of Organic Structures by Physical Methods [*A publication*]
DETERS ... Damage Tolerant/Easy Repair Structures (MCD)
DETES ...... Deep-Towed Explosive Source [*Seismology*]
DETEST.... Demystify the Established Standardized Tests [*Project*]
DETHERM ... DECHEMA [*Deutsche Gesellschaft fuer Chemisches Apparatewesen, Chemische Technik, und Biotechnologie e V*] Thermophysical Property Data Bank [*Federal Republic of Germany*] [*Information service or system*] (CRD)
DETHERM-SDC ... DECHEMA [*Deutsche Gesellschaft fuer Chemisches Apparatewesen, Chemische Technik, und Biotechnologie e V*] Thermophysical Property Data Bank - Data Evaluation System [*Database*]
DETHERM-SDR ... DECHEMA [*Deutsche Gesellschaft fuer Chemisches Apparatewesen, Chemische Technik, und Biotechnologie e V*] Thermophysical Property Data Bank - Data Retrieval System [*Database*]
DET INSP ... Detective Inspector [*Scotland Yard*] [*British*] (ADA)
DETJA ...... Defense Transportation Journal [*A publication*]
Det Law...... Detroit Lawyer [*A publication*]
Det Leg N .. Detroit Legal News [*A publication*] (DLA)

Det Lit........ Detskaja Literature [*A publication*]
Det LJ........ Detroit Law Journal [*A publication*] (DLA)
Det L Rev ... Detroit Law Review [*A publication*] (DLA)
DETM........ Determine (AABC)
Detmt......... Detachment [*British military*] (DMA)
DETN........ Detection (NASA)
DETN........ Detention (MSA)
DETN........ Determination
DETO........ Devils Tower National Monument
DETO........ Dyestuffs Environmental and Toxicology Organization
DETOC ..... Decision Table to COBOL [*Common Business-Oriented Language*] Processor [*Data processing*]
DETOL...... Directly Executable Test-Oriented Language [*1968*] [*Data processing*] (CSR)
DETOX ..... Detoxification (DSUE)
DETP........ Department of Environmental and Toxicologic Pathology [*An association*] (EA)
DETP........ Diethylenetriaminepentaacetic Acid [*Also, DETPA, DTPA*] [*Chelating agent*]
DETP........ Displaced Equipment Training Plan [*DoD*]
DETPA...... Diethylenetriaminepentaacetic Acid [*Also, DETP, DTPA*] [*Chelating agent*]
DETR .... Detector
DETR .... Detrimental (AABC)
DETRAH .. Detrahatur [*Let It, or Them, Be Drawn*] [*Pharmacy*] (ROG)
DETRAHAT ... Detrahatur [*Let It, or Them, Be Drawn*] [*Pharmacy*] (ROG)
DETRAN... Decision Table Translator [*Data processing*]
De Tranq Anim ... De Tranquillitate Animi [*of Plutarch*] [*Classical studies*] (OCD)
DETRESFA ... Distress Phase [*Aviation*]
DETRINS ... Detailed Routing Instructions (NATG)
Detr Med Ne ... Detroit Medical News [*A publication*]
Detr MJ ..... Detroit Medical Journal [*A publication*]
Detroit Acad Nat Sci Occasional Paper ... Detroit Academy of Natural Sciences. Occasional Papers [*A publication*]
Detroit BQ ... Detroit Bar Quarterly [*A publication*] (DLA)
Detroit Coll L ... Detroit College of Law [*Michigan*] (DLA)
Detroit Dent Bull ... Detroit Dental Bulletin [*A publication*]
Detroit Inst Bul ... Detroit Institute of Arts. Bulletin [*A publication*]
Detroit L .... Detroit Lawyer [*A publication*] (DLA)
Detroit Law ... Detroit Lawyer [*A publication*]
Detroit Leg N ... Detroit Legal News [*A publication*] (DLA)
Detroit L J ... Detroit Law Journal [*A publication*] (DLA)
Detroit L Rev ... Detroit Law Review [*A publication*] (DLA)
Detroit Med News ... Detroit Medical News [*A publication*]
Detroit Nw ... Detroit News [*A publication*]
Detroit Perspect ... Detroit in Perspective [*A publication*]
Detroit Rev Med and Pharm ... Detroit Review of Medicine and Pharmacy [*A publication*]
Detroit Sym ... Detroit Symphony Orchestra. Program Notes [*A publication*]
DETS......... Digital Element Test Set
DET SGT .. Detective Sergeant [*Scotland Yard*] [*British*] (ADA)
D'ETTE..... Dinette [*Classified advertising*] (ADA)
DETU........ Diethylthiourea [*Organic chemistry*]
DETW .... Detroit & Western [*Later, DW*] [*AAR code*]
DETX .... Detector Electronics Corp. [*NASDAQ symbol*] (NQ)
DEU........... Data Encoder Unit
DEU........... Data Encryption Unit
DEU........... Data Entry Unit
DEU........... Data Exchange Unit
deu............. Delaware [*MARC country of publication code*] [*Library of Congress*] (LCCP)
DEU........... Digital Evaluation Unit
DEU........... Display Electronics Unit (NASA)
DEU........... Duplicates Exchange Union (EA)
DEU........... Federal Republic of Germany [*ANSI three-letter standard code*] (CNC)
DeU........... University of Delaware, Newark, DE [*Library symbol*] [*Library of Congress*] (LCLS)
DEUA........ Digitronics Equipment Users Association
DeU-Ag...... University of Delaware, Agricultural Experiment Station, Newark, DE [*Library symbol*] [*Library of Congress*] (LCLS)
DEUC........ Division of End Use Conservation [*Energy Research and Development Administration*]
DEUCE ..... Digital Electronic Universal Calculating [*or Computing*] Engine
Deu E .... Deutschlands Erneuerung [*A publication*]
DEUPD7 ... Dermatology Update [*A publication*]
Deus........... Quod Deus Immutabilis Sit [*Philo*] (BJA)
DEUT .... Data Encoder Unit Transmitter
Deut .... Deuteronomy [*Old Testament book*]
Deut Agrartech ... Deutsche Agrartechnik [*A publication*]
Deut Ausschuss Stahlbeton ... Deutscher Ausschuss fuer Stahlbeton [*A publication*]
Deutch Archaeol Inst Jahrb ... Deutsches Archaeologisches Institut. Jahrbuch [*A publication*]
Deut Entomol Z ... Deutsche Entomologische Zeitschrift [*A publication*]
Deut Geod Komm Veroeff Reihe E Gesch Entwickl Geod ... Deutsche Geodaetische Kommission. Veroeffentlichungen. Reihe E. Geschichte und Entwicklung der Geodaesie [*A publication*]
Deut Geog Blaetter ... Deutsche Geographische Blaetter [*A publication*]

Deut Landwirt ... Deutsche Landwirtschaft [*A publication*]
Deut Lebensm Rundsch ... Deutsche Lebensmittel Rundschau [*A publication*]
Deut Luft Raumfahrt Forschungsber ... Deutsche Luft- und Raumfahrt. Forschungsbericht [*A publication*]
Deut Med Wo ... Deutsche Medizinische Wochenschrift [*A publication*]
Deut Mueller Ztg ... Deutsche Mueller Zeitung [*A publication*]
Deut Oesterr Alpen-Ver Zs ... Deutscher und Oesterreichischer Alpen-Verein. Zeitschrift [*A publication*]
Deut Papierwirtsch ... Deutsche Papierwirtschaft [*A publication*]
DeutR .... Deuteronomy Rabba　(BJA)
DeutR .... Deutsche Revue [*A publication*]
Deut Rundschau ... Deutsche Rundschau [*A publication*]
Deutsch Archaeol Inst Roem Mitt ... Deutsches Archaeologisches Institut. Mitteilungen. Roemische Abteilung [*A publication*]
Deutsch Dante Jahrb ... Deutsches Dante Jahrbuch [*A publication*]
Deutsch-Dominikan Tropenforschungsinstitut Veroeff ... Deutsch-Dominikanisches Tropenforschungsinstitut Veroeffentlichungen [*A publication*]
Deutsche Aerzte-Ztg ... Deutsche Aerztezeitung [*A publication*]
Deutsche Akad Wissen Berlin Schr ... Deutsche Akademie der Wissenschaften zu Berlin. Schriften der Sektion fuer Vor- und Fruehgeschichte [*A publication*]
Deutsche Bundesbank ... Monthly Report. Deutsche Bundesbank [*A publication*]
Deutsche Bundesbank Mo Rept ... Deutsche Bundesbank. Monthly Report [*A publication*]
Deutsche Entom Ztschr "Iris" ... Deutsche Entomologische Zeitschrift "Iris" [*A publication*]
Deutsche Geol Gesell Zeitschr ... Deutsche Geologische Gesellschaft. Zeitschrift [*A publication*]
Deutsche Keramische Gesell Ber ... Deutsche Keramische Gesellschaft. Berichte [*A publication*]
Deutsche Med Wochenschr ... Deutsche Medizinische Wochenschrift [*A publication*]
Deutsche Med-Ztg ... Deutsche Medizinal-Zeitung [*A publication*]
Deutsche Mineralog Gesell Fortschr Mineralogie ... Deutsche Mineralogische Gesellschaft. Fortschritte der Mineralogie [*A publication*]
Deutsche Oper ... Deutsche Oper am Rhein [*A publication*]
Deutscher Geographentag Verh ... Deutscher Geographentag Verhandlungen [*A publication*]
Deutsches Arch Klin Med ... Deutsches Archiv fuer Klinische Medizin [*A publication*]
Deutsche Schlacht-u Viehhof-Ztg ... Deutsche Schlacht- und Viehhof-Zeitung [*A publication*]
Deutsches Institut fuer Wirtschaftsforschung Econ Bul ... Deutsches Institut fuer Wirtschaftsforschung. Economic Bulletin [*A publication*]
Deutsche Tieraerztl Wochenschr ... Deutsche Tieraerztliche Wochenschrift [*A publication*]
Deutsche Ztschr Chir ... Deutsche Zeitschrift fuer Chirurgie [*A publication*]
Deutsche Ztschr Nervenh ... Deutsche Zeitschrift fuer Nervenheilkunde [*A publication*]
Deutsch Gesell Geol Wiss Ber ... Deutschen Gesellschaft fuer Geologische Wissenschaften. Berichte [*A publication*]
Deutsch Jahrb Musikw ... Deutsches Jahrbuch fuer Musikwissenschaft [*A publication*]
Deutsch Kam ... Deutsche Kameramann [*A publication*]
Deutsch Nationalbiblio Reihe A ... Deutsche Nationalbibliographie. Reihe A [*Leipzig*] [*A publication*]
Deutsch Nationalbiblio Reihe B ... Deutsche Nationalbibliographie. Reihe B [*Leipzig*] [*A publication*]
Deutschoesterr Spirit Ztg ... Deutschoesterreichische Spirituisen-Zeitung [*A publication*]
Deutschoesterr Tieraerztl Wchnschr ... Deutschoesterreichische Tieraerztliche Wochenschrift [*A publication*]
Deutsch Shakespeare Ges West Jahrb ... Deutsch Shakespeare Gesellschaft West. Jahrbuch [*A publication*]
Deutsch-Taschenb ... Deutsch-Taschenbuecher [*A publication*]
Deutsch Verein Kunstwis Z ... Deutscher Verein fuer Kunstwissenschaft. Zeitschrift [*A publication*]
Deutsch Zool Ges Verh ... Deutsche Zoologische Gesellschaft. Verhandlungen [*A publication*]
Deut Vier L ... Deutsche Vierteljahrsschrift fuer Literaturwissenschaft und Geistesgeschichte [*A publication*]
Deut Vier Lit ... Deutsche Vierteljahrsschrift fuer Literaturwissenschaft und Geistesgeschichte [*A publication*]
Deut Z Phil ... Deutsche Zeitschrift fuer Philosophie [*A publication*]
Deu Viertel ... Deutsche Vierteljahrsschrift fuer Literaturwissenschaft und Geistesgeschichte [*A publication*]
DEV .... Denver Silver [*Vancouver Stock Exchange symbol*]
DEV .... Design Evaluation Vehicle
DEV .... Deva [*Romania*] [*Seismograph station code, US Geological Survey*]　(SEIS)
DEV .... Develop [*or Development*]　(AFM)
DEV .... Development News [*A publication*]
Dev .... Devereux's North Carolina Law Reports [*A publication*]　(DLA)
Dev .... Devereux's Reports, United States Court of Claims [*A publication*]　(DLA)
DEV .... Deviation　(AAG)
DEV .... Device　(KSC)

DEV .... Devjo Industries, Inc. [*Toronto Stock Exchange symbol*]
DEV .... Devonian [*Geology*]
Dev .... Devotee [*A publication*]
DEV .... Director [*or Directorate*] of Evaluation [*Army*]
DEV .... Duck Egg Virus [*or Duck Embryo Vaccine*] [*Immunology*]
DEVA .... Death Valley National Monument
DEvA .... Deutsch-Evangelisch im Auslande [*A publication*]
DEVA .... Development Acceptance (AABC)
DEVA .... Development Validation Acceptance
Dev Agric Eng ... Developments in Agricultural Engineering [*A publication*]
DEVAIPR ... Development Acceptance in Process Review　(RDA)
Dev Anim Vet Sci ... Developments in Animal and Veterinary Sciences [*A publication*]
Dev Appl Spectrosc ... Developments in Applied Spectroscopy [*A publication*]
DEVAT ...... Depot Vehicle Automatic Tester
Dev & B ...... Devereux and Battle's North Carolina Equity Reports [*A publication*]　(DLA)
Dev & B ...... Devereux and Battle's North Carolina Law Reports [*A publication*]　(DLA)
DevB .... Devil's Box [*A publication*]
Dev & Bat ... Devereux and Battle's North Carolina Law Reports [*A publication*]　(DLA)
Dev & Bat Eq ... Devereux and Battle's North Carolina Equity Reports [*A publication*]　(DLA)
Dev & B Eq ... Devereux and Battle's North Carolina Equity Reports [*A publication*]　(DLA)
Dev Biochem ... Developments in Biochemistry [*A publication*]
Dev Biol ..... Developmental Biology [*A publication*]
Dev Biol Stand ... Developments in Biological Standardization [*A publication*]
Dev Biol Suppl ... Developmental Biology. Supplement [*A publication*]
Dev & BL (NC) ... Devereux and Battle's North Carolina Law Reports [*A publication*]　(DLA)
Dev Brain Res ... Developmental Brain Research [*A publication*]
DEVC .... Devcon International Corp. [*NASDAQ symbol*]　(NQ)
DEVC .... Development Change [*Aerospace*]　(AAG)
Dev CC .... Devereux's Reports, United States Court of Claims [*A publication*]　(DLA)
Dev Cell Biol .. Developmental and Cell Biology [*A publication*]
Dev Cell Biol (Amsterdam) ... Developments in Cell Biology (Amsterdam) [*A publication*]
Dev Change ... Development and Change [*A publication*]
DEVCO ..... Development Committee [*ISO*]　(DS)
Dev Comp Immunol ... Developmental and Comparative Immunology [*A publication*]
Dev Crop Sci ... Developments in Crop Science [*A publication*]
Dev Ct Cl ... Devereux's Reports, United States Court of Claims [*A publication*]　(DLA)
DEVCTR ... Development Center　(MCD)
DEVD .... Devilled [*Culinary*]　(ROG)
DEVD .... Devised　(ROG)
Dev Deeds ... Devlin on Deeds and Real Estate [*A publication*]　(DLA)
Dev Dialogue ... Development Dialogue [*A publication*]
Dev Disab Abstr ... Developmental Disabilities Abstracts [*A publication*]
DEVE .... Devise　(ROG)
DEVEAA ... Defense des Vegetaux [*A publication*]
Dev Econ ...... Developing Economies [*A publication*]
Dev Econ Geol ... Developments in Economic Geology [*A publication*]
Dev Educ ...... Developing Education [*A publication*]　(APTA)
DEVEL .... Development
Devel Biol .. Developmental Biology [*A publication*]
Devel Civ ..... Developpement et Civilisation [*A publication*]
Devel Dig ..... Development Digest [*A publication*]
Devel Ind Microbiol ... Developments in Industrial Microbiology [*A publication*]
Develop Bio ... Developmental Biology [*A publication*]
Develop Biol ... Developmental Biology [*A publication*]
Develop in Cell Biology ... Developments in Cell Biology [*A publication*]
Develop Cha ... Development and Change [*A publication*]
Develop and Change ... Development and Change [*A publication*]
Develop et Civilis ... Developpement et Civilisation [*A publication*]
Develop Dialogue ... Development Dialogue [*A publication*]
Develop Eco ... Developing Economies [*A publication*]
Develop Econ ... Developing Economies [*A publication*]
Develop Gr ... Development, Growth, and Differentiation [*A publication*]
Developing Ed ... Developing Education [*A publication*]
Develop in Mech ... Developments in Mechanics [*A publication*]
Develop Med ... Developmental Medicine and Child Neurology [*A publication*]
Develop Med Child Neurol ... Developmental Medicine and Child Neurology [*A publication*]
Development ... Development Forum [*General Edition*] [*A publication*]
Development & Materials Bull ... Development and Materials Bulletin [*A publication*]
Develop Psy ... Developmental Psychobiology [*A publication*]
Develop Psychol ... Developmental Psychology [*A publication*]
Develop in Statist ... Developments in Statistics [*A publication*]
Develop VIC ... Develop Victoria [*A publication*]　(APTA)
Develop VIC J ... Develop Victoria Journal [*A publication*]　(APTA)
Devel Psych ... Developmental Psychology [*A publication*]
Devel Psychobiol ... Development Psychobiology [*A publication*]

Dev Environ Biol Fishes ... Developments in Environmental Biology of Fishes [*A publication*]

Dev Eq .... Devereux's North Carolina Equity Reports [*A publication*] (DLA)

Dev Food Packag ... Developments in Food Packaging [*A publication*]

Dev Food Sci ... Development in Food Science [*A publication*]

Dev Forum ... Development Forum [*A publication*]

DevG .... Devisengesetz [*Law on Exchange Control*] [*German*] (DLA)

DEV GENC .. Federation of Turkish Revolutionary Youth

Dev Genet .. Developmental Genetics [*A publication*]

Dev Genet (Amsterdam) ... Developments in Genetics (Amsterdam) [*A publication*]

Dev Geochem ... Developments in Geochemistry [*A publication*]

Dev Geotech Eng ... Developments in Geotechnical Engineering [*A publication*]

Dev Geotectonics ... Developments in Geotectonics [*A publication*]

Dev Grow Differ ... Development, Growth, and Differentiation [*A publication*]

Dev Growth Differ ... Development, Growth, and Differentiation [*A publication*]

Dev Growth Differ (Nagoya) ... Development, Growth, and Differentiation (Nagoya) [*A publication*]

Dev Halophilic Microorganisms ... Developments in Halophilic Microorganisms [*A publication*]

DEV HGT ... Developed Height (MSA)

Dev Hydrobiol ... Developments in Hydrobiology [*A publication*]

Deviant Behav ... Deviant Behavior [*A publication*]

DEVIL .... Development of Integrated Logistics (NATG)

Dev Immunol ... Developments in Immunology [*A publication*]

Dev Ind Microbiol ... Developments in Industrial Microbiology [*A publication*]

Dev Ind Sci ... Developpement Industriel et Scientifique [*A publication*]

Dev Innovation Aust Process Ind Pap Aust Chem Eng Conf ... Development and Innovation for Australian Process Industries. Papers of the Australian Chemical Engineering Conference [*Newcastle, 1972*] [*A publication*] (APTA)

De Vir Ill.... De Viris Illustribus [*of St. Jerome*] [*Classical studies*] (OCD)

Dev Kin Bl ... Devereux's Kinne's Blackstone [*A publication*] (DLA)

Dev Kin Kent ... Devereux's Kinne's Kent [*A publication*] (DLA)

Dev L.......... Devereux's North Carolina Law Reports [*A publication*] (DLA)

Devl Biol .... Developmental Biology [*A publication*]

Devl Deeds ... Devlin on Deeds [*A publication*] (DLA)

DEVLPMT ... Development

DEVLPMTL ... Developmental

Dev Mamm ... Development in Mammals [*A publication*]

Dev Mat Bull ... Development and Materials Bulletin [*A publication*]

Dev Mech... Developments in Mechanics [*A publication*]

Dev Med Child Neurol ... Developmental Medicine and Child Neurology [*A publication*]

Dev Med Child Neurol Suppl ... Developmental Medicine and Child Neurology. Supplement [*A publication*]

Dev Miner Process ... Developments in Mineral Processing [*A publication*]

Dev Mol Cell Biochem ... Developments in Molecular and Cellular Biochemistry [*A publication*]

DEVN .... Deviation (MSA)

DEVN .... Devon Group, Inc. [*Stamford, CT*] [*NASDAQ symbol*] (NQ)

Dev Neurosci ... Developmental Neuroscience [*A publication*]

Dev Newsl ... Development Newsletter [*A publication*]

Dev Nucl Med ... Developments in Nuclear Medicine [*A publication*]

Dev Nutr Metab ... Developments in Nutrition and Metabolism [*A publication*]

DEVO .... De-Evolution [*Acronym is name of musical group*]

Dev Obstet Gynecol ... Developments in Obstetrics and Gynecology [*A publication*]

DEVON..... Devonshire [*County in England*]

Devon Hist ... Devon Historian [*A publication*]

Devonshire Assoc ... Devonshire Association [*A publication*]

Dev Ophthalmol ... Developments in Ophthalmology [*A publication*]

DEVPA...... Developmental Psychology [*A publication*]

DEVPA9...... Developmental Psychology [*A publication*]

Dev Pet Sci ... Developments in Petroleum Science [*A publication*]

Dev Pharmacol Ther ... Developmental Pharmacology and Therapeutics [*A publication*]

Dev Plant Biol ... Developments in Plant Biology [*A publication*]

Dev Plant Genet Breed ... Developments in Plant Genetics and Breeding [*A publication*]

Dev Plant Soil Sci ... Developments in Plant and Soil Sciences [*A publication*]

Dev Precambrian Geol ... Developments in Precambrian Geology [*A publication*]

Dev Psychobiol ... Developmental Psychobiology [*A publication*]

Dev Psychol ... Developmental Psychology [*A publication*]

Dev Psychol Monogr ... Developmental Psychology. Monograph [*A publication*]

Devpt.......... Development

DEVR .... Dever Explorations [*NASDAQ symbol*] (NQ)

DEVR .... Distortion-Eliminating Voltage Regulator

Dev Rev....... Developmental Review [*A publication*]

DEVS......... Devotions

DEVS......... DODAAC [*Department of Defense Activity Address Code*] Edit/Validation System [*Military*]

Devs Biol Standardiz ... Developments in Biological Standardization [*A publication*]

Dev Sedimentol ... Developments in Sedimentology [*A publication*]

DEVSIS..... Development Sciences Information System [*Information service or system*] [*Canada*] (IID)

Dev Soil Sci ... Developments in Soil Science [*A publication*]

Dev Stat ..... Developments in Statistics [*A publication*]

Dev Stud (Sthn Afr) ... Development Studies (Southern Africa) [*A publication*]

DEVT .... Development

Devt Assoc Bull ... Development Association. Bulletin [*A publication*]

DEVTOS... Developmental Tactical Operations Systems (MCD)

Dev Toxicol Environ Sci ... Developments in Toxicology and Environmental Science [*A publication*]

Devts Mfuring Ind ... Developments in Manufacturing Industry [*A publication*]

DEV WD ... Developed Width (MSA)

DEW.......... Delmarva Power & Light Co. [*NYSE symbol*] (SPSG)

Dew .... Dewey's Kansas Court of Appeals Reports [*A publication*] (DLA)

Dew .... Dewey's Reports [*60-70 Kansas*] [*A publication*] (DLA)

DEW.......... Digital Encyclopedia Workstation [*Medinfo 86*]

DEW.......... Directed Energy Warfare [*Army*] (INF)

DEW.......... Directed Energy Weapon

DEW.......... Distant Early Warning [*North American RADAR system*] [*Obsolete*]

DEWA .... Delaware Water Gap National Recreation Area

DeWAt....... Atlas Chemical Industries, Inc., Wilmington, DE [*Library symbol*] [*Library of Congress*] (LCLS)

DeWB .... Brandywine College, Wilmington, DE [*Library symbol*] [*Library of Congress*] (LCLS)

DEWCOM T & E ... Divisional Electronic Warfare Combat Model Test and Evaluation

DEWD....... Detailed Elementary Wiring Diagrams

Dew Div ..... Dewey on Divorce Law [*A publication*] (DLA)

DeWDJ....... E. I. Du Pont de Nemours & Co., Jackson Laboratory, Wilmington, DE [*Library symbol*] [*Library of Congress*] (LCLS)

DeWDL ..... E. I. Du Pont de Nemours & Co., Lavoisier Library, Wilmington, DE [*Library symbol*] [*Library of Congress*] (LCLS)

DeWDT ..... E. I. Du Pont de Nemours & Co., Technical Library, Wilmington, DE [*Library symbol*] [*Library of Congress*] (LCLS)

D'Ewes J.... D'Ewes' Journal and Parliamentary Collection [*A publication*] (DLA)

DeWH....... Hercules Powder Co. [*Later, Hercules, Inc.*], Experiment Station, Wilmington, DE [*Library symbol*] [*Library of Congress*] (LCLS)

DeWHI...... Hercules, Inc., Wilmington, DE [*Library symbol*] [*Library of Congress*] (LCLS)

DeWI .... Wilmington Institute Free Library and the New Castle County Free Library, Wilmington, DE [*Library symbol*] [*Library of Congress*] (LCLS)

DeWint ...... Henry Francis DuPont Winterthur Museum, Winterthur, DE [*Library symbol*] [*Library of Congress*] (LCLS)

DeWint-M ... Henry Francis DuPont Winterthur Museum, Joseph Downs Manuscript and Microfilm Collection, Winterthur, DE [*Library symbol*] [*Library of Congress*] (LCLS)

DeWitt ...... DeWitt's Reports [*24-42 Ohio State*] [*A publication*] (DLA)

DEWIZ...... Distant Early Warning Identification Zone [*North American RADAR system*] [*Obsolete*]

DEWK .... Dual Employed, with Kids [*Lifestyle classification*]

DEW LINE ... Distant Early Warning Line [*North American RADAR system*] [*Obsolete*]

DEWS........ Dews Laboratories, Inc. [*Minerals Wells, TX*] [*NASDAQ symbol*] (NQ)

Dew St........ Dewey's Compiled Statutes of Michigan [*A publication*] (DLA)

DEWSUM ... Distant Early Warning Summary (MCD)

DeWT .... Delaware Technical and Community College, Northern Campus, Wilmington, DE [*Library symbol*] [*Library of Congress*] (LCLS)

DEWTA .... DEW [*Deutsche Edelstahlwerke*] Technische Berichte [*A publication*]

DeWTC ..... Third Circuit Court of Appeals, Wilmington, DE [*Library symbol*] [*Library of Congress*] (LCLS)

DEW Tech Ber ... DEW [*Deutsche Edelstahlwerke*] Technische Berichte [*A publication*]

DEWTRG ... Dewatering (MSA)

DEW-V...... Directed Energy Weapons - Vehicle [*Army*]

DeWV .... United States Veterans Administration Center, Wilmington, DE [*Library symbol*] [*Library of Congress*] (LCLS)

DEWY .... [*The*] Dewey Electronics Corp. [*NASDAQ symbol*] (NQ)

DEX.......... Data Exchange

DEX.......... Decision Expediting [*Graphic Sciences, Inc., copying machine*]

DEX.......... Deferred Execution

DEX.......... Destroyer Escort Experimental (MCD)

DEX.......... Dexamethasone [*Also, D, DXM*] [*Antineoplastic drug*]

DEX.......... Dexamphetamine Sulfate Tablet [*Slang*] (DSUE)

DEX.......... Dexedrine

DEX.......... Dexter [*Right*] [*Latin*] (ROG)

DEX	[*The*] Dexter Corp. [*NYSE symbol*] (SPSG)
DEX	Dextran [*Organic chemistry*]
D Ex	Doctor of Expression
DEX	Double Exposure
DEXAN	Digital Experimental Airborne Navigator
DEXGAL	Dexamethasonyl Galactoside [*Biochemistry*]
DEXGLU	Dexamthasonyl Glucopyranoside [*Biochemistry*]
D/EXH	Dual Exhaust [*Automotive engineering*]
DEXIE	Dexedrine
DEXO	Dexon, Inc. [*NASDAQ symbol*] (NQ)
D Exp	Dairy Exporter [*A publication*]
DEXT	Dexter [*Right*] [*Latin*]
DEXTER	Dental X-Ray Teaching and Training Replica
DEXTOR	Deep Experimental Torpedo [*Also, DSWS*] [*Later, EXTOR*] (MCD)
DEZ	Deir Ez Zor [*Syria*] [*Airport symbol*] (OAG)
DEZ	Derekh 'Erets Zuta [*or Derek Erez Zuta*] (BJA)
DEZ	Diethyl Zinc [*Used for deacidification of paper to arrest book decay*]
DEZ	Docklands Enterprise Zone [*London, England*]
DEZB	Deutsche Entomologische Zeitschrift (Berlin) [*A publication*]
DF	Associate Directorate for Facilities and Systems Management [*Kennedy Space Center*] [*NASA*] (NASA)
DF	Condor Flugdienst [*Germany*] [*ICAO designator*] (FAAC)
DF	Daedalian Foundation (EA)
DF	Damage Free [*Business term*]
DF	Damping Factor
DF	Dandke Folkemaal [*A publication*]
DF	Danny Foundation (EA)
DF	Data Field [*Data processing*]
DF	Data Folder
DF	Date Filed [*IRS*]
DF	Dead Freight [*Shipping*]
DF	Dean of the Faculty
DF	Dean Foods Co. [*NYSE symbol*] (SPSG)
DF	Decapacitation Factor [*with reference to sperm*] [*Medicine*]
DF	Decimal Factor (MCD)
DF	Decimal Fraction (MDG)
DF	Decontamination Facility
DF	Decontamination Factor
DF	Defence Fellowship [*British*]
DF	Defensive Fire
DF	Defensor Fidei [*Defender of the Faith*] [*Latin*]
DF	Deferoxamine [*Also, Desferrioxamine*] [*Chelating agent*]
DF	Definition
DF	Deflection Factor (IEEE)
DF	Defogging (AAG)
DF	Degrees Fahrenheit (KSC)
DF	Degrees of Freedom [*of movement*]
DF	Deionization-Filtration
DF	Delay Fuse
DF	Democracy Fund (EA)
DF	Dense Flint (AAG)
D of F	Department of Finance (ADA)
DF	Depot Fixed (AAG)
DF	Depth of Field [*or Focus*] [*Photography*]
DF	Derating Factor
DF	Dermatology Foundation (EA)
DF	Describing Function
DF	Design Formula
DF	Destination Field
DF	Destroyer Flotilla [*Navy*]
DF	Detailed Forecast (MCD)
D & F	Determination and Findings
DF	Deutereium Fluoride (IEEE)
DF	Development Fixture (MCD)
DF	Development Flight (NASA)
DF	Development-Forward (MCD)
DF	Development Fund
DF	Device Flag [*Data processing*]
DF	Diabetic Father [*Medicine*]
DF	Dialogue Foundation (EA)
DF	Dialysis Fluid [*Physiology*]
DF	Dialyzable Fraction
DF	Diamond Flap [*Envelopes*]
df	Dias Fecha [*Days from Date*] [*Spanish*]
DF	Dicke-Fix [*Electronics*]
DF	Diesel Fuel (CINC)
DF	Dietary Fiber [*Nutrition*]
DF	Differentiation Factor [*Biochemistry*]
DF	Dilution Factor [*Also, Fd*] [*Nuclear energy*] (NRCH)
DF	Dimensional Flowcharting [*Data processing*]
DF	Dirac-Fock Theory [*Electrodynamics*]
DF	Direct Flight (MCD)
DF	Direct Flow
DF	Direct Fluorescence
DF	Direction Finder [*or Finding*] [*Radio aid to navigation*]
DF	Disaccommodation Factor
DF	Disassembly Facility [*NASA*] (NASA)
DF	Discharge Flow [*Chemical kinetics*]
DF	Discriminant Function [*Physiology*]

DF	Discrimination Filter (AAG)
DF	Disk File [*Data processing*] (BUR)
DF	Dislocated Farmer [*Job Training and Partnership Act*] (OICC)
D & F	Disposition and Findings (AAG)
DF	Disposition Form [*Army*]
DF	Disseminated Foci [*Medicine*]
DF	Dissipation Factor
DF	Distribution Factor
DF	Distribution Frame (KSC)
DF	Distribution Function [*Statistics*]
DF	Ditchley Foundation (EA)
DF	Diva Foundation (EA)
DF	Diversity Factor
DF	Diverted Force (CINC)
DF	Doctor of Forestry
DF	Door in Flat [*Theater*]
DF	Dorsal Fold
DF	Dorsiflexion [*Medicine*]
DF	Dose Factor [*Radioactivity calculations*]
DF	Double Feeder [*Line*] [*Technical drawings*]
DF	Double Foolscap [*Paper*] (ADA)
DF	Double Frequency
D-F	Double-Fronted
DF	Douglas Fir (MSA)
DF	Draft (ADA)
DF	Drag Friction
DF	Dream Factory (EA)
DF	Drinking Fountain (AAG)
DF	Drive Fit [*Technical drawings*]
DF	Drop Forge (KSC)
DF	Dual Facility
DF	[*Royal*] Dublin Fusiliers [*British military*] (DMA)
DF	Duty Factor [*Military*] (CAAL)
DF	Duty Free [*Customs*]
DF	Dye-Free [*Pharmacy*]
DF	Dynamic Fermenter [*Microbiology*]
DF	Dysautonomia Foundation (EA)
DF	Fallout Forecast Data [*Civil Defense*]
DF	I am connecting you to the station you request [*Telecommunications*] (FAAC)
D & F	Judgments of Divisional and Full Courts, Gold Coast [*A publication*] (DLA)
D & F 11-16	Divisional and Full Court Judgments [*1911-1916*] [*A publication*] (DLA)
DFA	Dance Films Association (EA)
DFA	Defence Force Advocate [*Australia*]
DFA	Defense Fisheries Administration [*Abolished, 1953*]
DFA	Department of Foreign Affairs (CINC)
DFA	Deposit Fund Account
DFA	Describing Function Analyzer [*NASA*]
DFA	Design for Automation [*Manufacturing technology*]
DFA	Design Fabrication Assembly
DFA	Designated Field Activity [*DoD*]
DFA	Diamonds Fields Artillery [*British military*] (DMA)
DFA	Dick Family Association (EA)
DFA	Die Forged Aluminum
DFA	Diesel Fuel with an Antarctic Additive
DFA	Digital Fault Analysis
DFA	Digital Frequency Analyzer
DFA	Diploma of Fine Art [*British*]
DFA	Diploma in Foreign Affairs (ADA)
DFA	Direct Fluorescent Antibody (Stain) [*Clinical medicine*]
DFA	Direct Immunofluorescent Assay [*Analytical biochemistry*]
DFA	Direction Finding Antenna
DFA	Distributed Function Architecture
DFA	Division Freight Agent
DFA	Doctor of Fine Arts
DFA	Doctors for Artists (EA)
DFA	Dominant Feature Analysis
DFA	Dried Fruit Association of California [*Later, DFA of California*] (EA)
DFA	Driver Fuel Assembly [*Nuclear energy*] (NRCH)
DFA	Droguerie Francaise. La Couleur [*A publication*]
DFA	Drop Forging Association [*Later, FIA*] (EA)
DFA	Dummy Fuel Assembly [*Nuclear energy*] (NRCH)
DFA	Dynamic Force Analysis
DFA	Partnership for a Drug Free America (EA)
DFAA	Dissolved Free Amino Acids
DFAA	United States Federal Aviation Administration, Washington, DC [*Library symbol*] [*Library of Congress*] (LCLS)
DFAC	Dining Facilities Administration Center (MCD)
DFAC	Dried Fruit Association of California [*Later, DFA of California*]
DFAD	Digital Feature Analysis Data [*Military*]
D & FA Daily	Defense and Foreign Affairs Daily [*A publication*]
DFAE	Director of Facilities and Engineering [*Military*] (AABC)
DFAED	Dated Forecast Authorization Equipment Data (MCD)
DFAI	Department of Foreign Affairs and Information [*South Africa*]
DFAIR	Defense Financial and Investment Review [*Pronounced "dee-fair"*] [*DoD*]
DFAMS	Defense Fuels Automated Management System [*DoD*]
DFAN	Dean of the Faculty, Aeronautics [*Air Force Academy*]

DFAn......... Discriminate Function Analysis
DFAO........ Food and Agricultural Organization of the United Nations, North American Regional Office, Washington, DC [*Library symbol*] [*Library of Congress*]   (LCLS)
DFAR .... Daily Field Activity Report
DFARS...... Defense Federal Acquisition Regulation Supplement   (RDA)
DFAST....... Dynamic File Allocation System
DFAT......... Department of Foreign Affairs and Trade [*Australia*]
DFAT........ Direct Fluorescent Antibody Technique [*Clinical chemistry*]
DFAW .... Direct Fire Antitank Weapon
D & FA Week ... Defense and Foreign Affairs Weekly [*A publication*]
DFB .... Deutsche Frauenbewegung [*German Women's Movement*] [*Federal Republic of Germany*]   (PPW)
DFB .... Diffusion Brazing
DFB .... Dinitrofluorobenzene [*Also, DNFB, FDNB*] [*Organic chemistry*]
DFB .... Distributed Feedback
DFB .... Distribution Fuse Board   (IEEE)
DFB .... Dry Film Binder
DFB-LD...... Distributed Feedback LASER Diode
DFBO Mitt ... DFBO [*Deutsche Forschungsgesellschaft fuer Blechverarbeitung und Oberflaechenbehandlung*] Mitteilungen [*A publication*]
DFBPT ...... Digital Force Balance Pressure Transducer
DFBW........ Digital Fly by Wire [*Aviation*]
DFC .... Data Flow Control   (IBMDP)
DFC .... Data Format Converter
DFC .... Desert Fishes Council   (EA)
DFC .... Design Field Change   (NRCH)
DFC .... Designs for Change   (EA)
DFC .... Development Finance Company [*Generic term*] [*Banking*]
DFC .... Devo Fan Club   (EA)
DFC .... Diagnostic Flow Chart [*Data processing*]   (IEEE)
DFC .... Di'anno Fan Club   (EA)
DFC .... Dictionnaire du Francais Contemporain [*Contemporary French Dictionary*] [*A publication*]
DFC .... Diesel Fuel and Coolant [*Nuclear energy*]
DFC .... Diffusion Formed Coating
DFC .... Digital Fire Control [*Military*]   (CAAL)
DFC .... Digital Flight Controller   (AAG)
DFC .... Disk File Check [*Data processing*]
DFC .... Disk File Control [*Data processing*]
DFC .... Distinguished Flying Cross [*Military decoration*] [*US and British*]
DFC .... Division Forms Control   (AAG)
DFC .... Dondino Fan Club   (EA)
DFC .... Doppler Frequency Converter   (MCD)
DFC .... Double Front Contact [*Photovoltaic energy systems*]
DFC .... Drop Forged Clamp
DFC .... Dry-Filled Capsules [*Pharmacy*]
DFC .... Dual-Feed Coupler
DFC .... Dust-Free Chamber
DFC .... Dynasty Fan Club   (EA)
DFC .... Federal City College [*Later, UDC*], Washington, DC [*Library symbol*] [*Library of Congress*] [*Obsolete*]   (LCLS)
DFC .... Headquarters Defense Communications Agency, Washington, DC [*OCLC symbol*]   (OCLC)
DFCA........ Dual Fault Correction Actuator
DFCA........ National Fire Prevention and Control Administration, Washington, DC [*Library symbol*] [*Library of Congress*]   (LCLS)
DFCC........ Digital Fire Control Computer [*Military*]   (MCD)
DFCC........ United States Federal Communications Commission, Washington, DC [*Library symbol*] [*Library of Congress*]   (LCLS)
DFCI......... Dana-Farber Cancer Institute [*Harvard Medical School*] [*Research center*]   (RCD)
DFCLS ...... Digital Flight Control and Landing System
DFCLT ...... Difficult   (FAAC)
DFCNV ..... Disk Data File Conversion Program [*IBM Corp.*]
DFCO........ Duty Flying Control Officer [*Navy*]
DFCP......... Division Funding Control Point
dFCS.......... Dialyzed Fetal Calf Serum
DFCS........ Digital Fire Control System [*Military*]   (CAAL)
DFCS........ Digital Flight Control Software [*NASA*]   (NASA)
DFCS........ Digital Flight Control System
DF/CS ...... Direction Finding Control Station   (MCD)
DFCS........ Director Fire Control System [*Air Force*]   (MCD)
DFCS........ Distinguished Federal Civilian Service [*Award*]   (RDA)
DFCS........ Drone Formation Control System [*Military*]
DFCU .... Disk File Control Unit [*Data processing*]
DFCU .... Dynamic Flow Control Unit [*Chromatography*]
DFD .... Dancers for Disarmament   (EA)
DFD .... Data for Development International Association [*See also DD*] [*Marseille, France*]   (EAIO)
DFD .... Data Flow Diagram
DFD .... Data Functional Diagram   (MCD)
DFD .... Demolition Firing Device
DFD .... Design-for-Discard [*Engineering*]
DFD .... Designed for Disassembly [*Product design*]
DFD .... Digital Flight Display

DFD .... Digital Frequency Discrimination [*Military*]   (CAAL)
DFD .... Digital Frequency Display
DFD .... Dogs for Defense [*Organization which trained dogs for armed services*] [*World War II*]
DFDA .... United States Food and Drug Administration, Bureau of Food, Washington, DC [*Library symbol*] [*Library of Congress*]   (LCLS)
DFDC .... Difluorodeoxycytidine [*Biochemistry*]
DFDC .... Disk File Descriptor Control [*Data processing*]
DFDD .... Difluorodiphenyldichloroethane [*Insecticide*]
DFDEL...... Deferred Delivery
DFDHIDWA ... Die Furcht des Herrn Ist der Weisheit Anfang [*Fear of the Lord Is the Beginning of Wisdom*] [(*Ps., CXI. 10) Motto of Dorothee Hedwig, Princess of Anhalt (1587-1608); Johann Sigismund, Elector of Brandenburg (1572-1619)*]
DFDI......... Diversifoods, Incorporated [*NASDAQ symbol*]   (NQ)
DFDL........ Dorsal Fin, Depressed Length [*Pisciculture*]
DFDNB .... Difluoro(dinitro)benzene [*Organic chemistry*]
DFDR .... Digital Flight Data Recorder   (MCD)
DFDSS ..... Data Facility Data Set Services
DFDT .... Difluorodiphenyltrichloroethane [*Insecticide*]
DFDT .... Dynamic Fault Diagnosis Technique   (MCD)
DFE .... Data Facility Extended
DFE .... Data Flow Engineer   (MCD)
DFE .... Debeye-Falkenhagen Effect [*Physics*]
DFE .... Derivative Fighter Engine
DFE .... Directed Fan Engine
DFE .... Direction Finding Equipment
DFE .... Directorate of Facilities Engineering [*Military*]
DFE .... Division Force Equivalents [*Army*]   (AABC)
DFE .... Doctor of Forest Engineering
DFEC........ Defense Finance Economic Committee   (NATG)
DFEC........ Douglas Fir Export Company [*Defunct*]   (EA)
DFED .... Dominion Federal Savings & Loan Association [*Tysons Corner, VA*] [*NASDAQ symbol*]   (NQ)
DF Eng...... Doctor of Forest Engineering
DFEU .... Disk File Electronics Unit [*Data processing*]
DFF........... Debbie Fox Foundation [*Later, NACH*]   (EA)
DFF........... Display Format Facility
DFF........... Division Final Fade
DFFC .... David Frizzell Fan Club   (EA)
DFFC .... Donna Fargo Fan Club [*Later, DFIFC*]   (EA)
DFFF .... Demokratiska Foerbundet av Finlands Folk [*Finnish People's Democratic League*]   (PPE)
DFFNAW ... Differentiation [*A publication*]
DFFR........ Dynamic Forcing Function [*Information*] Report [*Nuclear energy*]   (NRCH)
DFG .... Digital Function Generator
DFG .... Diode Function Generator
DFG .... Discrete Frequency Generator
DFG .... Display Format Generator   (MCD)
DFG .... Freer Gallery of Art, Washington, DC [*Library symbol*] [*Library of Congress*]   (LCLS)
DF/GA...... Day Fighter/Ground Attack [*British military*]   (DMA)
DFG Mitt... DFG Mitteilungen. Deutsche Forschungsgemeinschaft [*A publication*]
DFGS........ Digital Flight Guidance System   (IEEE)
DFH.......... Defense Family Housing [*Army*]   (AABC)
DFH.......... Deployable Field Headquarters
DFH.......... Developmental Fast Hydrofoil   (MCD)
DFH.......... Dollars per Flight Hour   (MCD)
DFH.......... Dual Filter Hybrid
DFHL .... United States Federal Home Loan Bank Board, Research Library, Washington, DC [*Library symbol*] [*Library of Congress*]   (LCLS)
DF Hom..... Diploma of the Faculty of Homoeopathy [*British*]
DFHS .... Dutch Family Heritage Society   (EA)
DFI........... Dark Field Illumination
DFI........... Decorative Fabrics Institute [*Defunct*]   (EA)
DFI........... Decreased Fuel Ingestion
DFI........... Deep Foundations Institute   (EA)
DFI........... Defiance, OH [*Location identifier*] [*FAA*]   (FAAL)
DFI........... Delegationen for Vetenskaplig och Teknisk Informationsforsorjning [*Swedish Delegation for Scientific and Technical Information*] [*Information service or system*] [*Defunct*]   (IID)
DFI........... Developmental Flight Instrumentation [*NASA*]
DFI........... Diabetes Foundation, Incorporated [*Later, JDC*]
DFI........... Dialogue with People of Living Faith and Ideologies [*A publication*]   (BJA)
DFI........... Digitally Fuel-Injected [*Automotive engineering*]
DFI........... Direct Foreign Investment
DFI........... Direct Fourier Inversion [*Mathematics*]
DFI........... Directorate for the Freedom of Information [*Formerly, Directorate for Security Review*] [*DoD*]
DFI........... Directory of Foreign Investors in the US [*A publication*]
DFI........... Disease-Free Intervals
DFI........... Disk File Interrogate [*Data processing*]
DFIB......... Data Function Information Book
DFIC......... Dehydrated Foods Industry Council [*Later, DCFC*]

DFIFAO .... Documents de Fouilles. Institut Francais d'Archeologie Orientale du Caire [*Cairo*] [*A publication*]
DFIFC .... Donna Fargo International Fan Club (EA)
DFII .... Duty Free International, Inc. [*NASDAQ symbol*] (NQ)
DFING ...... Direction Finding [*Radio*] [*Military*]
DFIRAP .... Deutsche Fischerei-Rundschau [*A publication*]
DFIS .... Digital Facsimile Interface System
DFIS .... Dual Filament Ion Source
DFISA .... Dairy and Food Industries Supply Association (EA)
DF & J ...... De Gex, Fisher, and Jones' English Chancery Reports [*A publication*] (DLA)
DFJ .... Dual Function Jammer
DFJ .... New Bedford, MA [*Location identifier*] [*FAA*] (FAAL)
DF & JB .... De Gex, Fisher, and Jones' English Bankruptcy Reports [*A publication*] (DLA)
DFL .... Daily Flight Log [*Aviation*] (FAAC)
DFL .... Deflating (MSA)
DFL .... Deflect (KSC)
DFL .... Degree of Financial Leverage
DFL .... Democrat-Farmer-Labor [*Party*] [*Minnesota*]
DFL .... Department of Family Life [*Later, Commission on Marriage and Family Life*] [*of NCC*] (EA)
DFL .... Deviation for Failure Location
DFL .... Display Formatting Language
DFL .... Doctor of Family Life
DFL .... Dry Film Lubricant
Dfl .... Dutch Florin [*Monetary unit*] (IMH)
DFL Ber ..... DFL [*Deutsche Forschungsanstalt fuer Luftfahrt*] Bericht [*A publication*]
DFLC .... Division of Foreign Labor Conditions [*Department of Labor*]
DFLD .... Distribution-Free Logic Design
DFLP .... Democratic Front for the Liberation of Palestine (PD)
DFLS .... Day Fighter Leaders School [*British military*] (DMA)
DFLX .... Dataflex Corp. [*NASDAQ symbol*] (NQ)
DFM .... Dansk Folkemal [*A publication*]
DFM .... Decorative Furniture Manufacturers Association [*Defunct*] (EA)
DFM .... Defiant Minerals [*Vancouver Stock Exchange symbol*]
DFM .... Design for Manufacturing
DFM .... Diesel Fuel, Marine (NVT)
DFM .... Digital Frequency Meter [*or Monitor*]
DFM .... Diploma in Forensic Medicine (ADA)
DFM .... Direct Flight Mode
DFM .... Director of Fleet Maintenance [*Navy*] [*British*]
DFM .... Director, Food Management [*Army*] (AABC)
DFM .... Distinguished Flying Medal [*British*]
DFM .... Double Failure Matrix [*Hazard quantification method*]
DFM .... Douglas Furnished Material [*DAC*]
DFM .... Dual-Frequency Method
DFM .... Franciscan Monastery, Washington, DC [*Library symbol*] [*Library of Congress*] (LCLS)
DFMA .... Design Failure-Mode Analysis
DFMA .... Difluoromethylarginine [*Organic chemistry*]
DFMA .... Director for Military Assistance (NATG)
DFMACH ... Drafting Machine
DFManS .... Director of Fleet Management Services [*Navy*] [*British*]
DFMhe ...... Deutsch-Franzoesische Monatshefte [*A publication*]
DFML .... Dictionary of Folklore, Mythology, and Legend [*A publication*]
DFMMS ..... Data File/Media Management System
DFMO .... Difluoromethylornithine [*Organic chemistry*]
DFMO .... Doppler Filter Mixer-Oscillator [*Electronics*] (AABC)
DFMR .... Daily Fetal Movements Record
DFMS .... Domestic and Foreign Missionary Society [*British*]
DFMSR ...... Directorate of Flight and Missile Safety Research [*Air Force*]
DFN .... Data File Number
DFNJ .... Descendants of Founders of New Jersey (EA)
DFNT .... Definite (FAAC)
DFNTN ..... Definition
DFO .... Danish Journal. A Magazine about Denmark [*A publication*]
DFO .... Defense Food Order [*Production and Marketing Administration*] [*Department of Agriculture*] (DLA)
DFO .... Deputy for Flight Operations [*NASA*] (KSC)
DFO .... Directed Format Option [*Rapid access management information system*]
DFO .... Director, Flight Operations [*NASA*] (KSC)
DFO .... Disk File Optimizer [*Data processing*] (BUR)
DFO .... Distilled Fuel Oil
DFO .... District Finance Officer
DFO .... Division Follow-On
DFO .... Dorsal Fold (Oesophagus)
DFo .... Folger Shakespeare Library, Washington, DC [*Library symbol*] [*Library of Congress*] (LCLS)
DFOA .... Deferoxamine [*Also, Desferrioxamine*] [*Chelating agent*]
DF-ODMR ... Delayed-Fluorescence Optically Detected Magnetic Resonance [*Physics*]
DFOLS ...... Depth of Flash Optical Landing System [*Navy*]
DFOM .... Deferoxamine Methanesulfonate [*or Desferrioxamine Mesylate*] [*Pharmacology*]
DFOM .... Difference Figure of Merit (MCD)
DFON .... Drivefone, Inc. [*NASDAQ symbol*] (NQ)
DForSc .... Doctor of Forest Science (ADA)

DFOS .... Diesel Fuel Oil System [*Nuclear energy*] (NRCH)
DFP .... Data Facility Product
DFP .... Davidon-Fletcher-Powell [*Method*]
DFP .... De Laurentiis Film Partnership [*AMEX symbol*] (SPSG)
DFP .... Define File Processor [*Data processing*]
DFP .... Demand Forecasting Program (BUR)
DFP .... Demokratische Fortschrittliche Partei [*Democratic Progressive Party*] [*Austria*] (PPE)
DFP .... Detroit Free Press [*A publication*]
DFP .... Deviant Flight Plan
DFP .... Diastolic Filling Period [*Medicine*]
DFP .... Diesel Fire Pump [*Nuclear energy*] (NRCH)
DFP .... Difluorophosphate [*Inorganic chemistry*]
DFP .... Diisopropyl Fluorophosphate [*or Diisopropyl Fluorophosphonate*] [*Also, DIFP*] [*Ophthalmic drug*]
DFP .... Diode Flat Pack
D-FP .... Diplomate, American Board of Family Practice (DHSM)
DFP .... Dipole Flat Plate
DFP .... Distribution Fuse Panel
DFP .... Dominica Freedom Party [*Political party*] (PPW)
DFP .... Dry Film Processor
DFP .... Dry Filter Processing
DFP .... Ductile Fracture Propagation [*Engineering*]
DFP .... Dun's Financial Profiles Report [*Dun & Bradstreet Credit Services*] [*Information service or system*] (CRD)
DFP .... Dynamic Flow Parameter
DFPA .... Douglas Fir Plywood Association [*Later, APA*] (EA)
DFPA .... National Society, Daughters of Founders and Patriots of America (EA)
DFPase ...... Di-isopropyl Phosphorofluoridase [*An enzyme*]
DFPC .... United States Federal Power Commission, Washington, DC [*Library symbol*] [*Library of Congress*] (LCLS)
DFPE .... Deflection Probable Errors (MCD)
DFPL .... Data Flow Programming Language
DFPS .... Digital Ferrite Phase Shifter
DFQ .... Day Frequency (FAAC)
DFQAO ...... Defense Fuel Quality Assurance Office [*DoD*]
DFQIS .... Dual Fuel Quantity Indicating System (MCD)
DFR .... Board of Governors, Federal Reserve System, Washington, DC [*Library symbol*] [*Library of Congress*] (LCLS)
DFR .... Decreasing Failure Rate
DFR .... Defense Fuel Region [*DoD*]
DFR .... Defer (AABC)
DFR .... Defrost (MSA)
DFR .... Degradation Failure Rate
DFR .... Delayed Free Recall
DFR .... Deutsch-Franzoesische Rundschau [*A publication*]
DFR .... Dihydroflavonol Reductase [*An enzyme*]
DFR .... Direction Finding Receiver
DFr .... Discophiles Francais [*Record label*] [*France*]
DFR .... Dofor Inc. [*Toronto Stock Exchange symbol*]
DFR .... Doppler Frequency Rate (MCD)
DFR .... Dounreay Fast Reactor [*British*]
DFR .... Dropped from Rolls
DFR .... Dual-Frequency Receiver
DFR .... Dun's Financial Records [*Dun's Marketing Services*] [*Parsippany, NJ*] [*Information service or system*] (IID)
DFR+ .... Dun's Financial Records Plus [*Dun's Marketing Services*] [*Information service or system*] (EISS)
DFR .... Durant Family Registry (EA)
DFR .... Dust-Free Room
DFRA .... Decreasing Failure Rate Average
DFRA .... Drop Forging Research Association [*British*]
DFRC .... Dairy Forage Research Center [*Department of Agriculture*] [*Madison, WI*] (GRD)
DFRC .... Distillers Feed Research Council (EA)
DFRC .... Dryden Flight Research Center [*NASA*]
DFRDP .... Dairy Farmers for Responsible Dairy Policy (EA)
DFRIF .... Defense Freight Railway Interchange Fleet [*Army*] (AABC)
DFRL .... Differential Relay (KSC)
DFRN .... Differential
DFRN .... Differential Velocity (NASA)
DFRP .... Deficiency and Replacement
DFRP .... Downcomer Flow Resistance Plate [*Nuclear energy*] (NRCH)
DFRS .... Differs (FAAC)
DFRT .... Demonstration Flight Rating Test (MCD)
DFS .... Dancer-Fitzgerald-Sample [*Advertising agency*]
DfS .... Dataflow Systems, Inc. [*Information service or system*] (IID)
DFS .... Defense Facsimile System (MCD)
DFS .... Demonstration Flight Satellite (MCD)
DFS .... Dental Fear Syndrome
DFS .... Deoxyfructoserotonin [*Antibacterial*]
DFS .... Depth-First Search
DFS .... Detail Finish Specification (MCD)
DFS .... Developments in Food Science [*Elsevier Book Series*] [*A publication*]
DFS .... [*A*] Dictionary of Forces' Slang [*A publication*]
DFS .... Digital Fascimile System (MCD)
DFS .... Digital Field System
DFS .... Digital Frequency Synthesizer
DFS .... Direct Fire Simulator

DFS............ Direct Fire System
DFS............ Direct Flow Sampler [Meteorology]
DFS............ Direct Forces Support [Military]
DFS............ Direction Finding Set [or System]
DFS............ Director of Flight Safety [Air Force]
DFS............ Display Formatting System
DFS............ Distance Finding Station
DFS............ Distributed File System
DFS............ Dividends from Space   (EA)
DFS............ Doctor of Foreign Science
DFS............ Doctor of Foreign Service
DFS............ Doctor of Forest Science
DFS............ Dofasco, Inc. [Toronto Stock Exchange symbol]
DFS............ Down Feeding Spindle
DFS............ Dragon Flight Simulator [Military]   (MCD)
DFS............ Dynamic Flight Simulator
DFSB......... Defense Force Section Base [Navy]
DFSC........ Defense Fuel Supply Center [Alexandria, VA]   (MCD)
DFSc........ Doctor of Financial Science
DFSCDX ... Developments in Food Science [A publication]
DFSD........ Directorate of Fleet Supply Duties [Navy] [British]
DFSE........ DFSoutheastern, Inc. [NASDAQ symbol]   (CTT)
DFSG........ Direct Formed Supergroup [Telecommunications]   (TEL)
DFSK........ Double Frequency Shift Keying [Radio]
DFSL........ Dallas Federal Savings & Loan [NASDAQ symbol]   (NQ)
DFSM........ Defence Force Service Medal [Military decoration] [Australia]
DFSP........ Defense Fuel Support Point [DoD]
DFSP........ Dermatofibrosarcoma Protuberans [Oncology]
DFSR........ Detailed Function System Requirement
DFSR........ Diffuser   (AAG)
DFSR........ Director [or Directorate] of Flight Safety Research [Air Force]
DFSS......... Democratic Front for the Salvation of Somalia   (PD)
DFSTN...... Direction Finding Station [Aviation]   (FAAC)
DFSU........ Disk File Storage Unit [Data processing]
DFSU........ Dual Frequency Signaling Units   (MCD)
DFSWO..... Department of the Financial Secretary of the War Office [British]
DFSZAV ... Deutsche Fischerei Zeitung [A publication]
DFT .... Deaerating Feed Tank
DFT .... Defendant
DFT .... Deployment for Training
DFT .... Design Feasibility Test
DFT .... Design for Testability [Military]
DFT .... Development Flight Test [Military]   (CAAL)
DFT .... Diagnostic Function Test [Data processing]
DFT .... Digital Facility Terminal [Telecommunications]   (TEL)
DFT .... Digital Filtering Technique
DFT .... Digital Fourier Transform [or Transformation] [Data processing]
DFT .... Direct Flight Test   (KSC)
DFT .... Director, Fleet Training
DFT .... Discrete Fourier Transform
DFT .... Distribution Function Terminal [Data processing]
DFT .... Draft
DFT .... Drift   (MSA)
DFT .... United States Federal Trade Commission, Washington, DC [Library symbol] [Library of Congress]   (LCLS)
DFT/A....... Draft Attached [Business term]
DFTA......... Dwarf Fruit Trees Association [Later, International Dwarf Fruit Trees Association]   (EA)
DFT/C ...... Clean Draft [Business term]
DFTG .... Drafting   (KSC)
DFTI.......... Dansk Fiskeriteknologisk Institut [Danish Fisheries Technology Institute] [Also, an information service or system]   (IID)
DFTM .... Douglas-Fir Tussock Moth
DFTMN .... Draftsman   (AFM)
DFTR......... Deflector   (MSA)
DFTSMN .. Draftsman   (KSC)
DFU .... Data File Utility [Data processing]   (IBMDP)
DFU .... Dead Fetus in Uterus
DFU .... Difluorourea [Organic chemistry]
DFU .... Dummy Firing Unit
DFUS........ Diffuse   (FAAC)
DFW .... Dallas/Fort Worth [Texas] [Airport symbol]
DFW .... Delegation for Friendship among Women   (EA)
DFW .... Diffusion Welding
DFW .... Director of Fortifications and Works [British]
DFW .... Dokumentation Fachbibliothek Werksbuecherei [A publication]
DFWM ...... Degenerate Four-Wave Mixing [Optical reflection]
DFWT........ Dallas Fort Worth Teleport Ltd. [Irving, TX] [Telecommunications]   (TSSD)
DFWU ...... Detroit Fast Food Workers' Union   (EA)
DFX .... Dicke-Fix [Electronics]   (CET)
DFY .... Dafrey Resources, Inc. [Vancouver Stock Exchange symbol]
DG............. Air Atlantique [Great Britain] [ICAO designator]   (FAAC)
DG............. Compagnie Gabonaise d'Affretement Aerien [ICAO designator]   (FAAC)
DG............. Daily Guardian [A publication]
DG............. Damaged Goods

DG............. Damianus Gulianus [Authority cited in pre-1607 legal work]   (DSA)
DG............. Dangerous Goods [Shipping]
DG............. Dansyl Glutamate [Biochemistry]
DG............. Danygraig [Welsh depot code]
DG............. Dark Green
DG............. Data General Corp. [Computer manufacturer]
DG............. Data Generator   (MCD)
DG............. Datagram [Telecommunications]
DG............. De Gex's English Bankruptcy Reports [A publication]   (DLA)
DG............. Decigram [Unit of measure]   (GPO)
DG............. Declaration de Guerre [Declaration of War] [French]   (ILCA)
DG............. Decreto Governatoriale [Governor's Decree] [Italian]   (ILCA)
DG............. Defense Guidance
DG............. Defensive Guard [Football]
DG............. Degaussing
DG............. Dei Gratia [By the Grace of God] [Latin]   (GPO)
DG............. Dekagram [Unit of measure]   (ROG)
DG............. Density Gradient
DG............. Dentate Granule Cell
DG............. Dentate Gyrus [Neuroanatomy]
DG............. Deo Gratias [Thanks Be to God] [Latin]   (GPO)
DG............. Deoxy-D-glucose [Also, DDG, DOG] [Biochemistry]
dG............. Deoxyguanylate [Biochemistry]
DG............. Destroyer, Guided Missile [Surface-to-air] [NATO]
DG............. Developments in Geotectonics [Elsevier Book Series] [A publication]
DG............. Diagnosis   (AABC)
Dg............. Dialog [Warsaw] [A publication]
DG............. Diastolic Gallop [Medicine]
DG............. Diesel Generator   (NRCH)
DG............. Differential Gain
DG............. Differential Generator
DG............. Differentially (Expressed) Gastrula [Genetics]
DG............. Digestive Gland
DG............. Diglyceride [Clinical chemistry]
DG............. Digoxigenin [Biochemistry]
DG............. Diode Gate
D & G........ Diprose and Gammon's Reports of Law Affecting Friendly Societies [1801-97] [England] [A publication]   (DLA)
DG............. Direct Grant
DG............. Directional Gyro
DG............. Director-General
DG............. Disc Grind [Technical drawings]
DG............. Displacement Gyro [Aerospace]
DG............. Display Generator   (NASA)
DG............. Distinguished Graduate [Military]
DG............. Distinguished Guest [Hotel term]
DG............. Distogingival [Dentistry]
DG............. District Guard [British military]   (DMA)
DG............. Disturbed Gum [Philately]
Dg............. Diving [British military]   (DMA)
D-G .... Divisional-General [British]
DG............. Documentation Group [Range Commanders Council] [NASA]
DG............. Dogged
DG............. Double Gear [Engineering]   (ROG)
DG............. Double Glass   (AAG)
DG............. Double Groove [Insulators]
DG............. Double-Gummed [Envelopes]
DG............. Downgrade   (NVT)
DG............. Dragoon Guards [Military unit] [British]
DG............. Dramatists Guild   (EA)
DG............. Dublin Gazette [A publication]
DG............. Dutch Guilder [Monetary unit]   (NATG)
DG............. Dynamogram
DG............. General Aviation Services Ltd. [United Kingdom] [ICAO designator]   (ICDA)
DGA.......... Damned Good Airplane
DGA.......... Dangriga [Belize] [Airport symbol]   (OAG)
DGA.......... Democratic Governors Association   (EA)
DGA.......... Deutsche Gesellschaft fuer Amerikastudien [German Association for American Studies]   (EA)
DGA.......... Diglycolamine [Organic chemistry]
DGA.......... Diploma in Government Administration [British]
DGA.......... Directors Guild of America   (EA)
DGA.......... Dog Grooming Association of Victoria [Australia]
DGA.......... Dummy Guide Assembly [Nuclear energy]   (NRCH)
DGA.......... Durum Growers Association of the United States   (EA)
DGAA........ Accra/Kotoka International [Ghana] [ICAO location identifier]   (ICLI)
DGABAC .. Deutsche Gartenbau [A publication]
DGAC....... Accra [Ghana] [ICAO location identifier]   (ICLI)
DGAD....... Ada [Ghana] [ICAO location identifier]   (ICLI)
DGAD....... Director-General of Army Development [Australia]
DGAE .... Director-General of Aircraft Equipment [Ministry of Aircraft Production] [British]
DGAE .... Director-General of Army Education [British]
DGAE .... Kete-Krachi [Ghana] [ICAO location identifier]   (ICLI)
DGAEM ... Director-General of Aerospace and Engineering Maintenance   (MCD)
DGAH .... Ho [Ghana] [ICAO location identifier]   (ICLI)

DGAHS..... Director-General of Army Health Services [*Australia*]
DGAK........ Akuse [*Ghana*] [*ICAO location identifier*]   (ICLI)
DGAMS .... Director-General of Army Medical Services [*British*]
DGA(N)..... Director-General of Aircraft (Naval) [*British military*]   (DMA)
DGANL ...... Digital to Analog   (MCD)
DGAO........ United States General Accounting Office, Washington, DC
        [*Library symbol*] [*Library of Congress*]   (LCLS)
DGAP .... Akatsi [*Ghana*] [*ICAO location identifier*]   (ICLI)
DGAP .... Development Group for Alternative Policies   (EA)
DGAQA..... Director-General of Army Quality Assurance [*Australia*]
DGAR........ Director-General of Army Requirements [*British*]
DGAS .... Delta Natural Gas Co., Inc. [*NASDAQ symbol*]   (NQ)
DGAS .... Diesel Generator Auxiliary System [*Nuclear energy*]   (NRCH)
DGAS .... Saltpond [*Ghana*] [*ICAO location identifier*]   (ICLI)
DGAT .... Director-General of Army Training [*Australia*]
DGAT .... Tema [*Ghana*] [*ICAO location identifier*]   (ICLI)
DGAV .... Director-General of Armoured Vehicles [*British*]
DGAVP ..... Desglycinamide-Arginine-Vasopressin [*Antidiuretic*]
DGAVS..... Director-General of the Army Veterinary Service [*British
        military*]   (DMA)
DGAW-A... Director-General of Accommodation and Works - Army
        [*Australia*]
DGB.......... Dangerous Goods Board [*IATA*]   (DS)
DGB.......... Deutscher Gewerkschaftsbund [*Confederation of German
        Trade Unions*] [*Federal Republic of Germany*]   (DCTA)
DGB.......... Diesel Generator Building [*Nuclear energy*]   (NRCH)
DGB.......... Disk Gap Band [*Parachute*]
DGB.......... Drogistenweekblad. Onafhankelijk Vakblad voor de
        Drogisterijbranche [*A publication*]
DGBA .... Diethylene Glycol Butyl Acetate [*Organic chemistry*]
DGBAW .... Der Grosse Baumeister aller Welten [*The Grand Architect of the
        Universe*] [*Freemasonry*] [*German*]
DGBC .... Digital Geoballistic Computer
DGBE .... Diethylene Glycol Butyl Ether [*Organic chemistry*]
DGBl......... Deutsche Geographische Blaetter [*A publication*]
DG Bl........ Deutsche Geschichtsblaetter [*A publication*]
DG BRIT REG FD ... Dei Gratia Britanniarum Regina, Fidei Defensor [*By
        the Grace of God, Queen of England, Defender of the
        Faith*] [*Latin*]   (ROG)
DGBUS ..... Digital Ground Bus
DGC.......... Data General Corporation [*Computer manufacturer*]
DGC.......... Data Graphics Corporation
DGC.......... Democratic Governors Conference   (EA)
DGC.......... Deutsche Gaststatte. Deutsche Hotelzeitung [*A publication*]
DGC.......... Developments in Geochemistry [*Elsevier Book Series*] [*A
        publication*]
DGC.......... Digital Geoballistic Computer
DGC.......... Diploma in Guidance and Counselling   (ADA)
DGC.......... Directors Guild of Canada
DGC.......... Durango [*Colorado*] [*Seismograph station code, US Geological
        Survey*] [*Closed*]   (SEIS)
DGC.......... Gallaudet College, Washington, DC [*Library symbol*] [*Library
        of Congress*]   (LCLS)
DGCA........ Director-General of Civil Aviation [*British*]
DGCAIES ... Diesel Generator Combustion Air Intake and Exhaust System
        [*Nuclear energy*]   (NRCH)
DGCC .... Director-General of Civilian Clothing [*British*]
DGCCP...... Dental Guidance Council for Cerebral Palsy   (EA)
DGCGO..... Dangerous Cargo   (FAAC)
DGC-K....... Gallaudet College, Kendall Demonstration School, Washington,
        DC [*Library symbol*] [*Library of Congress*]   (LCLS)
DGC-M...... Gallaudet College, Model Secondary School for the Deaf,
        Washington, DC [*Library symbol*] [*Library of
        Congress*]   (LCLS)
DGCO....... Director-General of Coordination and Organisation [*Australia*]
DGCStJ ..... Dame Grand Cross of the Order of Saint John of Jerusalem
        [*British*]   (ADA)
DGCWS..... Diesel Generator Cooling Water System [*Nuclear
        energy*]   (NRCH)
DGD.......... Deutsche Gesellschaft fuer Dokumentation [*German Society for
        Documentation*] [*Federal Republic of Germany*]
        [*Information service or system*]   (IID)
DGD.......... Diesel Geared Drive
DGD.......... Director of Ground Defence [*Military*] [*British*]
DGD.......... Director, Gunnery Division [*British military*]   (DMA)
DGD.......... Dogwood, MO [*Location identifier*] [*FAA*]   (FAAL)
DGD.......... Double Glass Door [*Classified advertising*]   (ADA)
DGD.......... Dynamic Gas Disengagement [*Chemical engineering*]
DGD.......... Dynamic Gravity Detector
DGDB........ Dipropylene Glycol Dibenzoate [*Organic chemistry*]
DGDC .... Deputy Grand Director of Ceremonies [*Freemasonry*]
DGDFA5 ... Development, Growth, and Differentiation [*A publication*]
DGDG....... Distributor-to-Group Display Generator
dGDP........ Deoxyguanosine Diphosphate [*Biochemistry*]
DGDP .... Double Groove, Double Petticoat [*Insulators*]
DGE.......... Davisson-Germer Experiment [*Physics*]
DGE.......... Density Gradient Electrophoresis
DGE.......... Design Engineer
DGE.......... Developments in Geotechnical Engineering [*Elsevier Book
        Series*] [*A publication*]
DGE.......... Director-General of Equipment [*Air Force*] [*British*]

DGE.......... Dual Gauge Expander
DGE.......... Dusty Gas Enveloped [*Astronomy*]
DGE.......... Mudgee [*Australia*] [*Airport symbol*]   (OAG)
DGEBA ..... Diglycidyl Ether of Bisphenol A [*Monomer*] [*Organic
        chemistry*]
D Ge E .... Doctor of Geological Engineering
D Ge Eng ... Doctor of Geological Engineering
D Gefl Ztg ... Deutsche Gefluegel-Zeitung [*A publication*]
DGEME .... Director-General of Electrical and Mechanical Engineering
        [*Australia*]
DGEMER ... Diglycidyl Ether of Methylolresorcinol [*Organic
        chemistry*]   (MCD)
DGEN........ Data Generation
DGEND...... Developments in Geotechnical Engineering [*A publication*]
D Geogr Bl .. Deutsche Geographische Blaetter [*A publication*]
DGEP .... Director-General of Engine Production [*British*]
DGES......... Division of Graduate Education in Science [*National Science
        Foundation*]
DGF .... Danmarks Gamle Folkeviser [*A publication*]
DGF .... Degrees Fahrenheit   (AAG)
DGF .... Dragonfly Distillers [*Vancouver Stock Exchange symbol*]
DGFC .... Accra [*Ghana*] [*ICAO location identifier*]   (ICLI)
DGFC .... Del Gray Fan Club   (EA)
DGFF .... Director-General of Filling Factories [*Formerly, DGOF(F)*]
        [*Ministry of Supply*] [*British*] [*World War II*]
DG F & J ... De Gex, Fisher, and Jones' English Chancery Reports [*A
        publication*]   (DLA)
DG F & JB ... De Gex, Fisher, and Jones' English Bankruptcy Reports [*A
        publication*]   (DLA)
DGFOSTS ... Diesel Generator Fuel Oil Storage and Transfer System
        [*Nuclear energy*]   (NRCH)
DGFV .... Director-General of Fighting Vehicles [*British military*]   (DMA)
DGFVE....... Director-General of Fighting Vehicles and Engineer Equipment
        [*British*]   (RDA)
DGG.......... Department of Geology and Geophysics [*MIT*]   (MCD)
DGG.......... Deutsche Grammophon Gesellschaft [*Phonograph recording
        company*]
DGG.......... Dynamic Gravity Generator
DGGB........ Directors Guild of Great Britain
DGGD....... Director-General of Ground Defence [*Military*] [*British*]
DGGE .... Denaturing Gradient-Gel Electrophoresis [*Analytical
        Biochemistry*]
DGGHP..... Deputy General Grand High Priest [*Freemasonry*]
DGGWL.... Director-General of Guided Weapons and Electronics
        [*British*]   (RDA)
DGH .... Diameter at Ground Height [*Botany*]
DGH .... Director-General of Health [*New Zealand*]
DGH .... District General Hospital
DGhE......... Embassy of Ghana, Washington, DC [*Library symbol*] [*Library
        of Congress*]   (LCLS)
DGHG .... Director-General, Home Guard [*British military*]   (DMA)
DGHP........ Deputy Grand High Priest [*Freemasonry*]
DGHP........ Drive-Gearhead Package
DGI........... Date Growers' Institute   (EA)
DGI........... Decision Graphics, Incorporated
DGI........... Dental Gold Institute   (EA)
DGI........... Direccion General de la Inteligencia [*Cuban intelligence
        service*]
DGI........... Disseminated Gonococcal Infection [*Clinical chemistry*]
DGI........... Duncan Gold Resources [*Vancouver Stock Exchange symbol*]
DGIA .... Director-General of Internal Audit [*British*]   (RDA)
DGIC .... Donegal Group, Incorporated [*Marietta, PA*] [*NASDAQ
        symbol*]   (NQ)
DGII .... Digi International, Inc. [*NASDAQ symbol*]   (NQ)
DGILLO..... Downgrade in Lieu of Layoff
DGIN .... Dagens Industri [*A publication*]
DGIS......... Direct Graphics Interface Specification
DGIS......... Director-General of Intelligence and Security   (MCD)
DGIS.......... DoD [*Department of Defense*] Gateway Information System
        [*Defense Technical Information Center*]   (TSSD)
DGIX .... Dyna Group International, Inc. [*NASDAQ symbol*]   (NQ)
DG & J....... De Gex and Jones' English Chancery Reports [*A
        publication*]   (DLA)
DGJ .... Donovan, Gerard J., Co., Inc., North Attleboro MA [*STAC*]
DG & JB .... De Gex and Jones' English Bankruptcy Reports [*1857-59*] [*A
        publication*]   (DLA)
DG J & S.... De Gex, Jones, and Smith's English Chancery Reports [*A
        publication*]   (DLA)
DG J & SB ... De Gex, Jones, and Smith's English Bankruptcy Reports [*A
        publication*]   (DLA)
DGK.......... Deutsche Gesellschaft fuer Kybernetik [*German Society for
        Cybernetics*] [*Federal Republic of Germany*]   (CSR)
DGKA........ Akim Oda [*Ghana*] [*ICAO location identifier*]   (ICLI)
DGKK........ Koforidua [*Ghana*] [*ICAO location identifier*]   (ICLI)
DGKRA ...... Denki Gakkai Ronbunshi. A [*A publication*]
DGL .... Dangling Construction [*Used in correcting manuscripts, etc.*]
DG/L .... Data General's System Programming Language
DGL .... Diffuse Galactic Light
DGL .... Doped Glass LASER
DGL .... Douglas, AZ [*Location identifier*] [*FAA*]   (FAAL)
DGL .... Douglas [*Arizona*] Municipal [*Airport symbol*]   (OAG)

DGLB .... Bole [*Ghana*] [*ICAO location identifier*] (ICLI)
DGLD .... Diaphragm Gland
DGLDP-A ... Director-General of Logistic Development and Plans - Army [*Australia*]
DGLE .... Tamale [*Ghana*] [*ICAO location identifier*] (ICLI)
DGLN .... Navrongo [*Ghana*] [*ICAO location identifier*] (ICLI)
DGLS .... Diesel Generator Lubrication System [*Nuclear energy*] (NRCH)
DGLS .... Missouri Division of Geology and Land Survey [*State of Missouri Department of Natural Resources*] [*Research center*] (RCD)
DGLW .... Wa [*Ghana*] [*ICAO location identifier*] (ICLI)
DGLY .... Yendi [*Ghana*] [*ICAO location identifier*] (ICLI)
DGM .... Data Gathering Monitoring [*System*]
dgm .... Decigram [*Unit of measure*]
DGM .... Defense Guidance Memorandum
DGM .... Deputy General Manager [*AEC*]
DGM .... Deputy Grand Marshal (ROG)
DGM .... Deputy Grand Master [*Freemasonry*]
DGM .... Destroyer, Guided Missile [*Surface-to-air/Surface-to-surface*] [*NATO*]
DGM .... Developments in Geomathematics [*Elsevier Book Series*] [*A publication*]
DGM .... Digital Group Multiplexer (MCD)
DGM .... Directional Gyro Mode
DGM .... Director-General of Manpower [*Ministry of Labour*] [*British*]
DGM .... Dissolved Gaseous Mercury [*Environmental chemistry*]
DGM .... Draco Gold Mines [*Vancouver Stock Exchange symbol*]
DGM .... Dummy Guided Missile
DGM .... Durable Goods Manufacturer [*DoD*]
DGMA .... Dental Group Management Association (EA)
DGMAT-A ... Director-General of Materiel - Army [*Australia*]
DGMechE(S) ... Director-General of Mechanical Engineering, Supply [*Ministry of Supply*] [*British*]
DG M & G ... De Gex, Macnaghten, and Gordon's English Chancery Reports [*A publication*] (DLA)
DG-MG ..... Diesel Geared - Motor Geared
DG M & GB ... De Gex, Macnaghten, and Gordon's English Bankruptcy Reports [*A publication*] (DLA)
dGMP .... Deoxyguanosine Monophosphate [*Biochemistry*]
DGMP .... Director-General of Munitions Production [*Ministry of Supply*] [*British*] [*World War II*]
DGMR .... Director-General of Military Railways [*British military*] (DMA)
DGMS .... Director-General of Medical Services [*British*]
DGMS .... Division of General Medical Sciences [*National Institutes of Health*]
DGMT .... Director-General of Military Training [*British*]
DGMTAO ... Deutsche Gewaesserkundliche Mitteilungen [*A publication*]
DGMW ...... Director-General of Military Works [*British military*] (DMA)
DGMW ...... Double-Gimbaled Momentum Wheel
DGN .... Dangerous Goods Note [*Shipping*] (DCTA)
DGN .... Data General Corp. [*NYSE symbol*] (SPSG)
DGN .... Design
DGN .... Direccion General de Normas [*National Standards Organization*] [*Mexico*]
DGN .... Dragoon Resources Ltd. [*Vancouver Stock Exchange symbol*]
DGNL .... Diagonal (FAAC)
DGNMT .... Director-General of Naval Manpower and Training [*British*]
DGNP .... Director-General of Naval Production [*Australia*]
DGNPS ...... Director-General of Naval Personnel Services [*British*]
DGNSAQ .. Diagnostica [*A publication*]
DGNSTC... Diagnostic
DGNTDW ... Developmental Genetics [*A publication*]
DGO .... Degaussing Officer [*Navy*]
DGO .... Diploma in Gynecology and Obstetrics [*British*]
DGO .... Directional Gyro Operation
DGO .... Director-General of Organization [*RAF*] [*British*]
DGO .... Domego Resources Ltd. [*Toronto Stock Exchange symbol*]
DGO .... Durango [*Mexico*] [*Airport symbol*] (OAG)
DGOA .... Director-General of [*Quality*] Assurance
DGOF .... Director-General of Ordnance Factories [*Ministry of Supply*] [*British*] [*World War II*]
DGOF(F)... Director-General of Ordnance Factories (Filling) [*Later, DGFF*] [*Ministry of Supply*] [*British*] [*World War II*]
DGOH .... Directorate General of Highways [*Vietnam*]
DGOP-A .... Director-General of Operations and Plans - Army [*Australia*]
DGOR .... Deutsche Gesellschaft fuer Operations Research [*German Society for Operational Research*] [*Federal Republic of Germany*] (CSR)
DGOS .... Director-General, Ordnance Systems [*Canada*]
DGP .... Dabrowa Gornicza [*Poland*] [*Seismograph station code, US Geological Survey*] (SEIS)
DGP .... Data Generating Program
DGP .... Deoxyglucose-Phosphate [*Biochemistry*]
DGP .... Design Guidance Package [*Military*] (CAAL)
DGP .... Destruction of Government Property
DGP .... Director-General of Personnel [*British*]
DGP .... Director-General of Production [*British Air Ministry*]
DGP .... Drive-Gearhead Package
DGP .... Dry Gas Pump

DGPA .... Deputy General Purchasing Agent [*Military*]
DGPL .... Downers Grove Public Library [*Illinois*]
DGPO .... United States Government Printing Office, Washington, DC [*Library symbol*] [*Library of Congress*] (LCLS)
DGPO-A .... Director-General of Personnel Operations - Army [*Australia*]
DGPO-S .... United States Government Printing Office, Serials Library, Alexandria, VA [*Library symbol*] [*Library of Congress*] (LCLS)
DGPS .... Differential Global Positioning System
DGPS(N)... Director-General, Personal Services (Naval) [*British military*] (DMA)
DGQA .... Director-General of Quality Assurance [*British*]
DGR .... Danger
DGR .... Degrease
DGR .... Director of Graves Registration [*British*]
DGR .... Directorate of Geophysics Research [*Air Research and Development Command*] (AAG)
DGR .... Division of Geothermal Research [*Energy Research and Development Administration*]
DGR .... Division of Government Research [*University of New Mexico*] [*Research center*] (RCD)
DGR .... Door Gunner [*Military*]
DGRA .... Diamond and Gemstone Remarketing Association (EA)
DGRAFMS ... Director-General of Royal Air Force Medical Services [*British*]
DGRBB .... Denki Gakkai Ronbunshi. B [*A publication*]
DGRCA .... Denki Gakkai Ronbunshi. C [*A publication*]
DGRD .... Director-General, Research and Development Policy [*Military*] [*Canada*]
DGRDS .... Director-General, Research and Development Services [*Military*] [*Canada*]
DGRHA ..... Doboku Gakkai Ronbun Hokokushu [*A publication*]
DGRM .... Director-General of Raw Materials [*Ministry of Supply*] [*British*]
DGRO .... Degaussing Range Officer [*Navy*]
DGRTP....... Death Gratuity Payment [*Army*] (AABC)
DGS .... Data Gathering System (MCD)
DGS .... Data Ground Station [*NASA*] (KSC)
DGS .... Degaussing System
DGS .... Density Gradient Sedimentation [*Analytical biochemistry*]
DGS .... Deputy General Secretary (DCTA)
DGS .... Destroyer, Guided Missile (Surface-to-Surface) [*NATO*]
DGS .... Digital Ground System
DGS .... Diploma in Graduate Studies [*British*]
DGS .... Director of Ground Safety [*Air Force*]
DGS .... Display Generation System
DGS .... Distributed Graphics System (MCD)
DGS .... Dominion Government Survey [*Canada*]
DGS .... Don't Give a Spit [*Slang*] [*Bowdlerized version*]
DGS .... Double Green Silk Covered [*Wire insulation*]
DGS .... Drill Guidance System
DGS .... University of Denver, Graduate School of Librarianship, Denver, CO [*OCLC symbol*] (OCLC)
DGSAA ..... Director-General of Small Arms Ammunition Production [*Ministry of Supply*] [*British*] [*World War II*]
DGSB........ Sefwi-Bekwai [*Ghana*] [*ICAO location identifier*] (ICLI)
DGSC .... Defense General Supply Center
DGSD .... Double Glass Sliding Doors [*Classified advertising*] (ADA)
DGSE........ Department of Geological Survey and Mineral Exploration [*Burma*] (DS)
DGSE........ Direction Generale de la Securite Exterieure [*Formerly, SDECE*] [*French intelligence agency*]
DGSFR ...... Degasifier
DGShips .... Director-General, Ships [*Navy*] [*British*]
DGSI.......... Digital Solutions, Inc. [*NASDAQ symbol*] (NQ)
DGSI.......... Kumasi [*Ghana*] [*ICAO location identifier*] (ICLI)
DGSJ .... Druggist's Guild of St. James [*Defunct*] (EA)
DGSM .... Director-General of Servicing and Maintenance [*RAF*] [*British*]
DGSN .... Sunyani [*Ghana*] [*ICAO location identifier*] (ICLI)
DGSP .... Director-General of Statistics and Planning [*Ministry of Supply*] [*British*]
DGSR .... Director-General, Ship Refitting [*Ministry of Defence*] [*British*]
DGSRD ..... Director-General of Scientific Research and Development [*Ministry of Supply*] [*British*]
DGSS .... Diesel Generator Starting System [*Nuclear energy*] (NRCH)
DGST .... Director-General, Supply and Transport [*British military*] (DMA)
DG/STAGE ... Data General's Standard Applications and Graphics Environment [*Engineering software*]
DGStJ .... Dame of Grace, Order of St. John of Jerusalem [*Later, D St J*] [*British*]
DGST(N)... Director-General of Supplies and Transport (Naval) [*British*]
DGSUP-A ... Director-General of Supply - Army [*Australia*]
DGSUP-N ... Director-General of Supply - Navy [*Australia*]
DGSW .... Wenchi [*Ghana*] [*ICAO location identifier*] (ICLI)
DGT .... Digit
DGT .... Digital Equipment Corp. [*Maynard, MA*] [*FAA designator*] (FAAC)
DGT .... Digitech Ltd. [*Toronto Stock Exchange symbol*]
DGT .... Direction Generale des Telecommunications [*Telecommunications administration*] [*France*] (TSSD)

DGT.......... Direction Generale des Telecommunications [*Gouvernement du Quebec*] [*Canada*]   (TSSD)
DGT.......... Director-General of Training [*British military*]   (DMA)
DGT.......... Director-General of Transportation [*British military*]   (DMA)
DGT.......... Directorate General of Telecommunications [*Taipei, Taiwan*]   (TSSD)
DGT.......... Dumaguete [*Philippines*] [*Airport symbol*]   (OAG)
DGT.......... Large German Telescope [*Acronym is based on German phrase*]
DGTA........ Director-General of the Territorial Army [*British*]
Dgt Bypass ... Digital Bypass Report [*A publication*]
DGTC........ Digitech, Inc. [*NASDAQ symbol*]   (NQ)
DGTF........ Director-General of the Territorial Force [*British military*]   (DMA)
DGTK....... Takoradi [*Ghana*] [*ICAO location identifier*]   (ICLI)
DGTL....... Digital   (MSA)
DG Tn....... Director-General of Transportation Services [*British*]
DGTO....... Degaussing Technical Officer [*Navy*]
DGTP....... Deoxyguanosine Triphosphate [*Biochemistry*]
DGTPA...... Diesel and Gas Turbine Progress [*Later, Diesel Progress North American*] [*A publication*]
DGTX....... Axim [*Ghana*] [*ICAO location identifier*]   (ICLI)
DGTZR...... Digitizer   (MSA)
DGU .... Boston, MA [*Location identifier*] [*FAA*]   (FAAL)
DGU .... Directional Gyro Unit
DGU .... Doctor of Griffith University [*Australia*]
DGU .... Downgrade to Unclassified [*Military*]   (MCD)
DGU .... Georgetown University, Washington, DC [*Library symbol*] [*Library of Congress*] [*OCLC symbol*]   (LCLS)
DGUAB8... Geological Survey of Denmark. Yearbook [*A publication*]
DGUADA ... Geological Survey of Denmark. Serie A [*A publication*]
D Guam...... United States District Court for the District of Guam   (DLA)
DGUBAA .. Geological Survey of Denmark. II Series [*A publication*]
DGUBDD ... Geological Survey of Denmark. Serie B [*A publication*]
DGUCAD ... Geological Survey of Denmark. III Series [*A publication*]
DGU (Geol Surv Den) Ser C ... DGU (Geological Survey of Denmark) Series C [*A publication*]
DGU-KIE .. Georgetown University, Kennedy Institute, Center for Bioethics, Washington, DC [*Library symbol*] [*Library of Congress*]   (LCLS)
DGU-L....... Georgetown University, Law Library, Washington, DC [*Library symbol*] [*Library of Congress*]   (LCLS)
DGU-M ..... Georgetown University, Medical, Dental, and Nursing Library, Washington, DC [*Library symbol*] [*Library of Congress*]   (LCLS)
DGU-Pop... Georgetown University, Kennedy Institute, Center for Population Research, Washington, DC [*Library symbol*] [*Library of Congress*]   (LCLS)
DGURBP... Geological Survey of Denmark. Report [*A publication*]
DGU-S....... Georgetown University, Science Library, Washington, DC [*Library symbol*] [*Library of Congress*]   (LCLS)
DGU-W ..... Georgetown University, Woodstock Theological Center, Washington, DC [*Library symbol*] [*Library of Congress*]   (LCLS)
DGV.......... Degaussing Vessel [*British military*]   (DMA)
DGV.......... Dextrose-Gelatin-Veronal [*Solution*] [*Microbiology*]
DGV.......... Dienst Grondwaterverkenning [*TNO Institute of Applied Geoscience*] [*Information service or system*]   (IID)
DGVA........ Delta-Guanidinovaleric Acid [*Biochemistry*]
DGVC....... Georgetown Visitation Preparatory School, Washington, DC [*Library symbol*] [*Library of Congress*]   (LCLS)
DGV/ZE.... Zeitschrift fuer Ethnologie. Deutsche Gesellschaft fuer Voelkerkunde [*A publication*]
DGW......... Director-General of Weapons [*British military*]   (DMA)
DGW......... Director-General of Works [*RAF*] [*British*]
DGW......... Double Gypsy Winch
DGW......... Douglas, WY [*Location identifier*] [*FAA*]   (FAAL)
DGW......... George Washington University, Washington, DC [*Library symbol*] [*Library of Congress*] [*OCLC symbol*]   (LCLS)
DGW(A).... Director-General of Weapons (Army) [*British military*]   (RDA)
DGW-C...... George Washington University, Carnegie Endowment for International Peace Collection, Washington, DC [*Library symbol*] [*Library of Congress*]   (LCLS)
DGWE....... Director General of Water Engineering   (DCTA)
DGWIP..... Director-General of Weapons and Instruments Production [*Military*] [*British*]
DGW-L...... George Washington University, Law Library, Washington, DC [*Library symbol*] [*Library of Congress*]   (LCLS)
DGW-M .... George Washington University, Medical Library, Washington, DC [*Library symbol*] [*Library of Congress*]   (LCLS)
DGW(N).... Director-General of Weapons Department (Naval) [*British*]
DGWO ...... Degaussing Wiping Officer [*Navy*]
DGW-PIP ... George Washington University, Medical Center, Population Information Program, Washington, DC [*Library symbol*] [*Library of Congress*]   (LCLS)
DGWS .... Division for Girls' and Women's Sports [*of American Association for Health, Physical Education, and Recreation; also used in a book title*] [*Later, NAGUS*]
DGX.......... Director-General of Explosives Production [*Ministry of Supply*] [*British*] [*World War II*]
DGX.......... Dungannon Explorations Ltd. [*Vancouver Stock Exchange symbol*]

DGZ.......... Designated Ground Zero   (MSA)
DGZ.......... Desired Ground Zero [*Bombing*]
DGZ.......... Deutsche Girozentrale - Deutsche Kommunalbank [*West German bank*]
DGZAA .... Denki Gakkai Zasshi [*A publication*]
DH .... Das Heisst [*That Is*] [*German*]
D & H .... Daughter and Heiress [*Genealogy*]
DH .... Day Hospital
DH .... Dayton-Hudson Corp. [*NYSE symbol*]   (SPSG)
DH .... De Havilland Aircraft of Canada Ltd. [*ICAO aircraft manufacturer identifier*]   (ICAO)
DH .... De Havilland Aircraft Co.
DH .... Dead Heat
DH .... Deadhead [*Freight*]
DH .... Decay Heat [*Nuclear energy*]   (NRCH)
DH .... Deccan Horse [*British military*]   (DMA)
D-H .... Decimal to Hexadecimal   (IEEE)
DH .... Decision Height [*Aviation*]
DH .... Dehydrogenase [*An enzyme*]
DH .... Delaware History [*A publication*]
D & H .... Delaware & Hudson Railway Co. [*Nickname: Delay and Hesitate*]
DH .... Delayed Hypersensitivity [*Immunology*]
DH .... Deliquescence Humidity
DH .... Demeure Historique [*An association*]   (EAIO)
DH .... Dental Hygienist [*British military*]   (DMA)
DH .... Dermatitis Herpetiformis [*Medicine*]
DH .... Design Handbook
DH .... Designated Hitter [*Formerly, DPH*] [*Also, DESI*] [*Baseball*]
DH .... Destination Hospital [*Aeromedical evacuation*]
D/H .... Deuterium/Hydrogen Ratio
DH .... Deutsches Handwerksblatt [*A publication*]
DH .... Device Handler
DH .... Diapause Hormone [*In insects*] [*Endocrinology*]
DH .... Difference in Height
DH .... Dignitatis Humanae [*Declaration on Religious Freedom*] [*Vatican II document*]
D/H .... Direct Hit
DH .... Directly Heated   (DEN)
DH .... Director of Hygiene [*British military*]   (DMA)
DH .... Dirham [*Monetary unit*] [*Morocco*]
DH .... Disc Harrowing [*Agriculture*]
DH .... Dislocated Homemaker [*Job Training and Partnership Act*]   (OICC)
DH .... Disorderly House
DH .... Display Hold
DH .... Disseminated Histoplasmosis [*Medicine*]
DH .... Diuretic Hormone [*Endocrinology*]
DH .... Doctor of Humanics
DH .... Doctor of Humanities
DH .... Documents d'Histoire [*A publication*]
DH .... Dominant Hand [*Psychometrics*]
DH .... Doors of Hope [*An association*]   (EA)
DH .... Double Helix [*Cytology, genetics*]
DH .... Double Heterostructure [*Physics*]
DH .... Double-Hung [*Construction*]
DH .... Double Hydrant [*On fire insurance maps*]
DH .... Dow Chemical Co. [*Research code symbol*]
DH .... Downhill [*Bicycle handlebars*]
D & H .... Dressed and Headed [*Lumber*]
DH .... Transair France [*France*] [*ICAO designator*]   (FAAC)
DHA .... Dairy Husbandry Adviser [*Ministry of Agriculture, Fisheries, and Food*] [*British*]
DHA .... Darling Harbour Authority [*Australia*]
DHA .... De Havilland Aircraft Proprietary Limited [*Australia*]
DHA .... Dehydroacetic Acid [*Pharmacology*]
DHA .... Dehydroascorbic Acid [*Also, DAA*] [*Oxidized form of Vitamin C*] [*Biochemistry*]
DHA .... Dehydroepiandrosterone [*Also, DEA, DHEA, DHIA*] [*Endocrinology*]
DHA .... Denver Handwriting Analysis [*Educational test*]
DHA .... Dependent Housing Area [*Army*]   (AABC)
DHA .... Design Hazard Analysis   (MCD)
DHA .... Dhahran [*Saudi Arabia*] [*Airport symbol*]   (OAG)
DHA .... Dialogos Hispanicos de Amsterdam [*A publication*]
DHA .... Dialogues d'Histoire Ancienne [*A publication*]
DHA .... Dihydroalprenolol [*Pharmacochemistry*]
DHA .... Dihydroanthracene [*Organic chemistry*]
DHA .... Dihydroxyacetone [*Organic chemistry*]
DHA .... District Health Authority [*British*]
DHA .... District Heating Association [*British*]
DHA .... Docosahexaenoic Acid
DHA .... Doctor of Hospital Administration
DHA .... Double Heave Amplitude
DHA .... Dutch Harbor [*Alaska*] [*Seismograph station code, US Geological Survey*] [*Closed*]   (SEIS)
DHAA .... Dehydroabietic Acid [*Organic chemistry*]
DHAD .... Dihydroxyanthracenedione [*Quinazarin*] [*Organic chemistry*]
DH Adm .... Doctor of Hospital Administration
DHAEMAE ... Disposable Hypodermic and Allied Equipment Manufacturers Association of Europe   (EAIO)

Dhaka Univ Stud Part B ... Dhaka University Studies. Part B [*A publication*]
DHAN .... Dihaloacetonitrile [*Organic chemistry*]
DHAP .... Dihydroxyacetone Phosphate [*Also, DAP*] [*Organic chemistry*]
DHAS .... Deborah Harry Appreciation Society   (EA)
DHAS .... Dehydroepiandrosterone Sulfate [*Biochemistry*]
D Hawaii .... United States District Court, District of Hawaii   (DLA)
DHB .... Daniel Hudson Burnham [*Architect and urban planner, 1846-1912*]
DHB .... Dihydroxybenzoic Acid [*Organic chemistry*]
DHBA .... Dihydroxybenzylamine [*Organic chemistry*]
DHBAA ..... Dock and Harbour Authority [*A publication*]
DHBG .... (Dihydroxybutyl)guanine [*Biochemistry*]
DHBV .... Duck Hepatic B Virus
DHC .... Air-Cushion Vehicle built by DeHavilland Aircraft Company of Canada [*Canada*] [*Usually used in combination with numerals*]
DHC .... Danielson Holding Corp. [*AMEX symbol*]   (SPSG)
DHC .... Data Handling Center   (KSC)
DHC .... Defense Homes Corporation [*World War II*]
DHC .... Dehydrocholesterol [*Organic chemistry*]
DHC .... Dehydrocholic Acid [*Organic chemistry*]
DHC .... Dihydrochalcone [*Sweetening agent*]
DHC .... Dilute Homogeneous Charge
DHC .... Documents Relatifs a l'Histoire des Croisades [*A publication*]
DHC .... Donohue, Inc. [*Toronto Stock Exchange symbol*]
DHCA .... Dihydroxycholestanoic Acid [*Biochemistry*]
DHCA .... Diversified Health Companies, Inc. [*NASDAQ symbol*]   (NQ)
DHCA .... Kaya [*Burkina Faso*] [*ICAO location identifier*]   (ICLI)
DHCB .... Barsalogho [*Burkina Faso*] [*ICAO location identifier*]   (ICLI)
DHCC .... Decay Heat Closed Cooling [*Nuclear energy*]   (IEEE)
DHCC .... Dihydroxycholecalciferol [*Vitamin D₃*]
DHCC .... Ouahigouya [*Burkina Faso*] [*ICAO location identifier*]   (ICLI)
DHCD .... Department of Housing and Community Development   (OICC)
DHCD .... Didyr [*Burkina Faso*] [*ICAO location identifier*]   (ICLI)
DHCE .... Batie [*Burkina Faso*] [*ICAO location identifier*]   (ICLI)
DHCF .... Holy Cross Foreign Mission Seminary, Washington, DC [*Library symbol*] [*Library of Congress*]   (LCLS)
DHCG .... Kongoussi [*Burkina Faso*] [*ICAO location identifier*]   (ICLI)
DHCHST .. Downey Hand Center Hand Sensitivity Test
DHCI .... Titao [*Burkina Faso*] [*ICAO location identifier*]   (ICLI)
DHCJ .... Djibo [*Burkina Faso*] [*ICAO location identifier*]   (ICLI)
DHCK .... Koudougou [*Burkina Faso*] [*ICAO location identifier*]   (ICLI)
DHCL .... Leo [*Burkina Faso*] [*ICAO location identifier*]   (ICLI)
DHCM ...... Manga [*Burkina Faso*] [*ICAO location identifier*]   (ICLI)
DHCO .... Boromo [*Burkina Faso*] [*ICAO location identifier*]   (ICLI)
DHCP .... Decentralized Hospital Computer Program [*Veterans Administration*]
DHCP .... Double Hexagonal Close-Packed [*Metallography*]
DHCP .... Po [*Burkina Faso*] [*ICAO location identifier*]   (ICLI)
DHCR .... Poura [*Burkina Faso*] [*ICAO location identifier*]   (ICLI)
DHCS .... Debbie Harry Collector's Society   (EA)
DHCS .... Department of Health and Community Services [*Northern Territory, Australia*]
DHCS .... Seguenega [*Burkina Faso*] [*ICAO location identifier*]   (ICLI)
DHCT .... Tenado [*Burkina Faso*] [*ICAO location identifier*]   (ICLI)
DHCU .... Data Handling and Control Unit
DHCU .... Gourcy [*Burkina Faso*] [*ICAO location identifier*]   (ICLI)
DHCY .... Division of Handicapped Children and Youth [*HEW*]
DHCY .... Yako [*Burkina Faso*] [*ICAO location identifier*]   (ICLI)
DHD .... Dihydrodigoxin [*Biochemistry*]
DHD .... Double Heat-Sink Diode   (CET)
DHD .... Drop-Hammer Die   (MSA)
DHD .... Durham Downs [*Australia*] [*Airport symbol*]   (OAG)
DHDAA ... Dihexadecyldimethylammonium Acetate [*Organic chemistry*]
DHDD .... Digital High-Definition Display   (KSC)
DHDI .... Drop-Hammer Die
DHDMI ..... Dihydroxy(dimethyl)imidazolidinone [*Organic chemistry*]
DH-DOC ... Dihydrodeoxycorticosterone [*Endocrinology*]
DHDS .... Data Handling and Display Subsystem
DHDSC ..... Dayton Hudson Department Store Company [*Division of Dayton-Hudson Corp.*]
DHE .... Data Handling Equipment
DHE .... Debye-Hueckel Equation [*Physics*]
DHE .... Department of Home Economics [*of NEA*] [*Later, HEEA*]   (EA)
DHE .... Dielectric Heating Equipment
DHE .... Dihematoporphyrin Ether [*Pharmacology*]
DHE .... Dihydroergocornine [*Endocrinology*]
DHE .... Dihydroergotamine [*Pharmacology*]
DHE .... Diploma in Horticulture, Royal Botanic Garden, Edinburgh [*British*]   (DBQ)
DHE .... Doctor of Church History
DHEA .... Boulsa [*Burkina Faso*] [*ICAO location identifier*]   (ICLI)
DHEA .... Dehydroepiandrosterone [*Also, DEA, DHA, DHIA*] [*Endocrinology*]
DHEAS ..... Dehydroepiandrosterone Sulfate [*Biochemistry*]
DHEB .... Bogande [*Burkina Faso*] [*ICAO location identifier*]   (ICLI)
DHEBA ..... (Dihydroxyethylene)bisacrylamide [*Organic chemistry*]
DHEC .... Dihydroergocryptine [*Organic chemistry*]
DH Ec .... Doctor of Home Economics
DH Ec .... Doctor of Household Economy

DHEC .... Komin-Yanga [*Burkina Faso*] [*ICAO location identifier*]   (ICLI)
DHED .... Diapaga [*Burkina Faso*] [*ICAO location identifier*]   (ICLI)
DHEE .... Dori [*Burkina Faso*] [*ICAO location identifier*]   (ICLI)
DHEF .... Fada N'Gourma [*Burkina Faso*] [*ICAO location identifier*]   (ICLI)
DHEG .... Di(hydroxyethyl)glycine [*Organic chemistry*]
DHEG .... Gorom-Gorom [*Burkina Faso*] [*ICAO location identifier*]   (ICLI)
DHEK .... Koupela [*Burkina Faso*] [*ICAO location identifier*]   (ICLI)
DHEL .... Kantchari [*Burkina Faso*] [*ICAO location identifier*]   (ICLI)
DHEM .... Tambao [*Burkina Faso*] [*ICAO location identifier*]   (ICLI)
DHEN .... Garango [*Burkina Faso*] [*ICAO location identifier*]   (ICLI)
DHEO .... Zorgo [*Burkina Faso*] [*ICAO location identifier*]   (ICLI)
DHEP .... Detailed Human Engineering Plan
DHEP .... Pama [*Burkina Faso*] [*ICAO location identifier*]   (ICLI)
DHER .... Arli [*Burkina Faso*] [*ICAO location identifier*]   (ICLI)
DHES .... Division of Health Examination Statistics [*HEW*]
DHES .... Sebba [*Burkina Faso*] [*ICAO location identifier*]   (ICLI)
DHESN ..... Dihydroergosine [*Biochemistry*]
DHET .... Tenkodogo [*Burkina Faso*] [*ICAO location identifier*]   (ICLI)
DHEW .... Department of Health, Education, and Welfare [*Later, DHHS*]
DHEW .... United States Department of Health, Education, and Welfare, Washington, DC [*Library symbol*] [*Library of Congress*]   (LCLS)
DHEY .... Ouargaye [*Burkina Faso*] [*ICAO location identifier*]   (ICLI)
DHEZ .... Zabre [*Burkina Faso*] [*ICAO location identifier*]   (ICLI)
DHF .... Dag Hammarskjold Foundation   (EAIO)
DHF .... Demand History File [*DoD*]
DHF .... Dengue Hemorrhagic Fever [*Medicine*]
DHF .... Dihydrofolate [*Biochemistry*]
DHF .... Dihydroxyflavone [*Organic chemistry*]
DHF .... Document History File   (MCD)
DHF .... Double Hollow Fork [*Bicycle part or a fool*] [*Slang*] [*British*]   (DSUE)
DHFA .... Double-Conductor, Heat and Flame-Resistant, Armored [*Cable*]
DHFC .... David Hasselhoff Fan Club   (EA)
DHFC .... David Heavener Fan Club   (EA)
DHFC .... David Hedison Fan Club   (EA)
DHFC .... Deidre Hall Fan Club   (EA)
DHFI .... Double Helix Films, Inc. [*NASDAQ symbol*]   (NQ)
DHFR .... Dihydrofolate Reductase [*An enzyme*]
DHFS .... Dengue Hemorrhagic Fever Syndrome [*Medicine*]
DHG .... Deutsche Handelsgesellschaft [*German Trading Company*]
DHG .... Di(hydroxyethyl)glycinate [*Organic chemistry*]
DHg .... Doctor of Hygiene
DHGE .... Dictionnaire d'Histoire et de Geographie Ecclesiastique [*A publication*]   (BJA)
DHH .... Deaf and Hard of Hearing
DHH .... Doctor of Honorary Humanities
DHHH ...... Ouagadougou (Airport) [*Burkina Faso*] [*ICAO location identifier*]   (ICLI)
DHHS .... Department of Health and Human Services
DHHS .... United States Department of Health and Human Services, Washington, DC [*Library symbol*] [*Library of Congress*]   (LCLS)
DHHV .... Ouagadougou [*Burkina Faso*] [*ICAO location identifier*]   (ICLI)
DHI .... Dental Health International   (EA)
DHI .... Department Head Instruction   (NRCH)
DHI .... Dhangarhi [*Nepal*] [*Airport symbol*]   (OAG)
DHI .... Dictionary of the History of Ideas [*A publication*]
DHI .... Dihydroxyindol
DHI .... Directional Horizon Indicator
DHI .... Door and Hardware Institute   (EA)
DHIA .... Dairy Herd Improvement Association [*Later, AIPL*]   (EA)
DHIA .... Dehydroisoandrosterone [*Also, DEA, DHA, DHEA*] [*Endocrinology*]
DHIC .... Dihydroisocodeine [*Pharmacology*]
DHIFC .... Doyle Holly International Fan Club   (EA)
DHIN .... Designhouse International, Inc. [*NASDAQ symbol*]   (NQ)
DHIR .... Dairy Herd Improvement Registry
DHIRS .... District Headquarters Induction and Recruiting Station [*Marine Corps*]
DHISF .... Document Handling and Information Services Facility [*General Accounting Office*]   (IID)
DHIY .... Devonshire Hussar Imperial Yeomanry [*Military*] [*British*]   (ROG)
DHK .... Dihydrokaempferol [*Botany*]
DHL .... David Herbert Lawrence [*British novelist, 1885-1930*]
DHL .... Davies Herbarium, University of Louisville [*Kentucky*]
DHL .... DHL Island Airways [*Honolulu, HI*] [*FAA designator*]   (FAAC)
DHL .... Diffuse Histiocytic Lymphoma [*Medicine*]
DHL .... Digital Equipment Corp., Hudson, Westboro, MA [*OCLC symbol*]   (OCLC)
DHL .... Doctor of Hebrew Letters
DHL .... Doctor of Hebrew Literature
DHL .... Doctor of Humane Letters
DHL .... House of Lords Appeals, in Dunlop's Court of Session Cases, from Vol. 13 [*1851-62*] [*A publication*]   (DLA)

D H Lawren ...	D. H. Lawrence Review [*A publication*]
D H Lawrence R ...	D. H. Lawrence Review [*A publication*]
DHLB	Dihydrolevobunolol [*Biochemistry*]
DH Lit	Doctor of Hebrew Literature
DH Litt	Doctor of Hebrew Letters [*or Literature*]
DHLLP	Direct High-Level Language Processor
DHLNL	Dihydroxylysinonorleucine [*Biochemistry*]
DHLR	D. H. Lawrence Review [*A publication*]
DHM	Daughters of the Heart of Mary [*Roman Catholic religious order*]
DHM	Debye-Huckel-Manning [*Theory*] [*Physical chemistry*]
DHM	Developments in Halophilic Microorganisms [*Elsevier Book Series*] [*A publication*]
DHM	Dexterous Hand Master [*Robotics*]
DHM	Dihydromorphine [*Analgesic compound*] [*Organic chemistry*]
DHM	Dihydromuscimol [*Biochemistry*]
DHM	Diocesan Home Missionary
DHM	Dry Honing Machine
DHM	Mokuleia, Oahu, HI [*Location identifier*] [*FAA*] (FAAL)
DHMA	Dihydroxymandelic Acid [*Also, DMA, DOMA*] [*Organic chemistry*]
DHMA	Drapery Hardware Manufacturers Association [*Defunct*] (EA)
DHMAA	Draft Horse and Mule Association of America (EA)
DHMPA	Dihydromycoplanecin A [*Biochemistry*]
DHMPA	Dihydroxymethoxyphenylalanine [*Biochemistry*]
DHMSA	Diploma in the History of Medicine, Society of Apothecaries of London [*British*] (DBQ)
DHMY	Dehumidify (MSA)
DHN	Displaced Homemakers Network (EA)
DHN	Dothan [*Alabama*] [*Airport symbol*] (OAG)
DHN	Dynamic Hardness Number
DHO	Dihydroouabain [*Biochemistry*]
DHO	Director of Home Operations [*Air Ministry*] [*British*] [*World War II*]
DHO	District Historical Office [*or Officer*] [*Navy*]
DHOA	Dano [*Burkina Faso*] [*ICAO location identifier*] (ICLI)
DHOB	Banfora [*Burkina Faso*] [*ICAO location identifier*] (ICLI)
DHOD	Dedougou [*Burkina Faso*] [*ICAO location identifier*] (ICLI)
DHOF	Safane [*Burkina Faso*] [*ICAO location identifier*] (ICLI)
DHOG	Gaoua [*Burkina Faso*] [*ICAO location identifier*] (ICLI)
DH/OH	Down Hours to Operating Hours Ratio [*Quality control*]
DHOH	Hounde [*Burkina Faso*] [*ICAO location identifier*] (ICLI)
DHOL	Loumana [*Burkina Faso*] [*ICAO location identifier*] (ICLI)
DHON	Nouna [*Burkina Faso*] [*ICAO location identifier*] (ICLI)
DHOO	Bobo-Dioulasso [*Burkina Faso*] [*ICAO location identifier*] (ICLI)
D Hor	Doctor of Horticulture
DHOR	Orodara [*Burkina Faso*] [*ICAO location identifier*] (ICLI)
DHOS	Sideradougou [*Burkina Faso*] [*ICAO location identifier*] (ICLI)
D Ho Sc	Doctor of Household Science
DHOT	Tougan [*Burkina Faso*] [*ICAO location identifier*] (ICLI)
DHOU	Diebougou [*Burkina Faso*] [*ICAO location identifier*] (ICLI)
DHOY	Aribinda [*Burkina Faso*] [*ICAO location identifier*] (ICLI)
DHP	Dehydrogenative Polymerization [*Biology*]
DHP	Dehydroproline [*Biochemistry*]
DHP	Demokratik Halk Partisi [*Democratic People's Party*] [*Turkish Cyprus*] [*Political party*] (PPE)
DHP	Deoxidized High-Residual Phosphorus [*Copper*]
DHP	Department Head Procedures (NRCH)
DHP	Deutsche Hannover Partei [*German Hanover Party*] (PPE)
DHP	Developed Horsepower
DHP	Dihexadecyl Phosphate [*Organic chemistry*]
DHP	Dihydroheptaprenol [*Biochemistry*]
DHP	Dihydropyridine [*Organic chemistry*]
DHP	Dihydroxyphenol [*Organic chemistry*]
DHP	Diploma in Hypnosis and Psychotherapy [*British*] (DBQ)
DHP	Document Handler Processor
DHPA	Degree of Honor Protective Association [*St. Paul, MN*] (EA)
DHPA	Dihydroxypropyladenine [*Biochemistry*]
DHPC	Dorsal Hippocampus [*Neuroanatomy*]
DHPE	Data Hardware Project Engineer [*NASA*]
DHPE	Dihydroxyphenylethanol [*Organic chemistry*]
DHPG	Dihydroxyphenethyleneglycol [*Organic chemistry*]
DHPG	Dihydroxyphenylglycol [*Also, DOPEG*] [*Organic chemistry*]
DHPG	(Dihydroxypropoxymethyl)guanine [*Biochemistry*]
DHPGTP	(Dihydroxypropoxymethyl)guanine Triphosphate [*Antiviral compound*]
DHPMA	Dihydroxypropyl Methacrylate [*Organic chemistry*]
DHPR	Dihydropteridine Reductase [*An enzyme*]
DHPR	Dihydropyridine Receptor [*Biochemistry*]
DHPTA	Diaminohydroxypropanetetraacetic Acid [*Also, DTA, DPTA*] [*Organic chemistry*]
dHpuA	Deoxyheptulosonic Acid [*Biochemistry*]
DHQ	Dihydroquercetin [*Botany*]
DHQ	Dihydroquinidine [*Organic chemistry*]
DHQ	District Headquarters
DHQ	Division Headquarters [*Military*]
DHQ	Mean Diurnal High-Water Inequality
DHQHS ...	Dihydroqinghaosu [*Organic chemistry*]
DHR	Danaher Corp. [*NYSE symbol*] (SPSG)
DHR	Decay Heat Removal [*Nuclear energy*] (NRCH)
DHR	Delayed Hypersensitivity Reaction [*Medicine*]
DHR	Delivery History Report (AFIT)
DHR	Double High-Resolution File [*Data processing*]
DHR	Duquesne Hispanic Review [*A publication*]
DHR	Holy Redeemer College, Washington, DC [*Library symbol*] [*Library of Congress*] (LCLS)
DHRA	Delta Houseboat Rental Association (EA)
DHRC	Douglas Hospital Research Centre [*McGill University, Douglas Hospital*] [*Canada*] [*Research center*] (RCD)
DHRS	Decay Heat Removal Service [*or System*] [*Nuclear energy*] (NRCH)
DHRS	Direct Heat Removal Service [*or System*] [*Nuclear energy*] (IEEE)
DHS	Dance History Scholars (EA)
DHS	Data Handling System
DHS	Daughters of the Holy Spirit [*Roman Catholic religious order*]
DHS	Decontamination Hot Shop [*Nuclear energy*] (NRCH)
DHS	Desert Hot Springs [*California*] [*Seismograph station code, US Geological Survey*] [*Closed*] (SEIS)
DHS	Despun Heat Shield
DHS	Destroyer Helicopter System (MCD)
DHS	Deutsches Handwerksblatt [*A publication*]
DHS	Dihydrostreptomycin [*Also, DHSM, DST*] [*Antimicrobial agent*]
DHS	Dinshah Health Society (EA)
DHS	Diploma in Horticultural Science (ADA)
DHS	Director of Health Services [*Army*] (AABC)
DHS	Director Historical Section [*World War I*] [*Canada*]
DHS	Discrete Horizon Sensor (MCD)
DHS	Dix-Huitieme Siecle [*A publication*]
DHS	Doctor of Health Science
DHS	Doctor of Hebrew Studies (BJA)
DHS	Doctor of Humanitarian Service
DHS	Dry Heat Sterilization
DHS	Dual-Hardness Steel
DHS	Duration of Hospital Stay
D/5HS	Dextrose (5%) in Hartman's Solution [*Medicine*]
DHSM	Dihydrostreptomycin [*Also, DHS, DST*] [*Antimicrobial agent*]
DHSS	Data Handling Subsystem (NATG)
DHSS	Department of Health and Social Security [*British*]
DHSS	Dihydrostreptomycin Sulfate [*Antimicrobial agent*]
DHSTEV ...	Data Handling in Science and Technology [*A publication*]
DHStL	Deutsch-Hebraeische Sterbeliste [*Berlin*] [*A publication*]
DHT	Dalhart, TX [*Location identifier*] [*FAA*] (FAAL)
DHT	Dihydrotachysterol [*Same as ATL-IO*] [*Biochemistry*]
DHT	Dihydrotestosterone [*Also, D*] [*Endocrinology*]
DHT	Dihydroxytryptamine [*Biochemistry*]
DHT	Discrete Hartley Transform (BYTE)
DHT	Discrete Hilbert Transform (IEEE)
DHT	Dvar Hashavua (Tel Aviv) [*A publication*]
DHTB	Dihydroteleocidin B [*Biochemistry*]
DHTK	DH Technology, Inc. [*San Diego, CA*] [*NASDAQ symbol*] (NQ)
DHTP	Dihydrotestosterone Propionate [*Endocrinology*]
DHTR	Delayed Hemolytic Transfusion Reaction [*Medicine*]
DHU	Deck Hand Uncertified [*Shipping*] (DS)
DHU	Disability Hearings Unit [*Social Security Administration*] (OICC)
D Hu	Doctor of Humanities
DHU	Document Handler Unit
DHU	Howard University, Washington, DC [*Library symbol*] [*Library of Congress*] [*OCLC symbol*] (LCLS)
DHUD	Department of Housing and Urban Development
DHUD	United States Department of Housing and Urban Development, Washington, DC [*Library symbol*] [*Library of Congress*] (LCLS)
D Hu L	Doctor of Humane Letters
DHUL	Dorchester Hugoton Limited [*NASDAQ symbol*] (NQ)
D Hum	Doctor of Humanities
DHumLitt ...	Doctor of Humane Letters
DHV	Design Hourly Volume [*Transportation*]
DHV	Duck Hepatitis Virus
DHVA	De Haas-van Alphen [*Effect*]
DHVM	Digital Hardware Voter Monitor (MCD)
DHW	Domestic Hot Water
DHW	Double-Hung Windows [*Technical drawings*]
DHW	Dyer Hill [*Washington*] [*Seismograph station code, US Geological Survey*] (SEIS)
DHX	Dump Heat Exchanger [*Nuclear energy*] (NRCH)
DHXCS	Dump Heat Exchanger Control System [*Nuclear energy*] (NRCH)
DHY	Deuterated Hydrogen Y [*Type of zeolite*]
DHY	Develet Hava Yollari [*Airline*]
DHY	Dhoney [*Ship's rigging*] (ROG)
D Hy	Doctor of Hygiene
D Hyg	Doctor of Hygiene
DHYZA7 ...	Deutsche Hydrographische Zeitschrift [*A publication*]
DHZ	Deutsche Handelszentrale [*German Trade Center*]
DHZ	Deutsche Hochschulzeitung [*A publication*]
D Hz	Die Holzzucht [*A publication*]
DHZ	Dihydralazine [*Antihypertensive agent*]

DI .... Argo, SA [*Dominican Republic*] [*ICAO designator*] (ICDA)
DI .... Daily Inspection [*Military*] (MCD)
DI .... Dark Ignition
DI .... Das Ist [*That Is*] [*German*]
DI .... Data Input [*Data processing*] (IEEE)
DI .... Data Integrator (MCD)
DI .... Data Interface
DI .... Data Item
DI .... Daylight Impression [*Psychical research*]
DI .... Dead Indian [*Careless man*] [*Army slang*]
DI .... Defective-Interfering [*Virology*]
DI .... Defence Intelligence [*British*]
DI .... Defense Industry
DI .... Defense Information (AFM)
DI .... Defense Instruction (ADA)
DI .... Deformability Index
DI .... Deicing
DI .... Deionization
DI .... Delay Indefinite [*Aviation*] (FAAC)
DI .... Demand Indicator (KSC)
DI .... [*The*] Democracy International (EA)
DI .... Density Indicator
DI .... Dental Information (EA)
DI .... Department of Industry [*British*] (DCTA)
D of I .... Department of the Interior
DI .... Department of the Interior (MCD)
DI .... Departmental Instruction (AAG)
DI .... Departure Approval Request for IFR [*Instrument Flight Rules*]
 Flight [*Aviation*] (FAAC)
DI .... Deputy Inspector [*British*] (ROG)
DI .... Deputy for Intelligence
DI .... Der Islam [*A publication*]
DI .... Description and Instructions
DI .... Design International (EA)
DI .... Designation Indicator
DI .... Desorption Ionization
DI .... Destination Index [*Data processing*]
DI .... Detective Inspector [*Scotland Yard*]
DI .... Deterioration Index [*Index of intellectual impairment on
 intelligence test*]
DI .... Development Integrated (MCD)
DI .... Development International (EA)
DI .... Developments in Immunology [*Elsevier Book Series*] [*A
 publication*]
DI .... Deviation Indicator
DI .... Device Independence
DI .... Diabetes Insipidus
DI .... Diagnostic Immunology [*A publication*]
Di .... Dial. A Magazine for Literature, Philosophy, and Religion [*A
 publication*]
Di .... Dialog [*A publication*]
Di .... Dialoghi [*A publication*]
DI .... Diameter
DI .... Diapason [*A publication*]
Di .... Diatoms [*Quality of the bottom*] [*Nautical charts*]
Di .... Didaskaleion [*A publication*]
DI .... Didymium [*Mixture of rare-earth elements*]
 [*Chemistry*] (ROG)
Di .... Diego [*Blood group*]
DI .... Dielectric Isolation
DI .... Difference Index [*Protein calculation*] [*Biochemistry*]
DI .... Differentiated Infiltrating Tumor [*Oncology*]
DI .... Diffusion Index [*Economics*]
DI .... Digital Input [*Data processing*]
Di .... Dinsdag [*Tuesday*] [*Afrikaans*]
Di .... Dinus de Mugello [*Flourished, 1278-98*] [*Authority cited in pre-
 1607 legal work*] (DSA)
di .... Diopside [*CIPW classification*] [*Geology*]
DI .... Diplomatic Immunity (ADA)
DI .... Direct-Indirect
DI .... Direct Injection [*Automotive engineering*]
DI .... Direct Investor
DI .... Direction Indicator
DI .... Directivity Index
D/I .... Director/Illuminator (CAAL)
DI .... Director of Infantry [*Military*] [*British*]
DI .... Director [*or Directorate*] of Installations [*Abolished 1953,
 functions transferred to Department of Defense*] [*Air
 Force*]
D of I .... Director of Intelligence [*RAF*] [*British*]
DI .... Directory Information [*Newsletter*]
DI .... Disability Income [*Insurance*]
DI .... Disability Insurance (AAG)
DI .... Disabled Individual [*Title XVI*] [*Social Security
 Administration*] (OICC)
DI .... Disc Harrowing and Ridging [*Agriculture*]
DI .... Discomfiture Index [*Weather*]
DI .... Discrete Input [*Data processing*] (KSC)
DI .... Disease Index [*Botany*]
DI .... Display Interface (NASA)
DI .... Disposition Instructions

DI .... Dissertationes Inaugurales [*A publication*]
Di .... Distal [*Medicine*]
DI .... Distillation [*Calorimetry*]
Di .... Distinctio [*Decretum Gratiani*] [*A publication*] (DSA)
DI .... Distinctive Insignia [*Military*]
DI .... Distoincisal [*Dentistry*]
DI .... Distribution of Industry [*British*]
DI .... District Inspector [*Navy*]
DI .... Diverting Ileostomy [*Medicine*]
DI .... Division Increment [*DoD*]
DI .... DOCARE International (EA)
DI .... Document Identifier [*Military*] (AFM)
DI .... Dolly In [*Films, television, etc.*]
DI .... Dominance Index [*Neurology*]
DI .... Doppler Inertial
DI .... Double Imperial [*Paper*] (ADA)
DI .... Double Indemnity [*Insurance*]
DI .... Double Injection
DI .... Dresser Industries, Inc. [*NYSE symbol*] (SPSG)
DI .... Drifters, Incorporated (EA)
DI .... Drill Instructor [*Marine Corps*]
DI .... Drug Information
DI .... Drug Interactions
DI .... Drvna Industrija [*A publication*]
DI .... Due In
DI .... Dvorak International (EAIO)
DI .... Dyskaryosis, Index of [*Cytopathology*]
DI .... Educational Documentation and Information Bulletin
 [*UNESCO*] [*A publication*]
DI .... Fighter [*Russian aircraft symbol*]
DI .... Flight Path Deviation Indicator [*Navigation*]
DI .... United States Department of the Interior, Washington, DC
 [*Library symbol*] [*Library of Congress*] (LCLS)
DIA .... Date of Initial Appointment
DIA .... Defense Intelligence Agency [*Formerly, JJ-2*] [*DoD*]
 [*Washington, DC*]
DIA .... Defense Intelligence Agency, Washington, DC [*OCLC
 symbol*] (OCLC)
DIA .... Deficiency in Allowance [*Military*] (MSA)
DIA .... Design and Industries Association [*British*]
DIA .... Deutscher Innen- und Aussenhandel [*Inner-German and
 Foreign Trade*]
DIA .... Diabetes [*Medicine*] (DHSM)
DIA .... Diagram (ADA)
DIA .... Dialect (ADA)
Dia .... Dialog [*A publication*]
Dia .... Dialoghi [*A publication*]
DIA .... Diameter
DIA .... Diamond
Dia .... Diaphon [*Record label*] [*Australia*]
DIA .... Diaphone [*Fog signal*]
DIA .... Diaphoretic [*Inducing Perspiration*] [*Pharmacy*] (ROG)
DIA .... Diasonics, Inc. [*AMEX symbol*] (SPSG)
DIA .... Diathermy [*Medicine*]
DIA .... Differentiation Inhibitory Activity [*Cytology*]
DIA .... Dig-In Angle
DIA .... Digital Imaging Australia
DIA .... Digital Interface Adapter [*Data processing*] (MCD)
DIA .... Digital Isolation Amplifier
DIA .... Diploma in International Affairs (ADA)
DIA .... Direct Interface Adapter
DIA .... Disabled in Action National (EA)
DIA .... Division of International Affairs [*An association*] (EA)
DIA .... Doctor of Industrial Arts
DIA .... Document Interchange Architecture
 [*Telecommunications*] (MCD)
DIA .... Documentation et Information Africaines [*African
 Documentation and Information*] [*Catholic News Agency*]
DIA .... Documents Information Accessing (BUR)
DIA .... Drug Information Association (EA)
DIA .... Drycleaning Institute of Australia
DIA .... Dual Interface Adapter
DIA .... Dubai International Airport
DIA .... Due in Assets
DIA .... Dulles International Airport [*FAA*]
DIA .... Dyadic Interaction Analysis
Diab .... Diabete [*Later, Diabete et Metabolisme*] [*A publication*]
DIAB .... Diabetes [*or Diabetic*]
DIAB .... Diamond-B Industries [*NASDAQ symbol*] (NQ)
Diab Abstr ... Diabetes Abstracts [*A publication*]
Diabet .... Diabetes [*A publication*]
Diabet .... Diabetologia [*A publication*]
Diabet Dig ... Diabetic Digest [*A publication*]
Diabete Met ... Diabete et Metabolisme [*A publication*]
Diabete Metab ... Diabete et Metabolisme [*A publication*]
Diabetes Educ ... Diabetes Educator [*A publication*]
Diabetes Lit Index ... Diabetes Literature Index [*A publication*]
Diabetes Metab Rev ... Diabetes/Metabolism Reviews [*A publication*]
Diabetes Metab Review ... Diabetes/Metabolism Reviews [*A publication*]
Diabetes Res ... Diabetes Research [*A publication*]

Diabetes Res Clin Prac ... Diabetes Research and Clinical Practice [*A publication*]
Diabetes Res Clin Pract ... Diabetes Research and Clinical Practice [*A publication*]
Diabetic J of Aust ... Diabetic Journal of Australia [*A publication*]　(APTA)
Diabet J ..... Diabetic Journal [*A publication*]
Diabetol Croat ... Diabetologia Croatica [*A publication*]
Diabetolog ... Diabetologia [*A publication*]
Diab Lit Ind ... Diabetes Literature Index [*A publication*]
DIA Bol Divulg ... DIA [*Division de Investigaciones Agropecuarias*] Boletin de Divulgacion [*A publication*]
DIA Bol Tec ... DIA [*Division de Investigaciones Agropecuarias*] Boletin Tecnico [*A publication*]
DIAC .... Data Interpretation and Analysis Center [*Canadian Navy*]
DIAC .... Defense Industry Advisory Council [*Later, IAC*]　(AFM)
DIAC .... Defense Information Analysis Center [*DoD*]
DIAC .... Diiodothyroacetic Acid [*Biochemistry*]
DIAC .... Directorate of Internal Affairs and Communications [*Allied German Occupation Forces*]
DIAD .... Adiake [*Ivory Coast*] [*ICAO location identifier*]　(ICLI)
DIAD .... Data Immediate Access Diagram
DIAD .... Diademed [*Numismatics*]
DIAD .... Donor-Insulator-Acceptor Device [*Electronics*]
DIAD .... Drum Information Assembler and Dispatcher
DIAD .... Inter-American Defense College, Fort McNair, Washington, DC [*Library symbol*] [*Library of Congress*]　(LCLS)
Diadora ...... Diadora Glasilo Arheoloskoga Muzeja u Zadru [*A publication*]
DIADS .... Digital Image Analysis and Display System [*Data processing*]
DIAE .... Agboville [*Ivory Coast*] [*ICAO location identifier*]　(ICLI)
DIAEAZ ..... Diabetes [*A publication*]
DIAG .... Diagnosis
DIAG .... Diagnostic Data [*NASDAQ symbol*]　(NQ)
DIAG .... Diagonal
Diag .... Diagonal Bands [*Navigation markers*]
DIAG .... Diagram　(KSC)
DIAGE ...... Defense Industry Advisory Group Europe [*Terminated, 1977*]
DIAGL .... Defense Intelligence Agency Guidance Letter　(MCD)
DIAGN ...... Diagnose　(NASA)
diagn .... Diagnostic　(BJA)
Diagn .... Diagnostica [*A publication*]
Diagn Cytopathol ... Diagnostic Cytopathology [*A publication*]
Diagn Gynecol Obstet ... Diagnostic Gynecology and Obstetrics [*A publication*]
Diagn Histopathol ... Diagnostic Histopathology [*A publication*]
Diagn Imag Clin Med ... Diagnostic Imaging in Clinical Medicine [*A publication*]
Diagn Imaging ... Diagnostic Imaging [*A publication*]
Diagn Imaging Clin Med ... Diagnostic Imaging in Clinical Medicine [*A publication*]
Diagn Immunol ... Diagnostic Immunology [*A publication*]
Diagn Intensivther ... Diagnostik und Intensivtherapie [*A publication*]
Diagn Lab .. Diagnostyka Laboratoryjna [*A publication*]
Diagn Lab Clin ... Diagnosi Laboratorio e Clinica [*A publication*]
Diagn Med ... Diagnostic Medicine [*A publication*]
Diagn Microbiol Infect Dis ... Diagnostic Microbiology and Infectious Disease [*A publication*]
Diagnosticos APEC ... Diagnosticos APEC. Associacao Promotora de Estudos de Economia [*A publication*]
Diagn Plazmy ... Diagnostika Plazmy [*USSR*] [*A publication*]
Diagn Radiol Ser ... Diagnostic Radiology Series [*A publication*]
Diagn Tec Lab ... Diagnostica e Tecnica di Laboratorio [*A publication*]
Diagn Ther ... Diagnosis and Therapy [*Japan*] [*A publication*]
Diagn Trait ... Diagnostics et Traitements [*A publication*]
Diagn Treat ... Diagnosis and Treatment [*Japan*] [*A publication*]
DIAGR ...... Diagrammatic
Diags .... Diagnostics
DIAI .... Defense Intelligence Agency Instruction　(MCD)
DIAL .... Data Independent Analysis Library　(CAAL)
DIAL .... Decimal Index of Art in the Lowlands [*A publication*]
DIAL .... Deficiencies in Allowance List [*Military*]　(NVT)
DIAL .... Developmental Indicators for the Assessment of Learning [*Education*]
DIAL .... Dialect
Dial .... Dialog [*Minneapolis*] [*A publication*]
Dial .... Dialoghi [*A publication*]
Dial .... Dialogi [*of Seneca the Younger*] [*Classical studies*]　(OCD)
Dial .... Dialogos. Problemi della Scuola Italiana [*A publication*]
DIAL .... Dialogue
Dial .... Dialogues. Cahiers de Litterature et de Linguistique [*A publication*]
Dial .... Dialogus de Oratoribus [*of Tacitus*] [*Classical studies*]　(OCD)
DIAL .... Differential-Absorption LIDAR [*Spectroscopy*]
DIAL .... Digital Image Analysis Laboratory [*University of Arizona*] [*Research center*]　(RCD)
DIAL .... Direct Information Access Link [*Data processing*]
DIAL .... Disablement Information Advice Lines [*British*]
DIAL .... Display Interactive Assembly Language [*Data processing*]　(IEEE)
DIAL .... Draper Industrial Assembly Language [*Data processing*]
DIAL .... Drum Interrogation, Alteration, and Loading System [*Honeywell, Inc.*]　(IEEE)

Dial Anthro ... Dialectical Anthropology [*A publication*]
Dial Ar .... Dialoghi di Archeologia [*A publication*]
Dial Arch ... Dialoghi di Archeologia [*A publication*]
DialB .... Dialektolohicnyi Bjuleten [*A publication*]
Dial Belg-Rom ... Dialectes Belgo-Romans [*A publication*]
Dial (Ch) .... Dial (Chicago) [*A publication*]
Dial D .... Dialogi Deorum [*of Lucian*] [*Classical studies*]　(OCD)
Dialec .... Dialectica [*A publication*]
Dial Ec .... Dialogo Ecumenico [*A publication*]
Dialec Hum ... Dialectics and Humanism [*A publication*]
DialEcum ..... Dialogo Ecumenico [*Salamanca*] [*A publication*]
Dialektika Ob'ekt Sub'ekt Poznanie Prakt Dejatel'nosti ... Dialektika Ob'ektivnogo i Sub'ektivnogo v Poznanie i Prakticeskoj Dejatel'nosti [*A publication*]
DIALGOL ... Dialect of Algorithmic Language
Dial Hist Anc ... Dialogues d'Histoire Ancienne [*A publication*]
Dial Meret ... Dialogi Meretricii [*of Lucian*] [*Classical studies*]　(OCD)
Dial Mort ... Dialogi Mortuorum [*of Lucian*] [*Classical studies*]　(OCD)
DIALOG ... Direction for Army Logistic　(MCD)
DIALOG ... On-Line Search Service [*Lockheed*]　(DLA)
Dialog Fairleigh Dickinson Univ Sch Dent ... Dialog. Fairleigh Dickinson University. School of Dentistry [*A publication*]
DIA-LOGICS ... Document Indexing and Listing of Graphic Information Codes System [*Jet Propulsion Laboratory, NASA*]
Dialogue C ... Dialogue. Canadian Philosophical Review [*A publication*]
Dialogue (Canada) ... Dialogue; Canadian Philosophical Review [*A publication*]
Dialogue (M) ... Dialogue (Milwaukee) [*A publication*]
Dialogue (PST) ... Dialogue (Phi Sigma Tau) [*A publication*]
Dialog (W) ... Dialog (Warsaw) [*A publication*]
DIAL-R ... Developmental Indicators for the Assessment of Learning - Revised [*Child development test*]
DIALS .... Defense Information Automated Locator System　(AABC)
DialS .... Dialog: Teatertidskrift (Stockholm) [*A publication*]
Dial Sc .... Dialogus de Scaccario [*Dialogue of the Exchequer*] [*A publication*]　(DLA)
Dial de Scacc ... Dialogus de Scaccario [*Dialogue of the Exchequer*] [*A publication*]　(DLA)
Dial Transplant ... Dialysis and Transplantation [*A publication*]
Dial Transplant Nephrol Pro Congr Eur Dial Transplant Assoc ... Dialysis, Transplantation, Nephrology. Proceedings. Congress of the European Dialysis and Transplant Association [*A publication*]
DIAM .... Data Independent Architecture Model
DIAM .... Defense Intelligence Acquisition Manual　(MCD)
DIAM .... Defense Intelligence Agency Manual　(MCD)
DIAM .... Defense Intelligence Agency Memorandum　(MCD)
DIAM .... Diameter
DIAMAT ... Dialektischer Materialismus
DIA Med ... DIA [*Division de Investigaciones Agropecuarias*] Medico [*A publication*]
DIA Med Urug ... DIA [*Division de Investigaciones Agropecuarias*] Medico Uruguayo [*A publication*]
DIAMON ... Diagnostic Monitor [*Data processing*]
Diamond News and SA Jeweller ... Diamond News and SA [*South African*] Jeweller [*A publication*]
Diamond Res ... Diamond Research [*A publication*]
DIAN .... Decca Integrated Airborne Navigator
DIAN .... Digital Analog [*Data processing*]　(IEEE)
Dian .... Hymmus in Dianam [*of Callimachus*] [*Classical studies*]　(OCD)
DIANA ...... Dusseldorf's Institution Art Network Application　(EISS)
DIAND ...... Department of Indian Affairs and Northern Development [*Canada*]
DIANE ...... Digital Integrated Attack and Navigation Equipment
DIANE ...... Direct Information Access Network for Europe [*Commission of the European Communities*] [*Information service or system*] [*Defunct*]　(IID)
DIANE ...... Distance Indicating Automatic Navigation Equipment
DIANE ...... Duct Integrity and Nozzle Efficiency　(MCD)
DIANM ...... Defense Intelligence Analytical Memorandum　(MCD)
DIAO .... Aboisso [*Ivory Coast*] [*ICAO location identifier*]　(ICLI)
DIAOB .... Defense Intelligence Air Order of Battle　(MCD)
DIAOLS .... Defense Intelligence Agency On-Line Information System　(MCD)
DIAP .... Abidjan/Port Bouet [*Ivory Coast*] [*ICAO location identifier*]　(ICLI)
Diap .... Diapason [*A publication*]
DIAP .... Diapason [*Octave*] [*Music*]
DIAPAS ..... Diabetes Personalized Alerting Service
DIAPH ...... Diaphragm　(MSA)
DIAR .... Defense Intelligence Agency Regulation
DIAR .... Development-Inhibitor Anchimeric Releasing [*Photography*]
DIAR .... Drew Institute for Archaeological Research [*Drew University*] [*Research center*]　(RCD)
DI Arch ...... Doctor of Interior Architecture
DI Arch E .. Doctor of Interior Architectural Engineering
DI Arch Eng ... Doctor of Interior Architectural Engineering
Diario Of Minist Mar ... Diario Oficial. Ministerio de Marina [*A publication*]
DIAS .... Diastolic [*Medicine*]
DIAS .... Digital Integrated Avionics System　(MCD)

DIAS......... Dublin Institute for Advanced Studies
DIAS......... DUNS [*Data Universal Numbering System*] Industrial Affiliations Service   (IID)
DIAS......... Dynamic Inventory Analysis System [*Data processing*]
DIATAC.... DIA [*Division de Investigaciones Agropecuarias*] Boletin Tecnico [*A publication*]
DIATH...... Diathermy [*Medicine*]
Diatomic Research Bull ... Diatomic Research Bulletin [*A publication*]
DIAU........ Abengourou [*Ivory Coast*] [*ICAO location identifier*]   (ICLI)
DIAV........ Abidjan [*Ivory Coast*] [*ICAO location identifier*]   (ICLI)
DIB .... Data Input Bus [*Data processing*]   (MDG)
DIB .... Data Inspection Board [*Europe*]
DIB .... Defense Industrial Base [*DoD*]
DIB .... Defense Industry Bulletin [*DoD*] [*A publication*]
DIB .... Defense Intelligence Board   (MCD)
DIB .... Department of Information and Broadcasting
DIB .... Department Information Bulletin
DIB .... Design Information Bulletin
DIB .... Dibrugarh [*India*] [*Airport symbol*]   (OAG)
DIB .... Dictionary of International Biography [*A publication*]
DIB .... Dielectric Infrared Beamsplitter
DIB .... Disability Insurance Benefits [*Social Security Administration*]   (OICC)
DIB .... Documentatie en Informatie over Toerisme [*A publication*]
DIB .... Dot Immunobinding Assay [*Immunology*]
DIB .... Dry Cleaning Information Bureau [*British*]   (CB)
DIBA .... Digital Integral Ballistic Analyzer   (NG)
DIBA .... Diisobutyl Adipate [*Organic chemistry*]
DIBA .... Diisobutylamine [*Organic chemistry*]
DIBA .... Domestic and International Business Administration [*Terminated 1977, functions assumed by Industry and Trade Administration*] [*Department of Commerce*]
DIBAC...... Diisobutylaluminum Chloride [*Organic chemistry*]
DIBAH...... Diisobutylaluminum Hydride [*Also, DBAH*] [*Organic chemistry*]
DIBC........ Bocanda [*Ivory Coast*] [*ICAO location identifier*]   (ICLI)
DIBHP ...... Diisopropylbenzene Hydroperoxide [*Organic chemistry*]
DIBI........ Boundiali [*Ivory Coast*] [*ICAO location identifier*]   (ICLI)
DIBIT .... Di-Binary Digit [*Two consecutive binary digits*]   (TEL)
DIBK........ Bouake [*Ivory Coast*] [*ICAO location identifier*]   (ICLI)
DIBK........ Diisobutyl Ketone [*Organic chemistry*]
DIBK........ Dime Financial Corp. [*NASDAQ symbol*]   (NQ)
DIBLAR ... Desert Institute. Bulletin ARE [*A publication*]
DIBN........ Bouna/Tehini [*Ivory Coast*] [*ICAO location identifier*]   (ICLI)
DIBOD5..... Dissertationes Botanicae [*A publication*]
DIBOL....... Digital Equipment's Business-Oriented Language [*Data processing*]
DIBRAC .... Direct Broadcast Access   (MCD)
DIBS........ Digital Integrated Business System [*Digital Equipment Corp.*]
DIBtn........ Defense Industry Bulletin [*DoD*] [*A publication*]
DIBU .... Bondoukou/Soko [*Ivory Coast*] [*ICAO location identifier*]   (ICLI)
DIC .... Automatic Door Isolating Cock [*British railroad term*]
DIC .... Dainippon Ink & Chemicals [*Japan*]
DIC .... Dairy Industry Committee   (EA)
DIC .... Data Input Clerk [*Data processing*]
DIC .... Data Input Consoles [*Data processing*]   (NVT)
DIC .... Data Insertion Converter
DIC .... Data Item Category
DIC .... Decision Industries Corporation [*NYSE symbol*]   (SPSG)
DIC .... Defense Identification Code   (NATG)
DIC .... Defense Intelligence Commentary   (MCD)
DIC .... Demand-Increasing Costs [*Economics*]
DIC .... Department of Industrial Cooperation [*University of Maine*] [*Research center*]   (RCD)
D & IC....... Dependency and Indemnity Compensation [*Military*]   (AFM)
DIC .... Dependency and Indemnity Compensation [*Military*]
DIC .... Designers d'Interieur du Canada [*Interior Designers of Canada - IDC*]
DIC .... Detailed Interrogation Center [*Navy*]
dic............. Dicembre [*December*] [*German*]
dic............. Diciembre [*December*] [*Spanish*]
Dic............. Dicta   (DLA)
DIC .... Dictionary
DIC .... Difference in Conditions
DIC .... Differential Interference Contrast [*Microscope*]
DIC .... Diffuse Intravascular Coagulation [*Hematology*]
DIC .... Digital Input [*or Integrating*] Computer [*Data processing*]
DIC .... Digital Integrated Circuit [*Data processing*]
DIC .... Digital Interface Component   (MCD)
DIC .... Diisopropylaminoethyl Chloride [*Organic chemistry*]
DIC .... (Dimethyltriazenyl)imidazolecarboxamide [*Dacarbazine*] [*Also, DTIC*] [*Antineoplastic drug*]
DIC .... Diploma of Membership of Imperial College of Science and Technology, University of London [*British*]
DIC .... Disseminated Intravascular Coagulation [*Hematology*]
DIC .... Dissolved Inorganic Carbon [*Also, DIOC*]
DIC .... Diving Information Center [*Navy*]
DIC .... Division of Industrial Cooperation [*MIT*]   (MCD)
DIC .... Document Identifier Code [*Military*]   (AFM)

DIC .... Documentacion Internacional de Carreteras [*International Road Research Documentation*] [*Database*] [*Ministerio de Obras Publicas y Urbanismo*] [*Spanish*] [*Information service or system*]   (CRD)
DIC .... Drunk in Charge
DIC .... United States Interstate Commerce Commission, Washington, DC [*Library symbol*] [*Library of Congress*]   (LCLS)
DICA .... Dance in Canada Association
DICA .... Defense Industry Cooperation Agreement [*Military*]
DICA .... Diagnostic Interview for Children and Adolescents
DICAB....... Directive Coordinated and Approved by Budget Director [*Air Force*]
DICAM .... Datasystem Interactive Communications Access Method [*Digital Equipment Corp.*]
DICAP....... Direct-Current Circuit Analysis Program [*Data processing*]
DICAS ...... Directional Command Activated Sonobuoy [*System*] [*Navy*]   (NVT)
DICASS..... Directional Command Activated Sonobuoy System [*Navy*]
DICBM...... Defense Intercontinental Ballistic Missile
DICBM...... Depressed-Trajectory Intercontinental Ballistic Missile   (MCD)
DICC......... Di-An Controls, Inc. [*NASDAQ symbol*]   (NQ)
DICC......... Digital Interface Code Converter [*Data processing*]
DICCAP .... Distributed Impressed Current Cathodic Protection [*Anticorrosion system*]
Dic Dom ..... Dicey. Law of Domicil [*A publication*]   (DLA)
Dice .... Dice's Reports [*79-91 Indiana*] [*A publication*]   (DLA)
DICE......... Digital Integrated Circuit Element [*Data processing*]
DICE......... Digital Intercontinental Conversion Equipment   (MCD)
DICE......... Digital Interface Countermeasures Equipment [*Air Force*]
DICE......... Digitally Implemented Communications Experiment   (MCD)
DICE......... Division of Improved Conversion Efficiency [*Energy Research and Development Administration*]
Dice .... Double [*or Dual*] Income, Children, and Everything [*Lifestyle classification*] [*Term coined by William F. Doescher, publisher of "D & B Reports"*]
DICEA....... Die Casting Engineer [*A publication*]
DICEF....... Digital Communications Experimental Facility [*Air Force*]
Dicey Confl Laws ... Dicey. Conflict of Laws [*A publication*]   (DLA)
Dicey Const ... Dicey's Lectures Introductory to the Study of the Law of the English Constitution [*A publication*]   (DLA)
Dicey Dom ... Dicey. Law of Domicil [*A publication*]   (DLA)
Dicey Domicil ... Dicey. Law of Domicil [*A publication*]   (DLA)
Dicey & Morris ... Dicey. Conflict of Laws [*A publication*]   (DLA)
DICHA....... Diseases of the Chest [*A publication*]
DICHAK ... Diseases of the Chest [*A publication*]
DIChem ..... Diploma of Industrial Chemistry   (ADA)
DICHLORAN ... Dichloronitroaniline [*Also, DCNA*] [*Fungicide*]
Dicht u Volkst ... Dichtung und Volkstum [*A publication*]
DICIFER... Digital Interactive Complex for Image Feature Extraction and Recognition [*Air Force*]
Dick........... Dickens' English Chancery Reports [*A publication*]   (DLA)
Dick........... Dickensian [*A publication*]
Dick........... Dickinson's New Jersey Equity Precedents [*A publication*]   (DLA)
Dick Black ... Dickson's Analysis of Blackstone's Commentaries [*A publication*]   (DLA)
Dick Ch...... Dickens' English Chancery Reports [*A publication*]   (DLA)
Dick Ch (Eng) ... Dickens' English Chancery Reports [*A publication*]   (DLA)
Dickens ...... Dickens' English Chancery Reports [*A publication*]   (DLA)
Dickens ...... Dickensian [*A publication*]
Dickens St ... Dickens Studies Newsletter [*A publication*]
Dicken Stud Newsl ... Dickens Studies Newsletter [*A publication*]
Dick Eq Pr ... Dickinson's New Jersey Equity Precedents [*A publication*]   (DLA)
Dick Ev ...... Dickson's Law of Evidence in Scotland [*A publication*]   (DLA)
Dickinson L Rev ... Dickinson Law Review [*A publication*]
DickinsonR ... Dickinson Review [*A publication*]
Dickinson S ... Dickinson Studies [*A publication*]
Dick Int'l L Ann ... Dickinson's International Law Annual [*A publication*]   (DLA)
Dick Just... Dickinson's Justice [*A publication*]   (DLA)
Dick Kent... Dickson's Analysis of Kent's Commentaries [*A publication*]   (DLA)
Dick L R..... Dickinson Law Review [*A publication*]
Dick L Rev ... Dickinson Law Review [*A publication*]
Dick (NJ)... Dickinson's New Jersey Equity Precedents [*A publication*]   (DLA)
DickQ .... Dickens Quarterly [*A publication*]
Dick Quar Ses ... Dickinson's Practical Guide to the Quarter Sessions [*A publication*]   (DLA)
DICM ...... Differential Interference Contrast Microscope
DICMD4 ... Diagnostic Imaging in Clinical Medicine [*A publication*]
DICN .... Diceon Electronics, Inc. [*NASDAQ symbol*]   (NQ)
DICNAVAB ... Dictionary of Naval Abbreviations [*A publication*]
DICO .... Discovery [*or Dissemination*] of Information through Cooperative Organization
DICODE ... Digital Correlation Demonstrator
DICOMSS ... Direct Commissary Support System [*DoD*]
DICOMTA ... Documentation Informatisee pour les Comptables [*CEDIC*] [*Database*]
DICORAP ... Directional Controlled Rocket-Assisted Projectile   (MCD)

DICOS...... Digital Communications System Evaluator (MCD)
DICOSE..... Digital Communications System Evaluator (MCD)
DICOSY.... Directional Coupler Synthesis (MCD)
DICP.......... Drop-In Care Partners (EA)
DICP Ann Pharmacother ... DICP (Drug Intelligence and Clinical Pharmacy) Annals of Pharmacotherapy [*A publication*]
Dic Par........ Dicey on Parties to Actions [*A publication*] (DLA)
DICPB......... Drug Intelligence and Clinical Pharmacy [*A publication*]
DICR .... Daily Inspection Call Record (MCD)
DICRA...... Diseases of the Colon and Rectum [*A publication*]
DICRAG...... Diseases of the Colon and Rectum [*A publication*]
Dic S......... Dickinson Studies [*A publication*]
DICS.......... Display Interface Computer System (MCD)
DICS.......... Down-Island Communication System [*Taiwan*] (CINC)
DICT.......... Dictaphone
DICT.......... Dictation
DICT.......... Dictator
DICT.......... Dictionary
Dicta.......... Dicta of Denver Bar Association [*A publication*] (DLA)
Dict Apol.... Dictionnaire Apologetique [*A publication*]
Dict C F.... Dictionnaire des Codes Francais [*A publication*] (DLA)
Dict Class Hist Nat ... Dictionnaire Classique d'Histoire Naturelle [*A publication*]
Dict Dr Com ... Dictionnaire de Droit Commercial [*French*] [*A publication*] (DLA)
Dict Droit Civil ... Dictionnaire de Droit Civil [*French*] [*A publication*] (DLA)
Dict de Jur ... Dictionnaire de Jurisprudence [*French*] [*A publication*] (DLA)
Dict Limb Rom ... Dictionarul Limbii Romane [*A publication*]
Dict Nat ..... Dictionnaire du Notariat [*French*] [*A publication*] (DLA)
DICU .... Digital Interface and Control Unit
DICY.......... Dicyanodiamide [*Also, DCD*] [*Organic chemistry*]
DID.......... Daily Intelligence Digest
DID.......... Dangerous Infectious Disease [*British*] (ROG)
DID.......... Data Identification
DID.......... Data Input Display [*Data processing*]
DID.......... Data Item Description
DID.......... Datamation Industry Directory (MCD)
DID.......... Delayed Ischemic Deficit [*Medicine*]
DID.......... Department of Commercial and Industrial Development [*Queensland, Australia*]
DID.......... Destron/Idi, Inc. [*Vancouver Stock Exchange symbol*]
DID.......... Detailed Issue Depot [*Military supply organization for Allied armies in Europe*] [*World War II*]
DID.......... Device Identifier
Did .... Didache (BJA)
DID.......... Didactic
Did .... Didaskaleion [*A publication*]
DID.......... Didcot [*British depot code*]
DID.......... Digital Information Display [*Data processing*]
DID.......... Direct Inward Dialing [*Telecommunications*]
DID.......... Director of the Intelligence Division [*British military*] (DMA)
DID.......... Discharge Ionization Detector
DID.......... Display Interface Device [*Telecommunications*] (TEL)
DID.......... Division of Innovation and Development [*Department of Education*]
DID.......... Division of Institutional Development [*Office of Education*]
DID.......... Division of Isotopes Development [*AEC*]
DID.......... Double Isotope Derivative
DID.......... Drug Induced Diseases [*Elsevier Book Series*] [*A publication*]
DID.......... Drum Information Display
DID.......... Dust Impact Detection System [*Astrophysics*]
DIDA .... Depository Institutions Deregulation and Monetary Control Act of 1980
DIDA .... Dignity in Death Alliance [*British*]
DIDA .... Diisodecyl Adipate [*Organic chemistry*]
DIDA .... Director of Intelligence, Division of the Admiralty [*British*]
DIDA .... Dynamic Instrumentation Digital Analyzer
DIDAC ...... Digital Data Computer
DIDACS.... Digital Data Communications System (MCD)
DIDAD ...... Digital Data Display
D Idaho...... United States District Court for the District of Idaho (DLA)
DIDAP...... Digital Data Processor
DIDAS...... Dynamic Instrumentation Data Automobile System [*Telemetering system for auto test tracks*]
Didasc........ Didascalia [*A publication*]
Dida de Segu ... Didacus de Segura [*Flourished, 16th century*] [*Authority cited in pre-1607 legal work*] (DSA)
Didask........ Didaskalos [*A publication*]
DIDB .... Dabou [*Ivory Coast*] [*ICAO location identifier*] (ICLI)
DIDB .... Inter-American Development Bank, Washington, DC [*Library symbol*] [*Library of Congress*] (LCLS)
DIDC .... Data Input Display Console [*Data processing*]
DIDC .... Depository Institutions Deregulation Committee [*Department of the Treasury*] [*Terminated, 1986*]
DIDD .... Dynamic Integrated Data Display
DIDDS...... Dynamic Integrated Data Display System
DI/DES...... Vessels Disposed of by Sinking, Burning, Abandoning, or Other Means of Destruction [*Navy*]
DIDF.......... Dual Input Describing Function [*Data processing*]
DIDG .... Diisodecyl Glutarate [*Organic chemistry*]

DIDIEW.... Digestive Diseases [*A publication*]
Did Iul........ Didius Iulianus [*of Scriptores Historiae Augustae*] [*Classical studies*] (OCD)
DIDK .... Dimbokro [*Ivory Coast*] [*ICAO location identifier*] (ICLI)
DIDL .... Daloa [*Ivory Coast*] [*ICAO location identifier*] (ICLI)
DIDL .... Digital Integrated Design Language [*Data processing*] (CSR)
DIDM......... Document Identification and Description Macros [*IBM Corp.*]
DI/DO .... Data Input/Data Output [*Data processing*]
DIDO......... Digital Input/Digital Output [*Data processing*]
DIDO......... Directional Doppler (MCD)
DIDOC .... Desired Image Distribution Using Orthogonal Constraints [*Illinois Institute of Technology*]
DIDOCS... Device Independent Display Operator Console Support (BUR)
dIDP .... Deoxyinosine Diphosphate [*Biochemistry*]
DIDP .... Diisodecyl Phthalate [*Organic chemistry*]
DIDS.......... Data Item Description System (MCD)
DIDS.......... Defense Information Distribution System [*Proposed in-home disaster warning system*]
DIDS.......... Defense Integrated Data System (AFM)
Did S.......... Diderot Studies [*A publication*]
DIDS.......... Digital Information Display System [*Data processing*]
DIDS.......... Diisothiocyano (Disulfonic Acid) Stilbene [*Organic chemistry*]
DIDS.......... DLSC [*Defense Logistics Services Center*] Integrated Data System [*Military*]
DIDS.......... Document Information Directory System [*NIOSH*] [*Database*]
DIDS.......... Domestic Information Display System [*Computer graphics*]
DIDS-CD... Decision Information Distribution System - Civil Defense [*Military*] (AABC)
DIDSIM .... Defense In-Depth Simulation
DIDSO ...... Defense Integrated Data System Program Management Office [*DoD*]
DIDSRS .... Defense Intelligence Dissemination, Storage, and Retrieval System (MCD)
DIDSY...... Dust Impact Detection System [*Astrophysics*]
DIDU......... Defense Item Data Utilization
DIDV .... Divo [*Ivory Coast*] [*ICAO location identifier*] (ICLI)
DIE .... Defense Intelligence Estimate (MCD)
DIE .... Developments in Endocrinology [*Elsevier Book Series*] [*A publication*]
DIE .... Diego Suarez [*Madagascar*] [*Airport symbol*] (OAG)
DIE .... Digital Image Enhancement [*Microscopy*]
DIE .... Diploma in Industrial Engineering (ADA)
DIE .... Diploma of the Institute of Engineering [*British*]
DIE .... Direct Injection Enthalpimetry
DIE .... Directors-in-Exile [*British*]
DIE .... Distance in Error
DIE .... Division of International Education [*Office of Education*]
DIE .... Doctor of Industrial Engineering
DIE .... Document of Industrial Engineering (KSC)
DIE .... Double Injection Effect
DIEA .... Department of Immigration and Ethnic Affairs [*Australia*]
DIEA .... Dictionary of Industrial Engineering Abbreviations [*A publication*] (KSC)
DIEA .... (Diisopropyl)ethylamine [*Organic chemistry*]
DIE (ACE) ... Division of International Education (of the American Council on Education) (EA)
DIEAG ...... Defense Industry Export Advisory Group
DIEB ALT ... Diebus Alternis [*Every Other Day*] [*Pharmacy*]
DIEB SECUND ... Diebus Secundis [*Every Second Day*] [*Pharmacy*]
DIEB TERT ... Diebus Tertiis [*Every Third Day*] [*Pharmacy*]
DIEC......... Defense Item Entry Control (AFIT)
DIECA...... Diethyldithiocarbonate [*Analytical chemistry*]
Die Cast Eng ... Die Casting Engineer [*A publication*]
Diecasting Met Moulding ... Diecasting and Metal Moulding [*A publication*]
Diecast Met Mould ... Diecasting and Metal Moulding [*A publication*]
DIECO ...... Defense Item Entry Control Office [*Military*]
DIECP ...... Defense Item Entry Control Program [*Military*] (AABC)
Diehlektr Poluprovodn ... Diehlektriki i Poluprovodniki [*A publication*]
DIEL......... Diesel Electric
DIELEC .... Dielectric
Dielectr Opt Aspects Intermol Interact ... Dielectric and Optical Aspects of Intermolecular Interactions [*A publication*]
Dielectr Relat Mol Processes ... Dielectric and Related Molecular Processes [*A publication*]
dien............ Diethylenediamine [*Organic chemistry*]
DI Eng .... Doctor of Industrial Engineering
DIEO .... Decennie Internationale d'Exploration des Oceans [*International Decade of Ocean Exploration*] (MSC)
DIEOB....... Defense Intelligence Electronic Order of Battle (MCD)
DIEP......... Diabetes in Early Pregnancy [*Medicine*]
DIEQA ...... Differential Equations [*A publication*]
DIER .... Department Instrument Equipment Reserve
Diergeneesk Memo ... Diergeneeskundig Memorandum [*A publication*]
DIES.......... Diesel
DIESA ...... Department of International Economic and Social Affairs [*United Nations*] [*Information service or system*] (IID)
Diesel .... Diesel and Gas Turbine Progress [*Later, Diesel Progress North American*] [*A publication*]
Diesel Eng ... Diesel Engineering [*England*] [*A publication*]
Diesel Eng Us Ass Report ... Diesel Engineers and Users Association. Reports [*A publication*]

Diesel Eng Users Ass Publ ... Diesel Engineers and Users Association. Publication [*A publication*]
Diesel Equip Supt ... Diesel Equipment Superintendent [*A publication*]
Diesel Gas Turbine Prog ... Diesel and Gas Turbine Progress [*Later, Diesel Progress North American*] [*A publication*]
Diesel Gas Turbine Progr ... Diesel and Gas Turbine Progress [*Later, Diesel Progress North American*] [*A publication*]
Diesel Gas Turbine Worldwide ... Diesel and Gas Turbine Worldwide [*A publication*]
Diesel Gas Turb Prog Worldwide ... Diesel and Gas Turbine Progress Worldwide [*Later, Diesel and Gas Turbine Worldwide*] [*A publication*]
Diesel Power Diesel Transp ... Diesel Power and Diesel Transportation [*A publication*]
Diesel Prog ... Diesel Progress [*A publication*]
Diesel Prog ... Diesel Progress North American [*A publication*]
Diesel Prog N Amer ... Diesel Progress North American [*A publication*]
Diesel Prog North Am ... Diesel Progress North American [*A publication*]
Dies Rail Tract ... Diesel Railway Traction [*A publication*]
DIET.......... American Health Companies, Inc. [*Rexburg, ID*] [*NASDAQ symbol*] (NQ)
DIET.......... Dietetics
DIET.......... Division of Integration and Environmental Testing [*Social Security Administration*]
Diet Collect ... Dietetique et Collectivites [*A publication*]
Diet Curr.... Dietetic Currents [*A publication*]
Diet Currents ... Dietetic Currents [*A publication*]
Diet Hyg Gaz ... Dietetic and Hygienic Gazette [*A publication*]
Diet et Nutr ... Dietetique et Nutrition [*A publication*]
Diet Nutr.... Dietetique et Nutrition [*A publication*]
Dietol Dietoter ... Dietologia e Dietoterapia [*A publication*]
Dietsk Med ... Dietskaia Meditsina [*A publication*]
DIF............. Data Interchange Format
DIF............. Decay in Flight [*Nuclear physics*]
DIF............. Defense Industrial Fund
DIF............. Deposit Insurance Fund [*Pronounced "diff"*]
DIF............. Descriptive Item File
DIF............. Device Input Format
dif.............. Differe [*Deferred Stock*] [*French*] [*Business term*]
DIF............. Difference (AFM)
DIF............. Differential (AFM)
DIF............. Differentiation Inducting Factor [*Immunology*]
DIF............. Difficulty-Importance-Frequency
DIF............. Diffuse
DIF............. Diffuser [*Freight*] [*Microbiology*]
DIF............. Diiodofluorescein [*Organic chemistry*]
DIF............. Direction Finder [*or Finding*] [*Radio aid to navigation*]
DIF............. Discrete Increment Filter (NASA)
DIF............. Discriminate Function [*Physiology*]
DIF............. Division of International Finance [*of FRS*]
DIF............. Document Interchange Format
DIF............. DOMSAT [*Domestic Satellite*] Interface Facility (MCD)
DIF............. Drug Information Fulltext [*American Society of Hospital Pharmacists*] [*Bethesda, MD*] [*Database*]
DIF............. Duty Involving Flying [*Military*]
DIF............. Dvorak International Federation (EA)
DIFA.......... Deposit Insurance Flexibility Act [*1982*]
DIFA.......... Differential Amplifier (MSA)
DIFA.......... Difurfurylideneacetone [*Organic chemistry*]
DIFAD...... Digitally Integrated Fleet Air Defense
DIFAR...... Direction-Finding and Ranging
DIFAR...... Directional Frequency Analysis and Recording System (MCD)
DIFC.......... Decommutator Interface Controller (MCD)
DIFCE........ Difference
DIFCLT..... Difficult
DIFCLTY ... Difficulty
DIFCREW ... Duty Involving Flying Crewman [*Military*] (NVT)
DIFCT....... Difficult (ROG)
DIFCTY .... Difficulty (ROG)
DIFD.......... Diversified Foods, Inc. [*NASDAQ symbol*] (NQ)
DIFDA....... Diffusion Data [*Later, Diffusion and Defect Data*] [*A publication*]
DIFDEN.... Duty in a Flying Status Not Involving Flying [*Air Force*] (NVT)
DIFET ...... Double Injection Field Effect Transistor [*Electronics*]
DIFF.......... Difference (KSC)
DIFF........ Differential (AABC)
DIFF .... Differential Blood Count
DIFFA ...... Design Industries Foundation for AIDS [*Acquired Immune Deficiency Syndrome*] (EA)
DIFFCE..... Difference (ROG)
DIFFER..... Difference (DSUE)
Differencial'nye Uravnenija i Vycisl Mat ... Differencial'nye Uravnenija i Vycislitelnaja Matematika [*A publication*]
Differentia ... Differentiation [*A publication*]
Differ Equations ... Differential Equations [*A publication*]
Differ Uravn ... Differentsial'nye Uravneniya [*A publication*]
Differ Uravn Primen ... Differentsial'nye Uravneniya i Ikh Primenenie [*A publication*]
DIFFR ...... Diffraction (MSA)
DIFF SENS ... Differential Sense [*Data processing*]

DIFFTR..... Differential Time Relay (IEEE)
DIFFUS..... Diffusing
Diffus Data ... Diffusion Data [*Later, Diffusion and Defect Data*] [*A publication*]
Diffus Defect Data ... Diffusion and Defect Data [*Switzerland*] [*A publication*]
Diffus Defect Monogr Ser ... Diffusion and Defect Monograph Series [*A publication*]
Diffuz Svarka Vak Met Splavov Nemet Mater ... Diffuzionnaya Svarka v Vakuume Metallov. Splavov i Nemetallicheskikh Materialov [*USSR*] [*A publication*]
DIFK.......... Ferkessedougou [*Ivory Coast*] [*ICAO location identifier*] (ICLI)
DI/FLC...... Vessels in Forward Areas Transferred to State Department Foreign Liquidation Corporation [*Navy*]
DIFM........ Due-In from Maintenance [*Military*] (AFM)
DIFO.......... Due-In from Overhaul [*Military*] (MCD)
DIFOPS .... Duty in a Flying Status Involving Operational or Training Flights [*Air Force*] (NVT)
DIFOT........ Duty Involving Operational or Training Flights [*Air Force*]
DIFOTECH ... Duty in a Flying Status Involving Operational or Training Flights as a Technical Observer [*Air Force*]
DIFOTINS ... Duty in a Flying Status Involving Operational or Training Flights under Instruction [*Air Force*]
DIFOTRELAS ... Duty in a Flying Status Involving Operational or Training Flights as His Relief [*Air Force*]
DIFOTRVK ... Duty in a Flying Status Involving Operational or Training Flights Revoked [*Air Force*]
DIFP.......... Diisopropyl Fluorophosphonate [*Also, DFP*] [*Toxic compound*]
DIFP.......... Diphenyliodonium Hexafluorophosphate [*Biochemistry*]
DIFP.......... International Food Policy Research Institute, Washington, DC [*Library symbol*] [*Library of Congress*] (LCLS)
DIFPP........ Defense Industrial Facilities Protection Program [*DoD*]
DIFPRO .... Duty in a Flying Status Involving Proficiency Flying [*Air Force*] (NVT)
DIFT.......... Dartford International Freight Terminal [*British*] (DS)
DIFT.......... Different
DI-FTMS .. Desorption Ionization Fourier Transform Mass Spectrometry
DIFU .... Deutsches Institut fuer Urbanistik [*Vereins fuer Kommunalwissenschaften e V*] [*Database producer*]
Difusion Econ ... Difusion Economica [*A publication*]
DIG............ Delivery Indicator Group (NATG)
DIG............ Departement Documentation et Information Geologique [*Geological Information and Documentation Department*] [*Bureau of Geological and Mining Research*] [*Information service or system*] (IID)
DIG............ Deputy Inspector-General
DIG............ Design Implementation Guide [*Telecommunications*] (TEL)
DIG............ Detonator Inspection Gauge
DIG............ Developments in Genetics [*Elsevier Book Series*] [*A publication*]
DIG............ Di Giorgio Corp. [*NYSE symbol*] (SPSG)
Dig............. Digeratur [*Let It Be Digested*] [*Pharmacy*]
Dig .... Digest [*1901-06*] [*Lahore, India*] [*A publication*] (DLA)
DIG .... Digest
Dig .... Digest of Justinian [*A publication*] (DLA)
Dig .... Digest of Writs [*A publication*] (DLA)
Dig .... Digesta [*Latin*] (OCD)
DIG .... Digital (AFM)
DIG .... Digital-Image-Generated [*Data processing*] (IEEE)
DIG .... Digital Input Gate
DIG .... Digitalis [*Foxglove*] [*Pharmacy*]
DIG .... Digitoxin
DIG .... Digoxin
DIG .... Disablement Income Group [*British*]
DIG .... Discussion in Groups
DIG .... Justinian Digesta [*Libri Pandectarum*] [*Legal*] (ROG)
DIGA .... Dynamics International Gardening Association (EA)
DIGA .... Gagnoa [*Ivory Coast*] [*ICAO location identifier*] (ICLI)
DIGAC .... Digital Avionics Control
DIGACC .... Digital Guidance and Control Computer
Dig Agric Econ ... Digest of Agricultural Economics [*A publication*]
DIGATEC ... Digital Gas Turbine Engine Control (MCD)
Digby RP ... Digby's History of the Law of Real Property [*A publication*] (DLA)
Dig Chiro Econ ... Digest of Chiropractic Economics [*A publication*]
Dig CLW ... Digest of Commercial Law of the World [*A publication*] (DLA)
DIGCOM .. Digital Computer (IEEE)
Dig Crim Proc ... Stephen's Digest of Criminal Procedure [*9th ed.*] [*1950*] [*A publication*] (DLA)
Dig Dis....... Digestive Diseases [*A publication*]
Dig Dis Sci ... Digestive Diseases and Sciences [*A publication*]
DIGEB....... Digestion [*A publication*]
DIGEBW... Digestion [*A publication*]
DIGEST ..... Diebold Generator for Statistical Tabulation (MUGU)
Digest......... Digest of Justinian [*A publication*] (DLA)
Digeste Soc ... Digeste Social [*A publication*]
Digest Mod Teach ... Digest of Modern Teaching [*A publication*] (APTA)
Dig Fla ...... Thompson's Digest of Laws [*Florida*] [*A publication*] (DLA)
DIGI .... Digital

DIGI .... DSC Communications Corp. [*Formerly, Digital Switch Corp.*] [*NASDAQ symbol*] (NQ)

DIGICOM ... Digital Communications

DIGIDOPS ... Digital Doppler System (MCD)

DIGINESS ... Digital Network Simulation System (MCD)

Dig Int Conf Med Biol Eng ... Digest. International Conference on Medical and Biological Engineering [*Sweden*] [*A publication*]

DIGIRAD ... Digital RADIAC

DIGIRALT ... Digital RADAR Altimeter (MUGU)

DIGISAT ... Digital Data Satellite Service [*Communications Satellite Corp.*]

DIGISMAC ... Digital Scene Matching Area Correlator [*Military*] (MCD)

DIGISPLAY ... Digitally Scanned Image Display (MCD)

DIGIT .... Digitalis [*Foxglove*] [*Pharmacy*] (ROG)

DIG-IT ...... Dramatic Interpretation of the Ghetto through Improvisational Theater [*Washington, DC*]

DIGITAC .. Digital Tactical Automatic Control (IEEE)

DIGITAL .. Digitalis [*Foxglove*] [*Pharmacy*] (ROG)

Digital DD ... Digital Design. Computer Compatible Directory and Technology Review [*A publication*]

Digital Dn .. Digital Design [*A publication*]

Digital Syst Ind Autom ... Digital Systems for Industrial Automation [*A publication*]

DIGITAR .. Digital Airborne Computer (IEEE)

Digit Comp Newsl ... Digital Computer Newsletter [*A publication*]

Digit Process ... Digital Processes [*A publication*]

DIGL .... Guiglo [*Ivory Coast*] [*ICAO location identifier*] (ICLI)

Dig Lit Dielec ... Digest of Literature on Dielectrics [*A publication*]

Dig Lit Dielect ... Digest of Literature on Dielectrics [*A publication*]

Dig LL ...... Digest Law of Libels [*A publication*]

DIGLYME ... Diethylene Glycol Dimethyl Ether [*Organic chemistry*]

DIGM .... Digimetrics, Inc. [*NASDAQ symbol*] (NQ)

Dig Metab Ruminant Proc Int Symp ... Digestion and Metabolism in the Ruminant. Proceedings of the International Symposium on Ruminant Physiology [*A publication*]

Digmo .... Dignissimo [*Most Dignified*] [*Portuguese*] [*Correspondence*]

DIGN .... Diagnon Corp. [*NASDAQ symbol*] (NQ)

DIGN .... Diagnostic (MSA)

DIGN .... Grand Bereby/Nero Mer [*Ivory Coast*] [*ICAO location identifier*] (ICLI)

Dig Neurol Psychiat ... Digest of Neurology and Psychiatry [*A publication*]

Dig Ophthal Otolaryng ... Digest of Ophthalmology and Otolaryngology [*A publication*]

Dig Ops JAG ... Digest of Opinions of Judge Advocate General, United States [*A publication*] (DLA)

Dig Pap IEEE Comput Soc Int Conf ... Digest of Papers. IEEE Computer Society International Conference [*A publication*]

Dig Pap Semicond Test Symp ... Digest of Papers. Semiconductor Test Symposium [*A publication*]

Dig Proem ... Digest of Justinian, Proem [*A publication*] (DLA)

DIGRD ...... Discipline and Grievances [*A publication*]

DIGRM ...... Digit/Record Mark [*Data processing*] (MDG)

DIGRMGM ... Digit/Record Mark Group/Mark [*Data processing*] (MDG)

DIGRO ...... Digital Readout [*Data processing*] (AAG)

Dig R Pr ..... Digby's Introduction to the History of Real Property [*A publication*] (DLA)

DIGS .... Delta [*or Digital*] Inertial Guidance System [*NASA*]

DIGS .... Deputy Inspector-General for Safety [*Air Force*]

DIGS .... Diggings [*i.e., Lodgings*] [*British*] (ROG)

DIGS .... Digital Inertial Guidance System

DI-GS .... United States Geological Survey, Reston, VA [*Library symbol*] [*Library of Congress*] (LCLS)

Dig Shares ... Digby's Sales and Transfer of Shares [*A publication*] (DLA)

Dig St .... English's Digest of the Statutes [*Arkansas*] [*A publication*] (DLA)

Dig Stat ICAO ... Digest of Statistics. International Civil Aviation Organization [*A publication*]

Dig Surg ..... Digestive Surgery [*A publication*]

DIGT .... Digitext, Inc. [*Thousand Oaks, CA*] [*NASDAQ symbol*] (NQ)

Dig Tech Pap IEEE Int Solid State Circuits Conf ... Digest of Technical Papers. IEEE International Solid State Circuits Conference [*A publication*]

Dig Tech Pap IEEE MTTS Int Microwave Symp ... Digest of Technical Papers. IEEE MTTS International Microwave Symposium [*A publication*]

DIGTL .... Digital (KSC)

Dig Treatm ... Digest of Treatment [*A publication*]

DIGTROPO ... [*Tactical*] Digital Troposcatter [*Radio terminal set*] (MCD)

Dig Vet ...... Digestum Vetus [*A publication*] (DSA)

DIH .... Deputy Inspector-General of Hospitals and Fleet [*Navy*] [*British*] (ROG)

DIH .... Diploma in Industrial Health [*British*]

DIH .... Discrete Input High (MCD)

DIHEA .... District Heating [*A publication*]

DIHEST ...... Direct-Induced High-Explosive Simulation Technique (MCD)

DIHIDH ...... Diagnostic Histopathology [*A publication*]

DIHL .... Declaration of Independence House and Library [*An association*] (EA)

DIHPPA ...... Diiodo(Hydroxyphenyl)pyruvic Acid [*Organic chemistry*]

DIHY .... Dihydrate

DII .... Decorator Industries, Incorporated [*AMEX symbol*] (SPSG)

DII .... Diode Ion Injector

DIIA .... Daily Industrial Index Analyzer [*News-a-tron Corp.*] [*Information service or system*] (CRD)

DIIC .... Daughters of Isabella, International Circle (EA)

DIIC .... Dielectrically Isolated Integration Circuit

DIII .... Abidjan [*Ivory Coast*] [*ICAO location identifier*] (ICLI)

DIIMD .... Diagnostic Imaging [*A publication*]

DIIMDY ...... Diagnostic Imaging [*A publication*]

DIIMEZ ...... Diagnostic Immunology [*A publication*]

DIIO .... District Industrial Incentive Office [*or Officer*] [*Navy*]

DIIP .... Defense Inactive Item Program (NG)

DIIP .... Defense Intelligence Interoperability Panel

DIIP .... Delinquency Investigation Inventory Profile [*IRS*]

DIIVS .... Defense Intransit Item Visibility System (MCD)

DiJ .... Dzis i Jutro [*A publication*]

DIK .... Dickinson [*North Dakota*] [*Airport symbol*] [*Obsolete*] (OAG)

DIK .... Dixon [*USSR*] [*Geomagnetic observatory code*]

Dik .... Double [*or Dual*] Income, Kids [*Lifestyle classification*]

DIK .... Drug Identification Kit

DIKNAA ..... Annual Report. National Veterinary Assay Laboratory [*A publication*]

DIKO .... Korhogo [*Ivory Coast*] [*ICAO location identifier*] (ICLI)

Dikorastushchie Introd Polezn Rast Bashk ... Dikorastushchie i Introdutsiruemye Poleznye Rasteniya v Bashkirii [*A publication*]

DIL .... Deliverable Items List (NASA)

Dil .... Dilantin [*Diphenylhydantoin*] [*Anticonvulsant*]

DIL .... Dilatus [*Dissolve*] [*Pharmacy*] (DHSM)

DIL .... Dili [*Indonesia*] [*Airport symbol*] (OAG)

DIL .... Dillard University, New Orleans, LA [*OCLC symbol*] (OCLC)

DIL .... Dillon (ROG)

DIL .... Dillon Ranch [*California*] [*Seismograph station code, US Geological Survey*] (SEIS)

Dil .... Dillon's United States Circuit Court Reports [*A publication*] (DLA)

DIL .... Dilloway (ROG)

DIL .... Diltiazem [*Pharmacology*]

DIL .... Dilute

DIL .... Director of International Logistics [*Military*]

DIL .... Disability Insurance Letter [*Social Security Administration*] (OICC)

DIL .... Discrete Input Low (MCD)

DIL .... Dispatch Inoperative List (MCD)

DIL .... Displayed Impact Line (MCD)

DIL .... Division of Insured Loans [*Office of Education*]

DIL .... Doctor of International Law

DIL .... Doppler Inertial LORAN

DIL .... Double Injection Luminescence

DIL .... Dual In-Line [*Electronic components*]

DILAG ...... Differential LASER Gyro (MCD)

DILAPD ..... Dilapidated (ROG)

DILAPIDN ... Dilapidation (ROG)

DILAT .... Dilation [*Medicine*]

Dil Cir Court Rep ... Dillon's United States Circuit Court Reports [*A publication*] (DLA)

DILD .... Diffuse Infiltrative Lung Disease [*Medicine*]

DILD .... Diluted

DILEP .... Digital Line Engineering Program [*Telecommunications*] (TEL)

DILET .... Dilettante (ROG)

DIL (Hack) ... Digest of International Law (Hackworth) [*A publication*] (DLA)

DILK .... Double [*or Dual*] Income, Lots of Kids [*Lifestyle classification*]

Dill .... Dillon's United States Circuit Court Reports [*A publication*] (DLA)

Dill Ir Jud A ... Dillon on the Irish Judicature Act [*A publication*] (DLA)

Dill Laws Eng & Am ... Dillon's Laws and Jurisprudence of England and America [*A publication*] (DLA)

Dill Mun Bonds ... Dillon on Municipal Bonds [*A publication*] (DLA)

Dill Mun Cor ... Dillon on Municipal Corporations [*A publication*] (DLA)

Dill Mun Corp ... Dillon on Municipal Corporations [*A publication*] (DLA)

Dillon .... Dillon's United States Circuit Court Reports [*A publication*] (DLA)

Dillon CC ... Dillon's United States Circuit Court Reports [*A publication*] (DLA)

Dillon Cir Court Rep ... Dillon's United States Circuit Court Reports [*A publication*] (DLA)

Dillon Mun Corp ... Dillon on Municipal Corporations [*A publication*] (DLA)

Dill Rem Caus ... Dillon on the Removal of Causes [*A publication*] (DLA)

Dill Rep ...... Dillon's United States Circuit Court Reports [*A publication*] (DLA)

DILMC ...... Defense International Logistics Management Course [*DoD*]

DIL (Moore) ... Digest of International Law (Moore) [*A publication*] (DLA)

DILN .... Dilution

DILO .... Digilog, Inc. [*NASDAQ symbol*] (NQ)

DILOT .... [*An*] Introduction to the Literature of the Old Testament [*S. R. Driver*] [*A publication*] (BJA)

DILP .... Dual In-Line Package [*Data processing*]

DilR .... Diliman Review [*A publication*]

DILS .... Doppler Inertial LORAN System

DILSUP .... Disposal List Ship Unit Portsmouth [*Navy*] [*British*]

DILUC...... Diluculo [At Daybreak] [Pharmacy]
DILUT....... Dilutus [Dilute] [Pharmacy]
DIL (White) ... Digest of International Law (Whiteman) [A publication]   (DLA)
DIM.......... Data Interpretation Module
DIM.......... Defense Information Memorandum   (NATG)
DIM.......... Dense Ionized Medium [Astrophysics]
DIM.......... Description, Installation, and Maintenance
DIM.......... Design Information Manual   (KSC)
DIM.......... Design Interface Meeting   (NASA)
DIM.......... Device Interface Module
DIM.......... Diamant. Maandelijks Tijdschrift voor de Studie van het Diamantbedrijf [A publication]
DIM.......... Digital Ignorant Mechanism [Pocket calculator facetiously described by T. R. Reid in his book, "The Chip"]
DIM.......... Digital Imaging Microscope
DIM.......... Digital Input Module [Data processing]
DIM.......... Digital Input Multiplexer   (CAAL)
DIM.......... Dimension   (KSC)
DIM.......... Dimidius [One-Half] [Pharmacy]
DIM.......... Diminished
DIM.......... Diminuendo [Getting Softer] [Music]
DIM.......... Diminutive
DIM.......... Dimissory [Ecclesiastical]   (ROG)
DIM.......... Dimitrovgrad [Bulgaria] [Seismograph station code, US Geological Survey]   (SEIS)
DIM.......... Dimmer
DIM.......... Diploma in Industrial Management   (ADA)
DIM.......... Direct Marketing [A publication]
DIM.......... Directory of International Mail [A publication]
DIM.......... District Industrial Manager [Navy]
DIM.......... District Inspector of Musketry [Military] [British]   (ROG)
DIM.......... Dorsal Intersegmental Muscles [Anatomy]
DIM.......... Drop-In-Maintenance   (MCD)
DIM.......... Dynamic Impedance Measurement
DIMA........ Direct Imaging Mass Analyzer
DIMACS... Center for Discrete Mathematics and Theoretical Computer Science [Rutgers University] [Research center]   (RCD)
DIMADC .. Diffusion in Metals and Alloys Data Center [National Institute of Standards and Technology]
DIMAP...... Digital/Modular Avionics Program [Aerospace]   (MCD)
DIMAPA... Dimethylaminopropylamine [Also, DMAPA] [Organic chemistry]
DIMATE... Depot-Installed Maintenance Automatic Test Equipment
DIMBOA .. Dihydroxymethoxybenzoxazinone [Organic chemistry]
DIMC....... Defense Inventory Management Course [DoD]
DIMCAL... Developments in Industrial Microbiology [A publication]
DIMDI ...... Deutsches Institut fuer Medizinische Dokumentation und Information [German Institute for Medical Documentation and Information] [Ministry for Youth, Family, and Health Affairs] [Database producer] [Information service or system]   (IID)
DIME .... Dialogue in Instrumental Music Education [A publication]
DIME .... Division of International Medical Education [Association of American Medical Colleges]
DIME .... Dual Independent Map Encoding [Transportation]
DIMEAR... DIA [Division de Investigaciones Agropecuarias] Medico [A publication]
Dim Econ Bourgogne ... Dimensions Economiques de la Bourgogne [A publication]
DIMEDONE ... Dimethylcyclohexanedione [Analytical chemistry]
DIMEDU .. Diabete et Metabolisme [A publication]
DIMEN ..... Dimension
Dimen NBS ... Dimensions. [US] National Bureau of Standards [A publication]
Dimens....... Dimensioni. Revista Abruzzese di Cultura e d'Arte [A publication]
Dimens Crit Care Nurs ... Dimensions of Critical Care Nursing [A publication]
Dimens Health Serv ... Dimensions in Health Service [A publication]
Dimension ... Canadian Dimension [A publication]
Dimensions NBS ... Dimensions. [US] National Bureau of Standards [A publication]
Dimens Oncol Nurs ... Dimensions in Oncology Nursing [A publication]
DIMEO ..... Defense Industrial and Management Engineering Office [DoD]
DIMES...... Defense Improved Management Engineering System [Military]
DIMES...... Defense Integrated Management Engineering System [Military]   (AFM)
DIMES...... Development of Improved Management Engineering Systems [Military]   (AABC)
DIMES...... Development of Integrated Management Engineering Systems [Military]
DIMES...... Digital Image Manipulation and Enhancement Systems
DIMIA...... Depository Institution Management Interlocks Act [1978]
DIMIA...... DIN [Deutsches Institut fuer Normung] Mitteilungen [A publication]
DIMID ...... Dimidius [One-Half] [Pharmacy]
DIMIS...... Depot Installation Management Information System [Army]
DIMM....... Defense Integrated Material Management   (MCD)
D Imm....... Deutsche Immobilien [A publication]
DIMN........ Man [Ivory Coast] [ICAO location identifier]   (ICLI)

DIMOA..... DM/Disease-a-Month [A publication]
DIMOAD ... Diabetes Insipidus, Diabetes Mellitus, Optic Atrophy, and Deafness [Medicine]
DIMOB .... Defense Intelligence Missile Order of Battle   (MCD)
DIMON..... Dimension   (ROG)
dIMP .... Deoxyinosine Monophosphate [Biochemistry]
DIMP .... Diisopropyl Methylphosphonate [Organic chemistry]
DIMPC..... Defense Item Management Coding Program [DoD]   (AFIT)
DIMPEA ... (Dimethoxyphenyl)ethylamine [Also, DMPE, DMPEA] [Psychomimetic compound]
DIMPLE ... Deuterium Moderated Pile Low Energy [Reactor]
DIMS......... Dimensions. Ontario Metis and Non-Status Indian Association [A publication]
DIMS......... Director, International Military Staff Memorandum [NATO]   (NATG)
DIMS......... Disorder of Initiating and Maintaining Sleep [Medicine]
DIMS......... Distributed Intelligence Microcomputer System
DIMSA...... Depot Integrated Maintenance Support Agreement [Air Force]
DIMSA...... Distribuidora de Impresos, Sociedad Anonima [Mexico]
DIMUS..... Digital Multibeam Steering
DIMUS..... Directional Multibeam Steering
DIN.......... Data Identification Number   (AFM)
DIN.......... Dedicated Intelligence Network   (MCD)
DIN.......... Defense Intelligence Notice   (MCD)
DIN.......... Deutsches Institut fuer Normung [German Institute for Standardization]   (IID)
DIN.......... Developments in Neurology [Elsevier Book Series] [A publication]
DIN.......... Devon Resource Investors [AMEX symbol]   (SPSG)
DIN.......... Dialogue North [A publication]
DIN.......... Digital Input [Data processing]   (KSC)
DIN.......... Dinar [Monetary unit] [Yugoslavia]
din .... Dinka [MARC language code] [Library of Congress]   (LCCP)
DIN.......... Dinner   (ADA)
DIN.......... Direct Injection Nebulization [For spectrometry]
DIN.......... Do It Now [Category of service call for maintenance or repair work] [Air Force]
DIN.......... Document Identification Number   (NG)
DINA........ Departamento de Inteligencia Nacional [National Intelligence Department] [Chilean secret police] [Superseded by CNI]
DINA........ Digital Network Analyzer
DINA........ Direct Internal Noise Amplification   (NG)
DINA........ Distributed Information Processing Network Architecture
DINA........ Japan Database Industry Association [Tokyo] [Information service or system]   (IID)
Dinamika Sploshn Sredy ... Dinamika Sploshnoj Sredy. Institut Gidrodinamiki Sibirskogo Otdeleniya Akademii Nauk SSSR [A publication]
DINB........ Dinner Bell Foods, Inc. [NASDAQ symbol]   (NQ)
DINC........ Dialogue North. Combined Edition [A publication]
Dinc......... Double [or Dual] Income, No Children [Lifestyle classification]
DInd.......... Doctor of Industrial Engineering
D Ind......... Doctor of Industry
DIN/DCSS ... Digital Network-Defense Special Security Communications System [National Security Agency]
DINE .... Dialogue North. Eastern Arctic Edition [A publication]
DINEE2..... Drug Interactions Newsletter [A publication]
DINF .... Do It Now Foundation   (EA)
DINFOS.... Defense Information School
DING........ Diversified Investment Group, Inc. [NASDAQ symbol]   (NQ)
D Ing .... Doctor Ingeniariae [Doctor of Engineering]
Dinglers Polytech J ... Dinglers Polytechnisches Journal [A publication]
Dink .... Double [or Dual] Income, No Kids [Lifestyle classification]
Dinky........ Double [or Dual] Income, No Kids Yet [Lifestyle classification]
DINM........ Developments in Nutrition and Metabolism [Elsevier Book Series] [A publication]
DIN Mitt ... DIN [Deutsches Institut fuer Normung] Mitteilungen [West Germany] [A publication]
DINN........ Dual Input Null Network
DINO........ Deputy Inspector of Naval Ordnance
DINO........ Dinosaur National Monument
DINOB ...... Defense Intelligence Naval Order of Battle   (MCD)
DINP .... Diisononyl Phthalate [Organic chemistry]
Din Prochn Mashin ... Dinamika i Prochnost Mashin [A publication]
DINS .... Directorate for Inspection Services [Assistant Secretary of Defense for Administration]   (CINC)
DINS .... Dormant Inertial Navigation System   (MCD)
Din Sploshn Sredy ... Dinamika Sploshnoj Sredy [A publication]
DIN Taschenb ... DIN [Deutsches Institut fuer Normung] Taschenbuch [West Germany] [A publication]
DINW........ Dialogue North. Western Arctic Edition [A publication]
DIO........... Data Input/Output [Data processing]
DIO........... Defence Arrangements for Indian Ocean [British] [World War II]
DIO........... Defense Intelligence Officer [Defense Intelligence Agency]   (MCD)
DIO........... Digital Input/Output [Data processing]
DIO........... Diocese
DIO........... Diode   (KSC)
DIO........... Diodes, Inc. [AMEX symbol]   (SPSG)
Dio .... Dionysius [Authority cited in pre-1607 legal work]   (DSA)

DIO........... Direct Input/Output [*Telecommunications*] (TEL)
DIO........... Director of Industrial Operations [*Military*] (AABC)
DI(O)......... Directorate of Intelligence (Operations) [*RAF*] [*British*]
DIO........... District Intelligence Officer
DIO........... Duty Intelligence Officer [*Air Force*]
DIOA........ Diisooctyl Adipate [*Organic chemistry*]
DIOA........ Dynamic Input-Output Analysis [*Economics*]
DIOB........ Digital Input/Output Buffer [*Data processing*]
DIOBS...... Defense Intelligence Order of Battle Systems (MCD)
DIOC........ Digital Input/Output Control [*Data processing*]
DIOC........ Dimethyloxacarbocyanine [*Organic chemistry*]
DIOC........ Diocese [*or Diocesean*]
DIOC........ Dissolved Inorganic Carbon [*Also, DIC*]
DIOC........ District Intelligence Operations Centers [*Vietnam*]
DIOC........ Ducati International Owners Club (EA)
Dio Cass.... Dio Cassius [*Third century AD*] [*Classical studies*] (OCD)
Dio Chrys... Dio Chrysostomus [*First century AD*] [*Classical studies*] (OCD)
DIOCN...... Diocesan (ROG)
Diod........... Diodorus Siculus [*First century BC*] [*Classical studies*] (OCD)
DIOD........ Odienne [*Ivory Coast*] [*ICAO location identifier*] (ICLI)
DIODE...... Digital Input/Output Display Equipment
Diod Sic.... Diodorus Siculus [*First century BC*] [*Classical studies*] (OCD)
DIOF........ Ouango Fitini [*Ivory Coast*] [*ICAO location identifier*] (ICLI)
DIOG........ Decylidenimino(octyl)guanidine [*Organic chemistry*]
Diog........... Diogene [*A publication*]
Diog Laert... Diogenes Laertius [*Third century AD*] [*Classical studies*] (OCD)
DIOH........ Due in from Overhaul (AFIT)
DIOI.......... Digital Input/Output Interface [*Data processing*] (KSC)
DIOLAMINE... Diethanolamine [*Also, DEA*] [*USAN*] [*Organic chemistry*]
Diomed Mari... Diomedes Mariconda [*Deceased, 1511*] [*Authority cited in pre-1607 legal work*] (DSA)
DION........ Dionics, Inc. [*NASDAQ symbol*] (NQ)
Dion........... Dioniso [*A publication*]
Dion Hal.... Dionysius Halicarnassensis [*First century BC*] [*Classical studies*] (OCD)
DIOP........ Defense Intelligence Objectives and Priorities (MCD)
DIOP........ Digital Input/Output Package [*Data processing*]
DIOPT........ Diisooctyl Phthalate [*Organic chemistry*]
DIOPT....... Diopter [*Also, D*] [*Optics*]
Diopt Optol Rev ... Dioptric and Optological Review [*A publication*]
Diopt Rev Br J Physiol Opt ... Dioptric Review and British Journal of Physiological Optics [*A publication*]
DIOS......... Diisooctyl Sebacate [*Organic chemistry*]
Dios........... Dionysius [*Authority cited in pre-1607 legal work*] (DSA)
DIOS......... Direct Memory Access Input/Output Subsystem (MCD)
DIOS......... Distributed Input/Output System
DIOX........ Dioxide [*Freight*]
DIP............ Data Input Processor [*Data processing*]
DIP............ Dead Item Purge [*Military*] (AFIT)
DIP............ Defamation, Identification, and Publication
DIP............ Defense Intelligence Plan (MCD)
DIP............ Design Improvement Program
DIP............ Design Internal Pressure [*Nuclear energy*] (NRCH)
DIP............ Designated Inspection Points (MCD)
DIP............ Desquamative Interstitial Pneumonia [*Medicine*]
DIP............ Destruction of Interstate Property
DIP............ Detailed Inspection Procedure (MCD)
DIP............ Developments in Psychiatry [*Elsevier Book Series*] [*A publication*]
DIP............ Diapaga [*Upper Volta*] [*Airport symbol*] (OAG)
DIP............ Digital Incremental Plotter
DIP............ Digital Instrumentation Programmer
DIP............ Diisopropylphenol [*Anesthetic*]
DIP............ Diphtheria [*Medicine*]
DIP............ Diploma
DIP............ Diplomat Resources [*Vancouver Stock Exchange symbol*]
Dip............. Diptera [*Entomology*]
DIP............ Dipyridyl [*Also, DIPY*] [*Organic chemistry*]
DIP............ Direct Insertion Probe
DIP............ Director of Industrial Planning [*War Office*] [*British*] [*World War II*]
DIP............ Directories in Print [*Formerly, DOD*] [*A publication*]
DIP............ Display Information Processor [*Air Force*]
DIP............ Display Input Processor (NASA)
DIP............ Display Interface Processing (MCD)
DIP............ Displayed Impact Point (MCD)
DIP............ Disposition of Inactive Parts List
DIP............ Dissolved Inorganic Phosphorus [*Chemistry*]
DIP............ Distal Interphalangeal [*Joint*] [*Anatomy*]
DIP............ Distributed Information Processing
DIP............ Dividend Investment Plan [*Stock purchase*] [*Investment term*]
DIP............ Division of Industrial Participation [*AEC*]
DIP............ Doctrine Improvement Program
DIP............ Document Image Processing [*Data processing*]
DIP............ Dokumentations- und Informationssystem fuer Parlamentsmaterial [*Documentation and Information System for Parliamentary Materials*] [*German Federal Diet Division of Scientific Documentation*] [*Information service or system*] (IID)

DIP............ Dormit in Pace [*Sleeps in Peace*] [*Latin*]
DiP............ Doswiadczenie i Przyclose [*Experience and the Future*] [*A publication*]
DIP............ Double In-Line Package [*Data processing*]
DIP............ Drip Infusion Pyelography [*Radiography*]
DIP............ Driver Improvement Program [*American Automobile Association*]
DIP............ Droit International Prive [*Private International Law*] [*French*] (DLA)
DIP............ Drug-Induced Pneumonitis [*Medicine*]
DIP............ Dual In-Line Package [*Data processing*]
DIP............ Dual In-Line Pin
DIP............ Dust Infall Predominant (AAG)
DIPA......... Diisopropanolamine [*Organic chemistry*]
DIPA......... Diisopropylamine [*Also, DIPAM*] [*Organic chemistry*]
DipA.......... Diploma in Analytical Chemistry
DipAcc....... Diploma in Accounting
Dip AD....... Diploma in Art and Design
DipAdmin(Nursing) ... Diploma in Administration (Nursing)
DipAdminSc ... Diploma in Administrative Science (ADA)
DipAdvAcc ... Diploma in Advanced Accounting (ADA)
DipAdvEd ... Diploma of Advanced Education (ADA)
DipAg......... Diploma in Agriculture (ADA)
DipAgEc.... Diploma in Agricultural Economics (ADA)
DipAgr....... Diploma in Agriculture
DipAgrChem ... Diploma in Agricultural Chemistry (ADA)
DipAgrEc.... Diploma in Agricultural Economics (ADA)
DipAgrEnt ... Diploma in Agricultural Entomology (ADA)
DipAgrExt ... Diploma in Agricultural Extension (ADA)
DipAgrExtn ... Diploma in Agricultural Extension (ADA)
DipAgrGen ... Diploma in Agricultural Genetics (ADA)
DipAgrMicro ... Diploma in Agricultural Microbiology (ADA)
DipAgrSc... Diploma in Agricultural Science (ADA)
DipALing.... Diploma in Applied Linguistics (ADA)
DIPAM...... Diisopropylamine [*Also, DIPA*] [*Organic chemistry*]
Dip AM...... Diploma in Applied Mechanics [*British*]
DipAnHus ... Diploma in Animal Husbandry (ADA)
DipAnth..... Diploma in Anthropology (ADA)
DipAnthrop ... Diploma in Anthropology (ADA)
DipAppMath ... Diploma in Applicable Mathematics
DipAppPsych ... Diploma in Applied Psychology (ADA)
DipAppSc .. Diploma of Applied Science (ADA)
DipAppSc(Nursing) ... Diploma in Applied Science (Nursing)
Dip Arch..... Diploma in Architecture [*British*]
DipArchComp ... Diploma in Architectural Computing
DipArchDes ... Diploma in Architectural Design (ADA)
DipArchivAdmin ... Diploma in Archives Administration (ADA)
DipArtEd.... Diploma in Art Education
DipArts...... Diploma in Arts (ADA)
DipAse(CofP) ... Graduate Level Specialist Diplomas in Advanced Study in Education, College of Preceptors [*British*] (DBQ)
DipAud...... Diploma in Audiology
DipAvMed ... Diploma in Avian Medicine
DipAvMed ... Diploma in Aviation Medicine (ADA)
DIPB......... Diisopropylbenzene [*Organic chemistry*]
Dip Bact..... Diploma in Bacteriology [*British*]
DipBdgSc... Diploma in Building Science
DipBdgSc(ECD) ... Diploma in Building Science (Energy-Conservative Design) (ADA)
DipBiom..... Diploma in Biometry (ADA)
DipBM....... Diploma in Business Management (ADA)
DipBMS..... Diploma in Basic Medical Sciences (ADA)
DipBuildSc ... Diploma of Building Science
DipBus....... Diploma in Business (ADA)
DipBusAdmin ... Diploma in Business Administration
DipBusMangt ... Diploma in Business Management (ADA)
DipBusStud ... Diploma in Business Studies (ADA)
DipBusStudies ... Diploma in Business Studies (ADA)
DIPC......... Digital Products Corporation [*NASDAQ symbol*] (NQ)
DipCAM.... Diploma of the Communication Advertising and Marketing Education Foundation [*British*] (DBQ)
DipCard..... Diploma in Cardiology (ADA)
DipCD........ Diploma in Civic Design [*British*]
DipCE........ Diploma of Civil Engineering (ADA)
DipCH....... Diploma in Clinical Hypnotherapy (ADA)
Dip Clin Path ... Diploma in Clinical Pathology [*British*]
DipClinSc .. Diploma in Clinical Science (ADA)
DipCoalGeol ... Diploma in Coal Geology
DipCom...... Diploma of Commerce (ADA)
DipCom & Con ... Diploma in Computers and Control
DipComm... Diploma in Commerce (ADA)
DipCommChildHealth ... Diploma in Community Child Health
DipCommSc ... Diploma in Community Science
DipComp.... Diploma in Computer Studies
DipCompSc ... Diploma in Computer Science (ADA)
DipCompSt ... Diploma in Computer Studies
DipContEd ... Diploma in Continuing Education (ADA)
Dip Cor...... Diplomatic Correspondence of the United States [*A publication*] (DLA)
DipCOT..... Diploma of the College of Occupational Therapists [*British*] (DBQ)

DipCrim.....	Diploma in Criminology (ADA)
DipDHus ...	Diploma in Dairy Husbandry (ADA)
DipDiet......	Diploma in Dietetics (ADA)
DipDiv	Diploma in Divinity
DIPDOP......	Disc and Drum Input/Output Routines [*Honeywell, Inc.*]
DIPE............	Diisopropyl Ether [*Organic chemistry*]
DIPEC.......	Defense Industrial Plant Equipment Center [*DoD*] (AFM)
DIPEC.......	Defense Industrial Production Equipment Center
DipEc.........	Diploma in Economics (ADA)
Dip Econ	Diploma of Economics (ADA)
DipEconGeog ...	Diploma of Economic Geography (ADA)
DipEconStats ...	Diploma in Economic Statistics (ADA)
DipEcStud ...	Diploma in Economic Studies
DIPED.......	Diisopropylethanediol [*Organic chemistry*]
DipEd.........	Diploma of Education [*British*] (EY)
DipEdAdmin ...	Diploma in Educational Administration (ADA)
DipEdPsych ...	Diploma in Educational Psychology (ADA)
DipEdSt.......	Diploma in Education Studies
DipEEng......	Diploma of Electrical Engineering (ADA)
DIPEF	Defense Industrial Plant Equipment Facility [*DoD*]
DipEF	Diploma in Executive Finance [*British*] (DBQ)
DipEH	Diploma in Environmental Health [*British*] (DBQ)
DipElecEng ...	Diploma of Electrical Engineering (ADA)
DipEMA....	Diploma in Executive Finance for Non-Accountants [*British*] (DBQ)
Dip Eng......	Diploma in Engineering [*British*]
DipEngGeol ...	Diploma in Engineering Geology
DipEngMgt ...	Diploma in Engineering Management (ADA)
DipEnvIA ..	Diploma in Environmental Impact Assessment
DipEnvironEng ...	Diploma in Environmental Engineering
DipEnvironStud ...	Diploma in Environmental Studies (ADA)
DipEnvSc..	Diploma in Environmental Science
DipEnvSt....	Diploma in Environmental Studies
DipEnvStud ...	Diploma in Environmental Studies
DipFA	Diploma in Fine Arts (ADA)
DipFD........	Diploma in Funeral Directing, National Association of Funeral Directors [*British*] (DBQ)
DipFDA	Diploma in Food and Drug Analysis (ADA)
DipFHS	Diploma in Family Historical Studies [*Australia*]
DipFIA	Diploma in Furniture and Interior Architecture
DipFinMangt ...	Diploma in Financial Management (ADA)
DipFor	Diploma of Forestry (ADA)
DipFrenchStud ...	Diploma in French Studies
DIPG	Port Gauthier [*Ivory Coast*] [*ICAO location identifier*] (ICLI)
DipGeog.....	Diploma in Geography
DipGeotEng ...	Diploma in Geotechnical Engineering
DipGerm....	Diploma in German
DipGraphicDes ...	Diploma of Graphic Design
DipGT........	Diploma in Glass Technology (ADA)
DIPH	Diphtheria [*Medicine*]
DIPH	Diphthong [*Linguistics*]
DipHA	Diploma in Health Administration (ADA)
DipHE	Diploma of Higher Education
DipHE	Diploma in Highway Engineering (ADA)
DipHealthSc ...	Diploma in Health Science
DipHigherEd ...	Diploma in Higher Education (ADA)
DipHortSc ...	Diploma in Horticultural Science (ADA)
DipHospAdmin ...	Diploma in Hospital Administration (ADA)
DipHPharm ...	Diploma in Hospital Pharmacy (ADA)
DipHSc	Diploma in Home Science (ADA)
DIPH/TET ...	Diphtheria/Tetanus [*Immunology*]
DIPH TOX ...	Diphtheria Toxoid [*Immunology*]
DIPH TOX AP ...	Diphtheria Toxoid, Alum Precipitated [*Immunology*]
DipHum......	Diploma in Humanities
DIPI...........	Diimidazolinophenylindole [*Biochemistry*]
DipIB(Scot) ...	Diplomate of the Institute of Bankers in Scotland [*British*] (DBQ)
DipIllumDes ...	Diploma in Illumination Design
DipIM-ArchivAd ...	Diploma in Information Management - Archives Administration (ADA)
DipIM-Lib ...	Diploma in Information Management - Librarianship (ADA)
DipImm......	Diploma in Immunology
Dip Ind Chem ...	Diploma in Industrial Chemistry [*British*]
DipInfmProcessing ...	Diploma in Information Processing (ADA)
DipIntAffs ...	Diploma in International Affairs (ADA)
DipIntDes..	Diploma of Interior Design (ADA)
DipIPharm ...	Diploma in Industrial Pharmacy (ADA)
DipIPSA	Diploma of the Institute of Private Secretaries (Australia) (ADA)
DipJ	Diploma of Journalism (ADA)
DipJ	Diploma of Jurisprudence
DIPJ	Distal Interphalangeal Joint [*Anatomy*]
DipJewDes ...	Diploma of Jewellery Design
DipJour......	Diploma in Journalism (ADA)
DipJourn....	Diploma in Journalism (ADA)
DipJur........	Diploma in Jurisprudence
DipJuris.....	Diploma of Jurisprudence (ADA)
DIPL...........	Diploma (EY)
DipL..........	Diploma of Law
dipl	Diplomat [*or Diplomacy*]
DIPL..........	Diplomatic (ADA)

DIPL..........	Display Initial Program Load (MCD)
DipLA..........	Diploma in Landscape Architecture
DipLabAnimSc ...	Diploma in Laboratory Animal Science
DipLabRelations and the Law ...	Diploma in Labour Relations and the Law
DipL(BAB) ...	Diploma of Law (Barristers' Admission Board)
Dipl Chem ...	Diploma in Chemistry [*British*]
DipLD........	Diploma of Landscape Design (ADA)
Dipl Dan	Diplomattirium Danicum [*A publication*]
DipLE.........	Diploma in Land Economy
DipLegStud ...	Diploma in Legal Studies
Dipl Eng.....	Diploma in Engineering [*British*]
Dipl Hist ...	Diplomatic History [*A publication*]
DipLib.........	Diploma in Librarianship (ADA)
DipLibStud ...	Diploma in Library Studies (ADA)
Dipl Kaufm ...	Diploma in Commerce [*German*]
Dipl Kfm ...	Diploma in Commerce [*German*]
Dipl Math ...	Diploma in Mathematics [*British*]
DIPLOM...	Diploma (ROG)
Dipl PA	Diploma in Public Administration [*British*]
Dipl Phys....	Diploma in Physics [*British*]
DipLS	Diploma of Legal Studies
DipL(SAB) ...	Diploma of Law (Solicitors' Admission Board)
DipLSc........	Diploma in Library Science (ADA)
DIPLXR	Diplexer [*Electronics*]
DipM	Diploma in Marketing, Institute of Marketing [*British*] (DBQ)
DipMatEng ...	Diploma in Materials Engineering
DipMathStud ...	Diploma in Mathematical Studies
DipMechE ...	Diploma of Mechanical Engineering (ADA)
DipMedSurg ...	Diploma in Medical Surgery (ADA)
DipMFOS ...	Diploma in Maxial, Facial, and Oral Surgery (ADA)
DipMicro...	Diploma in Microbiology
Dip Microbiol ...	Diploma in Microbiology [*British*]
DipMigTeach ...	Diploma in Migrant Teaching
DipMinSc..	Diploma in Mineral Science
DipMT.......	Diploma of Medical Technology (ADA)
DipMus.......	Diploma in Music (ADA)
DipMusComp ...	Diploma in Musical Composition
Dip (Mus Ed) RSAM ...	Diploma in Musical Education, Royal Scottish Academy of Music and Drama
DipMuseumStud ...	Diploma in Museum Studies
Dip of N	Diploma of Nursing (ADA)
DipNA & AC ...	Diploma in Numerical Analysis and Automatic Computing (ADA)
DipNAdmin ...	Diploma of Nursing Administration (ADA)
DipNatRes ...	Diploma in Natural Resources (ADA)
DipND	Diploma in Nutrition and Dietetics (ADA)
DipNEd.......	Diploma in Nursery School Education (ADA)
DipNucEng ...	Diploma in Nuclear Engineering (ADA)
DipNucSc...	Diploma in Nuclear Science (ADA)
DipNut & Diet ...	Diploma in Nutrition and Dietetics
DipNutrDiet ...	Diploma in Nutrition and Dietetics
DIPOA	Diesel Power [*A publication*]
DipOccHyg ...	Diploma of Professional Competence in Comprehensive Ocupational Hygiene [*British*] (DBQ)
DipOccThy ...	Diploma in Occupational Therapy (ADA)
Dip O & G ...	Diploma in Obstetrics and Gynaecology (ADA)
DipOL........	Diploma in Oriental Learning (ADA)
DIPOLES ...	Defense Intelligence Photoreconnaissance On-Line Exploitation System (MCD)
DipOpsRes ...	Diploma in Operations Research
DipOrth	Diploma in Orthodontics (ADA)
DipOT........	Diploma in Occupational Therapy
DIPP..........	Dairy Indemnity Payment Program [*Department of Agriculture*]
DIPP..........	Defence Industry Productivity Program [*Canada*]
DIPP..........	Defense Industrial Procurement Program [*Canada*]
DIPP..........	Defense Intelligence Projection for Planning (MCD)
DIPP.......	Diisopropyl Percarbonate [*Organic chemistry*]
DIPPA.......	Digital Parallel Processing Array
DipPA.......	Diploma of Practitioners in Advertising [*British*]
DipPaed......	Diploma in Paediatrics
Dip PE	Diploma in Physical Education [*British*]
DipPetResEng ...	Diploma in Petroleum and Reservoir Engineering
DipPharm ...	Diploma in Pharmacy (ADA)
DipPharmMed ...	Diploma in Pharmaceutical Medicine [*British*] (DBQ)
DipPhot	Diploma in Photogrammetry (ADA)
DipPhty......	Diploma in Physiotherapy (ADA)
DipPHus....	Diploma in Poultry Husbandry (ADA)
DipPhysEd ...	Diploma in Physical Education (ADA)
DipPhysio..	Diploma in Physiotherapy (ADA)
DipPlPath ...	Diploma in Plant Pathology (ADA)
DipPowEng ...	Diploma in Power Engineering
DIPPR.......	Design Institute for Physical Property Data [*AIChE*]
DipPrehistArch ...	Diploma of Prehistoric Archaeology (ADA)
DipProcessSystemsEng ...	Diploma in Process Systems Engineering
DipPSA......	Diploma in Public and Social Administration
Dip Psych ...	Diploma in Psychology [*British*]
DipPsyMed ...	Diploma in Psychological Medicine (ADA)
DipPubAd ...	Diploma in Public Administration (ADA)
DipPubAdmin ...	Diploma in Public Administration (ADA)
DipPubPol ...	Diploma in Public Policy

DipQS........ Diploma in Quantity Surveying (ADA)
DIPR......... Departmental Industrial Plant Reserve [*DoD*] (AFIT)
DIPR......... Detailed In-Process Review (MCD)
DIPR......... Direct Interaction with Product Repulsion [*Chemical kinetics*]
DIPRA...... Ductile Iron Pipe Research Association (EA)
DipRADA ... Diploma of Royal Academy of Dramatic Art [*British*] (EY)
DipRAM.... Diploma of the Royal Academy of Music [*British*] (DBQ)
DipRCM.... Diploma of the Royal College of Music [*British*] (DBQ)
DIPRDG.... Discourse Processes [*A publication*]
DipRE........ Diploma in Religious Education
DipResGeol ... Diploma in Resource Geology
DipRMS .... Diploma of the Royal Microscopical Society [*British*] (DBQ)
DIPROG.... Request Diagnosis, Prognosis, Present Condition
         [*Army*] (AABC)
DipRTP .... Diploma in Regional and Town Planning (ADA)
DipRurAcc ... Diploma in Rural Accounting (ADA)
DIPS......... Defection, Intercept-Passive Submarine (MCD)
DIPS......... Defense Intelligence Production Schedule (MCD)
DIPS......... Development Information Processing System
DIPS......... Diagnostic Inventory of Personality and Symptoms [*Personality*
         development test] [*Psychology*]
DIPS......... Digital Imagery Processing System (MCD)
DIPS......... Dynamic Isotope Power System
DipScAg ... Diploma in Science in Agriculture (ADA)
DIPSCAM ... Diploma Scam [*FBI investigation of mail-order colleges*]
DipSchoolAdmin ... Diploma in School Administration
DipSecEd ... Diploma in Secondary Education (ADA)
DipSoc ...... Diploma in Sociology (ADA)
Dip Soc Ad ... Diploma in Social Administration [*British*]
DipSocAdmin ... Diploma of Social Administration (ADA)
Dip Soc Med ... Diploma in Social Medicine [*British*]
DipSocSc ... Diploma in Social Science
DipSocSci .. Diploma of Social Science (ADA)
DipSocStud ... Diploma in Social Studies (ADA)
Dip Soc Studies ... Diploma in Social Studies [*British*]
DipSoilSc... Diploma in Soil Science
DipSP .... Diploma in Sound Preservation
DipS & PA ... Diploma in Social and Public Administration (ADA)
DipSpThy .. Diploma in Speech Therapy (ADA)
DipSS......... Diploma in Social Studies (ADA)
DipStructEng ... Diploma in Structural Engineering
DipStructFoundEng ... Diploma in Structural and Foundation Engineering
DipSurvSc ... Diploma in Surveying Science (ADA)
DipSW .... Diploma in Social Work (ADA)
DipT .... Diploma in Teaching (ADA)
DIPT......... Diplomate
DIPTAC .... DIFAR [*Directional Frequency Analyzing and Recording*]
         Pointing Tactic [*Military*] (CAAL)
DipTchg..... Diploma of Teaching
DipTchrLib .. Diploma in Teacher Librarianship (ADA)
DipT & CP ... Diploma of Town and Country Planning (ADA)
DipTCP .... Diploma in Town and Country Planning (ADA)
DipTE........ Diploma in Transportation Engineering [*British*] (DBQ)
DipTeach ... Diploma in Teaching
DipTeach(Nursing) ... Diploma in Teaching (Nursing)
DipTeach(Primary) ... Diploma in Teaching (Primary)
Dip Tech .... Diploma in Technology [*British*]
DipTech(Arch) ... Diploma in Technology (Architecture) (ADA)
DipTech(Buil) ... Diploma in Technology (Building) (ADA)
DipTech(Comm) ... Diploma in Technology (Commerce) (ADA)
Dip Tech (Eng) ... Diploma of Technology (Engineering) [*British*]
DipTech(InfProc) ... Diploma in Technology (Information
         Processing) (ADA)
DipTech(Mgt) ... Diploma in Technology (Management) (ADA)
DipTech(PubAdm) ... Diploma in Technology (Public
         Administration) (ADA)
DipTech(PubRel) ... Diploma in Technology (Public Relations) (ADA)
DipTech(Sci) ... Diploma in Technology (Science) (ADA)
DipTEFL ... Diploma in Teaching of English as a Foreign Language (ADA)
DipTelecomm ... Diploma in Telecommunications
DipTEM ..... Diploma in Teaching English to the Migrant (ADA)
DipTertiary Ed ... Diploma in Tertiary Education (ADA)
DipTESL .... Diploma of Teaching English as a Second Language (ADA)
DipTexInd ... Diploma of Textile Industry
DipTG........ Diploma of the Teachers Guild (ADA)
DipTh .... Diploma in Theology (ADA)
Dip Theol... Diploma of Theology (ADA)
DipTLiB .... Diploma in Teachers Librarianship (ADA)
DipTM....... Diploma in Training Management, the Institute of Training and
         Development [*British*] (DBQ)
DipTP .... Diploma of Teacher of Physiotherapy
DipTP .... Diploma in Town Planning [*British*]
DipTPT...... Diploma in Theory and Practice of Teaching [*British*]
DipTropAgron ... Diploma in Tropical Agronomy (ADA)
DipTRP ...... Diploma in Town and Regional Planning (ADA)
DipUrbDes(Arch) ... Diploma in Urban Design
DipUSP ..... Diploma in Urban and Social Planning
DipVA........ Diploma of Visual Arts
Dip Ven ..... Diploma in Venereology [*British*]
DipVetAn... Diploma in Veterinary Anaesthesia
DipVetClinStud ... Diploma in Veterinary Clinical Studies

DipVetPath ... Diploma in Veterinary Pathology (ADA)
DipVetRad ... Diploma in Veterinary Radiology
DipVFM .... Diploma in Valuation and Farm Management (ADA)
DipWildlifeMed & Hus ... Diploma in Wildlife Medicine and Husbandry
DIPX......... Diplex [*Electronics*] (MSA)
DIPY......... Dipyridyl [*Also, DIP*] [*Organic chemistry*]
DIQ........... Deviation Intelligence Quotient [*Education*]
DIQ........... Due-In Quantity
DIQ........... Las Vegas, NV [*Location identifier*] [*FAA*] (FAAL)
DIQD......... Disk-Insulated Quad [*Telecommunications*] (TEL)
DIR........... Data Input Register [*Data processing*]
DIR........... Data Item Requirement
DIR........... Defense Industrial Reserve [*DoD*]
DIR........... Defense Intelligence Report (MCD)
DIR........... Depot Inspection and Repair
DIR........... Development-Inhibitor-Releasing [*Photography*]
DIR........... Diamond Ranch [*California*] [*Seismograph station code, US*
         Geological Survey] (SEIS)
DIR........... Digital Instrumentation RADAR
DIR........... Dire Dawa [*Ethiopia*] [*Airport symbol*] (OAG)
DIR........... Direct
DIR........... Directive
DIR........... Director [*A publication*]
DIR........... Director [*or Directorate*] (AFM)
DI(R)......... Directorate of Intelligence (Research) [*RAF*] [*British*]
DIR........... Directory
DIR........... Dirigo [*I Guide*] [*Latin*] (ROG)
DIR........... Disassembly Inspection Report
DIR........... Doctrine of Incremental Reduction
DIR........... Document Information Record (KSC)
D & IR........ Duluth & Iron Range Railway Co.
DIR........... Florida Music Director [*A publication*]
DIRAM....... Digital Range Machine
Dir Ancient Monum Hist Bldgs Occas Pap ... Directorate of Ancient
         Monuments and Historic Buildings. Occasional Papers
         [*England*] [*A publication*]
Dirasat Nat Sci (Amman) ... Dirasat Natural Sciences (Amman) [*A*
         publication]
Dir Aut...... Diritti d'Autore [*A publication*]
Dir Aut...... Diritto Automobilistico [*A publication*]
DIRBE....... Diffuse Infrared Background Experiment [*Spectral*
         instrumentation]
Dir Boards ... Directors and Boards [*A publication*]
DIRBY....... When Directed By
DIRC .... Defense Intelligence Relay Center (MCD)
DIRC .... Defense Investigative Review Council
DIRC .... Dithered Infrared Configuration
DIRCARIBDOCKS ... Caribbean Division Naval Facilities Engineering
         Command
DIRCHESDOCKS ... Chesapeake Division Naval Facilities Engineering
         Command
Dir Cinem .. Diritto Cinematografico [*A publication*]
DIRCOL..... Direction Cosine Linkage
Dir Crim..... Diritto Criminale e Criminologia [*A publication*]
Dir fr Cu..... Direct from Cuba [*A publication*]
DIRD .... Director, International Research and Development [*Military*]
         [*Canada*]
DIRDET.... When Directed, Detach Duty Indicated
D Ir E......... Doctor of Irrigation Engineering
DIREC....... Direct Instant Response Electronic Composition
Direc......... Direction [*A publication*]
DIREC...... Director (ROG)
Dir Eccl...... Diritto Ecclesiastico [*A publication*]
Dir Ec Nucl ... Diritto ed Economia Nucleare [*A publication*]
DIR/ECT... Directory Project [*Bell Laboratories*]
Direct Brd .. Directors and Boards [*A publication*]
Direct Curr ... Direct Current [*A publication*]
Direct Curr & Power Electron ... Direct Current and Power Electronics [*A*
         publication]
Direct Inf Nuklearmed ... Direct Information. Nuklearmedizin [*A*
         publication]
Direct Inf Strahlenschutz ... Direct Information. Strahlenschutz [*A*
         publication]
Direct Mark ... Direct Marketing [*A publication*]
Direct Midrex ... Direct from Midrex [*A publication*]
Direct Mkt ... Magazine of Direct Marketing [*A publication*]
Directors and Bds ... Directors and Boards [*A publication*]
Direito Nucl ... Direito Nuclear [*A publication*]
D Ir Eng..... Doctor of Irrigation Engineering
DIREP....... Difficulty Report (AFIT)
DIREURDOCKS ... European Division Naval Facilities Engineering
         Command
DIRF......... Delinquent Investigation Research File [*IRS*]
DIRFLDSUPPACT ... Director, Field Support Activity
DIRFM...... Director Field Maintenance [*Army*] (AABC)
Dir Gen Agric (Peru) Divulg Inf ... Direccion General de Agricultura (Peru).
         Divulgaciones e Informaciones [*A publication*]
Dir Gen Bol ... Direccion General de Archivos y Bibliotecas. Boletin [*A*
         publication]
Dir Gen Inventario Nac For Publ ... Direccion General del Inventario
         Nacional Forestal. Publicacion [*A publication*]

Dir Gestion ... Direction et Gestion [*A publication*]

Dir et Gestion ... Direction et Gestion des Entreprises [*A publication*]

Dir Gestion Entr ... Direction et Gestion des Entreprises [*A publication*]

Dir e Giur ... Diritto e Giurisprudenza [*A publication*]

DIRGULFDOCKS ... Gulf Division Naval Facilities Engineering Command

DIRH .... Directions in Health, Physical Education, and Recreation. Monograph Series [*A publication*]

DIRH .... Dirham [*Monetary unit*] [*Iraq*]

DIRID .... Directional Infrared Intrusion Detector (MCD)

DIRINCO ... Direccion de Industria y Comercio [*Industry and Trade Directorate*] [*Chilean*]

Dir Indiana Crop Impr Ass Seed Certif Serv ... Directory. Indiana Crop Improvement Association. Seed Certification Service [*A publication*]

Dir Int .... Diritto Internazionale. Rivista Trimestrale di Dottrina e Documentazione [*A publication*]

Diritto Lav ... Diritto del Lavoro [*A publication*]

Dirl .... Dirleton's Decisions, Court of Sessions [*Scotland*] [*A publication*] (DLA)

DIRLANTDOCKS ... Director, Atlantic Division, Bureau of Yards and Docks [*Obsolete*]

DIRLAUTH ... Direct Liaison Authorized [*Military*] (NVT)

Dirl D .... Dirleton's Doubts and Questions in the Law [*A publication*] (DLA)

Dirl Dec ..... Dirleton's Decisions, Court of Sessions [*Scotland*] [*A publication*] (DLA)

DIRLINE .. Directory of Information Sources Online [*National Library of Medicine*] [*Database*]

Dir LR .... Directors Law Reporter [*A publication*] (APTA)

DIRM .... Defense Intelligence Requirement Manual (AFM)

Dir Mar ...... Diritto Marittimo [*A publication*] (DLA)

Dir Maritt ... Diritto Marittimo [*A publication*]

DIRMIDWESTDOCKS ... Midwest Division Naval Facilities Engineering Command

Dir Nac Propiedad Ind (Argent) ... Direccion Nacional de la Propiedad Industrial (Argentina) [*A publication*]

DIRNAVHIST ... Director of Naval History

DIRNAVPUBPRINTSERV ... Director, Navy Publication and Printing Service

DIRNSA .... Director, National Security Agency [*Pronounced "dern-za"*]

DIRO .... Deionization Reverse Osmosis [*Water treatment*]

DIRO .... District Industrial Relations Officer [*Navy*]

DIROCD ..... Director, Office of Civil Defense (AABC)

DIRON .... Direction

Dir Online Databases ... Directory of Online Databases [*United States*] [*A publication*]

DIROR ...... Director (ROG)

DIRPA .... Director of Personnel and Administration [*Army*] (AABC)

DIRPACALDOCKS ... Director, Pacific and Alaskan Divisions, Bureau of Yards and Docks [*Obsolete*]

DIRPACDOCKS ... Director, Pacific Division, Bureau of Yards and Docks [*Obsolete*]

Dir Prat Ass ... Diritto e Pratica dell'Assicurazione [*A publication*]

Dir e Prat Trib ... Diritto e Pratica Tributaria [*A publication*]

Dir Prat Trib ... Diritto e Pratica Tributaria [*A publication*]

DIRPRO .... When Directed Proceed

DIR PROP ... Directione Propria [*With Proper Direction*] [*Pharmacy*]

Dir Pubbl Reg Sicil ... Diritto Pubblico della Regione Siciliana [*A publication*]

Dir Publ Proc ... Directory of Published Proceedings [*United States*] [*A publication*]

Dir Publ Proc SEMT ... Directory of Published Proceedings. Series SEMT. Science, Engineering, Medicine, and Technology [*A publication*]

DIRS .... Departmental Industrial Reserve System

Dir San Mod ... Diritto Sanitario Moderno [*A publication*]

Dir Sc Int ... Diritto negli Scambi Internazionali [*A publication*] (DLA)

Dir Scol ...... Diritto Scolastico [*A publication*]

DIRSOEASTDOCKS ... Southeast Division Naval Facilities Engineering Command

DIRSOWESTDOCKS ... Southwest Division Naval Facilities Engineering Command

DIRSP/PROJMGRFBM ... Director, Special Projects/Project Manager, Fleet Ballistic Missile (MCD)

DIRSSP .... Director, Strategic Systems Project Office [*Navy*]

DIRT .... Defense Infrared Test (MCD)

DIRT .... Deposit Interest Retention Tax [*Ireland*]

DIRT .... Director's Instant Reversible Talkback [*Device enabling contact between director in control room and crew in studio*]

DIRT .... Dust Infrared Test (MCD)

DIRTY .... Darned Insulting, Rotten, Terrible Yarns [*Book title*]

Dir Unpubl Exp Ment Meas ... Directory of Unpublished Experimental Mental Measures [*A publication*]

DIRVIR ..... Directory Verification Processor [*Data processing*]

DIRW .... Director of Women Marines

DIRWESTDOCKS ... Western Division Naval Facilities Engineering Command

DIRWSEG ... Director, Weapons Systems Evaluation Group (CINC)

DIS .... Daily Issue Store [*British military*] (DMA)

DIS .... Data Input System [*Data processing*]

DIS .... Data Inspection Station

DIS .... Database Information System

DIS .... Decision Information Services Ltd. [*Information service or system*] (IID)

DIS .... Defence Information Sciences [*Australia*]

DIS .... Defence Intelligence Staff [*British*]

DIS .... Defense Institute of Security Assistance Management, Wright-Patterson AFB, OH [*OCLC symbol*] (OCLC)

DIS .... Defense Intelligence School

DIS .... Defense Intelligence Staff (MCD)

DIS .... Defense Intelligence Summary (MCD)

DIS .... Defense Investigative Service [*DoD*]

DIS .... Department of Defense Index of Specifications and Standards

DIS .... Department of Internal Security

DIS .... Design Improvement Study

DIS .... Design Integration Subsystem

DIS .... Development Information System [*United Nations*] [*Information service or system*] (IID)

DiS .... Diagnostic Interview Schedule [*Psychology*]

DiS .... Dickens Studies [*A publication*]

DIS .... Digital Identification Signal [*Data processing*]

DIS .... Digital Instrumentation Subsystem

DIS .... Digital Integration System (IEEE)

DIS .... Diploma in Industrial Studies, Loughborough University of Technology [*British*] (DBQ)

DIS .... Direct Ignition System [*Automotive engineering*]

DIS .... Directorate of Installation Services (MCD)

DI(S) .... Directorate of Intelligence (Security) [*RAF*] [*British*]

DIS .... Directory Information Service [*A publication*]

DIS .... Disability

DIS .... Disagree (NASA)

DIS .... Discharge

DIS .... Disciple

DIS .... Discipline

DIS .... Disconnect (DEN)

DIS .... Discontinued

DIS .... Discount

DIS .... Discrete (AAG)

DIS .... Discutient [*Dissolving*] [*Pharmacy*] (ROG)

DIS .... Disease

DIS .... Disintegration

DIS .... Dislocations in Solids [*Elsevier Book Series*] [*A publication*]

DIS .... [*The*] Disney [*Walt*] Co. [*NYSE symbol*] [*Wall Street slang name: "Mickey Mouse"*] (SPSG)

Dis .... Disney's Ohio Superior Court Reports [*A publication*] (DLA)

DIS .... Disorderly [*FBI standardized term*]

DIS .... Dispensed (ADA)

DIS .... Display (KSC)

DIS .... Disrotatory [*Chemistry*]

Dis .... Dissent [*A publication*]

DIS .... Dissertation Inquiry Service [*Xerox Corp.*]

Dis .... Dissolved

DIS .... Distance (MUGU)

DIS .... Distanced [*Horse racing*]

DIS .... Distant

Dis .... Distinctio [*Decretum Gratiani*] [*A publication*] (DSA)

DIS .... Distribute (ROG)

DIS .... Distributed Information System [*Data processing*]

DIS .... Distributor Gasket [*Automotive engineering*]

DIS .... District

DIS .... Distrifood. Weekblad voor de Betaillist en Groothandel in Food en Nonfood [*A publication*]

DIS .... Division of Information Services [*Council of State Governments*] [*Information service or system*] (EISS)

DIS .... Division of Information Services [*Council for Scientific and Industrial Research*] [*South Africa*] (EISS)

DIS .... Documentation Index System (MCD)

DIS .... Doppler Imaging System [*Physics*]

DIS .... Doppler Inertial System (AAG)

DIS .... Draft International Standard [*International Standards Organization*]

DIS .... Drilling Information Services [*Adams Engineering, Inc.*] [*Information service or system*] (IID)

DIS .... Drosophila Information Service [*Genetics*]

DIS .... Drug Information Service [*Memorial Medical Center of Long Beach*] [*Information service or system*] (IID)

DIS .... Drug Information Services [*University of Minnesota, Minneapolis*] (IID)

DIS .... Dual Image System

DIS .... Ductile Iron Society (EA)

DIS .... Loubomo [*Congo*] [*Airport symbol*] (OAG)

DISA .... Dairy Industries Supply Association [*Later, DFISA*]

DISA .... Dansk Industri Syndikat A/S [*Danish manufacturer of a machine gun mount being tested by US Army*] (RDA)

DISA .... Defense Institute of Security Assistance (MCD)

DisA .... Dissertation Abstracts [*Later, Dissertation Abstracts International*] [*A publication*]

DISA .... Division of International Security Affairs [*Energy Research and Development Administration*]

DISA .... Dwarf Iris Society of America (EA)

DISAB .... Disability (ADA)

DISAB .... DoD [*Department of Defense*] Information Security Advisory Board

Dis Abst ..... Dissertation Abstracts [*Later, Dissertation Abstracts International*] [*A publication*]
DISAC .... Digital Simulator and Computer   (IEEE)
DISACET ... Dissolution of Acetaminophen [*Clinical chemistry*]
DISAF ...... Delinquency Item Summary and Forecast   (MCD)
DISA Inf .... DISA [*Danske Industri Syndikat A/S*] Information [*A publication*]
DI/SAL ...... Vessels Disposed of by Sale through Navy Material Redistribution Agency [*Navy*]
DISALLCE ... Disallowance [*Legal*] [*British*]   (ROG)
DISALLD ... Disallowed [*Legal*] [*British*]   (ROG)
DISAM ...... Defense Institute of Security Assistance Management [*Air Force*]
DISAP ...... Disapprove   (AABC)
DISAPG ... Disappearing
Disappr ...... Disapproved In [*or Disapproving*] [*Legal term*]   (DLA)
Dis Aquat Org ... Diseases of Aquatic Organisms [*A publication*]
Disarm ...... Disarmament [*A publication*]
Disarm & Arms Control ... Disarmament and Arms Control [*A publication*]
DISASSM ... Disassemble
DISASSY .. Disassembly   (KSC)
Disaster Prev Res Inst Annu ... Disaster Prevention Research Institute. Annual [*Japan*] [*A publication*]
Disaster Prev Res Inst Kyoto Univ Bull ... Disaster Prevention Research Institute. Kyoto University. Bulletin [*A publication*]
DISB .... Defence Information Services Branch [*Australia*]
DISB .... Disburse   (AABC)
DISBMT ... Disbursement   (AFM)
DISBN .... Distribution   (DCTA)
DISBOFF ... Disbursing Officer
DISBS .... Disbursements [*Business term*]
DISC .... Daily Intelligence Summary Cable   (MCD)
DISC .... Data Index for Software Configuration   (MCD)
DISC .... Data Index for Software Control   (MCD)
DISC .... Data, Information, and System Control
DISC .... Data Information System for Management Control [*Military*]
DISC .... Data Processing and Information Science Contents [*BRS Information Technologies*] [*Online database*] [*Discontinued*]
DISC .... Decision Information Screening Center   (MCD)
DISC .... Defect Information and Servicing Control [*Aviation*]
DISC .... Defense Industrial Supply Center
DISC .... Defense Industrial Support Center   (MCD)
DISC .... Delay in Separation Code [*Military*]   (AABC)
DISC .... Diagnostic Interview Schedule for Children [*Psychology*]
DISC .... Differential Scatter [*Remote sensing technique*]
DISC .... Digital International Switching Center [*Telecommunications*]   (TEL)
DISC .... Direct-Injected Stratified Charge [*Engine*]   (RDA)
DISC .... Disability Insurance Sales Course [*LUTC*]
DISC .... Discharged [*Military*]
DISC .... Disciple   (ADA)
DISC .... Discone   (NASA)
DISC .... Disconnect   (KSC)
DISC .... Discontinue   (AFM)
DISC .... Discount
DISC .... Discourse   (ROG)
DISC .... Discover
Disc .... Discovery [*A publication*]
DISC .... Discrete   (KSC)
DISC .... Discus Corp. [*Bloomington, MN*] [*NASDAQ symbol*]   (NQ)
DISC .... District
DISC .... Divisional Interests Special Committee [*American Library Association*]
DISC .... Domestic International Sales Corporation [*See also Foreign Sales Corporation - FSC*]
DISC .... Drilling Information Service Company [*Houston, TX*] [*Telecommunications*]   (TSSD)
DISC4 .... Director of Information Systems for Command, Control, Communications, and Computers [*DoD*]
DISCA ...... Discovery [*England*] [*A publication*]
DISCAH ... Discovery [*New Haven*] [*A publication*]
DISCAS ... Defense Intelligence Special Career Automated System   (MCD)
DISCBI ...... Discovery [*London*] [*A publication*]
DISCCNC ... Declaration of Independence Second Centennial Commemorative National Committee   (EA)
Disc Excav (Scot) ... Discovery and Excavation (Scotland) [*A publication*]
Disc Far Soc ... Discussions. Faraday Society [*A publication*]
DISCH ...... Defense Intelligence School [*Air Force*]
DISCH ...... Discharge   (AFM)
DISCHE .... Discharge   (ROG)
Dis Chest ... Diseases of the Chest [*A publication*]
Disch Plann Update ... Discharge Planning Update [*A publication*]
DISCIP ...... Disciplinary   (DSUE)
Discip Grievances ... Discipline and Grievances [*A publication*]
Disc L and Proc Adv Sheets ... Disciplinary Law and Procedure Advance Sheets [*A publication*]
Discn Faraday Soc ... Discussions. Faraday Society [*A publication*]
DISCO ...... Defense Industrial Security Clearance Office
DISCO ...... Discotheque   (DSUE)
DISCO .... Dissertations on Chemical Oceanography

Disco Forum ... Discographical Forum [*A publication*]
DISCOID .. Direct Scan Operating with Integrated Delay   (MCD)
Discol .... Discolored
Dis Colon Rectum ... Diseases of the Colon and Rectum [*A publication*]
Dis Col Rec ... Diseases of the Colon and Rectum [*A publication*]
DISCOM ... Digital Selective Communications
DISCOM ... Division Support Command [*Army*]   (AABC)
DISCON .... Defense Integrated Secure Communications Network [*Australia*]   (TEL)
DISCON .... Disconnect   (KSC)
DISCON .... Discontinue
DISCON .... Discrepancy in Shipment Confirmation [*DoD*]
discontd ...... Discontinued
DISCORAP ... Directionally-Controlled Rocket-Assisted Projectile
DISCOS ...... Disturbance Compensation System [*Navy satellite navigation*]
Discoteca .... Discoteca alta Fedalta I [*A publication*]
Discount M ... Discount Merchandiser [*A publication*]
Discov .... Discovery [*A publication*]
DISCOVD ... Discovered   (ROG)
Discoveries Pharmacol ... Discoveries in Pharmacology [*A publication*]
Discovery Excav (Scot) ... Discovery and Excavation (Scotland) [*A publication*]
Discovery Rep ... Discovery Reports [*A publication*]
Discov Rep ... Discovery Reports [*A publication*]
DISCOVY ... Discovery   (ROG)
DISCOY ...... Discovery   (ROG)
DISC-P ...... Diagnostic Interview Schedule for Children - Parents Form [*Psychology*]
DI/SCP ...... Vessels Disposed of by Scrapping [*Navy*]
DISCR .... Discriminate   (AABC)
DISCREP ... Discrepancy Report
Discrete Appl Math ... Discrete Applied Mathematics [*A publication*]
Discrete Math ... Discrete Mathematics [*A publication*]
DISCRM ... Discriminate   (MUGU)
Discr Math ... Discrete Mathematics [*A publication*]
DISCRON ... Discretion
DISCRP ..... Discrepancy   (AABC)
DISCT .... Discount
DISCT .... District
Discur .... Discuriosities [*Record label*]
DISCUS .... Distilled Spirits Council of the United States   (EA)
Discuss Alphabet ... Discussion sur l'Alphabetisation [*A publication*]
Discuss Faraday Soc ... Discussions. Faraday Society [*A publication*]
Discuss Farad Soc ... Discussions. Faraday Society [*A publication*]
DISD .... Data and Information Systems Division [*IT & T*]
DISD .... Defense Industrial Supply Depot
DisDGM .... District Deputy Grand Master [*Freemasonry*]
DISDKB .... Descendants of the Illegitimate Sons and Daughters of the Kings of Britain   (EA)
DISE .... Development in Science Education [*National Science Foundation*]   (GRD)
DISE .... Distribution and Illumination System, Electrical [*Army*]   (INF)
DISECS ..... Defense Intelligence Space Exploitation and Correlation System   (MCD)
DISEM ...... Disseminate   (AABC)
DISEMB ... Disembark   (AABC)
DISENG .... Disengage
DISESTAB ... Disestablish
DISFREE .. Distribution-Free Statistics
DISG .... Seguela [*Ivory Coast*] [*ICAO location identifier*]   (ICLI)
DISGRAT ... Discharge Gratuity [*Military*]
DISH .... Data Interchange in the Shipping Industry
DISH .... Diffuse Idiopathic Skeletal Hyperostosis [*Medicine*]
Dish .... Double [*or Dual*] Income, Separate Homes [*Lifestyle classification*]
Dishek Alemi ... Dishekimligi Alemi [*A publication*]
Dishekim Derg ... Dishekimligi Dergisi [*A publication*]
DISHON ... Dishonorable   (ADA)
DISHOND ... Dishonored   (ROG)
DISI .... Defense Industrial Security Institute [*DoD*]
DISI .... Diode Ion Source Injector
DISI .... Door Insulating Systems Index
DISI .... Dorsal Intercalary Segment Instability [*Medicine*]
DISIDS ...... Display and Information Distribution System [*or Subsystem*]   (MCD)
DISIM .... Digital Input Simulator [*Data processing*]
DISJ .... Disjunctive   (ROG)
DISJUNCT ... Disjunctive [*Linguistics*]
DISK .... Devrimci Isci Sendikalari Konfederasyonu [*Confederation of Revolutionary Trade Unions of Turkey*]   (PD)
DISK .... Image Entertainment, Inc. [*NASDAQ symbol*]   (NQ)
DISKCOMP ... Disk Compare [*Data processing*]
Diskret Analiz ... Diskretnyi Analiz. Sbornik Trudov [*A publication*]
DISLOC ...... Dislocation [*Medicine*]
DISLVD .... Dissolved
DISM .... Dismantle   (MSA)
DISM .... Dismiss   (AABC)
Dis Marker ... Disease Markers [*A publication*]
DisMD .... Distal Muscular Dystrophy [*Medicine*]
DISMDG ... Documents. Institut Scientifique [*Rabat*] [*A publication*]
DISN .... Diiminosuccinonitrile [*Organic chemistry*]

Disn............ Disney's Superior Court of Cincinnati Reports [*Ohio*] [*A publication*] (DLA)
Dis Ner Sys ... Diseases of the Nervous System [*A publication*]
Dis Nerv Syst ... Diseases of the Nervous System [*A publication*]
Dis Nerv System ... Diseases of the Nervous System [*A publication*]
DISNET .... Defence Information Services Network [*Australia*]
Disn Gam... Disney. Gaming [*1806*] [*A publication*] (DLA)
Disn (Ohio) ... Disney's Ohio Superior Court Reports [*A publication*] (DLA)
DISO .... Dictionnaire des Inscriptions Semitiques de l'Ouest [*A publication*]
DISOAJ .... Difesa Sociale [*A publication*]
DISOD ...... Disodium
Dis Op........ Dissenting Opinion [*Legal term*] (DLA)
DISORD H ... Disorderly House [*Legal term*] (DLA)
DISOSS..... Distributed Office Support System [*IBM Corp.*]
DISP.......... Defense Industrial Security Program [*DoD*]
DISP.......... Defense Industry Studies Program (NG)
DISP.......... Dispatcher (MSA)
DISP.......... Dispensary (AFM)
DISP.......... Dispensation
DISP.......... Dispenser
DISP.......... Dispensetur [*Dispense*] [*Pharmacy*]
DISP.......... Disperse
DISP.......... Displacement
DISP.......... Display (KSC)
DISP.......... Disposal
DISP.......... Disproportionation
DISP.......... DoD [*Department of Defense*] Industrial Security Program (AABC)
DISP.......... San Pedro [*Ivory Coast*] [*ICAO location identifier*] (ICLI)
DISPAC .... Domestic and International Scientific Planning and Cooperation
DISPENS ... Dispensary (ADA)
DISPERSE ... Discretionary Population Effects for Riot and Stability Employment [*Crowd control*]
Dispersnye Sist Ikh Povedenie Elektr Magn Polyakh ... Dispersnye Sistemy i Ikh Povedenie v Elektricheskikh i Magnitnykh Polyakh [*A publication*]
DISPL........ Displacement (AAG)
DISPLAY ... Digital Service Planning Analysis [*Telecommunications*] (TEL)
DISPN....... Disposition (MSA)
DISPNSG ... Dispensing
Dispos Intern ... Disposables International and Nonwoven Fabric Review [*A publication*]
DISPOSN ... Disposition (ROG)
Disp Technol and Appl ... Displays. Technology and Applications [*A publication*]
DISQ .... Disquisition (ROG)
DISQUAL ... Disqualify (AABC)
Disquis Math Hungar ... Disquisitiones Mathematicae Hungaricae [*A publication*]
DISR.......... Daily Indicator Status Report (MCD)
DISR.......... Defense Indications Status Report (MCD)
DISR.......... Discrepant Item - Ships Record
Dis R .... Disney's Superior Court of Cincinnati Reports [*Ohio*] [*A publication*] (DLA)
DISRE .... Disregard (AABC)
DISREP..... Discrepancy in Shipment Report [*DoD*] (AABC)
DISS .... Digest of Intelligence and Security Services (MCD)
DISS .... Digital Interface Switching System
DISS .... Dissenter
DISS .... Dissertation
DISS .... Dissolve
DISS .... Sassandra [*Ivory Coast*] [*ICAO location identifier*] (ICLI)
Diss Abs..... Dissertation Abstracts [*Later, Dissertation Abstracts International*] [*A publication*]
Diss Abstr ... Dissertation Abstracts [*Later, Dissertation Abstracts International*] [*A publication*]
Diss Abstr A ... Dissertation Abstracts. A. Humanities and Social Sciences [*A publication*]
Diss Abstr B ... Dissertation Abstracts. B. Sciences and Engineering [*A publication*]
Diss Abstr B Sci Eng ... Dissertation Abstracts. B. Sciences and Engineering [*A publication*]
Diss Abstr Int ... Dissertation Abstracts International [*A publication*]
Diss Abstr Int B ... Dissertation Abstracts International. Section B. Sciences and Engineering [*A publication*]
Diss Abstr Int B Sci Eng ... Dissertation Abstracts International. Section B. Sciences and Engineering [*A publication*]
Diss Abstr Int Sec B ... Dissertation Abstracts International. Section B. Sciences and Engineering [*A publication*]
Diss Abstr Int Sect B ... Dissertation Abstracts International. Section B. Sciences and Engineering [*A publication*]
Diss Abstr Int Sect C ... Dissertation Abstracts International. Section C. European Dissertations [*A publication*]
DissadHRP ... Dissertationes ad Historiam Religionum Pertinentes [*A publication*] (BJA)
Diss Arch ... Dissertationes Archaeologicae [*A publication*]
Diss Arch Gand ... Dissertationes Archaeologicae Gandenses [*A publication*]

DISSCO .... DISSPLA [*Display Integrated Software System and Plotting Language*] and TELL-A-GRAF [*Programming language*] User Community [*Argonne National Laboratory*] [*Argonne, IL*] (CSR)
dissd .... Dissolved
DIS/SEC .... Disintegrations per Second
DISSEM.... Disseminated
DISSERT .. Dissertation
Dissert Abs Internat ... Dissertation Abstracts International [*A publication*]
Dissert Abstr Int ... Dissertation Abstracts International [*A publication*]
Dissertationes Math (Rozprawy Mat) ... Dissertationes Mathematicae (Rozprawy Matematyczny) [*A publication*]
Diss ad Flet ... Selden's Dissertatio ad Fletam [*A publication*] (DLA)
Diss Hohenheim Landwirt Hochsch ... Dissertation. Hohenheim Landwirtschaftliche Hochschule [*A publication*]
Diss Johannes Kepler Univ Linz ... Dissertationen der Johannes Kepler. Universitaet Linz [*A publication*]
DISSOC .... Dissociate
Diss Pan..... Dissertationes Pannonicae [*A publication*]
Diss Pharm ... Dissertationes Pharmaceuticae [*A publication*]
Diss Pharm Pharmacol ... Dissertationes Pharmaceuticae et Pharmacologicae [*A publication*]
DISSPLA .. Display Integrated Software System and Plotting Language [*Data processing*]
Diss Techn Univ Wien ... Dissertationen der Technischen Universitaet Wien [*A publication*]
DissUW ..... Dissertationen der Universitaet (Wien) [*A publication*]
DIST.......... Delegation for Scientific and Technical Information (IID)
DIST.......... Discount
DIST.......... Distal [*Medicine*]
DIST.......... Distance [*or Distant*] (AFM)
DIST.......... Distanced [*Horse racing*]
DIST.......... Distilla [*Distill*] [*Pharmacy*] (ROG)
DIST.......... Distilled [*or Distillery*]
Dist .... Distinctio [*Decretum Gratiani*] [*A publication*] (DSA)
DIST.......... Distinction (ROG)
DIST.......... Distinguish
DIST.......... Distribute
DIST.......... Distributed Time (KSC)
dist .... Distribution (IEEE)
DIST.......... Distributor (KSC)
DIST.......... District (AFM)
DIST.......... Disturbance [*FBI standardized term*]
DIST.......... Division of Information Science and Technology [*National Science Foundation*]
DISTAB .... Disestablish (NVT)
DISTAD.... District Administrator (CINC)
DISTAFF .. Directing Staff (NATG)
DISTAN .... Distributed Interactive Secure Telecommunications Area Network (MCD)
Distance Educ ... Distance Education [*A publication*] (APTA)
DISTAR .... Direct Instructional System for Teaching Arithmetic and Reading
Dist C......... District Court (DLA)
Dist Col App ... District of Columbia Court of Appeals (DLA)
Dist & Co Rep ... Pennsylvania District and County Reports [*A publication*] (DLA)
Dist Council Rev ... District Council Review [*A publication*]
Dist Ct........ District Court [*State*] (DLA)
Dist Ct App ... District Court of Appeal (DLA)
DISTD....... Distilled
Dist Drum ... Distant Drummer [*A publication*]
DISTENGR ... District Engineer [*Army*] (AABC)
Dist Heat ... District Heating [*A publication*]
Distill Feed Res Counc Conf Proc ... Distillers Feed Research Council. Conference Proceedings [*A publication*]
DISTING .. Distinguish
DISTING .. Distinguished (ROG)
Distinguished Lect Ser Soc Gen Physiol ... Distinguished Lecture Series. Society of the General Physiologists [*A publication*]
Dist Mem Geol Surv Botswana ... District Memoir. Geological Survey of Botswana [*A publication*]
Dist Mem Geol Surv Malaysia ... District Memoir. Geological Survey of Malaysia [*A publication*]
DISTN....... Distillation
DISTN....... Distortion (MSA)
DISTN....... Distribution (AAG)
Dist Nurs ... District Nursing [*A publication*]
DISTO....... Defense Industrial Security Education and Training Office (AABC)
Dist Proc.... Distributed Processing Newsletter [*A publication*]
DISTR ...... Distracted
DISTR ...... Distribution [*or Distributor*] (AFM)
Distr.......... Distribution [*A publication*]
DISTR ...... District (ROG)
Dist R........ Pennsylvania District Reports [*A publication*] (DLA)
DISTRA .... Distribution Authority [*Army*] (AABC)
DISTRAM ... Digital Space Trajectory Measurement System [*Raytheon Co.*]
DISTRB..... Distributes
Distrbutn.... Distribution [*A publication*]

Distr Col BAJ ... District of Columbia Bar Association. Journal [*A publication*] (DLA)
DISTREAT ... Upon Discharge Treatment [*Military*]
Dist Rep ..... District Reports [*A publication*] (DLA)
Dist Reports ... Pennsylvania District Reports [*A publication*] (DLA)
Dist Reps ... Pennsylvania District Reports [*A publication*] (DLA)
Distr Heat ... District Heating [*A publication*]
Distr Heat Ass J ... District Heating Association. Journal [*A publication*]
DISTRIB ... Distribution
Distrib Age ... Distribution Age [*A publication*]
Distrib El ... Distribution of Electricity [*A publication*]
Distrib Mgr ... Distribution Manager [*A publication*]
Distributive Wkr ... Distributive Worker [*A publication*]
Distrib Worldwide ... Distribution Worldwide [*A publication*]
District .... Pennsylvania District Reports [*A publication*] (DLA)
District Court LR ... District Court Law Reports [*Hong Kong*] [*A publication*] (DLA)
District Law ... District Lawyer [*A publication*]
District Law (DC) ... District Lawyer (District of Columbia) [*A publication*]
District Reps ... Pennsylvania District Reports [*A publication*] (DLA)
DISTRIPRESS ... Federation Internationale des Distributeurs de Presse [*International Federation of Wholesale Newspaper, Periodical, and Book Distributors*]
Distr Worldwide ... Distribution Worldwide [*A publication*]
DISU .... Digital International Switching Unit [*Telecommunications*] (TEL)
DISUB .... Duty Involving Underway Operations in Submarines
DISUD6 ...... Digestive Surgery [*A publication*]
DISUM ...... Daily Intelligence Summary [*Air Force*]
DISUS .... Disused (ROG)
DISV .... Discovery Oil Ltd. [*NASDAQ symbol*] (NQ)
DISY .... Dimokratikos Synagermos [*Democratic Rally*] [*Political party*] (EAIO)
DISY .... Disyllable
DISYLL ..... Disyllable (ROG)
DISYNDA ... Display of Synoptic Data
DIT .... Darwin Institute of Technology [*Australia*]
DIT .... Data Identification Table (MCD)
DIT .... Data Inquiry Terminal
DIT .... Defense Intelligence Thesaurus (MCD)
DIT .... Delay Ignition [*or Igniting*] Tracer [*Military*] (MCD)
DIT .... Delivery Issue Team (MCD)
DIT .... Department of Information Technology [*Commonwealth of Virginia*] [*Telecommunications service*] (TSSD)
DIT .... Detroit Institute of Technology
DIT .... Diiodotyrosine [*Biochemistry*]
DIT .... Director for Individual Training (MCD)
DIT .... Dithiothreitol [*Organic chemistry*]
DIT .... Diversified Techs Inc. [*Vancouver Stock Exchange symbol*]
DIT .... Documentation Implementation Team [*Deep Space Network, NASA*]
DIT .... Documentation Information Transmittal (NVT)
DIT .... Domestic Independent Tour [*or Travel*]
DIT .... Dorsal Intermediate Tract [*Anatomy*]
DIT .... Double Incidence Technique
DIT .... Drexel Institute of Technology [*Pennsylvania*] (MCD)
DIT .... Dual Input Transponder
DIT .... Dynamic Integrated Test (MCD)
DITA .... Diesel Tank Vessel
DITAC .... DIFAR [*Directional Frequency Analyzing and Recording*] Tactic [*Military*] (CAAL)
DITAR .... Digital Telemetry Analog Recording
DITB .... Digital Imagery Test Bed (MCD)
DITB .... Distribution Industry Training Board [*Terminated*] [*British*]
DITB .... Tabou [*Ivory Coast*] [*ICAO location identifier*] (ICLI)
DITC .... Disability Insurance Training Council [*Washington, DC*] (EA)
Ditchley J .. Ditchley Journal [*A publication*]
DITEC .... Digital Television Camera (MCD)
DITEC .... Digital Television Encoding
DI/TES ..... Vessels Disposed of by Using as Targets and Tests [*Navy*]
DITL .... [*A*] Day in the Life [*Series*] [*Photojournalism project*]
DITLA .... [*A*] Day in the Life of America [*Photojournalism project*]
DITLA .... [*A*] Day in the Life of Australia [*Photojournalism project*] (ADA)
DITLOHA ... [*A*] Day in the Life of Hawaii [*Photojournalism project*]
DITM .... Touba/Mahana [*Ivory Coast*] [*ICAO location identifier*] (ICLI)
DITMCO .. Data Information Test Material Checkout
dITP .... Deoxyinosine Triphosphate [*Biochemistry*]
DITP .... Detailed Individual Test Plan (MCD)
DITR .... Deutsches Informationszentrum fuer Technische Regeln [*German Information Center for Technical Rules*] [*German Institute for Standardization*] [*Information service or system*] (IID)
DITRAN .... Diagnostic FORTRAN [*Data processing*] (IEEE)
DI/TRN ..... Vessels Transferred to Other Government Agencies and Miscellaneous Activities [*Navy*]
DITS .... Digital Information Transfer Set (CAAL)
DITS .... Digital Television Spectrometer (NG)
DITTO .... Data Interfile Transfer, Testing, and Operations Utility [*IBM program product*]

DITU .... Digital Interface Test Unit [*Data processing*] (KSC)
DITY .... Committee for Do-It-Yourself Household Moving (EA)
DITY .... Do-It-Yourself (MCD)
DIU .... Data Interface Unit
DIU .... Destratification Impeller Unit
DIU .... Destruction Initiation Unit (CAAL)
DIU .... Digital Input Unit [*Data processing*]
DIU .... Digital Insertion Unit [*Data processing*]
DIU .... Digital Interface Unit [*Data processing*] (KSC)
DIU .... Diuretic [*Increasing Discharge of Urine*] [*Pharmacy*] (ROG)
DIU .... Diversion Investigative Unit [*Drug Enforcement Administration*]
DIU .... Office of Development Information and Utilization [*Agency for International Development*] [*Information service or system*] (IID)
Diu .... Sanol Arzneimittel Dr. Schwarz [*Germany*] [*Research code symbol*]
DIUP .... Director, Industry and University Programs [*Military*] [*Canada*]
DIV .... Data in Voice [*Telecommunications*]
Div. .... De Divinatione [*of Cicero*] [*Classical studies*] (OCD)
DIV .... Defense Intelligence Videocassettes (MCD)
DIV .... Devon Industries [*Vancouver Stock Exchange symbol*]
DIV .... Direction de l'Information de la Valorisation [*Information and Valorization Directorate*] [*National Institute of Agronomic Research*] [*Information service or system*] (IID)
Div. .... Divan [*A publication*]
DIV .... Divergence
Div. .... Diverse [*Various*] [*German*]
DIV .... Diverse (ROG)
DIV .... Diverter (KSC)
DIV .... Divide (MSA)
DIV .... Dividend [*Investment term*]
div .... Dividende [*Dividend*] [*French*] [*Business term*]
DIV .... Divine [*or Divinity*]
DIV .... Diving
Div. .... Divinitas [*A publication*]
Div. .... Divisi [*Divide*] [*Music*]
DIV .... Division (EY)
DIV .... Divisions [*A publication*]
DIV .... Divisor [*Mathematics*] (ROG)
Div. .... Divorce Proceedings [*Legal term*] (DLA)
DIV .... Divorced
DIV .... Dynamic Imagery Viewer
DIV .... Patriot Select Dividend Trust [*NYSE symbol*] (SPSG)
DIVA .... Digital Inquiry - Voice Answerback [*Touch-tone*] [*Bell System*] [*Telecommunications*]
DIVAD ..... Division Air Defense
DIVADA ... Division Air Defense Artillery (MCD)
DIVADS .... Division Air Defense Study (MCD)
Div Appl Chem Tech Pap CSIRO Aust ... Australia. Commonwealth Scientific and Industrial Research Organisation. Division of Applied Chemistry. Technical Paper [*A publication*] (APTA)
Div Appl Org Chem Tech Pap CSIRO Aust ... Australia. Commonwealth Scientific and Industrial Research Organisation. Division of Applied Organic Chemistry. Technical Paper [*A publication*] (APTA)
DIVAR .... Diving Instrumentation Vehicle for Environmental and Acoustic Research (MCD)
DIVART .... Division Artillery [*Army*]
DIVARTY ... Division Artillery [*Army*] (INF)
Div Atmos Phys Tech Pap Aust CSIRO ... Australia. Commonwealth Scientific and Industrial Research Organisation. Division of Atmospheric Physics. Technical Paper [*A publication*] (APTA)
DIVBASE ... Division Base [*Army*]
DIVC .... Diversicare Corp. of America [*NASDAQ symbol*] (NQ)
Div C .... Division Court [*Canada*] (DLA)
Div Caec ..... Divinatio in Caecilium [*of Cicero*] [*Classical studies*] (OCD)
Div Chem Technol Tech Pap CSIRO Aust ... Australia. Commonwealth Scientific and Industrial Research Organisation. Division of Chemical Technology. Technical Paper [*A publication*] (APTA)
DIVCOM .. Division Commander [*Navy*]
Div Ct .... Divisional Court Selected Judgments, Divisional Courts of the Gold Coast Colony [*A publication*] (DLA)
DIVD .... Dividend [*Investment term*]
Divde .... Dividende [*Dividend*] [*French*] [*Business term*] (ILCA)
DIVE .... Division Engineer (MCD)
DIVEMA ... Divinyl Ether-Maleic Anhydride [*Organic chemistry*]
DIVENGR ... Division Engineer [*Army*] (AABC)
DIVERTORD ... Diversion Order [*Military*] (NVT)
Div Fish Oceanogr Tech Pap Aust CSIRO ... Division of Fisheries and Oceanography. Technical Paper. Australia Commonwealth Scientific and Industrial Research Organisation [*A publication*]
DIVHED ... Division Headquarters [*Army*]
DIVIC .... Digital Variable Increment Computer
DIVID .... Divice [*A publication*]
DIVINFO ... Division of Information [*Marine Corps*]

Div Land Resour Manage Tech Pap CSIRO Aust ... Australia. Commonwealth Scientific and Industrial Research Organisation. Division of Land Resources Management. Technical Paper [*A publication*]   (APTA)

Div Land Res Tech Pap CSIRO Aust ... Australia. Commonwealth Scientific and Industrial Research Organisation. Division of Land Research. Technical Paper [*A publication*]   (APTA)

Div Land Use Res Tech Pap Aust CSIRO ... Division of Land Use Research. Technical Paper. Australia Commonwealth Scientific and Industrial Research Organisation [*A publication*]

Div Land Use Res Tech Pap CSIRO Aust ... Australia. Commonwealth Scientific and Industrial Research Organisation. Division of Land Use Research. Technical Paper [*A publication*]   (APTA)

DIVLEV .... Division Level [*Combat model*]   (MCD)

DIVLOGMOD ... Division Logistics Model   (MCD)

Divl Rep Dep Agric Br Guiana ... Divisional Reports. Department of Agriculture. British Guiana [*A publication*]

Div & Mat Ct ... Divorce and Matrimonial Causes Court   (DLA)

DIVN .... Division

DIVNL .... Divisional   (ADA)

DIVOO ...... Division Ordnance Officer

DIVOT ...... Digital-to-Voice Translator

DIVOTS .... Data Input Voice Output Telephone System

DIV in PAR AEQ ... Dividatur in Partes Aequales [*Divide into Equal Parts*] [*Pharmacy*]

DIVPAY .... Diving Pay [*Navy*]

DIV in PT AEQ ... Dividatur in Partes Aequales [*Divide into Equal Parts*] [*Pharmacy*]

Div Rep Div Soils CSIRO ... Divisional Report. Division of Soils. Commonwealth Scientific and Industrial Research Organisation [*A publication*]   (APTA)

DIV & S ..... Divorce and Separation   (DLA)

DIVS .... Signed Division [*Data processing*]

Div Soils Div Rep CSIRO Aust ... Australia. Commonwealth Scientific and Industrial Research Organisation. Division of Soils. Divisional Report [*A publication*]   (APTA)

Div Soils Tech Pap CSIRO Aust ... Australia. Commonwealth Scientific and Industrial Research Organisation. Division of Soils. Technical Paper [*A publication*]   (APTA)

Div Somn ... De Divinatione per Somnia [*of Aristotle*] [*Classical studies*]   (OCD)

DIVSP .... Division Supply Point

DIVTAG ..... Division through Army Group

Div Tech Conf Soc Plast Eng Tech Pap ... Divisional Technical Conference. Society of Plastics Engineers. Technical Papers [*A publication*]

DIVTOS .... Division Tactical Operations System   (MCD)

Div Trop Agron Tech Pap CSIRO (Aust) ... Division of Tropical Agronomy. Technical Paper. Commonwealth Scientific and Industrial Research Organisation (Australia) [*A publication*]

Div Trop Crops Pastures Tech Pap CSIRO (Aust) ... Division of Tropical Crops and Pastures. Technical Paper. Commonwealth Scientific and Industrial Research Organisation (Australia) [*A publication*]

Div Trop Pastures Tech Pap CSIRO Aust ... Australia. Commonwealth Scientific and Industrial Research Organisation. Division of Tropical Pastures. Technical Paper [*A publication*]   (APTA)

DIVU .... Unsigned Division [*Data processing*]

Divulg Pesq (Bogota) ... Divulgacion Pesquera (Bogota) [*A publication*]

Divulg Pesq Dir Gen Pesca (Bogota) ... Divulgacion Pesquera Direccion General de Pesca (Bogota) [*A publication*]

DIVWAG .. Division War Game   (MCD)

DIVY .... Discovery Associates, Inc. [*Encino, CA*] [*NASDAQ symbol*]   (NQ)

DIVYEO .... Diving Yeoman [*British military*]   (DMA)

DIW .... Dead in the Water [*Navy*]   (NVT)

DIW .... Design Information Worksheet

DIW .... Deutsches Institut fuer Wirtschaftsforschung [*Data Resources, Inc.*] [*Database*]

diw .... Diwidend [*Dividend*] [*Afrikaans*] [*Business term*]

DIW .... Visual Merchandising [*A publication*]

DIWAC ..... Digital Interface Weapon Aiming Computer   (MCD)

DI/WSA ..... Vessels Transferred to War Shipping Administration - Maritime Commission for Disposition [*Navy*]

DIWT .... Director of Inland Water Transport Service [*British*]

DIWT .... Dokumentations - und Informationsgesellschaft fuer Wirtschaft und Touristik mbH [*Database producer*]

DIWTM .... Dictionary of Initials - What They Mean [*A publication*]

DIX .... Discount [*Stock exchange*] [*British*]   (ROG)

DIX .... Dixon, CA [*Location identifier*] [*FAA*]   (FAAL)

DIX .... Grand Dixence [*Switzerland*] [*Seismograph station code, US Geological Survey*]   (SEIS)

Dix Av ...... Dixon on General Average [*A publication*]   (DLA)

Dix Dec ...... Dix's School Law Decisions [*New York*] [*A publication*]   (DLA)

Dix Dec (NY) ... Dix's School Law Decisions [*New York*] [*A publication*]   (DLA)

Dix Farm .... Dixon's Law of the Farm [*6th ed.*] [*1904*] [*A publication*]   (DLA)

Dix-Huit Siecle ... Dix-Huitieme Siecle [*A publication*]

DIXIT .... Delegation for Scientific and Technical Information, Communication, and Culture [*Information service or system*]   (IID)

Dix Mar Ins ... Dixon's Marine Insurance and Average [*A publication*]   (DLA)

Dix Mar Law ... Dixon's Abridgment of the Maritime Law [*A publication*]   (DLA)

Dix Part ..... Dixon on Partnership [*1866*] [*A publication*]   (DLA)

Dix Pr .... Dixon's Probate and Administration Law and Practice [*3rd ed.*] [*1912*] [*A publication*]   (DLA)

DIXS .... Dixson, Inc. [*NASDAQ symbol*]   (NQ)

Dix-Sept S ... Dix-Septieme Siecle [*A publication*]

Dix Ship .... Dixon's Law of Shipping [*A publication*]   (DLA)

Dix Subr .... Dixon's Law of Subrogation [*A publication*]   (DLA)

Dix Tit D .... Dixon on Title Deeds [*A publication*]   (DLA)

DIXY .... Dipole Xerography

DIY .... Derbyshire Imperial Yeomanry [*British military*]   (DMA)

DIY .... Diyarbakir [*Turkey*] [*Airport symbol*]   (OAG)

DIY .... Do-It-Yourself

D-I-Y .... Do-It-Yourselfer [*A publication*]

DIYE .... Do-It-Yourself Economics

DIYO .... Yamoussoukro [*Ivory Coast*] [*ICAO location identifier*]   (ICLI)

DIYRI .... Do-It-Yourself Research Institute [*Later, HIRI*]   (EA)

DIZ .... Defense Identification Zone

DIZ .... Deutsch-Israelitische Zeitung [*A publication*]

DIZ .... Deutsche Instrumentanbau Zeitung [*A publication*]

DIZ .... Deutsche Internierten Zeitung [*A publication*]

Diz Epigr .... Dizionario Epigrafico di Antichita Romana [*A publication*]   (OCD)

Dizion Vet ... Dizionario Veterinario [*A publication*]

DJ .... Air Djibouti [*ICAO designator*]   (FAAC)

DJ .... Daiichi Seiyaku Co. Ltd. [*Japan*] [*Research code symbol*]

DJ .... Dark-Eyed Junco [*Ornithology*]

D & J .... De Gex and Jones' English Chancery Reports [*A publication*]   (DLA)

D & J .... December and June [*Denotes semiannual payment of interest or dividends in these months*] [*Business term*]

DJ .... Denver Law Journal [*A publication*]

D of J .... Department of Justice

DJ .... Deutsches Dante-Jahrbuch [*A publication*]

DJ .... Die Justiz [*A publication*]

DJ .... Dieses Jahres [*Of This Year*] [*German*]   (ROG)

DJ .... Diffused Junction

DJ .... Digital Junction [*Telecommunications*]   (TEL)

DJ .... Dinner Jacket   (ADA)

DJ .... Diploma in Journalism   (ADA)

DJ .... Disc Jockey

DJ .... Disc Jockeys (Mobile) [*Public-performance tariff class*] [*British*]

DJ .... Discipleship Journal [*A publication*]

DJ .... Dishonest John [*In TV series "Time for Beany"*]

DJ .... Distributed Jamming   (MCD)

DJ .... District Judge

DJ .... District Office of Jurisdiction [*IRS*]

DJ .... Diversity-Joining [*Genetics*]

DJ .... Divorce Judge   (DAS)

DJ .... Djibouti [*ANSI two-letter standard code*] [*IYRU nationality code*]   (CNC)

DJ .... Doctor Juris [*Doctor of Law*]

DJ .... Double Jeopardy

DJ .... Dow Jones & Co., Inc. [*NYSE symbol*] [*Also, the stock market averages compiled by this company*]   (SPSG)

DJ .... Dragon Jump [*Pack*] [*Military*]   (MCD)

DJ .... Drill Jig   (MSA)

DJ .... Dust Jacket [*Paper cover for a hardbound book*]

DJ .... Dzis i Jutro [*A publication*]

DJ .... Recueil Dalloz. Section Jurisprudence [*French*] [*A publication*]   (DLA)

DJ .... United States Department of Justice, Washington, DC [*Library symbol*] [*Library of Congress*]   (LCLS)

DJA .... Djakarta [*Batavia*] [*Java*] [*Seismograph station code, US Geological Survey*]   (SEIS)

DJA .... Dow Jones Averages [*Information retrieval*]

DJAA .... Dog Judges Association of America [*Inactive*]   (EA)

DJAG .... Deputy Judge Advocate General

DJB .... Cleveland, OH [*Location identifier*] [*FAA*]   (FAAL)

D & JB .... De Gex and Jones' English Bankruptcy Reports [*1857-59*] [*A publication*]   (DLA)

DjB .... Dow Jones Books, Princeton, NJ [*Library symbol*] [*Library of Congress*]   (LCLS)

DJB .... Drill Jig Bushing

DJB .... Jambi [*Indonesia*] [*Airport symbol*]   (OAG)

DJB .... Joint Bank-Fund Library, Washington, DC [*OCLC symbol*]   (OCLC)

DJBF .... International Monetary Fund and International Bank for Reconstruction and Development, Joint Bank-Fund Library, Washington, DC [*Library symbol*] [*Library of Congress*]   (LCLS)

DJbN .... Deutsches Jahrbuch fuer Numismatik [*A publication*]

D Jb Num .. Deutsches Jahrbuch fuer Numismatik [*A publication*]

DJBR........ Development of the James Bay Region/Societe de Developpement de la Baie James [*A publication*]
DjbVk........ Deutsches Jahrbuch fuer Volkskunde [*A publication*]
DJC............ Application for Writ of Error Dismissed, Judgment Correct [*Legal term*] (DLA)
DJC............ Danville Junior College [*Illinois*]
DJC............ Delaware Journal of Corporate Law [*A publication*]
DJC............ Detroit Jazz Center (EA)
DJCB........ Dominican Junior College of Blauvelt [*Later, Dominican College*] [*New York*]
DJCC........ David Jamison Carlyle [*NASDAQ symbol*] (NQ)
DJC/JRI..... Detroit Jazz Center/Jazz Research Institute [*Later, DJC*] (EA)
DJCL........ Delaware Journal of Corporate Law [*A publication*]
DJCN........ Dow Jones Cable News [*Cable-television system*]
DJCO........ Daily Journal Corp. (SC) [*NASDAQ symbol*] (NQ)
DJD.......... Degenerative Joint Disease
DJD.......... Discoveries in the Judaean Desert [*A publication*]
DJD.......... Discoveries in the Judaean Desert of Jordan   (BJA)
DJDS........ Division of Juvenile Delinquency Service [*of SSA*]
DJE.......... Deflected Jet Exhaust
DJE.......... Demokratischer Jugendverband Europas [*Democrat Youth Community of Europe*] [*Political party*] (EAIO)
DJE.......... Dictionary of Jamaican English [*A publication*]
DJE.......... Djerba [*Tunisia*] [*Airport symbol*] (OAG)
DJF.......... Descriptor Justification Form [*ERIC*]
DJF.......... Divorced Jewish Female [*Classified advertising*]
DJG.......... Djanet [*Algeria*] [*Airport symbol*] (OAG)
DJGKN..... Doshida Joshidaigaku Gakujutsu Kenkyu Nenpo [*A publication*]
DJI.......... Designcraft Industries, Inc. [*Formerly, Designcraft Jewel Industries, Inc.*] [*AMEX symbol*] (SPSG)
DJI.......... Djibouti [*ANSI three-letter standard code*] (CNC)
DJI.......... Dow Jones Index [*Stock market*] [*Investment term*]
DJIA........ Dow Jones Industrial Average [*Stock market*] [*Investment term*]
DJIC.......... Dow Jones Index - Composite [*Stock market*] [*Investment term*]
DJII.......... Dow Jones Index - Industrials [*Stock market*] [*Investment term*]
DJIT........ Dow Jones Index - Transport [*Stock market*] [*Investment term*]
DJIU........ Dow Jones Index - Utilities [*Stock market*] [*Investment term*]
DJJ.......... Jayapura [*Indonesia*] [*Airport symbol*] (OAG)
DJK.......... Daughters of Jesus of Kermaria [*See also FJ*] [*Paris, France*] (EAIO)
DJL.......... Doctor of Jewish Literature (BJA)
DJM.......... Dentsu Japan Marketing Advertising [*A publication*]
DJM.......... Director, Joint Staff Memorandum [*Military*]
DJN.......... Delta Junction, AK [*Location identifier*] [*FAA*] (FAAL)
DJN.......... Demijohn [*Freight*]
DJN.......... Dow Jones News [*Dow Jones & Co., Inc.*] [*Information service or system*] (CRD)
DJNEWS.. Dow Jones News Wire [*A publication*]
DJNF........ Dow Jones Newspaper Fund (EA)
DJNR........ Dow Jones News/Retrieval [*Princeton, NJ*] [*Bibliographic database*] [*Information service or system*]
DJNR........ Dow Jones News Retrieval Service [*A publication*]
DJO.......... Daloa [*Ivory Coast*] [*Airport symbol*] (OAG)
DJOEO..... Development Job Outline Engineering Order [*DAC*]
DJOT........ Delayed Jam on Target
DJOWT..... District of Columbia Teachers College [*Later, University of the District of Columbia*], Washington, DC [*Library symbol*] [*Library of Congress*] [*Obsolete*] (LCLS)
DJP.......... Democratic Justice Party [*Republic of Korea*] [*Political party*] (PPW)
DJP.......... Doctor of Jewish Pedagogy
DJP.......... Dragon Jump Pack [*Military*] (MCD)
DJPC........ Deputy Justice of Peace Clerk [*British*] (ROG)
DJR.......... Marietta, GA [*Location identifier*] [*FAA*] (FAAL)
DJ & S...... De Gex, Jones, and Smith's English Chancery Reports [*A publication*] (DLA)
DJS.......... Deception Jamming System
DJS.......... Director, Joint Staff [*Military*] (AABC)
DJS.......... Doctor of Judicial Science
DJS.......... Doctor of Juridical Science
DJS.......... Slagersambacht [*A publication*]
DJ & SB..... De Gex, Jones, and Smith's English Bankruptcy Reports [*A publication*] (DLA)
DJSC........ Daily Journal of the Supreme Court
DJ Sc........ Doctor of Judicial Science
DJSM........ Director, Joint Staff Memorandum [*Military*] (AABC)
DJ St......... Deutsche Justiz-Statistik [*A publication*]
DJStJ........ Dame of Justice of St. John of Jerusalem [*Later, D St J*] [*British*]
DJT.......... Denver Jet, Inc. [*Englewood, CO*] [*FAA designator*] (FAAC)
DJT.......... Digest of Japanese Industry and Technology [*A publication*]
DJT.......... Doctor of Jewish Theology
DJTA........ Dow Jones Transportation Average [*Information retrieval*]
DJ Th........ Doctor of Jewish Theology
DJU.......... Diario de Justica da Uniao [*Brazil*] [*A publication*]
DJUA........ Dow Jones Utility Average [*Information retrieval*]

DJUOL...... Daily JUMPS [*Joint Uniform Military Pay System*] Update Output Listing (AABC)
D Jur........ Dalloz. Jurisprudence [*France*] [*A publication*]
D Jur........ Doctor of Jurisprudence
D Jurisp Gen ... Repertoire Dalloz de Jurisprudence Generale. Encyclopedie [*French*] [*A publication*] (DLA)
D Jur Sc..... Doctor of Juridical Science
DJV.......... Deshapremi Janatha Viyaparaya [*Patriotic People's Organisation*] [*Sri Lanka*] [*Political party*]
DJV.......... Deutsches Jahrbuch fuer Volkskunde [*A publication*]
DJZ.......... Deutsche Juristenzeitung [*A publication*]
DK.......... Dance Kaleidoscope [*Indiana*]
DK.......... Danish Krone [*Monetary unit*] (NATG)
DK.......... Dark
DK.......... Daughters of the King (EA)
DK.......... David Kaufmann Collection. Hungarian Academy of Sciences [*Budapest*] (BJA)
DK.......... Deca [*or Deka*] [*A prefix meaning multiplied by 10*] (KSC)
DK.......... Deck
DK.......... Degrees Kelvin (KSC)
DK.......... Democratic Kampuchea [*Pol Pot's regime in Cambodia*]
DK.......... Democratic People's Republic of Korea [*IYRU nationality code*] (IYR)
D i K........ Den'gi i Kredit [*A publication*]
DK.......... Denmark [*ANSI two-letter standard code*] (CNC)
dk.......... Denmark [*MARC country of publication code*] [*Library of Congress*] (LCCP)
DK.......... Deutscher Kulturbund [*German Cultural Federation*] [*German Democratic Republic*] (PPE)
DK.......... Devisa Kredit [*Credit Exchange*] [*Indonesian*] (IMH)
DK.......... Dezimal Klassifikation [*Netherlands*]
DK.......... Die Kultur [*A publication*]
DK.......... Diet Kitchen
DK.......... Disbursing Clerk [*Navy rating*]
DK.......... Display/Keyboard [*Data processing*] (MCD)
DK.......... Dock
DK.......... Don't Know
DK.......... Dorsal Kidney
DK.......... Duck
DK.......... Duct Keel [*of a ship*] (DS)
DK.......... Duke (ROG)
DK.......... Dukovna Kultura [*A publication*]
DK.......... Scanair Ltd. [*Denmark*] [*ICAO designator*] (FAAC)
DK1........ Disbursing Clerk, First Class [*Navy rating*]
DK2........ Disbursing Clerk, Second Class [*Navy rating*]
DK3........ Disbursing Clerk, Third Class [*Navy rating*]
DkA........ Deutschkundliche Arbeiten [*A publication*]
DKA.......... Diabetic Ketoacidosis [*Medicine*]
DKA.......... Diketogulonic Acid [*Organic chemistry*]
DKAI........ DAKA International, Inc. [*NASDAQ symbol*] (CTT)
DKAM...... Double Known Addition Method [*Analytical electrochemistry*]
D Kan........ United States District Court for the District of Kansas (DLA)
DKath........ De Katholick [*A publication*]
DKB.......... Dai-Ichi Kangyo Bank [*Japan*]
DKB.......... Decimal Keyboard [*Data processing*]
DKB.......... DeKalb, IL [*Location identifier*] [*FAA*] (FAAL)
Dk of Bay... Dock of the Bay [*A publication*]
D Kbl........ Deutsches Kunstblatt [*A publication*]
DKBSA...... Doklady Biological Sciences [*English Translation*] [*A publication*]
DKBSB...... Doklady Botanical Sciences [*English Translation*] [*A publication*]
DKC.......... Dickinson College, Carlisle, PA [*OCLC symbol*] (OCLC)
DKC.......... Disbursing Clerk, Chief [*Navy rating*]
DKCHA..... Doklady Chemistry [*English Translation*] [*A publication*]
DKCM...... Disbursing Clerk, Master Chief [*Navy rating*]
DKCS........ Disbursing Clerk, Senior Chief [*Navy rating*]
DKDI........ Dinking Die [*Tool*] (AAG)
DKDP........ Deutsche Kunst und Denkmalpflege [*A publication*]
DKE.......... Deck Edge
DKE.......... Delta Kappa Epsilon [*Society*]
DKEL........ Demokratikon Komma Ergazomenou Laou [*Democratic Party of Working People*] [*Greek*] (PPE)
DKESA...... Doklady. Earth Sciences Sections [*A publication*]
DKEY....... Datakey, Inc. [*NASDAQ symbol*] (NQ)
DKF.......... Dokumentation Kraftfahrwesen [*Motor Vehicle Documentation*] [*Federal Republic of Germany*] [*Information service or system*] (IID)
DKF.......... Dudley, Kenneth F., Ottumwa IA [*STAC*]
DKFC........ David Kirchner Fan Club (EA)
DKFC........ Dena Kaye Fan Club (EA)
Dkfm........ Diploma in Commerce [*German*]
DKG.......... Columbus, OH [*Location identifier*] [*FAA*] (FAAL)
DKG.......... Dekagram [*Unit of measure*] (GPO)
DKG.......... Diketogluconic Acid [*Organic chemistry*]
DKG.......... Docking [*Aerospace*] (KSC)
DKGM...... Dekagram [*Unit of measure*] (ROG)
DKHHD.... Denryoku Chuo Kenkyusho Hokoku. Sogo Hokoku [*A publication*]
DKI.......... Daniel K. Inouye [*US Senator from Hawaii*]

DKI .... Dart & Kraft, Incorporated [*Toronto Stock Exchange symbol*] (SPSG)
DKI .... Data Key Idle
DKI .... Deutsches Kunststoff-Institut [*German Plastics Institute*] [*Database producer*] [*Darmstadt*]
DKI .... Docking Initiate
DKI .... Don't Knock It [*Slang*]
DKI .... Dunk Island [*Australia*] [*Airport symbol*] (OAG)
D & K Int Rev ... Davidge and Kimball's Internal Revenue Laws [*A publication*] (DLA)
DKJC .... Dickey-John Corporation [*NASDAQ symbol*] (NQ)
DKK .... Dunkirk, NY [*Location identifier*] [*FAA*] (FAAL)
DKKIB ...... Denpa Kenkyusho Kiho [*A publication*]
DKL .... Dekaliter [*Unit of measure*] (GPO)
DKL .... Dickinson School of Law, Sheeley-Lee Law Library, Carlisle, PA [*OCLC symbol*] (OCLC)
Dk LR .... Dickinson Law Review [*A publication*] (DLA)
DKM .... Dekameter [*Unit of measure*] (GPO)
DKM .... Dickman Aviation Service [*Rolla, MO*] [*FAA designator*] (FAAC)
DKM .... Duke Minerals Ltd. [*Vancouver Stock Exchange symbol*]
DK Mitt .... DK Mitteilungen [*A publication*]
DKMN ...... Dakota Minerals, Inc. [*NASDAQ symbol*] (NQ)
DKN .... Dakon Metals, Inc. [*Vancouver Stock Exchange symbol*]
DKNFA ..... Dickenson Mines Cl A [*NASDAQ symbol*] (NQ)
DKNHDO ... Denryoku Chuo Kenkyusho Noden Kenkyusho Hokoku [*Agricultural Electricity Institute. Report*] [*A publication*]
DKNY .... Donna Karan New York [*Sportswear*]
DKO .... Ayer, Ft. Devens, MA [*Location identifier*] [*FAA*] (FAAL)
DKO .... Dankoe Mines Ltd. [*Vancouver Stock Exchange symbol*]
DKO .... Delay Key On
DKO .... Die Deutsche Kirche im Orient [*Cairo*] [*A publication*] (BJA)
DKP .... Dania Kommunista Partja [*Communist Party of Denmark*] [*Political party*]
DKP .... Danmarks Kommunistiske Parti [*Communist Party of Denmark*] (PPW)
DKP .... Democratic Korea Party [*Republic of Korea*] [*Political party*] (PPW)
DKP .... Deutsche Kommunistische Partei [*German Communist Party*] [*Federal Republic of Germany*] [*Political party*] (PPE)
DKP .... Dikalium Phosphate [*Pharmacology*]
DKP .... Diketopiperazine [*Organic chemistry*]
DKP .... DK Platinum Corp. [*Vancouver Stock Exchange symbol*]
DKPCA ...... Doklady Physical Chemistry [*English Translation*] [*A publication*]
DKPG .... Depth Keeping
DKR .... Dakar [*Senegal*] [*Airport symbol*] (OAG)
Dkr .... Dan Korona [*Danish Crown*] [*Monetary unit*] [*Hungarian*]
D KR .... Danish Krone [*Monetary unit*]
DKR .... Decker Resources Ltd. [*Vancouver Stock Exchange symbol*]
D Kred .... Den'gi i Kredit [*A publication*]
DKS .... Dekastere [*Unit of measure*]
DKS .... Deputy Keeper of the Signet (DLA)
DKS .... Direct Keying System
DKS .... Doniphan, Kensett & Searcy Railway [*AAR code*]
DKSA .... Seaman Apprentice, Disbursing Clerk, Striker [*Navy rating*]
DKSEN ...... Don King Sports and Entertainment Network [*Cable-television system*]
DKSN .... Seaman, Disbursing Clerk, Striker [*Navy rating*]
DKT .... Dahl-Kirkam Telescope
DKT .... Dakota Energy Corp. [*Vancouver Stock Exchange symbol*]
DKT .... Docket [*Law, Packaging*]
Dkt .... West Publishing Company's Docket [*1909-41*] [*A publication*] (DLA)
DKTC .... Dog Kidney Tissue Culture
DKTS .... Dakotas [*FAA*] (FAAC)
D Ku Denkm Pfl ... Deutsche Kunst und Denkmalpflege [*A publication*]
DKV .... Deer Kidney Virus
DKVS .... Det Kongelige Videnskapers Selskap [*A publication*]
DKW .... Das Kleine Wunder [*The Little Wonder*] [*Initialism used as name of German automobile, manufactured by Auto Union*]
DKWT .... De Kalb & Western Transportation R. R. [*AAR code*]
DKX .... Knoxville, TN [*Location identifier*] [*FAA*] (FAAL)
DKY .... Donkey Boiler [*of a ship*] (DS)
DKZ .... Deutsche Kolonialzeitung [*A publication*]
DL .... Associate Directorate for LPS [*Launch Processing System*] Development [*Kennedy Space Center*] [*NASA*] (NASA)
DL .... Dacron Braid Lacquered (MDG)
DL .... Dale
DL .... Damage Limitation [*Strategy*] [*Military*]
DL .... Danger List [*Medicine*]
DL .... Danske Lov [*Laws in Force*] [*Denmark*] (ILCA)
DL .... Dark on Light
DL .... Data Language
DL .... Data Link
DL .... Data List [*DoD*]
DL .... Datum Level
DL .... Davidson Laboratory [*Stevens Institute of Technology*]
DL .... Day Letter [*Telegraphy*]
DL .... Daylight (MSA)

DL .... Days Lost [*Military*]
DL .... Dead Light (AAG)
DL .... Dead Load
DL .... Deadline (AABC)
DL .... Deadweight Loss [*of grain*] [*Agriculture*]
DL .... Deciliter [*Unit of measure*] (GPO)
DL .... Decision Leaflets [*US Patent Office*]
DL .... Decret-Loi [*Decree-Law*] [*French*] (ILCA)
DL .... Decreto Legge [*Decree-Law*] [*Italian*] (ILCA)
DL .... Dedicated Landline
DL .... Defence Light [*British military*] (DMA)
DL .... Dekaliter [*Unit of measure*] (ROG)
DL .... Delay Line
DL .... D'Eldona Resources Ltd. [*Toronto Stock Exchange symbol*]
DL .... Delta Air Lines, Inc. [*ICAO designator*]
D/L .... Demand Loan
DL .... Dentate Line [*Anatomy*]
D/L .... Deorbit/Landing [*Aerospace*] (MCD)
DL .... Department of Labor
D of L .... Department of Labor
DL .... Departure Locator
DL .... Deputy Lieutenant [*British*]
DL .... Description of Leaf (ROG)
DL .... Destroyer Leader [*Navy*]
DL .... Detection Limit [*Analytical chemistry*]
DL .... Detskaya Literatura [*A publication*]
DL .... Deus Loci [*A publication*]
DL .... Deutsche Literaturzeitung [*A publication*]
DL .... Developed Length (AAG)
DL .... Development-Left (MCD)
dl .... Dextro-Levo(rotary) [*Also, r, rac*] [*Chemistry*]
DL .... Dial (FAAC)
DL .... Die Literatur [*A publication*]
DL .... Dielectric Loading Factor [*Electronics*] (MDG)
DL .... Difference of Latitude [*Navigation*] (MUGU)
DL .... Difference Limen [*Physiology, psychology*]
DL .... Diffraction Limited (MCD)
DL .... Diode Logic
DL .... Diogenes Laertius [*Third century AD*] [*Classical studies*] (OCD)
DL .... Direct Labor
DL .... Direct Line [*Followed by telephone number*]
DL .... Direct Listening (CAAL)
DL .... Direct Load
DL .... Director of Laboratories [*AFSC*]
DL .... Director of Labour [*Military*] [*British*]
DL .... Director Layer [*British military*] (DMA)
DL .... Disabled List [*Athletics*]
DL .... Disjunctively Linear
D/L .... Displacement to Length [*Ratio*]
D & L .... Distillate plus Loss
DL .... Distolingual [*Dentistry*]
DL .... Distributed Lab (MDG)
DL .... Distribution List
DL .... District Office of Location [*IRS*]
DL .... Doctor of Laws
DL .... Doctor of Letters
DL .... Doctor of Literature
DL .... Doctrine and Life [*A publication*]
DL .... Document Log (AABC)
DL .... Dominical Letter
D-L .... Donath-Landsteiner [*Hemolysin*] [*Hematology*]
DL .... Doppellafette [*Two-barreled mount*] [*German military - World War II*]
DL .... Dorsal Lip
DL .... Dorsal Longitudinal
DL .... Double Ledger [*Accounting*]
DL .... Douro Litoral [*A publication*]
DL .... Dow-Lepetit [*Research code symbol*]
D & L .... Dowling and Lowndes' English Bail Court Reports [*A publication*] (DLA)
DL .... Down Left [*The front left portion of a stage*] [*A stage direction*]
DL .... Down Link [*Data processing*]
D/L .... Downlist (NASA)
DL .... Drawing List [*Engineering*]
DL .... Drill Leader [*British military*] (DMA)
DL .... Driving Licence [*British*] (ADA)
DL .... Droit et Liberte, Contre le Racisme, l'Antisemitisme, pour la Paix [*Paris*] [*A publication*]
DL .... Dual Language
D of L .... Duchy of Lancaster [*British*] (ILCA)
dl .... Dull [*Philately*]
DL .... Dummy Load [*Military*] (MCD)
DL .... Duolateral
DL .... Dynamic Load Characteristic (MDG)
DL .... Frigate [*Navy symbol*]
DL .... Most Distal Leaf [*Botany*]
DL .... Recueil Dalloz. Section Legislation [*French*] [*A publication*] (DLA)
DL .... United States Department of Labor Library, Washington, DC [*Library symbol*] [*Library of Congress*] (LCLS)

DL/1 .... Data Language Version 1 [*Data processing*]
DLA .... Data Link Acquisition   (MCD)
DLA .... Data Link Adapter
DLA .... Data Link Address
DLA .... Declination of Launch Asymptote [*NASA*]   (KSC)
DLA .... Defense Logistics Agency [*Alexandria, VA*]
DLA .... Defense Logistics Area   (MCD)
DLA .... Delaware [*Ontario*] [*Seismograph station code, US Geological Survey*]   (SEIS)
DLA .... Delaware Law School of Widener College, Wilmington, DE [*OCLC symbol*]   (OCLC)
DLA .... Delay   (FAAC)
DLA .... Delay Line Assembly
DLA .... Delay Message [*Aviation code*]
DLA .... Democratic Labor Association [*Philippines*]
DLA .... Depot Level Activity   (NATG)
DLA .... Diffusion-Limited Aggregation [*Physical chemistry*]
DLA .... Dislocation Allowance [*Military*]
DLA .... Distolobial [*Dentistry*]
DLA .... Division of Library Automation [*University of California, Berkeley*] [*Information service or system*]   (IID)
DLA .... Divisional Land Agent [*Ministry of Agriculture, Fisheries, and Food*] [*British*]
DLA .... Doctor of Liberal Arts
DLA .... Dog Lymphocytotoxicity
DLA .... Douala [*Cameroon*] [*Airport symbol*]   (OAG)
DLAA .... DARCOM [*Development and Readiness Command, Army*] Logistics Assistance Activity   (MCD)
DLAB .... Defense Language Aptitude Battery [*Army*]   (INF)
DLAB .... Divisor Latch Access BIT [*Data processing*]
DLAC .... Delay Account of _____ [*Aviation*]   (FAAC)
DLAI .... Distolabioincisal [*Dentistry*]
DLAJ .... DeKalb Literary Arts Journal [*A publication*]
D La L .... Doctor of Latin Letters
D Landw Tz ... Deutsche Landwirtschaftliche Tierzucht [*A publication*]
D Lang ...... Doctor of Languages
DLAO .... Defense Logistics Analysis Office   (MCD)
DLaP .... Distolabiopulpal [*Dentistry*]
DL Arch ..... Doctor of Landscape Architecture
DLAT .... Defense Language Aptitude Test [*Army*]   (AABC)
DLAT .... Destructive Lot Acceptance Testing   (NASA)
DLAT .... Difference of Latitude [*Navigation*]
DLAT .... Discharge-Line Air Temperature [*Nuclear energy*]   (NRCH)
DLB .... Brandywine College of Widener University, Wilmington, DE [*OCLC symbol*]   (OCLC)
DLB .... Dannemiller, Lawrence B., Columbus OH [*STAC*]
DLB .... Delbancor Industry [*Vancouver Stock Exchange symbol*]
DLB .... Deposit Liquidation Board
DLB .... Dictionary of Literary Biography [*A publication*]
DLBI .... Differential Long-Baseline Interferometer [*Radio interferometry*]
DL Bl .... Deutsches Literaturblatt [*A publication*]
DLC .... Dalien [*China*] [*Airport symbol*]   (OAG)
DLC .... Data Link Control [*Data processing*]   (BUR)
DLC .... David Lipscomb College [*Tennessee*]
DLC .... Delay Line Case
DLC .... Delayed Clearance [*Aviation*]   (FAAC)
DLC .... Democratic Leadership Council   (EA)
DLC .... Dental Laboratory Conference   (EA)
DLC/1 .... Develcon Electronics Ltd. [*Toronto Stock Exchange symbol*]
DLC .... Development Loan Committee [*Department of State*]
DLC .... Diamondlike Carbon [*Materials science*]
DLC .... Differential Leukocyte Counts [*Hematology*]
DLC .... Digital Logic Circuit
DLC .... Dillon, SC [*Location identifier*] [*FAA*]   (FAAL)
DLC .... Diploma of Loughborough College [*British*]
DLC .... Direct Lift Control
DLC .... Disaster Loan Corporation [*Dissolved 1945, functions transferred to Reconstruction Finance Corporation*]
DLC .... Doctor of Celtic Literature
DLC .... Donation Land Claim [*Legal term*]   (DLA)
DLC .... Drummond Lighterage [*AAR code*]
DLC .... Duplex Line Control   (BUR)
DLC .... Dynamic Load Characteristic
DLC .... Library of Congress, Washington, DC [*Library symbol*] [*Library of Congress*] [*OCLC symbol*]   (OCLC)
DLC .... Osterhout Free Library [*Library network*]
DLCA .... Dairymen's League Cooperative Association [*Later, DC*]   (EA)
DLCA .... Diffusion-Limited Cluster Aggregation [*Physical chemistry*]
DLCA .... Driver Leasing Council of America   (EA)
DLCA .... Dynamic Logic Chassis Analyzer
DLCB .... Drifting Low-Capability Buoys [*National Oceanic and Atmospheric Administration*]   (MCD)
DLC-B .... Library of Congress, National Library Service for the Blind and Physically Handicapped, Washington, DC [*Library symbol*] [*Library of Congress*]   (LCLS)
DLC-BM ... Library of Congress, National Library Service for the Blind and Physically Handicapped, Music Library, Washington, DC [*Library symbol*] [*Library of Congress*]   (LCLS)
DLCC .... Division Logistics Control Center

DLCC .... FAO [*Food and Agriculture Organization of the United Nations*] Desert Locust Control Committee [*United Nations*]   (EA)
DLC(ESR) ... United States Library of Congress, Early State Records Collection, Washington, DC [*Library symbol*] [*Library of Congress*]   (LCLS)
DLCF .... Data Link Control Field [*Data processing*]
DLCF .... Develcon Electronics Ltd. [*Saskatoon, SK*] [*NASDAQ symbol*]   (NQ)
DLCH .... Delchamps, Inc. [*NASDAQ symbol*]   (NQ)
DLCM .... Drinker Library of Choral Music   (EA)
DLC-N .... United States Library of Congress, National Serials Data Program, Washington, DC [*Library symbol*] [*Library of Congress*]   (LCLS)
DLCO .... Deck Landing Control Officer [*British*]
DLCO .... Diffusing Capacity of the Lungs for Carbon Monoxide
DLCO .... Direct Labor Charges by Organization   (MCD)
DLCO-EA ... Desert Locust Control Organization for Eastern Africa   (EAIO)
DLCP .... Data Link Control Panel [*Data processing*]   (MCD)
DLC-P4 .... United States Library of Congress, Priority Four Collection, Washington, DC [*Library symbol*] [*Library of Congress*]   (LCLS)
DLCPP .... Depository Library Council to the Public Printer   (EA)
DLCS .... Data-Line Concentration System [*Bell System*]
DLD .... Data Link Decoder   (MCD)
DLD .... Deadline Date [*Air Force*]   (AFM)
DLD .... Delaware Technical and Community College, Wilmington, DE [*OCLC symbol*]   (OCLC)
DLD .... Delivered
DLD .... Diploma of Landscape Design   (ADA)
DLD .... Discount Long Distance [*Larose, LA*] [*Telecommunications*]   (TSSD)
DLD .... Division of Learning Disabilities [*Council for Exceptional Children*]
DLD .... Dromoland Development [*Vancouver Stock Exchange symbol*]
DLDED ..... Division Level Data Entry Device   (MCD)
DL Des ...... Doctor of Landscape Design
DLE .... Data Link Equipment
DLE .... Data Link Escape Character [*Keyboard*]   (CMD)
DLE .... Deflected Lamine Electrophoresis
DLE .... Delaware Technical and Community College, Stanton Campus, Newark, DE [*OCLC symbol*]   (OCLC)
DLE .... Delayed Light Emission [*Green plant phenomenon*]
DL & E ...... Design Limit and Endurance
DLE .... Detailed Labor Estimate   (MCD)
DLE .... Dialyzable Leukocyte Extract [*Hematology*]
DLE .... Direct Laboratories Estimate   (MCD)
DLE .... Discoid Lupus Erythematosus [*Medicine*]
DLE .... Disseminated Lupus Erythematosus [*Hematology*]
DLE .... Dole [*France*] [*Airport symbol*] [*Obsolete*]   (OAG)
DLE .... Dreaded Lake Effect [*Weather condition, resulting in increased precipitation, produced by Utah's Great Salt Lake*]
DLEA .... Double Leg Elbow Amplifier
DL Ec .... Doctor of Library Economics
DL Eng ...... Doctor of Landscape Engineering
DLEP .... Draft Local Environment Plan [*Australia*]
DLES .... Doctor of Letters in Economic Studies
D Let .... Doctor of Letters
DLevZ .... Deutsche Levante-Zeitung [*A publication*]
DLF .... Data List File
DLF .... Defense de la Langue Francaise [*A publication*]
DLF .... Del Rio, TX [*Location identifier*] [*FAA*]   (FAAL)
DLF .... Delaware Academy of Medicine, Wilmington, DE [*OCLC symbol*]   (OCLC)
DLF .... Designers Lighting Forum
DLF .... Deutschlandfunk [*Radio network*] [*Federal Republic of Germany*]
DLF .... Development Loan Fund [*Abolished 1961, functions redelegated to Agency for International Development*]
DLF .... Diffraction Limited Focusing
DLF .... Digitalis-Like Factor [*Biochemistry*]
DLF .... Digoxin-Like Factor [*Biochemistry*]
DLF .... Direct Lytic Factor [*Polypeptide from cobra venom*]
DLF .... Disability Living Foundation [*British*]
DLF .... Document Library Facility [*Data processing*]
DLF .... Dorsolateral Fascicle [*Muscular anatomy, neuroanatomy*]
DLF .... Dorsolateral Funiculus [*Neuroanatomy*]
DLF .... Drydock Launch Facility
DLFDU ..... Data Line Flight Direction Unit   (MCD)
DLFM .... Division Level Financial Management [*System*]   (MCD)
DLG .... Daddy's Little Girl
D Lg .... Decreto Legislativo [*Legislative Decree*] [*Italian*]   (ILCA)
DLG .... Defense Liaison Group   (CINC)
DLG .... Destroyer Leader, Guided Missile   (MCD)
DLG .... Digital Line Graph
DLG .... Dillingham [*Alaska*] [*Airport symbol*]   (OAG)
DLG .... Guided Missile Frigate [*Navy symbol*]
DLG .... Wilmington Medical Center, Wilmington, DE [*OCLC symbol*]   (OCLC)
DLG Mit Dtsch Landwirtsch Ges ... DLG. Mitteilungen. Deutsch Landwirtschafts Gesellschaft [*A publication*]

dLGN........ Dorsal Lateral Geniculate Nucleus [*Also, LGd*] [*Anatomy*]
DLGN....... Guided Missile Frigate (Nuclear Propulsion) [*Navy symbol*]
DLGS........ Doppler Landing Guidance System
DLH.......... Dalhousie [*India*] [*Seismograph station code, US Geological Survey*] [*Closed*]   (SEIS)
DLH.......... Deutsche Lufthansa AG [*German Lufthansa*] [*Airline*]
DLH.......... Docking Lock Handle
DLH.......... Duluth [*Minnesota*] [*Airport symbol*]   (OAG)
DLH.......... Henry Francis DuPont Winterthur Museum, Winterthur, DE [*OCLC symbol*]   (OCLC)
DLHC........ Diamondlike Hydrocarbon [*Coating material*]
DLI .... Deck-Launched Intercept   (MCD)
DLI .... Defense Language Institute [*DoD*] [*Washington, DC*]
DLI .... Del Laboratories, Incorporated [*AMEX symbol*]   (SPSG)
DLI .... Depolarized Light Intensity
DLI .... Diabetes Literature Index [*A publication*]
DLI .... Direct Liquid Inlet [*Interface*] [*Analytical instrumentation*]
DLI .... Distolinguoincisal [*Dentistry*]
DLI .... Distributorless Ignition [*Automotive engineering*]
DLI .... Do-List Item [*Military*]
DLI .... Doctor of Literary Interpretation
DLI .... Durham Light Infantry [*Military unit*] [*British*]
DLI .... E. I. Du Pont de Nemours & Co., Haskell Laboratory, Newark, DE [*OCLC symbol*]   (OCLC)
DLIC........ Detachments Left in Contact [*Military*]
DLIDC...... Defense Logistics Instructor Development Course [*Army*]
DLIEC...... Defense Language Institute, East Coast Center   (AABC)
DLIEL...... Defense Language Institute, English Language Center   (AABC)
DLIELC.... Defense Language Institute, English Language Center [*Military*]
DLIF......... Design Limit Load Factor
DLIF......... Digoxin-Like Immunoreactive Factor [*Laboratory analysis*]
DLIFLC.... Defense Language Institute, Foreign Language Center   (AABC)
DLILMN... Dial Illumination
DLIMP..... Descriptive Language Implemented by Macroprocessors
DLINDG ... Dial Indicating
DLine....... Direction Line [*A publication*]
DLIP......... Directory of Library and Information Professionals [*Gale Research, Inc.*] [*Information service or system*]   (CRD)
DLIR......... Depot Level Inspection Auto Repair   (MCD)
DLIR......... Downward-Looking Infrared [*Air Force*]
DLIS........ Department of Library and Information Studies [*Australia*]
DLIS........ Digoxin-Like Immunoreactive Substance [*Biochemistry*]
DLIS........ Dowlais Central [*Cardiff*] [*Welsh depot code*]
DLIS........ Downward-Looking Infrared System [*Air Force*]   (MCD)
DLISC-EP ... Defense Language Institute, Support Command - El Paso   (AABC)
DLISDA .... Defense Language Institute, Systems Development Agency   (AABC)
DLISW ..... Defense Language Institute, Southwest Branch   (AABC)
DLit.......... Deutsche Literatur [*A publication*]
D Lit......... Deutsche Literaturzeitung [*A publication*]
D Lit......... Doctor of Letters
D Lit......... Doctor of Literature
DLitt .... Doctor of Letters
DLitt .... Doctor of Literature
DLittS....... Doctor of Sacred Letters
DLIWC..... Defense Language Institute, West Coast Branch   (AABC)
DLJ.......... Donaldson Lufkin & Jenrette [*Investment bank*]   (ECON)
DLJ.......... University of Detroit. Law Journal [*A publication*]
DLJNAQ... Diagnostyka Laboratoryjna [*A publication*]
DLK .... Data Link   (KSC)
DLK .... Diamond Locking Knurl
DLK .... ICI Americas, Inc., Wilmington, DE [*OCLC symbol*]   (OCLC)
DLL .... Dalhousie University Law Library [*UTLAS symbol*]
DLL .... Dames of the Loyal Legion of the United States of America   (EA)
DLL .... Damietta-Latakia Line [*Nile river delta*] [*Geology*]
DLL .... Dells, WI [*Location identifier*] [*FAA*]   (FAAL)
DLL .... Design Load Limit   (MSA)
DLL .... Dial Long Line [*Bell System*]
DLL .... Dictionnaire de la Langue Louvite [*Paris*] [*A publication*]
DLL .... Discharge-Line Length [*Nuclear energy*]   (NRCH)
DLL .... Doctor of Late Laws
DLL .... Double Length Line
DLL .... Downline Loading
DLL .... Dynamic Link Library [*Software*] [*Data processing*]   (BYTE)
DLLF........ Design Limit Load Factor   (MCD)
DLLI........ Dulcitol Lysine Lactose Iron [*Agar*] [*Microbiology*]
DLLRS...... Dollars [*Monetary unit*]   (ROG)
DLM .... Dalaman [*Turkey*] [*Airport symbol*]   (OAG)
DLM .... Dalhousie University Health Sciences Library [*UTLAS symbol*]
DLM .... Data Line Monitor
DLM .... Delay Line Memory
DLM .... Democratic Labour Movement [*Guyana*] [*Political party*]   (PPW)
DLM .... Depot Level Maintenance [*Air Force*]   (AFM)
DLM .... Deputy Lord Mayor [*British*]
DLM .... Des Laufenden Monats [*Of the Current Month*] [*German*]
DLM .... Developments in Landscape Management and Urban Planning [*Elsevier Book Series*] [*A publication*]
DLM .... Digital Logic Module

DLM .... Director of Liaison and Munitions [*Military*] [*British*]
DLM .... Divine Light Mission [*A cult*]
DLM .... Doctor of Landscape Management
DLM .... Dorsal Longitudinal Muscle [*Anatomy*]
DLM .... Double Long Meter [*Music*]
DLM .... University of Delaware, Newark, DE [*OCLC symbol*]   (OCLC)
DLMA ...... Department of Labor, Manpower Administration
DLMA ...... Diocesan Lay Ministry Adviser [*Church of England*]
DLMCP.... Distributed Loop Message Communication Protocol
DLMF...... Depot Level Maintenance Facility   (MCD)
DLMH...... Direct Labor Man-Hours   (RDA)
DLMov ..... Doslidzennja z Literaturoznavstava ta Movoznavstva [*A publication*]
DLMP ...... Depot Level Maintenance Plant
DLMP ...... Down-Link Multipath   (MCD)
DLMRR.... Depot Level Maintenance Requirement Review   (AFIT)
DLMS....... Digital Land Mass Simulation   (MCD)
DLMS....... Digital Land Mass System [*Directorate of Military Survey*] [*British*]
DLMTB.... Defense Logistics Management Training Board   (AFM)
DLN .... Daily Legal News [*Pennsylvania*] [*A publication*]   (DLA)
DLN .... Dalton [*Australia*] [*Seismograph station code, US Geological Survey*] [*Closed*]   (SEIS)
DLN .... Dillon, MT [*Location identifier*] [*FAA*]   (FAAL)
DLN .... Document Locator Number [*Data processing*]
DLN .... Doris Lessing Newsletter [*A publication*]
DLN .... Dorsolateral Nucleus [*Neuroanatomy*]
DLN .... Double Length Number
DLNC....... Deputy Local Naval Commander
DLNC....... Document Locator Number Counter File [*IRS*]
DLO.......... Daleco Resources Corp. [*Vancouver Stock Exchange symbol*]
DLO.......... Daylight Opening
DLO.......... Dead Letter Office [*US Postal Service*]
DLO.......... Defense Liaison Office   (MCD)
DLO.......... Defense Logistics Agency, Alexandria, VA [*OCLC symbol*]   (OCLC)
DLO.......... Delano, CA [*Location identifier*] [*FAA*]   (FAAL)
DLO.......... Delayed Output [*Data processing*]
DLO.......... Deputy for Launch Operations [*NASA*]   (KSC)
DLO.......... Desired Learner Outcomes [*Education*]
DLO.......... Difference of Longitude [*Navigation*]
DLO.......... Diploma in Laryngology and Otolaryngology [*British*]
DLO.......... Direct Labor Organization
DLO.......... Director, Launch Operations [*NASA*]   (KSC)
DLO.......... Dirty Lubricating Oil   (AAG)
DLO.......... Dispatch Loading Only
DLO.......... Distolinguo-Occlusal [*Dentistry*]
DLO.......... District Legal Office [*or Officer*] [*Navy*]
DLO.......... Division Liaison Officer
DLO.......... Double Local Oscillator
DLO.......... Dual Loop Oscillator
DLO.......... Duke of Lancaster's Own [*British military*]   (DMA)
DLOA ...... Draft Letter of Agreement   (MCD)
DLOC ...... Daimler and Lanchester Owners' Club   (EA)
DLOC ...... Division Logistical Operation Center
DLOCK .... Dial Lock
DLOC of NA ... Daimler and Lanchester Owners Club of North America   (EA)
DLOG....... Distributed Logic Corp. [*NASDAQ symbol*]   (NQ)
DLOGS .... Division Logistics System   (MCD)
DLONG .... Difference of Longitude [*Navigation*]
DLOS .... Distributed Loop Operating System
DLOS .... Division Logistics Organization Structure   (MCD)
DLOV .... Daleco Resources Corp. [*Los Angeles, CA*] [*NASDAQ symbol*]   (NQ)
DLOY .... Duke of Lancaster's Own Yeomanry [*Military unit*] [*British*]
DLP .... CenTrust Bank [*AMEX symbol*]   (SPSG)
DLP .... Damage Limiting Program
DLP .... Data Link Processor [*Burroughs Corp.*] [*Data processing*]   (BUR)
DLP .... Data Link Programs   (MCD)
DLP .... Data Listing Programs   (IEEE)
DLP .... Date of Last Payment [*Insurance*]
DLP .... Defense Language Program   (AFM)
DLP .... Delcorp Resources, Inc. [*Vancouver Stock Exchange symbol*]
DLP .... Democratic Labor Party [*Australia*] [*Political party*]
DLP .... Democratic Labor Party [*Trinidad and Tobago*] [*Political party*]   (PPW)
DLP .... Democratic Labor Party [*Barbados*] [*Political party*]   (PPW)
DLP .... Democratic Left Party [*Political party*] [*Turkey*]   (MENA)
DLP .... Democratic Liberal Party [*Republic of Korea*] [*Political party*]   (ECON)
DLP .... Deoxidized Low-Residual Phosphorus [*Copper*]
DLP .... Direct Letter Perfect [*Actors' slang*]
DLP .... Director of Laboratory Programs [*Navy*]
DLP .... Display-List Processor [*Data processing*]
DLP .... Distolinguopulpal [*Dentistry*]
D/LP .... Dome Lamp [*Automotive engineering*]
DLP .... Dominica Labor Party [*Political party*]   (PPW)
DLP .... Double Large Post   (ADA)
DLP .... Douro Litoral (Portugal) [*A publication*]

DLP	Drone Launch Platform [Navy] (CAAL)
DLP	Dufour, Lacarriere, Pouget [Stockbroking firm] [France] (ECON)
DLPA........	Decorative Laminate Products Association (EA)
DLPA........	dl-Phenylalanine [Biochemistry]
DLPE........	Dilaurylphosphatidylethanolamine [Biochemistry]
DLPH	Delphi Information Systems, Inc. [NASDAQ symbol] (NQ)
Dl Planet....	Daily Planet [A publication]
DLPNAM ...	Delpinoa [A publication]
DLPP........	Data Link Pre-Processor [Ferranti Ltd.]
DLPR........	Defense Logistics Procurement Regulation (MCD)
DLPS........	Deck Landing Projector Sight [British military] (DMA)
DLPT........	Defense Language Proficiency Tests [Military]
DLQ	Drexel Library Quarterly [A publication]
DLQ	Mean Diurnal Low-Water Inequality
DLR	Data Link Receiver [Data processing] (MCD)
DLR	Dealer (MSA)
DLR	Delay Line Register
DLR	Depot Level Repairable (NVT)
DLR	Depot Logistics Report (MCD)
DLR	Developing Learning Readiness
DLR	Dickinson Law Review [A publication] (DLA)
DLR	Direct Labor Rate
DLR	Directors Law Reporter [A publication]
DLR	Division of Labor Relations [Energy Research and Development Administration]
DLR	Docklands Light Railway [British] (ECON)
DLR	Dollar [Monetary unit]
DLR	Dominion Law Reporter [India] [Usually with a province abbreviation, as DLR (AM), Ajmer-Merwara] [A publication] (DLA)
DLR	Dominion Law Reports [Database] [A publication]
DLR	Doppler LASER RADAR
DLR	Draft Letter Requirement (MCD)
DLR	Driving Licences Regulations [British] (ILCA)
DLR	Driving after License Revoked
DLR	Dynamic Line Regulation
DLR	Dynamic Load Regulation
DLRA	Department of Labor Recreation Association
DLRA	Door Lock Rotary Actuator
DLRB........	Digest of Decisions of the National Labor Relations Board [A publication]
DLR (Can) ...	Dominion Law Reports (Canada) [A publication]
DLRD	Design Layout Report Date [Telecommunications] (TEL)
DLR 2d	Dominion Law Reports. Second Series [A publication]
DLR 3d	Dominion Law Reports. Third Series [A publication]
DLR 2d (Can) ...	Dominion Law Reports. Second Series (Canada) [A publication]
DLRED......	Duquesne Law Review [A publication]
DL Rep......	DL [Dominion Laboratory] Report [A publication]
DLRF........	Direct Loan Revolving Fund [Department of Veterans Affairs]
DLRL	Diffraction Limited Raman LASER
DLRO	District Labor Relations Office [or Officer] [Navy]
DLRP........	Data Link Reference Point (NVT)
DLRU	Dryland Research Unit [Washington State University] [Research center] (RCD)
DLRUAJ ...	Deutsche Lebensmittel Rundschau [A publication]
DLRV	Dual Mode Lunar Roving Vehicle [NASA]
DLRWS.....	Dirty Liquid Radioactive Waste System [Nuclear energy] (NRCH)
DLS...........	Dallas [Texas] [Seismograph station code, US Geological Survey] [Closed] (SEIS)
DLS............	Dallas Corp. [NYSE symbol] (SPSG)
DLS............	Data Link Set
DLS............	Data Link Simulator
DLS............	Data Link Support
DLS............	Data Logging System
DLS............	Debt Liquidation Schedule
DLS............	Decoy Launching System [Navy] (CAAL)
DLS............	Deep Look Surveillance (MCD)
DLS............	Defence Light Section [British military] (DMA)
DLS............	Defense Legal Services Agency [DoD]
DLS............	Delay Line Synthesizer
DLS............	Deutsche Literatur und Sprachstudien [A publication]
DLS............	Differential Light Scattering
DLS............	Digital Library Systems, Inc. [Database producer] (IID)
DLS............	Digital Line System [Telecommunications] (TEL)
DLS............	Digital Logic System
DLS............	Direct Least Squares [Econometrics]
DLS............	Direct Logistical Support (RDA)
DLS............	Director of Legal Services [British military] (DMA)
DLS............	Distance Least-Squares [Mathematics]
DLS............	Divergent Lobed Suppressor [NASA]
DLS............	Division of Labor Studies [Indiana University] [Research center] (RCD)
DLS............	Doctor of Library Science
DLS............	Documents of Limited Significance (MCD)
DLS............	Dogwood Library System [Library network]
dls............	Dolares [Dollars] [Monetary unit] [Spanish]
DLS............	Dollars [Monetary unit]
DLS............	Dominion Land Surveyor [Canada]

DLS...........	Double Left Shift
DLS............	Driving after License Suspended
DLS............	DuPage Library System [Library network]
DLS............	Dynamic Light Scattering
DLS............	Dynamic Load Simulator (NASA)
DLS............	The Dalles, OR [Location identifier] [FAA] (FAAL)
DLS............	University of Pittsburgh, School of Librarianship and Information Science, Pittsburgh, PA [OCLC symbol] (OCLC)
DLSA........	Defense Legal Services Agency [DoD]
DLSA........	Digital Linear Slide Switch Assembly
DLSC........	Defense Logistics Service Center [Military] (AFIT)
DLSC........	Defense Logistics Support Center [Military]
DLSC........	Defense Logistics System Center
DLSC........	Differential Logistics Services Center [AEC]
DL Sc	Doctor of Library Science
DLSEF......	Division of Library Services and Educational Facilities [Office of Education]
DLSHLS ...	Dorothy L. Sayers Historical and Literary Society [British]
DLSI	Detectable Least Signal Increment [Instrumentation]
DLSIE	Defense Logistics Studies Information Exchange [Army]
DLSLD	Documents of Limited Significance - Limited Distribution (MCD)
DLSM.......	Data Link Summary Message (MCD)
D/LSM......	Directorate of Logistic Support Management [or Manager] (AAG)
DLSN	Dorsolateral Septal Nucleus [Neuroanatomy]
DLSO	Dial Line Service Observing [Telecommunications] (TEL)
DLSPDC ...	Distinguished Lecture Series. Society of the General Physiologists [A publication]
DLSS	Digital Linear Slide Switch (MCD)
DLSS	Direct Logistic Support System (MCD)
DLSSA	Digital Linear Slide Switch Assembly (MCD)
DLSSO	Defense Logistics Standards Systems Office
DLS Soc.....	Dorothy L. Sayers Society (EAIO)
DLST	Division Logistics System Test [Army] (AABC)
DLST/SEACAPS ...	Division Logistics System Test/Seventh Army Card Processor System
DLT	Dalton [California] [Seismograph station code, US Geological Survey] [Closed] (SEIS)
DLT	Darton, Longman & Todd [Publisher] [British]
DLT	Data Link Terminal
DLT	Data Link Translator
DLT	Data Loop Transceiver [Data processing]
DLT	Decision Logic Table [DoD]
DLT	Decision Logic Translator
DLT	Deck Landing Training
DLT	Delete (FAAC)
DLT	Delivery Lead Time [Army]
DLT	Delta Air Lines, Inc. (MCD)
DLT	Deltona Corp. [NYSE symbol] (SPSG)
DLT	Depletion-Layer Transistor (IEEE)
DLT	Development Land Tax [British]
DLT	Digital Line Termination [Telecommunications] (TEL)
DLT	Dihydroepiandrosterone Loading Test [Endocrinology]
DLT	Dilauryl Thiodipropionate [Also, DLTDP, DLTP] [Food preservative]
DLT	Direct Labor Time
DLT	Distributed Language Translation [Project being developed by BSO, a Dutch computer company]
DLT	Double Reduction-Locked Train
DLTA	DeltaUS Corp. [Formerly, Delta Drilling Co.] [NASDAQ symbol] (NQ)
DLTDP......	Dilauryl Thiodipropionate [Also, DLT, DLTP] [Food preservative]
DLTK........	Deltak Corp. [NASDAQ symbol] (NQ)
DLTM	Data Line Terminal Module [Military] (RDA)
DLTM	Data Link Test Message
DLTMA.....	Dynamic Load Thermo-Mechanical Analysis [Thermal analysis]
DLTOE......	Draft Living Table of Organization and Equipment [Military] (INF)
DLT/P.......	Deck-Landing Training/Practice [Navy] [British]
DLTP........	Dilauryl Thiodipropionate [Also, DLT, DLTDP] [Food preservative]
DLTPAE ...	Dialysis and Transplantation [A publication]
DLTR........	Data Link Terminal Repeater (NASA)
DLTR........	Data Link Transmission Repeater (NASA)
DLTRBL ...	Desert Locust Control Organization for Eastern Africa. Technical Report [A publication]
DLTS........	Deck Landing Training School
DLTS........	Deep Level Transient Spectroscopy
DLTS........	Defraction Limited Thermograph System (MCD)
DLTT........	Down-Link Television Terminal
DLTX........	Daltex Medical Sciences, Inc. [NASDAQ symbol] (NQ)
DLtz..........	Deutsche Literaturzeitung [A publication]
DLTZA......	DLZ. Die Landtechnische Zeitschrift [A publication]
DLU	Data Line Unit
DLU	Development Laboratory Unit (MCD)
DLU	Digital Line Unit [Telecommunications]
DLU	Digitizer Logic Unit

DLU..........	Display Logic Unit
DLV	Differential Lung Ventilation
DLV	Discharge-Line Volume [*Nuclear energy*] (NRCH)
DLV	Montgomery, AL [*Location identifier*] [*FAA*] (FAAL)
DLVD........	Delivered (NATG)
DLVO........	Derjaguin-Landau-Verwey-Overbeek [*Colloid science*]
DLVR	Deliver (AABC)
DLVY	Delivery (MSA)
DL & W	Delaware, Lackawanna & Western Railroad [*Nicknames: Delay, Linger & Wait; Darn Long & Winding; Dirty, Long & Weary*]
DLW	Delaware, Lackawanna & Western Railroad [*AAR code*]
DLW	Delaware Resources Corp. [*Vancouver Stock Exchange symbol*]
DLW	Delta Woodside Industries, Inc. [*NYSE symbol*] (CTT)
DLW	Deutsches Lesewerk [*A publication*]
DLWL.......	Discharge-Line Water-Leg Length [*Nuclear energy*] (NRCH)
D Lw Pr......	Deutsche Landwirtschaftliche Presse [*A publication*]
DL & WRR ...	Delaware, Lackawanna & Western Railroad
D Lwsch.....	Deutsche Landwirtschaft [*A publication*]
DLX	Deluxe (MSA)
DLX	DeLuxe Corp. [*NYSE symbol*] (SPSG)
DLX	Die Lock
DLX	Dylex Ltd. [*Toronto Stock Exchange symbol*]
DLX	Washington, DC [*Location identifier*] [*FAA*] (FAAL)
DLY	Daily
DLY	Delay (KSC)
DLY	Delivery (ROG)
DLY	Dillon Bay [*Vanuatu*] [*Airport symbol*] (OAG)
DLY	Dolly (MSA)
DLZ	Delaware, OH [*Location identifier*] [*FAA*] (FAAL)
DLZ	Deutsche Lehrerzeitung [*A publication*]
DLZ	Deutsche Literaturzeitung [*A publication*]
DLZ	Deutsche Lotto-Zeitung [*A publication*]
DLZ	Die Landtechnische Zeitschrift [*A publication*]
DLZ	Drop Landing Zone [*Air Force*] (AFM)
DLZ Die Landtech Z ...	DLZ. Die Landtechnische Zeitschrift [*A publication*]
DL Zg........	Deutsche Literarische Zeitung [*A publication*]
dm	Dahomey [*Benin*] [*MARC country of publication code*] [*Library of Congress*] (LCCP)
DM..............	Daily Mail [*United Kingdom*] [*A publication*]
DM..............	Dam
D of M.........	Dames of Malta (EA)
DM..............	Damien Ministries (EA)
DM..............	Dance Magazine [*A publication*]
D/M..........	Dance/Movement Therapy
DM..............	Danske Magazin [*A publication*]
DM..............	Dark Matter [*Astrophysics*]
DM..............	Data Management (KSC)
DM..............	Data Manager
DM..............	Data Master
DM..............	Data Memory
DM..............	Daughters of Mary of the Immaculate Conception [*Roman Catholic religious order*]
DM..............	Daughters of Our Lady of Mercy [*Roman Catholic religious order*]
DM..............	Daunomycin [*Antineoplastic drug*]
D & M........	Davison and Merivale's English Queen's Bench Reports [*A publication*] (DLA)
DM..............	Davison and Merivale's King's Bench Reports [*64 RR*] [*1843-44*] [*A publication*] (DLA)
DM..............	Deacon and Martyr [*Church calendars*]
DM..............	Deaf Missions (EA)
DM..............	Debater's Magazine [*A publication*]
DM..............	Debit Memorandum (MCD)
DM..............	Debugging Mode
DM..............	Decameter
DM..............	Decamired
DM..............	Deciduous (Primary) Molar [*Dentistry*]
DM..............	Decimal Multiply
DM..............	Decimeter [*Unit of measure*]
DM..............	Decision Maker
DM..............	Decreto Ministeriale [*Ministerial Decree*] [*Italian*] (ILCA)
DM..............	Dekameter [*Unit of measure*]
DM..............	Deletion Mutant [*Genetics*]
DM..............	Delta Ministry [*Later, DMM*] (EA)
DM..............	Delta Modulation
DM..............	Demand Meter
DM..............	Demineralized [*Water*] (NRCH)
D/M..........	Demodulate/Modulate
DM..............	Density Meter [*Instrumentation*]
DM..............	Dental Mechanic [*Ranking title*] [*British Royal Navy*]
DM..............	Depot Manufacture (MCD)
DM..............	Deputy Master [*Freemasonry*] (ROG)
DM..............	Deputy for Materiel
DM..............	Dermatomyositis [*Medicine*]
DM..............	Descriptive Method
DM..............	Design Manual
DM..............	Design Memorandum
DM..............	Destroyer Minelayer [*Navy symbol*] (MCD)
DM..............	Detector Mosaic
DM..............	Detroit & Mackinac Railway Co. [*AAR code*]
D & M........	Detroit & Mackinac Railway Co.
DM..............	Deutsche Mark [*Monetary unit*] [*Germany*]
DM..............	Development Milestone [*Aerospace*] (AAG)
DM..............	Development Motor (MCD)
DM..............	Developments in Mammals [*Elsevier Book Series*] [*A publication*]
DM..............	Devon Militia [*British military*] (DMA)
DM..............	Dextromethorphan [*Antitussive*] [*Pharmacy*]
DM..............	Diabetes Mellitus [*Medicine*]
DM..............	Diabetic Mother [*Medicine*]
DM..............	Diastolic Murmur [*Medicine*]
DM..............	Dichroic Mirror
DM..............	Die Musik [*A publication*]
DM..............	Diesel Mechanic [*or Mechanical*]
DM..............	Dieses Monats [*Of This Month*] [*German*] (ROG)
DM..............	Diffused Mesa
DM..............	Digital Module [*Telecommunications*] (TEL)
DM..............	Digital Music Tuner [*Cable television*]
DM..............	Diis Manibus [*To the Manes, i.e., Departed Souls*] [*Latin*]
DM..............	Dioxane-Methanol [*Scintillation solvent*] [*Bray solution*]
DM..............	Diphenylaminechloroarsine [*Tear gas*] [*Army symbol*]
D-M..........	Diplomate, American Board of Internal Medicine (DHSM)
DM..............	Direct Mail
DM..............	Direct Marketing
DM..............	Direct Marketing [*A publication*]
DM..............	Director of Management [*Military*]
D of M........	Director of Manning [*British military*] (DMA)
DM..............	Director of Mobilization [*British military*] (DMA)
DM..............	Director of Music [*British military*] (DMA)
DM..............	Directorate of Maintenance (AFIT)
DM..............	Disassembly Manual (MCD)
DM..............	Discard Message (CET)
DM..............	Disconnected Mode
DM..............	Disconnecting Manhole
DM..............	Diseased Mucosa [*Oncology*]
D/M..........	Disintegrations per Minute
DM..............	Dispersion Measure [*Astronomy*]
DM..............	Distribution Module [*Telecommunications*]
DM..............	District Manager
DM..............	District Members [*Also, EN for secrecy*] [*Fenian Brotherhood*] (ROG)
DM..............	Ditch Mile [*Newmarket Racecourse*] [*Horseracing*] [*British*]
DM..............	DM/Disease-a-Month [*A publication*]
DM..............	Docking Mechanism (MCD)
DM..............	Docking Module [*NASA*]
D & M........	Doctor and Martyr (ROG)
DM..............	Doctor of Mathematics
DM..............	Doctor of Medicine
DM..............	Doctor of Music
DM..............	Documenta et Monumenta [*A publication*] (BJA)
DM..............	Documentation Manager [*Air Force*] (AFM)
DM..............	Dome Mines Ltd. [*NYSE symbol*] [*Toronto Stock Exchange symbol*] (SPSG)
DM..............	Dominica [*ANSI two-letter standard code*] (CNC)
DM..............	Doppler Missile (MUGU)
DM..............	Dot Matrix
DM..............	Double Master [*LORAN stations*]
DM..............	Double Medium (ADA)
DM..............	Double Minute [*Cytology*]
DM..............	Drafting Manual (AABC)
DM..............	Dram (MCD)
D & M........	Dressed and Matched [*Technical drawings*]
DM..............	Drive Magnet
DM..............	Driver, Master
DM..............	Driver Mechanic [*British military*] (DMA)
DM..............	Drum
DM..............	Dry Mass
DM..............	Dry Matter
DM..............	Dublin Magazine [*A publication*]
DM..............	Dummy Round (MCD)
DM..............	Dungeon Master [*In game Dungeons and Dragons*]
DM..............	Illustrator Draftsman [*Navy rating*]
DM..............	Iran [*License plate code assigned to foreign diplomats in the US*]
DM..............	Light Minelayer [*Later, MMD*] [*Navy symbol*]
DM..............	Maersk Air I/S [*Denmark*] [*ICAO designator*] (FAAC)
DM..............	Magnetic Drum Module [*Data processing*]
DM..............	Master Diver [*Navy*]
DM..............	Master of Divinity
D of M........	Supreme Caldron, Daughters of Mokanna (EA)
DM..............	Vomiting Gas [*US Chemical Corps symbol*]
Dm²	Square Decimeter (ROG)
Dm³	Cubic Decimeter (ROG)
DMA..........	Dance Masters of America (EA)
DMA..........	Data Management Agent (MCD)
DMA..........	Data Management Analysis
DMA..........	Dealer Management Association [*Commercial firm*] [*Exeter, NH*]
DMA..........	Dean Martin Association (EAIO)
DMA..........	Debt Market Analysis [*MMS International*] [*Information service or system*] (CRD)

DMA......... Defence Manufacturers Association [*United Kingdom*] (DS)
DMA......... Defense Manpower Administration [*Superseded by Office of Manpower Administration, 1953*] [*Department of Labor*]
DMA......... Defense Mapping Agency [*Washington, DC*]
DMA......... Degraded Mission Assessment
DMA......... Dental Manufacturers of America (EA)
DMA......... Department of Memorial Affairs [*Veterans Administration*]
DMA......... Deployed Mechanical Assembly (MCD)
DMA......... Depot Maintenance Activity (MCD)
DMA......... Design Management Award [*Financial Times and London Business School*] [*British*]
DMA......... Designated Maintenance Activity (MCD)
DMA......... Designated Market Area [*Advertising*]
DMA......... Devil Mountain [*Alaska*] [*Seismograph station code, US Geological Survey*] (SEIS)
DMA......... Dietary Managers Association (EA)
DMA......... Digital Major Alarm (MCD)
DMA......... Dihydroxymandelic Acid [*Also, DHMA, DOMA*] [*Organic chemistry*]
DMA......... Dimethyl Adipimidate [*Biochemistry*]
DMA......... Dimethyl Arsonic Acid [*Organic chemistry*]
DMA......... Dimethylacetamide [*Also, DMAC*] [*Organic chemistry*]
DMA......... Dimethylamine [*Organic chemistry*]
DMA......... Dimethylaniline [*Organic chemistry*]
DMA......... Dimethylarginine [*Biochemistry*]
DMA......... Diploma in Municipal Accounting (ADA)
DMA......... Diploma in Municipal Administration [*British*]
DMA......... Direct Marketing Association [*New York, NY*] (EA)
DMA......... Direct Memory Access [*Computing method*]
DMA......... Direct Memory Address [*Data processing*]
DMA......... Director of Military Assistance
DMA......... District Manager's Assistant [*British*] (DCTA)
DMA......... Division of Military Application [*Energy Research and Development Administration*]
DMA......... Divisional Maintenance Area [*Military*] [*British*]
DMA......... Doctor of Municipal Administration
DMA......... Doctor of Musical Arts
DMA......... Dominica [*ANSI three-letter standard code*] (CNC)
DMA......... Double Motor Alternator
DMA......... Drive Motor Assembly (MCD)
DMA......... Drum Memory Assembly [*Data processing*]
DMA......... Dynamic Mechanical Analysis
DMA......... Tucson, AZ [*Location identifier*] [*FAA*] (FAAL)
DMA......... United States Maritime Administration, Washington, DC [*Library symbol*] [*Library of Congress*] (LCLS)
DMAA...... Dimethylarsenonic Acid [*Organic chemistry*]
DMAA...... Direct Mail Advertising Association [*Later, DMMA*]
DMAAC.... Defense Mapping Agency Aerospace Center [*Formerly, ACIC*]
DMAAC-TC ... Defense Mapping Agency Aerospace Center Technical Library/Translation Section
DMAB...... Defended Modular Array Basing [*Military*]
DMAB...... Dimethylaminobenzaldehyde [*Ehrlich's reagent*] [*Analytical chemistry*]
DMAB...... Dimethylaminoborane [*Organic chemistry*]
DMAC...... Dimethylacetamide [*Also, DMA*] [*Organic chemistry*]
DMAC...... Direct Memory Access Channel [*Pronounced "DEEmack"*] [*Data processing*]
DMAC...... Direct Memory Access Control [*Data processing*]
DMACC.... Direct Marketing Association Catalog Council [*New York, NY*] (EA)
DMACP.... Direct Memory Access Communications Processor
DMAD...... Diagnostic Machine Aids/Digital [*Raytheon Co.*] [*Programming language*] (CSR)
DMAD...... Dimethylacetylenedicarboxylate [*Organic chemistry*]
DM Adm... Doctor of Municipal Administration
DMAE...... Dimethylaminoethanol [*Antidepressant*]
D Ma E ...... Doctor of Marine Engineering
DMAEMA ... Dimethylaminoethyl Methacrylate [*Organic chemistry*]
D Ma Eng .. Doctor of Marine Engineering
DMAG...... Datamag, Inc. [*NASDAQ symbol*] (NQ)
DMAGAZ ... Durban Museum and Art Gallery. Annual Report [*A publication*]
DMAHC.... Defense Mapping Agency Hydrographic Center [*Later, DMAHTC*]
DMAHTC ... Defense Mapping Agency Hydrographic/Topographic Center [*Washington, DC*] [*Also, an information service or system*] (IID)
DMAI........ Direct Memory Access Interface
D/Maj........ Drum-Major [*British military*] (DMA)
DMAM...... Dimethyl Aminoethyl Methacrylate [*Organic chemistry*]
DMAM...... Di(methylamyl) Maleate [*Organic chemistry*]
DMaM...... United States Marine Corps Museum, Washington, DC [*Library symbol*] [*Library of Congress*] (LCLS)
DMAMDM ... Development in Mammals [*A publication*]
DMAMP... (Dimethylaminomethyl)phenol [*Organic chemistry*]
DMAMP... Dimethylamino(methyl)propanol [*Organic chemistry*]
DMAN...... Data Manager (KSC)
D Manage J ... Defense Management Journal [*A publication*]
DMANS.... Dimethylamino(nitro)stilbene [*Organic chemistry*]
DManSc.... Doctor of Management Sciences
DMAO...... Directorate of Military Aid Overseas [*British*]

DMAP...... DARCOM [*Development and Readiness Command, Army*] Modification Application Plan (MCD)
DMAP...... Digital Missile Autopilot (MCD)
DMAP...... Dimethylaminopyridine [*Organic chemistry*]
DMAP...... Direct Matrix Abstraction Process
DMAPA.... Dimethylaminopropylamine [*Also, DIMAPA*] [*Organic chemistry*]
DMAPMA ... Dimethylaminopropyl Methacrylamide [*Organic chemistry*]
DMAPN.... Dimethylaminopropionitrile [*Organic chemistry*]
DMAPP... Dimethylallyl Pyrophosphate [*Organic chemistry*]
DMAR...... Datamarine International, Inc. [*NASDAQ symbol*] (NQ)
DMAR...... Deferred Maintenance and Repair [*DoD*]
DMarC...... Marist College, Washington, DC [*Library symbol*] [*Library of Congress*] (LCLS)
DMARD.... Disease-Modifying Antirheumatic Drug [*Medicine*]
DMarS..... Marist Seminary, Washington, DC [*Library symbol*] [*Library of Congress*] (LCLS)
DMAS...... Defense Material Allotment System (AFIT)
DMAS...... Digital Modular Avionics System
DMAS..... Distribution Management Accounting System (IEEE)
D Mass..... United States District Court for the District of Massachusetts (DLA)
DMAT...... Digital Module Automatic Tester
DMATC.... Defense Mapping Agency Topographic Center [*Later, DMAHTC*]
DMATS.... Defense Metropolitan Area Telephone Service [*or System*] (MCD)
DMB......... Data Management Block
DMB......... Defense Mobilization Board [*Terminated, 1958*]
DMB......... Demineralized Bone [*Medicine*]
DMB......... Department of Management and Budget [*Australia*]
DMB......... Developments in Marine Biology [*Elsevier Book Series*] [*A publication*]
DMB......... Dibutanoylmorphine [*An analgesic*]
DMB......... Dihydro(methyl)benzodiazepinone [*Biochemistry*]
DMB......... Dimethoxybenzene [*Organic chemistry*]
DMB......... Dimethylbenzamil [*Organic chemistry*]
DMB......... Dimethylbusulfan [*Organic chemistry*]
DMB......... Dimethylmethylene Blue [*Organic chemistry*]
DMB......... Disconnect and Make Busy [*Telecommunications*] (TEL)
DMB......... Distinguished Marksmanship Badge
DMB......... Division Maintenance Battalion (MCD)
DmB......... Driemaandelijkse Bladen [*A publication*]
DMBA...... Dimethylbarbituric Acid [*Organic chemistry*]
DMBA...... Dimethylbenzanthracene [*Carcinogen*]
DMBA...... Dimethyl(butyl)amine [*Organic chemistry*]
DMBAO.... Dimethylbenzanthraceneoxide [*Organic chemistry*]
DMBAS.... Dimethoxy(amino)stilbene [*Organic chemistry*]
DMBC...... Dimethylbenzylcarbinol [*Organic chemistry*]
DMBC...... Double Mark Blank Column (BUR)
DMBCA.... Dimethylbenzylcarbinol Acetate [*Organic chemistry*]
DMBK...... Dominion Bankshares Corp. [*NASDAQ symbol*] (NQ)
DMBS...... Defense Material Billing System (AFIT)
DMBUA... Danish Medical Bulletin [*A publication*]
DMBZ..... Dimethylbenzimidazole [*Organic chemistry*]
DMC......... Chief Illustrator Draftsman [*Navy rating*]
DMC......... Darryl McDaniels [*A rap recording artist whose initials appear in the album title, "Run-D.M.C."*]
DMC......... Data Management Center (CAAL)
DMC......... Data Management Channel
DMC......... Data Management Computer (KSC)
DmC......... Data Microfilming Corp., Whittier, CA [*Library symbol*] [*Library of Congress*] (LCLS)
DMC......... Deck Motion Compensator (MCD)
DMC......... Defense Manpower Commission
DMC......... Defense Materiel Council [*DoD*]
DMC......... Degraded Mission Capability
DMC......... DeLorean Motor Company [*Initials used as name of its cars*]
DMC......... Demeclocycline [*Also, DMCT*] [*Antimicrobial compound*]
DMC......... Democratic Movement for Change [*Political party*] [*Israel*]
DMC......... Deputy Marshal of Ceremonies (ROG)
DMC......... Design, Manage, Construct
DMC......... Destination Management Company [*Generic term*]
DMC......... Developing Member Country [*Asian Development Bank*]
DMC......... Dichlorodiphenylmethylcarbinol [*Also, DCPC*] [*Insecticide*]
DMC......... Digital Microcircuit
DMC......... Digital Monitor Computer
DMC......... Dimethoxychalcone [*Organic chemistry*]
DMC......... Dimethyl Carbinol [*Organic chemistry*]
DMC......... Dimethyl Carbonate [*Organic chemistry*]
DMC......... Dimethylaminoethyl Chloride [*Organic chemistry*]
DMC......... Dimethylcysteine (Penicillamine) [*Pharmacology*]
DMC......... Direct Maintenance Cost (NASA)
DMC......... Direct Memory Channel
DMC......... Direct Microscopic Count
DMC......... Direct Multiplexed Control
DMC......... Direct Multiplexor Channel
DMC......... Discrete Memoryless Channel [*Data processing*]
DMC......... Disk Memory Controller [*Data processing*]
DMC......... Diversified Industries, Inc. [*NYSE symbol*] (SPSG)
DMC......... Dough-Molding Compound [*Plastics technology*]

DMC......... DSIF [*Deep Space Instrumentation Facility*] Monitor and Control Subsystem [*NASA*]
DMC......... Dull Men's Club (EA)
DMC......... Dynamic Matrix Control [*Chemical engineering*] [*Data processing*]
DMC......... Merkblaetter fuer den Aussenhandel [*A publication*]
DMC......... Metropolitan Club, Washington, DC [*Library symbol*] [*Library of Congress*] (LCLS)
DMC's....... Dialysis-Related Muscle Cramps [*Medicine*]
DMCA....... DeLorean Motor Club of America [*Commercial firm*] (EA)
DMCA....... Dependents' Medical Care Act [*HEW*]
DMCA....... Direct Marketing Computer Association [*Defunct*] (EA)
DMCA....... Direct Marketing Credit Association [*Stamford, CT*] (EA)
DMCB....... Data Measurement Corporation [*Gaithersburg, MD*] [*NASDAQ symbol*] (NQ)
DMCBAC ... Dimethylcetylbenzylammonium Chloride [*Antiseptic*] [*Organic chemistry*]
DMCBDX ... Developments in Molecular and Cellular Biochemistry [*A publication*]
DMCC....... Dean Martin Collector's Club [*Defunct*] (EA)
DMCC....... Depot Maintenance Control [*or Coordinator*] Center [*Army*] (AABC)
DMCC....... Dimethylcarbamoyl Chloride [*Organic chemistry*]
DMCC....... Direct Microscopic Clump Counts
DMCCC .... Deputy Missile Combat Crew Commander
DMCd....... Dimethylcadmium
DMCF....... Deservicing, Maintenance, and Checkout Facility [*NASA*] (NASA)
DMCG....... Direct Marketing Creative Guild [*New York, NY*] (EA)
DMCHA... Dimethylcyclohexamine [*Organic chemistry*]
DMCL....... Device Media Control Language [*CODASYL/Honeywell, Inc.*]
DMCL....... Digital MODEM Command Language [*Data processing*] (BYTE)
DMCM...... Double Density Modular Core Memory (MCD)
DMCM...... Master Chief Illustrator Draftsman [*Navy rating*]
DMCNA..... Developmental Medicine and Child Neurology [*A publication*]
DMCNAW .. Developmental Medicine and Child Neurology [*A publication*]
DMCOD.... Dimethylcyclooctadiene [*Organic chemistry*]
DMC/PC... Drives, Motors, Controls, and Programmable Controllers Exhibition [*British*] (ITD)
DMCR....... Director, Marine Corps Reserve
DMCS....... Data Med Clinical Support Services, Inc. [*NASDAQ symbol*] (NQ)
DMCS....... Dimethyldichlorosilane [*Organic chemistry*]
DMCS....... Senior Chief Illustrator Draftsman [*Navy rating*]
DMCSAD ... Developmental Medicine and Child Neurology. Supplement [*A publication*]
DMCT....... Demethylchlortetracycline [*Obsolete name*] [*Antimicrobial compound*] [*See DMC*]
DMCT....... Directorate of Missile Captive Test (AAG)
DMCU....... Display Monitor and Control Unit
DMCV....... Dairy Mart Convenience Stores, Inc. [*NASDAQ symbol*] (NQ)
DM & CW ... Diploma in Maternity and Child Welfare (ADA)
DMD......... Carrizo Springs, TX [*Location identifier*] [*FAA*] (FAAL)
DMD......... Data Model Diagramer [*Data processing*]
DMD......... Deformable Device [*Texas Instruments, Inc.*] [*Data processing*]
DMD......... Delmed, Inc. [*AMEX symbol*] (SPSG)
DMD......... Deployment Manning Document (MCD)
Dm/d......... Depth Molded (DS)
DMD......... Diamond (MSA)
DMD......... Diamond Resources [*Vancouver Stock Exchange symbol*]
DMD......... Digital Map Display
DMD......... Digital Message Device (AABC)
DMD......... Digital Muirhead Display (NOAA)
DMD......... Digoxigenin Monodigitoxoside [*Biochemistry*]
DMD......... Dimethadione [*Biochemistry*]
DMD......... Doctor of Dental Medicine
DMD......... Doctor of Mathematics and Didactics
DMD......... Doctor of Medical Dentistry
DMD......... Domodossola [*Italy*] [*Seismograph station code, US Geological Survey*] [*Closed*] (SEIS)
DMD......... Doomadgee Mission [*Australia*] [*Airport symbol*] (OAG)
DMD......... Dual Mode Display
DMD......... Duchenne Muscular Dystrophy
DMD......... Dynamic Map Display
DMD......... Dystonia Musculorum Deformans [*Medicine*]
D MD........ United States District Court for the District of Maryland (DLA)
DMDB....... Depot Maintenance Data Bank [*DARCOM*] (MCD)
DMDC....... Defense Manpower Data Center [*Alexandria, VA*]
DMDC....... Diffusion in Metals and Alloys Data Center [*National Institute of Standards and Technology*] (IID)
DMDC....... Dimethyl Dicarbonate [*Fungistatic agent*]
DMDC....... Dimethyldithiocarbamate [*Organic chemistry*]
DMDEL ... Dimethyldiethyllead [*Organic chemistry*]
DMDG....... Department of the Medical Director-General [*Navy*] [*British*]
DMDG....... Digital Message Device Group [*Later, SOICS*] [*Army*] (INF)
DMDGA..... DECHEMA [*Deutsche Gesellschaft fuer Chemisches Apparatewesen, Chemische Technik, und Biotechnologie eV*] Monographien [*A publication*]

DMDHEU ... Dimethylol Dihydroxyethyleneurea [*Used to provide durable press finish in fabrics*]
DM Dis Mon ... DM/Disease-a-Month [*A publication*]
DMDMH .. Dimethylol dimethylhydantoin [*Organic chemistry*]
DMDP....... Data Maintenance Diagnostic Program
DMD/PACT ... Digital Message Device/Processing and Communication Terminal (MCD)
DMDR....... (Demethoxy)daunorubicin [*Antineoplastic drug*]
DMDS....... Dimethyl Disulfide [*Organic chemistry*]
DMDSAI.... Drug Metabolism and Disposition [*A publication*]
DM & E..... Dakota, Minnesota & Eastern Railroad
DME......... Department of Mechanics [*JHU*]
DME......... Design Margin Evaluation (NG)
DME......... Design Mission Effect
DME......... Design Mission Evaluation
DME......... Diagnostic Monitor Executive [*Data processing*]
DME......... Digital Motor Electronics
DME......... Digital Multiplex Equipment [*Telecommunications*]
DME......... Dime Savings Bank of New York [*NYSE symbol*] (SPSG)
DME......... Dimethoxyethane [*Also known as GLYME*] [*Organic chemistry*]
DME......... Dimethyl Ether [*Organic chemistry*]
DME......... Dimethylethanolamine [*Organic chemistry*]
DME......... Diploma in Mechanical Engineering (ADA)
DME......... Direct Machine Environment
DME......... Direct Measurements Explorer [*Satellite*]
DME......... Director of Mechanical Engineering [*War Office*] [*British*] [*World War II*]
DME......... Director of Medical Education
DME......... Distance Measuring Equipment [*Navigation*]
DME......... Distance Monitoring Equipment [*Military*]
DME......... Doctor of Mechanical Engineering
D Me........ Doctor of Metaphysics
DME......... Dropping Mercury Electrode [*Electrochemistry*]
DME......... Dulbecco's Modified Eagle's Medium [*Also, DMEM, DMM*] [*Medium for cell growth*]
DME......... Durable Medical Equipment
DME......... Moscow [*USSR*] [*Airport symbol*]
DME......... Moscow [*USSR*] Domodedovo Airport [*Airport symbol*] (OAG)
DME......... United States Department of Commerce, National Oceanic and Atmospheric Administration, Marine and Earth Sciences Library, Rockville, MD [*Library symbol*] [*Library of Congress*] (LCLS)
D ME........ United States District Court for the District of Maine (DLA)
DMEA ...... Damage Modes and Effects Analysis (MCD)
DMEA ...... Defense Minerals Exploration Administration [*Department of the Interior*]
DME-A...... Direct Measurements Explorer A [*Satellite*]
D Mech ..... Doctor of Mechanics
DME/COTAR ... Distance Measuring Equipment/Correlation Tracking and Ranging
DMeCP...... Dimethylcarboxypsoralen [*Metabolite of TMeP*]
DMED....... Digital Message Entry Device [*Data processing*]
DMED....... Dimensional Medicine, Inc. [*Minnetonka, MN*] [*NASDAQ symbol*] (NQ)
D Med .... Doctor of Medicine
DM Ed .... Doctor of Musical Education
DMEDA .... Director of Medical Activities (AABC)
DMedRehab ... Diploma in Medical Rehabilitation [*British*] (DBQ)
DMEF .... Dannemiller Memorial Educational Foundation (EA)
DMEF .... Direct Marketing Educational Foundation [*New York, NY*] (EA)
DMEG ...... Discharge Multimedia Environmental Goals [*Environmental Protection Agency*]
DMEM...... Dulbecco's Minimum Essential Medium
DMEM...... Dulbecco's Modified Eagle's Medium [*Also, DME, DMM*] [*Medium for cell growth*]
DM Eng ..... Doctor of Mechanical Engineering
DMEP....... Data Network Modified Emulator Program [*Telecommunications*] (TEL)
D & Mer..... Davison and Merivale's English Queen's Bench Reports [*A publication*] (DLA)
DMES........ Digital Message Entry System
DMET .... Defense Management Educating and Training [*DoD*] (AFM)
DMET .... Digital Metcom, Inc. [*NASDAQ symbol*] (NQ)
DMET .... Distance Measuring Equipment TACAN [*Tactical Air Navigation*] (NG)
DMET .... Distance Measuring Equipment Terminal (CET)
D Met........ Doctor of Metallurgy
DMet........ Doctor of Meteorology (ADA)
DMETB...... Defense Management Education and Training Board [*DoD*]
D Met E ..... Doctor of Metallurgical Engineering
DMETEG ... Dimethyl Ether of Tetraethylene Glycol [*Organic chemistry*]
D Met Eng ... Doctor of Metallurgical Engineering
DMEU....... Dimethylolethyleneurea [*Organic chemistry*]
DMEV .... Distance Measuring Equipment-Collocated with VOR [*Very-High-Frequency Omnidirectional Range*] (FAAC)
DMEW ...... Deterministic Mix Evaluation Worldwide (MCD)
DMF.......... Dance Magazine Foundation (EA)
DMF.......... Data Management Facility

DMF .... Data Migration Facility [*Data processing*]
DMF .... Decayed, Missing, Filled [*Dentistry*]
DMF .... Deoxymorpholinofructose [*Biochemistry*]
DMF .... Digital Matched Filter
DMF .... Digital Multiplexing and Formatting [*Data processing*] (MCD)
DMF .... Dimethylformamide [*Also, DMFA*] [*Organic chemistry*]
DMF .... Disk Management Facility [*Data processing*]
DMF .... Dominican Mission Foundation (EA)
DMF .... Dose Modifying Factor [*Medicine*]
DMF .... Dreyfus Municipal Income, Inc. [*AMEX symbol*] (CTT)
DMF .... DSIF [*Deep Space Instrumentation Facility*] Maintenance Facility [*NASA*]
DMF .... Dummy Missile Firing
DMFA ...... Dimethylformamide [*Also, DMF*] [*Organic chemistry*]
DMFA ...... Direct Mail Fundraisers Association (EA)
DMFC ...... Debbie Myers Fan Club (EA)
DMFC ...... Direct Methanol Fuel Cell
DMFL .... Dimethylformal [*Organic chemistry*]
DMFS ...... Decayed, Missing, or Filled Surfaces [*Dentistry*]
DMFT ...... Decayed, Missing, and Filled Teeth [*Dentistry*]
DMG .... Damage (AFM)
DMG .... Data Management [*A publication*]
DMG .... Data Management Group (MCD)
D M & G .... De Gex, Macnaghten, and Gordon's English Chancery Reports [*A publication*] (DLA)
DMG .... De Maasgouw. Orgaan voor Limbrugsche Geschiedenis, Taal-en Letterkunde [*A publication*]
DMG .... Defense Marketing Group [*AMA*]
DMG .... Deputy Master-General [*Military*] [*British*]
DMG .... Deputy Military Governor [*US Military Government, Germany*]
DMG .... Deutsche Morgenlaendische Gesellschaft [*A publication*]
DMG .... Deutsches Mozartfest der Deutschen Mozart-Gesellschaft [*A publication*]
DMG .... Dimethylglycine [*Biochemistry*]
DMG .... Dimethylglyoxime [*Organic chemistry*]
DMG .... Distinguished Military Graduate
DMG .... Documents in Mycenaean Greek [*A publication*]
D M & GB ... De Gex, Macnaghten, and Gordon's English Bankruptcy Reports [*A publication*] (DLA)
DMGBL ..... Dimethyl-gamma-butyrolactone [*Biochemistry*]
DMG-DRS J ... DMG-DRS [*Design Methods Group - Design Research*] Journal [*A publication*]
DMGI .... Dumagami Mines Ltd. [*Toronto, ON*] [*NASDAQ symbol*] (NQ)
DMGMAF ... Mitteilungen der Deutschen Malakozoologischen Gesellschaft [*A publication*]
DMGO ...... Department of the Master General of the Ordnance [*British*]
DMGO ...... Divisional Machine Gun Officer [*British military*] (DMA)
DMGT .... Data Management (MSA)
DMGYA ..... Demography [*A publication*]
DMGZ .... Demagnetize
DMH .... Decimeter Height-Finder [*RADAR*]
DMH .... Department of Mental Health [*or Hygiene*]
DMH .... Dextromethorphan [*Antitussive*] [*Pharmacy*]
DMH .... Dimension House [*Vancouver Stock Exchange symbol*]
DMH .... Dimethylhexane [*Organic chemistry*]
DMH .... Dimethylhydrazine [*Rocket fuel base, convulsant poison*]
DMH .... Direct Man-Hours
DMH .... Drop Manhole [*Technical drawings*]
DMH .... Dual Mode Hydrazine
DMHF ...... Dimethylhydantoin Formaldehyde [*Organic chemistry*]
DMHR ...... Daughters of the Most Holy Redeemer [*Roman Catholic religious order*]
DMHS ...... Director of Medical and Health Services [*British*]
D/M/I .... Decision/Making/Information [*Information service or system*] (IID)
DMI .... Defense Material Item
DMI .... Defense Mechanisms Inventory [*Psychology*]
DMI .... Des Moines [*Iowa*] [*Seismograph station code, US Geological Survey*] [*Closed*] (SEIS)
DMI .... Design Management Institute (EA)
DMI .... Desmethylimipramine [*Antidepressant*]
DMI .... Destratification Motor Impeller
DMI .... Detroit, MI [*Location identifier*] [*FAA*] (FAAL)
DMI .... Diagnostic Mathematics Inventory
DMI .... Diamond Manufacturers and Importers Association of America
DMI .... Dimethyl Isosorbide [*Organic chemistry*]
DMI .... Dimethylimidazolidinone [*Organic chemistry*]
DMI .... Direct Memory Interface
DMI .... Director of Military Intelligence [*US, British*]
DMI .... Directorate of Military Intelligence [*Australia*]
DMI .... Distance Measuring Instrument
DMI .... Dumagami Mines Ltd. [*Toronto Stock Exchange symbol*]
DMI .... Dun's Market Identifiers [*Dun's Marketing Services*] [*Information service or system*] (CRD)
DMIA .... Dual Multiplexer Interface Adapter (NASA)
DMIAA ..... Diamond Manufacturers and Importers Association of America (EA)
DMIC .... Defense Metals Information Center [*Later, MCIC*] [*Battelle Memorial Institute*] (MCD)

DMIC .... Digital Microwave Corp. [*NASDAQ symbol*] (NQ)
DMIC .... Direct Marketing Insurance Council [*New York, NY*] (EA)
D Mic .... Doctor of Microbiology
DMICP ...... Danish Meteorological Institute. Climatological Papers [*Danske Meteorologiske Institut Klimatologiske Meddelelser*] [*A publication*]
DMID .... Diagnostic Microbiology and Infectious Disease [*A publication*]
DMIDDZ .. Diagnostic Microbiology and Infectious Disease [*A publication*]
DMIDF ...... Depot Master Item Data File [*Army*]
D Mi E .... Doctor of Mining Engineering
D Mi Eng .... Doctor of Mining Engineering
DMIF .... Depot Maintenance Industrial Fund (MCD)
DMIF .... DMI Furniture, Inc. [*NASDAQ symbol*] (NQ)
DMIFCUS ... Depot Maintenance Industrial Funding Customer (MCD)
DMII .... Descriptive Method Item Identification [*DoD*]
DMII .... Diagnostic Medical Instruments, Incorporated [*Syracuse, NY*] [*NASDAQ symbol*] (NQ)
D Mil S ..... Doctor of Military Science
DMIM .... Danske Meteorologiske Institut. Meddelelser [*A publication*]
DMIM .... Double Mannitol Isolation Method [*Microscopy*]
DMIM .... Dual Mode Imbedded Munitions (MCD)
D/MIN ...... Disintegrations per Minute
DMIN .... United States Bureau of Marine Inspection and Navigation, Washington, DC [*Library symbol*] [*Library of Congress*] [*Obsolete*] (LCLS)
D Minn ...... United States District Court for the District of Minnesota (DLA)
DMINS ..... Dual Miniature Inertial Navigation Systems (MCD)
DMIP .... Defense Materiel Interservicing Program [*DoD*]
DMIP .... Democratic Malaysia Indian Party [*Political party*] (FEA)
DMIP .... Dimethyl Isophthalate [*Organic chemistry*]
DMIR .... Designated Manufacturing Inspection Representative (MCD)
DMIR .... Duluth, Missabe & Iron Range Railway Co. [*AAR code*]
DM & IR .... Duluth, Missabe & Iron Range Railway Co.
DMIRR ...... Demand Mode Integral Rocket Ramjet (MCD)
DMIS .... Data Management Information System [*DoD*]
DMIS .... DATICO [*Digital Automatic Tape Intelligence Checkout*] Missile Interface Simulator
DMIS .... Dimis, Inc. [*NASDAQ symbol*] (NQ)
DMIS .... Director, Management Information Systems [*Later, ADD*] [*Army*] (AABC)
DMIS .... Donnelley Marketing Information Services [*Database producer*] (IID)
DMISA ...... Depot Maintenance Interservice Support Agreement [*Military*]
DMIU .... Destratification Motor Impeller Unit
DMIWAL ... Deutsche Milchwirtschaft [*A publication*]
DMIWSR ... Danish Meteorological Institute. Weather Service Report [*A publication*]
DMJ .... Daughters of Mary and Joseph [*Roman Catholic religious order*]
DMJ .... Defense Management Journal [*A publication*]
DMJ .... Deus Meumque Jus [*God and My Right*] [*Latin*] [*Freemasonry*]
DMJ .... Diploma in Medical Jurisprudence [*British*]
DMJ (Clin) ... Diploma in Medical Jurisprudence (Clinical) [*British*]
DMJO ...... Defense Management Journal Office [*DoD*]
DMJOA2 .. Deutsches Medizinisches Journal [*A publication*]
DMJOB ..... Defense Management Journal [*A publication*]
DMJP .... Door Mounted Junction Panel
DMJP .... Dragon Missile Jump Pack [*Military*] (MCD)
DMJ (Path) ... Diploma in Medical Jurisprudence (Pathological) [*British*]
DMJS .... December, March, June, September [*Denotes quarterly payments of interest or dividends in these months*] [*Business term*]
DMK .... Demirkoy [*Turkey*] [*Seismograph station code, US Geological Survey*] (SEIS)
DMK .... Dial Marking Kit
DMK .... Digital Equipment Corp., Merrimack, Merrimack, NH [*OCLC symbol*] (OCLC)
DMK .... Direct Action Marketing, Inc. [*AMEX symbol*] (SPSG)
DMK .... Dravida Munnetra Kazhagam [*India*] [*Political party*] (PPW)
DMKK ...... Deutsche Monatsschrift fuer Kolonialpolitik und Kolonisation [*A publication*]
DML .... Data Management Language [*Digital Equipment Corp.*]
DML .... Data Manipulation Language [*Digital Equipment Corp.*] [*Data processing*]
DML .... Demolition
DML .... Depot Maintenance Level
DML .... Depot Maintenance Literature (MCD)
DML .... Developmental Instrumentation Medium-Left
DML .... Dickenson Mines Ltd. [*AMEX symbol*] [*Toronto Stock Exchange symbol*] (SPSG)
DML .... Diffuse Mixed Lymphoma [*Oncology*]
DML .... Digitized Message Link
DML .... Dimyristoyl-Lecithin [*Biochemistry*]
DML .... Dock Mounted Loader (RDA)
DML .... Doctor Martin Luther College, New Ulm, MN [*OCLC symbol*] (OCLC)
DML .... Doctor of Modern Languages
DML .... Double Mars Loiter
DML .... Dry Matter Loss

DML......... Dual Mode LASER
DMLF......... Descending Medial Longitudinal Fasciculus
DMLIA...... Double-Modified Lysine Iron Agar [*Microorganism medium*]
DMLS...... Doppler Microwave Landing System
DMLT ...... Diploma in Medical Laboratory Technology (ADA)
DMM...... [*The*] Dansville & Mount Morris Railroad Co. [*AAR code*]
DM & M ... D'Arcy-MacManus & Masius [*Advertising agency*]
DMM...... Dark Mantling Material [*Lunar surface*]
DMM...... Data Manipulation Mode
DMM...... Dayton and Montgomery County Public Library, Dayton, OH
    [*OCLC symbol*] (OCLC)
DMM........ Dedicated Man/Months [*Jet Propulsion Laboratory, NASA*]
DMM........ Delta Ministry of Mississippi (EA)
dMM........ Deoxymannojirimycin [*Biochemistry*]
DMM........ Depleted MORB [*Mid-Ocean Ridge Basalt*] Mantle [*Geology*]
DMM........ Desmethylmetoxuron [*Organic chemistry*]
DMM........ Dia Met Minerals Ltd. [*Vancouver Stock Exchange symbol*]
DMM........ Digital Multimeter
DMM........ Digital Multiservice Module [*Telecommunications*]
DMM........ Dimethoxymethane [*Organic chemistry*]
DMM........ Dimethylmercury [*Toxicology*]
DMM........ Diploma in Manufacturing Management [*British*]
DMM........ Direct Mail Manager [*Software package*]
DMM........ Direct Metal Mastering [*System for manufacturing phonograph
    records*]
DMM........ Director of Mechanical Maintenance [*British military*] (DMA)
DMM........ Directorate of Materiel Management (MCD)
DMM........ Domestic Mail Manual [*US Postal Service*] [*A publication*]
DMM........ Dulbecco's Modified Eagle's Medium [*Also, DME, DMEM*]
    [*Medium for cell growth*]
DMMA...... Dimethylmuconic Acid [*Organic chemistry*]
DMMA...... Direct Mail/Marketing Association (EA)
DMMB...... Defense Medical Material Board (AFM)
DMMC...... Digital Multimeter Control
DMMC...... Division Materiel Management Center [*Military*] (AABC)
DMMCS...... Dimethylmonochlorosilane [*Organic chemistry*]
DMMEF...... Direct Mail/Marketing Educational Foundation (EA)
DMMF...... Dry and Mineral Matter Free [*Coal*]
DMMG...... Displacement Method Matrix Generator
DMMH/FH ... Direct Maintenance Man-Hours per Flight Hour
    [*Navy*] (NG)
DMMH/MA ... Direct Maintenance Man-Hours per Maintenance Action
DMMO...... Direct Marketing Minorities Opportunities [*Defunct*] (EA)
DMMP...... Dimethyl Methylphosphonate [*Organic chemistry*]
DMMP...... Direct Marketing Market Place [*A publication*]
DMMRB...... Daily Missouri-Mississippi River Bulletin [*A publication*]
DMM & SA ... Depot Materiel Maintenance and Support Activities [*Army*]
DMMU ..... Discrete Main Memory Unit [*Computer bus*]
DMN .... Damon Corp. [*NYSE symbol*] (SPSG)
DMN .... Data Model Normalizer [*Data processing*]
DMN .... Defective Material Notice (KSC)
DMN .... Deming, NM [*Location identifier*] [*FAA*] (FAAL)
DMN .... Dimension (AABC)
DMN .... Dimethylnaphthalene [*Organic chemistry*]
DMN .... Dimethylnitrosamine [*Also, DMNA, NDMA*] [*Organic
    chemistry*]
DMN .... Dimethynaphthidine [*An indicator*] [*Chemistry*]
DMn .... Dissolved Manganese [*Chemistry*]
DMN .... Dominion Explorers, Inc. [*Toronto Stock Exchange symbol*]
DMN .... Dominion Explorers, Inc. [*Vancouver Stock Exchange symbol*]
DMN .... Dorsal Motor Nucleus [*of the vagus*]
DMN .... Dorsomedial Nucleus [*Brain anatomy*]
DM & N ... Duluth, Missabe & Northern Railway
DMNA........ Dimethylnitrosamine [*Also, DMN, NDMA*] [*Organic
    chemistry*]
DMNA...... Distributed Microcomputer Network for Avionics (MCD)
DMND...... Diamond West Energy [*NASDAQ symbol*] (NQ)
DMNFA...... Daily Mail National Film Award [*British*]
DMNG ...... Damon Group [*NASDAQ symbol*] (SPSG)
DMNHA...... Dimensions in Health Service [*A publication*]
DMNI ...... Device Multiplexing Nonsynchronized Inputs [*Data processing*]
DMNO ...... Device Multiplexing Nonsynchronized Outputs [*Data
    processing*] (CET)
DMNOAM ... Durban Museum Novitates [*A publication*]
DMNRLZR ... Demineralizer
DMNT...... Dominant (FAAC)
DMO .... Data Management Office [*or Officer*] [*Air Force*] (AFM)
DMO .... Decision Making Organizer [*Test*]
DMO .... Defense Mobilization Order
DMO .... Demineralized Oil [*Petroleum Refining*]
DMO .... Dental Maintenance Organization
DMO .... Dependent Meteorological Office
DMO .... Dimethyloxazolidinedione [*Pharmacology*]
DMO .... Diode Microwave Oscillator
DMO .... Directives Management Officer [*FAA*] (FAAC)
DMO .... Director of Manpower and Organization [*Air Force*]
DMO .... Director of Maritime Operations [*RAF*] [*British*]
DMO .... Director Meteorological Officer, Ministry of Defence, London
    [*British*] (NATG)
DMO .... Director [*or Directorate*] of Military Operations
DMO .... Directory of Mortuary Operations [*Army*] (AABC)

DMO .... District Management Office
DMO .... District Marine Officer [*Navy*]
DMO .... District Material Officer [*Navy*]
DMO .... District Medical Officer [*Navy*]
DMO .... Divisional Medical Officer [*British*]
DMO .... Documentation Management Officer [*Air Force*] (AFM)
DMO .... Sedalia [*Missouri*] [*Airport symbol*] [*Obsolete*] (OAG)
DMOA...... Documenta et Monumenta Orientis Antiqui [*A publication*]
DMOB...... Defensive Missile Order of Battle (MCD)
DMOD...... Dimethyloctadiene [*Organic chemistry*]
DMOI...... Director of Military Operations and Intelligence
DMON ..... Discrete Monitoring (MCD)
DMon........ Montessori School, Washington, DC [*Library symbol*] [*Library
    of Congress*] (LCLS)
DMONBP ... Dermatologische Monatsschrift [*A publication*]
D Mont .... United States District Court for the District of Montana (DLA)
DMOR....... Distinguished Member of the Regiment
DMOS .... Data Management Operating System
DMOS .... Depletion Metal-Oxide Semiconductor (BUR)
DMOS .... Diffusion Metal-Oxide Semiconductor
    [*Telecommunications*] (TEL)
DMOS .... Diffusive Mixing of Organic Solutions [*Materials processing*]
DMOS .... Double-Diffused Metal-Oxide Semiconductor
    [*Microelectronics*] (MCD)
DMOS .... Duty Military Occupational Specialty
DMOS .... Dynamic Model Operations Section
DMOS(N) ... Director of Meteorological and Oceanographical Services
    (Naval) [*British*]
DMOT....... Dimethyloctatriene [*Organic chemistry*]
DMov......... Doslidzennja z Movoznavstva Zbirnyk Statej Aspirantiv i
    Dysertantiv [*A publication*]
DMP......... Data Management Plan [*Jet Propulsion Laboratory, NASA*]
DMP......... Data Management Program
DMP......... De Mortibus Persecutorum (BJA)
DMP......... Defense Manpower Policy
DMP......... Defense Materials Procurement Agency [*Abolished 1953,
    functions transferred to General Services
    Administration*] (DLA)
DMP......... Delayed Merge Package (MCD)
DMP......... Deployable Maintenance Platform (MCD)
DMP......... Dermatopathology [*Medical specialty*] (DHSM)
DMP......... DEU [*Display Electronics Unit*] Message Processor (NASA)
DMP......... Deutsche Mittelstandspartei [*German Middle Class Party*]
    [*Federal Republic of Germany*] (PPW)
DMP......... Developments in Mineral Processing [*Elsevier Book Series*] [*A
    publication*]
DMP......... Dimercaptopropanol [*Also, BAL: British Anti-Lewisite*]
    [*Detoxicant*] [*Organic chemistry*]
DMP......... Dimethoxypropane [*Organic chemistry*]
DMP......... Dimethyl Phthalate [*Organic chemistry*]
DMP......... Dimethylphenol [*Organic chemistry*]
DMP......... Dimethylpiperazine [*Also, DMPP*] [*Organic chemistry*]
DMP......... Dimethylpropanediol [*Organic chemistry*]
DMP......... Dimethylpyrrole [*Organic chemistry*]
DMP......... Diploma in Medical Psychology (ADA)
DMP......... Direct Memory Processor
DMP......... Director of Manpower Planning [*British*]
DMP......... Director of Military Personnel [*Air Force*]
DMP......... Disarmed Military Personnel
DMP......... Display Maintenance Program
DMP......... Documented Material Processed
DMP......... Dome Petroleum Ltd. [*AMEX symbol*] [*Toronto Stock
    Exchange symbol*] (SPSG)
DMP......... Dorsal Median Pallium [*Neuroanatomy*]
dMP......... Dorsal Midline Precursor [*Neuroanatomy*]
DMP......... Dump [*Data processing*]
DMP......... Pathfinder Regional Library Service System, Montrose, CO
    [*OCLC symbol*] (OCLC)
DMPA .... Defense Materials Procurement Agency [*Abolished 1953,
    functions transferred to General Services Administration*]
DMPA .... Depomedroxyprogesterone Acetate [*Contraceptive*]
DMPA .... (Dichlorophenyl) Methyl Isopropylphosphoramidothioate
    [*Herbicide*]
DMPA .... Dimethylolpropionic Acid [*Organic chemistry*]
DMPA .... Dimyristoyl Phosphatidic Acid [*Biochemistry*]
DMPA .... Distal Main Pulmonary Artery [*Anatomy*]
DMPC .... Dimethylaminopropyl Chloride [*Organic chemistry*]
DMPC .... Dimyristoyl Phosphatidylcholine [*Biochemistry*]
DMPD .... Defense Medical Purchase Description [*Defense Supply
    Agency*]
DMPD .... Dimethylphenylenediamine [*Organic chemistry*]
DMPD .... Director of Dockyard Manpower and Productivity [*Navy*]
    [*British*]
DMPDT .... Dimethylphosphorodithioate [*Organic chemistry*]
DMPE .... Depot Maintenance Plant Equipment (MCD)
DMPE .... (Dimethoxyphenyl)ethylamine [*Also, DIMPEA, DMPEA*]
    [*Psychomimetic compound*]
DMPE .... Dimyristoyl Phosphatidylethanolamine
DMPEA.... (Dimethoxyphenyl)ethylamine [*Also, DIMPEA, DMPE*]
    [*Psychomimetic compound*]
DMPG .... Dimyristoylphosphatidylglycerol [*Biochemistry*]

DMPG .... Dumping (MSA)
DMPI .... Desired Mean Point of Impact [*Military*]
DMPI .... Dimyristoyl Phosphatidylinositol
DMPIA ...... Dimethoxyphenylisopropylamine [*Organic chemistry*]
DMPO .... Data Management Policy Office [*Army*]
DMPO .... Dimethylpyrrolineoxide [*Organic chemistry*]
DMPP .... Dimethylpiperazine [*Also, DMP*] [*Organic chemistry*]
DMPR .... Damper (KSC)
DMPR .... Depot Maintenance Production Report
DMPS .... Deepwater Motion Picture System
DMPS .... Dimercaptopropanesulfonate [*Salt*] [*Organic chemistry*]
DMPS .... Dimethylpolysiloxane [*Organic chemistry*]
DMPU .... Dimethylolpropyleneurea [*Organic chemistry*]
DMQ .... Dimethylquinoline [*Organic chemistry*]
DMQ .... Direct Memory Queue [*Data processing*]
DMQ .... Director of Movements and Quartering [*British*]
DMQ. .... Dominco Industry Corp. [*Vancouver Stock Exchange symbol*]
DMQR .... Douglas Material Qualification Report [*DAC*]
DMR .... Daily Market Report [*Coffee, Sugar, and Cocoa Exchange*] [*A publication*]
DMR .... Daily Mechanical Report
DMR .... Data Management Routine
DMR .... Date Material Required
DMR .... Defective Materiel Report [*Air Force*]
DMR .... Demultiplexing/Mixing/Remultiplexing [*Device*] [*Telecommunications*] (TEL)
DMR .... Department of Mineral Resources [*Thailand*] (DS)
DMR .... Departmental Materiel Requisition
DMR .... Deutsche Motorrad Register [*German Motorcycle Register*] [*Defunct*] (EA)
DMR .... Developmental Instrumentation Medium-Right (NASA)
DMR .... Differential Microwave Radiometer [*Cosmic Background Explorer*] [*NASA*]
DMR .... Digital Equipment Corp., Marlboro, Marlboro, MA [*OCLC symbol*] (OCLC)
DMR .... Dimmer (MSA)
DMR .... Diploma in Medical Radiology [*British*]
DMR .... Direct Magnification Radiography
DMR .... Direct Metal Reaction [*Soap making*]
DMR .... Director of Materiel Readiness [*Army*]
DMR .... Directorate of Medical Research [*Army*]
DMR .... Distributor-Manufacturer-Representative
DMR .... Division of Materials Research [*National Science Foundation*]
DMR .... Drummer [*Military*] [*British*]
DMR .... Dual Mode Recognizer (MCD)
DMR .... Dynamic Module Replacement
DMRA .... DSA [*Defense Supply Agency*] Central Regional Audit Office
DMRD .... Davy McKee Research & Development [*British*] (IRUK)
DMRD .... Diploma in Medical Radio-Diagnosis [*British*]
DMRE .... Diploma in Medical Radiology and Electrology [*British*]
DMRE .... Division of Medical Radiation Exposure [*Bureau of Radiological Health*]
DMREEG ... Diabetes/Metabolism Reviews [*A publication*]
DMRF .... Dystonia Medical Research Foundation (EA)
DMRI .... Data Material Required, Increasing Urgency [*Navy*] (NG)
DMRL .... Decreasing Mean Residual Life
DMR(N) .... Director of Materials Research (Naval) [*British*]
DMRP .... Dredged Material Research Program [*Waterways Experiment Station*] [*Army*] (RDA)
D & MRR .. Detroit & Mackinac Railway Co.
DMRRDK .. Design and Management for Resource Recovery [*A publication*]
DMRS .... Data Management and Retrieval System
DMRT .... Diploma in Medical Radio-Therapy [*British*]
DMRTS ..... Dominion Mortgage & Realty [*NASDAQ symbol*] (NQ)
DmS .... Dakota Microfilm Service, Inc., Denver, CO [*Library symbol*] (LCLS)
DMS .... Data Management Service (IEEE)
DMS .... Data Management System [*Data processing*]
DMS .... Data Measuring System
DMS .... Data Monitoring System
DMS .... Data Multiplex System [*Data processing*]
DMS .... Database Management System [*Data processing*]
DMS .... Decision Making System
DMS .... Defense Management System (NATG)
DMS .... Defense Mapping School [*Army*] (AABC)
DMS .... Defense Marketing Survey (MCD)
DMS .... Defense Materials Service [*of GSA*]
DMS .... Defense Materials System
DMS .... Defense Missile Systems (KSC)
DMS .... Delayed Matching-to-Sample [*Psychology*]
DMS .... Delayed Muscle Soreness
DMS .... Delta Milliohm Sensor
DMS .... Delta Modulation System
DMS .... Denominational Ministry Strategy [*Later, CSM*] (EA)
DMS .... Density Manipulation Subsystem (MCD)
DMS .... Departmental Management System [*Department of Labor*]
DMS .... Depot Maintenance Service (AFIT)
DMS .... Depot Maintenance Support (AAG)
DMS .... Deputy Military Secretary [*British*]
DMS .... Dermatomyositis [*Medicine*]
DMS .... [*The*] Designer Menswear Show [*British*] (ITD)

DMS .... Destroyer Minesweeper [*Navy symbol*] [*Obsolete*]
DMS .... Development Management System [*IBM Corp.*]
DMS .... Deviation from Mean Standard (MUGU)
DMS .... Diagnostic Methodology Section [*National Institute of Dental Research*]
DMS .... Difference of Messing Subscription [*British military*] (DMA)
DMS .... Differential Maneuvering Simulator [*Aviation*]
DMS .... Differential Multiple Simulator (MCD)
DMS .... Digital Matrix Switch (MCD)
DMS .... Digital Motion System
DMS .... Digital Multiplex Switch
DMS .... Digital Multiplexing Synchronizer [*Data processing*]
DMS .... Diis Manibus Sacrum [*Sacred to the Manes, i.e., Departed Souls*] [*Latin*]
DMS .... Dimercaptosuccinic Acid [*Organic chemistry*]
DMS .... Dimethyl Silicone [*Organic chemistry*]
DMS .... Dimethyl Sulfide [*Organic chemistry*]
DMS .... Dimethyl Sulfoxide [*Also, DMSO*] [*Organic chemistry*]
DMS .... Dimethylstilbestrol [*Biochemistry*]
DMS .... Dimethylsuberimidate [*Organic chemistry*]
DMS .... Diminishing Manufacturing Service (MCD)
DMS .... Diminishing Manufacturing Sources
DMS .... Diploma in Management Studies [*British*]
DMS .... Direct Match Screening
DMS .... Direct Molded Sole [*Boot*] [*Military*]
DMS .... Director of Medical Services [*British*]
DMS .... Director for Mutual Security
DMS .... Directorate of Microgram Services [*RAF*] [*British*]
DMS .... Discount Merchandiser [*A publication*]
DMS .... Disk Monitor System [*Data processing*]
DMS .... Display Management System [*IBM Corp.*]
DMS .... Distance Measuring System
DMS .... Distinguished Military Students
DMS .... Docking Mechanism System [*or Subsystem*] [*NASA*] (NASA)
DMS .... Docking Module Subsystem (MCD)
DMS .... Doctor of Mechanical Science
DMS .... Doctor of Medical Science [*or Sciences*]
DMS .... Doctor of Military Science
DMs .... Doctor in Missionology
DMS .... Documentary Management System [*for citations*]
DMS .... Documentation of Molecular Spectroscopy
DMS .... Domini Sportswear [*Vancouver Stock Exchange symbol*]
DMS .... Doppler Measurement System
DMS .... Dragon [*Missile*] Maintenance Set [*Military*]
DMS .... Drum Memory System [*Data processing*]
DMS .... Dual Maneuvering Simulator (MCD)
DMS .... Dun's Marketing Services [*Dun & Bradstreet, Inc.*] [*Parsippany, NJ*] [*Information service or system*] (IID)
DMS .... Dynamic Mapping System [*Hewlett-Packard Co.*]
DMS .... Dynamic Missile Simulator
DMS .... Dynamic Motion Simulator (MCD)
DMS .... Dynamo Management System (AAG)
DMS .... High-Speed Minesweeper [*Navy symbol*] [*Obsolete*]
DMSA .... Dimercaptosuccinic Acid [*Organic chemistry*]
DMSA .... Diploma in Medical Services Administration [*British*]
DMSA .... Illustrator Draftsman, Seaman Apprentice [*Navy rating*]
DMSAFIF ... Depot Maintenance Service Air Force Industrial Fund (AFIT)
DMSC .... Defence Material Standardization Committee [*British military*] (DMA)
DMSC ...... Defense Medical Supply Center [*Later, Defense Personnel Support Center*]
DMSC .... Direct Simulation Monte Carlo Technique [*Statistics*]
DMSC .... Disinfected Mail Study Circle (EA)
DM Sc .... Doctor of Medical Science
DMSc .... Doctor of Missionary Science
DMS/CS .... Data Management System/Computer Subsystem [*Data processing*]
DMSDS ...... Direct Mail Shelter Development System [*Civil Defense*]
DMSE .... Direct Mission Support Equipment (MCD)
DMSELC .. Diatomic Molecule Spectra and Energy Levels Center
DMSH .... Diminish (FAAC)
DMS-HZ ... Dimethyl Sulfate-Hydrazine [*Organic chemistry*]
DMSM ...... Defense Manpower Static Model
DMSM ...... Defense Meritorious Service Medal [*Military decoration*]
DMSM ...... Diminishing Manufacturing Sources and Material Shortages (MCD)
DMS/MS .. Diminishing Manufacturing Sources/Material Shortages (MCD)
DMS(N) .... Director of Marine Services (Naval) [*British*]
DMSN .... Illustrator Draftsman, Seaman [*Navy rating*]
DmS-O .... Dakota Microfilm Service, Inc., Orlando, FL [*Library symbol*] [*Library of Congress*] (LCLS)
DMSO ...... Defense Materials Systems Office
DMSO ...... Dimethyl Sulfoxide [*Also, DMS*] [*Organic chemistry*]
DMSO ...... Director Major Staff Office (MCD)
DMSP .... Data Management Summary Processor (KSC)
DMSP .... Defense Meteorological Satellite Program [*Formerly, DAPP*] [*Air Force*]
DMSP .... Depot Maintenance Support Plan [*Air Force*] (AFM)
DMSP .... Dichroic Microspectrophotometer
DMSP .... Dimethylsulfoniopropionate [*Organic chemistry*]

DMSP.......	Dragon Missile Special Jump Pack [*Military*] (MCD)
DMSPSM ...	Data Management System Problem Specification Model [*Air Force*]
DMSR	Director of Missile Safety Research [*Air Force*]
DMSRD	Directorate of Materials and Structures Research and Development [*British*]
DMSS.......	Data Management System Simulator [*NASA*] (NASA)
DMSS.......	Data Multiplex Subsystem [*Data processing*]
DMSS.......	Defense Meteorological Satellite System [*Air Force*]
DMSS.......	Digital Multibeam Steering System
DMSS.......	Director of Medical and Sanitary Services [*British*]
DMSS.......	Directorate of Military Satellite Systems (AAG)
DMSSB	Direct Mail Services Standards Board [*British*]
DmS-SP	Dakota Microfilm Service, Inc., Saint Paul, MN [*Library symbol*] [*Library of Congress*] (LCLS)
DMST	Demonstrate (AFM)
DMSTN ...	Demonstration (AFM)
DMt	Dansk Musiktidsskrift [*A publication*]
DMT	Deep Mobile Target
DM & T	Defense Markets & Technology [*Predicasts, Inc.*] [*Database*]
DMT	Defense Mechanism Test [*Psychometrics*]
DMT	Demountable [*Technical drawings*]
DMT	Demycinosyltylosin [*Antibacterial*]
DMT	Detailed Maneuver Table
DMT	Dictaphone Machine Transcriber
DMT	Digital Message Terminal (MCD)
DMT	Dimensional Motion Time
dmt	Dimethoxytrityl [*As substituent on nucleoside*] [*Biochemistry*]
DMT	Dimethoxytryptamine [*Possible central nervous system neuroregulator*]
DMT	Dimethyl Terephthalate [*Organic chemistry*]
DMT	Dimethyltryptamine [*Hallucinogenic agent*]
DMT	Direct Memory Transfer [*Data processing*]
DMT	Direct Modulation Technique
DMT	Director of Machine Tools [*Ministry of Aircraft Production and Ministry of Supply*] [*British*]
DMT	Director of Military Training
DMT	Dispersive Mechanism Test (NRCH)
DMT	Doctor of Medical Technology
DMT	Dorsal Median Tract [*Anatomy*]
DMT	Dual Mode Tracker (MCD)
DMT	Dynamic Mechanical Testing
DMTA	Dynamic Mechanical Thermal Analysis
DMTB	Deployment Mobilization Troop Basis (AABC)
DMTC	Digital Magnetic Tape Controller (CAAL)
DMTC	Digital Message Terminal Computer (IEEE)
DMTCNQ ...	Dimethyl(Tetracyano)Quinodimethane
DMTF	Diffraction Limited Modulation Transfer Function (MCD)
DMTI	Digitized Moving Target Indicator (CET)
DMTM......	Detailed Monthly Trade Monitor [*Database*] [*Data Resources, Inc.*] [*Information service or system*] (CRD)
DMTPS.....	Digital Magnetic Tape Plotting System
D Mtr........	Defence Material [*A publication*]
DMTR	Dounreay Materials Testing Reactor [*British*]
DMTRA	Drug Metabolism Reviews [*A publication*]
DMTRAR ...	Drug Metabolism Reviews [*A publication*]
DMTS.......	Delayed Matching to Sample [*Psychology*]
DMTS.......	Department of Mines and Technical Survey [*Canada*]
DMTS.......	Digital Magnetic Tape System (CAAL)
DMTS.......	Digital Module Test Set
DMTS.......	Dimethyl Trisulfide [*Organic chemistry*]
DMTSF	Dimethyl(methylthio)sulfonium Fluoroborate [*Organic chemistry*]
DMTT	Dimethyltetrahydrothiadiazinethione [*Pesticide*] [*Organic chemistry*]
DMTU......	Digital Magnetic Tape Controller Unit
DMTU......	Digital Magnetic Tape Unit (MCD)
DMTU......	Dimethylthiourea [*Organic chemistry*]
DMTU......	Dual Modular Magnetic Tape Unit (CAAL)
DMTZR.....	Demagnetizer
DMU	Data Management Unit [*Data processing*]
DMU	Des Moines Union Railway Co. [*AAR code*]
DMU	Destratification Motor Unit
DMU	Device Mount Unit (MCD)
DMU	Diesel Multiple Unit
DMU	Digital Management Unit (MCD)
DMU	Digital Message Unit (MCD)
DMU	Digital Monitor Unit
DMU	Dimapur [*India*] [*Airport symbol*] (OAG)
DMU	Dimethylolurea [*Organic chemistry*]
DMU	Dimethyluracil [*Biochemistry*]
DMU	Distributed Microprocessor Unit
DMU	Dual Maneuvering Unit [*A spacecraft*]
DMU	Dynamic Mockup
DMUkrM ...	Doslidzennja i Materjaly z Ukrjins'koji Movy [*A publication*]
DMUP.......	Defense Materiel Utilization Program [*DoD*]
DMUS.......	Data Management Utility System
D Mus	Doctor of Music
D Mus A	Doctor of Musical Arts
DMusCantuar ...	Archbishop of Canterbury's Doctorate in Music [*British*] (DBQ)
D Mus Ed ..	Doctor of Musical Education
DMUX......	Demultiplexer [*Data processing*]
DM & V	Delaware, Maryland & Virginia Railroad
DMV.........	Delay Multivibrator
DMV.........	Delta Multivibrator
DMV.........	Department of Motor Vehicles
DMV.........	Deserted Medieval Village [*British*]
DMV.........	Digital Message Voice [*Device*] (MCD)
DMV.........	Disabled Motorists (Victoria) [*Australia*]
DMV.........	Division of Motor Vehicles (MCD)
DMV.........	Mount Vernon College, Washington, DC [*Library symbol*] [*Library of Congress*] (LCLS)
DMVC......	Dayton-Miami Valley Library Consortium - Library Division [*Library network*]
DMVS	Desert Mobility Vehicle System [*Army*]
DMW........	Demineralized Makeup Water [*Nuclear energy*] (NRCH)
DMW........	Demineralized Water
DMW........	Deutsche Medizinische Wochenschrift [*A publication*]
DMW........	Digital Milliwatt [*Telecommunications*] (TEL)
DMWG......	Direct Marketing Writers Guild [*Later, DMCG*] (EA)
DMWOAX ...	Deutsche Medizinische Wochenschrift [*A publication*]
DMWP.....	Depot Maintenance Workload Plan (MCD)
DMWR......	Depot Maintenance Work Request [*or Requirement*] [*Army*] (AABC)
DMWS	Direct Mineral Water Supply (ROG)
DMX........	Data Multiplex [*Computer*]
DMX........	Direct Memory Exchange
DM-XX.....	Douglas Missile - Model XX (MCD)
DMY.........	Dummy (KSC)
DMZ.........	Demilitarized Zone
DMZ.........	Drug Mending Zone [*Drug abuse center*]
DMZn........	Dimethylzinc
DN	Aerodespachos de El Salvador [*ICAO designator*] (FAAC)
DN	Dagens Nyheter [*A publication*]
DN	Daily Nation [*Nairobi*] [*A publication*]
DN	Daily News [*A publication*]
DN	Dance News [*A publication*]
Dn	Daniel [*Old Testament book*]
DN	Data Name
DN	Data Net (MCD)
DN	Data Number
DN	Date Number
DN	Day and Night [*Approach and landing charts*] [*Aviation*]
DN	Deacon (ROG)
DN	Debit Note [*Business term*]
DN	Decimal Number
dn	DeciNEM [*One-tenth of a NEM*] [*See NEM*]
dN	Decineper [*Physics*] (DEN)
DN	DekaNEM [*Ten NEM*] [*See NEM*]
D & N........	Dekker & Nordemann [*Publisher*]
DN	Delayed Neutron
D/N	Delivery Note (ADA)
D/N	Demand Note [*Banking*]
DN	Democrazia Nazionale - Constituente di Destra [*National Democracy - Right Constituent*] [*Italy*] [*Political party*] (PPE)
Dn	Denial [*Psychology*]
DN	Dentalman [*Nonrated enlisted man*] [*Navy*]
DN	Department of the Navy
DN	Departmental Notice (AAG)
DN	Descending Neuron [*Neurology*]
DN	Destra Nazionale [*National Right*] [*Italy*] [*Political party*] (PPE)
DN	Detail Networks (MCD)
DN	Detroit News [*A publication*]
DN	Deutsche Notenbank [*German Bank of Issue*]
DN	Developments in Neuroscience [*Elsevier Book Series*] [*A publication*]
D:N	Dextrose:Nitrogen Ratio
DN	Dialect Notes [*A publication*]
DN	Dibucaine Number [*Anesthesiology*]
DN	Dicrotic Notch [*Cardiology*]
DN	Dinitro-ortho-Cresol [*Also, DNOC*] [*Herbicide*]
DN	Diploma in Nursing
DN	Diploma in Nutrition [*British*]
DN	Direct Normalized [*Steel*]
DN	Directorate Notice (AAG)
DN	Discrepancy Notice [*NASA*] (NASA)
D/N	Dispatch Note [*Shipping*]
DN	Disposition Pennant [*Navy*] [*British*]
DN	Disraeli Newsletter [*A publication*]
DN	District Nurse [*British*]
DN	Divine Name (BJA)
DN	Division Notice (AAG)
DN	Doctor of Nursing
DN	Domino Nostro [*To Our Lord*] [*Latin*]
DN	Dominus [*The Lord*] [*Latin*]
DN	Dominus Noster [*Our Lord*] [*Latin*]
DN	Dore-Norbaska Resources, Inc. [*Toronto Stock Exchange symbol*]
DN	Dorsal Nerve [*Anatomy*]

DN .... Double Negation [*Rule of replacement*] [*Logic*]
DN .... Down
DN .... Dozen (ROG)
Dn .... Dragoon [*British military*] (DMA)
DN .... Dreiser Newsletter [*A publication*]
DN .... Druzba Narodov [*A publication*]
DN .... Dublin [*City and county in Ireland*] (ROG)
DN .... Duke of Northumberland [*British*] (ROG)
DN .... Duplicate Negative (MCD)
Dn .... Kongelige Bibliotek [*Royal Library*], Kobenhavn, Denmark [*Library symbol*] [*Library of Congress*] (LCLS)
DN .... United States Department of the Navy, Department Library, Washington, DC [*Library symbol*] [*Library of Congress*] (LCLS)
DNA........... Defense Nuclear Agency [*DoD*] [*Washington, DC*]
DNA........... Delta Nu Alpha Transportation Fraternity (EA)
DNA........... Deoxyribonucleic Acid [*Biochemistry, genetics*]
DNA........... Department of Native Affairs [*Australia*]
DNA........... Deputy for Nuclear Affairs (NATG)
DNA........... Dermatology Nurses' Association (EA)
DNA........... Designated National Agency [*for exchange of oceanographic data*] (MSC)
DNA........... Det Norske Arbeiderparti [*Norwegian Labor Party*] (PPE)
DNA........... Deutscher Normenausschuss [*German Standards Committee*] [*Later, DIN*]
DNA........... Diana Corp. [*NYSE symbol*] (SPSG)
DNA........... Did Not Arrive [*For no-show hotel reservation*]
DNA........... Did Not Attend
DNA........... Digital Network Architecture [*Digital Equipment Corp.*] [*Data processing*]
DNA........... DIMUS [*Digital Multibeam Steering*] Narrow-Band Accelerated (NVT)
DNA........... Director of Naval Accounts [*Obsolete*] [*British*]
dna .... Docena [*Dozen*] [*Spanish*]
D Na........... Doctor of Navigation
DNA........... Does Not Answer [*Telephone operator's designation*]
DNA........... Does Not Apply (MSA)
DNA........... Dynamar Energy Ltd. [*Toronto Stock Exchange symbol*]
DNA........... United States National Archives and Records Service, National Archives Library, Washington, DC [*Library symbol*] [*Library of Congress*] (LCLS)
DNAA....... Abuja/International [*Nigeria*] [*ICAO location identifier*] (ICLI)
DNAase ..... Deoxyribonuclease [*Preferred form, DNase*] [*An enzyme*]
DNACC .... Defense National Agency Check Center [*DoD*]
DNAD....... Director of Naval Air Division
DNADA..... Division of Narcotic Addiction and Drug Abuse [*National Institute of Mental Health*]
DN-Aer ...... United States Department of the Navy, Naval Air Systems Command, Arlington, VA [*Library symbol*] [*Library of Congress*] (LCLS)
DNAG........ Decade of North American Geology [*Geological Society of America*]
DNAL........ Diario de Noticias (Lisbon, Portugal) [*A publication*]
DNAL........ United States National Agricultural Library, Beltsville, MD [*Library symbol*] [*Library of Congress*] (LCLS)
DNAM....... Data Network Access Method
DNAM....... DNA Medical, Inc. [*NASDAQ symbol*] (NQ)
DNAME.... Department of Naval Architecture and Marine Engineering [*MIT*] (MCD)
DNAO .... Director of Naval Air Organization [*British*]
DNAp .... Deoxyribonucleic Acid Polymerase [*An enzyme*]
DNAP........ (Dinitrophenylazo)phenol [*Organic chemistry*]
DNAP........ Directorate of Naval Administration Planning [*British*]
DNAP........ DNA [*Deoxyribonucleic Acid*] Affinity Precipitation [*Analytical biochemistry*]
DNAP........ DNA Plant Technology Corp. [*Cinnaminson, NJ*] [*NASDAQ symbol*] (NQ)
DNAr........ United States National Arboretum, Washington, DC [*Library symbol*] [*Library of Congress*] (LCLS)
DN Arch .... Doctor of Naval Architecture
D Na S .... Doctor of Naval Science
DNASA ..... United States National Aeronautics and Space Administration, Washington, DC [*Library symbol*] [*Library of Congress*] (LCLS)
DNASA-G ... United States National Aeronautics and Space Administration, Goddard Space Flight Center, Greenbelt, MD [*Library symbol*] [*Library of Congress*] (LCLS)
D Na Sc...... Doctor of Naval Science
DNase........ Deoxyribonuclease [*An enzyme*]
DNAS-HRB ... National Academy of Sciences, Highway Research Board Library, Washington, DC [*Library symbol*] [*Library of Congress*] (LCLS)
DNAS-NAE ... National Academy of Sciences, National Academy of Engineering Library, Washington, DC [*Library symbol*] [*Library of Congress*] (LCLS)
D Nat .... Doctor of Naturopathy
D Natl .... Defense Nationale [*A publication*]
DNA-TP .... Defense Nuclear Agency Technical Publications [*DoD*]

DnAu.......... Statsbiblioteket i Arhus Universitetsbiblioteket [*State and Arhus University Library*], Arhus, Denmark [*Library symbol*] [*Library of Congress*] (LCLS)
DNav......... De Navorscher [*A publication*]
DNAW....... Directorate of Naval Air Warfare [*British*]
DNB........... Dance Notation Bureau (EA)
DNB........... Departure from Nucleate Boiling (NRCH)
DNB........... Deutsche Nationalbibliographie [*A publication*]
DNB........... Deutsche Notenbank [*German Bank of Issue*]
DNB........... Dictionary of National Biography [*A publication*] (APTA)
DNB........... Dinitrobenzene [*Organic chemistry*]
DNB........... Dinitrobenzidine [*Organic chemistry*]
DNB........... Distribution Number Bank
DNB........... Dun & Bradstreet, Inc. [*NYSE symbol*] (SPSG)
DNB........... Dunbar [*Australia*] [*Airport symbol*] [*Obsolete*] (OAG)
DNBA....... Di-normal-butylamine [*Organic chemistry*]
DNBA....... Dinitrobenzoic Acid [*Organic chemistry*]
DNBE........ Benin [*Nigeria*] [*ICAO location identifier*] (ICLI)
DNBI .... Bida [*Nigeria*] [*ICAO location identifier*] (ICLI)
DNBI .... Disease and Nonbattle Injury [*Military*] (NVT)
DNBJ........ Abuja [*Nigeria*] [*ICAO location identifier*] (ICLI)
DNBM....... Di-normal-Butylmagnesium [*Organic chemistry*]
DNBP .... Dinitro-ortho-secondary-butylphenol [*Also, DNOSBP, DNSBP*] [*Herbicide*]
DNBPG .... Dinitrobenzoylphenylglycine [*Biochemistry*]
DNBR........ Departure from Nucleate Boiling Ratio (NRCH)
DNBS .... Dinitrobenzenesulfonic [*Organic chemistry*]
DNBSB...... Dimensions. [*US*] National Bureau of Standards [*A publication*]
DNC........... Daon Centre Ltd. [*Partnership units*] [*Vancouver Stock Exchange symbol*]
DNC........... Data Name Card
DNC........... Day-Night Capability [*Aerospace*] (AAG)
DNC........... Delayed Neutron Counting
DNC........... Democratic National Committee (EA)
DNC........... Did Not Come
DNC........... Did Not Compete [*Yacht racing*] (IYR)
DNC........... Dinitrocarbanilide [*Organic chemistry*]
DNC........... Dinitrocellulose [*Organic chemistry*]
DNC........... Direct Notice of Cancellation [*Insurance*]
DNC........... Direct Numerical Control [*Automation method*] [*Data processing*]
DNC........... Director of Naval Construction [*British*]
DNC........... Director of Navy Communications
DNC........... Directorate of National Coordination (CINC)
DNC........... Disaster Nursing Chairman [*Red Cross*]
DNC........... Washington Cathedral, Washington, DC [*Library symbol*] [*Library of Congress*] (LCLS)
DNCA........ Calabar [*Nigeria*] [*ICAO location identifier*] (ICLI)
DNCB........ Dinitrochlorobenzene [*Organic chemistry*]
DNCCC .... Defense National Communications Control Center
DNCD........ National Society of Colonial Dames of America, Washington, DC [*Library symbol*] [*Library of Congress*] (LCLS)
DNCDCC .. Democratic National Committee - Department of Constituent Coordination (EA)
DNCG........ Digital Null Command Generator
DNCINST ... Director, Naval Communications Instruction
DNCNOTE ... Director, Naval Communications Notice
DNCPA ..... Dental Concepts [*A publication*]
DNCS .... Day/Night Camera System (MCD)
DNCS .... Distributed Network Control System
DNCT........ National Cable Television Association, Washington, DC [*Library symbol*] [*Library of Congress*] (LCLS)
DNCU........ Data Net Control Unit (NVT)
DNCW....... United States Catholic Conference, Washington, DC [*Library symbol*] [*Library of Congress*] (LCLS)
DNCWAD ... Democratic National Committee - Women's Affairs Division [*Later, DNCWD*] (EA)
DNCWD.... Democratic National Committee - Women's Division [*Formerly, DNCWAD*] (EA)
DND .... Danra Resources Ltd. [*Vancouver Stock Exchange symbol*]
DND .... Demodulator Neon Driver
DND .... Department of National Defence [*Canada*]
DND .... Development News Digest [*Later, Development Dossier*] [*A publication*] (APTA)
DND .... Died a Natural Death
DND .... Director of Navigation and Direction [*British military*] (DMA)
DND .... Directory of Numerical Databases [*Database*] [*NASA*] [*Information service or system*] (CRD)
DND .... Disqualification Not Discardable [*Yacht racing*] (IYR)
DND .... Do Not Duplicate
DND .... Dundee [*Scotland*] [*Airport symbol*] (OAG)
D ND.......... United States District Court for the District of North Dakota (DLA)
DNDAR..... Daughters of the American Revolution, Washington, DC [*Library symbol*] [*Library of Congress*] (LCLS)
DNDFT ..... Downdraft
DNDJA ..... Dainichi Nippon Densen Jiho [*A publication*]
DNDS........ Dinitrodiphenyl Disulfide [*Organic chemistry*]
DNDS........ Dinitrostilbenedisulfonic Acid [*Antimalarial*]
DNDS........ Director, Naval Dental Services [*British*]

DNE........... Department of Nuclear Engineering [*MIT*]   (MCD)
DNE........... Diffuse Neuroendocrine System [*Also, DNS*]
DNE........... Diploma in Nursing Education   (ADA)
DNE........... Director of Naval Equipment
DNE........... Director of Nursing Education
DNE........... Doctor of Naval Engineering
DNE........... Doron Exploration, Inc. [*Vancouver Stock Exchange symbol*]
DNE........... Duluth & Northeastern Railroad Co. [*AAR code*]
DNEA........ National Education Association, Washington, DC [*Library symbol*] [*Library of Congress*]   (LCLS)
DNED........ Deputy, Naval Education Development   (MCD)
DN Ed........ Doctor of Nursing Education
DNEDS ..... Director of Naval Education Service [*British*]
DNEN....... Enugu [*Nigeria*] [*ICAO location identifier*]   (ICLI)
DN Eng....... Doctor of Naval Engineering
DNES........ Director of Naval Education Service [*British*]   (DMA)
DNET........ Data-Net [*Data-Net, Inc.*] [*Rochester, NY*] [*Telecommunications*]   (TSSD)
DNET........ Director of Naval Engineering Training [*British military*]   (DMA)
DNET........ Division of Nuclear Education and Training [*AEC*]
D Nev........ United States District Court for the District of Nevada   (DLA)
DNEX........ Dionex Corp. [*NASDAQ symbol*]   (NQ)
DNEY........ Da Nang East Yard [*Vietnam*] [*Navy*]
DNF........... Denmark Review [*A publication*]
DNF........... Det Nye Folkepartiet [*New People's Party*] [*Norway*]   (PPE)
DNF........... Did Not Finish
DNF........... Disjunctive Normal Formula
DNF........... Dominion Naval Forces
DNFB........ Dinitrofluorobenzene [*Also, DFB, FDNB*] [*Organic chemistry*]
DNFC........ D & N Financial Corp. [*NASDAQ symbol*]   (SPSG)
DNFCT...... Director of Naval Foreign and Commonwealth Training [*British*]
DNFD........ Danielson Federal Savings and Loan Association [*NASDAQ symbol*]   (NQ)
DNFPS...... Director, Naval Future Policy Staff [*British*]
DNFST...... Department of Nutrition, Food Science, and Technology [*MIT*]   (MCD)
DNFV .... Dansk Naturhistorisk Forening. Videnskabelige Meddelelser [*A publication*]
DNFYP...... Department of the Navy Five-Year Program
DNG .... Danger
DNG .... Daru [*Papua New Guinea*] [*Seismograph station code, US Geological Survey*] [*Closed*]   (SEIS)
DNG .... De Nederlandse Gemeente [*A publication*]
DNG .... Dining
DNG .... Distinguished Naval Graduate
DNG .... Dorsal (Nephridial Gland)
DNG .... Dutch New Guinea [*Later, Irian Barat*]
DNG .... National Geographic Society, Washington, DC [*Library symbol*] [*Library of Congress*]   (LCLS)
DNGA........ National Gallery of Art, Washington, DC [*Library symbol*] [*Library of Congress*]   (LCLS)
DN-GF...... United States Department of the Navy, Naval Gun Factory, Washington, DC [*Library symbol*] [*Library of Congress*] [*Obsolete*]   (LCLS)
DNGS........ National Genealogical Society, Washington, DC [*Library symbol*] [*Library of Congress*]   (LCLS)
DNGU .... Gusau [*Nigeria*] [*ICAO location identifier*]   (ICLI)
DNGW ...... Director of Naval Guided Weapons [*British*]
DNH.......... Dunhuang [*China*] [*Airport symbol*]   (OAG)
D NH .... United States District Court for the District of New Hampshire   (DLA)
DN-HC...... United States Department of the Navy, Naval Historical Center, Operational Archives, Washington, DC [*Library symbol*] [*Library of Congress*]   (LCLS)
DNHM ...... Di-normal-Hexylmagnesium [*Organic chemistry*]
DN-HO...... United States Department of the Navy, Naval Oceanographic Office, Washington, DC [*Library symbol*] [*Library of Congress*]   (LCLS)
DNHS........ Di-Normal-Hexyl Sulfide [*Organic chemistry*]
DNHYAT ... Dental Hygiene [*A publication*]
DNI........... Damon Creations, Incorporated [*AMEX symbol*]   (SPSG)
DNI........... Digital Equipment Corp., Salem, Salem, NH [*OCLC symbol*]   (OCLC)
DNI........... Director of Naval Intelligence [*US, British*]
DNI........... Directorate of Naval Intelligence [*Australia*]
DNI........... Distributable Net Income
DNI........... Division of Naval Intelligence
DNI........... DNI Holdings, Inc. [*Vancouver Stock Exchange symbol*]
DNI........... Do Not Invite
DNI........... Sherman-Denison, TX [*Location identifier*] [*FAA*]   (FAAL)
DNIB........ Ibadan [*Nigeria*] [*ICAO location identifier*]   (ICLI)
DNIC........ Data Network Identification Code [*Telecommunications*]   (TEL)
DNIC........ Digital Network Interface Circuit [*Telecommunications*]
DNIE........ National Institute of Education, Washington, DC [*Library symbol*] [*Library of Congress*]   (LCLS)
DNIF .... Duty Not Involving Flying
DNigE........ Nigerian Embassy, Washington, DC [*Library symbol*] [*Library of Congress*]   (LCLS)

DNIH......... United States National Institutes of Health, Bethesda, MD [*Library symbol*] [*Library of Congress*]   (LCLS)
DNIH-HM ... United States National Institutes of Health, Bureau of Health Manpower, Bethesda, MD [*Library symbol*] [*Library of Congress*]   (LCLS)
DNIL .... Ilorin [*Nigeria*] [*ICAO location identifier*]   (ICLI)
DNIND4..... Drug-Nutrient Interactions [*A publication*]
DN-IS .... Defense Intelligence School, Washington, DC [*Library symbol*] [*Library of Congress*]   (LCLS)
DNJ .... Drone Noise Jammers [*Military*]
D NJ .... United States District Court for the District of New Jersey   (DLA)
DN-JAG .... United States Department of the Navy, Office of the Judge Advocate General, Law Library, Washington, DC [*Library symbol*] [*Library of Congress*]   (LCLS)
DNJC .... Dominus Noster Jesus Christus [*Our Lord Jesus Christ*] [*Latin*]
DNJO .... Jos [*Nigeria*] [*ICAO location identifier*]   (ICLI)
DNJS......... Descendants of the New Jersey Settlers   (EA)
DNK .... Denmark [*ANSI three-letter standard code*]   (CNC)
DNK .... Doklady na Naucnych Konferencijach [*A publication*]
DNKA........ Did Not Keep Appointment [*Medicine*]
DNKA........ Kaduna [*Nigeria*] [*ICAO location identifier*]   (ICLI)
DnKBO...... Bibliotekernes Oplysningskontor, Centre de Pret International, Kobenhavn, Denmark [*Library symbol*] [*Library of Congress*]   (LCLS)
DnKDR...... Center for Development Research, Koobenhavn, Denmark [*Library symbol*] [*Library of Congress*]   (LCLS)
DNKHAR ... Deltion tes Hellenikes Kteniatrikes Hetaireias [*A publication*]
DNKK........ Kano [*Nigeria*] [*ICAO location identifier*]   (ICLI)
DnKL......... Danmarks Laererhojskole [*Royal Danish School of Educational Studies*], Kobenhavn, Denmark [*Library symbol*] [*Library of Congress*]   (LCLS)
DnKN .... Kano/Mallam Aminu International [*Nigeria*] [*ICAO location identifier*]   (ICLI)
DnKP .... Danmarks Paedagogiske Bibliotek [*Danish National Library of Education*], Kobenhavn, Denmark [*Library symbol*] [*Library of Congress*]   (LCLS)
DnKU........ Kobenhavns Universitetsbibliotekets [*University of Copenhagen*], Afdeling, Norre Alle, Kobenhavn, Denmark [*Library symbol*] [*Library of Congress*]   (LCLS)
DnKU-S..... Kobenhavns Universitetsbiblioteks [*University of Copenhagen*], Afdeling, Fiolstraede, Kobenhavn, Denmark [*Library symbol*] [*Library of Congress*]   (LCLS)
DNL........... Augusta, GA [*Location identifier*] [*FAA*]   (FAAL)
DNL........... Det Norske Luftfartselskap AS [*Norwegian Airlines Ltd.*]   (EY)
DNL........... Diack Newsletter [*Database*] [*Diack, Inc.*] [*Information service or system*]   (CRD)
DNL........... Die Neue Literatur [*A publication*]
DNL........... Director of Naval Laboratories
DNL........... Do Not Like
DNL........... Do Not List
DNL........... Do Not Load [*Instruction re a freight car*]
DNL........... Dune Resources Limited [*Toronto Stock Exchange symbol*]
DNLA .... Dune Resources Limited [*Oklahoma City, OK*] [*NASDAQ symbol*]   (NQ)
DNLC .... Dixie National Corp. [*NASDAQ symbol*]   (NQ)
DNLCA .... Deoxynorlaudanosolinecarboxylic Acid [*Biochemistry*]
Dn LJ .... Denver Law Journal [*A publication*]
DnLK .... Downlink   (MCD)
DNLL .... Lagos App [*Nigeria*] [*ICAO location identifier*]   (ICLI)
DNLM .... United States National Library of Medicine, Bethesda, MD [*Library symbol*] [*Library of Congress*]   (LCLS)
DNLR .... National Labor Relations Board, Washington, DC [*Library symbol*] [*Library of Congress*]   (LCLS)
DNLT .... Downlist (NASA)
DNM .... Delayed Neutron Monitor [*Nuclear energy*]   (NRCH)
DNM .... Denham [*Australia*] [*Airport symbol*]   (OAG)
dNM .... Deoxynojirimycin [*Biochemistry*]
DNM .... Director of Naval Manning [*British military*]   (DMA)
DNM .... Distance to Nearest Male Plant [*Botany*]
DNM .... Dreyfus New York Municipal Income, Inc. [*AMEX symbol*]   (CTT)
DNM .... Dulce [*New Mexico*] [*Seismograph station code, US Geological Survey*] [*Closed*]   (SEIS)
D NM........ United States District Court for the District of New Mexico   (DLA)
DNMA....... Maiduguri [*Nigeria*] [*ICAO location identifier*]   (ICLI)
DNMC....... United States Naval Medical Center, Bethesda, MD [*Library symbol*] [*Library of Congress*]   (LCLS)
DN-MHi.... United States Department of the Navy, United States Marine Corps Historical Library, Washington, DC [*Library symbol*] [*Library of Congress*]   (LCLS)
DNMK....... Makurdi [*Nigeria*] [*ICAO location identifier*]   (ICLI)
DNMM ..... Division of Nuclear Materials Management [*AEC*]
DNMM ..... Lagos/Murtala Muhammed [*Nigeria*] [*ICAO location identifier*]   (ICLI)
DNMO ...... Director of Naval Management and Organization [*British military*]   (DMA)
DNMO ...... District Naval Material Office
DNMP .... Director of Naval Manpower Planning [*British*]

DNMR....... Director of Naval Manpower Requirements [*or Resources*] [*British*]
DNMR....... Dynamic Nuclear Magnetic Resonance
DN-MRC... United States Department of the Navy, Naval Regional Medical Center, San Francisco, CA [*Library symbol*] [*Library of Congress*] (LCLS)
DN-MRI.... United States Department of the Navy, Naval Medical Research Institute, Bethesda, MD [*Library symbol*] [*Library of Congress*] (LCLS)
DNMS....... Delayed Neutron Monitoring Subsystem [*Nuclear energy*] (NRCH)
DNMS....... Director of Naval Medical Services [*Royal Australian Navy*]
DNMS....... Division of Nuclear Materials Safeguards [*AEC*]
DN-MS...... United States Department of the Navy, Naval Medical School, Bethesda, MD [*Library symbol*] [*Library of Congress*] (LCLS)
DNMSP..... Director of Naval Manpower Structure Planning [*British military*] (DMA)
DNMT....... Director of Naval Manning and Training [*British*]
DNN.......... Dalton, GA [*Location identifier*] [*FAA*] (FAAL)
DNN.......... Dannevirke [*New Zealand*] [*Seismograph station code, US Geological Survey*] [*Closed*] (SEIS)
DNN.......... Dansk Normal Nul [*Oceanography*]
DN-NPG ... United States Department of the Navy, Naval Weapons Laboratory, Technical Library, Dahlgreen, VA [*Library symbol*] [*Library of Congress*] (LCLS)
DNNR....... Danners, Inc. [*NASDAQ symbol*] (NQ)
DNNS....... Dinitronaphtholsulfonic Acid [*Organic chemistry*]
DNNY........ [*The*] Frances Denney Companies, Inc. [*NASDAQ symbol*] (NQ)
DNO.......... Debit Note Only
DNO.......... Descending Node Orbit (MCD)
DNO.......... Director of Naval Operations
DNO.......... Director of Naval Ordnance [*Admiralty*] [*Obsolete*] [*British*]
DNO.......... District Naval Officer [*British*] (ADA)
DNO.......... District Nursing Officer
DNO.......... United States Naval Observatory, Washington, DC [*OCLC symbol*] (OCLC)
DNOA........ Director of Naval Officer Appointments [*British*]
DN-Ob....... United States Department of the Navy, Naval Observatory, Washington, DC [*Library symbol*] [*Library of Congress*] (LCLS)
DNOC........ Dinitro-ortho-Cresol [*Also, DN*] [*Herbicide*]
DNOCHP ... Dinitrocyclohexylphenol [*Insecticide*]
DN-OGC ... United States Department of the Navy, Office of the General Counsel, Arlington, VA [*Library symbol*] [*Library of Congress*] (LCLS)
DN-OL ...... United States Department of the Navy, Naval Ordnance Laboratory, White Oak, MD [*Library symbol*] [*Library of Congress*] (LCLS)
DNOM...... Director of Naval Oceanography and Meteorology [*British*]
DN-ONR... United States Department of the Navy, Office of Naval Research, Arlington, VA [*Library symbol*] [*Library of Congress*] (LCLS)
DNOP........ Director of Naval Officer Procurement
DNOR .... Directorate of Naval Operational Requirements [*British*]
DN-Ord ..... United States Department of the Navy, Naval Ordnance Systems Command, Arlington, VA [*Library symbol*] [*Library of Congress*] (LCLS)
DNOS........ Diagnostic, Inc. [*Minneapolis, MN*] [*NASDAQ symbol*] (NQ)
DNOS........ Director of Naval Operational Studies [*British*]
DNOS........ Oshogbo [*Nigeria*] [*ICAO location identifier*] (ICLI)
DNOSBP.... Dinitro-ortho-secondary-butylphenol [*Also, DNBP, DNSBP*] [*Herbicide*]
DNOT........ Directorate of Naval Operations and Trade [*British*]
DnOU .... Odense Universitet [*Odense University*], Odense, Denmark [*Library symbol*] [*Library of Congress*] (LCLS)
DNP........... Dai Nippon Printing Co. Ltd. [*Publisher*] [*Japan*]
DNP........... Dang [*Nepal*] [*Airport symbol*] (OAG)
DNP........... Declared National Program [*to share oceanographic data with other nations*]
DNP........... Deferred Nesting Program (MCD)
DNP........... Democratic Nationalist Party [*1959-1966*] [*Malta*] [*Political party*] (PPE)
DNP........... Denpasar [*Indonesia*] [*Seismograph station code, US Geological Survey*] (SEIS)
DNP........... Deoxyribonucleoprotamine [*Biochemistry*]
DNP........... Deoxyribonucleoprotein [*Biochemistry*]
DNP........... Did Not Play
DNP........... Diiodonitrophenol [*Pharmacology*]
DNP........... Dinitrophenol [*Organic chemistry*]
Dnp........... Dinitrophenyl [*Biochemistry*]
DNP........... Dinitrophenylhydrazine [*Also, DNPH*] [*Organic chemistry*]
DNP........... Dinonyl Phthalate [*Organic chemistry*]
DNP........... Do Not Publish
DNP........... Drill Nonpay Status [*Naval Reserve*]
DNP........... Duff/Phelps Utilities Income [*NYSE symbol*] (SPSG)
DNP........... Dummy Nose Plug
DNP........... Dynamic Nuclear Polarization
DNPA........ Di-normal-propylamine [*Organic chemistry*]
DNPA .... Dinitropropyl Acrylate [*An explosive*]

DNPC .... Denpac Corporation [*Hackensack, NJ*] [*NASDAQ symbol*] (NQ)
DNPC .... Dinitro-p-cresol [*Organic chemistry*]
DN-PC ...... United States Department of the Navy, Naval Photographic Center, Washington, DC [*Library symbol*] [*Library of Congress*] (LCLS)
DNPD........ Di(naphthyl)phenylenediamine [*Organic chemistry*]
DN-Pers..... United States Department of the Navy, Bureau of Naval Personnel, Washington, DC [*Library symbol*] [*Library of Congress*] (LCLS)
DNPG........ Defense Navigation Planning Group [*DoD*]
DNPH........ Dinitrophenylhydrazine [*Also, DNP*] [*Organic chemistry*]
DN-PIC ..... United States Department of the Navy, Naval Intelligence Support Center, Washington, DC [*Library symbol*] [*Library of Congress*] (LCLS)
DNP-KLK ... Dinitrophenylated Keyhole Limpet Hemocyanin [*Immunology*]
DNPlans.... Directorate of Naval Plans [*British*]
DNPO........ Port Harcourt [*Nigeria*] [*ICAO location identifier*] (ICLI)
DNPP .... Dinitrophenyl Phosphate [*Organic chemistry*]
DNPP .... Director, Navy Program Planning
DNPP .... Dominus Noster Papa Pontifex [*Our Lord the Pope*] [*Latin*]
DN-PP ...... United States Department of the Navy, Naval Ordnance Station, Indian Head, MD [*Library symbol*] [*Library of Congress*] (LCLS)
DNPPG ..... Department of the Navy Policy and Planning Guidance (MCD)
DNPR........ Director, Navy Petroleum Reserves
DNPr .... National Press Club, Washington, DC [*Library symbol*] [*Library of Congress*] (LCLS)
DNPS .... Dresden Nuclear Power Station (NRCH)
DNPS .... United States National Park Service, National Capital Park Library, Washington, DC [*Library symbol*] [*Library of Congress*] (LCLS)
DNPS-NR ... United States National Park Service, National Register Division, Washington, DC [*Library symbol*] [*Library of Congress*] (LCLS)
DNPT........ Dinitrosopentamethylenetetramine [*Organic chemistry*]
DNPTS...... Director of Naval Physical Training and Sport [*British*]
DNPV .... National Paint, Varnish, and Lacquer Association, Inc., Washington, DC [*Library symbol*] [*Library of Congress*] (LCLS)
DNPZ .... Dinitrosopiperazine [*Animal carcinogen*]
DNQ .... Deniliquin [*Australia*] [*Airport symbol*] (OAG)
DNQX......... Dinitroquinoxalinedione [*Organic chemistry*]
DNR........... Daunorubicin [*Daunomycin*] [*Also, D, DRB, R*] [*Antineoplastic drug*]
DNR........... Department of Natural Resources [*Department of Agriculture*] [*Sometimes facetiously referred to as Department of Nuts with Rifles*]
DNR........... Diana Resources Ltd. [*Vancouver Stock Exchange symbol*]
DNR........... Did Not Report (OICC)
DNR........... Digital Noise Reduction [*Television*]
DNR........... Dinard [*France*] [*Airport symbol*] (OAG)
DNR........... Director of Naval Recruiting [*British*]
D of NR...... Director of Naval Recruiting [*British*]
DNR........... Division of Naval Reactors [*Energy Research and Development Administration*]
DNR........... Do Not Reduce
DNR........... Do Not Renew [*A policy*] [*Insurance*]
DNR........... Do Not Resuscitate [*Medicine*]
DNR........... Does Not Run
dnr............ Donor [*MARC relator code*] [*Library of Congress*] (LCCP)
DNR........... Dovas Nordiske Rad [*Nordic Council for the Deaf - NCD*] (EAIO)
DNR........... Downrange [*NASA*] (KSC)
DNR........... Dynamic Noise Reduction [*Video technology*]
DNRC........ Democritus Nuclear Research Center [*Greece*]
DNRC........ United States Nuclear Regulatory Commission, Washington, DC [*Library symbol*] [*Library of Congress*] (LCLS)
DNRH........ Director of Naval Records and History
DNRIU...... Digital Net Radio Interface Unit (MCD)
DN-RL....... United States Department of the Navy, Naval Research Library, Arlington, VA [*Library symbol*] [*Library of Congress*] (LCLS)
DnRoU...... Roskilde Universitet [*Roskilde University*], Roskilde, Denmark [*Library symbol*] [*Library of Congress*] (LCLS)
DNRPAI.... Dana-Report. Carlsberg Foundation [*A publication*]
DNRQ........ Did Not Receive Questionnaire
DNRS .... Day/Night Reflex Sight [*Military*] (INF)
DN-RTPC ... United States Department of the Navy, Navy Training Publication Center, Pensacola, FL [*Library symbol*] [*Library of Congress*] (LCLS)
DNS .... DACOM-Net Service [*A packet-switching public data network*]
DNS .... Daily News [*Tanzania*] [*A publication*]
dns............. Dansyl [*As substituent on nucleoside*] [*Biochemistry*]
DNS .... Decentralized Data Processing Network System (BUR)
DNS .... Decimal Number System (AAG)
DNS .... Deflected Nasal Septum [*Medicine*]
DNS .... Denison, IA [*Location identifier*] [*FAA*] (FAAL)
DNS .... Denniston [*New Zealand*] [*Seismograph station code, US Geological Survey*] [*Closed*] (SEIS)
DNS .... Dense (FAAC)

DNS	Department of National Savings [*British*]
DNS	Diaphragm Nerve Stimulation
DNS	Did Not Show [*Medicine*]
DNS	Did Not Start [*Yacht racing*] (IYR)
DNS	Did Not Suit
DNS	Die Neueren Sprachen [*A publication*]
DNS	Diffuse Neuroendocrine System [*Also, DNE*]
DNS	Dimethylaminonaphthalenesulfonyl [*Also, Dansyl, dns*] [*Biochemical analysis*]
DNS	Dinitrosalicylic [*Organic chemistry*]
DNS	Dinonyl Sebacate [*Organic chemistry*]
D-NS	Diplomate, American Board of Neurological Surgery (DHSM)
DNS	Director of the Naval Service [*Canada, 1910-1926*]
DNS	Director of Naval Signals [*British military*] (DMA)
DNS	Director of Nuclear Safety [*Air Force*]
DNS	Directorate of Naval Signals [*British*]
DNS	Discrete Network Simulation
DNS	Distributed Network System
DNS	Doctor of Nursing Science
DNS	Doppler Navigation Sensor
DNS	Doppler Navigation System
DNS	Dow. New Series [*Dow and Clark, English House of Lords Cases*] [*A publication*] (DLA)
DNS	Dowling's English Bail Court Reports, New Series [*1841-43*] [*A publication*] (DLA)
DNS	Downs [*Maps and charts*] (ROG)
DNS	Dynamic Noise Suppression [*Electronics*]
DNS	Dysplastic Nevus Syndrome [*Medicine*]
DNSA	Dinitrosalicylate [*Organic chemistry*]
DNSA	Diploma in Nursing Administration (ADA)
DN-SA	United States Department of the Navy, Naval Supply Systems Command, Alexandria, VA [*Library symbol*] [*Library of Congress*] (LCLS)
DNSAP	Danmarks Nationalsocialistisk Arbejdersparti [*National Socialist Worker's Party of Denmark (or Danish NAZI Party)*] (PPE)
DNSAR	Sons of the American Revolution, National Society Library, Washington, DC [*Library symbol*] [*Library of Congress*] (LCLS)
DNSARC	Department of the Navy System Acquisition Review Council (MCD)
DNSB	D & N Savings Bank FSB [*Hancock, MI*] [*NASDAQ symbol*] (NQ)
DNSBP	Dinitro-ortho-secondary-butylphenol [*Also, DNBP, DNOSBP*] [*Herbicide*]
DNSC	Democratic National Strategy Council (EA)
DNSC	Dimethylaminonaphthalenesulfonyl Chloride [*Also, DANS*] [*Fluorescent reagent*]
DNSC	Director of Naval Service Conditions [*British*]
DN Sc	Doctor of Nursing Science
DNSDP	Defense Navigation Satellite Development Program (MCD)
DNSF	National Science Foundation, Washington, DC [*Library symbol*] [*Library of Congress*] (LCLS)
DN-Sh	United States Department of the Navy, Naval Ship Systems Command, Washington, DC [*Library symbol*] [*Library of Congress*] (LCLS)
DNSLP	Downslope (FAAC)
DNSO	Sokoto [*Nigeria*] [*ICAO location identifier*] (ICLI)
DNSPD	Divisions of Naval Staff Plans Division [*British*]
DNSPRB	DOC [*Department of Commerce*]/NASA Satellite Program Review Board (NOAA)
DNS-PS	Dimethylaminonaphthalenesulfonyl Phosphatidylserine [*Biochemistry*]
DNSR	Director of Nuclear Safety Research [*Air Force*]
DNSS	Defense Navigation Satellite System [*Formerly, SSPN*] (MCD)
D5/NSS	Dextrose (5%) in Normal Saline Solution [*Medicine*]
DNST	Daughters of the Nile, Supreme Temple (EA)
DNSTRM	Downstream (FAAC)
DNSW	Day Night Switching Equipment [*Telecommunications*]
DNSy	Directorate of Naval Security [*British*]
DNSYA	Diseases of the Nervous System [*A publication*]
DNSYAG	Diseases of the Nervous System [*A publication*]
DNT	De Nieuwe Taglalgids [*A publication*]
DNT	Denton [*Texas*] [*Seismograph station code, US Geological Survey*] [*Closed*] (SEIS)
DNT	Developing Nations Tractor [*Ford Motor Co.*]
DNT	Did Not Test [*Medicine*]
DNT	Digital Network Terminator
DNT	Dinitrotoluene [*Organic chemistry*]
DNT	Dinitrotrifluoromethyl [*Organic chemistry*]
DNT	Director of Naval Telecommunications
DNT	Director of Naval Training [*British military*] (DMA)
DNT	Downtime [*Data processing*] [*Telecommunications*]
DNT	Dragon Night Tracker [*Military*] (MCD)
DNT	National Trust for Historic Preservation, Washington, DC [*Library symbol*] [*Library of Congress*] (LCLS)
DNTA	Dinitrosoterephthalamide [*Organic chemistry*]
DNTh	Diploma in Natural Therapeutics [*British*]
DNTL	Dental (MSA)
DN-TMB	United States Department of the Navy, Naval Ship Research and Development Center, Carderock, MD [*Library symbol*] [*Library of Congress*]
DNTO	Divisional Naval Transport Officer [*British military*] (DMA)
DNTP	Deoxynucleoside Triphosphate [*Biochemistry*]
DNTP	Diethyl Nitrophenyl Phosphorothioate [*Insecticide*]
DNTRD	Denatured
DNTS	Director, Naval Transportation Service [*Later, CNTS*]
DNU	Denison University, Granville, OH [*OCLC symbol*] (OCLC)
DNU	Do Not Use
DNU	Dundee Resources [*Vancouver Stock Exchange symbol*]
D-NuM	Diplomate, American Board of Nuclear Medicine (DHSM)
DNUND	Dopovidi Akademii Nauk Ukrains'koi RSR. Seriya A. Fiziko-Matematichni ta Tekhnichni Nauki [*A publication*]
DNV	Danville [*Illinois*] [*Airport symbol*] (OAG)
DNVP	Deutschnationale Volkspartei [*German National People's Party*]
DNVS	Det Norske Videnskapers Selskap [*A publication*]
DNVT	Digital Nonsecure Voice Terminal (MCD)
DNW	Der Neue Weg [*A publication*]
DNW	Deutsch Niederlandischer Windkanal [*German*]
DNW	Directorate of Naval Warfare [*British*]
DNW	Duits-Nederlandse Windtunnel [*Netherlands*]
DNW	Dunoir, WY [*Location identifier*] [*FAA*] (FAAL)
DNW	United States National War College, Fort McNair, Washington, DC [*Library symbol*] [*Library of Congress*] (LCLS)
DNWC	Director of Naval Weapons Contracts [*British*]
DNWIND	Downwind (FAAC)
DNWS	Director of Naval Weather Service, Ministry of Defence [*British*] (NATG)
DNWS	Discrete Network Simulation
DNY	Delancey, NY [*Location identifier*] [*FAA*] (FAAL)
DNY	Dersam [*New York*] [*Seismograph station code, US Geological Survey*] (SEIS)
DNY	Destiny Resources Ltd. [*Vancouver Stock Exchange symbol*]
DNY	Donnelley [*R. R.*] & Sons Co. [*NYSE symbol*] (SPSG)
DN-YD	United States Department of the Navy, Naval Facilities Engineering Command, Washington, DC [*Library symbol*] [*Library of Congress*] (LCLS)
DNYO	Yola [*Nigeria*] [*ICAO location identifier*] (ICLI)
DNZA	Zaria [*Nigeria*] [*ICAO location identifier*] (ICLI)
DNZR	Danzar Investment Group, Inc. [*Dallas, TX*] [*NASDAQ symbol*] (NQ)
DO	Bearing Doubtful [*Aviation code*] (FAAC)
Do	Byk-Gulden Lomberg [*Germany*] [*Research code symbol*]
DO	Compania Dominicana de Aviacion SA [*ICAO designator*] (OAG)
DO	Dance Observer [*A publication*]
DO	Data Output [*Data processing*] (IEEE)
D/O	Daughter Of [*Genealogy*]
DO	Day-Old
DO	Day Order [*Investment term*]
DO	Decanter Oil [*Petroleum technology*]
D-O	Decimal to Octal [*Data processing*] (IEEE)
DO	Defence Operations [*British*] [*World War II*]
DO	Defense Order
DO	Deferred Ordinary (ADA)
DO	Delegation Order [*Legal term*] (DLA)
D/O	Delivery Order [*Business term*]
DO	Demi Official [*Military*] [*British*]
DO	Demolition Order (ROG)
DO	Dental Officer
D/O	Depot Overhaul (MCD)
DO	Depression Obvious [*Psychology*]
DO	Deputy for Operations
D & O	Description and Operations (NASA)
do.	Descuento [*Discount*] [*Spanish*]
DO	Design Objective (IEEE)
DO	Designated Official (NRCH)
DO	Desirable Objective (KSC)
DO	Deviating Oscillator
DO	Diamine Oxidase [*Also, DAO*] [*An enzyme*]
DO	Diesel Oil
D d O	Digest des Ostens [*A publication*]
DO	Digital Output [*Data processing*]
DO	Diploma in Ophthalmology
DO	Diploma in Osteopathy [*British*]
DO	Direct Obligation
DO	Direct Order
D-O	Directive-Organic [*Designation for biologically oriented, authoritarian psychiatrists*]
DO	Director of Operations
DO	Director's Office
D & O	Directors' and Officers' [*Liability insurance*]
DO	Disbursing Officer
DO	Disbursing Order
DO	Discrete Output [*Data processing*] (KSC)
DO	Dissolved Oxygen
DO	Disto-Occlusal [*Dentistry*]
DO	Distribution Office (DCTA)
DO	District Office [*or Officer*]

DO .... Ditto (AFM)
DO .... Divisional Officer [*Agricultural Development and Advisory Service*] [*British*]
DO .... Divisional Orders
DO .... Dock Office (ROG)
DO .... Dock Operations (DS)
DO .... Doctor of Ophthalmology
DO .... Doctor of Optometry
DO .... Doctor of Oratory
DO .... Doctor of Osteopathy
DO .... Doctor's Orders
DO .... Dollar [*Monetary unit*]
Do.............. Dominance [*Psychology*]
DO .... Dominican Republic [*ANSI two-letter standard code*] (CNC)
Do.............. Dominicus de Sancto Geminiano [*Flourished, 1407-09*] [*Authority cited in pre-1607 legal work*] (DSA)
DO .... Dominions Office [*British*]
DO .... Dora Explorations Ltd. [*Vancouver Stock Exchange symbol*]
DO .... Dornier [*German airplane type*]
DO .... Dornier-Werke GmbH [*Federal Republic of Germany*] [*ICAO aircraft manufacturer identifier*] (ICAO)
DO .... Draw Out (KSC)
D/O........... Drop Off
DO .... Dropout (AAG)
DO .... Due Out [*Army*]
DO .... Duty Officer [*Military*]
DO .... Oiselet [*Record label*] [*France*]
Do.............. Oligophranic Detail [*Psychology*]
DO .... Stock of the Item Requested Has Been Temporarily Exhausted; Your Order Has Been Recorded and Will Be Filled When Stock Becomes Available [*Advice of supply action code*] [*Army*]

DOA .... Abstracts on Tropical Agriculture [*A publication*]
DOA .... Dasher Owners of America (EA)
DOA .... Date of Availability [*Military*] (AFM)
DOA .... Day of Ammunition
DOA .... Dead on Arrival [*Medicine*]
DOA .... Dead on Arrival [*Rock music group*]
DOA .... Defeat Opiate Addiction [*An association*]
DOA .... Delegation of Authority (MCD)
DOA .... Department of Agriculture
DOA .... Department of the Army
DOA .... Digital Output Adapter
DOA .... Dioctyl Adipate [*Also, DEHA*] [*Organic chemistry*]
DOA .... Direction of Arrival
DOA .... Director of Officer Appointments [*British military*] (DMA)
DOA .... Disabled Officers Association (EA)
DOA .... Doany [*Madagascar*] [*Airport symbol*] (OAG)
DOA .... Documents on Acceptance [*Banking*]
DOA .... Dominant Obstacle Allowance (MCD)
DOA .... Organization of American States, Washington, DC [*OCLC symbol*] (OCLC)
DOAC....... Dubois Oleic Albumin Complex [*Microbiology*]
DOAE....... Defence Operational Analysis Establishment [*British*]
DOAK....... Doak Pharmacal Co., Inc. [*NASDAQ symbol*] (NQ)
DOAL....... Directorate of Airlift [*Air Force*] (MCD)
DOAMS .... Distant Object Attitude Measuring System (MCD)
Doane Inf Cent Index Syst Subj Index ... DICIS. Doane Information Center Indexing System. Subject Index [*A publication*]
Doanes Agr Rep ... Doane's Agricultural Report [*A publication*]
Doanes Bus Mag Amer Agr ... Doane's Business Magazine for American Agriculture [*A publication*]
DO/AO...... District Office/Area Office [*IRS*]
DOAO(FE) ... Defence Operational Analysis Organisation [*Far East*]
DOAP........ Daunorubicin, Oncovin [*Vincristine*], ara-C, Prednisone [*Antineoplastic drug regimen*]
DOAS .... Differential Optical Absorption Spectrometer
DOA/TOA ... Direction of Arrival/Time of Arrival (MCD)
DOB........... Data Output Bus [*Data processing*]
DOB........... Date of Birth
DOB........... Daughters of Bilitis [*Superseded by United Sisters*] (EA)
DOB........... Daughters of Bosses
DOB........... Decent Old Buffer [*British*] [*Slang*]
DOB........... Department of Energy, Bartlesville Energy Technology Center, Bartlesville, OK [*OCLC symbol*] (OCLC)
DOB........... Deployed Operating Base (MCD)
DOB........... Depth of Burial [*of explosives*]
DOB........... Depth of Burst (NATG)
DOB........... Detained on Board [*Referring to seamen*]
DOB........... Discrete Out Blockhouse [*NASA*] (KSC)
DOB........... Dispersed Operating Base [*Air Force*] (AFM)
DOB........... Doctor's Order Book
DOB........... Dombas [*Norway*] [*Geomagnetic observatory code*]
DOB........... Marietta, GA [*Location identifier*] [*FAA*] (FAAL)
DOBANIAN ... Descendants of Black African Natives in the American North [*Proposed appellation*]
DOBC........ Diesel Oil, Bentonite, Cement [*Oil well drilling technology*]
DOBIS....... Dortmunder Bibliothekssystem [*Dortmund Bibliographic Information System*] [*Cataloguing system developed in Germany*]
DOBP .... Dodecyloxyhydroxybenzophenone [*Organic chemistry*]

DOBQ....... Doughtie's Foods, Inc. [*NASDAQ symbol*] (NQ)
DObst .... Diploma in Obstetrics
D Obst RCOG ... Diploma in Obstetrics, Royal College of Obstetricians and Gynaecologists [*British*]
Dobuts Zasshi ... Dobutsugaku Zasshi [*Toyko*] [*A publication*]
Dobycha Obogashch Rud Tsvetn Met ... Dobycha i Obogashchenie Rud Tsvetnykh Metallov [*A publication*]
Dobycha Pererab Goryuch Slantsev ... Dobycha i Pererabotka Goryuchikh Slantsev [*USSR*] [*A publication*]
Dobycha Pererab Nerudn Stroit Mater ... Dobycha i Pererabotka Nerudnykh Stroitel'nykh Materialov [*A publication*]
DOC........... Catalogue of Byzantine Coins in the Dumbarton Oaks Collection and Whittemore Collection [*A publication*]
DOC........... DARCOM [*Development and Readiness Command, Army*] Operations Center (MCD)
DOC........... Data, Operations, and Control
DOC........... Data Optimizing Computer
DOC........... Data Output Channel (MSA)
DOC........... Date of Change
DOC........... Datsun Owners Club (EA)
DOC........... Decimal to Octal Conversion
DOC........... Deck of Cards (MCD)
DOC........... Degree of Control (MCD)
DOC........... Degree of Cooperation [*Military*] (NVT)
DOC........... Delayed Opening Chaff
DOC........... Denominazione di Origine Controllata [*Italian wine designation*]
DOC........... Deoxycholate [*Biochemistry*]
DOC........... Deoxycorticosterone [*Endocrinology*]
DOC........... Department of Commerce
DOC........... Department of Communications [*Canada*]
DOC........... Descend on Course [*Aviation*]
DOC........... Design Operation Capability (MCD)
DOC........... Dictionary of Organic Compounds [*A publication*]
DOC........... Died of Other Causes [*Medicine*]
DOC........... Digital Optical Cassette [*Information retrieval*]
DOC........... Digital Oscillator Chip [*Apple Computer, Inc.*]
DOC........... Digital Output Channel (MCD)
DOC........... Digital Output Control
DOC........... Direct Operating Cost [*Accounting*]
DOC........... Director of Camouflage [*British*]
DOC........... Director of Contracts [*Military*] [*British*]
DOC........... Dissolved Organic Carbon
DOC........... District Officer Commanding
DOC........... Divested Operating Company
DOC........... DOC (Doctors Ought to Care) (EA)
Doc............. Docent
DOC........... Docket
DOC........... Doctor (EY)
Doc............. Doctores Bononienses [*Latin*] (DSA)
DOC........... Document [*or Documentation*] (AFM)
DOC........... Douglas College Learning Resources Centre [*UTLAS symbol*]
DOC........... Drive Other Cars [*Insurance*]
DOC........... Dropout Connector
DOC........... Due-Out Cancellation [*Military*] (AFM)
DOC........... Dynamic Overload Controls [*Telecommunications*]
DOC........... Oblate College, Washington, DC [*Library symbol*] [*Library of Congress*] (LCLS)
DOCA........ Date of Change of Accountability [*Military*]
DOCA........ Date of Current Appointment [*Military*]
DOCA........ Defense Orientation Conference Association (EA)
DOCA........ Deoxycorticosterone [*or Desoxycorticosterone*] Acetate [*Also, DCA*] [*Endocrinology*]
DOCA........ Director of Overseas Civil Aviation [*British*]
Doc Abstr... Documentation Abstracts [*A publication*]
Doc Abstr Inf Sci Abstr ... Documentation Abstracts and Information Science Abstracts [*A publication*]
Doc Alb ..... Documenta Albana [*A publication*]
Doc A Merid ... Documents d'Archeologie Meridionale [*A publication*]
Doc Bibl ..... Documentacion Bibliotecologica [*A publication*]
Doc et Bibl ... Documentation et Bibliotheques [*A publication*]
Doc Biol ..... Documents on Biology [*A publication*]
Doc Biol Pract ... Documentation du Biologiste Practicien [*A publication*]
Doc Bon ..... Doctores Bononienses [*Latin*] (DSA)
Doc Bull Natl Res Cent (Egypt) ... Documentation Bulletin. National Research Centre (Egypt) [*A publication*]
Doc Bull Nat Res Cent (UAR) ... Documentation Bulletin. National Research Centre (United Arab Republic) [*A publication*]
DOCC........ Defense Communications Agency Operations Center Complex
DOCC........ Digital Optronics Corp. [*NASDAQ symbol*] (NQ)
DocC .... Documentation Catholique [*Paris*] [*A publication*]
DOCC........ Ducati Owners' Club of Canada (EA)
DOCC........ Office of the Comptroller of the Currency, Washington, DC [*Library symbol*] [*Library of Congress*] (LCLS)
Doc Cartogr Ecol ... Documents de Cartographie Ecologique [*A publication*]
Doc Cath .... Documentation Catholique [*A publication*]
Doc Centre Et Revenus Couts ... Documents. Centre d'Etude des Revenus et des Couts [*A publication*]
Doc CEPESS ... Documents CEPESS [*Centre d'Etudes Politiques, Economiques, et Sociales*] [*A publication*]

Doc Charleroi ... Documents et Rapports. Societe Paleontologique et Archeologique de l'Arrondissement Judiciaire de Charleroi [*A publication*]
Doc Chem Yugosl ... Documenta Chemica Yugoslavica [*A publication*]
Doc Combust Eng Assoc ... Document. Combustion Engineering Association [*England*] [*A publication*]
Doc Coop.... Documenti Cooperativi [*A publication*]
DOCDEL .. Document Delivery [*Information service or system*]
DOCE........ Date of Current Enlistment [*Military*]
Doc Eng .... Doctor of Engineering
Doc d'Et Droit Const ... Documents d'Etudes. Droit Constitutionnel et Institutions Politiques [*A publication*]
Doc d'Et Droit Internat Publ ... Documents d'Etudes. Droit International Public [*A publication*]
DOCG........ Denominazione di Origine Controllata e Garantita [*Italian wine designation*]
DOCG........ Deoxycorticosterone Glucoside [*Also, DCG*] [*Endocrinology*]
DOCGEN ... Document Generator
Doc Geogr.. Documentatio Geographica [*A publication*]
Doc Haematol (Bucharest) ... Documenta Haematologica (Bucharest) [*A publication*]
DOCHSIN ... District of Columbia Health Sciences Information Network [*Library network*]
Doc Inform Gestion ... Documents d'Information et de Gestion [*A publication*]
Doc Inst Sci (Rabat) ... Documents. Institut Scientifique (Rabat) [*A publication*]
Doc Invest Hidrol ... Documentos de Investigacion Hidrologica [*A publication*]
DOCK........ [*The*] Chicago Dock & Canal Trust [*Chicago, IL*] [*NASDAQ symbol*] (NQ)
DOCK........ Docket (DLA)
Docket........ Docket and the Barrister [*1889-98*] [*Canada*] [*A publication*] (DLA)
Docket........ West Publishing Company's Docket [*1909-41*] [*A publication*] (DLA)
Dock Harb Auth ... Dock and Harbour Authority [*A publication*]
Dock & Harbour ... Dock and Harbour Authority [*London*] [*A publication*]
DOCL........ Department of Commerce Library (IID)
Doc Lab Geol Fac Sci Lyon ... Documents des Laboratoires de Geologie de la Faculte des Sciences de Lyon [*A publication*]
Doc Med .... Documentation Medicale. Comite International de la Croix-Rouge [*A publication*]
Doc Med Geogr Trop ... Documenta de Medicina Geographica et Tropica [*A publication*]
DOCMOD ... Documentation Modernization [*Program*] [*Army*] (INF)
Doc Neerl Indones Morb Trop ... Documenta Neerlandica et Indonesica de Morbis Tropicis [*A publication*]
DOCO .... Director to Commissary Operations [*Military*] (AABC)
DOCO .... DOC Optics Corp. [*NASDAQ symbol*] (NQ)
Doc Ophthal ... Documenta Ophthalmologica [*A publication*]
Doc Ophthalmol ... Documenta Ophthalmologica [*A publication*]
Doc Ophthalmol Proc Ser ... Documenta Ophthalmologica. Proceedings Series [*A publication*]
DOCP .... Delaware Otsego Corp. [*NASDAQ symbol*] (NQ)
DOCPAL...... Sistema de Documentacion sobre Poblacion en America Latina [*Latin American Population Documentation System*] [*Economic Commission for Latin America and the Caribbean*] [*United Nations*] [*Information service or system*] (IID)
Doc Parl ..... Documents Parlementaires [*A publication*] (DLA)
Doc Phytosociol ... Documents Phytosociologiques [*A publication*]
Doc Polit .... Documentos Politicos [*A publication*]
Doc Public Adm ... Documentation in Public Administration [*A publication*]
DocRerPol... Doctor Rerum Politicarum [*Doctor of Political Science*]
Doc Rheum ... Documenta Rheumatologica [*A publication*]
DOCS .... Design Optimization Codes for Structures (MCD)
DOCS .... Dictionary of Organic Compounds [*A publication*]
DOCS .... Disk-Oriented Computer System (IEEE)
D Oc S........ Doctor of Ocular Science
Docs .... Doctores Bononienses [*Latin*] (DSA)
DOCS .... Doctors Officenters [*NASDAQ symbol*] (NQ)
DOCS .... Document Organization and Control System [*Telecommunications*] (TEL)
DOCS .... Documents
D Oc Sc...... Doctor of Ocular Science
Docs CEPESS ... Documents. CEPESS [*Centre d'Etudes Politiques, Economiques, et Sociales*] [*A publication*]
Doc Sci XVe Siecle ... Documents Scientifiques du XVe Siecle [*Geneva*] [*A publication*]
Doc Seance ... Document de Seance. Rapport Parlementaire au Parlement Europeen [*A publication*]
Doc Swed Counc Build Res ... Document. Swedish Council for Building Research [*A publication*]
DOCSYS ... Display of Chromosome Statistics System
Doct............ Doctor
Doct............ Doctores Bononienses [*Latin*] (DSA)
DOCT .... Doctrine (ROG)
DOCT .... Document
DoctArch ... Doctor of Christian Archeology
DoctCom.... Doctor Communis [*Rome*] [*A publication*]

Doct Comm ... Doctor Communis [*Rome*] [*A publication*]
Doct Dem... Doctrine of Demurrers [*A publication*] (DLA)
Doc Tech Charbon Fr ... Documents Techniques. Charbonnages de France [*A publication*]
Doc Tech Inst Natl Rech Agron Tunis ... Documents Techniques. Institut National de la Recherche Agronomique de Tunisie [*A publication*]
Doc Tech SCPA (Soc Commer Potasses Azote) ... Document Technique de la SCPA (Societe Commerciale des Potasses et de l'Azote) [*A publication*]
Doc To........ Doctores Tholosani [*Latin*] (DSA)
Doct Pl .... Doctrina Placitandi [*A publication*] (DLA)
Doct Plac.... Doctrina Placitandi [*A publication*] (DLA)
Doc Travail ... Document de Travail [*Besancon*] [*A publication*]
DoctrLife.... Doctrine and Life [*Dublin*] [*A publication*]
DOCU........ DocuCon, Inc. [*NASDAQ symbol*] (NQ)
DOCU........ Document (AABC)
Docum Adm ... Documentacion Administrativa [*A publication*]
Docum Admin ... Documentacion Administrativa [*A publication*]
Docum et Biblio ... Documentation et Bibliotheques [*A publication*]
Docum Cath ... Documentation Catholique [*A publication*]
Docum Centre Nat Rech For ... Document. Centre National de Recherches Forestieres [*A publication*]
Docum Econ ... Documentacion Economica [*Madrid*] [*A publication*]
Docum Econ Colombiana ... Documentacion Economica Colombiana [*A publication*]
Docum Econ (Paris) ... Documentation Economique (Paris) [*A publication*]
Documen.... Documentation Etc. [*A publication*]
Documents CEGM ... Documents. Centre d'Etudes Geologiques et Minieres [*A publication*]
Docum Europ ... Documentation Europeenne [*A publication*]
Docum Europe Centr ... Documentation sur l'Europe Centrale [*A publication*]
Docum Eur Ser Syndicale et Ouvriere ... Documentation Europeenne Serie Syndicale et Ouvriere [*A publication*]
Docum Franc Illustr ... Documentation Francaise Illustree [*A publication*]
Docum Inform Pedag ... Documentation et Information Pedagogiques [*A publication*]
Docum Jur ... Documentacion Juridica [*A publication*]
Docum Legis Afr ... Documentation Legislative Africaine [*A publication*]
Docum Paesi Est ... Documentazione sui Paesi de l'Est [*A publication*]
DOCUS ..... Display-Oriented Computer Usage System
Doc Ve........ Doctores Veteres [*Latin*] (DSA)
Doc Vet ...... Documenta Veterinaria [*A publication*]
Doc Vita It ... Documenti di Vita Italiana [*A publication*]
DOCX .... DocuGraphix, Inc. [*Cupertino, CA*] [*NASDAQ symbol*] (NQ)
DOD .... Date of Death
DoD........... Department of Defense [*Washington, DC*]
DOD .... Depth of Discharge
DOD .... Detroit Ordnance District [*Army*]
DOD .... Development Operations Division [*NASA*] (KSC)
DOD .... Died of Disease
DOD .... Dihydroxydiphenyl [*Antioxidant*] [*Organic chemistry*]
DOD .... Direct Outward Dialing [*Telecommunications*]
DOD .... Director of Dockyards [*Admiralty*] [*British*]
DOD .... Director of Operations Division [*Navy*] [*British*]
DOD .... Directory of Directories [*Later, DIP*] [*A publication*]
DOD .... Directory on Disk [*Information service or system*] (IID)
DOD .... Dissolved Oxygen Deficit [*Water pollution*]
DOD .... Dodoma [*Tanzania*] [*Airport symbol*] (OAG)
DOD .... Dodoma [*Tanzania*] [*Seismograph station code, US Geological Survey*] [*Closed*] (SEIS)
Dod............ Dod's Parliamentary Companion. Annual [*A publication*] (DLA)
Dod............ Dodson's English Admiralty Reports [*A publication*] (DLA)
DOD .... Draft on Demand [*Banking*] (ROG)
DOD .... Drop-on-Demand [*Computer printer*]
DOD .... United States Department of Energy, Regional Energy Information Center, Dallas, TX [*OCLC symbol*] (OCLC)
DODA .... Door and Operator Dealers Association (EA)
DODAAC ... Department of Defense Activity Address Code (AABC)
DODAAD ... Department of Defense Activity Address Designer (MCD)
DODAAD ... Department of Defense Activity Address Directory (AFM)
DODAAF .. Department of Defense Activity Address File
DODAAS .. Department of Defense Automatic Address System (MCD)
DODAC ..... Department of Defense Ammunition Code (AFM)
DODAC..... Dioctadecyldimethylammonium Chloride [*Organic chemistry*]
DODADL ... Department of Defense Authorized Data List
Dod Adm.... Dodson's English Admiralty Reports [*A publication*] (DLA)
DOD-AGFSRS ... Department of Defense Aircraft Ground Fire Suppression and Rescue Office
Dod Ant Parl ... Doderidge on the Antiquity and Power of Parliaments [*A publication*] (DLA)
DODAR..... Director of Drafting and Records [*British military*] (DMA)
DODAS ..... Digital Oceanographic Data Acquisition System (MCD)
DODCAPS ... Department of Defense Central Automated Personnel System (AFM)
DODCI ...... Department of Defense Computer Institute
DODCI ...... Diethyloxadicarbocyanine Iodide [*A dye*]
DODCLPMI ... Department of Defense Consolidated List of Principal Military Items
DODD .... Department of Defense Directive

DODDAC ... Department of Defense Damage Assessment Center
Dodd & Br Pr Pr ... Dodd and Brooks' Probate Court Practice [*A publication*] (DLA)
Dodd Bur Fees ... Dodd on Burial and Other Church Fees [*A publication*] (DLA)
DODDS ..... Department of Defense Dependents Schools
DODE .... Development Optical Diagnostic Equipment [*Military*]
Dod Eng Law ... Doderidge's English Lawyer [*A publication*] (DLA)
DODEP ..... Department of Defense Emergency Plans (AABC)
DODEP ..... Department of Defense Exercise Planning (AFM)
DOD(F) ...... Director of Operations Division (Foreign) [*Navy*] [*British*]
DODFCI ..... Department of Defense Foreign Counterintelligence Program
DODFDCO ... Department of Defense Foreign Disclosure Coordinating Office (AABC)
DODGE ..... Department of Defense Gravity Experiment [*Satellite*]
Dodge .... Dodge/Sweet's Construction Outlook [*A publication*]
DODGE-M ... Department of Defense Gravity Experiment, Multipurpose [*Satellite*]
DODH .... Department of Defense Handbook
DOD(H) .... Director of Operations Division (Home) [*Navy*] [*British*]
DODHBK .... Department of Defense Handbook
DODHGCSO ... Department of Defense Household Goods Commercial Storage Office
DODHGFO ... Department of Defense Household Goods Field Office
DODHSNS ... Department of Defense High School Newspaper Service
DODI .... Department of Defense Instruction
DODI .... District Office Direct Input [*Social Security computerized system*]
DODIC ...... Department of Defense Identification Code (AFM)
DODIC ...... Department of Defense Item Code
DODIDENTBAD ... Department of Defense Identification Badge
DODIEC .... Department of Defense Item Entry Control
DODIER .. Department of Defense Industrial Equipment Reserve (AABC)
DODIG ...... Department of Defense Inspector General
DODIIS ..... Department of Defense Intelligence Information System (MCD)
DODIM ..... Department of Defense Inventory Manager
DODINST .. Department of Defense Instruction
DODIS ..... Distribution of Oceanographic Data at Isentropic Levels System
DODISB .... Department of Defense Industrial Security Bulletin
DODISC .... Department of Defense Item Standardization Code
DODISL .... Department of Defense Industrial Security Letter
DODISM .. Department of Defense Industrial Security Manual
DODISPR ... Department of Defense Information Security Program Regulation (MCD)
DODISR ... Department of Defense Industrial Security Regulation
DODISS .... Department of Defense Index of Specifications and Standards
Dod Law L ... Doderidge's The Lawyer's Light [*A publication*] (DLA)
DODM ..... Department of Defense Manual
DODMDS ... Department of Defense Material Distribution System (MCD)
DODMERB ... Department of Defense Medical Examination Review Board
DOD/MIS ... Department of Defense Management Information System
DODMNL ... Department of Defense Manual
DODMPAC ... Department of Defense Military Pay and Allowance Committee
DODMPRC ... Department of Defense Military Personnel Records Center
DODMUL ... Department of Defense Master Urgency List (AFM)
DODNACC ... Department of Defense National Agency Check Center (AABC)
Dod Nobility ... Doderidge's Nobility [*A publication*] (DLA)
DOD NR ... Department of Defense. News Release [*A publication*]
DODO ...... Drain on Day One [*Classification for new newspaper*]
DOD-PEC ... Department of Defense Program Element Code (AFIT)
DODPM .... Department of Defense Military Pay and Allowance Entitlements Manual (AABC)
DODPMRP ... Department of Defense Precious Metals Recovery Program
DODPRO ... Department of Defense, Pacific Research Office (CINC)
DODPRT .. Date of Departure [*Military*] (AABC)
DODPSTR ... Department of Defense Poster
DODR .... Department of Defense Regulation
DODRE ..... Department of Defense Research and Engineering
DODS .... Definitive Orbit Determination System [*NASA*]
DODS .... Different Orbitals for Different Spins [*Atomic physics*]
Dods .... Dodson's English Admiralty Reports [*A publication*] (DLA)
DODSASP ... Department of Defense Small Arms Serialization Program
DodSO₄ ... Dodecyl Sulfate [*Organic chemistry*]
Dodson Adm (Eng) ... Dodson's English Admiralty Reports [*A publication*] (DLA)
DODSPBL ... Department of Defense Surplus Property Bidders List
DOD-SSP ... Department of Defense Single Stock Point (MCD)
DODT .... Design Option Decision Tree
DODT .... Display Octal Debugging Technique
DODX .... Department of Defense Oversized Flatcar (INF)
DOE .... Date of Enlistment [*Military*]
DOE .... Deep Ocean Environment
D-O-E .... Deoxyephedrine [*or Desoxyephedrine*] [*Pharmacology*]
DOE .... Department of Energy [*Washington, DC*]
DOE .... Department of the Environment [*Formerly, MPBW, MT*] [*British*]
DOE .... Design of Experiments [*Conference*] [*Army*] (RDA)
D Oe .... Deutsch-Oesterreich [*A publication*]

DOE .... Dictionary of Old English [*University of Toronto*] [*Canada*] [*Information service or system*] (IID)
DOE .... Dissolved Oxygen Electrode
DOE .... Djoemoe [*Surinam*] [*Airport symbol*] (OAG)
DOE .... Doctor of Oral English
DOE .... Dyspnea on Exercise [*or Exertion*] [*Medicine*]
DOE .... United States Department of Energy Library, Washington, DC [*OCLC symbol*] (OCLC)
D Oe B .... Der Oesterreichische Betriebswirt [*A publication*]
D Oec .... Doctor Oeconomiae [*Doctor of Economics*]
D Oe D .... Der Oeffentliche Dienst [*A publication*]
DOE/ET ...... Department of Energy/Assistant Secretary for Energy Technology [*Washington, DC*]
DOE Pat Available Licens ... DOE [*US Department of Energy*] Patents Available for Licensing [*United States*] [*A publication*]
DOE/RECON ... Department of Energy's Remote Console Information System [*Department of Energy*] [*Database*]
DOES .... Decision-Oriented Evaluation System
DOES .... Defense Organization Entity Standards [*DoD*]
DOES .... Defense Organization Entity System [*DoD*] (MCD)
DOES .... Disk-Oriented Engineering System [*Data processing*]
DOE-TIC .... Department of Energy Technical Information Center [*Oak Ridge, TN*] [*Database producer*]
DOE Transp Lib Bull ... DOE [*US Department of Energy*] and Transport Library Bulletin [*A publication*]
DOETS ...... Dual-Object Electronic Tracking System
DOE (US Dep Energy) Symp Ser ... DOE (US Department of Energy) Symposium Series [*A publication*]
DOF .... Deep Ocean Floor
DOF .... Defenders of Furbearers [*Later, Defenders of Wildlife*]
DOF .... Degree of Freedom
DOF .... Delivery on Field
DOF .... Demonstration of Operational Feasibility
DOF .... Depth of Focus [*Optics*]
DOF .... Device Output Format
DOF .... Dioctyl Fumarate [*Organic chemistry*]
DOF .... Direction of Fire [*Weaponry*] (INF)
DOF .... Direction of Flight (KSC)
DOF .... Director of Ordnance Factories [*Ministry of Supply*] [*British*] [*World War II*]
DOF .... United States Department of Energy NEICA, Albuquerque, NM [*OCLC symbol*] (OCLC)
DOFA .... Date of Full Availability
DOFA .... Details of Agreement [*NATO*] (NATG)
DOFAB ..... Damned Old Fool About Books [*Acronym created by Eugene Field*]
DOFC .... Defense Orthopedic Footwear Clinic [*Military*] (AABC)
DOFC .... Donny Osmond Fan Club (EA)
DOFD .... Date of First Demand [*Military*] (AFIT)
DOF(E) ...... Director of Ordnance Factories, Engineering Factories [*Ministry of Supply*] [*British*] [*World War II*]
DOFIC .... Domain-Originated Functional Integrated Circuit (IEEE)
DOFL .... Diamond Ordnance Fuze Laboratory [*Later, Harry Diamond Laboratories*] [*AMC*] [*Washington, DC*]
DOFS .... Day of Supply [*Military*]
DOFS .... Department of Organization and Field Services, AFL-CIO (EA)
DOFS .... Depot of Supplies [*Marine Corps*]
DOFTAB ... Dansk Ornithologisk Forenings Tidsskrift [*A publication*]
DOF(X) ...... Director of Ordnance Factories, Explosives Factories [*Ministry of Supply*] [*British*] [*World War II*]
DOG .... Days of Grace [*for payment*] [*Business term*]
DOG .... Deoxy-D-glucose [*Also, DDG, DG*] [*Biochemistry*]
DOG .... Dioctanoylglycerol [*Organic chemistry*]
D-OG .... Diplomate, American Board of Obstetrics and Gynecology (DHSM)
DOG .... Directory of Opportunities for Graduates [*A publication*]
DOG .... Disgruntled Old Graduate [*West Point*]
DOG .... Dissolver Off-Gas [*Nuclear energy*] (NRCH)
DOG .... Documentation sur l'Europe Centrale [*A publication*]
DOG .... Dog Owners' Guild
DOG .... Dongola [*Sudan*] [*Airport symbol*] (OAG)
DOG .... Double Chain Branch-Oblong Master Link-Grab Hook
DOG .... Drop Out Generator (NG)
DOG .... Due-Out of Group [*Military*] (MCD)
Doga Bilim Derg Seri A ... Doga Bilim Dergisi. Seri A [*A publication*]
Doga Bilim Derg Seri A1 ... Doga Bilim Dergisi. Seri A1 [*A publication*]
Doga Bilim Derg Seri A2 ... Doga Bilim Dergisi. Seri A2 [*A publication*]
Doga Bilim Derg Seri D ... Doga Bilim Dergisi. Seri D [*A publication*]
Doga Bilim Derg Seri D1 ... Doga Bilim Dergisi. Seri D1 [*A publication*]
Doga Bilim Derg Seri D2 ... Doga Bilim Dergisi. Seri D2 [*A publication*]
Doga Biyol Serisi ... Doga Biyoloji Serisi [*A publication*]
Doga Kim Serisi ... Doga Kimya Serisi [*A publication*]
Doga Ser A Math Phys Biol Sci ... Doga. Serie A. Mathematical, Physical, and Biological Sciences [*A publication*]
Doga Ser C Med Sci ... Doga. Serie C. Medical Sciences [*A publication*]
DOGI .... Dottrina Giuridica [*Consiglio Nazionale delle Ricerche*] [*Italy*] [*Information service or system*] (CRD)
DOGM ...... Dogmatic
DOGWV .... Wissenschaftliche Veroeffentlichungen der Deutschen Orientgesellschaft [*A publication*]

DOGYDY ... Developments in Obstetrics and Gynecology [*A publication*]
DOH .... Deutscher Orden der Harugari [*German Order of Harugari*] (EA)
DOH .... Diploma in Occupational Health
DOH .... Discrete Output High (MCD)
DOH .... Dock and Harbour Authority [*London*] [*A publication*]
DOH .... Doha [*Qatar*] [*Airport symbol*] (OAG)
DOH .... Dorchester Hotels, Inc. [*Vancouver Stock Exchange symbol*]
DOH .... Fort Bragg, NC [*Location identifier*] [*FAA*] (FAAL)
DOHC .... Double Overhead Camshaft [*Automotive term*]
DOHNA ..... Domestic Heating News [*A publication*]
DOHSA..... Death on the High Seas Act
DO Hyg ..... Diploma in Occupational Hygiene [*British*]
DOI........... Date of Information (MCD)
DOI........... Date of Injury [*Medicine*]
DOI........... Deep Ocean Installation
DOI........... Defence Oceanology International Exhibition [*Great Britain*] (ITD)
DOI........... Department of Industry [*British*] (DS)
DOI........... Department of the Interior (AABC)
DOI........... Department Operating Instruction
DOI........... Descent Orbit Insertion [*Aerospace*]
DOI........... Died of Injuries [*Military*] (AABC)
DOI........... Differential Orbit Improvement
DOI........... Directorate Office Instruction
DOI........... Distinctness of Image [*Mobay Corp.*]
DOI........... Division Operating Instruction [*Air Force*]
doi .... Dogri [*MARC language code*] [*Library of Congress*] (LCCP)
DOI........... Wing Director of Intelligence
Doi B .... Doitsu Bungaku [*A publication*]
DOIL .... Dallas Oil & Minerals, Inc. [*NASDAQ symbol*] (NQ)
DOIM....... Director [*or Directorate*] of Information Management [*DoD*]
DOIM....... Directory of International Mail [*A publication*]
DOIO .... Directly Operable Input/Output
DOIP .... Dioctyl Isophthalate [*Organic chemistry*]
DOIT .... Database Oriented Interrogation Technique [*Comserv Corp.*]
DO/IT ...... Digital Output/Input Translator [*Data processing*]
Doit Bung Ronko ... Doitsu Bungaku Ronko [*A publication*]
Doits........... Doitsugo [*A publication*]
DOJ.......... Department of Justice (AABC)
DOJ.......... Dominican Oblates of Jesus [*Roman Catholic women's religious order*]
DOJ .... United States Department of Justice Library, Washington, DC [*OCLC symbol*] (OCLC)
DOJb .... Deutsches Orient-Jahrbuch [*A publication*]
DOK........ De Odeon Kring [*The Odeon Club, for homosexuals*] [*Holland*]
DOK........ Die Ortskrankenkasse [*A publication*]
Dok .... Dokumentation [*A publication*]
DOK........ Donetsk [*USSR*] [*Airport symbol*] [*Obsolete*] (OAG)
DOK........ Oesterreich Nederland [*A publication*]
Dok Arbeitsmed ... Dokumentation Arbeitsmedizin [*A publication*]
DOKBA ..... Doklady Biophysics [*English Translation*] [*A publication*]
DOKDI ...... Documentation Service [*Swiss Academy of Medical Sciences*] [*Information service or system*] (IID)
DOKEA ..... Dokumenteshon Kenkyu [*A publication*]
Dok Fachbibl Werkbuech ... Dokumentation Fachbibliothek Werkbuecherei [*A publication*]
Dok/Inf...... Dokumentation/Information [*A publication*]
DOKK........ Dramatic Order Knights of Khorassan (EA)
Dokkyo J Med Sci ... Dokkyo Journal of Medical Sciences [*A publication*]
Dokl Acad Sci USSR Earth Sci Sect ... Doklady Academy of Sciences of the USSR. Earth Science Sections [*A publication*]
Dokl Akad Nauk Arm SSR ... Doklady Akademii Nauk Armyanskoi SSR [*A publication*]
Dokl Akad Nauk Azerb SSR ... Doklady Akademii Nauk Azerbajdzanskoj SSR [*A publication*]
Dokl Akad Nauk Az SSR ... Doklady Akademii Nauk Azerbaidzanskoj SSR [*A publication*]
Dokl Akad Nauk Beloruss SSR ... Doklady Akademii Nauk Belorusskoi SSR [*A publication*]
Dokl Akad Nauk B SSR ... Doklady Akademii Nauk Belorusskoi SSR [*A publication*]
Dokl Akad Nauk SSR Biochem Sect (Engl Transl) ... Doklady Akademii Nauk SSSR. Biochemistry Section (English Translation) [*A publication*]
Dokl Akad Nauk SSR Bot Sci Sect (Engl Transl) ... Doklady Akademii Nauk SSSR. Botanical Sciences Section (English Translation) [*A publication*]
Dokl Akad Nauk SSSR ... Doklady Akademii Nauk SSSR [*A publication*]
Dokl Akad Nauk SSSR Biochem Sect (Engl Transl) ... Doklady Akademii Nauk SSSR. Biochemistry Section (English Translation) [*A publication*]
Dokl Akad Nauk SSSR Biol Sci Sect (Engl Transl) ... Doklady Akademii Nauk SSSR. Biological Science Section (English Translation) [*A publication*]
Dokl Akad Nauk SSSR Bot Sci Sect (Engl Transl) ... Doklady Akademii Nauk SSSR. Botanical Sciences Section (English Translation) [*A publication*]
Dokl Akad Nauk SSSR Ser A ... Doklady Akademii Nauk SSSR. Seriya A [*A publication*]

Dokl Akad Nauk SSSR Ser Biol ... Doklady Akademii Nauk SSSR. Seriya Biologiya [*A publication*]
Dokl Akad Nauk SSSR Ser Geol ... Doklady Akademii Nauk SSSR. Seriya Geologiya [*USSR*] [*A publication*]
Dokl Akad Nauk SSSR Ser Khim ... Doklady Akademii Nauk SSSR. Seriya Khimiya [*A publication*]
Dokl Akad Nauk SSSR Ser Mat Fiz ... Doklady Akademii Nauk SSSR. Seriya Matematika Fizika [*A publication*]
Dokl Akad Nauk Tadzh SSR ... Doklady Akademii Nauk Tadzhikskoi SSR [*A publication*]
Dokl Akad Nauk Ukrain SSR Ser A ... Akademija Nauk Ukrainskoi SSR. Doklady. Serija A. Fiziko-Matematiceskie i Tehniceskie Nauki [*A publication*]
Dokl Akad Nauk Ukr SSR ... Doklady Akademii Nauk Ukrainskoi SSR [*Ukrainian SSR*] [*A publication*]
Dokl Akad Nauk Ukr SSR Ser B ... Doklady Akademii Nauk Ukrainskoi SSR. Seriya B [*A publication*]
Dokl Akad Nauk Ukr SSR Ser B Geol Khim Biol Nauki ... Doklady Akademii Nauk Ukrainskoi SSR. Seriya B. Geologicheskie, Khimicheskie, i Biologicheski Nauki [*A publication*]
Dokl Akad Nauk Uzbek SSR ... Doklady Akademii Nauk Uzbekskoi SSR [*A publication*]
Dokl Akad Nauk Uzb SSR ... Doklady Akademii Nauk Uzbekskoi SSR [*A publication*]
Dokl Akad Nauk UzSSR ... Doklady Akademii Nauk Uzbekskoi SSR [*A publication*]
Dokl Akad Pedagog Nauk RSFSR ... Doklady Akademii Pedagogicheskikh Nauk RSFSR [*A publication*]
Dokl Akad Skh Nauk Bolg ... Doklady Akademii Sel'skokhozyaistvennykh Nauk v Bolgarii [*A publication*]
Dokl Ak N Arm SSR ... Doklady Akademii Nauk Armjanskoj SSR [*A publication*]
Dokl Ak N Az SSR ... Doklady Akademii Nauk Azerbajdzanskoj SSR [*A publication*]
Dokl Ak N Bel SSR ... Doklady Akademii Nauk Belorusskoj SSR [*A publication*]
Dokl Ak SSSR ... Doklady Akademii Nauk SSSR [*A publication*]
Dokl Biochem (Engl Transl Dokl Akad Nauk SSSR Ser Biokhim) ... Doklady Biochemistry (English Translation of Doklady Akademii Nauk SSSR. Seriya Biokhimiya) [*A publication*]
Dokl Biol Sci ... Doklady Biological Sciences [*A publication*]
Dokl Biol Sci (Engl Transl Dokl Akad Nauk SSSR Ser Biol) ... Doklady Biological Sciences (English Translation of Doklady Akademii Nauk SSSR. Seriya Biologiya) [*A publication*]
Dokl Biophys ... Doklady Biophysics [*A publication*]
Dokl Biophys (Engl Transl Dokl Akad Nauk SSSR) ... Doklady Biophysics (English Translation of Doklady Akademii Nauk SSSR) [*A publication*]
Dokl Biophys (Engl Transl Dokl Akad Nauk SSSR Ser Biofiz) ... Doklady Biophysics (English Translation of Doklady Akademii Nauk SSSR. Seriya Biofizika) [*A publication*]
Dokl Bolg Akad Nauk ... Doklady Bolgarskoi Akademii Nauk [*A publication*]
Dokl Bot Sci ... Doklady Botanical Sciences [*A publication*]
Dokl Bot Sci (Engl Transl Dokl Akad Nauk SSSR Ser Bot) ... Doklady Botanical Sciences (English Translation of Doklady Akademii Nauk SSSR. Seriya Botanika) [*A publication*]
Dokl Chem ... Doklady Chemistry [*A publication*]
Dokl Chem Technol ... Doklady Chemical Technology. Academy of Sciences of the USSR. Chemical Technology Section [*A publication*]
Dokl Inst Geogr Sib Dal'nego Vostoka ... Doklady Instituta Geografii Sibiri i Dal'nego Vostoka [*A publication*]
Dokl Inst Geogr Sib Dal'n Vost ... Doklady Instituta Geografii Sibiri i Dal'nego Vostoka [*A publication*]
Dokl Irkutsk Protivochumn Inst ... Doklady Irkutskogo Protivochumnogo Instituta [*A publication*]
DoklIRuJa ... Doklady i Soobscenija Instituta Russkogo Jazyka [*A publication*]
Dokl Kom Aerosemki Fotogrametrii Geogr Obs SSR ... Doklady Komissii Aeros'emki i Fotogrametrii Geograficheskogo Obshchestva SSR [*A publication*]
Dokl Kom Aeros'emki Fotogr Geogr O-Va SSR ... Doklady Komissii Aeros'emki i Fotogrametrii Geograficheskogo Obshchestva SSR [*A publication*]
Dokl Konf Vopr Tsito Gistokhim ... Doklady Konferentsiya po Voprosam Tsito-i Gistokhimii [*A publication*]
Dokl L'vov Politekh Inst ... Doklady L'vovskogo Politekhnicheskogo Instituta [*A publication*]
Dokl L'vov Politekh Inst Khim Khim Tekhnol ... Doklady L'vovskogo Politekhnicheskogo Instituta Khimiya i Khimicheskaya Tekhnologiya [*A publication*]
Dokl Mosk Inst Inzh Skh Proizvod ... Doklady Moskovskogo Instituta Inzhenerov Sel'skokhozyaistvennogo Proizvodstva [*A publication*]
Dokl Mosk Ord Lenina Selskokhoz Akad Im Timiryazeva ... Doklady Moskovskaya Ordena Lenina Sel'skokhozyaistvennaya Akademiya Imeni K. A. Timiryazeva [*A publication*]
Dokl Mosk Ova Ispyt Prir Obshch Biol ... Doklady Moskovskogo Obshchestva Ispytatelei Prirody Obshchaya Biologiya [*A publication*]

Dokl Mosk Sel'Khoz Akad K A Timiryazeva ... Doklady Moskovskoi Sel'skokhozyaistvennoi Akademii Imeni K. A. Timiryazeva [*A publication*]

Dokl Mosk Skh Akad ... Doklady Moskovskaya Sel'skokhozyaistvennaya Akademiya Imeni K. A. Timiryazeva [*A publication*]

Dokl Mosk S-Kh Akad Im K A Timiryazeva ... Doklady Moskovskoi Sel'skokhozyaistvennoi Akademii Imeni K. A. Timiryazeva [*A publication*]

DoklMU .... Doklady i Soobscenija Filologoceskogo Fakul'teta Moskovskogo Universiteta [*A publication*]

Dokl Nauchn Konf Yarosl Gos Pedagog Inst ... Doklady na Nauchnykh Konferentsiyakh Yaroslavskii Gosudarstvennyi Pedagogicheskii Institut [*A publication*]

Dokl Nauchn Konf Yarosl Gosud Pedagog Inst ... Doklady na Nauchnykh Konferentsiyakh Yaroslavskii Gosudarstvennyi Pedagogicheskii Institut [*A publication*]

Dokl Otd Kom Geogr O-Va SSSR ... Doklady Otdelov i Komissii Geograficheskogo Obshchestva SSSR [*A publication*]

Dokl Ross S-Kh Akad Im K A Timiryazeva ... Doklady Rossiiskoi Sel'skokhozyaistvennoi Akademii Imeni K. A. Timiryazeva [*A publication*]

Dokl Sochinskogo Otd Geogr Ova SSSR ... Doklady Sochinskogo Otdela Geograficheskogo Obshchestva SSSR [*A publication*]

Dokl Soil Sci (Engl Transl) ... Doklady Soil Science (English Translation) [*A publication*]

Dokl Soobshch Kormoproizvod ... Doklady i Soobshcheniya po Kormoproizvodstvu [*A publication*]

Dokl Soobshch Uzhgorod Gos Univ Ser Biol ... Doklady i Soobshcheniya Uzhgorodskogo Gosudarstvennogo Universiteta. Seriya Biologicheskaya [*A publication*]

Dokl Soobshch Uzhgorod Gos Univ Ser Fiz Mat Khim ... Doklady i Soobshcheniya Uzhgorodskogo Gosudarstvennogo Universiteta. Seriya Fiziko. Matematicheskaya i Khimicheskaya [*A publication*]

Dokl Soobshch Uzhgorod Gos Univ Ser Fiz Mat Nauk ... Doklady i Soobshcheniya Uzhgorodskogo Gosudarstvennogo Universiteta. Seriya Fiziko. Matematicheskikh Nauk [*A publication*]

Dokl Soobshch Vses Nauch Issled Inst Ekon Selskokhoz ... Doklady i Soobshcheniya. Vsesoyuznyi Nauchno-Issledovatel'skii Institut Ekonomiki Sel'skogo Khozyaistva [*A publication*]

Dokl Sooshch Uzhgorod Gos Univ Ser Khim ... Doklady i Soobshcheniya Uzhgorodskogo Gosudarstvennogo Universiteta. Seriya Khimicheskaya [*A publication*]

Dokl Sov Geol Mezhdunar Geol Kongr ... Doklady Sovetskikh Geologov Mezhdunarodnyi Geologicheskii Kongress [*A publication*]

Dokl Tbilis Nauchn O-Va Anat Gistol Embriol ... Doklady Tbilisskogo Nauchnogo Obshchestva Anatomii, Gistologii, i Embriologii [*A publication*]

Dokl Timiryazevsk S-Kh Akad ... Doklady Timiryazevskaya Sel'skokhozyaistvennaya Akademiya [*A publication*]

Dokl TSKHA ... Doklady Timiryazevskaya Sel'skokhozyaistvennaya Akademiya [*A publication*]

Dokl TSKhA Timiriazevsk S-Kh Akad ... Doklady TSKhA. Timiriazevskaia Sel'skokhoziaistvennaia Akademiia [*A publication*]

Dokl Vses Akad Sel'khoz Nauk ... Doklady Vsesoyuznoi Akademii Sel'skokhozyaistvennykh Nauk Imeni V. I. Lenina [*A publication*]

Dokl Vses Akad Skh Nauk ... Doklady Vsesoyuznoi Akademii Sel'skokhozyaistvennykh Nauk [*A publication*]

Dokl Vses Akad S-Kh Nauk Im V I Lenina ... Doklady Vsesoyuznoi Akademii Sel'skokhozyaistvennykh Nauk Imeni V. I. Lenina [*USSR*] [*A publication*]

Dokl Vses Konf "Fiz Khrupkogo Razrusheniya" ... Doklady Vsesoyuznoi Konferentsii "Fizika Khrupkogo Razrusheniya" [*A publication*]

Dokl Vses Konf Teplofiz Svoistvam Veshchestv ... Doklady Vsesoyuznoi Konferentsii po Teplofizicheskim Svoistvam Veshchestv [*A publication*]

Dokl Vses Ordena Lenina Akad S-Kh Nauk Im V I Lenina ... Doklady Vsesoyuznoi Ordena Lenina Akademii Sel'skokhozyaistvennykh Nauk Imeni V. I. Lenina [*A publication*]

Dok Raum ... Dokumentation zur Raumentwicklung [*A publication*]

Dok Str ...... Dokumentation Strasse [*A publication*]

Doktorsavh Chalmers Tek Hoegsk ... Doktorsavhandlingar vid Chalmers Tekniska Hoegskola [*Sweden*] [*A publication*]

Dokum As Mitt ... Dokumentationsdienst Asien Mitteilungen [*A publication*]

Dokum Ostmitteleur (NF) ... Dokumentation Ostmitteleuropa (Neue Folge) [*A publication*]

Dokum Raumentwicklung ... Dokumentation zur Raumentwicklung [*A publication*]

DOKWA.... Dokumentation Wasser [*A publication*]

Dok Wasser ... Dokumentation Wasser [*West Germany*] [*A publication*]

Dok Zemed Lesn ... Dokumentace Zemedelska a Lesnicka [*A publication*]

DOL........... Daily Official List [*London Stock Exchange prices*]

DOL........... Daily Operating Log

DOL........... Degree of Operating Leverage [*Finance*]

DOL........... Department of Labor

DOL........... Detached Officer's List [*Army*]

DOL........... Director of Laboratories   (MCD)

DOL........... Director [*or Directorate*] of Logistics [*DoD*]

DOL........... Discrete Output Low   (MCD)

DOL........... Display-Oriented Language [*Data processing*]   (IEEE)

DOL........... Doctor of Oriental Languages

DOL........... Doctor of Oriental Learning

dol .... Dolar [*Dollar*] [*Monetary unit*] [*Portugal*]

DOL........... Dolce [*Sweet*] [*Music*]

DOL........... Dolichol [*Biochemistry*]

dol .... Dollar [*Dollar*] [*Monetary unit*] [*French*]

DOL........... Dollar [*Monetary unit*]   (AFM)

DOL........... Dolomite [*Lithology*]

Dol .... Dolphin

DOL........... Dynamic Octal Load

DOL........... Dynamic Oil Ltd. [*Vancouver Stock Exchange symbol*]

DOLA......... Dog Owners League of America [*Defunct*]   (EA)

DOLA/DOLD ... Date of Last Adjustment/Date of Last Demand [*Military*]   (AFIT)

DOLARS... Departmental On-Line Reporting System [*Military*]

DOLARS... Digital Offline Automatic Recording System

DOLARS... Doppler Location and Ranging System

DOLCE ..... Digital On-Line Cryptographic Equipment   (NATG)

DOLCEM ... Dolcemente [*Sweetly, Softly*] [*Music*]   (ROG)

Dolciani Math Exp ... [*The*] Dolciani Mathematical Expositions [*A publication*]

DOLCIS .... Dolcissimo [*Very Sweetly*] [*Music*]

DOLCISS ... Dolcissimo [*Very Sweetly*] [*Music*]   (ROG)

DOLCO..... Down-Link Communications [*Antisubmarine warfare*]   (MCD)

DOLDIS .... Directory of Online Databases Produced in Sweden [*Database*] [*Royal Institute of Technology Library*] [*Information service or system*]   (CRD)

DOLENT PART ... Dolenti Parti [*To the Afflicted Part*] [*Pharmacy*]

DOLF .... Date of Last Follow-Up   (AFIT)

DOLI .... Date of Last Inventory   (AFIT)

DOLICH ... Dolichos [*Plant commonly known as Cowitch*] [*Pharmacology*]   (ROG)

DOLITAC ... Department of Labor International Technical Assistance Corps

DOLL .... Dollar [*Monetary unit*]   (ROG)

Dollars ...... Dollars and Sense [*A publication*]

DOLLS ...... Delayed Opening Leaflet System [*Military propaganda*]

Doll & Sen ... Dollars and Sense [*A publication*]

DOLM....... College of Our Lady of Mount Carmel, Washington, DC [*Library symbol*] [*Library of Congress*]   (LCLS)

Dolmetsch B ... Bulletin: The Dolmetsch Foundation [*A publication*]

DOLO....... Disbursing Officers Liaison Office

DOLO....... Doloroso [*Mournfully*] [*Music*]   (ROG)

DOLR....... Dollar General Corp. [*NASDAQ symbol*]   (NQ)

DOLS .... DOL Resources, Inc. [*NASDAQ symbol*]   (NQ)

DOLT........ Date of Last Transaction   (AFIT)

DOL URG ... Dolore Urgente [*When the Pain Is Severe*] [*Pharmacy*]

DOM .... Data Output Multiplexer [*Data processing*]   (KSC)

DOM .... Database Options Menu

DOM .... Datur Omnibus Mori [*It Is Allotted unto All to Die*] [*Latin*]

Dom........... De Domo Sua [*of Cicero*] [*Classical studies*]   (OCD)

DOM .... Deo Optimo Maximo [*To God, Most Good, Most Great*] [*Latin*]

DOM .... Department of Medicine

DOM .... Depth of Modulation

DOM .... Description, Operation, and Maintenance

DOM .... Designing Out Maintenance

DOM .... Digital Ohmmeter

DOM .... Digital Output Multiplexer   (CAAL)

DOM .... Dimethoxymethylamphetamine [*A hallucinogenic drug, more commonly known as STP*]

DOM .... Diploma in Ophthalmic Medicine

DOM .... Dirty Old Man [*Slang*]

DOM .... Disk Operating Monitor [*Data processing*]

DOM .... Dissolved Organic Matter

DOM .... Division of Overseas Ministries [*National Council of Churches*]

DOM .... Doman Industries Ltd. [*Toronto Stock Exchange symbol*] [*Vancouver Stock Exchange symbol*]

DOM .... Domesday [*British*]   (ROG)

DOM .... Domestic   (AFM)

DOM .... Domicile

DOM .... Dominance [*Psychology*]

DOM .... Dominant

Dom........... Domingo [*Sunday*] [*Spanish*]

DOM .... Dominica [*West Indies*] [*Seismograph station code, US Geological Survey*]   (SEIS)

DOM .... Dominica [*West Indies*] [*Airport symbol*]   (OAG)

DOM .... Dominican Republic [*ANSI three-letter standard code*]   (CNC)

Dom........... Dominicana [*A publication*]

DOM .... Dominion

DOM .... Dominus [*The Lord*] [*Latin*]

DOM .... Dominus Omnium Magister [*God the Master, or Lord, of All*] [*Latin*] [*Motto of the Benedictine Order*]

Dom........... Domitianus [*of Suetonius*] [*Classical studies*]   (OCD)

DOM .... Drawn over Mandrel [*Tubes*]

DOM .... Quit for Domestic Reasons [*Unemployment insurance*]   (OICC)

DOMA....... Dihydroxymandelic Acid [*Also, DHMA, DMA*] [*Organic chemistry*]

DOMA....... Director, Operation and Maintenance, Army
DOMA....... Dokumentation Maschinenbau [*Mechanical Engineering Documentation*] [*Technical Information Center*] [*Information service or system*]
DOMAIN ... Distributed Operating Multi-Access Interactive Network [*Apollo Computer, Inc.*] [*Chelmsford, MA*] [*Telecommunications*] (TSSD)
DOMAR.... Doppler Martin RADAR [*Air Force*]
Domat Civ Law ... Domat's Civil Law [*A publication*] (DLA)
Domat Dr Pub ... Domat's Droit Publique [*A publication*] (DLA)
Domat Liv Prel ... Domat's Livres du Droit Public [*A publication*] (DLA)
DOMB....... Deep Ocean Moored Buoy [*Marine science*] (MSC)
Dom Book .. Domesday Book [*Census-like record of the lands of England, 1085-86*] [*A publication*] (DLA)
Dom Civ Law ... Domat's Civil Law [*A publication*] (DLA)
Dom Comm ... Domestic Commerce [*A publication*]
DOMD....... Digital Oxygen Metering Device [*Aerospace*]
DOME....... Development of Opportunities through Meaningful Education [*Project*]
DOME....... Diagnosis, Objectives, Method, Evaluation [*Formula*] [*LIMRA*]
Dom Eng .... Domestic Engineering [*A publication*]
Dom Engr.. Dominion Engineer [*A publication*]
DOMES .... Deep Ocean Mining Environmental Study [*National Oceanic and Atmospheric Administration*]
Domes .... Domesday Book [*Census-like record of the lands of England, 1085-86*] [*A publication*] (DLA)
DOMESD ... Domesday Book [*Census-like record of the lands of England, 1085-86*] (ROG)
Domesday .. Domesday Book [*Census-like record of the lands of England, 1085-86*] [*A publication*] (DLA)
Domest Anim Endocrinol ... Domestic Animal Endocrinology [*A publication*]
Domest Eng Heat Vent ... Domestic Engineering. Heat and Ventilation [*England*] [*A publication*]
Domest Heat News ... Domestic Heating News [*England*] [*A publication*]
DOMESTIC ... Development of Minicomputers in an Environment of Scientific and Technological Information Centers [*Data processing*]
Domestic Heat Air Cond News ... Domestic Heating and Air Conditioning News [*A publication*]
DOMF....... Darwin Overland Maintenance Force [*Australia*]
DOMF....... Dibromohydroxymercurifluorescein [*Antiseptic*]
Dom Foundrym ... Dominion Foundryman [*A publication*]
DOMH....... Dominion Holdings [*NASDAQ symbol*] (NQ)
Domi .... Dominicus de Sancto Geminiano [*Flourished, 1407-09*] [*Authority cited in pre-1607 legal work*] (DSA)
DOMI........ Domino Media, Incorporated [*NASDAQ symbol*] (NQ)
Dominion Observatory (Ottawa) Contr ... Dominion Observatory (Ottawa). Contributions [*A publication*]
Dominion Observatory Seismol Ser ... Dominion Observatory. Seismological Series [*A publication*]
Dominion Tax Cas CCH ... Dominion Tax Cases. Commerce Clearing House [*A publication*]
Domi de San Gemi ... Dominicus de Sancto Geminiano [*Flourished, 1407-09*] [*Authority cited in pre-1607 legal work*] (DSA)
DOMLIB... Domestic Library Automation Functions [*Data processing*]
Dom LR ..... Dominion Law Reports [*A publication*]
Dom Med ... Domus Medici [*A publication*]
Dom Med J ... Dominion Medical Journal [*A publication*]
Dom Mus Bull ... Dominion Museum Bulletin [*Wellington*] [*A publication*]
Dom Mus Monogr ... Dominion Museum Monographs [*New Zealand*] [*A publication*]
Dom Mus Rec Entomol (Wellington) ... Dominion Museum Records in Entomology (Wellington) [*A publication*]
Dom Mus Rec Ethnol ... Dominion Museum Records in Ethnology [*New Zealand*] [*A publication*]
Dom Mus Rec Zool (Wellington) ... Dominion Museum Records in Zoology (Wellington) [*A publication*]
DOMN ...... Domain Technology, Inc. [*NASDAQ symbol*] (NQ)
DOMO ...... Deep Ocean Mining Operations [*Marine science*] (MSC)
domo.......... Domingo [*Sunday*] [*Spanish*]
Dom Obs Pamph ... Dominion Observatory Pamphlet [*Canada*] [*A publication*]
DOMP....... Dope and Wimp [*Term used by Ross Thomas in his book, "Briarpatch"*]
DOMPRINT ... DOMESTIC [*Development of Microcomputers in an Environment of Scientific and Technological Information Centers*] Print Generator [*Data processing*]
DOM PROC ... Domus Procerum [*The House of Lords*] [*Latin*] (ROG)
DOMREP ... Dominican Republic (AFM)
DOMS....... Delayed-Onset Muscle Soreness
DOMS....... Depot Operation Management System [*Army*]
DOMS....... Diploma in Ophthalmic Medicine and Surgery [*British*]
DOMS....... Directorate of Military Support (AABC)
DOMS....... Doctor of Orthopaedic Medicine and Surgery
DOMSAT ... Domestic Satellite [*Communications satellite*] [*Australia*]
DOM SC .... Domestic Science [*Freight*]
Dom St .... Dominican Studies [*A publication*]
Domus Med ... Domus Medici [*A publication*]
DOMZ....... Dominguez Water Corp. [*Long Beach, CA*] [*NASDAQ symbol*] (NQ)

DON .... Delayed Order Notice [*Telecommunications*] (TEL)
DON .... Demand Order Number [*Army*] (AABC)
DON .... Deoxynivalenol [*A mycotoxin*]
DON .... Department of the Navy
DON .... Diazooxo-L-norleucine [*Antineoplastic drug*]
DON .... Dimensionality of Nations Project [*Hawaii*]
DON .... Director of Nursing
DON .... Dissolved Organic Nitrogen [*Analytical chemistry*]
DON .... Donative
DON .... Donec [*Until*] [*Pharmacy*] (ROG)
DON .... Donegal [*County in Ireland*]
DON .... Dongola [*Missouri*] [*Seismograph station code, US Geological Survey*] (SEIS)
DON .... Donnelly Corp. [*AMEX symbol*] (SPSG)
DON .... Doppler Optical Navigation
DONA ...... Decentralized Open Network Architecture (BUR)
Donaker .... Donaker's Reports [*165 Indiana*] [*A publication*] (DLA)
Donat .... Aelius Donatus [*Fourth century AD*] [*Classical studies*] (OCD)
Donauraum ... Zeitschrift fuer Donauraum-Forschung [*A publication*]
DONCS ...... Director of Operations Narcotics Control Reports [*CIA*]
DONEC ALV BIS DEJ ... Donec Alvus Bis Dejiciatur [*Until the Bowels Have Been Twice Evacuated*] [*Pharmacy*] (ROG)
DONEC ALV SOL FUER ... Donec Alvus Soluta Fuerit [*Until the Bowels Are Opened*] [*Pharmacy*] (ROG)
DONEC ALV SOL FUERIT ... Donec Alvus Soluta Fuerit [*Until the Bowels Are Opened*] [*Pharmacy*]
DONEC DOL NEPH EXULAV ... Donec Dolor Nephriticus Exulaverit [*Until the Nephritic Pain Is Removed*] [*Pharmacy*] (ROG)
DONEF ..... Donegal Resources Ltd. [*NASDAQ symbol*] (NQ)
DONEG..... Donegal [*County in Ireland*] (ROG)
Donell .... [*Hugo*] Donellus [*Deceased, 1591*] [*Authority cited in pre-1607 legal work*] (DSA)
Dong-A Ronchong Dong-A Univ ... Dong-A Ronchong. Dong-A University [*A publication*]
Dongguk J ... Dongguk Journal [*A publication*]
DONMICS ... Department of the Navy Management Information Control System
Donn .... Donnell's Irish Land Cases [*1871-76*] [*A publication*] (DLA)
Donn .... Donnelly's English Chancery Reports [*A publication*] (DLA)
Donnees Statist Limousin ... Donnees Statistiques du Limousin [*A publication*]
Donnelly .... Donnelly's English Chancery Reports [*A publication*] (DLA)
Donnelly (Eng) ... Donnelly's English Chancery Reports [*A publication*] (DLA)
Donn Eq ..... Donnelly's English Chancery Reports [*A publication*] (DLA)
Donn Ir Land Cas ... Donnell's Irish Land Cases [*1871-76*] [*A publication*] (DLA)
DONO .... Dimethyloctadecanamine N-Oxide [*Organic chemistry*]
DONOA .... Donovan Cos. [*NASDAQ symbol*] (NQ)
DONPIC .... Department of the Navy Program Information Center
DonSoc .... Donizetti Society (EA)
Don Tr........ Donovan's Modern Jury Trials [*A publication*] (DLA)
DOO .... Deep Ocean Ordnance
DOO .... Department Organization Order [*Department of Commerce*] (NOAA)
DOO........ Directing Ordnance Officer [*Military*] [*British*]
DOO .... Director, Office of Oceanography [*UNESCO*]
DOO .... Disposition One Only (MCD)
DOO .... District Operations Office [*or Officer*] [*Navy*]
DOO .... District Ordnance Office [*or Officer*] [*Navy*]
DOO .... Division Ordnance Officer
DOO .... Doolan Road [*California*] [*Seismograph station code, US Geological Survey*] (SEIS)
DOO .... Dorobisoro [*Papua New Guinea*] [*Airport symbol*] (OAG)
DOO .... Driver-Only Operation [*Railroad*] [*British*]
DOOF........ Driver-Only Operation, Freight [*Railroad*] [*British*]
DOOL........ Days of Our Lives [*NBC-TV daytime serial*]
DOOLAR .. Deep Ocean Object Location and Recovery [*Navy*]
DOOM .... Deep Ocean Optical Measurement
DOOP........ Driver-Only Operation, Passenger [*Railroad*] [*British*]
DOOPA ..... Documenta Ophthalmologica [*A publication*]
DOOPO..... Director of Operations, Operational Plans Officer (MUGU)
DOORS ..... Data on Occupations Retrieval System [*Great Britain Manpower Services Commission*] [*Information service or system*] (CRD)
DOORS ..... Development of Operational Reasoning Skills
DOORS ..... Directory of Outpatient Ostomy Resources and Services [*International Association for Enterostomal Therapy*]
DOP.......... Dermo-Optical Perception [*Parapsychology*]
DOP.......... Designated Overhaul Point
DOP.......... Desoctapeptide Insulin [*Medicine*]
DOP.......... Detachment of Patients
DOP.......... Detailed Operating Procedure
DOP.......... Detection Operational Program [*Military*] (CAAL)
DOP.......... Developing-Out Paper
DOP.......... Dilution of Precision
DOP.......... Dioctyl Phosphate [*Organic chemistry*]
DOP.......... Dioctyl Phthalate [*Also, DEHP*] [*Organic chemistry*]
D-OP.......... Diplomate, American Board of Ophthalmology (DHSM)
DOP.......... Director of Office of Programming [*Military*]
DOP.......... Disaster Operations Plan [*Nuclear energy*] (NRCH)

DOP.......... Dissolved Organic Phosphorus
DOP.......... Diver Operated Plug   (MCD)
DOP.......... Documents on Payment [*Banking*]
DOP.......... Dolpa [*Nepal*] [*Airport symbol*]   (OAG)
DOP.......... Doppler   (KSC)
DOP.......... Dumbarton Oaks Papers [*A publication*]
DOPA....... Dihydroxyphenylalanine [*Biochemistry*]
DOPAA...... Description of Proposed Actions and Alternatives [*Military*]
DOPAC..... Dihydroxyphenylacetic Acid [*Biochemistry*]
DOPACK .. Doppler Software Package   (ADA)
Dop Akad Nauk Ukr RSR ... Dopovidi Akademii Nauk Ukrains'koi RSR [*A publication*]
Dop Akad Nauk Ukr RSR Ser Fiz-Tekh Mat ... Dopovidi Akademii Nauk Ukrains'koi RSR. Seriya A. Fiziko-Tekhnichni ta Matematichni Nauki [*A publication*]
DOPapers ... Dumbarton Oaks Papers [*A publication*]
DOPDF ..... Doppler Direction-Finding Equipment   (FAAC)
DOPE .... Databank of Program Evaluations [*University of California, Los Angeles*]   (IID)
DOPE .... Dioleylphosphatidylethanolamine [*Organic chemistry*]
DOPE .... Display, Oral, Printed, and Electronic [*Media*]
DOPE .... Double Odd Pass Even [*System in game of bridge*]
DOPEG ..... Dihydroxyphenylglycol [*Also, DHPG*] [*Organic chemistry*]
DOPET...... Dihydroxyphenylethanol [*Organic chemistry*]
DOPF .... Duty Directed in Order Is Being Performed For
DOPGAM ... Deutsche Ophthalmologische Gesellschaft. Bericht [*A publication*]
DOPHDS.. Documents Phytosociologiques [*A publication*]
DOPHHH ... Division on Physically Handicapped, Homebound, and Hospitalized [*Later, DPH*]   (EA)
DOPI .... Overseas Private Investment Corp., Washington, DC [*Library symbol*] [*Library of Congress*]   (LCLS)
DOPIC...... Documentation of Programs in Core [*Data processing*]   (IEEE)
DOPIE....... Department of Primary Industries and Energy [*Australia*]
DOPLOC .. Doppler Phase Lock
DOPMA .... Defense Officer Personnel Management Act [*1980*]   (MCD)
DOPMS .... Defense Officer Personnel Management Study   (NVT)
DOPOA .... Dornier-Post [*English Edition*] [*A publication*]
Dopov Akad Nauk Ukr RSR ... Dopovidi Akademii Nauk Ukrains'koi RSR [*A publication*]
Dopov Akad Nauk Ukr RSR B ... Dopovidi Akademii Nauk Ukrains'koi RSR. Seriya B. Geologiya, Geofizika, Khimiya, ta Biologiya [*A publication*]
Dopov Akad Nauk Ukr RSR Ser B Heol Heofiz Khim Biol ... Dopovidi Akademiyi Nauk Ukrayins'koyi RSR. Seriya B. Heolohiya, Heofizyka, Khimiya, ta Biolohiya [*A publication*]
Dopov Akad Nauk Ukr RSR Ser B Heol Khim Biol Nauky ... Dopovidi Akademiyi Nauk Ukrayins'koyi RSR. Seriya B. Heolohichni, Khimichni, ta Biolohichni Nauky [*A publication*]
Dopov Akad Nauk Uk RSR Ser A ... Dopovidi Akademii Nauk Ukrains'koi RSR. Seriya A. Fiziko-Tekhnichni ta Matematichni Nauki [*A publication*]
Dopovidi Akad Nauk Ukrain RSR Ser A ... Dopovidi Akademii Nauk Ukrains'koi RSR. Seriya A. Fiziko-Tekhnichni ta Matematichni Nauki [*A publication*]
Dopovidi Akad Nauk Ukrain RSR Ser B ... Dopovidi Akademii Nauk Ukrains'koi RSR. Seriya B [*A publication*]
Dopov Povidomlenniya L'viv Derzh Univ ... Dopovidi ta Povidomlenniya L'vivs'koho Derzhavnoho Universytetu [*A publication*]
Dopov Povidomlennya L'viv Derzh Pedagog Inst Sekts Biol Khim ... Dopovidt ta Povidomlennya. L'vivs'kii Derzhvnii Institut. Sektsiya Biologii Khimii [*A publication*]
Dopov Povidom Lvivsk Derzh Univ ... Dopovidi ta Povidomiennia L'vivs'koho Derzhavnoho Universytetu [*A publication*]
Dopov Ukr Akad Sil's'kogospod Nauk ... Dopovidt Ukrains'koi Akademii Sil's'kogospodars'kikh Nauk [*A publication*]
DOPP .... Doppler   (MUGU)
DOPP PED ... Doppio Pedale [*Double Pedal*] [*Music*]
DOPS .... Digital Optical Projection System   (IEEE)
DOPS .... Dihydroxyphenylserine [*Biochemistry*]
DOpt......... Diploma in Ophthalmics   (ADA)
DOPTAR... Doppler Tracking and Ranging [*Military*]   (CAAL)
D Opth...... Doctor of Ophthalmology
Dop Ukr A ... Dopovidi Akademii Nauk Ukrains'koi RSR. Seriya A [*A publication*]
Dop Ukr B ... Dopovidi Akademii Nauk Ukrains'koi RSR. Seriya B [*A publication*]
DOR.......... Daily Operational Report
DOR.......... Data Output Register [*Data processing*]
DOR.......... Date of Rank [*Air Force*]
DOR.......... Date of Request   (AFM)
DOR.......... Design Objective Reliability
DOR.......... Digital Output Relay
DOR.......... Director of Operational Requirements [*Air Ministry*] [*British*]
DOR.......... Disaster Operations Room [*Public safety*]
DOR.......... Division of Research [*Indiana University*] [*Research center*]   (RCD)
D Or .... Doctor of Oratory

DOR.......... Document Ordres et Reglements Statutaires [*Statutory Orders and Regulations - SOR*] [*Database*] [*Federal Department of Justice*] [*Canada*] [*Information service or system*]   (CRD)
Dor .... Dorado [*Constellation*]
DOR.......... Dori [*Upper Volta*] [*Airport symbol*]   (OAG)
DOR.......... Doric
Dor .... Dorion's Quebec Reports [*A publication*]   (DLA)
DOR.......... Dormitory
DOR.......... Double Rotation [*Spectroscopy*]
DoR........... Downside Review [*A publication*]
DOR.......... Dropped Own Request [*Navy*]
DOR.......... Dundarave Resources [*Vancouver Stock Exchange symbol*]
DOR.......... Graduate School of Business Administration, Division of Research [*University of Michigan*] [*Research center*]   (RCD)
DOR.......... Reproduktie [*A publication*]
D OR......... United States District Court for the District of Oregon   (DLA)
DORA....... Defence of the Realm Act [*British*] [*World War I*]
DORA....... Directory of Rare Analyses [*A publication*]
DORA....... Disbursing Officers' Relief Act [*1982*]
Dora .... Dorado [*Constellation*]
DORA....... Double Roll Out Arrays   (MCD)
DORA....... Dynamic Operator Response Apparatus
DORAN..... Doppler Range and Navigation [*Electronics*]
Dor Bank ... Doria's Law and Practice in Bankruptcy [*2nd ed.*] [*1873*] [*A publication*]   (DLA)
DORCA..... Dynamic Operational Requirements and Cost Analysis [*Computer program*] [*NASA*]
DORCG..... Date of Rank, Current Grade [*Air Force*]   (AFM)
DORCH..... Dorchester [*City in England*]   (ROG)
DORCMA ... Door Operator and Remote Controls Manufacturers Association   (EA)
DORCSA... District Officer for Reserve Communication Supplementary Activities
DORE........ DoD [*Department of Defense*] Officer Record Examination
DORE........ Doran Energy Corp. [*NASDAQ symbol*]   (NQ)
DORF........ Diamond Ordnance Radiation Facility [*Nuclear reactor*]
DORFA ..... Subcommittee on Department Operations, Research, and Foreign Agriculture [*Congress*]
Dor Ins .... Dorsay's Law of Insolvency [*A publication*]   (DLA)
Dorion ...... Dorion's Quebec Queen's Bench Reports [*A publication*]   (DLA)
Dorion (Can) ... Dorion's Quebec Queen's Bench Reports (Canada) [*A publication*]   (DLA)
Dorion QB ... Dorion's Quebec Queen's Bench Reports [*A publication*]   (DLA)
DORIS....... Demographic Online Retrieval Information System [*CACI, Inc.*]
DORIS....... Development of Reasoning in Science
DORIS....... Direct Order Recording and Invoicing System [*A computer-based system of British petroleum companies*]
DORIS....... Doppler Ranging and Information System [*Navy*]   (MCD)
DORIS....... Dornier Recoverable Instrument Sonde   (MCD)
DORM....... Dormitory
Dor MD Laws ... Dorsey's Maryland Laws [*A publication*]   (DLA)
Do de Ro .... Domini de Rota [*Authority cited in pre-1607 legal work*]   (DSA)
DORPG ..... Date of Rank, Permanent Grade [*Air Force*]   (AFM)
Dor QB....... Dorion's Quebec Queen's Bench Reports [*A publication*]   (DLA)
DORS .... Davis Online Reference Services [*University of California, Davis*]   (OLDSS)
DORS .... Defence Operational Requirements [*British military*]   (DMA)
DORS .... Dorsetshire [*County in England*]   (ROG)
DORS .... Dynamic Operator Response System
D Or Sc ...... Doctor of the Science of Oratory
DORSET... Dorsetshire [*County in England*]
DOrth....... Diploma in Orthodontics [*British*]
D Orth........ Diploma in Orthoptics [*British*]
D Orth RCS Eng ... Diplomate in Orthodontics, Royal College of Surgeons of England
DORV........ Deep Ocean Research Vehicle   (IEEE)
DORV........ Double Outlet Right Ventricle [*Cardiology*]
DOS.......... Date of Separation [*Military*]
DOS.......... Day of Sale [*Business term*]   (ADA)
DOS.......... Days of Supply [*Rations*]
DOS.......... Decision Outstanding [*Data processing*]   (BUR)
DOS.......... Defense Occupational Specialties [*Army*]
DOS.......... Deferred Organic Supply   (MCD)
DOS.......... Degenerate Oscillating System
DOS.......... Deliverer of Services   (OICC)
DOS.......... Densities of States [*Photovoltaic energy systems*]
DOS.......... Density of States [*Physics*]
DOS.......... Deoxystreptamine [*Organic chemistry*]
DoS .... Department of Science [*Australia*]
DOS.......... Department of State
DOS.......... Department of State, Washington, DC [*OCLC symbol*]   (OCLC)
DOS.......... Department of Surgery
DOS.......... Dependents Overseas [*Military*]

DOS.......... Diabetes Opinion Survey [Child development test] [Psychology]
DOS.......... Digital Operation System (IEEE)
DOS.......... Dioctyl Sebacate [Organic chemistry]
DOS.......... Diploma in Orthopaedic Surgery (ADA)
D-OS.......... Diplomate, American Board of Orthopaedic Surgery (DHSM)
DOS.......... Director of Ordnance Services [Military] [British]
DOS.......... Director of Sales
DOS.......... Director of Stores [Navy] [British]
DOS.......... Director [or Directorate] of Support [Army]
DOS.......... Directorate of Overseas Surveys [Overseas Development Administration] [British] (DS)
DOS.......... Discrete Orthonormal Sequence
DOS.......... Disk Operating System [Data processing] (IID)
DOS.......... Division of Operational Safety [Energy Research and Development Administration] (MCD)
DOS.......... Doctor of Ocular Science
DOS.......... Doctor of Optical Science
DOS.......... Doctor of Optometric Science
DOS.......... Dos Bocas Dam [Puerto Rico] [Seismograph station code, US Geological Survey] (SEIS)
DOS.......... Dosage [Medicine]
DOS.......... Dosis [Dose] [Pharmacy] (ROG)
dos.......... Dosyn [Dozen] [Afrikaans]
DOS.......... Drum Out of Service (CET)
DOS.......... Dumbarton Oaks Studies [A publication]
DOSAAF... Dobrovol'noe Obshchestvo Sodeistviia Armii, Aviatsii, i Flotu [Voluntary Society for Cooperation with the Army, Aviation, and the Fleet] [USSR]
Do de San Gemi ... Dominicus de Sancto Geminiano [Flourished, 1407-09] [Authority cited in pre-1607 legal work] (DSA)
DOSAR ..... Dosimetry Applications Research Facility [AEC]
DOSC........ Dimensions of Self-Concept [Personality test]
DO Sc .... Doctor of Optometric Science
DOSC........ Dubois Oleic Serum Complex [Bacteriology]
DOSCA ..... Department of State Correspondents Association (EA)
DOSD .... Director of Organisation and Staff Duties [Australia]
DOSE .... Choice Drug Systems, Inc. [NASDAQ symbol] (NQ)
DOSE .... Disk Operating System - Enhanced [Data processing] (MCD)
DOSECC... Deep Observation and Sampling of the Earth's Continental Crust [National Science Foundation]
Doshisha L ... Doshisha Literature [A publication]
Doshisha LJ ... Doshisha Law Journal. International Edition [A publication] (DLA)
Doshisha L Rev ... Doshisha Law Review [A publication] (DLA)
DOSIM ..... Dosimeter (NASA)
DOSK .... Distributed Operating System Kernel [Data processing]
DOSK .... Doskocil Companies, Inc. [NASDAQ symbol] (NQ)
Dosl Tvarinnitstvi ... Doslidzhennya v Tvarinnitstvi [A publication]
DOS-LV ... Disk Operating System - Large Volumes [Data processing]
Dosl Zootekh L'vivskoho Zootekh Vet Inst ... Doslidzhennya Zootekhniki L'vivskoho Zootekhnicheskoho Veterinars'koho Instituta [A publication]
DOSM .... Desialylated Ovine Submaxillary Mucin [Biochemistry]
DOSN........ Disbursing Office Serial Number
DOSP .... Dalhousie Ocean Studies Programme [Dalhousie University] [Canada] [Research center] (RCD)
DOSP .... Deep Ocean Sediment Probe [Marine science] (MSC)
Dos Passos Stock-Brok ... Dos Passos on Stock-Brokers and Stock Exchanges [A publication] (DLA)
DOSPR...... Department of State Procurement Regulations
DOSS........ Decision-Oriented Scheduling System (MCD)
DOSS........ Distal Over-Shoulder Strap
DOSS........ Doppler Optical Surveillance System
Doss Alet ... Dossiers. Centre Regional Archeologique d'Alet [A publication]
Doss A (Paris) ... Dossiers de l'Archeologie (Paris) [A publication]
Doss Archeol ... Dossiers de l'Archeologie [A publication]
Doss Bis Jeune Afr Econ ... Dossiers Bis Jeune Afrique et Economia [A publication]
Doss Econ Lorraine ... Dossiers de l'Economie Lorraine [A publication]
Dossiers Archeol ... Dossiers Archeologiques [A publication]
Doss Mundo ... Dossier Mundo [A publication]
Doss Polit Agric Commune ... Dossiers de la Politique Agricole Commune [A publication]
DOSSU...... Dogs on Stamps Study Unit (EA)
DOS-SV..... Disk Operating System - Small Volumes [Data processing]
DOST .... Department of Science and Technology [Science and Technology Information Institute] [Philippines] (EISS)
DOST .... Dictionary of the Older Scottish Tongue [A publication]
DOst .... Diploma in Osteopathy [Australia]
Dostizh Nauki Tekh Peredovoi Opyt Promsti Stroit ... Dostizheniya Nauki i Tekhniki i Peredovoi Opyt v Promyshlennosti i Stroitel'stve [A publication]
DOSV .... Deep Oceanographic Survey Vehicle [Naval Oceanographic Office]
DOS/VS .... Disk Operating System/Virtual Storage [IBM Corp.] [Data processing] (MCD)
DOT.......... Daily Operability Test [Military] (CAAL)
DOT.......... Date of Trade [Investment term]
DOT.......... Deep Ocean Technology
DOT.......... Deep Ocean Transponder

DOT.......... Deep Oceanic Turbulence
DOT.......... Delayed on Target
DOT.......... Department of Overseas Trade [British]
DoT.......... Department of Trade [British]
DOT.......... Department of Transport [Canada]
DOT.......... Department of Transportation
DOT.......... Department of the Treasury (AFM)
DOT.......... Dependent Overseas Territory
DOT.......... Deployment Operations Team
DOT.......... Designated Order Turnaround [NYSE term]
DOT.......... Designating Optical Tracker [Telescope]
DOT.......... Dictionary of Occupational Titles [Department of Labor] [A publication]
DOT.......... Digital Optical Transceiver [Citifax Corp.]
DOT.......... Digital Output Timer [Data processing]
DOT.......... Diploma of Occupational Therapy
D-OT......... Diplomate, American Board of Otolaryngology (DHSM)
DOT.......... Director of Operational Training [RAF] [British]
DOT.......... Director on Target [Military] (CAAL)
DOT.......... Director [or Directorate] of Training [Army]
DOT.......... Discrete Ordinate Transport
DOT.......... Dorset Resources Ltd. [Toronto Stock Exchange symbol]
DOT.......... Dumbarton Oaks Texts [A publication]
DOT.......... Duplex One-Tape System
DOT.......... Dynamic Operation Test
DOT.......... Kansas City, MO [Location identifier] [FAA] (FAAL)
DoTA........ Department of Transport, Australia
DOTA........ Diakonia of the Americas (EA)
DOTC........ Data Observing Testing Console
DOTC........ Department of Transport (Canada) (FAAC)
DOTC........ Director, Office of Transport and Communications [Department of State] (AAG)
DOTCAB... Department of Transportation Contract Appeals Board
DOT/CIAP ... Department of Transportation/Climatic Impact Assessment Program (NASA)
DOTCOOP ... Department of Transportation Continuity of Operations Plan [Federal emergency plan]
DOTE........ OSD [Office of the Secretary of Defense] Operational Test and Evaluation (RDA)
DOTEO..... Department of Transportation's Emergency Organization
DOTG....... Di-ortho-toylguanidine [Organic chemistry]
DOTI........ Director of Operations, Training and Intelligence [Army] (AABC)
DOTIPOS ... Deep Ocean Test-in-Place and Observation System [Navy]
DOTM....... Director of Naval Ordnance, Torpedoes, and Mines [Royal Australian Navy]
DOTM....... Due-Out to Maintenance [Military] (MCD)
DOTP .... Deep Ocean Technology Project
DOTP .... Dental Officer Training Plan [Canada]
DOTP .... Dioctyl Terephthalate [Organic chemistry]
DOTP .... Duty Operational Test Director
DotR......... Dramatists of the Restoration [British] (ROG)
DOTS .... Digital Optical Technology System [3-D television system]
DOTS .... Diploma of Tertiary Studies
DOTS .... Direction of Trade Statistics [International Monetary Fund] [Information service or system] (CRD)
DOTS .... Division On-Line Tool System [Allan Collautt Associates, Inc.] [Automotive engineering]
DOTS .... Dredging Operations Technical Support (RDA)
DOTSP...... Distinctive Ovarian Tumor with Sexual Precocity
DOTSP...... Doctrinal and Organization Test Support Package [Army]
DOTT .... Decision-Oriented Templating Techniques
DOTT .... Di-o-tolylthiourea [Organic chemistry]
DOTT .... Documents from Old Testament Times [A publication] (BJA)
DOTT .... Duties Other than Teaching (ADA)
Dott Ing...... Dottore Ingenieur [Doctor of Engineering] [Italian]
Dottore Sci Agrar For ... Il Dottore in Scienze Agrarie Forestali [A publication]
DOTX........ Dotronix, Inc. [NASDAQ symbol] (NQ)
DOU.......... Dourados [Brazil] [Airport symbol] (OAG)
DOU.......... Dourbes [Belgium] [Geomagnetic observatory code]
DOU.......... Dourbes [Belgium] [Seismic station code, US Geological Survey] (SEIS)
DOUDDAS ... Deep Ocean Untended Digital Data Acquisition System [Marine science] (MSC)
Doug.......... Douglas' English Election Cases [A publication] (DLA)
Doug.......... Douglas' English King's Bench Reports [A publication] (DLA)
DOUG .... Douglas & Lomason Co. [NASDAQ symbol] (NQ)
Doug.......... Douglas' Michigan Supreme Court Reports [A publication] (DLA)
Doug.......... Douglas' Reports [A publication] (DLA)
Doug El Ca ... Douglas' English Election Cases [A publication] (DLA)
Doug El Cas ... Douglas' English Election Cases [A publication] (DLA)
DOUG FIR-L ... Douglas Fir Larch [Lumber]
Doug KB ... Douglas' English King's Bench Reports [A publication] (DLA)
Dougl El Cas ... Douglas' English Election Cases [A publication] (DLA)
Dougl KB ... Douglas' English King's Bench Reports [A publication] (DLA)
Dougl KB (Eng) ... Douglas' English King's Bench Reports [A publication] (DLA)
Dougl (Mich) ... Douglas' Michigan Supreme Court Reports [A publication] (DLA)

Doug (Mich) ... Douglas' Michigan Supreme Court Reports [*A publication*] (DLA)
DOULT ..... Doulton Ware [*Ceramics*] (ROG)
DOUSER ... Doppler Unbeamed Search RADAR
Dout Pr ...... Doutre. Procedure Civile de Bas Canada [*A publication*] (DLA)
douz .... Douzaine [*Dozen*] [*French*]
DOV .... Data over Voice [*Telecommunications*] (TEL)
DOV .... Diaphragm Operated Valve
DOV .... Disbursing Officer's Voucher
DOV .... Discharged on Visit [*Psychiatry*]
DOV .... Discrete Out Vehicle [*NASA*] (KSC)
DOV .... Distilled Oil of Vitriol
DOV .... Double Oil of Vitriol
DOV .... Dover Corp. [*NYSE symbol*] (SPSG)
DOV .... Dover, DE [*Location identifier*] [*FAA*] (FAAL)
DOV .... Dover Public Library, Dover, DE [*OCLC symbol*] (OCLC)
DOV .... Doverton Oils Ltd. [*Vancouver Stock Exchange symbol*]
DOVAP ..... Doppler, Velocity and Position [*NASA*]
DOVEB ..... Documenta Veterinaria (Brno) [*A publication*]
DOVETT ... Double Velocity Transit Time [*Physics*]
DOV PULV ... Doveri Pulvis [*Dover's Powder*] [*Pharmacy*] (ROG)
DOW .... Delivery on Wheels [*Shipping*] (DS)
DOW .... Density of Water
DOW .... Died of Wounds [*Military*]
DOW .... Dow Chemical Co. [*NYSE symbol*] [*Toronto Stock Exchange symbol*]
DOW .... Dow Chemical Co., Granville Research Center, Granville, OH [*OCLC symbol*] (OCLC)
DOW .... Dower [*or Dowager*]
Dow .... Dowling's English Practice Cases [*A publication*] (DLA)
Dow .... Dow's House of Lords (Parliamentary) Cases [*Same as Dow's Reports*] [*3 English Reprint*] [*A publication*] (DLA)
DOW .... Duration of War
DOWB ...... Deep Ocean Work Boat [*Marine science*] (MSC)
DOWB ...... Deep Operating Work Board (IEEE)
DOWB ...... Director of Works and Buildings [*British*]
Dow & C ... Dow and Clark's English House of Lords Cases [*A publication*] (DLA)
Dow & C (Eng) ... Dow and Clark's English House of Lords Cases [*A publication*] (DLA)
Dow & Cl .... Dow and Clark's English House of Lords Cases [*A publication*] (DLA)
Dowd Ins .... Dowdeswell on Life and Fire Insurance [*A publication*] (DLA)
Dow Inc ...... Dowell's Income Tax Acts [*9th ed.*] [*1934*] [*A publication*] (DLA)
Dow & L ..... Dowling and Lowndes' English Bail Court Reports [*A publication*] (DLA)
Dowl .... Dowling's English Bail Court (Practice) Cases [*A publication*] (DLA)
Dowl (Eng) ... Dowling's English Bail Court (Practice) Cases [*A publication*] (DLA)
Dowl & L .... Dowling and Lowndes' English Bail Court Reports [*A publication*] (DLA)
Dowl & Lownd ... Dowling and Lowndes' English Bail Court Reports [*A publication*] (DLA)
Dowl NS ..... Dowling's English Bail Court Reports, New Series [*1841-43*] [*A publication*] (DLA)
Dowl NS (Eng) ... Dowling's English Bail Court Reports, New Series [*1841-43*] [*A publication*] (DLA)
Dow & Lownd ... Dowling and Lowndes' English Practice Cases [*A publication*] (DLA)
Dowl PC ..... Dowling's English Bail Court (Practice) Cases [*A publication*] (DLA)
Dowl PC (Eng) ... Dowling's English Bail Court (Practice) Cases [*A publication*] (DLA)
Dowl PC NS ... Dowling's English Practice Cases, New Series [*A publication*] (DLA)
Dowl Pr ...... Dowling's Common Law Practice [*A publication*] (DLA)
Dowl PR ..... Dowling's Practice Reports [*A publication*] (DLA)
Dowl Pr Cas ... Dowling's English Practice Cases [*A publication*] (DLA)
Dowl Pr C NS ... Dowling's English Practice Cases, New Series [*A publication*] (DLA)
Dowl & R .... Dowling and Ryland's English King's Bench Reports [*A publication*] (DLA)
Dowl & R (Eng) ... Dowling and Ryland's English King's Bench Reports [*A publication*] (DLA)
Dowl & R Mag Cas (Eng) ... Dowling and Ryland's English Magistrates' Cases [*A publication*] (DLA)
Dowl & R NP ... Dowling and Ryland's English Nisi Prius Cases [*A publication*] (DLA)
Dowl & R NP (Eng) ... Dowling and Ryland's English Nisi Prius Cases [*A publication*] (DLA)
Dowl & Ryl ... Dowling and Ryland's English King's Bench Reports [*A publication*] (DLA)
Dowl & Ryl MC ... Dowling and Ryland's English Magistrates' Cases [*A publication*] (DLA)
Dowl & Ryl NP ... Dowling and Ryland's English Nisi Prius Cases [*A publication*] (DLA)

DOWM ..... Database of Off-Site Waste Management [*Public Data Access, Inc.*] [*Information service or system*] [*No longer available online*]
DOWN ...... Downing College [*Cambridge University*] (ROG)
Down Bt ..... Down Beat [*A publication*]
Down Earth ... Down to Earth [*A publication*]
Down & Lud ... Downton and Luder's English Election Cases [*A publication*] (DLA)
DownR .... Downside Review [*A publication*]
Dow NS ...... Dow and Clark's English House of Lords Cases [*A publication*] (DLA)
Dow NS ...... Dowling's English Bail Court Reports, New Series [*1841-43*] [*A publication*] (DLA)
Dow PC ...... Dowling's English Practice Cases [*A publication*] (DLA)
Dow PC ...... Dow's House of Lords (Parliamentary) Cases [*Same as Dow's Reports*] [*3 English Reprint*] [*A publication*] (DLA)
Dow PC (Eng) ... Dowling's English Practice Cases [*A publication*] (DLA)
Dow PC (Eng) ... Dow's House of Lords (Parliamentary) Cases [*Same as Dow's Reports*] [*3 English Reprint*] [*A publication*] (DLA)
Dow Pr ...... Dowling's English Practice Cases [*A publication*] (DLA)
DowR .... Downside Review [*Downside Abbey, Bath, England*] [*A publication*]
Dow & Ry ... Dowling and Ryland's English King's Bench Reports [*A publication*] (DLA)
Dow & Ry ... Dowling and Ryland's English Nisi Prius Cases [*A publication*] (DLA)
Dow & Ry KB ... Dowling and Ryland's English King's Bench Reports [*A publication*] (DLA)
Dow & Ry KB ... Dowling and Ryland's English Nisi Prius Cases [*A publication*] (DLA)
Dow & Ry MC ... Dowling and Ryland's English Magistrates' Cases [*A publication*] (DLA)
Dow & Ry NP ... Dowling and Ryland's English Nisi Prius Cases [*A publication*] (DLA)
Dow St .... Dowell's Stamp Duties [*1873*] [*A publication*] (DLA)
DOX .... Dolphin Explorations Ltd. [*Vancouver Stock Exchange symbol*] [*Toronto Stock Exchange symbol*]
DOX .... Dongara [*Australia*] [*Airport symbol*] (OAG)
DOX .... Doxology (ROG)
DOX .... Doxorubicin [*Also, D, DXR*] [*Formerly, ADR, Adriamycin*] [*Antineoplastic drug*]
Dox Graec ... Doxographi Graeci [*A publication*] (OCD)
DOXOL ..... Doxorubicinol [*Antineoplastic drug*]
DOY .... Day of Year
DOYL .... Doyle Dane Bernbach, Inc. [*NASDAQ symbol*] (NQ)
DOZ .... Dioctyl Azelate [*Organic chemistry*]
DOZ .... Dozen (AFM)
DP .... Air Sinai [*Egypt*] [*ICAO designator*] (FAAC)
DP .... By Direction of the President
DP .... Daily Penalty (ROG)
DP .... Dalloz Periodique [*French*] [*A publication*] (DLA)
D & P .... Damon and Pythias [*Fourth-century BC Greek philosophers renowned for their loyalty to one another*]
DP .... Damp-Proofing (AAG)
DP .... Dance Perspectives [*A publication*]
DP .... Dash Pot [*Relay*]
DP .... Data Pointer [*Computer memory*]
DP .... Data Printer
DP .... Data Processing
DP .... Data Processing and/or Computer Programming Programs [*Association of Independent Colleges and Schools specialization code*]
DP .... Data Processing Technician [*Navy rating*]
DP .... Data Protection Act [*1980's*] [*British*]
DP .... Date of Publication [*Online database field identifier*]
DP .... Datum Point
DP .... Daughters of Penelope (EA)
DP .... Dawson Packet [*A publication*]
DP .... Days' Purposes [*Shipping*]
DP .... De Profundis
DP .... Dead Point
DP .... Decision Package [*Military*]
DP .... Decision Point (CAAL)
DP .... Deck Piercing
DP .... Deed Poll
DP .... Deep (FAAC)
DP .... Deep Penetration [*Air Force*]
DP .... Deep Pulse [*Medicine*]
DP .... Defense Point
D/P .... Deferred Payment [*Business term*] (ADA)
DP .... Deflection Plate [*Technical drawings*]
DP .... Degradation Products [*Hematology*]
D of P .... Degree of Pocahontas
DP .... Degree of Polymerization
DP .... Delacorte Press [*Publisher*]
DP .... Delayed Procurement (NASA)
DP .... Delegation en Perse. Memoires [*A publication*]
D/P .... Delivery Against Payment [*Business term*] (ADA)
DP .... Delivery Point
DP .... Demand Meter, Printing

DP............	Dementia Praecox [*or a patient with this condition*] [*Medical slang*]
DP............	Demi-Pension [*Hotel rate*]
DP............	Democracy Project (EA)
DP............	Democratic Party [*Uganda*] [*Political party*] (PD)
DP............	Democratic Party [*Stronnictwo Demokratyczne*] [*Poland*] [*Political party*] (PPW)
DP............	Democratic Party [*Cook Island*] [*Political party*] (PPW)
DP............	Democratic Party [*Thailand*] [*Political party*] (PPW)
DP............	Democratische Partij - Bovenwinden [*Democratic Party - Windward Islands*] [*Netherlands Antilles*] [*Political party*] (PPW)
DP............	Democratische Partij van Curacao [*Democratic Party - Curacao*] [*Netherlands Antilles*] [*Political party*] (PPW)
DP............	Democrazia Proletaria [*Proletarian Democracy*] [*Italy*] [*Political party*] (PPE)
DP............	Demokratesch Partei [*Democratic Party*] [*Luxembourg*] [*Political party*] (PPE)
DP............	Demokraticheska Partiia [*Democratic Party*] [*Bulgaria*] [*Political party*] (PPE)
DP............	Demokratiki Parataksis [*Democratic Front*] [*Greek*] (PPE)
D & P........	Denison and Pearce's English Crown Cases [*1844-52*] [*A publication*] (DLA)
DP............	Dental Prosthetic Technician
DP............	Department of the Pacific [*Marine Corps*]
DP............	Departure Point (AFM)
DP............	Deployment Payload (MCD)
DP............	Deployment Pennant [*Navy*] [*British*]
D-P............	Depo-Provera [*Contraceptive*] [*The Upjohn Co.*]
DP............	Deposit
DP............	Deposited Plan (ADA)
DP............	Depth (MSA)
DP............	Deputy President [*Australia*]
DP............	Der Deutsche Pionier [*A publication*] (BJA)
Dp............	Dermatophagoides pteronyssinus [*House dust*]
DP............	Description Pattern
DP............	Desiderius Pastor [*Pseudonym used by Gerard Moultree*]
D & P........	Design and Production
DP............	Design Proof (NASA)
DP............	Design Proposal
DP............	Desktop Publishing [*Data processing*]
D/P............	Detained Pay
DP............	Detrucking Point
DP............	Deutsche Partei [*German Party*] [*Federal Republic of Germany*] (PPE)
DP............	Deutsche Philologie [*A publication*]
DP............	Developed Pressure [*Cardiology*]
D & P........	Developing and Printing
DP............	Developing Proboscis
DP............	Development Phase (NASA)
DP............	Development Plan
DP............	Development Proposal (NVT)
DP............	Development Prototype
DP............	Developmental Psychology [*A publication*]
DP............	Developments in Petrology [*Elsevier Book Series*] [*A publication*]
DP............	Devil Pups (EA)
DP............	Dew Point
DP............	Diagnostic Products Corp. [*NYSE symbol*] (SPSG)
DP............	Dial Pulse [*Telecommunications*]
DP............	Diametrical Pitch
d/p............	Dias Plazo [*Days' Time*] [*Spanish*]
DP............	Diastatic Power
DP............	Diastolic Pressure [*Medicine*]
DP............	Die Presse [*A publication*]
DP............	Diesel Particulate
DP............	Difference, Port [*Navigation*]
DP............	Difference of Potential
DP............	Difference in Pressure
DP............	Differential Phase [*Telecommunications*]
DP............	Differential Pressure
DP............	Differential Pulse
DP............	Diffused Planar
DP............	Diffusion Pressure
DP............	Diffusion Pump
DP............	Digit Present
DP............	Digital Plotter
DP............	Dining Permit [*Slang*]
DP............	Diphenyl [*Organic chemistry*]
DP............	Diphosgene [*Poison gas*] [*Army symbol*]
DP............	Diphosphate [*Biochemistry*]
D-P............	Diplomate, American Board of Pathology (DHSM)
DP............	Dipole (DEN)
DP............	Direct Participation (ADA)
DP............	Direct Path (NVT)
DP............	Direct Port [*Transportation*]
DP............	Direct Price
DP............	Directed Proliferation
DP............	Directing Point
DP............	Direction of President
DP............	Directione Propria [*With Proper Direction*] [*Pharmacy*]
DP............	Director of Pathology
DP............	Director of Personnel (MCD)
D of P........	Director of Planes [*Admiralty*] [*British*]
DP............	Director of Postings [*RAF*] [*British*]
DP............	Director of Programs [*Air Force, Army*]
DP............	Disabled Person (ADA)
DP............	Disaster Preparedness (NVT)
DP............	Disc Plowing [*Agriculture*]
DP............	Discharged Patient [*British*]
DP............	Disciple
DP............	Disconnection Pending [*Telecommunications*] (TEL)
DP............	Discourse Processes [*A publication*]
DP............	Discretionary Program (OICC)
DP............	Discussion Paper
DP............	Disk Pack [*Data processing*] (IEEE)
DP............	Disorderly Person
DP............	Dispatch Point
DP............	Dispensing Precaution
DP............	Dispersal Point
DP............	Displaced Person [*Post-World War II*]
DP............	Displacement
DP............	Display Package
DP............	Display Panel
DP............	Display Processor
DP............	Dissolution Patterns [*Physics*]
DP............	Distending Pressure
DP............	Distopulpal [*Dentistry*]
DP............	Distribution Plan (AFIT)
DP............	Distribution Point
DP............	Docking Protein [*Biochemistry*]
DP............	Doctor of Pharmacy
DP............	Doctor of Philosophy
D/P............	Documenti Contro Pagamento [*Documents Against Payment*] [*Italian*] [*Business term*]
D/P............	Documentos Contra Pago [*Documents Against Payment*] [*Spanish*] [*Business term*]
D/P............	Documents Against Payment [*Banking*]
D/P............	Documents Contre Paiement [*Documents Against Payment*] [*French*] [*Banking*]
DP............	Documents Presargoniques [*A publication*] (BJA)
D-P............	Dog Pound [*Multistory parking lot*] [*Slang*] [*British*]
DP............	Dom Perignon [*Champagne*]
DP............	Domestic Prelate
DP............	Domus Procerum [*The House of Lords*] [*Latin*]
DP............	Donor's Plasma [*Medicine*]
DP............	Doppelposten [*Double Sentry*] [*German military - World War II*]
DP............	Dorsal Pallium [*Neuroanatomy*]
DP............	Dorsal Pioneer Cell [*Cytology*]
DP............	Dorsal Pitt
DP............	Dorsalis Pedis [*Pulse*] [*Medicine*]
DP............	Double Paper [*Wire insulation*] (AAG)
DP............	Double Parallel [*Molecular biology*]
DP............	Double Petticoat [*Insulators*]
DP............	Double Plasma
DP............	Double Play [*Baseball*]
DP............	Double Pole [*Switch*]
DP............	Double Precision (NASA)
DP............	Double-Purpose Gun
DP............	Draft Proposal
DP............	Drain Panel (AAG)
D & P........	Drain and Purge (NASA)
DP............	Drill Pay
DP............	Drill Plate [*Tool*] (MSA)
DP............	Drill Purposes [*British military*] (DMA)
DP............	Drip-Proof (AAG)
DP............	Driving Power
DP............	Drop Point [*Air Force*] (AFM)
DP............	Drum Processor [*Data processing*] (IEEE)
D & P........	Drunk and Proud
DP............	Dry Point
DP............	Dual Pilot (MUGU)
DP............	Dual Purpose (NG)
DP............	Ducted Propellers [*Aviation*] (AAG)
DP............	Due Process
DP............	Dummy Part (MCD)
DP............	Dungpit (ROG)
DP............	Duplicate Positive (MCD)
DP............	Durable Press [*Textile technology*]
DP............	Duty Paid [*International trade*]
DP............	Duty Pay
DP............	Dynamic Programming [*Data processing*]
DP............	Dynamically Positioned
DP............	Maandblad de Pacht [*A publication*]
DP............	Potential Difference [*Electricity*] (ROG)
DP............	Two Pole (MSA)
DP............	United States Patent Office, Arlington, VA [*Library symbol*] [*Library of Congress*] (LCLS)
DP1............	Data Processing Technician, First Class [*Navy rating*]
DP2............	Data Processing Technician, Second Class [*Navy rating*]
DP3............	Data Processing Technician, Third Class [*Navy rating*]

DPA .... Black Data Processing Associates (EA)
DPA .... Chicago/West Chicago, IL [*Location identifier*] [*FAA*] (FAAL)
DPA .... D-Pantothenyl Alcohol [*Biochemistry*]
DPA .... Data Processing Activities
DPA .... Data Processing Agency
DPA .... Data Processing Algorithm
DPA .... Data Processing Area
DPA .... Data Processing Assembly (MCD)
DPA .... Data Protection Agency [*British*]
DPA .... Defense Production Act [*Obsolete*] (NG)
DPA .... Defense Production Administration [*Functions transferred to Office of Defense Mobilization*]
DPA .... Delegation of Procurement Authority
DPA .... Demonstration Programs Administration [*HUD*]
DPA .... Desert Pacific Airways [*Oxnard, CA*] [*FAA designator*] (FAAC)
DPA .... Designated Processing Agency (MCD)
DPA .... Destructive Part Analysis
DPA .... Destructive Physical Analysis
DPA .... Detailed Performance Analysis [*Bell System*]
DPA .... Deutsche Presse Agentur [*German Press Agency*] [*Federal Republic of Germany*]
DPA .... Dial Pulse Access [*Telecommunications*] (TEL)
DPA .... Dichloropropionanilide [*Also, DCPA*] [*Herbicide*]
DPA .... Different Premises Address [*Telecommunications*] (TEL)
DPA .... Diphenolic Acid [*Organic chemistry*]
DPA .... Diphenylamine [*Organic chemistry*]
DPA .... Diphenylanthracene [*Organic chemistry*]
DPA .... Dipicolinic Acid [*Organic chemistry*]
DPA .... Diploma in Public Administration [*British*]
DPA .... Dipropylacetic Acid [*Also, VPA*] [*Valproic acid*] [*Anticonvulsant compound*]
DPA .... Dipropylamine [*Organic chemistry*]
DPA .... Directorate of Policy [*Air Ministry*] [*British*]
DPA .... Discharged Prisoners' Aid [*British*]
DPA .... Displacements per Atom (MCD)
DPA .... Distribution Plan Authorization [*Military*] (AFIT)
D Pa .... Doctor of Painting
DPA .... Doctor of Public Administration
DPA .... Domestic Policy Association [*Later, NIF*] (EA)
DPA .... Double-Precision Arithmetic (AAG)
DPA .... Driving Point Admittance
DPA .... Dual Photon Absorptiometry [*Analytical chemistry*]
DPAA .... Data Processing, Analysis, and Archiving (NOAA)
DPAA .... Desktop Publishing Applications Association (EA)
DPAA .... Dissertazioni. Pontificia Accademia Roman di Archeologia [*A publication*]
DPAC .... Data Processing and Control (Unit) (CAAL)
DPAC .... Dense-Pac Microsystems, Inc. [*Garden Grove, CA*] [*NASDAQ symbol*] (NQ)
DPACCS ... Displaced Persons Assembly Center Camp Staffs [*Allied Military Government of Occupied Territory*] [*Post-World War II*]
DPACT ...... Defense Policy Advisory Committee on Trade [*DoD*]
DP Adm .... Doctor of Public Administration
DPAE .... Director of Program Analysis and Evaluation (RDA)
DPaed .... Doctor of Pedagogy
D in P AEQ ... Dividatur in Partes Aequales [*Divide into Equal Parts*] [*Pharmacy*]
DPAH........ Direct Product Actual Hours (MCD)
DPAHO..... Pan American Health Organization, Pan American Sanitary Bureau, Washington, DC [*Library symbol*] [*Library of Congress*] (LCLS)
DPAHO-FH ... Pan American Health Organization, Documentation Center, Division of Family Health, Washington, DC [*Library symbol*] [*Library of Congress*] (LCLS)
DPAI.......... (Dipropylaminoethyl)indole [*Organic chemistry*]
DPAIAI ..... Disregard Previous Assignment Instructions and Assign as Indicated [*Army*] (AABC)
DPALD....... DOE [*US Department of Energy*] Patents Available for Licensing [*A publication*]
DPAMMH ... Direct Productive Annual Maintenance Manhours (MCD)
DPANZ ..... Decorator and Painter for Australia and New Zealand [*A publication*]
DPAO........ Deputy Public Affairs Officer [*United States Information Service*]
DPAO........ District Public Affairs Officer [*Military*]
DPAP......... Dipeptidyl Aminopeptidase [*An enzyme*]
D-PARC .... Daigo Proving Ground and Research Centre [*Japan*]
DPARS...... Data Processing Automatic Record Standardization
DPAS........ Developments in Palaeontology and Stratigraphy [*Elsevier Book Series*] [*A publication*]
DPAS........ Discharged Prisoners' Aid Society [*British*]
DPASV...... Differential Pulse Anodic Stripping Voltammetry [*Electrochemistry*]
D-PAT ...... Drum-Programmed Automatic Tester
D Path....... Diploma in Pathology [*British*]
DPB .... Bucks County Free Library, Doylestown, PA [*OCLC symbol*] (OCLC)
DPB .... Dampier's Paper Book, Lincoln's Inn Library [*A publication*] (DLA)

DPB .... Data Plotting Board
DPB .... Data Processing Branch (IEEE)
DPB .... Defence Production Board [*NATO*] (NATG)
DPB .... Defence-Protected Build-Down [*Nuclear arms reduction strategy*] [*British*]
DPB .... Department of Plant Biology [*Carnegie Institution of Washington*] [*Research center*] (RCD)
DPB .... Deposit Passbook [*Banking*]
DPB .... Developments in Plant Biology [*Elsevier Book Series*] [*A publication*]
DPB .... Diphenylbutadiene [*Organic chemistry*]
DPB .... Disability Policy Board [*Veterans Administration*]
DPB .... Distinguished Pistol Badge
DPB .... Doctor of Physical Biology
DPB .... Document Processing Branch [*NTIS*]
DPB .... Dodecylpyridinium Bromide [*Organic chemistry*]
Dp BA .... Diploma in Business Administration [*British*]
DPBA .... Dr. Pepper Bottlers Association (EA)
DpBact....... Diploma in Bacteriology [*British*] (DBQ)
DPBC......... Depolarizing Bipolar Cell [*In the retina*]
DPBC......... Double-Pole, Both Connected [*Switch*]
DPBG .... Democratic Party for British Gibraltar (PPW)
DPBO .... Division Property Book Officer [*Military*] (AABC)
DPBSP ..... Drowning Prevention and Beach Safety Program (EA)
DPC .... Chief Data Processing Technician [*Formerly, MAC*] [*Navy rating*]
DPC .... Data Processing Center
DPC .... Data Processing Central
DPC .... Data Processing Computer (CAAL)
DPC .... Data Processing Control (AFM)
DPC .... Database Promotion Center, Japan [*Information service or system*] (EISS)
DPC .... Dataproducts Corporation [*AMEX symbol*] (SPSG)
DPC .... Dating Problems Checklist [*Psychology*]
DPC .... Defence Planning Committee [*NATO*] (NATG)
DPC .... Defence Production Chief [*British*]
DPC .... Defence Production Committee [*NATO*] (NATG)
DPC .... Defense Planning Council
DPC .... Defense Plant Corporation [*Obsolete*] [*Subsidiary of Reconstruction Finance Corp.*]
DPC .... Defense Procurement Circular [*DoD*]
DPC .... Delayed Primary Closure [*Medicine*]
DPC .... Democratic Policy Commission (EA)
DPC .... Desaturated Phosphatidylcholine [*Biochemistry*]
DPC .... Desert Protective Council (EA)
DPC .... Destination Point Code [*Telecommunications*] (TEL)
DPC .... Devotional and Practical Commentary [*A publication*]
DPC .... Diagnostic Products Corp.
DPC .... Differential Photocalorimetry [*Analytical technique*]
DPC .... Differential Pressure Control
DPC .... Digital Phase Comparator
DPC .... Digital Pressure Converter
DPC .... Digital Process Controller
DPC .... Diphenyl Carbonate [*Organic chemistry*]
DPC .... Diphenylaminecarboxylate [*Organic chemistry*]
DPC .... Diphenylcarbazide [*Organic chemistry*]
DPC .... Diphenylcarbene [*Organic chemistry*]
DPC .... Direct Patient Care [*Medicine*]
DPC .... Direct Power Conversion [*Nuclear energy*] (AAG)
DPC .... Direct Program Control (BUR)
DPC .... Directive Parental Counseling
DPC .... Displaced Persons' Camps
DPC .... Displaced Persons Commission [*Terminated, 1952*]
DPC .... Display Power Control
DPC .... Display Processor Code
DPC .... Distal Palmar Crease [*Anatomy*]
DPC .... Distribution Processing Center (MCD)
DPC .... Division of Physical Chemistry (EA)
DPC .... Documentation Processing Center [*British*]
DPC .... Dodecylpyridinium Chloride [*Also, LPC*] [*Organic chemistry*]
DPC .... Doklady Physical Chemistry
DPC .... Dollar Penny Coalition (EA)
DPC .... Double Paper-Covered [*Wire insulation*] (DEN)
DPC .... Dowling's English Practice Cases [*A publication*] (DLA)
DPC .... Dredging and Port Construction [*A publication*]
DPC .... Duke Primate Center [*North Carolina*]
DPCA .... Data Processing Control Area [*Space Flight Operations Facility, NASA*]
DPCA .... Diphenylcyclopentylamine [*Organic chemistry*]
DPCA .... Director of Personnel and Community Activities [*Army*] (AABC)
DPCA .... Displaced Phase Center Antenna
DPCA .... Doberman Pinscher Club of America (EA)
DPCC........ Data Processing Control Center [*or Console*] [*Space Flight Operations Facility, NASA*]
DPCC........ Director of Postal and Courier Communications [*British military*] (DMA)
DPCC........ Duneland Post Card Club [*Defunct*] (EA)
DPCCP..... Defective Parts and Components Control Program
DPCE........ Data Processing Customer Engineering (ADA)
DPCF........ Dorsal Peristomial Collar Fold

DPCI......... Distributed Processing Contractual Input [*Data processing*]
DPCM ...... Differential Pulse Code Modulation [*Transmission technique*]
DPCM ...... Distributed Processing Communications Module
DPCM .... Master Chief Data Processing Technician [*Formerly, MACM*] [*Navy rating*]
DPCN .... D-Penicillamine [*Pharmacology*]
DPCP........ Department of Prices and Consumer Protection [*British*]
DPCPDS ... Divulgacion Pesquera [*Bogota*] [*A publication*]
DPCR........ Departure Procedure (FAAC)
DPCS........ Desktop Page Composition System [*Vision Research*]
DPCS........ Difference Pressure Control Switch
DPCS........ Senior Chief Data Processing Technician [*Formerly, MACS*] [*Navy rating*]
DPCSMA .. Dry Process Ceramic and Steatite Manufacturers Association [*Later, TECMA*] (EA)
DPCT........ Differential Protection Current Transformer
DPCTE...... Data Processor and Computer Test Equipment
DPCTG...... Database Program Conversion Task Group [*CODASYL*]
DPCU .... Digital Processing and Control Unit
DPCX........ Distributed Processing Control Executive [*IBM Corp.*]
DPD.......... Data Processing Department
DPD.......... Data Processing Detachment
DPD.......... Data Processing Division [*IBM Corp.*]
DPD.......... Data Project Directive (AFM)
DPD.......... Deaminophenylalaninedehydroproline [*Biochemistry*]
DPD.......... Decontamination as Precursor to Decommissioning [*Nuclear energy*] (NRCH)
DPD.......... (Diethyl)phenylenediamine [*Organic chemistry*]
DPD.......... Diffuse Pulmonary Disease [*Medicine*]
DPD.......... Diffusion Pressure Deficit
DPD.......... Digit Plane Driver [*Data processing*] (IEEE)
DPD.......... Digital Phase Difference
DPD.......... Dignitary Protective Division [*US Secret Service*]
DPD.......... Diploma in Public Dentistry [*British*]
D-Pd.......... Diplomate, American Board of Pediatrics (DHSM)
DPD.......... Direct Payroll Deposit
DPD.......... Director, Personnel Department [*Marine Corps*]
DPD.......... Director of Plans Division [*Navy*] [*British*]
DPD.......... District Port Director [*Navy*]
D Pd.......... Doctor of Pedagogy
DPD.......... Domestic Presidential Directive [*Jimmy Carter Administration*]
DPDC .... Double Paper, Double Cotton [*Wire insulation*]
DPDD .... Defense Property Disposal Detachment (AFIT)
DPDI .... Dimple Die
DPDL .... Diffuse Poorly Differentiated Lymphocytic (Lymphoma) [*Oncology*]
DPDL .... Distributed Program Design Language
DPDM ...... Diphenyldiazomethane [*Organic chemistry*]
DPDM ...... Double Pulse Duration Modulation (KSC)
DPDM-R ... Defense Property Disposal Precious Metals Recovery [*DoD*] (AFIT)
DPDO .... Defense Property Disposal Office [*DoD*]
DPDPMRO-E ... Defense Property Disposal Precious Metals Recovery Office - Earle [*New Jersey*] [*DoD*]
D of PD(Q) ... Director of Plans Division (Quartering) [*Navy*] [*British*]
DPDR .... Defense Property Disposal Region [*DoD*]
DPDRAM ... Dual-Ported Dynamic Random Access Memory [*Data processing*]
DPDroh ..... Dopovidi ta Povidomlennja. Materialy Konferencij Drohobyc'koho Derzavnoho Pedahohicnoho Instytutu Imeni I. Ja. Franka. Serija Filolohicnych Nauk. Drohobyc [*A publication*]
DPDS......... DARC [*Description, Acquisition, Retrieval, and Conception*] Pluridata System [*Association for Research and Development of Chemical Informatics*] [*Information service or system*] (IID)
DPDS........ Defense Property Disposal Service [*DoD*]
DPDS......... Drustvo Prijatelja Dubrovacke Starine [*Society of the Friends of Ancient and Historical Dubrovnik - SFAHD*] (EAIO)
DP/DT....... Delta Pressure/Delta Time (MCD)
DPDT .... Double Pole, Double Throw [*Switch*]
DPDTSW .. Double-Pole, Double-Throw Switch
DPDU Dund ... Diploma in Public Dentistry, University of Dundee [*British*]
DPE .... Data Processing Equipment
DPE .... Demilitarization Protective Ensemble (RDA)
DPE .... Department for Professional Employees [*AFL-CIO*]
DPE .... Desktop Publishing Editor [*Computer program*]
DPE .... Detailed Plan Execution (MCD)
DPE .... Deuterated Polyethylene [*Organic chemistry*]
DPE .... Development Project Engineer (NRCH)
DPE .... Dieppe [*France*] [*Airport symbol*] [*Obsolete*] (OAG)
DPE .... Differential Paramagnetic Effect [*Low-temperature physics*]
DPE .... Diphenylethylene [*Organic chemistry*]
DPE .... Diphenyltrichloroethane [*Also, DPT*] [*Organic chemistry*]
DPE .... Diploma in Physical Education [*British*]
DPE .... Director Program Evaluation [*Navy*] (CAAL)
DPE .... Distributed Processing Environment
DPE .... Distributor-to-Printer Electronics
DPE .... District Power Equalizer [*Formula for school grants*]
DPE .... Doctor of Physical Education

DPE .... Duration of the Present Emergency [*British*] [*World War II*]
DPE .... Dynamic Phase Error
DPEc......... Doctor of Political Economy
D Ped .... Doctor of Pedagogy
D Pe E........ Doctor of Petroleum Engineering
D Pe Eng... Doctor of Petroleum Engineering
DPEK........ Differential Phase Exchange Keying (IEEE)
DPEM........ Depot Purchased Equipment Management [*DoD*]
DPEP......... Deoxophylloerythroetioporphyrin [*Biochemistry*]
DPERPLA ... Delegacion del Parlamento Europeo para las Relaciones con los Paises de Latinoamerica [*Europe-Latin America Interparliamentary Assembly - ELAIA*] [*Luxembourg, Luxembourg*] (EAIO)
DPESE....... Densely Packaged Encased Standard Element (AAG)
DPESO...... Department of Defense Product Engineering Services Office (MCD)
DPEWS ..... Design-to-Price Electronics Warfare System [*Military*]
DPEX........ Distributed Processing Executive Program
DPF.......... Data Processing Facility
DPF.......... Defatted Peanut Flour [*Food industry*]
DPF.......... Deferred Pay Fund
DPF.......... Denier per Filament [*Textile technology*]
DPF.......... Dense Plasma Focus
DPF.......... Dental Practitioner's Formulary
DPF.......... Depression Position-Finder
DPF.......... Differential Pressure Feedback (KSC)
DPF.......... Disciples Peace Fellowship (EA)
DPF.......... Diversified Processed Foods [*Vancouver Stock Exchange symbol*]
DPF.......... Drill Press Feed
DPF.......... Drug Policy Foundation (EA)
DPF.......... Dual Program Feature
DPF.......... Dynamic Pressure Feedback
DPfBl....... Deutsches Pfarrerblatt [*Essen, Germany*] [*A publication*]
dPFC........ Direct Plaque-Forming Cell [*Immunology*]
DPFC........ Dolly Parton Fan Club (EA)
DPFC........ Double Pole, Front Connected [*Switch*]
DPFD........ Deptford [*Region of London*]
DPFLP....... Democratic Popular Front for the Liberation of Palestine (BJA)
DPFO........ Data Processing Field Office (MCD)
DPFT........ Desk, Double-Pedestal Flat-Top
DPG.......... Damping (MSA)
DPG.......... Data Processing Group [*Army*] (AABC)
DPG.......... Date of Permanent Grade
DPG.......... Debutanized Pyrolysis Gasoline
DPG.......... Defense Policy Guidance [*Military*]
DPG.......... Defense Production Guarantees, Army
DPG.......... Desulfurize Pyrolysis Gasoline [*Petroleum refining*]
DPG.......... Developments in Precambrian Geology [*Elsevier Book Series*] [*A publication*]
DPG.......... Digital Pattern Generator
DPG.......... Diphenylguanidine [*Organic chemistry*]
DPG.......... Diphosphoglycerate [*Also, DPGA*] [*Biochemistry*]
DPG.......... Disodium Phosphoglycerate [*Organic chemistry*]
DPG.......... Dripolene Pyrolysis Gasoline [*Lummus Crest, Inc. process*]
DPG.......... Dugway Proving Ground [*Dugway, UT*] [*Army*] (AABC)
DPG.......... Dugway/Tooele, UT [*Location identifier*] [*FAA*] (FAAL)
DPG.......... Dumping
DPGA .... Diphosphoglycerate [*Also, DPG*] [*Biochemistry*]
DPGB .... Digest of Public General Bills [*Library of Congress*] [*A publication*]
DPGM....... Deputy Provincial Grand Master [*Freemasonry*] (ROG)
DPGM....... Diphosphoglyceromutase [*An enzyme*]
DPGN........ Diffuse Proliferative Glomerulonephritis [*Medicine*]
DPGp........ Data Processing Group [*Air Force*] (AFM)
DPGR .... Dugway Proving Ground [*Utah*] [*Army*]
DPH.......... Department of Public Health
DPH.......... Depth of Hold
DPH.......... Designated Pinch Hitter [*Later, DH*] [*Baseball*]
DPH.......... Diamond Penetrator Hardness
DPH.......... Diamond Pyramid Hardness (MSA)
DPH.......... Diphenylhexatriene [*A fluorophore*] [*Organic chemistry*]
DPH.......... Diphenylhydantoin [*Anticonvulsant*]
DPH.......... Diploma in Public Health [*British*]
DPH.......... Disintegrations per Hour
DPH.......... Division for Physically Handicapped (EA)
D Ph.......... Doctor of Philosophy
DPH.......... Doctor of Public Health
DPH.......... Doctor of Public Hygiene
DPHA........ Descripcion del Patrimonio Historico-Artistico Espanol [*Database*] [*Ministerio de Cultura*] [*Spanish*] [*Information service or system*] (CRD)
D Phar ..... Doctor of Pharmacy
D Phar C.... Doctor of Pharmaceutical Chemistry
DPharm .... Doctor of Pharmacy (ADA)
D Ph C ..... Doctor of Pharmaceutical Chemistry
D Phc .... Doctor of Pharmacology
DPHDent.... Diploma in Public Health Dentistry (ADA)
DPHE........ Doctor of Public Health Engineering
DPH Ed ..... Doctor of Public Health Education
DPH Eng ... Doctor of Public Health Engineering

DPHFA ..... Dissertationes Pharmaceuticae et Pharmacologicae [*A publication*]
D Phil........ Doctor of Philanthropy
D Phil........ Doctor of Philosophy
D Ph M ...... Doctor of Philosophy in Metaphysics
DPHN........ Diploma in Public Health Nursing   (ADA)
DPHN........ Doctor of Public Health Nursing
D Pho......... Doctor of Photography
DPHRCSEng ... Diploma in Dental Public Health, Royal College of Surgeons of England [*British*]   (DBQ)
D Ph S........ Doctor of Physical Science
D Ph Sc....... Doctor of Physical Science
DPHSDS... Drugs and the Pharmaceutical Sciences [*A publication*]
DPHU........ Dispersed Phase Hold Up [*Chemical engineering*]
DPhy.......... Doctor of Philosophy
D Phy......... Doctor of Physics
DPHy......... Doctor of Public Hygiene
DPhys........ Diploma of Physiotherapy [*British*]
D Phys Med ... Diploma in Physical Medicine [*British*]
DPHZ........ DATAPHAZ, Inc. [*NASDAQ symbol*]   (NQ)
DPI .... Data Processing Installation
DPI .... Data Publishing International [*Netherlands*] [*Information service or system*]   (IID)
DPI .... Deal Proneness Index [*Marketing*]
DPI .... Defense Plant Installation
DPI .... Delayed Procurement Item
DPI .... Department of Primary Industry [*Australia*]
DPI .... Department of Public Information [*United Nations*]
DPI .... Desired Point of Impact [*Military*]
DPI .... Detail Program Interrelationships   (NASA)
DPI .... Detected Pulse Interference   (CET)
DPI .... Different Premises Information [*Telecommunications*]   (TEL)
DPI .... Digital Process Instrument [*Data processing*]   (IEEE)
DPI .... Digital Pseudorandom Inspection   (IEEE)
DPI .... (Dihydroxyphenylimino)imidazolidine [*Biochemistry*]
DPI .... Diphosphoinositide [*Biochemistry*]
DPI .... Director of Public Instruction
DPI .... Disabled Peoples' International   (EAIO)
DPI .... Disposable Personal Income
dpi .... Dots-per-Inch [*Printing technology*]
DPI .... Duoplasmation Ion
DPI .... Dynamic Personality Inventory [*Psychology*]
DPIA......... Diethylenetriamine Producers Importers Alliance   (EA)
DPIB......... Disabled Persons' Information Bureau [*Australia*]
DPIBF........ Diphenylisobenzofuran [*Organic chemistry*]
DPIC......... Deputy Paymaster in Chief
DPIC......... Drug and Poison Information Centre [*University of British Columbia*] [*Information service or system*]   (IID)
DPICM..... Dual-Purpose Improved Conventional Munition   (AABC)
DPICS....... Dyadic Parent-Child Interaction Coding System [*Psychology*]
DPIE......... Department of Primary Industries and Energy [*Australia*]
DPIF.......... Drug Product Information File [*American Society of Hospital Pharmacists*] [*Information service or system*]   (IID)
DPII.......... Dairy Products Improvement Institute   (EA)
DPIO......... District Public Information Office [*or Officer*] [*Navy*]
DPIP......... Dichlorophenolindophenol [*Also, DCIP, DCPI, DCPIP*] [*Analytical reagent*]
DPIR......... Data Processing and Information Retrieval   (DIT)
DPIS......... Differential Pressure Isolation Switch   (IEEE)
DPIS......... Duoplasmation Ion Source
DPISPS ..... Department of Primary Industries [*Queensland*] Stock Permit System [*Australia*]   (ADA)
DPIUSA .... Disabled Peoples' International USA   (EA)
DPK .... Deer Park, NY [*Location identifier*] [*FAA*]   (FAAL)
DPK .... Delta Psi Kappa [*Society*]
DPK .... Democratic Party of Kurdistan [*Al-Hizb ad-Dimuqraati al-Kurid*] [*Iraq*] [*Political party*]   (PPW)
DPK .... Driscoll Play Kit [*Psychological testing*]
DPKG........ Data Packaging Corp. [*NASDAQ symbol*]   (NQ)
DP & L....... Dallas Power & Light Co.
DPL .... Data Processing Language
DPL .... De Proprietatibus Litterarum [*A publication*]
DPL .... Denver Public Library, Denver, CO [*OCLC symbol*]   (OCLC)
DPL .... Deploy   (AABC)
DPL .... Descriptor Privilege Level [*Data processing*]   (BYTE)
DPL .... Detroit Public Library
DPL .... Development Prototype Launcher
DPL .... Diagonal Proof Line [*Technical drawings*]
DPL .... Dipalmitoyl Lecithin [*Biochemistry*]
DPL .... Diploma   (ROG)
DPL .... Dipole   (KSC)
DPL .... Dipolog [*Philippines*] [*Airport symbol*]   (OAG)
DPL .... Distopulpolingual [*Dentistry*]
DPL .... Distribution Plot List
DPL .... Doctor of Patent Law
DPL .... Double [*or Dual*] Propellant Loading   (AFM)
DPL .... DPL, Inc. [*Formerly, Dayton Power & Light Co.*] [*NYSE symbol*]   (SPSG)
DPL .... Dual Propellant Loading
DPL .... Dunlop's Parochial Law [*A publication*]   (DLA)
DPL .... Dynex Petroleum Ltd. [*Toronto Stock Exchange symbol*]

DPL .... Kenansville, NC [*Location identifier*] [*FAA*]   (FAAL)
DPLa......... Distopulpolabial [*Dentistry*]
DPLCS ..... Digital Propellant Level Control System   (KSC)
DPLF......... Data [*or Digital*] Phone Line Formatter
DPLG .... Day Plane Guard [*Military*]   (NVT)
DPLL......... Digital Phase-Locked Loop [*Space communication*]
DPLM .... Domestic Public Land Mobile [*Telecommunications*]   (TEL)
DPLM .... Dual Pulse LASER Microwelder
DPLN .... Diffuse Proliferative Lupus Nephritis [*Medicine*]
DPLO .... District Postal Liaison Officer [*Navy*]
D in 2PLO ... Detur in Duplo [*Let Twice as Much Be Given*] [*Pharmacy*]   (ROG)
DPLOA ..... Draft Proposed Letter of Agreement
DPLR......... De Paul Law Review [*A publication*]
DPLR......... Doppler   (MCD)
D-PlS .... Diplomate, American Board of Plastic Surgery   (DHSM)
DPLXR ..... Duplexer   (MSA)
DPLY......... Deploy   (KSC)
DPM .... Data Preparation and Maintenance   (CAAL)
DPM .... Data Processing Machine   (AAG)
DPM .... Data Processing Manager
DPM .... Decays per Minute [*Radiochemistry*]
DPM .... Defense Program Memorandum   (AABC)
DPM .... Deflectable Photomultiplier
DPM .... Delhi Pacific Resources Ltd. [*Toronto Stock Exchange symbol*]
DPM .... Department Personnel Manual
DPM .... Depot Paymaster [*Military*] [*British*]   (ROG)
DPM .... Deputy Prime Minister [*British*]
DPM .... Deputy Project Manager
DPM .... Deputy Provost Marshal [*British*]
DPM .... Designated Project Manager
DPM .... Designated for Prompt Mobilization
DPM .... Development Planning Memo   (MCD)
DPM .... Development Program Manuals   (AFIT)
DPM .... Diaminopimelic Acid [*Also, DAP, DAPA*] [*An amino acid*]
DPM .... Dichroic Parametric Mirror
DPM .... Diesel Particulate Matter [*Environmental chemistry*]
DPM .... Digital Panel Meter [*Data processing*]
DPM .... Digital Plotter Map [*Military*] [*British*]
DPM .... Diploma in Psychological Medicine [*British*]
DPM .... Direct Procurement Method [*Personal property*]
DPM .... Discontinue Previous Medication [*Pharmacology*]
DPM .... Disintegrations per Minute
DPM .... Disruptive Pattern Material [*British military*]   (DMA)
DPM .... Doctor of Physical Medicine
DPM .... Doctor of Podiatric Medicine
DPM .... Doctor of Preventative Medicine
DPM .... Doctor of Psychiatric Medicine
DPM .... Documents per Minute [*Data processing*]   (BUR)
DPM .... Downtown People Mover
DPM .... Draft Presidential Memorandum [*DoD*]
DPM .... Drafting Practice Manual
DPM .... Dried Poultry Manure
DPM .... Dual Port Memory [*Data processing*]   (MCD)
DPM .... Dual Purpose Missile   (KSC)
DPM .... Dynamic Pressure Measurements
DPMA .... Data Processing Management Association   (EA)
DPMA .... Dictionary of Physics and Mathematics Abbreviations, Signs, and Symbols [*A publication*]
DPMA .... Distributive Principle of Multiplication over Addition [*Mathematics*]
DPMA .... Dummy Part Master   (MCD)
DPMAA .... Data Processing Magazine [*A publication*]
DPMAS..... Driver Performance Measurement and Analysis System   (MCD)
DPMC....... Defense Procurement Management Course [*DoD*]
DPMC....... Deli/Prepared Meats Committee   (EA)
DPMC....... Director of Personnel, Marine Corps
DPMC....... Dual Port Memory Control [*Data processing*]
DPMH....... Direct Productive Man-Hours   (AFIT)
DPMIAC... Defense Pest Management Information Analysis Center [*DoD*] [*Washington, DC*] [*Database*]
DPML .... Deputy Program Manager for Logistics   (AFIT)
DPMM ...... Dew Point Moisture Monitors [*Nuclear energy*]   (NRCH)
DPMM ...... Division of Production and Materials Management [*Energy Research and Development Administration*]
DPMO .... Defense Program Management Office [*DoD*]
DPMOAP ... National Society of Electronic Data Processing Machine Operators and Programmers [*Inactive*]
DPMP .... Depot Plant Modernization Plan [*Army*]
D-PMR...... Diplomate, American Board of Physical Medicine and Rehabilitation   (DHSM)
DPMR .... District Postmaster [*British*]   (DCTA)
DPMS........ Data Project Management System   (IEEE)
DPMS........ Departmental Property Management System
DPM/S..... Disintegrations per Minute/Second   (DEN)
DPN........... Diamond Pyramid Hardness Number
DPN .... Diphosphopyridine Nucleotide [*Also, ARPPRN, NAD*] [*Biochemistry*]
D-PN.......... Diplomate, American Board of Psychiatry and Neurology   (DHSM)

DPN..........	Dipropylnitrosamine [*Also, DPNA, NDPA*] [*Organic chemistry*]
DPNA.......	Dipropylnitrosamine [*Also, DPN, NDPA*] [*Organic chemistry*]
DPNase......	Diphosphopyridine Nucleotide Glycohydrolase [*Also, NaDase*] [*An enzyme*]
DPNC.......	Democratic Party of Nigeria and the Cameroons
DPNE.......	Division of Peaceful Nuclear Explosives [*AEC*]
DPNG.......	Deepening (FAAC)
DPNH.......	Diphosphopyridine Nucleotide, Reduced Form [*Biochemistry*]
DPNL.......	Distribution Panel
DPNR.......	Deproteinized Natural Rubber
DPO.......	Data Processing Operation
DPO.......	Defense Program Operation (AAG)
DPO.......	Delayed Pulse Oscillator
DPO.......	Demokratische Partei Oesterreichs [*Democratic Party of Austria*] (PPE)
DPO.......	Departure Prohibition Order [*Australia*]
DPO.......	Deployable Payloads Projects Office [*Kennedy Space Center*] [*NASA*] (NASA)
DPO.......	Depot (MCD)
DPO.......	Depot Property Officer
DPO.......	Deputy Principal Officer [*Foreign Service*]
DPO.......	Development Planning Objective
DPO.......	Development Project Officer (MCD)
DPO.......	Devonport [*Tasmania*] [*Australia*] [*Airport symbol*] (OAG)
DPO.......	Dial Pulse Originating [*Telecommunications*] (TEL)
DPO.......	Digital Processing Oscilloscope (MCD)
DPO.......	Diphenyl Oxide [*Organic chemistry*]
DPO.......	Diphenyloxazole [*Organic chemistry*]
DPO.......	Direct Purchasing Organisation [*Commercial firm*] [*British*]
DPO.......	Director, Planning and Operations (MCD)
DPO.......	Directory of Post Office (AFM)
DPO.......	Discontinued Post Office [*Deltiology*]
DPO.......	Distributing Post Office
DPO.......	District Personnel Office [*or Officer*] [*Navy*]
DPO.......	District Postal Office [*or Officer*] [*Navy*]
dpo.......	Dividend Payout Ratio [*Stock exchange term*]
DPO.......	Divisional Pests Officer [*Ministry of Agriculture, Fisheries, and Food*] [*British*]
DPO.......	Double Pulse Operation
DPO.......	Dripproof Open
DPO.......	Drop Out (KSC)
DPO.......	DSA [*Defense Supply Agency*] Planning Objective
DPO.......	Placid Oil Co., Exploration Library, Dallas, TX [*OCLC symbol*] (OCLC)
DPO.......	United States Postal Service, Washington, DC [*Library symbol*] [*Library of Congress*] (LCLS)
DPOA.......	Dissatisfied Peugeot Owners of America (EA)
DPOB.......	Date and Place of Birth
DPOC.......	Base de Documentos en Politica Criminal [*Criminal Law Documents Data Base*] [*United Nations Latin American Institute for Crime Prevention and Treatment of Offenders*] (IID)
DPOC.......	Dynamic Processor Overload Control [*Telephone technology*]
DPOD.......	DSA [*Defense Supply Agency*] Objective Document
DPODP.......	Double-Precision Orbit Determination Program [*NASA*]
DPOI.......	Delay-On-Pull-In
DPOIR.......	Dial Pulse Originating Incoming Register [*Telecommunications*]
DPOL.......	Political Directorate [*Allied German Occupation Forces*]
D Pol Sc....	Doctor of Political Science
DPopC.......	Population Crisis Committee, Washington, DC [*Library symbol*] [*Library of Congress*] (LCLS)
DPopI.......	Population Institute, Washington, DC [*Library symbol*] [*Library of Congress*] (LCLS)
DPopR.......	Population Reference Bureau, Washington, DC [*Library symbol*] [*Library of Congress*] (LCLS)
DPOS.......	District Planning Officers Society [*British*]
DPO-SA....	Development Project Office for Selected Ammunition [*Army*] (RDA)
DPOW.......	Prisoners of War and Displaced Persons Directorate [*Allied German Occupation Forces*]
DPOWA....	Distributive, Processing, and Office Workers Union of America
DPP.......	Dairy Produce Packers Ltd. [*British*]
DPP.......	Data Project Plan (AFIT)
DPP.......	Date of Prescribed Period [*Social Security Administration*] (OICC)
DPP.......	Days Postpollination [*Botany*]
DPP.......	Decentralized Printing Program [*Army*]
DPP.......	Decision Process Pattern (RDA)
DPP.......	Deep Pseudopupil [*Optical effect*]
DPP.......	Defense Procurement Program [*DoD*]
DPP.......	Deferred Payment Plan [*Banking, finance*]
DPP.......	Delayed Procurement Program
DPP.......	Delegate Production Policy (MCD)
DPP.......	Democratic Progressive Party [*Taiwan*] [*Political party*]
DPP.......	Democratic Progressive Party [*Transkei*] [*Political party*] (PPW)
DPP.......	Deployment Pointing Panels (NASA)
DPP.......	Detailed Project Plan
DPP.......	Development Program Plan

DPP.......	Diepdaume Mines [*Vancouver Stock Exchange symbol*]
DPP.......	Differential Pulse Polarography [*Analytical chemistry*]
DPP.......	Digital Parallel Processor
DPP.......	Diphenyl Phthalate [*Organic chemistry*]
DPP.......	Diphloretin Phosphate [*Biochemistry*]
DPP.......	Diphtheria Pertussis Prophylactic [*Medicine*]
DPP.......	Diploma in Plant Pathology (ADA)
DPP.......	Direct Product Profitability [*Analysis*]
DPP.......	Director of Personnel Planning [*Air Force*]
DP & P.......	Director of Plans and Programs [*Army*] (RDA)
DPP.......	Director of Procurement and Production [*Army*]
DPP.......	Director of Public Prosecutions [*British*]
DPP.......	Display Processor Program (MCD)
DPP.......	Disposable Plotter Pen [*Koh-I-Noor Rapidograph, Inc.*]
DPP.......	Distributed Phase Plate [*LASER technology*]
DPP.......	Division of Personnel Preparation [*Department of Education*]
DPP.......	Division of Polar Programs [*National Science Foundation*] [*Information service or system*] (IID)
DPP.......	Drip Pan Pot [*of closed-loop ex-vessel machine*] [*Nuclear energy*] (NRCH)
DPP.......	Dripproof Protected
DPP.......	Dry Photo Process
DPP.......	Duplicating Pattern Production (MCD)
DPPA.......	Diphenylphosphoryl Azide [*Organic chemistry*]
DPPA.......	Double Pumped Parametric Amplifier
DPPB.......	Disaster Preparedness Planning Board (AFM)
DPPC.......	Data Processing Products Contract
DPPC.......	Defense Planning and Programming Catalog (MCD)
DPPC.......	Defense Planning Programming Category
DPPC.......	Developmental Potential of Preschool Children [*Psychology*]
DPPC.......	Dipalmitoyl Phosphatidylcholine [*Biochemistry*]
DPPC.......	Diphenyl Phosphorochloridate [*or Diphenylphosphoric Acid Monochloride*] [*Organic chemistry*]
DPPD.......	Diphenylphenylenediamine [*Organic chemistry*]
DPPE.......	Data Processing Project Engineer
DPPE.......	Dipalmitoyl Phosphatidylethanolamine [*Biochemistry*]
DPPG.......	Defense Planning and Programming Guidance
DPPG.......	Defense Policy Planning Guidance (NVT)
DPPH.......	Diphenylpicrylhydrazyl [*Analytical chemistry*]
DPPNGL.....	Data Papers in Papua New Guinea Languages [*A publication*]
DPPNGS...	Douglas Point Project Nuclear Generating Station (NRCH)
DPPO.......	Deepwater Ports Project Office [*Marine science*] (MSC)
DPPO.......	Direct Procurement Petty Officer
DPPO.......	District Publications and Printing Office
DPPSA.......	Directory of Published Proceedings [*United States*] [*A publication*]
DPPSO.......	Data Processing Programming Support Office [*Military*]
DPPT.......	Director of Personnel Procurement and Training [*Air Force*]
DPPX.......	Distributed Processing Programming Executive Base [*IBM Corp.*]
DPQ.......	Defense Planning Questionnaire (MCD)
DPQ.......	Defense Position Questionnaire (MCD)
DPQ.......	Double-Precision Quantity
DPQCA.......	Dairy Products Quality Checked Association (EA)
DPQMR....	Draft Proposal Qualitative Materiel Requirement
DPQS.......	Draw-a-Person Quality Scale [*Psychology*]
D Pr.......	Darling. Practice of the Scotch Court of Session [*A publication*] (DLA)
DPR.......	Data Processing Request
DPR.......	Data Protection Registrar [*British*]
DPR.......	Decisiones de Puerto Rico [*A publication*] (DLA)
DPR.......	Defect Prevention Reports
DPR.......	Definition Phase Review (NASA)
DPR.......	Degrees per Revolution
DPR.......	Demonstration Power Reactor (NRCH)
DPR.......	Department Performance Rating
DPR.......	Department of Physical Research [*British*]
DPR.......	Deployment Position RADAR (MCD)
DPR.......	Depolymerized Rubber
DPR.......	Development Planning Reports (MCD)
DPR.......	Diaminopropanoic Acid [*An amino acid*]
DPR.......	Diazo Print
DPR.......	Dihydropyridine [*Organic chemistry*]
DPR.......	Director of Public Relations
DPR.......	Disabled Persons Railcard [*British*]
DPr.......	Discourse Processes [*A publication*]
DPR.......	Dispenser [*Technical drawings*]
DPR.......	District Probate Registry
DPR.......	Division of Physical Research [*Energy Research and Development Administration*]
DPR.......	Domestic Policy Review
DPR.......	Double Pulse Ranging (NG)
DPR.......	Drogue Parachute Deployment
DPR.......	Dual Pen Recorder
DPR.......	Dundee-Palliser Resources, Inc. [*Toronto Stock Exchange symbol*]
DPR.......	Dupree, SD [*Location identifier*] [*FAA*] (FAAL)
DPR.......	Economic Progress Report [*A publication*]
DPR.......	Puerto Rico Reports, Spanish Edition [*A publication*] (DLA)
D PR.......	United States District Court for the District of Puerto Rico (DLA)

DPRAC...... Delft Progress Report. Series A. Chemistry and Physics, Chemical and Physical Engineering [*A publication*]
DPRBA...... Delft Progress Report. Series B. Electrical, Electronic, and Information Engineering [*A publication*]
DPRC........ Defence Policy and Requirements Committee [*British military*] (DMA)
DPRC........ Defense Program Review Committee [*Military*] (CAAL)
DPRCB...... Delft Progress Report. Series C. Mechanical and Aeronautical Engineering and Shipbuilding [*A publication*]
DPRED...... Delft Progress Report [*A publication*]
DPREP....... Disk Preparation Processor [*Data processing*]
DPRF........ Drug Product Reference File [*US Public Health Service*] [*Information service or system*] (IID)
DPRF........ Dual Pulse Ranging Fuse
DPRM........ Diploma of Physical and Rehabilitation Medicine (ADA)
D-PrM .... Diplomate, American Board of Preventive Medicine (DHSM)
DPR(N)...... Directorate of Public Relations (Naval) [*British*]
DPRO........ Digital Projection Readout (CAAL)
DPRO........ District Public Relations Office [*or Officer*] [*Navy*]
DPROC ..... Draft Proposed Required Operational Capability (MCD)
DProGM.... Deputy Provincial Grand Master [*Freemasonry*]
DPRORM ... Drafting, Pay and Records Office, Royal Marines [*British*]
D PROV GM ... Deputy Provincial Grand Master [*Freemasonry*] (ROG)
DPRP........ Dripproof and Ratproof
DPRPB....... Delft Progress Report. Series A-F [*A publication*]
DPRS........ Default Proof Credit Card System, Inc. [*NASDAQ symbol*] (NQ)
DPRS........ Dynamic Preferential Runway System [*Aviation*]
DPRSD....... Depressed
DPRT........ Depart (AABC)
DPRT........ Drawing Parts Release Ticket (MCD)
DPRX........ Direct Pharmaceutical Corp. [*NASDAQ symbol*] (NQ)
DPS............ Data Package Set (CAAL)
DP(S)........ Data Packet (Subsystem) [*Telecommunications*] (TEL)
DPS............ Data Present Signal
DPS............ Data Processing Services Co. [*Information service or system*] (IID)
DPS............ Data Processing and Software (NASA)
DP & S .... Data Processing and Software (NASA)
DPS............ Data Processing Software System (NASA)
DPS............ Data Processing Standards [*NASA*] (KSC)
DPS............ Data-Processing Station
DPS............ Data Processing System [*or Subsystem*]
DPS............ Decision Package Sets
DPS............ Decision Program Set
DPS............ Dedicated Printer Share [*AC DataLink*] [*Data processing*]
DPS............ Deep Passive Sensors (MCD)
DPS............ Defence Policy Staff [*British*]
DPS............ Defense Planning Staff [*Military*] (AABC)
DPS............ Defense Printing Service
DPS............ Defense Priorities System [*DoD*]
DPS............ Degrees per Second
DPS............ Delayed Printer Simulator
DPS............ Delegate Production System (MCD)
DPS............ Demokratische Partei Saar [*Democratic Party of the Saar*] [*Federal Republic of Germany*] (PPE)
DPS............ Denison & Pacific Suburban Railway Co. [*AAR code*]
DPS............ Denpasar [*Indonesia*] [*Airport symbol*] (OAG)
DPS............ Dentures for Pensioners Scheme [*Australia*]
DPS............ Descent Power System [*NASA*]
D & PS .... Design and Performance Specification (MCD)
DPS............ Design and Procedure Standard [*NASA*]
DPS............ Destainer Power Supply [*Electrophoresis*]
DPS............ Development and Proof Services [*Aberdeen Proving Ground, MD*] (MCD)
DPS............ Developments in Petroleum Science [*Elsevier Book Series*] [*A publication*]
DPS............ Dewan Pengurus Sementara [*Provisional Management Board Section*] [*Indonesia*]
DPS............ Dialectic Problem Solver
DPS............ Different Premises Subscriber [*Telecommunications*] (TEL)
DPS............ Differential Power Switch
DPS............ Digital Phase Shifter
DPS............ Digital Plotter System
DPS............ Digital Power Supply
DPS............ Diode Phase Shifter
DPS............ Diphenyl Sulfone [*Organic chemistry*]
DPS............ Diphenylstilbene [*Organic chemistry*]
DPS............ Director of Personal Services [*Navy*] [*British*]
DPS............ Director of Postal Services [*British*]
D of PS...... Director of Public Service
DPS............ Disintegrations per Second
DPS............ Disk Programming System [*IBM Corp.*] (IEEE)
DPS............ Display Power Supply
DPS............ Distributed Presentation Services [*IBM Corp.*]
DPS............ Distributed Processing System [*Honeywell, Inc.*]
DPS............ Dividend per Share [*Investment term*] (ADA)
DPS............ Division Primary Standards (AAG)
DPS............ Doctor of Political Science
D Ps .... Doctor of Psychology
DPS............ Doctor of Public Service

DPS............ Document Processing System [*IBM Corp.*] [*Data processing*]
D & PS....... Dog and Pony Show
DPS............ Dripproof Semienclosed
DPS............ Dual Porosity Sinter
DPS............ Dynamic Philatelic Society
DPSA......... Dartmoor Pony Society of America (EA)
DPSA......... Data Processing Supplies Association [*Later, IOSA*] (MCD)
DPSA......... Deep Penetration Strike Aircraft
DPSA......... Deputy Public Service Arbitrator [*Australia*]
DPSA......... Diploma in Public and Social Administration (ADA)
DPSA......... Distinguished Public Service Award (MUGU)
DPSA......... Doctor of Public School Art
DPSA......... Seaman Apprentice, Data Processing Technician, Striker [*Navy rating*]
DPSB......... Defence Production Supply Board [*NATO*] (NATG)
DPSBad ..... Distinguished Pistol Shot Badge [*Military decoration*] (AABC)
DPSC......... Data Processing Service Center
DPSC......... Defense Personnel Support Center (AFM)
DPSC......... Defense Petroleum Supply Center
DPSC......... Detainees' Parents Support Committee [*South Africa*] (ECON)
DP Sc .... Doctor of Political Science
DPSC......... Double Paper, Single Cotton [*Wire insulation*] (AAG)
DPSD........ Dew Point Sensing Device
DPSD........ Dimensionless Power Spectral Density
DPSDR...... Douglas Process Standard Development Record [*DAC*]
DPSH........ Direct Product Standard Hours (AFIT)
DPSK........ Differential Phase Shift Keying
DPSM........ Diode Phase Shifter Module
DPSM........ Doctor of Public School Music
DPSN .... Seaman, Data Processing Technician, Striker [*Navy rating*]
DPSO........ Data Processing Systems Office [*Picatinny Arsenal, NJ*]
DPSO........ Defense Projects Support Office [*NASA*]
DPSP......... Diffuse Process Such as Pericarditis [*Cardiology*]
DPSPT....... Combat Consumption Support from D-Day to P-Day [*Military*] (AABC)
DPSR......... Data Processing Service Request (NVT)
DPSS......... Data Processing and Services Subsystem (NOAA)
DP & SS..... Data Processing and Software Subsystem (NASA)
DPSS......... Data Processing Subsystem
DPSS .... Data Processing Switching System [*Space Flight Operations Facility, NASA*]
DPSS .... Data Processing System Simulator (IEEE)
DPSS .... Deep Passive Sonobuoy System (MCD)
DPSS .... Department of Public Social Services
DPSS .... Director of Printing and Stationery Services [*Military*] [*British*]
DPsSc .... Doctor of Psychological Science (ADA)
DPSSO ...... DSA [*Defense Supply Agency*] Performance Standards Support Office
DPST......... Denver Post [*A publication*]
DPST......... Deposit
DPST......... Double Pole, Single Throw [*Switch*]
D Ps Th...... Doctor of Psycho-Therapy
DPSTK ...... Dipstick
DPSTSW.... Double-Pole, Single-Throw Switch
DPSW........ Differential Pressure Seawater
DPSW........ Double-Pole Switch
D Psych ...... Diploma in Psychiatry [*British*]
DPT .... Datapoint Corp. [*NYSE symbol*] (SPSG)
DPT .... Dedicated Planning Terminal (CAAL)
DPT .... Deep Pressure Touch
DPT .... Demerol-Phenergan-Thorazine [*Drug regime*]
DPT .... Depart
DPT .... Department
DPT .... Departure Control (MUGU)
DPT .... Deponent
DPT .... Deposit (ADA)
DPT .... Depot
DPT .... Depth
Dpt .... Dermatophagoides pteronyssinus [*House dust*]
DPT .... Descent Performance Test
DPT .... Design Proof Tests
DPT .... Development Project Team (MCD)
DPT .... Development Prototype (NG)
DPT .... Dew-Point Temperature [*Measure of humidity*]
DPT .... Dew Point Tester
DPT .... Diagnostic Prescriptive Teacher [*or Teaching*]
DPT .... Dial Pulse Terminating [*Telecommunications*] (TEL)
DPT .... Different Premises Telephone Number [*Telecommunications*] (TEL)
DPT .... Differential Pressure Transducer
DPT .... Digital Picture Terminal (NOAA)
DPT .... Digital Pressure Transducer
DPT .... Diphenyltrichloroethane [*Also, DPE*] [*Organic chemistry*]
DPT .... Diphosphothiamine [*Also, TDP, TPP*] [*Biochemistry*]
DPT .... Diphtheria, Pertussis, and Tetanus [*Also, DTP*] [*Immunology*]
DPT .... Diploma of Physio-Therapy [*British*]
DPT .... Dipropyltryptamine [*Hallucinogenic agent*]
D/P & T ..... Director of Personnel and Training [*Army*]
DPT .... Director of Plans and Training [*Military*] (AABC)
DPT .... Director, Polaris Technical [*Missiles*]
DPT .... Dissatisfied Parents Together (EA)

DPT .... Distributed Processing Technology [*Data processing*]
DPT .... Dripproof Totally Enclosed
DPT .... Dummy Part (MCD)
DPTA .... Diaminopropanoltetraacetic Acid [*Also, DTA, DHPTA*] [*Organic chemistry*]
dPTC.......... Dispersed Human Parathyroid Cell [*Clinical chemistry*]
DPTDR...... Draft Proposed Training Device Requirement (MCD)
DPTH .... Depth (FAAC)
DPTH .... Dipentamethylenethiuram Hexasulfide [*Organic chemistry*]
DPTH .... Diphenylthiohydantoin [*Organic chemistry*]
DPTHDL... Developmental Pharmacology and Therapeutics [*A publication*]
DPTM .... Director of Plans, Training, and Mobilization [*DoD*]
DPTO .... District Property Transportation Office [*or Officer*] [*Navy*]
DPTOE...... Draft Plan Table of Organization and Equipment (MCD)
DPTR........ Data Pointer [*Computer memory*]
DPTRAJ... Double-Precision Trajectory Program [*NASA*]
DPTRK...... Dumptruck (AABC)
DPTS......... Director of Physical Training and Sports [*Navy*] [*British*]
DPTSI .... Design Professions Technical Specialty Index [*National Society of Professional Engineers*] [*Information service or system*] (IID)
DPTT......... Double Pole, Triple Throw [*Switch*]
DPTW .... Desk, Double-Pedestal Typewriter
DPTY......... Deputy
DPU .... Data Path Unit [*Data processing*]
DPU .... Data Processing Unit
DPU .... Demand Processing Unit [*Military*]
DPU .... Design Proof Unit (KSC)
DPU .... Digital Patch Unit
DPU .... Digital Processing Unit
DPU .... Disk Pack Unit [*Data processing*]
DPU .... Driver Propulsion Unit
DPU .... Du Pont, Americus (Unit) [*AMEX symbol*] (SPSG)
DPU........... Organization of American States, Washington, DC [*Library symbol*] [*Library of Congress*] [*Obsolete*] (LCLS)
D Pub Adm ... Doctor of Public Administration
DP-UDC.... Democracia Popular - Union Democrata Cristiana [*People's Democracy - Christian Democratic Union*] [*Ecuador*] [*Political party*] (PPW)
DPUO........ Duty Directed Is Being Performed for Unit Issuing Order
DPV .... Design Point Vehicle
DPV .... Deutscher Verein zur Erforschung Palaestinas [*A publication*] (BJA)
DPV .... Differential Pulse Voltammetry [*Analytical chemistry*]
DPV .... Diffuse and Perivascular [*Medicine*]
DPV .... Dockside Proofing Vehicle
DPV .... Doppler Predict Voltage
DPV .... Dry Pipe Valve
DPV .... Duty Paid Value [*Business term*]
DPW .... Davis Polk & Wardwell, Library, New York, NY [*OCLC symbol*] (OCLC)
DPW .... Department of Public Welfare
DPW .... Department of Public Works
DPW .... Director of Prisoners of War [*British*] [*World War II*]
DPWG .... Defence Planning Working Group [*of Defense Ministers*] [*NATO*] (NATG)
DPWM ...... Double-Sided Pulse-Width Modulation [*Telecommunications*]
DPWO...... District Public Works Office
DPWP........ Director of Planning of War Production [*Air Ministry*] [*British*] [*World War II*]
DPWR .... Data Process Work Request (AAG)
DPWR .... Datapower, Inc. [*NASDAQ symbol*] (NQ)
DPWS........ Dual Purpose Weapon System
DPX .... Diethyl(phenyl)xanthine [*Organic chemistry*]
DPX .... Displaced Persons Executive [*Allied Military Government detachments, Red Cross teams, and UN Relief and Rehabilitation Administration Corps*] [*Post-World War II*]
DPX .... Duplex (ADA)
DPX .... Duplex Products, Inc. [*AMEX symbol*] (SPSG)
DPY .... Deploy (NASA)
DPZ .... Dale-Parizeau, Inc. [*Toronto Stock Exchange symbol*]
DQ .... Carib West Airways [*Barbados*] [*ICAO designator*] (FAAC)
DQ .... Deep Quest
DQ .... Definite Quantity (AFM)
DQ .... Deleted Quality Review Transaction [*IRS*]
DQ .... Denver Quarterly [*A publication*]
DQ .... Design Qualification (MCD)
DQ .... Design Quarterly [*A publication*]
DQ .... Destination Queues [*Data processing*] (MDG)
DQ .... Detention Quarters [*British*]
DQ .... Deterioration Quotient [*Medicine*]
DQ .... Development Quotient
DQ .... Direct Question [*Legal testimony*]
D of Q........ Director of Quartering [*British military*] (DMA)
DQ .... Directory Enquiry Service [*Telecommunications*] (TEL)
DQ .... Disqualified
dq .... Dominica [*MARC country of publication code*] [*Library of Congress*] (LCCP)
DQ .... Dornier GmbH [*West Germany*] [*ICAO designator*] (FAAC)

D-Q .... Drocourt-Queant Line [*World War I*] [*Canada*]
DQA .... Dairy Quality Assurance [*Australia*]
DQA .... Design Quality Assurance [*Telecommunications*] (TEL)
DQA .... Directorate of Quality Assurance [*Australia*]
DQA........... D'Or Val Mines Ltd. [*Toronto Stock Exchange symbol*] [*Vancouver Stock Exchange symbol*]
DQA........... Drawing Quality Audit (MCD)
DQAB........ Defence Quality Assurance Board [*British*] (RDA)
DQADO .... DCAS [*Defense Contract Administration Services*] Quality Assurance Staff Development Office
DQC........... Data Quality Control
DQC........... Definite Quantity Control
D-QC......... Drug-Quaternary Carrier [*Biochemistry*]
DQC........... Dynamic Quality Control
DQCM....... Data Quality Control Monitor
DQD .... Digital Quadrature Detection [*Instrumentation*]
DQE .... De Queen & Eastern Railroad Co. [*AAR code*]
DQE .... Detective Quantum Efficiency [*Photon device*]
DQE .... DQE, Inc. [*NYSE symbol*] (SPSG)
DQG .... Charlotte, NC [*Location identifier*] [*FAA*] (FAAL)
DQH .... Douglas, GA [*Location identifier*] [*FAA*] (FAAL)
DQM .... Data Quality Monitors (MDG)
DQM .... Depot Quartermaster [*Marine Corps*]
DQM .... Digital Quality Monitor
DQM .... Division Quartermaster
DQMG .... Deputy Quartermaster General
DQMS ...... Deputy Quartermaster-Sergeant [*British*]
DQN .... Depot Quartermaster, Norfolk, Virginia [*Marine Corps*]
DQN .... Diazonaphthoquinone-Sensitized Novolac [*Photoresist resin system*]
D of Q(N)... Directorate of Quartering (Navy) [*British*]
DQO .... Wilmington, DE [*Location identifier*] [*FAA*] (FAAL)
DQP.......... Depot Quartermaster, Philadelphia, Pennsylvania [*Marine Corps*]
DQP.......... Designated Qualified Person [*Department of Agriculture*]
DQP.......... Diode Qualification Program
DQPH........ Depot Quartermaster, Pearl Harbor, Hawaii [*Marine Corps*]
DQQ .... Depot Quartermaster, Quantico, Virginia [*Marine Corps*]
DQR .... Depot Quartermaster, Richmond, Virginia [*Marine Corps*]
DQR .... Design Qualification Requirement
DQR .... Dihydroquercetin Reductase [*An enzyme*]
DQR........... Dutch Quarterly Review of Anglo-American Letters [*A publication*]
DQS .... Index-Digest Quarterly System
DQSC .... Delta Queen Steamboat Company [*NASDAQ symbol*] (NQ)
DQSF........ Depot Quartermaster, San Francisco, California [*Marine Corps*]
DQSK .... Drawing Quality, Special-Killed [*Metallurgy*]
DQT .... Diode Qualification Test
DQTP .... Design Qualification Test Plan (MCD)
DQTP .... Diode Qualification Test Program
DQU .... Deganawidah-Quetzalcoatl University [*Initials preferred to spelled-out name*] [*California*]
DQU .... Dequincy, LA [*Location identifier*] [*FAA*] (FAAL)
DQU .... Duquesne Light Co. [*NYSE symbol*] [*Later, DQE*] (SPSG)
DQV .... Deckerville, MI [*Location identifier*] [*FAA*] (FAAL)
DR............. D-Related [*Antigen*] [*Immunology*]
DR............. Dacca Reports [*India*] [*A publication*] (DLA)
DR............. Dahlgren Rifle
DR.............. Daily Record [*Penny newspaper in "He Knew He Was Right" by Anthony Trollope*]
DR .... Daily Report
DR .... Daily Review
DR .... Dalhousie Review [*A publication*]
D-R .... Damp Rag [*Decontamination method*] [*Nuclear energy*] (NRCH)
DR .... Danish Reactor (NRCH)
DR............. Danmarks Retsforbund [*Justice Party of Denmark*] (PPE)
DR .... Dardanelle & Russellville Railroad Co. [*AAR code*]
DR .... Dark Red [*Philately*]
DR .... Darkroom [*Photography*]
DR .... Data Rate [*Telecommunications*] (TEL)
DR .... Data Receiver [*or Recorder*]
DR .... Data Reduction (KSC)
DR .... Data Register
DR .... Data Report
DR .... Data Request
DR .... Data Requirements [*NASA*]
D/R .... Database Reference [*A publication*]
DR .... Date of Rank [*Air Force*]
DR .... Daughter (ROG)
DR .... Daughters of the Revolution
DR .... De-Rating and Rating Appeals [*England and Scotland*] [*A publication*] (DLA)
DR .... Dead Reckoning [*Navigation*]
DR .... Dead Rise (DS)
DR .... Dear (ROG)
DR .... Death Rate
DR .... Death Row
DR............. Debit
DR.............. Debit Request
dr .... Debiteur [*Debtor*] [*French*]

DR............	Debtor
DR............	Decanus Ruralis [*Rural Dean*]
DR............	Decorator Remodeling [*A publication*]
DR............	Defence Regulation (DAS)
DR............	Defense [*or Disaster*] Readiness (OICC)
DR............	Defensive Response [*Psychology*]
DR............	Deficiency Report [*Air Force*] (AFM)
DR............	Degeneration Reaction
DR............	Degrees Rankine (KSC)
DR............	Delivery Rate [*DoD*]
DR............	Delivery Room [*Medicine*]
DR............	Demolition Rocket (NATG)
DR............	Density Report [*Army*]
DR............	Dental Recruit
DR............	Dependents Rate [*Air Force*] (AFM)
DR............	Deposit Receipt [*Banking*]
DR............	Deputy Remembrancer [*A publication*] (DLA)
DR............	Derrick (DS)
DR............	Design Requirement
DR............	Design Review (AAG)
DR............	Designator Register [*Data processing*]
DR............	Despatch Rider [*Military*] [*British*]
DR............	Destroyer Flag [*Navy*] [*British*]
DR............	Detailed Report
DR............	Detection RADAR
DR............	Deuteronomy Rabba (BJA)
DR............	Deutsche Reichsbahn [*German Democratic Republic Railway*] (DCTA)
DR............	Deutsche Reichspartei [*German National Party*] [*Federal Republic of Germany*] [*Political party*] (PPE)
DR............	Deutsche Rundschau [*A publication*]
DR............	Deutsches Recht [*German Law*] (ILCA)
DR............	Deutsches Reich [*German Empire*]
DR............	Development Report
DR............	Development-Right (MCD)
DR............	Deviation Range
DR............	Deviation Ratio
DR............	Devin Register [*An association*] (EA)
DR............	Diabetic Retinopathy [*Medicine*]
DR............	Diagnostic Radiology [*Medicine*]
DR............	Dial Real Estate Investment Trust [*NYSE symbol*] (SPSG)
DR............	Diesel Radial [*Aircraft engine*]
DR............	Dietary Restriction [*Medicine*]
DR............	Differential Rate
DR............	Differential Relay
DR............	Digital Radiography
DR............	Digital Rectal [*Proctoscopy*]
DR............	Digital Resolver
DR............	Dihydrotestosterone Receptor [*Endocrinology*]
DR............	Diliman Review [*A publication*]
DR............	Dining Room
DR............	Diploma in Radiology [*British*]
D-R............	Diplomate, American Board of Radiology (DHSM)
DR............	Direct Reading [*Spectroscopy*]
DR............	Direct Reduction [*Ironmaking process*]
DR............	Direct Repeat [*Genetics*]
D/R............	Direct/Reverse
DR............	Direct Route
D/R............	Directional Radio
DR............	Directive Antenna with Reflector
DR............	Director (ADA)
D of R........	Director of Remounts [*Military*] [*British*]
DR............	Disaster Representative [*Red Cross*]
DR............	Disc Ridge Splitting [*Agriculture*]
DR............	Discharging Resistor
DR............	Discount Rate [*Banking*]
DR............	Discrepancy Record [*or Report*] (KSC)
DR............	Discrete Register (MCD)
DR............	Discrimination RADAR
DR............	Discrimination Reversal [*Neurophysiology*]
DR............	Disk Recorder (DEN)
DR............	Dispatch Reliability (NASA)
D/R............	Dispatch Rider [*Marine Corps*]
DR............	Display Racks [*Freight*]
DR............	Display Result
DR............	Disposal Rate [*Of hormone metabolism*]
DR............	Disposition Record (NASA)
DR............	Dissociative Recombination [*Chemistry*]
DR............	Distant Range
D & R........	Distiller and Rectifier
DR............	Distribution Regulation [*Office of Price Stabilization*] (DLA)
DR............	Distribution Request
DR............	Distributor
DR............	District Railway [*London*]
DR............	District Registry
DR............	Division of Research [*Navy*]
DR............	Divisor [*Mathematics*]
DR............	DMR Group, Inc. [*Toronto Stock Exchange symbol*]
DR............	Dock Receipt
DR............	Doctor (EY)
DR............	Document Register (MCD)
DR............	Document Report
DR............	Dogger [*Ship's rigging*] (ROG)
DR............	Dollar [*Monetary unit*] (ROG)
dr............	Dominican Republic [*MARC country of publication code*] [*Library of Congress*] [*IYRU nationality code*] (LCCP)
DR............	Door
DR............	Dorsal Raphe [*Brain anatomy*]
DR............	Dorsal Root [*of spinal nerve*] [*Anatomy*]
DR............	Dose Ratio [*Medicine*]
DR............	Double Reduced [*Tinplate*]
Dr............	Double Reduction Gearing (DS)
DR............	Double Royal [*Paper*] (ADA)
D & R........	Dowling and Ryland's English King's Bench Reports [*A publication*] (DLA)
DR............	Down Right [*The front right portion of a stage*] [*A stage direction*]
D/R............	Downrange
DR............	Downside Review [*A publication*]
DR............	Drachma [*Monetary unit*] [*Greece*] (EY)
DR............	Draft
DR............	Draft Recommendation [*International Standards Organization*]
DR............	Draft Release (MCD)
DR............	Drafting Request (MSA)
DR............	Dragoon (ROG)
DR............	Drain (MSA)
DR............	Drake Law Review [*A publication*]
DR............	Dram
DR............	Drama (ADA)
DR............	Drama: The Quarterly Theatre Review [*A publication*]
DR............	Draped [*Numismatics*]
DR............	Draw Ratio [*Plastics technology*]
DR............	Drawer
DR............	Drawn (AABC)
DR............	Dress Rehearsal (MUGU)
DR............	Dressed [*Fish processing*]
DR............	Dresser
DR............	Dressing [*Medicine*]
Dr............	Drewry's English Vice Chancellors' Reports [*A publication*] (DLA)
DR............	Drift Rate
DR............	Drill (MSA)
DR............	Drill Regulations
DR............	Drill Rod
DR............	Drive [*or Driver*] (AFM)
DR............	Drum (MUGU)
DR............	Drum. Inuvik [*A publication*]
DR............	Drumworld [*A publication*]
Dr............	Drury's Irish Chancery Reports Tempore Napier [*1858-59*] [*A publication*] (DLA)
Dr............	Drury's Irish Chancery Reports Tempore Sugden [*A publication*] (DLA)
DR............	Dublin Review [*A publication*]
DR............	Dump Revenues [*Solid waste management*]
DR............	Dun's Review [*A publication*]
DR............	Duplicating Requisition (MCD)
DR............	Duquesne Review [*A publication*]
DR............	Dynamic Range
DR............	Increment of Response [*Psychology*]
Dr............	La Sainte Bible (1884) (Drioux) [*A publication*] (BJA)
DR............	Reaction of Degeneration [*Physiology*]
DR............	Robin Avions [*Pierre Robin*] [*France*] [*ICAO aircraft manufacturer identifier*] (ICAO)
DR............	Sociedade Brasileira de Turismo [*Brazil*] [*ICAO designator*] (FAAC)
DR & A.....	Data Reduction and Analysis
DRA...........	Data Reformatter Assembly
DR & A.....	Data Reporting and Accounting (AFM)
DR & A.....	Data Requirements and Analysis (MCD)
DRA...........	Data Research Associates, Inc. [*Information service or system*] (IID)
DRA...........	Data Resource Administrator
DRA...........	De-Rating Appeals [*England*] [*A publication*] (DLA)
DRA...........	Dead Reckoning Analyzer
DRA...........	Decision Risk Analysis [*Army*]
DRA...........	Defense [*or Disaster*] Relief Act (OICC)
DRA...........	Defense Reorganization Act
DRA...........	Dependent Relative Allowance (DLA)
DRA...........	Deputy Regional Administrator
DRA...........	Design Review Agreement (MCD)
DRA...........	Designated Responsible Activity (MCD)
DRA...........	Diagnosis-Rework Action (AAG)
DRA...........	Dielectric Rod Antenna
DRA...........	Diffuse Reflection Attachment [*Spectroscopy*]
DRA...........	Digital Read-In Assembly [*Data processing*]
DRA...........	Digital Recorder Analyzer [*Data processing*]
DRA...........	Direct Reckoning Analyzer (MUGU)
DRA...........	Directed Reading Activity [*Education*]
DRA...........	Director of Royal Artillery [*British*]

DRA.......... Discrete Recovery Area   (KSC)
DRA.......... DMR Group, Inc. Class A SV [*Toronto Stock Exchange symbol*]
DRA.......... Document Release Authorization   (KSC)
DRA.......... Doppler RADAR
Dra............ Draco [*Constellation*]
DRA.......... Drag Reducing Agent [*Petroleum pipeline transport*]
Dra............ Draper's Upper Canada King's Bench Reports [*A publication*]   (DLA)
dra............. Dravidian [*MARC language code*] [*Library of Congress*]   (LCCP)
DRA.......... Draw International Resources Corp. [*Formerly, Draw Resources Corp.*] [*Vancouver Stock Exchange symbol*]
DRA.......... Drawing Release Authorization
DRA.......... Drum-Read Amplifier [*Data processing*]   (CET)
DRA.......... Dude Ranchers' Association   (EA)
DRA.......... Mercury, NV [*Location identifier*] [*FAA*]   (FAAL)
DRA.......... Sandoz AG [*Germany*] [*Research code symbol*]
DRAAG..... Design Review and Acceptance Group [*Reviews nuclear weapon designs for DoD*]
DRA (BB & S) ... Decisions in Review and Appeal Cases (Basutoland, Bechuanaland, and Swaziland) [*A publication*]   (ILCA)
DRAC........ Defense Research Advisory Committee   (NATG)
DRAC........ Director of the Royal Armoured Corps [*British*]
DRAC........ Distributed Read Address Counter
DrAc.......... Doctor of Acupuncture [*British*]   (DBQ)
Drac.......... Draco [*Constellation*]
DRACO..... Dead Reckoning Automatic Computer [*Obsolete*]
DRAD........ Drill Adapter
Dr Ad......... Droit Administratif [*Administrative Law*] [*French*] [*A publication*]   (DLA)
D/RADEX ... Digitized RADAR Experiment
Dra Dow..... Draper on Dower [*A publication*]   (DLA)
DRADS...... Degradation of RADAR Defense System
DRAE .... Defence Research Analysis Establishment [*Canada*]
DRAE .... Diccionario de la Real Academia Espanola [*A publication*]
Dr Ae......... Doctor of Aviation
D Ra E .... Doctor of Radio Engineering
DRAEA ..... Draegerheft [*A publication*]
Draegerh.... Draegerheft. Mitteilungen der Draegerwerk AG Luebeck [*A publication*]
Draeger Rev ... Draeger Review [*West Germany*] [*A publication*]
D Ra Eng ... Doctor of Radio Engineering
Dr Ae S ...... Doctor of Aeronautical Science
Dr Ae Sc..... Doctor of Aeronautical Science
DRAFT...... Display Retrieval and Formatting Technique   (MCD)
DRAFT...... Document Read and Format Translator
Drag .... Dragonfly [*A publication*]
Dragns .... Dragoons [*Military unit*] [*British*]   (DMA)
Dragoco Ber (Engl Edn) ... Dragoco Berichte (English Edition) [*A publication*]
Dragoco Rep Engl Ed ... Dragoco Report. English Edition [*A publication*]
Dragoco Rep Ger Ed ... Dragoco Report. German Edition [*A publication*]
DRAGONAIR ... Hong Kong Dragon Airlines   (FEA)
Dr Agr........ Doctor of Agriculture
DRAI .... Dead Reckoning Analog [*or Analyzer*] Indicator
DRA/INED ... Development Research Associates, Inc., Institute for New Enterprise Development
Drake Att... Drake on Attachment [*A publication*]   (DLA)
Drake Attachm ... Drake on Attachment [*A publication*]   (DLA)
Drake Law R ... Drake Law Review [*A publication*]
Drake LR... Drake Law Review [*A publication*]
Drake L Rev ... Drake Law Review [*A publication*]
DRAM....... Detection RADAR Automatic Monitoring   (CET)
DRAM....... Drama   (ADA)
DRAM....... Dramatic
Dram.......... Drammaturgia [*A publication*]
DRAM....... Dynamic Random Access Mechanization
d-RAM...... Dynamic Random Access Memory [*Data processing*]
DRAMA .... Digital Radio and Multiplexer Acquisition   (MCD)
Drama R ... Drama Review [*A publication*]
Drama Rev ... Drama Review [*A publication*]
Drama Surv ... Drama Survey [*A publication*]
DramC ...... Drama Critique [*A publication*]
DRAMEDY ... Drama and Comedy [*Slice-of-life television show*]
DRAM PERS ... Dramatis Personae [*Characters of the Play*] [*Latin*]
DRAMS..... Digital Recording and Measuring System
DramS....... Drama Survey [*A publication*]
DRAN........ Dranetz Technologies, Inc. [*NASDAQ symbol*]   (NQ)
DRANS ..... Data Reduction and Analysis System
DRAO........ Dominion Radio Astrophysical Observatory [*Herzberg Institute of Astrophysics, National Research Council of Canada*] [*Research center*]   (RCD)
DRAP .... Deployment Readiness Assistance Program [*Military*]
DRAP .... Direct Reading Azimuth Protractor [*Bureau of Mines*]
DRAP .... Dram, Apothecary
DRAPE...... Data Recording and Processing Equipment
DRAPE...... Digital Recording and Playback Equipment   (MCD)
Draper........ Draper of Australasia [*A publication*]   (APTA)
Draper........ Draper's Upper Canada King's Bench Reports [*A publication*]   (DLA)

Draper (Can) ... Draper's Upper Canada King's Bench Reports [*A publication*]
Draper Fund Rep ... Draper Fund Report [*A publication*]
Draper Fund Rept ... Draper Fund Report [*A publication*]
Draper (Ont) ... Draper's Upper Canada King's Bench Reports [*A publication*]   (DLA)
Draper World Population Fund Rept ... Draper World Population Fund Report [*A publication*]
DRAS........ Django Reinhardt Appreciation Society [*Inactive*]   (EA)
DRASER ... Doppler RADAR and Storm Electricity Research Group [*Norman, OK*] [*Department of Commerce*]   (GRD)
DRAT .... Data Reduction Analysis Tape
DRAT .... Demonstration Reliability Acceptance Test
DRATE...... Difference of Rate
Dr Att......... Drake on Attachment [*A publication*]   (DLA)
DRAV....... Dram, Avoirdupois
DRAW....... Direct Read after Write [*Data processing*]
DRB .... Dartmouth College, Hanover, NH [*OCLC symbol*]   (OCLC)
DRB .... Data Review Board [*Military*]   (AFIT)
DRB .... Daunorubicin [*Daunomycin*] [*Also, D, DNR, R*] [*Antineoplastic drug*]
DRB .... Decade Resolver Bridge
DRB .... Decimal Register Binary
DRB .... Defence Research Board [*Canada*]
DRB .... Defense Resources Board
DRB .... Defense Review Board [*Aerospace*]
DRB .... Deficiency Review Board   (AFIT)
DRB .... Departmental Records Branch [*Military*]
DRB .... Derby [*Australia*] [*Airport symbol*]   (OAG)
DRB .... Design Requirements Baseline   (NASA)
DRB .... Design Review Board
DRB .... Deutsche Reichsbahn [*German State Railways*] [*Pre-1945*]
DRB .... Dichlororibofuranosylbenzimidazole [*Biochemistry*]
DRB .... Director. Journal of Business Leadership [*A publication*]
DRB .... Disability Retirement Branch [*BUPERS*]
DRB .... Discarding Rotating Band [*Military*]   (CAAL)
DRB .... Drainboard [*Technical drawings*]
DRB .... Dursunbey [*Turkey*] [*Seismograph station code, US Geological Survey*] [*Closed*]   (SEIS)
DRBA .... Dharma Realm Buddhist Association   (EA)
DRBC .... Delaware River Basin Commission [*Successor to INCODEL*]
DRBG .... Drill Bushing
DRBIA ...... Drill Bit [*A publication*]
Dr Bi Ch... Doctor of Biological Chemistry
Dr Bi Phy... Doctor of Biophysics
DrBl .... Dark Blend [*Philately*]
DrBusAdmin ... Doctor of Business Administration
DRC .... Damage Risk Contours
DRC .... Damage-Risk Criteria [*Tolerable limits for noise exposure*]
DRC .... Data Rate Changer
DRC .... Data Recording Camera
DRC .... Data Recording Controller [*Data processing*]   (BUR)
DRC .... Data Reduction Center [*or Complex*]
DRC .... Data Reduction Compiler [*or Computer*]   (MCD)
DRC .... Data Return Capsule [*or Container*]
DRC .... Defence Requirements Committee [*British military*]   (DMA)
DRC .... Defence Research Committee [*British*]
DRC .... Defence Review Committee [*NATO*]   (NATG)
DRC .... Deficit Reduction Coalition   (EA)
DRC .... Democratic Republic of China   (CINC)
DRC .... Democratic Republic of the Congo [*Later, Zaire*]
DRC .... Demographic Research Company, Inc. [*Information service or system*]   (IID)
DRC .... Deployment Readiness Condition [*Army*]   (AABC)
DRC .... Depot Repair Cycle   (MCD)
DRC .... Deputy Regional Commander
dr c .... Dernier Cours [*Closing Price*] [*French*]
DRC .... Design Research Center [*Carnegie-Mellon University*] [*Research center*]   (RCD)
DRC .... Design Rule Checker [*For integrated circuitry*]
DRC .... Diploma of the Royal College of Science and Technology, Glasgow [*British*]
DRC .... Direct-Reaction Calculation
DRC .... Disability Review Council [*Military*]   (AABC)
DRC .... Disability Rights Center   (EA)
DRC .... Disarmament Resource Center   (EA)
DRC .... Discoverer Recovery Capsule [*NASA*]
DRC .... Discrete Rate Command   (MCD)
DRC .... Distant Reading Compass
DRC .... District Recruiting Command [*Army*]   (AABC)
DRC .... Division of Rehabilitation Counseling [*of the APGA*]
DRC .... Document Record Card
DRC .... Documents Review Committee [*American Occupational Therapy Association*]
DRC .... Dolphin Research Center   (EA)
DRC .... Domaine de la Romanee-Conti [*French vintner*]
DRC .... Domestic Revenue Cost Coefficient [*Economics*]
DRC .... Donkey Red Cell[*s*]
DRC .... Dose Response Curve [*Medicine*]
DRC .... Drawing Record Card   (MCD)
DRC .... DRC Resources Corp. [*Vancouver Stock Exchange symbol*]

DRC........... DRCA Medical Corp. [*AMEX symbol*]   (SPSG)
DRC........... Dropped Rod Control [*Nuclear energy*]   (NRCH)
DRC........... Dry Rubber Content
DRC........... Dutch Reformed Church
DRC........... Dynamic Research Console
DRC........... Dynamics Research Corporation
Dr Can L...... Doctor of Canon Law
DRCCA...... Division of Resources, Centers, and Community Activities [*National Cancer Institute*]
DRCCC...... Defense Regional Communications Control Center
DRCCC-FE... Defense Regional Communications Control Center, Far East   (CINC)
DRCCC-SEA... Defense Regional Communications Control Center, Southeast Asia   (CINC)
DRCDE...... Development and Engineering Directorate [*Army*]   (RDA)
DRCDG...... Data Recording   (MSA)
Dr C Ec...... Droit Civil Ecclesiastique [*A publication*]   (DLA)
DR-CG....... Data Reduction and Computing Group [*Range Commanders Council*] [*NASA*]
DRCG......... Discrimination RADAR Control Group   (AAG)
DRCH....... Data Architects, Inc. [*NASDAQ symbol*]   (NQ)
DRCL........ Defence Research Chemical Laboratories [*Canada*]
DRCO......... Dynamics Research Corporation [*NASDAQ symbol*]   (NQ)
DRCOG...... Diploma of the Royal College of Obstetrics and Gynaecology [*British*]
Dr Com...... Doctor of Commerce
Dr Com...... Droit Commercial [*Commercial Law*] [*French*]   (DLA)
DrComSc... Doctor of Commercial Science
DRC Path.. Diploma of the Royal College of Pathologists [*British*]
DRCPE9....... Diabetes Research and Clinical Practice [*A publication*]
DRCPR....... Differential Reactive Current Project Relay
DR/CR...... Data Requirements/Change Request   (MCD)
Dr Cr Jus.... Doctor of Criminal Jurisprudence
DRCS......... Directorate of Reserve Component Support [*DoD*]
DRCS......... Distress Radio Call System [*Telecommunications*]   (TEL)
Dr CS......... Doctor of Commercial Science
DRCS......... Dynamically Redefinable Character Set [*Data processing*]
DRCSAB... Defence Research Centre, Salisbury, Administrative Branch [*Australia*]
DRCSMC.. Defence Research Centre, Salisbury, Management Committee [*Australia*]
DRCT........ Depot Repair Cycle Time
DRCT........ Direct   (AFM)
DRCTN...... Direction   (FAAC)
DRCTY...... Directly   (MSA)
DRCTY...... Directory   (AFM)
Dr Cul S...... Doctor of Cultural Science
Dr Cul Sc... Doctor of Cultural Science
DRCWDT... Colorado. Division of Wildlife. Division Report [*A publication*]
DR-CWG... Data Reduction and Computing Working Group [*Range Commanders Council*] [*NASA*]
DRD........... Data Recording Device [*Data processing*]   (BUR)
DRD........... Data Requirement Description [*NASA*]   (MCD)
DRD........... Data Requirements Document [*NASA*]   (NASA)
DRD........... Data Resources Directory Publications Subsystem [*Department of Energy*] [*Database*]
DRD........... Defence Research Directors [*NATO*]   (NATG)
DRD........... Deltawerken. Driemaandelijks Bericht [*A publication*]
DRD........... Demand Return Disposal
DRD........... Depressed Reticle Dive [*Military*]
DRD........... Design Requirement Drawing   (MCD)
DRD........... Detailed Requirements Document   (MCD)
DRD........... Diesel Reduction Drive
DRD........... Differenced-Range Doppler
DRD........... Director [*or Directorate*] of Research and Development [*Air Force*]
DRD........... Division of Reactor Development [*AEC*]
Dr D........... Doctor of Divinity
DRD........... Document Requirement Description   (KSC)
DRD........... Documentary Research Division [*Air Force*]
DRD........... Dorunda Station [*Australia*] [*Airport symbol*] [*Obsolete*]   (OAG)
DRD........... Draw Die [*Tool*]   (MCD)
DRD........... Drum-Read Driver [*Data processing*]
DRD........... Dual Readout Devices   (MCD)
DRDA........ Director, Research and Development, Air [*Military*] [*Canada*]
DRDA........ Division of Research Development and Administration [*University of Michigan*] [*Information service or system*]   (IID)
DRDCD..... Drilling - DCW [*Drilling Completion, Well Servicing*] [*A publication*]
DRDCN..... Data Reduction   (MSA)
DRDCS...... Director, Research and Development, Communications and Space [*Military*] [*Canada*]
DRDF........ Densified Refuse-Derived Fuel   (RDA)
DRDG RGE... Dredging Range [*Nautical charts*]
DRDHP..... Director, Research and Development, Human Performance [*Military*] [*Canada*]
DRDL........ Defense Research and Development Laboratory [*India*]
DRDL........ Director, Research and Development, Land [*Military*] [*Canada*]

DRDM....... Director, Research and Development, Maritime [*Military*] [*Canada*]
Dr Dobb's J... Dr. Dobb's Journal [*A publication*]
Dr Dobb's J Comput Calisthenics and Orthod... Dr. Dobb's Journal of Computer Calisthenics and Orthodontia [*Later, Dr. Dobb's Journal of Software Tools*] [*A publication*]
DRDP........ Detection RADAR Data Processing   (CET)
DRDP........ Director, Research and Development, Program Control [*Military*] [*Canada*]
DRDRCSEd... Diploma in Restorative Dentistry, Royal College of Surgeons of Edinburgh [*British*]   (DBQ)
DRDRM.... Director, Research and Development, Resource Management [*Military*] [*Canada*]
DRDS........ Degradation of RADAR Defense System
DRDT........ Division of Reactor Development and Technology [*AEC*]
DRDTO...... Detection RADAR Data Takeoff [*Air Force*]
DRE........... Data Reduction Equipment
DRE........... Dead Reckoning Equipment   (MSA)
DRE........... Defence Research Establishment [*Atlantic Canada*] [*UTLAS symbol*]
DR & E...... Defense Research and Engineering [*DoD*]
DRE........... Defense Research Establishment [*Israel*]
DRE........... Department of Resources and Energy [*Australia*]   (ADA)
DRE........... Department of Rural Education [*of NEA*] [*Later, REA*]   (EA)
DRE........... Destruction and Removal Efficiency [*Of waste incinerators*]
DRE........... Diploma in Remedial Electrolysis, Institute of Electrolysis [*British*]   (DBQ)
DRE........... Direct Reading Encoder
DRE........... Directional Reservation Equipment [*Telecommunications*]   (TEL)
DRE........... Director of Radio Equipment [*Navy*] [*British*]
DRE........... Director of Religious Education
DRE........... Director [*or Directorate*] of Research and Engineering [*Military*]
D/RE......... Disassembly/Reassembly Equipment [*Nuclear energy*]   (NRCH)
DRE........... District Reserve Equipment [*Army*]   (AABC)
DRE........... Diversity Reception Equipment
D Re........... Doctor of Religion
DRE........... Doctor of Religious Education
DRE........... Dokumentationsring Elektrotechnik [*Database*]
DRE........... Doppler RADAR Equipment
DRE........... Downrange Error [*NASA*]
DRE........... Drachma [*Monetary unit in Greece*]   (EY)
DRE........... Duke Realty Investments, Inc. [*NYSE symbol*]   (SPSG)
DREA........ Defence Research Establishment, Atlantic [*Canada*]
DREAM...... Data Retrieval, Entry, and Management
DREC........ Detection RADAR Electronic Component
Dr Ec......... Doctor of Economics
DRECP....... Design Release Engineering Change Proposal   (MCD)
DRED........ Daily Readiness [*Testing*]   (MCD)
DRED........ Data Routing and Error Detecting
DRED........ Detection RADAR Environmental Display [*Air Force*]
DRED........ Directed Rocket Engine Demonstrator
Dr Ed........ Doctor of Religious Education
DREDF...... Disability Rights Education and Defense Fund   (EA)
Dredged Mater Res... Dredged Material Research [*A publication*]
Dredging & Port Constr... Dredging and Port Construction [*A publication*]
DREE........ Department of Regional Economic Expansion [*Canada*]
D Re E........ Doctor of Refrigeration Engineering
D Re Eng.... Doctor of Refrigeration Engineering
D-REF....... Data Reference [*Environment Canada*] [*Information service or system*] [*Information service or system*]   (CRD)
DREF........ Distribution Research and Education Foundation   (EA)
DREG........ Data Regulations   (KSC)
DREG........ Dressing   (MSA)
DREGE....... Diabetes Retrieval Element Generator and Executor
DreiN........ Dreiser Newsletter [*A publication*]
DREK........ Dead Reckoning   (FAAC)
DRelEd...... Doctor of Religious Education
DREME..... Division of Research and Evaluation in Medical Education [*Ohio State University*] [*Research center*]   (RCD)
Dr En......... Doctor of English
Dr of Eng... Doctor of Engineering
Dr Eng....... Doctor of Engineering
Dr Ent....... Doctor of Entomology
DREO........ Defence Research Establishment, Ottawa [*Canada*]
DREO........ Defense Research and Engineering Office [*DoD*]
DREOR..... Defence Research Board of Canada. Defence Research Establishment Ottawa. Reports [*A publication*]
DREP........ Defence Research Establishment, Pacific [*Canada*]
DRep......... Ohio Decisions Reprint [*A publication*]   (DLA)
DREPO...... District Reserve Electronics Program Officer
DREPR...... Defence Research Board of Canada. Defence Research Establishment Pacific. Reports [*A publication*]
DRepr........ Ohio Decisions Reprint [*A publication*]   (DLA)
DRES........ DARCOM [*Development and Readiness Command, Army*] Readiness Evaluation System [*A publication*]
DRES........ Defence Research Establishment, Suffield [*Canada*]   (MCD)
DRES........ Direct Reading Emission Spectrograph   (NRCH)
DRES........ Dresden [*City in East Germany*]   (ROG)

Dresdner Kunstbl ... Dresdner Kunstblaetter. Monatsschrift. Staatliche Kunstsammlungen Dresden [*A publication*]
Dres Int Rev ... Dresse on Internal Revenue Laws [*A publication*]   (DLA)
DRESS ..... Depth Resolved Surface Coil Spectroscopy
DRESTC ... Defence Research Establishment, Suffield, Test Centre [*British*]   (NATG)
DRET .... Defence Research Establishment, Toronto [*Canada*]
DRET .... Direct Reentry Telemetry [*Air Force*]   (MCD)
DRETN ..... Defence Research Board of Canada. Defence Research Establishment Ottawa. Technical Note [*A publication*]
DRETS ...... Direct Reentry Telemetry System [*Air Force*]
Dr Europ ... Droit Europeen [*1958-63*] [*French*] [*A publication*]   (DLA)
DREV .... Defence Research Establishment, Valcartier [*Canada*]
DRev .... Deutsche Revue [*A publication*]
Drev Vysk .. Drevarsky Vyskum [*A publication*]
Drev Vyskum ... Drevarsky Vyskum [*A publication*]
DREW .... Drew Industries, Inc. [*NASDAQ symbol*]   (NQ)
Drew............ Drewry's English Vice Chancellors' Reports [*A publication*]   (DLA)
Drew............ Drew's Reports [*13 Florida*] [*A publication*]   (DLA)
Drew Ch F ... Drewry's Chancery Forms [*1876*] [*A publication*]   (DLA)
Drew (Eng) ... Drewry's English Chancery Reports [*A publication*]   (DLA)
Drew Eq Pl ... Drewry's Equity Pleading [*A publication*]   (DLA)
Drew Inj ..... Drewry on Injunctions [*1841*] [*A publication*]   (DLA)
Drew Pat .... Drewry's Patent Law Amendment Act [*1838*] [*A publication*]   (DLA)
DREWS..... Direct Readout Equatorial Weather Satellite
Drew & S ... Drewry and Smale's English Chancery Reports [*A publication*]   (DLA)
Drew & S (Eng) ... Drewry and Smale's English Chancery Reports [*A publication*]   (DLA)
Drew & Sm ... Drewry and Smale's English Chancery Reports [*A publication*]   (DLA)
Drew Tr M ... Drewry's Trade Marks [*1878*] [*A publication*]   (DLA)
Drexel Lib Q ... Drexel Library Quarterly [*A publication*]
Drexel Libr Q ... Drexel Library Quarterly [*A publication*]
Drexel Tech J ... Drexel Technical Journal [*A publication*]
Drex Lib Q ... Drexel Library Quarterly [*A publication*]
DREZ .... Dorsal Root Entry Zone [*Medicine*]
DRF .... Daily Replacement Factor [*Of lymphocytes*] [*Medicine*]
DRF .... Dairy Remembrance Fund   (EA)
DRF .... Dance Research Foundation   (EA)
DRF .... Data Reporting Form
DRF .... Data Request Form [*NASA*]   (NASA)
DRF .... Data Requirement Form   (KSC)
DRF .... Deafness Research Foundation   (EA)
DRF .... Depot Recovery Factor   (MCD)
DRF .... Depression Range Finder [*British military*]   (DMA)
DRF .... Destiny Research Foundation   (EA)
DRF .... Diamond Radiation Facility
DRF .... Differential Reinforcement [*Psychometrics*]
DRF .... Digital, Radio Frequency   (MCD)
DRF .... Direct Relief Foundation [*Later, DRI*]
DRF .... Dirty Rotten Form [*Slang*]   (ADA)
DRF .... Disaster Response Force [*Military*]
DRF .... Discharge Ringing Frequency
DRF .... Division Ready Force [*Army*]   (MCD)
Dr F............ Doctor of Forestry
DRF .... Doctorate Records File [*National Research Council*] [*Information service or system*]   (CRD)
DRF .... Documentation Request Form   (MCD)
DRF .... Dose Reduction Factor   (DEN)
DRF .... Dry Rectifier
DRF .... Dual Role Fighter   (MCD)
DRF .... Kenai, AK [*Location identifier*] [*FAA*]   (FAAL)
DRFA .... Dyslexia Research Foundation of Australia
DRFC .... David Rappaport Fan Club   (EA)
DRFC......... Del Reeves Fan Club   (EA)
Dr Fi........... Doctor of Finance
DRflmnBad ... Distinguished Rifleman Badge [*Military decoration*]   (AABC)
DRFN .... Driefontein Consolidated [*NASDAQ symbol*]   (NQ)
DRFO .... Danube River Field Organization [*Allied German Occupation Forces*]
DRFP......... Division of Retail Food Protection [*Food and Drug Administration*]
DRFP......... Draft Request for Proposal   (MCD)
DRFR........ Division of Research Facilities and Resources [*National Institutes of Health*]
DRFT........ Drift   (FAAC)
DRFUD4 ... Drugs of the Future [*A publication*]
DRFX......... Drill Fixture
DRG.......... Deering [*Alaska*] [*Airport symbol*]   (OAG)
DRG.......... Defense Research Group [*NATO*]
D & RG ..... Denver & Rio Grande Railroad
DR-G .... Deputy Registrar-General [*British*]
DRG.......... Diagnostic Related Group [*Medicine*]
DRG.......... Dickinson Robinson Group Ltd. [*British*]
DRG.......... Digital Ranging Generator [*Apollo*] [*NASA*]
DRG.......... Disaster Research Group [*National Academy of Sciences*]
DRG.......... Division of Research Grants [*National Institutes of Health*]
DRG.......... Dorsal Respiratory Group [*Medicine*]

DRG.......... Dorsal Root Ganglion [*Neuroanatomy*]
DRG.......... Drag
DRG.......... Drawing
DrG .... Drew Gateway [*A publication*]
DRG.......... DRG, Inc. [*Toronto Stock Exchange symbol*]
DRG.......... Drogue   (KSC)
DRG.......... During
DRGBAH.. Danish Review of Game Biology [*A publication*]
Dr Ge .... Doctor of Geology
Dr Geo........ Doctor of Geography
DRGM....... Deutsches-Reichsgebrauchsmuster [*German-Registered Design*]
Dr GP........ Doctor of Geopolitics
DRGR........ Dredger   (MSA)
DRGS .... Direct Readout Ground Station
DRGW....... [*The*] Denver & Rio Grande Western Railroad Co. [*AAR code*]
D & RGW .. [*The*] Denver & Rio Grande Western Railroad Co.
DRGX......... Diversified Retail Group, Inc. [*NASDAQ symbol*]   (NQ)
DRH .... Digital Readout Head [*Data processing*]
DRH .... Driver-Harris Co. [*AMEX symbol*]   (SPSG)
DRHD ...... Drill Head
Dr HL .... Doctor of Humanities of Learning
DRHM....... Durham [*City and county in England*]
Dr Hor .... Doctor of Horticulture
DRHP........ Diagnosis and Remediation of Handwriting Problems [*Educational test*]
Dr HS .... Doctor of Humanitarian Service
Dr Hy.......... Doctor of Hygiene
DRI .... Data Rate Indicator   (NASA)
DRI .... Data Recording Interface   (MCD)
DRI .... Data Reduction Interpreter
DRI .... Data Resources, Incorporated [*Database originator and operator*] [*Information service or system*]   (IID)
DRI .... Data Routing Indicator
DRI .... Davenport, Rock Island & North Western Railway Co. [*AAR code*]
DRI .... De Ridder, LA [*Location identifier*] [*FAA*]   (FAAL)
DRI .... De Rose Industries, Inc. [*AMEX symbol*]   (SPSG)
DRI .... Dead Reckoning Indicator   (MSA)
DRI .... Defense Research Institute [*Later, DRI - Defense Research and Trial Lawyers Association*]   (EA)
DRI .... Dental Research Institute [*University of California, Los Angeles*] [*Research center*]   (RCD)
DRI .... Denver Research Institute [*University of Denver*] [*Research center*]
DRI .... Descent Rate Indicator [*Aviation*]
DRI .... Desert Research Institute [*University of Nevada*] [*Research center*]
DRI .... Development of Regional Impact [*Land use*]
DRI .... Diabetes Research Institute [*University of Miami*] [*Research center*]   (RCD)
DRI .... Digital Research, Incorporated
DRI .... Direct Reduction Iron [*Ironmaking process*]
DRI .... Direct Relief International   (EA)
DRI .... Disaster Research Institute   (EAIO)
DRI .... Document Retrieval Index
DRI .... Dose Rate Instrumentation
DRI .... Drive
DRI .... Dual Roll Idler
DRI .... Dynamic Response Index
D RI .... United States District Court for the District of Rhode Island   (DLA)
DRI-BAS ... DRI [*Data Resources, Inc.*] Bank Analysis Service [*Information service or system*]   (CRD)
DRIC .... Defence Research Information Centre [*Great Britain*]
DRIC .... Dental Research Information Center   (DIT)
DRI-CEI .... DRI [*Data Resources, Inc.*] Current Economic Indicators Data Bank [*Information service or system*]   (CRD)
DRICOM .. DRI [*Data Resources, Inc.*] Commodities [*Information service or system*]   (CRD)
DRID .... Deflection Refractive Index Detector
DRID .... Direct Readout Image Dissector [*Camera system*]
DRIDAC.... Drum Input to Digital Automatic Computer
DRIE......... Department of Regional Industrial Expansion [*Canada*]
DRIF.......... Disposal Regional Inventory File [*Military*]
DRI-FACS ... DRI [*Data Resources, Inc.*] Financial and Credit Statistics [*Information service or system*]   (CRD)
DRIFT .... Diffuse Reflectance Infrared Fourier Transform [*Spectrometry*]
DRIFT .... Diversity Receiving Instrumentation for Telemetry
DRIFT .... Dynamic Reliability Instantaneous Forecasting Technique
DRIG .... Digital Rate-Integrating Gyro   (MCD)
DRIL.......... Directorio Revolucionario Iberico de Liberta [*Revolutionary Directorate for Iberian Liberation*]
DRIL.......... Drillstar Corp. [*NASDAQ symbol*]   (NQ)
DRILA........ Drilling [*A publication*]
DRILL....... Delaware Rapid Interlibrary Loan Project [*Library network*]
Drilling Contract ... Drilling Contractor [*A publication*]
Drill News ... Drilling News [*A publication*]
Drill Prod Pract ... Drilling and Production Practice [*A publication*]
DRILS .... Defense Retail Interservice Logistic Support [*Military*]
DRIMS...... Diagnostic Rifle Marksmanship Simulator   (MCD)
DRINA ...... Drvna Industrija [*A publication*]

DRINC ...... Dairy Research, Incorporated (EA)
Dr Ind .... Doctor of Industry
Dr Ing .... Doctor Ingeniariae [*Doctor of Engineering*]
Drink .... Drinkwater's English Common Pleas Reports [*1840-41*] [*A publication*] (DLA)
Drinkw .... Drinkwater's English Common Pleas Reports [*1840-41*] [*A publication*] (DLA)
Drinkwater ... Drinkwater's English Common Pleas Reports [*1840-41*] [*A publication*] (DLA)
Drinkw (Eng) ... Drinkwater's English Common Pleas Reports [*1840-41*] [*A publication*] (DLA)
DRIP .... Data Reduction Input Program [*Data processing*]
DRIP .... Digital Ray and Intensity Projector
DRIP .... Dividend Reinvestment Plan [*Also, DRP*]
DRIP .... Downspout Recharegment Infusion Program [*Energy development program*]
DRIPS .... Dynamic Real-Time Information Processing System (MCD)
DRIR .... Direct Readout Infrared Radiometer
DRIRU ...... Dry Rotor Inertial Reference Unit [*NASA*] (NASA)
DRIS .... Defense Retail Interservice Support [*Military*] (MCD)
DRIS .... Diagnosis and Recommended Integrated System [*Plant pathology*]
DRIS .... Diffuse Reflectance Infrared Spectroscopy [*Physics*]
DRI-SEC ... DRI [*Data Resources, Inc.*] US Equity and Debt Securities [*Information service or system*] (CRD)
DRISS .... Digital Read-In Subsystem [*Data processing*]
DRIT .... DTIC Retrieval and Indexing Terminology [*DoD*]
Dritte Welt Mag ... Dritte Welt Magazin [*A publication*]
Dr Iur .... Doctor of Laws
DRIV .... Drive [*Automotive engineering*]
DRIVE .... Democratic Republican Independent Voter Education Committee [*Political Action Committee*]
DRIVE .... Document Read, Information Verify, and Edit
DRIVER .... Division of Research and Improvement, Vocational Education, and Rehabilitation [*Department of Education*]
Driver Ed Bul ... Driver Education Bulletin [*A publication*]
Drives and Controls Int ... Drives and Controls International [*A publication*]
DRJ .... Data Requirements Justification [*Military*]
DrJ .... Doctor Juris [*Doctor of Law*]
DRJG .... Drill Jig
DRJI .... Drill Jig (AAG)
Dr JS .... Doctor of Judicial Science
Dr J Sc .... Doctor of Judicial Science
DrJU .... Doctor Juris Utriusque [*Doctor of Both Laws*]
Dr Jur .... Doctor Juris [*Doctor of Law*] (EY)
Dr Jur et Rer Pol ... Doctor of Laws and Political Science
DRK .... Data Request Keyboard
DRK .... Democratic People's Republic of Korea
DRK .... Derrick (MSA)
DRK .... Display Request Keyboard (KSC)
DRK .... Drunk [*FBI standardized term*]
DRKL .... Defence Research Kingston Laboratory [*Canada*] (MCD)
DRKN .... Durakon Industries, Inc. [*Lapeer, MI*] [*NASDAQ symbol*] (NQ)
DRL .... Data Reduction Laboratory
DRL .... Data Requirement List (KSC)
DRL .... Data Requirements Language
DRL .... Data Retrieval Language [*National Institute of Standards and Technology*]
DRL .... Date Required to Load (AABC)
DRL .... Daytime Running Lights [*Automotive engineering*]
DRL .... Defense Research Laboratory
DRL .... Derlan Industries Ltd. [*Toronto Stock Exchange symbol*]
DRL .... Design Review List (MCD)
DRL .... DI Industries [*Formerly, Drillers, Inc.*] [*AMEX symbol*] (SPSG)
DRL .... Differential Reinforcement of Low Rate [*Psychometrics*]
DRL .... Digital Readout Light [*Data processing*]
DRL .... Directional Reference Locator
DRL .... Division of Reactor Licensing [*AEC*]
DRL .... Document Requirement List (KSC)
DRLH .... Donated Records List [*Australia*]
DRLH .... Duralith Corp. [*NASDAQ symbol*] (NQ)
Dr Lit .... Doctor of Literature
Dr Litt .... Doctor of Letters
Dr LL .... Doctor of Laws
DRLMS ..... Digital RADAR Landmass Simulator
Dr LR .... Drake Law Review [*A publication*]
DRL/S .... Data Requirements List/Schedule
DRLS .... Despatch-Rider Letter-Service [*Military*] [*British*]
Dr LS .... Doctor of Library Science
DRLS .... Dragon Remote Launch System [*Military*] (MCD)
DRL/UT ...... Defense Research Laboratory/University of Texas (MUGU)
DRM .... Data Records Management (MCD)
DRM .... Decay Rate Meter
DRM .... Dental Repair Technician [*Navy*]
DRM .... Design Reference Mission [*NASA*]
DRM .... Design Reference Model (KSC)
DRM .... Detrital Remanent Magnetization [*Geophysics*]
DRM .... Development Reactor Mock-Up
DRM .... Diamond Shamrock Co. [*NYSE symbol*] (SPSG)

DRM .... Digital Radiometer
DRM .... Digital Range Machine
DRM .... Diploma in Resource Management (ADA)
DRM .... Direct Reduction Mortgage [*Banking*]
DRM .... Direction of Relative Movement [*Navigation*]
DRM .... Directorate for Resource Management [*CIA*]
DRM .... Drafting [*or Drawing*] Room Manual
DRM .... Drawing Requirements Manual [*NASA*] (NASA)
DRM .... Drum [*Shipping*]
DRM .... Drummond Island, MI [*Location identifier*] [*FAA*] (FAAL)
DRM .... Ducted Rocket Motor
DRM .... Dunraine Mines Ltd. [*Toronto Stock Exchange symbol*]
D & R Mag Cas ... Dowling and Ryland's English Magistrates' Cases [*A publication*] (DLA)
DRMAJ ..... Drum Major [*Marine Corps*]
Dr Marit .... Droit Maritime [*A publication*]
Dr Marit Franc ... Droit Maritime Francais [*A publication*]
D & RMC .. Dowling and Ryland's English Magistrates' Cases [*A publication*] (DLA)
DRMD .... Duramed Pharmaceutical, Inc. [*Cincinnati, OH*] [*NASDAQ symbol*] (NQ)
Dr Med ...... Doctor of Medicine
DRMF .... Damon Runyon Memorial Fund for Cancer Research [*Later, DRWWCF*] (EA)
DRMGAS ... Drugs Made in Germany [*A publication*]
DRMI .... Dual Radio Magnetic Indicator (MCD)
DRML .... Defence Research Medical Laboratory [*Canada*]
DRMO .... District Records Management Office [*or Officer*]
DRMS .... Data Resources Management System
DRMS .... Defense Reutilization and Marketing Service [*DoD*]
DRMS .... Department of Defense Resource Management System (NG)
Dr MT .... Doctor of Mechanotherapy
Dr Mus ...... Doctor of Music
DRN .... Daily Reports Notice [*Air Force*] (AFM)
DRN .... Data Record Number (MCD)
DRN .... Data Reference Number
DRN .... Dirranbandi [*Australia*] [*Airport symbol*] [*Obsolete*] (OAG)
DRN .... Document Release Notice [*Jet Propulsion Laboratory, NASA*]
DRN .... Document Revision Notice (MCD)
DRN .... Dorsal Raphe Nucleus [*Brain anatomy*]
DRN .... Dorsal Root Neurons [*Neuroanatomy*]
DRN .... Double-Round Nose
DRN .... Drain (NASA)
DRN .... Drawn [*Cricket*] (ROG)
DrN .... Druzba Narodov [*A publication*]
dRNA .... Ribonucleic Acid, Diverse [*Biochemistry, genetics*]
Dr & Nap ... Drury's Irish Chancery Reports Tempore Napier [*1858-59*] [*A publication*] (DLA)
DrNatSc ..... Doctor of Natural Science
DRNK .... Cable Car Beverage Corp. [*NASDAQ symbol*] (NQ)
DRNL .... Defence Research Northern Laboratory [*Canada*]
D & RNP .... Dowling and Ryland's English Nisi Prius Cases [*A publication*] (DLA)
D & RNPC ... Dowling and Ryland's English Nisi Prius Cases [*A publication*] (DLA)
Dr N Ph ..... Doctor of Natural Philosophy
Dr N Sc ...... Doctor of Natural Sciences
DRNT .... Diagnostic Roentgenology [*Medicine*]
DRO .... Daily Receipt of Obligation [*Military*]
DRO .... Daily Report of Obligation [*Navy*] (NG)
DRO .... Daily Routine Order
DRO .... Dancing Room Only
DRO .... Data Readout [*Navy*] (NVT)
DRO .... Day Room Orderly [*Army*]
DRO .... Desert Rose Resources [*Vancouver Stock Exchange symbol*]
DRO .... Destructive Readout
DRO .... Development Release Order
DRO .... Differential Reinforcement of Other Behavior [*Psychometrics*]
DRO .... Digital Readout [*Data processing*]
DRO .... Digital Readout Oscilloscope [*Data processing*]
dro .... Dinheiro [*Monetary unit*] [*Portugal*]
DRO .... Direct Recording Oscillograph
DRO .... Director of Recruiting and Organization [*Military*] [*British*]
DRO .... Disablement Resettlement Office [*or Officer*] [*Department of Education*] [*British*]
DRO .... Disposal Release Order [*DoD*]
DRO .... Divisional Records Office [*British military*] (DMA)
DRO .... Divisional Routine Order
DRO .... Document Release Order (NASA)
DRO .... Domestic Route Order
DRO .... Doubly Resonant Oscillator (IEEE)
DRO .... Drawing Requirement Outline
DRO .... Drogist. Vakblad voor Schoonheid, Gezondheid, en Hygiene [*A publication*]
DRO .... Durango [*Colorado*] [*Airport symbol*] (OAG)
DRO .... House Democratic Research Organization (EA)
DROAAK ... Deep Sea Research and Oceanographic Abstracts [*A publication*]
DROD .... Delayed Readout Detector [*Satellite instrument*]
DROFAZ ... Data Record of Oceanographic Observations and Exploratory Fishing [*Hokkaido*] [*A publication*]

DROG........ Drogue (NASA)
DROGA..... Drogownictwo [*A publication*]
Droit CC .... Droit Civil Canadien [*A publication*] (DLA)
Droit et Pratique Commer Internat ... Droit et Pratique du Commerce
　　　　International [*A publication*]
DROL........ Defense RDT & E [*Research, Development, Test, and
　　　　Evaluation*] Online System [*DTIC*] (MCD)
DRO-LA .... Defense Research Office, Latin America [*Army*] (AABC)
DROLS...... Defense RDT & E [*Research, Development, Test, and
　　　　Evaluation*] Online System [*DTIC*]
DROM....... Decoder Read-Only Memory
DROM....... Dromore [*District in Northern Ireland*] (ROG)
DROMDI.. Direct Readout Miss Distance Indicator
DRON .... Data Reduction (MCD)
Drone Cop ... Drone on Copyrights [*A publication*] (DLA)
DROO........ Digital Readout Oscilloscope [*Data processing*]
DROP........ Data Printout Program
DROP........ Distribution Register of Organic Pollutants [*In Water*]
　　　　[*Environmental Protection Agency*]
DROPS...... Demountable, Rack, Off-Loading, and Pick-Up System [*British
　　　　Army*]
DRORM .... Drafting and Records Office, Royal Marines [*British
　　　　military*] (DMA)
DROS .... Date Returned from Overseas [*Military*]
DROS .... Dead Reckoning Own Ship
DROS .... Direct Readout Satellite
DROS .... Disk Resident Operating System [*Data processing*] (IEEE)
Dr O Sc..... Doctor of the Science of Oratory
DROT........ Delayed Range on Target [*Air Force*]
Dr Ouvr...... Droit Ouvrier [*A publication*]
DROWS .... Direct Readout Weather Satellite
DRP .... Data Reception Process [*Telecommunications*] (TEL)
DRP .... Data Reduction Procedure [*or Program*]
DRP .... Data Retrieval Program (CAAL)
DRP .... Dead Reckoning Plotter
DRP .... Delayed Reenlistment Program [*Air Force*]
DRP .... Democratic Republican Party [*Minchu Kong Hwa Dang*]
　　　　[*Republic of Korea*] [*Political party*] (PPW)
DRP .... Densest Random Packing [*Solid state physics*]
DRP .... Designated Repair [*or Rework*] Point [*Military*] (CAAL)
DRP .... Detected Radiant Power
DRP .... Deutsche Rechtspartei [*German Party of the Right*] [*Federal
　　　　Republic of Germany*] [*Political party*] (PPE)
DRP .... Deutsches Reichspatent [*German State Patent*]
DRP .... Development Resources Panel [*United Nations Development
　　　　Program*]
DRP .... Digital Recording Process
DRP .... Digoxin Reduction Products [*Clinical chemistry*]
DRP .... Directional Radiated Power [*Telecommunications*] (TEL)
DRP .... Director of Radio Production [*Air Ministry*] [*British*] [*World
　　　　War II*]
DRP .... Disaster Recovery Plan [*Computer systems*]
DRP .... Discontinuously Reinforced Plastic
DRP .... Dissolved Reactive Phosphorus [*Environmental science*]
DRP .... Distribution Reinvestment Program [*Stock exchange term*]
DRP .... Distribution Resource Planning
DRP .... Dividend Reinvestment Plan [*Also, DRIP*]
DRP .... Doctor of Regional Planning
DRP .... Documentation Research Project [*American Institute of
　　　　Physics*]
DRP .... Dorsal Root Potential [*Anatomy*]
DRP .... Draft Requirements Package (MCD)
DRP .... Drill Plate [*Tool*] (MCD)
DRP .... Drone Recovery Platform (NVT)
DRP .... During Reporting Period
DRPA........ Delaware River Port Authority
Dr Pa........ Doctor of Painting
Dr PA........ Doctor of Public Administration
DRPC........ Defence Research Policy Committee [*British*]
DRPC........ Direct Reading Pocket Chamber
DRPC........ Division Reliability Policy Committee (AAG)
Dr of PE..... Doctor of Physical Education
DRPE........ Drill Plate [*Tool*] (AAG)
Dr PH .... Doctor of Public Health
Dr PH .... Doctor of Public Hygiene
Dr PH Hy .. Doctor of Public Health and Hygiene
Dr Phi .... Doctor of Philanthropy
Dr Phil ...... Doctor Philosophiae [*Doctor of Philosophy*]
Dr Phil Nat ... Doctor of Natural Philosophy
Dr Philos.... Doctor of Philosophy
Dr Pho....... Doctor of Photography
Dr Phy ...... Doctor of Physics
DRPI.......... Digital Rod Position Indication [*Nuclear energy*] (NRCH)
DRPL......... Drill Plate [*Tool*]
DRPO .... Defense Resources Planning Operation (AAG)
Dr Pol Sci.. Doctor of Political Science
DRPP .... Data Routing Patch Panel (MCD)
DRPPD5.... Deep-Sea Research. Part A. Oceanographic Research Papers
　　　　[*Later, Deep-Sea Research with Oceanographic Literature
　　　　Review*] [*A publication*]
DRPR .... Drawing Practice (NG)

Dr Pratique Com Int ... Droit et Pratique du Commerce International [*A
　　　　publication*]
DRPRB...... Druck Print [*A publication*]
Dr Pr M ...... Doctor of Preventative Medicine
DRPS......... Disk Real-Time and Programming System [*Data processing*]
DRPS......... Dry Reed Pushbutton Switch
Dr P Sc....... Doctor of Physical Science
DRQ........... Data Ready Queue [*IBM Corp.*] (IBMDP)
DRQ........... Data Request
DRR .... Data Recorder/Reproducer (MCD)
DRR .... Data Redundancy Reduction [*or Removal*] (KSC)
DRR .... Descent Rate RADAR
DRR .... Design Release [*or Request*] Review
DRR .... Design Requirements Review [*NASA*] (NASA)
DRR .... Development Revision Record (KSC)
DRR .... Digital RADAR Relay
DRR .... Direct Reading Receiver
DRR .... Disparity Reduction Rate [*Measures the progress a country has
　　　　made toward reconciling its current Physical Quality of
　　　　Life Index with its optimum projected PQLI for the year
　　　　2000*] [*Overseas Development Council*]
DRR .... Diversity Reception Receiver
DRR .... Division of Research Resources [*National Institutes of Health*]
　　　　[*Bethesda, MD*]
DRR .... Document Release Record (NRCH)
DRR .... Dorado Resources Ltd. [*Vancouver Stock Exchange symbol*]
DRR .... Dough Rate of Reaction [*Food science*]
DRR .... Drama Review [*A publication*]
DRR .... Drug Research Reports: The Blue Sheet [*A publication*]
DRR .... Durrie [*Australia*] [*Airport symbol*] [*Obsolete*] (OAG)
DRRA .... Tessaoua [*Niger*] [*ICAO location identifier*] (ICLI)
DRRB .... Data Requirements Review Board [*DoD*]
DRRC .... Dogondoutchi [*Niger*] [*ICAO location identifier*] (ICLI)
Dr RCA...... Doctor of the Royal College of Art
DRRD .... Division of Reactor Research and Development [*Energy
　　　　Research and Development Administration*]
DRRD .... Dosso [*Niger*] [*ICAO location identifier*] (ICLI)
DRRE .... Tera [*Niger*] [*ICAO location identifier*] (ICLI)
Dr of Rec... Doctor of Recreation
Dr Rer Nat ... Doctor Rerum Naturalium [*Doctor of Natural Science*]
Dr Rer Pol ... Doctor Rerum Politicarum [*Doctor of Political Science*]
Dr Rer Tech ... Doctor of Technical Science
DRRF .... Division Rapid Reaction Force [*Army*] (AABC)
DRRG .... Gaya [*Niger*] [*ICAO location identifier*] (ICLI)
DRRI .... Bilma [*Niger*] [*ICAO location identifier*] (ICLI)
DRRI .... Defense Race Relations Institute [*Air Force*]
DRRL .... Digital RADAR Relay Link
DRRL .... Tilabery [*Niger*] [*ICAO location identifier*] (ICLI)
DRRM....... Maradi [*Niger*] [*ICAO location identifier*] (ICLI)
DRRN....... Niamey Airport [*Niger*] [*ICAO location identifier*] (ICLI)
DRRP .... La Tapoa [*Niger*] [*ICAO location identifier*] (ICLI)
DRRR .... Niamey [*Niger*] [*ICAO location identifier*] (ICLI)
DRRT .... Data Reception, Recording, and Transmission (MCD)
DRRT .... Tahoua [*Niger*] [*ICAO location identifier*] (ICLI)
Dr R T Nap ... Drury's Irish Chancery Reports Tempore Napier [*1858-59*] [*A
　　　　publication*] (DLA)
Dr R T Sug ... Drury's Irish Chancery Reports Tempore Sugden [*A
　　　　publication*] (DLA)
DRRU....... Ouallam [*Niger*] [*ICAO location identifier*] (ICLI)
DRRV....... Niamey [*Niger*] [*ICAO location identifier*] (ICLI)
DRS .... Clarepine Industries, Inc. [*Toronto Stock Exchange symbol*]
DRS .... Daily River Stages (NOAA)
DRS .... Dar Es Salaam [*Tanzania*] [*Geomagnetic observatory code*]
DRS .... Data Rate Selector
DRS .... Data Reaction System (AAG)
DRS .... Data Receiving Station (KSC)
DRS .... Data Recording Set
DRS .... Data Recording System (MUGU)
DRS .... Data Reduction System [*Data processing*]
DRS .... Data Relay Satellite [*NASA*]
DRS .... Data Relay Station (NASA)
DRS .... Data Relay System (CAAL)
DRS .... Data Requirements Specification (KSC)
DRS .... Data Resources Series [*Elsevier Book Series*] [*A publication*]
DRS .... Data Retrieval System [*Data processing*] (BUR)
DRS .... Debtor Reporting System [*World Bank*]
DRS .... Defense Research Sciences
DRS .... Dementia Rating Scale [*Psychometric testing*]
DRS .... Detection and Ranging Set (CAAL)
DRs .... Deutsche Rundschau [*A publication*]
DRS .... Development Reference Service [*Society for International
　　　　Development*] (IID)
DRS .... Development Requirements Specification [*Nuclear
　　　　energy*] (NRCH)
DRS .... Diabetic Retinopathic Study [*National Eye Institute*]
DRS .... Diagnostic Reading Scales [*Education*]
DRS .... Diagnostic/Retrieval Systems, Inc. [*AMEX symbol*] (SPSG)
DRS .... Diagnostic Rework Sheets (AAG)
DRS .... Diffuse Reflection Spectroscopy
DRS .... Digital RADAR Simulator
DRS .... Digital RADAR System

DRS .... Digital Range Safety (NASA)
DRS .... Digital Readout System [*Data processing*]
DRS .... Digital Receiver Station [*Data processing*]
DRS .... Digital Recording System
DRS .... Dipping-Reflector Sequence [*Geology*]
DRS .... Director of Repair and Service [*British military*] (DMA)
D/RS .... Disassembly/Reassembly Station [*Nuclear energy*] (NRCH)
DRS .... Discrepancy Reporting System [*NASA*]
DRS .... Dissolved Reactive Silica [*Environmental science*]
DRS .... Division Reference Standards (AAG)
DRS .... Division of Research Services [*National Institutes of Health*]
　　　　　　 [*Bethesda, MD*]
DRS .... Django Reinhardt Society (EA)
Dr & S........ Doctor and Student [*A publication*] (DSA)
DRS .... Document Retrieval Services [*Information service or*
　　　　　　 system] (IID)
DRS .... Document Retrieval System
DRS .... Dominion Report Service [*Information service or system*] [*A*
　　　　　　 publication]
DRS .... Double Right Shift
DRS .... Dresden [*East Germany*] [*Airport symbol*] (OAG)
DRS .... Dressed [*Lumber*]
DRS .... Drowsiness (KSC)
DRS .... Dry Reed Switch
DRS .... Dynamic Reflectance Spectroscopy
DRSA....... Data Recording System Analyst (MUGU)
DRSAM..... Diploma of the Royal Scottish Academy of Music and Drama
Dr Sanit Soc ... Droit Sanitaire et Social [*A publication*]
DRSC......... Direct RADAR Scope Camera
Dr Sc .... Doctor of Science
Dr Sci......... Doctor of Science
Dr Sci Nat ... Doctor of Natural Sciences
Dr Sc Jur ... Doctor of the Science of Jurisprudence
Dr Sc Pol.... Doctor of Political Sciences (EY)
DRSCR....... Digital Range Safety Command Receiver [*NASA*] (KSC)
DRSCS ...... Digital Range Safety Command System [*NASA*] (MCD)
Dr Sc Techn ... Doctor of Technical Science
DRSD .... Dresdner Bank AG [*NASDAQ symbol*] (NQ)
DRSEDL..... Diagnostic Radiology Series [*A publication*]
DRSEM..... Deployable Receive Segment Engineering Model (MCD)
DRSG .... Digital Recorder Signal Generator [*Data processing*]
DRSG .... Division Restructuring Study Group [*TRADOC*]
　　　　　　 [*Army*] (RDA)
DRSG .... Dominican Republic Study Group (EA)
DRSG .... Dressing [*Medicine*]
DRSH .... Drill Shell
DRSHC ...... Deletion Reason/Supply History Code
Dr & Sm .... Drewry and Smale's English Vice Chancellors' Reports [*1860-*
　　　　　　 65] [*A publication*] (DLA)
DRSN .... Drifting Snow [*Meteorology*]
DRSN .... Drug Survival News [*A publication*]
DRSO .... Digital Recording [*NASDAQ symbol*] (NQ)
Dr So .... Doctor of Sociology
Dr Soc .... Droit Social [*A publication*]
Dr So Sc ..... Doctor of Social Science
DRSP......... Death Row Support Project (EA)
DRSP......... Defense Reconnaissance Support Program
DRSP........ Digital RADAR Signal Processor (MCD)
DRSPA ...... Druckspiegel [*A publication*]
DRSPAAJC ... Documents et Rapports. Societe Paleontologique et
　　　　　　 Archeologique de l'Arrondissement Judiciaire de Charleroi
　　　　　　 [*A publication*]
DRSR......... Direct RADAR Scope Recorder (MCD)
DRSR......... Dresser (MSA)
DRSS......... Data Relay Satellite System [*NASA*]
DRSS .... Discrepancy Report Squawk Sheet [*NASA*] (NASA)
DRSS .... Division of Retirement and Survivors Studies [*Social Security*
　　　　　　 Administration] (GRD)
DRSS .... Downrange Support Ship
Dr & Sug .... Drury's Irish Chancery Reports Tempore Sugden [*A*
　　　　　　 publication] (DLA)
DRSW .... Documentary Relations of the South West [*Arizona State*
　　　　　　 Museum] [*Tucson*] [*Information service or system*] (IID)
DRT .... Data Reckoning Tracer (MSA)
DRT .... Data Review Technician
DRT .... Daughters of the Republic of Texas (EA)
DRT .... Dead Reckoning Tracer [*RADAR*]
DRT .... Dead Reckoning Trainer
DRT .... Decade Ratio Transformer
DRT .... Decision Response Time
DRT .... Del Rio [*Texas*] [*Airport symbol*] [*Obsolete*] (OAG)
DRT .... Design Reference Timeline (MCD)
DRT .... Deviation for Replacement Time
DRT .... Device Reference Table
DRT .... Device Rise Time [*Photomultipliers for scintillation*
　　　　　　 counting] (IEEE)
DRT .... Diagnostic Rhyme Test
DRT .... Digital Readout Timer [*Data processing*]
DRT .... Digital Rotary Transducer
DRT .... Diode Recovery Tester
DRT .... Direct Reading Totalizer

DRT .... Director [*United Kingdom*] [*A publication*]
drt.............. Director [*MARC relator code*] [*Library of Congress*] (LCCP)
DRT .... Director of Railway Transport [*British military*] (DMA)
DRT .... Division Reconnaissance Team [*Warsaw Pact forces*] (INF)
DRT .... Dome Removal Tool
DRT .... Drawing Release Ticket (MCD)
DRT .... Drill Template (MCD)
DRTA .... Driptank
DRTBB ...... Drug and Therapeutics Bulletin [*A publication*]
DRTC .... Diabetes Research and Training Center [*University of Chicago*]
　　　　　　 [*Research center*] (RCD)
DRTC .... Diabetes Research and Training Center [*Washington*
　　　　　　 University] [*Research center*] (RCD)
DRTC .... Diabetes Research and Training Center [*Yeshiva University*]
　　　　　　 [*Research center*] (RCD)
DRTC .... Diploma of the Royal Technical College [*British*]
DRTC .... Documentation Research and Training Centre
DRTE .... Defence Research Telecommunication Establishment [*Canada*]
DRTE .... Doctor of Radio and Television Engineering
Dr Tech...... Doctor of Technology
DRT Eng.... Doctor of Radio and Television Engineering
Dr Theol..... Doctor of Theology
DRTI......... Dual Roll Trough Idler
DRTK .... Duratek Corp. [*NASDAQ symbol*] (NQ)
DRTL........ Diode Resistor Transistor Logic (MSA)
DRTM .... Disk Real-Time Monitor [*Data processing*]
Dr T Med... Doctor of Tropical Medicine
Dr T Nap ... Drury's Irish Chancery Reports Tempore Napier [*1858-59*] [*A*
　　　　　　 publication] (DLA)
DRTOBK... Drugs of Today [*A publication*]
DRTP......... Drill Template
DRTR .... Dead Reckoning Trainer
Dr Trav ..... Droit du Travail: Revue Mensuelle [*French*] [*A*
　　　　　　 publication] (DLA)
DRTRD ..... Director [*A publication*]
DRTSA ...... Defense Reconnaissance Tactical Support Activity (MCD)
Dr T Sug .... Drury's Irish Chancery Reports Tempore Sugden [*A*
　　　　　　 publication] (DLA)
DRU.......... Data Reference Unit
DRU.......... Data Reorganization Utility [*Data processing*]
DRU.......... Demolition Research Unit
DRu........... Deutsche Rundschau [*A publication*]
DRU.......... Digital Range Unit
DRU.......... Digital Register Unit
DRU.......... Digital Remote Unit [*Data processing*] (MCD)
DRU.......... Direct Reporting Unit
DRU.......... Disaccharide Repeating Unit [*Biochemistry*]
DRU.......... Document Retention Unit [*IRS*]
DRU.......... Drew University, Madison, NJ [*OCLC symbol*] (OCLC)
DRU.......... Drive Unit
DRU.......... Drummond, MT [*Location identifier*] [*FAA*] (FAAL)
DRU.......... Drummond Petroleum Ltd. [*Toronto Stock Exchange symbol*]
Dru........... Drury's Irish Chancery Reports Tempore Sugden [*A*
　　　　　　 publication] (DLA)
DRUB .... Digital Remote Unit Buffer [*Data processing*] (MCD)
DRUC........ Disposition Record Unsatisfactory Condition (MCD)
D Ru E .... Doctor of Rural Engineering
D Ru Eng ... Doctor of Rural Engineering
DRUG........ Drug Screening Systems, Inc. [*NASDAQ symbol*] (NQ)
Drug Abu MS ... Drug Abuse Council. Monograph Series [*A publication*]
Drug Abu PPS ... Drug Abuse Council. Public Policy Series [*A publication*]
Drug Abuse & Alcohol Rev ... Drug Abuse and Alcoholism Review [*A*
　　　　　　 publication]
Drug Abuse LR ... Drug Abuse Law Review [*A publication*] (DLA)
Drug Abuse L Rev ... Drug Abuse Law Review [*A publication*] (DLA)
Drug Abuse Prev Rep ... Drug Abuse Prevention Report [*A publication*]
Drug Action Drug Resist Bact ... Drug Action and Drug Resistance in Bacteria
　　　　　　 [*A publication*]
Drug Alcohol Depend ... Drug and Alcohol Dependence [*A publication*]
Drug Alert ... Nurse's Drug Alert [*A publication*]
Drug Allied Ind ... Drug and Allied Industries [*A publication*]
Drug Chem Exports ... Drug and Chemical Exports [*A publication*]
Drug Chem Toxicol ... Drug and Chemical Toxicology [*A publication*]
Drug Circ ... Druggists Circular [*A publication*]
Drug Cosmet ... Drug and Cosmetic Industry [*A publication*]
Drug and Cosmetic Ind ... Drug and Cosmetic Industry [*A publication*]
Drug Cosmet Ind ... Drug and Cosmetic Industry [*A publication*]
Drug Dev C ... Drug Development Communications [*A publication*]
Drug Dev Commun ... Drug Development Communications [*A publication*]
Drug Dev Ind Pharm ... Drug Development and Industrial Pharmacy [*A*
　　　　　　 publication]
Drug Dev Res ... Drug Development Research [*A publication*]
Drug Dig ... Drug Digests [*A publication*]
Drug Enf .... Drug Enforcement [*A publication*]
Drug Enforce ... Drug Enforcement [*A publication*]
Drug Forum J Human Issues ... Drug Forum. Journal of Human Issues [*A*
　　　　　　 publication]
Drug Induced Dis ... Drug Induced Diseases [*A publication*]
Drug Inf Bull ... Drug Information Bulletin [*A publication*]
Drug Inf Health Prof ... Drug Information for the Health Professions [*A*
　　　　　　 publication]

Drug Inf J .. Drug Information Journal [*A publication*]
Drug Intel .. Drug Intelligence and Clinical Pharmacy [*A publication*]
Drug Intell ... Drug Intelligence [*Later, Drug Intelligence and Clinical Pharmacy*] [*A publication*]
Drug Intell Clin Pharm ... Drug Intelligence and Clinical Pharmacy [*A publication*]
Drug Interact Newsl ... Drug Interactions Newsletter [*A publication*]
Drug Merch ... Drug Merchandising [*A publication*]
Drug Metab ... Drug Metabolism Reviews [*A publication*]
Drug Metab Dispos ... Drug Metabolism and Disposition [*A publication*]
Drug Metab Disposition ... Drug Metabolism and Disposition [*A publication*]
Drug Metab Rev ... Drug Metabolism Reviews [*A publication*]
Drug Meta D ... Drug Metabolism and Disposition [*A publication*]
Drug Nutr .. Drug-Nutrient Interactions [*A publication*]
Drug-Nutrient Interact ... Drug-Nutrient Interactions [*A publication*]
Drug-Nutr Interact ... Drug-Nutrient Interactions [*A publication*]
Drug Res .... Drug Research [*A publication*]
Drugs Exp Clin Res ... Drugs under Experimental and Clinical Research [*A publication*]
Drugs Health Care ... Drugs in Health Care [*A publication*]
Drugs Made Ger ... Drugs Made in Germany [*A publication*]
Drugs Pharm Sci ... Drugs and the Pharmaceutical Sciences [*A publication*]
Drug Stand ... Drug Standards [*A publication*]
Drug Stor N ... Drug Store News [*A publication*]
Drug Ther .. Drug Therapy [*A publication*]
Drug Ther Bull ... Drug and Therapeutics Bulletin [*A publication*]
Drug Ther Hosp Ed ... Drug Therapy. Hospital Edition [*A publication*]
Drug Ther Prescr Pract Probl ... Drug Therapy. Prescribing Practices and Problems [*A publication*]
Drug Ther Rev ... Drug Therapy. Reviews [*A publication*]
Drug Topic A ... Annual Consumer Expenditures Survey (Supplement to Drug Topics) [*A publication*]
Drug Vitam Allied Ind ... Drug, Vitamin, and Allied Industries [*A publication*]
DRUIA ...... Drug Intelligence [*Later, Drug Intelligence and Clinical Pharmacy*] [*A publication*]
DRUID ...... Digital Readout Unit and Interactive Displays   (MCD)
DRUIDS .... Diffuse Reflectance Using Infrared Dispersive Spectrophotometry
DRUJ .... Distal Radioulnar Joint [*Anatomy*]
DRUL .... Downrange Up Link [*Apollo*] [*NASA*]
DRUM .... Deep Reflections from the Upper Mantle [*Geology*]
Dru & Nap ... Drury's Irish Chancery Reports Tempore Napier [*1858-59*] [*A publication*]   (DLA)
D Rund .... Deutsche Rundschau [*A publication*]
DR UNIV PAR ... Doctor of the University of Paris   (ROG)
DRurSc ...... Doctor of Rural Science   (ADA)
Drury .... Drury's Irish Chancery Reports [*A publication*]   (DLA)
Drury Coll Bradley G Field Sta B ... Drury College. Bradley Geological Field Station. Bulletin [*A publication*]
Drury (Ir) ... Drury's Irish Chancery Reports [*A publication*]   (DLA)
Drury T Nap ... Drury's Irish Chancery Reports Tempore Napier [*1858-59*] [*A publication*]   (DLA)
Drury T Sug ... Drury's Irish Chancery Reports Tempore Sugden [*A publication*]   (DLA)
Drury & Wal ... Drury and Walsh's Irish Chancery Reports [*1837-40*] [*A publication*]   (DLA)
Drury & Wal (Ir) ... Drury and Walsh's Irish Chancery Reports [*1837-40*] [*A publication*]   (DLA)
Drury & War ... Drury and Warren's Irish Chancery Reports [*1841-43*] [*A publication*]   (DLA)
Drury & War (Ir) ... Drury and Warren's Irish Chancery Reports [*1841-43*] [*A publication*]   (DLA)
Dru & Sug .. Drury's Irish Chancery Reports Tempore Sugden [*A publication*]   (DLA)
Dru T Nap ... Drury's Irish Chancery Reports Tempore Napier [*1858-59*] [*A publication*]   (DLA)
Dru T Sug .. Drury's Irish Chancery Reports Tempore Sugden [*A publication*]   (DLA)
Dru T Sugden ... Drury's Irish Chancery Reports Tempore Sugden [*A publication*]   (DLA)
Dru & Wal ... Drury and Walsh's Irish Chancery Reports [*1837-40*] [*A publication*]   (DLA)
Dru & War ... Drury and Warren's Irish Chancery Reports [*1841-43*] [*A publication*]   (DLA)
Druzh N ..... Druzhba Narodov. Ezhemesiachnyi Literaturno-Khudozhestvennyi i Obshchestvenno-Politicheskii Zhurnal [*A publication*]
DRV .... Data Recovery Vehicle
DRV .... Deep-Diving Research Vehicles   (KSC)
DRV .... Deep Research Vehicle [*or Vessel*] [*NOO*]
DRV .... Democratic Republic of Vietnam [*North Vietnam*]
D Rv .... Deutsche Revue [*A publication*]
DRV .... Dravo Corp. [*NYSE symbol*]   (SPSG)
DRV .... Dumont D'Urville [*Pointe Geologie, Adelie*] [*Antarctica*] [*Seismograph station code, US Geological Survey*]   (SEIS)
DRVID ...... Differenced-Range Versus Integrated Doppler [*Charged particle measurement*]
DRVN .... Democratic Republic of Vietnam [*North Vietnam*]
DRVN .... Driven [*Automotive engineering*]
Drvna Ind ... Drvna Industrija [*A publication*]
DRVR .... Driver   (MSA)

DRVS .... Diabetic Retinopathy Vitrectomy Study [*National Eye Institute*]
DRVS .... Doppler RADAR Velocity Sensor
DRVS .... Drill Vise
DRVYA ..... Drevarsky Vyskum [*A publication*]
DRW .... Darwin [*Australia*] [*Airport symbol*]   (OAG)
DRW .... Defensive Radio Warfare   (NATG)
DRW .... Dennis R. Williams [*Designer's mark on US bicentennial dollar*]
dRW .... Deutsche Reichswaehrung [*German Standard Currency*] [*German*]
DRW .... Dirty RADWASTE [*Nuclear energy*]   (NRCH)
DRW .... Repro en Druk [*A publication*]
Dr & Wal ... Drury and Walsh's Irish Chancery Reports [*1837-40*] [*A publication*]   (DLA)
Dr & War ... Drury and Warren's Irish Chancery Reports [*1841-43*] [*A publication*]   (DLA)
DRWAW ... Distillery, Rectifying, Wine, and Allied Workers International Union of America [*Later, DWAW*]   (EA)
DRWEA ..... Draht-Welt [*A publication*]
DRWG .... Drawing   (NATG)
DR WIND ... Door or Window [*Freight*]
DRWN .... Drew National Corp. [*NASDAQ symbol*]   (NQ)
DRWWCF .. Damon Runyon-Walter Winchell Cancer Fund   (EA)
DRX .... Datarex Systems [*AMEX symbol*]   (SPSG)
DRX .... Drachma [*Monetary unit*] [*Greece*]
DRX .... Drexel University, School of Library and Information Science, Philadelphia, PA [*OCLC symbol*]   (OCLC)
DRX .... Drucox Petroleum [*Vancouver Stock Exchange symbol*]
DRXR .... Drexler Technology Corp. [*NASDAQ symbol*]   (NQ)
DRY .... Dreyfus Corp. [*NYSE symbol*]   (SPSG)
DRY .... Dryden Resources Corp. [*Vancouver Stock Exchange symbol*]
DRY .... Manchester, NH [*Location identifier*] [*FAA*]   (FAAL)
DRYR .... Dreyer's Grand Ice Cream, Inc. [*NASDAQ symbol*]   (NQ)
Dry Valley Drill Proj Bull ... Dry Valley Drilling Project. Bulletin. Northern Illinois University. Department of Geology [*A publication*]
DRZ .... Deep Reconnaissance Zone [*Army*]   (AABC)
DRZA .... Agades-Sud [*Niger*] [*ICAO location identifier*]   (ICLI)
DRZD .... Dirkou [*Niger*] [*ICAO location identifier*]   (ICLI)
DRZG .... Goure [*Niger*] [*ICAO location identifier*]   (ICLI)
DRZI .... Iferouane [*Niger*] [*ICAO location identifier*]   (ICLI)
DRZL .... Arlit [*Niger*] [*ICAO location identifier*]   (ICLI)
DRZL .... Drizzle [*Meteorology*]   (FAAC)
DRZM .... Maine-Soroa [*Niger*] [*ICAO location identifier*]   (ICLI)
DRZN .... N'Guigmi [*Niger*] [*ICAO location identifier*]   (ICLI)
DRZR .... Zinder [*Niger*] [*ICAO location identifier*]   (ICLI)
DRZT .... Tanout [*Niger*] [*ICAO location identifier*]   (ICLI)
DS .... Compagnie Senegalaise de Transports Aeriens [*Senegal*] [*ICAO designator*]   (ICDA)
D-S .... Dada-Surrealism
DS .... Dairy Shrine   (EA)
DS .... Dajnavna Sigurnost [*Bulgarian Secret Police affiliated with the KGB*]
DS .... Dal Segno [*Repeat from the Sign*] [*Music*]
DS .... Dallas Semiconductor [*NYSE symbol*]   (SPSG)
DS .... Dalton on Sheriffs [*A publication*]   (DLA)
DS .... Dance Tuition Schools [*Public-performance tariff class*] [*British*]
D & S .... Dangerous and Suspicious
DS .... Danmarks Statistik [*Denmark*]
DS .... Dansk Samling [*Danish Union*]   (PPE)
DS .... Danske Studier [*A publication*]
DS .... Dantrolene Sodium [*Muscle relaxant*]
DS .... Daoist Sanctuary   (EA)
DS .... Dark Shadows [*Television program*]
DS .... Data Scanning   (BUR)
DS .... Data Segment
DS .... Data Set [*Data processing*]
DS .... Data Sheet   (NATG)
DS .... Data Station [*Spectroscopy*]
DS .... Data Storage [*Data processing*]   (NASA)
DS .... Data Synchronization   (DEN)
DS .... Data System
DS .... Data Systems Technician [*Navy rating*]
DS .... Date of Service [*Military*]
DS .... Daughters of Scotia   (EA)
D of S .... Daughters of Scotia [*Bayonne, NJ*]
D of S .... Day of Supply [*Military*]
DS .... Days after Sight [*Business term*]
D & S .... De Gex and Smale's English Chancery Reports [*63-64 English Reprint*] [*1846-52*] [*A publication*]   (DLA)
D & S .... Deane and Swabey's English Ecclesiastical Reports [*A publication*]   (DLA)
DS .... Dead Air Space [*Physiology*]
DS .... Debenture Stock [*Investment term*]   (ADA)
DS .... Debugging System
DS .... Decade Scaler   (MSA)
DS .... Decanning Scuttle
DS .... Decimal Subtract
DS .... Decision Sheet   (NATG)
DS .... Decision and Switching

DS .... Decistere [*Unit of measure*] (ROG)
DS .... Decomposition Sintering (RDA)
DS .... Decontamination Shop [*Nuclear energy*] (NRCH)
DS .... Deepstar [*A manned, self-propelled submersible vehicle built by Western Electric Corp.*]
DS .... Defence Secretariat [*Ministry of Defence*] [*British*]
DS .... Defense Support (CINC)
DS .... Define Storage
DS .... Define Symbol
DS .... Degree of Substitution
DS .... Dekastere [*Unit of measure*] (ROG)
DS .... Delius Society (EA)
DS .... Delivery Schedule
DS .... Delphian Society
DS .... Delphinium Society (EA)
DS .... Delta Society (EA)
DS .... Demokraticheska Sgovor [*Democratic Alliance*] [*Bulgaria*] [*Political party*] (PPE)
DS .... Demokraticka Strana [*Democratic Party*] [*Czechoslovakia*] [*Political party*] (PPE)
DS .... Demokratikos Sinaspismos [*Democratic Coalition*] [*Greece*] [*Political party*] (PPE)
DS .... Demokratikos Synagermos [*Democratic Rally*] [*Greek Cyprus*] [*Political party*] (PPE)
DS .... Dental Surgery [*or Surgeon*] [*Medical Officer designation*] [*British*]
D of S .... Department of State
DS .... Department of State
DS .... Depolarization Shift [*Electrophysiology*]
D of S .... Depot of Supplies [*Marine Corps*]
DS .... Depression Subtle [*Psychology*]
DS .... Depth Sounder
DS .... Deputy-Secretary [*British*]
DS .... Deputy Sheriff (DLA)
DS .... Dermatan Sulfate [*Biochemistry*]
DS .... Descent Stage [*NASA*] (KSC)
D/S .... Descent State [*NASA*] (KSC)
DS .... Descent System
DS .... Design Sheet
DS .... Design Specification (MCD)
DS .... Design Standards
DS .... Destroyer Surface-Effect Ship (MCD)
DS .... Detached Service [*Army*]
DS .... Detail Specification (MCD)
DS .... Detective Sergeant [*Scotland Yard*]
D et S .... Detur et Signatur [*Let It Be Given and Labeled*] [*Pharmacy*]
DS .... Deutsche Studien [*A publication*]
DS .... Developments in Sedimentology [*Elsevier Book Series*] [*A publication*]
DS .... Device Selector
D/S .... Dextrose and Saline [*Medicine*]
DS .... Dial System
D/S .... Diastolic/Systolic [*Ratio*] [*Cardiology*]
DS .... Dickens Society (EA)
DS .... Dictionnaire de Spiritualite Ascetique et Mystique, Doctrine et Histoire [*Paris*] [*A publication*] (BJA)
DS .... Diderot Studies [*A publication*]
DS .... Dielectric Spectroscopy
DS .... Difference Sensation [*Psychology*]
DS .... Difference Spectroscopy
DS .... Difference, Starboard [*Navigation*]
DS .... Differential Spacing [*Typography*]
DS .... Digit Select (BUR)
DS .... Digit Symbol [*Psychometrics*]
DS .... Digital Signal
DS .... Digital System
DS .... Dilute Strength [*Chemistry*]
DS .... Diode Switch
DS .... Dioptric Strength
DS .... Dip Soldering
D-S .... Diplomate, American Board of Surgery (DHSM)
DS .... Diplomatic Service [*or Servant*] [*British*]
DS .... Direct Sequence [*Telecommunications*] (TEL)
D/S .... Direct Ship (MCD)
DS .... Direct Steamer
DS .... Direct Support [*Army*]
DS .... Directing Staff
DS .... Direction Sports (EA)
DS .... Directionally Solidified [*Metallurgy*]
DS .... Director of Services [*Air Force*]
DS .... Director of Signals [*British military*] (DMA)
DS .... Disabled Spouse [*Title XVI*] [*Social Security Administration*] (OICC)
DS .... Disaster Services [*Red Cross*]
DS .... Discarding Sabot [*Navy*]
DS .... Disconnect Switch (MSA)
DS .... Discontinue (BUR)
D/S .... Disintegrations per Second
DS .... Disjunctive Syllogism [*Rule of inference*] [*Logic*]
DS .... Disk Storage [*Data processing*] (NASA)
DS .... Disk System

DS .... Dispersion Staining [*Analytical chemistry*]
DS .... Dispersion Strengthened [*Metallurgy*]
DS .... Display Screen
DS .... Display Section
D & S .... Display and Storage (MSA)
DS .... Display Subsystem (MCD)
DS .... Disseminated Sclerosis [*Medicine*]
Ds .... Dissimulation [*Psychology*]
DS .... Dissociator [*Genetics*]
DS .... Dissolved Solids
DS .... Distant Surveillance
D/S .... Distributed/Stand-Alone [*Pricing*]
DS .... Distributed System
DS .... Distribution Space
DS .... District Secretary [*British*]
DS .... Diver, Salvage [*Navy rating*]
DS .... Diving Saucer
DS .... Divisional Superintendent [*British police*]
DS .... Divorce Support [*An association*] (EA)
DS .... Dock Service
DS .... Docking Survey
DS .... Docking System
DS .... Doctor of Science
D & S .... Doctor and Student [*A publication*] (DLA)
DS .... Doctor of Surgery (ADA)
DS .... Document Signed
D & S .... Documentation and Status (AAG)
DS .... Documented Sample (KSC)
DS .... Dokumentation Schweisstechnik [*Welding Documentation*] [*Federal Institute for Materials Testing*] [*Information service or system*] (IID)
D & S .... Dollars & Sense [*Economic Affairs Bureau*] [*A publication*]
DS .... Dolphin Society (EA)
DS .... Domesday Survey [*Census-like record of the lands of England, 1085-86*]
DS .... Domestic Service [*Equipment specification*]
D & S .... Dominance and Submission
DS .... Dominican Studies [*A publication*]
DS .... Dominion Securities Ltd. [*Toronto Stock Exchange symbol*] [*Vancouver Stock Exchange symbol*]
DS .... Dominus [*The Lord*] [*Latin*]
DS .... Donor's Serum [*Medicine*]
DS .... Double Sandwich
D/S .... Double-Screened [*Coal*]
DS .... Double-Sided [*Disks*] [*Data processing*]
DS .... Double Silk [*Wire insulation*] (AAG)
DS .... Double Slave [*LORAN stations*]
DS .... Double Stitch [*Bookbinding*]
DS .... Double Stout [*Brewing*] (ROG)
DS .... Double Strength [*Medicine*]
DS .... Double Subdominance [*Ethology*]
DS .... Down's Syndrome [*Medicine*]
DS .... Downspout (AAG)
DS .... Downstage [*Toward audience*] [*A stage direction*]
DS .... Downstream (AAG)
DS .... Downtime between Sorties [*Military*] (AFIT)
DS .... Dracula Society (EA)
DS .... Draft Stop [*Technical drawings*]
DS .... Drama Survey [*A publication*]
DS .... Drawing Society (EA)
DS .... Drawing Summary (AAG)
D & S .... Drewry and Smale's English Chancery Reports [*A publication*] (DLA)
DS .... Drill Sergeant [*Army*]
DS .... Drive System
DS .... Drop Siding
DS .... Drugstore [*US maps*]
DS .... Drum Storage [*Data processing*] (IEEE)
DS .... Drum Switch
DS .... Dry Sunk (ROG)
DS .... Dry Swallow [*Medicine*]
DS .... Dudley Herbarium of Stanford University [*San Francisco, CA*]
DS .... Durham & Southern Railway Co. [*AAR code*]
DS .... Dust Storm [*Astronomy*]
DS .... Duty Section [*Air Force*] (AFM)
DS .... Duty Status [*Air Force*] (AFM)
DS .... Dwarf Shoot [*Botany*]
DS .... Dyestuffs
D/S .... Dynamic to Static
DS .... Dynamic Stories [*A publication*]
DS .... Societe Nationale de Transport Aerien Air Senegal [*Senegal*] [*ICAO designator*] (FAAC)
DS .... United States Department of State Library [*Division of Library and Reference Services*], Washington, DC [*Library symbol*] [*Library of Congress*] (LCLS)
DS1 .... Data Systems Technician, First Class [*Navy rating*]
DS2 .... Data Systems Technician, Second Class [*Navy rating*]
DS-2 .... Decontaminating Solution Number Two [*Chemical defense*] [*Army*] (RDA)
DS3 .... Data Systems Technician, Third Class [*Navy rating*]
DS4 .... Direct Support Unit Standard Supply System [*Army*] (AABC)

D5/S	Dextrose (5%) in Saline [*Medicine*]
DSA	Dairy Science Abstracts [*Database*] [*Commonwealth Bureau of Dairy Science and Technology*] [*Information service or system*] (CRD)
DSA	Dalcroze Society of America (EA)
DSA	Dante Society of America (EA)
DSA	Data Set Adapter [*Data processing*]
DSA	Data Systems Administration (NVT)
DSA	Dataroute Serving Area [*TransCanada Telephone System/ Computer Communications Group*]
DSA	Day Sailer Association (EA)
DSA	Defense Shipping Authority
DSA	Defense Supply Agency [*Later, Defense Logistics Agency*] [*Alexandria, VA*]
DSA	Defense Supply Association [*Later, ALA*] (EA)
DSA	Defense Support Agency
DSA	Defense Systems Analysis [*DoD*]
DSA	Delay Study Analysis
DSA	Democratic Socialists of America [*Political party*] (EA)
DSA	Dental Surgery Assistant [*British*]
DSA	Deployable Solar Array
DSA	Deputy Scientific Adviser [*British*]
DSA	Deputy-Secretary to the Admiralty [*British*]
DSA	Deputy Sector Advisor
DSA	Deputy Senior Advisor
DSA	Desert Air, Inc. [*Seattle, WA*] [*FAA designator*] (FAAC)
DSA	Design Schedule Analysis
DSA	Designated Security Agency (NATG)
DSA	Development Signature Approval
DSA	Developmental Sentence Analysis [*Education*]
DSA	Dial Service Analysis [*Telecommunications*] (TEL)
DSA	Dial Service Assistance [*Telecommunications*] (CET)
DSA	Dickens Studies Annual [*A publication*]
DSA	Diffusion Self-Alignment
DSA	Digital Serving Area [*Telecommunications*] (TEL)
DSA	Digital Signal Analyzer (IEEE)
DSA	Digital Spectrum Analyzer (NVT)
DSA	Digital Storage Architecture
DSA	Digital Subtraction Angiography [*Medicine*]
DSA	Dimensionally Stabilized Anode
DSA	Diploma in Social Administration
DSA	Direct Selling Association (EA)
DSA	Direct Service Activities (MCD)
DSA	Direct Storage Access
DSA	Discrete Sample Analyzer
DSA	Dispersal Anchorage [*Navy*] (NVT)
DSA	District Senior Advisory (MCD)
DSA	Division Service Area [*Army*]
DSA	Division Support Area (AABC)
DSA	Documentation Staging Area [*Military*]
DSA	Dodecylsuccinic Anhydride [*Organic chemistry*]
DSA	Doppler Spectrum Analyzer
DSA	Down's Syndrome Association [*British*]
DSA	Dozenal Society of America (EA)
DSA	Drillsite Supervisors Association (EA)
DSA	Drum Seiners Association (EA)
DSA	Duluth, South Shore & Atlantic Railroad [*AAR code*] [*Obsolete*]
DSA	Dynamic Signal Analyzer
DSA	Dynamic Spring Analysis
DSA	Dynamic Storage Area (CMD)
DSA	Spectro-Angular Density Method of Forecasting Ocean Waves [*Marine science*] (MSC)
DSA	Supreme Lodge of the Danish Sisterhood of America (EA)
DSAA	Defense Security Assistance Agency
DSAA	Driving School Association of America (EA)
DSA/AAO	Development Signature Approval - Advanced Assembly Outline
DSAB	Dictionary of South African Biography [*A publication*]
DSABL	Disable (AABC)
DSABLSEVP	Disability Severance Pay
DSAC	Deputy Supreme Allied Commander (AABC)
DSAC	Diaper Service Accreditation Council (EA)
DSAC	Dixon Springs Agricultural Center [*University of Illinois*] [*Research center*] (RCD)
DSACAS	Defense Supply Agency Contract Administration Services [*DoD*]
DSACEL	Defense Supply Agency Contractor Experience List [*DoD*]
DSACEUR	Deputy Supreme Allied Commander, Europe (NATG)
DSAD	Data Systems and Analysis Directorate (MCD)
DSAD	Data Systems Application Division [*Agricultural Research Service*]
DSAD	Data Systems Authorization Directory (AFIT)
DSAD	Destruct Safe Arm Device
D-SAFE	Depot System Support Activity Far East [*US Army Materiel Command*]
DSA/FO	Development Signature Approval - Fabrication Order
DSAFSM	Deputy Safeguard [*Missile defense*] System Manager (AABC)
DSAFSM	Deputy System Manager [*Army*] (AABC)
DSAG	Defence Systems Analysis Group [*Canada*]
DSAH	Defense Supply Agency Handbook [*DoD*]

DSAHBK	Defense Supply Agency Handbook [*DoD*]
DSAIER	Defense Supply Agency Industrial Equipment Reserve [*DoD*]
DS-AIK	Demokratiske Sosialister - Arbeidernes Informasjon Kommitte [*Democratic Socialists - Workers' Information Committee*] [*Norway*] [*Political party*] (PPE)
DSAM	Defense Supply Agency Manual [*DoD*]
DSAM	Dual-Surface Attenuation Module (MCD)
DSAMOS	Diffusion Self-Aligned Metal-Oxide Semiconductor (BUR)
DSAN	Debug Syntax Analysis [*Telecommunications*] (TEL)
DSAO	Data Systems Automation Office [*Columbus, Ohio*] [*Military*]
DSAO	Diplomatic Service Administration Office [*British*]
DSAP	Data Systems Automation Program
DSAP	Dee Scofield Awareness Program (EA)
DSAP	Defense Security Assistance Program (NVT)
DSAP	Defense Supply Agency Poster [*DoD*] (MCD)
DSAP	Defense Systems Application Program [*DoD*]
DSAP	Destination Service Access Point
DSAP	Directory Scope Analysis Program [*Bell System*]
DSAR	Defense Supply Agency Regulation [*DoD*]
DSARC	Defense Systems Acquisition Review Council [*Pentagon board*] (MCD)
DSARDS	Dante Studies with the Annual Report of the Dante Society [*A publication*]
DSAS	Del Shannon Appreciation Society (EAIO)
DSAS	Dial Service Assistance Switchboard [*Telecommunications*] (CET)
DSAS	Direct Support Aviation Section [*Army*]
DSAS	Discrete Subaortic Stenosis [*Medicine*]
DSASC	Defense Supply Agency Administrative Support Center [*DoD*]
D Sa Sc	Doctor of Sacred Sciences
DSASDE	Alabama. Agricultural Experiment Station. Auburn University. Agronomy and Soils Departmental Series [*A publication*]
DSASO	Deputy Senior Air Staff Officer [*British military*] (DMA)
DSAT	Defensive Satellite (MCD)
DSAT	Disk Storage Allocation Table (MCD)
DSATC	Descend so as to Cross [*Aviation*] (FAAC)
DSATR	Descend so as to Reach [*Aviation*] (FAAC)
DSAW	Dispersive Surface Acoustic Wave (MCD)
DSA-WRAO	Defense Supply Agency - Western Regional Audit Office [*DoD*]
DSB	Dahlgren Smoothbore
DSB	Danske Statsbaner [*Danish State Railways*]
DSB	Data Set Block
DSB	Debit sans Brene [*Charge without Abatement*] [*French*] [*Business term*]
DSB	Debit sans Brevet [*Debt without Writ*] [*French*] [*Legal term*] (DLA)
DSB	Debitum Sine Brevi [*Debt without Writ*] [*Latin*] [*Legal term*] (DLA)
DSB	Decade Synchronic Bridge
DSB	Defence Signal Board [*British*]
DSB	Defense Science Board [*DoD*]
DSB	Denominational Schools Board [*Australia*]
DSB	Department of State. Bulletin [*A publication*]
DSB	Device Status Byte [*Data processing*] (BUR)
DSB	Diagnostic Skills Battery [*Educational test*]
DSB	Dictionary of Scientific Biography [*A publication*]
DSB	Diplomatic Services Bureau
DSB	Direct Sound Broadcast
DSB	Distribution Switchboard
DSB	Divine Science Bachelor
DSB	Document Status Bulletin (MCD)
DSB	Double Sideband
DSB	Double Strand Break [*Genetics*]
DSB	Drill Spacer Block (MCD)
DSB	Drug Supervisory Body
DSB	Duty Steam Boat [*British military*] (DMA)
DS in BA	Doctor of Science in Business Administration
DSBAM	Double-Sideband Amplitude Modulation [*Telecommunications*] (TEL)
DSBAMRC	Double-Sideband Amplitude Modulation Reduced Carrier [*Telecommunications*] (IEEE)
DSBC	DS Bancor, Inc. [*NASDAQ symbol*] (NQ)
DSBCO	Defense Surplus Bidders Control Office
DSBE	Dasibi Environmental Corp. [*Glendale, CA*] [*NASDAQ symbol*] (NQ)
DSBE	Di-secondary-butyl Ether [*Organic chemistry*]
DSBEC	Double-Sideband Emitted Carrier [*Telecommunications*] (TEL)
DSBG	Disbursing (AFM)
DSBL	Disable (MSA)
DSBLTY	Disability
DSBRC	Double-Sideband Reduced Carrier [*Telecommunications*] (TEL)
DSBS	Defense Science Board Subcommittee [*DoD*]
DSBSC	Double-Sideband Suppressed Carrier [*Modulation*]
DSBTC	Double-Sideband Transmitted Carrier [*Telecommunications*]
DSB (UN)	Drug Supervisory Body of the United Nations
DSBV	Double-Sealed Ball Valve
DSC	Danish Shippers Council (DS)
DSC	Data Separator Card (MCD)

DSC .... Data Services Center [*International City Management Association*] [*Information service or system*]   (IID)
DSC .... Data Set Controller
DSC .... Data Statistics Comparison Software [*Data processing*]
DSC .... Data Synchronizer Channel
DSC .... Data System Console   (CAAL)
DSC .... Data Systems Controller   (MCD)
DSC .... Data Systems Technician, Chief [*Navy rating*]
DSC .... Debye-Sears Cell [*Physics*]
DSC .... [A] Decade of Study of the Constitution   (EA)
DSC .... Decent Suit of Civvies [*British slang military decoration*] [*World War I*]
DSC .... Decision Sciences Corporation   (IID)
DSC .... Dedicated Signal Conditioner   (MCD)
DSC .... Defense Shipping Council [*NATO*]   (NVT)
DSC .... Defense Supply Center   (AABC)
DSC .... Defense Supply Corporation [*World War II*]
DSC .... Defensiveness Scale for Children [*Psychology*]
DSC .... Delaware State College [*Dover*]
DSC .... Depot Supply Center
DSC .... Deputy Sheriff Clerk   (ROG)
DSC .... Design Safety Criteria [*Nuclear energy*]   (NRCH)
DSC .... Differential Scanning Calorimeter [*or Calorimetry*] [*Instrumentation*]
DSC .... Differential Signal Control
DSC .... Digital Scan Converter   (MCD)
DSC .... Digital Selective Calling
DSC .... Digital Signal Conditioner   (MCD)
DSC .... Digital Sound Corporation [*Telecommunications service*]   (TSSD)
DSC .... Digital Stabilization Console
DSC .... Digital Subscriber Controller [*Telecommunications*]
DSC .... Direct Satellite Communications
DSC .... Disappearance of Single Cell [*Assay*] [*Cytology*]
DSC .... Discone Antenna
DSC .... Discrete System Concept
DSC .... Discrete Timesystems, Inc. [*Toronto Stock Exchange symbol*]
DSC .... Disk Storage Controller [*Data processing*]   (CMD)
DSC .... Disodium Cromoglycate [*Pharmacology*]
DSC .... Distant Station Connected [*Data processing*]   (BUR)
DSC .... Distinguished Service Cross [*Military decoration*] [*US and British*]
DSC .... Distribution of Stockage Code   (AABC)
DSC .... District Switching Center [*Telecommunications*]
DSC .... DIVAD Systems Controller   (MCD)
DSC .... Divided Spouses Coalition   (EA)
DSC .... Doctor of Christian Science
DSC .... Doctor of Commercial Science
D Sc............ Doctor of Science
D Sc............ Doctor Scientiae [*Doctor of Science*] [*Latin*]
DSC .... Doctor of Surgical Chiropody
DSC .... Document Service Center
DSC .... Documentation Standards Committee [*British*]   (DIT)
DSC .... Doppler Shift Compensation [*Physics*]
DSC .... Double Silk Covered [*Wire insulation*]
DSC .... Down's Syndrome Congress [*Later, NDSC*]   (EA)
DSC .... Downstage Center [*Toward audience*] [*A stage direction*]
DSC .... Drain Saturation Current
DSC .... Duns Scotus College [*Detroit, MI*]
DSC .... Dynamic Sequential Control   (AAG)
DSC .... Dynamic Slide Compensator
DSC .... Dynamic Standby Computer   (KSC)
DSC .... International Die Sinkers' Conference
DSC .... Scottish Rite of Freemasonry, Southern Jurisdiction USA, Supreme Council Library, Washington, DC [*Library symbol*] [*Library of Congress*]   (LCLS)
DSC .... South Carolina State Library, Columbia, SC [*OCLC symbol*]   (OCLC)
D SC.......... United States District Court for the District of South Carolina   (DLA)
DSCA........ Department of State Correspondents Association   (EA)
DScA........ Doctor of Science in Agriculture
DScAdm .... Doctor in Administrative Sciences
DSCAEF.... Deputy Supreme Commander, Allied Expeditionary Force
DScAg....... Doctor of Science in Agriculture   (ADA)
D Sc Agr .... Doctor of Science in Agriculture
DSc(Agric) ... Doctor of Science in Agriculture   (ADA)
D'scape ...... Designscape [*A publication*]
DSCAPRS ... Dental Suction Apparatus
DSCB........ Data Set Control Block [*Data processing*]
DSCC........ Datasouth Computer Corporation [*NASDAQ symbol*]   (NQ)
DSCC........ Deep Space Communications Complex   (MCD)
DSCC........ Democratic Senatorial Campaign Committee [*Commercial firm*]   (EA)
DSCC........ Desiccant [*Chemistry*]
DSCC........ Division Support Control Center [*Army*]
D Sc Com ... Doctor of Science in Commerce
DSCD .... Directorate of Stores and Clothing Development [*British*]
DScD .... Doctor of Science and Didactics   (ADA)
DScE........ Doctor of Science in Engineering
D Sc Econ .. Doctor of Science in Economics

D Sc (Eng) ... Doctor of Science (Engineering)   (EY)
DSCF......... Doppler-Shifted Constant Frequency [*Biosonar research*]
DScFin....... Doctor of Financial Science
DScFor....... Doctor of Science in Forestry   (ADA)
DSCG .... Disodium Cromoglycate [*Pharmacology*]
DSCH .... Dark Skies for Comet Halley [*Defunct*]   (EA)
D Sch Mus ... Doctor of School Music
D Sc Hyg.... Doctor of Science in Hygiene
D Sci .... Doctor of Science
D Sci H ...... Doctor of Science and Hygiene
DSCIM ...... Display System Computer Input Multiplexer [*NASA*]   (NASA)
D Sc L .... Doctor of the Science of Law
DSCLO....... Disclosure-Online [*Information service or system*]
DSCM .... Data Systems Technician, Master Chief [*Navy rating*]
DSCM .... Display Components, Inc. [*Westford, MA*] [*NASDAQ symbol*]   (NQ)
DScMil ...... Doctor of Military Science   (ADA)
D Scn......... Doctor of Scientology
DSCNT...... Descent   (FAAC)
D Sc O .... Doctor of the Science of Oratory
DSCOA9 ... Duquesne Science Counselor [*A publication*]
DSCONT... Discontinue   (MSA)
D Sc Os...... Doctor of the Science of Osteopathy
DSCP........ Datascope Corp. [*NASDAQ symbol*]   (NQ)
DSCP........ Defense Satellite Communications Program   (MCD)
DSCP........ Defense Suppression Concept Plan   (MCD)
DSCP........ Division Supply Control Point
DScP......... Doctor of Political Science
DSCR........ District Sub-Chief Ranger [*Ancient Order of Foresters*]
DSCRM...... Discriminator   (MSA)
DSCRP...... Descriptor [*Data processing*]
DSCS .... Data Systems Technician, Senior Chief [*Navy rating*]
DSCS .... Defense Satellite Communications System [*DoD*]
DSCS .... Desk Side Computer System [*General Electric Co.*]
DSCS .... Digital Simulator Computer System
DScS .... Doctor of Social Science
DSCS NCF ... Defense Satellite Communications System Network Control Facility   (MCD)
DScSoc....... Doctor of Social Science
DSCS OCE ... Defense Satellite Communications System Operations Control Element   (MCD)
DSc(Social Sciences) ... Doctor of Science in the Social Sciences, University of Southampton [*British*]   (DBQ)
DSCS PO... Defense Satellite Communications System Program Office   (MCD)
DSCT........ Double Secondary Current Transformer   (MSA)
D Sc Tech .. Doctor of Technical Science
D Sc in VM ... Doctor of Science in Veterinary Medicine
DSD .... Data Set Definition [*Data processing*]   (IBMDP)
DSD .... Data Status Display
DSD .... Data Storage Device
DSD .... Data Structure Diagram
DSD .... Data Systems Designator   (AFM)
DSD .... Dead Sea Scrolls: Manual of Discipline   (BJA)
DSD .... DECHEMA [*Deutsche Gesellschaft fuer Chemisches Appartewesen, Chemische Technik, und Biotechnologie eV*] Stoffdaten Dienst [*DECHEMA Physical Property Data Service*] [*Information service or system*]   (IID)
DSD .... Deep Submergence Device   (NVT)
DSD .... Deep Suspended DIFAR [*Military*]   (CAAL)
DSD .... Demographic Surveys Division [*Census*]   (OICC)
DSD .... Departmental Science Development [*National Science Foundation*]
DSD .... Depression Sine Depression [*Psychology*]
DSD .... Deputy Secretary of Defense
dsd.............. Diamond-Square-Diamond [*Lipscomb polyhedral rearrangement in borane anion and carborane series*]
DSD .... Digital System Design   (IEEE)
DSD .... Digital System Diagram
DSD .... Diode Semiconductor Device
DSD .... Diplomatic Service Department [*Brunei*]   (DS)
DSD .... Director of Signal Department [*Obsolete*] [*Navy*] [*British*]
DSD .... Director of Staff Duties [*Military*] [*British*]
DSD .... Disk Storage Device [*Data processing*]
DSD .... Divine Science Doctor
DSD .... Doctrine and Systems Directorate [*Army*]   (RDA)
DSD .... Double-Single-Dummy [*in game of bridge*]
DSD .... Dry Sterile Dressing [*Medicine*]
DSD .... DSIF [*Deep Space Instrumentation Facility*] Supply Depot [*NASA*]
DSD .... Dual-Speed Drive
DSD .... La Desirade [*Guadeloupe*] [*Airport symbol*]   (OAG)
D SD .... United States District Court for the District of South Dakota   (DLA)
DSD .... United States Superintendent of Documents, Washington, DC [*Library symbol*] [*Library of Congress*]   (LCLS)
DSDAR...... Deputy and Scientific Director of Army Research
DSDC .... Data Systems Design Center [*Air Force*]
DSDD .... Defense Subsystem Development and Demonstration   (MCD)
DSDD .... Double-Sided, Double-Density Disk [*Data processing*]
DS & DH ... Data Switching and Data Handling   (AFM)

DSDI......... Descendants of the Signers of the Declaration of Independence (EA)
DS Di........ Doctor of Scientific Didactics
DSDIO....... Director, Strategic Defense Initiative Organization [*Military*] (SDI)
DSDL......... Data Storage Description Language
dsDNA....... Deoxyribonucleic Acid, Double-Stranded [*Biochemistry*] [*Genetics*]
DSDP........ Data System Development Plan
DSDP........ Deep Sea Drilling Project [*Later, IPOD*] [*National Science Foundation*]
DSDR........ Design Section Drawing Record (MCD)
DSDRS...... DoD [*Department of Defense*] Standard Data Repository System
DSDS........ Dataphone Switched Digital Service [*AT & T*]
DSDS........ Digital Synchro Data Source
DSDS........ Document Survey Data Sheet (KSC)
DSDS........ Dynamic Synchro Data Service [*or Source*] (MCD)
DSDS....... Naval School Deep Sea Divers
DSDT........ Data-Set Definition Table [*Data processing*]
DSDT........ Deformographic Storage Display Tube [*IBM Corp.*]
DSDT........ Discrete Space and Discrete Time
DSDU........ Data Storage Distribution Unit (MCD)
DSDVOR .. Double-Sideband Doppler Very-High-Frequency Omnidirectional Range [*FAA*]
DSE.......... Data Set Extension [*IBM Corp.*] [*Data processing*] (BUR)
DSE.......... Data Storage Equipment
DSE.......... Data Support Element (MCD)
DSE.......... Data Switching Exchange [*Telecommunications*]
DSE.......... Data Systems Engineering [*A publication*]
DSE.......... Data Systems Engineering
DSE.......... Debye-Sears Effect [*Physics*]
DSE.......... Dessie [*Ethiopia*] [*Airport symbol*] (OAG)
DSE.......... Detector, Selector, and Effector [*Social science*]
DSE.......... Development Student Engineer (MCD)
DSE.......... Development Support Equipment
DSE.......... Digital Shaft Encoder
DSE.......... Dimensionally Stabilized Electrode [*Electrochemistry*]
DSE.......... Direct Support Element [*Military*] (NVT)
DSE.......... Directorate of Systems Engineering (AAG)
DSE.......... Distal Sequence Element [*Genetics*]
DSE.......... Distributed Systems Environment [*Honeywell, Inc.*] (BUR)
DSE.......... Doctor of Sanitary Engineering
DSE.......... Doctor of Science in Economics
DSE.......... Draft Safety Evaluation (NRCH)
DSE.......... Driver Screening Evaluator
DSE.......... Dyad Symmetry Element [*Genetics*]
DSE.......... Dynamic System Electronics
DSEA........ Data Storage Electronics Assembly [*Apollo*] [*NASA*]
DSEA........ Davis Submerged Escape Apparatus [*British military*] (DMA)
D Se A...... Doctor of Secretarial Arts
DSEB........ Defense Shipping Executive Board [*NATO*] (NVT)
DSec......... Degre Second. Studies in French Literature [*A publication*]
DSEC........ Director of Security (AABC)
DSECEL..... DGU [*Geological Survey of Denmark*] Series C [*A publication*]
DSECT...... Dummy Control Section [*Data processing*]
DSED........ Defense Suppression Expendable Drone (MCD)
DSEE........ Designated Special Emphasis Engineering (KSC)
DSEF........ Direct Selling Education Foundation (EA)
DSE/FAD ... Data Systems Environment Functions and Application Design [*Course*] [*Data processing*]
DSEG........ Data Systems Engineering Group (MCD)
DSEG........ Design Studies Evaluation Group [*NATO*] (NATG)
DSEG........ Developments in Solid Earth Geophysics [*Elsevier Book Series*] [*A publication*]
DSEI......... Daily Summary of Enemy Intelligence [*World War II*]
DSEL........ Doctor of Science and English Literature
DS Eng....... Doctor of Sanitary Engineering
DSENGA..... Disengaging
DSENGR... Data Systems Engineer
DSEP........ Defense Science and Engineering Program (MCD)
DSES........ Defense Systems Evaluation Squadron [*Air Force*] (AFM)
D Se Sc...... Doctor of Secretarial Science
DSESq....... Defense System Evaluation Squadron [*Air Force*]
D Se St....... Doctor of Secretarial Studies
DSF........... Dairy Suppliers Foundation [*Defunct*] (EA)
DSF........... Data Scanning and Formatting
DSF........... Daughters of St. Francis of Assisi [*Roman Catholic religious order*]
DSF........... Day-Second-Foot [*Measurement*]
DSF........... Defense Stock Fund [*DoD*]
DSF........... Delancey Street Foundation (EA)
D & SF ...... Denver & Santa Fe Railway
DSF..........., Departmental Square Feet (MCD)
DSF........... Design Safety Factor
DSF........... Deutsch-Sowjetische-Freundschaft [*German-Soviet Friendship*] [*Common street name in East Germany*]
DSF........... Development Stimulating Factor [*Biochemistry*]
DSF........... Directional Solidification Furnace
DSF........... Disk Storage Facility [*Data processing*]
DSF........... Disulfiram [*Organic chemistry*]

DSF........... Doctor of the Science of Forestry
DSF........... Dynamic Science Fiction [*A publication*]
DSFA........ Defense Solid Fuels Administration [*Terminated, 1954*]
DSFC........ Dark Shadows Fan Club (EA)
DSFC........ Dinah Shore Fan Club (EA)
DSFC........ Direct Side Force Control [*Aviation*]
DSFC........ Dogman and the Shepherds Fan Club (EA)
DSFF........ Downflow Stationary Fixed-Film [*Chemical engineering*]
DSFG........ Diamond Setters Fraternal Guild (EA)
DSFI......... Derogatis Sexual Functioning Inventory [*Psychology*]
DSFI......... Divine Science Federation International (EA)
DSFNS...... Deutsche-Slawische Forschungen zur Namenkunde und Siedlungsgeschichte [*A publication*]
DSFR........ Detailed System Functional Requirements
DSFT........ Dansk Skovforenings Tidsskrift [*A publication*]
DSFT......... Detection Scheme with Fixed Thresholds [*Communication signal*]
DSFTA...... Dansk Skovforenings Tidsskrift [*A publication*]
DSFTA5.... Dansk Skovforenings Tidsskrift [*A publication*]
DSFU........ Danish Sailors' and Firemen's Union (EA)
DSG.......... Danzig Study Group [*German Philatelic Society*] (EA)
DSG.......... Decision Support Graphics [*Hewlett-Packard Co.*]
DSG.......... Deep Submergence Group
DSG.......... Defense Suppression Group [*DoD*] (MCD)
DSG.......... Defense Systems Group
DSG.......... Democratic Study Group (EA)
DSG.......... Deoxyspergualin [*Antineoplastic drug*]
DSG.......... Deputy Secretary General (NATG)
DSG.......... Desaguadero [*Bolivia*] [*Seismograph station code, US Geological Survey*] [*Closed*] (SEIS)
DSG.......... Designate (AABC)
DSG.......... Designatronics, Inc. [*AMEX symbol*] (SPSG)
DSG.......... Designer Shoe Guild (EA)
DSG.......... Deutsche Studien zur Geistesgeschichte [*A publication*]
DSG.......... Digital Signal Generator
DSG.......... Direct Support Group [*Army*] (AABC)
DSG.......... Directed Studies Group [*Air Force*] (AFM)
dsg........... Dressing [*Medicine*]
DSGEAX... Desinfektion und Gesundheitswesen [*A publication*]
DS in Ge Engr ... Doctor of Science in Geological Engineering
DSGM....... Director Standing Group Memorandum [*NATO*] (NATG)
DSGN........ Design (AFM)
DSGN........ Designate (AFM)
DSGND..... Designated (FAAC)
Dsgn Eng ... Design Engineering [*A publication*]
dsgnr.......... Designator
DSGp........ Directed Studies Group [*Air Force*] (AFM)
DS in Gp Engr ... Doctor of Science in Geophysical Engineering
DSGRD7 ... Delaware Sea Grant. Technical Report Del-SG [*A publication*]
DSGS(CAR) ... Deputy Secretary of the General Staff (Coordination and Reports) [*Army*] (AABC)
D/Sgt .... Drill Sergeant [*British military*] (DMA)
DSGW .... Deutsche Shakespeare-Gesellschaft (West Germany) [*A publication*]
DSH.......... Deactivated Shutdown Hours [*Electronics*] (IEEE)
DSH.......... Deliberate Self-Harm Syndrome
DSH.......... DSH [*Deafness, Speech, and Hearing*] Abstracts [*A publication*]
DSH.......... Dushanbe [*Stalinabad*] [*USSR*] [*Seismograph station code, US Geological Survey*] (SEIS)
DSHA........ DSH [*Deafness, Speech, and Hearing*] Abstracts [*A publication*]
DSH Abstr ... DSH [*Deafness, Speech, and Hearing*] Abstracts [*A publication*]
DSHE........ Downstream Heat Exchanger (AAG)
DSHIP....... Digest of Selected Health and Insurance Plans [*A publication*]
D/SHLD..... Dust Shield [*Automotive engineering*]
DSHMRA ... Deep Seabed Hard Mineral Resources Act
DSHP........ Disodium Hydrophosphate [*Inorganic chemistry*] [*Also, DSP*]
DSHR........ Dish-Rinsing
DSI........... Dairy Society International (EA)
DSI............ Danish Scientific Investigations in Iran [*A publication*]
DSI............ Data Set Identifier
DSI............ Data Submitted Information (KSC)
DSI............ Data System Integration [*NASA*]
DSI............ Data Systems Inquiry (AABC)
DSI............ Dead Sea Isaiah Scroll (BJA)
DSI............ Decision Sciences [*A publication*]
DSI............ Decision Sciences Institute (EA)
DSI............ [*Air*] Defense Suppression Integration (MCD)
DSI............ Delivery to Surgery Interval [*Gynecology*]
DSI............ DeSales Secular Institute (EA)
DSI............ Design Science Institute
DSI............ Digital Speech Interpolation [*Telephone channels*]
DSI............ Digital Strain Indicator
DSI............ Direct Support Item [*Army*]
DSI............ Dissociative Surface Ionization [*Organic chemistry*]
DSI............ Distilled Spirits Institute [*Later, DISCUS*] (EA)
DSI............ Distribution Sciences, Inc. [*Information service or system*] (IID)
DSI............ Division of Science Information [*National Science Foundation*] (IID)

DSI............ Divisional Safety Inspector [*Ministry of Agriculture, Fisheries, and Food*] [*British*]
DSI............ Domini Social Index [*Stock exchange term*]
DSI............ Dominion-Scottish Investments Ltd. [*Toronto Stock Exchange symbol*]
DSI............ Double Sandwich Indirect
DSI............ Down's Syndrome International   (EA)
DSI............ Dreyfus Strategic Government [*NYSE symbol*]   (SPSG)
DSI............ Drinking Straw Institute [*Defunct*]   (EA)
DSI............ Dwelling Sculpture Institute   (EA)
DSI............ Smithsonian Institution, Washington, DC [*Library symbol*] [*Library of Congress*]   (LCLS)
DSIA......... Defense Suppression Integration Analysis   (MCD)
DSIA......... Diaper Service Industry Association [*Later, NADS*]   (EA)
DSI-AAA... Smithsonian Institution, Archives of American Art, Washington, DC [*Library symbol*] [*Library of Congress*]   (LCLS)
DSIATP..... Defense Sensor Interpretation and Application Training Program   (AFM)
DSI Bull..... DSI [*Dairy Society International*] Bulletin [*A publication*]
DSIC.......... Diagnostic Sciences, Inc. [*NASDAQ symbol*]   (NQ)
DSID.......... Data Set Identification [*Data processing*]   (IBMDP)
DSID.......... Disposable Seismic Intrusion Detector   (MCD)
DSID.......... Divergence Source-Image Distortion [*Crystal*]
DSIdentBad ... Drill Sergeant Identification Badge [*Military decoration*]   (AABC)
DSIF.......... Deep Space Instrumentation Facility
DSI-HMS ... Smithsonian Institution, Hirshhorn Museum and Sculpture Garden, Washington, DC [*Library symbol*] [*Library of Congress*]   (LCLS)
DSII.......... Decom Systems, Incorporated [*NASDAQ symbol*]   (NQ)
DSIIR........ Direct Support Imagery Interpretation Report   (MCD)
DSIJa........ Doklady i Soobscenija Instituta Jazykoznanija Akademii Nauk SSSR [*A publication*]
DSIM......... Doctor of Science in Industrial Medicine
DSI-MAA ... Smithsonian Institution, Museum of African Art, Washington, DC [*Library symbol*] [*Library of Congress*]   (LCLS)
DSI-MHT ... Smithsonian Institution, National Museum of History and Technology, Washington, DC [*Library symbol*] [*Library of Congress*]   (LCLS)
DSI-Mus... Smithsonian Institution, Museum Reference Center, Washington, DC [*Library symbol*] [*Library of Congress*]   (LCLS)
DSI-NAS... Smithsonian Institution, National Space and Air Museum, Washington, DC [*Library symbol*] [*Library of Congress*]   (LCLS)
DSI-NCF ... Smithsonian Institution, National Collection of Fine Arts, Washington, DC [*Library symbol*] [*Library of Congress*]   (LCLS)
DSI-NPG... Smithsonian Institution, National Portrait Gallery, Washington, DC [*Library symbol*] [*Library of Congress*]   (LCLS)
DSIP.......... Delta-Sleep-Inducing Peptide
DSIPT .... Dissipate   (FAAC)
DSIR.......... Department of Scientific and Industrial Research [*of the Privy Council for Scientific and Industrial Research*] [*Later, SRC*] [*British*]
DSIS .... Defence Scientific Information Service [*Canada*] [*Information service or system*]   (IID)
DSIS .... Defense Communications System SCF [*Satellite Control Facility*] Interface System   (MCD)
DSIS .... Director [*or Directorate*] of Scientific Information Service [*Canada*]
DSI-SOA ... Smithsonian Institution, National Museum of Natural History, Office of Anthropology, Washington, DC [*Library symbol*] [*Library of Congress*]   (LCLS)
DSJ........... Discrete Sonic Jet
DSJ........... Doctor of the Science of Jurisprudence
DSJOA...... Defence Science Journal [*New Delhi*] [*A publication*]
DSJOAA..... Defence Science Journal [*A publication*]
DS Jur....... Dalloz-Sirey. Jurisprudence [*France*] [*A publication*]
DSK .... Daur Schutzluft Klimasystem [*German*]
DSK .... Demokratikon Sosialistikon Komma [*Democratic Socialist Party*] [*Greece*] [*Political party*]   (PPE)
DSK .... Deputy Seal Keeper [*British*]   (ROG)
DSK .... Dera Ismail Khan [*Pakistan*] [*Airport symbol*]   (OAG)
DSK .... Disk [*Data processing*]
DSK .... Disk Island [*Alaska*] [*Seismograph station code, US Geological Survey*]   (SEIS)
DSK .... Dvorak Simplified Keyboard [*Typewriter keyboard developed by August Dvorak in the 1920's*]
DSKSAR ... Denki Seirigaku Kenkyu [*Electrophysiology*] [*A publication*]
DSKY........ Display and Keyboard [*Data processing*]
DSL........... Danske Sprog-og Literaturselskab [*A publication*]
DSL........... Data Set Label [*Data processing*]
DSL........... Data Simulation Language
DSL........... Data Structures Language [*Data processing*]   (BUR)
DSL........... Decalogue Society of Lawyers   (EA)
DSL........... Deep Scattering Layer [*Undersea populations*]
DSL........... Defence Standards Laboratories [*British*]
DSL........... Denver & Salt Lake Railroad [*AAR code*]
D & SL....... Denver & Salt Lake Railroad

DSL........... Department of Supply Laboratories [*Australia*]
DSL........... Depressed Sight Line   (MCD)
DSL........... Detailed Ship Loading
DSL........... Detroit Signal Laboratory [*Army*]
DSL........... Dickinson School of Law [*Pennsylvania*]
DSL........... Diesel   (MSA)
DSL........... Digital Simulation Language [*Data processing*]   (CSR)
DSL........... Directory of Special Libraries and Information Centers [*A publication*]
DSL........... Doctor of Sacred Literature
DSL........... Downey Savings & Loan Association [*NYSE symbol*]   (SPSG)
DSL........... Downstage Left [*Toward audience*] [*A stage direction*]
DSL........... Downwind Safety Limit
DSL........... Drawing and Specification Listing   (NRCH)
DSLL......... Duquesne Studies in Language and Literature [*A publication*]
DSLO .... Distributed Systems Licensing Option [*IBM Corp.*]
DSLP .... Diary of Social Legislation and Policy [*Australia*] [*A publication*]
DSLT .... Deck Surface Light   (AAG)
DSLT .... Detection Scheme with Learning of Thresholds [*Communication signal*]
DSLT .... Diamond Crystal Salt Co. [*NASDAQ symbol*]   (NQ)
DSLTR ...... Desalter   (MSA)
DSLV .... Dissolved   (NVT)
DSM .... Danziger Statistische Mitteilungen [*Danzig*] [*A publication*]
DSM .... Data Status Messages   (KSC)
DSM .... Data Storage Memory
DSM .... Data Systems Modernization
D & Sm ...... De Gex and Smale's Reports Tempore Knight-Bruce and Parker, Vice-Chancellor's Court [*1846-52*] [*England*] [*A publication*]   (DLA)
DSM .... Deep Space Measurement   (KSC)
DSM .... Defence Studies Methodology [*British*]
DSM .... Defense Standardization Manual [*DoD*]
DSM .... Defense Suppression Missile
DSM .... Dense-Staining Material [*Cytology*]
DSM .... Des Moines [*Iowa*] [*Airport symbol*]   (OAG)
DSM .... Design Standards Manual   (AAG)
DSM .... Development of Substitute Materials
DSM .... Diagnostic and Statistical Manual of Mental Disorders [*A publication*]
DSM .... Digital Scanning Electron Microscope
DSM .... Digital Select Matrix
DSM .... Digital Select Module   (KSC)
DSM .... Digital Simulation Model   (KSC)
DSM .... Diploma in Social Medicine [*British*]
DSM .... Diploma in State Medicine   (ROG)
DSM .... Direct Signal Monitoring [*Telecommunications*]   (TEL)
DSM .... Direct Support Maintenance [*Army*]
DSM .... Direction of Systems Management
DSM .... Director of Supply and Maintenance [*Army*]
DSM .... Discovery Mines Ltd. [*Toronto Stock Exchange symbol*]
DSM .... Disk Space Management [*Data processing*]
DSM .... Distinguished Service Medal [*Military decoration*] [*US and British*]
DSM .... District Sales Manager
DSM .... District Scout Master [*Scouting*]
DSM .... Divisional Sergeant-Major [*British military*]   (DMA)
DSM .... Doctor of Sacred Music
DSM .... Double Short Meter [*Music*]
D & Sm ...... Drewry and Smale's English Chancery Reports [*A publication*]   (DLA)
DSM .... Dreyfus Strategic Municipals, Inc. [*NYSE symbol*]   (SPSG)
DSM .... Dried Skim Milk
DSM .... Dutch State Mines
DSM .... Dynamic Scattering Mode   (IEEE)
DSM .... United States Department of the Interior, Office of Surface Mining, Washington, DC [*Library symbol*] [*Library of Congress*]   (LCLS)
DSMA .... Defense Supply Management Agency
DSMA .... Direct Support Maintenance Activity [*Army*]   (MCD)
DSMA .... Disodium Methyl Arsonate [*Herbicide*]
DSMA .... Divine Science Ministers Organization   (EA)
DSMA .... Division of Small Manufacturers Assistance [*FDA*]
DSMA .... Doll Supply Manufacturers Association   (EA)
DSMA .... Door and Shutter Manufacturers' Association [*British*]
DSMAC.... Digital Scene Matching Area Correlator [*Military*]
DSMB....... Data Safety Monitoring Board [*Generic term*]
DSMC .... Dealers Safety and Mobility Council   (EA)
DSMC .... Defense Specification Management Course [*Army*]
DSMC .... Defense Systems Management College [*Fort Belvoir, VA*] [*Army*]   (RDA)
DSMC .... Defense Systems Management Course [*Air Force*]
DSMD .... Discount Schedule and Marketing Data
DSMD .... Draft Ships Manpower Document [*Navy*]   (CAAL)
DS in Met Engr ... Doctor of Science in Metallurgical Engineering
DSMG .... Designated Systems Management Group [*Military*]
DSMGP.... Designated Systems Management Group [*Military*]
DSMHA .... Discrete Mathematics [*A publication*]
DSM-III-R ... Diagnostic and Statistical Manual of Mental Disorders [*A publication*]

DSMJA ..... Delaware Medical Journal [*A publication*]
DSMJBB ... Dar Es Salaam Medical Journal [*A publication*]
DSMP .... Daughters of St. Mary of Providence [*Roman Catholic religious order*]
DSMS .... Data Systems and Mathematics Staff [*Bureau of Radiological Health*] (IID)
DSMS .... Defense Systems Management School [*Fort Belvoir, VA*] (AABC)
DSMS .... Drawing Submittal Monitoring System [*MAC*]
DSMSB ...... Die Set Manufacturers Service Bureau (EA)
DSMT .... Dual-Speed Magnetic Transducer
DSMTD ..... Dismounted
DSN .... Dance Services Network
DSN .... Data Set Name
DSN .... Data Smoothing Network [*Telecommunications*]
DSN .... Deep Space Network [*NASA*]
DSN .... Defense Secure Network [*Military*]
DSN .... Defense Switched [*or Switchboard*] Network
DSN .... Dennison Manufacturing Co. [*NYSE symbol*] (SPSG)
DSN .... Detroit Suburban Network [*Radio*]
DSN .... Dickens Studies Newsletter [*A publication*]
DSN .... Digital Switching Network [*Telecommunications*]
DSN .... Distributed Sensor Network (MCD)
DSN .... Distributed Systems Network [*Hewlett-Packard Co.*]
DSN .... Dusing [*New York*] [*Seismograph station code, US Geological Survey*] [*Closed*] (SEIS)
DSN .... Marquette, MI [*Location identifier*] [*FAA*] (FAAL)
DSNA .... Dictionary Society of North America (EA)
DSNADNS ... Dihydroxy(hydroxydisulfonaphthylazo)naphthalenedisulfonic Acid [*An indicator*] [*Chemistry*]
DSND .... Descend [*Aviation*] (FAAC)
DSNDI ...... Descend Immediately [*Aviation*] (FAAC)
DSNGA6 .... Denkschriften. Schweizerische Naturforschende Gesellschaft [*A publication*]
DSNI .... [*The*] DocketSearch Network, Incorporated [*Information service or system*] (IID)
DSNJDI .... Dirasat Natural Sciences [*Amman*] [*A publication*]
DSNQ .... Design Quarterly [*A publication*]
DSNS .... Division of Space Nuclear Systems [*Energy Research and Development Administration*]
DSNT .... Descent (KSC)
DSNT .... Distant (FAAC)
DSNTZ ...... Desensitize (MSA)
DSO .... Data Services Operations [*Informatics, Inc.*] (IID)
DSO .... Data Set Optimizer [*Boole & Babbage, Inc.*]
DSO .... Data Systems Office
DSO .... De Soto, Inc. [*NYSE symbol*] (SPSG)
DSO .... Defence Sales Organisation [*Ministry of Defence*] [*British*]
DSO .... Defense Sciences Office [*Arlington, VA*] [*DoD*] (GRD)
DSO .... Defense Subsistence Office [*DoD*]
DSO .... Defense System Operator [*ECM operator*]
DSO .... Dependents Schooling Office [*Military*]
DSO .... Design Stop Order
DSO .... Detailed Secondary Objective (MCD)
DSO .... Detailed Supplementary Objective (MCD)
DSO .... Digital Storage Oscilloscope [*Gould, Inc.*]
DSO .... Direct Shipment Order (AAG)
DSO .... Direct System Output [*Data processing*] (MCD)
DSO .... Director of Site Operations [*Nuclear energy*] (NRCH)
DSO .... Directorate of Supply Operations (AFIT)
DSO .... Display Switching Oscilloscope
DSO .... Distinguished Service Order [*British*]
DSO .... District Sales Office
DSO .... District Security Office [*or Officer*] [*Navy*]
DSO .... District Service Office [*or Officer*] [*Navy*]
DSO .... District Sorting Office [*British*] (ROG)
DSO .... District Staff Officer [*British*] (ROG)
DSO .... District Supply Office [*or Officer*] [*Navy*]
DSO .... Division Signal Officer [*Army*]
DSO .... Division Supply Officer [*Army*]
DSO .... Doctor of the Science of Oratory
D So .... Doctor of Sociology
DSO .... Donora Southern R. R. [*AAR code*]
DSO .... Drawing Sign Out (MCD)
DSO .... Evansville, IN [*Location identifier*] [*FAA*] (FAAL)
DSOAG ..... Deputy Senior Officer, Assault Group [*British military*] (DMA)
DSOB .... Dirksen Senate Office Building [*Washington, DC*] (DLA)
DSOC .... Democratic Socialist Organizing Committee [*Later, DSA*] (EA)
DSOC .... Division Support Operations Center (MCD)
DSocS .... Doctor of Social Science
D Soc Sc .... Doctor of Social Science
DSocSci ..... Doctor of Social Science
DSODS ...... Drug Specific Oral Delivery System [*Pharmacy*]
DSOFC ...... David Selby Official Fan Club (EA)
DSOL .... Defects in Solids [*Elsevier Book Series*] [*A publication*]
DSOM .... Digital Systems Operations Panel (MCD)
DSomm ..... Recueil Dalloz. Section Sommaires [*French*] [*A publication*] (DLA)
DSOPS ...... Direct Support Operations (NVT)
DSORDRS ... Disorders
DSOS .... Data Switch Operating System

D So Sc ...... Doctor of Social Science
D So Se ...... Doctor of Social Service
DSOT .... Daily Systems Operability Test [*for surface-to-air missiles*]
DSOTS ...... Demonstration Site Operational Test Series
DSOW ...... Denmark Strait Overflow Water [*Oceanography*]
DSP .... Data Source Panel (MCD)
DSP .... Data Standardization Project [*DoD*]
DSP .... Daughters of St. Paul, Missionary Sisters of the Catholic Editions [*Roman Catholic religious order*]
DSP .... Decessit sine Prole [*Died without Issue*] [*Latin*]
DSP .... Deep-Sea Particles
DSP .... Deep South Petroleum [*Vancouver Stock Exchange symbol*]
DSP .... Deep Space Probe
DSP .... Deep Submergence Program (MCD)
DSP .... Defense Development Sharing Program [*US and Canada*] (RDA)
DSP .... Defense Satellite Program (MCD)
DSP .... Defense Science Program
DSP .... Defense Standardization Program [*DoD*]
DSP .... Defense Support Program
DSP .... Democratic Socialist Party [*Ireland*] [*Political party*] (PPW)
DSP .... Democratic Socialist Party [*Republic of Korea*] [*Political party*] (PPW)
DSP .... Democratic Socialist Party [*India*] [*Political party*] (PPW)
DSP .... Democratic Socialist Party [*Minshushakaito*] [*Japan*] [*Political party*] (PPW)
DSP .... Deployable Solar Panel
DSP .... Derogatis Stress Profile [*Personality development test*] [*Psychology*]
DSP .... Designated Stock Point
Dsp .... Dessertspoon (ADA)
DSP .... Deutsche Sex Partei [*German*] [*Political party*]
DSp .... Deutsche Sprache [*A publication*]
DSP .... Diamond Shamrock Offshore [*NYSE symbol*] (SPSG)
DSP .... Digital Signal Processor [*Data processing*]
DSP .... Digital Strip Printer
DSP .... Direct Support Plan (MCD)
DSP .... Direct Support Platoon
DSP .... Director of Selection and Personnel [*British*]
DSP .... Director Selector Panel
DSP .... Disadvantaged Schools Program [*Australia*]
DSP .... Disodium Phosphate [*or Dibasic Sodium Phosphate*] [*Also, DSHP*] [*Inorganic chemistry*]
DSP .... Display Simulation Program
DSP .... Distilled Spirits Plant
DSP .... Distributed System Program [*Data processing*]
DSP .... Distribution Point
DSP .... Dithiobis(succinimidylpropionate) [*Organic chemistry*]
DSP .... Division Standard Practice (AAG)
D Sp .... Doctor of Speech
DSP .... Doppler Spectrum Processor
DSP .... Double Silver Plate
DSP .... Dual Speed
DSP .... Dynamic Speaker
DSP .... Dynamic Subscription Promotion
DSP .... Dynamic Support Program [*Data processing*]
DSPC .... Disaturated Phosphatidylcholine [*Biochemistry*]
DSPC .... Distearoyl Phosphatidylcholine [*Biochemistry*]
DSPCH ...... Dispatch (AABC)
DSPD .... Disalicylidenepropanediamine [*Organic chemistry*]
DSPE .... Division of Scientific Personnel and Education [*National Science Foundation*]
DS in PE .... Doctor of Science in Petroleum Engineering
DSPEC ...... Design Specification
DSPF .... Data Services Planning Form
DSPG .... Defense Special Projects Group (MCD)
DSPH .... Diopter Spherical
DSpir .... Dictionnaire de Spiritualite [*Paris*] [*A publication*]
DSPL .... Decessit sine Prole Legitima [*Died without Legitimate Issue*] [*Latin*]
DSPL .... Definitized Spare Parts List (AAG)
DSPL .... Disciplinary
DSPL .... Display
DSPL .... Disposal
DSPL .... Douglas Space Physics Laboratory (MUGU)
DSPLC ...... Displace (FAAC)
DSPLCD .... Displaced
DSPLN ...... Discipline (AFM)
DSPM .... Decessit sine Prole Mascula [*Died without Male Issue*] [*Latin*]
DSPM .... Designated Subsystems Project Manager [*NASA*] (NASA)
DSPM .... Double Strokes per Minute (MSA)
DSPMO ..... Defense SAAMS [*Special Airlift Assignment Missions*] Program Management Office [*DoD*]
DSPMS ..... Decessit sine Prole Mascula Superstita [*Died without Surviving Male Issue*] [*Latin*]
DSPN .... Disposition (AFM)
DSPNSG ... Dispensing
DSPO .... Dispose (AABC)
DSPP .... Digest of Selected Pension Plans [*Bureau of Labor Statistics*] [*A publication*]
DSPR .... Defense Supply Procurement Regulation [*Military*]

DS in PRE ... Doctor of Science in Petroleum Refining Engineering
DSPRL ...... Dispersal (FAAC)
DSPS .... Decessit sine Prole Superstita [*Died without Surviving Issue*] [*Latin*]
DSPS .... Delayed Sleep Phase Syndrome
DSPS .... Digital Signal Processing System
DSPS ...... Duquesne Studies. Philological Series [*A publication*]
DSPT .... Diagnostic Spelling Potential Test [*Educational test*]
DSPT .... DSP Technology, Inc. [*Fremont, CA*] [*NASDAQ symbol*] (NQ)
DSPV .... Decessit sine Prole Virile [*Died without Male Issue*] [*Latin*] (ADA)
DSQ .... Director of Supplies and Quartering [*British military*] (DMA)
DSQ .... Discharged to Sick Quarters
DSQ .... Disqualified [*Yacht racing*] (IYR)
DSQD .... Double-Sided Quad-Density [*Disk drive*] [*Scottsdale Systems*] [*Data processing*]
DSR .... Daily Service Report
DSR .... Daily Status Report (AAG)
DSR .... Danmarks Radio (EY)
DSR .... Dasher Resources [*Vancouver Stock Exchange symbol*]
DSR .... Data Scanning and Routing
DSR .... Data Set Ready [*Model signal*]
DSR .... Data Specification Request
DS & R .... Data Storage and Retrieval (MSA)
DSR .... Data Storage and Retrieval (MCD)
DSR .... Data Survey Report (AAG)
DSR .... Daughters of St. Rita of the Immaculate Heart [*Roman Catholic religious order*]
DSR .... De Ridder, LA [*Location identifier*] [*FAA*] (FAAL)
DSR .... Defense Source Register (MCD)
DSR .... Defense Subsistence Region [*DoD*]
DSR .... Defense Suppression Rocket
DSR .... Delayed Sound Reinforcement
DSR .... Depolymerized Scrap Rubber [*Waste recycling*]
DSR .... Desire (FAAC)
DSR .... Differentiation with Symmetrical Reinforcement
DSR .... Digit Storage Relay
DSR .... Digital Shift Register
DSR .... Digital Stepping Recorder
DSR .... Direct Ship Release (MCD)
DSR .... Direct Ship Requirements (MCD)
DSR .... Direct Space Refinement
DSR .... Direct Stage Recorder (MCD)
DSR .... Direct Storage Recorder
DSR .... Director of Scientific Research [*British*]
DSR .... Director of Surveillance and Reconnaissance [*Army*]
DSR .... Discriminating Selector Repeater (DEN)
DSR .... Distributed State Response
DSR .... Division of Solar Research [*Energy Research and Development Administration*]
DSR .... Division of Sponsored Research [*University of Florida*] [*Research center*] (RCD)
DSR .... Division of Sponsored Research [*MIT*] (MCD)
DSR .... Division of Sponsored Research [*University of South Florida*] [*Research center*] (RCD)
DSR .... Document Status Report [*Military*]
DSR .... Downstage Right [*Toward audience*] [*A stage direction*]
DSR .... Dresher, Inc. [*NYSE symbol*] (CTT)
DSR .... Dummy Stowage Receptacle
DSR .... Dynamic Shift Register
DSR .... Dynamic Sideband Regulator
DSR .... Dynamic Spatial Reconstructor [*X-ray scanning machine*]
DSRA .... Dockyard Ship Riggers' Association [*A union*] [*British*]
DSRAB9 ...... Desarrollo Rural en las Americas [*A publication*]
DSRC .... David Sarnoff Research Center [*RCA*] (MCD)
DSRD .... Data Systems Research and Development [*Oak Ridge National Laboratory*]
DSRE .... Defense Subsistence Region - Europe (AABC)
DSRK .... Deutsche Schiffs Revision und Klassifikation [*German ship classification society*] (DS)
DSR/LOC ... Debt Service Reserve/Letter of Credit Program [*Investment term*]
dsRNA .... Double-Stranded Ribonucleic Acid [*Biochemistry, genetics*]
dsRNase ..... Double-Stranded Ribonuclease
DS/RPIE .... Direct Support Real Property Installed Equipment (AFIT)
DSRS .... Deep Submergence Rescue System [*Navy*] (NVT)
DSRS .... Direct Scope Recording System (MCD)
DSRS .... Distal Splenorenal Shunt [*Medicine*]
DSRT .... Desert [*Board on Geographic Names*]
DSR-TKA ... Delta Sigma Rho-Tau Kappa Alpha (EA)
DSRV .... Deep Submergence Rescue Vehicle [*Navy*]
DSRV .... Deep Submergence Research Vessel
DSS .... Data Storage System
DSS .... Data Summary Sheets (MCD)
DSS .... Data Switching System
DSS .... Data Systems Specification
DS & S .... Data Systems and Statistics (AFM)
DSS .... Data Systems Supervisor (MCD)
DSS .... Dead Sea Scrolls (BJA)
DSS .... Decision and Simulation System [*Data processing*]

DSS .... Decision Support System
DSS .... Decorstone Industry [*Vancouver Stock Exchange symbol*]
DSS .... Deep Seismic Sounding [*Geophysics*]
DSS .... Deep Seismic Sounding Program [*USSR*]
DSS .... Deep Space Station [*NASA*]
DSS .... Deep Submergence Systems [*Navy*]
DSS .... Defense Signals Staff (NATG)
DSS .... Defense Supply Service [*DoD*]
DSS .... Dengue Shock Syndrome [*Medicine*]
DSS .... Department of Social Services [*in various governmental agencies*]
DSS .... Department Summary Schedule [*NASA*] (NASA)
DSS .... Department of Supply and Service [*Canada*] (IMH)
DSS .... Depot Supply System [*Army*]
DSS .... Deputy of Space Systems [*Air Force*]
DSS .... Design Studies [*A publication*]
DSS .... Developmental Sentence Scoring [*for the hearing-impaired*]
DSS .... Developments in Soil Science [*Elsevier Book Series*] [*A publication*]
DSS .... Diagnostic Simulation System
DSS .... Digital Signal Synchronizer
DSS .... Digital Simulator System
DSS .... Digital Storage System
DSS .... Digital Subset [*or Subsystem*]
DSS .... Digital Switching System [*Telecommunications*] (TEL)
DSS .... Dimethylsilapentane Sulfonate [*Organic chemistry*]
DSS .... Dioctyl Sodium Sulfosuccinate [*Organic chemistry*]
DSS .... Diploma in Sanitary Science (ROG)
DSS .... Direct Station Selection [*Telecommunications*]
DSS .... Direct Subsystem (MCD)
DSS .... Direct Supply Support [*Military*]
DSS .... Direct Support System [*Army*]
DSS .... Directed Stationing System [*DoD*]
DSS .... Director [*or Directorate*] of Statistical Services [*Air Force*]
DSS .... Distributed System Simulator
DSS .... Disuccinimydyl Suberate [*Organic chemistry*]
DSS .... Division of Safeguards and Security [*Energy Research and Development Administration*]
DSS .... Doctor Sacrae Scripturae [*Doctor of Holy Scripture*]
DSS .... Doctor of Sanitary Science
DSS .... Doctor of Science in Surgery
DSS .... Doctor of Secretarial Science
DSS .... Doctor of Social Service
DSS .... Documentation Support Services (NASA)
DSS .... Documents Signed
DSS .... Double Spot System
DSS .... Drill Sergeant School [*Army*] (AABC)
DSS .... Drum Storage System
DSS .... Duchess (ROG)
DSS .... Dynamic Science Stories [*A publication*]
DSS .... Dynamic Simulation System (MCD)
DSS .... Dynamic Steady State
DSS .... Dynamic Support System (MCD)
DSS .... Dynamic System Synthesizer
DSS .... Dyslexia Screening Survey [*Psychology*]
DSS .... XVIIe Siecle [*A publication*]
DSSA .... Development Society of Southern Africa (EAIO)
DSSA .... Direct Supply Support Activity [*Army*] (AABC)
Dssa .... Dottoressa [*Female Doctor*] [*Italian*]
DSS & A .... Duluth, South Shore & Atlantic Railroad [*Nickname: Damned Slow Service and Abuse*] [*Obsolete*]
DSSB .... Double Single-Sideband (MSA)
DSSC .... Defense Subsistence Supply Center [*Later, Defense Personnel Support Center*]
DSSc .... Diploma in Sanitary Science [*British*]
DS Sc .... Doctor of Social Science
DSSC .... Double-Sideband Suppressed Carrier [*Modulation*] (IEEE)
DSSCDM .. Developments in Soil Science [*A publication*]
DSSCS .... Defense Special Security Communications System [*Pronounced "discus"*]
DssCSA ..... Deaconess Community of St. Andrew [*Anglican religious community*]
DSSD .... Direct Supply Support Depot [*Military*] (AFM)
DSSD .... Double-Sided Single-Density Disk [*Data processing*]
DSSE .... Design Selection Specification Engineer
DSSI .... Digital Storage Systems Interconnect
DSSJ .... Deceptive Self-Screening Jammer (MCD)
DSSM .... Dedicated Solar Sortie Mission [*Aerospace*] (MCD)
DSSM .... Defense Superior Service Medal [*Military decoration*]
DSSM .... Division of State Systems Management [*Social and Rehabilitation Service, HEW*]
DSSM .... Drawing Stimulus Strategy Measure
DSSN .... Disbursing Station Symbol Number [*Military*] (AFM)
DSSN .... Seaman, Data Systems Technician, Striker [*Navy rating*]
DS & SO ..... Data Systems and Statistics Officer [*Air Force*]
DSSO .... Defense Surplus Sales Office
DSSO .... District Ships Service Office [*or Officer*] [*Navy*]
DSSO .... Duty Space Surveillance Officer [*Air Force*] (AFM)
DSSP .... Deep Submergence Systems Project [*Navy*]
DSSP .... Defense Standardization and Specification Program [*DoD*] (RDA)

DSSP .... Depot Support Supply Plan (AFIT)
DSSP .... Direct Supply Support Point [*Military*]
DSSP .... Division Support Slice Program (MCD)
DSSPO ...... Deep Submergence Systems Project Office [*Navy*]
DSSP/SSD ... Department Supply Storage Point/Stock Storage Depot [*DoD*]
DSSPTO ... Deep Submergence Systems Project Technical Office [*San Diego, CA*] [*Navy*]
DSSR .... Deep Space Surveillance RADAR (MCD)
DSS & R .... Document Storage Search and Retrieval [*Air Force*]
DSSRG ...... Deep Submergence Systems Review Group [*Navy*]
DSSS .... Deep Space Surveillance Satellite [*Military*]
DSSS .... Defense Special Security System (MCD)
DSSS .... Division of Special Schools and Services (OICC)
DSSS .... Division of Supplemental Security Studies [*Department of Health and Human Services*] (GRD)
DSSSP ...... Division of Student Support and Special Programs [*Office of Education*]
DSSSS ...... Developments in Solar System and Space Science [*Elsevier Book Series*] [*A publication*]
DSST .... Director of Supply and Secretariat Training [*British military*] (DMA)
DSST .... Driver Stage Silicon Transistor
DSSV .... Deep Submergence Search Vehicle [*Research submarine*] [*Navy*]
DSS-W ...... Defense Supply Service - Washington [*DoD*]
DST .... Dansk Skovforenings Tidsskrift [*A publication*]
DSt .... Danske Studier [*A publication*]
DST .... Danstar Resources Ltd. [*Vancouver Stock Exchange symbol*]
DST .... Data Source Terminal (MCD)
DST .... Data Storage Terminal
DST .... Data Systems Test [*Formerly, DAT*]
DST .... Daylight Saving Time
DST .... Deep Sleep Therapy
D St .... Dermatologische Studien [*A publication*]
DST .... Dermatology and Syphilology Technician [*Navy*]
DST .... Desensitization Test [*Allergy*]
DST .... Design Support Test (MCD)
DST .... Destructor [*Military*]
DST .... Detailed System Test
DSt .... Deutsche Studien [*A publication*]
DST .... Development Suitability Test (MCD)
DST .... Dexamethasone Suppression Test [*Clinical chemistry*]
DST .... Dielectric Strength Test
DST .... Differential Skin Surface Temperature
DST .... Digit-Symbol Substitution Test [*Psychiatry*]
DST .... Digital Subscriber Terminal
DST .... Dihydrostreptomycin [*Also, DHS, DHSM*] [*Antimicrobial agent*]
DST .... Dimensional Special Tooling (NASA)
DST .... Direct Screw Transfer
DST .... Direct Sounding Transmission [*Meteorology*]
DST .... Direct-Viewing Storage Tube
DST .... Direction de la Surveillance du Territoire [*Directorate of Territorial Surveillance*] [*France*]
DST .... Director of Sea Transport [*British military*] (DMA)
DST .... Director of Supplies and Transport [*British*]
DS/T .... Discarding Sabot/Training [*British military*] (DMA)
DST .... Display Storage Tube (CET)
DST .... Distort (FAAC)
dst............. Distributor [*MARC relator code*] [*Library of Congress*] (LCCP)
DST .... District
DST .... Doctor of Sacred Theology
D St .... Doctor of Statistics
DST .... Dodecanoylsarcosyltaurine [*Crustacean detergent*]
DST .... Donor Specific Transfusion
DST .... Door Stop (AAG)
DST .... Double Spot Tuning
DST .... Double Summer Time [*Daylight Saving Time two hours ahead of Standard Time*] [*British*]
DST .... Douglas Sleeper Transport [*Aviation*]
DST .... Drill Stem Test (ADA)
DST .... Drop Survival Time
DST .... Dursunbey [*Turkey*] [*Seismograph station code, US Geological Survey*] (SEIS)
DST .... Dust [*Tea trade*] (ROG)
DST .... Dynamic Stability Test (NASA)
DST .... Missoula, MT [*Location identifier*] [*FAA*] (FAAL)
DSTA........ Diagnostic Screening Test: Achievement [*Educational test*]
DSTA........ Distribution Assembly [*Ground Communications Facility, NASA*]
DStAP ...... Saint Anselm's Abbey, Washington, DC [*Library symbol*] [*Library of Congress*] (LCLS)
DSTB........ Danmarks Statistiks TidsseriedataBank [*Danmarks Statistik*] [*Denmark*] [*Information service or system*] (CRD)
DSTC........ Daylight Saving Time Coalition [*Inactive*] (EA)
DSTC........ Disc Technology Corporation [*Billerica, MA*] [*NASDAQ symbol*] (NQ)
DSTC........ Distance (FAAC)
DSTD .... Double-Sided, Triple-Deposit
DST & DD ... Developing Systems Training and Devices Directorate [*Army*]

DSTDP...... Distearyl Thiodipropionate [*Organic chemistry*]
DSTE........ Defense System Terminal Equipment (MCD)
DSTE........ Digital Subscriber Terminal Equipment (AFM)
D St E .... Doctor of Structural Engineering
D St Eng .... Doctor of Structural Engineering
DSTF .... Delta Spin Test Facility (MCD)
DSTI .... Directorate of Scientific and Technical Intelligence [*British*]
DSTI......... Division of Scientific and Technical Information [*International Atomic Energy Agency*] (DIT)
D St J .... Dame of Justice/Grace of the Order of St. John of Jerusalem [*British*]
DStJ........... Saint Joseph Seminary, Washington, DC [*Library symbol*] [*Library of Congress*] (LCLS)
DSTL......... Diagnostic Screening Test: Language [*Educational test*]
DSTL........ Distill
DSTLD........ Distilled
DSTLT .... Distillate
DSTM........ Diagnostic Screening Test: Math [*Educational test*]
DSTN........ Destination (KSC)
DSTO .... Defence Science and Technology Organisation [*Australia*] (RDA)
DSTO .... District Supply and Transport Officer [*British military*] (DMA)
DSTP .... Data Self-Test Program
DSTP .... Director of Strategic Target Planning [*Military*]
DStPC........ Saint Paul's College, Washington, DC [*Library symbol*] [*Library of Congress*] (LCLS)
DSTPS........ Director of Strategic Target Planning Staff [*Offutt AFB*] [*Military*] (CINC)
DSTR........ Deserter [*Military*] (AABC)
DSTR........ Destructor [*Military*]
D St R .... Deutsche Steuer-Rundschau [*A publication*]
D St R .... Deutsches Steuerrecht [*A publication*]
DSTR........ Diagnostic Screening Test: Reading [*Educational test*]
DSTR........ Distribution (MCD)
DSTR........ Dorsal Striatum [*Neuroanatomy*]
DSTR........ Dynamic Systems Test Rig [*Helicopters*] [*Army*] (RDA)
DSTS .... Desk Side Time Shared [*Data processing*] [*General Electric Co.*]
DSTS .... Destruct System Test Set
DSTS .... Diagnostic Screening Test: Spelling [*Educational test*]
DSTS .... Dockside Training Simulator
DSTS .... DST Systems, Inc. [*NASDAQ symbol*] (NQ)
DSTS .... Duquesne Studies. Theological Series [*A publication*]
D Studies ... Dostoevsky Studies. Journal of the International Dostoevsky Society [*A publication*]
D St Z .... Deutsche Steuerzeitung [*A publication*]
D St Zt .... Deutsche Steuerzeitung [*A publication*]
DSU .... Data Service Unit [*Telecommunications*]
DSU .... Data Storage Unit
DSU .... Data Synchronization [*or Synchronizer*] Unit
D & SU ...... Daughters and Sons United (EA)
DSU .... Decoder Switching Unit
DSU .... Deutsche Soziale Union [*German Social Union*] [*Federal Republic of Germany*] (PPW)
DSU .... Device-Switching Unit
DSU .... Digital Service Unit [*Signal converting device*] [*Telecommunications*] (TSSD)
DSU .... Digital Storage Unit (DIT)
DSU .... Direct Support Unit [*Army*]
DSU .... Disk Storage Unit [*Data processing*] (MSA)
DSU .... Display Support Unit (MCD)
DSU .... Drum Storage Unit
DSUE .... [*A*] Dictionary of Slang and Unconventional English [*A publication*]
DSU/GSU ... Direct Support Unit/General Support Unit [*Computer system*]
DSUH........ Direct Suggestion under Hypnosis
DSUPHTR ... Desuperheater
D-SUPT..... Detective Superintendent
D Sur .... Doctor of Surgery
DSUzU ...... Doklady i Soobscenija Uzgorodskogo Universiteta [*A publication*]
DSV .... Damping Structural Vibrations
DSV .... Dansville, NY [*Location identifier*] [*FAA*] (FAAL)
DSV .... Deep Submergence Vehicle [*Navy symbol*]
DSV .... Detected Safety Violation
DSV .... Digital Sum Variation [*Telecommunications*]
DSV .... Diving Support Vessel (DS)
DSV .... Double Silk Varnish [*Wire insulation*] (AAG)
DSV .... Douglas Space Vehicle
DSV .... Drum Safety Valve (DS)
DS/VD...... Director of Salvage Department [*Navy*] [*British*]
DSVG .... Dollar Savings Association [*NASDAQ symbol*] (NQ)
DSVL........ Doppler SONAR Velocity Log (MCD)
DSVP......... Director of Small Vessels Pool [*Admiralty*] [*British*]
DSVT........ Digital Secure Voice Telephone [*Telecommunications*] (TEL)
DSVT........ Digital Subscriber Voice Terminal (MCD)
DSVY........ Director of Survey [*British military*] (DMA)
DSW ...... Data Status Word
D & Sw ...... Deane and Swabey's English Ecclesiastical Reports [*A publication*] (DLA)
DSW .... Deep Sea Winch
DSW .... Delivered with Standard Wiring

DSW	Device Status Word (CMD)
D/SW.........	Dimmer Switch [*Automotive engineering*]
DSW	Direct-Step-on-the-Wafer [*Microelectronics*]
DSW	Director of Special Weapons [*Army*]
D of S (W) ...	Director of Stores (Washington) [*Navy*]
DSW	Discovery West Corp. [*Toronto Stock Exchange symbol*]
DSW	Doctor of Social Welfare
DSW	Doctor of Social Work
DSW	Door Switch
DSW	Drum Switch
DSWP	Director of Surface Weapons Projects [*Navy*] [*British*]
DSWS.......	Deep Submergence Weapon System [*Also, DEXTOR*] (MCD)
DSWS.......	Direct Support Weapon System (MCD)
DSWS.......	Division Support Weapon System (MCD)
DSWV	Director of Special Weapons and Vehicles [*Military*] [*British*]
DSX	Digital Signal Cross-Connect [*Telecommunications*]
DSX	Distributed Systems Executive [*IBM Corp.*]
DSXBT	Deep Shipboard Expendable Bathythermograph [*Oceanography*]
DSYG	Deputy Secretary General (NATG)
D Sy Th......	Doctor of Systematic Theology
DSZ	Madison, WI [*Location identifier*] [*FAA*] (FAAL)
DT.............	Daily Telegraph [*A publication*] (APTA)
DT.............	Daily Times [*Lagos*] [*A publication*]
DT.............	Dakota Territory (ROG)
DT.............	Dark Trace
DT.............	Data Tabulation (OICC)
DT.............	Data Terminal
DT.............	Data Transcriber
DT.............	Data Translator (IEEE)
DT.............	Data Transmission
DT.............	Date (AFM)
DT.............	Daughter
DT.............	Daylight Time
DT.............	Days after Transplanting [*Botany*]
DT.............	Dead Time
DT.............	Debits Tax (ADA)
DT.............	Decay Time (MSA)
DT.............	Deccan Trap [*Geology*]
DT.............	Decision Table [*Data processing*]
DT.............	Deduction Theorem [*Logic*]
DT.............	Deep Tank (MSA)
DT.............	Defensive Tackle [*Football*]
DT.............	Defensive Target [*Military*]
DT.............	Deferred Telegram
DT.............	Delayed Time (KSC)
DT.............	Delirium Tremens [*Also, DT's*] [*Hallucinatory condition of advanced alcoholism*]
DT.............	Delivery Time
D & T	Demonstration and Training
DT.............	Dental Technician [*Navy rating*]
DT.............	Deoxythymidine [*Organic chemistry*]
DT.............	Department of Trade [*British*] (DS)
DT.............	Department Training
D of T	Department of the Treasury [*Commonly TD, Treasury Department*]
DT.............	Desk Top
DT.............	Detecting Heads [*JETDS nomenclature*] [*Military*] (CET)
DT.............	Detection Threshold (CAAL)
D/T............	Detection/Tracker (NVT)
DT.............	Detroit Terminal Railroad Co. [*AAR code*]
D-T............	Deuterium-Tritium Reaction [*Fusion program*]
Dt	Deuteronomy [*Old Testament book*]
DT.............	Deutsche Tagespost [*A publication*]
DT.............	Deutsche Theologie [*A publication*] (BJA)
DT.............	Developed Template (MCD)
D & T	Development and Technology
DT.............	Development Test [*or Testing*] (MCD)
DT.............	Development Type (AABC)
DT.............	Developments in Toxicology and Environmental Science [*Elsevier Book Series*] [*A publication*]
DT.............	Dial Tone [*Telecommunications*] (TEL)
DT.............	Die Template (MSA)
DT.............	Differential Time (IEEE)
DT.............	Digit Tube (IEEE)
DT.............	Digital Technique
DT.............	Digital Test Measurement System (NASA)
DT.............	Digital Tracker
DT.............	Digroup Terminal [*Telecommunications*] (TEL)
D/T............	Dilutions to Threshold [*Olfactory*]
D-T............	Dinner Theater
DT.............	Dip Tube
DT.............	Diphtheria, Tetanus [*Medicine*]
DT.............	Diphtheria Toxin [*Biochemistry*]
D of T	Director of Traffic
DT.............	Director of Transport [*British military*] (DMA)
DT.............	Disconnector Trap
DT.............	Discrepancy Tag
D/T............	Disk Tape [*Data processing*] (IEEE)
DT.............	Disk Technician [*Data processing*]
DT.............	Dispersion Time (NATG)

DT.............	Displacement Transducer (KSC)
DT.............	Display Translator (MCD)
DT.............	Distance Test
DT.............	Distributive Trades [*Department of Employment*] [*British*]
DT.............	District Trust Co. [*Toronto Stock Exchange symbol*]
DT.............	Diver, Second Class [*Navy rating*]
DT.............	Divus Thomas [*A publication*]
DT.............	Doctor of Theology
DT.............	Document Type [*Online database field identifier*]
DT.............	Doit [*Debit*] [*French*]
DT.............	Double Tachycardia [*Cardiology*]
DT.............	Double Throw [*Switch*]
DT.............	Double Time
DT.............	Double Tube
DT.............	Dow Theory [*Stock market analysis*]
DT.............	Down Through [*Clairvoyance experiment*]
DT.............	Downtime [*Data processing*] [*Telecommunications*] (AAG)
DT.............	Drain Tile [*Technical drawings*]
D & T	Drama and Theatre [*A publication*]
DT.............	Drama Tree (EA)
DT.............	Draught
DT.............	Dressed or Tanned [*Freight*]
DT.............	Dressing Table [*Classified advertising*] (ADA)
DT.............	Drive Tube
DT.............	Drop Tank (KSC)
DT.............	Drop Test Report
DT.............	Drum Transfer (CET)
DT.............	Dry Toned [*Copier*] [*Reprography*]
DT.............	Dual Tires
DT.............	Dump Telemetry
DT.............	Duration of Tetany [*Medicine*]
DT.............	Duscepoleznie Tchtenie [*A publication*]
DT.............	Dust-Tight (MSA)
DT.............	Dwell Time (AAG)
DT.............	Dye Testing
DT.............	Dynamic Tester
DT.............	TAAG Linhas Aereas de Angola [*Angola*] [*ICAO designator*] (ICDA)
DT.............	Telefunken (Pressed by Decca) [*Record label*] [*Great Britain*]
DT.............	United States Department of the Treasury, Washington, DC [*Library symbol*] [*Library of Congress*] (LCLS)
DT1	Dental Technician, First Class [*Navy rating*]
DT2...........	Dental Technician, Second Class [*Navy rating*]
DT3...........	Dental Technician, Third Class [*Navy rating*]
DT's	Delirium Tremens [*Also, DT*] [*Hallucinatory condition of advanced alcoholism*]
DTA	Data File [*Data processing*]
DTA	Data Transfer Area [*Data processing*]
DTa	Deep Tank Aft (DS)
DTA	Deep Transverse Arrest [*Obstetrics*]
DTA	Default Transfer Area [*Data processing*] (PCM)
DTA	Defense Transport Administration [*Terminated, functions transferred to Interstate Commerce Commission*]
DTA	Delta, UT [*Location identifier*] [*FAA*] (FAAL)
DTA	Dental Therapy Assistant (RDA)
DTA	Dentonia Resources Ltd. [*Vancouver Stock Exchange symbol*]
DTA	Detailed Traffic Analysis [*Telecommunications*] (TEL)
DTA	Detroit Tooling Association (EA)
DTA	Development Test Article
DTA	Diaminopropanoltetraacetic Acid [*Also, DPTA, DHPTA*] [*Organic chemistry*]
DTA	Diethylenetriamine [*Also, DETA*] [*Organic chemistry*]
DTA	Differential Thermal [*or Thermogravimetric*] Analysis [*or Analyzer*]
DTA	Diphtheria Toxin, A Strain [*Immunology*]
DTA	Diploma in Tropical Agriculture (ADA)
DTA	Disk Transfer Area [*Data processing*] (BYTE)
DTA	Disk Turbine Assembly
DTA	Distributing Terminal Assembly [*Electronics*]
DTA	District Traffic Agent
DTA	Divisao de Exploracao dos Transportes Aereos [*Angolan airline*]
DTA	Division Tactical Area [*Army*]
DTA	Dominion Traffic Association [*Canada*]
DTA	Double Tape Armored [*Heavy-duty telephone buried cable*]
DTA	Dovetail Anchor [*Technical drawings*]
DTA	Dual Trace Amplifier
DTA	Due to Arrive
DTAA	Diamond Trade Association of America [*Later, DTPSAA*] (EA)
DTAB	Datatab, Inc. [*NASDAQ symbol*] (NQ)
DTAB	Dodecyltrimethylammonium Bromide [*Organic chemistry*]
DTABL......	Decision Table Processor [*IBM Corp.*]
DTAC	Dodecyltrimethylammonium Chloride [*Organic chemistry*]
DTACCS ...	Director/Telecommunications and Command and Control System (MCD)
DTACK......	Data Transfer Acknowledge [*Computer memory management*]
DTAF.........	(Dichlorotriazinyl)aminofluorescein [*Also, DCTAF*] [*Analytical biochemistry*]
DTAF.........	Dynamic Tactical Area File [*Military*] (CAAL)
DTAM	Daily Traffic Assignment Model [*Aviation*]

DTAM ...... Descend to and Maintain [*Aviation*] (FAAC)
DTAO ...... During the Temporary Absence Of [*Military*]
Dt Apoth .... Deutsche Apotheker [*A publication*]
Dt Apoth Post ... Deutsche Apotheker Post [*A publication*]
Dt ApothZtg ... Deutsche Apotheker-Zeitung [*A publication*]
Dt Arb Univ Koeln ... Deutsche Arbeiten der Universitaet Koeln [*A publication*]
Dt Arch Klin Med ... Deutsches Archiv fuer Klinische Medizin [*A publication*]
DTARS ...... Digital Transmitting and Routing System (IEEE)
DTAS .... Data Transmission and Switching
DTAS .... Diagnostic Test of Arithmetic Strategies
DTAS .... Division of Tropical Animal Science [*Australia*]
DTASW ...... Director, Torpedo, Anti-Submarine, and Mine Warfare [*British military*] (DMA)
DTAT .... Depot Turn-Around Time (MCD)
DTAX .... Descend to and Cross [*Aviation*] (FAAC)
D Tax .... Dominion Tax Cases [*CCH Canadian Ltd.*] [*Information service or system*] [*A publication*] (DLA)
DTB .... Danmarks Tekniske Bibliotek [*National Technological Library of Denmark*] [*Information service or system*] (IID)
DTB .... Decimal to Binary [*Data processing*] (BUR)
DTB .... Destroyer Tactical Bulletin [*Navy*]
DTB .... Deutsche Terminboerse [*Derivatives market*] [*Federal Republic of Germany*]
DTB .... Deviation Test Bridge
DTB .... Distribution [*A publication*]
DTB .... Ditaurobilirubin [*Biochemistry*]
DTB .... Dynamic Translation Buffer
dtba .... Date to Be Agreed (AIA)
DTBA .... (Dimethyltriazenol)benzoic Acid [*Antineoplastic drug*]
Dt Bauern Techn ... Deutsche Bauerntechnik [*A publication*]
DTBC .... Di-tert-butylcatechol [*Organic chemistry*]
DTBC .... Di-tert-butylcresol [*Organic chemistry*]
DTBC .... Lower Canada Reports (Decisions des Tribunaux du Bas-Canada) [*1850-67*] [*A publication*] (DLA)
Dt Beitr ...... Deutsche Beitraege. Eine Zweimontsschrift [*A publication*]
DTBHQ ..... Di-tert-butylhydroquinone [*Organic chemistry*]
Dt Bienenkal ... Deutsche Bienenkalender [*A publication*]
Dt Bienenztg ... Deutsche Bienenzeitung [*A publication*]
Dt Bienenzucht ... Deutsche Bienenzucht [*A publication*]
DT BIOL ... Deutsche Biologische Literatur [*German Biological Literature*] [*Also, DBL*] [*Database*] [*Forschungsinstitut Senckenberg*] [*Information service or system*]
DTBN .... Di-tert-butylnaphthalene [*Organic chemistry*]
DTBP .... Dedicated Total Buried Plant [*Telecommunications*] (TEL)
DTBP .... Di-tert-butyl Peroxide [*Organic chemistry*]
DTBP .... Di-Tert-Butylphenol [*Biochemistry*]
DTBSD ...... Database [*United States*] [*A publication*]
DTBWAZ ... Deutsche Bienenwirtschaft [*A publication*]
dTC .... d-Tubocurarine [*Muscle relaxant*]
DTC .... Data Technology Corp.
DTC .... Data Terminals & Communications, Inc.
DTC .... Data Test Center [*Telecommunications*] (TEL)
DTC .... Data Transmission Center (KSC)
DTC .... Data Transmission Channel (CMD)
DTC .... Dead Time Correction
DTC .... Decision Threshold Computer
DTC .... Defense Technical Center
DTC .... Dental Technician, Chief [*Navy rating*]
DTC .... Department of Technical Cooperation [*British*]
DTC .... Department of Transport and Construction [*Australia*]
DTC .... Deposit-Taking Company [*Generic term that originated in Hong Kong*]
DTC .... Depository Transfer Check [*Banking*]
DTC .... Depository Trust Company
DTC .... Depot Training Center
DTC .... Desert Test Center [*Fort Douglas, UT*] [*Army*] (AABC)
DTC .... Desert Tortoise Council (EA)
DTC .... Desert Training Center [*Army*]
DTC .... Design to Cost (MCD)
DTC .... Design/Test Contractor (KSC)
DTC .... Desk Top Computer
DTC .... Detection Threshold Computer [*Telecommunications*] (TEL)
DTC .... Developmental Training Center [*Indiana University*] [*Research center*] (RCD)
DTC .... Dextro-Tubocurarine [*Organic chemistry*]
DTC .... Dictionnaire de Theologie Catholique [*Paris*] [*A publication*]
DTC .... Differential Throttle Control
DTC .... Digital Tape Conversion
DTC .... Digital Television Camera
DTC .... Digital to Tone Converter
DTC .... Diploma in Textile Chemistry (ADA)
DTC .... Direct-to-Consumer [*Sales*]
DTC .... Direct Trading Corporation [*Thailand*] (DS)
DTC .... Disciplinary Training Center
DTC .... Display Test Chamber
DTC .... Display Timing Control
DTC .... Doctor of Textile Chemistry
DTC .... Document de Transport Combine [*Combined Transport Document*] [*French*] [*Business term*]

DTC .... Documento de Transporte Combinado [*Combined Transport Document*] [*Spanish*] [*Business term*]
DTC .... Documento di Trasporto Combinato [*Combined Transport Document*] [*Italian*] [*Business term*]
DTC .... Dominion Tax Cases [*CCH Canadian Ltd.*] [*Information service or system*] [*A publication*] (DLA)
DTC .... Domtar, Inc. [*NYSE symbol*] [*Toronto Stock Exchange symbol*] [*Vancouver Stock Exchange symbol*] (SPSG)
DTC .... Doppler Translation Channel
DTC .... Downtime Code [*Military*] (AFIT)
DTC .... DSIF [*Deep Space Instrumentation Facility*] Telemetry and Command Subsystem [*NASA*]
DTC .... International Trade Commission, Washington, DC [*Library symbol*] [*Library of Congress*] (LCLS)
DTC .... United States International Trade Commission, Washington, DC [*OCLC symbol*] (OCLC)
DTCCS ...... Defense Telecommunications Command and Control System (MCD)
DTCD .... Diploma in Tuberculosis and Chest Diseases [*British*]
DTCFA ...... Documents Techniques. Charbonnages de France [*A publication*]
DTCH .... Detached
DTCH .... Diploma in Tropical Child Health [*British*]
DT Ch .... Doctor of Textile Chemistry
DTCI .... Data Technology Corp. [*NASDAQ symbol*] (NQ)
DTCM .... Dental Technician, Master Chief [*Navy rating*]
DTCR .... Data Transfer and Certification Record (KSC)
DTCS .... Data Transmission and Control System (AAG)
DTCS .... Dental Technician, Senior Chief [*Navy rating*]
DTCS .... Digital Test Command System
DTCS .... Drone Target Control System [*Military*] (MCD)
DTCS .... Drone Tracking and Control System [*Military*] (MCD)
DTC(STC) ... Deaf Teachers Certificate (Sydney Teachers College) [*Australia*]
DTCU .... Data Transmission Control Unit [*Burroughs Corp.*]
DTCW .... Data Transfer Command Word (NASA)
DTD .... Data Terminal Display
DTD .... Data Transfer Done
DTD .... Dated (AFM)
DTD .... Dekoratie voor Trouwe Dienst [*Decoration for Devoted Service*] [*South Africa*]
DTD .... Dentur Tales Doses [*Give in Such Doses*] [*Pharmacy*]
DTD .... Department of Tank Design [*British*] (MCD)
DTD .... Detailed Test Description (MCD)
DTD .... Difficult to Deliver [*US Postal Service*]
DTD .... Digital Terrain Data [*Army*]
DTD .... Digital Topographic Data (MCD)
DTD .... Diploma in Tuberculous Diseases [*British*]
D of TD ...... Director of Tactical Division [*Navy*] [*British*]
DTD .... Directorate of Technical Development (MCD)
DTD .... Directorate of Training Developments [*Army*]
DTD .... Dismounted Training Day [*Military*] (INF)
DTD .... Doctor of Textile Dyeing
DTD .... Documentatieblad. Nieuwe Reeks [*A publication*]
DTD .... Dual Trace Display
DTD .... Washington, DC [*Location identifier*] [*FAA*] (FAAL)
DTDC .... Desolventizer-Toaster-Dryer-Cooler [*Oil technology*]
DT Des .... Doctor of Textile Design
DTDMA ...... Distributed Time Division Multiple Access [*System*] [*DoD*]
dTDP .... Deoxyribosylthymine Diphosphate [*Biochemistry*]
DTDP .... Deoxythymidine Diphosphate [*Biochemistry*]
DTDP .... Ditridecyl Phthalate [*Organic chemistry*]
DTDR .... Draft Training Device Requirement (MCD)
DTDRA ..... Denki Tsushin Daigaku Gakuho [*A publication*]
DTDS .... Digital Television Display System
DT/DT .... Drop Tube/Drop Tower [*Facility*]
DTDU .... Dichloro-bis(trifluoromethyl)diphenylurea [*Insectproofing agent for wool*]
DT/DV ...... Deposit Ticket/Debit Voucher [*Data processing*]
DTE .... Data Terminal Equipment [*Data processing*]
DTE .... Data Transmitting Equipment
DTE .... Database [*A publication*]
DTE .... Datatracker International [*Vancouver Stock Exchange symbol*]
DTE .... Dayton, TN [*Location identifier*] [*FAA*] (FAAL)
dte .... Dedicatee [*MARC relator code*] [*Library of Congress*] (LCCP)
DTE .... Defence Technology Enterprises Ltd. [*British*] (IRUK)
DTE .... Depot Tooling Equipment
DTE .... Detroit Edison Co. [*NYSE symbol*] (SPSG)
DT & E .... Development, Test, and Evaluation (AFM)
DTE .... Diamond Tool Engineering Co.
DTE .... Digital Television Encoder
DTE .... Digital Television System (KSC)
DTE .... Diplomacy Test of Empathy [*Psychology*]
DTE .... Dithioerythritol [*Organic chemistry*]
DTE .... Doctor of Textile Engineering
DTE .... Down to Earth [*A publication*] (ADA)
DTE .... Dual Track Etcher
DTEA .... Data Telemetry Exploitation Aid (MCD)
DTEAS ...... Detection Track Evaluation and Assignment Systems [*Navy*] (NG)
DTEC .... Department of Technical and Economic Cooperation [*Thailand*] (DS)

D Tech .... Doctor of Technology
D Tech Chem ... Doctor of Technical Chemistry (EY)
DTED .... Digital Terrain Elevation Data [*Military*]
DTEE......... Division of Technology and Environmental Education [*Office of Education*]
DTEGA2 ..... Dermatologia Tropica et Ecologia Geographica [*A publication*]
D Tel .... Daily Telegraph [*London*] [*A publication*]
D Telegraph ... Daily Telegraph [*London*] [*A publication*]
DT Eng .... Doctor of Textile Engineering
Dt Ent Z...... Deutsche Entomologische Zeitschrift [*A publication*]
Dteol T .... Dansk Teologisk Tidsskrift [*A publication*]
DTER .... Dither
DTESD...... Developments in Toxicology and Environmental Science [*A publication*]
DTEV .... Deutsche Telecom eV [*Federal Republic of Germany*] [*Telecommunications*] (TSSD)
DTF .... Daily Transaction File
DTF .... Dairy Trade Federation [*British*] (ECON)
DTF .... Data Transmission Factor
DTF .... Data Transmission Feature
DTF .... Data Transmission Function
DTF .... Data Transmittal Form (MCD)
DTF .... Date to Follow [*Telecommunications*] (TEL)
DTF .... Dedicated Terminal Facility [*Telecommunications*] (TSSD)
DTf........... Deep Tank Forward [*Shipping*] (DS)
DTF .... Define the File [*Data processing*] (BUR)
DTF .... Dial Tone First [*Telecommunications*] (TEL)
DTF .... Diamond Thin-Film [*Coating technology*]
DTF .... Dicyanomethylenetrinitrofluorene [*Organic chemistry*]
DTF .... Division of Training and Facilities [*Office of Education*]
DTF .... Dow Chemical Co., Texas Division, Freeport, TX [*OCLC symbol*] (OCLC)
DTF .... Drone Target Facility [*Military*]
DTF .... Drone Test Facility [*Military*]
DTF .... Dry Tortugas Island, FL [*Location identifier*] [*FAA*] (FAAL)
DTF .... Dynamic Test Fixture [*Military*] (MCD)
DTF .... Dynamic Track Following [*Electronics*]
DTFAA...... Dansk Tidsskrift foer Farmaci [*A publication*]
DTFAAN... Dansk Tidsskrift foer Farmaci [*A publication*]
DTFDW...... Deciduous Tree Fruit Disease Workers [*An association*] (EA)
DTG .... Data Transmission Generator (MCD)
DTG .... Date-Time Group [*Group of figures at head of radio or Teletype message indicating filing time*]
DTG .... Derivative Thermogravimetry
DTG .... Display Transmission Generator
DTG .... Dual Track Geneva
DTG .... Dwight, IL [*Location identifier*] [*FAA*] (FAAL)
DTG .... Dynamically Tuned Gyro [*Inertial sensor*] (IEEE)
DTGDA ..... Denshi Tsushin Gakkai Rombunshi. Part D [*A publication*]
DTGHD...... Denshi Tsushin Gakkai Gijutsu Kenkyu Hokoku [*A publication*]
DTGS....... Deuterated Triglycine Sulfate [*Organic chemistry*]
DTGW...... Director of Guided Weapons Trials [*British military*] (DMA)
DTGZA ..... Denki Tsushin Gakkai Zasshi [*A publication*]
DTH......... Dance Theater of Harlem
DTH......... Death Valley [*California*] [*Airport symbol*] (OAG)
DTH......... Delayed-Type Hypersensitivity [*Immunology*]
DTh.......... Deutsche Theologie: Monatsschrift fuer die Deutsche Evangelische Kirche [*A publication*]
DTH......... Diploma in Tropical Hygiene [*British*]
DTH......... Direct to Home [*Satellite broadcast mode*] [*Canada*]
DTh.......... Divus Thomas [*A publication*]
D Th .... Doctor of Theology
D Theol...... Diploma in Theology [*British*]
D Theol...... Doctor of Theology
DTheolC ..... Sulpician Seminary Theological College, Washington, DC [*Library symbol*] [*Library of Congress*] (LCLS)
DTH Ith..... Dis Ticaret Hacmi ve Ithalat [*Foreign Trade Volume and Imports*] [*Turkish*]
DThom....... Divus Thomas [*Piacenza*] (BJA)
DThomP .... Divus Thomas [*Piacenza*] (BJA)
DThPT....... Diploma in Theory and Practice of Teaching (Durham University) [*British*]
DTHy........ Sandoz [*Italy*] [*Research code symbol*]
DTI .... Data-Tech Institute [*Clifton, NJ*] (TSSD)
DTI .... Defense Technical Information Center, Alexandria, VA [*OCLC symbol*] (OCLC)
DTI .... Department of Trade and Industry [*British*]
DTI .... Department of the Treasury, Internal Revenue Service, Washington, DC [*Library symbol*] [*Library of Congress*] (LCLS)
DTI .... Deposit-Taking Institution (ADA)
DTI .... Design Technical Information [*or Instruction*] (KSC)
DTI .... Detroit, Toledo & Ironton Railroad Co. [*AAR code*]
DT & I....... Detroit, Toledo & Ironton Railroad Co. [*Nickname: Damned Tough and Independent*]
DTI .... Development through Industry
DTI .... Development Test Instrumentation (NASA)
DTI .... Dial Test Indicator
DTI .... Direct Trader Input [*Customs term*] (DCTA)
DTI .... Director of Tactical Investigation [*Military*] [*British*]

DTI .... Director Train Indicator
DTI .... Display Terminal Interchange
DTI .... Distortion Transmission Impairment [*Telecommunications*] (TEL)
DTI .... Division of Technical Information [*AEC*]
DTI .... Domestic Technology Institute (EA)
DTI .... Drug and Therapeutic Information [*Later, Medical Letter*] (EA)
DTI .... Durham Technical Institute [*Durham, NC*]
DTIB......... Distribuco, Inc. [*NASDAQ symbol*] (NQ)
DTIC........ Defense Technical Information Center [*Formerly, DDC*] [*DoD*] [*Information service or system*] [*Alexandria, VA*]
DTIC........ (Dimethyltriazenyl)imidazolecarboxamide [*Dacarbazine*] [*Also, DIC*] [*Antineoplastic drug*]
DTIC-ACT-D ... DTIC [*Dacarbazine*], Actinomycin D [*Dactinomycin*] [*Antineoplastic drug regimen*]
DTID .... Disposal Turn-In Document [*Military*]
DTIE......... Division of Technical Information Extension [*Later, Technical Information Center*] [*AEC*]
Dt Ill Bienenztg ... Deutsche Illustrierte Bienenzeitung [*A publication*]
DTIM .... DTI Medical Corp. [*NASDAQ symbol*] (NQ)
DTIMD9 ... INTA [*Instituto Nacional de Tecnologia Agropecuaria*] Divulgacion Tecnica [*A publication*]
Dt Imkerfuehrer ... Deutsche Imkerfuehrer [*A publication*]
Dt Imkerkal ... Deutscher Imkerkalender [*A publication*]
Dt Imkerztg ... Deutsche Imkerzeitung [*A publication*]
DTIN .... Digital Transmission, Inc. [*NASDAQ symbol*] (NQ)
Dt Indinst Ber Wirtpol ... Berichte. Deutsches Industrielinstitut zur Wirtschaftspolitik [*A publication*]
Dt Inst Wirtschaftsforsch Wochenber ... Deutsches Institut fuer Wirtschaftsforschung. Wochenbericht [*A publication*]
DTIR........ Defense Technical Intelligence Report (MCD)
DtIs .... Deutero-Isaiah (BJA)
DtIsrZtg..... Deutsche Israelitische Zeitung [*Regensburg*] [*A publication*]
DTK .... Datatech Systems Ltd. [*Toronto Stock Exchange symbol*]
DTK .... Dietrich, AK [*Location identifier*] [*FAA*] (FAAL)
DTKR .... Developmental Tasks for Kindergarten Readiness [*Child development test*]
DTKTA...... Dansk Teknisk Tidsskrift [*A publication*]
DTL .... Datel Industries Ltd. [*Toronto Stock Exchange symbol*] [*Vancouver Stock Exchange symbol*]
DTL .... Dead Time Log
DTL .... Deep Trench Latrine [*British military*] (DMA)
DTL .... Degree of Total Leverage [*Finance*]
DTL .... Delta Teen-Lift (EA)
DTL .... Detail (AABC)
DTL .... Detroit Lakes [*Minnesota*] [*Airport symbol*] [*Obsolete*] (OAG)
DTL .... Diode-Transistor Logic
DTL .... Direct to Licensee
DTL .... Duct Transmission Loss [*Facility*] (MCD)
DTL .... United States Department of the Treasury, Washington, DC [*OCLC symbol*] (OCLC)
DTLA .... Detroit Tests of Learning Aptitude [*Education*]
Dt Landwirt ... Deutsche Landwirtschaft [*A publication*]
Dt Landwirt (Berlin) ... Deutsche Landwirtschaft (Berlin) [*A publication*]
Dtl Arch .... Deutschland Archiv [*A publication*]
DTLCC...... Design to Life-Cycle Cost
Dt LebensmittRdsch ... Deutsche Lebensmittel Rundschau [*A publication*]
DTLG .... Department of Territories and Local Government [*Australia*]
DTLN .... Data Transmission Network Corp. [*NASDAQ symbol*] (NQ)
DTLN .... International Date Line (FAAC)
DTM......... Carnegie Institution of Washington [*District of Columbia*] [*Seismograph station code, US Geological Survey*] [*Closed*] (SEIS)
DTM......... Dataram Corp. [*AMEX symbol*] (SPSG)
DTm......... Deep Tank Midship [*Shipping*] (DS)
DTM......... Delay Timer Multiplier (IEEE)
DTM......... Design Test Model
DTM......... Desktop Manufacturing
DTM......... Deutsche Texte des Mittelalters [*A publication*]
DTM......... Developmental Test Model
DTM......... Digital Television Monitor
DTM......... Digital Troposcatter MODEM (MCD)
DTM......... Digital Trunk Module [*Telecommunications*]
DTM......... Diocesan Travelling Mission [*Roman Catholic*]
DTM......... Diploma in Tropical Medicine [*British*]
DTM......... Director of Telecommunications Management [*Air Force*] [*Abolished, 1970*]
DTM......... Director of Transport and Movements [*British military*] (DMA)
DTM......... Directory of Texas Manufacturers [*University of Texas at Austin*] [*Information service or system*] (CRD)
DTM......... Doctor of Tropical Medicine
DTM......... Dortmund [*West Germany*] [*Airport symbol*] (OAG)
DTM......... Draft Technical Manual
DTM......... Dual Transport Module (NOAA)
DTM......... Dynamic Tensile Modulus [*Materials testing*]
DTM......... Dynamic Test Model [*Spacecraft*]
DTma....... Deep Tank Midship Aft [*Shipping*] (DS)
DTMB .... David W. Taylor Model Basin [*Also, DATMOBAS, TMB*] [*Later, DTNSRDC, NSRDC*] [*Washington, DC*]

DTMB .... Monastir/Habib Bourgiba [*Tunisia*] [*ICAO location identifier*]
DTMC .... Di(p-chlorophenyl)trichloromethylcarbinol [*Miticide*] (ICLI)
DTMD ...... Dento-Med Industries, Inc. [*NASDAQ symbol*] (NQ)
DTMD ...... Determined (NVT)
DTMD ...... Differential Temperature Measuring Device
Dt Med J.... Deutsches Medizinisches Journal [*A publication*]
Dt Med Wschr ... Deutsche Medizinische Wochenschrift [*A publication*]
DTmf......... Deep Tank Midship Forward [*Shipping*] (DS)
DTMF .... Dual Tone Modulated Frequency [*Telecommunications*]
DTMF .... Dual-Tone Multifrequency [*Telecommunications*]
DTM & H .... Diploma in Tropical Medicine and Hygiene [*British*]
DTMI .... Dairy Training and Merchandising Institute [*Later, MTI*] (EA)
DTMI .... Diversified Technology Management [*NASDAQ symbol*] (NQ)
Dt Milchwirt ... Deutsche Milchwirtschaft [*A publication*]
DTMNA ...... Datamation [*A publication*]
DTMO....... Design [*or Development*], Test, and Mission Operations [*NASA*]
dTMP .... Deoxyribosylthymine Monophosphate [*Biochemistry*]
DTMP .... Deoxythymidine Monophosphate [*Biochemistry*]
DTMS....... Data Base and Transaction Management System [*IBM Corp.*]
DTMS....... Defense Traffic Management Service
DTMS....... Delivery and Transport Management System [*Software package*] [*British*]
DTMS....... Development, Test, and Mission Support (MCD)
DTMS....... Digital Test Measurement [*or Monitor*] System
DTN.......... [*The*] Daily Times of Nigeria [*A publication*]
DTN.......... Dalmatian Resources Ltd. [*Vancouver Stock Exchange symbol*]
DTN.......... Data Transporting Network
DTN.......... Defence Telecommunications Network [*British military*] (DMA)
DTN.......... Defense Teleprinter Network (NATG)
DTN.......... Detain (AABC)
DTN.......... Digital Equipment Corp., Spit Brook, Nashua, NH [*OCLC symbol*] (OCLC)
DTN......... Diphtheria Toxin Normal [*Medicine*]
DTN......... Diploma of Teaching (Nursing)
DTN......... Drug Trade News [*A publication*]
DTN......... DuMont Television Network [*1946-55*]
DTN......... Shreveport, LA [*Location identifier*] [*FAA*] (FAAL)
DTNB .... Dithiobis(nitrobenzoic acid) [*Analytical biochemistry*]
DT (Newspr) (Tas) ... Daily Telegraph Reports (Newspaper) (Tasmania) [*A publication*] (APTA)
DTNHEB .. Dithiobis(nitrohydroxyethylbenzamide) [*Biochemistry*]
DTNS .... Dragon Terminal Night Sight [*Military*] (MCD)
DTNSRDC ... David W. Taylor Naval Ship Research and Development Center [*Later, DTRC*] [*Bethesda, MD*]
DTO......... Data Takeoff [*Air Force*]
DTO......... Data Terminal Operator [*Data processing*]
DTO......... Decentralized Toll Office [*Telecommunications*] (TEL)
dto .... Dedicator [*MARC relator code*] [*Library of Congress*] (LCCP)
DTO......... Defense Transportation Order [*Department of Commerce*]
DTO......... Denton, TX [*Location identifier*] [*FAA*] (FAAL)
DTO......... Deodorized Tincture of Opium [*Pharmacy*]
dto .... Descuento [*Discount*] [*Spanish*]
DTO......... Detailed Test Objective [*NASA*]
DTO......... Digital Testing Oscilloscope (IEEE)
DTO......... Direct Termination Overflow [*MCI Communications Corp.*] [*Telecommunications*]
DTO......... Direct Turn-Over (NG)
DTO......... District Training Office [*or Officer*] [*Navy*]
DTO......... District Transportation Officer
DTO......... Division Transportation Office [*or Officer*]
DTOC....... Division Tactical Operations Center
DTOE .... Draft Table of Organization and Equipment [*Military*] (INF)
DTOM....... DeTomaso Industries, Inc. [*Red Bank, NJ*] [*NASDAQ symbol*] (NQ)
DTOP....... Daily Turn On Procedures [*Data processing*] (MCD)
DT/OT ...... Development Test/Operational Test
DTP.......... Dairy Termination Program [*Department of Agriculture*]
DTP.......... Dance Touring Program [*National Endowment for the Arts*]
DTP.......... Data Transfer Protocol
DTp.......... Department of Transport [*United Kingdom*] (DS)
DTP.......... Depth Telemetering Pinger
DTP.......... Design to Price (NVT)
DTP.......... Desktop Publishing [*Data processing*]
DTP.......... Detailed Test Plan [*or Procedure*]
DTP.......... Development Threat Package
DTP.......... Developmental Therapeutics Program [*National Cancer Institute*]
dtp .... Diethyldithiophosphate [*Organic chemistry*]
DTP.......... Diode Test Program
DTP.......... Diphtheria, Tetanus, Pertussis [*Also, DPT*] [*Immunology*]
DTP.......... Diphtheria, Tetanus, Poliovirus [*Vaccine*] [*Medicine*]
DTP.......... Directory Tape Processor
DTP.......... Display Translator Program (MCD)
DTP.......... Distal Tingling on Percussion [*Medicine*]
DTP.......... Dolph-Tchebyscheff Pattern
DTP.......... Doppler Techniques Proposal

DTP.......... Double Test Position
DTP.......... Driver Training Platoon [*British military*] (DMA)
DTP.......... Drum Timing Pulse
DTP.......... Dynamic Test Panel
DTP.......... Dynamic Testing Program (AAG)
DTPA .... Diethylenetriaminepentaacetic Acid [*Also, DETP, DETPA*] [*Chelating agent*]
DTPC........ Desert Tortoise Preserve Committee (EA)
DTPEW ...... Design-to-Price Electronic Warfare [*Military*] (CAAL)
DTPEWS .. Design-to-Price Electronic Warfare Suite [*Navy*] (MCD)
Dt PH .... Deutsch-Polnische Hefte [*A publication*]
DTPH........ Diploma in Tropical Public Health [*British*]
DTPL........ Domain Tip Propagation Logic (MCD)
DTPR........ Detailed Test Procedures (NASA)
DTPS........ Diffusion Transfer Processing System [*Reprography*]
DTPSAA .... Diamond Trade and Precious Stone Association of America (EA)
DTPT........ Dedicated Theater Planning Terminal [*Military*] (MCD)
DTR .... Daily Transaction Registering [*or Reporting*] [*Data processing*]
DTR .... Data Telemetering Register
DTR .... Data Terminal Reader
DTR .... Data Terminal Ready
DTR .... Data Transfer Rate
DTR .... Data Transfer Register
DTR .... Data Translator (MCD)
DTR .... Deep Tendon Reflex [*Physiology*]
DTR .... Defense Test Range (MCD)
DTR .... Definite-Time Relay (MSA)
DTR .... Demand Totalizing Relay (KSC)
DTR .... Department of Trade [*British*] (ADA)
Dtr .... Deuteronomy Rabba (BJA)
DTR .... Diamond T Register (EA)
DTR .... Diatec Resources Ltd. [*Vancouver Stock Exchange symbol*]
DTR .... Diffusion Transfer [*Reprography*]
DTR .... Diffusion Transfer Reversal [*Reprography*]
DTR .... Digital Tape Recorder
DTR .... Digital Telemetering Register
DTR .... Diploma in Therapeutic Radiology [*British*]
DTR .... Directorate of Technical Research [*Navy*] [*Canada*]
DTR .... Disposable Tape Reel [*Data processing*]
DTR .... Distribution Tape Reel [*Data processing*]
DTR .... Division of Tax Research
DTR .... Document Transmittal Record (NRCH)
DTR .... Downtime Ratio [*Data processing*] [*Telecommunications*] (TEL)
DTR .... Drug Therapy. Reviews [*Elsevier Book Series*] [*A publication*]
DTr .... Trinity College, Washington, DC [*Library symbol*] [*Library of Congress*] (LCLS)
DTRA .... Defense Technical Review Activity [*or Agency*] [*Military*] (AABC)
DTRC .... David W. Taylor Research Center [*Bethesda, MD*] [*United States Space and Naval Warfare Systems Command*] (GRD)
DTRD .... Development Test Requirements Document [*NASA*] (NASA)
DTRE .... Defence Telecommunications Research Establishment [*British*]
DTREDU .. Drug Therapy Reviews [*A publication*]
DTREM..... Dust, Thermal, and Radiation Engineering Measurements Package [*NASA*]
Dt Rev .... Deutsche Revue [*A publication*]
DTRF........ Daily Transaction Register File [*Data processing*]
DTRF........ Data Transmittal and Routing Form (NRCH)
DTRH........ DRX, Inc. [*NASDAQ symbol*] (NQ)
DTRK .... DataTrak, Inc. [*NASDAQ symbol*] (NQ)
DTRM .... Determine (FAAC)
DTRM .... Dual Thrust Rocket Motor
DTRN .... Datatron, Inc. [*NASDAQ symbol*] (NQ)
D Trns J .... Defense Transportation Journal [*A publication*]
DTRP........ Diploma in Town and Regional Planning (ADA)
Dt Rs......... Deutsche Rundschau [*A publication*]
DTRS........ Development Test Requirement Specification (NRCH)
DTRS........ Digital TranService Corp. [*Norcross, GA*] [*NASDAQ symbol*] (NQ)
DTRS........ Distress (MSA)
DT/RSS .... Data Transmission/Recording Subsystem
DTRT........ Deteriorate
DTRT .... Do the Right Thing [*Also, DWIM*] [*In data processing context, translates as "Guess at the meaning of poorly worded instructions"*]
DTRX .... Detrex Corp. [*NASDAQ symbol*] (NQ)
DTS .... Data Terminal Set (NVT)
DTS .... Data Test Station
DTS .... Data Transfer System [*Army*] (AABC)
DTS .... Data Transmission System [*Air Force*]
DTS .... Defense Telephone Service [*DoD*]
DTS .... Defense Transportation System [*DoD*]
DTS .... Defensive Technology Study [*Military*] (SDI)
DTS .... Delaware Technical and Community College, Southern Campus, Georgetown, DE [*OCLC symbol*] (OCLC)
DTS .... Dense Tubular System
DTS .... Department of Technology and Society (EA)
DTS .... Detailed Test Specification

DTS .... Detailed Type Specification (MCD)
DTS .... Detector Tracker Switch
DTS .... [*The*] Detroit & Toledo Shore Line Railroad Co. [*AAR code*]
DTS .... Development Test Satellite
DTS .... Development and Test Support
DTS .... Diarium Terrae Sanctae [*Jerusalem*] [*A publication*]
DTS .... Differential Temperature Switch (NRCH)
DTS .... Digital Tandem Switch
DTS .... Digital Telemetry System
DTS .... Digital Television System (MCD)
DTS .... Digital Termination Service [*Data transmission*]
DTS .... Digital Termination System [*Telecommunications*]
DTS .... Digital Test System (MCD)
DTS .... Digital Titration System
DTS .... Digital Tracking System [*or Subsystem*]
D-TS .... Diplomate, American Board of Thoracic Surgery (DHSM)
DTS .... Diplomatic Telecommunications Service (FAAC)
DTS .... District Traffic Superintendent [*British railroad term*]
DTS .... Doctor of Textile Science
DTS .... Domestic Transmission System [*ITT*] [*Telecommunications*] (TEL)
DTS .... Doppler Tracking Station
DTS .... Double Throw Switch
DTS .... Dovetail Anchor Slot [*Technical drawings*]
DTS .... DSIF [*Deep Space Instrumentation Facility*] Tracking and Monitor-Control Subsystem [*NASA*]
DTSA .... Dynamic Test System
DTSA .... Defense Technology Security Administration
DTSC .... DARCOM [*Development and Readiness Command, Army*] Technical Steering Committee (MCD)
Dtsch Aerztebl ... Deutsches Aerzteblatt. Aerztliche Mitteilungen [*A publication*]
Dtsch Agrartech ... Deutsche Agrartechnik [*West Germany*] [*A publication*]
Dtsch Akad Landwirtschaftwiss Berl Tagungber ... Deutsche Akademie der Landwirtschaftwissenschaften zu Berlin. Tagungsberichte [*A publication*]
Dtsch Akad Wiss Berlin Vortr Schr ... Deutsche Akademie der Wissenschaften zu Berlin. Vortraege und Schriften [*A publication*]
Dtsch Akad Wiss Berlin Zentralinst Phys Erde Veroeff ... Deutsche Akademie der Wissenschaften zu Berlin. Zentralinstituts Physik der Erde. Veroeffentlichungen [*A publication*]
Dtsch Apoth ... Deutsche Apotheker [*A publication*]
Dtsch Apoth-Ztg ... Deutsche Apotheker-Zeitung [*A publication*]
Dtsch Apoth Ztg Beil Neue Arzneim Spez ... Deutsche Apotheker-Zeitung. Beilage. Neue Arzneimittel und Spezialitaeten [*A publication*]
Dtsch Archit ... Deutsches Architektenblatt [*West Germany*] [*A publication*]
Dtsch Arch Klin Med ... Deutsches Archiv fuer Klinische Medizin [*A publication*]
Dtsch Aussenpolitik ... Deutsche Aussenpolitik [*East Germany*] [*A publication*]
Dtsch Baumsch ... Deutsche Baumschule [*A publication*]
Dtsch Bauz ... Deutsche Bauzeitschrift. Fachblatt fuer Entwurf und Ausfuehrung [*A publication*]
Dtsch Bauz Fachbl Entwurf Ausfuhrung ... Deutsche Bauzeitschrift. Fachblatt fuer Entwurf und Ausfuehrung [*West Germany*] [*A publication*]
Dtsch Beitr Geotech ... Deutsche Beitraege zur Geotechnik [*A publication*]
Dtsch Bibliogr Halbjahres Verzeichnis ... Deutsche Bibliographie. Halbjahres-Verzeichnis [*West Germany*] [*A publication*]
Dtsch Bibliogr Woech Verzeichnis A ... Deutsche Bibliographie. Woechentliches Verzeichnis. Reihe A [*West Germany*] [*A publication*]
Dtsch Bibliogr Woech Verzeichnis B ... Deutsche Bibliographie. Woechentliches Verzeichnis. Reihe B [*West Germany*] [*A publication*]
Dtsch Bibliogr Woech Verzeichnis C ... Deutsche Bibliographie. Woechentliches Verzeichnis. Reihe C [*West Germany*] [*A publication*]
Dtsch Bienenwirtsch ... Deutsche Bienenwirtschaft [*A publication*]
Dtsch Chem Z ... Deutsche Chemiker-Zeitschrift [*A publication*]
Dtsch Dendrol Ges Kurzmitt ... Deutsche Dendrologische Gesellschaft. Kurzmitteilungen [*A publication*]
Dtsch Destill Ztg ... Deutsche Destillateur Zeitung [*A publication*]
Dtsch Druckgewerbe ... Deutsche Druckgewerbe [*A publication*]
Dtsche A .... Deutsche Annalen [*A publication*]
Dtsche Aussenpolit ... Deutsche Aussenpolitik [*A publication*]
Dtsche Ges Mineraloelwiss Kohlechem ... Deutsche Gesellschaft fuer Mineraloelwissenschaft und Kohlechemie [*A publication*]
Dtsch Eisenbahntech ... Deutsche Eisenbahntechnik [*A publication*]
Dtsch Elektrotech ... Deutsche Elektrotechnik [*East Germany*] [*A publication*]
Dtsch Engl Med Rundsch ... Deutsche-Englische Medizinische Rundschau [*A publication*]
Dtsch Entomol Z ... Deutsche Entomologische Zeitschrift [*A publication*]
Dtsche Stud ... Deutsche Studien. Vierteljahreshefte fuer Vergleichende Gegenwartskunde [*A publication*]
Dtsche Z Philos ... Deutsche Zeitschrift fuer Philosophie [*A publication*]
Dtsch Farben Z ... Deutsche Farben Zeitschrift [*A publication*]

Dtsch Faserst Spinnpflanzen ... Deutsche Faserstoffe und Spinnpflanzen [*A publication*]
Dtsch Fischereirundsch ... Deutsche Fischereirundschau [*A publication*]
Dtsch Fisch Rundsch ... Deutsche Fischerei-Rundschau [*A publication*]
Dtsch Fischwirtsch ... Deutsche Fischwirtschaft [*A publication*]
Dtsch Fisch Ztg ... Deutsche Fischerei Zeitung [*A publication*]
Dtsch Flungtec ... Deutsche Flungtechnik [*A publication*]
Dtsch Forschungsdienst Sonderber Kernenerg ... Deutscher Forschungsdienst. Sonderbericht Kernenergie [*West Germany*] [*A publication*]
Dtsch Forschungsgem Farbst Komm Mitt ... Deutsche Forschungsgemeinschaft Farbstoff Kommission Mitteilung [*A publication*]
Dtsch Forschungsgem Komm Erforsch Luftverunreinigung Mitt ... Deutsche Forschungsgemeinschaft Kommission zur Erforschung der Luftverunreinigung. Mitteilung [*West Germany*] [*A publication*]
Dtsch Forschungsgem Komm Geowiss Gemeinschaftsforsch Mitt ... Deutsche Forschungsgemeinschaft Kommission fuer Geowissenschaftliche Gemeinschaftsforschung Mitteilung [*West Germany*] [*A publication*]
Dtsch Forschungsgem Komm Pruef Fremder Stoffe Lebensm Mitt ... Deutsche Forschungsgemeinschaft Kommission zur Pruefung Fremder Stoffe bei Lebensmitteln Mitteilung [*A publication*]
Dtsch Forschungsgem Mitt ... Deutsche Forschungsgemeinschaft Mitteilungen [*West Germany*] [*A publication*]
Dtsch Forsch Versuchsanst Luft Raumfahrt Nachr ... Deutsche Forschungs- und Versuchsanstalt fuer Luft und Raumfahrt. Nachrichten [*West Germany*] [*A publication*]
Dtsch Forstm ... Deutsche Forstmann [*A publication*]
Dtsch Gaertnerboerse ... Deutsche Gaertnerboerse [*A publication*]
Dtsch Gartenbau ... Deutsche Gartenbau [*A publication*]
Dtsch Geod Komm Bayer Akad Wiss Reihe C ... Deutsche Geodaetische Kommission bei der Bayerischen Akademie der Wissenschaften. Reihe C. Dissertationen [*A publication*]
Dtsch Geod Komm Veroeff Reihe B ... Deutsche Geodaetische Kommission. Veroeffentlichungen. Reihe B. Angewandte Geodaesie [*A publication*]
Dtsch Geol Ges Nachr ... Deutsche Geologische Gesellschaft. Nachrichten [*A publication*]
Dtsch Ges Arbeitsmed Jahrestag ... Deutsche Gesellschaft fuer Arbeitsmedizin. Jahrestagung [*A publication*]
Dtsch Ges Holzforsch Ber ... Deutsche Gesellschaft fuer Holzforschung Bericht [*A publication*]
Dtsch Ges Metallkd Fachber ... Deutsche Gesellschaft fuer Metallkunde Fachberichte [*West Germany*] [*A publication*]
Dtsch Ges Mineraloelwiss Kohlechem Compend ... Deutsche Gesellschaft fuer Mineraloelwissenschaft und Kohlechemie. Compendium [*West Germany*] [*A publication*]
Dtsch Gesundheitsw ... Deutsche Gesundheitswesen [*A publication*]
Dtsch Gesundheitswes ... Deutsche Gesundheitswesen [*A publication*]
Dtsch Gewaesserkd Mitt ... Deutsche Gewaesserkundliche Mitteilungen [*A publication*]
Dtsch Goldschmiede Z ... Deutsche Goldschmiede-Zeitung [*A publication*]
Dtsch Hebe Foerdertech ... Deutsche Hebe und Foerdertechnik [*A publication*]
Dtsch Hydrogr Inst Jahresber ... Deutsches Hydrographisches Institut. Jahresbericht [*A publication*]
Dtsch Hydrogr Z ... Deutsche Hydrographische Zeitschrift [*A publication*]
Dtsch Inst Wirtschaftsforsch Wochenber ... Deutsches Institut fuer Wirtschaftsforschung. Wochenbericht [*A publication*]
Dtsch Kaelte Klimatech Ver Abh ... Deutscher Kaelte und Klimatechnischer Verein. Abhandlungen [*A publication*]
Dtsch Kaeltetech Ver Abh ... Deutscher Kaeltetechnischer Verein. Abhandlungen [*A publication*]
Dtsch Kongr Perinat Med ... Deutscher Kongress fuer Perinatale Medizin [*A publication*]
Dtsch Kraftfahrtforsch Strassenverkehrstech ... Deutsche Kraftfahrtforschung Strassenverkehrstechnik [*A publication*]
Dtsch Krankenpflegez ... Deutsche Krankenpflegezeitschrift [*A publication*]
Dtsch Kunstseiden Ztg Spezialorgan Zellwolle ... Deutsche Kunstseiden Zeitung und Spezialorgan fuer Zellwolle [*A publication*]
Dtsch Landwirtsch ... Deutsche Landwirtschaft [*A publication*]
Dtsch Landwirtsch Ges Mitt ... Deutsche Landwirtschafts-Gesellschaft Mitteilungen [*A publication*]
Dtsch Landwirtsch Rundsch ... Deutsche Landwirtschaftliche Rundschau [*A publication*]
Dtsch Landwirtsch Tierz ... Deutsche Landwirtschaftliche Tierzucht [*A publication*]
Dtsch Lebensm Rundsch ... Deutsche Lebensmittel Rundschau [*A publication*]
Dtsch Licht Wasserfach Ztg ... Deutsche Licht- und Wasserfach Zeitung [*A publication*]
Dtsch Luftfahrt Raumfahrt Forschungsber ... Deutsche Luft- und Raumfahrt. Forschungsbericht [*A publication*]
Dtsch Luftfahrt Raumfahrt Mitt ... Deutsche Luft- und Raumfahrt. Mitteilung [*A publication*]
Dtsch Luft Raumfahrt Mitt ... Deutsche Luft- und Raumfahrt. Mitteilung [*A publication*]

Dtschl-Union-Dienst ... Deutschland-Union-Dienst [*West Germany*] [*A publication*]

Dtsch Med Forsch ... Deutsche Medizinische Forschung [*A publication*]

Dtsch Med J ... Deutsches Medizinisches Journal [*A publication*]

Dtsch Med Wochenschr ... Deutsche Medizinische Wochenschrift [*A publication*]

Dtsch Med Wschr ... Deutsche Medizinische Wochenschrift [*A publication*]

Dtsch Metallwaren Ind ... Deutsche Metallwaren Industrie [*A publication*]

Dtsch Milchwirtsch ... Deutsche Milchwirtschaft [*A publication*]

Dtsch Milchwirtsch (Gelsenkirchen) ... Deutsche Milchwirtschaft (Gelsenkirchen) [*West Germany*] [*A publication*]

Dtsch Milchwirtsch (Leipzig) ... Deutsche Milchwirtschaft (Leipzig) [*A publication*]

Dtsch Molkerei Ztg ... Deutsche Molkerei-Zeitung [*A publication*]

Dtsch Molk Fettwirtsch ... Deutsche Molkerei- und Fettwirtschaft [*A publication*]

Dtsch Molk Ztg ... Deutsche Molkerei-Zeitung [*A publication*]

Dtsch Mot Z ... Deutsche Motor-Zeitschaft [*A publication*]

Dtsch Muellerei ... Deutsche Muellerei [*A publication*]

Dtsch Mus Abh Ber ... Deutsches Museum. Abhandlungen und Berichte [*A publication*]

Dtsch Nahrungsm Rundsch ... Deutsche Nahrungsmittel. Rundschau [*A publication*]

Dtsch Ophthalmol Ges Ber ... Deutsche Ophthalmologische Gesellschaft. Bericht [*A publication*]

Dtsch Ophthalmol Ges Heidelberg Ber Zusammenkunft ... Deutsche Ophthalmologische Gesellschaft in Heidelberg. Bericht ueber die Zusammenkunft [*A publication*]

Dtsch Opt Wochenschr Cent Ztg Opt Mech ... Deutsche Optische Wochenschrift und Central-Zeitung fuer Optik und Mechanik [*A publication*]

Dtsch Opt Wochenschrift ... Deutsche Optische Wochenschrift [*A publication*]

Dtsch Pelztierz ... Deutsche Pelztierzuchter [*A publication*]

Dtsch Roheisen ... Deutsches Roheisen [*A publication*]

Dtsch Schiffahrtsarch ... Deutsches Schiffahrtsarchiv [*A publication*]

Dtsch Schwarzbunte ... Deutsche Schwarzbunte [*A publication*]

Dtsch Stomatol ... Deutsche Stomatologie [*A publication*]

Dtsch Tab Ztg ... Deutsche Tabak Zeitung [*A publication*]

Dtsch Tech ... Deutsche Technik [*A publication*]

Dtsch Textilgewerbe ... Deutsche Textilgewerbe [*A publication*]

Dtsch Textiltech ... Deutsche Textiltechnik [*A publication*]

Dtsch Textilwirtsch ... Deutsche Textilwirtschaft [*A publication*]

Dtsch Tieraerztl Wochenschr ... Deutsche Tieraerztliche Wochenschrift [*A publication*]

Dtsch Tieraerztl Wochenschr Tieraerztl Rundsch ... Deutsche Tieraerztliche Wochenschrift Tieraerztliche Rundschau [*A publication*]

Dtsch Tierarztebl ... Deutsches Tierarzteblatt [*A publication*]

Dtsch Toepfer Ziegler Ztg ... Deutsche Toepfer und Ziegler Zeitung [*A publication*]

Dtsch Tropenmed Z ... Deutsche Tropenmedizinische Zeitschrift [*A publication*]

Dtsch Tuberk Bl ... Deutsches Tuberkulose-Blatt [*A publication*]

Dtsch Ver Gas Wasserfachmaennern Schriften Gas ... Deutscher Verein von Gas- und Wasserfachmaennern. Schriftenreihe. Gas [*A publication*]

Dtsch Versuchsanst Luft Raumfahrt Ber ... Deutsche Versuchsanstalt fuer Luft- und Raumfahrt. Bericht [*A publication*]

Dtsch Verwaltungsbl Verwaltungsarch ... Deutsches Verwaltungsblatt und Verwaltungsarchiv [*A publication*]

Dtsch Weinbau ... Deutsche Weinbau [*A publication*]

Dtsch Wein Ztg ... Deutsche Wein-Zeitung [*A publication*]

Dtsch Wirker Ztg ... Deutsche Wirker Zeitung [*A publication*]

Dtsch Wollen Gewerbe ... Deutsche Wollen Gewerbe [*A publication*]

Dtsch Zahnaerztl Wochenschr ... Deutsche Zahnaerztliche Wochenschrift [*A publication*]

Dtsch Zahnaerztl Z ... Deutsche Zahnaerztliche Zeitschrift [*A publication*]

Dtsch Zahn- Mund- Kieferheilkd ... Deutsche Zahn- Mund- und Kieferheilkunde [*A publication*]

Dtsch Zentralbl Krankenpfl ... Deutsches Zentralblatt fuer Krankenpflege [*A publication*]

Dtsch Z Gesamte Gerichtl Med ... Deutsche Zeitschrift fuer die Gesamte Gerichtliche Medizin [*A publication*]

Dtsch Z Mund Kiefer Gesichtschir ... Deutsche Zeitschrift fuer Mund-, Kiefer-, und Gesichtschirurgie [*A publication*]

Dtsch Z Nervenheilkd ... Deutsche Zeitschrift fuer Nervenheilkunde [*A publication*]

Dtsch Z Verdau Stoffwechselkr ... Deutsche Zeitschrift fuer Verdauungs und Stoffwechselkrankheiten [*A publication*]

DTSD .... Director of Tactical and Staff Duties Division [*British military*] (DMA)

DTSD .... Director of Training and Staff Duties Division [*Navy*] [*British*]

DTS Direct ... DTS [*Digital Termination Systems*] Directory [*A publication*]

DTSERD ... Driver and Traffic Safety Education Research Digest [*A publication*]

DTSG .... Data Transmission Study Group [*Military*]

DTSI .... Datron Systems, Incorporated [*Simi Valley, CA*] [*NASDAQ symbol*] (NQ)

D-Ts/ka ..... Debit Account

D & TSL .... [*The*] Detroit & Toledo Shore Line Railroad Co.

DTSP .... Dataspeed, Inc. [*NASDAQ symbol*] (NQ)

DTSP .... Down through Sealed Packs [*Clairvoyance experiment*]

DTSS .... Dartmouth Time-Sharing System [*Data processing*]

DTSS .... Digital Topographic Support System [*Army*] (RDA)

DTSS .... Dynamic Tracking Suspension System [*Automotive engineering*]

Dt Studien ... Deutsche Studien [*A publication*]

DTS-W .... Defense Telephone Service - Washington [*DoD*]

DTSY .... Digital Transmission System

DTT .... Dansk Teologisk Tidsskrift [*Copenhagen*] [*A publication*]

DTT .... Data Transfer Timing

DTT .... Data Transition Tracking

DTT .... Design Thermal Transient [*Nuclear energy*] (NRCH)

DTT .... Design Transition Temperature (NRCH)

DTT .... Detent [*Mechanical engineering*]

DTT .... Detroit [*Michigan*] [*Airport symbol*] (OAG)

DTT .... Developmental Technician Team (MCD)

DTT .... Difficult to Test [*Audiology*]

DTT .... Diphtheria-Tetanus Toxoid [*Medicine*]

DTT .... Director of Technical Training [*British military*] (DMA)

DTT .... Dithiothreitol [*Organic chemistry*]

DTT .... Doctor of Textile Technology

DTT .... Doctrinal and Tactical Training [*Army*] (INF)

DTT .... Double Twin Tube [*Fluorescent lighting*]

DTT .... Drag Disk-Turbine Transducer [*Nuclear energy*] (NRCH)

DTT .... Duplicate Title Transferred [*Library science*]

DTT .... Dynamic Test Target [*Military*] (CAAL)

DTTA .... Tunis/Carthage [*Tunisia*] [*ICAO location identifier*] (ICLI)

DTTAC ...... Distributive Trades Technology Advisory Centre [*University of Stirling*] [*British*] (CB)

DTTB .... Bizerte/Sidi Ahmed [*Tunisia*] [*ICAO location identifier*] (ICLI)

DTTC .... Diethylthiatricarbocyanine [*Organic chemistry*]

DTTC .... Tunis [*Tunisia*] [*ICAO location identifier*] (ICLI)

DTTD .... Dedicated Test Training Detachment (MCD)

DTTD .... Remada [*Tunisia*] [*ICAO location identifier*] (ICLI)

DTTF .... Gafsa [*Tunisia*] [*ICAO location identifier*] (ICLI)

DTTG .... Gabes [*Tunisia*] [*ICAO location identifier*] (ICLI)

Dt Th .... Deutsche Theologie [*A publication*]

DTTI .... Bordj El Amri [*Tunisia*] [*ICAO location identifier*] (ICLI)

DTTIAF ...... Deutsche Tieraerztliche Wochenschrift [*A publication*]

DTTid .... Dansk Teologisk Tidsskrift [*A publication*]

Dt Tieraerztl Wschr ... Deutsche Tieraerztliche Wochenschrift [*A publication*]

DTTJ .... Jerba/Zarzis [*Tunisia*] [*ICAO location identifier*] (ICLI)

DTTK .... Kairouan [*Tunisia*] [*ICAO location identifier*] (ICLI)

DTTL .... Data Transition Tracking Loop

DTTL .... Kelibia [*Tunisia*] [*ICAO location identifier*] (ICLI)

DT/TM ...... Delayed Time/Telemetry (KSC)

DTTN .... Jendouba [*Tunisia*] [*ICAO location identifier*] (ICLI)

dTTP .... Deoxyribosylthymine Triphosphate [*Biochemistry*]

DTTP .... Deoxythymidine Triphosphate [*Biochemistry*]

DTTP .... Documents to the People [*A publication*]

DTTR .... El Borma [*Tunisia*] [*ICAO location identifier*] (ICLI)

DTTU .... Data Transmission Terminal Unit [*Burroughs Corp.*]

Dt Tub Bl ... Deutsches Tuberkulose-Blatt [*A publication*]

DTTV .... Tunis [*Tunisia*] [*ICAO location identifier*] (ICLI)

DTTX .... Sfax/El Maou [*Tunisia*] [*ICAO location identifier*] (ICLI)

DTTY .... Digital-to-Teletype

DTTZ .... Tozeur/Nefta [*Tunisia*] [*ICAO location identifier*] (ICLI)

DTU .... Data Terminal Unit [*Telecommunications*]

DTU .... Data Terminating Unit (TEL)

DTU .... Data Transfer Unit

DTU .... Data Transmission Unit

DTU .... Dial Terminal Unit (CAAL)

DTU .... Digital Tape Unit (IEEE)

DTU .... Digital Telemetry Unit

DTU .... Digital Transmission Unit (IEEE)

DTU .... Display Terminal Unit (CMD)

DTUC .... David Thompson University Centre [*Nelson, BC*] [*Canada*] [*Pronounced "dee-tuck"*]

DTUL .... Deflection Temperature under Load [*Plastics technology*]

DTUN .... Detroit & Canada Tunnel Corp. [*NASDAQ symbol*] (NQ)

Dt Unterr ... Deutschunterricht. Arbeitshefte zu Seiner Praktischen Gestaltung [*A publication*]

DTUPC ...... Design to Unit Production Cost [*Army*]

DTUTF ...... Digital Tape Unit Test Facility [*NASA*]

DTV .... Day Television [*Sensing equipment*]

DTV .... Deutscher Taschenbuch Verlag [*Publisher*]

DTV .... Digital Television (MSA)

DTV .... Disney Television [*Animated music video program*] [*Cable-television*]

DTV .... Driver's Thermal Viewer [*Tank technology*] [*Army*]

DTV .... Dynamic Test Vehicle

DT/VAC .... Diphtheria-Tetanus Vaccine [*Medicine*]

DTVC .... Digital Transmission and Verification Converter (KSC)

Dt Verw Bl ... Deutsches Verwaltungsblatt [*A publication*]

DtVis .... Deutsche Vierteljahrsschrift fuer Literaturwissenschaft und Geistesgeschichte [*A publication*]

Dt Vischr ... Deutsche Vierteljahrsschrift fuer Literaturwissenschaft und Geistesgeschichte [*A publication*]

DTVM .... Differential Thermocouple Voltmeter

DTVM .... Diploma in Tropical Veterinary Medicine [*British*]

DTVP........ Developmental Test of Visual Perception [*Frostig*]
DTVS........ Distributor Thermo-Vacuum Switch [*Automotive engineering*]
DTW.......... Dance Theater Workshop (EA)
DTW.......... Dealer Tankwagon [*Gasoline*]
DTW.......... Detroit [*Michigan*] [*Airport symbol*]
DTW.......... Digital Equipment Corp., Tewkesbury, Tewkesbury, MA [*OCLC symbol*] (OCLC)
DTW.......... Dry Tank Weight
DTW.......... DTW. Deutsche Tierarztliche Wochenschrift [*A publication*]
DTW.......... Dual Tandem Wheels [*Aviation*]
DTW.......... Dynamic Time Warping
Dt Waldenser ... Deutsche Waldenser [*A publication*]
Dt Wass Wirt ... Deutsche Wasserwirtschaft [*A publication*]
DTWBA9 .. Deutsche Weinbau [*A publication*]
Dt Wein Rd ... Deutsche Weinrundschau [*A publication*]
Dt Wein Zt ... Deutsche Weinzeitung [*A publication*]
Dt Wirtinst Forschhft ... Deutsches Wirtschaftsinstitut Forschungshefte [*A publication*]
DTWX .... Dial Teletypewriter Exchange
DTX.......... Dedicated Terminal Facility [*Telecommunications*] (TSSD)
DTX.......... Dominion Textile, Inc. [*Toronto Stock Exchange symbol*]
DTXG........ Detroit-Texas Gas Gathering [*NASDAQ symbol*] (NQ)
DTYD....... Development Trust for the Young Disabled [*British*] (IRUK)
DTYO....... Duty Officer [*Military*]
DTZ.......... Deutsche Tonkuenstlerzeitung [*A publication*]
DTZ.......... Division Tactical Zone [*Army*] (AABC)
Dt Zahnaerztebl ... Deutsches Zahnaerzteblatt [*A publication*]
Dt Zahnhkd ... Deutsche Zahnheilkunde [*A publication*]
Dt Z Chir ... Deutsche Zeitschrift fuer Chirurgie [*A publication*]
D T Zg....... Deutsche Tiefbauzeitung [*A publication*]
Dt Z f Ph ... Deutsche Zeitschrift fuer Philosophie [*A publication*]
Dt Zs Akup ... Deutsche Zeitschrift fuer Akupunktur [*A publication*]
Dt Zs Philos ... Deutsche Zeitschrift fuer Philosophie [*A publication*]
DU .... Chess Wing Ltd. [*Great Britain*] [*ICAO designator*] (FAAC)
DU .... Dansk Udsyn [*A publication*]
DU .... Decision Unit [*Management*] (RDA)
D/U........... Delay Unit [*Telecommunications*] (TEL)
DU .... Deleted Unpostable [*IRS*]
DU .... Demarcation Unit (MCD)
DU .... Denatured Uranium [*Nuclear reactor technology*]
DU .... Depleted Uranium
DU .... Deutschunterricht [*A publication*]
DU .... Devisa Umum [*General Exchange*] [*Indonesia*] (IMH)
DU .... Diagnosis Undetermined [*or Unknown*] [*Medicine*]
DU .... Diazouracil [*Pharmacology*]
DU .... Diazyme Unit [*Of hydrolytic enzyme activity*]
DU .... [A] Dictionary of the Underworld [*A publication*]
DU .... Digital Unit
DU .... Dimensioning Unit [*Telecommunications*] (TEL)
D-U........... Diplomate, American Board of Urology (DHSM)
DU .... Display Unit (NASA)
DU .... Display, Upper
DU .... Distribution Unit (KSC)
DU .... Dobson Unit [*Measure of ozone*]
DU .... Dockers' Union [*British*]
DU .... Doctor of the University
DU .... Documentation Unit
DU .... Dog Unit [*Veterinary medicine*]
DU .... Double Uptake [*Boilers*]
Du .... Dual (BJA)
DU .... Duchy
DU .... Ducks Unlimited (EA)
Du .... Due
DU .... Duke
DU .... Duodenal Ulcer [*Medicine*]
DU .... Duplex [*Radio*] (NATG)
DU .... Dutch
DU .... Dwelling Unit [*Household census*]
DU .... Philips-Duphar NV [*Netherlands*] [*Research code symbol*]
DU .... Position Not Guaranteed [*Aviation code*] (FAAC)
DUA......... Deer Unlimited of America (EA)
DUA......... Deutschunterricht fuer Auslaender [*A publication*]
DUA......... Digital Uplink Assembly
DUA......... Digitronics Users Association [*Later, IUA*] (EA)
DUA......... Disaster Unemployment Assistance [*Disaster Relief Act*]
DUA......... Doctor of the University of Adelaide [*Australia*]
DUAX........ Dual Resources Ltd. [*Vancouver Stock Exchange symbol*]
dua............. Duala [*MARC language code*] [*Library of Congress*] (LCCP)
DUA......... Durant, OK [*Location identifier*] [*FAA*] (FAAL)
DUABA8 ... Delaware. Agricultural Experiment Station. Bulletin [*A publication*]
DUAL....... Dual Lite, Inc. [*NASDAQ symbol*] (NQ)
DUAL........ Dynamic Universal Assembly Language [*Data processing*]
DUAL-COMM ... Data Use and Access Laboratories - Communications, Inc. [*Information service or system*] (IID)
DUALEXTAC ... Dual Salvo Attack Tactic [*Navy*] (NVT)
Duane Nat ... Duane on the Law of Nations [*A publication*] (DLA)
Duane Road L ... Duane's Road Laws of Pennsylvania [*A publication*] (DLA)
Duar........... [*Franciscus*] Duarenus [*Deceased, 1559*] [*Authority cited in pre-1607 legal work*] (DSA)

Duaren .... [*Franciscus*] Duarenus [*Deceased, 1559*] [*Authority cited in pre-1607 legal work*] (DSA)
DUART ..... Dual Universal Asynchronous Receiver/Transmitter [*Motorola, Inc.*]
DUAS .... Uralic and Altaic Studies Department [*Indiana University*] [*Research center*] (RCD)
DUB.......... Dubious (ADA)
DUB.......... Dubitans [*or Dubius*] [*Doubting or Dubious*] [*Latin*]
DUB........... Dubitatur [*It Is Doubted*] [*Legal term*] (DLA)
DUB.......... Dublin [*City and county in Ireland*]
DUB.......... Dublin [*Ireland*] [*Airport symbol*] (OAG)
DUB.......... Dublin Rathfarnham Castle [*Ireland*] [*Seismograph station code, US Geological Survey*] [*Closed*] (SEIS)
DUB.......... Dysfunctional Uterine Bleeding [*Medicine*]
DUBDD..... Director of Unexploded Bomb Disposal Department [*Navy*] [*British*]
DUBID3 .... Dutch Birding [*A publication*]
DUBL........ Double
DUBL........ Dublin [*City and county in Ireland*]
Dublin J Med Sci ... Dublin Journal of Medical Science [*A publication*]
Dublin Med Press ... Dublin Medical Press [*A publication*]
Dublin Q J Med Sc ... Dublin Quarterly Journal of Medical Science [*A publication*]
Dublin Q J Sc ... Dublin Quarterly Journal of Science [*A publication*]
DublinRev ... Dublin Review [*A publication*]
Dublin ULJ ... Dublin University. Law Journal [*A publication*]
Dublin UL Rev ... Dublin University. Law Review [*A publication*]
Dubl J Med Sci ... Dublin Journal of Medical Science [*A publication*]
Dubl Mag... Dublin Magazine [*A publication*]
Dubl Re ...... Dublin Review [*A publication*]
Dubl Univ Mag ... Dublin University Magazine [*A publication*]
DUBMAC ... Deutsche Baumschule [*A publication*]
Dub Mag.... Dublin Magazine [*A publication*]
DubR.......... Dublin Review [*A publication*]
Dub Rev ..... Dublin Review [*A publication*]
DUBSDX... Dhaka University Studies. Part B [*A publication*]
Dub Univ... Dublin University Magazine [*A publication*]
DUC.......... Data Utilization Center [*Navy*] (NVT)
DUC.......... Data Utilization Console
DUC.......... Dense Upper Cloud (FAAC)
DUC.......... Digital Uplink Command (MCD)
DUC.......... Distinguished Unit Citation [*Military decoration*]
DUC.......... Division of Unemployment Compensation [*A publication*] (DLA)
DUC.......... Doctor of the University of Calgary
DUC.......... Dragon under Cover (MCD)
DUC.......... Duarte [*California*] [*Seismograph station code, US Geological Survey*] (SEIS)
DUC.......... Duchess
DUC.......... Duncan [*Oklahoma*] [*Airport symbol*] [*Obsolete*] (OAG)
DUC.......... University Club, Washington, DC [*Library symbol*] [*Library of Congress*] (LCLS)
DUCA....... United States Court of Appeals for the District of Columbia, Washington, DC [*Library symbol*] [*Library of Congress*] (LCLS)
Du Cange ... Du Cange's Glossarium [*A publication*] (DLA)
DUCC....... Deep Underground Command Center (MCD)
DUCE .... Denied Usage Channel Evaluator [*Telecommunications*] (TEL)
DUCE .... Distinguished Unit Citation Emblem [*Military decoration*]
Duc Gl....... Ducange's Glossarium [*A publication*] (DLA)
DUCH .... Duchess (ROG)
Ducio.......... [*Bertrandus de*] Deucio [*Deceased, 1355*] [*Authority cited in pre-1607 legal work*] (DSA)
DUCK....... Duckwall-Alco Stores [*NASDAQ symbol*] (NQ)
DUCO....... Durham Corporation [*NASDAQ symbol*] (NQ)
DUCOM.... Defence Union Catalogue of Monographs [*Australia*]
DUCON .... Duty Connection
DUCOR..... Defence Union Catalogue of Reports [*Australia*]
DUCOS ..... Defence Union Catalogue of Serials [*Australia*]
DUCS .... Deep Underground Communications System (AFM)
DUCS .... Defense Unit Classification System
DUCS .... Department of University Computer Systems [*University of Connecticut*] [*Research center*] (RCD)
DUD .... Design under Design
Dud .... Dudley's Georgia Reports [*A publication*] (DLA)
Dud .... [*C. W.*] Dudley's South Carolina Law Reports [*1837-38*] [*A publication*] (DLA)
DUD .... Dunedin [*New Zealand*] [*Airport symbol*] (OAG)
DUDAT..... Due Date
DUDC........ University of the District of Columbia, Washington, DC [*Library symbol*] [*Library of Congress*] (LCLS)
Dud Ch....... [*C. W.*] Dudley's South Carolina Equity Reports [*A publication*] (DLA)
Dud Eq .... [*C. W.*] Dudley's South Carolina Equity Reports [*A publication*] (DLA)
Dud Eq (SC) ... [*C. W.*] Dudley's South Carolina Equity Reports [*A publication*] (DLA)
Dud (GA) ... Dudley's Georgia Reports [*A publication*] (DLA)
Dud (Geo) .. Dudley's Georgia Reports [*A publication*] (DLA)
Dudl .... Dudley's Georgia Reports [*A publication*] (DLA)

Dudl .... [*C. W.*] Dudley's South Carolina Equity Reports [*A publication*] (DLA)

Dud L .... [*C. W.*] Dudley's South Carolina Law Reports [*1837-38*] [*A publication*] (DLA)

Dudl .... [*C. W.*] Dudley's South Carolina Law Reports [*1837-38*] [*A publication*] (DLA)

Dud Law..... [*C. W.*] Dudley's South Carolina Law Reports [*1837-38*] [*A publication*] (DLA)

Dudley Ednl J ... Dudley Educational Journal [*A publication*]

Dudley (GA) ... Dudley's Georgia Reports [*A publication*] (DLA)

Dud LSC.... [*C. W.*] Dudley's South Carolina Law Reports [*1837-38*] [*A publication*] (DLA)

dUDP........ Deoxyuridine Diphosphate [*Biochemistry*]

Dud R........ Dudley's Georgia Reports [*A publication*] (DLA)

Dud SC...... [*C. W.*] Dudley's South Carolina Law Reports [*1837-38*] [*A publication*] (DLA)

DUDST & K'S BART ... Dudstone and King's Barton [*England*]

DUE.......... Detection of Unauthorized Equipment [*Bell Laboratories*]

DuE........... Dichtung und Erkenntnis [*A publication*]

DUE.......... Distinguished Unit Emblem [*Military decoration*]

DUE.......... Dundo [*Angola*] [*Airport symbol*] (OAG)

DUEGG..... Dual Energy Gamma Group [*Nuclear energy*] (NRCH)

DUEL......... Data Update Edit Language [*Data processing*]

Duelmener Hb ... Duelmener Heimatblaetter [*A publication*]

DUEMEV ... Directory of Unpublished Experimental Mental Measures [*A publication*]

Duer .... Duer's New York Superior Court Reports [*A publication*] (DLA)

Duer Const Jur ... Duer's Constitutional Jurisprudence [*A publication*] (DLA)

Duer Gesch Bl ... Duerener Geschichtsblaetter [*A publication*]

Duer Ins ..... Duer on Insurance [*A publication*] (DLA)

Duer Mar Ins ... Duer on Marine Insurance [*A publication*] (DLA)

Duer (NY) ... Duer's New York Superior Court Reports [*A publication*] (DLA)

Duer Rep.... Duer on Representation [*A publication*] (DLA)

Duesseldorfer Jahrb ... Duesseldorfer Jahrbuch [*A publication*]

DUET .... Distance University Education via Television [*Mount Saint Vincent University*] [*Halifax, NS*] [*Telecommunications service*] (TSSD)

DUET .... Dual Emitter Transistor [*Electronics*]

DUETS...... Duo-Mode Electric Transport System, Inc.

DUF .... Chavis, KY [*Location identifier*] [*FAA*] (FAAL)

DUF .... Diffusion under [*Epitaxial*] Film (IEEE)

Duff........... Duff's Feudal Conveyancing [*Scotland*] [*A publication*] (DLA)

Duff Conv.... Duff's Feudal Conveyancing [*Scotland*] [*A publication*] (DLA)

DUFLY....... Duty Involving Flying [*Military*]

DUFLYTECH ... Duty Involving Flying as a Technical Observer [*Military*]

DUFM....... Durr-Fillauer Medical, Inc. [*NASDAQ symbol*] (NQ)

Dufresne .... Dufresne's Glossary [*A publication*] (DLA)

DUG .... Douglas [*Arizona*] [*Airport symbol*] (OAG)

DUG .... Dugway [*Utah*] [*Seismograph station code, US Geological Survey*] (SEIS)

Dugd.......... Dugdale's Origines Juridiciales [*A publication*] (DLA)

Dugd Orig Jur ... Dugdale's Origines Juridiciales [*A publication*] (DLA)

Dug Mon.... Dugdale's Monasticon [*A publication*] (DLA)

Dug Orig.... Dugdale's Origines Juridiciales [*A publication*] (DLA)

Dug Sum .... Dugdale on Summons [*A publication*] (DLA)

DUI........... Data Use Identifier (AFM)

DUI........... Distinctive Unit Insignia [*Military*] (INF)

DUI........... Driving under the Influence (DHSM)

DUI........... Drug Use Index [*Psychology*]

DUIL......... Driving under the Influence of Liquor

Duinen .... De Duinen. Bulletin du Centre Scientifique et Culturel de l'Abbaye des Dunes et du Westhoek [*A publication*]

DUINS ...... Duty under Instruction

DUJ .... Du Bois [*Pennsylvania*] [*Airport symbol*] (OAG)

DUJ .... Durham University. Journal [*A publication*]

DUJ .... E. I. Du Pont de Nemours & Co., Jackson Laboratory, Wilmington, DE [*OCLC symbol*] (OCLC)

DUJ .... Juris Utriusque Doctor [*Doctor of Both Laws; i.e., Canon and Civil Law*]

DUK.......... Duke, Nat, New York NY [*STAC*]

DUK.......... Duke Power Co. [*NYSE symbol*] (SPSG)

DUKAB..... Dopovidi Akademii Nauk Ukrains'koi RSR. Seriya A. Fiziko-Tekhnichni ta Matematichni Nauki [*A publication*]

Duke.......... Duke's Law of Charitable Uses [*A publication*] (DLA)

Duke BAJ ... Duke Bar Association. Journal [*A publication*] (DLA)

Duke BA Jo ... Duke University Bar Association. Journal [*A publication*] (DLA)

Duke Bar J ... Duke Bar Journal [*A publication*]

Duke B Ass'n J ... Duke Bar Association. Journal [*A publication*] (DLA)

Duke B J.... Duke Bar Journal [*A publication*]

Duke Ch Us ... Duke on Charitable Uses [*1676*] [*A publication*] (DLA)

Duke Div R ... Duke Divinity School. Review [*A publication*]

Duke Law J ... Duke Law Journal [*A publication*]

Duke L J ... Duke Law Journal [*A publication*]

Duke Math J ... Duke Mathematical Journal [*A publication*]

Duke Univ Mar Stn Bull ... Duke University. Marine Station Bulletin [*A publication*]

Duke Univ Math Ser ... Duke University Mathematics Series [*A publication*]

DUKRA ..... Dopovidi Akademii Nauk Ukrains'koi RSR [*A publication*]

Du Kunstz .. Du Kunstzeitschrift [*A publication*]

DUKW...... Amphibious Truck, 2 1/2-ton Cargo

DUL........... Diffuse Undifferentiated Lymphoma [*Oncology*]

DUL........... Duluth [*Minnesota*] [*Seismograph station code, US Geological Survey*] [*Closed*] (SEIS)

DULC........ Dulcis [*Sweet*] [*Pharmacy*]

Dulck .... Dulcken's Eastern District Reports [*Cape Colony, South Africa*] [*A publication*] (DLA)

Du LJ .... Duke Law Journal [*A publication*]

DULN....... Duke University Library Notes [*A publication*]

DULR .... Dublin University. Law Review [*A publication*]

DULR .... Duquesne University. Law Review [*A publication*]

DUM .... Died Unmarried [*Genealogy*]

DUM .... Dublin University Mission

DUM .... Dummy (MSA)

DUM .... Dumont D'Urville [*France*] [*Geomagnetic observatory code*]

dum .... Dutch, Middle [*MARC language code*] [*Library of Congress*] (LCCP)

DUMA...... Dubai Marine Areas (BJA)

DUMAND ... Deep Underwater Muon and Neutrino Detection [*Astrophysics*]

DUMB....... Deep Underground Missile Basing

Dumbarton OP ... Dumbarton Oaks Papers [*A publication*]

DumbOaksP ... Dumbarton Oaks Papers [*Cambridge, MA*] [*A publication*]

DUMF .... Dumfriesshire [*County in Scotland*]

Dumfriesshire Galloway Nat Hist Antiq Soc Trans ... Dumfriesshire and Galloway Natural History Antiquarian Society. Transactions [*A publication*]

DUMJA .... Duke Mathematical Journal [*A publication*]

DUML .... Diabetic Ulcer Meal [*Airline notation*]

dUMP........ Deoxyuridine Monophosphate [*Biochemistry*]

DUMP HEAP ... Journal of Diverse Unsung Miracle Plants for Healthy Evolution among People [*A publication*]

DUMR....... Dust and Moisture

DUMS .... Deep Unmanned Submersibles

DUN .... Data Users' Note [*NASA*] (MCD)

DUN .... Death of Ur-Nammu (BJA)

DUN .... Douglas United Nuclear, Inc. (KSC)

DUN .... Dundo [*Angola*] [*Seismograph station code, US Geological Survey*] (SEIS)

DUN .... Dunedin [*New Zealand*] (ROG)

DUN .... Dunnage

DUN .... Dun's Business Month [*A publication*]

DUNB....... Dunbartonshire [*County in Scotland*]

DUNBL..... Dunblane (ROG)

DUNC....... Deep Underwater Nuclear Counting

Dunc Eccl L ... Duncan's Scotch Parochial Ecclesiastical Law [*A publication*] (DLA)

Dunc Ent Cas ... Duncan's Scotch Entail Cases [*A publication*] (DLA)

Dunc Ev ..... Duncombe on the Law of Evidence [*A publication*] (DLA)

Dunc Man ... Duncan's Manual of Summary Procedure [*A publication*] (DLA)

Dunc Mer Cas ... Duncan's Mercantile Cases [*1885-86*] [*Scotland*] [*A publication*] (DLA)

Dunc Merc Cas ... Duncan's Mercantile Cases [*1885-86*] [*Scotland*] [*A publication*] (DLA)

Dunc NP .... Duncombe's Nisi Prius [*A publication*] (DLA)

Dun & Cum ... Dunphy and Cummins' Remarkable Trials [*A publication*] (DLA)

Dund LC .... Dundee Law Chronicle [*1853-58*] [*A publication*] (DLA)

DUNELM ... Bishop of Durham [*British*]

DUNELM ... Dunelmensis [*Of Durham*] [*Signature of Bishops of Durham*] [*Latin*] (ROG)

Dungl Med Dict ... Dunglison. Dictionary of Medical Science and Literature [*A publication*] (DLA)

DUNIS ...... Directory of United Nations Information Systems [*Database*] [*Inter-Organisation Board of the United Nations*] [*Information service or system*] (CRD)

DUniv .... Doctor of the University

DUNK....... Dunkeld (ROG)

DUNK....... Dunkeswell [*England*]

DUNK........ Dunkin Donuts, Inc. [*NASDAQ symbol*] (NQ)

Dunl .... Dunlop, Bell, and Murray's Scotch Court of Session Cases, Second Series [*1838-62*] [*A publication*] (DLA)

Dunl Abr .... Dunlap's Abridgment of Coke's Reports [*A publication*] (DLA)

Dunl Adm Pr ... Dunlop's Admiralty Practice [*A publication*] (DLA)

Dunl B & M ... Dunlop, Bell, and Murray's Scotch Court of Session Cases, Second Series [*1838-62*] [*A publication*] (DLA)

Dunl (Ct of Sess) ... Dunlop, Bell, and Murray's Scotch Court of Session Cases, Second Series [*1838-62*] [*A publication*] (ILCA)

Dunl F .... Dunlap's Forms [*A publication*] (DLA)

Dunl L PA ... Dunlop's Laws of Pennsylvania [*A publication*] (DLA)

Dunl L US ... Dunlop's Laws of the United States [*A publication*] (DLA)

Dunlop .... Dunlop, Bell, and Murray's Scotch Court of Session Cases, Second Series [*1838-62*] [*A publication*] (DLA)

Dunl Paley Ag ... Dunlap's Paley on Agency [*A publication*] (DLA)

Dunl Par .... Dunlop on Parochial Law [*Scotland*] [*A publication*] (DLA)

Dunl Pr ...... Dunlop's Admiralty Practice [*A publication*] (DLA)

Dun L & T ... Dun's Landlord and Tenant in Ireland [*A publication*] (DLA)

Dunn .... Dunning's English King's Bench Reports [*1753-54*] [*A publication*] (DLA)

Dunning ..... Dunning's English King's Bench Reports [*1753-54*] [*A publication*] (DLA)

DunR .... [*The*] Dunwoodie Review [*A publication*]

DUNS .... Data Universal Numbering System [*Dun's number*] [*Business term*]

Duns .... Dun's Business Month [*A publication*]

Dun's .... Dun's Review [*A publication*]

Duns Bus M ... Dun's Business Month [*A publication*]

Dun's Bus Mon ... Dun's Business Month [*A publication*]

Dun's Int R ... Dun's International Review [*A publication*]

Dun's R ...... Dun's Review [*A publication*]

Dun's Rev ...... Dun's Review [*A publication*]

Dun's Stat R ... Dun's Statistical Review [*A publication*]

DUNST ..... Dunstable [*Municipal borough in England*]

DUO .... Datatron Users' Organization

DUO .... DOS [*Disk Operating System*] under OS [*Operating System*]

DUO .... Duetto [*Duet*] [*Music*] (ROG)

DUO .... Duodecimo [*Book up to 20 centimeters in height*]

DUOD .... Duodenum [*Anatomy*]

DUODA ..... Duodecim [*A publication*]

DUODAG ... Duodecim [*A publication*]

DUP .... Democratic Unification Party [*Minjutongil Dang*] [*Republic of Korea*] [*Political party*] (PPW)

DUP ..... Democratic Unionist Party [*Sudan*] [*Political party*] (PD)

DUP ..... Democratic Unionist Party [*Northern Ireland*] [*Political party*]

DUP .... Diploma of the University of Paris

DUP .... Disk Utility Program [*IBM Corp.*] [*Data processing*]

DUP .... Distinguished University Professor

DUP .... Diundecyl Phthalate [*Organic chemistry*]

DUP .... Du Pont Canada, Inc. [*Toronto Stock Exchange symbol*]

DUP .... Duplex [*Watchmaking*] (ROG)

DUP .... Duplicate (AFM)

DUP .... Dupont Canada, Inc. [*Toronto Stock Exchange symbol*]

DUP .... E. I. DuPont de Nemours & Co., Lavoisier Library, Wilmington, DE [*OCLC symbol*] (OCLC)

DUP .... National Society, Daughters of Utah Pioneers (EA)

DUP .... Ulster Democratic Unionist Party [*Northern Ireland*] [*Political party*] (PPW)

DUPAC ..... Duke University Preventive Approach to Cardiovascular Disease

DuPage Busi ... DuPage Woodfield Business News [*A publication*]

DUPC .... Displayed under Program Control

Dup Const ... Duponceau on the Constitution [*A publication*] (DLA)

DUPE .... Duplicate (AABC)

DUP-FIL ... Duplicate Filing [*IRS*]

Dup Jur ...... Duponceau on Jurisdiction of United States Courts [*A publication*] (DLA)

dupl .... Duplicate (BJA)

DUPLX .... Duplex (NASA)

DUPLXR ..... Duplexer (NASA)

DUPMA .... Du Pont Magazine [*A publication*]

Duponceau US Cts ... Duponceau on Jurisdiction of United States Courts [*A publication*] (DLA)

DuPont .... DuPont Magazine [*A publication*]

Du Pont Mag ... Du Pont Magazine [*A publication*]

Du Pont Mag Eur Edn ... Du Pont Magazine. European Edition [*A publication*]

DUPPA ...... Dual Path Protection Arrangement [*AT & T*]

DUQ .... Duncan/Quamichan Lake [*Canada*] [*Airport symbol*] [*Obsolete*] (OAG)

Duq .... Duquesne Law Review [*A publication*]

DUQ .... Duquesne University Library, Pittsburgh, PA [*OCLC symbol*] (OCLC)

Duq LR ...... Duquesne Law Review [*A publication*]

Duq L Rev ... Duquesne Law Review [*A publication*]

DUQN .... Duquesne Systems, Inc. [*Pittsburgh, PA*] [*NASDAQ symbol*] (NQ)

Duq R .... Duquesne Review [*A publication*]

Duquesne L Rev ... Duquesne Law Review [*A publication*]

Duquesne Sci Couns ... Duquesne Science Counselor [*A publication*]

Duquesne U L Rev ... Duquesne University. Law Review [*A publication*]

DUR .... Duration

DUR .... Durban [*South Africa*] [*Airport symbol*] (OAG)

DUR .... Durham [*City and county in England*]

DUR .... Durham [*England*] [*Seismograph station code, US Geological Survey*] (SEIS)

DUR .... Durham Resources, Inc. [*Toronto Stock Exchange symbol*]

DUR .... During

Dur .... Durium [*Record label*] [*Italy*]

DUR .... Duro-Test Corp. [*AMEX symbol*] (SPSG)

DUR .... Durus [*Hard*] [*Pharmacy*]

DURA .... Durability (MCD)

Duran .... [*Guillelmus*] Durandi [*Deceased, 1296*] [*Authority cited in pre-1607 legal work*] (DSA)

Durand .... [*Guillelmus*] Durandi [*Deceased, 1296*] [*Authority cited in pre-1607 legal work*] (DSA)

Durand Spec Jur ... Durandi. Speculum Judiciale [*A publication*] (DLA)

Durban Mus Art Gallery Annu Rep ... Durban Museum and Art Gallery. Annual Report [*A publication*]

Durban Mus Novit ... Durban Museum Novitates [*A publication*]

DUR DOL ... Durante Dolore [*While Pain Lasts*] [*Pharmacy*]

DUR DOLOR ... Durante Dolore [*While Pain Lasts*] [*Pharmacy*]

Dur Dr Fr ... Duranton's Droit Francais [*A publication*] (DLA)

Durf .... Durfee's Reports [*2 Rhode Island*] [*A publication*] (DLA)

Durfee .... Durfee's Reports [*2 Rhode Island*] [*A publication*] (DLA)

Durferrit Hausmitt ... Durferrit Hausmitteilungen [*A publication*]

DURG .... During (FAAC)

DURGC ..... During Climb [*Aviation*] (FAAC)

DURGD ..... During Descent [*Aviation*] (FAAC)

DURH ...... Durham [*City and county in England*]

Durham Res ... Durham Research Review [*A publication*]

Durham Univ ... Durham University. Journal [*A publication*]

Durham Univ Biol Soc J ... Durham University Biological Society. Journal [*A publication*]

Durham Univ Dep Geogr Occas Publ New Ser ... Durham University. Department of Geography. Occasional Publications. New Series [*A publication*]

Durham Univ J ... Durham University. Journal [*A publication*]

DURH LI ... Durham Light Infantry [*Military unit*] [*British*] (ROG)

DURI .... [*The*] Duriron Co., Inc. [*NASDAQ symbol*] (NQ)

DUrI .... Urban Institute, Washington, DC [*Library symbol*] [*Library of Congress*] (LCLS)

Durie .... Durie's Scotch Court of Session Decisions [*1621-42*] [*A publication*] (DLA)

DURN .... Duration (FAAC)

Durn & E .... Durnford and East's (Term) Reports [*1785-1800*] [*England*] [*A publication*] (DLA)

Dur Newc Res Rev ... Durham and Newcastle Research Review [*A publication*]

DURS .... Dursley [*England*]

DurUJ .... Durham University. Journal [*A publication*]

Durzh Vestn ... Durzhaven Vestnik [*Bulgaria*] [*A publication*]

DUS .... Dacca University. Studies [*A publication*]

DUS .... Data Utilization Station

DUS .... Diagnostic Utility System

DUS .... Diploma of the University of Southampton [*British*]

DUS .... Dockside Underway Replenishment Simulator [*Navy*] (NVT)

DUS .... Dollar Unit Sampling (ADA)

DUS .... Driver Units Speaker

DUS .... Dusheti [*USSR*] [*Seismograph station code, US Geological Survey*] (SEIS)

DUS .... Dusseldorf [*West Germany*] [*Airport symbol*] (OAG)

DUS .... Dusty Mac Mines Ltd. [*Vancouver Stock Exchange symbol*]

DUS .... Marshfield, WI [*Location identifier*] [*FAA*] (FAAL)

DUSA .... Deputy Under Secretary of the Army (AABC)

DUSA .... Dryclean USA, Inc. [*Miami, FL*] [*NASDAQ symbol*] (NQ)

DUSAA ...... Davison United States Army Airfield (AABC)

DUSAM ..... Dummy Surface-to-Air Missile

Dusanbin Gos Ped Inst Ucen Zap ... Dusanbinskii Gosudarstvennyi Pedagogiceskii Institut Imeni T. G. Sevcenko Ucenyi Zapiski [*A publication*]

DUSB .... United States Brewers Association, Washington, DC [*Library symbol*] [*Library of Congress*] (LCLS)

DUSC .... Deep Underground Support Center [*Air Force*]

DUSC .... United States Supreme Court, Washington, DC [*Library symbol*] [*Library of Congress*] (LCLS)

DUSD .... Data Services Division [*Census*] (OICC)

DUSD .... Deputy Under Secretary of Defense (RDA)

DUSDRE(C³I) ... Deputy Under Secretary of Defense for Research and Engineering (Communications, Command, Control, and Intelligence) [*Military*]

DUSEA5 .... Dusenia [*A publication*]

DUSFC .... Deputy Undersecretary for Field Coordination [*HUD*]

DUSIGN ..... To Duty Assigned By [*Military*]

DUSN .... Diffuse Unilateral Subacute Neuroretinitis [*Ophthalmology*]

DUSNWS ... Director, United States Naval Weather Service

DUSO .... Developing Understanding of Self and Others [*Educational tool*]

DUSODA .. For Duty or Such Other Duty as [*Command or Activity Indicated*] May Assign [*Military*]

DUSS .... Deep Underground Sanguine System [*Navy*] (MCD)

DUST .... Dusty Mac Mines Ltd. [*Vancouver, BC*] [*NASDAQ symbol*] (NQ)

DUSTA ...... Duty Station [*Navy*]

DUSW .... Director of Undersea Warfare, Ministry of Defence, London (NATG)

Du Sz .... Dunantuli Szemle [*A publication*]

DuszpPZ .... Duszpasterz Polski Zagranica [*Rome*] [*A publication*]

DUT .... Deutsche Umsiedlungstreuhandgesellschaft [*A publication*] (BJA)

DUT .... Device under Test

DUT .... Duplication Technician, Photolithography [*Navy rating*]

dut .... Dutch [*MARC language code*] [*Library of Congress*] (LCCP)

DUT .... Dutch

DUT .... Dutch Harbor [*Alaska*] [*Airport symbol*] (OAG)

DUTA .... Display Unit Test Assembly (MCD)

D Utah ...... United States District Court for the District of Utah (DLA)

DUTC .... Dallas Union Terminal [*AAR code*]

Dutch .... Dutcher's Law Reports [*25-29 New Jersey*] [*A publication*] (DLA)

Dutch Art & Archre Today ... Dutch Art and Architecture Today [*A publication*]
Dutch Q Rev ... Dutch Quarterly Review of Anglo-American Letters [*A publication*]
DutchS .... Dutch Studies [*A publication*]
Dutch S (The Hague Netherlands) ... Dutch Studies (The Hague, Netherlands) [*A publication*]
Dut & Cowd Rev ... Dutton and Cowdrey's Revision of Swift's Digest of Connecticut Laws [*A publication*]   (DLA)
DUTE .... Digital Universal Test Equipment   (MCD)
DUTOUT ... [*For*] Duty Outside the Continental Limits of the United States
dUTP .... Deoxyuridine Triphosphate [*Biochemistry*]
DUTS .... Decision Unit Tracking System [*Nuclear energy*]   (NRCH)
DUULD5 ... Annual Research Reviews. Duodenal Ulcer [*A publication*]
DUV .... Data Under Voice [*Bell System*]
DUV .... Daughters of Union Veterans of the Civil War, 1861-1865   (EA)
DuV .... Dichtung und Volkstum [*A publication*]
Duv .... Duvall's Canada Supreme Court Reports [*A publication*]   (DLA)
Duv .... Duvall's Reports [*62, 63 Kentucky*] [*A publication*]   (DLA)
Duval .... Duvall's Canada Supreme Court Reports [*A publication*]   (DLA)
Duvall .... Duvall's Canada Supreme Court Reports [*A publication*]   (DLA)
DUVAS ..... Derivative Ultraviolet Absorption Spectrometer [*Instrumentation*]
Duv (Can)... Duvall's Canada Supreme Court Reports [*A publication*]   (DLA)
DuW .... Dichtung und Wirklichkeit [*A publication*]
DUW .... Director of Underwater Weapons [*British*]
DUWCAL ... Duluth Weapons Calibration System
DUWP .... Director of Underwater Weapons Projects [*Navy*] [*British*]
DUX .... Dumas, TX [*Location identifier*] [*FAA*]   (FAAL)
Dux .... Duxbury's High Court Reports [*South African Republic*] [*1895*] [*A publication*]   (DLA)
DUZ .... Deutsche Universitaetszeitung [*A publication*]
DV .... Air Vendee [*France*] [*ICAO designator*]   (FAAC)
DV .... Damage and Vulnerability   (MCD)
DV .... Data Vetting
DV .... Death Valley Resources [*Vancouver Stock Exchange symbol*]
DV .... Defective Vision   (ADA)
DV .... Dei Verbum [*Dogmatic Constitution on Divine Revelation*] [*Vatican II document*]
DV .... Delta Velocity   (KSC)
DV .... Demonstration and Validation   (MCD)
DV .... Deo Volente [*God Willing*] [*Latin*]
DV .... Dependent Vehicle
DV .... Designee for Verification [*NASA*]   (NASA)
DV .... Deutsche Vierteljahrsschrift [*A publication*]
DV .... Device
DV .... Diana Vreeland [*Fashion editor, 1903-1989*]
D & V .... Diarrhea and Vomiting [*Medicine*]
DV .... Dichtung und Volkstum [*A publication*]
DV .... Dieu Vivant [*Paris*] [*A publication*]
DV .... Different Version
DV .... Differential Velocity   (KSC)
DV .... Differential Voltage   (IEEE)
DV .... Digital Video
DV .... Digital Voice   (MCD)
DV .... Dilute Volume [*Chemistry*]
DV .... Diploma in Venereology   (ADA)
DV .... Direct Vision [*Aviation*]
DV .... Directed Verdict [*Legal term*]
D of V .... Director of Victualling [*British military*]   (DMA)
DV .... DirectVision [*Home-information service of KPIX-TV*]
DV .... Disbursement Voucher   (AFM)
DV .... Disease Variable [*Medicine*]
DV .... Distemper Virus
DV .... Distinguished Visitor
DV .... Distressed Vehicle   (KSC)
DV .... Diverter Valve   (KSC)
DV .... Divide
DV .... Divinitas   (BJA)
DV .... Division [*Mathematics*]   (ROG)
DV .... Division Flag [*Navy*] [*British*]
DV .... Division Piece [*Rotary piston meter*]
DV .... Division of Validation [*Social Security Administration*]
DV .... Divisionsverfuegung [*or Divisionsverordnung*] [*Divisional Order*] [*German military - World War II*]
DV .... Divorce [*Facetious translation of DV, Deo Volente (God Willing)*]   (DSUE)
DV .... Divorced
DV .... Domiciliary Visit [*Medicine*]
DV .... Dorsoventral [*Anatomy*]
DV .... Douay Version [*Bible*]
DV .... Double Vibrations [*Cycles*]
DV .... Double Vision
DV .... Doubtful-Very [*Theatrical term*] [*Facetious translation of DV, Deo Volente (God Willing)*]   (DSUE)
DV .... Drift Voltage
DV .... Dual Valve

DV .... Dump Valve   (IEEE)
DV .... Durchgangsvermittlung [*Long-distance telephone exchange*] [*German military - World War II*]
DV .... Dutch RCA [*Victor*] [*Record label*]
DVA .... Adams County School District No. 12, Northglenn, CO [*OCLC symbol*]   (OCLC)
DVA .... Davis Airlines [*Bryan, TX*] [*FAA designator*]   (FAAC)
DVA .... Department of Veterans Affairs [*Canada*]
DVA .... Department of Veterans Affairs [*Formerly, Veterans Administration*]
DVA .... Designed, Verified, and Assigned Date [*Telecommunications*]   (TEL)
DVA .... Deutsche Verlags-Anstalt [*Publishing company*]
DVA .... Development and Change [*A publication*]
DVA .... Differential Voltage Amplifier
DVA .... Diploma in Veterinary Anaesthesia [*British*]
DVA .... Directory of Visual Arts Organizations [*Arts Midwest*] [*Information service or system*]   (CRD)
DVA .... Discovery Value Accounting   (ADA)
DVA .... Distance Visual Acuity [*Ophthalmology*]
DVA .... Divinylacetylene [*Organic chemistry*]
DVA .... Document Validation Audit [*NASA*]   (MCD)
DVA .... Dunkirk Veterans Association [*Leeds, England*]   (EAIO)
DVA .... Duration of Voluntary Apnea [*Physiology*]
DVA .... Dynamic Visual Acuity   (IEEE)
DVA .... United States Veterans Administration, Washington, DC [*Library symbol*] [*Library of Congress*]   (LCLS)
DVAB .... Defense Vocational Aptitude Battery [*Military*]   (NVT)
DVAD .... Dollar Value of Annual Demands   (AFIT)
DVAL .... Demonstration and Validation   (MCD)
DVARS ...... Doppler Velocity Altimeter RADAR Set [*Military*]   (CAAL)
DVASA ...... Doklady Vsesoyuznoi Akademii Sel'skokhozyaistvennykh Nauk Imeni V. I. Lenina [*A publication*]
DVAV .... Dorsoventral Abdominal Vibration [*Entomology*]
DVB .... Department of Veterans Benefits [*Veterans Administration*]
DVB .... Device Base Control Block [*Data processing*]   (IBMDP)
DVB .... Diamminedichloroplatinum [*Cisplatin*], Vindesine, Bleomycin [*Antineoplastic drug regimen*]
DVB .... Digital Video Bandwidth
DVB .... Divinylbenzene [*Organic chemistry*]
DVB .... Volta Bureau for the Deaf, Washington, DC [*Library symbol*] [*Library of Congress*]   (LCLS)
DVBD .... Diesel V-Belt Drive
DVBSA3 .... Developments in Biological Standardization [*A publication*]
DVC .... Community College of Denver, North Campus, Westminster, CO [*OCLC symbol*]   (OCLC)
DVC .... Device   (MSA)
DVC .... Digital Video Communication [*Military*]   (CAAL)
DVC .... Digital Voice Communications
DVC .... Direct Variable Cost
DVC .... Direct View Console   (MCD)
DVC .... Divanillylidenecyclohexanone [*or Divanillalcyclohexanone*] [*Pharmacology*]
DVC .... Dove Creek, CO [*Location identifier*] [*FAA*]   (FAAL)
DVCBAP .... Developmental and Cell Biology [*A publication*]
DVCCS ...... Differential Voltage-Controlled Current Source   (IEEE)
DVCMF ...... Doxorubicin [*Adriamycin*], Vincristine, Cyclophosphamide, Methotrexate, Fluorouracil [*Antineoplastic drug regimen*]
DVCS .... Devices
DVCS .... Digital Voice Communications System   (MCD)
D/VD .... Data/Voice Data   (MCD)
DVD .... Delta Velocity Display
DVD .... Design Verification Demonstration
DVD .... Detail Velocity Display   (IEEE)
DV & D ...... Diploma in Venereology and Dermatology   (ADA)
DVD .... Direct Vendor Delivery [*DoD*]
DVD .... Direct-View Device [*Night vision*]
DVD .... Dissociated Vertical Deviation [*Ophthalmology*]
DVD .... Thurmont, MD [*Location identifier*] [*FAA*]   (FAAL)
DVDALV... Double Vessel Disease with an Abnormal Left Ventricle [*Cardiology*]
DVDC .... Divisional Vendor Data Coordinator   (MCD)
DVDP .... Dry Valley Drilling Project [*National Science Foundation*]
DVDS .... Digital Video Display System
DVDSAD .. Davidsonia [*A publication*]
DVDY .... Diving Duty [*Military*]
DVE .... Community College of Denver, North AEC Project, Westminster, CO [*OCLC symbol*]   (OCLC)
DVE .... Developing Economies [*A publication*]
DVE .... Devnic Energy, Inc. [*Toronto Stock Exchange symbol*]
DVE .... Differential Vector Equation
Dve .... Drive
DVE .... Duck Virus Enteritis
DVEC-A .... Developing Economics [*A publication*]
DVECC ...... Disease Vector Ecology and Control Center [*Military*]   (NVT)
DV Ed .... Doctor of Vocational Education
DVENA3 ... Dermatologiya i Venerologiya [*A publication*]
DVEO .... Defense Value Engineering Services Officer
DVESO ...... DoD [*Department of Defense*] Value Engineering Services Office   (IEEE)
D Vet Med ... Doctor of Veterinary Medicine

DVetSc....... Doctor of Veterinary Science (ADA)
DVF .... Diane Von Furstenberg [*Couturiere*]
DVF .... Dualbowl Vibratory Feeder
DVF .... Society of the Descendants of Washington's Army at Valley
            Forge (EA)
DVFC........ Danny Vann Fan Club (EA)
DVFE........ Director, Vehicle and Field Engineering [*Military*] [*Canada*]
DVFO .... Digital Variable-Frequency Oscillator (IEEE)
DVFR........ Defense Visual Flight Rules
DVG.......... Digital Video Generator [*Data processing*]
DVGL........ Dimensional Visions Group, Inc. [*NASDAQ symbol*] (NQ)
DVH .... Dental, Visual, and Hearing Insurance
DVH .... Diploma in Veterinary Hygiene [*British*]
DVH .... Divi Hotels NV [*AMEX symbol*] (SPSG)
DVH .... Division for the Visually Handicapped (EA)
DVI .... Development Forum. Business Edition [*A publication*]
DVI .... Device-Independent Format [*Data processing*]
DVI .... Digital Vascular Imaging [*Roentgenology*]
DVI .... Digital Video Interactive [*CD-ROM technology*] [*General
            Electric Co.*]
DVI .... Dover Industries Ltd. [*Toronto Stock Exchange symbol*]
DVI .... Dust Veil Index [*of atmosphere*]
DVI .... Information Management Specialists, Denver, CO [*OCLC
            symbol*] (OCLC)
D VI .... United States District Court for the District of the Virgin
            Islands [*DLA*]
DVIC .... DVI Financial Corporation [*NASDAQ symbol*] (NQ)
Dvigateli Vnutr Sgoraniya (Kharkov) ... Dvigateli Vnutrennego Sgoraniya
            (Kharkov) [*Ukrainian SSR*] [*A publication*]
DVIOJ........ Deutsche Vereinigung fuer die Interessen der Osteuropaeischen
            Juden [*A publication*]
DVIP......... Digital Video Integrator and Processor (MCD)
DVIS.......... Datavision, Inc. [*NASDAQ symbol*] (NQ)
DVIS.......... Digital Vascular Imaging System [*Roentgenology*] (MCD)
DVJ........... Colorado Supreme Court Library, Denver, CO [*OCLC
            symbol*] (OCLC)
DVJB........ Danmarks Veterinaer- og Jordbrugsbase [*Danish Veterinary
            and Agricultural Library Catalogue*] [*Information service
            or system*]
DVJS........ Deutsche Vierteljahrsschrift fuer Literaturwissenschaft und
            Geistesgeschichte [*A publication*]
DVK .... Danville, KY [*Location identifier*] [*FAA*] (FAAL)
DVK .... Davis-Keays Mining [*Vancouver Stock Exchange symbol*]
DVL .... Del-Val Financial Corp. [*NYSE symbol*] (SPSG)
DVL .... Delta Velocity Launch
DVL .... Develop (MSA)
DVL .... Devils Lake [*North Dakota*] [*Airport symbol*] (OAG)
DVL .... Direct Voice Line (CET)
DVL .... Distance Velocity Laboratory
DVL .... Dorsal Velar Lobe
DVLC .... Driver and Vehicle Licensing Centre [*British*] (DCTA)
DVLG .... Deutsche Vierteljahrsschrift fuer Literaturwissenschaft und
            Geistesgeschichte [*A publication*]
DVLP........ Development
Dvlpmt .... Development
DVM.......... Decessit Vita Matris [*Died during the Lifetime of the Mother*]
            [*Latin*]
DVM......... Digital Velocity Meter
DVM......... Digital Voltmeter
DVM......... Directional Variable Microphone
DVM......... Discontinuous Variational Method
DVM......... Displaced Virtual Machine
DVM......... Doctor of Veterinary Medicine
DVM......... Doxurubicin [*Adriamycin*], Vincristine, Methotrexate
            [*Antineoplastic drug regimen*]
DVMA........ Direct Virtual Memory Access [*Data processing*]
DVME........ Dulbecco-Vogt Modified Eagle's [*Medium for cell growth*]
DVMMB7 ... Datenverarbeitung in der Medizin [*A publication*]
DVMR .... Division of Veterinary Medical Research [*Department of
            Health and Human Services*] (GRD)
DVMS ...... Doctor of Veterinary Medicine and Surgery
DVN.......... Community College of Denver, North Campus, Westminster,
            CO [*OCLC symbol*] (OCLC)
DVN.......... Davenport, IA [*Location identifier*] [*FAA*] (FAAL)
DVN.......... Devisavit Vel Non [*Issue of fact as to whether a will in question
            was made by the testator*] [*Latin*] [*Legal term*] (DLA)
DVN.......... Devon Energy Corp. [*AMEX symbol*] (CTT)
DVN.......... Devonion Resources [*Vancouver Stock Exchange symbol*]
DVNA........ Direct-View Navigation Aid
DVO.......... Davao [*Philippines*] [*Airport symbol*] (OAG)
DVO.......... Davenport Industries Ltd. [*Vancouver Stock Exchange symbol*]
DVO.......... Decimal Voltage Output
DVO.......... Delta Velocity On/Off
DVO.......... Devoe Airlines [*Miami, FL*] [*FAA designator*] (FAAC)
DVO.......... Direct View Optics
DVO.......... Divisional Veterinary Officer [*Ministry of Agriculture,
            Fisheries, and Food*] [*British*]
DVO.......... Durchfuehrungsverordnung [*Executive Decree*]
            [*German*] (ILCA)
DVOM....... Digital Volt-Ohmmeter
DVON .... Devon Stores Corp. [*NASDAQ symbol*] (NQ)

DVOP........ Disabled Veterans Outreach Program [*Department of Labor*]
DVOR........ Doppler VHF [*Very High Frequency*] Omnirange
DVOT........ Dog Vomit on Toast [*Creamed beef or tuna on toast*] [*Military
            slang*]
DVP .... Data Validation Program [*NASA*]
DVP .... Decessit Vita Patris [*Died during the Lifetime of the Father*]
            [*Latin*]
DVP .... Delivery Versus Payment
DVP .... Delta Velocity Planet
DVP .... Demokratische Volkspartei [*Democratic People's Party*]
            [*Federal Republic of Germany*] (PPE)
DVP .... Design Verification Period (MCD)
DVP .... Design Verification Program (MCD)
DVP .... Deutsche Volkspartei [*German People's Party (1919-
            1933)*] (PPE)
DVP .... Devran Petroleum Ltd. [*Vancouver Stock Exchange symbol*]
DVP .... Differential Value Profile [*Psychology*]
DVP .... Digital Voice Privacy [*Telecommunications*]
DVP .... Domestic Violence Project (EA)
DVP .... University of Denver, Denver, CO [*OCLC symbol*] (OCLC)
DVPDF ...... Dry Vacuum Pump Discharge Filter
DVPF........ Dry Vacuum Pump Filter
DVPH........ Diploma in Veterinary Public Health (ADA)
DVPL-ASP ... Daunorubicin, Vincristine, Prednisone, L-Asparaginase
            [*Antineoplastic drug regimen*]
DVPMAL ... Developmental Psychology. Monograph [*A publication*]
DVPPI....... Daylight View Plan Position Indicator (CET)
DVPSD8 ... Developments in Plant and Soil Sciences [*A publication*]
DVR .... Community College of Denver, Red Rocks Campus, Golden,
            CO [*OCLC symbol*] (OCLC)
DVR .... Department [*or Division*] of Vocational Rehabilitation (OICC)
DVR .... Design Verification Rig (MCD)
DVR .... Devco Railway [*Cape Breton Development Corp. - Coal Div.*]
            [*AAR code*]
DVR .... Diver (MSA)
DVR .... Division of Vocational Rehabilitation [*Later, DTVE*] [*Office of
            Education*]
DVR .... Doctor in Veterinary Radiology
DVR .... Document Validation Report
DVR .... Driver (AABC)
DVR .... Jet Way, Inc. [*Ypsilanti, MI*] [*FAA designator*] (FAAC)
DVR .... Lebanon, NH [*Location identifier*] [*FAA*] (FAAL)
DVR .... Van Riebeeck Decoration [*British military*] (DMA)
DVRABAD ... Driver Badge, Amphibious Vehicles [*Military decoration*]
DVRF........ Dover Regional Financial Shares [*Philadelphia, PA*] [*NASDAQ
            symbol*] (NQ)
DVRG .... Deja Vu Research Group (EAIO)
DVRG .... Diverge (FAAC)
DVRI .... Direct View RADAR Indicator [*Military*] (CAAL)
DVRMBAD ... Driver Badge, Motorcycles [*Military decoration*]
DvrMechBadA ... Driver and Mechanic Badge, Amphibious Vehicles
            [*Military decoration*] (AABC)
DvrMechBadM ... Driver and Mechanic Badge, Motorcycles [*Military
            decoration*] (AABC)
DvrMechBadMech ... Driver and Mechanic Badge, Mechanic [*Military
            decoration*] (AABC)
DvrMechBadOp ... Driver and Mechanic Badge, Operator [*Military
            decoration*] (AABC)
DvrMechBadT ... Driver and Mechanic Badge, Tracked Vehicles [*Military
            decoration*] (AABC)
DvrMechBadW ... Driver and Mechanic Badge, Wheeled Vehicles [*Military
            decoration*] (AABC)
DVRS........ Diversco, Inc. [*NASDAQ symbol*] (NQ)
DVRSN ..... Diversion (FAAC)
DVRTBAD ... Driver Badge, Tracked Vehicles [*Military decoration*]
DVRWBAD ... Driver Badge, Wheeled Vehicles [*Military decoration*]
DVRY........ DeVry, Inc. [*NASDAQ symbol*] (NQ)
DVS .... Davis [*Australia*] [*Geomagnetic observatory code*]
DVS .... Delta Valley & Southern Railway Co. [*AAR code*]
DVS .... Denver Special Librarians, Denver, CO [*OCLC
            symbol*] (OCLC)
DVS .... Descriptive Video Services [*for the sight-impaired*] [*Public
            Broadcasting Service*]
DVS .... Design Verification Specification (NASA)
DVS .... Development Forum [*A publication*]
DVS .... Digital Voice System (MCD)
DVS .... Digital Voltage Source
DVS .... Director of Veterinary Services [*Military*] [*British*]
DVS .... Doctor of Veterinary Science
DVS .... Doctor of Veterinary Surgery
DVS .... Doppler Velocity Sensor
DVS .... Dynamic Vacuum Seal
DVSA........ Dierkundige Vereniging van Suidelike Afrika [*Zoological
            Society of Southern Africa - ZSSA*] [*Port Elizabeth, South
            Africa*] (EAIO)
DVSB........ Danske Videnskabernes Selskabs Biologiske. Skrifter [*A
            publication*]
DVS Ber..... DVS [*Deutscher Verband fuer Schweisstechnik*] Berichte [*West
            Germany*] [*A publication*]
DV Sc ...... Doctor of Veterinary Science
DVSC........ Doctor of Veterinary Surgery

DV Sci........	Doctor of Veterinary Science
DVSI........	Digital Vibration Survey Instrument
DVSM	Det Kongelige Danske Videnskabernes Selskab. Historisk-Filologiske Meddelelser [*Copenhagen*] [*A publication*]
DVSM	Diploma in Veterinary State Medicine
DVSS........	Danske Videnskabernes Selskabs Skrifter [*A publication*]
DVST........	Direct-View Storage Tube [*Princeton Electronic Products*]
DVT..........	Davic Enterprise, Inc. [*Vancouver Stock Exchange symbol*]
DVT..........	Deep Venous Thrombosis [*Medicine*]
DVT..........	Dejiny Ved a Techniky [*A publication*]
DVT..........	Design Verification Test
DVT..........	Development Verification Testing (RDA)
DVT..........	Phoenix, AZ [*Location identifier*] [*FAA*] (FAAL)
D VT	United States District Court for the District of Vermont (DLA)
DVT-Dejiny Ved a Techniky ... Dejiny Ved a Techniky. Spolecnost pro Dejiny Ved a Techniky [*A publication*]
DVTE	Division of Vocational and Technical Education [*Formerly, DVR*] [*Office of Education*]
DVTI.........	Diversified Tech, Inc. [*NASDAQ symbol*] (NQ)
DVTL........	Dovetail (MSA)
DVTMDS ...	(Divinyl)tetramethyldisilazane [*Organic chemistry*]
DVU..........	Delta Velocity Ullage
DVU..........	Deutsche Volksunion [*German People's Union*] [*Federal Republic of Germany*] [*Political party*] (PD)
DVV..........	Downward Vertical Velocity [*Meteorology*] (FAAC)
DVW..........	Davenport [*Washington*] [*Seismograph station code, US Geological Survey*] (SEIS)
DVX..........	Data Voice Exchange (MCD)
DVX..........	Denver Area Project, Denver, CO [*OCLC symbol*] (OCLC)
DVX..........	Digital Voice Exchange [*Telecommunications*] (TEL)
DVZ..........	Arapahoe Community College, Littleton, CO [*OCLC symbol*] (OCLC)
DVZ..........	Mocksville, NC [*Location identifier*] [*FAA*] (FAAL)
DVZ Dtsch Verkehrs-Ztg ... DVZ Deutsche Verkehrs-Zeitung [*West Germany*] [*A publication*]
DW..........	Association of Drinkwatchers International [*Defunct*] (EA)
DW..........	Daily Wear Contact Lenses
DW..........	Daisy Wheel [*Printer*]
DW..........	Damage Waiver [*Insurance*]
DW..........	Dangerous Weapon
DW..........	Data Word (NASA)
DW..........	Data Word Buffer [*Data processing*] (MDG)
DW..........	Daughters of Wisdom [*Montfort Sisters*] [*Roman Catholic religious order*]
DW..........	Deadweight
DW..........	Decentralized Warehouse (AFIT)
DW..........	Deck Watch [*A small chronometer*] [*Navy*]
DW..........	Deep Water [*Nautical charts*]
DW..........	Delayed Weather
DW..........	Delivered Weight [*Business term*] (ADA)
DW..........	Demineralized Water (NRCH)
D of W	Department of Works [*Military*] [*British*]
D & W	Detection and Warning
DW..........	Detroit & Western [*AAR code*]
DW..........	Deutsche Welle [*Radio network*] [*Federal Republic of Germany*]
DW..........	Deutsche Woche [*A publication*]
DW..........	Developed Width (AAG)
D/W........	Dextrose in Water [*Medicine*]
D d W........	Dialectes de Wallonie [*A publication*]
DW..........	Die Welt [*A publication*]
DW..........	Die Weltliteratur [*A publication*]
D/W........	Direct Writing (MUGU)
DW..........	Director of Works [*Air Ministry*] [*British*]
DW..........	Disabled Widow [*or Widower*] [*Social Security Administration*] (OICC)
DW..........	Disc Width [*Pisciculture*]
DW..........	Dishwasher [*Classified advertising*]
DW..........	Dislocated Worker [*Job Training and Partnership Act*] (OICC)
DW..........	Display Write [*Software*]
DW..........	Distilled Water
DW..........	Dividend Warrant (ROG)
DW..........	DLT Luftverkehrsgesellschaft mbH [*Federal Republic of Germany*] [*ICAO designator*] (ICDA)
DW..........	Dock Warehouse [*Shipping*] (ROG)
DW..........	Dock Warrant
DW..........	Domestic Water (AAG)
DW..........	Don't Want [*Telecommunications*] (TEL)
DW..........	Double Wall
DW..........	Double Weight
DW..........	Double Word [*Data processing*]
DW..........	Downy Woodpecker [*Ornithology*]
DW..........	Drinking Water (AAG)
DW..........	Drop and Block Wire [*Telecommunications*] (TEL)
DW..........	Drop Wire
DW..........	Drum Write [*Data processing*]
D & W	Drury and Walsh's Irish Chancery Reports [*1837-40*] [*A publication*] (DLA)
D & W	Drury and Warren's Irish Chancery Reports [*1841-43*] [*A publication*] (DLA)
DW..........	Dry Weight
DW............	Drywell (NRCH)
DW............	Dual Wheels [*Aviation*]
DW............	Duke of Wellington's West Riding Regiment [*Military unit*] [*British*]
DW............	Dumbwaiter (MSA)
DW............	Durbin-Watson [*Procedure*] [*Statistics*]
DW............	Dust Wrapper [*Paper cover for a hardbound book*]
DW............	Sandoz AG [*Switzerland*] [*Research code symbol*]
D5/W........	Dextrose (5%) in Water [*Medicine*]
DWA..........	Daily Weighted Average [*Data sampling*]
DWA..........	Deadly Weapon Act
DWA..........	Delaware Division of Libraries, Dover, DE [*OCLC symbol*] (OCLC)
DWA..........	Died of Wounds Resulting from Action with Enemy [*Military*]
DWA..........	Digital Watch Association (EA)
DWA..........	Director of War Archives [*British*]
DWA..........	Dirty Writers of America [*Satirical*]
DWA..........	Double-Wire Armor
DWA..........	Drug Wholesalers Association [*Later, NWDA*] (EA)
DWA..........	Dutch Warmblood Association (EA)
DWAA.......	Dog Writers' Association of America (EA)
DWAAF	Director of Women's Auxiliary Air Force [*British*]
DWAC.......	Director, Women's Army Corps (AABC)
DWAC.......	Distributed Write Address Counter
D-Wagen....	Durchgangswagen [*Through Carriage*] [*German*]
D & Wal.....	Drury and Walsh's Irish Chancery Reports [*1837-40*] [*A publication*] (DLA)
D & War.....	Drury and Warren's Irish Chancery Reports [*1841-43*] [*A publication*] (DLA)
Dwar	Dwarris on Statutes [*A publication*] (DLA)
DWARN...	Dakota Women of All Red Nations (EA)
Dwar St	Dwarris on Statutes [*A publication*] (DLA)
DWAT	Deadweight All Told [*Shipping*]
DWAW.......	Distillery, Wine, and Allied Workers International Union (EA)
DWB..........	Designers' Workbench (TEL)
DWB..........	Deutsche Warande en Belfort [*A publication*]
DWB..........	Disabled Widow [*or Widower*] Benefits [*Social Security Administration*] (OICC)
DWB..........	Dismissed for Want of Bond [*Legal term*] (DLA)
DWB..........	Doctors without Borders [*See also MSF*] (EAIO)
DWB..........	Double with Bath [*Hotel room*]
DWB..........	Soalala [*Madagascar*] [*Airport symbol*] (OAG)
DWBA	Direct Wire Burglar Alarm
DWBA	Distorted Wave-Borne Approximation
DWBO......	District War Bond Office [*or Officer*] [*Navy*]
DWC..........	Deadweight Capacity
DWC..........	Democratic Workers' Congress [*Ceylon*]
DWC........	Detroit, MI [*Location identifier*] [*FAA*] (FAAL)
DWC........	Discolored Wood Columns [*Plant pathology*]
DWC........	Dislocated Worker Center [*Job Training and Partnership Act*] (OICC)
DWC........	Dissolved Water Color [*Environmental chemistry*]
D3WCA......	Davis 3-Wheel Club of America (EA)
DWCC	Deadweight Cargo Capacity [*Shipping*]
DWCOORD(N) ... Director of Weapons Coordination (Naval) [*British*]
DWD..........	Deep Water Dump
DWD..........	Deepest Working Depth
DWD..........	Deutsche Wissenschaftlicher Dienst [*A publication*]
DWD..........	Died with Disease [*Medicine*]
DWD..........	Director of Wreck Disposal
DWD..........	Dream World [*A publication*]
DWD..........	Driving While Drugged
DWD..........	Driving While Drunk [*Police term*]
DWD..........	Drum Write Driver [*Data processing*]
DWD..........	Dumbwaiter Door
DWD..........	Dynamic Weather Display
DWDI......	Draw Die [*Tool*] (AAG)
DWDL......	Diffuse Well-Differentiated Lymphocytic [*Oncology*]
DWDL......	Donald W. Douglas Laboratory [*McDonnell Douglas Corp.*]
DWE.......	Delivery with Equipment (MCD)
DWE.......	Tulsa, OK [*Location identifier*] [*FAA*] (FAAL)
DWED......	Drywell Equipment Drain (IEEE)
DWEDS.....	Drywell Equipment Drain Sump (NRCH)
DWEL......	Dwelling (MSA)
DWEM......	Dead White European Males [*Derogatory appellation for Western culture*]
DWER	Directorate of Weapons and Engineering Research [*Canada*]
DWES.......	Director of Weapons Equipment, Surface [*British military*] (DMA)
DWEST....	Deep Water Environmental Survival Training [*Navy*]
DWET	Directorate of Weapons Effect Tests (MCD)
DWEU.......	Director of Weapons Equipment, Underwater [*British military*] (DMA)
DWEV.......	Deutsche Wissenschaft, Erziehung, und Volksbildung [*A publication*]
DWF..........	Directional Warhead Fuze
DWF..........	Divorced White Female [*Classified advertising*]
Dwf...........	Dwarf [*Horticulture*]
DWFD......	Drywell Floor Drain (IEEE)
DWFDS.....	Drywell Floor Drain Sump (NRCH)
DWFM......	Draw Form [*Tool*] (AAG)

DWG.......... Deadweight Gauge
DWG.......... Diamond Walnut Growers (EA)
DWG.......... Digital Waveform Generator (MCD)
DWG.......... Drawing (AFM)
DWG.......... Dwelling (ADA)
DWG.......... DWG Corp. [*AMEX symbol*] (SPSG)
DWH.......... Houston, TX [*Location identifier*] [*FAA*] (FAAL)
DWH .... Washington Hall Junior College, Washington, DC [*Library symbol*] [*Library of Congress*] (LCLS)
DWHC....... Washington Hospital Center, Medical Library, Washington, DC [*Library symbol*] [*Library of Congress*] (LCLS)
DWHO...... Washington Hospital Center, Medical Library, Washington, DC [*Library symbol*] [*Library of Congress*] (LCLS)
DWI.......... Danish West Indies
DWI.......... Data Word In (MCD)
DWI.......... Descriptor Word Index
DWI.......... Died without Issue (DLA)
DWI.......... Differential Wave Impedance (DEN)
DWI.......... Directional Wireless Installation [*British military*] (DMA)
DWI.......... Driving While Intoxicated [*Legal term*]
DWI.......... Durable Woods Institute (EA)
DWI.......... Durum Wheat Institute [*Later, MNF*] (EA)
DWI.......... Dutch West Indies
DWI.......... Washington International College, Washington, DC [*Library symbol*] [*Library of Congress*] (LCLS)
DWIA .... Distorted Wave Impulse Approximation
DWIC .... Disaster Welfare Inquiry Center [*Federal disaster planning*]
DWIC .... DWI Corporation [*NASDAQ symbol*] (NQ)
DWICA ..... Deep Water Isotopic Current Analyzer [*TVA*] (MSC)
DWIFC...... Doctor Who International Fan Club [*Australia*]
Dwight ...... Dwight's Charity Cases [*England*] [*A publication*] (DLA)
DWIM....... Division for Women in Medicine [*Defunct*] (EA)
DWIM....... Do What I Mean [*Also, DTRT*] [*In data processing context, translates as "Guess at the meaning of poorly worded instructions"*]
DWIN........ Doctor Who Information Network [*Toronto, ON*] (EAIO)
DWINAU ... Defenders of Wildlife News [*A publication*]
D-WIP ...... Defense-Wide Intelligence Plan [*DoD*]
DWL.......... Depressed Water Leg [*Nuclear energy*] (NRCH)
DWL.......... Designed Water Line [*Technical drawings*]
DWL.......... Desired Work Load
DWL.......... Displacement Water Line
DWL.......... Dominant Wavelength
DWL.......... Dowel
DWL.......... Drywell (NRCH)
DWLD....... Dental World Center [*NASDAQ symbol*] (NQ)
DWLFBD.. Double-Wall Fiberboard
DWLG....... Dwelling (AABC)
DWLIAU... Defenders of Wildlife Magazine [*Later, Defenders*] [*A publication*]
DWM........ Deputy Worshipful Master [*Freemasonry*] (ROG)
DWM........ Destination Warning Marker
DWM........ Destination Word Marker (CMD)
DWM........ Deutsche Waffen- und Munitionsfabriken [*German Weapons and Munitions Factory*] [*World War II*]
DWM........ Divine Word Missionaries [*See also SVD*] [*Rome, Italy*] (EAIO)
DWM........ Divorced White Male [*Classified advertising*]
DWM........ Dogwood [*Missouri*] [*Seismograph station code, US Geological Survey*] (SEIS)
DWMC..... Dedicated Wooden Money Collectors (EA)
DWMI....... Diamond Wheel Manufacturers Institute (EA)
Dw Mil...... Dwyer on the Militia Laws [*A publication*] (DLA)
DWML...... Due West Motor Line [*AAR code*]
DWMS...... Demineralized Water Makeup System [*Nuclear energy*] (NRCH)
DWMSTDP ... Defense Work Measurement Standard Time Data Program [*Air Force*] (AFM)
DWMT...... Division of Waste Management and Transportation [*Energy Research and Development Administration*]
DWN .... Darwin, MN [*Location identifier*] [*FAA*] (FAAL)
DWN .... Down (KSC)
DWN......... Drawn (MSA)
DWNAV(N) ... Director of Weapons Navigation (Naval) [*British*]
DWNDFTS ... Downdrafts (FAAC)
DWO .... Delta Wing Orbiter (KSC)
DWO .... Department Work Order (MCD)
DWO .... Development Work Order
DWO .... Direct Writing Oscillograph
DWO .... Directorate of War Organization [*RAF*] [*British*]
DWP.......... Deep Water Port [*Marine science*]
DWP.......... Director of Weapons Production [*British military*] (DMA)
DWP.......... Dismissed for Want of Prosecution [*Legal term*] (DLA)
DWP.......... Displaced Worker Program (OICC)
DWP.......... District of Columbia Public Library, Washington, DC [*OCLC symbol*] (OCLC)
DWP.......... Duluth, Winnipeg & Pacific Railway [*AAR code*]
DW & P .... Duluth, Winnipeg & Pacific Railway
DWP.......... Public Library of the District of Columbia, Martin Luther King Memorial Library, Washington, DC [*Library symbol*] [*Library of Congress*] (LCLS)

DWPA .... Deep Water Ports Act [*1974*] (MSC)
DWPF....... Defense Waste Processing Facility [*Department of Energy*]
DWP(N) .... Director of Weapons Production (Naval) [*British*]
DWPNT..... Dew Point (FAAC)
DWPO....... District War Plans Officer
DWPROD(N) ... Director of Weapons Production (Naval) [*British*]
DWQRC.... Drinking Water Quality Research Center [*Florida International University*]
DWR.......... Development Work Request
DWR.......... Digital Wired Recorder
DWR.......... Dirty Word Remover [*Graffiti-removing chemical*]
DWR.......... Divisional Work Request (AAG)
DWR.......... Drawer (MSA)
DWR.......... Du-Well Resources Ltd. [*Vancouver Stock Exchange symbol*]
DWR.......... Duke of Wellington's Regiment [*Military unit*] [*British*]
DWR.......... United States Walter Reed Army Medical Center, Post/Patient Library, Washington, DC [*Library symbol*] [*Library of Congress*] (LCLS)
DWRA .... Defense Western Regional Audit Office [*DoD*]
DWRA .... Dry Wrinkle Recovery Angle [*Textile technology*]
DWRAF..... Director of the Women's Royal Air Force [*British military*] (DMA)
DW & RB... Daily Weather and River Bulletin [*A publication*]
DWRC....... Denver Wildlife Research Center [*Colorado*] [*Department of Agriculture*] (GRD)
DWRC....... Descend Well to Right of Course [*Aviation*] (FAAC)
DWRDS .... Director, Weapons Research and Development, Surface [*British military*] (DMA)
DWRDU.... Director, Weapons Research and Development, Underwater [*British military*] (DMA)
DWRGLU ... Dock, Wharf, Riverside, and General Labourers' Union [*British*]
DWR-I....... United States Walter Reed Army Medical Center, Research Institute, Washington, DC [*Library symbol*] [*Library of Congress*] (LCLS)
DWRI .... Walter Reed Army Institute of Research, Washington, DC [*Library symbol*] [*Library of Congress*] (LCLS)
DWR-M..... United States Walter Reed Army Medical Center, Medical Library, Washington, DC [*Library symbol*] [*Library of Congress*] (LCLS)
DWRNS .... Department of the Director, Women's Royal Naval Service [*British*]
DWRP .... Director of Weapons Resources and Programmes [*British military*] (DMA)
DWR-P...... Walter Reed Army Medical Biomechanical Research Center, Forest Glen, MD [*Library symbol*] [*Library of Congress*] (LCLS)
DWRTO .... Defense Western Regional Telecommunications Office [*DoD*]
DWS .... Deck Working Space
DWS .... Defense Weapons System
DWS .... Depot Working Standards
DWS .... Design Work Study
DWS .... Detailed Work Statement (MCD)
DWS .... Detroit Waldhorn Society (EA)
DWS .... Development Work Statement (NRCH)
DWS .... Developments in Water Science [*Elsevier Book Series*] [*A publication*]
DWS .... Disaster Warning Satellite [*NASA*] (NASA)
DWS .... Disaster Warning System [*National Weather Service*]
DWS .... Dorcas Welfare Society [*Later, Community Services*] (EA)
DWS .... Double White Silk Covered [*Wire insulation*]
DWS .... Drinking Water Standard
DWS .... Drop Wood Siding [*Technical drawings*]
DWS .... Dry Workshop [*NASA*] (KSC)
DWS .... Orlando, FL [*Location identifier*] [*FAA*] (FAAL)
DWS .... Washington Star, Washington, DC [*Library symbol*] [*Library of Congress*] (LCLS)
DWSA .... Director of Weapon Systems Analysis [*Army*] (AABC)
DWSC .... Director of Welfare and Service Conditions [*British military*] (DMA)
DWSI........ Doug Wilson Studios, Inc. [*NASDAQ symbol*] (NQ)
DWSMC... Defense Weapons System Management Center
DWSN....... Dawson Geophysical Co. [*NASDAQ symbol*] (NQ)
DWSO....... Drainage and Water Supply Officer [*Ministry of Agriculture, Fisheries, and Food*] [*British*]
DWSP(N) ... Director of Weapons Surface Projects (Naval) [*British*]
DWSR .... Dodge Wayfarer Sportabout Registry (EA)
DWSS....... Double Wipe Slide Switch
DWST....... Demineralized Water Storage Tank [*Nuclear energy*] (NRCH)
Dw Stat ..... Dwarris on Statutes [*A publication*] (DLA)
DWStK .... Deutsche Waffen Stillstandkommission [*German Armistice Commission, in France*] [*World War II*]
DWT.......... Deadweight
DWT.......... Deadweight Tester
DWT.......... Deadweight Tons [*Shipping*]
DWT.......... Deck Watch Time [*Navigation*]
DWT.......... Denarius Weight [*Pennyweight*]
DWT.......... Dog Wags Tail [*Airspace effects*]
DWT.......... Double-Weight [*Paper*]
DWT.......... Drop-Weight Test [*Nuclear energy*] (NRCH)

DWT.........	Wesley Theological Seminary, Washington, DC [*Library symbol*] [*Library of Congress*] [*OCLC symbol*] (LCLS)
DWTF.......	Daily and Weekly till Forbidden [*Advertising*]
D & WTF...	Daily and Weekly till Forbidden [*Advertising*]
DWTM......	Office of Defense Waste and Transportation Management [*Washington, DC*] [*Department of Energy*] (GRD)
DWTMC ...	Domestic Water Tank Manufacturers Council [*Defunct*]
DWTR.......	Descend Well to Right [*Aviation*] (FAAC)
DWTS.......	Digital Wideband Transmission System (MCD)
DWTT	Drop-Weight Tear Test
DWU	Dakota Wesleyan University [*South Dakota*]
DWUC......	Democratic Women's Union of Canada
DWUI	Driving While under the Influence (OICC)
DWV.........	Deutsche Warenvertriebsgesellschaft [*German Commodity Trading Company*]
DWV.........	Dielectric Withstand Voltage (MCD)
DWV.........	Drain, Waste, and Vent [*System*]
DWW........	Davis Water & Waste Industries, Inc. [*NYSE symbol*] (SPSG)
DWW........	Distillery, Wine, and Allied Workers International Union
DWW........	Jet Courier Service, Inc. [*Cincinnati, OH*] [*FAA designator*] (FAAC)
DWW........	Wilmington Institute Free Library and the New Castle County Free Library, Wilmington, DE [*OCLC symbol*] (OCLC)
DWW........	Woodrow Wilson International Center for Scholars, Washington, DC [*Library symbol*] [*Library of Congress*] (LCLS)
DWWB......	Del E. Webb Corp. [*NASDAQ symbol*] (NQ)
DWWBFC ...	Don Winters and the Winters Brothers Fan Club [*Defunct*] (EA)
DWY.........	Gadsden, AL [*Location identifier*] [*FAA*] (FAAL)
D Wyo........	United States District Court for the District of Wyoming (DLA)
DWYT.......	Dwight Health Care [*NASDAQ symbol*] (NQ)
DWZP	Deutsche Wissenschaftliche Zeitschrift fuer Polen [*A publication*]
DX.............	Danair A/S [*Denmark*] [*ICAO designator*] (FAAC)
DX.............	Data Extraction (CAAL)
DX.............	Data Transfer [*Data processing*]
DX.............	Destroyer Experimental (MCD)
Dx	Diagnosis
DX.............	Direct Exchange [*Army*] (AABC)
DX.............	Direct Expansion
DX.............	Distance [*Radio term*] (EA)
DX.............	Double Cash Ruled [*Stationery*]
DX.............	Duplex [*Signaling*] [*Telecommunications*] (MSA)
DXA..........	Direct Exchange Activity (AABC)
DXAK	Atakpame/Akpaka [*Togo*] [*ICAO location identifier*] (ICLI)
DXB.........	Dubai [*United Arab Emirates*] [*Airport symbol*] (OAG)
DXBS........	Bassari [*Togo*] [*ICAO location identifier*] (ICLI)
DXC..........	Data Exchange Control
DXD..........	Dixie [*Australia*] [*Airport symbol*] [*Obsolete*] (OAG)
DXD..........	Drexore Developments, Inc. [*Vancouver Stock Exchange symbol*]
DXDP	Dapango [*Togo*] [*ICAO location identifier*] (ICLI)
dXDP	Deoxyxanthosine Diphosphate [*Biochemistry*]
DX/DXG ...	ASW [*Antisubmarine Warfare*], Gun, and Missile Escort Ship [*Navy symbol*]
DXE..........	Data Transmitting Equipment (MSA)
DXE..........	Dexter, MO [*Location identifier*] [*FAA*] (FAAL)
DXE..........	Dixylylethane [*Organic chemistry*]
DXF	Data Exchange Format (PCM)
DXF	Drawing Exchange File [*Data processing*] (PCM)
DXG..........	Dyonix Greentree Technologies, Inc. [*Vancouver Stock Exchange symbol*]
DXG..........	Guided Missile Destroyer [*Navy symbol*]
DXGN........	Guided Missile Destroyer, Nuclear-Propulsion [*Navy symbol*]
DXH	Dexleigh Corp. [*Toronto Stock Exchange symbol*]
DXHO.......	Hahotoe [*Togo*] [*ICAO location identifier*] (ICLI)
DXI...........	Direct Exchange Item [*Army*] (AABC)
DXK..........	Diagnostek, Inc. [*NYSE symbol*] (SPSG)
DXKP	Anie/Kolokope [*Togo*] [*ICAO location identifier*] (ICLI)
DXL..........	Dorset Exploration Ltd. [*Toronto Stock Exchange symbol*]
DXM.........	Dexamethasone [*Also, D, DEX*] [*Antineoplastic drug*]
DXMG.......	Sansanne-Mango [*Togo*] [*ICAO location identifier*] (ICLI)
dXMP	Deoxyxanthosine Monophosphate [*Biochemistry*]
DXN.........	Dixons Group ADR [*NYSE symbol*] (SPSG)
DXNG.......	Niamtougou [*Togo*] [*ICAO location identifier*] (ICLI)
DXP.........	Detroit, MI [*Location identifier*] [*FAA*] (FAAL)
DXR.........	Danbury [*Connecticut*] [*Airport symbol*] [*Obsolete*] (OAG)
DXR.........	Daxor Corp. [*AMEX symbol*] (SPSG)
DXR.........	Deep X-Ray
DXR.........	Deex Resources Corp. [*Vancouver Stock Exchange symbol*]
DXR.........	Doxorubicin [*Also, D, DOX*] [*Formerly, ADR, Adriamycin*] [*Antineoplastic drug*]
DXRD........	Dynamic X-Ray Diffraction [*Physics*]
DXRT	Deep X-Ray Therapy
DXS..........	Data Exchange System [*Texas Instruments, Inc.*]
DXS..........	Dextran Sulfate [*Organic chemistry*]
DXSK........	Sokode [*Togo*] [*ICAO location identifier*] (ICLI)
DXSST	Data Exchange System Statement Translator [*Texas Instruments, Inc.*]

DXT	Dalton, MA [*Location identifier*] [*FAA*] (FAAL)
DXT	Deep X-Ray Therapy
DXT	Dextrose [*Freight*]
DXT	Dixon Ticonderoga Co. [*AMEX symbol*] (SPSG)
DXTA	Tabligbo [*Togo*] [*ICAO location identifier*] (ICLI)
DXTK	Diagnostek, Inc. [*NASDAQ symbol*] (NQ)
dXTP	Deoxyxanthosine Triphosphate [*Biochemistry*]
DXU...........	Drexel University, Philadelphia, PA [*OCLC symbol*] (OCLC)
DX-W.........	Direct Exchange - Wholesale (MCD)
DXX..........	Madison, MN [*Location identifier*] [*FAA*] (FAAL)
DXXX........	Lome/Tokoin [*Togo*] [*ICAO location identifier*] (ICLI)
DXYN........	Dixie Yarns, Inc. [*Chattanooga, TN*] [*NASDAQ symbol*] (NQ)
Dy.............	Catholic Douay Version [*of the Bible*] [*1609*] (BJA)
DY.............	Daf Yomi (BJA)
DY.............	Daily (ROG)
DY.............	Dandy [*Ship's rigging*] (ROG)
DY.............	Day (MSA)
DY.............	Deflection Yoke
DY.............	Delinquent Year [*IRS*]
DY.............	Delivery
DY.............	Democratic Yemen Airlines (ALYEMDA) [*People's Democratic Republic of Yemen*] [*ICAO designator*] (ICDA)
DY.............	Demy [*Half*] [*Size of paper*] (ROG)
DY.............	Density
Dy.............	Dependency [*Psychology*]
DY.............	Deputy
DY.............	Deputy Director [*KSC Directorate*] (MCD)
DY.............	Derbyshire Yeomanry [*British military*] (DMA)
DY.............	Design Year [*DoD*]
DY.............	Dockyard
DY.............	Duty (AFM)
DY.............	Dycom Industries, Inc. [*NYSE symbol*] (SPSG)
Dy.............	Dyer's English King's Bench Reports [*73 English Reprint*] [*A publication*] (DLA)
DY.............	Dynamotors [*JETDS nomenclature*] [*Military*] (CET)
Dy.............	Dyne [*Unit of force*] [*Also, D, dyn*] [*Preferred unit is N, Newton*]
Dy.............	Dysprosium [*Chemical element*]
DY1...........	Dyersburg [*Tennessee*] [*Seismograph station code, US Geological Survey*] [*Closed*] (SEIS)
DY2...........	Lassiter [*Tennessee*] [*Seismograph station code, US Geological Survey*] [*Closed*] (SEIS)
DY3...........	Tiptonville [*Tennessee*] [*Seismograph station code, US Geological Survey*] [*Closed*] (SEIS)
DY4...........	Samburg [*Tennessee*] [*Seismograph station code, US Geological Survey*] [*Closed*] (SEIS)
DY5...........	Lassiter Corners [*Tennessee*] [*Seismograph station code, US Geological Survey*] [*Closed*] (SEIS)
DYA..........	Deflection Yoke Amplifier
DYA..........	Dynamics Corp. of America [*NYSE symbol*] (SPSG)
DYA..........	Dysart [*Australia*] [*Airport symbol*] (OAG)
DYAN........	Dyansen Corp. [*NASDAQ symbol*] (NQ)
DYANA	Dynamic Analyzer
Dyason House Pap ...	Dyason House Papers [*A publication*]
Dyason H P ...	Dyason House Papers [*A publication*] (APTA)
DYB...........	Dynamic Braking
DYB...........	Dynamic Business [*A publication*]
DYC...........	Dalmys (Canada) Ltd. [*Toronto Stock Exchange symbol*]
Dyche & P Dict ...	Dyche and Pardon's Dictionary [*A publication*] (DLA)
DYCON......	Dynamic Control
DYCONTR ...	Duty Controller [*Air Force*]
DYCOP	Dynamic Console for Operations Planners
DYD...........	Dockyard
D & YE.......	Diabetes and Your Eyes [*National Eye Institute*] [*A publication*]
Dye Ind	Dyeing Industry [*Japan*] [*A publication*]
Dyer	Dyer's English King's Bench Reports [*73 English Reprint*] [*A publication*] (DLA)
Dyer (Eng) ...	Dyer's English King's Bench Reports [*73 English Reprint*] [*A publication*] (DLA)
Dyer Text Printer Bleacher Finish ...	Dyer, Textile Printer, Bleacher, and Finisher [*A publication*]
Dyes Chem Tech Bull ...	Dyes and Chemicals Technical Bulletin. Paper Industry Issue [*A publication*]
Dyes Chem Tech Bull Pap Ind Issue ...	Dyes and Chemicals Technical Bulletin. Paper Industry Issue [*A publication*]
DYET.........	Diet Institute, Inc. [*NASDAQ symbol*] (NQ)
DYF	Damned Young Fools [*Officers under the age of thirty*] [*British naval slang*]
DYFUS......	Dynamic Fuze Simulator [*RADAR*]
DYG..........	Discovery Gold Explorations Ltd. [*Vancouver Stock Exchange symbol*]
DYG..........	Drying
DYHBIFC ...	Don Youngblood and the Hoosier Bears International Fan Club (EA)
DYHM	Dynamic Homes, Inc. [*NASDAQ symbol*] (NQ)
DYHR........	Dehydrator (MSA)
DYL..........	Doylestown, PA [*Location identifier*] [*FAA*] (FAAL)
DYLEX......	Damn Your Lame Excuses [*Facetious translation for the name of a Toronto-based specialty store chain*]

Dym Death Dut ... Dymond's Death Duties [*15th ed.*] [*1973*] [*A publication*] (DLA)
DYN.......... Detectability of Yes-No
DYN.......... Drives You Nuts [*Coined by Erma Bombeck*]
DYN.......... Dynamic
Dyn .... Dynamite [*A publication*]
DYN.......... Dynamiting [*FBI standardized term*]
DYN.......... Dynamo (MSA)
DYN.......... Dynamometer [*Engineering*] (DEN)
Dyn .... Dynasty (BJA)
DYN.......... Dynasty Resources, Inc. [*Vancouver Stock Exchange symbol*]
DYN.......... DynCorp [*NYSE symbol*] (SPSG)
dyn .... Dyne [*Unit of force*] [*Also, D*] [*Preferred unit is N, Newton*] (DEN)
DYNA....... Dynaflow [*Automotive engineering*]
DYNA....... Dynamic Analyzer (MCD)
DYNA....... Dynascan Corp. [*NASDAQ symbol*] (NQ)
DYNAL ..... Dynamic Analysis (NRCH)
Dynamic Econom Theory and Appl ... Dynamic Economics. Theory and Applications [*A publication*]
DYNAMO ... Dynamic Action Management Operations [*BSD*]
DYNAMO ... Dynamic Automatic Monitoring (CET)
DYNAMO ... Dynamic Model Continuous Time Simulation (BUR)
Dynam Psych ... Dynamische Psychiatrie [*A publication*]
DYNARM ... Dynamic Arm Programmer [*Data processing*]
DYNASAR ... Dynamic Systems Analyzer [*General Electric Co.*] (IEEE)
DYNA-SOAR ... Dynamic Soaring [*Space flight*]
DYNAT ..... Dynamic Accuracy Tester [*General Electric Co.*]
Dyn Atmos & Oceans ... Dynamics of Atmospheres and Oceans [*A publication*]
Dyn Brain Edema Pro Int Workshop ... Dynamics of Brain Edema. Proceedings of the International Workshop on Dynamic Aspects of Cerebral Edema [*A publication*]
DYNC .... Dynamic Classics Ltd. [*NASDAQ symbol*] (NQ)
DYN/CM .. Dynes per Centimeter
DYN/CM² .. Dynes per Square Centimeter
DYNI .... Dynatrend, Incorporated [*NASDAQ symbol*] (NQ)
DYNM....... Dynamotor
Dyn Mass Spectrom ... Dynamic Mass Spectrometry [*A publication*]
DYNMT .... Dynamite (MSA)
DYNMT .... Dynamometer [*Engineering*]
DYNO .... Dynamometer [*Engineering*] (KSC)
DYNO .... Dynapac, Inc. [*Santa Clara, CA*] [*NASDAQ symbol*] (NQ)
DYNP .... DynCorp [*NASDAQ symbol*] (NQ)
Dyn Psychiatr ... Dynamische Psychiatrie [*A publication*]
Dyn Psychiatry ... Dynamic Psychiatry [*A publication*]
DYNS .... Dynamic Sciences International, Inc. [*NASDAQ symbol*] (NQ)
Dyn Solids Liq Neutron Scattering (1977) ... Dynamics of Solids and Liquids by Neutron Scattering (1977) [*A publication*]
Dyn Supervision ... Dynamic Supervision [*A publication*]
DYNT .... Dynatronics Laser Corp. [*NASDAQ symbol*] (NQ)
DYNTACS .. Dynamical Tactical Simulator
DYNTACS-X ... Dynamic Tactical Simulator - Enhanced
DYNX........ Dynatec International, Inc. [*Salt Lake City, UT*] [*NASDAQ symbol*] (NQ)
DYO.......... Diocesan Youth Officer [*Church of England*]
DYO.......... Duke of York's Own [*British military*] (DMA)
DYO.......... Rutland, VT [*Location identifier*] [*FAA*] (FAAL)
DYOL........ Dynamic Oil Ltd. [*NASDAQ symbol*] (NQ)
DYP .... Directory Yellow Pages [*Telecommunications*] (TEL)
DYP .... Dogru Yol Partisi [*Correct Way Party*] [*Turkey*] [*Political party*] (EY)
DYPSAQ... Dynamic Psychiatry [*A publication*]
DYPSAQ... Dynamische Psychiatrie [*A publication*]
DYQ.......... Greeneville, TN [*Location identifier*] [*FAA*] (FAAL)
DYR.......... Dyersburg, TN [*Location identifier*] [*FAA*] (FAAL)
DYR.......... Dynamo Resources [*Vancouver Stock Exchange symbol*]
DYR.......... Dyneer Corp. [*AMEX symbol*] (SPSG)
DYRAD ..... Dynamic Resolver Angle Digitizer
DYRQRPRCHT ... Duties Require Parachuting [*Army*] (AABC)
DYS .... Abilene, TX [*Location identifier*] [*FAA*] (FAAL)
DYS .... Duke of York's Royal Military School [*British military*] (DMA)
DYS .... Dysgerminoma [*Oncology*]
DYSAC..... Digital Simulated Analog Computer (MCD)
DYSAC..... Dynamic Storage Analog Computer (IEEE)
DYSEAC.. Digital High-Speed Standard Eastern Automatic Computer
DYSM ...... Dysmenorrhea [*Medicine*]
DYSN .... Dysan Corp. [*NASDAQ symbol*] (NQ)
DYSTAC... Dynamic Storage Analog Computer
DYSTAL ... Dynamic Storage Allocation Language [*in FORTRAN*] [*Data processing*]
DYSUD ..... Dynamic Supervision [*A publication*]
Dy Sum Proc ... Dyett's Summary Proceedings [*A publication*] (DLA)
DYT .... Dynatronics Laser Corp. [*Vancouver Stock Exchange symbol*]
DYTAPS ... Dynamic Tongue and Palatometric Shapes [*System to help the deaf speak*]
DYTC .... Dynatech Corporation [*NASDAQ symbol*] (NQ)
DYTM .... Dynatem, Inc. [*Irvine, CA*] [*NASDAQ symbol*] (NQ)
DYTR .... Dyatron Corp. [*NASDAQ symbol*] (NQ)
DYU.......... Dushanbe [*USSR*] [*Airport symbol*] (OAG)
DYV.......... Dolly Varden Minerals [*Vancouver Stock Exchange symbol*]

D-YWHF ... Dozen-Year White House Foul-Up Cycle [*Reference to the 1949 "mess in Washington," 1961 Bay of Pigs disaster, 1973 Watergate scandal, and 1985 Iran-CONTRA affair*] [*Term coined by William Safire*]
DYWIDAG Ber ... DYWIDAG [*Dyckerhoff und Widmann AG*] Berichte [*West Germany*] [*A publication*]
DYZO........ Dror Young Zionist Organization [*Later, YKM*] (EA)
DZ............. Algeria [*ANSI two-letter standard code*] (CNC)
DZ............. Definitive Zone
DZ............. Diazepam [*Also, D, DAP*] [*A sedative*]
DZ............. Dizygotic [*Genetics*]
DZ............. Dizziness (KSC)
DZ............. Doctor of Zoology
DZ............. Douglas Airways [*Pty.*] Ltd. [*Papua-New Guinea*] [*ICAO designator*] (FAAC)
DZ............. Dozen
DZ............. Drizzle [*Meteorology*]
DZ............. Drop Zone [*For parachute troops and gliders*] [*Military*]
DZ............. Druckzuender [*Pressure Igniter*] [*German military - World War II*]
dz............. Duzia [*Dozen*] [*Portuguese*]
DZA.......... Algeria [*ANSI three-letter standard code*] (CNC)
DZA.......... Dizygotic Twins Reared Apart [*Genetics*]
DZA.......... Doppler Zeeman Analyser [*British*]
DZA.......... Drop Zone Area [*Military*]
DZA.......... Dzaoudzi [*Comoro Islands*] [*Airport symbol*] (OAG)
DZAAS....... Drop Zone Assembly Aid System [*Military*] (INF)
DZaE .... Embassy of Zaire, Washington, DC [*Library symbol*] [*Library of Congress*] (LCLS)
DZCO........ Drop Zone Control Officer [*Military*] (AFM)
DzD.......... Dzejas Diena [*A publication*]
DZF .... Dokumentationszentrale Feinwerktechnik [*Precision Technology Documentation Center*] [*Originator, operator, and database*] [*Federal Republic of Germany*] [*Information service or system*] (IID)
DZGGAK .. Deutsche Zeitschrift fuer die Gesamte Gerichtliche Medizin [*A publication*]
DZH.......... Dzhafr [*USSR*] [*Seismograph station code, US Geological Survey*] [*Closed*] (SEIS)
DZI .... Zuckerindustrie. Landwirtschaft, Technik, Chemie, Wirtschaft [*A publication*]
DzKarSt ..... Dzveli Kartuli Enis K'atedris Stomebi [*A publication*]
DZKR .... Deutsche Zeitschrift fuer Kirchenrecht [*A publication*]
Dz Lit .... Dziennik Literacki [*A publication*]
DZM......... Miami-Dade Public Library System, Miami, FL [*OCLC symbol*] (OCLC)
DZMKAS ... Deutsche Zahn- Mund- und Kieferheilkunde [*A publication*]
DZNE .... Douzaine [*Dozen*] [*French*]
DZNEAF... Deutsche Zeitschrift fuer Nervenheilkunde [*A publication*]
DZ Nh....... Deutsche Zeitschrift fuer Nervenheilkunde [*A publication*]
D Zoll B .... Deutsche Zollbeamte [*A publication*]
DZool........ Doctor of Zoology (ADA)
Dz P .... Dziennik Polski [*A publication*]
DZ Ph .... Deutsche Zeitschrift fuer Philosophie [*A publication*]
DZR .... Double Zigzag Rectifier
DZS .... Drop Zone Study [*Military*] (MCD)
D Zs N Hk ... Deutsche Zeitschrift fuer Nervenheilkunde [*A publication*]
DZSO .... Drop Zone Safety Officer [*Military*] (AABC)
DZT .... Deutsche Zeitschrift [*A publication*]
DZT .... Deutsche Zeitung [*A publication*]
DZT .... Deutsche Zentrale fuer Tourismus eV [*German National Tourist Board*] [*Federal Republic of Germany*] (EY)
DZT .... Dzhergetal [*USSR*] [*Seismograph station code, US Geological Survey*] [*Closed*] (SEIS)
Dz Z .... Dziennik Zachodni [*A publication*]
DZZEA...... Deutsche Zahnaerztliche Zeitschrift [*A publication*]
DZZEA7.... Deutsche Zahnaerztliche Zeitschrift [*A publication*]

E

E...............	Air Evacuation [*Military aircraft identification prefix*] (FAAC)
E...............	Air Force Training Category [*Inactive duty training periods and 30 days active duty training per year*]
E...............	Amphibian [*Russian aircraft symbol*]
E...............	Awarded by US Government to firms which have increased exports substantially [*Beginning early 1960's*]
E...............	Cases in the Eastern District's Local Division of the Supreme Court [*1910-46*] [*South Africa*] [*A publication*] (DLA)
E...............	Church of England School [*British*]
E...............	Color Excess [*Astronomy*]
E...............	Ear, Nose, and Throat [*Medical Officer designation*] [*British*]
E...............	Earl
E...............	Early [*Genetics*]
E...............	Earnings [*Finance*]
E...............	Earth [*Wind triangle problems and relative movement problems*]
E...............	Easily
E...............	East [*or Eastern*]
E...............	Easter
E...............	Eastern Standard Time
E...............	East's English King's Bench Term Reports [*A publication*] (DLA)
E...............	Easy [*Phonetic alphabet*] [*World War II*] (DSUE)
E...............	Easy to Move [*Horticulture*]
e...............	Eccentricity [*of application of load*] [*Aerospace*] (AAG)
E...............	Ecclesiastical (DLA)
E...............	Ecclesiastical District [*Maps*] (ROG)
E...............	Echo [*Phonetic alphabet*] [*International*] (DSUE)
E...............	Eclairage [*Illumination*] [*French*] (IEEE)
E...............	Economics (ADA)
E...............	Economist [*A publication*]
E...............	Ecstacy [*Synthetic stimulant*]
E...............	Edge [*Lumber*]
E...............	Edinburgh [*City in Scotland*] (ROG)
E...............	Edition
E...............	Edrophonium [*A cholinergic*] [*Anesthesiology*]
E...............	Educated
E...............	Edward [*Phonetic alphabet*] [*Royal Navy*] [*World War I*] [*Pre-World War II*] (DSUE)
E...............	Effectiveness (CAAL)
E...............	Effector [*Biology*]
E...............	Efficiency [*or Efficient*]
E...............	Egyptian
E...............	Eighteen "Great" Choral Preludes [*Bach*]
E...............	Einheit [*A publication*]
E...............	Einspritz [*Fuel-injection*] [*As in 280 E, the model number of a Mercedes-Benz automobile*]
E...............	Einsteinium [*Also see Es*] [*Chemical element*]
E...............	Elaborate [*Used in correcting manuscripts, etc.*]
E...............	[*Modulus of*] Elasticity [*Young's modulus*] [*Symbol*] [*IUPAC*] [*See also Y, YME*]
E...............	Eldest
E...............	Eldisine [*Also, VDS*] [*Antineoplastic drug*]
E...............	Electric (ADA)
E...............	Electric Field Strength [*Symbol*]
E...............	Electric Field Vector
E...............	Electrode Potential
E...............	Electromotive Force [*Symbol*] [*See also EMF, V*] [*Electrochemistry*]
e...............	Electron [*A nuclear particle*]
E...............	Electronic [*Automotive engineering*]
E...............	Electronic Capability [*Designation for all US military aircraft*]
E...............	Electronic Countermeasures [*Military*]
E...............	Electronics Program [*Association of Independent Colleges and Schools specialization code*]
E...............	Electrophoretic Analysis [*Botany*]
e...............	Elementary Charge [*of a proton*] [*Symbol*] [*IUPAC*]
E...............	Elevation Angle (NASA)
E...............	Ell
E...............	Elocution
E...............	Elohist Source [*Biblical scholarship*]
E...............	Elysium Mons [*A filamentary mark on Mars*]
E...............	Embassy
E...............	EMBRAER [*Empresa Brasileira Aeronautica SA*] [*Brazil*] [*ICAO aircraft manufacturer identifier*] (ICAO)
E...............	Embroidery [*Quilting*]
E...............	Embryo [*Botany*]
E...............	Embryonic
E...............	Emergency [*Symbol placed in neighborhood windows to indicate that resident will aid passing schoolchildren in the event of an emergency*]
E...............	Eminence (DLA)
E...............	Eminent [*Freemasonry*]
E...............	Emitter (MSA)
E...............	Emma [*Novel by Jane Austen*]
E...............	Emmetropia [*Also, EM*] [*Ophthalmology*]
E...............	Emperor (ROG)
E...............	Empfindichkeit [*Susceptibility to Stimulation*] [*Psychology*]
e...............	Emphatic [*Linguistics*]
E...............	Empty
E...............	Enamel (AAG)
E...............	Encounter [*Time*]
E...............	End [*Football*]
E...............	Ending of Precipitation [*Meteorology*] (FAAC)
E...............	Endocrinology
E...............	Endoplasmic [*Freeze etching in microscopy*]
E...............	Endotoxin [*Microbiology*]
E...............	Enema [*Medicine*]
E...............	Enemy (ADA)
E...............	Energy [*Symbol*] [*IUPAC*]
E...............	Enflurane [*Also, ENF*] [*An anesthetic*]
E...............	Engine
E...............	Engineer [*or Engineering*]
E...............	England (ROG)
E...............	English [*A publication*]
E...............	English
E...............	Enlisted [*Often in combination with numbers to denote serviceman's grade*]
E...............	Entering [*FBI standardized term*]
(E)............	Entgegen [*Opposed*] [*German*] [*Chemistry*]
E...............	Entrance
E...............	Entry [*Horse racing*]
E...............	Entscheidung [*Decision, Judgment*] [*German*] (ILCA)
E...............	Entwurf [*Draft*] [*German*] (ILCA)
E...............	Environment [*Psychology*]
E...............	Enzyme, Free [*Enzyme kinetics*]
e...............	Eodem [*In the Same Place, Title Explained*] [*Latin*] (ILCA)
E...............	Eolus. A Review for New Music [*A publication*]
E...............	Eos. Commentarii Societatis Philologae Polonorum [*A publication*]
E...............	Eosinophil [*Hematology*]
E...............	Epidermis
E...............	Epinephrine [*Endocrinology*]
E...............	Epistle
E...............	Epithelium [*Anatomy*]
E...............	Equation of Time (ROG)
E...............	Equatorial [*Air mass*]
E...............	Equity (DLA)
E...............	Equivalent
E...............	Erasmus [*A publication*]
E...............	Erbium [*Chemical element*] [*Symbol is ER*] (ROG)
E...............	Erg [*Unit of work*] (GPO)
E...............	Ergobank [*Greek*]
E...............	Eriodictyol [*Organic chemistry*]
E...............	Erlang [*Unit*] [*Statistics*] [*Telecommunications*]
E...............	Erogenic
E...............	Error [*Data processing*] (BUR)
E...............	Errors [*Baseball*]
E...............	Erythrocyte [*Hematology*]
E...............	Erythromycin [*Also, ERY, ERYC, ETM*] [*Antibacterial compound*]
E...............	Escape (ROG)

E................	Escherichia [*Bacterial strain*]
E................	Escorial [*A publication*]
E................	Escudo [*Monetary unit*] [*Chile, Portugal*]
E................	Esophagus [*Anatomy*]
E................	Esophoria for Distance [*Ophthalmology*]
E................	Espana [*Spain*]
E................	Especial [*Designation on brandy labels*]
E................	Esprit [*A publication*]
E................	Estate Agency [*London Stock Exchange*]
E................	Estimate
E................	Ethanol
e................	Ethyl [*As substituent on nucleoside*] [*Biochemistry*]
E................	Etnografija [*A publication*]
E................	Euler Number [*Fluid mechanics*]
E................	Eurocard [*Credit card*] [*British*]
E------------	Europa [*A publication*]
e-----........	Europe [*MARC geographic area code*] [*Library of Congress*] (LCCP)
E................	European [*British military*] (DMA)
E................	Euston Railway Station [*British*] (ROG)
E................	Evangelist [*Church calendars*]
E................	Evaporation
E................	Evening
E................	Evensong
E................	Evidence [*Law*]
E................	Exa [*A prefix meaning multiplied by 10^{18} SI symbol*]
E................	"Excellence in Production" [*Army-Navy "E" awarded manufacturers*] [*World War II*]
E................	Excellency
E................	Excellent
E................	Excellent Skiing Conditions
E................	Exchequer [*British*] (DLA)
E................	Excitatory Tendency [*Psychology*]
E................	Exclusion
E................	Execution [*DoD*]
E................	Exempt [*from traceability*] [*NASA*] (NASA)
E................	Exoplasmic [*Freeze etching in microscopy*]
E................	Expectation
E................	Expenditure [*Economics*]
E................	Expenses
E................	Experience
E................	Experiment Compartment
E................	Experimental
E................	Experimental [*When preceding vessel classification*] [*Navy symbol*]
E................	Experimenter [*Psychology*]
E................	Expert Slope [*Skiing*]
E................	Expired [*Gas*] [*Medicine*]
E................	Explained [*Statement of import of decision in cited case, not merely a restatement of the facts*] [*Legal term*] (DLA)
E................	Explicit
E................	Exponent
E................	Export
E................	Export Service [*Queen's award*] [*British*]
E................	Exposure
E................	Extinction [*Neurophysiology*]
E................	Extra Wide [*Women's shoe width*] [*More than one "E" indicates increasing wideness, up to EEE*]
E................	Extralymphatic [*Medicine*]
E................	Extraordinary Ray [*Direction of*]
E................	Eye
E................	Eye Infection [*Classification system used by doctors on Ellis Island to detain, re-examine, and possibly deny entry to certain immigrants*]
E................	Farbenfabriken Bayer [*Germany*] [*Research code symbol*]
E................	Glutamic Acid [*One-letter symbol; see Glu*] [*An amino acid*]
E................	Hotels and Restaurants [*Public-performance tariff class*] [*British*]
E................	Irradiance [*Symbol*] [*IUPAC*]
E................	Medium Wide [*Men's shoe width*] [*More than one "E" indicates increasing wideness, up to EEEE*]
E................	Modulus of Elasticity [*Mechanics*]
e................	Naperian [*or Natural*] Logarithm Base [*2.7182818*]
E................	Second Class Ship on Lloyd's Register (ILCA)
E................	Sleet [*Meteorology*]
E................	Spain [*IYRU nationality code*] (IYR)
E................	Special Electronics Installation [*Aviation designation used by all US military services*]
E................	Torpedo Boat [*German symbol*]
E................	Transco Energy Co. [*NYSE symbol*] (SPSG)
E................	Unreliable Source of Intelligence [*Military*]
E................	Voltage (CET)
E................	Water Vapor Pressure
E1...............	Basic Airman [*Air Force*]
E₁...............	Estrone [*Endocrinology*]
E1...............	Private [*Marine Corps*]
E1...............	Recruit [*Army*]
E1...............	Seaman Recruit [*Navy*]
E2...............	Airman [*Air Force*]
E2...............	Estradiol [*Also, E-diol, ES*] [*Endocrinology*]
E2...............	Private 2 [*Army*]

E2...............	Private First Class [*Marine Corps*]
E2...............	Seaman Apprentice [*Navy*]
E3...............	Airman, First Class
E³...............	Education and Experience in Engineering [*Illinois Institute of Technology program*]
E³...............	Electromagnetic Environmental Effect (CAAL)
E₃...............	Estriol [*Endocrinology*]
E3...............	Lance Corporal [*Marine Corps*]
E3...............	Private First Class [*Army*]
E3...............	Seaman [*Navy*]
E4...............	Corporal [*Army, Marine Corps*]
E-4...............	Petty Officer, Third Class [*Navy*]
4-E.............	Selective Service Class [*for a Conscientious Objector Available for, Assigned to, or Released from Work of National Importance*] [*Obsolete*]
E4...............	Sergeant [*Air Force*]
E4...............	Specialist 4 [*Army*]
E5...............	Petty Officer, Second Class [*Navy*]
E5...............	Sergeant [*Army, Marine Corps*]
E5...............	Specialist 5 [*Obsolete*] [*Army*]
E5...............	Staff Sergeant [*Air Force*]
E6...............	Petty Officer, First Class [*Navy*]
E6...............	Specialist 6 [*Obsolete*] [*Army*]
E6...............	Staff Sergeant [*Army, Marine Corps*]
E6...............	Technical Sergeant [*Air Force*]
E7...............	Chief Petty Officer [*Navy*]
E7...............	Gunnery Sergeant [*Marine Corps*]
E7...............	Master Sergeant [*Air Force*]
E7...............	Platoon Sergeant
E7...............	Specialist 7 [*Obsolete*] [*Army*]
E8...............	First Sergeant [*Army, Marine Corps*]
E8...............	Master Sergeant [*Army, Marine Corps*]
E8...............	Senior Chief Petty Officer [*Navy*]
E8...............	Senior Master Sergeant [*Air Force*]
E8...............	Specialist 8 [*Obsolete*] [*Army*]
E9...............	Chief Master Sergeant [*Air Force*]
E9...............	Command Sergeant Major [*Army*]
E9...............	Master Chief Petty Officer [*Navy*]
E9...............	Master Gunnery Sergeant [*Marine Corps*]
E9...............	Sergeant Major [*Marine Corps*]
E9...............	Sergeant Major of the Army
E9...............	Specialist 9 [*Obsolete*] [*Army*]
E9...............	Staff Sergeant Major [*Army*]
E (Date).......	Effective Date [*Military*] (AABC)
E (Layer)....	Layer of the ionosphere from above 55 miles to approximately 85 miles (AAG)
E (Mail).....	Electronic Mail [*Telecommunications*]
E (Meter)....	Electropsychometer [*Device for measuring emotional response through electrical conductivity of subject's skin*]
EA.............	Airbus Industrie [*France*] [*ICAO aircraft manufacturer identifier*] (ICAO)
ea-----........	Alps Region [*MARC geographic area code*] [*Library of Congress*] (LCCP)
EA.............	Each
EA.............	Early (ROG)
EA.............	Early American
EA.............	Early Antigen [*Immunochemistry*]
EA.............	Earphone Amplifier
EA.............	East Africa
EA.............	East Anglia [*England*] (ROG)
EA.............	Eastern Africa Law Reports [*A publication*] (DLA)
EA.............	Eastern Air Lines, Inc. [*ICAO designator*]
EA.............	Eastern Anthropologist [*A publication*]
EA.............	Eastern Area
Ea.............	East's English King's Bench Term Reports [*A publication*] (DLA)
Ea.............	East's Notes of Cases [*1785-1821*] [*Bengal, India*] [*A publication*] (DLA)
EA.............	Ebstein's Anomaly [*Cardiology*]
E & A	Ecclesiastical and Admiralty Reports [*1853-55*] [*A publication*] (DLA)
EA.............	Economic Adviser
EA.............	Economic Analysis
EA.............	Economie Appliquee [*A publication*]
EA.............	Edge Act [*Banking*]
EA.............	Edgewood Arsenal [*Aberdeen Proving Ground, MD*] [*Army*]
EA.............	Editorial Assistant [*Publishing*]
EA.............	Educational Advisor
EA.............	Educational Age
EA.............	Educational Alliance (EA)
EA.............	Educational Art
EA.............	Educators to Africa [*Later, ETAA*] (EA)
EA.............	Effective Address [*Data processing*] (MDG)
E-A.............	Egg Albumin
EA.............	Egyptian Army
EA.............	Eidgenoessische Abschiede [*A publication*]
EA.............	Eighth Army (MCD)
EA.............	Ekklesiastike Aletheia [*A publication*]
EA.............	El-Amarna (BJA)
EA.............	Eleanor Association (EA)
EA.............	Electrical Artificer [*Navy*] [*British*]

EA .... Electrocardiographic Amplifier
EA .... Electron Affinity [Chemistry]
EA .... Electronic Arts
EA .... Electronic Assembly
EA .... Electronic Associates, Inc. [NYSE symbol]   (SPSG)
EA .... Ellagic Acid
EA .... Emergency Action   (MCD)
EA .... Emergency Addressee [Aeromedical evacuation]
EA .... Emergency Area   (AFM)
EA .... Emirates Airlines [United Arab Emirates]   (MENA)
EA .... Emotions Anonymous   (EA)
EA .... Employers' Association [British]   (DCTA)
EA .... Employment Act   (OICC)
EA .... Encyclopedia Americana [A publication]
EA .... Encyclopedia of Associations [Information service or system]
               [A publication]
EA .... Endometriosis Association   (EA)
EA .... Enemy Aircraft
EA .... Energy Absorption   (AAG)
EA .... Enforcement Action [Nuclear energy]   (NRCH)
EA .... Engagement Area [Military]   (INF)
EA .... Engelbert's Aquarians   (EA)
EA .... Engine Assembly
EA .... Engineer Rear-Admiral [Navy] [British]
E & A .... Engineering and Acquisition
EA .... Engineering Aid [Navy rating]
EA .... English Actors [A publication]
E in A .... English in Africa [A publication]
EA .... English Association [London, England]   (EAIO)
EA .... English-Pressed Allegro [Record label]
EA .... Enlistment Allowance [Military]
EA .... Enquiry Agency [British]
EA .... Enrolled Agent [IRS]
EA .... Entered Apprentice [Freemasonry]
EA .... Enterprise America   (EA)
EA .... Enterprise Australia   (ADA)
EA .... Entertaining Allowance [British military]   (DMA)
EA .... Enthalpimetric Analysis [Analytical chemistry]
EA .... Entwicklungsalter [Developmental Age] [Psychology]
EA .... Enumeration Area [Statistics]
EA .... Environmental Abstracts [A publication]
EA .... Environmental Action   (EA)
EA .... Environmental Assessment   (MCD)
EA .... Ephemeris Archaiologike [A publication]
EA .... Epidural Anesthesia [Medicine]
EA .... Equinox Association   (EAIO)
EA .... Equipment Alignment
EA .... Erbe und Auftrag [A publication]
E & A .... Errata and Addenda   (NRCH)
E & A .... Error and Appeal [Legal term]   (DLA)
EA .... Erythrocyte-Antibody [Complex] [Immunochemistry]
EA .... Erythromycin Acistrate [Antibacterial]
EA .... Erythromycilamine [Antibacterial]
EA .... Escort Aircraft   (CINC)
EA .... Estivoautumnal [Malaria]
EA .... Estonian Aid   (EA)
EA .... Estudios Afrocubanos [A publication]
EA .... Estudios Americanos [A publication]
EA .... Ethanolamine [Also, Etn, OLAMINE] [Organic chemistry]
EA .... Ethyl Acrylate [Organic chemistry]
EA .... Ethylene-Diamine Dinitrate/Ammonium Nitrate Explosive
EA .... Etudes Anglaises [A publication]
EA .... Etudes Asiatiques [A publication]
EA .... Europa-Archiv. Europaeischer Austauschdienst [A publication]
EA .... Eusko Alkartasuna [Basque Solidarity] [Political party] [Spain]
EA .... Evolutionary Acquisition Strategy [Army]
EA .... Examining for Aphasia [Psychology]
E and A ...... Exchequer and Audit Department [British government]
EA .... Excise Act [Canada]
EA .... Executive Assistant
EA .... Expectancy Age [Education]
EA .... Experiment Assembly   (KSC)
EA .... Export Authorisation System [Hong Kong]
EA .... Extended Aeration Process [Sludge treatment]
EA .... Extended Attribute [Data processing]
EA .... External Affairs Department [Canada]
EA .... Parke, Davis & Co. [Research code symbol]
E & A .... Spinks' English Ecclesiastical and Admiralty Reports [A
               publication]   (DLA)
E & A .... Upper Canada Error and Appeal Reports [A
               publication]   (DLA)
EA1 .... Engineering Aid, First Class [Navy rating]
EA2 .... Engineering Aid, Second Class [Navy rating]
EA3 .... Engineering Aid, Third Class [Navy rating]
e-aa--- .... Albania [MARC geographic area code] [Library of
               Congress]   (LCCP)
EAA .... Eagle [Alaska] [Airport symbol]   (OAG)
EAA .... East Africa Association   (EA)
EAA .... East African Airways Corp. [African airline]
EAA .... East African Artillery [British military]   (DMA)
EAA .... Economic Activity Analysis

EAA .... Ecuadorean American Association   (EA)
EAA .... Educational Administration Abstracts [A publication]
EAA .... Electric Auto Association   (EA)
EAA .... Electrical Aerosol Analyzer [Instrumentation]
EA(A) .... Electrical Artificer, Air [British military]   (DMA)
EAA .... Enciclopedia dell'Arte Antica, Classica, e Orientale [A
               publication]
EAA .... Encyclopedia of American Associations [Later, EA] [A
               publication]
EAA .... Engineer in Aeronautics and Astronautics
EAA .... Engineering and Architects Association
EAA .... Entertainment Agents Association [British]
EAA .... Epilepsy Association of America [Later, EFA]
EAA .... Equipment Approval Authority   (AFM)
EAA .... Equity Access Account [Revolving mortgage-credit account]
               [Merrill Lynch & Co.]
E Aa .... Erhvervshistorisk Aarbog [A publication]
EAA .... Essential Amino Acids [Nutrition]
EAA .... Estudos Anglo-Americanos [A publication]
EAA .... Ethyl Acetoacetate [Organic chemistry]
EAA .... Ethyleneacrylic Acid [Organic chemistry]
EAA .... Euro-American Alliance   (EA)
EAA .... European Academy of Anaesthesiology   (EA)
EAA .... European Accounting Association [Brussels, Belgium]   (EAIO)
EAA .... European Aluminium Association [Federal Republic of
               Germany]   (EA)
EAA .... European Athletic Association [Paris, France]
EAA .... Evrytanian Association of America   (EA)
EAA .... Excitatory Amino Acid [Neurophysiology]
EAA .... Excretory Amino Acid
EAA .... Experimental Aircraft Association   (EA)
EAA .... Export Administration Act [1979]
EAA .... Extrinsic Allergic Alveolitis [Medicine]
EAAA .... European Association of Advertising Agencies
EAAACD... EAA [Experimental Aircraft Association] Antique/Classic
               Division   (EA)
EAAAF...... EAA [Experimental Aircraft Association] Aviation
               Foundation   (EA)
EA(A)APP ... Electrical Artificer (Air), Apprentice [British military]   (DMA)
EAABSH... English Association of American Bond and Share Holders
               [Commercial firm]   (EA)
EAAC .... East African Airways Corporation [African airline]
EAAC .... East African Armoured Corps [British military]   (DMA)
EAAC .... European Agricultural Aviation Centre [Later, International
               Agricultural Aviation Centre]
EAAC .... European Association of Audiophonological Centres   (EA)
EAACI....... European Academy of Allergology and Clinical
               Immunology   (EAIO)
EAAE....... European Association of Agricultural Economists   (EA)
EAAEC...... East African Army Educational Corps [British military]   (DMA)
EAAED...... Electrotehnica, Electronica, si Automatica. Seria Automatica si
               Electronica [A publication]
EAAFR...... European Academic Association for Financial Research   (EAIO)
EAAFRO... East African Agriculture and Forestry Research Organization
EAAH....... Essential Amino Acids plus Histidine [Nutrition]
EAAJ....... East African Agricultural and Forestry Journal [A publication]
EAAJA5.... East African Agricultural Journal [A publication]
EAAM ...... European Association for Aquatic Mammals   (EA)
EAAMC .... East African Army Medical Corps [British military]   (DMA)
EAANAH ... Eastern Anthropologist [A publication]
EAAOC ..... East African Army Ordnance Corps [British military]   (DMA)
EA-AP .... Encyclopedia of Associations: Association Periodicals [A
               publication]
EAAP........ European Association for Animal Production [Rome, Italy]
EAAPAN... European Association for Animal Production. Publication [A
               publication]
EAAS........ European Association for American Studies [Venice,
               Italy]   (EAIO)
EAASH ...... European Academy of Arts, Sciences, and Humanities   (EAIO)
EAASN...... EAAS [European Association for American Studies] Newsletter
               [A publication]
EAAUA ..... EAA [Experimental Aircraft Association] Ultralight Association
               [Defunct]   (EA)
EAB .... Abbse [Yemen Arab Republic] [Airport symbol]   (OAG)
EAB .... Aberfoyle [Scotland] [Seismograph station code, US Geological
               Survey]   (SEIS)
EAB .... Economic Advisory Board [Department of Commerce]
               [Washington, DC]   (EGAO)
EAB .... Economic Affairs Bureau   (EA)
EAB .... Educational Advisory Board [British]
EAB .... Elongation-at-Break [Textile technology]
EAB .... Emergency Actions Book
EAB .... Enemy Activities Branch [British military]   (DMA)
EAB .... Energy Absorption
EAB .... Era of Arnold Bennett [A publication]
EAB .... Esperanto-Asocio de Britujo [British]
EAB .... Ethics Advisory Board [HEW]
EAB .... Exclusion Area Boundary [Nuclear energy]   (NRCH)
EABC........ European Amateur Baseball Confederation   (EA)
EABC........ European/ASEAN [Association of Southeast Asian Nations]
               Business Council   (DS)

EABMD .... Energy Advisory Bulletin for Texas Manufacturers [*A publication*]
EABN .... Engineer Aviation Battalion [*Military*]
EABR .... East Asia Blocking Ridge [*Meteorology*]
EABRD ..... Electrically Activated Bank Release Device (IEEE)
EABS .... Erotic Art Book Society [*Commercial firm*] (EA)
EABS .... Euro-Abstracts [*Commission of the European Communities*] [*Information service or system*]
EABT .... European Association for Behavior Therapy (EA)
EABUB ..... Electronic Applications Bulletin [*A publication*]
E Abul .... Estudios Abulenses [*A publication*]
EABV .... Effective Arterial Blood Volume
EAC .... EAC Industries, Inc. [*AMEX symbol*] (SPSG)
EAC .... Early American Coppers (EA)
EAC .... East African Community [*Formed in 1967*] [*Formerly, EACSO*]
EAC .... East Australian Current [*Oceanography*]
EAC .... Eastern Air Command [*CBI Theater*] [*World War II*]
EAC .... Eastern Arizona College [*Formerly, EAJC*] [*Thatcher*]
EAC .... Echelon Above Corps [*Military*] (RDA)
EAC .... Economic Adjustment Committee (MCD)
EAC .... Educational Advisory Committee [*AIAA*]
EAC .... Educational Assessment Center [*University of Washington*] [*Research center*] (RCD)
EAC .... Effective Acoustic Center
EAC .... Effective Atomic Charge
EAC .... Ehrlich Ascites Carcinoma [*Cells*] [*Oncology*]
EAC .... Eire Army Corps
EAC .... Electro-Optical Area Correlator [*Missile guidance system*]
EAC .... Electronic Air Cleaner
EAC .... Emergency Action Communications (MCD)
EAC .... Emergency Action Console [*Navy*] (CINC)
EAC .... Enciclopedia di Autori Classici [*A publication*]
EAC .... End-Around Carry
EAC .... Energy Absorbing Capacity (NASA)
EAC .... Energy Absorption Characteristics (AAG)
EAC .... Engineer Amphibian Command [*World War II*]
EAC .... Engineering Aid, Chief [*Navy rating*]
EAC .... Engineering Applications Centre [*University of Strathclyde*] [*United Kingdom*] (CB)
EAC .... Environmental Action Coalition (EA)
EAC .... Environmentally Assisted Crack [*Metallurgy*]
EAC .... Epiphany Apostolic College [*New York*]
EAC .... EPRI [*Electric Power Research Institute*] Journal [*A publication*]
EAC .... Equipment Availability Constant (MCD)
EAC .... Equity Appreciation Certificate [*Investment term*]
EAC .... Erythrocyte-Antibody Complement [*Immunochemistry*]
EAC .... Estimate at Completion (NASA)
EAC .... Estimated Acquisition Cost [*of drug products*] [*HEW*]
EAC .... Estimated Arrival Carrier (MCD)
EAC .... Ethnic American Coalition (of Eastern Europeans) (EA)
EAC .... Ethyl Acetamidocinnamate [*Organic chemistry*]
EAC .... Etudes d'Archeologie Classique [*A publication*]
EAC .... Euro-Asia Capital Ltd. [*Vancouver Stock Exchange symbol*]
EAC .... European Advisory Committee [*Allied German Occupation Forces*]
EAC .... European Advisory Council (EAIO)
EAC .... European Association for Co-Operation
EAC .... European Association of Conservatories (EA)
EAC .... European Atomic Commission (NATG)
EAC .... Evangelical Association of the Caribbean (EAIO)
EAC .... Executive Air Charter [*Honolulu, HI*] [*FAA designator*] (FAAC)
EAC .... Exhibitors Advisory Council
EAC .... Expected Approach Clearance [*Aviation*] (AFM)
EAC .... Expedition Advisory Centre [*Royal Geographical Society*] [*British*] (CB)
EAC .... Experiment Apparatus Container
EAC .... Extended Arithmetic Chip
EAC .... External Auditory Canal [*Anatomy*]
EACA .... Constructionman Apprentice, Engineering Aid, Striker [*Navy rating*]
EACA .... Epsilon-Aminocaproic Acid [*Pharmacology*]
EACA .... European Association of Charter Airlines (EAIO)
EACA .... European Athletics Coaches Association (EAIO)
EACA .... Law Reports, Court of Appeals of Eastern Africa [*A publication*] (DLA)
EAC-AIA ... EEC Advisory Council of the Asbestos International Association (EAIO)
EACC .... East Asia Christian Conference [*Later, Christian Conference of Asia - CCA*]
EACC .... Egyptian American Chamber of Commerce (EA)
EACC .... Electronic Asset Control Center (AFM)
EACC .... Emergency Alternate Command Center (CINC)
EACC .... Environmental Assessment Command Center [*Nuclear energy*] (NRCH)
EACC .... Error Adaptive Control Computer (IEEE)
EACD .... Eczematous Allergic Contact Dermatitis [*Dermatology*]
EACE .... Euro American Cultural Exchange (EA)
EACE .... European Association of Cognitive Ergonomics (EAIO)

EACF .... Employer Identification Number Assignment Control Card File [*IRS*]
EA/CG ...... Ecology Action/Common Ground [*An association*]
EACH .... East Camden & Highland Railroad Co. [*AAR code*]
Ea Ch Qu ... Eastern Churches Quarterly [*A publication*]
EACL .... Energie Atomique du Canada, Limitee [*Atomic Energy of Canada Limited - AECL*]
EACL .... European Association for Chinese Law (EAIO)
EACM .... East African Common Market
EACM .... Engineering Aid, Master Chief [*Navy rating*]
EACMFS ... European Association for Cranio-Maxillo-Facial Surgery (EAIO)
EACN .... Constructionman, Engineering Aid, Striker [*Navy rating*]
EACN .... Equivalent Alkane Carbon Number [*of crude oil*]
EACN .... European Air Chemistry Network
EACNG ..... Emergency Advisory Committee for Natural Gas [*Department of the Interior*] [*Terminated, 1977*] (EGAO)
EACNLT .... Expect Approach Clearance Not Later Than [*Aviation*] (FAAC)
EACO .... EA Engineering, Science & Technology, Inc. [*NASDAQ symbol*] (NQ)
EACOS ...... European Air Combat Operations Staff [*Military*]
EACP .... European Area Communications Plan [*Military*] (AABC)
EACPI ...... European Association of Country Planning Institutions (EAIO)
EACR .... European Association for Cancer Research (EAIO)
EACRP ...... European-American Committee on Reactor Physics
EACS .... East Asian Cultural Studies [*A publication*]
EACS .... Engineering Aid, Senior Chief [*Navy rating*]
EACS .... EP/EO [*Employee Plans/Exempt Organization*] Application Control System [*IRS*]
EACS .... European Allied Contacts Section [*Supreme Headquarters, Allied Expeditionary Force*] [*World War II*]
EACS .... European Association of Chinese Studies (EA)
EACSO ...... East African Common Services Organization [*Later, EAC*]
EACT .... Emergency Action Coordination Team [*Department of Energy*]
EACTA ..... European Association of Cardiothoracic Anaesthesiologists [*Cambridge, England*] (EAIO)
EACVD ..... Electron-Assisted Chemical Vapor Deposition [*Coating technology*]
EAD .... Eadem [*The Same*] [*Pharmacy*]
EAD .... Earliest Arrival Date (AABC)
EAD .... Echelon Above Division [*Military*] (MCD)
EAD .... Economic Analysis Division [*Federal Emergency Management Agency*] [*Information service or system*] (IID)
EAD .... Effective Air Distance
EAD .... Electrically Alterable Device (NASA)
EAD .... Endo-Atmospheric Decoy
EAD .... Engineering Aid, Draftsman [*Navy rating*] [*Obsolete*]
EAD .... Engineers Australian Database
EAD .... Entry Acceptance Data (DS)
EAD .... Entry on Active Duty [*Army*]
EAD .... Equilibrium Air Distillation (AAG)
EAD .... Equipment Allocation Document (MCD)
EAD .... Equipment Availability Date (MCD)
EAD .... Equivalent Air Depth [*Deep-sea diving*]
EAD .... Estimated Availability Date [*Military*] (AFM)
EAD .... Ethyl Azodicarboxylate [*Organic chemistry*]
E & AD ...... Exchequer and Audit Department [*British government*] (RDA)
EAD .... Expected Availability Date (MCD)
EAD .... Expendable Acoustic Device [*Military*] (CAAL)
EAD .... Extended Active Duty
EAD .... External Aerodynamic Diffusion
EAD .... Nevada, MO [*Location identifier*] [*FAA*] (FAAL)
EADA .... Eighth Armored Division Association (EA)
EADAS ..... Engineering and Administrative Data Acquisition System [*Bell System*]
EADB .... East African Development Bank
EADB .... Experimental Arctic Data Buoy (MSC)
EADC .... Energy Analysis and Diagnostic Center [*Department of Energy*]
EADC .... Ethylaluminum Dichloride [*Organic chemistry*]
EADCU ..... Enemy Ammunition Disposal and Collection Unit [*Military*] [*British*]
EADF .... Eastern Air Defense Force
EaDI .... Easy Access Data Interchange [*Unisys Corp.*] (IT)
EADI .... Electronic Attitude and Direction Indicator
EADI .... European Association of Development Research and Training Institutes (EAIO)
EADIZ ...... Entering Air Defense Identification Zone (FAAC)
EADL .... Erlanger Arbeiten zur Deutschen Literatur [*A publication*]
EADP .... European Association of Directory Publishers (EA)
EADRI .... European Association of Development Research and Training Institutes
EADS .... Echelons Above Division Study [*Military*] (AABC)
EADS .... Engineering Administrative Data Systems (MCD)
EADS .... Engineering Analysis Data System
EADS .... Environmental Assessment Data Systems [*Environmental Protection Agency*] [*Information service or system*] [*Discontinued*] (IID)
EADT .... East Anglia Daily Times [*A publication*]
EADX .... Echelons Above Division - Expanded [*Military*] (MCD)
EAE .... Ecology Action East [*An association*] (EA)
EAE .... Economic Bulletin for Asia and the Pacific [*A publication*]

EAE .... Emae [*Vanuatu*] [*Airport symbol*]   (OAG)
EAE .... Energy and the Environment [*A publication*]
EAE .... Ethylaminoethanol [*Organic chemistry*]
EAE .... Excavaciones Arqueologicas en Espana [*A publication*]
EAE .... Experimental Autoimmune Encephalomyelitis [*Medicine*]
EAE .... Extended Arithmetic Element
EAEBP ...... European Association of Editors of Biological Periodicals   (DIT)
EAEC........ East African Economic Community
EAEC........ European Airlines Electronic Committee
EAEC........ European Atomic Energy Community [*Also, EURATOM*]   (DCTA)
EAECA..... Eastern Economist [*A publication*]
EAEE......... Evangelische Arbeitsgemeinschaft fuer Erwachsenenbildung in Europa [*Protestant Association for Adult Education in Europe*]   (EAIO)
EAEF........ Energy Action Educational Foundation [*Later, EAEP*]   (EA)
EAEG .... European Association of Exploration Geophysicists   (EAIO)
EAEHL...... Encyclopaedia of Archaeological Excavations in the Holy Land [*Jerusalem*] [*A publication*]
EAEI......... Ecology Action Educational Institute   (EA)
EA/EIS...... Environmental Assessment/Environmental Impact Statement [*Army*]   (RDA)
EAEME..... East African Electrical and Mechanical Engineers [*British military*]   (DMA)
EAENA3 ... Advances in Anatomy, Embryology, and Cell Biology [*A publication*]
EAEP........ Energy Action Educational Project of C/LEC [*Defunct*]   (EA)
EAER........ Eastern Africa Economic Review [*A publication*]
EAES .... European Atomic Energy Society
EAESP ...... European Association of Experimental Social Psychology   (EA)
EAETLFFM ... European Association for the Exchange of Technical Literature in the Field of Ferrous Metallurgy [*Luxembourg*]   (EA)
EAEWAU ... Edinburgh School of Agriculture. Experimental Work [*A publication*]
EAF........... Earth Awareness Foundation   (EA)
EAF........... Educational Accountability Function   (OICC)
EAF........... Egyptian Air Force
EAF........... Electric Arc Furnace [*Steelmaking*]
EAF........... Emergency Action File [*Air Force*]   (AFM)
EAF........... Emery Air Freight Corp. [*NYSE symbol*]   (SPSG)
EAF........... Environmental Action Foundation   (EA)
EAF........... Eosinophil-Activating Factor [*Immunology*]
EAF........... Equivalent Availability Factor   (IEEE)
EAF........... Ethnographisch-Archaeologische Forschungen [*A publication*]
EAF........... Exhaust Air Filter
EAF........... Expeditionary Airfield   (MCD)
EAF........... Experiment Analysis Form   (KSC)
EAF........... Fairbanks, AK [*Location identifier*] [*FAA*]   (FAAL)
EAFB........ Edwards Air Force Base [*California*]
EAFB........ Eglin Air Force Base [*Florida*]
EAFB........ Elison Air Force Base [*Alaska*]   (KSC)
EAFB........ Ellington Air Force Base [*Texas*]   (KSC)
EAFC........ Eastern Area Frequency Coordinator
EAFC........ Eastland Financial Corporation [*NASDAQ symbol*]   (NQ)
EAFE........ Europe, Australia, and Far East
EAFFRO ... East African Freshwater Fisheries Research Organization
EAFHS...... Eighth Air Force Historical Society   (EA)
EAFJAU ... East African Agricultural and Forestry Journal [*A publication*]
EAFNA8... East African Agriculture and Forestry Research Organization. Forestry Technical Note [*A publication*]
EAFOAB... East African Common Services Organization. East African Marine Fisheries Research Organization. Annual Report [*A publication*]
EAFOBC... East African Freshwater Fisheries Research Organization. Annual Report [*A publication*]
EAFORD... International Organisation for the Elimination of All Forms of Racial Discrimination [*Geneva, Switzerland*]   (EAIO)
E Afr .... East Africa
E Afr Agr Forest J ... East African Agricultural and Forestry Journal [*A publication*]
E Afr Agric For J ... East African Agricultural and Forestry Journal [*A publication*]
E Afr Agric J ... East African Agricultural Journal [*A publication*]
E Afr Annu ... East African Annual [*A publication*]
E Afr Econ ... Eastern Africa Economic Review [*A publication*]
E Afr Farmer Plant ... East African Farmer and Planter [*A publication*]
E Afric Agric & For J ... East African Agricultural and Forestry Journal [*A publication*]
E African LJ ... East African Law Journal [*A publication*]   (DLA)
E Afr LR .... East Africa Law Reports [*A publication*]   (DLA)
E Afr L Rev ... Eastern Africa Law Review [*A publication*]   (DLA)
E Afr Med J ... East African Medical Journal [*A publication*]
E Afr Stud ... East African Studies [*A publication*]
E Afr Wildlife J ... East African Wildlife Journal [*A publication*]
E Afr Wildl J ... East African Wildlife Journal [*A publication*]
EAFS .... European Academy of Facial Surgery   (EAIO)
EAG.......... Eagle Financial Corp. [*AMEX symbol*]   (SPSG)
EAG........... Eaglet Mines Ltd. [*Toronto Stock Exchange symbol*] [*Vancouver Stock Exchange symbol*]

EAG .... Economic Analysis Group [*Washington, DC*] [*General Accounting Office*]   (GRD)
EAG .... Electroantennogram [*Entomology*]
EAG .... ELINT [*Electronic Intelligence*] Advisory Group   (AABC)
EAG .... Equipment Advisory Group
EAG .... Evaluation and Analysis Group [*Bureau of Ordnance*] [*Washington, DC*] [*Navy*]   (MCD)
EAG .... Experimental Miscellaneous Auxiliary [*Navy symbol*]
EAG .... Ministry of External Affairs, Government Documents [*UTLAS symbol*]
EAGA .... Episcopal Actor's Guild of America   (EA)
EAGAB9.... Escola de Agronomia da Amazonia. Boletim [*A publication*]
EAGE .... Electrical Aerospace Ground Equipment   (TEL)
EAGER ...... Electronic Audit Gauger
EAGF........ Electrically Augmented Gravity Filter [*Chemical engineering*]
EAGGF.... European Agricultural Guidance and Guarantee Fund [*Also known as FEOGA*]
EAGLE...... Elevation Angle Guidance Landing Equipment
EAGLE...... Environmental Assessment of Great Lakes Ecosystems [*United States Fish and Wildlife Service*]   (ASF)
EAGLE...... European Association for Grey Literature Exploitation [*Database producer*] [*Address unknown*]   (EAIO)
EAGLE...... Experiment and Guidance Loop Evaluator
EAGLE...... Extended Application of Ground LASER Equipment   (MCD)
Eag Mag Com ... Eagle's Magistrate's Pocket Companion [*A publication*]   (DLA)
EAGR .... East African Geographical Review [*A publication*]
EAGRD ..... Experimental Aging Research [*A publication*]
EAGS........ English and Germanic Studies [*A publication*]
Eag T......... Eagle's Law of Tithes [*2nd ed.*] [*1836*] [*A publication*]   (DLA)
Eag & Y.... Eagle and Younge's English Tithe Cases [*A publication*]   (DLA)
Eag & Yo.... Eagle and Younge's English Tithe Cases [*A publication*]   (DLA)
EAH.......... Epochs of Ancient History [*A publication*]
EAH .... Essex Archaeology and History [*A publication*]
EAH .... European Academy of History   (EA)
EAHA .... European Association of Hospital Administrators   (EA)
EAHCCL... Educators' Ad Hoc Committee on Copyright Law   (EA)
EAHF .... Eczema, Asthma, Hay Fever [*Medicine*]
EAHHFC . Engel's Angels in Humperdinck Heaven Fan Club   (EA)
EAHIL....... European Association of Health Information and Libraries [*Stockholm, Sweden*]   (EAIO)
EAHILC.... Erie Area Health Information Library Cooperative [*Library network*]
EAHP .... European Association of Hospital Pharmacists   (EAIO)
EAHQ....... Ethylanthrahydroquinone [*Organic chemistry*]
EAHY .... European Architectural Heritage Year [*1975*]
EAI .... Education Audit Institute [*Washington, DC*]
EAI .... Electronic Associates, Incorporated
EAI .... Emphysema Anonymous, Incorporated   (EA)
EAI .... Emulsifying Activity Index [*Food analysis*]
EAI .... Engineers and Architects Institute [*Defunct*]
EAI .... England-Amerika-Institut [*A publication*]
EAI .... Ethyl Acetimidate [*Biochemistry*]
EAIA .... Early American Industries Association   (EA)
EAIABJ.... East African Institute for Medical Research. Annual Report [*A publication*]
EAIC........ Electronic Air Inlet Controller   (MCD)
EAIC........ Energy Assets International Corporation [*NASDAQ symbol*]   (NQ)
EAID .... Engine Air Intake Duct [*Hovercraft*]
EAID .... Equipment Authorization Inventory Data [*Air Force*]   (AFM)
EAID .... ESRO [*European Space Research Organization*] Advanced Imaging Detector [*Satellite*]
EAIDL....... Equipment Authorization Inventory Data Listing [*Air Force*]   (AFM)
EAIDS....... Equipment Authorization Inventory Data System [*Air Force*]   (AFIT)
EAIM .... End Article Item Manager   (AFIT)
EAIND ...... Electronique et Applications Industrielles [*A publication*]
EA-IO .... Encyclopedia of Associations: International Organizations [*A publication*]
EAIR.......... Empire Airlines [*NASDAQ symbol*]   (NQ)
EAIR......... End Article Identity Record
EAIR......... Extended Area Instrumentation RADAR   (MCD)
EAIS......... Columbia University. East Asian Institute. Studies [*A publication*]
EAIS......... Extended Area Instrumentation System   (MCD)
EAJ.......... East Africa Journal [*A publication*]
EAJA .... Equal Access to Justice Act [*1980*]
EAJC .... Eastern Arizona Junior College [*Later, EAC*]
EAJCC ...... European Association of Jewish Community Centres   (EAIO)
EAJ Criminol ... East African Journal of Criminology [*A publication*]   (DLA)
EAJKAJ.... East African Agricultural Journal of Kenya, Tanganyika, Uganda, and Zanzibar [*A publication*]
EAJP .... East Asia Journalism Program   (EA)
EAK .... East Kootenay Community College Library [*UTLAS symbol*]
EAK .... Einleitung in die Assyrischen Koenigsinschriften [*A publication*]   (BJA)
EAK .... Ethyl Amyl Ketone [*Organic chemistry*]
EAK .... Executive Air Link [*Spring, TX*] [*FAA designator*]   (FAAC)
EAL .... Eagle Industry [*Vancouver Stock Exchange symbol*]

EAL .... Early American Life Insurance Association   (EA)
EAL .... Early American Literature [*A publication*]
EAL .... Eastern Air Lines, Inc. [*AMEX symbol*] [*Air carrier designation symbol*]   (SPSG)
EAL .... Ehrenfest Adiabatic Law [*Physics*]
EAL .... Electromagnetic Amplifying Lens
EAL .... Emergency Action Level [*Nuclear energy*]   (NRCH)
EAL .... Environmental Acoustics Laboratory [*Pennsylvania State University*] [*Research center*]   (RCD)
EAL .... Equalized Assessed Valuation
EAL .... Equipment Air Lock [*Nuclear energy*]   (NRCH)
EAL .... Equipment Applications List   (MCD)
EAL .... Estimated [*or Expected*] Average Life
EAL .... Ethiopia Air Lines
EALB .... East African Literature Bureau
EALCAE ... Ecumenical Association of Laity Centres and Academies in Europe [*See also OVATE*] [*Bad Boll, Federal Republic of Germany*]   (EAIO)
EALG .... Ealing Corp. [*NASDAQ symbol*]   (NQ)
EALJ .... East African Law Journal [*A publication*]   (DLA)
EALM .... European Association of Livestock Markets [*See also AEMB*] [*Brussels, Belgium*]   (EAIO)
EALN .... Early American Literature. Newsletter [*A publication*]
EALR .... East Africa Law Reports [*A publication*]   (DLA)
EAL Rev .... Eastern Africa Law Review [*A publication*]
EAM .... Electrically Alterable Memory [*Data processing*]
EAM .... Electronic Accounting Machine [*Data processing*]
EAM .... Electronic Automatic Machinery
EAM .... Emergency Action Message [*Navy*]   (NVT)
EAM .... Entered Apprentice Mason [*Freemasonry*]   (ROG)
EAm .... Estudios Americanos [*Sevilla*] [*A publication*]
EAM .... Ethnikon Apelephtherotikon Metopon [*National Liberation Front*] [*Greek*]   (PPE)
EAM .... Evanescent Access Method [*Sperry UNIVAC*]
EAM .... External Auditory Meatus [*Anatomy*]
EAM .... Nejran [*Saudi Arabia*] [*Airport symbol*]   (OAG)
EAMA .... Etats Africains et Malgache Associes [*Associated African and Malagasy States*]
EAM/AIF ... Expense Appropriation Management/Army Industrial Fund
EAMAS .... Emergency Action Message Authentication System [*Military*]
EAMC .... Eastern Atlantic and Mediterranean Command [*Military*]
EAMCAHS ... European Association of Music Conservatories, Academies, and High Schools   (EAIO)
EAMCBP .. European Association of Makers of Corrugated Base Papers   (EAIO)
EAMD .... Equivalent Aerodynamic Median Diameter [*of atmospheric particulates*]
E-A-ME ...... European-African-Middle Eastern [*Communications area*] [*NASA*]   (KSC)
EAMECM ... European-African-Middle Eastern Campaign Medal [*Military decoration*]
EAMEDPM ... Electric Accounting Machine and Electronic Data Processing Machine
EAMF .... European Association of Music Festivals   (EA)
EAMFS ..... European Association for Maxillo-Facial Surgery   (EA)
EAMG .... Electric Arc Metallizing Gun
EAMG .... Experimental Autoimmune Myasthenia Gravis [*Medicine*]
EAMHD .... Engineering Aspects of Magnetohydrodynamics [*A publication*]   (MCD)
EAMHMS ... European Association of Museums of the History of Medical Sciences [*See also AEMHSM*]   (EAIO)
EAMI .... Expansion Anchor Manufacturers Institute   (EA)
EAMJ .... East African Management Journal [*A publication*]
EAMJA ...... East African Medical Journal [*A publication*]
EAMJAV .. East African Medical Journal [*A publication*]
EAmL .... Early American Literature [*A publication*]
EAMLS ..... East African Military Labour Service [*British military*]   (DMA)
EAMP .... Engine Analytical Maintenance Program [*Navy*]   (NVT)
EAMR .... Engineering Advance Material Release   (KSC)
EAMRAL ... East African Common Services Organization. East African Institute for Medical Research. Annual Report [*A publication*]
EAMT .... Expanded Alternative Minimum Tax
EAMTC ...... European Association of Management Training Centres
EAMTMC ... Eastern Area Military Traffic Management Command   (AFIT)
EAMTMTS ... Eastern Area, Military Traffic Management and Terminal Service   (AABC)
EAMU .... Electric Accounting Machine Unit
e-an---......... Andorra [*MARC geographic area code*] [*Library of Congress*]   (LCCP)
EAN .... Association Internationale de Numerotation des Articles [*International Article Numbering Association*]   (EAIO)
EAN .... Eastern Mines Ltd. [*Vancouver Stock Exchange symbol*]
EAN .... Effective Atomic Number
EAN .... Emergency Action Notification [*Civil Defense*]
EAN .... Equivalent Atomic Number
EAn .... Etudes Anglaises [*A publication*]
EAN .... European Article Number [*Equivalent of Universal Product Code*]
EAN .... Expenditure Account Number
EAN .... Experimental Allergic Neuritis [*Medicine*]

EAN .... Experimental Autoimmune Neuritis [*Medicine*]
EAN .... Wheatland, WY [*Location identifier*] [*FAA*]   (FAAL)
EANA .... Esperanto Association of North America [*Defunct*]   (EA)
EANA .... European Alliance of News Agencies
EANC .... Estonian American National Council   (EA)
EANCO ...... Emergency Actions Noncommissioned Officer [*Army*]   (AABC)
EANDC ..... Edgewood Arsenal Nuclear Defense Center [*Maryland*] [*Army*]
EANDC ..... European-American Nuclear Data Committee [*OECD*]
E Anglian Archaeol ... East Anglian Archaeology [*A publication*]
EANGUS ... Enlisted Association of the National Guard of the United States
EANHAU ... EANHS [*East Africa Natural History Society*] Bulletin [*A publication*]
EANHS ..... East African Natural History Society   (EAIO)
EANHS Bull ... EANHS [*East Africa Natural History Society*] Bulletin [*A publication*]
EANPC ...... European Association for National Productivity Centers [*See also AECNP*]   (EAIO)
EANS .... Emergency Action Notification System [*White House Teletype network*] [*Civil Defense*]
EANS .... European Association of Neurosurgical Societies   (EAIO)
E Anthropol ... Eastern Anthropologist [*A publication*]
EANWA .... Energieanwendung [*A publication*]
EAO .... Economy Act Order
EAO .... Egyptian Antiquities Organization   (EA)
EAO .... Emergency Actions Officer [*Army*]   (AABC)
EAO .... Etudes d'Archeologie Orientale [*Clermont-Ganneau*] [*A publication*]
EAOA .... Eastern Authorities Orchestral Association [*British*]
EAOG .... European Association of Organic Geochemists   (EAIO)
EAON .... Except as Otherwise Noted
EAORAV .. East African Common Services Organization. East African Agricultural and Forestry Research Organization. Record of Research [*A publication*]
EAOS .... Expiration of Active Obligated Service [*Military*]
EAP .... East Africa Protectorate [*Later, Kenya*]
EA & P .... East Asian and Pacific [*Series*] [*A publication*]
EAP .... Easton Area Public Library, Easton, PA [*OCLC symbol*]   (OCLC)
EAP .... Ecole Europeenne des Affaires [*European School of Management*] [*Paris*]
EAP .... Ecological Agriculture Projects [*See also PAE*] [*Sainte Anne De Bellevue, PQ*]   (EAIO)
EAP .... Economie Appliquee [*A publication*]
EAP .... Edgar Allan Poe [*Initials used as pseudonym*]
EAP .... Educational Awareness Project   (EA)
EAP .. Effective Air Path
eap.............. Effet a Payer [*Bill Payable*] [*French*] [*Business term*]
EAP ...... Electroacupuncture
EAP .... Electronics Assembly Plant [*College Station, TX*] [*Westinghouse Electric Corp.*]
EAP .... Emergency Action Procedure [*Military*]   (NVT)
EAP .... Employee Assistance Program
EAP .... Employment Access Program [*Australia*]
EAP .... English for Academic Purposes [*Australia*]
EAP .... English Association Pamphlets [*A publication*]
EAP .... Entered Apprentice [*Freemasonry*]   (ROG)
EAP .... Epiallopregnanolone [*Endocrinology*]
EAP .... Equipment Alignment Procedure   (MCD)
EAP .... Equivalent Air Pressure
EAP .... Erythrocyte Acid Phosphatase [*Hematology*]
EAP .... Esophageal Atrial Pacing [*Medicine*]
EAP .... Europaeische Arbeiterpartei [*European Workers' Party*] [*Federal Republic of Germany*] [*Political party*]   (PPE)
EAP .... Evoked Action Potential [*Neurophysiology*]
EAP .... Expenditure Analysis Plan   (TEL)
EAP .... Experimental Activity Proposal [*Nuclear energy*]   (NRCH)
EAP .... Experimental Aircraft Programme [*British*]
EAP .... Eye Artifact Potential
EAPA .... Embedded-Alumina-Particle Aluminide [*Chemical coating*]
EAPA .... Energy Abstracts for Policy Analysis [*National Science Foundation*] [*A publication*]   (MCD)
EAPA .... European Asphalt Pavement Association   (EA)
EAPAUS ... Employment Agencies Protective Association of the United States [*Later, National Employment Association*]
EAPC .... East African Pioneer Corps [*British military*]   (DMA)
EAPCC ...... European Association of Poison Control Centers   (EAIO)
EAPD .... EAP [*Employee Assistance Program*] Digest [*A publication*]
EAPD .... Eastern Air Procurement District
EAPF .... Electrically Augmented Pressure Filter [*Chemical engineering*]
EAPFBO ... European Association of Professional Fire Brigade Officers   (EA)
EAPG .... Eastern Atlantic Planning Guidance [*NATO*]   (NATG)
EAPH .... East African Publishing House [*Kenya*]
EAPHSS ... European Association of Programmes in Health Services Studies   (EAIO)
EAPI .... East-West Environment and Policy Institute [*East-West Center*] [*Research center*]   (RCD)
EAPL .... Engineering Assembly Parts List
EAPLR ...... East Africa Protectorate Law Reports [*A publication*]   (DLA)
EAPM .... European Association of Perinatal Medicine   (EAIO)

EAPM........ European Association of Personnel Management [*Paris, France*] (EA)
EAPP........ Engineered Australia Plan Party
EAPP........ European Association for the Promotion of Poetry (EA)
EAPR........ East Asian Pastoral Review [*A publication*]
EAPR........ European Association for Potato Research (EAIO)
EAPROM ... Electrically Alterable Programmable Read-Only Memory [*Data processing*]
EA Prot LR ... East Africa Protectorate Law Reports [*A publication*] (DLA)
EAPS........ Engine Air Particle Separator
EAPS........ European Association for Population Studies (EA)
EAPS........ European Association of Professional Secretaries [*Paris, France*] (EAIO)
EAPSB ..... Edgar Allan Poe Society of Baltimore (EA)
EAPSS...... Electronic Intelligence Analysis Processing Subsystem (MCD)
EAPTA8 ... INTA [*Instituto Nacional de Tecnologia Agropecuaria*]. Estacion Experimental Regional Agropecuaria [*Pergamino*]. Informe Tecnico [*A publication*]
EAQ.......... Ethylanthraquinone [*Organic chemistry*]
EAQNA..... Earthquake Notes [*A publication*]
EAQUDJ... Eau du Quebec [*A publication*]
EAR .... China Market [*A publication*]
EAR .... EAR. Edinburgh Architectural Research [*A publication*]
ear .... Effet a Recevoir [*Bill Receivable*] [*French*] [*Business term*]
EAR .... Electronic Audio Recognition
EAR .... Electronically Agile RADAR
EAR .... Employee Appraisal Record
EAR .... Employee Attitude Research (IEEE)
EAR .... Encyclopedia of American Religions [*A publication*]
EAR .... Energy Audit Report [*Navy*]
EAR .... Engineering Abstract Report [*Defense Supply Agency*]
EAR .... Engineering Analysis Report (KSC)
E & AR...... Error and Appeal Reports [*Canada*] [*A publication*] (DLA)
EAR .... Escape and Rescue
EAR .... Estimated Assumed Resources [*Minerals*]
EAR .... European Association of Radiology (EA)
EAR .... Experimental Alcoholic Rhabdomyolysis [*Medicine*]
EAR .... Experimental Array RADAR [*Army*]
EAR .... Expired Air Resuscitation (ADA)
EAR .... Export Administration Regulation [*Department of Commerce*]
EAR .... Extravehicular Aerospace Routing
EAR .... Kearney [*Nebraska*] [*Airport symbol*] (OAG)
EARA .... Equipment Authorization Review Activity (MCD)
EARB .... European Airlines Research Bureau
EARB........ Export Administration Review Board
EARC........ East African Reconnaissance Corps [*British military*] (DMA)
EARC........ Eastern Aerospace Rescue and Recovery Center [*Air Force*]
EARC........ Eastern Association of Rowing Colleges (EA)
EARC........ Educational Administration Resource Centre [*Information service or system*] (EISS)
EARC........ Elemental Analysis Research Center [*Department of Health and Human Services*] (GRD)
EARC........ Extraordinary Administrative Radio Conference [*ITU*]
EARCCUS ... East African Regional Committee for Conservation and Utilisation of Soil
EArch........ Etudes Archeologiques [*A publication*]
Ear Clin Int ... Ear Clinics International [*A publication*]
EARCOS ... East Asia Regional Council of Overseas Schools (EA)
EARFLAP ... Emergency Action Reporting for Logistics Action Programming [*Military*] (AFM)
Ear Hear .... Ear and Hearing [*A publication*]
EARI.......... Engineer Agency for Resources Inventories [*Army Corps of Engineers*]
EARI.......... Equipment Acceptance Requirements and Inspections (AAG)
EARL......... Environmental Awareness Reading List [*Department of the Interior*]
Earlham Coll Sci Bull ... Earlham College. Science Bulletin [*A publication*]
EARLPRADATE ... Earliest Practicable Date
Early Am L ... Early American Literature [*A publication*]
Early Am Lit ... Early American Literature [*A publication*]
Early Child Bull ... Early Childhood Bulletin [*A publication*] (APTA)
Early Child Dev Care ... Early Child Development and Care [*A publication*]
Early Child Ed ... Early Childhood Education [*A publication*]
Early Hum Dev ... Early Human Development [*A publication*]
EarlyM ...... Early Music [*A publication*]
Early Mus ... Early Music [*A publication*]
Early Mus G ... Early Music Gazette [*A publication*]
Early Mus Gaz ... Early Music Gazette [*A publication*]
Early Yrs.... Early Years [*A publication*]
EArmS....... Erevanskij Armjanskij Gosudarstvennyk Pedagogiceskij Institut Imeni Chacatur Abovjana. Sbornik Naucnych Trudov. Serija Russkogo Jazyka [*A publication*]
Earn .... Earnshaw's Gold Coast Judgments [*1909-10*] [*Ghana*] [*A publication*] (DLA)
EARN .... European Academic Research Network [*A computer network*]
Ear Nose Throat J ... Ear, Nose, and Throat Journal [*A publication*]
Earnshaw... Gold Coast Judgments, by Earnshaw [*1909-10*] [*Ghana*] [*A publication*] (DLA)
EAROM .... Electrically Alterable Read-Only Memory [*Data processing*]
EAROPH .. East Asia Regional Organization for Planning and Housing
EAROS...... Electrically Alterable Read-Only Store [*Data processing*]

EARP......... Equipment Antiriot Projector [*British*] (MCD)
EARRD..... European Applied Research Reports. Nuclear Science and Technology Section [*A publication*]
EARRS ..... Engineering Automated Release and Record System (MCD)
EARS......... East African Reconnaissance Squadron [*British military*] (DMA)
EARS......... Emergency Airborne Reaction System (MCD)
EARS......... Emergency Automated Response Subsystem [*National Oceanic and Atmospheric Administration*]
EARS......... Entry to Anesthesia Record by Speech
EARS......... Environmental Analog Recording System
EARS....... Executive Audial Rehabilitation Society
EARS......... HEARx Ltd. [*NASDAQ symbol*] (NQ)
EARSEL.... European Association of Remote Sensing Laboratories (EA)
EA-RSL.... Encyclopedia of Associations: Regional, State, and Local Organizations [*A publication*]
Earth Evol Sci ... Earth Evolution Sciences [*A publication*]
Earth Extraterr Sci ... Earth and Extraterrestrial Sciences. Conference Reports and Professional Activities [*A publication*]
Earth G ...... Earth Garden [*A publication*]
Earth Gar... Earth Garden [*A publication*] (APTA)
Earth Inf Bul ... Earthquake Information Bulletin [*A publication*]
Earth Law J ... Earth Law Journal [*Netherlands*] [*A publication*]
Earth Life Sci Ed ... Earth and Life Science Editing [*A publication*]
Earth L J.... Earth Law Journal [*A publication*]
Earth Miner Sci ... Earth and Mineral Sciences [*A publication*]
Earthmover & Civ Contrac ... Earthmover and Civil Contractor [*A publication*] (APTA)
Earth Plan ... Earth and Planetary Science Letters [*A publication*]
Earth Planetary Sci Lett ... Earth and Planetary Science Letters [*A publication*]
Earth Planet Sci Lett ... Earth and Planetary Science Letters [*A publication*]
Earth and Planet Sci Lett ... Earth and Planetary Science Letters [*A publication*]
Earthq Engng Struct Dynam ... Earthquake Engineering and Structural Dynamics [*A publication*]
Earthquake Engng & Struct Dyn ... Earthquake Engineering and Structural Dynamics [*A publication*]
Earthquake Eng Struct Dyn ... Earthquake Engineering and Structural Dynamics [*A publication*]
Earthquake Inf Bull ... Earthquake Information Bulletin [*A publication*]
Earthquake Not ... Earthquake Notes [*A publication*]
Earthqu Inf Bull ... Earthquake Information Bulletin [*A publication*]
Earthqu Notes ... Earthquake Notes [*A publication*]
Earth S....... Earth Science [*A publication*]
Earth Sci.... Earth Science [*A publication*]
Earth Sci Bull ... Earth Science Bulletin [*A publication*]
Earth Sci Digest ... Earth Science Digest [*A publication*]
Earth Sci Inst Special Pub ... Earth Science Institute. Special Publication [*A publication*]
Earth Sci J ... Earth Science Journal [*A publication*]
Earth Sci Jour ... Earth Science Journal [*A publication*]
Earth Sci R ... Earth Science Reviews [*A publication*]
Earth Sci Relat Inf Sel Annot Titles ... Earth Science and Related Information. Selected Annotated Titles [*A publication*]
Earth Sci Rep Alberta Res Counc ... Earth Sciences Report. Alberta Research Council [*A publication*]
Earth Sci Rev ... Earth Science Reviews [*A publication*]
Earth Shelter Dig Energy Rep ... Earth Shelter Digest and Energy Report [*A publication*]
Earth Surf Process ... Earth Surface Processes [*A publication*]
Earth Surf Processes ... Earth Surface Processes [*A publication*]
Earth Surf Processes and Landforms ... Earth Surface Processes and Landforms [*A publication*]
EARTS ...... En Route Automated RADAR Tracking System [*Aviation*] (FAAC)
Earw.......... Earwalker's Manchester Court-Leet Records [*England*] [*A publication*] (DLA)
EAS............ Early American Society (EA)
EAS............ Earth Aspect Sensor
EAs .... East African Shilling [*Monetary unit*]
EAS............ Eastern Analytical Symposium
EAS............ Eastern Apicultural Society of North America (EA)
EAS............ Eastern College, St. Davids, PA [*OCLC symbol*] (OCLC)
EAS............ Educational Analog Simulator
EAS............ Electronic Article Surveillance
EAS............ Employee Auxiliary Services (MCD)
EAS............ End-Around Shift
EAS............ Engert Aviation Services, Inc. [*Kansas City, MO*] [*FAA designator*] (FAAC)
EAS............ Engineering Aid, Surveyor [*Navy rating*] [*Obsolete*]
EAS............ Engineering Automated Systems (MCD)
EAS............ Enlisted Assignment System
EAS............ Enterprise Allowance Scheme [*for the self-employed*] [*British*]
EAS............ Environmental Assessment Scale [*Occupational therapy*]
EAS............ Equipment Acquisition Strategy (ADA)
EAS............ Equivalent Air Speed
EAS............ Error Analysis Study
EAS............ Essays in Arts and Sciences [*A publication*]
EAS............ Essential Air Servicer [*Department of Transportation*]
EAS............ Essential Auxiliary Support [*Nuclear energy*] (NRCH)

EAS........... Estimated Air Speed (MCD)
EAS........... Europe Aero Service
EAS........... European Aquaculture Society (EA)
EAS........... European Atherosclerosis Society (EA)
EAS........... Evaluation and Analysis Staff [*Bureau of Ordnance*] [*Washington, DC*] [*Navy*] (MCD)
EAS........... Executive Agreement Series [*A publication*] (DLA)
EAS........... Executive Air Services Proprietary Ltd. [*Australia*] (ADA)
EAS........... Executive Assignment Service [*Civil Service Commission*]
EAS........... Experiment Assurance System [*Nuclear energy*] (NRCH)
EAS........... Experimenter-Administered Stimulation [*Psychology*]
EAS........... Expiration of Active Service [*Marine Corps*]
EAS........... Extended Area Service [*Telecommunications*]
EAS........... Extensive Air Shower [*Cosmic ray physics*]
EAS........... External Agency Simulator (MCD)
EAS........... San Sebastian [*Spain*] [*Airport symbol*] (OAG)
EASA........ Electrical Apparatus Service Association (EA)
EASA........ Emergency Air Staff Actions (AFM)
EASA........ Engineer Automation Support Activity [*Army Corps of Engineers*]
EASB........ Electronic Area Support Base [*Air Force*]
EASC........ EAS Technologies, Inc. [*New York, NY*] [*NASDAQ symbol*] (NQ)
EASC........ East African Service Corps [*British military*] (DMA)
EASC........ East Asian Studies Center [*Indiana University*] [*Research center*] (RCD)
EASC........ Ethylaluminum Sesquichloride [*Organic chemistry*]
EASC........ Exploration of Alternative Concepts (MCD)
EASCD...... Earth Sciences [*A publication*]
EASCO...... European Association of Schools and Colleges of Optometry (EA)
EASCOM ... Eastern Command [*World War II*]
EASCOMINT ... Extended Air Surveillance Communications Intercept [*Air Force*]
EASCON.... Electronics and Aerospace Systems Convention (MCD)
EASD......... European Association for the Study of Diabetes [*See also AEED*] (EAIO)
EASE......... Easement [*Legal term*] (DLA)
EASE......... Econolite Automatic Sensing Equipment
EASE......... Editing, Arranging, and Sequencing Environment [*Data processing*] (BYTE)
EASE......... Elastic Analysis for Structural Engineering (NRCH)
EASE......... Electrical Automatic Support Equipment
EASE......... Electronic Analog Simulating Equipment [*Data processing*]
EASE......... Emigrant's Assured Savings Estate [*Banking program*]
EASE......... Engineering Automatic System for Solving Equations
EASE......... European Association of Science Editors [*Formed by a merger of European Association of Earth Science Editors and European Life Sciences Editors*] (EAIO)
EASE......... European Association for Special Education
EASE......... Experimental Assembly of Structures in Extravehicular Activity [*Space technology*]
EASel........ Engineers Adhesive Selector Program
EASEMT .. Easement [*British*] [*Legal term*] (ROG)
EASEP...... Early Apollo Scientific Experiments Package [*or Payload*] [*NASA*]
EASH .... Shilling [*Monetary unit in Tanzania*]
EASI .... East Asia Strategy Initiative [*Military*]
EASI .... Electrical Accounting for the Security Industry [*IBM Corp.*] (IEEE)
EASI .... Engineered Support Systems, Incorporated [*St. Louis, MO*] [*NASDAQ symbol*] (NQ)
EASI .... Estimate of Adversary Sequence Interruption [*Nuclear energy*] (NRCH)
EASI .... European Association of Shipping Informatics [*Brussels, Belgium*] (EAIO)
EASI .... Expanded Additional Skill Identifier [*Military*] (AABC)
EASI .... Expected Amount of Sample Information [*Statistics*]
E Asian Executive Rep ... East Asian Executive Reports [*A publication*]
EASIC .... Evaluating Acquired Skills in Communication [*Language ability test*]
EASJ Th.... East Asia Journal of Theology [*A publication*]
EASL .... Electroacoustic Systems Laboratory
EASL .... Engineering Analysis and Simulation Language [*Data processing*]
EASL .... European Association for the Study of the Liver
EASL .... Experimental Assembly and Sterilization Laboratory [*NASA*]
EASMD..... Engineering Aspects of Magnetohydrodynamics [*A publication*]
EASM/RSF ... External Armament Stores Management/Remote Set Fuze (MCD)
EASMT..... Easement [*British*] [*Legal term*] (ROG)
EASNA...... Employee Assistance Society of North America (EA)
EASP........ Edgewood Arsenal Special Publication [*Army*]
EASP........ Employee Auxiliary Service Personnel (MCD)
EASP........ European Association for Signal Processing [*Lausanne, Switzerland*] (MCD)
EAST .... East Australian Standard Time (DEN)
EAST .... Eastern Academy of Sexual Therapy [*Later, SSTAR*] (EA)
East........... Eastern Reporter [*A publication*] (ILCA)
EAST .... Eastover Corp. [*NASDAQ symbol*] (NQ)

East .... East's English King's Bench Term Reports [*A publication*] (DLA)
East .... East's Notes of Cases in Morley's East Indian Digest [*A publication*] (DLA)
EAST .... Electric Arc Shock Tunnel [*NASA*]
EAST .... Experimental Army Satellite Tactical
EAST .... External Rotation, Abduction Stress Test [*Medicine*]
East Af .... East Africa Court of Appeals Reports [*A publication*] (DLA)
EASTAF.... Eastern Transport Air Force
East Afr Agric For J ... East African Agricultural and Forestry Journal [*A publication*]
East Afr Agric For Res Organ Annu Rep ... East African Agricultural and Forestry Research Organization. Annual Report [*A publication*]
East Afr Agric For Res Organ For Tech Note ... East African Agriculture and Forestry Research Organization. Forestry Technical Note [*A publication*]
East Afr Agric For Res Organ Rec Res Annu Rep ... East African Agriculture and Forestry Research Organization. Record of Research. Annual Report [*A publication*]
East Afr Agric J ... East African Agricultural Journal [*A publication*]
East Afr Agric J Kenya Tanganyika Uganda Zanzibar ... East African Agricultural Journal of Kenya, Tanganyika, Uganda, and Zanzibar [*A publication*]
East Afr Common Serv Organ East Afr Inst Med Res Annu Rep ... East African Common Services Organization. East African Institute for Medical Research. Annual Report [*A publication*]
East Afr Freshw Fish Res Org Annu Rep ... East African Freshwater Fisheries Research Organization. Annual Report [*A publication*]
East Afr Geogr R ... East African Geographical Review [*A publication*]
East Afr Inst Malaria Vector-Borne Dis Annu Rep ... East African Institute of Malaria and Vector-Borne Diseases. Annual Report [*A publication*]
East Afr Inst Med Res Annu Rep ... East African Institute for Medical Research. Annual Report [*A publication*]
East Afr J Criminol ... East African Journal of Criminology [*A publication*] (DLA)
East Afr J Med Res ... East African Journal of Medical Research [*A publication*]
East Afr J Rur Develop ... Eastern Africa Journal of Rural Development [*A publication*]
East Afr LJ ... East African Law Journal [*A publication*] (DLA)
East Afr LR ... Eastern Africa Law Review [*A publication*]
East Afr L Rep ... East Africa Law Reports [*A publication*] (DLA)
East Afr L Rep ... Eastern Africa Law Reports [*Durban*] [*A publication*] (DLA)
East Afr L Rev ... Eastern Africa Law Review [*A publication*]
East Afr Med J ... East African Medical Journal [*A publication*]
East Afr Nat Resour Res Counc Annu Rep ... East African Natural Resources Research Council. Annual Report [*A publication*]
East Afr Rep Trade Ind ... East African Report on Trade and Industry [*A publication*]
East Afr Trypanosomiasis Res Organ Annu Rep ... East African Trypanosomiasis Research Organization. Annual Report [*A publication*]
East Afr Trypanosomiasis Res Organ Rep ... East African Trypanosomiasis Research Organization. Report [*A publication*]
East Afr Tuberc Invest Cent Annu Rep ... East African Tuberculosis Investigation Centre. Annual Report [*A publication*]
East Afr Vet Res Organ Annu Rep ... East African Veterinary Research Organization. Annual Report [*A publication*]
East Afr Virus Res Inst Rep ... East African Virus Research Institute. Report [*A publication*]
East Afr Wildl J ... East African Wildlife Journal [*A publication*]
East Anthro ... Eastern Anthropologist [*A publication*]
East Anthropol ... Eastern Anthropologist [*A publication*]
EASTASAC ... East African Society of African Culture
East As Cult Stud ... East Asian Cultural Studies [*A publication*]
East Asian R ... East Asian Review [*A publication*]
East As R... East Asian Review [*A publication*]
East Bay..... East Bay Voice [*A publication*]
East Buddhist ... Eastern Buddhist [*A publication*]
East Cent Eur ... East Central Europe [*A publication*]
EastChQ.... Eastern Churches Quarterly [*Ramsgate, London*] [*A publication*]
East Ch R... Eastern Churches Review [*A publication*]
EASTCO... East Coast
EASTCOBASE ... East Coast Base
EASTCOMMRGN ... Eastern Communications Region [*Military*] (AFM)
EASTCON ... Eastern Sea Frontier Control Local of Shipping in Gulf of Maine
EASTCON ... Eastern States International Construction Expo and Conference [*Associated General Contractors of America - Carolinas Branch*] (TSPED)
EASTCON ... Electronic Aerospace Systems Convention
East DC ..... Eastern District Court Reports [*South Africa*] [*A publication*] (DLA)
East DL...... Eastern Districts, Local Division, South African Law Reports [*A publication*] (DLA)
East Econ... Eastern Economist [*A publication*]

East End Environ ... East End Environment [*A publication*]
East (Eng) ... East's English King's Bench Term Reports [*A publication*] (DLA)
Eastern Africa Econ R ... Eastern Africa Economic Review [*A publication*]
Eastern Africa J Rural Development ... Eastern Africa Journal of Rural Development [*A publication*]
Eastern Anthropol ... Eastern Anthropologist [*A publication*]
Eastern Eur Econ ... Eastern European Economics [*A publication*]
Eastern J of Internat L ... Eastern Journal of International Law [*A publication*] (DLA)
Eastern J Int L ... Eastern Journal of International Law [*A publication*] (ILCA)
Eastern J In'tl L ... Eastern Journal of International Law [*A publication*] (DLA)
East Europe ... International Market Letter: East Europe [*A publication*] (DLA)
East Europ Quart ... East European Quarterly [*A publication*]
East Eur Q ... East European Quarterly [*A publication*]
East For Prod Lab (Can) Rep ... Eastern Forest Products Laboratory (Canada). Report [*A publication*]
East Fruit Grow ... Eastern Fruit Grower [*A publication*]
East Grape Grow Winery News ... Eastern Grape Grower and Winery News [*A publication*]
EASTH ...... Easthamstead [*England*]
East Horiz ... Eastern Horizon [*A publication*]
East J Int L ... Eastern Journal of International Law [*A publication*] (DLA)
EASTLANT ... Eastern Atlantic Area [*NATO*]
EASTLANTMEDCOM ... Eastern Atlantic and Mediterranean Command [*Military*]
East Librn ... Eastern Librarian [*A publication*]
East LR ...... Eastern Law Reporter [*Canada*] [*A publication*] (DLA)
East LR (Can) ... Eastern Law Reporter [*Canada*] [*A publication*] (DLA)
East Malays Geol Surv Rep ... East Malaysia Geological Survey. Report [*A publication*]
East Malling Res Stn Annu Rep ... East Malling Research Station. Annual Report [*A publication*]
East Malling Res Stn (Maidstone England) Rep ... East Malling Research Station (Maidstone, England). Report [*A publication*]
Eastman Org Chem Bull ... Eastman Organic Chemical Bulletin [*A publication*]
East Met Rev ... Eastern Metals Review [*A publication*]
East Midl Geogr ... East Midland Geographer [*A publication*]
EASTN ...... Eastern
East N of C ... East's Notes of Cases in Morley's East Indian Digest [*A publication*] (DLA)
EASTOMP ... East-Ocean Meeting Point
EASTPAC ... Eastern Pacific Area (MUGU)
East PC ...... East's Pleas of the Crown [*A publication*] (DLA)
East PC (Eng) ... East's Pleas of the Crown (England) [*A publication*] (DLA)
East Pharm ... Eastern Pharmacist [*A publication*]
East Pharmst ... Eastern Pharmacist [*A publication*]
East Pl Cr .. East's Pleas of the Crown [*A publication*] (DLA)
East Punjab ... All India Reporter, East Punjab [*1948-50*] [*A publication*] (DLA)
East Rep ..... Eastern Reporter [*A publication*] (DLA)
EASTROPAC ... Eastern Tropical Pacific [*Oceanographic expedition*]
EASTROPIC ... Cooperative Survey of the Eastern Tropical Pacific (MSC)
EASTSEAFRON ... Eastern Sea Frontier
EASTT ...... Experimental Army Satellite Tactical Terminals
East Tenn Hist Soc Publ ... East Tennessee Historical Society. Publications [*A publication*]
East Underw ... Eastern Underwriter [*A publication*]
East US Bus L Rev ... Eastern United States Business Law Review [*A publication*] (DLA)
East West ... East West Journal [*A publication*]
East West Perspect ... East West Perspectives [*A publication*]
East Wkr ... Eastern Worker [*A publication*]
EASY .... Caucus Committee on Education, Arts, Science, and Youth [*Australia*]
EASY .... Early Acquisition System [*Army*] (AABC)
EASY .... Efficient Assembly System [*Honeywell, Inc.*] [*Assembler language*]
EASY .... Engine Analyzer Systems [*Air Force*] (MCD)
EASY .... Evasive Aircraft System (MCD)
EAT .... Chili's, Inc. [*NYSE symbol*] (SPSG)
EAT .... Earliest Arrival Time
EAT .... Eastern Air Transport
EAT .... Economic Inquiry [*A publication*]
EAT .... Economic Review. Federal Reserve Bank of Atlanta [*A publication*]
EAT .... Ehrlich Ascites Tumor [*Oncology*]
EAT .... Electroaerosol Therapy [*Medicine*]
EAT .... Employment Appeal Tribunal [*British*]
EAT .... Encoder Address Translator
EAT .... End-Around Test
EAT .... Engineering Analysis Team [*NASA*]
EAT .... Environmental Acceptance Test (NASA)
EAT .... Estimated [*or Estimating*] Approach Time [*Aviation*] (FAAC)
EAT .... Ethiopia Aid Tonight [*Australia*]
EAT .... European Advertising Tripartite [*Brussels, Belgium*] (EA)
EAT .... European Association of Teachers [*See also AEDE*] (EAIO)

EAT .... Expected Approach Time [*Aviation*] (FAAC)
EAT .... Experimental Autoimmune Thymitis [*Medicine*]
EAT .... Experiments in Art and Technology (EA)
EAT .... External Air Transportability (MCD)
EAT .... PNR Food Industries Ltd. [*Toronto Stock Exchange symbol*]
EAT .... Wenatchee [*Washington*] [*Airport symbol*] (OAG)
EATA .... East Asia Travel Association (EAIO)
EATA .... Enhanced AT Attachment [*Data processing*]
EATB .... East Anglia Tourist Board [*British*] (DCTA)
EATBA8 ..... East African Tuberculosis Investigation Centre. Annual Report [*A publication*]
EATC .... Ecology and Analysis of Trace Contaminants [*Program*] [*Oak Ridge National Laboratory*] (IID)
EATC .... Ehrlich Ascites Tumor Cell [*Oncology*]
EATC .... Electronic Automatic Temperature Control [*Automotive engineering*]
EATCAB ..... Estacion Experimental Agricola de Tucuman. Circular [*A publication*]
Eat Cont ..... Eaton's Supplement to Chipman on Contracts [*A publication*] (DLA)
EATCS ...... European Association for Theoretical Computer Science (EAIO)
EATD .... Expanded Advanced Terminal Defense Study
EATDS .... Expanded Advanced Terminal Defense Study (MCD)
EATI .... Equipment and Tool Institute [*Glenview, IL*]
EATJP .... European Association for the Trade in Jute Products (EA)
EATM .... Edgewood Arsenal Technical Memorandum [*Army*]
EATMA7 ... Estacion Experimental Agricola de Tucuman. Publicacion Miscelanea [*A publication*]
EATMS ..... Electroacoustic Transmission Measuring System [*Telecommunications*] (TEL)
EATN .... Bank of East Tennessee [*Knoxville, TN*] [*NASDAQ symbol*] (NQ)
EATO .... Eaton Financial Corp. [*NASDAQ symbol*] (NQ)
EATO .... Euro-Asia Trade Organisation
EATP .... European Association for Textile Polyolefins (EAIO)
EATR .... Edgewood Arsenal Technical Report [*Army*]
EATR .... Enroute Air Traffic Regulation (MCD)
EATR .... Equilibrium Air Total Radiation
EATRAM ... East African Trypanosomiasis Research Organization. Annual Report [*A publication*]
EATS .... Eateries, Inc. [*Oklahoma City, OK*] [*NASDAQ symbol*] (NQ)
EATS .... Empire Air Training Scheme [*British military*] (DMA)
EATS .... Engine Acceleration Temperature Schedule
EATS .... Equipment Accuracy Test Station
EATS .... European Air Transport Service
EATS .... Extended Area Test System [*Navy*]
EATTA ...... East African Tea Trade Association (EA)
EAU .... American University, Washington, DC [*OCLC symbol*] (OCLC)
EAU .... Auchinoon [*Scotland*] [*Seismograph station code, US Geological Survey*] (SEIS)
e-au--- .... Austria [*MARC geographic area code*] [*Library of Congress*] (LCCP)
EAU .... Eau Claire [*Wisconsin*] [*Airport symbol*] (OAG)
EAU .... Emergency Accommodation Unit (ADA)
EAU .... Energy Absorbing Unit [*Automotive engineering*]
EAU .... Experimental Allergic Uveitis [*Ophthalmology*]
EAU .... Experimental Autoimmune Uveoretinitis [*Immunology*]
Eau Amenag Reg Provencale ... Eau et Amenagement de la Region Provencale [*A publication*]
E & AUC .... Grant's Error and Appeal Reports [*A publication*] (DLA)
EAUG .... European Atex Users Group [*Deventer, Netherlands*] (EAIO)
Eau Ind ...... Eau et l'Industrie [*A publication*]
EAUMAC ... Ecological Society of Australia. Memoirs [*A publication*]
EA-UPDS ... Encyclopedia of Associations: Updating Service [*A publication*]
Eau Que ...... Eau du Quebec [*A publication*]
EAUS .... Enterprise Association of the United States (EA)
EAUTC .... Engineer Aviation Unit Training Center [*Military*]
EAUXCP ... East Auxiliary Airborne Command Post (MCD)
EAV .... Bettles, AK [*Location identifier*] [*FAA*] (FAAL)
EAV .... Effective Angular Velocity
EAV .... Engine Assembly Vehicle
EAV .... Explosive-Actuated Valve
EAV .... Viner [*E. A.*] Holdings [*Toronto Stock Exchange symbol*]
EAVA .... European Association of Veterinary Anatomists (EA)
EAVC .... Edinburgh Artillery Volunteer Corps [*British military*] (DMA)
EAVE .... Experimental Autonomous Vehicle [*Underwater robot*]
EAVES ..... Eavesdropping (DLA)
EAVF .... Electrically Augmented Vacuum Filter [*Chemical engineering*]
EAVK .... Viner [*E. A.*] Holdings Ltd. [*Toronto, ON*] [*NASDAQ symbol*] (NQ)
EAVN .... Eaton Vance Corp. [*NASDAQ symbol*] (NQ)
EAVRBX ... East African Veterinary Research Organization. Annual Report [*A publication*]
EAW .... Easy Washer [*Laboratory science*]
EAW .... Electric Arc Weld
EAW .... Electrical Association for Women [*British*]
EAW .... Employment at Will
EAW .... Environmental Policy and Law [*A publication*]

EAWA	East Africa Wins Again [*Used by US Diplomatic Corps in Nairobi, Kenya, to express dispair at bureaucratic obstacles*]
EAWJAD..	East African Wildlife Journal [*A publication*]
EAWP.......	Eastern Atlantic War Plan [*NATO*] (NATG)
EAWR	Employment at Will Reporter [*A publication*] (DLA)
EAWS.......	East African Wildlife Society (EA)
EAX	Electronic Automatic Exchange [*See also ESS*] [*General Telephone & Electronics*] [*Telecommunications*]
EAZ	Empfindlicher Aufschlagzuender [*Superquick impact fuze*] [*German military - World War II*]
EAZ	Ethnographisch-Archaeologische Zeitschrift [*A publication*]
eb-----	Baltic States [*MARC geographic area code*] [*Library of Congress*] (LCCP)
EB	Die Heilige Schrift in Deutscher Uebersetzung. Echter-Bibel [*Wuerzburg*] [*A publication*] (BJA)
EB	Early Bargain [*Stock exchange term*] [*British*] (DCTA)
EB	Early Bronze [*Age*]
EB	Early Burst [*Premature explosion of a warhead*]
EB	EarthBank Association of North America (EA)
EB	Eastbound
EB	Eastern Buddhist [*A publication*]
EB	Educational Broadcasting [*A publication*]
EB	Ehrlich-Bober Financial Corp. [*AMEX symbol*] (SPSG)
EB	Electric Boat (MCD)
EB	Electricity Board [*British*]
EB	Electron Beam
EB	Elementary Body
E & B........	Ellis and Blackburn's English Queen's Bench Reports [*118-120 English Reprint*] [*A publication*] (DLA)
EB	Emergency Box (MCD)
EB	Emphysematous Bullae [*Pulmonary medicine*]
EB	Encyclopaedia Biblica [*A publication*]
EB	Encyclopaedia Britannica [*A publication*] (APTA)
EB	Encyclopaedia Britannica, Inc.
EB	Engine Bulletin (MCD)
EB	Engine Burn [*NASA*]
EB	Engineer Battalion [*Military*]
EB	Engineering Bulletin (MCD)
EB	English Baron (ROG)
EB	English Bible
EB	Enlistment Bonus [*Military*] (AABC)
EB	Environment and Behavior [*A publication*]
EBX	Environmental Buoy [*Marine science*] (MSC)
EB	Epidermolysis Bullosa [*Dermatology*]
EB	Epstein-Barr [*Virus*]
EB	Equipment Bay (KSC)
EB	Equipment Branch [*Air Force*] [*British*]
EB	Equipment Building (AAG)
EB	Erbium [*Chemical element*] [*Symbol is Er*] (ROG)
E-B	Estate-Bottling [*Wine*]
EB	Estradiol Benzoate [*Endocrinology*]
EB	Estudios Biblicos [*A publication*]
EB	Ethidium Bromide [*Trypanocide*] [*Also, ETB, Etd Br*] [*Biochemical analysis*]
EB	Ethylbenzene [*Organic chemistry*]
EB	Ethylene Bromide [*Same as DBE, EDB*] [*Organic chemistry*]
EB	Etudes Balzaciennes [*A publication*]
EB	Etudes Bibliques [*Paris*] [*A publication*]
EB	Evaluation Branch [*BUPERS*]
EB	Evan's Blue [*Fluorescent dye*]
EB	Everybody's Magazine [*A publication*] (APTA)
EB	Executive Board
EB	Executive Bulletin
EB	Expansion Bolt [*Technical drawings*]
EB	Experimental Buoy [*Marine science*] (MSC)
EB	[*The*] Expositor's Bible [*A publication*]
EB	Extended Benefits [*Unemployment insurance*]
EB	External Burning (RDA)
EB	Eyepiece Box
EB	Force Aerienne Belge [*Belgium*] [*ICAO designator*] (FAAC)
EB	L'Equilibre Biologique [*France*] [*Research code symbol*]
EB	Pennsylvania Commuter Airlines [*Airline code*]
EBA	Early Birds of Aviation (EA)
EBA	Ecole des Beaux Arts [*Paris, France*]
EBA	Edison Birthplace Association (EA)
EBA	Elba Island [*Italy*] [*Airport symbol*] [*Obsolete*] (OAG)
EBA	Electron Beam Accelerator
EBA	Emergency Breathing Apparatus
EBA	English Bowling Association
EBA	Enriched Brucella Blood Agar [*Culture media*]
EBA	Epizootic Bovine Abortion
EBA	Erythrocyte Binding Antigen [*Immunology*]
EBA	Ethoxybenzoic Acid [*Dental cement*]
EBA	Ethyl Bromoacetate [*Organic chemistry*]
EBA	Ethyl(butyl)amine [*Organic chemistry*]
EBA	Experimental Ballistics Associates (EA)
EBA	Experimental Behavioral Analyzer
EBAA	European Business Aviation Association (EAIO)
EBAA........	Eye Bank Association of America (EA)
EBADAS ...	Endocrine Bioassay Data [*A publication*]

EBAE........	European Bureau of Adult Education (EAIO)
EBAFE	Economic Bulletin for Asia and the Far East [*Later, Economic Bulletin for Asia and the Pacific*] [*A publication*]
EBAILL.....	European Bureau for the Allocation of International Long Lines (NATG)
EBAL........	Aalst [*Belgium*] [*ICAO location identifier*] (ICLI)
EBALD.......	Energy at Booz-Allen [*A publication*]
EBAM........	Amougies [*Belgium*] [*ICAO location identifier*] (ICLI)
EBAM	Electron-Beam-Addressed Memory [*Air Force*]
EBAP.........	Eldisine [*Vindesine*], BCNU [*Carmustine*], Adriamycin, Prednisone [*Antineoplastic drug regimen*]
EBAPS	Engine Bleed Air Precooler System
EBAW	Antwerp-Anvers [*Belgium*] [*ICAO location identifier*] (ICLI)
EBB...........	Economic Analysis and Workers' Management (Belgrade) [*A publication*]
EBB...........	Economic Bulletin Board [*Information service or system*] (EISS)
EBB...........	Eibei Bungaku [*British and American Literature: The Rikkyo Review of Arts and Letters*] [*A publication*]
EBB...........	Electronic Bulletin Board [*Department of Commerce*] [*Washington, DC*] [*Information service or system*] (IID)
EBB...........	Entebbe/Kampala [*Uganda*] [*Airport symbol*] (OAG)
EBB...........	European Brazilian Bank [*London, England*]
EBB...........	Evangelische Blaetter aus Bethlehem [*A publication*]
EBB...........	Extra Best Best [*Steel wire*]
EBBA........	Eastern Bird Banding Association (EA)
EBBA........	English Basket Ball Association
EBBA........	(Ethoxybenylidene)butylaniline [*Organic chemistry*]
EBBB........	Brussels [*Belgium*] [*ICAO location identifier*] (ICLI)
EB & BB	Eastbound Basing and Billing Book
EBBD........	Central Data Bank, EUROCONTROL [*Belgium*] [*ICAO location identifier*] (ICLI)
EBBE........	Beauvechain [*Belgium*] [*ICAO location identifier*] (ICLI)
EBBF	Equitable Benefit-Based Financing
EBBL	Klein Brogel [*Belgium*] [*ICAO location identifier*] (ICLI)
EBBR	Brussels/National [*Belgium*] [*ICAO location identifier*] (ICLI)
EBBS	Brussels [*Belgium*] [*ICAO location identifier*] (ICLI)
EBBS	Engineering Bulletin Board System
EBBSAA....	Entomologische Blaetter fuer Biologie und Systematik der Kaefer [*A publication*]
EBBT	Brasschaat [*Belgium*] [*ICAO location identifier*] (ICLI)
EBBU........	Brussels [*Belgium*] [*ICAO location identifier*] (ICLI)
EBBV........	Brussels [*Belgium*] [*ICAO location identifier*] (ICLI)
EBBX........	Bertrix [*Belgium*] [*ICAO location identifier*] (ICLI)
EBC...........	Bay Area Library and Information System [*Library network*]
EBC...........	Brevard Community College, Cocoa, FL [*OCLC symbol*] (OCLC)
EBC...........	Economic Bulletin/Warta Cafi [*A publication*]
EBC...........	Educational Broadcasting Corporation (EA)
EBC...........	Electron Beam Control
EBC...........	Electron Beam Curing [*Chemical technology*]
EBC...........	Electron Beam Cutting [*Engraving*] [*Welding*]
EBC...........	Electronic Batch Control
EBC...........	Employee Benefits Cases (DLA)
EBC...........	Emulated Buffer Computer (MCD)
EBC...........	Enamel Bonded Single Cotton [*Wire insulation*] (AAG)
EBC...........	End Breguet Cruise [*SST*]
EBC...........	Eugene Ballet Company [*Eugene, OR*]
EBC...........	European Bibliographical Center
EBC...........	European Billiards Confederation
EBC...........	European Brewery Convention
EBC...........	Expositor's Bible Commentary [*A publication*]
EBCA........	(Ethoxybenzylidene)cyanoaniline [*Also, PEBAB*] [*Organic chemistry*]
EBCA........	External Branch Condition Address [*Telecommunications*] (TEL)
EBCD........	Extended Binary-Coded Decimal [*Data processing*]
EBCDIC	Extended Binary-Coded Decimal Interchange Code [*Data processing*]
EBCE.........	Electron Beam Control Electronics
EBCE.........	Experience-Based Career Education
EBCE-MD ...	Experience-Based Career Education for Mentally Disabled Students (OICC)
EBCG.........	Experimental Buried Collector Gauge
EBCI.........	Charleroi/Gosselies [*Belgium*] [*ICAO location identifier*] (ICLI)
EBCI..........	Eagle Bancorp, Incorporated [*NASDAQ symbol*] (NQ)
EBCI..........	External Branch Condition Input [*Telecommunications*] (TEL)
EBCS.........	Electronic Business Communications System
EBCT.........	Empresa Brasileira de Correios e Telegrafos [*State enterprise*] [*Brazil*] (EY)
EBCT.........	Extended Battlefield Contact Team (MCD)
EBCV.........	Chievres [*Belgium*] [*ICAO location identifier*] (ICLI)
ebd.............	Ebenda (BJA)
EBD...........	Economic Batch Determination
EBD	Effective Billing Date (TEL)
EBD	El Obeid [*Sudan*] [*Airport symbol*] (OAG)
EBD	Epidermolysis Bullosa Dystrophia [*Dermatology*]
EBD	Equivalent Binary Digit
EBD	Eucaloric Balanced Diet
EBD	Eye Ball Down (MCD)

EBDC......... Enamel Bonded Double Cotton [*Wire insulation*]
EBDC......... Ethylenebis(dithiocarbamate) [*Organic chemistry*]
EBDD......... Epidermolysis Bullosa Dystrophic Dominant [*Dermatology*]
EBDI......... Electronic Business Document Interchange
EBDI......... External Breathing Direct Injection [*Chrysler Corp.*] [*Automotive engineering*]
EBDP......... Enamel Bonded Double Paper [*Wire insulation*]
EBDR........ Epidermolysis Bullosa Dystrophic Recessive [*Dermatology*]
EBDS........ Enamel Bonded Double Silk [*Wire insulation*]
e-be---......... Belgium [*MARC geographic area code*] [*Library of Congress*]   (LCCP)
EBE............ Economic Bulletin for Europe [*A publication*]
EBE............ Economic Outlook [*A publication*]
EBE............ Electron Beam Evaporator
EBE............ Electron Binding Energy
EB & E....... Ellis, Blackburn, and Ellis' English Queen's Bench Reports [*1858*] [*A publication*]   (DLA)
EBE............ Experimental Bridging Establishment [*British*]
EBEC......... Encyclopaedia Britannica Educational Corporation
EBEE......... Electron Beam Evaporation Equipment
EBEH........ Environment and Behavior [*A publication*]
EBEM........ Electron Beam Evaporation Module
EBERAS.... Event-by-Event Recording and Sorting [*Electronics*]
Ebersole..... Ebersole's Reports [*59-80 Iowa*] [*A publication*]   (DLA)
Ebersole (IA) ... Ebersole's Reports [*59-80 Iowa*] [*A publication*]   (DLA)
EbertRV..... Reallexikon der Vorgeschichte [*M. Ebert*] [*A publication*]   (BJA)
EBES .... Electric Beam Exposure System [*Integrated circuit*] [*Bell Laboratories*]
EBEUA...... Economic Bulletin for Europe [*A publication*]
EBF............ Economic and Business Foundation
EBF............ Electric Bomb Fuze   (NG)
EBF............ Electron-Bombardment Furnace
EBF............ Ennis Business Forms, Inc. [*NYSE symbol*]   (SPSG)
EB & F .... Equipment Blockages and Failures [*Telecommunications*]   (TEL)
EBF............ Erythroblastosis Fetalis [*Hematology*]
EBF............ Europaeische Baptistische Foderation [*European Baptist Federation - EBF*]   (EAIO)
EBF............ Europaeische Baptistische Frauenunion [*European Baptist Women's Union - EBWU*] [*Federal Republic of Germany*]   (EAIO)
EBF............ Externally Blown Flap [*Aviation*]
EBFA........ Electron Beam Fusion Accelerator
EBFBRG ... European Bank of Frozen Blood of Rare Groups [*Amsterdam, Netherlands*]   (EAIO)
EBFC........ Ed Bruce Fan Club   (EA)
EBFC......... Elvis Brothers Fan Club   (EA)
EBFC........ Eric Braeden Fan Club   (EA)
EBFG........ East Bay Fan Guild   (EA)
EBFN........ Koksijde [*Belgium*] [*ICAO location identifier*]   (ICLI)
EBFS .... Enclosure Building Filtration System   (IEEE)
EBFS .... Florennes [*Belgium*] [*ICAO location identifier*]   (ICLI)
EBFYC ...... European Baptist Federation Youth Committee   (EAIO)
EBG .... Economic Bulletin of Ghana [*A publication*]
EBG .... El Bagre [*Colombia*] [*Airport symbol*]   (OAG)
EBG .... Electron Beam Generator
EBG .... Electron Beam Gun
EBG .... Engin Blinde du Genie [*French*]
EBGB........ Brussels/Grimbergen [*Belgium*] [*ICAO location identifier*]   (ICLI)
EBGL........ Glons [*Belgium*] [*ICAO location identifier*]   (ICLI)
EBGT........ Gent/St. Denijs Westrem [*Belgium*] [*ICAO location identifier*]   (ICLI)
EBH........... Black Hill [*Scotland*] [*Seismograph station code, US Geological Survey*]   (SEIS)
EBH........... Epibromohydrin [*Organic chemistry*]
EBHN........ Hoevenen [*Belgium*] [*ICAO location identifier*]   (ICLI)
EBHP .... Ethylbenzene Hydroperoxide [*Organic chemistry*]
EBI............ Educational Broadcasting International [*A publication*]
EBI............ Effective Buying Income [*Portion of gross income after subtracting taxes, food, clothing, and housing expenditures*]
EBI............ Electronic Business [*A publication*]
EBI............ Emetine Bismuth Iodide [*Pharmacology*]
EBI............ Encyclopaedia Biblica [*A publication*]   (BJA)
EBI............ Energy Bibliography and Index [*Gulf Publishing Co.*] [*Houston, TX*] [*Information service or system*] [*A publication*]
EBI............ Equivalent Background Input
EBI............ Ergosterol Biosynthesis Inhibitor [*Biochemistry*]
EBI............ Estudios Biblicos [*A publication*]
EBI............ Everly Brothers International   (EA)
EBI............ Expanded Background Investigation   (AFM)
EBI............ Experience and Background Inventory [*Management and supervision test*]
EBI............ Eye Ball In
EBIB......... Encyclopaedia Biblica [*A publication*]
EBIB......... Energy Bibliography and Index [*Center for Energy and Mineral Resources - Texas A & M University*] [*College Station, TX*] [*Bibliographic database*]
EBib........... Estudios Biblicos [*A publication*]

E Bibl .... Estudios Biblicos [*A publication*]
EBIC .... EFTA [*European Free Trade Association*] Brewing Industry Council   (EAIO)
EBIC .... Electron-Beam-Induced Current [*Photovoltaic energy systems*]
EBIC .... Electron-Bombardment-Induced Conductivity
EBICON...... Electron-Bombardment-Induced Conductivity
EBIFC........ Elmer Bird International Fan Club   (EA)
EBII .... Electro-Biology, Incorporated [*NASDAQ symbol*]   (NQ)
EBIP .... European Biotechnology Information Project [*British Library*] [*Information service or system*]   (IID)
EBIPA ...... Enka Biniiru To Porima [*A publication*]
EBIS .... East Bay Information Service [*Library network*]
EBIS .... Electron Beam Ion Source   (IEEE)
EBIS .... Employee Benefits Infosource [*International Foundation of Employee Benefit Plans*] [*Information service or system*]   (CRD)
EBIS .... Employment Barrier Identification Scale [*Employment test*]
EBIS .... Encyclopedia of Business Information Sources [*A publication*]
EBIS .... ESCAP [*Economic and Social Commission for Asia and the Pacific*] Bibliographic Information System [*United Nations*] [*Thailand*] [*Information service or system*]   (IID)
EBIS .... Ethylenebisisothiocyanate Sulfide [*Organic chemistry*]
EBIS .... Exothermic Bimetallic Ignition System   (MCD)
EBIST........ Expert Bradley Infantry Squad Training Test [*Army*]   (INF)
EBIT......... Earnings before Interest and Taxes [*Accounting*]
EBIT......... Electron Beam Ion Trap [*Developed at Lawrence Livermore and Lawrence Berkeley National Laboratories*] [*Atomic physics*]
EBITS........ Estimated Earnings before Interest and Taxes
EBIV........ Electron-Beam-Induced Voltage [*Photovoltaic energy systems*]
EBJ .... Employee Benefits Journal [*A publication*]
EBJ .... Esbjerg [*Denmark*] [*Airport symbol*]   (OAG)
EBJ .... European Business Journal [*A publication*]
EBK .... Eastern Bakeries Ltd. [*Toronto Stock Exchange symbol*]
EBK .... Easy Bleaching Kraft [*Pulp and paper technology*]
EBK .... Embryonic Bovine Kidney
EBKC .... Eliot Savings Bank [*NASDAQ symbol*]   (NQ)
EBKH .... Balen/Keiheuvel [*Belgium*] [*ICAO location identifier*]   (ICLI)
EBKT .... Kortrijk-Wevelgem [*Belgium*] [*ICAO location identifier*]   (ICLI)
EBL........... Austin, TX [*Location identifier*] [*FAA*]   (FAAL)
EBL........... Broadlaw [*Scotland*] [*Seismograph station code, US Geological Survey*]   (SEIS)
EBL........... Eastern Basketball League
EBL........... Electric Heated Back Light [*Automotive engineering*]
EBL........... Electronic Bearing Line [*RADAR technology*]
EBL........... Encyclopaedia Biblica [*A publication*]   (ROG)
EBL........... Endemic Burkitt's Lymphoma [*Medicine*]
EBL........... Enzootic Bovine Leukemia
EBL........... Estimated Blood Loss [*Medicine*]
EBL........... European Bridge League   (EAIO)
EBL........... Event-Based Language [*1979*] [*Data processing*]   (CSR)
EBL........... Eye Ball Left   (MCD)
EBLAN...... Eblanencis [*Signature of the Bishops of Dublin*]   (ROG)
EBLB .... Elsenborn [*Belgium*] [*ICAO location identifier*]   (ICLI)
EBLG .... Liege/Bierset [*Belgium*] [*ICAO location identifier*]   (ICLI)
EBLH .... Liege/Bierset [*Belgium*] [*ICAO location identifier*]   (ICLI)
EBLUL...... European Bureau for Lesser Used Languages   (EA)
EBM .... Early-Break-Make [*Data processing*]
EBM .... Electron Beam Machining [*Manufacturing term*]
EBM .... Electron Beam Method
EBM .... Electron Beam Microanalysis
EBM .... Energy Balance Model [*Climatology*]
EBM .... Esen Bulak [*Mongolia*] [*Seismograph station code, US Geological Survey*] [*Closed*]   (SEIS)
EBM .... Estimation-before-Modeling   (MCD)
EBM .... Europaeische Baptistische Mission [*European Baptist Mission*] [*Federal Republic of Germany*]   (EAIO)
EBM .... European Baptist Mission   (EAIO)
EBM .... Expressed Breast Milk [*Medicine*]
EBM .... Extended Branch Mode
EBMA .... Elastic Braid Manufacturers Association [*Later, EFMC or EFMCNTA*]   (EA)
EBMA ...... Engine, Booster Maintenance Area
EBMB........ Melsbroek [*Belgium*] [*ICAO location identifier*]   (ICLI)
EBMD........ Electron Beam Mode Discharge
EBME........ Eagle's Basal Medium with Earle's Salts [*Culture medium*]
EBMI......... Brussels [*Belgium*] [*ICAO location identifier*]   (ICLI)
EBMI......... E & B Marine, Inc. [*NASDAQ symbol*]   (NQ)
EBMLM...... Electron Beam Membrane Light Modulator [*Army*]   (MCD)
EBMO........ Moorsele [*Belgium*] [*ICAO location identifier*]   (ICLI)
EBMOA .... Elektronika Bol'shikh Moshchnostei [*A publication*]
EBMT........ Munte [*Belgium*] [*ICAO location identifier*]   (ICLI)
EbN........... East by North
EBn .... Enchiridion Biblicum. Editionis Napoli/Roma [*A publication*]
EBN .... Endosperm Balance Number [*Genetics*]
EBN .... Essobron [*A publication*]
EBNA .... EBV [*Epstein-Barr Virus*] Nuclear Antigen [*Immunochemistry*]
EBNA .... Economisch Bulletin Nederlandse Antillen [*A publication*]
EBNA .... Epstein-Barr Nuclear Antigen [*Virus*] [*Immunology*]

EBNC .... Equitable Bancorporation [*NASDAQ symbol*]   (NQ)
EBND .... Eastbound   (FAAC)
EBNM .... Namur-Suarlee [*Belgium*] [*ICAO location identifier*]   (ICLI)
EBNY .... Edition Bookbinders of New York   (EA)
EBO .... Extrahepatic Biliary Obstruction [*Medicine*]
EBO .... Eye Ball Out
E/BOD ...... Electrolytic Biological Oxygen Demand
EBONTA .. (Ethylenebis(oxyethylenenitrilo))tetraacetic Acid [*Also, EGTA*] [*Organic chemistry*]
EBOR .... Eboracensis [*Signature of the Bishop of York*]   (ROG)
EBOR .... Eboracum [*York*] [*County in England*] [*Latin*]   (ROG)
EBOR .... Experimental Beryllium Oxide Reactor [*Later, BORE*]
EBOS .... Oostende [*Belgium*] [*ICAO location identifier*]   (ICLI)
EBP .... Electric Bilge Pump
EBP .... Epidural Blood Patch [*Medicine*]
EBP .... Estradiol-Binding Protein [*Biochemistry*]
EBP .... Explanation of Benefit Payment [*Insurance*]
EBP .... Extended Basal Period
EBPA .... Electron Beam Parametric Amplifier
EBPA .... Ethylbenzene Producers Association   (EA)
EBPG .... Electron Beam Pattern Generator
EBPI .... Employee Benefit Plans, Inc. [*NASDAQ symbol*]   (NQ)
EBPN .... Early Babylonian Personal Names [*A publication*]   (BJA)
EBPR .... Employee Benefit Plan Review [*A publication*]
EBPS .... European Baptist Press Service [*of the European Baptist Federation*]   (EAIO)
EBPSUSA ... El Bireh Palestine Society of the USA   (EA)
EBQ .... Experience and Background Questionnaire [*Test*]
Ebr .... De Ebrietate [*Philo*]   (BJA)
EBR .... Ebro [*Spain*] [*Geomagnetic observatory code*]
EBR .... Ebro Roquetas [*Tarragona*] [*Spain*] [*Seismograph station code, US Geological Survey*]   (SEIS)
EBR .... Educational Broadcasting Review [*A publication*]
EBR .... Electron Beam Readout
EBR .... Electron Beam Recorder [*or Recording*]
EBR .... Electron Beam Regulator
EBR .... Emergency Bomb Release   (CINC)
EBR .... Employee Benefit Research Institute. Research Report [*A publication*]
EBR .... Emulsion Butadiene Rubber
E BR .... Encyclopaedia Britannica [*A publication*]   (ROG)
EBR .... Epoxy Bridge Rectifier
EBR .... Experimental Breeder Reactor
EBR .... Eye Ball Right   (MCD)
EBRA .... Emergency Banking Relief Act
EBRA .... Engineer Buyers' and Representatives' Association [*British*]
EBra .... Estudos Brasileiros [*A publication*]
EBRD .... European Bank for Reconstruction and Development [*Economic assistance for Eastern Europe*] [*Proposed*]
EBRD .... Export Business Relations Division [*Department of Commerce*]
EBRG .... Earth-Based Radio Guidance
EBRI .... Employee Benefit Research Institute   (EA)
EBRS .... European Businessmen Readership Study [*Database*] [*Research Services Ltd.*] [*Information service or system*]   (CRD)
EBRSDP .... Experimental Brain Research. Supplementum [*A publication*]
EBS .... CANEBSCO Subscription Service Ltd. [*ACCORD*] [*UTLAS symbol*]
EBS .... Eagle Butte [*South Dakota*] [*Seismograph station code, US Geological Survey*]   (SEIS)
EbS .... East by South
EBS .... Eastern Baptist Theological Seminary, Philadelphia, PA [*OCLC symbol*]   (OCLC)
EBS .... Eastern Base Section [*Mediterranean and England*] [*Army*] [*World War II*]
EBS .... Eastern Bering Sea
EBS .... Edison Brothers Stores, Inc. [*NYSE symbol*]   (SPSG)
EBS .... Educational Broadcast Satellite   (MCD)
EBS .... Electric Brain Stimulator
EBS .... Electron Beam Semiconductor
EBS .... Electron Beam System
EBS .... Electron-Bombarded Semiconductor
EBS .... Electron-Bombardment Silicon   (KSC)
EBS .... Electronic Band Spectra
EB & S .... Ellis, Best, and Smith's English Queen's Bench Reports [*A publication*]   (DLA)
EBS .... Emergency Bed Service [*Medicine*]
EBS .... Emergency Borating System   (IEEE)
EBS .... Emergency Breathing Subsystem   (MCD)
EBS .... Emergency Broadcast System [*Formerly, CONELRAD*]
EBS .... Enamel Bonded Single Silk [*Wire insulation*]   (AAG)
EBS .... Engine Breather Separator
EBS .... Epidermolysis Bullosa Simplex [*Dermatology*]
EBS .... Ernest Bloch Society   (EA)
EBS .... Ethylene Bistearamide [*Organic chemistry*]
EBS .... Extruded Bar Solder
EBS .... Webster City, IA [*Location identifier*] [*FAA*]   (FAAL)
EBSA .... Estuarine and Brackish-Water Sciences Association   (EAIO)
EBS Bulletin ... Bulletin. Experimental Building Station [*A publication*]   (APTA)
EBSC .... Eibungaku Shicho [*Current Thoughts in English Literature*] [*A publication*]

Ebsco Bull Ser Changes ... Ebsco Bulletin of Serials Changes
EBSD .... European Business Services Directory [*A publication*]
EBSF .... National Black Survival Fund [*Acronym is based on former name, Emergency Black Survival Fund*]   (EA)
EBSH .... Saint-Hubert [*Belgium*] [*ICAO location identifier*]   (ICLI)
EBSI .... Eagle Bancshares, Incorporated [*Tucker, GA*] [*NASDAQ symbol*]   (NQ)
Ebs Inf .... Ebsworth on the Law of Infants [*A publication*]   (DLA)
EBSK .... Epidermolysis Bullosa Simplex-Koebner [*Dermatology*]
EBSK .... Erlanger Beitrage zur Sprach- und Kunstwissenschaft [*A publication*]
EBSL .... Zutendaal [*Belgium*] [*ICAO location identifier*]   (ICLI)
EBSLG ...... European Business School Librarians Group [*London Business School*] [*Information service or system*]   (IID)
EBSP .... Spa/La Sauveniere [*Belgium*] [*ICAO location identifier*]   (ICLI)
EBSR .... Engineer Boat and Shore Regiment [*Army*]
EB & SR ..... Engineer Boat and Shore Regiment [*Army*]
EBSR .... Eye-Bank for Sight Restoration   (EA)
EBSRVR .... East Bengal State Railway Volunteer Rifles [*British military*]   (DMA)
EBSS .... Education and Behavioral Sciences Section [*Association of College and Research Libraries*]
EBST .... Edinburgh Bibliographical Society. Transactions [*A publication*]
EBST .... Sint-Truiden [*Belgium*] [*ICAO location identifier*]   (ICLI)
EBSU .... Saint-Hubert [*Belgium*] [*ICAO location identifier*]   (ICLI)
EBSZ .... Semmerzake [*Belgium*] [*ICAO location identifier*]   (ICLI)
EBT .... Earth-Based Tug [*NASA*]
EBT .... Echelons Below Theater [*Military*]   (MCD)
EBT .... Electron Beam [*Fluorescence*] Technique
EBT .... Electron Beam Transmission
EBT .... Elmo Bumpy Torus [*Nuclear energy*]
EBT .... Enid Board of Trade   (EA)
EBT .... Epicardial Breakthrough [*Cardiology*]
EBT .... Etudes Balkaniques Tchecoslovaques [*A publication*]
EBT .... Examination Before Trial   (DHSM)
EBT .... Executive Business Transport [*Aircraft*]
EBT-1 .... Elmo Bumpy Torus-One   (MCD)
EBTA J .... EBTA [*Eastern Business Teachers Association*] Journal [*A publication*]
EBTA Y ..... EBTA [*Eastern Business Teachers Association*] Yearbook [*A publication*]
E B Tch ...... Etudes Balkaniques Tchecoslovaques [*A publication*]
EBTF .... ECC [*Emergency Control Center*] Bypass Test Facility [*Nuclear energy*]   (NRCH)
EBTG .... Everything But the Girl [*British band*]
EBTN .... Goetsenhove [*Belgium*] [*ICAO location identifier*]   (ICLI)
EBT-P .... Elmo Bumpy Torus-Proof of Principle   (MCD)
EBTR .... Electronic Bearing-Time Recorder
EBT-S .... Elmo Bumpy Torus-Scale   (MCD)
EBTTC ...... European Baptist Theological Teachers' Conference [*Hamburg, Federal Republic of Germany*]   (EAIO)
EBTX .... Theux-Verviers [*Belgium*] [*ICAO location identifier*]   (ICLI)
EBTY .... Tournai/Maubray [*Belgium*] [*ICAO location identifier*]   (ICLI)
e-bu--- .... Bulgaria [*MARC geographic area code*] [*Library of Congress*]   (LCCP)
EBU .... Economic Bulletin for Europe [*A publication*]
EBU .... Electronic Business [*A publication*]
EBU .... European Badminton Union   (EA)
EBU .... European Blind Union   (EA)
EBU .... European Boxing Union
EBU .... European Broadcasting Union [*Switzerland*]
EBU .... Eye Ball Up   (MCD)
EBU .... St. Etienne [*France*] [*Airport symbol*]   (OAG)
E Buddhist ... Eastern Buddhist [*A publication*]
EBUL .... Ursel [*Belgium*] [*ICAO location identifier*]   (ICLI)
EBUM .... Brussels [*Belgium*] [*ICAO location identifier*]   (ICLI)
EBUR .... Brussels [*Belgium*] [*ICAO location identifier*]   (ICLI)
EBU Rev ..... EBU [*European Broadcasting Union*] Review [*A publication*]
EBU Rev A ... EBU [*European Broadcasting Union*] Review. Part A [*A publication*]
EBU Rev Part A ... EBU [*European Broadcasting Union*] Review. Part A. Technical [*Switzerland*] [*A publication*]
EBU Rev Tech ... EBU [*European Broadcasting Union*] Review. Part A. Technical [*A publication*]
EBURN ..... Eburneus [*Made of Ivory*] [*Pharmacy*]   (ROG)
EBV .... Efferent Branchial Vein [*Anatomy*]
EBV .... Electron-Bombardment Vehicle
EBV .... Epstein-Barr Virus
EBV .... Estimated Blood Volume [*Hematology*]
EBVA .... Brussels [*Belgium*] [*ICAO location identifier*]   (ICLI)
EBVP .... Epidoxorubicin, Bleomycin, Vinblastine, Prednisone [*Antineoplastic drug regimen*]
EBVT .... Exterior Ballistic Verification Projectile   (MCD)
EBW .... Effective Bandwidth
EBW .... Electron Beam Welding   (MUGU)
EBW .... Exploding Bridge-Wire
EBWE .... Weelde [*Belgium*] [*ICAO location identifier*]   (ICLI)
EBW-HV ... Electron Beam Welding - High Vacuum
EBWM ...... Brussels [*Belgium*] [*ICAO location identifier*]   (ICLI)
EBW-MV .. Electron Beam Welding - Medium Vacuum

EBW-NV ...	Electron Beam Welding - Nonvacuum
EBWR.......	Experimental Boiling Water Reactor
EBWS.......	Exploding Bridge-Wire System [KSC]
EBWU	European Baptist Women's Union (EAIO)
EBY	European Blue Cross Youth Association (EAIO)
EBY	Neah Bay, WA [Location identifier] [FAA] (FAAL)
EBYC........	European Bureau for Youth and Childhood
EBYLA2	Embryologia [A publication]
EByz..........	Etudes Byzantines [A publication]
EBZ...........	Exercise Benefit Zone [Aerobic dance]
EBZH	Hasselt [Belgium] [ICAO location identifier] (ICLI)
EBZR.......	Zoersel [Belgium] [ICAO location identifier] (ICLI)
EBZW........	Genk/Zwartberg [Belgium] [ICAO location identifier] (ICLI)
EC	Ear Clamp [Medicine]
EC	Early Childhood (ADA)
EC	Early-Closing Day [British]
EC	Earth Closet [British] (ROG)
EC	East Carolina Railway [AAR code]
EC	East Central [Refers especially to London postal district]
EC	East Coast
EC	Eastern Cedar [Utility pole] [Telecommunications] (TEL)
EC	Eastern Central
EC	Eastern Command [British]
Ec	Ecclesiastes [Old Testament book] (BJA)
EC	Ecclesiastical Commissioner [British] (DAS)
EC	Echo-Cancellation [Data transmission] (BYTE)
EC	Echo Controller [Telecommunications] (TEL)
EC	Eclipse
EC	Eco Corp. [Toronto Stock Exchange symbol]
EC	Ecology [A publication]
EC	Ecology Center (EA)
EC	Economic Analysis [Program] [Department of State]
EC	Economica [A publication]
EC	Economics
EC	Economist [A publication]
Ec	Ecossais [Scottish] [French] [Freemasonry]
Ec	Ectoparasitic [Biology]
ec	Ecuador [MARC country of publication code] [Library of Congress] [IYRU nationality code] (LCCP)
EC	Ecuador [ANSI two-letter standard code] (CNC)
EC	Ecumenical Celebrations (EA)
EC	Eddy Current [Electromagnetism] (NRCH)
EC	Edge Connector
EC	Education Code (OICC)
EC	Education and Culture [A publication]
EC	Effective Concentration [Instrumentation]
EC	Effective Conductivity
EC	Ego Control [Psychology]
EC	Egypte Contemporaine [A publication]
EC	Ejection Click [Cardiology]
EC	Elder Craftsmen (EA)
EC	Election Cases [A publication] (DLA)
EC	Electric Cipher [or Coding] Machine Repairman [Navy rating]
EC	Electric Current
EC	Electrical Conductivity
EC	Electricity Commission [British] (DAS)
EC	Electricity Council [British]
EC	[The] Electrification Council
EC	Electrochemical [or Electrochemistry]
EC	Electrocoagulate
EC	Electroconductivity
EC	Electron Capture [Radioactivity]
EC	Electron Coupled (DEN)
EC	Electronic Calculator [or Computer] (BUR)
EC	Electronic Calibration
EC	Electronic Coding
EC	Electronic Combat
EC	Electronic Comparator
EC	Electronic Computer (MCD)
EC	Electronic Conductivity
EC	Electronic Counter
EC	Electronics Chassis
EC	Electronics and Control
EC	Element Contractor (NASA)
EC	Elevation Console
EC	Elvis in Canada [An association] (EAIO)
EC	Embarkation Commandant [Military] [British]
EC	Embryonal Carcinoma [Medicine]
EC	Emergency Capability
EC	Emergency Chaplain [Army] [British]
E/C	Emergency Charges
EC	Emergency Commission [British]
EC	Emergency Coordinator (CET)
EC	Eminent Chaplain [Freemasonry] (ROG)
EC	Eminent Commander [Freemasonry] (ROG)
EC	Eminent Conductor [Freemasonry] (ROG)
EC	Employment Code [IRS]
EC	Employment Counseling (OICC)
EC	Emulsible Concentrate
EC	Emulsifying Capacity [Food technology]
EC	En Cuenta [On Account] [Spanish] [Business term]

EC	Enamel Covered
EC	Enamel Single Cotton [Wire insulation] (AAG)
EC	Enciclopedia Cattolica [Vatican City] [A publication] (BJA)
E/C	Encoder Coupler (NASA)
EC	Encyclopedia Canadiana [A publication]
EC	Endothelial Cell [Medicine]
EC	Enemy Capabilities (MCD)
EC	Energy Charge
EC	Energy Corporation [Philippines] (DS)
EC	Engagement Controller [Navy] (NVT)
EC	Engelhard Corporation [Formerly, ENG] [NYSE symbol] (SPSG)
EC	Engine Change (MCD)
EC	Engine Control (MCD)
EC	Engine Cutoff [Aerospace] (MCD)
EC	Engineer Captain [Navy] [British]
E in C	Engineer-in-Charge [Army]
E in C	Engineer-in-Chief
EC	Engineer Circular [Army Corps of Engineers]
EC	Engineering Change (MCD)
EC	Engineering Cognizant Authority (MCD)
EC	Engineering Construction
E & C	Engineering and Construction
EC	Engineering Corps
EC	Engineering Critical (MCD)
EC	English Chancery (DLA)
EC	English Chancery Reports [American Reprint] [A publication] (DLA)
EC	English Conditions [Insurance]
EC	English Constitution (ADA)
EC	Entente Council [See also CE] (EAIO)
EC	Enteric Coated [Pharmacy]
EC	Entering Complaint [Medicine]
EC	Enterochromaffin Cells [Medicine]
EC	Entorhinal Cortex [Brain anatomy]
EC	Entries Closed (ROG)
EC	Entry Code [Data processing]
EC	Entry Controller
EC	Environment Canada
EC	Environment Condition (CAAL)
EC	Environmental Chamber (KSC)
EC	Environmental Complexity
EC	Environmental Control (KSC)
EC	Enzyme Commission [of the International Union of Biochemistry]
EC	EPCOT [Experimental Prototype Community of Tomorrow] Center [Walt Disney World]
EC	Epidermal Cell
EC	Epilepsy Concern Service Group (EA)
EC	Episcopal Church
EC	Episcopal Communicators (EA)
EC	Equation Cruncher [Data processing]
E/C	Equipment or Component
EC	Equipment Controller (CET)
EC	Erection Computer
EC	Ergocryptine [Organic chemistry]
EC	Erosion Control [Type of water project]
EC	Error Code [Data processing]
E/C	Error Correcting [or Correction] [Data processing]
EC	Erythrocyte Creatine [Clinical chemistry]
EC	Escherichia Coli [Microorganism]
EC	Escort Convoy (CINC)
EC	Essays in Criticism [A publication]
EC	Essentiality Code (NASA)
EC	Established Church
EC	Estudios Clasicos [A publication]
E-C	Ether-Chloroform [Mixture]
EC	Ethyl Corporation (KSC)
EC	Etling Clearinghouse (EA)
EC	Eton College [Great Britain] (ROG)
EC	Etudes Celtiques [A publication]
EC	EURAIL [Eoropean Railway] Community (EAIO)
EC	Euro-Children (EAIO)
EC	Eurocard [Credit card] [British] (ADA)
EC	Eurocheque [Credit card] [British]
EC	EuroCity [Railroad]
ec-----	Europe, Central [MARC geographic area code] [Library of Congress] (LCCP)
EC	European Cellars [Commercial firm] [British]
EC	European Commission
EC	European Communities [An association] (EAIO)
EC	European Community [Collective name given to the consolidation of the European Coal and Steel Community, the Common Market, and the European Atomic Energy Community] (KSC)
EC	European Companions (EAIO)
EC	Evaluation Center (NATG)
EC	Evangelicals Concerned (EA)
EC	Events Controller (MCD)
EC	Events Coupler (MCD)
EC	Ex Commissione [Upon Order]

EC .... Ex-Coupon [*Investment term*]
EC .... Examining Circulars
EC .... Excellent Companion [*Freemasonry*] (ROG)
EC .... Excellent Condition [*Doll collecting*]
EC .... Exceptional Children Abstracts [*A publication*] (IID)
EC .... Exchange Chromatography
E-C .... Excitation-Contraction [*Physiology*]
EC .... Excretory Cell
EC .... Executive Committee (NATG)
EC .... Executive Council (ADA)
EC .... Exempli Causa [*For the Sake of Example*] [*Latin*]
EC .... Exercise Commander [*NATO*] (NATG)
EC .... Exhaust Closes [*Valve position*]
EC .... Expansive Classification
EC .... Experiment Canister (MCD)
EC .... Experiment Computer (MCD)
EC .... Experimentation Command [*Army*] (MCD)
EC .... Expiratory Center [*Physiology*]
EC .... Explorers Club (EA)
EC .... Extended Control [*Mode*] [*Data processing*]
EC .... Extended Coverage [*Insurance*]
EC .... Extension and Conversion [*Public buildings*]
EC .... Extension Course
EC .... Exterior Closet (ADA)
EC .... External Combustion
EC .... Extra Control [*Wire*] [*Telecommunications*] (TEL)
EC .... Extra Coordination
EC .... Extracellular [*Hematology*]
EC .... Extracranial [*Medicine*]
EC .... Eye Care (EA)
EC .... Eyes Closed [*Ataxia*]
EC .... Journal of Educational Computing Research [*A publication*]
EC .... Ontario Election Cases [*1884-1900*] [*Canada*] [*A publication*] (DLA)
EC .... Spain [*Aircraft nationality and registration mark*] (FAAC)
EC .... Travelair GmbH & Co. KG [*West Germany*] [*ICAO designator*] (FAAC)
EC .... Worthington Biochemical Corp. [*Research code symbol*]
EC-1 .... Emission Control 1 Gasoline [*ARCO*]
EC$_{50}$ .... Effective Concentration at which Light Emission Is Reduced by 50% [*Instrumentation*]
EC$_{50}$ .... Effective Concentration, Median Value
ECA .... Department of Economic Affairs of the United Nations
ECA .... Eagle Commuter Airlines [*Brownwood, TX*] [*FAA designator*] (FAAC)
ECA .... Early Closing Association [*British*]
ECA .... Early Comparability Analysis (RDA)
ECA .... Earth Central Angle
ECA .... Eastern Central Motor Carriers Association, Agent, Akron OH [*STAC*]
ECA .... Economic Commission for Africa [*Addis Ababa, Ethiopia*] [*See also CEA*] [*United Nations*] (EAIO)
ECA .... Economic Control Agency [*Allied German Occupation Forces*]
ECA .... Economic Cooperation Act [*of 1948*]
ECA .... Economic Cooperation Administration [*Administered aid under Marshall Plan; abolished, 1951*]
ECA .... Economic Information on Argentina [*A publication*]
Eca .... Economica [*A publication*]
ECA .... Ecumenical Clergy Association [*Later, AGEI*] (EA)
ECA .... Educational Centres Association [*British*]
ECA .... Educational Communication Association (EA)
ECA .... Eigenvalue Change Analysis
ECA .... El Cajon [*California*] [*Seismograph station code, US Geological Survey*] [*Closed*] (SEIS)
ECA .... El Camino Resources, Inc. [*Vancouver Stock Exchange symbol*]
ECA .... Electrical Control Activity (MCD)
ECA .... Electronic Confusion Area
ECA .... Electronic Control Amplifier (MCD)
ECA .... Electronic Control Assembly [*Ford Motor Co.*]
ECA .... Elsa Clubs of America (EA)
ECA .... Embroidery Council of America (EA)
ECA .... Engine Computer Assembly [*Automotive engineering*]
ECA .... Engineering Change Analysis
ECA .... Engineering Change Announcement
ECA .... Engineering Change Authorization
ECA .... Engineering Contractors Association (EA)
ECA .... English Curling Association
ECA .... Ensign Class Association (EA)
ECA .... Enter Control Area [*Aviation*]
ECA .... Environmental Control Administration [*Later, EPA*]
ECA .... Epoxy Curing Agent
ECA .... Equipment Condition Analysis (MSA)
ECA .... Ericson Class Association (EA)
ECA .... Estudios Centroamericanos [*A publication*]
ECA .... Ethacrynic Acid [*Biochemistry*]
ECA .... Ethylcarboxylate Adenosine [*Biochemistry*]
ECA .... Europe China Association (EA)
ECA .... European Choral Association (EA)
ECA .... European Civil Affairs
ECA .... European Commission on Agriculture [*FAO*] [*United Nations*]
ECA .... European Communications Area [*Military*]

ECA .... European Confederation of Agriculture
ECA .... Evangelical Church Alliance (EA)
ECA .... Exceptional Circumstances Allowance [*Legal term*] (DLA)
ECA .... Exchange Carrier Association (EA)
ECA .... Executive Chef Association [*Defunct*] (EA)
ECA .... Explosives Corporation of America (MCD)
ECA .... Export Control Act (MCD)
ECAB .... Employees' Compensation Appeals Board [*Department of Labor*]
ECAB .... Engineering Committee for the American Bicentennial
ECAB .... Executive Committee of the Army Board [*British*]
ECAC .... Eastern College Athletic Conference (EA)
ECAC .... Electromagnetic Compatibility Analysis Center [*Illinois Institute of Technology*] [*Annapolis, MD*]
ECAC .... Engineering College Administrative Council
ECAC .... European Civil Aviation Conference [*See also CEAC*] (EAIO)
ECAD .... Electronic Computer-Aided Design [*Data processing*] (BYTE)
ECAD .... Engineer Control and Advisory Detachment [*Air Force*]
ECAD .... European Civil Affairs Division [*US Military Government, Germany*]
ECAD .... Existing Chemical Assessment Division [*Environmental Protection Agency*]
ECADR ...... Nordic Council for Alcohol and Drug Research (EA)
ECAE .... Educational Center for Applied Ekistics (EA)
ECAF .... Excess Cost Adjudication Function [*Army*]
ECAFE ...... Economic Commission for Asia and the Far East [*Later, ESCAP*] [*United Nations*]
ECAHTI .... European Committee for Agricultural and Horticultural Tools and Implements (EA)
ECAL .... Equipment Calibration [*Military*] (NVT)
E (Callao).. Estudios (Callao, Argentina) [*A publication*]
ECAM .... Electronic Centralized Aircraft Monitoring System
ECAMA .... European Citric Acid Manufacturers Association [*of the European Council of Chemical Manufacturers' Federations*] (EAIO)
ECAMWP ... European Committee of Associations of Manufacturers of Welding Products (EA)
Ec An .... Economic Analysis [*A publication*]
ECAN .... Electronic Calibration and Normalization (KSC)
ECAN .... Electronic Consumer Advertising Network [*Data Corporation of America*]
Ec Ant Nimes ... Ecole Antique de Nimes. Bulletin Annuel [*A publication*]
ECAO .... Environmental Criteria and Assessment Office [*Environmental Protection Agency*] (GRD)
ECAO/CIN ... Environmental Criteria and Assessment Office, Cincinnati [*Ohio*] [*Environmental Protection Agency*] (GRD)
ECAO/RTP ... Environmental Criteria and Assessment Office, Research Triangle Park [*North Carolina*] [*Environmental Protection Agency*] (GRD)
ECAP .... Electric Companies' Advertising Program
ECAP .... Electrical [*or Electronic*] Circuit Analysis Program
ECAP .... Electronic Control Analyzer and Programmer [*Automotive engineering*]
ECAP .... Energy Crisis Assistance Program [*Federal government*]
ECAP .... Enhanced Cobra Armament Program [*Military*]
ECAP .... Environmental Compatibility Assurance Program [*Navy*]
ECAPE ...... Exploratory Committee on Assessing the Progress of Education [*Later, NAEP*]
Ec Appl ...... Economie Appliquee [*A publication*]
ECAR .... East Central Area Reliability Coordination Agreement [*Regional power council*]
ECAR .... Electronic Control Assembly - Roll (KSC)
ECAR .... European Civil Affairs Regiment
ECARL ...... Expendable Cluster Aircraft Rocket Launcher
ECarm .... Ephemerides Carmeliticae [*A publication*]
ECARS ...... Electronic Coordinatograph and Readout System
ECAS .... Energy Conversion Alternatives Study [*NASA*]
ECAS .... Enhanced Cobra/TOW [*Tube-Launched, Optically-Tracked, Wire-Guided*] Armament System [*Military*] (MCD)
ECAS .... Experiment Computer Application Software (MCD)
ECASS ...... Electronically Controlled Automatic-Switching System (DEN)
ECASS ...... Export Control Automated Support System [*Department of Commerce*]
ECASTAR ... Energy Conservation Assessment of Systems, Technologies, and Requirements
ECAT .... Ecole d'Appui Tactique [*French*]
EC-AT .... Electronically Controlled Automatic Transmission [*Mazda*] [*Automotive engineering*]
ECAT .... Emergency Committee for American Trade (EA)
ECAT .... Emission Computerized Axial Tomography
ECAT .... Equipment Category
ECATRA ... European Car and Truck Rental Association (EA)
ECATS ...... Expandable Computerized Automatic Test System (MCD)
E Catt .... Enciclopedia Cattolica [*A publication*]
ECAW .... European Council for Animal Welfare (EA)
ECB .... Echelons Corps Level and Below [*Military*]
ECB .... Echo de la Bourse [*A publication*]
ECB .... Eddy Current Brake [*Mechanical engineering*]
ECB .... Electrically Controlled Birefringence [*Telecommunications*] (TEL)

ECB............	Encontros com a Civilizacao Brasileira Editora Civilizacao Brasileira [*A publication*]
ECB............	Engineer Construction Battalion (CINC)
ECB............	Engineering Control Board (AAG)
ECB............	Environment Coordination Board [*United Nations*]
ECB............	Equipment Control Board (KSC)
ECB............	Estudos de Castelo Branco [*A publication*]
ECB............	Etched Circuit Board
ECB............	European Central Bank
ECB............	European Congress of Biotechnology
ECB............	European Coordination Bureau for International Youth Organizations [*See also BEC*] (EAIO)
ECB............	European Corn Borer [*Agronomy*]
ECB............	Event Control Block [*Data processing*] (BUR)
ECB............	Events Control Buffer [*NASA*] (NASA)
ECB............	Export Control Bulletin [*Department of Commerce*]
ECB............	Newcombe, KY [*Location identifier*] [*FAA*] (FAAL)
ECB............	Quarterly Review of Economics and Business [*A publication*]
ECBA.........	Eastern Coast Breweriana Association (EA)
ECBA.........	Eastern College Basketball Association (EA)
ECBA.........	European Communities Biologists Organization [*University of Bremen*] (EAIO)
ECBC.........	Empress Chinchilla Breeders Cooperative (EA)
ECBF.........	E. C. Brown Foundation (EA)
ECBF.........	Episcopal Church Building Fund (EA)
ECBM........	Episcopal Commission for Black Ministries (EA)
ECBMD......	Emergency Committee to Boycott Mother's Day
ECBO........	Enterocytopathogenic Bovine Virus
ECBO........	European Cell Biology Organization (EAIO)
ECBOA......	Economic Botany [*A publication*]
ECBOA5....	Economic Botany [*A publication*]
ECB-P........	Excellence-in-Competition Badge (Pistol) [*Military decoration*]
ECB-R........	Excellence-in-Competition Badge (Rifle) [*Military decoration*]
ECBS.........	Engineer Combat Battalions (CINC)
E & CB1S...	Edge and Center Bead on One Side [*Technical drawings*]
E & CB2S...	Edge and Center Bead on Two Sides [*Technical drawings*]
ECBTE.......	European Committee for Building Technical Equipment [*See also CEETB*] (EAIO)
ECBU	Economic Bulletin. Bank of Norway [*A publication*]
ECBUAN ..	Eczacilik Bulteni [*A publication*]
ECBUDQ ..	Ecological Bulletins - NFR [*Statens Naturvetenskapliga Forskningsrad*] [*A publication*]
Ec Bul Eur ...	Economic Bulletin for Europe [*A publication*]
ECBV.........	Effective Circulating Blood Volume [*Physiology*]
ECC	East Carolina College [*Later, ECU*] [*North Carolina*]
ECC	East Coast Carriers Conference, New York NY [*STAC*]
ECC	Eastern Claims Conference (EA)
ECC	ECC International Ltd. [*Formerly, Educational Computer Corp.*] [*NYSE symbol*] (SPSG)
ECC	Eccentric (AAG)
Ecc.............	Ecclesiastes [*Old Testament book*] (BJA)
ECC	Economic Commentary. Federal Reserve Bank of Cleveland [*A publication*]
ECC	Economic Council of Canada
ECC	Eddy Current Clutch [*Mechanical engineering*]
ECC	Effective Creep Compliance
ECC	El Camino College [*Torrance, CA*]
ECC	El Centro [*California*] [*Seismograph station code, US Geological Survey*] [*Closed*] (SEIS)
ECC	Electricity Consumers' Council [*British*]
ECC	Electrocardiocorder [*Medicine*]
ECC	Electrochemical Cathodes (MCD)
ECC	Electronic Calibration Center [*National Institute of Standards and Technology*]
ECC	Electronic Carburetor Control [*Automotive engineering*]
ECC	Electronic Common Control [*Telecommunications*] (TEL)
ECC	Electronic Components Code (NATG)
ECC	Electronic Components Conference
ECC	Elgin Community College [*Illinois*]
ECC	Ellsworth Community College [*Iowa*] [*Formerly, EJC*]
ECC	Emergency Cardiac Care
ECC	Emergency Combat Capability
ECC	Emergency Conservation Committee [*Defunct*]
ECC	Emergency Control Center (CINC)
ECC	Emergency Core Cooling [*or Coolant*] [*Nuclear energy*]
ECC	Employees' Compensation Commission
ECC	End Conscription Campaign [*South African*]
ECC	Energy Conservation Caucus (EA)
ECC	Energy Conservation Coalition (EA)
ECC	Energy Conservation Council
ECC	Energy Content Curve (NOAA)
ECC	Engineering Casualty Control [*Military*] (NVT)
ECC	Engineering Change Control
ECC	Engineering Change Coordination (MCD)
ECC	Engineering Critical Component (KSC)
ECC	English Ceramic Circle [*London, England*]
ECC	English Chamber Choir
ECC	English China Clays PLC (ECON)
ECC	Enlisted Classification Code
ECC	Enlisted Correspondence Course
ECC	Environmental Control Canister
ECC	Equatorial Communications Company [*Mountain View, CA*] [*Telecommunications*] (TSSD)
ECC	Equatorial Countercurrent [*Oceanography*]
ECC	Equipment Category Code [*Military*] (AABC)
ECC	Equipment Configuration Control (AAG)
ECC	Eras of the Christian Church [*A publication*]
ECC	Error Checking and Correction [*Data processing*]
ECC	Error Correction Capability [*Computer software quality*]
ECC	Error Correction Code
ECC	Ertl Collectors Club [*Commercial firm*] (EA)
ECC	Escherichia Coli [*Microorganism*]
ECC	Esperanto Cultural Centre (EAIO)
ECC	Essex Community College, James A. Newpher Library, Baltimore, MD [*OCLC symbol*] (OCLC)
ECC	Estimated Correction Cost (MCD)
ECC	Ethiopian Collectors Club (EA)
ECC	Eton College Chronicle [*A publication*] [*British*]
ECC	Eurasian Communist Countries (MCD)
ECC	European Communist Countries (MCD)
ECC	European Community Commission (MCD)
ECC	European Coordinating Committee
ECC	European Corsetry Commission (EAIO)
ECC	European Cultural Centre [*Geneva, Switzerland*]
ECC	Everett Community College [*Formerly, EJC*] [*Washington*]
ECC	Ex-Communist Country
ECC	Exceptional Child Center [*Utah State University*] [*Research center*] (RCD)
ECC	Exchange Control Copy [*Business term*] (DS)
ECC	Excitement, Choreiform Movements, and Circling [*Characterizations of a medical syndrome*]
ECC	Expanded Community Calling [*Telecommunications*] (TEL)
ECC	Experimental Computer Complex
ECC	Exposition and Conference Council (EA)
ECC	External Chest Compression [*Medicine*]
ECC	Extracorporeal Circulation [*Medicine*]
ECCA........	Electronic Component Checkout Area (AAG)
ECCA........	European Coil Coating Association
ECCAA......	Executive Chefs de Cuisine Association of America [*Later, Chefs de Cuisine Association of America*] (EA)
Ecc & Ad	Spinks' English Ecclesiastical and Admiralty Reports [*1853-55*] [*A publication*] (DLA)
ECCAD5....	EORTC [*European Organization for Research on Treatment of Cancer*] Cancer Chemotherapy Annual [*A publication*]
ECCAI.......	European Coordinating Committee for Artificial Intelligence (EAIO)
ECCANE...	East Coast Conference on Aerospace and Navigational Electronics (MCD)
ECCAS	Economic Community of Central African States [*See also CEEAC*] [*Bangui, Central African Republic*] (EAIO)
ECCAS	Engineer Command and Control Automation System [*Army*] (RDA)
ECCB.........	Eastern Caribbean Central Bank (EAIO)
ECCB.........	Electronic Components Certification Board (EA)
ECCB.........	Engineering Change Control Board (NASA)
ECCC.........	Ecology Center Communications Council [*Defunct*] (EA)
ECCC.........	European Command Coordination Committee [*Military*] (AABC)
ECCC.........	European Communities Chemistry Committee (EA)
ECCCS	Emergency Command Control Communications System
ECCCS	European Command and Control Console System [*DoD*]
ECCDA......	Eastern Connecticut Clam Diggers Association [*Defunct*] (EA)
ECCE.........	ECC Energy Corp. [*NASDAQ symbol*] (NQ)
ECCE.........	Extracapular Cataract Extraction [*Ophthalmology*]
ECCFD......	European Commission for the Control of Foot-and-Mouth Disease
ECC HOM ...	Ecce Homo [*Behold the Man*] [*Latin*] (ROG)
ECCI..........	Experimental Consultative Conference of Industrialists (NATG)
ECCJ	European Communities Court of Justice (DLA)
Eccl	Ecclesiastes [*Old Testament book*]
ECCL.........	Ecclesiastical
Eccl	Ecclesiazusae [*of Aristophanes*] [*Classical studies*] (OCD)
ECCL.........	Essex County Cooperating Libraries [*Library network*]
ECCL.........	Scriptores Ecclesiastici [*Ecclesiastical Authors*] [*Latin*] (ROG)
Eccl & Ad	Ecclesiastical and Admiralty [*Legal term*] (DLA)
Eccl & Ad	Spinks' English Ecclesiastical and Admiralty Reports [*A publication*] (DLA)
Eccl & Adm ...	Spinks' Ecclesiastical and Admiralty [*Upper Canada*] [*A publication*] (DLA)
Eccles	Ecclesiastes [*Old Testament book*]
ECCLES....	Ecclesiastical
EcclesR	Ecclesiastes Rabbah (BJA)
Eccl R.........	English Ecclesiastical Reports [*A publication*] (DLA)
Eccl Rep......	Ecclesiastical Reports [*England*] [*A publication*] (DLA)
Eccl Rev	Ecclesiastical Review [*A publication*]
ECCLS.......	European Committee for Clinical Laboratory Standards [*Kent, England*]
Eccl Stat....	Ecclesiastical Statutes [*A publication*] (DLA)
Ecclus.........	Ecclesiasticus [*Old Testament book*] [*Apocrypha*]
ECCM	East Caribbean Common Market (DS)
ECCM	Electronic Counter-Countermeasures [*Military*]

ECCMO .... Electronic Counter-Countermeasures Operator
          [*Military*]   (CET)
ECCND ..... Electric Comfort Conditioning News [*A publication*]
ECCO .... European Conference of Conscripts Organisations   (EAIO)
ECCO .... European Culture Collections' Organization   (EAIO)
ECCOIL .... Eastern Construction Company in Laos   (CINC)
ECCP .... East Coast Coal Port [*Shipping*] [*British*]
ECCP .... Engineering Concepts Curriculum Project
ECCP .... European Chamber of Commerce of the Philippines   (DS)
ECCP .... European Committee on Crime Problems
ECCP .... Executive Committee on Commercial Policy [*Abolished, 1944*]
Ec Cred ..... Economia e Credito [*A publication*]
ECCS .... Economic Hundred Call Seconds [*Telecommunications*]   (TEL)
ECCS .... Electronic Concentrated Control System [*Computerized car fuel
          system*]
ECCS .... Emergency Core-Cooling System [*Nuclear energy*]
ECCS .... Engineer Command and Control System [*Software*]
ECCS .... European Committee for Consultant Services   (EA)
ECCSL...... Emitter-Coupled Current-Steered Logic [*Electronics*]   (MSA)
ECCTIS ..... Educational Counselling and Credit Transfer Information
          Service [*Information service or system*]   (IID)
ECCTO...... European Community Cocoa Trade Organization   (EAIO)
ECCTT ...... Engineering Casualty Control Training Team [*Navy*]
ECCVBW .. Ecologie et Conservation [*A publication*]
ECCVBW .. Ecology and Conservation [*A publication*]
ECD .... Early-Closing Day [*British*]
ECD .... Educational and Cultural Development Program
ECD .... Effective Cutoff Diameter [*Particulate measurement*]
ECD .... Efficiency of Conversion of Digested Material [*Physiology*]
ECD .... Electric Control Drive
ECD .... Electrochemical Deburring
ECD .... Electrochromic Display [*Instrumentation*]
EC & D...... Electromagnetic Cover and Deception   (MCD)
ECD .... Electron-Capture Detection [*Instrumentation*]
ECD .... Electronic Communications Division [*Air Force*]   (AFM)
ECD .... Elk Chute Ditch [*Missouri*] [*Seismograph station code, US
          Geological Survey*]   (SEIS)
ECD .... Emergency Category Designation
ECD .... Endocardial Cushion Defect
ECD .... Endothelial Cell Density [*Anatomy*]
ECD .... Energy Conversion Devices, Inc.
E-in-CD ..... Engineer-in-Chief's Department [*British military*]   (DMA)
ECD .... Engineering Control Drawing   (MCD)
ECD .... Enhanced Color Display [*Computer monitor*]
ECD .... Enhanced Console Driver [*Data processing*]
ECD .... Entry Corridor Display   (KSC)
ECD .... Environmental Conditions Determination   (AAG)
ECD .... Episcopal Conference of the Deaf   (EA)
ECD .... Equal Charge Displacement [*Fission*]
ECD .... Equivalent Current Dipole [*Magnetism*]
ECD .... Error Control Device   (TEL)
ECD .... Estimated Completion Date
ECD .... Ethoxycoumarin Deethylase [*An enzyme*]
ECD .... European Communications Division [*Military*]
ECD .... Except Change Departure to Read [*Aviation*]   (FAAC)
ECD .... Prospect, AK [*Location identifier*] [*FAA*]   (FAAL)
ECDA .... Engine Control Development Area   (KSC)
EC & DB.... Encourage Coughing and Deep Breathing [*Medicine*]
ECDC .... Early Child Development and Care [*A publication*]
ECDC .... Economic Cooperation among Developing Countries [*United
          Nations*]
ECDC .... Electrochemical Diffused-Collector Transistor
ECDC .... Energy Capital Development Corporation [*NASDAQ
          symbol*]   (NQ)
ECDC .... Engineering Configuration Data Control   (AAG)
ECDC .... External Countdown Clock
ECDCAD... Early Child Development and Care [*A publication*]
ECDCC...... Early Childhood Day Care Center [*University of Alabama*]
          [*Research center*]   (RCD)
Ec Dev Cult Change ... Economic Development and Cultural Change [*A
          publication*]
ECDFTT ... Employment-Corrected Double Factorial Terms of Trade
          [*Economics*]
ECDG .... Electrochemical Discharge Grinding [*Manufacturing term*]
ECDGF...... Embryonal Carcinoma Derived Growth Factor [*Biochemistry*]
ECDGF...... Endothelial Cell-Derived Growth Factor [*Biochemistry*]
ECDIN ...... Environmental Chemicals Data and Information Network
          [*Commission of the European Communities*] [*Chemical
          databank*]   (IID)
ECDMMRL ... European Committee for the Development of the Meuse and
          Meuse/Rhine Links   (EAIO)
ECDO .... Electronic Community Deal Office
          [*Telecommunications*]   (TEL)
ECDO .... Enterocytopathogenic Dog Orphan Virus
ECDU .... Electrical Coupling Display Unit   (KSC)
ECDU .... European Christian Democratic Union [*Brussels, Belgium*]
          [*Political party*]   (EAIO)
ECE.......... Early Childhood Education
ECE.......... Echo Control Equipment [*Telecommunications*]   (TEL)
ECE.......... Economic Commission for Europe [*United Nations*]
          [*Switzerland*]   (IRC)

ECE.......... Economic Coverage Endorsement
ECE.......... Eddy Current Energy
ECE.......... El Campo, TX [*Location identifier*] [*FAA*]   (FAAL)
ECE.......... Electrical Checkout Equipment   (KSC)
ECE.......... Electrochemical, Chemical, Electrochemical [*Chemical
          mechanism*]
ECE.......... Element Characteristics Equation
ECE.......... Engineering Capacity Exchange   (IEEE)
ECE.......... Environmental Contaminant Evaluation [*Fish and Wildlife
          Service program*]
ECE.......... Environmental Control Equipment
ECE.......... Episcopal Center for Evangelism   (EA)
ECE.......... European Commodities Exchange [*of the European Economic
          Community*]   (EA)
ECE.......... Experiment Checkout Equipment   (MCD)
ECE.......... Export Council for Europe   (ILCA)
ECE.......... Extended Coverage Endorsement [*Insurance*]
ECE.......... External Combustion Engine [*Steam bus*]
ECEA .... Exceptional Child Education Abstracts [*Later, ECER*] [*A
          publication*]
ECEBA ..... Energy Conservation in Existing Buildings Act of 1976
ECEC........ Effective Cation and Exchange Capacity [*Soil science*]
ECE Chem ... Annual Review of the Chemical Industry, 1981. Economic
          Commission for Europe [*A publication*]
ECEF .... Earth-Centered, Earth-Fixed
ECEFP....... Executive Committee on Economic Foreign Policy
          [*Terminated*]   (EGAO)
ECEJAETA ... European Chamber of Extra-Judicial Adjudicators and Expert
          Technical Advisers [*See also CEASPECT*]   (EA)
ECEL........ Epithermal Critical Experiment Laboratory [*Nuclear energy*]
ECELL ...... Electrochemical Cell   (MCD)
ECelt .... Etudes Celtiques [*A publication*]
ECENGR... Electronic Engineer   (FAAC)
E Cent .... Eighteenth Century [*A publication*]
E Cent Eur ... East Central Europe [*A publication*]
ECEP .... Equivalent CEP
ECEP .... Experiment Checkout Equipment Processor   (NASA)
ECER........ Exceptional Child Education Resources [*Formerly, ECEA*]
          [*Council for Exceptional Children*] [*Bibliographic
          database*] [*A publication*]
ECES .... Evaluation Contractors Estimating System
ECET........ Electronic Control Assembly - Engine Thrust   (KSC)
Ec Ete Phys Part ... Ecole d'Ete de Physique des Particules [*A publication*]
ECETOC... [*The*] European Chemical Industry Ecology and Toxicology
          Center [*Brussels, Belgium*]
ECF........... Earth Crust Formation
ECF........... East Coast Fever [*Veterinary medicine*]
ECF........... Echo Control Factor [*Telecommunications*]   (TEL)
ECF........... Effective Cutoff Frequency
ECF........... Electrically Conductive Film   (MCD)
ECF........... Electrochemical Fluorination [*Chemical synthesis*]
ECF........... Element Change Factor   (MCD)
ECF........... Eleventh Commandment Fellowship   (EA)
ECF........... Ellsworth Convertible Growth & Income Fund, Inc. [*AMEX
          symbol*]   (SPSG)
ECF........... Emergency Cooling Function [*Nuclear energy*]   (NRCH)
ECF........... Employees' Compensation Fund   (NG)
ECF........... Engineering Central Files
ECF........... Eosinophil Chemotactic Factor [*Hematology*]
ECF........... Equivalency Capability File   (MCD)
ECF........... European Caravan Federation   (EA)
ECF........... European Coffee Federation   (EAIO)
ECF........... European Cultural Foundation   (EAIO)
ECF........... "Evangelize China" Fellowship   (EA)
ECF........... Excess Chiasma Frequency [*Genetics*]
ECF........... Expended Core Facility [*Nuclear energy*]
ECF........... Experimental Cartographic Facility [*Air Force*]
ECF........... Export Cargo Form [*Shipping*]
ECF........... Extended Care Facility [*Medicine*] [*Obsolete*]
ECF........... Externally Caused Failure
ECF........... Extracellular Fluid [*Physiology*]
ECFA .... Emergency Community Facilities Act of 1970
ECF-A........ Eosinophil Chemotactic Factor of Anaphylaxis
          [*Immunochemistry*]
ECFA .... European Committee on Future Accelerators [*Nuclear energy*]
ECFA .... Evangelical Council for Financial Accountability   (EA)
ECFB .... Ethyl Cellulose Perfluorobutyrate
ECFC .... Eastchester Financial Corp. [*NASDAQ symbol*]   (NQ)
ECFC .... Employers Council on Flexible Compensation   (EA)
ECFD........ Executive Council on Foreign Diplomats   (EA)
ECFI .... Electronic Company Filing Index [*Disclosure Information
          Group*] [*Information service or system*]   (IID)
ECF-IUF ... European Committee of Food, Catering, and Allied Workers'
          Unions within the IUF [*International Union of Food and
          Allied Workers' Associations*]   (EAIO)
ECFM........ Eddy Current Flow Meter [*Nuclear energy*]   (NRCH)
ECFMG.... Educational Commission for Foreign Medical Graduates   (EA)
ECFNBN... Ecology of Food and Nutrition [*A publication*]
ECFSA...... Episcopal Churchpeople for a Free Southern Africa   (EA)
ECFSOV ... Episcopal Council for Foreign Students and Other Visitors
          [*Defunct*]   (EA)

ECFTU ...... European Confederation of Free Trade Unions [Later, ETUC]
ECFV .... Electrical Contractors Federation of Victoria [Australia]
ECFV .... Extracellular Fluid Volume [Physiology]
ECG .... Eco Corp. [AMEX symbol] (SPSG)
ECG .... Ecosystem Conservation Group [Marine science] (MSC)
ECG .... Egyptian Cotton Gazette [Alexandria] [A publication]
ECG .... Electro-Epitaxial Crystal Growth [Materials processing]
ECG .... Electrocardiogram [Also, EK, EKG] [Medicine]
ECG .... Electrocardiograph [Also, EKG] (MSA)
ECG .... Electrochemical Grinding (IEEE)
ECG .... Electronic Component Group
ECG .... Elizabeth City, NC [Location identifier] [FAA] (FAAL)
ECG .... Energy Coordinating Group [Twelve-nation coalition]
ECG .... Engineering Craftsmen's Guild [A union] [British]
ECG .... Environmental Control Group (CAAL)
ECG .... Equine Chorionic Gonadotropin [Endocrinology]
ECG .... European Contact Group on Urban Industrial Mission (EAIO)
ECG .... European Cooperation Grouping (DCTA)
ECG .... Evaporative Cooling Garment [Spacesuit] [NASA]
ECG .... Export Credit Guarantee (DLA)
ECGAI ...... Education Council of the Graphic Arts Industry [Later, GATF] (EA)
ECGB .... East Coast of Great Britain [Shipping]
ECGC .... Electron-Capture Gas Chromatography
ECGC .... Essex County Gas Company [NASDAQ symbol] (NQ)
ECGD .... Export Credits Guarantee Department [British]
ECGEA ...... Economic Geography [A publication]
ECGF .... Endothelial Cell Growth Factor [Cytochemistry]
ECGF .... European Container Glass Federation (EA)
ECGI .... Environmental Control Group, Incorporated [NASDAQ symbol] (NQ)
ECGLA ...... Economic Geology and the Bulletin of the Society of Economic Geologists [A publication]
ECGLC ...... Economic Community of the Great Lakes Countries [See also CEPGL] [Gisenye, Rwanda] (EAIO)
ECGLC ...... Electron Capture Gas-Liquid Chromatography
ECGS .... Endothelial Cell Growth Supplement [Cytochemistry]
ECGS .... Evaporative Cooling Garment System [NASA]
ECGT .... Ecologist [A publication]
ECGWAK ... Empire Cotton Growing Corporation. Review [A publication]
ECGYA ...... Ecology [English Translation] [A publication]
ECH .... Earth Coverage Horn [Satellite communications]
ech .... Echantillon [Sample] [Business term] [French]
ECH .... Echelon
ECH .... Echery [France] [Seismograph station code, US Geological Survey] (SEIS)
ECH .... Echlin, Inc. [NYSE symbol] (SPSG)
ECH .... Electrochemical Honing [Manufacturing term]
ECH .... Electron Cyclotron Heating [Nuclear energy]
ECH .... Engine Compartment Heater (AAG)
ECh .... Enseignement Chretien [A publication]
ECH .... Epichlorohydrin [Organic chemistry]
ECH .... Epochs of Church History [A publication]
ECH .... Ketchikan, AK [Location identifier] [FAA] (FAAL)
ECHA .... Eastern College Hockey Association (EA)
Echanges Int Develop ... Echanges Internationaux et Developpement [A publication]
Echang Univ ... Echangiste Universel. Revue Mensuelle des Collectionneurs de Timbres et des Numismates [A publication]
ECHC .... Etudes Carmelitaines Historiques et Critiques [A publication]
ECHC .... European Colloquium on Heterocyclic Chemistry
ECHE .... Ealing College of Higher Education [England]
Echinoderm Stud ... Echinoderm Studies [A publication]
Ec Hist R ... Economic History of Rome [A publication]
ECHMB ... Electrochemistry [A publication]
ECHMBU ... Specialist Periodical Reports. Electrochemistry [A publication]
ECHO .... Each Community Helps Others [Environmental Protection Agency]
ECHO .... Early Childhood Organisation [Australia]
ECHO .... East Coast Hazards Observation [Sampling program]
Echo .... Echo Magazine [A publication]
ECHO .... Echocardiogram [Cardiology]
ECHO .... Echoencephalogram [Neurology]
EchO .... Echos d'Orient [A publication]
ECHO .... Educational Concern for Hunger Organization (EA)
ECHO .... Elder Cottage Housing Opportunity
ECHO .... [The] Electonic Clearing House, Inc. [NASDAQ symbol] (NQ)
ECHO .... Electronic Communications for the Home and Office [Marina Del Ray, CA] [Telecommunications service] (TSSD)
ECHO .... Electronic Computing, Hospital-Oriented (IEEE)
ECHO .... Enterocytopathogenic Human Orphan Virus
E Ch O ...... Ergebnisse der Chirurgie und Orthopaedie [A publication]
ECHO .... Etoposide, Cyclophosphamide, Hydroxydaunomycin [Adriamycin], Oncovin [Vincristine] [Antineoplastic drug regimen]
ECHO .... European Commission Host Organization [Commission of the European Communities] [Information service or system] [Host system] [Luxembourg] (IID)
ECHO .... Evolution of Competing Hierarchical Organizations
ECHO .... Experimental Contract Highlight Operation [NASA]
ECHO .... Expo Collectors - Historians Organization (EA)

ECHO .... Hungarian Economic Information Service (EISS)
Echo Brass ... Echo de la Brasserie [A publication]
Echo Mines Metall ... Echo des Mines et de la Metallurgie [France] [A publication]
Echo Min Met ... Echo des Mines et de la Metallurgie [A publication]
Echo Rech ... Echo des Recherches [A publication]
Echos Med ... Echos de la Medecine [A publication]
Echo Vet .... Echo Veterinaire [A publication]
E Ch Q ...... Eastern Churches Quarterly [A publication]
ECHR .... Emergency Coalition for Haitian Refugees (EA)
EChr .... Enseignement Chretien [A publication]
ECHR .... European Commission of Human Rights (EA)
ECI .... Earth-Centered Inertial [System]
ECI .... East Coast of Ireland [Shipping]
ECI .... Eastern Carolina Aviation, Incorporated [Richlands, NC] [FAA designator] (FAAC)
ECI .... ECI Environmental [AMEX symbol] (SPSG)
ECI .... Economist [A publication]
ECI .... Edgell Communications, Inc. [Database producer] (IID)
ECI .... Efficiency of Conversion of Ingested Material [Physiology]
ECI .... Electrical Circuit Interrupter (KSC)
ECI .... Electronic Cascade Impactor [For aerosol analysis]
ECI .... Electronic Communications, Incorporated
ECI .... Electronic Computer Ignition [Automotive engineering]
ECI .... Electronic Control Instrumentation
ECI .... Electronic Controlled Injection [Automotive engineering]
ECI .... Emergency Coolant Injection [Nuclear energy] (NRCH)
ECI .... Employee Cost Index
ECI .... Employment Cost Index (OICC)
ECI .... Encor Energy Corp. Inc. [Toronto Stock Exchange symbol] [Vancouver Stock Exchange symbol]
ECI .... Enemy Countries Intelligence [Ministry of Economic Warfare] [British] [World War II]
ECI .... Engineering Change Incorporation (AAG)
ECI .... Engineering Change Information
ECI .... Engineering Change Instruction
ECI .... Environmental Carcinogen Information [Department of Energy] [Information service or system] (IID)
ECI .... Environmental Clearinghouse, Incorporated [An association] (EA)
ECI .... Equipment Change Information
ECI .... Equity Capital for Industry [British]
ECI .... Error Cause Identification [Military] (AFM)
ECI .... Essential Controls and Instrumentation [Nuclear energy] (NRCH)
ECI .... EURATOM [European Atomic Energy Community] Classified Information
ECI .... European Federation of Trade Unions for Energy, Chemical, and Miscellaneous Industries (EA)
ECI .... Evangelism Center International (EA)
ECI .... Executives Consultants, Incorporated [An association] (EA)
ECI .... Experimental Cities, Incorporated (EA)
ECI .... Export Consignment Identifying Number (DS)
ECI .... Extension Course Institute [Air Force]
ECI .... Extracorporeal Irradiation [Medicine]
ECIA .... Education Consolidation and Improvement Act [1981]
ECIB .... Extracorporeal Irradiation of Blood [Medicine]
ECIC .... Electric Consumers Information Committee (EA)
ECIC .... Electronic Components Information Center [Battelle Memorial Institute]
ECIC .... Export Credits Insurance Corporation [Canada]
ECIC .... Extracranial-Intracranial [Medicine]
ECID .... Emission Circular Intensity Differential [Spectroscopy]
ECID .... En Route Computer Identification (KSC)
ECIEL .... Estudios Conjuntos sobre Integracion Economica Latinoamericana [Program]
ECIEL .... Programa de Estudios Conjuntos sobre la Integracion Economica Latinoamericana [Program of Joint Studies for Latin American Economic Integration] (EAIO)
ECIF .... Electronic Components Industry Federation [British]
ECIIB .... Enemy Civilian Internee Information Bureau [Military] (AABC)
ECIIB(Br) ... Enemy Civilian Internee Information Bureau (Branch) [Military] (AABC)
ECIL .... ECI Telecom Ltd. [Formerly, Electronics Corporation of Israel] [NASDAQ symbol] (NQ)
ECIL .... Expected Confidence Interval Length [Statistics]
ECIME4 ..... Experimental and Clinical Immunogenetics [A publication]
ECIMOT ... European Central Inland Movements of Transport
ECIN .... Economic Indicators [A publication]
ECIN .... Electronics, Missiles & Communications, Inc. [NASDAQ symbol] (NQ)
ECIND ...... Economic Inquiry [A publication]
ECINE7 ..... Ear Clinics International [A publication]
ECIO .... Experiment Computer Input/Output (NASA)
EC-IOA ..... European Committee of the International Ozone Association [See also CEAIO] (EA)
ECIP .... Energy Conservation Investment Program [DoD] (MCD)
ECIPL .... Engineering Change Identity Parts List [McDonnell Douglas Aircraft Corp.]

ECIS .... Elvis Costello Information Service [*Purmerend, Netherlands*] (EAIO)
ECIS .... Emory Center for International Studies [*Emory University*] [*Research center*] (RCD)
ECIS .... Engineering Careers Information System
ECIS .... Error Correction Information System [*NASA*]
ECIS .... European Community Information Service (EA)
ECIS .... European Council of International Schools (EA)
ECIS .... Extension and Change of Immigration Status (ADA)
ECITO .... European Central Inland Transport Organization
ECIWDSS ... Environment Canada. Inland Waters Directorate. Scientific Series [*A publication*]
ECIY .... Earl of Chester's Imperial Yeomanry [*British military*] (DMA)
ECJ .... Court of Justice of the European Communities (DLA)
ECJ .... Economic Journal [*United Kingdom*] [*A publication*]
ECJ .... Etudes Publies par des Peres de la Compagnie de Jesus [*A publication*] (BJA)
ECJC .... East Central Junior College [*Decatur, MS*]
ECJCS .... European Council of Jewish Community Services (EA)
ECJF .... Emergency Council of Jewish Families (EA)
ECJOA ...... Economic Journal [*A publication*]
ECJPA .... Endocrinologia Japonica [*A publication*]
ECJPAE .... Endocrinologia Japonica [*A publication*]
ECJS .... East Coast Joint Service, Stock [*Railroad*] [*British*] (ROG)
Eck .... Eckart [*Berlin*] [*A publication*]
ECK .... Economic and Commercial News [*A publication*]
ECK .... Embryonic Chicken Kidney
ECK .... Emergency Communications Key
ECK .... Epidermal Cytokeratin [*Cytology*]
ECK .... Peck, MI [*Location identifier*] [*FAA*] (FAAL)
Eckart J ..... Eckart Jahrbuch [*Witten*] [*A publication*]
ECL .... East Coast Laboratory [*Environmental Science Services Administration*]
ECL.......... Eclipse Mining [*Vancouver Stock Exchange symbol*]
Ecl .... Eclogues [*of Vergil*] [*Classical studies*] (OCD)
ECL.......... Ecolab, Inc. [*NYSE symbol*] (SPSG)
ECL.......... Eddy Current Loss [*Electromagnetism*]
ECL.......... Egyptian Confederation of Labor
ECL.......... Electrochemiluminescence
ECL.......... Electronic Components Laboratory
ECL.......... Emerson College, Boston, MA [*OCLC symbol*] (OCLC)
ECL.......... Emitter-Coupled Logic [*Electronics*]
ECL.......... Energy Conversion Laboratory [*MIT*] (MCD)
ECL.......... Engineering Change List (MCD)
ECL.......... Engineering Computer Laboratory [*University of Southern California*] [*Research center*] (RCD)
ECL.......... Engineering Configuration List (MCD)
ECL.......... English China Clays International PLC [*British*] (IRUK)
ECL.......... English Church Leaders [*A publication*]
ECL.......... English Comprehension Level [*Army*] (AABC)
ECL.......... Enterochromaffin-Like [*Biochemistry*]
ECL.......... Entry Closed Loop (NASA)
ECL.......... Environmental Conservation Law [*New York, NY*] [*A publication*]
ECL.......... Equipment Component List [*Army*] (AABC)
ECL.......... Equivalent Chain Length [*of fatty acids*] [*Biochemistry*]
E Cl .... Etudes Classiques [*A publication*]
ECL.......... Euglobulin Clot Lysis [*Hematology*]
ECL.......... European Calibration Line
ECL.......... Eurotec Consultants Limited [*Information service or system*] (IID)
ECL.......... Evets Communications Ltd. [*Telecommunications service*] (TSSD)
ECL.......... Exchange Control Logic (KSC)
ECL.......... Executive Control Language [*Data processing*]
ECLA .... Economic Commission for Latin America [*Database originator*] [*Later, ECLAC*] [*United Nations*]
ECLA .... Etudes Classiques [*A publication*]
ECLA .... Evangelical Church Library Association (EA)
ECLAC ...... Economic Commission for Latin America and the Caribbean [*See also CEPAL*] [*United Nations*] [*Santiago, Chile*] (EAIO)
EClas .... Estudios Clasicos [*A publication*]
EClass........ Les Etudes Classiques [*Namur*] [*A publication*]
ECLAY ...... ECC Group ADR [*Formerly, English China Clays ADR*] [*NASDAQ symbol*] (SPSG)
ECLC .... Emergency Civil Liberties Committee [*Later, NECLC*] (EA)
ECLE .... European Centre for Leisure and Education (EA)
ECLEC ...... Eclectic (ROG)
ECLED ...... Economics Letters [*A publication*]
Ecl Engin ... Eclectic Engineering Magazine [*Van Nostrand's*] [*A publication*]
Eclet Quim ... Ecletica Quimica [*A publication*]
ECLG......... European Consumer Law Group (EA)
E-C Life .... Eighteenth-Century Life [*A publication*]
ECLIPS ...... Expanded Calculator Link Processing System [*Data processing*]
Ecl M .... Eclectic Magazine [*A publication*]
ECLM........ Economic Community for Livestock and Meat [*See also CEBV*] (EAIO)
Ecl Mus...... Eclectic Museum [*A publication*]
ECLO .... Emitter-Coupled Logic Operator [*Electronics*]

ECLOF ...... Ecumenical Church Loan Fund
Eclogae Geol Helv ... Eclogae Geologicae Helvetiae [*A publication*]
Ecl R .... Eclectic Review [*A publication*]
ECLR........ European Competition Law Review [*A publication*] (DLA)
ECLS .... Environmental Control and Life Support [*NASA*] (NASA)
ECLSS....... Environmental Control and Life Support Subsystem [*NASA*] (MCD)
ECLSS....... Extended Campus Library Services Section [*Association of College and Research Libraries*]
ECLT .... English Comprehensive Level Test [*DoD*]
ECLT .... Euglobulin Clot Lysis Time [*Clinical chemistry*]
ECM .... ECM Paytel [*Vancouver Stock Exchange symbol*]
ECM .... Econometrica [*A publication*]
ECM .... Effective Complex Modulus
ECM .... Electric [*or Electronic*] Cipher [*or Coding*] Machine
ECM .... Electrochemical Machining
ECM .... Electronic Control Module [*Instrumentation*]
ECM .... Electronic Countermeasure [*Military*]
ECM .... Elementary Circulation Mechanism
ECM .... Ellipsoid Collector Mirror
ECM .... Embryonic Chicken Muscle
ECM .... Emergency Conservation Measures
ECM .... Emission Characteristics Monitor
ECM .... Engine Condition Monitoring
ECM .... Engine Control Module [*General Motors' computer system*]
ECM .... Engineering Change Memo (KSC)
ECM .... Error Correction Mode [*Data processing*]
ECM .... Erythema Chronicum Migrans [*Dermatology*]
ECM .... Estudios de Cultura Maya [*A publication*]
ECM .... Etude en Commun de la Mediterranee [*Cooperative Investigations in the Mediterranean - CIM*] [*French*] (MSC)
ECM .... European Christian Mission
ECM .... European Common Market
ECM .... Evangelical and Catholic Mission (EA)
ECM .... Evasive Combat Maneuver (MCD)
ECM .... Event Control Module [*Chromatography*]
ECM .... Exco Capital Markets [*Money brokers*] [*British*]
ECM .... Extended Conventional Memory [*Data processing*]
ECM .... Extended Core Memory [*Data processing*] (MCD)
ECM .... External Cardiac Massage [*Medicine*] (ADA)
ECM .... External Crystalline Massif [*Geology*]
ECM .... Extracellular Material [*Physiology*]
ECM .... Extracellular Matrix [*Cytology*]
ECMA .... East Coast Magnetic Anomaly [*Geophysics*]
ECMA .... Eastern Cosmetic Manufacturers Association
ECMA .... Embalming Chemical Manufacturers Association [*Westport, CT*] (EA)
ECMA .... Engineering College Magazines Associated (EA)
ECMA .... Ethylcholine Mustard Aziridinium [*Picrate*] [*Biochemistry*]
ECMA .... European Catalysts Manufacturers Association [*of the European Council of Chemical Manufacturers' Federation*] (EAIO)
ECMA .... European Collectors and Modellers Association (EAIO)
ECMA .... European Computer Manufacturers Association [*Switzerland*]
ECMAA .... Economie et Medecine Animales [*France*] [*A publication*]
ECMAA .... Ethiopian Community Mutual Assistance Association (EA)
ECMAAI... Economie et Medecine Animales [*A publication*]
ECMALGOL ... European Computer Manufacturers Association Algorithmic Language
Ec & Mar ... Notes of Cases, English Ecclesiastical and Maritime Courts [*1844-50*] [*A publication*] (DLA)
ECMB........ Economic Consequences of Marriage Breakdown [*Survey*] [*Australia*]
ECMB........ European Committee for Mini-Basketball [*See also CEMB*] [*Munich, Federal Republic of Germany*] (EAIO)
ECMB........ European Conference on Molecular Biology
ECMBR..... European Committee on Milk-Butter-Fat Recording
ECMC ...... Episcopal Church Missionary Community (EA)
ECMC ...... European Container Manufacturers Committee (EA)
ECMCA..... Eastern Central Motor Carriers Association
EC-MCA ... External Carotid - Middle Cerebral Artery [*Anatomy*]
ECMCC..... Encyclopedie Medico-Chirurgicale [*A publication*]
ECMCS ..... European Conference on Mixing and Centrifugal Separation
ECM-D...... Engineering Change Management-Development
ECME........ Economic Commission for the Middle East [*United Nations*] (DS)
ECME........ Electronic Circuit-Making Equipment [*Data processing*]
ECMEA...... Electronic Countermeasures Environment [*Military*]
ECMEA...... European Conference of Meteorological Experts for Aeronautics
ECMEX...... Electronic Countermeasures Exercise [*Military*] (NVT)
ECMF........ European Community Mortgage Federation [*Brussels, Belgium*] (EA)
ECMHP...... East Coast Migrant Health Project (EA)
ECMM ...... Etudes Carmelitaines Mystiques et Missionnaires [*A publication*]
ECMM ...... Extracts from China Mainland Magazines [*US Consulate*] [*Hongkong*] [*A publication*]
ECMO .... Electronic Countermeasures Officer [*Navy*] (NVT)
ECMO .... Enterocytopathogenic Monkey Orphan Virus
ECMO .... Extracorporeal Membrane Oxygenator [*Respirator*]
ECMOA .... Ecological Monographs [*A publication*]

ECMOAQ ... Ecological Monographs [*A publication*]
ECMob ...... Electronic Countermeasures Observer [*Military*]
ECMODT ... Ecological Modelling [*A publication*]
ECMP........ Electronic Countermeasures Program [*Military*]
ECMP........ Enteric-Coated Microspheres of Pancrelipase
ECMR .... Eastern Contract Management Region [*Air Force*]
ECMR .... Equipment Calibration Maintenance Record   (MCD)
ECMRA..... European Chemical Market Research Association [*West Wickham, Kent, England*]
ECMS........ Engine Configuration Management System
ECMSA ..... Electronics Command Meteorological Support Agency [*Army*]   (MCD)
ECMSC6 ... Estuarine and Coastal Marine Science [*A publication*]
ECMSN..... Electronic Countermeasures Mission [*Military*]
ECMT....... European Conference of Ministers of Transport   (EAIO)
ECMTA ..... Econometrica [*A publication*]
ECMTNG ... Electronic Countermeasures Training [*Military*]   (NVT)
ECMU .... Extended Core Memory Unit [*Data processing*]   (NVT)
ECMWF.... European Center for Medium-Range Weather Forecasting
ECMY .... Economy Savings Bank, PaSA [*NASDAQ symbol*]   (NQ)
ECN .... Ecogen, Inc. [*AMEX symbol*]   (SPSG)
ECN .... Economist [*A publication*]
ECN .... Effective Carbon Number [*Chemistry*]
ECN .... El Condor Resources [*Vancouver Stock Exchange symbol*]
ECN .... Emergency Communication Network [*Highway*] [*Telecommunications*]   (TEL)
ECN .... Engineering Change Notice
ECN .... Environmental Communications Network [*Proposed environmental information exchange network*]
ECN .... Epoxy Creosol Novolac [*Resin*]
ECN .... Equipage Category Number   (MSA)
ECN .... Ercan [*Cyprus*] [*Airport symbol*]   (OAG)
ECN .... Estudios de Cultura Nahuatl [*A publication*]
ECN .... European Chemical News [*Reed Business Publishing Ltd.*] [*Information service or system*]   (CRD)
ECNAMP ... East Caribbean Natural Area Management Program   (EAIO)
Ec N Bulg.. Economic News of Bulgaria [*A publication*]
ECNDT ..... European Council for Nondestructive Testing   (EA)
ECNEA...... Electroencephalography and Clinical Neurophysiology [*A publication*]
ECNEAZ... Electroencephalography and Clinical Neurophysiology [*A publication*]
EC Nebr Univ Coop Ext Serv ... EC. Cooperative Extension Service. University of Nebraska [*A publication*]
ECNF......... European Central NOTAM [*Notice to Airmen*] Facility [*Military*]
ECNG .... East Central Nuclear Group
ECNOS...... Eastern Atlantic, Channel and North Sea Orders for Ships [*NATO*]   (NATG)
ECNP........ Environmental Coalition on Nuclear Power   (EA)
ECNR .... European Council for Nuclear Research   (DCTA)
ECNRT...... Emitter-Controlled Negative Resistance Triode
ECNSB ...... Electrical Consultant [*A publication*]
ECN Sup.... European Chemical News. Supplement [*A publication*]
ECO .... East Central Oklahoma State University, Ada, OK [*OCLC symbol*]   (OCLC)
ECO .... Eastern Counties Omnibus Co. Ltd. [*British*]
ECO .... Echo Bay Mines Ltd. [*AMEX symbol*] [*Toronto Stock Exchange symbol*]   (SPSG)
ECO .... Economic Cooperation Organization
ECO .... Economica [*A publication*]
ECO .... Ecumenical Committee on the Andes   (EA)
ECO .... Effective Citizens Organization [*Later, PAC*]   (EA)
ECO .... Electron-Coupled Oscillator
ECO .... Electronic Central Office [*Within network*] [*Telecommunications*]   (TEL)
ECO .... Electronic Checkout
ECO .... Electronic Contact Operate
ECO .... Emergency Commissioned Officer [*British military*]   (DMA)
ECO .... Energy Conservation Opportunities [*Federal Energy Administration*]
ECO .... Engine Checkout System [*Aerospace*]   (AAG)
ECO .... Engine Combustion   (NASA)
ECO .... Engine Cutoff [*Aerospace*]   (MCD)
ECO .... Engineering Change Order
ECO .... Engineering Control Office [*Telecommunications*]   (TEL)
ECO .... English Chamber Orchestra
ECO .... Entry Clearance Officer [*Immigration*]   (DLA)
ECO .... Environment Centre Outlook [*A publication*]   (APTA)
ECO .... Environmental Control Organization [*Proposed in 1970 by Walter J. Hickel, Secretary of the Interior*]
ECO .... Environmental Crisis Operation [*University of British Columbia*]
ECO .... Epichlorohydrin Ethylene Oxide [*Organic chemistry*]   (RDA)
ECO .... Equipment Control Officer [*Air Force*]   (AFM)
Eco .... Escherichia Coli [*Microorganism*]
ECO .... European Coal Organization
ECO .... Exempted by Commanding Officer
ECO .... Experience Critique Orgel [*Nuclear reactor*] [*Italy*]
ECOA .... Equal Credit Opportunity Act [*1974, 1976*]
ECOA .... Equipment Company of America [*NASDAQ symbol*]   (NQ)

Eco Argent ... Economic Information on Argentina [*A publication*]
ECOBDY... Eisenhower Consortium. Bulletin [*A publication*]
ECOC .... Eastern Counties Omnibus Company Ltd. [*British*]   (DCTA)
ECOCAB... Economic Cabinet [*British*]
Eco Cient.... Eco Cientifico [*A publication*]
ECOCOM ... Economic Commission for Europe [*United Nations*]   (DS)
ECOD .... Error Classification, Omission, or Deficiency   (MCD)
ECOD .... Estimated Cost of Damage   (MCD)
ECOD .... Ethoxycoumarin O-Deethylase [*An enzyme*]
ECODU ...... European Control Data User's Organization   (EA)
ECOF .... Engineering Change Order Factor   (MCD)
Eco Farm.... Eco Farmaceutico [*A publication*]
Eco Forcst .. Economic Forecasts. A Worldwide Survey [*A publication*]
ECOG .... Eastern Cooperative Oncology Group [*Research center*]   (RCD)
ECOG .... Electrocorticogram [*or Electrocorticographic*]
ECOGA ..... Ecologist [*A publication*]
ECOGAC .. Ecologist [*A publication*]
ECOGDF ... Ecologia [*Buenos Aires*] [*A publication*]
ECOIN ...... European Core Inventory of Existing Substances [*Chemicals which are exempt from new product regulations*]
ECOL .... American Ecology Corp. [*Agoura Hills, CA*] [*NASDAQ symbol*]   (NQ)
ECOL .... Ecology [*A publication*]
ECOL .... Ecology
ECOLA...... Ecology [*United States*] [*A publication*]
Ecol Abstr ... Ecological Abstracts [*A publication*]
Ecol Action Newsl ... Ecology Action Newsletter [*A publication*]
ECOLAR .... Ecology [*A publication*]
Ecol Bull .... Ecological Bulletins [*Sweden*] [*A publication*]
Ecol Bull - NFR (Statens Naturvetensk Forskningsrad) ... Ecological Bulletins - NFR (Statens Naturvetenskapliga Forskningsrad) [*A publication*]
Ecol Conserv ... Ecology and Conservation [*A publication*]
Ecol Dis.... Ecology of Disease [*A publication*]
Ecol Ent ..... Ecological Entomology [*A publication*]
Ecol Entom ... Ecological Entomology [*A publication*]
Ecol Entomol ... Ecological Entomology [*A publication*]
Ecol Food Nutr ... Ecology of Food and Nutrition [*A publication*]
Ecol Law Q ... Ecology Law Quarterly [*A publication*]
Ecol LQ..... Ecology Law Quarterly [*A publication*]
Ecol L Quart ... Ecology Law Quarterly [*A publication*]
Ecol Mediterr ... Ecologia Mediterranea [*A publication*]
Ecol Model ... Ecological Modelling [*A publication*]
Ecol Monogr ... Ecological Monographs [*A publication*]
Ecolo .... Parti Ecologiste [*Ecologist Party*] [*Belgium*]   (PPW)
Ecology (Engl Transl Ekologiya) ... Ecology (English Translation of Ekologiya) [*A publication*]
Ecology L Q ... Ecology Law Quarterly [*A publication*]
Ecol Q .... Ecologist Quarterly [*Later, Ecologist*] [*England*] [*A publication*]
Ecol Res Comm Bull ... Ecological Research Committee. Bulletin [*A publication*]
Ecol Rev ..... Ecological Review [*Deutsche Schwarzbunte*] [*A publication*]
Ecol Rev ..... Ecology Review [*A publication*]
Ecol Soc Aust Mem ... Ecological Society of Australia. Memoirs [*A publication*]
Ecol Soc Aust Proc ... Ecological Society of Australia. Proceedings [*A publication*]   (APTA)
Ecol Stud.... Ecological Studies [*A publication*]
Ecol Stud Anal Synth ... Ecological Studies, Analysis, and Synthesis [*A publication*]
E Com .... Echos du Commonwealth [*A publication*]
ECOM....... Economica [*A publication*]
E-COM...... Electronic Computer-Originated Mail [*Postal Service*]
ECOM....... Electronics Command [*Fort Monmouth, NJ*] [*Army*]
ECOM....... En Route Communications [*Aviation*]   (FAAC)
ECOM....... Especialidades Consumidas por la Seguridad Social [*Ministerio de Sanidad y Consumo*] [*Spain*] [*Information service or system*]   (CRD)
ECOMA .... Electrical Construction and Maintenance [*A publication*]
ECOMA .... European Computer Measurement Association
ECOMCON ... Emergency Communications Control [*Fictitious military unit in film "Seven Days in May"*]
ECOMINAS Bol Mens ... ECOMINAS [*Empresa Colombiana de Minas*] Boletin Mensual [*Bogota*] [*A publication*]
ECOMMRGN ... Eastern Communications Region [*Air Force*]
ECOMOG ... Economic Community Monitoring Group [*West Africa*]
E COMP.... Excellent Companion [*Freemasonry*]
ECOMS..... Early Capability Orbital Manned Station
ECOM SA ... Empresa Nacional de Computacion y Informatica Sociedad Anonima [*Santiago, Chile*]   (TSSD)
Econ .... Econometrica [*A publication*]
Econ .... Economia [*A publication*]
ECON....... Economics   (EY)
ECON....... Economics Laboratory, Inc. [*NASDAQ symbol*]   (NQ)
Econ .... Economist [*A publication*]
ECON....... Economy   (AFM)
ECON........ Electromagnetic Emission Control   (IEEE)
EconAb ..... Economic Abstracts [*A publication*]
Econ Abstr ... Economic Abstracts [*A publication*]
Econ Act..... Economic Activity [*A publication*]
Econ Activ ... Economic Activity [*A publication*]

Econ Activity ... Economic Activity in Western Australia [*A publication*]
Econ Activity in WA ... Economic Activity in Western Australia [*A publication*] (APTA)
Econ Activity WA ... Economic Activity in Western Australia [*A publication*] (APTA)
Econ Act West Aust ... Economic Activity in Western Australia [*A publication*] (APTA)
ECONADS ... Economic Advisers
Econ Aff..... Economic Affairs [*A publication*]
Econ Afr..... Economic Bulletin for Africa [*A publication*]
Econ Agric ... Economiste Agricole [*A publication*]
Econ Agr (Paris) ... Economie Agricole (Paris) [*A publication*]
Econ Anal & Policy ... Economic Analysis and Policy [*A publication*] (APTA)
Econ Analys ... Economic Analysis [*A publication*]
Econ Analysis (Belgrade) ... Economic Analysis and Workers' Management (Belgrade) [*A publication*]
Econ Analysis and Policy (NS) ... Economic Analysis and Policy (New Series) [*A publication*]
Econ Ann ... Economic Annalist [*A publication*]
Econ Appl.. Economie Appliquee [*A publication*]
Econ Appliq ... Economie Appliquee [*A publication*]
Econ Appliquee ... Economie Appliquee [*A publication*]
ECONB..... Electrical Contracting [*United States*] [*A publication*]
Econ (BA).. Economica (Buenos Aires) [*A publication*]
Econ B Afr ... Economic Bulletin for Africa [*A publication*]
Econ B Asia Far East ... Economic Bulletin for Asia and the Far East [*Later, Economic Bulletin for Asia and the Pacific*] [*A publication*]
Econ B Asia Pacific ... Economic Bulletin for Asia and the Pacific [*A publication*]
Econ B (Athens) ... Economic Bulletin. Commercial Bank of Greece (Athens) [*A publication*]
Econ B (Cairo) ... Economic Bulletin. National Bank of Egypt (Cairo) [*A publication*]
Econ B Europe ... Economic Bulletin for Europe [*A publication*]
Econ B Latin Amer ... Economic Bulletin for Latin America [*A publication*]
Econ B (Oslo) ... Economic Bulletin (Oslo) [*A publication*]
Econ Bot..... Economic Botany [*A publication*]
Econ Botan ... Economic Botany [*A publication*]
Econ Bul A ... Economic Bulletin for Asia and the Pacific [*A publication*]
Econ Bul Asia and Far East ... Economic Bulletin for Asia and the Far East [*Later, Economic Bulletin for Asia and the Pacific*] [*A publication*]
Econ Bul Asia and Pacific ... Economic Bulletin for Asia and the Pacific [*A publication*]
Econ Bul Europe ... Economic Bulletin for Europe [*A publication*]
Econ Bull ... Economic Bulletin [*A publication*]
Econ Bull Eur ... Economic Bulletin for Europe [*A publication*]
Econ Bull for Europe ... Economic Bulletin for Europe [*A publication*]
Econ Bull Lat Am ... Economic Bulletin for Latin America [*A publication*]
Econ Bus R ... Economic and Business Review [*A publication*]
Econ Centre-Est ... Economie du Centre-Est [*A publication*]
Econ Cienc Soc ... Economia y Ciencias Sociales [*A publication*]
Econ Colombiana 4a Epoca ... Economia Colombiana. Cuarta Epoca [*A publication*]
Econ Comp and Econ Cyb Stud and Res ... Economic Computation and Economic Cybernetics Studies and Research [*A publication*]
Econ Comput and Econ Cybern Stud and Res ... Economic Computation and Economic Cybernetics Studies and Research [*A publication*]
Econ Comput Econ Cybern Stud Res ... Economic Computation and Economic Cybernetics Studies and Research [*A publication*]
Econ Cont .. Contents of Recent Economics Journals [*A publication*]
Econ e Credito ... Economia e Credito [*A publication*]
ECOND..... Energy Consumer [*A publication*]
Econ y Desarrollo ... Economia y Desarrollo [*A publication*]
Econ Dev Cu ... Economic Development and Cultural Change [*A publication*]
Econ Dev & Cul Change ... Economic Development and Cultural Change [*A publication*]
Econ Dev Cult Change ... Economic Development and Cultural Change [*A publication*]
Econ Devel Cult Ch ... Economic Development and Cultural Change [*A publication*]
Econ Devel Cult Change ... Economic Development and Cultural Change [*A publication*]
Econ Devel and Cult Change ... Economic Development and Cultural Change [*A publication*]
Econ Develop Cult Change ... Economic Development and Cultural Change [*A publication*]
Econ Development and Cultural Change ... Economic Development and Cultural Change [*A publication*]
Econ EC..... Economia EC [*A publication*]
Econ Educ Bul ... Economic Education Bulletin [*A publication*]
Econ El....... Economie Electrique [*A publication*]
Econ Eye ... Economic Eye [*A publication*]
Econ Financial Surv Aust ... Economic and Financial Survey of Australia [*A publication*] (APTA)
Econ & Financial Survey Aust ... Economic and Financial Survey of Australia [*A publication*] (APTA)

Econ Financ R Central Bank Nigeria ... Economic and Financial Review. Central Bank of Nigeria [*A publication*]
Econ Finan Surv Aust ... Economic and Financial Survey of Australia [*A publication*]
Econ y Fin Esp ... Economia y Finanzas Espanolas [*A publication*]
Econ et Fins Agrics ... Economie et Finances Agricoles [*A publication*]
Econ Forum ... Economic Forum [*A publication*]
Econ Geog ... Economic Geography [*A publication*]
Econ Geogr ... Economic Geography [*A publication*]
Econ-Geogr ... Economie-Geographie [*A publication*]
Econ Geography ... Economic Geography [*A publication*]
Econ Geol... Economic Geology [*A publication*]
Econ Geol... Economic Geology and the Bulletin of the Society of Economic Geologists [*A publication*]
Econ Geol Bull Soc Econ Geol ... Economic Geology and the Bulletin of the Society of Economic Geologists [*A publication*]
Econ Geology Mon ... Economic Geology. Monograph [*A publication*]
Econ Geol Rep Alberta Res Counc ... Economic Geology Report. Alberta Research Council [*A publication*]
Econ Geol Rep Miner Resour Div (Manitoba) ... Economic Geology Report. Mineral Resources Division (Manitoba) [*A publication*]
Econ Geol Rep Res Counc Alberta ... Economic Geology Report. Research Council of Alberta [*A publication*]
Econ Geol VT Geol Surv ... Economic Geology. Vermont Geological Survey [*A publication*]
Econ e Gestao ... Economia e Gestao [*A publication*]
Econ Hist... Economic History [*A publication*]
Econ Hist... Economy and History [*A publication*]
Econ Hist R ... Economic History Review [*A publication*]
Econ Hist Rev ... Economic History Review [*A publication*]
Econ Hist Rev Second Ser ... Economic History Review. Second Series [*A publication*]
EconHR..... Economic History Review [*A publication*]
Econ et Human ... Economie et Humanisme [*A publication*]
Econ et Humanisme ... Economie et Humanisme [*A publication*]
Econ Ind..... Economia Industrial [*A publication*]
Econ & Ind Democ ... Economic and Industrial Democracy [*A publication*]
Econ Indic ... Economic Indicators [*A publication*]
Econ Indicators ... Economic Indicators [*A publication*]
Econ Inf Argentina ... Economic Information on Argentina [*A publication*]
Econ Info Argentina ... Economic Information on Argentina [*A publication*]
Econ Inf Rep Food Resour Econ Dep Univ Fla Agric Exp Stns ... Economic Information Report. University of Florida. Food and Resource Economics Department. Agricultural Experiment Stations [*A publication*]
Econ Inq..... Economic Inquiry [*A publication*]
Econ Inquiry ... Economic Inquiry [*A publication*]
Econ Internaz ... Economia Internazionale [*A publication*]
Econ Internaz Fonti Energia ... Economia Internazionale delle Fonti di Energia [*A publication*]
Econ Int Fonti Energia ... Economia Internazionale delle Fonti di Energia [*A publication*]
Econ Int (Genova) ... Economia Internazionale (Genova) [*A publication*]
Econ Issues Dep Agric Econ Coll Agric Life Sci Univ Wis ... Economic Issues. Department of Agricultural Economics. College of Agricultural and Life Sciences. University of Wisconsin [*A publication*]
Econ Istruzione e Formazione Professionale ... Economia. Istruzione e Formazione Professionale [*A publication*]
Econ Italy... Economic News from Italy [*A publication*]
Econ J .... Economic Journal [*A publication*]
Econ e Lav ... Economia e Lavoro [*A publication*]
Econ Leaf... Economic Leaflets [*Florida*] [*A publication*]
Econ Leaflets ... Economic Leaflets [*A publication*]
Econ Lett.... Economics Letters [*Netherlands*] [*A publication*]
Econ (Lisbon) ... Economia (Lisbon) [*A publication*]
Econ (London) ... Economica (London) [*A publication*]
Econ Marche ... Economia Marche [*A publication*]
Econ Med Anim ... Economie et Medecine Animales [*A publication*]
Econ Meridionale ... Economie Meridionale [*A publication*]
Econ Mex... Economista Mexicano [*A publication*]
Econ Mex... Review of the Economic Situation of Mexico [*A publication*]
Econ Microbiol ... Economic Microbiology [*A publication*]
Econ Monog ... Economic Monographs [*A publication*]
Econ Monographs ... Economic Monographs [*Sydney*] [*A publication*] (APTA)
Econ Monograph (Vic) ... Economic Monograph (Melbourne, Victoria) [*A publication*]
Econ Monogr Econ Soc Aust NZ ... Economic Society of Australia and New Zealand. Economic Monograph [*A publication*]
Econ N .... Economic News [*A publication*]
Econ News ... Economic News [*A publication*] (APTA)
ECONOMAN ... Effective Control of Manpower (AFM)
Econom Anc Gr ... [*The*] Economics of Ancient Greece [*A publication*] (OCD)
Econom Comp Econom Cybernet Stud Res ... Economic Computation and Economic Cybernetics Studies and Research [*Bucharest*] [*A publication*]
Econom Comput Econom Cybernet Stud Res ... Economic Computation and Economic Cybernetics Studies and Research [*Bucharest*] [*A publication*]

Econometrics Oper Res ... Econometrics and Operations Research [*A publication*]
Economic Activity in WA ... Economic Activity in Western Australia [*A publication*] (APTA)
Econom Lett ... Economics Letters [*Netherlands*] [*A publication*]
Econom Oper Res ... Econometrics and Operations Research [*A publication*]
Econom Theory Econometrics Math Econom ... Economic Theory, Econometrics, and Mathematical Economics [*A publication*]
Econ Out (CA) ... Economic Outlook (California) [*A publication*]
Econ Outlk ... Economic Outlook [*A publication*]
Econ Outlook ... Economic Outlook USA [*A publication*]
Econ Outlook (London) ... Economic Outlook (London) [*A publication*]
Econ Outlook USA ... Economic Outlook USA [*A publication*]
Econ Out US ... Economic Outlook USA [*A publication*]
Econ Out W ... Economic Outlook World [*A publication*]
Econ Panorama (Bancomer) ... Economic Panorama (Bancomer) [*A publication*]
Econ Pap.... Economic Papers [*A publication*]
Econ Papers ... Economic Papers [*A publication*] (APTA)
Econ Paps .. Economic Papers [*A publication*]
Econ Pas (Australia and NZ) ... Economic Papers (Australia and New Zealand) [*A publication*]
Econ Pas (Warsaw) ... Economic Papers (Warsaw) [*A publication*]
Econ Pays Arabes ... Economie des Pays Arabes [*A publication*]
Econ Perspectives ... Economic Perspectives [*A publication*]
Econ Planning ... Economics of Planning [*A publication*]
Econ Planning (Helsinki) ... Economic Planning (Helsinki) [*A publication*]
Econ Plann J Agric Relat Ind ... Economic Planning. Journal for Agriculture and Related Industries [*A publication*]
Econ et Pol ... Economie et Politique [*A publication*]
Econ Pol 2a Epoca ... Economia Politica. Segunda Epoca [*A publication*]
Econ Policy Issues ... Economic Policy Issues [*A publication*]
Econ et Polit ... Economie et Politique [*A publication*]
Econ Polit Wkly ... Economic and Political Weekly [*A publication*]
Econ Pol W ... Economic and Political Weekly [*A publication*]
Econ Pres... Economic Report of the President [*Council of Economic Advisors*] [*United States*] [*A publication*]
Econ et Prevision ... Economie et Prevision [*A publication*]
Econ Priorities Rep ... Economic Priorities Report [*A publication*]
Econ Proc R Dublin Soc ... Economic Proceedings. Royal Dublin Society [*A publication*]
Econ Progress Rep ... Economic Progress Report [*A publication*]
Econ Pubblica ... Economia Pubblica [*A publication*]
Econ R........ Economic Review [*A publication*] (APTA)
Econ R Bank Israel ... Economic Review. Bank of Israel [*A publication*]
Econ R (Colombo) ... Economic Review (Colombo) [*A publication*]
Econ Rec.... Economic Record [*A publication*]
Econ Rep Dep Agric Appl Econ Univ Minn ... Economic Report. Department of Agricultural and Applied Economics. University of Minnesota [*A publication*]
Econ Rep Edinburgh Sch Agr ... Economic Report. Edinburgh School of Agriculture [*A publication*]
Econ Rep Geol Surv Dep (Zambia) ... Economic Report. Geological Survey Department (Zambia) [*A publication*]
Econ Reporter ... Economic Reporter [*A publication*]
Econ Rep Univ Fla Agric Exp Stns ... Economics Report. University of Florida. Agricultural Experiment Stations [*A publication*]
Econ Res .... Economic Research [*Nagoya, Japan*] [*A publication*]
Econ Rev.... Economic Review [*A publication*] (APTA)
Econ Rev Bank Leumi ... Economic Review. Bank Leumi [*Tel Aviv*] [*A publication*]
Econ R Kansallis Osake-Pankki ... Economic Review. Kansallis Osake-Pankki [*A publication*]
Econ R (Karachi) ... Economic Review (Karachi) [*A publication*]
Econ Rur .... Economie Rurale [*A publication*]
Econ Rurale ... Economie Rurale [*A publication*]
Econ Salvad ... Economia Salvadorena [*A publication*]
Econ et Sante ... Economie et Sante [*A publication*]
Econ Situation Rep ... Economic Situation Report [*A publication*]
Econ and Soc ... Economy and Society [*A publication*]
Econ Soc Aust NZ NSW Br Econ Monog ... Economic Society of Australia and New Zealand. New South Wales Branch. Economic Monograph [*A publication*] (APTA)
Econ e Socialismo ... Economia e Socialismo [*A publication*]
Econ and Social R (Dublin) ... Economic and Social Review (Dublin) [*A publication*]
Econ and Social Research Inst Q Econ Commentary ... Economic and Research Institute. Quarterly Economic Commentary [*A publication*]
Econ Societ ... Economy and Society [*A publication*]
Econ e Sociol ... Economia e Sociologia [*A publication*]
Econ Soc Issues Calif Univ Berkeley Coop Ext Serv ... Economic and Social Issues. University of California, Berkeley. Cooperative Extension Service [*A publication*]
Econ Soc R ... Economic and Social Review [*A publication*]
Econ Soc Tijds ... Economisch en Sociaal Tijdschrift [*A publication*]
Econs et Socs ... Economies et Societes [*A publication*]
Econ-Sta Ber ... Economisch-Statistische Berichten [*A publication*]
Econ Stand (CCH) ... Economic Standards (Commerce Clearing House) [*A publication*] (DLA)

Econ and Statis R (East Africa) ... Economic and Statistical Review (East Africa) [*A publication*]
Econ et Statist ... Economie et Statistique [*A publication*]
Econ-Statist Ber ... Economisch-Statistische Berichten [*A publication*]
Econ e Storia (2a Ser) ... Economia e Storia (Seconda Serie) [*A publication*]
Econ Stud... Economic Studies [*A publication*]
Econ Survey ... Economic Survey of Ancient Rome [*A publication*] (OCD)
Econ Surv Lat Am ... Economic Survey of Latin America [*A publication*]
Econ Tech Rev Rep EPS (Can) ... Economic and Technical Review. Report EPS [*Environmental Protection Service*] (Canada) [*A publication*]
Econ Tiers-Monde ... Economiste du Tiers-Monde [*A publication*]
Econ Trend ... Tendances/Trends. Economie et Finances [*A publication*]
Econ Trends ... Economic Trends [*A publication*]
Econ Trentina ... Economia Trentina [*Italy*] [*A publication*]
Econ W ...... Economic World [*A publication*]
ECOO N.... Educational Computing Organization of Ontario. Newsletter [*A publication*]
Eco Out (UK) ... Economic Outlook (United Kingdom) [*A publication*]
ECOP .... Extension Committee on Organization and Policy [*Department of Agriculture*] (EA)
ECOPD ..... Engineering Conference. Proceedings [*United States*] [*A publication*]
ECOQD ..... Electricity Conservation Quarterly [*India*] [*A publication*]
ECOR .... Engineer Change Order Request (AAG)
ECOR .... Engineering Committee on Oceanic Resources [*Later, SUT*] [*United Nations*]
ECOS........ Experiment Computer Operating System (MCD)
ECOSAL ... Equipo de Conferencias Sindicales de America Latina [*Committee for Latin American Trade Union Conferences*]
ECOSEC ... European Cooperation Space Environment Committee
ECOSOC... Economic and Social Council [*ICSU*] [*United Nations*]
EcoSSP ..... Escherichia Coli Single-Stranded Protein
Eco Sur LA ... Economic Survey of Latin America [*A publication*]
Ecosyst World ... Ecosystems of the World [*A publication*]
ECOTAGE ... Ecological Sabotage [*Tactic used by radical environmentalists*]
Ecotoxicol Environ Qual ... Ecotoxicology and Environmental Quality [*A publication*]
Ecotoxicol Environ Saf ... Ecotoxicology and Environmental Safety [*A publication*]
Ecotoxicol Environ Safety ... Ecotoxicology and Environmental Safety [*A publication*]
Eco Turkey ... General Economic Conditions in Turkey [*A publication*]
E of Cov...... Trial of the Earl of Coventry [*A publication*] (DLA)
ECOWAS ... Economic Community of West African States [*Treaty signed May 28, 1975*]
ECOX .... Educational Communications on Exhibit [*Commercial firm*]
ECP........... Central Newspapers, Inc. Class A [*NYSE symbol*] (SPSG)
ECP........... Congolese Progressive Students [*Zaire*] (PD)
ECP........... Early Churches in Palestine [*A publication*] (BJA)
ECP........... East Cleveland Public Library, East Cleveland, OH [*OCLC symbol*] (OCLC)
ECP........... Eclipse Capital Corp. [*Toronto Stock Exchange symbol*]
ECP........... Economic Perspectives [*Federal Reserve Bank of Chicago*] [*A publication*]
ECP........... Edinburgh County Police [*British*] (ROG)
ECP........... Education Center Publications (MCD)
ECP........... Egyptian Communist Party [*Political party*] (PD)
ECP........... Electric Current Perturbation [*Method*] [*Southwest Research Institute*]
ECP........... Electrical Contact Plate
ECP........... Electrical Control Package
ECP........... Electrically Compensated Pyrometer
ECP........... Electromagnetic Compatibility Program [*Air Force*]
ECP........... Electromagnetic Containerless Processing [*Materials processing*]
ECP........... Electronic Calculating Punch
ECP........... Electronic Circuit Protector
ECP........... Electronic Control Products (MUGU)
ECP........... Elliptical Cavity Pump
ECP........... Endogenous Circadian Phase [*Physiology*]
ECP........... Energy Charge Potential
ECP........... Engineering Change Program
ECP........... Engineering Change Proposal
ECP........... Engineering Control Proposal
ECP........... Engineering Costs and Production Economics [*A publication*]
ECP........... English Centre of PEN (EAIO)
ECP........... Enkephalin-Containing Polypeptide [*Physiological chemistry*]
ECP........... Entry Control Point (MCD)
ECP........... Eosinophil Cationic Protein [*Immunology*]
ECP........... Equipment Collecting Point [*Military*] [*British*]
ECP........... Equipment Conversion Package [*Telecommunications*] (TEL)
ECP........... Escherichia Coli Polypeptides
ECP........... Estimated Critical Position [*Nuclear energy*] (NRCH)
ECP........... Estradiol Cyclopentanepropionate [*Endocrinology*]
ECP........... Ethiopian Communist Party [*Political party*] (PD)
ECP........... Euro-Commercial Paper [*Finance*]
ECP........... European Committee of Crop Protection
ECP........... European Organization for Cooperation in Cancer Prevention Studies (EA)

ECP............ Evangeli Christi Proedicatur [*Preacher of the Gospel of Christ*] [*Latin*] (ROG)
ECP............ Evaporative Cooling Processor
ECP............ Executive Control Program [*Data processing*]
ECP............ Explicitly Coded Program (MCD)
ECP............ External Control Panel
ECP............ External Counterpulsation [*Medicine*]
ECP............ Extracellular Products
ECPA........ Effective Cell Pair Area [*Electrochemistry*]
ECPA........ Electric Consumer Protection Act of 1986
ECPA........ Electronic Communications Piracy Act of 1986
ECPA........ Energy Conservation and Production Act [*1976*] (MCD)
ECPA........ Energy Consumers and Producers Association (EA)
ECPA........ Evangelical Christian Publishers Association (EA)
ECPA........ Expert Committee on Post Adjustments [*United Nations*]
ECPC........ Edge Connector Programmable Cartridge
ECPC........ Enlarged Committee for Program and Coordination [*United Nations Development Program*]
ECPC........ Ethnic Cultural Preservation Council [*Also known as Association of North American Museums, Libraries, Archives, Cultural Centers, and Fraternal Organizations*] (EA)
ECPC........ European Communist Party Conference
ECPCDP ... Euro-Commercial Paper and Certificates of Deposit Programme [*Finance*]
ECPD........ Engineers Council for Professional Development [*Later, ABET*] (EA)
ECPD........ Export Cargo Packing Declaration (DS)
ECPE........ European Centre of Public Enterprise (EAIO)
ECPED...... Engineering Costs and Production Economics [*A publication*]
ECPGR...... Expert Committee on Plant Gene Resources [*Canadian Agricultural Services Coordinating Committee*]
ECPI.......... Electronic Computer Programming Institute [*Ceased operation, 1976*]
ECPIP........ Electric Companies' Public Information Program
ECPIU....... Electronic Circuit Plug-In Unit
ECPMAOA ... Executive Committee's Panel on Meteorological Aspects of Ocean Affairs [*WMO*] (MSC)
ECPO .... Eastern College Personnel Officers
ECPO .... Enteric Cytopathogenic Porcine Orphan Virus
ECPOG....... Electrochemical Potential Gradient
ECPR......... Electrically Calibrated Pyroelectric Radiometer
ECPR......... European Consortium for Political Research [*Colchester, Essex, England*] (EAIO)
ECPRAG ... Empire Cotton Growing Corporation. Progress Reports from Experiment Stations [*A publication*]
Ec Prat Hautes Etud Inst Montp Mem Trav ... Ecole Pratique des Hautes Etudes. Institut de Montpellier. Memoires et Travaux [*A publication*]
ECPRD...... European Centre for Parliamentary Research and Documentation [*See also CERDP*] [*Luxembourg, Luxembourg*] (EAIO)
ECP Rep ... ECP [*Energy Conservation Project*] Report [*United States*] [*A publication*]
ECPS .... Environment and Consumer Protection Service [*EEC*] (DS)
ECPS .... European Centre for Population Studies (EA)
ECPS .... Extended Control Program Support [*IBM Corp.*]
ECPT......... Ethylcamptothecin [*Antineoplastic drug*]
ECPT......... European Confederation for Physical Therapy (EAIO)
ECPWS .... Engineering Change Proposal Work Statement (AAG)
ECPY........ Electronic Control Assembly - Pitch and Yaw (KSC)
ECQUA ..... Engineering. Cornell Quarterly [*A publication*]
ECQUDX .. Ecletica Quimica [*A publication*]
ECR .... Canada Law Reports, Exchequer Court [*A publication*] (DLA)
ECR .... Eastern Churches Review [*A publication*]
ECR .... Eastern Counties Railway [*British*] (ROG)
ECR .... Economic Record [*A publication*]
ECR .... Economic Review. Federal Reserve Bank of Atlanta [*A publication*]
ECR .... Economy Cylinder Rating [*Engine technology*]
Ec R.......... Ecumenical Review [*A publication*]
ECR .... Electrochemical Reaction
ECR .... Electron Cyclotron Resonance (IEEE)
ECR .... Electronic Cash Register
ECR .... Electronic Control Relay (IEEE)
ECR .... Electronic Countermeasures and Reconnaissance
ECR .... Embedded Computer Resources (MCD)
ECR .... Embossed Character Reader [*Banking*]
ECR .... Emergency Combat Readiness (AAG)
ECR .... Emergency Coolant Recirculation [*Nuclear energy*] (NRCH)
ECR .... Emitted Coherent Radiation
ECR .... Enemy Contact Report [*NATO*] (NATG)
ECR .... Energy Consumption Rate
ECR .... Energy Control Report [*Navy*]
E CR .... Engineer Commander [*Navy*] [*British*] (ROG)
ECR .... Engineering Change Report (KSC)
ECR .... Engineering Change [*or Correction*] Request [*or Requirement*]
ECR .... Engineering Concept Review
ECR .... Entry Control Roster (MCD)
ECR .... Environmental Control Report [*A publication*] (EAAP)
ECR .... Equipment Control Record (MCD)

ECR .... Error Cause Removal [*Quality control*]
ECR .... Error Control Receiver (IEEE)
ECr.......... Esprit Createur [*A publication*]
ECr .... Essays in Criticism [*A publication*]
ECR .... Estimate Change Request (NRCH)
ECR .... European Court Reports [*European Communities*] [*A publication*] (DLA)
ECR .... European Economic Review [*A publication*]
ECR .... Except Change Route to Read [*Aviation*] (FAAC)
ECR .... Exchequer Court Reports [*Canada Department of Justice*] [*Information service or system*] (CRD)
ECR .... Execute Command Request (KSC)
ECR .... Executive Control Routines
ECR .... Export Control Regulations [*Department of Commerce*]
ECR .... External Channels Ratio
ECRA........ Electric Car Racing Association
ECR/A....... Engineering Change Request/Authorization (AFM)
ECRA........ Excess and Casualty Reinsurance Association (EA)
Ecran.......... Ecran 79 [*France*] [*A publication*]
ECRB........ Export Control Review Board
ECRB........ Extensor Carpi Radialis Brevis [*Anatomy*]
ECRC........ Early Childhood Resource Center
ECRC........ Elderly Care Research Center [*Case Western Reserve University*] [*Research center*] (RCD)
ECRC........ Electricity Council Research Center [*British*] (MCD)
ECRC........ Electronic Component Reliability Center [*Battelle Memorial Institute*] (MCD)
ECRC........ Employers Casualty Company [*NASDAQ symbol*] (NQ)
ECRC........ Engineering College Research Council (EA)
ECRC........ Equipment Category Rollup Code [*Army*]
ECRC........ European Community Research Council
ECRCA..... Echo des Recherches [*A publication*]
ECRDA..... Economic Record (Australia) [*A publication*]
ECRDG ..... Electronic Component Research and Development Grant [*Canada*]
ECRE........ Edinburgh Centre of Rural Economy [*British*] (CB)
ECRE........ European Consultation on Refugees and Exiles
ECREA...... European Conference of Radiotelegraphy Experts for Aeronautics
Ec Rec ...... Economic Record [*A publication*]
Ec Rev ..... Ecumenical Review [*A publication*]
ECRF........ Edited Collections Report File [*IRS*]
ECRF........ Externally Coupled Resonator Filter (MCD)
ECRH........ Electron Cyclotron Resonance Heating (MCD)
ECRI........ East Central Reservoir Investigation [*Department of the Interior*] (GRD)
ECRI........ Emergency Care Research Institute (EA)
ECRIM...... Engineering Construction and Related Industries Manpower [*British*]
ECRL........ East Central Regional Library System [*Library network*]
ECRM....... Euronorm Certified Reference Material
ECRO .... Erection Counter Readout
ECRO .... European Chemoreception Research Organization (EAIO)
ECRQDQ .. Conseil de la Recherche et du Developpement Forestiers du Quebec. Etude [*A publication*]
ECRR........ Engineering Change Request and Record (MCD)
ECRS........ Earthwork/Center for Rural Studies (EA)
ECRS........ Economic and Contingency Reserve Stock [*Military*]
ECRS........ Equipment Control Record System [*Army*]
ECRT........ European Confederation of Retail Tobacconists [*Luxembourg*] (EA)
ECRU .... Emergency Communications Research Unit [*Carleton University*] [*Canada*] [*Research center*] (RCD)
e-cs--- ...... Czechoslovakia [*MARC geographic area code*] [*Library of Congress*] (LCCP)
ECS............ Early Childhood Services (ADA)
ECS............ Echantillons Commerciaux/Commercial Samples [*International trade*] [*French*]
ECS............ Echo Control Subsystem [*Telecommunications*] (TEL)
ECS............ Economic Census Staff [*Census*] (OICC)
ECS............ Economy-Class Syndrome [*Medicine*]
ECS............ Ecos Resources [*Vancouver Stock Exchange symbol*]
ECS............ Education Commission of the States (EA)
ECS............ Educational Career Service [*Later, EHCS*] [*An association*] (EA)
ECS............ Eighteenth-Century Studies [*A publication*]
ECS............ Elective Cosmetic Surgery
ECS............ Electrical Connector Subassembly
ECS............ Electrocardioscanner
ECS............ Electrochemical Society (EA)
ECS............ Electroconvulsive Shock
ECS............ Electronic Composing System
ECS............ Electronic Control Sensor (MCD)
ECS............ Electronic Control Switch (IEEE)
ECS............ Electronic Countermeasures System [*Military*]
ECS............ Electronic Courier Systems [*Eatontown, NJ*] (TSSD)
ECS............ Electronically Controlled Suspension [*Mitsubishi*] [*Automotive engineering*]
ECS............ Electronics Control System
ECS............ Embedded Computer Systems
ECS............ Emergency Call System [*AT & T*]

ECS............ Emergency Control Station [*Nuclear energy*]   (NRCH)
ECS............ Emergency Coolant System   (MSA)
ECS............ Emission Control System   (MCD)
ECS............ Emperor's Clothes Syndrome
ECS............ Empty Coaching Stock [*Railway term*]   (DCTA)
ECS............ Enable Control System
ECS............ [*PATRIOT*] Engagement Control Station [*Army*]
ECS............ Engagement Control System [*Navy*]   (MCD)
ECS............ Engine Control System
ECS............ Engineering Change Schedule   (AAG)
ECS............ Engineering Change Sheet   (NATG)
ECS............ Engineering Change Summary
ECS............ Engineering Control System
ECS............ English Citizen Series [*A publication*]
ECS............ Environmental Conservation Service [*Canada*]
ECS............ Environmental Control Shroud [*Nuclear energy*]   (NRCH)
ECS............ Environmental Control System [*NASA*]
ECS............ Equipment Concentration Sites [*Military*]   (AABC)
ECS............ Equipment Construction Site   (MCD)
ECS............ Error Correction Servo [*or Signals*]   (AAG)
ECS............ Established Church of Scotland   (ROG)
ECS............ Etched Circuit Society [*Defunct*]   (EA)
ECS............ European Communication Satellite
ECS............ European Company Statute [*A publication*]   (DLA)
ECS............ European Confederation of Scouts   (EAIO)
ECS............ Evaporation Control System [*Automobile antipollution device*]
ECS............ Exact Cubic Search [*Mathematics*]
ECS............ Executive Compensation Service
ECS............ Executive Control System [*Data processing*]
ECS............ Exhaust Control System
ECS............ Exospheric Composition Studies   (MUGU)
ECS............ Experimental Communications Satellite [*NASA*]
ECS............ Exploder Control Sensor   (MCD)
ECS............ Extended Character Set [*Data processing*]   (PCM)
ECS............ Extended Core Storage [*Data processing*]
ECS............ Exterior Communications System [*Military*]   (CAAL)
ECS............ External Calling Sequence [*Data processing*]
ECS............ Extracapillary Space
ECS............ Extracellular-Like, Calcium-Free Solution [*Medicine*]
ECS............ IEEE Electromagnetic Compatability Society   (EA)
ECS............ Newcastle, WY [*Location identifier*] [*FAA*]   (FAAL)
ECS............ Tijdschrift voor Economie en Management [*A publication*]
ECSA......... Eastern College Soccer Association   (EA)
ECSA......... Episcopal Churchmen for South Africa   (EA)
ECSA......... European Chlorinated Solvent Association   (EAIO)
ECSA......... European Communication Security Agency
ECSA......... European Computing Services Association
ECSA......... Exceptional Civilian Service Award   (RDA)
ECSA......... Exchange Carriers Standards Association   (EA)
ECSA......... Expanded Clay and Shale Association [*Later, LAPA*]   (EA)
ECSAMR.. Emergency Committee to Save America's Marine
            Resources   (EA)
ECS/API ... Enhanced Character Set/All Purpose Interface [*Xerox Corp.*]
ECSBA...... Economisch-Statistische Berichten [*A publication*]
ECSC......... East Central State College [*Later, East Central Oklahoma State
            University*]
ECSC......... Energy Conservation and Solar Centre [*British*]   (CB)
ECSC......... European Coal and Steel Community [*France, West Germany,
            Italy, BENELUX*]
ECSC......... European Conference on Satellite Communications   (MCD)
ECSCA...... English Cocker Spaniel Club of America   (EA)
ECSDA...... Electromechanical Components and Systems Design [*A
            publication*]
ECSE......... Advisory Committee for Electrical, Computer, and Systems
            Engineering [*Terminated, 1985*]   (EGAO)
ECSF......... European Civil Service Federation   (EAIO)
ECSG......... Electronic Connector Study Group
ECSH........ Edgewood College of the Sacred Heart [*Wisconsin*]
ECSHAZ... Ecosphere [*Berkeley*] [*A publication*]
ECS/HCS ... Educational Career Service/Health Career Service [*Later,
            EHCS*] [*An association*]   (EA)
ECSI......... Electronic Control Security, Inc. [*NASDAQ symbol*]   (NQ)
ECSI......... Emergency Committee to Suspend Immigration   (EA)
ECSI......... Export Cargo Shipping Instruction   (DS)
ECSIL....... Experimental Cross Section Information Library [*University of
            California, Livermore*]
Ec Sit EEC ... Economic Situation in the Community. European Economic
            Community [*A publication*]
ECSLA ...... European Centre of Studies on Linear Alkylbenzene   (EAIO)
ECSMA...... European Copper Sulphate Manufacturers' Association   (EAIO)
ECSMB...... Environmental Control and Safety Management [*A publication*]
ECSO......... Effective Concentration of Substance for 50% Survival of
            Organism
ECSO......... Enterocytopathogenic Swine Orphan Virus
ECSOB...... Eastern College Soccer Officials Bureau [*Later, ECSA*]
ECSP......... Electronic Command Signal Programmer   (MCD)
ECSP......... Electronic Specialist
ECSP......... Electronics Control Signal Processor [*HELLFIRE*]
ECSP......... Enhanced Consumer Spending Patterns [*National Planning
            Data Corp.*] [*Information service or system*]   (CRD)
ECSP......... Extended Corresponding States Principle [*Physical chemistry*]

ECSS .... Equipment Concentration Site System [*Army*]
ECSS .... European Committee for the Study of Salt   (EA)
ECSS .... Extendable Computer System Simulator [*Programming
            language*] [*1973*]
ECSSA...... European Centre for Studies of Sulfuric Acid   (EAIO)
ECSSD ..... Estuarine, Coastal, and Shelf Science [*A publication*]
ECSSD3 ... Estuarine, Coastal, and Shelf Science [*A publication*]
ECSSL...... [*A*] programming language   (CSR)
ECST .... Emergency Condensate Storage Tank [*Nuclear
            energy*]   (NRCH)
ECSTA ...... Economist [*London*] [*A publication*]
ECSTASY ... Economical Storage and Access System [*Data processing*]
ECSTC...... Electrocomponent Science and Technology [*A publication*]
ECSTD6 ... Echinoderm Studies [*A publication*]
Ec Stor ...... Economia e Storia; Rivista Italiana di Storia Economica e
            Sociale [*A publication*]
Ec Super Agric Suede Ann ... Ecole Superieure d'Agriculture de la Suede.
            Annales [*A publication*]
Ec Svy Eur ... Economic Survey of Europe [*A publication*]
Ec Svy Fin ... Economic Survey of Finland [*A publication*]
Ec Svy Jpn ... Economic Survey of Japan [*A publication*]
ECSWTR .. European Centre for Social Welfare Training and Research [*See
            also CEFRAS*] [*United Nations*]   (EAIO)
ECT............ Earth-Centered True
ECT............ Ecopress Italia [*A publication*]
ECT............ Eddy Current Test [*Nuclear energy*]   (NRCH)
ECT............ Edge Crush Test [*Packaging*]
ECT......... [*The*] Egyptian Coffin Texts [*A publication*]   (BJA)
ECT............ Electrochemical Turning [*Manufacturing term*]
ECT............ Electroconvulsive Therapy [*or Treatment*] [*Medicine*]
ECT............ Electronically Controlled Transmission [*Automotive
            engineering*]
ECT............ Ellsworth [*Connecticut*] [*Seismograph station code, US
            Geological Survey*]   (SEIS)
ECT............ Emergency Cooling Tower [*Nuclear energy*]   (NRCH)
ECT............ Emission Computed Tomography
ECT............ Encyclopedia of Chemical Technology [*A publication*]
ECT............ Engine Coolant Temperature [*Automotive engineering*]
ECT............ Engine Cutoff Timer [*Aerospace*]   (KSC)
ECT............ Enteric Coated Tablet [*Pharmacology*]
ECT............ Environmental Control Table
ECT............ Error Control Translator
ECT............ Error Control Transmitter
ECT............ Estimated Cloud Time [*Drinking slang*]
ECT............ Estimated Completion Time [*Business term*]
ECT............ Evaporative Cooling Techniques
ECT............ Executive Career Trac [*A publication*]
ECT............ Exposure Control Technique
ECT............ Extortionate Credit Transactions [*FBI standardized term*]
ECTA......... Electronics Component Test Area   (AAG)
ECTA......... Error-Correcting Tree Automation [*Data processing*]
ECTA......... European Cutting Tools Association   (EA)
ECTAA...... Electra [*Rijswijk*] [*A publication*]
ECTAA...... Group of National Travel Agents' Associations within the
            EEC   (EAIO)
ECTAR...... Electronic Tactical Action Report   (AFM)
ECTC......... East Coast Telecommunications Center [*Defense
            Communications System*]   (RDA)
ECTC......... Eastern Coal Transportation Conference   (EA)
ECTEL ...... European Telecommunications and Professional Electronics
            Industry [*Formed by a merger of European Conference of
            Associations of Telecommunications Industries and
            European Conference of Radio and Electronic Equipment
            Associations*]   (EAIO)
ECTEOLA ... Epichlorohydrin Triethanolamine [*Organic chemistry*]
ECTFE ...... Ethylene-Chlorotrifluoroethylene [*Organic chemistry*]
ECTG......... European Channel Tunnel Group [*Planning a proposed tunnel
            between England and France under the English Channel*]
ECTH .... Electro-Catheter Corp. [*NASDAQ symbol*]   (NQ)
ECTI......... Eddy Current Testing Instrument
ECTI......... Erie County Technical Institute [*New York*]
ECTL......... Elcotel, Inc. [*Sarasota, FL*] [*NASDAQ symbol*]   (NQ)
ECTL......... Emitter-Coupled Transistor Logic [*Electronics*]
Ecto .... Ectoparasitic [*Biology*]
ECTPWF... European Confederation for Trade in Paint, Wall- and
            Floorcoverings   (EAIO)
ECTS .... Electric Circuit Test Set
ECTS .... Electrical Cable Test Set
ECTS .... Electronic Custom Telephone Set [*or System*]   (NRCH)
ECTS .... European Calcified Tissue Society   (EA)
ECTS .... European Conference on Telecommunications by Satellite
ECTTA...... Economia Trentina [*A publication*]
ECTWT.... Ecumenical Coalition on Third World Tourism   (EA)
ECU .... East Carolina University [*Formerly, ECC*] [*Greenville, NC*]
ECU .... Economia Internazionale [*A publication*]
ECU .... Ecuador [*ANSI three-letter standard code*]   (CNC)
ECU .... Electrical Conversion Unit
ECU .... Electrochemical Unit
ECU .... Electronic Cabling Unit
ECU .... Electronic Control Unit
ECU .... Electronic Conversion Unit   (IEEE)

ECU .... Electronic Coupling Unit (MCD)
ECU .... Energy Conservation Update [*A publication*]
ECU .... Engine Change Unit (MCD)
ECU .... Engine Control Unit
ECU .... English Church Union
ECU .... Entry Computer
ECU .... Environment Conditioning Unit (MCD)
ECU .... Environmental Control Unit
ECU .... Equipment Control Unit (AFIT)
ECU .... Euclid Public Library, Euclid, OH [*OCLC symbol*] (OCLC)
ECU .... European Chiropractors' Union (EAIO)
ECU .... European Currency Unit [*European monetary system*]
ECU .... Extended Care Unit [*Medicine*] (DHSM)
ECU .... Extreme Close-Up [*Television*]
ECUA .... Ecuador
Ecuador Dir Gen Geol Minas Publ ... Ecuador. Direccion General de Geologia y Minas. Publication [*A publication*]
ECUC .... Education Credit Union Council (EA)
ECUK .... East Coast of the United Kingdom [*Shipping*]
Ecumenical R ... Ecumenical Review [*A publication*]
Ecumen Rev ... Ecumenical Review [*A publication*]
Ecum R...... Ecumenical Review [*A publication*]
Ecum St Hist ... Ecumenical Studies in History [*A publication*]
EcuR .... Ecumenical Review [*Geneva*] [*A publication*]
ECUSAT ... Ecumenical Satellite Commission
ECUT .... Energy Conversion and Utilization Technologies Program [*Department of Energy*]
ECV .... Economic Review. Federal Reserve Bank of Cleveland [*A publication*]
ECV .... Electric Clock Valve
ECV .... Enamel Single Cotton Varnish [*Wire insulation*] (AAG)
ECV .... Energy Conservation Vehicle [*British Leyland*]
ECV .... Esperantist Club of Veterans [*See also VEK*] [*Wolfhagen, Federal Republic of Germany*] (EAIO)
ECV .... External Cephalic Version [*Gynecology*]
ECV .... Extracellular Volume [*Hematology*]
ECVAC..... Endorsers Conference for Veterans Affairs Chaplaincy (EA)
E & CV1S .. Edge and Center V on One Side [*Technical drawings*]
E & CV2S .. Edge and Center V on Two Sides [*Technical drawings*]
ECVT........ Electro-Continuously Variable Transmission [*Subaru*] [*Automotive engineering*]
ECVT .... Electronically Controlled Continuously Variable Transmission
ECW .... Eastern Coach Works [*British*] (DCTA)
Ec W .... Economic Weekly [*A publication*]
ECW .... Emergency Conservation Work [*Succeeded by CCC, 1937, now obsolete*]
ECW .... Emergency Cooling Water [*Nuclear energy*] (NRCH)
ECW .... Envipco Canada [*Vancouver Stock Exchange symbol*]
ECW .... Episcopal Church Women
ECW .... Essays on Canadian Writing [*A publication*]
ECW .... Extracellular Water [*Physiology*]
ECWA .... Economic Commission for Western Asia [*Later, ESCWA*] [*United Nations*]
ECWA .... Economic Community of West Africa
ECWAS..... Economic Community of West African States [*Treaty signed May 28, 1975*]
ECWC....... Extended Cold/Wet Clothing Systems [*Military*] (INF)
ECWCS..... Extended Cold Weather Clothing System [*Army*] (INF)
ECWG .... Emergency Communications Working Group [*DoD*]
ECWG .... Environmental Characterization Working Group
ECWIM..... European Committee of Weighing Instrument Manufacturers (EAIO)
EC WIRE .. Extra Control Wire (MSA)
ECWODB ... Ecosystems of the World [*Elsevier Book Series*] [*A publication*]
Ec World ... Economic World [*A publication*]
ECWP........ Egyptian Communist Workers' Party [*Political party*] (PD)
ECWP........ Emergency Cooling Water Pond [*Nuclear energy*] (NRCH)
ECWPH ... Emergency Cooling Water Pumphouse [*Nuclear energy*] (NRCH)
ECWS........ European Centre for Work and Society (EA)
ECWU .... Energy and Chemical Workers Union [*See also STEC*]
ECX .... Echos. Le Quotidien de l'Economie [*A publication*]
ECX .... Electronically Controlled Telephone Exchange (DEN)
Ec Xaver..... Ecclesiastica Xaveriana [*A publication*]
ECY .... Economy Inns, Inc. [*Vancouver Stock Exchange symbol*]
ECYC........ Earl of Chester's Yeomanry Cavalry [*British military*] (DMA)
ECYC........ European Confederation of Youth Clubs (EA)
ECYFC.... European Committee for Young Farmers and 4H Clubs (EA)
ECYO........ European Community Youth Orchestra (EAIO)
ECYU .... Elizabethan Club of Yale University (EA)
ECZ .... East Cape [*New Zealand*] [*Seismograph station code, US Geological Survey*] (SEIS)
Eczac Bul ... Eczacilik Bulteni [*A publication*]
Eczacilik Bul ... Eczacilik Bulteni [*A publication*]
ED.............. Aerolineas Nacionales del Ecuador SA [*ICAO designator*] (FAAC)
ED.............. Consolidated Edison Co. of New York, Inc. [*NYSE symbol*] (SPSG)
Ed.............. Department of Education [*Cabinet department*]
ED.............. Doctor of Engineering
ED.............. Eastern District [*ATSC*]

ED............. Eastern District Court Reports [*South Africa*] [*A publication*] (DLA)
ED............. Economic Development [*A publication*]
ED............. Economically Disadvantaged (OICC)
ED............. Economics Division [*US Military Government, Germany*]
ED............. Ectodermal Dysplasia [*Medicine*]
Ed............. Edda. Revue de Litterature [*A publication*]
Ed............. Eden's English Chancery Reports Tempore Northington [*28 English Reprint*] [*1757-66*] [*A publication*] (DLA)
Ed............. Edgar's Decisions, Scotch Court of Session [*1724-25*] [*A publication*] (DLA)
ED............. Edge Distance
ED............. Edinburgh [*City in Scotland*]
ED............. Edit [*or Edited*]
ED............. Edition (AFM)
ED............. Editor (EY)
ED............. Education
Ed............. Education [*A publication*]
ED............. Education Department [*British military*] (DMA)
E & D........ Education and Development
ED............. Educational Drama
ED............. Edulcorata [*Sweetened*] [*Pharmacy*] (ROG)
'Ed............. 'Eduyyoth (BJA)
ED............. Effective Dose
ED............. Efficiency Decoration [*Military*] [*British*]
ED............. Egg Diameter [*Pisciculture*]
ED............. El Derecho [*Argentina*] [*A publication*]
ED............. Elasticity of Demand [*Economics*] (DCTA)
E/D............. Elbow Disarticulation [*Orthopedics*]
ED............. Election District
ED............. Electric Dynamic [*Motors*]
ED............. Electrical Department [*Navy*] [*British*]
ED............. Electrical Differential
ED............. Electrochemical Detector [*Instrumentation*]
ED............. Electrodialysis [*Medicine*]
ED............. Electrodynamic (DEN)
ED............. Electron Device (MCD)
ED............. Electron Diffraction
ED............. Electronic Development (MCD)
ED............. Electronic Differential [*Analyzer*]
ED............. Electronic Digital [*Analyzer*]
ED............. Electronic Display
E/D............. Embarkation/Disembarkation
ED............. Embryonic Day
ED............. Emergency Department [*of a hospital*]
ED............. Emergency Destruction (MCD)
ED............. Emotional Disturbance
ED............. Emotionally Deprived
ED............. Emotionally Disabled (OICC)
ED............. [*The*] Emphatic Diaglott [*1942*] [*A publication*] (BJA)
ED............. Employability Development (OICC)
E d D.......... Enciclopedia del Diritto [*A publication*]
ED............. End Door
ED............. Enemy Dead
ED............. Engine Designer (DS)
ED............. Engine Drive (MSA)
ED............. Engineering Data
ED............. Engineering Department [*Navy*] [*British*]
ED............. Engineering Depot
ED............. Engineering Design
ED............. Engineering Development
E & D........ Engineering and Development Directorate [*Johnson Space Center*] [*NASA*] (NASA)
ED............. Engineering Directive (NASA)
ED............. Engineering Division
ED............. Engineering Document
ED............. Engineering Draftsman
ED............. Engineering Duty [*Navy*]
ED............. English Duke (ROG)
ED............. Entertainment Duty (DLA)
ED............. Entner-Doudoroff [*Hexose metabolic pathway*]
ED............. Enumeration District [*Census*]
ED............. Envelope Drawing (MSA)
ED............. Environmental Disruption
ED............. Enzymatic Deficiencies
ED............. Ephemeris Dacoromana [*A publication*]
ED............. Epidural [*Brain anatomy*]
ED............. Equilibrium Dialysis [*Analytical chemistry*]
ED............. Equipment Delay (CAAL)
ED............. Erase Digital [*Signal*]
ED............. ERIC [*Educational Resources Information Center*] Document
ED............. Error Detecting [*or Detection*] [*Data processing*]
ED............. Erythema Dose [*Medicine*]
ED............. Esquerra Democratica [*Democratic Left*] [*Spain*] [*Political party*] (PPE)
ED............. Establishment Date [*IRS*]
ED............. Estate Duty (DLA)
ED............. Estimated Date (AAG)
ED............. Ethynodiol [*Pharmacology*]
ED............. Etudes Dahomeennes [*A publication*]

ED............ Etudes et Documents du Conseil d'Etat [French] [A publication] (DLA)
ED............ Euclidean Distance Matrix [Statistics]
ED............ Euntes Docete [A publication]
ED............ Eurodefence
ed---- .... Europe, Southeastern [MARC geographic area code] [Library of Congress] (LCCP)
ED............ Every Day
ED............ Evolutionary Distance
ED............ Ex-Dividend [Without the right to dividend] [Finance]
ED............ Excess Distribution (ADA)
ED............ Exchequer Division, English Law Reports [A publication] (DLA)
ED............ Excused from Duty
ED............ Executive Director
ED............ Exhaust Dampers [Nuclear energy] (NRCH)
ED............ Existence Doubtful [Navigation charts]
ED............ Expanded Display
E-D........... Expansion Deflection (AAG)
E & D .... Experimental and Demonstration Projects
ED............ Experimental Design
ED............ Exploratory Development [Military]
ED............ Explosive Device
ED............ Exports Directorate [British]
ED............ Exposure Draft [Business term]
ED............ Extended Definition Television [in ED Beta] [Sony Corp.]
ED............ Extended Duration (OICC)
ED............ Extensive Disease [Medicine]
ED............ External Device [Data processing]
ED............ Extra Dividend [Banking] (ADA)
ED............ Extra Duty [Marine Corps]
ED............ Extra-Low Dispersion [Instrumentation]
ED............ Extraction Dialysis [For separation of mixtures]
ED............ Extrusion Die (MCD)
ED$_{50}$........... Effective Dose, Median
EDA .... Early Departure Authorized
EDA .... Eating Disorders Association (EAIO)
EDA .... Economic Development Administration [Formerly, Office of Appalachian Assistance] [Terminated] [Department of Commerce]
EDA .... Economic Development and Cultural Change [A publication]
EDA .... Education Development Associates [Information service or system]
EDA .... Educational Drama Association (EAIO)
EDA .... Electrodermal Audiometry [Otolaryngology]
EDA .... Electronic Dental Anesthesia
EDA .... Electronic Design Automation [Data processing]
EDA .... Electronic Differential Analyzer
EDA .... Electronic Digital Analyzer (MCD)
EDA .... Electronic Display Assembly (NASA)
EDA .... Elevation Drive Assembly (MCD)
EDA .... Emergency Declaration Area [Environmental Protection Agency]
EDA .... Emergency Distance Available [Aviation] (AIA)
EDA .... Encoder/Decoder Assembly (MCD)
EDA .... End-Diastolic Area [Cardiology]
EDA .... Equipment Design Agent
EDA .... Equipment Disposition Authorization
EDA .... Erection Digital Assembly
EDA .... Error Detector Assembly
EDA .... Error and Dispersion Analysis (MCD)
EDA .... Estimated Date of Arrival (NG)
EDA .... Estimated Date of Availability (AAG)
EDA .... Ethylene Diacrylate [Organic chemistry]
EDA .... Ethylenediamine [Organic chemistry]
EDA .... European Demolition Association (EA)
EDA .... European Desalination Association [Glasgow, Scotland] (EAIO)
EDA .... Excess Defense Article (AFIT)
EDA .... Exhaust Deflection Angle
EDA .... Exploratory Data Analysis [Statistics]
EDA .... Explosive Distributors Association (EA)
EDA .... Extensive-Dilatancy Anisotropy [Geology]
Ed A2 .... Advanced Degree in Education
EDAA .... Frankfurt Am Main, USAFE [United States Air Force in Europe] [Federal Republic of Germany] [ICAO location identifier] (ICLI)
EDAB .... Bitburg [Federal Republic of Germany] [ICAO location identifier] (ICLI)
EDAB .... Early Deploying Armored Bridge (MCD)
EdAb.......... Education Abstracts [A publication]
EDA Bull ... EDA [British Electrical Development Association] Bulletin [A publication]
EDAC .... Edac Technologies Corp. [Marinette, WI] [NASDAQ symbol] (NQ)
EDAC .... Electron Donor Acceptor Complex
EDAC .... Electronic Dive Angle Control
EDAC .... Equipment Distribution and Condition [Statistical reporting system] [Military] (AFM)
EDAC .... Error Detection and Correction

EDAC .... Ethyl(dimethylaminopropyl)carbodiimide [Also, EDC, EDCI] [Organic chemistry]
EDAC .... Exhibit and Display Association of Canada
EDAC .... Kindsbach [Federal Republic of Germany] [ICAO location identifier] (ICLI)
EdAd.......... Educational Administration Abstracts [A publication]
EDAD .... Spangdahlem [Federal Republic of Germany] [ICAO location identifier] (ICLI)
Ed Adm Q .. Educational Administration Quarterly [A publication]
Ed Adm & Sup ... Educational Administration and Supervision [A publication]
EDAF........ Rhein-Main Air Base [Federal Republic of Germany] [ICAO location identifier] (ICLI)
EDAH .... Etudes Dahomeennes [A publication]
EDAH .... Hahn [Federal Republic of Germany] [ICAO location identifier] (ICLI)
EDAK .... Kindsbach [Federal Republic of Germany] [ICAO location identifier] (ICLI)
EDAL .... Engineering Design and Analysis Laboratory [University of New Hampshire] [Research center] (RCD)
EDAL .... Sollingen [Federal Republic of Germany] [ICAO location identifier] (ICLI)
EDALHAB ... Engineering Design and Analysis Laboratory Habitat
EDAM .... Experiments, Drill, and Maintenance
EDAM .... Zweibrucken [Federal Republic of Germany] [ICAO location identifier] (ICLI)
EDAN .... Lahr [Federal Republic of Germany] [ICAO location identifier] (ICLI)
EDANA ..... European Disposables and Nonwovens Association (EAIO)
EDAO........ Gates [Federal Republic of Germany] [ICAO location identifier] (ICLI)
EDAP .... Environmental Design Alignment Process
EDAP .... May [Federal Republic of Germany] [ICAO location identifier] (ICLI)
EDAPS..... Electronic Data Processing System
EDAQ........ Rotz [Federal Republic of Germany] [ICAO location identifier] (ICLI)
EDAR .... Ramstein [Federal Republic of Germany] [ICAO location identifier] (ICLI)
ED Ark ...... United States District Court for the Eastern and Western Districts of Arkansas (DLA)
Ed Arn........ Editiones Arnamagnaenae [A publication]
EDARR....... Engineering Drawing and Assembly Release Record (AAG)
EDAS......... Enlisted Distribution and Assignment System [DoD]
EDAS......... ERIC [Educational Resources Information Center] Data Access System [Search system]
EDAS......... Sembach [Federal Republic of Germany] [ICAO location identifier] (ICLI)
Ed Asia Oceania ... Education in Asia and Oceania [A publication]
Ed Asia Pacif ... Education in Asia and the Pacific [A publication]
Ed Ass........ Eddis. Administration of Assets [1880] [A publication] (DLA)
EDAT .... Electronic Data Technologies [NASDAQ symbol] (NQ)
EDAV .... Siegenberg [Federal Republic of Germany] [ICAO location identifier] (ICLI)
EDAVR ..... Enlisted Distribution and Verification Report
EDAW .... Wiesbaden [Federal Republic of Germany] [ICAO location identifier] (ICLI)
EDAX .... Energy Dispersive Analysis by X-Ray [Photovoltaic energy systems]
EDAX .... Ramstein [Federal Republic of Germany] [ICAO location identifier] (ICLI)
Ed B .... Bachelor of Education
EDB .... Broward Community College, Fort Lauderdale, FL [OCLC symbol] (OCLC)
EDB .... Early Dry Breakfast [Medicine]
EDB .... Econometric Data Bank [University of Melbourne] [Australia] [Information service or system] (CRD)
EDB .... Economic Defense Board [Later, Board of Economic Warfare] [World War II]
EDB .... Economic Development Board [Generic term] (DS)
EDB .... Educational Data Bank (IEEE)
EDB .... El Debba [Sudan] [Airport symbol] [Obsolete] (OAG)
EDB .... Elongated Die Bushing
EDB .... Emergency Dispersal Bases (NATG)
EDB .... Emily Dickinson Bulletin [A publication]
EDB .... End of Data Block [Data processing] (CET)
EDB .... Energy Database [Department of Energy] [Information service or system]
EDB .... Engineering Data Bank [GIDEP]
EDB .... Environmental Data Book (NASA)
EDB .... Ethylene Dibromide [Same as DBE, EB] [Organic chemistry]
EDB .... Excise Duty Bulletins [Revenue Canada - Customs and Excise] [Information service or system] (CRD)
EDB .... Extensor Digitorum Brevis [Anatomy]
EDB .... Extradimensional Being
EDBA .... Berlin [Federal Republic of Germany] [ICAO location identifier] (ICLI)
EDBAR...... Edith and Dana Bennett Agricultural Roundtable (EA)
EDBB........ Berlin/Tempelhof [Federal Republic of Germany] [ICAO location identifier] (ICLI)

EDBCA...... Electricite de France. Bulletin de la Direction des Etudes et Recherches. Serie C. Mathematiques-Informatique [*A publication*]

EDBD .... Environmental Data Base Directory [*National Oceanographic Data Center*] [*Database*]   (MSC)

EDBE........ Export Development Bank of Egypt

EDBG .... Berlin/Gatow [*Federal Republic of Germany*] [*ICAO location identifier*]   (ICLI)

EDBHPA... Ethylenediaminebis(hydroxyphenylacetic acid) [*Also, EDDHA, EDHPA*] [*Organic chemistry*]

Ed Bills ...... Eddis on Bills of Exchange [*A publication*]   (DLA)

Ed Bi-Mo.. Educational Bi-Monthly [*A publication*]

Ed B Int...... Educational Broadcasting International [*United Kingdom*] [*A publication*]

Ed BL......... Eden's Bankrupt Law [*A publication*]   (DLA)

Ed Books and Equip ... Educational Books and Equipment [*A publication*]   (APTA)

EDBP......... Epidemiology, Demography, and Biometry Program [*National Institute on Aging*] [*Department of Health and Human Services*]

Ed Bro .... Eden's Edition of Brown's English Chancery Reports [*1757-66*] [*A publication*]   (DLA)

EDBT........ Berlin/Tegel [*Federal Republic of Germany*] [*ICAO location identifier*]   (ICLI)

EDC .... Eastern Defense Command [*Army*]

EDC .... Eastern District Court Reports [*South Africa*] [*A publication*]   (DLA)

EDC .... Eastman Dental Center [*University of Rochester*] [*Research center*]   (RCD)

EDC .... Economic Development Committee [*Nickname: "Little Neddie"*] [*British*]

EDC .... Economic Development and Cultural Change [*A publication*]

EdC .... EDCO, Springfield, MO [*Library symbol*] [*Library of Congress*]   (LCLS)

EDC .... Edincik [*Turkey*] [*Seismograph station code, US Geological Survey*]   (SEIS)

EDC .... Education Development Center [*Defunct*]   (EA)

EDC .... Effective Date of Change   (MCD)

EDC .... Electrode Dark Current

EDC .... Electronic Data Communications

EDC .... Electronic Desk Calculator   (IEEE)

EDC .... Electronic Digital Computer

EDC .... Electronic Discharge LASER   (MCD)

EDC .... Electronics Design Center [*Case Western Reserve University*] [*Research center*]   (RCD)

EDC .... Emergency Decontamination Center [*Nuclear energy*]   (NRCH)

EDC .... Emergency Digital Computer

EDC .... Enamel Double Cotton [*Wire insulation*]   (AAG)

EDC .... End-Detonating Cartridge [*Explosive*]

EDC .... End-Diastolic Count [*Cardiology*]

EDC .... Energy Distribution Curve [*Electron*]

EDC .... Engineering Data Control

EDC .... Engineering Design Change

EDC .... Engineering Documentation Center [*NASA*]   (KSC)

EDC .... EROS [*Earth Resources Observation Systems*] Data Center [*Marine science*]   (MSC)

EDC .... Error Detecting Code

EDC .... Error Detection and Correction   (NATG)

EDC .... Escalation during Construction   (MCD)

EDC .... Estimated Date of Completion

EDC .... Estimated [*or Expected*] Date of Confinement [*Obstetrics*]

EDC .... Ethyl(dimethylaminopropyl)carbodiimide [*Also, EDAC, EDCI*] [*Organic chemistry*]

EDC .... Ethylene Dichloride [*Organic chemistry*]

EDC .... European Defense Community [*NATO*]

EDC .... European Disarmament Conference

EDC .... European Documentation Centre [*University of Dundee*] [*Dundee, Scotland*]   (DLA)

EDC .... Evaluation Documentation Center [*Department of Health and Human Services*] [*Information service or system*]   (IID)

EDC .... Expect Departure Clearance [*Aviation*]   (FAAC)

EDC .... Expected Date of Confinement [*Medicine*]   (DHSM)

E/DC .... Expected/Dual-Command Travel Time

EDC .... Experiment Development Center [*NASA*]   (KSC)

EDC .... Experimental Display Concept [*Space shuttle*] [*NASA*]

EDC .... Explosive Disposal Control

EDC .... Export Development Corporation [*Canada*]

EDC .... External-Device Code [*Data processing*]   (MDG)

EDC .... External Disk/Drum Channel

EDC .... Extra Dark Color   (ADA)

EDC .... Extractive Distillation Column [*Chemical engineering*]

EDCA .... Employment Department Clerks' Association [*A union*] [*British*]

EDCA .... Executive Director for Conventional Ammunition

EDCA .... Gluecksburg [*Federal Republic of Germany*] [*ICAO location identifier*]   (ICLI)

ED Cal .... United States District Court for the Eastern District of California   (DLA)

Ed Can .... Education Canada [*A publication*]

Ed Cat .... Ediciones Catedra [*A publication*]

EDCB .... Bueckeburg [*Federal Republic of Germany*] [*ICAO location identifier*]   (ICLI)

EDCC .... Economic Development and Cultural Change [*A publication*]

EDCC .... Goch [*Federal Republic of Germany*] [*ICAO location identifier*]   (ICLI)

EDCCA ..... Economic Development and Cultural Change [*A publication*]

EDC Ch ..... Economic Development and Cultural Change [*A publication*]

EDCE......... Etudes et Documents du Conseil d'Etat [*French*] [*A publication*]   (DLA)

EDCE......... Rheine-Bentlage [*Federal Republic of Germany*] [*ICAO location identifier*]   (ICLI)

EDCEN ..... Education Center [*Army*]   (AABC)

EDCG .... Eggebek [*Federal Republic of Germany*] [*ICAO location identifier*]   (ICLI)

EDCG .... Error Detection Code Generator

Ed Ch .... Edwards' New York Chancery Reports [*A publication*]   (DLA)

EDCH .... Hurth [*Federal Republic of Germany*] [*ICAO location identifier*]   (ICLI)

EDCHA ..... Education in Chemistry [*A publication*]

Ed in Chem ... Education in Chemistry [*A publication*]

Ed Ch R ..... Edwards' New York Chancery Reports [*A publication*]   (DLA)

EDCI.......... Ethyl(dimethylaminopropyl)carbodiimide [*Also, EDAC, EDC*] [*Organic chemistry*]

EDCI.......... Itzehoe Hungriger Wolf [*Federal Republic of Germany*] [*ICAO location identifier*]   (ICLI)

Ed Circ WA ... Education Circular. Education Department of Western Australia [*A publication*]   (APTA)

EDCK .... Kiel-Holtenau [*Federal Republic of Germany*] [*ICAO location identifier*]   (ICLI)

EDCL......... Celle [*Federal Republic of Germany*] [*ICAO location identifier*]   (ICLI)

EDCL......... Electric-Discharge Convection LASER [*Navy*]

EDCLMDA ... Eastern Dry Cleaning and Laundry Machinery Distributors Association [*Defunct*]   (EA)

EDCM .... Aachen/Merzbruck [*Federal Republic of Germany*] [*ICAO location identifier*]   (ICLI)

EDCM .... Educom Corp. [*NASDAQ symbol*]   (NQ)

EDC(M)..... Electrochemical Depolarized Carbon Dioxide (Module) [*NASA*]   (NASA)

EDCMR .... Effective Date of Change of Morning Report [*Military*]

EDCN .... Education   (ADA)

EDCN .... Engineering Drawing Change Notice [*Nuclear energy*]   (NRCH)

EDCN .... Experimental Data Communications Network   (MCD)

EDCN .... Nordholz [*Federal Republic of Germany*] [*ICAO location identifier*]   (ICLI)

EDCO .... Edison Control Corp. [*Piscataway, NJ*] [*NASDAQ symbol*]   (NQ)

EDCo .... Educational Development Corporation [*Defunct*]   (EA)

EDCOM .... Editor and Compiler

Ed Comment ... Editorial Comment   (DLA)

EDCP .... Engineering Design Change Proposal

E/DCP....... Equipment/Document Change Proposal   (NATG)

EDCP .... Ethyl Dichlorophosphate [*Organic chemistry*]

EDCP .... External Data Channel Processor   (NOAA)

EDCPF ...... Environmental Data Collection and Processing Facility [*Tucson, AZ*] [*Army*]   (AABC)

Ed CR......... Edwards' New York Chancery Reports [*A publication*]   (DLA)

EDCR .... Engineering Design Change Request   (MCD)

EDCR .... Rotenburg/Wumme [*Federal Republic of Germany*] [*ICAO location identifier*]   (ICLI)

EDCS......... Ecumenical Development Cooperative Society   (EAIO)

EDCS......... Engineering Design Change Schedule

EDCS......... Extended Defense Communication System   (CINC)

EDCS......... Schleswig [*Federal Republic of Germany*] [*ICAO location identifier*]   (ICLI)

EDCSA...... Effective Date of Change of Strength Accountability [*Military*]

EDCT......... Estimated Departure Clearance Time [*Aviation*]   (FAAC)

EDCTU ..... Electronic Development and Compatibility Test Unit

EDCU .... Butzweilerhof [*Federal Republic of Germany*] [*ICAO location identifier*]   (ICLI)

EDCV .... Enamel Double Cotton Varnish [*Wire insulation*]

EDCW .... External-Device Control Word [*Data processing*]

EDCW .... Werl [*Federal Republic of Germany*] [*ICAO location identifier*]   (ICLI)

Ed D.......... Doctor of Education

EDD.......... Earliest Due Date

EDD.......... Eastern Development Division [*Air Force*]

EDD.......... Economic Development District [*EDA*]

EDD.......... Editions   (ROG)

EDD.......... Editors   (ROG)

EDD.......... Electric Displacement Density

EDD.......... Electrodermal Diagnosis [*Controversial medical technique*]

EDD.......... Electronic Data Display

EDD.......... Electronic Dehydration Dryer

EDD.......... Electronic Document Delivery [*Software*]

EDD.......... End Delivery Date   (AAG)

EDD.......... End-Diastolic Diameter [*Cardiology*]

EdD........... End-Diastolic Dimension [*Cardiology*]

EDD.......... Engagement Data Display   (MCD)

EDD.......... Engineering Data Depository   (MSA)

EDD.......... Engineering Design Data   (AAG)

EDD........... Engineering and Development Directorate [*Johnson Space Center*] [*NASA*]
EDD........... English Dialect Dictionary [*A publication*]
EDD........... Envelope Delay Distortion
EDD........... Enzyme-Digested Delta Endotoxin [*of Bacillus thuringiensis*] [*Biological control*]
EDD........... Equipment Development Division [*Britain's national phone-tapping center*]
EDD........... Essential Data Duplicator [*Utilico Microware*]
EDD........... Estimated Delivery Date
EDD........... Event Data Distributor　(MCD)
EDD........... Expected Date of Delivery [*Obstetrics*]
EDD........... Expert Database Designer [*Data processing*]
EDD........... Extra Deep Drawing [*Metal industry*]
EDDA........ Bonn, Frankfurt Am Main [*Federal Republic of Germany*] [*ICAO location identifier*]　(ICLI)
EDDA..,..... Ethylenediaminediacetic Acid [*Organic chemistry*]
EDDC........ East Coast Documents Distribution Center
EDDD........ Expanded Direct Distance Dialing [*Telecommunications*]
EDDD........ Frankfurt Am Main [*Federal Republic of Germany*] [*ICAO location identifier*]　(ICLI)
Ed for Dev ... Education for Development [*A publication*]
EDDF........ Error Detection and Decision Feedback
EDDF........ Frankfurt Am Main [*Federal Republic of Germany*] [*ICAO location identifier*]　(ICLI)
EDDFEC ... Estimated Date of Departure Far East Command [*Military*]
EDDH........ Hamburg [*Federal Republic of Germany*] [*ICAO location identifier*]　(ICLI)
EDDHA..... Ethylenediaminedi-O-Hydroxyphenylacetate [*or -hydroxyphenylacetic Acid*] [*Also, EDBHPA, EDHPA*] [*Organic chemistry*]
EDDI .... Ethylenediamine Dihydriodide [*Organic chemistry*]
EDDID ...... Energy and Development Digest [*A publication*]
Ed Digest ... Education Digest [*A publication*]
EDDK........ Koeln-Bonn [*Federal Republic of Germany*] [*ICAO location identifier*]　(ICLI)
EDDL .... Duesseldorf [*Federal Republic of Germany*] [*ICAO location identifier*]　(ICLI)
EDDM....... Muenchen [*Federal Republic of Germany*] [*ICAO location identifier*]　(ICLI)
EDDN........ Nuernberg [*Federal Republic of Germany*] [*ICAO location identifier*]　(ICLI)
EDDP........ Electron Dipole-Dipole Polarization
EDDP........ Engineering Design Data Package　(AAG)
EDDP........ Engineering Design Documentation Procedures　(MCD)
EDDR........ Electron Dipole-Dipole Reservoir　(NASA)
EDDS .... Electron Devices Data Service [*National Institute of Standards and Technology*]
EDDS .... Emergency Detection and Decision System
EDDS .... Ethylenediaminedisuccinic [*Organic chemistry*]
EDDS .... Stuttgart [*Federal Republic of Germany*] [*ICAO location identifier*]　(ICLI)
EDDU........ Rhein [*Federal Republic of Germany*] [*ICAO location identifier*]　(ICLI)
EDDV .... Hannover [*Federal Republic of Germany*] [*ICAO location identifier*]　(ICLI)
EDDW....... Bremen [*Federal Republic of Germany*] [*ICAO location identifier*]　(ICLI)
EDDY .... Maastricht [*Federal Republic of Germany*] [*ICAO location identifier*]　(ICLI)
EDDZ........ Frankfurt Am Main [*Federal Republic of Germany*] [*ICAO location identifier*]　(ICLI)
EDE .... Edenton, NC [*Location identifier*] [*FAA*]　(FAAL)
EDE .... Electrical Design Engineering
EDE .... Electronic Defense Evaluator
EDE .... Elliptic [*or Exact*] Differential Equation
EDE .... Emergency Decelerating [*Relay*]　(IEEE)
EDE .... Emitter Dip Effect　(IEEE)
EDE .... Empire District Electric Co. [*NYSE symbol*]　(SPSG)
EDE .... Environmental Data and Ecological Parameters Data Base [*International Society of Ecological Modelling*] [*Information service or system*]　(IID)
EDE .... Esquerda Democratica Estudantil [*Democratic Student Left*] [*Portugal*] [*Political party*]　(PPE)
EDE .... Experimental Demolition Establishment [*British*]
EDEA .... Amberg [*Federal Republic of Germany*] [*ICAO location identifier*]　(ICLI)
EDEAC...... EPRI [*Electric Power Research Institute*] Database for Environmentally Assisted Cracking [*Battelle Memorial Institute*] [*Information service or system*]　(IID)
EDEB......... Ansbach [*Federal Republic of Germany*] [*ICAO location identifier*]　(ICLI)
EDEC......... Aschaffenburg [*Federal Republic of Germany*] [*ICAO location identifier*]　(ICLI)
EDECWS .. Emergency Diesel Engine Cooling Water System [*Nuclear energy*]　(NRCH)
EDED .... Error Detection Encoder-Decoder [*Ground Communications Facility, NASA*]
EDED .... Kaiserlautern [*Federal Republic of Germany*] [*ICAO location identifier*]　(ICLI)

EDEE......... Heidelberg, United States Army [*Federal Republic of Germany*] [*ICAO location identifier*]　(ICLI)
EDEF......... Babenhausen [*Federal Republic of Germany*] [*ICAO location identifier*]　(ICLI)
EDEG .... Bad Kissingen [*Federal Republic of Germany*] [*ICAO location identifier*]　(ICLI)
EDEH........ Bad Kreuznach [*Federal Republic of Germany*] [*ICAO location identifier*]　(ICLI)
EDEI......... Miesau-West [*Federal Republic of Germany*] [*ICAO location identifier*]　(ICLI)
EDEJ......... Bamberg [*Federal Republic of Germany*] [*ICAO location identifier*]　(ICLI)
EDEK .... Baumholder [*Federal Republic of Germany*] [*ICAO location identifier*]　(ICLI)
EDEK .... Ethniki Demokratiki Enosi Kyprou [*Socialist Party of Cyprus*] [*Political party*]　(PPW)
EDEL .... Bayreuth [*Federal Republic of Germany*] [*ICAO location identifier*]　(ICLI)
EDELS ...... Emergency Diesel Engine Lubrication System [*Nuclear energy*]　(NRCH)
EDEM ...... Muenchen, Hospital, Perlacher Forst [*Federal Republic of Germany*] [*ICAO location identifier*]　(ICLI)
Eden........... Eden's English Chancery Reports [*28 English Reprint*] [*A publication*]　(DLA)
EDEN .... Emma Dorothy Eliza Nevitte Southworth [*American novelist, 1818-99*] [*Acronym used as pseudonym*]
EDEN .... Evaluated Disposition toward the Environment [*Student attitude test*]
EDEN .... Maurice Rose [*Federal Republic of Germany*] [*ICAO location identifier*]　(ICLI)
EDENA ..... Educator [*A publication*]
Eden Bankr ... Eden's Bankrupt Law [*A publication*]　(DLA)
Eden (Eng) ... Eden's English Chancery Reports [*28 English Reprint*] [*A publication*]　(DLA)
Eden Pen Law ... Eden's Principles of Penal Law [*A publication*]　(DLA)
Eden's Prin PL ... Eden's Principles of Penal Law [*A publication*]　(DLA)
EDEO .... Bremerhaven [*Federal Republic of Germany*] [*ICAO location identifier*]　(ICLI)
EDEP......... Budingen [*Federal Republic of Germany*] [*ICAO location identifier*]　(ICLI)
EDER .... Crailsheim [*Federal Republic of Germany*] [*ICAO location identifier*]　(ICLI)
EDES......... Darmstadt [*Federal Republic of Germany*] [*ICAO location identifier*]　(ICLI)
EDES......... Ethnikos Demokratikos Ellinikos Stratos [*National Democratic Greek Army*]　(PPE)
EDESA ..... Economic Development of Equatorial and Southern Africa
EDESA ..... Ediciones Espanolas Sociedad Anonima [*A publication*]
EDESS ...... Emergency Diesel Engine Starting System [*Nuclear energy*]　(NRCH)
EDET........ Elevation Data Edit Terminals　(RDA)
EDET........ Engine Detector　(MCD)
EDET......... Erlangen [*Federal Republic of Germany*] [*ICAO location identifier*]　(ICLI)
EDETATE ... Ethylenediaminetetraacetate [*Also, EDTA, enta*] [*Organic chemistry*] [*USAN*]
EDETD..... Energy Detente [*A publication*]
EDEU........ Giebelstadt [*Federal Republic of Germany*] [*ICAO location identifier*]　(ICLI)
E Deusto .... Estudios de Deusto [*A publication*]
EDEV .... Friedberg [*Federal Republic of Germany*] [*ICAO location identifier*]　(ICLI)
EDEW .... Enhanced Distant Early Warning
EDEW .... Fuerth [*Federal Republic of Germany*] [*ICAO location identifier*]　(ICLI)
EDEX .... Fulda [*Federal Republic of Germany*] [*ICAO location identifier*]　(ICLI)
Ed Exec Overview ... Educational Executive's Overview [*A publication*]
EDEY .... Zweibrucken [*Federal Republic of Germany*] [*ICAO location identifier*]　(ICLI)
EDEZ......... Germersheim [*Federal Republic of Germany*] [*ICAO location identifier*]　(ICLI)
EDF .... Anchorage, AK [*Location identifier*] [*FAA*]　(FAAL)
EDF .... Earthquake Data File [*Marine science*]　(MSC)
EDF .... East Daggafontein [*Vancouver Stock Exchange symbol*]
EDF .... Economics of Distribution Foundation　(EA)
Ed F............ Educational Forum [*A publication*]
EDF .... Electric Depth Finder
EDF .... Electricite de France [*Information service or system*]　(IID)
EDF .... Electrophoresis Duplicating Film [*For analytical chemistry*]
EDF .... Elongatable Dow Fiber [*Dow Chemical Co.*]
EDF .... Elongation, Derotation, and Lateral Flexion [*Medicine*]
EDF .... Emergency Decontamination Facility [*Energy Research and Development Administration*]
EDF .... Empirical Distribution Function [*Statistics*]
EDF .... Engineering Data File
EDF .... Enlisted Dining Facility [*Military*]
EdF............ Enroles de Force [*Forced Conscripts*] [*Luxembourg*]　(PPE)
EDF .... Environmental Defense Fund　(EA)
EDF .... Erythroid Differentiation Factor [*Endocrinology*]
EDF .... European Defense Force　(NATG)

EDF .... European Development Fund (EY)
EDF .... Experiment Data Facility [*NASA*] (KSC)
EDF .... External Delay Factor [*Data processing*]
EDFA .... Electronic Differential Analyzer (MSA)
EDFB .... Eastern Deciduous Forest Biome [*Ecological biogeographic study*]
EDFB .... Reichelsheim [*Federal Republic of Germany*] [*ICAO location identifier*] (ICLI)
EDFC .... Aschaffenburg-Grossostheim [*Federal Republic of Germany*] [*ICAO location identifier*] (ICLI)
EDF-DOC ... Electricite de France [*Bibliographic database*] [*French*]
EDFE .... Egelsbach [*Federal Republic of Germany*] [*ICAO location identifier*] (ICLI)
EDFE .... Engineer District, Far East (CINC)
EDFF .... Frankfurt [*Federal Republic of Germany*] [*ICAO location identifier*] (ICLI)
EDFG .... Extended Data Flow Graph
EDFG .... Gelnhausen [*Federal Republic of Germany*] [*ICAO location identifier*] (ICLI)
EDFK .... Bad Kissingen [*Federal Republic of Germany*] [*ICAO location identifier*] (ICLI)
EDFM .... Mannheim-Neuostheim [*Federal Republic of Germany*] [*ICAO location identifier*] (ICLI)
EDFN .... Marburg-Schoenstadt [*Federal Republic of Germany*] [*ICAO location identifier*] (ICLI)
EDFO .... Economic Development Financing Organization [*Greece*]
EDFO .... Michelstadt [*Federal Republic of Germany*] [*ICAO location identifier*] (ICLI)
Ed Forum ... Educational Forum [*A publication*]
EDFORUM ... Educators Forum [*Columbus, OH*] [*Information service or system*] (IID)
EDFP .... Engine Driven Fire Pump (IEEE)
EDFQ .... Allendorf/Eder [*Federal Republic of Germany*] [*ICAO location identifier*] (ICLI)
EDFR .... Effective Date of Federal Recognition [*Military*]
EDFR .... Rothenburg [*Federal Republic of Germany*] [*ICAO location identifier*] (ICLI)
EDFS .... Schweinfurt-Sud [*Federal Republic of Germany*] [*ICAO location identifier*] (ICLI)
ED-FTGA ... Eastern Dark-Fired Tobacco Growers Association (EA)
EDFU .... Mainbullau [*Federal Republic of Germany*] [*ICAO location identifier*] (ICLI)
EDFV .... Worms [*Federal Republic of Germany*] [*ICAO location identifier*] (ICLI)
EDFW .... Wuerzburg-Schenkenturm [*Federal Republic of Germany*] [*ICAO location identifier*] (ICLI)
EDFX .... Fuldatal [*Federal Republic of Germany*] [*ICAO location identifier*] (ICLI)
Edg .... Edgar's Reports, Scotch Court of Session [*1724-25*] [*A publication*] (DLA)
EDG .... Edgewood Arsenal, MD [*Location identifier*] [*FAA*] (FAAL)
EDG .... Electrical Discharge Grinding [*Manufacturing term*]
EDG .... Electrodynamic Gradient Freeze [*Crystal growing technique*]
EDG .... Electrodynogram [*For evaluation of walking gait*]
EDG .... Electronic Development Group [*Military*] (AFIT)
EDG .... Emergency Diesel Generator (NRCH)
EDG .... Exploratory Development Goal [*Military*]
Edg All News ... Edgar Allen News [*A publication*]
Edgar .... Edgar's Reports, Scotch Court of Session [*1724-25*] [*A publication*] (DLA)
EDGAR ..... Electronic Data Gathering, Analysis, and Retrieval [*Securities and Exchange Commission pilot project*] (IID)
EDGAR ..... Experimental Data Gathering and Reduction (MCD)
Ed Gaz NSW ... Education Gazette. New South Wales Department of Education [*A publication*] (APTA)
Ed Gaz SA ... Education Gazette. South Australia Department of Education [*A publication*] (APTA)
Ed Gaz & Teach Aid (Vic) ... Education Gazette and Teachers Aid (Victoria) [*A publication*] (APTA)
EDGB .... Breitscheid/Dillkreis [*Federal Republic of Germany*] [*ICAO location identifier*] (ICLI)
Edg C .... Canons Enacted under King Edgar [*A publication*] (DLA)
EDGC .... Edgcomb Corporation [*New York, NY*] [*NASDAQ symbol*] (NQ)
EDGCAIES ... Emergency Diesel Generator Combustion Air Intake and Exhaust System [*Nuclear energy*] (NRCH)
EDGE .... Electronic Data Gathering Equipment
EDGE .... Ergonomic Digitally Generated Environments [*Chrysler Corp.*]
EDGE .... Experimental Display Generator
EDGEDA .. Educational Gerontology [*A publication*]
EDGEP ...... European Democratic Group in the European Parliament [*Brussels, Belgium*] [*Political party*] (EAIO)
Edgerton Germeshausen & Grier Rept ... Edgerton, Germeshausen, and Grier Report [*A publication*]
EDGF .... Endothelial-Derived Growth Factor [*Biochemistry*]
EDGF .... Eye-Derived Growth Factor [*Biochemistry*]
EDGK .... Korbach [*Federal Republic of Germany*] [*ICAO location identifier*] (ICLI)
EDGL .... Ludwigshafen-Unfallklinik [*Federal Republic of Germany*] [*ICAO location identifier*] (ICLI)
Edg Leas .... Edges' Forms of Leases [*A publication*] (DLA)

EDGM .... Mosbach-Lohrbach [*Federal Republic of Germany*] [*ICAO location identifier*] (ICLI)
EDGN .... Nordenbeck [*Federal Republic of Germany*] [*ICAO location identifier*] (ICLI)
EDGO .... Oedheim [*Federal Republic of Germany*] [*ICAO location identifier*] (ICLI)
EDGW .... Edgewise (MSA)
EDGW .... Wolfhagen/Granerberg [*Federal Republic of Germany*] [*ICAO location identifier*] (ICLI)
EdH .... Educational Horizons [*A publication*]
EDH .... Efficient Deck Hand (NATG)
EDH .... Engineering Design Handbook (MCD)
EDH .... Essays by Divers Hands [*A publication*]
EDH .... Sturgeon Bay, WI [*Location identifier*] [*FAA*] (FAAL)
EDHA .... Hamburg [*Federal Republic of Germany*] [*ICAO location identifier*] (ICLI)
EDHASA .. Editora y Distribuidora Hispano-Americana Sociedad Anonima [*Publisher's imprint*] [*Spain*]
EDHB .... Grube [*Federal Republic of Germany*] [*ICAO location identifier*] (ICLI)
EDHC .... Luchow/Rehbeck [*Federal Republic of Germany*] [*ICAO location identifier*] (ICLI)
EDHE .... Experimental Data Handling Equipment
EDHE .... Uetersen [*Federal Republic of Germany*] [*ICAO location identifier*] (ICLI)
Ed Heidelb ... Editiones Heidelbergenses [*A publication*]
EDHG .... Luneburg [*Federal Republic of Germany*] [*ICAO location identifier*] (ICLI)
EDHI .... Hamburg/Finkenwerder [*Federal Republic of Germany*] [*ICAO location identifier*] (ICLI)
EDHK .... Enose Demokratikou Hellinikou Kentrou [*Union of the Greek Democratic Center*] (PPE)
EDHL .... Luebeck/Blankensee [*Federal Republic of Germany*] [*ICAO location identifier*] (ICLI)
EDHM .... Hartenholm [*Federal Republic of Germany*] [*ICAO location identifier*] (ICLI)
EDHN .... Neumuenster [*Federal Republic of Germany*] [*ICAO location identifier*] (ICLI)
Ed Horiz .... Educational Horizons [*A publication*]
EDHP .... Engine Driven Hydraulic Pump (MCD)
EDHPA ..... Ethylenediaminedi-O-Hydroxyphenylacetic Acid [*Also, EDBHPA, EDDHA*] [*Organic chemistry*]
EDHS .... Engineering Design Handbook Series (MCD)
EDHX .... Bad Bramstedt [*Federal Republic of Germany*] [*ICAO location identifier*] (ICLI)
Edi .... Diaphragmatic Electrical Activity
EDI .... Eating Disorder Inventory [*Psychology*]
EDI .... Economic Development Institute [*of the International Bank for Reconstruction and Development*]
EDI .... Economically Disadvantaged Income (ADA)
EDI .... Edinburgh [*Scotland*] [*Airport symbol*] (OAG)
EDI .... Edinburgh [*Scotland*] [*Seismograph station code, US Geological Survey*] (SEIS)
EDI .... Edingtonite [*A zeolite*]
EDI .... Editor [*Data processing*]
EdI .... Education Index [*A publication*]
EDI .... Educational Data Information Ltd. [*Information service or system*] (IID)
EDI .... Educational Documentation and Information [*A publication*]
EDI .... Electrical Deflection Indicator
EDI .... Electron Diffraction Instrument
EDI .... Electronic Data Interchange
EDI .... Electronic Document Interchange
EDI .... Endocrinology Index [*A publication*]
EDI .... Engineering Demonstrated Inspection (AAG)
ED & I .... Engineering, Design, and Inspection
EDI .... Ensured Data Integrity
EDI .... Environmental Diagnostics, Inc.
EDI .... Eponyms Dictionaries Index [*A publication*]
EDIA .... Electronic Data Interchange Association (EA)
EDIA .... Giessen [*Federal Republic of Germany*] [*ICAO location identifier*] (ICLI)
EDIAC .... Engineering Decision Integrator and Communicator
EDIB .... Goeppingen [*Federal Republic of Germany*] [*ICAO location identifier*] (ICLI)
EDIC .... Economic Documentation and Information Centre Ltd. [*British*] [*Database producer*] (IID)
EDIC .... Equipment Dictionary [*Navy*] (MCD)
EDIC .... Grafenwoehr [*Federal Republic of Germany*] [*ICAO location identifier*] (ICLI)
Edict .... Edicts of Justinian [*A publication*] (DLA)
EDICT .... Engineering Department Interface Control Task [*or Technique*]
EDICT .... Engineering Document [*or Drawing*] Information Collection Task [*or Technique*]
EDICUDA ... Editorial Cuadernos para el Dialogo [*A publication*]
EDID .... Hanau [*Federal Republic of Germany*] [*ICAO location identifier*] (ICLI)
EDIE .... Heidelberg [*Federal Republic of Germany*] [*ICAO location identifier*] (ICLI)
EDIF .... Electronic Design Interchange Format [*Data processing*]

EDIF......... Heilbronn [*Federal Republic of Germany*] [*ICAO location identifier*] (ICLI)
EDIFC...... Ethel Delaney International Fan Club (EA)
EDIG......... Feucht [*Federal Republic of Germany*] [*ICAO location identifier*] (ICLI)
EDIGA...... Engineering Digest [*A publication*]
EDIGD...... Energy Digest [*Colorado Springs, CO*] [*A publication*]
EDIH......... Hohenfels [*Federal Republic of Germany*] [*ICAO location identifier*] (ICLI)
EDII.......... Augsburg Hospital [*Federal Republic of Germany*] [*ICAO location identifier*] (ICLI)
EDIJ......... Bohmer [*Federal Republic of Germany*] [*ICAO location identifier*] (ICLI)
EDIK......... Illesheim [*Federal Republic of Germany*] [*ICAO location identifier*] (ICLI)
EDIL......... Karlsruhe [*Federal Republic of Germany*] [*ICAO location identifier*] (ICLI)
ED Ill........ United States District Court for the Eastern District of Illinois (DLA)
Edil Mod.... Edilizia Moderna [*A publication*]
EDIM....... Epidemic [*or Epizootic*] Diarrhea of Infant Mice
EDIM........ Equipment Design Information Memo
EDIM........ Kirchgons [*Federal Republic of Germany*] [*ICAO location identifier*] (ICLI)
EDIMB...... Edimbourg [*Edinburgh*] (ROG)
EDIN......... Economic Development Information Network [*Indiana University*] [*Information service or system*] (IID)
EDIN......... Edinburgh [*City in Scotland*]
EDIN........ Ediner, Inc. [*Edina, MN*] [*NASDAQ symbol*] (NQ)
EDIN........ Engineering Design Integration System [*NASA*] (MCD)
EDIN........ Kitzingen [*Federal Republic of Germany*] [*ICAO location identifier*] (ICLI)
Edinb Dent Hosp Gaz ... Edinburgh Dental Hospital. Gazette [*A publication*]
Edinb G Soc Tr ... Edinburgh Geological Society. Transactions [*A publication*]
Edinb J Sci Technol Photogr Art ... Edinburgh Journal of Science, Technology, and Photographic Art [*A publication*]
Edinb LJ .... Edinburgh Law Journal [*A publication*] (DLA)
Edinb Math Notes ... Edinburgh Mathematical Notes [*A publication*]
Edinb Med J ... Edinburgh Medical Journal [*A publication*]
Edinb Med and S J ... Edinburgh Medical and Surgical Journal [*A publication*]
Edinb Sch Agric Annu Rep ... Edinburgh School of Agriculture. Annual Report [*A publication*]
Edinb Sch Agric Exp Work ... Edinburgh School of Agriculture. Experimental Work [*A publication*]
EDINBURG ... Edinburgensis [*Signature of Bishops of Edinburgh*] (ROG)
Edinburgh Bibliogr Soc Trans ... Edinburgh Bibliographical Society. Transactions [*A publication*]
Edinburgh Geol Soc Trans ... Edinburgh Geological Society. Transactions [*A publication*]
Edinburgh J Sci ... Edinburgh Journal of Science [*A publication*]
EDI-NET... Electronic Data Interchange Network (TSSD)
Ed Inj........ Eden on Injunctions [*1821*] [*A publication*] (DLA)
Edin Rev...... Edinburgh Review [*A publication*]
EDIO......... Butzbach (Schloss) [*Federal Republic of Germany*] [*ICAO location identifier*] (ICLI)
E-Diol........ Estradiol [*Also, E2, ES*] [*Endocrinology*]
EDIP......... European Defense Improvement Program [*NATO*] (MCD)
EDIP......... Landstuhl [*Federal Republic of Germany*] [*ICAO location identifier*] (ICLI)
EDIQ......... Herzo Base [*Federal Republic of Germany*] [*ICAO location identifier*] (ICLI)
EDIR......... Ludwigsburg [*Federal Republic of Germany*] [*ICAO location identifier*] (ICLI)
EDIS......... Edison National Historic Site
EDIS......... Engineering Data Information System (IEEE)
EDIS......... Environmental Data and Information Service [*Later, NESDIS*]
EDIS......... Executive Directorate Industrial Security (MCD)
EDIS......... Nellingen [*Federal Republic of Germany*] [*ICAO location identifier*] (ICLI)
EDISD...... EDIS. Environmental Data and Information Service [*A publication*]
Edison Electr Inst Bull ... Edison Electric Institute. Bulletin [*A publication*]
Edison Electr Inst Stat Yearb Electr Util Ind ... Edison Electric Institute. Statistical Yearbook. Electric Utility Industry [*A publication*]
EDIT......... Edited (ROG)
EDIT......... Edition
EDIT......... Editor (ROG)
EDIT......... Engineering Development Integration Test
EDIT......... Environmental Diagnostics, Inc. [*Burlington, NC*] [*NASDAQ symbol*] (NQ)
EDIT......... Error Deletion by Iterative Transmission
EDIT......... Estate Duties Investment Trust (DLA)
EDIT......... Eye-Slaved Display Integration and Test
EDIT......... Nuernberg, Hospital [*Federal Republic of Germany*] [*ICAO location identifier*] (ICLI)
EDITAR..... Electronic Digital Tracking and Ranging
EDITH...... Emergency Drill in the Home [*Fire Department drill exercise*]
EDITH...... Estate Duties Investment Taxes [*British*]
Editorial Research Repts ... Editorial Research Reports [*A publication*]

Edit Publ.... Editor and Publisher [*A publication*]
EDITS....... Educational and Industrial Testing Service
EDITS....... Electronic Data Information Technical Service (DIT)
EDITS....... Electronic [*Warfare*] Data Integration Test System (MCD)
EDITS....... Experimental Digital Television System
EDITSPEC ... Editing Specifications (MCD)
EDIU......... Heidelberg [*Federal Republic of Germany*] [*ICAO location identifier*] (ICLI)
EDIV......... Pirmasens [*Federal Republic of Germany*] [*ICAO location identifier*] (ICLI)
EDIW......... Wuerzburg, Hospital [*Federal Republic of Germany*] [*ICAO location identifier*] (ICLI)
EDIX......... Schwaebisch Gmuend [*Federal Republic of Germany*] [*ICAO location identifier*] (ICLI)
EDIZ......... Schwabach [*Federal Republic of Germany*] [*ICAO location identifier*] (ICLI)
Ed J Sci..... Edinburgh Journal of Science, Technology, and Photographic Art [*A publication*]
e-dk--- .... Denmark [*MARC geographic area code*] [*Library of Congress*] (LCCP)
EDK.......... Enose Demokratikou Kentrou [*Union of the Democratic Center*] [*Greek*] (PPW)
EDK.......... Handels Rundschau [*A publication*]
EDKB........ Bonn/Hangelar [*Federal Republic of Germany*] [*ICAO location identifier*] (ICLI)
EDKD........ Altena/Hegenscheid [*Federal Republic of Germany*] [*ICAO location identifier*] (ICLI)
EDKE........ Dierdorf/Wienau [*Federal Republic of Germany*] [*ICAO location identifier*] (ICLI)
EDKF........ Bergneustadt/Auf Dem Dumpel [*Federal Republic of Germany*] [*ICAO location identifier*] (ICLI)
EDKI........ Betzdorf/Kirchen [*Federal Republic of Germany*] [*ICAO location identifier*] (ICLI)
EDKL......... Leverkusen [*Federal Republic of Germany*] [*ICAO location identifier*] (ICLI)
EDKM....... Meschede/Schuren [*Federal Republic of Germany*] [*ICAO location identifier*] (ICLI)
EDKN....... Wipperfurth/Neye [*Federal Republic of Germany*] [*ICAO location identifier*] (ICLI)
EDKS......... Siegerland [*Federal Republic of Germany*] [*ICAO location identifier*] (ICLI)
EDKV....... Dahlemer Binz [*Federal Republic of Germany*] [*ICAO location identifier*] (ICLI)
EDKW....... Werdohl/Kuntrop [*Federal Republic of Germany*] [*ICAO location identifier*] (ICLI)
ED KY....... United States District Court for the Eastern District of Kentucky (DLA)
EDKZ........ Meinerzhagen [*Federal Republic of Germany*] [*ICAO location identifier*] (ICLI)
EDL.......... Economic Dislocation Loans [*Small Business Administration*]
EDL.......... Edition Deluxe
EDL.......... Educational Developmental Laboratories [*of McGraw Hill, Inc.*]
EdL.......... Educational Leadership [*A publication*]
EDL.......... Eldoret [*Kenya*] [*Airport symbol*] [*Obsolete*] (OAG)
EDL.......... Electric Delay Line
EDL.......... Electric Double Layer
EDL.......... Electrical Discharge LASER (MCD)
EDL.......... Electrodeless Discharge Lamp
EDL.......... Electron Devices Laboratory
EDL.......... Electronic Defense Laboratory
EDL.......... End-Diastolic Length [*Cardiology*]
EDL.......... Engineering Development Laboratory
EdL.......... Engineering Drawing List
EdL.......... Etudes de Lettres [*Universite de Lausanne*] [*A publication*]
EDL.......... Every-Day Life [*Psychological testing*]
EDL.......... Executive Data Link [*IBM Corp.*]
EDL.......... Extensor Digitorum Longus [*Anatomy*]
EDL.......... South African Law Reports, Eastern Districts Local Division [*South Africa*] [*A publication*] (DLA)
EDLA........ Arnsberg [*Federal Republic of Germany*] [*ICAO location identifier*] (ICLI)
EDLA........ Estudios de Linguistica Aplicada [*A publication*]
EDLA........ Exotic Dancers League of America (EA)
ED LA....... United States District Court for the Eastern District of Louisiana (DLA)
EDLB........ Borkenberge [*Federal Republic of Germany*] [*ICAO location identifier*] (ICLI)
EDLC......... Edwardian Drama and Literature Circle (EA)
EDLC......... Kamp/Lintfort [*Federal Republic of Germany*] [*ICAO location identifier*] (ICLI)
EDLCC...... Electronic Data Local Communications Central [*or Complex*]
EDLD........ Dinslaken/Schwarze Heide [*Federal Republic of Germany*] [*ICAO location identifier*] (ICLI)
ED/LD....... Emotionally Disturbed/Learning Disabled
EDLD......... Employee Daily Labor Distribution (AAG)
EDLE......... Essen/Muelheim [*Federal Republic of Germany*] [*ICAO location identifier*] (ICLI)
Ed Lead...... Educational Leadership [*A publication*]
EDLF........ Endogenous Digitalis-Like Factor [*Biochemistry*]

EDLF......... Grefrath/Niershorst [*Federal Republic of Germany*] [*ICAO location identifier*] (ICLI)

EDLG .... Muenster/Osnabruck [*Federal Republic of Germany*] [*ICAO location identifier*] (ICLI)

EDLH........ Hamm/Lippewiesen [*Federal Republic of Germany*] [*ICAO location identifier*] (ICLI)

EDLI.......... Bielefeld/Windelsbleiche [*Federal Republic of Germany*] [*ICAO location identifier*] (ICLI)

Ed Lib Bulletin ... Education Libraries Bulletin [*A publication*]

Ed LJ .... Edinburgh Law Journal [*A publication*] (DLA)

EDLK........ Krefeld/Egelsberg [*Federal Republic of Germany*] [*ICAO location identifier*] (ICLI)

EDLL......... Duesseldorf [*Federal Republic of Germany*] [*ICAO location identifier*] (ICLI)

EDLM .... Marl/Loemuhle [*Federal Republic of Germany*] [*ICAO location identifier*] (ICLI)

EDLN .... Engineering Development Logic Network (NASA)

EDLN .... Moenchengladbach [*Federal Republic of Germany*] [*ICAO location identifier*] (ICLI)

EDLO .... Oerlinghausen [*Federal Republic of Germany*] [*ICAO location identifier*] (ICLI)

EDLP......... Engineering Development Laboratory Program (KSC)

EDLP......... Paderborn/Lippstadt [*Federal Republic of Germany*] [*ICAO location identifier*] (ICLI)

EDLQ .... Essen [*Federal Republic of Germany*] [*ICAO location identifier*] (ICLI)

EDLS......... Stadtlohn/Wenningfeld [*Federal Republic of Germany*] [*ICAO location identifier*] (ICLI)

EDLT......... Muenster/Telgte [*Federal Republic of Germany*] [*ICAO location identifier*] (ICLI)

EDLW .... Dortmund/Wickede [*Federal Republic of Germany*] [*ICAO location identifier*] (ICLI)

EDLX......... Wesel/Romerwardt [*Federal Republic of Germany*] [*ICAO location identifier*] (ICLI)

EDM.......... Early Diastolic Murmur [*Medicine*]

EDM.......... Edgar Dale Media Center, Columbus, OH [*OCLC symbol*] (OCLC)

EDM.......... Edmonton [*Alberta*] [*Seismograph station code, US Geological Survey*] (SEIS)

EdM........... Education Media [*A publication*]

EDM.......... Electric Drive Mechanism (KSC)

EDM.......... Electrical Discharge [*or Electrodischarge*] Machine [*or Machining*]

EDM.......... Electrical Disintegration Machining [*Nuclear energy*] (NRCH)

EDM.......... Electron Density Map [*Crystallography*]

EDM.......... Electronic Distance Measuring

EDM.......... Electronic Drafting Machine

EDM.......... Employability Development Model (OICC)

EDM.......... Encyclopedic Dictionary of Mathematics [*A publication*]

EDM.......... Enforced Dipole Moment

EDM.......... Engineering Data Management

EDM.......... Engineering Design Machine

EDM.......... Engineering Design Memorandum

EDM.......... Engineering Development Model

EDM.......... Engineering Drafting Machine

EDM.......... Engineering Drafting Manual [*Air Force*]

EDM.......... Engineering Drawing Microfilm (MCD)

EDM.......... Equipment Code Department Master (MCD)

EDM.......... Equipment Deadlined for Maintenance [*Army*] (AABC)

EDM.......... Exploratory Development Model [*Military*]

Ed M .... Master of Education

EDMA .... Augsburg/Muehlhausen [*Federal Republic of Germany*] [*ICAO location identifier*] (ICLI)

EDMA .... Empresa de Desenvolvimento Mineiro do Alentejo [*Nationalized industry*] [*Portugal*] (EY)

EDMA .... Ethylene Dimethacrylate [*Organic chemistry*]

EDMA .... Ethylene Glycol Dimethacrylate [*Organic chemistry*]

EDMA .... European Direct Marketing Association [*Jona/SG, Switzerland*] (EAIO)

EDMA .... Extended Direct Memory Access [*Data processing*]

Ed Mag ...... Educational Magazine [*A publication*] (APTA)

EDMALC ... European Direct Marketing Association List Council [*Jona/SG, Switzerland*] [*Inactive*] (EA)

Ed Man...... Education Manitoba [*A publication*]

EDMARS ... Educational Document Management and Retrieval System [*Japan*] [*Database*]

EDMB .... Biberach Aerodrome Riss [*Federal Republic of Germany*] [*ICAO location identifier*] (ICLI)

Ed M in BT Ed ... Master of Education in Business Teacher Education

EDMC .... Eldorado Motor Corporation [*Minneapolis, KS*] [*NASDAQ symbol*] (NQ)

EDMC .... Energy Data and Modeling Center [*Institute of Energy Economics*] [*Japan*] [*Database producer*] (IID)

EDME .... Eggenfelden, Nieder Bayern [*Federal Republic of Germany*] [*ICAO location identifier*] (ICLI)

EDME .... Electronic Distance Measuring Equipment (MCD)

Ed Meth..... Educational Method [*A publication*]

Edm Exch Pr ... Edmund's Exchequer Practice [*A publication*] (DLA)

EDMF .... Extended Data Management Facility

EDMF .... Fuerstenzell Bei Passau [*Federal Republic of Germany*] [*ICAO location identifier*] (ICLI)

EDMG....... Gunzburg/Donauried [*Federal Republic of Germany*] [*ICAO location identifier*] (ICLI)

EDMH....... Gunzenhausen [*Federal Republic of Germany*] [*ICAO location identifier*] (ICLI)

EDMI .... Electron-Dense Mitochondrial Inclusions [*Oncology*]

EDMI .... Employees of Diplomatic Missions [*A publication*]

EDMI .... European Dun's Market Identifiers [*Information service or system*] (EISS)

EDMI .... Illertissen [*Federal Republic of Germany*] [*ICAO location identifier*] (ICLI)

ED Mich .... United States District Court for the Eastern District of Michigan (DLA)

EDMICS ... Engineering Data Management Information Control System [*DoD*]

ED MJ .... Edinburgh Medical Journal [*A publication*]

EDMJ........ Jesenwang [*Federal Republic of Germany*] [*ICAO location identifier*] (ICLI)

EDMK....... Kempten/Durach [*Federal Republic of Germany*] [*ICAO location identifier*] (ICLI)

EDML .... Landshut [*Federal Republic of Germany*] [*ICAO location identifier*] (ICLI)

EDMM....... Muenchen [*Federal Republic of Germany*] [*ICAO location identifier*] (ICLI)

Ed Mo .... Edinburgh Monthly Review [*A publication*]

EDMO....... Oberpfaffenhofen [*Federal Republic of Germany*] [*ICAO location identifier*] (ICLI)

ED MO...... United States District Court for the Eastern District of Missouri (DLA)

Ed Mod ..... Edilizia Moderna [*A publication*]

Edmonds' St at Large ... Edmonds' New York Statutes at Large [*A publication*] (DLA)

Edmontn Jl ... Edmonton Journal [*A publication*]

Edmonton Geol Soc Q ... Edmonton Geological Society. Quarterly [*A publication*]

Edmonton Geol Soc Quart ... Edmonton Geological Society. Quarterly [*A publication*]

Edmonton J ... Edmonton Journal [*A publication*]

Edmonton P L News Notes ... Edmonton Public Library. News Notes [*A publication*]

Edmonton Rep ... Edmonton Report [*A publication*]

EDMP .... Ethyl (Diisopropylamino)ethylmethyl-phosphonite [*Nerve gas intermediate*] [*Organic chemistry*]

EDMP .... Vilsbiburg [*Federal Republic of Germany*] [*ICAO location identifier*] (ICLI)

Ed M in Phy Ed ... Master of Education in Physical Education

EDMQ....... Donauworth/Genderkingen [*Federal Republic of Germany*] [*ICAO location identifier*] (ICLI)

EDMR .... Ottobrunn [*Federal Republic of Germany*] [*ICAO location identifier*] (ICLI)

EDMS........ Electra Data Management System

EDMS........ Engineering Data Management System [*Jet Propulsion Laboratory, NASA*]

EDMS........ Engineering Data Microreproduction System [*DoD*]

EDMS....... Extended Data Management System [*Xerox Corp.*]

EDMS........ Straubing/Wallmuehle [*Federal Republic of Germany*] [*ICAO location identifier*] (ICLI)

EDMSAB .. Educacion Medica y Salud [*A publication*]

Edm Sel Ca ... Edmonds' New York Select Cases [*A publication*] (DLA)

Edm Sel Cas ... Edmonds' New York Select Cases [*A publication*] (DLA)

Edm Stat .... Edmonds' New York Statutes at Large [*A publication*] (DLA)

EDMT .... Tanheim [*Federal Republic of Germany*] [*ICAO location identifier*] (ICLI)

EDMU....... Muenchen [*Federal Republic of Germany*] [*ICAO location identifier*] (ICLI)

Ed Mus ...... Educazione Musicale [*A publication*]

Ed Mus Mag ... Education Music Magazine [*A publication*]

EDMV .... Vilshofen [*Federal Republic of Germany*] [*ICAO location identifier*] (ICLI)

EDMW ...... Deggendorf/Steinkirchen [*Federal Republic of Germany*] [*ICAO location identifier*] (ICLI)

EDMX .... Oberschleissheim [*Federal Republic of Germany*] [*ICAO location identifier*] (ICLI)

EDMY .... Muehldorf [*Federal Republic of Germany*] [*ICAO location identifier*] (ICLI)

EDN.......... Edition

EdN........... Editors' Notes [*A publication*]

EDN.......... Education

EDN.......... Electrodesiccation [*Medicine*]

EDN.......... Engine Deflector Nozzle

EDN.......... Engineering Department Notice (AAG)

EDN.......... Engineering Discrepancy Notice [*Nuclear energy*] (NRCH)

EDN.......... Enterprise, AL [*Location identifier*] [*FAA*] (FAAL)

EDN.......... Eosinophil Derived Neurotoxin [*Immunology*]

EDNA........ Ahlhorn [*Federal Republic of Germany*] [*ICAO location identifier*] (ICLI)

EDNA........ Emergency Department Nurses Association [*Later, ENA*] (EA)

EDNB........ Koeln-Wahn [*Federal Republic of Germany*] [*ICAO location identifier*] (ICLI)

EDNC........ United States District Court for the Eastern District of North Carolina (DLA)

EDND........ Diepholz [*Federal Republic of Germany*] [*ICAO location identifier*] (ICLI)

Ed New Philos J ... Edinburgh New Philosophical Journal [*A publication*]

Ed News..... Education News [*A publication*] (APTA)

EDNF .... Ehlers Danlos National Foundation (EA)

EDNF .... Fassberg [*Federal Republic of Germany*] [*ICAO location identifier*] (ICLI)

EDNG........ Geilenkirchen [*Federal Republic of Germany*] [*ICAO location identifier*] (ICLI)

EDNH .... Husum [*Federal Republic of Germany*] [*ICAO location identifier*] (ICLI)

EDNJ......... Jever [*Federal Republic of Germany*] [*ICAO location identifier*] (ICLI)

EDNK........ Koeln-Bonn [*Federal Republic of Germany*] [*ICAO location identifier*] (ICLI)

EDNL .... Leck [*Federal Republic of Germany*] [*ICAO location identifier*] (ICLI)

Ednl Administration Bull ... Educational Administration Bulletin [*A publication*]

Ednl Broadcasting International ... Educational Broadcasting International [*A publication*]

Ednl Change and Dev ... Educational Change and Development [*A publication*]

Ednl Dev .... Educational Development [*A publication*]

Ednl Dev Centre R ... Educational Development Centre Review [*A publication*]

Ednl Dev International ... Educational Development International [*A publication*]

Ednl Documentation and Information ... Educational Documentation and Information [*A publication*]

Ednl R........ Educational Review [*A publication*]

Ednl Research ... Educational Research [*A publication*]

Ednl Sciences ... Educational Sciences [*A publication*]

Ednl Studies ... Educational Studies [*A publication*]

Ednl Studies in Maths ... Educational Studies in Mathematics [*A publication*]

EDNM....... Muenster [*Federal Republic of Germany*] [*ICAO location identifier*] (ICLI)

EDNN........ Norvenich [*Federal Republic of Germany*] [*ICAO location identifier*] (ICLI)

EDNO........ Oldenburg [*Federal Republic of Germany*] [*ICAO location identifier*] (ICLI)

Ed in the North ... Education in the North [*A publication*]

EDNP .... Ethyl Dinitropentanoate [*An explosive*]

EDNP .... Hopsten [*Federal Republic of Germany*] [*ICAO location identifier*] (ICLI)

EDNQ........ Hohn [*Federal Republic of Germany*] [*ICAO location identifier*] (ICLI)

Edns .... Editions [*A publication*]

Ed NS .... Education Nova Scotia [*A publication*]

Ed NSW..... Education. New South Wales Teachers Federation [*A publication*] (APTA)

EDNT .... Wittmundhafen [*Federal Republic of Germany*] [*ICAO location identifier*] (ICLI)

EDNV .... Kalkar [*Federal Republic of Germany*] [*ICAO location identifier*] (ICLI)

EDNW .... Wunstorf [*Federal Republic of Germany*] [*ICAO location identifier*] (ICLI)

EDNX .... Goch [*Federal Republic of Germany*] [*ICAO location identifier*] (ICLI)

EDNY .... United States District Court for the Eastern District of New York (DLA)

EDO........... Economic Development Operations

EDO........... Edgewood, NM [*Location identifier*] [*FAA*] (FAAL)

EDO........... EDO Corp. [*NYSE symbol*] (SPSG)

EDO........... Effective Diameter of Objective [*Optics*]

EDO........... Employee Development Officer

EDO........... Engineering Duty Officer [*Military*]

EDO........... Engineering Duty Only [*Aerospace*]

EDO........... Error Demodulator [*or Determination*] Output (MCD)

EDO........... Estate Duty Office [*British*]

E & DO ...... Experimental and Development Operations (MCD)

EDO........... Exploratory Development Objective [*Military*]

EDO........... Export Development Office [*Department of Commerce*] (IMH)

EDO........... Office of Executive Director for Operations [*Nuclear energy*] (NRCH)

EDOA........ Schweinfurt [*Federal Republic of Germany*] [*ICAO location identifier*] (ICLI)

EDOB .... Garlstedt/Clay Kaserne [*Federal Republic of Germany*] [*ICAO location identifier*] (ICLI)

EDOC .... Echterdingen [*Federal Republic of Germany*] [*ICAO location identifier*] (ICLI)

EDOC .... Economic Development Opportunity Committee [*Department of Labor*]

EDOC .... Effective Date of Change (AFM)

EDOE .... Ulm [*Federal Republic of Germany*] [*ICAO location identifier*] (ICLI)

EDOF .... Wertheim [*Federal Republic of Germany*] [*ICAO location identifier*] (ICLI)

Ed Off Gaz Qld ... Education Office Gazette. Queensland Department of Education [*A publication*] (APTA)

EDOG....... Bad Cannstatt Hospital [*Federal Republic of Germany*] [*ICAO location identifier*] (ICLI)

EDOH .... Emery [*Federal Republic of Germany*] [*ICAO location identifier*] (ICLI)

EDOI .... Vilseck [*Federal Republic of Germany*] [*ICAO location identifier*] (ICLI)

EDOJ........ Bonn (Bad Godesberg-Plittersdorf) [*Federal Republic of Germany*] [*ICAO location identifier*] (ICLI)

EDOK........ Frankfurt-North [*Federal Republic of Germany*] [*ICAO location identifier*] (ICLI)

ED Okla.... United States District Court for the Eastern District of Oklahoma (DLA)

EDOL .... Frankfurt City [*Federal Republic of Germany*] [*ICAO location identifier*] (ICLI)

EDOM....... Worms [*Federal Republic of Germany*] [*ICAO location identifier*] (ICLI)

EDOMP .... Educational Development of Military Personnel

EDON........ Kaiserslautern [*Federal Republic of Germany*] [*ICAO location identifier*] (ICLI)

Ed Ont ...... Education Ontario [*A publication*]

EDOP .... Schwaebisch Hall/Hessental [*Federal Republic of Germany*] [*ICAO location identifier*] (ICLI)

EDOQ....... Heidelberg, United States Army [*Federal Republic of Germany*] [*ICAO location identifier*] (ICLI)

EDOR........ Coleman [*Federal Republic of Germany*] [*ICAO location identifier*] (ICLI)

Ed et Ord ... Edits et Ordonnances [*Lower Canada*] [*A publication*] (DLA)

EDOS .... Effective Date of Supply

EDOS .... Estimated Delivery Dates of Supply [*Army*] (INF)

EDOS .... Extended Disk Operating System [*Data processing*] (BUR)

EDOS .... Kaiserslautern (Kapaun) [*Federal Republic of Germany*] [*ICAO location identifier*] (ICLI)

EDOT .... Finthen [*Federal Republic of Germany*] [*ICAO location identifier*] (ICLI)

EDOU........ Wiesbaden [*Federal Republic of Germany*] [*ICAO location identifier*] (ICLI)

Ed Outl ..... Educational Outlook [*A publication*]

EDOV........ Bad Tolz [*Federal Republic of Germany*] [*ICAO location identifier*] (ICLI)

EDOW....... Wildflecken [*Federal Republic of Germany*] [*ICAO location identifier*] (ICLI)

EDOX .... Augsburg/Gablingen [*Federal Republic of Germany*] [*ICAO location identifier*] (ICLI)

EDOY........ Leighton Barracks [*Federal Republic of Germany*] [*ICAO location identifier*] (ICLI)

EDOZ .... Bad Hersfeld [*Federal Republic of Germany*] [*ICAO location identifier*] (ICLI)

EDP .... Early Decision Plan [*Medical school entrance program*]

EDP .... Earth Dynamics Program [*Smithsonian Astrophysical Observatory*]

EDP .... Economic Development Program

EDP .... EDP [*Electronic Data Processing*] Industry Report [*A publication*]

EDP .... Effective Directives and Plans (MUGU)

EDP .... Electron Decay Profile

EDP .... Electronic Data Processing

EDP .... Electronic Digital Pipette [*Instrumentation*]

EDP .... Electronic Display Panel

EDP .... Electrophoresis Duplicating Paper [*For analytical chemistry*]

EDP .... Emergency Defense Plan [*Later, GDP*] (NATG)

EDP .... Emergency Distribution Plan [*DoD*] (AFIT)

EDP .... Employment Development Plan [*Job Training and Partnership Act*] (OICC)

EDP .... End-Diastolic Pressure [*Cardiology*]

EDP .... Energy Development Partnership [*AMEX symbol*] (SPSG)

EDP .... Engineering Data Package [*Air Force*] (AFIT)

EDP .... Engineering Design Plan

EDP .... Engineering Design Proposal (AAG)

EDP .... Engineering Development Phase (OAG)

EDP .... Epatite "Degenerative-Proliferativa" [*A strain of mouse hepatitis virus*]

EDP .... Equipment Deadlined for Parts [*Army*]

EDP .... Equipment Distribution Plan (MCD)

EDP .... Estimated Date of Publication (AAG)

EDP .... Expeditious Discharge Program [*Army*]

EDP .... Experimental Development

EDP .... Experimental Dynamic Processor (MUGU)

EDPA .... Erhardt Development Prehension Assessment

EDPA .... Exhibit Designers and Producers Association (EA)

ED PA........ United States District Court for the Eastern District of Pennsylvania (DLA)

EDPAA...... EDP [*Electronic Data Processing*] Analyzer [*A publication*]

EDPAA...... EDP [*Electronic Data Processing*] Auditors Association (EA)

EDPAC...... Estimated Departure from Pacific (CINC)

EDP A C S ... EDP [*Electronic Data Processing*] Audit, Control, and Security Newsletter [*A publication*]

EDP Anal .. EDP [*Electronic Data Processing*] Analyzer [*A publication*]

EDP Aud.... EDP [*Electronic Data Processing*] Auditor [*A publication*]

EDPC........ Electronic Data Processing Center

EDPE........ Electronic Data Processing Equipment

EDP Europa ... EDP [*Electronic Data Processing*] Europa Report [*A publication*]

EDPF .... Fritzlar [*Federal Republic of Germany*] [*ICAO location identifier*] (ICLI)

EDPH .... Neuhausen Ob Eck [*Federal Republic of Germany*] [*ICAO location identifier*] (ICLI)

Ed Philos J ... Edinburgh Philosophical Journal [*A publication*]

EDP In-Depth Rep ... EDP [*Electronic Data Processing*] In-Depth Reports [*A publication*]

EDP Indus Rep ... EDP [*Electronic Data Processing*] Industry Report [*A publication*]

EDP/IR ..... Electronic Data Processing/Industry Report

EDP-IR ...... Electronic Data Processing - Information Retrieval

EDPITAF ... Education Development Projects Implementing Task Force [*Philippines*] (DS)

EDP Japan ... EDP [*Electronic Data Processing*] Japan Report [*A publication*]

EDPKA2 .... Endokrynologia Polska [*A publication*]

EDPL .... Altenstadt [*Federal Republic of Germany*] [*ICAO location identifier*] (ICLI)

Ed PL .... Eden's Principles of Penal Law [*A publication*] (DLA)

EDPL .... Eminent Domain Procedure Law [*New York, NY*] [*A publication*]

EDPLOT ... Engineering Data Plotting [*Data processing*]

EDPM ...... Electronic Data Processing Machine [*Also translated by some users of such equipment as "Every Damn Problem Multiplied"*]

EDPM .... Electronic Data Processing Magnetic [*Tape*]

EDPM .... Laupheim [*Federal Republic of Germany*] [*ICAO location identifier*] (ICLI)

EDPN .... Mendig [*Federal Republic of Germany*] [*ICAO location identifier*] (ICLI)

EDP Performance Rev ... EDP [*Electronic Data Processing*] Performance Review [*A publication*]

EDP Perf Rev ... EDP [*Electronic Data Processing*] Performance Review [*A publication*]

EDPR .... Engineering Development Part Release (KSC)

EDPR .... Roth [*Federal Republic of Germany*] [*ICAO location identifier*] (ICLI)

EDPRESS ... Educational Press Association of America (EA)

EDPRICE ... Energy Detente International Price/Tax Series [*Lundberg Survey, Inc.*] [*Information service or system*] [*No longer available online*] (CRD)

Ed Prod Rep ... Educational Product Report [*A publication*]

EDPS .... Electronic Data Processing System

EDPS .... Electronic Dew Point Sensor

EDPS .... Equipment Distribution Planning Studies [*Army*] (AABC)

EDPS .... Exploratory Development Program Summary [*Military*]

EDPS .... Straubing/Mitterharthausen [*Federal Republic of Germany*] [*ICAO location identifier*] (ICLI)

EDPSG ...... European Diabetes Pregnancy Study Group [*of the European Association for the Study of Diabetes*] (EAIO)

Ed & Psychol M ... Educational and Psychological Measurement [*A publication*]

EDPT .... Electronic Data Processing Test (AFM)

EDPT .... Niederstetten/Bad Mergentheim [*Federal Republic of Germany*] [*ICAO location identifier*] (ICLI)

Ed & Pub ... Editor and Publisher [*A publication*]

Ed Publ Fourth Estate ... Editor and Publisher - the Fourth Estate [*A publication*]

EDPW .... Ethylenediamine-Pyrocatechol-Water [*Mixture for etching silicon sensors*]

EDP Weekly ... EDP (Electronic Data Processing) Weekly [*A publication*]

EDQ .... Economic Distribution Quantity (AFIT)

EDQA .... Electronic Devices Quality Assurance

EDQC .... Coburg/Brandensteinsebene [*Federal Republic of Germany*] [*ICAO location identifier*] (ICLI)

EDQD .... Bayreuth [*Federal Republic of Germany*] [*ICAO location identifier*] (ICLI)

EDQE .... Burg Feuerstein [*Federal Republic of Germany*] [*ICAO location identifier*] (ICLI)

EDQF .... Ansbach/Petersdorf [*Federal Republic of Germany*] [*ICAO location identifier*] (ICLI)

EDQH .... Herzogenaurach [*Federal Republic of Germany*] [*ICAO location identifier*] (ICLI)

EDQK .... Kulmbach [*Federal Republic of Germany*] [*ICAO location identifier*] (ICLI)

EDQL .... Lichtenfels [*Federal Republic of Germany*] [*ICAO location identifier*] (ICLI)

EDQM ...... Hof [*Federal Republic of Germany*] [*ICAO location identifier*] (ICLI)

EDQN .... Neumarkt, Oberpfalz [*Federal Republic of Germany*] [*ICAO location identifier*] (ICLI)

EDQP .... Rosenthal-Field Plossen [*Federal Republic of Germany*] [*ICAO location identifier*] (ICLI)

EDQT .... Hassfurt/Mainwiesen [*Federal Republic of Germany*] [*ICAO location identifier*] (ICLI)

Ed Que ...... Education Quebec [*A publication*]

EDQW .... Weiden, Oberpfalz [*Federal Republic of Germany*] [*ICAO location identifier*] (ICLI)

EDQY .... Coburg/Steinrucken [*Federal Republic of Germany*] [*ICAO location identifier*] (ICLI)

EDR .... Economic Development Review [*A publication*]

EDR .... Edgemont Resources [*Vancouver Stock Exchange symbol*]

Ed R .... Edinburgh Review [*A publication*]

EdR .... Educational Record [*A publication*]

Ed R .... Educational Review [*United Kingdom*] [*A publication*]

EDR .... Educator's Desk Reference [*A publication*]

EDR .... Edward River [*Australia*] [*Airport symbol*] (OAG)

EDR .... Effective Direct Radiation

EDR .... Electrical Distance Recorder [*British military*] (DMA)

EDR .... Electrodermal Response

EDR .... Electrodialysis Reversing

EDR .... Electron Decay Rate

EDR .... Electron-Dense Region [*in Microorganisms*]

EDR .... Electronic Decoy Rocket

EDR .... Emergency Distance Required [*Aviation*] (AIA)

EDR .... Employee Data Record

EDR .... Encyclopedic Dictionary of Religion

EDR .... Engineering Data Requirements (AAG)

EDR .... Engineering Department [*or Division*] Report

EDR .... Engineering Design Review (NASA)

EDR .... Engineering Drawing Release

EDR .... Environmental Data Records

EDR .... Equivalent Direct Radiation

EDR .... Estimated Date of Resumption (AAG)

EDR .... Ethanol-Disulfiram Reaction [*Pharmacology*]

EDR .... European Depositary Receipt [*Investment term*]

EDR .... [*The*] Executive Desk Register [*Information service or system*] (IID)

EDR .... Expect Departure Release [*Aviation*] (FAAC)

EDR .... Experiment Data Record

EDR .... Experimental Development Requirements (CINC)

EDR .... Exploratory Development Request [*Military*]

EDR .... Exploratory Development Requirement [*Military*]

EDR .... Roscoe's Eastern District Reports [*Cape Of Good Hope*] [*A publication*] (DLA)

EDRA .... Engineering Drawing Release Authorization

EDRA .... Environmental Design Research Association (EA)

EDR Anthrc ... Energy Data Reports. Distribution of Pennsylvania Anthracite [*A publication*]

EDRAS ...... Economic Data Retrieval and Application System (BUR)

EDR B Coal ... Energy Data Reports. Bituminous Coal and Lignite Distribution [*A publication*]

EDRC .... Engineering Design Research Center [*Pittsburgh, PA*] [*National Science Foundation*] (GRD)

EDRCAM ... Endocrine Research Communications [*A publication*]

EDRCC ...... Electronic Data Remote Communications Complex

Ed R (China) ... Educational Review (China) [*A publication*]

EDR Coal B & L ... Energy Data Reports. Coal, Bituminous and Lignite [*A publication*]

Ed RD .... Doctor of Religious Education

EDRE .... Emergency Deployment Readiness Exercise [*Army*] (INF)

EdReAn ...... Educational Research Analysts (EA)

Ed Rec .... Educational Record. Tasmania Education Department [*A publication*] (APTA)

Ed Rec Bur Bul ... Educational Records Bureau. Bulletins [*Greenwich, Connecticut*] [*A publication*]

Ed Res .... Educational Research [*Oxford*] [*A publication*]

Ed Res B .... Educational Research Bulletin [*A publication*]

Ed Res Perspectives ... Education Research and Perspectives [*A publication*]

Ed Res Record ... Educational Research Record [*A publication*]

Ed Res Rep (Wash DC) ... Editorial Research Reports (Washington, DC) [*A publication*]

EDRF .... Bad Duerkheim [*Federal Republic of Germany*] [*ICAO location identifier*] (ICLI)

EDRF .... Endothelium-Derived Vascular Relaxant Factor [*Biochemistry*]

EDRF .... Experience Demand Replacement Factor [*Navy*]

EDR F Oils ... Energy Data Reports. Fuel Oils by Sulphur Content [*A publication*]

EDRI .... Electronic Distributors' Research Institute

EDRJ .... Saarlouis/Dueren [*Federal Republic of Germany*] [*ICAO location identifier*] (ICLI)

EDRK .... Koblenz/Winningen [*Federal Republic of Germany*] [*ICAO location identifier*] (ICLI)

EDR Ker .... Energy Data Reports. Sales of Fuel Oil and Kerosene [*A publication*]

EDRL .... Effective Damage Risk Level

EDRL .... Lachen/Speyerdorf [*Federal Republic of Germany*] [*ICAO location identifier*] (ICLI)

EDR LPS ... Energy Data Reports. Liquefied Petroleum Sales [*A publication*]

EDR N Gas ... Energy Data Reports. Natural Gas [*A publication*]

EDRO .... Office of Executive Director of Regional Operations [*Nuclear energy*] (NRCH)

EDR Pet St ... Energy Data Reports. Petroleum Statement [*A publication*]

EDRRA ...... Editorial Research Reports [*A publication*]

EDRS .... Education Document Reproduction Service

EDRS .... Engineering Data Retrieval System [*Military*]

EDRS .... ERIC [*Educational Resources Information Center*] Document Reproduction Service [*Department of Education*] [*Alexandria, VA*]

EDRS......... Saarbruecken [*Federal Republic of Germany*] [*ICAO location identifier*] (ICLI)
EDRSA2.... Elma Dill Russell Spencer Foundation Series [*A publication*]
EDRT .... Effective Date of Release from Training
EDRT .... Trier/Foehren [*Federal Republic of Germany*] [*ICAO location identifier*] (ICLI)
EDRY .... Speyer [*Federal Republic of Germany*] [*ICAO location identifier*] (ICLI)
EDRZ .... Pirmasens/Zweibruecken [*Federal Republic of Germany*] [*ICAO location identifier*] (ICLI)
EDS .... Echo Depth Sounder
EDS .... Economic Digest [*A publication*]
EdS .... Ecrits des Saints [*A publication*]
EDS .... Edisto Resources [*AMEX symbol*] (SPSG)
EDS .... Editorial Data Systems
EDS .... Educational Delivery System (OICC)
Ed S........... Educational Specialist
EDS .... Ehlers-Danlos Syndrome [*Medicine*]
EDS .... El Dorado Systems Canada [*Vancouver Stock Exchange symbol*]
EDS .... Electrical Distribution System (MCD)
EDS .... Electron Devices Society (EA)
EDS .... Electronic Data Switching System [*Data processing*] (TEL)
EDS .... Electronic Data System (IEEE)
EDS .... Electronic Data Systems Federal Corp.
EDS .... Electronic Data Systems Ltd. [*Information service or system*] (IID)
EDS .... Electronic Distribution Show (ITD)
EDS .... Electronic Distribution System (MCD)
EDS .... Electronic Document Service
EDS .... Emergency Deorbit System [*NASA*] (KSC)
EDS .... Emergency Detection System
EDS .... Emergency Disablement System
EDS .... Emergency Distribution System (MCD)
EDS .... Employability Development Services [*US Employment Service*] [*Department of Labor*]
EDS .... Enamel Double Silk [*Wire insulation*] (AAG)
EDS .... Energy Data System [*Environmental Protection Agency*] [*Databank*] (IID)
EDS .... Energy Depot Systems
EDS .... Energy Dispersive Spectroscopy
EDS .... Energy Dispersive System [*Microscopy*]
EDS .... Engine Diagnostic System
EDS .... Engineering Data Sheet
EDS .... Engineering Data Software
EDS .... Engineering Data Systems [*DoD*]
EDS .... English Dance and Song [*A publication*]
EDS .... English Dialect Society
EDS .... Entry Data Subsystem
EDS .... Environmental Data Service [*Later, NESDIS*] [*Washington, DC*] [*National Oceanic and Atmospheric Administration*] (EA)
EDS .... Equatorial Dynamics Study [*Marine science*] (MSC)
EDS .... Equipment Decontamination Station [*Military*]
EDS .... Error Detection System (KSC)
EDS .... Estimated Date of Separation
EDS .... European Distribution System [*DoD*]
EDS .... Excess Disposition System (MCD)
EDS .... Excessive Daytime Sleepiness
EDS .... Exchangeable Disk Storage [*Data processing*]
EDS .... Experiment Data System
EDS .... Explosive Device System (KSC)
EDS .... Express Delivery Service
EDS .... Extradimensional Shift [*Psychometrics*]
EDS .... Exxon Donor Solvent Process [*Coal liquefaction*]
EDS .... IEEE Electron Devices Society (EA)
EDS .... Orangeburg, SC [*Location identifier*] [*FAA*] (FAAL)
EDS .... [*E. D.*] Smith's New York Common Pleas Reports [*A publication*] (DLA)
EDSA......... Effective Date of Change in Station Assignment [*Military*]
EDSA......... Epifanio de los Santos [*Avenue where Philippine President Marcos' government tanks were stopped by unarmed citizens*] [*In the EDSA Revolution of February, 1986*]
EDSA......... European Distribution System Aircraft [*DoD*]
EDSA......... Landsberg [*Federal Republic of Germany*] [*ICAO location identifier*] (ICLI)
EDSAC...... Electronic Delay Storage Automatic Calculator [*or Computer*] [*1949*]
EDSAC...... Electronic Discrete Sequential Automatic Computer [*University of Manchester, 1949*] [*British*] (IEEE)
EDSAI....... Educational Dealers and Suppliers Association International (EA)
Ed San........ Education Sanitaire [*A publication*]
EDSAT...... [*Center for*] Educational Diffusion and Social Application of Satellite Telecommunications [*University of Wisconsin*]
EDSB......... Buchel [*Federal Republic of Germany*] [*ICAO location identifier*] (ICLI)
EDSC......... Engineering Data Service Center [*Air Force*]
EDSC......... Engineering Data Support Center [*Air Force*] (CET)
EDSC......... European Deaf Swimming Championships [*London, England*]
Ed in Science ... Education in Science [*A publication*]

Ed Screen... Educational Screen [*A publication*]
Ed Screen AV G ... Educational Screen and Audiovisual Guide [*Later, AV Guide: The Learning Media Magazine*] [*A publication*]
EDSD .... Engineering and Development Services Department [*Naval Air Development Center*]
EDSD .... Leipheim [*Federal Republic of Germany*] [*ICAO location identifier*] (ICLI)
EDSE......... Erding [*Federal Republic of Germany*] [*ICAO location identifier*] (ICLI)
EDSE......... ESELCO, Inc. [*Formerly, Edison Sault Electric Co.*] [*NASDAQ symbol*] (SPSG)
Ed Ser Fla Dep Nat Resour Mar Res Lab ... Educational Series. Florida Department of Natural Resources. Marine Research Laboratory [*A publication*]
EDSF......... Fuerstenfeldbruck [*Federal Republic of Germany*] [*ICAO location identifier*] (ICLI)
EDSFC ...... Electronic Data Systems Federal Corporation
EDSG......... Bremgarten [*Federal Republic of Germany*] [*ICAO location identifier*] (ICLI)
EDSI.......... Ingoldstadt [*Federal Republic of Germany*] [*ICAO location identifier*] (ICLI)
EDSIL .... Engineering Development Systems Integration Laboratory
ED SK .... Engineering Department Sketch (MSA)
EDSK......... Kaufbeuren [*Federal Republic of Germany*] [*ICAO location identifier*] (ICLI)
EDSL......... End-Diastolic Segment Length [*Cardiology*]
EDSL......... Lechfeld [*Federal Republic of Germany*] [*ICAO location identifier*] (ICLI)
EDSM........ Memmingen [*Federal Republic of Germany*] [*ICAO location identifier*] (ICLI)
E D Smith .. [*E. D.*] Smith's New York Common Pleas Reports [*A publication*] (DLA)
E D Smith (NY) ... [*E. D.*] Smith's New York Common Pleas Reports [*A publication*] (DLA)
E D Smith R ... [*E. D.*] Smith's New York Common Pleas Reports [*A publication*] (DLA)
E D Smith's CPR ... [*E. D.*] Smith's New York Common Pleas Reports [*A publication*] (DLA)
E D Smith's R ... [*E. D.*] Smith's New York Common Pleas Reports [*A publication*] (DLA)
EDSN .... Neubiberg [*Federal Republic of Germany*] [*ICAO location identifier*] (ICLI)
EDS-NWT ... Eskimo Dog Society of the Northwest Territories [*Defunct*] (EA)
Ed & Social Science ... Education and Social Science [*A publication*]
Ed Sp......... Education Specialist
EDSP......... Engineering Design Support to Production (MCD)
EDSP......... Pferdsfeld [*Federal Republic of Germany*] [*ICAO location identifier*] (ICLI)
Ed Spec ... Education Specialist
EDS & R .... Engineering Data Storage and Retrieval [*Military*]
EDSR......... Exploratory Development Summary Report [*Military*]
EDSS .... Engineering and Development Support Services (KSC)
EDST .... Eastern Daylight Saving Time
EDST .... Elastic Diaphragm Switch Technology [*IBM Corp.*] (MCD)
EDSTAT ... Educational Statistics [*Search system*]
EDSTM..... Environmental Data Service Technical Memoranda [*National Oceanic and Atmospheric Administration*] (NOAA)
Ed Studies ... Educational Studies [*A publication*]
Ed Stud Math ... Educational Studies in Mathematics [*Dordrecht*] [*A publication*]
EDSU .... Neuburg [*Federal Republic of Germany*] [*ICAO location identifier*] (ICLI)
Ed Survey... Educational Survey [*A publication*]
EDSV........ Enamel Double Silk Varnish [*Wire insulation*]
EDSV......... Mebstetten [*Federal Republic of Germany*] [*ICAO location identifier*] (ICLI)
EDT .... Eastern Daylight Time
EDT .... Editor
EdT .... Educational Technology [*A publication*]
ED T .... Educational Times [*A publication*]
EDT .... Effective Date of Training
EDT .... Effective Diagenetic Temperature [*Geology*]
EDT .... Electrical Discharge Tube (MSA)
EDT .... Electrodeless Discharge Tube
EDT .... Electronic Data Transmission (AAG)
EDT .... Employability Development Team (OICC)
EDT .... Energy Dissipation Tests (NRCH)
EDT .... Engineering Design Test
EDT .... Engineering Development Test
EDT .... Engineering Drawing Tree
ED & T ...... Equipment Development and Test Report [*Forest Service*]
EDT .... Equipment Downtime
EDT .... Equipment Drain Tank [*Nuclear energy*] (NRCH)
EDT .... Estimated Delivery Times
EDT .... Estimated Departure Time
EDT .... Estimated Discharge Time
EDT .... Ethylenediamine Tartrate [*Organic chemistry*]
EDTA .... Aalen-Heidenheim/Elchingen [*Federal Republic of Germany*] [*ICAO location identifier*] (ICLI)
EDTA .... Edudata Corp. [*Far Hills, NJ*] [*NASDAQ symbol*] (NQ)

EDTA .... Ethylenediaminetetraacetate [*Also, EDETATE, enta*] [*Organic chemistry*]

EDTA .... Ethylenedinitrilo Tetraacetic Acid [*Organic chemistry*] (NRCH)

EDTAN ..... Ethylenediaminetetraacetonitrile [*Also, EDTN*] [*Organic chemistry*]

EDTB........ Baden-Baden [*Federal Republic of Germany*] [*ICAO location identifier*] (ICLI)

EDTC........ Engineering Design Test, Contractor (MCD)

EDTC........ Engineering Development and Test Center [*Mack Trucks, Inc.*] [*Allentown, PA*]

EDTCC...... Electronic Data Traffic Control Center [*or Complex*]

EDTCC...... Electronic Data Transmission Communications Central

E D Tch ...... Etudes et Documents Tchadiens [*A publication*]

EDTD .... Donaueschingen/Villingen [*Federal Republic of Germany*] [*ICAO location identifier*] (ICLI)

EDTE........ Effective Date [*Military*] (AFIT)

EDTE........ Schwenningen Am Nickar [*Federal Republic of Germany*] [*ICAO location identifier*] (ICLI)

Ed for Teaching ... Education for Teaching [*A publication*]

Ed Tech..... Educational Technology [*A publication*]

ED Tenn .... United States District Court for the Eastern District of Tennessee (DLA)

ED Tex...... United States District Court for the Eastern District of Texas (DLA)

EDTF........ Freiburg/Breisgau [*Federal Republic of Germany*] [*ICAO location identifier*] (ICLI)

EDTG........ Engineering Design Test, Government (MCD)

EDTH........ Heubach, Wurttemberg [*Federal Republic of Germany*] [*ICAO location identifier*] (ICLI)

Ed Theatre J ... Educational Theatre Journal [*A publication*]

Ed Theory .. Educational Theory [*A publication*]

EDTK .... Karlsruhe/Forchheim [*Federal Republic of Germany*] [*ICAO location identifier*] (ICLI)

EDTM .... Mengen [*Federal Republic of Germany*] [*ICAO location identifier*] (ICLI)

EDTN .... Ethylenediaminetetraacetonitrile [*Also, EDTAN*] [*Organic chemistry*]

EDTN .... Nabern/Teck [*Federal Republic of Germany*] [*ICAO location identifier*] (ICLI)

EDTNA/ERCA ... European Dialysis and Transplant Nurses Association/ European Renal Care Association [*Formerly, European Dialysis and Transplant Nurses Associaton*] (EA)

EDTO .... Offenburg/Baden [*Federal Republic of Germany*] [*ICAO location identifier*] (ICLI)

Ed Today.... Education Today [*A publication*]

EDTPO...... Ethylenediaminetetra(methylenephosphonic Acid) [*Organic chemistry*]

EDTR .... Experimental, Developmental, Test, and Research

Ed & Training ... Education and Training [*A publication*]

Ed & Train Men Retard ... Education and Training of the Mentally Retarded [*A publication*]

EDTRED... Endodontics and Dental Traumatology [*A publication*]

EDTS........ Equipment Drain Treatment System [*Nuclear energy*] (NRCH)

EDTSR...... Electronic Dial Tone Speed Register [*Bell System*]

EDTV........ Enhanced Definition Television (PCM)

Ed TV Int... Educational Television International [*A publication*]

EDTX .... Schwaebisch Hall/Weckrieden [*Federal Republic of Germany*] [*ICAO location identifier*] (ICLI)

EDTY .... Friedrichshafen-Lowental [*Federal Republic of Germany*] [*ICAO location identifier*] (ICLI)

EDTZ........ Konstanz [*Federal Republic of Germany*] [*ICAO location identifier*] (ICLI)

EDU........... Dundee [*Scotland*] [*Seismograph station code, US Geological Survey*] (SEIS)

EDU........... Early Deploying Unit (MCD)

EDU........... Education (ADA)

Edu........... Educo [*Record label*]

EDU........... Electrical Distribution Unit

EDU........... Electronic Display Unit

EDU........... Electronic Distributor Unit [*Automotive engineering*]

EDU........... Engineering Development Unit [*NASA*] (NASA)

EDU........... Environmental Diving Unit [*Marine science*] (MSC)

EDU........... Ethiopian Democratic Union [*Political party*] (PD)

EDU........... Europaeische Demokratische Union [*European Democratic Union*] (EAIO)

EDU........... European Democrat Union [*Austria*] (PPE)

EDU........... Experimental Diving Unit

EDU........... Ministry of Education, Information Centre [*Ontario*] [*UTLAS symbol*]

EDUC........ Educated [*or Education*] (AFM)

Educ.......... Education [*A publication*]

EDUC........ Educational Development Corporation [*NASDAQ symbol*] (NQ)

EDUC .... Eductor (MSA)

Educa........ Education [*A publication*]

Educ Adm .. Educational Administration [*A publication*] (APTA)

Educ Adm .. Educational Administrator [*A publication*]

Educ Adm Abstr ... Educational Administration Abstracts [*A publication*]

Educ Admin ... Educational Administration Quarterly [*A publication*]

Educ Admin Abstr ... Educational Adminstration Abstracts [*A publication*]

Educ Admin Supervision ... Educational Administration and Supervision [*A publication*]

Educ Adm Q ... Educational Administration Quarterly [*A publication*]

Educ Adm & Sup ... Educational Administration and Supervision [*A publication*]

Educa R...... Educational Review [*A publication*]

Educational Bldg Digest ... Educational Building Digest [*A publication*]

Education M ... Education Musicale [*A publication*]

Educatn 89 ... Projections of Education Statistics to 1988-89 [*A publication*]

EDUCATSS ... Education Cataloguing Support System [*UTLAS symbol*]

Educazione M ... Educazione Musicale [*A publication*]

Educ Brdcstng ... Educational Broadcasting [*A publication*]

Educ Broadcast Int ... Educational Broadcasting International [*A publication*]

Educ Broad Int ... Educational Broadcasting International [*A publication*]

Educ Bull .... Education Bulletin [*A publication*]

Educ Can.... Education Canada [*A publication*]

Educ Cap.... Education Capital [*A publication*] (APTA)

Educ Change Dev ... Educational Change and Development [*A publication*]

Educ Chem ... Education in Chemistry [*A publication*]

Educ Comm & Tech J ... Educational Communication and Technology Journal [*A publication*]

Educ Comput ... Educational Computing [*A publication*]

Educ Cult ... Education and Culture [*A publication*]

Educ et Cult ... Education et Culture [*A publication*]

Educ Dent (Ica) ... Educacion Dental (Ica, Peru) [*A publication*]

Educ et Develop ... Education et Developpement [*A publication*]

Educ Dig .... Education Digest [*A publication*]

Educ Digest ... Education Digest [*A publication*]

Educ Dir Dent Aux ... Educational Directions for Dental Auxiliaries [*A publication*]

Educ Dir Dent Hyg ... Educational Directions in Dental Hygiene [*A publication*]

Educ Doc & Inf ... Educational Documentation and Information [*A publication*]

EducF........ Educational Forum [*A publication*]

Educ Film Guide ... Educational Film Guide [*A publication*]

Educ Foc .... Educational Focus [*A publication*]

Educ Focus ... Educational Focus [*A publication*]

Educ For .... Educational Forum [*A publication*]

Educ Forum ... Educational Forum [*A publication*]

Educ Found Am Soc Plast Reconstr Surg Proc Symp ... Educational Foundation. American Society of Plastic and Reconstructive Surgeons. Proceedings of the Symposium [*A publication*]

Educ Gaz.... Education Gazette [*A publication*] (APTA)

Educ Gazette ... Education Gazette [*Sydney*] [*A publication*] (APTA)

Educ Gaz SA ... Education Gazette. South Australia Department of Education [*A publication*] (APTA)

Educ Gerontol ... Educational Gerontology [*A publication*]

Educ Guard ... Education Guardian [*A publication*]

Educ Horiz ... Educational Horizons [*A publication*]

Educ Ind..... Education Index [*A publication*]

Educ Index ... Education Index [*A publication*]

Educ Ind Telev ... Educational and Industrial Television [*A publication*]

Educ Innovations ... Educational Innovations [*A publication*] (APTA)

Educ J .... Education Journal [*A publication*]

EDUCL...... Educational

Educ Lead .. Educational Leadership [*A publication*]

Educ Leadersh ... Educational Leadership [*A publication*]

Educ Lg Cit ... Education in Large Cities [*A publication*]

Educ Libr Bull ... Education Libraries Bulletin [*A publication*]

Educ Libr Serv Bull ... Education Library Service Bulletin [*A publication*] (APTA)

Educ L Rep (West) ... Education Law Reporter (West) [*A publication*]

Educ Mag.... Educational Magazine [*A publication*] (APTA)

Educ Manage Admin ... Educational Management and Administration [*A publication*]

Educ Media ... Educational Media [*A publication*]

Educ Media Int ... Educational Media International [*A publication*]

Educ and Medicine ... Education and Medicine [*A publication*]

Educ Med Salud ... Educacion Medica y Salud [*A publication*]

Educ Mus Mag ... Educational Music Magazine [*A publication*]

EDUCN...... Education

Educ N .... Education News [*A publication*] (APTA)

Educ Nat.... Education Nationale [*A publication*]

Educ News ... Education News [*A publication*] (APTA)

Educnl........ Educational

Educ NSW ... Education. New South Wales Teachers Federation [*A publication*] (APTA)

EDUCOM ... EDUCOM [*Educational Communications*] Bulletin [*A publication*]

EDUCOM ... Interuniversity Communications Council (EA)

EDUCOM Bull ... EDUCOM [*Educational Communications*] Bulletin [*A publication*]

Educ Ont.... Education Ontario [*A publication*]

Educ Outl.... Educational Outlook [*A publication*]

Educ Perm ... Education Permanente [*A publication*] (APTA)

Educ Philos Theory ... Educational Philosophy and Theory [*A publication*]

Educ Phil Theor ... Educational Philosophy and Theory [*A publication*] (APTA)

Educ Plan... Educational Planning [*A publication*]

Educ Policy Bull ... Education Policy Bulletin [*A publication*]
Educ Prod Rept ... Educational Product Report [*A publication*]
Educ Psychol ... Educational Psychologist [*A publication*]
Educ & Psychol M ... Educational and Psychological Measurement [*A publication*]
Educ & Psychol Meas ... Educational and Psychological Measurement [*A publication*]
Educ Psychol Measmt ... Educational and Psychological Measurement [*A publication*]
Educ Psychol Measure ... Educational and Psychological Measurement [*A publication*]
Educ Psyc M ... Educational and Psychological Measurement [*A publication*]
Educ Q ...... Education Quarterly [*A publication*]
Educ Q Nepal ... Education Quarterly. Katmandu, Nepal College of Education [*A publication*]
Educ R....... Educational Review [*A publication*]
Educ Rec .... Educational Record [*A publication*]
Educ Rec Bur Bull ... Educational Records Bureau. Bulletins [*Greenwich, Connecticut*] [*A publication*]
Educ Recd .. Educational Record [*A publication*]
Educ Record ... Educational Record [*A publication*] (APTA)
Educ Res .... Educational Research [*A publication*]
Educ Res .... Educational Researcher [*A publication*]
Educ Res Bul ... Educational Research Bulletin [*A publication*]
Educ Researcher ... Educational Researcher [*A publication*]
Educ Res News ... Educational Research News [*A publication*]
Educ Res Perspect ... Education Research and Perspectives [*A publication*] (APTA)
Educ Res Q ... Educational Research Quarterly [*A publication*]
Educ Res Quart ... Educational Research Quarterly [*A publication*]
Educ Rev .... Education Review [*A publication*]
Educ Sanit ... Educazione Sanitaria [*A publication*]
Educ Sci ... Education in Science [*A publication*]
Educ Screen ... Educational Screen [*A publication*]
Educ Ser Miner Resour Div (Manitoba) ... Educational Series. Mineral Resources Division (Manitoba) [*A publication*]
Educ Sordomuti ... Educazione dei Sordomuti [*A publication*]
Educ Stat ... Projections of Education Statistics to 1992-93 [*A publication*]
Educ Stud ... Educational Studies [*A publication*]
Educ Stud Math ... Educational Studies in Mathematics [*A publication*]
Educ Suppl Yorks Beekprs Ass ... Educational Supplement. Yorkshire Beekeepers Association [*A publication*]
Educ Tech .. Educational Technology [*A publication*]
Educ Techn ... Educational Technology [*A publication*]
Educ Technol ... Educational Technology [*A publication*]
Educ Theatre J ... Educational Theatre Journal [*A publication*]
Educ Theor ... Educational Theory [*A publication*]
Educ Theory ... Educational Theory [*A publication*]
Educ Through Technol ... Education through Technology [*A publication*] (APTA)
Educ and Train ... Education and Training [*A publication*]
Educ & Training ... Education and Training [*A publication*]
Educ & Train Men Retard ... Education and Training of the Mentally Retarded [*A publication*]
Educ & Train Mentally Retard ... Education and Training of the Mentally Retarded [*A publication*]
Educ TV ..... Educational and Industrial Television [*A publication*]
Educ Urban ... Education and Urban Society [*A publication*]
Educ & Urban Soc ... Education and Urban Society [*A publication*]
Educ and Urban Society ... Education and Urban Society [*A publication*]
Educ Urb Soc ... Education and Urban Society [*A publication*]
Educ Vict ... Education for Victory [*A publication*]
Educ Visual ... Education of the Visually Handicapped [*A publication*]
Educ (WA) ... Education (Perth, Western Australia) [*A publication*] (APTA)
EDUD........ Detmold [*Federal Republic of Germany*] [*ICAO location identifier*] (ICLI)
Edu D........ Educational Digest [*A publication*]
EDUG........ European Datamanager Users Group [*London, England*] (CSR)
EDUH .... Hildesheim [*Federal Republic of Germany*] [*ICAO location identifier*] (ICLI)
EDUK........ Rheindahlen [*Federal Republic of Germany*] [*ICAO location identifier*] (ICLI)
EDUL .... Laarbruch [*Federal Republic of Germany*] [*ICAO location identifier*] (ICLI)
EDUN........ Nordhorn Range [*Federal Republic of Germany*] [*ICAO location identifier*] (ICLI)
EDUNET .. Education Network [*EDUCOM*]
EDUO........ Guetersloh [*Federal Republic of Germany*] [*ICAO location identifier*] (ICLI)
EDUR........ Bruggen [*Federal Republic of Germany*] [*ICAO location identifier*] (ICLI)
EDUR........ Engineering Drawing Usage Record [*DAC*]
EDUS .... Soest [*Federal Republic of Germany*] [*ICAO location identifier*] (ICLI)
Ed USA...... Education USA [*A publication*]
EDUSAT.... Educational Satellite (KSC)
EDUW........ Wildenrath [*Federal Republic of Germany*] [*ICAO location identifier*] (ICLI)
'Eduy......... 'Eduyyoth (BJA)
EDV........... Eastern Diverging Volcanism [*Geology*]

EDV .... Economic Development Review [*A publication*]
EDV .... Electronic Depressurizing Valve (MCD)
EDV........... Elektronische Datenverarbeitung [*Electronic Data Processing - EDP*] [*German*]
EDV .... End-Diastolic Volume [*Cardiology*]
EDV .... Epidermodysplasia Verruciformis [*Medicine*]
EDVA .... Bad Gandersheim [*Federal Republic of Germany*] [*ICAO location identifier*] (ICLI)
ED VA .... United States District Court for the Eastern District of Virginia (DLA)
EDVAC...... Electronic Discrete Variable Automatic Calculator [*or Computer*] (MCD)
EDVAP...... Electronic Digital-Vernier Analog Plotter (MUGU)
EDVB .... Braunschweig [*Federal Republic of Germany*] [*ICAO location identifier*] (ICLI)
EDVBD8 ... EDV [*Elektronische Datenverarbeitung*] in Medizin und Biologie [*A publication*]
EDVC .... Celle/Arloh [*Federal Republic of Germany*] [*ICAO location identifier*] (ICLI)
EDVE .... Braunschweig [*Federal Republic of Germany*] [*ICAO location identifier*] (ICLI)
EdVENT.... Educational Events [*Timeplace, Inc.*] [*Waltham, MA*] [*Information service or system*] (IID)
EDVH........ Hodenhagen [*Federal Republic of Germany*] [*ICAO location identifier*] (ICLI)
EDVI......... Hoxter/Holzminden [*Federal Republic of Germany*] [*ICAO location identifier*] (ICLI)
Ed Vis Hand ... Education of the Visually Handicapped [*A publication*]
EDVK .... Kassel/Calden [*Federal Republic of Germany*] [*ICAO location identifier*] (ICLI)
EDVL......... Holleberg [*Federal Republic of Germany*] [*ICAO location identifier*] (ICLI)
EDVM .... Kassel-Mittelfeld [*Federal Republic of Germany*] [*ICAO location identifier*] (ICLI)
EDV Med Biol ... EDV [*Elektronische Datenverarbeitung*] in Medizin und Biologie [*A publication*]
EDVN........ Northeim [*Federal Republic of Germany*] [*ICAO location identifier*] (ICLI)
EDVP........ Peine/Eddesse [*Federal Republic of Germany*] [*ICAO location identifier*] (ICLI)
EDVR .... Enlisted Distribution and Verification Report
EDVR .... Rinteln [*Federal Republic of Germany*] [*ICAO location identifier*] (ICLI)
EDVS .... Salzgitter/Drutte [*Federal Republic of Germany*] [*ICAO location identifier*] (ICLI)
EDVU .... Uelzen [*Federal Republic of Germany*] [*ICAO location identifier*] (ICLI)
EDVV .... Hannover [*Federal Republic of Germany*] [*ICAO location identifier*] (ICLI)
EDVX .... Gifhorn [*Federal Republic of Germany*] [*ICAO location identifier*] (ICLI)
EDVY .... Porta Westfalica [*Federal Republic of Germany*] [*ICAO location identifier*] (ICLI)
EDW .... Earth Departure Window [*Aerospace*]
EDW .... Edwards [*California*] [*Airport symbol*] [*Obsolete*] (OAG)
EDW .... Edwards Air Force Base [*California*] [*TACAN station*] (NASA)
Edw .... Edwards' Chester Palatine Courts [*England*] [*A publication*] (DLA)
Edw .... Edwards' English Admiralty Reports [*A publication*] (DLA)
Edw .... Edwards' New York Chancery Reports [*A publication*] (DLA)
Edw .... Edwards' Reports [*2, 3 Missouri*] [*A publication*] (DLA)
EDW .... El Dorado & Wesson Railway Co. [*AAR code*]
Ed (WA).... Education (Western Australia) [*A publication*] (APTA)
EDWA .... Norden-Hage [*Federal Republic of Germany*] [*ICAO location identifier*] (ICLI)
EDWAA .... Economic Dislocation and Worker Adjustment Assistance [*Department of Labor*]
Edw Abr..... Edwards' Abridgment of Prerogative Court Cases [*A publication*] (DLA)
Edw Abr..... Edwards' Abridgment, Privy Council [*A publication*] (DLA)
Edw Adm ... Edwards' English Admiralty Reports [*A publication*] (DLA)
Edw Adm (Eng) ... Edwards' English Admiralty Reports [*A publication*] (DLA)
Edw Adm Jur ... Edwards' Admiralty Jurisdiction [*1847*] [*A publication*] (DLA)
Edwards' Chr R ... Edwards' New York Chancery Reports [*A publication*] (DLA)
Edwards' Rep ... Edwards' New York Chancery Reports [*A publication*] (DLA)
ED Wash ... United States District Court for the Eastern District of Washington (DLA)
EDWB .... Bremerhaven/Am Luneort [*Federal Republic of Germany*] [*ICAO location identifier*] (ICLI)
Edw Bail..... Edwards on the Law of Bailments [*A publication*] (DLA)
Edw Bailm ... Edwards on the Law of Bailments [*A publication*] (DLA)
Edw Bills.... Edwards on Bills and Notes [*A publication*] (DLA)
Edw Bills & N ... Edwards on Bills and Notes [*A publication*] (DLA)
Edw Brok & F ... Edwards on Factors and Brokers [*A publication*] (DLA)
EDWC .... Damme [*Federal Republic of Germany*] [*ICAO location identifier*] (ICLI)
EDWC .... Electrical Discharge Wire Cutting [*Manufacturing term*]

Edw Ch ...... Edwards' New York Chancery Reports [*A publication*] (DLA)
Edw Chan .. Edwards' New York Chancery Reports [*A publication*] (DLA)
Edw Ch (NY) ... Edwards' New York Chancery Reports [*A publication*] (DLA)
Edw Conf .. Edward the Confessor (King of England) (DLA)
EDWD....... Lemwerder [*Federal Republic of Germany*] [*ICAO location identifier*] (ICLI)
EDWE ...... Emden [*Federal Republic of Germany*] [*ICAO location identifier*] (ICLI)
Edw Eccl Jur ... Edwards on Ecclesiastical Jurisdiction [*A publication*] (DLA)
EDWF........ Leer-Nuttermoor [*Federal Republic of Germany*] [*ICAO location identifier*] (ICLI)
Edw Fac ..... Edwards on Factors and Brokers [*A publication*] (DLA)
EDWG....... Wangerooge [*Federal Republic of Germany*] [*ICAO location identifier*] (ICLI)
Edw Gam ... Edwards' Law of Gaming [*A publication*] (DLA)
EDWH....... Oldenburg/Hatten [*Federal Republic of Germany*] [*ICAO location identifier*] (ICLI)
EDWI .... Wilhelmshaven/Mariensiel [*Federal Republic of Germany*] [*ICAO location identifier*] (ICLI)
ED Wis ...... United States District Court for the Eastern District of Wisconsin (DLA)
EDWJ........ Juist [*Federal Republic of Germany*] [*ICAO location identifier*] (ICLI)
Edw Jur..... Edwards' Juryman's Guide [*A publication*] (DLA)
EDWL .... Langeoog [*Federal Republic of Germany*] [*ICAO location identifier*] (ICLI)
Edw Lead Dec ... Edwards' Leading Decisions in Admiralty [*Edwards' Admiralty Reports*] [*A publication*] (DLA)
EDWM ...... Weser-Wumme [*Federal Republic of Germany*] [*ICAO location identifier*] (ICLI)
Edw MO .... Edwards' Reports [*2, 3 Missouri*] [*A publication*] (DLA)
EDWN....... Nordhorn/Klausheide [*Federal Republic of Germany*] [*ICAO location identifier*] (ICLI)
Edw (NY)... Edwards' New York Chancery Reports [*A publication*] (DLA)
EDWO....... Osnabruck/Atterheide [*Federal Republic of Germany*] [*ICAO location identifier*] (ICLI)
Ed World ... Education Around the World [*A publication*]
Edw Part .... Edwards on Parties in Chancery [*A publication*] (DLA)
Edw PC ..... Edwards' English Prize Cases [*A publication*] (DLA)
Edw Pleas .. Edwards' Pleasantries of the Courts of New York [*A publication*] (DLA)
Edw Pr Cas ... Edwards' English Prize Cases [*A publication*] (DLA)
Edw Pr Ct Cas ... Edwards' Abridgment of Prerogative Court Cases [*A publication*] (DLA)
EDWQ....... Ganderkesee-Atlas Aerodrome [*Federal Republic of Germany*] [*ICAO location identifier*] (ICLI)
EDWR ...... Borkum [*Federal Republic of Germany*] [*ICAO location identifier*] (ICLI)
ED/WR...... Edge Wear [*Deltiology*]
EDWR .... Edwards Industries, Inc. [*NASDAQ symbol*] (NQ)
Edw Rec .... Edwards on Receivers in Equity [*A publication*] (DLA)
Edw Ref..... Edwards on the Law of Referees [*A publication*] (DLA)
Edw Rep..... Edwards' New York Chancery Reports [*A publication*] (DLA)
EDWS........ Norden/Norddeich [*Federal Republic of Germany*] [*ICAO location identifier*] (ICLI)
Edw St Act ... Edwards on the Stamp Act [*A publication*] (DLA)
EDWT .... Nordenham-Einswarden [*Federal Republic of Germany*] [*ICAO location identifier*] (ICLI)
EDWTH ...... End-Diastolic Wall Thickness [*Cardiology*]
Edw (Tho).. Edwards' English Admiralty Reports [*A publication*] (DLA)
EDWU....... Varrelbusch [*Federal Republic of Germany*] [*ICAO location identifier*] (ICLI)
EDWV .... Verden/Scharnhorst [*Federal Republic of Germany*] [*ICAO location identifier*] (ICLI)
EDWW ...... Bremen [*Federal Republic of Germany*] [*ICAO location identifier*] (ICLI)
EDWY .... Norderney [*Federal Republic of Germany*] [*ICAO location identifier*] (ICLI)
EDX .... Edna, TX [*Location identifier*] [*FAA*] (FAAL)
EDX .... Electrodiagnosis [*Medicine*]
EDX .... Energy Dispersive X-Ray
EDX .... Event Driven Executive [*IBM Corp.*]
EDXA .... Energy Dispersive X-Ray Analysis [*or Analyzer*] [*Also, EDXRA*]
EDXB .... Heide/Busum [*Federal Republic of Germany*] [*ICAO location identifier*] (ICLI)
EDXC .... European DX Council [*Huntingdon, Cambridgeshire, England*] (EAIO)
EDXD .... Energy Dispersive X-Ray Diffraction [*Atomic structure determination*]
EDXE .... Rheine/Eschendorf [*Federal Republic of Germany*] [*ICAO location identifier*] (ICLI)
EDXF........ Energy Dispersive X-Ray Fluorescence [*Spectrometry*]
EDXF........ Flensburg/Schaferhaus [*Federal Republic of Germany*] [*ICAO location identifier*] (ICLI)
EDXH........ Helgoland/Dune [*Federal Republic of Germany*] [*ICAO location identifier*] (ICLI)
EDXM .... St. Michaelisdonn [*Federal Republic of Germany*] [*ICAO location identifier*] (ICLI)

EDXO........ St. Peter/Ording [*Federal Republic of Germany*] [*ICAO location identifier*] (ICLI)
EDXR .... Rendsburg/Schachtholm [*Federal Republic of Germany*] [*ICAO location identifier*] (ICLI)
EDXRA...... Energy Dispersive X-Ray Analysis [*or Analyzer*] [*Also, EDXA*]
EDXRF........ Energy Dispersive X-Ray Fluorescence [*Spectrometry*]
EDXRS........ Energy Dispersive X-Ray Spectrometry
EDXS........ Energy Dispersive X-Ray Spectrum
EDXW .... Westerland/Sylt [*Federal Republic of Germany*] [*ICAO location identifier*] (ICLI)
EDXY .... Wyk Auf Fohr [*Federal Republic of Germany*] [*ICAO location identifier*] (ICLI)
EDYA .... Ampfing/Waldkraiburg [*Federal Republic of Germany*] [*ICAO location identifier*] (ICLI)
EDYB .... Arnbruck [*Federal Republic of Germany*] [*ICAO location identifier*] (ICLI)
EDYG .... Beilingries [*Federal Republic of Germany*] [*ICAO location identifier*] (ICLI)
EDYL........ Leutkirch/Unterzeil [*Federal Republic of Germany*] [*ICAO location identifier*] (ICLI)
EDYN .... Nittenau/Bruck [*Federal Republic of Germany*] [*ICAO location identifier*] (ICLI)
EDYNMT ... Electric Dynamometer [*Engineering*]
EDYR .... Regensburg-Oberhub [*Federal Republic of Germany*] [*ICAO location identifier*] (ICLI)
EDYV .... Vogtareuth [*Federal Republic of Germany*] [*ICAO location identifier*] (ICLI)
EDZA .... Mittenwald-Luttensee [*Federal Republic of Germany*] [*ICAO location identifier*] (ICLI)
EDZB......... Bergen-Hohne [*Federal Republic of Germany*] [*ICAO location identifier*] (ICLI)
EDZD .... Ulm [*Federal Republic of Germany*] [*ICAO location identifier*] (ICLI)
EDZE........ Sengwarden [*Federal Republic of Germany*] [*ICAO location identifier*] (ICLI)
EDZF......... Fuerstenfeldbruck [*Federal Republic of Germany*] [*ICAO location identifier*] (ICLI)
EDZG .... Oldenburg [*Federal Republic of Germany*] [*ICAO location identifier*] (ICLI)
EDZH........ Garmersdorf [*Federal Republic of Germany*] [*ICAO location identifier*] (ICLI)
EDZI......... Trier [*Federal Republic of Germany*] [*ICAO location identifier*] (ICLI)
EDZJ......... Idar-Oberstein [*Federal Republic of Germany*] [*ICAO location identifier*] (ICLI)
EDZK .... Karlsruhe [*Federal Republic of Germany*] [*ICAO location identifier*] (ICLI)
EDZL .... Flensburg [*Federal Republic of Germany*] [*ICAO location identifier*] (ICLI)
EDZM .... Muenster-Gievenbeck [*Federal Republic of Germany*] [*ICAO location identifier*] (ICLI)
EDZN .... Koblenz [*Federal Republic of Germany*] [*ICAO location identifier*] (ICLI)
EDZO .... Motne-Centre, Offenbach [*Federal Republic of Germany*] [*ICAO location identifier*] (ICLI)
EDZQ .... Quickborn [*Federal Republic of Germany*] [*ICAO location identifier*] (ICLI)
EDZR .... Aurich [*Federal Republic of Germany*] [*ICAO location identifier*] (ICLI)
EDZS......... Bredstedt [*Federal Republic of Germany*] [*ICAO location identifier*] (ICLI)
EDZT .... Altenstadt [*Federal Republic of Germany*] [*ICAO location identifier*] (ICLI)
EDZU .... Appenweiler [*Federal Republic of Germany*] [*ICAO location identifier*] (ICLI)
EDZW .... Offenbach [*Federal Republic of Germany*] [*ICAO location identifier*] (ICLI)
EDZX .... Traben-Trarbach [*Federal Republic of Germany*] [*ICAO location identifier*] (ICLI)
EDZY .... Weiden [*Federal Republic of Germany*] [*ICAO location identifier*] (ICLI)
EE .... Early English [*Language, etc.*]
EE .... East Europe [*A publication*]
EE .... Eastern Economist [*A publication*]
EE .... Eastern Establishment [*Politics*]
EE .... Edit Error [*Military*] (AFIT)
EE .... Edward Elgar [*Publisher*] [*British*]
E/E............. Electrical/Electronic
EE .... Electrical Engineer [*or Engineering*]
EE .... Electrodynamic Explorer [*NASA*]
EE .... Electronic Editing [*Telecommunications*]
EE .... Electronic Editions [*Cowles Publishing Co.*] [*Information service or system*] (IID)
EE .... Electronic Engineering
EE .... Electronics to Electronics
EE .... Electronics Engineering Division [*Coast Guard*]
EE .... Elementary English [*A publication*]
EE .... Elements of Expense [*Army*] (AABC)
E & E........ Ellis and Ellis' English Queen's Bench Reports [*A publication*] (DLA)
EE .... Embassador Extraordinary [*Diplomacy*] [*British*] (ROG)

EE	Embryo Extract
EE	Emergency Establishment [*Military*] (NATG)
EE	Employee (OICC)
EE	Enantiomeric Excess [*Organic chemistry*]
EE	End Effector (MCD)
E-E	End to End [*Technical drawings*] (NASA)
E to E	End to End [*Telecommunications*]
EE	Enentarzid (BJA)
EE	Energy Efficiency [*Electrochemistry*]
EE	Energy Enterprises [*Information service or system*] (IID)
EE	Engagement Effectiveness [*Army*] (AABC)
EE	Enge's Entourage (EA)
EE	Engineering Economics
EE	English Earl (ROG)
EE	English Electric [*Commercial firm*] [*British*]
EE	English Ell [*Unit of measure*] (ROG)
EE	English Estates [*British*] (GEA)
EE	English Exchequer Reports [*A publication*] (DLA)
EE	Enki and Eridu (BJA)
EE	Enlightenment Essays [*A publication*]
EE	Enter Exponent [*Data processing*]
EE	Envoy Extraordinary [*Department of State*]
EE	Ephemeris Epigraphica [*A publication*]
EE	Equine Encephalitis
EE	Equity Earnings [*Accounting*]
EE	Equity Exchequer [*Legal term*] (DLA)
EE	Erasmus in English [*A publication*]
EE	Errors Excepted [*Business term*]
E-E	Erythematous-Edematous [*Reaction*] [*Medicine*]
E & E	Escape and Evasion
EE	Esquire Radio & Electronics, Inc. [*AMEX symbol*] (SPSG)
EE	Estudios Eclesiasticos [*A publication*]
EE	Estudios Eruditos en Memoriam de Bonilla y San Martin [*A publication*]
e e	Eterorrythmos Etaireia [*Limited or Registered Partnership*] [*Greek*]
EE	Ethniki Enosis [*National Unity Party*] [*Greek*] (PPE)
EE	Ethynyl Estradiol [*Endocrinology*]
EE	Euer Ehrwuerden [*Your Reverence*] [*German*]
EE	Eurocity Express [*Airline*] [*British*]
EE	Eurofly Co. [*Italy*] [*ICAO designator*] (FAAC)
ee----	Europe, Eastern [*MARC geographic area code*] [*Library of Congress*] (LCCP)
EE	Euzkadiko Ezkerra [*Basque Left*] [*Spain*] [*Political party*] (PPE)
E & E	Evacuation and Evasion
E & E	Evasion and Escape [*Military*]
EE	Evreiskaia Entsiklopediia [*A publication*] (BJA)
EE	Executair Ltd. [*Nigeria*] [*ICAO designator*] (ICDA)
EE	Executive Engineer [*British*] (DCTA)
EE	Expenditure and Employment (OICC)
EE	Experimental Establishment [*RAF*] [*British*]
EE	Expiration of Enlistment
E of E	Expiration of Enlistment
EE	Extended Edition [*IBM Corp.*] (BYTE)
EE	External Entity
EE	External Environment
EE	Eye and Ear
EE	Journal of Environmental Engineering [*A publication*]
EEA	Adrian College, Adrian, MI [*OCLC symbol*] (OCLC)
E & EA	Each and Every Accident [*Insurance*] (AIA)
EEA	Eastern Economic Association
EEA	Educational Administration Abstracts [*A publication*]
EEA	Electric Energy Association [*Later, EEI*] (EA)
EEA	Electrical and Electronics Abstracts [*United Kingdom*] [*Information service or system*] [*A publication*]
EEA	Electrical Engineering Abstracts [*A publication*]
EEA	Electromagnetic Environment Analysis
EEA	Electronic Engineering Association [*British*]
EEA	Emergency Employment Act [*1971*]
EEA	End-to-End Anastomosis [*Medicine*]
EEA	Engineering Evaluation Article (AAG)
EEA	Equal Employment Act
EEA	Essential Elements of Analysis
EEA	Estimated Expenditure of Ammunition (AABC)
EEA	Ethylene-Ethyl Acetate [*Organic chemistry*]
EEA	Ethylene-Ethyl Acrylate [*Copolymer*] [*Organic chemistry*]
EEA	Europaeische Evangelische Allianz [*European Evangelical Alliance - EEA*] (EAIO)
EEA	Evaluation Elements of Analysis (MCD)
EEAC	Equal Employment Advisory Council (EA)
EEAP	Emergency Egress Air Pack [*NASA*] (KSC)
EEAT........	Emotional-Ethical Attitudes Test [*Psychometrics*]
EEAT........	End, Evening Astronomical Twilight (MCD)
EEAVA......	Elektroenergetika i Avtomatika [*A publication*]
EEB...........	Bendix Engineering Development Center, Southfield, MI [*OCLC symbol*] (OCLC)
EEB...........	Eastern Electricity Board [*British*]
EEB...........	Economic Engineering Branch [*Army Tank Automotive Command*] [*Warren, MI*]
EEB...........	Effective External Boundary [*Forestry*]
EEB..........	European Environmental Bureau [*Brussels, Belgium*]
EEB..........	European Trends [*A publication*]
EEB..........	Exports to Europe Branch [*British Overseas Trade Board*] (DS)
EEBCS......	Electrical Equipment Bay Cooling System
EEBD........	Emergency Escape Breathing Device [*Navy*] (CAAL)
EEBM.......	Eastern Europe Bible Mission (EA)
EEC.......	East Erie Commercial Railroad [*AAR code*]
EEC.......	Economic Education for Clergy (EA)
EEC.......	Ectrodactylia, Ectodermal Dysplasia, Cleft Lip and Palate
EEC.......	Education Exploration Center
EEC.......	Educational Equity Concepts [*An association*] (EA)
EEC.......	EECO, Inc. [*AMEX symbol*] (SPSG)
EEC.......	Electrical and Electronics Commission
EEC.......	Electrical Export Corporation [*Defunct*]
EEC.......	Electronic Engine Control
EEC.......	Electronic Equipment Committee [*NASA*] (KSC)
EEC.......	Emerson Electric Company
EEC.......	Encased Elastic Cylinder
EEC.......	End of Equilibrium Cycle [*Nuclear energy*] (NRCH)
EEC.......	Enemy Exports Committee [*British*] [*World War II*]
EEC.......	Engine Electronic Control (MCD)
EEC.......	Engineering Economist [*A publication*]
EEC.......	Enlisted Evaluation Center [*Army*]
EEC.......	Enough Is Enough Club (EA)
EEC.......	Enteropathogenic Escherichia coli [*Also, EPEC*] [*Medicine*]
EEC.......	Europa Esperanto-Centro [*European Esperanto Centre - EEC*] (EAIO)
EEC.......	European Economic Community [*Common Market*]
EEC.......	European Esperanto Centre (EA)
EEC.......	Evaporation [*or Evaporative*] Emission Control [*Automobile antipollution device*]
EEC.......	EXAMETNET [*Experimental Inter-American Meteorological Rocket Network*] Executive Committee [*NASA*]
EEC.......	Exhaust Emission Control [*Automotive engineering*]
EEC.......	Expected Environmental Concentration [*Environmental science*]
EEC...........	Extendable Exit Cone (MCD)
EEC...........	St. Clair Community College, Port Huron, MI [*OCLC symbol*] (OCLC)
EECA........	Emergency Energy Conservation Act [*1979*]
EECA........	Engineering Economic Cost Analysis (MCD)
EECA........	European Electronic Component Manufacturers Association (EAIO)
EEC Bull....	European Economic Community. Bulletin of the European Communities [*A publication*]
EEC Bull S ...	European Economic Community. Bulletin of the European Communities. Supplement [*A publication*]
EECC........	Environmental Epidemiology and Cancer Centre [*United Kingdom*] (IRUK)
EECCS	European Ecumenical Commission for Church and Society [*Formerly, Ecumenical Commission for Church and Society*] (EA)
EECE........	Emergency Economic Committee for Europe [*A "Western Nation" organization*] [*Post-World War II*]
EECGDR...	Entente Europeenne du Commerce en Gros des Deux-Roues (EA)
EECIS.......	Electrical, Environmental Control, and Instrumentation Systems Specialist [*NASA*]
EECIT	Estudios Escenicos. Cuadernos del Instituto del Teatro [*A publication*]
EECL........	Emitter-Emitter Coupled Logic [*Electronics*] (IEEE)
EECL........	Encyclopedia of European Community Law [*A publication*] (DLA)
EEC-LCM ...	EEC [*European Economic Community*] Liaison Committee of Midwives [*London, England*] (EAIO)
EECM.......	East European Chemical Monitor [*Business International*] [*Vienna, Austria*] [*Information service or system*] (IID)
EECM.......	Electronic Engine Control Module
EECN	Ecogen, Inc. [*NASDAQ symbol*] (SPSG)
EECO	Enerco, Inc. [*Formerly, Energy Environmental*] [*NASDAQ symbol*] (NQ)
EECOD	European Ecumenical Organization for Development [*Brussels, Belgium*] (EAIO)
EECOM	CSM [*Command and Service Module*] Environmental and Electrical Systems Engineer [*NASA*]
EECOM	Electrical, Environmental, and Communications
EECOM	Electrical, Environmental, Consumables, and Mechanical Systems (MCD)
EECP........	Emergency Energy Conservation Program (OICC)
EEC Prot PI ...	Protocol on Privileges and Immunities of the European Economic Community [*A publication*] (DLA)
EECS	Electronic Engine Control System [*OC Johnson & Associates, Inc.*] [*Automotive engineering*]
EECS	Equal Employment Compliance Section [*Employment and Training Administration*] (OICC)
EECSB3.....	Electroencephalography and Clinical Neurophysiology. Supplement [*A publication*]
EEC-SLC...	European Economic Community - Shipbuilders' Linking Committee [*Brussels, Belgium*] (EAIO)
EECT........	End, Evening Civil Twilight [*Navigation*]
EECW........	Emergency Exchanger Cooling Water (IEEE)

EED .... Eastern Economist [*A publication*]
EED .... Electroexplosive Device
EED .... Electronic Engineering Division [*Coast Guard*]
EED .... Electronic Explosive Device (NVT)
EED .... Emergency Escape Device
EED .... Energy Efficient Design
E & ED .... English and Empire Digest [*A publication*] (DLA)
EED .... European Enterprises Development Co. [*Luxembourg*]
EED .... Needles, CA [*Location identifier*] [*FAA*] (FAAL)
EED .... Wayne State University, Division of Library Science, Detroit, MI [*OCLC symbol*] (OCLC)
EEDB .... Energy and Environment Data Base [*Oak Ridge National Laboratory*] [*Database*]
EEDC .... Encino Energy & Development [*NASDAQ symbol*] (NQ)
EEDID .... Energy Executive Directory [*A publication*]
E & E Dig... English and Empire Digest [*A publication*] (DLA)
EEDM .... External Event Detection Module [*Data processing*] (MDG)
EEDND ..... Energy Educator Newsletter [*A publication*]
EEDP .... Evaluation, Experimental and Development Projects (OICC)
EEDQ .... Ethoxycarbonylethoxydihydroquinone [*Pharmacology*]
EEE .... Brainerd, MN [*Location identifier*] [*FAA*] (FAAL)
EEE .... Detroit Edison Co., Information Services, Detroit, MI [*OCLC symbol*] (OCLC)
EEE .... Eastern Equine Encephalomyelitis [*Virus*]
EEE .... Eastern European Economics [*A publication*]
EEE .... Electrical, Electronic, and Electromechanical
EEE .... Electrical Engineering Exposition
EEE .... Electromagnetic Environment Experiment [*NASA*] (MCD)
EEE .... Electronic Equipment Engineering [*A publication*]
EEE .... Energy Efficient Engine
E in EE..... Engineer in Electrical Engineering
EEE .... Ensource, Inc. [*NYSE symbol*] (SPSG)
EEE .... Environmental-Ecological Education [*Office of Education program*]
EEE .... Equal, Effective, Elected [*Canada's Triple E Senate movement*]
EEE .... Error [*Aviation code*] (FAAC)
EEE .... External Ear Effect [*Audiology*]
EEEC .... Electromagnetic Energy Environment Criteria [*Army*] (AABC)
EEEC .... Extraepithelial Enterochromaffin Cells [*Cytology*]
EEEE .... Ektelestiki Epitropi Exoterikou Emboriou [*Foreign Trade Executive Committee*] [*Greek*]
EEEEE ...... Erase [*British naval signaling*]
EEEI .... Energy, Economics and Environment Institute (EA)
EEES .... Electronic Equipment Environment Survey (AFM)
EEEU .... End Effector Electronics Unit (MCD)
EEEVAL ... East End Environment [*A publication*]
EEF .... Earth Ecology Foundation (EA)
EEF .... Egypt Exploration Fund [*A publication*]
EEF .... Egyptian Expeditionary Force [*Military*] [*British*]
EEF .... Eisenhower Exchange Fellowships (EA)
EEF .... Engineering Employers' Federation [*British*] (DCTA)
EEF .... Erickson Educational Foundation [*Later, J2CP Information Services*]
EEF .... Exoerythrocytic Form [*Phase of malaria parasite*]
EEF .... Export Expansion Facility [*Export-Import Bank of the US*]
EEF .... Exxon Education Foundation
EEF .... Ford Motor Co., Engineering and Research Library, Dearborn, MI [*OCLC symbol*] (OCLC)
EEF .... Sisters Island, AK [*Location identifier*] [*FAA*] (FAAL)
EEFC .... Economic Education Foundation for Clergy [*Later, EEC*] (EA)
EEFF .... Electrostatically Enhanced Fabric Filtration
EEFHA ...... East European Family History Association (EA)
EEFI .... Essential Elements of Friendly Information [*Army*] (AABC)
EEFIS .... Evasion and Escape Fingerprint Identification System
EEFM .... Egyptian Exploration Fund. Memoirs [*A publication*] (ROG)
EEG .... Electroencephalogram [*or Electroencephalography*] [*Medicine*]
EEG .... Employee Exposure Guidelines [*General Motors Corp.*]
EEG .... Environmental Education Group [*Inactive*] (EA)
EEG .... Environmental Effects Group [*Army*] (RDA)
EEG .... European Expedition Guild (EA)
EEG .... Europese Economische Gemeenschap [*European Economic Community*]
EEG .... Great Lakes Bible College, Lansing, MI [*OCLC symbol*] (OCLC)
EEG Cl Neur ... Electroencephalography and Clinical Neurophysiology [*A publication*]
EEGEA ...... EEG/EMG; Zeitschrift fuer Elektroenzephalographie, Elektromyographie, und Verwandte Gebiete [*West Germany*] [*A publication*]
EEGL .... Eagle Entertainment, Inc. [*NASDAQ symbol*] (NQ)
EEH .... EMU [*Extra-Vehicular Mobility Unit*] Electrical Harness
EEH .... European Economic Review [*A publication*]
EEH .... Explorations in Economic History [*A publication*]
EEH .... Siena Heights College, Adrian, MI [*OCLC symbol*] (OCLC)
EEHA/AEA ... Anuario de Estudios Americanos. Consejo Superior de Investigaciones Científicas y Universidad de Sevilla, Escuela de Estudios Hispano-Americanos [*A publication*]
EEHA/HBA ... Historiografía y Bibliografía Americanistas. Escuela de Estudios Hispano-Americanos de Sevilla [*A publication*]
EEI .... EBSCO Electronic Information [*EBSCO Industries, Inc.*] [*Information service or system*] (IID)

EEI .... Ecology/Environment [*AMEX symbol*] (SPSG)
EEI .... Edison Electric Institute (EA)
EEI .... Edison Electric Institute. Bulletin [*A publication*]
EEI .... Educational Expeditions International [*Later, Earthwatch*]
EEI .... Electrical and Electromagnetic Interference (KSC)
EEI .... Electronic Emission Intelligence [*Military*]
EEI .... Ellis Enterprises, Inc. (EISS)
EEI .... Environmental Equipment Institute [*Defunct*] (EA)
EEI .... Essential Elements of Information [*Military*]
EEI .... Evans Economics, Incorporated [*Database producer*] [*Information service or system*] (IID)
EEI .... Excel Energy, Inc. [*Toronto Stock Exchange symbol*]
EEI .... Hillsdale College, Mossey Learning Center, Hillsdale, MI [*OCLC symbol*] (OCLC)
EEIB .... Enemy Equipment Intelligence Branch [*World War II*]
EEIB .... Environmental Engineering Intersociety Board
EEIBA ...... EEI [*Edison Electric Institute*] Bulletin [*A publication*]
EEI Bul ..... Edison Electric Institute. Bulletin [*A publication*]
EEIC .... Electrical/Electronics Insulation Conference (EA)
EEIC .... Element of Expense/Investment Code (AFM)
EEIC .... European Electronic Intelligence Center (MCD)
EEI Elec P ... Edison Electric Institute. Electric Perspectives [*A publication*]
EEII .... Eby Elementary Identification Instrument [*Educational test*]
EEIND....... Energy and the Environment: Interactions [*A publication*]
EE-IS........ Basque Left - Left for Socialism (PPW)
EEIS .... End-to-End Information System (NASA)
EEIS .... Enemy Equipment Identification Service [*World War II*]
EEIS .... Evanston Early Identification Scale [*Psychology*]
EEISD ...... EIS. Environmental Impact Statements [*A publication*]
EEIST .... Enemy Equipment Intelligence Service Team [*World War II*]
EEJ .... Capital Library Cooperative, Mason, MI [*OCLC symbol*] (OCLC)
EEJ .... Eastern Economic Journal [*A publication*]
EEJ .... Equatorial Electrojet
EEK .... Economisch en Sociaal Instituut voor de Middenstand. Informatieblad [*A publication*]
EEK .... Eek [*Alaska*] [*Airport symbol*] (OAG)
EEK .... Epoxy Experimental Kit
EEK .... Kellogg Community College, Battle Creek, MI [*OCLC symbol*] (OCLC)
E & EL .... Each and Every Loss [*Insurance*] (AIA)
EEL .... Electrical Equipment List (MCD)
EEL .... Electromagnetic Effects Laboratory [*Army*] (RDA)
EEL .... Emergency Exposure Limits (AFM)
EEL .... Energy Policy [*A publication*]
EEL .... Engineering Electronics Laboratory
EEL .... Environmental Effects Laboratory [*Army*]
EEL .... Evans Electroselenium Limited [*as in EEL analyzer, used in biochemical analysis*] [*British*]
EEL .... Exclusive Exchange Line [*Telecommunications*]
EEL .... Lansing Community College, Lansing, MI [*OCLC symbol*] (OCLC)
EELC .... Ethnic Employees of the Library of Congress (EA)
EELMA ...... Electricite-Electronique Moderne [*A publication*]
EELOAZ... Eesti Loodus [*A publication*]
EELR .... Extended Emission Line Region [*Spectrometry*]
EELS .... Electron Energy Loss Spectroscopy [*Also, ELS*]
EELS .... Electronic Emitter Location System (MCD)
EELUT...... Eastern Energy and Land Use Team [*Kearneysville, WV*] [*Department of the Interior*] (GRD)
EEM .... Earth Entry Module [*NASA*] (KSC)
EEM .... Eastern European Mission [*Later, SGA*]
EEM .... Effective Elastic Modulus
EEM .... Effective Engineering Management
EEM .... Effective Exposure Method (KSC)
EEM .... Electronic Engineers Master (MUGU)
EEM .... Electronic Equipment Modification
EEM .... Electronic Equipment Monitoring (IEEE)
EEM .... Electrostatic Electron Microscope
EEM .... Engineering Evaluation Model (KSC)
EEM .... Engineering Experimental Memo
EEM .... Ensemble for Early Music
EEM .... Excess Exchange Material (AFIT)
EEM .... Excitation-Emission Matrix [*Fluorometry*]
EEM .... Expendable Electronic Markers (NVT)
EEM .... Experienced Export Manager [*Designation awarded by American Society of International Executives*]
EEM .... Extrapolated End-Point Method [*Nuclear energy*] (NRCH)
EEM .... Michigan State University, East Lansing, MI [*OCLC symbol*] (OCLC)
EEMA .... Eglise et l'Etat au Moyen Age [*A publication*]
EEMB .... Emanu-El Men's Bulletin [*A publication*]
EEMB .... Estudios Eruditos en Memoriam de Bonilla y San Martin [*A publication*]
EEMCA ..... Estudios de Edad Media de la Corona de Aragon [*A publication*]
EEMD .... Electronic Equipment Maintainability Datebook (MCD)
EEMDA ..... Electrical-Electronics Materials Distributors Association [*Later, LEMDA*] (EA)
EEMJEB... Electrical and Electronic Manufacturers Joint Education Board
EEMK .... Electronic Equipment Maintenance Kit

EEMM ...... [*The*] Egyptian Expedition. Metropolitan Museum of Art [*New York*] [*A publication*] (BJA)
EE & MP ... Envoy Extraordinary and Minister Plenipotentiary [*Department of State*]
EEMS........ Enhanced Expanded Memory Specifications [*AST, Quadram*]
EEMS........ European Environmental Mutagen Society [*Leiden, Netherlands*] (EAIO)
EEMT........ Electronic Equipment Maintenance Trainer (MCD)
EEMTIC .... Electrical and Electronic Measurement and Test Instrumentation Conference (MCD)
EEMTR..... Enhanced Enlisted Master Tape Record (AABC)
EEMUA .... Engineering Equipment and Materials User's Association [*British*]
EEN .... Eastern Educational Television Network [*Boston, MA*] [*Telecommunications service*] (TSSD)
EEN .... Eden Resources Ltd. [*Vancouver Stock Exchange symbol*]
EEN .... Emergency Engineering Notice (MCD)
EEN .... Environment [*A publication*]
EEN .... Even-Even Nucleus
E'EN .... Evening (ROG)
EEN .... Keene [*New Hampshire*] [*Airport symbol*] (OAG)
E End News ... East End News [*A publication*]
EENGR ...... Electrical Engineer (FAAC)
EENMA .... Electrical Engineer and Merchandiser [*A publication*]
EENT .... Early Evening Nautical Twilight (MCD)
EENT .... End, Evening Nautical Twilight [*Navigation*]
EENT .... Eyes, Ears, Nose, and Throat [*Medicine*]
EENTA..... Eye, Ear, Nose, and Throat Journal [*A publication*]
EENTDT ... Ecological Entomology [*A publication*]
E & EO ...... Each and Every Occurrence [*Insurance*] (AIA)
EEO .... Ealing Electro-Optics [*British*]
EEO .... Effective Equal Opportunity
EEO .... Electroendosmosis [*Analytical biochemistry*]
EEO .... Elliptical Earth Orbit
EEO .... Equal Employment Officer
EEO .... Equal Employment Opportunity
EEO .... Expedite Engineering Order (MCD)
EEOA .... Equal Employment Opportunity Act (OICC)
EEOA .... Equal Employment Opportunity Agency
EEOC .... Equal Employment Opportunity Commission
EEOC Compl Man ... Equal Employment Opportunity Commission Compliance Manual [*Commerce Clearing House*] (DLA)
EEOC Compl Man BNA ... EEOC [*Equal Employment Opportunity Commission*] Compliance Manual. Bureau of National Affairs [*A publication*]
EEOC Compl Man CCH ... EEOC [*Equal Employment Opportunity Commission*] Compliance Manual. Commerce Clearing House [*A publication*]
EEOED ..... Emergency Earth Orbital Escape Device (KSC)
EEOO....... Equal Employment Opportunity Officer [*DoD*]
EEOOA ..... Equal Employment Opportunity Officer Activity
EEOP........ Equal Educational Opportunities Program [*HEW*]
EEOP........ Equal Employment Opportunity Program (MCD)
EEOS........ Equality of Educational Opportunity Survey [*1965*]
EEO Spotl ... EEO [*Equal Employment Opportunity*] Spotlight [*A publication*]
EEP........... Earth Equatorial Plane
EEP........... Economic Education Project [*Public Media Center*] (EA)
EEP........... Einstein Equivalence Principle [*Gravity*]
EEP........... Electrode Electrostatic Precipitator
EEP........... Electroencephalophony [*Medical electronics*] (IEEE)
EEP........... Elliptical Error Probability (CAAL)
EEP........... Emergency Essential Personnel (AFM)
EEP........... End Exercise Point (FAAC)
EEP........... Energy Engineering Program [*Navy*]
EEP........... Engineering Experimental Phase [*National Data Buoy Project*]
EEP........... Enormously Entertaining Prodigy
EEP........... Environmental Experiments Program [*National Science Foundation*]
EEP........... Epsilon Eta Phi [*Later, Phi Chi Theta*]
EEP........... Esperanza Explorations Ltd. [*Vancouver Stock Exchange symbol*]
EEP........... Experimental Education Program
EEP........... Explorations in Eastern Palestine [*A publication*] (BJA)
EEP........... Export Enhancement Program [*Department of Agriculture*]
EEP........... External Economic Policy [*British*]
EEP........... Lansing Public Library, Lansing, MI [*OCLC symbol*] (OCLC)
EEPA........ Electromagnetic Energy Policy Alliance (EA)
EEPC......... Energy and Environmental Policy Center [*Harvard University*] [*Research center*] (RCD)
EEPC......... India Engineering Export Promotion Council (EA)
EEPI......... Extraretinal Eye Position Information [*Ophthalmology*]
EEPM........ Electrical and Electronic Properties of Materials
EEPMD..... Energy Economics, Policy, and Management [*A publication*]
EEPNL...... Estimated Effective Perceived Noise Level
EEPROM ... Electrically Erasable, Programmable, Read-Only Memory [*Data processing*]
EEPS .... Emergency Electrical Power System (MCD)
EEPSAPT ... Epistemonike Epeteris tes Philosophikes Scholes tou Aristoteleiou Panepistemiou Thessalonikes [*A publication*]

EEPSPA .... Epistemonike Epeteris tes Philosophikes Scholes tou Panepistemiou Athenon [*A publication*]
EEPVS...... Electrical Equipment Protection Room Ventilation System [*Nuclear energy*] (NRCH)
EEQEA...... Electronic Equipment Engineering [*A publication*]
EEQNA ..... Electronic Equipment News [*A publication*]
EER .... Electronic Equipment Representative (MCD)
EER .... Elevated Electric Railway [*South London Railway*] (ROG)
EER .... Encounter Energy Resources Ltd. [*Toronto Stock Exchange symbol*]
EER .... Energy Efficiency Ratio [*Home appliance electric output*]
EER .... English Ecclesiastical Reports [*A publication*] (DLA)
EER .... Entered Employment Rate [*Job Training and Partnership Act*] (OICC)
EER .... Envelope Elimination and Restoration
EER .... Equipment Evaluation Report (NG)
EER .... European Economic Review [*A publication*]
E'ER .... Ever (ROG)
EER .... Expendable-Expendable-Reusable
EER .... Experimental Ecological Reserves [*Project*] [*National Science Foundation*]
EER .... Explosive Echo Ranging
EER .... Extended Endocardial Resection [*Medicine*]
EER .... University of Michigan, School of Library Science, Ann Arbor, MI [*OCLC symbol*] (OCLC)
EERA........ Electrical Equipment Representatives Association (EA)
EERA........ Explosive Excavation Research Agency [*Formerly, NCG*] [*Army*] (RDA)
EERC......... Earthquake Engineering Research Center [*University of California, Berkeley*] (IID)
EERC......... Explosive Echo Ranging Charge (NG)
EERD .... Electronic Equipment Reliability Databook (MCD)
EERF .... Eastern Environmental Radiation Facility [*Environmental Protection Agency*] (IID)
EERGD...... Energy (Ottawa) [*A publication*]
EERI.......... Earthquake Engineering Research Institute (EA)
EERL......... Eastern Environmental Radiation Laboratory [*Environmental Protection Agency*]
EERL......... Electrical Engineering Research Laboratory (KSC)
EERL......... Explosive Excavation Research Laboratory [*Army Engineer Waterways Experiment Station*] [*Livermore, CA*]
EE & RM ... Elementary Electrical and Radio Material [*Training School*] [*Navy*]
EERO .... European Environmental Research Organization
EERO .... Explosive Excavation Research Office [*Livermore, CA*] [*Army*]
EEROA ..... Elektro [*A publication*]
EEROM .... Electrically Erasable Read-Only Memory [*Data processing*] (MDG)
EERS .... Earthquake Early Reporting System [*Marine science*] (MSC)
EERS .... Expeditionary Equipment Report System
EERWA..... Enlisted Efficiency Report Weighted Average [*Army*]
EES .... E-Section Escape Suit [*Military*]
EES .... Eco-Energy System
EES .... Educational Employment Service
EES .... Effectiveness Evaluation System
EES .... Egypt Exploration Society (EA)
EES .... Ejection Escape Suit (NASA)
EES .... Electrical Equipment Shelter
EES .... Electromagnetic Environment Simulator
EES .... Electronic Emission Security (NATG)
EES .... Electronic Environment Simulator
EES .... Emergency Ejection Suits (MCD)
EES .... Emergency Establishment Supplements (NATG)
EES .... Emergency Evacuation Study [*Military*] (MCD)
EES .... Endoscopic Esophageal Sclerotherapy [*Medicine*]
EES .... Energy Extension Service [*Department of Energy*]
EES .... Engineering Equation Solver [*Macintosh*] [*Data processing*]
EES .... Engineering Experiment Station [*University of Missouri, Columbia*] [*Research center*] (RCD)
EES .... Enlisted Evaluation System [*Army*]
E & ES ...... Environmental and Energy Systems
EES .... Environmental Engineering Section
EES .... Erythromycin Ethylsuccinate [*Antimicrobial compound*]
EES .... European Economic Space
EES .... European Exchange System
EES .... Evangelical Education Society of the Protestant Episcopal Church (EA)
EES .... Examining and Entrance Station [*Air Force*]
EES .... Spring Arbor College, Spring Arbor, MI [*OCLC symbol*] (OCLC)
EESA......... Education for Economic Security Act [*1988*]
EESA......... Electrical and Engineering Staff Association [*British*]
EESADV..... Ecotoxicology and Environmental Safety [*A publication*]
EESB......... Electrical and Electronics Standards Board [*American National Standards Institute*] [*Telecommunications*]
EESB......... Expression. Journal of the English Society [*A publication*]
EESC......... East European Solidarity Committee (EAIO)
EESC......... Environmental and Energy Study Conference (EA)
EESc.......... Estudis Escenics. Quaderns de l'Institut del Teatre de la Diputacio de Barcelona [*A publication*]

EESGRM .. Egypt Exploration Society. Graeco-Roman Memoirs [*A publication*]
EESI .... Eastern Environmental Services, Inc. [*NASDAQ symbol*] (NQ)
EESMB ..... Electrical and Electronics Standards Management Board
EES/NCFR ... Education and Enrichment Section of the National Council on Family Relations (EA)
EESR .... Egypt Exploration Society. Report [*A publication*]
EESS .... Environmental Effects on Space Systems
Eesti NSV Tead Akad ... Eesti NSV Teaduste Akadeemia. Toimetised [*USSR*] [*A publication*]
Eesti NSV Tead Akad Fuus Astronoom Inst Uurim ... Eesti NSV Teaduste Akadeemia. Fuusika ja Astronoomia Instituudi Uurimused [*A publication*]
Eesti NSV Tead Akad Fuus Inst Uurim ... Eesti NSV Teaduste Akadeemia. Fuusika Instituudi Uurimused [*A publication*]
Eesti NSV Tead Akad Tartu Astronoom Observ Publ ... Eesti NSV Teaduste Akadeemia. Tartu Astronoomia Observatooriumi Publikatsioonik [*A publication*]
Eesti NSV Tead Akad Toim Biol ... Eesti NSV Teaduste Akadeemia. Toimetised. Bioloogia [*A publication*]
Eesti NSV Tead Akad Toim Biol Ser ... Eesti NSV Teaduste Akadeemia. Toimetised. Bioloogiline Seeria [*Estonian SSR*] [*A publication*]
Eesti NSV Tead Akad Toim Fuus Mat ... Eesti NSV Teaduste Akadeemia. Toimetised. Fuusika. Matemaatika [*A publication*]
Eesti NSV Tead Akad Toim Fuus Mat Tehnikatead Seer ... Eesti NSV Teaduste Akadeemia. Toimetised. Fuusika. Matemaatika ja Tehnikateaduste Seeria [*A publication*]
Eesti NSV Tead Akad Toim Geol Izv Akad Nauk Est SSR Geol ... Eesti NSV Teaduste Akadeemia. Toimetised. Geoloog Izvestiia Akademii Nauk Estonskoi SSR Geologiia [*A publication*]
Eesti NSV Tead Akad Toim Izv Ser Geol ... Eesti NSV Teaduste Akadeemia. Toimetised. Izvestiya. Seria Geoloogia [*Estonian SSR*] [*A publication*]
Eesti NSV Tead Akad Toim Izv Ser Keem ... Eesti NSV Teaduste Akadeemia. Toimetised. Izvestiya. Seria Keemia [*Estonian SSR*] [*A publication*]
Eesti NSV Tead Akad Toim Keem Geol ... Eesti NSV Teaduste Akadeemia. Toimetised. Keemia. Geoloogia [*A publication*]
Eesti NSV Tead Akad Toim Keem Izv Akad Nauk Est SSR Khim ... Eesti NSV Teaduste Akadeemia. Toimetised. Keemia. Izvestiia Akademii Nauk Estonskoi SSR Khimiia [*A publication*]
Eesti Vabariigi Tartu Ulik Toim A ... Eesti Vabariigi Tartu Ulikooli Toimetised A. Mathematica, Physica, Medica [*A publication*]
Eesti Vabariigi Tartu Ulik Toim C ... Eesti Vabariigi Tartu Ulikooli Toimetised C. Annales [*A publication*]
EEST/PD .. Emergency Establishment Supplement Table of Personnel Distribution [*NATO*] (NATG)
EESWS ...... Emergency Equipment Service Water System [*Nuclear energy*] (NRCH)
EE/Systems Eng ... EE/Systems Engineering Today [*A publication*]
E/E Syst Eng Today ... E/E Systems Engineering Today [*A publication*]
EET............ Eastern European Time (DCTA)
EET............ Education Equivalency Test
Ee T............ Eglise et Theologie [*A publication*]
EET............ Electrical Equipment Trailer
EET............ Electronic Exposure Timer (KSC)
EET............ Energy Efficient Transport (MCD)
EET............ Engage Enemy Target
EET............ Engineering Evaluation Test (NG)
EET............ Entry Elapsed Time (MCD)
EET............ Epoxy-Encapsulated Transistor
EET............ Equator Earth Terminal
EET............ Equipment Engaged Tone [*Telecommunications*] (TEL)
EET............ Equivalent Exposure Time (KSC)
EET............ Estimated Elapsed Time [*Aviation*] (FAAC)
EET............ Etruscan Enterprises Ltd. [*Vancouver Stock Exchange symbol*]
EET............ Event Elapsed Time (MCD)
EET............ Explosive-to-Electric Transducer
EETAD...... ETA. Elektrowaerme im Technischen Ausbau [*A publication*]
EETB........ Electronic Electrical Termination Building [*NASA*] (NASA)
EETC........ Electronic Equipment Technical Committee [*NASA*] (KSC)
EETCB...... Eternally Elvis TCB [*Taking Care of Business*] (EA)
EETED...... Elektrische Energie-Technik [*A publication*]
EETF........ Electronic Environmental Test Facility (MUGU)
EETPU...... Electrical, Electronic, Telecommunication, and Plumbing Union [*British*] (DCTA)
EETS........ Early English Text Society [*Oxford, England*]
EEU.......... East European Markets [*A publication*]
EEU.......... European Esperanto Union (EA)
EEU.......... University Microfilms International, Ann Arbor, MI [*OCLC symbol*] (OCLC)
E Eur........ East Europe [*A publication*]
E Eur Econ ... Eastern European Economics [*A publication*]
E Eur Mkts ... East European Markets [*A publication*]
E Europe Q ... East European Quarterly [*A publication*]
E Eur Q...... East European Quarterly [*A publication*]
EEV.......... Encircling Endocardial Ventriculotomy [*Cardiology*]
EEV .... English Electric Valve [*Electronics company*]

EEVeTec.... Equipment, Environment, Velocity, Technique, Conditioning [*Sports medicine*]
EEVF......... East Eifel Volcanic Field [*Geology*] [*Federal Republic of Germany*]
EEVT........ Electrophoresis Equipment Verification Test
EE & W ..... Emperor of the East and West [*Freemasonry*] (ROG)
EEW .... Extraordinary Electromagnetic Wave
EEW .... Neenah, WI [*Location identifier*] [*FAA*] (FAAL)
EEW .... Willard Library, Battle Creek, MI [*OCLC symbol*] (OCLC)
EEX .... Electronic Egg Exchange [*Computer program*]
EEX .... Essex Petroleum [*Vancouver Stock Exchange symbol*]
EEX .... Excess Exception Code [*Air Force*] (AFIT)
EEX .... Michigan State Library Services, Lansing, MI [*OCLC symbol*] (OCLC)
EEY .... Winchester, VA [*Location identifier*] [*FAA*] (FAAL)
EEZ.......... Exclusive Economic Zone [*Offshore sovereignty*] [*ICSU*]
EF .... Each Face [*Technical drawings*]
EF .... Eagle Forum (EA)
EF .... Ear Foundation (EA)
EF .... Early Finish
EF .... Earth First (EA)
EF .... East Florida [*Obsolete*] (ROG)
E & F........ Economic and Financial [*Plans*] [*British*]
EF .... Ectopic Focus [*Cardiology*]
EF .... Edema Factor [*Medicine*]
EF .... Eglin Field [*Florida*] [*Air Force*] (MCD)
E u F........ Ehe und Familie im Privaten und Oeffentlichen Recht [*A publication*]
EF .... Ejection Fraction [*Cardiology*]
EF .... Eksportfinans [*Export Finance*] [*Commercial firm*] [*Norway*]
E & F........ Elder and Fyfes Ltd. [*Shipping*] (ROG)
EF .... Elect of Fifteen [*Freemasonry*] (ROG)
EF .... Eleftherofronon [*Free Opinion Party*] [*Greek*] (PPE)
EF .... Elevation Finder [*Military*]
EF .... Elongation Factor [*Biochemistry, genetics*]
EF .... Embedded Figures [*Psychometrics*]
EF .... Emergency Facilities (AAG)
EF .... Emergency Fix
EF .... Emitter Follower [*Electronics*] (MCD)
EF .... Employed Full Time [*Chiropody*] [*British*]
EF .... En Foco [*An association*] (EA)
EF .... Ending Flag Value for Data Input [*Data processing*]
EF .... Endoplasmic Fracture [*Freeze etching in microscopy*]
E/F........... Enemy/Friendly (MCD)
EF .... Engineering Foundation (EA)
EF .... English Finish [*Paper*]
EF .... Enterprise Foundation (EA)
EF .... Environmental Factor
EF .... Eosinophilic Fasciitis [*Medicine*]
EF .... Epithelial Force (Assay) [*Oncology*]
EF .... Equilibrium Field (MCD)
EF .... Equipment Factor (CAAL)
EF .... Equivalent Focal Length [*Optics*]
EF .... Error Factor (IEEE)
EF .... Estudis Franciscans [*A publication*]
EF .... Ethos Foundation (EA)
EF .... Etruscan Foundation (EA)
EF .... Etudes Franciscaines [*A publication*]
EF .... Eurodata Foundation (EAIO)
EF .... [*The*] Europe Fund [*NYSE symbol*] (SPSG)
EF .... European Foundation (DS)
EF .... Eurotransplant Foundation (EA)
EF .... Evangelische Freiheit [*A publication*] (BJA)
EF .... Everyman's Fiction [*Series published by J. M. Dent & Sons*] [*British*]
EF .... Executive Forum (EA)
EF .... Exhaust Fan (AAG)
EF .... Exoplasmic Fracture [*Freeze etching in microscopy*]
EF .... Expeditionary Force
EF .... Experimental Flight
EF .... Experiments in Fluids [*A publication*]
EF .... Expressional Fluency [*Research test*] [*Psychology*]
EF .... Extended Facility [*IBM Corp.*]
E/F........... Extension/Flexion [*Medicine*]
EF .... External Flaps (AAG)
EF .... Extra Fine [*Threads*]
EF .... Extractable Fluorescence
EF .... Extremely Fine [*Condition*] [*Antiquarian book trade and numismatics*]
EF .... Extrinsic Factor [*Vitamin B_{12} Also, APA, APAF, LLD*]
EF .... Eye Focus
EFA.......... Category E Flying Accident [*British military*] (DMA)
EFA.......... Eastern Finance Association (EA)
EFA.......... [*African*] Economic Affairs, Allied [*World War II*]
EFA.......... Eddy Family Association (EA)
EFA.......... Editorial Freelancers Association (EA)
EFA.......... Effective Filtration Area
EFA.......... Electrinium Foundation of America (EA)
EFA.......... Electronics Field Activity
EFA.......... Engineering Field Activity (MCD)
EFA.......... Enginemen and Firemen's Association [*A union*] [*British*]

EFA............ Entire Field Available [*Aviation*]   (FAAC)
EFA............ Environmental Financing Authority [*Expired, 1975*] [*Environmental Protection Agency*]
EFA............ Epilepsy Foundation of America   (EA)
EFA............ Equestrian Federation of Australia
EFA............ Equilibrium Float Altitude [*Balloon flight*]
EFA............ Eskridge Family Association   (EA)
EFA............ Essential Fatty Acid [*Biochemistry*]
EFA............ European Fairytale Association [*See also EMG*] [*Rheine, Federal Republic of Germany*]   (EAIO)
EFA............ European Fighter Aircraft
EFA............ European Finance Association   (EAIO)
EFA............ European Free Alliance [*See also ALE*] [*Brussels, Belgium*] [*Political party*]   (EAIO)
EFA............ Evangelical Friends Alliance [*Later, EFI*]   (EA)
EFA............ Experiment Flight Applications   (NASA)
EFA............ Eyepiece Focusing Adjustment [*Optics*]   (ROG)
EFAA........ Aavahelukka [*Finland*] [*ICAO location identifier*]   (ICLI)
EFAC........ Energy Factors, Inc. [*NASDAQ symbol*]   (NQ)
EFACF ...... European Folk Art and Craft Federation [*Zurich, Switzerland*]   (EAIO)
EFAD........ Essential Fatty Acid Deficiency [*Medicine*]
EFAD........ European Federation of the Associations of Dietitians   (EAIO)
EFAG........ Emergency Field Arresting Gear   (MCD)
EFAI......... Educational Foundation for the Apparel Industry [*Later, EFFI*]   (EA)
EFAID...... Energie Fluide, l'Air Industriel [*A publication*]
EFAL........ Alavus [*Finland*] [*ICAO location identifier*]   (ICLI)
EFAPA ..... Electronica y Fisica Aplicada [*A publication*]
EFAPIT.... Euromarket Federation of Animal Protein Importers and Traders   (EAIO)
EFAPP...... Enrico Fermi Atomic Power Plant [*Decommissioned*]   (NRCH)
EFAR........ Economic Feeder Administration and Relief   (TEL)
EFAR........ Error Factor Analysis and Reduction   (ADA)
EFAS........ Electronic Flash Approach System
EFAS .... Emergency Feedwater Actuation Signal [*Nuclear energy*]   (NRCH)
EFAS .... En Route Flight Advisory Services [*FAA*]
EFATCA ... European Federation of Air Traffic Controllers Association
EFATD...... Energia del Fuego al Atomo [*A publication*]
EFB............ EFTA [*European Free Trade Association*] Bulletin [*A publication*]
EFB............ Eight Fathom Bight [*Alaska*] [*Airport symbol*]   (OAG)
EFB............ Electric Feedback
EFB............ Electrode Film Barrier
EFB............ Electrofluidized Bed [*Chemical engineering*]
EFB............ Engineering Field Bulletin   (MCD)
EFB............ Europaeische Foderation Biotechnologie [*European Federation of Biotechnology*] [*Federal Republic of Germany*]   (EAIO)
EFB............ Experimental Fighting Biplane [*British military*]   (DMA)
EFBD........ Emergency Feed Baron Detector   (IEEE)
EFBPBI ..... European Federation of the Brush and Paint Brush Industries   (EA)
EFBS .... E. F. Benson Society   (EAIO)
EFBS .... European Federation of Building Societies   (EAIO)
EFBSA....... Bulletin. Direction des Etudes et Recherches. Serie A. Supplement (France) [*A publication*]
EFBWW .... European Federation of Building and Woodworkers   (EA)
EFC............ Earth-Fixed Coordinate   (MCD)
EFC............ Eastern Football Conference
EFC............ Effective Full-Charge [*Weaponry*]   (RDA)
EFC............ Electrical Field Current
EFC............ Electrochemical Fuel Cell
EFC............ Electrofluid Converter
EFC............ Electronic Frequency Control
EFC............ Elfquest Fan Club   (EA)
EFC............ Elvira Fan Club   (EA)
EFC............ Emergency Fleet Corporation [*Defunct, 1936*]
EFC............ Emergency Foster Care   (ADA)
EFC............ Encampment for Citizenship [*An association*]   (EA)
EFC............ Engineering Field Change   (MSA)
EFC............ Equipment Functional Check   (KSC)
EFC............ Equivalent Full Charge
EFC............ Ernest Fan Club   (EA)
EFC............ Escort Force Commander [*NATO*]   (NATG)
EFC............ Estimated Final Cost
EFC............ Etched Flexible Circuitry
EFC............ European Federation of Corrosion   (EA)
EFC............ European Forestry Commission
EFC............ Eurythmics Fan Club   (EA)
E & FC...... Examined and Found Correct   (ADA)
EFC............ Exile Fan Club   (EA)
EFC............ Expected Fraction of Casualties   (MCD)
EFC............ Expected Further Clearance [*Aviation*]   (FAAC)
EFC............ Expeditionary Force Canteens [*Official supply organization*] [*British*] [*World War I*]
EFC............ Experiment Farm Cottage [*Australia*]
EFCAT ...... European Football Commentators Association Television   (EA)
EFCB .... Emergency Financial Control Board
EFCCCI..... Early Four Cylinder Chevrolet Club, International   (EA)

EFCE......... European Federation of Chemical Engineering [*See also EFCIW*]   (EAIO)
EFCEM ..... European Federation of Catering Equipment Manufacturers   (EA)
EFCGU...... European Federation of Chemical and General Workers Unions   (EAIO)
EFCIW ...... Europaeische Foderation fuer Chemie-Ingenieur-Wesen [*European Federation of Chemical Engineering - EFCE*]   (EAIO)
EFCPA ...... Electric Furnace Conference Proceedings [*A publication*]
EFCR .... Experimental Fast Ceramic Reactor
EFCS .... Earth-Fixed Coordinate System   (MCD)
EFCS .... Electronic Flight Control System
EFCS .... Electronic Fuel Control System
EFCS .... European Federation for Company Sports   (EAIO)
EFCS .... European Federation of Cytology Societies   (EAIO)
EFCSM ..... European Federation of Ceramic Sanitaryware Manufacturers   (EA)
EFCT .... Effect   (FAAC)
EFCUA...... Extreme Fuel - Critical, Unspecified Area [*NASA*]
EFCV .... Excess Flow Check Valve [*Nuclear energy*]   (NRCH)
EFD .... Earliest Finish Date
EFD .... Early Failure Detection
EFD .... Education for Development [*A publication*]
EFD .... Electric Flux Density
EFD .... Electrofluid Dynamic [*Process*]   (MCD)
EFD .... Enemy Forward Disposition [*Military*]
EFD .... Energy Flux Density
EFD .... Enfield Resources [*Vancouver Stock Exchange symbol*]
EFD .... Engineered Fasteners Division [*Townsend Co.*]
EFD .... Engineering Facilities Depot
EFD .... Engineering Field Divisions [*Military*]
EFD .... Engineering Flow Diagram   (NRCH)
EFD .... European Energy Report [*A publication*]
EFD .... European Faculty Directory [*A publication*]
EFD .... Excused from Duty
EFD .... Executive Flight Detachment   (AAG)
EFD .... Houston, TX [*Location identifier*] [*FAA*]   (FAAL)
EFDA........ Epoxyfarnesyl Diazoacetate [*Organic chemistry*]
EFDA........ European Formula Drivers Association   (EAIO)
EFDA........ European Funeral Directors' Association   (EAIO)
EFDA........ Expanded Function Dental Auxiliary [*HEW program*]
EFDARS ... Electronic Flight Data and Recording System   (MCD)
EFDAS ...... Electronic Flight Data Accumulation Service
EFDBA ...... Bulletin. Direction des Etudes et Recherches. Serie B (France) [*A publication*]
EFDNA ..... Bulletin. Direction des Etudes et Recherches. Serie A (France) [*A publication*]
EFDS .... Equipment and Floor Drainage System [*Nuclear energy*]   (NRCH)
EFDSS .... English Folk Dance and Song Society [*British*]
EFE........... Early Fuel Evaporation [*Automotive technology*]
EFE........... EFTA [*European Free Trade Association*] Bulletin [*A publication*]
EFE........... Endocardial Fibroelastosis [*Medicine*]
EFE........... External Field Emission
EFEA .... European Free Exchange Area   (NATG)
EFEHV ...... Educational Fund to End Handgun Violence   (EA)
EFEM........ Energy Filtering Electron Microscope
EFEMA...... Association des Fabricants Europeens d'Emulsifants Alimentaires [*Association of European Manufacturers of Food Emulsifiers*]   (EAIO)
EFES .... Tampere [*Finland*] [*ICAO location identifier*]   (ICLI)
EFET .... Enontekio [*Finland*] [*ICAO location identifier*]   (ICLI)
EFET .... Epoxy Field Effect Transistor
EFEU......... Eura [*Finland*] [*ICAO location identifier*]   (ICLI)
EFF .... Eastern Fishermen's Federation [*See also FPE*] [*Canada*]
EFF .... Educational Freedom Foundation   (EA)
EFF .... Effect   (AFM)
Eff .... Effective [*Legal term*]   (DLA)
eff .... Effektiv [*Effective*] [*Business term*] [*German*]
EFF .... Efferent [*Anatomy*]
EFF .... Effervescent [*Pharmacy*]   (ROG)
EFF .... Efficiency
EFF .... Effigy   (ROG)
EFF .... Effluent
EFF .... Electric Flow Field
EFF .... Electronic Frontier Foundation   (EA)
EFF .... Emerald Airlines [*Austin, TX*] [*FAA designator*]   (FAAC)
EFF .... English for Foreigners
EFF .... Enterprise, Family, and Freedom [*Australia*] [*Political party*]
EFF .... European Furniture Federation
EFF .... European Taxation [*A publication*]
EFF .... Extended Fund Facility [*International Monetary Fund*]
EFFAS .... European Federation of Financial Analysts' Societies   (EA)
EFFBR ...... Enrico Fermi Fast Breeder Power Reactor
EFFCY....... Efficiency   (AABC)
EFFE .... Environmentalists for Full Employment   (EA)
EFFE .... European Federation of Flight Engineers

Eff Environ Cells Tissues Proc World Congr Anat Clin Pathol ... Effects of Environment on Cells and Tissues. Proceedings. World Congress of Anatomic and Clinical Pathology [*A publication*]

EFFF.......... Electrical Field-Flow Fractionation [*Electrochemical separation method*]

EFFG.......... Effectuating (ROG)

EFFGRO ... Efficient Growth [*Computer program*] (NASA)

Eff Health Care ... Effective Health Care [*A publication*]

EFFI .... Educational Foundation for the Fashion Industries (EA)

EFFI .... Electronic Fiber Fineness Indicator

EFFI .... Electronic Forum for Industry [*British*]

EFFIC........ Efficiency (ROG)

Effic Text ... Efficience Textile [*A publication*]

EFFIG........ Effigies (ROG)

Effi Text..... Efficience Textile [*A publication*]

Effluent Water Treat J ... Effluent and Water Treatment Journal [*A publication*]

EFFO.......... Forssa [*Finland*] [*ICAO location identifier*] (ICLI)

EFFORPA ... Elliptic Function First-Order Ripple Phase Approximation

EFFoST ...... European Federation of Food Science and Technology (EA)

EF Foundation ... Educational Foundation for Foreign Study (EA)

Eff a P .... Effet a Payer [*Bill Payable*] [*Accounting*] [*French*]

Eff a R .... Effet a Recevoir [*Bill Receivable*] [*Accounting*] [*French*]

EFFU.......... Epithelial Focus-Forming Unit [*Oncology*]

Eff Udobr.... Effectivnost Udobrenii [*A publication*]

EFFUNDAT ... Effundatur [*Let It Be Poured Out*] [*Pharmacy*] (ROG)

Eff Wat Tre ... Effluent and Water Treatment Journal [*A publication*]

EFG .... Economic Forestry Group [*British*]

EFG .... Edge-Defined Film-Fed Growth [*Photovoltaics*]

EFG .... Efogi [*Papua New Guinea*] [*Airport symbol*] (OAG)

EFG .... Electric Field Gradient [*of crystals*]

EFG .... Entscheidungen der Finanzgerichte [*Reports of the Fiscal Courts*] [*German*] [*A publication*] (DLA)

EFG .... Equitec Financial Group, Inc. [*NYSE symbol*] (SPSG)

EFGRAQ... Eastern Fruit Grower [*A publication*]

EFGS .... Easterling Family Genealogical Society (EA)

EFGTF ...... Entrained-Flow Gasification Test Facility

EFGUAZ... Escuela de Farmacia Guatemala [*A publication*]

EFH .... Earth Far Horizon [*NASA*] (KSC)

EFH .... Enge's Flaming Hearts (EA)

EFH .... Engine Flight Hours

EFH .... [*The*] Hutton [*E. F.*] Group, Inc. [*NYSE symbol*] (SPSG)

EFHA .... Esperanto Family History Association [*Later, EEFHA*] (EA)

EFHA .... Halli [*Finland*] [*ICAO location identifier*] (ICLI)

EFHC .... Emanuel Foundation for Hungarian Culture (EA)

EFHF.......... Helsinki/Helsinki-Malmi [*Finland*] [*ICAO location identifier*] (ICLI)

EFHK .... Helsinki/Vantaa [*Finland*] [*ICAO location identifier*] (ICLI)

EFHL........ Hailuoto [*Finland*] [*ICAO location identifier*] (ICLI)

EFHM .... Hameenkyro [*Finland*] [*ICAO location identifier*] (ICLI)

EFHN .... Hanko [*Finland*] [*ICAO location identifier*] (ICLI)

EFHP......... Haapavesi [*Finland*] [*ICAO location identifier*] (ICLI)

EFHT......... Ahtari [*Finland*] [*ICAO location identifier*] (ICLI)

EFHV .... Hyvinkaa [*Finland*] [*ICAO location identifier*] (ICLI)

EFI............. Educational Futures, Inc. (EA)

efi .... Efik [*MARC language code*] [*Library of Congress*] (LCCP)

EFI .... Electronic Flash Illuminator

EFI .... Electronic Fuel Injection

EFI .... Emissary Foundation International (EA)

EF & I .... Engineer, Furnish, and Install

EFI .... Enrico Fermi Institute [*University of Chicago*]

EFI .... Enrico Fermi International Summer School of Physics [*Elsevier Book Series*] [*A publication*]

EFI .... Environic Foundation International (EA)

EFI .... Estadisticas Financieras Internacionales [*A publication*]

EFI .... Euromarkt Nieuws [*A publication*]

EFI .... Evangelical Friends International (EA)

EFI .... Expeditionary Force Institutions [*Military*] [*British*]

e-fi--- .... Finland [*MARC geographic area code*] [*Library of Congress*] (LCCP)

EFIA .... European Fertilizer Importers' Associations (EAIO)

EFIB .... Eastern Freight Inspection Bureau

EFIC .... EFI Electronics Corp. [*NASDAQ symbol*] (NQ)

EFIC .... Export Finance Insurance Corporation [*Australia*] (ADA)

EFICO .... Electrical Fitting Inventory Control Branch

EFICON.... Electronic Financial Control

EFICP........ Electronic Flight Instrument Control Panel (MCD)

EFII .... I Salmi [*Finland*] [*ICAO location identifier*] (ICLI)

EFIK .... Kiikala [*Finland*] [*ICAO location identifier*] (ICLI)

EFil............ Estudios Filologicos [*A publication*]

EFIL .... European Federation for Intercultural Learning (EAIO)

EFIL .... Ilmajoki [*Finland*] [*ICAO location identifier*] (ICLI)

EFI (M) ..... Electronic Fuel Injection (Metering) [*Automotive engineering*]

EFIM......... Immola [*Finland*] [*ICAO location identifier*] (ICLI)

EFIR .... Educational Fund for Individual Rights (EA)

Efird........... Efird's Reports [*45-56 South Carolina*] [*A publication*] (DLA)

EFIS........... Electronic Flight Instrument System

EFISGA..... England, France, Ireland, Scotland, Germany, and Aborigines [*See also TUPONA*] [*Suggested early name for Canada*]

EFIT .... Electronic Facial Identification Technique

EFIV .... Ivalo [*Finland*] [*ICAO location identifier*] (ICLI)

EFJC.......... Europaische Federation Junger Chore [*European Federation of Young Choirs*] (EAIO)

EFJG .... Educational Foundation for Jewish Girls [*Later, Jewish Foundation for Education of Women*] (EA)

EFJM .... Jamijarvi [*Finland*] [*ICAO location identifier*] (ICLI)

EFJO .... Joensuu [*Finland*] [*ICAO location identifier*] (ICLI)

EFJP .... Jakalapaa [*Finland*] [*ICAO location identifier*] (ICLI)

EFJY .... Jyvaskyla [*Finland*] [*ICAO location identifier*] (ICLI)

EFK............ Newport, VT [*Location identifier*] [*FAA*] (FAAL)

EFKA .... Kauhava [*Finland*] [*ICAO location identifier*] (ICLI)

EFKE .... Kemi [*Finland*] [*ICAO location identifier*] (ICLI)

EFKG........ Kumlinge [*Finland*] [*ICAO location identifier*] (ICLI)

EFKH .... Kuhmo [*Finland*] [*ICAO location identifier*] (ICLI)

EFKI .... Kajaani [*Finland*] [*ICAO location identifier*] (ICLI)

EFKJ .... Kauhajoki [*Finland*] [*ICAO location identifier*] (ICLI)

EFKK .... Kruunupyy [*Finland*] [*ICAO location identifier*] (ICLI)

EFKL........ Helsinki [*Finland*] [*ICAO location identifier*] (ICLI)

EFKM........ Kemijarvi [*Finland*] [*ICAO location identifier*] (ICLI)

EFKR .... Karsamaki [*Finland*] [*ICAO location identifier*] (ICLI)

EFKS .... Kuusamo [*Finland*] [*ICAO location identifier*] (ICLI)

EFKT .... Kittila [*Finland*] [*ICAO location identifier*] (ICLI)

EFKU........ Kuopio [*Finland*] [*ICAO location identifier*] (ICLI)

EFKV .... Kivijarvi [*Finland*] [*ICAO location identifier*] (ICLI)

EFKY .... Kymi [*Finland*] [*ICAO location identifier*] (ICLI)

EFL .... Argostolion [*Greece*] [*Airport symbol*] (OAG)

EFL .... Educational Facilities Laboratories (EA)

EFL .... Effective Focal Length [*Optics*]

EFL .... Effluent (MSA)

E FL .... Ell, Flemish [*Unit of measure*] (ROG)

EFL .... Emitter Follower Logic [*Electronics*]

EFL .... English as a Foreign Language

EFL .... Equivalent Focal Length [*Optics*]

EFL .... Essays in French Literature [*University of Western Australia*] [*A publication*]

EFL .... Explosion and Flame Laboratory [*British*] (IRUK)

EFL .... External Finance Limit

EFL .... Folkways (Ethnic Folkways Library) [*Record label*]

EFLA .... Education for Librarianship - Australia [*A publication*]

EFLA .... Educational Film Library Association (EA)

EFLA .... Vesivehmaa [*Finland*] [*ICAO location identifier*] (ICLI)

EFLL .... Essays in Foreign Languages and Literature [*A publication*]

EFLP .... Lappeenranta [*Finland*] [*ICAO location identifier*] (ICLI)

EF & LTC ... Enemy Fuels and Lubricants Technical Committee

EFL-UAR ... Egyptian Federation of Labor - United Arab Republic [*Obsolete*]

EFM .... Electric Field Meter

EFM .... Electronic Fetal Monitoring [*Medicine*]

EFM .... Electronics for Medicine

EFM .... Engineering Feasibility Model (MCD)

EFM .... Epifluorescence Microscopy

EFM .... European Federalist Movement

EFM .... Evangelistic Faith Missions (EA)

EFM .... Expeditionary Force Message [*Low-rate cable or radio message selected from a list of standard wordings*]

EFM .... Extensive Field Maintenance [*Military*] (NG)

EFM .... Palm Beach Junior College, Lake Worth, FL [*OCLC symbol*] (OCLC)

EFMA .... Emergency Farm Mortgage Act of 1933

EFMA....... European Fertilizer Manufacturers Association (EAIO)

EFMA....... European Financial Management and Marketing Association (EAIO)

EFMA .... European Fittings Manufacturers Association [*London, England*] (EAIO)

EFMA .... Evangelical Foreign Missions Association (EA)

EFMA....... Mariehamn [*Finland*] [*ICAO location identifier*] (ICLI)

EFMB........ Expert Field Medical Badge [*Military decoration*] (AABC)

EFMBB9 ... Einfuehrungen zur Molekularbiologie [*A publication*]

EFMC........ Educators Fund Management Corporation [*of NEA*]

EFMC........ Elastic Fabric Manufacturers Council of the Northern Textile Association

EFMC........ European Federation of Medicinal Chemistry (EAIO)

EFMCNTA ... Elastic Fabric Manufacturers Council of the Northern Textile Association (EA)

EFMD .... European Foundation for Management Development (EAIO)

EFME .... Menkijarvi [*Finland*] [*ICAO location identifier*] (ICLI)

EFMEA..... Engineering Fracture Mechanics [*A publication*]

EFMG........ Electric Fuse Manufacturers Guild [*Defunct*] (EA)

EFMI......... Elastic Fabric Manufacturers Institute [*Later, EFMC or EFMCNTA*] (EA)

EFMI......... European Federation for Medical Informatics (EAIO)

EFMI......... Mikkeli [*Finland*] [*ICAO location identifier*] (ICLI)

EFMO........ Effigy Mounds National Monument

EFMP........ Emergency Food and Medical Program

EFMP....... Exceptional Family Member Program [*Army*] (INF)

EFN .... Euro-American Financial [*Vancouver Stock Exchange symbol*]

EFN .... Extrafloral Nectary [*Botany*]

EFN .... Palm Beach Junior College, North Campus Library, Lake Worth, FL [*OCLC symbol*] (OCLC)

EFNED...... Energy Forum in New England [*A publication*]

EFNEP ...... Expanded Food and Nutrition Education Program [*Department of Agriculture*]

EFNRA......	Educational Foundation of the National Restaurant Association (EA)	
EFNS........	Educational Foundation for Nuclear Science (EA)	
EFNU	Nummela [*Finland*] [*ICAO location identifier*] (ICLI)	
EFO	East Fork, AK [*Location identifier*] [*FAA*] (FAAL)	
EFO	Error, Freak, Oddity	
EFOA	European Fuel Oxygenates Association (EAIO)	
EFOCC.....	Errors, Freaks and Oddities Collector's Club (EA)	
EFOC Fiber Opt Commun Proc ...	EFOC [*European Fiber Optics and Communications*] Fiber Optics and Communications. Proceedings [*A publication*]	
EFOC/LAN ...	European Fiber Optic Communications and Local Area Network Exposition [*Information Gatekeepers, Inc.*] (TSPED)	
EFOP........	Oripaa [*Finland*] [*ICAO location identifier*] (ICLI)	
EFOR........	Equivalent Forced Outage Rate (IEEE)	
EFOR........	Oritkari [*Finland*] [*ICAO location identifier*] (ICLI)	
EFOSS......	Engineer Family of Systems Study (MCD)	
EFOU	Oulu [*Finland*] [*ICAO location identifier*] (ICLI)	
EFP..........	Economiste Arabe. L'Economie et les Finances des Pays Arabes [*A publication*]	
EFP..........	Effective Filtration Pressure [*Physiology*]	
EFP..........	Electric Fire Pump [*Nuclear energy*] (NRCH)	
EFP..........	Electronic Field Production (IEEE)	
EFP..........	Emergency Firing Panel	
EFP..........	End Forming Press	
EFP..........	Error-Free Performance	
EFP..........	Escaped Federal Prisoner	
EFP..........	Europaeische Foederalistische Partei [*European Federalist Party*] [*Austria*] (PPE)	
EFP..........	European Federation of Parasitologists (EAIO)	
EFP..........	Exchange for Physicals [*Commodities exchange*]	
EFPA........	European Food Phosphates Producers' Association (EAIO)	
EFPD........	Effective Full Power Day (KSC)	
EFPE........	Pello [*Finland*] [*ICAO location identifier*] (ICLI)	
EFPH........	Equivalent Full Power Hour [*FCC*]	
EFPH........	Evaluating Fallout Protection in Homes [*Later, HFPS*] [*Civil Defense*]	
EFPI	European Federation of the Plywood Industry (EA)	
EFPI	Piikajarvi [*Finland*] [*ICAO location identifier*] (ICLI)	
EFPIA........	European Federation of Pharmaceutical Industries' Associations (EA)	
EFPK	Pieksamaki [*Finland*] [*ICAO location identifier*] (ICLI)	
EFPL	English and Foreign Philosophical Library [*A publication*]	
EFPM	Effective Full Power Month (NRCH)	
EFPO........	Pori [*Finland*] [*ICAO location identifier*] (ICLI)	
EFPOD......	Electric Farm Power [*United States*] [*A publication*]	
EFPPA.......	European Federation of Professional Psychologists Associations (EA)	
EFPRA3	Estudos sobre a Fauna Portuguesa [*A publication*]	
EFPS..........	Elsevier Series in Forensic and Police Science [*Elsevier Book Series*] [*A publication*]	
EFPS..........	European Federation of Productivity Services [*Stockholm, Sweden*] (EA)	
EFPS..........	Rovaniemi [*Finland*] [*ICAO location identifier*] (ICLI)	
EFPSD9.....	Annual Research Reviews. Effects of Psychotherapy [*A publication*]	
EFPU	Pudasjarvi [*Finland*] [*ICAO location identifier*] (ICLI)	
EFPV	Eisenhower Foundation for the Prevention of Violence [*Later, Milton S. Eisenhower Federation*] (EA)	
EFPW	European Federation for the Protection of Waters	
EFPWCM ...	European Federation of Pallet and Wooden Crate Manufacturers (EA)	
EFPY	Effective Full-Power Years (NRCH)	
EFPY	Pyhasalmi [*Finland*] [*ICAO location identifier*] (ICLI)	
EFPZ	Export Free Processing Zone	
EFR..........	Echo Free Room	
EFR..........	Editeurs Francais Reunis [*A publication*]	
EFR..........	Effective Filtration Rate [*Physiology*]	
EFR..........	Electro-Flux Remelting [*Metal industry*]	
EFR..........	Electronic Failure Report	
E FR	Ell, French [*Unit of measure*] (ROG)	
EFR..........	Emergency Fund Request	
EFR..........	Empire Forestry Review [*A publication*]	
EFR..........	Engine Firing Rate (NVT)	
EFR..........	Engine Flat Rate	
EFR..........	Entrained-Flow Reactor [*Chemical engineering*]	
EFR..........	Equipment Failure Rate	
EFR..........	Exact Finite Range	
EFR..........	Expect Further Routing [*Aviation*] (FAAC)	
EFR..........	Extended-Field Radiotherapy [*Radiology*]	
e-fr---..........	France [*MARC geographic area code*] [*Library of Congress*] (LCCP)	
EFRA........	Rautavaara [*Finland*] [*ICAO location identifier*] (ICLI)	
EFran........	Etudes Franciscaines [*A publication*]	
EFRAP......	Exchange Feeder Route Analysis Program [*Bell System*]	
EFRC........	Education Funding Research Council (EA)	
EFRC........	Edwards Flight Research Center [*NASA*]	
EFRH........	Pattijoki [*Finland*] [*ICAO location identifier*] (ICLI)	
EFRIS.......	External Finished Reports Information Subsystem [*Data processing*]	
EFRN........	Rantasalmi [*Finland*] [*ICAO location identifier*] (ICLI)	
EFRO........	Electronic Failure Report Only	
EFRO........	Rovaniemi Airport [*Finland*] [*ICAO location identifier*] (ICLI)	
EFRV........	Kiuruvesi [*Finland*] [*ICAO location identifier*] (ICLI)	
EFRY........	Rayskala [*Finland*] [*ICAO location identifier*] (ICLI)	
EFS	Earth-Fixed System	
EFS	Electric Field-Induced Spectra	
EFS	Electric Field Strength	
EFS	Electronic Firing Switches [*Military*] (NG)	
EFS	Electronic Frequency Selection (IEEE)	
EFS	Emergency Feeding Service [*Civil Defense*]	
EFS	Emergency Feedwater System [*Nuclear energy*] (NRCH)	
EFS	Error Free Seconds (TEL)	
EFS	Experimental Firing Ship	
EFS	External File System (BYTE)	
EFSA	European Federation of Sea Anglers (EAIO)	
EFSA	Savonlinna [*Finland*] [*ICAO location identifier*] (ICLI)	
EFSB	Elmwood Federal Savings Bank [*NASDAQ symbol*] (NQ)	
EFSE	Selanpaa [*Finland*] [*ICAO location identifier*] (ICLI)	
EFSH........	Equine Follicle Stimulating Hormone [*Endocrinology*]	
EFSIA.......	Electronic Financial Systems Cl A [*NASDAQ symbol*] (NQ)	
EFSJ	Sonkajarvi-Jyrkka [*Finland*] [*ICAO location identifier*] (ICLI)	
EFSO	Sodankyla [*Finland*] [*ICAO location identifier*] (ICLI)	
EFSORPA ...	Elliptic Function Second-Order Ripple Phase Approximation	
EFSP.........	Electrolytic Fused-Salt Process	
EFSP.........	Electronic Family Security Program [*of Sun Life Assurance Company of Canada*]	
EFSP.........	Emergency Food and Shelter Program [*FEMA*]	
EFSPA.......	L'Economie et la Finance de la Syrie et de Pays Arabes [*Damascus*] [*A publication*]	
EFSS.........	E. F. Schumacher Society (EA)	
EFSS.........	Emergency Food Supply Scheme [*World Food Program*]	
EFSSS	Engine Failure Sensing and Shutdown System [*NASA*] (KSC)	
EFSU	Suomussalmi [*Finland*] [*ICAO location identifier*] (ICLI)	
EFSUMB ..	European Federation of Societies of Ultrasound in Medicine and Biology (EAIO)	
EFT...........	Early Finish Time	
EFT...........	Effect (MSA)	
EFT...........	Electronic Fund Tape [*Banking*]	
EFT...........	Electronic Funds Transfer [*Banking*]	
EFT...........	Electrostatically Focused Tube	
EFT...........	Embedded Figures Test [*Psychology*]	
EFT...........	Emergency Flight Termination (AFM)	
EFT...........	Engineering Feasibility Test (CAAL)	
EFT...........	Engineering Flight Test	
EFT...........	English Fiction in Transition, 1880-1920 [*Later, English Literature in Transition, 1880-1920*] [*A publication*]	
EFT...........	Eno Foundation for Transportation (EA)	
EFT...........	Etchingham Family Tree (EA)	
EFT...........	Experimental Flight Test	
EFT...........	External Function Translator	
EFT's........	Expanded Field [*Prism*] Telescopes [*Instrumentation*]	
EFTA........	Electronic Fund Transfer Act [*1978*]	
EFTA........	Electronic Funds Transfer Association [*Washington, DC*] (EA)	
EFTA........	Enrolled Federal Tax Accountant [*Designation awarded by EFTA Institute*]	
EFTA........	ERADCOM [*Electronics Research and Development Command*] Flight Test Activity	
EFTA.........	European Free Trade Area (DS)	
EFTA.........	European Free Trade Association [*Known as the "Outer Seven" as opposed to the "Inner Six" Common Market nations*] [*Switzerland*]	
EFTA.........	European Free Trade Association. Bulletin [*A publication*]	
EFTA Bull ...	EFTA [*European Free Trade Association*] Bulletin [*A publication*]	
EFTC	Edwards Flight Test Center [*NASA*]	
EFTC	Elementary Flying Training College [*British*]	
EFTC	European Fluorocarbon Technical Committee [*of the European Council of Chemical Manufacturers' Federations*] [*Belgium*] (EAIO)	
EFTC	European Freight Timetable Conference (EAIO)	
EFTCBFC ...	Elvis Forever TCB [*Taking Care of Business*] Fan Club (EA)	
EFTE.........	Tervola [*Finland*] [*ICAO location identifier*] (ICLI)	
EFTEC	European Fluorocarbon Technical Committee [*of the European Council of Chemical Manufacturers' Federations*] (EAIO)	
EFTI	Engineering Flight Test Inspector	
EFTI	Engineering Flight Test Instrumentation (AAG)	
EFTO........	Encrypt for Transmission Only [*Military*]	
EFTO........	Encrypted for Transmission Overseas (MCD)	
EFTP.........	Tampere-Pirkkala [*Finland*] [*ICAO location identifier*] (ICLI)	
EFTPOS.....	Electronic Funds Transfer at Point-of-Sale	
EFTR.........	Engineering Flight Test Report	
EFT Report ...	EFT Report. The Newsletter of Electronic Funds Transfer [*A publication*]	
EFTRO.......	European Federation of Tobacco Retail Organizations (EAIO)	
EFTS	Electronic Funds Transfer System [*Banking*] [*National Science Foundation*]	
EFTS	Elementary Flying Training School [*British*]	
EFTS	Teisko [*Finland*] [*ICAO location identifier*] (ICLI)	
EFTTA	European Fishing Tackle Trade Association (EAIO)	
EFTU.........	Turku [*Finland*] [*ICAO location identifier*] (ICLI)	

EFTV .... Effectivity
EFU .... Eastern Enterprises [*NYSE symbol*]   (SPSG)
EFU .... Equivalent Fatality Unit [*National Highway Traffic Safety Administration*]
EFUT .... Utti [*Finland*] [*ICAO location identifier*]   (ICLI)
EFV .... Electric Field Vector
EFV .... Extracellular Fluid Volume [*Physiology*]
EFVA .... Educational Foundation for Visual Arts [*British*]
EFVA .... European Federation of Vending Associations   (EA)
EFVA .... Vaasa [*Finland*] [*ICAO location identifier*]   (ICLI)
EFVC .... Expiratory Flow-Volume Curve [*Medicine*]
EFVI .... Viitasaari [*Finland*] [*ICAO location identifier*]   (ICLI)
EFVL .... Vaala [*Finland*] [*ICAO location identifier*]   (ICLI)
EFVP .... El Salvador Film and Video Projects [*Later, El Salvadore Media Projects*]   (EA)
EFVR .... Varkaus [*Finland*] [*ICAO location identifier*]   (ICLI)
EFVU .... Vuotso [*Finland*] [*ICAO location identifier*]   (ICLI)
EFW .... Emergency Feedwater [*System*] [*Nuclear energy*]   (NRCH)
EFW .... Executive Financial Woman [*National Association of Bank Women*] [*A publication*]
EFW .... Jefferson, IA [*Location identifier*] [*FAA*]   (FAAL)
EFWB .... Wredeby [*Finland*] [*ICAO location identifier*]   (ICLI)
EFWS .... Emergency Feedwater System [*Nuclear energy*]   (NRCH)
EFWS .... Evaluation of Foreign Weapons Systems   (MCD)
EFWST ..... Emergency Feedwater Storage Tank [*Nuclear energy*]   (NRCH)
EFX .... Equifax, Inc. [*Formerly, Retail Credit Co.*] [*NYSE symbol*]   (SPSG)
EFY .... End of Fiscal Year   (AFM)
EFYC .... European Federation of Young Choirs [*See also EFJC*]   (EAIO)
EFYL .... Ylivieska-Raudaskyla [*Finland*] [*ICAO location identifier*]   (ICLI)
EFZ .... Electronic Final Zero
EG .... Economic Geography [*A publication*]
EG .... Economics and Government [*Office of Management and Budget*]
EG .... Edge Grain
Eg .... Egidius de Fuscarariis [*Deceased, 1289*] [*Authority cited in pre-1607 legal work*]   (DSA)
EG .... Egypt [*ANSI two-letter standard code*]   (CNC)
EG .... Egyptian   (ROG)
E u G .... Eiszeitalter und Gegenwart [*A publication*]
EG .... Ejusdem Generis [*Of the Same Kind*] [*Latin*]
EG .... Electrogalvanizing [*Automotive engineering*]
EG .... Electronic Guidance   (AAG)
EG .... Else Good [*In good condition except for defects mentioned*] [*Antiquarian book trade*]
EG .... Emergency Gear   (FAAC)
EG .... Emergency Generator   (NRCH)
EG .... Emergency Grade [*Automotive engineering*] [*Polymer Steel Corp.*]
EG .... Employment Gazette [*A publication*]
EG .... Employment Guide   (CAAL)
EG .... Engelbert's "Goils" [*An association*]   (EA)
E/G .... Engine-Generator
EG .... Engineering Geologist
EG .... English and Germanic Studies [*A publication*]
EG .... Enteric Ganglion [*Neurology*]
EG .... Entry Guidance [*NASA*]   (NASA)
EG .... Environment Generator
EG .... Enziklopedyah Shel Galuyot   (BJA)
EG .... Eosinophilic Granuloma [*Medicine*]
eg .... Equatorial Guinea [*MARC country of publication code*] [*Library of Congress*]   (LCCP)
EG .... Escort Group
EG .... Esophagogastrectomy [*Medicine*]
EG .... Esquerra Gallega [*Galician Left*] [*Political party*]   (PPW)
EG .... Estate Gazette [*A publication*]   (DLA)
EG .... Estrone Glucuronide [*Endocrinology*]
EG .... Estudios Geograficos [*A publication*]
EG .... Ethylene Glycol [*Organic chemistry*]
EG .... Etudes Germaniques [*A publication*]
EG .... European Greens [*Brussels, Belgium*] [*Political party*]   (EAIO)
EG .... Evangelisches Gemeindeblatt fuer Galizien [*A publication*]
EG .... Ex Grege [*Among the Rest*] [*Latin*]
EG .... Executive Generator
EG .... Exempli Gratia [*For Example*] [*Latin*]
EG .... Existential Generalization [*Rule of quantification*] [*Logic*]
EG .... Experimental Assistant, Gunnery [*British military*]   (DMA)
EG .... Experimental Glider
EG .... Experimental Group
EG .... Expert Gunner [*Army*]
EG .... Exploratory Group   (NATG)
EG .... Japan Asia Airways Co. Ltd. [*ICAO designator*]   (FAAC)
EGA .... Agnes Scott College, Decatur, GA [*OCLC symbol*]   (OCLC)
EGA .... Die Entwicklung der Glyptik Waehrend der Akkad-Zeit [*A publication*]   (BJA)
EGA .... East German Army   (CINC)
EGA .... Edge Gradient Analysis
EGA .... Effluent [*or Evolved*] Gas Analysis
EGA .... Embroiderers' Guild of America   (EA)
EGA .... Eminent Grand Almoner [*Freemasonry*]   (ROG)

EGA .... End Game Analysis
EGA .... Engineering Assistant
EGA .... Enhanced Graphics Adapter [*Computer technology*]
EGA .... EQK Green Acres LP [*NYSE symbol*]   (SPSG)
EGA .... Estimated Gestational Age
EGA .... Evolved Gas Analysis [*Chemistry*]
EGA .... Exhaust Gas Analyzer   (MCD)
EGA .... Export Guarantees Act
EGAA .... Belfast/Aldergrove [*United Kingdom*] [*ICAO location identifier*]   (ICLI)
EGAA .... Emergency General Account of Advances
EGAA .... Enhanced Graphics Acquisition and Analysis [*Data processing*]
EGAABL .... Eley Game Advisory Station. Annual Review [*A publication*]
EGAAE ..... European Group of Artists of the Ardennes and the Eifel   (EAIO)
EGAB .... Enniskillen/St. Angelo [*United Kingdom*] [*ICAO location identifier*]   (ICLI)
EGAC .... Belfast Harbour [*United Kingdom*] [*ICAO location identifier*]   (ICLI)
EGAD .... Electric Power Generation and Distribution   (MCD)
EGAD .... Electronegative Gas Detector
EGAD .... Electronic Ground Automatic Destruct [*Air Force*]
EGAD .... Newtownards [*United Kingdom*] [*ICAO location identifier*]   (ICLI)
EGADS ...... Electronic Ground Automatic Destruct Sequencer [*Air Force*]
EGAE .... Londonderry/Eglinton [*United Kingdom*] [*ICAO location identifier*]   (ICLI)
EGAL .... Egalitarian
EGAL .... Elevation Guidance for Approach and Landing [*Aviation*]
EGAL .... Langford Lodge [*United Kingdom*] [*ICAO location identifier*]   (ICLI)
EGAMS ..... Evolved Gas Analysis Mass Spectrometry   (MCD)
Egan Bills .. Egan. Bills of Sale [*4th ed.*] [*1882*] [*A publication*]   (DLA)
EGAO .... Encyclopedia of Governmental Advisory Organizations [*A publication*]
EGAP .... End Game Analysis Program   (MCD)
EGAPBW ... Egyptian Journal of Animal Production [*A publication*]
EGAS .... European Group for Atomic Spectroscopy   (EAIO)
EGASA6 .... Eley Game Advisory Service. Booklet [*A publication*]
EGASCAC ... Educational Guidance Associates School and College Advisory Center [*Formerly, SCAC*]   (EA)
EGAT .... Electricity Generating Authority of Thailand   (DS)
EGB .... Episcopal Guild for the Blind   (EA)
EGB .... Expected Gentlemanly Behavior   (DSUE)
EGBAR ...... Everything's Going to Be All Right
EGBB .... Birmingham [*United Kingdom*] [*ICAO location identifier*]   (ICLI)
EGBDF ...... Every Good Boy Deserves Favour [*Title of play by Tom Stoppard*]
EGBDF ...... Every Good Boy Does Fine [*or Deserves Favor*] [*Mnemonic guide to notes on the treble clef*]
EGBE .... Coventry [*United Kingdom*] [*ICAO location identifier*]   (ICLI)
EGBG .... Leicester [*United Kingdom*] [*ICAO location identifier*]   (ICLI)
EGBJ .... Gloucester and Cheltenham/Staverton [*United Kingdom*] [*ICAO location identifier*]   (ICLI)
EGBK .... Northampton/Sywell [*United Kingdom*] [*ICAO location identifier*]   (ICLI)
EGBM .... Tatenhill [*United Kingdom*] [*ICAO location identifier*]   (ICLI)
EGBN .... Nottingham [*United Kingdom*] [*ICAO location identifier*]   (ICLI)
EGBO .... Halfpenny Green [*United Kingdom*] [*ICAO location identifier*]   (ICLI)
EGBP .... Pailton [*United Kingdom*] [*ICAO location identifier*]   (ICLI)
EGBS .... Shobdon [*United Kingdom*] [*ICAO location identifier*]   (ICLI)
EGBW .... Wellesbourne Mountford [*United Kingdom*] [*ICAO location identifier*]   (ICLI)
EGC .... Bergerac [*France*] [*Airport symbol*] [*Obsolete*]   (OAG)
EGC .... Eagle [*Colorado*] [*Seismograph station code, US Geological Survey*] [*Closed*]   (SEIS)
EGC .... Ebony Gold Corp. [*Vancouver Stock Exchange symbol*]
EGC .... Educational Guidance Center for the Mentally Retarded [*Defunct*]   (EA)
EGC .... Effective Government Committee   (EA)
EgC .... Egypte Contemporaine [*A publication*]
EGC .... Electronic Governor Control [*Automotive engineering*]
EGC .... Electronic Gyro Compass
EGC .... Eminent Grand Commander [*Freemasonry*]   (ROG)
EGC .... Engineer Group, Construction [*Military*]
EGC .... Experiments Ground Computer [*NASA*]   (NASA)
EGC .... Exposure Growth Curve
EGCA .... Coal Aston [*United Kingdom*] [*ICAO location identifier*]   (ICLI)
EGCB .... Manchester/Barton [*United Kingdom*] [*ICAO location identifier*]   (ICLI)
EGCC .... Manchester International [*United Kingdom*] [*ICAO location identifier*]   (ICLI)
EGCD .... Woodford [*United Kingdom*] [*ICAO location identifier*]   (ICLI)
EGCE .... Wrexham/Borras [*United Kingdom*] [*ICAO location identifier*]   (ICLI)
EGCF .... Sandtoft [*United Kingdom*] [*ICAO location identifier*]   (ICLI)

EGCG .... Epigallocatechin Gallate [*Biochemistry*]
EGCG .... Strubby [*United Kingdom*] [*ICAO location identifier*] (ICLI)
EGCH .... Holyhead [*United Kingdom*] [*ICAO location identifier*] (ICLI)
EGCI.......... Doncaster [*United Kingdom*] [*ICAO location identifier*] (ICLI)
EGCI.......... Export Group for the Construction Industries [*British*]
EGCJ .... Sherburn-In-Elmet [*United Kingdom*] [*ICAO location identifier*] (ICLI)
EGCL .... Eagle Corporation Limited [*NASDAQ symbol*] (NQ)
EGCL .... Fenland [*United Kingdom*] [*ICAO location identifier*] (ICLI)
EGCM .... European Group of Cellulose Manufacturers [*Defunct*] (EA)
EGCMC..... European Glass Container Manufacturers' Committee [*Great Britain*] (EAIO)
EGCN .... Northern Area Maintenance Unit [*United Kingdom*] [*ICAO location identifier*] (ICLI)
Eg Cont ...... Egypte Contemporaine [*A publication*]
EGCPM..... European Group of Corrugated Paper Makers (EAIO)
EGCR .... Experimental Gas-Cooled Reactor
E/GCR....... Extended Group Coded Recording [*Data processing*] (IBMDP)
EGCS......... Empire Gas Corporation [*Lebanon, MO*] [*NASDAQ symbol*] (NQ)
EGCS......... English Guernsey Cattle Society [*British*]
EGCS......... Sturgate [*United Kingdom*] [*ICAO location identifier*] (ICLI)
EGD .... Economic News of Bulgaria [*A publication*]
EGD .... Effluent Guidelines Division [*Environmental Protection Agency*]
EGD .... Electrogasdynamic [*Generator*]
EGD .... Esophagogastroduodenoscopy [*Medicine*]
EGD .... Estates Gazette Digest of Cases [*A publication*] (DLA)
EGD .... Evolved Gas Detection [*Chemistry*]
EGDA .... Brawdy [*United Kingdom*] [*ICAO location identifier*] (ICLI)
EGDA .... Ethylene Glycol Diacetate [*Organic chemistry*]
EGDB .... Plymouth (Mount Wise) [*United Kingdom*] [*ICAO location identifier*] (ICLI)
EGDC .... Chivenor [*United Kingdom*] [*ICAO location identifier*] (ICLI)
EGDC .... Estates Gazette Digest of Cases [*A publication*] (DLA)
EGDD........ Royal Air Force Supervisory Centre Communications [*United Kingdom*] [*ICAO location identifier*] (ICLI)
EGDE .... Ethylene Glycol Dimethyl Ether [*Also, DME, GLYME*] [*Organic chemistry*]
EGDF .... Embryonic Growth and Development Factor [*Biochemistry*]
EGDG........ St. Mawgan [*United Kingdom*] [*ICAO location identifier*] (ICLI)
EGDH........ Royal Air Force 1 Group [*United Kingdom*] [*ICAO location identifier*] (ICLI)
EGDJ .... Upavon [*United Kingdom*] [*ICAO location identifier*] (ICLI)
EGDJAS ... Egyptian Dental Journal [*A publication*]
EGDK .... Kemble [*United Kingdom*] [*ICAO location identifier*] (ICLI)
EGDL .... Lyneham [*United Kingdom*] [*ICAO location identifier*] (ICLI)
EGDM .... Boscombe Down [*United Kingdom*] [*ICAO location identifier*] (ICLI)
EGDN .... Ethylene Glycol Dinitrate [*Organic chemistry*]
EGDN........ Netheravon [*United Kingdom*] [*ICAO location identifier*] (ICLI)
EGDP .... Portland [*United Kingdom*] [*ICAO location identifier*] (ICLI)
EGDR .... Culdrose [*United Kingdom*] [*ICAO location identifier*] (ICLI)
EGDS......... Bulford/Salisbury Plain [*United Kingdom*] [*ICAO location identifier*] (ICLI)
EGDS......... Equipment Group Design Specifications (NATG)
EGDT .... Wroughton [*United Kingdom*] [*ICAO location identifier*] (ICLI)
EGDV .... Hullavington [*United Kingdom*] [*ICAO location identifier*] (ICLI)
EGDX .... St. Athan [*United Kingdom*] [*ICAO location identifier*] (ICLI)
EGDY .... Yeovilton [*United Kingdom*] [*ICAO location identifier*] (ICLI)
EGE .... Eagle, CO [*Location identifier*] [*FAA*] (FAAL)
EGE .... Elevated Glandular Epidermis
EGE .... Emergency Ground Egress (MCD)
EGE .... Engelbert's Golden Eagles (EA)
EGE .... Eosinophilic Gastroenteropathy [*Medicine*]
e-ge--- .... Germany, East [*MARC geographic area code*] [*Library of Congress*] (LCCP)
EGE Actual ... EGE [*Eau-Gaz-Electricite et Applications*] Actualites [*A publication*]
EGECON .. Electronic Geographic Coordinate Navigation (MCD)
E GER....... East Germany (DLA)
EGERDQ .. Entomologica Germanica [*A publication*]
EGerm....... Etudes Germaniques [*A publication*]
E & Ger St ... English and Germanic Studies [*A publication*]
Egerton Coll Agric Bull ... Egerton College. Agricultural Bulletin [*A publication*]
EGESA ...... Egeszsegtudomany [*A publication*]
Egesz.......... Egeszsegtudomany [*A publication*]
Ege Univ Fen Fak Ilmi Rap Ser ... Ege Universitesi Fen Fakultesi Ilmi Raporlar Serisi [*A publication*]
Ege Univ Ziraat Fak Derg Seri A ... Ege Universitesi Ziraat. Fakultesi Dergisi. Seri A [*A publication*]
Ege Univ Ziraat Fak Yayin ... Ege Universitesi Ziraat. Fakultesi Yayinlari [*A publication*]
EGEX......... Energex Minerals Ltd. [*NASDAQ symbol*] (NQ)
Eg Ext .... Egan on Extradition [*1846*] [*A publication*] (DLA)

EGF .... Electrical Grapple Fixture (MCD)
EGF .... Energy Guideline Factors
EGF .... Englefield Resources [*Vancouver Stock Exchange symbol*]
EGF .... Epicorum Graecorum Fragmenta [*A publication*] (OCD)
EGF .... Epidermal Growth Factor [*Endocrinology*]
EGF .... Europaeische Go Foderation [*European Go Federation - EGF*] [*Austria*] (EAIO)
EGF .... European Go Federation (EAIO)
EGF .... European Grassland Federation (EA)
EGFC .... Cardiff/Tremorfa [*United Kingdom*] [*ICAO location identifier*] (ICLI)
EGFE......... Haverfordwest [*United Kingdom*] [*ICAO location identifier*] (ICLI)
EGFF .... Cardiff [*United Kingdom*] [*ICAO location identifier*] (ICLI)
EGFH .... Swansea [*United Kingdom*] [*ICAO location identifier*] (ICLI)
EGFI .... Weston-Super-Mare [*United Kingdom*] [*ICAO location identifier*] (ICLI)
EGFR .... Epidermal Growth Factor Receptor [*Biochemistry*]
EGFRK...... Epidermal Growth Factor Receptor Kinase [*An enzyme*]
EGF-URO ... Epidermal Growth Factor - Urogastrone [*Endocrinology*]
EGG .... EG & G, Inc. [*NYSE symbol*] (SPSG)
EGG .... Eggerton [*England*]
EGG .... Egyptian Gazette [*A publication*]
EGG .... Electric Glue Gun
EGG .... Electrogastrogram [*Medicine*]
EGGA .... European General Galvanizers Association (EA)
EGGA .... London [*United Kingdom*] [*ICAO location identifier*] (ICLI)
EGGB .... London [*United Kingdom*] [*ICAO location identifier*] (ICLI)
EGGC .... London [*United Kingdom*] [*ICAO location identifier*] (ICLI)
EGGD .... Bristol/Lulsgate [*United Kingdom*] [*ICAO location identifier*] (ICLI)
Egg Dam .... Eggleston on Damages [*A publication*] (DLA)
EGGE .... Bletchley [*United Kingdom*] [*ICAO location identifier*] (ICLI)
EGGF .... Uxbridge [*United Kingdom*] [*ICAO location identifier*] (ICLI)
EGGN........ United Kingdom International NOTAM Office [*ICAO location identifier*] (ICLI)
EGGO .... London [*United Kingdom*] [*ICAO location identifier*] (ICLI)
EGGOA ..... Engineering Geology (Amsterdam) [*A publication*]
Eg Gov School Med Rec ... Egyptian Government School of Medicine. Records [*A publication*]
EGGP .... Liverpool [*United Kingdom*] [*ICAO location identifier*] (ICLI)
Egg Prod .... Egg Producer [*A publication*]
EGGQ........ Liverpool [*United Kingdom*] [*ICAO location identifier*] (ICLI)
EGGR .... Redhill [*United Kingdom*] [*ICAO location identifier*] (ICLI)
EGGS......... Egghead, Inc. [*NASDAQ symbol*] (NQ)
EGGVG ..... Einfuehrungsgesetz zum Gerichtsverfassungsgesetz [*A publication*]
EGGW .... Luton [*United Kingdom*] [*ICAO location identifier*] (ICLI)
EGGX .... Shanwick [*United Kingdom*] [*ICAO location identifier*] (ICLI)
EGGY .... United Kingdom MOTNE Centre [*ICAO location identifier*] (ICLI)
EGH.......... Europaische Gesellschaft fuer Herbologie [*European Weed Research Society*] (EAIO)
EGHA .... Compton Abbas [*United Kingdom*] [*ICAO location identifier*] (ICLI)
EGHC........ Land's End/St. Just [*United Kingdom*] [*ICAO location identifier*] (ICLI)
EGHD........ Plymouth/Roborough [*United Kingdom*] [*ICAO location identifier*] (ICLI)
EGHE........ Scilly Isles/St. Mary's [*United Kingdom*] [*ICAO location identifier*] (ICLI)
EGHG........ Yeovil [*United Kingdom*] [*ICAO location identifier*] (ICLI)
EGHH........ Bournemouth/Hurn [*United Kingdom*] [*ICAO location identifier*] (ICLI)
EGHI .... Southampton [*United Kingdom*] [*ICAO location identifier*] (ICLI)
EGHJ .... Bembridge [*United Kingdom*] [*ICAO location identifier*] (ICLI)
EGHK........ Penzance/Eastern Green [*United Kingdom*] [*ICAO location identifier*] (ICLI)
EGHL .... Lasham [*United Kingdom*] [*ICAO location identifier*] (ICLI)
EGHM .... Hamble [*United Kingdom*] [*ICAO location identifier*] (ICLI)
EGHN .... Sandown (Isle Of Wight) [*United Kingdom*] [*ICAO location identifier*] (ICLI)
EGHO .... Thruxton [*United Kingdom*] [*ICAO location identifier*] (ICLI)
EGHR........ Chichester/Goodwood [*United Kingdom*] [*ICAO location identifier*] (ICLI)
EGHS .... East Gippsland Historical Society [*Australia*]
EGHS .... Henstridge [*United Kingdom*] [*ICAO location identifier*] (ICLI)
EGHVA ...... Eclogae Geologicae Helvetiae [*A publication*]
EGHVAG .. Eclogae Geologicae Helvetiae [*A publication*]
Egi............. Egidius de Losano [*Authority cited in pre-1607 legal work*] (DSA)
EGI .... Egilsstadir [*Iceland*] [*Seismograph station code, US Geological Survey*] (SEIS)
EGI .... Explosive Gas Indicator
e-gi--- .... Gibraltar [*MARC geographic area code*] [*Library of Congress*] (LCCP)
EGI .... Industrial Egypt [*A publication*]
EGI .... Valparaiso, FL [*Location identifier*] [*FAA*] (FAAL)

Egid............ Egidius de Fuscarariis [*Deceased, 1289*] [*Authority cited in pre-1607 legal work*] (DSA)

Egid Bellam ... Egidius Bellamera [*Deceased, 1407*] [*Authority cited in pre-1607 legal work*] (DSA)

EGIF.......... Equipment Group Interface

EGIL.......... Electrical, General Instrumentation, and Lighting Engineer (MCD)

EGIL.......... Environmental, General Instrumentation, Life Support [*NASA*] (KSC)

EGIND ...... Energinfo [*A publication*]

EGIS.......... Encyclopedia of Geographic Information Sources [*A publication*]

EGIS.......... Executive Guide to Information Sources [*Later, EBIS*] [*A publication*]

EGJA........ Alderney, Channel Islands [*United Kingdom*] [*ICAO location identifier*] (ICLI)

EGJB........ Guernsey, Channel Islands [*United Kingdom*] [*ICAO location identifier*] (ICLI)

EGJBAY ... Egyptian Journal of Botany [*A publication*]

EGJC........ Eagle Grove Junior College [*Iowa*]

EGJCA3 .... Egyptian Journal of Chemistry [*A publication*]

EGJGAF ... Egyptian Journal of Geology [*A publication*]

EGJJ.......... Jersey, Channel Islands [*United Kingdom*] [*ICAO location identifier*] (ICLI)

EGK.......... Dayton, OH [*Location identifier*] [*FAA*] (FAAL)

EGK.......... Ein Grosser Komponist [*A Great Composer*] or Ein Genialer Komponist [*A Great Genius of a Composer*] [*Suggested interpretations for the adopted surname of German composer Werner Egk. Egk maintained that he chose the name in honor of his wife, Elisabeth Karl*]

EGKA .... Shoreham [*United Kingdom*] [*ICAO location identifier*] (ICLI)

EGKAA ..... Energetika [*A publication*]

EGKB .... Biggin Hill [*United Kingdom*] [*ICAO location identifier*] (ICLI)

EGKC .... Bognor Regis [*United Kingdom*] [*ICAO location identifier*] (ICLI)

EGKE .... Challock [*United Kingdom*] [*ICAO location identifier*] (ICLI)

EGKH........ Lashenden/Headcorn [*United Kingdom*] [*ICAO location identifier*] (ICLI)

EGKK .... London/Gatwick [*United Kingdom*] [*ICAO location identifier*] (ICLI)

EGKM .... West Malling [*United Kingdom*] [*ICAO location identifier*] (ICLI)

EGKO .... Einfuehrungsgesetz zur Konkursordnung [*A publication*]

EGKR .... Redhill [*United Kingdom*] [*ICAO location identifier*] (ICLI)

EGKS......... Europaeische Gemeinschaft fuer Kohle und Stahl [*European Coal and Steel Community*] [*German*] (DCTA)

EGKT .... Early Grand Knight Templar [*Freemasonry*] (ROG)

EGKZA..... Engei Gakkai Zasshi [*A publication*]

EGKZA9.... Engei Gakkai Zasshi [*A publication*]

EGL .... Eagle Aviation [*Long Beach, CA*] [*FAA designator*] (FAAC)

EGL .... Eagle Clothes, Inc. [*AMEX symbol*] (SPSG)

EGL .... Eagle Precision Technologies, Inc. [*Toronto Stock Exchange symbol*]

EGL .... Eclectic Grand Lodge [*Freemasonry*] (ROG)

EGL .... Encyclopedia of Georgia Law [*A publication*] (DLA)

EGL .... Eosinophilic Granuloma of the Lung [*Medicine*]

EGL .... Equipment Guide List (NVT)

EGL .... Expected Grade Level [*Education*]

EGL .... Extragalactic Light

EGL .... Gala Law [*Scotland*] [*Seismograph station code, US Geological Survey*] (SEIS)

EGLA........ Bodmin [*United Kingdom*] [*ICAO location identifier*] (ICLI)

EGLA........ Eagle Telephonics, Inc. [*NASDAQ symbol*] (NQ)

EGLB........ Brooklands [*United Kingdom*] [*ICAO location identifier*] (ICLI)

EGLC........ Eagle Computer, Inc. [*NASDAQ symbol*] (NQ)

EGLD........ Denham [*United Kingdom*] [*ICAO location identifier*] (ICLI)

EGLE........ Eagle Food Centers, Inc. [*NASDAQ symbol*] (NQ)

EGLG .... Panshanger [*United Kingdom*] [*ICAO location identifier*] (ICLI)

EGLI.......... Esperantista Go-Ligo Internacia [*International Esperantist League for Go - IELG*] (EAIO)

EGLI.......... Essay and General Literature Index [*A publication*]

Eglise Th.... Eglise et Theologie [*A publication*]

EGLJ .... Chalgrove [*United Kingdom*] [*ICAO location identifier*] (ICLI)

EGLK........ Blackbushe [*United Kingdom*] [*ICAO location identifier*] (ICLI)

EGLL......... London City [*United Kingdom*] [*ICAO location identifier*] (ICLI)

EGLM .... Exchangeable General Linear Model [*Statistics*]

EGLM .... White Waltham [*United Kingdom*] [*ICAO location identifier*] (ICLI)

EGLMA9... Estudios Geologicos [*Madrid*] [*A publication*]

EGLMSFCMS ... Elves', Gnomes', and Little Men's Science Fiction, Chowder, and Marching Society (EA)

EGLMT..... Ejector-Launcher, Guided Missile, Transporter

EGLN .... London/Heathrow [*United Kingdom*] [*ICAO location identifier*] (ICLI)

EGLS......... Old Sarum [*United Kingdom*] [*ICAO location identifier*] (ICLI)

Egl Th........ Eglise et Theologie [*A publication*]

Egl Viv ...... Eglise Vivante [*A publication*]

EGLW .... London [*United Kingdom*] [*ICAO location identifier*] (ICLI)

EGM.......... Egyptian Mail [*A publication*]

EGM.......... El Golfo De Santa Clara [*Mexico*] [*Seismograph station code, US Geological Survey*] (SEIS)

EGM.......... Electronic Governor Module (IEEE)

EGM.......... Empire Gallantry Medal [*British*]

EGM.......... Enhanced Graphics Monitor [*Computer technology*]

EGM.......... European Glass Container Manufacturers' Committee [*London, England*]

EGM.......... Excellent Grand Master [*Freemasonry*] (ROG)

EGM.......... Extraordinary General Meeting [*British*] (ADA)

EGM.......... Sege [*Solomon Islands*] [*Airport symbol*] (OAG)

eGmbH ...... Eingetragene Gesellschaft mit Beschraenkter Haftung [*Registered Company with Limited Liability*] [*German*] (ILCA)

EGM of C .. Excellent Grand Master of Ceremonies [*Freemasonry*] (ROG)

EGMC........ Southend [*United Kingdom*] [*ICAO location identifier*] (ICLI)

EGMD....... Lydd [*United Kingdom*] [*ICAO location identifier*] (ICLI)

EGME .... Ethylene Glycol Monomethyl Ether [*A poison*] [*Organic chemistry*]

EGMEX ..... Eastern Gulf of Mexico

EGMF........ Edvard Grieg Memorial Foundation (EA)

EGMH....... Manston [*United Kingdom*] [*ICAO location identifier*] (ICLI)

EGMR .... East Griqualand Mounted Rifles [*British military*] (DMA)

EGMT .... Elapsed Greenwich Mean Time (KSC)

EGMTR.... Eglin Gulf Missile Test Range [*Florida*] [*Air Force*]

EGN........... Eagle's Nest [*New York*] [*Seismograph station code, US Geological Survey*] (SEIS)

EGN.......... El Geneina [*Sudan*] [*Airport symbol*] (OAG)

EGN.......... Ellen Glasgow Newsletter [*A publication*]

EGN.......... Energen Corp. [*NYSE symbol*] (SPSG)

EGN.......... Experimental Glomerulonephritis [*Medicine*]

EGN.......... Express Group Newspapers [*British*]

EGNA .... Eucharistic Guard for Nocturnal Adoration (EA)

EGNA .... Hucknall [*United Kingdom*] [*ICAO location identifier*] (ICLI)

EGNB .... Brough [*United Kingdom*] [*ICAO location identifier*] (ICLI)

EGNC .... Carlisle [*United Kingdom*] [*ICAO location identifier*] (ICLI)

EGND........ Huddersfield/Crosland Moor [*United Kingdom*] [*ICAO location identifier*] (ICLI)

EGNE .... Repton/Gamston [*United Kingdom*] [*ICAO location identifier*] (ICLI)

EGNF .... Nether Thorpe [*United Kingdom*] [*ICAO location identifier*] (ICLI)

EGNG .... Preston and Blackburn/Samlesbury [*United Kingdom*] [*ICAO location identifier*] (ICLI)

EGNH .... Blackpool [*United Kingdom*] [*ICAO location identifier*] (ICLI)

EGNI .... Skegness/Ingoldmells [*United Kingdom*] [*ICAO location identifier*] (ICLI)

EGNJ......... Humberside [*United Kingdom*] [*ICAO location identifier*] (ICLI)

EGNL .... Barrow/Walney Island [*United Kingdom*] [*ICAO location identifier*] (ICLI)

EGNM....... Leeds and Bradford [*United Kingdom*] [*ICAO location identifier*] (ICLI)

EGNO........ Warton [*United Kingdom*] [*ICAO location identifier*] (ICLI)

E/GNP....... Energy/Gross National Product [*Fuel use ratio*]

EGNR........ Hawarden [*United Kingdom*] [*ICAO location identifier*] (ICLI)

EGNS .... Isle Of Man/Ronaldsway [*United Kingdom*] [*ICAO location identifier*] (ICLI)

EGNT .... Expositer's Greek New Testament [*A publication*]

EGNT .... Newcastle [*United Kingdom*] [*ICAO location identifier*] (ICLI)

EGNV .... Tees-Side [*United Kingdom*] [*ICAO location identifier*] (ICLI)

EGNW .... Wickenby [*United Kingdom*] [*ICAO location identifier*] (ICLI)

EGNX........ East Midlands [*United Kingdom*] [*ICAO location identifier*] (ICLI)

EGO........... Eccentric Geophysical Observatory [*Also, EOGO*] [*NASA*]

EGO.......... Ego Resources Ltd. [*Toronto Stock Exchange symbol*]

EGO.......... Electronic Grading Operator

EGO.......... Excellent Grand Orator [*Freemasonry*] (ROG)

EGO.......... Exhaust Gas Oxygen [*Automotive engineering*]

EGO.......... Experimental Geophysical Orbiting [*Vehicle*]

EGOB .... Burtonwood [*United Kingdom*] [*ICAO location identifier*] (ICLI)

EGOBOO ... Ego Boost

EGOC .... Bishops Court [*United Kingdom*] [*ICAO location identifier*] (ICLI)

EGOD....... Llanbedr [*United Kingdom*] [*ICAO location identifier*] (ICLI)

EGOE........ Ternhill [*United Kingdom*] [*ICAO location identifier*] (ICLI)

EGOMAC ... Effect of Gravity on Methane-Air Combustion

EGOPA ...... Engineering Optimization [*A publication*]

EGOQ........ Mona [*United Kingdom*] [*ICAO location identifier*] (ICLI)

EGOR........ Ego Resources, Inc. [*NASDAQ symbol*] (NQ)

EGOS .... European Group for Organizational Studies (EAIO)

EGOS .... Shawbury [*United Kingdom*] [*ICAO location identifier*] (ICLI)

EGOTH..... Egyptian Government Organization for Tourism and Hotels

EGOV — Valley [*United Kingdom*] [*ICAO location identifier*]   (ICLI)
EGOW — Woodvale [*United Kingdom*] [*ICAO location identifier*]   (ICLI)
EGOY — West Freugh [*United Kingdom*] [*ICAO location identifier*]   (ICLI)
EGP — Eagle Pass [*Texas*] [*Airport symbol*] [*Obsolete*]   (OAG)
EGP — Eagle Pass Resources [*Vancouver Stock Exchange symbol*]
EGP — Early Greek Philosophy [*1930*] [*A publication*]   (OCD)
EGP — EastGroup Properties SBI [*AMEX symbol*]   (SPSG)
EGP — Economic Geography [*A publication*]
EGP — Egypt   (ROG)
EGP — Ejercito Guerrillero de los Pobres [*Guerrilla Army of the Poor*] [*Guatemala*]
EGP — Elliptical Gear Planetary
EGP — Embezzlement of Government Property
EGP — Eminentra Granularis Posterior [*Anatomy*]
EGP — Energy Policy [*A publication*]
EGP — Exhaust Gas Pressure
EGP — Experimental Geodetic Payload [*Japan*]
EGP — Experimental GOES [*Goestationary Operational Environmental Satellite*] Platform [*Marine science*]   (MSC)
EGP — Extended Guide Projectile [*Navy*]   (MCD)
EGPA — European Group of Public Administration [*See also GEAP*] [*Brussels, Belgium*]   (EAIO)
EGPA — Export Grape and Plum Act [*1960*]
EGPA — Kirkwall [*United Kingdom*] [*ICAO location identifier*]   (ICLI)
EGPACOM — Environmental Group, Pacific Command   (CINC)
EGPB — Sumburgh [*United Kingdom*] [*ICAO location identifier*]   (ICLI)
EGPBAU — Egyptian Pharmaceutical Bulletin [*A publication*]
EGPC — Egyptian General Petroleum Corporation
EGPC — English Greenhouse Products Corp. [*NASDAQ symbol*]   (NQ)
EGPC — Wick [*United Kingdom*] [*ICAO location identifier*]   (ICLI)
EGPD — Aberdeen/Dyce [*United Kingdom*] [*ICAO location identifier*]   (ICLI)
EGPE — Inverness/Dalcross [*United Kingdom*] [*ICAO location identifier*]   (ICLI)
EGPF — East Greenland Polar Front [*Oceanography*]
EGPF — Glasgow [*United Kingdom*] [*ICAO location identifier*]   (ICLI)
EGPH — Edinburgh [*United Kingdom*] [*ICAO location identifier*]   (ICLI)
EGPI — Islay/Port Ellen [*United Kingdom*] [*ICAO location identifier*]   (ICLI)
EGPJ — Fife/Glenrothes [*United Kingdom*] [*ICAO location identifier*]   (ICLI)
EGPJBL — Egyptian Pharmaceutical Journal [*A publication*]
EGPK — Prestwick [*United Kingdom*] [*ICAO location identifier*]   (ICLI)
EGPL — Benbecula [*United Kingdom*] [*ICAO location identifier*]   (ICLI)
EGPM — Scatsta [*United Kingdom*] [*ICAO location identifier*]   (ICLI)
EGPMF — Error Gap Probability Mass Function
EGPN — Dundee (Riverside Park) [*United Kingdom*] [*ICAO location identifier*]   (ICLI)
EGPO — Stornoway [*United Kingdom*] [*ICAO location identifier*]   (ICLI)
EGPQ — Edinburgh [*United Kingdom*] [*ICAO location identifier*]   (ICLI)
EGPR — Barra [*United Kingdom*] [*ICAO location identifier*]   (ICLI)
EGPS — Electric Ground Power System [*Aerospace*]   (AAG)
EGPS — Extended General Purpose Simulator [*National Electronics Conference*]   (IEEE)
EGPS — Peterhead/Longside [*United Kingdom*] [*ICAO location identifier*]   (ICLI)
EGPT — Perth/Scone [*United Kingdom*] [*ICAO location identifier*]   (ICLI)
EGPU — Tiree [*United Kingdom*] [*ICAO location identifier*]   (ICLI)
EGPW — Unst (Shetland Isles) [*United Kingdom*] [*ICAO location identifier*]   (ICLI)
EGPX — Scottish Air Traffic Control Centre [*United Kingdom*] [*ICAO location identifier*]   (ICLI)
EGPY — Dounreay/Thurso [*United Kingdom*] [*ICAO location identifier*]   (ICLI)
EGQ — Emmetsburg, IA [*Location identifier*] [*FAA*]   (FAAL)
EGQB — Ballykelly [*United Kingdom*] [*ICAO location identifier*]   (ICLI)
EGQJ — Machrihanish [*United Kingdom*] [*ICAO location identifier*]   (ICLI)
EGQK — Kinloss [*United Kingdom*] [*ICAO location identifier*]   (ICLI)
EGQL — Leuchars [*United Kingdom*] [*ICAO location identifier*]   (ICLI)
EGQM — Boulmer [*United Kingdom*] [*ICAO location identifier*]   (ICLI)
EGQN — Buchan [*United Kingdom*] [*ICAO location identifier*]   (ICLI)
EGQP — Edinburgh [*United Kingdom*] [*ICAO location identifier*]   (ICLI)
EGQQ — Prestwick [*United Kingdom*] [*ICAO location identifier*]   (ICLI)
EGQR — Saxa Vord [*United Kingdom*] [*ICAO location identifier*]   (ICLI)
EGQS — Lossiemouth [*United Kingdom*] [*ICAO location identifier*]   (ICLI)
EGQT — Edinburgh [*United Kingdom*] [*ICAO location identifier*]   (ICLI)
EGR — Eagle River Mines [*Vancouver Stock Exchange symbol*]

EgR — Egyptian Religion [*A publication*]
EGR — Electrographic Recorder   (CAAL)
EGR — Electronic Governor Regulator   (IEEE)
EGR — Embossed Groove Recording
EGR — Empire Grade Road [*California*] [*Seismograph station code, US Geological Survey*]   (SEIS)
egr — Engraver [*MARC relator code*] [*Library of Congress*]   (LCCP)
EGR — Enhanced Guardrail   (MCD)
EGR — Erythrocyte Glutathione Reductase [*An enzyme*]
EGR — Excellent Grand Recorder [*Freemasonry*]   (ROG)
EGR — Exhaust Gas Recirculation [*Engines*]
e-gr--- — Greece [*MARC geographic area code*] [*Library of Congress*]   (LCCP)
EGRA — Glasgow [*United Kingdom*] [*ICAO location identifier*]   (ICLI)
EGRB — London [*United Kingdom*] [*ICAO location identifier*]   (ICLI)
EGRC — Manchester [*United Kingdom*] [*ICAO location identifier*]   (ICLI)
EGRD — Bristol [*United Kingdom*] [*ICAO location identifier*]   (ICLI)
EGRD — Eye Guard
EGRE — Malvern [*United Kingdom*] [*ICAO location identifier*]   (ICLI)
EGREAF — Egretta [*A publication*]
EGRESS — Emergency Global Rescue, Escape, and Survival System [*NASA*]
EGRESS — Evaluation of Glide Reentry Structural Systems
EGRET — Energetic Gamma Ray Experiment Telescope [*NASA*]
EGRG — Cardiff City [*United Kingdom*] [*ICAO location identifier*]   (ICLI)
EGRH — High Wycombe [*United Kingdom*] [*ICAO location identifier*]   (ICLI)
Egr High — Egremont on the Law of Highways [*A publication*]   (DLA)
EGRI — Southampton [*United Kingdom*] [*ICAO location identifier*]   (ICLI)
Egri Muz Ev — Az Egri Muzeum Evkoenyve [*A publication*]
EGRJ — Upavon [*United Kingdom*] [*ICAO location identifier*]   (ICLI)
EGRK — Ocean Station Vessel Romeo [*United Kingdom*] [*ICAO location identifier*]   (ICLI)
EGRL — East Gippsland Regional Library [*Australia*]
EGRL — Ocean Station Vessel Lima [*United Kingdom*] [*ICAO location identifier*]   (ICLI)
EGRM — Ocean Station Vessel Mike [*United Kingdom*] [*ICAO location identifier*]   (ICLI)
EGRN — Norwich [*United Kingdom*] [*ICAO location identifier*]   (ICLI)
EGRP — Plymouth [*United Kingdom*] [*ICAO location identifier*]   (ICLI)
EGRR — Bracknell [*United Kingdom*] [*ICAO location identifier*]   (ICLI)
EGRS — Egress   (KSC)
EGRS — Extragalactic Radio Source
EGRS — Sullom Voe [*United Kingdom*] [*ICAO location identifier*]   (ICLI)
EGRT — Newcastle [*United Kingdom*] [*ICAO location identifier*]   (ICLI)
EGRTA — Energy Report (Alton, England) [*A publication*]
EGRU — Ocean Station Vessel Charlie [*United Kingdom*] [*ICAO location identifier*]   (ICLI)
EGRW — Nottingham [*United Kingdom*] [*ICAO location identifier*]   (ICLI)
EGRY — Leeds [*United Kingdom*] [*ICAO location identifier*]   (ICLI)
EGS — Economic General Staff [*British*]
EGS — Edge Guide System
EGS — Egilsstadir [*Iceland*] [*Airport symbol*]   (OAG)
EGS — Electrical Galvanic Stimulation [*Physiology*]
EGS — Electrogalvanized Steel
EGS — Electrographic Seizure [*Neurophysiology*]
EGS — Electronic-Glide Slope   (NG)
EGS — Elementary Gliding School [*British military*]   (DMA)
EGS — Emil Gilels Society   (EA)
EGS — English and Germanic Studies [*A publication*]
EGS — English Goethe Society [*British*]
EGS — Equity Guard Stock Fund [*AMEX symbol*]   (SPSG)
EGS — Ethylene Glycol Succinate [*Organic chemistry*]
EGS — Europaeische Gesellschaft fuer Schriftpsychologie und Schriftexpertise [*European Society of Handwriting Psychology - ESHP*]   (EAIO)
EGS — European Geophysical Society   (EAIO)
EGS — Excellent Grand Secretary [*Freemasonry*]   (ROG)
EGS — Exhaust Gas System
EGS — Extension of the Gastric Shield
EGSA — Electrical Generating Systems Association   (EA)
EGSA — Shipdham [*United Kingdom*] [*ICAO location identifier*]   (ICLI)
EGSB — Bedford/Castle Mill [*United Kingdom*] [*ICAO location identifier*]   (ICLI)
EGSC — Cambridge [*United Kingdom*] [*ICAO location identifier*]   (ICLI)
EGSC — Eastern Group Supply Council [*Australia*]
EGSD — Great Yarmouth/North Denes [*United Kingdom*] [*ICAO location identifier*]   (ICLI)
EGSE — Electrical [*or Electronic*] Ground-Support Equipment
EGSE — Ipswich [*United Kingdom*] [*ICAO location identifier*]   (ICLI)
EGSF — Peterborough (Conington) [*United Kingdom*] [*ICAO location identifier*]   (ICLI)

EGSG......... Stapleford [*United Kingdom*] [*ICAO location identifier*] (ICLI)
EGSH........ Norwich [*United Kingdom*] [*ICAO location identifier*] (ICLI)
EGSIPS..... Electronic Guides for Standardizing Items of Procurement and Supply (MCD)
EGSJ......... Polstead [*United Kingdom*] [*ICAO location identifier*] (ICLI)
EGSK........ Hethel [*United Kingdom*] [*ICAO location identifier*] (ICLI)
EGSL......... Andrewsfield [*United Kingdom*] [*ICAO location identifier*] (ICLI)
EGSM........ Beccles [*United Kingdom*] [*ICAO location identifier*] (ICLI)
EGSMA..... Electrical Generating Systems Marketing Association [*Later, EGSA*] (EA)
EGSMA..... Energomashinostroenie [*A publication*]
EGSN......... Bourn (Cambs) [*United Kingdom*] [*ICAO location identifier*] (ICLI)
EGSP......... Peterborough/Sibson [*United Kingdom*] [*ICAO location identifier*] (ICLI)
EGSR......... Earls Colne [*United Kingdom*] [*ICAO location identifier*] (ICLI)
EGSS......... London/Stansted [*United Kingdom*] [*ICAO location identifier*] (ICLI)
EGST......... Elmsett [*United Kingdom*] [*ICAO location identifier*] (ICLI)
E and G Stud ... English and Germanic Studies [*A publication*]
EGSW........ Weeley [*United Kingdom*] [*ICAO location identifier*] (ICLI)
EGT.......... Egypt
EGT.......... Elapsed Ground Time (MCD)
EGT.......... Eminent Grand Treasurer [*Freemasonry*] (ROG)
EGT.......... Equivalent Gear Train
EGT.......... Estates, Gifts, and Trusts Journal [*A publication*]
EGT.......... Estimated Ground Time (MCD)
EGT.......... Excellent Grand Tabernacle [*Freemasonry*] (ROG)
EGT.......... Exhaust Gas Temperature
EGT.......... [*The*] Expositor's Greek Testament [*A publication*] (BJA)
EGT.......... Wellington, KS [*Location identifier*] [*FAA*] (FAAL)
EGTA........ Aylesbury/Thame [*United Kingdom*] [*ICAO location identifier*] (ICLI)
EGTA........ Esophageal Gastric Tube Airway [*Medicine*]
EGTA........ Ethylene Glycol Bis(aminoethyl ether)tetraacetic Acid [*Also, EBONTA*] [*Organic chemistry*]
EGTA........ European Group of Television Advertising (EA)
EGTB........ Wycombe Air Park/Booker [*United Kingdom*] [*ICAO location identifier*] (ICLI)
EGTC......... Cranfield [*United Kingdom*] [*ICAO location identifier*] (ICLI)
EGTD........ Dunsfold [*United Kingdom*] [*ICAO location identifier*] (ICLI)
EGTE......... Exeter [*United Kingdom*] [*ICAO location identifier*] (ICLI)
EGTF......... Fairoaks [*United Kingdom*] [*ICAO location identifier*] (ICLI)
EGTG........ Bristol/Filton [*United Kingdom*] [*ICAO location identifier*] (ICLI)
EGTH........ Hatfield [*United Kingdom*] [*ICAO location identifier*] (ICLI)
EGTI......... Exhaust Gas Temperature Indicator
EGTI......... Leavesden [*United Kingdom*] [*ICAO location identifier*] (ICLI)
EGTK........ Oxford/Kidlington [*United Kingdom*] [*ICAO location identifier*] (ICLI)
EGTKA..... Energetik [*A publication*]
EGTO........ Rochester [*United Kingdom*] [*ICAO location identifier*] (ICLI)
EGTR......... Eglin Gulf Test Range [*Florida*] [*Air Force*]
EGTR......... Elstree [*United Kingdom*] [*ICAO location identifier*] (ICLI)
EGTS......... Emergency Gas Treatment System [*Nuclear energy*] (NRCH)
EGTT......... London Air Traffic Control Center [*United Kingdom*] [*ICAO location identifier*] (ICLI)
EGUA........ Upper Heyford [*United Kingdom*] [*ICAO location identifier*] (ICLI)
EGUB........ Benson [*United Kingdom*] [*ICAO location identifier*] (ICLI)
EGUC........ Aberporth [*United Kingdom*] [*ICAO location identifier*] (ICLI)
EGUD........ Abingdon [*United Kingdom*] [*ICAO location identifier*] (ICLI)
EGUF........ Farnborough [*United Kingdom*] [*ICAO location identifier*] (ICLI)
EGUH........ High Wycombe [*United Kingdom*] [*ICAO location identifier*] (ICLI)
EGUHM.... Extra Gentleman Usher to His Majesty [*British*]
Eguin Baro ... Eguinarius Baro [*Deceased, 1550*] [*Authority cited in pre-1607 legal work*] (DSA)
EGUK........ Waterbeach [*United Kingdom*] [*ICAO location identifier*] (ICLI)
EGUL........ Lakenheath [*United Kingdom*] [*ICAO location identifier*] (ICLI)
EGUM........ Manston [*United Kingdom*] [*ICAO location identifier*] (ICLI)
EGUN........ Fast Pulse Electron Gun [*NASA*] (NASA)
EGUN........ Mildenhall [*United Kingdom*] [*ICAO location identifier*] (ICLI)
EGUO........ Oakington [*United Kingdom*] [*ICAO location identifier*] (ICLI)
EGUP........ Sculthorpe [*United Kingdom*] [*ICAO location identifier*] (ICLI)
EGUS........ Lee-On-Solent [*United Kingdom*] [*ICAO location identifier*] (ICLI)
EGUU........ Uxbridge [*United Kingdom*] [*ICAO location identifier*] (ICLI)
EGUW........ Wattisham [*United Kingdom*] [*ICAO location identifier*] (ICLI)

EGUY........ Wyton [*United Kingdom*] [*ICAO location identifier*] (ICLI)
EGV.......... Eagle River, WI [*Location identifier*] [*FAA*] (FAAL)
EGV.......... Exit Guide Vane
EGVA........ Fairford [*United Kingdom*] [*ICAO location identifier*] (ICLI)
EGVB........ Bawdsey [*United Kingdom*] [*ICAO location identifier*] (ICLI)
EGVC........ Northolt [*United Kingdom*] [*ICAO location identifier*] (ICLI)
EGVG........ Woodbridge [*United Kingdom*] [*ICAO location identifier*] (ICLI)
EGVI......... Greenham Common [*United Kingdom*] [*ICAO location identifier*] (ICLI)
Eg Vic Or ... Egitto e Vicino Oriente [*A publication*]
EGVJ......... Bentwaters [*United Kingdom*] [*ICAO location identifier*] (ICLI)
EGVN........ Brize Norton [*United Kingdom*] [*ICAO location identifier*] (ICLI)
EGVO........ Odiham [*United Kingdom*] [*ICAO location identifier*] (ICLI)
EGVP......... Middle Wallop [*United Kingdom*] [*ICAO location identifier*] (ICLI)
E & GVR.... Ellesmere & Glyn Valley Railway [*Later, GVR*] [*Wales*]
EGVT........ Wethersfield [*United Kingdom*] [*ICAO location identifier*] (ICLI)
EGVW........ Bedford [*United Kingdom*] [*ICAO location identifier*] (ICLI)
EGW.......... Edgewater Resources Ltd. [*Vancouver Stock Exchange symbol*]
EGW.......... Electrogas Welding
EGW.......... Enamel Guild: West (EA)
EGW.......... Engineering Writer
e-gw---........ Germany, West [*MARC geographic area code*] [*Library of Congress*] (LCCP)
EGWB........ Ministry of Defence, United Kingdom [*ICAO location identifier*] (ICLI)
EGWC........ Cosford [*United Kingdom*] [*ICAO location identifier*] (ICLI)
EGWD........ West Drayton [*United Kingdom*] [*ICAO location identifier*] (ICLI)
EGWE........ Henlow [*United Kingdom*] [*ICAO location identifier*] (ICLI)
EGWI......... London [*United Kingdom*] [*ICAO location identifier*] (ICLI)
EGWL........ North Luffenham [*United Kingdom*] [*ICAO location identifier*] (ICLI)
EGWN........ Halton [*United Kingdom*] [*ICAO location identifier*] (ICLI)
EGWS........ Stanmore Park [*United Kingdom*] [*ICAO location identifier*] (ICLI)
EGWU........ Northolt [*United Kingdom*] [*ICAO location identifier*] (ICLI)
EGWX........ CINCFLEETWOC [*United Kingdom*] [*ICAO location identifier*] (ICLI)
EGWZ........ Alconbury [*United Kingdom*] [*ICAO location identifier*] (ICLI)
EGX.......... Egegik [*Alaska*] [*Airport symbol*] (OAG)
EGX.......... Energex Minerals Ltd. [*Toronto Stock Exchange symbol*] [*Vancouver Stock Exchange symbol*]
EGX.......... Engex, Inc. [*AMEX symbol*] (SPSG)
e-gx---........ Germany [*MARC geographic area code*] [*Library of Congress*] (LCCP)
EGXB........ Binbrook [*United Kingdom*] [*ICAO location identifier*] (ICLI)
EGXC........ Coningsby [*United Kingdom*] [*ICAO location identifier*] (ICLI)
EGXE........ Leeming [*United Kingdom*] [*ICAO location identifier*] (ICLI)
EGXG........ Church Fenton [*United Kingdom*] [*ICAO location identifier*] (ICLI)
EGXH........ Honington [*United Kingdom*] [*ICAO location identifier*] (ICLI)
EGXI......... Finningley [*United Kingdom*] [*ICAO location identifier*] (ICLI)
EGXJ......... Cottesmore [*United Kingdom*] [*ICAO location identifier*] (ICLI)
EGXN........ Newton [*United Kingdom*] [*ICAO location identifier*] (ICLI)
EGXP........ Scampton [*United Kingdom*] [*ICAO location identifier*] (ICLI)
EGXS......... Swinderby [*United Kingdom*] [*ICAO location identifier*] (ICLI)
EGXT........ Wittering [*United Kingdom*] [*ICAO location identifier*] (ICLI)
EGXU........ Linton-On-Ouse [*United Kingdom*] [*ICAO location identifier*] (ICLI)
EGXV........ Leconfield [*United Kingdom*] [*ICAO location identifier*] (ICLI)
EGXW........ Waddington [*United Kingdom*] [*ICAO location identifier*] (ICLI)
EGXZ......... Topcliffe [*United Kingdom*] [*ICAO location identifier*] (ICLI)
EGY.......... Economic Geography [*A publication*]
EGY.......... Egypt [*ANSI three-letter standard code*] (CNC)
egy............. Egyptian [*MARC language code*] [*Library of Congress*] (LCCP)
EGY.......... Egyptian (ROG)
EGY.......... Egyptology
EGY.......... English Bay, AK [*Location identifier*] [*FAA*] (FAAL)
EGY.......... Triton Energy Corp. [*Toronto Stock Exchange symbol*]
EGYAA.... Energetyka [*A publication*]
EGYB......... Brampton [*United Kingdom*] [*ICAO location identifier*] (ICLI)
EGYC........ Coltishall [*United Kingdom*] [*ICAO location identifier*] (ICLI)
EGYD........ Cranwell [*United Kingdom*] [*ICAO location identifier*] (ICLI)
EGYDA.... Energy Digest [*Washington, DC*] [*A publication*]
EGYE........ Barkston Heath [*United Kingdom*] [*ICAO location identifier*] (ICLI)
EGYH........ Holbeach [*United Kingdom*] [*ICAO location identifier*] (ICLI)

EGYK .... Elvington [*United Kingdom*] [*ICAO location identifier*] (ICLI)
EGYM ...... Marham [*United Kingdom*] [*ICAO location identifier*] (ICLI)
EGYP .... Egyptian (ROG)
EGYP .... Mount Pleasant [*United Kingdom*] [*ICAO location identifier*] (ICLI)
EGYPT ...... Eager to Grab Your Pretty Top [*Correspondence*] [*Bowdlerized version*] (DSUE)
EGYPT ...... Egyptian (ROG)
Egypt Agric Organ Bahtim Exp Stn Tech Bull ... Egyptian Agricultural Organization. Bahtim Experiment Station Technical Bulletin [*A publication*]
Egypt Agric Rev ... Egyptian Agricultural Review [*A publication*]
Egypt Comput J ... Egyptian Computer Journal [*A publication*]
Egypt Cott Gaz ... Egyptian Cotton Gazette [*A publication*]
Egypt Dent J ... Egyptian Dental Journal [*A publication*]
Egypte Contemp ... Egypte Contemporaine [*A publication*]
Egypt Geol Surv Ann ... Egypt Geological Survey. Annals [*A publication*]
Egypt Geol Surv Min Auth Pap ... Egyptian Geological Survey and Mining Authority. Paper [*A publication*]
Egypt Geol Surv Pap ... Egypt Geological Survey. Paper [*A publication*]
Egyptian Statist J ... Egyptian Statistical Journal [*A publication*]
Egypt J Agron ... Egyptian Journal of Agronomy [*A publication*]
Egypt J Anim Prod ... Egyptian Journal of Animal Production [*A publication*]
Egypt J Bilharz ... Egyptian Journal of Bilharziasis [*A publication*]
Egypt J Bilharziasis ... Egyptian Journal of Bilharziasis [*A publication*]
Egypt J Biomed Eng ... Egyptian Journal of Biomedical Engineering [*A publication*]
Egypt J Bot ... Egyptian Journal of Botany [*A publication*]
Egypt J Ch ... Egyptian Journal of Chemistry [*A publication*]
Egypt J Chem ... Egyptian Journal of Chemistry [*A publication*]
Egypt J Chest Dis Tuberc ... Egyptian Journal of Chest Diseases and Tuberculosis [*A publication*]
Egypt J Dairy Sci ... Egyptian Journal of Dairy Science [*A publication*]
Egypt J Food Sci ... Egyptian Journal of Food Science [*A publication*]
Egypt J Genet Cytol ... Egyptian Journal of Genetics and Cytology [*A publication*]
Egypt J Geol ... Egyptian Journal of Geology [*A publication*]
Egypt J Hortic ... Egyptian Journal of Horticulture [*A publication*]
Egypt J Microbiol ... Egyptian Journal of Microbiology [*A publication*]
Egypt J Neurol Psychiat Neurosurg ... Egyptian Journal of Neurology, Psychiatry, and Neurosurgery [*A publication*]
Egypt J Pharm Sci ... Egyptian Journal of Pharmaceutical Sciences [*A publication*]
Egypt J Phyopathol ... Egyptian Journal of Phytopathology [*A publication*]
Egypt J Phys ... Egyptian Journal of Physics [*A publication*]
Egypt J Physiol Sci ... Egyptian Journal of Physiological Sciences [*A publication*]
Egypt J Phytopathol ... Egyptian Journal of Phytopathology [*A publication*]
Egypt J Psychiatry ... Egyptian Journal of Psychiatry [*A publication*]
Egypt J Psychol ... Egyptian Journal of Psychology [*A publication*]
Egypt J Soc Med ... Egyptian Journal of Social Medicine [*A publication*]
Egypt J Soil Sci ... Egyptian Journal of Soil Science [*A publication*]
Egypt J Vet Sci ... Egyptian Journal of Veterinary Science [*A publication*]
EGYPTOL ... Egyptology (ROG)
Egypt Orthop J ... Egyptian Orthopaedic Journal [*A publication*]
Egypt Pharm Bull ... Egyptian Pharmaceutical Bulletin [*A publication*]
Egypt Pharm J ... Egyptian Pharmaceutical Journal [*A publication*]
Egypt Pharm Rep ... Egyptian Pharmaceutical Reports. Pharmaceutical Society of Egypt and the Syndicate of Pharmacists [*A publication*]
Egypt Popul Fam Plann Rev ... Egyptian Population and Family Planning Review [*A publication*]
Egypt Revs Sci ... Egyptian Reviews of Science [*A publication*]
Egypt Sugar Distill Co Sugar Cane Dep Res Bull ... Egyptian Sugar and Distillation Company. Sugar Cane Department. Research Bulletin [*A publication*]
Egypt Sugar Distill Co Sugar Cane Dep Tech Bull ... Egyptian Sugar and Distillation Company. Sugar Cane Department. Technical Bulletin [*A publication*]
EGYR .... Watton [*United Kingdom*] [*ICAO location identifier*] (ICLI)
EGYSA ...... Energy Sources [*New York*] [*A publication*]
EGYSAO... Energy Sources [*A publication*]
Egyt Trav Mag ... Egypt Travel Magazine [*A publication*]
EH.............. Aer Arann Teoranta [*Ireland*] [*ICAO designator*] (FAAC)
EH.............. Early Hebrew (BJA)
EH.............. Eastern Horizon [*Hong Kong*] [*A publication*]
EH.............. Eclosion Hormone [*Entomology*]
EH.............. Economic History [*A publication*]
EH.............. Economie et Humanism [*Economy and Humanism*] [*An association*] (EAIO)
E & H .... Economy and History [*A publication*]
EH.............. Editiones Heidelbergenses [*A publication*]
EH.............. Educationally Handicapped
EH.............. Eggs in Hatching [*Parcel Post*]
EH.............. Electric Heater (AAG)
EH.............. Electrohydraulic [*Nuclear energy*] (NRCH)
EH.............. Electrohydrodynamic Ionization
EH.............. Eminent Herald [*Freemasonry*] (ROG)
EH.............. Emotionally Handicapped [*Psychology*]
EH.............. Encyclopaedia Hebraica [*Jerusalem*] [*A publication*] (BJA)
EH.............. Engine Hoods

EH............. English Horn
EH............. English Hymnal [*Episcopalian*]
EH............. Enlarged Heart [*Medicine*]
EH............. Enlil Hymn (BJA)
E & H .... Environment and Heredity
EH............. Environmental Health [*A publication*]
EH............. Epochs of History [*A publication*]
EH............. Epoxide Hydrolase [*An enzyme*]
EH............. Equitable Handicap [*Sailing*]
EH............. Eridu Hymn (BJA)
EH............. Escort Helicopter (CINC)
EH............. Essential Hypertension [*Medicine*]
EH............. Ethiopian Herald [*A publication*]
EH............. Ets Haim Seminary [*Amsterdam*] (BJA)
EH............. Europaeische Hochschulschriften [*A publication*]
EH............. Even ha-'Ezer, Shulhan 'Arukh (BJA)
EH............. Everlasting Heritage [*A variety of sweet corn*]
EH............. Exegetisches Handbuch zum Alten Testament [*Muenster*] [*A publication*] (BJA)
EH............. Exercise Head
EH............. Extended Hueckel [*Molecular orbit*] [*Atomic physics*]
EH............. Extra Hazardous (AAG)
EH............. Western Sahara [*ANSI two-letter standard code*] (CNC)
EHA .... Early History of Assyria [*A publication*] (BJA)
EHA .... East Hampton Aire [*East Hampton, NY*] [*FAA designator*] (FAAC)
EHA .... Economic History Association (EA)
EHA .... Education of the Handicapped Act [*1968*]
EHA .... Edward Hamilton Aitken [*Author*] [*Initials used as pseudonym*]
EHA .... Einzelhandelsberater [*A publication*]
EHA .... Electric Heating Association (EA)
EHA .... Electrical Harness Assembly (KSC)
EHA .... Electrohydraulic Actuator
EHA .... Elkhart, KS [*Location identifier*] [*FAA*] (FAAL)
EHA .... Emotional Health Anonymous (EA)
EHA .... En Route High Altitude
EHA .... Environmental Hygiene Agency [*Army*] (MCD)
EHA .... Environmental Protection Agency, Region I Library, Boston, MA [*OCLC symbol*] (OCLC)
EHA .... Enziklopedyah la-Hafirot ha-Arkheologiyot be-Erez Yisrael [*A publication*] (BJA)
EHA .... Equipment Handover Agreement [*Shipping*] (DS)
EHA .... Ethylhexyl Acrylate [*Organic chemistry*]
EHA .... Expect Higher Altitude [*Aviation*] (FAAC)
EHAA ...... Amsterdam [*Netherlands*] [*ICAO location identifier*] (ICLI)
EHAA ...... Epidemic Hepatitis-Associated Antigen [*Immunochemistry*]
EHAA ...... Every Hand an Adventure [*Bridge bidding method*]
EHAF .... Employee Health and Fitness [*A publication*]
EHAL .... Ameland [*Netherlands*] [*ICAO location identifier*] (ICLI)
EHAM ...... Amsterdam/Schiphol [*Netherlands*] [*ICAO location identifier*] (ICLI)
EHA-MR... Equitable Handicap Associated-Measured Rating [*Boating*]
E Handel... Elektro-Handel [*A publication*]
EHAS .... East Hertshire Archaeological Society [*British*]
EHAT .... Exegetisches Handbuch zum Alten Testament [*Muenster*] [*A publication*] (BJA)
EHB .... Environmental Protection Agency, Environmental Research Laboratory, Narragansett, RI [*OCLC symbol*] (OCLC)
EHB .... Extra Hard Black [*Pencil leads*] (ROG)
EHB .... Modern Power Systems [*A publication*]
EHBA .... Extrahepatic Biliary Atresia [*Medicine*]
EHBD .... Weert/Budel [*Netherlands*] [*ICAO location identifier*] (ICLI)
EHBF........ Estimated Hepatic Blood Flow [*Medicine*]
EHBF........ Extrahepatic Blood Flow [*Medicine*]
EHBK .... Maastricht/Zuid-Limburg [*Netherlands*] [*ICAO location identifier*] (ICLI)
EHBS........ Epeteris tes Hetaireias Byzantinon Spoudon [*A publication*]
EHC .... Elastic Hysteresis Constant
EHC .... Electrical Heating Control (MCD)
EHC .... Electrohydraulic Control (NRCH)
EHC .... Emergency Housing Corporation
EHC .... Emory and Henry College [*Virginia*]
EHC .... Enterohepatic Circulation [*Medicine*]
EHC .... Enterohepatic Clearance [*Medicine*]
EHC .... Extended Health Care [*Insurance*]
EHC .... Extra-Heavy Crude [*Petroleum technology*]
EHC .... Extrahepatic Cholestasis [*Medicine*]
EHCA .... Education for All Handicapped Children Act
EHCD........ Department of Environment, Housing, and Community Development [*Australia*]
EHCLS..... Encapsulated Harpoon Command and Launch System (MCD)
EHCM....... Editor "Hebrew Christians' Magazine" [*Pseudonym used by Nathan Davis*]
EHCS .... Educational and Health Career Services (EA)
EHD .... Elastohydrodynamic
EHD .... Electrohemodynamics
EHD .... Electrohydrodimerization [*Organic chemistry*]
EHD .... Electrohydrodynamics
EHD .... Electron-Hole Drop [*Semiconductor physics*]
EHD .... Engineer Historical Division [*Army*]

EHD.......... English Historical Documents [*A publication*]
EHD.......... Epizootic Hemorrhagic Disease [*Veterinary medicine*]
EHDA........ Electrical Housewares Distributors Association (EA)
EHDA........ Ethylhexadecyldimethylammonium Bromide [*Blood count diluent*]
EHDB........ De Bilt [*Netherlands*] [*ICAO location identifier*] (ICLI)
EHDEDN ... Early Human Development [*A publication*]
EHDHP...... Electrodynamic Heat Pipe [*NASA*]
EHDL........ Deelen [*Netherlands*] [*ICAO location identifier*] (ICLI)
EHDP........ Ethanehydroxydiphosphonate [*or -diphosphonic Acid*] [*Also, HEDP*] [*Organic chemistry*]
EHDP........ Ethylenehydroxydiphosphonate [*Organic chemistry*]
EHDP........ Venraij/De Peel [*Netherlands*] [*ICAO location identifier*] (ICLI)
EHDPP...... Ethylhexyl Diphenyl Phosphate [*Organic chemistry*]
EHDR........ Drachten [*Netherlands*] [*ICAO location identifier*] (ICLI)
EHDR........ Erection, Holddown, and Release [*Aerospace*] (AAG)
EHE.......... Embassy Home Entertainment [*Video distributor*]
EHEC........ Ethyl(hydroxyethyl)cellulose [*Organic chemistry*]
EHECA ..... Emergency Highway Energy Conservation Act [*1974*]
EheG......... Ehegesetz [*Marriage Law*] [*German*] (ILCA)
Ehe G........ Ehegesetz [*A publication*]
Ehe Ges G ... Ehegesundheitsgesetz [*A publication*]
EHEH........ Eindhoven [*Netherlands*] [*ICAO location identifier*] (ICLI)
EHES......... Environmental Health Engineering Services [*Army*] (AABC)
EHF.......... Electrical Historical Foundation [*Inactive*] (EA)
EHF .... Electrohydraulic Forming
EHF .... End Half
EHF .... Epidemic Hemorrhagic Fever [*Disease encountered by American troops during the Korean Conflict. The disease was suspected of being caused by the North Koreans in an early use of biological warfare.*]
EHF .... Experimental Husbandry Farm [*British*]
EHF .... Exponential Hazard Function
EHF .... Extremely High Frequency [*Electronics, radio wave*]
EHFA .... Electric Home and Farm Authority [*Terminated, 1947*]
EHFC .... Emmylou Harris Fan Club (EA)
EHG.......... Edinburgh Home Guard [*British military*] (DMA)
EHGG........ Groningen/Eelde [*Netherlands*] [*ICAO location identifier*] (ICLI)
EHGR........ Gilze-Rijen [*Netherlands*] [*ICAO location identifier*] (ICLI)
EHGV........ 'S Gravenhage [*Netherlands*] [*ICAO location identifier*] (ICLI)
EHH .... Ever Heard of Him? [*Facetious criterion for determining insignificance of Supreme Court Justices*] [*Proposed by University of Chicago professor David P. Currie*]
EHHD .... Epeteris tou Kentrou Ereunes tes Historias tou Hellenikou Dikaiou [*A publication*]
EHHO .... Hoogeveen [*Netherlands*] [*ICAO location identifier*] (ICLI)
EHHV .... Hilversum [*Netherlands*] [*ICAO location identifier*] (ICLI)
EHI........... Electronic Height Indicator (MCD)
EHI........... Emergency Homes, Incorporated
EHI........... Employee Health Insurance
EHI........... Environmental Health Institute [*Pittsfield, MA*]
EHIA .... European Herbal Infusions Association (EA)
EHIC .... Emergency Hurricane Information Center [*Marine science*] (MSC)
EHIL .... E-H International, Inc. [*NASDAQ symbol*] (NQ)
Ehime Daigaku Nogaku Kiyo Mem Coll Agric Ehime Univ ... Ehime Daigaku Nogakubu Kiyo. Memoirs of the College of Agriculture. Ehime University [*A publication*]
EHIP .... Employee Health Insurance Plan (DHSM)
EHIS.......... Emission History Information System [*Environmental Information Agency*]
EHIS.......... Encyclopedia of Health Information Sources [*A publication*]
EHJ .... Economisch-Historisch Jaarboek [*A publication*]
EHJIA .... Ehara Jiho [*A publication*]
EHJODF.... European Heart Journal [*A publication*]
E H K........ Eine Heilige Kirche [*A publication*]
EHK.......... Electrode Heater Kit
EHK.......... Ermlaendischer Hauskalender [*A publication*]
EHKD........ De Kooy (Den Helder) [*Netherlands*] [*ICAO location identifier*] (ICLI)
EHKM....... Epeteris Hetaireias Kykladikon Meleton [*A publication*]
Ehkon Neft Prom-St ... Ehkonomika Neftyanoj Promyshlennosti [*A publication*]
Ehksp Khir Anesteziol ... Ehksperimental'naya Khirurgiya i Anesteziologiya [*A publication*]
Ehksp Onkol ... Ehksperimental'naya Onkologiya [*A publication*]
Ehkspress-Inf Lab Tekhnol Issled Obogashch Miner Syr'ya ... Ehkspress-Informatsiya. Laboratornye Tekhnologicheskie Issledovaniya i Obogashchenie Mineral'nogo Syr'ya [*A publication*]
Ehkspress-Inf Montazh Oborudovaniya Tepl Ehlektrostn ... Ehkspress-Informatsiya. Montazh Oborudovaniya na Teplovykh Ehlektrostantsiyakh [*A publication*]
Ehkspress-Inf Neftegazov Geol Geofiz ... Ehkspress-Informatsiya. Neftegazovaya Geologiya i Geofizika [*A publication*]
Ehkspress-Inf Ser Reg Razved Promysl Geofiz ... Ehkspress-Informatsiya. Seriya. Regional'naya. Razvedochnaya i Promyslovaya Geofizika [*A publication*]

Ehkspress-Inf Stroit Tepl Ehlektrostn ... Ehkspress-Informatsiya. Stroitel'stvo Teplovykh Ehlektrostantsij [*A publication*]
Ehkspress-Inf Svar Rab ... Ehkspress-Informatsiya. Svarochnye Raboty [*A publication*]
EHL.......... Eastern Hockey League
EHL.......... Effective Halflife [*Nuclear science*]
EHL.......... El Bolson [*Argentina*] [*Airport symbol*] (OAG)
EHL.......... Elastohydrodynamic Lubrication
EHL.......... Environmental Health Laboratory [*Air Force*]
EHL.......... Extensor Hallucis Longus [*Anatomy*]
EHLD .... Etudes d'Histoire Litteraire et Doctrinale [*A publication*]
EHLE .... Lelystad [*Netherlands*] [*ICAO location identifier*] (ICLI)
Ehlektrofiz Appar ... Ehlektrofizicheskaya Apparatura [*A publication*]
Ehlektrokhim ... Ehlektrokhimiya. Akademiya Nauk SSSR. Ezhemesyachnyj Zhurnal [*A publication*]
Ehlektron Ionnye Protsessy Tverd Telakh ... Ehlektronnye i Ionnye Protsessy v Tverdykh Telakh [*A publication*]
Ehlektron Obrab Mater ... Ehlektronnaya Obrabotka Materialov [*A publication*]
Ehlektrosvyaz' Radiotekh ... Ehlektrosvyaz' i Radiotekhnika [*A publication*]
Ehlektr Stn ... Ehlektricheskie Stantsii [*A publication*]
EHL(K)...... Environmental Health Laboratory, Kelly Air Force Base
EHL-M....... Environmental Health Laboratory, McClellan Air Force Base
EHLS........ Environmental Health Laboratory Sciences Division [*Atlanta, GA*] [*Department of Health and Human Services*] (GRD)
EHLW .... Leeuwarden [*Netherlands*] [*ICAO location identifier*] (ICLI)
EHM.......... Advisory Committee for Earthquake Hazard Mitigation [*Washington, DC*] [*National Science Foundation*] (EGAO)
EHM.......... Cape Newenham [*Alaska*] [*Airport symbol*] (OAG)
EHM.......... Electrohydraulic Motor
EHM.......... Engine Health Monitoring (MCD)
EHM.......... Environmental Hazards Management Institute [*University of New Hampshire*] [*Research center*] (RCD)
EH/M........ Extension Hose/Mouthpiece (MCD)
EHMA .... European Healthcare Management Association (EAIO)
EHMA....... European Hotel Managers Association (EA)
EHMA....... Evangelism and Home Missions Association (EA)
EHMC....... Nieuw Milligen [*Netherlands*] [*ICAO location identifier*] (ICLI)
EHME....... Employee Health Maintenance Examination
EHML....... Nieuw Milligen [*Netherlands*] [*ICAO location identifier*] (ICLI)
EHMO ...... Extended Hueckel Molecular Orbit [*Atomic physics*]
EHMS ...... Electrohydrodynamic Ionization Mass Spectrometry
EHMS ...... Engine Health Monitoring System
EHMZ....... Middelburg/Midden Zeeland [*Netherlands*] [*ICAO location identifier*] (ICLI)
EHN .... End Hunger Network (EA)
EHN .... Environmental Health Network (EA)
EHN .... Environmental Health News [*Database*] [*Occupational Health Services, Inc.*] [*Information service or system*] (CRD)
EHN .... European Host Network [*Data processing*]
EHN .... Exploring Human Nature [*National Science Foundation project*]
EHNA........ Erythro(hydroxynonyl)adenine [*Biochemistry*]
Ehnerg Ehlektrif ... Ehnergetika i Ehlektrifikatsiya [*A publication*]
Ehnerg Stroit ... Ehnergeticheskoe Stroitel'stvo [*A publication*]
Ehnerg Stroit Rubezhom ... Ehnergeticheskoe Stroitel'stvo za Rubezhom [*A publication*]
EHNP........ Edwin I. Hatch Nuclear Plant (NRCH)
EHNP........ Emmeloord/Noord-Oostpolder [*Netherlands*] [*ICAO location identifier*] (ICLI)
Ehntomol Obozr ... Ehntomologicheskoe Obozrenie [*A publication*]
EHO .... Early Hebrew Orthography [*A publication*] (BJA)
EHO .... Environmental Health Officer [*British*] (DCTA)
EHO .... Extrahepatic Obstruction [*Medicine*]
EHO .... Shelby, NC [*Location identifier*] [*FAA*] (FAAL)
EHOG .... European Host Operators Group [*EURONET*] [*Luxembourg*]
EHOT .... External Hydrogen/Oxygen Tank (NASA)
EHP.......... Effective Horsepower
EHP.......... Electric Horsepower
EHP.......... Electrical Hull Penetration
EHP.......... Electron-Hole Potential Method [*Physics*]
EHP.......... Emerald Homes LP [*NYSE symbol*] (SPSG)
EHP.......... Estimated Horsepower
EHP.......... Extra-High Potency
EHP.......... Extra-High Pressure (ROG)
EHP.......... Extrinsic Hyperpolarizing Potential
EHPAC ..... Emergency Health Preparedness Advisory Committee [*Terminated, 1973*] (EA)
EHPF........ European Health Policy Forum (EAIO)
EHPG .... Ethylenebis(hydroxyphenylglycine) [*Organic chemistry*]
EHPh R ..... Etudes d'Histoire et de Philosophie Religieuses [*A publication*]
EHPM .... Electrohydraulic Pulse Motor
EHPM .... European Federation of Associations of Health Product Manufacturers (EAIO)
EHPR .... Etudes d'Histoire et de Philosophie Religieuses [*A publication*]
EHPRG ..... European High Pressure Research Group (EA)
EHPRUS... Etudes d'Histoire et de Philosophie Religieuses. Universite de Strausbourg [*A publication*]

EHR.........	Earned Hour Ratio (NASA)
EHR.........	Economic History Review [*A publication*]
EHR.........	Emergency Heat Removal [*Nuclear energy*] (NRCH)
EHR.........	English Historical Review [*A publication*]
EHR.........	European Human Rights (EAIO)
EHR.........	Europese Documentatie [*A publication*]
EHR.........	Events History Recorder (MCD)
EHR.........	Extra-High Reliability
EHRA......	Endurance Horse Registry of America (EA)
EHRC.......	European Humanities Research Centre [*University of Warwick*] [*British*] (CB)
EHRD.......	Rotterdam [*Netherlands*] [*ICAO location identifier*] (ICLI)
EHRR	European Human Rights Reports [*A publication*]
EHRS	European Histamine Research Society (EAIO)
EHS	Earth Horizon Scanner
EHS	Earth-Lunar Horizon Sensor
EHS	Ecclesiastical History Society (EAIO)
EHS	Electrical Horology Society (EA)
EHS	Elongating Hypocotyl Section [*Botany*]
EHS	Emergency Health Service [*HEW*]
EHS	Emergency Hospital Scheme
EH & S......	Environmental, Health, and Safety
EHS	Environmental Health Service [*US Government*]
EHS	Environmental Health Specialist
EHS	Estonian Educational Society (EA)
EHS	Experimental Horticulture Station [*British*]
EHS	Extra-High Strength [*Steel*] [*Telecommunications*] (TEL)
EHS	Extremely Hazardous Substances
EHSB.......	Soesterberg [*Netherlands*] [*ICAO location identifier*] (ICLI)
EHSDS......	Experimental Health Services Delivery Systems [*HEW*]
EHSE.......	Estudios de Historia Social de Espana [*A publication*]
EHSE.......	Hoeven/Seppe [*Netherlands*] [*ICAO location identifier*] (ICLI)
EHSI........	Electronic Horizontal Situation Indicator
EHSM	Epeteris Hetaireias Stereoelladikon Meleton [*A publication*]
EHSQ	Emergency Health Services Quarterly [*A publication*]
EHSRE2....	Emergency Health Services Review [*A publication*]
EHST.......	Engellireth-Holm Swarm Tumor [*Medicine*]
EHST.......	Stadskanaal [*Netherlands*] [*ICAO location identifier*] (ICLI)
EHT.........	East Hartford, CT [*Location identifier*] [*FAA*] (FAAL)
EHT.........	Effective Hydration Temperature [*Archeology, geology*]
EHT.........	Electrothermal Hydrazine Thruster
EHT.........	Extra-High Tension
EHTD.......	Equivalent Heat Transfer Dimensionality [*Process engineering*]
EHTE	Deventer/Teuge [*Netherlands*] [*ICAO location identifier*] (ICLI)
EHTED	Energie Alternative [*A publication*]
EHTR	Emergency Highway Traffic Regulation [*Federal disaster planning*]
EHTRC	Emergency Highway Traffic Regulation Center [*Federal disaster planning*] (AABC)
EHTW	Enschede/Twenthe [*Netherlands*] [*ICAO location identifier*] (ICLI)
EHTX	Texel [*Netherlands*] [*ICAO location identifier*] (ICLI)
EHU	Economie et Humanisme [*A publication*]
EHU	Electric Heating Unit
e-hu---	Hungary [*MARC geographic area code*] [*Library of Congress*] (LCCP)
EHV.........	El Hato [*Venezuela*] [*Seismograph station code, US Geological Survey*] (SEIS)
EHV.........	Electric Heart Vector [*Cardiology*]
EHV.........	Electric and Hybrid Vehicles
EHV.........	Electrohydraulic Valve (MCD)
EHV.........	Equine Herpes Virus
EHV.........	Extra-High Voltage [*FPC*]
EHVB	Valkenburg [*Netherlands*] [*ICAO location identifier*] (ICLI)
EHVK.......	Volkel [*Netherlands*] [*ICAO location identifier*] (ICLI)
EHW........	Extreme High Water
EHWO	Woensdrecht [*Netherlands*] [*ICAO location identifier*] (ICLI)
EHWS	Electric Hot Water Service [*Classified advertising*] (ADA)
EHX.........	Experiment Dedicated Heat Exchanger (MCD)
EHY.........	Engage High Yield
E Hy..........	Weichardts Ergebnisse der Hygiene, Bakterien-, Immunitaetsforschung, und Experimentellen Therapie [*A publication*]
EHYB	Ypenburg [*Netherlands*] [*ICAO location identifier*] (ICLI)
EI	Aer Lingus Teoranta [*Ireland*] [*ICAO designator*] (FAAC)
EI	Early Iron Age [*Archeology*] (BJA)
EI	Earned Income
E/I.............	Earned Premium to Incurred Loss Ratio [*Insurance*]
EI	East India (ROG)
EI	East Indies
EI	Eat-In [*Kitchen*] [*Classified advertising*]
EI	Economia Internazionale [*A publication*]
EI	Ecumenical Institute [*World Council of Churches*] (EA)
EI	Education Index [*A publication*]
EI	Educationally Impaired
EI	Effectiveness Index (MCD)
EI	Eisenhower Institute (EA)
EI	Elderhostel, Inc. (EA)
EI	Electrical Insulation (MCD)
EI	Electrolyte Imbalance [*Physiology*]

EI	Electromagnetic Interference
EI	Electron Impact [*Mass spectrometry*]
EI	Electron Ionization [*Spectrometry*]
EI	Electronic Ignition [*Automotive engineering*]
EI	Electronic Imaging Conference and Exposition (ITD)
EI	Electronic Installation
EI	Electronic Instruction (MCD)
EI	Electronic Interface (MCD)
EI	Electronic Interference
EI	Elet es Irodalom [*A publication*]
EI	Eligible Individual [*Social Security Administration*]
EI	Elmwood Institute (EA)
EI	Emaus Internacional [*Emmaus International*] (EA)
EI	Emergency Injection [*Nuclear energy*] (NRCH)
EI	Emergency International (EA)
EI	Emigrant Institute [*Sweden*]
EI	Emission Index
EI	Emotionally Impaired
EI	Empathy Inventory [*Teacher evaluation test*]
EI	Enciclopedia Italiana [*A publication*]
EI	Encyclopaedia of Islam [*A publication*]
EI	Encyclopedie de l'Islam [*A publication*]
EI	End Injection (IEEE)
EI	End Item
EI	Endevco, Incorporated [*AMEX symbol*] (SPSG)
E/I.............	Endorsement Irregular [*Banking*]
EI	Enemy Intelligence
Ei..............	Engineering Index [*A publication*]
Ei..............	Engineering Information [*An association*] [*Also, an information service or system*] (EA)
E-I	Engineering-Installation (AFM)
EI	Engineering Instruction
EI	Engineering Investigation (MCD)
EI	English Illustrated Magazine [*A publication*]
EI	English Institute (EA)
E & I..........	English and Irish Appeals, House of Lords [*A publication*] (DLA)
EI	Entayant Institute (EA)
EI	Entry Interface (NASA)
EI	Entsiklopedyah 'Ivrit [*or Enziklopedyah 'Ivrit*] (BJA)
EI	Environmental Impact (NASA)
EI	Environmentally Ill [*Medicine*]
EI	Enzyme Inhibitor [*Biochemistry*]
EI	Epigraphia Indica [*A publication*]
EI	Epilepsy International (EAIO)
E & I..........	Equip and Install (MSA)
EI	Equipment Item (MCD)
EI	Eretz - Israel [*A publication*]
EI	Error Indicator [*Data processing*]
EI	Esalen Institute (EA)
EI	Essential Information [*An association*] (EA)
EI	Establishment Inspection [*Federal government*]
EI	Estudios Ibericos [*A publication*]
EI	Estudios Italianos [*A publication*]
EI	Ethyleneimine [*Organic chemistry*]
EI	Etudes Irlandaises [*A publication*]
EI	Etudes Italiennes [*A publication*]
EI	Evaluation Instrumentation (AAG)
EI	Ex-Interest [*Without the right to interest*] [*Finance*]
EI	Exact Interest [*Banking*]
EI	Exaltation of Inanna [*A publication*] (BJA)
E & I..........	Examination and Inventory (AFIT)
EI	Excerpta Indonesica [*A publication*]
EI	Excessively Included [*Colored gemstone grade*]
EI	Executive Instruments [*Ghana*] [*A publication*] (DLA)
EI	Existential Instantiation [*Rule of quantification*] [*Logic*]
E/I.............	Expiration-Inspiration [*Ratio*] [*Physiology*]
EI	Exponential Integral
EI	Exposure Index [*Photography*]
EI	Extensions for Independence [*An association*] (EA)
EI	Extra-Illustrated
E-I	Extraversion-Introversion [*Psychology*]
ei----	Iberian Peninsula [*MARC geographic area code*] [*Library of Congress*] (LCCP)
EI	Ireland [*Aircraft nationality and registration mark*] (FAAC)
EI	Journal of Professional Issues in Engineering [*A publication*]
EI	L'Educatore Israelita [*A publication*]
EI	L'Egypte Industrielle [*Cairo*] [*A publication*]
EIA	Early Iron Age [*Archeology*]
EIA	Economic Impact Assessment
EIA	Education Improvement Act of 1984
EIA	Education Industries Association [*Later, NSSEA*] (EA)
EIA	Electroimmunoassay [*Clinical medicine*]
EIA	Electronic Industries Association [*Formerly, RETMA*] (EA)
EIA	End Item Application (MCD)
EIA	Energy Independence Authority
EIA	Energy Information Administration [*Department of Energy*] (IID)
EIA	Engineering Industries Association [*London, England*] (EAIO)
EIA	Engineering Inspectors' Association [*A union*] [*British*]
EiA...........	English in Action (EA)

EIA .... Envelope Institute of America
EIA .... Environment Information Abstracts [*A publication*]
EIA .... Environmental Impact Assessment [*Environmental Protection Agency*]   (MCD)
EIA .... Environmental Protection Agency, Region II Library, New York, NY [*OCLC symbol*]   (OCLC)
EIA .... Enzyme-Linked Immunosorbent Assay [*Clinical chemistry*]
EIA .... Equine Infectious Anemia
EIA .... Equipment Interchange Association   (EA)
EIA .... Estudos Ibero-Americanos [*A publication*]
EIA .... Eucalyptus Improvement Association   (EA)
EIA .... Euskal Iraultzako Alderdia [*Basque Revolutionary Party*]   (PPW)
EIA .... Exercise-Induced Anaphylaxis [*Medicine*]
EIA .... Exercise-Induced Asthma [*Medicine*]
EIAA .... Shannon/Ballygirreen [*Ireland*] [*ICAO location identifier*]   (ICLI)
EIAC........ Ecological Information and Analysis Center
EIAC........ Electronic Industries Association of Canada
EIAC........ Energy Information Administration Clearinghouse
EIAC........ Environmental Information Analysis Center [*Battelle Memorial Institute*]   (IID)
EIAC........ Ergonomics Information Analysis Centre [*University of Birmingham*] [*British*]   (CB)
EIAD .... End Item Allocation Document   (AAG)
EIAEA ...... Equipement Industriel. Achats et Entretien [*A publication*]
EIA/EIS ... Environmental Impact Assessment/Environmental Impact Statement
EIA/EPUB ... Energy Information Administration Electronic Publication System [*Database*] [*Department of Energy*] [*Information service or system*]   (CRD)
EIA-J .... Electronic Industries Association - Japan
EIALC ...... Environmental Impact Assessment for Life Cycle [*Army*]
EIAP.......... Environmental Impact Analysis Program [*or Project*] [*Department of the Interior*]   (GRD)
E & I App... Law Reports, House of Lords, English and Irish Appeals [*1866-75*] [*A publication*]   (DLA)
EIA Publ New Releases ... EIA [*Electronics Industries Association*] Publications. New Releases [*United States*] [*A publication*]
EIASA .... Energia e Industrias Aragonesas Sociedad Anonima [*Spain*]
EIASM ...... European Institute for Advanced Studies in Management [*Information service or system*]   (IID)
EIASN ...... End Item Assembly Sequence Number   (NASA)
EIAV.......... Early Intervention Association of Victoria [*Australia*]
EIAV.......... Equine Infectious Anemia Virus
EIB............ Earthquake Information Bulletin [*A publication*]
EIB............ Economic Impact Budget
EIB............ Edinboro State College, Edinboro, PA [*OCLC symbol*]   (OCLC)
EIB............ Educational/Instructional Broadcasting [*A publication*]
EIB............ Egyptian International Bank   (IMH)
EIB............ Eigen Huis en Interieur [*A publication*]
EIB............ Electrical Interface Building [*NASA*]   (KSC)
EIB............ Electronic Information Bulletin [*Navy*]
EIB............ Electronics Information Branch [*Navy*]   (MCD)
EIB............ Electronics Installation Bulletin
EIB............ Engineering Instruction Bulletin   (KSC)
EIB............ European Investment Bank
EIB............ Exercise-Induced Bronchiospasm [*Medicine*]
EIB............ Expert Infantryman Badge [*Military decoration*]
E-IB .... Export-Import Bank
EIB............ External Intelligence Bureau   (MCD)
EIBA.......... Ethylene-(Isobutyl Acrylate) [*Organic chemistry*]
EIBA.......... European International Business Association [*Brussels, Belgium*]   (EA)
EIBAD....... Expert Infantryman Badge [*Military decoration*]
EIBUS .... Export-Import Bank of the United States [*Formerly, EIB(W)*]
EIB(W)...... Export-Import Bank (of Washington) [*Later, EIBUS*]
EIC............ Earned Income Credit
EIC............ Earth Inductor Compass
EIC............ Earth-Ionosphere Cavity
EIC............ East India Company [*1600-1858*] [*British*]
EIC............ Easter Island [*Seismograph station code, US Geological Survey*]   (SEIS)
EIC............ Easter Island Committee   (EA)
EIC............ Education Information Center [*Georgia State Department of Education*] [*Information service or system*]   (IID)
EIC............ Educational Information Center [*Office of Education*]
EIC............ Elastase Inhibitory Capacity [*Physiology*]
EIC............ Electrical Insulation Conference [*Later, EEIC*]   (MCD)
EIC............ Electrically Insulated Coating
EIC............ Electron Ionization Cross Section
EIC............ Electrostatic Ion Cyclotron [*Seismology*]
EIC............ Embar Information Consultants [*Information service or system*]   (IID)
EIC............ Emplaced Instrument Complex [*Aerospace*]
EIC............ Employer Identification Code   (AABC)
EIC............ Employment and Immigration Canada Library [*UTLAS symbol*]
EIC............ Enamel Insulating Compound
EIC............ End Item Contract
EIC............ Energy Industries Council [*United Kingdom*]   (DS)

EIC............ Energy Information Center [*Battelle Memorial Institute*]   (IID)
EIC............ Engineer-in-Charge
EIC............ Engineering Information Center
EIC............ Engineering Installation Center [*Military*]
EIC............ Engineering Institute of Canada
EIC............ Entertainment Industries Council   (EA)
EIC............ Environment Information Center, Inc. [*Database producer*]
EIC............ Environmental Industry Council   (EA)
EIC............ Environmental Protection Agency, Region II Field Office, Edison, NJ [*OCLC symbol*]   (OCLC)
EIC............ Enzyme Immunochromatography
EIC............ Ephemerides Iuris Canonici [*A publication*]
EIC............ Equipment Identification Code
EIC............ Equipment Installation and Checkout   (MUGU)
EIC............ Equipment Interstage Container
EIC............ Essays in Criticism [*A publication*]
EIC............ European Independents Confederation   (EAIO)
EIC............ European Insurance Committee [*Paris, France*]   (EA)
EIC............ Exercise Intelligence Center [*Military*]   (CINC)
EIC............ Exhibitors in Cable [*An association*]   (EA)
EIC............ Experiment Integration Center   (MCD)
EIC............ Experimental Intercom   (NASA)
e-ic---.......... Iceland [*MARC geographic area code*] [*Library of Congress*]   (LCCP)
EICA.......... Experimental Integrated Conformed Array
EICAS .... Engine Indication and Crew Alerting System   (MCD)
EICBL ...... Eastern Independent Collegiate Basketball League
EICC.......... Echuca Inspectorate Camp Committee [*Education Department*] [*Victoria, Australia*]
EICC.......... Emergency Information and Coordination Center [*Federal Emergency Management Agency*]
EICDT ...... Ego-Ideal and Conscience Development Test [*Personality development test*] [*Psychology*]
EICG.......... Electromagnetic Interference Control Group   (AAG)
Eich O........ Eichordnung [*A publication*]
Eichsfelder Heimath ... Eichsfelder Heimathefte [*A publication*]
Eichstaedter Bienenztg ... Eichstaedter Bienenzeitung [*A publication*]
EICK.......... Cork [*Ireland*] [*ICAO location identifier*]   (ICLI)
Eickhogg-Mitt ... Eickhogg-Mitteilungen [*West Germany*] [*A publication*]
EICM.......... Employer's Inventory of Critical Manpower
EICMS........ Engine In-Flight Condition Monitoring System   (MCD)
EIC-NE...... Educational Improvement Center - Northeast [*Information service or system*]
EIC Ne...... EIC [*Engineering Institute of Canada*] News [*A publication*]
EI CO........ East India Company [*1600-1858*] [*British*]   (ROG)
EICS .... East India Civil Service [*British*]   (ROG)
EICS .... East India Company's Service [*British*]
EICS .... Electromagnetic Intelligence Collection System
EICS .... Environmental Impact Computer System [*Database*] [*Army Corps of Engineers*]
EIC Trans ... EIC [*Engineering Institute of Canada*] Transactions [*A publication*]
EICW.......... Electrostatic Ion Cyclotron Waves [*Seismology*]
EID .... East India Dock
EID .... Economic and Industrial Democracy [*A publication*]
EID .... Egg-Infective Dose [*Clinical chemistry*]
EID .... Eider Resources Minieres, Inc. [*Toronto Stock Exchange symbol*]
Eid............ Eidos. A Journal of Painting, Sculpture, and Design [*A publication*]
EID .... Electromagnetic Impulse Deicing [*System under development by NASA*]
EID .... Electron Impact [*or Induced*] Desorption
EID .... Electronic Instrument Digest [*A publication*]
EID .... Electronic Intrusion Detection
EID .... Embryo Infective Dose
EID .... Emergency Infusion Device [*Medicine*]
EID .... Emitter Identification   (MCD)
EID .... End Item Delivery   (AAG)
EID .... End Item Description   (AAG)
EID .... End Item Designators
EID .... End Item Documentation   (MCD)
E-ID .... Energy-Information Database [*International Research and Evaluation*] [*Information service or system*]   (CRD)
EID .... Engineering Item Description   (AAG)
EID .... Environmental Information Division [*Air Force Air Training Command*]   (IID)
EID .... Equipment Interface Document   (CAAL)
EID .... Eugenic Insemination by Donor
EID .... Export Insurance Division [*of the Ministry of International Trade and Industry*] [*Japan*]
EID .... Research Laboratory for Equine Infectious Diseases [*Cornell University*] [*Research center*]   (RCD)
EIDAA....... Electrical India [*A publication*]
EIDAP....... Emitter Isolated Difference Amplifier Paralleling [*Bell System*]
EIDB.......... Dublin [*Ireland*] [*ICAO location identifier*]   (ICLI)
EIDC.......... East Indian Defence Committee
EIDCT ...... Educational Institute of Design, Craft, and Technology [*British*]
EIDD .... Experiment Interface Definition Document   (MCD)
EIDED....... Escuela Interamericana de Educacion Democratica

Eidg Anst Forstl Versuchswes Mitt ... Eidgenoessische Anstalt fuer das Forstliche Versuchswesen. Mitteilungen [*A publication*]

Eidge Tech Hochsch Versuchsans Wasserbau Erdbau Mitt Zurich ... Eidgenoessische Technische Hochschule. Versuchsanstalt fuer Wasserbau und Erdbau. Mitteilungen (Zurich) [*A publication*]

Eidg Tech Hochsch Versuchsanst Wasserbau Erdbau Mitt ... Eidgenoessische Technische Hochschule. Versuchsanstalt fuer Wasserbau und Erdbau. Mitteilungen (Zurich) [*A publication*]

Eidikai Meletai Geol Ellados ... Eidikai Meletai Edi tes Geologias tes Ellados [*A publication*]

EIDL.......... Economic Injury Disaster Loan [*Small Business Administration*]

EIDLT .... Emergency Identification Light [*Aerospace*] (AAG)

EIDOS....... Electronic Information Delivery Online System [*Information retrieval*]

EIDP.......... Ecumenical Institute for the Development of Peoples (EAIO)

EIDP.......... End Item Data Package (NASA)

EIDS.......... Electronic Information Delivery System [*Individual learning center equipped with head sets and video monitors*]

EIDS.......... Equipment Integration Design Section

EIDSO....... Engineer Information and Data Systems Office [*Army*] (AABC)

EIDW .... Dublin [*Ireland*] [*ICAO location identifier*] (ICLI)

EIE............. Economia Industrial [*A publication*]

EIE............. Electronic Information Exchange [*National Message Center, Inc.*] [*Overland Park, KS*] [*Telecommunications service*] (TSSD)

EIE............. End Item Equipment

EIE............. English Institute. Essays [*A publication*]

e-ie---.......... Ireland [*MARC geographic area code*] [*Library of Congress*] (LCCP)

EIEAD....... Elektrowaerme International. Edition A. Elektrowaerme im Technischen Ausbau [*A publication*]

EIE-AF ...... Experienced International Executive - Air Forwarding [*Designation awarded by American Society of International Executives, Inc.*]

EIEB.......... Experienced International Executive - Banking [*Designation awarded by American Society of International Executives, Inc.*]

EIEBD .... Elektrowaerme International. Edition B. Industrielle Elektrowaerme [*A publication*]

EIEC.......... Emergency Incident of Environmental Contamination [*Environmental Protection Agency*]

EIEC.......... English Industrial Estates Corporation

EIEC.......... European Institute of Ecology and Cancer [*Formerly, European Institute of Cancerology*] (EA)

EIE-C......... Experienced International Executive - Credit [*Designation awarded by American Society of International Executives, Inc.*]

EIED.......... Electrically Initiated Explosive Device

EIE-EM..... Experienced International Executive - Export Management [*Designation awarded by American Society of International Executives, Inc.*]

EIE-F......... Experienced International Executive - Forwarding [*Designation awarded by American Society of International Executives, Inc.*]

EIEM........ Environmental Interference Effects Model (MCD)

EIE-M .... Experienced International Executive - Marketing [*Designation awarded by American Society of International Executives, Inc.*]

EIES .... Electron Impact Emission Spectroscopy [*Photovoltaic energy systems*]

EIES .... Electronic Information Exchange System [*Pronounced "eyes"*] [*New Jersey Institute of Technology*] [*Computer network*] [*Telecommunications*]

EIE-TM..... Experienced International Executive - Traffic Management [*Designation awarded by American Society of International Executives, Inc.*]

EIF............ Electrochemical Industries (Frutarom) Ltd. [*AMEX symbol*] (SPSG)

EIF............. Electronic Industries Foundation (EA)

EIF............. Erythema-Inducing Factor [*Hematology*]

EIF............. Erythrocyte Initiation Factor

EIF............. Executive Inventory File [*Civil Service Commission*]

EIF............. Pittsfield, MA [*Location identifier*] [*FAA*] (FAAL)

EIFA.......... Element Interface Functional Analysis (NASA)

EIFAC .... European Inland Fisheries Advisory Commission [*UN Food and Agriculture Organization*] [*Italy*]

EIFAC Occas Pap ... EIFAC [*European Inland Fisheries Advisory Commission*] Occasional Paper [*A publication*]

EIFAC Tech Pap ... EIFAC [*European Inland Fisheries Advisory Commission*] Technical Paper [*A publication*]

EIFDC .... Eterna International Foundation for Disabled Children (EA)

EIFEB....... Economia Internazionale delle Fonti di Energia [*A publication*]

EIFF .... Enemy Identification Friend or Foe

Eif Jud Act ... Eiffe on the Irish Judicature Act [*A publication*] (DLA)

EIFOV....... Effective Instantaneous Field of View

EIFPA2...... EIFAC [*European Inland Fisheries Advisory Commission*] Technical Paper [*A publication*]

EIFS.......... Economic Impact Forecast System [*Army*] (RDA)

EIFS.......... Exterior Insulation and Finish System [*Sto Industries*]

Eig............. Eigse [*A publication*]

EIG .... Electronic Image Generator

EIG .... Elephant Interest Group (EA)

EIG .... Emitter Identification Guide (NG)

EIG .... Exchange Information Group (NATG)

EIG .... Voltage Inner Gimbal

EIGA .... Ethics in Government Act

Eight Century Curr Bibliogr ... Eighteenth Century: a Current Bibliography [*A publication*]

Eight Ct...... Eighteenth Century. Theory and Interpretation [*A publication*]

Eight-Ct L ... Eighteenth-Century Life [*A publication*]

Eight-Ct St ... Eighteenth-Century Studies [*A publication*]

Eighteenth Cent Life ... Eighteenth-Century Life [*A publication*]

Eighteenth-Cent Stud ... Eighteenth-Century Studies [*A publication*]

EIGL .... Eastern Intercollegiate Gymnastic League (EA)

EIGM .... Gormanston County Meath [*Ireland*] [*ICAO location identifier*] (ICLI)

Eigo S........ Eigo Seinen [*A publication*]

EIGR.......... Empire Insurance Co. [*NASDAQ symbol*] (NQ)

EIH .... East India House (ROG)

EIHC.......... Essex Institute. Historical Collections [*A publication*]

EIHCA7 .... Essex Institute. Historical Collections [*A publication*]

Eih Pbl....... Eichstaetter Pastoralblatt [*A publication*]

EIHR.......... Eisenhower Institute for Historical Research [*Smithsonian Institution*]

EIHSW...... European Institute of Hunting and Sporting Weapons (EAIO)

EII .... E-II Holdings [*NYSE symbol*] (SPSG)

EII .... Earth Island Institute (EA)

EII .... Electronically Invisible Interconnect [*Data processing*]

EII .... Encoded Item Identifier (CAAL)

EII .... Engineering Item Identification

EII .... Equity in Industry [*Australia*]

EII .... Ethnic Identification Index (BJA)

EIIA.......... European Information Industry Association [*Database producer*] (EISS)

EIIS .... Energy Industry Information System (IEEE)

EIIV .... Electronics Interface Integrated Validation (KSC)

EIJID........ Ebara Infiruko Jiho [*A publication*]

EIK............ Eat-In Kitchen [*Classified advertising*]

EIK............ Elektronische Informationsverarbeitung und Kybernetik [*A publication*]

EIKN .... Connaught Regional Airport [*Ireland*] [*ICAO location identifier*] (ICLI)

EIKON ...... Gesellschaft der Freunde der Ikonenkunst (EAIO)

EIL............ Echo de l'Industrie. Revue Luxembourgeoise de la Vie Economique et Sociale [*A publication*]

EIL............ Egyptian International Line (DS)

EIL............ Eilat [*Israel*] [*Seismograph station code, US Geological Survey*] (SEIS)

EIL............ Electron Injection LASER

EIL............ Electronic Instruments Limited [*as in EIL electrode, used in biochemistry*] [*British*]

EIL............ Environmental Impairment Liability

EIL............ Essays on International Law [*A publication*] (ILCA)

EIL............ Essays in Literature [*A publication*]

EIL............ Event Index Log [*NASA*] (KSC)

EIL............ Experiment in International Living/School for International Training (EA)

EIL............ Explosive Investigative Laboratory [*Navy*]

EiL............ Ezik i Literatura [*A publication*]

EIL............ Fairbanks, AK [*Location identifier*] [*FAA*] (FAAL)

EILI .... EIL Instruments, Inc. [*NASDAQ symbol*] (NQ)

Eil Wom..... Eiloart's Laws Relating to Women [*1878*] [*A publication*] (DLA)

EIM .... Elastomeric Insulation Material

EIM .... Electronic Imaging in Medicine [*Computer graphics*]

EIM .... Elite Insurance Management Ltd. [*Toronto Stock Exchange symbol*] [*Vancouver Stock Exchange symbol*]

EIM .... End Item Manager (AFIT)

EIM .... Engine Inventory Manager [*Air Force*] (AFIT)

EIM .... European Institute for the Media (EA)

EIM .... European Interactive Media [*Joint venture of Philips International and PolyGram BV International*]

EIM .... Excitability-Inducing Material [*Biochemistry*]

EIM .... Explosives Investigation Memorandum [*Navy*] (MCD)

EIM .... Eyelet-Installing Machine

EIMA .... Exterior Insulation Manufacturers Association (EA)

EIMB......... Electronics Installation and Maintenance Bulletin

EIMC......... English Institute Materials Center

EIME......... Electronic Instrument Manufacturers Exhibit (MUGU)

EIME......... Mhic Easmuinn Baldonnel, County Dublin [*Ireland*] [*ICAO location identifier*] (ICLI)

EIMF......... End Item Maintenance Form

EIMKH ..... Ergebnisse der Inneren Medizin und Kinderheilkunde [*A publication*]

EIMOB...... Ekspress-Informatsiya. Montazh Oborudovaniya na Teplovykh Elektrostantsiyakh [*A publication*]

EIMR........ Equipment Item Material Requirements

EIMS......... Electron Ionization Mass Spectrometry

EIMS......... End Item Maintenance Sheets (MCD)

EIMS......... Engineering Installation Management System [*Air Force*] (CET)
EIMS......... Environmental Information Management System
EIMTS ..... End Item Maintenance Transmittal Sheet
EIN .... Educational Information Network [*Princeton, NJ*]
EIN .... Eindhoven [*Netherlands*] [*Airport symbol*] (OAG)
EIN .... Employer Identification Number [*IRS*]
EIN .... Engineer Intelligence Note
EIN .... Equipment Installation Notice (AAG)
EIN .... Eulerian Iterative Nonsteady [*Method*] [*Mathematics*]
EIN .... Europa Informatie, Buitenlandse Betrekkingen [*A publication*]
EIN .... European Information Network [*Telecommunications*] (TEL)
EIN .... Excitatory Interneuron [*Neurophysiology*]
EIN .... Experimental Integrated Network
EIN .... External Interlace
EinA........... English in Africa [*A publication*]
E Ind .... East Indies
EINDA ...... Electrified Industry [*A publication*]
EINECS .... European Inventory of Existing Commercial Chemical Substances [*Which will be exempt from new product regulations*]
Einfuehr Molekularbiol ... Einfuehrungen zur Molekularbiologie [*A publication*]
Einfuehrungen Molekularbiol ... Einfuehrungen zur Molekularbiologie [*A publication*]
Einfuehrung Molekularbiol ... Einfuehrungen zur Molekularbiologie [*A publication*]
Einh .... Einheit. Theoretische Zeitschrift des Wissenschaftlichen Sozialismus [*A publication*]
EINIS .... European Integrated Network of Image and Services (EAIO)
EINN .... Shannon [*Ireland*] [*ICAO location identifier*] (ICLI)
E INS .... Engineer Inspector [*Navy*] [*British*] (ROG)
EINS.......... Etudes/Inuit/Studies [*A publication*]
EINSD....... Eau et l'Industrie [*A publication*]
Einspr......... Einspruch [*Objection, Opposition, Caveat*] [*German*] (ILCA)
Einstein QJ Biol Med ... Einstein Quarterly Journal of Biology and Medicine [*A publication*]
E Int .... Equal Interval [*Isophase navigation light*]
Einzelv .... Einzelveroeffentlichungen des Seewetteramtes [*A publication*]
EIO .... Electric Induction Oven
EIO .... Emergency Information Officer [*Civil Defense*]
EIOBL....... Equipment Item Out of Balance (AFIT)
EIOC .... Early Initial Operational Capability (MCD)
EIOC .... Equivalent Input Offset Current
EIOD .... Equivalent Instruction or Duty
EIOI........... Expedition Internationale de l'Ocean Indien [*International Indian Ocean Expedition - IIOE*] [*French*] (MSC)
EIO-IMS... Early Initial Operational-Information Management System (MCD)
EIOPAD... EIFAC [*European Inland Fisheries Advisory Commission*] Occasional Paper [*A publication*]
EIOV .... Equivalent Input Offset Voltage
EIP .... Association Mondiale pour l'Ecole Instrument de Paix [*World Association for the School as an Instrument of Peace*] [*Geneva, Switzerland*] (EAIO)
EIP............. Economic Inventory Policy
EIP............. Economic Inventory Procedures [*Army*] (AABC)
EIP............. Educational Incentive Plan [*Red Cross*]
EIP............. Electronic Installation Plan (NG)
EIP............. Emergency Implementation Procedure (NRCH)
EIP............. Emitter Identification Program [*RADAR*] (MCD)
EIP............. Employment Initiatives Program [*Australia*]
EIP............. End-Inspiratory Pause [*Respiration*]
EIP............. End Item Parameter
EIP............. Engineering Installation Plan (CET)
EIP............. Equipment Installation Procedure [*Telecommunications*] (TEL)
EIP............. Equipment in Place (MCD)
EIP............. ERA [*Equal Rights Amendment*] Impact Project (EA)
EIP............. Estudos Italianos em Portugal [*A publication*]
EIP............. Ethylene Interpolymer Alloy
EIP............. Exoatmospheric Interceptor Propulsion (MCD)
EIP............. Experiment Implementation Plan [*NASA*]
EIP............. Extensor Indicis Proprius [*Anatomy*]
EIPA.......... Ethyl(isopropyl)amiloride [*Organic chemistry*]
EIPA.......... Ethylisopropylaniline [*Organic chemistry*]
EIPA.......... European Institute of Public Administration (EA)
EIPC.......... European Institute of Printed Circuits (EA)
EIPGA .... Ekspress-Informatsiya. Seriya: Regional'naya, Razvedochnaya, i Promyslovaya Geofizika [*A publication*]
EIPH .... Exercise-Induced Pulmonary Hemorrhage [*Veterinary medicine*]
EIPM.......... EIP Microwave, Inc. [*NASDAQ symbol*] (NQ)
EIPS .... Endogenous Inhibitor of Prostaglandin Synthase [*Biochemistry*]
EIPT .... Electronic Industry Production and Test Equipment (IMH)
EIR............. East Indian Railway
Eir .... Eirene. Studia Graeca et Latina [*A publication*]
EIR............. Either (ROG)
EIR............. Electron-Ion Recombination
EIR............. Emerald Isle Resources, Inc. [*Vancouver Stock Exchange symbol*]

EIR............. Emergency Information Readiness [*Civil Defense*]
EIR............. Employee Incident Report (MCD)
EIR............. End Item Requirement (AAG)
EIR............. Energy Information Resource (MCD)
EIR............. Engineering Information Report [*Telecommunications*] (TEL)
EIR............. Engineering Information Request [*Nuclear energy*] (NRCH)
EIR............. Engineering Investigation Request
EIR............. Environmental Impact Report [*Environmental Protection Agency*]
EIR............. Environmental Impact Review
EIR............. Equipment Improvement Recommendations [*Military*]
EIR............. Equipment Improvement Report [*DoD*]
EIR............. Equipment Inoperable Record [*Nuclear energy*] (NRCH)
EIR............. Equipment Installation Record (MCD)
EIR............. Establishment Inspection Report [*Federal government*]
EIR............. European Industrial Relations Review [*A publication*]
Eir .... Lambard's Eirenarcha [*A publication*] (DLA)
EIRAC........ Entertainment Industry Referral and Assistance Center (EA)
EIR-Ber ..... Eidgenoessisches Institut fuer Reaktorforschung. Bericht [*A publication*]
EIR-Ber (Wuerenlingen) ... EIR-[*Eidgenoessisches Institut fuer Reaktorforschung*] Bericht (Wuerenlingen) [*A publication*]
EIRC.......... Exploration in Renaissance Culture [*A publication*]
EIRD.......... Economics Information Resources Directory [*A publication*]
EIRD.......... Engineering Information Report Date [*Telecommunications*] (TEL)
EIRD.......... Engineering Instrumentation Requirements Document
EIRD.......... Experiment Integration Requirements Document [*NASA*]
Eire .... Ireland. A Journal of Irish Studies [*A publication*]
EIRI........... Early Intervention Research Institute [*Utah State University*] [*Research center*] (RCD)
EIRI........... Energy Information Resources Inventory [*Database*] [*Department of Energy*] [*Information service or system*] (CRD)
EIRIS......... Ethical Investment Research Service [*London, England*] [*Information service or system*]
EIRJa .... Etimologiceskie Issledovanija po Russkomu Jazyku [*A publication*]
EIRMA...... European Industrial Research Management Association [*France*]
EIRP.......... Effective Instantaneous [*or Isotropic*] Radiated Power [*Telecommunications*]
EIRP.......... Equivalent Isotropically Radiated Power [*Microwave transmission*]
EIRR.......... European Industrial Relations Review [*A publication*]
EIRS.......... Engineering and Industrial Research Station [*Mississippi State University*] [*Research center*] (RCD)
EIRS.......... Ethical Investment Research Service [*London, England*] [*Information service or system*] (IID)
EIRT.......... Executive Independent Review Team (MCD)
EIRU .... Early Intervention Resource Unit [*Victoria, Australia*]
EIS............. Digest of Environmental Impact Statements [*A publication*]
EIS............. Economic Information System [*International Monetary Fund*] [*Information service or system*] (IID)
EIS............. Educational Institute of Scotland
EIS............. Effluent Inventory System [*Nuclear energy*] (NRCH)
EIS............. Electrical and Instrument Shop (NRCH)
EIS............. Electrical Integration System (NASA)
EIS............. Electromagnetic Intelligence System
EIS............. Electronet Information Systems, Inc. [*Information service or system*] (IID)
EIS............. Electronic Imaging System [*Computer graphics*]
EIS............. Electronic Information Series [*Information service or system*] (IID)
EIS............. Electronic Information Services [*Industry*] (IT)
EIS............. Emergency Information System [*Software package*] [*Research Alternatives, Inc.*]
EIS............. Emergency Injection System [*Nuclear energy*] (NRCH)
EIS............. Employee Information System (MCD)
EIS............. End Interruption Sequence [*Data processing*]
EIS............. End Item Specification (AAG)
EIS............. Engineering Information System (MCD)
EIS............. Entered in Service [*Military*]
EIS............. Environmental Impact Statement [*Environmental Protection Agency*]
EIS............. Environmental Impact Study
EIS............. Environmental Information System [*National Science Foundation*]
EIS............. Epidemic Intelligence Service [*of the Centers for Disease Control*]
EIS............. Epidemiology Information System [*Database*] [*Oak Ridge National Laboratory*] [*Information service or system*] (CRD)
EIS............. Excelsior Income Shares, Inc. [*NYSE symbol*] (SPSG)
EIS............. Executive Information Service [*or Software or System*]
EIS............. Executive Information Software
EIS............. Expanded Inband Signaling [*Telecommunications*] (TEL)
EIS............. Expendable Instrument System
EIS............. Experiment Information System
EIS............. Export Inspection Service [*Australia*]
EIS............. Export Intelligence Service (DS)

EIS.............	Extended Instruction Set [*Honeywell, Inc.*]
EIS.............	Eyes in the Sky
EIS.............	Tortola [*British Virgin Islands*] [*Airport symbol*] (OAG)
EISA..........	EEG Aperiodic-Interval Spectrum Analysis [*Neurology*]
EISA..........	European Independent Steelworks Association (EAIO)
EISA..........	Extended Industry Standard Architecture [*Data processing*]
EISB	Electrical Industry Study Board (EA)
EISC	Eastern Illinois State College [*Later, EIU*]
EISC	Electronic Industry Show Corporation (EA)
EISC	Entertainment Industry Support Committee (EA)
EISCAT....	European Incoherent Scattering Scientific Association
EISD..........	Engineering and Industrial Software Directory [*Engineering Information, Inc.*] [*Information service or system*] (CRD)
Eisei Dobutsu/Jap J Sanit Zool ... Eisei Dobutsu/Japanese Journal of Sanitary Zoology [*A publication*]
Eisei Shikenjo Hokoku/Bull Nat Inst Hyg Sci ... Eisei Shikenjo Hokoku/ Bulletin. National Institute of Hygienic Sciences [*A publication*]
Eisenbahn-Ing ... Eisenbahn-Ingenieur [*A publication*]
Eisenbahntech Rundsch ... Eisenbahntechnische Rundschau [*A publication*]
Eisenhower Consortium Bull ... Eisenhower Consortium. Bulletin [*A publication*]
Eisenhower Consortium Bull Rocky Mt For Range Exp ... Eisenhower Consortium. Bulletin. United States Rocky Mountain Forest and Range Experiment Station [*A publication*]
EISF..........	Elastic Incoherent Structure Factor [*of spectra*]
EISG	Energy Information Systems Group [*Department of Energy*] [*Also, an information service or system*] (IID)
EISIM	Electron Impact Selected Ion Monitoring [*Instrumentation*]
E Isl	Encyclopedie de l'Islam [*A publication*]
EISL	Shannon [*Ireland*] [*ICAO location identifier*] (ICLI)
EISN..........	Experimental Integrated Switched Network
EISO..........	Environmental Information System Office [*National Science Foundation*]
EISOAU....	Eiyo To Shokuryo [*A publication*]
EISRA	Ekspress-Informatsiya. Svarochyne Raboty [*A publication*]
EISS...........	Encyclopedia of Information Systems and Services [*Later, IID*] [*A publication*]
Eis Shik Hok ... Eisei Shikenjo Hokoku [*Bulletin. National Institute of Hygienic Sciences*] [*A publication*]
EISU	Shannon [*Ireland*] [*ICAO location identifier*] (ICLI)
EISV	Extrinsic Irradiated Silicon Vidicon
Eiszeitalter Gegenw ... Eiszeitalter und Gegenwart [*A publication*]
Eisz Geg ... Eiszeitalter und Gegenwart [*A publication*]
EIT.............	Electrical Information Test
EIT.............	Electrical Installation Test [*or Technician*]
EIT.............	Electrical Insulation Tape
EIT.............	Electrical Intersystems Test
EIT.............	Electromagnetic Interference Testing
EIT.............	Electron-Bombardment Ion Thrustor
EIT.............	Electronic Information Technology [*Hardware manufacturer*]
EIT.............	Electronic Installation Technician
EI & T	Emplacement, Installation, and Test (CET)
EIT.............	Engineer-in-Training
EIT.............	Engineering Index Thesaurus [*A publication*]
EIT.............	Entry Interface Time (MCD)
EIT.............	(Erythrofuranosyl)imidazolinethione [*Antineoplastic drug*]
EIT.............	Erythroid Iron Turnover [*Hematology*]
EIT.............	Europe Industry and Technology Division [*Department of Trade*] [*British*]
EIT.............	European Institute of Technology [*International Consortium of Industrial Firms*]
EIT.............	European Institute for Trans-National Studies in Group and Organizational Development (EA)
EIT.............	Ezhegodnik Imperatorskikh Teatrov [*A publication*]
e-it---	Italy [*MARC geographic area code*] [*Library of Congress*] (LCCP)
EITB	Engineering Industry Training Board [*British*]
EITB	Enzyme-Linked Immunoelectrotransfer Blot (Technique) [*Clinical chemistry*]
EITBA	Engelhard Industries. Technical Bulletin [*A publication*]
EITC..........	Earned Income Tax Credit
EITEA	Ekspress-Informatsiya. Stroitel'stvo Teplovykh Elektrostantsii [*A publication*]
EITP	End Item Test Plan (MCD)
EITR..........	Ecumenical Institute for Theological Research (EAIO)
EITS	East Integrated Test Stand (KSC)
EITS	Educational and Industrial Testing Service
E & ITV	Education and Industrial Television [*A publication*]
EITZ..........	English Inshore Traffic Zone (DS)
EIU	Eastern Illinois University [*Formerly, EISC*] [*Charleston*]
EIU	Economist Intelligence Unit [*British*]
EIU	Electronic Interface Unit
EIU	Engine Interface Unit (NASA)
EIU	Enid, OK [*Location identifier*] [*FAA*] (FAAL)
EIU	Equipment Inventory Update [*Telecommunications*] (TEL)
EIUES	English Institute of the University of Uppsala. Essays and Studies on English Language and Literature [*A publication*]
EIV.............	Effective Initial Value
EIV.............	Engine Installation Vehicle
EIV.............	Entsiklopedyah 'Ivrit [*or Enziklopedyah 'Ivrit*] (BJA)
EIVKA	Elektronische Informatsionsverarbeitung und Kybernetik [*A publication*]
EIVR..........	Exchange of Information, Visits, and Reports
EIVT..........	Electrical and Instrumentation Verification Tests [*NASA*] (NASA)
EIVT..........	Electrical Interface Verification Test [*NASA*] (NASA)
EIVT..........	Electronic Installation Verification Test [*NASA*] (NASA)
EIW	Enamel Insulated Wire
EIW	European Institute for Water (EAIO)
EIW	New Madrid, MO [*Location identifier*] [*FAA*] (FAAL)
EIWS	Engineering Installation Workload Schedule (CET)
EIX.............	Elders IXL Canada, Inc. [*Toronto Stock Exchange symbol*]
EIY.............	Economic Inquiry [*A publication*]
EIY.............	Ein Yahav [*Israel*] [*Airport symbol*] [*Obsolete*] (OAG)
Eiyogaku Zasshi Jap J Nutr ... Eiyogaku Zasshi/Japanese Journal of Nutrition [*A publication*]
Eiyo Syok Gak ... Eiyo Syokuryo Gakkai [*A publication*]
EJ..............	Die Entstehung des Judentums [*A publication*] (BJA)
EJ..............	Economic Journal [*A publication*]
EJ..............	Edoth (Jerusalem) [*A publication*]
E u J...........	Einst und Jetzt [*A publication*]
EJ..............	Eject (KSC)
EJ..............	Ejus [*Of Him, or Of Her*] [*Latin*]
EJ..............	Elbow Jerk [*Medicine*]
EJ..............	Electronic Jamming
EJ..............	Electronic Journalism
EJ..............	Elizabeth Jones [*Designer's mark, when appearing on US coins*]
EJ..............	Encyclopaedia Judaica [*A publication*]
EJ..............	English Journal [*A publication*]
EJ..............	Eranos-Jahrbuch [*A publication*]
EJ..............	Estudios Josefinos [*A publication*]
EJ..............	European Judaism [*A publication*]
EJ..............	Eusko-Jakintza. Revue des Etudes Basques [*A publication*]
EJ..............	Everest & Jennings International [*AMEX symbol*] (SPSG)
EJ..............	Expansion Joint
EJ..............	Gestair Executive Jet [*Spain*] [*ICAO designator*] (FAAC)
EJ..............	Ireland [*Aircraft nationality and registration mark*] (FAAC)
EJA............	Barrancabermeja [*Colombia*] [*Airport symbol*] (OAG)
EJA............	Engineering Job Analysis (KSC)
EJA............	Environmental Protection Agency, Region III Library, Philadelphia, PA [*OCLC symbol*] (OCLC)
EJA............	Executive Jet Aviation, Inc. [*Columbus, OH*] [*FAA designator*] (FAAC)
EJABDD ...	Applied Microbiology and Biotechnology [*A publication*]
EJAGDS ...	Egyptian Journal of Agronomy [*A publication*]
EJAMA......	European Journal of Applied Microbiology [*A publication*]
EJAPC......	European Journal of Applied Physiology and Occupational Physiology [*A publication*]
EJAPCK....	European Journal of Applied Physiology and Occupational Physiology [*A publication*]
EJASA......	Engineering Journal [*New York*] [*A publication*]
EJB	Ectopic Junctional Beat [*Cardiology*]
EJB	Engineering Industries of Japan [*A publication*]
EJB	Environmental Protection Agency, Headquarters Library, Washington, DC [*OCLC symbol*] (OCLC)
EJb.............	Eranos-Jahrbuch [*Zurich*] [*A publication*]
EJBCAI	European Journal of Biochemistry [*A publication*]
EJBLAB	Egyptian Journal of Bilharziasis [*A publication*]
EJC............	Eccles-Jordan Circuit [*Electronics*]
EJC............	Ellsworth Junior College [*Iowa*] [*Later, ECC*]
EJC............	Ely Junior College [*Minnesota*] [*Later, Vermilion Community College*]
EJC............	Enciclopedia Judaica Castellana [*A publication*] (BJA)
EJC............	Endicott Junior College [*Beverly, MA*]
EJC............	Engineers Joint Council [*Superseded by AAES*] (EA)
EJC............	Environmental Protection Agency, Law Library, Washington, DC [*OCLC symbol*] (OCLC)
EJC............	Ephemerides Juris Canonici [*A publication*]
EJC............	Espoir de la Jeunesse Camerounaise [*Hope of the Cameroonese Youth*]
EJC............	Estherville Junior College [*Iowa*]
EJC............	Eveleth Junior College [*Later, Mesabi Community College*] [*Minnesota*]
EJC............	Everett Junior College [*Later, ECC*] [*Washington*]
EJC............	Owen Sound Air Services Ltd. [*Toronto, ON*] [*FAA designator*] (FAAC)
EJCAAH ...	European Journal of Cancer [*A publication*]
EJCBDN ...	European Journal of Cell Biology [*A publication*]
EJCC	Eastern Joint Computer Conference
EJCDAQ ...	Egyptian Journal of Chest Diseases and Tuberculosis [*A publication*]
EJCDBR....	European Journal of Cardiology [*A publication*]
EJCIB8	European Journal of Clinical Investigation [*A publication*]
EJCNC	Engineers Joint Council Nuclear Congress (IEEE)
EJCOD	European Journal of Cancer and Clinical Oncology [*A publication*]
EJCODS ...	European Journal of Cancer and Clinical Oncology [*A publication*]
EJCPA.......	European Journal of Clinical Pharmacology [*A publication*]
EJCPAS	European Journal of Clinical Pharmacology [*A publication*]

EJCT .... Eject
EJCTR .... Ejector
EJD .... Environmental Protection Agency, Region III Field Office, Annapolis, MD [OCLC symbol]   (OCLC)
EJDPD ...... European Journal of Drug Metabolism and Pharmacokinetics [A publication]
EJDPD2 .... European Journal of Drug Metabolism and Pharmacokinetics [A publication]
EJE .... Chicago Outer Belt R. R. [AAR code]
EJE .... Electric Junction Equation
EJE .... Elgin, Joliet & Eastern Railway Co. [AAR code]
EJE .... Environmental Protection Agency, OTS [Office of Toxic Substances] Technical Information Center, Washington, DC [OCLC symbol]   (OCLC)
EJEA .... Empire Journal of Experimental Agriculture [A publication]
EJEAAR .... Empire Journal of Experimental Agriculture [A publication]
EJEV .... Eusko-Jakintza. Revista de Estudios Vascos [A publication]
EJF .... Equal Justice Foundation   (EA)
EJF .... Estimated Junction Frequency [Telecommunications]   (TEL)
EJFPA ...... European Journal of Forest Pathology [A publication]
EJFPA9 ..... European Journal of Forest Pathology [A publication]
EJFSAI ..... Egyptian Journal of Food Science [A publication]
EJGCA9 .... Egyptian Journal of Genetics and Cytology [A publication]
EJGS .... Eminent Junior Grand Steward [Freemasonry]   (ROG)
EJH .... Wedjh [Saudi Arabia] [Airport symbol]   (OAG)
EJHCAE ... Egyptian Journal of Horticulture [A publication]
EJI .... Expansion Joint Institute
EJIMAF ..... European Journal of Immunology [A publication]
EJ Korvette ... Eugene [Ferkauf], Joseph [Zwillenberg], Corvettes [Names from which the E. J. Korvettes discount department store moniker was derived. They refer, respectively, to the store's founder, his former business partner, and a type of Canadian submarine chaser used during World War II]
EJM .... Etudes sur le Judaisme Medieval [A publication]   (BJA)
EJM .... European Journal of Marketing [A publication]
EJMA .... Educational Jewelry Manufacturers Association [Defunct]   (EA)
EJMA .... Expansion Joint Manufacturers Association   (EA)
EJMBA2 .... Egyptian Journal of Microbiology [A publication]
EJMCA5 ... European Journal of Medicinal Chemistry. Chimie Therapeutique [A publication]
EJMED ..... Eizo Joho. Medikaru [A publication]
EJN .... Ejection
EJNMD9 ... European Journal of Nuclear Medicine [A publication]
EJN ST ...... Ejection Seat   (MSA)
EJO .... Earp, Joseph O., Seattle WA [STAC]
EJO .... Engineering Job Order   (MCD)
EJOB .... European Joint Optical Bistability Programme [To develop an optical computer]
EJOODK ... European Journal of Orthodontics [A publication]
EJOR .... European Journal of Operational Research [A publication]
E Jos .... Estudios Josefinos [A publication]
EJP .... European Journal of Parapsychology [A publication]
EJP .... Exchange Jump
EJP .... Excitatory Junctional Potential [Neurophysiology]
EJPC .... European Justice and Peace Commissions   (EAIO)
EJPEA .... Emergency Jobs Programs Extension Act of 1976
EJPEDT .... European Journal of Pediatrics [A publication]
EJPHAZ ... European Journal of Pharmacology [A publication]
EJPLAD .... Egyptian Journal of Physiological Science [A publication]
EJPSBZ .... Egyptian Journal of Pharmaceutical Sciences [A publication]
EJR .... Detroit, MI [Location identifier] [FAA]   (FAAL)
EJR .... East Jersey Railroad & Terminal Co. [AAR code]
EJRDD2 .... European Journal of Respiratory Diseases [A publication]
EJRMG ..... Edmond James Rothschild Memorial Group [Foundation]
EJRSDD.... European Journal of Respiratory Diseases. Supplement [A publication]
EJS .... East Jordan & Southern R. R. [AAR code]
EJS .... Engineering Job Sheet   (MCD)
EJS .... Enhanced JTIDS [Joint Tactical Information Distribution System] System [Air Force]
EJSEDA .... European Journal of Science Education [A publication]
EJSSAF .... Egyptian Journal of Soil Science [A publication]
EJT .... Eccles-Jordan Trigger [Electronics]
EJT .... Engineering Job Ticket
EJT .... Extended Joint Test   (MCD)
EJTX .... Energetics, Inc. [NASDAQ symbol]   (NQ)
EJU .... European Judo Union   (EAIO)
EJU .... Exports to Japan Unit [British Overseas Trade Board]   (DS)
EJUAA ...... Emergency Jobs and Unemployment Assistance Act
EJud .... Encyclopaedia Judaica: Das Judentum in Geschichte und Gegenwart [Berlin] [A publication]   (BJA)
EJUSD ...... Ejusdem [Of the Same] [Latin]
EJV .... External Jugular Vein [Anatomy]
EJVSAU.... Egyptian Journal of Veterinary Science [A publication]
EJWG .... Eco-Justice Working Group [Joint Strategy and Action Committee and National Council of the Churches of Christ in the USA]   (EA)
EJW Gibb Mem Ser ... Elias John Wilkinson Gibb Memorial Series [A publication]
EK .... Eastern Knight [Freemasonry]   (ROG)

EK .... Eastman Kodak Co. [NYSE symbol]   (SPSG)
EK .... Eerste Kwartier [First Quarter] [Afrikaans]
EK .... Einschluss-Korper [Inclusion body] [Medicine]
EK .... Einzelkommentar [A publication]   (BJA)
EK .... Electrocardiogram [Also, ECG, EKG] [Medicine]
EK .... Euralair International [France] [ICAO designator]   (FAAC)
EK .... Evangelische Kirchenzeitung [Berlin] [A publication]
EK .... Evangelische Kommentare [A publication]
EKA .... Environmental Protection Agency, Region IV Library, Atlanta, GA [OCLC symbol]   (OCLC)
EKA .... Eskdalemuir Array [Scotland] [Seismograph station code, US Geological Survey]   (SEIS)
EKA .... Eureka Aero Industries [Eureka, CA] [FAA designator]   (FAAC)
EKA .... Eureka/Arcata [California] Murray Field [Airport symbol] [Obsolete]   (OAG)
EKAE .... Aero [Denmark] [ICAO location identifier]   (ICLI)
EKAH .... Tirstrup [Denmark] [ICAO location identifier]   (ICLI)
EkahR .... Ekah Rabbah   (BJA)
EKANA ..... Elektro-Anzeiger [A publication]
EKAT .... Anholt [Denmark] [ICAO location identifier]   (ICLI)
EKAV .... Avno [Denmark] [ICAO location identifier]   (ICLI)
EKB .... Electronic Keyboard
EKB .... Electronic Knowledge Bank
EKB .... Environmental Protection Agency, Library Services, Research Triangle Park, NC [OCLC symbol]   (OCLC)
EKBI .... Billund [Denmark] [ICAO location identifier]   (ICLI)
EKBRD5... Ekologia-CSSR [Ecology-CSSR] [A publication]
EKBS .... Electronic Keyboard System
EKC .... East Kansas City Aviation, Inc. [Grain Valley, MO] [FAA designator]   (FAAC)
EKC .... Eastman Kodak Company
EKC .... Economic Review. Federal Reserve Bank of Kansas City [A publication]
EKC .... Environmental Protection Agency, Environmental Research Laboratory, Gulf Breeze, FL [OCLC symbol]   (OCLC)
EKC .... Epidemic Keratoconjunctivitis [Ophthalmology]
EKC .... Ethylketocyclazocine [Biochemistry]
EKCA .... Kobenhavn [Denmark] [ICAO location identifier]   (ICLI)
EKCH .... Kobenhavn/Kastrup [Denmark] [ICAO location identifier]   (ICLI)
EKD .... Economic Titles/Abstracts [A publication]
EKD .... Environmental Protection Agency, Environmental Research Laboratory, Athens, GA [OCLC symbol]   (OCLC)
EKD .... Epic Data, Inc. [Toronto Stock Exchange symbol] [Vancouver Stock Exchange symbol]
EKD .... Eucaloric Ketogenic Diet
EKD .... Evangelische Kirche Deutschlands
EKDK .... Kobenhavn [Denmark] [ICAO location identifier]   (ICLI)
EKE .... Biloxi, MS [Location identifier] [FAA]   (FAAL)
EKE .... Ekereku [Guyana] [Airport symbol]   (OAG)
EKE .... Environmental Protection Agency, Library, Research Triangle Park, NC [OCLC symbol]   (OCLC)
EKEB .... Esbjerg [Denmark] [ICAO location identifier]   (ICLI)
EKEEK ...... Epeteris tou Kentrou Epistemonikon Ereunon Kyprou [A publication]
EKEHL...... Epeteris tou Kentrou Ereunes tes Hellenikes Laographias [A publication]
E KENT R ... East Kent Regiment [Military unit] [British]   (ROG)
EKF........... Environmental Protection Agency, ESRL [Environmental Sciences Research Laboratory], Meteorology Laboratory, Research Triangle Park, NC [OCLC symbol]   (OCLC)
EKFC .... Elvis Is King Fan Club   (EAIO)
EKG .... Carlsbad, CA [Location identifier] [FAA]   (FAAL)
EKG .... Effective Kilogram   (NRCH)
EKG .... Electrocardiogram [Also, ECG, EK] [Medicine]
EKG .... Electrocardiograph [Also, ECG]   (NASA)
EKGF........ Gormfelt [Denmark] [ICAO location identifier]   (ICLI)
EKGH........ Gronholt [Denmark] [ICAO location identifier]   (ICLI)
EKH .... Elkhorn Ranch [California] [Seismograph station code, US Geological Survey]   (SEIS)
EKHAA ..... Eksperimental'naya Khirurgiya i Anesteziologiya [A publication]
EKHAAF... Eksperimental'naya Khirurgiya i Anesteziologiya [A publication]
EKHG........ Herning/Skinderholm [Denmark] [ICAO location identifier]   (ICLI)
EKHO....... Lindtorp [Denmark] [ICAO location identifier]   (ICLI)
EKHS........ Hadsund [Denmark] [ICAO location identifier]   (ICLI)
EKHV........ Haderslev [Denmark] [ICAO location identifier]   (ICLI)
EKI........... Corpus Christi, TX [Location identifier] [FAA]   (FAAL)
EKI........... Ekaton Industries, Inc. [Toronto Stock Exchange symbol]
EKI........... Ekistic Index [A publication]
EKI........... Ekonomi dan Keuangan Indonesia [A publication]
EKI........... Electronic Keyboarding, Incorporated [Information service or system]   (IID)
EKI........... Elkhart [Indiana] [Airport symbol]   (OAG)
EKI........... Esperanto en Komerco Kaj Industrio [Institute for Esperanto in Commerce and Industry]   (EA)
EKIAAK.... Ekologiya [A publication]
EKIF .... Employer Identification Number Key Index File [IRS]
EKISA .... Ekistics [A publication]

Ekist........... Ekistics [*A publication*]
Ekistics Probl Sci Hum Settl ... Ekistics; the Problems and Science of Human Settlements [*A publication*]
Ekist Ind .... Ekistic Index [*A publication*]
EKK .... Evangelisch-Katholischer Kommentar zum Neuen Testament [*A publication*] (BJA)
EKK .... Evangelische-Katholischer Kommentar zum Neuen Testament [*A publication*]
EKKA .... Karup [*Denmark*] [*ICAO location identifier*] (ICLI)
EKKE........ Epanastatiko Kommunistiko Komma Ellados [*Revolutionary Communist Party of Greece*] (PPW)
EKKL........ Kalundborg [*Denmark*] [*ICAO location identifier*] (ICLI)
EKKM .... Arhus/Kirstinesminde [*Denmark*] [*ICAO location identifier*] (ICLI)
EKL........... Evangelisches Kirchenlexikon. Kirchlich-Theologisches Handwoerterbuch [*A publication*] (BJA)
EKL........... Evangelisches Kirchenlexikon. Kirchlichtheologisches Handwoerterbuch [*A publication*]
EKLS .... Laeso [*Denmark*] [*ICAO location identifier*] (ICLI)
EKLV........ Lemvig [*Denmark*] [*ICAO location identifier*] (ICLI)
EKM .... Edwald-Kornfeld Method
EKM .... Elkhart, IN [*Location identifier*] [*FAA*] (FAAL)
EKMA .... Empirical Kinetic Modeling Approach [*Air pollution research*]
EKMB .... Maribo [*Denmark*] [*ICAO location identifier*] (ICLI)
EKMC .... Karup [*Denmark*] [*ICAO location identifier*] (ICLI)
EKMI........ Danish Meteorological Institute [*Denmark*] [*ICAO location identifier*] (ICLI)
EKMK .... Karup [*Denmark*] [*ICAO location identifier*] (ICLI)
EKMMA8 ... Eksperimentalna Meditsina i Morfologiya [*A publication*]
EKMN .... Koster Vig [*Denmark*] [*ICAO location identifier*] (ICLI)
EKMZAD ... Conference Europeenne sur la Microcirculation/Conferenza Europea di Microcircolazione [*A publication*]
EKMZAD ... European Conference on Microcirculation [*A publication*]
EKN .... Ecology of Knowledge Network (EA)
EK of N ...... Election Knight of Nine [*Freemasonry*] (ROG)
EKN .... Elkins [*West Virginia*] [*Airport symbol*] (OAG)
EKN .... Eta Kappa Nu [*Fraternity*]
EKN .... Exportkreditnamnden [*Export Credit Agency*] [*Sweden*]
EKNE .... Department of Elementary, Kindergarten, and Nursery Education [*of NEA*] [*Later, American Association of Elementary, Kindergarten, Nursery Educators*]
EKNM .... Morso [*Denmark*] [*ICAO location identifier*] (ICLI)
EK/NOD ... Eastman Kodak/Navy Ordnance District (AAG)
EKNPA....... Ekonomika Neftianoi Promyshlennosti [*A publication*]
EKNS........ Nakskov [*Denmark*] [*ICAO location identifier*] (ICLI)
EKNTB....... Elektronika [*A publication*]
EKO .... Ekco Group [*NYSE symbol*] (SPSG)
Eko............ Eko [*Record label*] [*France*]
EKO........... Elko [*Nevada*] [*Airport symbol*] (OAG)
EKO........... Elko [*Nevada*] [*Seismograph station code, US Geological Survey*] [*Closed*] (SEIS)
EKOD........ Odense/Beldringe [*Denmark*] [*ICAO location identifier*] (ICLI)
EKOL .... European Kompass Online [*Reed Information Services Ltd.*] [*Information service or system*]
EKOLDI.... Ekologiya [*Sofia*] [*A publication*]
Ekol Fiziol Osob Rast Yuzhn Urala Ikh Resur ... Ekologicheskie i Fiziologicheskie Osobennosti Rastenii Yuzhnogo Urala i Ikh Resursy [*A publication*]
Ekol Pol ..... Ekologia Polska [*A publication*]
Ekol Pol Pol J Ecol ... Ekologia Polska/Polish Journal of Ecology [*A publication*]
Ekol Pol Ser A ... Ekologia Polska. Seria A [*A publication*]
Ekol Pol Ser B ... Ekologia Polska. Seria B [*A publication*]
Ekol Polska ... Ekologia Polska [*A publication*]
Ekon Cas..... Ekonomicky Casopis [*A publication*]
Ekon Forsknstift Skogsarb ... Ekonomi. Forskningsstiftelsen Skogsarbeten [*A publication*]
Ekon Gaz ... Ekonomicheskaya Gazeta [*A publication*]
Ekon Keuangan ... Ekonomi dan Keuangan Indonesia [*A publication*]
Ekon Matemat Met ... Ekonomika i Matematiceskie Metody [*A publication*]
Ekon Matem Metody ... Ekonomika i Matematiceskie Metody [*A publication*]
Ekon-Mate O ... Ekonomicko-Matematicky Obzor [*A publication*]
Ekon-Mat Obz ... Ekonomicko-Matematicky Obzor [*A publication*]
Ekon Nauki ... Ekonomiceskie Nauki [*A publication*]
Ekon Neft Prom-Sti ... Ekonomika Neftianoi Promyshlennosti [*USSR*] [*A publication*]
Ekonom i Mat Metody ... Ekonomika i Matematiceskie Metody [*A publication*]
Ekonom-Mat Obzor ... Ceskoslovenska Akademie Ved. Ekonomicko-Matematicky Obzor [*A publication*]
Ekon Org Promysl Proizvodstva ... Ekonomika i Organizacija Promyslennogo Proizvodstva [*A publication*]
Ekon Poljopr ... Ekonomika Poljoprivrede [*A publication*]
Ekon Poljopriv ... Ekonomika Poljoprivrede [*A publication*]
Ekon Probl Effekt ... Ekonomiceskie Problemy Effektivnosti Proizvodstva [*A publication*]
Ekon R (Ljubljana) ... Ekonomska Revija (Ljubljana) [*A publication*]
Ekon R (Stockholm) ... Ekonomisk Revy (Stockholm) [*A publication*]
Ekon Samf T ... Ekonomiska Samfundets Tidskrift [*A publication*]
Ekon Samfund Ts ... Ekonomiska Samfundets Tidskrift [*A publication*]

Ekon Sel' Khoz ... Ekonomika Sel'skogo Khozaistva [*A publication*]
Ekon Sel'sk Choz ... Ekonomika Sel'skogo Chozjajstva [*A publication*]
Ekon Sel'sk Khoz ... Ekonomika Sel'skogo Khozyaistva [*A publication*]
Ekon Sov Ukr ... Ekonomika Sovetskoi Ukrainy [*A publication*]
Ekon Stavebnictva ... Ekonomika Stavebnictva [*Czechoslovakia*] [*A publication*]
Ekon Stroit ... Ekonomika Stroitel'stva [*A publication*]
Ekon Zemed ... Ekonomika Zemedelstvi [*A publication*]
EKOPO ...... Evreiskii Komitet Pomoshchi [*Shanghai*] (BJA)
EKOSB...... Ekonomika Stavebnictva [*A publication*]
EKP........... Eestimaa Kommunistlik Partei
EKP........... Epikeraprosthesis [*Ophthalmology*]
EKP........... Evreiskaia Kommunisticheskaia Partiia [*Political party*] (BJA)
EKP........... Wisconsin Rapids, WI [*Location identifier*] [*FAA*] (FAAL)
EKPB......... Krusa-Padborg [*Denmark*] [*ICAO location identifier*] (ICLI)
EKPOAT...... Ekologia Polska. Seria A [*A publication*]
EKQ........... Monticello, KY [*Location identifier*] [*FAA*] (FAAL)
EKR .... East Kent Regiment [*Military unit*] [*British*]
Ekr .... Ekran [*A publication*]
EKR .... Eksportkreditradet [*Export Credit Agency*] [*Denmark*]
EKR .... EQK Realty Investors I SBI [*NYSE symbol*] (SPSG)
EKR .... Meeker, CO [*Location identifier*] [*FAA*] (FAAL)
EKRC......... Elisabeth Kubler-Ross Center (EA)
EKRD......... Randers [*Denmark*] [*ICAO location identifier*] (ICLI)
EKRK........ Kobenhavn/Roskilde [*Denmark*] [*ICAO location identifier*] (ICLI)
EKRKA....... Elektronik [*A publication*]
EKRN .... Ronne [*Denmark*] [*ICAO location identifier*] (ICLI)
EKRR........ Ro [*Denmark*] [*ICAO location identifier*] (ICLI)
EKRS......... Ringsted [*Denmark*] [*ICAO location identifier*] (ICLI)
eks............ Eksemplaar [*Copy*] [*Afrikaans*]
EKS .... Electrocardiogram Simulator
EKS .... Electronic Keyboard System
EKS .... Elks, Inc. [*Toronto Stock Exchange symbol*]
EKSB .... Sonderborg [*Denmark*] [*ICAO location identifier*] (ICLI)
EKSC........ Eastern Kentucky State College [*Later, EKU*]
EKSD........ Spjald [*Denmark*] [*ICAO location identifier*] (ICLI)
EKSI .... Electro-Kinetic Systems, Incorporated [*Trainer, PA*] [*NASDAQ symbol*] (NQ)
EKSM........ Evreiskii Kommunisticheskii Soiuz Molodezhi (BJA)
EKSN........ Sindal [*Denmark*] [*ICAO location identifier*] (ICLI)
EKSODD... Eksperimental'naya Onkologiya [*A publication*]
EKSP......... Skrydstrup [*Denmark*] [*ICAO location identifier*] (ICLI)
Eksp Bot ... Eksperimental'naja Botanika [*A publication*]
Eksp Chir... Eksperimental'naja Chirurgija [*A publication*]
Eksp Chir Anest ... Eksperimental'naja Chirurgija i Anesteziologija [*A publication*]
Eksp Issled Fiziol Biofiz Farmakol ... Eksperimental'nye Issledovaniya po Fiziologii, Biofizike, i Farmakologii [*A publication*]
Eksp Khir .. Eksperimental'naja Khirurgiya [*A publication*]
Eksp Khir Anesteziol ... Eksperimental'naya Khirurgiya i Anesteziologiya [*A publication*]
Eksp Klin Farmakoter ... Eksperimental'naya i Klinicheskaya Farmakoterapiya [*A publication*]
Eksp Klin Radiol ... Eksperimental'naya i Klinicheskaya a Radiologiya [*Ukrainian SSR*] [*A publication*]
Eksp Klin Stomatol ... Eksperimentalnaia Klinicheskaia Stomatologiia [*A publication*]
Eksp Med .. Eksperimentalna Meditsina [*A publication*]
Eksp Med Morfol ... Eksperimentalna Meditsina i Morfologiya [*A publication*]
Ekspress-Inf Lab Tekhnol Issled Obogashch Miner Syr'ya ... Ekspress-Informatsiya Laboratornye Tekhnologicheskie Issledovaniya i Obogashchenie Mineral'nogo Syr'ya [*USSR*] [*A publication*]
Ekspress-Inf Montazh Oborudovaniya Teplovykh Elektrosn ... Ekspress-Informatsiya. Montazh Oborudovaniya na Teplovykh Elektrostantsiyakh [*USSR*] [*A publication*]
Ekspress Inf Morsk Gidrofiz Inst Akad Nauk Ukr SSR ... Ekspress-Informatsiya. Morskoi Gidrozicheskii Institut Akademiya Nauk Ukrainskoi SSR [*A publication*]
Ekspress-Inf Nauchno-Issled Inst Sel Khoz Severn Zaural'ya ... Ekspress-Informatsiya Nauchno-Issledovatel'skii Institut Sel'skogo Khozyaistva Severnogo Zaural'ya [*A publication*]
Ekspress-Inf Neftegazov Geol Geofiz ... Ekspress-Informatsiya. Neftegazovaya Geologiya i Geofizika [*USSR*] [*A publication*]
Ekspress-Inf Ser Reg Razved Prom Geofiz ... Ekspress-Informatsiya. Seriya: Regional'naya, Razvedochnaya, i Promyslovaya Geofizika [*USSR*] [*A publication*]
Ekspress-Inf Stroit Tepl Elektrostn ... Ekspress-Informatsiya. Stroitel'stvo Teplovykh Elektrostantsii [*USSR*] [*A publication*]
Ekspress-Inf Svar Rab ... Ekspress-Informatsiya. Svarochnye Raboty [*USSR*] [*A publication*]
Eksp Tekh Svoistva Primen Avtomob Top Smaz Mater Sperszhidk ... Ekspluatatsionno Tekhnicheskie Svoistva i Primenenie Avtomobil'nykh Topliv. Smazochnykh Materialov i Sperszhidkostei [*A publication*]
Eksp Vodn Toksikol ... Eksperimental'naya Vodnaya Toksikologiya [*A publication*]
EKSS .... Samso [*Denmark*] [*ICAO location identifier*] (ICLI)
EKST .... Sydfyn/Tasinge [*Denmark*] [*ICAO location identifier*] (ICLI)

EKSTA ...... Electricheskie Stantsii [*A publication*]
EKSTB ...... Ekonomiska Samfundets Tidskrift [*A publication*]
EKSV .... Skive [*Denmark*] [*ICAO location identifier*] (ICLI)
EKT .... Eskilstuna [*Sweden*] [*Airport symbol*]
EKTCB ...... Elektrotechnik [*A publication*]
EKTD .... Tonder [*Denmark*] [*ICAO location identifier*] (ICLI)
EKTKA ...... Elektrotechnik [*A publication*]
EKTMA ...... Elektroteknikeren [*A publication*]
EKTRA ...... Elektrie [*A publication*]
EKTRB ...... Elektrotechnik [*A publication*]
EKTS .... Electronic Key Telephone System
EKTS .... Thisted [*Denmark*] [*ICAO location identifier*] (ICLI)
EKU .... Eastern Kentucky University [*Formerly, EKSC*] [*Richmond*]
eKv .... Electron Kilovolt (EY)
EKV .... Weeksville, NC [*Location identifier*] [*FAA*] (FAAL)
EKVA .... Vandel [*Denmark*] [*ICAO location identifier*] (ICLI)
EKVB .... Viborg [*Denmark*] [*ICAO location identifier*] (ICLI)
EKVD .... Vamdrup [*Denmark*] [*ICAO location identifier*] (ICLI)
EKVF .... East Kent Volunteer Fencibles [*British military*] (DMA)
EKVG .... Vagar, Faroe Islands [*Denmark*] [*ICAO location identifier*] (ICLI)
EKVH .... Vesthimmerland [*Denmark*] [*ICAO location identifier*] (ICLI)
EKVJ .... Stauning [*Denmark*] [*ICAO location identifier*] (ICLI)
EKVL .... Vaerlose [*Denmark*] [*ICAO location identifier*] (ICLI)
EKW .... Eisenbahnkesselwagen [*Railway tank car*] [*German military - World War II*]
EKW .... Electrical Kilowatts
EKW .... Worcester, MA [*Location identifier*] [*FAA*] (FAAL)
EKY .... Electrokymogram
EKYT .... Alborg [*Denmark*] [*ICAO location identifier*] (ICLI)
EKZVA ...... Elektrizitaetsverwertung [*A publication*]
EKZVA ...... Elktrosvyaz [*A publication*]
EKZWA ..... Elektrizitaetswirtschaft [*A publication*]
el----- .... Benelux Countries [*MARC geographic area code*] [*Library of Congress*] (LCCP)
EL .... Each Layer [*Technical drawings*]
EL .... Early Latent [*Medicine*]
EL .... East Longitude (ROG)
EL .... Eastern League [*Baseball*]
EL .... Eastern Lines
EL .... Economic League [*British*]
EL .... Economics Laboratory, Inc.
EL .... Education Level
EL .... Education Library [*A publication*]
EL .... Educational Leadership [*A publication*]
EL .... Egg Length
EL .... Einfache Lafette [*Single-barreled mount*] [*German military - World War II*]
El .... Elamite (BJA)
EL .... Elastic Limit
El .... Elberfelder Bibel [*1905*] (BJA)
El .... Elchies' Dictionary of Decisions, Scotch Court of Session [*A publication*] (DLA)
EL .... Eldest (ROG)
EL .... Election
EL .... Election Laws
El .... Electra [*of Sophocles*] [*Classical studies*] (OCD)
El .... Electra [*of Euripides*] [*Classical studies*] (OCD)
EL .... Electric
EL .... Electric LASER (MCD)
EL .... Electric Light
EL .... Electrician [*British military*] (DMA)
EL .... Electrohome Ltd. [*Toronto Stock Exchange symbol*]
EL .... Electroluminescence
El .... Electronics [*A publication*]
El .... Electronics Laboratory
El .... Electrotechnics [*A publication*]
El .... Electrum [*Numismatics*]
El .... Elektricestvo [*A publication*]
EL .... Element
EL .... Elementary
EL .... Elevated [*Railway*] [*Also, L*]
EL .... Elevation (AAG)
EL .... Eli Lilly & Co. [*Research code symbol*]
El .... Eline
EL .... Elsevier Lexica [*Elsevier Book Series*] [*A publication*]
EL .... Emergency Legislation
EL .... Emergency Librarian [*A publication*]
EL .... EMILY's List (EA)
EL .... Engineer Lieutenant [*Navy*] [*British*]
EL .... Engineering Laboratories [*Army*] (MCD)
E & L .... Engineering and Laboratory (KSC)
EL .... Engineering Letter [*Telecommunications*] (TEL)
E/L .... Entry/Landing (NASA)
EL .... Entry Lock [*Diving apparatus*]
EL .... Ephemerides Liturgicae [*A publication*]
EL .... Ephemerides Lovanienses (BJA)
EL .... Epidemiological Laboratory [*Air Force*]
E & L .... Equity & Law [*Brokerage group*] [*British*]
EL .... Equivalent Length [*Engineering*]

EL .... Erie-Lackawanna Railway Co. [*AAR code*] [*Absorbed into Consolidated Rail Corp.*]
EL .... Etudes de Lettres [*A publication*]
EL .... Europa Letteraria [*A publication*]
EL .... Europaeische Literatur [*A publication*]
EL .... Evangelical Lutheran (ROG)
EL .... Even Lot [*Investment term*]
EL .... Excess Limit
EL .... Exchange Line [*Telecommunications*] (TEL)
EL .... Exercise Limit [*Medicine*]
EL .... Expected Loss
EL .... Exploration Lease (ADA)
EL .... Eye Lens (MSA)
EL .... Eymard League (EA)
EL .... Ezik i Literatura [*A publication*]
EL .... Liberia [*Aircraft nationality and registration mark*] (FAAC)
EL2 .... Elongation in Two Inches
ELA .... Eagle Lake, TX [*Location identifier*] [*FAA*] (FAAL)
ELA .... Eighth Lively Art [*Advertising award*]
ELA .... Elazig [*Turkey*] [*Seismograph station code, US Geological Survey*] [*Closed*] (SEIS)
ELA .... Electron Linear Accelerator
ELA .... Electronic Library Association [*Defunct*] (EA)
ELA .... En Route Low Altitude
ELA .... English Language Amendment [*Proposed*]
ELA .... Enmekar and the Lord of Aratta (BJA)
ELA .... Environmental Protection Agency, Region V Library, Chicago, IL [*OCLC symbol*] (OCLC)
ELA .... Equilibrium-Line Altitude [*Glaciation*]
ELA .... Equine Lymphocyte Alloantigen [*Genetics, immunochemistry*]
ELA .... Ernest K. Lehmann & Associates, Inc. [*Also, an information service or system*] (IID)
ELA .... Ethical Library [*A publication*]
ELA .... Etudes de Linguistique Appliquee [*A publication*]
ELA .... European Laser Association (EA)
ELA .... Expressive Language Age [*of the hearing-impaired*]
ELA .... Extra Large Apertures [*Optics*] (ROG)
ELABB ..... Electroanalytical Abstracts [*A publication*]
Elabuz Gos Ped Inst Ucen Zap ... Elabuzskii Gosudarstvennyi Pedagogiceskii Institut. Ucenye Zapiski [*A publication*]
ELACS ...... Extended Life Attitude Control System [*NASA*]
E LACT ..... E Lacte [*With Milk*] [*Pharmacy*]
ELADS ...... Early Launch Air Defense System (MCD)
ELAFB ...... Ellsworth Air Force Base [*South Dakota*] (KSC)
ELAIA .... Europe-Latin America Interparliamentary Assembly [*See also DPERPLA*] [*Luxembourg, Luxembourg*] (EAIO)
EL AL .... Every Landing, Always Late [*Humorous interpretation of El Al Airlines*]
ELAM .... Endothelial Leukocyte Adhesion Molecule [*Cytology*]
ELAMS ...... Electronic Laboratory Animal Monitoring System
ELAN .... Extended Local Area Network [*Defunct*] (TSSD)
E LANC R ... East Lancashire Regiment [*Military unit*] [*British*] (ROG)
E Lang T .... English Language Teaching [*Later, English Language Teaching Journal*] [*A publication*]
E Lan R ...... East Lancashire Regiment [*Military unit*] [*British*] (DAS)
El Anz .... Elektro-Anzeiger [*A publication*]
ELAP .... Emergency Legal Assistance Project
El App Bull ... Electronic Applications Bulletin [*A publication*]
ELAS .... Earth Laboratory Applications Software
ELAS .... Earth Resources Laboratory Application Software
ELAS .... Elastic (MSA)
ELAS .... Electronics Assembly Services, Inc. [*NASDAQ symbol*] (NQ)
ELAS .... Ellenikos Laikos Apeleutherotikos Stratos [*Hellenic People's Army of Liberation*] [*Military arm of EAM*] [*Greek*]
ELAS .... Equilibrium Problems of Linear Structures
ELAS .... Extended Lymphadenopathy Syndrome [*Medicine*]
Elast .... Elastomerics [*A publication*]
Elast Xtra ... Elastomerics Extra [*A publication*]
ELAT .... Elaterium [*To Stimulate or Incite*] [*Pharmacy*] (ROG)
ELAT .... Estimated Latitude (FAAC)
ELATE ...... Engineers' Language for Automatic Test Equipment
ELB .... Bachelor of English Literature
ELB .... Early Light Breakfast [*Medicine*]
ELB .... El Banco [*Colombia*] [*Airport symbol*] (OAG)
ELB .... Elbow (MSA)
ELB .... Eldorado Bancorp [*AMEX symbol*] (SPSG)
ELB .... Electronic Lean Burn (ADA)
El & B .... Ellis and Blackburn's English Queen's Bench Reports [*118-120 English Reprint*] [*A publication*] (DLA)
ELB .... Emergency Locator Beacon
ELB .... Environmental Law Bulletin [*A publication*] (APTA)
ELB .... Environmental Protection Agency, Library, Environmental Research Center, Cincinnati, OH [*OCLC symbol*] (OCLC)
ELB .... Export Licensing Branch [*British Overseas Trade Board*] (DS)
ELBA .... English Language Books Abroad [*A publication*]
ELBAA ...... Elektrische Bahnen [*A publication*]
El B & E ...... Ellis, Blackburn, and Ellis' English Queen's Bench Reports [*A publication*] (DLA)
El B & El ...... Ellis, Blackburn, and Ellis' English Queen's Bench Reports [*A publication*] (DLA)
El a Bl .... Ellis and Blackburn Queen's Bench Cases [*A publication*]

El & Bl .... Ellis and Blackburn's English Queen's Bench Reports [*118-120 English Reprint*] [*A publication*] (DLA)
El Bl & El... Ellis, Blackburn, and Ellis' English Queen's Bench Reports [*A publication*] (DLA)
El Bl & El (Eng) ... Ellis, Blackburn, and Ellis' English Queen's Bench Reports [*A publication*] (DLA)
El & Bl (Eng) ... Ellis and Blackburn's English Queen's Bench Reports [*118-120 English Reprint*] [*A publication*] (DLA)
ELBOWS .. No Erasures, No Leaves Torn Out, No Blank Spaces, No Overturning, No Writing between Lines, Statements to Be in Exact Words [*Directions for written reports*] [*Scotland Yard*]
El (Bruessel) ... Electricite (Bruessel) [*A publication*]
El B & S ..... Ellis, Best, and Smith's English Queen's Bench Reports [*A publication*] (DLA)
ELBS .... English Language Book Society [*British*]
El B & S (Eng) ... Ellis, Best, and Smith's English Queen's Bench Reports [*A publication*] (DLA)
ELBT .... Elbit Computers Ltd. [*NASDAQ symbol*] (NQ)
ELBT .... English Language Books by Title [*A publication*]
ELBUA..... Electrical Business [*A publication*]
ELBW....... Extremely Low Birth Weight [*Obstetrics*] (ADA)
ELC........... Early Landed Cognac [*British*]
ELC........... El Coco Explorations Ltd. [*Vancouver Stock Exchange symbol*]
ELC........... Elcho Island [*Australia*] [*Airport symbol*] (OAG)
ELC........... Elco [*Illinois*] [*Seismograph station code, US Geological Survey*] (SEIS)
ELC........... Electronic Level Control [*General Motors Corp.*] [*Automotive engineering*]
ELC........... Electronic Load Controller
ElC........... Elevator Code
ELC........... Entrepreneurial Leadership Center (EA)
ELC........... Environment Liaison Centre [*Later, ELCI*] (EAIO)
ELC........... Environmental Protection Agency, Motor Vehicle Emission Laboratory, Ann Arbor, MI [*OCLC symbol*] (OCLC)
ELC........... Essential Light Chain
ELC........... Europe's Largest Companies [*ELC International*] [*Information service or system*] (CRD)
ELC........... Evangelical Lutheran Church [*Later, ELCA*]
ELC........... Expression-Linked Extra Copy [*Genetics*]
ELC........... External Locus of Control [*Psychology*]
ELC........... Extra-Low Carbon
ELCA........ Earth Landing Control Assembly [*NASA*] (KSC)
ELCA........ Enzyme-Linked Coagulation Assay [*Clinical chemistry*]
ELCA........ European Landscape Contractors Association (EAIO)
ELCA........ Evangelical Lutheran Church in America [*Formed by merger of ALC, ELC, and LCA*]
ELCA........ Evangelical Lutheran Church of Australia
ELCAA...... Electrochimica Acta [*A publication*]
ELC Acts ... Expiring Law Continuance Acts (DLA)
ELCAG..... ELINT [*Electronic Intercept*] Collection/Analysis Guide [*Air Force*]
ELCAR...... [*The*] Elkhart Carriage & Motor Car Co. [*Automobile manufacturer (1909-1915), later, Elcar Motor Co. (1916-1931)*] [*Acronym also used as car name*]
El Cas........ Election Cases [*A publication*] (DLA)
ELCAS ..... Elevated Causeway System (CAAL)
El Cas........ New York Election Cases (Armstrong's) [*A publication*] (DLA)
El Cas (NY) ... New York Election Cases (Armstrong's) [*A publication*] (DLA)
ELCB........ Earth Leakage Circuit Breaker
ELCCA...... Electronic Components [*A publication*]
ELCD........ Electrolytic Conductivity Detector
ELCD........ Evaporative Loss Control Device [*Automobile antipollution device*]
ELCFR ...... English Linguistics, 1500-1800: A Collection of Facsimile Reprints [*A publication*]
Elch........... Elchies. Court of Session Cases [*Scotland*] [*A publication*] (DLA)
Elchies .... Elchies. Court of Session Cases [*Scotland*] [*A publication*] (DLA)
Elchies' Dict ... Elchies' Dictionary of Decisions, Scotch Court of Session [*A publication*] (DLA)
El Chim...... Elektrochimija [*A publication*]
El Chim Acta ... Electrochimica Acta [*A publication*]
ELCI .... Environment Liaison Centre International (EAIO)
ELCIA....... Electronics and Instrumentation [*A publication*]
ELCINA..... Electronic Component Industries Association
ELCMA..... Electrical Communication [*A publication*]
ELCN....... Elco Industries, Inc. [*NASDAQ symbol*] (NQ)
ELCNC4.... Electron [*Brussels*] [*A publication*]
ELCO .... Electrolytic Capacitor (DEN)
ELCO .... Eliminate and Count [*Coding*] [*Data processing*]
ELCO .... European Liaison Committee for Osteopaths (EA)
ELCOM..... Electronics and Computers [*Cambridge Scientific Abstracts*] [*Bethesda, MD*] [*Bibliographic database*]
El Commun ... Electrical Communication [*A publication*]
El Commun Lab Rep ... Electrical Communication Laboratory Reports [*A publication*]
El Comp ..... Electronic Components [*A publication*]
ELCON ..... Electricity Consumers Resource Council (EA)

ELCON ..... Equipment Loss Consolidator
El Constr.... Electrical Construction and Maintenance [*A publication*]
El Contract ... Electrical Contracting [*A publication*]
ELCR........ Engineer Lieutenant-Commander [*Navy*] [*British*]
ELCRD...... Electro Conference Record [*A publication*]
ELCS........ Electronic Control Systems, Inc. [*NASDAQ symbol*] (NQ)
ELCSMI.... European Liaison Committee for the Sewing Machine Industries (EA)
ELCT........ Electronic (AABC)
ELCTC ...... Electric Contact
ELCTCBR ... Electric Contact Brush
ELCTD...... Electrode (MSA)
ELCTDN .... Electrophoresis [*A publication*]
ELCTLT.... Electrolyte
ELCTRG ... Electric Contact Ring
ELCTRN ... Electron [*A nuclear particle*]
ELCWA..... Electronics World [*A publication*]
ELD .... Earth Launch Date [*Aerospace*]
ELD .... East Longitude Date
ELD .... Economic Load Dispatching (BUR)
ELD .... Edge-Lighted Display
ELD .... Egg Lethal Dose
ELD .... Ehrlich-Lettre Hyperdiploid [*Mouse ascites tumor*]
ELD .... El Dorado [*Arkansas*] [*Airport symbol*] (OAG)
ELD .... Elder Tech Ltd. [*Vancouver Stock Exchange symbol*]
ELD .... Eldest
ELD .... Eldon Industrials, Inc. [*NYSE symbol*] (SPSG)
ELD .... Electroluminescent Diode
ELD .... Electroluminescent Display [*Data processing*]
ELD .... Electronic Lie Detector
ELD .... Energy Level Diagram
ELD .... Engineering Logic Diagram
ELD .... Environmental Protection Agency, Library, Environmental Research Laboratory, Duluth, MN [*OCLC symbol*] (OCLC)
ELD .... Error Logging Device
ELD .... Extra-Long Distance
ELD .... Federation of Liberal and Democratic Parties of the European Community [*Brussels, Belgium*] [*Political party*] (EAIO)
ELD .... Office of the Executive Legal Director [*Nuclear energy*] (NRCH)
ELDATRAWP ... Electronic Data Transmission Working Party [*Army*] (AABC)
ELDC........ Eldec Corp. [*Lynnwood, WA*] [*NASDAQ symbol*] (NQ)
ELDC........ Equivalent Load Duration Curve
ELDC........ European Lead Development Committee (EA)
ELDDA..... Electricidade [*A publication*]
Elders W .... Elders Weekly [*A publication*] (APTA)
ELDG .... Eldorado Gold & Exploration, Inc. [*NASDAQ symbol*] (NQ)
El Dict........ Elchies' Dictionary of Decisions, Scotch Court of Session [*A publication*] (DLA)
EL DIEFF ... Lew David Feldman [*New York bookseller; phonetic spelling of his initials forms name of company*]
El Dig........ Eller's Minnesota Digest [*A publication*] (DLA)
ELDISC..... Electrical Disconnect (MCD)
El Distrib ... Electrical Distribution [*A publication*]
ELDMK..... Earth Landmark [*NASA*]
ELDNB..... Elektrodienst [*A publication*]
ELDO .... European Launcher Development Organization [*Superseded by European Space Agency*]
ELDO/ESRO Bull ... ELDO/ESRO [*European Launcher Development Organization/European Space Research Organization*] Bulletin [*France*] [*A publication*]
ELDO/ESRO Sci Tech Rev ... ELDO/ESRO [*European Launcher Development Organization/European Space Research Organization*] Scientific and Technical Review [*France*] [*A publication*]
ELDOR ..... Electron Electron Double Resonance [*Physics*]
ELDR........ [*The*] Elder-Beerman Stores Corp. [*NASDAQ symbol*] (NQ)
ELDR........ European Federation of Liberal, Democratic, and Reform Parties (EAIO)
ELDS........ Editorial Layout Display System
ELDV........ Electrically Operated Depressurization Valve (MCD)
ELE.......... El Paso Energy Corp. [*Vancouver Stock Exchange symbol*]
ELE.......... El Real [*Panama*] [*Airport symbol*] (OAG)
ELE.......... Electronic Launching Equipment
Ele........... Eledoisin [*Biochemistry*]
ELE.......... Emergency Lighting Equipment
ELE.......... Empresa Nacional de Electricidad SA ADS [*NYSE symbol*] (SPSG)
ELE.......... Engine Life Expectancy (NG)
ELE.......... Equivalent Logic Element
ELE.......... Estimated Life Expectancy (MCD)
ELE.......... European Electronics [*A publication*]
ELEA........ Evangelical Lutheran Education Association (EA)
ELEC .... Election (ROG)
ELEC .... Electorate (ROG)
ELEC .... Electric (AFM)
Elec .... [*The*] Electrician [*A publication*]
Elec .... Electro [*Record label*] [*Finland*]
ELEC......... Electronic (NASA)

ELEC .... Electronics
ELEC .... Electrospace Systems [*NASDAQ symbol*]   (NQ)
ELEC .... Electuarium [*Electuary*] [*Pharmacy*]   (ROG)
ELEC .... English Language Education Council. Bulletin [*A publication*]
ELEC .... Etudes de Litterature Etrangere et Comparee [*A publication*]
ELEC .... European League for Economic Cooperation
ELECA ...... Electronics [*A publication*]
ELECAD .... Electronics [*A publication*]
Elec Aust.... Electronics Australia [*A publication*]   (APTA)
Elec Austr .. Electronic Australia [*A publication*]
Elec Bldg.... Electricity in Building [*A publication*]
Elec Busns .. Electronic Business [*A publication*]
Elec C .... Elections Code [*A publication*]   (DLA)
Elec Com .... Electrical Communication [*A publication*]
Elec Comft ... Electric Comfort Conditioning News [*A publication*]
Elec Comm ... Electrical Communication [*A publication*]
Elec Commun ... Electrical Communication [*A publication*]
Elec Constr Maint ... Electrical Construction and Maintenance [*A publication*]
Elec Contractor ... Electrical Contractor [*A publication*]   (APTA)
ELECD ...... Element Code   (MCD)
Elec Data ... Advance Release of Data for the Statistical Year Book of the Electric Utility Industry [*A publication*]
Elec Des ..... Electronic Design [*A publication*]
Elec Desgn ... Electronic Design [*A publication*]
Elec Ed .... Electronic Education [*A publication*]
Elec & Electron Abstr ... Electrical and Electronic Abstracts [*A publication*]
Elec Eng..... Electrical Engineer [*A publication*]   (APTA)
Elec Eng..... Electrical Engineering [*A publication*]
Elec Eng..... Electronic Engineering [*A publication*]
Elec Eng Abstr ... Electrical Engineering Abstracts [*A publication*]
Elec Eng Japan ... Electrical Engineering in Japan [*A publication*]
Elec Eng (Melbourne) ... Electrical Engineer (Melbourne) [*A publication*]
Elec Eng & Merchandiser ... Electrical Engineer and Merchandiser [*A publication*]   (APTA)
Elec Engr ... Electrical Engineer [*A publication*]
Elec Eng Rev ... Electrical Engineering Review [*A publication*]
Elec Engrg Electron ... Electrical Engineering and Electronics [*A publication*]
Elec Engrg and Electronics ... Electrical Engineering and Electronics [*A publication*]
Elec Eng T ... Electronic Engineering Times [*A publication*]
Elec En Jap ... Electrical Engineering in Japan [*A publication*]
Elec Fact .... Electronic News Financial Fact Book and Directory [*A publication*]
Elec Farm Mag ... Electricity on the Farm Magazine [*A publication*]
Elec Fr Bull Dir Etud Rech Ser A Nucl Hydraul Therm ... Electricite de France. Bulletin de la Direction des Etudes et Recherches. Serie A. Nucleaire, Hydraulique, Thermique [*A publication*]
Elec Fr Bull Dir Etud Rech Ser B Reseaux Elec Mater Elec ... Electricite de France. Bulletin de la Direction des Etudes et Recherches. Serie B. Reseaux Electriques, Materiels Electriques [*A publication*]
Elec Furnace Conf Proc AIME ... Electric Furnace Conference Proceedings. Metallurgical Society of AIME. Iron and Steel Division [*A publication*]
Elec Ind ...... Electronics Industry, Incorporating Electronic Components [*A publication*]
Elec J .... Electrical Journal [*A publication*]
Elec LR ...... Election Law Reports [*India*] [*A publication*]   (DLA)
Elec Manuf ... Electrical Manufacturing [*A publication*]
Elec Merch ... Electrical Merchandising [*A publication*]
Elec Merch W ... Electrical Merchandising Week [*A publication*]
Elec Mkt .... Electronic Market Data Book [*A publication*]
Elec Mkt T ... Electronic Market Trends [*A publication*]
Elec M & M Sys ... Electronic Mail and Message Systems [*A publication*]
Elec Mus R ... Electronic Music Review [*A publication*]
ELECN ...... Electrician   (AFM)
Elec News ... Electronic News [*A publication*]
Elec News Eng ... Electrical News and Engineering [*A publication*]
ELECOM ... Electronic Computing
Elec Outlk ... US Electric Utility Industry Outlook to the Year 2000 [*A publication*]
Elec Powr A ... Electric Power Annual [*A publication*]
Elec Powr M ... Electric Power Monthly [*A publication*]
Elec Prod ... Electronic Products [*A publication*]
Elec Prog.... Electronic Progress [*A publication*]
Elec Publ Rev ... Electronic Publishing Review [*A publication*]
Elec Pub Rv ... Electronic Publishing Review [*A publication*]
Elec R .... Electrical Review [*A publication*]
Elec Res Ass ERA Rep ... Electrical Research Association. ERA Report [*A publication*]
Elec Retail ... Electronics Retailing [*A publication*]
Elec Rev ..... Electrical Review [*A publication*]
Elec Revw... Electrical Review [*A publication*]
Elec Ry J.... Electric Railway Journal [*A publication*]
ELECSYSCOM ... Electronic Systems Command [*Also, NESC*] [*Navy*]
ELECT ...... Election   (AABC)
ELECT ...... Electrical
ELECT ...... Electrolyte   (KSC)
ELECT ...... Electronic   (MCD)

ELECT ...... Electuarium [*Electuary*] [*Pharmacy*]
ELECTC.... Electronic Control
Elect Cas.... Election Cases [*A publication*]   (DLA)
Elect Cas NY ... New York Election Cases (Armstrong's) [*A publication*]   (DLA)
Elect Contractor ... Electrical Contractor [*A publication*]
Elec Technol (USSR) ... Electric Technology (USSR) [*A publication*]
Elect Electron Mfr ... Electrical and Electronics Manufacturer [*A publication*]
Elect Electron Trader ... Electrical and Electronic Trader [*A publication*]
Elect Engng Trans Instn Engrs Aust ... Electrical Engineering Transactions. Institution of Engineers of Australia [*A publication*]   (APTA)
Elect Engr (Melb) ... Electrical Engineer (Melbourne) [*A publication*]   (APTA)
Elect Equip ... Electrical Equipment [*A publication*]
ELECTHYDR ... Electrohydraulic   (KSC)
Elec Times ... Electric Times [*A publication*]
Elec T Intnl ... Electronics Today International [*A publication*]
Elect J .... Electric Journal [*A publication*]
ELECTL.... Electrical
ELECTL.... Electrolytic
Electl Engr ... Electrical Engineer [*A publication*]
Electl Wkly ... Electrical Weekly [*A publication*]
ELECTLY ... Electrically
ELECTMECH ... Electromechanical   (KSC)
Elect Mech Engng Trans ... Institution of Engineers of Australia. Electrical and Mechanical Engineering Transactions [*A publication*]   (APTA)
ELECTMG ... Electromagnetic
Elec Tod..... Electronics Today International [*A publication*]   (APTA)
Elect Pwr.... Electrical Power Engineer [*A publication*]
Elect Pwr Engr ... Electrical Power Engineer [*A publication*]
ELECTR.... Electronics   (NASA)
Electr Act... Electrochimica Acta [*A publication*]
Elec Traction ... Electric Traction [*A publication*]   (APTA)
Electr App ... Electrical Apparatus [*A publication*]
Electr Automob ... Electricite Automobile [*A publication*]
Electr Calculation ... Electrical Calculation [*Japan*] [*A publication*]
ELECTRCL ... Electrical
Electr Co J ... Electronics and Communications in Japan [*A publication*]
Electr Comf Cond J ... Electric Comfort Conditioning Journal [*A publication*]
Electr Comf Cond News ... Electric Comfort Conditioning News [*A publication*]
Electr Commun ... Electrical Communication [*A publication*]
Electr Commun Lab Tech J ... Electrical Communication Laboratories. Technical Journal [*A publication*]
Electr Conserv Q ... Electricity Conservation Quarterly [*India*] [*A publication*]
Electr Constr and Maint ... Electrical Construction and Maintenance [*A publication*]
Electr Consult ... Electrical Consultant [*A publication*]
Electr Contract ... Electrical Contracting [*A publication*]
Electr Contract ... Electrical Contractor [*A publication*]
Electr Dig... Electrical Digest [*Canada*] [*A publication*]
Electr Distrib ... Electrical Distribution [*England*] [*A publication*]
Electr and Electron ... Electrical and Electronics Technician Engineer [*A publication*]
Electr Electron Abstr ... Electrical and Electronics Abstracts [*A publication*]
Electr-Electron Mod ... Electricite-Electronique Moderne [*A publication*]
Electr Energ Electron ... Electricidade, Energia, Electronica [*A publication*]
Electr Eng ... Electrical Engineer [*A publication*]
Electr Eng.. Electronic Engineering [*London*] [*A publication*]
Electr Eng Jap ... Electrical Engineering in Japan [*A publication*]
Electr Eng (Johannesburg) ... Electrical Engineer (Johannesburg) [*A publication*]
Electr Eng Jpn ... Electrical Engineering in Japan [*A publication*]
Electr Eng (Melb) ... Electrical Engineer (Melbourne) [*A publication*]
Electr Eng Merch ... Electrical Engineer and Merchandiser [*Australia*] [*A publication*]
Electr Eng Rev ... Electrical Engineering Review [*A publication*]
Electr Eng Trans ... Electrical Engineering Transactions [*Australia*] [*A publication*]
Electr Eng Trans Inst Eng Aust ... Electrical Engineering Transactions. Institution of Engineers of Australia [*A publication*]   (APTA)
Elect Rep.... Election Reports [*Ontario*] [*A publication*]   (DLA)
Electr Equip ... Electrical Equipment [*A publication*]
Elect Rev ... Electrical Review [*A publication*]
ELECTREX ... International Electrotechnical Exhibition [*British Electrical and Allied Manufacturers Association*]   (TSPED)
Electr Farm Power ... Electric Farm Power [*A publication*]
Electr Forum ... Electric Forum [*A publication*]
Electr Fr Bull Dir Etud et Rech Ser A Nucl Hydraul Therm ... Electricite de France. Bulletin de la Direction des Etudes et Recherches. Serie A. Nucleaire, Hydraulique, Thermique [*A publication*]
Electr Fr Bull Dir Etud Rech Ser A Nucl Hydraul Therm ... Electricite de France. Bulletin de la Direction des Etudes et Recherches. Serie A. Nucleaire, Hydraulique, Thermique [*A publication*]
Electr Furn Conf Proc ... Electric Furnace Conference Proceedings [*A publication*]

Electr Furn Proc Metall Soc AIME ... Electric Furnace Conference Proceedings. Metallurgical Society of AIME. Iron and Steel Division [*A publication*]
Electr Furn Steel Proc ... Electric Furnace. Steel Proceedings [*A publication*]
Electr Heat J ... Electric Heating Journal [*A publication*]
Electric....... Electrician and Electrical Engineer [*A publication*]
Electric Comp ... Electric Company Magazine [*A publication*]
Electricte.... Revue Generale de l'Electricite [*A publication*]
Electrified Ind ... Electrified Industry [*A publication*]
Electr Ind... Electricien Industriel [*A publication*]
Electr India ... Electrical India [*A publication*]
Electr Inf... Electrical Information [*Japan*] [*A publication*]
Electrique.. Industries Electriques et Electroniques [*A publication*]
Electr Lett ... Electronics Letters [*A publication*]
Electr Light & Power ... Electric Light and Power [*A publication*]
Electr Light Power (Boston) ... Electric Light and Power (Boston) [*A publication*]
Electr Light Power Energy/Gener ... Electric Light and Power. Energy/Generation [*A publication*]
Electr Light Power Transm/Distrib ... Electric Light and Power. Transmission/Distribution [*A publication*]
Electr Mach and Electromech ... Electric Machines and Electromechanics [*A publication*]
Electr Mach Electromech ... Electric Machines and Electromechanics [*A publication*]
Electr Mach and Power Syst ... Electric Machines and Power Systems [*A publication*]
Electr Mag Ohm ... Electrical Magazine Ohm [*Japan*] [*A publication*]
Electr Mech Eng Trans Inst Eng Aust ... Electrical and Mechanical Engineering Transactions. Institution of Engineers of Australia [*A publication*] (APTA)
Electr and Mech Executive Eng ... Electrical and Mechanical Executive Engineer [*A publication*]
Electrnc Wk ... Electronics Week [*Later, Electronics*] [*A publication*]
Electr News Eng ... Electrical News and Engineering [*A publication*]
Electr Nucl Technol ... Electrical and Nuclear Technology [*A publication*]
ELECTRO ... Electronics (KSC)
ELECTRO ... Electrotype (ROG)
Electroanal Abstr ... Electroanalytical Abstracts [*A publication*]
Electroanal Chem ... Electroanalytical Chemistry [*A publication*]
ELECTROCHEM ... Electrochemistry
Electrochem ... Electrochemistry [*A publication*]
Electrochem Ind Phys Chem ... Electrochemistry and Industrial Physical Chemistry [*Japan*] [*A publication*]
Electrochem Ind Process and Biol ... Electrochemistry in Industrial Processing and Biology [*A publication*]
Electrochem Ind Process Biol (Engl Transl) ... Electrochemistry in Industrial Processing and Biology (English Translation) [*A publication*]
Electrochem Metall Ind ... Electrochemical and Metallurgical Industry [*A publication*]
Electrochem Molten and Solid Electrolytes ... Electrochemistry of Molten and Solid Electrolytes [*A publication*]
Electrochem Soc J ... Electrochemical Society. Journal [*A publication*]
Electrochem Tech ... Electrochemical Technology [*A publication*]
Electrochem Technol ... Electrochemical Technology [*A publication*]
Electrochim Acta ... Electrochimica Acta [*A publication*]
Electrochim Metal ... Electrochimica Metallorum [*A publication*]
Electrocomponent Sci Technol ... Electrocomponent Science and Technology [*A publication*]
Electrocompon Sci and Technol ... Electrocomponent Science and Technology [*A publication*]
Electrocompon Sci Technol ... Electrocomponent Science and Technology [*A publication*]
Electrodeposition and Surf Treat ... Electrodeposition and Surface Treatment [*A publication*]
Electroencephalogr and Clin Neurophysiol ... Electroencephalography and Clinical Neurophysiology [*A publication*]
Electroencephalogr Clin Neurophysiol ... Electroencephalography and Clinical Neurophysiology [*A publication*]
Electroencephalogr Clin Neurophysiol Suppl ... Electroencephalography and Clinical Neurophysiology. Supplement [*A publication*]
Electroenceph Clin Neurophysiol ... Electroencephalography and Clinical Neurophysiology [*A publication*]
Electromech Compon Syst Des ... Electromechanical Components and Systems Design [*A publication*]
Electromech Des ... Electromechanical Design [*A publication*]
Electromed ... Electromedica [*A publication*]
Electromet Met Alloys Rev ... Electromet Metals and Alloys Review [*A publication*]
Electromet Rev ... Electromet Review [*A publication*]
Electromyography and Clin Neurophysiol ... Electromyography and Clinical Neurophysiology [*A publication*]
Electromyogr Clin Neurophysiol ... Electromyography and Clinical Neurophysiology [*A publication*]
Electron...... Electronics [*A publication*]
Electron Abstr J ... Electronics Abstracts Journal [*A publication*]
Electron Appl ... Electronic Applications [*A publication*]
Electron Appl Bull ... Electronic Applications Bulletin [*A publication*]
Electron Appl Components Mater ... Electronic Applications. Components and Materials [*Netherlands*] [*A publication*]

Electron Appl Ind ... Electronique et Applications Industrielles [*France*] [*A publication*]
Electron Aust ... Electronics Australia [*A publication*]
Electron Bus ... Electronic Business [*A publication*]
Electron Comm Japan ... Electronics and Communications in Japan [*A publication*]
Electron Commun ... Electronic Communicator [*A publication*]
Electron Commun Abstr J ... Electronics and Communications Abstracts Journal [*A publication*]
Electron & Communic Abstr J ... Electronics and Communications Abstracts Journal [*A publication*]
Electron Commun Japan ... Electronics and Communications in Japan [*A publication*]
Electron and Commun Jpn ... Electronics and Communications in Japan [*A publication*]
Electron Commun Jpn ... Electronics and Communications in Japan [*A publication*]
Electron Compon ... Electronic Components [*A publication*]
Electron Components ... Electronic Components [*A publication*]
Electron Components Appl ... Electronic Components and Applications [*Netherlands*] [*A publication*]
Electron Components and Appl ... Electronic Components and Applications [*A publication*]
Electron and Comput Mon ... Electronics and Computing Monthly [*A publication*]
Electron Des ... Electronic Design [*A publication*]
Electron Device Lett ... Electron Device Letters [*A publication*]
Electron Electro-Optic Infrared Countermeas ... Electronic, Electro-Optic, and Infrared Countermeasures [*A publication*]
Electron Electro-Opt Infrared Countermeas ... Electronic, Electro-Optic, and Infrared Countermeasures [*A publication*]
Electron Eng (Lond) ... Electronic Engineering (London) [*A publication*]
Electron Eng (Phila) ... Electronic Engineering (Philadelphia) [*A publication*]
ELECTRONENGR ... Electronics Engineer
Electron Equip Eng ... Electronic Equipment Engineering [*A publication*]
Electron Equip News ... Electronic Equipment News [*A publication*]
Electron Fis Apl ... Electronica y Fisica Aplicada [*A publication*]
Electronic. ... Electronics [*A publication*]
Electronic Ind & Tele-Tech ... Electronic Industries and Tele-Tech [*A publication*]
Electronic Libr ... Electronic Library [*A publication*]
Electronic N ... Electronic News [*A publication*]
Electronic & Radio Eng ... Electronic and Radio Engineer [*A publication*]
Electronics Aust ... Electronics Australia [*A publication*] (APTA)
Electronics Today ... Electronics Today International [*A publication*] (APTA)
Electron Ind ... Electronic Industries [*A publication*]
Electron Ind ... Electronics Industry [*A publication*]
Electron Ind ... Electronique Industrielle [*A publication*]
Electron Ind Electron Instrum ... Electronic Industries and Electronic Instrumentation [*A publication*]
Electron Inf Plann ... Electronics Information and Planning [*A publication*]
Electron Inf and Plann ... Electronics Information and Planning [*A publication*]
Electron Instrum ... Electronics and Instrumentation [*A publication*]
Electron Learn ... Electronic Learning [*A publication*]
Electron Lett ... Electronics Letters [*A publication*]
Electron Libr ... Electronic Library [*A publication*]
Electron Library ... Electronic Library [*A publication*]
Electron Mag ... Electronics Magazine [*A publication*]
Electron Meas ... Electronic Measuring [*A publication*]
Electron Med ... Electronique Medicale [*A publication*]
Electron Meten ... Electronisch Meten [*A publication*]
Electron Mfr ... Electronics Manufacturer [*A publication*]
Electron Microelectron Ind ... Electronique et Microelectronique Industrielles
Electron et Microelectron Ind ... Electronique et Microelectronique Industrielles [*A publication*]
Electron Microsc Soc Am Annu Meet Proc ... Electron Microscopy Society of America. Annual Meeting. Proceedings [*A publication*]
Electron Microsc Soc South Afr Proc ... Electron Microscopy Society of Southern Africa. Proceedings [*A publication*]
Electron Micros Soc Southern Afr Proc ... Electron Microscopy Society of Southern Africa. Proceedings [*A publication*]
Electron News ... Electronic News [*A publication*]
Electron Nouv ... Electronique Nouvelle [*A publication*]
Electron Packag Prod ... Electronic Packaging and Production [*A publication*]
Electron Packag and Prod ... Electronic Packaging and Production [*A publication*]
Electron Power ... Electronics and Power [*A publication*]
Electron & Power ... Electronics and Power [*A publication*]
Electron and Power ... Electronics and Power. Journal of the Institution of Electrical Engineers [*A publication*]
Electron Prod ... Electronic Products Magazine [*A publication*]
Electron Prod Des ... Electronic Product Design [*A publication*]
Electron Prod Methods & Equip ... Electronic Production Methods and Equipment [*A publication*]
Electron Prog ... Electronic Progress [*A publication*]
Electron Publ Abstr ... Electronic Publishing Abstracts [*A publication*]
Electron Publishing Rev ... Electronic Publishing Review [*A publication*]
Electron Publ Rev ... Electronic Publishing Review [*A publication*]
Electron Pwr ... Electronics and Power [*A publication*]

Electron and Radio Tech ... Electronic and Radio Technician [*A publication*]
Electron Reliab Microminiaturization ... Electronics Reliability and Microminiaturization [*England*] [*A publication*]
Electron Rep ... Electronics Report [*A publication*]
Electron Rev (Tokyo) ... Electronics Review (Tokyo) [*A publication*]
Electron Sound and RTE ... Electronic Sound and RTE [*A publication*]
Electron Spectrosc Theory Tech Appl ... Electron Spectroscopy Theory, Techniques, and Applications [*A publication*]
Electron Struct Magnet Inorg Comp ... Electronic Structure and Magnetism of Inorganic Compounds [*A publication*]
Electron Surv Comput ... Electronic Survey Computing [*A publication*] (APTA)
Electron Surv Computing ... Electronic Survey Computing [*A publication*] (APTA)
Electron Technol ... Electron Technology [*A publication*]
Electron Technol Q ... Electron Technology. Quarterly [*A publication*]
Electron Technol Rep ... Electronic Technology Reports [*South Korea*] [*A publication*]
Electron Test ... Electronics Test [*A publication*]
Electron Times ... Electronic Times [*A publication*]
Electron Today ... Electronics Today [*A publication*]
Electron Today Int ... Electronics Today International [*A publication*]
Electron Warf Def Electron ... Electronic Warfare Defense Electronics [*A publication*]
Electron Wkly ... Electronics Weekly [*A publication*]
Electron World ... Electronics World [*A publication*]
Electro-Opt ... Electro-Optics [*A publication*]
Electro Opt Ser ... Electro-Optics Series [*A publication*]
Electro-Opt Syst Des ... Electro-Optical Systems Design [*A publication*]
Electro-Opt Systems ... Electro-Optical Systems Design [*A publication*]
Electrophotogr ... Electrophotography [*A publication*]
Electroplat Met Finish ... Electroplating and Metal Finishing [*A publication*]
Electroplat and Met Finish ... Electroplating and Metal Finishing [*A publication*]
Electroquim Corrasao ... Electroquimica e Corrasao [*A publication*]
Electro-Rev ... Electro-Revue [*A publication*]
Electro-Tech ... Electro-Techniek [*A publication*]
Electro-Tech ... Electro-Technology [*A publication*]
Electrotech J Jpn ... Electrotechnical Journal of Japan [*A publication*]
Electro-Technol ... Electro-Technology [*A publication*]
Electro-Technol (Bangalore India) ... Electro-Technology (Bangalore, India) [*A publication*]
Electro-Technol (NY) ... Electro-Technology (New York) [*A publication*]
Electroteh Electron Autom Electroteh ... Electrotehnica, Electronica, si Automatica. Serie Electrotehnica [*Romania*] [*A publication*]
Electrothermie Int Ed B ... Electrothermie International. Edition B. Applications Industrielles de l'Electrothermie [*A publication*]
Electr Perspect ... Electric Perspectives [*A publication*]
Electr Pow ... Electronics and Power [*A publication*]
Electr Power Commun ... Electric Power Communicator [*Canada*] [*A publication*]
Electr Power Energy Syst ... Electrical Power and Energy Systems [*England*] [*A publication*]
Electr Power Mon ... Electric Power Monthly [*Japan*] [*A publication*]
Electr Power Res Inst (Rep) EPRI AF ... Electric Power Research Institute (Report) EPRI AF [*A publication*]
Electr Power Res Inst (Rep) EPRI EA ... Electric Power Research Institute (Report) EPRI EA [*A publication*]
Electr Power Res Inst (Rep) EPRI EL ... Electric Power Research Institute (Report) EPRI EL [*A publication*]
Electr Power Res Inst (Rep) EPRI EM ... Electric Power Research Institute (Report) EPRI EM [*A publication*]
Electr Power Res Inst (Rep) EPRI ER ... Electric Power Research Institute (Report) EPRI ER [*A publication*]
Electr Power Res Inst (Rep) EPRI ER (Palo Alto Calif) ... Electric Power Research Institute (Report) EPRI ER (Palo Alto, California) [*A publication*]
Electr Power Res Inst (Rep) EPRI FP ... Electric Power Research Institute (Report) EPRI FP [*A publication*]
Electr Power Res Inst (Rep) EPRI FP (Palo Alto Calif) ... Electric Power Research Institute (Report) EPRI FP (Palo Alto, California) [*A publication*]
Electr Power Res Inst (Rep) EPRI NP ... Electric Power Research Institute (Report) EPRI NP [*A publication*]
Electr Power Res Inst (Rep) EPRI SR (Palo Alto Calif) ... Electric Power Research Institute (Report) EPRI SR (Palo Alto, California) [*A publication*]
Electr Power Syst Res ... Electric Power Systems Research [*A publication*]
Electr Prod ... Electronic Products Magazine [*A publication*]
Electr Rev ... Electrical Review [*A publication*]
Electr Rev Int ... Electrical Review International [*A publication*]
Electr Superv ... Electrical Supervisor [*A publication*]
Electr Technol (USSR) ... Electric Technology (USSR) [*A publication*]
Electr Times ... Electrical Times [*A publication*]
Electr Util & Energy Abs ... Electrical Utilization and Energy Abstracts [*A publication*]
Electr Veh ... Electric Vehicles [*A publication*]
Electr Veh Batteries ... Electric Vehicles and Batteries [*England*] [*A publication*]

Electr Veh Dev ... Electric Vehicle Developments [*England*] [*A publication*]
Electr Veh News ... Electric Vehicle News [*A publication*]
Electr Week ... Electrical Week [*A publication*]
Electr World ... Electrical World [*A publication*]
Elect Supervis ... Electrical Supervisor [*A publication*]
Elect Times ... Electrical Times [*A publication*]
Elect Tract ... Electric Traction [*A publication*] (APTA)
Elect World ... Electrical World [*A publication*]
ELECTY.... Electricity
Elec Veh..... Electric Vehicle News [*A publication*]
Elec W........ Electrical Weekly [*A publication*] (APTA)
Elec War D ... Electronic Warfare Digest [*A publication*]
Elec Week ... Electronics Weekly [*A publication*]
Elec West ... Electrical West [*A publication*]
Elec World ... Electrical World [*A publication*]
ELEGA...... Electronic Engineering [*A publication*]
ELEGC...... Electric Light and Power. Energy/Generation [*A publication*]
ELEK........ Electronic (MSA)
Elek........... Elektra [*Record label*]
ELEKA...... Elektrichestvo [*A publication*]
Elek Bahnen ... Elektrische Bahnen [*A publication*]
Elek Tech... Elektrotechniek [*A publication*]
Elekt Ind.... Elektronik Industrie [*A publication*]
Elektr Ausruestung ... Elektrische Ausruestung [*A publication*]
Elektr Bahnen ... Elektrische Bahnen [*A publication*]
Elektr Energ-Tech ... Elektrische Energie-Technik [*A publication*]
Elektr Masch ... Elektrische Maschinen [*A publication*]
Elektr Muhendisligi ... Elektrik Muhendisligi [*A publication*]
Elektr Nachrichtenwes ... Elektrisches Nachrichtenwesen [*A publication*]
Elektr Nachr Tech ... Elektrische Nachrichten Technik [*A publication*]
Elektro-Anz ... Elektro-Anzeiger [*A publication*]
Elektrochem Z ... Elektrochemische Zeitschrift [*A publication*]
Elektroenerget i Avtomat ... Elektroenergetika i Avtomatika [*A publication*]
Elektrofiz Appar ... Elektrofizicheskaya Apparatura [*A publication*]
Elektrofiz App Sb Statei ... Electrofizicheskaya Apparatura Sbornik Statei [*USSR*] [*A publication*]
Elektroizolacna Kablova Tech ... Elektroizolacna a Kablova Technika [*Czechoslovakia*] [*A publication*]
Elektro-Jahrb ... Elektro-Jahrbuch [*Switzerland*] [*A publication*]
Elektrok Tidsskr ... Elektroteknisk Tidsskrift [*A publication*]
Elektro Med Biomed und Tech ... Elektro Medizin, Biomedizin, und Technik [*A publication*]
Elektromeister & Dtsch Elektrohandwerk ... Elektromeister und Deutsches Elektrohandwerk [*A publication*]
Elektron Anz ... Elektronik-Anzeiger [*A publication*]
Elektron Appl ... Elektronik Applikation [*A publication*]
Elektron Bol'shikh Moshch ... Elektronika Bol'shikh Moshchnostei [*USSR*] [*A publication*]
Elektron Datenverarb ... Elektronische Datenverarbeitung [*A publication*]
Elektron Entwickl ... Elektronik Entwicklung [*A publication*]
Elektron Heute ... Elektronik Heute [*A publication*]
Elektronik ... Elektronik - Technologie - Anwendungen - Marketing [*A publication*]
Elektronik ... Elektronik-Zeitung [*A publication*]
Elektron Ind ... Elektronik Industrie [*A publication*]
Elektron Inf ... Elektronik Informationen [*A publication*]
Elektron Informationsverarbeit Kybernetik ... Elektronische Informationsverarbeitung und Kybernetik [*A publication*]
Elektron Informationsverarb Kybern ... Elektronische Informationsverarbeitung und Kybernetik [*A publication*]
Elektron Informationsverarb Kybernet ... Elektronische Informationsverarbeitung und Kybernetik [*Berlin*] [*A publication*]
Elektron Int ... Elektron International [*A publication*]
Elektron Ionnye Protsessy Tverd Telakh ... Elektronnye i Ionnye Protsessy v Tverdykh Telakh [*A publication*]
Elektron J ... Elektronik Journal [*A publication*]
Elektron Khim Kardiol ... Elektronika i Khimiya v Kardiologii [*A publication*]
Elektronmikroskopiever Suidelike Afr Verrig ... Elektronmikroskopievereniging van Suidelike Afrika. Verrigtings [*Electron Microscopy Society of Southern Africa. Proceedings*] [*A publication*]
Elektron Model ... Elektronnoe Modelirovanie [*Ukrainian SSR*] [*A publication*]
Elektron (Muenchen) ... Elektronik (Muenchen) [*A publication*]
Elektronnaya Obrab Mater ... Elektronnaya Obrabotka Materialov [*A publication*]
Elektron Obrab Mater ... Elektronnaya Obrabotka Materialov [*A publication*]
Elektron Prax ... Elektronik Praxis [*A publication*]
Elektron Radio Telev ... Elektroniikka Radio Televisio [*Finland*] [*A publication*]
Elektron Rechenanlagen ... Elektronische Rechenanlagen [*A publication*]
Elektron Rechenanlagen Comput Prax ... Elektronische Rechenanlagen mit Computer Praxis [*A publication*]
Elektron Rechnen und Regeln ... Elektronisches Rechnen und Regeln [*A publication*]
Elektron Rechnen Regeln Sonderband ... Elektronisches Rechnen und Regeln. Sonderband [*A publication*]
Elektron Rechnen und Regeln Sonderband ... Elektronisches Rechnen und Regeln. Sonderband [*A publication*]
Elektron Rech Regeln ... Elektronisches Rechnen und Regeln [*A publication*]

Elektron Tekh Ser 12 ... Elektronnaya Tekhnika. Seriya 12 [*A publication*]
Elektron Tekh Ser 1 Elektron ... Elektronnaya Tekhnika. Seriya 1. Elektronika [*USSR*] [*A publication*]
Elektron Wiss Tech ... Elektron in Wissenschaft und Technik [*A publication*]
Elektron-Ztg ... Elektronik-Zeitung [*West Germany*] [*A publication*]
Elektro-Prakt ... Elektro-Praktiker [*East Germany*] [*A publication*]
Elektroprom-St Priborostr ... Elektropromishlenost i Priborostroene [*Bulgaria*] [*A publication*]
Elektro Prom-St i Priborostroene ... Elektro Promishlenost i Priborostroene [*A publication*]
Elektrotec .. Elektrotechniek Elektronica [*A publication*]
Elektrotech Cas ... Elektrotechniky Casopis [*A publication*]
Elektrotech und Maschinenbau ... Elektrotechnik und Maschinenbau [*A publication*]
Elektrotech Maschinenbau ... Elektrotechnik und Maschinenbau [*A publication*]
Elektrotech Obz ... Elektrotechnicky Obzor [*A publication*]
Elektrotech Z A ... Elektrotechnische Zeitschrift. Ausgabe A [*A publication*]
Elektrotech Z Ausg A ... Elektrotechnische Zeitschrift. Ausgabe A [*A publication*]
Elektrotech Z Ausg B ... Elektrotechnische Zeitschrift. Ausgabe B [*A publication*]
Elektrotech Z B ... Elektrotechnische Zeitschrift. Ausgabe B [*A publication*]
Elektrotech Zeit ... Elektrotechnische Zeitschrift [*A publication*]
Elektrotech Z ETZ A ... Elektrotechnische Zeitschrift. ETZ A [*A publication*]
Elektrotech Z ETZ B ... Elektrotechnische Zeitschrift. ETZ B [*A publication*]
Elektroteh Ind Pogonu ... Elektrotehnika u Industriji Pogonu [*A publication*]
Elektroteh Vestn ... Elektrotehniski Vestnik [*A publication*]
Elektrotek Tidsskr ... Elektroteknisk Tidsskrift [*A publication*]
Elektrowaerme A ... Elektrowaerme im Technischen-Ausbau [*A publication*]
Elektrowaerme Int ... Elektrowaerme International [*A publication*]
Elektrowaerme Int A ... Elektrowaerme International. Edition A. Elektrowaerme im Technischen Ausbau [*A publication*]
Elektrowaerme Int A Elektrowaerme Tech Ausbau ... Elektrowaerme International. Edition A. Elektrowaerme im Technischen Ausbau [*A publication*]
Elektrowaerme Int B ... Elektrowaerme International. Edition B. Elektrowaerme im Technischen Ausbau [*A publication*]
Elektrowaerme Int B Elektrowaerme ... Elektrowaerme International. Edition B. Industrielle Elektrowaerme [*A publication*]
Elektrowaerme Int Ed A ... Elektrowaerme International. Edition A. Elektrowaerme im Technischen Ausbau [*A publication*]
Elektrowaerme Int Ed B ... Elektrowaerme International. Edition B. Industrielle Elektrowaerme [*A publication*]
Elektrowrm Tech-Ausbau ... Elektrowaerme im Technischen-Ausbau [*A publication*]
Elektr Stantsii ... Elektricheskie Stantsii [*A publication*]
Elektr Stn .. Elektricheskie Stantsii [*A publication*]
Elektr & Teplovoznaya Tyaga ... Elektricheskaya i Teplovoznaya Tyaga [*A publication*]
Elektr Teplovoz Tyaga ... Elektricheskaya i Teplovoznaya Tyaga [*A publication*]
Elektr Z B ... Elektrotechnische Zeitschrift. Ausgabe B [*A publication*]
Elek Zeit .... Elektrotechnische Zeitschrift [*A publication*]
El & El .... Ellis and Ellis' English Queen's Bench Reports [*A publication*] (DLA)
El & El (Eng) ... Ellis and Ellis' English Queen's Bench Reports [*A publication*] (DLA)
Elelmez Ipar ... Elelmezesi Ipar [*A publication*]
Elelm Ipar ... Elelmezesi Ipar [*A publication*]
Elelmiszervizgalati Kozl ... Elelmiszervizgalati Kozlemenyek [*A publication*]
Elelmiszerviz Kozl ... Elelmiszervizgalati Kozlemenyek [*A publication*]
Elelmiszerv Kozl ... Elelmiszervizgalati Kozlemenyek [*A publication*]
ELEM........ Element (MSA)
ELEM........ Elementary (MSA)
ELEMA..... Electrical Engineer (Melbourne) [*A publication*]
Elem Chastitsy Kosm Luchi ... Elementarnye Chastitsy i Kosmicheskie Luchi [*A publication*]
ElemE .... Elementary English [*A publication*]
Elem Engl .. Elementary English [*A publication*]
Elem Math ... Elemente der Mathematik [*A publication*]
Elem Math Suppl ... Elemente der Mathematik. Supplement [*A publication*]
Elem Met Clim ... Elementos Meteorologicos e Climatologicos [*A publication*]
Elem Sch J ... Elementary School Journal [*A publication*]
Elem School J ... Elementary School Journal [*A publication*]
ELENA...... Electrical Engineering. American Institute of Electrical Engineers [*A publication*]
El Enc Clin Neurophys ... Electroencephalography and Clinical Neurophysiology [*A publication*]
Elenchus Bibliogr Biblicus ... Elenchus Bibliographicus Biblicus [*A publication*]
ELEND...... Electrical Engineer [*A publication*]
El Energ..... Electrical Energy [*A publication*]
El and Energi Elektrotek ... El and Energi Elektroteknikeren [*A publication*]
El Eng........ Electrical Engineer [*A publication*]
El Eng .... Electrical Engineering. American Institute of Electrical Engineers [*A publication*]
El Engl........ Elementary English [*A publication*]
El Engl R ... Elementary English Review [*A publication*]
EL & Eq .... English Law and Equity Reports [*American Reprint*] [*A publication*] (DLA)

ELEQB...... Electric Equipment [*A publication*]
ELES .... Extended Linear Expenditure System
ELet .... Esperienze Letterarie. Rivista Trimestrale di Critica e Cultura [*A publication*]
ELet .... Etudes de Lettres [*A publication*]
ELet .... Europa Letteraria [*A publication*]
ELETB ...... Electrical Engineering Transactions [*A publication*]
Elettron Oggi ... Elettronica Oggi [*A publication*]
Elettron & Telecomun ... Elettronica e Telecomunicazioni [*A publication*]
Elettrotecn ... Elettrotecnica [*A publication*]
Elettrotecnica Suppl ... Elettrotecnica. Supplemento [*Italy*] [*A publication*]
ELEV........ Elevation (AFM)
ELEV........ Elevator
ELEV........ Elevon [*Aviation*] (NASA)
ElevenYBB ... Eleven Years of Bible Bibliography [*A publication*] (BJA)
Elev Insemination ... Elevage Insemination [*A publication*]
Elev Kosmos ... Elevtheros Kosmos [*A publication*]
Elev Porcin ... Elevage Porcin [*A publication*]
ELEWA..... Electrical West [*United States*] [*A publication*]
ELEX........ Electronics (MSA)
ELEX........ Electronics Exercise [*Military*] (NVT)
ELEX........ Elexis Corp. [*NASDAQ symbol*] (NQ)
Eley Game Advis Serv Annu Rep ... Eley Game Advisory Service. Annual Report [*A publication*]
Eley Game Advis Serv Bookl ... Eley Game Advisory Service. Booklet [*A publication*]
Eley Game Advis Stn Annu Rep ... Eley Game Advisory Station. Annual Report [*A publication*]
ELF.......... E-L Financial Corp. Ltd. [*Toronto Stock Exchange symbol*]
ELF.......... Early Lunar Flare
ELF.......... Education Liberation Front
ELF.......... El Fasher [*Sudan*] [*Airport symbol*] (OAG)
ELF.......... Electroluminescent Ferroelectric
ELF.......... Electron LASER Facility [*Physics*]
ELF.......... Electronic Location Finder
ELF.......... Elginfield [*Ontario*] [*Seismograph station code, US Geological Survey*] (SEIS)
ELF.......... Eliminate Legal-Size Files [*An association*]
ELF.......... Ellipsometry, Low Field [*Microscopy*]
ELF.......... Elvish Linguistic Fellowship (EA)
ELF.......... Emergency Land Fund [*Later, FSC/LAF*] (EA)
ELF.......... Engine Lube Filter
ELF.......... Eritrean Liberation Front [*Ethiopia*] (PD)
ELF.......... Esperanto-Ligo Filatelista [*Philatelic Esperanto League - PEL*] (EAIO)
ELF.......... Etude de la Langue Francaise [*A publication*]
ELF.......... European Landworkers Federation
ELF.......... Everybody Loves Fudge [*in Keebler Co. brand of cookies "E. L. Fudge"*]
ELF.......... Expeditionary Logistics Facility (MCD)
ELF.......... Explosive-Actuated Light Filter (NG)
ELF.......... Explosive Lens Flashbinder
ELF.......... Extensible Language Facility [*Data processing*] (IEEE)
ELF.......... Extremely Low Frequency [*Electronics, radio wave*]
ELFA .... Enzyme-Linked Fluorescence Assay
ELFC .... Electroluminescent Ferroelectric Cell
ELFC .... Elvis Lives On Fan Club (EA)
ELFCA ...... Ecole de Langue Francaise de la Cote D'Azur [*France*] (ECON)
ELF-ERAP ... Essences et Lubrifiants de France - Entreprise de Recherches et d'Activites Petrolieres [*French oil company*]
ELFIS .... Ernaehrungs-, Land-, und Forstwissenschaftliches Informations-System [*German Information System on Food, Agriculture, and Forestry*] [*Zentralstelle fuer Agrardokumentation und -Information*] [*Information service or system*]
ELFOD...... Electric Forum [*United States*] [*A publication*]
ELF-PLF ... Eritrean Liberation Front - Popular Liberation Forces [*Ethiopia*] (PD)
ELF-RC ..... Eritrean Liberation Front - Revolutionary Command [*Ethiopia*] (PD)
ELG .... El Cap Gold Mines [*Vancouver Stock Exchange symbol*]
ELG .... Electrolytic Grinding (IEEE)
ELG .... Emergency Landing Ground
ELG .... Equal Life Group [*Depreciation class*]
ELG .... European Liaison Group [*Army*] (AABC)
ELG .... European Lymphology Group [*See also GEL*] [*Brussels, Belgium*] (EAIO)
ELGB........ Emergency Loan Guarantee Board
EL-GIEU ... Erector-Launcher Ground Interface Electronics Unit (MCD)
ELGMT..... Erector-Launcher, Guided Missile, Transportable
ELGSS....... Ev. [*Evangelical*] Lutheran Good Samaritan Society (EA)
ELGT........ Electric & Gas Technology, Inc. [*Dallas, TX*] [*NASDAQ symbol*] (NQ)
ELH .... Egg-Laying Hormone [*Endocrinology*]
ELH .... Equine Luteinizing Hormone [*Endocrinology*]
ELH .... Journal of English Literary History [*A publication*]
e-lh--- .... Liechtenstein [*MARC geographic area code*] [*Library of Congress*] (LCCP)
ELH .... North Eleuthera [*Bahamas*] [*Airport symbol*] (OAG)
ELH Engl L ... ELH. English Literary History [*A publication*]

ELHI .... Elementary and High School [*Acronym refers to books published for this market*]
ELHILL .... Lister Hill System [*Search system*]
ELHWS..... Electric Hot Water Service [*Classified advertising*] (ADA)
ELHYD ..... Electrohydraulic
ELI............. Early Latent Infection [*Medicine*]
ELI............. Economic Literature Index [*American Economic Association*] [*Information service or system*] (IID)
ELI............. Educational Leadership Institute (EA)
ELI............. ELE Energy, Incorporated [*Vancouver Stock Exchange symbol*]
ELI............. Electronic Line Indicator [*Tennis*]
ELI............. Elim [*Alaska*] [*Airport symbol*] (OAG)
Eli............. Elite [*Record label*] [*Europe*]
ELI............. Elizabethville [*Zaire*] [*Later, KVA*] [*Geomagnetic observatory code*]
ELI............. Elizabethville [*Karavia*] [*Zaire*] [*Seismograph station code, US Geological Survey*] [*Closed*] (SEIS)
ELI............. Emitter Location and Identification
ELI............. Endomorphin-Like Immunoreactivity
ELI............. Energy Law Institute (EA)
ELI............. English Language Institute [*University of Michigan*] [*Research center*] (RCD)
ELI............. Environmental Law Institute (EA)
ELI............. Equitable Life Interpreter [*Computer*]
ELI............. European Light Infantry [*British military*] (DMA)
ELI............. Extended Lubrication Interval [*Automotive engineering*]
ELI............. Extensible Language I [*Data processing*]
ELI............. Extra-Low Impurity [*Metals*]
ELI............. Extra-Low Interstitial [*Alloy*]
ELIA......... Elementary Imprint Assistance [*Writing system for the blind*]
ELIA......... Enhanced Luminescent Immunoassay [*Analytical biochemistry*]
ELIAS........ Entry Level Interactive Applications Systems [*Data processing*]
ELIAS........ Environment Libraries Automated System [*Environment Canada*] [*Database*] [*Information service or system*] (IID)
ELIC......... Early Literacy in Childhood [*Australia*]
ELIC......... Early Literacy Inservice Course [*Australia*]
ELICIANT ... Eliciantur [*Let Be Drawn*] [*Pharmacy*] (ROG)
ELIDA .... Electronic Industries [*A publication*]
ELIEDA .... Enzyme-Linked Immunoelectric Diffusion Assay [*Clinical chemistry*]
ELIFE....... Enhancement of Life Support, Europe (MCD)
ELIG......... Eligible (AFM)
ELIM........ Eliminate (AFM)
ELIM........ Eliminator [*Automotive engineering*]
ELIM........ Enlisted Loss Inventory Model (MCD)
ELIM........ Evangelical Lutherans in Mission [*Group opposing the Missouri Synod of the Lutheran Church*]
ELIN........ Exhibit Line Item Number (MCD)
El Ind .... Electrical Industry [*A publication*]
ELIND........ Electricien Industriel [*A publication*]
ELing .... Etudes Linguistiques [*A publication*]
ELINT .... Electronic Intelligence [*or Intercept*] [*Meaning of ELINT determined by reference to before (Intercept) and after (Intelligence) analysis of reconnaissance mission results*]
ELINT TGU ... Electronic Intelligence Technical Guidance Unit (MCD)
Elin-Z......... Elin- Zeitschrift [*A publication*]
ELIP......... Electrostatic Latent Image Photography (IEEE)
ELIP......... Elliptical (FAAC)
ELIPA .... Experienced Librarians and Information Personnel in the Developing Countries of Asia and Oceania [*Korea Advanced Institute of Science and Technology*] [*Seoul*] [*Information service or system*] (IID)
ELIS .... Electronic Library Information System [*Library network*] (IT)
ELIS .... Eli Scientific, Inc. [*NASDAQ symbol*] (NQ)
ELIS .... Encyclopedia of Legal Information Sources [*A publication*]
ELISA........ Enzyme-Linked [*or -Labeled*] Immunosorbent Assay [*Immunochemistry*]
Elisha Mitchell Sci Soc J ... Elisha Mitchell Scientific Society. Journal [*A publication*]
ELIT .... Electronics Information Test
ELiT......... English Literature in Transition, 1880-1920 [*A publication*]
ELit......... Estafeta Literaria [*A publication*]
ELit......... Etudes Litteraires [*A publication*]
ELITE....... Executive Level Interactive Terminal Environment (RDA)
ELIX......... Elixir [*Pharmacology*]
ELIZ......... Elizabethan (ROG)
Eliz............. Queen Elizabeth (DLA)
ElizS......... Elizabethan Studies [*A publication*]
ELJ .... El Recreo [*Colombia*] [*Airport symbol*] (OAG)
ELJ .... Eljer Industries, Inc. [*NYSE symbol*] (SPSG)
ELJ .... Executive-Legislative-Judicial
ELJAA ...... Elektro-Jahrbuch [*A publication*]
ELK........... Elcor Corp. [*NYSE symbol*] (SPSG)
ELK........... Elk City, OK [*Location identifier*] [*FAA*] (FAAL)
ELK........... Elko [*Nevada*] [*Seismograph station code, US Geological Survey*] (SEIS)
ELK........... Emerald Lake Resources, Inc. [*Toronto Stock Exchange symbol*]

ELK........... Enosis Laikou Kommatos [*Union of Populist Parties*] [*Greek*] (PPE)
ELK........... Ethniko Laiko Komma [*National Populist Party*] [*Greek*] (PPE)
ELKCA ..... Elektrotechnicky Casopis [*A publication*]
ELKE........ Elevated Kinetic Energy Weapon
ELKHA ..... Elektro-Handel [*A publication*]
ELKOA..... Elektronik [*A publication*]
ELKRD..... Elektronik-Centralen. Report. ECR [*A publication*]
ELKt........ Epitheorese Logou Kai Technes [*A publication*]
ELKTA ..... Elektrotekhnika [*A publication*]
ELKTD..... Elektronikk [*A publication*]
ELKWA..... Elektrowirtschaft [*A publication*]
ELKZ........ Evangelisch-Lutherische Kirchenzeitung [*Berlin*] [*A publication*]
ELL........... Ellipsometry [*Surface analysis*]
ELL........... Elmali [*Turkey*] [*Seismograph station code, US Geological Survey*] (SEIS)
ELL........... English Language Laboratory
ELL........... English Language and Literature [*A publication*]
ELL........... Equivalent Loudness Level
ELL........... Excimer LASER Lithography
ELL........... Huntsville, AL [*Location identifier*] [*FAA*] (FAAL)
ELLA........ Eastern Lamp and Lighting Association (EA)
ELLA........ European Long Lines Agency [*NATO*]
Ell Ann .... Ellison. Law of Annuities [*A publication*] (DLA)
Ell B & Ell ... Ellis, Blackburn, and Ellis' English Queen's Bench Reports [*A publication*] (ILCA)
Ell & Bl .... Ellis and Blackburn's English Queen's Bench Reports [*118-120 English Reprint*] [*A publication*] (DLA)
Ell Bl & Ell ... Ellis, Blackburn, and Ellis' English Queen's Bench Reports [*A publication*] (DLA)
Ell B & S ... Ellis, Best, and Smith's English Queen's Bench Reports [*A publication*] (DLA)
Ell D & Cr ... Ellis. Debtor and Creditor [*1822*] [*A publication*] (DLA)
Ell Deb .... Elliot's Debates on the Federal Constitution [*A publication*] (DLA)
Ell Dig........ Eller's Minnesota Digest [*A publication*] (ILCA)
Ell Dip Code .... Elliot's American Diplomatic Code [*A publication*] (DLA)
ELLEA....... Electronics Letters [*A publication*]
Ell & Ell ..... Ellis and Ellis' English Queen's Bench Reports [*A publication*] (DLA)
Ellesm Post N ... Ellesmere's Post Nati [*A publication*] (DLA)
ELLF .... Etudes de Langue et de Litterature Francaises [*A publication*]
Elli .... Ellipse [*A publication*]
Ell Ins .... Ellis on Fire and Life Insurance and Annuities [*A publication*] (DLA)
Elliot Deb Fed Const ... Elliot's Debates on the Federal Constitution [*A publication*] (DLA)
Elliott App Proc ... Elliott's Appellate Procedure [*A publication*] (DLA)
Elliott Roads & S ... Elliott on Roads and Streets [*A publication*] (DLA)
Elliott Soc N H Charleston Pr ... Elliott Society of Natural History of Charleston. Proceedings [*A publication*]
Elliott Supp ... Elliott's Supplement to the Indiana Revised Statutes [*A publication*] (DLA)
ELLIPT ..... Elliptical
Ellis............ Ellis on Insurance [*A publication*] (DLA)
ELLIS........ European Legal Literature Information Service [*London, England*]
Ellis & Bl ... Ellis and Blackburn's English Queen's Bench Reports [*118-120 English Reprint*] [*A publication*] (DLA)
Ellis Dr & Cr ... Ellis. Debtor and Creditor [*1822*] [*A publication*] (DLA)
Ellis Horwood Ser Comput Appl ... Ellis Horwood Series. Computers and Their Applications [*A publication*]
Ellis Horwood Ser Math Appl ... Ellis Horwood Series. Mathematics and Its Applications [*A publication*]
ELLL........ Electrosensory Lateral Line [*Invertebrate zoology*]
ELLM........ Ellman's, Inc. [*NASDAQ symbol*] (NQ)
ELLPA ..... Electric Light and Power [*A publication*]
ELLS .... English Literature and Language [*Tokyo, Japan*] [*A publication*]
ELLSA....... Enzyme-Linked Ligand Sorbent Assay [*Analytical biochemistry*]
Ells Cop Man ... Ellsworth's Copyright Manual [*A publication*] (DLA)
Ell Trade.... Ellet on the Laws of Trade [*A publication*] (DLA)
Ellwanger Jb ... Ellwanger Jahrbuch: Ein Volksbuch fuer Heimatpflege in Virngau und Ries [*A publication*]
ELLX .... Luxembourg/Luxembourg [*ICAO location identifier*] (ICLI)
ELM .... Eastern Atlantic and Mediterranean [*Military*]
ELM .... El Urogallo (Madrid) [*A publication*]
ELM .... Element (AABC)
ELM .... Element Load Model
ELM .... Elma [*New York*] [*Seismograph station code, US Geological Survey*] [*Closed*] (SEIS)
ELM .... Elmira [*New York*] [*Airport symbol*] (OAG)
ELM .... Emitter Location Method
ELM .... Emulsion Liquid Membrane [*Chemical separation technology*]
ELM .... Endings [*of nerves*] to Lip Muscle
ELM .... Expendable Light Markers (NVT)
ELM .... Extended Length Methods (MCD)
ELM .... Extended Lunar Mission [*NASA*] (KSC)

ELM .... External Limiting Membrane
ELM .... La-Rouche-Sur-Yon [*France*] [*Airport symbol*]
ELMA .... Emergency Lighting Manufacturers Association [*Defunct*] (EA)
ELMAA ..... Electrical Manufacturing [*A publication*]
Elma Dill Russell Spencer Found Ser ... Elma Dill Russell Spencer Foundation Series [*A publication*]
ELMAP ..... Exchange Line Multiplexing Analysis Program (TEL)
Elm Arch Jur ... Elmes on Architectural Jurisprudence [*A publication*] (DLA)
ELMCBK .... Electromedica [*English Edition*] [*A publication*]
ELMCH .... Electromechanical
ELMD .... Electromedics, Inc. [*NASDAQ symbol*] (NQ)
Elm Dig ..... Elmer's New Jersey Digest of Laws [*A publication*] (DLA)
Elm Dilap... Elmes on Ecclesiastical Civil Dilapidation [*A publication*] (DLA)
ELME .... Emitter Location Method
ELMECH ... Electromechanical (NASA)
Elmer Lun ... Elmer's Practice in Lunacy [*A publication*] (DLA)
Elm Exec Dep ... Elmes' Executive Departments of the United States [*A publication*] (DLA)
ELMG .... Electromagnetic Sciences, Inc. [*NASDAQ symbol*] (NQ)
ELMG .... Engine Life Management Group [*Navy*]
ELMINT .... Electromagnetic Intelligence
Elm Lun ..... Elmer's Practice in Lunacy [*A publication*] (DLA)
ELMMA .... Elemente der Mathematik [*A publication*]
ELMN(A) ... Electrical Mechanician (Air) [*Navy rating*] [*British*]
ELMN(AW) ... Electrical Mechanician (Air Weapon) [*British military*] (DMA)
Elm NJ Laws ... Elmer's New Jersey Digest of Laws [*A publication*] (DLA)
ELMO .... El Morro National Monument
ELMO .... Engineering and Logistics Management Office [*MERDC*] [*Army*]
ELMO .... European Laundry and Dry Cleaning Machinery Manufacturers Organization (EA)
ELMOD .... Elektronnoe Modelirovanie [*A publication*]
ELMS .... Earth Limb Measurement Satellite [*NASA/Air Force*]
ELMS .... Educators of Library Media Specialists Section [*American Association of School Librarians*]
ELMS .... Elastic Loop Mobility System [*NASA*]
ELMS .... Elmer's Restaurants, Inc. [*Portland, OR*] [*NASDAQ symbol*] (NQ)
ELMS .... Engineering Lunar Model Surface
ELMS .... Experimental Library Management System
ELMT .... Electronic Mechanic Technician
ELMYA ..... Electromyography [*Later, Electromyography and Clinical Neurophysiology*] [*A publication*]
ELMYAH ... Electromyography [*Later, Electromyography and Clinical Neurophysiology*] [*A publication*]
ELMZA .... Elelmiszertudomany [*A publication*]
ELN .... Ejercito de Liberacion Nacional [*National Liberation Army*] [*Peru*] (PD)
ELN .... Ejercito de Liberacion Nacional [*National Liberation Army*] [*Colombia*] (PD)
ELN .... Ejercito de Liberacion Nacional [*National Liberation Army*] [*Bolivia*] (PD)
ELN .... Elan Corp. PLC ADS [*AMEX symbol*] (SPSG)
ELN .... Electronic Laboratory Notebook
ELN .... Ellensburg, WA [*Location identifier*] [*FAA*] (FAAL)
ELN .... English Language Notes [*A publication*]
ELN .... Environmental Law Newsletter [*A publication*] (APTA)
ELNA .... Esperanto League for North America (EA)
ELND .... Elective Node Dissection [*Medicine*]
ELNEO ..... Elastase-Neomycin Gene [*Genetics*]
ELNES ..... Electron Loss Near Edge Structure [*Electron microscopy*]
ELNG .... Elongate (MSA)
ELNGT...... Elongate (FAAC)
ELNS .... European League for a New Society [*See also LIENS*] [*Paris, France*] (EAIO)
ELO .... Eldorado Minerals & Petroleum [*Vancouver Stock Exchange symbol*]
ELO .... Electric Light Orchestra [*Rock music group*]
ELO .... Ely, MN [*Location identifier*] [*FAA*] (FAAL)
ELO .... Epoxidized Linseed Oil [*Organic chemistry*]
ELO .... Evangelical Literature Overseas (EA)
ELO .... Eye Lens Obsolescence [*Ophthalmology*]
ELO .... Logiealmond [*Scotland*] [*Seismograph station code, US Geological Survey*] (SEIS)
ELOC .... Eastern Line of Communication [*World War II*]
Eloc .... Elocution
ELOCARS ... Electro-Optical Collection and Analysis Reporting System (MCD)
ELO-CATS ... Electro-Optical Collection and Analysis Targeting System
ELODA ..... Electronic Design [*A publication*]
ELOG .... European Landowning Organization Group (EAIO)
ELOI .... Emergency Letter of Instructions
ELOISE..... European Large Orbiting Instrumentation for Solar Experiments
ELONG ..... Elongation (MSA)
ELONG ..... Estimated Longitude (FAAC)
ELOP......... El-De Electro-Optic Development Ltd. [*NASDAQ symbol*] (NQ)

ELOQ .... Eloquence [*or Eloquent*] (ROG)
ELOR .... Extended Lunar Orbital Rendezvous [*NASA*] (KSC)
ELORM .... Extended Lunar Orbital Rendezvous Mission [*NASA*] (KSC)
ELOS........ Extended Line-of-Sight (CAAL)
ELOSA9 .... Elsevier Oceanography Series [*Elsevier Book Series*] [*A publication*]
ELOTARLOCS ... Electro-Optical Target Locating System (MCD)
ELOWA .... Electro-Technology [*New York*] [*A publication*]
ELOX .... Electrical Spark Erosion
ELP........... El Pangue [*Chile*] [*Seismograph station code, US Geological Survey*] (SEIS)
ELP........... El Paso [*Texas*] [*Airport symbol*] (OAG)
ELP........... El Paso Refinery Preferred LP [*NYSE symbol*] (SPSG)
ELP........... El Paso, TX [*Location identifier*] [*FAA*] (FAAL)
ELP........... Electronic Label Printing [*Diagraph Corp.*]
ELP........... Electronic Printer (MCD)
ELP........... Elliptical (MSA)
ELP........... Emergency Loading Procedure
ELP........... Emerson, Lake & Palmer [*Rock music group*]
ELP........... Emulsified Liquid Propellant
ELP........... Endogenous Limbic Potentials [*Neurophysiology*]
ELP........... Engine Lube and Purge [*System*]
ELP........... English Language Program (MCD)
ELP........... Estimated Learning Potential
ELP........... Extreme Limb Photometer [*Instrumentation*]
ELPA .... El Paso Electric Co. [*NASDAQ symbol*] (NQ)
El Pal ...... El Palacio [*A publication*]
El Paso Econ R ... El Paso Economic Review [*A publication*]
El Paso Geol Soc Annu Field Trip (Guideb) ... El Paso Geological Society. Annual Field Trip (Guidebook) [*A publication*]
El Paso Trial Law Rev ... El Paso Trial Lawyers Review [*A publication*] (DLA)
ELPB .... Engine Logistics Planning Board [*Air Force*] (AFIT)
ELPBA ..... Elektropromishlenost i Priborostroene [*A publication*]
EL-PC....... Electroluminescent-Photoconductive (MCD)
ELPE .... Electroluminescent-Photoelectric
ELPG .... Electric Light and Power Group
ELPGA ..... European Liquefied Petroleum Gas Association (EA)
ELPH........ Elliptical Head (IEEE)
Elph .... Elphinstone, Norton, and Clark. Interpretation of Deeds [*1885*] [*A publication*] (DLA)
Elph Conv .. Elphinstone's Introduction to Conveyancing [*A publication*] (DLA)
Elph Interp Deeds ... Elphinstone's Rules for Interpretation of Deeds [*A publication*] (DLA)
ELPHR....... Experimental Low-Temperature Process Heat Reactor
ELPLBS ..... Ekologia Polska [*A publication*]
ELPLD ...... Electronics Information and Planning [*A publication*]
ELPNEU ... Electropneumatic
ELPOA ...... Electronic Products [*A publication*]
ELPPA ...... Electronic Packaging and Production [*A publication*]
ELPVA ...... Elektroprivreda [*A publication*]
ELPWA ..... Electronics and Power [*A publication*]
ELQ .... El Quisco [*Chile*] [*Seismograph station code, US Geological Survey*] [*Closed*] (SEIS)
ELQ .... Gassim [*Saudi Arabia*] [*Airport symbol*] (OAG)
ELQC........ Electroluminescent Quantum Counter
ELR........... Earned Loss Ratio [*Insurance*]
ELR........... East London Railway (ROG)
ELR........... Eastern Law Reporter [*Canada*] [*A publication*] (DLA)
ELR........... Educational Lending Right [*Australia*]
ELR........... Eldon Resources Ltd. [*Vancouver Stock Exchange symbol*]
ELR........... Election Law Reports [*India*] [*A publication*] (DLA)
ELR........... Engineering Laboratory Report
ELR........... Engineering Liaison Request (KSC)
ELR........... English Literary Renaissance [*A publication*]
ELR........... Environmental Law Reporter [*Environmental Law Institute*] [*A publication*]
ELR........... Environmental Law Reporter of New South Wales [*A publication*] (APTA)
ELR........... Equal Listener Response [*Scale*]
ELR........... European Law Review [*A publication*]
ELR........... Expected Loss Ratio [*Insurance*]
ELR........... Rapid City, SD [*Location identifier*] [*FAA*] (FAAL)
ELRA .... Electronic RADAR
elra .... European Leisure and Recreation Association (EAIO)
ELRAA ..... Elektronische Rechenanlagen [*A publication*]
ELRAC...... Electronic Reconnaissance Accessory
ELRC........ Electro Rent Corporation [*NASDAQ symbol*] (NQ)
ELREA ..... Electrical Review [*London*] [*A publication*]
ELRen....... English Literary Renaissance [*A publication*]
EL Rev ...... European Law Review [*A publication*]
ELRFTD.... Eye-Safe LASER Range Finder Training Device (MCD)
ELRIC ...... Employers Labor Relations Information Committee (EA)
ELRMD..... Electric Ratemaking [*A publication*]
ELRN .... Elron Electronic Industries Ltd. [*NASDAQ symbol*] (NQ)
ELRO .... Electronics Logistics Research Office
ELRPA ...... Environmental Law Reporter [*A publication*]
ELRPD ...... ELCON [*Electricity Consumers Resource Council*] Report [*A publication*]
ELS........... Early Lunar Shelter [*NASA*] (KSC)

ELS............ Earth Landing System [*or Subsystem*] [*NASA*]
ELS............ East London [*South Africa*] [*Airport symbol*]   (OAG)
ELS............ Eastern Launch Site   (MCD)
ELS............ Electric Limit Switch
ELS............ Electrical System
ELS............ Electron Energy Loss Spectroscopy [*Also, EELS*]
EL & S........ Electronic Laboratories and Services
ELS............ Electrophoretic Light Scattering [*Analytical chemistry*]
ELS............ Electrostatic Loudspeaker   (DEN)
ELS............ Elevon Load System [*Aviation*]   (MCD)
ELS............ Elizabeth Linington Society   (EA)
ELS............ Elm Leaf Scorch [*Plant pathology*]
ELS............ Elsevier [*Published by the Elsevier family*]   (ROG)
Els............. Elsinore [*A publication*]
ELS............ Elsinore Corp. [*AMEX symbol*]   (SPSG)
ELS............ Emitter Location System [*Air Force*]
ELS............ Enchiridion Locorum Sanctorum [*A publication*]   (BJA)
ELS............ Energy-Loss Spectroscopy
ELS............ English Literary Studies [*A publication*]
ELS............ Entry Level System [*Data processing*]
ELS............ Eosinophilic Lymphfolliculosis of the Skin [*Kimura disease*] [*Dermatology*]
ELS............ Error Likely Situation   (IEEE)
ELS............ Escanaba & Lake Superior Railroad Co. [*AAR code*]
ELS............ Evangelical Lutheran Synod
ELS............ Extra-Long Staple [*Cotton*]
ELS............ Harvard Environmental Law Society   (EA)
ELSA......... Compania de Alumbrado Electrica San Salvador SA [*NASDAQ symbol*]   (NQ)
ELSA......... Electronic Selective Archives [*Swiss News Agency*] [*Information service or system*]   (IID)
ELSA......... English Language Skills Assessment in a Reading Context [*Educational test*]
ELSA......... Environmental Life-Support Assembly [*NASA*]   (KSC)
ELSA......... Estonian Learned Society of America   (EA)
ELSA......... Evangelical Lutheran Synod in Australia
El Salv....... El Salvador
El Salvador Servicio Geol Nac Anales Bol Bol Sismol ... El Salvador. Servicio Geologico Nacional. Anales. Boletin. Boletin Sismologico [*A publication*]
El Salvador Univ Inst Tropical Inv Cient Anuario Comun ... El Salvador. Universidad. Instituto Tropical de Investigaciones Cientificas. Anuario Comunicaciones [*A publication*]
El Salv Dir Gen Invest Agron Secc Agron Bol Tec ... El Salvador. Direccion General de Investigaciones Agronomicas. Seccion de Agronomia. Boletin Tecnico [*A publication*]
El Salv Dir Gen Invest Agron Secc Entomol Bol Tec ... El Salvador. Direccion General de Investigaciones Agronomicas. Seccion de Entomologia. Boletin Tecnico [*A publication*]
El Salv M... Banco Central de Reserra de El Salvador. Revista Mensual [*A publication*]
ELSAP....... Elektronische Schiessanlace fuer Panzer [*German*]
ELSASSER ... Elsaess-Lothringen Partei [*Alsace-Lorraine Party*] [*German*]   (PPE)
ELSB......... Edge-Lighted Status Board [*Navy*]
ELSC......... Earth Landing Sequence Controller [*NASA*]   (NASA)
El Sch Guid & Counsel ... Elementary School Guidance and Counseling [*A publication*]
El Sch J...... Elementary School Journal [*A publication*]
El School T ... Elementary School Teacher [*A publication*]
ELSE......... Electrical Launch Support Equipment [*NASA*]   (KSC)
ELSE......... Electro-Sensors, Inc. [*NASDAQ symbol*]   (NQ)
ELSEC...... Electronic Security [*Air Force*]
Elsevier Oceanogr Ser ... Elsevier Oceanography Series [*Elsevier Book Series*] [*A publication*]
Elsevier Oceanogr Ser (Amsterdam) ... Elsevier Oceanography Series (Amsterdam) [*Elsevier Book Series*] [*A publication*]
ELSEWH .. Elsewhere [*Manuscripts*]   (ROG)
ELSI......... Electrosource, Inc. [*NASDAQ symbol*]   (NQ)
ELSI......... Extra-Large-Scale Integration [*Data processing*]   (TEL)
ELSIE....... Electronic Letter Sorting and Indicator Equipment
ELSIE....... Electronic Signaling and Indicating Equipment   (IEEE)
ELSIE....... Electronic Speech Information Equipment [*System developed by Britain's Department of Transport to facilitate bus transit*]
ELSIE....... Emergency Life-Saving Instant Exit [*Aircraft*] [*Air Force*]
ELSM....... Els Marges [*Barcelona*] [*A publication*]
ELSO....... El Nino-Southern Oscillation [*Experiment*]
ELSOR...... Education Libraries Sharing of Resources [*Network*]
ELSP .... Economic Lot Scheduling Problem
ELSPA...... Elektricheskie Seti i Sistemy [*A publication*]
ELSRB...... Electrotechnical Laboratory. Summaries of Reports [*Japan*] [*A publication*]
ELSS......... Electronic Legislative Search System [*Commerce Clearing House, Inc.*] [*Information service or system*]
ELSS......... Emergency Life Support System
ELSS......... Emplaced Lunar Scientific Station [*Aerospace*]
ELSS......... EVA [*Extravehicular Activity*] Life-Support System [*NASA*]
EL-SSC...... Electronic Switching System Control [*Telecommunications*]   (TEL)
ELSSE....... Electronic Sky Screen Equipment [*Air Force*]

ELSUA ..... Electrical Supervisor [*A publication*]
ELSUR...... Electronic Surveillance Index [*FBI file of persons overheard on wiretaps*]
ELSW .... Elsewhere   (FAAC)
Els W Bl.... Elsley's Edition of William Blackstone's English King's Bench Reports [*A publication*]   (DLA)
Elsyn Parl .. Elsynge on Parliaments [*A publication*]   (DLA)
ELT........... Each Less Than
ELT........... Eagle's Law of Tithes [*2nd ed.*] [*1836*] [*A publication*]   (ILCA)
ELT........... East London Telecommunications [*Commercial firm*] [*British*]
ELT........... Electra [*A publication*]
ELT........... Electrocardiography and Basal Metabolism Technician [*Navy*]
ELT........... Electrometer   (DEN)
ELT........... Electronic Technician
ELT........... Element
ELT........... Elscint Ltd. [*NYSE symbol*]   (SPSG)
ELT........... Eltsovka [*USSR*] [*Seismograph station code, US Geological Survey*]   (SEIS)
ELT........... Emergency Locator Transmitter
ELT........... Enforcement of Laws and Treaties [*Program*] [*Coast Guard*]
ELT........... Engineering Laboratory Technician
ELT........... English Language Teaching [*Later, English Language Teaching Journal*] [*A publication*]
ELT........... English Language Teaching
ELT........... English Literature in Transition, 1880-1920 [*A publication*]
ELT........... Entry Level Training
ELT........... Environmental Team Leader [*Nuclear energy*]   (NRCH)
ELT........... Euglobulin Lysis Time [*Clinical chemistry*]
ELT........... European Letter Telegram
ELTC......... English Language Teaching Centre [*Royal Melbourne Institute of Technology*] [*Australia*]
ELTC......... Enlisted Loss to Commissioned Status [*Military*]
ELTCA ..... Electricite [*A publication*]
Elt Com ..... Elton on Commons and Waste Lands [*A publication*]   (DLA)
Elt Copyh ... Elton on Copyholds [*A publication*]   (DLA)
ELTD........ Eurobike Limited   (EA)
ELTEA ...... Electro-Technology [*Bangalore, India*] [*A publication*]
Eltec......... Electronic Technology [*Automotive engineering*]
ELTEC ...... Electronics Technician   (NOAA)
El Techn..... Elektrotehnika [*A publication*]
El Techn Cas ... Elektrotechnicky Casopis [*A publication*]
El Technol (USSR) ... Electric Technology (USSR) [*A publication*]
El Techn Zs ... Elektrotechnische Zeitschrift [*A publication*]
Eltek Aktuell Elektron ... Elteknik Med Aktuell Elektronik [*A publication*]
Eltek Aktuell Elektron A ... Elteknik Med Aktuell Elektronik. Edition A [*A publication*]
Elteknik Med Aktuel Elektron ... Elteknik Med Aktuell Elektronik [*A publication*]
ELTG........ European Logistics Task Group   (MCD)
ELTGA ..... Electric Technology (USSR) [*English Translation*] [*A publication*]
ELTHB...... Elektrotehnika [*A publication*]
ELTI .... Elapsed-Time Indicator   (MCD)
ELTIA ...... Electrical Times [*A publication*]
ELTJ......... English Language Teaching Journal [*A publication*]
ELTKA ..... Elektrotechniek [*A publication*]
Elton Com ... Elton on Commons and Waste Lands [*A publication*]   (DLA)
Elton Copyh ... Elton on Copyholds [*A publication*]   (DLA)
ELTPA ..... Electronic Progress [*A publication*]
ELTR........ Emergency Locator Transmitter Receiver
ELTRD...... Elektronikschau [*A publication*]
ELTRN...... Electron [*A nuclear particle*]
ELTRNC ... Electronic
ELTS .... English Language Testing Service [*Australia*]
ELTSA ...... Elettrotecnica. Supplemento [*A publication*]
ELTSA ...... End Loans to Southern Africa [*An association*]   (EAIO)
ELTTA ...... Electrotehnica [*A publication*]
Elt Ten of Kent ... Elton's Tenures of Kent [*A publication*]   (DLA)
ELTV......... Ejection Launch Test Vehicle   (NG)
ELTW....... Enlisted Loss to Warrant Status [*Military*]
ELTZA ...... Elettrificazione [*A publication*]
ELU .... El Oued [*Algeria*] [*Airport symbol*]   (OAG)
ELu .... Estudios Lulianos [*A publication*]
e-lu--- .... Luxembourg [*MARC geographic area code*] [*Library of Congress*]   (LCCP)
ELul .... Estudios Lulianos [*A publication*]
ELUX........ Electrolux AB [*NASDAQ symbol*]   (NQ)
ELV.......... Earth Launch Vehicle [*NASA*]
ELV.......... Electrically Operated Valve
ELV.......... Elfin Cove [*Alaska*] [*Airport symbol*]   (OAG)
ELV.......... Elfin Cove, AK [*Location identifier*] [*FAA*]   (FAAL)
ELV.......... Enclosed-Frame Low Voltage   (IEEE)
ELV.......... Expendable Launch Vehicle [*NASA*]   (KSC)
ELV.......... Extension Lay Volunteers   (EA)
ELV.......... Extra-Low Voltage
ELVEA ...... Elektrontehniski Vestnik [*A publication*]
El Verw ..... Elektrizitaetsverwertung [*A publication*]
ELVIS....... Electroluminescent Vertical Indication System
ELVIS....... Electrovisual System   (MUGU)
ELVN .... Eleven   (NASA)
ELW .... Anderson, SC [*Location identifier*] [*FAA*]   (FAAL)

ELW .... Earth Launch Window [*Aerospace*] (AAG)
ELW .... Electronic Warfare (CAAL)
ELW .... Extreme Low Water
ELW .... Webster College, Eden Theological Seminary, Webster Groves, MO [*OCLC symbol*] (OCLC)
ELWAR..... Electronic Warfare
ELWD .... Extra-Long Working Distance [*Microscopy*]
El Wi .... Elektrizitaetswirtschaft [*A publication*]
El Wiss Techn ... Elektron in Wissenschaft und Technik [*A publication*]
ELWIU...... Essays in Literature. Western Illinois University [*A publication*]
ELWLA..... Elektrowelt [*A publication*]
Elw Mal .... Elwell on Malpractice and Medical Jurisprudence [*A publication*] (DLA)
Elw Med Jur ... Elwell on Malpractice and Medical Jurisprudence [*A publication*] (DLA)
ELWOA .... Electrical World [*A publication*]
ELWS....... Extreme Low Water of Spring Tide
ELWYA..... Electronics Weekly [*A publication*]
elx........... Elamite [*MARC language code*] [*Library of Congress*] (LCCP)
ELX.......... Exol Industries Ltd. [*Vancouver Stock Exchange symbol*]
ELX.......... Keeler, MI [*Location identifier*] [*FAA*] (FAAL)
ELXS........ ELXSI Corp. [*NASDAQ symbol*] (NQ)
ELXT........ Elbow Extension [*Sports medicine*]
ELY.......... Easterly
ELY.......... Ely [*Nevada*] [*Seismograph station code, US Geological Survey*] [*Closed*] (SEIS)
ELY.......... Ely [*Nevada*] [*Airport symbol*] (OAG)
ELY.......... Ely, NV [*Location identifier*] [*FAA*] (FAAL)
ELYC........ East Lothian Yeomanry Cavalry [*British military*] (DMA)
ELZ.......... Elazig [*Turkey*] [*Seismograph station code, US Geological Survey*] (SEIS)
El Z .... Elektrotechnische Zeitschrift [*A publication*]
ELZ.......... Elizabethtown College, Elizabethtown, PA [*OCLC symbol*] (OCLC)
ELZ.......... Elzevir [*Elsevier*] [*Published by the Elsevier family*] (ROG)
ELZ.......... Wellsville, NY [*Location identifier*] [*FAA*] (FAAL)
ELZC........ Emergency Lead-Zinc Committee [*Later, Lead-Zinc Producers Committee*] (EA)
EM............ Die Evangelischen Missionen (BJA)
EM............ E. Merck [*Laboratories*]
EM............ Earl Marshal [*British*]
EM............ Early Minoan [*Archeology*] (BJA)
EM............ Earth Mass
EM............ East Midlands [*England*]
EM............ Eastern Megalopolis [*Proposed name for possible "super-city" formed by growth and mergers of other cities*]
EM............ Easton Minerals [*Vancouver Stock Exchange symbol*]
EM............ Ebony Man [*Johnson Publishing Co., Inc.*] [*A publication*]
EM............ Ecological Monographs [*A publication*]
EM............ Econometrica [*A publication*]
EM............ Economical Methods [*A line of Varian spectrometers*]
EM............ Edgmoor & Manetta Railway [*AAR code*]
EM............ Education Manual [*Military*]
EM............ Educational Marketer [*A publication*]
EM............ Edward Medal [*British*]
E & M .... Effectiveness and Maintainability (MCD)
EM............ Efficiency Medal
EM............ Efficiency Modulation
EM............ Egyptian Mysteries [*Freemasonry*] (ROG)
EM............ Ehrverskonomiske Meddelelser [*A publication*]
EM............ Ejection Murmur [*Cardiology*]
EM............ Elective Masonry [*Freemasonry*] (ROG)
e/m .... Electric Charge to Mass (IEEE)
/EM .... Electric Motors (MCD)
E & M .... Electrical and Mechanical (KSC)
EM............ Electrician's Mate [*Navy rating*]
EM............ Electrodeposition Memo
EM............ Electromagnetic
EM............ Electromechanical
EM............ Electromicroscopic
EM............ Electron Microprobe
EM............ Electron Microscope
EM............ Electronic Magnetic Slip Couplings (DS)
EM............ Electronic Mail [*Telecommunications*]
EM............ Electrophoretic Mobility [*Analytical biochemistry*]
E und M .... Elektrotechnik und Maschinenbau [*A publication*]
EM............ Elektrotechnik und Maschinenbau [*A publication*]
E u M .... Elektrotechnik und Maschinenbau [*A publication*]
EM............ Elevation Model (NRCH)
EM............ Em Mao [*In Hand*] [*Portuguese*]
EM............ Emanation (ADA)
EM-M......... Embargo (ADA)
E-M........... Embden-Meyerhof [*Glycolytic pathway*] [*Biochemistry*]
Em............ Emergence [*Biology*]
EM............ Emergency (NASA)
EM............ Emergency Maintenance (BUR)
EM............ Emergency Management
EM............ Emergency Medicine [*Medical specialty*] (DHSM)
EM............ Emergency Message (CINC)
Em............ Emerita [*A publication*]
EM............ Eminence

EM............ Eminent (ROG)
EM............ Emission
EM............ Emission Monochromator [*Spectroscopy*]
EM............ Emitter (MSA)
EM............ Emmetropia [*Also, E*] [*Ophthalmology*]
EM............ Emotionally Disturbed
EM............ Empirical Studies of the Arts [*A publication*]
Em............ Emuna [*A publication*]
EM............ End Matched
EM............ End of Medium [*Data processing*]
EM............ Endocrinology and Metabolism [*A publication*]
EM............ Endosteal Marrow [*Hematology*]
EM............ Energy Management
EM............ Energy Maneuverability (MCD)
EM............ Engine Maintenance
EM............ Engineer Manager
EM............ Engineer Manual [*Army Corps of Engineers*]
EM............ Engineer of Mines [*or Mining*]
EM............ Engineering Management (MCD)
EM............ Engineering Manual (IEEE)
EM............ Engineering Mechanician
EM............ Engineering Memorandum
EM............ Engineering Model
EM............ Engineering Module (NASA)
EM............ English Market
EM............ English Marquess (ROG)
EM............ English Miscellany [*A publication*]
EM............ Engraving Master (MCD)
EM............ Enlisted Man [*or Men*]
EM............ Enlisted Member (AABC)
EM............ Entertainment Marketing, Inc. [*AMEX symbol*] (SPSG)
EM............ Entity Module [*Data processing*]
EM............ Entsiqlopedia Miqra'it-Encyclopaedia Biblica [*Jerusalem*] [*A publication*] (BJA)
EM............ Environmental Management (NRCH)
EM............ Environmental Monitoring
EM............ Ephemerides Mariologicae (BJA)
EM............ Epigraphical Museum [*Epigraphic notation*]
EM............ Episcopus et Martyr [*Bishop and Martyr*] [*Latin*]
EM............ Epitaxial Mesa
EM............ Equitum Magister [*Master of the Horse*] [*British*]
EM............ Erasable Memory [*Data processing*] (KSC)
E & M .... Erection and Maintenance
EM............ Error Multiplier
EM............ Escape Motor
EM............ Espana Misionera [*A publication*]
E-M........... Etat-Major [*Headquarters*] [*French military*]
EM............ Ethnikon Mouseion [*A publication*]
Em............ Ethnomusicology [*A publication*]
EM............ Etna & Montrose R. R. [*AAR code*]
EM............ Etudes Mauritaniennes [*A publication*]
EM............ Etymologicum Magnum [*A publication*]
EM............ European Movement
EM............ Evaluation Model (NRCH)
EM............ Evangelist and Martyr [*Church calendars*]
EM............ Evans Medical Ltd. [*Great Britain*] [*Research code symbol*]
EM............ Excavation Memoirs [*London*] [*A publication*]
EM............ Excellent Masons [*Freemasonry*] (ROG)
EM............ Exception Monitor (NASA)
EM............ Excerpta Medica [*Amsterdam*] [*A publication*]
EM............ Excerpta Medica Foundation [*Database producer*]
EM............ Executive Jet Aviation, Inc. [*Great Britain*] [*ICAO designator*] (FAAC)
EM............ Executive Memorandum
EM............ Expanded Memory Manager (BYTE)
EM............ Expanded Metal
EM............ Experimental Memo
EM............ External Memorandum
EM............ Extra Milers [*Later, EMC*] (EA)
EM............ Heli-Air-Monaco [*Monaco*] [*ICAO designator*] (ICDA)
EM............ Journal of Engineering Mechanics [*A publication*]
EM............ Merlot International Aviation Ltd. [*Great Britain*] [*ICAO designator*] [*Obsolete*] (FAAC)
EM1........... Electrician's Mate, First Class [*Navy rating*]
EM2........... Electrician's Mate, Second Class [*Navy rating*]
EM3........... Electrician's Mate, Third Class [*Navy rating*]
EM/A .... Arstryck. Etnografiska Museum [*A publication*]
EMA .... East Midlands [*England*] [*Airport symbol*] (OAG)
EMA .... East Midlands Airport [*England*]
EMA .... Effective Mass Approximation
EMA .... Effective Mechanical Advantage [*Bone-muscle physiology*]
EM(A)....... Electrical Mechanic (Air) [*British military*] (DMA)
EMA .... Electromagnetic Accelerometer [*Navigation*]
EMA .... Electromagnetic Analysis (NASA)
EMA .... Electromantle
EMA .... Electron Microprobe Analyzer [*Also, EMPA*]
EMA .... Electronic Mail Association (EA)
EMA .... Electronic Maintenance Assembly
EMA .... Electronic Missile Acquisition
EMA .... Electronics Manufacturers Association [*Defunct*] (EA)
EMA .... Electronics Materiel Agency [*Army*]

EMA .... Elm [*Alabama*] [*Seismograph station code, US Geological Survey*] (SEIS)
EMA .... Emergency Minerals Administration [*Department of the Interior*]
EMA .... Emergency Movements Atomic [*Military*] (AABC)
EMA .... Employment Management Association (EA)
EMA .... Engine Maintenance Area (AAG)
EMA .... Engine Manufacturers Association (EA)
EMA .... Engineered Materials Abstracts [*Materials Information*] [*Information service or system*] [*A publication*]
EMA .... Engineering Methods Analysis (MCD)
EMA .... Engineers' and Managers' Association [*A union*] [*British*] (DCTA)
EMA .... English Men of Action [*A publication*]
EMA .... Envelope Manufacturers Association [*Later, EMAA*] (EA)
EMA .... Environmental Management Association (EA)
EMA .... Environmental Monitoring and Assessment [*A publication*]
EMA .... Environmental Protection Agency, Region VI Library, Dallas, TX [*OCLC symbol*] (OCLC)
EMA .... Epeteris tou Mesaionikou Archeiou [*A publication*]
EMA .... Epithelial Membrane Antigen [*Immunology*]
EMA .... Equal Mental Age [*Psychometrics*]
EMA .... Equipment Maintenance Agreement
EMA .... Equity Market Analysis [*MMS International*] [*Information service or system*] (CRD)
EMA .... Essential Maintenance Action (MCD)
EMA .... Ethyl Methacrylate [*Organic chemistry*]
EMA .... Ethylene-Maleic Anhydride [*Copolymer*] [*Organic chemistry*]
EMA .... Ethylene Methyl Acrylate [*Photovoltaic energy systems*]
EMA .... Europe in the Middle Ages. Selected Studies [*Elsevier Book Series*] [*A publication*]
EMA .... European Marketing Association [*Brixham, Devonshire, England*] (EA)
EMA .... European Monetary Agreement
EMA .... European Motorcycle Association (EA)
EMA .... Evangelical Missionary Alliance [*British*]
EMA .... Evaporated Milk Association (EA)
EMA .... Exchequer Master's Associate [*British*] (ROG)
EMA .... Expediting Management Association (EA)
EMA .... Exposition Management Association (EA)
EMA .... Extended Mercury Autocoder (IEEE)
EMA .... Extended Mission Apollo [*NASA*]
EMA .... Ezegodnik Muzeja Architektury [*A publication*]
EMAA ...... Envelope Manufacturers Association of America (EA)
EMAA ...... European Mastic Asphalt Association (EA)
EMAAA .... Epeteris Mesaionikou Archeiou Akademias Athenon [*A publication*]
EmAb .... Employment Relations Abstracts [*A publication*]
EMAC ...... Educational Media Association of Canada
EMAC ...... Electromechanical Averaging Circuit
EMAC ...... Equipment Maintenance and Control [*Online database*]
EMAC ...... European Marketing Academy (EAIO)
EMAC ...... European and Mediterranean Association of Coloproctology (EAIO)
E-MAD ...... Engineer-Maintenance Assembly-Disassembly [*NERVA program*]
EMAE ...... Electrical and Mechanical Assistant Engineer [*British military*] (DMA)
Emailletech Mon Bl ... Emailletechnische Monats Blaetter [*A publication*]
EM/AM .... Emergency Message - Alert Message (CINC)
EMAP ...... Evoked Muscle Action Potential [*Neurophysiology*]
Em App ...... Emergency Court of Appeals [*United States*] (DLA)
EMAR ...... Experimental Memory - Address Register
E Maria ..... Estudios Marianos [*A publication*]
EMARL ..... Edit Master and Activity Review List (MCD)
EMAS .... Electro-Acoustic Music Association of Great Britain (EAIO)
EMAS .... Emergency Message Authentication System [*USEUCOM*] (AABC)
EMAS .... Employment Medical Advisory Service [*Department of Employment*] [*British*]
EMAS .... Energy Management Advisory Service [*Australia*]
EMASD ..... Environmental Monitoring and Assessment [*A publication*]
EMAT ...... Electromagnetic Acoustic Transducer [*Engineering*]
EMAT ...... Expendable Mobile Acoustic Target (MCD)
EMATS ..... Emergency Message Automatic Transmission System [*Military*]
EMATS-AF ... Emergency Message Automatic Transmission System - Air Force
EMATS-JCS ... Emergency Message Automatic Transmission System - Joint Chiefs of Staff
EMATT ..... Expendable Mobile ASW [*Antisubmarine Warfare*] Tracking Target [*Navy*] (CAAL)
EM(AW).... Electrical Mechanic (Air Weapon) [*British military*] (DMA)
EMB .... Early-Make-Break [*Data processing*]
EMB .... Electronic Material Bulletin [*Army*] (MCD)
EMB .... Emballages Magazine [*A publication*]
EMB .... Embankment
EMB .... Embargo (ADA)
EMB .... Embark (AABC)
EMB .... Embassy (AFM)
EMB .... Emboss (MSA)
EMB .... Embroidered

EMB .... Embryology (ROG)
EMB .... Empire Marketing Board [*For motion pictures in England*]
EMB .... Endomyocardial Biopsy [*Medicine*]
EMB .... Energy Mobilization Board
EMB .... Engineering Manpower Bulletin [*Engineers' Joint Council*] [*A publication*]
EMB .... Engineering in Medicine and Biology (MCD)
EMB .... Environmental Medicine Branch [*NASA*] (KSC)
EMB .... Environmental Protection Agency, R. S. Kerr Environmental Research Laboratory, Ada, OK [*OCLC symbol*] (OCLC)
EMB .... Eosin-Methylene Blue [*Dye combination*]
EMB .... Ethambutol [*An antituberculosis drug*]
EMB .... Experimental Model Basin [*Navy*]
EMB .... Explosive Motor Behavior [*Neurochemistry*]
EMBA ...... Emba Mink Breeders Association (EA)
Emballage Dig ... Emballage Digest [*A publication*]
EMBARK ... Embarkation (DSUE)
EMBASE .. Excerpta Medica Database [*Trademark*] [*Elsevier*] [*Bibliographic database*]
EMBD .... Embedded in a Layer [*To indicate cumulonimbus embedded in layers of other clouds*] [*Aviation code*] (FAAC)
EMBDD ..... Embedded [*Meteorology*] (FAAC)
EMBDU .... Ethnic Minority Business Development Unit [*British*]
Em Benefit ... Employee Benefit Plan Review [*A publication*]
Emberiza Vogelschutz Vogelkd Rheinl Pfalz ... Emberiza Vogelschutz und Vogelkunde in Rheinland Pfalz [*A publication*]
EMBERS .. Emergency Bed Request System [*Data processing*]
EMBEZ ..... Embezzlement (DLA)
EMB of GP ... Elected Members Board of General Purposes [*Freemasonry*] (ROG)
EMBKMT ... Embankment
embl .... Embalagem [*Package*] [*Portuguese*]
EMBL .... Eniwetok Marine Biological Laboratory [*Marine science*] (MSC)
EMBL .... European Molecular Biology Laboratory [*Research center*] [*Federal Republic of Germany*] (IRC)
EMBO .... Embarkation Officer [*Marine Corps*]
EMBO .... Embarkation Order [*Marine Corps*]
EMBO .... European Molecular Biology Organization [*Federal Republic of Germany*]
EMBO (Eur Mol Biol Organ) J ... EMBO (European Molecular Biology Organization) Journal [*A publication*]
EMBOFF .. Embassy Officer
EMBO J ... EMBO [*European Molecular Biology Organization*] Journal [*A publication*]
Embouteillage Cond ... Embouteillage Conditionnement [*A publication*]
EMBR .... Embroidery
EMBR .... Embryo
Embr .... Embryologia [*A publication*]
EMBR .... Equipment Management Balance Register (AFIT)
EMBRAC ... Embracery [*Legal term*] (DLA)
EMBRAPA Empresa Bras Pesqui Agropecu ... EMBRAPA. Empresa Brasileira de Pesquisa Agropecuaria [*A publication*]
EMBRATEL ... Empresa Brasileira de Telecomunicacoes [*Brazilian Telecommunications Enterprises*] (TSSD)
EMBRATUR ... Empresa Brasileira de Turismo [*Brazilian Tourism Company*]
EMBRY ..... Embryology
EMBRYOL ... Embryology
EMBS .... Embossed [*Deltiology*]
EMBS .... Energy Management Bumper System [*Automobile safety*]
EMBS .... IEEE Engineering in Medicine and Biology Society (EA)
EMBTEL .. Embassy Telegram (NATG)
EMBZA6 .. Emberiza [*A publication*]
EMC .... Canada Centre for Remote Sensing Library [*UTLAS symbol*]
EMC .... Eastern Mennonite College [*Virginia*]
EMC .... Educational Media Council [*Defunct*] (EA)
EMC .... Educational Media and Technology Center
EMC .... Educational Modulation Center
EMC .... El Monte Carmelo [*A publication*]
EMC .... El Museo Canario [*A publication*]
EMC .... Electrician's Mate, Chief [*Navy rating*]
EMC .... Electromagnetic Compatibility
EMC .... Electromagnetic Control
EMC .... Electromagnetic Cyclotron
EMC .... Electromechanochemical
EMC .... Electron Microscopy Center for Materials Research [*Argonne, IL*] [*Argonne National Laboratory*] [*Department of Energy*] (GRD)
EMC .... Electronic Mail Courier
EMC .... Electronic Manifold Card [*Clippard Instrument Laboratory, Inc.*] [*Cincinnati, OH*]
EMC .... Electronic Material Change
EMC .... Electronic Music Consortium (EA)
EMC .... EMC Corp. [*NYSE symbol*] (SPSG)
EMC .... Emergency Management Coordinator [*Nuclear energy*] (NRCH)
EMC .... Emergency Medical Center
EMC .... Emergency Message Changes (MCD)
EMC .... Emmanuel College, Boston, MA [*OCLC symbol*] (OCLC)
EMC .... Employee-Management Cooperation

EMC .... Encephalomyocarditis [*Virus*]
EMC .... Energy Management Center
EM & C...... Engelhard Minerals & Chemicals Corp. [*Later, Engelhard Corp.*]
EMC .... Engine Maintenance Center　(AAG)
EMC .... Engine Manufacturers' Committee　(EAIO)
EMC .... Engine Monitor Computer
EMC .... Engineer Maintenance Center
EMC .... Engineer Maintenance Control [*Army*]
EMC .... Engineered Military Circuit [*Leased long lines established in continental US*] [*Military*]
EMC .... Engineering Manpower Commission　(EA)
EMC .... Engineering Mock-Up Critical Experiment [*Nuclear energy*]　(NRCH)
EMC .... Enzyme-Modified Cheese
EMC .... Equilibrium Moisture Content
EMC .... Equipment Maintenance Council [*Inactive*]　(EA)
EMC .... Equipment Management Code [*Air Force*]　(AFIT)
EMC .... Equivalent Mission Cycle
EMC .... Etched Metal Circuit
EMC .... European Mathematical Council　(EA)
EMC .... European Mechanics Committee
EMC .... European Military Communication　(IEEE)
EMC .... European Muon Collaboration [*Nuclear research*]
EMC .... Exercise Monitoring and Control　(MCD)
EMC .... Experiment Mock-Up Converters　(KSC)
EMC .... Export Management Company
EMC .... Extended Math Coprocessor [*Data processing*]
EMC .... Extended Model Checker [*Data processing*]
EMC .... Extra Miler Club　(EA)
EMC .... Eye-Motion Camera
e-mc--- ..... Monaco [*MARC geographic area code*] [*Library of Congress*]　(LCCP)
EMC .... Winnemucca, NV [*Location identifier*] [*FAA*]　(FAAL)
Emc² .... Electronic Mail Communication Center [*Naples, FL*] [*Telecommunications service*]　(TSSD)
EMCA ...... Electronic Mail Corporation of America [*NASDAQ symbol*]　(NQ)
EMCA ...... Electronic Motion Control Association　(EA)
EMCAB..... Electromagnetic Compatibility Advisory Board　(MCD)
EMCAE8.. Environmental Mutagens and Carcinogens [*A publication*]
EMCB....... Electrician's Mate, Construction Battalion [*Navy rating*] [*Obsolete*]
EMCBC..... Electrician's Mate, Construction Battalion, Communications [*Navy rating*] [*Obsolete*]
EMCBD..... Electrician's Mate, Construction Battalion, Draftsman [*Navy rating*] [*Obsolete*]
EMCBG..... Electrician's Mate, Construction Battalion, General [*Navy rating*] [*Obsolete*]
EMCBL..... Electrician's Mate, Construction Battalion, Line and Station [*Navy rating*] [*Obsolete*]
EMCC ...... Easy Magic Cookery Council　(EA)
EMCC ...... Electromagnetic Control Compatibility
EMCC ...... Emergency Medicine and Crisis Care [*Database*]
EMCC ...... Emergency Mission Control Center [*NASA*]
EMCC ...... Emett and Chandler Corporation [*NASDAQ symbol*]　(NQ)
EMCC ...... Essential Motor Control Center　(AAG)
EMCC ...... European Municipal Credit Community
EMCCC..... European Military Communications Co-Ordinating Committee [*NATO*]
EMCCS..... Emergency Medical Command and Communications System
EMCD....... Electromechanical Control Diagram　(MCD)
EMCE....... EMC Energies, Inc. [*NASDAQ symbol*]　(NQ)
EMCEE..... Master of Ceremonies
EMCF....... Employer Master Control File [*State Employee Security Agency*]　(OICC)
EMCF....... European Monetary Co-Operation Fund [*Bank for International Settlements*]　(EY)
EMCFOM ... Electromagnetic Compatibility Figure of Merit [*Telecommunications*]　(TEL)
EMCI........ EMC Insurance Group, Incorporated [*NASDAQ symbol*]　(NQ)
EMCI........ Engineering Model Configuration Inspection　(MCD)
EMCIS...... Experimental Military Command Information System　(MCD)
EMCM ...... Electrician's Mate, Master Chief [*Navy rating*]
EMCMF.... Embarked Mine Countermeasures Force
EMCNA9 .. Electromyography and Clinical Neurophysiology [*A publication*]
EMCO ...... Engineering Measurements Company [*Longmont, CO*] [*NASDAQ symbol*]　(NQ)
EMCON..... Electron Microscopy Congress
EMCON..... Emission Control　(CAAL)
EMCP....... Electromagnetic Compatibility Program [*Air Force*]　(AFM)
EMCP....... Emergency Military Construction Program
EMC & R... Emergency Medical Care and Rescue
EMCRF.... European and Mediterranean Cereal Rusts Foundation　(EAIO)
EMCRO.... Experimental Medical Care Review Organization [*Program of the National Center for Health Services Research and Development*]
EMCS....... Electrician's Mate, Senior Chief [*Navy rating*]

EMCS....... Electromagnetic Compatibility Standardization [*Program*] [*Telecommunications*]　(IEEE)
EMCS....... Energy Management and Control System
EMCS....... Energy Management and Controls Society　(EA)
Em Ct App ... Emergency Court of Appeals [*United States*]　(DLA)
EMCTP..... Electromagnetic Compatibility Test Plan　(IEEE)
EMC USA ... Estonian Music Center, USA　(EA)
EMCV ...... Encephalomyocarditis Virus
EMCWP.... European Mediterranean Commission on Water Planning　(EA)
EMCX ...... Engineering Measurements [*NASDAQ symbol*]　(NQ)
EMD........ Electric Motor Driven
EMD........ Electro-Motive Division [*General Motors Corp.*]
EMD........ Electrolytic Manganese Dioxide [*For use in batteries*]
EMD........ Electromagnetic Defense　(CAAL)
EMD........ Electromechanical Dissociation
EMD........ Electronic Map Display
EMD........ Emerald [*Australia*] [*Airport symbol*]　(OAG)
EMD........ Emory University School of Dentistry, Atlanta, GA [*OCLC symbol*]　(OCLC)
EMD........ Engine Management Display　(MCD)
EMD........ Engine Monitor Display　(MCD)
EMD........ Engineering Master Drawing　(MCD)
EMD........ Engineering Mechanics Division [*American Society of Civil Engineers*]　(MCD)
EMD........ English Miscellany. St. Stephen's College (Delhi) [*A publication*]
EMD........ Entry Monitor Display　(KSC)
EMD........ Equipment Manufacturers Design
EMD........ Esophageal Motility Disorder [*Medicine*]
EMD........ European Market Development
EMD........ Exploration Map Data　(RDA)
EMD........ Export Market Digest [*A publication*]
EMD........ Eye-Movement Device
EMD........ Marshalltown, IA [*Location identifier*] [*FAA*]　(FAAL)
EMD........ Valley Commuter [*Eugene, OR*] [*FAA designator*]　(FAAC)
Emder Jb ... Emder Jahrbuch [*A publication*]
EMDG....... Export Market Development Grants [*Australia*]
EMDI....... Energy Management Display Indicator
EMDJA2... Ethiopian Medical Journal [*A publication*]
EM & D J Eng Mater Compon Des ... EM and D [*Engineering Materials and Design*] Journal of Engineering Materials, Components, and Design [*A publication*]
EM D J Mater Components Des ... EM and D [*Engineering Materials and Design*] Journal of Engineering Materials, Components, and Design [*A publication*]
EMDL .... East Midlands [*England*]
EMDO....... Engineering and Manufacturing District Office [*FAA*]　(FAAC)
EM DOM ... Eminent Domain [*Legal term*]　(DLA)
EMDP .... Electromotive Difference of Potential
EM & D Prod Data ... EM and D [*Engineering Materials and Design*] Product Data [*A publication*]
EMDS........ Electronic Material Data Service　(MUGU)
EME .... CEMR [*Canada Energy Mines and Resources*] Headquarters Library [*UTLAS symbol*]
EME .... Earth-Mars-Earth
EME .... Earth-Moon-Earth [*Extraterrestrial communications*]
EME .... Ecgonine Methyl Ester [*Organic chemistry*]
EME .... [*National Council of Churches*] Ecumenical Ministries in Education　(EA)
EME .... Electrical and Mechanical Engineering [*or Engineers*]
EME .... Electromagnetic Energy　(IEEE)
EME .... Electromantle Extraction
EME .... Emden [*West Germany*] [*Airport symbol*]　(OAG)
EME .... Emerson Radio Corp. [*Formerly, ERP*] [*NYSE symbol*]　(SPSG)
EME .... Emetic [*Pharmacy*]　(ROG)
EME .... Emetine [*Antiamebic compound*]
EME .... Energy and Man's Environment [*Utility-funded curriculum program*]
E in ME ... Engineer in Mechanical Engineering
EME .... Environmental Measurements Experiment
EME .... Euromoney [*A publication*]
EMEA ...... Electronic Maintenance Engineering Association
EMEA ...... Employment and Earnings [*A publication*]
EMEC........ Electromagnetic Effects Capability　(NASA)
EMEC........ Electromagnetic Effects Compatibility [*NASA*]　(NASA)
EMEC........ Electronic Maintenance Engineering Center [*Military*]　(IEEE)
EMEC........ Engineers Manual for Emergency Construction [*Army Corps of Engineers*]
EM Econ Mocambique ... EM. Economia de Mocambique [*A publication*]
EMEDDQ ... Ecologia Mediterranea [*A publication*]
EMEED..... Electrical and Mechanical Executive Engineer [*England*] [*A publication*]
EMEG....... Electromagnetic Environment Generator
EMEI........ Equipment Management Exception Indicator　(AFIT)
EMELD.... Electric Machines and Electromechanics [*A publication*]
EMEM ...... Eagle's Minimum Essential Medium [*Culture medium*]
EMEND.... Emendatio [*Emendation*] [*Latin*]
EMEP....... European Monitoring and Evaluation Programme [*Environmental research*]
EMER........ Electromagnetic Environment Recorder　(MCD)

emer .... Emerald [*Philately*]
EMER....... Emergency (KSC)
Emer....... Emerita [*A publication*]
EMER....... Emeritus
EMer.......... Mercury [*Record label*] [*Great Britain*]
E Mercks Jahresber ... E Merck's Jahresberichte [*A publication*]
Emer Ct App ... Emergency Court of Appeals [*United States*] (DLA)
EMERG..... Emergency (AABC)
Emerg Dep News ... Emergency Department News [*A publication*]
Emergency Lib ... Emergency Librarian [*A publication*]
Emergency Libn ... Emergency Librarian [*A publication*]
EMERGE STAT ... Information available this office indicates that service
     member requested his/her return on leave through local
     chapter, American Red Cross. Advise by message action
     taken and, if applicable, place of entry and estimated time
     of arrival in United States or territory of residence. If
     denied, advise reasons (AABC)
Emerg Health Serv Q ... Emergency Health Services Quarterly [*A publication*]
Emerg Health Serv Rev ... Emergency Health Services Review [*A publication*]
Emerg Lib .. Emergency Librarian [*A publication*]
Emerg Med ... Emergency Medicine [*A publication*]
Emerg Med Annu ... Emergency Medicine Annual [*A publication*]
Emerg Med Clin North Am ... Emergency Medicine Clinics of North America
     [*A publication*]
Emerg Med Serv ... Emergency Medical Services [*A publication*]
Emerg Med Tech Legal Bull ... Emergency Medical Technician Legal Bulletin
     [*A publication*]
Emerg Nurse Legal Bull ... Emergency Nurse Legal Bulletin [*A publication*]
Emerg Plann Dig ... Emergency Planning Digest [*A publication*]
Emerg Serv News ... Emergency Services News [*A publication*]
Emerig Assur ... Emerigon. Traite des Assurances et des Contrats a la Grosse
     [*A publication*] (DLA)
Emerig Ins ... Emerigon on Insurance [*A publication*] (DLA)
Emerig Mar Loans ... Emerigon on Maritime Loans [*A publication*] (DLA)
Emerig Traite des Assur ... Emerigon. Traite des Assurances et des Contrats a
     la Grosse [*A publication*] (DLA)
Emerig Tr des Ass ... Emerigon. Traite des Assurances et des Contrats a la
     Grosse [*A publication*] (DLA)
Emerig Tr des Assur ... Emerigon. Traite des Assurances et des Contrats a la
     Grosse [*A publication*] (DLA)
Emer Ins .... Emerigon on Insurance [*A publication*] (DLA)
Emer Libr .. Emergency Librarian [*A publication*]
Emer Mar Lo ... Emerigon on Maritime Loans [*A publication*] (DLA)
Emerson & Haber Pol & Civ Rits ... Emerson and Haber's Political and Civil
     Rights in the United States [*A publication*] (DLA)
EMES........ Electrical, Mechanical, and Environmental Systems (MCD)
EM/ES ...... Emergence and Establishment [*Agriculture*]
EMET....... Eastmet Corp. [*NASDAQ symbol*] (NQ)
E Met .... Engineer of Metallurgy
EMETD..... Energy Meetings [*A publication*]
EMETF ..... Electromagnetic Environmental Test Facility [*Fort Huachuca,
     AZ*] [*Army*] (AABC)
EMEX........ Equatorial Mesoscale Experiment [*National Oceanic and
     Atmospheric Administration*]
Emexcon .... Empresa Exportadora de la Construccion [*Construction Export
     Company*] [*Cuba*] (GEA)
EMF .... Electro-Machine Fixture (MCD)
EMF .... Electromagnetic Flow [*or Florometer*] [*Cardiology*]
EMF .... Electromotive Force [*See also E, V*] [*Electrochemistry*]
EMF .... Electronic Mail Facility [*Postal Service*]
EMF .... Eletromagnetic Force (NASA)
EMF .... Emergency Medicine Foundation (EA)
EMF .... Endomyocardial Fibrosis [*Cardiology*]
EMF .... Enlisted Master File [*Army*] (INF)
EMF .... Equipment Maintenance Facility [*Deep Space Instrumentation
     Facility, NASA*]
EMF .... Erythrocyte Maturation Factor [*Hematology*]
EMF .... Europaeische Motel Foderation [*European Motel
     Federation*] (EA)
EMF .... European Missionary Fellowship
EMF .... European Monetary Fund [*Proposed*]
EMF .... Event Marketing Funds [*Business term*]
EMF .... Every Morning Fixum [*An old car*] [*Slang*]
EMF .... Excerpta Medica Foundation [*Database producer*] (EA)
EMF .... Explosive Metal Forming
EMF .... Templeton Emerging Markets Fund, Inc. [*NYSE
     symbol*] (SPSG)
EMFA....... Electrician's Mate, Fireman Apprentice [*Navy rating*]
Emfac........ Emery Industries, Inc. [*Research code symbol*]
EMFC....... EMF Corporation [*NASDAQ symbol*] (NQ)
EMFF .... Edward Mulhare's Foundation of Friends (EA)
EMFF .... Electromagnetic Form Factor
EMFIA ...... Electroplating and Metal Finishing [*A publication*]
EMFJ .... Europees Muziekfestival voor de Jeugd [*European Music
     Festival for the Youth*] (EAIO)
EMFM....... Electromagnetic Flowmeter
EMFN....... Electrician's Mate, Fireman [*Navy rating*]
EMFP....... Electromagnetic Flow Probe [*Analytical biochemistry*]
EMFRA2... Empire Forestry Review [*A publication*]
EMFT....... Early-Morning Fuzzy Thinking
EMFU .... Ethoxymethylfluorouracil [*Antineoplastic drug*]

EMG.......... Eastmaque Gold Mines Ltd. [*Toronto Stock Exchange symbol*]
     [*Vancouver Stock Exchange symbol*]
EMG.......... Electromagnetic Gyro
EMG.......... Electromyogram [*or Electromyographic*]
EMG.......... Equipment Management Group
E-MG......... Etat-Major General [*General Headquarters*] [*French military*]
EMG.......... Europaeische Maerchengesellschaft [*European Fairytale
     Association - EFA*] [*Rheine, Federal Republic of
     Germany*] (EAIO)
EMG.......... Executive Mansion and Grounds [*i.e., the White House and its
     grounds*] [*Executive Office of the President*]
EMG.......... Exomphalos, Macroglossia, and Giantism [*Syndrome*]
     [*Medicine*]
EMG.......... Exponentially Modified Gaussian [*Mathematical function*]
EMG.......... Eye-Movement Gauge
EMG.......... Shreveport, LA [*Location identifier*] [*FAA*] (FAAL)
EMGB .... Engine-Mounted Gear Box (MCD)
EMGBL.... Ethyl(methyl)-Gamma-Butyrolactone [*Biochemistry*]
EMGE .... Electronic Maintenance Ground Equipment (KSC)
EM in Geol ... Mining Engineer in Geology
EMGORS ... Electromyogram Sensors [*For control of artificial limbs*]
EMGTN ... Equivalent Megatonnage [*Military weapon index*] (MCD)
EMGV .... Eastmaque Gold Mines Ltd. [*NASDAQ symbol*] (NQ)
EMGWS.... Electromagnetic Gun Weapon System
EMH......... Educable Mentally Handicapped
EMH......... Efficient Market Hypothesis (ADA)
EMH......... Electronic Mail Handling
EMH......... Emhart Corp. [*Formerly, EMM*] [*NYSE symbol*] (SPSG)
EMH......... Epochs of Modern History [*A publication*]
EMH......... Estimated Man-Hours (AFIT)
EMHO ...... Emons Holdings, Inc. [*NASDAQ symbol*] (NQ)
EMHR....... Estimated Maximum Heart Rate [*Aerobic dance*]
EMI .... Eastern Microwave, Inc. [*Telecommunications service*] (TSSD)
EMI .... Educationally Mentally Impaired
EMI .... Electrical & Musical Industries Ltd. [*British*]
EMI .... Electromagnetic Interference
EMI .... Electronic Maintenance Inspector
EMI .... Emergency Management Institute
EMI .... Emergency Medical Information
EMI .... EMI [*formerly, Electric & Musical Industries Ltd.*] Special
     Issues [*Record label*] [*Great Britain*]
EMI .... Emirau [*Papua New Guinea*] [*Airport symbol*] (OAG)
EMI .... Engineering Management International [*A publication*]
EMI .... Engineering and Manufacturing Instructions (NRCH)
EMI .... Environmental Mediation International (EA)
EMI .... Environmental Mutagen Information [*Department of Energy*]
     [*Information service or system*] (IID)
EMI .... Enzyme and Microbore Immobilization [*Biochemistry*]
EMI .... Evangelical Ministries, Incorporated (EA)
EMI .... Excavation Engineering and Earth Mechanics Institute
     [*Colorado School of Mines*] [*Research center*] (RCD)
EMI .... Exchange of Medical Information [*Program*] [*Veterans
     Administration*]
EMI .... Expressible Moisture Index
EMI .... External Muon Identifier [*Atomic physics*]
EMI .... Extra Military Instruction
EMI .... Extractive Metallurgy Institute (EA)
EMI .... Westminster, MD [*Location identifier*] [*FAA*] (FAAL)
EMIA .... Enzyme Membrane Immunoassay [*Biochemistry*]
EMIAC..... Electric & Musical Industries [*later, EMI Ltd.*] Analogue
     Computer (DEN)
EMIB........ European Master's in International Business
EMIC........ Electromagnetic Interference and Compatibility
EMIC........ Emergency Maternity and Infant Care
EMIC........ Environmental Mutagen Information Center [*Environmental
     Information System Office*]
EMICE ..... Electromagnetic Interference Control Engineer (IEEE)
EMID .... Electromagnetic Intrusion Detector (NVT)
EMID .... Emergency Medical Information Devices
EMIDD .... Environment Midwest [*A publication*]
EMIDEC.... EMI [*formerly, Electric & Musical Industries Ltd.*] Data
     Electronic Computer [*Great Britain*]
E Midl Geogr ... East Midland Geographer [*A publication*]
EMIE........ Educational Media Institutes Evaluation [*Project*]
EMIERT ... Ethnic Materials and Information Exchange Round Table
     [*American Library Association*] (EA)
EMIETF.... Ethnic Materials Information Exchange Task Force [*Later,
     EMIERT*] (EA)
EMILAS.... Energy Management in Lighting Award Scheme [*British*]
Emilia Pr Rom ... Emilia Preromana [*A publication*]
EMILY ...... Early Money Is Like Yeast [*Political fund raising campaign for
     female Democrats running for the US Senate*]
EMIMA..... Electrical and Mechanical Instrument Makers' Association [*A
     union*] [*British*]
EMIN........ Eminent (ROG)
EMINT..... Electromagnetic Intelligence (MSA)
EMIP........ Equivalent Means Investment Period
EMIPA..... Elelmezesi Ipar [*A publication*]
EMIqr .... Entsiqlopedia Miqra'it-Encyclopaedia Biblica [*Jerusalem*] [*A
     publication*] (BJA)

EMIR......... EDP [*Electronic Data Processing*]-Microfilm-Integrated-Retrieval [*German Patent Office*]
EMIRA...... Ezegodnik Muzeja Istorii i Ateizma [*Moscow*] (BJA)
EMIRS ...... Electrochemically Modulated Infrared Reflectance Spectroscopy
EMIRTEL ... Emirates Telecommunications Corp. Ltd. (TEL)
EMIS......... Ecosystem of Machines Information System
EMIS......... Educational Management Information System
EMIS......... Electromagnetic Intelligence System
EMIS......... Electronic Markets and Information Systems, Inc. [*Information service or system*]
EMIS......... Electronic Materials Information Service [*Institution of Electrical Engineers*] [*Database*] (IID)
EMIS......... Emission (KSC)
EMIS......... Engineering Management Information System [*Defense Supply Agency*]
EMIS......... Evangelical Missions Information Service (EA)
EMIS......... Extension Management Information System [*Department of Agriculture*]
EMISEC.... Emission Security (AFM)
EMISS...... Electromolecular Instrument Space Simulator
EMIT......... Electromagnetic Induction Tweeter
EMIT......... Electromagnetic Interference Testing
EMIT......... Emergency Message Initiation Terminal (MCD)
EMIT......... Engineering Management Information Technique
EMIT......... Enzyme Multiplied Immunoassay Technique [*Clinical chemistry*] [*Syva Company trademark*]
EMIT......... Enzyme Multiplied Immunoassay Test [*Clinical chemistry*] [*Generic*]
EMITS ...... Electromagnetic Interference Test System [*Navy*] (MCD)
EMITT...... Emittatur [*Let It Be Discharged*] [*Pharmacy*] (ROG)
EMJ......... Engineering and Mining Journal [*A publication*]
EMJC........ East Mississippi Junior College [*Scooba, MS*]
EMJH .... Ellinghausen, McCullough, Johnson, Harris [*Medium*] [*Microbiology*]
EMJODG ... EMBO [*European Molecular Biology Organization*] Journal [*A publication*]
E & M Jour ... Engineering and Mining Journal [*A publication*]
EMK .... Edward Moore Kennedy [*American politician*]
EMK .... Electrical Meter Kit
EMK .... Electro-Motorische Kraft [*Electromotive Force*] [*German*]
EMK .... Emergency Medical Kit (MCD)
EMK .... Emmonak [*Alaska*] [*Airport symbol*] (OAG)
EML .... Eastern Co. [*AMEX symbol*] (SPSG)
EML .... Educational Materials Laboratory
EML .... Electromagnetic Launcher [*Military*] (SDI)
EML .... Electromagnetic Levitator
EML .... Electromechanical Laboratories (MUGU)
E-ML .... Electronic-Media Literacy [*or Literate*]
EML .... Elementary Math Library [*IBM Corp.*]
EML .... Emco Limited [*Toronto Stock Exchange symbol*]
EML .... Emergency Manning Level (CET)
EML .... Emory University Division of Librarianship, Atlanta, GA [*OCLC symbol*] (OCLC)
EML .... Empire Lines, Inc.
EML .... Engineering Materials List [*Nuclear energy*]
EML .... Engineering Mechanics Laboratory [*National Institute of Standards and Technology*] (IEEE)
EML .... English Men of Letters [*A publication*]
EML .... Environmental Measurements Laboratory [*Department of Energy*] (GRD)
E & ML...... Environmental and Morale Leave [*Military*]
EML .... Equipment Maintenance Log [*Army*] (AABC)
EML .... Equipment Modification List (MCD)
EML .... Estimated Month of Loss
EML .... Expanded Metal Lath
EML .... Expected Measured Loss [*Telecommunications*] (TEL)
EML .... Experimental Meteorology Laboratory
EML .... Extended Media List [*British*]
EMLA........ Electromechanical Linear Actuator
EMLC........ Experimental Manpower Laboratory for Corrections (OICC)
EMLD ...... Emerald (ROG)
EMLF .... Eastern Mineral Law Foundation (EA)
EMLI......... Environmental Measurements Laboratory Impactor [*Sampling instrument*]
Em LJ ...... Emory Law Journal [*A publication*]
EMLR....... Engineering Manufacturing Liaison Release (KSC)
EMLX....... Emulex Corp. [*NASDAQ symbol*] (NQ)
EMM......... CANMET [*Canada Centre for Mineral and Energy Technology*] Library [*Canada Energy, Mines, and Resources*] [*UTLAS symbol*]
EMM......... East Machias [*Maine*] [*Seismograph station code, US Geological Survey*] (SEIS)
EMM......... Electromagnetic Measurement (IEEE)
EMM......... Electromechanical Machining [*Manufacturing term*]
EMM......... Electromechanical Mockup (KSC)
E & MM .... Electronics & Music Maker Magazine [*British*] [*A publication*]
EMM......... Emmanuel College [*Boston, MA*] (ROG)
EMM......... Emmenagogue [*Promoting Menstruation*] [*Pharmacy*] (ROG)
EMM......... Emory University, A. W. Calhoun Medical Library, Atlanta, GA [*OCLC symbol*] (OCLC)
EMM......... Engineering Management Manual

EMM......... Entente Medicale Mediterraneenne [*Mediterranean Medical Entente*] (EAIO)
EMM......... Etudes de Metaphysique et de Morale [*A publication*]
EMM......... Expanded Memory Manager
EMM......... Experiences in Marketing Management (MCD)
EMM......... Extended Midcourse Mode [*Navy*] (CAAL)
EMM......... Kemmerer, WY [*Location identifier*] [*FAA*] (FAAL)
e-mm--- ...... Malta [*MARC geographic area code*] [*Library of Congress*] (LCCP)
EMMA ...... Electron Microscopy and Microanalysis (IEEE)
EMMA ...... Emergency Medicine Management Association [*Defunct*] (EA)
EMMA ...... Engineering Mock-Up and Manufacturing Aid (MCD)
EMMA ...... Exceptional Merit Media Awards [*National Women's Political Caucus*]
EMMA ...... Expanded Metal Manufacturers Association [*Defunct*] (EA)
EMMA ...... Expeditious Monitor and Maintenance Analyst [*Computer*] [*NASA*]
EMMA ...... Eye-Movement Measuring Apparatus
EMMC ...... Corps of Engineers Manual for Military Construction [*Army*]
EMMCC...... Erection Mechanism Motor Control Center
EMMGB ..... Eaton's Motor Machine Gun Battery [*British military*] (DMA)
EMMP ..... Equipment Maintenance Management Program [*Air Force*]
EMMPS ... Emergency Military Manpower Procurement System (MCD)
EMMPS ... Enhanced MEECN [*Minimum Essential Emergency Communications Network*] Message Processing System
EMMR ...... Eastern Museum of Motor Racing (EA)
EMMRIT .. Electronic Warfare Signal Intelligence Material Management Realignment Implementation Task Group
EMMS....... Electronic Mail and Message Systems
EMMTAC ... Executive Manpower Management Technical Assistance Center [*Civil Service Commission*]
EMMTAP ... Executive Manpower Management Technical Assistance Plan [*Civil Service Commission*]
EMMY ...... Derivative of IMMY, Image Orthicon Camera. An Emmy is awarded by the National Academy of Television Arts and Sciences for excellence in television.
EMN......... Eastman Resources, Inc. [*Toronto Stock Exchange symbol*]
EMN......... Eleanor [*Roosevelt*], Marion [*Dickerman*], and Nancy [*Cook*] [*Democratic Party activists*]
EMN......... Engineering Management Network (NASA)
EMN......... Escuadron de la Muerte Nuevo [*New Death Squad*] [*El Salvador*] (PD)
EMN......... Nema [*Mauritania*] [*Airport symbol*] (OAG)
EMNE ...... Early Modern English [*Language, etc.*]
EMNED.... Energy Management News [*A publication*]
EMNGD.... Environmental Management [*A publication*]
EMO......... Earth Physics Library [*Canada Energy Mines and Resources*] [*UTLAS symbol*]
EMO......... Electric Motor-Operated (NRCH)
EMO......... Electromechanical Optical (AAG)
EMO......... Electronics Material Officer
EMO......... Embarkation Medical Official [*Military*] [*British*]
EMO......... Emergency Measures Organization [*Canada*]
EMO......... Emo [*Papua New Guinea*] [*Airport symbol*] (OAG)
EMO......... Emollient (ROG)
EMO......... Emosson [*Switzerland*] [*Seismograph station code, US Geological Survey*] (SEIS)
EMO......... Engage Missile Orders [*Military*] (CAAL)
EMO......... Environmental Medicine Officer [*Military*]
EMO......... Equipment Management Office [*Air Force*] (AFIT)
EMO......... Equipment Move Order (AAG)
EMOA...... Encyclopedia of Medical Organizations and Agencies [*A publication*]
EMOD...... Electronic Modules Corp. [*NASDAQ symbol*] (NQ)
EMOD...... Erasable Memory Octal Dump [*Data processing*]
EMODA.... EMO [*Emergency Measures Organization*] Digest [*Canada*] [*A publication*]
EMO (Emerg Meas Organ) Dig ... EMO (Emergency Measures Organization) Digest (Canada) [*A publication*]
EMOFICO ... Committee for Environmental Monitoring of Forest Insect Control Operations
EMOG....... Enstatite, Magnesite, Olivine, Graphite [*Geology*]
emol............ Emolumentos [*Profits*] [*Portuguese*]
EMOLL..... Emolliens [*Mollifying, Healing*] [*Pharmacy*] (ROG)
EMON....... Environmental Monitoring & Testing Corp. [*NASDAQ symbol*] (NQ)
EMON....... Exception Monitoring (MCD)
E Mong ...... Etudes Mongoles [*A publication*]
Emory L J ... Emory Law Journal [*A publication*]
Emory Univ Quart ... Emory University Quarterly [*A publication*]
EMOS ...... Earth Mean Orbital Speed
EMOS .... English for Migrant and Overseas Students [*Program*] [*Australia*]
EMOS .... Enhancement Metal-Oxide Semiconductor (BUR)
EMOS .... Entry Military Occupational Specialty (AABC)
EMOT .... Emotional
EMOT .... Estimated Minimum Operating Temperature [*Engineering*]
EMOV....... Electromagnetically Operated Valve (NRCH)
EMP .... Electromagnetic Power [*or Pulse*]
EMP .... Electromagnetic Propagation
EMP .... Electromechanical Power [*or Pulse*]

EMP .... Electromolecular Propulsion [*Electrochemistry*]
EMP .... Electron Microprobe
EMP .... Electronic Manuscript Project [*Association of American Publishers*] [*Information service or system*] (IID)
EMP .... Electronic Multiplying Punches (DEN)
EMP .... Em Mao Propria [*Portuguese*]
EMP .... Embden-Meyerhof-Parnas [*Hexose metabolic pathway*] [*Biochemistry*]
EMP .... Emergency Medical Personnel (MCD)
EMP .... Empennage [*Aerospace engineering*]
EMP .... Emperor [*or Empress*]
EMP .... Empire
EMP .... Empire Airlines [*Oriskany, NY*] [*FAA designator*] (FAAC)
EMP .... Empire of Carolina, Inc. [*AMEX symbol*] (SPSG)
EMP .... Empire of Carolina Warrants [*AMEX symbol*] (SPSG)
EMP .... Empire Co. Ltd. [*Toronto Stock Exchange symbol*]
EMP .... Emplastrum [*Plaster*] [*Pharmacy*]
EMP .... Employables (OICC)
EMP .... Employee [*or Employer*] (DCTA)
Emp .... Employer [*A publication*]
EMP .... Emporia, KS [*Location identifier*] [*FAA*] (FAAL)
EMP .... End of Month Payment [*Business term*]
EMP .... Energy Management Plan (MCD)
EMP .... Engineering, Mathematics, and Physical Sciences [*Military*]
EMP .... Engineering Modification Proposal (NG)
EMP .... Epidermal Melanin Pigmentation [*Dermatology*]
EMP .... Equipment Mounting Plate (NASA)
EMP .... Erasable Memory Program [*Data processing*]
EMP .... Evaluated Maintenance Programming
EMP .... Ex Modo Praescripto [*In the Manner Prescribed*] [*Pharmacy*]
EMP .... Experimental and Molecular Pathology [*A publication*]
EMP .... External Power Monitor
EMPA .... Electron Microprobe Analysis [*Also, EMA*]
EMPA .... Etudes Mensuelles sur l'Economie et les Finances de la Syrie et des Pays Arabes [*Damascus*] [*A publication*]
EMPAC ..... Ethnic Millions Political Action Committee (EA)
EMPASS ... Electromagnetic Performance of Air and Ship Systems
EMPB .... Effervescent Magnetic Peroxoborate
EMPB .... Embroidery Manufacturers Promotion Board [*Later, SEMPB*] (EA)
EMPB .... Emergency Mobilization Preparedness Board [*DoD*]
EMPB .... Ethyl(methyl)(piperidyl)barbituric Acid [*Biochemistry*]
EMPC .... Educational Media Producers Council [*of the National Audio-Visual Association*] [*Later, NAVA Materials Council*]
EMPC .... Empire-Crown Auto [*NASDAQ symbol*] (NQ)
EMPC .... Equipment Modification Procurement Costs (MCD)
Emp Cott Grow Corp R ... Empire Cotton Growing Corporation. Review [*A publication*]
Emp Cott Grow Rev ... Empire Cotton Growing Corporation. Review [*A publication*]
Emp Cotton Grow Corp Prog Rep Exp Stn ... Empire Cotton Growing Corporation. Progress Reports from Experiment Stations [*A publication*]
Emp Cotton Grow Rev ... Empire Cotton Growing Corporation. Review [*A publication*]
EMPD .... Ethoxy-meta-phenylenediamine [*Organic chemistry*]
EMPDAC ... Educational Media Producers and Distributors Association of Canada
Emp For Handb ... Empire Forestry Handbook [*A publication*]
Emp For J ... Empire Forestry Journal [*A publication*]
Emp For Rev ... Empire Forestry Review [*A publication*]
EMPG .... Electrical/Mechanical Power Generation Subsystem
EMPG .... Excerpta Medica/EMBASE Publishing Group (EISS)
EMPGS ..... Electrical/Mechanical Power Generation Subsystem (MCD)
EMPH .... Emphysema [*Medicine*]
EMPHAS ... Emphysema plus Asthma [*Medicine*]
EMPHASIS ... Evaluation Management Using Past History Analysis for Scientific Inventory Simulation
Emphasis Nurs ... Emphasis. Nursing [*A publication*]
EMPI .... Empi, Inc. [*NASDAQ symbol*] (NQ)
EMPI .... Engineering Manual Preparation Instruction [*Army Materiel Command*]
EMPIRE ... Early Manned Planetary-Interplanetary Round Trip Experiment
Empire For J ... Empire Forestry Journal [*A publication*]
Empire J Exp Agr ... Empire Journal of Experimental Agriculture [*A publication*]
Empire Prod ... Empire Producer [*A publication*]
EMPIRES ... Excerpta Medica Physicians Information Retrieval and Education Service [*Elsevier Science Publishers*] [*Information service or system*]
Empire State Rept ... Empire State Report [*A publication*]
Empirical Econ ... Empirical Economics [*A publication*]
Empir Res T ... Empirical Research in Theatre [*A publication*]
Emp J Exp Ag ... Empire Journal of Experimental Agriculture [*A publication*]
Emp J Exp Agric ... Empire Journal of Experimental Agriculture [*A publication*]
EMPL .... Emplacement (AABC)
EMPL .... Emplane [*British*]
EMPL .... Emplastrum [*Plaster*] [*Pharmacy*] (ROG)
EMPL .... Employ [*or Employee*] (AABC)
EMPL .... Employer (ROG)

EMPL .... Engineering Master Parts List (KSC)
EMPLAST ... Emplastrum [*Plaster*] [*Pharmacy*] (ROG)
Empl Benefit Plan Rev ... Employee Benefit Plan Review [*A publication*]
Empl Benefits J ... Employee Benefits Journal [*A publication*]
Empl B Jrl ... Employee Benefits Journal [*A publication*]
Empl Comp App Bd ... Decisions of the Employees' Compensation Appeals Board [*Department of Labor*] (DLA)
Empl Coordinator Research Inst Am ... Employment Coordinator. Research Institute of America [*A publication*]
EMPLEE... Employee
Empl Gaz ... Employment Gazette [*A publication*]
EMPLMNT ... Employment
Empl News ... Employment News [*A publication*]
Employ Benefit Plan Rev ... Employee Benefit Plan Review [*A publication*]
Employ Benefits J ... Employee Benefits Journal [*A publication*]
Employee Benefits Cas BNA ... Employee Benefits Cases. Bureau of National Affairs [*A publication*]
Employee Health Fitness Newsl ... Employee Health and Fitness Newsletter [*A publication*]
Employee Rel ... Employee Relations [*A publication*]
Employers R ... Employers' Review [*A publication*] (APTA)
Employers' Rev ... Employers' Review [*A publication*]
Employ Gaz ... Employment Gazette [*A publication*]
Employment ... Employment and Earnings [*A publication*]
Employ Rel Abstr ... Employment Relations Abstracts [*A publication*]
Employ Relat Abstr ... Employment Relations Abstracts [*A publication*]
Employ Relat Law J ... Employee Relations Law Journal [*A publication*]
Empl Prac Dec ... Employment Practices Decisions [*Commerce Clearing House*] [*A publication*] (DLA)
Empl Prac Dec CCH ... Employment Practices Decisions. Commerce Clearing House [*A publication*]
Empl Prac Guide ... Employment Practices Guide [*Commerce Clearing House*] [*A publication*] (DLA)
Empl Prac Guide CCH ... Employment Practices Guide. Commerce Clearing House [*A publication*]
EMPLR ..... Employer
Empl R .... Employers' Review [*A publication*]
Empl RA .... Employment Relations Abstracts [*A publication*]
Empl Relat Law J ... Employee Relations Law Journal [*A publication*]
Empl Rel LJ ... Employee Relations Law Journal [*A publication*]
Empl Rep ... Employment Report [*A publication*]
Empl'rs Liab ... Employers' Liability (DLA)
Empl Safety & Health Guide CCH ... Employment Safety and Health Guide. Commerce Clearing House [*A publication*]
Empl Saf'y & Health Guide ... Employment Safety and Health Guide [*A publication*] (DLA)
Empl Serv R ... Employment Service Review [*A publication*]
Empl & Training Rep BNA ... Employment and Training Reporter. Bureau of National Affairs [*A publication*]
Emplymnt S ... Employment and Earnings. Supplement [*A publication*]
EMPNO .... Employee Number (MCD)
Emporia St Res Stud ... Emporia State Research Studies [*A publication*]
Emp Prod ... Empire Producer [*A publication*]
EMPR .... Empire Financial Corp. [*NASDAQ symbol*] (NQ)
Emp R .... Empire Review [*A publication*]
Emp Rel ... Employee Relations [*A publication*]
Emp Rel LJ ... Employee Relations Law Journal [*A publication*]
EMPRESS ... Electromagnetic Pulse Radiation Environment Simulator for Ships [*Navy*] (MCD)
EMPRO ..... Emergency Proposal (NATG)
EMPS .... Electromagnetic Pulse Simulator (MCD)
EMPS .... Emergency Power Supply (MSA)
EMPSA ..... Experimental and Molecular Pathology. Supplement [*A publication*]
EMPSKD .. Employment Schedule (NVT)
EMPSKED ... Employment Schedule (NVT)
Emp Surv Rev ... Empire Survey Review [*A publication*]
EMPT .... Electronic Maintenance Proficiency Test
Emp Vesic ... Emplastrum Vesicatorium [*A Blister*] [*Medicine*]
EMQ .... Economic Manufacturing Quality
EMQ .... Electromagnetic Quiet
EMQ .... Ethoxyquin [*Antioxidant*] [*Organic chemistry*]
EMQ .... Evangelical Missions Quarterly [*A publication*]
EMR .... Augusta, GA [*Location identifier*] [*FAA*] (FAAL)
EMR .... Eastern & Midlands Railway [*British*] (ROG)
EMR .... Echo Mountain Resources Ltd. [*Vancouver Stock Exchange symbol*]
EMR .... Educable Mentally Retardate [*or Retarded*]
EMR .... Effective Management Responsibility
EMR .... Electromagnetic Radiation (AFM)
EMR .... Electromechanical Relay [*Power switchgear*] (IEEE)
EMR .... Electromechanical Research (IEEE)
EMR .... Electronic Module Retard [*Automotive engineering*]
EMR .... Electronic Moisture Recorder
EMR .... Emergency Medical Responders
EMR .... Emerson Electric Co. [*NYSE symbol*] (SPSG)
EMR .... Emotionally Mentally Retarded [*Psychology*]
EMR .... Employee Relations [*A publication*]
E & MR ... Energy & Mineral Resources [*Business Publishers, Inc.*] [*No longer available online*] [*Information service or system*] (CRD)

EMR .... Energy, Mines, and Resources [*Canadian government department*]
EMR .... Engine Maintenance Reminder [*Automotive engineering*]
EMR .... Engine Mixture Ratio
EMR .... Engineering Malfunction Report (MCD)
EMR .... Engineering Modification Requirements (MCD)
EMR .... Enlisted Manning Report [*Air Force*]
EMR .... Equipment Maintenance Record [*Army*] (AABC)
EMR .... Error Monitor Register (KSC)
EMR .... Executive Management Responsibility (MCD)
EMR .... Executive Management Review (NG)
EMR .... Geological Survey of Canada Library [*Canada Energy Mines and Resources*] [*UTLAS symbol*]
EMRA .... Electronics Materiel Readiness Activity [*Army*]
EMRA .... Emergency Medicine Residents' Association (EA)
EMRB .... European Marketing Research Board [*British*]
EMRC .... Electronic Media Rating Council (EA)
EMRC .... European Medical Research Council (EAIO)
EMREL ..... Emission Release (NVT)
EMRETIREAUTH ... This message authority for retirement [*Military*] (AABC)
EMRF .... European Monetary Reserve Fund [*Common Market*]
EMRG .... Electromagnetic Radiation Generator
EMRH .... Electromagnetic Radiation Hazard (MCD)
EMRH .... Emergency Manual Release Handle (MCD)
EMRIC .... Educational Media Research Information Center
EMRIWTB ... Canada. Department of Energy, Mines, and Resources. Inland Waters Branch. Technical Bulletin [*A publication*]
EMRL .... Equipment Maintenance Requirements List (MCD)
EMRLD ..... Excimer, Mid-Range [*or Moderate-Power*], Raman-Shifted LASER Device
EMRLS ..... Eastern Massachusetts Regional Library System [*Information service or system*] (EISS)
EMRO .... Eastern Mediterranean Regional Office [*World Health Organization*] [*Information service or system*] (IID)
EMROD .... Ekspluatatsiya, Modernizatsiya i Remont Oborudovaniya v Neftepererabatyvayushchei i Neftekhimicheskoi Promyshlennosti [*A publication*]
EMRODA ... Electronic MRO [*Maintenance Repair Operation*] Distributors Association (EA)
EMRP .... Effective Monopole-Radiated Power (TEL)
EMRPO .... Electromagnetic Radiation Project Office [*Naval Medical Research and Development Command*] [*Bethesda, MD*]
EMRRI ...... Energy and Mineral Resources Research Institute [*Iowa State University*] [*Research center*] (RCD)
EMRS .... East Malling Research Station [*British*] (ARC)
EMRS .... Electromagnetic Radiation System (MCD)
EMRS .... Emergency Medicine Research Society [*Manchester, England*] (EAIO)
EMRS .... Engineering Management Requirements Special [*McAir*]
E-MRS ..... European-Materials Research Society (EAIO)
EMRSAV .. East Malling Research Station. Annual Report [*A publication*]
EMRT .... Electronic Market-Research Terminal
EMRY .... Emery Energy, Inc. [*NASDAQ symbol*] (NQ)
EMS .... Earl Marshal's Secretary [*Pseudonym used by James Dalloway*]
EMS .... Early Morning Specimen [*Medicine*]
EMS .... Earthquake Monitoring System (NRCH)
EMS .... East Malaysia Shipping Ent. Pty. Ltd. (DS)
EMS .... Elaine Music Shop [*Record label*]
EMS .... Electrical Muscle Stimulation [*Physiology*]
EMS .... Electromagnetic Submarine [*Navy*]
EMS .... Electromagnetic Surveillance [*Air Force*]
EMS .... Electromagnetic Susceptibility (IEEE)
EMS .... Electromyosignal [*Data processing*]
EMS .... Electron-Momentum Spectrometer
EMS .... Electron Multiplex Switch
EMS .... Electronic Mail Service [*Telecommunications*]
EMS .... Electronic Mail System [*Postal Service*]
EMS .... Electronic Management System
EMS .... Electronic Medical System
EMS .... Electronic Meeting Services [*Clinton, MD*] [*Telecommunications*] (TSSD)
EMS .... Electronic Message System
EMS .... Elephant Memory System [*Data processing*]
EMS .... Elvis Presley Memorial Society of Syracuse, New York (EA)
EMS .... Embessa [*Papua New Guinea*] [*Airport symbol*] (OAG)
EMS .... Emergency Medical Service
EMS .... Emergency Mission Support [*Air Force*]
EMS .... Emergency Signal (BUR)
EMS .... Emission Spectrograph
EMS .... EMS Systems Ltd. [*Vancouver Stock Exchange symbol*]
EMS .... Energy Management System
EMS .... Enforcement Management Subsystem [*Environmental Protection Agency*]
EMS .... Engine Management System [*Army*]
EMS .... Engineering Master Schedule
EMS .... English Market Selection [*Cigars*]
EMS .... English Men of Science [*A publication*]
EMS .... Enhanced Memory Specifications [*Data processing*]
EMS .... Enhanced Mobility System [*LTV Aerospace and Defense Co.*]
EMS .... Entry Monitor System [*or Subsystem*] [*NASA*]

EMS .... Environmental Mutagen Society (EA)
EMS .... Eosinophilia Myalgia Syndrome [*Medicine*]
EMS .... Equilibrated Metal Surface [*Catalyst science*]
EMS .... Equilibrium Mode Simulator (TEL)
EMS .... Equipment Maintenance Squadron [*POMO*] (MCD)
EMS .... Ericsson Manufacturing Systems [*Commercial firm*] [*British*]
EMS .... Error Mean Square
EMS .... Ethyl Methanesulfonate [*or Ethyl Methanesulfonic Acid*] [*Experimental mutagen*]
EMS .... European Mariculture Society (EAIO)
EMS .... European Monetary System
EMS .... Exception Management System
EMS .... Expanded Memory Specification [*Data processing*]
EMS .... Experimental Monitoring Satellite (MCD)
EMS .... Export Marketing Service [*Department of Agriculture*]
EMS .... Express Mail Service [*Generic term*]
EMS .... IEEE Engineering Management Society (EA)
EMS .... Surveys and Mapping Library [*Canada Energy Mines and Resources*] [*UTLAS symbol*]
EMSA .... Eastern Marathon Swimming Association (EA)
EMSA .... Electrician's Mate, Seaman Apprentice [*Navy rating*]
EMSA .... Electron Microscopy Society of America (EA)
EMSA .... Electronics Materiel Support Agency [*Army*]
EMSA .... Electrophoretic Mobility Shift Assay [*Analytical biochemistry*]
EmSA .... Emakeele Seltsi Aastaraamat [*A publication*]
EMSC .... Educational Media Selection Center [*National Book Committee*]
EMSC .... Electromechanical Stop Clock
EMSCD .... English Miscellany. St. Stephen's College (Delhi) [*A publication*]
EMSD .... Electrical Measurements and Standards Division [*National Institute of Standards and Technology*] (GRD)
EMSD .... Equipment Major Subdivision
EMSEC ..... Emanations Security (AABC)
EMSI .... EMS Systems Ltd. [*Dallas, TX*] [*NASDAQ symbol*] (NQ)
EMSIB ...... Eastern Mediterranean Special Service Intelligence Bureau [*British*] [*World War I*]
EM/SIM ... Emulator/Simulator (MCD)
EMSKED .. Employment Schedule
EMSL .... Electronic Material Sciences Laboratory
EMSL/CIN ... Environmental Monitoring and Support Laboratory, Cincinnati [*Ohio*] [*Environmental Protection Agency*] (GRD)
EMSL/LV ... Environmental Monitoring Systems Laboratory, Las Vegas [*Nevada*] [*Environmental Protection Agency*] (GRD)
EMSL/RTP ... Environmental Monitoring Systems Laboratory, Research Triangle Park [*North Carolina*] [*Environmental Protection Agency*] (GRD)
EMSM ...... Employee Services Management [*A publication*]
EMSN .... Electrician's Mate, Seaman [*Navy rating*]
EMSN .... Emission (MSA)
EMSN .... External-Mix Spray Nut
EMS Newsl ... EMS [*Environmental Mutagen Society*] Newsletter [*A publication*]
EMSO .... Education Society [*Later, Psychology Society - PS*] (EA)
EMSO .... Electronic Memory Systems Organization [*Burroughs Corp.*]
EMSO .... Emergency Medical Services Organisation [*South Australian Health Commission*]
EMSO .... European Mobility Service Office [*Army*] (AABC)
EMSP .... Enhanced Modular Signal Processor (MCD)
EMSq .... Equipment Maintenance Squadron [*Air Force*]
EMSR .... Electrician's Mate, Ship Repair [*Navy rating*] [*Obsolete*]
EMSR .... Electronic Material Shipment Request [*Navy*]
EMSR .... Employment Service Review [*A publication*]
EMSRG ..... Electrician's Mate, Ship Repair, General Electrician [*Navy rating*] [*Obsolete*]
EMSRS ..... Electrician's Mate, Ship Repair, Shop Electrician [*Navy rating*] [*Obsolete*]
EMSRT ..... Electrician's Mate, Ship Repair, I.C. Repairman [*Navy rating*] [*Obsolete*]
EMSS .... Electromagnetic Servoactuator System (NASA)
EMSS .... Electronic Message Service System [*Telecommunications*] (TEL)
EMSS .... Emergency Medical Service System
EMSS .... Emergency Mission Support System [*Air Force*]
EMSS .... Experimental Manned Space Station [*Air Force*]
EMSTRP... Equipment Management System Training Requirements Program [*Navy*] (NG)
EMSU .... Electromagnetic Simulation Unit (MCD)
EMSU .... Environmental Meteorological Support Unit [*National Weather Service*]
EMT .... Each More Than
EMT .... Early Missile Test
EMT .... Econometrica [*A publication*]
EMT .... El Monte, CA [*Location identifier*] [*FAA*] (FAAL)
EMT .... Elapsed Maintenance Time
EMT .... Elapsed Method of Training (MCD)
EMT .... Electrical Mate Test (KSC)
EMT .... Electrical Mechanical Tubing
EMT .... Electrical Metallic Tubing
EMT .... Electrician's Mate, Telephone [*Coast Guard rating*] [*Obsolete*]

EMT .... Electromagnetic Thrust [*Propulsion for ship or submarine*]
EMT .... Electromechanical Team
EMT .... Electromechanical Technology
EMT .... Electromechanical Test (NASA)
EMT .... Electron Microscope Tomography
EMT .... Electronic Maintenance Technician [*FAA*]
EMT .... Electronic Mind Tester
EMT .... Elemental Method of Training
EMT .... Embalmer [*Navy rating*]
EMT .... Emergency Medical Tag
EMT .... Emergency Medical Technician
EMT .... Emergency Medical Treatment [*Military*] (AABC)
EMT .... Emerging Medical Technology Fund, Inc. [*AMEX symbol*] (SPSG)
EMT .... Emmet [*California*] [*Seismograph station code, US Geological Survey*] (SEIS)
EMT .... Emory University, Pitts Theological Library, Atlanta, GA [*OCLC symbol*] (OCLC)
EMT .... Empire Resources [*Vancouver Stock Exchange symbol*]
Em T .... Employment Taxes, Social Security Act Rulings [*Internal Revenue Service*] [*A publication*] (DLA)
EMT .... Empty
EMT .... End of Magnetic Tape [*Data processing*] (MDG)
EMT .... Engineering Model Transport
EMT .... Equivalent Megatonnage [*Military weapon index*]
EMT .... European Mediterranean Troposphere (IEEE)
EMT .... Evaluation Modality Test [*Psychology*]
EMT .... Evaluation Monitoring Team (MCD)
EMT .... Executive Management Team (NRCH)
EMT .... Expanded Mobility Truck (MCD)
EMT-A ...... Emergency Medical Technician, Ambulance (DHSM)
EMTA .... Endomethylenetetrahydrophthalic Acid [*Organic chemistry*]
EMTAC..... Emergency Machine Tool Armament Corps [*British*] [*World War II*]
EMTDA .... Engineering Materials and Design [*A publication*]
EMTDP..... Environmental Mutagen Test Development Program [*National Institute of Environmental Health Sciences*]
EMTE....... Electromagnetic Test Environment
EMTECH ... Electromagnetic Technology
EMTED2... Enzyme and Microbial Technology [*A publication*]
EMTEDS .. Electromagnetic Test Environment Data System (MCD)
EMTF .... Estimated Mean Time to Failure
EMTH .... Energy Methods Corp. [*NASDAQ symbol*] (NQ)
EMTI .... Edge-Mounted Threaded Inserts
EMT-I .... Emergency Medical Technician, Intermediate [*Also, IEMT*] (DHSM)
EMT J ...... EMT [*Emergency Medical Technician*] Journal [*A publication*]
EMT Legal Bull ... Emergency Medical Technician Legal Bulletin [*A publication*]
EMT-P ..... Emergency Medical Technician, Paramedic (DHSM)
EMTR....... Emitter (MSA)
EMTR....... Enlisted Master Tape Record [*Army*] (AABC)
EMTRA..... Eastern Metals Review [*A publication*]
EMTS....... Electronic Money Transfer System
EMTS....... Ethylmercury-P-Toluenesulfonamide [*Organic chemistry*]
EMTT....... Expanded Mobility Tactical Truck (MCD)
EMTTF ...... Equivalent Mean Time to Failure
EMTU .... Enhanced Master Terminal Unit
EMU......... Eastern Michigan University [*Ypsilanti*]
EMU......... Economic and Monetary Union
EMU......... Electric Multiple Unit [*Passenger trains*] (DCTA)
EMU......... Electromagnetic Unit
EMU......... Emory University, Atlanta, GA [*OCLC symbol*] (OCLC)
EMU......... Emulator (MSA)
EMU......... Engine Multiplexing Unit (MCD)
EMU......... Engineering Mock-Up
EMU......... Engineering Model Unit [*NASA*] (NASA)
EMU......... Environmental Measurement Unit (MCD)
EMU......... Europaische Musikschul-Union [*European Union of Music Schools*] (EAIO)
EMU......... European Mineworkers' Union [*Zambia*]
EMU......... European Monetary Union
EMU......... European Monetary Unit [*Proposed*]
EMU......... Experimental Military Unit [*Australia*]
EMU......... Extended Memory Unit (NASA)
EMU......... Extravehicular Mobility Unit [*NASA*] (KSC)
EMUA...... European Monetary Unit of Account
EMUG...... European MAP [*Manufacturing Automation Protocol*] Users Group [*Automotive engineering*]
EMUL ...... Emulsion (MSA)
EMULS...... Emulsum [*Emulsion*] [*Medicine*] (ROG)
Em Univ Q ... Emory University Quarterly [*A publication*]
EMUX ...... Electrical Multiplex
EMV .... Egress Maintenance Vehicle
EMV .... Electromagnetic Velocity (KSC)
EMV .... Electromagnetic Voltage (CAAL)
EMV .... Electromagnetic Vulnerability
eMv .... Electron Megavolt (EY)
EMV .... Emporia, VA [*Location identifier*] [*FAA*] (FAAL)
EMV .... Expected Monetary Value
EMV .... Eyes, Motor, Voice [*Glasgow Coma Scale*] [*Medicine*]

EMVJ........ Etched Multiple Vertical Junction [*Photovoltaic energy systems*]
EMVP....... Electro-Magnetic Velocity Profiler [*Oceanography*] (MSC)
EMVW ..... Enquetes du Musee de la Vie Wallonne [*A publication*]
EMW .... Electrical Megawatt
EMW .... Electromagnetic Warfare (MCD)
EMW .... Electromagnetic Wave
EMW .... Electromagnetic Window
EMW .... Enquetes. Musee de la Vie Wallonne [*A publication*]
EMW .... Equipment Manufacturers Workmanship
EMW .... Evangelical Magazine of Wales [*A publication*]
EMW .... Evangelical Movement of Wales
EM Wash State Univ Coop Ext Serv ... EM. Washington State University. Cooperative Extension Service [*A publication*]
EMWF....... Electromagnetic Wave Form
EMWO...... Engineering Mock-Up Work Order
EMWP ...... Esperantist Movement for World Peace [*See also MEM*] [*Tours, France*] (EAIO)
EMWS....... Ethnic Minorities and Women in Science [*National Science Foundation*]
EMX .... El Maiten [*Argentina*] [*Airport symbol*] (OAG)
EMX .... Electron Microprobe X-Ray Analyzer
EMXA ...... Electron Microprobe X-Ray Analyzer
EMXRF .... Electron Microprobe X-Ray Fluorescence
Emy......... Emergency (DS)
EMY .... Emergency List [*Navy*] [*British*]
EMZ......... Evangelische Missionszeitschrift [*A publication*]
EMZMAJ ... Entomologische Mitteilungen. Zoologischen Museum [*Hamburg*] [*A publication*]
EMZSA3 ... Entomologische Mitteilungen. Zoologischen Staatsinstitut und Zoologischen Museum [*Hamburg*] [*A publication*]
EN .... Early Negative
EN .... Earth Vote Network (EA)
EN .... Earthcare Network (EA)
EN .... Eastern Airways [*United Kingdom*] [*ICAO designator*] (ICDA)
EN .... Economic News [*A publication*]
EN .... Education Nationale [*A publication*]
EN .... Electronic News [*A publication*]
EN .... Element Number [*Data processing*]
En........... Encounter [*A publication*]
EN .... Endo Laboratories, Inc. [*Research code symbol*]
En........... Endosperm [*Botany*]
EN .... Enema [*Medicine*]
EN .... Enemy (AABC)
EN .... Enforcement Notification (NRCH)
EN .... Engineering Note [*or Notice*]
EN .... Engineman [*Navy rating*]
EN .... Enki and Ninhursag (BJA)
En........... Enoch (BJA)
EN .... Enrolled Nurse
en........... Enstatite [*CIPW classification*] [*Geology*]
EN .... Entanglement Network (EA)
EN .... Enterra Corp. [*NYSE symbol*] (SPSG)
EN .... Eras of Nonconformity [*A publication*]
EN .... Ere Nouvelle [*A publication*]
EN .... Erythema Nodosum [*Medicine*]
EN .... Esquimalt & Nanaimo Railway Co. [*AAR code*]
EN .... Ethylenediamine [*Organic chemistry*]
EN .... Etudes Numismatiques [*A publication*]
EN .... Euro-Nevada Mining Corp. Ltd. [*Toronto Stock Exchange symbol*]
EN .... Europa Nostra [*Historic preservation organization*] (EA)
en----- .... Europe, Northern [*MARC geographic area code*] [*Library of Congress*] (LCCP)
EN .... European Norm [*Standards*]
EN .... European Numismatics [*A publication*]
EN .... Exception Noted
EN .... Experimental Neurology [*A publication*]
EN .... Export Network [*Great Britain*] [*Information service or system*] (CRD)
EN .... Ezrat Nashim [*Inactive*] (EA)
EN .... Genair Ltd. [*Great Britain*] [*ICAO designator*] (FAAC)
EN1........... Engineman, First Class [*Navy rating*]
EN2........... Engineman, Second Class [*Navy rating*]
EN3........... Engineman, Third Class [*Navy rating*]
ENA......... Eastern News Agency [*Bangladesh*] (FEA)
ENA......... Electronic Networking Association [*Information service or system*] (IID)
ENA......... Elkan N. Adler Collection [*Jewish Theological Seminary of America, New York*] (BJA)
ENA......... Emergency Nurses Association (EA)
ENA......... Enable (NASA)
ENA......... Engineering Next Assembly (MCD)
ENA......... English Newspaper Association
ENA......... Enrolled Nursing Aide (ADA)
ENA......... Environmental Protection Agency, Region VII Library, Kansas City, MO [*OCLC symbol*] (OCLC)
ENA......... Ethiopian News Agency
ENA......... Ethylnitrolic Acid [*Organic chemistry*]
ENA......... Euro-National Australia Limited
ENA......... European Neuroscience Association (EAIO)

ENA.......... Evening News Association
ENA.......... Experimental Negotiating Agreement [*Steelworkers contract*]
ENA.......... Extractable Nuclear Antigen [*Immunology*]
ENA.......... Kenai [*Alaska*] [*Airport symbol*] (OAG)
ENA.......... Kenai, AK [*Location identifier*] [*FAA*] (FAAL)
ENAA........ Epithermal Neutron Activation Analysis [*Analytical chemistry*]
ENAAD..... Energetika (Alma-Ata) [*A publication*]
ENAB........ Evening Newspaper Advertising Bureau [*Business term*]
ENAB........ Exports to North America Branch [*British Overseas Trade Board*] (DS)
ENABLE... Education and Neighborhood Action for Better Living Environment
ENABOL... Empresa Naviera Boliviana [*Shipping company*] [*Bolivia*] (EY)
ENAC........ Electronic Numerical Integrator and Calculator [*Early computer, 1946*] (DCTA)
ENAC........ Expanded National Agency Check [*DoD*]
ENACD..... Environmental Action [*A publication*]
ENACT...... Environmental Action for Survival (EA)
ENADS...... Enhanced Network Administration System [*Telecommunications*] (TEL)
ENAEA ..... Electrical News and Engineering [*A publication*]
ENAF........ Employer Identification Number Name and Address File [*IRS*]
ENAGDM ... Energia Nuclear e Agricultura [*A publication*]
ENAL........ Alesund/Vigra [*Norway*] [*ICAO location identifier*] (ICLI)
ENALD...... Energy and Alternatives Magazine [*A publication*]
ENAM....... Enamel (KSC)
ENAMA3.. Entomologica Americana [*A publication*]
ENAMD..... Enameled (ROG)
ENAN....... Andoya [*Norway*] [*ICAO location identifier*] (ICLI)
ENANB ..... Enteric [*or Epidemic*] NANB [*Non-A, Non-B*] Hepatitis [*Medicine*]
ENAS......... Ny Alesund (Svalbard) [*Norway*] [*ICAO location identifier*] (ICLI)
ENAT .... Alta [*Norway*] [*ICAO location identifier*] (ICLI)
ENAT .... En Route Air Traffic Control [*A publication*]
ENATA ..... Energia es Atomtechnika [*A publication*]
ENB .... Eneabba [*Australia*] [*Airport symbol*] (OAG)
ENB .... Energiebesparing in Bedrijf en Instelling [*A publication*]
ENB .... English National Board Careers Advisory Centre [*British*] (CB)
ENBA .... Economics News Broadcasters Association (EA)
ENBD .... Bodo [*Norway*] [*ICAO location identifier*] (ICLI)
ENBJ .... Bjornoya [*Norway*] [*ICAO location identifier*] (ICLI)
ENBL........ Enable (MSA)
ENBL........ Forde/Bringeland [*Norway*] [*ICAO location identifier*] (ICLI)
ENBM .... Bomoen [*Norway*] [*ICAO location identifier*] (ICLI)
ENBN .... Bronnoysund/Bronnoy [*Norway*] [*ICAO location identifier*] (ICLI)
ENBO .... Bodo [*Norway*] [*ICAO location identifier*] (ICLI)
ENBR .... Bergen/Flesland [*Norway*] [*ICAO location identifier*] (ICLI)
ENBS........ Batsfjord [*Norway*] [*ICAO location identifier*] (ICLI)
ENBV .... Berlevag [*Norway*] [*ICAO location identifier*] (ICLI)
ENC .... Eastern Nazarene College, Wollaston, MA [*OCLC symbol*] (OCLC)
ENC .... Electroencephalography Technician [*Navy*]
ENC .... Els Nostres Classics [*A publication*]
ENC .... Emergency National Council Against US Intervention in Central America/The Caribbean (EA)
ENC .... Enclose [*Technical drawings*]
ENC .... Enclosure
ENC .... Encode (NASA)
ENC .... Encounter [*A publication*]
ENC .... Encyclopedia
ENC .... Engineering Command (AAG)
ENC .... Engineman, Chief [*Navy rating*]
ENC .... Enlistment Canceled [*Military*]
ENC .... Enteral Nutrition Council (EA)
ENC .... Equivalent Noise Charge
ENC .... Euromin Canada Ltd. [*Vancouver Stock Exchange symbol*]
ENC .... Exhaust Nozzle Control
ENCa .... Nancy [*France*] [*Airport symbol*] (OAG)
EnCa .... Endometrial Carcinoma [*Oncology*]
ENCA .... European Naval Communications Agency [*NATO*]
ENCA .... Oslo Caa [*Norway*] [*ICAO location identifier*] (ICLI)
ENCAP...... Encapsulation (MSA)
ENCAR ..... Enclosed Cryocondenser for Air Recovery
Enc Arch ... Gwilt's Encyclopedia of Architecture [*A publication*] (DLA)
EncBibl...... Encyclopaedia Biblica [*Jerusalem*] [*A publication*] (BJA)
Enc Brit...... Encyclopaedia Britannica [*A publication*]
Enc Buddh ... Encyclopaedia of Buddhism [*A publication*]
ENCC .... Emergency Network Control Center (MCD)
ENCC .... Encore Computer Corp. [*NASDAQ symbol*] (NQ)
Enc Catt .... Enciclopedia Cattolica [*A publication*]
ENCD .... Encode (MSA)
Enc Dict .... Encyclopedia Dictionary, Edited by Robert Hunter [*1879-88*] [*A publication*] (DLA)
ENCDR ..... Encoder (MSA)
ENCE .... Extendable Nozzle Cone
ENCEA...... Encephale [*A publication*]
ENCEAN .. Encephale [*A publication*]
Enceph .... Encephale [*A publication*]

Enc Forms ... Encyclopedia of Forms [*A publication*] (DLA)
Ench B ...... Enchiridion Biblicum [*A publication*]
ENCHDZ .. Specialist Periodical Reports. Environmental Chemistry [*A publication*]
Ench Symb ... Enchiridion Symbolorum [*A publication*]
EncI.......... Encounter (Indianapolis) [*A publication*]
Enc I.......... Encyclopedie de l'Islam [*A publication*]
Enc Ins US ... Insurance Year-Book [*A publication*] (DLA)
Enc Is .... Encyclopaedia of Islam [*A publication*]
EncJud....... Encyclopaedia Judaica [*Jerusalem*] [*A publication*] (BJA)
Enc Jur D... Encyclopedie Juridique Dalloz [*French*] [*A publication*] (DLA)
ENCL........ EnClean, Inc. [*NASDAQ symbol*] (NQ)
ENCL........ Enclose (KSC)
ENCL........ Enclosure (ROG)
EncL.......... Encounter (London) [*A publication*]
Enc Law .... American and English Encyclopedia of Law [*A publication*] (DLA)
ENCLD...... Enclosed (ROG)
ENCLD...... Energy Clearinghouse [*A publication*]
Enc Lik Umj ... Enciklopedija Likovnik Umjetnosti [*A publication*]
ENCLO ..... Enclosure
ENCLOD ... Enclosed (ROG)
ENCLOSG ... Enclosing (ROG)
ENCM .... Engineman, Master Chief [*Navy rating*]
ENCMD .... Energy Dollars and Sense of Conservation [*A publication*]
Enc Mens O Mer ... Encyclopedie Mensuelle d'Outre-Mer [*A publication*]
ENCMP..... Economists' National Committee on Monetary Policy (EA)
Enc Mus..... Encyclopedie de la Musique [*A publication*]
ENCN .... Kristiansand/Kjevik [*Norway*] [*ICAO location identifier*] (ICLI)
ENCO .... Energy Company [*Slogan and brand name used by Humble Oil & Refining Co.*] [*Later, Exxon*]
ENCO .... Environmental Conservation [*A publication*]
ENCOM .... Engineer Construction Command [*Army*]
En Conserv ... Energy Conservation News [*A publication*]
Encore....... Encore American and Worldwide News [*A publication*]
Encore Aust ... Encore Australia [*A publication*]
Encount...... Encounter [*A publication*]
Encounter (Chr Theol Sem) ... Encounter (Christian Theological Seminary) [*A publication*]
ENCP........ ENERCAP Corp. [*NASDAQ symbol*] (NQ)
ENCP........ European Naval Communications Plan [*NATO*] (NATG)
Enc Pamphl Ser ... Encounter Pamphlet Series [*A publication*]
Enc Pl & Pr ... Encyclopedia of Pleading and Practice [*A publication*] (DLA)
Enc Psych .. Encyclopedia of Psychology [*A publication*]
ENCR .... Encrypted (MCD)
ENCR .... Enscor, Inc. [*NASDAQ symbol*] (NQ)
ENCR .... Environmental Carcinogenesis Reviews [*A publication*]
ENCS........ Engineman, Senior Chief [*Navy rating*]
ENCSD...... Encased (MSA)
Enc SEI...... Enciclopedia SEI [*Societa Editrice Internazionale*] [*A publication*]
Enc Spett.... Enciclopedia dello Spettacolo [*A publication*]
ENCTR...... Encounter (FAAC)
ENCU .... Environmental Control Unit (MCD)
Enc Unif Sci ... Encyclopedia of Unified Science [*A publication*]
Enc US Sup Ct Rep ... Encyclopedia of United States Supreme Court Reports [*A publication*] (DLA)
ENCY .... Encyclopedia
ENCYA ..... Engineering Cybernetics [*English Translation*] [*A publication*]
Ency Amer ... Encyclopaedia Americana [*A publication*]
Ency Brit.... Encyclopaedia Britannica [*A publication*]
ENCYC...... Encyclopedia
Encyc........ Encyclopedia of the Laws of England [*2 eds.*] [*1897-1919*] [*A publication*] (DLA)
Encyc Brit .. Encyclopaedia Britannica [*A publication*]
Encycl Biol (Paris) ... Encyclopedie Biologique (Paris) [*A publication*]
Encycl Chem Technol ... Encyclopedia of Chemical Technology [*A publication*]
Encycl Chem Technol ... Kirk-Othmer Encyclopedia of Chemical Technology [*A publication*]
Encycl Entomol ... Encyclopedie Entomologique [*A publication*]
Encycl Med-Chir ... Encyclopedie Medico-Chirurgicale [*A publication*]
Encycl Mycol ... Encyclopedie Mycologique [*A publication*]
Encyclopedia Math Appl ... Encyclopedia of Mathematics and Its Applications [*A publication*]
Encycl Ornithol (Paris) ... Encyclopedie Ornithologique (Paris) [*A publication*]
Encycl Plant Anat ... Encyclopedia of Plant Anatomy [*A publication*]
Encycl Plant Physiol New Ser ... Encyclopedia of Plant Physiology. New Series [*A publication*]
Encycl Urol ... Encyclopedia of Urology [*A publication*]
Encycl Vet Med Surg and Obst ... Encyclopaedia of Veterinary Medicine, Surgery, and Obstetrics [*A publication*]
ENCYDI.... Encyclia [*A publication*]
Ency of Ev ... Encyclopedia of Evidence [*A publication*] (DLA)
Ency of Forms ... Encyclopedia of Forms and Precedents [*A publication*] (DLA)
Ency Law ... American and English Encyclopedia of Law [*A publication*] (DLA)

Ency L & P ... American and English Encyclopedia of Law and Practice [*A publication*] (DLA)
Ency of L & Pr ... Encyclopedia of Law and Practice [*A publication*] (DLA)
Ency of Pl & Pr ... Encyclopedia of Pleading and Practice [*A publication*] (DLA)
Ency P & P ... Encyclopedia of Pleading and Practice [*A publication*] (DLA)
Ency US Sup Ct ... Encyclopedia of United States Supreme Court Reports [*A publication*] (DLA)
Ency US Sup Ct Rep ... Encyclopedia of Pleading and Practice. Supplement [*A publication*] (DLA)
END.......... Earth Net Dial
END.......... Electronic Null Detector
END.......... Eliminate the National Debt (EA)
END.......... Endocrinology [*Medical specialty*] (DHSM)
END.......... Endorsed [*or Endorsement*] [*Business term*]
END.......... Endowed (ROG)
END.......... Endurance Minerals [*Vancouver Stock Exchange symbol*]
END.......... Enid, OK [*Location identifier*] [*FAA*] (FAAL)
END.......... Entente Nationale Democratique [*National Democratic Entente*] [*Monaco*] [*Political party*] (PPE)
END.......... Environment News Digest [*A publication*] (EAAP)
END.......... Equipes Notre-Dame [*Teams of Our Lady - TOOL*] [*Paris, France*] (EAIO)
END.......... European Nuclear Disarmament [*London, England*]
END.......... Exaltation Newcastle Disease
ENDA....... ENDA [*Enviroment and Development*] Caribe [*An association*] (EAIO)
ENDA-TM ... Environnement et Developpement du Tiers Monde [*Environment and Development of the Third World*] (EAIO)
End Bdg Ass ... Endlich on Building Associations [*A publication*] (DLA)
ENDC........ Eighteen-Nation Disarmament Committee [*or Conference*] [*Later, CCD*] [*Convened March 14, 1962; actually attended by 17 nations, with France absent*]
ENDCA..... Endoscopy [*A publication*]
ENDCAM ... Endoscopy [*A publication*]
ENDCE..... Endurance (FAAC)
ENDE........ Empresa Nacional de Electricidad SA [*State electricity company*] [*Bolivia*] (EY)
ENDE........ Endeavour [*A publication*]
ENDEA...... Endeavour [*A publication*]
ENDEAS... Endeavour [*Oxford*] [*A publication*]
Endeavour New Ser ... Endeavour. New Series [*A publication*]
ENDECJA ... Stronnictwo Narodowej Demokracji [*Nationalist Democratic Party*] [*Poland*] (PPE)
ENDED..... Energy Development [*A publication*]
Endem Dis Bull Nagasaki Univ ... Endemic Diseases Bulletin. Nagasaki University [*A publication*]
ENDEX..... End Date of an Exercise (MCD)
ENDEX..... Environmental Data Index [*National Oceanic and Atmospheric Administration*] (MCD)
ENDF........ Evaluated Nuclear Data File [*National Nuclear Data Center*] [*Information service or system*]
ENDG........ Ending (FAAC)
ENDGA..... Engineers' Digest [*A publication*]
ENDGD..... Energy Digest [*Bombay*] [*A publication*]
ENDI......... Dagali [*Norway*] [*ICAO location identifier*] (ICLI)
Endicott 86 ... Northwestern Endicott Report, 1986. Employment Trends for College Graduates in Business [*A publication*]
ENDID...... Energy Dialog [*A publication*]
End Interp St ... Endlich's Commentaries on the Interpretation of Statutes [*A publication*] (DLA)
End Interp Stat ... Endlich's Commentaries on the Interpretation of Statutes [*A publication*] (ILCA)
ENDKA..... Endokrinologie [*A publication*]
ENDKAC .. Endokrinologie [*A publication*]
Endl Bldg Ass'ns ... Endlich on Building Associations [*A publication*] (DLA)
ENDO........ Endotronics, Inc. [*NASDAQ symbol*] (NQ)
ENDOA...... Endocrinology [*A publication*]
ENDOAO ... Endocrinology [*A publication*]
ENDOC..... Environmental Information and Documentation Centres Database [*Commission of the European Communities*] [*Information service or system*] (CRD)
Endocr Bioassay Data ... Endocrine Bioassay Data. United States Department of Health, Education, and Welfare [*A publication*]
Endocr Exp ... Endocrinologia Experimentalis [*A publication*]
ENDOCRIN ... Endocrinology
Endocrinol ... Endocrinologie [*A publication*]
ENDOCRINOL ... Endocrinology
Endocrinol Exp ... Endocrinologia Experimentalis [*A publication*]
Endocrinol Ind ... Endocrinology Index [*A publication*]
Endocrinol Jpn ... Endocrinologia Japonica [*A publication*]
Endocrinol Jpn Suppl ... Endocrinologia Japonica. Supplement [*A publication*]
Endocrinol Metab Ser ... Endocrinology and Metabolism Series [*A publication*]
Endocrinol Sci Cost ... Endocrinologia e Scienza della Costituzione [*A publication*]
Endocr Jap ... Endocrinologia Japonica [*A publication*]
Endocr Res ... Endocrine Research Communications [*A publication*]
Endocr Res Commun ... Endocrine Research Communications [*A publication*]

Endocr Rev ... Endocrine Reviews [*A publication*]
Endocr Soc Aust Proc ... Endocrine Society of Australia. Proceedings [*A publication*]
Endod & Dent Traumatol ... Endodontics and Dental Traumatology [*A publication*]
Endod Dent Traumatol ... Endodontics and Dental Traumatology [*A publication*]
endo-H .... Endoglucosaminidase-H [*An enzyme*]
Endok Mekh Regul Prisposobleniya Org Myshechnoi Deyat ... Endokrinnye Mekhanizmy Regulyatsii Prisposobleniya Organizma k Myshechnoi Deyatel'nosti [*A publication*]
Endokr....... Endokrinologie [*A publication*]
Endokrinol ... Endokrinologie [*A publication*]
Endokr Pol ... Endokrynologia Polska [*A publication*]
Endokrynol Pol ... Endokrynologia Polska [*A publication*]
ENDOMET ... Endometrium [*Anatomy*]
ENDO-PAC ... Endo-Atmospheric Penetration Aids Concept
ENDOR..... Electron-Nuclear Double Resonance
ENDORPHIN ... Endogenous Morphine [*or Endomorphin*] [*Also, ENM*] [*Brain peptide*]
ENDORST ... Endorsement (ROG)
ENDOW.... Endowment (ROG)
ENDP........ Endpaper (ADA)
ENDPRM ... Endpaper Map [*Publishing*]
ENDRD ...... Energy Directory [*A publication*]
ENDS .... Environmental Data Services [*Publisher*] [*British*]
ENDS .... European Nuclear Documentation System [*Information service or system*]
ENDT .... Endorsement
ENDU........ Bardufoss [*Norway*] [*ICAO location identifier*] (ICLI)
ENE .... East-Northeast
ENE .... Ende [*Indonesia*] [*Airport symbol*] (OAG)
ENE .... Energy Economics [*A publication*]
ene............. Enero [*January*] [*Spanish*]
ENE .... Enron Corp. [*NYSE symbol*] [*Toronto Stock Exchange symbol*] (SPSG)
ENE .... * Ethylnorepinephrine [*Also, ENS*] [*Pharmacology*]
ENE .... Kennebunk, ME [*Location identifier*] [*FAA*] (FAAL)
e-ne---........ Netherlands [*MARC geographic area code*] [*Library of Congress*] (LCCP)
ENEA .... Ente Nazionale per l'Energia Atomica [*Italy*] (EY)
ENEA .... European Nuclear Energy Agency (DS)
ENEAD ..... Energy in Agriculture [*A publication*]
ENEC .... Energy and Economics Data Bank [*IAEA*] [*Information service or system*]
ENEC .... Extendable Nozzle Exit Cone (MCD)
ENECA...... Engineering Economist [*A publication*]
ENEDD ..... Energy and Education [*A publication*]
ENEGA ..... Energies [*A publication*]
ENEIB....... Energy International [*A publication*]
ENEK .... Ekofisk [*Norway*] [*ICAO location identifier*] (ICLI)
ENEL......... Ente Nazionale per l'Energia Elettrica [*Italian Electricity Board*] [*Information service or system*] (IID)
EnEl.......... Enuma Elis (BJA)
ENELA...... Energia Elettrica [*A publication*]
ENEM .... Enema [*Medicine*] (ROG)
ENEO .... Ebrei nell'Europa Orientale (BJA)
ENER .... Energize (AAG)
ENER .... Energy Conversion Devices, Inc. [*NASDAQ symbol*] (NQ)
ENER .... Energy Directory [*Database*] [*Australia*]
ENERA....... Energie [*A publication*]
ENERB....... Energy Conversion [*A publication*]
ENERD ..... Energy [*A publication*]
ENERG ..... Energicamente [*With Energy*] [*Music*]
Energa Atom ... Energia es Atomtechnika [*A publication*]
Energ Alternative ... Energie Alternative [*Italy*] [*A publication*]
Energa Nu ... Energia Nucleare [*Milan*] [*A publication*]
Energa Nucl ... Energia Nucleare [*Milan*] [*A publication*]
Energ es Atomtech ... Energia es Atomtechnika [*A publication*]
Energ Atomtech ... Energia es Atomtechnika [*A publication*]
Energ Avtom ... Energetika i Avtomatika [*A publication*]
Energ-Brief ... Energie-Brief [*A publication*]
Energ Bull ... Energeticeskij Bjulleten [*A publication*]
Energ Byull ... Energeticheskii Byulleten [*A publication*]
Energ Commun ... Energy Communications [*A publication*]
ENERGE ..... Energicamente [*With Energy*] [*Music*] (ROG)
Energ El..... Energia Elettrica [*A publication*]
Energ Elektrif ... Energetika i Elektrifikatsiya [*A publication*]
Energ Elektrif (Kiev) ... Energetika i Elektrifikatsiya (Kiev) [*A publication*]
Energ Elektrotekh Prom ... Energetika i Elektrotekhnicheskaya Promyshlennost [*A publication*]
Energ Elet ... Energia Elettrica [*A publication*]
Energ Elettr ... Energia Elettrica [*A publication*]
Energ Elettr A ... Energia Elettrica. A [*A publication*]
Energ Elettr B ... Energia Elettrica. B [*A publication*]
Energeteknol Ispol'z Topl ... Energetekhnologicheskow Ispol'zovanie Toplova [*USSR*] [*A publication*]
Energ Fluide ... Energie Fluide [*A publication*]
Energ Fluide et Lubr Hydraul Pneum Asservissements ... Energie Fluide et Lubrification et Hydraulique Pneumatique Asservissements [*A publication*]

Energ Fontes Altern ... Energia. Fontes Alternativas [*A publication*]
Energ Fuego At ... Energia del Fuego al Atomo [*A publication*]
Energ Hidroteh ... Energetica si Hidrotehnica [*A publication*]
Energia....... Publicacion sobre Energia [*A publication*]
Energieonder Cent Ned Rep ... Energieonderzoek Centrum Nederland Report [*A publication*]
Energietech ... Energietechnik [*A publication*]
Energiewirtsch Tagesfragen ... Energiewirtschaftliche Tagesfragen [*A publication*]
Energ Ind ... Energia e Industria [*A publication*]
Energ Inst Im G M Krzhizhanovskogo Sb Tr ... Energeticheskii Institut Imeni G. M. Krzhizhanovskogo. Sbornik Trudov [*A publication*]
Energ Manage ... Energy Management [*A publication*]
Energ Mashinostr ... Energeticheskoe Mashinostroenie [*A publication*]
Energ Metall Phenom ... Energetics in Metallurgical Phenomena [*A publication*]
Energ Nucl ... Energia Nuclear [*A publication*]
Energ Nucl Agric ... Energia Nuclear e Agricultura [*A publication*]
Energ Nucl (Lisbon) ... Energia Nuclear. Boletim Informativo do Forum Atomico Portugues (Lisbon) [*A publication*]
Energ Nucl (Madrid) ... Energia Nuclear (Madrid) [*A publication*]
Energ Nucl Mag ... Energie Nucleaire Magazine [*Later, Energie Magazine*] [*A publication*]
Energ Nucl (Milan) ... Energia Nucleare (Milan) [*A publication*]
Energ Nucl (Paris) ... Energie Nucleaire (Paris) [*A publication*]
Energotekhnol Ispol'z Topl ... Energotekhnologicheskoe Ispol'zovante Topliva [*A publication*]
Energ Pol Con Rep ... Energy Policy and Conservation Report [*A publication*]
Energ Polic ... Energy Policy [*A publication*]
Energ Reg Dig ... Energy Regulation Digest [*A publication*]
Energ Stroit ... Energeticheskoe Stroitel'stvo [*USSR*] [*A publication*]
Energ Stroit Rubezhom ... Energeticheskoe Stroitel'stvo za Rubezhom [*USSR*] [*A publication*]
Energ Szakirod Tajek ... Energiaipari Szakirodalmi Tajekoztato [*A publication*]
Energ Tech ... Energie und Teknik [*A publication*]
Energ Techn ... Energietechnik [*A publication*]
Energ Technik ... Energie und Teknik [*A publication*]
Energ Trans ... Energetika i Transport [*A publication*]
Energ Transp ... Energetika i Transport [*USSR*] [*A publication*]
Energy........ Energy User News [*A publication*]
Energy Abstr Policy Anal ... Energy Abstracts for Policy Analysis [*National Science Foundation*] [*A publication*]
Energy Advis Bull Tex Manuf ... Energy Advisory Bulletin for Texas Manufacturers [*A publication*]
Energy Agric ... Energy in Agriculture [*A publication*]
Energy Alternatives Mag ... Energy and Alternatives Magazine [*A publication*]
Energy in Bldgs ... Energy in Buildings [*A publication*]
Energy Bldgs ... Energy and Buildings [*A publication*]
Energy Bldgs ... Energy in Buildings [*A publication*]
Energy Build ... Energy and Buildings [*A publication*]
Energy and Build ... Energy and Buildings [*A publication*]
Energy Bus ... Energy Business. The Future of Coal, 1981 and Beyond [*A publication*]
Energy Clgh ... Energy Clearinghouse [*A publication*]
Energy Cnvers & Manage ... Energy Conversion and Management [*A publication*]
Energy Comm ... Energy Communications [*A publication*]
Energy Commun ... Energy Communications [*A publication*]
Energy Conserv Dig ... Energy Conservation Digest [*A publication*]
Energy Conserv Rep ... Energy Conservation Report [*Canada*] [*A publication*]
Energy Conserv Update ... Energy Conservation Update [*A publication*]
Energy Consum ... Energy Consumer [*A publication*]
Energy Cont (P-H) ... Energy Controls (Prentice-Hall, Inc.) [*A publication*] (DLA)
Energy Conv ... Energy Conversion [*A publication*]
Energy Convers ... Energy Conversion [*A publication*]
Energy Convers Intl J ... Energy Conversion. An International Journal [*A publication*]
Energy Convers Manage ... Energy Conversion and Management [*A publication*]
Energy Convers and Manage ... Energy Conversion and Management [*A publication*]
Energy Convers Tech Rep Aust Natl Univ Dep Eng Phys ... Australian National University. Department of Engineering Physics. Energy Conversion Technical Report [*A publication*] (APTA)
Energy Dev ... Energy and Development Journal [*A publication*]
Energy Dev ... Energy Developments [*A publication*]
Energy Dev Jpn ... Energy Developments in Japan [*A publication*]
Energy Dev (New York) ... Energy Development (New York). IEEE Power Engineering Society Papers [*A publication*]
Energy Dig ... Energy Digest [*A publication*]
Energy Dig (Colo Spring Colo) ... Energy Digest (Colorado Springs, Colorado) [*A publication*]
Energy Dig (London) ... Energy Digest (London) [*A publication*]
Energy Dig (Wash DC) ... Energy Digest (Washington, DC) [*A publication*]
Energy Dly ... Energy Daily [*A publication*]
Energy Dollars Sense Conserv ... Energy Dollars and Sense of Conservation [*A publication*]

Energy Econ ... Energy Economics [*A publication*]
Energy Econ Policy Manage ... Energy Economics, Policy, and Management [*A publication*]
Energy Educ ... Energy and Education [*A publication*]
Energy Educ Newsl ... Energy Educator Newsletter [*A publication*]
Energy Eng ... Energy Engineering [*A publication*]
Energy Enging ... Energy Engineering [*A publication*]
Energy Environ ... Energy and Environment [*South Africa*] [*A publication*]
Energy Environ (NY) ... Energy and the Environment (New York) [*A publication*]
Energy Environ (Oak Ridge Tenn) ... Energy and the Environment (Oak Ridge, Tennessee) [*A publication*]
Energy Environ Proc Nat Conf ... Energy and the Environment. Proceedings of the National Conference [*A publication*]
Energy Exec Dir ... Energy Executive Directory [*A publication*]
Energy Explor Exploit ... Energy Exploration and Exploitation [*A publication*]
Energy F & F ... World Energy. The Facts and the Future [*A publication*]
Energy Forum N Engl ... Energy Forum in New England [*A publication*]
Energy Ind ... Energy Index [*A publication*]
Energy Ind Commerce Q Bull ... Energy for Industry and Commerce. Quarterly Bulletin [*A publication*]
Energy Inf Abstr ... Energy Information Abstracts [*A publication*]
Energy Int ... Energy International [*A publication*]
Energy Int J ... Energy. The International Journal [*A publication*]
Energy J..... Energy Journal [*New Zealand*] [*A publication*]
Energy Law J ... Energy Law Journal [*A publication*]
Energy LJ .. Energy Law Journal [*A publication*]
Energy L Serv ... Energy Law Service [*A publication*] (DLA)
Energy M... Energy Magazine [*A publication*]
Energy Manage ... Energy Management [*A publication*]
Energy Manage (Cleveland Ohio) ... Energy Management (Cleveland, Ohio) [*A publication*]
Energy Manage (India) ... Energy Management (India) [*A publication*]
Energy Manage News ... Energy Management News [*A publication*]
Energy Meet ... Energy Meetings [*United States*] [*A publication*]
Energy Mgmt (CCH) ... Energy Management (Commerce Clearing House) [*A publication*] (DLA)
Energy Mgr ... Energy Manager [*A publication*]
Energy Miner Resour ... Energy and Minerals Resources [*A publication*]
Energy Newsl ... Energy Newsletter [*United States*] [*A publication*]
Energy Perspect ... Energy Perspectives [*A publication*]
Energy Pipelines Syst ... Energy Pipelines and Systems [*A publication*]
Energy Plann Network ... Energy Planning Network [*United States*] [*A publication*]
Energy Pol ... Energy Policy [*A publication*]
Energy Pollut Control ... Energy and Pollution Control [*Japan*] [*A publication*]
Energy Process (Can) ... Energy Processing (Canada) [*A publication*]
Energy Prog ... Energy Progress [*A publication*]
Energy Q.... Energy Quarterly [*Taiwan*] [*A publication*]
Energy Rep (Alton Engl) ... Energy Report (Alton, England) [*A publication*]
Energy Rep States ... Energy Report to the States [*A publication*]
Energy Res ... Energy Research [*England*] [*A publication*]
Energy Res Abstr ... Energy Research Abstracts [*A publication*]
Energy Res Dig ... Energy Research Digest [*A publication*]
Energy Resourc Technol ... Energy Resources and Technology [*A publication*]
Energy Resour (Osaka) ... Energy and Resources (Osaka) [*A publication*]
Energy Res Rep ... Energy Research Reports [*A publication*]
Energy Rev ... Energy Review [*A publication*]
Energy Systems Pol ... Energy Systems and Policy [*A publication*]
Energy Syst Policy ... Energy Systems and Policy [*A publication*]
Energy Syst and Policy ... Energy Systems and Policy [*A publication*]
Energy Technol Conf Proc ... Energy Technology Conference. Proceedings [*A publication*]
Energy Technol Rev ... Energy Technology Review [*A publication*]
Energy Technol (Wash DC) ... Energy Technology (Washington, DC) [*A publication*]
Energy Top ... Energy Topics [*A publication*]
Energy Users Rep (BNA) ... Energy Users Reports (Bureau of National Affairs) [*A publication*] (DLA)
Energy Wld ... Energy World [*A publication*]
ENERN ..... East-Northeastern [*Meteorology*] (FAAC)
ENET .... Evaluation Network [*An association*] (EA)
ENETD ..... Environmental Ethics [*A publication*]
ENEV .... Evenes [*Norway*] [*ICAO location identifier*] (ICLI)
ENEWD .... East-Northeastward [*Meteorology*] (FAAC)
ENEWD .... European Network for East-West Dialogue (EA)
ENEWS ..... Effectiveness of Navy Electronic Warfare Systems
ENEX .... Enex Resources Corp. [*NASDAQ symbol*] (NQ)
ENEXA ..... Endocrinologia Experimentalis [*A publication*]
ENEXAM ... Endocrinologia Experimentalis [*A publication*]
ENEX-ASIA ... International Electrical and Electronic Engineering Exhibition [*Interfama Pte. Ltd.*] (TSPED)
EnF .... Encontro com o Folclore [*A publication*]
ENF .... Enfield Corp. Ltd. [*Toronto Stock Exchange symbol*]
ENF .... Enflurane [*Also, E*] [*An anesthetic*]
ENF .... Enforcement (DCTA)
ENF .... Equipment Not Operationally Ready to Fire [*Military*] (MCD)
ENF .... Omaha, NE [*Location identifier*] [*FAA*] (FAAL)
ENFA .... Fireman Apprentice, Engineman, Striker [*Navy rating*]
ENFAD ..... Fusion Power Associates. Executive Newsletter [*A publication*]

Enfant Milieu Trop ... Enfant en Milieu Tropical [*A publication*]
ENFB........ Oslo/Fornebu [*Norway*] [*ICAO location identifier*] (ICLI)
ENFC........ Elvis Now Fan Club (EA)
ENFD .... Enfield [*Borough of London*]
Enf'd .... Enforced [*Legal term*] (DLA)
ENFD .... Forde [*Norway*] [*ICAO location identifier*] (ICLI)
Enferm Torax ... Enfermedades del Torax [*A publication*]
Enferm Torax Tuberc ... Enfermedades del Torax y Tuberculosis [*A publication*]
ENFET ...... Enzyme Field Effect Transistor [*Electrochemistry*]
ENFG .... Fagernes/Leirin [*Norway*] [*ICAO location identifier*] (ICLI)
ENFIA....... Exchange Network Facilities Interconnecting Arrangement [*Tariffs*] [*Telecommunications*]
ENFL........ Energy File [*Vancouver, British Columbia*] [*A publication*]
ENFL........ Floro [*Norway*] [*ICAO location identifier*] (ICLI)
ENFLA...... Energie Fluide [*A publication*]
ENFN .... Fireman, Engineman, Striker [*Navy rating*]
ENFO .... Forus [*Norway*] [*ICAO location identifier*] (ICLI)
ENFOR ..... Energy from the Forest Program [*Canada*]
ENFP......... Extrovert, Intuitive, Feeling, Perceptive [*Meyers-Briggs Type Indicator*]
ENFR......... Frigg [*Norway*] [*ICAO location identifier*] (ICLI)
ENFTAF ... Enfermedades del Torax [*A publication*]
ENFUEM ... Energy & Fuels [*A publication*]
ENFY......... Fyresdal [*Norway*] [*ICAO location identifier*] (ICLI)
ENFZ......... Fritzoe [*Norway*] [*ICAO location identifier*] (ICLI)
ENG.......... Electronic News Gathering [*Television news coverage*]
ENG.......... Electronystagmography [*Medicine*]
ENG.......... Empty Net Goals [*Hockey*]
ENG.......... Engagement (ADA)
ENG.......... Engine (AFM)
ENG.......... Engineer [*or Engineering*] (EY)
Eng............ [*The*] Engineer [*A publication*]
ENG.......... Engineer Hill [*Alaska*] [*Seismograph station code, US Geological Survey*] (SEIS)
ENG.......... Engineer Officer [*Navy*] [*British*]
Eng............ Engineering [*A publication*]
ENG.......... England [*or English*]
eng............. English [*MARC language code*] [*Library of Congress*] (LCCP)
Eng............ English [*A publication*]
Eng............ English Reports (N. C. Moak) [*A publication*] (DLA)
Eng............ English's Reports [*6-13 Arkansas*] [*A publication*] (DLA)
ENG.......... Engrave
ENG.......... Engraver (ROG)
EN(G)........ Enrolled Nurse (General) [*British*] (DBQ)
ENGA........ Emergency Natural Gas Act of 1977
ENGA........ Engage (MSA)
Eng Adm.... English Admiralty Reports [*A publication*] (DLA)
Eng Adm R ... English Admiralty Reports [*A publication*] (DLA)
Engage/Soc Act ... Engage/Social Action [*A publication*]
ENGAGMT ... Engagement (ROG)
Eng Agric... Engenharia Agricola [*A publication*]
Eng Apprent ... Engineer Apprentice [*A publication*]
Eng Aspects Magnetohydrodyn ... Engineering Aspects of Magnetohydrodynamics [*A publication*]
Eng As South Tr ... Engineering Association of the South. Transactions [*A publication*]
Eng Aust .... Engineers Australia [*A publication*] (APTA)
Eng in Aust ... English in Australia [*A publication*] (APTA)
ENGBAT... Engineer Battalion [*Military*]
ENGBCA... Corps of Engineers Board of Contract Appeals [*Army*]
Eng Boilerhouse Rev ... Engineering and Boilerhouse Review [*A publication*]
Eng Boil H Rev ... Engineering and Boiler House Review [*A publication*]
Eng Build ... Engineer and Builder [*A publication*]
Eng Bull ..... Engineering Bulletin [*A publication*]
Eng Bull Purdue Univ ... Engineering Bulletin. Purdue University [*A publication*]
Eng Bull Purdue Univ Eng Ext Ser ... Engineering Bulletin. Purdue University. Engineering Extension Series [*A publication*]
Eng & Bu Rec ... Engineering and Building Record [*USA*] [*A publication*]
Eng Buy Guide ... Engineer Buyers Guide [*A publication*]
Eng CC....... English Crown Cases [*American Reprint*] [*A publication*] (DLA)
Eng Cem World ... Engineering and Cement World [*A publication*]
Eng Ch .... English Chancery [*Legal term*] (DLA)
Eng Ch .... English Chancery Reports [*American Reprint*] [*A publication*] (DLA)
Eng Chem Dig ... Engineering and Chemical Digest [*A publication*]
Eng CL....... English Common Law Reports [*A publication*] (DLA)
Eng Club Phila Pr ... Engineers' Club of Philadelphia. Proceedings [*A publication*]
ENGCOM ... Engineering Command (MCD)
ENGCOMDC ... Engineer Commissioner, District of Columbia [*Military*] (AABC)
Eng Com LR ... English Common Law Reports [*A publication*] (DLA)
Eng Comput ... Engineering Computers [*A publication*]
Eng Constr World ... Engineering Construction World [*A publication*]
Eng Contract Rec ... Engineering and Contract Record [*A publication*]
Eng Cornell Q ... Engineering. Cornell Quarterly [*A publication*]
Eng Costs Prod Econ ... Engineering Costs and Production Economics [*Netherlands*] [*A publication*]

Eng Cr Cas ... English Crown Cases [*American Reprint*] [*A publication*] (DLA)
Eng Cybern ... Engineering Cybernetics [*A publication*]
Eng Cyc..... English Cyclopaedia [*A publication*]
Eng D......... Doctor of Engineering
ENGD........ Engrossed (ROG)
Eng Dance ... English Dance and Song [*A publication*]
Eng Design ... Engineering Materials and Design [*A publication*]
Eng Dig...... Engineers' Digest [*A publication*]
Eng Dig (London) ... Engineers' Digest (London) [*A publication*]
Eng Dig (NY) ... Engineering Digest (New York) [*A publication*]
Eng Dig (Toronto) ... Engineering Digest (Toronto) [*A publication*]
Eng Dom M ... Englishwoman's Domestic Magazine [*A publication*]
Eng Eccl.... English Ecclesiastical Reports [*A publication*] (DLA)
Eng Ecc R .. English Ecclesiastical Reports [*A publication*] (DLA)
Eng Econ.... Engineering Economist [*A publication*]
Eng Economist ... Engineering Economist [*A publication*]
Eng Educ.... Engineering Education [*A publication*]
Eng Educ.... English Education [*A publication*]
Eng Educ (Lancaster PA) ... Engineering Education (Lancaster, Pennsylvania) [*A publication*]
Engei Gakkai Zasshi J Jap Soc Hortic Sci ... Engei Gakkai Zasshi/Journal of the Japanese Society for Horticultural Science [*A publication*]
Engelhard Ind Tech Bull ... Engelhard Industries. Technical Bulletin [*A publication*]
Engenh Min Met ... Engenharia, Mineracao, Metalurgia [*A publication*]
Engenh Quim ... Engenharia e Quimica [*A publication*]
Eng Exch ... English Exchequer Reports [*A publication*] (DLA)
Eng Exp Stat News ... Engineering Experiment Station News [*A publication*]
Eng FD & S Soc Jl ... English Folk Dance and Song Society. Journal [*A publication*]
Eng Found ... Engineering Foundation [*A publication*]
Eng Found Conf ... Engineering Foundation Conference [*A publication*]
Eng Foundryman ... Engineer and Foundryman [*A publication*]
Eng Fract Mech ... Engineering Fracture Mechanics [*A publication*]
Eng'g......... Engineering [*A publication*] (DLA)
ENGGD..... Ekspress-Informatsiya. Neftegazovaya Geologiya i Geofizika [*A publication*]
Eng Geol .... Engineering Geology [*A publication*]
Eng Geol (Amsterdam) ... Engineering Geology (Amsterdam) [*A publication*]
Eng Geol Case Hist ... Engineering Geology Case Histories [*A publication*]
Eng Geol (Sacramento) ... Engineering Geology (Sacramento) [*A publication*]
Eng Geol Soils Eng Symp Proc ... Engineering Geology and Soils Engineering Symposium. Proceedings [*A publication*]
Eng Graphics ... Engineering Graphics [*A publication*]
ENGH .... Engraph, Inc. [*NASDAQ symbol*] (NQ)
Eng His R .. English Historical Review [*A publication*]
Eng Hist Bul ... English History Bulletin for Teachers in Secondary Schools [*A publication*] (APTA)
Eng Hist R ... English Historical Review [*A publication*]
Eng Hist Rev ... English Historical Review [*A publication*]
EngI .... Engineering Index [*A publication*]
ENGIA ...... [*The*] Engineer [*A publication*]
ENGID........ Engine Identification Report [*Air Force*]
Eng Illust ... English Illustrated Magazine [*A publication*]
ENGIN ...... Engineering
Eng Ind ...... Engineering Index [*A publication*]
Eng Index... Engineering Index [*A publication*]
Eng Index Annu ... Engineering Index Annual [*A publication*]
Eng Index Bioeng Abstr ... Engineering Index. Bioengineering Abstracts [*A publication*]
Eng Index Energy Abstr ... Engineering Index. Energy Abstracts [*A publication*]
Eng Index Mon ... Engineering Index Monthly [*A publication*]
Eng Index Mon Author Index ... Engineering Index Monthly and Author Index [*A publication*]
Eng Index Monthly Author Index ... Engineering Index Monthly and Author Index [*A publication*]
Eng Ind India ... Engineering Index of India [*A publication*]
Eng Ind (Iraq) ... Engineering Industries (Iraq) [*A publication*]
ENGINE ... Australian Engineering Database [*Information service or system*] (IID)
Engineers' Bull ... Engineers' Bulletin [*A publication*]
Engineers Gaz ... Engineers' Gazette [*A publication*] (APTA)
ENGING ... Engineering
Engin M..... Engineering Magazine [*A publication*]
Engin Medic ... Engineering in Medicine [*A publication*]
Engin N..... Engineering News-Record [*A publication*]
Eng Insp..... Engineering Inspection [*A publication*]
Eng Inst Can ... Engineering Institute of Canada [*A publication*]
Eng Inst Canada Trans ... Engineering Institute of Canada. Transactions [*A publication*]
Eng & Instrumentation ... Engineering and Instrumentation [*A publication*]
ENG INT... Engage Intercept (CAAL)
Eng & Ir App ... Law Reports, English and Irish Appeal Cases [*A publication*] (DLA)
Eng Ir App ... Law Reports, English and Irish Appeal Cases [*A publication*] (DLA)
Eng Issues ... Engineering Issues [*A publication*]
Eng J.......... Engineering Journal [*A publication*]

Eng J .... English Journal [*A publication*]
Eng J Am Inst Steel Constr ... Engineering Journal. American Institute of Steel Construction [*A publication*]
Eng J (Montreal) ... Engineering Journal (Montreal) [*A publication*]
Eng J (NY) ... Engineering Journal (New York) [*A publication*]
Eng J Singapore ... Engineering Journal of Singapore [*A publication*]
Eng Judg .... Scotch Court of Session Cases Decided by the English Judges [*1655-61*] [*A publication*]   (DLA)
ENGL .... England
ENGL .... English   (ROG)
Engl Abstr Sel Art Sov Bloc Mainland China Tech J Ser 1 ... English Abstracts of Selected Articles from Soviet Bloc and Mainland China Technical Journals. Series 1. Physics and Mathematics [*A publication*]
Engl Abstr Sel Art Sov Bloc Mainland China Tech J Ser 2 ... English Abstracts of Selected Articles from Soviet Bloc and Mainland China Technical Journals. Series 2. Chemistry [*A publication*]
Engl Abstr Sel Art Sov Bloc Mainland China Tech J Ser 3 ... English Abstracts of Selected Articles from Soviet Bloc and Mainland China Technical Journals. Series 3. Metals [*A publication*]
Engl Abstr Sel Art Sov Bloc Mainland China Tech J Ser 5 ... English Abstracts of Selected Articles from Soviet Bloc and Mainland China Technical Journals. Series 5. Electronics and Electrical Engineering [*A publication*]
Engl Abstr Sel Art Sov Bloc Mainland China Tech J Ser 6 ... English Abstracts of Selected Articles from Soviet Bloc and Mainland China Technical Journals. Series 6. Bio-Sciences [*A publication*]
Engl Afr ..... English in Africa [*A publication*]
Engl Alive .. English Alive [*A publication*]
Eng Lang Notes ... English Language Notes [*A publication*]
Eng Lang Teach J ... English Language Teaching Journal [*A publication*]
Engl Aust ... English in Australia [*A publication*]   (APTA)
Eng Law & Eq ... English Law and Equity Reports [*American Reprint*] [*A publication*]   (DLA)
Engl Educ ... English in Education [*A publication*]
Engl Elec J ... English Electric Journal [*A publication*]
Engl El J ... English Electric Journal [*A publication*]
Eng L & Eq ... English Law and Equity Reports [*American Reprint*] [*A publication*]   (DLA)
Eng L & Eq R ... English Law and Equity Reports [*American Reprint*] [*A publication*]   (DLA)
Engl Heritage Monit ... English Heritage Monitor [*A publication*]
Engl Hist R ... English Historical Review [*A publication*]
Engl Hist Rev ... English Historical Review [*A publication*]
Engl Hist Rev ... English History Review [*A publication*]
Engl Inst Ann ... English Institute. Annual [*A publication*]
Engl Inst N ... English Institute. New Series [*A publication*]
English .... English's Reports [*6-13 Arkansas*] [*A publication*]   (DLA)
English Church M ... English Church Music [*A publication*]
English in Ed ... English in Education [*A publication*]
English His ... English Historical Review [*A publication*]
English History Bul ... English History Bulletin for Teachers in Secondary Schools [*A publication*]   (APTA)
English Hist Rev ... English Historical Review [*A publication*]
English Language Teaching J ... English Language Teaching Journal [*A publication*]
English MJ ... English Music Journal [*A publication*]
English R ... English Review [*A publication*]
Eng Lit in Trans ... English Literature in Transition, 1880-1920 [*A publication*]
Eng LJ .... Energy Law Journal [*A publication*]
Engl J .... English Journal [*A publication*]
Engl J (Col Ed) ... English Journal (College Edition) [*A publication*]
Engl J (HS Ed) ... English Journal (High School Edition) [*A publication*]
Engl Lang Lit ... English Language and Literature [*A publication*]
Engl Lang N ... English Language Notes [*A publication*]
Engl Lang Not ... English Language Notes [*A publication*]
Engl Lang Notes ... English Language Notes [*A publication*]
Engl Lang Teach ... English Language Teaching [*Later, English Language Teaching Journal*] [*A publication*]
Engl Lit Lang ... English Literature and Language [*A publication*]
Engl Lit Re ... English Literary Renaissance [*A publication*]
Engl Lit Renaissance ... English Literary Renaissance [*A publication*]
Engl Lit Tr ... English Literature in Transition, 1880-1920 [*A publication*]
Engl Lit Transition ... English Literature in Transition, 1880-1920 [*A publication*]
Engl Misc .. English Miscellany. A Symposium of History [*A publication*]
Engl NZ ..... English in New Zealand [*A publication*]
Engl Place-Name Soc ... English Place-Name Society. Annual Volume [*A publication*]
Engl Q .... English Quarterly [*A publication*]
Engl Rec ..... English Record [*A publication*]
Engl Rev ..... English Review [*A publication*]
Engl St .... English Studies. A Journal of English Letters and Philology [*A publication*]
Engl St Afr ... English Studies in Africa [*A publication*]
Engl St Can ... English Studies in Canada [*A publication*]
Engl Stud ... Englische Studien [*A publication*]
Engl Stud ... English Studies [*A publication*]
Engl Stud Afr ... English Studies in Africa [*A publication*]
ENG-LT .... Engineer Lieutenant [*Navy*] [*British*]   (ROG)

Eng L T ...... English Language Teaching [*Later, English Language Teaching Journal*] [*A publication*]
Engl Teach Assoc NSW Newsl ... English Teachers Association of New South Wales. Newsletter [*A publication*]
Engl Teach For ... English Teaching Forum [*A publication*]
Engl Usage Sthn Afr ... English Usage in Southern Africa [*A publication*]
Eng M .... Engineering Magazine [*A publication*]
ENGM .... Oslo/Gardermoen [*Norway*] [*ICAO location identifier*]   (ICLI)
Eng Mag .... Engineering Magazine [*A publication*]
Eng Man .... Engineering Management and Equipment Digest [*A publication*]
Eng Mat ..... Engineering Materials [*A publication*]
Eng Mat Des ... Engineering Materials and Design [*A publication*]
Eng Mater ... Engineering Materials [*Japan*] [*A publication*]
Eng Mater & Des ... Engineering Materials and Design [*A publication*]
Eng Mater Des ... Engineering Materials and Design [*A publication*]
Eng Mater Process Methods ... Engineering Materials and Processing Methods [*A publication*]
Eng Med .... Engineering in Medicine [*A publication*]
Eng Mineracao Met ... Engenharia, Mineracao, Metalurgia [*A publication*]
Eng Mining J ... Engineering and Mining Journal [*A publication*]
Eng Min J ... Engineering and Mining Journal [*A publication*]
Eng & Min J ... Engineering and Mining Journal [*A publication*]
Eng Min J Press ... Engineering and Mining Journal Press [*A publication*]
Eng Min Metal ... Engenharia, Mineracao, Metalurgia [*A publication*]
Eng Min World ... Engineering and Mining World [*A publication*]
ENGN .... Engineering
Eng N .... Engineering News-Record [*A publication*]
ENGN .... Grimsmoen [*Norway*] [*ICAO location identifier*]   (ICLI)
ENGNA .... Engineering [*A publication*]
ENGND5 ..... Entomologia Generalis [*A publication*]
Eng New-Rc ... Engineering News-Record [*A publication*]
Eng News .... Engineering News [*A publication*]
Eng News (NY) ... Engineering News (New York) [*A publication*]
Eng News-Rec ... Engineering News-Record [*A publication*]
Eng News (Tokyo) ... Engineering News (Tokyo) [*A publication*]
ENGNG ..... Engineering
Engng .... Engineering [*A publication*]
Engng Des ... Engineering Designer [*A publication*]
Engng Des Int ... Engineering Design International [*A publication*]
Engng Educ ... Engineering Education [*A publication*]
Engng Geol ... Engineering Geology [*A publication*]
Engng J .... Engineering Journal [*A publication*]
Engng J (Can) ... Engineering Journal (Canada) [*A publication*]
Engng Mat Des ... Engineering Materials and Design [*A publication*]
Engng Mater Des ... Engineering Materials and Design [*A publication*]
Engng Med ... Engineering in Medicine [*A publication*]
Engng Min J ... Engineering and Mining Journal [*A publication*]
Engng Outlook ... Engineering Outlook [*A publication*]
Engng Prod ... Engineering Production [*A publication*]
Engng Struct ... Engineering Structures [*A publication*]
Engng Thermophys China ... Engineering Thermophysics in China [*A publication*]
Engng Today ... Engineering Today [*A publication*]
ENG-NMCS ... Engine Not Mission Capable - Supply   (AFIT)
ENGNR ..... Engineer
Eng Optim ... Engineering Optimization [*A publication*]
Eng Optimization ... Engineering Optimization [*A publication*]
ENGORC .. Engineer Officers Reserve Corps
Eng Outlook Univ Ill ... Engineering Outlook. University of Illinois [*A publication*]
Eng Pews ... English on Church Pews [*A publication*]   (DLA)
Eng Pl .... English Pleader [*A publication*]   (DLA)
Eng Pr Cas ... Roscoe's English Prize Cases [*A publication*]   (DLA)
Eng Process Econ ... Engineering and Process Economics [*A publication*]
Eng Prod ..... Engineering Production [*A publication*]
Eng Progr Univ Fla Bull ... Engineering Progress. University of Florida. Bulletin [*A publication*]
Eng Progr Univ Fla Tech Progr Rep ... Engineering Progress. University of Florida. Technical Progress Report [*A publication*]
Eng Quim ... Engenharia e Quimica [*A publication*]
Engr .... [*The*] Engineer [*A publication*]
ENGR .... Engineer
EngR .... English Record [*A publication*]
EngR .... English Review [*A publication*]
ENGR .... Engraved
ENGR .... Engraver   (ROG)
ENGR .... Engravings   (ROG)
ENGRBN .. Engineer Battalion [*Military*]
Eng R & C Cas ... English Railway and Canal Cases [*A publication*]   (DLA)
ENGRCEN ... Engineering Center
Engr D .... Doctor of Engineering
ENGRE ..... Engineer Element
Eng Re .... English Reports, Full Reprint [*A publication*]   (DLA)
Eng Rep ..... English Reports, Full Reprint [*A publication*]   (DLA)
Eng Rep ..... English Reports (N. C. Moak) [*American Reprint*] [*A publication*]   (DLA)
Eng Rep ..... English's Reports [*6-13 Arkansas*] [*A publication*]   (DLA)
Eng Rep Anno ... English Reports, Annotated [*A publication*]   (DLA)
Eng Rep R ... English Reports, Full Reprint [*A publication*]   (DLA)

Eng Rep Re ... English Reports, Full Reprint [*A publication*]   (DLA)
Eng Res Bull ... Engineering Research Bulletin [*A publication*]
Eng Res Bull Rutgers Univ Coll Eng ... Engineering Research Bulletin. Rutgers
        University. College of Engineering [*A publication*]
Eng Rev...... English Review. Salem State College [*A publication*]
ENGRFAC ... Engineering Facility
ENGRG ..... Engineering
Engrg Cybernetics ... Engineering Cybernetics [*A publication*]
ENGRING ... Engineering
Eng RR Ca ... English Railway and Canal Cases [*A publication*]   (DLA)
Engrs Aust ... Engineers Australia [*A publication*]
Engrs Dig... Engineers' Digest [*A publication*]
Engrs' Digest ... Engineers' Digest [*London*] [*A publication*]
Eng Ru Ca ... English Ruling Cases [*A publication*]   (DLA)
Eng Rul Cas ... English Ruling Cases [*A publication*]   (DLA)
ENGRV ..... Engrave
Eng Ry & C Cas ... English Railway and Canal Cases [*A publication*]   (DLA)
EngS .... English Studies [*Amsterdam*] [*A publication*]
ENGS .... Engross   (ROG)
Eng Sc D .... Doctor of Engineering Science
Eng Sc Ecc ... English and Scotch Ecclesiastical Reports [*A
        publication*]   (DLA)
Eng Sci...... Engineering and Science [*A publication*]
Eng and Sci ... Engineering and Science [*A publication*]
Eng-Sci News ... Engineering-Science News [*A publication*]
Eng Soc Libr ESL Bibliogr ... Engineering Societies Library. ESL Bibliography
        [*A publication*]
Eng Soc W Pa ... Engineers' Society of Western Pennsylvania. Proceedings [*A
        publication*]
Eng Soc York Pr ... Engineering Society of York. Proceedings [*A publication*]
ENGSS...... Engineering Schoolship [*Navy*]   (NVT)
Eng St .... English Studies [*A publication*]
ENGSTAT ... Engine Status Report [*Air Force*]
Eng Struct ... Engineering Structures [*A publication*]
Eng Stud .... English Studies [*A publication*]
Eng T .... Engineering Times [*A publication*]
ENGT....... Engrossment   (ROG)
ENGTB...... Energetika (Sofia, Bulgaria) [*A publication*]
Eng Teach ... English Teacher [*A publication*]   (APTA)
Eng Teach Assn NSW News ... English Teachers Association of New South
        Wales. Newsletter [*A publication*]   (APTA)
Eng Teach Assoc NSW Newsl ... English Teachers Association of New South
        Wales. Newsletter [*A publication*]   (APTA)
Eng and Technol ... Engineering and Technology [*A publication*]
Eng Technol (Osaka) ... Engineering and Technology (Osaka) [*Japan*] [*A
        publication*]
Eng Times ... Engineering Times [*A publication*]
Eng Times (Calcutta) ... Engineering Times (Calcutta) [*A publication*]
Eng Today ... Engineering Today [*A publication*]
ENGV........ Engine V-Belt
Eng Week .. Engineering Week [*A publication*]
Eng WR ..... Englishwomen's Review [*A publication*]
ENGY........ Energy   (MSA)
ENGY .... Energy Ventures, Inc. [*NASDAQ symbol*]   (NQ)
Engy (Austl) ... Forecasts of Energy Demand and Supply (Australia). 1982-83
        to 1991-92 [*A publication*]
Engy Bsns.. Energy Business [*A publication*]
Engy Insidr ... Energy Insider [*A publication*]
Engy Supply ... Energy Supply to the Year 2000 [*A publication*]
ENH .... Carrosserie [*A publication*]
ENH .... Earth Near Horizon [*NASA*]   (KSC)
ENH .... Educable Neurologically Handicapped
ENH .... Enshi [*China*] [*Airport symbol*]   (OAG)
Enh............ Hymnal Prayer of Enheduanna   (BJA)
ENHA....... Hamar/Stafsberg [*Norway*] [*ICAO location identifier*]   (ICLI)
Enhanced Oil-Recovery Field Rep ... Enhanced Oil-Recovery Field Reports [*A
        publication*]
ENHB....... Heggebakken [*Norway*] [*ICAO location identifier*]   (ICLI)
ENHBA5... Ehime Daigaku Nogakubu Enshurin Hokoku [*A publication*]
ENHD .... Haugesund/Karmoy [*Norway*] [*ICAO location
        identifier*]   (ICLI)
ENHE .... Encounter in Health Education
ENHEA ..... Environmental Health [*Nagpur*] [*A publication*]
ENHF........ Hammerfest [*Norway*] [*ICAO location identifier*]   (ICLI)
ENHID...... Energy Highlights [*A publication*]
ENHK .... Hasvik [*Norway*] [*ICAO location identifier*]   (ICLI)
ENHN .... Harnmoen [*Norway*] [*ICAO location identifier*]   (ICLI)
ENHO .... Hopen [*Norway*] [*ICAO location identifier*]   (ICLI)
ENHS........ European Natural Hygiene Society   (EAIO)
ENHS........ Hokksund [*Norway*] [*ICAO location identifier*]   (ICLI)
ENHV........ Honningsvag/Valan [*Norway*] [*ICAO location
        identifier*]   (ICLI)
ENI .... Effective Networks, Inc. [*Telecommunications service*]   (TSSD)
ENI .... Elan Industries, Inc. [*Vancouver Stock Exchange symbol*]
ENI .... Enemy Initiated Incident [*Vietnam*]
ENI .... Engineering Index [*A publication*]
ENI .... Equivalent Noise Input   (DEN)
ENIAC....... Electronic Numerical Integrator and Calculator [*Early
        computer, 1946*]

ENIAL....... Entreprise Nationale de Developpement et de Coordination des
        Industries Alimentaires [*Nationalized industry*]
        [*Algeria*]   (EY)
ENIG .... Electronic Nuclear Instrumentation Group   (MCD)
ENIRF....... Enemy Initiated Incident Responded to by Friendly Forces
        [*Vietnam*]
ENIT......... Ente Nazionale Italiano per il Turismo [*Italian*]
ENJA........ Jan Mayen [*Norway*] [*ICAO location identifier*]   (ICLI)
ENJB........ Jarlsberg [*Norway*] [*ICAO location identifier*]   (ICLI)
ENJJPT .... Euro-NATO Joint Jet Pilot Training
En Jnl........ Energy Journal [*A publication*]
ENJOA...... Engineering Journal [*Montreal*] [*A publication*]
ENJOD ..... Energy Journal [*A publication*]
ENJOYT ... Enjoyment   (ROG)
EnJu.......... Encyclopaedia Judaica [*Jerusalem*] [*A publication*]   (BJA)
EnJuYB .... Encyclopaedia Judaica Year Book [*A publication*]
ENK .... Enerteck Energy Technologies Corp. [*Vancouver Stock
        Exchange symbol*]
enk .... England [*MARC country of publication code*] [*Library of
        Congress*]   (LCCP)
ENK .... Enkephalin [*Brain peptide, subclass of ENDORPHIN*]
ENK .... Expected Number of Kills [*Military*]   (MCD)
ENKA .... Kautokeino [*Norway*] [*ICAO location identifier*]   (ICLI)
ENKB .... Kristiansund/Kvernberget [*Norway*] [*ICAO location
        identifier*]   (ICLI)
ENKJ .... Kjeller [*Norway*] [*ICAO location identifier*]   (ICLI)
ENKR .... Kirkenes/Hoybuktmoen [*Norway*] [*ICAO location
        identifier*]   (ICLI)
ENL .... Centralia, IL [*Location identifier*] [*FAA*]   (FAAL)
ENL .... Ejercito Nacional de Liberacion [*National Liberation Army*]
        [*Nicaragua*]   (PD)
ENL .... Enamel   (ROG)
En L .... Engineer Lieutenant [*Navy*] [*British*]   (DMA)
ENL .... Enlarged
ENL .... Enlistment   (AFM)
ENL .... Equivalent Noise Level
ENL .... Erythema Nodosum Leproticum [*Medicine*]
ENL .... Eye Notochord Length [*Fish anatomy*]
ENLB .... Emergency Nurse Legal Bulletin [*A publication*]
En L Cr ...... Engineer Lieutenant-Commander [*Navy*] [*British*]   (DMA)
Enl E .... Enlightenment Essays [*A publication*]
ENLF .... Eelam National Liberation Front [*Sri Lanka*]
ENLG .... Enlarge   (MSA)
ENLGD ..... Enlarged
ENLI .... Lista [*Norway*] [*ICAO location identifier*]   (ICLI)
ENLIBD .... Entomologicke Listy [*A publication*]
ENLK .... Leknes [*Norway*] [*ICAO location identifier*]   (ICLI)
ENLN .... Eastern Nigeria Legal Notice [*A publication*]   (DLA)
ENLR .... Eastern Nigeria Law Reports [*1956-60*] [*A publication*]   (DLA)
ENM .... Economie [*A publication*]
ENM .... Emmonak, AK [*Location identifier*] [*FAA*]   (FAAL)
ENM .... Endogenous Morphine [*or Endomorphin*] [*Also,
        ENDORPHIN*] [*Brain peptide*]
enm............ English, Middle [*MARC language code*] [*Library of
        Congress*]   (LCCP)
EN(M) .... Enrolled Nurse (Mental) [*British*]   (DBQ)
ENMAA .... Enseignement Mathematique [*A publication*]
En Manag .. Energy Management [*A publication*]
ENMCC .... Expanded National Military Command Center   (MCD)
ENMGD.... Energy Management [*A publication*]
EN(MH)..... Enrolled Nurse (Mental Handicap) [*British*]   (DBQ)
ENMH .... Mehamn [*Norway*] [*ICAO location identifier*]   (ICLI)
ENMI .... Olso [*Norway*] [*ICAO location identifier*]   (ICLI)
ENMJA..... Engineering and Mining Journal [*A publication*]
ENMK .... Ener-Mark Corp. [*NASDAQ symbol*]   (NQ)
ENML .... End Mill
ENML .... Molde/Aro [*Norway*] [*ICAO location identifier*]   (ICLI)
ENMLD .... Enameled
ENMOD.... Environmental Modification
ENMR .... Environmental Management Review [*A publication*]
ENMR .... Executive for National Military Representatives [*Supreme
        Headquarters Allied Powers Europe*]   (NATG)
ENMS .... Environments. Journal of Interdisciplinary Studies [*A
        publication*]
ENMS .... European Nuclear Medical Society   (EAIO)
ENMS .... Mosjoen/Kjaerstad [*Norway*] [*ICAO location
        identifier*]   (ICLI)
ENMU .... Eastern New Mexico University
Enn............ Enneades [*of Plotinus*] [*Classical studies*]   (OCD)
ENN .... Ennisteel Corp. [*Toronto Stock Exchange symbol*]
ENN .... Export News (New Zealand) [*A publication*]
ENN .... Nenana, AK [*Location identifier*] [*FAA*]   (FAAL)
ENNA .... Banak [*Norway*] [*ICAO location identifier*]   (ICLI)
ENNCA ..... Energia Nuclear [*A publication*]
ENNE .... Environment News. Alberta Department of the Environment [*A
        publication*]
ENNEDD .. Essays in Neurochemistry and Neuropharmacology [*A
        publication*]
ENNG .... Ethyl-nitronitrosoguanidine [*Organic chemistry*]
ENNI .... EnergyNorth, Incorporated [*NASDAQ symbol*]   (NQ)
ENNK........ Narvik/Framnes [*Norway*] [*ICAO location identifier*]   (ICLI)

ENNLA ..... Energia Nucleare [*A publication*]
ENNLAV .. Energia Nuclear [*A publication*]
ENNM....... Namsos [*Norway*] [*ICAO location identifier*] (ICLI)
ENNO .... Notodden [*Norway*] [*ICAO location identifier*] (ICLI)
ENNOD .... Energy News Notes. CERI [*Colorado Energy Research Institute*] [*A publication*]
ENNSD ..... Energy News [*Pakistan*] [*A publication*]
ENNUA..... Energie Nucleaire [*A publication*]
En Nucl...... Energie Nucleaire [*A publication*]
ENNWD.... Energy News [*United States*] [*A publication*]
ENO .... Econotities [*A publication*]
ENO.......... English National Opera
ENO.......... Enolase [*An enzyme*]
ENO.......... Enough
ENO.......... Extraordinary Nuclear Occurrence (NRCH)
ENO.......... Kenton, DE [*Location identifier*] [*FAA*] (FAAL)
e-no--- ...... Norway [*MARC geographic area code*] [*Library of Congress*] (LCCP)
ENOB .... Bodo Oceanic [*Norway*] [*ICAO location identifier*] (ICLI)
ENOC .... Association of the European National Olympic Committees [*See also ACNOE*] [*Brussels, Belgium*] (EAIO)
ENOCC ..... Emergency Network Operations Control Center (MCD)
ENOL .... Enology
ENOL........ Orland [*Norway*] [*ICAO location identifier*] (ICLI)
ENORAK .. Encyclopedie Ornithologique [*Paris*] [*A publication*]
ENORS ...... Engine Not Operationally Ready - Supply [*Air Force*]
ENOS .... Oslo [*Norway*] [*ICAO location identifier*] (ICLI)
ENOV........ Orsta-Volda/Hovden [*Norway*] [*ICAO location identifier*] (ICLI)
ENOWD.... Europaeisches Netzwerk fuer den Ost-West-Dialog [*European Network for East-West Dialogue - ENEWD*] (EAIO)
ENP .... Electroless Nickel Plating
ENP .... Energy Programs [*Database*] [*Energy, Mines, and Resources, Canada*] [*Information service or system*] (CRD)
ENP .... Enerplus Resources Corp. [*Toronto Stock Exchange symbol*]
ENP .... Exceptional Needs Payment [*Legal term*] (DLA)
ENP .... Extractable Nucleoprotein [*Biochemistry*]
ENP .... Nouvel Economiste (Paris) [*A publication*]
En Pas....... En Passant [*A publication*]
ENPBB...... Environmental Physiology and Biochemistry [*A publication*]
ENPC........ Energy Production Company [*NASDAQ symbol*] (NQ)
ENPED...... Energy Perspectives [*A publication*]
ENPGD..... Energy Progress [*A publication*]
En Profile.. Energy in Profile [*A publication*]
ENQ.......... Enquiry [*Transmission control character*]
Enquete Mens Conjonct ... Enquete Mensuelle de Conjoncture [*A publication*]
Enquetes Mus Vie Wallonne ... Enquetes. Musee de la Vie Wallonne [*A publication*]
Enqu Musee Vie Wall ... Enquetes. Musee de la Vie Wallonne [*A publication*]
ENR .... Effort Net Return [*Motivation model*] [*Business term*]
ENR .... Emissora Nacional de Radiodifusao [*Radio network*] [*Portugal*]
ENR .... En Route (NVT)
ENR .... Energy and Natural Resources (DLA)
ENR .... Enertec Corp. [*Toronto Stock Exchange symbol*]
ENR .... Engineering Narrative Report [*Defense Supply Agency*]
ENR .... Engineering News-Record [*A publication*]
ENR .... Enrollment (ROG)
ENR .... Eosinophilic Nonallergic Rhinitis [*Medicine*]
ENR .... Epoxidized Natural Rubber
ENR .... Equivalent Noise Ratio [*or Resistance*] [*Electronics*] (IEEE)
ENR .... Excess Noise Ratio
E/NR .... Exercised/Not Repositioned [*Sports medicine*]
ENR .... Extrathyroidal Neck Radioactivity [*Radiology*]
ENRA .... Mo I Rana/Rossvoll [*Norway*] [*ICAO location identifier*] (ICLI)
ENRAT...... En Route, Arrival at _____ [*Military*] (NVT)
ENRE .... Energy Report. Community Information Center. Fairbanks North Star Borough [*A publication*]
ENREA...... Engineering News-Record [*A publication*]
ENREB...... Entomological Review [*English Translation*] [*A publication*]
ENREP...... Directory of Environmental Research Projects in the European Communities [*Information service or system*] [*EURONET*]
ENRFOSCOMD ... En Route This Station from Oversea Command
ENRG .... DEKALB Energy Co. [*NASDAQ symbol*] (NQ)
ENRGD..... Energies [*A publication*]
ENRGZ..... Energize (MSA)
ENRL .... Enrollment (AABC)
ENRM .... Rorvik/Ryum [*Norway*] [*ICAO location identifier*] (ICLI)
ENRO .... Roros [*Norway*] [*ICAO location identifier*] (ICLI)
ENRPAE ... En Route to/from Public Affairs Event [*Military*] (NVT)
ENRPD ..... Energy Report (Denver, Colorado) [*A publication*]
ENRS........ Rost [*Norway*] [*ICAO location identifier*] (ICLI)
ENRSD..... Energy Research [*A publication*]
ENRSE8 .... Endocrine Research [*A publication*]
ENRSVC ... En Route and Provide Service to Units Indicated [*Military*] (NVT)
ENRT .... En Route
ENRY .... Rygge [*Norway*] [*ICAO location identifier*] (ICLI)
ENRYD ..... Energy [*A publication*]

ENS .... Electron News Service [*Evans Economics, Inc.*] [*Information service or system*] (CRD)
ENS .... Emergency Notification System [*Nuclear energy*] (NRCH)
ENS .... Employer Nomination Scheme [*Australia*]
ENS .... Energy Nova Scotia [*Database*] [*Nova Scotia Research Foundation Corp.*] [*Information service or system*] (CRD)
ENS .... Enschede [*Netherlands*] [*Airport symbol*] (OAG)
ENS .... Ensemble [*Together*] [*French*]
ENS .... ENSERCH Corp. [*NYSE symbol*] [*Toronto Stock Exchange symbol*]
ENS .... Ensign (AABC)
ENS .... Enteric Nervous System [*Neurobiology*]
ENS .... Ethylnorsuprarenin [*Also, ENE*] [*Pharmacology*]
ENS .... Europaeische Kernenergie-Gesellschaft [*European Nuclear Society - ENS*] (EAIO)
ENS .... European Nervous System
ENS .... Experimental Navigation Ship
ENS .... Extended Nylon Shaft
ENSA........ Entertainments National Service Association [*Facetiously translated as "Every Night Something Awful"*] [*Military*] [*British*]
ENSABO... Anais. Escola Nacional de Saude Publica e de Medicina Tropical [*A publication*]
Ensaios FEE ... Ensaios FEE. Fundacao de Economia e Estatistica [*A publication*]
Ensay Estud ... Ensayos y Estudios [*A publication*]
Ensayos Econs ... Ensayos Economicos [*A publication*]
Ensayos Pol Econ ... Ensayos sobre Politica Economica [*A publication*]
ENSB........ Equivalent Noise Sideband
ENSB........ Svalbard/Longyear [*Norway*] [*ICAO location identifier*] (ICLI)
ENSCA...... European Natural Sausage Casings Association (EA)
ENSCE...... Enemy Situation Correlation Element [*DoD*]
ENSD .... Sandane/Anda [*Norway*] [*ICAO location identifier*] (ICLI)
ENSDF...... Evaluated Nuclear Structure Data File [*National Nuclear Data Center*] [*Information service or system*]
Enseignement Math ... Enseignement Mathematique [*A publication*]
Enseign Math ... Enseignement Mathematique [*A publication*]
Enseign Math 2 ... Enseignement Mathematique. Revue Internationale. 2e Serie [*A publication*]
Enseign Techn ... Enseignement Technique [*A publication*]
Ensenanza Invest Psicol ... Ensenanza e Investigacion en Psicologia [*A publication*]
ENSF........ Statfjord-A [*Norway*] [*ICAO location identifier*] (ICLI)
ENSG .... Ensuing (ROG)
ENSG .... Sogndal/Haukasen [*Norway*] [*ICAO location identifier*] (ICLI)
ENSH .... Svolvaer/Helle [*Norway*] [*ICAO location identifier*] (ICLI)
ENSHBB.... Engei Shikenjo Hokoku. C. Morioka [*A publication*]
Enshurin Shuho/Rep Kyushu Univ Forests ... Enshurin Shuho/Reports. Kyushu University Forests [*A publication*]
ENSI .... Equivalent Noise Sideband Input (MCD)
ENSIC...... Environmental Sanitation Information Center [*Asian Institute of Technology*] [*Information service or system*] (IID)
ENSIGC .... Ecole Nationale Superieure d'Ingenieurs de Genie Chimique [*France*] (ECON)
ENSIT .... Enemy Situation (MCD)
ENSK........ Stokmarknes/Skagen [*Norway*] [*ICAO location identifier*] (ICLI)
En SL......... Engineer Sub-Lieutenant [*Navy*] [*British*] (DMA)
ENSN........ Ensun Corp. [*NASDAQ symbol*] (NQ)
ENSN........ Skien/Geiteryggen [*Norway*] [*ICAO location identifier*] (ICLI)
ENSO .... El Nino and Southern Oscillation [*Coupled oceanic-atmospheric change*]
ENSO .... Envirosource, Inc. [*NASDAQ symbol*] (NQ)
ENSO .... Stord [*Norway*] [*ICAO location identifier*] (ICLI)
ENSOD ..... Energy Sources [*A publication*]
ENSP........ Engineering Specification [*Air Force*]
ENSR........ Sorkjosen [*Norway*] [*ICAO location identifier*] (ICLI)
ENSS........ Svartnes [*Norway*] [*ICAO location identifier*] (ICLI)
ENST........ Enstar Group, Inc. [*NASDAQ symbol*] (NQ)
ENST........ Sandnessjoen/Stokka [*Norway*] [*ICAO location identifier*] (ICLI)
ENSURE... Engineering Surveillance Report (MCD)
ENSURE... Expedited Non-Standard Urgent Requirements for Equipment [*Army*] (AABC)
ENSV........ Stavanger [*Norway*] [*ICAO location identifier*] (ICLI)
ENSYN..... Electromagnetic Environment Synthesizer (NVT)
ENT .... Canadian Pacific Enterprises, Inc. [*NYSE symbol*] [*Toronto Stock Exchange symbol*] [*Vancouver Stock Exchange symbol*] (SPSG)
Ent............. Coke's Book of Entries [*1614*] [*England*] [*A publication*] (DLA)
EN & T..... Ears, Nose, and Throat
ENT .... Ears, Nose, and Throat
ENT .... Electrical Nonmetallic Tubing
ENT .... Emergency Negative Thrust
ENT .... Eniwetok [*Marshall Islands*] [*Airport symbol*] (OAG)
ENT .... Entebbe [*Uganda*] [*Seismograph station code, US Geological Survey*] [*Closed*] (SEIS)
ENT .... Enter (MUGU)
ENT .... Entering [*FBI standardized term*]

Ent............. Enterprise
ENT.......... Entertainment
ENT.......... Entertainment Publishing, Inc. [*AMEX symbol*]   (CTT)
Ent............. Entire [*Philately*]
ENT.......... Entity
Ent............. Entomologist [*A publication*]
Ent............. Entomologiste [*A publication*]
ENT.......... Entomology
ENT.......... Entrance   (ROG)
ENT.......... Entry   (NASA)
ENT.......... Environmental Science and Technology [*A publication*]
ENT.......... Environmental Test   (MCD)
ENT.......... Equivalent Noise Temperature [*Electronics*]
ENT.......... Exhaust Nozzle Temperature   (KSC)
Ent............. Rastell's Entries [*A publication*]   (DLA)
enta .... Ethylenediaminetetraacetate [*Also, EDETATE, EDTA*] [*Organic chemistry*]
ENTAC...... Engin Teleguide Anti-Char [*Antitank Missile*] [*French*]
ENTAC...... Entrance National Agency Check [*Military*]   (AABC)
ENTAD ..... Energy News [*United States*] [*A publication*]
Ent Arb Mus GF ... Entomologische Arbeiten. Museum Georg Frey [*A publication*]
ENTBAV... Entomologische Berichten [*Berlin*] [*A publication*]
Ent Ber...... Entomologische Berichten [*A publication*]
Ent Ber (Amst) ... Entomologische Berichten (Amsterdam) [*A publication*]
Ent Ber (Berlin) ... Entomologische Berichten (Berlin) [*A publication*]
ENTC .... Engine Negative Torque Control   (MSA)
ENTC .... Entronics Corp. [*NASDAQ symbol*]   (NQ)
ENTC .... Tromso/Langnes [*Norway*] [*ICAO location identifier*]   (ICLI)
ENTCE...... Entrance   (ROG)
Ent Circ Dep Agric (Br Columb) ... Entomological Circular. Department of Agriculture (British Columbia) [*A publication*]
Ent Circ Div Pl Ind Fla Dep Agric Consumer Serv ... Entomology Circular. Division of Plant Industry. Florida Department of Agriculture and Consumer Services [*A publication*]
ENTD .... Entered
ENTEA...... Energie und Technik [*A publication*]
En Techn.... Energietechnik [*A publication*]
ENTELEC ... Energy Telecommunications and Electrical Association   (EA)
ENTER...... Enterprise   (DLA)
Enterp Western Aust ... Enterprise Western Australia [*A publication*]   (APTA)
Entertain Law Report ... Entertainment Law Reporter [*A publication*]
Entertainment LJ ... Entertainment Law Journal [*A publication*]   (DLA)
Ent Exp App ... Entomologia Experimentalis et Applicata [*A publication*]
Ent Exper Appl ... Entomologia Experimentalis et Applicata [*A publication*]
Ent Fact Sheet Univ Minn ... Entomology Fact Sheet. University of Minnesota [*A publication*]
ENTG .... Entering   (ROG)
ENTG .... Entourage International, Inc. [*Houston, TX*] [*NASDAQ symbol*]   (NQ)
ENTG .... Euro-NATO Training Group [*An association*]   (EAIO)
Ent Gaz...... Entomologist's Gazette [*A publication*]
Ent Germ ... Entomologica Germanica [*A publication*]
ENTI.......... Intercontinental Enterprises, Inc. [*NASDAQ symbol*]   (NQ)
ENT J .... Ear, Nose, and Throat Journal [*A publication*]
Ent Jber ..... Entomologischer Jahresbericht [*A publication*]
ENTJDO.... Ear, Nose, and Throat Journal [*A publication*]
ENTK .... Enertech, Inc. [*NASDAQ symbol*]   (NQ)
ENTL........ Entitle   (AABC)
Ent Leafl Univ MD ... Entomology Leaflet. University of Maryland [*A publication*]
Ent Listy .... Entomologicke Listy [*A publication*]
Ent Medd... Entomologiske Meddelelser [*A publication*]
Ent Meddr ... Entomologiske Meddelelser [*A publication*]
Ent Meded Ned Indiee ... Entomologische Mededeelingen van Nederlandsch-Indiee [*A publication*]
ENTMEY ... Entomography [*A publication*]
Ent Mitt ..... Entomologische Mitteilungen [*A publication*]
Ent Mitt Zool Mus (Hamburg) ... Entomologische Mitteilungen. Zoologischen Museum (Hamburg) [*A publication*]
Ent Mitt Zool St Inst ... Entomologische Mitteilungen. Zoologischen Staatsinstitut und Zoologischen Museum [*A publication*]
Ent Mon Mag ... Entomologist's Monthly Magazine [*A publication*]
ENTNAC .. Entrance National Agency Check [*Military*]   (NVT)
Ent Nachr .. Entomologische Nachrichten [*A publication*]
ENTND2... ISSCT [*International Society of Sugarcane Technologists*] Entomology Newsletter [*A publication*]
Ent News... Entomological News [*A publication*]
ENTO .... Entomology   (AABC)
ENTO .... Torp [*Norway*] [*ICAO location identifier*]   (ICLI)
Ent Obozr .. Entomologicheskoe Obozrenie [*A publication*]
ENTOM ... Entomology
Entom Month Mag ... Entomologist's Monthly Magazine [*A publication*]
Entom N..... Entomological News [*A publication*]
Entom News ... Entomological News [*A publication*]
ENTOMOL ... Entomologic
Entomol...... Entomologist [*A publication*]
Entomol Abh (Dres) ... Entomologische Abhandlungen (Dresden) [*A publication*]
Entomol Abstr ... Entomology Abstracts [*A publication*]
Entomol Am ... Entomologica Americana [*A publication*]

Entomol Arb Mus G Frey (Tutzing-bei Muench) ... Entomologische Arbeiten. Museum Georg Frey (Tutzing-bei Muenchen) [*A publication*]
Entomol Arb Mus G Frey (Tutzing Muenchen) ... Entomologische Arbeiten. Museum Georg Frey (Tutzing-bei Muenchen) [*A publication*]
Entomol Ber (Amst) ... Entomologische Berichten (Amsterdam) [*A publication*]
Entomol Ber (Berl) ... Entomologische Berichten (Berlin) [*A publication*]
Entomol Bl ... Entomologische Blaetter [*A publication*]
Entomol Bl Biol Syst Kaefer ... Entomologische Blaetter fuer Biologie und Systematik der Kaefer [*A publication*]
Entomol Bull Brit Mus (Natur Hist) ... Entomology Bulletin. British Museum (Natural History) [*A publication*]
Entomol Exp Appl ... Entomologia Experimentalis et Applicata [*A publication*]
Entomol Gaz ... Entomologist's Gazette [*A publication*]
Entomol Gen ... Entomologia Generalis [*A publication*]
Entomol Ger ... Entomologica Germanica [*A publication*]
Entomol Listy ... Entomologicke Listy [*A publication*]
Entomol Medd ... Entomologiske Meddelelser [*A publication*]
Entomol Mimeo Ser Utah State Univ Agr Ext Serv ... Entomology Mimeo Series. Utah State University. Agricultural Extension Service [*A publication*]
Entomol Mitt Zool Mus (Hamb) ... Entomologische Mitteilungen. Zoologischen Museum (Hamburg) [*A publication*]
Entomol Mitt Zool Staatsinst Zool Mus (Hamb) ... Entomologische Mitteilungen. Zoologischen Staatsinstitut und Zoologischen Museum (Hamburg) [*A publication*]
Entomol Mon Mag ... Entomologist's Monthly Magazine [*A publication*]
Entomol Nachr ... Entomologische Nachrichten [*A publication*]
Entomol Nachr Ber ... Entomologische Nachrichten und Berichte [*A publication*]
Entomol News ... Entomological News [*A publication*]
Entomol Newsl ... Entomologists' Newsletter [*A publication*]
Entomol Obozr ... Entomologicheskoe Obozrenie [*A publication*]
Entomologia Exp Appl ... Entomologia Experimentalis et Applicata [*A publication*]
Entomologia Gen ... Entomologia Generalis [*A publication*]
Entomologie Phytopath Appl ... Entomologie et Phytopathologie Appliquees [*A publication*]
Entomologist's Gaz ... Entomologist's Gazette [*A publication*]
Entomologist's Mon Mag ... Entomologist's Monthly Magazine [*A publication*]
Entomologists Newsl ... Entomologists' Newsletter [*A publication*]
Entomologist's Rep Dep Agric Tanganyika ... Entomologist's Report. Department of Agriculture. Tanganyika [*A publication*]
Entomol Phytopathol Appl ... Entomologie et Phytopathologie Appliquees [*A publication*]
Entomol Probl ... Entomologicke Problemy [*A publication*]
Entomol Rec J Var ... Entomologist's Record and Journal of Variation [*A publication*]
Entomol Rev ... Entomological Review [*A publication*]
Entomol Rev (Engl Transl Entomol Obozr) ... Entomological Review (English Translation of Entomologicheskoye Obozreniye) [*A publication*]
Entomol Scand ... Entomologica Scandinavica [*A publication*]
Entomol Scand Suppl ... Entomologica Scandinavica. Supplementum [*A publication*]
Entomol Sin ... Entomologia Sinica [*A publication*]
Entomol Soc Amer N Cent State Br Proc ... Entomological Society of America. North Central State Branch. Proceedings [*A publication*]
Entomol Soc Nigeria Occas Publ ... Entomological Society of Nigeria. Occasional Publication [*A publication*]
Entomol Soc NZ Bull ... Entomological Society of New Zealand. Bulletin [*A publication*]
Entomol Soc Ont Annu Rep ... Entomological Society of Ontario. Annual Report [*A publication*]
Entomol Tidskr ... Entomologisk Tidskrift [*A publication*]
Entomol Z ... Entomologische Zeitschrift [*A publication*]
Entomol Zs ... Entomologische Zeitschrift [*A publication*]
Entomoph .. Entomophaga [*A publication*]
Entomophaga Mem Hors Ser ... Entomophaga. Memoire Hors Serie [*A publication*]
Entom Soc Am Ann ... Entomological Society of America. Annals [*A publication*]
ENTPA...... Entropie [*A publication*]
Ent Problemy ... Entomologicke Problemy [*A publication*]
ENTPROL ... (Ethylenedinitrilo)tetrakis(propanol) [*Organic chemistry*]
ENTPS ...... Expanded Near-Term Prepositioning Ships
ENTR .... Enterprise Technology [*NASDAQ symbol*]   (NQ)
ENTR .... Entire
ENTR .... Entrance [*Maps and charts*]   (MSA)
ENTR .... Trondheim [*Norway*] [*ICAO location identifier*]   (ICLI)
ENTRACE .. Entrance   (ROG)
En Trends .. Energy Trends [*A publication*]
Entrep .... Entrepreneur [*A publication*]
Entrepteneur ... Entrepreneur Magazine [*A publication*]
Entret Bichat Med Biol ... Entretiens de Bichat Medecine et Biologie [*A publication*]

Entretiens Bichat Chir Spec ... Entretiens de Bichat Chirurgie Specialites [*A publication*]

Entretiens Bichat Med Biol ... Entretiens de Bichat Medecine et Biologie [*A publication*]

Entretiens Bichat Stomatol ... Entretiens de Bichat Stomatologie [*France*] [*A publication*]

Entretiens Bichat Ther ... Entretiens de Bichat Therapeutique [*A publication*]

Entretiens Chize Ser Ecol Ethol ... Entretiens de Chize. Serie Ecologie et Ethologie [*A publication*]

Entretiens Chize Ser Physiol ... Entretiens de Chize. Serie Physiologie [*A publication*]

Entries Antient ... Rastell's Old Entries [*So cited in Rolle Abridgment*] [*A publication*] (DLA)

Entr Psych ... Entretiens Psychiatriques [*A publication*]

ENT/SAT ... Entertainment Satellite [*Proposed*] (MCD)

Ent Scand... Entomologica Scandinavica [*A publication*]

Entsch.......... Entscheidung [*Decision, Judgment*] [*German*] (ILCA)

ENTSD...... Energy Times [*India*] [*A publication*]

Entsikl Izmer Kontrolya Avtom ... Entsiklopediya Izmerenii. Kontrolya i Avtomatizatsii [*A publication*]

Ent & Sports Law ... Entertainment and Sports Lawyer [*A publication*] (DLA)

ENTSPR ... Entsprechend [*Corresponding*] [*German*]

Ent Tidskr ... Entomologisk Tidskrift [*A publication*]

ENTURSA ... Empresa Nacional de Turismo [*Spain*] (EY)

ENTW .... [*The*] Entwistle Co. [*NASDAQ symbol*] (NQ)

Entw.......... Entwurf [*Draft*] [*German*] (ILCA)

Entw Ber Siemens ... Entwicklungsberichte der Siemens [*A publication*]

Entwicklungsber Siemens und Halske ... Entwicklungsberichte der Siemens und Halske Aktiengesellschaft [*A publication*]

Entwicklungsgesch Syst Pflanz ... Entwicklungsgeschichte und Systematik der Pflanzen [*A publication*]

Ent Z.......... Entomologische Zeitschrift [*A publication*]

Ent Z (Frankf A M) ... Entomologische Zeitschrift (Frankfurt Am Main) [*A publication*]

ENU.......... Enugu [*Nigeria*] [*Airport symbol*] (OAG)

ENU.......... Essential/Nonessential/Update [*Telecommunications*] (TEL)

ENU.......... Ethylnitrosourea [*Organic chemistry*]

ENUC........ Electro-Nucleonics, Inc. [*NASDAQ symbol*] (NQ)

ENUM....... Enumeration (MSA)

ENUN....... Enunciation (ROG)

ENUP........ Environment Update. Environment Canada [*A publication*]

ENUSA ..... Experimental Neurology. Supplement [*A publication*]

En Users Rep ... Energy Users Report [*Commerce Clearing House*] [*A publication*] (DLA)

ENV.......... Envelope (KSC)

ENV.......... Environ [*About*] [*French*]

Env............ Environment [*A publication*]

Env............ Environment/Ecology [*A publication*]

Env............ Environment Information Access [*A publication*]

ENV.......... Environmental Safety Systems, Inc. [*Toronto Stock Exchange symbol*]

ENV.......... Enviropact, Inc. [*AMEX symbol*] (SPSG)

ENV.......... Envoy (ROG)

ENV.......... Equivalent Noise Voltage

ENV.......... Erdbeernekrosevirus

ENV.......... Wendover, UT [*Location identifier*] [*FAA*] (FAAL)

ENVA....... Environmental Affairs [*A publication*]

ENVA .... Trondheim/Vaernes [*Norway*] [*ICAO location identifier*] (ICLI)

Env Action ... Environment Action Bulletin [*A publication*]

Env Aff....... Environmental Affairs [*A publication*]

ENVANAL ... Environmental Analysis [*Program*]

Env Biol F .. Environmental Biology of Fishes [*A publication*]

ENVD........ Vadso [*Norway*] [*ICAO location identifier*] (ICLI)

Env Data Serv ... Environmental Data Service [*A publication*]

Env Entomol ... Environmental Entomology [*A publication*]

ENVEX....... Environmental Extremists

Env Exp Bot ... Environmental and Experimental Botany [*A publication*]

Env Extr..... Envoy Extraordinary (DLA)

ENVG......... Efferent Vein from Nephridial Gland [*Anatomy*]

ENVG......... Environment and Planning. A [*A publication*]

ENVHA..... Environmental Health [*London*] [*A publication*]

Env Health Persp ... Environmental Health Perspectives [*A publication*]

EnvI.......... Environment Index [*A publication*]

ENVI......... Envirosafe Services, Inc. [*NASDAQ symbol*] (NQ)

Envir.......... Environment [*A publication*]

ENVIR....... Environmental (MSA)

Envir Action ... Environmental Action [*A publication*]

Envir Behav ... Environment and Behavior [*A publication*]

Envir Conserv ... Environmental Conservation [*A publication*]

Envir Ent... Environmental Entomology [*A publication*]

Envir & Exper Bot ... Environmental and Experimental Botany [*A publication*]

Envir Geol ... Environmental Geology [*A publication*]

Envir Hlth Persp ... Environmental Health Perspectives [*A publication*]

Envir Lett... Environmental Letters [*A publication*]

Envir L Rep ... Environmental Law Reporter [*A publication*]

ENVIRN... Environment

Envir News ... Environment News [*A publication*]

Envirn Sci .. Environmental Science and Technology [*A publication*]

ENVIROBIB ... Environmental Periodicals Bibliography [*Environmental Studies Institute*] [*Information service or system*]

ENVIROFATE ... Environmental Fate [*Environmental Protection Agency*] [*Information service or system*] (CRD)

ENVIROLINE ... Environment Information On-Line [*Database*] [*Environment Information Center, Inc.*] [*New York, NY*]

ENVIRON ... Environmental

ENVIRON ... Environmental Information Retrieval On-Line [*Environmental Protection Agency*]

Environ ...... Environnement [*A publication*]

Environ Abstr ... Environmental Abstracts [*A publication*]

Environ Action ... Environmental Action [*A publication*]

Environ Aff ... Environmental Affairs [*A publication*]

Environ Awareness ... Environmental Awareness [*A publication*]

Environ Behav ... Environment and Behavior [*A publication*]

Environ & Behavior ... Environment and Behavior [*A publication*]

Environ Biol ... Environmental Biology [*A publication*]

Environ Biol Fishes ... Environmental Biology of Fishes [*A publication*]

Environ Biol Med ... Environmental Biology and Medicine [*A publication*]

Environ Can Annu Rep ... Environment Canada. Annual Report [*A publication*]

Environ Can For Pest Manage Inst Rep FPM-X ... Environment Canada. Forest Pest Management Institute. Report FPM-X [*A publication*]

Environ Can Rapp Annu ... Environnement Canada. Rapport Annuel [*A publication*]

Environ Change ... Environment and Change [*A publication*]

Environ Chem ... Environmental Chemistry [*A publication*]

Environ Chem Hum Anim Health ... Environmental Chemicals. Human and Animal Health. Proceedings of Annual Conference [*A publication*]

Environ Comment ... Environmental Comment [*A publication*]

Environ Conser ... Environmental Conservation [*A publication*]

Environ Conserv ... Environmental Conservation [*A publication*]

Environ Conserv Eng ... Environmental Conservation Engineering [*Japan*] [*A publication*]

Environ Contr Manage ... Environmental Control Management [*A publication*]

Environ Control Biol ... Environment Control in Biology [*Japan*] [*A publication*]

Environ Contr Safety Manage ... Environmental Control and Safety Management [*A publication*]

Environ Creation ... Environmental Creation [*Japan*] [*A publication*]

Environ Data Serv ... Environmental Data Service [*A publication*]

Environ Data Serv Rep ... Environmental Data Services Report [*A publication*]

Environ Educ ... Environmental Education [*A publication*]

Environ Eng ... Environmental Engineering [*A publication*]

Environ Engrg ... Environmental Engineering [*A publication*]

Environ Entomol ... Environmental Entomology [*A publication*]

Environ Ethics ... Environmental Ethics [*A publication*]

Environ and Exp Bot ... Environmental and Experimental Botany [*A publication*]

Environ Exp Bot ... Environmental and Experimental Botany [*A publication*]

Environ & Exper Bot ... Environmental and Experimental Botany [*A publication*]

Environ Forum ... Environmental Forum [*A publication*]

Environ Geochem Health ... Environmental Geochemistry and Health [*A publication*]

Environ Geol ... Environmental Geology [*A publication*]

Environ Geol Bul ... Environmental Geology Bulletin [*A publication*]

Environ Geol Colorado Geol Surv ... Environmental Geology. Colorado Geological Survey [*A publication*]

Environ Geol Notes Ill State Geol Surv ... Environmental Geology Notes. Illinois State Geological Survey [*A publication*]

Environ Geol Water Sci ... Environmental Geology and Water Sciences [*A publication*]

Environ Geol Wat Sci ... Environmental Geology and Water Science [*A publication*]

Environ Health ... Environmental Health [*London*] [*A publication*]

Environ Health Criter ... Environmental Health Criteria [*A publication*]

Environ Health (Lond) ... Environmental Health (London) [*A publication*]

Environ Health (Nagpur) ... Environmental Health (Nagpur) [*A publication*]

Environ Health Perspect ... Environmental Health Perspectives [*A publication*]

Environ Health Ser Radiol Health ... Environmental Health Series. Radiological Health [*A publication*]

Environ Hlth ... Environmental Health [*A publication*]

Environ Hlth Perspectives ... Environmental Health Perspectives [*A publication*]

Environ Impact Assess Rev ... Environmental Impact Assessment Review [*A publication*]

Environ Impact News ... Environmental Impact News [*A publication*]

Environ Index ... Environment Index [*A publication*]

Environ India ... Environment India [*A publication*]

Environ Int ... Environment International [*A publication*]

Environ L... Environmental Law [*A publication*]

Environ Law ... Environmental Law [*A publication*]

Environ Law Rep ... Environmental Law Reporter [*A publication*]

Environ Law Rev ... Environment Law Review [*A publication*]

Environ Lett ... Environmental Letters [*A publication*]

Environ L Rev ... Environment Law Review [*A publication*]
Environ Man ... Environment and Man [*A publication*]
Environ Manage ... Environmental Management [*A publication*]
Environ Meas Lab Environ Rep US Dep of Energy ... Environmental Measurements Laboratory. Environmental Report. United States Department of Energy [*A publication*]
Environ Med ... Environmental Medicine. Annual Report of the Research Institute of Environmental Medicine. Nagoya University [*A publication*]
Environ Med (Nagoya) ... Environmental Medicine (Nagoya) [*A publication*]
Environ Midwest ... Environment Midwest [*A publication*]
Environm L ... Environmental Law [*A publication*]
Environ Monit Assess ... Environmental Monitoring and Assessment [*Netherlands*] [*A publication*]
Environm Policy & L ... Environmental Policy and Law [*A publication*]
Environmt .. Environmental Action [*A publication*]
Environ Mutagen ... Environmental Mutagenesis [*A publication*]
Environ Mutagen Carcinog ... Environmental Mutagens and Carcinogens [*A publication*]
Environ Mutagenesis ... Environmental Mutagenesis [*A publication*]
Environ News ... Environment News [*A publication*]
Environ Newsl ... Environmental Newsletter [*A publication*]
Environ Nutr Newsl ... Environmental Nutrition Newsletter [*A publication*]
Environ Per Bibl ... Environmental Periodicals Bibliography [*A publication*]
Environ Period Bibliogr ... Environmental Periodicals Bibliography [*A publication*]
Environ Physiol ... Environmental Physiology [*A publication*]
Environ Physiol Biochem ... Environmental Physiology and Biochemistry [*A publication*]
Environ Plann A ... Environment and Planning. A [*A publication*]
Environ and Planning ... Environment and Planning [*A publication*]
Environ Policy Law ... Environmental Policy and Law [*A publication*]
Environ Pol Law ... Environmental Policy and Law [*A publication*]
Environ Pollut ... Environment and Pollution [*Republic of Korea*] [*A publication*]
Environ Pollut ... Environmental Pollution [*A publication*]
Environ Pollut ... Environnement et Pollution [*A publication*]
Environ Pollut (Barking) ... Environmental Pollution (Barking) [*A publication*]
Environ Pollut Manage ... Environmental Pollution Management [*A publication*]
Environ Pollut Mgmt ... Environmental Pollution Management [*A publication*]
Environ Pollut Ser A ... Environmental Pollution. Series A. Ecological and Biological [*A publication*]
Environ Pollut Ser B ... Environmental Pollution. Series B. Chemical and Physical [*A publication*]
Environ Pollut Ser B Chem Phys ... Environmental Pollution. Series B. Chemical and Physical [*A publication*]
Environ Prof ... Environmental Professional [*A publication*]
Environ Prog ... Environmental Progress [*A publication*]
Environ Prot Agency (US) Publ AP Ser ... Environmental Protection Agency (US). Publication. AP [*Air Pollution*] Series [*A publication*]
Environ Prot Agency (US) Publ APTD Ser ... Environmental Protection Agency (US). Publication. APTD [*Air Pollution Technical Data*] Series [*A publication*]
Environ Prot Eng ... Environment Protection Engineering [*A publication*]
Environ Prot Surv ... Environmental Protection Survey [*England*] [*A publication*]
Environ Prot Technol Ser ... Environmental Protection Technology Series [*A publication*]
Environ Prot Technol Ser EPA ... Environmental Protection Technology Series. EPA [*Environmental Protection Agency*] [*A publication*]
Environ Psychol Nonverbal Behav ... Environmental Psychology and Nonverbal Behavior [*A publication*]
Environ Q .. Environmental Quarterly [*A publication*]
Environ Qual ... Environmental Quality [*A publication*]
Environ Qual Abstr ... Environmental Quality Abstracts [*A publication*]
Environ Qual Saf ... Environmental Quality and Safety [*A publication*]
Environ Qual Saf Suppl ... Environmental Quality and Safety. Supplement [*A publication*]
Environ Quart ... Environmental Quarterly [*A publication*]
Environ Radiat Bull ... Environmental Radiation Bulletin [*A publication*]
Environ Rep Environ Meas Lab US Dep Energy ... Environmental Report. Environmental Measurements Laboratory. United States Department of Energy [*A publication*]
Environ Res ... Environmental Research [*A publication*]
Environ Res Inst Mich Annu Rep ... Environmental Research Institute of Michigan. Annual Report [*A publication*]
Environ Resour ... Environmental Resource [*A publication*]
Environ Sanit Abstr ... Environmental Sanitation Abstract [*A publication*]
Environ Sanit Eng Res ... Environmental and Sanitary Engineering Research [*A publication*]
Environ Sanit Rev ... Environmental Sanitation Review [*A publication*]
Environ Sci Appl ... Environmental Sciences and Applications [*A publication*]
Environ Sci Res ... Environmental Science Research [*A publication*]
Environ Sci & Tech ... Environmental Science and Technology [*A publication*]
Environ Sci and Technol ... Environmental Science and Technology [*A publication*]

Environ Sci Technol ... Environmental Science and Technology [*A publication*]
Environ Sc Tech ... Environmental Science and Technology [*A publication*]
Environ Southwest ... Environment Southwest [*A publication*]
Environ Space Sci ... Environmental Space Sciences [*A publication*]
Environ Space Sci (Engl Transl Kosm Biol Med) ... Environmental Space Sciences (English Translation of Kosmicheskaya Biologiya i Meditsina) [*A publication*]
Environ Technol Econ ... Environmental Technology and Economics [*A publication*]
Environ Technol Lett ... Environmental Technology Letters [*A publication*]
Environ This Mon ... Environment This Month [*A publication*]
Environ Toxicol Chem ... Environmental Toxicology and Chemistry [*A publication*]
Environm Toxin Ser ... Environmental Toxin Series [*A publication*]
Environ Views ... Environment Views [*A publication*]
Envir Plann ... Environment and Planning [*A publication*]
Envir Poll Control ... Environmental Pollution Control [*A publication*]
Envir Pollu ... Environmental Pollution [*A publication*]
Envir Qual ... Environmental Quality. Annual Report of the Council of Environmental Quality [*A publication*]
Envir Rep ... Environment Reporter [*Bureau of National Affairs*] [*A publication*]   (DLA)
Envir Res ... Environmental Research [*A publication*]
Envir Sci & Tech ... Environmental Science and Technology [*A publication*]
Envir Sci Techn ... Environmental Science and Technology [*A publication*]
Envir Sc Technol ... Environmental Science and Technology [*A publication*]
Env L ... Environmental Law [*A publication*]
Env L Rev .. Environmental Law Review [*A publication*]
Env L Rptr ... Environmental Law Reporter [*A publication*]
ENVMT ..... Environment   (AFM)
ENVMTL ..... Environmental
ENVN .... Tromso [*Norway*] [*ICAO location identifier*]   (ICLI)
ENVPA ..... Environmental Pollution [*A publication*]
ENVPD .... Environmental Progress [*A publication*]
Env Phys Bi ... Environmental Physiology and Biochemistry [*A publication*]
Env Plann .. Environment and Planning [*A publication*]
ENVPREDRSCHF ... Environmental Prediction Research Facility [*Monterey, CA*] [*Navy*]
ENVPREDRSCHFAC ... Naval Environmental Prediction Research Facility [*Marine science*]   (MSC)
Envpsych ... Environmental Psychology [*City University of New York*] [*Defunct*] [*Information service or system*]   (CRD)
ENVQA ..... Environmental Quarterly [*A publication*]
ENVR .... Envirodyne Industries, Inc. [*NASDAQ symbol*]   (NQ)
ENVR .... Environmental   (KSC)
ENVRA ..... Environmental Research [*A publication*]
ENVRB .... Environmental Report [*A publication*]
ENVRNMTL ... Environmental
ENVS .... Environment Views. Alberta Department of the Environment [*A publication*]
ENVS .... Envirosure Management Corp. [*Buffalo, NY*] [*NASDAQ symbol*]   (NQ)
Env Sci Tec ... Environmental Science and Technology [*A publication*]
ENV-SYS .. Environmental System   (MCD)
ENVT .... Environmental
ENVTA ..... Environment [*A publication*]
ENVTAR ..... Environment [*Washington, DC*] [*A publication*]
Envtl Affairs ... Environmental Affairs [*A publication*]   (DLA)
Envtl F .... Environmental Forum [*A publication*]   (DLA)
Envtl L .... Environmental Law [*A publication*]
Envtl LQ Newsl ... Environmental Law Quarterly Newsletter [*A publication*]
Envtl L Rep ... Environmental Law Reporter [*A publication*]
Envtl L Rep Envtl L Inst ... Environmental Law Reporter. Environmental Law Institute [*A publication*]
Envtl L Rev ... Environmental Law Review [*A publication*]   (DLA)
Envtl L Rptr ... Environmental Law Reporter [*A publication*]   (DLA)
Envtl Pol'y & L ... Environmental Policy and Law [*A publication*]   (DLA)
Env't Reg Handbook ... Environment Regulation Handbook [*A publication*]   (DLA)
Envt Reg Handbook Envt Information Center ... Environment Regulation Handbook. Environment Information Center [*A publication*]
Env't Rep (BNA) ... Environment Reporter (Bureau of National Affairs) [*A publication*]   (DLA)
Envt Rep Cas BNA ... Environment Reporter Cases. Bureau of National Affairs [*A publication*]
ENVV .... Bergen [*Norway*] [*ICAO location identifier*]   (ICLI)
ENVY .... Vaeroy [*Norway*] [*ICAO location identifier*]   (ICLI)
ENW .... Economic News [*A publication*]
ENW .... Effects of Nuclear Weapons [*AEC-DoD book*]
ENW .... Elgin National Industries, Inc. [*Formerly, Elgin National Watch Co.*] [*NYSE symbol*]   (SPSG)
ENW .... Kenosha, WI [*Location identifier*] [*FAA*]   (FAAL)
En Watch ... Energy Watch [*A publication*]
ENWSD ..... Energy Newsletter [*A publication*]
ENX .... Enexco International Ltd. [*Vancouver Stock Exchange symbol*]
ENX .... ENSR Corp. [*AMEX symbol*]   (SPSG)
ENY .... Ashland, WI [*Location identifier*] [*FAA*]   (FAAL)
ENY .... Energy [*A publication*]

ENY .... European Original New York Seltzer Ltd. [*Vancouver Stock Exchange symbol*]
ENY .... Yanan [*China*] [*Airport symbol*]   (OAG)
ENZ .... Enscor, Inc. [*Toronto Stock Exchange symbol*]
ENZ .... Enzo Biochem, Inc. [*AMEX symbol*]   (SPSG)
ENZ .... Nogales, AZ [*Location identifier*] [*FAA*]   (FAAL)
ENZN .... Enzon, Inc. [*South Plainfield, NJ*] [*NASDAQ symbol*]   (NQ)
ENZO .... Ethernet Needing Zero Overhead
ENZV .... Stavanger/Sola [*Norway*] [*ICAO location identifier*]   (ICLI)
ENZYA .... Enzymologia [*A publication*]
Enzym Biol Clin ... Enzymologia Biologica et Clinica [*A publication*]
Enzyme Eng ... Enzyme Engineering [*A publication*]
Enzyme Microb Technol ... Enzyme and Microbial Technology [*A publication*]
Enzymes Med ... Enzymes in Medicine [*A publication*]
Enzyme Technol Rotenburg Ferment Symp ... Enzyme Technology. Rotenburg Fermentation Symposium [*A publication*]
Enzymol Biol Clin ... Enzymologia Biologica et Clinica [*A publication*]
Enzymologia ... Enzymologia Acta Biocatalytica [*A publication*]
EO .... Aero America, Inc. [*ICAO designator*]   (ICDA)
eo----- .... Danube River and Basin [*MARC geographic area code*] [*Library of Congress*]   (LCCP)
EO .... Earth Observation
EO .... Earth Orbit [*NASA*]   (KSC)
EO .... Easter Offerings [*to a church*]
EO .... Eastern Orthodox
EO .... Echos d'Orient [*A publication*]
EO .... Education Officer [*Military*]
EO .... Ego Overcontrol [*Psychology*]
EO .... Elbow Orthosis [*Medicine*]
EO .... Electro-Optical
EO .... Elliptical Orbit [*Aerospace*]   (AAG)
EO .... Emergency Officer [*Nuclear energy*]   (NRCH)
EO .... Employers Organization   (DCTA)
EO .... End Office [*Telecommunications*]   (TEL)
EO .... Engine Oil
EO .... Engine Out   (NASA)
EO .... Engineer Officer [*Navy*] [*British*]
E/O .... Engineering/Operations [*NASA*]   (NASA)
E/O .... Engineering Opportunities [*A publication*]
EO .... Engineering Order
EO .... English [*Communion*] Office [*Episcopalian*]
EO .... Entertainments Officer [*Military*] [*British*]
E/O .... Eocene/Oligocene [*Geological boundary zone*]
eo .... Eosinophil [*Hematology*]
Eo .... Eotvos Number [*Fluid mechanics*]
EO .... Equal Opportunity
EO .... Equal Opportunity Program Office [*Kennedy Space Center Directorate*] [*NASA*]   (NASA)
EO .... Equipment Operator [*Navy rating*]
EO .... Errors and Omissions [*Insurance*]
EO .... Est et Ouest [*A publication*]
EO .... Ethylene Oxide [*Organic chemistry*]
EO .... Europaeische Osten [*A publication*]
EO .... Europe and Oil [*A publication*]
EO .... Europe Orientale [*A publication*]
EO .... Ex Officio [*By Virtue of Office*] [*Latin*]
EO .... Examining Officer   (ROG)
EO .... Excise Officer   (ROG)
EO .... Exclusive Or [*Gates*] [*Data processing*]
EO .... Executive Office [*or Officer*]
EO .... Executive Order [*Rule or regulation having the force of law, issued by the President with congressional authorization*]
EO .... Exempt Organization [*IRS*]
EO .... Exhaust Opens [*Valve position*]
EO .... Expected Output
EO .... Experimental Officer [*Also, ExO, XO*] [*Ministry of Agriculture, Fisheries, and Food*] [*British*]
EO .... Explosive Ordnance [*Military*]   (AFM)
EO .... Export Office   (ROG)
EO .... Extended Operations
EO .... Extra Executive Transport [*Federal Republic of Germany*] [*ICAO designator*]   (FAAC)
EO .... Eyes Open [*Ataxia*]
EO1 .... Edge Oya [*Norway*] [*Seismograph station code, US Geological Survey*]   (SEIS)
EO1 .... Equipment Operator, First Class [*Navy rating*]
EO2 .... Equipment Operator, Second Class [*Navy rating*]
EO3 .... Equipment Operator, Third Class [*Navy rating*]
EOA .... Economic Opportunity Act [*1964*] [*Repealed, 1974*]
EOA .... Effective On or About [*Business term*]
EOA .... Empire American Federal Savings [*AMEX symbol*]   (SPSG)
EOA .... End of Address [*Data processing*]
EOA .... Energy Office [*Department of Agriculture*]   (OICC)
EOA .... Environmental Protection Agency, Region VIII Library, Denver, CO [*OCLC symbol*]   (OCLC)
EOA .... Epithelioma [*Medicine*]
EOA .... Equal Opportunity Advisor [*DoD*]
EOA .... Erosive Osteoarthritis [*Medicine*]
EOA .... Essential Oil Association of the United States   (EA)
EOA .... Examination, Opinion, and Advice [*Medicine*]

EOA .... Exercise Operating Area   (NVT)
EOAD .... Educational Organizations and Agencies Directory [*A publication*]
EOAE .... Earth-Orientated Applications Experiment   (MCD)
EOAP .... Earth Observations Aircraft Program [*NASA*]
EOAP .... Equipment Oil Analysis Program [*Air Force*]   (MCD)
EOAR .... European Office of Aerospace Research
EOARD ..... European Office of Aerospace Research and Development
EOATD ..... Earth-Oriented Applications of Space Technology [*Formerly, Advances in Earth-Oriented Applications of Space Technology*] [*A publication*]
EOAU .... Electro-Optical Alignment Unit   (AAG)
EOB .... Educational Opportunity Bank
EOB .... Electronic Order of Battle   (MSA)
EOB .... Emergency Observation Bed [*Medicine*]
EOB .... End of Battle [*Time*]   (MCD)
EOB .... End of Block [*Data processing*]
EOB .... End of Bombardment
EOB .... End of Buffer   (MCD)
EOB .... Enemy Order of Battle   (AFM)
EOB .... Engineering and Operations Building [*NASA*]
EOB .... Environmental Protection Agency, NEIC Library, Denver, CO [*OCLC symbol*]   (OCLC)
EOB .... Estimated on Berth
EOB .... Executive Office Building [*Washington, DC*]
EOB .... Expense Operating Budget   (AFM)
EOB .... Explanation of Benefits
EOBC .... Edmonton Oilers Booster Club [*Defunct*]   (EA)
EOBCC ...... End of Battle Control Center   (MCD)
EOBK .... Eastover Bank for Savings [*Jackson, MS*] [*NASDAQ symbol*]   (NQ)
EOBMA .... Elektronnaya Obrabotka Materialov [*A publication*]
EOBMAF ... Elektronnaya Obrabotka Materialov [*A publication*]
EOBP .... Explanation of Benefit Payment [*Insurance*]
EOBT & T ... [*Armed Forces*] End of Battle Technology and Training Center   (MCD)
EOC .... Eastern Oregon College
EOC .... Edge of Cutter   (MSA)
EOC .... Edsel Owner's Club   (EA)
EOC .... Educational Opportunity Center [*Higher Education Act*]
EOC .... Electronic Operations Center [*Military*]
EOC .... Elva Owners Club [*Worthing, West Sussex, England*]   (EAIO)
EOC .... Emergency Operating Center [*Civil Defense*]
EOC .... Emergency Operational Capability   (AAG)
EOC .... Emergency Operations Center [*Military*]
EOC .... End of Card [*Data processing*]   (CMD)
EOC .... End of Construction   (NG)
EOC .... End of Contract   (AAG)
EOC .... End of Conversion
EOC .... End of Course   (AFM)
EOC .... End of Cycle   (NRCH)
EOC .... Enemy Oil Committee [*US*]
EOC .... Engine Order Capability   (NASA)
EOC .... Engine Out Capability   (MCD)
EOC .... Engineered Operating Cycle
EOC .... Engineering Operations Control   (MCD)
EOC .... Equal Opportunities Commission [*British*]
EOC .... Equal Opportunity Cases [*Australia*] [*A publication*]
EOC .... Equipment Operational Control
EOC .... Erbium Oxide Crystal
EOC .... Ercoupe Owners Club   (EA)
EOC .... Error of Closure
EOC .... Executive Officers Council of the National Association of Real Estate Boards   (EA)
EOC .... Experimental Operations Center
EOC .... Explosive Ordnance Components [*Military*]   (MCD)
EOC .... Extended Overhaul Cycle   (NVT)
EOCA .... Constructionman Apprentice, Equipment Operator, Striker [*Navy rating*]
EOCA .... Early Onset Cerebellar Ataxia [*Medicine*]
EOCA .... Electronic Office Centers of America, Inc. [*Schaumburg, IL*] [*Telecommunications*]   (TSSD)
EOCC .... Emergency Operations Control Center [*Environmental Protection Agency*]
EOCC .... Engineering Operational Casualty Control   (NVT)
EOCCM .... Electro-Optical Counter-Countermeasures   (MCD)
EOCCT ..... End-of-Course Comprehensive Testing
EOCD .... Error, Omission, Clarification, or Deficiency   (MCD)
EOCI .... Electric Overhead Crane Institute [*Later, Crane Manufacturers Association of America*]   (EA)
EOCM .... Electro-Optical Countermeasures   (MCD)
EOCM .... Equipment Operator, Master Chief [*Navy rating*]
EOCN .... Constructionman, Equipment Operator, Striker [*Navy rating*]
EOCP .... Emergency Out of Commission for Parts
EOCP .... Engine Out of Commission for Parts
EOCR .... Experimental Organic Cooled Reactor
EOCS .... Equipment Operator, Senior Chief [*Navy rating*]
EOCT .... End-of-Cycle Test [*Army training*]   (INF)
EOC and WPA ... Editors Organizing Committee and Writers' and Publishers' Alliance for Disarmament   (EA)
EOCY .... End of Calendar Year

EOD.......... Date of Entering Office
EOD.......... Earth Observations Division [*Johnson Space Center*] [*NASA*]
EOD.......... Economic Objectives Department [*Ministry of Economic Warfare*] [*British*] [*World War II*]
EOD.......... Education Outcomes Division [*Washington, DC*] [*Department of Education*]   (GRD)
EOD.......... Electric Organ Discharge [*Electrophysiology*]
EOD.......... Electro-Optic Display
EOD.......... Elements of Data   (MSA)
EOD.......... Emergency Ordnance Disposal
EOD.......... End of Data [*Data processing*]
EOD.......... End of Day   (AFM)
EOD.......... End of Dialing [*Telecommunications*]   (TEL)
EOD.......... Engineering Operating Directives   (MCD)
EOD.......... Entry on Duty   (MUGU)
EOD.......... Established Onset of Disability   (OICC)
EOD.......... Estimated on Dock   (KSC)
EOD.......... Estimated Operational Date   (CINC)
EOD.......... Every Other Day
EOD.......... Expected Occupancy Date
EOD.......... Explosive Ordnance Detachment [*Army*]   (RDA)
EOD.......... Explosive Ordnance Device [*Military*]   (MCD)
EOD.......... Explosive Ordnance Disposal [*Military*]
EODB....... End of Data Block [*Data processing*]   (MCD)
EODB....... Explosive Ordnance Disposal Bulletin [*Military*]
EODC....... Explosive Ordnance Disposal Center [*DoD*]
EODC....... Explosive Ordnance Disposal Control [*Military*]   (AABC)
EODCC..... EOD Control Center
EODD....... Electro-Optic Digital Deflector   (IEEE)
EODE....... Explosive Ordnance Disposal Evaluator
EODG....... Explosive Ordnance Disposal Group [*Military*]   (NVT)
EODGRU ... Explosive Ordnance Disposal Group [*Military*]
EODGRULANT ... Explosive Ordnance Disposal Group, Atlantic [*Military*]
EODGRUPAC ... Explosive Ordnance Disposal Group, Pacific [*Military*]
EODN....... Explosive Ordnance Disposal, Nuclear [*Military*]   (NVT)
EODP....... Engineering Order Delayed for Parts
EODPP...... Epidemiology and Oral Disease Prevention Program [*Bethesda, MD*] [*National Institute of Dental Research*] [*Department of Health and Human Services*]   (GRD)
EODS....... Electro-Optic Direction Sensor
EODS....... Explosive Ordnance Disposal School [*Indian Head, MD*] [*Military*]
EODSBad ... Explosive Ordnance Disposal Specialist Badge [*Military decoration*]   (AABC)
EODSupvBad ... Explosive Ordnance Disposal Supervisor Badge [*Military decoration*]   (AABC)
EODTC..... Electro-Optic Display Test Chamber
EODU....... Explosive Ordnance Disposal Unit [*Military*]   (NVT)
EOE.......... Earth Orbit Ejection [*Aerospace*]   (MCD)
EOE.......... Earth Orbit Equipment [*Aerospace*]
EOE.......... Element of Expense
EOE.......... End of Extent [*Data processing*]   (IBMDP)
EOE.......... Enemy Occupied Europe [*World War II*]
EOE.......... Equal Opportunity Employer
EOE.......... Errors and Omissions Excepted [*Insurance*]
E and OE ... Errors and Omissions Excepted [*Insurance*]
EOE.......... Ethiodized Oil Emulsion [*Clinical chemistry*]
EOE.......... Ethyloxaergoline [*Biochemistry*]
EOE.......... European Options Exchange [*Netherlands*]
EOE.......... Newberry, SC [*Location identifier*] [*FAA*]   (FAAL)
EOEC....... End of Equilibrium Cycle [*Nuclear energy*]   (NRCH)
EOED....... Earth Orbit Escape Device [*Aerospace*]
EOEM....... Electronic Original Equipment Market
EOE M/F .. Equal Opportunity Employer, Male/Female   (OICC)
EOF.......... Earth Orbital Flight [*Aerospace*]   (AAG)
EOF.......... Electro-Optic Force
EOF.......... Emergency Operating Facility [*Civil Defense*]
EOF.......... Emergency Operations Facility [*Nuclear energy*]   (NRCH)
EOF.......... Empirical Orthogonal Function [*Statistics*]
EOF.......... End of File [*Data processing*]
EOF.......... Expected Operations Forecast [*Aviation*]   (FAAC)
EOFCS..... Electro-Optical Fire Control System [*Military*]   (CAAL)
EOFEA..... Equal Opportunity and Full Employment Act   (OICC)
EOFY....... End of Fiscal Year
EOG.......... Educational Opportunity Grant
EOG.......... Effect on Guarantees
EOG.......... Electrograph   (KSC)
EOG.......... Electrooculogram [*or Electrooculography*] [*Medicine*]
EOG.......... Electroolfactogram [*Medicine*]
EOG.......... Enron Oil & Gas [*NYSE symbol*]   (SPSG)
EOG.......... Voltage Outer Gimbal
EOGB....... Electro-Optical Glide Bomb   (MCD)
EOGO....... Eccentric Orbital Geophysical Observatory [*Also, EGO*] [*NASA*]   (MUGU)
EOGRAL... European Journal of Obstetrics, Gynecology, and Reproductive Biology [*A publication*]
EO/GW..... Electro-Optical Guided Weapons
EOH.......... Emergency Operation Headquarters [*Army*]   (AABC)
EOH.......... End of Overhaul
EOH.......... Equipment on Hand   (AABC)
EOH.......... Equipment Operator, Hauling [*Navy rating*]

EOH.......... Experiment Operations Handbook   (KSC)
EOHP....... Except as Otherwise Herein Provided
EOHT....... External Oxygen and Hydrogen Tanks   (NASA)
EOI.......... Earth Orbit Insertion [*NASA*]   (KSC)
EOI.......... Eday [*Orkney Islands*] [*Airport symbol*]   (OAG)
EOI.......... End of Input [*Data processing*]
EOI.......... End of Inquiry [*Data processing*]
EOIC....... Ethylene Oxide Industry Council   (EA)
EOID....... Electro-Optical Ion Detection [*Spectroscopy*]
EOIG....... Enemy Oil Intelligence Group [*Ministry of Economic Warfare*] [*British*] [*World War II*]
EOIL....... Energy Oil [*NASDAQ symbol*]   (NQ)
E/O-IMS... Engineering/Operations - Information Management System   (NASA)
EOIS....... Electro-Optical Imaging System   (IEEE)
EOITS....... Electro-Optical Identification and Tracking System   (MCD)
EOJ.......... End of Job [*Data processing*]
EOK.......... Keokuk, IA [*Location identifier*] [*FAA*]   (FAAL)
EOKA....... Ethnike Organosis Kypriakou Agonos [*National Organization of Cypriot Fighters*] [*Greece*]
EOL.......... Earth Orbit Launch [*NASA*]   (KSC)
EOL.......... Economic Opportunity Act Loan
EOL.......... Electro-Optics and Laser International Exhibition and Conference [*Great Britain*]   (ITD)
EOL.......... Emir Oils Limited [*Vancouver Stock Exchange symbol*]
EOL.......... End of Life
EOL.......... End of Line [*Telecommunications*]   (FAAC)
EOL.......... Ex Oriente Lux [*A publication*]   (BJA)
EOL.......... Expression-Oriented Language [*Data processing*]
EOL.......... Neola, IA [*Location identifier*] [*FAA*]   (FAAL)
EOLAB..... Electro-Optics Laboratory [*University of Michigan*] [*Research center*]   (RCD)
EOLAS...... [*The*] Irish Science and Technology Agency [*Information service or system*]   (IID)
EOLAS - ISTA ... EOLAS - the Irish Science and Technology Agency   (EAIO)
EOLB....... End of Line Block [*Data processing*]   (CET)
EOLC....... Earth Orbital Launch Configuration [*NASA*]   (KSC)
EOLES..... Escourteur Oceanque Leger a Effet de Surface [*Light Ocean-Going Surface Effects Ship*] [*French*]
EOLL...... Ernest Orland Lawrence Livermore Laboratory [*University of California*]   (KSC)
EOLM....... Electro-Optical Light Modulator
EOLM....... End of Line Marker [*Data processing*]
EOLR....... Electrical Objective Loudness Rating   (IEEE)
EOLT....... End of Logical Tape [*Data processing*]
EOLV....... Electro-Optic Light Valve
EOM.......... Earth Observation Mission [*NASA*]
EOM.......... Earth Orbital Mission [*NASA*]
EOM.......... Egyptian Order of Merit
EOM.......... Electro-Optical Modulator
EOM.......... Employment Office Manager   (ADA)
EOM.......... End of Medium [*Data processing*]   (BUR)
EOM.......... End of Message [*Data processing*]
EOM.......... End of Mission
EOM.......... End of Month [*Business term*]
EOM.......... Energize Output M [*Symbol language*]
EOM.......... Engineering Operations Manual [*NASA*]   (NASA)
EOM.......... Enjoyment of Music Series, EMI [*Record label*] [*Great Britain*]
EOM.......... Equation of Motion   (NASA)
EOM.......... European Options Market   (DCTA)
EOM.......... Every Other Month   (ADA)
EOM.......... Executives on the Move [*A publication*]
EOM.......... External Ocular Movement [*Medicine*]
EOM.......... Extractable Organic Matter [*Environmental chemistry*]
EOM.......... Extraocular Movements [*Ophthalmology*]
EOM.......... Extraocular Muscles [*Ophthalmology*]
EOMA...... Emergency Oxygen Mask Assembly   (KSC)
EOMB...... Explanation of Medicare [*or Medical*] Benefits
EOMC...... Estudios Orientales (Mexico City) [*A publication*]
EOMF...... End of Minor Frame   (MCD)
EOMF...... Exempt Organization Master File [*IRS*]
EOMS...... End of Message Sequence [*Data processing*]   (CET)
EOMSF..... Earth Orbital Military Space Force   (MCD)
EOMTC.... Eugene O'Neill Memorial Theater Center   (EA)
EON.......... Equipment Operator, Construction Equipment [*Navy rating*]
EON.......... Ethylene Oxide Number [*Surfactant technology*]
EON.......... Eugene O'Neill Newsletter [*A publication*]
EON.......... Peotone, IL [*Location identifier*] [*FAA*]   (FAAL)
EONE........ Eastern Offshore News. Eastcoast Petroleum Operators' Association [*A publication*]
EOO.......... Erasmi Opera Omnia [*Elsevier Book Series*] [*A publication*]
EOOE........ Erreur ou Omission Exceptee [*Error or Omission Excepted*] [*French*]
EOOW....... Engineering Officer of the Watch [*Navy*]   (NVT)
EOP.......... Earth Observations Programs [*NASA*]
EOP.......... Earth and Ocean Physics [*NASA*]   (NASA)
EOP.......... Earth Orbit Plane [*Aerospace*]   (AAG)
EOP.......... Economics of Planning [*A publication*]
EOP.......... Efficiency of Plating [*Microbiology*]
EOP.......... Electro-Optic Projector
EOP.......... Electronic Overload Protection

EOP .... Emergency Operating Procedure [*Nuclear energy*]   (NRCH)
EOP .... Emergency Operating Program   (OICC)
EOP .... Emergency Operations Plan [*Civil Defense*]
EOP .... Emergency Oxygen Pack [*NASA*]   (KSC)
EOP .... Encyclopedia of Occultism and Parapsychology [*A publication*]
EOP .... End Output [*Data processing*]   (IEEE)
EOP .... End of Paragraph
EOP .... End of Part   (MCD)
EOP .... End of Period
EOP .... End of Procedure [*Data processing*]
EOP .... End of Program [*Data processing*]
EOP .... End of Push [*Spectroscopy*]
EOP .... Engineering Operating Procedure   (MCD)
EOP .... Equal Opportunity Policy   (OICC)
EOP .... Equal Opportunity Programs   (MCD)
EOP .... Equipment Operating [*or Operational*] Procedure   (AAG)
EOP .... Executive Office of the President
EOP .... Executive Office of the President, Washington, DC [*OCLC symbol*]   (OCLC)
EOP .... Experiment Operations Panel
EOP .... Experiments of Opportunity   (NASA)
EOP .... Extraoptic Photoreceptors
EOPAP ...... Earth and Ocean Physics Applications Program [*NASA*]
EOPC .... Electro-Optic Phase Change   (IEEE)
EOPF .... End of Powered Flight
EOPP .... Employment Opportunities Pilot Program [*Department of Labor*]
EOPPA ...... Ekonomika i Organizatsiya Promyshlennogo Proizvodstva [*A publication*]
EOPS .... Equal Opportunity Program Specialist [*Navy*]   (NVT)
EOPT .... Energy Optics, Inc. [*NASDAQ symbol*]   (NQ)
EOPTO ..... Electro-Optical Technology Program Office [*Navy*]   (GRD)
EOQ .... Economic Order Quantity
EOQ .... End of Quarter   (AFM)
EOQC .... European Organization for Quality [*Switzerland*]
EOQI .... Equal Opportunity Quality Indicator [*Navy*]   (NVT)
EOR .... Earth Orbit Rendezvous [*NASA*]
E Or .... Echos d'Orient [*A publication*]
EOR .... Electro-Optical Research
EOR .... End of Record [*Data processing*]
EOR .... End of Reel
EOR .... End of Run [*Telecommunications*]   (TEL)
EOR .... Engine Order
EOR .... Enhanced Oil Recovery [*Petroleum engineering*]
EOR .... Equipment Operationally Ready   (AABC)
EOR .... Exclusive Or [*Gates*] [*Data processing*]
EOR .... Explosive Ordnance Reconnaissance [*Military*]
EORA .... Explosive Ordnance Reconnaissance Agent [*Military*]   (AABC)
EORBS ...... Earth Orbiting Recoverable Biological Satellite
EORC .... Emergency Operations Research Center
EORC .... Engineering Officers Reserve Corps
EORC .... Equal Opportunities Resource Centre [*Perth, Australia*]
EORF .... Electron Optical Recording Facility
EORL .... Emergency Officers' Retired List [*Army*]
EORR .... Empire-Orr, Inc. [*New York, NY*] [*NASDAQ symbol*]   (NQ)
EO/RR ...... Equal Opportunity/Race Relations [*Navy*]   (NVT)
EORSA ...... Episcopalians and Others for Responsible Social Action   (EA)
EORSAT ... ELINT [*Electronic Intelligence*] - Ocean Reconnaissance Satellite   (MCD)
EORT .... Equipment Operational Readiness Trends [*Report*]   (MCD)
EORTC ...... European Organization for Research on the Treatment of Cancer [*Research center*] [*Switzerland*]   (IRC)
EORTC Cancer Chemother Annu ... EORTC [*European Organization for Research on Treatment of Cancer*] Cancer Chemotherapy Annual [*A publication*]
E Orth .... Eastern Orthodox
EOS .... Earth Observatory Satellite [*NASA*]
EOS .... Earth Observing System [*NASA*]
EOS .... Earth Orbit Station
EOS .... Earth Orbital Shuttle [*NASA*]   (KSC)
EOS .... Efficiency of Survival [*Genetics*]
EOS .... Electro-Optical Systems, Inc. [*Subsidiary of Xerox Corp.*]
EOS .... Electrophoretic Operations in Space [*Without gravity*]
EOS .... Eligible for Overseas Service
EOS .... Elsevier Oceanography Series [*Elsevier Book Series*] [*A publication*]
EOS .... Emergency Operations Simulation [*Civil Defense*]
EOS .... Emergency Operations Staff   (MCD)
EOS .... Emergency Operations System
EOS .... Emergency Oxygen Supply [*or System*]
EOS .... Enclosed Operating Station [*Military*]   (CAAL)
EOS .... End of Season [*Business term*]
EOS .... End of Service   (MCD)
EOS .... Energy of State
EOS .... Engineering Operating Station [*Military*]   (CAAL)
EOS .... Engineering Operating System
EOS .... Eosinophils [*Hematology*]
EOS .... Equation of State
EOS .... Eugene O'Neill Society   (EA)
EOS .... European Orthodontic Society   (EAIO)
EOS .... Expiration of Obligated Service [*Military*]

EOS .... Extended Operating System [*DoD*]
EOS .... Neosho, MO [*Location identifier*] [*FAA*]   (FAAL)
EOSA .... Explosive Ordnance Safety Approval [*Military*]   (MUGU)
E-O SAEL ... Electro-Optical Sensors Atmospheric Effects Library   (RDA)
EOSAT ...... Earth Observation Satellite Co. [*Joint venture of RCA Corp. and Hughes Aircraft Co.*]
EOSC .... Eastern Oregon State College
EOSCOR ... Extended Observation of Solar and Cosmic Radiation [*National Center for Atmospheric Research*]
EOSD .... Emergency Operations Systems Development [*Civil Defense*]
EOSD .... Equipment on Station Date [*Army*]   (AABC)
EOSDIS .... Earth Observing System Data and Information System
EOS/ESD .. Electrical Overstress/Electrostatic Discharge Association   (EA)
EOSO .... Escort Oilers Supervising Officer [*Navy*]
EO & SP .. Economic Order and Stockage Policy   (AFIT)
EOSP .... Economic Order and Stockage Procedure
EOSS .... Earth Orbital Space Station [*NASA*]   (MCD)
EOSS .... Electro-Optical Sensor System [*Navy*]   (MCD)
EOSS .... Electro-Optical Simulation System [*for missiles*] [*Army*]   (MCD)
EOSS .... Emergency Operational Sequencing System   (MCD)
EOST .... Emergency Operations Simulation Techniques [*Civil Defense*]
Eos Trans Am Geophys Union ... Eos. Transactions of the American Geophysical Union [*A publication*]
EOT .... Earth-Observed Time [*NASA*]
EOT .... Economic Impact. A Quarterly Review of World Economics [*A publication*]
EOT .... Electric Overhead Travelling
EOT .... End of Tape [*Data processing*]
EOT .... End of Task [*Data processing*]
EOT .... End of Test [*Data processing*]
EOT .... End of Text [*Data processing*]
EOT .... End of Tour [*Air Force*]   (AFM)
EOT .... End of Track
EOT .... End of Transmission [*Data processing*]
E & OT ...... Enemy and Occupied Territories Department [*Ministry of Economic Warfare*] [*British*] [*World War II*]
EOT .... Enemy-Occupied Territory
EOT .... Energy Optimized Technology [*German-manufactured car tire*] [*Continental Gummi-Werke AG*]
EOT .... Equal Opportunity and Treatment [*Army program*]
EO(T)A ...... Engineering Officers' (Telecommunications) Association [*British*]
EOTC .... Electro-Optic Test Chamber
EOTD .... Electro-Optical Tracking Device
EOTF .... Electro-Optics Test Facility
EOTS .... Earth Orbiting Teleoperator System [*Spacecraft*] [*NASA*]
EOTS .... Electron Optic Tracking System   (MUGU)
EOU .... Electro-Optical Unit
EOU .... Enemy Objective Unit [*of US*] [*in London*]
EOU .... Epidemic Observation Unit [*Medicine*]
EOUPD ..... Ekonomika, Organizatsiya i Upravlenie v Neftepererabatyvayushchei i Neftekhimicheskoi Promyshlennosti [*A publication*]
EOUSA ..... Executive Office for United States Attorneys [*Department of Justice*]
EOUSD ..... Economic Outlook USA [*A publication*]
EOV .... Columbia, SC [*Location identifier*] [*FAA*]   (FAAL)
EOV .... Economic Order Van   (AABC)
EOV .... Electrically Operated Valve
EOV .... End of Volume [*Data processing*]
EOVS .... Electro-Optical Viewing System   (MCD)
EOW .... End of Word [*Data processing*]
EOW .... Energy over Weight   (MCD)
EOW .... Engine over the Wing
EOW .... Engineering Order Worksheet
EOW .... Engineer's Order Wire
EOW .... Every Other Week
EOWA .... English Olympic Wrestling Association
EOWPVT ... Expressive One-Word Picture Vocabulary Test [*Intelligence test*]
EOWPVT:UE ... Expressive One-Word Picture Vocabulary Test: Upper Extension [*Intelligence test*]
EOWS .... Electro-Optical Weapons System
EOY .... End of Year
EOZ .... Elorza [*Venezuela*] [*Airport symbol*]   (OAG)
EP .... Early Philosophies [*A publication*]
EP .... Early Positive
EP .... Earned Premium [*Insurance*]
EP .... Earning Power [*Business term*]
EP .... Earnings Price [*Investment term*]
E & P .... Earnings and Profit   (ADA)
EP .... Earth Penetrator [*Weapon*]
EP .... Eastward Position
EP .... Ebury Press [*Publisher*] [*Great Britain*]
EP .... Ecclesiastical Parish
EP .... Economic Papers [*A publication*]
EP .... Economic Planning   (MCD)
EP .... Economic Planning. Journal for Agriculture and Related Industries [*A publication*]
EP .... Economic Policy [*British*]

EP	Ectopic Pregnancy [*Obstetrics*]
EP	Edible Portion [*of a food*]
E & P..........	Editor and Publisher [*A publication*]
EP	Editor and Publisher [*A publication*]
EP	Educational Publication [*NASA*]
EP	Effective Par [*Investment term*]
EP	Effective Production
EP	Egyptian Pattern [*British military*] (DMA)
EP	Egyseg Partja [*Party of Unity*] [*Hungary*] (PPE)
EP	El Pais [*Spain*] [*A publication*]
EP	Elbow Pitch (MCD)
EP	Electric Power (NRCH)
EP	Electric Primer
EP	Electrical Panel (NG)
E/P..............	Electrical-to-Pneumatic [*Converter*] (NRCH)
EP	Electrical Propulsion (AAG)
EP	Electrical Prototype
EP	Electrically Polarized [*Relay*]
EP	Electrode Plasma [*Energy source*]
EP	Electron Paramagnetic
EP	Electron Photon
E/P..............	Electron/Proton (MCD)
EP	Electronic and Desktop Publishing
EP	Electronic Package
EP	Electronic Post [*Defunct*] [*British Post Office*] (TSSD)
EP	Electronic Printer
EP	Electronics Panel
EP	Electrophoresis
EP	Electrophysiology
EP	Electroplate
EP	Electropneumatic
EP	Electrostatic Powder
EP	Electrostatic Precipitator [*Also, ESP*]
EP	Elephantine Papyri (BJA)
EP	Eligible Participant (OICC)
EP	Elongated Punch
EP	Emergency Planning (NATG)
EP	Emergency Preparedness [*Nuclear energy*] (NRCH)
EP	Emergency Procedures (MCD)
EP	Emission Policy (NATG)
EP	Employee Participation (ADA)
EP	Employee Plan [*IRS*]
EP	Employment Protection [*Act*] [*British*]
EP	Empowerment Project (EA)
EP	Emulation Program [*IBM Corp.*] (BUR)
EP	En Passant [*In Passing*] [*Chess*]
EP	En Route Penetration [*Aviation*] (FAAC)
E/P..............	End-Paper [*Bibliography*]
EP	End Point [*Distilling*]
EP	End of Program [*Data processing*]
EP	Ending Period (AABC)
EP	Endogenous Pyrogen [*Immunology*]
EP	Endorser Potential [*Advertising term*]
EP	Endothia parasitica [*Plant pathology*]
EP	Enemy Position
EP	Engineer Pamphlet [*Army Corps of Engineers*]
EP	Engineer Personnel [*Marine Corps*]
EP	Engineering Paper
EP	Engineering Personnel [*Coast Guard*]
EP	Engineering Phase (MCD)
EP	Engineering Practice (NG)
EP	Engineering Print (KSC)
EP	Engineering Procedure
EP	Engineering Project
EP	Engineering Proposal
EP	Enlisted Personnel (AABC)
EP	Enserch Exploration Partnership Ltd. [*NYSE symbol*] (SPSG)
EP	Entrainment Pressure
EP	Entrucking Point [*Military*]
EP	Entry Point (BUR)
EP	Environmental Pollution [*A publication*] (NOAA)
EP	Environmental Protective Plan (MCD)
EP	Enzyme Presoak [*for laundry*]
EP	Enzyme-Product Complex [*Enzyme kinetics*]
EP	Eparchy (ROG)
Ep	Ephesians [*New Testament book*] (BJA)
EP	Epiotic [*Ear anatomy*]
EP	Episcopalian
EP	Episcopus [*Bishop*] [*Latin*]
EP	Epistle
EP	Epistola [*Epistle, Letter*] [*Latin*] (ROG)
Ep	Epistulae [*of Epicurus*] [*Classical studies*] (OCD)
Ep	Epistulae [*of Julian*] [*Classical studies*] (OCD)
Ep	Epistulae [*of Augustine*] [*Classical studies*] (OCD)
Ep	Epistulae [*of Seneca the Younger*] [*Classical studies*] (OCD)
Ep	Epistulae [*of St. Jerome*] [*Classical studies*] (OCD)
Ep	Epistulae [*of Pliny the Younger*] [*Classical studies*] (OCD)
EP	Epitaxial Planar [*Electronics*]
EP	Epithelial Proliferation [*Histology*]
EP	Epping [*Urban district in England*]
EP	Equipment Piece (NRCH)
EP	Equipment Practice [*Telecommunications*] (TEL)
EP	Equipment Publication (AABC)
EP	Erasmus Press, Lexington, KY [*Library symbol*] [*Library of Congress*] (LCLS)
EP	Erythrocyte Protoporphyrin [*Hematology*]
EP	Erythrophagocytosis [*Hematology*]
EP	Erythropoietic Porphyria [*A genetic disorder*]
Ep	Erythropoietin [*Also, EPO*] [*Hematology*]
EP	Estate Planning [*A publication*]
EP	Estimated Position [*Navigation*]
EP	Etched Plate
EP	Etudes Papyrologiques [*A publication*]
EP	Etudes Philosophiques [*A publication*]
EP	European Parliament
EP	European Plan [*Hotel room rate*]
EP	Europrime Capital [*Vancouver Stock Exchange symbol*]
EP	Evening Prayer
EP	Evoked Potential [*Neurophysiology*]
EP	Excess Profits
EP	Executive Pension [*British*]
EP	Executive Program (MCD)
E & P..........	Exercise and Plans (CINC)
EP	Expanded Polystyrene (ADA)
EP	Expectancy Phenomenon
EP	Expected Pay-Off
EP	Experienced Playgoer [*Theatrical*]
E & P..........	Exploration and Production [*In organization name Oil Industry International Exploration & Production Forum*]
EP	Explosion-Proof
EP	Extended Play
EP	Extension Pay [*British military*] (DMA)
EP	External Phloem [*Botany*]
EP	External Pressure
EP	External Publication
EP	Externally Powered [*Gun*] (MCD)
EP	Extra Point [*Football*]
EP	Extraction Procedure [*Chemical engineering*]
E & P..........	Extraordinary and Plenipotentiary
EP	Extreme Pressure (MSA)
EP	Iran [*Aircraft nationality and registration mark*] (FAAC)
E & P..........	Oil Industry International Exploration and Production Forum (EAIO)
EP	Pelita Air Service [*ICAO designator*] (FAAC)
EP	Presbyterian, Church of England [*Military*] (ROG)
ep----	Pyrenees Region [*MARC geographic area code*] [*Library of Congress*] (LCCP)
EPA	Earth's Polar Axis (KSC)
EPA	Eastern Provincial Airways [*Labrador*]
EPA	Eastern Psychological Association
EPA	Economic Price Adjustment
EPA	Educational Paperback Association (EA)
EPA	Educational Publishers Association
EPA	Eicosapentaenoic Acid [*Biochemistry*]
EPA	Eire Philatelic Association (EA)
EPA	Electron Probe Analyzer
EPA	Emergency Powers Act [*British*] [*World War II*]
EPA	Empire Parliamentary Association [*Later, CPA*]
EPA	Employee Plan Administrators
EPA	Employee Promotion Appraisal [*FAA*] (FAAC)
EPA	Employment Protection Act [*1975*] [*British*] (DCTA)
EPA	Energetic Particles Analyzer [*Astrophysics*]
EPA	Engineering Practice Amendment (AAG)
EPA	Environment Planning Assessment Act [*Australia*]
EPA	Environment Pollutions Agency [*British*]
EPA	Environmental Protection Agency [*Government agency formed in 1970*]
EPA	Epidermolysis Bullosa Acquisita [*Dermatology*]
EPA	Equal Pay Act [*US*] (OICC)
EPA	Equatorial Pitch Angle [*Geophysics*]
EPA	Erect Posterior-Anterior
EPA	Erythroid Potentiating Activity [*Hematology*]
EPA	Estimated Position Arc [*Navy*] (NVT)
EPA	Ether-Isopentane-Ethanol [*Solvent system*]
EPA	Ethnic Party of Australia [*Political party*] (ADA)
EPA	Ethylbenzene Producers Association (EA)
EPA	Europaeisches Patentamt [*European Patent Office - EPO*] (EAIO)
EPA	European Photochemistry Association (EAIO)
EPA	European Productivity Agency
EPA	Evangelical Press Association (EA)
EP & A	Exercise Plans and Analysis Division (MCD)
EPA	Exoatmospheric Penetration Aid
EPA	Export Pound Account [*Special type of currency*] [*United Arab Republic*]
EPA	Extended Planning Annex
EPA	Extrinsic Plasminogen Activator [*Hematology*]
EPA	Eyre Peninsula Airways [*Australia*]
EPA	L'Economie des Pays Arabes [*A publication*] (BJA)
EPAA........	Educational Press Association of America [*Later, EDPRESS*] (EA)
EPAA........	Emergency Petroleum Allocation Act

EPAA......... Employing Printers Association of America [*Defunct*] (EA)
EPAA......... European Primary Aluminum Association [*Later, European Aluminium Association - EAA*] (IID)
EPA/ARB ... Environmental Protection Agency/Air Resources Board
EPABX...... Electronic Private Automatic Branch Exchange [*Telecommunications*] (MCD)
EPAC........ Entraineurs en Patinage Artistique du Canada [*Figure Skating Coaches of Canada - FSCC*]
EPACASR ... Environmental Protection Agency Chemical Activities Status Report [*Environmental Protection Agency*] [*Database*]
EPA Cit Bul ... EPA [*Environmental Protection Agency*] Citizens' Bulletin [*A publication*]
EPAD .... Enlisted Personnel Assignment Document [*Navy*] (NVT)
EPA (Environ Prot Agency) Environ Prot Technol Ser ... EPA (Environmental Protection Agency) Environmental Protection Technology Series [*A publication*]
EPAGM..... Environmental Protection Agency Grants Administration Manual
EPAI......... El Pollo Asado, Incorporated [*Phoenix, AZ*] [*NASDAQ symbol*] (NQ)
EPAIS........ Encyclopedia of Public Affairs Information Sources [*A publication*]
EPA J .... EPA [*Environmental Protection Agency*] Journal [*A publication*]
EPAM....... Elementary Perceiver and Memorizer [*University of California*] [*Learning theory*] [*Computer device*]
EPAM....... Emergency Priorities and Allocations Manual [*DoD*]
Epam......... Epaminondas [*of Nepos*] [*Classical studies*] (OCD)
EPAMS..... Experimental Prototype Automatic Meteorological System (MCD)
EPAN .... Electronic Purchasing Agent Network [*Service of Data Corp. of America*]
EPANY...... Export Packers Association of New York [*Defunct*] (EA)
EPap .... Etudes de Papyrologie [*A publication*]
EPA-PRD ... Environmental Protection Agency - Pesticide Regional Division
E-PAR .... Electronic Warfare/Radioelectronic Parity Study
EPAS .... Energetic Particle Anisotropy Spectrometer
EPAS .... Experimental Project Apollo-Soyuz [*Acronym used as name of a cologne created to commemorate the first joint US/Russian manned space flight*]
EPASA ...... Electron Probe Analysis Society of America [*Later, MAS*] (EA)
EPAT........ Earliest Possible Arrival Time (MCD)
EPB........... Economic Policy Board [*Department of the Treasury*]
EPB........... Editorial Production Branch [*BUPERS*]
EPB........... Ejercito Popular Boricua [*Puerto Rican Popular Army*] (PD)
EPB........... Electronic Publishing and Bookselling [*A publication*]
EPB........... Electronic Publishing Business [*Electronic Publishing Ventures, Inc.*] [*Information service or system*] (IID)
EPB........... Employee Benefit Plan Review [*A publication*]
EPB........... Energy Pulse Bonding [*Electronics*]
EPB........... Engineering Process Bulletin
EPB........... Enlisted Programs Branch [*BUPERS*]
EPB........... Environmental Periodicals Bibliography [*Environmental Studies Institute*] [*Information service or system*]
EPB........... Equipment Parts Bin
EPB........... Equivalent Passband (MCD)
EPB........... Equivalent Pension Benefit [*British*]
EPB........... Ethylpyridinium Bromide [*Organic chemistry*]
EPB........... Export Promotion Bureau [*Pakistani*] (GEA)
EPB........... Extensor Pollicis Brevis [*Anatomy*]
EPB........... External Proton Beam
EpBarn...... Epistle of Barnabas (BJA)
EPBCA ...... Ergebnisse der Physiologie, Biologischen Chemie, und Experimentellen Pharmakologie [*A publication*]
EPBCAQ ... Ergebnisse der Physiologie, Biologischen Chemie, und Experimentellen Pharmakologie [*A publication*]
EPBGPN ... Environment Protection Board. Gas Pipeline Newsletter [*A publication*]
EPBLFC .... Elvis Presley Burning Love Fan Club (EA)
EPBM....... Earth Pressure Balance Machine [*Excavation*]
EPBX........ Electronic Private Branch Exchange [*Telecommunications*]
EPC.......... Earth Potential Compensation [*Telecommunications*] (TEL)
EPC.......... Earth Prelaunch Calibration [*NASA*] (KSC)
EPC........... Eastern Pilgrim College [*Later, United Weslayan College*] [*Pennsylvania*]
EPC.......... East's Pleas of the Crown [*A publication*] (DLA)
EPC.......... Easy Processing Channel
EPC........... Economic Policy Committee [*OECD*]
EPC........... Economic Policy Council [*UNA-USA*]
EPC........... Editorial Processing Center
EPC........... Editor's Presentation Copy
EPC........... Educational Policies Commission [*Defunct*] (EA)
EPC........... Educational Publishers Council [*British*]
EPC........... Effective Production Coefficient
EPC........... Ejercito Popular Catalan [*Catalan Popular Army*] [*Spain*] (PD)
EPC........... Ejercito del Pueblo Costarricense [*Political party*] [*Costa Rica*] (EY)
EPC........... Elastic Performance Coefficient [*Textile testing*]
EPC........... Elder Flowers, Peppermint, and Composition Essense [*Patent medicine ingredients*] [*British*]
EPC........... Electric Power Corporation [*Burma*] (DS)

EPC........... Electron Photon Cascade
EPC........... Electronic Power Conditioner
EPC........... Electronic Program Control
EPC........... Electronic Publishing Committee [*Association of American Publishers*] [*Information service or system*] (IID)
EPC........... Elementary Processing Centers
EPC........... Emergency Planning Canada
EPC........... Emergency Propaganda Committee [*London*] [*World War II*]
EPC........... End Plate Current
EPC........... End Products Committee [*of WPB*] [*World War II*]
EPC........... Engineering Part Card
EPC........... English Prize Cases [*Legal*]
EPC........... Environmental Policy Center (EA)
EPC........... Environmental Pollution Control
EPC........... Epilepsy Partialis Continua [*Medicine*]
EPC........... Equipotential Cathode
EPC........... Error Protection Code (NASA)
Epc........... Erythrocyte Particle Counter [*Hematology*]
EPC........... Erythroid Progenitor Cells [*Hematology*]
EPC........... Ethyl Phenylcarbamate [*Plant regulator*] [*Organic chemistry*]
EPC........... European Patent Convention
EPC........... European Political Community (NATG)
EPC........... European Political Cooperation
EPC........... European Popular Circle (EAIO)
EPC........... Evaluation and Planning Centre for Health Care [*London School of Hygiene and Tropical Medicine*] [*British*] (CB)
EPC........... Evaporative Pattern Casting [*Automotive engineering*]
EPC........... Excess Profits Tax Council Ruling or Memorandum [*Internal Revenue Bureau*] [*A publication*] (DLA)
EPC........... Experiment Point Control [*NASA*]
EPC........... External Pneumatic Compression [*Medicine*]
EPC........... External Power Contractor (NASA)
EPC........... Extra-Pair Copulation [*Biology*]
EPC........... Honolulu, HI [*Location identifier*] [*FAA*] (FAAL)
EPC........... Roscoe's English Prize Cases [*A publication*] (DLA)
EPCA........ Electronic Pest Control Association (EA)
EPCA........ Emergency Price Control Act of 1942
EPCA........ Employment Protection Consolidation Act [*1978*] [*British*] (DLA)
EPCA........ Energy Policy and Conservation Act [*1975*]
EPCA........ European Petrochemical Association [*Database producer*]
EPCA........ External Pressure Circulatory Assist [*Cardiac treatment*]
EPCAC...... Ecumenical Program on Central America and the Caribbean (EA)
EPCAG...... Electronic Publishing Consultative and Advisory Group [*Australia*]
EPCCFC.... Elvis Presley Circle City Fan Club (EA)
EPCCS....... Emergency Positive Control Communications System
EPCCT ...... Emergency Planning Committee for Civil Transportation [*US and Canada*]
EPCDC..... Electrical Power Conditioning, Distribution, and Control (MCD)
EPCER ...... Experimental Patrol Craft, Escort and Rescue
EPCI .... Enhanced Peripheral Communication Interface [*Motorola, Inc.*]
EPCO .... Emergency Power Cutoff [*NASA*] (KSC)
EPCO .... Engine Parts Coordinating Office [*Navy*]
EPCO .... Engineer Procurement Office [*Army*]
EPCOT...... Experimental Prototype Community of Tomorrow [*Disney World*] [*Facetious translation: "Every Person Comes Out Tired"*]
EPCP .... Electric Plant Control Panel
EPCRA ...... Emergency Planning and Community Right-to-Know Act [*1986*]
EPCRTK ... Emergency Planning and Community Right-to-Know Act [*1986*]
EPCS .... Earnings and Profits Calculation System
EPCS .... Engineer Functional Components System (AABC)
EPCS .... Experiment Point Control System [*or Subsystem*] [*NASA*] (KSC)
EPCU........ Electrical Power Control Unit (MCD)
EPD .... Earliest Possible Date
EPD .... Earliest Practicable Date (AFIT)
EPD .... Eastern Procurement Division [*Navy*]
EPD .... Eastern Production District [*Navy*]
EPD .... Electric Power Database [*Electric Power Research Institute*] [*Information service or system*] (IID)
EPD .... Electric Power Distribution
EP & D....... Electrical Power and Distribution (CET)
EPD .... Electronic Proximity Detector (MCD)
EPD .... Emergency Procedures Document (MCD)
EPD .... Energetic Particles Detector [*Geophysics*]
EPD .... Engineering Planning Document
EPD .... Enlisted Personnel Directorate [*Army*]
EPD .... Enlisted Personnel Division [*Navy*]
EPD .... Environmental Protection Devices (MCD)
EPD .... Eplett Dairies Ltd. [*Toronto Stock Exchange symbol*]
EPD .... European Progressive Democrats (PPE)
EPD .... Excess Profits Duty
EPD .... Exchange Parameter Definitions [*Telecommunications*] (TEL)
EPD .... Exponential Power Distribution [*Statistics*]
EPD .... Extra Police Duty [*Extra cleaning chores*] [*Military*]

EPDA .... Education Professions Development Act [*1965*]
EPDA .... Educational Professional Development Assistance [*Office of Education*]
EPDA .... Emergency Powers Defence Act [*British*] [*World War II*]
EPDB........ Electrical Power Distribution Box   (MCD)
EPDB........ Environmental Protection Data Base [*Environmental Protection Agency*]
EPDB........ Experiment Power Distribution Box   (NASA)
EPDC........ Economic Power Dispatch Computer
EPDC........ Electrical Power Distribution and Control   (NASA)
EPDCC...... Elementary Potential Digital Computing Component
EPDCC...... European Pressure Die Casting Committee   (EA)
EPDCS ...... Electrical Power Distribution and Control System   (KSC)
EPDF........ Engineer Performance Description Form [*Test*]
EPDM .... Ethiopian People's Democratic Movement [*Political party*]
EPDM .... Ethylene-Propylene-Diene Monomer [*Rubber, ASTM nomenclature*]
EPDML..... Epidemiological
EPDMLGY ... Epidemiology
EPDO .... Enlisted Personnel Distribution Office [*Navy*]
EPDOCONUS ... Enlisted Personnel Distribution Office, Continental United States [*Navy*]
EPDOLANT ... Enlisted Personnel Distribution Office, Atlantic Fleet [*Navy*]
EPDOPAC ... Enlisted Personnel Distribution Office, Pacific Fleet [*Navy*]   (MUGU)
EPDP........ Engineering Program Definition Plan   (MCD)
EPD/RDIS ... Electric Power Database/Research and Development Information System [*Electric Power Research Institute*] [*Information service or system*]   (IID)
EPDS........ Electrical Power Distribution System [*or Subsystem*]   (KSC)
EPDS........ Electronic Parts Distributors' Show
EPDT........ Estimated Project Duration Time
EPDU .... Ethiopian People's Democratic Union   (EA)
EPDWO ...... Engineering and Product Development Work Order
EPE............ Economic Policy towards Eire [*British*]
EPE............ Editorial Projects in Education   (EA)
EPE............ Electronic Parts and Equipment   (NATG)
EPE............ Electrophoresis Experiment [*NASA*]   (MCD)
EPE............ Electrostatic Probe Experiment
EPE............ Emergency Passenger Exit
EPE............ Emergency Preparedness Evaluation [*Nuclear energy*]   (NRCH)
EPE............ Energetic Particles Explorer [*Satellite*] [*NASA*]
EPE............ Ethniki Politiki Enosis [*National Political Union*] [*Greek*]   (PPE)
EPE............ Experimental and Proving Establishment [*Canada*]   (MCD)
EPE............ Explosion-Proof Enclosure
EPE............ Export Direction [*A publication*]
EPE............ Pellston, MI [*Location identifier*] [*FAA*]   (FAAL)
EPEA........ Electrical Power Engineers' Association [*A union*] [*British*]
EPEA........ Experiment Pointing Electronic Assembly [*NASA*]
EPEA........ Exploratory Project for Economic Alternatives   (EA)
EPEAA...... Employing Photo-Engravers Association of America [*Defunct*]   (EA)
EPEBD7 .... Environmental Pollution. Series A. Ecological and Biological [*A publication*]
EPEC........ Emerson Programmer-Evaluator-Controller [*Data processing*]
EPEC........ Enteropathogenic Escherichia coli [*Also, EEC*] [*Medicine*]
EPEEA ...... Enlisted Personnel Enlistment Eligibility Activity [*Army*]
EPEN........ Greek National Political Society   (PPW)
EP/EO....... Employee Plans/Exempt Organization [*IRS*]
EPEOD...... Energy People [*A publication*]
EPER .... Emergency Project for Equal Rights   (EA)
E-PERM.... Electret-Passive Environmental Radon Monitor [*Rad-Elec, Inc.*]
EPESA ...... Ediciones y Publicaciones Espanolas Sociedad Anonima [*A publication*]
Epet.......... Epeteris tes Hetaireias Byzantinon Spoudon [*A publication*]
EPF.......... Education Projects Fund [*British Council/Overseas Development Administration*]   (DS)
EPF.......... Emergency Plant Facilities
EPF.......... End of Programmed Flight   (MCD)
EPF.......... Endothelial Proliferating Factor [*Biochemistry*]
EPF.......... Episcopal Peace Fellowship   (EA)
EPF.......... Esparros [*France*] [*Seismograph station code, US Geological Survey*]   (SEIS)
EPF.......... Established Program Financing
EPF.......... European Packaging Federation   (EAIO)
EPF.......... European Psycho-Analytical Federation   (EA)
EPF.......... Exophthalmos-Producing Factor [*Endocrinology*]
EPF.......... Expected Provident Fund
EPF.......... Exploitation Products File   (MCD)
EPF.......... Extra-Pair Fertilization [*Biology*]
EPFBA ...... Florida. University. Engineering and Industrial Experiment Station. Bulletin Series [*A publication*]
EPFCL....... Elvis Presley Fan Club of Luxembourg   (EAIO)
E & P Forum ... Oil Industry International Exploration and Production Forum   (EA)
EPFSU ...... Earth's Physical Features Study Unit   (EA)
EPFTR....... Expert Panel on the Facilitation of Tuna Research [*Marine science*]   (MSC)
EPG .... Ecole Polytechnique, Publications Officielles [*UTLAS symbol*]

EPG .... Economic Policy Group
EPG .... Economic Pressure on Germany Committee [*War Cabinet*] [*British*] [*World War II*]
EPG .... Edit Program Generator
EPG .... Eggs per Gram [*Parasitology*]
EPG .... Electrical Power Generator   (NASA)
EPG .... Electrolytic Plunge Grinder
EPG .... Electronic Program Guide [*Cable-television system*]
EPG .... Electronic Proving Ground [*Army*]   (MCD)
EPG .... Electropneumogram [*Medicine*]
EPG .... Electrostatic Power Generator
EPG .... Emergency Power Generator
EPG .... Eminent Persons Group [*Group of elder statesmen from Commonwealth countries*]
EPG .... Empire Gold Resources Ltd. [*Vancouver Stock Exchange symbol*]
EPG .... Employee Participation Group
EPG .... Eniwetok Proving Ground [*AEC*]
EpG .... EP Group of Companies, Microform Division, Wakefield, Yorkshire, United Kingdom [*Library symbol*] [*Library of Congress*]   (LCLS)
EPG .... European Participating Governments [*In the F-16 fighter program*]
EPG .... European Press Group
EPG .... European Programme Group [*NATO*]   (RDA)
EPG .... Weeping Water, NE [*Location identifier*] [*FAA*]   (FAAL)
EPGA .... Emergency Petroleum and Gas Administration [*Department of the Interior*]
EPGCR...... Experimental Prototype Gas-Cooled Reactor
EPGD .... Gdansk/Rebiechowo [*Poland*] [*ICAO location identifier*]   (ICLI)
EPGR........ Electrical Potential Gradient Radiosonde [*Meteorology*]
EPGRS ...... Employment Policy Grievance Review Staff [*OSA*]
EPGS .... Electric Power Generation System
EPh .... Ecclesiasticos Pharos [*A publication*]
EPH .... Electric Process Heating   (MCD)
EPH .... Electronic Package Housing
EPH .... Employ the Physically Handicapped
EpH .... Epeirotike Hestia [*A publication*]
Eph............ Ephesians [*New Testament book*]
EPH .... Ephraim
EPH .... Ephrata, WA [*Location identifier*] [*FAA*]   (FAAL)
EPH .... Epoch Capital Corp. [*Vancouver Stock Exchange symbol*]
EPh .... Etudes Philosophiques [*A publication*]
EPH .... Explosion-Proof Housing
EPHC .... Eastern Pacific Hurricane Center [*San Francisco*] [*National Weather Service*]   (NOAA)
EphC .... Ephemerides Carmeliticae [*A publication*]
EphCarm ... Ephemerides Carmeliticae. Cura Pontificiae Facultatis Theologicae S. Teresiae a Jesu et Ionnis a Cruce [*Rome*] [*A publication*]
Eph Dac ..... Ephemerides Dacoromana [*A publication*]
EPHE .... Ecole Pratique des Hautes Etudes [*A publication*]
EPHE/H ... Homme. Revue Francaise d'Anthropologie. La Sorbonne, l'Ecole Pratique des Hautes Etudes [*A publication*]
Eph Ep ...... Ephemeris Epigraphica [*A publication*]
Eph Epigr .. Ephemeris Epigraphica [*A publication*]   (OCD)
Ephes .... Ephesians [*New Testament book*]   (ROG)
EPHESHPhA ... Ecole Pratique des Hautes Etudes. IVe Section. Sciences Historiques et Philologiques. Annuaire [*A publication*]
EPHESRA ... Ecole Pratique des Hautes Etudes. Ve Section. Sciences Religieuses. Annuaire [*A publication*]
EPhi........... English Philips [*Record label*]
EPhK .... Egyetemes Philologiai Koezloeny [*A publication*]
EPHL......... Eastern Professional Hockey League
EphL.......... Ephemerides Liturgicae [*A publication*]
EphLitg...... Ephemerides Liturgicae [*Rome*] [*A publication*]
EphMar ..... Ephemerides Mariologicae [*Madrid*] [*A publication*]
EPhMRA... European Pharmaceutical Marketing Research Association   (EAIO)
EPHO .... Ephemeris - Orbit
EPHR .... Ephemeris - Reentry
Ephr .... Ephraim   (BJA)
EPHSOC... Ephemera Society [*British*]
Eph Th L ... Ephemerides Theologicae Lovanienses [*A publication*]
EPI............ Eagle-Picher Industries, Inc. [*NYSE symbol*]   (SPSG)
EPI............ Earth Path Indicator
EPI............ Economic Performance Indicator [*New York Stock Exchange*]
EPI............ Economic Policy Institute   (EA)
EPI............ Economic Procurement Item   (NATG)
EPI............ Educational Planning Institute   (EA)
EPI............ Edwards Personality Inventory [*Psychology*]
EPI............ Ehrenreich Photo-Optical Industries, Inc.
EPI............ Electron Photon Interaction
EPI............ Electronic Position Indicator
EPI............ Elevation Position Indicator [*Aviation*]
EPI............ Emergency Public Information [*Civil Defense*]
EPI............ Emulsion Polymers Institute   (EA)
EPI............ Engine Performance Indicator   (NG)
EPI............ Environmental Policy Institute   (EA)
EPI............ Epidote [*Petrology*]

EPI............ Epilogue (ROG)
EPI............ Epinephrine [*Endocrinology*]
EPI............ Epistilbite [*A zeolite*]
EPI............ European Paper Institute [*Research center*]
EPI............ Evoked Potential Index [*Neurophysiology*]
EPI............ Expanded Plan Indicator
EPI............ Expanded Position Indicator
EPI............ Expanded Programme on Immunization [*World Health Organization*]
EPI............ Extension Producing Interneuron [*Neurology*]
EPI............ Eysenck Personality Inventory [*Psychology*]
EPIA......... Electric Power Industry Abstracts [*Utility Data Institute*] [*Information service or system*]
EPIA......... End Poverty in America Society (EA)
EPIAI....... EP [*Elvis Presley*] Impersonators Association International (EA)
EPIC......... Earth-Pointing Instrument Carrier [*A satellite*]
EPIC.....,... El Paso [*Texas*] Intelligence Center [*Drug Enforcement Administration; Border Patrol; US Customs Service; Bureau of Alcohol, Tobacco, and Firearms; FAA; US Coast Guard*]
EPIC......... Electronic Photochromic Integrating Cathode-Ray [*Tube*]
EPIC......... Electronic Portable Information Center [*Data processing*]
EPIC......... Electronic Product Information Center [*Buick's computerized information network and database*]
EPIC......... Electronic Properties Information Center [*DoD*]
EPIC......... Embedded Post-Beamformer Interference Canceler (CAAL)
EPIC......... Emergency Programs Information Center [*Database*]
EPIC......... End Poverty in California [*Slogan used by Upton Sinclair during campaign as Democratic candidate for governor of California, 1934*]
EPIC......... Energy Conservation Program Guide for Industry and Commerce [*Department of Commerce*]
EPIC......... Energy Policy Information Center [*Defunct*] (EA)
EPIC......... Enhanced Performance Implanted CMOS [*Texas Instruments, Inc.*]
EPIC......... Environmental Photographic Interpretation Center [*Environmental Protection Agency*]
EPIC......... EPIC Health Group, Inc. [*NASDAQ symbol*] (NQ)
EPIC......... Epitaxial Passivated Integrated Circuits (MCD)
EPIC......... Estates Property Investment Co. [*British*]
EPIC......... Estimate of Properties for Industrial Chemistry [*Universite de Liege*] [*Database*]
EPIC......... European Proliferation Information Centre [*British*] (CB)
EPIC......... Evaluator Programmer Integrated Circuit [*NASA*]
EPIC......... Evidence Photographers International Council (EA)
EPIC......... Exchange Price Indicators [*Database*] [*British*]
EPIC......... Exhaust Plume Interference Characterization [*NASA*] (KSC)
EPIC......... Export Processing Industry Coalition
EPIC......... Extended Performance and Increased Capability
EPIC......... External Pneumatic Intermittent Compression
EPIC......... Extraterrestrial Photographic Information Center [*NASA*]
EPICA....... Ecumenical Program for Inter American Communication and Action [*Later, EPCAC*] (EA)
EPICS....... Enlisted Personnel Individualized Career System [*Military*] (MCD)
EPICS....... European Petrochemical Industry Computerized System [*Parpinelli Tecnon*] [*Italy*] [*Information service or system*] (IID)
Epict Diss .. Epicteti Dissertationes [*of Arrian*] [*Classical studies*] (OCD)
EPID......... Epidemic
EPIDEM ... Epidemiological (ADA)
Epidemiol Community Health ... Epidemiology and Community Health [*A publication*]
Epidemiol Mikrobiol Infekts Boles ... Epidemiologiya Mikrobiologiya i Infektsiozni Bolesti [*A publication*]
Epidemiol Rev ... Epidemiologic Reviews [*A publication*]
Epidemiol Rev (Engl Transl Przegl Epidemiol) ... Epidemiological Review (English Translation of Przeglad Epidemiologiczny) [*A publication*]
Epidem Mikrobiol ... Epidemiologiya Mikrobiologiya i Infektsiozni Bolesti [*A publication*]
EPIE......... Educational Products Information Exchange
EPIEI....... Educational Products Information Exchange Institute [*Later, EPIE Institute*] (EA)
EPIGAS..... Epigastrium [*The part above the stomach*] [*Pharmacy*] (ROG)
Epig Indica ... Epigraphia Indica [*A publication*]
Epigr......... Epigrammata [*of Theocritus*] [*Classical studies*] (OCD)
Epigr......... Epigrammata [*of Callimachus*] [*Classical studies*] (OCD)
Epigr......... Epigrammata Super Exilio [*of Seneca the Younger*] [*Classical studies*] (OCD)
Epigraph Stud ... Epigraphische Studies [*A publication*]
Epigr Gr ..... Epigrammata Graeca ex Lapidibus Conlecta [*A publication*] (OCD)
Epigr Vostok ... Epigrafika Vostoka. Sbornik Statei [*A publication*]
EPIL......... Epilepsy
EPIL......... Epilogue
EPILA....... Epilepsia [*A publication*]
EPIN......... Electronic Personnel Information Network [*Data Corp. of America*]
Epin........... Epinomis [*of Plato*] [*Classical studies*] (OCD)

EPINT....... Executive Program Initialize
EPIO......... Employment Prospects by Industry and Occupation [*A publication*] (ADA)
EPIP .... Emergency Plan Implementing Procedure [*Nuclear energy*] (NRCH)
EPIPH...... Epiphany
EPIRB ...... Emergency Position-Indicating Radio Beacon (MCD)
EPIREPT .. Epidemiological Report
EPIS .... Episcopal
EPIS .... Episiotomy [*Obstetrics*]
EPIS .... Epistle
EPIS .... Exchange Price Information Service [*Finance*] [*British*]
Epist.......... Epistulae [*of Sidonius Apollinaris*] [*Classical studies*] (OCD)
Epist.......... Epistulae [*of Horace*] [*Classical studies*] (OCD)
Epistemon Epeteris Kteniatr Sch ... Epistemonike Epeteris Kteniatrikes Scholes [*A publication*]
Epistolog Graec ... Epistolographi Graeci [*A publication*] (OCD)
EPISTOM ... Epistomium [*A Stopper*] [*Pharmacy*]
EPIT .... Epitaph
Epit .... Epitomae [*of Livy*] [*Classical studies*] (OCD)
Epit .... Epitome [*of Apollodorus*] [*Classical studies*] (OCD)
EPIT .... Epitome
EPITH...... Epithelium [*Medicine*]
EPITH...... Epithet (ROG)
Epit Oxyrh ... Epitome Oxyrhynchica [*of Livy*] [*Classical studies*] (OCD)
EPIX .... EPI International, Inc. [*NASDAQ symbol*] (NQ)
EPJ .... Essay-Proof Journal [*A publication*]
EpJer .... Epistle of Jeremy [*Apocrypha*] (BJA)
EPK.......... Egyetemes Philologiai Koezloeny [*A publication*]
EPK.......... Electronic Press Kit
EPK.......... Entwicklungspolitische Korrespondenz [*A publication*]
EPK.......... Epitek International, Inc. [*Toronto Stock Exchange symbol*]
EPK.......... Equipotential Kathode
EPK.......... Ethnikon Phileleftheron Komma [*National Liberal Party*] [*Greek*] (PPE)
EPK.......... Partido Comunista de Euzkadi/Euzkadiko Partidu Komunista [*Basque Communist Party*] (PPW)
EPKE........ Epitheoresis Koinonikon Ereunon [*A publication*]
EPKK........ Krakow/Balice [*Poland*] [*ICAO location identifier*] (ICLI)
EPKL........ European Pan-Keltic League (EA)
EPL.......... Early Programming Language [*Data processing*]
EPL.......... Edmonton Public Library [*UTLAS symbol*]
EPL.......... Effective Privilege Level [*Data processing*]
EPL.......... Ejercito Popular de Liberacion [*Popular Liberation Army*] [*El Salvador*] (PD)
EPL.......... Ejercito Popular de Liberacion [*Popular Liberation Army*] [*Colombia*]
EPL.......... Electrical Power Level (MCD)
EPL.......... Electronic, Electrical, and Electromechanical Parts List (NASA)
EPL.......... Electronic Intelligence Parameter Limits
EPL.......... Electroplate (MSA)
EPL.......... Elliptically Polarized Light
EPL.......... Emergency Power Level (KSC)
EPL.......... Emitter Position Location
EPL.......... Emitter Program Library (CAAL)
EPL.......... Encoder Programming Language [*Data processing*]
EPL.......... Engineering Parts List (KSC)
E & PL ...... Entry and Postlanding [*NASA*] (KSC)
EPL.......... Environmental Protection Limit (NRCH)
EPL.......... Equipment Performance Log
EPL.......... Erie County Library, Erie, PA [*OCLC symbol*] (OCLC)
EPL.......... Excess Profits Levy [*British*]
EPL.......... Extensor Pollicis Longus [*Anatomy*]
e-pl--- .... Poland [*MARC geographic area code*] [*Library of Congress*] (LCCP)
EPLA........ Electronics Precedence List Agency
EPLAF....... European Planning Federation [*London, England*] (EA)
EPLANS ... Engineering, Planning, and Analysis Systems [*Telecommunications*] (TEL)
EPLD........ Electrically Programmable Logic Device [*Data processing*]
EPL/DRL ... Engineering Parts List/Drawing Release List (KSC)
EPLF........ Eritrean People's Liberation Front [*Ethiopia*] (PD)
EPLN........ Epolin, Inc. [*NASDAQ symbol*] (NQ)
EPLRS....... Enhanced Position Location Reporting System [*Army*] (INF)
EPLS .... Eastern Peninsula Library System [*Library network*]
EPLT .... Electrocon International, Inc. [*NASDAQ symbol*] (NQ)
EPM .... Earth-Probe-Mars [*Angle*]
EPM .... Ecole Polytechnique, Bibliotheque [*Montreal*] [*UTLAS symbol*]
EPM .... Economic Planning Machine [*British*]
EPM .... Education for Public Management [*Program*] [*Civil Service Commission*] (RDA)
EPM .... Educational and Psychological Measurement [*A publication*]
EPM .... Educator's Purchasing Master [*A publication*]
EPM .... Elastic Plastic Membrane
EPM .... Electron Probe Microanalysis [*Also, EPMA*]
EPM .... Electronic Parts Manual
EPM .... Emigration Portfolio Manager [*Investment term*]
EPM .... Empirical Pseudopotential Method [*Physics*]
EPM .... Energy-Protein Malnutrition
EPM .... Engineering Procedures Manual

EPM .... Environmental Pollution Management [*A publication*]
EPM .... Environmental Project Manager (NRCH)
EPM .... Etudes de Philosophie Medievale [*A publication*]
EPM .... External Polarization Modulation (IEEE)
EPMA........ Electron Probe Microanalysis [*Also, EPM*]
EPMAC..... Enlisted Personnel Management Center [*Navy*] (NVT)
EPMARKUP ... European Publishers' Markup User Group
EPMaRV ... Earth Penetrating Maneuverable Reentry Vehicle [*Military*]
EPMAU ... Expected Present Multiattribute Utility (IEEE)
EPMCC..... Enesco Precious Moments Collectors' Club (EA)
EPMD .... Enlisted Personnel Management Directorate
EPMD .... Eric and Parrish Making Dollars [*Rap recording group*]
EPMEA..... Educational and Psychological Measurement [*A publication*]
EPMF .... Employees' Plan Master File [*IRS*]
EPMP........ Ethyl(para-Nitrophenyl)methylphosphonate [*Biochemistry*]
EPMS .... Engine Performance Monitoring System (MCD)
EPMS .... Engineering Performance Management System (NASA)
EPMS .... Engineering Performance Measurement System (MCD)
EPMS .... Engineering Project Management System (MCD)
EPMS .... Enlisted Personnel Management System [*Army*] (AABC)
EPMSR ..... Environment Canada. Pacific Marine Science Reports [*A publication*]
EPN .... Effective Perceived Noise [*Aviation*]
EPN .... Engineering Program Notice (AFIT)
EPN .... Epena [*Congo*] [*Airport symbol*] (OAG)
EPN .... Ethyl para-Nitrophenyl Phenylphosphonothioate [*Insecticide*]
EPN .... European Plastics News [*A publication*]
EPN .... Excitatory Premotor Neuron [*Neurology*]
EPN .... Expansion [*A publication*]
EPNdB..... Effective-Perceived-Noise Decibel Level [*Aviation*]
EPNED...... Energy Planning Network [*A publication*]
EPNL........ Effective-Perceived-Noise Level [*Aviation*]
EPNP........ Epoxy(nitrophenoxy)propane [*Organic chemistry*]
EPNS........ Electroplated Nickel Silver
EPNS........ English Place-Name Society
EPO .... Earth Parking Orbit [*Apollo*] [*NASA*]
EPO .... Elected Public Official
EPO .... Electron Plasma Oscillation [*Astrophysics*]
EPO .... Electrostatic Plasma Oscillator
EPO .... Element Project Office [*NASA*] (NASA)
EPO .... Emergency Planning Officer [*Army*]
EPO .... Emergency Power Off
EPO .... Energy Policy Office [*Formerly, National Energy Office*] [*Executive Office of the President*] [*Abolished, 1974*]
EPO .... Engine Project Office [*NASA*] (KSC)
EPO .... Engine Propeller Order (MSA)
EPO .... Environmental, Population, and Organismic Biology
EPO .... Eosinophil Peroxidase [*An enzyme*]
EPO .... Epidemiology Program Office [*Department of Health and Human Services*] (GRD)
EPO .... Erythropoietin [*Also, Ep*] [*Hematology*]
EPo .... Esperienza Poetica [*A publication*]
EPO .... Estuarine Programs Office [*National Oceanic and Atmospheric Administration*]
EPO .... European Patent Office [*Federal Republic of Germany*] (EY)
EPO .... Examination Procedure Outline [*Weighing equipment*]
EPO .... Experiment Performance Option
EPO .... Expo Oil [*Vancouver Stock Exchange symbol*]
e-po---......... Portugal [*MARC geographic area code*] [*Library of Congress*] (LCCP)
EPOA .... Eastcoast Petroleum Operators' Association [*Canada*]
EPOA .... Exercise Plan of Analysis (MCD)
EPOBAK.. EPPO [*European and Mediterranean Plant Protection Organization*] Publications. Series C [*A publication*]
EPOC .... Eastern Pacific Oceanic Conference
EPOC .... Employment Policy and Organization Committee [*British*] (DCTA)
EPOC .... Equity Policy Center (EA)
EPOC .... Evening Primrose Oil Capsules [*Trade name*] [*British*]
EPOC .... External Payload Operations Center
EPOCA..... Environmental Project on Central America (EA)
EPOCS ..... Equatorial Pacific Ocean Climate Studies [*National Oceanic and Atmospheric Administration*]
Epod.......... Epodi [*of Horace*] [*Classical studies*] (OCD)
EPOE........ End Piece of Equipment
EPOI........ Ehrenreich Photo-Optical Industries, Inc.
EPOP........ Each Pays Own Postage
EPOS........ Electronic Point-of-Sale [*Data processing*]
EPP........... Concord, NH [*Location identifier*] [*FAA*] (FAAL)
EPP........... Earth Physics Program
EPP........... Editions Phonographiques Parisiennes - Allegro Label [*Record label*] [*France*]
EPP........... Effective Program Projections
EPP........... Electric Power Plant (MCD)
EPP........... Electrical Power Panel (MCD)
EPP........... Emergency Power Package (NG)
EPP........... End Plate Potential
EPP........... End Point Prediction
EPP........... Engineering and Public Policy [*Graduate program, Carnegie-Mellon University*]
EPP........... Environmental Protection Program (CAAL)

EPP........... Epistolae [*Epistles, Letters*] [*Latin*] (ROG)
EPP........... Equal Payment Plan
EPP........... Erythropoietic Protoporphyria [*A genetic disorder*]
EPP........... Estimating Price Policy
EPP........... Estonian Papers in Phonetics [*A publication*]
EPP........... European People's Party - Federation of Christian Democratic Parties of the European Community [*Brussels, Belgium*]
EPP........... European Producer Price
EPP........... Excess Personal Property
EPP........... Exchangeable-Potassium-Percentage
EPP........... Executive Promotion Program [*FAA*] (FAAC)
EPPA .... Employee Polygraph Protection Act of 1988
EPPA .... Established Pattern of Psychodynamic Adaptation
EPPAPA..... European Pure Phosphoric Acid Producers' Association (EAIO)
EPPASF .... Elvis Presley Performing Arts Scholarship Foundation (EA)
EPPASFV ... Elvis Presley Performing Arts Scholarship Foundation of Virginia [*Later, EPPASF*] (EA)
EPPB .... Export Promotion Programme Budget [*British*]
EPPC .... Ethics and Public Policy Center (EA)
EPPHI....... Educators of Professional Personnel for the Hearing Impaired
EPPI .... Eastern Pennsylvania Psychiatric Institute
EPPI .... Electronic Programmed Procurement Information (NG)
EPPIC........ Educate People - Protect Innocent Children (EA)
EPPL .... Electronic Preferred Parts List [*Jet Propulsion Laboratory, NASA*]
EPPL .... Emergency Production Planning List [*Army*]
EPPO........ Earth Physics and Physical Oceanography Program [*NASA*]
EPPO........ European and Mediterranean Plant Protection Organization [*See also OEPP*] (EAIO)
EPPO........ Poznan/Lawica [*Poland*] [*ICAO location identifier*] (ICLI)
EPPO Bull ... EPPO [*European and Mediterranean Plant Protection Organization*] Bulletin [*A publication*]
EPPO (Eur Mediterr Plant Prot Organ) Publ Ser C ... EPPO (European and Mediterranean Plant Protection Organization) Publications. Series C [*A publication*]
EPPO Plant Health Newsl Publ Ser B ... EPPO [*European and Mediterranean Plant Protection Organization*] Plant Health Newsletter Publications. Series B [*A publication*]
EPPO Publ Ser C ... EPPO [*European and Mediterranean Plant Protection Organization*] Publications. Series C [*A publication*]
EPPP .... Emergency Production Planning Program [*Navy*] (NG)
EPPS .... Edwards Personal Preference Scale [*or Schedule*] [*Psychology*]
EPPS .... Electrical Power/Pyro Sequential System (MCD)
EPPT/S ..... Electrical Power Production Technician/Specialist (AAG)
EPPVS....... Emergency Propulsive Propellant Venting System
EPQ .... Embarrassing Personal Question [*National Security Agency screening procedure*]
EPQ .... Eysenck Personality Questionnaire [*Personality development test*] [*Psychology*]
EPR........... Earnings Price Ratio
EPR........... Earthquake Prediction Research [*A publication*]
EPR........... East Pacific Rise [*Geology*]
EPR........... Eastern Pakistan Rifles [*British military*] (DMA)
EPR........... Economic Production Rate (MCD)
EPR........... Economische Politierechter [*A publication*]
EPR........... Einstein-Podolsky-Rosen [*Quantum mechanics*]
EPR........... El Paraiso Resources Ltd. [*Vancouver Stock Exchange symbol*]
EPR........... Electrical Pressure Regulator (IEEE)
EPR........... Electrochemical Potentiokinetic Reactivation [*Metallurgical test*]
EPR........... Electromechanical Potentiokinetic Reactivation Test [*Nuclear energy*] (NRCH)
EPR........... Electron Paramagnetic Resonance [*Also, ESR*] [*Physics*]
EPR........... Electronic Parts Reliability
EPR........... Electronic Procurement Regulation [*Defense Supply Agency*]
EPR........... Electronic Publishing Review [*A publication*]
EPR........... Electrophrenic Respiration [*Medicine*]
EPR........... Elimination of Purchase Requirement [*Department of Agriculture*]
EPR........... Emergency Parts Requisition (KSC)
EPR........... Engine Power [*or Pressure*] Ratio
EPR........... Engineer Photographic and Reproduction [*Marine Corps*]
EPR........... Engineering Parts Release (KSC)
EPR........... Engineering Power Reactor
EPR........... Equipment Performance Report
EPR........... Equipotential Region
EPR........... Equivalent Parallel Resistance (DEN)
EPR........... Error Pattern Register
EPR........... Esperance [*Australia*] [*Airport symbol*] (OAG)
EPR........... Essential Performance Requirements (NATG)
EPR........... Estimated Price Request (MCD)
EPR........... Ethylene Propylene Rubber [*Organic chemistry*]
EPr........... Etudes de Presse [*A publication*]
EPR........... Evaluation Project Report [*Air Force*]
EPR........... Exhaust Pressure Ratio
EPR........... Exhaust Pressure Regulator [*Automotive engineering*]
EPR........... Experimental Power Reactor (MCD)
EPR........... Explosion-Proof Relay
EPR........... External Power Relay (MCD)
EPR........... Extreme Pressure Ratio [*Military*]
EPR........... Eye Point of Regard [*NASA*]

EPRA........	Early Planning for Retirement Association [*Australia*]
EPRA........	Eastern Psychiatric Research Association (EA)
EPRA........	Electronic Production Resources Agency [*Military*]
EPRAD......	Elektro-Praktiker [*A publication*]
ePRAI.......	Escherichia Coli Phosphoribosyl Anthranilate Isomerase
EPRC........	European Policies Research Centre [*University of Strathclyde*] [*Glasgow, Scotland*] [*Database producer*] (IID)
EPRCD......	Electric Power Research Institute (Report) EPRI CS [*A publication*]
EPRD........	Electrical Power Requirements Data
EPRD........	Emergency Plans and Readiness Division [*of OEP*] [*Terminated*]
EPRDA7....	Economic Proceedings. Royal Dublin Society [*A publication*]
EPRDB8....	Ekologia Polska. Seria B [*A publication*]
EPRF........	Environmental Prediction Research Facility [*Monterey, CA*] [*Navy*]
EPRF........	Exhausted Publications Reference File (MCD)
EPRG........	Emergency Planning Review Guideline [*Nuclear energy*] (NRCH)
EPR/G.......	End-Paper Rubbed, Else Good [*Condition*] [*Antiquarian book trade*]
EPRI........	Electric Power Research Institute [*Information service or system*] (IID)
EPRI........	Engine Pressure Ratio Indicator
EPRI........	Environmental Protection Research Institute
EPRI J.......	EPRI [*Electric Power Research Institute*] Journal [*A publication*]
EPRI Rep NP ...	EPRI [*Electric Power Research Institute*] Report. NP [*United States*] [*A publication*]
EPRJD......	EPRI [*Electric Power Research Institute*] Journal [*A publication*]
EPRL........	Electric Power Research Laboratory [*Arizona State University*] [*Research center*] (RCD)
EPRL........	Warszawa [*Poland*] [*ICAO location identifier*] (ICLI)
EPRLF.......	Eelam People's Revolutionary Liberation Front [*Sri Lanka*] [*Political party*]
EPRM........	Equipment Performance Report Management System (MCD)
EPRN........	Emergency Program Release Notice [*NASA*] (NASA)
EPRO........	Eastern Professional River Outfitters Association (EA)
EPRO........	Etudes Preliminaires aux Religions Orientales dans l'Empire Romain [*A publication*] (BJA)
EPROER....	Etudes Preliminaires aux Religions Orientales dans l'Empire Romain [*A publication*]
EPROM....	Erasable Programmable Read-Only Memory [*Data processing*] (MCD)
EPRP........	Ethiopian People's Revolutionary Party [*Political party*] (PD)
EPRS........	Electron Paramagnetic Resonance Spectroscopy
EPRTCS....	Emergency Power Ride-Through Capability System [*Nuclear energy*] (NRCH)
ePrv..........	Enolpyruvate [*Biochemistry*]
EPRZ........	Rzeszow/Jasionka [*Poland*] [*ICAO location identifier*] (ICLI)
EPS............	Early Prolific Straightneck Summer Squash
EPS............	Earnings per Share [*Finance*]
EPS............	Earth-Probe-Sun [*Angle*]
EPS............	El Paso Southern Railway Co. [*AAR code*]
EPS............	Elastosis Perforans Serpiginosa [*Medicine*]
EPS............	Electric Power Source (MCD)
EPS............	Electric Power Steering System [*Automotive engineering*]
EPS............	Electric Power System [*or Subsystem*] (NRCH)
EPS............	Electric Propulsion System
EPS............	Electrical Power Storage (ROG)
EPS............	Electrical Power Supply
EPS............	Electrical Power System [*or Subsystem*]
EPS............	Electrochemical Photocapacitance Spectroscopy
EPS............	Electromagnetic Position Sensor
EPS............	Electron-Proton Spectrometer
EPS............	Electronic Payments System
EPS............	Electronic Power Steering [*Mitsubishi*] [*Automotive engineering*]
EPS............	Electronic Publishing System (BYTE)
EPS............	Electrophysiologic Study
EPS............	Electropneumatic Gear Shift [*System*]
EPS............	Embossing Press Station
EPS............	Emergency Power Supply
EPS............	Emergency Power System
EPS............	Emergency Pressurization System
EPS............	Emergency Procurement Service [*Later, Defense Materials Service*]
EPS............	Encapsulated Post-Script [*Data processing*]
EPS............	Encoder Power Supply
EPS............	Endoscopic Paravariceal Sclerotherapy [*Medicine*]
EPS............	Energetic Particles Satellite [*NASA*] (MUGU)
EPS............	Engineering Performance Standards
EPS............	Engineering Planning Skeleton (MCD)
EPS............	Engineering Print System [*Xerox*]
EPS............	Engineering Procedures Services (MCD)
EPS............	Engineering Purchase Specification
EPS............	English Philological Studies [*A publication*]
EPS............	Entertainment Production Services [*British*]
EPS............	Environmental Protection Service, West Vancouver [*Environment Canada*] [*Research center*] (RCD)

EPS............	Environmental Protection Shelter (MCD)
EPS............	Environmental Protection System (AAG)
EPS............	Environmental Purification Systems, Inc.
EPS............	Equilibrium Problem Solver (IEEE)
EPS............	Equipment Policy Statement [*Army*] (AABC)
EPS............	Equipotential Surface
EPS............	Equivalent Prior Sample [*Information*] [*Statistics*]
EPS............	Essay-Proof Society (EA)
EPS............	Ethiopian Philatelic Society (EA)
EPS............	European Physical Society (EAIO)
EPS............	Even Parity Select
EPS............	Event Processing System
EPS............	Excitation Power Supply (MCD)
EPS............	Executive Planning Section [*British military*] (DMA)
EPS............	Executive Profile Survey [*Management and supervision test*]
EPS............	Executive Protective Service [*Formerly, White House Police; later, USSS/UD*]
EPS............	Exercise Planning Staff [*NATO*] (NATG)
EPS............	Exophthalmos-Producing Substance [*Endocrinology*]
EPS............	Exotic Pathology Society [*Paris, France*] (EAIO)
EPS............	Expandable Polystyrene [*Plastics technology*]
EPS............	Experiment Pointing System [*NASA*]
EPS............	Experimental Power Supply (NASA)
EPS............	Experimental Procurement Service
EPS............	Experimental Psychology Society [*British*]
EPS............	Experimental Publications System [*Defunct*]
EPS............	Expressed Prostatic Secretion [*Physiology*]
EPS............	Extensible Programming System [*Data processing*] (CSR)
EPS............	External Page Storage [*Data processing*] (BUR)
EPS............	Extrapyramidal Symptoms [*Medicine*]
EPS............	Eye Protection Shutter
EPS............	Ezra Pound Society (EA)
EPSA........	Educational Program in Systems Analysis (RDA)
EPSA........	Electrostatic Particle Size Analyzer
EPS3AP....	Environment Protection Service. Air Pollution Report [*A publication*]
EPSC........	Emergency Petroleum Supply Committee [*Terminated, 1976*] (EA)
EPSC.........	EPSCO, Inc. [*NASDAQ symbol*] (NQ)
EPSC.........	Excitatory Postsynaptic Current [*Neurophysiology*]
EPSCG......	Groupe de Contact Parlementaire et Scientifique [*European Parliamentary and Scientific Contact Group*] (EA)
EPSCoR.....	Experimental Program to Stimulate Competitive Research [*National Science Foundation*]
EPSCS.......	Enhanced Private Switched Communications Service [*Pronounced "ep-sis"*] [*AT & T*]
EPSDT......	Early and Periodic Screening, Diagnosis, and Treatment
EPSDU......	Experimental Process System Development Unit [*Photovoltaic energy systems*]
EPSEIS.....	Encyclopedia of Physical Sciences and Engineering Information Sources [*A publication*]
EPSF.........	Early Postsurgical Fitting [*Medicine*]
EPSF.........	Employee Profile Security File [*IRS*]
EPSF.........	Encapsulated Post-Script Draw Format [*Data processing*]
EPSG.........	European Pineal Study Group (EAIO)
EPSI.........	Earnings per Share Issued [*Finance*]
EPSI.........	Epsilon Data Management, Inc. [*Burlington, MA*] [*NASDAQ symbol*] (NQ)
EPSI.........	Erikson Psychosocial Stage Inventory [*Psychology*]
EPSIA........	Eastern Professional Ski Instructors Association [*Formerly, EPSTI*] (EA)
EPSIG.......	Electronic Publishing Special Interest Group [*Association of American Publishers*]
EPSL........	Eastern Primary Standards Laboratory
EPSL........	Emergency Power Switching Logic (NRCH)
EPSLA......	Earth and Planetary Science Letters [*A publication*]
EPsM........	Educational and Psychological Measurement [*A publication*]
EPSMD......	Elektrotekhnicheskaya Promyshlennost. Seriya. Elektrotekhnicheskie Materialy [*A publication*]
EPSNA......	Sbornik Nauchnykh Trudov Estonskoi Sel'skokhozyaistvennoi Akademii [*A publication*]
EPSnEC.....	Environment Protection Service. Environmental Impact Control Directorate. Surveillance Report [*A publication*]
EPSnES.....	Environmental Protection Service. Environmental Strategies Directorate. Economic and Technical Review [*A publication*]
EPSnNW ...	Environment Protection Service. Northwest Region. Department of the Environment. Reports [*A publication*]
EPS NR ...	Environmental Protection Service. Report Series. Northern Regions [*A publication*]
EPS4NW ...	Environment Protection Service. Northwest Region. Technology Development Report [*A publication*]
EPSOC......	Earth-Physics Satellite Observation [*or Observing*] Campaign [*Smithsonian Astrophysical Observatory*]
EPSOC......	Ephemera Society of America (EA)
EPSP.........	Enolpyruvylshikimic Acid Phosphate [*Organic chemistry*]
EPSP.........	Excitatory Postsynaptic Potential [*Neurophysiology*]
EPSP.........	Experiment Power Switching Panel (MCD)
EPSPDH ...	Environmental Pollution. Series B. Chemical and Physical [*A publication*]
EPSPS.......	Enolpyruvylshikimatephosphate Synthase [*An enzyme*]

EPSRD ...... Electric Power Systems Research [*A publication*]
EPSS .... Experimental Packet Switching System [*Telecommunications*]
EPST .... Electric Power Statistics [*A publication*]
EPST .... Encyclopedia of Polymer Science and Technology [*A publication*]
Epst Cat ..... Catalogue of the Epstean Collection [*A publication*]
EPSTF .... Electrical Power System Test Facility [*NASA*] (KSC)
EPSTI .... Eastern Professional Ski Touring Instructors [*Later, EPSIA*] (EA)
EPS3WP .... Environment Protection Service. Water Pollution Report [*A publication*]
EPT .... Early Pregnancy Test
EPT .... Economic Power Transmission
EPT .... El Paso [*Texas*] [*Seismograph station code, US Geological Survey*] (SEIS)
EPT .... Electric Power Transmission (ADA)
EP & T ...... Electronic Products & Technology [*Canada*] [*A publication*]
EPT .... Electrostatic Printing Tube
EPT .... Emergency Procedure Trainer [*NASA*] (NASA)
EPT .... Endoscopic Papillotomy [*Medicine*]
EPT .... English Placement Test [*Education*]
EPT .... Epitope, Inc. [*AMEX symbol*] (SPSG)
EPT .... Epsilon Pi Tau (EA)
EPT .... Ethylene Propylene Terpolymer [*Organic chemistry*]
EPT .... Euro Petroleum Corp. [*Toronto Stock Exchange symbol*] [*Vancouver Stock Exchange symbol*]
EPT .... Evoked Potential Technique [*Neurophysiology*]
EPT .... Examination Division Planning Tape [*IRS*]
EPT .... Excess Profits Tax
EPT .... Experimental Prototype Test (MCD)
EPT .... External Pipe Thread [*Technical drawings*]
EPTA .... Electric Propulsion Trajectory Analysis
EPTA .... Electrophysiological Technologists' Association (EAIO)
EPTA .... European Piano Teachers Association (EAIO)
EPTA .... European Power Tool Association (EAIO)
EPTA .... Expanded Program of Technical Assistance [*United Nations*]
EPTAQ .... Executive Program Task Assignment Queue Manager (MCD)
EPTC .... Ethyl Dipropylthiocarbamate [*Organic chemistry*]
EPTC .... Extraction Procedure Toxicity Characteristic [*Environmental Protection Agency*]
EPTD .... Ethylphosphonothioicdichloride [*Organic chemistry*]
EPTDA ...... Electric Light and Power. Transmission/Distribution [*A publication*]
EPTE .... Existed Prior to Enlistment [*Especially, dependency or physical defect*] [*Military*]
EPTE .... Existed Prior to Entry [*Military*]
EPTFC .... Elvis Presley Tribute Fan Club (EA)
EPTFE .... Expanded Polytetrafluoroethylene [*Organic chemistry*]
EPTG .... Electronic Publication Technology Group [*Inactive*] (EA)
EPTI .... Existed Prior to Induction [*Especially, dependency or physical defect*] [*Military*]
EPTL .... Estates, Powers, and Trusts Law [*A publication*]
EPTO .... Engineer Packaging Technical Office [*Merged with General Equipment Command*]
EPTQAM ... Etudes Psychotherapiques [*A publication*]
Ep ad Tryph ... Epistula ad Tryphonem [*of Quintilian*] [*Classical studies*] (OCD)
EPTS .... Engine Power Trim System
EPTS .... Existed Prior to Entry Service [*Military*]
EPTSB .... Environmental Protection Technology Series [*A publication*]
EPTTC .... European Passenger Train Timetable Conference (EA)
EPTU .... Events per Time Unit (NASA)
EPTW .... Educational Programs that Work [*Department of Education*] [*Information service or system*] (IID)
EPU .... East Promontory [*Utah*] [*Seismograph station code, US Geological Survey*] (SEIS)
EPU .... Economic Planning Unit [*Generic term*] (DS)
EPU .... Electrical Power Unit
EPU .... Emergency Power Unit
EPU .... Entry Processing Unit [*Data processing*] (DCTA)
EPU .... Environmental Physiology Unit [*Simon Fraser University*] [*Canada*] [*Research center*] (RCD)
EPU .... European Payments Union
EPU .... Evropska Platna Unija [*European Payments Union*]
EPU .... Executive Processing Unit
EPUB .... Electronic Publishing System [*ITT Dialcom*] [*Database*]
EPubl .... Enseignement Public [*A publication*]
EPUBS ...... Electronic Publishing Abstracts [*The Research Association for the Paper and Board, Printing and Packaging Industries*] [*Database*]
EPUS .... Episcopus [*Bishop*] [*Latin*]
EPUT .... Events per Unit Time
EPUTS ...... Emergency Power Unit Test Set
EPUU .... Enhanced PLRS [*Position Location Reporting System*] User Unit [*Air Force*]
EPV .... Earth Probe near Limb of Venus [*Angle*]
EPV .... Electric Polarization Vector
EPV .... Electric Powered Vehicle
EPV .... Electropneumatic Valve
EPV .... Emergency Pressurization Valve (MCD)

EPV .... Evangelische Progressieve Volkspartij [*Evangelical Progressive People's Party*] [*Netherlands*] (PPW)
EPV .... External Pressure Vessel
EPVS .... Emergency Propellant Venting System
EPVTS ...... English Picture Vocabulary Tests [*Educational test*]
EPW .... Earth-Penetrating Warhead (RDA)
EPW .... Earth Penetrator Weapon (MCD)
EPW .... Economic and Political Weekly [*A publication*]
EPW .... Electric Pressure Wave
EPW .... Elektra Power, Inc. [*Vancouver Stock Exchange symbol*]
EPW .... Elliptically Polarized Wave
EPW .... Enemy Prisoner of War [*Army*] (AABC)
EPW .... Ephrata [*Washington*] [*Seismograph station code, US Geological Survey*] (SEIS)
EPWA .... Warszawa/Okecie [*Poland*] [*ICAO location identifier*] (ICLI)
EPWG ...... Electromagnetic Propagation Working Group [*Army*]
EPWG ...... Environmental Projects Working Group [*NASA*] (NASA)
EPWIB ...... Enemy Prisoner of War Information Bureau [*Army*] (AABC)
EPWIB(Br) ... Enemy Prisoner of War Information Bureau (Branch) [*Army*] (AABC)
EPWR .... Emergency Power
EPWS .... Emergency Production Weapons Schedule [*Navy*] (NG)
EPX .... Electronic Patrol, Experimental (MCD)
EPXMA ..... Electron Probe X-Ray Microanalyzer
EPZ .... Electron Polar Zone
EPZ .... Emergency Planning Zone [*Nuclear emergency planning*]
EPZ .... Export Processing Zone (ECON)
EPZA .... Export Processing Zone Authority
EQ .... Economic Quotient
EQ .... Education Quarterly [*New Delhi*] [*A publication*]
EQ .... Educational Quotient [*Psychology*]
EQ .... Emo Questionnaire [*Psychology*]
EQ .... Encephalization Quotient
EQ .... Energy Quotient
EQ .... Engineering Quality
EQ .... Enquiries [*Telecommunications*] (TEL)
EQ .... Environmental Quality
EQ .... Equal
EQ .... Equality (ROG)
EQ .... Equalization [*Electronics*]
EQ .... Equalizer
EQ .... Equation (KSC)
EQ .... Equatorial
EQ .... Equerry
EQ .... Eques [*Knight*] [*Latin*] (ROG)
EQ .... Equestrian (ROG)
EQ .... Equipment (BUR)
EQ .... Equipment Qualification (NRCH)
Eq .... Equitable [*Legal term*] (DLA)
Eq .... Equites [*Knights*] [*of Aristophanes*] [*Classical studies*] (OCD)
EQ .... Equity
Eq .... Equity Court [*or Division*] [*Legal term*] (DLA)
Eq .... Equity Reports [*A publication*] (DLA)
EQ .... Equivalent
EQ .... Ethnic Quotient
EQ .... Evangelical Quarterly [*A publication*]
EQ .... Transportes Aereos Nacionales Ecuatorianos [*Ecuador*] [*ICAO designator*] (FAAC)
EQA .... El Dorado, KS [*Location identifier*] [*FAA*] (FAAL)
EQA .... Environmental Quality Abstracts [*A publication*]
EQA .... [*Secretary of the Army*] Environmental Quality Award (MCD)
EQA .... Equipment Quality Analysis
EQA .... Eurodoc [*A publication*]
EQA .... OCLC [*Online Computer Library Center*] Europe, Birmingham, England [*OCLC symbol*] (OCLC)
Eq Ab .... Abridgment of Cases in Equity [*1667-1744*] [*A publication*] (DLA)
EQAU .... Equity AU, Inc. [*NASDAQ symbol*] (NQ)
EQ AUR .... Eques Auratus [*Knight Bachelor*] [*Latin*] (ROG)
EQB .... Chambersburg, PA [*Location identifier*] [*FAA*] (FAAL)
EQBK .... [*The*] Equity Bank [*NASDAQ symbol*] (NQ)
EQBLE ...... Equitable [*Legal term*] (ROG)
EQC .... Environmental Quality Control
EQC .... Environmental Quality Council [*Terminated, 1970*] (MCD)
EQC .... Externally Quenched Counter
EQCA .... Equestrian Centers of America [*NASDAQ symbol*] (NQ)
Eq Ca Ab.... Equity Cases Abridged [*A publication*]
Eq Ca Abr .. Abridgment of Cases in Equity [*1667-1744*] [*A publication*] (DLA)
Eq Cas........ Equity Cases [*A publication*] (DLA)
Eq Cas........ Gilbert's English Equity Cases [*A publication*] (DLA)
Eq Cas Abr ... Equity Cases Abridged [*2 vols.*] [*21, 22 English Reprint*] [*A publication*] (DLA)
Eq Cas Abr (Eng) ... Equity Cases Abridged [*2 vols.*] [*21, 22 English Reprint*] [*A publication*] (DLA)
Eq Cas Mod ... Equity Cases [*A publication*] (DLA)
EQCC .... Entry Query Control Console [*Data processing*]
EQCM .... Master Chief Equipmentman [*Navy rating*]
EQ CONV ... Equitable Conversion (DLA)
EQCRT ...... Equipment Certified (FAAC)
EQD .... Electrical Quality Assurance Directorate [*British*]

EQD.......... Established Quarter of Disability [*Social Security Administration*] (OICC)
EQDD....... Equipment Density Data (AABC)
Eq Draft..... Equity Draftsman (Van Heythuysen's, Edited by Hughes) [*A publication*] (DLA)
EQE.......... Equivalent Quantum Efficiency (MCD)
EQE.......... Event Queue Element [*Data processing*] (MCD)
Eq Empl Compl Man ... Equal Employment Compliance Manual [*A publication*]
EQF.......... Elswick Quick-Firing Gun
EQFI.......... Equity Finance Group, Inc. [*NASDAQ symbol*] (NQ)
EQGC........ Equity Growth Corporation [*NASDAQ symbol*] (NQ)
EqI.......... Equity Income [*Finance*]
EQIA........ Environmental Quality Improvement Act of 1970
EQIC........ Equitable of Iowa Companies [*NASDAQ symbol*] (NQ)
EQIN........ Equities International Life Insurance Co. [*Fort Worth, TX*] [*NASDAQ symbol*] (NQ)
EQIX........ Equinox Solar, Inc. [*NASDAQ symbol*] (NQ)
Eq Judg...... Equity Judgments, by A'Beckett [*New South Wales*] [*A publication*] (DLA)
EQK.......... Equimark Corp. [*NYSE symbol*] (SPSG)
EQL.......... Environmental Quality Laboratory [*California Institute of Technology*]
EQL.......... Equal (MSA)
EQL.......... Expected Quality Level
EQL Memo Calif Inst Technol Environ Qual Lab ... EQL Memorandum. California Institute of Technology. Environmental Quality Laboratory [*A publication*]
EQLY........ Equally [*Legal term*] (ROG)
EQM.......... Environmental Quality Magazine [*A publication*]
EQM.......... Equitable Real Estate Shoping [*NYSE symbol*] (SPSG)
EQMM...... Ellery Queen's Mystery Magazine [*A publication*]
EQN.......... Equation
EQN.......... Equine Resources Ltd. [*Vancouver Stock Exchange symbol*]
EQNT....... Equinetics, Inc. [*NASDAQ symbol*] (NQ)
EQNX....... Equinox [*A publication*]
EQO.......... Environmental Quality Objective [*British*] (DCTA)
EQO.......... Environmental Quality Office [*HUD*] (OICC)
EQP.......... Englehard, NC [*Location identifier*] [*FAA*] (FAAL)
EQP.......... Equipment (CINC)
EQP.......... Equity Preservation Corp. [*Toronto Stock Exchange symbol*] [*Vancouver Stock Exchange symbol*]
EQP.......... Health Equity Properties [*NYSE symbol*] (SPSG)
Eq PA....... Equal Pay Act [*1970*] [*British*] (DCTA)
EQPFOR... Equipment Foreman
EQPMT.... Equipment (MDG)
EQPRDF ... Equine Practice [*A publication*]
EQPT....... Equipment
EQQ.......... Electric Quadrupole-Quadrupole
Eq R .... Common Law and Equity Reports [*1853-55*] [*A publication*] (DLA)
EQR.......... Equity Reserve Corp. [*Toronto Stock Exchange symbol*]
Eq R .... Gilbert's English Equity Reports [*1705-27*] [*A publication*] (DLA)
Eq R .... Harper's South Carolina Equity Reports [*A publication*] (DLA)
Eq R (Eng) ... Equity Reports [*England*] [*A publication*] (DLA)
EQREP...... Equipment Report (MCD)
Eq Rep .... Equity Reports [*A publication*] (DLA)
Eq Rep .... Equity Reports, Published by Spottiswoode [*A publication*] (DLA)
Eq Rep .... Gilbert's English Equity Reports [*1705-27*] [*A publication*] (DLA)
Eq Rep .... Harper's South Carolina Equity Reports [*A publication*] (DLA)
EQS.......... Environmental Quality Staff [*Tennessee Valley Authority*] [*Knoxville, TN*] (GRD)
EQS.......... Environmental Quality Standard [*British*] (DCTA)
EQS.......... Equatorial Scatter
EQS.......... Esquel [*Argentina*] [*Airport symbol*] (OAG)
EQS.......... Exact Quadratic Search [*Mathematics*]
EQSA........ Extended Quasi-Static Approximation [*Materials research*]
EQSF........ Equity Strategies Fund [*NASDAQ symbol*] (NQ)
EQT.......... Engineering Qualification Test
EQT.......... Environmental Qualification Test
EQT.......... Equation of Time [*Navigation*]
EQT.......... Equitable Resources, Inc. [*Formerly, Equitable Gas Co.*] [*NYSE symbol*] (SPSG)
EQT.......... Equivalent Training (AFM)
EQTR........ Equitable Resources, Inc. [*NASDAQ symbol*] (NQ)
EQTX....... Equitex, Inc. [*NASDAQ symbol*] (NQ)
EQTY....... Equity Oil Co. [*NASDAQ symbol*] (NQ)
EQU.......... Equate (MDG)
Equ.......... Equity [*Business term*]
Equ.......... Equuleus [*Constellation*]
EQU.......... Equus Petroleum [*Vancouver Stock Exchange symbol*]
EQUA....... Equatorial Communications Co. [*NASDAQ symbol*] (NQ)
EQUALANT ... Equatorial Atlantic (MSC)
Equal Now ... Equality Now [*A publication*]
Equal Opportunities Int ... Equal Opportunities International [*A publication*]
EQUAPAC ... Equatorial Pacific
EQUAT ..... Equatorial (ROG)

EQUATE... Electronic Quality Assurance Test Equipment [*System*] [*Army*] (RDA)
EQUI .... [*The*] Equion Corp. [*New Haven, CT*] [*NASDAQ symbol*] (NQ)
EQUIL....... Equilibrium (MSA)
EQUIMPEX ... China National Machinery and Equipment Import & Export Corp. [*People'sRepublic of China*] (IMH)
Equine Pract ... Equine Practice [*A publication*]
Equine Vet J ... Equine Veterinary Journal [*A publication*]
EQUIP....... Equipment
Equip Dev Test Rep US For Serv Equip Dev Ctr San Dimas Calif ... Equipment Development and Test Report. United States Forest Service. Equipment Center (San Dimas, California) [*A publication*]
Equipement ... Equipement - Logement - Transports [*A publication*]
Equip Ind Achats & Entretien ... Equipement Industriel. Achats et Entretien [*A publication*]
Equip Mec ... Equipement Mecanique [*France*] [*A publication*]
Equip Preview Chem Process Ind ... Equipment Preview of Chemical Process Industries [*A publication*]
Equip Tips US Dep Agric For Serv Equip Dev Cent ... Equip Tips. United States Department of Agriculture. Forest Service Equipment Development Center [*A publication*]
Equit Distr Rep ... Equitable Distribution Reporter [*A publication*]
Equity Rep ... Common Law and Equity Reports [*1853-55*] [*A publication*] (DLA)
Equity Rep ... Equity Reports (Gilbert) [*England*] [*A publication*] (DLA)
Equity Rep ... Harper's South Carolina Equity Reports [*A publication*] (DLA)
EQUIV ...... Equivalent (AFM)
equiv wt ...... Equivalent Weight [*Chemistry*]
EQUL........ Employment in Queensland Libraries [*Australia*]
E QUOL VEH ... E Quolibet Vehiculo [*In Any Vehicle*] [*Pharmacy*]
E QUOV LIQ ... E Quovis Liquido [*In Any Liquid*] [*Pharmacy*]
EQV .... Equivest International Financial Corp. [*Vancouver Stock Exchange symbol*]
EQX .... Equinox Resources Ltd. [*Toronto Stock Exchange symbol*] [*Vancouver Stock Exchange symbol*]
EQY .... Monroe, NC [*Location identifier*] [*FAA*] (FAAL)
EQZ .... Seymour, IN [*Location identifier*] [*FAA*] (FAAL)
ER .... [*The*] Earlham Review [*A publication*]
ER .... Early Release (MCD)
ER .... Earned Run [*Baseball*]
ER .... Earnings Report [*Business term*]
ER .... Earth Radii
ER .... Earth Rate
ER .... Earth Resources (MCD)
ER .... East Riding of Yorkshire [*Administrative county in England*]
ER .... East River [*New York*]
ER .... Eastern Rite News Service
ER .... East's English King's Bench Term Reports [*A publication*] (DLA)
ER .... Easy to Reach [*Telecommunications*] (TEL)
ER .... Ecclesiastical Review [*A publication*]
ER .... Echo Ranging
ER .... Ecole Rabbinique [*France*] (BJA)
ER .... Economic Record [*A publication*]
ER .... Economic Regulations [*Civil Aeronautics Board*]
ER .... Ecumenical Review [*A publication*]
ER .... Edinburgh Review [*A publication*]
ER .... Educational Ratio
ER .... Educational Resources [*Auckland, NZ*]
ER .... Educational Review [*A publication*]
ER .... Edwardus Rex [*King Edward*] [*Latin*]
ER .... Effectiveness Ratio (MCD)
ER .... Effectiveness Report [*Military*]
ER .... Efficiency Review [*DoD*]
ER .... Ego Resiliency [*Psychology*]
ER .... Egyptian Railways (DCTA)
ER .... Eisenbahntechnische Rundschau [*A publication*]
ER .... Ejection Rate [*Medicine*]
ER .... Ekonomska Revija [*Ljubljana*] [*A publication*]
ER .... Elder
ER .... Eleanor Roosevelt [*1884-1962*]
ER .... Election Reports [*Ontario*] [*A publication*] (DLA)
ER .... Electrical Resistance (MSA)
ER .... Electro-Rheological
ER .... Electronic Reconnaissance
ER .... Electrorheology [*Physics*]
ER .... Elektronische Rechenanlagen [*A publication*]
ER .... Elizabeth Regina [*Queen Elizabeth*] (DLA)
ER .... Elizabetha Regina [*Queen Elizabeth*] [*Latin*]
ER .... Embryo Replacement [*Gynecology*]
ER .... Emergency Request
ER .... Emergency Rescue
ER .... Emergency Reserve
ER .... Emergency Response [*Nuclear energy*] (NRCH)
ER .... Emergency Room [*Medicine*]
ER .... Employer (OICC)
E/R .... En Route
ER .... Endoplasmic Reticulum [*Cytology*]
E & R.......... Ends and Rings [*Architecture*] (ROG)

ER	Energy Research [*Elsevier Book Series*] [*A publication*]
ER	Energy Review [*A publication*]
ER	Engine Room [*Force*]
ER	Engineering Regulations [*A publication*]
ER	Engineering Release (MCD)
E & R	Engineering and Repair [*Department*] [*Navy*]
ER	Engineering Report
ER	Engineering Route [*Telecommunications*] (TEL)
ER	Englische Rundschau [*A publication*]
ER	English Reports [*Legal*]
ER	English Reports, Full Reprint [*A publication*] (DLA)
ER	English Review [*A publication*]
ER	English Revised Version [*of the Bible*] [*A publication*] (BJA)
ER	Enhanced Radiation Weapon
ER	Enhancement Ratio
ER	Environmental Report (NRCH)
ER	Environmental Resistance
ER	Episcopal Recorder [*A publication*]
ER	Equipment Readiness [*DoD*]
ER	Equipment Record
ER	Equipment Repairer [*British military*] (DMA)
ER	Equipment Requirement
ER	Equivalent Roentgen
ER	Equivalent Round (MCD)
Er	Eranos [*A publication*]
Er	Erasmus [*A publication*]
Er	Erbium [*Chemical element*]
Er	Erevna [*A publication*]
Er	Eriu [*A publication*]
ER	Errata
ER	Erroneous
ER	Error [*Baseball*]
ER	Error Rate [*Statistics*]
ER	Error Recorder
ER	Error Recovery (BUR)
ER	Error Relay
ER	Erskine Register (EA)
'Er	'Erubin [*or 'Eruvin*] (BJA)
ER	Erythrocyte [*Hematology*]
ER	Erythrocyte Rosette [*Hematology*]
ER	Espera Resposta [*Awaiting Reply*] [*Portuguese*]
ER	Established Reliability (MCD)
ER	Estimated Rental (ROG)
ER	Estimating Relationship (AFIT)
ER	Estradiol Receptor [*Endocrinology*]
ER	Estrogen Receptor [*Endocrinology*]
ER	Estudis Romanics [*A publication*]
ER	Eternelle Revue [*A publication*]
ER	Etudes Rabelaisiennes [*A publication*]
ER	Etudes Rhodaniennes [*A publication*]
ER	European Report [*A publication*]
E/R	Evacuation/Replacement [*Jar technique*] [*Microbiology*]
ER	Evaluation Record [*LIMRA*]
ER	Evaluation Report
ER	Evergreen Review [*A publication*]
ER	Evoked Response [*Neurophysiology*]
ER	Ex-Rights [*Without Rights*] [*Investment term*]
ER	Exchange Ratio (MCD)
E/R	Exchange and Repair (FAAC)
ER	Exchange Rolls
ER	Executive Request [*Data processing*]
ER	Executive Reserve
E/R	Exercised/Repositioned [*Sports medicine*]
ER	Exodus Rabbah (BJA)
ER	Expedite Requirement (KSC)
ER	Expense Report (AAG)
ER	Expert Rifleman
ER	Explanation Report [*NASA*] (NASA)
ER	Explosives Report
ER	Extended Range
ER	Extended Release [*Pharmacy*]
ER	External Report
ER	External Resistance [*Physics*]
ER	External Rotation [*Myology*]
ER	Extra Restricted (ADA)
ER	Eye Research (EA)
ER	Here [*or Herewith*] [*Aviation code*] (FAAC)
ER	[*The*] Item Requested Cannot Be Identified as an Item Currently Stocked [*Supply action error code*] [*Army*]
er-----	Rhine River and Basin [*MARC geographic area code*] [*Library of Congress*] (LCCP)
ER	Sundor International Air Services Ltd. [*Israel*] [*ICAO designator*] (FAAC)
ERA	Earned Run Average [*Baseball*]
ERA	Eastern Railroad Association [*Defunct*] (EA)
ERA	Economic Record (Australia) [*A publication*] (APTA)
ERA	Economic Regulatory Administration (MCD)
ERA	Education and Religious Affairs [*US Military Government, Germany*]
ERA	Education Research Assistant (ADA)
ERA	Educational Rankings Annual [*A publication*]

ERA	Effective Rate of Assistance [*International trade*]
ERA	Egypt Research Account [*A publication*]
ERA	Egyptian Research Account [*London*] [*A publication*] (BJA)
ERA	Electric Railroaders Association (EA)
ERA	Electrical [*or Electronic*] Replaceable Assembly
ERA	Electrical Research Association [*British*]
ERA	Electrical Response Activity
ERA	Electron Ring Accelerator
ERA	Electronic Reading Automation [*Information retrieval*]
ERA	Electronic Representatives Association (EA)
ERA	Electronic Research Association [*British*]
ERA	Electroshock Research Association [*Later, International Psychiatric Library Service*]
ERA	Ellison, R. A., Cincinnati OH [*STAC*]
ERA	Emergency Relief Administration
ERA	Energy Reorganization Act [*1974*]
ERA	Energy Research Abstracts [*A publication*]
ERA	Engine-Room Artificer [*Obsolete*] [*Navy*] [*British*]
ERA	Engineer Rear-Admiral [*Navy*] [*British*]
ERA	Engineering Release Authorization
ERA	Engineering Request Authorization (AAG)
ERA	Engineering Research Associates (MCD)
ERA	English Racing Automobiles Ltd. [*British*]
ERA	English Reports, Annotated [*A publication*] (DLA)
ERA	Environmental Protection Agency, Region IX Library, San Francisco, CA [*OCLC symbol*] (OCLC)
ERA	Enzyme Rate Analyzer
ERA	Enzymic Radiochemical Assay [*Clinical chemistry*]
ERA	Equal Rights Advocates (EA)
ERA	Equal Rights Amendment [*Proposed constitutional amendment which supports equal rights regardless of sex*]
ERA	Equipment Rental Agreement
ERA	Equitable Reserve Association [*Neenah, WI*] (EA)
ERA	ERA. Education Research Abstracts [*A publication*] (APTA)
Era	Erato [*Record label*] [*France*]
ERA	Estrogen Receptor Assay [*Clinical chemistry*]
ERA	European Ramblers' Association (EAIO)
ERA	European Research Associates
ERA	European Rum Association (EAIO)
ERA	Evaporative Rate Analysis [*Surface technology*]
ERA	Evoked Response Audiometry [*Neurophysiology*]
ERA	Excess Rent Allowance [*British*]
ERA	Exchange Rate Agreement [*Banking*] [*British*]
ERA	Expense for Return of Absentee [*Military*]
ERA	Explosive Reactive Armor [*Tank design*]
ERA	Extended Range Ammunition (MCD)
ERA	Extended-Range ASROC [*Antisubmarine Rocket*] [*Navy*] (NVT)
ERA	Extra-Regimental Assignment [*Army*] (INF)
ERAA	Equipment Review and Authorization Activity [*Military*] (AFM)
ERA Abstr ...	ERA [*British Electrical and Allied Industries Research Association*] Abstracts [*A publication*]
ERAB	Energy Research Advisory Board [*Department of Energy*]
ERab	Etudes Rabelaisiennes [*A publication*]
ERAC	Economics Research Advisory Committee [*Australia*]
ERAC	Electromagnetic Radiation Advisory Council
ERAC	Electronic Random Action Control
ERAC	Energy Research and Advisory Centre [*Australia*]
ERAC	Environmental Research Assessment Committee [*National Research Council*]
ERAD	En Route Radial [*Aviation*] (FAAC)
ERAD	Erie Army Depot
ERADCOM ...	Electronics Research and Development Command [*Later, LABCOM*] [*Adelphi, MD*] [*Army*]
ERADCOM/ASL ...	Electronics Research and Development Command Atmospheric Sciences Laboratory [*Army*]
ERAF	Earth Resources Aircraft Facility [*NASA*]
ERA Foeren Elektr Ration Anvaendning ...	ERA. Foerening foer Elektricitetens Rationella Anvaendning [*A publication*]
ERAI	Electronic Research Associates, Inc. [*NASDAQ symbol*] (NQ)
ERAM	Earth Resources Applications Mission [*NASA*] (KSC)
ERAM	Extended Range Antiarmor Munition
ERAM	Extended Range Antitank Mine (MCD)
ERAMS	Environmental Radiation Ambient Monitoring System [*Environmental Protection Agency*]
ERAN	Examine and Repair as Necessary
EranJb	Eranos-Jahrbuch [*A publication*]
Eranos	Eranos-Jahrbuch [*A publication*]
Eranos-Jb ..	Eranos-Jahrbuch [*A publication*]
ERAP	Earth Resources Aircraft Program [*NASA*]
ERAP	Economic Research Action Project [*Students for a Democratic Society*] [*Defunct*]
ERAPS	Expendable Reliable Acoustic Path Sensor [*or Sonar or Sonobuoy*] (MCD)
ERAS	Educational Resources Allocation Systems
ERAS	EIN [*Employer Identification Number*] Research and Assignment System [*IRS*]
ERAS	Electronic Reconnaissance Access Set
ERAS	En Route Advisory Service [*Aeromedical evacuation*]
ERASE	Eat Right and Slim Easily [*Weight Watchers, Inc., competition*]

ERASE ..... Electromagnetic Radiation Source Elimination   (NVT)
ERASER .... Elevated Radiation Seeking Rocket
Erasmus E ... Erasmus in English [*A publication*]
ErasmusR .. Erasmus Review [*A publication*]
Erasmus Rev ... Erasmus Review [*A publication*]
Era Social .. Era Socialista [*A publication*]
ErasR .... Erasmus Review [*A publication*]
ERATO ..... Exploratory Research for Advanced Technology [*Japan*]
Eratosth ..... Eratosthenes [*275-194BC*] [*Classical studies*]   (OCD)
E-RAU .... Embry-Riddle Aeronautical University [*Formerly, ERSA*] [*Daytona Beach, FL*]
ERB .... Earth's Radiation Budget [*Meteorology*]
ERB .... Ecclesiastical Relations Branch [*BUPERS*]
ERB .... Edgar Rice Burroughs [*1875-1950*] [*Author of Tarzan books*]
ERB .... Educational Records Bureau   (EA)
ERB .... Educational Research Bulletin [*A publication*]
ERB .... Educational Rewards Bureau
ERB .... Edwards Rocket Base   (MUGU)
ERB .... Electronic Recording Beam   (MDG)
ERB .... Emergency Radio Beacon
ERB .... Employment Relations Board [*Usually preceded by abbreviation of state name*]
ERB .... Engineering Reference Branch [*Department of the Interior*]
ERB .... Engineering Review Board [*NASA*]   (NASA)
ERB .... Engineers Registration Board [*Council of Engineering Institutions*] [*British*]
ERB .... Enlisted Record Brief [*Army*]   (AABC)
ERB .... Environmental Protection Agency, Environmental Monitoring and Support Laboratory, Las Vegas, NV [*OCLC symbol*]   (OCLC)
ERB .... Epic Resources (BC) Ltd. [*Vancouver Stock Exchange symbol*]
ERB .... Erbamont, NV [*NYSE symbol*]   (SPSG)
ERB .... Etudes Romanes de Brno [*A publication*]
ERB .... Experiment Review Board [*Nuclear Regulatory Commission*]   (NRCH)
ERB .... Key to Economic Science [*A publication*]
ErbAuf .... Erbe und Auftrag [*Beuron*] [*A publication*]
ERB-Dom .. Edgar Rice Burroughs Domain [*as in organization, Friends of ERB-Dom*]
ERBE .... Earth Radiation Budget Experiment [*NASA*]
Erbe der V ... Erbe der Vergangenheit [*A publication*]
ERBF .... Effective Renal Blood Flow [*Medicine*]
ERBI .... Earth Radiation Budget Instrument
ERBL .... Erb Lumber Co. [*NASDAQ symbol*]   (NQ)
ERBM .... Extended-Range Ballistic Missile
ERBP .... Equilibrium Reflux Boiling Point [*Brake fluid*]
ERBr .... Etudes Romanes de Brno [*A publication*]
ERBS .... Earth Radiation Budget Satellite [*NASA*]   (MCD)
ERBS .... Expanded Range Bench Stock
ERBSS .... Earth Radiation Budget Satellite System [*NASA*]   (MCD)
Erb St G ..... Erbschaftssteuergesetz [*A publication*]
ERC .... Earth Rate Compensation
ERC .... Echo-Rhino-Coryza [*Virus*] [*Usage obsolete*]
ERC .... Economic Research Council [*Research center*] [*British*]   (IRC)
ERC .... Economic Resources Corporation [*OEO-Department of Labor project*]   (EA)
ERC .... Economic Review. Federal Reserve Bank of Cleveland [*A publication*]
ERC .... Ecosystems Research Center [*Cornell University, EPA*] [*Research center*]   (RCD)
ERC .... Edge Reading Controller
ERC .... Educational Reference Center [*National Institute of Education*]
ERC .... Educational Research Center [*New Mexico State University*] [*Research center*]   (RCD)
ERC .... Eject Rocket Container
ERC .... El Reno College [*Oklahoma*]
ERC .... Elections Research Center   (EA)
ERC .... Electric Regulation Company
ERC .... Electrical Rule Checker [*For integrated circuitry*]
ERC .... Electron Reflection Coefficient
ERC .... Electronics Research Center [*NASA*]
ERC .... Emergency Relocation Center   (NRCH)
E-R-C .... Employee Relocation Council   (EA)
ERC .... En Route Chart [*Aviation*]
ERC .... Endoscopic Retrograde Cholangiography [*Medicine*]
ERC .... Energy Resources Center [*University of Illinois at Chicago*] [*Research center*]   (RCD)
ERC .... Energy Resources Council [*Terminated, 1977*]
ERC .... Engineering Research Center [*University of Maryland*] [*Research center*]   (RCD)
ERC .... Engineering Research Center [*New Mexico State University*] [*Research center*]   (RCD)
ERC .... Engineering Research Council   (NRCH)
ERC .... English Ruling Cases [*A publication*]   (DLA)
ERC .... Enlisted Reserve Corps [*Later, Army Reserve*]
ERC .... Environmental Reporter Cases [*Bureau of National Affairs*] [*A publication*]   (DLA)
ERC .... Environmental Research Center [*Environmental Protection Agency*]
ERC .... Environmental Resources Center
ERC .... Environmental Response Center [*Department of Energy*]   (IID)

ERC .... Epic Record Company [*Record label*] [*New York*]
ERC .... Epilepsy Research Center [*Baylor College of Medicine*] [*Research center*]   (RCD)
ERC .... Epping Realty Corp. [*Vancouver Stock Exchange symbol*]
ERC .... Equal Rights Congress   (EA)
ERC .... Equatorial Ring Current   (IEEE)
ERC .... Equipage Repair Part Consumable   (AFIT)
ERC .... Equipment Readiness Codes [*or Criteria*]   (MCD)
ERC .... Equipment Record Card   (AAG)
ERC .... ERC International [*NYSE symbol*]   (SPSG)
ERC .... Eritrean Relief Committee   (EA)
ERC .... Erythropoietin-Responsive Cell [*Hematology*]
ERC .... Esquerra Republicana de Catalunya [*Catalan Republican Left*] [*Spain*] [*Political party*]   (PPE)
ERC .... Essentials Review Committee [*American Occupational Therapy Association*]
ERC .... ESSO [*Standard Oil*] Resources Canada Ltd. [*UTLAS symbol*]
ERC .... Estonian Relief Committee   (EA)
ERC .... Estrogen Receptor, Cytosolic [*Endocrinology*]
ERC .... Ethics Resource Center   (EA)
ERC .... European Registry of Commerce   (DS)
ERC .... Evaluation Research Center [*University of Virginia*] [*Research center*]   (RCD)
ERC .... Event Recorder   (NASA)
ERC .... Events Recorder Console   (MCD)
ERC .... Exemplary Rehabilitation Certificate [*Department of Labor*]
ERC .... Expatriate Resources Co. [*British*]
ERC .... Expendability Repair Classification   (AAG)
ERC .... Expenditure Review Committee [*Australia*]
ERC .... Explosives Research Center [*Bruceton, PA*] [*Bureau of Mines*]
ERCA .... Educational Research Council of America   (EA)
ERCA .... Electrochemically Regenerable Carbon Dioxide Absorber   (NASA)
ERCA .... Emergency Relief and Construction Act
ER CAM .... Eremitarum Camaldulensium [*Monk Hermits of Camaldoli*] [*Roman Catholic religious order*]
ERCB .... Exploitation de Renseignements Contenus dans les Brevets [*Patent Information Exploitation - PIE*] [*Canadian Patent Office*]
ERCBA8 .... Ecological Research Committee. Bulletin [*A publication*]
ERCC .... Error Checking and Correction [*Data processing*]
ERCC .... Expendability, Recoverability Cost Code   (AAG)
ERCE .... ERC Environmental & Energy Services Co., Inc. [*NASDAQ symbol*]   (CTT)
ERCEW ..... Ethical and Religious Classics of East and West [*A publication*]
ERCF .... Eglin RADAR Control Facility [*Florida*] [*Air Force*]   (MCD)
ERCG .... Erecting
ERCHCW ... European Regional Clearing House for Community Work   (EAIO)
ERCHD ..... Energy Report from Chase [*A publication*]
ERCI .... ERC Industries, Inc. [*NASDAQ symbol*]   (NQ)
ERCIA ...... Egg Research and Consumer Information Act [*1974*]
Erck .... Erck's Ecclesiastical Register [*1608-1825*] [*England*] [*A publication*]   (DLA)
ERCMIS .... Environmental Requirements/Capabilities Management Information System   (MCD)
ERCMS .... ELINT [*Electronic Intelligence*] Requirements and Capabilities Management System   (MCD)
ERCN .... Employee Record Change Notice
ERCOCFA ... Eleanor Roosevelt's Centennial Observance Committee of Friends and Admirers   (EA)
ERCOT ...... Electric Reliability Council of Texas [*Regional power council*]
ERCP .... Endoscopic Retrograde Cholangiopancreatographic [*Exam*] [*Medicine*]
ERCR .... Electronic Retina Computing Reader
ERCR .... Erector
ERCS .... Emergency Rocket Communications System
ERCW .... Emergency [*or Essential*] Raw Cooling Water [*Nuclear energy*]   (NRCH)
ERD .... Eastern Recruiting Division
ERD .... Economic Review. Federal Reserve Bank of Dallas [*A publication*]
ERD .... Elastic Recoil Detection
ERD .... Electronic Research Directorate [*Air Force*]
ERD .... Emergency Recovery Display [*Bell System*]
ERD .... Emergency Reserve Decoration [*British*]
ERD .... Emergency Return Device [*Aerospace*]
ER & D ...... Energy Research and Development
ERD .... Entity-Relationships Diagram [*Data processing*]
ERD .... Equipment Readiness Date [*Army*]   (AABC)
ERD .... Equipment Readiness Drawing [*Army*]
ERD .... Equipment Requirements Data [*Army*]
ERD .... Equivalent Residual Dose
ERD .... Erdek [*Turkey*] [*Seismograph station code, US Geological Survey*]   (SEIS)
ERD .... Erdoel und Kohle, Erdgas, Petrochemie [*A publication*]
ERD .... Error Recording Device
ERD .... Estimated Receival Date   (KSC)
ERD .... Estimated Release Date   (AAG)
ERD .... Evoked Response Detector [*Neurophysiology*]   (MCD)
ERD .... Expense for Return of Deserter [*Military*]

ERD .... Experiment Requirements Document (KSC)
ERD .... Exponentially Retrograded Diode
ERDA .... Electronic Resources Development Agency
ERDA .... Electronics Research and Development Activity [*Army*]
ERDA .... Energy Research and Development Administration [*Superseded by Department of Energy, 1977*]
ERDAA ..... Electronics Research and Development Activity Analysis [*Army*] (MCD)
ERDAC ...... Energy Research and Development Advisory Council
ERDA (Energy Res Dev Adm) Symp Ser ... ERDA (Energy Research and Development Administration) Symposium Series [*A publication*]
ERDAM .... Energy Research and Development Administration Manual [*A publication*] (IEEE)
ERDC .... Earth Resources Data Center [*NASA*]
ERDC .... East Region Development Corporation
ERDC .... Electronic Research and Development Command [*Army*]
ERDC .... Engineering Research and Development Center [*University of Nevada, Reno*] [*Research center*] (RCD)
ERDC .... Ergonomic Research and Design Centre [*Australia*]
ERDE .... Explosive Research and Development Establishment [*British*]
Erdeszeti Faipari Egy Tud Kozl ... Erdeszeti es Faipari Egyetem Tudomanyos Kozlemenyei [*A publication*]
Erdeszeti Faipari Tud Kozl ... Erdeszeti es Faipari Tudomanyos Kozlemenyek [*A publication*]
Erdeszeti Kut ... Erdeszeti Kutatasok [*A publication*]
Erdeszettud Kozl ... Erdeszettudomanyi Kozlemenyek [*A publication*]
Erdesz Faipari Egyetem Kiad ... Erdeszeti es Faipari Egyetem Kiadvanyai [*A publication*]
Erdesz Faipari Egyetem Tud Kozl ... Erdeszeti es Faipari Egyetem Tudomanyos Kozlemenyei [*A publication*]
Erdesz Kutat ... Erdeszeti Kutatasok [*A publication*]
Erdesz Kutatas ... Erdeszeti Kutatasok [*A publication*]
ERDF .... European Regional Development Fund [*See also FEDER*] [*Brussels, Belgium*] (EAIO)
ERDI .... Energy Research and Development Inventory [*Marine science*] (MSC)
ERDI .... Energy and Resource Development Institute [*Clemson University*] [*Research center*] (RCD)
ERDIC .... Energy Research, Development, and Information Centre [*University of New South Wales*] [*Australia*]
ERDIP .... Experimental Research and Development Incentives Program [*National Science Foundation*]
Erdk .... Erdkunde [*A publication*]
Erd Kh ...... Erdoel und Kohle [*A publication*]
Erd Koh EPB ... Erdoel und Kohle, Erdgas, Petrochemie Vereinigt mit Brennstoff-Chemie [*A publication*]
ERDL .... Engineering Research and Development Laboratory [*Army*]
ERDL .... Extended Range Data Link [*Bomb*] (MCD)
ERDL .... Exxon Research and Development Laboratories [*Formerly, Esso Research Laboratory*]
Erdmagn Ber ... Erdmagnetische Berichte [*A publication*]
Erd Muz ..... Erdelyi Muzeum [*A publication*]
Erdoel-Erdgas Z ... Erdoel-Erdgas Zeitschrift [*A publication*]
Erdoel Erdgas Z Int Ed ... Erdoel-Erdgas Zeitschrift. International Edition [*A publication*]
Erdoel Kohle ... Erdoel und Kohle, Erdgas, Petrochemie [*A publication*]
Erdoel Kohle Erdgas Petrochem ... Erdoel und Kohle, Erdgas, Petrochemie [*West Germany*] [*A publication*]
Erdoel Kohle Erdgas Petrochem Brennst-Chem ... Erdoel und Kohle, Erdgas, Petrochemie Vereinigt mit Brennstoff-Chemie [*A publication*]
Erdoel Kohle Erdgas Petrochem Ver Brennst Chem ... Erdoel und Kohle, Erdgas, Petrochemie Vereinigt mit Brennstoff-Chemie [*A publication*]
Erdoel-Z ..... Erdoel-Zeitschrift [*A publication*]
Erdoel Z Bohr Foerdertech ... Erdoel-Zeitschrift fuer Bohr- und Foerdertechnik [*A publication*]
Erdol & Kohl ... Erdoel und Kohle, Erdgas, Petrochemie [*A publication*]
ERDR .... Earth Rate Directional Reference
ERDS .... Equipment Recall Data System (MCD)
ERDSDX ... ERDA [*Energy Research and Development Administration*] Symposium Series [*A publication*]
ERE .... East Carolina University, Greenville, NC [*OCLC symbol*] (OCLC)
ERE .... Echo Range Equipment
ERE .... Edison Responsive Environment [*Automated learning system*]
ERE .... Elite Resources Corp. [*Vancouver Stock Exchange symbol*]
ERE .... Emergency Rescue Equipment
ERE .... Encyclopaedia of Religion and Ethics [*A publication*]
ERE .... Erave [*Papua New Guinea*] [*Airport symbol*] (OAG)
ERE .... Erevan [*USSR*] [*Seismograph station code, US Geological Survey*] (SEIS)
ERE .... Erie Airways, Inc. [*Erie, PA*] [*FAA designator*] (FAAC)
ERE .... Estrogen-Responsive Element [*Endocrinology*]
ERE .... Extra-Regimentally Employed [*List*] [*Military*] [*British*]
EREC .... Electronic Reconnaissance (MCD)
ERec .... English Record [*A publication*]
EREC .... Enlisted Records and Evaluation Center [*Fort Benjamin Harrison, IN*] [*Army*]
EREC .... Erection (ROG)

EREC .... Exxon Research and Engineering Company [*Information service or system*] (IID)
ERECT ...... Erection
ERECTN ... Erection (ROG)
EREF .... Energy Research and Education Foundation
EREND ..... Energy and the Environment [*A publication*]
EREP .... Earth Resources Experiment Package [*Skylab*] [*NASA*]
EREP .... Earth Resources Package [*NASA*] (NASA)
EREP .... End Results Evaluation Program [*Later, SEER*] [*National Cancer Institute*]
EREP .... Environmental Recording, Editing, and Printing Program (BUR)
EREP .... Equipment Replacement and Enhancement Program [*Data processing*]
EREPP ...... Earth Resources Experiment Package Program [*Skylab*] [*NASA*]
ERes .... Education Research [*A publication*]
ERES .... Electronic Reflected Energy System [*Acoustics*]
ERES .... Energy Reserve, Inc. [*NASDAQ symbol*] (NQ)
ERES .... Erie Western Railway Co. [*AAR code*]
ERES .... Erlanger Rechner-Entwurfs-Sprache [*Programming language*] [*1974*] (CSR)
Erevan Gos Univ Ucen Zap Estesv Nauki ... Erevanskii Gosudarstvennyi Universitet. Ucenye Zapiski. Estestvennye Nauki [*A publication*]
ERF .... Early Renal Failure [*Medicine*]
ERF .... Electro-Rheological Fluids [*American Cyanamid Co.*]
ERF .... Emergency Recovery Force
ERF .... Emergency Response Facility (MCD)
ERF .... Employer's Return File [*IRS*]
ERF .... Enerplus Resources Fund Series 'B' Trust Units [*Toronto Stock Exchange symbol*]
ERF .... Entrainment Release Factor [*Nuclear energy*] (NRCH)
ERF .... Erfurt [*East Germany*] [*Airport symbol*] (OAG)
ERF .... Error Function
ERF .... Estuarine Research Federation (EA)
ERF .... European Redistribution Facility
ERF .... Exchange Reference File (ADA)
ERF .... Excitatory Receptive Field [*Physiology*]
ERF .... Explosion Release Factor [*Nuclear energy*] (NRCH)
ERF .... Exponential Reliability Function
ERFA .... European Radio Frequency Agency [*Later, ARFA*] [*NATO*]
Erfahr Denk ... Erfahrung und Denken [*A publication*]
Erfahrungswiss Bl ... Erfahrungswissenschaftliche Blaetter [*A publication*]
ERFC .... Eddie Rabbitt Fan Club (EA)
ERFC .... Error Function Complementary
ERFC .... Erythrocyte Rosette-Forming Cells [*Hematology*]
ERFDP ...... Earth Resources Flight Data Processor [*NASA*]
Erf Hlkd ...... Erfahrungsheilkunde [*A publication*]
ERFI .... Error Function, Inverse
ERFIS .... Emergency Response Facility Information System [*Nuclear energy*] (NRCH)
ERFPI .... Extended-Range Floating Point Interpretive System
E & RFTS .. Elementary and Reserve Flying Training School [*British military*] (DMA)
ERG .... Electromagnetic Radiation Generator
ERG .... Electronic Rentals Group [*Commercial firm*] [*British*]
ERG .... Electroretinogram [*Medicine*]
ERG .... Emergency Recovery Group
ERG .... Emergency Response Guidelines [*Nuclear energy*] (NRCH)
ERG .... Employment Resources Group [*British*]
ERG .... Endocrine Research Group [*University of Calgary*] [*Research center*] (RCD)
ERG .... Endoplasmic Reticulum of Golgi [*Cytology*]
ERG .... Energy-Related General [*National Science Foundation research office*]
ERG .... Energy-Related Graduate [*National Science Foundation trainee program*]
ERG .... Energy Research for the Governors
ERG .... Engineer Reactors Group [*Army*]
ERG .... Engineering Release Group (AAG)
ERG .... Environmental Research Group
ERG .... Erase Gap [*Data processing*]
ERG .... ERG Resources, Inc. [*Formerly, Energy & Resources (CAM) Ltd.*] [*Toronto Stock Exchange symbol*]
Erg .... Ergaenzung [*Amendment, Supplement*] [*German*] (DLA)
Erg .... Ergebenst [*Truly*] [*Correspondence*] [*German*]
ERG .... Ergometer (MCD)
ERG .... Existence, Relatedness, and Growth [*Basic human needs suggested by Clayton P. Alderfer*]
ERG .... Exportrisikogaraantie [*Export credit agency*] [*Swiss*]
Erg Allg Path ... Ergebnisse der Allgemeinen Pathologie und Pathologischen Anatomie [*West Germany*] [*A publication*]
Erg Ang Math ... Ergebnisse der Angewandten Mathematik [*A publication*]
Erg Bl AZ .. Ergaenzungsblaetter zur Allgemeinen Zeitung [*A publication*]
Erg Blut Transf Forsch ... Ergebnisse der Bluttransfusionsforschung [*A publication*]
Erg Chir Orthop ... Ergebnisse der Chirurgie und Orthopaedie [*A publication*]
ERG/(CM² S) ... Ergs per Square Centimeter Second [*Unit of work*]

Ergeb Allgem Pathol Pathol Anat ... Ergebnisse der Allgemeinen Pathologie und Pathologischen Anatomie [*West Germany*] [*A publication*]

Ergeb Anat Entwicklungsgesch ... Ergebnisse der Anatomie und Entwicklungsgeschichte [*A publication*]

Ergeb Angiol ... Ergebnisse der Angiologie [*A publication*]

Ergeb Biol ... Ergebnisse der Biologie [*A publication*]

Ergeb Exakten Naturwiss ... Ergebnisse der Exakten Naturwissenschaften [*West Germany*] [*A publication*]

Ergeb Exp Med ... Ergebnisse der Experimentellen Medizin [*A publication*]

Ergeb Inn Med Kinderheilkd ... Ergebnisse der Inneren Medizin und Kinderheilkunde [*A publication*]

Ergeb Limnol ... Ergebnisse der Limnologie [*A publication*]

Ergeb Math Grenzgeb ... Ergebnisse der Mathematik und Ihrer Grenzgebiete [*A publication*]

Ergeb Mikrobiol Immunitaetsforsch ... Ergebnisse der Mikrobiologie und Immunitaetsforschung [*A publication*]

Ergebn Allg Path u Path Anat ... Ergebnisse der Allgemeinen Pathologie und Pathologischen Anatomie des Menschen und der Tiere [*A publication*]

Ergebn Biol ... Ergebnisse der Biologie [*A publication*]

Ergebn Physiol ... Ergebnisse der Physiologie, Biologischen Chemie, und Experimentellen Pharmakologie [*A publication*]

Ergeb Pathol ... Ergebnisse der Pathologie [*A publication*]

Ergeb Physiol Biol Chem Exp Pharmakol ... Ergebnisse der Physiologie, Biologischen Chemie, und Experimentellen Pharmakologie [*A publication*]

Ergeb Plasmaphys Gaselektron ... Ergebnisse der Plasmaphysik und der Gaselektronik [*A publication*]

Ergeb Plasmaphysik Gaselektronik ... Ergebnisse der Plasmaphysik und der Gaselektronik [*A publication*]

Ergeb Tech Roentgenkd ... Ergebnisse der Technischen Roentgenkunde [*A publication*]

Ergeb Vitam Hormonforsch ... Ergebnisse der Vitamin und Hormonforschung [*A publication*]

Erg Exakt Naturw ... Ergebnisse der Exakten Naturwissenschaften [*A publication*]

ERGMF ..... Erickson Gold Mines [*NASDAQ symbol*]   (NQ)

Ergnzngsbde Ztschr Veterinaerk ... Ergaenzungsbaende zur Zeitschrift fuer Veterinaerkunde [*A publication*]

ERGOA ..... Ergonomics [*A publication*]

ERGOAX .. Ergonomics [*A publication*]

ERGODATA ... Banque de Donnees Internationales de Biometrie Humaine et d'Ergonomie [*International Database of Human Biometrics and Ergonomics*] [*Universite Rene Descartes*] [*France*] [*Information service or system*]   (CRD)

ERGON ..... Ergonomics   (ADA)

Ergon Abstr ... Ergonomics Abstracts [*A publication*]

Ergonomics Abstr ... Ergonomics Abstracts [*A publication*]

ERGP .... Extended Range Guided Projectiles   (MCD)

ERGS .... Earth Geodetic Satellite [*Air Force*]

ERGS .... En Route Guidance System   (IEEE)

ERGS .... Energy Reserves Group [*NASDAQ symbol*]   (NQ)

ERG/S .... Ergs per Second [*Unit of work*]

ERGS .... ETC: A Review of General Semantics [*A publication*]

ERGTB ...... Engineering Times [*A publication*]

ERGWD .... Energiewesen [*A publication*]

ERGYA ...... Energy [*A publication*]

ERGYD ...... Energyline [*A publication*]

ERH .... Egg-Laying Release Hormone [*Endocrinology*]

ERH .... Elastomeric Rotary-Wing Head [*Military*]   (CAAL)

ERH .... ERA Helicopter, Inc. [*Lake Charles, LA*] [*FAA designator*]   (FAAC)

ERH .... Erith Herbarium [*Borough Museum*] [*British*]

ERH .... Ethiopian Refugee Help-Line   (EAIO)

ERH .... Euronet News [*A publication*]

ERHAD ..... Elektro Radio Handel [*A publication*]

ERHPA ...... Efficient Reliable High-Power Amplifier   (MCD)

ERHS .... Evangelical and Reformed Historical Society

ERHSA-UCC ... Evangelical and Reformed Historical Society and Archives, United Church of Christ   (EA)

ERHS-UCC ... Evangelical and Reformed Historical Society, United Church of Christ [*Later, ERHSA-UCC*]   (EA)

ERI .... Ear Research Institute [*Later, HEI*]   (EA)

ERI .... Economic Research Institute [*Utah State University*] [*Research center*]   (RCD)

ERI .... Education and Research Institute [*Washington, DC*]   (EA)

ERI .... Educational Research Information

ER et I .... Edwardus Rex et Imperator [*Edward King and Emperor*] [*Latin*]

ERI .... EGFR [*Epidermal Growth Factor Receptor*] Related Inhibitor [*Biochemistry*]

ERI .... Eleanor Roosevelt Institute   (EA)

ERI .... Electronics Research Laboratory [*Montana State University*] [*Research center*]   (RCD)

ERI .... Ellef Ringnes Island [*Canada*]

ERI .... Elm Research Institute   (EA)

ERI .... Employee Benefit Research Institute. Policy Forum [*A publication*]

ERI .... Employee Relations Index

ERI .... End of Recorded Information [*Data processing*]

ERI .... Energy Research Institute   (EA)

ERI .... Energy Resources Institute [*University of Oklahoma*] [*Research center*]   (RCD)

ERI .... Engineering Research Institute [*Iowa State University*] [*Research center*]   (AAG)

ERI .... Enterprise Resources [*Vancouver Stock Exchange symbol*]

ERI .... Entomological Research Institute

ERI .... Environmental Research Institute   (EA)

ERI .... Environmental Response Inventory [*Research test*] [*Psychology*]

Eri .... Eridamus [*Constellation*]

ERI .... Erie [*Pennsylvania*] [*Airport symbol*]   (OAG)

ERI .... Erie, PA [*Location identifier*] [*FAA*]   (FAAL)

ERI .... Erindale Campus Library, University of Toronto [*UTLAS symbol*]

ERI .... Erionite [*A zeolite*]

ERI .... Eureka Ridge [*Idaho*] [*Seismograph station code, US Geological Survey*] [*Closed*]   (SEIS)

ERI .... Executive Resources International [*British*]

ERI .... Expressive-Regressive Index

ERI .... Extravehicular Reference Information [*NASA space program*]

ERI .... Eyes Right   (EA)

ERIA .... Electroradioimmunoassay [*Clinical chemistry*]

ERIAD .... Electric Power Research Institute (Report) EPRI AP [*A publication*]

ERIC .... Educational Resources [*formerly, Research*] Information Center [*Department of Education*] [*Bibliographic database*] [*Washington, DC*]

ERIC .... Electronic Remote and Independent Control

ERIC .... Electronic Retailing Investment Corporation [*Acronym is also the name of an electronic vending kiosk*]

ERIC .... Energy Rate Input Controller   (IEEE)

ERIC .... Ericsson [*L. M.*] Telephone Co. [*NASDAQ symbol*]   (NQ)

ERIC .... ERISA [*Employee Retirement Income Security Act*] Industry Committee   (EA)

ERICA .... European Research into Consumer Affairs [*Research center*] [*England*]   (IRC)

ERICA .... Experiment on Rapidly Intensifying Cyclones over the Atlantic [*National Oceanic and Atmospheric Administration*]

ERICA .... Eye-Gaze Response Interface Computer Aid [*Computer designed for the physically handicapped that responds to user's eye movements*] [*Designed by Thomas Hutchinson*]

ERIC Abstr ... ERIC [*Educational Resources Information Center*] Abstracts [*A publication*]

ERIC/ACVE ... Educational Resources Information Center/Clearinghouse on Adult, Career, and Vocational Education [*Department of Education*]   (IID)

ERIC/CAPS ... Educational Resources Information Center/Clearinghouse on Counseling and Personnel Services [*Department of Education*] [*University of Michigan*] [*Research center*]   (IID)

ERIC/CE ... Educational Resources Information Center/Clearinghouse in Career Education [*Ohio State University*]   (IID)

ERIC/CEM ... Educational Resources Information Center/Clearinghouse on Educational Management [*Department of Education*] [*University of Oregon*] [*Eugene*] [*Research center*]

ERIC/CHE ... Educational Resources Information Center/Clearinghouse on Higher Education   (IID)

ERIC/CHESS ... Educational Resources Information Center/Clearinghouse for Social Studies/Social Science Education [*Department of Education*] [*Information service or system*]   (IID)

ERIC/CLIS ... Educational Resources Information Center/Clearinghouse for Library Information Sciences

ERIC/CLL ... Educational Resources Information Center/Clearinghouse on Languages and Linguistics [*Department of Education*] [*Center for Applied Liguistics*]   (IID)

ERIC/CRESS ... Educational Resources Information Center/Clearinghouse on Rural Education and Small Schools [*Department of Education*] [*New Mexico State University*] [*Research center*]   (IID)

ERIC/CUE ... Educational Resources Information Center/Clearinghouse on Urban Education [*Department of Education*] [*Columbia University*]   (IID)

ERIC Curr Index J Educ ... ERIC [*Educational Resources Information Center*] Current Index to Journals in Education [*A publication*]

ERIC/EC ... Educational Resources Information Center/Clearinghouse on Handicapped and Gifted Children [*Department of Education*] [*Information service or system*]   (IID)

ERIC/EECE ... Educational Resources Information Center/Clearinghouse on Elementary and Early Childhood Education [*Department of Education*] [*University of Illinois*]   (IID)

ERIC/HE .. Educational Resources Information Center/Clearinghouse on Higher Education [*George Washington University*] [*Research center*]   (EA)

ERIC/IR .... Educational Resources Information Center/Clearinghouse for Information Resources [*Department of Education*] [*Syracuse University*] [*Research center*]   (IID)

ERICR .... Eleanor Roosevelt Institute for Cancer Research

ERIC/RCS ... Educational Resources Information Center/Clearinghouse on Reading and Communication Skills [*Department of Education*] [*Urbana, IL*]

ERIC/SMEAC ... Educational Resources Information Center/Clearinghouse for Science, Mathematics, and Environmental Education [*Department of Education*] [*Information service or system*] (IID)

ERIC/SP ... Educational Resources Information Center/School Personnel [*Department of Education*] [*Washington, DC*]

Ericsson Rev ... Ericsson Review [*A publication*]

Ericsson Te ... Ericsson Technics [*A publication*]

Ericsson Tech ... Ericsson Technics [*A publication*]

ERIC/TE... Educational Resources Information Center/Clearinghouse on Teacher Education

ERIC/TM ... Educational Resources Information Center/Clearinghouse on Tests, Measurement, and Evaluation [*Department of Education*] [*Educational Testing Service*] (IID)

ERICZC .... Educational Reptiles in Captivity Zoological Compound (EA)

Erid .... Eridamus [*Constellation*]

E Riding Archaeol ... East Riding Archaeologist [*A publication*]

ERIE......... Eastern Regional Institute for Education

ERIE......... Environmental Resistance Inherent in Equipment

Erie .... Erie County Legal Journal [*Pennsylvania*] [*A publication*] (DLA)

ERIE.......... Erie Lackawanna, Inc. [*NASDAQ symbol*] (NQ)

Erie Co Leg J ... Erie County Legal Journal [*Pennsylvania*] [*A publication*] (DLA)

Erie Co L J (PA) ... Erie County Law Journal (Pennsylvania) [*A publication*] (DLA)

Erie LJ .... Erie County Legal Journal [*Pennsylvania*] [*A publication*] (DLA)

ERILCO .... Exchange of Ready for Issue in Lieu of Concurrent Overhaul

ERIM........ Environmental Research Institute of Michigan [*Research center*] (RCD)

ERIND ...... Electrical Review International [*A publication*]

ERINT...... Extended-Range Intercept Technology Missile [*Army*]

ERIP......... Energy-Related Inventions Program [*Department of Energy and National Bureau of Standards*]

ERIP......... Engineering Research Initiation Program [*National Science Foundation*]

ERIPS....... Earth Resources Image [*or Interactive*] Processing System

ERIS .... Earth-Reflecting Ionospheric Sounder [*Air Force*] (MCD)

ERIS .... Engineering Resins Information System [*General Electric Co.*]

ERIS .... Equipe de Recherche Interdisciplinaire en Sante [*Universite de Montreal, Quebec*] [*Canada*]

Er Is .... Eretz - Israel [*A publication*]

ERIS .... Exoatmospheric Reentry Vehicle Interceptor Subsystem [*Army*] (RDA)

ERISA ...... Employee Retirement Income Security Act of 1974 [*Also facetiously translated as Every Ridiculous Idea Since Adam*]

ERISTAR ... Earth Resources Information Storage, Transformation, Analysis, and Retrieval

Erit .... Eritrea

ERJ........... Alexandria, LA [*Location identifier*] [*FAA*] (FAAL)

ERJ........... Economic Research Journal [*A publication*]

ERJ........... Extended-Range Juno [*Survey meter for radiation*]

ERJ........... External Ramjet

ERJE .... Extended Remote Job Entry

Erjedesipari Kut Intez Kozl ... Erjedesipari Kutato Intezet Koslemenyei [*A publication*]

ERK .... Ethniko Rizospastiko Komma [*National Radical Party*] [*Greek*] (PPE)

ERK .... Experimental Research Kit

ERK .... Maandschrift Economie [*A publication*]

ERKUA3 ... Erdeszeti Kutatasok [*A publication*]

ERL........... Earth Resources Laboratory [*Later, NSTL*] [*NASA*] (KSC)

ERL........... Echo Return Loss [*Telecommunications*]

ERL........... Economic Retention Level (AFIT)

ERL........... Electronics Research Laboratory [*MIT*] (MCD)

ERL........... Electronics Research Laboratory [*University of California, Berkeley*] [*Research center*] (RCD)

ERL........... Emergency Reference Level [*Nuclear energy*] (NRCH)

ERL........... Employee Relations Law Journal [*A publication*]

ERL........... Environmental Research Laboratories [*Boulder, CO*] [*National Oceanic and Atmospheric Administration*]

ERL........... Equipment Requirement List (MCD)

Erl .... Erlass [*Deree, Edict, Order*] [*German*] (ILCA)

ERL........... ESSA [*Environmental Science Services Administration*] Research Laboratories

ERL........... Etudes Romanes de Lund [*A publication*]

ERL........... European Requirements List [*Military*] (AABC)

ERL........... Event Record Log

ERL........... Extended-Range Lance [*Missile*] (MCD)

ERL........... Eye Research Laboratories [*University of Chicago*] [*Research center*] (RCD)

ERLANG... Erlangen [*Federal Republic of Germany*] (ROG)

Erlanger Forsch Reihe B ... Erlanger Forschungen. Reihe B. Naturwissenschaften [*A publication*]

Erlanger Geol Abh ... Erlanger Geologische Abhandlungen [*A publication*]

Erlanger Jb Bienenk ... Erlanger Jahrbuch fuer Bienenkunde [*A publication*]

ERL/ATH ... Athens Environmental Research Laboratory [*Athens, GA*] [*Environmental Protection Agency*] (GRD)

ERL/COR ... Corvallis Environmental Research Laboratory [*Corvallis, OR*] [*Environmental Protection Agency*] (GRD)

ERL/DUL ... Duluth Environmental Research Laboratory [*Minnesota*] [*Environmental Protection Agency*] (GRD)

ERLE......... Echo Return Loss Enhancement

Erle Tr Un ... Erle on the Law of Trade-Unions [*A publication*] (DLA)

ERL/GB .... Gulf Breeze Environmental Research Laboratory [*Gulf Breeze, FL*] [*Environmental Protection Agency*] (GRD)

ERLIA6 ..... Ergebnisse der Limnologie [*A publication*]

ERLL......... Enhanced Run Length Limited [*Data processing*] (BYTE)

ERL/NARR ... Narragansett Environmental Research Laboratory [*Narragansett, RI*] [*Environmental Protection Agency*] (GRD)

ERLR........ Eastern Region of Nigeria Law Reports [*A publication*] (DLA)

ERLTM..... ESSA [*Environmental Science Services Administration*] Research Laboratories. Technical Memorandum [*A publication*]

ERL-UCB ... University of California, Berkeley Electronics Research Laboratory [*Research center*] (RCD)

ERLY........ Erly Industries, Inc. [*Formerly, Early California Industries*] [*NASDAQ symbol*] (NQ)

ERM .... Earth Re-Entry Module (MCD)

ERM .... Earth Resistivity Meter

ERM .... Earth Return Module [*NASA*] (KSC)

ERM .... Edge Reading Meter

ERM .... Effective Relaxation Modulus

ERM .... Electrical Research Memorandum

ERM .... Electrochemical Relaxation Methods

ERM .... Emergency Radiation Monitor

ERM .... Energy Research Management (MCD)

ERM .... Engine Room

ERM .... Environmental Resources Management, Inc. [*Database producer*] (IID)

ERM .... Epiretinal Membrane [*Ophthalmology*]

ERM .... Erimo [*Japan*] [*Seismograph station code, US Geological Survey*] (SEIS)

ERM .... Ermine [*Heraldry*]

ERM .... Euromoney [*A publication*]

ERM .... European Red Mite [*Insect*]

ERM .... Exchange Rate Mechanism [*Finance*]

ERM .... Explosives Research Memorandum

e-rm--- ...... Romania [*MARC geographic area code*] [*Library of Congress*] (LCCP)

ERMA ...... Electronic Recording Machine Accounting

ERMA ...... Engineering Reprographic Management Association [*Later, ERS*]

ERMA ...... Expansion Rate Measuring Apparatus

ERMA ...... Extended Red Multialkali [*Cathode*]

ERMAC..... Echo-Ranging Masked Acoustic Communications

ERMAC..... Electromagnetic Radiation Management Advisory Council [*US Government*]

ERMBE..... Energy-Related Minority-Owned Business Enterprise

ERMCO..... European Ready Mixed Concrete Organization (EAIO)

ERMES.... European Radio Messaging System

ERMING.... Ermington [*England*]

ERMISS.... Explosion-Resistant Multi-Influence Sweep System (NATG)

ERMP....... Energy Research Management Project [*Federal interagency group*]

ER/MRT ... Equipment Removal/Material Review Tag [*Military*] (MCD)

ERMU...... Experimental Remote Maneuvering Unit

ERN .... Eastern

ERN .... Educational Radio Network

ERN .... Engineering Reference Number

ERN .... Engineering Release Notice (MSA)

ERN .... Ernestine [*Alaska*] [*Seismograph station code, US Geological Survey*] [*Closed*] (SEIS)

ERN .... Explosives Research Note

ERN .... Installatie Journaal [*A publication*]

ERNA ...... Engineer, Royal Naval Artillery [*Navy*] [*British*] (ROG)

Ernaehr Umsch ... Ernaehrungs-Umschau [*A publication*]

Ernaehrungsforsch Inst Ernaehr (Potsdam) ... Ernaehrungsforschung. Institut fuer Ernaehrung (Potsdam) [*A publication*]

Ernaehrungsl Prax ... Ernaehrungslehre und- Praxis [*A publication*]

Ernaehrungswirtsch Lebensmitteltech (Hamburg) ... Ernaehrungswirtschaft. Lebensmitteltechnik (Hamburg) [*A publication*]

Ernahrungsforsch Wiss Prax ... Ernaehrungsforschung Wissenschaft und Praxis [*A publication*]

ERNAS...... European Review of Native American Studies [*A publication*]

ERNFA7.... Ernaehrungsforschung [*A publication*]

ERNIC....... Earnings-Related National Insurance Contribution [*British*] (DCTA)

ERNIE....... Electronic Random Number and Indicating Equipment [*Used for selecting winning premium bond numbers*] [*British*]

ERNK .... Enlya Ruzgariya Netwa Kurdistan [*National Front for the Liberation of Kurdistan*] [*Turkey*] [*Political party*]

ERNLR...... Eastern Region of Nigeria Law Reports [*A publication*] (DLA)

ERNO....... European Research National Organization (MCD)

ERNSDF ... Ernstia [*A publication*]

ERO .... Early Retirement Opportunity [*Business term*]

ERO	Eldred Rock, AK [*Location identifier*] [*FAA*] (FAAL)	
ERO	Emergency Repair Overseer [*Navy*]	
ERO	Energy Research Office [*Department of Energy*] (OICC)	
ERO	Engineering Release Operations (NASA)	
ERO	Engineering Release Order [*Formerly, ROD*]	
ERO	Ero Industries, Inc. [*AMEX symbol*] (SPSG)	
ERO	European Regional Organization of the ICFTU	
ERO	European Regional Organization of the International Dental Federation (EAIO)	
ERO	European Research Office [*British*]	
EROD	Ethoxyresorufin O-Deethylase [*An enzyme*]	
E Rodenwaldt Arch	Ernst Rodenwaldt Archiv [*A publication*]	
Eroeterv Koezl	Eroeterv Koezlemenyek [*A publication*]	
EROI	Energy Return on Investment	
EROM	Electron Readout Measurement (MCD)	
EROM	Erasable Read-Only Memory [*Data processing*]	
EROMDA	Eastern Regional Office Machine Dealers Association Convention (TSPED)	
EROP	Executive Review of Overseas Programs [*Army*] (AABC)	
EROP	Extensions and Restrictions of Operators (IEEE)	
EROPA	Eastern Regional Organization for Public Administration [*Manila, Philippines*] [*See also OROAP*]	
EROQ	ENVIROQ Corp. [*NASDAQ symbol*] (SPSG)	
EROS	Earth Resources Observation Systems [*US Geological Survey*]	
EROS	Eelam Revolutionary Organization [*Sri Lanka*] [*Political party*]	
EROS	Elimination of Range Zero System [*Aviation*]	
EROS	Environment and RADAR Operations Simulator	
EROS	Equipment Required on Site (MCD)	
EROS	Experimental Reflector Orbital Shot [*NASA project*]	
EROW	Executive Right of Way [*Telecommunications*] (TEL)	
EROWS	Expendable Remote Operating Weather Station [*Air Force*]	
ERP	Early Receptor Potential [*of the eye*]	
ERP	Earthquake Reporting and Prediction (NOAA)	
ERP	Econometric Research Program [*Princeton University*] [*Research center*] (RCD)	
ERP	Economic Rights Program [*Later, WERP*] (EA)	
ERP	Effective Radiated Power [*Radio transmitting*]	
ERP	Effective Refractory Period	
ERP	Ejercito Revolucionario del Pueblo [*People's Revolutionary Army*] [*Argentina*] (PD)	
ERP	Ejercito Revolucionario del Pueblo [*People's Revolutionary Army*] [*El Salvador*] (PD)	
ERP	Electronic Requirement Plan [*Navy*]	
ERP	Electrostatic Reversal Printing	
ERP	Elevated Release Point [*Nuclear energy*] (NRCH)	
ERP	Eligibility Review and Reemployment Assistance Program [*Employment Service*] [*Department of Labor*]	
ERP	Emergency Rubber Project [*National Research Council*]	
ERP	End Reporting Period	
ERP	Endocardial Resection Procedure [*Cardiology*]	
ERP	Endoscopic Retrograde Pancreatography [*Medicine*]	
ERP	Engineered Restoration Procedure	
ERP	Engineering Release Package	
ERP	Engineering Requirements Plan [*for Military Assistance Programs*]	
ERP	Environmental Research Papers (MCD)	
ERP	Environmental Responsibility Program [*An association*] (EA)	
ERP	Equipment Repair Parts	
ERP	Equipment Replacement Program [*Data processing*]	
ERP	Equipment Requirement Program (MCD)	
ERP	Error-Recovery Package [*Data processing*] (MDG)	
ERP	Error-Recovery Procedure [*Data processing*]	
ERP	Estrogen Receptor Protein [*Endocrinology*]	
ERP	Euler-Rodrigues Parameter [*Physics*]	
ERP	European Recovery Program	
ERP	Event-Related Potential [*Neurophysiology*]	
ERP	Extended-Range Projectile	
ERP	Eye Reference Point [*NASA*] (KSC)	
ERPA	Office of Exploratory Research and Problem Assessment [*National Science Foundation*]	
ERPAL	Electronic Repair Parts Allowance List [*Navy*]	
ERPC	Eastern Railroad Presidents Conference [*Later, ERA*] (EA)	
ERPC	Eglin Refugee Processing Center [*Florida*] [*Air Force*] (MCD)	
ERPC	Emerson Radio & Phonograph Corporation [*Later, Emerson Radio Corporation*]	
ERPD	Electronic Reconnaissance Procurement Division	
ERPD	Experimental RADAR Prediction Device (MCD)	
ERPF	Effective Renal Plasma Flow [*Medicine*]	
ERPL	Equipment Repair Parts List	
ERPLD	Extended-Range Phase-Locked Demodulator (IEEE)	
ERPM	Engineering Requirements and Procedures Manual (MCD)	
ERPN	Eastern Region Public Notice [*Nigeria*] [*A publication*] (DLA)	
ERPO	Earth Resources Project Office (MCD)	
ERPPO	Engineer Repair Parts Packaging Office [*Merged with General Equipment Command*]	
ER-PR	Effectiveness Report - Performance Report [*Air Force*] (AFM)	
ERPR	Exponentially Restored, Poisson-Released	
ERPS	Equipment Release Priority System [*DoD*]	
ERPSL	Essential Repair Part Stockage List [*Military*] (AABC)	
ERQ	Economic Reorder Quantity (ADA)	
ERQ	Economic Repair Quantity	

ERQC	Engineering Reliability and Quality Control (AAG)	
Err	[*The*] Comedy of Errors [*Shakespearean work*]	
ERR	Eagle Ridge Resources Ltd. [*Vancouver Stock Exchange symbol*]	
ERR	Economic Retention Requirement (AFIT)	
ERR	Economic Review. Federal Reserve Bank of Richmond [*A publication*]	
ERR	Elk River Reactor	
ERR	Employer Relations Representative	
ERR	Engine Removal Report	
ERR	Engineering Release Record (AAG)	
ERR	Engineering Reliability Review (MCD)	
ERR	Engineering Research Report	
ERR	Erie Railroad	
ERR	Errata (NVT)	
ERR	Errol, NH [*Location identifier*] [*FAA*] (FAAL)	
ERR	Error (MCD)	
err	Estonian Soviet Socialist Republic [*MARC country of publication code*] [*Library of Congress*] (LCCP)	
ERR	Estrogen Receptor-Related	
Err & App	Error and Appeal Reports [*Canada*] [*A publication*] (DLA)	
ER/RB	Enhanced Radiation/Reduced Blast	
ERRC	Eastern Regional Research Center [*Department of Agriculture*] [*Philadelphia, PA*] (GRD)	
ERRC	Error Correction	
ERRC	Expendability/Recoverability/Repair Capability (NASA)	
ERRC	Expendability, Recoverability, Repairability Cost (NASA)	
ERRCC	Expendability, Recoverability, Repairability Cost Category	
ERRDEP	Error Variance Dependent on Level [*Statistical test*]	
ERRDF	Earth Resources Research Data Facility	
ERREAC	Employee Relocation Real Estate Advisory Council [*Later, E-R-C*] (EA)	
ERRET	Error Return Point (MCD)	
ERRI	Environmental Resources Research Institute [*Pennsylvania State University*] [*Information service or system*] (IID)	
ERRN	Expedite Release Request Notice (MCD)	
ERRON	Erroneous	
ERRP	EGF [*Epidermal Growth Factor*] Receptor-Related Protein [*Biochemistry*]	
ERRS	Environmental Response and Referral Service [*Oak Ridge National Laboratory*] (IID)	
ERRT	Economic Research Round Table (EA)	
ERS	Earnings-Related Supplement [*British*]	
ERS	Earth Recovery Subsystem [*NASA*] (KSC)	
ERS	Earth Regeneration Society (EA)	
ERS	Earth Resources Satellite [*NASA*]	
ERS	Earth Resources Survey [*NASA*]	
ERS	Eastern Range Ships	
ERS	Economic Research Service [*Department of Agriculture*] [*Washington, DC*]	
ERS	Economic Research Service. Reports [*A publication*]	
ERS	Economic Retention Stock	
ERS	Educational Research Service (EA)	
ERS	Electoral Reform Society [*British*]	
ERS	Electric Railway Society (EAIO)	
ERS	Electronic Reconnaissance Set	
ERS	Electronic Reconnaissance System	
ERS	Electronic Register-Sender [*Telecommunications*] (TEL)	
ERS	Electronic Remote Switching (MCD)	
ERS	Electronic Rig Stats [*Pennwell Publishing Co.*] [*Information service or system*] (IID)	
ERS	Elevated Radio System	
ERS	Emergency Recovery Section	
ERS	Emergency Relocation Site [*Military*]	
ERS	Emergency Reporting System [*Telecommunications*] (TEL)	
ERS	Emergency Road Service [*American Automobile Association*]	
ERS	En Route Supplement [*A publication*] (APTA)	
ERS	Endoscopic Retrograde Sphincterotomy [*Medicine*]	
ERS	Energy Return System [*In ERS 2000, brand name of Reebok International Ltd.*]	
ERS	Engineering Release System	
ERS	Engineering Reprographic Society (EA)	
ERS	Engineering Research Station [*British*]	
ERS	English Reprint Series [*A publication*]	
ERS	Entry and Recovery Simulation (MCD)	
ERS	Environmental Research Satellite [*NASA*]	
ERS	Equilibrium Radiation Spectra	
ERS	Equipment Record System (KSC)	
ERS	Equipment Requirement Specification	
ERS	Erased (MSA)	
ERS	Eros Resources [*Vancouver Stock Exchange symbol*]	
ERS	ESA [*European Space Agency*] Remote Sensing Satellite	
ERS	Estimated Release Schedule (AAG)	
ERS	Ethnic and Racial Studies [*A publication*]	
ERS	European Research [*A publication*]	
ERS	European Rhinologic Society (EA)	
ERS	Expanded RADAR Service (AFM)	
ERS	Experimental RADAR System	
ERS	Experimental Research Society [*Defunct*] (EA)	
ERS	External Reflection Spectroscopy	
ERS	External Regulation System (IEEE)	

ERS........... Windhoek-Eros [*Namibia*] [*Airport symbol*] (OAG)
ERSA........ Electronic Research Supply Agency
ERSA........ Embry-Riddle School of Aviation [*Later, E-RAU*] [*Florida*]
ERSA........ Emergency Relocation Site Afloat (MCD)
ERSA........ Extended-Range Strike Aircraft [*for low-level missions*] [*Air Force*]
ERSAL...... Environmental Remote Sensing Applications Laboratory [*Oregon State University*] [*Research center*] (RCD)
ERSC........ Extended-Range and Space Communication (MCD)
ERSD........ Electronic Range Scoring Device (MCD)
ERSD........ Engineering Research Services Division [*North Carolina State University*] [*Research center*] (RCD)
ERSER...... Expanded Reactance Series Resonator
ERSFF...... Eastern Region SEATO [*Southeast Asia Treaty Organization*] Field Forces (CINC)
ERSFP...... Earth Resources Survey Flights Program [*NASA*]
ERSI......... Elastomeric Reusable Surface Insulation (NASA)
ERSIR...... Earth Resources Shuttle Imaging RADAR
Ersk.......... Erskine's Institutes of the Law of Scotland [*A publication*] (DLA)
Ersk.......... Erskine's Principles of the Law of Scotland [*A publication*] (DLA)
Ersk Dec .... Erskine's United States Circuit Court, Etc., Decisions [*35 Georgia*] [*A publication*] (DLA)
Erskine I .... Erskine's Institutes of the Law of Scotland [*8 eds.*] [*1773-1871*] [*A publication*] (DLA)
Erskine Inst ... Erskine's Institutes of the Law of Scotland [*8 eds.*] [*1773-1871*] [*A publication*] (DLA)
Ersk Inst .... Erskine's Institutes of the Law of Scotland [*8 eds.*] [*1773-1871*] [*A publication*] (DLA)
Ersk Prin ... Erskine's Principles of the Law of Scotland [*A publication*] (DLA)
Ersk Speech ... Erskine's Speeches [*A publication*] (DLA)
Ersk Speeches ... Erskine's Speeches [*A publication*] (DLA)
ERSNA...... Efferent Renal Sympathetic Nerve Activity [*Physiology*]
ERSOS ..... Earth Resource Survey Operational System (TEL)
ERSP........ Earth Resources Survey Program [*NASA*]
ERSP........ Event-Related Slow-Brain Potential [*Neurophysiology*]
ERSP......... Expendable Recoverable Sound Projector [*Navy*] (CAAL)
ERSPRC.... Earth Resources Survey Program Review Committee [*NASA*] (NOAA)
ERSR........ Equipment Reliability Status Report
ERSS .... Earth Resources Satellite System (IEEE)
ERS Staff Rep US Dep Agric Econ Res Serv ... ERS Staff Report. United States Department of Agriculture. Economic Research Service [*A publication*]
ERSTD...... Energy Report to the States [*A publication*]
ERT .... Earth Received Time [*Astronomy*]
ERT .... Educational Requirements Test
ERT .... Effective Reference Time
ERT .... Egyptian Religious Texts and Representations [*New York*] [*A publication*] (BJA)
ERT .... Electrical Resistance Temperature
ERT .... Elektroniikka Radio Televisio [*A publication*]
ERT .... Elementary Renewal Theorem
ERT .... Emergency Response Team (NRCH)
ERT .... Encoder-Receiver-Transmitter [*Telecommunications*]
ERT .... Enershare Technology Corp. [*Vancouver Stock Exchange symbol*]
ERT .... Engine Rotor Tester
ERT .... Engineering Release Ticket
ERT .... Ente de Radiodifusion y Television [*Radio and television network*] [*Argentina*]
ERT .... Environmental Research and Technology, Inc. [*Concord, MA*] (MCD)
ERT .... Environmental Research and Technology, Information Center, Concord, MA [*OCLC symbol*] (OCLC)
ERT .... Environmental Response Team [*Environmental Protection Agency*]
ERT .... Equipment Removal Tag (MCD)
ERT .... Equipment Repair Time
ERT .... Estimated Repair Time [*Telecommunications*] (TEL)
ERT .... Estrogen Replacement Therapy [*Medicine*]
ERT .... European Round Table (EAIO)
ERT .... Evangelical Review of Theology [*A publication*]
ERT .... Execute Reference Time (MCD)
ERT .... Exhibits Round Table [*American Library Association*]
ERT .... Expected Run-Time
ERT .... Extended-Range TOW [*Tube-Launched, Optically Tracked Wire-Guided (Weapon)*] (MCD)
ERT .... Extended Research Telescope
ERT .... External Radiation Therapy [*Medicine*]
ERT .... Roundtable of European Industrialists [*Paris, France*] (EAIO)
ERTA........ Economic Recovery Tax Act [*1981*]
ERTA........ Emergency Railroad Transportation Act, 1933
ERTA........ European Road Transport Agreement (ILCA)
ERTAT...... Expressway and Rapid Transit Authority of Thailand (DS)
ERTC........ Emergency Rescue Team Chief [*Air Force*]
ERTC........ Engineer Replacement Training Center
ERTC........ European Regional Test Center (NATG)

ERTE........ Name used by clothing designer Romain de Tirtoff, derives from the French pronunciation of his initials, "RT"
ERT (Energy Resour Technol) ... ERT (Energy Resources and Technology) [*Formerly, Energy Resources Report*] [*A publication*]
ERTG........ Economic [*or Economical*] Radioisotope Thermoelectric Generator
ERTH .... Earth [*Freight*]
ERTI......... Electron-Ray Tuning Indicator (DEN)
ERTLA...... Elektroniikka Radio Televisio [*A publication*]
ERTS .... Earth Resources Technology Satellite [*Later, LANDSAT*] [*NASA*]
ERTS .... Edwards Rocket Test Site (KSC)
ERTS .... Electronic Arts [*Commercial firm*] (NQ)
ERTS .... ELINT [*Electronic Intelligence*] Receiver Test System (MCD)
ERTS .... Environmental Radiological Technical Specifications [*Nuclear energy*] (NRCH)
ERTS .... Environmental Resources Technology Satellite (NRCH)
ERTS .... Error Rate Test Set (TEL)
ERU .... Earth Rate Unit [*NASA*] (KSC)
ERU .... Eastern Rugby Union of America (EA)
ERU .... Electronic Reconnaissance Unit (MCD)
ERU .... Emergency Recovery Unit
ERU .... English Rugby Union
ERU .... Erume [*Papua New Guinea*] [*Airport symbol*] (OAG)
'Erub .... 'Erubin (BJA)
ERUHG...... External Representation of the Ukrainian Helsinki Group (EA)
ERUMAT ... Ernaehrungs-Umschau [*A publication*]
ERUN........ Education Research Unit News [*Australian Union of Students*] [*A publication*] (ADA)
ERV .... ECM [*Electronic Countermeasures*] - Resistant Voice
ERV .... Efferent Renal Vein [*Anatomy*]
ERV .... Electrical Review [*A publication*]
ERV .... Electromagnetic Relief Valve [*Engineering instrumentation*]
ERV .... English Revised Version [*of the Bible*] [*A publication*] (BJA)
ERV .... Entry Research Vehicle
ERV .... Expiratory Reserve Volume [*Physiology*]
ERV .... Extract Release Volume [*Food technology*]
ERV .... Kerrville, TX [*Location identifier*] [*FAA*] (FAAL)
ERVAD ..... Engineering Release for Vendor Article Data [*Later, PRVD*] (AAG)
ERVm .... English Revised Version [*of the Bible*], Margin
ERVSC ...... Engineer and Railway Volunteer Staff Corps [*Army*] [*British*]
ERW .... Economic Review [*A publication*]
ERW .... Electrical Resistance Weld
ERW .... Enhanced Radiation Weapon
ERW .... European Research. Marketing, Opinion, Advertising [*A publication*]
ERWP........ European Railway Wagon Pool (EA)
ER(WR)..... Earnings Record (Wage Record) [*Social Security Administration*] (OICC)
ERWRE...... Earthenware [*Freight*]
ERWS........ Engineering Release Work Sheet (AAG)
ERY .... Early (FAAC)
ERY .... East Riding Yeomanry [*Military unit*] [*British*]
ERY .... East Riding of Yorkshire [*Administrative county in England*] (ROG)
ERY .... Erysipelas [*Medicine*]
ERY .... Erythromycin [*Also, E, ERYC, ETM*] [*Antibacterial compound*]
ERY .... Newberry, MI [*Location identifier*] [*FAA*] (FAAL)
ERYC........ Erythromycin [*Also, E, ERY, ETM*] [*Antibacterial compound*]
ERYIY .... East Riding of Yorkshire Imperial Yeomanry [*British military*] (DMA)
ERZ .... Eastern Rift Zone [*Geology*]
ERZ .... Erzurum [*Turkey*] [*Seismograph station code, US Geological Survey*] (SEIS)
ERZ .... Erzurum [*Turkey*] [*Airport symbol*] (OAG)
ERZ .... Extended Reconnaissance Zone [*Army*] (AABC)
ES .... Abbott Laboratories Ltd. [*Great Britain*] [*Research code symbol*]
ES .... Eagle Squadron [*British military*] (DMA)
ES .... Early Shock [*Medicine*]
ES .... Early Successional [*Botany*]
ES .... Earned Surplus
ES .... Earth Sciences Division [*Army Natick Laboratories*]
ES .... Earth Station
ES .... Eastern States (ADA)
ES .... Ebenezer Society (EA)
ES .... Echo Sounding
ES .... Echo Suppressor [*Telecommunications*] (TEL)
ES .... Econometric Society (EA)
ES .... Economic Studies [*Bureau of the Census*]
ES .... Edge Salicornia Zone [*Ecology*]
ES .... Edinaya Systema [*Unified System*] [*Russian*] [*Data processing*]
ES .... Edison Screw
ES .... Educational Services [*Publisher*]
ES .... Educational Specialist
ES .... Educational Studies [*A publication*]
Es .... Ego Strength [*Psychology*]
ES .... Einheitliche Systematik [*Library science*]

Es	Einsteinium [*Preferred form, but also see E*] [*Chemical element*]
ES	Ejection Sound [*Cardiology*]
es	El Salvador [*MARC country of publication code*] [*Library of Congress*] (LCCP)
ES	Elastic Suspensor
ES	Elasticities of Substitution [*Statistics*]
ES	Elasticity of Supply [*Economics*] (DCTA)
ES	Eldest Son
ES	Electric Starting (ADA)
ES	Electrical Stimulus
ES	Electrochemical Society
E/S	Electrode Signalling [*British military*] (DMA)
ES	Electromagnetic Storage
ES	Electromagnetic Switching (IEEE)
ES	Electron Synchrotron [*Nuclear energy*]
ES	Electronic Section [*National Weather Service*]
ES	Electronic Shop Major [*Coast Guard*]
ES	Electronic Standard
ES	Electronic Switching [*Telecommunications*]
ES	Electronic Systems
ES	Electroshock [*Psychology*]
ES	Electrospray [*Ionization*] [*Physics*]
ES	Electrostatic
ES	Electrostatic Spraying
ES	Electrostatic Storage
ES	Elenchus Suppletorius ad Elenchum Bibliographicum Biblicum [*A publication*] (BJA)
ES	Eligible for Separation
ES	Eligible Spouse [*Social Security Administration*]
ES	Ellis Air Lines
ES	Ells Scotch (ROG)
ES	Embryo Sac [*Botany*]
ES	Embryo Stem Cell
ES	Embryonal Stem [*Cell line*]
ES	Embryonic Shield
E(S)	Emergency Service
e(S)	Emergent S Wave [*Earthquakes*]
ES	Emission Spectrum [*Spectroscopy*]
ES	Employee Suggestion (AAG)
ES	Employer Services [*State Employee Security Agency*] (OICC)
ES	Employment Service [*US*] (KSC)
ES	Emulsifying Salts [*Food technology*]
E-S	En Route Supplement
E/S	En Suite (ADA)
ES	Enamel Single Silk [*Wire insulation*] (AAG)
ES	Enamelist Society (EA)
ES	End Sheet [*Publishing*]
ES	End Strength
ES	End of Study
ES	Endocrine Society (EA)
ES	Endogenous Substance [*Biology*]
ES	Endoplasmic Surface [*Freeze etching in microscopy*]
ES	Endoscopic Sclerotherapy [*Medicine*]
ES	Endoscopic Sphincterotomy [*Medicine*]
ES	Enema Saponis [*Medicine*]
ES	Enemy Status (MCD)
ES	Engagement Simulation [*Military*] (INF)
ES	Engine-Sized [*Paper*]
E/S	Engineer/Service [*Aerospace*] (AAG)
ES	Engineered Safeguards [*Nuclear energy*] (NRCH)
ES	Engineering and Society
ES	Engineering Standard
ES	Engineering Study
ES	Enginesmith [*British military*] (DMA)
ES	Englische Studien [*A publication*]
ES	Englisches Seminar [*A publication*]
ES	English Studies [*A publication*]
ES	Enterprise Statistics [*A publication*]
ES	Environmental Safety (EA)
ES	Enzyme-Substrate Complex [*Enzyme kinetics*]
ES	Ephphatha Services (EA)
ES	Epigraphic Society (EA)
ES	Eprova Ltd. [*Switzerland*] [*Research code symbol*]
ES	Equal Section [*Technical drawings*]
ES	Equipment Section
ES	Equipment Serviceability (MCD)
ES	Equipment Specialist [*Military*] (AFIT)
ES	Equipment Specification
ES	Equipment Status (MCD)
ES	Ergonomics Society [*British*]
ES	Erkennungssignal [*Recognition signal*] [*German military - World War II*]
ES	Escape System (MCD)
Es	Escorial [*A publication*]
ES	Escort Ship (CINC)
E & S	Essays and Studies [*London*] [*A publication*]
E & S	Essays and Studies [*London*] [*A publication*]
ES	ESSO Magazine [*A publication*]
ES	Estimate (ROG)
ES	Estimated Tax [*IRS*]
ES	Estradiol [*Also, E₂ E-diol*] [*Endocrinology*]
ES	Estudios Segovianos [*A publication*]
ES	Eureka Society (EA)
es-----	Europe, Southern [*MARC geographic area code*] [*Library of Congress*] (LCCP)
ES	Evangelization Society (EA)
ES	Eversley Series [*A publication*]
E & S	Excess and Surplus Business [*Insurance*]
ES	Exclusive of Sheeting
ES	Excretory-Secretory
ES	Executive Secretary
ES	Exempt Security
ES	Existential Study [*Psychology*]
ES	Exoplasmic Surface [*Freeze etching in microscopy*]
ES	Experiment Segment (MCD)
ES	Experimental Station
ES	Expert System [*Data processing*]
E of S	Expiration of Service
ES	Export Surpluses [*British*]
ES	Extended Sleeper [*In truck name Aero ES*] [*Volvo White Truck Corp.*] [*Automotive engineering*]
ES	Extension Service [*Department of Agriculture*]
ES	Exterior Surface
ES	External Services [*British Broadcasting Corp.*]
ES	External Store
ES	Extra Segment [*Data processing*]
ES	Extra Series
ES	Extraction Steam [*System*] [*Nuclear energy*] (NRCH)
ES	Eye Stalk
ES	IEEE Education Society (EA)
ES	Journal of Environmental Systems [*A publication*]
ES	Seagreen Air Transport [*Antigua, Barbuda*] [*ICAO designator*] (FAAC)
ES	Spain [*ANSI two-letter standard code*] (CNC)
ES²	European Silicon Structures [*Proposed Pan-European manufacturer of semiconductors*]
E/S³	Engineering and Scientific Support System [*IBM Corp.*]
ESA............	Earth Station - Arabia
ESA............	Eastern Ski Association [*Later, USSA*] (EA)
ESA............	Eastern Surfing Association (EA)
ESA............	Ecole Superieure des Affaires [*High Business School*] [*Information service or system*] (EISS)
ESA............	Ecological Society of America (EA)
ESA............	Economic Stabilization Act [*Wage-price controls*] [*Expired April 30, 1974*]
ESA............	Economic Stabilization Administration
ESA............	Economic Stabilization Agency [*Terminated, 1953*]
ESA............	Ejercito Salvadoreno Anticomunista [*Salvadoran Anti-Communist Army*] (PD)
ESA............	Ejercito Segredo Anti-Comunista [*Secret Anti-Communist Army*] [*Guatemala*] (PD)
ESA............	Electrical Stress Analysis
ESA............	Electrically Supported [*or Suspended*] Accelerometer
ESA............	Electrolysis Society of America [*Later, SCME*] (EA)
ESA............	Electron Scan Antenna [*FAA*]
ESA............	Electronic Security Alarm [*Automobile theft preventive*]
ESA............	Electronic Subsystems Analysis (MCD)
ESA............	Electronic Surge Arrester
ESA............	Electrostatic Analyzer
ESA............	Emakeele Seltsi Aastaraamat [*A publication*]
ESA............	Emergency Safe Altitude (MCD)
ESA............	Employee Standards Administration
ESA............	Employment Service Agency [*Department of Employment*] [*British*]
ESA............	Employment Standards Administration [*Department of Labor*]
ESA............	End-Systolic Areas [*Cardiology*]
ESA............	Endangered Species Act [*1973*]
ESA............	Energy Security Act [*1980*]
ESA............	Energy-Separating Agent [*Chemical engineering*]
ESA............	Engine Service Association (EA)
ESA............	Engineer Stores Assignment [*British*]
ESA............	Engineer Surveyors' Association [*A union*] [*British*]
ESA............	Engineering Study Authorization Division [*NASA*] (KSC)
ESA............	Engineering Supply Area (NASA)
ESA............	Engineering Support Activity [*Military*]
ESA............	Engineering Support Assembly (NASA)
ESA............	Engineers and Scientists of America [*Defunct*]
ES & A	English, Scottish & Australian Bank Ltd. (ADA)
ESA............	English, Scottish & Australian Bank Ltd. (ADA)
ESA............	English Studies in Africa [*A publication*]
ESA............	Entomological Society of America (EA)
ESA............	Environmental Protection Agency, Region X Library, Seattle, WA [*OCLC symbol*] (OCLC)
ESA............	Environmental Study Area
ESA............	Environmentally Sensitive Area [*British*]
ESA............	Epigraphic South Arabian (BJA)
ESA............	Epiphyllum Society of America (EA)
ESA............	Episcopal Synod of America (EA)
ESA............	Equalized Sidelobe Antenna
ESA............	Equipment Service Association (EA)
ESA............	Equivalent Snowline Altitude

ESA............ Esa Ala [*Papua New Guinea*] [*Airport symbol*]   (OAG)
ESA............ Esa Ala [*D'Entrecasteaux Islands*] [*Seismograph station code, US Geological Survey*]   (SEIS)
E/SA......... ESA. Engage/Social Action [*A publication*]
ESA............ Eurasia Septentrionalis Antiqua [*A publication*]
ESA............ European Space Agency [*See also ASE*]   (EAIO)
ESA............ European Space Association
ESA............ European Strabismological Association   (EAIO)
ESA............ European Supply Agency   (NATG)
ESA............ Euthanasia Society of America [*Later, SRD*]   (EA)
ESA............ Evangelicals for Social Action   (EA)
ESA............ Exer-Safety Association   (EA)
ESA............ Expiration of Service Agreement [*Military*]   (AABC)
ESA............ Explosive Safe Area [*NASA*]
ESA............ Explosive Safety Approval   (MUGU)
ESA............ Extended Service Agreement
ESA............ Externally Specified Address   (CAAL)
ESA............ Economic Stimulus Appropriations Act   (OICC)
ESAA....... Emergency School Aid Act [*1972*]
ESAA....... Employment Security Administration Account
ESAA....... English Setter Association of America   (EA)
ESAA....... European Special Activities Area [*Military*]
ESAB........ Energy Supplies Allocation Board
ESA Bull.... ESA [*European Space Agency*] Bulletin [*France*] [*A publication*]
ESAC......... Electronic Systems Assistance Center [*Telecommunications*]   (TEL)
ESAC......... Environmental Systems Applications Center [*NASA*]
ESAC......... Evangelical Social Action Commission   (EA)
ESACT...... Engineering and Systems Analysis for the Control of Toxics Technology Center [*University of California at Los Angeles*] [*Research center*]   (RCD)
ESACT...... European Society for Animal Cell Technology   (EA)
ESADA...... Empire State Atomic Development Associates, Inc.
ESADS...... Earth Science and Applications Data System [*National Oceanic and Atmospheric Administration*]
ESAE........ European Society of Association Executives   (EA)
ESAF........ Enhanced Structural Adjustment Facility [*IMF*]   (ECON)
ESAFA...... Employment Security Administrative Financing Act of 1954
ESAfr....... English Studies in Africa [*A publication*]
ESAFT...... Electrically Steerable Antenna Feed Techniques   (NG)
ESAIRA.... Electronically Scanning Airborne Intercept RADAR Antenna
ESA-IRS.... European Space Agency Information Retrieval Service [*Italy*]
ESA J........ ESA [*European Space Agency*] Journal [*A publication*]
ESAJD...... ESA [*European Space Agency*] Journal [*A publication*]
Esakia Occas Pap Hikosan Biol Lab Entomol ... Esakia Occasional Papers of the Hikosan Biological Laboratory in Entomology [*A publication*]
ESAL......... Eastern Air Lines, Inc. [*NASDAQ symbol*]   (NQ)
ESAL......... Engine Start after Launch [*Navy*]   (CAAL)
ESAL......... Equivalent Single Axle Load
ESAM....... Extendable Stiff Arm Manipulator [*NASA*]
ESAMS...... Elliott Automation Space and Advanced Military Systems
ESAO .... Earth Sciences Assistance Office [*Department of the Interior*]   (GRD)
ESAO .... European Society for Artificial Organs   (EA)
ESAOA...... Eastern Ski Area Operators Association   (EA)
ESAP........ Emergency School Assistance Program
ESAP......... Employment Security Automation Project [*Department of Labor*]
ESAP........ Evoked Sensory Action Potential [*Neurophysiology*]
ESAPDG ... Environmental Sciences and Applications [*A publication*]
ESAR........ Electromagnetic Spectrum Allocation Request [*Army*]   (RDA)
ESAR........ Electronically Scanned Array RADAR   (IEEE)
ESAR........ Electronically Steerable Array RADAR
ESARBICA ... Eastern and Southern African Regional Branch of the International Council on Archives [*Nairobi, Kenya*]   (EAIO)
ESARCC ... Endangered Species Act Reauthorization Coordinating Committee   (EA)
ESARCL.... Edinburgh School of Agriculture. Annual Report [*A publication*]
Esarh.......... Esarhaddon   (BJA)
ESARIPO ... Industrial Property Organization for English-Speaking Africa [*Nairobi, Kenya*]   (EAIO)
ESARS...... Earth Surveillance and Rendezvous Simulator
ESARS...... Employment Service Automated [*or Automatic*] Reporting System [*Department of Labor*]
ESAS .... Electronically Steerable Antenna System [*Navy*]   (CAAL)
ESAS .... Engineered Safeguards Actuation System [*Nuclear energy*]   (NRCH)
ESASAM .. Ecological Studies Analysis and Synthesis [*A publication*]
ESASC...... Elementary School Administrative Supervisory Certificate
ESA Sci and Tech Rev ... ESA [*European Space Agency*] Scientific and Technical Review [*A publication*]
ESAT......... Employee Satisfaction
ESATA...... Executive Subroutines for Afterheat Temperature Analysis [*Computer program*] [*NASA*]
ESAUAS ... Endocrine Society of Australia. Proceedings [*A publication*]
ESA (UN) ... Department of Economic and Social Affairs of the United Nations [*Later, Department of Social Affairs*]

ESAUSA ... Estonian Student Association in the United States of America   (EA)
ESAWC..... Evaluation Staff, War College [*Air Force*]
ESAWR..... Early Settlers Association of the Western Reserve   (EA)
ESAX........ East Saxon [*Dialect of Old English*] [*Language, etc.*]
ESB............ Ankara-Esenboga [*Turkey*] [*Airport symbol*]   (OAG)
ESB............ Earth Station - Brazil
ESB............ Eastern Seaboard [*Thailand*]   (DS)
ESB............ Economic Stabilization Board [*World War II*]
ESB............ Economisch-Statistische Berichten [*A publication*]
ESB............ Educational Service Branch [*BUPERS*]
ESB............ Effective School Battery [*Educational test*]
ESB............ Eigen Schoon en de Brabander [*A publication*]
ESB............ Electric Storage Battery
ESB............ Electrical Stimulation of the Brain
ESB............ Electrical Systems Branch [*NASA*]   (KSC)
ESB............ Empennage Support Beam [*Aerospace engineering*]   (MCD)
ESB............ Engineer Special Brigade [*Military*]
ESB............ English-Speaking Background   (ADA)
ESB............ English-Speaking Board (International) [*British*]
ESB............ Environmental Protection Agency, ERC [*Environmental Research Center*] Library, Corvallis, OR [*OCLC symbol*]   (OCLC)
ESB............ Environmental Studies Board [*National Academy of Sciences*]
ESB............ [*Ralph*] Eppel, [*Gregg*] Simpson, [*Bob*] Bell [*Music group*] [*Canada*]
ESB............ Esa Ala [*D'Entrecasteaux Islands*] [*Seismograph station code, US Geological Survey*]   (SEIS)
ESB............ Esselte Business Systems, Inc. [*NYSE symbol*]   (SPSG)
ESB............ Essential Switching Box   (MCD)
ESB............ European Schoolbooks Ltd. [*British*]
ESB............ European Society of Biomechanics   (EA)
ESB............ Executive for Small Business
ESB............ Experiments Systems Branch [*NASA*]   (KSC)
ESB............ Extra Strong Bitter [*Beer*] [*British*]
ESBA........ Eastern Sovereign Base Area [*British military*]   (DMA)
ESBA........ Ethyl-sec-butylamiline [*Organic chemistry*]
ESBC........ Electronics Small Business Council
ESBCY...... European Society for Blue Cross Youth   (EA)
ESBFCOA ... Eastern States Blast Furnace and Coke Oven Association   (EA)
ESBFS...... East of Scotland Brass Founders' Society [*A union*]
ESBGA...... Eisenbahn-Ingenieur [*A publication*]
ESBIAV..... Essays in Biochemistry [*A publication*]
ESBK........ [*The*] Elmira Savings Bank FSB [*Elmira, NY*] [*NASDAQ symbol*]   (NQ)
ESBL........ Engine Start before Launch [*Navy*]   (CAAL)
ESBO......... Environmental and Safety Business Opportunities [*Bureau of National Affairs*]
ESBP......... Ezik i Stil na Balgarskite Pitsateli [*A publication*]
ESBR........ Electronic Stacked Beam RADAR   (FAAC)
ESBRS...... Elementary School Behavior Rating Scale [*Devereaux*] [*Psychology*]
ESBUAX ... Estuarine Bulletin [*A publication*]
ESBVM .... Ecumenical Society of the Blessed Virgin Mary   (EA)
ESC........... Earth Station - Congo
ESC........... Earthspirit Community   (EA)
ESC........... Eastern Simulation Council
ESC........... Eastern Snow Conference Annual Meetings. Proceedings [*A publication*]
ESC........... Echo Suppressor Control [*Telecommunications*]   (TEL)
ESC........... Ecological Study Center [*Oak Ridge National Laboratory*]
ESC........... Economic Sciences Corporation [*Information service or system*]   (IID)
ESC........... Economic and Social Council [*United Nations*]
ESC........... Educational Systems Corporation [*Defunct*]   (EA)
ESC........... El Salvador [*Chile*] [*Seismograph station code, US Geological Survey*] [*Closed*]   (SEIS)
ESC........... Electric Surface Current
ESC........... Electromechanical Stop Clock
ESC........... Electronic Scan Converter
ESC........... Electronic Security Command   (MCD)
ESC........... Electronic Shop Computer
ESC........... Electronic Spark Control [*Automotive*]
ESC........... Electronic Still Camera
ESC........... Electronic Supervisory Control   (MCD)
ESC........... Electronic Switching Center   (CET)
ESC........... Electronic Systems Center [*Air Force*]
ESC........... Electronic Systems Command [*Also, NESC*] [*Navy*]
ESC........... Electrostatic Collector
ESC........... Electrostatic Compatibility   (IEEE)
ESC........... Elementary School Center [*An association*]   (EA)
ESC........... Embryonic Stem Cell [*Cytology*]
ESC........... Enamel Single-Covered [*Wire insulation*]   (DEN)
ESC........... End-Systolic Count [*Cardiology*]
ESC........... Energy Systems Center [*University of Nevada*] [*Research center*]   (RCD)
ESC........... Engine Start Command   (KSC)
ESC........... Engineer Studies Center   (MCD)
ESC........... Engineering Sequential Camera   (KSC)
ESC........... Engineering Service Circuit
ESC........... English Shakespeare Company   (ECON)

ESC............	English Shepherd Club (EA)
ESC............	English Studies in Canada [*A publication*]
ESC............	Environmental Stress Crack [*or Cracking*] [*Plastics*]
ESC............	Environmental Studies Center [*State University of New York at Buffalo*] [*Research center*] (RCD)
ESC............	Environmental Study Conference [*House of Representatives*]
ESC............	Environmental Systems Corporation [*NYSE symbol*] (SPSG)
ESC............	Epoxy Spray Coater
ESC............	Equipment Section Container
ESC............	Equipment Serviceability Criteria [*Military*]
ESC............	Equipment Storage Container (KSC)
ESCM............	Erythropoietin-Sensitive Stem Cell [*Hematology*]
ESC............	Escalator [*Technical drawings*]
ESC.........	Escanaba [*Michigan*] [*Airport symbol*] (OAG)
ESC............	Escanaba, MI [*Location identifier*] [*FAA*] (FAAL)
ESC.........	Escape (NASA)
ESC.........	Escape Character [*Keyboard*] (KSC)
ESC............	Escobilla [*Little Broom*] [*Spanish*] [*Flamenco dance term*]
ESC............	Escompte [*Discount, Rebate*] [*French*]
Esc............	Escorial [*A publication*]
Esc.............	Escort [*Record label*]
ESC............	Escort (AABC)
Esc..............	Escrow [*Legal term*] (DLA)
ESC............	Escudo [*Monetary unit*] [*Chile, Portugal*]
ESC............	Escutcheon
ESC............	Esplanade Centre Holdings [*Vancouver Stock Exchange symbol*]
EsC............	Esprit Createur [*A publication*]
ESC............	European Security Conference [*Soviet-sponsored*]
ESC............	European Seismological Commission (EAIO)
ESC............	European Shippers' Councils [*Netherlands*] (DS)
ESC............	European Society of Cardiology (MCD)
ESC............	European Society of Climatotherapy [*See also FEC*] [*Briancon, France*] (EAIO)
ESC............	European Society of Culture [*See also SEC*] (EAIO)
ESC............	European Space Conference
ESC............	European Sport Shooting Confederation (EAIO)
ESC............	Ex Senatus Consulto [*By Decree of the Senate*] [*Latin*]
ESCOS............	Exchange Servicing Center [*Telecommunications*] (TEL)
ESC............	Executive Search Council (EA)
ESC............	Executive Seminar Center [*Civil Service Commission*]
ESC............	Executive Systems Corporation [*An association*] [*Defunct*] (EA)
ESC............	Expandable Shelter Containers (MCD)
E/SC............	Expected/Single-Command Travel Time
ESC............	Extended Service Coverage [*Automotive engineering*]
ESCA............	Electron Spectroscopy for Chemical Analysis
ESCA.........	Endangered Species Conservation Act of 1969
ESCA.........	Escalade, Inc. [*NASDAQ symbol*] (NQ)
ESCA.........	Executive Stewards' and Caterers' Association [*Later, IFSEA*]
ESCA.........	Exposition Service Contractors Association (EA)
ESCA.........	Extended Source Calibration Area [*Nuclear energy*] (NRCH)
Esc Agron Amazonia Bol ...	Escola de Agronomia da Amazonia. Boletim [*A publication*]
ESCAP	Economic and Social Commission for Asia and the Pacific [*Information service or system*] (EISS)
ESCAP	European Society of Child and Adolescent Psychiatry (EA)
ESCAP	United Nations Economic and Social Commission for Asia and the Pacific [*Bangkok, Thailand*] (EAIO)
ESCAPE.....	Expansion Symbolic Compiling Assembly Program for Engineers
ESCAPE....	Expeditious Sales, Catalog, and Property Evaluation [*Defense Logistics Services Center project*] [*DoD*]
ESCAPER ...	Emergency System of Control Allowing Pilot Escape and Recovery (MCD)
ESCAR	Experimental Superconducting Accelerating Ring [*Atomic physics*]
ESCARFOR ...	Escort Carrier Force
ESCAT	Emergency Security Control of Air Traffic (AFM)
ESCBA	Earth Science Bulletin [*A publication*]
ESCC	Engineering Sequential Camera Coverage (KSC)
ESCC	Evans & Sutherland Computer Corp. [*NASDAQ symbol*] (NQ)
ESCC	Stockholm [*Sweden*] [*ICAO location identifier*] (ICLI)
ESCCP........	Engineering and Scientific Career Continuation Pay [*Air Force*]
ESCD........	Engineering Specification Control Document (AAG)
Esc Eng Univ Minas Gerais Inst Pesqui Radioat Publ ...	Escola de Engenharia. Universidade de Minas Gerais. Instituto de Pesquisas Radioativas. Publicacao [*A publication*]
ESCES.......	Experimental Space Communication Earth Station [*Telecommunications*] (TEL)
ESCF	Electronic Systems Compatibility Facility [*NASA*]
ESCF	Linkoping/Malmen [*Sweden*] [*ICAO location identifier*] (ICLI)
Esc Farm....	Escuela de Farmacia [*A publication*]
Esc Farm Guatem ...	Escuela de Farmacia Guatemala [*A publication*]
ESCG.........	Energy Sciences Corporation [*NASDAQ symbol*] (NQ)
ESCH	Earth Station - Chile
ESCH	Escherichia [*Bacterial strain*]
ESCHAT...	Eschatological (ADA)
E School L Rev ...	Eastern School Law Review [*A publication*] (DLA)
ESCHR......	El Salvador Committee for Human Rights (EAIO)

ESCI	Earth Sciences, Incorporated [*NASDAQ symbol*] (NQ)
ESCI	European Society for Clinical Investigation (EAIO)
ESCIS.......	Encyclopedia of Senior Citizens Information Sources [*A publication*]
ESCK	Norrkoping/Bravalla [*Sweden*] [*ICAO location identifier*] (ICLI)
ESCL	Electronic Systems Compatibility Laboratory [*NASA*]
ESCL	Escalator (MSA)
EsCl	Estudios Clasicos [*A publication*]
ESCL	Soderhamn [*Sweden*] [*ICAO location identifier*] (ICLI)
ESCLBC....	Estomatologia e Cultura [*A publication*]
ESCM........	Uppsala [*Sweden*] [*ICAO location identifier*] (ICLI)
ESCN.........	Electrolyte and Steroid-Produced Cardiopathy Characterized by Necrosis [*Medicine*]
ESCN.........	Stockholm/Tullinge [*Sweden*] [*ICAO location identifier*] (ICLI)
Esc Nac Agric (Chapingo) Monogr ...	Escuela Nacional de Agricultura (Chapingo). Monografias [*A publication*]
Esc Nac Agric (Chapingo) Rev ...	Escuela Nacional de Agricultura (Chapingo). Revista [*A publication*]
Esc Nac Agric (Chapingo) Ser Apuntes ...	Escuela Nacional de Agricultura (Chapingo). Serie de Apuntes [*A publication*]
Esc Nac Agric (Chapingo) Ser Invest ...	Escuela Nacional de Agricultura (Chapingo). Serie de Investigaciones [*A publication*]
ESCO.........	Earth Station - Colombia
ESCO.........	Engineers Supply Control Office [*Army*]
ESCO.........	European Satellite Consulting Organization [*France*] [*Telecommunications*] (TSSD)
ESCOE......	Engineering Societies Commission on Energy [*Defunct*] (EA)
ESCOMO ...	Escort Cost Model
ESCON......	Estimated Consumption [*of gasoline*] [*Computer model*]
ESCOP......	Experimental Stations Committee on Organization and Policy [*National Association of State Universities and Land-Grant Colleges*]
ESCORON ...	Escort-Scouting Squadron
ESCORT ...	Electronic System for Control of Receipt Transactions (MCD)
ESCORTDIV ...	Escort Division
ESCORTFIGHTRON ...	Escort Fighter Squadron
ESCOS	Electronic Security Combat Operations Staff [*Military*]
ESCP	Earth Science Curriculum Project [*Education*]
ESCP	Expendable Surface Current Probe [*Coast Guard*]
ESCPB.......	European Society of Comparative Physiology and Biochemistry (EAIO)
ESCR	Environmental Stress-Crack Resistance [*Plastics*]
ESCRG	Escort Guard
Escriche	Escriche's Diccionario Razonado de Legislacion y Jurisprudencia [*A publication*] (DLA)
Escriche Dic Leg ...	Escriche's Diccionario Razonado de Legislacion y Jurisprudencia [*A publication*] (DLA)
Escriche Dict ...	Escriche's Dictionary of Jurisprudence [*A publication*] (DLA)
ESCRTC....	Eastern Signal Corps Replacement Training Center
ESCRU......	Episcopal Society for Cultural and Racial Unity [*Defunct*] (EA)
ESCS	Eccentrically Stiffened Cylindrical Shell
ESCS	Economics, Statistics, and Cooperatives Service [*Later, ERS, SRS*] [*Department of Agriculture*]
ESCS	Emergency Satellite Communications System
ESCS	Enlisted Signal Corps School
ESCSI.......	Expanded Shale, Clay, and Slate Institute (EA)
Esc Super Agric Luiz De Queiroz (Sao Paulo) Bol ...	Escola Superior de Agricultura "Luiz De Queiroz" (Sao Paulo). Boletim [*A publication*]
ESCT	Elapsed Spacecraft Time
escte	Escompte [*Discount, Rebate*] [*Business term*] [*French*]
ESCU.........	Extended Service and Cooling Umbilical (NASA)
ESCVS.......	European Society for Cardiovascular Surgery (EAIO)
ESCWA	Economic and Social Commission for Western Asia [*United Nations*] [*Research center*] [*Iraq*] (IRC)
ESCWS	Essential Service Cooling Water System [*Nuclear energy*] (NRCH)
ESD	Earliest Start Date
ESD	Earth Sciences Division [*Army Natick Laboratories*] (NOAA)
ESD	Eastsound [*Washington*] [*Airport symbol*] (OAG)
ESD	Echo Sounding Device [*Navigation*]
ESD	Ecological Sciences Division [*Oak Ridge National Laboratory*]
ESD	Economic Surveys Division [*Census*] (OICC)
ESD	Effective Standard Deviation [*of chemical standardized solutions*]
ESD	Electron Spectrographic Diffraction
ESD	Electron-Stimulated Desorption [*Spectroscopy*]
ESD	Electronic Systems Division [*Hanscom Air Force Base, MA*]
ESD	Electrooptic Symbol Display
ESD	Electrostatic Discharge (MCD)
ESD	Electrostatic Storage Deflection
ESD	Elongated Single Domain
ESD	Emergency Shutdown (MCD)
ESD	End of Screening Date [*DoD*]
ESD	End-Systolic Diameter [*or Dimension*] [*Cardiology*]
ESD	Ending Sequence Done
ESD	Energy Systems and Policy [*A publication*]

ESD .... Engineered Systems & Development Corp. [*AMEX symbol*] (SPSG)
ESD .... Engineering Society of Detroit   (EA)
ESD .... Engineering Standardization Directives
ESD .... English as a Secondary Dialect
ESD .... Environmental Sciences Division [*Oak Ridge National Laboratory*]
ESD .... Environmental Sex Determination [*Biology*]
ESD .... Equipment Statistical Data
ESD .... Equipment Supply Depot [*British military*]   (DMA)
ESD .... Equivalent Spherical Diameter [*of a particle*]
ESD .... Equivalent Stylized Day [*Of wartime combat*]
Esd .... Esdras [*Apocrypha*]   (BJA)
ESD .... Esterase D [*An enzyme*]
ESD .... Estimated Shipping Date
ESD .... Estimated Standard Deviation [*Mathematics*]
ESD .... Ex-Stock Dividend [*Investment term*]
ESD .... Experiment Systems Division   (MCD)
ESD .... Exponential-Slope Difference [*Statistics*]
ESD .... Extension Shaft Disconnect [*Nuclear energy*]   (NRCH)
ESD .... External Symbol Dictionary [*A publication*]
ESD .... Extra Soil Defense [*Fabric treatment*]
ESDA .... Ljungbyhed [*Sweden*] [*ICAO location identifier*]   (ICLI)
ESDAC .... European Space Data Center   (MCD)
ESDB .... Angelholm [*Sweden*] [*ICAO location identifier*]   (ICLI)
ESDBAK ... Eisei Dobutsu [*Japanese Journal of Sanitary Zoology*] [*A publication*]
ESDC .... Equipment Sliding Drawer Cabinet
ESDC .... Equipment Statistical Data Card
ESDC .... Extended Salvage Depth Capability   (MCD)
ESDCA ...... Endocrinologia e Scienze della Costituzione [*A publication*]
ESDD .... Regional Military Command Subcenter South [*Sweden*] [*ICAO location identifier*]   (ICLI)
ESDE .... Electrostatic Discharge Effects   (MCD)
ESDF .... Ronneby [*Sweden*] [*ICAO location identifier*]   (ICLI)
ESDI .... Enhanced Small Device [*or Disk*] Interface [*Data processing*]
ES:DI .... Extra Segment:Destination Index [*Data processing*]
ESDIAD .... Electron-Stimulated Desorption Ion Angular Distribution [*For study of surfaces*]
ESDR .... Electrical System Design Report
ESDRP ...... Evreiskaia Sotsialdemokraticheskaia Rabochaia Partiia   (BJA)
ESDS .... Economic and Social Data System [*Agency for International Development*] [*Database*]
ESDS .... Elemental Standard Data System   (NG)
ES-DSMA ... Ephphatha Services - Division for Service and Mission in America   (EA)
ESD TDR .. Electronic Systems Division, Technical Documentary Reports [*AFSC*]
ESDU .... Engineering Sciences Data Unit
ESDU .... Event Storage and Distribution Unit
ESDU Data Items ... Engineering Sciences Data Unit. Data Items [*A publication*]
ESE .... East-Southeast
ESE .... Electrical Support Equipment
ESE .... Electron Spin Echo [*Physics*]
ESE .... Electronic Stock Evaluator Corp.
ESE .... Electronic Support Equipment   (MCD)
ESE .... Electronic System Evaluator
ESE .... Emergency Strike Effort [*Military*]
ESE .... Engineering Associate of the Society of Engineers, Inc. [*British*]   (DBQ)
ESE .... Engineering Support Equipment   (KSC)
ESE .... Ephemeris fuer Semitische Epigraphik [*A publication*]   (BJA)
ESE .... ESCO Electronics [*NYSE symbol*]   (SPSG)
ESE .... Estec Systems [*Vancouver Stock Exchange symbol*]
ESE .... European Stock Exchange
ESE .... EVA [*Extravehicular Activity*] Support Equipment [*NASA*]   (NASA)
ESE .... Experiment Support Equipment
ESE .... Review of the Economic Situation of Mexico [*A publication*]
ESE .... SFO Helicopter Airlines, Inc. [*Oakland, CA*] [*FAA designator*]   (FAAC)
ESEA .... Elementary and Secondary Education Act [*1965*]
ESEC .... Earth Station - Ecuador
ESEC .... En Route Secondary RADAR Beacon [*Aviation*]   (FAAC)
E Sec .... L'Enseignement Secondaire [*A publication*]
ESECA ...... Energy Supply and Environmental Coordination Act of 1974
ESED .... Environmental System and Effects Division [*NASA*]
ESEE .... European Society for Engineering Education
ESEEM .... Electron Spin Echo Envelope Modulation [*Physics*]
E Sef .... Estudios Sefardies [*A publication*]
ESEG .... Earth Station - Egypt
ESELL ...... Essays and Studies in English Language and Literature [*A publication*]
ESEM .... Electron Spin Echo Modulation [*Physics*]
ESEM .... Environmental Scanning Electron Microscope
ESEM .... Eski Sark Eserleri Muezesi [*Istanbul*]   (BJA)
ESERN ...... East-Southeastern [*Meteorology*]   (FAAC)
ESES .... Earth-Moon Space Exploration Study
ESE/VM ... Expert System Environment/Virtual Machine [*Data processing*]
ESEWD .... East-Southeastward [*Meteorology*]   (FAAC)

ESEX .... Essex Corp. [*NASDAQ symbol*]   (NQ)
ESF .... Alexandria [*Louisiana*] [*Airport symbol*]   (OAG)
ESF .... Alexandria, LA [*Location identifier*] [*FAA*]   (FAAL)
ESF .... Earth Society Foundation   (EA)
ESF .... Eastern Sea Frontier
ESF .... Ecoles Sans Frontieres [*Education Without Frontiers*] [*An association*]   (EAIO)
ESF .... Economic Support Fund [*Agency for International Development*]
ESF .... Electrostatic Focusing [*Electronics*]
ESF .... Engineered Safety Feature [*Nuclear energy*]   (NRCH)
ESF .... Engineering Specification Files
ESF .... Engineering Structural Foam
ESF .... Erythropoietic Stimulating [*or Erythropoietin Switching*] Factor [*Hematology*]
ESF .... Esperantic Studies Foundation   (EA)
ESF .... European Schools Federation   (EA)
ESF .... European Science Foundation   (EAIO)
ESF .... European Security Forum
ESF .... European Simmental Federation   (EAIO)
ESF .... European Social Fund
ESF .... European Surfing Federation   (EAIO)
ESF .... Even Side Flat
ESF .... Explosive-Safe Facility
ESF .... Extended Super Frame [*Telecommunications*]
ESFA .... Emergency Solid Fuels Administration
ESFA .... Engineered Safety Feature Actuation [*Nuclear energy*]   (NRCH)
ESFAS ...... Engineered Safety Features Actuation System [*Nuclear energy*]   (NRCH)
ESFC .... Equivalent Specific Fuel Consumption   (NG)
ESFH .... Hasslosa [*Sweden*] [*ICAO location identifier*]   (ICLI)
ESFI .... Epitaxial Silicon Films on Insulators   (MCD)
ESFI .... Knislinge [*Sweden*] [*ICAO location identifier*]   (ICLI)
ESFJ .... Sjobo [*Sweden*] [*ICAO location identifier*]   (ICLI)
ESFM .... Moholm [*Sweden*] [*ICAO location identifier*]   (ICLI)
ESFO .... Engineering Support Field Office [*Federal disaster planning*]
ESFQ .... Kosta [*Sweden*] [*ICAO location identifier*]   (ICLI)
ESFR .... Early Suppression Fast Response [*Sprinkler program for fire protection*]
ESFR .... Rada [*Sweden*] [*ICAO location identifier*]   (ICLI)
ESFS .... Engineered Safety Features System [*Nuclear energy*]   (NRCH)
ESFSWR ... Extra-Special Flexible Steel Wire Rope [*British*]
ESFU .... Vaxjo/Urasa [*Sweden*] [*ICAO location identifier*]   (ICLI)
ESFVS ...... Engineered Safety Feature Ventilation System [*Nuclear energy*]   (NRCH)
ESFY .... Byholma [*Sweden*] [*ICAO location identifier*]   (ICLI)
ESG .... Earth Station - Greece
ESG .... Edith Stein Guild   (EA)
ESG .... Education Service Group [*Bibliographic Retrieval Services*] [*Information service or system*]   (IID)
ESG .... Electrically [*or Electrostatically*] Suspended Gyro   (MSA)
ESG .... Electronic Sweep Generator
ESG .... ElectroSound Group, Inc. [*AMEX symbol*]   (SPSG)
ESG .... Electrostatic Gyroscope   (IEEE)
ESG .... Engineer Studies Group [*Office of the Chief of Engineers*]
ESG .... Engineering Service [*or Support*] Group   (AAG)
ESG .... English Standard Gauge
ESG .... Environmental Sciences Group [*Boulder, CO*] [*Department of Commerce*]   (GRD)
ESG .... Ethnobotany Specialist Group   (EA)
ESG .... Exchange Software Generator   (TEL)
ESG .... Expanded Sweep Generator   (CET)
ESGA .... Backamo [*Sweden*] [*ICAO location identifier*]   (ICLI)
ESGA .... Electrically Supported [*or Suspended*] Gyro Accelerometer
ESGC .... Alleberg [*Sweden*] [*ICAO location identifier*]   (ICLI)
ESGG .... Goteborg/Landvetter [*Sweden*] [*ICAO location identifier*]   (ICLI)
ESGH .... Herrljunga [*Sweden*] [*ICAO location identifier*]   (ICLI)
ESGI .... Alingsas [*Sweden*] [*ICAO location identifier*]   (ICLI)
ESGJ .... Jonkoping [*Sweden*] [*ICAO location identifier*]   (ICLI)
ESGK .... Falkoping [*Sweden*] [*ICAO location identifier*]   (ICLI)
ESGL .... Lidkoping [*Sweden*] [*ICAO location identifier*]   (ICLI)
ESGLD ...... European Study Group on Lysosomal Diseases   (EAIO)
ESGLNLA ... European Support Groups for Liberation and Nonviolence in Latin America   (EAIO)
ESGM .... Electrostatically Supported Gyro Monitor [*Navy*]
ESGM .... Eta Sigma Gamma [*A publication*]
ESGM .... European Society of Gastrointestinal Motility [*Louvain, Belgium*]   (EAIO)
ESGN .... Electrically Suspended Gyro Navigation
ESGO .... Vargarda [*Sweden*] [*ICAO location identifier*]   (ICLI)
ESGP .... Emergency Shelter Grant Program [*HUD*]
ESGP .... Goteborg/Save [*Sweden*] [*ICAO location identifier*]   (ICLI)
ESGQ .... Skovde [*Sweden*] [*ICAO location identifier*]   (ICLI)
ESGR .... Employer Support of the Guard and Reserve
ESGS .... Stromstad/Nasinge [*Sweden*] [*ICAO location identifier*]   (ICLI)
ESGT .... Trollhattan/Vanersborg [*Sweden*] [*ICAO location identifier*]   (ICLI)
ESGU .... Experimental Sheet Growth Unit [*Photovoltaic energy systems*]
ESGV .... Varberg [*Sweden*] [*ICAO location identifier*]   (ICLI)
ESGX .... Boras-Viared [*Sweden*] [*ICAO location identifier*]   (ICLI)

ESGY .... Saffle [*Sweden*] [*ICAO location identifier*]   (ICLI)
ESH .... Equivalent Solar Hour [*NASA*]
ESH .... Equivalent Standard Hours   (MCD)
ESH .... Harbor Defense SONARman [*Navy*]
ESH .... Human Resources, Institutions, and Agrarian Reform Division [*FAO*] [*United Nations*] [*Italy*] [*Information service or system*]   (IID)
ESH .... Scheib [*Earl*], Inc. [*AMEX symbol*]   (SPSG)
ESH .... Shoreham-By-Sea [*England*] [*Airport symbol*]   (OAG)
ESH .... Western Sahara [*ANSI three-letter standard code*]   (CNC)
ESHA .... Abisko [*Sweden*] [*ICAO location identifier*]   (ICLI)
ESHAA3 ... Engei Shikenjo Hokoku. A. Hiratsuka [*A publication*]
ESHAC ...... Electric Space Heating and Air Conditioning   (MCD)
ESHB .... Electrical Stimulation - Hot Boning [*Meat processing*]
ESHB .... Goteborg/Eastern Hospital [*Sweden*] [*ICAO location identifier*]   (ICLI)
ESHBA6 .... Engei Shikenjo Hokoku. B. Okitsu [*A publication*]
ESHC .... Stockholm/Southern Hospital [*Sweden*] [*ICAO location identifier*]   (ICLI)
ESHDAC ... Engei Shikenjo Hokoku. D. Kurume [*A publication*]
ESHE .... Landskrona [*Sweden*] [*ICAO location identifier*]   (ICLI)
ESHG .... Etudes Suisses d'Histoire Generale [*A publication*]
ESHG .... Stockholm/Gamla Stan [*Sweden*] [*ICAO location identifier*]   (ICLI)
ESHH .... Enthronement of the Sacred Heart in the Home   (EA)
ESHH .... Helsingborg/Harbour [*Sweden*] [*ICAO location identifier*]   (ICLI)
ESHI .... Ingmarso [*Sweden*] [*ICAO location identifier*]   (ICLI)
ESHK .... Earth Station - Hong Kong
ESHL .... Stockholm/Huddinge Hospital [*Sweden*] [*ICAO location identifier*]   (ICLI)
ESHLY ...... Energy Systems Holding ADR [*NASDAQ symbol*]   (NQ)
ESHM .... Malmo/Harbour [*Sweden*] [*ICAO location identifier*]   (ICLI)
ESHN .... Nacka [*Sweden*] [*ICAO location identifier*]   (ICLI)
ESHO .... Skovde/Hospital [*Sweden*] [*ICAO location identifier*]   (ICLI)
ESHP .... Empire State Historical Publications [*Series*]
ESHP .... Equivalent Shaft Horsepower [*Air Force*]
ESHP .... European Society of Handwriting Psychology   (EAIO)
ESHPH ..... European Society for the History of Photography   (EA)
ESHR .... Akersberga [*Sweden*] [*ICAO location identifier*]   (ICLI)
ESHS .... Sandhamn [*Sweden*] [*ICAO location identifier*]   (ICLI)
ESHU .... Emergency Ship Handling Unit [*Navy*]
ESHU .... Uppsala/Akademiska [*Sweden*] [*ICAO location identifier*]   (ICLI)
ESHV .... Vaxholm [*Sweden*] [*ICAO location identifier*]   (ICLI)
ESHW .... Vastervik Hospital [*Sweden*] [*ICAO location identifier*]   (ICLI)
ESI .... Early Screening Inventory [*Child development test*]
ESI .... Earth Station - Iran
ESI .... Edizioni Scientifiche Italiane [*A publication*]
ESI .... Educational Services, Incorporated [*Later, EDC*]
ESI .... Educational Services, International   (EA)
ESI .... Educational Sport Institute   (EA)
ESI .... Educreative Systems, Incorporated
ESI .... Electrical System Integration   (MCD)
ESI .... Electron Spectroscopic Imaging
ESI .... Electronic System Integration   (KSC)
ESI .... Electrospray Ionization [*Physics*]
ESI .... Elementary and Secondary School Index [*Research test*] [*Psychology*]
ESI .... Emergency Stop Indicator [*Aerospace*]   (AAG)
ESI .... Emulsion Stability Index [*Food analysis*]
ESI .... Engineering and Scientific Interpreter   (IEEE)
ESI .... Entertainment Systems International [*Database producer*]   (IID)
ESI .... ESI Industries Corp. [*AMEX symbol*] [*Vancouver Stock Exchange symbol*]
ESI .... Espinosa [*Brazil*] [*Airport symbol*]   (OAG)
ESI .... Ethiopian Standards Institution
ESI .... Executive Security International [*Institute for training bodyguards*] [*Aspen, CO*]
ESI .... Executives' Secretaries, Incorporated [*Later, EWI*]   (EA)
ESI .... Externally Specified Index
ESI .... Extremely Sensitive Information [*Army*]   (AABC)
ESIA .... Karlsborg [*Sweden*] [*ICAO location identifier*]   (ICLI)
ESIAC ...... Electronic Satellite Image Analysis Console [*NASA*]
ESIB .... Satenas [*Sweden*] [*ICAO location identifier*]   (ICLI)
ESIBEEP ... Electricity Supply Industry Building Energy Estimating Program [*Electricity Council*] [*British*]
ESIC .... Earth Station - Ivory Coast
ESIC .... Ecological Sciences Information Center [*Oak Ridge National Laboratory*]
ESIC .... Environmental Science Information Center [*National Oceanic and Atmospheric Administration*]
Esic-Market Estud Gestion Com Empr ... Esic-Market, Estudios de Gestion Comercial y Empresa [*A publication*]
ESIG .... Environmental and Societal Impacts Group [*National Center for Atmospheric Research*]
ESIG .... Eugenics Special Interest Group   (EA)
ESII .... Regional Military Command Subcenter West [*Sweden*] [*ICAO location identifier*]   (ICLI)

ESIIO .... European Symposium of Independent Inspecting Organizations   (EA)
ESIL .... Essential Support Items List
ESIL .... European Standard Inventory List   (NATG)
ESIO .... Electro Scientific Industries, Inc. [*NASDAQ symbol*]   (NQ)
ESIP .... Employment Service Improvement Program [*Department of Labor*]
ESIR .... Electronically Stimulated Incarnation Recall
ESIS .... Earth Station - Israel
ESIS .... European Shielding Information Service [*EURATOM*] [*Databank*]   (IID)
ESIS .... Executive Selection Inventory System
ESISD .... ESIS Newsletter [*A publication*]
ESITB .... Electricity Supply Industry Training Board [*Australia*]
ESITC .... Electricity Supply Industry Training Committee [*Australia*]
ESJ .... Earth Station - Jordan
ESJ .... Epithelial Stromal Junction [*Anatomy*]
ESJ .... Escort Jamming [*Military*]   (CAAL)
ESK .... Earth Station - Kenya
ESK .... Electrostatic Klystron
ESK .... Engineering Sketch
ESK .... Environmental Sensor Kit   (MCD)
ESK .... Eskdalemuir [*Scotland*] [*Geomagnetic observatory code*]
ESK .... Eskdalemuir [*Scotland*] [*Seismograph station code, US Geological Survey*]   (SEIS)
ESK .... Eskimo [*Language, etc.*]
esk .... Eskimo [*MARC language code*] [*Library of Congress*]   (LCCP)
ESK .... Telecommunications Censorship Technician [*Navy*]
ESKA .... Ekranolytny Spassatyelny Kater Amphibiya [*Screen-Effect Amphibious Lifeboat*] [*USSR*]
ESKA .... Gimo [*Sweden*] [*ICAO location identifier*]   (ICLI)
ESKB .... Stockholm/Barkarby [*Sweden*] [*ICAO location identifier*]   (ICLI)
ESKC .... Sundbro [*Sweden*] [*ICAO location identifier*]   (ICLI)
ESKC .... Telecommunications Censorship Technician, Chief [*Navy*]
ESKCM ..... Telecommunications Censorship Technician, Master Chief [*Navy*]
ESKCS .... Telecommunications Censorship Technician, Senior Chief [*Navy*]
ESKD .... Dala-Jarna [*Sweden*] [*ICAO location identifier*]   (ICLI)
ESKGA ...... Eisei Kagaku [*A publication*]
ESKGA2 .... Eisei Kagaku [*A publication*]
ESKH .... Eksharad [*Sweden*] [*ICAO location identifier*]   (ICLI)
ESKHA ...... Eisei Shikenjo Hokoku [*Bulletin. National Institute of Hygienic Sciences*] [*A publication*]
ESKHA5 .... Eisei Shikenjo Hokoku [*Bulletin. National Institute of Hygienic Sciences*] [*A publication*]
ESKI .... Eskimo [*A publication*]
ESKI .... Stockholm [*Sweden*] [*ICAO location identifier*]   (ICLI)
ESKK .... Karlskoga [*Sweden*] [*ICAO location identifier*]   (ICLI)
ESKL .... Norrkoping [*Sweden*] [*ICAO location identifier*]   (ICLI)
ESKM .... Mora/Siljan [*Sweden*] [*ICAO location identifier*]   (ICLI)
ESKN .... Nykoping/Oxelosund [*Sweden*] [*ICAO location identifier*]   (ICLI)
ESKO .... Munkfors [*Sweden*] [*ICAO location identifier*]   (ICLI)
ESKR .... Stockholm Radio [*Sweden*] [*ICAO location identifier*]   (ICLI)
ESKRM ..... Evreiskii Soiuz Kommunisticheskoi Rabochei Molodezhi   (BJA)
ESKS .... Strangnas [*Sweden*] [*ICAO location identifier*]   (ICLI)
ESKT .... Tierp [*Sweden*] [*ICAO location identifier*]   (ICLI)
ESKTD ...... Elektrotekhnicheskaya Promyshlennost. Seriya. Khimicheskie i Fizicheskie Istochniki Toka [*A publication*]
ESKU .... Sunne [*Poland*] [*ICAO location identifier*]   (ICLI)
ESKV .... Arvika [*Sweden*] [*ICAO location identifier*]   (ICLI)
ESKW .... Gavle/Avan [*Sweden*] [*ICAO location identifier*]   (ICLI)
ESKX .... Bjorkvik [*Sweden*] [*ICAO location identifier*]   (ICLI)
ESL .... Earth Sciences Laboratory [*Boulder, CO*] [*National Oceanic and Atmospheric Administration*]
ESL .... Earth Station - Libya
ESL .... Eastern Shipping Lines   (DS)
ESL .... Egg Stalk Length
ESL .... Electro Science Laboratory [*Ohio State University*]
ESL .... Electromagnetic Systems Laboratories, Inc.
ESL .... Electronic Support Laboratory
ESL .... Electronic Systems Laboratory   (MCD)
ESL .... Electroscience Laboratory [*Ohio State University*] [*Research center*]   (RCD)
ESL .... End-Systolic Length [*Cardiology*]
ESL .... Engineer Sub-Lieutenant [*Navy*] [*British*]   (ROG)
ESL .... Engineering and Services Laboratory [*Air Force*] [*Tyndall Air Force Base, FL*]   (GRD)
ESL .... Engineering Societies Library   (MCD)
ESL .... English as a Second Language
ESL .... Environmental Systems Laboratory [*Virginia Polytechnic Institute and State University*] [*Research center*]   (RCD)
ESL .... Essential Service Line [*Telecommunications*]   (TEL)
ESL .... Esterline Corp. [*NYSE symbol*]   (SPSG)
ESL .... Etac Sales Ltd. [*Toronto Stock Exchange symbol*]
ESI .... Etudes Slaves et Est-Europeennes [*A publication*]
ESL .... European Studies in Law [*Elsevier Book Series*] [*A publication*]
ESL .... Evans Signal Laboratory [*Army*]

ESL............ Exceeding Speed Limit
ESL............ Extended Service Life [*Military*] (CAAL)
ESL............ Eye Standard Length [*Fish anatomy*]
ESL............ Kessel, WV [*Location identifier*] [*FAA*] (FAAL)
ESLAB...... European Space Laboratory
ESLE......... Equivalent Station Location Error
ES/LES...... Equipment Section/Loaded Equipment Section
ESLH........ Electrical Stimulation of the Lateral Hypothalamus [*Medicine*]
ESLI......... Empire State Life Insurance Co. [*NASDAQ symbol*] (NQ)
ESLI......... Esperantista Sak-Ligo Internacia [*International Esperantist Chess League - IECL*] (EAIO)
ESLJ......... [*The*] East St. Louis Junction R. R. [*AAR code*]
ESLO........ European Satellite Launching Organization (MCD)
ESLO........ European Space Launcher Organization
ESLR........ Etudes Slaves et Roumaines [*A publication*]
ESLR........ Events Select Logic and Rates (MCD)
ESLT........ Equipment Section Leakage Test
ESM........... Earth Station - Mexico
ESM........... East Surrey Militia [*British military*] (DMA)
ESM........... Edible Structure Material
ESM........... Edmund Sixtus Muskie [*American politician*]
ESM........... Effectiveness Simulation Model
ESM........... Ejection Systolic Murmur [*Cardiology*]
ESM........... Elastomeric Shield Material [*Plastic technology*]
ESM........... Elastomeric Solid Material
ESM........... Electrical Stimulation of the Midbrain
ESM........... Electronic Shop Minor [*Coast Guard*]
ESM........... Electronic Support Measures [*Instrumentation*] (IEEE)
ESM........... Electronic Surveillance Measures
ESM........... Electronic Switch Module
ESM........... Electronic Warfare Support Measures [*Formerly, EWSM*] (AABC)
ESM........... Emerald Star Mining [*Vancouver Stock Exchange symbol*]
ESM........... Employment Security Manual (OICC)
ESM........... Energy Storage Modulator
ESM........... Engineering Schedule Memorandum
ESM........... Engineering Service Memorandum (MCD)
ESM........... Escort Mission
ESM........... Esmeraldas [*Ecuador*] [*Airport symbol*] (OAG)
ESM........... European Society for Microcirculation (EA)
ESM........... European Society for Mycobacteriology (EA)
ESM........... Experiments Systems Monitor [*NASA*] (KSC)
e-sm---........ San Marino [*MARC geographic area code*] [*Library of Congress*] (LCCP)
ESM........... Underwater Mechanic [*Obsolete*] [*Navy*]
ESM........... Winston-Salem State University, Winston-Salem, NC [*OCLC symbol*] (OCLC)
ESMA........ Electrical Sign Manufacturers Association
ESMA........ Electronic Sales-Marketing Association [*Defunct*] (EA)
ESMA........ Emmaboda [*Sweden*] [*ICAO location identifier*] (ICLI)
ESMA........ Engraved Stationers Manufacturers Association (EA)
ESMA........ Episcopal Society for Ministry on Aging (EA)
ESMB........ Borglanda [*Sweden*] [*ICAO location identifier*] (ICLI)
ESMC........ Eastern Space and Missile Center [*Air Force*] [*Patrick Air Force Base, FL*] [*Also, ETR*]
ESMC........ Environmental System Management Controller (MCD)
ESMC........ Karlshamn [*Sweden*] [*ICAO location identifier*] (ICLI)
ESME........ Eslov [*Sweden*] [*ICAO location identifier*] (ICLI)
ESME........ Excited State Mass Energy
ESMED9... Ethics in Science and Medicine [*A publication*]
ESMF........ Eleanor Steber Music Foundation (EA)
ESMF........ Fagerhult [*Sweden*] [*ICAO location identifier*] (ICLI)
ESMG........ Ljungby/Feringe [*Sweden*] [*ICAO location identifier*] (ICLI)
ESMH........ Hoganas [*Sweden*] [*ICAO location identifier*] (ICLI)
ESMI......... Sovdeborg [*Sweden*] [*ICAO location identifier*] (ICLI)
ESMJ........ Kagerod [*Sweden*] [*ICAO location identifier*] (ICLI)
ESMK........ Kristianstad/Everod [*Sweden*] [*ICAO location identifier*] (ICLI)
ESML........ Expendable Supplies and Materials List (MCD)
ESML........ Landskrona/Viarp [*Sweden*] [*ICAO location identifier*] (ICLI)
ESMM........ Equivalent Square Miles of Mapping (NOAA)
ESMM........ Malmo [*Sweden*] [*ICAO location identifier*] (ICLI)
ESMN........ Lund [*Sweden*] [*ICAO location identifier*] (ICLI)
ESMO........ Earth Station - Morocco
ESMO........ Electronics System Measures Operator (MCD)
ESMO........ European Society for Medical Oncology (EA)
ESMO........ Oskarshamn [*Sweden*] [*ICAO location identifier*] (ICLI)
ESMP........ Anderstorp [*Sweden*] [*ICAO location identifier*] (ICLI)
ESMP........ El Salvador Media Projects (EA)
ESMQ........ Kalmar [*Sweden*] [*ICAO location identifier*] (ICLI)
ESMR........ Electrically Scanned Microwave Radiometer [*NASA*]
ESMR........ Trelleborg [*Sweden*] [*ICAO location identifier*] (ICLI)
ESMRI...... Engraved Stationery Manufacturers Research Institute (EA)
ES-MS....... Electrospray Ionization Mass Spectrometry
ESMS........ Environment and Special Measurement System (MCD)
ESMS........ Eta Sigma Gamma. Monograph Series [*A publication*]
ESMS........ Malmo/Sturup [*Sweden*] [*ICAO location identifier*] (ICLI)
ESMSA...... 18 Square Meter Sailing Association (EA)
ESMSLCC ... Edward Sapir Monograph Series in Language, Culture, and Cognition [*A publication*]
ESMST...... European Society of Membrane Science and Technology (EA)

ESMT........ Electronic Shop Minor Telephone and Teletype [*Coast Guard*]
ESMT........ Halmstad [*Sweden*] [*ICAO location identifier*] (ICLI)
ESMU ...... Electronic Systems Mockup (KSC)
ESMV........ Hagshult [*Sweden*] [*ICAO location identifier*] (ICLI)
ESMWT... Engineering, Science, and Management War Training
ESMX........ Vaxjo/Kronoberg [*Sweden*] [*ICAO location identifier*] (ICLI)
ESMY........ Smalandsstenar [*Sweden*] [*ICAO location identifier*] (ICLI)
ESMZ........ Olanda [*Sweden*] [*ICAO location identifier*] (ICLI)
ESN .... Earth-Sun Coordinate System
ESN .... Easton, MD [*Location identifier*] [*FAA*] (FAAL)
ESN .... Educationally Subnormal
ESN .... Elastic Stop Nut [*Hardware*]
ESN .... Encyclopaedia Sefardica Neerlandica [*A publication*] (BJA)
ESN .... Engineering Shipping Notice (AAG)
ESN .... Engineers Society of Norway
ESn .... Englische Studien [*A publication*]
ESN .... English-Speaking Nations [*of NATO*]
ESN .... Error Sequence Number [*Data processing*]
ESN .... Escagenetics Corp. [*AMEX symbol*] (SPSG)
ESN .... Essence Biotech [*Vancouver Stock Exchange symbol*]
ESN .... Essential (AABC)
ESN .... Estrogen-Stimulated Neurophysin [*Endocrinology*]
ESN .... European Scientific Notes [*Navy*] (MCD)
ESN .... European Society of Nematologists (EAIO)
ESN .... European Society for Neurochemistry (EA)
ESN .... European Society of Neuroradiology (EA)
ESN .... Executive Suite Network [*An association*] (EA)
ESNA........ Economic Security Employees' National Association [*Canada*]
ESNA........ Elastic Stop Nut Corp. of America
ESNA........ Electrical Survey-Net Adjuster
ESNA........ Hallviken [*Sweden*] [*ICAO location identifier*] (ICLI)
ESNAAX... Essex Naturalist [*London*] [*A publication*]
ESNB........ Solleftea [*Sweden*] [*ICAO location identifier*] (ICLI)
ESNC........ Educational Statistics, National Center (OICC)
ESNC........ Hede/Hedlanda [*Sweden*] [*ICAO location identifier*] (ICLI)
ESNCD..... European Society for Noninvasive Cardiovascular Dynamics (EA)
ESND .... Sveg [*Sweden*] [*ICAO location identifier*] (ICLI)
ESNETT ... Engineering and Science Network on Thinking (EA)
ESNF........ Farila [*Sweden*] [*ICAO location identifier*] (ICLI)
ESNG .... Gallivare [*Sweden*] [*ICAO location identifier*] (ICLI)
ESNH........ Hudiksvall [*Sweden*] [*ICAO location identifier*] (ICLI)
ESNI......... Kubbe [*Sweden*] [*ICAO location identifier*] (ICLI)
ESNICVD ... European Society for Noninvasive Cardiovascular Dynamics (EAIO)
ESNJ .... Jokkmokk [*Sweden*] [*ICAO location identifier*] (ICLI)
ESNK........ Kramfors [*Sweden*] [*ICAO location identifier*] (ICLI)
ESNL........ Lycksele [*Sweden*] [*ICAO location identifier*] (ICLI)
ESNM........ Optand [*Sweden*] [*ICAO location identifier*] (ICLI)
ESNN .... Sundsvall-Harnosand [*Sweden*] [*ICAO location identifier*] (ICLI)
ESNO........ Ornskoldsvik [*Sweden*] [*ICAO location identifier*] (ICLI)
ESNP........ Pitea [*Sweden*] [*ICAO location identifier*] (ICLI)
ESNQ........ Kiruna [*Sweden*] [*ICAO location identifier*] (ICLI)
ESNR........ Orsa [*Sweden*] [*ICAO location identifier*] (ICLI)
ESNS .... Skelleftea [*Sweden*] [*ICAO location identifier*] (ICLI)
ESNSW..... Entomological Society of New South Wales [*Australia*]
ESNT .... Sattna [*Sweden*] [*ICAO location identifier*] (ICLI)
ESNTL ...... Essential
ESNU .... Umea [*Sweden*] [*ICAO location identifier*] (ICLI)
ESNV........ Vilhelmina [*Sweden*] [*ICAO location identifier*] (ICLI)
ESO .... Echo Suppressor, Originating End [*Telecommunications*] (TEL)
ESO .... Economic Stabilization Office (OICC)
ESO .... Educational Services Office [*or Officer*] [*Navy*]
ESO .... Electrical Spinal Orthosis
ESO .... Electronic Standards Office [*Navy*]
ESO .... Electronics Supply Office [*or Officer*]
ESO .... Embarkation Staff Officer [*Military*] [*British*]
ESO .... Emergency Security Operations (AFM)
ESO .... Emergency Support Organization (NRCH)
ESO .... Engineering Service Order (AAG)
ESO .... Engineering Stop Order (AAG)
ESO .... Epoxidized Soybean Oil [*Organic chemistry*]
Eso .... Esoteric [*Record label*]
ESO .... European Southern Observatory (EAIO)
ESO .... Event Sequence Override
ESOA .... Epiphyllum Society of America
ESOA .... European Society of Osteoarthrology (EAIO)
ESOAA..... Eight Sheet Outdoor Advertising Association [*Independence, MO*] (EA)
ESOB........ Eastern Soccer Officials Bureau [*Later, ECSA*] (EA)
ESOC........ Emergency Supply Operations Center [*Defense Supply Agency*] (MCD)
ESOC........ European Space Operations Center
ESOD........ Erythrocyte Superoxide Dismutase [*An enzyme*]
ESOE........ Orebro [*Sweden*] [*ICAO location identifier*] (ICLI)
ESOFC ...... Erika Slezak Official Fan Club (EA)
ESO-FHWA ... Emergency Standby Order - Federal Highway Administration [*Federal disaster planning*]
ESOH .... Hagfors [*Sweden*] [*ICAO location identifier*] (ICLI)

ESOL......... English to Speakers of Other Languages [Program]
ESOMAR ... European Society for Opinion and Market Research [Netherlands]
ESONE...... European Standards on Nuclear Electronics Committee [Switzerland]
ESOP........ Employee Stock Option [or Ownership] Plan [Tax plan]
ESOP........ Engineering Student Officer Program [Air Force]
ESOPH...... Esophagus [Anatomy]
ESOPRS.... European Society of Ophthalmic Plastic and Reconstructive Surgery [London, England]   (EAIO)
ESOPS ...... Employment Service Online Placement System [Data processing]
ESOR........ Emergency Standoff Range   (NVT)
ESOR........ Rescue Coordination Center [Sweden] [ICAO location identifier]   (ICLI)
ESOS........ Stockholm [Sweden] [ICAO location identifier]   (ICLI)
ESOT........ Employee Stock Ownership Trust
ESOUA ..... Ekonomika Sovetskoi Ukrainy [A publication]
ESov.......... Etudes Sovietiques [A publication]
ESOW .... Engineering Statement of Work   (NASA)
ESOW .... Vasteras/Hasslo [Sweden] [ICAO location identifier]   (ICLI)
ESP........... Earth-Surface Potential
ESP........... East Stroudsburg, PA [Location identifier] [FAA]   (FAAL)
ESP........... Eastern Special Passenger [Eastern Airlines]
ESP........... Economic Stabilization Program [Internal Revenue Service]
ESP........... Economic Sufficiency Plan   (OICC)
ESP........... Edge-Supported Pulling [Photovoltaic energy systems]
ESP........... Einzelhandelsspanne [Retail Markup] [See also EHS]
ESP........... Electrical Systems Panel [Apollo Spacecraft Program Office] [NASA]
ESP........... Electro Sensor Panel [Toyota]
ESP........... Electron Spin Polarization
ESP........... Electron Stream Potential   (MSA)
ESP........... Electronic Security Profile [of Equitable Life Assurance Society]
ESP........... Electronic Seismic Photography
ESP........... Electronic Server Pad [Restaurant computer device manufactured by Remanco Systems, Inc.]
ESP........... Electronic Standard Procedure   (MCD)
ESP........... Electronic Supervisory Panel   (MCD)
ESP........... Electronic Systems Planning   (RDA)
ESP........... Electroselective Pattern Metering [Olympus cameras]
ESP........... Electrosensitive Programming
ESP........... Electroshock Protection   (MCD)
ESP........... Electrosonic Profiler
ESP........... Electrostatic Precipitator [Also, EP]
ESP........... Elevated Stabilized Platform [Aircraft]
ESP........... Elimination of Solvation Procedure [Chemistry]
ESP........... Elsevier Science Publishers
ESP........... [The] Emanu El Single Person   (BJA)
ESP........... Employee Savings Program
ESP........... Employee Share Plan [Australia]
ESP........... Employee Stock Purchase [Software]
ESP........... Employer School Program   (OICC)
ESP........... Employment Service Potential [Department of Labor]
ESP........... Emulation Sensing Processor [Quality Micro Systems]
ESP........... End Systolic Pressure [Cardiology]
ESP........... Energetic Storm Particle
ESP........... Energy Services Planning
ESP........... Energy Systems and Policy [A publication]
ESP........... Engine Sequence Panel   (AAG)
ESP........... Engine Service Platform   (KSC)
ESP........... Engine Start Panel
ESP........... Engineering Schedule Plan
ESP........... Engineering Service Project   (MCD)
ESP........... Engineering Service Publications   (AAG)
ESP........... Engineering Signal Processor
ESP........... Engineering Software Package
ES & P ...... Engineering Systems and Procedures   (MCD)
ESP........... English for Scientific Purposes [Education] [British]
ESP........... English Symposium Papers [A publication]
ESP........... Enhanced Service Provider [Online database service]
ESP........... Environmental Sketches in Perspective [Computer program]
E & SP ...... Equipment and Spare Parts
ESP........... Equipment Status Panel   (AAG)
ESP........... Equipment Support Plan   (MCD)
ESP........... Especially
esp .... Esperanto [MARC language code] [Library of Congress]   (LCCP)
ESP........... Esperanto [Language, etc.]
ESP........... Espey Manufacturing & Electronics Corp. [AMEX symbol]   (SPSG)
Esp .... Espinasse's English Nisi Prius Reports [1793-1810] [A publication]   (DLA)
ESP........... Espionage [FBI standardized term]
ESP........... Espressivo [With Expression] [Music]
ESP........... Estate Planning [A publication]
ESP........... European Society of Pathology   (EAIO)
ESP........... Evoked Synaptic Potential [Neurophysiology]
ESP........... Exchange Sale Property
ESP........... Exchangeable-Sodium-Percentage
ESP........... Expandable Stored Program

ESP........... Expanded Spread Profile [Seismology]
ESP........... Experiment Sensing Platform   (NASA)
ESP........... Extended Self-Contained PROLOG [Programming language]
ESP........... Extended Service Plan [Ford Motor Co.]
ESP........... Extended Storage Platelet Pack [Hematology]
ESP........... Extended Streamflow Prediction   (NOAA)
ESP........... External Standard Pulse [Instrumentation]
ESP........... Extrasensory Perception
ESP........... Extravehicular Support Pack [or Package] [NASA]
ESP........... Spain [ANSI three-letter standard code]   (CNC)
e-sp--- ...... Spain [MARC geographic area code] [Library of Congress]   (LCCP)
ESP-1........ Elizabeth S. Priori-1 [Virus named after one of the scientists who isolated it]
ESPA .... Electronically Steerable Phased Array [SPADATS]   (MCD)
ESPA .... Elvis Special Photo Association   (EA)
EspA .... Espanol Actual [A publication]
ESPA .... Evening Student Personnel Association [Later, Evening Student Association]   (EA)
ESPA .... Exhaust Systems Professional Association   (EA)
ESPA .... Lulea/Kallax [Sweden] [ICAO location identifier]   (ICLI)
Espace Geogr ... Espace Geographique [A publication]
Espaces et Soc ... Espaces et Societes [A publication]
Esp Act ...... Espinasse. Actions on Statutes [A publication]   (ILCA)
ESPAR .... Electronically Steerable Phased Array RADAR [SPADATS]
ESPAWS... Enhanced Self-Propelled Artillery Weapon System   (MCD)
ESPAWSS ... Enhanced Self-Propelled Artillery Weapon System Study   (MCD)
Esp Bank ... Espinasse's Law of Bankrupts [1825] [A publication]   (DLA)
ESPC .... Education Systems & Publications Corporation [Belleville, NJ] [NASDAQ symbol]   (NQ)
ESPC .... Emergency Status Precedence Code [DoD]
ESPC .... Ostersund/Froson [Sweden] [ICAO location identifier]   (ICLI)
ESPD........ Export Services and Promotions Division [British Overseas Trade Board]   (DS)
ESPD........ Gunnarn [Sweden] [ICAO location identifier]   (ICLI)
Esp Dig ...... Espinasse's Digest of the Law of Actions at Nisi Prius [1812] [A publication]   (ILCA)
ESPE .... European Society for Pediatric Endocrinology   (EAIO)
ESPE .... United Socialist Alliance of Greece   (PPW)
ESPE .... Vidsel [Sweden] [ICAO location identifier]   (ICLI)
ESPEC...... Electrical Specification
E-Spec....... Equipment Specification [Nuclear energy]   (NRCH)
ESPEC...... Especially
ESPEN ...... Estimated Tax Penalty [IRS]
Esper Ricer Ist Agr Gen Colt Erbacee Univ Pisa ... Esperienza e Ricerche. Istituto di Agronomia Generale e Coltivazioni Erbacee. Universita di Pisa [A publication]
ESPES....... Especialidades Farmaceuticas Espanolas Data Bank [Spanish Pharmaceutical Specialities Data Bank] [Spanish Drug Information Center] [Information service or system]   (IID)
Esp Ev....... Espinasse on Penal Evidence [A publication]   (DLA)
ESPG........ Boden [Sweden] [ICAO location identifier]   (ICLI)
ESPG........ Espionage   (AABC)
Esp Ganad ... Espana Ganadera [A publication]
ESP/GC & EE ... Equipment Spare Package/Ground Communications and Electronic Equipment
ESPHI ...... European Society for Paediatric Haematology and Immunology   (EAIO)
ESPI .... Etched Sensitized Projected Image [Circuit board manufacture]
ESPJ........ Heden [Sweden] [ICAO location identifier]   (ICLI)
ESPL .... Electronic Switching Programming Language
ESPL .... Extensible Structure Processing Language [1969-71] [Data processing]   (CSR)
ESPM .... Energy Supply Planning Model [National Science Foundation]
ESPN........ Entertainment and Sports Programming Network [Television]
ESPN........ European Society for Pediatric Nephrology   (EAIO)
Esp NP....... Espinasse's English Nisi Prius Reports [1793-1810] [A publication]   (DLA)
ESPOD...... Electronic System Precision Orbit Determination [Air Force]   (MCD)
ESPOL...... Executive System Problem-Oriented Language [Burroughs Corp.] [Data processing]   (BUR)
ESPP .... Regional Military Command Subcenter North [Sweden] [ICAO location identifier]   (ICLI)
Esp Pen Ev ... Espinasse on Penal Evidence [A publication]   (DLA)
ESPPI........ Expanding and Specialty Paper Products Institute [Defunct]   (EA)
Esp P St ..... Espinasse on Penal Statutes [A publication]   (DLA)
ESPQ........ Early School Personality Questionnaire [Psychology]
Espr.......... Espressivo [With Expression] [Music]
ESPR .... European Society of Paediatric Radiology   (EA)
ESPRAF.... ESP [Extrasensory Perception] Research Associates Foundation [Defunct]   (EA)
Espres .... Espressivo [With Expression] [Music]
ESPRESS ... Espressivo [With Expression] [Music]
ESPRI........ Empire State Paper Research Institute [College of Environmental Science and Forestry at Syracuse] [Research center]   (RCD)

ESPRIT..... European Strategic Program for Research and Development in Information Technology and Telecommunications [*Research center*] [*Belgium*] (TSSD)
ESPRIT..... Eye-Slaved Projected Rafter Inset [*Simulator*]
Esprit Cr .... Esprit Createur [*A publication*]
Esprit des Lois ... Montesquieu's Esprit des Lois [*Spirit of Laws*] [*A publication*] (DLA)
ESPRP....... Energy Systems and Policy Research Program [*University of Wisconsin - Madison*] [*Research center*] (RCD)
ESPS.......... Experiment Segment and Pallet Simulator [*NASA*] (NASA)
ESPSL....... O Estado de Sao Paulo. Suplemento Literario [*A publication*]
ESPT......... Esprit Systems, Inc. [*NASDAQ symbol*] (NQ)
ESPWO..... Exigencies of the Service Having Been Such as to Preclude the Issuance of Competent Written Orders in Advance
ESQ .... Emerson Society. Quarterly [*A publication*]
Esq .... Esquire [*A publication*]
ESQ .... Esquire
Esq .... Esquire [*Record label*] [*Great Britain*]
ESQ .... Extra-Special Quality [*Steel cable*] [*Ship's equipment*] (DS)
Esq Ins ..... Esquirol on Insanity [*A publication*] (DLA)
ESQO .... Arboga [*Sweden*] [*ICAO location identifier*] (ICLI)
ESQP........ Berga [*Sweden*] [*ICAO location identifier*] (ICLI)
ESQR .... Esquire
ESQRE ...... Esquire [*Gentleman*] (ROG)
ESQST ...... Ego Strength Q-Sort Test [*Psychology*]
ESQT........ Extended Sterilization Qualification Test
Esquisses Math ... Esquisses Mathematiques [*A publication*]
ESQV........ Visby [*Sweden*] [*ICAO location identifier*] (ICLI)
ESR........... Early Site Review [*Nuclear energy*] (NRCH)
ESR........... Early Storage Reserve
ESR........... East Surrey Regiment [*Military unit*] [*British*]
ESR........... Economic and Social Review [*A publication*]
ESR........... Economic Subregion [*Bureau of the Census*]
ESR........ Edge-Stabilized Ribbon [*Photovoltaic energy systems*]
ESR........... Editorial Status Report
ESR........... Educators for Social Responsibility (EA)
ESR........... Effective Search Radius (MCD)
ESR........... Effective Signal Radiated
ESR........... Effective SONAR Range [*Navy*] (NVT)
ESR........... Effective Sunrise
ESR........... Egyptian State Railway (ROG)
ESR........... El Salvador [*Chile*] [*Airport symbol*] (OAG)
ESR........... Electron Spin Resonance [*Also, EPR*] [*Physics*]
ESR........... Electronic Scanning RADAR
ESR........... Electronic Send/Receive
ESR........... Electronic Systems Reliability (MCD)
ESR........... Electroslag Remelting [*Steel alloy*]
ESR........... Emory Sources and Reprints [*A publication*]
ESR........... Employment Service Representative
ESR........... Engineering Service Requests (MUGU)
ESR........... Engineering Summary Report
ESR........... Engineering Support Request (NASA)
ESR........... Enstar Indonesia, Inc. [*AMEX symbol*] (SPSG)
ESR........... Environmental System Resources [*National Science Foundation*] (MCD)
ESR........... Equipment Status Report [*Air Force*]
ESR........... Equipment Supervisory Rack [*Telecommunications*] (TEL)
ESR........... Equivalent Series Resistance
ESR........... Equivalent Service Rounds [*A standard for indicating gun erosion*]
ESR........... Erythrocyte Sedimentation Rate [*Hematology*]
ESR........... Escape Road [*Hawaii*] [*Seismograph station code, US Geological Survey*] (SEIS)
ESR........... Essex Scottish Regiment of Canada [*Military unit*]
ESR........... [*The*] Ethnic Studies Report [*A publication*]
ESR........... Etudes Slaves et Roumaines [*A publication*]
ESR........... European Security Region [*Military*]
ESR........... European Studies Review [*A publication*]
ESR........... Executive Service Requests (MCD)
ESR........... Executive Summary Requirements (MCD)
ESR........... Expedite Shipping Request (MCD)
ESR........... Experimental Superheat Reactor
ESR........... Extension Service Review [*A publication*]
ESR........... External Standard Ratio
ESR........... Extrahepatic Shunt Ratio [*Medicine*]
ESRA........ Eastern Ski Representatives Association (EA)
ESRA........ Emergency Ship Repair Act of 1954
ESRA........ European Society of Regional Anaesthesia (EA)
ESRANGE ... European Space Range [*Sweden*] (MCD)
ESRB......... European Society for Radiation Biology [*Formerly, Association of Radiobiologists from EURATOM Countries*] (EA)
ESRBB ...... Energeticheskoe Stroitel'stvo za Rubezhom [*A publication*]
ESRC........ Economic and Social Research Council [*British*]
ESRD........ End Stage Renal Disease [*Medicine*]
ESRD........ Equipment Shipment Ready Date [*Army*] (AABC)
ESREA ...... Earth Science Reviews [*A publication*]
ESREAV ... Earth-Science Reviews [*A publication*]
ESREDY ... Estuarine Research [*A publication*]
ESRF .... Easter Seal Research Foundation of the National Easter Seal Society (EA)
ESRF .... Electrical Systems Repair Facilities (MCD)

ESRF .... End Stage Renal Failure [*Medicine*]
ESRF .... European Squash Rackets Federation (EA)
ESRFR...... Environmental Studies Revolving Funds Report [*A publication*]
ESRI .... Earth Sciences and Resources Institute [*University of South Carolina at Columbia*] [*Research center*] (RCD)
ESRI .... Engineering and Statistical Research Institute [*Canada*] (ARC)
ESRIN ...... European Space Research Institute
ESRL .... Eastern Shore Regional Library Resource Center [*Library network*]
ESRL .... Environmental Sciences Research Laboratory [*Environmental Protection Agency*] (GRD)
ESRL/RTP ... Environmental Sciences Research Laboratory/Research Triangle Park [*Environmental Protection Agency*]
ESRN........ ESSO Resources News [*A publication*]
ESRNBP ... Specialist Periodical Reports. Electron Spin Resonance [*A publication*]
ESRO........ Engineering Stop and Release Order [*Aerospace*]
ESRO........ European Space Research Organization [*Superseded by ESA*]
ESRO/ELDO Bull ... ESRO/ELDO [*European Space Research Organization/European Launcher Development Organization*] Bulletin [*A publication*]
ESRP .... Emergency Substitute in a Regular Position [*Education*]
ESRP .... Environmental Standard Review Plan (NRCH)
ESRP .... Evreiskaia Sotsialisticheskaia Rabochaia Partiia (BJA)
ESRR .... Early Site Review Report [*Nuclear energy*] (NRCH)
ESRS .... Early Sites Research Society (EA)
ESRS .... Electronic Scanning RADAR System (MCD)
ESRS .... Emporia State Research Studies [*A publication*]
ESRS .... European Society for Rural Sociology
ESRS .... European Synchrotron Radiation Source [*High-energy physics*]
ESRU........ Electrical Stimulating and Recording Unit
ESS .... Earth-Sighting Simulator [*NASA*]
ESS .... Earth Station - Sudan
ESS .... Echo Suppression Subsystem [*Telecommunications*] (TEL)
ESS .... Educational Services Section [*Navy*]
ESS .... Educational Subscription Service, Inc.
ESS .... Effective Sunset
ESS .... Electrical Standards Set
ESS .... Electronic Scanning Spectrometer
ESS .... Electronic Security Surveillance
ESS .... Electronic Security System
ESS .... Electronic Sequence Switching
ESS .... Electronic Surveillance System
ESS .... Electronic Switching System [*See also EAX*] [*Telecommunications*]
ESS .... Electronics Systems Source (MCD)
ESS .... Electropneumatic Service System [*Truck engineering*]
ESS .... Elementary Science Study [*National Science Foundation*]
ESS .... Emergency Ship Service [*Navy*] (MSA)
ESS .... Emergency Short Stay [*in hospital*] [*British*]
ESS .... Emergency Social Services [*Civil Defense*]
ESS .... Emergency Survival System
ESS .... Emplaced Scientific Station [*Aerospace*]
ESS .... Employment Security System [*Department of Labor*]
ESS .... Empty Sella Syndrome [*Medicine*]
ESS .... Encyclopedia of the Social Sciences [*A publication*]
ESS .... Energy Storage System
ESS .... Engine Speed Synchronizer
ESS .... Engine Start Signal
ESS .... Engineer Specialized Services
ESS .... Engineered Safety System (IEEE)
ES & S....... Engineering Services and Safety (NRCH)
ESS .... Engineering Source Selection
ESS .... Engineering Standard Specification (MCD)
ESs............ English Studies [*A publication*]
ESS .... Entry Survival System
ESS .... Environmental Science Series [*Elsevier Book Series*] [*A publication*]
ESS .... Environmental Stress Screening (MCD)
ESS .... Environmental Support System (MCD)
ESS .... Equipment Section Shell
ESS .... Erection Subsystem
ESS .... Erythrocyte-Sensitizing Substance [*Hematology*]
ESS .... Essence
Ess............. Essence [*A publication*]
ESS .... Essential
ESS .... Essex [*County in England*]
ESS .... Esstra Industries Corp. [*Vancouver Stock Exchange symbol*]
ESS .... European Special Situations Fund [*EEC*]
ESS .... Evaporation/Solidification System [*Nuclear energy*] (NRCH)
ESS .... Event Scheduling System
ESS .... Evolutionary Stable Strategy
ESS .... Excited Skin Syndrome [*Dermatology*]
ESS .... Executive Suites and Services [*Business term*]
ESS .... Executive Support System
ESS .... Executive's Shopping Service
ESS .... Expendable Second Stage [*Space shuttle*] [*NASA*]
ESS .... Expendable Sound Source
ESS .... Experiment Subsystem Simulator [*NASA*] (NASA)
ESS .... Experiment Support System (MCD)

ESS .... Experimental SAGE [*Semi-Automatic Ground Environment*] Sector
ESS .... Expert Statistical System
ESS .... Explosive Safety Survey (NVT)
ESS .... Middleton Island, AK [*Location identifier*] [*FAA*] (FAAL)
ESS .... Northern Essex Community College, Haverhill, MA [*OCLC symbol*] (OCLC)
ESSA .... Earth Station - South Africa
ESSA .... Economists', Sociologists', and Statisticians' Association
ESSA .... Electronic Scanning and Stabilizing Antenna
ESSA .... Embassy Social Secretaries Association (EA)
ESSA .... Emergency Safeguards System Activation (IEEE)
ESSA .... Endangered Species Scientific Authority [*US Fish and Wildlife Service*] [*Terminated 1979, functions transferred to Department of the Interior*]
ESSA .... Environmental Science Services Administration [*Later, National Oceanic and Atmospheric Administration*]
ESSA .... Environmental and Social Systems Analysts Ltd.
ESSA .... Environmental Survey Satellite (TEL)
ESSA .... European Single Service Association (EA)
ESSA .... Stockholm/Arlanda [*Sweden*] [*ICAO location identifier*] (ICLI)
Ess Ang Sax Law ... Essays on Anglo-Saxon Law [*A publication*] (DLA)
ESSAR........ Early Site Safety Analysis Report [*Nuclear energy*] (NRCH)
ESSAR........ EBASCO Standard Safety Analysis Report [*Nuclear energy*] (NRCH)
Essay Gen Lit Index ... Essay and General Literature Index [*A publication*]
Essay Phys ... Essays in Physics [*A publication*]
Essays Biochem ... Essays in Biochemistry [*A publication*]
Essays Can Wri ... Essays on Canadian Writing [*A publication*]
Essays Chem ... Essays in Chemistry [*A publication*]
Essays Crit ... Essays in Criticism [*A publication*]
Essays Fr L ... Essays in French Literature [*A publication*]
Essays Fundam Immunol ... Essays in Fundamental Immunology [*A publication*]
Essays Lit .. Essays in Literature [*A publication*]
Essays Neurochem Neuropharmacol ... Essays in Neurochemistry and Neuropharmacology [*A publication*]
Essays Pap ... Essays and Papers. Soong Jun University [*Korea*] [*A publication*]
Essays Pap Soong Jun Univ ... Essays and Papers. Soong Jun University [*A publication*]
Essays Phys ... Essays in Physics [*A publication*]
Essays Poet ... Essays in Poetics [*A publication*]
Essays Stud ... Essays and Studies [*A publication*]
Essays Stud Fac Hiroshima Jogakuin Coll ... Essays and Studies by the Faculty of Hiroshima Jogakuin College [*A publication*]
Essays Toxicol ... Essays in Toxicology [*A publication*]
ESSB .... Electronic Supply Support Base [*Air Force*]
ESSB .... Stockholm/Bromma [*Sweden*] [*ICAO location identifier*] (ICLI)
ESSBR....... Electronically Scanned Stacked Beam RADAR [*Program*]
ESSC .... Earth Station - Scandinavia
ESSC .... Earth System Science Committee [*US governmental interagency group*]
ESSC .... Eskilstuna/Ekeby [*Sweden*] [*ICAO location identifier*] (ICLI)
ESSC .... European Sport Shooting Confederation (EAIO)
ESSCIRC .. European Solid-State Circuits Conference (MCD)
Ess Crit ...... Essays in Criticism [*A publication*]
ESSD .... Borlange [*Sweden*] [*ICAO location identifier*] (ICLI)
ESSD .... Environment Supply Sensing Device (MCD)
ESSE .... Earth Station - Senegal
ESSE .... EBASCO Services, Inc. Site Support Engineering [*Nuclear energy*] (NRCH)
ESSE .... Stockholm/Ska-Edeby [*Sweden*] [*ICAO location identifier*] (ICLI)
ESSEN ...... Essential
Essenze Deriv Agrum ... Essenze e Derivati Agrumari [*A publication*]
ESSEX....... Effects of Subsurface Explosions [*Project*] [*Army and DNA*] (RDA)
ESSEX....... Experimental Solid-State Exchange [*Communication system*] (MCD)
Essex Archaeol Hist ... Essex Archaeology and History [*A publication*]
Essex Arch Hist ... Essex Archaeology and History [*A publication*]
Essex Co N H Soc J ... Essex County Natural History Society. Journal [*A publication*]
Essex I His ... Essex Institute. Historical Collections [*A publication*]
Essex Inst B ... Essex Institute. Bulletin [*A publication*]
Essex Inst Coll ... Essex Institute. Historical Collections [*A publication*]
Essex Inst Hist Coll ... Essex Institute. Historical Collections [*A publication*]
Essex Inst Hist Collect ... Essex Institute. Historical Collections [*A publication*]
Essex Inst Pr ... Essex Institute. Proceedings [*A publication*]
Essex J .... Essex Journal [*A publication*]
Essex Nat (Lond) ... Essex Naturalist (London) [*A publication*]
Essex Natur ... Essex Naturalist [*A publication*]
ESSF.......... ESSEF Corp. [*NASDAQ symbol*] (NQ)
ESSF.......... Hultsfred [*Sweden*] [*ICAO location identifier*] (ICLI)
ESSFL........ Electron Steady-State Fermi Level
ESSFLO .... Electronic Switching System Flow Chart

ESSFNR.... Exercise Simulation System for Flexible Nuclear Response (MCD)
ESSFTA .... English Springer Spaniel Field Trial Association (EA)
ESSG .... Engineer Strategic Studies Group [*Army*] (AABC)
ESSG .... Ludvika [*Sweden*] [*ICAO location identifier*] (ICLI)
ESSH .... Laxa [*Sweden*] [*ICAO location identifier*] (ICLI)
ESSI........... Employment Security Systems Institute
ESSI........... Visingso [*Sweden*] [*ICAO location identifier*] (ICLI)
ESSK .... Gavle-Sandviken [*Sweden*] [*ICAO location identifier*] (ICLI)
ESSL.......... Eastern Secondary Standards Laboratory
ESSL.......... Linkoping/SAAB [*Sweden*] [*ICAO location identifier*] (ICLI)
ESSLR....... Eye-Safe Simulated LASER Range Finder (MCD)
ESSM .... Brattforsheden [*Sweden*] [*ICAO location identifier*] (ICLI)
ESSM .... Emergency Ship Salvage Material [*Navy*] (NG)
ESSN .... ESSO North [*A publication*]
ESSNSS .... Electronic Supply Segment of the Navy Supply System
ESSO .... Elected Spanish Speaking Officials (EA)
ESSO .... Embarkation Supply and Stores Officer [*Military*] [*British*]
ESSO .... Standard Oil [*Trademark in foreign use only; superseded in US, 1973, by Exxon*]
Esso Agr .... Esso Agricola [*A publication*]
ESSO Mag ... ESSO Magazine [*A publication*]
ESSO Oilways Int ... ESSO [*Standard Oil*] Oilways International [*A publication*]
ESSOR ...... Essai Orgel [*Orgel test reactor*] [*Italy*]
Essor Frigorif Fr ... Essor Frigorifique Francais [*A publication*]
ESSP.......... Earliest Scram Set Point [*Nuclear energy*] (NRCH)
ESSP.......... Elementary School Science Project
ESSP.......... Norrkoping/Kungsangen [*Sweden*] [*ICAO location identifier*] (ICLI)
ESSPO ...... Electronic Supporting Systems Project Office [*Air Force*]
ESSQ .... Karlstad [*Sweden*] [*ICAO location identifier*] (ICLI)
Ess R.......... Essex Review [*A publication*]
ESSR .... Expected Sample Size Ratio [*Statistics*]
ESSRA....... Economic and Social Science Research Association [*British*]
ESSS.......... External Stores Support System [*or Subsystem*] (MCD)
ESSS.......... Stockholm Aeronautical Fixed Telecommunication Network Center [*Sweden*] [*ICAO location identifier*] (ICLI)
ESSSD....... Ekonomicheskoe Sotrudnichestvo Stran-Chlenov SEV [*A publication*]
ESST .... Eastern Equatorial Pacific Sea Surface Temperature [*Oceanography*]
ESST .... Torsby/Fryklanda [*Sweden*] [*ICAO location identifier*] (ICLI)
ESSU .... Electronic Selective Switching Unit
ESSU .... Eskilstuna [*Sweden*] [*ICAO location identifier*] (ICLI)
ESSV .... Visby [*Sweden*] [*ICAO location identifier*] (ICLI)
ESSW .... Vastervik [*Sweden*] [*ICAO location identifier*] (ICLI)
ESSWACS ... Electronic Solid-State Wide-Angle Camera System (MCD)
ESSX .... Essex Communications Corp. [*Greenwich, CT*] [*NASDAQ symbol*] (NQ)
ESSX .... Vasteras/Johannisberg [*Sweden*] [*ICAO location identifier*] (ICLI)
ESSY .... Earth Station - Syria
ESSZ .... Vangso [*Sweden*] [*ICAO location identifier*] (ICLI)
EST............ Boundary Estimate Message [*Aviation code*]
EST............ Early Start Time
EST............ Earth Station - Turkey
EST............ Eastern Standard Time
EST............ Echo Suppressor, Terminating End [*Telecommunications*] (TEL)
EST............ Economisch en Sociaal Tijdschrift [*A publication*]
EST............ Effective Study Test [*Study skills test*]
EST............ Electronic Sequencer Timer
EST............ Electronic Shop Major Telephone and Teletype [*Coast Guard*]
EST............ Electronic Social Transformation
EST............ Electronic Spark Timing [*Automotive engineering*]
EST............ Electronics Sea Trials (MCD)
EST............ Electroshock Therapy [*Psychology*]
EST............ Electrostatic Storage Tube
EST............ Elmo Snakey Torus (MCD)
EST............ Embedded Sensor Technique
E & ST .... Employment and Suitability Test [*Aerospace*] (AAG)
EST............ En Route Support Team [*Military*] (AFIT)
EST............ Endodermal Sinus Tumor [*Oncology*]
EST............ Endoscopic Sphincterotomy [*Medicine*]
EST............ Engineer/Service Test [*Aerospace*] (MCD)
EST............ Engineering Sub Task (MCD)
EST............ Engineering Support Team (KSC)
ESt............ English Studies [*A publication*]
EST............ Enlistment Screening Test [*Military*]
ES & T .... Environmental Science and Technology [*A publication*]
EST............ Epidemiology and Sanitation Technician [*Navy*]
EST............ Equilibrium Surface Thermochemistry
EST............ Equity Silver Mines Ltd. [*Toronto Stock Exchange symbol*] [*Vancouver Stock Exchange symbol*]
est.............. Erhard Seminars Training
ESt............ Erlanger Studien [*A publication*]
EST............ Established (EY)
EST............ Estancia [*New Mexico*] [*Seismograph station code, US Geological Survey*] (SEIS)
EST............ Estate

EST............ Esteemed (ADA)
EST............ Esterase [*An enzyme*]
Est.............. Esther [*Old Testament book*]
EST............ Estherville, IA [*Location identifier*] [*FAA*] (FAAL)
EST............ Estimate (EY)
EST............ Estonia
est.............. Estonian [*MARC language code*] [*Library of Congress*] (LCCP)
EST............ Estuary [*Maps and charts*]
Est.............. Estudios [*A publication*]
EST............ European Society of Toxicology (EAIO)
EST............ Exhaust System Terminal (KSC)
EST............ Expanded Service Testing
EST............ University of New Hampshire, Jackson Estuarine Laboratory, Durham, NH [*OCLC symbol*] (OCLC)
ESTA......... Electroshock Therapy Apparatus [*Psychology*]
ESTA......... Escape System Test Article (MCD)
ESTA......... European Security Transport Association (EA)
Est A Alava ... Estudios de Arqueologia Alavesa [*A publication*]
ESTAB...... Establish [*or Establishment*] (KSC)
ESTABD ... Established (ROG)
ESTABLT ... Establishment (ROG)
Estac Cent Ecol Bol (Spain) ... Estacion Central de Ecologia. Boletin (Spain) [*A publication*]
Estac Exp Agric Tucuman Bol ... Estacion Experimental Agricola de Tucuman. Boletin [*A publication*]
Estac Exp Agric Tucuman Circ ... Estacion Experimental Agricola de Tucuman. Circular [*A publication*]
Estac Exp Agric Tucuman Publ Misc ... Estacion Experimental Agricola de Tucuman. Publicacion Miscelanea [*A publication*]
Estac Exp Agropecu Pergamino Bol Divulg ... Estacion Experimental Agropecuaria Pergamino. Boletin de Divulgacion [*A publication*]
Estac Exp Agropecu Pergamino Publ Tec ... Estacion Experimental Agropecuaria Pergamino. Publicacion Tecnico [*A publication*]
Estac Exp Aula dei Zaragoza Bol ... Estacion Experimental de Aula dei Zaragoza. Boletin [*A publication*]
Estac Exp Aula dei Zaragoza Dep Mejora Ens ... Estacion Experimental de Aula dei Zaragoza. Departamento de Mejora Ensayos [*A publication*]
Estac Exp Reg Agropecu Parana Ser Notas Tec ... Estacion Experimental Regional Agropecuaria Parana. Serie Notas Tecnicas [*A publication*]
Estadist Espanola ... Estadistica Espanola [*A publication*]
Estadistica Esp ... Estadistica Espanola [*A publication*]
Est Ag .... Estudio Agustiniano [*A publication*]
ESTAR...... Estimated Arrival Date
Estates Gaz ... Estates Gazette [*A publication*]
Estates Q ... Estates and Trusts Quarterly [*A publication*]
Estates Times Rev ... Estates Times Review [*A publication*]
ESTB......... Establish [*or Establishment*] (AFM)
ESTB......... Esteban's Mexican Foods [*NASDAQ symbol*] (NQ)
EstB.......... Estudios Biblicos [*Madrid*] [*A publication*]
ESTBD...... Established
EstBib........ Estudios Biblicos [*Madrid*] [*A publication*]
ESTC......... Eighteenth Century Short Title Catalogue [*British Library*] [*Bibliographic database*] [*London, England*]
ESTC......... European Space Technology Center [*Netherlands*] (KSC)
ESTCA...... Empire State Tattoo Club of America (EA)
ESTCA...... Error-Sensitive Test Case Analysis (MCD)
Est Coas M ... Estuarine and Coastal Marine Science [*A publication*]
Est Contrib Int Biol Programme Prog Rep ... Estonian Contributions to the International Biological Programme. Progress Report [*A publication*]
Est Cult Maya ... Estudios de Cultura Maya [*A publication*]
ESTD........ Electronic Standard (MSA)
ESTD........ Established (ADA)
ESTD........ Estimated
EstD.......... Estudios. Duquesne University [*A publication*]
EstdH......... Estudios de Hispanofila [*A publication*]
ESTE........ Engineering Special Test Equipment (AAG)
ESTE .... Estate
EstE .... Estudios Eclesiasticos [*Madrid*] [*A publication*]
EstE .... Estudios Escenicos [*A publication*]
ESTEC...... European Space Research and Technology Center [*Netherlands*] (IID)
ESTEC...... European Space Technology Center [*Netherlands*] (NASA)
EstEcl........ Estudios Eclesiasticos [*Madrid*] [*A publication*]
Estee .... Estee's District Court of Hawaii [*A publication*] (DLA)
Estee (Hawaii) ... Estee's District Court of Hawaii [*A publication*] (DLA)
ESTEEM... Empower Self through Education and Eating Management
Estel-Ber Forsch Entwickl Unserer Werke ... Estel-Berichte aus Forschung und Entwicklung Unserer Werke [*A publication*]
Est Europ... Est Europeen [*A publication*]
ESTF .... Environmental Systems Test Facility (KSC)
EstF........... Estudios Franciscanos [*A publication*]
EstFilRelOr ... Estudios de Filosofia y Religion Orientales [*Buenos Aires*] [*A publication*]
EstFr .... Estudios Franciscanos [*Barcelona*] [*A publication*]
EstFranc .... Estudios Franciscanos [*Barcelona*] [*A publication*]
EStG .... Einkommensteuergesetz [*Income Tax Law*] [*German*] (DLA)

Est Gaz....... Estates Gazette [*A publication*]
Est Gaz Dig ... Estates Gazette Digest of Land and Property Cases [*A publication*]
Est Gifts & Tr J ... Estates, Gifts, and Trusts Journal [*A publication*] (DLA)
Esth........... Esther [*Old Testament book*]
ESTH......... Esthetic
ESTHA...... Environmental Science and Technology [*A publication*]
EstHM...... Estudios de Historia Moderna [*A publication*]
EsthR........ Esther Rabbah (BJA)
E/S TIEP... Engineering/Service Test and Independent Evaluation Program [*Army*] (AABC)
ESTIMD ... Estimated (ROG)
ESTK........ EasTek Corp. [*NASDAQ symbol*] (NQ)
ESTL .... Electronic Systems Test Laboratory [*NASA*]
ESTL .... European Space Tribology Laboratory
EstLit .... Estafeta Literaria [*A publication*]
Estm.......... Estimated (DLA)
EstMar...... Estudios Marianos [*Madrid*] [*A publication*]
ESTN........ Eastern
ESTN........ Endstone [*Horology*]
EStn .... Englische Studien [*A publication*]
ESTN........ Estimation
ESTO........ Eastco Industrial Safety Corp. [*NASDAQ symbol*] (NQ)
ESTO........ Engineer/Service Test Office [*Aerospace*]
ESTO........ Estonian World Festival
ESTO........ Europaeische Studentenvereinigung in Osterreich
Estomatol Cult ... Estomatologia e Cultura [*A publication*]
ESTOPL.... Easy Search of Topical Law [*Australia*]
ESTOP & W ... Estoppel and Waiver [*Legal term*] (DLA)
EstOr .... Estudios Orientales [*A publication*]
Est-Ouest... Est et Ouest. Bulletin de l'Association d'Etudes et d'Informations Politiques Internationales [*A publication*]
ESTP .... Electronic Systems Test Program [*NASA*]
Est Plan ..... Estate Planning [*A publication*]
Est Plan Rev ... Estate Planning Review [*A publication*] (DLA)
Est Powers & Trusts ... Estates, Powers, and Trusts [*Legal term*] (DLA)
Est Prac ..... Estee's Code Pleading, Practice, and Forms [*A publication*] (DLA)
Est Prac Pl ... Estee's Code Pleading, Practice, and Forms [*A publication*] (DLA)
ESTR .... Educational Services and Teaching Resources Unit [*Murdoch University*] [*Australia*]
EstR .... Esther Rabbah (BJA)
ESTRA ...... Experimental STOL Transport Research
ESTRACK ... European Space Tracking and Telemetry Network (MCD)
ESTRIFF... Encryptic Secure Tracking RADAR Identification Friend or Foe (NATG)
ESTRO...... European Society for Therapeutic Radiology and Oncology (EAIO)
ESTS .... Early Scottish Text Society [*A publication*]
ESTS .... Echo Suppressor Testing System [*Telecommunications*] (TEL)
ESTS .... Electronic Systems Test Set (MCD)
EstSSR ...... Estonian Soviet Socialist Republic
Estt............ Establishment [*British military*] (DMA)
Est and Tr Q ... Estates and Trusts Quarterly [*A publication*]
Est and Tr Rep ... Estates and Trusts Reports [*A publication*]
Est & Trusts ... Estates and Trusts [*Legal term*] (DLA)
ESTU........ Electronic System Test Unit
Estuarine Bull ... Estuarine Bulletin [*A publication*]
Estuarine Coastal Mar Sci ... Estuarine and Coastal Marine Science [*A publication*]
Estuarine Coastal Shelf Sci ... Estuarine, Coastal, and Shelf Science [*England*] [*A publication*]
Estuarine Res ... Estuarine Research [*A publication*]
EStud .... English Studies [*A publication*]
Estud Agron ... Estudos Agronomicos [*A publication*]
Estud Agron Missao Estud Agron Ultramar ... Estudos Agronomicos. Missao de Estudos Agronomicos do Ultramar [*A publication*]
Estud Andin ... Estudios Andinos [*A publication*]
Estud As Afr ... Estudios de Asia y Africa [*A publication*]
Estud Cl ..... Estudios Clasicos [*A publication*]
Estud Clas ... Estudios Clasicos [*A publication*]
Estud Coop ... Estudios Cooperativos [*A publication*]
Estud Cult Nahuatl ... Estudios de Cultura Nahuatl [*A publication*]
Estud Derecho 2a Epoca ... Estudios de Derecho. Segunda Epoca [*A publication*]
Estud Econ ... Estudios de Economia [*A publication*]
Estud Econ Argentina ... Estudios sobre la Economia Argentina [*A publication*]
Estud Econs ... Estudos Economicos [*A publication*]
Estud Empresar ... Estudios Empresariales [*A publication*]
Estud Empresariales ... Estudios Empresariales [*A publication*]
Estud Ensaios Doc Junta Invest Cient Ultramar (Port) ... Estudos, Ensaios, e Documentos. Junta de Investigacoes Cientificas do Ultramar (Portugal) [*A publication*]
Estud Esteril ... Estudios sobre Esterilidad [*A publication*]
Estud Extremenos ... Estudios Extremenos; Revista Historica, Literaria, y Artistica [*A publication*]
Estud Fauna Port ... Estudos sobre a Fauna Portuguesa [*A publication*]
Estud Filosof ... Estudios Filosoficos [*A publication*]
Estud Geogr ... Estudios Geograficos [*A publication*]

Estud Geogr Inst Juan Sebastian Elcano ... Estudios Geograficos. Instituto "Juan Sebastian Elcano" [*A publication*]

Estud Geol Inst Invest Geol "Lucas Mallada" ... Estudios Geologicos. Instituto de Investigaciones Geologicas "Lucas Mallada" [*A publication*]

Estud Geol (Madr) ... Estudios Geologicos (Madrid) [*A publication*]

Estud Hist Agrar ... Estudis d'Historia Agraria [*A publication*]

Estud Ib-Am ... Estudos Ibero-Americanos [*A publication*]

E Studies .... English Studies [*A publication*]

Estud Inform Serv Flor Aquic (Portugal) ... Estudos e Informacao. Servicos Florestais e Aquicolas (Portugal) [*A publication*]

Estud Int .... Estudios Internacionales [*A publication*]

Estud Internac ... Estudios Internacionales [*A publication*]

Estudios Geol ... Estudios Geologicos [*A publication*]

Estudios Teol (Guatemala) ... Estudios Teologicos (Guatemala) [*A publication*]

Estud Legis ... Estudios Legislativos [*A publication*]

Estud Leopold ... Estudos Leopoldenses [*A publication*]

Estud Notas Trab Serv Fom Min (Port) ... Estudos. Notas e Trabalhos do Servico de Fomento Mineiro (Portugal) [*A publication*]

ESTUDO ... Estuaries [*A publication*]

Estudos Agron ... Estudos Agronomicos [*A publication*]

Estudos Teol (Brazil) ... Estudos Teologicos (Brazil) [*A publication*]

Estud Parag ... Estudios Paraguayos [*A publication*]

Estud Quim Inst Nac Invest Ind (Port) ... Estudos de Quimica. Instituto Nacional de Investigacao Industrial (Portugal) [*A publication*]

Estud Segov ... Estudios Segovianos [*A publication*]

Estud Sindic ... Estudios Sindicales [*A publication*]

Estud Sindicales ... Estudios Sindicales [*A publication*]

Estud Sindicales y Coops ... Estudios Sindicales y Cooperativos [*A publication*]

Estud Soc ... Estudios Sociales. Revista de Ciencias Sociales [*A publication*]

Estud Soc C ... Estudios Sociales Centroamericanos [*A publication*]

Estud Soc Centroam ... Estudios Sociales Centroamericanos [*A publication*]

Estud Soc Centroamer ... Estudios Sociales Centroamericanos [*A publication*]

ESTV .... Error Statistics by Tape Volume [*Data processing*] (IBMDP)

Est Zaragoza ... Estudios. Seminario de Prehistoria, Arqueologia, e Historia Antigua. Facultad de Filosofia y Letras de Zaragoza [*A publication*]

ESU .... Efficiency Scrutiny Unit [*Australia*]

ESU .... Electricity Supply Union [*British*]

ESU .... Electronic Sequencing Unit [*for helicopters*] [*Army*] (RDA)

ESU .... Electronic Services Unlimited [*New York, NY*] [*Telecommunications*] (TSSD)

ESU .... Electronic Switching Unit [*Telecommunications*] (MCD)

ESU .... Electrostatic Unit

ESU .... Electrosurgical Unit [*Medicine*]

ESU .... Empty Signal Unit [*Telecommunications*] (TEL)

ESU .... Engine Service Unit (AAG)

ESU .... English Speaking Union [*London, England*] (EAIO)

ESU .... English-Speaking Union of the United States (EA)

ESU .... Enormous State University [*Fictitious school often featured in comic strip "Tank McNamara"*]

ESU .... Esutoru [*Uglegorsk*] [*USSR*] [*Seismograph station code, US Geological Survey*] [*Closed*] (SEIS)

ESU .... Europa Study Unit (EA)

ESUA .... Amsele [*Sweden*] [*ICAO location identifier*] (ICLI)

ESUB .... Arbra [*Sweden*] [*ICAO location identifier*] (ICLI)

ESU Bus Rev ... Emporia State University. Business Review [*A publication*]

ESUC .... English Speaking Union of the Commonwealth [*London, England*] (EAIO)

ESUE .... Idre [*Sweden*] [*ICAO location identifier*] (ICLI)

ESUF .... Fallfors [*Sweden*] [*ICAO location identifier*] (ICLI)

ESUG .... Gargnas [*Sweden*] [*ICAO location identifier*] (ICLI)

ESUH .... Harnosand/Myran [*Sweden*] [*ICAO location identifier*] (ICLI)

ESUIC .... English Speaking Union International Council [*London, England*] (EAIO)

ESUK .... Kalixfors [*Sweden*] [*ICAO location identifier*] (ICLI)

ESUL .... Ljusdal [*Sweden*] [*ICAO location identifier*] (ICLI)

ESUM .... Mohed [*Sweden*] [*ICAO location identifier*] (ICLI)

ESUN .... Sundsvall [*Sweden*] [*ICAO location identifier*] (ICLI)

ESUNA ..... Ethiopian Students Union of North America

ESUR .... Ramsele [*Sweden*] [*ICAO location identifier*] (ICLI)

E SURR R ... East Surrey Regiment [*Military unit*] [*British*] (ROG)

ESUS .... Asele [*Sweden*] [*ICAO location identifier*] (ICLI)

ESUT .... Evaluation of Small Unit Training (MCD)

ESUT .... Hemavan [*Sweden*] [*ICAO location identifier*] (ICLI)

ESU/UFE ... European Showmen's Union/Union Foraine Europeenne (EA)

ESUV .... Alvsbyn [*Sweden*] [*ICAO location identifier*] (ICLI)

ESUY .... Edsbyn [*Sweden*] [*ICAO location identifier*] (ICLI)

ESV .... Earth Satellite Vehicle [*Air Force*]

ESV .... Earth Station - Venezuela

ESV .... Ego Support Value [*Psychology*]

ESV .... Elastic Space Vehicle

ESV .... Electrostatic Voltmeter (DEN)

ESV .... Emergency Shutoff Valve (KSC)

ESV .... Enamel Single Silk Varnish [*Wire insulation*] (AAG)

ESV .... End-Systolic Volume [*Cardiology*]

ESV .... Energy Services [*AMEX symbol*] (SPSG)

ESV .... Enserv Corp. [*Toronto Stock Exchange symbol*]

ESV .... Error Statistics by Volume [*Data processing*] (BUR)

ESV .... Esophageal Valve [*Anatomy*]

ESV .... Essential Service Value [*Telecommunications*] (IEEE)

ESV .... Expanded Service Volume (FAAC)

ESV .... Experimental Safety Vehicle [*Later, Research Safety Vehicle*] [*Department of Transportation*]

ESV .... Extension Society Volunteers [*Defunct*]

ESVA .... Avesta [*Sweden*] [*ICAO location identifier*] (ICLI)

ESVF .... Frolunda [*Sweden*] [*ICAO location identifier*] (ICLI)

ESVG .... Gagnef [*Sweden*] [*ICAO location identifier*] (ICLI)

ESVH .... Hallefors [*Sweden*] [*ICAO location identifier*] (ICLI)

ESVK .... Katrineholm [*Sweden*] [*ICAO location identifier*] (ICLI)

ESVM .... Malung [*Sweden*] [*ICAO location identifier*] (ICLI)

ESVP .... European Society of Veterinary Pathology (EA)

ESVQ .... Koping [*Sweden*] [*ICAO location identifier*] (ICLI)

ESVR .... Examination Status Verification Report (NVT)

ESVS .... Escape Suit Ventilation System (MCD)

ESVS .... Escape System Ventilation System (NASA)

ESVS .... Siljansnas [*Sweden*] [*ICAO location identifier*] (ICLI)

ESW .... Economic and Sector Work

ESW .... Electroslag Welding

ESW .... Emergency Service Water [*Nuclear energy*] (NRCH)

ESW .... Engine Status Word (MCD)

ESW .... Engineering Statement of Work (MCD)

ESW .... Error Status Word [*Data processing*] (BUR)

ESW .... ESSA [*Environmental Science Services Administration*] World [*A publication*]

ESW .... Essential Service Water [*Nuclear energy*] (NRCH)

ESW .... Ethical Society of Washington (EA)

e-sw--- .... Sweden [*MARC geographic area code*] [*Library of Congress*] (LCCP)

ESWD .... Emergency Service Water Discharge [*Nuclear energy*] (NRCH)

ESWI .... Emergency Service Water Intake [*Nuclear energy*] (NRCH)

ESWI .... Norrkoping [*Sweden*] [*ICAO location identifier*] (ICLI)

ESWL .... Equivalent Single Wheel Load (MCD)

ESWL .... Estimated Surface Wheel Load (CINC)

ESWL .... Extracorporeal Shockwave Lithotripsy [*Medicine*]

ESWS .... Earth Satellite Weapon Systems

ESWS .... Emergency Service Water Screening [*Nuclear energy*] (NRCH)

ESWS .... Emergency Service Water System [*Nuclear energy*] (IEEE)

ESWS .... Essential Service Water System [*Nuclear energy*] (NRCH)

ESWSS ...... Emergency Service Water Supply System [*Nuclear energy*] (NRCH)

ESX .... Essex Chemical Corp. [*NYSE symbol*] (SPSG)

ESX .... Essex County College, Newark, NJ [*OCLC symbol*] (OCLC)

ESX .... Essex Financial Partners LP (Unit) [*AMEX symbol*] (SPSG)

ESY .... E-Systems, Inc. [*NYSE symbol*] (SPSG)

ESY .... Earth Station - Yugoslavia

ESY .... Economisch en Sociaal Tijdschrift [*A publication*]

ESY .... Episcopal Service for Youth (EA)

ESY .... Extended School Year

ESY .... West Yellowstone, MT [*Location identifier*] [*FAA*] (FAAL)

ESYA .... Extended School Year Aid

e-sz--- .... Switzerland [*MARC geographic area code*] [*Library of Congress*] (LCCP)

ET .... Easter Term

ET .... Eastern Time (GPO)

ET .... Eaton Trust Co. [*Toronto Stock Exchange symbol*]

ET .... Eddy-Current Testing [*Electromagnetism*]

ET .... Edge Thickness [*Technical drawings*]

ET .... Edge-Triggered (IEEE)

E & T .... Education and Training [*Navy*]

ET .... Educational and Industrial Television [*A publication*]

ET .... Educational Television [*A publication*]

ET .... Educational Test [*British military*] (DMA)

ET .... Educational Therapy

ET .... Educational Training

ET .... Effective Temperature

ET .... Egypt

ET .... Eildon Tree [*A publication*]

ET .... Ekonomisk Tidskrift [*A publication*]

ET .... Elapsed Time

ET .... Electric Telegraph

ET .... Electrical Time

ET .... Electrical Transcription

ET .... Electrical Typewriter (CMD)

ET .... Electrode Track

ET .... Electron Transfer

ET .... Electron [*or Electronic*] Tube (MCD)

ET .... Electronic Technician

ET .... Electronic Test

ET .... Electronic Time [*Fuze*] (MCD)

ET .... Electronic Transformers (MCD)

ET .... Electronic Typewriter

ET .... Electronics Technician [*Navy rating*]

ET .... Elevated Temperature (MCD)

ET .... Embedded Training [*Army*] (RDA)

ET .... Embryo Transfer

ET .... EMCLASS Terms [*Online database field identifier*]

ET .... Emergency Takeover

ET .... Emergency Tank [*Nuclear energy*] (NRCH)

ET .... Emergency Treatment [*Dentistry*]
ET .... Emerging Technology
ET .... Emissions Trading [*Environmental Protection Agency*]
ET .... Empathy Test [*Psychology*]
E & T .... Employment and Training
ET .... Employment Training [*British*]
ET .... End of Tape [*Data processing*]   (CET)
ET .... End of Text [*Data processing*]
ET .... End-Tidal [*Physiology*]
ET .... Endogenous Transcript [*Genetics*]
ET .... Endotoxin [*Microbiology*]
ET .... Endotracheal Tube [*Medicine*]
ET .... Engaged Tone [*Telecommunications*]   (TEL)
ET .... Engine Turned [*Watchmaking*]   (ROG)
ET .... Engineer Training
ET .... Engineering Technology   (MCD)
ET .... Engineering Test
ET .... English Text
ET .... English Title [*Online database field identifier*]
ET .... English Translation
ET .... Enterically Transmitted [*Medicine*]
ET .... Enterostomal Therapist [*Gastroenterology*]
ET .... Entertainment Tax   (DLA)
ET .... Entertainment Tonight [*Television program*]
ET .... Environmental Test
ET .... Enziklopedyah [*or Entsiklopedyah*] Talmudit   (BJA)
ET .... Ephemeris Time [*Astronomy*]
ET .... Epitheorese Technes [*A publication*]
ET .... Equation of Time [*Navigation*]
ET .... Equipment Test
ET .... Equipment Time
ET .... Equivalent Training   (AABC)
ET .... Erimaki Tokage [*Japanese name for the Australian frill-necked
                  lizard, a national favorite that figured in one of
                  Mitsubishi's advertising campaigns*]
E/T .... Escape Tower [*NASA*]   (KSC)
ET .... Escort Trains   (CINC)
ET .... Esotropia for Distance [*Ophthalmology*]
ET .... Essential Thrombocythemia [*Hematology*]
ET .... Essential Tremor [*Neurophysiology*]
ET .... Estate and Gift Tax Ruling [*A publication*]   (DLA)
ET .... Estate Tax
ET .... Estimated Time
Et .... Ethics [*A publication*]
ET .... Ethiopia [*Aircraft nationality and registration mark*]   (FAAC)
ET .... Ethiopia [*ANSI two-letter standard code*]   (CNC)
et .... Ethiopia [*MARC country of publication code*] [*Library of
                  Congress*]   (LCCP)
ET .... Ethiopian Airlines Corp. [*Ethiopia*] [*ICAO designator*]   (FAAC)
ET .... Ethnomusicology [*A publication*]
Et. .... Ethyl [*Organic chemistry*]
ET .... Ethyltoluene [*Organic chemistry*]
Et. .... Etoiles [*A publication*]
Et. .... Etudes [*A publication*]
ET .... Etudes Traditionnelles [*A publication*]
ET .... Etudes et Travaux. Travaux du Centre d'Archeologie
                  Mediterraneenne de l'Academie Polonaise de Sciences
                  [*Warsaw*] [*A publication*]
et----- .... Europe, East Central [*MARC geographic area code*] [*Library of
                  Congress*]   (LCCP)
ET .... European Taxation [*A publication*]
ET .... European Theater
ET .... European Trends [*A publication*]
ET .... Eustachian Tube [*Anatomy*]
ET .... Evangelische Theologie [*A publication*]
ET .... Evapotranspiration [*Hydrology*]
ET .... Event Timer   (NASA)
ET .... Ex-Tapol [*Political Prisoner*] [*Indonesia*]
ET .... Exchange Termination [*Telecommunications*]
ET .... Excise Tax [*Canada*]
ET .... Executive Team   (NRCH)
ET .... Exodus Trust   (EA)
ET .... Expander Tube
ET .... Expenditure Targets [*Medical care proposal*]
ET .... Explosive Technology
ET .... Expository Times [*A publication*]
ET .... Extended Take [*Recording term*]
ET .... External Tank [*NASA*]
ET .... Extraterrestrial [*Also used in film title "ET - The Extra-
                  Terrestrial"*]
ET .... Eye Travel
ET .... Foreign Economic Trends and Their Implications for the
                  United States [*A publication*]
ET .... Journal of Educational Technology [*A publication*]
ET1 .... Electronics Technician, First Class [*Navy rating*]
ET2 .... Electronics Technician, Second Class [*Navy rating*]
ET3 .... Electronics Technician, Third Class [*Navy rating*]
ETA .... Education through Aviation
ETA .... Educational Television Association   (EAIO)
ETA .... Educational Theater Association   (EA)
ETA .... Effectiveness Training Associates

ETA .... Effects Test Area [*Army*]
ETA .... Ejector Thrust Augmentation [*Air Force*]
ETA .... Electra North West [*Vancouver Stock Exchange symbol*]
ETA .... Electrical Thermal Analysis
ETA .... Electrothermal Atomization [*For spectrometry*]
ETA .... Emanation Thermal Analysis
ETA .... Embroidery Trade Association   (EA)
ETA .... Employment and Training Administration [*Formerly,
                  Manpower Administration*] [*Department of Labor*]
ETA .... Energy Tax Act [*1978*]
ETA .... Engineering Task Assignment
ETA .... Entertainment Trades Alliance [*British*]
ETA .... Environmental Test Article   (NASA)
ETA .... Equipment Transfer Aisle   (NRCH)
ETA .... Equivalent Target Area   (MCD)
ETA .... Esperanto Teachers Association [*British*]
ETA .... Estimated Target Assurance
ETA .... Estimated Time of Acquisition   (KSC)
ETA .... Estimated [*or Expected*] Time of Arrival
Eta .... Eterna [*Record label*] [*German Democratic Republic*]
ETA .... Etudes Administratives [*A publication*]
EtA .... Etudes Anglaises [*A publication*]
ETA .... European Taxpayers Association   (EA)
ETA .... European Tennis Association   (EAIO)
ETA .... European Throwsters Association   (EA)
ETA .... European Thyroid Association   (EAIO)
ETA .... European Tropospheric-Scatter Army [*Communications
                  system*]
ETA .... European Tugowners Association [*London, England*]   (EAIO)
ETA .... Euzkadi ta Azkatasuna [*Basque Fatherland and Freedom*]
                  [*Spain*]   (PD)
ETA .... Evangelical Training Association   (EA)
ETA .... Exception Time Accounting
ETA .... Excise Tax Act [*Canada*]
ETA .... Expect to Arrive
ETA .... Expected Turnaround [*Data processing*]
ETA .... Experimental Test Accelerator [*Nuclear physics*]
ETA .... Explosive Transfer Assembly   (MCD)
ETA .... External Tank Attachment   (MCD)
ETA .... Extraterrestrial Activity
ETA .... Extraterrestrial Actuality
ETAA .... Educators to Africa   (EA)
ETAA .... Eelam Tamils Association of America   (EA)
ETAA .... Electrothermal Atomic Absorption [*Analytical technique*]
ETAAS .... Electrothermal Atomic Absorption Spectrometry
ETAb .... English Teaching Abstracts [*A publication*]
ETAB .... Environmental Testing Advisory Board [*Dow Chemical Co.*]
Etab. .... Etablissement [*Establishment*] [*Business term*] [*French*]
ETAB .... Expanded Technical Assistance Board [*United Nations*]
Etabl .... Etablissement [*Establishment*] [*Business term*]
                  [*French*]   (CED)
ETAC .... Electrically Tuned Antenna Coupler
ETAC .... Electronics Technical Applications Center [*Air Force*]
ETAC .... Environment Technical Advisory Committee [*Australia*]
ETAC .... Environmental Technical Applications Center [*Air Force*]
ETACCS ..... European Theater Air Command and Control Study [*DoD*]
ETACS ...... Electronic Time and Alarm Control System [*Mitsubishi*]
                  [*Automotive engineering*]
ETAD .... Ecological and Toxicological Association of the Dyestuffs
                  Manufacturing Industry [*Basel, Switzerland*]   (EAIO)
ETADS ...... Enhanced Transportation Automated Data System [*Air Force*]
ETA Elektrowaerme Tech Ausbau Ed A ... ETA. Elektrowaerme im
                  Technischen Ausbau. Edition A [*A publication*]
ETAFF .... European Technical Association for Furniture Finishes
                  [*Defunct*]
ETA-I .... Electronics Technicians Association, International   (EA)
ETAIRS .... Employment and Training Automated Information and
                  Retrieval System [*Department of Labor*] [*Database*]
ET AL .... Et Alia [*And Others*] [*Latin*]
ET AL .... Et Alibi [*And Elsewhere*] [*Latin*]
et al .... Et Alii [*or Et Aliae or Et Alia*] [*And Others*] [*Latin*]   (GPO)
ET AL FREQ ... Et Alii Frequentis [*And in Many Other (Passages)*]
                  [*Latin*]   (ROG)
ETAM .... Anklam [*German Democratic Republic*] [*ICAO location
                  identifier*]   (ICLI)
ETA-M ...... Euzkadi ta Azkatasuna [*Basque Fatherland and Freedom*]
                  Military Front [*Spain*]
ETAM .... Experimental Transmitting Antenna Modular Model   (MCD)
ETAMS ..... Employment and Training Administration Management System
                  [*Department of Labor*]
Et Angl .... Etudes Anglaises [*A publication*]
ETANSW News ... English Teachers Association of New South Wales.
                  Newsletter [*A publication*]   (APTA)
ETAP .... Expanded Technical Assistance Program [*United Nations*]
ETAPC ...... European Technical Association for Protective
                  Coatings   (EAIO)
ETA-PM.... Euzkadi ta Azkatasuna [*Basque Fatherland and Freedom*]
                  Political-Military Front [*Spain*]
Et Ar .... Etudes Arabes [*A publication*]
ETARAQ... Entomologische Arbeiten. Museum G. Frey (Tutzing-bei
                  Muenchen) [*A publication*]

ETARO ..... Employment and Training Administration Regional Office [*Department of Labor*]
ETAS........ Effective True Airspeed (AFM)
ETAS........ Elevated Target Acquisition System
ETAS........ Escort Towed Array Sensor [*Later, TACTAS*] [*Navy*] (MCD)
ETASS...... Evaluation of the Army Study System (MCD)
ETAT........ Education and Training Advisory Team (CINC)
ETAT........ Eesti NSV Teaduste Akadeemia Toimetised. Uhiskonnateaduste Seeria [*A publication*]
ETATA...... Eesti NSV Teaduste Akadeemia. Toimetised. Bioloogia [*A publication*]
ETATAW ... Eesti NSV Teaduste Akadeemia. Toimetised. Bioloogia [*A publication*]
Etat San Animaux Belgique ... Etat Sanitaire des Animaux de la Belgique [*A publication*]
ETB........... Elastic Top and Bottom [*Military-issue clothing*] [*British*] [DSUE]
ETB........... Electrical Time Base
ETB........... Electronic Test Block
ETB........... Elvis Teddy Bears (EA)
ETB........... End of Transmission Block [*Data processing*]
ETB........... Engineering Test Basis (KSC)
ETB........... English Tourist Board
ETB........... Enlisted Training Branch [*BUPERS*]
ETB........... Equipment Transfer Bag [*NASA*]
ETB........... Estimated Time of Berthing [*Navigation*]
ETB........... Ethidium Bromide [*Trypanocide*] [*Also, EB, Etd Br*] [*Biochemical analysis*]
ETB........... Etobicoke Public Library [*UTLAS symbol*]
ETB........... Experimental Test Bed (MCD)
ETB........... West Bend, WI [*Location identifier*] [*FAA*] (FAAL)
ETBA....... Hellenike Trapeza Biomechanikes Anaptyxeos
EtBalk....... Etudes Balkaniques [*A publication*]
Et Balkan... Etudes Balkaniques [*A publication*]
ETBC....... East Texas Baptist College
ETBE........ Ethyl Tertiary-Butyl Ether [*Fuel additive*]
ETBH .... Barth [*German Democratic Republic*] [*ICAO location identifier*] (ICLI)
ETBKAV ... Entomologische Berichten [*Amsterdam*] [*A publication*]
ETBN .... Berlin/Schonefeld [*German Democratic Republic*] [*ICAO location identifier*] (ICLI)
ETBO .... Engineering Test Base Office (AAG)
ETBPR ...... European Theater Bureau of Public Relations [*World War II*]
ETBS .... Berlin/Schonefeld [*German Democratic Republic*] [*ICAO location identifier*] (ICLI)
ETB TUG .. ETB - TUG. Equipement Technique du Batiment - Technische Uitrusting van het Gebouw [*A publication*]
EtByz .... Etudes Byzantines [*A publication*]
ETC........... Early Typewriter Collectors Association (EA)
ETC........... Earth Terminal Complex
ETC........... Earth Terrain Camera [*NASA*] (MCD)
ETC........... Educational Technology Center [*Department of Education*] [*Harvard University*] [*Research center*] (RCD)
ETC........... Educational Travel Connection [*Oracle Corp.*] [*Information service or system*] (IID)
ETC........... El Centro [*Colombia*] [*Seismograph station code, US Geological Survey*] (SEIS)
ETC........... Electra Title Corporation [*Vancouver Stock Exchange symbol*]
ETC........... Electrical Trade Council (EA)
ETC........... Electroacoustic Torpedo Countermeasure (MCD)
ETC........... Electronic Temperature Control
ETC........... Electronic Text Corp. [*Information service or system*] (IID)
ETC........... Electronic Toll Center [*AT & T*]
ETC........... Emergency Training Centre [*British*]
ETC........... Empresario de Transporte Combinado [*Combined Transport Operator*] [*Business term*] [*Spanish*]
ETC........... Enclosed Track Conveyor
ETC........... Energy Transfer Center
ETC........... Energy Transfer Control [*Aviation*]
ETC........... Engine Technical Commission
ETC........... Engine Test Chamber (MCD)
ETC........... Engineering Test Capsule
ETC........... Engineering Test Center (MCD)
ETC........... Engineering and Training Center [*NASA*] (KSC)
ETC........... Entrepreneur de Transport Combine [*Combined Transport Operator*] [*Business term*] [*French*]
ETC........... Environmental Tectonics Corp. [*AMEX symbol*] (SPSG)
ETC........... Environmental Test Chamber
ETC........... Environmental Toxicology and Chemistry [*A publication*]
ETC........... Equal-Time Commutation
ETC........... Equipment Trust Certificate
ETC........... Estimated Time of Completion
ETC........... Estimated Time of Correction
ETC........... Et Cetera [*And So Forth*] [*Latin*]
ETC........... Euro Travellers Cheque [*Thomas Cook International*]
ETC........... European Tax Confederation (EAIO)
ETC........... European Tea Committee (EA)
ETC........... European Tool Committee (EA)
ETC........... European Trade Committee [*British Overseas Trade Board*] (DS)
ETC........... European Traffic Committee

ETC........... European Translations Centre [*Later, International Translations Centre*]
ETC........... European Travel Commission (EA)
ETC........... Expected Total Cost
ETC........... Experimental Techniques Centre [*Brunel University*] [*British*] (CB)
ETC........... Explosion of the Total Contents [*Insurance*] (DS)
ETC........... Explosive Transient Camera [*Astronomy*]
ETC........... Export Trading Company [*Department of Commerce*]
ETC........... Extended Text Compositor [*Applied Data Research, Inc.*]
ETC........... Extraterrestrial Civilization
ETCA........ Edge Tool Cutters' Association [*A union*] [*British*]
ETCA........ Emergency Terrain Clearance Altitude
ETCA........ Etudes Techniques et Constructions Aerospatiales [*Belgium*]
ETCA........ Export Trading Company Act of 1982
Et Camer.... Etudes Camerounaises [*A publication*]
Et Carm..... Etudes Carmelitaines [*A publication*]
ETCC........ Eastern Tank Carrier Conference
ETCC........ Environmental Test Control Center (AAG)
ETCD........ Estimated Task Completion Date (AAG)
ETCE........ Energy Sources Technology Conference and Exhibition (ITD)
Et Celt....... Etudes Celtiques [*A publication*]
ETCF .... European Technical Committee for Fluorine [*of the European Council of Chemical Manufacturers' Federations*] [*Belgium*] (EAIO)
ETCFC ...... Earl Thomas Conley Fan Club (EA)
ETCG........ Elapsed-Time Code Generator
ETCH........ Etching (MSA)
Et Chypr .... Etudes Chypriotes [*A publication*]
ETCI......... Electronic Tele-Communications, Incorporated [*Waukesha, WI*] [*NASDAQ symbol*] (NQ)
ETCI......... Engineering Technologist Certification Institute (EA)
EtCl........... Etudes Classiques [*A publication*]
Et Cl Aix ... Etudes Classiques. Faculte des Lettres et Sciences Humaines d'Aix [*A publication*]
Et Class...... Etudes Classiques [*A publication*]
ETCM....... Electronics Technician, Master Chief [*Navy rating*]
ETCO .... Cottbus [*German Democratic Republic*] [*ICAO location identifier*] (ICLI)
ETCO .... [*The*] Earth Technology Corp. (USA) [*NASDAQ symbol*] (NQ)
ETCO .... Emergency Traffic Coordinating Officer [*Army*] (AABC)
ETCO .... Equipment Transfer or Change Order (NASA)
Et Cong ..... Etudes Congolaises [*A publication*]
Et Conj ..... Etudes et Conjoncture [*A publication*]
Et et Conj ... Etudes et Conjoncture [*A publication*]
ETCP .... Engineering Technical Change Package (MCD)
ETC Quart Index ... European Translations Centre. Quarterly Index [*A publication*]
ETCR........ Estimated Time of Crew's Return
EtCr .... Etudes Creoles [*A publication*]
Et Cret....... Etudes Cretoises [*A publication*]
ETC Rev Gen ... ETC: A Review of General Semantics [*A publication*]
ETCRRM .. Electronic Teleprinter Cryptographic Regenerative Repeater Mixer (NATG)
ETCS .... Electronics Technician, Senior Chief [*Navy rating*]
ETD .... Effective Transfer Date [*Military*] (AFM)
ETD .... Electrical Terminal Distributor (KSC)
ETD .... Electronic Tactical Display [*Military*]
ETD .... Electronic Time Delay
ETD .... Engineering Test Directive
ETD .... Environments and Threats Directorate [*Army*]
ETD .... Equipment Technical Director (MCD)
ETD .... Estimated [*or Expected*] Time of Departure
ETD .... Estimated Turnover Date (MCD)
ETD .... Event Time Digitizer
ETD .... External Tank Door (MCD)
Et Dahom... Etudes Dahomeennes [*A publication*]
Etd Br......... Ethidium Bromide [*Trypanocide*] [*Also, EB, ETB*] [*Biochemical analysis*]
ETDC........ EADAS [*Engineering and Administrative Data Acquisition System*] Traffic Data Center [*Bell System*]
ETDCFRL ... European Training and Development Centre for Farming and Rural Life (EA)
ETDE......... Experimental Target Designation Equipment
ETDI......... Eurasian Target Data Inventory [*File*] (MCD)
ETDL......... Electronics Technology and Devices Laboratory [*Army*] [*Fort Monmouth, NJ*] (RDA)
ETDN .... Dresden [*German Democratic Republic*] [*ICAO location identifier*] (ICLI)
Et Doc Cons d'Etat ... Etudes et Documents. Conseil d'Etat [*A publication*]
Et et Doc (Educ Nat) ... Etudes et Documents (Education Nationale) [*A publication*]
ETDP......... Emergency Traffic Disposition Plan [*Military*]
ETDP......... Estimated Time and Point of DEWIZ [*Distant Early Warning Identification Zone*] Penetration (FAAC)
Et de Droit Contemp ... Etudes de Droit Contemporain [*French*] [*A publication*] (DLA)
ETDRS ...... Early Treatment Diabetic Retinopathy Study
ETDS .... Elapsed Time Distribution System (MCD)
ETDT......... Extrusion Trim and Drill Template

ETE............ Educational and Training Establishment [*Military*] [*British*]
ET/E.......... Electrical Technician/Electrician (AAG)
ETE............ Electromagnetic Test Environment (MCD)
ETE............ Electronic Test Equipment
ETE............ Electrothermal Engine
ETE............ Emergency Transceiver Equipment
ETE............ End to End (NASA)
ETE............ Engineering Support Test Equipment [*Deep Space Instrumentation Facility, NASA*]
ETE............ Engineering Test Equipment (CAAL)
ET & E....... Engineering Test and Evaluation (MCD)
ETE............ Engineering Test Evaluation (AAG)
ETE............ Engineering Time Estimate
ETE............ Enhanced Tactical Fighter Engineering (MCD)
ET & E....... Environmental Technology and Economics [*A publication*]
ETE............ Estimated Time En Route
Ete............. Eterna [*Record label*] [*German Democratic Republic*]
ETE............ Expendable Turbine Engine
ETE............ Experimental Tunneling Establishment [*British*]
ETE............ Metemma [*Ethiopia*] [*Airport symbol*] (OAG)
ETEAA...... Entomologia Experimentalis et Applicata [*A publication*]
ETEAAT ... Entomologia Experimentalis et Applicata [*A publication*]
Et Eburn..... Etudes Eburneennes [*A publication*]
ETEC......... Effective Thermal Expansion Coefficient
ETEC........ Electronic Truck Engine Control System [*Automotive engineering*]
ETEC........ Energy Technology Engineering Center [*Department of Energy*] [*Canoga Park, CA*] (GRD)
ETEC........ Enterotoxigenic Escherichia coli [*Water pollution indicator*]
Et Ec .... Etudes Economiques [*A publication*]
ETECG...... Electronics Test Equipment Coordination Group [*Military*]
Et Econ (Mons) ... Etudes Economiques (Mons, Belgium) [*A publication*]
Et Ec Rur ... Etudes d'Economie Rurale [*A publication*]
ETEDS ...... Electromagnetic Test Environment Data System
ETEF......... Erfurt [*German Democratic Republic*] [*ICAO location identifier*] (ICLI)
E Tenn Hist Soc Pub ... East Tennessee Historical Society. Publications [*A publication*]
Eter .... Eternity Magazine [*A publication*]
ETERD...... Energy Technology Review [*A publication*]
ETEX......... Eastex Energy, Inc. [*NASDAQ symbol*] (NQ)
Et Ex .... Etudes et Expansion (EA)
ETF............ Eastern Task Force
ETF............ Eastfield Resources [*Vancouver Stock Exchange symbol*]
ETF............ Education Task Force [*Government Documents Round Table*] [*American Library Association*]
ETF............ Eglin Test Facility [*Florida*] [*NASA*] (KSC)
ETF............ Electron-Transferring Flavoprotein [*Biochemistry*]
ETF............ Electronic Tuning Fork
ETF............ Electronically Tunable Filter
ETF............ Electrothermal Filter
ETF............ Engine Test Facility [*Air Force*] [*Arnold Air Force Base, TN*] (MCD)
ETF............ Enhanced Tactical Fighter (MCD)
ETF............ Enhanced-Technology Fighter (MCD)
ETF............ Environmental Task Force (EA)
ETF............ Environmental Test Facility [*Fort Huachuca, AZ*] [*United States Army Electronic Proving Ground*] (GRD)
ETF............ Estimated Time of Flight
EtF............ Etudes Franciscaines [*A publication*]
ETF............ Eustachian Tube Function [*Medicine*]
ETF............ Evaluation Task Force (EA)
ETF............ Export Task Force (EA)
ETFC......... Ernest Tubb Fan Club (EA)
ETFE......... Ethylene-Tetrafluoroethylene [*Organic chemistry*]
ETFIR....... Emergency Task Force for Indochinese Refugees [*Defunct*] (EA)
ETFL......... Each Thousand-Foot Level [*Aviation*] (FAAC)
ETFL......... Friedland [*German Democratic Republic*] [*ICAO location identifier*] (ICLI)
ETFO......... Electronics Technical Field Office [*FAA*]
Et Fr.......... Etudes Francaises [*A publication*]
EtFranc..... Etudes Franciscaines [*Blois*] [*A publication*]
Et Francisc ... Etudes Franciscaines. Revue Mensuelle [*A publication*]
ETG .... Eatonton [*Georgia*] [*Seismograph station code, US Geological Survey*] (SEIS)
ETG .... Electrical Test Group (NRCH)
ETG .... Electrical Thermal Generators (KSC)
ETG .... Electronic Truck Governor [*Cummins Engine*] [*Automotive engineering*]
ETG .... Electronic Turbine Governor
ETG .... External Thermal Garment
ETG .... Keating, PA [*Location identifier*] [*FAA*] (FAAL)
ETGAA5.... Entomologist's Gazette [*A publication*]
Et Gaul....... Etudes Gaulliennes [*A publication*]
ETGCR...... Exogenous Triglyceride Clearance Rate [*Medicine*]
Et Germ ..... Etudes Germaniques [*A publication*]
Et Greg....... Etudes Gregoriennes [*A publication*]
ETGS........ Edge Tool Grinders' Society [*A union*] [*British*]
ETGT........ Equal To or Greater Than
ETGTS ...... Electronic Text and Graphics Transfer System

Et Guin...... Etudes Guineennes [*A publication*]
E & Th ...... Eglise et Theologie [*A publication*]
ETH.......... Eidgenoessische Technische Hochschule [*Federal Technical University*] (IID)
ETH .... Elat [*Israel*] [*Airport symbol*] (OAG)
ETH .... Elixir Terpin Hydrate [*Pharmacy*]
E Th .... Elizabethan Theatre [*A publication*]
ETH .... Ethics
Eth .... Ethics. An International Journal of Social, Political, and Legal Philosophy [*A publication*]
ETH .... Ethiopia [*ANSI three-letter standard code*] (CNC)
eth .... Ethiopic [*MARC language code*] [*Library of Congress*] (LCCP)
Eth .... Ethnos [*A publication*]
ETH .... Etudes de Theologie et d'Histoire de la Spiritualite [*A publication*]
ETH .... Extraterrestrial Hypothesis
ETH.......... Wheaton, MN [*Location identifier*] [*FAA*] (FAAL)
ETH/C....... Elixir Terpin Hydrate with Codeine [*Pharmacy*]
ETHD....... Heringsdorf [*German Democratic Republic*] [*ICAO location identifier*] (ICLI)
EthEnoch... Ethiopic Book of Enoch [*A publication*] (BJA)
Eth Eud...... Ethica Eudemia [*of Aristotle*] [*Classical studies*] (OCD)
EthF......... Ethnologia Fennica [*Finnish Studies in Ethnology*] [*A publication*]
Ethics Animals ... Ethics and Animals [*A publication*]
Ethics Sci Med ... Ethics in Science and Medicine [*A publication*]
ETHIOP.... Ethiopic [*Language, etc.*] (ROG)
Ethiop Geol Surv Annu Rep ... Ethiopia Geological Survey. Annual Report [*A publication*]
Ethiop Geol Surv Bull ... Ethiopia Geological Survey. Bulletin [*A publication*]
Ethiop Inst Agric Res Rep ... Ethiopian Institute of Agricultural Research. Report [*A publication*]
Ethiop Med J ... Ethiopian Medical Journal [*A publication*]
Et Hist Mod ... Etudes d'Histoire Moderne et Contemporaine [*A publication*]
EThL.......... Ephemerides Theologicae Lovanienses [*A publication*]
ETHM........ Econo-Therm Energy Systems [*NASDAQ symbol*] (NQ)
Eth Mus..... Ethno-Musicologica [*A publication*]
Ethmus....... Ethnomusicology [*A publication*]
Ethmus Sel Repts ... Ethnomusicology. Selected Reports [*A publication*]
Ethn .... Ethnographia [*A publication*]
Ethn .... Ethnohistory [*A publication*]
Eth Nic....... Aristotle's Nicomachean Ethics [*A publication*] (DLA)
Eth Nic....... Ethica Nicomachea [*of Aristotle*] [*Classical studies*] (OCD)
Ethnic & Racial Stud ... Ethnic and Racial Studies [*A publication*]
Ethnic Stud ... Ethnic Studies [*A publication*]
Ethnic Stud Bibliogr ... Ethnic Studies Bibliography [*A publication*]
Ethno .... Ethnohistory [*A publication*]
EthnoE....... Ethnologia Europaea [*A publication*]
EthnoF....... Ethnologie Francaise [*A publication*]
ETHNOG ... Ethnography (ADA)
Ethnogr AZ ... Ethnographisch-Archaeologische Zeitschrift [*A publication*]
Ethnogr Mus Univ Oslo Yb ... Ethnographic Museum. University of Oslo. Yearbook [*A publication*]
Ethnohist ... Ethnohistory [*A publication*]
ETHNOL... Ethnology
Ethnol Amer ... Ethnologia Americana [*A publication*]
Ethnol Anz ... Ethnologischer Anzeiger [*A publication*]
Ethnol Europ ... Ethnologia Europaea [*A publication*]
Ethnol Fennica ... Ethnologia Fennica [*Finnish Studies in Ethnology*] [*A publication*]
Ethnol Fr.... Ethnologie Francaise [*A publication*]
Ethnol Franc ... Ethnologie Francaise [*A publication*]
Ethnol Scand ... Ethnologia Scandinavica [*A publication*]
Ethnol Z..... Ethnologische Zeitschrift [*A publication*]
Ethnomedizin ... Ethnomedizin. Ethnomedizine Zeitschrift fuer Interdisziplinare Forschung [*A publication*]
Ethnomusic ... Ethnomusicology [*A publication*]
Ethnomusicol ... Ethnomusicology [*A publication*]
Ethno-Psych ... Ethno-Psychologie [*A publication*]
Ethno-Psychol ... Ethno-Psychologie [*A publication*]
Ethno Z...... Ethnologisch Zeitschrift [*Zuerich*] [*A publication*]
Ethn Racial Stud ... Ethnic and Racial Studies [*A publication*]
Ethn Stud... Ethnic Studies [*A publication*] (APTA)
ETHO........ Ethylene Oxide [*Organic chemistry*] (KSC)
ethol .... Ethology
EThR......... Etudes Theologiques et Religieuses [*A publication*]
ETHRC...... East Timor Human Rights Committee (EA)
Eth Rec ..... Ethical Record [*A publication*]
Eth S .... Ethnologia Slavica [*A publication*]
Eth Sc.......... Ethnologia Scandinavica [*A publication*]
ETI............ Economics & Technology, Inc. [*Telecommunications service*] (TSSD)
ETI............ Educational Travel, Incorporated
ETI............ Elapsed-Time Indicator
ETI............ Electric Test Installation
ETI............ Electric Tool Institute [*Later, Power Tool Institute*] (EA)
ETI............ Electrochemical Time Indicator [*Army*] (MCD)
ETI............ Electronic Technical Institute (EA)
ETI............ Electronics Today International [*A publication*] (APTA)
ETI............ En Terre d'Islam [*A publication*]
ETI............ Encapsulated Toroidal Inductor

ETI............ Engine Test Information
ETI............ Environmental Teratology Information [*Department of Energy*] [*Information service or system*] (IID)
ETI............ Equipment and Tool Institute (EA)
ETI............ Estimated Information [*Aviation*] (FAAC)
ETI............ Estimated Time of Interception
ETI............ European Toy Institute (EAIO)
ETI............ European Transuranium Institute [*Federal Republic of Germany*]
ETI............ Exhaust Trail Indicator [*Military*] (NVT)
ETI............ Extraction Tool Insert
ETI............ Extraterrestrial Intelligence
ETI............ Foreign Economic Trends and Their Implications for the United States [*A publication*]
ETIC........ Environmental Teratology Information Center [*Department of Energy*] (IID)
ETIC........ Estimated Time in Commission [*Army*] (AABC)
EtIE .... Etudes Indo-Europeennes [*A publication*]
ETIF.......... Employer Identification Number Taxpayer Information File [*IRS*]
ETIH........ Error Terminate Interrupt Handler (MCD)
ETII.......... External-to-Internal Interface (MCD)
ETiM........ Echo Teatrolne i Muzyczne [*A publication*]
ETIM........ Elapsed Time (FAAC)
ETINA....... Electronique Industrielle [*A publication*]
Et Int........ Etudes Internationales [*A publication*]
ET INT AL ... Et Inter Alia [*And Among Others*] [*Latin*] (ROG)
ETIOL....... Etiology
ETIP.......... Experimental Technology Incentives Program [*National Institute of Standards and Technology*]
ETIS .... Environmental Technical Information System [*Army*] [*Information service or system*] (IID)
ETISALAT ... Emirates Telecommunications Corp. Ltd. [*Telecommunications service*] (TSSD)
ETITA ...... Energetekhnologicheskow Ispol'zovanie Toplova [*A publication*]
ETIYRA .... [*El*] Toro International Yacht Racing Association (EA)
ETJ.......... Educational Theatre Journal [*A publication*]
ET J .... ET [*Enterostomal Therapy*] Journal [*A publication*]
ETJC......... Engineering Trades' Joint Council [*British*] (DCTA)
ETK .... Eicosanoyl(trifluoroacetyl)kanamycin [*Antiviral*]
ETK .... Electron Tube Klystron
ETK .... Embryonic Turkey Kidney
ETK .... Entek Oil & Gas [*Vancouver Stock Exchange symbol*]
EtK.......... Epeteris tou Kalabryton [*A publication*]
ETK .... Epitesugyi Tajekoztatasi Kozpont [*Information Center of Building*] [*Ministry for Building and Urban Development*] [*Information service or system*] (IID)
ETK .... Explosive Testing Kit (MCD)
ETKKA ...... Elteknik [*A publication*]
ETKZ......... Kyritz [*German Democratic Republic*] [*ICAO location identifier*] (ICLI)
ETL........... Earliest Time to Launch [*Navy*] (CAAL)
ETL........... Eastern Lights Resources Ltd. [*Vancouver Stock Exchange symbol*]
ETL........... Effective Testing Loss [*Telecommunications*] (TEL)
ETL........... Electrical Testing Laboratory [*Portsmouth Naval Shipyard, NH*]
ETL........... Electronic Technology Laboratory [*Air Force*] (MCD)
ETL........... Electrotechnical Laboratory (MCD)
ETL........... Emergency Time Limit
ETL........... Ending Tape Label [*Data processing*] (BUR)
ETL........... Engineer Technical Letter [*Army Corps of Engineers*]
ETL........... Engineer Topographic Laboratories [*Army*] [*Fort Belvoir, VA*] (MCD)
ETL........... Engineering Test Laboratory (AAG)
ETL........... Environmental Test Laboratory [*Jet Propulsion Laboratory, NASA*]
ETL........... Ephemerides Theologicae Lovanienses [*A publication*]
ETL........... [*The*] Essex Terminal Railway Co. [*AAR code*]
ETL........... Etching by Transmitted Light
EtL........... Etudes de Lettres [*A publication*]
ETL........... Explicacion de Textos Literarios [*A publication*]
ETLA........ Epeteris tou Laographikov Arkheiov [*A publication*]
ETLM....... Leipzig/Mockau [*German Democratic Republic*] [*ICAO location identifier*] (ICLI)
ETLO........ Equipment Transfer or Loan Order
Et Loire..... Etudes Prehistoriques et Protohistoriques des Pays de la Loire [*A publication*]
ETLOW..... External Tank Lift-Off Weight [*NASA*] (NASA)
ETLS .... Leipzig [*German Democratic Republic*] [*ICAO location identifier*] (ICLI)
ETLT........ Equal To or Less Than
ETM .... Educational Training Material (MCD)
ETM .... Elapsed-Time Meter
ETM .... Electrical Tactical Map
ETM .... Electrical Time Measurement
ETM .... Electrically Transmitted Message
ETM .... Electronic Test and Measurement (MCD)
ETM .... Electronics Technician's Mate [*Navy rating*]

ETM .... Emery Testing Machine [*Nineteenth-century hydraulic testing machine*] (RDA)
ETM .... Energy Transfer Module [*Aviation*] (MCD)
ETM .... Engineering Test Model (KSC)
ETM .... Enhanced Timing Module (IEEE)
ETM .... Erythromycin [*Also, E, ERY, ERYC*] [*Antibacterial compound*]
ETM .... Excise Tax Memoranda [*Revenue Canada - Customs and Excise*] [*Information service or system*] (CRD)
ETM .... Export Turkey Magazine [*A publication*]
ETM .... Extension Training Management [*Military*] (INF)
ETM .... Extension Training Materials [*Army*]
ETM .... Extension Training Memorandum [*Civil Defense*]
ETM .... External Technical Memorandum
ETM .... External Tympaniform Membrane [*Zoology*]
ETM .... Extraterrestrial Material
ETMA ...... Educational Television for the Metropolitan Area
ETMA ...... Elapsed Time/Maintenance Action (MCD)
Et Mal...... Etudes Maliennes [*A publication*]
EtMar........ Etudes Mariales [*Paris*] [*A publication*]
ETMB....... Electrical Techniques in Medicine and Biology (MCD)
ETMC....... European Telephone Marketing Council [*of the European Direct Marketing Organization*] [*Jona, Switzerland*] (EA)
ETMD....... Essential Technical Medical Data
ETMD....... Extendable Tubular Member Device [*Aerospace*]
ETMDAA ... Entomologiske Meddelelser [*A publication*]
ETME........ [*The*] European Turf Management Exhibition [*Great Britain*] (ITD)
ETMF........ Elapsed Time Multiprogramming Factor
ETMG .... Magdeburg [*German Democratic Republic*] [*ICAO location identifier*] (ICLI)
ETMNA .... Entomological News [*A publication*]
ETMS....... Ernst Toller Memorial Society [*Later, ISSE*] (EA)
ETMSB .... Ethnomusicology [*A publication*]
ETMSR .... Electronics Technician's Mate, Ship Repair [*Navy rating*]
ETMT....... Ethoxy(trichloromethyl)thiadiazole [*Fungicide*]
ETMWG ... Electronic Trajectory Measurements Working Group [*IRIG*] [*Range Commanders Council*] [*White Sands Missile Range, NM*]
ETN .... Eastern Technical Net [*Air Force*]
ETN .... Eastland, TX [*Location identifier*] [*FAA*] (FAAL)
ETN .... Eaton Corp. [*NYSE symbol*] (SPSG)
ETN .... Educational Telecommunications Network
ETN .... Educational Telephone Network [*University of North Dakota*] [*Grand Forks*] (TSSD)
ETN .... Electrical Terminal Nut
ETN .... Electronics Technician, Communications [*Navy rating*]
ETN .... Elektrotechniek; Technisch-Economisch Tijdschrift [*A publication*]
ETN .... Equipment Table Nomenclature (AFM)
Etn........... Ethanolamine [*Also, EA, OLAMINE*] [*Organic chemistry*]
ETN .... Extension Teleconferencing Network [*Texas A & M University*] [*College Station, TX*] [*Telecommunications service*] (TSSD)
ETNA ...... East Timor News Agency
ETNAM .... European Theater Network Analysis Model (MCD)
ET-NANBH ... Enterically Transmitted Non-A, Non-B Hepatitis [*Medicine*]
ETNF........ Estimated Time to Next Failure (MCD)
ETNKA ..... Energietechnik [*A publication*]
ETNLB6.... Ethnology [*A publication*]
Etnogr Polska ... Etnografia Polska [*A publication*]
Etnol Antropol Cult ... Etnologia Antropologia Culturale [*A publication*]
Etnol Stud ... Etnologiska Studier [*A publication*]
Et Normandes ... Etudes Normandes [*A publication*]
Et Notes Inform Batiment ... Etudes et Notes d'Information. Direction du Batiment et des Travaux Publics et de la Conjoncture [*A publication*]
ETNSA...... Electronics Technician, Communications Seaman Apprentice [*Navy rating*]
ETNSAQ... Etnologiska Studier [*A publication*]
ETNSN...... Electronics Technician, Communications Seaman [*Navy rating*]
ETNVT...... Edinaia Tovarnaia Nomenklatura Vneshney Torgovli [*Commodity nomenclature system used in international trade*]
ETO .... Electronic Temperature Offset
ETO .... Emergency Test Operation
ETO .... Energy Technology Office [*Department of Energy*] (OICC)
ETO .... Ephemeris-Tuned Oscillator
ETO .... ESSO [*Standard Oil*] Turbo Oil
ETO .... Estimated Takeoff (KSC)
ETO .... Estimated Time Off
ETO .... Estimated Time of Operations [*NASA*] (KSC)
ETO .... Estimated Time Over [*Aviation*] (FAAC)
ETO .... Estimated Time of Ovulation [*Gynecology*]
ETO .... Ethylene Oxide [*Organic chemistry*]
ETO .... European Theater of Operations [*World War II*]
ETO .... European Transport Organization [*ECE*]
ETO .... Eustachian Tube Obstruction [*Medicine*]
ETO .... Evadale, TX [*Location identifier*] [*FAA*] (FAAL)
ETO .... Expiration of Term of Obligation [*Military*]
ETO .... Express Transportation Order [*Army*] (AABC)
ETOC .... Emergency Technical Operations Center [*DoD*]

ETOC .... Estimated Time of Correction [*NASA*]   (KSC)
ETOC .... Estimated Time Out of Commission
ETOCDK... Environmental Toxicology and Chemistry [*A publication*]
ETOFY...... Elvis, This One's for You Fan Club   (EA)
ETOG........ European Technical Operations Group
ETOH........ Ethyl Alcohol
ETOM .... Electron Trapping Optical Memory [*Data processing*]
ETOMA .... Environmental Threshold of Measurement Accuracy
ETONU..... E-Tron Corp. Uts [*NASDAQ symbol*]   (NQ)
ETOP........ Engineering Technical Operating Procedure
ETOP........ Environmental Threat and Opportunity Profile
ETOPBN... Etizenia [*A publication*]
ETOPD...... Energy Topics [*A publication*]
ETOS........ Extended Tape Operating System   (BUR)
ETOT .... Estimated Time Over Target
ETOUSA... European Theater of Operations, United States Army
          [*Pronounced "ee-too-sah"*] [*World War II*]
ETOV .... Estimated Time Over [*Aviation*]   (FAAC)
ETOXAC... Essays in Toxicology [*A publication*]
ETP........... East Timor Project [*Defunct*]   (EA)
ETP........... Eastern Tennis Patrons   (EA)
ETP........... Eastern Tropical Pacific Ocean
ETP........... Electrical Tough Pitch [*Copper*]
ETP........... Electrolytic Tough-Pitch [*Copper grade*]
ETP........... Electron Temperature Probe
ETP........... Electron Transfer [*or Transporting*] Particle
ETP........... Electron Tube Panel
ETP........... Elevated Training Platform
ETP........... Eligible Termination Payment   (ADA)
ETP........... Eltopia [*Washington*] [*Seismograph station code, US Geological
          Survey*]   (SEIS)
ETP........... Emergency Technology Program [*Oak Ridge National
          Laboratory*]
ETP........... Engine Test Panel [*Aerospace*]   (AAG)
ETP........... Engineering Test Program [*NASA*]   (KSC)
ETP........... Engineering Thermoplastic [*Plastics technology*]
ETP........... Entire Treatment Period [*Medicine*]
ETP........... Environmental Test Program   (AAG)
ETP........... Equal Time Point
ETP........... Equipment Test Plan   (NASA)
ETP........... Equivalent Top Product
ETP........... Estimated Time of Penetration [*Aviation*]   (FAAC)
ETP........... Estimated Turnaround Point
EtP........... Etnoloski Pregled [*A publication*]
Et P........... Etudes de Papyrologie [*A publication*]
ETP........... European Training Programme in Brain and Behavior Research
          [*of the European Science Foundation*] [*France*]   (EA)
ETP........... Evaluation Test Plan
ETP........... Excise Tariff Proposals [*A publication*]   (APTA)
ETP........... Experimental Test Procedure   (MCD)
ETP........... Extended Term Plan   (BUR)
ETP........... Potential Evapotranspiration [*Hydrology*]
ETPA........ Electronically Tunable Parametric Amplifier
ETPA........ Emergency Technical Provisions Act of 1976
ETPAE ..... Ethyl-Terminated Polyarylene Ether [*Organic chemistry*]
EtPapyr.... Etudes de Papyrologie [*Cairo*] [*A publication*]
ETPBBR.... European Training Programme in Brain and Behavior Research
          [*of the European Science Foundation*] [*France*]   (EAIO)
ETPD........ Essential Tremor and Parkinson's Disease [*Neurophysiology*]
ETPD........ Estimated Time of Parachute Deployment   (MUGU)
Et Pezenas ... Etudes sur Pezenas et l'Herault [*A publication*]
ETPI .... Eastern Telecommunications Philippines, Incorporated
          [*Manila*]   (TSSD)
Et Planning Familial ... Etudes de Planning Familial [*A publication*]
ET-PNL..... Engine Test Panel [*Aerospace*]   (AAG)
ETPO........ European Trade Promotion Organization   (DS)
EtPol........ Etnografia Polska [*A publication*]
Et Polemol ... Etudes Polemologiques [*A publication*]
Et Pr Hist .. Etudes Prehistoriques [*A publication*]
ETPS .... Empire Test Pilots' School [*British*]
ETQ .... Estates and Trusts Quarterly [*A publication*]
ETQAP...... Education and Training in Quality Assurance Practices
          [*American Society for Quality Control*]   (NRCH)
ETR .... Early Token Release [*Data processing*]
ETR .... East Timor Report [*A publication*]   (APTA)
ETR .... Eastern Test Range [*See also ESMC*] [*Air Force*]
ETR .... Education, Training and Research Associates   (EA)
ETR .... Effective Thyroxine Ratio [*Medicine*]
ETR .... Electron Tube Rectifier
ETR .... Electronic Trouble Report
ETR .... Electronically Tuned Receiver
ETR .... Electronics Technician, (RADAR) [*Navy rating*]
ETR .... Emergency Tension Retractor [*Mercedes Benz*] [*Automotive
          engineering*]
ETR .... Employment Review [*A publication*]
ETR .... Encrypted Traffic Report   (CET)
ETR .... Energy Test Reactor
ETR .... Engine Transaction Report   (NVT)
ETR .... Engineering Test Reactor
ETR .... Engineering Test Request [*NASA*]   (KSC)
ETR .... Entergy Corp. [*NYSE symbol*]   (SPSG)

ETR .... Environmental Test Report
ETR .... Equipment Temporarily Removed   (MCD)
ETR .... Erient Resources, Inc. [*Vancouver Stock Exchange symbol*]
ETR .... Estates and Trusts Reports [*A publication*]
ETR .... Estimated Time of Repair   (NG)
ETR .... Estimated Time of Return
etr .... Etcher [*MARC relator code*] [*Library of Congress*]   (LCCP)
Etr .... Eternity [*A publication*]
ETR .... Ethylthioribose [*Biochemistry*]
ETR .... ETR. Eisenbahntechnische Rundschau [*A publication*]
ETR .... Etudes Rurales: Revue Trimestrielle d'Histoire, Geographie,
          Sociologie, et Economie des Campagnes [*A publication*]
ETR .... Etudes Theologiques et Religieuses [*A publication*]
ETR .... European Trends [*A publication*]
ETR .... Expected Time of Response
ETR .... Export Traffic Release
ETR .... Export Transport Release
ETR .... External Technical Report
ETR .... External Timing Register
ET₄R .... Effective T_4 Ratio [*Endocrinology*]
ETRA........ Eastern Test Range [*Formerly, Atlantic Missile Range*] [*Air
          Force*]
ETRA........ Estimated Time to Reach Altitude
ETRA........ Excise Tax Reduction Act
ETRC........ Educational Television and Radio Center [*Later, EBC*]
ETRC........ Engineering Test Reactor Critical Facility
ETRC........ Entree Corp. [*NASDAQ symbol*]   (NQ)
ETRC........ Expected Total Remnant Costs
Etr Cities.... [*The*] Etruscan Cities and Rome [*A publication*]   (OCD)
ETRE......... Entre' Computer Centers, Inc. [*NASDAQ symbol*]   (NQ)
Et Region Paris ... Etudes de la Region Parisienne [*A publication*]
E T Rel ...... Etudes Theologiques et Religieuses [*A publication*]
ETRL......... Environmental Toxicology Research Laboratory [*National
          Environmental Research Center*]
ETRM....... External Tank Rocket Motor
ETRMD..... Electromagnetics [*A publication*]
ETRO .... Estimated Time of Return to Operation [*Military*]   (AFM)
ETROD..... Eastern Test Range Operations Directive [*Air Force*]   (NASA)
ETRSA ..... Electronics Technician, (RADAR) Seaman Apprentice [*Navy
          rating*]
ETRSD...... Electronic Technology Reports [*A publication*]
ETRSN...... Electronics Technician, (RADAR) Seaman [*Navy rating*]
ETRT .... Electronically Tuned Receiver Tuner
ETRTA...... Elettrotecnica [*A publication*]
ETRTO...... European Tyre and Rim Technical Organisation [*Belgium*]
ETRU........ Emergency Target Relay Unit   (MCD)
ETRUA...... Eisenbahntechnische Rundschau [*A publication*]
Et Rur .... Etudes Rurales [*A publication*]
ETS........... Board of Education for the City of Etobicoke [*UTLAS symbol*]
ETS........... East Stroudsburg State College, East Stroudsburg, PA [*OCLC
          symbol*]   (OCLC)
ETS........... Econometric Time-Series [*Computer program*]   (PCM)
ETS........... Educational Talent Search   (EA)
ETS........... Educational Teleconference System [*University of Missouri -
          Columbia*] [*Telecommunications*]   (TSSD)
ETS........... Educational Testing Service   (EA)
ETS........... Educational TV Services [*Oklahoma State University*]
          [*Stillwater*]   (TSSD)
ETS........... Edwards Test Station [*NASA*]
ETS........... Electrical Test Setup [*NASA*]   (KSC)
ETS........... Electron Transmission Spectroscopy
ETS........... Electron Transport System
ETS........... Electronic Tandem Switching [*Telecommunications*]   (TEL)
ETS........... Electronic Telegraph System
ETS........... Electronic Test Set
ETS........... Electronic Test Stand
ETS........... Electronic Test Station
ETS........... Electronic Timing Set
ETS........... Electronic Translator System [*Bell System*]
ETS........... Elucidatio Terrae Sanctae   (BJA)
ETS........... Emergency Telephone Service
ETS........... Emergency Temporary Standard [*OSHA*]
ETS........... Empire Telecommunications [*British*] [*World War II*]
ETS........... Employment Transfer Scheme [*British*]
ETS........... Endless Tangent Screw
ETS........... Energy Transfer System   (MCD)
ETS........... Energy Transmission System [*Automotive engineering*]
ETS........... Engine Test Stand [*Nevada*] [*Seismograph station code, US
          Geological Survey*] [*Closed*]   (SEIS)
ETS........... Engine Test Stands [*NERVA program*]
ETS........... Engineered Time Standards   (NG)
ETS........... Engineering Tactical System
ETS........... Engineering and Technical Service   (AFM)
ETS........... Engineering Test Satellite
ETS........... Engineering Time Standards [*Navy*]   (NVT)
ETS........... Engineering Time Study   (MCD)
ETS........... Enquiry Terminal System [*International Computers Ltd.*]
ETS........... Environmental Technical Specifications   (NRCH)
ETS........... Environmental Technology Seminar   (EA)
ETS........... Environmental Test Specification   (IEEE)

ETS........... Environmental Testing Section [*Social Security Administration*]
ETS........... Environmental Tobacco Smoke
ETS........... Episcopal Theological School
ETS........... Equal Time Spacing
ETS........... Estimated Time of Sailing [*Navigation*]
ETS........... Estimated Time of Separation [*Military*] [*Slang*]
et s............. Et Suivants [*And Following*] [*French*] (ILCA)
ETS........... ETS International, Inc. [*Vancouver Stock Exchange symbol*]
ETs............ Etudes Tsiganes [*A publication*]
ETS........... European Telephone System [*DoD*]
ETS........... European Teratology Society (EA)
ETS........... European Treaty Series [*Council of Europe*] [*A publication*] (DLA)
ETS........... Evaluation Test Specification
ETS........... Evaluation Trainers
ETS........... Evangelical Theological Society (EA)
ETS........... Expeditionary Test Set (MCD)
ETS........... Expiration of Term of Service [*Military*]
ETS........... External Tank System (MCD)
ETS........... External Transcribed Spacer [*Genetics*]
ETS........... Extra Telecoms Service [*British*]
ETS........... Journal. Evangelical Theological Society [*A publication*]
ETS........... Scandinavian Journal of Economics [*A publication*]
ETSA........ Seaman Apprentice, Electronics Technician, Striker [*Navy rating*]
ETSAL...... Electronic Terms for Space Age Language
ETSC........ East Tennessee State College [*Later, East Tennessee State University*]
ETSC........ East Texas State College [*Later, East Texas State University*]
ETSC........ Employment and Training Service Center (EA)
ETSCA...... English Toy Spaniel Club of America (EA)
ETSD........ Enhanced Thermionically Supported Discharge [*Materials technology*]
ETSEP....... External Tank Separation [*NASA*] (NASA)
ET SEQ ..... Et Sequens [*or Et Sequentes, Et Sequentia*] [*And the Following*] [*Latin*]
ETSG........ Elevated Temperature Strain Gauge
ETSI.......... Energy Transportation Systems, Incorporated
ETSI......... European Telecommunications Standards Institute
ETSI.......... Executive Telecom System, Incorporated [*Database producer*] (IID)
ETSL........ East Texas Savings & Loan Association [*Tyler, TX*] [*NASDAQ symbol*] (NQ)
ETSN........ Seaman, Electronics Technician, Striker [*Navy rating*]
Et Soc (Paris) ... Etudes Sociales (Paris) [*A publication*]
ETSP........ Entitled to Severance Pay
ETSPL....... Equivalent Threshold Sound Pressure Level
ETSQ........ Electrical Time, Superquick
ET SQQ..... Et Sequens [*or Et Sequentes, Et Sequentia*] [*And the Following*] [*Latin*]
ETSS .... Electronic Telecommunication Switching System (MCD)
ETSS .... Entry Time-Sharing System [*Data processing*] [*IBM Corp.*]
ETSS .... Evaluation of Total System Survivability (MCD)
ETSS .... External Tank Separation Subsystem [*NASA*] (NASA)
ETSSD ...... Elektronnaya Tekhnika. Seriya 1. Elektronika [*A publication*]
ETST .... Electronic Technical Suitability Test
ET/ST .... Engineer Test/Service Test [*Aerospace*]
Et Statist Banque Etats Afr Centr ... Etudes et Statistiques. Banque des Etats de l'Afrique Centrale. Bulletin Mensuel [*A publication*]
ETSTC...... Educational Testing Service Test Collection (IID)
ETSU........ East Tennessee State University [*Formerly, East Tennessee State College*]
ETSU........ East Texas State University [*Formerly, East Texas State College*]
ETSU........ Energy Technology Support Unit at Harwell [*British*]
ETT........... Early Thrust Termination
ETT........... Easy to Test [*Audiology*]
ETT........... Einheitlicher Transittarif [*Uniform Transit Tariff*] [*Business term*] [*German*]
ETT........... Electromagnetic Thickness Tool [*Gas well*]
ETT........... Electron Tube, Triode
ETT........... Electronic Tensile Tester
ETT........... Electronically Tuned Tuner
ETT........... End of Tape Test [*Data processing*]
ETT........... Endotracheal Tube [*Medicine*]
ETT........... Equipment Task Time
ETT........... Estimated Time of Track
ETT........... Estimated Travel Time [*Army*] (AABC)
ETT........... Etaiyapuram [*India*] [*Geomagnetic observatory code*]
ETT........... Etana Tech Corp. [*Vancouver Stock Exchange symbol*]
ETT........... Evasive Target Tank [*Army*] (RDA)
ETT........... Exercise Tolerance Test [*Medicine*]
ETT........... Expected Test Time
ETT........... Extended Time Tests
ETT........... Extrusion Trim Template
ETTA........ English Table Tennis Association
ETTA........ Evangelical Teacher Training Association [*Later, ETA*] (EA)
Ett Ad........ Etting's American Admiralty Jurisdiction [*A publication*] (DLA)
ETTC........ Engine Test Technology Centre [*Worcester, England*]

ETTC........ Estimated Total Target Cost
ETTCA...... Elektrotechniker [*A publication*]
ETTCB ...... Elettronica e Telecomunicazioni [*A publication*]
ETTO .... Extractor Tool
Ettore Majorana Internat Sci Ser Phys Sci ... Ettore Majorana International Science Series. Physical Sciences [*A publication*]
Ettore Majorana Int Sci Ser Life Sci ... Ettore Majorana International Science Series. Life Sciences [*A publication*]
Ettore Majorana Int Sci Ser Phys Sci ... Ettore Majorana International Science Series. Physical Sciences [*A publication*]
ETTP........ Etch Template [*Tool*] (AAG)
Et Trav...... Etudes et Travaux [*Studia i Prace*]. Travaux du Centre d'Archeologie Mediterraneenne de l'Academie Polonaise de Sciences [*A publication*]
ETTS .... Edge Tool Trade Society [*A union*] [*British*]
ETTU........ European Table Tennis Union (EA)
ETU .... East Traverse Mountains [*Utah*] [*Seismograph station code, US Geological Survey*] (SEIS)
ETU .... Economie et Statistique [*A publication*]
ETU .... Electrical Trades Union [*British*]
ETU .... Electronic Translator Unit [*Telecommunications*]
ETU .... Emergency and Trauma Unit
ETU .... Emergency Treatment Unit
ETU .... Employment and Training Unit [*Work Incentive Program*]
ETU .... Engineering Test Unit
ETU .... Enhanced Telephone Unit
ETU .... Erection Timing Unit
ETU .... Ethylene Thiourea [*Organic chemistry*]
Etu............ Etude [*Record label*]
ETU .... European Triathlon Union (EA)
ETU .... Expected Total Utility
ETUC........ European Trade Union Confederation [*Formerly, ECFTU*]
Etud Ang.... Etudes Anglaises [*A publication*]
Etud Angl.... Etudes Anglaises [*A publication*]
Etud Anglaises ... Etudes Anglaises [*A publication*]
Etud Balk... Etudes Balkaniques [*A publication*]
Etud Cinema ... Etudes Cinematographiques [*A publication*]
Etud Class... Etudes Classiques [*A publication*]
Etud Classiq ... Etudes Classiques [*A publication*]
Etude CEE Ser Agr ... Etudes CEE [*Communaute Economique Europeenne*]. Serie Agriculture [*A publication*]
Etude Cent Nat Etude Experim Machin Agr ... Etude. Centre National d'Etudes et d'Experimentation de Machinisme Agricole [*A publication*]
Etud Ecol ... Etudes Ecologiques [*A publication*]
Etud Econs et Fins ... Etudes Economiques et Financieres [*A publication*]
Etud Econs (Mons) ... Etudes Economiques (Mons, Belgium) [*A publication*]
Etud Econs (Paris) ... Etudes Economiques (Paris) [*A publication*]
Etudes Cin ... Etudes Cinematographiques [*A publication*]
Etude Spec Minist Richesses Nat Que ... Etude Speciale. Ministere des Richesses Naturelles du Quebec [*A publication*]
Etude Stat Inst Nat Stat ... Etudes Statistiques. Institut National de la Statistique et des Etudes Economiques [*A publication*]
Etude Trav ... Etude du Travail [*A publication*]
Etud et Expansion ... Etudes et Expansion [*A publication*]
Etud Fran... Etudes Francaises [*A publication*]
Etud Ger .... Etudes Germaniques [*A publication*]
Etud Germaniques ... Etudes Germaniques [*A publication*]
Etud Hist Droit Canon ... Etudes Historiques de Droit Canonique [*A publication*]
Etud Int ... Etudes Internationales [*A publication*]
Etud Internat ... Etudes Internationales [*A publication*]
Etud Irland ... Etudes Irlandaises [*A publication*]
Etud Ital..... Etudes Italiennes [*A publication*]
Etud Limousines ... Etudes Limousines [*A publication*]
Etud Lit...... Etudes Litteraires [*A publication*]
Etud Mar ... Etudes Mariales [*A publication*]
Etud Phil.... Etudes Philosophiques [*A publication*]
Etud Philos ... Etudes Philosophiques [*A publication*]
Etud Psychother ... Etudes Psychotherapiques [*A publication*]
Etud Rech Inst Meteorol Part 2 ... Etudes et Recherches. Institut de Meteorologie. Part 2. Hydrologie [*A publication*]
Etud Reg Paris ... Etudes de la Region Parisienne [*A publication*]
Etud Rur .... Etudes Rurales [*A publication*]
Etud Rurales ... Etudes Rurales [*A publication*]
Etud Slav E ... Etudes Slaves et Est-Europeennes [*A publication*]
Etud Socs ... Etudes Sociales [*A publication*]
Etud Statis (Brussels) ... Etudes Statistiques (Brussels) [*A publication*]
Etud Tech Econ Ser E (Inst Geol Geophys) ... Etudes Techniques et Economiques. Seria E. Hydrogeologie (Institut de Geologie et Geophysique) [*A publication*]
Etud Theol ... Etudes Theologiques et Religieuses [*A publication*]
Etud Trad... Etudes Traditionnelles [*A publication*]
Etud Trav Ec Maroc Agric Publ ... Etudes et Travaux. Ecole Marocaine d'Agriculture. Publication [*A publication*]
ETUI........ European Trade Union Institute (DCTA)
ET UX........ Et Uxor [*And Wife*] [*Latin*]
ETV .... Educational Television
ETV .... Ejection Test Vehicle (NG)
ETV .... Electric Test Vehicle [*Department of Energy*]
ETV .... Electrothermal Vaporization

ETV .... Engineering Television Mode
ETV .... Engineering Test Vehicle (KSC)
ETV .... Epitaxial Tuning Varactor
ETV .... Europaeischer Tabakwaren-Grosshandels-Verband [*European Tobacco Wholesalers' Union*] (EAIO)
ETVA........ External Tank Vent Arm (MCD)
ETVG .... European Tumour Virus Group (EAIO)
Et Vir .... Et Viri [*And Husband*] [*Latin*]
ETVM .... Electrostatic Transistorized Voltmeter
ETW .... Effectiveness Training for Women [*A course of study*]
ETW .... End of Tape Warning [*Data processing*] (CET)
ETW .... Entertainment This Week [*TV program*]
ETW .... Equipment Trials Wing [*Military*] [*British*]
ETW .... Error Time Word (KSC)
ETW .... Executive Television Workshop [*New York, NY*]
ETW .... New Town, ND [*Location identifier*] [*FAA*] (FAAL)
ETWN .... East Tennessee & Western North Carolina Railroad Co. [*AAR code*]
ETWN .... Wriezen [*German Democratic Republic*] [*ICAO location identifier*] (ICLI)
ETX .... East Texas, PA [*Location identifier*] [*FAA*] (FAAL)
ETX .... Eburnetoxin [*Biochemistry*]
ETX .... End of Text [*Data processing*]
ETX .... Entex, Inc. [*Formerly, UG*] [*NYSE symbol*] (SPSG)
Ety .... Eternity [*A publication*]
ETYA........ Eicosatetraynoic Acid [*Organic chemistry*]
ETYM........ Etymology
Etym Mag ... Etymologicum Magnum [*A publication*]
Etym Magn ... Etymologicum Magnum [*Twelfth century AD*] [*Classical studies*] (OCD)
Etymol........ Etymology
ETZ............ Elektrotechnische Zeitschrift [*A publication*]
ETZ............ Etz Lavud Ltd. [*AMEX symbol*] (SPSG)
ETZ............ Nantucket, MA [*Location identifier*] [*FAA*] (FAAL)
Et Zair........ Etudes Zairoises [*A publication*]
ETZ Arch .. ETZ. Elektrotechnische Zeitschrift. Archiv [*A publication*]
ETZ Elektrotech Z ... ETZ. Elektrotechnische Zeitschrift [*A publication*]
ETZ Elektrotech Z Ausg A ... ETZ. Elektrotechnische Zeitschrift. Ausgabe A [*West Germany*] [*A publication*]
EU............ Compania Ecuatoriana de Aviacion [*Ecuador*] [*ICAO designator*] (FAAC)
Eu............ East Europe [*A publication*]
EU............. Ehrlich Units [*Clinical chemistry*]
EU............. Ejector Unit (MCD)
EU............. Electronic Unit
EU............. Elms Unlimited [*Superseded by ERI*]
EU............. Empresa Ecuatoriana de Aviacion [*Ecuador*] [*ICAO designator*] (ICDA)
EU............. End-User [*Data processing*]
EU............. Endotoxin Unit [*Clinical chemistry*]
E/U............. Engineer/User [*Aerospace*] (AAG)
EU............. Engineering Unit (MCD)
EU............. Entropy Unit
EU............. Enzyme Unit [*Analytical biochemistry*]
EU............. Episcopalians United (EA)
eU............. Equivalent Uranium
EU............. Erection Unit
EU............. Error Unavoidable
EU............. Estudos Universitarios [*Recife*] [*A publication*]
E-U .... Etats-Unis [*United States*] [*French*]
EU............. Ethyleneurea [*Organic chemistry*]
Eu............. Euclides [*A publication*]
Eu............. Euler Number [*IUPAC*] [*Fluid mechanics*]
Eu............. Euphorion [*A publication*]
EU............. Euromoney [*A publication*]
EU............. Europe
Eu............. Europium [*Chemical element*]
EU............. Evacuation Unit [*Army*]
EU............. Evangelical Union [*British*]
EU............. Execution Unit [*Data processing*]
EU............. Expected Utility
EU............. Experience Unit
EU............. Experimental Unit (NASA)
Eu............. Norwich Pharmacal Co. [*Research code symbol*]
EU............. Office of Assistant Administrator for Europe, Africa, and Middle East [*FAA*] (FAAC)
EUA.......... Eastern Underwriters Association [*Later, ISO*]
EUA.......... Eastern Utilities Associates [*NYSE symbol*] (SPSG)
EUA.......... Estados Unidos Americanos [*United States of America*] [*Spanish*]
EUA.......... Eua Tonga Island [*South Pacific*] [*Airport symbol*] (OAG)
EUA.......... European Area Headquarters [*Red Cross*]
EUA.......... European Units of Account [*Economics*]
EUA.......... Examination under Anesthesia [*Medicine*]
EUA.......... Exchange Users Association (EA)
EUA.......... Extended User Area [*Data processing*]
EUA.......... Faculty of Library Science, University of Alberta [*EDUCATSS*] [*UTLAS symbol*]
EUAC........ Equivalent Uniform Annual Cost
EUAIS....... European Union of Arab and Islamic Studies [*See also UEAI*] (EAIO)

EUAM....... Euro American Goup, Inc. [*NASDAQ symbol*] (NQ)
EUB........ Emergency Utility Building (NRCH)
EUB.......... Estados Unidos do Brasil [*United States of Brazil*] [*Portuguese*]
EUB.......... Evangelical United Brethren [*Church*]
EUB.......... School of Library Service, Dalhousie University [*EDUCATSS*] [*UTLAS symbol*]
EUBS........ European Underseas Bio-Medical Society (EAIO)
EUC......... Emergency Unemployment Compensation [*Account*]
EUC......... End Use Check
EUC......... End User Computing [*AT & T*]
EUC......... Equatorial Undercurrent [*Marine science*] (MSC)
EUC......... Estudis Universitaris Catalans [*A publication*]
Euc......... Euclid [*Second century BC*] [*Classical studies*] (OCD)
EUC......... Euclid R. R. [*AAR code*]
EUC......... Euclidean [*Mathematics*]
EUC......... Eureka Canyon [*California*] [*Seismograph station code, US Geological Survey*] (SEIS)
EUC......... European Union of Coachbuilders (EA)
EUC.......... Library Studies Program, Concordia University [*EDUCATSS*] [*UTLAS symbol*]
EUCA .... European Federation of Associations of Coffee Roasters (EA)
EUCA .... Extended Unemployment Compensation Account
EUCADT... Euphoria et Cacophoria [*International Edition*] [*A publication*]
EUCARPIA ... European Association for Research on Plant Breeding (EAIO)
EUCARPIA Congr Assoc Eur Amelior Plant ... EUCARPIA [*European Association for Research on Plant Breeding*] Congres. Association Europeenne pour l'Amelioration des Plantes [*A publication*]
EUCC .... Computing Center [*Emory University*] [*Research center*] (RCD)
EUCC .... Employers' Unemployment Compensation Council (EA)
EUCEPA ... Europaeischer Verband fuer Zellstoff und Papiertechnik [*European Liaison Committee for Pulp and Paper*] (EAIO)
EUCF........ Equivalent Uniform Cash Flow
EUCH........ Eucharist (ROG)
EUCLB..... Euroclay [*A publication*]
EUCLID... Experimental Use Computer, London Integrated Display
EUCOFEL ... Union Europeenne du Commerce de Gros en Fruits et Legumes [*European Union of the Fruit and Vegetable Wholesale, Import, and Export Trade*] [*Brussels, Belgium*] (EAIO)
EUCOLAIT ... Union Europeenne du Commerce des Produits Laitiers et Derives [*European Union of Importers, Exporters, and Dealers in Dairy Products*] (EAIO)
EUCOM ... European Command [*Military*]
EUCOMED ... European Confederation of Medical Suppliers Associations (EA)
EUCORG .. European Cooperation Research Group [*European parliamentarians*]
EUCP........ Emergency Urgent Change Package [*Army*] (AABC)
EUCRA9 ... EUCARPIA [*European Association for Research on Plant Breeding*] Congres. Association Europeenne pour l'Amelioration des Plantes [*A publication*]
EUCUS..... Emergency Unitized Cargo Unloading System [*Navy*] (CAAL)
EUD.......... Extended Upper Deck
EUD.......... Library Techniques, Sheridan College [*EDUCATSS*] [*UTLAS symbol*]
EUDAC .... European Defense Analysis Center (MCD)
EUDAC ..... European Distribution and Accounting Agency of the Military Committee, London [*US Army*] (AABC)
EUDEBA... Editorial Universitaria de Buenos Aires [*A publication*]
EUDISED ... European Documentation and Information System for Education [*Council of Europe*] [*Database*] (IID)
EUDS .... Electronic Unit Design Section
EUE.......... Europeen, Europaer. Magazine de l'Economie et de la Culture [*A publication*]
EUE.......... Universite de Montreal, Ecole de Bibliotheconomie [*EDUCATSS*] [*UTLAS symbol*]
EUE .... University of Essex Library, Colchester, England [*OCLC symbol*] (OCLC)
Euer.......... Euer. Doctrina Placitandi [*England*] [*A publication*] (DLA)
EUF.......... Electroultrafiltration
EUF .... End User Facility
EUF .... Equivalent Unavailability Factor (IEEE)
EUF .... Eufaula, AL [*Location identifier*] [*FAA*] (FAAL)
EUF .... Euromoney Trade Finance Report [*A publication*]
EUF .... European Union of Federalists
EUF .... Library Technician Program, Fraser Valley College [*EDUCATSS*] [*UTLAS symbol*]
EUFA........ European Union Football Associations
EUFID...... European File [*A publication*]
EUFSAR ... Ege Universitesi Fen Fakultesi Ilmi Raporlar Serisi [*A publication*]
EUG.......... CEGEP [*College d'Enseignement General et Professionnel*], Trois-Rivieres, Bibliotheque [*EDUCATSS*] [*UTLAS symbol*]
EUG.......... Eugene [*Oregon*] [*Airport symbol*] (OAG)
EUG.......... Eugene, OR [*Location identifier*] [*FAA*] (FAAL)
Eu G .... Europaeisches Gespraech [*A publication*]
EUG.......... European Industrial Relations Review [*A publication*]
EUG.......... European Union of Geosciences [*Strasbourg, France*]

EUGEN..... Eugenics (ADA)
Eugen Lab Lect Ser ... Eugenics Laboratory. Lecture Series [*A publication*]
Eugen Lab Mem ... Eugenics Laboratory. Memoirs [*A publication*]
Eugen News ... Eugenical News [*A publication*]
Eugen Q ..... Eugenics Quarterly [*A publication*]
Eugen Rev ... Eugenics Review [*A publication*]
Eugen Soc Symp ... Eugenics Society Symposia [*A publication*]
EUGQAQ ... Eugenics Quarterly [*A publication*]
Eug R .... Eugenics Review [*A publication*]
Euh............ Euhemer [*A publication*]
EUH .... Expected Utility Hypothesis
EUH .... Library Technician Program, Mohawk College [*EDUCATSS*] [*UTLAS symbol*]
EUI .... Electronic Unit Injector [*Automotive engineering*]
EUI .... SAIT [*Southern Alberta Institute of Technology*] Library Technician Program [*UTLAS symbol*]
EUIPA...... Electric Utility Industrial Power Association (EA)
EUJ........... Georgian College [*EDUCATSS*] [*UTLAS symbol*]
EUJS .... European Union of Jewish Students (EA)
EUK........... Eureka Resources, Inc. [*Vancouver Stock Exchange symbol*]
EUK .... Library Technician Program, Kelsey Institute [*EDUCATSS*] [*UTLAS symbol*]
e-uk--- .... United Kingdom [*MARC geographic area code*] [*Library of Congress*] (LCCP)
Eukleides A Agymnasio NS ... Eukleides. Ekdose tes Ellenikes Mathemates Etairias. A. Agymnasio. Nea Seira [*A publication*]
e-uk-en ...... England [*MARC geographic area code*] [*Library of Congress*] (LCCP)
e-uk-ni........ Northern Ireland [*MARC geographic area code*] [*Library of Congress*] (LCCP)
e-uk-st .... Scotland [*MARC geographic area code*] [*Library of Congress*] (LCCP)
e-uk-ui .... United Kingdom Miscellaneous Islands [*MARC geographic area code*] [*Library of Congress*] (LCCP)
e-uk-wl ...... Wales [*MARC geographic area code*] [*Library of Congress*] (LCCP)
EUL .... Europa van Morgen [*A publication*]
Eu L .... Europe Letteraria [*A publication*]
EUL .... Expected Upper Limit [*Clinical psychology*]
EUL .... School of Library Technology, Lakehead University [*EDUCATSS*] [*UTLAS symbol*]
EULA .... Euro-Latin American Bank Ltd.
EULABANK ... Euro-Latin America Bank Ltd. [*London, England*] (EY)
EULAR...... European League Against Rheumatism (EAIO)
EULEP Newsl ... EULEP [*European Late Effects Project Group*] Newsletter [*A publication*]
Eul J .... Eulenspiegel-Jahrbuch [*A publication*]
Eul Ji Med J ... Eul Ji Medical Journal [*A publication*]
EUM .... Entraide Universitaire Mondiale [*World University Service - WUS*] (EAIO)
Eum............ Eumenides [*of Aeschylus*] [*Classical studies*] (OCD)
EUM.......... Eureka Mesa [*New Mexico*] [*Seismograph station code, US Geological Survey*] (SEIS)
EUM.......... European-Mediterranean [*Military*]
EUM.......... Graduate School of Library Science, McGill University [*EDUCATSS*] [*UTLAS symbol*]
EUMABOIS ... Comite Europeen des Constructeurs de Machines a Bois [*European Committee of Woodworking Machinery Manufacturers*] (EAIO)
EUMAPRINT ... European Committee of Associations of Printing and Paper Converting Machinery (EA)
EUMC .... Entraide Universitaire Mondial du Canada [*World University Service of Canada - WUSC*]
EUMC .... European Microwave Conference and Exhibition [*Great Britain*] (ITD)
EUMETSAT ... European Meteorological Satellite (MCD)
EUMETSAT ... European Organization for the Exploitation of Meteorological Satellites
EUMR .... Emergency Unsatisfactory Material Report (MCD)
EUMS .... European Union of Music Schools [*See also EMU*] (EA)
EUMT .... Europaeische Union Gegen den Missbrauch der Tiere [*European Union for the Prevention of Cruelty to Animals*] [*Switzerland*] (EAIO)
EUN.......... Electronic University Network [*TeleLearning Systems*] [*San Francisco, CA*] [*Data processing*]
Eun........... Eunuchus [*of Terence*] [*Classical studies*] (OCD)
EUN.......... European Plastics News [*A publication*]
EUN.......... Laayoune [*Morocco*] [*Airport symbol*] (OAG)
EUN.......... Library Technician Program, Niagara College [*EDUCATSS*] [*UTLAS symbol*]
EUN.......... University of Newcastle, Newcastle-Upon-Tyne, England [*OCLC symbol*] (OCLC)
Eun........... Wynne's Eunomus [*A publication*] (DLA)
EUNICEF ... European Command Nuclear Interface Element Fastbreak (MCD)
EUNMWSCM ... European Union of Natural Mineral Water Sources of the Common Market (EAIO)
EuntDoc..... Euntes Docete [*Rome*] [*A publication*]
EUO........... Emergency Use Only (FAAC)
EUO........... Library Technician Program, Algonquin College [*EDUCATSS*] [*UTLAS symbol*]

EUP .... Edinburgh Paperback [*A publication*]
EUP .... Edinburgh University Press [*Publisher*] [*Scotland*]
EUP .... Electric Utility Pump
EUP .... English Universities Press
EUP .... Equipment Upgrade Program [*Army*]
EUP .... Estimated Unit Price (MCD)
Eup........... Eupolis [*Fifth century BC*] [*Classical studies*] (OCD)
EUP .... Europa Petroleum [*Vancouver Stock Exchange symbol*]
EUP .... Europe [*A publication*]
EUP .... Experimental Use Permit [*Environmental Protection Agency*]
EUP .... Extension [*O Intercambio*] Universitaria de la Plata [*A publication*]
EUPH .... Euphonium [*Musical instrument*]
Euph........... Euphorion [*A publication*]
EUPHAA .. Euphytica [*A publication*]
EUPHEM ... Euphemism (ROG)
Euphoria Cacophoria (Int Ed) ... Euphoria et Cacophoria (International Edition) [*A publication*]
Euphyt .... Euphytica. Netherlands Journal of Plant Breeding [*A publication*]
EUPJ .... Experimental Underwater Pump Jet
EUPJA ...... European Polymer Journal [*A publication*]
EUPNA ..... Europhysics News [*A publication*]
EUPNB...... European Plastics News [*A publication*]
EUPRAC... European Public Relations Advisory Committee
EUPRISO ... European Union of Public Relations - International Service Organization [*See also UERP*] (EAIO)
EUPSA ...... European Union of Paediatric Surgical Associations (EAIO)
EUQ.......... Emory University Quarterly [*A publication*]
EUQ.......... John Abbott College Library [*EDUCATSS*] [*UTLAS symbol*]
EUR.......... Electrically Transmitted Unsatisfactory Report
EUR.......... Emergency Unsatisfactory Report [*Military*] (AFM)
EUR.......... Engineering Unsatisfactory Report [*Military*] (AFIT)
EUR.......... Equipment Unsatisfactory Report
EUR.......... Eureka [*Nevada*] [*Seismograph station code, US Geological Survey*] (SEIS)
EUR.......... Eureka, MT [*Location identifier*] [*FAA*] (FAAL)
Eur .... Euripides [*Fifth century BC*] [*Classical studies*] (OCD)
EUR.......... Eurocan Ventures Ltd. [*Vancouver Stock Exchange symbol*]
Eur .... Eurochord [*Record label*] [*France*]
EUR.......... Euromoney [*A publication*]
EUR.......... Europe (AFM)
EUR.......... Library Technician Program, Red River Community College [*EDUCATSS*] [*UTLAS symbol*]
e-ur--- .... USSR [*Union of Soviet Socialist Republics*] [*MARC geographic area code*] [*Library of Congress*] (LCCP)
Eur A.......... Europa-Archiv [*A publication*]
EURA.......... European Renderers Association (EAIO)
EURAC ..... European Requirements and Army Capabilities (AABC)
EurACS ..... European Association of Classification Societies (EAIO)
EURAFRICA ... Europe and Africa
Eurafr Trib Tiers-Monde ... Eurafrica et Tribune de Tiers-Monde [*A publication*]
EURAG ..... Federation Europeenne des Personnes Agees [*European Federation for the Welfare of the Elderly*] (EAIO)
e-ur-ai........ Armenian Soviet Socialist Republic [*MARC geographic area code*] [*Library of Congress*] (LCCP)
EURAILPASS ... European Railway Passenger [*Ticket*]
e-ur-aj........ Azerbaijan Soviet Socialist Republic [*MARC geographic area code*] [*Library of Congress*] (LCCP)
EURAL....... European Air Lines
EURALARM ... Association des Constructeurs Europeens de Systemes d'Alarme Incendie et Vol [*Association of European Manufacturers of Fire and Intruder Alarm Systems*] (EAIO)
EURAM .... European Research on Advanced Materials
Eur Appl Res Rep ... European Applied Research Reports [*A publication*]
Eur Appl Res Rep Environ Nat Resour Sect ... European Applied Research Reports. Environment and Natural Resources Section [*A publication*]
Eur Appl Res Rep-Nucl Sci Technol Sect ... European Applied Research Reports. Nuclear Science and Technology Section [*A publication*]
Eur Arb ...... European Arbitration [*A publication*] (DLA)
Eur Arch .... Europa-Archiv [*A publication*]
Eur Arch Psychiatry Neurol Sci ... European Archives of Psychiatry and Neurological Sciences [*A publication*]
EURAS...... Association Europeenne l'Anodisation [*European Anodisers' Association*] (EA)
EURASAFRICA ... Europe, Asia, and Africa
EURASAP ... European Association for the Science of Air Pollution (EAIO)
EURASIP ... European Association for Signal Processing (EAIO)
Eur Ass Arb ... European Assurance Arbitration [*1872-75*] [*A publication*] (DLA)
Eur Assoc Anim Prod Publ ... European Association for Animal Production. Publication [*A publication*]
EURATOM ... European Atomic Energy Community [*Also, EAEC*]
EURATOM Bull ... EURATOM [*European Atomic Energy Community*] Bulletin [*Belgium*] [*A publication*]
EURATOM Bull Eur At Energy Community ... EURATOM. Bulletin of the European Atomic Energy Community [*A publication*]

EURATOM Rev Eur At Energy Community ... EURATOM Review. European Atomic Energy Community [*Belgium*] [*A publication*]

Eur Biophys J ... European Biophysics Journal [*A publication*]

Eur Brew Conv Proc Congr ... European Brewery Convention. Proceedings of the Congress [*A publication*]

e-ur-bw .... Belorussian Soviet Socialist Republic [*MARC geographic area code*] [*Library of Congress*] (LCCP)

e-urc-- .... Central Black Soil Region, RSFSR [*MARC geographic area code*] [*Library of Congress*] (LCCP)

Eur Chem N ... European Chemical News [*A publication*]

Eur Chem Ne ... European Chemical News [*A publication*]

Eur Chem News ... European Chemical News [*England*] [*A publication*]

Eur Chir Forsch ... Europaeische Chirurgische Forschung [*A publication*]

EURCO ... European Composite Unit [*European Economic Community*]

Eur Coal Util Conf Proc ... European Coal Utilisation Conference. Proceedings [*A publication*]

EURCOM ... European Command [*Military*]

Eur Commun Bull ... European Communities Bulletin [*A publication*]

Eur Commun Econ Soc Comm Bull ... European Communities Economic and Social Committee. Bulletin [*A publication*]

Eur Community ... European Community [*A publication*]

Eur Community (Engl Ed) ... European Community (English Edition) [*A publication*]

Eur Conf Anim Blood Groups Biochem Polymorph ... European Conference on Animal Blood Groups and Biochemical Polymorphism [*A publication*]

Eur Conf Anim Blood Groups Biochem Polymorphism ... European Conference on Animal Blood Groups and Biochemical Polymorphism [*A publication*]

Eur Conf Microcirc ... European Conference on Microcirculation [*A publication*]

Eur Congr Sleep Res ... European Congress on Sleep Research [*A publication*]

Eur Conslt Ass Deb ... Council of Europe, Debates of the Consultative Assembly [*A publication*] (DLA)

Eur Cos Mkt ... European Cosmetic Markets [*A publication*]

EURCUP ... Estudos Universitarios: Revista de Cultura da Universidade de Pernambuco [*A publication*]

EURDA ..... Etudes d'Urbanisme de Developpement et d'Amenagement [*du Territoire*]

Eur Demographic Info Bul ... European Demographic Information Bulletin [*A publication*]

Eur Demographic Info Bul (Hague) ... European Demographic Information Bulletin (The Hague) [*A publication*]

Eur Dial Transplant Assoc Eur Renal Assoc Proc ... European Dialysis and Transplant Association - European Renal Association. Proceedings [*A publication*]

Eur Dial Transplant Assoc Proc ... European Dialysis and Transplant Association. Proceedings [*A publication*]

Eur Domani ... Europa Domani [*A publication*]

e-ure-- .... East Siberian Region, RSFSR [*MARC geographic area code*] [*Library of Congress*] (LCCP)

EUREA ...... Eugenics Review [*A publication*]

EUREAB ... Eugenics Review [*A publication*]

EUREAU .. Union des Associations des Distributeurs d'Eau de Pays Membres des Communautes Europeennes [*Union of the Water Supply Associations from Countries of the European Communities*] (EAIO)

EURECA ... European Retrievable Carrier [*Space shuttle experiment*]

Eur Economy ... European Economy [*A publication*]

Eur Econ R ... European Economic Review [*A publication*]

EUREKA ... European Research Cooperation Agency [*Non-defense research study group including eighteen European countries*]

EUREL ...... Association Europeenne des Reserves Naturelles Libres [*European Association for Free Nature Reserves*] [*Inactive*] (EAIO)

EUREL ...... Convention of National Societies of Electrical Engineers of Western Europe (EAIO)

EUREMAIL ... Conference Permanente de l'Industrie Europeenne de Produits Emailles

Eur Energy ... European Energy Prospects to 1990 [*A publication*]

e-ur-er .... Estonian Soviet Socialist Republic [*MARC geographic area code*] [*Library of Congress*] (LCCP)

Eur Ethn .... Europa Ethnica [*A publication*]

EURF .... Experience Usage Replacement Factor [*Navy*]

e-urf-- .... Far Eastern Region, RSFSR [*MARC geographic area code*] [*Library of Congress*] (LCCP)

Eur File ...... European File [*Luxembourg*] [*A publication*]

Eur en Formation ... Europe en Formation [*A publication*]

Eur France OM ... Europe France Outremer [*A publication*]

Eur Fr Outremer ... Europe France Outremer [*A publication*]

Eur Geophys Soc Meet Abstr ... European Geophysical Society. Meeting. Abstracts [*A publication*]

Eur Grundrechte ... Europaeische Grundrechte [*A publication*]

e-ur-gs .... Georgian Soviet Socialist Republic [*MARC geographic area code*] [*Library of Congress*] (LCCP)

EurH .... Europaeische Hochschulschriften [*A publication*]

Eur Heart J ... European Heart Journal [*A publication*]

Euriam Bul ... Euriam Bulteni [*A publication*]

Eur Ind Rel R ... European Industrial Relations Review [*A publication*]

Eur Intellectual Property Rev ... European Intellectual Property Review [*A publication*]

Eur Intell Prop R ... European Intellectual Property Review [*A publication*]

Eur Int Pr R ... European Intellectual Property Review [*A publication*]

EURIPA .... European Information Industry Association [*Formerly, European Information Providers Association*] [*Information retrieval*] (IID)

Euristop Off Inf Bookl ... Eurisotop Office Information Booklet [*A publication*]

EURJA ...... European Rubber Journal [*A publication*]

Eur J Anaesthesiol ... European Journal of Anaesthesiology [*A publication*]

Eur J A Phy ... European Journal of Applied Physiology and Occupational Physiology [*A publication*]

Eur J Appl Microbiol ... European Journal of Applied Microbiology [*A publication*]

Eur J Appl Microbiol Biotechnol ... European Journal of Applied Microbiology and Biotechnology [*A publication*]

Eur J Appl Physiol ... European Journal of Applied Physiology and Occupational Physiology [*A publication*]

Eur J Appl Physiol Occup Physiol ... European Journal of Applied Physiology and Occupational Physiology [*A publication*]

Eur J App M ... European Journal of Applied Microbiology [*A publication*]

Eur J Bioch ... European Journal of Biochemistry [*A publication*]

Eur J Biochem ... European Journal of Biochemistry [*A publication*]

Eur J Canc ... European Journal of Cancer [*A publication*]

Eur J Cancer ... European Journal of Cancer [*A publication*]

Eur J Cancer Clin Oncol ... European Journal of Cancer and Clinical Oncology [*A publication*]

Eur J Cardiol ... European Journal of Cardiology [*A publication*]

Eur J Cell Biol ... European Journal of Cell Biology [*A publication*]

Eur J Cell Biol Suppl ... European Journal of Cell Biology. Supplement [*A publication*]

Eur J Chiro ... European Journal of Chiropractic [*A publication*]

Eur J Cl In ... European Journal of Clinical Investigation [*A publication*]

Eur J Clin Biol Res ... European Journal of Clinical and Biological Research [*France*] [*A publication*]

Eur J Clin Invest ... European Journal of Clinical Investigation [*A publication*]

Eur J Clin Microbiol ... European Journal of Clinical Microbiology [*A publication*]

Eur J Clin Microbiol Infect Dis ... European Journal of Clinical Microbiology and Infectious Diseases [*A publication*]

Eur J Clin Pharmacol ... European Journal of Clinical Pharmacology [*A publication*]

Eur J Cl Ph ... European Journal of Clinical Pharmacology [*A publication*]

Eur J Comb ... European Journal of Combinatorics [*A publication*]

Eur J Drug Metab Pharmacokinet ... European Journal of Drug Metabolism and Pharmacokinetics [*A publication*]

Eur J Educ ... European Journal of Education [*A publication*]

Eur J Eng Educ ... European Journal of Engineering Education [*A publication*]

Eur J Epidemiol ... European Journal of Epidemiology [*A publication*]

Eur J For Pathol ... European Journal of Forest Pathology [*A publication*]

Eur J Gynaecol Oncol ... European Journal of Gynaecological Oncology [*A publication*]

Eur J I Car ... European Journal of Intensive Care Medicine [*A publication*]

Eur J Immun ... European Journal of Immunology [*A publication*]

Eur J Immunol ... European Journal of Immunology [*A publication*]

Eur J Intensive Care Med ... European Journal of Intensive Care Medicine [*A publication*]

Eur J Mass Spectrom Biochem Med Environ Res ... European Journal of Mass Spectrometry in Biochemistry, Medicine, and Environmental Research [*A publication*]

Eur J Med Chem ... European Journal of Medicinal Chemistry [*A publication*]

Eur J Med Chem Chim Ther ... European Journal of Medicinal Chemistry. Chimica Therapeutica [*A publication*]

Eur J Mktg ... European Journal of Marketing [*A publication*]

Eur J Nucl Med ... European Journal of Nuclear Medicine [*A publication*]

Eur J Obstet Gynecol ... European Journal of Obstetrics and Gynecology [*Later, European Journal of Obstetrics, Gynecology, and Reproductive Biology*] [*A publication*]

Eur J Obstet Gynecol Reprod Biol ... European Journal of Obstetrics, Gynecology, and Reproductive Biology [*A publication*]

Eur J Oper Res ... European Journal of Operational Research [*A publication*]

Eur J Orthod ... European Journal of Orthodontics [*A publication*]

Eur J Ped ... European Journal of Pediatrics [*A publication*]

Eur J Pediatr ... European Journal of Pediatrics [*A publication*]

Eur J Pharm ... European Journal of Pharmacology [*A publication*]

Eur J Pharmacol ... European Journal of Pharmacology [*A publication*]

Eur J Phys ... European Journal of Physics [*A publication*]

Eur J Popul ... European Journal of Population [*A publication*]

Eur J Radiol ... European Journal of Radiology [*A publication*]

Eur J Respir Dis ... European Journal of Respiratory Diseases [*A publication*]

Eur J Respir Dis Suppl ... European Journal of Respiratory Diseases. Supplement [*A publication*]

Eur J Rheumatol Inflamm ... European Journal of Rheumatology and Inflammation [*A publication*]

Eur J Rheumatol Inflammation ... European Journal of Rheumatology and Inflammation [*A publication*]

Eur J Sci Educ ... European Journal of Science Education [*A publication*]

Eur J Sociol ... European Journal of Sociology [*A publication*]

Eur J Soc P ... European Journal of Social Psychology [*A publication*]
Eur J Steroids ... European Journal of Steroids [*A publication*]
Eur J Surg Oncol ... European Journal of Surgical Oncology [*A publication*]
Eur J Toxicol ... European Journal of Toxicology [*A publication*]
Eur J Toxicol Environ Hyg ... European Journal of Toxicology and Environmental Hygiene [*A publication*]
e-urk-- .... Caucasus [*MARC geographic area code*] [*Library of Congress*] (LCCP)
e-ur-kg .... Kirghiz Soviet Socialist Republic [*MARC geographic area code*] [*Library of Congress*] (LCCP)
Eur Konf Mikrozirk ... Europaeische Konferenz ueber Mikrozirkulation [*A publication*]
e-ur-kz .... Kazakh Soviet Socialist Republic [*MARC geographic area code*] [*Library of Congress*] (LCCP)
e-url-- .... Central Region, RSFSR [*MARC geographic area code*] [*Library of Congress*] (LCCP)
Eur L Dig ... European Law Digest [*A publication*] (DLA)
Eur L Facs ... European Linguistics. A Collection of Facsimile Reprints [*A publication*]
e-ur-li .... Lithuanian Soviet Socialist Republic [*MARC geographic area code*] [*Library of Congress*] (LCCP)
Eur L Newsl ... European Law Newsletter [*A publication*] (DLA)
Eur L Rev ... European Law Review [*A publication*] (DLA)
e-ur-lv .... Latvian Soviet Socialist Republic [*MARC geographic area code*] [*Library of Congress*] (LCCP)
Eur Mediterr Plant Prot Organ Publ Ser A ... European and Mediterranean Plant Protection Organization. Publications. Series A [*A publication*]
Eur Mediterr Plant Prot Organ Publ Ser D ... European and Mediterranean Plant Protection Organization. Publications. Series D [*A publication*]
Eur Meet Wildfowl Conserv Proc ... European Meeting on Wildfowl Conservation. Proceedings [*A publication*]
e-ur-mv .... Moldavian Soviet Socialist Republic [*MARC geographic area code*] [*Library of Congress*] (LCCP)
e-urn-- .... Northwestern Region, RSFSR [*MARC geographic area code*] [*Library of Congress*] (LCCP)
EURNAVFACENGCOM ... European Division Naval Facilities Engineering Command
Eur Neurol ... European Neurology [*A publication*]
Eur Nouv ..... Europe Nouvelle [*A publication*]
Eur Nucl ..... Europa Nucleare [*A publication*]
EURO .... Eurocapital Corp. [*NASDAQ symbol*] (NQ)
e-uro-- .... Soviet Central Asia [*MARC geographic area code*] [*Library of Congress*] (LCCP)
Euro Abstr Sec 1 ... Euro Abstracts. Section 1. EURATOM [*European Atomic Energy Community*] and EEC [*European Economic Community*] Research [*Luxembourg*] [*A publication*]
Euro Abstr Sect 2 ... Euro Abstracts. Section 2. Coal and Steel [*Luxembourg*] [*A publication*]
EUROBA .. European Professional Fair for Industry and Handicraft of Bakery, Confectionery, Pastry, Biscuits, Chocolate, and Ice Cream Making (TSPED)
EUROBAT ... Association of European Battery Manufacturers (EA)
EUROBIT ... European Association of Manufacturers of Business Machines and Data Processing Equipment [*Frankfurt, Federal Republic of Germany*] (EAIO)
EUROBITUME ... European Bitumen Association (EA)
EUROBRAZ ... European Brazilian Bank
EUROBUILD ... European Organization for the Promotion of New Techniques and Methods in Building (EA)
EUROCAE ... European Organization for Civil Aviation Electronics [*France*] (MCD)
EUROCAT ... European Registry of Congenital Abnormalities and Twins
EUROCEAN ... European Oceanic Association [*Monaco, Monaco*] (EAIO)
EUROCENTRES ... Foundation for European Language and Educational Centres (EA)
EURO CHEMIC ... European Company for the Chemical Processing of Irradiated Fuels (DS)
EUROCHOR ... Arbeitsgemeinschaft Europaeischer Chorverbaende [*European Choral Association - ECA*] (EA)
EUROCOM ... European Communications
EUROCOM ... Union Europeenne des Negociants en Combustibles [*European Fuel Merchants Union*]
EUROCOMP ... European Computing Congress (IEEE)
EUROCOMSAT ... European Consortium Communications Satellite (MCD)
EUROCONTROL ... European Organization for the Safety of Air Navigation
EURO COOP ... Communaute Europeenne des Cooperatives de Consommateurs [*European Consumers' Cooperation Committee*] [*Common Market*]
Euro Coop .. Euro Cooperation [*A publication*]
EUROCORD ... Federation des Industries de Ficellerie et Corderie de l'Europe Occidentale [*Federation of Western European Rope and Twine Industries*] (EA)
EURODICAUTOM ... European Automated Dictionary
EUROFEDOP ... European Federation of Employees in Public Services (EAIO)
EUROFEU ... Comite Europeen des Constructeurs de Materiels d'Incendie et de Secours [*European Committee of the Manufacturers of Fire Protection and Safety Equipment and Fire Fighting Vehicles*] (EAIO)

EUROFORGE ... European Committee of Forging and Stamping Industries (EAIO)
EUROGLACES ... Association des Industries de Glaces Alimentaires de la CEE [*Association of the Ice Cream Industries of the European Economic Community*]
EUROGYPSUM ... Working Community of the European Gypsum Industry (EAIO)
EURO-HKG ... European High Temperature Nuclear Power Stations Society (EAIO)
Eur Oil .... Europe and Oil [*West Germany*] [*A publication*]
Eur Oil Gas Mag ... European Oil and Gas Magazine [*West Germany*] [*A publication*]
Eurolaw Com Intel ... Eurolaw Commercial Intelligence [*A publication*] (DLA)
EUROLOC ... Locate in Europe Information Retrieval System [*University of Strathclyde*] [*Glasgow, Scotland*] [*Information service or system*] (IID)
EUROMAISIERS ... Groupement des Associations des Maisiers des Pays de la CEE [*Group of the Maize Processors Associations in the European Economic Community Countries*] [*Brussels, Belgium*]
EUROMALT ... Comite de Travail des Malteries de la CEE [*Working Committee of European Economic Community Malters*]
EUROMART ... European Common Market
EUROMECH ... European Mechanics Committee [*ICSU*]
EUROMICRO ... European Association for Microprocessing and Microprogramming
Euromicro J ... Euromicro Journal [*Netherlands*] [*A publication*]
Euromicro Newsl ... Euromicro Newsletters [*A publication*]
EUROMIL ... Europaeische Organisation der Militarverbande [*European Organization of Military Associations*] (EAIO)
Euro Mon ... EuroMonitor Review [*A publication*]
EUROMOT ... European Committee of Associations of Manufacturers of Internal Combustion Engines (EA)
Eurom Surveys Aust NZ Series ... Euromarket Surveys. Australian/New Zealand Series [*A publication*] (APTA)
EURONEM ... European Association of Netting Manufacturers (EA)
EURONET ... European On-Line Information Network [*Commission of the European Communities*] [*Information service or system*] (IID)
Europ Busin ... European Business [*A publication*]
Europ Chem ... Europa Chemie [*A publication*]
Europ Demogr Inform B ... European Demographic Information Bulletin [*A publication*]
European Assocn for Archtl Education Newsheet ... European Association for Architectural Education. Newsheet
European Ind Relations Rev ... European Industrial Relations Review [*A publication*]
European Inf Serv ... European Information Service [*A publication*]
European J Combin ... European Journal of Combinatorics [*A publication*]
European J Ed ... European Journal of Education [*A publication*]
European J Engineering Ed ... European Journal of Engineering Education [*A publication*]
European J Oper Res ... European Journal of Operational Research [*A publication*]
European J Phys ... European Journal of Physics [*A publication*]
European J of Science Ed ... European Journal of Science Education [*A publication*]
European L Rev ... European Law Review [*A publication*]
European Photogr ... European Photography [*A publication*]
European Rubber J ... European Rubber Journal [*A publication*]
European Sm Bus J ... European Small Business Journal [*A publication*]
EUROPECHE ... Association des Organisations Nationales d'Entreprises de Peche de la CEE [*Association of National Organizations of Fishing Enterprises in the European Economic Community*] [*Federal Republic of Germany*]
Europe Com ... European Community [*A publication*]
Europe Communities Comm ... European Communities Commission [*A publication*]
Europ Econ and Pol Survey ... European Economic and Political Survey [*A publication*]
Europ Econ R ... European Economic Review [*A publication*]
Europe Daily Bull ... Europe Daily Bulletin [*A publication*]
Europe O Mer ... Europe Outremer [*A publication*]
EUROPHOT ... Association Europeenne des Photographes Professionnels [*European Association of Professional Photographers*]
Europhys Conf Abstr ... Europhysics Conference Abstracts [*Switzerland*] [*A publication*]
Europhys Conf Macromol Phys Proc ... Europhysics Conference on Macromolecular Physics. Proceedings [*A publication*]
Europhys News ... Europhysics News [*A publication*]
Europ Intell Prop Rev ... European Intellectual Property Review [*A publication*]
Europ J Polit Res ... European Journal of Political Research [*A publication*]
Europ J Soc Psychol ... European Journal of Social Psychology [*A publication*]
EUROPLANT ... European Plantmakers Committee (EA)
Europlas Mon ... Europlastics Monthly [*England*] [*A publication*]
Europlast Mon ... Europlastics Monthly [*A publication*]
EUROPLATE ... European Registration Plate Association (EA)

EUROPMAISERS ... Groupement des Associations des Maisiers des Pays de la CEE [*Group of Associations of Maize Processors of EEC Countries*] (EAIO)

EUROPMI ... Comite de Liaison des Petites et Moyennes Entreprises Industrielles des Pays de la CEE [*Liaison Committee for Small and Medium-Sized Industrial Enterprises in the EEC*] [*Brussels, Belgium*] (EAIO)

Europ R Agric Econ ... European Review of Agricultural Economics [*A publication*]

Europ Rdsch ... Europaeische Rundschau [*A publication*]

EUROPS ... European Air Operations Staff [*Military*]

Europ Stud Newsl ... European Studies Newsletter [*A publication*]

Europ Stud R ... European Studies Review [*A publication*]

Europ TS .... European Treaty Series [*Council of Europe*] [*A publication*] (DLA)

EUROPUMP ... Comite Europeen des Constructeurs de Pompes [*European Committee of Pump Manufacturers*] (EAIO)

EUROPUMP ... European Committee of Pump Manufacturers (EA)

EUROPUR ... Association Europeenne des Fabricants de Blocs de Mousse Souple de Polyurethane [*European Association of Flexible Foam Block Manufacturers*] (EAIO)

Europ Wehrkunde ... Europaeische Wehrkunde [*A publication*]

Europ YB ... European Yearbook [*A publication*]

EURORAD ... European Association of Manufacturers of Radiators (EA)

Euro Rep Stud ... Euro Reports and Studies [*A publication*]

Euro Res ... European Research [*A publication*]

Euro Rev .... Eurostat Review [*A publication*]

Eur Organ Res Fluorine Dent Caries Prev Proc Congr ... European Organization for Research on Fluorine and Dental Caries Prevention. Proceedings of the Congress [*A publication*]

Eur Organ Res Treat Cancer (EORTC) Monogr Ser ... European Organization for Research on Treatment of Cancer (EORTC). Monograph Series [*A publication*]

Eur Organ Res Treat Cancer Monog Ser ... European Organization for Research on the Treatment of Cancer. Monograph Series [*A publication*]

Eur Organ Treat Cancer Monogr Ser ... European Organization for Research on the Treatment of Cancer. Monograph Series [*A publication*]

EUROSAC ... Federation Europeenne des Fabricants de Sacs en Papier a Grande Contenance [*European Federation of Multiwall Paper Sacks Manufacturers*] (EAIO)

EUROSAT ... European Application Satellite Systems

EUROSPACE ... European Industrial Space Study Group

Euro Space Agency (Spec Publ) ESA SP ... European Space Agency (Special Publication). ESA SP [*France*] [*A publication*]

Euro Spectr ... Euro-Spectra [*A publication*]

EUROSTAT ... [*The*] European Static Protection and Shielding Exhibition [*Great Britain*] (ITD)

EUROSTAT ... Statistical Office of the European Communities [*Commission of the European Communities*] (EAIO)

EUROTALC ... Association Scientifique de l'Industrie Europeenne du Talc [*Scientific Association of European Talc Industry*] (EAIO)

Eurotest Tech Bull ... Eurotest Technical Bulletin [*A publication*]

EUROTOX ... Comite Europeen Permanent de Recherches sur la Protection des Populations contre les Risques de Toxicite a Long Terme [*Permanent European Research Committee for the Protection of the Population against the Hazards of Chronic Toxicity*]

Eur Outremer ... Europe Outremer [*A publication*]

EUROVISION ... European Television

e-urp-- .... Povolzhskii Region, RSFSR [*MARC geographic area code*] [*Library of Congress*] (LCCP)

Eur Paed H ... European Paediatric Haematology and Oncology [*A publication*]

Eur Paediatr Haematol Oncol ... European Paediatric Haematology and Oncology [*A publication*]

Eur Parl Deb ... European Parliamentary Assembly Debates [*A publication*] (DLA)

Eur Parl Doc ... European Parliament Working Documents [*A publication*] (DLA)

Eur Parl Docs ... European Parliament Working Documents [*A publication*] (DLA)

EURPISO ... European Union of Public Relations - International Service Organization [*Hungary*] (EA)

Eur Plas N ... European Plastics News [*A publication*]

Eur Plast News ... European Plastics News [*A publication*]

Eur Polym J ... European Polymer Journal [*A publication*]

Eur Potato J ... European Potato Journal [*A publication*]

Eur Pot J .... European Potato Journal [*A publication*]

e-urr-- .... North Caucasus, RSFSR [*MARC geographic area code*] [*Library of Congress*] (LCCP)

Eur Rdsch .. Europaeische Rundschau [*A publication*]

Eur Res ...... European Research [*A publication*]

Eur Research ... European Research [*A publication*]

Eur Respir J ... European Respiratory Journal [*A publication*]

Eur Rev Agric Econ ... European Review of Agricultural Economics [*A publication*]

Eur Rev Endocrinol ... European Review of Endocrinology [*A publication*]

Eur Rev Endocrinol Suppl ... European Review of Endocrinology. Supplement [*A publication*]

Eur Rev Lit ... Europe. Revue Litteraire Mensuelle [*A publication*]

Eur Rev Med Pharmacol Sci ... European Review for Medical and Pharmacological Sciences [*A publication*]

e-ur-ru .... Russian SFSR [*MARC geographic area code*] [*Library of Congress*] (LCCP)

Eur Rubber J ... European Rubber Journal [*A publication*]

Eur Rubb J ... European Rubber Journal [*A publication*]

Eur Rub Jl ... European Rubber Journal [*A publication*]

e-urs-- .... Siberia [*MARC geographic area code*] [*Library of Congress*] (LCCP)

Eur Semicond Prod ... European Semiconductor Production [*A publication*]

Eur Shipbldg ... European Shipbuilding [*A publication*]

Eur Solid State Device Res Conf ... European Solid State Device. Research Conference [*A publication*]

Eur South Obs Bull ... European Southern Observatory. Bulletin [*West Germany*] [*A publication*]

Eur Space Agency Sci Tech Rev ... European Space Agency. Scientific and Technical Review [*A publication*]

Eur Space Res Organ Contract Rep ... European Space Research Organization. Contractor Report [*A publication*]

Eur Stud R ... European Studies Review [*A publication*]

Eur Sud-Est 5e Ser ... Europe Sud-Est. Cinquieme Serie [*A publication*]

Eur Surg Re ... European Surgical Research [*A publication*]

Eur Surg Res ... European Surgical Research [*A publication*]

EUR/SV/LDO ... European Space Vehicle Launcher Development Organization (MCD)

Eur Symp Calcif Tissues Proc ... European Symposium on Calcified Tissues. Proceedings [*A publication*]

Eur Symp Chem React Eng ... European Symposium on Chemical Reaction Engineering [*A publication*]

Eur Symp Enhanced Oil Recovery ... European Symposium on Enhanced Oil Recovery [*A publication*]

Eur Symp Horm Cell Regul ... European Symposium on Hormones and Cell Regulation [*A publication*]

Eur Symp Lindane ... European Symposium on Lindane [*A publication*]

Eur Symp Powder Metall Prepr ... European Symposium for Powder Metallurgy. Preprints [*A publication*]

Eur Symp Pulvermetall Vorabdrucke ... Europaeisches Symposium fuer Pulvermetallurgie. Vorabdrucke [*A publication*]

e-ur-ta .... Tajik Soviet Socialist Republic [*MARC geographic area code*] [*Library of Congress*] (LCCP)

Eur Tax ...... European Taxation [*A publication*]

Eur Taxation ... European Taxation [*A publication*]

Eur Tech Dig ... European Technical Digests [*A publication*]

e-ur-tk .... Turkmen Soviet Socialist Republic [*MARC geographic area code*] [*Library of Congress*] (LCCP)

Eur TL .... European Transport Law [*Belgium*] [*A publication*] (DLA)

Eur Trans L ... European Transport Law [*Belgium*] [*A publication*] (DLA)

Eur Transp L ... European Transport Law [*Belgium*] [*A publication*] (DLA)

e-uru-- .... Ural Region, RSFSR [*MARC geographic area code*] [*Library of Congress*] (LCCP)

e-ur-un .... Ukrainian Soviet Socialist Republic [*MARC geographic area code*] [*Library of Congress*] (LCCP)

Eur Urol ..... European Urology [*A publication*]

e-ur-uz .... Uzbek Soviet Socialist Republic [*MARC geographic area code*] [*Library of Congress*] (LCCP)

e-urv-- .... Volgo-Viatskii Region, RSFSR [*MARC geographic area code*] [*Library of Congress*] (LCCP)

e-urw-- .... West Siberian Region, RSFSR [*MARC geographic area code*] [*Library of Congress*] (LCCP)

Eur Wehrkunde ... Europaeische Wehrkunde [*A publication*]

EURYB ...... Europa Year Book [*A publication*]

Eur YB .... European Yearbook [*A publication*] (DLA)

EURYDICE ... Education Information Network in the European Community [*Commission of the European Communities*] [*Belgium*] [*Information service or system*] (IID)

Eur Z Forstpathologie ... Europaeische Zeitschrift fuer Forstpathologie [*A publication*]

Eur Z Kartoffelforsch ... Europaeische Zeitschrift fuer Kartoffelforschung [*A publication*]

EUS .... Eastern United States

EUS .... Economic Outlook USA [*A publication*]

Eus .... Eusebius [*Ecclesiastical historian, c. 260-340AD*] [*Classical studies*] (OCD)

EUS .... External Urethral Sphincter [*Anatomy*]

EUS .... Library Techniques, Seneca College [*EDUCATSS*] [*UTLAS symbol*]

EUS .... Market Research Europe [*A publication*]

EUSA .... Eighth United States Army

EUSAK ...... Eighth United States Army in Korea

EUSAR ...... Eighth United States Army Rear

EUSC .... Effective United States Control Fleet

EUSEB ...... Eusebius [*Ecclesiastical historian, c. 260-340AD*] [*Classical studies*] (ROG)

EUSEC ...... Conference des Societes d'Ingenieurs de l'Europe Occidental et des Etats-Unis d'Amerique [*Conference of Engineering Societies of Western Europe and the United States of America*]

EUSEC ...... European Communications Security and Evaluation Agency of the Military Committee, London [*US Army*] (AABC)

EUSIDIC... European Association of Information Services [*Formerly, European Association of Scientific Information Dissemination Centers*] [*Information service or system*] (IID)

EUSIREF.. European Scientific Information Referral [*EUSIDIC*] [*Information service or system*] (IID)

EUSJA...... European Union of Science Journalists Associations (EAIO)

EUSM...... European Union of Social Medicine (EA)

EUSND...... Energy User News [*A publication*]

EUSRBM.. Europaeische Chirurgische Forschung [*A publication*]

EUSSBP... Eugenics Society Symposia [*A publication*]

EUSSG...... European Union for the Scientific Study of Glass (EA)

EUT........... Equipment under Test

Eut............ Euterpe [*Record label*]

EUT........... Faculty of Library and Information Science, University of Toronto [*EDUCATSS*] [*UTLAS symbol*]

EUTE......... Early User Test and Experimentation [*DoD*]

EUTELSAT ... European Telecommunications Satellite Organization [*France*] [*Telecommunications*] (TSSD)

Euthphr...... Euthyphro [*of Plato*] [*Classical studies*] (OCD)

EUTO........ European Union of Tourist Officers (EAIO)

EUU.......... Faculty of Library Science, University of British Columbia [*EDUCATSS*] [*UTLAS symbol*]

EUU.......... Smithfield, NC [*Location identifier*] [*FAA*] (FAAL)

EUV.......... Europa-Archiv [*A publication*]

EUV.......... Extreme Ultraviolet

EUV.......... Library Technician Program, Vancouver Community College [*EDUCATSS*] [*UTLAS symbol*]

EUVE........ Extreme Ultraviolet Explorer

EUVEPRO ... European Vegetable Protein Federation (EAIO)

EUVP........ Extreme Ultraviolet Photometer (MCD)

EUVSH ..... Equivalent Ultraviolet Solar Hour [*NASA*]

EUVT........ Extended Ultraviolet Transmission

EUVT........ Extreme Ultraviolet Telescope

EUW.......... Eureka [*Washington*] [*Seismograph station code, US Geological Survey*] (SEIS)

EUW.......... European Union of Women [*Stockholm, Sweden*]

EUW.......... School of Library and Information Science, University of Western Ontario [*EDUCATSS*] [*UTLAS symbol*]

Eu W N ..... Eudora Welty Newsletter [*A publication*]

EUX........... Saint Eustatius [*Antilles*] [*Airport symbol*] (OAG)

EUYCD ..... European Union of Young Christian Democrats [*Belgium*] (EY)

EUZ........... European Chemical News [*A publication*]

EV........... Economic Value [*Accounting*]

EV........... Ecos de Valvanera [*A publication*]

EV........... Educt Vent

EV........... Efferent Vessel [*Anatomy*]

EV........... Efficient Vulcanizing [*Rubber processing*]

EV........... Eigenvalue [*Mathematics*]

EV........... Eingang Vorbehalten [*Rights reserved, i.e., copyrighted*] [*German*]

EV........... Electric Vehicle

eV............ Electron Volt

EV........... Electronic Viewfinder [*Photography*]

EV........... Elektrotehniski Vestnik [*A publication*]

EV........... Emotional Violence

EV........... Engineer Volunteers [*British military*] (DMA)

EV........... English Version

EV........... English Viscount (ROG)

EV........... Entrained Air Volume

EV........... Epegrafika Vostika [*A publication*]

EV........... Erdelyi Vilagszovetseg [*Transylvanian World Federation - TWF*] (EAIO)

EV........... Ere Vulgaire [*Common Era*] [*French*] [*Freemasonry*] (ROG)

EV........... Escort Vessel [*Enemy*]

EV........... Esophageal Varices [*Medicine*]

EV........... EuroVision [*Later, SGA*] (EA)

EV........... Evaluate

EV........... Evangelist

Ev........... Evangile [*Paris*] [*A publication*] (BJA)

EV........... Evaporator Vessel (NRCH)

EV........... Evening

EV........... [*The*] Everett Railroad Co. [*AAR code*]

EV........... Evergreen International Airlines, Inc. [*ICAO designator*] (FAAC)

EV........... Evergreen Review [*A publication*]

EV........... Everted [*or Eversion*] [*Medicine*]

EV........... Every

Ev........... Evidence [*Legal term*] (DLA)

EV........... Evolution

EV........... Ex Voto [*In Fulfillment of a Vow*] [*Latin*]

EV........... Exhaust Valve [*Nuclear energy*] (NRCH)

EV........... Expected Value [*Statistics*]

EV........... Expendable Vehicle (MCD)

EV........... Experimental Version (SDI)

EV........... Explosive Valve (KSC)

EV........... Exposure Value [*System*] [*Photography*]

EV........... Extracellular Virus

EV........... Extravascular [*Anatomy*]

EV........... Extravehicular (MCD)

EV........... Exudative Vitreoretinopathy [*Ophthalmology*]

ev-----......... Scandinavia [*MARC geographic area code*] [*Library of Congress*] (LCCP)

EVA........... Early Valve Actuation [*Nuclear energy*] (NRCH)

EVA........... Earned Value Analysis (NASA)

EVA........... Einzelspaltrohrversuchsanlage [*Hydrogen generating reactor*]

EVA........... Electronic Velocity Analyzer

EVA........... Electronic Voice Alert [*Automotive engineering*]

EVA........... Electronic Vote Analysis [*Election poll*]

EVA........... Engineer Vice-Admiral [*British*]

EVA........... English Volleyball Association

EVA........... Error Volume Analysis [*Data processing*] (IBMDP)

EVA........... Escort Vessel Administration [*World War II*]

EVA........... Esperantlingva Verkista Asocio [*Esperanto Writers Association - EWA*] (EA)

EVA........... Essex Volunteer Artillery [*British military*] (DMA)

EVA........... Ethyl Violet-Azide [*Broth*] [*Microbiology*]

EVA........... Ethylene-Vinyl Acetate [*Copolymer*] [*Organic chemistry*]

EVA........... Europaeische Vereinigung der Allgemeinarzte [*European Union of General Practitioners*] (EAIO)

EVA........... European Review of Agricultural Economics [*A publication*]

EVA........... European Vaccine Against AIDS [*Acquired Immune Deficiency Syndrome*] [*Medicine*]

EVA........... Evadale, TX [*Location identifier*] [*FAA*] (FAAL)

EVA........... Extravehicular Activity [*Aerospace*]

EVAA....... Electric Vehicle Association of the Americas (EA)

EVAC....... Electric Vehicle Association of Canada

EVAC....... Etoposide (VP-16), Vincristine, Adriamycin, Cyclophosphamide [*Antineoplastic drug regimen*]

EVAC....... Evacuation (AFM)

EVAC....... Evacuator (MSA)

EVACSHIP ... Evacuation Ship [*Navy*] (NVT)

EVADE...... Evaluation of Air Defense Effectiveness

EVAF........ International Association for Business Research and Corporate Development [*West Wickham, Kent, England*] (EAIO)

Ev Ag .... Evans on Agency [*A publication*] (DLA)

EVAL........ Earth Viewing Applications Laboratory (MCD)

EVAL........ Evaluate [*or Evaluation or Evaluator*] (AFM)

Eval Eng..... Evaluation Engineering [*A publication*]

Eval & Exper ... Evaluation and Experiment. Some Critical Issues in Assessing Social Programs [*A publication*]

Eval Health Prof ... Evaluation and the Health Professions [*A publication*]

Eval Newsletter ... Evaluation Newsletter [*A publication*]

Eval Program Plann ... Evaluation and Program Planning [*A publication*]

Eval Q .... Evaluation Quarterly [*A publication*]

Eval Rev..... Evaluation Review [*A publication*]

Evaluation in Ed ... Evaluation in Education [*A publication*]

Evaluation Health Professions ... Evaluation and the Health Professions [*A publication*]

Evaluation Q ... Evaluation Quarterly [*A publication*]

Evaluation R ... Evaluation Review [*A publication*]

Evaluatn.... Evaluation: A Forum for Human Services Decision-Makers [*A publication*]

Evalu Stu.... Evaluation Studies. Review Annual [*A publication*]

EVAN....... Electronic Verification of Account Number [*Social Security*]

EVAN....... Evangelical [*or Evangelist*]

Evan........... Evangile [*Paris*] [*A publication*] (BJA)

EVAN....... Evans, Inc. [*NASDAQ symbol*] (NQ)

EVAN-G.... End Violence Against the Next Generation (EA)

EVANG ..... Evangelical [*or Evangelist*]

Evang........... Evangelical Quarterly [*A publication*]

Evang Komment ... Evangelische Kommentare [*West Germany*] [*A publication*]

Evang Q .... Evangelical Quarterly [*A publication*]

Evang R..... Evangelical Review [*A publication*]

Evang Th ... Evangelische Theologie [*A publication*]

Evan Kirchor ... Evangelische Kirchenchor [*A publication*]

Evans .... Evans' King's Bench Reports [*1756-88*] [*A publication*] (DLA)

Evans .... Lord Mansfield's Decisions [*1799-1814*] [*England*] [*A publication*] (DLA)

EVAP........ Evaporate (KSC)

EVAPTR ... Evaporator [*Freight*]

EVARS...... Experimental Vehicle for Avionics Research (MCD)

EVATA...... Electronic-Visual-Auditory Training Aid

EVATA...... Extravehicular Activity Translational Aid (NASA)

EVATP...... Experimental Volunteer Army Training Program (RDA)

EVATRON ... Eccentric Variable-Angle Thermionic Rheostat

EVB........... Extruded Vinyl Bumper

EVBAA..... Electric Vehicles and Batteries [*A publication*]

EVBHA ..... Environment and Behavior [*A publication*]

EVBMA ..... Environmental Biology and Medicine [*A publication*]

EVC........... Educational Video Corporation

EVC........... Electric Vehicle Council [*Defunct*] (EA)

EVC........... Endatcom Ventures [*Vancouver Stock Exchange symbol*]

EVC........... Engineer Volunteer Corps [*British*]

EVC........... Error Vector Computer (NG)

EVC........... Executive Volunteer Corps

EVC........... Extravehicular Communications [*Aerospace*] (NASA)

EVC........... Extravehicular Communicator [*NASA*] (KSC)

e-vc---......... Vatican City [*MARC geographic area code*] [*Library of Congress*] (LCCP)

EVCA......... European Venture Capital Association   (EAIO)

EVCC......... Ex-Vessel Core Catcher [*Nuclear energy*]   (NRCH)

EVCE......... Evidence

EVCl......... Ethylene-Vinyl Chloride [*Fire-retardant resin*] [*Organic chemistry*]

EVC-O...... Electronic Vibration Cutoff [*Aerospace*]   (AAG)

EVCON...... Events Control [*Subsystem*] [*NASA*]   (NASA)

EVCS......... Extravehicular Communications System [*NASA*]

EVCS......... Extruded Vinyl Chamfer Strip

EVCT........ Extravehicular Crew Transfer [*NASA*]   (MCD)

EVCTD...... Extravehicular Crew Transfer Device [*NASA*]   (KSC)

EVCU .... Extravehicular Communications Umbilical [*Aerospace*]   (MCD)

EVD.......... Economische Voorlichtingsdienst [*Economic Information Service*] [*Information service or system*]   (IID)

EVD.......... Electrovacuum Drive

EVD.......... Exportmededelingen [*A publication*]

EVD.......... Extended Voluntary Departure [*Temporary status sometimes granted by the State Department as protection against deportation*]

EVD.......... External Visual Display   (MCD)

EVDE........ External Visual Display Equipment [*Used in Apollo mission*] [*NASA*]

EVDF........ Eugene V. Debs Foundation   (EA)

EVDG........ Electric Vehicle Development Group Ltd. [*British*]

EVDS........ Electronic Visual Display Subsystem

EVDS........ Explosive Vapor Detector Systems   (MCD)

EVE.......... Eagle Valley Environmentalists   (EA)

EVE.......... Economic Verification Experiments [*Marine science*]   (MSC)

EVE.......... Education, Volunteerism, Employment Opportunities

EVE.......... Einstein Viscosity Equation

EVE.......... Electric Vehicle Exposition   (ADA)

EVE.......... Ethyl Vinyl Ether [*Organic chemistry*]

EVE.......... Evenes [*Norway*] [*Airport symbol*]   (OAG)

EVE.......... Evening

EVEA........ Extravehicular Engineering Activity [*Aerospace*]

EVECW..... Extravascular Extracellular Water [*Medicine*]

EVEN........ Evening   (ROG)

EVEN........ Evensong   (ROG)

EVER........ Everglades National Park

EVER........ Evergreen Resources, Inc. [*NASDAQ symbol*]   (NQ)

Everday Sci ... Everyday Science [*A publication*]

Everglades Nat History ... Everglades Natural History [*A publication*]

Everybody's LM ... Everybody's Law Magazine [*A publication*]   (DLA)

EVERY M ... Everybody's Magazine [*A publication*]   (ROG)

Everyman's Sci ... Everyman's Science [*A publication*]

EVESR ...... ESADA [*Empire State Atomic Development Associates, Inc.*] Vallecitos Experimental Superheat Reactor

EVETB ...... Environmental Entomology [*A publication*]

EVF........... Electromagnetic Vibrating Feeder

EVF........... Equipment Visibility File   (NASA)

EVF........... Tendance des Ventes du Vetement Masculin pour Hommes et Juniors [*A publication*]

EVFM........ Ex-Vessel Flux Monitor [*Nuclear energy*]   (NRCH)

EVG.......... Electric Vacuum Gyro

EVG.......... Electrostatic Vector Grid

EVG.......... Evening

EVG.......... Evergold Resources [*Vancouver Stock Exchange symbol*]

EVG.......... Extravehicular Glove [*NASA*]   (KSC)

EVGA .... Extended Video Graphics Array   (PCM)

EVGD........ Evergood Products Corp. [*NASDAQ symbol*]   (NQ)

EVGN........ Evergreen Bancorp, Inc. [*Glens Falls, NY*] [*NASDAQ symbol*]   (NQ)

EVH.......... Esophageal Varices Hemorrhage [*Medicine*]

EVH.......... Wereldmarkt [*A publication*]

EVHA........ English Villages Housing Association   (ECON)

EVHA........ Europese Vereniging voor Haveninformatica [*European Port Data Processing Association*] [*Belgium*]   (EA)

Ev Harr ...... Evans' Edition of Harris' Modern Entries [*A publication*]   (DLA)

EVHM....... Ex-Vessel Handling Machine [*Later, CLEM*] [*Nuclear energy*]   (NRCH)

EVI........... Cedar Crest and Muhlenberg Colleges, Allentown, PA [*OCLC symbol*]   (OCLC)

EVI........... Early Vendor Involvement Program [*Automotive engineering*]

EVI........... Education Voucher Institute   (EA)

EVI........... Encapsulated Variable Inductor

EVI........... Evergreen International Corp. [*Toronto Stock Exchange symbol*]

EVI........... Evington, VA [*Location identifier*] [*FAA*]   (FAAL)

EVIA......... [*The*] Enchanted Village, Inc. [*NASDAQ symbol*]   (NQ)

EVID......... Evidence

Evid .... Evidences [*Paris*] [*A publication*]   (BJA)

EVIF......... Emergency Virus Isolation Facility [*National Cancer Institute*]

EVIL......... Eastern Verbal Investigators League

EVIL......... Elevation Versus Integrated Log

EVIL......... Extensible Video Interactive Language [*Data processing*]

E VIN........ E Vino [*In Wine*] [*Pharmacy*]

EVIST........ Ethics and Values in Science and Technology [*National Science Foundation*]

Ev Jud Pr ... Evans' Practice of the Supreme Court of Judicature [*A publication*]   (DLA)

EvK .... Evangelische Kommentare [*Stuttgart*] [*A publication*]

EVKOD...... Evangelische Kommentare [*A publication*]

EvKom....... Evangelische Kommentare [*Stuttgart*] [*A publication*]

EvKoMoe... Evreiskii Kommunisticheskii Soiuz Molodezhi   (BJA)

EVL........... Cleveland, OK [*Location identifier*] [*FAA*]   (FAAL)

EVL........... Everyman's Library [*A publication*]

EVLSS....... Extravehicular Life Support System [*NASA*]

EVLTA ...... Environmental Letters [*A publication*]

EVLTN...... Evaluation   (MSA)

EVLW....... Extravascular Lung Water [*Medicine*]

EVLWA..... Environmental Law [*A publication*]

EVM .... Earth Viewing Module

EVM .... Electronic Voltmeter   (IEEE)

EVM .... Elektronno-Vychislitel'naya Mashina [*Electronic Calculating Machine*] [*Russian*]

EVM .... Engine Vibration Monitor   (MCD)

EVM .... Epitesugyi es Varosfejlesztesi Miniszterium [*Ministry for Building and Urban Development*] [*Information service or system*]   (IID)

EVM .... Errors-in-Variables Model [*Statistics*]

EVM .... Evacuation Mission [*Air Force*]

EVM .... Evangelie en Maatschappij [*A publication*]

EVM .... Evasive Maneuvering

EVM .... Eveleth, MN [*Location identifier*] [*FAA*]   (FAAL)

EVM .... Extended Virtual Machine

EvM .... Inscriptions of the Reigns of Evil-Merodach, Neriglissar, and Laborosoarchod   (BJA)

Ev Md Pr ... Evans' Maryland Practice [*A publication*]   (DLA)

Ev MQ ...... Evangelical Missions Quarterly [*A publication*]

EVMS........ Emil Verban Memorial Society   (EA)

EVMU....... Extravehicular Mobility Unit [*NASA*]   (NASA)

EVN .... Erevan [*USSR*] [*Airport symbol*]   (OAG)

EVN .... Even Resources [*Vancouver Stock Exchange symbol*]

EVNG .... Evangeline Railway Co. [*AAR code*]

EVNG .... Evening

EVNSA...... Electric Vehicle News [*A publication*]

EVO .... East Liverpool, OH [*Location identifier*] [*FAA*]   (FAAL)

EVO .... Eisenbahn-Verkehrsordnung [*Germany*]

EVO .... Electronic Variable Orifice [*Automotive engineering*]

EVO .... Engineering Verification Order   (MCD)

EVO .... Extravehicular Operation [*Aerospace*]

EvObshchestKom ... Evreiskii Obshchestvennyi Komitet Pomoshchi Pogromlennym   (BJA)

EVOC .... Excerpta Medica Vocabulary [*Elsevier Science Publishers BV*] [*Netherlands*] [*Information service or system*]   (CRD)

Evol .... Evolution [*A publication*]

EVOL .... Evolved

Evol Biol .... Evolutionary Biology [*A publication*]

Evol Genet Res Rep ... Evolutionary Genetics Research Reports [*A publication*]

Evol Med ... Evolution Medicale [*A publication*]

Evol Psychiatr ... Evolution Psychiatrique [*A publication*]

Evol Theory ... Evolutionary Theory [*A publication*]

EVOM .... Electronic Voltohmmeter   (IEEE)

EVOP .... Evaluation and Optimization

EVOP .... Evolutionary Operation [*Statistical technique*]

EVox .... English Vox [*Record label*]

EVP........... Electronic Voice Phenomena [*Parapsychology*]

EVP........... Enhanced VERDIN [*Antijam Modem, Very-Low Frequency*] Processor [*Military*]   (CAAL)

EVP........... Evangelische Volkspartei der Schweiz [*Swiss Evangelical People's Party*] [*Political party*]   (PPW)

EVP........... Evangelische Volkspartij [*Evangelical People's Party*] [*Netherlands*] [*Political party*]   (EY)

EVP........... Evoked Visual Potential [*Neurophysiology*]

EVP........... Executive Vice President

EVPD........ Evaporated

EVPHB...... Environmental Physiology [*A publication*]

EVPHI...... Europese Vereniging voor Pediatrische Hematologie en Immunologie [*European Society for Paediatric Haematology and Immunology - ESPHI*]   (EAIO)

EVPI .... Expected Value of Perfect Information [*Statistics*]

Ev Pl .... Evans on Pleading [*A publication*]   (DLA)

Ev Poth ..... Evans' Translation of Pothier on Obligations [*A publication*]   (DLA)

Ev Pr & Ag ... Evans on the Law of Principal and Agent [*A publication*]   (DLA)

EVPSA ...... Evolution Psychiatrique [*A publication*]

EVPTD...... Energy Viewpoint [*A publication*]

Ev Q .... Evangelical Quarterly [*A publication*]

EVQMA..... Environmental Quality [*A publication*]

EVR .... Electronic Video Recording [*CBS Laboratories' brand name for tape cartridges of TV programs*]

EVR .... Everest Resources Ltd. [*Vancouver Stock Exchange symbol*]

EvR .... Evergreen Review [*A publication*]

EVR .... Evoked Vascular Response [*Physiology*]

EVR .... External Visual Reference [*Motion sickness*]

EVRC........ Eton Volunteer Rifle Corps [*British military*]   (DMA)

EVRCL...... Evaluation Research Corporation Uts [*NASDAQ symbol*] (NQ)
EVRD........ Excellentissime Vestre Reverendissime Dominationis [*Of Your Most Excellent and Reverend Lordship*] [*Latin*] (ECON)
Ev RL........ Evans' Road Laws of South Carolina [*A publication*] (DLA)
EVRLK...... Ever-Lock
EVRO........ EVRO Financial Corp. [*Formerly, Envirosearch Corp.*] [*NASDAQ symbol*] (NQ)
EVRX........ Everex Systems, Inc. [*NASDAQ symbol*] (NQ)
EVS........... Economische Voorlichting Suriname [*A publication*]
EVS........... Ecumenical Voluntary Service [*Defunct*]
EVS........... Electro-Optical Viewing System
EVS........... Electro-Optical Visual Sensors [*Hughes Aircraft Co.*]
EVS........... Electronic Valve Specification (MCD)
EVS........... Electronic Voice Switching (AFM)
EVS........... Emergency Venting System
EVS........... Endoscopic Variceal Sclerosis [*Medicine*]
EVS........... Engine Vertical Scale
EVS........... Enhanced VERDIN [*Antijam Modem, Very-Low Frequency*] System [*Military*] (CAAL)
EVS........... Environmental Science (AABC)
EVS........... Equi Ventures, Inc. [*Vancouver Stock Exchange symbol*]
EVS........... Equipment Visibility System (NASA)
E-V-S........ Expected Value-Variance-Skewness [*Statistics*]
EVS........... Extravehicular Suit [*Aerospace*] (MCD)
EVS........... Extravehicular System [*Aerospace*]
EVS........... Extreme Value Statistics
EVS........... Eye-Voice Span
EVSA........ Electronic Variable Shock Absorber [*Automotive engineering*]
Ev Sat........ Every Saturday [*A publication*]
EVSB........ Evansville Federal Savings Bank [*NASDAQ symbol*] (NQ)
EVSC........ Extravehicular Suit Communications [*Aerospace*]
EVSCB...... Everyman's Science [*A publication*]
EVSD........ Electronic Vision Systems Development
EVSD........ Energy-Variant Sequential Detection (CET)
EvSektsiia ... Evreiskaia Sektsiia (BJA)
EVSI......... Expected Value of Sample Information [*Statistics*]
EVSS........ Extravehicular Space Suit [*Aerospace*] (MCD)
EVSSAV.... Environmental Space Sciences [*English translation of Kosmicheskaya Biologiya i Meditsina*] [*A publication*]
EVSt......... Einfuhr- und Vorratsstelle fuer Getreide und Futtermittel [*German*] [*A publication*] (DLA)
EVST........ Ex-Vessel Storage Tank [*Nuclear energy*] (NRCH)
Ev Stat....... Evans' Collection of Statutes [*A publication*] (DLA)
EVSTC...... Extravehicular Suit Telemetry Communications [*Aerospace*]
EVSU........ Extravehicular Space Unit [*Aerospace*] (MCD)
EVT.......... Earth Venus Transit [*Aerospace*]
EVT.......... Economic Investment Trust Ltd. [*Toronto Stock Exchange symbol*]
EVT.......... Education and Vocational Training [*British military*] (DMA)
EVT.......... Effective Visual Transmission (NATG)
EVT.......... Elasticity, Viscosity, and Thixotropy
EVT.......... Emergency Veterinary Tag
EVT.......... End Viewing Tube
EVT.......... Engineering Verification Test
EVT.......... Evaluation Vector Table
EvT.......... Evangelische Theologie [*Munich*] [*A publication*]
EVT.......... Expect Vector To [*Aviation*] (FAAC)
EvTC........ Extravehicular Transfer [*NASA*] (KSC)
EvTC........ Evangelizing Today's Child [*A publication*]
Ev Th........ Evangelische Theologie [*A publication*]
EvThB........ Evangelische Theologie (Beiheft) [*A publication*]
EVTM........ Ex-Vessel Transfer Machine [*Nuclear energy*] (NRCH)
Ev Tr......... Evans' Trial [*A publication*] (DLA)
E/VTS....... Engine/Vehicle Test Stand
EVTV........ Extravascular Thermal Volume [*Medicine*]
EVU.......... Maryville, MO [*Location identifier*] [*FAA*] (FAAL)
EVV.......... English Versions
EVV.......... Evansville [*Indiana*] [*Airport symbol*] (OAG)
EVVA........ Europaeische Vereinigung der Veterinaranatomen [*European Association of Veterinary Anatomists - EAVA*] (EAIO)
EVVA........ Extravehicular Visor Assembly [*NASA*]
EVW.......... European Voluntary Worker
EVW.......... Evanston, WY [*Location identifier*] [*FAA*] (FAAL)
EvWelt....... Evangelische Welt. Bethel bei Bielefeld [*Germany*] [*A publication*]
EVX.......... Electronic Voice Exchange [*Commterm, Inc.*] [*Billerica, MA*] [*Telecommunications*] (TSSD)
EVY.......... Every
EW............ Each Way (MSA)
EW............ Early Warning [*Air Force*]
EW............ Earthenware
EW............ Earthwatch [*United Nations Environment Program*]
EW............ East Washington Railway Co. [*AAR code*]
EW............ East and West [*A publication*]
E & W........ East and West [*A publication*]
EW............ East-West
EW............ East-West Airlines Ltd. [*Australia*] [*ICAO designator*] (FAAC)
EW............ Eastern World [*A publication*]
EW............ Eave-to-Eave Width [*of boxcar*]
EW............ Eco/Log Week [*A publication*]

EW............ Economic Warfare [*British*]
EW............ Economic Week [*A publication*]
EW............ Ecosystems of the World [*Elsevier Book Series*] [*A publication*]
EW............ Edinger-Westphal Nucleus [*Neuroanatomy*]
EW............ Edmund Walker [*Car parts distribution company*] [*British*]
EW............ Egg Width
EW............ Eingetragenes Warenzeichen [*Registered Trademark*] [*German*]
EW............ Electronic Warfare
EW............ Emergency Ward
EW............ Eminent Women [*A publication*]
EW............ Empty Weight
EW............ End Wall [*Of a cell*] [*Botany*]
EW............ Energy-to-Weight Ratio (MCD)
EW............ Engineer's Writer [*British military*] (DMA)
E & W........ England and Wales
EW............ Enlisted Woman [*or Women*]
EW............ Equivalent Weapons [*Military*]
EW............ Euer [*Your*] [*German*]
EW............ Europaeische Wandervereinigung [*European Ramblers' Association - ERA*] [*Federal Republic of Germany*] (EAIO)
ew-----......... Europe, Western [*MARC geographic area code*] [*Library of Congress*] (LCCP)
EW............ Ex-Warrants [*Without Warrants*] [*Finance*]
EW............ Extended-Wear Lenses [*Optometry*]
EW............ Extensive Wound
EW............ External Work
EW............ Extreme Width [*of flight deck*]
EW............ Sleet Showers [*Meteorology*] (FAAC)
EWA.......... Early Warning/Attack Assessment
EWA.......... East-West Acceleration
EWA.......... East-West Airlines Ltd. [*Australia*]
EWA.......... Edgewood Arsenal [*Maryland*] [*Army*] (AABC)
EWA.......... Education and World Affairs [*Later, ICED*]
EWA.......... Education Writers Association (EA)
EWA.......... Emunah Women of America (EA)
EWA.......... End Warning Area [*Data processing*] (BUR)
EWA.......... Engineering Work Assignment
EWA.......... Engineering Work Authorization [*Aerospace*]
EWA.......... Esperanto Writers Association (EA)
EWA.......... Estimated Warehouse Arrival (NASA)
EWA.......... Europaeische Wahrungsabkommen [*European Monetary Agreement*] [*German*] (DCTA)
EWA.......... European Wax Association (EAIO)
EWA.......... European Welding Association (EAIO)
EWA.......... Kewanee, MS [*Location identifier*] [*FAA*] (FAAL)
EWAA-USA ... Elsa Wild Animal Appeal - USA (EA)
EWABL/AAU ... Eastern Women's Amateur Basketball League of the AAU [*Amateur Athletic Union of the United States*] (EA)
EWAC....... Early Warning Aircraft (MCD)
EWAC....... Electronic Warfare Anechoic Chamber
EWACS..... Electronic Wide-Angle Camera System
EWAD....... Early Warning Air Defense (NATG)
EWAG....... Exploding Wire Aerosol Generator [*Liquid suspension*]
EWAHA.... East West Academy of Healing Arts (EA)
EWAI........ Eisenhower World Affairs Institute [*Later, EI*] (EA)
EWAN....... Enterprise-Wide Application Network
EWASER .. Electromagnetic Wave Amplification by Stimulated Emission of Radiation
EWAT....... E'Town Corp. [*Formerly, Elizabethtown Water*] [*NASDAQ symbol*] (NQ)
EWB.......... Earl Weaver Baseball [*Computer game*]
EWB.......... Embedded Wiring Board (MSA)
EWB.......... Emergency Warnings Branch [*National Weather Service*]
EWB.......... Encyclopedia of World Biography [*A publication*]
EWB.......... Ernaehrungswirtschaft [*A publication*]
EWB.......... Estrogen Withdrawal Bleeding [*Medicine*]
EWB.......... New Bedford [*Massachusetts*] [*Airport symbol*] (OAG)
EWB.......... New Bedford, MA [*Location identifier*] [*FAA*] (FAAL)
EWBS........ Exportwarenbegleitschein [*Export Bill of Lading*] [*German*]
EWC.......... East-West Center (EA)
EWC.......... Eastern Women's Center (EA)
EWC.......... Edward Waters College [*Jacksonville, FL*]
EWC.......... Electric Water Cooler
EWC.......... Electronic Warfare Center (MCD)
EWC.......... Electronic Warfare Coordinator (NVT)
EWC.......... Ellwood City, PA [*Location identifier*] [*FAA*] (FAAL)
EWC.......... Episcopal Women's Caucus (EA)
EWCAS..... Early Warning and Control Aircraft System (IEEE)
EW/CAS ... Electronic Warfare/Close-Air Support (MCD)
EW-CAS-JTF ... Electronic Warfare, Close-Air Support, Joint Task Force (MCD)
EWCC....... East-West Cultural Center (EA)
EWCC....... Electronic Warfare Coordination Center
EWCC....... Elvis We Care Campaign [*Later, EPIAI*] (EA)
EWCD .... Electronic Warfare Cover and Deception (MCD)
EWCDMS ... Electronic Warfare Cover and Deception Management Subsystem (MCD)
EWCI......... East-West Communication Institute [*Later, East-West Institute of Culture and Communication*] [*Research center*] (RCD)
EWCI......... Evangelical Women's Caucus, International (EA)

EWCL........ Electromagnetic Warfare and Communications Laboratory
EW-CLI..... East-West Institute of Culture and Communication [*Research center*] (RCD)
EWCP........ Early Warning Change Proposal (MCD)
EWCR....... East-West Center Review [*A publication*]
EW/CRP ... Early Warning/Control and Reporting Post
EWCS....... Electronic Warfare Control Ship [*Navy*] (NVT)
EWCS....... Electronic Warfare Coordinating Staff
EWCS....... European Wideband Communications System [*Army*]
EW & CSq ... Early Warning and Control Squadron [*Air Force*]
EWD......... Elementary Wiring Diagram
EWD......... Elseviers Weekblad [*A publication*]
EWD......... Europaeischer Wissenschaftsdienst [*A publication*]
EWDD....... European Wholesalers and Distributors Directory [*Pronounced "eewed"*] [*A publication*]
EWDI .... Electronic Wind Direction Indicator
EWDT .... Early Warning Data Transmission (NATG)
EWE......... Electronic Warfare Element (AABC)
EWE......... Emergency Window Escape [*NASA*] (NASA)
ewe .... Ewe [*MARC language code*] [*Library of Congress*] (LCCP)
EWEA .... European Wind Energy Association (EAIO)
EWEC........ Electromagnetic Wave Energy Converter [*Solar energy conversion*]
Ewell Bl.... Ewell's Edition of Blackstone [*A publication*] (DLA)
Ewell Cas Inf ... Ewell's Leading Cases on Infancy, Etc. [*A publication*] (DLA)
Ewell Ess ... Ewell's Essentials of the Law [*A publication*] (DLA)
Ewell Evans Ag ... Ewell's Edition of Evans on Agency [*A publication*] (DLA)
Ewell Fix ... Ewell on the Law of Fixtures [*A publication*] (DLA)
Ewell LC .... Ewell's Leading Cases on Infancy, Etc. [*A publication*] (DLA)
EWEPS...... Environmental Weapons Effects Prediction System (MCD)
EWES........ Electronic Warfare Evaluation Simulator
EWES........ Engineering Waterways Experiment Station [*Army*]
EWEX....... Electronic Warfare Exercise (NVT)
EWEXIPT ... Electronic Warfare Exercise in Port (NVT)
EWF.......... Early Warning Fighter
EWF.......... Earth, Wind, and Fire [*Rock music group*]
EWF.......... Education Without Frontiers [*An association*] (EAIO)
EWF.......... Electromagnetic Wave Filter
EWF.......... Electronic Warfare
EWF.......... Equivalent-Weight Factor
EWF.......... European Warrant Fund [*NYSE symbol*] (SPSG)
EWF.......... European Weightlifting Federation (EA)
EWF.......... Wake Forest University, Winston-Salem, NC [*OCLC symbol*] (OCLC)
EWFH ...... East-West Fine, Hundreds
EWFT....... East-West Fine, Tens
EWFU....... East-West Fine, Units
EWG .... Equipment Working Group
EWG .... Ernaehrungswissenschaften Giessen [*Nutrition Sciences - Giessen University*] [*Database*]
EWG .... Euromissiles Working Group (EA)
EWG .... Europaeische Wirtschaftsgemeinschaft [*European Economic Community*]
EWG .... Executive Working Group [*NATO*]
EW/GCI.... Early Warning/Ground Control Intercept [*RADAR*]
EWGETS .. Electronic Warfare Ground Environment Threat Simulator
EWHA ...... Eastern Women's Headwear Association [*Later, AMMA*] (EA)
EWHO ...... Elbow-Wrist-Hand-Orthosis [*Medicine*]
EWI .... Ecologist [*A publication*]
EWI .... Edison Welding Institute (EA)
EWI .... Education with Industry
EW & I...... Electronic Warfare and Intelligence [*Military*]
EW/I......... Electronic Warfare/Intercept (MCD)
EWI .... Electronic Wiring Intercommunication
EWI .... Enarotali [*Indonesia*] [*Airport symbol*] (OAG)
EWI .... Entered without Inspection [*Usually applies to aliens who enter at other than a port of entry*]
EWI .... Executive Women International [*Salt Lake City, UT*] (EA)
EWI .... Experiential World Inventory [*Psychodiagnostic questionnaire*]
EWICB...... Electronic Warfare Interface Connection Box
E & WIDC ... East and West India Dock Company [*Shipping*] (ROG)
EWIF .... Electronic Warfare Intelligence Facility [*Fort Huachuca, AZ*] [*United States Army Electronic Proving Ground*] (GRD)
Ewing Just ... Ewing's Justice [*A publication*] (DLA)
EWIOC...... Electronic Warfare and Intelligence Operations Center [*Military*] (MCD)
EWIP......... Edinburgh University. Department of Linguistics. Work in Progress [*A publication*]
EWIRC...... Electronic Warfare Integrated Reprogramming Concept (MCD)
EWIS........ Electronic Warfare Information System (MCD)
EWITA...... Evaluation of Women in the Army (MCD)
EWJC........ European Women's Judo Championships [*London, England*]
EWK........ Newton, KS [*Location identifier*] [*FAA*] (FAAL)
EWL .... Earliest Work Listed
EWL .... Effective Wavelength
EWL .... Electronic Warfare Laboratory [*Army*]
EWL .... Evaporative Water Loss
EWL .... Exchange Work List [*Telecommunications*] (TEL)
EWL .... Wake Forest University, Law Library, Winston-Salem, NC [*OCLC symbol*] (OCLC)

EWLD ...... Engineering Weekly Labor Distribution (AAG)
E & WLR ... East and West London Railway [*British*] (ROG)
EWLTP .... Earl Warren Legal Training Program (EA)
EWM........ Edgewise Meter
EWM........ Electrical Welding Machine
EWM........ Elseviers Magazine [*A publication*]
EWM........ Episcopal World Mission (EA)
EWM........ MSU [*Michigan State University*] and WSU [*Wayne State University*] Union List of Serials, Detroit, MI [*OCLC symbol*] (OCLC)
EWM........ Newman, TX [*Location identifier*] [*FAA*] (FAAL)
EWMA ..... Exponentially Weighted Moving Average [*Statistics*]
EWMB ..... Enemy War Materials Branch [*Supreme Headquarters, Allied Expeditionary Force*] [*World War II*]
EWMC ..... Eli Whitney Metrology Center
EWMD...... European Women's Management Development Network (EAIO)
EWMFC.... Elvis Worldwide Memorial Fan Club (EA)
EWMIS..... Electronic Warfare Management Information System [*Air Force*] (MCD)
EWN......... Evelyn Waugh Newsletter [*A publication*]
EWN......... New Bern [*North Carolina*] [*Airport symbol*] (OAG)
EWN......... New Bern, NC [*Location identifier*] [*FAA*] (FAAL)
EWO......... Electrical and Wireless Operators [*Air Force*] [*British*]
EWO......... Electronic Warfare Office [*or Officer*]
EWO......... Emergency War Operations
EWO......... Emergency War Order [*Air Force*]
EWO......... Engineering Work Order
EWO......... Enki and the World Order [*A publication*] (BJA)
EWO......... Essential Work Order
EWO......... Ewo [*Congo*] [*Airport symbol*] (OAG)
EWO......... New Hope, KY [*Location identifier*] [*FAA*] (FAAL)
EWODS .... Engineering Work Order - Drawing Summary (AAG)
EWO & HP ... Electric Wall Oven and Hot Plates [*Classified advertising*] (ADA)
EWOPS..... Electronic Warfare Operations (NVT)
E World .... Eastern World [*A publication*]
EWOS ...... Electronic Warfare Operational System [*Air Force*]
EWOT ...... Electronic Warfare Officer Training (AFM)
EWOTS..... Early Warning Observation Teams (CINC)
E-WOW..... Explore the World of Work [*Vocational guidance test*]
EWP .... Electronic Warfare Plans [*NATO*] (NATG)
EWP .... Emergency War Plan
EWP .... Exploding Wire Phenomena
EWP .... Newport, AR [*Location identifier*] [*FAA*] (FAAL)
EWPCA..... European Water Pollution Control Association (EAIO)
EWPI........ East-West Population Institute
EWPI........ Eysenck-Withers Personality Inventory [*Psychology*]
EWQ......... Enlisted Women's Quarters [*Military*]
EWQ......... Exceptionally Well Qualified (AFM)
EWQOS..... Environmental and Water Quality Operational Studies [*Army Corps of Engineers*]
EWQRC .... Electronic Warfare Quick Reaction Capability (MCD)
EWR......... Early Warning RADAR [*Air Force*]
EWR......... East West Resources [*Vancouver Stock Exchange symbol*]
EWR......... East-West Review [*A publication*]
E & WR .... Elmira and Williamsport Railway [*British*] (ROG)
EWR......... Engineering Work Report [*or Request*]
EWR......... Estimated Weight Report
EWR......... New York [*New York*] Newark [*Airport symbol*] (OAG)
EWR......... Newark, NJ [*Location identifier*] [*FAA*] (FAAL)
EWRC....... European Weed Research Council [*Later, EWRS*]
EWR & I.... Emergency Welfare Registration and Inquiry [*Civil Defense*]
EWRL....... Estimated Weapon Release (MCD)
EWRS....... European Weed Research Society [*See also EGH*] [*Research center*] [*Federal Republic of Germany*] (IRC)
EWRSI Newsl ... EWRSI [*East-West Resource Systems Institute*] Newsletter [*A publication*]
EW/RSTA ... Center for Electronic Warfare/Reconnaissance, Surveillance, and Target Acquisition [*Fort Monmouth, NJ*] [*United States Army Communications-Electronics Command*] (GRD)
EWRT........ Electrical Women's Round Table (EA)
EWS.......... Early Warning System
EWS.......... East-West Speed
EWS.......... Edgar Wallace Society (EAIO)
EWS.......... Eduworld Society [*Later, CFB*] (EA)
EWS.......... Egg White Serum [*Immunology*]
EWS.......... Electronic Warfare System (MCD)
EWS.......... Emergency Water Supply
EWS.......... Emergency Welfare Service [*Civil Defense*]
EWS.......... Engineering Work Schedule (MCD)
EWS.......... Engineering Work Statement (MCD)
EWS.......... Engineering Work-Station [*Yokogawa Hewlett Packard Ltd.*] [*Japan*]
EWS.......... Engineering Writing and Speech (MCD)
EWS.......... English Westerners Society [*British*]
EWS.......... Estimated Will Ship
EWS.......... Evelyn Waugh Society (EA)
EWS.......... Experienced Worker Standard

EWSA........ EEC Wheat Starch Manufacturers Association
        [*Defunct*] (EAIO)
EWSB........ East Weymouth Savings Bank [*Weymouth, MA*] [*NASDAQ
        symbol*] (NQ)
EWSC........ Electric Water Systems Council
EWSC........ Scripps [*E. W.*] Co. [*NASDAQ symbol*] (NQ)
EWSCL ..... Extended-Wear Soft Contact Lens [*Optometry*]
EWSF........ Electric Wave Section Filter
EWSI........ Electronic Wind Speed Indicator
EW/SIGINT ... Electronic Warfare/Signal Intelligence (MCD)
EWSLA ...... East-West Sign Language Association
EWSM....... Electronic Warfare Support Measures [*Later, ESM*] (AABC)
EWST........ Elevated Water Storage Tank [*Nuclear energy*] (NRCH)
EWSTP ..... Emergency War Surgery Training Program [*Army*]
EWT .... Eastern War Time [*World War II*]
EWT .... Edible Whip Technology [*Aerosol technology*]
EWT .... Electronic Warfare Technology (MCD)
EWT .... Electronic Warfare Trainer
EWT .... Evaluation and Warning Team (CINC)
EWT .... Expandable Wing Tank
EWTA .... East Wind Trade Associates (EA)
EWTA .... Expo West Trade Association (EA)
EWTAD .... Early Warning Threat Analysis Display
EWTAP..... Electronic Warfare Tactics Analysis Program
        [*Military*] (CAAL)
EWTC....... East-West Trade Council [*Defunct*] (EA)
EWTES ..... Electronic Warfare Tactical [*or Threat*] Environment
        Simulation (NG)
EWTFA ...... Energiewirtschaftliche Tagesfragen [*A publication*]
EWTJA ..... Effluent and Water Treatment Journal [*A publication*]
EWTJAG .. Effluent and Water Treatment Journal [*A publication*]
EWTMI..... European Wideband Transmission Media Improvement
        Program (IEEE)
EWTN .... Eternal Word Television Network [*Cable-television system*]
EWTNGSq ... Electronic Warfare Training Squadron [*Air Force*]
EWTPC ..... East-West Trade Policy Committee
EWTR....... Electronic Warfare Test Range [*Military*]
EWTS .... Expandable Wing Tank Structure
EWTT........ Electronic Warfare Tactics Trainer
EWW........ Extended Work Week
EWWRS.... Eric's Wasted Worldwide Repair Society (EA)
EWWS....... Electronic Warfare Warning System
EWWS....... ESSA [*Environmental Science Services Administration*]
        Weather Wire Service
Ex.............. Citation in Examiner's Decision [*Legal term*] (DLA)
Ex.............. Court of Exchequer [*England*] [*Legal term*] (DLA)
Ex.............. English Exchequer Reports [*A publication*] (DLA)
EX .... Examined
Ex.............. Examiner [*Quezon City*] [*A publication*]
Ex.............. Examiner's Decision [*Legal term*] (DLA)
EX .... Example
EX .... Exceeding
EX .... Excellent [*Condition*] [*Deltiology*]
EX .... Except
EX .... Excess (AABC)
EX .... Exchange
EX .... Exchequer [*British*]
EX .... Exchequer Reports [*A publication*]
EX .... Excise (DSUE)
EX .... Excluding
EX .... Exclusive (ADA)
EX .... Excudit [*Made*] [*Latin*] (ROG)
EX .... Excursion
EX .... Excursus (ROG)
EX .... Execute
EX .... Executed Out Of [*Business term*]
EX .... Execution (ROG)
EX .... Executive
EX .... Executive Express [*ICAO designator*] (FAAC)
EX .... Executive Management Office [*Kennedy Space Center
        Directorate*] [*NASA*] (NASA)
EX .... Executive Schedule [*Job classification for certain Presidentially
        appointed executives*]
EX .... Executor (ROG)
EX .... Exempt
ex.............. Exercice [*Financial Year*] [*French*]
EX .... Exercise (NVT)
EX .... Exerque [*Numismatics*]
EX .... Exeunt [*They Go Out*] [*Latin*] (ROG)
EX .... Exhaust [*Automotive engineering*]
EX .... Exhibit
EX .... Exhibition (DSUE)
EX .... Exit [*He, or She, Goes Out*] [*Latin*] (ROG)
Ex.............. Exodus [*Old Testament book*]
EX .... Experimental Station [*ITU designation*] (CET)
EX .... Expert
EX .... Explanation
Ex.............. Explicator [*A publication*]
EX .... Export
EX .... Export [*New York*] [*A publication*]

EX .... Exposure
EX .... Express
EX .... Extension (ADA)
EX .... Extra
EX .... Extra Gilt [*Bookbinding*] (ROG)
EX .... Extractum [*Extract*] [*Latin*]
EX .... Extravaganza (ROG)
Ex.............. Extraversion [*Psychology*]
EX .... Lakeside Laboratories, Inc. [*Research code symbol*]
EX .... Without
EXA .... Albion College, Albion, MI [*OCLC symbol*] (OCLC)
EXA .... Executing Agency Identifier (CINC)
EXA .... Exmar Resources Ltd. [*Vancouver Stock Exchange symbol*]
EXACCT ... Expenditure Account
EXACT..... Energy Dispersive X-Ray Analysis Computation Technique [*X-
        Ray fluorescence software*] [*Kevex Corp.*]
EXACT...... Exchange of Authenticated Electronic Component Performance
        Test Data [*European counterpart of GIDEP*]
EX & AD.... Executor and Administrator (DLA)
EX AFF..... Ex Affinis [*Of Affinity*] [*Latin*]
EXAFS ...... Extended X-Ray Absorption Fine Structure [*Spectrometry*]
EXAG .... Exaggeration
EXAGT...... Executive Agent
EXAM .... Elemental X-Ray Analysis of Materials
ExAM....... Ex Air Ministry [*British*] (DEN)
EXAM .... Examination (AFM)
Exam.......... Examiner [*Legal term*] (DLA)
EX-AM ..... Expedited Air Munitions
EXAM .... Experimental Aerospace Multiprocessor
EXAMD .... Examined
EXAMETNET ... Experimental Inter-American Meteorological Rocket
        Network [*NASA*]
EXAMINA ... Examination (DSUE)
EXAMN.... Examination
EXAMR.... Examiner
EXAMS ..... Exposure Analysis Modeling System [*Environmental
        chemistry*]
Exam Sit Econ Mexico ... Examen de la Situacion Economica de Mexico [*A
        publication*]
EXAPT ...... Extended Subset of Automatically Programmed Tools
        [*Manufacturing term*]
EX AQ .... Ex Aqua [*In Water*] [*Pharmacy*]
EXAR........ Exar Corp. [*NASDAQ symbol*] (NQ)
Ex Aut........ Ex Authenticis Pandectis [*Digest of Justinian*] [*A
        publication*] (DSA)
EXav .... Ecclesiastica Xaveriana [*Bogota*] [*A publication*]
EXB .... Grand Rapids Baptist College and Seminary, Grand Rapids, MI
        [*OCLC symbol*] (OCLC)
EXBEDCAP ... Expanded Bed Capacity
ex-bon .... Ex-Bonification [*Ex-Bonus*] [*Finance*] [*French*]
EXBRA...... Experimental Brain Research [*A publication*]
EXBT........ Exabyte Corp. [*NASDAQ symbol*] (NQ)
EXC .... Calvin College and Seminary, Grand Rapids, MI [*OCLC
        symbol*] (OCLC)
ex c .... Ex-Coupon [*Ex-Coupon*] [*Finance*] [*French*]
EXC .... Excavate (MSA)
EXC .... Exceeding [*Weight*] [*Postage*] [*British*] (ROG)
EXC .... Excel Industries, Inc. [*AMEX symbol*] (SPSG)
EXC .... Excellency
EXC .... Excellent (AABC)
EXC .... Except
EXC .... Exchange
EX/C .... Exchange Certificate [*Rate*] [*Value of the English pound*]
EXC .... Exchange Key [*Word processing*]
EXC .... Excision [*Medicine*]
EXC .... Excitation (MSA)
EXC .... Exclude
EXC .... Excudit [*Made*] [*Latin*]
EXC .... Excursion (ROG)
EXC .... Experiment Computer (MCD)
Ex C .... Expert Comptable [*A publication*]
EXCA....... Excalibur Technology Corp. [*NASDAQ symbol*] (NQ)
EXCA....... Excavate [*Technical drawings*]
EXCAP ..... Expanded Capability (CAAL)
EXCC........ Exercise Control Center [*Military*] (AABC)
EXCCA...... Exceptional Children [*A publication*]
EXCELL.... Excellent (ADA)
EXCELS.... Expanded Communications - Electronics System [*DoD*]
Excep Child ... Exceptional Children [*A publication*]
Except Chil ... Exceptional Children [*A publication*]
Except Child ... Exceptional Child [*A publication*] (APTA)
Except Child Educ Abstr ... Exceptional Child Education Abstracts [*A
        publication*]
Except Child Educ Resour ... Exceptional Child Education Resources [*A
        publication*]
Except Infant ... Exceptional Infant [*A publication*]
Except Parent ... Exceptional Parent [*A publication*]
Excerp Bot ... Excerpta Botanica [*A publication*]
Excerp Criminol ... Excerpta Criminologica [*A publication*]
EXCERP e ROT FIN ... Excerpta e Rotulis Finium [*Extracts of Boundary
        Records*] [*A publication*] (ROG)

Excerpta Bot Sect A Taxon Chorol ... Excerpta Botanica. Sectio A. Taxonomica et Chorologica [*A publication*]
Excerpta Crim ... Excerpta Criminologica [*A publication*] (DLA)
Excerpta Criminol ... Excerpta Criminologica [*A publication*]
Excerpta Med (Amst) ... Excerpta Medica (Amsterdam) [*A publication*]
Excerpta Med Int Congr Ser ... Excerpta Medica. International Congress Series [*Amsterdam*] [*A publication*]
Excerpta Med Sect 1 ... Excerpta Medica. Section 1. Anatomy, Anthropology, Embryology, and Histology [*A publication*]
Excerpta Med Sect 2 ... Excerpta Medica. Section 2. Physiology [*A publication*]
Excerpta Med Sect 3 ... Excerpta Medica. Section 3. Endocrinology [*A publication*]
Excerpta Med Sect 4 ... Excerpta Medica. Section 4. Medical Microbiology and Hygiene [*A publication*]
Excerpta Med Sect 5 ... Excerpta Medica. Section 5. General Pathology and Pathological Anatomy [*A publication*]
Excerpta Med Sect 6 ... Excerpta Medica. Section 6. Internal Medicine [*A publication*]
Excerpta Med Sect 7 ... Excerpta Medica. Section 7. Pediatrics [*A publication*]
Excerpta Med Sect 8 ... Excerpta Medica. Section 8. Neurology and Psychiatry [*A publication*]
Excerpta Med Sect 9 ... Excerpta Medica. Section 9. Surgery [*A publication*]
Excerpta Med Sect 10 ... Excerpta Medica. Section 10. Obstetrics and Gynecology [*A publication*]
Excerpta Med Sect 11 ... Excerpta Medica. Section 11. Oto-Rhino-Laryngology [*A publication*]
Excerpta Med Sect 12 ... Excerpta Medica. Section 12. Ophthalmology [*A publication*]
Excerpta Med Sect 13 ... Excerpta Medica. Section 13. Dermatology and Venereology [*A publication*]
Excerpta Med Sect 14 ... Excerpta Medica. Section 14. Radiology [*A publication*]
Excerpta Med Sect 15 ... Excerpta Medica. Section 15. Chest Diseases, Thoracic Surgery, and Tuberculosis [*A publication*]
Excerpta Med Sect 16 ... Excerpta Medica. Section 16. Cancer [*A publication*]
Excerpta Med Sect 17 ... Excerpta Medica. Section 17. Public Health, Social Medicine, and Hygiene [*A publication*]
Excerpta Med Sect 23 ... Excerpta Medica. Section 23. Nuclear Medicine [*A publication*]
Excerpta Med Sect 29 ... Excerpta Medica. Section 29. Clinical Biochemistry [*A publication*]
Excerpta Med Sect 30 ... Excerpta Medica. Section 30. Pharmacology and Toxicology [*A publication*]
Excerpta Med Sect 2A ... Excerpta Medica. Section 2A. Physiology [*A publication*]
Excerpta Med Sect 2B ... Excerpta Medica. Section 2B. Biochemistry [*A publication*]
Excerpta Med Sect 2C ... Excerpta Medica. Section 2C. Pharmacology and Toxicology [*A publication*]
Excerpta Med Sect 4 Med Microbiol Immunol Serol ... Excerpta Medica. Section 4. Medical Microbiology, Immunology, and Serology [*A publication*]
Excg .... Exchange
EXCG .... Exchange Bancorp, Inc. [*NASDAQ symbol*] (NQ)
EXCG .... Exercise Control Group [*Military*] (AABC)
Exch .... Court of Exchequer [*England*] [*Legal term*] (DLA)
Exch .... English Exchequer Reports [*A publication*] (DLA)
Exch .... English Law Reports, Exchequer [*1866-75*] [*A publication*] (DLA)
EXCH .... Exchange [*Telecommunications*] (AFM)
EXCH .... Exchequer [*British*]
Exch .... Exchequer Division, High Court [*1875-80*] [*A publication*] (DLA)
Exch .... Exchequer Reports (Welsby, Hurlstone, and Gordon) [*A publication*] (DLA)
ExChAb ..... Exceptional Child Education Abstracts [*Later, ECER*] [*A publication*]
Exch C .... Canada Law Reports, Exchequer Court [*A publication*] (DLA)
Exch Can ... Canada Law Reports, Exchequer Court [*A publication*] (DLA)
Exch Cas .... Exchequer Cases [*Legacy duties, etc.*] [*Scotland*] [*A publication*] (DLA)
EXCH CHAM ... Exchequer Chamber [*Legal term*] (DLA)
Exch CR ..... Canada Law Reports, Exchequer Court [*A publication*] (DLA)
Exch Ct (Can) ... Canada Law Reports, Exchequer Court [*A publication*] (DLA)
Exch Div .... Exchequer Division, English Law Reports [*A publication*] (DLA)
Exch Div (Eng) ... Exchequer Division, English Law Reports [*A publication*] (DLA)
Exch Flower Nursery Gard Cent Trade ... Exchange for the Flower, Nursery, and Garden Center Trade [*A publication*]
EXCHO ..... Exchange Officer [*Air Force*]
EXCH P ..... Exchange of Property (DLA)
Exch Rep .... English Exchequer Reports [*A publication*] (DLA)
Exch Rep .... Exchequer Reports (Welsby, Hurlstone, and Gordon) [*A publication*] (DLA)
Exch Rep WH & G ... Exchequer Reports (Welsby, Hurlstone, and Gordon) [*A publication*] (DLA)
EXCIPLEX ... Excited State Complex [*LASER*] (IEEE)
EXCITE ..... Expanded with Computers and Information Technology

EXCL .... Exclamation
EXCL .... Exclude (MSA)
EXCL .... Excluding (EY)
EXCL .... Exclusive (AFM)
EXCLAM .. Exclamatory (ROG)
EXCLD ...... Exclude
EXCLG ...... Excluding (ROG)
EXCLU ...... Exclusive (MDG)
EXCLV ...... Exclusive (FAAC)
EXCO .... Executive Committee (IEEE)
EXCO .... Executive Council (ADA)
EXCOA ..... Explosives Corporation of America
EXCOM ..... Executive Committee [*National Security Council*]
EX COM ..... Extravagantes Communes [*A publication*] (DLA)
EXCOMM ... Exterior Communications [*Military*] (CAAL)
EXCOMMS ... Extended Communications Search [*Navy*] (NVT)
EXCOMP ... National Executive Compensation Database [*Information service or system*] (EISS)
EXCP .... Except (FAAC)
EXCP .... Execute Channel Program [*Data processing*]
EXCPT ...... Exception
Ex CR .... Canada Exchequer Court Reports [*1875-1922*] [*A publication*] (DLA)
Ex CR .... Canada Law Reports, Exchequer Court [*A publication*] (DLA)
Ex C R .... Exchequer Court Reports [*Canada*] [*A publication*]
EXCSV ...... Excessive (MSA)
EXCT .... Execute (FAAC)
EXCTR ...... Exciter [*Electricity*]
Exctr .... Executor
EXCUR ...... Excursion (KSC)
Excursions Rec Math Ser ... Excursions in Recreational Mathematics Series [*A publication*]
ex d .... Ex-Dividende [*Ex-Dividend*] [*Finance*] [*French*]
EX D .... Ex Dividendum [*Without the right to dividend*] [*Finance*] (ROG)
EXD .... Examined
EXD .... Expeditor Resource Group Ltd. [*Vancouver Stock Exchange symbol*]
EXD .... External Device [*Data processing*]
Ex D .... Law Reports, Exchequer Division [*England*] [*A publication*] (DLA)
EXDAMS ... Extendable Debugging and Monitoring System [*Data processing*]
EXDIR ...... Exercise Director (CINC)
EXDIS ...... Exclusive Distribution [*Military security classification*] (AFM)
EX DIV ...... Ex-Dividend [*Without the right to dividend*] [*Finance*]
EXDIV ...... Experimental Division
Ex Div .... Law Reports, Exchequer Division [*England*] [*A publication*] (ILCA)
EXDLVY .... Expedite Delivery (FAAC)
ex dr .... Ex-Droits [*Ex-Rights*] [*Finance*] [*French*]
EXE .... Executable Program File [*Data processing*]
EXE .... Execute (ROG)
EXE .... Executive [*A publication*]
EXE .... Exeter [*British depot code*]
EXE .... Kent County Library and Kent County Library System, Grand Rapids, MI [*OCLC symbol*] (OCLC)
EXEC .... Execute (MSA)
EXEC .... Executive (EY)
Exec .... Executive [*A publication*]
EXEC .... Executive Appointments [*Database*] [*Australia*]
EXEC .... Executor
EXEC1 .... President on Board Civil Aircraft [*Aviation designator*] (FAAC)
EXEC2 .... Vice President on Board Civil Aircraft [*Aviation designator*] (FAAC)
Exec Disclosure Guide CCH ... Executive Disclosure Guide. Commerce Clearing House [*A publication*]
Exec Doc .... Executive Document [*Legal term*] (DLA)
EXEC1F .... President's Family on Board Civil Aircraft [*Aviation designator*] (FAAC)
EXEC2F .... Vice President's Family on Board Civil Aircraft [*Aviation designator*] (FAAC)
Exec Female ... Executive Female [*A publication*]
Exec Fit Newsl ... Executive Fitness Newsletter [*A publication*]
Exec Housekeeper ... Executive Housekeeper [*A publication*]
Exec Housekeeping Today ... Executive Housekeeping Today [*A publication*]
Exec Mem Jogger ... Executive's Memory Jogger [*A publication*]
EXECO ...... Executive Officer
Exec Reprt ... Executive Report [*A publication*]
Exec Sci Inst ... Executive Sciences Institute [*A publication*]
Executive Eng ... Executive Engineer [*A publication*]
EXECX ...... Executrix
EXED .... Executed (ROG)
EXEL .... Excel Interfinancial Corp. [*NASDAQ symbol*] (NQ)
EXELFS ..... Extended Electron Loss Fine Structure [*Spectrometry*]
EXEMP ..... Exemption (DLA)
Exempt Org Rep CCH ... Exempt Organizations Reports. Commerce Clearing House [*A publication*]
EXEOD ..... Expects to Enter on Duty (NOAA)
EXER .... Exercise (AABC)

Exercise Sport Sci Rev ... Exercise and Sport Sciences Reviews [A publication]
Exerc Sport Sci Rev ... Exercise and Sport Sciences Reviews [A publication]
Exer Pat..... Exercices de la Patience [A publication]
EXES........ Expenses (ROG)
EXET........ Exeter College [Oxford University] (ROG)
Exeter Papers Econ Hist ... Exeter Papers on Economic History [A
          publication]
EXF........... Executive Female [A publication]
EXF........... External Function
EXF........... Toledo, OH [Location identifier] [FAA] (FAAL)
EXFAS ...... Extended Fine Auger Structure [Physics]
EXFINCO .... Export Finance Co. [British]
EXFOD....... Explosive Foxhole Digger [Army] (INF)
EXG.......... Air Exchange, Inc. [Dallas, TX] [FAA designator] (FAAC)
EX G .... Ex Grege [Among the Rest] [Latin] (ROG)
EXG.......... Exchange Two Registers [Data processing]
EX G .... Exempli Gratia [For Example] [Latin] (ROG)
EXG.......... Exhibition Bulletin [A publication]
EXG.......... Existing [Technical drawings]
EXG.......... Grand Valley State College, Allendale, MI [OCLC
          symbol] (OCLC)
EXGA .... External Gauge
EXGEA..... Experimental Gerontology [A publication]
EXGO....... Export Guarantee Office [Export credit agency] [New Zealand]
EX GR .... Exempli Gratia [For Example] [Latin]
EXH.......... Exhaust (KSC)
EXH.......... Exhibit
EXH.......... Hope College, Holland, MI [OCLC symbol] (OCLC)
Exhaust Gas Air Pollut Abs ... Exhaust Gas and Air Pollution Abstracts [A
          publication]
EXHBN ..... Exhibition
EXHBNR .. Exhibitioner (ROG)
EXHE....... Executive Health [A publication]
EXHEB...... Experimental Hematology [A publication]
EXHIB...... Exhibetur [Let It Be Given] [Pharmacy]
EXHIB...... Exhibited [or Exhibition]
EXHIB...... Exhibitioner (ROG)
Exhib & Conf Gaz ... Exhibitions and Conferences Gazette [A publication]
Exhibition Bull ... Exhibition Bulletin [A publication]
Ex H Lec.... Exeter Hall Lectures [A publication]
EXHN....... Exhibition
EXHS........ Executive House, Inc. [NASDAQ symbol] (NQ)
EXHST...... Exhaust
EXHV....... Exhaust Vent
EXI........... Excursion Inlet [Alaska] [Airport symbol] (OAG)
EXI........... Excursion Inlet, AK [Location identifier] [FAA] (FAAL)
EXI........... Whirlpool Corp., Technical Information Center, Benton
          Harbor, MI [OCLC symbol] (OCLC)
EXID........ Exidyne, Inc. [NASDAQ symbol] (NQ)
EX IDON CRASS LIQ ... Ex Idoneo Crasso Liquido [In a Suitable Thick
          Liquid] [Pharmacy]
EX IDON LIQ ... Ex Idoneo Liquido [In a Suitable Liquid] [Pharmacy]
Ex Il .... Express Ilustrowany [A publication]
EXIM........ Export-Import Bank
EXIMBANK ... Export-Import Bank
EXIMBK ... Export-Import Bank
EXIS .... Expert Information Systems Ltd. [Information service or
          system] (IID)
EXIST....... Existing
Exist Psychiat ... Existential Psychiatry [A publication]
EXIX......... Executrix (ROG)
EXJAM...... Expendable Communications Jammer [Army] (INF)
EXJO........ Explorers Journal [A publication]
EXK .... Kalamazoo College, Kalamazoo, MI [OCLC symbol] (OCLC)
EXKTA ..... Exaktn [A publication]
EXL........... Exall Resources Ltd. [Toronto Stock Exchange symbol]
EXL........... Western Michigan University, School of Librarianship,
          Kalamazoo, MI [OCLC symbol] (OCLC)
EX LIB...... Ex Libris [From the Library Of] [Book plate] [Latin] (ROG)
EXLL .... Excel Energy Corp. [NASDAQ symbol] (NQ)
EXLN .... Excelan, Inc. [NASDAQ symbol] (NQ)
EXLST...... Exit List [Data processing]
EXLV........ Excess Leave [Military]
EXM .... Exempt
EXM .... Exhaust Muffler
EXM .... Expense Management and Control, Inc. [Vancouver Stock
          Exchange symbol]
EXM .... Export Markt [A publication]
EX Mag ..... EX Magazine [A publication]
EXMDA ...... International Congress Series. Excerpta Medica [A publication]
EX-MER ... Ex-Meridian [Navigation]
EXMETNET ... Experimental Meteorological Sounding Rocket Research
          Network (IEEE)
EXMOVREP ... Expedited Movement Report [Army] (AABC)
EXMP........ Expanded Metal Plate [Technical drawings]
EXMR .... Examiner
EXN .... Andrews University, Berrien Springs, MI [OCLC
          symbol] (OCLC)
EXNEA...... Experimental Neurology [A publication]
EXO .... Executive Officer
Exo............ Exodus [Old Testament book] (DSA)

EXO........... Exonuclease [An enzyme]
EXO........... Experiment Operator (MCD)
ExO........... Experimental Officer [Also, EO, XO] [Ministry of Agriculture,
          Fisheries, and Food] [British]
EXO........... Extotal Resources, Inc. [Vancouver Stock Exchange symbol]
EXO........... Olivet College, Olivet, MI [OCLC symbol] (OCLC)
Exod.......... Exodus [Old Testament book]
EX OFF ..... Ex Officio [By Virtue of Office] [Latin] (ROG)
EX OFFICIN ... Ex Officina [From the Workshop Of] [Latin] (ROG)
EXOIII........ Exonuclease III [An enzyme]
EXON........ Execution (ROG)
EXON........ Exonia [Exeter] [British]
Exon.......... Exoniensis [Of Exeter] [Latin] (ILCA)
EXON........ Exxon USA [A publication]
EXON D.... Exeter Domesday Book [A publication] (ROG)
EXOP .... Executive Office of the President
EXOP .... Experiment and Operations (KSC)
EXOR .... Exclusive Or [Gates] [Data processing]
EXOR .... Executor (ROG)
EXORD ..... Exercise Order [Military] (AFM)
EXOS .... Executive Office of the Secretary [Navy]
EXOS .... Executive Operating System [Military] (CAAL)
EXOS .... Exospheric Satellite [Japan]
EXOX........ Executrix
EXP........... Du Pont [E. I.] De Nemours & Co., Inc. [Research code
          symbol]
EX P........... Ex Parte [One-Sided Statement] [Latin] [Legal term] (ROG)
EXP........... Expand (NASA)
EXP........... Expansion (KSC)
EXP........... Expect
EXP........... Expectorant [Pharmacy] (ROG)
EXP........... Expectorated [Medicine]
Exp........... Expedie [Shipped] [Business term] [French]
EXP........... Expedition (ADA)
EXP........... Expend
EXP........... Expense (AABC)
EXP........... Experienced
Exp........... Experientia [A publication]
EXP........... Experiment (KSC)
Exp........... Experiment [A publication]
EXP........... Expert
EXP........... Expired (ROG)
Exp........... Explained [Legal term] (DLA)
Exp........... Explicator [A publication]
EXP........... Explosive
EXP........... Exponential
EXP........... Export
EXP........... Export [A publication]
EXP........... Expose (KSC)
EXP........... Exposition of the Blessed Sacrament [Roman Catholic]
Exp........... Expositor [A publication]
Exp........... Express [A publication]
EXP........... Express (AABC)
Exp........... Expropriation [Legal term] (DLA)
EXP........... Expulsion (KSC)
EXP........... Expurgated
EXP........... Orgue Expressif [Swell Organ] [Music]
EXP........... Portage Public Schools, Portage, MI [OCLC symbol] (OCLC)
EXP........... Transco Exploration Partnership Ltd. [NYSE symbol] (SPSG)
Exp Ag ...... Experimental Agriculture [A publication]
Exp Aging Res ... Experimental Aging Research [A publication]
Exp Agric... Experimental Agriculture [A publication]
Exp An....... Experimental Animals [A publication]
Exp Anim... Experimentation Animale [A publication]
Exp Anim (Tokyo) ... Experimental Animals (Jikken Dobutsu) (Tokyo) [A
          publication]
Expansion Reg ... Expansion Regionale [A publication]
Expans Region ... Expansion Regionale [A publication]
Expans Region (Paris) ... Expansion Regionale (Paris) [A publication]
Exp & Appl Acarol ... Experimental and Applied Acarology [A publication]
Ex Paras ... Experimental Parasitology [A publication]
EXPAT ...... Expatriate (DSUE)
ExpB......... [The] Expositor's Bible [A publication] (BJA)
Exp Biol ... Experimental Biology [A publication]
Exp Biol (Berl) ... Experimental Biology (Berlin) [A publication]
Exp Biol Med ... Experimental Biology and Medicine [A publication]
Exp Bot ...... Experimental Botany [A publication]
Exp Bot Int Ser Monogr ... Experimental Botany: An International Series of
          Monographs [A publication]
Exp Brain R ... Experimental Brain Research [A publication]
Exp Brain Res ... Experimental Brain Research [A publication]
Exp Brain Res Suppl ... Experimental Brain Research. Supplementum [A
          publication]
EXPC......... Expect (FAAC)
EXPC......... Experience (AABC)
Exp Cell Biol ... Experimental Cell Biology [A publication]
Exp Cell Re ... Experimental Cell Research [A publication]
Exp Cell Res ... Experimental Cell Research [A publication]
Exp Cell Res Suppl ... Experimental Cell Research. Supplement [A
          publication]
Exp Cereb .. Experimentation Cerebrale [A publication]

Exp Chem Thermodyn ... Experimental Chemical Thermodynamics [*A publication*]

Exp Clin Endocrinol ... Experimental and Clinical Endocrinology [*A publication*]

Exp Clin Im ... Experimental and Clinical Immunogenetics [*A publication*]

Exp Clin Immunogenet ... Experimental and Clinical Immunogenetics [*A publication*]

Exp CR ...... Experimental Cell Research [*A publication*]

EXPD......... Expeditors International of Washington, Inc. [*Seattle, WA*] [*NASDAQ symbol*] (NQ)

EXPD......... Expired (ROG)

EXPD......... Exposed

EXPDIVUNIT ... Experimental Diving Unit

EXPDN ..... Expedition

EXPEA ...... Experientia [*A publication*]

EXPED...... Expediting

Exped........ Expedition [*A publication*]

EXPED...... Expeditionary

Expedition ... Expedition Bulletin. University Museum. University of Pennsylvania [*A publication*]

EXPELS.... Expandable Precision Emitter Location System (MCD)

Exp Embryol Teratol ... Experimental Embryology and Teratology [*A publication*]

EXPEN...... Expendable (MSA)

EXPEND... Expenditure

EXPER ...... Experienced

Exper .... Experientia [*A publication*]

EXPER ...... Experiment (AFM)

Exper .... Experimental Light [*Navigation signal*]

Exper Agric ... Experimental Agriculture [*A publication*]

Experien..... Experiences. Bulletin. Section Belgoluxembourgeoise du Centre International de Recherches et d'Information sur l'Economie Collective [*A publication*]

Experiment Tech Phys ... Experimentelle Technik der Physik [*A publication*]

Exper Mech ... Experimental Mechanics [*A publication*]

Exper Med Surg ... Experimental Medicine and Surgery [*A publication*]

Exper Neurol ... Experimental Neurology [*A publication*]

Exper Parasitol ... Experimental Parasitology [*A publication*]

Exper Suppl ... Experientia Supplementum [*A publication*]

Exper Suppl (Basel) ... Experientia Supplementum (Basel) [*A publication*]

EXPERT.... Expanded Program Evaluation and Review Technique

Exp Eye Res ... Experimental Eye Research [*A publication*]

Exp Fluids ... Experiments in Fluids [*A publication*]

Exp Geront ... Experimental Gerontology [*A publication*]

Exp Gerontol ... Experimental Gerontology [*A publication*]

ExPGN ...... Extracapillary Proliferative Glomerulonephritis [*Nephrology*]

ExpGT .... [*The*] Expositor's Greek Testament [*A publication*] (BJA)

Exp Hemat ... Experimental Hematology [*A publication*]

Exp Hematol ... Experimental Hematology [*Lawrence, Kansas*] [*A publication*]

Exp Hematol (Copenh) ... Experimental Hematology (Copenhagen) [*A publication*]

Exp Hematol (NY) ... Experimental Hematology (New York) [*A publication*]

Exp Hematol (Oak Ridge Tenn) ... Experimental Hematology (Oak Ridge, Tennessee) [*A publication*]

Exp Hirnforsch ... Experimentelle Hirnforschung [*A publication*]

EXPHO ..... Expedite Delivery by Telephone (FAAC)

Exp Hort .... Experimental Horticulture [*A publication*]

Exp Hortic ... Experimental Horticulture [*A publication*]

Exp Husb... Experimental Husbandry [*A publication*]

EXPIR .... Expiration [*or Expiratory*] [*Medicine*]

EXPL......... Explanation

Expl........... Explicator [*A publication*]

EXPL......... Explore. Alberta's Outdoor Magazine [*A publication*]

EXPL......... Explorer

EXPL......... Explosive (KSC)

Expl Agric ... Experimental Agriculture [*A publication*]

EXPLAN ... Exercise Plan [*Military*] (AFM)

EXPLAN ... Explanatory (ADA)

Explan Leafl Intervention Bd Agric Prod ... Explanatory Leaflet. Intervention Board for Agricultural Produce [*A publication*]

Exp Lap ..... Exploratory Laparatomy [*Medicine*]

Expl Brain Res ... Experimental Brain Research [*A publication*]

Expl Cell Res ... Experimental Cell Research [*A publication*]

EXPLD...... Explained (ROG)

EXPLD...... Explode (MSA)

Expl Ec His ... Explorations in Economic History [*A publication*]

EXPLET ..... Expletive (ROG)

Expl Gerontol ... Experimental Gerontology [*A publication*]

Expl Hort... Experimental Horticulture [*A publication*]

Expl Husb ... Experimental Husbandry [*A publication*]

EXPLN ...... Explosion (MSA)

EXPLO...... Explosive (AABC)

Explo Econ Hist ... Explorations in Economic History [*A publication*]

EXPLOR ... Explicit 2-D Patterns Local Operations and Randomness [*Programming language*] [*1975*] (CSR)

Explor .... Explorations [*A publication*]

Explorations Econ Hist ... Explorations in Economic History [*A publication*]

Explorations Econ Research ... Explorations in Economic Research [*A publication*]

Explor Econ Hist ... Explorations in Economic History [*A publication*]

Explor Econ Pet Ind ... Exploration and Economics of the Petroleum Industry [*A publication*]

Explor Econ Petrol Ind ... Exploration and Economics of the Petroleum Industry [*A publication*]

Explor Econ Res ... Explorations in Economic Research [*A publication*]

Explor Entrep Hist ... Explorations in Entrepreneurial History [*A publication*]

Explor Geophys ... Exploration Geophysics [*A publication*]

Explor Geophys (USSR) ... Exploration Geophysics (USSR) [*A publication*]

Explor J ..... Explorers Journal [*A publication*]

Explor Parc Nat A ... Exploration du Parc National Albert [*A publication*]

explos......... Explosive

Explos Anch ... Explosive Anchorage [*Buoy*]

Explos Eng ... Explosives Engineer [*A publication*]

Explosives Eng ... Explosives Engineer [*A publication*]

Explosivst.. Explosivstoffe [*A publication*]

Expl Parasit ... Experimental Parasitology [*A publication*]

Expl Path... Experimental Pathology [*A publication*]

EXPLR ...... Exploder

Expl Rec Dep Agric S Aust ... Experimental Record. Department of Agriculture. South Australia [*A publication*] (APTA)

Expl Text L ... Explicacion de Textos Literarios [*A publication*]

Exp Lung Res ... Experimental Lung Research [*A publication*]

Exp Mech .. Experimental Mechanics [*A publication*]

Exp Med Microbiol ... Experimental Medicine and Microbiology [*A publication*]

Exp Med Microbiol (Engl Transl Med Dosw Mikrobiol) ... Experimental Medicine and Microbiology (English Translation of Medycyna Doswiadczalna i Mikrobiologia) [*A publication*]

Exp Med Pathol Klin ... Experimentelle Medizin, Pathologie, und Klinik [*A publication*]

Exp Med Surg ... Experimental Medicine and Surgery [*A publication*]

Exp Molec Path ... Experimental and Molecular Pathology [*A publication*]

Exp Molecul Pathol ... Experimental and Molecular Pathology [*A publication*]

Exp Mol Pat ... Experimental and Molecular Pathology [*A publication*]

Exp Mol Pathol ... Experimental and Molecular Pathology [*A publication*]

Exp Mol Pathol Suppl ... Experimental and Molecular Pathology. Supplement [*A publication*]

Exp Mycol ... Experimental Mycology [*A publication*]

EXPN .... Expansion [*Automotive engineering*]

EXPN .... Expiration (ROG)

EXPN .... Exposition

EXPND ..... Expenditure (AFM)

Exp Neurol ... Experimental Neurology [*A publication*]

Exp Neurol Suppl ... Experimental Neurology. Supplement [*A publication*]

EXPNT...... Exponent (MSA)

EXPNT...... Exponential (MSA)

Exp Nucl Phys ... Experimental Nuclear Physics [*A publication*]

Exp (NY) ... Export (New York) [*A publication*]

EXPO .... Experimental Order (MSA)

EXPO .... Exposition

EXPO .... Expressivo [*With Expression*] [*Music*] (ROG)

EXPO .... Extended-Range Poseidon [*Missile*] [*Navy*]

EXPO .... Insteel Industries, Inc. [*NASDAQ symbol*] (NQ)

Expo Annu Biochim Med ... Exposes Annuels de Biochimie Medicale [*A publication*]

Export Dir ... Export Direction [*A publication*]

Export Nws ... Export News [*A publication*]

Export Rev Br Drug Chem Ind ... Export Review of the British Drug and Chemical Industries [*A publication*]

Exports of Aust ... Exports of Australia [*A publication*] (APTA)

Exports of Aust & NZ ... Exports of Australia and New Zealand [*A publication*] (APTA)

Expos .... Expositor [*A publication*]

Expos Ann Biochim Med ... Exposes Annuels de Biochimie Medicale [*A publication*]

Expos Annu Biochim Med ... Exposes Annuels de Biochimie Medicale [*A publication*]

EXPOSE ... Ex-Partners of Servicemen (Women) for Equality (EA)

Exposit Tim ... Expository Times [*A publication*]

Expos T...... Expository Times [*A publication*]

Exp Parasit ... Experimental Parasitology [*A publication*]

Exp Parasitol ... Experimental Parasitology [*A publication*]

Exp Path.... Experimentelle Pathologie [*A publication*]

Exp Pathol ... Experimentelle Pathologie [*A publication*]

Exp Pathol (Jena) ... Experimental Pathology (Jena) [*A publication*]

Exp Pathol Suppl ... Experimental Pathology. Supplement [*A publication*]

Exp Physiol Biochem ... Experiments in Physiology and Biochemistry [*A publication*]

Exp Progr Grassland Res Inst (Hurley) ... Experiments in Progress. Grassland Research Institute (Hurley) [*A publication*]

ExpQualBad ... Expert Qualification Badge [*Military decoration*] (AABC)

Exp R .... Expatriate Review [*A publication*]

EXPR........ Expire (AABC)

EXPR........ Expression

EXPR........ Orgue Expressif [*Swell Organ*] [*Music*]

Exp Rec Dep Agric S Aust ... Experimental Record. Department of Agriculture. South Australia [*A publication*]

Exp Rep Equine Health Lab ... Experimental Reports of Equine Health Laboratory [*A publication*]

Exp Rep Min Agr Natur Resour (Nigeria) Midwest Reg ... Experiment Report. Ministry of Agriculture and Natural Resources (Nigeria). Midwest Region [*A publication*]

EXPRES.... Experimental Research in Electronic Submission of Scientific Documents Program [*Washington, DC*] [*National Science Foundation*]

Express-Ne ... Express-News [*A publication*]

Express Transl Serv List ... Express Translation Service List [*A publication*]

EXPRO...... Experiment Procedures (KSC)

ExPro ...... Exploratory Project on the Conditions of Peace (EA)

EXPS........ Expenses (ROG)

EXPS........ Express (FAAC)

EXPSAS.... Engineering Change Proposal Service Action Status (AAG)

Exp Ship Guide ... Export Shipping Guide [*A publication*] (APTA)

EXPSN...... Expansion

EXPSR...... Exposure (MSA)

Exp Sta Record ... Experiment Station Record [*A publication*]

Exp Stn Rec ... Experiment Station Record. United States Department of Agriculture [*A publication*]

Exp St Rec ... Experiment Station Record [*Washington, DC*] [*A publication*]

EXPT........ Expect (AABC)

EXPT........ Expectorant [*Pharmacy*]

EXPT........ Experiment

ExpT........ Expository Times [*A publication*]

EXPTE...... Ex Parte [*One-Sided Statement*] [*Latin*] [*Legal term*] (ROG)

Exp Tech... Experimental Techniques [*A publication*]

Exp Tech Phys ... Experimentelle Technik der Physik [*East Germany*] [*A publication*]

ExpTim...... Expository Times [*Edinburgh*] [*A publication*]

EXPTL...... Experimental

EXPTO...... Expedite Travel Order (NOAA)

EXPTR...... Exporter (ADA)

EXPURG... Expurgated (ADA)

Exp Veterinaermed ... Experimentelle Veterinaermedizin [*A publication*]

EXPY........ Expressway (MCD)

EXQ.......... Aquinas College, Grand Rapids, MI [*OCLC symbol*] (OCLC)

EXQ.......... Ex Quay [*Seller's responsibility is to make goods available on the wharf at destination named*] [*"INCOTERM," International Chamber of Commerce official code*]

EXR .... Chapman Air, Inc. [*Oviedo, FL*] [*FAA designator*] (FAAC)

Ex R .... Ex-Rights [*Without Rights*] [*Investment term*]

EXR .... Execute and Repeat

EXR .... Executor

ExR .... Exodus Rabbah (BJA)

EXR .... Express Resources Ltd. [*Vancouver Stock Exchange symbol*]

EXR .... Grand Rapids Public Library, Grand Rapids, MI [*OCLC symbol*] (OCLC)

EXRAY...... [*Audio*] Expendable Relay (MCD)

EXREDCON ... Exercise Readiness Condition [*Military*] (AABC)

EX REL...... Ex Relatione [*On the Report Of*] [*Latin*] (ADA)

EXREM..... External REM [*Roentgen-Equivalent-Man*] [*Radiology*]

EXREP...... Expedite Mail Reply (FAAC)

EXREQ...... Extract of Requisition

EXRX...... Executrix

Exs............ De Exsecrationibus [*Philo*] (BJA)

EXS.......... Ex Ship [*Seller's responsibility is to make goods available on board ship at destination named*] [*"INCOTERM," International Chamber of Commerce official code*]

EXS.......... Executive Skills [*A publication*]

ExS .... Exogenous Substance [*Biology*]

EXS.......... Expenses

EXS.......... Extrastrong [*Technical drawings*]

EXS.......... Western Theological Seminary, Holland, MI [*OCLC symbol*] (OCLC)

EX SC ...... Ex Senatus Consulto [*By Decree of the Senate*] [*Latin*] (ROG)

EX SD...... Ex Senatus Decreto [*By Decree of the Senate*] [*Latin*] (ROG)

EXSEC...... Extra Section (FAAC)

EXSH .... Expeditionary Shelters [*Marine Corps*] (MCD)

EXSHI....... Expedite Shipment (NOAA)

EXSL .... Exhibition of Sports and Leisure [*British*] (ITD)

EXSP .... Extracts from the Soviet Press on the Soviet North and Antarctic [*A publication*]

EXSPEC.... Exercise Specification [*NATO*] (NATG)

EXST .... Existing (MSA)

EXSTA ..... Experimental Station

EXSUM..... Executive Summary (MCD)

EXT .... Except (ROG)

EXT .... Exeter [*England*] [*Airport symbol*] (OAG)

EXT .... Experiment Terminal (MCD)

Ex T .... Expository Times [*A publication*]

EXT .... Extant

EXT .... Extend [*or Extension*] (AFM)

EXT .... Extende [*Spread*] [*Pharmacy*]

EXT .... Extension

EXT .... Extensor [*Anatomy*]

EXT .... Exterior (AABC)

EXT .... External (AABC)

EXT .... Extinct

EXT .... Extinguish (KSC)

EXT .... Extortion [*FBI standardized term*]

EXT .... Extra

EXT .... Extract [*or Extracted*]

EXT .... Extractum [*Extract*] [*Latin*]

EXT .... Extraordinary

Ext............ Extrapolation [*A publication*]

EXT .... Extreme

EXT .... Extremity [*Medicine*]

Ext Abstr Conf Solid State Devices Mater ... Extended Abstracts. Conference on Solid State Devices and Materials [*A publication*]

EXTAC...... Experimental Tactic (NVT)

Ext Affairs ... External Affairs [*A publication*]

EXTAL...... Extra Time Allowance

EXT sup ALUT MOLL ... Extende super Alutum Mollem [*Spread upon Soft Leather*] [*Pharmacy*] (ROG)

Ext Amer ... Extension en las Americas [*A publication*]

Ext Bull Agric Ext Serv Univ Minn ... Extension Bulletin. Agriculture Extension Service. University of Minnesota [*A publication*]

Ext Bull Cornell Agric Exp Stn ... Extension Bulletin. Cornell Agricultural Experiment Station [*A publication*]

Ext Bull Del Univ Agr Ext Serv ... Extension Bulletin. Delaware University. Agricultural Extension Service [*A publication*]

Ext Bull Dep Agric S Aust ... Extension Bulletin. Department of Agriculture. South Australia [*A publication*] (APTA)

Ext Bull Dept Agric South Aust ... Extension Bulletin. Department of Agriculture and Fisheries. South Australia [*A publication*] (APTA)

Ext Bull E Coop Ext Serv Mich State Univ ... Extension Bulletin E. Cooperative Extension Service. Michigan State University [*A publication*]

Ext Bull Flor Agric Exp St ... Extension Bulletin. Florida Agricultural Experiment Station [*A publication*]

Ext Bull Ind Agric Exp Stn ... Extension Bulletin. Indiana Agricultural Experiment Station [*A publication*]

Ext Bull Iowa State Univ ... Extension Bulletin. Iowa State University [*A publication*]

Ext Bull MD Univ Coop Ext Serv ... Extension Bulletin. Maryland University. Cooperative Extension Service [*A publication*]

Ext Bull Mich State Univ Coop Ext Serv ... Extension Bulletin. Michigan State University. Cooperative Extension Service [*A publication*]

Ext Bull Mich St Coll ... Extension Bulletin. Michigan State College [*A publication*]

Ext Bull Ohio State Univ Coll Agr Coop Ext Serv ... Extension Bulletin. Ohio State University. College of Agriculture. Cooperative Extension Service [*A publication*]

Ext Bull Ohio St Univ ... Extension Bulletin. Ohio State University [*A publication*]

Ext Bull Oreg State Univ Coop Ext Serv ... Extension Bulletin. Oregon State University. Cooperative Extension Service [*A publication*]

Ext Bull Purdue Univ Dep Agric Ext ... Extension Bulletin. Purdue University. Department of Agricultural Extension [*A publication*]

Ext Bull Univ MD Coop Ext Serv ... Extension Bulletin. University of Maryland. Cooperative Extension Service [*A publication*]

Ext Bull Univ Minn Agr Ext Serv ... Extension Bulletin. University of Minnesota. Agricultural Extension Service [*A publication*]

Ext Bull Univ Minn Agric Ext Serv ... Extension Bulletin. University of Minnesota. Agricultural Extension Service [*A publication*]

Ext Bull US Dep Agric ... Extension Bulletin. United States Department of Agriculture [*A publication*]

Ext Bull Wash State Univ Coll Agr Ext Serv ... Extension Bulletin. Washington State University. College of Agriculture. Extension Service [*A publication*]

Ext Bull Wash St Coll ... Extension Bulletin. Washington State College [*A publication*]

Ext Circ Ark Coll Agric ... Extension Circular. Arkansas College of Agriculture [*A publication*]

Ext Circ Ill Univ ... Extension Circular. Illinois University [*A publication*]

Ext Circ N Carol Agric Exp Stn ... Extension Circular. North Carolina Agricultural Experiment Station [*A publication*]

Ext Circ NC State Univ Agr Ext Serv ... Extension Circular. North Carolina State University. Agricultural Extension Service [*A publication*]

Ext Circ Oreg State Univ Ext Serv ... Extension Circular. Oregon State University. Extension Service [*A publication*]

Ext Circ PA St Coll Agric ... Extension Circular. Pennsylvania State College. School of Agriculture [*A publication*]

Ext Circ P Auburn Univ Agr Ext Serv ... Extension Circular P. Auburn University. Agricultural Extension Service [*A publication*]

Ext Circ Purdue Univ Coop Ext Serv ... Extension Circular. Purdue University. Cooperative Extension Service [*A publication*]

Ext Circ Purdue Univ Dept Agr Ext ... Extension Circular. Purdue University. Department of Agricultural Extension [*A publication*]

Ext Circ S Dak Coll Agric ... Extension Circular. South Dakota College of Agriculture [*A publication*]

Ext Circ S Dak State Univ Coop Ext Serv ... Extension Circular. South Dakota State University. Cooperative Extension Service [*A publication*]

Ext Circ Utah Agric Coll ... Extension Circular. Utah Agricultural College [*A publication*]

Ext Circ Wash State Univ Coll Agr Ext Serv ... Extension Circular. Washington State University. College of Agriculture. Extension Service [*A publication*]

Ext Circ Wash State Univ Coop Ext Serv ... Extension Circular. Washington State University. Cooperative Extension Service [*A publication*]

Ext Course Lect Ak Prim Assoc ... Extension Course Lectures. Auckland Primary Principals Association [*A publication*]

EXTD .... Extend [*or Extended*] (KSC)

EXTD .... Extracted

EXTD .... Extrude (MSA)

EXT D & C ... External Drug and Cosmetic [*Color*]

Ext Dev Unit Rep ... Extension Development Unit Report [*A publication*]

EXTEL ...... Exchange Telegraph [*Press agency*] [*British*] (DCTA)

Extel Handbook Mark Leaders ... Extel Handbook of Market Leaders [*A publication*]

Extended Abstr Program Bienn Conf Carbon ... Extended Abstracts and Program. Biennial Conference on Carbon [*A publication*]

EXTENL ... Extension of Enlistment [*Military*]

Extensn ...... Extension [*A publication*]

EXTER ...... External (KSC)

Exter Ca ..... Lobingier's Extra-Territorial Cases [*United States Court for China*] [*A publication*] (DLA)

Exterm Log ... Exterminators' Log [*A publication*]

External Stud Gaz ... External Studies Gazette [*A publication*] (APTA)

External Studies Gaz ... External Studies Gazette [*A publication*] (APTA)

Externer Ber Kernforschungszentr Karlsruhe ... Externer Bericht. Kernforschungszentrum Karlsruhe [*A publication*]

Externer Ber Kernforschungszentrum Karlsruhe ... Externer Bericht. Kernforschungszentrum Karlsruhe [*A publication*]

EXTERRA ... Extraterrestrial Research Agency [*Army*] (IEEE)

Ext Facts Coop Ext Serv Oklahoma State Univ ... Oklahoma State University. Cooperative Extension Service. Extension Facts [*A publication*]

Ext Folder Mich State Univ Agr Appl Sci Coop Ext Serv ... Extension Folder. Michigan State University of Agriculture and Applied Science. Cooperative Extension Service [*A publication*]

Ext Folder Mich St Univ ... Extension Folder. Michigan State University [*A publication*]

Ext Folder NC Agric Ext Serv ... Extension Folder. North Carolina Agricultural Extension Service [*A publication*]

Ext Folder NC State Univ Agr Ext Serv ... Extension Folder. North Carolina State University. Agricultural Extension Service [*A publication*]

Ext Folder Univ Minn Agr Ext Serv ... Extension Folder. University of Minnesota. Agricultural Extension Service [*A publication*]

Ext Folder Univ NH Coll Agr Ext Serv ... Extension Folder. University of New Hampshire. College of Agriculture. Extension Service [*A publication*]

EXTFP .... Experienced Teacher Fellowship Program

EXTG .... Extinguish (AAG)

EXTG .... Extracting (MSA)

EXTGH ..... Extinguish

EXTGR ...... Extinguisher (AAG)

EXTHEO .. Extra-Theoretical [*Telecommunications*] (TEL)

EXTIN .... Extinguish (ROG)

EXTING .... Extinguish (KSC)

Exting .... Extinguished Light [*Navigation signal*]

EXTL .... Executive TeleCard Ltd. [*NASDAQ symbol*] (NQ)

ExTL .... Explicacion de Textos Literarios [*A publication*]

EXTL .... External (DLA)

Ext Leafl Ohio State Univ Coll Agr Coop Ext Serv ... Extension Leaflet. Ohio State University. College of Agriculture. Cooperative Extension Service [*A publication*]

Ext Leafl Utah State Univ Agr Ext Serv ... Extension Leaflet. Utah State University. Agricultural Extension Service [*A publication*]

Ext Leafl Utah St Univ ... Extension Leaflet. Utah State University [*A publication*]

EXT LRCP ... Extra Licentiate of the Royal College of Physicians [*British*] (ROG)

EXTLV ...... Extension of Leave [*Military*] (AABC)

EXTM .... Ex Testamento [*In Accordance with the Testament Of*] [*Latin*]

EXTM .... Extended Telecommunications Modules

EXTM .... Extreme

Ext Mimeogr Circ S Dak State Univ Coop Ext Serv ... Extension Mimeographed Circular. South Dakota State University. Cooperative Extension Service [*A publication*]

Ext Mimeo Wash State Univ Coll Agr Ext Serv ... Extension Mimeo. Washington State University. College of Agriculture. Extension Service [*A publication*]

EXTN .... Extension

EXTN .... Extraction

EXTND ..... Extended

EXTND ..... Extender (MSA)

EXTNL ...... External

EXTNR ...... Extender

EXTNS ...... Extension

Exton Mar Dic ... Exton's Maritime Dicaeologie [*A publication*] (DLA)

EXTOR ...... External Torpedo [*Formerly, DEXTOR*] (MCD)

EXTORP ... Exercise Torpedo (NVT)

EXT P .... Extra Parochial [*Geographical division*] [*British*]

Ext Publ Ill Univ N Cent Reg ... Extension Publication. Illinois University. North Central Region [*A publication*]

Ext Publ LA State Univ Agr Ext Serv ... Extension Publication. Louisiana State University. Agricultural Extension Service [*A publication*]

Ext Publ Wash St Coll ... Extension Publication. Washington State College [*A publication*]

EXTR .... Executor [*Business term*]

EXTR .... External (ROG)

EXTR .... Extra (ROG)

EXTR .... Extract

EXTR .... Extraordinary (ROG)

EXTR .... Extravagant (ROG)

extr .... Extreme

EXTR .... Extrude (MSA)

EXTRA ...... Export Tender Risk Advance [*British*]

Extra Ca ..... Lobingier's Extra-Territorial Cases [*United States Court for China*] [*A publication*] (DLA)

EXTRACONUS ... Outside Continental United States [*Military*] (AFIT)

EXTRAD ... Extradition (ADA)

EXTRADOP ... Extended-Range Doppler

EXTRADOVAP ... Extended-Range Doppler Velocity and Position (CET)

EXTRAH .... Extrahatur [*Draw Out*] [*Pharmacy*] (ROG)

EXTRAOR ... Extraordinary (ROG)

EXTRAP ... Extrapolate (FAAC)

Extrap .... Extrapolation [*A publication*]

Extrapolat ... Extrapolation [*A publication*]

Extra Sess ... Extraordinary Session [*A publication*] (DLA)

EXTRAV ... Extravaganza (ROG)

Extrav Com ... Extravagantes Communes [*A publication*] (DSA)

Extrav Joann XXII ... Extravagantes Johannes XXII [*A publication*] (DSA)

Extr Comm ... Extravagantes Communes [*A publication*] (DSA)

EXTRIX ..... Executrix

Extr Joann XXII ... Extravagantes Johannes XXII [*A publication*] (DSA)

EXTRM ..... Extreme (FAAC)

EXTRN ...... External Reference (BUR)

EXTRN ...... Extrusion (MSA)

Extr Or Med ... Extreme-Orient Medical [*A publication*]

EXTRX ...... Executrix [*Business term*]

Ext Serv Bull IA St Coll Agric ... Extension Service Bulletin. Iowa State College of Agriculture [*A publication*]

Ext Service R ... Extension Service Review [*A publication*]

Ext Serv Leafl Coll Agric Rutgers Univ ... Extension Service Leaflet. College of Agriculture. Rutgers University [*A publication*]

Ext Serv R ... Extension Service Review [*A publication*]

Ext Serv Rev ... Extension Service Review [*A publication*]

EXTSN ...... Extension (MDG)

Ext Stud PA State Univ Ext Serv ... Extension Studies. Pennsylvania State University. Extension Service [*A publication*]

EXTSV ...... Extensive (FAAC)

EXTV ...... Extensive

EXTVE ...... Executive

EXU .... Upjohn Co., Technical Library, Kalamazoo, MI [*OCLC symbol*] (OCLC)

EXUD .... Excudit [*Made*] [*Latin*] (ROG)

EXUP .... Exhaust Ultimate Power Valve [*Yamaha Motor Co.*]

EXW .... Europa Chemie [*A publication*]

Ex W .... Ex-Warrants [*Without Warrants*] [*Finance*]

EXW .... Ex Works [*Seller's only responsibility is to make goods available at his premises*] [*"INCOTERM," International Chamber of Commerce official code*]

EXW .... Explosion Welding

Ex W .... Express Wieczorny [*A publication*]

EXW .... Extreme Width

EXW .... Martinsburg, WV [*Location identifier*] [*FAA*] (FAAL)

EXW .... Western Michigan University, Kalamazoo, MI [*OCLC symbol*] (OCLC)

EXWEP ..... Exercise Weapon (NVT)

EXX .... Exador Resources, Inc. [*Toronto Stock Exchange symbol*]

EXX .... Examples

EXX .... Executrix

EXX .... Expo Data [*A publication*]

EXX .... Lexington, NC [*Location identifier*] [*FAA*] (FAAL)

Exxon Monogr Ser ... Exxon Monograph Series [*A publication*]

EXY .... Excerpta Indonesica [*A publication*]

EXZ .... Ezellenz [*Excellency*] [*German*]

EXZ .... Kalamazoo Library System, Kalamazoo, MI [*OCLC symbol*] (OCLC)

E & Y .... Eagle and Younge's English Tithe Cases [*A publication*] (DLA)

EY .... East Yorkshire Militia [*British military*] (DMA)

EY .... Eastern Yiddish (BJA)

EY .... Eger's Yellow

EY .... Egg Yolk

EY .... Electron Yield

EY .... Elvisly Yours [*Fan club*] (EAIO)

EY .... Equilibrium Yield [*Fishery management*] (MSC)

EY .... Essex Yeomanry [*British military*] (DMA)

EY .... Ethyl Corp. [*NYSE symbol*] [*Toronto Stock Exchange symbol*] (SPSG)

EY .... Europe Aero Service [*France*] [*ICAO designator*] (FAAC)

EY .... European Yearbook [*A publication*]

EY .... Journal of Energy Engineering [*A publication*]

EYA .... Washtenaw Community College, Ann Arbor, MI [*OCLC symbol*] (OCLC)
EYB .... Macomb County Library, Mt. Clemens, MI [*OCLC symbol*] (OCLC)
EYBIA5 ..... Encyclopedie Biologique [*Paris*] [*A publication*]
EYBSOYB ... Examine Your Birthday Suit on Your Birthday [*To detect potentially malignant moles*] [*Skin Cancer Foundation*]
EYC .... European Youth Campaign
EYC .... European Youth Centre [*Council of Europe*] (EY)
EYC .... Michigan Library Consortium, Wayne State University, Detroit, MI [*OCLC symbol*] (OCLC)
EYCD .... European Young Christian Democrats [*Formerly, European Union of Young Christian Democrats*] (EA)
EYCE........ Ecumenical Youth Council in Europe (EAIO)
EYCO .... Estimated Yearly Cost of Operation [*of electrical appliance*]
EYD .... Engineering Youth Day
EYD .... University of Michigan, Dearborn Campus, Dearborn, MI [*OCLC symbol*] (OCLC)
EYDIDI ..... Ecology of Disease [*A publication*]
EYE .... Eastern Michigan University, Ypsilanti, MI [*OCLC symbol*] (OCLC)
EYE .... European Year of the Environment [*Beginning March 23, 1987*]
EYE .... Indianapolis, IN [*Location identifier*] [*FAA*] (FAAL)
EYE .... Sterling Optical [*NYSE symbol*] (SPSG)
Eye Ear Nos ... Eye, Ear, Nose, and Throat Monthly [*A publication*]
Eye Ear Nose Throat Mon ... Eye, Ear, Nose, and Throat Monthly [*A publication*]
Eye Ear Nose Throat Month ... Eye, Ear, Nose, and Throat Monthly [*A publication*]
EYENAZ... Encyclopedie Entomologique [*A publication*]
EYES .... Salvatori Ophthalmics, Inc. [*NASDAQ symbol*] (NQ)
EYETD ...... Energy Economist [*A publication*]
Eyewit .... Eyewitness [*A publication*]
EYF .... European Youth Foundation (EA)
EYF.......... Henry Ford Hospital, Medical Library, Detroit, MI [*OCLC symbol*] (OCLC)
EYG .... General Motors Corp., Research Laboratory, Warren, MI [*OCLC symbol*] (OCLC)
EYGZAD... Eiyogaku Zasshi [*Japanese Journal of Nutrition*] [*A publication*]
EYH.......... Huron Valley Library System, Ann Arbor, MI [*OCLC symbol*] (OCLC)
EYI........... Livonia Public Schools, Livonia, MI [*OCLC symbol*] (OCLC)
EYJ........... John Wesley College Library, Owosso, MI [*OCLC symbol*] [*Inactive*] (OCLC)
EYL.......... Lawrence Institute of Technology, Southfield, MI [*OCLC symbol*] (OCLC)
EY Loc Hist Ser ... East Yorkshire Local History Series [*A publication*]
EYLT .... Eyelet (MSA)
EYM .... Electron Yield Measurement
EYM .... University of Michigan, Ann Arbor, MI [*OCLC symbol*] (OCLC)
EYMS........ Electron Yield Measurement System
EYMYA6... Encyclopedie Mycologique [*A publication*]
EYOC .... Estimated Yearly Operating Cost [*of electrical appliance*]
E YORK R ... East Yorkshire Regiment [*Military unit*] [*British*] (ROG)
EYP.......... Detroit Public Library, Detroit, MI [*OCLC symbol*] (OCLC)
EYP.......... East York Public Library [*UTLAS symbol*]
EYP.......... El Yopal [*Colombia*] [*Airport symbol*] (OAG)
EYP.......... El Yunque [*Puerto Rico*] [*Seismograph station code, US Geological Survey*] [*Closed*] (SEIS)
EYP.......... Electronic Yellow Pages [*Dun's Marketing Services*] [*Information service or system*] (IID)
EYP.......... Port Huron, MI [*Location identifier*] [*FAA*] (FAAL)
EYPC........ Eyepiece (MSA)
EYPSB....... Energy Pipelines and Systems [*A publication*]
EYQ .... Detroit Cooperative Cataloging Center, Detroit, MI [*OCLC symbol*] (OCLC)
EYR .... East Yorkshire Regiment [*Military unit*] [*British*]
EYR .... Eyrewell [*New Zealand*] [*Geomagnetic observatory code*]
EYR .... Oakland University, Rochester, MI [*OCLC symbol*] (OCLC)
Eyre.......... Eyre's English King's Bench Reports Tempore William III [*A publication*] (DLA)
Eyre MS .... Eyre's Manuscript Notes of Cases, King's Bench [*New York Law Institute Library*] [*A publication*] (DLA)
EYS.......... Board of Education for the Borough of East York [*UTLAS symbol*]
EYS.......... Experimental Yacht Society [*Defunct*] (EA)
EYS.......... St. Clair County Library System, Port Huron, MI [*OCLC symbol*] (OCLC)
EYS.......... World Council of Churches Ecumenical Youth Service (EA)
EYT .... Detroit Institute of Arts, Research Library, Detroit, MI [*OCLC symbol*] (OCLC)
EYTK........ Eye Technology, Inc. [*St. Paul, MN*] [*NASDAQ symbol*] (NQ)
EYU .... University of Detroit, Detroit, MI [*OCLC symbol*] (OCLC)
e-yu---......... Yugoslavia [*MARC geographic area code*] [*Library of Congress*] (LCCP)
EYV .... Wayne County Community College, Detroit, MI [*OCLC symbol*] (OCLC)
EYW .... Key West [*Florida*] [*Airport symbol*] (OAG)
EYW .... Key West, FL [*Location identifier*] [*FAA*] (FAAL)

EYW .... Wayne State University, Detroit, MI [*OCLC symbol*] (OCLC)
EYY .... Mercy College of Detroit, Detroit, MI [*OCLC symbol*] (OCLC)
EYZ .... Madonna College, Livonia, MI [*OCLC symbol*] (OCLC)
EZ .... Eastern Zone
EZ .... Easy [*Slang*]
EZ .... Eczema [*Medicine*]
EZ .... Ehuzu [*Benin*] [*A publication*]
EZ .... Eineiige Zwillinge [*Monozygotic Twins*] [*Psychology*]
EZ .... Electrical Zero
EZ .... Elektronik-Zeitung fuer Industrie, Wirtschaft, Wissenschaft, und Verwaltung [*A publication*]
EZ .... Enterprise Zone [*British*]
E/Z........... Equal Zero (MDG)
EZ .... Euroair Transport Ltd. [*Great Britain*] [*ICAO designator*] (FAAC)
EZ .... Extraction Zone [*Military*] (AFM)
Ez .... Ezekiel [*Old Testament book*]
Ez .... Ezra [*Old Testament book*]
EZA .... Alma College, Alma, MI [*OCLC symbol*] (OCLC)
EZA .... Newark, NJ [*Location identifier*] [*FAA*] (FAAL)
EZB.......... Cloverland Processing Center, Escanaba, MI [*OCLC symbol*] (OCLC)
EZB.......... Oakland, CA [*Location identifier*] [*FAA*] (FAAL)
EZC .... Central Michigan University, Mount Pleasant, MI [*OCLC symbol*] (OCLC)
EZC .... European Zone Charge (DS)
EZCO .... Extraction Zone Control Officer [*Military*] (AFM)
EZD .... Enziklopedyah shel ha-Ziyonut ha-Datit [*A publication*] (BJA)
EZE.......... Buenos Aires [*Argentina*] Ezeiza [*Airport symbol*] (OAG)
EZECH....... Ezechiel [*Old Testament book*] [*Douay version*]
Ezeg Muz Ist Rel At Ak N SSSR ... Ezhegodnik Muzeja Istorii Religii i Ateizma Akademii Nauk SSSR [*A publication*]
Ezek .... Ezekiel [*Old Testament book*]
EZEM........ E-Z-EM, Inc. [*NASDAQ symbol*] (NQ)
EZF.......... Ferris State College, Big Rapids, MI [*OCLC symbol*] (OCLC)
Ezheg Geol Mineral Ross ... Ezhegodnik po Geologii i Mineralogii Rossii [*A publication*]
Ezheg Inst Geokhim Sib Otd Akad Nauk SSSR ... Ezhegodnik Instituta Geokhimii Sibirskogo Otdeleniya Akademii Nauk SSSR [*A publication*]
Ezheg Inst Geol Geokhim Akad Nauk SSSR Ural Fil ... Ezhegodnik. Institut Geologii i Geokhimii. Akademiya Nauk SSSR Ural'skii Filial [*A publication*]
Ezheg Inst Geol Geokhim Akad Nauk SSSR Ural Nauchn Tsentr ... Ezhegodnik. Institut Geologii i Geokhimii. Akademiya Nauk SSSR Ural'skii Nauchnyi Tsentr [*A publication*]
Ezheg Nauchn Rab Alma-At Inst Usoversh Vrachei ... Ezhegodnik Nauchnykh Rabot Alma-Atinskii Institut Usovershenstvovaniya Vrachei [*A publication*]
Ezheg Nauchn Rab Inst Usoversh Vrachei Kaz SSR ... Ezhegodnik Nauchnykh Rabot Instituta Usovershenstvovaniya Vrachei Kazakhskoi SSR [*A publication*]
Ezhegodnik GIM ... Ezhegodnik Gosudarstvennyi Istoricheskii Muzei [*A publication*]
Ezhegodnik Zool Muz Akad Nauk SSSR ... Ezhegodnik Zoologicheskogo Muzeia Akademii Nauk Sofuza Sovetskikh Sotsialisticheskikh Respublik [*A publication*]
Ezhegodnik Zool Muz Ross Akad Nauk ... Ezhegodnik Zoologicheskogo Muzeia Rossiiskoi Akademii Nauk [*A publication*]
Ezheg O-Va Estestvoispyt Akad Nauk Est SSR ... Ezhegodnik Obshchestva Estestvoispytatelei Akademiya Nauk. Estonskoi SSR [*A publication*]
Ezheg Sib Inst Geokhim ... Ezhegodnik Sibirskogo Instituta Geokhimii [*A publication*]
Ezhe Inst Geokhim Sib Otd Akad Nauk SSSR ... Ezhegodnik Instituta Geokhimii Sibirskogo Otdeleniya Akademii Nauk SSSR [*A publication*]
EZI........... European Zinc Institute (EA)
EZI........... Kewanee, IL [*Location identifier*] [*FAA*] (FAAL)
EZI........... Mid-Peninsula Library Cooperative, Iron Mountain, MI [*OCLC symbol*] (OCLC)
EZK .... Ezekiel [*Old Testament book*]
EZL.......... Lake Superior State College, Sault Ste. Marie, MI [*OCLC symbol*] (OCLC)
Ez Lit .... Ezik i Literatura [*A publication*]
EZM .... Muskegon County Library, Muskegon, MI [*OCLC symbol*] (OCLC)
EZN .... Ezine [*Turkey*] [*Seismograph station code, US Geological Survey*] (SEIS)
EZN .... Northern Michigan University, Marquette, MI [*OCLC symbol*] (OCLC)
EZP .... Superiorland Library Cooperative, Marquette, MI [*OCLC symbol*] (OCLC)
Ezr........... Ezra [*Old Testament book*]
EZR .... Gulf of Alaska/Bering Sea, AK [*Location identifier*] [*FAA*] (FAAL)
EZS........... Edgar Z. Steever IV [*Designer's mark when appearing on US coins*]
EZS........... Elazig [*Turkey*] [*Airport symbol*] (OAG)
EZS........... Saginaw Valley State College, University Center, MI [*OCLC symbol*] (OCLC)

EZT............ Elizabethton, TN [*Location identifier*] [*FAA*]   (FAAL)
EZT............ Michigan Technological University, Houghton, MI [*OCLC symbol*]   (OCLC)
EZV .... Erlanger Zeitschriften-Verzeichnis [*A publication*]
EZV .... EZ Ventures Ltd. [*Vancouver Stock Exchange symbol*]
EZW .... White Pine Library System, Saginaw, MI [*OCLC symbol*]   (OCLC)
EZY .... Elk City, OK [*Location identifier*] [*FAA*]   (FAAL)
EZZ............ Ethnologische Zeitschrift (Zurich) [*A publication*]
EZZ............ Michigan North Processing Center, Cadillac, MI [*OCLC symbol*]   (OCLC)

F

f .... Acceleration [*Symbol*]   (DEN)
f------ .... Africa [*MARC geographic area code*] [*Library of Congress*]   (LCCP)
F .... Air Force Training Category [*No inactive duty periods and 4 months minimum initial active duty training per year*]
F .... Cleared to the Fix [*Aviation*]   (FAAC)
F .... College of Future Education [*British*]
F .... Consuetudines Feudorum [*The Book of Feuds*] [*Latin*] [*A publication*]   (DLA)
°F .... Degrees Fahrenheit   (MCD)
F .... Dominion Rubber Co. [*Canada*] [*Research code symbol*]
F .... Eaton Laboratories, Inc. [*Research code symbol*]
F .... Fac [*Let There Be Made*] [*Pharmacy*]
F .... Face
F .... Facial Rash [*Classification system used by doctors on Ellis Island to detain, re-examine, and possibly deny entry to certain immigrants*]
F .... Facial Surface [*Dentistry*]
F .... Facies [*Medicine*]
F .... Faculty of Advocates Collection of Decisions, Scotch Court of Sessions [*A publication*]   (DLA)
F .... Fahrenheit
F .... Failure
F .... Fair
F .... Fair Skiing Conditions
F .... Falck [*When used in identifying W. F. Bach's compositions, refers to cataloging of his works by musicologist Falck*]
F .... Falls   (ROG)
F .... False
F .... Family
F .... Family [*Suitable for all*] [*Movie rating*] [*Canada*]
F .... Farad [*Symbol*] [*Unit of electric capacitance*]   (GPO)
F .... Faraday Constant [*Electrochemistry*]
F .... Farce   (ROG)
f .... Fardo [*Package*] [*Spanish*]
F .... Farthing [*Monetary unit*] [*Great Britain*]
F .... Fast
F .... Fasting [*Test*] [*Medicine*]
F .... Fat
F .... Father
F .... Fathom
F .... [*Johannes*] Faventinus [*Deceased circa 1187*] [*Authority cited in pre-1607 legal work*]   (DSA)
F .... Feast
F .... February [*A publication*]
F .... February
F .... Feces
F .... Fecit [*He, or She, Did It*] [*Latin*]
F .... Federal League [*Major league in baseball, 1914-15*]
F .... Federal Reporter [*A publication*]   (DLA)
F .... Feedback
F .... Feet [*or Foot*]
F .... Feldspar Subgroup [*Orthoclase, albite, anorthite*] [*CIPW classification*] [*Geology*]
F .... Feliciter [*Happily*]
F .... Fell [*Horse racing*]
F .... Fellow
F .... Felon
F .... Female
F .... Feminine
F .... Femmes [*or Feminin*] [*Initial used as title of a publication*]
f .... Femto [*A prefix meaning divided by 10 to the 15th power*] [*SI symbol*]
F .... Fen [*Monetary unit*] [*China*]
F .... Fendi [*Italian couturier*]
F .... Fennia [*A publication*]
F .... Fenoterol [*Pharmacology*]
F .... Fermentation [*Biology*]
F .... Fermi [*Later, Femtometer*] [*Unit of length*] [*Nuclear physics*]
F .... Ferrosan [*Sweden*] [*Research code symbol*]
F .... Fertile [*Medicine*]

F .... Fertility Factor [*Genetics*]
F .... Fertilized
F .... Fetal [*Medicine*]
F .... Fetch [*Data processing*]
F .... Fiat [*Make*] [*Pharmacy*]
F .... Fibre [*Classification key in textile printing*]
F .... Fibrous
F .... Fiction
F .... Field
F .... Field of Vision [*Medicine*]
F .... Fighter [*Designation for all US military aircraft*]
F .... Filament   (AAG)
F .... File [*Data processing*]
F .... Filial Generation [*Biology*]
F .... Filius [*Son*] [*Latin*]
F .... Filly [*Thoroughbred racing*]
F .... Filter
F .... Final [*Telecommunications*]   (TEL)
F .... Final Approach [*Aviation*]   (FAAC)
F .... Final Target
F .... Finance [*or Financial*]
F .... Fine [*Condition*] [*Antiquarian book trade, numismatics, etc.*]
F .... Fine [*Designation on brandy labels*]
F .... Fine [*End*] [*Music*]
F .... Finger
F .... Finish
F .... Fire
F .... Fireman [*Navy rating*]
F .... Firm
F .... First Class [*Airline fare code*]
F' .... First Focal Distance [*Symbol*] [*Optics*]   (ROG)
F .... Fischer [*Rat strain*]
F .... Fitted as Flagship [*Suffix to plane designation*]
F .... Fitter [*Navy rating*] [*British*]
F .... Fitzherbert's Abridgment [*1516*] [*A publication*]   (DSA)
F .... Fixed Light [*Navigation signal*]
F .... Flag [*Data processing*]
F .... Flash [*Precedence*] [*Telecommunications*]   (TEL)
F .... Flat
F .... Flat Band Metallic Armor   (AAG)
F .... Flat-Tainers [*British*]   (DCTA)
F .... Fleet
F .... Fletcher Challenge Investments, Inc. [*Toronto Stock Exchange symbol*] [*Vancouver Stock Exchange symbol*]
F .... Flied Out [*Baseball*]
F .... Flight Inspection   (FAAC)
F .... Flint   (AAG)
F .... Floods
F .... Flora oder Allgemeine Botanische Zeitung [*A publication*]
F .... Florida State Library, Tallahassee, FL [*Library symbol*] [*Library of Congress*]   (LCLS)
F .... Florin [*Monetary unit*] [*Netherlands*]
F .... Floryn [*Florin*] [*Monetary unit*] [*Afrikaans*]
F .... Flow [*of blood*] [*Medicine*]
F .... Flower
F .... Fluency [*A factor ability*] [*Psychology*]
F .... Flugzeug [*Airplane*] [*German military*]
F .... Fluid
F .... Fluid Ounce
F .... Fluorine [*Chemical element*]
F .... Fluorouracil [*Also, FU*] [*Antineoplastic drug*]
F .... Flying [*Officer qualified as both pilot and observer*] [*British*]
F .... Focal Length [*Photography*]
F .... Fog [*Meteorology*]
F .... Foil [*Dentistry*]
F .... Folge [*Series*] [*German*]   (ILCA)
F .... Folio [*Book 30 centimeters and over in height*]
F .... Folio [*A publication*]
F .... Follow-Up
F .... Following [*Pages*] [*Also, FF*]   (MUGU)
F .... Font

F .... Fontaine [*A publication*]
F .... Foord's Cape Of Good Hope Reports [*South Africa*] [*A publication*]   (DLA)
F .... Foord's Supreme Court Reports [*Cape Colony, South Africa*] [*A publication*]   (DLA)
F .... For
F .... Foraging [*Ornithology*]
F .... Force [*Symbol*] [*IUPAC*]
F .... Ford Motor Co. [*NYSE symbol*] [*Wall Street slang names: "Tin Lizzy" or "Flivver"*]   (SPSG)
F .... Forecastle
F .... Forint [*Monetary unit*] [*Hungary*]
F .... Form [*Of*]
F .... Form [*Rorschach*] [*Psychology*]
F .... Forma [*Also, f*]
F .... Formality
F .... Formed
F .... Formula
f .... Formyl [*As substituent on nucleoside*] [*Biochemistry*]
F .... Fornix [*Neuroanatomy*]
F .... Forretningbanken A/S [*Bank*] [*Norway*]
F .... Fort   (ROG)
F .... Fortasse [*Perhaps*] [*Latin*]
F .... Forte [*Loud*] [*Music*]
F .... Fortnightly [*A publication*]
F .... Forum [*A publication*]
F .... Forward
F .... Forward Compartment
F .... Foul
F .... Founded   (EY)
F .... Fox [*Phonetic alphabet*] [*World War II*]   (DSUE)
F .... Foxtrot [*Phonetic alphabet*] [*International*]   (DSUE)
F .... Fracture
F .... Fragile
f .... Fragment   (BJA)
F .... Fragmentation
F .... Frame Construction
F .... Franc [*Monetary unit*] [*France*]
F .... Francais [*French*]
F .... France [*Aircraft nationality and registration mark*]   (FAAC)
F .... France [*IYRU nationality code*]
F .... Fraser [*James E.*] [*Designer's mark, when appearing on US coins*]
F .... Fraser, Inc. [*Toronto Stock Exchange symbol*]
F .... Fraser's Scotch Court of Sessions Cases, Fifth Series [*A publication*]   (DLA)
F .... Frater [*Brother*] [*Latin*]
F .... Freddie [*Phonetic alphabet*] [*Pre-World War II*]   (DSUE)
F .... Freddy [*Phonetic alphabet*] [*Royal Navy*] [*World War I*]   (DSUE)
F .... Free
F .... Free [*Rate*] [*Value of the English pound*]
F .... Freehold [*Legal term*]   (ROG)
F .... Freeway   (ADA)
F .... Fremskridtspartiet [*Progress Party*] [*Denmark*] [*Political party*]   (PPE)
F .... French
F .... Frequency
f .... Frequency [*Symbol*] [*IUPAC*]
F .... Frequency of Fading [*Broadcasting*]
F .... Frequent [*In mention of occurrence of species*]
F .... Freshwater [*Load line mark*]
F .... Friar
F .... Friction
F .... Friday
F .... Frogerius [*Rogerius Beneventanus*] [*Flourished, 12th century*] [*Authority cited in pre-1607 legal work*]   (DSA)
F .... From
F .... Front   (KSC)
F .... Froude Number [*IUPAC*]
F .... Fuchsia [*Genotype of Phlox paniculata*]
F .... Fuel
F .... Fueler [*Aircraft designation*]
f .... Fugacity [*Thermodynamics*]
F .... Full
F .... Full Load [*Displacement*]
F .... Function
f .... Furanose [*One-letter symbol*] [*Biochemistry*]
F .... Furlong [*Unit of distance*]
F .... Furlough [*Military*]   (ADA)
F .... Fusarium Wilt [*Plant pathology*]
F .... Fuse   (DEN)
F .... Fuss [*Feet of organ stops*]
F .... Goals For [*Hockey*]
F .... Helmholtz Function [*Symbol*]   (DEN)
F .... Individual [*Missile launch environment symbol*]
F .... Intelligence for which the Source Reliability Cannot be Judged
F .... Interceptor [*Aircraft*]
F .... Lab. Funai [*Japan*] [*Research code symbol*]
F .... Libri Feudorum [*A publication*]   (DSA)
F .... Luminous Flux [*Physics*]

F .... Mutuel Field [*Horse racing*]
F .... Phenylalanine [*One-letter symbol*] [*Also, Phe*]
F .... Photoreconnaissance [*Aircraft designation*]
f .... Polar Flattening [*Symbol*] [*Physics*]
F .... Requires Food and Water [*Search and rescue symbol that can be stamped in sand or snow*]
F" .... Second Focal Distance [*Symbol*] [*Optics*]   (ROG)
F .... Ship being built by US for a foreign nation, when precedes vessel classification [*Navy symbol*]
F_1 .... Filial Generation, First [*Biology*]
F1 .... First Folio Edition [*1623*] [*Shakespearean work*]
F_2 .... Filial Generation, Second [*Biology*]
F2 .... Second Folio Edition [*1632*] [*Shakespearean work*]
2F .... Two-Seater Fighter Aircraft [*Navy*]
F^3 .... Form-Fit-Function [*Pronounced "f-cubed"*]
4F .... Fair, Fat, Fertile, and Forty [*Medical slang describing women most susceptible to gallbladder attacks*]
4-F .... Selective Service Class [*for Man Not Qualified for Military Service*]
3F's .... Fashion, Features, and Fluff [*Subject assignments to which female journalists were once limited*]
3F's .... Fixity of Tenure, Fair Rents, and Free Sale [*Phrase used in Parliamentary discussions of Irish affairs, 1880-1882; opposition translated the initials as Fraud, Force, and Folly*]
F (Layer) .... Layer of the ionosphere from above 90 miles to approximately 300 miles   (MUGU)
F (Plan) ...... Fiber Plan [*Used in title of book advocating a high-fiber diet*]
FA .... Aeronautical Station [*ITU designation*]   (CET)
FA .... Area Forecast [*Aviation code*]   (FAAC)
fa----- .... Atlas Mountain Region [*MARC geographic area code*] [*Library of Congress*]   (LCCP)
FA .... Fabrication Assembly   (MCD)
Fa .... Fabula [*A publication*]
FA .... Face Amount [*Business term*]
FA .... Facilitating Agency [*Business term*]
FA .... Factor Analysis [*Mathematics*]
FA .... Factory Act [*British*]   (ILCA)
FA .... Factory Automation
fa .... Factura [*Bill*] [*Spanish*]
FA .... Faculty of Advocates [*British*]   (ILCA)
FA .... Failure Analysis   (AAG)
FA .... Fairchild Aircraft
FA .... Fairchild Aircraft Ltd. [*Canada*], Fairchild/Republic [*ICAO aircraft manufacturer identifier*]   (ICAO)
FA .... Fairchild Corp. Class A [*NYSE symbol*]   (SPSG)
FA .... Faith Alive   (EA)
FA .... Families Anonymous   (EA)
FA .... Family Agency
FA .... Family Allowance [*Navy*]
FA .... Family America [*An association*]   (EA)
FA .... Fanconi's Anemia [*Medicine*]
FA .... Fanny Adams [*Canned mutton stew*] [*Slang*]   (DSUE)
FA .... Fantastic Adventures [*A publication*]
FA . ... Fantasy Association   (EA)
FA .... Farm Aid   (EA)
FA .... Farnesynic Acid [*Juvenile hormone analog*]
fa .... Faroe Islands [*MARC country of publication code*] [*Library of Congress*]   (LCCP)
FA .... Fascicular Area [*Neurology*]
FA .... Fashion Aid   (EA)
FA .... Fasti Archaeologici [*A publication*]
FA .... Father   (DSUE)
FA .... Fatty Acid [*Biochemistry*]
FA .... Fawcett Association [*A union*] [*British*]
fa .... Fayalite [*CIPW classification*] [*Geology*]
F & A .... February and August [*Denotes semiannual payments of interest or dividends in these months*] [*Business term*]
FA .... Feet Apart [*Dance terminology*]
FA .... Felonious Assault
FA .... Femoral Artery [*Anatomy*]
fA .... Femtoampere   (IEEE)
FA .... [*The*] Ferroalloys Association   (EA)
FA .... Ferrocarriles Argentinos [*Railway*] [*Argentina*]   (EY)
FA .... Fertilization Antigen [*Immunology*]
FA .... Ferulic Acid [*Biochemistry*]
FA .... Fibonacci Association   (EA)
FA .... Fibrinolytic Activity [*Hematology*]
FA .... Fibroadenoma [*Oncology*]
FA .... Field Accelerating Contactor or Relay [*Industrial control*]   (IEEE)
F/A .... Field Activities
FA .... Field Address
FA .... Field Allowance [*British military*]   (DMA)
FA .... Field Ambulance [*Military*]
FA .... Field Army
FA .... Field Artillery
FA .... Field Audit [*IRS*]
FA .... Field Goals Attempted [*Football, basketball*]
FA .... Fielding Average [*Baseball*]
FA .... Fifth Avenue Ventures [*Vancouver Stock Exchange symbol*]

FA	Fighter Alert (NATG)	
FA	Fighter Allocator (NATG)	
FA	Filologiskt Arkiv [*A publication*]	
FA	Filterable Agent [*Virology*]	
FA	Final Address Register [*Data processing*] (MDG)	
FA	Final Approach [*Aviation*] (FAAC)	
FA	Final Assembly (MSA)	
F & A	Finance and Accounting	
FA	Finance and Accounting (MCD)	
FA	Finance Act [*British*] (DCTA)	
F & A	Finance and Audit Committee [*American Library Association*]	
FA	Financial Adviser	
FA	[*The*] Financial Australian [*A publication*] (APTA)	
FA	Finanzarchiv [*A publication*]	
FA	Fine Alignment	
FA	Fine Arts	
FA	Finite Automation	
FA	Fire Alarm (ROG)	
F & A	Fire and Allied Lines [*Insurance*]	
FA	Fireman Apprentice [*Navy rating*]	
Fa	Firma [*Legal term*] (DLA)	
FA	First Access	
FA	First Aid [*Medicine*]	
FA	First Announcement	
FA	First Article	
FA	First Attack [*Men's lacrosse position*]	
FA	Fixed Asset [*Business term*]	
FA	Flag Allowance (CINC)	
FA	Fleet Auxiliary [*British*]	
FA	Flight Acceptance	
FA	Flight Aft (NASA)	
FA	Flight Attendant	
FA	Floating Airfields [*British*] [*World War II*]	
FA	Floating Asset [*Business term*]	
FA	Florida (ROG)	
FA	Fluorenamine [*Also, AF*] [*Carcinogen*]	
FA	Fluorescent Angiography	
FA	Fluorescent Antibody [*Clinical chemistry*]	
FA	Fluoroalanine [*Organic chemistry*]	
FA	Folia Archaeologica [*A publication*]	
FA	Folic Acid [*Also, PGA, PteGlu*] [*Biochemistry*]	
FA	Folklore Americano [*A publication*]	
FA	Folklore Americas [*A publication*]	
FA	Food Additive	
FA	Food and Agriculture (NATG)	
FA	Football Association [*Controlling body of British soccer*]	
FA	Forage Acre	
FA	Foragers of America (EA)	
FA	Forced Air (MSA)	
FA	Forced-Air-Cooled [*Transformer*] (IEEE)	
FA	Forces Aeriennes Francaises [*ICAO designator*] (FAAC)	
F & A	Fore and Aft	
FA	Forecaster Aid [*Military*]	
FA	Foreign Affairs [*A publication*]	
FA	Foreign Agriculture Including Foreign Crops and Markets [*A publication*]	
FA	Foreign Agriculture. United States Department of Agriculture [*A publication*]	
FA	Forestry Abstracts [*Oxford, England*] [*A publication*]	
FA	Forestry Act [*Town planning*] [*British*]	
FA	Formal Advertising (MCD)	
fa	Formylaminoacyl [*As substituent on nucleoside*] [*Biochemistry*]	
FA	Forstarchiv [*A publication*]	
FA	Fortified Aqueous [*Pharmacology*]	
F/A	Forward/Aft (KSC)	
FA	Forward America (EA)	
FA	Found Abandoned	
FA	Foundation of America (EA)	
FA	Four Arrows (EA)	
FA	Frame Analyzer (MCD)	
FA	France-Amerique [*A publication*]	
FA	Frankford Arsenal [*Pennsylvania*] [*Army*] [*Closed*]	
FA	Frater Anselm [*Pseudonym used by Anselm Baker*]	
F & A	Free and Accepted [*Freemasonry*] (ROG)	
FA	Free of All Average [*Insurance*]	
FA	Free Alongside [*Shipping*]	
FA	Free America [*In the movie "Red Dawn"*]	
FA	Free Aperture [*Technical drawings*]	
FA	Free Astray	
FA	Freight Agent	
FA	Freight Allowal	
FA	Freight Astray	
FA	Freight Auditor	
FA	French Army (NATG)	
FA	Frente Amplio [*Broad Front*] [*Uruguay*] [*Political party*] (PD)	
FA	Frequency Agility	
FA	Freund's Adjuvant [*Immunology*]	
FA	Friedenwald Archives (BJA)	
FA	Friedreich's Ataxia [*Medicine*]	
FA	Friendly Aircraft	

FA	Friends of Astrology (EA)	
FA	Friendship Ambassadors Foundation (EA)	
FA	Front Axle [*Automotive engineering*]	
FA	Frontal Aviation [*Soviet tactical air force*] [*World War II*]	
FA	Frozen Asset [*Business term*]	
F/A	Fuel-Air [*Ratio*]	
F/A	Fuel Assembly (NRCH)	
FA	Full Action	
FA	Full Adder [*Data processing*]	
FA	Full Arc (NRCH)	
FA	Fully Automatic (KSC)	
FA	Fulvic Acid [*Organic chemistry*]	
FA	Functional Analysis	
FA	Functional Area	
FA	Functional Assembly (MCD)	
FA	Fundamentalists Anonymous (EA)	
FA	Furfuryl Alcohol [*Organic chemistry*]	
FA	Fuse Alarm (TEL)	
FA	Fuzed Alloy	
FAA	False Alarm Avoidance	
FAA	Family Allowance, Class A [*Navy*]	
FAA	Fatty Acid Alkanolamide [*Organic chemistry*]	
FAA	Federal Aviation Act [*1958*]	
FAA	Federal Aviation Administration [*Formerly, Federal Aviation Agency*] [*Department of Transportation*]	
FAA	Federation of Australian Accountants (ADA)	
FAA	Fellow of the American Association for the Advancement of Science	
FAA	Fellow of the Australian Academy of Science	
FAA	Field Artillery Airborne	
FAA	Film Artistes' Association [*A union*] [*British*] (DCTA)	
FAA	Fireplace Association of America [*Later, WHA*]	
FAA	First Article Approval [*or Audit*]	
FAA	Flameless Atomic Absorption	
FAA	Fleet Air Arm [*British*]	
FAA	Fluorenylacetamide [*Also, AAF, AcNHFln*] [*Organic chemistry*]	
FAA	Flying Apache Association (EA)	
FAA	For an Approach To [*Aviation*] (FAAC)	
FAA	Foreman's Association of America [*Defunct*] (EA)	
FAA	Formalin-Acetic Acid-Alcohol [*Fixative*] [*Botany*]	
FAA	Foundation for the Advancement of Artists (EA)	
FAA	Foundation for American Agriculture [*Later, FAAPFF*] (EA)	
FAA	Fraternal Actuarial Association [*Defunct*] (EA)	
FAA	Free of All Average [*Insurance*]	
FAA	Free Amino Acid [*Biochemistry*]	
FAA	French Australian Association of Victoria [*Australia*]	
FAA	Fresh Acid Add [*Nuclear energy*] (NRCH)	
FAA	Friends of Africa in America (EA)	
FAA	Fulbright Alumni Association [*Later, Fulbright Association*] (EAIO)	
FAA	Functional Analysis and Its Applications [*A publication*]	
FAA	Functional Area Assessment	
FAA	National Aviation Facilities Experimental Center, Atlantic City, NJ [*OCLC symbol*] (OCLC)	
FAA	Office of Aviation Medicine. Report [*Federal Aviation Administration*] [*A publication*]	
FAAA	Federation for American Afghan Action (EA)	
FAAA	Fellow of the American Academy of Allergy	
FAAA	First Allied Airborne Army [*World War II*]	
FAA-AAF	Federal Aviation Administration Airway Facilities Service	
FAA-AAP	Federal Aviation Administration Office of Airports Programs	
FAA-AC	Federal Aviation Administration Aeronautical Center	
FAA-ADS	Federal Aviation Administration Aircraft Development Service	
FAA-AEE	Federal Aviation Administration Office of Environment and Energy	
FAA-AEM	Federal Aviation Administration Office of Systems Engineering Management	
FAA-AEQ	Federal Aviation Administration Office of Environmental Quality	
FAA-AF	Federal Aviation Administration Airway Facilities Service	
FAA-AFS	Federal Aviation Administration Flight Standards Service	
FAA-AFTN	Federal Aviation Administration Aeronautical Fixed Telecommunications Network (NOAA)	
FAA-AM	Federal Aviation Administration Office of Aviation Medicine	
FAA-AP	Federal Aviation Administration Office of Airports Programs	
FAA-ARD	Federal Aviation Administration Systems Research and Development Service	
FAA-AS	Federal Aviation Administration Airports Service	
FAAAS	Fellow of the American Academy of Arts and Sciences	
FAAAS	Fellow of the American Association for the Advancement of Science	
FAA-ASP	Federal Aviation Administration Office of Aviation Systems Plans	
FAA-AT	Federal Aviation Administration Air Traffic Service	
FAA-ATS	Federal Aviation Administration Air Traffic Service (NOAA)	
FAA-AV	Federal Aviation Administration Office of Aviation Policy	
FAA Aviat Ne	FAA [*Federal Aviation Administration*] Aviation News [*A publication*]	
FAAB	Alexander Bay [*South Africa*] [*ICAO location identifier*] (ICLI)	
FAAB	Family Allowance, Class A and B [*Navy*]	

FAABiol..... Fellow of the Australian Academy of Biology
FAAC......... Airspace Control Command [*South Africa*] [*ICAO location identifier*] (ICLI)
FAAC......... FARO [*Federation of AIDS Related Organizations*] AIDS [*Acquired Immune Deficiency Syndrome*] Action Council (EA)
FAAC......... Fellow of the American Association of Criminology
FAAC......... French-American Aid for Children (EA)
FAA/CAS ... Federal Aviation Administration Canadian Air Services Committee
FAACB...... Friends in Art of American Council of the Blind (EA)
FAACE...... Forces Aeriennes Alliees Centre-Europe [*Allied Air Forces Central Europe*] [*NATO*] (NATG)
FAACS...... Fully Automated Accounting Computer System (MCD)
FAAD .... Adelaide [*South Africa*] [*ICAO location identifier*] (ICLI)
FAAD .... Forward Area Air Defense
FAADC...... Fleet Accounting and Disbursing Center [*Navy*] (NVT)
FAADC²I... Forward Area Air Defense Command and Control Intelligence System [*Army*]
FAADS...... Federal Assistance Award Data System [*Bureau of the Census*] [*Washington, DC*] [*Information service or system*]
FAA-DS..... Federal Aviation Administration Development Services
FAADS...... Field Army Air Defense System (MCD)
FAADS...... Forward Area Air Defense System
FAADW...... Forward Area Air Defense Weapon
FAAE....... Fellow of the Association of Automotive Engineers [*Australia*]
FAA-EE..... Federal Aviation Administration Office of Environment and Energy
FAA-EM ... Federal Aviation Administration Office of Systems Engineering Management
FAA-EQ .... Federal Aviation Administration Office of Environmental Quality
FAAF........ Forney Army Airfield [*Fort Leonard Wood, MO*]
FAA-FS ..... Federal Aviation Administration Flight Standards Service
FAA-FS-NFID ... Federal Aviation Administration Flight Standards Service National Flight Inspection Division
FAAG .... Aggeneys [*South Africa*] [*ICAO location identifier*] (ICLI)
FAAG .... First Advertising Agency Group
FAA Gen Av N ... FAA [*Federal Aviation Administration*] General Aviation News [*A publication*]
FAAH .... South African Air Force Headquarters [*ICAO location identifier*] (ICLI)
FAAI......... Fellow of the Institute of Administrative Accounting and Data Processing [*British*] (DCTA)
FAAIECE ... Fulbright Association of Alumni of International Educational and Cultural Exchange (EA)
FAALS ...... Field Artillery Acoustic Locating System (MCD)
FAALS ...... Forward-Area Armored Logistics System [*Military*]
FAAMC..... Federation des Associations d'Antiquaires du Marche Commun (EA)
FAA-MS.... Federal Aviation Administration Office of Management Systems
FAAN .... Aliwal North [*South Africa*] [*ICAO location identifier*] (ICLI)
FAAN .... Fellow of the American Academy of Nursing
FAAN .... First Advertising Agency Network [*Later, First Network of Affiliated Advertising Agencies*] [*Defunct*] (EA)
FAA-NA .... Federal Aviation Administration National Aviation Facilities Experimental Center
FAANaOS ... Fellowship of the American Academy of Neurological and Orthopaedic Surgeons (EA)
FAANE...... Forces Aeriennes Alliees Nord-Europe [*Allied Air Forces Northern Europe*] [*NATO*] (NATG)
FAA-NO.... Federal Aviation Administration Office of Noise Abatement
FAA-NS..... Federal Aviation Administration National Airspace System Program Office
FAAO .... Federation of American Arab Organizations (EA)
FAAO .... Field Artillery Aerial Observer
FAAO .... Finance and Accounts Office [*Army*]
FAAO .... Fleet Aviation Accounting Office
FAA Order ... Federal Aviation Administration Orders [*A publication*] (DLA)
FAAOS...... Fellow of the American Academy of Orthopedic Surgeons
FAAP....... Federal Aid to Airports Program [*FAA*]
FAAP......... Fixed Asset Accounting Package [*Data processing*]
FAAPFF.... Foundation for American Agriculture Program of the Farm Foundation [*Formerly, FAA*] (EA)
FAAPS ...... Fine Art, Antique, and Philatelic Squad [*Scotland Yard*] [*British*]
FAAQS...... Federal Ambient Air Quality Studies
FAA-QS..... Federal Aviation Administration Quiet Short-Haul Air Transportation Systems Office
FAAR........ Arandis [*Namibia*] [*ICAO location identifier*] (ICLI)
FAAR........ Federal Aviation Administration Requirements (FAAC)
FAAR........ Feminist Alliance Against Rape (EA)
FAAR........ Forward Area Alerting RADAR
FAAR........ Friends of American Art in Religion (EA)
FAA-RD .... Federal Aviation Administration Systems Research and Development Service
FAARO ...... Federal Aviation Administration Regional Office (NOAA)
FAARP...... Forward Area Aiming and Refueling Point [*Military*] (MCD)
FAAS........ Family of Army Aircraft System

FAAS......... Fellow of the Academy of Arts and Sciences
FAAS......... Flame Atomic Absorption Spectrometry
FAAS......... Flameless Atomic Absorption Spectrophotometry
FAAS......... Forward Area Alerting System (AABC)
FAASE ...... Forces Aeriennes Alliees Sud-Europe [*Allied Air Forces Southern Europe*] [*NATO*] (NATG)
FAA-SST... Federal Aviation Administration Office of Supersonic Transport Development
FAASTU ... Fleet Air Arm Service Trials Unit [*British*]
FAASV ...... Field Artillery Ammunition Support Vehicle
FAAT........ First Article Acceptance Test (MCD)
FAAT........ French Australian and Antarctic Territories
FA1AT....... Fecal Alpha 1 - Antitrypsin [*Clinical chemistry*]
FAATD...... Fundamental and Applied Toxicology [*A publication*]
FAATDC ... Federal Aviation Administration Technical Development Center
FAAW .... Federation of Arab Agricultural Workers (EAIO)
FAAWC...... Fleet Antiair Warfare Coordinator [*Navy*] (CAAL)
FAAWTC .. Fleet Antiair Warfare Training Center
FAAWTRACEN ... Fleet Antiair Warfare Training Center
FAB............ Aeronautical Broadcast Station [*ITU designation*] (CET)
Fab............. Antigen-Binding Fragment [*Immunology*]
FAB........... Bradley Air Service [*Carp, ON*] [*FAA designator*] (FAAC)
Fab .... Fabius Accorambonus [*Deceased, 1559*] [*Authority cited in pre-1607 legal work*] (DSA)
FAB........... Fable (ROG)
FAB........... Fabric
FAB........... Fabricate
fab .... Fabrication [*Manufacture*] [*Business term*] [*French*]
FAB........... Fabrichnaya [*USSR*] [*Seismograph station code, US Geological Survey*] [*Closed*] (SEIS)
Fab .... Fabrik [*Factory*] [*Business term*] [*German*]
Fab .... Fabula [*A publication*]
FAB........... Fabulous (ROG)
FAB........... Facilities Advisory Board (AAG)
FAB........... Family Allowance, Class B [*Navy*]
FAB........... Fast Atom Bombardment [*Mass spectrometry*]
FAB........... Features, Advantages, Benefits [*of clothing*] [*Retailing*]
FAB........... Federal Aborigines Board [*Churches of Christ*] [*Australia*]
FAB........... Feline Advisory Bureau [*British*] (CB)
FAB........... Festschrift fuer Alfred Bertholet [*Tuebingen*] [*A publication*]
FAB........... Field Artillery Brigade (AABC)
FAB........... Film Advisory Board (EA)
FAB........... First-Aid Box (AAG)
FAB........... Fixed Action Button (NVT)
FAB........... Fleet Air Base
FAB........... Fleet Air Broadcast (NATG)
FAB........... Forca Aerea Brasileira [*Brazilian Air Force*]
FAB........... Foreign Affairs Bulletin [*Thailand*] [*A publication*]
F Ab .... Forestry Abstracts [*A publication*]
FAB........... Formalin-Ammonium Bromide [*Fixative*]
FAB........... Forwarder Air Waybill [*Shipping*] (DS)
Fab .... Fragment, Antigen-Binding [*Immunochemistry*]
Fab .... Franco de Bord [*Free on Board - FOB*] [*French*]
fab .... Franco a Bordo [*Free on Board - FOB*] [*Spanish*]
FAB........... Free Association Books [*Publisher*] [*British*]
fab .... Frei an Bord [*Free on Board - FOB*] [*German*]
FAB........... Functional Adhesive Bonding
FAB........... Functional Area Breakdown
FAB........... Functional Arm Brace [*Medicine*]
FABA........ Firing Attachment Blank Ammunition (MCD)
FABAC...... Fellow of the Association of Business and Administrative Computing [*British*] (DBQ)
FABB........ Brakpan [*South Africa*] [*ICAO location identifier*] (ICLI)
FABB........ Filene's [*Boston*] Automatic Bargain Basement
FABC........ First Alabama Bancshares, Inc. [*NASDAQ symbol*] (NQ)
FABCFFS ... Feline Advisory Bureau and Central Fund for Feline Studies (EAIO)
FABD........ Burgersdorp [*South Africa*] [*ICAO location identifier*] (ICLI)
FABE........ Fellow of the Association of Business Executives [*British*] (DCTA)
FABERE.... Flexion, Abduction, External Rotation, Extension [*Orthopedics*]
FABF .... Fellows of the American Bar Foundation (EA)
FABI........ Federazione Autonoma Bancari Italiana [*Bank Workers Federation*] [*Italy*] (EY)
FABI........ Folk Artists Bibliographical Index [*A publication*]
FABIS....... Filmless Automatic Bond Inspection System
FABL........ Bloemfontein/J. B. M. Hertzog [*South Africa*] [*ICAO location identifier*] (ICLI)
FABL........ Fire Alarm Bell
FABM........ Bethlehem [*South Africa*] [*ICAO location identifier*] (ICLI)
FABM........ Fellowship of American Baptist Musicians (EA)
FABMDS .. Field Army Ballistic Missile Defense System [*Later, AADS*] [*Antimissile missile*]
FABMIDS ... Field Army Ballistic Missile Defense System [*Later, AADS*] [*Antimissile missile*]
FABMS ..... Fast Atom Bombardment Mass Spectroscopy
FABN........ Barberton [*South Africa*] [*ICAO location identifier*] (ICLI)
FABP........ Fatty Acid Binding Protein [*Biochemistry*]
FABR........ Bredasdorp [*South Africa*] [*ICAO location identifier*] (ICLI)

FABR.........	Fabricated
F Abr.........	Fitzherbert's Abridgment [*1516*] [*A publication*] (DLA)
F & ABR	Food and Agriculture Branch [*US Military Government, Germany*]
FABRIC.....	Florida Architecture and Building Research Center [*University of Florida*] [*Research center*] (RCD)
FABRIC.....	Frequency Assignment by Reference to Interference Charts (MCD)
FABS	Brits [*South Africa*] [*ICAO location identifier*] (ICLI)
FABS	Fabulous Inns of America [*NASDAQ symbol*] (NQ)
FABSAE....	FAO [*Food and Agriculture Organization of the United Nations*] Fisheries Biology Synopsis [*A publication*]
FABTECH ...	Fabrication Technology (MCD)
Fab Tr	Fabian Tract [*A publication*]
FABU.........	Fleet Air Base Unit
FABU.........	Fuel Additive Blender Unit
FA (Bud)....	Folia Archaeologica (Budapest) [*A publication*]
FABV.........	Brandvlei [*South Africa*] [*ICAO location identifier*] (ICLI)
FABW	Beaufort West [*South Africa*] [*ICAO location identifier*] (ICLI)
FABWH	Flush Armor Balance Watertight Hatch
FABX	Beatrix Mine [*South Africa*] [*ICAO location identifier*] (ICLI)
FABX	Fire Alarm Box
FABY	Beaufort West/Wes Town [*South Africa*] [*ICAO location identifier*] (ICLI)
FABZAZ ...	Flora oder Allgemeine Botanische Zeitung [*Jena*] [*A publication*]
FAC...........	Airport Control Station [*ITU designation*] (DEN)
FAC...........	Facial [*Chemistry*]
FAC...........	Facilities Associate Contractor
FAC...........	Facility (AAG)
FAC...........	Facsimile
FAC...........	Factor (MSA)
FAC...........	Factory
FAC...........	Factum Similis [*Facsimile*] [*Latin*]
FAC...........	Faculty (AABC)
Fac	Faculty of Advocates Collection of Decisions, Scotch Court of Sessions [*A publication*] (DLA)
FAC...........	Failure Analysis Coordinator
FAC...........	Familial Adenamatosis Coli [*Medicine*]
FAC...........	Farm Advisory Committee [*MAFF*] [*British*]
FAC...........	Fast Affinity Chromatography
FAC...........	Fast Attack Craft
FAC...........	Fast as Can [*Business term*]
FAC...........	Federal Advisory Council [*Department of Labor*]
FAC...........	Federal Airports Corporation [*Australia*]
FAC...........	Federal Aviation Commission [*Terminated, 1935*]
FAC...........	Femoral Ash per Centimeter
FAC...........	Field Accelerator
FAC...........	File Access Channel
FAC...........	Filter Address Correction
FAC...........	Final Acceptance Criteria (NRCH)
FAC...........	Financial Administrative Control (AFM)
FAC...........	Fine Alignment Complete
FAC...........	First Air Courier, Inc. [*El Reno, OK*] [*FAA designator*] (FAAC)
FAC...........	First Alert Capability [*Military*]
FAC...........	First Amendment Congress (EA)
FAC...........	First Atlanta Corporation [*NYSE symbol*] (SPSG)
FAC...........	Fiscal Advisory Committee [*American Occupational Therapy Association*]
FAC...........	Fixed Air Capacitor
FAC...........	Fleet Activities Command [*Navy*]
FAC...........	Fleet Augmentation Component
FAC...........	Fletcher Aviation Corporation
FAC...........	Flettner Aircraft Corporation (MCD)
FAC...........	Floating Accumulator
FAC...........	Fluorescent Analog Cytochemistry [*Microscopic technique*]
FAC...........	Fluorouracil, Adriamycin, Cyclophosphamide [*Antineoplastic drug regimen*]
FAC...........	Flying Activity Category (AFM)
FAC...........	Food Advisory Committee [*British*]
FAC...........	Food Aid Committee (EAIO)
FAC...........	Footwear and Accessories Council (EA)
FAC...........	Ford Aerosports Club (EA)
FAC...........	Foreign Adoption Center [*Later, FCVN*] (EA)
FAC...........	Foreign Agricultural Club (EA)
FAC...........	Foreign Allowable Catch [*Fishery management*] (MSC)
FAC...........	Forward Air Control [*or Controller*] [*Air Force*]
fac...............	Forwarding Agents Commission [*Shipping*] (DS)
FAC...........	Fragments of Attic Comedy [*A publication*] (OCD)
FAC...........	France au Combat [*A publication*]
F de Ac	Franciscus de Accursio [*Deceased, 1293*] [*Authority cited in pre-1607 legal work*] (DSA)
FAC...........	Free Alongside Carrier [*Business term*]
FAC...........	Free Available Chlorine [*Analytical chemistry*]
FAC...........	Freedom to Advertise Coalition (EA)
FAC...........	French-American Committee for the Statue of Liberty (EA)
FAC...........	Frequency Allocation Committee
FAC...........	Frequency Analysis and Control
FAC...........	Front d'Alliberament Catala [*Spain*]
FAC...........	Front des Artistes Canadiens [*Canadian Artists' Representation - CAR*]

FAC...........	Fuel Adjustment Clause
FAC...........	Functional Area Code
FAC...........	Fund for Advancement of Camping (EA)
FAC...........	Fund for Artists' Colonies (EA)
FACA........	Federal Advisory Committee Act
FACA........	Federal Alcohol Control Administration [*Established, 1933; abolished, 1935*]
FAcA........	Fellow of the Acupuncture Association [*British*] (DBQ)
FACA........	Fellow of the American College of Angiology
FACA........	Fellow of the American College of Apothecaries
FAC(A).....	Forward Air Controller (Airborne) (NVT)
FACA........	Monte Carlo [*South Africa*] [*ICAO location identifier*] (ICLI)
Fac Agron Montevideo Publ Misc ...	Facultad de Agronomia de Montevideo. Publicacion Miscelanea [*A publication*]
FACAl.......	Fellow of the American College of Allergists
FACAn.......	Fellow of the American College of Anesthesiologists
FACAT.....	First Article Capability Assessment Test (MCD)
FACB........	Colesburg [*South Africa*] [*ICAO location identifier*] (ICLI)
FACC........	Federation Africaine des Chambres de Commerce [*Federation of African Chambers of Commerce*] [*Ethiopia*] (EAIO)
FACC........	Fellow of the American College of Cardiology
FACC........	Food Additives and Contaminants Committee [*British*]
FACC........	Force Associated Control Communications [*Military*] (AFM)
FACC........	Ford Aerospace and Communications Corporation (MCD)
FACC........	French-American Chamber of Commerce (EA)
FACCA......	Fellow of the Association of Certified and Corporate Accountants [*British*] (EY)
Fac Cienc Agrar Para Bol ...	Faculdade de Ciencias Agrarias do Para. Boletim [*A publication*]
Fac Cienc Agrar Univ Austral Chile Bol ...	Facultad de Ciencias Agrarias. Universidad Austral de Chile. Boletin [*A publication*]
FAC/CO	Facility Checkout
FAC Cocoa ...	Foreign Agriculture Circular. Cocoa [*A publication*]
FAC Coffee ...	Foreign Agriculture Circular. Coffee [*A publication*]
Fac Coll......	Faculty of Advocates Collection of Decisions, Scotch Court of Sessions, First and Second Series [*38 vols.*] [*A publication*] (DLA)
Fac Coll NS ...	Faculty of Advocates Collection of Decisions, Scotch Court of Sessions [*A publication*] (DLA)
FACCON.....	Facilities Control [*Radio Central*] [*Navy*] (CAAL)
FACCONCEN ...	Facilities Control Center [*Army*] (AABC)
FAC Cotton ...	Foreign Agriculture Circular. Cotton [*A publication*]
FACCP	Fellow of the American College of Chest Physicians
FACD........	Cradock [*South Africa*] [*ICAO location identifier*] (ICLI)
FACD........	Fellow of the American College of Dentists
FACD........	Foreign Area Consumer Dialing [*Telecommunications*]
FAC Dairy ...	Foreign Agriculture Circular. Dairy Products [*A publication*]
Fac Dec	Faculty of Advocates Collection of Decisions, Scotch Court of Sessions, First and Second Series [*38 vols.*] [*A publication*] (DLA)
Fac Derecho R Univ Zulia ...	Facultad de Derecho. Revista. Universidad de Zulia [*A publication*]
FAC DLP...	Foreign Agriculture Circular. Livestock and Poultry Export Trade [*A publication*]
FACE........	Facelifters Home Systems, Inc. [*Brooklyn, NY*] [*NASDAQ symbol*] (NQ)
FACE........	Facilities and Communication Evaluation [*Army*] (AABC)
FACE........	Factory Automatic Checkout Equipment
FACE........	Families Adopting Children Everywhere (EA)
FACE........	Federal Advertising Committee on Ethics (MCD)
FACE........	Federally Assisted Code Enforcement [*Proposed HUD program*]
FACE........	Federation of Associations on the Canadian Environment
FACE........	Federation des Associations Canadiennes sur l'Environnement [*Federation of Associations on the Canadian Environment*]
FACE........	Federation des Associations de Chasseurs de la CEE [*Federation of Hunters' Associations of the European Economic Community*] [*Brussels, Belgium*]
FACE........	Fellow of the Australian College of Education
FACE........	Fellowship of Artists for Cultural Evangelism (EA)
FACE........	Field Alterable Control Element (MDG)
FACE........	Field Artillery Computer Equipment
FACE........	Financial Advertising Committee on Ethics
FACE........	Florida Area Cumulus Experiment [*National Science Foundation*]
FACE........	Folk Arts for Communication and Education
FACE........	Forward Area Collection and ECM [*Electronic Countermeasures*]
FACE........	Forward Area Collection Equipment (MCD)
FACE........	Foundation for Accredited Chiropractic Education [*Later, FCER*] (EA)
FACE........	International Federation of Associations of Computer Users in Engineering Architecture and Related Fields (EAIO)
FACE........	Saint Francis Association for Catholic Evangelism (EA)
FACE IT....	Foreign Agents Compulsory Ethics in Trade Act [*Proposed*]
FACENGCOM ...	Facility Engineering Command
FACEP......	Fellow of American College of Emergency Physicians (DHSM)
FACES.......	Family Adaptability and Cohesion Evaluation Scale [*Psychology*]
FACES.......	Federal Advisory Council on Employment Security

FACES...... FORTRAN [*Formula Translating System*] Automatic Code Evaluation System [*NASA*] [*Data processing*]
FACET ...... Facetious
FACET ...... Fluid Amplifier Control Engine Test
FACETS.... Franco American Committee for Educational Travel and Studies [*Later, FACETS Tour France*]
FACETS.... Fraud and Abuse Clearinghouse for Effective Technology Sharing [*Department of Health and Human Services*]
FACETS.... Future Anti-Air Concepts Experimental Technology Seeker [*Military aircraft research program*] [*British*]
FACF .... Facility Chief [*Aviation*] (FAAC)
FACFI........ Federal Advisory Committee on False Identification [*Department of Justice*] [*Terminated, 1976*]
FACFP....... Fellow of the American College of Family Physicians
FACFS....... Fellow of the American College of Foot Surgeons
FACG........ Fellow of the American College of Gastroenterology
FACGD...... Federation of American Citizens of German Descent [*Later, DANK*] (EA)
FAC GrainS ... Foreign Agriculture Circular. World Grain Situation [*A publication*]
FACH .... Cookhouse [*South Africa*] [*ICAO location identifier*] (ICLI)
FACH .... Family and Community Health [*A publication*]
FACH .... Forceps to After-Coming Head [*Obstetrics*]
FACHA ..... Fellow of the American College of Health Administrators
Fachausschussber Dtsch Glastech Ges ... Fachausschussbericht der Deutschen Glastechnischen. Gesellschaft [*A publication*]
Fachber Huettenpraxis Metallweiterverarb ... Fachberichte Huettenpraxis Metallweiterverarbeitung [*A publication*]
Fachber Oberflaechentech ... Fachberichte fuer Oberflaechentechnik [*A publication*]
Fachbuchreihe Schweisstech ... Fachbuchreihe Schweissentechnik [*West Germany*] [*A publication*]
FACHCA... Fellow of American College of Health Care Administrators (DHSM)
FACHCA... Foundation of American College of Health Care Administrators (EA)
FACHE...... Fellow of American College of Healthcare Executives (DHSM)
Fachh Chemigr ... Fachhefte fuer Chemigraphie, Lithographie, und Tiefdruck [*A publication*]
Fachh Chemigr Lithogr Tiefdruck ... Fachhefte fuer Chemigraphie, Lithographie, und Tiefdruck [*A publication*]
Fach Inf Energ-Versorg Schwaben AG ... Fach-Informationen. Energie-Versorgung Schwaben AG [*A publication*]
Fachliche Mitt Oesterr Tabakregie ... Fachliche Mitteilungen der Oesterreichischen Tabakregie [*A publication*]
FAC Hort... Foreign Agriculture Circular. Horticultural Products [*A publication*]
FACHPER ... Fellow of the Australian College of Health, Physical Education, and Recreation
FACHRES-CA ... Faculty for Human Rights in El Salvador and Central America (EA)
FACI.......... Fellow of the Australian Chemical Institute [*Later, FRACI*]
FACI.......... First Article Configuration Inspection [*Gemini*] [*NASA*] (AFM)
FACI.......... Folklore Americano; Organo del Comite Interamericano de Folklore [*A publication*]
Facial Orthop Temporomandibular Arthrol ... Facial Orthopedics and Temporomandibular Arthrology [*A publication*]
Facial Plast Surg ... Facial Plastic Surgery [*A publication*]
FACIL .... Facility
FACILE..... Fire and Casualty Insurance Library Edition
FACIM ...... Foundation for a Course in Miracles (EA)
Fac Ingen Agrimens (Montevideo) Publ Didact Inst Mat Estadis ... Facultad de Ingenieria y Agrimensura (Montevideo). Publicaciones Didacticas del Instituto de Matematica y Estadistica [*A publication*]
FACISCOM USA ... Finance and Comptroller Information Systems Command, United States Army
Fack .... Fackel [*A publication*]
FACL......... Carolina [*South Africa*] [*ICAO location identifier*] (ICLI)
FACLC ...... Federation of American Cultural and Language Communities (EA)
Fac Lett Sc NS ... Faculte des Lettres et Sciences Humaines. Universite de Clermont-Ferrand. Nouvelle Serie [*A publication*]
FAC-LEV ... Fluorouracil, Adriamycin, Cyclophosphamide, Levamisole [*Antineoplastic drug regimen*]
Fac of LR ... Faculty of Law Review. University of Toronto [*A publication*]
Fac L Rev ... Faculty of Law Review [*A publication*]
FAC MAT ... Facilities Matrix (MCD)
FACMD..... Fluoroactinomycin D [*Antineoplastic drug*]
FACMN .... Fleet Chief Aircraft Mechanician [*British military*] (DMA)
FACMS ..... Foundation for Advances in Clinical Medicine and Science [*Later, FAMS*] (EA)
FACMTA .. Federal Advisory Council on Medical Training Aids
FACNHA .. Foundation of American College of Nursing Home Administrators [*Later, FACHCA*] (EA)
FACO .... Copperton [*South Africa*] [*ICAO location identifier*] (ICLI)
FACO .... FA Computer Technologies, Inc. [*NASDAQ symbol*] (NQ)
FACO .... Fabrication and Acceptance Checkout (MCD)
FACO .... Factory Acceptance Checkout (MCD)
FACO .... Factory Assembly and Checkout

FACO .... Fellow of American College of Organists
FACO .... Fellow of the American College of Otolaryngology
FACO .... Final Assembly Checkout [*NASA*] (NASA)
FACOEB .. Food Additives and Contaminants [*A publication*]
FACOG ..... Fellow of the American College of Obstetricians and Gynecologists
FACOGAZ ... Union des Fabricants Europeens de Compteurs de Gaz [*Union of European Manufacturers of Gas Meters*] (EAIO)
FAC Oil ..... Foreign Agriculture Circular. Oilseeds and Products [*A publication*]
FACOM .... Fellow of the Australian College of Occupational Medicine
FACOSH.. Federal Advisory Committee on Occupational Safety and Health [*Department of Labor*] [*Washington, DC*]
FA/COSI... Final Assembly and Closeout System Installation (MCD)
FACP .... Fellow of the American College of Physicians
FACP........ Fellow of the Association of Computer Professionals [*British*] (DBQ)
FACP........ Forward Air Control Party [*Military*] (CAAL)
FACP........ Forward Air Control Post (AFM)
FACP........ Ftorafur [*Tegafur*], Adriamycin, Cyclophosphamide, Platinol [*Cisplatin*] [*Antineoplastic drug regimen*]
FACP........ Fully Automated Computer Program (AAG)
FACP........ Functional Assignment Control Panel (MCD)
FACPM .... Fellow of the American College of Preventive Medicine
FACR........ Carletonville [*South Africa*] [*ICAO location identifier*] (ICLI)
FACR........ Fellow of the American College of Radiology
FACR........ First Article Configuration Review [*Army*] (AABC)
FACR........ Force Assessment in the Central Region [*NATO*] (NATG)
FACRED... Federal Advisory Council on Regional Economic Development
Fac Res Pap ... Faculty Research Papers [*South Korea*] [*A publication*]
Fac Res Pap Hanyang Women's Jr Coll ... Faculty Research Papers. Hanyang Women's Junior College [*A publication*]
FACS .... Facilities (ADA)
FACS .... Facsimile (KSC)
FACS .... Fast Atom Capillaritron Source [*Instrumentation*]
FACS .... Fast Attack Class Submarine [*Navy*]
FACS .... Federal Automated Career System
FACS .... Federation of American Controlled Shipping [*New York, NY*] (EA)
FACS .... Fellow of the American College of Surgeons
FACS .... Field Army Communication System (AABC)
FACS .... Finance and Control System (NASA)
FACS .... Financial Accounting and Control System
FACS .... Fine Attitude Control System [*Aerospace*]
FACS .... Flexible Accounting Control System [*Data processing*] (BUR)
FACS .... Flight Augmentation Control System [*Aviation*]
FACS .... Floating Decimal Abstract Coding System
FACS .... Fluid Amplifier Control System
FACS .... Fluorescence-Activated Cell Sorter [*Becton, Dickinson Electronics Laboratory*] [*Instrumentation*]
FACS .... Force Automation and Communications [*Military*]
FACS .... Foundation for American Communications (EA)
FACS .... Frederick A. Cook Society (EA)
FACS .... Friendship Association of Chinese Students and Scholars (EA)
FACS .... Fully Automatic Compiling System
FACS .... Future Armored Combat System [*Military*]
FACSC ...... Frequency Allocation Coordinating Subcommittee [*Canada*]
FACSEA.... Society for French American Cultural Services and Educational Aid (EA)
FACSFAC ... Fleet Air Control and Survey Facility
FACSFAX ... Fleet Air Control and Surveillance Facility (MCD)
FACSI........ Federal Advisory Council on Scientific Information
FACSIM.... Facsimile
FACSIMILE ... FAMECE [*Family of Military Engineer Construction Equipment*] Computer Simulator [*or Simulation*] for Independent and Logical Evaluation (MCD)
Facsimile Repr Herpetol ... Facsimile Reprints in Herpetology [*A publication*]
Facsimile Repr Soc Study Amphibians Reptiles ... Facsimile Reprint. Society for the Study of Amphibians and Reptiles [*A publication*]
Facsim Repr Herpetol ... Facsimile Reprints in Herpetology [*A publication*]
Facsim Repr Soc Study Amphibians Reptiles ... Facsimile Reprint. Society for the Study of Amphibians and Reptiles [*A publication*]
FACSM ..... Fellow of the American College of Sports Medicine
FACSO ...... Facilities Supply Office
FAC/SPC .. Fisheries Advisory Committee of the South Pacific Commission
FACSS....... Federation of Analytical Chemistry and Spectroscopy Societies (EA)
FACSTEAM ... Facilities Installation Study Program [*Navy*] (NVT)
FAC Sugar ... Foreign Agriculture Circular. Sugar, Molasses, and Honey [*A publication*]
FACT......... Cape Town [*South Africa*] [*ICAO location identifier*] (ICLI)
FACT......... Facility for the Analysis of Chemical Thermodynamics [*McGill University*] [*Information service or system*] (IID)
FACT......... Factor Analysis Chart Technique [*Business term*]
FACT......... Factory [*Automotive engineering*]
FACT......... Factory Automation, Control, and Test Facility
FACT......... Factual Compiler
FACT......... Fairchild Advanced CMOS Technology [*Fairchild Semiconductor Corp.*]
FACT......... Faith and Atheism in Communist Territories [*Australia*]
FACT........ Fast Access Current Text

FACT........ Fast Asymptotic Coherent Transmission (NVT)
FACT........ Federation Against Copyright Theft [*British*]
FACT........ Federation of American Consumers and Travelers (EA)
FACT........ Federation of Automated Coding Technologies (EA)
FACT........ Feminist Anti-Censorship Task Force
FACT........ Festival of American Community Theatre [*American Community Theatre Association*]
FACT........ Field Audit and Completion Test [*Market research*]
FACT........ Fingerprint Automatic Classification Technique [*Data processing*]
FACT........ First Albany Companies, Inc. [*Albany, NY*] [*NASDAQ symbol*] (NQ)
FACT........ First American Congress of Theater
FACT........ Flanagan Aptitude Classification Test [*Psychology*]
FACT........ Flexible Automatic Circuit Tester
FACT........ Flight Acceptance Composite Test [*NASA*]
FACT........ Food Additive Campaign Team [*British*]
FACT........ Food Animal Concerns Trust (EA)
FACT....... Foreign Access to Computer Technology [*USIA*]
FACT........ Foundation for Advanced Computer Technology
FACT........ Foundation for Advancement in Cancer Therapy (EA)
FACT........ Fuel Abstracts and Current Titles [*A publication*]
FACT........ Fully Automatic Calibration Technology [*Analytical balances*]
FACT........ Fully Automatic Cataloging Technique [*Data processing*] (MCD)
FACT........ Fully Automatic Compiler [*or Computer*]-Translator [*Data processing*]
FACT........ Fully Automatic Compiling Technique [*Data processing*]
FACT........ Fully Automatically Controlled Train [*British*]
facta .... Factura [*Bill*] [*Spanish*]
FAC Tea .... Foreign Agriculture Circular. Tea and Spices [*A publication*]
Fact Equip Mater ... Factory Equipment and Materials [*South Africa*] [*A publication*]
FACTER.... Forward Air Controller Terminal
FACTEX.... Fast Asymptotic Coherent Transmission Extended (MCD)
Fact Mag.... Fact Magazine [*A publication*]
Fact Manage (NY) ... Factory Management (New York) [*A publication*]
Fact Man Maint ... Factory Management and Maintenance [*A publication*]
Fact Mut Bull Loss Prev ... Factory Mutual Bulletin of Loss Prevention [*A publication*]
FAC Tobac ... Foreign Agriculture Circular. Tobacco [*A publication*]
FACTOR ... Foundation to Assist Canadian Talent on Records
Factory and Ind Management ... Factory and Industrial Management [*A publication*]
Factory Mgt ... Factory Management and Maintenance [*A publication*]
Fact Pl........ Factory and Plant [*A publication*] (APTA)
Fact Plant .. Factory and Plant [*A publication*]
FACTRO.... Factory Mechatronics (TSPED)
FACTS...... Facilities Action Control Target System [*US Postal Service*]
FACTS...... Facilities Administration Consolidated Tape System (MCD)
FACTS...... Facilities Administration Control and Time Schedule
FACTS...... Facilities Assets Catalog and Tracking System [*Army*]
FACTS...... Facsimile Transmission System [*Telecommunications*]
FACTS...... Family and Community Treatment Services
FACTS...... Fast Access to Computerized Technical Sources [*Information service or system*] (IID)
FACTS...... Fast Action on Comments of Technical Significance
FACTS...... Fast Agricultural Communication Terminal System [*Purdue University*] [*Information service or system*]
FACTS...... Field Army Calibration Team Support
FACTS...... Financial Accounting and Control Techniques for Supply [*Army*]
FACTS...... Financial Analysis Capability through Scanning
FACTS...... Financing Analysis Cost and Testing Service [*LIMRA*]
FACTS...... First Amendment Consumer and Trade Society (EA)
FACTS....... FLIR [*Forward-Looking Infrared RADAR*] Augmented Cobra TOW [*Tube-Launched, Optically-Tracked, Wire-Guided Weapon*] Sight
FACTS...... FORTRAN [*Formula Translating System*] Analytical Cross Reference Tabulation System [*Data processing*]
FACTS....... Foundation for the Advancement of Chiropractic Tenets and Science (EA)
FACTS....... Free Available Chlorine Test with Syringaldazine [*Analytical chemistry*]
FACTS....... National Food and Conservation through Swine (EA)
Facts & Figures ... Australian in Facts and Figures [*A publication*] (APTA)
Facts (Finl) ... Facts about Film (Finland) [*A publication*]
Fact Sheet Coop Ext Serv Univ MD ... Fact Sheet. Cooperative Extension Service. University of Maryland [*A publication*]
Fact Sheet Oreg State Univ Coop Ext Serv ... Fact Sheet. Oregon State University. Cooperative Extension Service [*A publication*]
Fact Sheet S Dak State Univ Coop Ext Serv ... Fact Sheet. South Dakota State University. Cooperative Extension Service [*A publication*]
Fact Sheets Swed ... Fact Sheets on Sweden [*A publication*]
Fact Sheet Univ MD Coop Ext Serv ... Fact Sheet. University of Maryland. Cooperative Extension Service [*A publication*]
Fact Sheet USDA ... Fact Sheet. United States Department of Agriculture [*A publication*]
Fact Sh Univ Wis Ext ... Fact Sheet. University of Wisconsin - Extension [*A publication*]

Facts Methods Sci Res ... Facts and Methods for Scientific Research [*A publication*]
Facty .... Factory
FACUI....... Federal Advisory Council on Unemployment Insurance
FACV........ Calvinia [*South Africa*] [*ICAO location identifier*] (ICLI)
FACW........ Clanwilliam [*South Africa*] [*ICAO location identifier*] (ICLI)
FAC WCP ... Foreign Agriculture Circular. World Crop Production [*A publication*]
FAD .... Faculty Author Development [*Software development program*]
FAD .... Familial Alzheimer's Disease [*Medicine*]
FAD .... Family Assessment Device
FAD .... Fantastic Adventures [*1939-1953*] [*A publication*]
FAD .... Federal Anti-Trust Decisions [*A publication*] (DLA)
FAD .... Ferrite Array Demonstration [*RADAR*]
FAD .... Fetal Activity Determination
FAD .... Fighter Air Director [*Military*] (NVT)
FAD .... Final Approach Display (MCD)
FAD .... Financial Accounting Data
FAD .... Fine Art Development [*British*]
FAD .... First Appearance Datum [*Geology*]
FAD .... First Article Demonstration
FAD .... Fish Aggregating Device [*Pisciculture*]
FAD .... Flavin-Adenine Dinucleotide [*Biochemistry*]
FAD .... Flea Allergy Dermatitis [*Medicine*]
FAD .... Fleet Air Defense (MCD)
FAD .... Fleet Air Detachment [*Navy*]
FAD .... Flexible Automatic Depot
FAD .... Floating Add [*Data processing*] (IEEE)
FAD .... Fonds Africain de Developpement [*African Development Fund*]
F/AD........ Force/Activity Designator [*Military*]
FAD .... Foreign Affairs and Defence Committee [*Australia*]
FAD .... Free Air Delivered
FAD .... Fuel Advisory Departure Procedures [*Aviation*] (FAAC)
FAD .... Fuerzas Armadas Democraticas [*Democratic Armed Forces*] [*Nicaragua*] (PD)
FAD .... Functional Area Description
FAD .... Funding Authorization Document (AABC)
FADA .... De Aar [*South Africa*] [*ICAO location identifier*] (ICLI)
FADA .... Federal Assets Disposition Association [*Functions transferred to FDIC and RTC, 1989*]
FADA .... Fourth Armored Division Association (EA)
FADA .... Fuerzas de Accion Armada [*Armed Action Forces*] [*Guatemala*] (PD)
FADAC...... Field Artillery Digital Automatic Computer (IEEE)
FADALA ... Failure Detection and Location Analysis (MCD)
FADAP...... Fleet Antisubmarine Data Analysis Program
FADC........ Douglas Colliery [*South Africa*] [*ICAO location identifier*] (ICLI)
FADC........ Fighter Air Direction Center
FADD .... Dundee [*South Africa*] [*ICAO location identifier*] (ICLI)
FADD .... Fight Against Dictating Designers [*Group opposing below-the-knee fashions introduced in 1970*]
F Addit Contr Ser FAO ... Food Additive Control Series. Food and Agriculture Organization of the United Nations [*A publication*]
FADEAC ... Federacion Argentina de Entidades Empresarias de Autotransporte de Cargas [*Transportation service*] [*Argentina*] (EY)
FADEC...... Full Authority Digital Engine Control
FADEM..... Flower of Friendship and Development of Macau [*Political party*] (EY)
FADES ...... Fuselage Analysis and Design Synthesis
FADH........ Durnacol [*South Africa*] [*ICAO location identifier*] (ICLI)
FADH₂....... Flavin-Adenine Dinucleotide [*Reduced*] [*Biochemistry*]
FADICA .... Foundations and Donors Interested in Catholic Activities (EA)
FADINAP ... Fertilizer Advisory Development Information Network for Asia and the Pacific
FADIR....... Flexion, Adduction, Internal Rotation [*Orthopedics*]
FADL........ Delareyville [*South Africa*] [*ICAO location identifier*] (ICLI)
FADM....... Fleet Admiral
FADM....... Functional Area Documentation Manager [*Air Force*] (AFM)
FADN....... Durban/Louis Botha [*South Africa*] [*ICAO location identifier*] (ICLI)
FADN .... Frente Anti-Comunista de Defensa Nacional [*Anti-Communist Front for National Defense*] [*Ecuador*]
FADO .... Fellow of the Association of Dispensing Opticians [*British*] (DBQ)
FADOA ..... Family Coordinator [*A publication*]
FADO(Hons) ... Fellow of the Association of Dispensing Opticians with Honours Diploma [*British*] (DBQ)
FADO(Hons)CL ... Fellow of the Association of Dispensing Opticians with Honours Diploma and Diploma in Contact Lens Fitting [*British*] (DBQ)
FADP........ Finnish Association for Data Processing
FADPUG... Federal ADP [*Automatic Data Processing*] Users Group
FADR....... Dunnottar [*South Africa*] [*ICAO location identifier*] (ICLI)
FADR .... Foreign Animal Disease Report [*A publication*]
FADS........ Dordabis [*Namibia*] [*ICAO location identifier*] (ICLI)
FADS........ Force Administration Data System [*Bell System*]

FADS......... FORTRAN [*Formula Translating System*] Automatic Debugging System [*Data processing*]
FADS......... Forward Area Deployment, Spain
FADSID .... Fighter-Aircraft-Delivered Seismic Intrusion Detector   (NVT)
FADV .... Devon [*South Africa*] [*ICAO location identifier*]   (ICLI)
f-ae--- .... Algeria [*MARC geographic area code*] [*Library of Congress*]   (LCCP)
FAE............ Dayton, OH [*Location identifier*] [*FAA*]   (FAAL)
FAE............ Faenza [*Italy*] [*Seismograph station code, US Geological Survey*] [*Closed*]   (SEIS)
FAE............ Faroe Islands [*Denmark*] [*Airport symbol*]   (OAG)
FAE............ Fellow of the Accountants' and Executives' Corporation of Canada
FAE............ Fetal Alcohol Effect [*Medicine*]
FAE............ Field Advisory Element   (CINC)
FAE............ Field Application Engineer   (IEEE)
FAE............ Final Approach Equipment [*Aviation*]
FAE............ Final Average Earnings
FAE............ Fine Alignment Equipment
FAE............ Fondation Archives Europeennes   (EA)
FAE............ Foundation for Accounting Education   (EA)
FAE............ Frei aber Einsam [*Free but Lonely*] [*Motto of Joseph Joachim, 19th century German violinist*]   (ECON)
FAE............ Fuel Air Explosive   (MCD)
FAE............ Fund for the Advancement of Education [*Defunct*]   (EA)
FAEA......... Ellisras Control Reporting Point [*South Africa*] [*ICAO location identifier*]   (ICLI)
FAEC......... Estcourt [*South Africa*] [*ICAO location identifier*]   (ICLI)
FAEC......... Foundation of the American Economic Council   (EA)
FAEC......... Full Authority Electronic Control   (MCD)
FAECF ...... Federation des Associations Europeennes des Constructeurs de Fenetres [*Federation of European Window Manufacturers Associations - FEWMA*]   (EA)
Fa Econ ..... Farm Economics [*A publication*]
Fa Econ ..... Farm Economist [*A publication*]
FAEE......... Fatty Acid Ethyl Ester
FAEJ .... Fonds d'Action et d'Education Juridiques pour les Femmes [*Women's Legal Education and Action Fund - LEAF*] [*Canada*]
FAEL......... East London/Ben Schoeman [*South Africa*] [*ICAO location identifier*]   (ICLI)
Faellesudvalget Statens Mejeri-Husdyrbrugsfors Beret ... Faellesudvalget foer Statens Mejeri-og Husdyrbrugsforsog Beretning [*A publication*]
FAEO .... Ermelo [*South Africa*] [*ICAO location identifier*]   (ICLI)
FAEPC ...... Federation des Associations d'Editeurs de Periodiques de la CE [*Brussels, Belgium*]   (EAIO)
FAER......... Ellisras [*South Africa*] [*ICAO location identifier*]   (ICLI)
FAER......... Foreign Agricultural Economic Reports
Faerber Ztg .. Faerber-Zeitung [*A publication*]
FAES......... Eshowe [*South Africa*] [*ICAO location identifier*]   (ICLI)
FAES......... Flame Atomic Emission Spectrometry
FAES .... Foreign Affairs Executive Seminar [*Department of State*]
FAESHED ... Fuel Air Explosive System Helicopter Delivered
FAET......... Elliot [*South Africa*] [*ICAO location identifier*]   (ICLI)
FAETU...... Fleet Airborne Electronic Training Unit [*Navy*]
FAETUA ... Fleet Airborne Electronic Training Unit, Atlantic
FAETUDET ... Fleet Airborne Electronic Training Unit Detachment
FAETULANT ... Fleet Airborne Electronic Training Unit, Atlantic
FAETUP ... Fleet Airborne Electronic Training Unit, Pacific   (IEEE)
FAETUPAC ... Fleet Airborne Electronic Training Unit, Pacific [*Later, FASOTRAGRUPAC, FASOTRAGRUPACFLT*]
FAF............ Family of the Americas Foundation   (EA)
FAF............ Fast-Acting Fuse
FAF............ Fathers Are Forever   (EA)
FAF............ Fatty Acid-Free [*Biochemistry*]
FAF............ Fibroblast Activating Factor [*Biochemistry*]
FAF............ Film Arts Foundation   (EA)
FAF............ Final Approach Fix [*Aviation*]   (AFM)
FAF............ Financial Accounting Foundation [*Stamford, CT*]   (EA)
FAF............ Financial Aid Form [*Of College Board*]
FAF............ Financial Analysts Federation [*Later, AIMR*]   (EA)
FAF............ Financing Adjustment Factor
FAF............ Fine Arts Foundation   (EA)
FAF............ First Aerodynamic Flight   (NASA)
F/AF .... FishAmerica Foundation   (EA)
FAF............ Fleet Amenities Fund [*Navy*] [*British*]
FAF............ Flyaway Factory
FAF............ Fort Eustis, VA [*Location identifier*] [*FAA*]   (FAAL)
FAF............ Free Asia Foundation   (EA)
FAF............ Free at Factory [*Business term*]
FAF............ French Air Force
FAF............ French-American Foundation   (EA)
FAF............ Fund for America's Future   (EA)
FAF............ Fuzing, Arming, and Firing
FAF............ Philippine Development [*A publication*]
FAFB......... Fairchild Air Force Base [*Washington*]   (AAG)
FAFB......... Ficksburg [*South Africa*] [*ICAO location identifier*]   (ICLI)
FAFBAH ... FAO [*Food and Agriculture Organization of the United Nations*] Fisheries Biology Technical Paper [*A publication*]

FAFCAK ... FAO [*Food and Agriculture Organization of the United Nations*] Fisheries Circular [*A publication*]
F & A Feed ... Journal of Flour and Animal Feed Milling [*A publication*]
FAFF .... Frankfort [*South Africa*] [*ICAO location identifier*]   (ICLI)
F Affairs..... Foreign Affairs [*A publication*]
FAFK .... Fisantekraal [*South Africa*] [*ICAO location identifier*]   (ICLI)
FAFLBE .... Fauna and Flora [*Transvaal*] [*A publication*]
FAFN......... Fauna Fennica [*A publication*]
FAFO......... FAFCO, Inc. [*NASDAQ symbol*]   (NQ)
FAFP .... Foreign Area Fellowship Program [*Later, SSRC*]
FAFPIC .... Forestry and Forest Products Industry Council [*Australia*]
FAFR......... Fatal Accident Frequency Rate
FAFR .... Fraserburg [*South Africa*] [*ICAO location identifier*]   (ICLI)
FAFRAV ... Faune de France [*A publication*]
FAFROTSKIES ... [*Things that*] Fall from the Skies [*Meteorological phenomena*]
FAFS .... Farm and Food Society [*British*]
FAFS .... Flame Atomic Fluorescence Spectrometry
FAFSBZ ... FAO [*Food and Agriculture Organization of the United Nations*] Fisheries Synopsis [*A publication*]
FAFT .... First Article Factory Tests   (NATG)
FAFT .... First Article Flight Test
FAFT .... Free Air Facility Track [*Edwards Air Force Base*]   (AAG)
FAFTAH ... First a Friend, Then a Host [*Safety slogan encouraging partygivers to prevent guests' overindulgence in alcohol*]
FAFWC ..... Fuchu Air Force Weather Central   (CINC)
F-Ag........... F Antigen [*Immunochemistry*]
FAG .... Faggot [*Derogatory term for male homosexual*] [*Slang*]   (DSUE)
FAG .... Fagotto [*Bassoon*] [*Music*]
FAG .... Fatigue [*Slang*]   (DSUE)
FAG .... Finance and Accounting Group [*Air Force*]   (AFM)
FAG .... Fiscal Activities Guide [*Department of Labor*]   (OICC)
FAG .... Fleet Assistance Group
FAG .... Foreign Agriculture [*A publication*]
FAG .... Forward Air Guide   (NVT)
FAG .... Fraud Against the Government
FAG .... Free-Air Gradient [*Geophysics*]
FAGA .... Friedreich's Ataxia Group in America   (EA)
FAGAAS ... Frankfurter Arbeiten aus dem Gebiete der Anglistik und der Amerika-Studien [*A publication*]
FAGAIRTRANS ... First Available Government Air Transportation [*Navy*]
FAGB......... Gobabis [*Namibia*] [*ICAO location identifier*]   (ICLI)
FAGC......... Fast Automatic Gain Control
FAGC......... Grand Central [*South Africa*] [*ICAO location identifier*]   (ICLI)
FAGCA...... Fenton Art Glass Collectors of America   (EA)
FAGE........ Factory Aerospace Ground Equipment   (MCD)
FAGE........ Fluorescence Assay with Gas Expansion [*Analytical chemistry*]
FAGE........ Future Age [*A publication*]   (ADA)
FAGE........ Gough Island [*South Africa*] [*ICAO location identifier*]   (ICLI)
FAGF .... Grootfontein [*Namibia*] [*ICAO location identifier*]   (ICLI)
FAGG .... George/P. W. Botha [*South Africa*] [*ICAO location identifier*]   (ICLI)
FAGI .... Giyani [*South Africa*] [*ICAO location identifier*]   (ICLI)
FAGL........ Groblersdal [*South Africa*] [*ICAO location identifier*]   (ICLI)
FAGLA ...... Furylacryloylglycylleucine Amide [*Biochemistry*]
FAGLAI ..... Farmaceutski Glasnik [*A publication*]
FAGLANT ... Fleet Assistance Group, Atlantic [*Navy*]
FAGM .... Johannesburg/Rand [*South Africa*] [*ICAO location identifier*]   (ICLI)
FAGMS..... Field Artillery Guided Missile [*Air Force*]
FAGO .... Fellow of the American Guild of Organists
FAGp......... Finance and Accounting Group [*Air Force*]   (AFM)
FAGPAC ... Fleet Assistance Group, Pacific [*Navy*]
FAGR......... Graaff Reinet [*South Africa*] [*ICAO location identifier*]   (ICLI)
F Agric ...... Food and Agriculture [*A publication*]
FAGS......... Federation of Astronomical and Geophysical Data Analysis Services [*ICSU*] [*Paris, France*]   (EAIO)
FAGS........ Federation of Astronomical and Geophysical Services [*Research center*] [*France*]   (IRC)
FAGS........ Fellow of the American Geographical Society
FAGS........ Flinders Association of Graduate Students [*Australia*]
FAGT........ First Available Government Transportation
FAGT........ Grahamstown [*South Africa*] [*ICAO location identifier*]   (ICLI)
FAGTRANS ... First Available Government Transportation
FAGU .... Fleet Air Gunnery Unit
FAGUPAC ... Fleet Air Gunnery Unit, Pacific   (MUGU)
FAGV .... Gravelotte [*South Africa*] [*ICAO location identifier*]   (ICLI)
FAGY......... Greytown [*South Africa*] [*ICAO location identifier*]   (ICLI)
FAH........... Facilitation Awards for Handicapped Scientists and Engineers Program [*Washington, DC*] [*National Science Foundation*]   (GRD)
FAH........... Fahrenheit   (KSC)
FAH........... Farrah Resources [*Vancouver Stock Exchange symbol*]
FAH........... Federation of American Hospitals [*Later, FAHS*]
FAH........... Folklore of American Holidays [*A publication*]
fah .... Frei aus Hier [*Free at Factory, Free from Here*] [*Business term*] [*German*]
FAH........... Sheboygan, WI [*Location identifier*] [*FAA*]   (FAAL)
FAHA .... Fellow of the Australian Academy of the Humanities
FAHA .... Finnish-American Historical Archives   (EA)
FAHA .... Harmony [*South Africa*] [*ICAO location identifier*]   (ICLI)

FAHAA ..... Family Handyman [*A publication*]
FAHB .... Hartebeespoortdam [*South Africa*] [*ICAO location identifier*] (ICLI)
FAHC .... First American Health Concepts, Inc. [*Mesa, AZ*] [*NASDAQ symbol*] (NQ)
FAHD .... Forum on Allied Health Data [*American Occupational Therapy Association*]
FAHD .... Humansdorp [*South Africa*] [*ICAO location identifier*] (ICLI)
FAHE .... Friends Association for Higher Education (EA)
FAHE .... Pullenshope (Hendrina) [*South Africa*] [*ICAO location identifier*] (ICLI)
FAHG .... Heidelberg [*South Africa*] [*ICAO location identifier*] (ICLI)
FAHI .... Halali [*Namibia*] [*ICAO location identifier*] (ICLI)
FAHM .... Hermanus [*South Africa*] [*ICAO location identifier*] (ICLI)
FAHN .... Fahnestock Viner Holdings, Inc. [*NASDAQ symbol*] (NQ)
FAHN .... Henties Bay [*Namibia*] [*ICAO location identifier*] (ICLI)
FAHO .... Heilbrond [*Namibia*] [*ICAO location identifier*] (ICLI)
FAHQ .... Pretoria [*South Africa*] [*ICAO location identifier*] (ICLI)
FAHQMT ... Fully Automatic High-Quality Machine Translation [*Data processing*] (DIT)
FAHQT ..... Fully Automatic High-Quality Translation [*Data processing*]
FAHR .... Fahrenheit
FAHR .... Formosan Association for Human Rights (EA)
FAHR .... Harrismith [*South Africa*] [*ICAO location identifier*] (ICLI)
FAHRB ...... Federation of Associations of Health Regulatory Boards [*Later, FARB*] (EA)
FAH Rev .... FAH [*Federation of American Hospitals*] Review [*A publication*]
FAHS .... Farm & Home Financial Corp. [*NASDAQ symbol*] (NQ)
FAHS .... Federation of American Health Systems (EA)
FAHS .... Franco-American Historical Society (EA)
FAHS .... Hoedspruit [*South Africa*] [*ICAO location identifier*] (ICLI)
FAHSM ...... Finnish American Historical Society of Michigan (EA)
FAHSW ...... Finnish-American Historical Society of the West (EA)
FAHT .... Hoedspruit Civil/Burgerlike [*South Africa*] [*ICAO location identifier*] (ICLI)
FAHV .... Hendrik Verwoerddam [*South Africa*] [*ICAO location identifier*] (ICLI)
FAI .... FAI Insurances Ltd. [*NYSE symbol*] [*Toronto Stock Exchange symbol*] (CTT)
FAI .... Fail As-Is [*Nuclear energy*] (NRCH)
FAI .... Fairbanks [*Alaska*] [*Airport symbol*] (OAG)
FAI .... Fairbanks, AK [*Location identifier*] [*FAA*] (FAAL)
FAI .... Fairplay International Shipping Weekly [*A publication*]
FAI .... Falcon Airways, Incorporated [*Addison, TX*] [*FAA designator*] (FAAC)
FAI .... Federal Acquisitions Institute [*Formerly, FPI*] (MCD)
FAI .... Federation Abolitionniste Internationale [*International Abolitionist Federation*] [*India*]
FAI .... Federation Aeronautique Internationale [*International Aeronautical Federation*] [*France*]
FAI .... Fellow of the Chartered Auctioneers' and Estate Agents' Institute [*British*]
FAI .... Financial Accounting Institute [*Tenafly, NJ*] [*Telecommunications service*] (TSSD)
FAI .... First-Aid Instructor [*Red Cross*]
FAI .... First Article Inspection [*NASA*] (KSC)
FAI .... Flight Anomaly Investigation [*NASA*] (KSC)
FAI .... Fly as Is (MCD)
FAI .... Fonds d'Activites Internationales [*International Activities Fund*] [*Canadian Labour Congress*]
FAI .... Frequency Application Index
FAI .... Frequency-Azimuth Intensity [*RADAR*]
FAI .... Fresh Air Inlet (MSA)
FAI .... Fresh Air Input
FAI .... Fuel Air Incendiary Concussion Bomb (MCD)
FAI .... Fujitsu America, Incorporated [*Hillsboro, OR*]
FAIA .... 550th Airborne Infantry Association (EA)
FAIA .... Fellow of the American Institute of Actuaries
FAIA .... Fellow of the American Institute of Architects
FAIA .... Fellow of the Association of International Accountants [*British*]
FAIAA .... Fellow of the American Institute of Aeronautics and Astronautics [*Formerly, FIAes, FIAS*]
FAIAS .... Fellow of the Australian Institute of Agricultural Science
FAIAT .... Federazione delle Associazioni Italiane Alberghi e Turismo [*Hotels and Tourism Federation*] [*Italy*] (EY)
FAIAU .... Fleet Air Intelligence Augmenting Unit (CINC)
FAIB .... Federation des Associations Internationales Etablies en Belgique [*Federation of International Associations Established in Belgium*]
FAIBM ...... Fellow of the Australian Institute of Building Management
FAIC .... Fellow of Agricultural Institute of Canada
FAIC .... Fellow of the American Institute of Criminology
FAIC .... Fellow Associate of the Institute of Chemistry
FAIC .... Fellow of the Australian Institute of Cartographers
FAICAZ ..... Folia Allergologica et Immunologica Clinica [*A publication*]
FAIDS .... Feline Acquired Immune Deficiency Syndrome [*Pathology*]
FAIE .... Fellow of the British Association of Industrial Editors (DBQ)
FAIEE .... Fellow of the American Institute of Electrical Engineers
FAIEE .... Fellow of the Australian Institute of Electrical Engineers
FAIF .... Field Automated Intelligence File (AFM)

FAIHA ...... Fellow of the Australian Institute of Hospital Administration
FAII .... Fellow of the Australian Insurance Institute
FAIL .... Failure
FAILCLEA ... Federazione Autonoma Italiana Lavoratori Cemento Legno, Edilizia, ed Affini [*Workers in Cement, Wood, Construction, and Related Industries Federation*] [*Italy*] (EY)
FAILE .... Federazione Autonoma Italiana Lavoratori Elettrici [*Electrical Workers Federation*] [*Italy*] (EY)
Failure Modes Compos ... Failure Modes in Composites. Proceedings of the Symposium [*A publication*]
FAIM .... Fellow of the Australian Institute of Management
Faim-Develop ... Faim-Developpement [*A publication*]
FAIME ...... Foreign Affairs Information Management Effort [*Computer*] [*Department of State*]
FAIN .... Fellow of the Australian Institute of Navigation
FAINT .... File of Administrative Interests [*Australia*]
FAIO .... Field Army Issuing Office
FAIO .... Field Artillery Intelligence Officer [*Military*] (AABC)
FAIP .... Fellow of the Australian Institute of Physics
FAIPA .... Faipar [*A publication*]
FAIPA .... Fellow of the Australian Institute of Public Administration
Faip Kutatas ... Faipari Kutatasok [*A publication*]
FA/IPT ...... First Article/Initial Production Testing [*Army's Combat System Test Activity*] (INF)
FAIR .... Fabrication, Assembly, and Inspection Record [*NASA*] (NASA)
FAIR .... Fair Access to Insurance Requirements [*Government insurance program*]
FAIR .... Fair and Impartial Random Selection [*System*] [*Military draft*]
FAIR .... Fair Lanes, Inc. [*NASDAQ symbol*] (NQ)
FAIR .... Fairing
FAIR .... Fairness and Accuracy in Reporting (EA)
FAIR .... Fans Against Indian Racism (EA)
FAIR .... Fast Access Information Retrieval
FAIR .... Federal Assistance Information Reporting
FAIR .... Federation for American Immigration Reform (EA)
FAIR .... Firearms and Individual Rights [*A California organization*]
FAIR .... Fleet Air [*Wing*]
FAIR .... Fly-Along Infrared Program [*Army*] (RDA)
FAIR .... Focus on Arms Information and Reassurance
FAIR .... Free from Tax, Affordable, Insured Rewarding [*Savings certificate*] [*Savings and Loan Association*]
FAIR .... Fund for Assuring an Independent Retirement (EA)
FAIR .... Irene [*South Africa*] [*ICAO location identifier*] (ICLI)
FAIRC .... Faircross [*England*]
FAIRDEX ... Fleet Air Defense Exercise [*Navy*] (NG)
FAIRE .... Fellow of the Australian Institute of Radio Engineers
FAIREC ..... Fruits Agro-Industrie Regions Chaudes [*Institut de Recherches sur les Fruits et Agrumes*] [*Database*]
FAIRECONRON ... Fleet Air Reconnaissance Squadron
FAIRELM ... Fleet Air Eastern Atlantic and Mediterranean (NATG)
Fair Empl Prac Cas ... Fair Employment Practices Cases (DLA)
Fair Empl Prac Cas BNA ... Fair Employment Practice Cases. Bureau of National Affairs [*A publication*]
Fairf .... Fairfield's Reports [*10-12 Maine*] [*A publication*] (DLA)
Fairfield ..... Fairfield's Reports [*10-12 Maine*] [*A publication*] (DLA)
Fairf (ME) ... Fairfield's Reports [*10-12 Maine*] [*A publication*] (DLA)
Fair M & D ... Fairbanks' Marriage and Divorce Laws of Massachusetts [*A publication*] (DLA)
FAIR Newsl ... Fast Access Information Retrieval. Newsletter [*A publication*]
FAIRS .... Fairchild Automatic Intercept and Response System (MCD)
FAIRS .... Federal Aviation Information Retrieval System
FAIRSHIPS ... Fleet Airships
FAIRSHIPWING ... Fleet Airship Wing
Fair Tr .... Fair Trade Laws [*A publication*] (DLA)
FAIRTRANS ... First Available Air Transportation
FAIRWESTPAC ... Fleet Air Wing, Western Pacific Area
FAIRWING ... Fleet Air Wing
FAIS .... Federation d'Associations d'Ingenieurs et de Scientifiques [*Federation of Engineering and Scientific Associations*] [*Canada*] (EAIO)
FAIS .... Force Air Intelligence Study [*Air Force*]
FAIS .... Foreign Affairs Interdepartmental Seminar [*Military*]
FAIS .... Isithebe [*South Africa*] [*ICAO location identifier*] (ICLI)
Faisneis .... Faisneis Raithiuil Quarterly Bulletin [*A publication*]
FAIST .... Fellow of the Australian Institute of Science and Technology
FAIT .... First-Aid Instructor Trainer [*Red Cross*]
FAITE .... Final Acceptance Inspection Test Equipment (MCD)
FAIUS .... Fellow of the Australian Institute of Urban Studies
FAIX .... Fairways Corp. [*Air carrier designation symbol*]
FAJ .... Fajardo [*Puerto Rico*] [*Airport symbol*] (OAG)
FAJ .... Fajardo, PR [*Location identifier*] [*FAA*] (FAAL)
FAJ .... Friends of Ann Jillian (EA)
FAJAAY ..... Folia Anatomica Japonica [*A publication*]
FAJB .... Johannesburg [*South Africa*] [*ICAO location identifier*] (ICLI)
FAJF .... Jagersfontein [*South Africa*] [*ICAO location identifier*] (ICLI)
FAJS .... Johannesburg/Jan Smuts [*South Africa*] [*ICAO location identifier*] (ICLI)
FAK .... Flat Rock, VA [*Location identifier*] [*FAA*] (FAAL)
FAK .... Fly-Away Kit (MCD)

FAK .... Fondation Aga Khan [*Aga Khan Foundation*]   (EAIO)
FAK .... Freight, All Kinds [*Railroad*]
FAK .... Full-Aperture Kicker [*Synchrotron*]
FAKA........ Karibib [*Namibia*] [*ICAO location identifier*]   (ICLI)
FAKB........ Karasburg [*Namibia*] [*ICAO location identifier*]   (ICLI)
FAKD .... Klerksdorp [*South Africa*] [*ICAO location identifier*]   (ICLI)
FAKG .... Komati Power Station/Kragsentrale [*South Africa*] [*ICAO location identifier*]   (ICLI)
FAKH........ Kenhardt [*South Africa*] [*ICAO location identifier*]   (ICLI)
FAKJ .... Kamanjab [*Namibia*] [*ICAO location identifier*]   (ICLI)
FAKK........ Kakamas [*South Africa*] [*ICAO location identifier*]   (ICLI)
FAKL........ Kriel [*South Africa*] [*ICAO location identifier*]   (ICLI)
FAKM .... Kimberley/B. J. Vorster [*South Africa*] [*ICAO location identifier*]   (ICLI)
Fak Mat Univ Kiril Metodij Skopje Godisen ... Skopje Univezitetot Kiril i Metodij Fakultet na Matematicka Godisen Zbornik (Skopje) [*A publication*]
FAKN .... Klippan Control Reporting Point [*South Africa*] [*ICAO location identifier*]   (ICLI)
FAKP........ Komatipoort [*South Africa*] [*ICAO location identifier*]   (ICLI)
FAKR........ Krugersdorp [*South Africa*] [*ICAO location identifier*]   (ICLI)
FAKS........ Kroonstad [*South Africa*] [*ICAO location identifier*]   (ICLI)
Fakt........... Faktura [*Invoice*] [*Business term*] [*German*]
fakt........... Faktuur [*Invoice*] [*Business term*] [*Afrikaans*]
FAKT........ Keetmanshoop/J. G. H. Van Der Wath [*Namibia*] [*ICAO location identifier*]   (ICLI)
Faktory Vneshn Sredy Ikh Znach Zdorov ya Naseleniya ... Faktory Vneshnei Sredy i Ikh Znachenie dlya Zdorov ya Naseleniya [*A publication*]
Fakt Vneshn Sred Znach Zdor Nasel Resp Mezhved Sb ... Faktory Vneshnykh Sred Znachenie Zdorov'ya Naseleniya Respublikanskii Mezhvedomstvennyi Sbornik [*A publication*]
FAKU .... Kuruman [*South Africa*] [*ICAO location identifier*]   (ICLI)
FAKX........ Khorixas [*Namibia*] [*ICAO location identifier*]   (ICLI)
FAKZ......... Kleinsee [*South Africa*] [*ICAO location identifier*]   (ICLI)
FAL........... Facilitation of International Air Transport [*Aviation*]
FAL........... Facilities Laboratory [*National Center for Atmospheric Research*]
FAL........... Failure Analysis Laboratory   (MCD)
FAL........... Falcon Cable Systems LP [*AMEX symbol*]   (SPSG)
FAL........... File Access Listener
FAL........... Financial Analysis Language [*Data processing*]   (MCD)
FAL........... Finite Automation Language [*Data processing*]
FAL........... First Approach and Landing [*Test*] [*NASA*]   (NASA)
FAL........... Food and Agricultural Legislation [*A publication*]
FAL........... Forces Armees Laotiannes [*Federated Army of Laos*]   (CINC)
FAL........... Fractional Allelic Loss [*Genetics*]
FAL........... Frequency Allocation List
FAL........... Frontier Airlines, Inc. [*Air carrier designation symbol*]
FAL........... Fuerzas Armadas de Liberacio [*Argentina*]
FAL........... Function of Astronaut Location [*NASA*]   (KSC)
FAL........... Roma, TX [*Location identifier*] [*FAA*]   (FAAL)
FALA........ First Amendment Lawyers Association   (EA)
FALA........ Lanseria [*South Africa*] [*ICAO location identifier*]   (ICLI)
FALAA...... Farbe und Lack [*A publication*]
FALB .... Falstaff Brewing Corp. [*NASDAQ symbol*]   (NQ)
FALB .... Ladybrand [*South Africa*] [*ICAO location identifier*]   (ICLI)
FALC .... Armed Forces for the Liberation of Cabinda [*Angola*]   (PD)
FALC .... Falconbridge Ltd. [*NASDAQ symbol*]   (NQ)
Falc .... Falconer's Scotch Court of Session Cases [*1744-51*] [*A publication*]   (DLA)
FALC......... Lime Acres [*South Africa*] [*ICAO location identifier*]   (ICLI)
Falc Co Cts ... Falconer's English County Court Cases [*A publication*]   (DLA)
Falc & F ..... Falconer and Fitzherbert's English Election Cases [*1835-39*] [*A publication*]   (DLA)
Falc & Fitz ... Falconer and Fitzherbert's English Election Cases [*1835-39*] [*A publication*]   (DLA)
Falc Marine Dict ... Falconer's Marine Dictionary [*A publication*]   (DLA)
FALCRI..... Federazione Autonoma Lavoratori Casse di Risparmio Italiane [*Savings Banks Workers Federation*] [*Italy*]   (EY)
FALD........ Finnish American League for Democracy   (EA)
FALG........ Fowl Antimouse Lymphocyte Globulin [*Immunochemistry*]
FALH .... Lohathla [*South Africa*] [*ICAO location identifier*]   (ICLI)
FALI .... Fund Alabama, Incorporated [*NASDAQ symbol*]   (NQ)
FALI .... Lichtenburg [*South Africa*] [*ICAO location identifier*]   (ICLI)
FALJC .... Federal Administrative Law Judges Conference   (EA)
Falke Monatsschr Ornithol ... Falke Monatsschrift fuer Ornithologie und Vivarienkunde [*A publication*]
Falke Monatsschr Ornithol Vivarienkd Ausg A ... Falke Monatsschrift fuer Ornithologie und Vivarienkunde. Ausgabe A [*A publication*]
FALK I...... Falkland Islands   (ROG)
FALKLD I ... Falkland Islands   (ROG)
Falkl Isl Depend Surv Sci Rep ... Falkland Islands Dependencies Survey. Scientific Reports [*A publication*]
Falk Symp ... Falk Symposium [*England*] [*A publication*]
FALL......... Lydenburg [*South Africa*] [*ICAO location identifier*]   (ICLI)
FALLEX..... Fall [*Autumn*] Exercise [*Military*] [*NATO*]   (NATG)
FALM........ Falmouth [*Municipal borough in England*]
FALM........ Loraine Mine [*South Africa*] [*ICAO location identifier*]   (ICLI)

FALN........ Fuerzas Armadas de Liberacion Nacional [*Armed Forces of National Liberation*] [*Venezuela*]   (PD)
FALN........ Fuerzas Armadas de Liberacion Nacional Puertorriquena [*Armed Forces of Puerto Rican National Liberation*]   (EA)
FALO........ Louis Trichardt [*South Africa*] [*ICAO location identifier*]   (ICLI)
FALOP ...... Forward Area Limited Observing Program   (MCD)
FALPA ...... Fellow of the Incorporated Society of Auctioneers and Landed Property Agents [*British*]
FALR .... Florida Administrative Law Reports [*A publication*]
FALS .... Foreign Area and Language Study
FALSET..... Falsetto [*Music*]
FALSTAF ... Forward Area LASER Systems - Tactical and Fiscal [*Military*]
FALT .... FADAC [*Field Artillery Digital Automatic Computer*] Automatic Logic Tester
FALT .... Field Artillery Logic Tester [*Army*]   (AABC)
FALT .... Louis Trichardt [*South Africa*] [*ICAO location identifier*]   (ICLI)
FALTRAN ... FORTRAN [*Formula Translating System*]-to-ALGOL [*Algorithmic language*] Translator [*Data processing*]   (IEEE)
FALW........ Forward Area LASER Weapon
FALW........ Langebaanweg [*South Africa*] [*ICAO location identifier*]   (ICLI)
FALY......... Ladysmith [*South Africa*] [*ICAO location identifier*]   (ICLI)
FALZ......... Luderitz [*Namibia*] [*ICAO location identifier*]   (ICLI)
Fam .... Epistulae ad Familiares [*of Cicero*] [*Classical studies*]   (OCD)
FAM .... Facilities Analysis Model [*Data processing*]
FAM .... Familiar   (AABC)
FAM .... Family   (AFM)
Fam .... Family Division, High Court, England and Wales   (DLA)
FAM .... Farmington, MO [*Location identifier*] [*FAA*]   (FAAL)
FAM .... Fast Aerial Mine [*British military*]   (DMA)
FAM .... Fast Auxiliary Memory   (IEEE)
FAM .... Fathom Oceanology Ltd. [*Toronto Stock Exchange symbol*]
FAM .... Federation of Apparel Manufacturers   (EA)
FAM .... Feed Assembly Modification
FAM .... Field Artillery Missile
FAM .... File Access Manager
FAM .... Filter Assembly Machine   (MCD)
FAM .... Final Address Message [*Telecommunications*]   (TEL)
FAM .... Fluorouracil, Adriamycin, Mitomycin [*Antineoplastic drug regimen*]
FAm .... Folklore Americano [*A publication*]
FAm .... Folklore Americas [*A publication*]
FAM .... Fontes Artis Musicae [*A publication*]
FAM .... Foreign Air Mail
F & AM ...... Free and Accepted Masons
FAM .... Free and Accepted Masons
FAM .... Free at Mill [*Business term*]
FAM .... Frequency Modulation and Advanced Memory [*Yamaha International Corp.*]
FAM .... Full Army Mobilization War Reserves   (AABC)
FAMA .... Federal Agricultural Marketing Authority
FAMA ...... Federal Association of Management Analysts [*Defunct*]
FAMA .... Fellow of the American Medical Association
FAMA ...... Fire Apparatus Manufacturers Association   (EA)
FAMA ...... First Amarillo Bancorporation, Inc. [*NASDAQ symbol*]   (NQ)
FAMA ...... Flota Aerea Mercane Argentina
FAMA ...... Fluorescent Antibody-Membrane Antigen [*Immunochemistry*]
FAMA ...... Fondation pour l'Assistance Mutuelle en Afrique au Sud du Sahara [*Foundation for Mutual Assistance in Africa South of the Sahara*]
FAMA ...... Forward Airhead Maintenance Area [*Military*] [*British*]
FAMA ...... Matatiele [*South Africa*] [*ICAO location identifier*]   (ICLI)
Fam Adv..... Family Advocate [*A publication*]
Fam Advocate ... Family Advocate [*A publication*]
FAMAE..... Following Amendment Authorized Effective [*Followed by date*]   (FAAC)
Fa Man ...... Farm Management [*A publication*]
FAMAS..... Field Artillery Meteorological Acquisition System   (MCD)
FAMAS..... Flutter and Matrix Algebra System [*Data processing*]
FAMA Surv Rep Malays Fed Agric Mark Auth ... FAMA Survey Report. Republic of Malaysia Federal Agricultural Marketing Authority [*A publication*]
FAMB........ 1st American Bancorp, Inc. [*Boston, MA*] [*NASDAQ symbol*]   (NQ)
F Amb .... Field Ambulance [*British military*]   (DMA)
FAMB........ Friends of the American Museum in Britain   (EA)
FAMB........ Middelburg [*South Africa*] [*ICAO location identifier*]   (ICLI)
Fam Bibl .... Familiengeschichtliche Bibliographie [*A publication*]
FAMBSA .. Farmers and Manufacturers Beet Sugar Association
FAMC....... Federal Agricultural Mortgage Corp. [*NASDAQ symbol*]   (NQ)
FAMC....... Fitzsimons Army Medical Center   (AABC)
FAMC........ Foreign Affairs Manual Circular [*A publication*] [*Department of State*]
FAMC........ Middelburg [*South Africa*] [*ICAO location identifier*]   (ICLI)
Fam Cas Cir Ev ... Famous Cases of Circumstantial Evidence, by Phillips [*A publication*]
Fam Com Hlth ... Family and Community Health [*A publication*]
Fam Community Health ... Family and Community Health [*A publication*]

Fam Coord ... Family Coordinator [*A publication*]
FAMD .... Malamala [*South Africa*] [*ICAO location identifier*] (ICLI)
FAMDEC .... Family Court of Australia Decisions [*Database*]
Fam Dev .... Famille et Developpement [*A publication*]
FAME .... Farmers' Allied Meat Enterprises Cooperative
FAME .... Fatty Acid Methyl Ester [*Biochemistry*]
FAME .... Field Activity Missile Engineering (MCD)
FAME .... Financial Analysis of Management Effectiveness [*Department of Agriculture*]
FAME .... [*The*] Flamemaster Corp. [*Sun Valley, CA*] [*NASDAQ symbol*] (NQ)
FAME .... Florida Association of Marine Explorers
FAME .... Fluorouracil, Adriamycin, MeCCNU [*Semustine*] [*Antineoplastic drug regimen*]
FAME .... Forecasts, Appraisals, and Management Evaluations (MCD)
FAME .... Fund for the Advancement of Music Education (EA)
FAME .... Future American Magical Entertainers
FAME .... Marion Island [*South Africa*] [*ICAO location identifier*] (ICLI)
FAMECE .. Family of Military Engineer Construction Equipment
FAMECE/UET ... Family of Military Engineer Construction Equipment/Universal Engineer Tractor (RDA)
Fa Mechan ... Farm Mechanization [*A publication*]
Fam Ec Rev ... Family Economics Review [*A publication*]
FAMEX ...... Familiarization Exercise [*Military*] (NVT)
FAMF .... First AmFed Corp. [*NASDAQ symbol*] (NQ)
FAMF .... Floating Aircraft Maintenance Facility [*Army*] (AABC)
FAMG .... Margate [*South Africa*] [*ICAO location identifier*] (ICLI)
FAMH .... Maltahohe [*Namibia*] [*ICAO location identifier*] (ICLI)
Fam Handy ... Family Handyman [*A publication*]
Fam Health ... Family Health [*A publication*]
FAMI .... Famiglia Brands, Inc. [*NASDAQ symbol*] (NQ)
FAMI .... Marble Hall [*South Africa*] [*ICAO location identifier*] (ICLI)
F Am IEE ... Fellow of the American Institute of Electrical Engineers
Family Econ R ... Family Economics Review [*A publication*]
Family Hlth ... Family Health [*A publication*]
Family Law Rev ... Family Law Review [*A publication*]
Family LQ ... Family Law Quarterly [*A publication*]
Family Plann Digest ... Family Planning Digest [*A publication*]
Family Pract ... Family Practice [*A publication*]
FAMINE ... Families Against Meat in New England [*Worcester, Massachusetts, group protesting high cost of food, 1973*]
FamIS .... Family Impact Seminar [*Australia*]
FAMIS ...... Financial and Management Information System [*Naval Oceanographic Office*]
FAMK .... Mafikeng [*South Africa*] [*ICAO location identifier*] (ICLI)
Fam L .... Family Law [*A publication*]
FAML .... Mariental [*Namibia*] [*ICAO location identifier*] (ICLI)
Fam Law .... Family Law [*A publication*]
Fam Law Q ... Family Law Quarterly [*A publication*]
Fam L Coord ... Family Life Coordinator [*A publication*]
FAMLI ...... Family Medicine Literature Index [*A publication*]
FAMLI Fam Med Lit Index ... FAMLI. Family Medicine Literature Index [*A publication*]
Fam LN ...... Family Law Notes [*A publication*] (APTA)
Fam L Newsl ... Family Law Newsletter [*A publication*]
Fam LQ ...... Family Law Quarterly [*A publication*]
Fam LR ...... Family Law Reports [*A publication*] (APTA)
Fam LR ...... Family Law Review [*A publication*]
Fam L Rep ... Family Law Reporter [*A publication*]
Fam L Rep BNA ... Family Law Reporter. Bureau of National Affairs [*A publication*]
Fam L Rev ... Family Law Review [*A publication*]
Fam L Tax Guide CCH ... Family Law Tax Guide. Commerce Clearing House [*A publication*]
FAMM ...... Family Medical Treatment Centers of America [*NASDAQ symbol*] (NQ)
FAMM ...... Mmabatho International [*South Africa*] [*ICAO location identifier*] (ICLI)
FAMMe ..... Fluorouracil, Adriamycin, Mitomycin C, MeCCNU [*Semustine*] [*Antineoplastic drug regimen*]
FAMMM .. Familial Atypical Multiple Mole Melanoma [*Oncology*]
FAMN .... Malalane [*South Africa*] [*ICAO location identifier*] (ICLI)
fam nov .... Familia Nova [*New Family*] [*Biology*]
FAMO .... Forward Airfield Maintenance Organization
FAMO .... Mossel Bay/Baai [*South Africa*] [*ICAO location identifier*] (ICLI)
FAMOS ..... Fast Multitasking Operating System [*MVT Microcomputer Systems, Inc.*]
FAMOS ..... Fleet Application of Meteorological Observations from Satellites (IEEE)
FAMOS ..... Flight Acceleration Monitor Only System (NASA)
FAMOS ..... Floating-Gate Avalanche-Injection Metal-Oxide Semiconductor [*Data processing*]
FAMOUS ... French-American Mid-Ocean Undersea Study [*Joint undersea program*]
FAMP .... Fire Alarm Monitoring Panel (IEEE)
FAMP .... Foreign Army Material Production (MCD)
FAMP .... Frontier Armed and Mounted Police [*British government*]
FAMP .... Mpacha [*Namibia*] [*ICAO location identifier*] (ICLI)
Fam Physician ... Family Physician [*A publication*]
Fam Plan N ... Family Planning News [*A publication*]

Fam Plann Inf Serv ... Family Planning Information Service [*A publication*]
Fam Plann (Lond) ... Family Planning (London) [*A publication*]
Fam Plann Perspect ... Family Planning Perspectives [*A publication*]
Fam Plann Popul Rep ... Family Planning/Population Report [*US*] [*A publication*]
Fam Plann Resume ... Family Planning Resume [*A publication*]
Fam Plann Today ... Family Planning Today [*A publication*]
Fam Plan Pe ... Family Planning Perspectives [*A publication*]
Fam Prac Surv ... Family Practice Survey [*A publication*]
Fam Pract .. Family Practice [*A publication*]
Fam Pract News ... Family Practice News [*A publication*]
Fam Pract Res J ... Family Practice Research Journal [*A publication*]
Fam Proc .... Family Process [*A publication*]
Fam Process ... Family Process [*A publication*]
FAMR .... Family Relations [*A publication*]
FAMR .... First American Financial Corp. [*NASDAQ symbol*] (NQ)
FAMR .... Mariepskop [*South Africa*] [*ICAO location identifier*] (ICLI)
FAMRA .... Fleet Air Mediterranean Repair Area (MCD)
Fam Relat .. Family Relations [*A publication*]
Fam RZ ...... Zeitschrift fuer das Gesamte Familienrecht [*German*] [*A publication*] (DLA)
FAMS .... Failure Analysis of Material Systems (MCD)
FAMS .... Famous Restaurants, Inc. [*Scottsdale, AZ*] [*NASDAQ symbol*] (NQ)
FAMS .... Farfield Acoustic Measuring System (KSC)
FAMS .... Fellow of the Ancient Monuments Society [*British*]
FAMS .... Fellow of the Association of Medical Secretaries, Practice Administrators, and Receptionists [*British*] (DBQ)
FAMS .... Field Army Messenger Service (AABC)
FAMS .... Field Artillery Missile System (RDA)
FAMS .... First Article Master Schedule (MCD)
FAM-S .... Fluorouracil, Adriamycin (Doxorubicin), Mitomycin C, and Streptozotocin [*Antineoplastic drug regimen*]
FAMS .... Forecasting and Modeling System [*Data processing*] (BUR)
FAMS .... Foundation for Advances in Medicine and Science (EA)
FAMS .... Free-Agent Market Simulator [*Computer programmed to calculate the market value of free agents in the National Basketball Association*]
FAMS .... Messina [*South Africa*] [*ICAO location identifier*] (ICLI)
FAmSCE ... Fellow of the American Society of Civil Engineers
FAMSEG .. Field Artillery Missile Systems Evaluation Group (RDA)
FAMSL ...... Fleet Aviation Material Support List [*Navy*] (AFIT)
FAM-T ...... Fluorouracil, Doxorubicin [*Adriamycin*], Mitomycin, Triazinate [*Antineoplastic drug regimen*]
FAMT .... Meyerton [*South Africa*] [*ICAO location identifier*] (ICLI)
FAMTO .... First Aid Mechanical Transport Outfit [*A vehicle standard pack for immediate repairs*] [*Military*] [*British*]
FAMU .... Fleet Aircraft Maintenance Unit
FAMU .... Florida Agricultural and Mechanical University [*Tallahasse, FL*]
FAMU ...... Fuel Additive Mixture Unit
FAMY .... Family (ROG)
FAMY .... Malmesbury [*South Africa*] [*ICAO location identifier*] (ICLI)
FAMZ .... Msauli [*South Africa*] [*ICAO location identifier*] (ICLI)
fan .... Fang [*MARC language code*] [*Library of Congress*] (LCCP)
FAN .... Fanning Island [*Line Islands*] [*Seismograph station code, US Geological Survey*] [*Closed*] (SEIS)
FAN .... Fantasy Fiction [*A publication*]
FAN .... Farsund [*Norway*] [*Airport symbol*] (OAG)
FAN .... Fighter Automatic Navigator
FAN .... Forces Armees Neutralistes [*Neutralist Armed Forces*] [*Laos*]
Fa N .... Francais au Nigeria [*A publication*]
FANA .... Fan Association of North America (EA)
FANA .... Fantasiae [*A publication*]
FANA .... Fellow of the American Neurological Association
FANA .... Fluorescent Antinuclear Antibody Test [*Serology*]
FANA .... Forex Association of North America (EA)
FANA .... Futon Association of North America (EA)
FANA .... Namatoni [*Namibia*] [*ICAO location identifier*] (ICLI)
FANAF ...... Federation des Societes d'Assurances de Droit National Africains [*Federation of African National Insurance Companies*] [*Dakar, Senegal*] (EAIO)
F Anal Jrl .. Financial Analysts Journal [*A publication*]
FANC .... Newcastle [*South Africa*] [*ICAO location identifier*] (ICLI)
FANCAP .... Fluids, Aeration, Nutrition, Communication, Activity, and Pain [*Medicine*]
FANCAS ... Fluids, Aeration, Nutrition, Communication, Activity, and Stimulation [*Medicine*]
FANDT ..... Fuel and Transportation [*Navy*]
FANE .... Federation d'Action Nationale et Europeene [*Federation of National and European Action*] [*France*] [*Political party*] (PPE)
FANEL ...... Federation for Accessible Nursing Education and Licensure (EA)
FANES ...... Furnace Atomic Nonthermal Excitation Spectrometry
FanF .... Fantasy Fiction [*A publication*]
FANFT ...... Formamidonitrofurylthiazole [*Organic chemistry*]
FANG .... Flechette Area Neutralizing Gun
FANH .... New Hanover [*South Africa*] [*ICAO location identifier*] (ICLI)
FANI .... Food, Agriculture, and Nutrition Inventory [*Department of Agriculture*] [*Discontinued*]

FANK .... Forces Armees Nationales Khmeres [*Cambodian National Armed Forces*] [*Replaced Royal Cambodian Armed Forces*]

FANL .... New Largo [*South Africa*] [*ICAO location identifier*] (ICLI)

FANNDE .. Forward Addition Algorithm Using the Nearest-Neighbor Distance Error Criteria [*Algorithm*]

FANO .... Fauna Norrlandica. Department of Ecological Zoology. Umea University [*A publication*]

FANO .... Frente Anticomunista del Nororiente [*Northeastern Anticommunist Front*] [*Guatemala*] (PD)

FANPT ...... Freeman Anxiety, Neurosis, and Psychosomatic Test [*Psychology*]

Fan Rom Law ... Fanton's Tables of Roman Law [*A publication*] (DLA)

Fans .... Fantasy: The Magazine of Science Fiction [*A publication*]

FanS .... Fantasy Stories [*A publication*]

FANS .... Fellow of the American Neurological Society

FANS .... Fight to Advance the Nation's Sports [*Defunct*] (EA)

FANS .... Food and Nutritional System [*Military*] (AABC)

FANS .... Forgotten Americans Need Support (EA)

FANS .... Franchise of Americans Needing Sports (EA)

FANS .... Future Air Navigation Systems [*Aviation*]

FANS .... Nelspruit [*South Africa*] [*ICAO location identifier*] (ICLI)

FANSY ...... Frequency Analysis and Synthesis [*Computer program*]

Fant .... Fantasy [*A publication*]

FANT .... Forces Armees Nationales Tchadiennes [*Chad*] (PD)

FANT .... French Atmospheric Nuclear Test (MCD)

FANTAC ... Fighter Analysis Tactical Air Combat

Fant & Sci Fict ... Fantasy and Science Fiction [*A publication*]

FANV .... Nieuwoudtville [*South Africa*] [*ICAO location identifier*] (ICLI)

FANX .... Friendship [*Airport*] Annex [*National Security Agency*]

FANY .... First-Aid Nursing Yeomanry [*British women's organization formed to do medical transport work for the army; later did general transport work*]

FANY .... Nylstroom [*South Africa*] [*ICAO location identifier*] (ICLI)

FANYS ...... First Aid Nursing Yeomanry Service [*British military*] (DMA)

FANZCP ... Fellow of the Australian and New Zealand College of Psychiatrists

FANZINE ... Fan Magazine [*Generic term for a publication of interest to science fiction fans*]

f-ao--- .... Angola [*MARC geographic area code*] [*Library of Congress*] (LCCP)

FAO .... Fabrication Assembly Order (MCD)

FAO .... Faro [*Portugal*] [*Airport symbol*] (OAG)

FAO .... Fatty Amine Oxide [*Organic chemistry*]

FAO .... Field Audit Office

FAO .... Finance and Accounts Office [*or Officer*] [*Army*]

FAO .... Finish All Over [*Technical drawings*]

FAO .... Fleet Accountant Officer [*British*]

FAO .... Fleet Administration Office

FAO .... Flight Activities Officer [*NASA*]

FAO .... Food and Agriculture Organization [*United Nations*] [*Italy*] [*Information service or system*] (IID)

FAO .... Foreign Agricultural Organization

FAO .... Foreign Area Officer [*Army*] (INF)

FAO .... Free Albania Organization (EA)

FAO .... Fumaramido Oripavine [*Biochemistry*]

FAOA .... Funk Aircraft Owners Association (EA)

FAOA .... Ondangua [*Namibia*] [*ICAO location identifier*] (ICLI)

FAOAC ..... Field Artillery Officer Advanced Course [*Military*] (INF)

FAO Ag Bul ... Food and Agriculture Organization of the United Nations. Monthly Bulletin of Agriculture [*A publication*]

FAO Agric Dev Pap ... FAO [*Food and Agriculture Organization of the United Nations*] Agricultural Development Papers [*A publication*]

FAO Agric Serv Bull ... FAO [*Food and Agriculture Organization of the United Nations*] Agricultural Services Bulletin [*A publication*]

FAO Agric Stud ... FAO [*Food and Agriculture Organization of the United Nations*] Agricultural Studies [*A publication*]

FAO/APS ... FAO [*Food and Agriculture Organization of the United Nations*] Association of Professional Staff [*Rome, Italy*] (EAIO)

FAO At Energy Ser ... FAO [*Food and Agriculture Organization of the United Nations*] Atomic Energy Series [*A publication*]

FAO Atom En Ser ... FAO [*Food and Agriculture Organization of the United Nations*] Atomic Energy Series [*A publication*]

FAOBA ..... Farmaceuticky Obzor [*A publication*]

FAOBAS .... Farmaceuticky Obzor [*A publication*]

FAOD .... Odendaalsrus [*South Africa*] [*ICAO location identifier*] (ICLI)

FAO Dev Program ... FAO [*Food and Agriculture Organization of the United Nations*] Development Program [*A publication*]

FAO Doc .... FAO [*Food and Agriculture Organization of the United Nations*] Documentation [*A publication*]

FAOE .... Omega [*Namibia*] [*ICAO location identifier*] (ICLI)

FAO Econ Soc Dev Ser ... FAO [*Food and Agriculture Organization of the United Nations*] Economic and Social Development Series [*A publication*]

FAO Fish Biol Synop ... FAO [*Food and Agriculture Organization of the United Nations*] Fisheries Biology Synopsis [*A publication*]

FAO Fish Biol Tech Pap ... FAO [*Food and Agriculture Organization of the United Nations*] Fisheries Biology Technical Paper [*A publication*]

FAO Fish Bull ... FAO [*Food and Agriculture Organization of the United Nations*] Fisheries Bulletin [*A publication*]

FAO Fish Circ ... FAO [*Food and Agriculture Organization of the United Nations*] Fisheries Circular [*A publication*]

FAO Fish Rep ... FAO [*Food and Agriculture Organization of the United Nations*] Fisheries Reports [*A publication*]

FAO Fish Ser ... FAO [*Food and Agriculture Organization of the United Nations*] Fisheries Series [*A publication*]

FAO Fish Synop ... FAO [*Food and Agriculture Organization of the United Nations*] Fisheries Synopsis [*A publication*]

FAO Fish Tech Pap ... FAO [*Food and Agriculture Organization of the United Nations*] Fisheries Technical Paper [*A publication*]

FAO Food Nutr Pap ... FAO [*Food and Agriculture Organization of the United Nations*] Food and Nutrition Paper [*A publication*]

FAO Food Nutr Ser ... FAO [*Food and Agriculture Organization of the United Nations*] Food and Nutrition Series [*A publication*]

FAO For Developm Pap ... FAO [*Food and Agriculture Organization of the United Nations*] Forestry Development Papers [*A publication*]

FAO For & For Prod Stud ... FAO [*Food and Agriculture Organization of the United Nations*] Forestry and Forest Products Studies [*A publication*]

FAOG .... Oranjemund [*Namibia*] [*ICAO location identifier*] (ICLI)

FAO Gen Fish Counc Mediterr Circ ... FAO [*Food and Agriculture Organization of the United Nations*] General Fisheries Council for the Mediterranean. Circular [*A publication*]

FAO Gen Fish Counc Mediterr Stud Rev ... FAO [*Food and Agriculture Organization of the United Nations*] General Fisheries Council for the Mediterranean. Studies and Reviews [*A publication*]

FAOH .... Oudtshoorn [*South Africa*] [*ICAO location identifier*] (ICLI)

FAO Indo-Pac Fish Comm Proc ... FAO [*Food and Agriculture Organization of the United Nations*] Indo-Pacific Fishery Commission. Proceedings [*A publication*]

FAO Inf Serv Bull ... FAO [*Food and Agriculture Organization of the United Nations*] Information Service Bulletin [*A publication*]

FAO Irrig Drain Pap ... Food and Agriculture Organization of the United Nations. Irrigation and Drainage Paper [*A publication*]

FAOJ .... Outjo [*Namibia*] [*ICAO location identifier*] (ICLI)

FAOK .... Okakarara [*Namibia*] [*ICAO location identifier*] (ICLI)

FAOLU ...... Federation of All Okinawan Labor Unions

FAO Man Fish Sci ... FAO [*Food and Agriculture Organization of the United Nations*] Manuals in Fisheries Science [*A publication*]

FAOMELU ... Federation of All Okinawan Military Employees' Labor Unions

FAO Mo Bul Ag Econ & Stat ... FAO [*Food and Agriculture Organization of the United Nations*] Monthly Bulletin of Agricultural Economics and Statistics [*Later, FAO Monthly Bulletin of Statistics*] [*A publication*]

FAOMS ..... Foreign Area Officer Management System [*Army*]

FAON .... Okahandja [*Namibia*] [*ICAO location identifier*] (ICLI)

FAO Nutr Meet Rep Ser ... FAO [*Food and Agriculture Organization of the United Nations*] Nutrition Meetings. Report Series [*A publication*]

FAO Nutr Stud ... FAO [*Food and Agriculture Organization of the United Nations*] Nutritional Studies [*A publication*]

FAOO .... Okaukuejo [*Namibia*] [*ICAO location identifier*] (ICLI)

FAOP .... Foreign Area Officer Program [*Army*] (MCD)

FAOP .... Opuwa [*Namibia*] [*ICAO location identifier*] (ICLI)

FAOPA2 .... FAO [*Food and Agriculture Organization of the United Nations*] Plant Protection Bulletin [*A publication*]

FAO Pasture Fodder Crop Stud ... FAO [*Food and Agriculture Organization of the United Nations*] Pasture and Fodder Crop Studies [*A publication*]

FAO Paturages Cult Fourrageres ... FAO [*Food and Agriculture Organization of the United Nations*] Paturages et Cultures Fourrageres [*A publication*]

FAO Plant ... FAO [*Food and Agriculture Organization of the United Nations*] Plant Protection Bulletin [*A publication*]

FAO Plant Prod Prot Ser ... FAO [*Food and Agriculture Organization of the United Nations*] Plant Production and Protection Series [*A publication*]

FAO Plant Prot Bull ... FAO [*Food and Agriculture Organization of the United Nations*] Plant Protection Bulletin [*A publication*]

FAO Pl Prot Bull ... FAO [*Food and Agriculture Organization of the United Nations*] Plant Protection Bulletin [*A publication*]

FAO Prod Yb ... FAO [*Food and Agriculture Organization of the United Nations*] Production Yearbook [*A publication*]

FAOR .... Olifants River Bridge [*South Africa*] [*ICAO location identifier*] (ICLI)

FAO Rep .... FAO [*Food and Agriculture Organization of the United Nations*] Report [*A publication*]

FAOS .... Oshakati [*Namibia*] [*ICAO location identifier*] (ICLI)

FAO Soils Bull ... FAO [*Food and Agriculture Organization of the United Nations*] Soils Bulletin [*A publication*]

FAOTA ...... Fellow of the American Occupational Therapy Association

FAO Timber ... Food and Agriculture Organization of the United Nations. Timber Bulletin for Europe [*A publication*]

FAOU	Fellow of the American Ornithologists Union
FAOUSA...	Finance and Accounts Office [*or Officer*], United States Army
FAOV	Otavi [*Namibia*] [*ICAO location identifier*] (ICLI)
FAOW	Otjiwarongo [*Namibia*] [*ICAO location identifier*] (ICLI)
FAOY	Orkney [*South Africa*] [*ICAO location identifier*] (ICLI)
FAP............	Facilities Assistance Program
FAP............	Facility Analysis Plan [*Telecommunications*] (TEL)
FAP............	Failure Analysis Program
FAP............	Familial Adenomatous Polyposis [*Formerly, FPC*] [*Medicine*]
FAP............	Familial Amyloid Polyneuropathy [*Medicine*]
FAP............	Family Assistance Plan [*or Program*] [*Proposed during Nixon administration*]
FAP............	Family Auto Policy [*Insurance*]
FAP............	Fast Action Procedures (NVT)
FAP............	Fast Atmospheric Pulsation
FAP............	Fault Analysis Process (TEL)
FAP............	Federal Art Project
FAP............	Fibrillating Action Potential [*Neurophysiology*]
FAP............	Field Application Panel (IEEE)
FAP............	Final Anthropic Principle [*Term coined by authors John Barrow and Frank Tipler in their book, "The Anthropic Cosmological Principle"*]
FAP............	Final Approach Path [*or Plane*] [*Aviation*]
FAP............	Finance and Accounting Policy [*Army*] (AABC)
FAP............	Financial Analysis Program [*IBM Corp.*]
FAP............	Financial Assistance Program (AFM)
FAP............	Fine Arts Philatelists (EA)
FAP............	First-Aid Post
FAP............	Fiscale en Administratieve Praktijkvragen [*A publication*]
FAP............	Fixed Action Pattern
FAP............	Flexible Accelerator Path [*Economic theory*]
FAP............	Flight Acceptance Profile (KSC)
FAP............	Floating-Point Arithmetic Package [*Data processing*]
FAP............	Food Additive Petition
FAP............	Force Alignment Plan [*Military*] (INF)
FAP............	Foreign Air Program
FAP............	FORTRAN [*Formula Translating System*] Assembly Program [*Data processing*]
FAP............	Fos-Associated Protein [*Biochemistry*]
FAP............	Foundation for the Arts of Peace (EA)
FAP............	Franc d'Avarie Particuliere [*Free of Particular Average*] [*Business term*] [*French*]
FAP............	Franco d'Avaria Particolare [*Free of Particular Average*] [*Business term*] [*Italian*]
FAP............	Frequency Allocation Panel
FAP............	Fuerzas Armadas Peronistas [*Argentina*]
FAP............	Full American Plan [*Hotel room rate*]
FAP............	(Furfurylamino)purine [*Plant hormone*] [*Organic chemistry*]
FAPA.........	F-15 Adapted Place Atlas Program (MCD)
FAPA.........	Family Aide Projects Association [*Australia*]
FAPA.........	Fantasy Amateur Press Association
FAPA.........	Federation of Asian Pharmaceutical Associations
FAPA.........	Federation of Asian Photographic Art
FAPA.........	Fellow of the American Psychiatric Association
FAPA.........	Fellow of the American Psychoanalytic Association
FAPA.........	Fellow of the American Psychological Association
FAPA.........	Filipino American Political Association
FAPA.........	Flight Accrual Payment Action [*Air Force*]
FAPA.........	Formosan Association for Public Affairs (EA)
FAPA.........	Fred Astaire Performing Arts Association
FAPA.........	Future Aviation Professionals of America (EA)
FAPA.........	Port Alfred [*South Africa*] [*ICAO location identifier*] (ICLI)
FAPABS....	FORSCOM [*Forces Command*] Automatic Program and Budget System [*Army*] (MCD)
FAPAP	Federation des Personnels Africains de Police [*Federation of African Police*]
FAPB.........	Pietersburg [*South Africa*] [*ICAO location identifier*] (ICLI)
FAPBBY....	Fortschritte im Acker- und Pflanzenbau [*Advances in Agronomy and Crop Science*] [*A publication*]
FAPC.........	Familial Adenomatous Polyposis Coli [*Medicine*]
FAPC.........	Fatty Acid Producers' Council (EA)
FAPC.........	Federal Area Port Controller
FAPC.........	Food and Agriculture Planning Committee [*NATO*] (NATG)
FAPC.........	Prince Albert [*South Africa*] [*ICAO location identifier*] (ICLI)
FAPCC......	Film, Air, and Package Carriers Conference (EA)
FAPCES....	Fundamental Aspects of Pollution Control and Environmental Science [*Elsevier Book Series*] [*A publication*]
FAPE.........	Free Appropriate Public Education
FAPE.........	Port Elizabeth/H. F. Verwoerd [*South Africa*] [*ICAO location identifier*] (ICLI)
FA Peguy ...	Feuillets Mensuels d'Information de l'Amitie Charles Peguy [*A publication*]
FAPF	Piet Retief [*South Africa*] [*ICAO location identifier*] (ICLI)
FAPFAB....	FAO [*Food and Agriculture Organization of the United Nations*] Pasture and Fodder Crop Studies [*A publication*]
FAPG.........	Fleet Air Photographic Group
FAPG.........	Plettenberg Bay [*South Africa*] [*ICAO location identifier*] (ICLI)
FAPH	Fluoroaldehyde Pyridylhydrazone [*Organic chemistry*]
FAPH	Phalaborwa/Hendrik Van Eck [*South Africa*] [*ICAO location identifier*] (ICLI)
FAPHA......	Fellow of the American Public Health Association
FAPI	Fellow of the Australian Planning Institute
FAPI	First Article Production Inspection (MCD)
FAPI	Pietersburg [*South Africa*] [*ICAO location identifier*] (ICLI)
FAPIG	First Atomic Power Industry Group [*Japan*]
FAPJ.........	Port St. Johns [*South Africa*] [*ICAO location identifier*] (ICLI)
FAPL	Pongola [*South Africa*] [*ICAO location identifier*] (ICLI)
FAPM........	Pietermaritzburg [*South Africa*] [*ICAO location identifier*] (ICLI)
FAPN........	Pilansberg [*South Africa*] [*ICAO location identifier*] (ICLI)
FAPO.........	Field Army Petroleum Office (AABC)
FAPOA......	Farmacja Polska [*A publication*]
FAPP.........	Potgietersrus [*South Africa*] [*ICAO location identifier*] (ICLI)
FAPPEC....	Federation of Associations of Periodical Publishers in the EC (EAIO)
FAPPS.......	First Article Preproduction Sample [*DoD*]
FA-PPT	First Article - Preproduction Test (MCD)
FAPR.........	Federal Aviation Procurement Regulations
FAPR.........	Pretoria [*South Africa*] [*ICAO location identifier*] (ICLI)
FAPRA......	Federation of African Public Relations Associations (EAIO)
FAPRON...	Fleet Air Photo Squadron
FAPRS.......	Federal Assistance Programs Retrieval System [*General Services Administration*] [*Information service or system*] (MCD)
FAPS	Fate of Atmospheric Pollutants Study [*National Science Foundation*]
FAPS	Fellow of the American Physical Society
FAPS	Financial Aid Planning Service [*College Scholarship Service*]
FAPS	Foreign Affairs Programming System (CINC)
FAPS	Potchefstroom [*South Africa*] [*ICAO location identifier*] (ICLI)
FAPSEK....	Fundamental Aspects of Pollution Control and Environmental Science [*Elsevier Book Series*] [*A publication*]
FAPSIM.....	Food and Agricultural Policy Simulator
FAPsS........	Fellow of the Australian Psychological Society
FAPT	Postmasburg [*South Africa*] [*ICAO location identifier*] (ICLI)
FAPTU	Farm Animal Practice Teaching Unit [*Royal Veterinary College*] [*British*] (IRUK)
FAPUS	Fabrication Performance Utilization System (MCD)
FAPUS	Frequency Allocation Panel, United States (NVT)
FAPUSMCEB ...	Frequency Allocation Panel, United States Military Communications Electronics Board
FAPV	Petrusville [*South Africa*] [*ICAO location identifier*] (ICLI)
FAPY	Parys [*South Africa*] [*ICAO location identifier*] (ICLI)
FAPZ.........	Progress [*South Africa*] [*ICAO location identifier*] (ICLI)
FAQ	Fair Average Quality
FAQ	Free at Quay [*Business term*]
FAQS........	Fair Average Quality of Season [*Business term*]
FAQS........	Fast Queuing System [*Data processing*]
FAQT........	Queenstown [*South Africa*] [*ICAO location identifier*] (ICLI)
FAR	Failure Analysis Report
FAR	False Alarm Rate
FAR	Farad [*Unit of electric capacitance*] (ROG)
FAR	Fargo [*North Dakota*] [*Airport symbol*] (OAG)
FAR	Fargo, ND [*Location identifier*] [*FAA*] (FAAL)
FAR	Farina [*Flour*] [*Pharmacy*] (ROG)
FAR	Farmer (ROG)
FAR	Farmington Public Library, Farmington, NM [*OCLC symbol*] (OCLC)
FAR	Faro [*Portugal*] [*Seismograph station code, US Geological Survey*] (SEIS)
far.............	Faroese [*MARC language code*] [*Library of Congress*] (LCCP)
Far.............	Farresley's Cases in Holt's King's Bench Reports [*A publication*] (DLA)
Far.............	Farresley's Reports [*7 Modern Reports*] [*87 English Reprint*] [*1733-45*] [*A publication*] (DLA)
FAR	Farrier (ROG)
FAR	Farrington Aircraft Corp. [*Paducah, KY*] [*FAA designator*] (FAAC)
FAR	Farthing [*Monetary unit*] [*Great Britain*]
FAR	Federal Acquisition Regulation
FAR	Federal Air Regulations [*FAA*]
FAR	Federal Airworthiness Regulation
FAR	Federal Assistance Review [*Program*]
FAR	Federal Aviation Regulation
FAR	Federation des Associations Roumaines du Canada [*Federation of Romanian Associations of Canada*]
FAR	Field Activity Report
FAR	Field Analysis Report
FAR	Field Assessment Review [*Military*]
FAR	Fighter, Attacker, Reconnaissance [*Requirements*] [*Air Force*]
FAR	File Address Register
FAR	Final Acceptance Review [*NASA*] (NASA)
FAR	Financial Accounts Receivable
FAR	First Alarm Register
FAR	Fixed Acoustic Range
FAR	Fixed Amount Reimbursement [*Agency for International Development*]
FAR	Fixed Array RADAR
FAR	Flight Acceptance Review (MCD)
FAR	Flight Aptitude Rating

FAR .... Floor Area Ratio [*in office buildings*]
FAR .... Force d'Action Rapide [*Rapid Deployment Force*] [*French*]
FAR .... Forces Armees Royales [*Royal Armed Forces*] [*Laos*]
FAR .... Foreign Affairs Research Documentation Center [*Department of State*]
FAR .... Foreign Agricultural Relations Office
FAR .... Foreign Agriculture Report [*Department of Agriculture*]
FAR .... Foreign Area Research Coordination Group [*Department of State*]
FAR .... Forward Acquisition RADAR
FAR .... Foundation for Administrative Research (MCD)
FAR .... Foundation for Agronomic Research [*University of Pittsburgh*] [*Research center*] (RCD)
FAR .... Fowler, A. R., Saint Paul MN [*STAC*]
FAR .... French American Review [*A publication*]
FAR .... Frequency Adjusting Rheostat
FAR .... Fuerzas Armadas Rebeldes [*Rebel Armed Forces*] [*Guatemala*] (PD)
FAR .... Functional Area Review [*Military*]
FAR .... Fund for an American Renaissance (EA)
FARA........ Faradyne Electronics Corp. [*NASDAQ symbol*] (NQ)
FARA........ Federal Agents Registration Act (OICC)
FARA........ Flexible Automation for Robotic Analysis
FARA........ Foreign Affairs Recreation Association (EA)
FARA........ Foreign Agents Registration Act of 1938
FARAC...... Fuerzas Armadas Anticomunistas [*Anti-Communist Armed Forces*] [*Nicaragua*] (PD)
FARADA... Failure Rate Data Program [*Navy*] (NG)
Faraday Dis ... Faraday Discussions of the Chemical Society [*A publication*]
Faraday Discuss ... Faraday Discussions of the Chemical Society [*A publication*]
Faraday Discuss Chem Soc ... Faraday Discussions of the Chemical Society [*A publication*]
Faraday Soc Trans ... Faraday Society. Transactions [*A publication*]
Faraday Spec Discuss Chem Soc ... Faraday Special Discussions of the Chemical Society [*A publication*]
Faraday Symp Chem Soc ... Faraday Symposia of the Chemical Society [*A publication*]
FARB........ Federation of Associations of Regulatory Boards (EA)
FARB........ Richard's Bay [*South Africa*] [*ICAO location identifier*] (ICLI)
Farbe & Lack ... Farbe und Lack [*A publication*]
Farben Ztg ... Farben Zeitung [*A publication*]
FARC........ Farr Company [*NASDAQ symbol*] (NQ)
FARC........ Fast Accurate Refraction Correction [*NASA*] (KSC)
FARC........ Federal Archives and Records Center [*Regional depository of the National Archives and Records Service*]
FARC........ Field Artillery Replacement Center
FARC........ Fuerzas Armadas Revolucionarias Colombianas [*Revolutionary Armed Forces of Colombia*]
FARCA...... Farm Chemicals [*A publication*]
FARCAC... Farm Chemicals [*A publication*]
FARD .... Riversdale [*South Africa*] [*ICAO location identifier*] (ICLI)
FARE .... FARED Robot Systems, Inc. [*NASDAQ symbol*] (NQ)
FARE........ Fatal Accident Reduction Effort [*or Enforcement*] [*Department of Transportation*]
FARE........ Foreign Assignment Resources Employees [*FAA*]
FARE........ Forward Area Refueling Equipment [*Army*]
FARE........ Full Access and Rights to Education Coalition
FAREAI .... Farmaceutisk Revy [*A publication*]
Far East Ass Trop Med ... Far Eastern Association of Tropical Medicine [*A publication*]
Far East Ceram Bull ... Far Eastern Ceramic Bulletin [*A publication*]
Far East Econ R ... Far Eastern Economic Review [*A publication*]
Far Eastern Econ Rev ... Far Eastern Economic Review [*A publication*]
Far East J Anesth ... Far East Journal of Anesthesia [*A publication*]
Far East LR ... Far Eastern Law Review [*A publication*]
Far East L Rev ... Far Eastern Law Review [*A publication*] (DLA)
Far East Med J ... Far East Medical Journal [*A publication*]
Far East Q ... Far Eastern Quarterly [*A publication*]
Far East R ... Far Eastern Review [*A publication*]
Far East S.. Far Eastern Survey [*A publication*]
Far East Surv ... Far Eastern Survey [*A publication*]
Far East Univ Fac J ... Far Eastern University. Faculty Journal [*A publication*]
Far E Econ R ... Far Eastern Economic Review [*A publication*]
FAREGAZ ... Union des Fabricants Europeens de Regulateurs de Pression du Gaz [*Union of European Manufacturers of Gas Pressure Controllers*] (EAIO)
FARELF.... Far East Land Forces (CINC)
FARET ...... Fast Reactor Experiment Test [*Proposed but never built*] [*Nuclear energy*]
FAREX ...... Fleet Analysis and Reconstruction of Exercise [*Navy*] (MCD)
FARF........ Fairfield-Noble Corp. [*NASDAQ symbol*] (NQ)
FARG........ Farmington [*New Mexico*] [*Seismograph station code, US Geological Survey*] (SEIS)
FARG........ Rustenburg [*South Africa*] [*ICAO location identifier*] (ICLI)
FARGO ..... Forty Automatic Report Generating Operation (MCD)
FARH .... Rehoboth [*Namibia*] [*ICAO location identifier*] (ICLI)
FAR Horiz ... Foreign Area Research Horizons [*A publication*]
FARI.......... First Amendment Research Institute (EA)

FARK........ First Federal Savings of Arkansas FA [*Little Rock, AR*] [*NASDAQ symbol*] (NQ)
FARK........ Forces Armees Royales Khmeres [*Royal Cambodian Armed Forces*] [*Replaced by FANK*]
FARK........ Rooikop [*South Africa*] [*ICAO location identifier*] (ICLI)
FARM....... Farm Animal Reform Movement (EA)
Farm.......... Farmacia [*A publication*]
Farm.......... Farmacija [*A publication*]
Farm.......... Farmaco [*A publication*]
Farm.......... Farmalecta [*A publication*]
FARM....... Farmer Brothers Co. [*NASDAQ symbol*] (NQ)
FARM....... Farmers Assistance Relief Mission (EA)
Farmac...... Farmacognosia [*A publication*]
Farmacihist Ars ... Farmacihistoriska Saellskapets Arsskrift [*A publication*]
Farmaco Ed Prat ... Farmaco. Edizione Pratica [*A publication*]
Farmaco Ed Sci ... Farmaco. Edizione Scientifica [*Italy*] [*A publication*]
Farmaco Ed Scient ... Farmaco. Edizione Scientifica [*A publication*]
Farmaco Pra ... Farmaco. Edizione Pratica [*A publication*]
Farmaco Sci ... Farmaco. Edizione Scientifica [*A publication*]
Farm Aikak ... Farmaseuttinen Aikakauslehti [*A publication*]
Farmakol T ... Farmakologiya i Toksikologiya [*A publication*]
Farmakol Toksikol ... Farmakologiya i Toksikologiya [*A publication*]
Farmakol Toksikol (Kiev) ... Farmakologiya i Toksikologiya (Kiev) [*Ukrainian SSR*] [*A publication*]
Farmakol Toksikol (Mosc) ... Farmakologiya i Toksikologiya (Moscow) [*A publication*]
Farmakol Toksikol Resp Mezhved Sb ... Farmakologiya i Toksikologiya Respublikanskii Mezhvedomstvennyi Sbornik [*A publication*]
Farmak Toks ... Farmakologiya i Toksikologiya [*A publication*]
Farmatsevt Zh (Kiev) ... Farmatsevtychnyi Zhurnal (Kiev) [*A publication*]
Farm Bldg Progress ... Farm Building Progress [*A publication*]
Farm Bldg R & D Studies ... Farm Building R and D Studies [*A publication*]
Farm Bldgs Digest ... Farm Buildings Digest [*A publication*]
Farm Bldgs Topics ... Farm Buildings Topics [*A publication*]
Farm Bras ... Farmaceutico Brasileiro [*A publication*]
Farm Bull US Dep Agric ... Farmers' Bulletin. US Department of Agriculture [*A publication*]
FARMC..... Frankfurt Army Regional Medical Center [*US Army 97th General Hospital*] [*Federal Republic of Germany*]
Farm Chem ... Farm Chemicals [*A publication*]
Farm Clin... Farmacia Clinica [*A publication*]
Farm Coop ... Farmer Cooperatives [*A publication*]
Farm Delt Ed Sci ... Farmakeftikon Deltion. Edition Scientifique [*A publication*]
Farm Dhelt Epistim Ekdosis ... Farmakevtikon Dheltion Epistimoniki Ekdosis [*A publication*]
Farm Econ ... Farm Economics [*A publication*]
Farm Econ ... Farm Economist [*A publication*]
Farm Econ Facts Opin Ill Univ Coop Ext Serv ... Farm Economics. Facts and Opinions. Illinois University. Cooperative Extension Service [*A publication*]
Farm Econ PA State Univ Coop Ext Serv ... Farm Economics. Pennsylvania State University. Cooperative Extension Service [*A publication*]
Farm Ed Prat ... Farmaco. Edizione Pratica [*A publication*]
Farm Ed Sci ... Farmaco. Edizione Scientifica [*A publication*]
Farm Eng ... Farm Engineering [*A publication*]
Farm Eq ..... Farm Equipment News [*A publication*]
Farm Equip Dealer ... Farm Equipment Dealer [*A publication*]
Farmer Coop US Dep Agric Econ Stat Coop Serv ... Farmer Cooperatives. United States Department of Agriculture. Economics Statistics and Cooperatives Service [*A publication*]
FARMERS ... Frequency Agility RADAR Modifications to Existing RADAR Systems [*DoD*]
Farmer's Advocate Can Countryman ... Farmer's Advocate and Canadian Countryman [*A publication*]
Farmers' B ... Farmers' Bulletin [*A publication*]
Farmers Bull ... Farmers' Bulletin [*A publication*]
Farmers Bull USDA ... Farmers' Bulletin. United States Department of Agriculture [*A publication*]
Farmers Leafl Natl Inst Agric Bot ... Farmers Leaflet. National Institute of Agricultural Botany [*A publication*]
Farmers Newsl ... Farmers' Newsletter [*A publication*] (APTA)
Farmers Rep Leeds Univ Dept Agr Econ Sect ... Farmers' Report. Leeds University. Department of Agriculture. Economics Section [*A publication*]
Farmers' Sci Joint Conf ... Farmers' and Scientists' Joint Conference [*A publication*]
Farmer Stockbr ... Farmer and Stockbreeder [*A publication*]
Farmers Wkly ... Farmers Weekly [*South Africa*] [*A publication*]
Farmers Wkly (Bloemfontein S Afr) ... Farmers Weekly (Bloemfontein, South Africa) [*A publication*]
Farm Farmakol ... Farmatsiya i Farmakologiya [*A publication*]
Farm Food Res ... Farm and Food Research [*A publication*]
Farm For ... Farm Forestry [*A publication*]
Farm & Garden Ind ... Farm and Garden Index [*A publication*]
Farm Gard Index ... Farm and Garden Index [*A publication*]
Farm Glas ... Farmaceutski Glasnik [*A publication*]
Farm Glasn ... Farmaceutski Glasnik [*A publication*]
Farm & Home Sci ... Farm and Home Science [*A publication*]

Farm Home Sci ... Farm and Home Science [*A publication*]
Farm In ...... Farm Index [*A publication*]
Farming Bus ... Farming Business [*A publication*]
Farming Dig ... Farming Digest [*A publication*]
Farming Mech ... Farming Mechanization [*A publication*]
Farming Progr ... Farming Progress [*A publication*]
Farming Rev ... Farming Review [*A publication*]
Farming S Afr ... Farming in South Africa [*A publication*]
Farm J ...... Farm Journal [*A publication*]
Farm J Brit Guiana ... Farm Journal of British Guiana [*A publication*]
Farm J (Calcutta) ... Farm Journal (Calcutta) [*A publication*]
Farm J (E Ed) ... Farm Journal (Eastern Edition) [*A publication*]
Farmkoter Zpr ... Farmakoterapeuticke Zpravy [*A publication*]
Farmkoter Zpr Suppl ... Farmakoterapeuticke Zpravy. Supplementum [*A publication*]
Farmline US Dep Agric Econ Stat Coop Serv ... Farmline. United States Department of Agriculture. Economics Statistics and Cooperatives Service [*A publication*]
Farm Mach ... Farm Machinery [*A publication*]
Farm Manage ... Farm Management [*A publication*]
Farm Manage Notes ... Farm Management Notes [*A publication*]
Farm Manage Rep USDA Coop Ext Serv ... Farm Management Report. United States Department of Agriculture. Cooperative Extension Service [*A publication*]
Farm Manage Rev ... Farm Management Review [*A publication*]
Farm Mech ... Farm Mechanization [*A publication*]
Farm Mech Stud ... Farm Mechanization Studies [*A publication*]
Farm Ne ..... Farming News and North British Agriculturist [*A publication*]
Farmnote West Aust Dep Agric ... Farmnote. Western Australian Department of Agriculture [*A publication*]
Farm Nuova ... Farmacia Nuova [*A publication*]
Farm Obz ... Farmaceuticky Obzor [*A publication*]
Farmos Med News ... Farmos Medical News [*A publication*]
Farm Pol .... Farm Policy [*A publication*]   (APTA)
Farm Pol .... Farmacja Polska [*A publication*]
Farm Pol (1902-1914) ... Farmaceuta Polski (1902-1914) [*A publication*]
Farm Policy Rev Conf ... Farm Policy Review Conference [*A publication*]
Farm Power Equip ... Farm and Power Equipment [*A publication*]
Farm Q .... Farm Quarterly [*A publication*]
Farm Quart ... Farm Quarterly [*A publication*]
Farm y Quim ... Farmacia y Quimica [*A publication*]
Farm R .... Farmacevtisk Revy [*A publication*]
Farm Ranch Home Q ... Farm, Ranch, and Home Quarterly [*A publication*]
Farm Ranch Home Q Nebr Agric Exp Stn ... Farm, Ranch, and Home Quarterly. Nebraska Agricultural Experiment Station [*A publication*]
Farm Res .... Farm Research [*A publication*]
Farm Res News ... Farm Research News [*A publication*]
Farm Revy ... Farmacevtisk Revy [*A publication*]
FARMS ..... Farm Audience Readership Measurement Service [*Starch INRA Hooper, Inc.*] [*Information service or system*]   (IID)
Farm Safety Rev ... Farm Safety Review [*A publication*]
Farm S Afr ... Farming in South Africa [*A publication*]
Farm Sci e Tec ... Farmaco Scienza e Tecnica [*A publication*]
Farm Technol ... Farm Technology [*A publication*]
Farm Tid ... Farmaceutisk Tidende [*A publication*]
Farm Tijdschr Belg ... Farmaceutisch Tijdschrift voor Belgie [*A publication*]
Farm Today ... Farming Today [*A publication*]
Farm Toks ... Farmakologija i Toksikologija [*A publication*]
Farm i Toksik ... Farmakologija i Toksikologija [*A publication*]
Farm Vestn ... Farmacevtski Vestnik [*A publication*]
Farm Week ... Farmers' Weekly [*A publication*]
Farm Z .... Farmatsevtychnyi Zhurnal [*A publication*]
Farm Zh ..... Farmatsevtychnyi Zhurnal [*A publication*]
Farm Zh (Kharkov) ... Farmatsevticheskii Zhurnal (Kharkov) [*A publication*]
Farm Zh (Kiev) ... Farmatsevtychnyi Zhurnal (Kiev) [*A publication*]
Farm Zh (Leningrad) ... Farmatsevticheskii Zhurnal (Leningrad) [*A publication*]
Farm Zpr ... Farmakoterapeuticke Zpravy [*A publication*]
FARN .... Fuerzas Armadas de Resistencia Nacional [*Armed Forces of National Resistance*] [*El Salvador*]   (PD)
FARN .... Fuerzas Armadas Revolucionarias Nicaraguenses [*Nicaraguan Armed Revolutionary Forces*]   (PD)
FARO .... Flare-Activated Radiobiological Observatory
FAROES ... Fleet Automatic Reconstruction and Opportunity Evaluation System [*Navy*]   (CAAL)
FARP .... Forward Area Resupply Point
FARP .... Rosh Pinah [*Namibia*] [*ICAO location identifier*]   (ICLI)
FARPO ...... Federal Acquisition Regulation Project Office   (MCD)
Farq Chy .... Farquharson's Court of Chancery [*A publication*]   (DLA)
FARR .... Failure and Rejection Report   (MCD)
FARR .... Farragut Mortgage Co., Inc. [*Waltham, MA*] [*NASDAQ symbol*]   (NQ)
Farr .... Farresley's Reports [*7 Modern Reports*] [*87 English Reprint*] [*1733-45*] [*A publication*]   (DLA)
FARR .... Forward Area Refuelling and Rearming
FARRA ...... Farm Research [*Switzerland*] [*A publication*]
FARRAN .... Farm Research [*A publication*]
Farrant .... Digest of Manx Cases [*1925-47*] [*A publication*]   (DLA)
Farr Bill ..... Farren's Bill in Chancery [*A publication*]   (DLA)

Farr Const ... Farrar's Manual of the United States Constitution [*A publication*]   (DLA)
Farresley .... Farresley's Reports [*7 Modern Reports*] [*87 English Reprint*] [*1733-45*] [*A publication*]   (DLA)
Farr Life Ass ... Farren on Life Assurance [*A publication*]   (DLA)
Farr Mas .... Farren's Masters in Chancery [*A publication*]   (DLA)
Farr Med Jur ... Farr's Medical Jurisprudence [*A publication*]   (DLA)
FARRP ...... Forward Area Rearm and Refuel Point
FARRS ...... Forward Area Rearm and Refuel Site   (MCD)
FARS .... Failure Analysis Report Summary [*Bell System*]
FARS .... Fatal Accident Reporting System [*National Highway Traffic Safety Administration*] [*Washington, DC*]   (GRD)
FARS .... Field Army Replacement System   (AABC)
FARS .... Forward Area RAWINSONDE [*RADAR Wind Sounding and Radiosonde*] Set [*Army*]
FARS .... Fuel and Ammunition Resupply Study
FARS .... Robertson [*South Africa*] [*ICAO location identifier*]   (ICLI)
Far Seas Fish Res Lab S Ser ... Far Seas Fisheries Research Laboratory. S Series [*A publication*]
F Artil J .... Field Artillery Journal [*A publication*]
F Arts Q .... Fine Arts Quarterly [*A publication*]
FARU .... Rundu [*Namibia*] [*ICAO location identifier*]   (ICLI)
FARUA ...... Farumashia [*A publication*]
FARV .... Future Armored Resupply Vehicle [*Army*]
FARV .... Riverview [*South Africa*] [*ICAO location identifier*]   (ICLI)
Farwell ...... Farwell on Powers [*3 eds.*] [*1874-1916*] [*A publication*]   (DLA)
FARWG ...... Federal Acquisition Regional Work Group [*Army*]
Farw Pow ... Farwell on Powers [*3 eds.*] [*1874-1916*] [*A publication*]   (DLA)
FAS .... Facility Activation [*or Activity*] Schedule
FAS .... Facility Air Supply
FAS .... Faculty of Architects and Surveyors [*British*]   (DAS)
FAS .... Failure Analysis Section
FAS .... Fairbanks Air Service [*Alaska*]   (FAAC)
FAS .... Fallout Assessment System
FAS .... Family Action Section   (EA)
FAS .... Family Allowance Supplement [*Australia*]
FAS .... Famous Artists Schools [*Later, FAS International, Inc.*]
FAS .... Fantastic Stories [*A publication*]
FAS .... Fast Announcement Service [*NTIS publication*]
FAS .... Fasten [*Technical drawings*]
FAS .... Feature Analysis System [*Image analysis*]
FAS .... Federal Airport Service
FAS .... Federal Aviation Service
FAS .... Federation des Affaires Sociales, Inc. [*Federation of Social Affairs*] [*Canada*]
FAS .... Federation of American Scientists   (EA)
FAS .... Feel Augmentation System [*Helicopters*]
FAS .... Fellow of the Actuarial Society
FAS .... Fellow of the Anthropological Society [*British*]   (DAS)
FAS .... Fellow of the Antiquarian Society [*British*]
FAS .... Fellow of the Society of Arts [*British*]   (DAS)
FAS .... Fellows in American Studies
FAS .... Fetal Alcohol Syndrome [*Medicine*]
FAS .... Field Alert Status [*Army*]   (AABC)
FAS .... Field Artillery School   (MCD)
FAS .... File Access Subsystem [*Data processing*]   (TEL)
FAS .... Film Availability Services [*British Film Institute*]
FAS .... Final Asset Screen [*DoD*]
FAS .... Final Average Salary
FAS .... Financial Accounting Standard
FAS .... Finnish-American Society [*Later, LFAS*]   (EA)
FAS .... Fire Support Aerial System
FAS .... First Assistant Secretary   (ADA)
FAS .... Firsts and Seconds [*Lumber trade*]
FAS .... Fixed Airlock Shroud [*NASA*]
FAS .... Flame Absorption Spectroscopy
FAS .... Fleet Attack Submarine [*Navy*]   (CAAL)
FAS .... Flexible Access System
FAS .... Flight Advisory Service [*FAA*]
FAS .... Flight Analysis Section
FAS .... Flight Assistance Service
FAS .... Focusing Array Study
FAS .... Follow-Up Alarm System
FAS .... Force Accounting Structure
FAS .... Force Accounting System [*Army*]   (AABC)
FAS .... Forces Aerienne Strategiques [*French*]
FAS .... Foreign Agricultural Service [*Department of Agriculture*] [*Washington, DC*]
FAS .... Foreign Aid Society [*British*]
FAS .... Foreign Area Specialist [*Army*]
FAS .... Forward Acquisition Sensor
FAS .... Forward Acquisition System
FAS .... Foundation for Aggregate Studies
FAS .... Frame Alignment Signal [*Telecommunications*]   (TEL)
FAS .... Frankfurter Althistorische Studien [*A publication*]
FAS .... Free Alongside Ship ["*INCOTERM*," *International Chamber of Commerce official code*]
FAS .... Free-Association Strength [*Psychometrics*]
FAS .... Frequency Allocation [*or Assignment*] Subcommittee   (AFM)
FAS .... Fueling-at-Sea [*Navy*]   (MSA)
FAS .... Functional Address Symbol [*Military*]   (AFIT)

FAS............ Fund for American Studies   (EA)
FASA......... Federation of ASEAN [*Association of South East Asian Nations*] Shipowners' Associations [*Kuala Lumpur, Malaysia*]   (EAIO)
FASA .... Fellow, American Society of Appraisers [*Designation awarded by American Society of Appraisers*]
FASA .... Fellow of the American Sociological Association
FASA .... Fellow of the Australian Society of Accountants
FASA .... Field Army Service Area   (AABC)
FASA .... Fixed Area Scanning Alarm
FASA .... Fleet Airships, Atlantic
FASA .... Freestanding Ambulatory Surgery Association   (EA)
FASA .... Sani Pass [*South Africa*] [*ICAO location identifier*]   (ICLI)
FASAB ...... Front Autonomiste et Socialiste Autogestionnaire Bretonne [*Breton Autonomist and Socialist Self-Rule Front*] [*France*] [*Political party*]   (PPE)
FASAC ...... Foreign Applied Sciences Assessment Center
FASAF....... Filipinas Americas Science and Art Foundation   (EA)
FASAS....... Federation of Asian Scientific Academies and Societies [*India*]   (EY)
FASB .... Fellow of the Asiatic Society of Bengal
FASB .... Financial Accounting Standards Board [*Formerly, Accounting Principles Board*] [*American Institute of Certified Public Accountants*]
FASB .... First American Savings Bank FSB [*NASDAQ symbol*]   (NQ)
FASB .... Springbok [*South Africa*] [*ICAO location identifier*]   (ICLI)
FASBB....... Soils Bulletin [*A publication*]
FASBDH... FAO [*Food and Agriculture Organization of the United Nations*] Agricultural Services Bulletin [*A publication*]
FASC .... Fascicle
Fasc............ Fascicule [*Installment*] [*A publication*]   (DLA)
FASC .... Fasciculus [*Little Bundle*] [*Latin*]   (ROG)
FASC .... Foreign Affairs Specialist Corps [*Department of State*]
FASC .... Foreign Agricultural Service Club [*Later, Foreign Agricultural Club*]   (EA)
FASC .... Forward Area Signal Center   (MCD)
FASC .... Forward Area Support Center   (MCD)
FASC .... Free-Standing Ambulatory Surgical Center
FASC .... Secunda [*South Africa*] [*ICAO location identifier*]   (ICLI)
FASCA ...... Federation of Armenian Students Clubs of America   (EA)
FASCAM .. Family of Scatterable Mines [*Army*]   (RDA)
FASCAP.... Fast-Payback Capital Investment Program [*Air Force*]
FASCE....... Fellow of the American Society of Civil Engineers
Fasc Math ... Fasciculi Mathematici [*A publication*]
FASCNA ... Federation of Alpine and Schuhplattler Clubs in North America   (EA)
FASCO ...... Fast Scan Cutoff   (CAAL)
FASCO ...... Forward Area Support Company [*Military*]
FASCO ...... Forward Area Support Coordination Officer [*Army*]   (AABC)
FASCOM .. Field Army Support Command
FASCOS.... Flight Acceleration Safety Cutoff System   (MCD)
FASCS....... Federated Antisubmarine Combat System [*Navy*]   (CAAL)
FASCWS... First-Aid, Small Craft, and Water Safety [*Red Cross*]
FASD.......... Flameless Alkali Sensitized Detector [*Instrumentation*]
FASD......... Saldanha [*South Africa*] [*ICAO location identifier*]   (ICLI)
FASE .... Federation of Acoustical Societies of Europe   (EAIO)
FASE .... Federation Europeenne des Societes d'Acoustique [*Federation of Acoustical Societies of Europe*]   (EAIO)
FASE .... Fellow of the Antiquarian Society of Edinburgh   (ROG)
FASE .... Fundamentally Analyzable Simplified English [*Data processing*]
FASE .... Sanae [*South Africa*] [*ICAO location identifier*]   (ICLI)
FASEB....... Federation of American Societies for Experimental Biology   (EA)
FASEB Monogr ... FASEB [*Federation of American Societies for Experimental Biology*] Monographs [*A publication*]
FASEC....... Foundation for America's Sexually Exploited Children   (EA)
Faserforsch Textiltech ... Faserforschung und Textiltechnik [*A publication*]
Faserf T ..... Faserforschung und Textiltechnik [*A publication*]
Faserst Spinnpflanzen ... Faserstoffe und Spinnpflanzen [*A publication*]
FASF .... Fantastic Science Fiction [*A publication*]
FASF .... Southern Air Command [*South Africa*] [*ICAO location identifier*]   (ICLI)
FAS/FA ..... Florida Anthropologist. Florida Anthropological Society [*A publication*]
FASG......... Fanconi's Anemia Support Group   (EA)
FASG......... Schweizer Reneke [*South Africa*] [*ICAO location identifier*]   (ICLI)
FASH........ Forward Area Support Helicopter
FASH........ Fraternal Association of Steel Haulers   (EA)
FASH........ Stellenbosch [*South Africa*] [*ICAO location identifier*]   (ICLI)
FASI .... Fellow of the Ambulance Service Institute [*British*]   (DBQ)
FASI .... Friedreich's Ataxia Society of Ireland   (EAIO)
FASI .... Springs [*South Africa*] [*ICAO location identifier*]   (ICLI)
FASID .... Fellow of the Society of Interior Designers
FASK .... Swartkop [*South Africa*] [*ICAO location identifier*]   (ICLI)
FASKAP... Field Artillery Survey Knowledge Acquisition Program [*Army*]
FASL .... Fellow of the Anthropological Society, London   (ROG)
FASL .... Fellow of the Antiquarian Society, London   (ROG)
FASL .... Sutherland [*South Africa*] [*ICAO location identifier*]   (ICLI)
FASLA ...... Filmstrip and Slide Laboratory
FASM........ Swakopmund [*Namibia*] [*ICAO location identifier*]   (ICLI)

FASMDG ... FASEB [*Federation of American Societies for Experimental Biology*] Monographs [*A publication*]
FASN......... [*The*] Fashion Channel Network, Inc. [*NASDAQ symbol*]   (NQ)
FASN......... Senekal [*South Africa*] [*ICAO location identifier*]   (ICLI)
FASO......... Field Aviation Supply Office
FASO......... Forward Airfield Supply Organization
FASOC...... Forward Air Support Operations Center   (NATG)
FASOLA ... Fa, Sol, and La [*Musical notation system*]
FASOR...... Forward Area SONAR Research [*Navy*]
FASOTRAGRUPAC ... Fleet Aviation Specialized Operational Training Group, Pacific [*Formerly, FAETUPAC*] [*Later, FASOTRAGRUPACFLT*] [*Navy*]
FASOTRAGRUPACFLT ... Fleet Aviation Specialized Operational Training Group, Pacific Fleet [*Formerly, FASOTRAGRUPAC, FAETUPAC*] [*Navy*]
FASP .... Facility for Automatic Software Production [*Data processing*]   (CAAL)
FASP .... Fleet Airships, Pacific
FASP .... Frequency Analysis of System Program [*NASA*]
FASP .... Sir Lowry's Pass [*South Africa*] [*ICAO location identifier*]   (ICLI)
FASPA ...... Federation Africaine des Syndicats du Petrole et Assimiles [*African Federation of Trade Unions of Oil and Petrochemicals*] [*Tripoli, Libya*]   (EAIO)
FASR .... Standerton [*South Africa*] [*ICAO location identifier*]   (ICLI)
FASRA ...... Foundation to Assist Scientific Research in Africa   (EAIO)
FASRON ... Fleet Air [*or Aircraft*] Service Squadron [*Obsolete*]
FASS .... Fine Alignment Subsystem
FASS .... Flight Activities Scheduling System [*NASA*]
FASS .... Forward Acquisition Sensor   (IEEE)
FASS .... Free Air Suspension System
FASS .... Sishen [*South Africa*] [*ICAO location identifier*]   (ICLI)
FASSA ...... Fellow of the Academy of the Social Sciences in Australia
FASSC....... Ford Aerospace Satellite Services Corporation [*Arlington, VA*] [*Telecommunications*]   (TSSD)
FASSN ...... Fast Attack Submarine   (MCD)
FASST....... Federation of Americans Supporting Science and Technology
FASST....... Fly America's Supersonic Transport [*Student group*]
FASST....... Fly Around Saturated Sectors and Terminals [*National Business Aircraft Association*] [*Database*]
FAST .... [*To*] Facilitate Acceleration through Special Techniques [*Federal Highway Administration*]
FAST .... Facility for Accelerated Service Testing
FAST .... Facility for Analyzing Surface Texture [*National Bureau of Standards*]   (MCD)
FAST .... Facility for Automatic Sorting and Testing
FAST .... Factory Automation Systems Technology [*British*]
FAST .... Failure Analysis by Statistical Techniques [*Data processing code*]
FAST .... Fair and Simple Tax [*Type of flat tax proposed by Rep. Jack Kemp and Sen. Bob Kasten*]
FAST .... Falcon and SOPAC Air Transport [*Australia*]
FAST .... Fans Against the Strike   (EA)
FAST .... Fare Automated Search Technique [*Airline travel service information system*]
FAST .... Fast Access Scan Talker [*Occupational therapy*]
FAST .... Fast Acquisition Search and Track   (MCD)
FAST .... Fast Automatic Shuttle Transfer [*System*] [*Navy*]
FAST .... Fast at Sea Transfer [*Equipment*]
FAST .... Fastenal Co. [*NASDAQ symbol*]   (NQ)
FAST .... Fastening [*or Fastener*] [*Automotive engineering*]
Fast .... Fasti [*of Ovid*] [*Classical studies*]   (OCD)
Fa St .... Faulkner Studies [*A publication*]
FAST .... Federal Advanced Superconducting Transportation Act
FAST .... Federal Assistance for Staff Training [*Education*]
FAST .... Federal Assistance Streamlining Taskforce [*HEW*]
FAST .... Federation Against Software Theft
FAST .... Fence Against Satellite Threats
FAST .... Fiduciary Activity Simulation Training [*Investment banking simulation game*]
FAST .... Field Artillery Survey Team
FAST .... Field Artillery Survey Test   (MCD)
FAST .... Field Assistance in Science and Technology Program [*US Army Materiel Command*]
FAST .... Field Assistance Support Team   (MCD)
FAST .... Field Data Applications, Systems, and Techniques [*Data processing*]
FAST .... File Analysis and Selection Technique [*Data processing*]
FAST .... Finite Area Solids Technology   (MCD)
FAST .... First Atomic Ship Transport, Inc.
FAST .... Fixed Abrasive Slicing [*Semiconductor technology*]
FAST .... Fleet-Sizing Analysis and Sensitivity Technique [*Bell System*]
FAST .... Flexible Algebraic Scientific Translator [*NCR Corp.*]
FAST .... Flight Advisory Service Test [*FAA*]
FAST .... Flight Aptitude Selection Test [*Army*]
FAST .... Fluorescent Antibody Staining Technique [*Clinical chemistry*]
FAST .... Food and Allied Service Trades Department [*of AFL-CIO*]   (EA)
FAST .... Foolproof Auditing and Sale of Tickets [*in motion picture theaters*]

FAST .... Forecasting and Assessment in Science and Technology [*Commission of the European Communities program, 1978-1983*]
FAST .... Forecasting and Scheduling Technique
FAST .... Foreign Area Specialist Training [*Army*]
FAST .... Formal Auto-Indexing of Scientific Texts [*Data processing*] (IEEE)
FAST .... Formula and Statement Translator [*Data processing*] (MCD)
FAST .... Forward Air Strike Task (CINC)
FAST .... Forward Airborne Surveillance and Tracking
FAST .... Forward Area Support Team [*Military*] (INF)
FAST .... Foundation for Applied Science and Technology [*University of Pittsburgh*] [*Research center*] (RCD)
FAST .... Four-Address to SOAP [*Self-Optimizing Automatic Pilot*] Translator [*Data processing*] (IEEE)
FAST .... Freight Accounting Shipment Tracing System (MCD)
FAST .... Freight Automated System for Traffic Management (AABC)
FAST .... Frequency Agile Search and Track Seeker
FAST .... Friction Assessment Screening Test [*for brake linings*]
FAST .... Fuel Aerosol Simulation Test [*Nuclear energy*] (NRCH)
FAST .... Fuel Assembly Stability Test (NRCH)
FAST .... Fuel and Sensor, Tactical (MCD)
FAST .... Fully Automated Scoring Target [*System*] (MCD)
FAST .... Functional Analysis System Technique
FAST .... Fundamentals of Application and System Training [*Course*] [*Data processing*]
FAST .... Somerset East [*South Africa*] [*ICAO location identifier*] (ICLI)
FASTA ...... Federal Aviation Science and Technological Association (EA)
FASTAC .... Flame/Furnace Autosampling Technique with Automatic Calibration [*Spectroscopy*]
FASTALS ... Force Analysis Simulation of Theater Administrative and Logistics Support [*Military*]
FASTAR .... Frequency Angle Scanning, Tracking, and Ranging
FASTBAC's ... First Automotive Short-Term Bonds and Certificates [*Drexel Burnham Lambert, Inc.*] [*Finance*]
FASTBACCS ... Field Artillery System Training for the Common Battalion Command and Control System (MCD)
FASTEL .... Fast Economic Language [*Data processing*] (BUR)
FASTEL .... Files for Agricultural Science and Technology Literature [*Database*] [*Agricultural Science Information Center*] [*Information service or system*] (CRD)
FASTEP .... Files for Agricultural Science and Technology Personnel [*Database*] [*Agricultural Science Information Center*] [*Information service or system*] (CRD)
FASTFIRE ... Field Artillery System Training Fire Direction Centers (MCD)
FASTI .... Fast Access to Systems Technical Information
FAST J ...... FAST Journal [*A publication*]
FASTLODS ... Fighter Aircraft Structural Loads [*Program*] [*Air Force*]
FAST-OB .. Officer Battery Flight Aptitude Selection Test [*Military*] (INF)
FASTOP .... Flutter and Strength Optimization Program for Lifting Surface Structures (MCD)
FASTP .... Foreign Area Specialist Training Program [*Army*]
FASTPACK ... Fuel and Sensor Tactical Package (MCD)
FASTRACK ... Force Accounting System Track [*Army*] (MCD)
FASTRAM ... Falling Sphere Trajectory Measurement (MUGU)
FAST RIPSAW ... Financial Automation Systems Team for Writing Programs for Standardized Army-Wide Applications
FASTRON ... Fleet Aircraft Service Squadron (MUGU)
FASTS .... Federation of Australian Scientific and Technological Societies
FASTSUPPORT ... Field Artillery System Training for the Fire Support Officer (MCD)
FASTULANT ... Fleet Ammunition Ship Training Unit, Atlantic
FASTUPAC ... Fleet Ammunition Ship Training Unit, Pacific
FASTV ...... First Artillery Ammunition Resupply Vehicle [*Army*] (RDA)
FAST-VAL ... Forward Air Strike Evaluation
FASU .... Fleet Aviation Support Unit (MCD)
FASU .... Sace [*South Africa*] [*ICAO location identifier*] (ICLI)
FASUS ...... Freight Assurance Storage, United States
FASV .... Field Alert Status Verification [*Army*] (MCD)
FASV .... Silvermine [*South Africa*] [*ICAO location identifier*] (ICLI)
F/ASVS ...... Fighter/Attack Simulator Visual System [*Military*]
FASW .... South West Africa Air Force Headquarters [*Namibia*] [*ICAO location identifier*] (ICLI)
FASWC ...... Fleet Antisubmarine Warfare Command (IEEE)
FASWOC .. Food and Service Workers of Canada
FASWSCHOOL ... Fleet Antisubmarine Warfare School
FASX .... Fairbanks Air Service [*Alaska*] [*Air carrier designation symbol*]
FASX .... Swellendam [*South Africa*] [*ICAO location identifier*] (ICLI)
FASY .... Syferfontein [*South Africa*] [*ICAO location identifier*] (ICLI)
FASZ .... Skukuza [*South Africa*] [*ICAO location identifier*] (ICLI)
Fat .... De Fato [*of Cicero*] [*Classical studies*] (OCD)
FAT .... Factory Acceptance Test
FAT .... Family Adjustment Test [*Psychology*]
FAT .... Family Assessment Tool [*Kit*] [*Medicine*]
FAT .... Fast Automatic Transfer
FAT .... Fast Axonal Transport [*Neurobiology*]
FAT .... Fathom (NATG)
FAT .... Fatphobia Awareness Training
FAT .... Federation of Arab Teachers (EAIO)
FAT .... Field Artillery Tractor [*British*]
FAT .... File Allocation Table [*Data processing*]

FAT .... Final Acceptance, Assembly Tests
FAT .... Final Aerospace Trial
FAT .... Final Assembly Test
FAT .... First Article Test
FAT .... Fischer Athenaeum Taschenbuecher [*A publication*]
FAT .... Fixed Asset Transfer [*Business term*]
FAT .... Flight Acceptance Test
FAT .... Flight Attitude Table [*NASA*] (NASA)
FAT .... Flight Test Station [*ITU designation*] (CET)
FAT .... Fluorescent Antibody Test [*Clinical medicine*]
FAT .... Food Awareness Training
FAT .... Forces Armees Tchadiennes [*Chad Armed Forces*] (PD)
FAT .... Foreign Area Toll [*Telecommunications*] (TEL)
FAT .... Foreign Area Translation [*Telecommunications*] (TEL)
FAT .... Formula Assembler Translator [*Data processing*] (BUR)
FAT .... Forward Area Trace (MCD)
FAT .... Foundation for Anglican Traditions (EA)
FAT .... Free Air Temperature (NG)
FAT .... Fresno [*California*] [*Airport symbol*] (OAG)
FAT .... Friends of Appropriate Technology (EA)
Fatab .... Fataburen [*A publication*]
FATAB ..... Field Artillery Target Acquisition Battalion [*Army*] (AABC)
Fataburen ... Fataburen. Nordiska Museets och Skansens Arsbok [*A publication*]
FATAG ...... Field Artillery Target Acquisition Group [*Army*] (AABC)
FATAL ...... FADAC [*Field Artillery Digital Automatic Computer*] Automatic Test Analysis Language (IEEE)
FATAR ...... Fast Analysis of Tape and Recovery
FATB .... Floor Ataxia Test Battery
FATC .... Field Artillery Training Centre [*British military*] (DMA)
FATC .... Fleet Area Telecommunications Center [*Navy*] (MCD)
FATC .... Tristan De Cunha [*South Africa*] [*ICAO location identifier*] (ICLI)
FATCAT ... Film and Television Correlation Assessment Technique (MCD)
FATCAT ... Frequency and Time Circuit Analysis Technique [*NASA*]
FAT-COI ... Federation Americaine du Travail et Congres des Organisations Industrielles [*American Federation of Labor and Congress of Industrial Organizations - AFL-CIO*] [*Canada*]
FATCP ...... Forum for the Advancement of Toxicology in Colleges of Pharmacy (EA)
FATD .... Federal Applied Technology Database [*National Technical Information Service*] [*Information service or system*] (CRD)
FATDAD ... Fermanagh, Armagh, Tyrone, Derry, Antrim, Down [*The six counties of Northern Ireland*]
FATDL ...... Frequency and Time-Division Data Link
FATDOC ... Film and Television Documentation Center [*State University of New York at Albany*] [*Information service or system*] (IID)
FATDS ...... Field Artillery Tactical Data Systems [*Army*] (RDA)
FATE .... Fuze Arming Test Experiment
FATES ...... Flow-Through Aquatic Toxicology Exposure System [*Evaluation of sediment contaminants*]
FATF .... Free Air Test Facility
FATFL ...... FSS [*Flight Service Station*] Assumes Control of Tower Frequencies and Lights [*Aviation*] (FAAC)
FATH .... Fathom
FATH .... Thohoyandou [*South Africa*] [*ICAO location identifier*] (ICLI)
Fatigue Eng Mater and Struct ... Fatigue of Engineering Materials and Structures [*A publication*]
Fatigue Eng Mater Struct ... Fatigue of Engineering Materials and Structures [*A publication*]
Fatigue Eng Mat Struct ... Fatigue of Engineering Materials and Structures [*A publication*]
FATIPEC .. Federation d'Associations de Techniciens des Industries de Peintures, Vernis, Emaux, et Encres d'Imprimerie de l'Europe [*Federation of the Associations of Technicians of the Paint, Varnish, and Ink Industries of Continental Europe*] (EAIO)
FATIS .... FATIS [*Food and Agriculture Technical Information Service*] Publications [*A publication*]
FATIS Rev ... FATIS [*Food and Agriculture Technical Information Service*] Review [*A publication*]
FATK .... Tsumkwe [*Namibia*] [*ICAO location identifier*] (ICLI)
FATLAD ... Fermanagh, Armagh, Tyrone, Londonderry, Antrim, Down [*Unionist mnemonic for the six counties of Northern Ireland*]
FATM .... Tsumeb [*Namibia*] [*ICAO location identifier*] (ICLI)
FATMAT .. Field Artillery Turret Maintenance Trainer (MCD)
FATMS ..... Field Artillery Turret Maintenance Simulator (MCD)
FATN .... First American Corp. [*NASDAQ symbol*] (NQ)
FATOA ...... Farmakologiya i Toksikologiya [*Moscow*] [*A publication*]
FATOAO .. Farmakologiya i Toksikologiya [*Moscow*] [*A publication*]
FATOBP ... Farmakologiya i Toksikologiya Respublikanskii Mezhvedomstvennyi Sbornik [*A publication*]
FATOC ...... Field Army Tactical Operation Center
FATOLA ... Flexible Aircraft Takeoff and Landing Analysis (MCD)
FATP .... Bloemfontein/New Tempe [*South Africa*] [*ICAO location identifier*] (ICLI)
FATP .... Factory Acceptance Test Procedure

FATPAC.... Fishing/Tourist Port Advisory Committee [*New South Wales, Australia*]
FATR........ Fixed Auto Transfer (MCD)
FATR........ Fixed Autotransformer
FATRACS ... Field Army Tactical Random Access Communications System
FATRANS ... First Available Transportation
Fat Rev.... Fatis Review [*A publication*]
FATS .... Factory Acceptance Test Specification
FATS .... Fight to Advertise the Truth about Saturates [*Student legal action organization*]
FATS .... FORTRAN [*Formula Translating System*] Automatic Timing System [*Data processing*]
FATS .... South African Air Force Tactical Support Command [*ICAO location identifier*] (ICLI)
FATSA ...... Flowers Auditory Test of Selective Attention
FATSO ...... First Aid Technical Stores Outfit [*Military*] [*British*]
FATT .... Forward Area Tactical Teletype (MCD)
FATT .... Fracture Appearance Transition Temperature
FATT .... Tutuka [*South Africa*] [*ICAO location identifier*] (ICLI)
FATTS ...... Forward Area Tactical Teletypewriter Set
FATTY ...... Forward Area Tactical Typewriter
FATU........ Fleet Air Tactical Unit
FATV .... First Ameri-Cable Corp. [*Columbus, OH*] [*NASDAQ symbol*] (NQ)
FATZ .... Tzaneen [*South Africa*] [*ICAO location identifier*] (ICLI)
FAU .... Fairfield University, Fairfield, CT [*OCLC symbol*] (OCLC)
FAU .... Fairview, OK [*Location identifier*] [*FAA*] (FAAL)
FAU .... Falmouth Petroleum [*Vancouver Stock Exchange symbol*]
FAU .... Faujasite [*A zeolite*]
FAU .... Fine Alignment Unit
FAU .... Fixed Asset Utilization [*Business term*] (ADA)
FAU .... Flag Administrative Unit
FAU .... Florida Atlantic University [*Boca Raton*]
FAU .... Freeport McMoRan Gold Co. [*NYSE symbol*] (SPSG)
FAU .... Frequency Allocation and Uses
FAU .... Friends Ambulance Unit [*British military*] (DMA)
FAUC........ Ulco [*South Africa*] [*ICAO location identifier*] (ICLI)
FAUCAR... Folia Anatomica Universitatis Conimbrigensis [*Coimbra*] [*A publication*]
FAUH........ Uitenhage [*South Africa*] [*ICAO location identifier*] (ICLI)
FAUK .... Usakos [*Namibia*] [*ICAO location identifier*] (ICLI)
FAUL........ Five Associated University Libraries [*State University of New York at Buffalo and Binghamton, Cornell University, Syracuse University, University of Rochester*]
FAUL........ Ulundi [*South Africa*] [*ICAO location identifier*] (ICLI)
Faulkner St ... Faulkner Studies [*A publication*]
FAULT........ Families Against Legal Trauma [*Australia*]
Faun Abh (Dres) ... Faunistische Abhandlungen (Dresden) [*A publication*]
Faun Abh Staatl Mus Tierk Dresden ... Faunistische Abhandlungen. Staatliches Museum fuer Tierkunde in Dresden [*A publication*]
Fauna Entomol Scand ... Fauna Entomologica Scandinavica [*A publication*]
Fauna Fenn ... Fauna Fennica [*A publication*]
Fauna Flora (Stockh) ... Fauna och Flora (Stockholm) [*A publication*]
Fauna Flora (Transvaal) ... Fauna and Flora (Transvaal) [*A publication*]
Fauna Hung ... Fauna Hungariae [*A publication*]
Fauna Ital .. Fauna d'Italia [*A publication*]
Fauna Norv Ser A ... Fauna Norvegica. Series A [*A publication*]
Fauna Norv Ser C ... Fauna Norvegica. Series C [*A publication*]
Fauna NZ... Fauna of New Zealand [*A publication*]
Fauna Pol... Fauna Polski [*A publication*]
Faune Fr..... Faune de France [*A publication*]
Faune Que ... Faune du Quebec [*A publication*]
Faune Que Rapp Spec ... Faune du Quebec. Rapport Special [*A publication*]
Faunistische Abh ... Faunistische Abhandlungen [*A publication*]
Faun Maerkm ... Faunistilisi Maerkmeid [*A publication*]
Faun-Oekol Mitt ... Faunistisch-Oekologische Mitteilungen [*A publication*]
Faun Rec Univ Qu ... Faunistic Records. University of Queensland Papers [*A publication*]
FAUP........ Upington/Pierre Van Ryneveld [*South Africa*] [*ICAO location identifier*] (ICLI)
FAUS........ Federal Aid Urban System [*Road improvement program*] [*Federal Highway Administration*]
FAUS........ Feingold Association of the United States (EA)
FAUS........ Uis [*Namibia*] [*ICAO location identifier*] (ICLI)
FAUSST.... French-Anglo-United States Supersonic Transport
FAUST........ Far Ultraviolet Space Telescope
Faust .... Faust's Compiled Laws [*Scotland*] [*A publication*] (DLA)
Faust B....... Faust Blaetter [*A publication*]
FAUT........ Umtata (K. D. Matanzima) [*South Africa*] [*ICAO location identifier*] (ICLI)
FAV .... Fakarava [*French Polynesia*] [*Airport symbol*] (OAG)
FAV .... Fan Air Valve (MCD)
FAV .... Fast Attack Vehicle [*Army*] (INF)
FAV .... Favorable (AFM)
FAV .... Favorite (ADA)
FAV .... Fayetteville [*Arkansas*] [*Seismograph station code, US Geological Survey*] (SEIS)
FAV .... Fire Ant Venom [*Immunology*]
FAV .... Fixed-Angle Variable

FAV .... Forfar Artillery Volunteers [*British military*] (DMA)
FAV .... Frog Adenovirus
FAV .... Full Analog Video
FAVA .... Fixed Asset Valuation Adjustment [*Business term*] (ADA)
FAVB .... Vryburg [*South Africa*] [*ICAO location identifier*] (ICLI)
FAVC........ Flight Attendant Volunteer Corps (EA)
FAVD .... Vrede [*South Africa*] [*ICAO location identifier*] (ICLI)
FAVE .... Ventersdorp [*South Africa*] [*ICAO location identifier*] (ICLI)
FAVG .... Durban/Virginia [*South Africa*] [*ICAO location identifier*] (ICLI)
FAVN .... Fluorescent-Antibody Virus Neutralization Test [*Immunology*]
FAVO .... Fleet Aviation Officer [*British*]
FAVP........ Vanderbijlpark [*South Africa*] [*ICAO location identifier*] (ICLI)
FAVR .... Vredendal [*South Africa*] [*ICAO location identifier*] (ICLI)
FAVS........ Family of Army Vehicles Study
FAVU .... Volksrust [*South Africa*] [*ICAO location identifier*] (ICLI)
FAVUA ...... Fiziologicheski Aktivnye Veshchestva [*Ukrainian SSR*] [*A publication*]
FAVV .... Vereeniging [*South Africa*] [*ICAO location identifier*] (ICLI)
FAVW .... Victoria West [*South Africa*] [*ICAO location identifier*] (ICLI)
FAVY .... Vryheid [*South Africa*] [*ICAO location identifier*] (ICLI)
FAW .... Faith at Work (EA)
FAW .... Fighter, All Weather [*British military*] (DMA)
FAW .... First Automotive Works [*Chinese manufacturer*]
FAW .... Fleet Air Wing [*Navy*]
FAW .... Fleet All Weather
FAW .... Forward Area Weapons [*Military*]
FAW .... Friends of American Writers (EA)
FAW .... Friends Around the World [*An association*] (EA)
FAW .... Northampton, MA [*Location identifier*] [*FAA*] (FAAL)
FAWA .... Federation of Asian Women's Associations [*San Marcelino, Philippines*]
FAWA .... Warmbaths [*South Africa*] [*ICAO location identifier*] (ICLI)
FAWAF ..... Fleet Air Wing, Atlantic Fleet (MCD)
FAWB .... Pretoria/Wonderboom [*South Africa*] [*ICAO location identifier*] (ICLI)
FAWBE ...... Fire Ant Whole Body Extract [*Immunology*]
Fawc.......... Fawcett on Landlord and Tenant [3 eds.] [1870-1905] [*A publication*] (DLA)
FAWC........ Federation of Army Wives Clubs [*British*]
FAWC........ Franciscan Apostolate of the Way of the Cross (EA)
FAWC........ Worcester [*South Africa*] [*ICAO location identifier*] (ICLI)
Fawcett....... Fawcett on Landlord and Tenant [3rd ed.] [1905] [*A publication*] (ILCA)
Fawc L & T ... Fawcett on Landlord and Tenant [3 eds.] [1870-1905] [*A publication*] (DLA)
FAWCO ..... Federation of American Women's Clubs Overseas (EA)
Fawc Ref .... Fawcett. Court of Referees [1866] [*A publication*] (DLA)
FAWD .... Warden [*South Africa*] [*ICAO location identifier*] (ICLI)
FAWE .... Windhoek/Eros [*Namibia*] [*ICAO location identifier*] (ICLI)
FAWEA ...... Farmers Weekly [*London*] [*A publication*]
FAWEB .... Farmers Weekly (Bloemfontein, South Africa) [*A publication*]
FAWEP...... Field Activity War Emergency Program [*DoD*]
FAWESP.. Field Activity War and Emergency Support Plan [*DoD*] (MCD)
FAWG .... Flight Assignment Working Group [*NASA*] (NASA)
FAWH....... Windhoek/J. G. Strijdom [*Namibia*] [*ICAO location identifier*] (ICLI)
FAWI....... Witbank [*South Africa*] [*ICAO location identifier*] (ICLI)
FAWK....... Waterkloof [*South Africa*] [*ICAO location identifier*] (ICLI)
FAWL....... Williston [*South Africa*] [*ICAO location identifier*] (ICLI)
FAWM .... Welkom [*South Africa*] [*ICAO location identifier*] (ICLI)
FAWNT..... Fellowship of Australian Writers, Northern Territory Chapter
FAWO .... Willowmore [*South Africa*] [*ICAO location identifier*] (ICLI)
FAWOD ..... Furnish Assignment Instructions without Delay
FAWP .... Wepener [*South Africa*] [*ICAO location identifier*] (ICLI)
FAWPRA .. Fleet Air Western Pacific Repair Area (MCD)
FAWPSC... Frequency Allocation and Wave Propagation Subcommittee (NATG)
FAWPSS... Forward Area Water Point Supply System
FAWS....... First-Aid and Water Safety [*Red Cross*]
FAWS....... Flight Advisory Weather Service
FAWSHMOTRON ... Fast Wave Simple Harmonic Motion [*A microwave tube device*]
FAWT........ For Address, Write To
FAWT........ Kingwilliamstown [*South Africa*] [*ICAO location identifier*] (ICLI)
FAWTC...... Fleet Antiwarfare Training Center (MUGU)
FAWTU...... Fleet All-Weather Training Unit
FAWTULANT ... Fleet All-Weather Training Unit, Atlantic
FAWTUPAC ... Fleet All-Weather Training Unit, Pacific
FAWW .... Windhoek [*South Africa*] [*ICAO location identifier*] (ICLI)
FAWY .... Wolseley [*South Africa*] [*ICAO location identifier*] (ICLI)
FAX .... Aeronautical Fixed Station [*ITU designation*] (CET)
FAX .... Facsimile (AFM)
FAX .... Facsimile Transmission [*Telecommunications*] (MCD)
FAX .... Fast Anion Exchange [*Chromatography*]
FAX .... First Australia Prime [*AMEX symbol*] (SPSG)
FAX .... Friedreich's Ataxia Group (EAIO)
FAX .... Fuel Air Explosive

FAX .... Midwest Air Freighter [*Kansas City, KS*] [*FAA designator*]   (FAAC)

FAXDIN.... Facsimile Transmission over AUTODIN [*Telecommunications*]

FAXM........ Hotelcopy, Inc. [*NASDAQ symbol*]   (NQ)

FAXPAK .. Facsimile Packet [*ITT*] [*Telecommunications*]   (TEL)

FAXTM..... Facsimile Transmission [*Telecommunications*]   (NOAA)

FAY .... Fantastic Adventures Yearbook [*A publication*]

FAY .... Fayetteville [*Arkansas*] [*Seismograph station code, US Geological Survey*] [*Closed*]   (SEIS)

FAY .... Fayetteville [*North Carolina*] [*Airport symbol*]   (OAG)

FAY .... Fayetteville, NC [*Location identifier*] [*FAA*]   (FAAL)

FAY .... Fay's, Inc. [*NYSE symbol*]   (SPSG)

FAY .... Field-Collected Aster Yellows [*Plant pathology*]

FAY .... Friends and Associates for Yaddo   (EA)

Fayette Leg J (PA) ... Fayette Legal Journal [*Pennsylvania*] [*A publication*]   (DLA)

Fay LJ........ Fayette Legal Journal [*Pennsylvania*] [*A publication*]   (ILCA)

FAYP........ Ysterplaat [*South Africa*] [*ICAO location identifier*]   (ICLI)

FAYT........ Fayette Federal Savings Bank [*NASDAQ symbol*]   (NQ)

FAZ.......... Frankfurter Allgemeine Zeitung [*A publication*]

FAZA........ Zastron [*South Africa*] [*ICAO location identifier*]   (ICLI)

FAZR........ Zeerust [*South Africa*] [*ICAO location identifier*]   (ICLI)

fb----- .... Africa, Sub-Saharan [*MARC geographic area code*] [*Library of Congress*]   (LCCP)

FB .... Bartow Public Library, Bartow, FL [*Library symbol*] [*Library of Congress*]   (LCLS)

FB .... Base Station [*ITU designation*]   (CET)

FB .... Bursa Airlines, Inc. [*Turkey*] [*ICAO designator*]   (ICDA)

FB .... Fabula [*A publication*]

FB .... Face Brick [*Technical drawings*]

FB .... Facility Board [*Air Force*]   (CET)

FB .... Faculty of Building [*British*]

FB .... Family Bible [*Genealogy*]

FB .... Fantasy Book [*A publication*]

FB .... Farbenfabriken Bayer [*Germany*] [*Research code symbol*]

FB .... Farmers' Bulletin [*A publication*]

FB .... Fast Blue [*Biological stain*]

FB .... Feedback   (AAG)

FB .... Fenian Brotherhood [*Irish political movement, c. 1858-1914*]   (ROG)

FB .... Fermentation Biomass

FB .... Ferranti Ltd. [*Great Britain*] [*ICAO designator*]   (FAAC)

FB .... Fiber-in-Bending [*Lumber*]

FB .... Fiberboard [*Technical drawings*]

FB .... Fiberoptic Bronchoscopy [*Also, FOB*] [*Medicine*]

FB .... Fibroblast [*Medicine*]

FB .... Fidelity Bond [*Business term*]

FB .... Fighter Bomber

FB .... File Block

FB .... Film Badge   (IEEE)

FB .... Film Bulletin

FB .... Final Braking   (MCD)

FB .... Fine Business [*i.e., excellent*] [*Amateur radio*]

FB .... Finger Breadth [*Medicine*]

F & B .... Fire and Bilge

FB .... Fire Brigade

FB .... Firing Battery   (AABC)

FB .... First Break [*A publication*]

FB .... First Brochure

FB .... Fishery Board

FB .... Fixed Block

FB .... Flashbulb [*Photography*]

FB .... Flat Bar [*Technical drawings*]

F-B .... Florida State Library, Bureau of Book Processing, Tallahassee, FL [*Library symbol*] [*Library of Congress*]   (LCLS)

FB .... Flow Block

FB .... Fluidized Bed

FB .... Flying Boat

FB .... Fog Bell [*Navigation charts*]

FB .... Foldback [*Genetics*]

FB .... Folklore Brabancon [*A publication*]

FB .... Fondation de Bellerive [*Bellerive Foundation - BF*]   (EAIO)

FB .... Fontane Blaetter [*A publication*]

F & B .... Food and Beverage

FB .... Food Brokers Ltd. [*British*]

FB .... Foreign Body [*Medicine*]

FB .... Foreign [*or French*] Brandy [*British*]   (ROG)

FB .... Form Block   (MCD)

FB .... Forschungen und Berichte [*Graz*] [*A publication*]

FB .... Forward Body

fb .... Foul Bottom [*Navigation signal*]

FB .... Found Brothers Aviation Ltd. [*Canada*] [*ICAO aircraft manufacturer identifier*]   (ICAO)

FB .... Fraenkische Blaetter fuer Geschichtsforschung und Heimatpflege [*A publication*]

FB .... Franc Belge [*Belgian Franc*] [*Monetary unit*]

FB .... Franse Boek [*A publication*]

FB .... Free Baptist

FB .... Freight Bill [*Business term*]

FB .... Friends of Buddhism   (EA)

FB .... Friendship Book [*Address list circulated by Beatles fans*]

FB .... Full Bench

FB .... Fullback [*Football*]

F & B .... Fumigation and Bath [*Military*]

FB .... Fumigation and Bath [*Military*]

FB .... Function Button [*Data processing*]

FB .... Furnace Brazing

FB .... Fuse Block   (KSC)

FBA.......... Fanned Beam Antenna

FBA.......... Farbenfabriken Bayer [*Germany*] [*Research code symbol*]

FBA.......... Farm Bankruptcy Act [*1933*]

FBA.......... Farm Buildings Association [*British*]

FBA.......... FBA Pharmaceuticals Ltd. [*Great Britain*] [*Research code symbol*]

FBA.......... Federal Bar Association   (EA)

FBA.......... Fellow of the British Academy   (ROG)

FBA.......... Fellow of the British Arts Association   (DBQ)

FBA.......... Fibre Box Association   (EA)

FBA.......... Fighter Bomber Aircraft   (NATG)

FB/A.......... Fighter Bomber Attack   (NATG)

FBA.......... Figural Bottle Association [*Defunct*]

FBA.......... Financial and Business Administration Department [*American Occupational Therapy Association*]

FBA.......... Fixed Block Architecture

FBA.......... Flexible Benefit Account [*Business term*]

FBA.......... Foundation Beefmaster Association   (EA)

FBA.......... Freshwater Biological Association [*British*]   (ARC)

FBA.......... Fur Breeders Association of the United Kingdom [*British*]

FBA.......... State Library of Florida, Tallahassee, FL [*OCLC symbol*]   (OCLC)

FBAA........ Fellow of the British Association of Accountants and Auditors   (EY)

FBAA........ Flying Boat Alighting Area

FBAA........ Frankfurter Beitraege zur Anglistik und Amerikanistik [*A publication*]

FBAA........ Fur Brokers Association of America   (EA)

FBAC........ Fair Budget Action Campaign   (EA)

FBAC........ First National Bancorp of Gainesville [*Gainesville, GA*] [*NASDAQ symbol*]   (NQ)

FBACSI .... Fur Buyers Association, Coat and Suit Industry   (EA)

FBAN........ FNB Corp. [*NASDAQ symbol*]   (NQ)

FBAO .... Farm Buildings Advisory Officer [*Ministry of Agriculture, Fisheries, and Food*] [*British*]

FBAP .... Federal Bureau of Advanced Paranoia [*Agency in film "Last Embrace"*]

FBARAD ... Freshwater Biological Association. Annual Report [*A publication*]

FBAS .... Fellow of the British Association of Secretaries [*British*]   (DAS)

FBAS .... Fixed Base Aft Station   (MCD)

FBASDJ ... Fundacion Bariloche Series [*A publication*]

FBB............ Fabrimetal [*A publication*]

FBB............ Fast-Burn Booster [*Rocketry*]

FBB............ Functional Breadboard System [*Skylab*] [*NASA*]

FB:BC .... First Battle: Battalion through Corps [*DoD*]

FBBGAJ ... Folia Biochimica et Biologica Graeca [*A publication*]

FBBO .... Fellow of the British Ballet Organisation

FBBS .... Facts Bulletin Board System [*Database*] [*Fast Agricultural Communications Terminal System*] [*Information service or system*]   (CRD)

FBC............ Barry College, North Miami, FL [*OCLC symbol*]   (OCLC)

FBC............ Fallen Building Clause

FBC............ Fat Binding Capacity [*Food technology*]

FBC............ Filesmiths' Benefit Club [*A union*] [*British*]

FBC............ First Boston Corporation [*NYSE symbol*]   (SPSG)

FBC............ Fixed Bathtub Capacitor

FBC............ Florence Babylonian Collection   (BJA)

FBC............ Fluidized-Bed Combustion   (NASA)

FBC............ Fonblanque's Bankruptcy Cases [*1849-52*] [*A publication*]   (DLA)

FBC............ Foundation for Books to China   (EA)

FBC............ Fox Broadcasting Company

FBC............ Free-Binding Capacity [*Serology*]

FBC............ Friends Bible College [*Haviland, KS*]

FBC............ Friends of Books and Comics   (EA)

FBC............ Frobisher Bay [*Northwest Territories*] [*Seismograph station code, US Geological Survey*] [*Closed*]   (SEIS)

FBC............ Full Blood Count [*Medicine*]   (ADA)

FBC............ Fully Buffered Channel

FBCA........ Fusion Bonded Coaters Association [*Absorbed by CRSI*]   (EA)

FBCE .... Federation Bancaire de la Communaute Europeenne [*Banking Federation of the European Community*]   (EAIO)

FBCE .... Fellowship of British Christian Esperantists

FBCICSR .. Fairbanks North Star Borough. Community Information Center. Special Report [*A publication*]

FBCK .... Firebrick

FBCN .... Federation of British Columbia Naturalists. Newsletter [*A publication*]

FBCO........ Camp Okavango [*Botswana*] [*ICAO location identifier*]   (ICLI)

FBCO........ Fellow of the British College of Ophthalmic Opticians   (DBQ)

FBCOD...... Foreign Body Cornea Right Eye [*Medicine*]

FBCOS ...... Foreign Body Cornea Left Eye [*Medicine*]

FBCS .... Fellow of the British Computer Society
FBCS .... Fixed-Base Crew Station [*NASA*]   (NASA)
FBCT .... Form Block Check Template   (MCD)
FBCV .... First Bancorp [*NASDAQ symbol*]   (NQ)
FBCW .... Fallen Building Clause Waiver [*Legal term*]   (DLA)
f-bd--- .... Burundi [*MARC geographic area code*] [*Library of Congress*]   (LCCP)
FBD .... Fibreboard Corp. [*AMEX symbol*]   (CTT)
FBD .... Fibrocystic Breast Disease [*Medicine*]
FBD .... Film: British Documentary
FBD .... Flow Block Diagram
FBD .... Free Board
FBD .... Free Body Diagram
FBD .... Full Business Day   (TEL)
FBD .... Functional Block Diagram [*Telecommunications*]   (TEL)
FBDB .... Federal Business Development Bank [*See also BFD*] [*Canada*] [*Database producer*]
FBDC......... Fiberboard, Corrugated
FBDCA ...... French Bulldog Club of America   (EA)
FBDLR ...... Forschungsbericht. Deutsche Luft und Raumfahrt [*A publication*]
FBDS .... Fiberboard, Solid
FBE........... Federation of Bank Employers [*British*]   (DCTA)
FBE........... Folding Boat Equipment [*British military*]   (DMA)
FBE........... Fortschrittliche Betriebsfuehrung und Industrial Engineering [*A publication*]
FBEA .... Fellow of the British Esperanto Association   (DAS)
FBEI .... Fellow of the Institution of Body Engineers [*British*]   (DBQ)
FBE Not..... Noticiario das Actividades Sociais da Federacao Brasileira de Engenheiros [*A publication*]
F Ber Bad Wuert ... Forschungen und Berichte zur Vor- und Fruehgeschichte in Baden-Wuerttemberg [*A publication*]
FBF .... Federal Buildings Fund [*General Services Administration*]
FBF .... Femoral Blood Flow [*Physiology*]
FBF .... Film: British Feature
FBF .... First Boston Income Fund, Inc. [*NYSE symbol*]   (SPSG)
FBF .... Forearm Blood Flow [*Medicine*]
FBF .... Frame by Frame
FBF .... Francis Bacon Foundation   (EA)
FBFC .... Florence Ballard Fan Club   (EA)
FBFI .... Frederic Burk Foundation, Incorporated [*San Francisco State University*] [*Research center*]   (RCD)
FBFM .... Feedback Frequency Modulation
FBFO .... Federation of British Fire Organisations
FBFR .... Fluidized-Bed Film Reactor [*For water purification*]
FBFS .... Fuel Building Filter System [*Nuclear energy*]   (NRCH)
FBFT .... Flow Bias Functional Test   (IEEE)
FBFT .... Francistown [*Botswana*] [*ICAO location identifier*]   (ICLI)
FBG .... Fayetteville/Fort Bragg, NC [*Location identifier*] [*FAA*]   (FAAL)
FBG .... Federal Barge Lines, Inc., St. Louis MO [*STAC*]
FBG .... Fibrinogen [*Factor I*] [*Hematology*]
FBG .... Finsbury Group Ltd. [*Vancouver Stock Exchange symbol*]
FBG .... Fluidized-Bed Gasifier [*Coal gasification*]
FBG .... Frankfurter Beitraege zur Germanistik [*A publication*]
FBGA......... First Bancgroup of Alabama [*NASDAQ symbol*]   (NQ)
FBGHA ..... 483rd Bombardment Group (H) Association   (EA)
FBGI .... Financial Benefit Group, Incorporated [*Boca Raton, FL*] [*NASDAQ symbol*]   (NQ)
FBGM........ Gomare [*Botswana*] [*ICAO location identifier*]   (ICLI)
FBGZ......... Ghanzi [*Botswana*] [*ICAO location identifier*]   (ICLI)
FBH .... Federal Board of Hospitalization [*Coordinated hospitalization activities of Army, Navy, and various agencies; terminated, 1948*]
FBH .... Fichero Bibliografico Hispano-Americano [*A publication*]
FBH .... Fire Brigade Hydrant
FBH .... Fluidized-Bed Hydrogenator [*Chemical engineering reactor*]
FBH .... Free on Board in Harbor [*Business term*]
FBH .... Hall [*Frank B.*] & Co., Inc. [*NYSE symbol*]   (SPSG)
FBHA .... Fellow of the British Hypnotherapy Association   (DBQ)
FBHC .... Fortified Benzene Hexachloride [*Insecticide*]
FBHC .... Franciscan Brothers of the Holy Cross [*See also FFSC*] [*Hausen, Federal Republic of Germany*]   (EAIO)
FBHDA ..... Friends and Buddies of the Hour Glass Division Association [*Later, FBHGA*]   (EA)
FBHDL...... Force Beachhead Line [*Navy*]
FBHGA ..... Friends and Buddies of the Hour Glass Association   (EA)
FBHI......... Fellow of the British Horological Institute
FBHL........ Force Beachhead Line [*Navy*]   (NVT)
FBHQ........ Gaborone Civil Aviation Headquarters [*Botswana*] [*ICAO location identifier*]   (ICLI)
FBHS......... Fellow of the British Horse Society   (DBQ)
FBI........... Federal Bureau of Investigation
FBI........... Federation of British Industries [*Later, CBI*]
FBI........... First Boston Strategic [*NYSE symbol*]   (SPSG)
FBI........... Flossing, Brushing, and Irrigation [*Dentistry*]
FBI........... Foreign Body Ingestion [*Medicine*]
FBI........... Foreign-Born Irish
FBI........... Full Bench Decisions [*India*] [*A publication*]   (DLA)
FBI's .... Forgotten Boys of Iceland [*Nickname for US soldiers in Iceland*] [*World War II*]

FBIC .... Farm Buildings Information Centre Ltd. [*British*]   (CB)
FBIC .... Firstbank of Illinois Company [*Springfield, IL*] [*NASDAQ symbol*]   (NQ)
FBIC .... Free Beaches Information Center [*Later, The Naturists*]   (EA)
FBICC .... Flow Blue International Collectors Club   (EA)
FBID .... Fellow of the British Institute of Interior Design   (DBQ)
FBIE .... Fellow of the British Institute of Embalmers   (DBQ)
FBIICR...... Fairbanks North Star Borough. Impact Information Center. Report [*A publication*]
FBIICSR... Fairbanks North Star Borough. Impact Information Center. Special Reports [*A publication*]
FBIL .... Foreign Business and Investments Law [*1973*] [*Oman*]   (IMH)
FBI Law Enf Bul ... FBI [*Federal Bureau of Investigation*] Law Enforcement Bulletin [*A publication*]
FBILEB ..... FBI [*Federal Bureau of Investigation*] Law Enforcement Bulletin [*A publication*]
FBIM......... Fellow of the British Institute of Management [*Formerly, FIIA*]
FBIOAA .... Feuillets de Biologie [*A publication*]
FBIPP........ Fellow of the British Institute of Professional Photography   (DBQ)
FBIS.......... Fellow of the British Interplanetary Society
FBIS.......... Foreign Broadcast Information System
FBIS.......... Foreign Broadcast Intelligence Service [*FCC*] [*World War II*]
FBIST........ Fellow of the British Institute of Surgical Technologists   (DBQ)
FBIU .... Freshwater Biological Investigation Unit [*Department of Agriculture for Northern Ireland*] [*United Kingdom*]   (IRUK)
FBJW .... Jwaneng [*Botswana*] [*ICAO location identifier*]   (ICLI)
FBK...... Fairbanks [*Alaska*] [*Seismograph station code, US Geological Survey*] [*Closed*]   (SEIS)
FBK........... Fairbanks/Wainwright, AK [*Location identifier*] [*FAA*]   (FAAL)
FBK........... Fantasy Book [*A publication*]
FBK........... Flat Back
FBKE........ Kasane [*Botswana*] [*ICAO location identifier*]   (ICLI)
FBKG........ Kang [*Botswana*] [*ICAO location identifier*]   (ICLI)
FBKKW...... Flugbetriebsstoff-Kesselkraftwagen
FBKP........ First Bank of Philadelphia [*NASDAQ symbol*]   (NQ)
FBKR........ Khwai River Lodge [*Botswana*] [*ICAO location identifier*]   (ICLI)
FBKRA...... Fiziologiya i Biokhimiya Kul'turnykh Rastenii [*A publication*]
FBKY........ Kanye [*Botswana*] [*ICAO location identifier*]   (ICLI)
FBL........... Farbe und Lack. Zentralblatt der Farbenindustrie und Lackindustrie und des Handels [*A publication*]
FBL........... Faribault, MN [*Location identifier*] [*FAA*]   (FAAL)
FBL........... Fecal Blood Loss [*Medicine*]
FBL........... Federal Barge Lines, Inc. [*AAR code*]
FBL........... Fly-by-Light
FBL........... Folicular Basal Lamina [*Medicine*]
FBL........... Form Block Line   (MCD)
FBL........... Foundation for Better Living   (EA)
FBL........... Light [*Used to qualify icing, turbulence, interference, or static reports*] [*Aviation code*]   (FAAC)
FBLA .... First Bancshares of Louisiana [*NASDAQ symbol*]   (NQ)
FBLA-PBL ... Future Business Leaders of America - Phi Beta Lambda [*Washington, DC*]   (EA)
FBLC .... Fibroblast-Like Cell [*Cytology*]
FBLO .... Lobatse [*Botswana*] [*ICAO location identifier*]   (ICLI)
FBM .... Biscayne College, Miami, FL [*OCLC symbol*]   (OCLC)
FBM .... Feet Board Measure
FBM .... Ferber Mining Corp. [*Vancouver Stock Exchange symbol*]
FBM .... Fetal Breathing Movements [*Gynecology*]
FBM .... Financial and Business Management Division [*American Occupational Therapy Association*]
FBM .... Flavor-by-Mouth [*Sensory testing*]
FBM .... Fleet Ballistic Missile
FBM .... Fluorobenzyl(methylaminopurine) [*Biochemistry*]
FBM .... Foot Board Measure   (MSA)
FBM .... Foreground and Background Monitor
fBm........... Fractional Brownian Motion [*Mathematics*]
FBM .... Lubumbashi [*Zaire*] [*Airport symbol*]   (OAG)
FBMG........ Machaneng [*Botswana*] [*ICAO location identifier*]   (ICLI)
FBMIDF.... Folia Botanica Miscellanea [*A publication*]
FBML........ Molepolole [*Botswana*] [*ICAO location identifier*]   (ICLI)
FBMM....... Makalamabedi [*Botswana*] [*ICAO location identifier*]   (ICLI)
FBMN........ Maun [*Botswana*] [*ICAO location identifier*]   (ICLI)
FBMP........ Fleet Ballistic Missile Program
FBMR........ Fleet Ballistic Missile Requisition [*Navy*]   (AFIT)
FBMS .... Fleet Ballistic Missile System
FBMS .... Mosetse [*Botswana*] [*ICAO location identifier*]   (ICLI)
FBMSTLL ... Fleet Ballistic Missile Submarine Tender Load List
FBMWS ...... Fleet Ballistic Missile Weapon System
FBN .... Federal Bureau of Narcotics
FBN .... Feedback Network
FBN .... Food Business Network [*Information service or system*]   (EISS)
FBN .... Fuel-Bound Nitrogen
FBN .... State Library of Florida, Bureau of Book Processing, Tallahassee, FL [*OCLC symbol*]   (OCLC)
FBNC........ First Bancorp [*NASDAQ symbol*]   (NQ)
FBNCC...... Fall Back Network Control Center   (MCD)
FBNML..... Francis Bitter National Magnet Laboratory [*MIT*]

FBNN .... Nokaneng [*Botswana*] [*ICAO location identifier*]   (ICLI)
FBNT .... Nata [*Botswana*] [*ICAO location identifier*]   (ICLI)
FBNW .... Gaborone Notwane [*Botswana*] [*ICAO location identifier*]   (ICLI)
FBo............ Boca Raton Public Library, Boca Raton, FL [*Library symbol*] [*Library of Congress*]   (LCLS)
FBO .... Federal Paper Board Co., Inc. [*NYSE symbol*]   (SPSG)
FBO .... Field Bake Oven [*Military*]
FBO .... Fixed-Base Operator [*Provider of nonairline aviation services to users of airports*]
FBO .... For the Benefit Of
FBO .... Foreign Building Office [*Department of State*]
FBO .... Furnished by Others [*Technical drawings*]
FBOA .... Fellow of the British Optical Association
FBOC .... Figural Bottle Openers Collectors Club   (EA)
FBOE .... Frequency Band of Emission   (CET)
FBOH .... First Bancorporation of Ohio [*NASDAQ symbol*]   (NQ)
FBOK .... Okwa [*Botswana*] [*ICAO location identifier*]   (ICLI)
FBOOM .... Fort Benning Officers' Open Mess [*Pronounced "fuhboom"*]
FBOR .... Orapa [*Botswana*] [*ICAO location identifier*]   (ICLI)
FBOU .... Fellow of the British Ornithologists' Union   (ROG)
FBoU .... Florida Atlantic University, Boca Raton, FL [*Library symbol*] [*Library of Congress*]   (LCLS)
FBP........... Federal Bonding Program
FBP........... Femoral Blood Pressure [*Medicine*]
FBP........... Fibonacci Benchmark Program [*Data processing*]   (BYTE)
FBP........... Fibrin Breakdown Products [*Hematology*]
FBP........... Fibrinopeptide B [*Biochemistry*]
FBP........... Fighter Bomber Program
FBP........... Filtered Back-Projection [*Data processing*]
FBP........... Final Boiling Point
FBP........... Financial Business Package [*Data processing*]
FBP........... Fleet Boat Pool
FBP........... Fluidized-Bed Process
FBP........... Folate-Binding Protein [*Biochemistry*]
FBP........... Fortschrittliche Buergerpartei [*Progressive Citizens' Party*] [*Liechtenstein*]   (PPW)
FBP........... Fructose bisphosphate [*Also, FDP*] [*Biochemistry*]
FBP........... Fuel Booster Pump
FBPA .... Pandamatenga [*Botswana*] [*ICAO location identifier*]   (ICLI)
FBPase....... Fructose bisphosphatase [*An enzyme*]
FBPC .... Foreign Bondholders Protective Council   (EA)
FBPCS....... Federation of Behavioral, Psychological, and Cognitive Sciences   (EA)
FBPG .... Forschungen zur Brandenburgisch-Preussischen Geschichte [*A publication*]
FBPN .... Feminist Business and Professional Network   (EA)
FBPsS....... Fellow of the British Psychological Society
FBPY .... Palapye [*Botswana*] [*ICAO location identifier*]   (ICLI)
FBQ .... Fibrequest International Ltd. [*Formerly, Trawler Petroleum Explorations Ltd.*] [*Vancouver Stock Exchange symbol*]
FBR........... Broward County Libraries Division, Pompano Beach, FL [*OCLC symbol*]   (OCLC)
FBR........... Fabra [*Barcelona*] [*Spain*] [*Seismograph station code, US Geological Survey*]   (SEIS)
FBR........... Fast Breeder Reactor [*Nuclear energy*]
FBR........... Fast Burn Rate
FBR........... Fast Burst Reactor [*Nuclear energy*]
FBR........... Feedback Report   (NVT)
FBR........... Feedback Resistance   (IEEE)
FBR........... Ferric-Leach Bacterial Regeneration [*Uranium extraction process*]
FBR........... Fiber   (KSC)
FBR........... Fireball Radius [*Military*]   (AABC)
FBR........... First Brands Corp. [*NYSE symbol*]   (SPSG)
FBR........... Flat Board Reach [*Test*] [*Occupational therapy*]
FBR........... Fluidized-Bed Reactor   (MCD)
FBR........... Forschungsberichte Bundesrepublik Deutschland [*Fachinformationszentrum Karlsruhe GmbH*] [*Federal Republic of Germany*] [*Information service or system*]   (CRD)
FBR........... Fort Bridger, WY [*Location identifier*] [*FAA*]   (FAAL)
FBR........... Foundation for Biomedical Research   (EA)
FBR........... Foundation for Blood Research [*Research center*]   (RCD)
FBR........... Foundation for Business Responsibilities [*British*]
FbR .... Fred B. Rothman & Co., South Hackensack, NJ [*Library symbol*] [*Library of Congress*]   (LCLS)
FBR........... Frobisher Resources Ltd. [*Vancouver Stock Exchange symbol*]
FBR........... Full Bench Rulings [*Bengal, India*] [*A publication*]   (DLA)
FBr............ Manatee County Library System, Bradenton, FL [*Library symbol*] [*Library of Congress*]   (LCLS)
F Brab ...... Folklore Brabancon [*A publication*]
FBRBD ...... Fiberboard
FBRC........ Fabricland, Inc. [*NASDAQ symbol*]   (NQ)
FBRC........ Frederick Burk Foundation Research Center
F/BRD ...... Floor Board [*Automotive engineering*]
FBRD .... Flying Boat Repair Depot [*British military*]   (DMA)
FBRF .... Fast Burst Reactor Facility [*Nuclear energy*]
FBritIRE.... Fellow of the British Institution of Radio Engineers
FBRK........ Fire Brick [*Technical drawings*]
FBRK........ Rakops [*Botswana*] [*ICAO location identifier*]   (ICLI)

FBRL......... Final Bomb Release Line
FBrM .... Manatee Junior College, Bradenton, FL [*Library symbol*] [*Library of Congress*]   (LCLS)
FBRNWP.. Full Bench Rulings, Northwest Provinces [*India*] [*A publication*]   (DLA)
FBro .... Frederick Eugene Lykes, Jr., Memorial County Library, Brooksville, FL [*Library symbol*] [*Library of Congress*]   (LCLS)
FBRS .... Fibrous
FBRS .... Fleet Broadcast Receive Subsystem [*Navy*]   (CAAL)
FBRSU ..... Full-Boiling Range High-Sensitivity Unleaded [*Motor fuel*]
FBRT......... Francis Bacon Research Trust [*British*]
FBRU......... Full-Boiling Range Unleaded [*Motor fuel*]
FBRX........ Fibronics International, Inc. [*NASDAQ symbol*]   (NQ)
f-bs--- .... Botswana [*MARC geographic area code*] [*Library of Congress*]   (LCCP)
FBS............ Facsimile Broadcast Service
FBS............ Fan Beam Scatterometer
FBS............ Farm Bureau Services
FBS............ Fasting Blood Sugar [*Physiology*]
FBS............ Feedback Signal
FBS............ Feedback System
FBS............ Fellow of the Botanical Society [*British*]   (ROG)
FBS............ Fellow of the Building Societies Institute [*British*]
FBS............ Fetal Blood Sample [*Hematology*]
FBS............ Fetal Bovine Serum [*Medicine*]
FB/S.......... Fighter Bomber Strike   (NATG)
FBS............ Film: British Series
FBS............ Fine Bearing Servo
FBS............ Firefighter Breathing System [*NASA*]
FBS............ First Bank System, Inc. [*NYSE symbol*]   (SPSG)
FBS............ Flare Build-Up Study [*Meteorology*]
FBS............ Flash/Bang/Smoke   (MCD)
FBS............ Fortified Barrier System   (MCD)
FBS............ Forward-Based Systems [*US aircraft based outside the US and capable of carrying nuclear weapons to the USSR*]
FBS............ Francis Bacon Society   (EA)
FBS............ Franco Belgian Services   (DS)
FBSA .... Filter-Band Suppressor Assembly
FBSC .... Fellow of the British Society of Commerce
FBSC .... Fred Bear Sports Club   (EA)
FBSComm ... Fellow of the British Society of Commerce
FBSD .... Serondela [*Botswana*] [*ICAO location identifier*]   (ICLI)
FBSE .... Fellow of the Botanical Society, Edinburgh   (ROG)
FBSH......... First Bankshares Corp. of South Carolina [*NASDAQ symbol*]   (NQ)
FBSI.......... All Indonesian Labor Federation   (IMH)
FBSI.......... Fellow of the Boot and Shoe Institution [*British*]
FBSI.......... First Banc Securities, Incorporated [*Morgantown, WV*] [*NASDAQ symbol*]   (NQ)
FBSI.......... Furniture and Bedding Spring Institute [*Defunct*]   (EA)
FBSK .... Gaborone/Sir Seretse Khama [*Botswana*] [*ICAO location identifier*]   (ICLI)
FBSM .... Fellow of the Birmingham School of Music [*British*]
FBSP......... Selebi-Phikwe [*Botswana*] [*ICAO location identifier*]   (ICLI)
FBSR .... Serowe [*Botswana*] [*ICAO location identifier*]   (ICLI)
FBSSD....... Fushoku Boshoku Shinpojumu Shiryo [*A publication*]
FBSV .... Savuti [*Botswana*] [*ICAO location identifier*]   (ICLI)
FBSW .... Shakawe [*Botswana*] [*ICAO location identifier*]   (ICLI)
FBT........... Fibertech Industries Corp. [*Formerly, Essex Petroleum Corp.*] [*Vancouver Stock Exchange symbol*]
FBT........... First City Bancorporation of Texas, Inc. [*NYSE symbol*]   (SPSG)
F/Bt........... Flying Boat [*British military*]   (DMA)
FBT........... Form Block Template   (MSA)
FBT........... Forward Ballast Tank   (MSA)
FBT........... Fringe Benefits Tax
FBT........... Full Berth Terms [*Shipping*]
FBTC......... FB & T Corp. [*NASDAQ symbol*]   (NQ)
FBTD .... Food and Beverage Trades Department [*of AFL-CIO*]   (EA)
FBTE .... Tshane [*Botswana*] [*ICAO location identifier*]   (ICLI)
FBTL .... Tuli Lodge [*Botswana*] [*ICAO location identifier*]   (ICLI)
FBTR .... Fast Breeder Test Reactor [*Nuclear energy*]
FBTR .... For Better Living, Inc. [*NASDAQ symbol*]   (NQ)
FBTS .... Form Block Template Set   (MCD)
FBTS .... Tshabong [*Botswana*] [*ICAO location identifier*]   (ICLI)
FBTX .... First Bancshares of Texas, Inc. [*NASDAQ symbol*]   (NQ)
FBU .... Federation of Broadcasting Unions [*British*]
FBU .... Fire Brigade Union
FBU .... Franc Burundaise [*Burundi Franc*] [*Monetary unit*]
FBU .... Fraternite Blanche Universelle [*Universal White Brotherhood*]   (EAIO)
FBU .... Freie-Buerger-Union [*Free Citizens' Union*] [*Federal Republic of Germany*]   (PPW)
FBU .... Fully Built-Up [*Manufacturing*]
F (Buc) ...... Forschungen zur Volks- und Landeskunde (Bucuresti) [*A publication*]
F Bul .... Film Bulletin [*A publication*]
FBUS........ Fisher Business Systems, Inc. [*NASDAQ symbol*]   (NQ)
FBV .... Field Base Visit   (NASA)
FBV .... Friends of Bobby Vee   (EA)

FBV............ Fuel Bleed Valve (NASA)
FBV............ Fuel Building Ventilation [*Nuclear energy*] (NRCH)
FBVBA ...... Fortschritt-Berichte. VDI [*Verein Deutscher Ingenieure*] Zeitschriften. Reihe 4. Bauingenieurwesen [*A publication*]
FBVF .... Fiberglass Backed Vacuum Forming [*Fiberglass production*]
FBW........... Fly by Wire
FB WD....... Fibreboard and Wood [*Freight*]
FBWU .... Fire Brick Workers' Union [*British*]
FBX........... Fighter Bomber [*Advanced*]
FBX........... France, BENELUX
FBXC........ FBX Corporation [*Hauppauge, NY*] [*NASDAQ symbol*] (NQ)
FBXG........ Xugana [*Botswana*] [*ICAO location identifier*] (ICLI)
FBXX .... Xaxaba [*Botswana*] [*ICAO location identifier*] (ICLI)
f-by--- .... Biafra [*MARC geographic area code*] [*Library of Congress*] (LCCP)
FBY........... Fairbury, NE [*Location identifier*] [*FAA*] (FAAL)
FBY........... Future Budget Year (AFM)
FBYB .... Fly Before You Buy [*Aerospace industry slogan*]
FBypV....... United States Veterans Administration Center, Bay Pines, FL [*Library symbol*] [*Library of Congress*] (LCLS)
FBZ........... Forward Battle Zone [*British*]
fc---- .... Africa, Central [*MARC geographic area code*] [*Library of Congress*] (LCCP)
FC .... All India Reporter, Federal Court [*1947-50*] [*A publication*] (DLA)
FC .... British Guiana Full Court Reports (Official Gazette) [*A publication*] (DLA)
FC .... Canada Law Reports, Federal Court [*A publication*] (DLA)
FC .... Coast Station [*ITU designation*] (CET)
FC .... Compound Fracture [*Medicine*]
FC .... Congregatio Fratrum Caritate [*Brothers of Charity*] [*Roman Catholic religious order*]
FC .... Critical Frequency (CET)
FC .... Daughters of the Cross of Liege [*Roman Catholic religious order*]
FC .... Face-Centered [*Crystallography*]
FC .... Facilities Construction (AAG)
FC .... Facilities Contract
F/C .... Facilities Control [*Military*]
FC .... Faciundum Curavit [*He Caused To Be Made*] [*Latin*]
FC .... Faculty of Advocates Collection of Decisions, Scotch Court of Sessions [*A publication*] (DLA)
FC .... Fail Closed [*Nuclear energy*] (NRCH)
FC .... Failure Count
fc................ Fair Condition [*Doll collecting*]
FC .... Fairchild Club (EA)
FC .... Fairflight Ltd. [*Great Britain*] [*ICAO designator*] (FAAC)
FC .... False Cape [*NASA*] (KSC)
FC .... Family Circle [*A publication*]
F & C .... Family and Commercial [*Hotels*] [*British*] (ROG)
FC .... Fast Component
FC .... Fathers of the Church [*A publication*]
FC .... FCA International Ltd. [*Toronto Stock Exchange symbol*]
FC .... Feature Count [*Data processing*]
FC .... Fecal Coli [*Microbiology*]
FC .... Federal Cabinet [*Australia*]
FC .... Federal Cases [*A publication*] (DLA)
FC .... Federal Court Reports [*A publication*]
FC .... Federalist Caucus (EA)
FC .... Federation Council (EA)
FC .... Feed the Children (EA)
FC .... Feint and Cash [*of account book rulings*]
FC .... Fellow Craft [*Freemasonry*] (ROG)
FC .... Ferrite Core
FC .... Ferrocement
FC .... Ferrochelatase [*An enzyme*]
FC .... Ferromagnetic Contamination [*Medicine*]
FC .... Ferry Command [*RAF*] [*British*]
FC .... Fiberglass Covers (DCTA)
FC .... Fibro Cement (ADA)
FC .... Fidei Commissum [*Bequeathed in Trust*] [*Latin*]
FC .... Field Camera
FC .... Field Change
FC .... Field Circular [*Military*] (INF)
FC .... Field Command [*Military*]
FC .... Fielder's Choice [*Baseball*]
FC .... Fieri Curavit [*Caused to Be Made*] [*Latin*]
FC .... Fighter Catapult [*Ship*]
FC .... Fighter Command [*Air Force*]
FC .... File Cabinet (AAG)
FC .... File Code [*Data processing*] (IEEE)
FC .... File Control (AFIT)
FC .... File Conversion [*Data processing*] (BUR)
FC .... File Copy
FC .... Film-Coated [*Pharmacy*]
FC .... Film Comment [*A publication*]
FC .... Filson Club (EA)
FC .... Filter Center
FC .... Finance Charge
FC .... Finance Committee [*UN Food and Agriculture Organization*]
FC .... Finance Corps

FC .... Financial Controller
FC .... Find Called [*or Calling*] Party [*Telecommunications*] (TEL)
FC .... Fine Champagne
FC .... Fine Cognac
FC .... Fine Control (DEN)
FC .... Finger Counting [*See also CF*]
FC .... Fire Clay
FC .... Fire Cock [*British*] (ROG)
FC .... Fire Commander [*British military*] (DMA)
FC .... Fire Control [*of guns*]
FC .... Fire Control Armourer [*British military*] (DMA)
FC .... Fire Controlman [*Navy rating*] [*Obsolete*]
FC .... Firing Channel [*Military*] (CAAL)
FC .... Fishery Council (EA)
FC .... Fit Check [*NASA*] (NASA)
FC .... Fixed Camera (KSC)
FC .... Fixed Capital [*Business term*]
FC .... Fixed Charge [*Business term*]
FC .... Fixed Cost [*Economics*]
FC .... Flight Capsule
F/C .... Flight Certificate
FC .... Flight Charts
FC .... Flight Computer [*NASA*] (NASA)
FC .... Flight Control
F/C .... Flight Controller (NASA)
FC .... Flight Crew
FC .... Flight Critical (MCD)
FC .... Floating Capital [*Business term*]
FC .... Flood Control
FC .... Flow Coating
FC .... Flow Controller [*Nuclear energy*] (NRCH)
FC .... Fluorocytosine [*Antifungal compound*]
FC .... Flying Colonels [*Delta Air Lines' club for frequent flyers*] (EA)
FC .... Foaming Capacity [*Food technology*]
FC .... Foley Catheter [*Urology*]
FC .... Folin-Ciocalteau [*Clinical chemistry*]
FC .... Follow Copy [*Printing*]
FC .... Font Change [*Data processing*] (BUR)
FC .... Food Controller [*British*] [*World War II*]
FC .... Foot-Candle [*Illumination*]
FC .... Football Club [*British*]
FC .... Football Committee [*British*]
FC .... Footwear Caucus (EA)
FC .... Footwear Council [*Defunct*] (EA)
FC .... Forage Corps [*British military*] (DMA)
FC .... Forage Crop [*Agriculture*]
FC .... Force Control (MCD)
FC .... Ford Motor Co. of Canada Ltd. [*AMEX symbol*] (SPSG)
FC .... Forecast Center Station [*Telecommunications*] (TEL)
FC .... Foreign Classics [*A publication*]
FC .... Foreign Consul (ROG)
FC .... Foreign Currency
FC .... Forestry Commission [*British*]
FC .... Formal Conference on Weights and Measures [*Australia*]
F/C .... Format Code [*Data processing*]
FC .... Forward Chaining [*Psychology*]
FC .... Foundation Center (EA)
FC .... Foundation Code [*IRS*]
FC .... Fraction Collector [*Chromatography*]
FC .... Fractocumulus [*Meteorology*]
Fc .... Fragment, Crystallizable [*of an antibody*] [*Immunochemistry*]
FC .... Franc [*Monetary unit*] [*France*] (ROG)
fc................ Franco [*Shipping Costs Paid*] [*French*]
FC .... Free of Cells [*Medicine*]
FC .... Free Choice [*Psychology*]
FC .... Free Cholesterol [*Clinical chemistry*]
FC .... Free Church
FC .... Frequency Converter
FC .... Freres de la Charite [*Brothers of Charity*] (EAIO)
FC .... Friars Club (EA)
FC .... Friendly Capabilities (MCD)
FC .... Friends of Community (EA)
FC .... Front-Connected
FC .... Frozen Cell
FC .... Fuel Cell (KSC)
FC .... Fuel Controller (DAS)
FC .... Fuel Cycle (NRCH)
F & C......... Full and Change (ADA)
FC .... Full Charge [*Accounting*]
FC .... Full Corner [*Philately*]
FC .... Full Court (ADA)
FC .... Full Court Judgments [*Ghana*] [*A publication*] (DLA)
FC .... Functional Chief [*of a civilian career program*] [*Military*]
FC .... Functional Code
FC .... Fund Campaign [*Red Cross*]
FC .... Fund Code (AABC)
FC .... Funding Cycle (OICC)
FC .... Funnel Cloud
FC .... Fuse Chamber (TEL)
FC .... Futures Contract [*Investment term*]
FC .... Fuze Committee [*Military*]

FC .... Hard Filled Capsules [*Pharmacy*]
FC .... Selected Judgments of the Full Court, Accra and Gold Coast [*A publication*]   (DLA)
FC .... Subcutaneous Fat Class
FC .... Union of Soviet Socialist Republics [*Formerly, SX*] [*License plate code assigned to foreign diplomats in the US*]
FC '22........ Full Court Judgments [*1922*] [*Ghana*] [*A publication*]   (DLA)
FC '20-1 ..... Full Court Judgments [*1920-21*] [*Ghana*] [*A publication*]   (DLA)
FC '23-25 ... Selected Judgments of the Full Court [*1923-25*] [*Ghana*] [*A publication*]   (DLA)
FC '26-29 ... Selected Judgments of the Full Court [*1926-29*] [*Ghana*] [*A publication*]   (DLA)
FC's........... False Calves [*Padding worn under tights by actors, to improve shape of their legs*]
FCa .... Cape Canaveral Public Library, Cape Canaveral, FL [*Library symbol*] [*Library of Congress*]   (LCLS)
FCA............ Fabri-Centers of America, Inc. [*NYSE symbol*]   (SPSG)
FCA............ Facility Change Authorization   (AAG)
FCA............ Fairlane Club of America   (EA)
FCA............ Falcon Club of America   (EA)
FCA............ Fan Club Associates [*Later, IFCA*]   (EA)
FCA............ Farm Credit Administration [*Independent government agency*]
FCA............ Fast Critical Assembly [*Nuclear reactor*] [*Japan*]
FCA............ Federal Code, Annotated [*A publication*]   (DLA)
FCA............ Federal Committee on Apprenticeship [*Department of Labor*]
FCA............ Federal Communications Act
FCA............ Federal Council on the Aging [*Succeeded by President's Council on Aging, 1962*]
FCA............ Federated Council of Academics [*Australia*]
FCA............ Federation of Canadian Archers
FCA............ Federation of Canadian Artists
FCA............ Federation Canadienne de l'Agriculture [*Canadian Federation of Agriculture - CFA*]
FCA............ Federation Canadienne des Archers [*Federation of Canadian Archers*]
FCA............ Federation of Commodity Associations   (EAIO)
FCA............ Feiten en Cijfers. Economisch, Financieel, Sociaal, Fiscaal, Juridisch [*A publication*]
FCA............ Fellow of the Institute of Chartered Accountants [*British*]   (ROG)
FCA............ Fellow of the Institute of Chartered Architects [*British*]
FCA............ Fellowship of Christian Athletes   (EA)
FCA............ Ferrari Club of America   (EA)
FCA............ Ferrite Control Amplifier
FCA............ Fiat Club of America   (EA)
FCA............ Field Change Analysis
FCA............ Field Change Authorization [*Nuclear energy*]   (NRCH)
FCA............ Fighter Control Area [*Military*]
FCA............ Films for Christ Association   (EA)
FCA............ Financial Corp. of America   (ECON)
FCA............ Fire Control Area [*Army*]
FCA............ First Chair of America   (EA)
FCA............ Fixed Coaxial Attenuator
FCA............ Fleet Chief Armourer [*British military*]   (DMA)
FCA............ Flight Control Assemblies
FCA............ Fluids Control Assembly   (NASA)
FCA............ Fluorocytosine Arabinoside [*Also, ara-FC*] [*Antitumor compound*]
FCA............ Flying Chiropractors Association   (EA)
FCA............ Force Cost Assessor   (MCD)
FCA............ Foundation for the Community of Artists   (EA)
FCA............ Fraternity of Canadian Astrologers
FCA............ Free China Assistance   (EA)
FCA............ Freight Claim Agent
FCA............ Freight Claim Association
FCA............ French Computing Association
FCA............ Frequency Control and Analysis
FCA............ Freund's Complete Adjuvant [*Immunology*]
FCA............ Friendly Contacts Associates   (EA)
FCA............ Fuel Capsule [*or Cell*] Assembly   (MCD)
FCA's......... Full Circle Associates   (EA)
FCA............ Full-Coverage Area [*Radio and TV*]
FCA............ Functional Compatibility Analysis   (MCD)
FCA............ Functional Configuration Audit
FCA............ Kalispell [*Montana*] [*Airport symbol*]   (OAG)
FCA............ Kalispell, MT [*Location identifier*] [*FAA*]   (FAAL)
F5CA.......... Force 5 Class Association   (EA)
FCAA......... Fleet Chief Aircraft Artificer [*British military*]   (DMA)
FCAA......... Florence Crittenton Association of America [*Later, CWLA*]   (EA)
FCA(Aust) ... Fellow of the Institute of Chartered Accountants in Australia
FCAC......... Folklore Studies Association of Canada
FCAC........ Forward Control and Analysis Center   (MCD)
FCA(Can).. Fellow of the Institute of Chartered Accountants in Canada
FCACMN ... Fleet Chief Aircrewman [*British military*]   (DMA)
FCAD........ Field Contract Administration Division [*of ONM*]
FCADD...... Fondation Canadienne sur l'Alcool et la Dependance aux Drogues [*Canadian Foundation on Alcohol and Drug Dependencies - CFADD*]
FCAF .... Fleet Chief Air Fitter [*British military*]   (DMA)

FCAF .... Flight Crew Accommodations Facility   (MCD)
FCaF .... Florida Solar Energy Center, Cape Canaveral, FL [*Library symbol*] [*Library of Congress*]   (LCLS)
FCAF .... Frequency Control Analysis Facility
FCAIM ...... Fundamental and Clinical Aspects of Internal Medicine [*Elsevier Book Series*] [*A publication*]
FCAM....... Fellow of the Communication Advertising and Marketing Education Foundation [*British*]   (DBQ)
FCAME..... Fellowship of Christians in the Arts, Media, and Entertainment   (EA)
FCANA..... Federation of Cambodian Associations in North America   (EA)
FCA(NZ) ... Fellow Chartered Accountant of New Zealand
FCAP........ Fellow of the College of American Pathologists
FCAP........ Fellowship of Christian Airline Personnel   (EA)
FCAP........ Flight Control Applications Program [*NASA*]   (NASA)
FCAP........ Fluor Chrome Arsenate Phenol [*Wood preservative*]
FCAP........ Foolscap [*Paper*]
FCap .... French Capitol [*Record label*]
FCAP (Fac Cienc Agrar Para) Inf Tec ... FCAP (Faculdade de Ciencias Agrarias do Para) Informe Tecnico [*A publication*]
FCAR........ First Carolina Investors, Inc. [*NASDAQ symbol*]   (NQ)
FCAR........ Foreign Currency Agriculture Research Program [*Department of Agriculture*]
FCAR........ Free of Claim for Accident Reported [*Shipping*]   (DS)
F Carr Cas ... Federal Carriers Cases [*Commerce Clearing House*] [*A publication*]   (DLA)
F Carrier Cas ... Federal Carriers Cases [*Commerce Clearing House*] [*A publication*]   (DLA)
F Cas.......... Federal Cases [*A publication*]   (DLA)
FCAS .... Fellow of the Casualty Actuarial Society [*Designation awarded by Casualty Actuarial Society*]
FCAS .... Frequency Coded Armaments System
FCAS .... Frequency Control Analysis Subsystem   (MCD)
FCas........... Seminole County Public Library System, Casselberry, FL [*Library symbol*] [*Library of Congress*]   (LCLS)
FCASI....... Fellow of the Canadian Aeronautics and Space Institute
F Cas No .... Federal Case Number [*Legal term*]   (DLA)
FCAT .... Flight Composite Acceptance Test
Fcath .... Foley Catheter [*Urology*]
FCAW....... Flux Cored Arc Welding
FCAW....... Foundation for Citizens Against Waste   (EA)
FCb .... Cocoa Beach Public Library, Cocoa Beach, FL [*Library symbol*] [*Library of Congress*]   (LCLS)
FCB........... Facility Clearance Board [*WPB*]
FCB........... Fast Capacitor Bank
FCB........... Fenedexpress [*A publication*]
FCB........... File Control Block [*Data processing*]   (BUR)
FCB........... Fluocortin Butyl [*Pharmacology*]
FCB........... Foote, Cone & Belding Communications, Inc. [*Advertising agency*] [*NYSE symbol*]   (SPSG)
FC & B .... Foote, Cone & Belding Communications, Inc. [*Advertising agency*]
FCB........... Foreign Clearance Base
FCB........... Forms Control Buffer [*Data processing*]   (IBMDP)
FCB........... Foundation for Commercial Banks   (EA)
FCB........... Free Cutting Brass
FCB........... Freight Container Bureau [*AAR*]
FCB........... Frequency Control Board [*British*]   (AIA)
FCB........... Frequency Coordinating Body
FCB........... Friends of Clara Barton   (EA)
FCB........... Fuel Cell Battery
FCB........... Function Control Block [*Data processing*]   (IBMDP)
FCB........... Marine Broadcast Station [*ITU designation*]   (CET)
FCBA......... Fair Credit Billing Act
FCBA......... Federal Communications Bar Association   (EA)
FCBA......... Fellow of the Canadian Bankers' Association
FCBA......... Foreign Currency Borrowers' Association [*Australia*]
FCBA......... Lalouila [*Congo*] [*ICAO location identifier*]   (ICLI)
FCBB......... Brazzaville/Maya Maya [*Congo*] [*ICAO location identifier*]   (ICLI)
FCBC .... First Connecticut Bancorp Inc. [*NASDAQ symbol*]   (NQ)
FCBC .... Foreign Countries and British Colonies [*A publication*]
FCBCD ...... For Carter Before Camp David [*Refers to Israeli-Egyptian agreements of 1978*]
FCBD........ Djambala [*Congo*] [*ICAO location identifier*]   (ICLI)
FCBFL .... Feminists Concerned for Better Feminist Leadership   (EA)
FCBG........ Federation of Children's Book Groups [*British*]
FCBG........ Madingou [*Congo*] [*ICAO location identifier*]   (ICLI)
FCBI .... First Commerce Bancshares, Incorporated [*Lincoln, NE*] [*NASDAQ symbol*]   (NQ)
FCBJS .... Federated Council of Beth Jacob Schools   (EA)
FCBK........ Fairfield County Bancorp, Inc. [*NASDAQ symbol*]   (NQ)
FCBK........ Kindamba [*Congo*] [*ICAO location identifier*]   (ICLI)
FCBL........ Lague [*Congo*] [*ICAO location identifier*]   (ICLI)
FCBM........ Mouyondzi [*Congo*] [*ICAO location identifier*]   (ICLI)
FCBN........ Furon Co. [*NASDAQ symbol*]   (NQ)
FCBO........ M'Pouya [*Congo*] [*ICAO location identifier*]   (ICLI)
FCBP .... M'Passa [*Congo*] [*ICAO location identifier*]   (ICLI)
FCBS .... Sibiti [*Congo*] [*ICAO location identifier*]   (ICLI)
FCBSI........ Fellow of the Chartered Building Societies Institute [*British*]   (DBQ)

FCBT	Loutete [*Congo*] [*ICAO location identifier*] (ICLI)
FCBU	Aubeville [*Congo*] [*ICAO location identifier*] (ICLI)
FCBUSA ...	Finance Corps Board, United States Army
FCBV	Brazzaville [*Congo*] [*ICAO location identifier*] (ICLI)
FCBY	N'Kay/Yokangassi [*Congo*] [*ICAO location identifier*] (ICLI)
FCBZ	Zanaga [*Congo*] [*ICAO location identifier*] (ICLI)
FCC	Face-Centered Cubic [*Crystallography*]
FCC	Facilities Control Console (AAG)
FCC	Falsely Claiming [*US*] Citizenship
FCC	Family Communion Crusade [*Defunct*] (EA)
FCC	Farm Credit Corporation [*Canada*]
FCC	Farm Credit Council (EA)
FCC	Farm Crisis Committee (EA)
FCC	Federal City College [*Later, UDC*] [*Washington, DC*]
FCC	Federal Communications Commission [*Independent government agency*]
FCC	Federal Communications Commission, Washington, DC [*OCLC symbol*] (OCLC)
FCC	Federal Construction Council (EA)
FCC	Federal Consultative Council of South African Railways and Harbors Staff Association
FCC	Federal Council of Churches
FCC	Federation Canadienne des Communications [*Canadian Federation of Communications Workers - CFCW*]
FCC	Fellowship of Companies for Christ [*Later, FCCI*] (EA)
FCC	Fellowship of Concerned Churchmen (EA)
F/CC	Fermentation/Cell Culture [*Biology*]
F/cc	Fibers per Cubic Centimeter
FCC	Field Camera Control
FCC	Field Control Center
FCC	Field Controller Component (MCD)
FCC	Fighter Control Center (MUGU)
F & CC	Fire and Casualty Cases [*Commerce Clearing House*] [*A publication*] (DLA)
FCC	Fire Collectors Club (EA)
FCC	Fire Control Code
FCC	Fire Control Computer
FCC	Fire Control Console (NATG)
FCC	First Central Financial Corporation [*AMEX symbol*] (SPSG)
FCC	First-Class Certificate
FCC	Fixed Ceramic Capacitor
FCC	Fixed Communications Cabinet (MCD)
FCC	Flat Conductor Cable
FCC	Fleet Command Center [*Navy*] (CAAL)
FCC	Fletcher Challenge Canada Ltd. [*Toronto Stock Exchange symbol*] [*Vancouver Stock Exchange symbol*]
FCC	Flight Communications Center
FCC	Flight Control Center
FCC	Flight Control Computer (KSC)
FCC	Flight Control Console
FCC	Flight Control Container
FCC	Flight Coordination Center (AFM)
FCC	Flight Crew Compartment (MCD)
FCC	Florida Christian College
FCC	Florida Citrus Commission [*Later, Florida Department of Citrus*]
FCC	Fluid Catalytic Cracking [*Fuel technology*]
FCC	Fluid Convection Cathode
FCC	Fluorochlorocarbon [*Organic chemistry*]
FCC	Follicular Center Cell [*Cytology*]
FCC	Fontana Corrosion Center [*Ohio State University*] [*Research center*] (RCD)
FCC	Food Chemicals Codex [*National Academy of Sciences*] [*A publication*]
FCC	Forbidden Combination Check
FCC	Foreign Commerce Club of New York (EA)
FCC	Forms Control Center (OICC)
FCC	Fort Churchill [*Manitoba*] [*Seismograph station code, US Geological Survey*] (SEIS)
FCC	Fort Churchill [*Manitoba*] [*Geomagnetic observatory code*]
FCC	Foundation for a Christian Civilization (EA)
FCC	Foundation for Community Creativity (EA)
FCC	Free Church Council [*British*] (DAS)
FCC	French Chamber of Commerce (DCTA)
FCC	Fuel Cell Catalyst
FCC	Fuel Control Computer
FCC	Fuels Control Center (AFIT)
FCC	Fully Cellular Containership (DS)
FCC	Future Characteristics Change [*Military*] (CAAL)
FCCA	Farmers Chinchilla Cooperative of America [*Later, ECBC*] (EA)
FCCA	Federal Court Clerks Association (EA)
FCCA	Fleet Chief Caterer [*British military*] (DMA)
FCCA	Forestry, Conservation Communications Association (EA)
FCCA	Four Cylinder Club of America
FCCADG ...	Focus on Critical Care [*A publication*]
FCCB	Field Change Control Board
FCCB	Field Configuration Control Board [*Army*] (AABC)
FCCC	Brazzaville [*Congo*] [*ICAO location identifier*] (ICLI)
FCCC	Farm Credit Corporation Canada [*Ottawa, ON*]
FCCC	Federal Complaint Coordinating Center [*US Office of Consumer Affairs*]
FCCC	Federation Canadienne des Cine-Clubs [*Canada*]
FCCC	Federation des Clubs Cooperatifs de Consommation [*Federation of Consumer Cooperative Associations*] [*Canada*]
FCCC	Fire Control Control Console
FCCC	Flight Coordination Control Central
FC & CE ...	Flight Crew and Crew Equipment
FCCEA	Fleet Chief Control Electrical Artificer [*British military*] (DMA)
FCCEL	Fleet Chief Control Electrician [*British military*] (DMA)
FCCEMN ...	Fleet Chief Control Electrical Mechanician [*British military*] (DMA)
FCCFA	Fraternite des Commis de Chemins de Fer, de Lignes Aeriennes, et de Navigation, Manutentionaires de Fret, Employes de Messageries et de Gares [*Brotherhood of Railway, Airline, and Steamship Clerks, Freight Handlers, Express and Station Employees*] [*Canada*]
FCCI	Federal Clean Car Incentive Program [*Environmental Protection Agency*] (MCD)
FCCI	Fellowship of Companies for Christ International (EA)
FCCIM	Federal Coordination Committee on Instrumentation and Measurement
FCCIP	Federal Clean Car Incentive Program [*Environmental Protection Agency*]
FCCJ	Foreign Correspondents' Club of Japan
FCCK	Fire Control Check [*Military*] (NVT)
FCCK	Fleet Chief Cook [*British military*] (DMA)
FCCN	Federal Communications Commission Network
FCCO	Fellow of the Canadian College of Organists
FCCO	Flight Change Control Order
FCCOP	Fire Control Computer Operational Program (MCD)
FCCP	Fellow of the American College of Chest Physicians
FCCP	Firm Contract Cost Proposal (NASA)
FCCP	Friends Coordinating Committee on Peace [*Defunct*] (EA)
FCCPO	Federal Contract Compliance Program Office [*Department of Labor*] (IEEE)
FCCS	Fellow of the Corporation of Certified Secretaries [*British*] (EY)
FCCS	Forces Correspondence Courses Scheme [*Military*] [*British*]
FCCSET	Federal Coordinating Council for Science, Engineering, and Technology [*Pronounced "fix it"*] [*Office of Science and Technology Policy*]
FCCSS	Fire Control Control Subsystem
FCCSSAT ...	Federal Council on Computer Storage Standards and Technology [*General Services Administration*]
FCCST	Federal Coordinating Council for Science and Technology
FCCT	Fellow of the Canadian College of Teachers
FCCT	Flight Controller Confidence Test (KSC)
FCCTS	Federal COBOL [*Common Business-Oriented Language*] Compiler Testing Service [*National Institute of Standards and Technology*]
FCCU	Fluid Catalytic Cracking Unit [*Fuel technology*]
FCCUS	French Chamber of Commerce of the United States [*Later, French-American Chamber of Commerce*]
FCCV	Future Close Combat Vehicle
FCCVP	Future Close Combat Vehicle Program
FCCVS	Future Close Combat Vehicle System (MCD)
FCCY	Fleet Chief Communication Yeoman [*British military*] (DMA)
f-cd---	Chad [*MARC geographic area code*] [*Library of Congress*] (LCCP)
F & CD	Failure and Consumption Data (AAG)
FCD	Fecal Collection Device [*NASA*]
FCD	Femoral Cortical Density
FCD	Fine Chemicals Directory Data Base [*Molecular Design Ltd.*] [*Information service or system*]
FCD	Fine Control Damper [*Nuclear energy*] (NRCH)
FCD	Fixed Center Drive
FCD	Flight Control Division [*Johnson Space Center*] [*NASA*] (NASA)
FCD	Flood Control District [*Florida*]
FCD	Food Control Diet
FCD	Foundation for Child Development (EA)
FCD	Four-Bar Cutter Device
FCD	Frente Civico Democratico [*Civilian Democratic Front*] [*Guatemala*] [*Political party*] (PPW)
FCD	Frequency Compression Demodulator
FCD	Fuel Cut Defenser [*Automotive engineering*]
FCD	Function Circuit Diagram
FCD	Functional Control Diagram (NRCH)
FCD	Fuze Control Device (MCD)
FCDA	Federal Civil Defense Administration [*Transferred to Office of Defense and Civilian Mobilization, 1958; to Department of Defense and Office of Emergency Preparedness, 1961*]
FCDA	First Cavalry Division Association (EA)
FCDA	First Federal Savings & Loan of Coeur D'Alene [*Coeur D'Alene, ID*] [*NASDAQ symbol*] (NQ)
FCDA	Fuel Control Diaphragm Assembly
FC/DASA ...	Field Command, Defense Atomic Support Agency
FCDB	Flight Control Data Bus (MCD)

FCDC......... Fire Control Data Converter (MCD)
FCDC......... Fixed Ceramic Disk Capacitor
FCDF......... Failure and Consumption Data Form (AAG)
FCDG .... Federal Civil Defense Guide
F & CD/IR ... Failure and Consumption Data Inspection Report (AAG)
FCDivBad ... First Class Diver Badge [Military decoration] (AABC)
FCDL......... Forsyth County Defense League (EA)
FCDN .... Ferrocarril de Nacozari [AAR code]
FCDNA ..... Field Command, Defense Nuclear Agency [DoD]
FCDR........ Failure Cause Data Report
FCDSSA.... Fleet Combat Direction Systems Support Activity [Navy] (MCD)
FCDSSA/SD ... Fleet Combat Direction Systems Support Activity, San Diego [California] [Navy]
FCDSTC.... Fleet Combat Direction System Training Center [Navy] (CAAL)
FCDSTCL ... Fleet Combat Direction System Training Center, Atlantic [Navy] (MCD)
FCDT........ Four-Coil Differential Transformer
FCDU .... Foreign Currency Deposit Units
FCE.......... Facilities Capital Employed [DoD]
FCE.......... Factory Checkout Equipment (MCD)
FCE.......... Federation Canadienne des Echecs [Chess Federation of Canada]
FCE.......... Federation Canadienne des Enseignants [Canadian Teachers' Federation - CTF]
FCE.......... Federation Canadienne des Etudiants [Canadian Federation of Students]
FCE.......... Field Checkout Equipment
FCE.......... Fire Control Electronics (MCD)
FCE.......... Fire Control Element (MCD)
FCE.......... Fire Control Equipment
FCE.......... Fleet Civil Engineer
FCE.......... Flexible Critical Experiment
FCE.......... Flight Control Electronics
FCE.......... Flight Control Equipment [NASA] (NASA)
FCE.......... Flight Crew Equipment [NASA] (NASA)
FCE.......... Fondo de Cultura Economica [Mexico] [A publication]
FCE.......... Forest City Enterprises, Inc. [AMEX symbol] (SPSG)
FCE.......... Foundation for Character Education (EA)
FCE.......... Foundation for Credit Education [Nazareth, PA] (EA)
FCE.......... Frequency Converter Excitation
FCE.......... Friends Council on Education (EA)
FCE.......... Functional Capacities Evaluation [Test] [Occupational therapy]
FCEA......... Fellow of the Association of Cost and Executive Accountants [British] (DBQ)
FCEA......... Fleet Chief Electrical Artificer [British military] (DMA)
FCEC......... Fire Control Engagement Controller [Military] (CAAL)
FCEF .... Flight Crew Equipment Facility [NASA] (NASA)
FCEH .... Federation Canadienne des Etudes Humaines [Canadian Federation for the Humanities - CFH]
FCEI .... Facility Contract End Item
FCEL(A).... Fleet Chief Electrician (Air) [British military] (DMA)
FCEL(AW) ... Fleet Chief Electrician (Air Weapon) [British military] (DMA)
FCELMN(A) ... Fleet Chief Electrical Mechanician (Air) [British military] (DMA)
FCELMN(AW) ... Fleet Chief Electrical Mechanician (Air Weapon) [British military] (DMA)
FCEM........ Femmes Chefs d'Entreprises Mondiales [World Association of Women Entrepreneurs] (EAIO)
FCEM........ Foreign Capital Export Manufacturing
FCEMN..... 14th Century English Mystics Newsletter [A publication]
FCEPC...... Flight Control Electrical Package Container
FCER........ Foundation for Chiropractic Education and Research (EA)
FCES .... Flight Control Electronic Set (MCD)
FCES(Aust) ... Fellow of the Commercial Education Society of Australia
FCEU........ Flight Control Electronics Unit
f-cf--- .... Congo [MARC geographic area code] [Library of Congress] (LCCP)
FCF.......... Facility Capital Funds (AAG)
FCF.......... Family Camping Federation [Later, FCFA] (EA)
FCF.......... Feline and Canine Friends (EA)
FCF.......... Fellowship of Christian Firefighters, International (EA)
FCF.......... First Captive Flight [NASA] (NASA)
FCF.......... Fishermen's Compensation Fund [National Oceanic and Atmospheric Administration]
FCF.......... Flag Correlation Facility (MCD)
FCF.......... Flight Critical Forward (NASA)
FCF.......... For Colouring of Food [British]
FCF.......... Free China Fund for Medical and Refugee Aid
FCF.......... Frequency Compressive Feedback
FCF.......... Fuel Cycle Facility [Nuclear energy]
FCF.......... Functional Check Flight [Air Force] (AFM)
FCFA......... Family Camping Federation of America [Formerly, FCF] [Defunct] (EA)
FCFA .... Florida Commercial Fisheries Association (EA)
FCFC........ Film Council Film Circuit [Library network]
FCFC........ Free Church Federal Council
FCFC........ Full-Coverage Film Cooling
FCFD......... Fluorescence Capillary Fill Device [Instrumentation]

FCFDU...... Federation Canadienne des Femmes Diplomees des Universites [Canadian Federation of University Women]
FCFI .... First Capitol Financial Corp. [NASDAQ symbol] (NQ)
FCFK .... Fondation Canadienne de la Fibrose Kystique [Canadian Cystic Fibrosis Foundation]
FCFM........ Flight Combustion Facility Monitor (MCD)
FCFN........ First City Financial Corp. Ltd. [NASDAQ symbol] (NQ)
FCFO......... Full Cycling File Organization
FCFS......... First Come, First Served [Data processing]
FCFS......... Frequency Coded Firing System (MCD)
FCF SE ...... Facility Checking Flight - Service Evaluation [Air Force] (MCD)
FCFT .... Fixed Cost, Fixed Time (IEEE)
f-cg--- .... Congo (Kinshasa) [Zaire] [MARC geographic area code] [Library of Congress] (LCCP)
FCG .... Facility Change Group (KSC)
FCG .... Facing
FCG .... Falconbridge Gold Corp. [Toronto Stock Exchange symbol]
FCG .... Federation for Constitutional Government [Defunct] (EA)
FCG .... Fernwood, Columbia & Gulf R. R. [AAR code]
FCG .... Field Coordination Group
FCG .... Fire Control Group
FCG .... First Communications Group, Inc. [Coral Gables, FL] (TSSD)
FCG .... Fleet Composite Group [Navy] (CAAL)
FCG .... Flight Control Group (MCD)
FCG .... Foreign Clearance Guide (AFM)
FCG .... Fragmenta Comicorum Graecorum [A publication] (OCD)
FCG .... Friction Cam Gear
FCG .... Fuel Contents Gauge (MSA)
FCG .... Fund for Constitutional Government (EA)
FCGA........ Facility Gauge (AAG)
FCGC........ Flight Control Gyro Container
FCGCMA ... Federation of Cash Grain Commission Merchants Associations [Defunct] (EA)
FCgDH ...... Doctors Hospital, Medical Library, Coral Gables, FL [Library symbol] [Library of Congress] (LCLS)
FCGI.......... Fellow of the City and Guilds of London Institute [British] (ROG)
FCGM .... Frammenti della Commedia Greca e del Mimo nella Sicilia e nella Magna Grecia [A publication] (OCD)
FCgM .... United States Department of Commerce, National Oceanic and Atmospheric Administration, Miami Branch Library, Coral Gables, FL [Library symbol] [Library of Congress] (LCLS)
FCGP......... Fellow of the College of General Practitioners
FCGPC...... Flight Control Gyro Package Container
FCGR........ Fatigue Crack Growth Rate [Metals]
FCGRS ...... Federation Canadienne de Gymnastique Rythmique Sportive [Canadian Modern Rhythmic Gymnastics Federation - CMRGF]
FCGS......... Freight Classification Guide System
FCH .... Federal Cataloging Handbook
FCH .... Fellow of the Coopers Hill College [British]
FCh .... Field Champion [Dog show term]
FCH .... Film Carrousel Handle
FCH .... Fircrest Resources [Vancouver Stock Exchange symbol]
FCH .... First Capital Holdings Corp. [NYSE symbol] (SPSG)
FCH .... Flight Controllers Handbook
FCH .... Foundation for Cooperative Housing [Later, CHF]
FCH .... Freightlines and Construction Holdings [Australia]
FCH .... Fresno, CA [Location identifier] [FAA] (FAAL)
FCHC .... Fellow of Catherine Hall, Cambridge [British] (ROG)
FCHC .... Newberry Library Family and Community History Center [Research center] (RCD)
FCHCA...... Foreign Car Haters Club of America (EA)
FChemSoc ... Fellow of the Chemical Society [British]
FCHG .... Formal Change (MCD)
FCHGD .... Feminist Center for Human Growth and Development (EA)
FChH......... Florida State Hospital, Chattahoochee, FL [Library symbol] [Library of Congress] (LCLS)
FCHL........ Flight Control Hydraulics Laboratory [NASA] (NASA)
FCHO........ Federation Canadienne de Handball Olympique [Canadian Team Handball Federation - CTHF]
FCHQ........ Filson Club History Quarterly [A publication]
FCHR .... Functional Cost Hour Report (MCD)
FChrLDG .. Forschungen zur Christlichen Literatur- und Dogmengeschichte [A publication]
FChS .... Fellow of the Society of Chiropodists [British]
Fchse.......... Franchise
FCHT .... First Chattanooga Financial Corp. [NASDAQ symbol] (NQ)
FCI .... Defense Foreign Counterintelligence [Program] [DoD]
FCI .... Fairfield Communities, Inc. [NYSE symbol] (SPSG)
FCI............ Fan Circle International (EA)
FCI............ Fashion Coordination Institute [Defunct] (EA)
FCI............ Fast Coastal Interceptor [US Coast Guard vessel]
FCI............ Federal Crime Insurance
FCI............ Federal Crop Insurance
FCI............ Federation Colombophile Internationale [International Pigeon Federation - IPF] (EAIO)
FCI............ Federation Cynologique Internationale [International Federation of Kennel Clubs] [Thuin, Belgium] (EA)

FCI............	Fellow of the Canadian Credit Institute
FCI............	Fellow of the Institute of Commerce [British]
FCI............	Fire Control Instruments (MCD)
FCI............	First China Investment Corp. [Vancouver Stock Exchange symbol]
FCI............	First Communications, Incorporated [Atlanta, GA] (TSSD)
FCI............	Flight Command Indicator (MCD)
FCI............	Flight Control Indicator (MCD)
FCI............	Flight Control Integration [Apollo] [NASA]
FCI............	Flight Critical Items (MCD)
FCI............	Florida Computer, Incorporated [Information service or system] (IID)
FCI............	Fluid Conductivity Indicator
FCI............	Fluid Controls Institute (EA)
FCI............	Flux Changes per Inch [Data processing]
F & CI........	Food and Container Institute
FCI............	Food Corporation of India
FCI............	Foreign Counterintelligence
FCI............	Franklin College of Indiana
FCI............	Fraud Control Institute [Communications Fraud Control Association] (TSSD)
FCI............	Freedom Communications International News Agency [London, England] (EAIO)
FCI............	Fuel Coolant Interaction [Nuclear energy] (NRCH)
FCI............	Functional Configuration Identification (KSC)
FCIA..........	Federal Criminal Investigators Association (EA)
FCIA..........	Fellow of the Canadian Institute of Actuaries
FCIA..........	Fellow of the Corporation of Insurance Agents [British]
FCIA..........	Foreign Credit Insurance Association [New York, NY] (EA)
FCIA..........	Franchise Consultants International Association (EA)
FCIA..........	Friends of Cast Iron Architecture (EA)
FCIArb........	Fellow of the Chartered Institute of Arbitrators [British] (DBQ)
FCIB..........	Fellow of the Corporation of Insurance Brokers [British]
FCIB..........	Foreign Credit Interchange Bureau (EA)
FCIBS........	Fellow of the Chartered Institution of Building Services [British] (DBQ)
FCIC..........	Fairchild Camera & Instrument Corporation (MCD)
FCIC..........	Federal Crop Insurance Corporation [Department of Agriculture]
FCIC..........	Fellow of the Chemical Institute of Canada
FCIC..........	Foreign Credit Insurance Corporation [Business term]
FCICA........	Floor Covering Installation Contractors Association (EA)
FCIF..........	Flight Crew Information File (AFM)
FCII..........	Federated Council of Israel Institutions (EA)
FCII..........	Fellow of the Chartered Insurance Institute [British] (EY)
FCIL..........	Finance Corporation for Industry Ltd. [British]
FCILA........	Fellow of the Chartered Institute of Loss Adjusters [British] (DBQ)
FCIM..........	Federation des Concours Internationaux de Musique [Federation of International Music Competitions - FIMC] (EAIO)
FCIM..........	Flight Control Interface Module (MCD)
FCIN..........	Frankfort & Cincinnati Railroad Co. [AAR code]
FCIOB........	Fellow of the Chartered Institute of Building [British] (DBQ)
FCIP..........	Field Cable Installation Platoon [Army] (AABC)
FCIP..........	Flight Cargo Implementation Plan (MCD)
FCIP..........	Foreign Counterintelligence Program [DoD]
FCIPA........	Fellow of the Chartered Institute of Patent Agents [British]
FCIQ..........	Fairbanks North Star Borough. Community Information Center. Quarterly [A publication]
FCIR..........	Facility Change Initiation Request
F-CIR........	Failure and Consumption Inspector's Report (AAG)
FCIS..........	Fellow of the Chartered Institute of Secretaries [British] (ROG)
FCIS..........	Force Cost Information System (MCD)
FCIS..........	Foreign Counterintelligence System [Federal Bureau of Investigation]
FCISA........	Fellow of the Institute of Chartered Secretaries and Administrators [Australia]
FCIT..........	Fellow of the Chartered Institute of Transport [British]
FCIT..........	First Citizens Financial Corp. [NASDAQ symbol] (NQ)
FCIU..........	Family Crisis Intervention Unit [New York Police Department]
FCJ............	Federal Chief Justice [Nigeria] [A publication] (DLA)
FCJ............	Federal Court Judgements [Canada Department of Justice] [Information service or system] (CRD)
FCJ............	Foreign Criminal Jurisdiction (AABC)
FCJ............	Society of the Sisters, Faithful Companions of Jesus [Roman Catholic religious order]
FCK............	Field Change Kit
FCK............	Filter Change Kit
FCK............	Fuel Charge Kit
FCl............	Clearwater Public Library, Clearwater, FL [Library symbol] [Library of Congress] (LCLS)
FCL............	Federal Communications Law Journal [A publication]
FCL............	Feedback Control Loop [Data processing] (BUR)
FCL............	Femme Couleur Libre [French] (DLA)
FCL............	Film Capability Laboratories [Bell System]
FCL............	Final Coordination Line [Military]
FCL............	Fire Coordination Line [Military] (AABC)
FCL............	Fleet Control List [Navy] (AFIT)
FCL............	Flight Control Laboratory
FCL............	Flux Current Loop

FCL............	Format Control Language
FCL............	Fort Collins, CO [Location identifier] [FAA] (FAAL)
FCL............	Foundation for Christian Living (EA)
FCL............	Freon Coolant Line [NASA] (NASA)
FCL............	Freon Coolant Loop [Space shuttle] [NASA]
FCL............	Frick Chemical Laboratory (KSC)
FCL............	Fuel Cell (KSC)
FCL............	Full Container Load [Shipping]
FCL............	Fuze Cavity Liner [Projectile] (NG)
FCL............	Sarbah's Fanti Customary Laws [Ghana] [A publication] (DLA)
FCLA.........	Family Centered Learning Alternatives (EA)
FCLA.........	Florida Center for Library Automation [Florida State University System] [Information service or system] (IID)
FCLAA.......	Federal Coal Leasing Amendments Act [1976]
FCLBAR.....	Folia Clinica et Biologica [A publication]
FCLC.........	First Centennial Corporation [NASDAQ symbol] (NQ)
FCLD.........	Foundation for Children with Learning Disabilities [Later, NCLD] (EA)
FCLF.........	First Columbia Financial Corp. [NASDAQ symbol] (NQ)
FCLI..........	Fordham University School of Law, Corporate Law Institute (DLA)
FClM.........	Morton F. Plant Hospital, Clearwater, FL [Library symbol] [Library of Congress] (LCLS)
FC/LOS.....	Fire Control, Line-of-Sight
FCLP.........	Field Carrier Landing Passes [or Practice]
FCLR.........	First Commercial Corp. [NASDAQ symbol] (NQ)
FCLTY......	Facility (AFM)
FCLTYCHECKINGSq ...	Facility Checking Squadron [Air Force]
f-cm---	Cameroon [MARC geographic area code] [Library of Congress] (LCCP)
FCM..........	Faculty of Community Medicine [British]
FCM..........	Farrier Corporal-Major [British military] (DMA)
FCM..........	Fat-Corrected Milk
FCM..........	Fault Control Module (TEL)
FCM.	FCMI Financial Corp. [Toronto Stock Exchange symbol]
FCM..........	Federal Class Manager (AFIT)
FCM..........	Federation of Canadian Municipalities
FCM..........	Federation Canadienne des Municipalites [Federation of Canadian Municipalities]
FCM..........	Fellowship of Christian Magicians (EA)
FCM..........	Fellowship of Christian Motorcyclists [Welwyn Garden City, England] (EAIO)
FCM..........	Fellowship of Christian Musicians (EA)
FCM	Ferrocarril Mexicano [AAR code]
FCM	Fiber Composite Material
FCM	Filament Composite Material
FCM	Firmware Control Memory
FCM	First-Class Mail [Postal Service]
FCM	Flight Combustion Monitor [NASA] (KSC)
FCM	Florida Agricultural and Mechanical University, Tallahassee, FL [OCLC symbol] (OCLC)
FCM	Florida Citrus Mutual (EA)
FCM	Flow Cytometry [Analytical biochemistry]
FCM	Food, Clothing, Maintenance [Red Cross]
FCM	Forged Chrom-Moly
FCM	Framing Camera Mopper
FCM	Friends of Cathedral Music (EA)
FCM	Fuel Cell Module
FCM	Fund for a Conservative Majority (EA)
FCM	Futures Commission Merchant
FCM	Minneapolis, MN [Location identifier] [FAA] (FAAL)
FCMA.......	Fellow of the Institute of Cost and Management Accountants [British]
FCMA.......	Field Cashier Military Accounts [British military] (DMA)
FCMA.......	Fishery Conservation and Management Act [1976] [Also, MFCMA]
FCMA.......	Fleet Chief Medical Assistant [British military] (DMA)
FCMA.......	Mavinza [Congo] [ICAO location identifier] (ICLI)
FCMB.......	First City Merchant Bank Ltd.
FCMB.......	N'Ziba [Congo] [ICAO location identifier] (ICLI)
FCMD	Fire Command (KSC)
FCMD	Vouka/Sidetra [Congo] [ICAO location identifier] (ICLI)
FCMEA.....	Fleet Chief Marine Engineering Artificer [British military] (DMA)
FCMEM.....	Fleet Chief Marine Engineering Mechanic [British military] (DMA)
FCMF........	Loufoula [Congo] [ICAO location identifier] (ICLI)
FCMG	Gokango [Congo] [ICAO location identifier] (ICLI)
FCMI.........	Irogo [Congo] [ICAO location identifier] (ICLI)
FCMK.......	Kele/Kibangou [Congo] [ICAO location identifier] (ICLI)
FCML.......	Leboulou [Congo] [ICAO location identifier] (ICLI)
FCMM	Federation Canadienne des Maires et des Municipalites [Canadian Federation of Mayors and Municipalities]
FCMM	Mossendjo [Congo] [ICAO location identifier] (ICLI)
FCMN	N'Gongo [Congo] [ICAO location identifier] (ICLI)
FCMO	Vouka/Mandoro [Congo] [ICAO location identifier] (ICLI)
FCMPU.....	Female Cigar Makers' Protective Union [British]
FCMR.......	Marala [Congo] [ICAO location identifier] (ICLI)
FCMS........	Facilities Computer Monitoring System [Johnson Controls, Inc.]

FCMS........ Fellow of the College of Medicine and Surgery [British]
F/CMS ...... Financial/Cost Management System (MCD)
FCMS........ Flight Crew Mission Simulator [NASA] (KSC)
FCMS........ Force Capability Management System [Military]
FCMS........ Nyanga [Congo] [ICAO location identifier] (ICLI)
FCMSBR... Federal Coal Mine Safety Board of Review [Independent government agency] [Inactive, 1970]
FCMS & SR ... Federal Committee for Meteorological Services and Supporting Research
FCMT........ Bekol/Thomas [Congo] [ICAO location identifier] (ICLI)
FCMT........ Fleet Chief Medical Technician [British military] (DMA)
FCMT........ Flight Configuration Mode Test [Gemini] [NASA]
FCMU........ Foot-Controlled Maneuvering Unit [Skylab] [NASA]
FCMV....... Fuel Consuming Motor Vehicle
FCMW ...... Foundation for Child Mental Welfare (EA)
FCMY........ Mayoko/Legala [Congo] [ICAO location identifier] (ICLI)
FCMZ........ N'Zabi [Congo] [ICAO location identifier] (ICLI)
FCN .... FC Financial Corp. [Vancouver Stock Exchange symbol]
FCN .... Federal Catalog Number
FCN .... Field Change Notification (KSC)
FCN .... Fire Control Notes [A publication]
FCN .... Frijoles Canyon [New Mexico] [Seismograph station code, US Geological Survey] [Closed] (SEIS)
FCN .... Function (NASA)
FCN .... Treaty of Friendship, Commerce, and Navigation [Indonesia] (IMH)
FCNA .... Florida Citrus Nurserymen's Association (EA)
FCN(Aust) ... Fellow of the College of Nursing (Australia)
FCNC........ First Citizens Bancshares, Inc. [Raleigh, NC] [NASDAQ symbol] (NQ)
FCNEEG ... Frontiers of Clinical Neuroscience [A publication]
FCNL......... French Committee of National Liberation [World War II]
FCNL......... Frequently-Called-Numbers List [Bell System]
FCNL......... Friends Committee on National Legislation (EA)
FCNP........ Fire Control Navigation Panel (IEEE)
FCNPC...... Film Culture Non-Profit Corporation (EA)
FCNS .... Fairchild Communications Networks & Services Co. [Chantilly, VA] [Telecommunications service] [Later, FCS] (TSSD)
FCNSI .... Federation Canadienne Nationale des Syndicats Independants [Canadian National Federation of Independent Unions - CNFIU]
FCNTL...... Function Timeline
FCO .... Cleanout Flush with Finished Floor
FCO .... Facility Change Order (AAG)
FCO .... Facility Coordination Offices [FAA] (FAAC)
FCO .... Fair Copy
FCO .... Federal Career Opportunities [A publication]
FCO .... Federal Coordinating Officer [Federal disaster planning]
FCO .... Fellow of the College of Organists [British] (ROG)
FCO .... Fellow of the College of Osteopathy [British]
FCO .... Field Change Order
F Co........... Field Company [British military] (DMA)
FCO .... Files Control Office
FCO .... Final Checkout (MCD)
FCO .... Fire Control Operator [Army]
FCO .... First Connecticut Small Business Investment Co. [AMEX symbol] (SPSG)
FCO .... Fixed Cycle Operation
FCO .... Flag Communications Officer [Navy]
FCO .... Fleet Communications Officer [Navy] [British]
FCO .... Flight Clearance Office
FCO .... Flight Communications Operator
FCO .... Flight Crew Operations [NASA]
FCO .... Flying Control Officer [Navy]
FCO .... Foreign and Commonwealth Office [British]
fco.............. Franco [Free of Charge] [Shipping] [French]
FCO .... Franco [Free of Charge] [Shipping] [Italian] [Spanish]
FCO .... Frequency Control Officer (MUGU)
FCO .... Functional Checkout
FCO .... Rome [Italy] Leonardo Da Vinci (Fium) Airport [Airport symbol] (OAG)
FCoa......... Cocoa Public Library, Cocoa, FL [Library symbol] [Library of Congress] (LCLS)
FCOA .... Federation of Chinese Organizations in America (EA)
FCOA .... Foremost Corporation of America [NASDAQ symbol] (NQ)
FCoaB........ Brevard Community College, Cocoa, FL [Library symbol] [Library of Congress] (LCLS)
FCOAC...... Furnish Copies of Orders to Appropriate Commanders
FCOB........ Boundji [Congo] [ICAO location identifier] (ICLI)
FCOB........ First Commercial Bancorp [NASDAQ symbol] (NQ)
FCOB........ Flight Control Operations Branch [NASA] (MCD)
FCOD........ Flight Crew Operations Directorate [NASA] (KSC)
FCOE........ Ewo [Congo] [ICAO location identifier] (ICLI)
FCOEA...... Fleet Chief Ordnance Electrical Artificer [British military] (DMA)
FCOEL...... Fleet Chief Ordnance Electrician [British military] (DMA)
FCOEMN ... Fleet Chief Ordnance Electrical Mechanician [British military] (DMA)
FCOG .... Fellow of the British College of Obstetricians and Gynaecologists (DAS)
FCOG .... Fellow of the College of Obstetricians and Gynecologists

FCOG .... Gamboma [Congo] [ICAO location identifier] (ICLI)
FCOH........ Flight Controllers Operations Handbook [NASA] (KSC)
FCOI......... Fire Control Optical Instrument
FCOI......... Impfondo [Congo] [ICAO location identifier] (ICLI)
FCOJ .... Frozen Concentrated Orange Juice
FCOK .... Kelle [Congo] [ICAO location identifier] (ICLI)
FCOL........ First Colonial Bancshares Corp. [Chicago, IL] [NASDAQ symbol] (NQ)
FCOL........ Loukolela [Congo] [ICAO location identifier] (ICLI)
F Com........ Film Comment [A publication]
FCOM .... First Commerce Corp. [NASDAQ symbol] (NQ)
FCOM .... Flight Crew Operating Manual (MCD)
FCOM .... Makoua [Congo] [ICAO location identifier] (ICLI)
F Comm ..... Full Commission
F Comment ... Film Comment [A publication]
FCON .... First Constitution Finance Corp. [NASDAQ symbol] (NQ)
FCOO .... Owando [Congo] [ICAO location identifier] (ICLI)
FCoS .... Fetal Cord Serum [Gynecology]
FCOS......... Flight Computer Operating System [NASA] (NASA)
FCOS......... Flight Control Operating System [NASA] (NASA)
FCOS......... Flight Control Operational Software (MCD)
FCOS......... Souanke [Congo] [ICAO location identifier] (ICLI)
FCOT........ Betou [Congo] [ICAO location identifier] (ICLI)
FCO-T .... Flight Communications Operator in Training
FCOU .... Ouesso [Congo] [ICAO location identifier] (ICLI)
FCOV .... Facility Checkout Vehicle [NASA] (KSC)
F/COV ...... Floor Covering (ADA)
FCP........... Failure Correction Panel (NASA)
FCP........... Falls City Press, Louisville, KY [Library symbol] [Library of Congress] (LCLS)
FCP........... Federal Cataloging Program
FCP........... Fellow of the College of Preceptors [British] (ROG)
FCP........... Ferrocarril del Pacifico, SA de CV [AAR code]
FCP........... Ferry Command Police [British military] (DMA)
FCP........... Field Change Package [Nuclear energy] (NRCH)
FCP........... Field Change Proposal
FCP........... Field Command Post
FCP........... File Control Processor [Data processing] (BUR)
FCP........... File Control Program [Data processing]
FCP........... Final Common Pathway [Neurology]
FCP........... Fire Control Panel (MCD)
FCP........... Fire Control Personnel [Marine Corps]
FCP........... Fire Control Platoon [Army]
FCP........... Firm Cost Proposal (NASA)
FCP........... First Calgary Petroleums Ltd. [Toronto Stock Exchange symbol]
FCP........... Fixed Code Processor
FCP........... Flight Control Panel (MCD)
FCP........... Flight Control Programmer
FCP........... Flight Correction Proposal (MCD)
FCP........... Florida Citrus Packers (EA)
FCP........... Fluorouracil, Cyclophosphamide, Prednisone [Antineoplastic drug regimen]
FCP........... Fonds Commun de Placement [Mutual Fund] [French]
FCP........... Foolscap [Paper]
FCP........... Foreign Corporation Project [IRS]
FCP........... Forward Command Post (NATG)
FCP........... Foundation for Creative Philosophy (EA)
FCP........... French Communist Party
FCP........... Frequency Control Panel (MCD)
FCP........... Friends of the Conservative Party (EA)
FCP........... Fuel Cell Power Plant
FCP........... Full Couterpoise Procedure [Physical chemistry]
FCP........... Function Control Package [Data processing]
FCPA .... Fabricants Canadiens de Produits Alimentaires [Grocery Products Manufacturers of Canada - GPMC]
FCPA .... Fellow of the Canadian Psychological Association
FCPA .... Fellow of the Institute of Certified Public Accountants [British] (DAS)
FCPA .... Foreign Corrupt Practices Act [1977]
FCPA .... Makabana [Congo] [ICAO location identifier] (ICLI)
FCPAC ...... Free Congress Political Action Committee (EA)
FC Path...... Fellow of the College of Pathologists [Later, Royal College of Pathologists] [British]
FCPB .... Bangamba [Congo] [ICAO location identifier] (ICLI)
FCPC .... Fair Campaign Practices Committee (EA)
FCPC .... Federal Committee on Pest Control
FCPC .... Fleet Computer Programming Center (MUGU)
FCPCL....... Fleet Computer Programming Center, Atlantic [Navy]
FCPCLANT ... Fleet Computer Programming Center, Atlantic [Navy]
FCPCNA ... First Czechoslovak Philatelic Club of North America (EA)
FCPCP....... Fleet Computer Programming Center, Pacific [Navy]
FCPCPAC ... Fleet Computer Programming Center, Pacific [Navy] (MCD)
FCPD........ Loudima [Congo] [ICAO location identifier] (ICLI)
FC/PDL..... Freight Classification Packaging Data List (AFIT)
FCPE .... Leganda [Congo] [ICAO location identifier] (ICLI)
FCPG .... Federation of Catholic Physicians Guilds
FCPG .... Kibangou [Congo] [ICAO location identifier] (ICLI)
FCPI .... Flux Changes per Inch [Data processing]
FCPI .... Frequency Control [NASDAQ symbol] (NQ)
FCPI .... Vounda/Loubetsi [Congo] [ICAO location identifier] (ICLI)

FCPJA3....   Fragmenta Coleopterologica Japonica [*A publication*]
FCPK........   N'Komo [*Congo*] [*ICAO location identifier*]   (ICLI)
FCPL.........   Loubomo [*Congo*] [*ICAO location identifier*]   (ICLI)
F/CPLG.....   Fluid Coupling [*Automotive engineering*]
FCPM........   Fellow of the Confederation of Professional Management [*British*]   (DBQ)
FCPM........   Free Cuba Patriotic Movement   (EA)
FCPM........   M'Baya [*Congo*] [*ICAO location identifier*]   (ICLI)
FCPN........   Noumbi [*Congo*] [*ICAO location identifier*]   (ICLI)
FCPO.........   Fellowship of Christian Peace Officers   (EA)
FCPO.........   First Class Post Office
FCPO.........   Fleet Chief Petty Officer [*Navy*] [*British*]
FCPO.........   Pemo [*Congo*] [*ICAO location identifier*]   (ICLI)
FCPP ....   Pointe-Noire [*Congo*] [*ICAO location identifier*]   (ICLI)
FCPPS ......   Fuel Cell Power Plant System   (KSC)
FCPRC ......   Federal Cultural Policy Review Committee [*Canada*]
FCPS ....   Fellow of the Cambridge Philological Society [*British*]
FCPS ....   Fellow of the Cambridge Philosophical Society [*British*]   (ROG)
FCPS ....   Fellow of the College of Physicians and Surgeons [*British*]
FCPS ....   Firewood Cutters' Protective Society [*A union*] [*British*]
FCPS ....   FOSIC [*Fleet Ocean Surveillance Information Center*] Communications Processing Subsystem   (MCD)
FCPS ....   France and Colonies Philatelic Society   (EA)
FCPS ....   Fuel Cell Power System [*or Subsystem*]
FCP(SA)....   Fellow of the College of Physicians of South Africa
FCP(SoAf) ...   Fellow of the College of Physicians of South Africa
FCPSO (SoAf) ...   Fellow of the College of Physicians and Surgeons and Obstetricians of South Africa
FCPT ....   Fleet Chief Physical Trainer [*British military*]   (DMA)
FCPY ....   Loukanyi [*Congo*] [*ICAO location identifier*]   (ICLI)
FCR...........   Facility Capability Report [*Military*]
FCR...........   Facility Capability Review
FCR...........   Facility Change Request
FCR...........   False Contact Rate   (CAAL)
FCR............   Farm Costs and Returns [*A publication*]
FCR............   Fast Ceramic Reactor [*Program*]
FCR............   Fast Conversion Ratio   (NRCH)
FCR............   Fearne on Contingent Remainders [*1722-1844*] [*A publication*]   (DLA)
FCR............   Federal Court Reporter [*A publication*]   (APTA)
FCR............   Federal Court Reports [*A publication*]   (DLA)
FCR............   Federal Court Reports [*Canada Department of Justice*] [*Information service or system*]   (CRD)
FCR............   Federal Court Rules [*A publication*]
FCR............   Fellowship of Christian Racers [*Defunct*]   (EA)
FCR............   Field Change Request [*Nuclear energy*]   (NRCH)
FCR............   Filmcritica [*A publication*]
FCR............   Final Configuration Review   (KSC)
FCR............   Fine Crushed Rock   (ADA)
FCR............   Fire Control RADAR
FCR............   Fire Controlman, Range-Finder Operator [*Navy rating*] [*Obsolete*]
FCR............   Firstcorp, Inc. [*AMEX symbol*]   (SPSG)
FCR............   Fixed Change Rate
FCR............   Flight Condition Recognition [*Army aviation*]
FCR............   Flight Configuration Review   (MCD)
FCR............   Flight Control Room
FCR............   Floating Control Regulator
FCR............   Food and Cookery Review [*A publication*]
FCR............   Forward Calculation Request
FCR............   Forwarders Certificate of Receipt [*Shipping*]
FCR............   Fractional Catabolic Rate [*Clinical chemistry*]
FCR............   France Cables & Radio Co. [*France*] [*Telecommunications*]   (TSSD)
FCR............   Frederick Cancer Research Center, Frederick, MD [*OCLC symbol*]   (OCLC)
FCR............   Free China Review [*A publication*]
FCR............   Front Communiste Revolutionnaire [*France*]
FCR............   Fruitlet Core Rot [*of pineapple*]
FCR............   Fuel Core Reserve [*Nuclear energy*]
FCR............   Full Cold Rolled [*Steel*]
FCR............   Functional Configuration Review   (MCD)
FCR.........   Fuse Current Rating
FCRA........   Fabric Care Research Association [*British*]   (IRUK)
FCRA........   Fair Credit Reporting Act [*1971*]
FCRA........   Fecal Collection Receptacle Assembly [*NASA*]   (KSC)
FCRA........   Fellow of the College of Radiologists of Australia
FCRA........   Fellow of the Corporation of Registered Accountants [*British*]   (DAS)
FCRAA ......   Folding Chair Rental Association of America [*Later, RSA*]
FCRAO......   Five College Radio Astronomy Observatory
FCRAP .....   Federation of Cattle Raisers Association of the Philippines   (DS)
FCRC........   Federal Contract Research Center
FCRC........   Four Corners Regional Commission [*Department of Commerce*]
FCRC........   Frederick Cancer Research Center   (RDA)
FCRD........   Feline Central Retinal Degeneration [*Animal pathology*]
FCRD........   Firstcorp, Inc. [*NASDAQ symbol*]   (NQ)
FCRE........   First Continental REIT [*Houston, TX*] [*NASDAQ symbol*]   (NQ)

FCRE........   Foundation for Cotton Research and Education [*Later, The Cotton Foundation*]   (EA)
FCREA ......   Fleet Chief Radio Electrical Artificer [*British military*]   (DMA)
FCREF......   Free Congress Research and Education Foundation   (EA)
FCREL(A) ...   Fleet Chief Radio Electrician (Air) [*British military*]   (DMA)
FCREMN ...   Fleet Chief Radio Electrical Mechanician [*British military*]   (DMA)
FCRF........   Fire Control Reference Frame   (MCD)
FCRF ....   Frederick Cancer Research Facility [*Frederick, MD*] [*Department of Health and Human Services*]   (GRD)
FC (RFC)...   Functional Capacity (Residual Functional Capacity) [*Social Security Administration*]   (OICC)
FCRG........   Food Chain Research Group [*University of California*] [*Research center*]   (RCD)
F Criticism ...   Film Criticism [*A publication*]
FCRL.........   Fish Culture Research Laboratory [*Kearneysville, WV*] [*Fish and Wildlife Service*] [*Department of the Interior*]   (GRD)
FCRL.........   Flight Control Ready Light System
FCRLS.......   Flight Control Ready Light System
FCRN........   Fund Classification Reference Number [*Military*]   (AFIT)
FCRP ....   Final CAPE [*Capability and Proficiency Evaluation*] Review Period
FCRPS......   Federal Columbia River Power System
FCRSA......   Flat-Coated Retriever Society of America   (EA)
FCRS(S) ....   Fleet Chief Radio Supervisor (Special) [*British military*]   (DMA)
FCRS(W)...   Fleet Chief Radio Supervisor (Warfare) [*British military*]   (DMA)
FCRT ....   Flight Display Cathode-Ray Tube   (NASA)
FCRU........   Facilities Control Relay Unit [*Army*]   (AABC)
FCRV ....   Front Commun pour le Respect de la Vie [*Common Front for the Respect of Life*] [*Canada*]
FCS ....   Facsimile Communications System [*Telecommunications*]
FCS ....   Failure and Consumption Sheets   (AAG)
FCS ....   Fairchild Communications Services Company [*Washington, DC*]   (TSSD)
FCS ....   Fairchild Semiconductor
FCS ....   Farm Credit System [*of FCA*]
FCS ....   Farmer Cooperative Service [*Later, ESCS*] [*Department of Agriculture*]
FCS ....   Fecal Containment System [*NASA*]
FCS ....   Federal Catalog System [*of GSA*]
FCS ....   Federal Communications Systems   (MCD)
FCS ....   Federation of Communication Services [*London, England*]   (TSSD)
FCS ....   Feedback Control System
FCS ....   Fellow of the Chemical Society [*British*]   (ROG)
FCS ....   Fellowship of Catholic Scholars   (EA)
FCS ....   Fetal Calf [*or Cow*] Serum [*Medicine*]
FCS ....   Fetal Cord Serum [*Embryology*]
FCS ....   Fifteenth-Century Studies [*A publication*]
FCS ....   Fighter Catapult Ship [*British military*]   (DMA)
FCS ....   Fighter Command School [*Air Force*]
FCS ....   File Control Services [*Digital Equipment Corp.*]
FC & S ....   Final Command and Sequencing [*Viking lander mission*] [*NASA*]
FCS ....   Fire Control Simulator
FCS ....   Fire Control System
FCS ....   Fire Controlman, Submarine [*Navy rating*] [*Obsolete*]
FCS ....   First Customer Shipment [*IBM Corp.*] [*Data processing*]
FCS ....   Fiscal Studies [*United Kingdom*] [*A publication*]
FCS ....   Fish Culture Section [*American Fisheries Society*]   (EA)
FCS ....   Fisheries Conservation Zone
FCS ....   Fixed Control Storage
FCS ....   Flag Cancel Society   (EA)
FCS ....   Flame Control System
FCS ....   Flight Command School
FCS ....   Flight Command Subsystem [*Spacecraft*]
FCS ....   Flight Control Set
F/CS ....   Flight Control System   (AAG)
FCS ....   Flight Crew System [*NASA*]   (NASA)
FCS ....   Flowmeter Calibration Stand
FCS ....   Fluorescence Correlation Spectroscopy
FCS ....   Food Containment System
FCS ....   Forces Courier Services [*Military*] [*British*]
FCS ....   Foreign Commercial Service [*International Trade Administration*]
FCS ....   Forged Carbon Steel
FCS ....   Fort Calhoun Station [*Nuclear energy*]   (NRCH)
FCS ....   Fort Carson, CO [*Location identifier*] [*FAA*]   (FAAL)
FCS ....   Frame Check Sequence [*Data processing*]   (IBMDP)
FCS ....   Frederic Chopin Society [*Later, IFCF*]   (EA)
FC & S ....   Free of Capture and Seizure [*Insurance*]
FCS ....   Free of Capture and Seizure [*Insurance*]
FCS ....   Free Crystalline Silica
FCS ....   French Chemical Society [*See also SFC*]   (EAIO)
FCS ....   Frequency Coded System   (MCD)
FCS ....   Friends of Creation Spirituality   (EA)
FCS ....   Fuel Computer System   (MCD)
FCSA ....   Federation Canadienne du Sport Automobile [*Canadian Automobile Sport Clubs*]

FCSA .... Fleet Chief Stores Accountant [*British military*] (DMA)
FCSA .... Flight Control Servo Assembly
FCSA .... Forest Conservation Society of America
FCSA .... Frequency Coordination System Association [*Ottawa, ON*] [*Telecommunications service*] (TSSD)
FCSAD ..... Free of Capture, Seizure, Arrest, and Detainment [*Insurance*]
FCSB .... Federation Canadienne du Sport Boules [*An association*] (EAIO)
FCSB .... Fellowship of Conservative Southern Baptists (EA)
FCSB .... Fire Control Switchboard
FCSB .... Fluid Circulation Storage Battery [*Automotive engineering*]
FCSC .... Federal Conversion Support Center (MCD)
FCSC .... Fire Control System Console [*Military*] (CAAL)
FCSC .... Fire Control System Coordinator
FCSC .... Fleet Command Support Center [*Navy*] (CAAL)
FCSC .... Foreign Claims Settlement Commission
FCSC Ann Rep ... Foreign Claims Settlement Commission. Annual Report [*A publication*] (DLA)
FCSC Dec & Ann ... Foreign Claims Settlement Commission. Decisions and Annotations [*A publication*] (DLA)
FCSCDG ... Fleet Command Support Center Development Group [*Navy*] (MCD)
FCSCJ .... Filiae a Caritate Sacri Corde Jesus [*Daughters of Charity of the Sacred Heart of Jesus*] [*Roman Catholic religious order*]
FC (Scott) .. Faculty of Advocates Collection of Decisions, Scotch Court of Sessions [*A publication*] (DLA)
FCSCUS... Federal Claims Settlement Commission of the United States
FCSCWO .. Fleet Command Support Center Watch Officer [*Navy*] (MCD)
FC & SCWSL ... Fire Control and Small Caliber Weapon Systems Laboratory [*Picatinny Arsenal, Dover, NJ*] [*Army*] (RDA)
FCSD .... Flight Crew Support Division [*NASA*] (KSC)
FCSG .... Fire Control Sensor Group
FCSG .... Flight Control Sensor Group
FCSG .... Focusing
FCSI .... FCS Laboratories, Inc. [*NASDAQ symbol*] (NQ)
FCSI .... Fellow of the Construction Surveyors' Institute [*British*] (DBQ)
FCSI .... Foodservice Consultants Society International (EA)
FCSL .... Fire Control System Laboratory
FCSLA ...... First Catholic Slovak Ladies Association (EA)
FCSLE....... Forecastle (KSC)
FCSLU ...... First Catholic Slovak Ladies Union [*Later, FCSLA*] (EA)
FCSM .... Fire Control System Module
FCSM .... Flight Combustion-Stability Monitor [*Apollo*] [*NASA*]
FCSN........ Federation for Children with Special Needs (EA)
FCSO .... Full Career Seaman Officer [*Navy*] [*British*]
FCSP .... Fellow of the Chartered Society of Physiotherapy [*British*]
FCSP .... Sisters of Charity of Providence [*Religious order*]
FCSPASTU ... Federation of Civil Service and Primary Aided School Teachers' Unions [*Mauritius*]
FCSRCC.... Free of Capture, Seizure, Riots, and Civil Commotions [*Insurance*]
FCSRT....... Fellow of the Canadian Society of Radiological Technicians
FCSS.......... Federal Civil Service System
FCSS.......... Federation Canadienne des Sciences Sociales [*Social Science Federation of Canada - SSFC*]
FCSS.......... Federation Canadienne de Sport Scolaire [*Canadian Federation of Provincial School Athletic Associations*]
FCSS.......... Fire Control Sight System [*Military*]
FCSS.......... Flight Control Systems Section
FCSS.......... Frost, Cog, and Screwmakers' Society [*A union*] [*British*]
FCSS.......... Fuel Cell Servicing System (MCD)
FCS(SA) .... Fellow of the College of Surgeons of South Africa
FCS(SoAf) ... Fellow of the College of Surgeons of South Africa
FCST .... Federal Council for Science and Technology [*Later, FSPC, FCCSET*] [*Executive Office of President*]
FCST .... Fellow of the College of Speech Therapists [*British*]
FCST .... Flat Cable Stripping Tool
FCST .... Forecast (AFM)
FCST-CORR ... Federal Council for Science and Technology - Committee on Water Resources Research (NOAA)
FCSTD ...... Fleet Chief Steward [*British military*] (DMA)
FCSU......... Fire Control Simulator Unit
FCSU......... Fire Control Switching Unit
FCSU......... First Catholic Slovak Union of the USA and Canada (EA)
FCSU......... Freon Coolant Servicing Unit (MCD)
FCSUM..... Federation of Civil Service Unions of Mauritius
FCSUS....... Foundation of California State University, Sacramento [*Research center*] (RCD)
FCSWB .... Fire Control Switchboard
FCSWBD .. Fire Control Switchboard
FCT........... Face-Centered Tetragonal [*Crystallography*]
FCT........... Facet Enterprises, Inc. [*NYSE symbol*] (SPSG)
FCT........... Factory (KSC)
FCT........... Fatigue Cracking Test
FCT........... Federal Capital Territory [*Later, ACT*] [*Australia*]
FCT........... Federal Court of Canada
FCT........... Federation Canadienne du Travail [*Canadian Federation of Labour - CFL*]
FCT........... Filament Center Tap
FCT........... Final Contract Trials [*Navy*]
FCT........... Financial Correlation Table

FCT........... Fire Control Technician [*Navy rating*] [*Obsolete*]
FCT........... Fire Control Trainer
FCT........... First City Trust Co. [*Toronto Stock Exchange symbol*]
FCT........... Flight Control Team (MCD)
FCT........... Flight Crew Trainer [*NASA*] (KSC)
FCT........... Flux-Corrected Transport [*Algorithm*]
FCT........... Food Composition Table
FCT........... Foreign Currency Translation (ADA)
FCT........... Foundation for Christian Theology (EA)
FCT........... Fraction Thereof
FCT........... Fragment Connection Table [*Chemistry*]
FCT........... Fuel Cell Test (MCD)
FCT........... Full Cleanliness Training
FCT........... Function
FCT........... Yakima, WA [*Location identifier*] [*FAA*] (FAAL)
FCTA........ Flow Control Time of Arrival [*Aviation*] (FAAC)
FCTB .... Featherston Camp Trumpet Band [*British military*] (DMA)
FCTB .... Fellow of the College of Teachers of the Blind
FCTB .... Financial Center Bancorp [*NASDAQ symbol*] (NQ)
FCTB .... Flight Crew Training Building [*NASA*] (KSC)
FCTC .... Fleet Combat Training Center [*Navy*] (NVT)
FCTCA ...... Federal Capital Territory Cricket Association [*Australia*]
FCTCAA .... Flowers-Costello Test of Central Auditory Abilities
FCTCSC.... Flue-Cured Tobacco Cooperative Stabilization Corporation (EA)
FCTE .... Fire Control Test Equipment
FCTF .... Five Civilized Tribes Foundation (EA)
FCTF .... Flue-Cured Tobacco Farmer [*A publication*]
FCTF .... Fuel Cell Test Facility (MCD)
FCTGA ...... Flue-Cured Tobacco Growers Association (EA)
FCTN........ First Federal Savings & Loan Association [*NASDAQ symbol*] (NQ)
FCTN........ Function (MSA)
FCTOD7.... Food and Chemical Toxicology [*A publication*]
FCTP .... Field Challenge Test Plan
FCTP .... Fire Control Test Package
FCTR .... First Charter Corp. [*NASDAQ symbol*] (NQ)
FCTRL ...... Final Contractor's Trial (NVT)
FCTS .... Fire Control Test Set
FCTS .... Firing Circuit Test Set
FCTS .... Flight Control Test Stand [*Aviation*]
FCTS .... Flight Crew Trainer Simulator [*NASA*] (KSC)
F Ct Sess ... Fraser's Scotch Court of Sessions Cases [*A publication*] (DLA)
FCTT .... Fuel Cladding Transient Tester [*Nuclear energy*] (NRCH)
FCTXAV ... Food and Cosmetics Toxicology [*A publication*]
FCTY .... Factory (MUGU)
FCTYA ...... Factory [*A publication*]
FCU .... Fan Coil Unit (NRCH)
FCU .... Fare Construction Unit [*Airlines*]
FCU .... Federal Credit Unions Bureau
FCU .... Field Communication Unit [*Military*]
FCU .... Fighter Control Unit [*Military*] [*British*]
FCU .... File Control Unit
FCU .... Fire Control Unit
FCU .... Flight Control Unit
FCU .... Fluid Checkout Unit (MCD)
FCU .... Force Control Unit
FCU .... Format Conversion Unit [*Data processing*]
FCU .... Frequency Converter Unit
FCU .... Fuel Consumption Unit (NATG)
FCUA .... Federal Credit Union Administration
FCUA .... Federated Clerks' Union of Australia
FCUA .... Fuel-Critical, Unspecified Area
F CUL .... Film Culture [*A publication*]
F Cultura.... Filme Cultura [*A publication*]
F Culture.... Film Culture [*A publication*]
FCUMS...... Federation of Computer Users in the Medical Sciences (EA)
FCUSA ...... Finance Center, United States Army
FCV........... Facility Checkout Vehicle [*NASA*] (KSC)
FCV........... Feline Calicivirus
FCV........... Fellow of College of Violinists [*British*] (ROG)
FCV........... Flight Checkout Vehicle
FCV........... Flow Control Valve
FC²V .... Future Command and Control Vehicle
FCVN......... Friends of Children of Vietnam (EA)
FCVRE ...... Funders Committee for Voter Registration and Education (EA)
FCVS .... FORTRAN [*Formula Translating System*] Compiler Validation System [*Data processing*]
FCW .... Fire Control Workshop
FCW .... Flight Crew Workload [*Navy*]
FCW .... Flyer Coil Winder
FCW .... Format Control Word (NASA)
FCWA........ Fellow of the Chartered Institute of Cost and Work Accountants [*British*] (EY)
FCWBWU ... Fancy Cane, Wicker, and Bamboo Workers' Union [*British*]
FCWG .... Frequency Coordination Working Group (MUGU)
FCWRENAF ... Fleet Chief WREN [*Women's Royal Naval Service*] Air Fitter [*British military*] (DMA)
FCWRENCINE ... Fleet Chief WREN [*Women's Royal Naval Service*] Cinema Operator [*British military*] (DMA)

FCWRENCK ... Fleet Chief WREN [*Women's Royal Naval Service*] Cook [*British military*] (DMA)
FCWRENDHYG ... Fleet Chief WREN [*Women's Royal Naval Service*] Dental Hygienist [*British military*] (DMA)
FCWRENDSA ... Fleet Chief WREN [*Women's Royal Naval Service*] Dental Surgery Assistant [*British military*] (DMA)
FCWRENEDUC ... Fleet Chief WREN [*Women's Royal Naval Service*] Education Assistant [*British military*] (DMA)
FCWRENMET ... Fleet Chief WREN [*Women's Royal Naval Service*] Meteorological Observer [*British military*] (DMA)
FCWRENPHOT ... Fleet Chief WREN [*Women's Royal Naval Service*] Photographer [*British military*] (DMA)
FCWRENQA ... Fleet Chief WREN [*Women's Royal Naval Service*] Quarters Assistant [*British military*] (DMA)
FCWREN(R) ... Fleet Chief WREN [*Women's Royal Naval Service*] (RADAR) [*British military*] (DMA)
FCWRENREG ... Fleet Chief WREN [*Women's Royal Naval Service*] Regulating [*British military*] (DMA)
FCWRENREL ... Fleet Chief WREN [*Women's Royal Naval Service*] Radio Electrician [*British military*] (DMA)
FCWRENRS(M) ... Fleet Chief WREN [*Women's Royal Naval Service*] Radio Supervisor (Morse) [*British military*] (DMA)
FCWRENSA ... Fleet Chief WREN [*Women's Royal Naval Service*] Stores Accountant [*British military*] (DMA)
FCWRENSTD ... Fleet Chief WREN [*Women's Royal Naval Service*] Steward [*British military*] (DMA)
FCWRENTEL ... Fleet Chief WREN [*Women's Royal Naval Service*] Telephonist [*British military*] (DMA)
FCWRENTSA ... Fleet Chief WREN [*Women's Royal Naval Service*] Training Support Assistant [*British military*] (DMA)
FCWRENWA ... Fleet Chief WREN [*Women's Royal Naval Service*] Weapon Analyst [*British military*] (DMA)
FCWRENWTR(G) ... Fleet Chief WREN [*Women's Royal Naval Service*] Writer (General) [*British military*] (DMA)
FCWRENWTR(P) ... Fleet Chief WREN [*Women's Royal Naval Service*] Writer (Pay) [*British military*] (DMA)
FCWRENWW ... Fleet Chief WREN [*Women's Royal Naval Service*] Welfare Worker [*British military*] (DMA)
FCWTC ..... Friends Committee on War Tax Concerns (EA)
f-cx--- .... Central African Republic [*MARC geographic area code*] [*Library of Congress*] (LCCP)
FCX........... Freeport McMoRan Copper & Gold [*NYSE symbol*] (SPSG)
FCx .... Frontal Cortex [*Neuroanatomy*]
FCY........... Fancy (ROG)
FCY........... Federation Canadienne de Yachting [*Canadian Yachting Association*]
FCY........... First City Financial Corp. Ltd. [*Toronto Stock Exchange symbol*] [*Vancouver Stock Exchange symbol*]
FCY........... First City Industries, Inc. [*NYSE symbol*] (SPSG)
FCY........... Forrest City, AR [*Location identifier*] [*FAA*] (FAAL)
FCYP .... Florida Cypress Gardens [*NASDAQ symbol*] (NQ)
FCZ........... Fishery Conservation Zone
FCZ........... Forward Combat Zone (NATG)
Fd .... Dilution Factor [*Also, DF*] [*Nuclear energy*] (NRCH)
FD .... Face of Drawing (AAG)
FD .... Facilities and Design (MCD)
F & D .... Facilities and Design (KSC)
FD .... Facility Drawing
FD .... Failure Definition (MCD)
FD .... Familial Dysautonomia [*Medicine*]
FD .... Fan Douche [*Medicine*]
FD .... Fanfulla della Domenica [*A publication*]
Fd .... Fantail Darter [*Ichthyology*]
FD .... Fascia Dentata [*Brain anatomy*]
FD .... Fatal Dose
FD .... Fault Detection (MCD)
FD .... Fault Directory
FD .... Federal Directive
FD .... Federal Document (AFM)
FD .... Feed (MSA)
FD .... Female Domination
FD .... Female Treated with DOC [*Deoxycorticosterone*]
Fd .... Ferredoxin [*Biochemistry*]
FD .... Fiber Duct [*Telecommunications*] (TEL)
FD .... Fidei Defensor [*Defender of the Faith*] [*Latin*]
FD .... Field
FD .... Field Decelerating Contactor or Relay [*Industrial control*] (IEEE)
FD .... Field Desorption
FD .... Field Director
FD .... Field of Drawing (AAG)
FD .... Fighter Direction
FD .... File Definition [*Data processing*]
FD .... File Description
FD .... File Directory
FD .... Fill/Drain (MCD)
F & D .... Fill and Drain (AAG)
F a D .... Film a Divadio [*A publication*]
FD .... Filosofska Dumka [*A publication*]
F/D .... Filter/Demineralizer (NRCH)
FD .... Finance Department

F and D ...... Finance and Development [*A publication*]
FD .... Finance Docket
FD .... Financial Director
FD .... Financieel Dagblad [*A publication*]
F & D .... Findings and Determination (AFM)
FD .... Finished Dialing [*Telecommunications*] (TEL)
FD .... Fire Department
FD .... Fire Detector
FD .... Fire Direction
FD .... Fire District [*Australia*]
FD .... Fire Drop (AABC)
FD .... First Day [*Philately*]
FD .... First Defense [*Men's lacrosse position*]
FD .... First Down [*Football*]
Fd .... Fjord [*Maps and charts*]
FD .... Flame Deflector
FD .... Flange Focal Distance (IEEE)
FD .... Fleet Duties [*British military*] (DMA)
FD .... Flexible Disk
FD .... Flight Day (MCD)
FD .... Flight Deck (MCD)
FD .... Flight Delay (MCD)
FD .... Flight Director [*NASA*] (KSC)
FD .... Floor Drain [*Technical drawings*]
FD .... Floppy Disk [*Data processing*] (BUR)
FD .... Fluctuation-Dissipation [*Theorem*] [*Statistical mechanics*]
FD .... Fluorescence Detection [*Spectrometry*]
FD .... Focal Diameter
FD .... Focal Distance
FD .... Fog Diaphone [*Navigation charts*]
FD .... Fold
FD .... Folin-Denis [*Analytical chemistry*]
FD .... Fonetica si Dialectologie [*A publication*]
F & D .... Fonetica si Dialectologie [*A publication*]
FD .... Food
FD .... Food Distribution Division [*of AMS, Department of Agriculture*]
FD .... Foot Drape [*Medicine*]
FD .... Forbush Decrease [*Geophysics*]
FD .... Force Development
FD .... Force Displacement [*Sports medicine*]
FD .... Forced Draft
FD .... Forceps Delivery [*Obstetrics*]
FD .... Ford (ROG)
FD .... Ford of Europe, Inc. [*United Kingdom*] [*ICAO designator*] (ICDA)
FD .... Ford Motor Co. Ltd. [*Great Britain*] [*ICAO designator*] (FAAC)
FD .... Formal Decorative [*Horticulture*]
FD .... Fort Detrick [*Maryland*] [*Army*] (MCD)
FD .... Forward (ADA)
FD .... Found (MSA)
FD .... Fourth Dimension [*Time*] (AAG)
FD .... Fractional Destraction [*Supercritical distillation*]
FD .... Frame Difference
FD .... Framed [*Construction*]
FD .... Framework Density [*Crystallography*]
FD .... Franc [*Monetary unit*] [*French Somaliland*]
FD .... Franc Djibouti [*Monetary unit*]
FD .... Franco Domicile [*Shipping*] (DS)
FD .... Free Delivery
FD .... Free Discharge
FD .... Free Dispatch
FD .... Free Dock [*Business term*]
FD .... Free Drop
FD .... Freeze-Dried
F & D .... Freight and Demurrage [*Shipping*]
FD .... Freight Department
FD .... Frequency Demodulator
FD .... Frequency Discrimination [*Neurophysiology*]
FD .... Frequency Distance [*Telecommunications*] (TEL)
FD .... Frequency Diversity
FD .... Frequency Division
FD .... Frequency Doubler
FD .... Frequency Drift
FD .... Front of Dash [*Technical drawings*]
FD .... Front Door [*Shipping*]
FD .... Full Dress [*Colloquial reference to formal dress*]
FD .... Full Duplex [*Telecommunications*]
FD .... Function Designator (NASA)
FD .... Functional Description
FD .... Fund (ROG)
FD .... Fuze Delay
fd----- .... Sahara Desert [*MARC geographic area code*] [*Library of Congress*] (LCCP)
FD .... Winds and Temperatures Aloft Forecast [*Symbol*] [*National Weather Service*]
F 2d .... Federal Reporter, Second Series [*A publication*] (DLA)
FDA .... Fault Detection and Annunciation (NASA)
FDA .... Feather and Down Association (EA)

FDA .... Federal Domestic Assistance [*Catalog*] (OICC)
FDA .... Federal Drug Administration
FDA .... Federal Drug Administration. Publications [*A publication*]
FDA .... Ferrite Driver Amplifier
FDA .... Ferrocenedicarboxylic Acid [*Organic chemistry*]
FDA .... Fertilizer Dealers Association [*Defunct*] (EA)
FDA .... Final Delivered Article
FDA .... Final Design Acceptance [*or Approval or Authorization*]
FDA .... First Division Association [*British*]
FDA .... Flight Deck Assembly (MCD)
FDA .... Flight Detection and Annunciation (MCD)
FDA .... Florida Airlines, Inc. [*Tampa, FL*] [*FAA designator*] (FAAC)
FDA .... Florida State University, Tallahassee, FL [*OCLC symbol*] (OCLC)
FDA .... Fluorescein Diacetate [*Organic chemistry*]
FDA .... Flying Dentists Association (EA)
FDA .... Folded Dipole Antenna
FDA .... Food Distribution Administration [*Terminated, 1945*]
FDA .... Food and Drug Administration [*Rockville, MD*] [*Department of Health and Human Services*]
FDA .... Foreign Demographic Analysis Division [*Census*] (OICC)
FDA .... Freiburger Diozesanarchiv [*A publication*]
FDA .... Fremdenverkehr + das Reiseburo. Tourismus und Kongress [*A publication*]
FDA .... Frequency Distortion Analyzer
FDA .... Fronto-Dextra Anterior [*A fetal position*] [*Obstetrics*]
FDA .... Functional Demonstration and Acceptance (AAG)
FDA .... Functional Design Activity [*Army*]
FDA .... Functional Design Agency (MCD)
FDA .... Funeral Directors Association [*Australia*]
FDA .... Furniture Deliverers' Association
FDA .... Southern International Airways [*Tampa, FL*] [*FAA designator*] (FAAC)
FDAA .... Federal Disaster Assistance Administration [*FEMA*]
FDACB ..... FDA [*Food and Drug Administration*] Consumer [*A publication*]
FDA Clin Exp Abstr ... FDA [*Food and Drug Administration*] Clinical Experience Abstracts [*A publication*]
FDA Cons .. FDA [*Food and Drug Administration*] Consumer [*A publication*] (DLA)
FDA Consum ... FDA [*Food and Drug Administration*] Consumer [*A publication*]
FDA Consum Food Drug Adm ... FDA (Food and Drug Administration) Consumer [*A publication*]
FDADA ..... FDA [*Food and Drug Administration*] Drug Bulletin [*A publication*]
FDA Drug Bull ... FDA [*Food and Drug Administration*] Drug Bulletin [*A publication*]
FDA-EDRO ... Food and Drug Administration, Office of Executive Director of Regional Operations (NRCH)
FDAI .... Flight Direction and Altitude Indicator
FDAI......... Flight Director Attitude Indicator [*NASA*] (NASA)
FDANSW ... Funeral Directors Association of New South Wales [*Australia*]
FDA Pap.... FDA [*Food and Drug Administration*] Papers [*A publication*]
FDAS........ Field Depot Aviation Squadron [*Air Force*]
FDAS........ Flight Data Acquisition System
FDAS........ Frequency Distribution Analysis Sheet
FDAT........ Flight Data (FAAC)
FDATC..... Flying Division Air Training Command
FDAU .... Flight Data Acquisition Unit
FDB .... Fahrenheit Dry Bulb (KSC)
FDB .... Ferrari Data Bank (EA)
FDB .... Field Descriptor Block
FDB .... Field Dynamic Braking
FDB .... Fighter Dive-Bomber
FDB .... File Data Block [*Data processing*]
FDB .... Fleet Data Base [*Navy*] (CAAL)
FDB .... Flight Dynamics Branch [*NASA*] (KSC)
FDB .... Forced-Draft Blower
FDB .... Full Data Block (KSC)
FDB .... Functional Description Block [*Telecommunications*] (TEL)
FDb........... Volusia County Public Libraries, Daytona Beach, FL [*Library symbol*] [*Library of Congress*] (LCLS)
FDbBC...... Bethune-Cookman College, Daytona Beach, FL [*Library symbol*] [*Library of Congress*] (LCLS)
FDBC........ Flight Director Bombing Computer (MCD)
FDBK........ Feedback (MSA)
FDBK........ Founders Bank [*New Haven, CT*] [*NASDAQ symbol*] (NQ)
FDBLR...... Frequency Doubler (MSA)
FDBPS...... Fleet Database Production System [*Navy*] (MCD)
FDbY .... S. Cornelia Young Memorial Library, Daytona Beach, FL [*Library symbol*] [*Library of Congress*] (LCLS)
FDC .... Facility Design Criteria (AAG)
FDC .... Failure Diagnostic Code [*Military*] (AFIT)
FDC .... Fathers Day Council (EA)
FDC .... Federacion Democrata Cristiana [*Christian Democratic Federation*] [*Spain*] [*Political party*] (PPE)
FDC .... Federal Design Council (EA)
FDC .... Field Data Computer
FDC .... Field Discharge Chip

FDC .... Filiae Divinae Caritatis [*Daughters of Divine Charity*] [*Roman Catholic religious order*]
FDC .... Final Design Criteria
FDC .... Fire-Department Connection [*Technical drawings*]
FDC .... Fire Detection Center
FDC .... Fire Direction Center [*Military*]
FDC .... First-Day Cover [*Philately*]
FDC .... Fishery Data Center [*FAO*] (MSC)
FDC .... Fixed Decade Capacitor
FDC .... Fleur de Coin [*Mint state*] [*Numismatics*]
FDC .... Flight Data Center (FAAC)
FDC .... Flight Director Computer (MCD)
FDC .... Floppy Disk Controller [*Data processing*] (MDG)
FDC .... Florida Department of Citrus (EA)
FDC .... Fluid Digital Computer
FDC .... Follicular Dendritic Cell
FDC .... Food, Drug, and Cosmetic [*Act*]
FDC .... Formation Drone Control [*Navy*] (NG)
FDC .... Forward Direction Center [*Air Force*]
FDC .... Frederick Air Taxi Service, Inc. [*Frederick, MD*] [*FAA designator*] (FAAC)
FDC .... Freedom Defence Committee [*National Council for Civil Liberties*] [*British*]
FDC .... Frequency of Dividing Cells [*Bacteriology*]
FDC .... Frequency Domain Coding
FDC .... Functional Data Coordinator (MCD)
FDC .... Functional Design Criteria (NRCH)
FDCA...... Flying Disc Collectors Association (EA)
Fd Can ..... Food in Canada [*A publication*]
FDCCC...... First Day Cover Collectors Club (EA)
FDC Cont Newsl ... FDC [*Food, Drug, and Cosmetics*] Control Newsletter [*A publication*]
FDCD .... Facility Design Criteria Document (AAG)
FDCD .... Fluorescence-Detected Circular Dichroism [*Spectroscopy*]
Fd Chem News Guide ... Food Chemical News Guide [*A publication*]
Fd Chem Toxic ... Food and Chemical Toxicology [*A publication*]
FDCO .... Defense Foreign Disclosure Coordinating Office
FDCOA .... Fundicao [*A publication*]
Fd Cosmet Toxicol ... Food and Cosmetics Toxicology [*A publication*]
FD Cosm L Rep ... Food, Drug, Cosmetic Law Reporter [*Commerce Clearing House*] [*A publication*] (DLA)
FDCPA...... Fair Debt Collection Practices Act
FDCPA...... Food, Drug, and Consumer Product Agency [*Proposed successor to FDA*] [*HEW*]
FDCS......... Fighter Director Control Schools [*Navy*]
FDCS......... Flight Deck Communication System [*Navy*] (CAAL)
FDCS......... Functionally Distributed Computing System
FDCSB7 .... Faraday Discussions of the Chemical Society [*A publication*]
FDCT......... Fast Discrete Cosine Transform (MCD)
FDCT......... Franck Drawing Completion Test [*Psychology*]
FDCT......... Frequency Domain Coding Technique
FDCU .... Fire Detector Control Unit (MCD)
FDD .... Flexible Disk Drive
FDD .... Floating Digital Drive
FDD .... Floating Dry Dock [*Navy*]
FDD .... Floppy Disk Drive [*Data processing*]
FDD .... Food and Drug Directorate [*Canada*]
FDD .... Foreign Document Division [*of CIA*]
FdD .... Fouilles de Delphes [*A publication*]
FDD .... Franc de Droits [*Free of Charge*] [*Business term*] [*French*]
FD & D ...... Freight, Demurrage, and Defense [*Shipping*] (DS)
FDDB .... Function Designator Database (MCD)
FDDC .... Ferric Dimethyldithiocarbamate [*A fungicide*]
FDDC .... Flight Deck Debarkation Control [*Navy*] (CAAL)
FDDI......... Fiber Distributed Data Interface [*AMP Products Corp.*]
FDDL........ Frequency-Division Data Link [*Radio*]
FDDM .... Fort Dodge, Des Moines & Southern Railway Co. [*AAR code*]
FDDM & S ... Fort Dodge, Des Moines & Southern Railway Co.
FDDR........ Field Deviation Disposition Request [*Nuclear energy*] (NRCH)
FDDS........ Federation of Dental Diagnostic Sciences (EA)
FDDS........ Federation of Digestive Disease Societies [*Defunct*] (EA)
FDDS........ FLAG [*FORTRAN Load and Go*] Data Display System (MCD)
FDDS........ Flight Data Distribution System
FDE .... Federal Express Corp. [*Little Rock, AR*] [*FAA designator*] (FAAC)
FDE .... Female-Day-Equivalent [*Entomology*]
FDE .... Field Decelerator
FDE .... Flaw Detection Equipment
FD & E ...... Follow-On Development Test and Evaluation (MCD)
FDE .... Forde [*Norway*] [*Airport symbol*] (OAG)
FDE .... Frente Democratico Eleitoral [*Democratic Electoral Front*] [*Portugal*] [*Political party*] (PPE)
FDE .... Functional Differential Equation
FDEC........ Fluidyne Engineering Corporation (KSC)
FDEC........ Forum for Death Education and Counseling [*Later, ADEC*] (EA)
FDEC........ Forum for Death Education and Counseling. Newsletter [*A publication*]
FDEN .... Females, Density Of [*Ecology*]
FDEO .... Flight Development Engineering Order (MCD)

FDEP........... Final Draft Equipment Publication (MCD)
FDEP........... Flight Data Entry Panel
FDEP........... Flight Data Entry and Printout [Aviation] (FAAC)
FDEP........... Formatted Data Entry Program [Mohawk Data Systems]
FDET........... Force Development Experimentation Testing (MCD)
FDEVDS ... Food Development [A publication]
FDF........... Failure Density Function
FDF........... Fast Death Factor [Medicine]
FDF........... Flame Deflector Firex
FDF........... Flight Data File [NASA] (NASA)
FDF........... Flush Door Fastener
FDF........... Food Defense Fund (EA)
FDF........... Food and Drink Federation [England and Belgium]
FDF........... Form Die Forge (MCD)
FDF........... Fort-De-France [Martinique] [Airport symbol] (OAG)
FDF........... Fort-De-France [Morne Des Cadets] [Martinique]
              [Seismograph station code, US Geological Survey] (SEIS)
FDF........... Front Democratique des Bruxellois Francophones [French-
              Speaking Democratic Front] [Belgium] [Political
              party] (PPW)
F & DF....... Fuel and Defueling (MSA)
FDF........... Fundamentally Different Factors [Environmental Protection
              Agency]
FDF........... Further Differentiated Fibroblast [Cytology]
FD/FF....... Flux Delta/Flux Flow (IEEE)
FD/FL....... Fault Detection/Fault Location [Military] (CAAL)
FDFL......... Fluid Flow
Fd Flavs Ingredients Process Packag ... Food: Flavouring Ingredients
              Processing and Packaging [A publication]
FDG........... Feeding
FDG........... Fermi-Dirac Gas
FDG........... Flight Director Group (MCD)
FDG........... Flight Dynamics Group [NASA] (KSC)
FDG........... Fluorodeoxyglucose [Organic chemistry]
FDG........... Fly Dressers Guild [Pinner, Middlesex, England] (EAIO)
FDG........... Folk Dance Guide [A publication]
FDG........... Fractional Doppler Gate
FDG........... Funding
FDG........... Fur Dressers Guild (EA)
FDGB........ Freier Deutscher Gewerkschaftsbund [Free German Trade
              Union Federation] [German Democratic Republic]
              [Political party] (PPE)
FDGC........ Federated Guaranty Corporation [Montgomery, AL]
              [NASDAQ symbol] (NQ)
FDGD........ Nhlangano [Swaziland] [ICAO location identifier] (ICLI)
FDGK........ Fukui Daigaku Gakugeigakubu Kiyo [A publication]
FDGL........ Lavumisa [Swaziland] [ICAO location identifier] (ICLI)
FDGM....... Final Defense Guidance Memorandum [Navy]
FDH........... Familial Dysalbuminemic Hyperthyroxinemia [Medicine]
FDH........... Floating Divide or Halt
FDH........... Formate Dehydrogenase [An enzyme]
FDH........... Friedrichshafen [West Germany] [Airport symbol] (OAG)
FDHD........ Floppy Disk High-Density [Data processing]
FDHDB.... Flight Deck Hazardous Duty Billet [Navy]
FDHDP.... Flight Deck Hazardous Duty Pay [Navy]
FDHE........ Faculty Directory of Higher Education [A publication]
FDHRS..... Freies Deutsches Hochstift: Reihe der Schriften [A publication]
FDI........... Failure Detection and Isolation (MCD)
FDI........... Failure Detector Indicator (NASA)
FDI........... Fault Detection and Identification (MCD)
FDI........... Fault Detection and Isolation (NASA)
FDI........... Federal Deposit Insurance Corp., Washington, DC [OCLC
              symbol] (OCLC)
FDI........... Federation Dentaire Internationale [International Dental
              Federation] [London, England] (EA)
FDI........... Feeder Distribution Interface [Bell System]
FDI........... Field Discharge
FDI........... Field Displacement Isolator
FDI........... Field Disposition Instruction [Nuclear energy] (NRCH)
FDI........... First Day of Issue [Philately]
FDI........... First Devonian Explorations [Vancouver Stock Exchange
              symbol]
FDI........... First Dorsal Interosseous Muscle [Myology]
FDI........... Flight Direction Indicator
FDI........... Follicle Development Index [Gynecology]
FDI........... Food and Disarmament International [Brussels,
              Belgium] (EAIO)
FDI........... Food Engineering [A publication]
FDI........... Foreign Direct Investment
FDI........... Form Die Impact (MCD)
FDI........... Formal Documents Issued [Federal Power Commission]
FDI........... Fuel Desulphurization, Incorporated
FDI........... Poplar Bluff, MO [Location identifier] [FAA] (FAAL)
FDIA......... Fellow of the Design Institute of Australia
FDIADJ .... Frontiers in Diabetes [A publication]
FDIC......... Federal Deposit Insurance Corporation [Independent
              government agency] [Database]
FDIC......... Fire Department Instructors Conference (EA)
FDIC......... Flying Days per Inspection Cycle [Air Force] (AFIT)
FDIC......... Food and Drink Industries Council [British]
FDICA....... Foundations and Donors Interested in Catholic Activities (EA)

F Dict .... Kames and Woodhouselee's Folio Dictionary, Scotch Court of
              Session [A publication] (DLA)
FDIF .... Federation Democratique Internationale des Femmes
              [Women's International Democratic Federation - WIDF]
              [Berlin, German Democratic Republic] (EAIO)
FDIIA6 ...... Food Irradiation Information [A publication]
FDIIR .... Fault Detection, Isolation, Identification, and
              Recompensation (NASA)
FDIM......... Federacion Democratica Internacional de Mujeres [Women's
              International Democratic Federation]
F-DIM ...... Fluorescence Digital Imaging Microscopy
Fd Inds....... Food Industries [A publication]
FDIR.......... Fault Detection Identification/Isolation and Recovery/
              Recognition (NASA)
FDIR.......... Fronteer Directory Co., Inc. [NASDAQ symbol] (NQ)
F Directions ... Film Directions [A publication]
FDIS.......... Flight Displays and Interface System (NVT)
FDIS.......... Freeway Driver Information System
FDIU .... Fetal Death in Utero [Medicine]
FDJ............ Filles de Jesus [Sons of Jesus] [Religious order]
FDj............ Franc Djibouti [Monetary unit]
FDJ............ Free Diffusion Junction [Electrochemistry]
FDJ............ Freie Deutsche Jugend [Free German Youth] [German
              Democratic Republic] [Political party] (PPE)
FDK........... Frederick, MD [Location identifier] [FAA] (FAAL)
FDKNEF ... Bulletin. Fukuoka University of Education. Part 3.
              Mathematics, Natural Sciences, and Technology [A
              publication]
FDL........... Fast Deployment Logistics Ship [Navy symbol]
FDL........... Ferndale [Cardiff] [Welsh depot code]
FDL........... Fick Diffusion Law
FDL........... Fish Disease Leaflet
FDL........... Fixed Delay Line
FDL........... Fleur-de-Lys [Heraldry]
FDL........... Flight Determination Laboratory [WSMR]
FDL........... Flight Director Loop (MCD)
FDL........... Flight Dynamic Laboratory [Air Force]
FDL........... Foremost [or Forward] Defended Localities [or Locations]
              [British]
FdL............ Forum der Letteren [A publication]
FDL........... Forward Defended Locality [Military] [British]
FDL........... Frequency Double LASER
FDL........... Fuehrer der Luft [Air liaison officer with Navy] [German
              military - World War II]
FDlb.......... Delray Beach Library, Delray Beach, FL [Library symbol]
              [Library of Congress] (LCLS)
FDLB......... Faraday Laboratories, Inc. [NASDAQ symbol] (NQ)
FDLD......... Frequency Doubling LASER Device
FDLH......... Flight Determination Laboratory, Holloman Air Force Base
FDLI .... Food and Drug Law Institute
FDLJAO ... Food, Drug, Cosmetic Law Journal [A publication]
FDLN .... Feedline (NASA)
FDLN .... Food Lion, Inc. [NASDAQ symbol] (NQ)
FDLN .... Forced-Draft, Low-Nitrogen Oxide [Combustion engineering]
FDLS .... Fast Deployment Logistics Ship [Navy]
FD/LS....... Fault Detection/Location Subsystem
FDLUQ ..... Fronte Democratica Liberale dell'Uomo Qualunque [Liberal
              Democratic Front of the Common Man] [Italy] [Political
              party] (PPE)
f-dm--- .... Dahomey [Benin] [MARC geographic area code] [Library of
              Congress] (LCCP)
FDM .... Faraday Disc Machine
FDM .... Feasibility Demonstration Model
FDM .... Flight Data Manager (MCD)
FDM .... Formal Development Method [Data processing]
FDM .... Freedom Airlines, Inc. [Binghamton, NY] [FAA
              designator] (FAAC)
FDM .... Frequency Data Multiplexer (NASA)
FDM .... Frequency Deviation Meter
FDM .... Frequency-Division Multiplex [Telecommunications]
FDM .... Full Descriptive Method
FDM .... Functional Development Model (MCD)
FDM .... Fund for a Democratic Majority (EA)
FDM .... Fundamental Design Method
FDM .... Furniture Design and Manufacturing [A publication]
FDMA ...... Ferrocarril de Minatitlan al Carmen [AAR code]
FDMA ...... Fibre Drum Manufacturers Association [Defunct]
FDMA ...... Frequency-Division Multiple Access
              [Telecommunications] (MCD)
FDMB ...... Mbabane [Swaziland] [ICAO location identifier] (ICLI)
FDMC ...... First Data Management Company, Inc. [NASDAQ
              symbol] (NQ)
FDMC ...... Fiscal Director of the Marine Corps
FDMD ...... Foundation for Depression and Manic Depression (EA)
Fd Mf........ Food Manufacture [A publication]
FDM/FM .. Frequency Division Multiplex/Frequency Modulation
              [Telecommunications] (TEL)
FDMH ...... Mhlume [Swaziland] [ICAO location identifier] (ICLI)
FDMHA ... Frederick Douglass Memorial and Historical Association (EA)
FDMIS ...... Force Development Management Information System [Army]
FDMR ...... Fluorescence-Detected Magnetic Resonance [Physics]

FD-MS ...... Field Desorption - Mass Spectrometry
FDMS........ Flight Data Management System [*Air Force*]   (AFM)
FDMS........ Force Development Management Information System [*Army*]   (MCD)
FDMS........ Frequency-Division Multiplexing System [*Radio*]   (MCD)
FDMS........ Manzini/Matsapa [*Swaziland*] [*ICAO location identifier*]   (ICLI)
FDMVC..... Frequency-Division Multiplex Voice Communication
FDN......... Field Designator Number [*Air Force*]   (AFM)
Fdn........... Fonodan [*Record label*] [*Denmark*]
FDN.......... Foreign Directory Name [*Telecommunications*]   (TEL)
FDN.......... Foundation   (KSC)
FDN.......... Fuerza Democratica Nicaraguense [*Nicaraguan Democratic Force*]   (PD)
FDN.......... Future Digital Network   (MCD)
FDNB........ Fluorodinitrobenzene [*Also, DFB, DNFB*] [*Organic chemistry*]
FDNC........ Frequency Dependent Negative Conductance [*Physics*]
FDNET....... Fighter Direction Net [*Navy*]
FDNG........ Feeding
FDNR........ Frequency Dependent Negative Resistance [*Physics*]
Fd Nutr ...... Food and Nutrition [*A publication*]
Fd Nutr Notes Rev ... Food and Nutrition. Notes and Reviews [*A publication*]   (APTA)
Fd Nutr Notes Revs ... Food and Nutrition. Notes and Reviews [*A publication*]   (APTA)
FDO.......... Faculty of Dispensing Opticians [*British*]
FDO.......... Family Dollar Stores, Inc. [*NYSE symbol*]   (SPSG)
FDO.......... Fee Determination Official   (NASA)
FDO.......... Field Director Overseas [*Red Cross*]
FDO.......... Fighter Director Officer [*Navy*]
FDO.......... Fighter Duty Officer
FDO.......... Fire Direction Officer [*Army*]   (AABC)
FDO.......... Fleet Aircraft Direction Officer [*Navy*] [*British*]
FDO.......... Fleet Dental Officer
FDO.......... Flight Deck Officer [*British military*]   (DMA)
FDO.......... Flight Duty Officer [*Air Force*]   (AFM)
FDO.......... Flight Dynamics Officer [*NASA*]   (KSC)
FDO.......... Food Distribution Order
F Doba ..... Film a Doba [*A publication*]
F & Doba.... Film a Doba [*A publication*]
FDOI......... First Day of Issue [*Philately*]
FDOK........ Fidelity of Oklahoma [*NASDAQ symbol*]   (NQ)
FDOP .... Filtered Detection Only Processor   (CAAL)
F Dope....... Film Dope [*A publication*]
FDOR........ Flight Design Operations Review   (MCD)
FDOS........ Floppy Disk Operating System [*Data processing*]   (IEEE)
FDP........... Fast Digital Processor [*Data processing*]
FDP........... Fibrin [*or Fibrinogen*] Degradation Products [*Hematology*]
FDP........... Field Data Processing
FDP........... Field Development Program [*LIMRA*]
FDP........... Fighter Director Post
FDP........... Filii Divinae Providentiae [*Sons or Daughters of Divine Providence*] [*Roman Catholic religious order*]
FDP........... Final Design Presentation   (NOAA)
FDP........... Flare Dispenser Pod
FDP........... Flexor Digitorum Profundus [*Anatomy*]
FDP........... Flight Data Processing   (KSC)
FDP........... Flight Demonstration Program   (MCD)
FDP........... Flood Damage Prevention [*Type of water project*]
FDP........... Food Distribution Program [*Department of Agriculture*]
FDP........... Foodpress, Economisch, en Technisch Weekblad voor de Voedingsmiddelenindustrie en Genotmiddelenindustrie en Groothandel in de Benelux [*A publication*]
FDP........... Foreign Duty Pay
FDP........... Form Die Press   (MCD)
FDP........... Forward Defense Post   (NATG)
FDP........... Forward Director Post
FDP........... Forward Distribution Point [*Military*]
FDP........... Four Decades of Poetry 1890-1930 [*A publication*]
FDP........... Free Democrat Party [*Turkey*] [*Political party*]
FDP........... Freedom Democratic Party [*in Mississippi*]
FDP........... Freeze Desalination Plant
FDP........... Freie Demokratische Partei [*Free Democratic Party*] [*Federal Republic of Germany*] [*Political party*]   (EAIO)
FDP........... Freisinnig-Demokratische Partei der Schweiz [*Radical Democratic Party of Switzerland*]   (PPW)
FDP........... Fronto-Dextra Posterior [*A fetal position*] [*Obstetrics*]
FDP........... Frontul Democratic Popular [*Democratic Popular Front*] [*Romania*] [*Political party*]   (PPE)
FDP........... Fructose Diphosphate [*Biochemistry*]
FDP........... Full Dog Point   (MSA)
FDP........... Funded Delivery Period [*DoD*]
FDPC........ FDP Corporation [*NASDAQ symbol*]   (NQ)
FDPC........ Federal Data Processing Centers
FDPC........ Fluorimetric Determination of Plasma Cortisol [*Clinical chemistry*]
F & D Pkg .. Food and Drug Packaging [*A publication*]
FDPL........ Fluid Pressure Line   (MSA)
FDPM........ Final Draft, Presidential Memorandum [*DoD*]
FDPO........ Field Post Office [*Military*] [*British*]
FDPO .... Foreign Disclosure Policy Office [*Military*]   (AFIT)

FDPRBZ.... FAO [*Food and Agriculture Organization of the United Nations*] Development Program [*A publication*]
Fd Process ... Food Processing [*A publication*]
Fd Process Ind ... Food Processing Industry [*A publication*]
Fd Process Market ... Food Processing and Marketing [*Chicago*] [*A publication*]
Fd Process Packag ... Food Processing and Packaging [*A publication*]
Fd Prod Dev ... Food Product Development [*A publication*]
FDPS........ Field Developed Programs [*Data processing*]
FD/PSK..... Frequency-Differential/Phase-Shift Keyed System [*Data processing*]
FDQ......... Florida Designers Quarterly [*A publication*]
FDQA .... Flight Development Quality Assurance   (MCD)
FDQTA..... Fields and Quanta [*A publication*]
FDR .... Facility Data Report [*Nuclear energy*]
FDR .... Fact, Discussion, Recommendations
FDR .... Fahrdienstregelement [*Traffic Service Regulations*] [*German*]
F & DR...... Failure and Discrepancy Reporting   (KSC)
FDR .... Fairleigh Dickinson University, Rutherford, NJ [*OCLC symbol*]   (OCLC)
FDR .... Federal Document Retrieval [*Information service or system*]   (IID)
FDR .... Feeder
FDR .... File Data Register [*Data processing*]
FDR .... Final Data Report
FDR .... Final Design Review   (MCD)
FDR .... Finder   (MSA)
FDR .... Fire Door   (AAG)
FDR .... First Allied Resources Corp. [*Vancouver Stock Exchange symbol*]
FDR .... First Degree Relatives
FDR .... Flight Data Recorder
FDR .... Fluorogenic Drug Reagent [*Clinical chemistry*]
FDR .... Formal Design Review
FDR .... Founder
FDR .... Framework-Determining Region [*Immunogenetics*]
FDR .... Franklin Delano Roosevelt [*US president, 1882-1945*]
FDR .... Frederick, OK [*Location identifier*] [*FAA*]   (FAAL)
FDR .... Frente Democratico Contra la Represion [*Democratic Front Against Repression*] [*Guatemala*] [*Political party*]   (PD)
FDR .... Frequency Dependent Rejection [*Telecommunications*]   (TEL)
FDR .... Frequency Diversity RADAR
FDR .... Frequency Domain Reflectometry
F/DR......... Front Door [*Automotive engineering*]
FDR .... Functional Demonstration Requirement   (AAG)
FDR .... Functional Design Requirements   (NRCH)
FDR .... Functional Design Review   (MCD)
FDRA .... Footwear Distributors and Retailers of America   (EA)
FDRC........ Federal Resources Corporation [*Salt Lake City, UT*] [*NASDAQ symbol*]   (NQ)
FDRE........ Fondation Denis de Rougemont pour l'Europe [*Geneva, Switzerland*]   (EAIO)
Fd Res .... Food Research [*A publication*]
FDRF........ Financial Data Records Folder   (MUGU)
FDRFA ...... Flight Data Recorder and Fault Analyzer [*Military*]
FDRFC ...... Friends of Debbie Reynolds Fan Club   (EA)
FDRG .... Fluid Dynamics Research Group [*MIT*]   (MCD)
FDRI......... Family and Demographic Research Institute [*Brigham Young University*] [*Research center*]   (RCD)
FDRI......... First Data Resources [*NASDAQ symbol*]   (NQ)
FDRI......... Flight Director Rate Indicator   (KSC)
FDRL......... Fluid Dynamics Research Laboratory [*MIT*]   (MCD)
FDRL......... Franklin D. Roosevelt Library
FDRMA..... Flooring Division, Rubber Manufacturers Association   (EA)
FDRPS ...... Franklin D. Roosevelt Philatelic Society   (EA)
FDRS........ Flight Data Recording System
FDRS........ Flight Display Research System
FDRS........ Food Distribution Research Society   (EA)
FDRT........ Flexible Digital Receiving Terminal
FDRY........ Foundry   (KSC)
FDS........... Faraday Dark Space
FDS........... Fast Diode Switch
FDS........... Fathometer Depth Sounder
FDS........... Federated Department Stores, Inc. [*NYSE symbol*]   (SPSG)
FDS........... Fellow of Dental Surgery [*British*]
FDS........... Feminine Deodorant Spray [*Initialism used as brand name*]
FDS........... Fence Disturbance System [*Military*]
FDS........... Fermi-Dirac Statistics
FDS........... Field Dressing Station [*Military*]   (NATG)
FDS........... Fighter Director Ship [*Navy*]
FDS........... Finance Disbursing Section [*Army*]
FDS........... Finsbury Data Services Ltd. [*Database*] [*London, England*]
FDS........... Fire Detection System
FDS........... Fire Distribution System
FDS........... First Development System   (MCD)
FDS........... Fixed Distributed Subsystem [*Antisubmarine warfare*]   (MCD)
FDS........... Flare Detection System   (KSC)
FDS........... Fleet Dental Surgeon [*Navy*] [*British*]
FDS........... Fleet Digital System   (MCD)
FDS........... Flexible Disk System
FDS........... Flexible Display System

FDS........... Flexible Drive Shaft
FDS........... Flexor Digitorum Superficialis [*Anatomy*]
FDS........... Flight Data System [*NASA*]
FDS........... Flight Design and Scheduling   (MCD)
FDS........... Flight Design System (NASA)
FDS........... Flight Director System (NATG)
FDS........... Flight Dynamics Simulator   (MCD)
FDS........... Flight Dynamics Software [*or System*]   (MCD)
FDS........... Floppy Disk System [*Data processing*]
FDS........... Fluid Distribution System   (KSC)
FDS........... Flying Doctor Service [*Australia*]
FDS........... Forward Delivery Squadron [*British military*]   (DMA)
FDS........... Forward Dressing Station [*Military*] [*British*]
FDS........... Fountainwell Drama Series [*A publication*]
FDS........... Frame Difference Signal
FDS........... Frequency Division Separator [*Multiplexing*]
FDS........... Frequency Division Switching [*Radio and television
              broadcasting*]
FDS........... Friends Disaster Service   (EA)
FDS........... Functional Design Specifications   (MCD)
FDS........... Stetson University, De Land, FL [*Library symbol*] [*Library of
              Congress*]   (LCLS)
FDSA........ Force Development System Agency [*DoD*]
FD/SC....... Failure Definitions/Scoring Criteria   (AABC)
FDSC........ Flight Dynamics Simulation Complex   (MCD)
FDSC........ Flight Dynamics Situation Complex   (NASA)
FDSD........ Forschungen zur Deutschen Sprache und Dichtung [*A
              publication*]
FDSG........ Freeze-Dried (Allogenic) Skin Graft [*Medicine*]
FDSIS....... Flight Deck System Integration Simulator
FDS-L....... Stetson University College of Law, St. Petersburg, FL [*Library
              symbol*] [*Library of Congress*]   (LCLS)
FDSR........ Floppy Disk Send/Receive [*Data processing*]
FDSRCPSGlas ... Fellow in Dental Surgery of the Royal College of Physicians
              and Surgeons of Glasgow
FDSRCPS Glasg ... Fellow in Dental Surgery of the Royal College of
              Physicians and Surgeons of Glasgow
FDSRCS.... Fellow in Dental Surgery of the Royal College of Surgeons of
              England
FDSRCSE ... Fellow in Dental Surgery of the Royal College of Surgeons of
              Edinburgh
FDSRCSEd ... Fellow in Dental Surgery of the Royal College of Surgeons of
              Edinburgh
FDSRCS Edin ... Fellow in Dental Surgery of the Royal College of Surgeons of
              Edinburgh
FDSRCS Eng ... Fellow in Dental Surgery of the Royal College of Surgeons of
              England
FDSSR....... Flight Dynamics Staff Support Room [*Apollo*] [*NASA*]
FDST........ Siteki [*Swaziland*] [*ICAO location identifier*]   (ICLI)
FDSTA...... Feedstuffs [*A publication*]
FDSU........ Flight Data Storage Unit
FDSUDR... Folia Dendrologica. Supplementum [*A publication*]
FDSVC ...... Food Service   (MSA)
FDT .... Failure Diagnostic Team [*Aerospace*]   (AAG)
FDT .... Fault Detection Tester
FDT .... Fidelity Trust Co. [*Toronto Stock Exchange symbol*]
FDT .... Fighter Director Tender [*Navy*]
FDT .... Figure Drawing Test [*Psychology*]
FDT .... First Destination Transportation [*Military*]   (AFM)
FDT .... Flexible Digital Terminal
FDT .... Flight Demonstration Team   (MCD)
FDT .... Floor Drain Tank [*Nuclear energy*]   (NRCH)
FDT .... Flowing Gas Detonation Tube
FDT .... Food, Drink, Tobacco [*Department of Employment*] [*British*]
FDT .... Formatted Data Tapes
FDT .... Fountainwell Drama Texts [*A publication*]
FDT .... Fronto-Dextra Transversa [*A fetal position*] [*Obstetrics*]
FDT .... Full Duplex Teletype
FDT .... Functional Description Table
FDTA........ Fisheries Development Trust Account [*Australia*]
FDTB........ Foreign and Domestic Teachers' Bureau   (EA)
FDTC........ Fibre Drum Technical Council   (EA)
FDT & E .... Field Development Test and Evaluation   (MCD)
FDTE........ Final Development Test and Evaluation   (MCD)
FDTE........ Force Development Testing and Experimentation
              [*Military*]   (AABC)
Fd Technol ... Food Technology [*A publication*]
Fd Technol Aust ... Food Technology in Australia [*A publication*]   (APTA)
FDTF........ Federal Documents Task Force [*Government Documents
              Round Table*] [*American Library Association*]
FDTK........ Floating Drift Tube Klystron
FDTM .... Tambankulu [*Swaziland*] [*ICAO location identifier*]   (ICLI)
FDTMDRC ... FORSCOM [*Forces Command*]/DARCOM [*Development
              and Readiness Communications*]/TRADOC [*Training and
              Doctrine Command*] Material Development and Readiness
              Council [*Army*]   (MCD)
Fd Trade Rev ... Food Trade Review [*A publication*]
FDTS........ Firing Device Test Set [*Military*]   (CAAL)
FDTS........ Floor Drain Treatment System [*Nuclear energy*]   (NRCH)
FDTS........ Tshaneni [*Swaziland*] [*ICAO location identifier*]   (ICLI)

FDTSC ...... Folger Documents of Tudor and Stuart Civilization [*A
              publication*]
FDTU .... Federation of Danish Trade Unions
FDU .... Bandundu [*Zaire*] [*Airport symbol*]   (OAG)
FDu .... Dunedin Public Library, Dunedin, FL [*Library symbol*]
              [*Library of Congress*]   (LCLS)
FDU .... Fairleigh Dickinson University [*New Jersey*]
FDU .... Fairleigh Dickinson University, Teaneck, NJ [*OCLC
              symbol*]   (OCLC)
FDU .... Flight Development Unit   (MCD)
FDU .... Fluid Distribution Unit   (MCD)
FDU .... Flying Dutchman [*A publication*]
FDU .... Frequency Determining Unit
FDU .... Frequency Doubling Unit
FDU(A)..... Fleet Diving Unit (Atlantic) [*Canadian Navy*]
FDUB .... Ubombo [*Swaziland*] [*ICAO location identifier*]   (ICLI)
FDU(P)..... Fleet Diving Unit (Pacific) [*Canadian Navy*]
FDV .... Fault Detect Verification
FDV .... Flow-Diversion Valve
FDV .... Friend Disease Virus [*Also, FLV, FV*]
FDV .... Full Duplex VOCODER [*Voice Coder*]
FDV .... Nome, AK [*Location identifier*] [*FAA*]   (FAAL)
FDVS........ Field Depot Veterinary Stores [*British military*]   (DMA)
FDW .... Feed Water   (AAG)
FDW .... Fine [*Condition*] in Dust Wrapper [*Antiquarian book trade*]
FDW .... Flat Data Wing
FDW .... Winnsboro, SC [*Location identifier*] [*FAA*]   (FAAL)
FDWL........ Fiberboard, Double Wall
FD WMR.. Food Warmer   (NASA)
FDX .... Federal Express Corp. [*NYSE symbol*] [*Toronto Stock
              Exchange symbol*]   (SPSG)
FDX .... Foodex, Inc. [*Toronto Stock Exchange symbol*]
FDX .... Full Duplex [*Telecommunications*]
FDY .... Fidelity Financial Corp. [*NYSE symbol*]   (SPSG)
FDY .... Findlay, OH [*Location identifier*] [*FAA*]   (FAAL)
FDZ .... Fetal Death Zone [*Medicine*]
fe----- .... Africa, East [*MARC geographic area code*] [*Library of
              Congress*]
FE .... Air Jet [*France*] [*ICAO designator*]   (FAAC)
FE .... Eustis Memorial Library, Eustis, FL [*Library symbol*] [*Library
              of Congress*]   (LCLS)
FE .... Extended Forecasts [*Symbol*] [*National Weather Service*]
FE .... Facilities Engineer   (MCD)
F & E......... Facilities and Equipment
F & E......... Facility and Environment   (NASA)
FE .... Failure to Eject   (MCD)
FE .... Failure Equation
FE .... Far East
FE .... Farm Economics Research Division [*of ARS, Department of
              Agriculture*]
FE .... Farman Experimental [*British military*]   (DMA)
FE .... February   (ADA)
FE .... Fecal Emesis
FE .... Fecal Energy [*Nutrition*]
FE .... Feliciana Eastern Railroad Co. [*Later, FERR*] [*AAR code*]
FE .... Female with Eggs [*Pisciculture*]
FE .... Ferroelectric
Fe .... Ferrum [*Iron*] [*Chemical element*]
FE .... Fetal Erythroblastosis [*Medicine*]
FE .... Fibrinogen Equivalent [*Hematology*]
FE .... Field Engineer [*or Engineering*]
FE .... Field Expedient   (AABC)
FE .... Fighter Escort
F und E....... Finanzierung und Entwicklung [*A publication*]
FE .... Fine Erection
FE .... Fire Extinguisher   (AAG)
FE .... First Edition   (ADA)
FE .... First Entry [*British military*]   (DMA)
FE .... Fit for Service Everywhere [*British military*]   (DMA)
FE .... Flame Emission
FE .... Fleet Engineer [*Navy*] [*British*]   (ROG)
FE .... Flemish Ell [*Unit of length*]   (ROG)
F/E............ Flexion/Extension [*Orthopedics*]
FE .... Flexor Exciter [*Neurology*]
FE .... Flight Engineer [*or Engineering*]
FE .... Flight Examiner [*Aeromedical evacuation*]
FE .... Flow Element [*Nuclear energy*]   (NRCH)
FE .... Fluid Extract [*Pharmacy*]
FE .... Fluoresceinated Estrogen [*Clinical chemistry*]
FE .... Fonetic English [*for spelling words the way they sound*]
FE .... For Example   (ROG)
FE .... Foreign Exchange [*Investment term*]
FE .... Forest Engineer
FE .... Format Effector [*Data processing*]
FE .... France-Eurafrique [*A publication*]
F/E............ Fraudulent Enlistment
FE .... Free End [*Dentistry*]
FE .... Friedensengel [*Angel of Peace*] [*Torpedo auxiliary equipment*]
              [*German military - World War II*]
FE .... Friends for Education [*Later, FFE*]   (EA)
FE .... Friends of the Everglades   (EA)

FE	Fries Entertainment, Inc. [*AMEX symbol*] (SPSG)
FE	Front End (ADA)
FE	Fuel Economy [*In automobile model name "Honda Civic 1300 FE"*]
F/E	Full Empty (NASA)
FE	Functional Entity [*Telecommunications*] (TEL)
FE	Funding Exchange (EA)
FE	Furnace Explosion [*Insurance*]
FE	Further Education
FE	Futures Exchange [*Investment term*]
FE	Office of Fossil Energy
FE	Organo de Falange Espanola [*A publication*]
FEA	Eglin Air Force Base, Eglin, FL [*OCLC symbol*] (OCLC)
FEA	Failure Effect Analysis
FEA	Far East and Australasia [*A publication*]
FEA	Farmstead Equipment Association (EA)
FEA	Feather Falls [*California*] [*Seismograph station code, US Geological Survey*] [*Closed*] (SEIS)
FEA	Federal Editors Association [*Later, NAGC*] (EA)
FEA	Federal Electoral Assembly [*Australia*]
FEA	Federal Energy Administration [*Formerly, FEO*] [*Superseded by Department of Energy, 1977*]
FEA	Federal Executive Association
FEA	Federation Europeenne des Associations Aerosols [*Federation of European Aerosol Associations*] (EA)
FEA	Federation Internationale pour l'Education Artistique
FEA	Fetlar [*Shetland Islands*] [*Airport symbol*] (OAG)
FEA	Fiber-Embedding Approximation
FEA	Field Effect Amplifier
FEA	Field Evaluation Agency [*Army*]
FEA	Filarial Excretory Antigen [*Immunology*]
FEA	Financieel Economisch Magazine (Amsterdam) [*A publication*]
FEA	Finite Element Analysis [*Engineering*]
FEA	Follow-Up Error Alarm
FEA	Foreign Economic Administration [*World War II*]
FEA	Formal Environmental Assessment (MCD)
FEA	Fraternity Executives Association (EA)
FEA	French Equatorial Africa
FEA	Front End Analysis
FEA	Full Employment Act [*1946*] (OICC)
FEA	Functional Economic Area
FEA	Further Education Association [*South Australia*]
FEA	Future Engineers of America (EA)
FEA	St. Anthony's College. Far Eastern Affairs [*A publication*]
FEAA	Federal Employees' Appeal Authority [*Civil Service Commission*]
FEAA	Folk Education Association of America (EA)
FEAA	Free Enterprise Awards Association (EA)
FEAAES	Far East Army and Air Force Exchange Service
FEAAF	Federation Europeenne des Associations d'Analystes Financiers [*European Federation of Financial Analysts' Societies - EFFAS*] (EAIO)
FEAB	Federacion Espanola de Industrias de la Alimentacion y Bebidas [*Industrial association*] [*Spain*] (EY)
FEABL	Finite Element Analysis Basic Library [*MIT*]
FEAC	Fairchild Engine & Airplane Corporation
FEAC	Far Eastern Advisory Council
FEAC	Freelance Editors' Association of Canada
FEAC	Full Employment Action Council (EA)
FEACCI	Far-East-America Council of Commerce and Industry [*Defunct*] (EA)
FEACO	Federation Europeenne des Associations de Conseils en Organisation [*European Federation of Management Consultants Associations*] [*France*]
FEAD	Federation Europeenne des Associations de Dieticiens [*European Federation of the Associations of Dietitians - EFAD*] (EAIO)
FEAD	Fondo Especial de Asistencia para el Desarrollo (de la OEA) [*Organizacion de Estados Americanos*] [*Washington, DC*]
FEAF	Far East Air Force
FEA(I)	Federal Employees Association (Independent)
FEAICS	Federation Europeenne des Associations d'Ingenieurs de Securite et de Chefs de Service de Securite [*European Federation of Associations of Engineers and Heads of Industrial Safety Services*]
FEAIE	Federation Europeenne des Associations d'Instruments a Ecrire [*Federation of European Writing Instruments Associations*] (EAIO)
FEAKA	Fel'dsher i Akusherka [*A publication*]
FEAKAD	Fel'dsher i Akusherka [*A publication*]
FEALC	Federacion Espeleologica de America Latina y el Caribe [*Speleological Federation of Latin America and the Caribbean*] (EAIO)
FEALOGFOR	Far East Air Logistical Force
FEAMCOM	Far East Air Materiel Command
FEAN	Federation des Enseignants d'Afrique Noire [*Federation of Teachers of Black Africa*]
FeAn	Ferroan Anorthosite [*Lunar geology*]
FEANI	Federation Europeenne d'Associations Nationales d'Ingenieurs [*European Federation of National Engineering Associations*] (EAIO)

FEAO	Federation of European American Organizations (EA)
FEAOA	Far East Auto Owners Association (EA)
FEAP	Facilities Engineer Apprentice Program [*Army*] (MCD)
FEAP	Far East/Pacific (AIA)
FEAP	Federation Europeenne des Associations des Psychologues [*European Federation of Professional Psychologists Associations - EFPPA*] (EA)
Fea Posth	Fearne's Posthumous Works [*A publication*] (DLA)
FEAPW	Federal Emergency Administration of Public Works [*Consolidated into Federal Works Agency and administered as PWA, 1939*]
FEAR	Federal Employment Activity Report
FEAR	Field Engineering Assistance Request (MCD)
FEAREA	Far East Area (CINC)
FEARO	Federal Environmental Assessment Review Office [*Canada*]
Fear Rem	Fearne on Contingent Remainders [*1722-1844*] [*A publication*] (DLA)
FEARTR	Federal Environmental Assessment Review Office. Technical Report [*A publication*]
FEAST	Fab Eating at School Today [*Nutritional improvement group*] [*British*]
FEAST	Food Education and Service Training
FEAST	Food Equipment and Additives Suppliers and Traders [*Leatherhead Food Research Association*] [*Information service or system*] (CRD)
F East Ship	Far East Shipping [*A publication*]
FEAT	Final Engineering Acceptance Test [*Apollo*] [*NASA*]
FEAT	Formal Evaluation Acceptance Test [*Apollo*] [*NASA*]
FEAT	Frequency of Every Allowable Term [*Data processing*]
FEATA	Far East Air Transport Association
FEAU	Fluoro(ethyl)arabinosyluracil [*Biochemistry*]
FEB	FABS Electronic Bible [*FABS International, Inc.*] [*Information service or system*] (CRD)
FEB	Fair Employment Board [*of Civil Service Commission*] [*Abolished, 1955*]
FEB	Febrifuge [*Allaying Fever Heat*] [*Pharmacy*] (ROG)
FEB	Febris [*Fever*] [*Pharmacy*]
FEB	February (EY)
FEB	Federal Executive Board
FEB	Field Engineering Bulletin
FEB	Financial and Economic Board (NATG)
FEB	Finite Elastic Body
FEB	Flying Evaluation Board
FEB	Forca Expedicionaria Brasileira [*Brazilian Expeditionary Force, 1944-1955*]
FEB	Forward Equipment Bay (MCD)
FEB	Functional Electronic Block
FEB	Functional Exploration of Bone
FEB	Sanfebagar [*Nepal*] [*Airport symbol*] (OAG)
FEBA	Far East Broadcasting Association
FEBA	Federal Energy Bar Association (EA)
FEBA	Foreign Exchange Brokers Association [*British*]
FEBA	Forward Edge of the Battle Area [*Army*] (AABC)
FEBAC	Federal Education Broadcasts Advisory Committee [*Australia*]
FEBANCOOP	Federacion de Bancos Cooperativos de la Republica Argentina [*Bankers' association*] [*Argentina*] (EY)
FEBC	Far East Broadcasting Company
FEBC	First Eastern Corporation [*NASDAQ symbol*] (NQ)
FEB DUR	Febre Durante [*During the Fever*] [*Pharmacy*] (ROG)
FeBe	Federation de l'Industrie du Beton [*Precast Concrete Federation*] [*Belgium*] (EY)
FEBECA	Federation Belge du Commerce Alimentaire [*Foodstuffs Trade Federation*] [*Belgium*] (EY)
FEBELGRA	Federation Belge des Industries Graphiques [*Graphic Industries Federation*] [*Belgium*] (EY)
FEBIA	Federal Employees Benefits Improvement Act of 1986
FEBIC	Federation Belge de l'Industrie de la Chaussure [*Footwear Federation*] [*Belgium*] (EY)
FEBJA	Federal Bar Journal [*Later, Federal Bar News and Journal*] [*A publication*]
FEBLAL	FEBS [*Federation of European Biochemical Societies*] Letters [*A publication*]
FEBMA	Federation of European Bearing Manufacturers Associations (EA)
FEBMA	Forged Eye Bolt Manufacturers Association [*Inactive*] (EA)
FEBNYC	Foreign Exchange Brokers of New York City (EA)
FEBOSCO	Federation des Scouts du Congo
FEBP	Fetoneonatal Estrogen-Binding Protein
FEBPBY	FEBS [*Federation of European Biochemical Societies*] Proceedings of the Meeting [*A publication*]
FEBS	Federation of European Biochemical Societies [*France*]
FEBS Lett	FEBS [*Federation of European Biochemical Societies*] Letters [*A publication*]
FEBS Proc Meet	FEBS [*Federation of European Biochemical Societies*] Proceedings of the Meeting [*A publication*]
FEC	Eckerd College, St. Petersburg, FL [*OCLC symbol*] (OCLC)
FEC	Facilities Engineering Command [*Also, NFEC*] [*Formerly, Bureau of Yards and Docks*] [*Navy*]
FEC	Faculty Exchange Center (EA)
FEC	Far East Command [*Military*]
FEC	Far East Conference [*Defunct*] (EA)

FEC............ Far Eastern Commission
FEC............ Far Eastern Economic Review [*A publication*]
FEC............ Fecerunt [*They Did It*] [*Latin*]   (ADA)
FEC............ Fecit [*He, or She, Did It*] [*Latin*]
FEC............ Federal Elections Commission [*Formerly, OFE*]
FEC............ Federal Electric Company   (KSC)
FEC............ Federal Executive Committee   (OICC)
FEC............ Federation of Egalitarian Communities   (EA)
FEC............ Federation of the European Cutlery and Flatware
                 Industries   (EA)
FEC............ Federation Europeenne de Climatotherapie [*European Society
                 of Climatotherapy - ESC*] [*Briancon, France*]   (EAIO)
FEC............ Ferroelectric Ceramic
FEC............ Field Engineering Change   (KSC)
FEC............ Field Error Correction   (MCD)
FEC............ Fine Erection Complete
FEC............ Finnish Export Credit [*Export credit agency*] [*Finland*]
FEC............ Fire Extinguisher Cabinet [*Technical drawings*]
FEC............ Fixed Electrolytic Capacitor
FEC............ Floating Error Code [*Digital Equipment Corp.*]
FEC............ Florida East Coast Railway Co. [*AAR code*]
FEC............ Fondation d'Etudes du Canada [*Canada Studies Foundation -
                 CSF*]
FEC............ Fondation Europeenne de la Culture [*European Cultural
                 Foundation - ECF*] [*Netherlands*]
FEC............ Food and Energy Council   (EA)
FEC............ [*Office of*] Foreign Economic Coordination
FECU.......... Foreign Exchange Certificate [*People's Republic of China*]
FEC............ Foreign Exchange Cost   (AFM)
FEC............ Forward End Cap
FEC............ Forward Error Correction [*Computer code*]
FEC............ Forward Events Controller   (MCD)
FEC............ Foundation for Exceptional Children   (EA)
FEC............ Franciscan Educational Conference [*Defunct*]
FEC............ Free Energy Change
FEC............ Free Europe Committee [*Later, RFE/RL*]   (EA)
FEC............ Free-Standing Emergency Center
FEC............ Freestanding Emergency Clinic
FEC............ French Expeditionary Corps
FEC............ [*Henry C.*] Frick Educational Commission
FEC............ Friedl Expert Committee   (EA)
FEC............ Front-End Computer
FECA........ Facilities Engineering and Construction Agency [*HEW*]
FECA........ Federal Election Campaign Act of 1971
FECA........ Federal Employees Compensation Act [*1908*]   (AFM)
FECA........ Fully Enclosed Covered Area   (ADA)
FECB........ Far East Combined Bureau [*Singapore, 1940*] [*Military*]
FECB........ Far Eastern Ceramic Bulletin [*A publication*]
FECB........ Federation des Employes Congolais des Banques [*Federation of
                 Congolese Bank Clerks*]
FECB........ File Extended Control Block [*Data processing*]   (BUR)
FECC........ Federal Employees Coordinating Committee   (EA)
FECC........ Federation Europeenne du Commerce Chimique [*Federation of
                 European Chemical Merchants - FECM*]   (EAIO)
FECEGC ... Federation Europeenne des Constructeurs d'Equipement de
                 Grandes Cuisines [*European Federation of Catering
                 Equipment Manufacturers - EFCEM*]   (EA)
FECEP....... Federation Europeenne des Constructeurs d'Equipement
                 Petrolier [*European Federation of Petroleum Equipment
                 Manufacturers*]
FECF .... Food Executives Club of Florida   (EA)
FECG........ Fetal Electrocardiography [*Medicine*]
FECI .... Fellow of the Institute of Employment Consultants
                 [*British*]   (DBQ)
FECL .... Federal Constitutional Law
FECL .... Fleet Electronics Calibration Laboratory
FECM....... Federation of European Chemical Merchants   (EA)
FECMA..... Federation of European Coin-Machine Associations   (EAIO)
FECMDW ... Forest Ecology and Management [*A publication*]
FECOM..... Far East Command [*Military*]
FECOM..... Fonds Europeen de Cooperation Monetaire [*European
                 Monetary Cooperation Fund*]
FECOMZ ... Forward Echelon, Communications Zone [*Europe*] [*Army*]
FECP .... Facility Engineering Change Proposal
FECP .... Field Engineering Change Proposal
FECP .... Formal Engineering Change Proposal   (MSA)
FECP .... Front End Communications Processor
FECR .... Far East Communications Region [*Air Force*]   (MCD)
FECS .... Federation of European Chemical Societies   (EAIO)
FECS .... Federation Europeenne des Fabricants de Ceramiques
                 Sanitaires [*European Federation of Ceramic Sanitaryware
                 Manufacturers - EFCSM*]   (EAIO)
FECT .... Federation of European Chemical Trade   (EAIO)
FECT .... Fibroelastic Connective Tissue [*Medicine*]
FECU .... Flutter Exciter Control Unit   (MCD)
FECUA...... Farmers' Educational and Cooperative Union of America   (EA)
FECZ .... Forward Echelon, Communications Zone [*Europe*] [*Army*]
FED .... Army Engineer District, Far East
FED .... Federal   (AFM)
Fed .... Federal Reporter [*A publication*]   (DLA)
FED .... Federal Reserve Bulletin [*A publication*]

FED .... Federal Reserve System [*Banking*]
FED .... Federal Specification
FED .... Federalist
Fed .... [*The*] Federalist, by Hamilton [*A publication*]   (DLA)
FED .... Federation   (EY)
FED .... Field Effect Device
FED .... Field Emission Deposition [*Coating technique*]
FED .... Final Estimation of Data [*Data processing*]
FED .... FirstFed Financial [*NYSE symbol*]   (SPSG)
FED .... Five-Inch Evasion Device   (MCD)
FED .... Fleetwood Petroleum [*Vancouver Stock Exchange symbol*]
FED .... Flight Events Demonstration [*NASA*]   (KSC)
FED .... Foundation for Ethnic Dance   (EA)
FED .... Fusion Engineering Device [*Nuclear energy*]
FEDA........ Federated Engine Drivers' Association [*Australia*]
FEDA........ Foodservice Equipment Distributors Association   (EA)
FEDA........ Foundation for Ecological Development Alternatives   (EAIO)
FEDAC...... Federal Education Data Acquisition Council   (OICC)
FEDAC...... Federal Executive Drug Abuse Council
FEDAC...... Forward Error Detection and Correction
Fed Accountant ... Federal Accountant [*A publication*]   (APTA)
FEDAL...... Failed Element Detection and Location [*In nuclear power
                 reactors*]
Fed Am Hosp Rev ... Federation of American Hospitals. Review [*A
                 publication*]
Fed Anti-Tr Cas ... Federal Anti-Trust Cases, Decrees, and Judgments [*1890-
                 1918*] [*A publication*]   (DLA)
Fed Anti-Tr Dec ... Federal Anti-Trust Decisions [*A publication*]   (DLA)
FEDAPT ... Foundation for Extension and Development of the American
                 Professional Theatre   (EA)
Fed Atlant ... Federal Reserve Bank of Atlanta. Economic Review [*A
                 publication*]
Fed Audit Guide CCH ... Federal Audit Guide. Commerce Clearing House [*A
                 publication*]
Fed Aust Music Teach Assoc Q Mag ... Federation of Australian Music
                 Teachers' Associations. Quarterly Magazine [*A
                 publication*]   (APTA)
FEDB........ Failure Experience Data Bank [*GIDEP*]
Fed BAJ..... Federal Bar Association. Journal [*A publication*]
Fed BA Jo ... Federal Bar Association. Journal [*A publication*]
Fed Banking L Rep ... Federal Banking Law Reports [*Commerce Clearing
                 House*] [*A publication*]   (DLA)
Fed Bar J ... Federal Bar News and Journal [*A publication*]
Fed B J....... Federal Bar Journal [*Later, Federal Bar News and Journal*] [*A
                 publication*]
Fed BN...... Federal Bar News [*Later, Federal Bar News and Journal*] [*A
                 publication*]
Fed Bull...... Federation Bulletin [*A publication*]
FEDC........ Federal Economic Development Co-Ordinator [*Canada*]
FEDC........ Field Exercise Data Collection [*Army*]   (RDA)
FEDC........ Fusion Energy Design Center   (MCD)
Fed Can M Inst J ... Federated Canadian Mining Institute. Journal [*A
                 publication*]
Fed Carr Cas ... Federal Carriers Cases [*Commerce Clearing House*] [*A
                 publication*]   (DLA)
Fed Carr Cas CCH ... Federal Carriers Cases. Commerce Clearing House [*A
                 publication*]
Fed Carr Rep ... Federal Carriers Reporter [*Commerce Clearing House*] [*A
                 publication*]   (DLA)
Fed Carr Rep CCH ... Federal Carriers Reports. Commerce Clearing House [*A
                 publication*]
Fed Cas ...... Federal Cases [*A publication*]   (DLA)
Fed Cas No ... Federal Case Number [*Legal term*]   (DLA)
Fed Com B J ... Federal Communications Bar Journal [*Later, Federal
                 Communications Law Journal*] [*A publication*]
Fed Com LJ ... Federal Communications Law Journal [*A publication*]
Fed Comm BJ ... Federal Communications Bar Journal [*Later, Federal
                 Communications Law Journal*] [*A publication*]
Fed Comm LJ ... Federal Communications Law Journal [*A
                 publication*]   (DLA)
Fed Cont Rep (BNA) ... Federal Contracts Report (Bureau of National Affairs)
                 [*A publication*]   (DLA)
Fed Council Bull ... Federal Council of University Staff Associations. Bulletin
                 [*A publication*]
Fed Ct .... Federal Court of Australia
Fed Ct .... Indian Rulings, Federal Court [*A publication*]   (DLA)
FEDD .... For Early Domestic Dissemination   (MCD)
Fed 2d .... Federal Reporter, Second Series [*A publication*]   (DLA)
Fed Dallas ... Federal Reserve Bank of Dallas. Farm and Ranch Bulletin [*A
                 publication*]
FEDDEC..... Federal Court of Australia Decisions [*Database*]
Feddes Repert ... Feddes Repertorium [*A publication*]
Feddes Repert Specierum Nov Regni Veg ... Feddes Repertorium. Specierum
                 Novarum Regni Vegetabilis [*A publication*]
Feddes Repert Specierum Nov Regni Veg Beih ... Feddes Repertorium.
                 Specierum Novarum Regni Vegetabilis. Beihefte [*A
                 publication*]
Feddes Repert Z Bot Taxon Geobot ... Feddes Repertorium. Zeitschrift fuer
                 Botanische Taxonomie und Geobotanik [*A publication*]
Feddes Reprium Z Bot Taxon Geobot ... Feddes Repertorium. Zeitschrift fuer
                 Botanische Taxonomie und Geobotanik [*A publication*]

FEDE .... Federation Europeenne des Ecoles [*European Schools Federation - ESF*] (EAIO)

FEDEAU ... Federation pour le Developpement de l'Artisanat Utilitaire [*Federation for the Development of Utilitarian Crafts*] [*Defunct*] (EAIO)

FEDECAME ... Federacion Cafetalera de America [*Central American Coffee Growers' Federation*]

FEDECO ... Federacion de Comunidades Judias de Centroamerica y Panama [*Federation of Jewish Communities of Central America and Panama*] (EAIO)

FEDEFAM ... Federacion Latinoamericana de Asociaciones de Familiares de Detenidos-Desaparecidos [*Federation of Associations of Families of Disappeared-Detainees*] (EAIO)

Fed Election Camp Fin Guide (CCH) ... Federal Election Campaign Financing Guide (Commerce Clearing House) [*A publication*] (DLA)

FEDEMO ... Federal Democratic Movement [*Political party*] [*Uganda*]

Fed Energy Reg Commn Rep CCH ... Federal Energy Regulatory Commission Reports. Commerce Clearing House [*A publication*]

FEDER ...... Fonds Europeen de Developpement Regional [*European Regional Development Fund - ERDF*] [*Brussels, Belgium*] (EAIO)

Federacion Latinoam Bancos R ... Federacion Latinoamericana de Bancos. Revista [*A publication*]

Federal Home Loan Bank Bd J ... Federal Home Loan Bank Board. Journal [*A publication*]

Federal Law Rev ... Federal Law Review [*A publication*] (APTA)

Federal L Rev ... Federal Law Review [*A publication*]

Federal Reserve Mo Chart Bk ... Federal Reserve Monthly Chart Book [*A publication*]

Federation Ins Couns Q ... Federation of Insurance Counsel. Quarterly [*A publication*]

Federation Proc ... Federation Proceedings [*A publication*]

FEDERSINDAN ... Federazione dei Sindacati Dipendenti Aziende di Navigazione [*Italy*] (EY)

FEDES ...... Federation Europeenne de l'Emballage Souple (EAIO)

Fede de Sen ... Federicus Petrucius de Senis [*Flourished, 1321-43*] [*Authority cited in pre-1607 legal work*] (DSA)

Fed Est & Gift Tax Rep ... Federal Estate and Gift Tax Reports [*Commerce Clearing House*] [*A publication*]

Fed Est & Gift Tax Rep CCH ... Federal Estate and Gift Tax Reports. Commerce Clearing House [*A publication*]

Fed Eur Biochem Soc Meet Proc ... Federation of European Biochemical Societies. Meeting Proceedings [*England*] [*A publication*]

Fed Eur Biochem Soc Symp (Berl) ... Federation of European Biochemical Societies. Symposium (Berlin) [*A publication*]

Fed Evid R ... Federal Rules of Evidence [*A publication*] (DLA)

FEDEX ...... [*The*] Federal Energy Data Index [*Department of Energy*] [*Information service or system*] [*Defunct*] (CRD)

Fed-Ex .... Federal Express Corp.

Fed Ex Tax Rep ... Federal Excise Tax Reporter [*Commerce Clearing House*] [*A publication*] (DLA)

Fed Ex Tax Rep CCH ... Federal Excise Tax Reports. Commerce Clearing House [*A publication*]

FEDF .... Federated Financial Savings & Loan Association [*NASDAQ symbol*] (NQ)

Fed Fr Soc Sci Nat Bull Trimest ... Federation Francaise des Societes de Sciences Naturelles. Bulletin Trimestriel [*A publication*]

FEDG .... Federated Guaranty Life [*NASDAQ symbol*] (NQ)

FEDGE ...... Finite Element Data Generation [*Data processing*]

Fed Home Loan Bank Bd J ... Federal Home Loan Bank Board. Journal [*A publication*]

Fed Home Loan Bank Board J ... Federal Home Loan Bank Board. Journal [*A publication*]

Fed Home Loan Bk Bd J ... Federal Home Loan Bank Board. Journal [*A publication*]

FEDIAF ..... Federation Europeenne de l'Industrie des Aliments pour Animaux Familiers [*European Petfood Industry Federation*] (EAIO)

FEDICER ... Federation des Industries Ceramiques de Belgique et du Luxembourg [*Ceramics Federation*] [*Belgium*] (EY)

FEDIMA ... Federation des Industries de Matieres Premieres et des Ameliorants pour la Boulangerie et la Patisserie dans la CEE [*European Federation of Manufacturers of Bakers' and Confectioners' Ingredients and Additives*] [*Common Market*]

Fed Inc Gift & Est Taxn MB ... Federal Income Gift and Estate Taxation. Matthew Bender [*A publication*]

Fed Ins Counsel Q ... Federal Insurance Counsel Quarterly [*A publication*] (DLA)

Fed Inst M Eng Tr ... Federated Institution of Mining Engineers. Transactions [*A publication*]

Fed Inter-Agency Sediment Conf Proc ... Federal Inter-Agency Sedimentation Conference. Proceedings [*A publication*]

Fed Int Lait Bull Annu ... Federation Internationale de Laiterie. Bulletin Annuel [*A publication*]

FEDIOL .... Federation de l'Industrie de l'Huilerie de la CEE [*EEC Seed Crushers and Oil Processors' Federation*] [*Brussels, Belgium*] (EAIO)

FEDIS .... Federation Belge des Entreprises de Distribution [*Belgium*] (EY)

Fed KC .... Federal Reserve Bank of Kansas City. Monthly Review [*A publication*]

FEDL .... Federal

Fed Law Rev ... Federal Law Review [*A publication*]

FEDLINK ... Federal Library and Information Network [*Formerly, FLECC*] [*Library of Congress*] [*Washington, DC*] [*Library network*]

Fed LJ .... Federal Law Journal of India [*A publication*] (DLA)

Fed LJ Ind ... Federal Law Journal of India [*A publication*] (DLA)

Fed LQ .... Federal Law Quarterly [*A publication*] (DLA)

Fed LR .... Federal Law Reports [*A publication*] (APTA)

Fed LR .... Federal Law Review [*A publication*]

Fedl Register ... Federal Register [*A publication*]

Fed L Rep .. Federal Law Reports [*A publication*]

Fed L Rev ... Federal Law Review [*A publication*] (APTA)

Fed Malaya Dep Agric Bull ... Federation of Malaya. Department of Agriculture. Bulletin [*A publication*]

Fed Malaya Dep Agric Econ Ser ... Federation of Malaya. Department of Agriculture. Economic Series [*A publication*]

Fed Malaya Dep Agric Gen Ser ... Federation of Malaya. Department of Agriculture. General Series [*A publication*]

Fed Malaya Dep Agric Sci Ser ... Federation of Malaya. Department of Agriculture. Scientific Series [*A publication*]

FEDN .... Federation

FEDNET ... Federal Information Network

Fed'n Ins Counsel Q ... Federation of Insurance Counsel. Quarterly [*A publication*]

Fedn Proc Fedn Am Socs Exp Biol ... Federation Proceedings. Federation of American Societies for Experimental Biology [*A publication*]

FEDOLIVE ... Federation de l'Industrie de l'Huile d'Olive de la CEE [*Federation of the European Economic Community Olive Oil Industry*]

FEDOM .... Fonds Europeen de Developpement pour les Pays et Territoires d'Outre-Mer [*European Development Fund for Overseas Countries and Territories*]

FEDP .... Facility and Equipment Design Plan (MCD)

FEDP .... Federal Executive Development Program [*Civil Service Commission*]

FEDP .... Federated Purchaser, Inc. [*NASDAQ symbol*] (NQ)

Fed P .... Federation Proceedings [*A publication*]

Fed Phila .... Federal Reserve Bank of Philadelphia. Business Review [*A publication*]

Fed Power Serv MB ... Federal Power Service. Matthew Bender [*A publication*]

Fed Prac ..... Federal Practice and Procedure [*A publication*] (DLA)

Fed Prob ..... Federal Probation [*A publication*]

Fed Probat ... Federal Probation [*A publication*]

Fed Probation ... Federal Probation [*A publication*]

Fed Prob NL ... Federal Probation Newsletter [*A publication*] (DLA)

Fed Proc ..... Federation Proceedings [*A publication*]

Fed Proc ..... Proceedings. Federation of American Societies for Experimental Biology [*A publication*]

Fed Proc Fed Am Soc Exp Biol ... Federation Proceedings. Federation of American Societies for Experimental Biology [*A publication*]

Fed Proc Transl Suppl ... Federation Proceedings. Translation Supplement [*United States*] [*A publication*]

FED Publ Am Soc Mech Eng Fluids Eng Div ... FED Publication. American Society of Mechanical Engineers. Fluids Engineering Division [*A publication*]

Fed Pub Serv J ... Federal Public Service Journal [*A publication*] (APTA)

Fed R .... Federal Reporter [*A publication*] (DLA)

Fed R App P ... Federal Rules of Appellate Procedure [*A publication*] (DLA)

Fed R Civil P ... Federal Rules of Civil Procedure [*A publication*] (DLA)

Fed R Civ P ... Federal Rules of Civil Procedure [*A publication*] (DLA)

Fed R Crim P ... Federal Rules of Criminal Procedure [*A publication*] (DLA)

Fed R D ...... Federal Rules Decisions [*A publication*]

Fed Reg ...... Federal Register [*A publication*]

FEDREG ... Federal Register Abstracts [*Capitol Services, Inc.*] [*Washington, DC*] [*Database*]

Fed Reg Empl Serv ... Federal Regulation of Employment Service [*A publication*]

Fed Regist ... Federal Register [*A publication*]

Fed Regist (Wash DC) ... Federal Register (Washington, DC) [*A publication*]

Fed Rep ...... Federal Reporter [*A publication*] (DLA)

Fed Res Bank NY ... Federal Reserve Bank of New York. Quarterly Review [*A publication*]

Fed Res Bull ... Federal Reserve Bulletin [*A publication*]

Fed Reserve B ... Federal Reserve Bulletin [*A publication*]

Fed Reserve Bank NYQ Rev ... Federal Reserve Bank of New York. Quarterly Review [*A publication*]

Fed Reserve Bank St Louis Rev ... Federal Reserve Bank of St. Louis. Review [*A publication*]

Fed Reserve Bull ... Federal Reserve Bulletin [*A publication*]

Fed Revenue Forms (P-H) ... Federal Revenue Forms (Prentice-Hall, Inc.) [*A publication*] (DLA)

Fed R Evid ... Federal Rules of Evidence [*A publication*] (DLA)

Fed R Evid Serv ... Federal Rules of Evidence Service [*A publication*] (DLA)

Fed Richmd ... Federal Reserve Bank of Richmond. Monthly Review [*A publication*]

FEDRIP..... Federal Research in Progress [*NTIS*] [*Department of Commerce*] [*Information service or system*] (IID)
Fed R Serv 2d (Callaghan) ... Federal Rules Service, Second Series [*A publication*] (DLA)
Fed Rules Civ Proc ... Federal Rules of Civil Procedure [*A publication*] (DLA)
Fed Rules Cr Proc ... Federal Rules of Criminal Procedure [*A publication*] (DLA)
Fed Rules Dec ... Federal Rules Decisions [*A publication*]
Fed Rules Serv ... Federal Rules Service [*A publication*] (DLA)
Fed Rules Serv 2d ... Federal Rules Service, Second Series [*A publication*] (DLA)
FEDS........ Federal Employees for a Democratic Society [*Defunct*]
FEDS........ Federal Employment Decision Search [*Database*] [*Labor Relations Press*] [*Information service or system*] (CRD)
FEDS........ Field Experimenter Detection [*or Detector*] Survivability (MCD)
FEDS........ Fixed/Exchangeable Disk Store
FEDS........ Foreign Economic Development Service [*Abolished 1972, functions transferred to the Economic Research Service*] [*Department of Agriculture*]
Fed Sci Prog ... Federal Science Progress [*A publication*]
Fed Sec L Rep ... Federal Securities Law Reporter [*Commerce Clearing House*] [*A publication*] (DLA)
Fed Ser Coat Technol ... Federation Series on Coating Technology [*A publication*]
Fed SF BFL ... Federal Reserve Bank of San Francisco. Business and Financial Letter [*A publication*]
FEDSIM.... Federal Computer Performance Evaluation and Simulation Center [*General Services Administration*]
FEDSPEC ... Federal Specification
FED-STAN ... Standards Referenced in Federal Legislation [*Standards Council of Canada*] [*Information service or system*] (CRD)
Fed Stat...... Federal Reserve Statistical Release. Industrial Production [*A publication*]
Fed Stat Ann ... Federal Statutes, Annotated [*A publication*] (DLA)
Fed Stat R ... Federal Reserve Statistical Release. Industrial Production [*A publication*]
FEDSTD ... Federal Standard
Fed St L ..... Federal Reserve Bank of St. Louis. Monthly Review [*Later, Federal Reserve Bank of St. Louis. Review*] [*A publication*]
FEDSTRIP ... Federal Standard Requisitioning and Issue Procedure
Fed Sup...... Federal Supplement [*A publication*] (DLA)
Fed Supp..... Federal Supplement [*A publication*] (DLA)
Fed Tax Artic ... Federal Tax Articles [*A publication*]
Fed Tax Coordinator 2d Res Inst Am ... Federal Tax Coordinator Second. Research Institute of America [*A publication*]
Fed Tax Coordinator 2d (RIA) ... Federal Tax Coordinator Second (Tax Research Institute of America) [*A publication*] (DLA)
Fed Tax Enf ... Federal Tax Enforcement [*A publication*] (DLA)
Fed Taxes .. Federal Taxes [*Prentice-Hall, Inc.*] [*A publication*] (DLA)
Fed Taxes Est & Gift ... Federal Taxes: Estate and Gift Taxes [*Prentice-Hall, Inc.*] [*A publication*] (DLA)
Fed Taxes (P-H) ... Federal Taxes (Prentice-Hall, Inc.) [*A publication*] (DLA)
Fed Tax Guide Rep CCH ... Federal Tax Guide Reports. Commerce Clearing House [*A publication*]
Fed Times .. Federal Times [*United States*] [*A publication*]
Fed Tr Rep ... Federal Trade Reporter [*A publication*] (DLA)
FEDU .... Fluoroethyl(deoxyuridine) [*Biochemistry*]
Fed Yellow Book ... Federal Yellow Book [*United States*] [*A publication*]
FEE............ Far Eastern Economic Review [*A publication*]
FEE............ Field Engineering and Equipment [*Military*]
FEE............ Fill Exit Entry [*Data processing*]
F & EE ...... Film and Equipment Exchange [*Army*] (AABC)
FEE............ Fondation Europeenne pour l'Economie
FEE............ Forced Equilibrating Expiration [*Physiology*]
FEE............ Foundation for Economic Education
FEE............ Freeway Resources Ltd. [*Vancouver Stock Exchange symbol*]
FEEA........ Federal Employee Education and Assistance Fund
FEEA........ Federal Energy Emergency Administration (MCD)
FEEC......... Field Enterprises Educational Corporation [*Later, World Book-Childcraft International, Inc.*]
FEECA...... Federation Europeenne pour l'Education Catholique des Adultes [*European Associaton for Catholic Adult Education*] (EAIO)
FEED......... Field Exploitation of Elevation Data (RDA)
Feed Addit Compend ... Feed Additive Compendium [*A publication*]
Feed Bag Mag ... Feed Bag Magazine [*A publication*]
Feed Feed Dig ... Feed and Feeding Digest [*A publication*]
Feed Illus ... Feeds Illustrated [*A publication*]
Feed Ind Rev ... Feed Industry Review [*A publication*]
Feedlot Manage ... Feedlot Management [*A publication*]
Feed Manage ... Feed Management [*A publication*]
Feed Manage E Ed ... Feed Management. Eastern Edition [*A publication*]
FEEDS ...... Fire Emergency Equipment Dispatch System
Feed Situation USDA Econ Res Serv ... Feed Situation. US Department of Agriculture. Economic Research Service [*A publication*]
FE-EL........ Ferroelectric-Electroluminescent
FEEM........ Field Electron Emission Microscope [*or Microscopy*]

FEEMS ..... Facilities Engineer Equipment Maintenance System [*Army*]
FEER........ Far Eastern Economic Review [*A publication*]
FEER........ Fast Eigensolution Extraction Routine [*Computer program*]
FEER......... Fundamental Equilibrium Exchange Rate [*Economics*]
FEF............ Fast Extrusion Furnace
FEF............ Feline Embryonic Fibroblast
FEF............ Flight Engineering Facility (MCD)
FEF............ Forced Expiratory Flow [*Physiology*]
FEF............ Foundation for Educational Futures (EA)
FEF............ Foundry Educational Foundation [*Inactive*] (EA)
FEF............ Free Energy Function
FEF............ Freedom of Expression Foundation (EA)
FEF............ French Expeditionary Force
FEF............ Friends of the Earth Foundation (EA)
FEF............ Frontal Eye Field [*Neuroanatomy*]
FEF............ Frozen Equilibrium Flow
FEF............ Fuel Examination Facility [*Nuclear energy*] (NRCH)
FEF............ Fusion Energy Foundation (EA)
FEFA........ Alindao [*Central African Republic*] [*ICAO location identifier*] (ICLI)
FEFAC ...... Federation Europeenne des Fabricants d'Aliments Composes [*European Federation of Compound Animal Feedingstuff Manufacturers*] (EAIO)
FEFANA ... Federation Europeenne des Fabricants d'Adjuvants pour la Nutrition Animale [*European Federation of Manufacturers of Feed Additives*] (EAIO)
FEFB .... Obo [*Central African Republic*] [*ICAO location identifier*] (ICLI)
FEFC........ Far Eastern Freight Conference
FEFCO ...... Federation Europeenne des Fabricants de Carton Ondule [*European Federation of Manufacturers of Corrugated Board*] [*France*]
FEFF......... Bangui/M'Poko [*Central African Republic*] [*ICAO location identifier*] (ICLI)
FEFG .... Bangassou [*Central African Republic*] [*ICAO location identifier*] (ICLI)
FEFI .... Birao [*Central African Republic*] [*ICAO location identifier*] (ICLI)
FEFL........ Bossembele [*Central African Republic*] [*ICAO location identifier*] (ICLI)
FEFM .... Bambari [*Central African Republic*] [*ICAO location identifier*] (ICLI)
FEFM .... Federazione Europea Fabbricanti Matite [*Federation of Eraser Pencil Manufacturers Associations*] (EAIO)
FEFN .... N'Dele [*Central African Republic*] [*ICAO location identifier*] (ICLI)
FEFO........ Bouar [*Central African Republic*] [*ICAO location identifier*] (ICLI)
FEFO........ First-Ended, First-Out [*Data processing*]
FEFP......... Fuel Element Failure Propagation [*Nuclear energy*]
FEFPEB..... Federation Europeenne des Fabricants de Palettes et Emballages en Bois [*European Federation of Pallet and Wooden Crate Manufacturers - EFPWCM*] (EAIO)
FEFPL....... Fuel Element Failure Propagation Loop [*Nuclear energy*] (NRCH)
FEFR......... Bria [*Central African Republic*] [*ICAO location identifier*] (ICLI)
FEFS.......... Bossangoa [*Central African Republic*] [*ICAO location identifier*] (ICLI)
FEFT .... Berberati [*Central African Republic*] [*ICAO location identifier*] (ICLI)
FEFV .... Bangui [*Central African Republic*] [*ICAO location identifier*] (ICLI)
FEFY .... Yalinga [*Central African Republic*] [*ICAO location identifier*] (ICLI)
FEFZ .... Zemio [*Central African Republic*] [*ICAO location identifier*] (ICLI)
f-eg--- .... Equatorial Guinea [*MARC geographic area code*] [*Library of Congress*] (LCCP)
FEG .... First Canadian Energy Corp. [*Vancouver Stock Exchange symbol*]
FEgAD...... United States Air Force, Armament Development and Test Center, Technical Library, Eglin Air Force Base, FL [*Library symbol*] [*Library of Congress*] (LCLS)
FEGADG... Fern Gazette [*A publication*]
FEGLI .... Federal Employees' Group Life Insurance
FEGP......... [*The*] Federated Group, Inc. [*NASDAQ symbol*] (NQ)
FEgRH ...... United States Air Force, Eglin Regional Hospital, Eglin Air Force Base, FL [*Library symbol*] [*Library of Congress*] (LCLS)
FEGS......... Federation Employment and Guidance Service (EA)
FEGZ......... Bozoum [*Central African Republic*] [*ICAO location identifier*] (ICLI)
FEH .... Federation Europeenne Halterophile [*European Weightlifting Federation - EWF*] (EA)
FEHA........ Federal Hall National Memorial
FEHB......... Federal Employees Health Benefits
FEHBA...... Federal Employees Health Benefits Act
FEHBP....... Federal Employees Health Benefits Program (AFM)
FEHE......... Feed-Effluent Heat Exchanger [*Chemical engineering*]
FEHTA7.... Florists' Exchange [*A publication*]

FEHVA...... Federation of European Heating and Ventilating Associations (EA)
FEI............. Facilities Engineering Items [Military] (AABC)
FEI............. Farm Equipment Institute [Later, FIEI] (EA)
FEI............. Federal Executive Institute
FEI............. Federation Equestre Internationale [International Equestrian Federation] [Berne, Switzerland] (EAIO)
FEI............. Financial Executives Institute (EA)
F & EI .... Fire and Explosion Index [Hazard analysis]
FEI............. Firing Effectiveness Indicator [Military] (CAAL)
FEI............. Firing Error Indicator
FEI............. For Engineering Information (AAG)
FEI............. Force Effectiveness Indicator [COEA] (MCD)
FEI............. Foreign Investment Review [A publication]
FEI............. Foundation Europalia International (EAIO)
FEI............. Free Europe, Incorporated [Later, RFE/RL]
FEI............. Frequency Electronics, Incorporated [AMEX symbol] (SPSG)
FEI............. Frontend International Technologies, Inc. [Vancouver Stock Exchange symbol]
FEIA.......... Flight Engineers' International Association (EA)
FEIA.......... Foreign Earned Income Act [1978]
FEIBP........ Federation Europeenne de l'Industrie de la Brosserie et de la Pinceuterie [European Federation of the Brush and Paint Brush Industries - EFBPBI] (EAIO)
FEIC.......... Federation Europeenne de l'Industrie du Contreplaque [European Federation of the Plywood Industry - EFPI] (EA)
FEIC.......... Fellow of the Engineering Institute of Canada
FEIC.......... Fossil Energy Information Center [ORNL] (GRD)
FEICA........ Federation Europeenne des Industries de Colles et Adhesifs [Association of European Adhesives Manufacturers] (EA)
FEICC .... Foundation for the Establishment of an International Criminal Court (EA)
FEICRO .... Federation of European Industrial Co-Operative Research Organizations (EA)
FEICUS..... Family Education and Information Council of the United States (EA)
FEID.......... Flight Equipment Interface Device [NASA] (NASA)
FEID.......... Functional Engineering Interface Device [NASA] (NASA)
FEIEA .... Federation of European Industrial Editors' Associations
FEIG.......... Fossil Energy Information Group [Department of Energy] [Information service or system] (IID)
FEILS........ Federal Energy Information Locator Systems
FEIM......... Federation Europeenne des Importateurs de Machines et d'Equipements de Bureau [European Federation of Importers of Business Equipment] (EAIO)
FEIN.......... Federal Employer Identification Number
Feingeraete Tech ... Feingeraete Technik [A publication]
Feinwerktech Messtech ... Feinwerktechnik und Messtechnik [A publication]
Feinwerktech und Messtech ... Feinwerktechnik und Messtechnik [A publication]
Feinwerktech & Micronic ... Feinwerktechnik und Micronic [A publication]
FEIPP........ Fantastic Entertainment in Public Places [Melbourne, Victoria, Australia]
FEIS.......... Fellow of the Educational Institute of Scotland
FEIS.......... Final Environmental Impact Statement
FEITC........ Federation Europeenne des Industries Techniques du Cinema
FEIZ......... Fellow of the Engineering Institution of Zambia
FEJ .... Far East Journal [A publication]
FE de las JONS ... Falange Espanola de las Juntas de Ofensiva Nacional Sindicalista [Spanish Phalange of the Syndicalist Juntas of the National Offensive] [Political party] (PPE)
FEK........... Frequency Exchange Keying
FEKG......... Fetal Electrocardiogram [Medicine]
FEKTA ...... Forum foer Ekonomi och Teknik [A publication]
FEL........... Familial Erythrophagocytic Lymphohistocytosis [Medicine]
FEL........... Feldberg In Schwarzwald [Federal Republic of Germany] [Seismograph station code, US Geological Survey] (SEIS)
Fel .... Felinus Sandeus [Deceased, 1503] [Authority cited in pre-1607 legal work] (DSA)
FEL........... Fellis [Gall] [Pharmacy] (ROG)
FEL........... Fellow
FEL........... Felony [FBI standardized term]
Fel............ Felsted [Record label] [Great Britain, etc.]
FEL........... Felucca [Ship's rigging] (ROG)
FeL .... Filologia e Letteratura [A publication]
FEL........... Fisheries Engineering Laboratory [Marine science] (MSC)
FEL........... Flight Engineer's Licence [British] (AIA)
FEL........... Food Engineering Laboratory [Army]
FEL........... Free Electron LASER
FEL........... Frequency Engineering Laboratory (MCD)
FEL........... Friend Erythroleukemia Cell [Oncology]
FEL........... Fritz Engineering Laboratory [Lehigh University]
FEL........... Front End Loader (ADA)
FEL........... Full Employment League
FELA .... Federal Employers' Liability Act (Railroads) [1906]
FELABAN ... Federacion Latinoamericana de Bancos [Latin American Banking Federation - LABF] [Bogota, Colombia] (EAIO)
FELACUTI ... Federacion Latinoamericana de Usuarios del Transporte [Latin American Federation of Shippers' Councils] (EAIO)
FELAP....... Finite Element Analysis Program [Nuclear energy] (NRCH)

FELATRAP ... Federacion Latinoamericana de Trajabadores de la Prensa [Latin American Federation of Press Workers] (EAIO)
FELCO ...... Federation of English Language Course Organisation [British]
FELDF...... Free Enterprise Legal Defense Fund [Bellevue, WA] (EA)
Fel'dsher Akush ... Fel'dsher i Akusherka [A publication]
Feld Wald Wasser Schweiz Jagdztg ... Feld, Wald, Wasser. Schweizerische Jagdzeitung [A publication]
FELE .... Franklin Electric Co., Inc. [NASDAQ symbol] (NQ)
FELF......... Far East Land Forces [British military] (DMA)
FELG........ Far East Liaison Group (CINC)
Feli .... Felinus Sandeus [Deceased, 1503] [Authority cited in pre-1607 legal work] (DSA)
Felin .... Felinus Sandeus [Deceased, 1503] [Authority cited in pre-1607 legal work] (DSA)
FELINE..... Frederick Engineering's Dataline Monitor/Protocol Analyzer [Data processing]
Feline Pract ... Feline Practice [A publication]
FELL .... Federal Labor Laws
FELL .... Fellow
Fell........... Fellowship [A publication]
Fell Guar ... Fell on Guaranty and Suretyship [A publication] (DLA)
FELM....... Felmersham [England]
FEL MEM ... Felicis Memoriae [Of Happy Memory] [Latin]
FELPBG..... Feline Practice [A publication]
FELR........ Far Eastern Law Review [A publication]
FELR .... Feeler
Fel Rav .... Felix Ravenna [A publication]
Felsmech Ingenieurgeol ... Felsmechanik und Ingenieurgeologie [Austria] [A publication]
FELV .... Feline Leukemia Virus [Also, FLV]
FEM .... Federation Europeenne de la Manutention [European Federation of Handling Industries] (EAIO)
FEM .... Federation Europeenne des Motels [European Motel Federation]
FEM .... Female [or Feminine] (KSC)
FEM .... Femoral [Anatomy]
FEM .... Ferguson Library, Stamford, CT [OCLC symbol] (OCLC)
FEM .... Field-Effect Modified (IEEE)
FEM .... Field Electron Microscope [or Microscopy]
FEM .... Field Emission Microscope [or Microscopy]
FEM .... Field Engineering Maintenance
FEM .... Field Evaluation Model
FEM .... Finite-Element Meshing [or Modeling] [Data processing] (PCM)
FEM .... Finite Element Method
FEM .... Flame Emission Spectroscopy
FEM .... Flexion-Extension Motion [Orthopedics]
FEM .... Flyable Engineering Model (KSC)
FEMA....... Farm Equipment Manufacturers Association (EA)
FEMA....... Federal Emergency Management Agency [Independent government agency]
FEMA....... Fire Equipment Manufacturers Association (EA)
FEMA....... Flavor and Extract Manufacturers Association of the USA (EA)
FEMA....... Food Equipment Manufacturers Association (EA)
FEMA....... Foundry Equipment and Materials Association [Later, CISA] (EA)
FEMAA..... Feed Management [A publication]
FE Magazin ... FE. The Magazine for Financial Executives [A publication]
FEMAP..... Finite Element Mold-Filling Analysis Program [General Electric Co.]
FEMAS..... Far East Merchants Association [Defunct] (EA)
FEMCO..... National Federation of Export Management Companies (EA)
FEMCPL... Facilities and Environmental Measurement Components Parts List [NASA] (NASA)
FEMED..... Feinwerktechnik und Messtechnik [A publication]
FEMF....... Floating Electronic Maintenance Facility (MCD)
FEMF....... Foreign Electromotive Force (TEL)
FEM (Fact Equip Mater) ... FEM (Factory Equipment and Materials) [South Africa] [A publication]
FEMFM .... Federation of European Manufacturers of Friction Materials (EA)
FEMIB ...... Federation Europeenne des Syndicats de Fabricants de Menuiseries Industrielles de Batiment [European Federation of Building Joinery Manufacturers] (EAIO)
FEMIDE ... Federacion Mundial de Instituciones Financieras de Desarrollo [World Federation of Development Financing Institutions - WFDFI] [Madrid, Spain] (EAIO)
Feminist..... Feminist Studies [A publication]
Feminist Rev ... Feminist Review [A publication]
Feminist Stud ... Feminist Studies [A publication]
FEM INTERN ... Femoribus Internis [To the Inner Part of the Thigh] [Pharmacy] (ROG)
FEMIPI..... Federation Europeenne des Mandataires de l'Industrie en Propriete Industrielle [European Federation of Agents of Industry in Industrial Property] (EAIO)
Femip Kut Intez Kozl ... Femipari Kutato Intezet Kozlemenyei [A publication]
Femip Kut Intez Kozlem ... Femipari Kutato Intezet Kozlemenyei [Hungary] [A publication]
Fem Issues ... Feminist Issues [A publication]
FEMK........ Federation Europeenne des Masseurskinesitherapeutes Praticiens en Physiotherapie

FEMKSF ... Frauendienst der Evangelisch-Methodistischen Kirche in der Schweiz und in Frankreich [*United Methodist Women in Switzerland and in France*] (EAIO)
FEMO ...... Finite Element Modeling Optimization
FEMOSI ... Federation Mondiale des Syndicats d'Industries [*World Federation of Industrial Workers' Unions*]
FEMP .... Free Energy Minimization Procedure [*Data processing*]
Fem R .... Feminist Review [*A publication*]
FEMR .... Fleet Electromagnetic Radiation [*Team*] [*Navy*] (NVT)
Fem Rview ... Feminist Review [*A publication*]
FEMS .... Facilities Engineering Management System (MCD)
FEMS .... Facilities and Environmental Measuring System [*NASA*] (KSC)
FEMS .... Federation of the European Microbiological Societies (EAIO)
FEMS .... Field Electronic Maintenance Section [*National Weather Service*]
FEMS (Fed Eur Microbiol Soc) Microbiol Ecol ... FEMS (Federation of European Microbiological Societies) Microbiology-Ecology [*A publication*]
FEMS (Fed Eur Microbiol Soc) Microbiol Rev ... FEMS [*Federation of European Microbiological Societies*] Microbiology Reviews [*A publication*]
FEMS (Fed Eur Microbiol Soc) Symp ... FEMS (Federation of European Microbiological Societies) Symposium [*A publication*]
FEMS Mic Ec ... FEMS [*Federation of European Microbiological Societies*] Microbiology-Ecology [*A publication*]
FEMS Microbiol Lett ... FEMS [*Federation of European Microbiological Societies*] Microbiology Letters [*A publication*]
Fem Stud .... Feminist Studies [*A publication*]
FEMUSI ... Federacion Mundial de Sindicatos de Industrias [*World Federation of Industrial Workers' Unions*]
FE & MV ... Fremont, Elkhorn & Missouri Valley Railroad
FEMXAA .. Folia Entomologica Mexicana [*A publication*]
FEN .... Antara Financial and Economic News [*Jakarta*] [*A publication*]
FEN .... Fairchild Industries, Inc. [*NYSE symbol*] (SPSG)
FEN .... Far East Network [*US Armed Forces radio station*] [*Japan*]
FEN .... FEN. Factory Equipment News [*A publication*] (APTA)
FEN .... Fengtien [*Hoten, Shenyang*] [*Republic of China*] [*Seismograph station code, US Geological Survey*] (SEIS)
FEN .... Frequency-Emphasizing Network (IEEE)
Fenarete ..... Fenarete-Letture d'Italia [*A publication*]
FENASYCOA ... Federation Nationale des Syndicats du Commerce Ouest Africain [*National Federation of Commerce Unions - West Africa*]
FENC .... Fencing (ROG)
FENDRE ... Forces to Eliminate No-Deposit/No-Return
FENEA ...... Fertiliser News [*A publication*]
FEN Finite Elem News ... FEN. Finite Element News [*England*] [*A publication*]
FEng .... Fellow [*or Fellowship*] of Engineering
F/Eng. .... Flight Engineer (AIA)
F Eng .... Forest Engineer
FENIT ...... Federazione Nazionale Imprese Trasporti [*Transport Undertakings Federation*] [*Italy*] (EY)
FENKIN ... Fuel Supply Unknown [*Aviation*] (FAAC)
FENLAI .... Federazione Nazionale Lavoratori Auto-Ferrotramvieri e Internavigatori [*Transportation industry*] [*Italy*] (EY)
FENN .... Fennia [*A publication*]
FENNAJ ... Fennia [*A publication*]
FENP .... Fluoro(ethyl)norprogesterone [*Endocrinology*]
FENPB ...... Full Employment and National Purposes Budget (OICC)
Fent .... Fenton's Important Judgments [*New Zealand*] [*A publication*] (DLA)
Fent .... Fenton's New Zealand Reports [*A publication*] (DLA)
Fent Imp Judg ... Fenton's Important Judgments [*New Zealand*] [*A publication*] (DLA)
FENTL ...... Fuel Supply Until [*Followed by time*] [*Aviation*] (FAAC)
Fent (New Zealand) ... Fenton's New Zealand Reports [*A publication*] (DLA)
Fent NZ ..... Fenton's New Zealand Reports [*A publication*] (DLA)
FeNTO ...... Federation of the Scientific and Technical Organizations of the Socialist Countries [*Formerly, Permanent Council of Scientific and Technical Organizations of Socialist Countries*] (EA)
Fenton .... Fenton's Important Judgments [*New Zealand*] [*A publication*] (DLA)
FENUD ..... Fusion Energy Update [*A publication*]
Fenway C ... Fenway Court [*A publication*]
FEO .... Facility Emergency Organization [*Nuclear energy*] (NRCH)
FEO .... Federal Energy Office [*Later, FEA*]
FEO .... Feodosiya [*USSR*] [*Seismograph station code, US Geological Survey*] [*Closed*] (SEIS)
FEO .... Field Engineering Order (KSC)
FEO .... Field Extension Office [*DoD*]
FEO .... Flag Engineering Officer [*British*]
FEO .... Fleet Engineer Officer [*Obsolete*] [*British*]
FEO .... Flora Europaea Organization [*British*]
FEO .... Fuel-Efficient Oil
FEODT ...... Federation Europeenne des Organisations des Detaillants en Tabacs [*European Federation of Tobacco Retail Organizations*] (EAIO)
FEOF .... Foreign Exchange Operations Fund

FEOGA .... Fonds European d'Orientation et de Garantie Agricole [*Also known as EAGGF*]
FEORA2 .... Fertilite Orthogenie [*A publication*]
FEORP ...... Federal Equal Opportunity Recruitment Program
FEOS .... Forward Engineering Operating Station [*Navy*] (CAAL)
FEP .... Fair Employment Practice
FEP .... Federal Education Project [*Defunct*] (EA)
FEP .... Federal Employee Program
FEP .... Federation Europeenne de Psychanalyse [*European Psycho-Analytical Federation - EPF*] (EAIO)
FEP .... Fermented Egg Product [*Animal repellent*]
FEP .... Financial Evaluation Program [*IBM Corp.*]
FEP .... Flash Evaporator Plant
FEP .... Fluorinated Ethylene-Propylene [*Copolymer*]
FEP .... Fore Edges Painted [*Paper*]
FEP .... Foundation for Education with Production (EA)
FEP .... Free Enterprise Personnel (MCD)
FEP .... Free Erythrocyte Protoporphyrin [*Hematology*]
FEP .... Freeport, IL [*Location identifier*] [*FAA*] (FAAL)
FEP .... Front-End Processor [*Computer*] (NASA)
FEP .... Fuse Enclosure Package (IEEE)
FEPA .... Fair Educational Practice Act [*New York, New Jersey, Massachusetts*]
FEPA .... Fair Employment Practices Act [*1964*]
FEPA .... Far-Eastern Prehistory Association [*Later, IPPA*] (EA)
FEPA .... Federal Employees Pay Act
FEPA .... Federal Executive Pay Act, 1956
FEPA .... Federal Executive and Professional Association (EA)
FEPA .... Federation Europeenne des Fabricants de Produits Abrasifs [*European Federation of the Manufacturers of Abrasive Products*] [*France*]
FEPACE .... Federation Europeenne des Producteurs Autonomes et des Consommateurs Industriels d'Energie [*European Federation of Autoproducers and Industrial Consumers of Energy*] (EAIO)
FEPACI ..... Federation of Pan-African Cinema [*of the Organization of African Unity*]
FEPAFEM ... Federacion Panamericana de Asociacions de Facultades de Medicina [*Pan American Federation of Associations of Medical Schools - PAFAMS*] [*Caracas, Venezuela*] (EAIO)
FEPC .... Fair Employment Practices Code
FEPC .... Fair Employment Practices Committee [*or Commission*]
FEPCA .... Federal Environmental Pesticide Control Act [*1972*]
FEPD .... Federation Europeenne des Parfumeurs Detaillants [*European Federation of Perfumery Retailers*] (EAIO)
FEPD .... Forward Environmental Protection Device (MCD)
FEPE .... Europaeische Vereinigung der Briefumschlagfabrikanten [*European Association of Envelope Manufacturers*] (EAIO)
FEPE .... Federation Europeenne de la Publicite Exterieure [*European Federation of Outdoor Advertising*] [*France*]
FEPEM ...... Federation of European Petroleum Equipment Manufacturers [*Netherlands*]
FEPF .... European Federation of Earthenware, China and Tableware, and Ornamental Ware (EAIO)
FEPI .... Filipino Employment Policy Instruction (CINC)
FEPMA ...... Federation of European Pencil Manufacturers Associations [*See also FEFM*] (EA)
FEPNDW ... Forest Environmental Protection. United States Forest Service. Northern Region [*A publication*]
FEPO .... For Examination Purposes Only [*Education*]
FEPOW ..... Far East Prisoner of War
FEPP .... Foreign Excess Personal Property
FEPP .... Full Employment and Production Program (OICC)
FEPRA .... Federation Proceedings [*A publication*]
FEPRA7 ..... Federation Proceedings [*A publication*]
FEPRB8 ..... Feuillets du Praticien [*A publication*]
FEPS .... Far-Encounter Planet Sensor
FEPS .... Flight Envelope Protection System [*Aviation*]
FEPTO ...... Front Engine Power-Take-Off [*Automotive engineering*]
FEPU .... Frente Eleitoral do Povo Unido [*United People's Electoral Front*] [*Portugal*] [*Political party*] (PPE)
FEPXA .... Fernmelde-Praxis [*A publication*]
FEQ .... Failure Equation
FEQ .... Far Eastern Quarterly [*A publication*]
FER .... Fathers for Equal Rights (EA)
FER .... Fear [*A publication*]
FER .... Federacion de Estudiantes Revolucionarios [*Federation of Revolutionary Students*] [*Uruguay*] (PD)
FER .... Federal Economic Review [*A publication*]
FER .... Federation of Engine Re-Manufacturers [*Chigwell, Essex, England*] (EAIO)
FER .... Federation des Etudiants Revolutionnaires [*Federation of Revolutionary Students*] [*France*]
FER .... Feed Efficiency Ratio
FER .... Ferndale [*California*] [*Seismograph station code, US Geological Survey*] (SEIS)
FER .... Ferrierite [*A zeolite*]
FER .... Ferrum [*Iron*] [*Pharmacy*]
FER .... Ferry
FER .... Field Engineering Representative

FER............ Final Engineering Report
FER............ Fleet Employment Reports (MCD)
FER............ Force Exchange Ratio (MCD)
FER............ Forest Environment Research [*Department of Agriculture*] (GRD)
FER............ Forward Engine Room
FER............ Friends of Eye Research [*Formerly, FERRAT*] (EA)
FER............ Fusion Engineering Reactor [*Japan*]
FERA.......... Federal Emergency Relief Act of 1933
FERA.......... Federal Emergency Relief Administration [*Liquidated, 1937*]
Ferard Fixt ... Amos and Ferard on Fixtures (DLA)
FERC.......... Federal Energy Regulatory Commission [*Department of Energy*]
FERD.......... Facility and Equipment Requirements Document (NASA)
FERD.......... Foreign Economic Relations Department [*Burma*] (DS)
FERD.......... Fuel Element Rupture Detection [*Nuclear energy*] (NRCH)
FERES........ Federation Internationale des Instituts de Recherches Socio-Religieuses [*International Federation of Institutes for Socio-Religious Research*]
FERF.......... Financial Executives Research Foundation (EA)
Fer Fixt...... Ferard on Fixtures [*A publication*] (DLA)
Ferg........... Consistorial Decisions, Scotland, by George Ferguson, Lord Hermand [*A publication*] (DLA)
FERG........ Family Economics Research Group [*Department of Agriculture*] (GRD)
Ferg........... Fergusson's Consistorial Decisions [*Scotland*] [*A publication*] (DLA)
Ferg Cons... Fergusson's Consistorial Reports [*Scotland*] [*A publication*] (DLA)
Ferg M & D ... Fergusson's Divorce Decisions by Consistorial Courts [*Scotland*] [*A publication*] (DLA)
Ferg Proc ... Ferguson's Common Law Procedure Act [*Ireland*] [*A publication*] (DLA)
Ferg Ry Cas ... Fergusson's Five Years' Railway Cases [*A publication*] (DLA)
Fergusson... Fergusson's Consistorial Decisions [*Scotland*] [*A publication*] (DLA)
Fergusson... Fergusson's Scotch Session Cases [*1738-52*] [*A publication*] (DLA)
FERIC .... False Entries in Records of Interstate Carriers [*FBI standardized term*]
FERIC .... Forest Engineering Research Institute of Canada [*Vancouver, BC*]
FERIC (For Eng Res Inst Can) Tech Rep ... FERIC (Forest Engineering Research Institute of Canada) Technical Report [*A publication*]
FERM........ Fast Escape Recallable Missile
FERM........ Fermanagh [*County in Northern Ireland*] (ROG)
FERMA2... Fermentatio [*A publication*]
FERMANH ... Fermanagh [*County in Northern Ireland*]
Ferment Ind ... Fermentation and Industry [*A publication*]
Fermentn Spirt Promst ... Fermentnaya i Spirtovaya Promyshlennost [*A publication*]
Fermes Mod ... Fermes Modernes [*A publication*]
FERMILAB ... Fermi National Accelerator Laboratory [*Also, FNAL*] [*Batavia, IL*] [*Department of Energy*]
FERN......... Federal Employee/Retiree Newsletter [*A publication*] [*Information service or system*] (IID)
Fernald Eng Synonyms ... Fernald's English Synonyms [*A publication*] (DLA)
Fern Dec .... Decretos del Fernando [*Mexico*] [*A publication*] (DLA)
Fern Gaz .... Fern Gazette [*A publication*]
Fern Internat ... Fernwaerme International [*A publication*]
Fernmelde-Ing ... Fernmelde-Ingenieur [*A publication*]
Fernmelde-Prax ... Fernmelde-Praxis [*A publication*]
Fernmeldetech Z ... Fernmeldetechnische Zeitschrift [*West Germany*] [*A publication*]
Fernsehen & B ... Fernsehen und Bildung [*A publication*]
Fernseh- & Kino- Tech ... Fernseh- und Kino- Technik [*A publication*]
Fernwaerme Int ... Fernwaerme International [*A publication*]
FERO......... Far East Research Office
FERO......... Ferrofluidics Corp. [*NASDAQ symbol*] (NQ)
FEROA...... Ferroelectrics [*A publication*]
Ferodo Int Tech News ... Ferodo International Technical News [*A publication*]
FERPA ...... Family Educational Rights and Privacy Act [*1974*]
FERPIC..... Ferroelectric Ceramic Picture Device (IEEE)
FERR........ Feliciana Eastern Railroad Co. [*Formerly, FE*] [*AAR code*]
FERR........ Ferrum [*Iron*] [*Pharmacy*] (ROG)
Ferrar......... [*Johannes Petrus de*] Ferrariis [*Flourished, 14th-15th century*] [*Authority cited in pre-1607 legal work*] (DSA)
Ferrara Univ Ann Sez 9 ... Ferrara. Universita. Annali. Sezione 9. Scienze Geologiche e Paleontologiche [*A publication*]
FERRAT ... Friends of Eye Research, Rehabilitation, and Treatment [*Later, FER*] (EA)
Ferret .... [*Aemilius*] Ferretus [*Deceased, 1552*] [*Authority cited in pre-1607 legal work*] (DSA)
Ferriere ...... Ferriere's Dictionnaire de Droit et de Pratique [*A publication*] (DLA)
Ferriere Dict de Jr ... Ferriere's Dictionary of Jurisprudence [*A publication*] (DLA)
FERROD... Ferrite-Rod Antenna (IEEE)

Ferroelectr ... Ferroelectrics [*A publication*]
Ferroelectr Lett ... Ferroelectrics Letters [*United Kingdom*] [*A publication*]
Ferroelectr Lett Sect ... Ferroelectrics Letters Section [*A publication*]
Ferroelectr Relat Phenom ... Ferroelectricity and Related Phenomena [*A publication*]
Ferron .... [*Arnaldus*] Ferronus [*Deceased, 1563*] [*Authority cited in pre-1607 legal work*] (DSA)
FERS .... Federal Employees' Retirement System
FERSA ...... Federal Employees' Retirement System Act of 1986
FERSI........ Flat Earth Research Society International (EA)
FERST....... Freight and Equipment Reporting System for Transportation [*IBM Corp.*]
FERST/VS ... Freight and Equipment Reporting System for Transportation/ Virtual Storage [*IBM Corp.*]
FERT .... Fertilizer
FERT .... Fortitudo Eius Rhodum Tenuit [*His Strength Keeps Rhodes*] [*Motto of Lodovico family. Initials were used on gold coin struck by Duke Lodovico (1439-1465)*]
FERT .... Nu-West Industries, Inc. [*NASDAQ symbol*] (NQ)
Fert Abstr .. Fertilizer Abstracts [*A publication*]
Fert Agric.. Fertilizers and Agriculture [*A publication*]
Fert Assoc India Proc ... Fertiliser Association of India. Proceedings [*A publication*]
FERTD...... Fertilized
Fert Data.... Fertilizer Summary Data [*A publication*]
Fert Embryog Ovulated Plants Proc Int Cytoembryol Symp ... Fertilization and Embryogenesis in Ovulated Plants. Proceedings. International Cytoembryological Symposium [*A publication*]
Fert Farming Food ... Fertiliser, Farming, and Food [*A publication*]
Fert Feed Stuffs J ... Fertilizer and Feeding Stuffs Journal [*A publication*]
Fert Focus .. Fertilizer Focus [*A publication*]
Fert Green Bk ... Fertilizer Green Book [*A publication*]
Fertigungstech Betr ... Fertigungstechnik und Betrieb [*A publication*]
Fertil Contracept ... Fertility and Contraception [*A publication*]
Fertil Feed Stuffs J ... Fertilizer and Feeding Stuffs Journal [*A publication*]
Fertil Orthogenie ... Fertilite Orthogenie [*A publication*]
Fertil Steril ... Fertility and Sterility [*A publication*]
Fertil Steril Proc World Congr ... Fertility and Sterility. Proceedings. World Congress on Fertility and Sterility [*A publication*]
Fert Inst (Delhi) Proc ... Fertiliser Institute (Delhi). Proceedings [*A publication*]
Fert Int...... Fertilizer International [*A publication*]
Fert Intnl.... Fertilizer International [*A publication*]
Fert Issues ... Journal of Fertilizer Issues [*A publication*]
Fert Mark News ... Fertilizer Marketing News [*A publication*]
Fert News... Fertilizer News [*A publication*]
Fert Prog.... Fertilizer Progress [*A publication*]
Fert R........ Fertilizer Review [*A publication*]
Fert Res...... Fertilizer Research [*A publication*]
Fert Sci Technol Ser ... Fertilizer Science and Technology Series [*A publication*]
Fert Soc S Afr J ... Fertilizer Society of South Africa. Journal [*A publication*]
Fert Solutions ... Fertilizer Solutions [*A publication*]
Fert Steril... Fertility and Sterility [*A publication*]
Fert Technol ... Fertilizer Technology [*A publication*]
FERTZ ...... Fertilizer
FERV........ Fervens [*Hot*] [*Pharmacy*]
FERV........ Foundation for Education and Research in Vision (EA)
FERVY ...... Ferrovanadium Corp. ADR [*NASDAQ symbol*] (NQ)
FES............ Asian Survey [*A publication*]
FES............ Family Environment Scale
FES............ Family Expenditure Survey [*Department of Employment*] [*British*]
FES............ Far Eastern Survey [*A publication*]
FES............ Fast Erect System
FES............ Federal Executive Service
FES............ Federal Extension Service [*Department of Agriculture*]
FES............ Federation of Eastern Stars (EA)
FES............ Federation Europeenne de la Salmoniculture [*Federation of the European Trout and Salmon Industry*] [*Formerly, European Salmon Breeding Federation*] (EA)
FES............ Fellow of the Entomological Society [*British*]
FES............ Fellow of the Ethnological Society [*British*]
FES............ Festus, MO [*Location identifier*] [*FAA*] (FAAL)
FES............ Field Emission Spectroscopy
FES............ Field Emitting Surface
FES............ Field Engineering Service
FES............ Final Environmental Statement [*Bureau of Outdoor Recreation*]
FES............ Fine Error Sensor (KSC)
FES............ First Empire State Corp. [*AMEX symbol*] (SPSG)
FES............ Flame Emission Spectrometry
FES............ Flash Evaporator System (MCD)
FES............ Flight Element Set (MCD)
FES............ Flower Essence Society (EA)
FES............ Fluid to Electric Switch
FES............ Fluidic Environmental Sensor (RDA)
FES............ Fluorescence Excitation Spectrum
FES............ Food Education Society [*British*]

FES .... Forced Expiratory Spirogram [*Medicine*]
FES .... Forms Entry System
FES .... Front-End Screening [*DoD*]
FESA .... Facilities Engineering Support Agency [*Army*]   (MCD)
FESA .... Federal Employees Salary Act of 1970
FESA .... Federal Employment Service Act [*1933*]
FESA .... Federal Executive Salary Act of 1964
FESA .... Federation of Engineering and Scientific Associations
FESA .... Fonetic English Spelling Association
FESAC ...... Fondation de l'Enseignement Superieur en Afrique Centrale
FESAP .... Finite Element Structures Analysis Program [*Data processing*]
FESC .... Far East Science Center
FESC .... Federation Europeenne des Sports Corporatifs [*European Federation for Company Sports - EFCS*]   (EAIO)
FESCID ..... Federation Europeenne des Syndicats de la Chimie et des Industries Diverses[*European Federation of Chemical and General Workers Unions*]   (EAIO)
FESCO ...... Far Eastern Shipping Company [*USSR*]
FESCO ...... Foreign Enterprise Service Corporation [*People's Republic of China*]
FESE .... Field-Enhanced Secondary Emission
FESFP .... Federation Europeenne des Syndicats de Fabricants de Parquets [*European Federation of Parquet Manufacturers Unions*]
FeSFV .... Feline Syncytium-Forming Virus
FESI .... Federation Europeenne des Syndicats d'Entreprises d'Isolation [*European Federation of Associations of Insulation Contractors*]   (EA)
FESIA .... Federal Employees Salary Increase Act
FESL .... Failure Effects Summary List   (NASA)
FESO .... Federal Employment Stabilization Office [*Functions transferred to National Resources Planning Board, 1939*]
FESP .... (Fluoroethyl)spiperone [*Biochemistry*]
FESPIC ..... Far East and South Pacific   (ADA)
FESR .... Finite Energy Sum Rules [*Physics*]
FESR .... Further Education Statistical Record [*Department of Education and Science*] [*British*]
FESS .... Facilities Engineer Supply System [*Army*]
FESS .... Fleet Environmental Support System [*Navy*]
FESS .... Flight Experiment Shielding Satellite
FESS .... Flywheel Energy Storage System
Fessen Pat .. Fessenden on Patents [*A publication*]   (DLA)
Fess Pat ..... Fessenden on Patents [*A publication*]   (DLA)
FEST .... Festival
Fest .... Festival [*Record label*]
FESTA ...... Fertility and Sterility [*A publication*]
FESTAC .... World Black and African Festival of Arts and Culture
FESTAS ..... Fertility and Sterility [*A publication*]
FestF .... Festival (France) [*Record label*]
Festkoerperprobl ... Festkoerperprobleme [*A publication*]
FESTUK.... Federation of Engineering and Shipbuilding Trades of the United Kingdom [*A union*]
FESV .... Feline Sarcoma Virus [*Also, FeSV*]
FESW .... Federation of Eastern Stars of the World   (EA)
FESX .... First Essex Bancorp, Inc. [*NASDAQ symbol*]   (NQ)
FESYP .... Federation Europeenne des Syndicats de Fabricants de Panneaux de Particules [*European Federation of Associations of Particleboard Manufacturers*]   (EAIO)
f-et--- .... Ethiopia [*MARC geographic area code*] [*Library of Congress*]   (LCCP)
FET .... Federal Estate Tax   (DLA)
FET .... Federal Excise Tax
FET .... Federation of Environmental Technologists   (EA)
FET .... Field Effect Transistor
FET .... Financieel Ekonomische Tijd [*A publication*]
FET .... Fleet Evaluation Trial [*Navy*]   (NG)
FET .... Flight Elapsed Time   (MCD)
FET .... Flight Engineer in Training
FET .... Fluidic Emergency Thruster [*Aviation*]
FET .... Fluorescence Energy Transfer [*Physics*]
FET .... Foldable Elastic Tube [*Satellite hinge*]
FET .... Forced Expiratory Time [*Physiology*]
FET .... Foreign Economic Trends [*A publication*]
FET .... Foreign Escorted Tour [*Travel*]
FET .... Foundation on Economic Trends   (EA)
FET .... Freeze-Etch Technique
FET .... Fremont, NE [*Location identifier*] [*FAA*]   (FAAL)
FET .... Functional Element Test
FET .... Milling Feed and Fertilizer [*A publication*]
FETAC ...... Foreign Economic and Trade Arbitration Commission [*Chinese*]   (GEA)
FETAP ...... Federation Europeenne des Transports Aeriens Prives [*European Federation of Independent Air Transport*]
FETBB....... Federation Europeenne des Travailleurs du Batiment et du Bois [*European Federation of Building and Woodworkers - EFBWW*]   (EAIO)
FETC .... Federal Excise Tax Council [*Defunct*]   (EA)
FETEDP.... Fertilizer Technology [*A publication*]
FETF .... Flight Engine Test Facility
FETI .... Fluorescence Energy Transfer Immunoassay [*Analytical biochemistry*]
FETID .... Federal Times [*A publication*]

FET de las JONS ... Falange Espanola Tradicionalista y de las Juntas de Ofensiva Nacional Sindicalista [*Traditionalist Spanish Phalange of the Syndicalist Juntas of the National Offensive*] [*Political party*]   (PPE)
FETO......... Factory Equipment Transfer Order
FETO......... Field Engineering Theory of Operations
FETRA ...... Federation des Industries Transformatrices de Papier et Carton [*Paper and Board Federation*] [*Belgium*]   (EY)
FETS .... Forced Expiratory Time, in Seconds [*Physiology*]
Fet Sei Ans ... Fette - Seifen - Anstrichmittel. Verbunden mit der Zeitschrift die Ernaehrungs Industrie [*A publication*]
FETS/SEA ... Federal Emission Test Sequence and Selective Enforcement Audit [*General Motors Corp.*]
FETT .... First Engine to Test
Fett Carr .... Fetter's Treatise on Carriers of Passengers [*A publication*]   (DLA)
Fettchem Umsch ... Fettchemische Umschau [*A publication*]
Fette Seife ... Fette - Seifen - Anstrichmittel [*A publication*]
Fette Seifen Anstrichm ... Fette - Seifen - Anstrichmittel [*A publication*]
Fette Seifen Anstrmittel ... Fette - Seifen - Anstrichmittel [*A publication*]
FETU......... Far Eastern Technical Unit [*World War II*]
FEU.......... Federated Engineering Union
FEU .... Fire Experimental Unit [*British Fire Service*]   (IRUK)
FEU .... Fossil Energy Update [*A publication*]
FEU .... Fuel Equivalent Unit
FEU .... Further Education Unit [*British*]
FEUBAI .... Annali. Universita di Ferrara. Sezione IV. Botanica [*A publication*]
FEUD .... Feudal
Feud Lib.... Feudorum Liber [*Book of Feuds*] [*Latin*] [*A publication*]   (DLA)
FEUFJ....... Far Eastern University. Faculty Journal [*A publication*]
Feuill Biol .. Feuillets de Biologie [*A publication*]
Feuill Prat .. Feuillets du Praticien [*A publication*]
FEUPF ...... Federation Europeenne des Unions Professionelles de Fleuristes [*European Federation of Professional Florists' Unions*]   (EAIO)
FEURS ...... Fabrication Equivalent Unit Reporting System   (MCD)
FEUS......... French Engineers in the United States   (EA)
FEV........... Familial Exudative Vitreoretinopathy [*Ophthalmology*]
FEV........... Forced Expiratory Volume [*Physiology*]
FEVA .... Federal Employees Veterans Association [*Later, NAGE*]   (EA)
FEVAC...... Ferroelectric Variable Capacitor
FEVE .... Federation Europeenne du Verre d'Emballage [*European Container Glass Federation - ECGF*]   (EA)
Feversham Cttee ... Committee on Human Artificial Insemination. Report [*1960*] [*A publication*]   (ILCA)
FEVIR .... Federation of European Veterinarians in Industry and Research   (EA)
FEVSD ...... Federation Europeenne pour la Vente et le Service a Domicile [*European Direct Selling Federation*] [*Brussels, Belgium*]   (EA)
FEW.......... Cheyenne, WY [*Location identifier*] [*FAA*]   (FAAL)
FEW.......... Federally Employed Women
FEWA .... Farm Equipment Wholesalers Association   (EA)
FEWC....... Force Electronic Warfare Coordinator   (NVT)
FEWG....... Flight Evaluation Working Group   (MCD)
FEWIA ...... Federation of European Writing Instruments Associations [*See also FEAIE*]   (EA)
FEWITA ... Federation of European Wholesale and International Trade Associations [*Common Market*] [*Belgium*]
FEWMA ... Federation of European Window Manufacturers Associations   (EA)
FEWO .... Fund for Education in World Order [*Later, FFP*]   (EA)
FEWS........ Famine Early Warning System [*US Agency for International Development*]
FEWSG ..... Fleet Electronic Warfare Support Group
FEWT....... Functional Equipment Withholding Tab [*Obsolete*]
FEWTS...... Force Electronic Warfare/Tactical SIGINT
FEX........... Fabien Exploration, Inc. [*Toronto Stock Exchange symbol*]
FEX........... Field Exercise [*Military*]   (NVT)
FEX........... Financial Executive [*A publication*]
FEX........... Fleet Exercise [*Navy*]
FEX........... FLIGHTEXEC Ltd. [*London, ON, Canada*] [*FAA designator*]   (FAAC)
FEX........... Foreign Exchange [*Telecommunications*]   (TEL)
FEX........... Fort Worth, TX [*Location identifier*] [*FAA*]   (FAAL)
FEXA .... Florida Express, Inc. [*Orlando, FL*] [*NASDAQ symbol*]   (NQ)
FEXC........ First Executive Corporation [*NASDAQ symbol*]   (NQ)
FEXHA..... Fuel Supply Exhausted [*Aviation*]   (FAAC)
FEXT........ Far-End Crosstalk [*Telecommunications*]
FEXT .... Fire Extinguisher
FEY........... Forever Yours
FEYI .... Fey Industries [*NASDAQ symbol*]   (NQ)
FEZ........... Federation Europeenne de Zootechnie [*European Federation for Animal Production*] [*Rome, Italy*]
FEZ........... Fez [*Morocco*] [*Airport symbol*]   (OAG)
FEZ........... Fighter Engagement Zone [*Military*]   (NVT)
ff----- .... Africa, North [*MARC geographic area code*] [*Library of Congress*]   (LCCP)
FF.............. Africair Service [*Senegal*] [*ICAO designator*]   (FAAC)

F-F	Face to Face
F to F	Face to Face [Technical drawings]
FF	Facility Forecast (MCD)
FF	Factory Finish [Technical drawings]
F on F	Facts on File [A publication]
FF	Failure Factor (NG)
FF	Failure to Feed (MCD)
FF	Fairness Fund (EA)
FF	Faith and Form [A publication]
FF	Fanfare [A publication]
FF	Fanny Fern [Pseudonym used by Sara Payson Parton]
FF	Farm Foundation (EA)
FF	Fast Fatigue [Type of muscle contraction]
FF	Fast Flow
FF	Fast Food [A publication]
FF	Fast Forward [Audio-visual technology]
FF	Fat Free [Biochemistry]
FF	Fecerunt [They Did It] [Latin]
FF	Fee Factor (MCD)
FF	Felicissimi Fratres [Most Fortunate Brothers] [Latin]
FF	Felicissimus [Most Happy] [Latin] (ROG)
FF	Feuille Federale [Switzerland] [A publication]
FF	Fianna Fail [Warriors of Destiny] [Political party] [Ireland]
F of F	Field of Fire [Military] (AABC)
FF	Field Forces [Military]
FF	Field Function [Telecommunications] (TEL)
FF	Fieri Fecit [Caused to Be Made] [Latin]
FF	Fighting French
FF	File Finish (MSA)
FF	Fill Factor [Photovoltaic energy systems]
F/F	Fill/Full [or Full/Fill] (MCD)
FF	Filmfacts [A publication]
F & F	Films and Filming [A publication]
FF	Films and Filming [A publication]
FF	Filter Factor (NRCH)
FF	Filtration Fraction [Physiology]
FF	Fimbria-Fornix [Neuroanatomy]
FF	Finagle-Factor
FF	Finger to Finger [Medicine]
FF	Finlandia Foundation (EA)
FF	Fir-Fast [Forestry]
FF	Fire Fighting (MSA)
F & F	Fire and Flushing (KSC)
F & F	Fire-and-Forget (MCD)
FF	Firefinder
FF	First Families [i.e., the aristocracy] [Slang]
FF	First Fandom (EA)
FF	First Financial Fund, Inc. [NYSE symbol] (SPSG)
F of F	Firth of Forth (DAS)
F & F	Fittings and Fixtures (ADA)
FF	Fixed Fee [Business term] (AAG)
FF	Fixed Focus [Photography]
FF	Fixing Fluid [Histology]
FF	Flat Face [Diamonds]
FF	Flat Feet
FF	Fleet Fighter [Air Force]
FF	Fleet Flagship
ff	Fleurs [Flowers] [Pharmacy]
FF	Flexi-Filament
FF	Flight Forward (MCD)
F-F	Flip-Flop [Data processing]
FF	Florida Facility [NASA] (KSC)
FF	Fluorine Facility [Nuclear energy] (NRCH)
FF	Flush Fitting
FF	Fog Factor
FF	Foglio Federale Svizzero [A publication]
FF	Folded File
FF	Folded Flat [Freight]
FF	Folgende [And the Following Pages, Verses, etc.] [German] (ROG)
FF	Folios [Leaves]
FF	Folklore [A publication]
FF	Folklore Forum [A publication]
FF	Following [Pages] [Also, F]
FF	Force Feed (MSA)
FF	Force Field
FF	Force Flagship
FF	Force [or Forced] Fluid [Medicine]
FF	Ford Foundation
FF	Foreign Flag
FF	Foremanship Foundation [Defunct] (EA)
FF	Forgotten Fantasy [A publication]
FF	Form Feed [Data processing]
FF	Forschungen und Fortschritte [A publication]
F & F	Forschungen und Fortschritte [A publication]
FF	Fortissimo [Very Loud] [Music]
FF	Forward Fuselage
FF	Fossil Fuels
FF	Foster Father
F & F	Foster and Finlason's English Nisi Prius Reports [175, 176 English Reprint] [A publication] (DLA)
FF	Foul Fly [Baseball]
FF	Fraenkische Forschungen [A publication]
FF	Fragrance Foundation (EA)
FF	Franc [Monetary unit] [Marie Galente]
FF	France Franciscaine [A publication]
FF	Francs Francais [French Francs] [Monetary unit]
FF	Franklin Furnace (EA)
F-F	Frasnian-Famennian [Boundary] [Geophysics]
FF	Frate Francesco [A publication]
FF	Fratres [Brothers] [Latin]
FF	Fredspolitisk Folkeparti [People's Peace Policy Party] [Denmark] (PPE)
FF	Free-Fall
FF	Free the Fathers (EA)
FF	Free Flight
FF	Free Flood
FF	Free Fraction
FF	Free French [World War II]
FF	Freedom Federation [Defunct] (EA)
FF	Freedom Fund [An association] (EA)
FF	Freedom's Friends (EA)
FF	Freight Forwarder
FF	French Fourragere [Military decoration]
FF	French Franc [Monetary unit]
FF	French Fried
FF	Fresh Frozen
FF	Frie Folkevalgte [Freely Elected Representatives] [Norway] (PPE)
FF	Friends of the Farm [An association] (EA)
FF	Friendship Force (EA)
FF	Frigate [Navy symbol]
FF	Front Focal Length [Optics]
FF	Frontier Force
FF	Fruit Frost (NOAA)
FF	Fuel Flow (AAG)
FF	Full Face [Photography]
FF	Full-Fashioned
FF	Full Field
FF	Function of a Quantity [Mathematics] (ROG)
F & F	Furniture and Fixtures [Insurance]
FF	Thick Fog [Navigation]
FFA	Air-Cushion Vehicle built by Flygtekniska Forsoksanstalen [Sweden] [Usually used in combination with numerals]
FFA	Fast Fourier Analyzer (MCD)
FFA	Federal Firearms Act
FFA	Fellow of the Faculty of Actuaries [British]
FFA	Fellow of the Faculty of Anesthetists [British]
FFA	Fiberglass Fabrication Association (EA)
FFA	FirstFed America [AMEX symbol] (SPSG)
FFA	Flammable Fabrics Act [1953]
FFA	Flexible Factory Automation
FFA	Florida Foliage Association (EA)
FFA	For Further Assignment
FFA	Forces Francaises en Allemagne [French Forces in Germany] (MCD)
FFA	Foreign Freight Agent
FFA	Forest Farmers Association (EA)
FFA	Foundation for Foreign Affairs (EA)
FFA	Frankford Arsenal [Pennsylvania] [Army] [Closed] (AABC)
FFA	Frankfurter Allgemeine Zeitung fuer Deutschland [A publication]
FFA	Free-for-All (ADA)
FFA	Free from Alongside [Shipping]
FFA	Free from Average [Insurance]
FFA	Free Fatty Acid [Biochemistry]
FFA	Free Field Analysis
FFA	Free Fire Area (AABC)
FFA	Free Foreign Agency [or Agent] [Business term]
FFA	Friends of Frank Ashmore (EA)
FFA	Friends of French Art (EA)
FFA	Full Freight Allowed
FFA	Funds Flow Analysis
FFA	Future Farmers of America [Later, NFFAO] (EA)
FFA	Kill Devil Hills, NC [Location identifier] [FAA] (FAAL)
FFA	South Pacific Forum Fisheries Agency [Australia]
FFAA	4th Field Artillery (Mountain Pack) Association (EA)
FFAC	Federal Food Advisory Committee [Cost of Living Council]
FFAC	Forward Forward Air Controller [Military]
FFACCRR	Freedom of Faith: A Christian Committee for Religious Rights (EA)
FFACT	Fiber, Fabric, and Apparel Coalition for Trade (EA)
FFACT	Frozen Foods Action Communications Team (EA)
FFACTS	Flammable Fabric Accident Case and Testing System [National Institute of Standards and Technology]
FFAG	Fixed-Field Alternating Gradient [Accelerator] [Nuclear energy]
FFAGHS	Federation of Franco-American Genealogical and Historical Societies (EA)
FFAIS	Full Frontal Area Impact Switch (MCD)
FFAL	First Federal of Alabama FSB [Jasper, AL] [NASDAQ symbol] (NQ)

FFAR......... Folding Fin Aircraft Rocket
FFAR......... Forward Fighting Aircraft Rocket
FFAR......... Forward Firing Aircraft
FFARACS ... Fellow of the Faculty of Anaesthetists of the Royal Australian College of Surgeons
FFARCS.... Fellow of the Faculty of Anaesthetists of the Royal College of Surgeons of England
FFARCS Eng ... Fellow of the Faculty of Anaesthetists of the Royal College of Surgeons of England
FFARCSI .. Fellow of the Faculty of Anaesthetists of the Royal College of Surgeons in Ireland
FFARCSIrel ... Fellow of the Faculty of Anaesthetists of the Royal College of Surgeons in Ireland [*British*]   (DBQ)
FFARP....... Fleet Fighter Acoustic Countermeasures Readiness Program [*Navy*]   (MCD)
FFAS .... Fellow of the Faculty of Architects and Surveyors, London [*British*]
FFAS .... Flash Flood Alarm System [*National Weather Service*]
FFAS .... Flickinger Foundation for American Studies   (EA)
FFAS .... Free Flight Analysis Section
FFAST....... Fire and Forget Antitank System Technology   (MCD)
FFAT .... First Federal Bank FSB [*NASDAQ symbol*]   (NQ)
FFAUS ...... Federation of French Alliances in the United States [*Later, FIAF*]   (EA)
FFAZ......... First Federal Savings & Loan of Arizona [*NASDAQ symbol*]   (NQ)
FFB........... Fact-Finding Bodies
FFB........... Fat-Free Body
FFB........... Federal Farm Board [*Name changed to Farm Credit Administration, 1933*]
FFB........... Federal Financing Bank
FFB........... Fertilizer International [*A publication*]
FFB........... First Fidelity Bancorp. [*NYSE symbol*]   (SPSG)
FFB........... Fixed-Film Biological [*Process for wastewater treatment*]
FFB........... Flexible Fiber-Optic Bronchoscopy [*Medicine*]
FFB........... Fluid Film Bearing
FFB........... Food from Britain
FFB........... Friends of Fritz Busch [*Record label*]
FFB........... Functional Flow Block
FFBA .... Fellow of the Corporation of Executives and Administrators [*British*]   (DBQ)
FFBA .... Foundation of the Federal Bar Association   (EA)
FFBC .... First Financial Bancorp [*NASDAQ symbol*]   (NQ)
FFBD......... Functional Flow Block Diagram
FFBI .... Foundation for Blood Irradiation   (EA)
FFBJ .... Federation of Free Byelorussian Journalists   (EA)
FFBK .... First Florida Banks, Inc. [*NASDAQ symbol*]   (NQ)
FFBM .... Fat-Free Body Mass
FFBN......... First Federal Bank FSB [*Nashua, NH*] [*NASDAQ symbol*]   (NQ)
FFBT .... Forward Fuel Ballast Tank
FFBV .... First Federal Savings & Loan Association of Brooksville [*Brooksville, FL*] [*NASDAQ symbol*]   (NQ)
FFC........... Family Fitness Council
FFC........... Farmers Federation Cooperative
FFC........... Federal Facilities Corporation [*Dissolved, 1961*]
FFC........... Federal Fire Council [*Defunct*]   (EA)
FFC........... Fellowship of Fire Chaplains   (EA)
FFC........... Ferret Fanciers Club   (EA)
FFC........... Film Finance Corporation [*Australia*]
FFC........... Films for Christ Association
FFC........... Final Flight Certification [*Aerospace*]
FFC........... Financial Funds Control
FFC........... Firm Fan Club [*Defunct*]   (EA)
FFC........... First Families of Carolina [*See also FFV*]
FFC........... First Flight Cover [*Philately*]
FFC........... Firstfund Capital Corp. [*Vancouver Stock Exchange symbol*]
FFC........... Fixed Film Capacitor
FFC........... Flagler College, St. Augustine, FL [*OCLC symbol*]   (OCLC)
FFC........... Flin Flon [*Manitoba*] [*Seismograph station code, US Geological Survey*]   (SEIS)
FFC........... Flip-Flop Complementary [*Data processing*]   (MSA)
FFC........... Folklore Fellows Communications [*A publication*]
FFC........... For Further Clearance [*Aviation*]   (FAAC)
FFC........... Ford Forestry Center [*Michigan Technological University*] [*Research center*]   (RCD)
FFC........... Foreign Funds Control
FFC........... Foundation for Cure   (EA)
FFC........... Free from Chlorine
FFC........... Free from Foreign Capture   (ROG)
FFC........... Full Faith and Credit [*Finance*]
FFC........... Fund American Companies [*Formerly, Fireman's Fund Corp.*] [*NYSE symbol*]   (SPSG)
FFC........... Fund for the Future Committee   (EA)
FFC........... Futures for Children   (EA)
FFC........... Fuze Firing Circuit   (RDA)
FFCA .... Carolina Bancorp, Inc. [*NASDAQ symbol*]   (NQ)
FFCAA ...... Federation Francaise des Cooperatives Agricoles d'Approvisionnement
FFC Abstr ... Forest Fire Control Abstracts [*A publication*]
FFCAC ...... Federation Francaise des Cooperatives Agricoles de Cereales

FFCB .... Federal Farm Credit Board [*of FCA*]
FFCBB...... Fred's Fan Club - Burstein's Buffalos   (EA)
FFCF......... Federation des Femmes Canadiennes-Francaises [*Federation of French-Canadian Women*]
FFCH........ First Financial Holdings, Inc. [*NASDAQ symbol*]   (NQ)
FFCI .... Fellow of the Faculty of Commerce and Industry [*British*]   (DBQ)
FFCM .... Fellow of the Faculty of Community Medicine [*British*]
F F Commun ... F F Communications [*A publication*]
FFCR .... Freight Forwarders Certificate of Receipt [*Shipping*]   (DS)
FFCS......... Federal Farm Credit System
FFCS......... Fellow of the Faculty of Secretaries [*British*]   (DBQ)
FFCS.......... First Colorado Financial Corp. [*Colorado Springs, CO*] [*NASDAQ symbol*]   (NQ)
FFCS.......... Food Facilities Consultants Society [*Later, FCSI*]   (EA)
FFCSA....... Florida Fresh Citrus Shippers Association [*Later, FCP*]   (EA)
FFCT .... FFB Corp. [*New Haven, CT*] [*NASDAQ symbol*]   (NQ)
FFD.......... Fairfield Minerals Ltd. [*Vancouver Stock Exchange symbol*]
FFD.......... Fellow in the Faculty of Dentistry [*British*]
FFD.......... Field Forcing (Decreasing)
FFD.......... Film: Foreign Documentary
FFD.......... Fixed Format Display   (MCD)
FFD.......... Flange Focal Distance   (MCD)
FFD.......... Focus Film Distance [*Radiology*]
FFD.......... Formation Flight Display
FFD.......... Forward Floating Depot [*Army*]
FFD.......... Free Flight Data
FFD.......... Friendly Forward Disposition
FFD.......... Fuel Failure Detection
FFD.......... Functional Flow Diagram
FFD of A ... Federated Funeral Directors of America [*Commercial firm*]
FFDA......... Federated Funeral Directors of America [*Commercial firm*]   (EA)
FFDA......... Fiber Fineness Distribution Analyzer   (ADA)
FFDA......... Flying Funeral Directors of America   (EA)
FFDCA ..... Federal Food, Drug, and Cosmetic Act
FFDK......... Fixed Flexion Deformity of the Knee [*Orthopedics*]
FFDO........ Fellow of the Faculty of Dispensing Opticians [*British*]   (DBQ)
FFDO........ Force Fighter Director Officer
FFDRCSI .. Fellow of the Faculty of Dentistry of the Royal College of Surgeons in Ireland
FFDRCS Irel ... Fellow of the Faculty of Dentistry of the Royal College of Surgeons in Ireland
FFDS .... Fleet Flag Data System [*Navy*]   (MCD)
FFDW........ Fat-Free Dry Weight
FFE........... Blick durch die Wirtschaft [*A publication*]
FFE........... Falling Film Evaporation
FFE........... Finished Floor Elevation [*Technical drawings*]
FFE........... Fire for Effect [*Army*]   (INF)
FFE........... Fire-Fighting Equipment   (AAG)
FFE........... Forced Fault Entry [*Data processing*]
FFE........... Friends for Education   (EA)
FF & E .... Furniture, Fixtures, and Equipment [*Insurance*]
FFEC .... Field-Free Emission Current
FFED .... Fidelity Federal Savings & Loan Association [*Philadelphia, PA*] [*NASDAQ symbol*]   (NQ)
FFEJWW .. Future Farm Experts of the Junior Woodchucks of the World [*Subgroup of Junior Woodchucks organization mentioned in Donald Duck comic by Carl Barks*]
FFEM .... Freeze-Fracture Electron Microscopy
FFEP.......... Finlands Folks Enhetsparti [*Finnish People's Unity Party*]   (PPE)
F & Fernsehen ... Film und Fernsehen [*A publication*]
FFES.......... First Federal Savings & Loan Association of East Hartford [*NASDAQ symbol*]   (NQ)
FFES.......... Food Facilities Engineering Society [*Later, FFCS*]   (EA)
FFEX .... Field Firing Exercise [*Military*]   (NVT)
FFF .... Fairly Fearless Flier
FFF .... Faith for the Family [*A publication*]
FFF .... Family of Faith Foundation [*Later, FFM*]   (EA)
FFF .... Famous Fone Friends   (EA)
FFF .... Farm Film Foundation [*Later, Grange-Farm Film Foundation*]   (EA)
FFF .... Fast Fission Factor
FFF .... Federation of Fly Fishers   (EA)
FFF .... Federation of Free Farmers [*Philippines*]
FFF .... Fellowship of First Fleeters
FFF .... Field-Flow Fractionation [*Chemical separation method*]
FFF .... Film: Foreign Feature
FFF .... Fine French Furniture
FFF .... Fission-Fusion-Fission [*Bomb*]   (DEN)
FFF .... Fitness for the Future [*Nursing Services Course*] [*Red Cross*]
FFF .... Flat or Folded Flat [*Freight*]
FFF .... Flicker Fusion Frequency [*Ophthalmology*]
FFF .... Flight Facilities Flight
FFF .... Flight Freedoms Foundation   (EA)
FFF .... Form, Fit, and Function   (MCD)
FFF .... Fortississimo [*As Loud as Possible*] [*Music*]
FFF .... Foundation for a Future   (EA)
FFF .... Free Flight Facility   (MCD)
FFF .... Free French Forces [*World War II*]

FFF .... Fuel Failure Fraction [*Nuclear energy*] (NRCH)
FFF .... Future Fisherman Foundation (EA)
FFFA .... Federation Feminine Franco-Americaine [*Federation of French American Women*] (EA)
FFFA .... Federation of French American Women (EA)
FFFC .... Franklin First Financial Corp. [*NASDAQ symbol*] (CTT)
FFFC .... Freddy Fender Fan Club
FFFCA ...... Fabulous Fifties Ford Club of America (EA)
FFFFM ...... Full-Face Fire-Fighters' Mask (MCD)
FFFG .... FFO Financial Group, Inc. [*NASDAQ symbol*] (CTT)
FFG .... First Families of Georgia 1733-1797 (EA)
FFG .... Form and Finish Grinding
FFG .... Foundation Faith of God (EA)
FFG .... Foundation for Future Generations (EA)
FFG .... Free-Fall Grab [*Marine geology*]
FFG .... Freshbake Foods Group [*British*]
FFG .... Friendly Foreign Government
FFG .... Guided Missile Frigate [*Navy symbol*]
FFGA .... 1st Fighter Group Association (EA)
FFGI .... Food and Feed Grain Institute [*Kansas State University*] [*Research center*] (RCD)
ffGn .... Fast Fractional Gaussian Noise [*Mathematics*]
FFGT .... Firefighter [*Army*] (AABC)
FFGT .... First Federal Savings & Loan Association of Georgetown [*NASDAQ symbol*] (NQ)
FFH .... Fairfax Financial Holdings Ltd. [*Toronto Stock Exchange symbol*]
FFH .... Families for the Homeless (EA)
FFH .... Fast-Frequency Hopping (MCD)
FFH .... Formerly Fat Housewife [*Weight Watchers, International; advertising*]
FFH .... Foundation for Health (EA)
FFH .... Freedom from Hunger Foundation [*UN Food and Agriculture Organization*]
FFHAET ... Flora and Fauna Handbook [*A publication*]
FFHC .... First Financial Corp. [*Stevens Point, WI*] [*NASDAQ symbol*] (NQ)
FFHC .... Freedom from Hunger Campaign [*UN Food and Agriculture Organization*]
FFHC/AD ... Freedom from Hunger Campaign - Action for Development [*UN Food and Agriculture Organization*]
FFHC Basic Stud ... FFHC [*Freedom from Hunger Campaign*] Basic Studies [*A publication*]
FF Hom ...... Fellow of the Faculty of Homoeopathy [*British*]
FFHP .... First Harrisburg Bancorp, Inc. [*NASDAQ symbol*] (NQ)
FFHR .... Fusion-Fission Hybrid Reactor
FFHS .... Federation of Family History Societies (EA)
FFHS .... First Franklin Corp. [*NASDAQ symbol*] (NQ)
FFHS .... Forby Family Historical Society (EA)
FFI .... Fairmont Financial, Incorporated [*AMEX symbol*] (SPSG)
FFI .... Faisal Finance Institution [*Turkey*]
FFI .... Family Functioning Index
FFI .... Fellow of the Faculty of Insurance [*French Forces of the Interior*] (DAS)
FFI .... Field Forcing (Increasing)
FFI .... Film Four International [*Commercial firm*] [*British*]
FFI .... Finance for Industry [*Later, Investors in Industry International - 3I*] [*British*]
FFI .... Fit for Issue [*Navy*]
FFI .... Fluid Flow Indicator
FFI .... Flying Fifteen International (EA)
FFI .... For Further Information
FFI .... For Further Instructions (DS)
FFI .... Forces Francaises de l'Interieur [*French Forces of the Interior*] [*World War II*]
FFI .... Foundation for Fluency (EA)
FFI .... Free from Infection [*Medicine*]
FFI .... Freeman Fox International [*Commercial firm*] [*British*]
FFI .... Freight Forwarders Institute [*Defunct*] (EA)
FFI .... French Forces of the Interior [*World War II*] (MCD)
FFI .... Friend Finders International [*Commercial firm*] (EA)
FFI .... Frozen Food Institute
FFI .... Fuel Flow Indicator
FFI .... Full Field Investigation (NRCH)
FFIA .... Fellow of the Federal Institute of Accountants [*Australia*]
FFIEC .... Federal Financial Institutions Examination Council (OICC)
FFI (Forsvarets Forskningsints) Mikrosk ... FFI (Forsvarets Forskningsinstitutt) Mikroskopet [*Norway*] [*A publication*]
FFII .... Falls Financial, Inc. [*NASDAQ symbol*] (NQ)
FFIIG......... Federation Francaise de l'Imprimerie et des Industries Graphiques [*France*] (EY)
FFII-MS .... Fission Fragment-Induced Ionization - Mass Spectroscopy
FFILH .... Flat Fillister Head [*Screws*]
F/FILT ...... Fuel Filter [*Automotive engineering*]
FFI Mikrosk ... FFI [*Forsvarets Forskningsinstitutt*] Mikroskopet [*Norway*] [*A publication*]
FFIN .... First Financial Savings & Loan [*NASDAQ symbol*] (NQ)
FFIN-L ...... Nova University, Law Library, Fort Lauderdale, FL [*Library symbol*] [*Library of Congress*] (LCLS)
FFIR .... Foundation for Financial Institutions Research [*Rolling Meadows, IL*] (EA)

F & Fitz ...... Falconer and Fitzherbert's English Election Cases [*1835-39*] [*A publication*] (DLA)
F & FIY ...... Fife and Forfar Imperial Yeomanry [*British military*] (DMA)
FFJ .... Friends for Jamaica (EA)
FFJF .... Federation of Former Jewish Fighters (EA)
FFK .... Fixed Function Keyboard (MCD)
FFKL .... Freiburger Forschungen zur Kunst und Literaturgeschichte [*A publication*]
FFKT .... Farmers Capital Bank Corp. [*Frankfort, KY*] [*NASDAQ symbol*] (NQ)
FFKY .... First Federal Savings Bank Elizabethtown [*NASDAQ symbol*] (NQ)
FFKZ .... First Federal Savings & Loan of Kalamazoo [*Kalamazoo, MI*] [*NASDAQ symbol*] (NQ)
FFL .... Fairfield, IA [*Location identifier*] [*FAA*] (FAAL)
FFL .... Fast Freight Line [*Shipping*]
FFL .... Federal Fiscal Liability
FFL .... Federation of Free Labor [*Philippines*]
FFL .... Female Flared
FFL .... Feminists for Life of America (EA)
FFL .... Field Failure (AAG)
FFL .... Fiji Federation of Labor
FFL .... Finished Floor Line [*Technical drawings*]
FFL .... First Financial Language [*Data processing*]
FFL .... Fitness for Life (EA)
FFL .... Fixed and Flashing Light [*Navigation signal*]
FFL .... Flip-Flop Latch [*Data processing*] (MSA)
FFL .... Forces Francaises Libres [*Free French Forces*]
FFl .... Fort Lauderdale Public Library, Fort Lauderdale, FL [*Library symbol*] [*Library of Congress*] (LCLS)
FFL .... Front Focal Length [*Optics*]
FFL .... Fuel Fill Line (AAG)
FFL .... Light Frigate
FFLA .... Federal Farm Loan Act [*1916*]
FFLA .... Fellow of the Faculty of Fire Loss Adjusters [*British*] (DAS)
FFLA .... Ferromagnetic Fluid Levitation Accelerometer
FFlB .... Broward Community College, Fort Lauderdale, FL [*Library symbol*] [*Library of Congress*] (LCLS)
FFlBL .... Broward County Libraries Division, Fort Lauderdale, FL [*Library symbol*] [*Library of Congress*] (LCLS)
FFlN .... Nova University, Fort Lauderdale, FL [*Library symbol*] [*Library of Congress*] (LCLS)
FFlN-O ...... Nova University, Physical Oceanographic Laboratory Library, Dania, FL [*Library symbol*] [*Library of Congress*] (LCLS)
FFLOP ...... Field Fresnel Lens Optical Platform
FFLR .... Florida Foreign Language Reporter [*A publication*]
FFLS .... Failed Fuel Location Subsystem [*Nuclear energy*] (NRCH)
FFLT .... Familiarization Flight [*Aviation*] (FAAC)
FFLY .... Faithfully
FFM .... Family Farm Movement (EA)
FFM .... Famous Fantastic Mysteries [*A publication*]
FFM .... Fast Food Management [*A publication*]
FFM .... [*The*] Fellowship for Freedom in Medicine [*British*]
FFM .... Fergus Falls, MN [*Location identifier*] [*FAA*] (FAAL)
FFM .... Film Fan Monthly [*A publication*]
FFM .... First Financial Management Corp. [*NYSE symbol*] (SPSG)
FFM .... Foundation for Microbiology (EA)
FFM .... Free-Flying [*Experiment*] Module [*NASA*] (NASA)
FFM .... Fuel Failure Mock-Up [*Nuclear energy*]
FFM .... Fuel Fill to Missile [*Aerospace*] (AAG)
FFM .... Full Face Mask [*Military*] (CAAL)
FFM .... Fund for the Feminist Majority (EA)
FFm .... Lee County Public Library, Fort Meyers, FL [*Library symbol*] [*Library of Congress*] (LCLS)
FFMA .... Folklore and Folk Music Archivist [*A publication*]
FFMA .... Fraternal Field Managers' Association [*Appleton, WI*] (EA)
FFMAS ..... Furniture Factories' Marketing Association of the South [*Later, IHFMA*] (EA)
FFMC .... Federal Farm Mortgage Corporation [*Established, 1934; assets transferred to Secretary of the Treasury, 1961*]
FFMC .... Freshwater Fish Marketing Corporation [*See also OCPED*]
FFMDAP .. Folia Facultatis Medicae Universitatis Comenianae Bratislaviensis [*A publication*]
FFmE .... Edison Community College, ECC/USF Learning Resources, Fort Meyers, FL [*Library symbol*] [*Library of Congress*] (LCLS)
FFMED ..... Fixed Former Message Entry Device (MCD)
FFMG .... Foundry Facings Manufacturers Group [*Later, FSMG*] (EA)
FFMIP .... Foreign Military Sales Financial Management Improvement Program (MCD)
FFMN .... Fixed Federal Monitoring Network [*Aviation*] (FAAC)
FFMY .... First Federal Savings & Loan Association of Fort Myers [*NASDAQ symbol*] (NQ)
FFN .... Fantasy Stories [*A publication*]
FFN .... Fleet Flash Network [*Navy*]
FFN .... Folded Flat or Nested [*Freight*]
FFN .... FreeLance Finders Network (EA)
FFNC .... First Fix Not Converted
FF-NM ...... Flip-Flop - National Module [*Data processing*] (AAG)
FFNPA ...... Fund for New Priorities in America (EA)

FFNPE2 .... FAO [*Food and Agriculture Organization of the United Nations*] Food and Nutrition Paper [*A publication*]
FFNS .... First Savings Bancorp [*NASDAQ symbol*]   (NQ)
FFO............ Dayton, OH [*Location identifier*] [*FAA*]   (FAAL)
FFO............ Forces Francaises de l'Ouest
FFO............ Formation Flight Operation
FFO............ Forward Firing Ordnance   (MCD)
FFO............ French Family Association   (EA)
FFO............ Fullam Family Organization   (EA)
FFO............ Furnace Fuel Oil   (NATG)
FFOB........ Flexible Fiber-Optic Borescope
FFOB........ Forward Fighting Operating Base [*Military*]   (AFM)
FFOD........ First Federal Savings Bank [*NASDAQ symbol*]   (NQ)
FFODAZ... Forstlige Forsogsvaesen i Danmark [*A publication*]
FFOF .... Foreign Fishing Observer Fund [*National Oceanic and Atmospheric Administration*]
FFOM........ FirstFed Michigan Corp. [*NASDAQ symbol*]   (NQ)
FFORCEV ... Field Force, Vietnam   (CINC)
F Form .... Film Form [*A publication*]
FForum ..... Folklore Forum [*A publication*]
FForumB.... Folklore Forum. Bibliographic and Special Series [*A publication*]
FFOS .... Facilities Forecast Obligations Summary
FFOT......... Fast Frequency on Target
FFP .... Consolidated First Fund [*Vancouver Stock Exchange symbol*]
FFP .... Far-Field Pressure
FFP .... Fast Field Program   (KSC)
FFP .... Fast Floating Point [*Data processing*]
FFP .... Federal Financial Participation
FFP .... Federation for Progress   (EA)
FFP .... Feminists Fighting Pornography   (EA)
FFP .... FFP Partners LP [*AMEX symbol*]   (SPSG)
FFP .... Finite Flat Plate
FFP .... Firm-Fixed Price [*Government contracting*]
FFP .... Fleet Frequency Plans
FFP .... Floating Foundation of Photography
FFP .... Food for Peace [*Overseas food donation program*]
FFP .... Food for Poland [*Later, Food for Peace*]   (EA)
F & FP ..... Force and Financial Program   (AFM)
FFP .... Forte Piano [*Loud, then Soft*] [*Music*]
FFP .... Fouilles Franco-Polonaises [*Cairo*] [*A publication*]
FFP .... Foundation for Peace   (EA)
FFP .... Founding Fathers Papers   (EA)
FFP .... Free Flight Plan [*Northwest Airlines, Inc.*]
FFP .... Fresh Frozen Plasma [*Medicine*]
FFP .... Friends of Family Planning   (EA)
FFP .... Friends of the Filipino People   (EA)
FFP .... Fuel Fabrication Plant [*Nuclear energy*]   (NRCH)
FFP .... Fuel Fill to Fuel Prefab   (AAG)
FFP .... [*The*] Fund for Peace [*An association*]   (EA)
FFp............. Saint Lucie-Okeechobee Regional Library, Fort Pierce, FL [*Library symbol*] [*Library of Congress*]   (LCLS)
FFPA .... Free from Prussic Acid
FFPBAY.... Folia Forestalia Polonica. Seria B (Drzewnictwo) [*A publication*]
FFPC .... Firm-Fixed Price Contract
FFPC .... Florida First Federal Savings Bank [*NASDAQ symbol*]   (NQ)
FFPE......... Federation de la Fonction Publique Europeenne [*European Civil Service Federation*]   (EAIO)
FFPh .... Fellow of the Faculty of Physiotherapists
FFPI.......... Fixed-Fee-plus-Incentive [*Business term*]   (MCD)
FFPI.......... Flip-Flop Position Indicator [*Data processing*]
FFpI .... Indian River Community College, Fort Pierce, FL [*Library symbol*] [*Library of Congress*]   (LCLS)
FFPLE....... Firm-Fixed Price Letter [*Government contracting*]   (MCD)
FFPOA5.... Folia Forestalia Polonica. Seria A (Lesnictwo) [*A publication*]
FFPR......... First Federal Savings Bank [*NASDAQ symbol*]   (NQ)
FFPS......... Fauna and Flora Preservation Society   (EA)
FFPS......... Fellow of the Faculty of Physicians and Surgeons [*British*]
FFR........... Failure Frequency Report [*Military*]   (AFIT)
FFR........... Falfurrias, TX [*Location identifier*] [*FAA*]   (FAAL)
FFR........... Fellow of the Faculty of Radiologists [*British*]
FFR........... Film Forum Review [*A publication*]
FFR........... Fission-Fusion Ratio
FFR........... Fit for Role [*Military*] [*British*]
FFR........... Fitted for Radio [*Military*] [*British*]
FFR........... Fixed Frequency Receiver
FFR........... Fleet Fighter Reconnaissance [*Air Force*]
FFR........... Folded Flow Reactor
FFR........... Foreign Force Reduction   (NATG)
FFR........... Forsvarets Forskningsrad [*Defense Board*] [*Denmark*]
FFR........... Fosterlaendska Folkroerelsen [*Patriotic People's Movement*] [*Finland*]   (PPE)
FFR........... Foundation for Field Research   (EA)
F Fr .... (Frater) Johannes de Freiburg [*Deceased, 1314*] [*Authority cited in pre-1607 legal work*]   (DSA)
FFR........... Free Field Room
FFR........... Free Flight Rocket   (NATG)
FFR........... Free French [*World War II*]
FFr............ French Franc [*Monetary unit*]
FFR........... Frequency-Following Response [*Neurophysiology*]

FFR............ Frontier Force Rifles [*British military*]   (DMA)
FFR............ RADAR Picket Frigate [*Navy symbol*]   (NVT)
FFRATS .... Full Flight Regime Auto Throttle System   (ADA)
FFRC .... Fossil Fuel Resources Committee
FFRD......... Flip-Flop Relay Driver [*Data processing*]
FFRDC ...... Federally Funded Research and Development Center [*National Science Foundation*]
FFRED ...... Farm and Food Research [*A publication*]
FFRF......... Freedom from Religion Foundation   (EA)
FFRR .... Full-Frequency Range Recording
FFRRCSIrel ... Fellow of the Faculty of Radiologists, Royal College of Surgeons of Ireland [*British*]   (DBQ)
FFRSA...... Fondation pour Favoriser les Recherches Scientifiques en Afrique [*Foundation to Assist Scientific Research in Africa*]   (EAIO)
FFRV .... Fidelity Federal Savings Bank [*NASDAQ symbol*]   (NQ)
FFS .... Family Financial Statement
FFS .... Fast Foodservice [*A publication*]
FFS .... Fat-Free Solids
FFS .... Fat-Free Supper [*Medicine*]
FFS .... Feeder Fault Sensing   (MCD)
FFS .... Fellow of the Faculty of Architects and Surveyors [*British*]   (DBQ)
FFS .... Fellow of the Franklin Society [*British*]
FFS .... Film: Foreign Series
FFS .... First Federal Bancorp [*AMEX symbol*]   (SPSG)
FFS .... First Flight Society   (EA)
FFS .... Flame Fluorescence Spectroscopy
FFS .... Flight Following Service [*FAA*]
FFS .... Florida Department of Agriculture [*Tallahassee, FL*] [*FAA designator*]   (FAAC)
FFS .... Formation Flying Simulator
FFS .... Formatted File System [*Data processing*]
FFS .... Foundation for Fire Safety   (EA)
FFS .... Free-Fall Sensor
FFS .... Front des Forces Socialistes [*Front of Socialist Forces*] [*Algeria*] [*Political party*]   (PD)
FFSA .... Field Functional System Assembly and Checkout
FFSA .... First Federal Savings, FA [*NASDAQ symbol*]   (NQ)
FFSA & C .. Field Functional System Assembly and Checkout   (KSC)
FFSB.......... Federation des Foires et Salons du Benelux [*Federation of Fairs and Trade Shows of Benelux - FFTSB*]   (EA)
FFSB.......... Fulton Federal Savings Bank [*NASDAQ symbol*]   (NQ)
FFSC.......... [*From the Latin for*] Franciscan Brothers of the Holy Cross [*Roman Catholic religious order*]
FFSCDL .... Folia Facultatis Scientiarum Naturalium Universitatis Purkynianae Brunensis: Chemia [*A publication*]
FFSCUG.... Formatted File System Commercial Users' Group [*Data processing*]
FFSD .... First Federal Savings Bank [*Decatur, AL*] [*NASDAQ symbol*]   (NQ)
FFSD .... Free Foil Switching Device
FFSEDR.... FAO [*Food and Agriculture Organization of the United Nations*] Fisheries Series [*A publication*]
FFS & FP... Five-Year Force Structure and Financial Program [*Navy*]   (AFIT)
FFSH .... Farm Fresh, Inc. [*NASDAQ symbol*]   (NQ)
FFSJA5 ..... Fertilizer and Feeding Stuffs Journal [*A publication*]
FFSK.......... Fast Frequency Shift Keying   (MCD)
FFSM .... Federation des Fondations pour la Sante Mondiale [*Federation of World Health Foundations - FWHF*] [*Geneva, Switzerland*]   (EA)
FFSM .... First Federal Savings Bank of Montana [*Kalispell, MT*] [*NASDAQ symbol*]   (NQ)
FFSP......... Fossil Fired Steam Plant   (IEEE)
FFSR......... First Federal Savings & Loan Association of Raleigh [*NASDAQ symbol*]   (NQ)
FFSR......... Fund for Stockowners Rights   (EA)
FFSS.......... Full-Frequency Stereophonic Sound   (DEN)
FFSW .... First Financial Services Corp. [*NASDAQ symbol*]   (NQ)
FFT .... Fast Fourier Transform [*Mathematics*]
FFT .... Finite Fourier Transform
FFT .... Flicker Fusion Threshold [*Ophthalmology*]
FFT .... Floor-to-Floor Time [*Engineering*]
FFT .... For Further Transfer [*to*] [*Military*]
FFT .... Formation Flight Trainer [*Air Force*]
FFT .... Frankfort, KY [*Location identifier*] [*FAA*]   (FAAL)
FFT .... Freight Forwarders Tariff Bureau, Inc., New York NY [*STAC*]
f-ft---........ French Territory of the Afars and Issas [*Djibouti*] [*MARC geographic area code*] [*Library of Congress*]   (LCCP)
FFT .... Fuel Flow Totalizer [*Aerospace*]
FFT .... Full Free Triple [*Lift truck*]
FFTA .... Foundation of the Flexographic Technical Association [*Later, FTA*]   (EA)
FFTA .... Frozen Fish Trades Association   (EA)
FFTB .... Freight Forwarders Tariff Bureau   (EA)
FFTC .... Fixed Feed Through Capacitor
FFTC/ASPAC ... Food and Fertilizer Technology Center for the Asian and Pacific Region   (EAIO)
FFTCom .... Fellow of the Faculty of Teachers in Commerce [*British*]   (DBQ)

FFTF.........	Fast Flux Test Facility [*Nuclear energy*]
FFTG........	Firefighting [*Army*] (AABC)
FFTN........	Fidelity Bancshares, Inc. [*Formerly, Fidelity Federal Savings & Loan of Tennessee*] [*NASDAQ symbol*] (NQ)
FFTO........	Free-Flying Teleoperator [*Program*] [*Electronics*]
FF/TOT.....	Fuel Flow Totalizer [*Aerospace*] (AAG)
FFTPAS	Forests Commission Victoria. Forestry Technical Papers [*A publication*]
FFTPBT	FAO [*Food and Agriculture Organization of the United Nations*] Fisheries Technical Paper [*A publication*]
FFTR	Firefighter (AFM)
FFTSB	Federation of Fairs and Trade Shows of Benelux [*Formerly, Federation of Fairs and Exhibitions in Benelux - FFSB*] (EA)
FFTV	Free Flight Test Vehicle
FFU...........	Federation of Film Unions [*British*]
FFU...........	Federation du Francais Universel [*Federation for Universal French - FUF*] (EAIO)
FFU...........	Focus-Forming Unit [*Medical/biochemical research*]
FFU...........	Provo, UT [*Location identifier*] [*FAA*] (FAAL)
FFUBAP....	Folia Facultatis Scientiarum Naturalium Universitatis Purkynianae Brunensis: Biologia [*A publication*]
F/FURN	Fully Furnished (ADA)
FFUT	First Federal Savings Bank [*Formerly, First Federal Savings & Loan Association of Salt Lake City*] [*NASDAQ symbol*] (NQ)
FFV...........	Far-Field Visibility [*Aviation*]
FFV...........	Fast Flying Vestibule [*Old railroad term for a deluxe coach*]
FFV...........	Field Failure Voltage (IEEE)
FFV...........	Field Force, Vietnam
FFV...........	Finest Foods of Virginia [*Brand name*]
FFV...........	Flexible-Fuel Vehicle [*Operable by either gasoline or methanol*] [*Ford Motor Co.*]
FF & V......	Fresh Fruits and Vegetables
FFV's	First Families of Virginia [*Supposedly elite society*] [*Slang*]
FFVA........	Florida Fruit and Vegetable Association (EA)
FFVF........	Freedoms Foundation at Valley Forge (EA)
FFVIB.......	Fresh Fruit and Vegetable Information Bureau [*British*] (CB)
FFVS.........	Free Field Voltage Sensitivity
FFW..........	Failure Free Warranty [*Military*] (AFIT)
FFW..........	Federation of Free Workers [*Philippines*]
FFW..........	Filoil Free Workers [*Philippines*]
FFW..........	Fitted for Wireless [*British military*] (DMA)
FFW..........	Foreign Free World (MCD)
FFWCB	Federation of Flatmen, Watermen, and Canal Boatmen [*A union*] [*British*]
FFWH	First Federal Savings & Loan Association of Winter Haven [*NASDAQ symbol*] (NQ)
FFWHC.....	Federation of Feminist Women's Health Centers (EA)
FFWP	First Federal of Western Pennsylvania [*NASDAQ symbol*] (NQ)
FFWS	First Farwest Corp. [*NASDAQ symbol*] (NQ)
FFWT	Final Feedwater Temperature [*Nuclear energy*] (NRCH)
FFWV	Federation of French War Veterans (EA)
FFWV	First Fidelity Bancorp, Inc. [*NASDAQ symbol*] (NQ)
FFWW	Fat-Free Wet Weight
FFY..........	Faithfully
F & FY	Fife and Forfar Yeomanry [*British military*] (DMA)
FFYQ........	Federal Fiscal Year Quarters (OICC)
FFY/SH.....	Fife and Forfar Yeomanry/Scottish Horse [*British military*] (DMA)
FFZ..........	Fiji Fracture Zone [*Geology*]
FFZ..........	Forzatissimo [*Extremely Loud*] [*Music*] (ROG)
FFZ..........	Free Fire Zone [*Army*] (AABC)
FG...........	Ariana Afghan Airline Co. Ltd. [*Afghanistan*] [*ICAO designator*] (FAAC)
fg-----	Congo River and Basin [*MARC geographic area code*] [*Library of Congress*] (LCCP)
FG...........	Fallschirmjaeger-Gewehr [*Parachutist's rifle*] [*German military - World War II*]
FG...........	Family Groups [*Aid to Families with Dependent Children*] (OICC)
FG............	Fashion Group [*Later, TFG*] (EA)
FG............	Fast Glycolytic [*Muscle*]
FG............	February Group [*An association*] (EA)
F-G...........	Feeley-Gorman [*Agar*] [*Microbiology*]
FG............	Feldenkrais Guild [*An association*] (EA)
fg............	Felsic Granulite [*Geology*]
FG............	Female Groove
FG............	Ferrosan [*Sweden*] [*Research code symbol*]
FG............	Fiberglass (ADA)
Fg............	Fibrinogen [*Factor 1*] [*Hematology*]
FG............	Field Goal [*Football, basketball*]
FG............	Field Grade
FG............	Field Gun
FG............	Filament Ground (MSA)
FG............	File Gap [*Data processing*] (BUR)
FG............	Filter Gate
FG............	Financial Gazette [*South Africa*] [*A publication*]
FG............	Finanzgericht [*Tax Court*] [*German*] (ILCA)
FG............	Fine Grain

FG	Fire Guardsman [*British*] [*World War II*]
FG	Firegreen Ltd. [*Food-processing and distributing company*] [*British*]
FG	Fiscal Guidance (AABC)
FG	Fission Gas (NRCH)
FG	Flashgun [*Photography*]
FG	Flat Grain [*Lumber*]
FG	Floated Gyro [*Aerospace*] (AAG)
FG	Flow Gauge
FG	Fog
FG	Fog Gong [*Navigation charts*]
FG	Fog Gun [*Navigation charts*]
F & G........	Folded and Gathered Sheets [*Printing*]
FG	Folding
FG	Foodservice Group [*Atlanta, GA*] (EA)
FG	Foot Groove
FG	Foot Guards [*British*]
FG	Football Grounds [*Public-performance tariff class*] [*British*]
FG	Foreground [*Data processing*]
FG	Foreign Geneva [*Alcohol*] (ROG)
FG	Forgotten Generation (EA)
FG	Form und Geist [*A publication*]
F u G	Form und Geist [*A publication*]
FG	Formula Grants [*Vocational education*] (OICC)
FG	Forward Gate
FG	Foundation for Grandparenting (EA)
FG	Frame Ground [*Data processing*] (BUR)
FG	Franc Guineen [*Monetary unit*]
FG	Frank Gasperro [*Designer's mark, when appearing on US coins*]
fg	French Guiana [*MARC country of publication code*] [*Library of Congress*] (LCCP)
FG	Friction Glaze
FG	Frog [*Engineering*]
FG	Fuel Gas
FG	Full Gilt [*Bookbinding*] (ADA)
FG	Fully Good
FG	Function Generator [*Data processing*] (IEEE)
FG	Fundamentals Graduate
FG	Future Generations [*An association*] (EA)
FG	Gainesville Public Library, Gainesville, FL [*Library symbol*] [*Library of Congress*] (LCLS)
FG	USF & G Corp. [*NYSE symbol*] (SPSG)
FGA	Fasting Glycocholic Acid [*Clinical chemistry*]
FGA	Fellow of the Gemmological Association [*British*]
FGA	Field Goals Attempted [*Football, basketball*]
FGA	Fighter Ground Attack (NATG)
FGA	First General Resources Co. [*Vancouver Stock Exchange symbol*]
FGA	Font Graphics Accelerator [*Toshiba*]
FGA	Foreign General Agent [*Insurance*]
FGA	Foreign General Average [*Insurance*]
FGA	Fort Garland, CO [*Location identifier*] [*FAA*] (FAAL)
FGA	Free of General Average
FGA	Fresh Garlic Association (EA)
F/GA	Fuel Gage [*Automotive engineering*]
FGAA	Federal Government Accountants Association [*Later, AGA*] (EA)
FGADL......	Forschungen zur Geschichte der Aelteren Deutschen Literatur [*A publication*]
FGAN	Fertilizer Grade Ammonium Nitrate
FGAR........	Foreign Governments or Their Authorized Representatives (MCD)
FGAS	Fountain Oil & Gas, Inc. [*Denver, CO*] [*NASDAQ symbol*] (NQ)
FGB	Fast Gunboat [*Navy*] [*British*]
FGB	Fiberglass Brush
FGB	Foliage-Gleaning Bat [*Zoology*]
FGB	Foundation for Global Broadcasting (EA)
FGBC	First Golden Bancorporation [*NASDAQ symbol*] (NQ)
FGBI	First Granite Bancorporation, Incorporated [*Granite City, IL*] [*NASDAQ symbol*] (NQ)
FGBMFI....	Full Gospel Business Men's Fellowship International (EA)
FGBT........	Bata [*Equatorial Guinea*] [*ICAO location identifier*] (ICLI)
FGC	Facility Group Control [*Military*] (AFM)
FGC	Federation Generale du Congo [*Congolese General Federation*]
FGC	FGIC Corporation [*NYSE symbol*] (SPSG)
FGC	Fiberglass Curtain
FGC	Finished Goods Control
FGC	Fiscal Guidance Category [*Military*] (CAAL)
FGC	Fixed Gain Control
FGC	Fixed Glass Capacitor
FGC	Freemont Gold [*Vancouver Stock Exchange symbol*]
FGC	Friends General Conference (EA)
FGC	Friends of Guy Clark (EA)
FGC	Functional Group Code (MCD)
FGC	Futures Guarantee Corp. [*Hong Kong*] (ECON)
FGCA........	Ford Galaxie Club of America (EA)
FGCB	Fiberglass Cone Brush
FGcC..........	Clay County Public Library, Green Cove Springs, FL [*Library symbol*] [*Library of Congress*] (LCLS)
FGCC........	Foundation for Gifted and Creative Children (EA)

FGCL......... Fellow of the Guild of Cleaners and Launderers [*British*] (DBQ)
FGCM .... Field General Court-Martial
FGCS......... Fifth-Generation Computer Systems
FGCS......... Flight Guidance and Control Systems
FGD .... Ferri-Gas Duplexer
FGD .... Fine Grain Data [*Equipment*] [*RADAR*]
FGD .... Fishguard [*Goodwick*] [*British depot code*]
FGD .... Flue-Gas Desulfurization
FGD .... Forged
FGD .... Formaldehyde-Glutaraldehyde-Dichromate [*Fixative*]
FGD .... Fuel Gas Desulfurization
FGDF......... Fidelco [*Fidelity Cooperative*] Guide Dog Foundation (EA)
FGDI......... Forging Die [*Tool*] (AAG)
FGE .... Factory Ground Equipment (KSC)
FGE .... Fitchburg Gas & Electric Light Co. [*AMEX symbol*] (SPSG)
FGE .... Fractographic Examination [*Metallurgy*]
FGEA......... Full Gospel Evangelistic Association (EA)
FGF .... Fibroblast Growth Factor [*Cytochemistry*]
FGF .... Filament-Wound Glass Fiber
FGF .... Fishermen's Guarantee Fund [*National Oceanic and Atmospheric Administration*]
FGF .... Fresh Gas Flow
FGF .... Fully Good, Fair [*Business term*]
FGF .... Future Germany Fund [*NYSE symbol*] (SPSG)
FGFC......... Fixed Gas-Filled Capacitor
FGFSA ..... Florida Gift Fruit Shippers Association (EA)
FGGE......... First GARP [*Global Atmospheric Research Program*] Global Experiment [*National Academy of Sciences*]
FGGHA ..... Fukushima Daigaku Gakugei Gakubu Rika Hokoku [*A publication*]
FGGM .... Fort George G. Meade [*Maryland*]
FGGYA...... Fortschritte der Geburtshilfe und Gynaekologie [*A publication*]
FGGYAV... Advances in Obstetrics and Gynaecology [*A publication*]
FGH .... Fans of General Hospital (EA)
FGH .... Fiberglass Hull
FGH .... Flameless Gas Heater
FGH .... Flexible Gyro Header
FGH .... Fort Garry Horse [*Military unit*] [*World War I*] [*Canada*]
f-gh---......... Ghana [*MARC geographic area code*] [*Library of Congress*] (LCCP)
FGHA .... Flexible Gyro Header Assembly
FGHC .... First Georgia Holding, Inc. [*NASDAQ symbol*] (NQ)
FGH-JWB ... Florence G. Heller - JWB [*Jewish Welfare Board*] Research Center [*Research center*] (RCD)
FGI........... Fashion Group International (EAIO)
FGI........... Federation of German Industries (EA)
FGI........... Federation Graphique Internationale [*International Graphical Federation - IGF*] [*Berne, Switzerland*] (EAIO)
FGI........... Fellow of the Institute of Certificated Grocers [*British*]
FGI........... [*The*] Foothill Group, Incorporated [*NYSE symbol*] (SPSG)
FGIC......... Financial Guaranty Insurance Corporation
FGIM........ Figures or Images [*Freight*]
FGIPCI...... Federation of Government Information Processing Councils, Incorporated (EA)
FGIS .... Federal Grain Inspection Service [*Department of Agriculture*]
FGJ........... Freezing Gas Jet
FGJA .... Flat Glass Jobbers Association [*Later, FGMA*]
FGL........... Fiberglass [*Technical drawings*]
FGL........... Financial General Ledger
FGL........... FMC Gold [*NYSE symbol*] (SPSG)
FGLFS ...... Florida Gulf Realty Trust [*NASDAQ symbol*] (NQ)
FGLOA..... Figyelo [*A publication*]
FGLP .... Forschungen zur Geschichte und Lehre des Protestantismus [*Munich*] [*A publication*]
FGLS .... Florida Glass Industries, Inc. [*NASDAQ symbol*] (NQ)
FGLS .... Force Generation Levels [*Military*] (NVT)
FGM .... Field Goals Made [*Football, basketball*]
FGM .... First General Mine Management & Gold Corp. [*Vancouver Stock Exchange symbol*]
FGM .... Fiscal Guidance Memorandum [*Navy*]
FGM .... Fission Gas Monitor (NRCH)
FGM .... Florida Atlantic University, Boca Raton, FL [*OCLC symbol*] (OCLC)
FGM .... Fluxgate Magnetometer
FGM .... Freunde Guter Musik Club [*Record label*] [*Germany*]
FGM .... Functionally Gradient Material [*Materials science and technology*]
f-gm---........ Gambia [*MARC geographic area code*] [*Library of Congress*] (LCCP)
FGMA ...... Flat Glass Marketing Association (EA)
FGMDSS .. Future Global Maritime Distress and Safety System
FGN .... Family Group Number
FGN .... Federal German Navy
FGN .... First Generation Resources Ltd. [*Vancouver Stock Exchange symbol*]
FGN .... Foreign (AFM)
FGNCC..... Foreign Claims Commission [*Canada*]
FGNL .... First General Resources Co. [*NASDAQ symbol*] (NQ)
FGO .... Fellow of the Guild of Organists [*British*]
FGO .... Finance Group Office

FGO .... Flag Gunnery Officer
FGO .... Fleet Gunnery Officer [*Obsolete*] [*British*]
FGO .... Forschungen zur Geschichte Oberoesterreichs [*A publication*]
FGO .... Fuego [*Guatemala*] [*Seismograph station code, US Geological Survey*] (SEIS)
f-go---......... Gabon [*MARC geographic area code*] [*Library of Congress*] (LCCP)
Fg Off........ Flying Officer [*British military*] (DMA)
FGOG........ Foregoing (ROG)
FGOLF...... Federation des Gynecologues et Obstetriciens de Langue Francaise [*Federation of French-Language Gynaecologists and Obstetricians*] [*Paris, France*] (EAIO)
FGP........... Fetch, Generate, and Project Machine [*Computer program*]
F & GP....... Finance and General Purposes Committee [*British*] (DCTA)
FGP........... First Guardian [*Vancouver Stock Exchange symbol*]
FGP........... Foster Grandparents Program (EA)
FGP........... Frontal Groove of Pinnule
FGP........... Fundic Gland Polyposis [*Medicine*]
FGPBA7 .... Folia Geobotanica et Phytotaxonomica [*A publication*]
FGPFL....... Fixed and Group Flashing Light [*Navigation signal*]
FGR .... Feline Gardner-Rasheed Virus
FGR .... Fellowship of the Golden Rule (EA)
FGR .... Filmograph [*A publication*]
FGR .... Finger (MSA)
FGR .... Flue Gas Recirculation [*Combustion engineering*]
FGR .... Foundation for Giraffe Rescue
FGR .... Foundation for Glaucoma Research (EA)
FGR .... Freehold Ground Rent (ROG)
FGRAAL ... FORTRAN [*Formula Translating System*] Extended Graph Algorithmic Language [*1972*] [*Data processing*] (CSR)
FGRF......... Forest Genetics Research Foundation (EA)
FGrH .... Fragmente der Griechischen Historiker [*A publication*] (OCD)
FGrHist ..... Fragmente der Griechischen Historiker [*A publication*]
FGRI......... Fixed Ground Radio Installations
FGRNA ..... Fortschritte auf dem Gebiete der Roentgenstrahlen und der Nuklearmedizin [*A publication*]
FGRP......... Farmers Group, Inc. [*NASDAQ symbol*] (NQ)
FGRTA...... Feingeraete Technik [*A publication*]
F & G Rundsch ... F und G [*Felten und Guilleaume*] Rundschau [*A publication*]
FGS........... Fancy Goods Store [*British military*] (DMA)
FGS........... Fashion Glamour Set
FGS........... Federation of Genealogical Societies (EA)
FGS........... Fellow of the Geographical Society
FGS........... Fellow of the Geological Society [*British*]
FGS........... Fischerei-Geraete-Station
FGS........... Flight Guidance System (MCD)
FGS........... Flowing Gas Stream
FGS........... Focal Glomerulosclerosis [*Medicine*]
FGS........... Francis Grose Society [*Defunct*] (EA)
FGS........... Friends of George Sand (EA)
FGS........... Friends of Georges Sadoul (EAIO)
FGS........... Friends of the Golden State
FGS........... Fulton Generating Station [*Nuclear energy*] (NRCH)
FGS........... Palmer, AK [*Location identifier*] [*FAA*] (FAAL)
FGS........... Santa Fe Community College, Gainesville, FL [*Library symbol*] [*Library of Congress*] (LCLS)
FGSA .... Fellow of the Geographical Society of America
FGSA .... Fellow of the Geological Society of America
FGSA .... Fostoria Glass Society of America (EA)
FGSF .... Full Gospel Student Fellowship (EA)
FGSL .... Malabo, Isla De Macias, Nguema Biyoga [*Equatorial Guinea*] [*ICAO location identifier*] (ICLI)
FGSM....... Fellow of Guildhall School of Music [*British*] (EY)
FGSS .... Flexible Guidance Software System (MCD)
FGST .... First Grade Screening Test [*To detect learning disabilities*]
FGT .... Farmington, MN [*Location identifier*] [*FAA*] (FAAL)
FGT .... Federal Gift Tax (DLA)
FGT .... Flue-Gas Treatment
FGT .... Freight
FGTB........ Federation Generale du Travail de Belgique [*A union*] [*Belgium*] (DCTA)
FGTO .... French Government Tourist Office
FGTSA ..... Fur Garment Traveling Salesmen's Association
FGU .... Fangatau [*French Polynesia*] [*Airport symbol*] (OAG)
FGU .... Flaming Gorge [*Utah*] [*Seismograph station code, US Geological Survey*] [*Closed*] (SEIS)
FGU .... Forearm Glucose Uptake [*Clinical chemistry*]
FGULS ...... Florida Union List of Serials, Gainesville, FL [*Library symbol*] [*Library of Congress*] (LCLS)
f-gv---......... Guinea [*MARC geographic area code*] [*Library of Congress*] (LCCP)
FGV .... United States Veterans Administration Hospital, Gainesville, FL [*Library symbol*] [*Library of Congress*] (LCLS)
FGWC ...... First Greatwest Corporation [*NASDAQ symbol*]
FGX .... Flemingsburg, KY [*Location identifier*] [*FAA*] (FAAL)
FGY .... Foggy (MSA)
FH............. C. H. Boehringer Sohn, Ingelheim [*Germany*] [*Research code symbol*]
FH............. Clin-Byla [*France*] [*Research code symbol*]

fh----- East African Horn [*MARC geographic area code*] [*Library of Congress*] (LCCP)

FH ...... Familial Hypercholesteremia [*or Hypercholesterolemia*] [*Medicine*]

FH ...... Family History [*Medicine*]

FH ...... Family of Humanists [*An association*] (EA)

FH ...... Fane's Horse [*British military*] (DMA)

FH ...... Federation of Homemakers (EA)

FH ...... Fetal Head [*Medicine*]

FH ...... Fetal Heart [*Medicine*]

FH ...... Feuilles d'Histoire [*A publication*]

FH ...... Fiat Haustus [*Let a Drink Be Made*] [*Pharmacy*]

FH ...... Ficoll-Hypaque [*Clinical hematology*]

FH ...... Fides et Historia [*A publication*]

F et H ... Fides et Historia [*A publication*]

FH ...... Field Hospital [*British military*] (DMA)

FH ...... Field Howitzer [*British military*] (DMA)

FH ...... Fighter (NATG)

FH ...... Fire Hose (AAG)

FH ...... Fire Hydrant

FH ...... First Half [*of month*] (DCTA)

FH ...... Fixed Hub [*Rotary piston meter*]

FH ...... Flag Hoist

FH ...... Flat Head [*Screw*]

FH ...... Flex Hose (MCD)

FH ...... Flight Hour

FH ...... Floating Hospital (EA)

FH ...... Flying Hour

FH ...... Fog Horn [*Navigation charts*]

FH ...... Foodservice and Hospitality [*A publication*]

FH ...... Force Headquarters [*Allied forces*] [*World War II*]

FH ...... Fore Hatch [*Shipping*]

FH ...... Foundation for Health (EA)

FH ...... Foundation Health Corp. [*AMEX symbol*] (SPSG)

FH ...... Frankfort Horizontal [*Eye-ear plane*] [*Anatomy*]

FH ...... Frankfurter Hefte [*A publication*]

FH ...... Free Harbor

FH ...... Freedom House (EA)

FH ...... French Horn

FH ...... Frequency Hopping [*Modulation*]

FH ...... Friends of Hibakusha (EA)

FH ...... Friendship House (EA)

FH ...... Fuji Heavy Industries Ltd. [*Japan*] [*ICAO aircraft manufacturer identifier*] (ICAO)

FH ...... Full Hard (MSA)

FH ...... Fulminant Hepatitis [*Medicine*]

FH ...... Fumarate Hydratase [*An enzyme*]

FHA ...... Farmers Home Administration [*Later, FmHA*] [*Department of Agriculture*]

FHA ...... Fault Hazard Analysis [*Hazard quantification method*]

FHA ...... Federal Highway Administration [*Department of Transportation*]

FHA ...... Federal Housing Administration [*HUD*]

FHA ...... Fellow of the Institute of Health Service [*formerly, Hospital*] Administrators [*British*]

FHA ...... Finance Houses Association [*British*]

FHA ...... Fine Hardwoods Association [*Later, FHAWA*] (EA)

FHA ...... Fitzgerald-Hemingway Annual [*A publication*]

FHA ...... Flexible Header Assembly

FHA ...... Floating Homes Association (EA)

FHA ...... Free-Heave Amplitude

FHA ...... Friends Historical Association (EA)

FHA ...... Future Homemakers of America (EA)

FHA ...... Future Horsemen of America

FHAA ...... Field Hockey Association of America (EA)

FHAAO ... Force Headquarters, Antiaircraft [*World War II*]

FHAEB ... Force Headquarters, North African Economic Board [*World War II*]

FHAG ...... Force Headquarters, Adjutant General [*World War II*]

FHAGG ... Force Headquarters, Adjutant General, Executive [*World War II*]

FHAGM ... Force Headquarters, Adjutant General, Miscellaneous [*World War II*]

FHAGP ... Force Headquarters, Adjutant General, Personnel [*World War II*]

FHAGR ... Force Headquarters, Adjutant General, Mail and Records [*World War II*]

FHA (HERO) ... Future Homemakers of America (Home Economics Related Occupations) (OICC)

FHAI ...... Federal Housing Authority Insurance (AABC)

FHAIR ... Force Headquarters, Air Commander-in-Chief, Mediterranean [*World War II*]

FHAM ...... Federal Housing Administration Matters [*FBI standardized term*]

FHAP ...... Fair Housing Assistance Program [*HUD*]

FHAS ...... Federation of Hellenic American Societies of Greater New York (EA)

FHAS ...... Fellow of the Highland and Agricultural Society of Scotland

FHAW ... Wideawake [*Ascension Island*] [*ICAO location identifier*] (ICLI)

FHAWA ... Fine Hardwoods American Walnut Association (EA)

FHB ...... Family Hold Back [*Indicates family should take small portions at a meal where guests are present*]

FHB ...... Federal Home Bank

FHB ...... Fine Homebuilding [*A publication*]

FHB ...... Fremantle Harbour Board [*Australia*]

FHB ...... Fuel-Handling Building [*Nuclear energy*] (NRCH)

FHBVI ... Fuel-Handling Building Ventilation Isolation [*Nuclear energy*] (NRCH)

FHC ...... Fairchild-Hiller Corporation [*Later, Fairchild Industries, Inc.*] (KSC)

FH & C ... Faith, Hope, and Charity [*Freemasonry*] (ROG)

FHC ...... Faith, Hope, and Charity [*Freemasonry*]

FHC ...... Federal Housing Commission [*HUD*] (OICC)

FHC ...... Federal Housing Corporation

FHC ...... Fickle Hill [*California*] [*Seismograph station code, US Geological Survey*] (SEIS)

FHC ...... Fire Hose Cabinet (KSC)

FHC ...... First Hospitality [*Vancouver Stock Exchange symbol*]

FHC ...... Fish Creek, AK [*Location identifier*] [*FAA*] (FAAL)

FHC ...... Flight Half Coupling (MCD)

FHC ...... Four-Horse Club [*British*]

FHC ...... Freed-Hardeman College [*Tennessee*]

FHC ...... Fuel-Handling Cell [*Nuclear energy*] (NRCH)

FHC ...... University of South Florida, Sarasota Campus, Sarasota, FL [*OCLC symbol*] (OCLC)

FHCAO ... Force Headquarters, Chief Administrative Officer [*World War II*]

FHCAS ... Federal Highway Cost Allocation Study [*Also, HCAS*]

FHCCH ... Force Headquarters, Claims and Hirings [*World War II*]

FHCE ...... Foundation for Health Care Evaluation (EA)

FHCIC ... Force Headquarters, Commander-in-Chief [*World War II*]

FHCIMA ... Fellow of the Hotel, Catering, and Institutional Management Association [*British*] (DBQ)

FHCIV ... Force Headquarters, Civil Affairs [*World War II*]

FHCOS ... Force Headquarters, Chief of Staff [*World War II*]

FHCP ...... Footscray Home Care Project for Elderly People [*Australia*]

FHCRC ... Fred Hutchinson Cancer Research Center [*University of Washington*] [*Research center*] (RCD)

FHCWS ... Force Headquarters, Chemical Warfare [*World War II*]

FHCYAI ... Folia Histochemica et Cytochemica [*Later, Folio Histochemica et Cytobiologica*] [*A publication*]

FHCYEM ... Folia Histochemica et Cytobiologica [*A publication*]

FHD ...... Family Housing Division [*Army*] (AABC)

FHD ...... First-Hand Distribution

FHD ...... Fixed-Head Disk [*Data processing*]

FHD ...... Friends of Holly Dunn (EA)

FHD ...... Fund for Human Dignity (EA)

FHDA ...... Fir and Hemlock Door Association [*Defunct*] (EA)

FHDCC ... Force Headquarters, Deputy Allied Commander-in-Chief [*World War II*]

FHDHC ... Force Headquarters, Director of Harbor Craft [*World War II*]

FHDMS ... Force Headquarters, Military Secretary Section [*World War II*]

FHDO ...... Field Handling Design Objective

FHDSC ... Force Headquarters, Deputy Chief of Staff [*World War II*]

FHE ...... Family Home Entertainment [*Division of International Video Entertainment*]

FHE ...... Fast Hydrofoil Escort

FHE ...... Forward Headquarters Element

FHE ...... Foundation for Handgun Education [*Later, EFEHV*] (EA)

F & HE ... Fridays and Holidays Excepted

FHE ...... Fuel-Handling Equipment [*Nuclear energy*] (NRCH)

FHEFI ... Force Headquarters, Expeditionary Forces Institute [*World War II*]

FHENG ... Force Headquarters, Engineer [*World War II*]

FHENW ... Force Headquarters, Works [*World War II*]

FHEO ...... Fair Housing and Equal Opportunity [*HUD*] (OICC)

FHEPFC ... For the Heart Elvis Presley Fan Club (EA)

F Her ...... Film Heritage [*A publication*]

FHES ...... Fuel-Handling Equipment System [*Nuclear energy*] (NRCH)

FHEx ...... Fridays and Holidays Excepted (DS)

FHF ...... First Horizontal Flight [*NASA*] (KSC)

FHF ...... Friendly Hand Foundation (EA)

FHF ...... Fulminant Hepatic Failure [*Medicine*]

FHF ...... University of South Florida, Fort Myers Campus, Fort Myers, FL [*OCLC symbol*] (OCLC)

FHFA ...... Four-Conductor, Heat-and-Flame-Resistant, Armor [*Cable*]

FHFB ...... Federal Housing Finance Board [*Pronounced "foof-ba"*]

FHFC ...... Farm House Foods Corporation [*NASDAQ symbol*] (NQ)

FHFF ...... Fleet Hurricane Forecast Facility

FHFLD ... Force Headquarters, Field Artillery Section [*World War II*]

FHG ...... Fellow of the Institute of Heraldic and Genealogical Studies [*British*] (DBQ)

FHG ...... Fragmenta Historicorum Graecorum [*A publication*] (OCD)

FHG ...... Mueller. Fragmenta Historicorum Graecorum [*A publication*]

FhG Ber ... FhG [*Fraunhofer-Gesellschaft*] Berichte [*A publication*]

FHGDM ... Force Headquarters, Movements and Transportation [*World War II*]

FHGDQ ... Force Headquarters, "Q" Maintenance [*World War II*]

FHGDT ... Force Headquarters, Supply and Transport [*World War II*]

FHH ...... Female Headed Household

FHH ...... Fetal Heart Heard [*Medicine*]

FHH .... Foundation for Hospice and Homecare (EA)
FHHDC..... Force Headquarters, Headquarters Commandant [World War II]
FHI .... Federation Halterophile Internationale [International Weightlifting Federation - IWF] (EAIO)
FHI .... Fine Homes International, Inc. [NYSE symbol] (SPSG)
FHi............. Florida Historical Society, University of South Florida, Tampa, FL [Library symbol] [Library of Congress] (LCLS)
FHI .... Folk Heritage Institute (EA)
FHI .... Food for the Hungry, Incorporated (EA)
FHI .... Fuji Heavy Industries Ltd.
FHiaC........ Coulter Diagnostics, Inc., Hialeah, FL [Library symbol] [Library of Congress] (LCLS)
FHIC......... Flying Hours per Inspection Cycle [Air Force] (AFIT)
FHIC......... Franciscan Hospitaller Sisters of the Immaculate Conception [Roman Catholic religious order]
FHIF......... Frequenting House of Ill Fame
FHIID........ Fast Heavy Ion Induced Desorption [Analytical chemistry]
FHI/IFRP ... Family Health International [Acronym is based on former name, Family Health International/International Fertility Research Program] (EA)
FHINC ...... Force Headquarters, Information and Censorship [World War II]
FHIP......... Family Health Insurance Plan
FHIP......... Federal Health Insurance Plan [Proposed] (DHSM)
FHist.......... Fides et Historia [A publication]
FHL .... Federal Home Loan Bank Board. Journal [A publication]
FHL .... Forest Hydrology Laboratory [Forest Service]
FHL .... Forward Half-Line [Feed]
FHL .... Fraser's House of Lords Reports [Scotland] [A publication] (DLA)
FHLB........ Federal Home Loan Bank
FHLBA...... Family Health Bulletin [A publication]
FHLBB...... Federal Home Loan Bank Board [Functions transferred to Office of Thrift Supervision, 1989]
FHLBB Jrl ... Federal Home Loan Bank Board. Journal [A publication]
FHLBS ...... Federal Home Loan Bank System
FHLD .... Freehold [Legal term]
FHLIA .... Force Headquarters, Liaison [World War II]
FHLMC.... Federal Home Loan Mortgage Corporation [Federal Home Loan Bank Board] [Nickname: "Freddie Mac"]
FHLS......... First Hungarian Literary Society (EA)
FHLT......... Force (Fleet) High-Level Terminal [Navy] (CAAL)
FHM .... Faith Mines Ltd. [Vancouver Stock Exchange symbol]
FHM .... Fargo House Movement [Trinidad and Tobago] [Political party] (PPW)
FHM .... Fat Head Minnow
FHM .... Feed Water Heater Management
FHM .... Franciscan Handmaids of the Most Pure Heart of Mary [Roman Catholic religious order]
FHM .... University of South Florida, Tampa, FL [OCLC symbol] (OCLC)
FHMA....... Family Housing Management Account [Army] (AABC)
FHMA....... Family Housing Management Appropriation
FHMED..... Force Headquarters, Surgeon [World War II]
FHMGS .... Force Headquarters, Military Government Section [World War II]
FHMO....... Friends of the Hop Marketing Order (EA)
FHMO....... Fully Hydrogenated Menhaden Oil [Food science]
FHMS .... Flat Head Machine Screw [Technical drawings]
FHN .... Fund for Human Need [British]
FHNH .... Fetal Heart Not Heard [Medicine]
FHNL........ Far Horizons Newsletter [A publication]
FHNP........ United States National Park Service, Everglades National Park, Homestead, FL [Library symbol] [Library of Congress] (LCLS)
FHO........... Failed Handover [NASA] (NASA)
FHO........... Family Hands Off [Indicates that a certain dish is not to be eaten by members of the family at a meal where guests are present]
FHO........... Family Hold Off [Indicates that a certain dish is not to be eaten by members of the family at a meal where guests are present]
FHO........... Frederick's of Hollywood, Inc. [AMEX symbol] (SPSG)
FHONF ..... Facing History and Ourselves National Foundation (EA)
FHORD..... Force Headquarters, Ordnance [World War II]
FHP.......... Family History Project [University of Melbourne Archives] [Australia]
FHP.......... Flying Hour Program [Army]
FHP.......... Fort Hare Papers [A publication]
FHP.......... Fort Howard Corp. [Formerly, Fort Howard Paper] [NYSE symbol] (SPSG)
FHP.......... Fractional Horsepower (MSA)
FHP.......... Free Hepatic Venous Pressure [Medicine]
FHP.......... Friction Horsepower
FHP.......... Friends of Historical Pharmacy (EA)
FHP.......... Fuel Handling Procedure [Nuclear energy] (NRCH)
FHP.......... Fuel High Pressure (NASA)
FHPAD ...... Fort Hare Papers [A publication]
FHPC........ FHP International Corp. [NASDAQ symbol] (NQ)
FHPC......... Fuel-Handling and Preparation Cell [Nuclear energy] (NRCH)

FHPET...... Force Headquarters, Petroleum [World War II]
FHPRO ..... Force Headquarters, Public Relations [World War II]
FHPS........ Federal Health Programs Service [Health Services and Mental Health Administration, HEW]
FHPSGI ... Funeral Home Public Service Group International (EA)
FHPWO .... Force Headquarters, Psychological Warfare Office [World War II]
FHQ.......... Florida Historical Quarterly [A publication]
FHQAE ..... Force Headquarters, "Q" Army Equipment Branch [World War II]
FHR .... Familial Hypophosphatemic Rickets
FHR .... Federal Housing Representative [Australia]
FHR .... Fetal Heart Rate [Medicine]
FHR .... Fire Hose Rack
FHR .... Fire Hose Reel
FHR .... Fisher Foods, Inc. [NYSE symbol] (SPSG)
FHR .... Foundation for Hand Research
FHR .... Foundation for Homeopathic Research (EA)
FHR .... Friends of Haitian Refugees (EA)
FHR .... Fund for Human Rights [Later, WDL] (EA)
FHR .... Further
FH-RDC .... Family History-Research Diagnostic Criteria [Medicine, Psychiatry]
FHR FNSHD T PRMD ... Further Finished Than Primed [Freight]
FHR FNSHD T RGH ... Further Finished Than Rough [Freight]
FH & RM .. Fuel Handling and Radioactive Maintenance (NRCH)
FHRNA ..... Force Headquarters, Commander-in-Chief, Mediterranean [World War II]
FHS .... Family and Health Section (EA)
FHS .... Fatal Heart Sound [Medicine] (DHSM)
FHS .... Fellow of the Horticultural Society [British]
FHS .... Feminine Hygiene Spray
FHS .... Fetal Heart Sounds [Medicine]
FHS .... Fetal Hydantoin Syndrome [Medicine]
FHS .... Fire Hose Station [Technical drawings]
FHS .... Flame Hardness Standard (MCD)
FHS .... Football Hall of Shame (EA)
FHS .... Forest History Society (EA)
FHS .... Forward Heat Shield [NASA] (KSC)
FHS .... French Historical Studies [A publication]
FHS .... Frequency Hopping Signal
FHS .... Fuel-Handling System [Nuclear energy] (NRCH)
FHS .... Furniture History Society (EA)
FHS .... University of South Florida, St. Petersburg Campus, St. Petersburg, FL [OCLC symbol] (OCLC)
FHSA......... Federal Hazardous Substances Act
FHSC........ Fellow of the Heraldry Society of Canada
FHSCAW ... Farm and Home Science [A publication]
FHSF........ Fixed-Head Storage Facility [Data processing]
FHSG .... Family Housing [Army] (AABC)
FHSGS...... Force Headquarters, Secretary General Staff [World War II]
FHSIG ...... Force Headquarters, Signal [World War II]
FH & SL .... Furnished Hardware and Services List (MCD)
FHSR........ Final Hazards Summary Report [Nuclear energy] (NRCH)
FHSR........ Foundation for Health Services Research (EA)
FHSS......... Forward Heat-Shield Separation [NASA] (KSC)
FHSUP...... Force Headquarters, Quartermaster [World War II]
FHSY......... Family Health Systems [NASDAQ symbol] (NQ)
FHT .... Fast Hartley Transform (BYTE)
FHT .... Fetal Heart Tone [Obstetrics]
FHT .... Field Handling Trainer [Army] (INF)
FHT .... Fingerhut Companies, Inc. [NYSE symbol] (SPSG)
FHT .... Fisher-Hirschfelder-Taylor [Molecular model]
FHT .... Francs Hoc Tempore [Francs at the Current Value] [Business term] [French]
FHT .... Free-Heave Test
FHT .... Friedrich Technologies, Inc. [Vancouver Stock Exchange symbol]
FHT .... Fully Heat Treated (IEEE)
FHTC .... Fixed High-Temperature Capacitor
FHTNC .... Fleet Home Town News Center
FHTTA...... Fellow of the Highway and Traffic Technicians Association [British] (DBQ)
FHU.......... Fort Huachuca/Sierra Vista [Arizona] [Airport symbol] (OAG)
FHU.......... Fort Huachuca/Sierra Vista, AZ [Location identifier] [FAA] (FAAL)
FHU.......... Foundation of Human Understanding (EA)
FHUSN ..... Force Headquarters, United States Naval Staff [World War II]
FHV .... Fahnestock Viner Holdings, Inc. [Toronto Stock Exchange symbol] [Vancouver Stock Exchange symbol]
FHV .... Flockhouse Virus
FHVC .... Fixed High-Volt Capacitor
FHVN .... Fairhaven Savings Bank [Fairhaven, MA] [NASDAQ symbol] (NQ)
FHVP .... Free Hepatic Venous Pressure [Medicine]
FHWA .... Federal Highway Administration [Department of Transportation]
FH-WC ..... Fellow of Heriot-Watt College, Edinburgh
FHWN ...... First Hawaiian, Inc. [NASDAQ symbol] (NQ)
FHWS .... Flat Head Wood Screw [Technical drawings]
FHY .... Fire Hydrant

FI...............	Daughters of Jesus [*Roman Catholic religious order*]
FI...............	Fabrication Instruction (NG)
FI...............	Facilities Item
FI...............	Fade In [*Films, television, etc.*]
FI...............	Fail in Place [*Nuclear energy*] (NRCH)
F/I.............	Failed Item (AAG)
FI...............	Fairplay Information [*Fairplay Publications Ltd.*] [*Information service or system*] (IID)
FI...............	Falkland Islands
FI...............	Farm Index [*A publication*]
FI...............	Farmitalia [*Italy*] [*Research code symbol*]
FI...............	Farmland Industries (EA)
FI...............	Faroe Islands
FI...............	Fatigue Index [*Aircraft strain/fatigue scale*] [*British*]
FI...............	Fault Identification (MCD)
FI...............	Fault Isolation
FI...............	[*The*] Fertilizer Institute
FI...............	Fidelity [*to Living Condition*] Index [*Botany*]
Fi...............	Fidell's Precedents [*A publication*] (DLA)
FI...............	Field Intensity
FI...............	Field Interview
FI...............	Field Ionization
FI...............	Fieseler [*Federal Republic of Germany*] [*ICAO aircraft manufacturer identifier*] (ICAO)
FI...............	Fighter Interceptor
FI...............	Films, Incorporated
Fi...............	Filologia [*A publication*]
FI...............	Final Issue
FI...............	Finished Intelligence (MCD)
fi...............	Finland [*MARC country of publication code*] [*Library of Congress*] (LCCP)
FI...............	Finland [*ANSI two-letter standard code*] (CNC)
FI...............	Fireball International [*Axminster, Devonshire, England*] (EAIO)
FI...............	First Idaho Resources [*Vancouver Stock Exchange symbol*]
FI...............	Fiscal (AFIT)
FI...............	Fisher Institute [*Dallas, TX*] (EA)
FI...............	Fixed Interval [*Reinforcement schedule*]
FI...............	Flight Instructor
FI...............	Flight Instrumentation (MCD)
FI...............	Flood Insurance [*HUD*]
FI...............	Flow Indicator
FI...............	Flow Injection [*Chemical processing*]
FI...............	Folklore Italiano [*A publication*]
FI...............	Foodbanking, Inc. [*An association*] (EA)
FI...............	For Instance
FI...............	Force Integrator [*DoD*]
FI...............	Forecasting International Ltd. [*Information service or system*] (IID)
FI...............	Foreign Intelligence (MCD)
FI...............	Foreign Investment [*Business term*]
FI...............	Foresight Institute (EA)
FI...............	Formal Inspection (MCD)
FI...............	Formaldehyde Institute (EA)
FI...............	Formula Internationale [*Agreement of Unification of Formulae*] [*Medicine*] (ROG)
FI...............	Forsttechnische Informationen [*A publication*]
FI...............	Forum Institute (EA)
FI...............	Forum Italicum [*A publication*]
FI...............	France Info [*Radio France*]
FI...............	Free In [*Shipping*] (ADA)
FI...............	Freemen Institute (EA)
FI...............	Front Independantiste [*Independence Front*] [*New Caledonia*] [*Political party*] (PPW)
FI...............	Frontiers International (EA)
FI...............	Fuel Injection [*Automotive engineering*]
F & I..........	Furnished and Installed (KSC)
FI...............	Icelandair [*Iceland*] [*ICAO designator*] (FAAC)
fi-----.........	Niger River and Basin [*MARC geographic area code*] [*Library of Congress*] (LCCP)
FIA.............	Factory Insurance Association [*Later, Industrial Risk Insurers*]
FIA.............	Families in Action [*Later, NFA*] (EA)
FIA.............	Fashion Industries of Australia
FIA.............	Fault Isolation Analysis (MCD)
FIA.............	Federacion Interamericana de Abogados [*Washington, DC*]
FIA.............	Federal Insurance Administration [*HUD*]
FIA.............	Federal Inventory Accounting
FIA.............	Federated Ironworkers' Association of Australia
FIA.............	Federation Internationale des Acteurs [*International Federation of Actors*] (EAIO)
FIA.............	Federation Internationale de l'Artisanat [*International Federation of Master-Craftsmen*]
FIA.............	Federation Internationale de l'Automobile [*International Automobile Federation*] (EAIO)
FIA.............	Federation Internationale des Aveugles [*International Federation of the Blind*]
FIA.............	Federation of Islamic Associations in the US and Canada (EA)
FIA.............	Fellow of the Institute of Actuaries [*British*]
FIA.............	Fellow of the Institute of Auctioneers [*British*]
FIA.............	Fiat SpA [*NYSE symbol*] (CTT)

FIA.............	Financial Analysts Journal [*A publication*]
FIA.............	Financial Inventory Accounting
FIA.............	Fixed Income Account
FIA.............	Flatware Importers Association [*Defunct*]
FIA.............	Flight Information Area
FIA.............	Floating-Point Instruction Address [*Data processing*]
FIA.............	Florida Commuter Airlines, Inc. [*West Palm Beach, FL*] [*FAA designator*] (FAAC)
FIA.............	Flow Injection Analyzer [*Chemical analyses*]
FIA.............	Fluorescence Indicator Analysis
FIA.............	Fluorescent Immunoassay [*Analytical biochemistry*]
FIA.............	Footwear Industries of America (EA)
FIA.............	Force Integration Analysis [*DoD*]
FIA.............	Foreign Investment Application [*Taiwan*] (IMH)
FIA.............	Forging Industry Association (EA)
FIA.............	Free Interstitial Atom
FIA.............	Freedom of Information Act [*1966*] (AFM)
FIA.............	Freund's Incomplete Adjuvant [*Immunology*]
FIA.............	Full Interest Admitted
FIA.............	Futures Industry Association (EA)
FIA.............	Socorro, NM [*Location identifier*] [*FAA*] (FAAL)
FIAA.........	Federation Internationale d'Athletisme Amateur [*International Amateur Athletic Federation - IAAF*] [*London, England*] (EAIO)
FIAA.........	Fellow of the Incorporated Association of Architects and Surveyors [*British*] (DBQ)
FIAA.........	Fellow of the Institute of Affiliate Accountants [*Australia*]
FIAA.........	Fellow of the Institute of Arbitrators of Australia
FIAA.........	Fencing Industry Association of Australia
FIAA & S...	Fellow of the Incorporated Association of Architects and Surveyors [*British*]
FIAAS........	Fellow of the Institute of Australian Agricultural Science
FIAB.........	Federation Internationale des Associations de Bibliothecaires [*International Federation of Library Associations*]
FIAB.........	Fellow of the International Association of Bookkeepers [*British*] (DCTA)
FIAB.........	Foreign Intelligence Advisory Board (CINC)
FIABCI......	Federation Internationale des Professions Immobilieres [*International Real Estate Federation*] (EAIO)
FIAC.........	Federation of International American Clubs [*Oslo, Norway*] (EAIO)
FIAC.........	Federation Internationale Amateur de Cyclisme [*International Amateur Cycling Federation*] [*Rome, Italy*] (EA)
FIAC.........	Fellow of the Institute of Company Accountants [*British*] (DAS)
FIAC.........	Flight Information Advisory Committee [*Terminated, 1977*] [*FAA*]
FIAC.........	Fluorodeoxyiodoara-C [*An antiviral compound*]
FIAC.........	Fluoroiodoarabinosylcytosine
FIAC.........	Foreign Investments Assistance Center [*Board of Investment*] [*Philippines*] (DS)
FIACAT	Federation Internationale de l'Action des Chretiens pour l'Abolition de la Torture [*International Federation of Action of Christians for the Abolition of Torture*] (EAIO)
FIACC	Five International Associations Coordinating Committee [*Budapest, Hungary*] (EAIO)
FIACTA	Federation Internationale des Associations de Controleurs du Trafic Aerien [*International Federation of Air Traffic Controllers' Associations*] (EAIO)
FIACTC.....	Federation Internationale des Associations des Chimistes du Textile et da la Couleur
FIAD.........	Federation Internationale des Associations de Distributeurs de Films [*International Federation of Associations of Film Distributors*] (EAIO)
FIAD.........	Flame Ionization Analyzer and Detector
FIAE.........	Food Industry Association Executives (EA)
FIAEA	Fellow of the Institute of Automotive Engineer Assessors [*British*] (DBQ)
FIAEM	Federation Internationale des Associations d'Etudiants en Medecine [*International Federation of Medical Students Associations - IFMSA*] [*Vienna, Austria*] (EAIO)
FIAEP........	Federation Internationale des Associations d'Entrepots Publics [*International Federation of Public Warehousing Associations - IFPWA*] (EAIO)
FIAeS.........	Fellow of the Institute of Aeronautical Sciences [*Later, FAIAA*] [*British*] (EY)
FIAESTA ..	Federation Internationale des Associations de l'Electronique de Securite du Trafic Aerien [*International Federation of Air Traffic Safety Electronic Associations*] (EAIO)
FIAF	Federation Internationale des Archives du Film [*International Federation of Film Archives*] (EAIO)
FIAF	French Institute/Alliance Francaise (EA)
FIAgrE.......	Fellow of the Institution of Agricultural Engineers [*British*]
FIAI	Federation Internationale des Associations d'Instituteurs [*International Federation of Teachers' Associations - IFTA*] (EAIO)
FIAI	Fellow of the Institute of Industrial and Commercial Accountants [*British*]
FIAJ	Federation Internationale des Auberges de la Jeunesse [*International Youth Hostel Federation - IYHF*] [*Welwyn Garden City, Hertfordshire, England*] (EAIO)

FIAJF .... Federation Internationale des Amies de la Jeune Fille
FIAJY .... Fellowship in Israel for Arab-Jewish Youth   (EA)
FIAL .... Fellow of the International Institute of Arts and Letters
FIAM .... Fellow of the International Academy of Management
FIAM .... First American Bank and Trust [*NASDAQ symbol*]   (NQ)
FIAMA ...... Fellow of the Incorporated Advertising Managers Association
            [*British*]   (DAS)
FIAMC ...... Federation Internationale des Associations Medicales
            Catholiques [*International Federation of Catholic Medical
            Associations*]   (EA)
FIAMS ...... Fellow of the Indian Academy of Medical Sciences
FIAMS ...... Flinders Institute for Atmospheric and Marine Sciences
            [*Australia*]
FIANATM ... Federation Internationale des Associations Nationales de
            Negociants en Aciers, Tubes, et Metaux [*International
            Federation of Associations of Steel, Tube, and Metal
            Merchants*]   (EAIO)
FIANDIC .. Families in Action National Drug Information Center [*Later,
            NFA*]   (EA)
FIANEI ..... Federation Internationale des Associations Nationales d'Eleves
            Ingenieurs [*International Federation of National
            Associations of Engineering Students*]
FIANZ .... Fellow of the Institute of Actuaries of New Zealand
FIAP .... Federation Internationale de l'Art Photographique
            [*International Federation of Photographic Art*]   (EAIO)
FIAP .... Fellow of the Institution of Analysts and Programmers
            [*British*]   (DBQ)
FIAPA .... Federation Internationale des Associations de Chefs de Publicite
            d'Annonceurs [*International Federation of Advertising
            Managers Associations*]
FIAPF .... Federation Internationale des Associations de Producteurs de
            Films [*International Federation of Film Producers'
            Associations*]
FIAPL .... Federation Internationale des Associations de Pilotes de Ligne
FIAPN .... Federation Internationale des Associations de Patrons de
            Navires [*International Federation of Shipmasters
            Associations*]   (EAIO)
FIAPS .... Federation Internationale des Associations de Professeurs de
            Sciences [*International Council of Associations for Science
            Education - ICASE*]   (EAIO)
FIAR .... Failed Item Analysis Report   (MCD)
FIAR .... Failure Investigation Action Report [*NASA*]   (NASA)
FIArb .... Fellow of the Institute of Arbitrators
FIARE ...... Flight Investigation of Apollo Reentry Environment   (MUGU)
FIAS .... Federacion Interamericana de Asociaciones de Secretarias
            [*Inter-American Federation of Secretaries*] [*San Salvador,
            El Salvador*]   (EAIO)
FIAS .... Federation Internationale Amateur de Sambo [*Anglet,
            France*]   (EAIO)
FIAS .... Fellow of the Incorporated Association of Architects and
            Surveyors [*British*]   (DBQ)
FIAS .... Fellow of the Institute of Aeronautical Sciences [*Later, FAIAA*]
            [*British*]
Fias .... Free in and Stowed [*Shipping*]   (DS)
FIAS .... Frontiers in Aging Series [*A publication*]
FIASC .... Federal Inter-Agency Sedimentation Conference [*Department
            of Agriculture*]
FIAT .... Fabbrica Italiana Automobile, Torino [*Italian automobile
            manufacturer; acronym is used as name of its cars and is
            sometimes facetiously translated "Fix It Again, Tony," a
            reference to the alleged frequency of repair*]
FIAT .... Federation Internationale des Archives de Television
            [*International Federation of Television Archives -
            IFTA*]   (EAIO)
FIAT .... Federation Internationale des Associations de Thanatopraxie
            [*International Federation of Thanatopractic Associations*]
FIAT .... Fellow of the Institute of Animal Technicians [*British*]   (DBQ)
FIAT .... Fellow of the Institute of Asphalt Technology [*British*]   (DBQ)
FIAT .... Field Information Agency, Technical [*Under G-2, SHAEF*]
FIAT .... Film Inspection Apply Template   (MCD)
FIAT .... First Installed Article, Tests [*NATO*]   (NATG)
FIATA ...... Federation Internationale des Associations de Transitaires et
            Assimilies [*International Federation of Freight Forwarders
            Associations*] [*Zurich, Switzerland*]   (EAIO)
FIATC ...... Federation Internationale des Associations Touristiques de
            Cheminots [*International Federation of Railwaymen's
            Travel Associations - IFRTA*] [*France*]
FIATE ...... Federation Internationale des Associations de Travailleurs
            Evangeliques
FIAU .... Fluorodeoxyiodoara-U [*An antiviral compound*]
FIAV .... Federation Internationale des Agences de Voyages
            [*International Federation of Travel Agencies*]
FIAV .... Federation Internationale des Associations de Vexillologie
            [*International Federation of Vexillological
            Associations*]   (EA)
FIA(V) ...... Forum of Information Associations (Victoria) [*Australia*]
FIAWOL ... Fandom Is a Way of Life [*Science-fiction-fan slogan*]
FIAWS ...... Fellow of the International Academy of Wood Sciences
FIAX .... Fiesta-Air [*Air carrier designation symbol*]
FIB .... Bulletin. Federation des Industries Belges [*A publication*]
FIB .... Fast Ion Bombardment

FIB .... Federation Internationale de Badminton [*International
            Badminton Federation - IBF*]   (EA)
FIB .... Federation Internationale de Baseball [*International Baseball
            Federation*]
FIB ....:...... Federation Internationale de Boules [*International Bocce
            Federation*] [*Turin, Italy*]   (EAIO)
FIB .... Fellow of the Institute of Bankers [*British*]   (EY)
FIB .... Fellow of the Institute of Builders [*British*]
FIB .... Fiber
fib .... Fibrillation [*Medicine*]
FIB .... Fibrinogen [*Factor 1*] [*Hematology*]
FIB .... Fibrositis [*Medicine*]
FIB .... Fibula [*Medicine*]
FI B .... Fide Bona [*In Good Faith*] [*Latin*]   (ROG)
FIB .... File Information Block
FIB .... Fish Industry Board. Bulletin [*New Zealand*] [*A publication*]
FIB .... Fisherman's Information Bureau [*Chicago, IL*]
FIB .... Fixed Interim Baseline
FIB .... Fleet Installation Budget [*Navy*]
FIB .... Flight Information Bulletin   (AABC)
FIB .... Fluidics Inertial Bomb
FIB .... Force-in-Being   (ADA)
FIB .... Foreground Initiated Batch [*Data processing*]
FIB .... Foreign Investment Board [*Honiara, Solomon Islands*]   (GEA)
FIB .... FORTRAN [*Formula Translating System*] Information Bulletin
            [*Data processing*]   (IEEE)
FIB .... Forward Indicator BIT [*Binary Digit*]   (TEL)
FIB .... Free into Barge [*Shipping*]
FIB .... Free into Bunker
FIB .... Kodiak, AK [*Location identifier*] [*FAA*]   (FAAL)
FIBA .... Federation Internationale de Basketball Amateur [*International
            Amateur Basketball Federation*] [*Munich, Federal
            Republic of Germany*]   (EA)
FIBA .... Federazione Italiana Bancari e Assicuratori [*Italy*]   (EY)
FIBA .... Fellow of the Institute of Banking Associations
FIBA .... Fellow of the Institute of Business Administration [*British*]
FIBBD ...... F + I Bau [*A publication*]
FIBC .... Federal Interagency Broadcast Committee
FIBC .... Flexible Intermediate Bulk Container [*Shipping*]
FIBCA .... Flexible Intermediate Bulk Container Association   (EA)
FIBCO ...... Fellow of the Institution of Building Control Officers   (DBQ)
FIBD .... Fellow of the Institute of British Decorators
FIBD .... Ford International Business Development [*Ford Motor Co.*]
FIBEP .... Federation Internationale des Bureaux d'Extraits de Presse
            [*International Federation of Press Cutting Agencies -
            IFPCA*]   (EAIO)
FIBEP .... Fundo de Financiamento de Importacao de Bens de Producao
            [*Fund for Financing Capital Goods Imports*] [*Brazil*]
FIBER .... Fund for Integrative Biomedical Research
Fiber and Integrated Opt ... Fiber and Integrated Optics [*A publication*]
Fiber Integr Opt ... Fiber and Integrated Optics [*A publication*]
Fiber Laser ... Fiber Laser News [*A publication*]
Fiber Opt ... Fiber Optics News [*A publication*]
Fiber Opt Commun ... Fiber Optics and Communications [*A publication*]
Fiberoptcs .. Fiberoptics Report [*A publication*]
Fiber Prod ... Fiber Producer [*A publication*]
FIBEX .... First International BIOMASS Experiment [*ICSU*]   (MSC)
FIBF .... Fellow of the Institute of British Foundrymen   (DBQ)
FIBI .... Filed but Impracticable [*to transmit*]   (FAAC)
FIBI .... First International Bank of Israel Ltd.   (BJA)
FIBID9 ...... Freshwater Invertebrate Biology [*A publication*]
FI Biol .... Fellow of the Institute of Biology [*Formerly, FInstBiol*]
            [*British*]
FIBK .... First Interstate Corp. of Alaska [*NASDAQ symbol*]   (NQ)
Fibonacci Q ... Fibonacci Quarterly [*A publication*]
Fibonacci Quart ... Fibonacci Quarterly [*A publication*]
FIBP .... Fellow of the Institute of British Photographers
FIBQA .... Fibonacci Quarterly [*A publication*]
FIBR .... American Fiber Optics Corp. [*NASDAQ symbol*]   (NQ)
FIBRD ...... Fibreboard [*Freight*]
Fibre Chem ... Fibre Chemistry [*A publication*]
Fibre Containers ... Fibre Containers and Paperboard Mills [*A publication*]
Fibre Fabr ... Fibre and Fabric [*A publication*]
Fibre Sci Technol ... Fibre Science and Technology [*A publication*]
Fibres Fabr Cordage ... Fibres, Fabrics, and Cordage [*A publication*]
Fibres Fabr J ... Fibres and Fabrics Journal [*A publication*]
Fibres Plast ... Fibres and Plastics [*A publication*]
Fibres & Polym ... Fibres and Polymers [*A publication*]
fibrin .... Fibrinogen [*Factor 1*] [*Hematology*]
Fibr Text Ind ... Fibres and Textile Industries [*A publication*]
FIB(Scot) ... Fellow of the Institute of Bankers in Scotland [*British*]   (DBQ)
FIBT .... Federation Internationale de Bobsleigh et de Tobogganing
            [*International Bobsledding and Tobogganing Federation*]
            [*Milan, Italy*]   (EAIO)
FIBTP .... Federation Internationale du Batiment et des Travaux Publics
FIBUA .... Fighting in Built-Up Areas [*Military*]   (INF)
FIBV .... Federation Internationale des Bourses de Valeurs [*International
            Federation of Stock Exchanges*]   (EAIO)
FIBW .... First Interstate Bank of Washington, DC, NA [*NASDAQ
            symbol*]   (NQ)

FIC............ Congregatio Fratrum Immaculatae Conceptionis Beatae Mariae Virginis [*Brothers of the Immaculate Conception of the Blessed Virgin Mary*] (EAIO)

FIC............ Family Information Centre [*Australian Institute of Family Studies*] [*Information service or system*] (IID)

FIC............ Fast-Moving Industrializing Country

FIC............ Fault Isolation Code

FIC............ Federal Information Center Program (EA)

FIC............ Federation of Insurance Counsel (EA)

FIC............ Federation Internationale de Canoe [*International Canoe Federation - ICF*] [*Florence, Italy*] (EAIO)

FIC............ Federation Internationale des Chronometreurs [*Rome, Italy*] (EAIO)

FIC............ Federation Internationale de Cremation [*International Cremation Federation*] (EAIO)

FIC............ Fellow of the Institute of Chemistry [*Later, FRIC*] [*British*]

FIC............ Fellow of the Institute of Commerce

FIC............ Field Installed Connector

FIC............ Film Integrated Circuit

FIC............ Financial Inventory Control

FIC............ First-in-Chain [*Data processing*]

FIC............ Fleet Intelligence Center [*Navy*] (NVT)

FIC............ Fleet Issue Control [*Navy*] (NVT)

FIC............ Flight Information Center

FIC............ Foam Inhibiting Conjugate [*Chemical engineering*]

FIC............ Focus-Inducing Cell [*Population*] [*Immunochemistry*]

FIC............ [*John E.*] Fogarty International Center for Advanced Study in the Health Sciences [*Department of Health and Human Services*] [*Bethesda, MD*]

FIC............ Food Industries Center [*Ohio State University*] [*Research center*] (RCD)

FIC............ Foodstuff Industries Corporation [*Burma*] (DS)

FIC............ Force Indicator Code (MCD)

FIC............ Foreign Investment Committee [*Malaysia*] (IMH)

FIC............ Forest Industries Council (EA)

FIC............ Foundation for International Cooperation (EA)

FIC............ Fraternal Insurance Counselor [*Designation awarded by Fraternal Field Managers' Association*]

FIC............ Fratrum Instructionis Christianae [*Brothers of Christian Instruction*] [*La Mennais Brothers*] [*Roman Catholic religious order*]

FIC............ Free Insurance and Carriage [*Shipping*] (DS)

FIC............ Freedom of Information Clearinghouse [*An association*] (EA)

FIC............ Freight, Insurance, Carriage

FIC............ Frequency Interference Control

FIC............ Friends of Imperial Cancer [*London, England*]

FIC............ Funding Information Center [*Spokane Public Library*] [*Information service or system*] (IID)

FIC............ Fur Institute of Canada

FICA.......... Federal Insurance Contributions Act [*1954*] [*Under which collections are made from employers and employees for OASDI benefits*]

FICA.......... Federation Internationale des Cheminots Antialcooliques [*International Railway Temperance Union*]

FICA.......... Fellow of the Commonwealth Institute of Accountancy

FICA.......... Forest Industries Campaign Association [*Australia*]

FICA.......... Fraternal Insurance Counsellors Association [*Later, NAFIC*] (EA)

FICAAL..... Flore Illustree des Champignons d'Afrique Centrale [*A publication*]

FICAC....... Federation Internationale des Corps et Associations Consulaires [*Federation of International Consular Corps and Associations*] (EAIO)

FICAP....... Federation of International Country Air Personalities (EA)

FICAP....... Furniture Industry Consumer Advisory Panel [*Defunct*] (EA)

FICB......... Federal Intermediate Credit Bank

FICC......... Federation of Insurance and Corporate Counsel [*Marblehead, MA*] (EA)

FICC......... Federation Internationale de Camping et de Caravanning [*International Federation of Camping and Caravanning*] [*Brussels, Belgium*] (EA)

FICC....... Federation Internationale de Chimie Clinique [*International Federation of Clinical Chemistry*]

FICC....... Federation Internationale des Cine-Clubs [*International Federation of Film Societies*]

FICC......... Fixed Income Consumer Counseling [*ACTION*]

FICC......... Frequency Interference Control Center [*Air Force*]

FICCA....... False Identification Crime Control Act of 1982

FICCC....... Federation Internationale des Clubs de Camping-Cars [*Montreuil, France*] (EAIO)

FICCI....... Federation of Indian Chambers of Commerce and Industries

FICCIA...... Federation Internationale des Cadres de la Chimie et des Industries Annexes

FICD......... Fellow of the Indian College of Dentists

FICD......... Fellow of the Institute of Canadian Dentists

FICD......... Fellow of the Institute of Civil Defence [*British*]

FICD......... Fellow of the International College of Dentists

FICE......... Federacion de Industriales del Calzado Espanol [*Industrial association*] [*Spain*] (EY)

FICE......... Federal Interagency Committee on Education

FICE......... Federation Internationale des Choeurs d'Enfants [*International Federation of Children's Choirs*] (EA)

FICE......... Federation Internationale des Communautes Educatives [*International Federation of Educative Communities*] [*Zurich, Switzerland*] (EAIO)

FICE......... Federation Internationale des Communautes d'Enfants [*International Federation of Children's Communities*]

FICE......... Fellow of the Institution of Civil Engineers [*British*]

FICEMEA ... Federation Internationale des Centres d'Entrainement aux Methodes d'Education Active [*International Federation of Training Centres in Methods of Active Education*] (EAIO)

FICEP....... Federation Internationale Catholique d'Education Physique et Sportive [*Catholic International Federation for Physical and Sports Education - CIFPSE*] [*Paris, France*] (EAIO)

FICeram..... Fellow of the Institute of Ceramics [*British*]

FICEUR .... Fleet Intelligence Center, Europe [*Navy*]

FICEURLANT ... Fleet Intelligence Center, Europe and Atlantic [*Navy*] (MCD)

FICF .... Federation Internationale Culturelle Feminine [*Women's International Cultural Federation - WICF*] (EAIO)

FIChemE ... Fellow of the Institution of Chemical Engineers [*British*]

Fichero Med Ter Purissimus ... Fichero Medico Terapeutico Purissimus [*A publication*]

Fiches Identif Zooplancton ... Fiches d'Identification du Zooplancton [*A publication*]

Fiches Phytopathol Trop ... Fiches de Phytopathologie Tropicale [*A publication*]

Fichier Micropaleontol Gen ... Fichier Micropaleontologique General [*A publication*]

FIChor .... Fellow of the Benesh Institute of Choreology [*British*] (DBQ)

FICI .... Fair, Isaac & Co., Inc. [*NASDAQ symbol*] (NQ)

FICI .... Fellow of the Institute of Chemistry of Ireland

FICI .... Fellow of the International Colonial Institute [*British*]

FICIC........ Federation Internationale du Commerce et des Industries du Camping

FICICA...... Federation Internationale du Personnel d'Encadrement des Industries et Commerces Agricoles et Alimentaires [*International Federation of Managerial Staff of Agricultural and Alimentary Industry and Commerce*] (EAIO)

Fic Int........ Fiction International [*A publication*]

FICJA....... Fellow of the International Criminal Justice Association

FICJF .... Federation Internationale des Conseils Juridiques et Fiscaux [*International Federation of Legal Fiscal Consultants*]

FICM........ [*From the Latin for*] Brothers of the Immaculate Heart of Mary [*Roman Catholic religious order*]

FICM........ Federation of International Music Competitions (EA)

FICM........ Federation Internationale des Cadres des Mines

FICM........ Fellow of the Institute of Credit Management [*British*] (DCTA)

FICM........ Fleet Intelligence Collection Manual (MCD)

FICO......... Fellow of the Institute of Careers Officers [*British*] (DBQ)

FICO......... Field Installation Change Order (MCD)

FICO......... File Control [*Microfilm*] (MCD)

FICO......... Financing Corporation [*Created by the Reagan administration in 1987 for the Federal Savings and Loan Insurance Corporation*]

FICO......... Fireweed Country. Magazine of the Yukon [*A publication*]

FICO......... Flight Information and Control of Operations

FICO......... Ford Instrument Company (MCD)

FICO......... Franchiselt Corp. [*NASDAQ symbol*] (NQ)

FICOD....... Force Identification Code [*Military*]

FICON...... Fighter Conveyor

FICON...... File Conversion [*Data processing*]

FICorrST... Fellow of the Institution of Corrosion Science and Technology [*British*] (DBQ)

FICP .... Federation Internationale des Clubs de Publicite [*International Federation of Advertising Clubs*] [*Lille, France*] (EAIO)

FICP .... Federation Internationale du Cyclisme Professionel [*International Federation of Professional Cycling*]

FICP .... Freres de l'Instruction Chretienne de Ploermel [*Brothers of Christian Instruction of Ploermel*] [*Rome, Italy*] (EAIO)

FICPAC..... Fleet Intelligence Center, Pacific [*Navy*] (CINC)

FICPACFAC ... Fleet Intelligence Center, Pacific Facility [*Navy*]

FICPI........ Federation Internationale des Conseils en Propriete Industrielle [*International Federation of Industrial Property Attorneys*] (EAIO)

FICQ......... Federation of Insurance Counsel. Quarterly [*A publication*]

FICR........ Fidelcor, Inc. [*NASDAQ symbol*] (NQ)

FICR........ Financial Inventory Control Report

FICS .... Fault Isolation Checkout System

FICS .... Federation Internationale des Chasseurs de Son [*International Federation of Sound Hunters - IFSH*] (EAIO)

FICS .... Fellow of the Institute of Chartered Shipbrokers [*British*]

FICS .... Fellow of the International College of Surgeons

FiCS.......... Financial Clearing and Services Ltd. [*Information service or system*] (IID)

FICS .... Financial Information Control System

FICS .... Fire Control Simulation (MCD)

FICS .... Forecasting and Inventory Control System

FICSA....... Federation of International Civil Servants' Associations [*Geneva, Switzerland*] (EA)

FICT .... Federation Internationale de Centres Touristiques [*International Federation of Tourist Centres*] (EAIO)
FICT .... Fictilis [*Made of Pottery*] [*Latin*]
FICT .... Fiction
FICTIONZINE ... Fiction Magazine [*Generic term for a publication covering science fiction*]
FICU .... Folklore. Boletin del Departmento de Folklore del Instituto de Cooperacion Universitaria [*A publication*]
FICU .... Fonds Internationale de Cooperation Universitaire [*International Fund for University Cooperation*] [*Montreal, PQ*] (EAIO)
FICW .... Fellow of the Institute of Clerks of Works of Great Britain, Inc. (DBQ)
FID .... Failure Identification (MCD)
FID .... Far-Infrared Detector
FID .... Fault Isolation Detection (MCD)
FID .... Fault Isolation Diagnostics (MCD)
FID .... Federacion Internacional de Documentacion [*International Federation for Documentation - IFD*] [*Spanish*] [*Information service or system*] (ASF)
FID .... Federation Internationale du Diabete [*International Diabetes Federation - IDF*] [*Brussels, Belgium*] (EAIO)
FID .... Federation Internationale d'Information et de Documentation [*International Federation for Information and Documentation*] [*Netherlands*] [*Information service or system*] (IID)
FID .... Fellow of the Institute of Directors [*British*]
FID .... Fidata Corp. [*AMEX symbol*] (SPSG)
FID .... Fides [*Faith*] [*Latin*] (ROG)
FID .... Fiduciary (ADA)
FID .... Field Intelligence Department
FID .... Finance and Development [*A publication*]
FID .... Flame Ionization Detector
FID .... Flight Implementation Directive (MCD)
FID .... Foolproof Identification [*System*]
FID .... Force Identification [*Military*] (NVT)
FID .... Format Identification [*Data processing*] (IBMDP)
FID .... Free into Container Depot [*Business term*]
FID .... Free Induction Delay
FID .... Port Fidalgo [*Alaska*] [*Seismograph station code, US Geological Survey*] (SEIS)
FIDA .... Fellow of the Institute of Directors in Australia
FIDA .... Formyliminodiacetic Acid [*Organic chemistry*]
FIDAC .... Federation Interalliee des Anciens Combattants [*World War I*] [*French*] (DAS)
FIDAC .... Film Input to Digital Automatic Computer
FIDACSYS ... Film Input to Digital Automatic Computer System
FIDADT .... US Forest Service. Forest Insect and Disease Leaflet [*A publication*]
FIDAF .... Federacion Internacional de Asociaciones de Ferreteros y Almacenistas de Hierros [*International Federation of Ironmongers and Iron Merchants Associations*]
FIDAQ .... Federation Internationale des Associations de Quincailliers et Marchands de Fer [*International Federation of Ironmongers and Iron Merchants Associations - IFIA*] (EAIO)
FIDAS .... Formularorientiertes Interaktives Datenbanksystem [*Forms-Oriented Interactive Database System*] [*Federal Republic of Germany*]
FIDASE .... Falkland Islands and Dependencies Aerial Survey Expedition [*1955-57*]
FIDCR .... Federal Interagency Day Care Requirements
FID DEF .... Fidei Defensor [*Defender of the Faith*] [*Latin*] (ROG)
FIDE .... Federation de l'Industrie Dentaire en Europe [*Federation of the European Dental Industry*]
FIDE .... Federation Internationale pour le Droit Europeen [*International Federation for European Law*] (EAIO)
FIDE .... Federation Internationale des Echecs [*International Chess Federation*] [*Switzerland*]
FIDEGEP ... Federation Interalliee des Evades de Guerre et des Passeurs
FIDEM .... Federation Internationale des Editeurs de Medailles [*International Federation of Medal Producers*]
FIDEM .... Federation Internationale d'Etudes Medievales (EAIO)
FIDER .... Foundation for Interior Design Education Research (EA)
FIDES .... Fonds d'Investissement pour le Developpement Economique et Social [*1946*] [*United Nations*]
Fides H ...... Fides et Historia [*A publication*]
FIDF .... Financial Institutions Data File [*Rand McNally & Co.*] [*Information service or system*] (CRD)
FIDH .... Federation Internationale des Droits de l'Homme [*International Federation for Human Rights*] [*Paris, France*] (EA)
FIDI .... Federation Internationale des Demenageurs Internationaux [*International Federation of International Furniture Removers - IFIFR*] (EAIO)
FIDIA .... Federation Internationale des Intellectuels Aveugles
FIDIA .... Fellow of the Industrial Design Institute of Australia
Fidia Res Found Symp Ser ... Fidia Research Foundation Symposium Series [*A publication*]
FIDIC .... Federation Internationale des Ingenieurs Conseils [*International Federation of Consulting Engineers*] (EAIO)
Fi Dis .... Fight Against Disease [*A publication*]

FIDJC .... Federation Internationale des Directeurs de Journaux Catholiques
Fid L Chron ... Fiduciary Law Chronicle [*A publication*] (DLA)
FIDMDV ... US Forest Service. Forest Insect and Disease Management. Northern Region Report [*A publication*]
FID News Bull ... Federation Internationale de Documentation. News Bulletin [*A publication*]
FIDO .... Facility for Integrated Data Organization
FIDO .... Fallout Intensity Detector Oscillator
FIDO .... Flight Dynamics Officer [*NASA*]
FIDO .... Flight Inspection District Office [*FAA*]
FIDO .... Fog, Intense, Dispersal Of [*NASA*]
FIDO .... Fog Investigation and Dispersal Operation [*System used on airfield landing strips*] [*World War II*]
FIDO .... Freaks, Irregulars, Defects, and Oddities [*Numismatics*]
FIDO .... Fugitive Information Data Organizer [*Database*]
FIDOF .... Federation Internationale des Organisateurs de Festivals [*International Federation of Festival Organizations*] (EAIO)
FIDP .... Foreign Internal Defense Plan (MCD)
FID Publ .... Federation Internationale de Documentation. Publication [*A publication*]
FID R Doc ... Federation Internationale de Documentation. Revue de la Documentation [*A publication*]
FIDS .... Facility Intrusion Detection System (RDA)
FIDS .... Falkland Islands Dependencies Survey [*1943-62*]
FIDS .... Flight Information Data System [*United Airlines*]
FIDS .... Flight Information Display System [*Information service or system*] (IID)
FIDTA .... Fellow of the International Dance Teachers' Association [*British*] (DBQ)
Fiduciary .... Fiduciary Reporter [*Pennsylvania*] [*A publication*] (DLA)
Fiduciary R (PA) ... Fiduciary Reporter [*Pennsylvania*] [*A publication*] (DLA)
Fiduciary Rptr ... Fiduciary Reporter [*Pennsylvania*] [*A publication*] (DLA)
Fiduc Rep ... Fiduciary Reporter [*Pennsylvania*] [*A publication*] (DLA)
FIE .... Fair Isle [*Scotland*] [*Airport symbol*] (OAG)
FIE .... Fault Isolation Equipment (MCD)
FIE .... Federation Internationale des Echecs [*International Chess Federation*]
FIE .... Federation Internationale d'Escrime [*International Fencing Federation*]
FIE .... Fellow of the Institute of Engineers [*British*]
FIE .... Fiesta Airlines [*Mesa, AZ*] [*FAA designator*] (FAAC)
FIE .... Flight Instrumentation Engineer (MCD)
FIE .... Florida Industries Exposition
FIE .... Foundation for Integrative Education (EA)
FIE .... Fourier Integral Estimate
FIEA .... Federation Internationale des Experts en Automobiles [*International Federation of Automobile Experts*] [*Rhode St. Genese, Belgium*] (EAIO)
FIEAust ..... Fellow of the Institution of Engineers of Australia
FIEC .... Federation de l'Industrie Europeenne de la Construction [*European Construction Industry Federation*] (EAIO)
FIEC .... Federation Internationale des Associations d'Etudes Classiques [*International Federation of the Societies of Classical Studies*] (EAIO)
FIEC .... Fellowship of Independent Evangelical Churches
Fie Cr Abstr ... Field Crop Abstracts [*A publication*]
FIED .... Fellow of the Institution of Engineering Designers [*British*] (DBQ)
FIEDA .... Fondation Internationale pour l'Enseignement du Droit des Affaires [*Canada*]
FIEE .... Federation des Industries Electriques et Electroniques [*France*] (EY)
FIEE .... Fellow of the Institute of Electrical Engineers [*British*]
FIEEE .... Fellow of the Institute of Electrical and Electronic Engineers
FIEF .... Federation Internationale pour l'Economie Familiale [*International Federation for Home Economics - IFHE*] (EAIO)
FIEI .... Farm and Industrial Equipment Institute (EA)
FIEI .... Fellow of the Institution of Engineering Inspection [*British*]
FIE(India) ... Fellow of the Institution of Engineers, India
FIEJ .... Federation Internationale des Editeurs de Journaux [*International Federation of Newspaper Publishers*] [*Paris, France*] (EAIO)
Field .... Fieldiana [*A publication*]
Field Anal .. Field's Analysis of Blackstone's Commentaries [*A publication*] (DLA)
Field Col Mus Pub G S Zool S ... Field Columbian Museum. Publications. Geological Series. Zoological Series [*A publication*]
Field Columbian Mus Publ Geol Ser ... Field Columbian Museum. Publications. Geological Series [*A publication*]
Field Com Law ... Field on the Common Law of England [*A publication*] (DLA)
Field Conf Guideb NM Geol Soc ... Field Conference Guidebook. New Mexico Geological Society [*A publication*]
Field Corp ... Field on Corporations [*A publication*] (DLA)
Field Crop Abstr ... Field Crop Abstracts [*A publication*]
Field Crops Res ... Field Crops Research [*A publication*]

Field Cur .... Field on Protestant Curates and Incumbents [*A publication*] (DLA)
Field Dam .. Field on the Law of Damages [*A publication*] (DLA)
Field & D Ch Pr ... Field and Dunn's Chancery Practice [*A publication*] (DLA)
Field Dev N ... Field Development Newsletter [*A publication*]
Field Drain ... Field Drainage [*A publication*]
Field Ev ...... Field's Law of Evidence in British India [*A publication*] (DLA)
Field w Fie ... Fields within Fields within Fields [*A publication*]
Fieldiana Anthropol ... Fieldiana Anthropology [*A publication*]
Fieldiana Bot ... Fieldiana Botany [*A publication*]
Fieldiana Geol ... Fieldiana Geology [*A publication*]
Fieldiana Geol Mem ... Fieldiana Geology. Memoirs [*A publication*]
Fieldiana Geology Mem ... Fieldiana Geology. Memoirs [*A publication*]
Fieldiana Tech ... Fieldiana Technique [*A publication*]
Fieldiana Zool ... Fieldiana Zoology [*A publication*]
Fieldiana Zool Mem ... Fieldiana Zoology. Memoirs [*A publication*]
Fieldiana Zoology Mem ... Fieldiana Zoology. Memoirs [*A publication*]
Field Il .... Field Illustrated [*A publication*]
Field on Inh ... Field on the Hindu and Mohammedan Laws of Inheritance [*A publication*] (DLA)
Field Int Code ... Field's International Code [*A publication*] (DLA)
Field & Lab ... Field and Laboratory [*A publication*]
Field Lab .... Field and Laboratory [*A publication*]
Field Mus Nat Hist Publ Bot Ser ... Field Museum of Natural History Publications. Botanical Series [*A publication*]
Field Mus Nat Hist Publ Geol Ser ... Field Museum of Natural History Publications. Geological Series [*A publication*]
Field Mus Nat Hist Publ Zool Ser ... Field Museum of Natural History Publications. Zoological Series [*A publication*]
Field Nat .... Field Naturalist [*A publication*]
Fieldnotes Arizona Bur Geol Miner Technol ... Fieldnotes. Arizona Bureau of Geology and Mineral Technology [*A publication*]
Field Notes US For Serv ... Field Notes. United States Forest Service [*A publication*]
Field Pen L ... Field's Penal Law [*A publication*] (DLA)
Field Pr Cor ... Field on Private Corporations [*A publication*] (DLA)
Field Res Proj Man Nat Ser ... Field Research Projects. Man and Nature Series [*A publication*]
Field Res Proj Nat Area Stud ... Field Research Projects. Natural Area Studies [*A publication*]
Field & S .... Field and Stream [*A publication*]
Field Seed Certif Guide Ill Crop Impr Ass ... Field Seed Certification Guide. Illinois Crop Improvement Association [*A publication*]
Field Stat Rec Div Plant Ind CSIRO ... Field Station Record. Division of Plant Industry. Commonwealth Scientific and Industrial Research Organisation [*A publication*] (APTA)
Field Stn Rec ... Field Station Record. Division of Plant Industry. Commonwealth Scientific and Industrial Research Organisation [*A publication*] (APTA)
Field Stn Rec Aust CSIRO Div Plant Ind ... Australia. Commonwealth Scientific and Industrial Research Organisation. Division of Plant Industry. Field Station Record [*A publication*] (APTA)
Field Stn Rec Div Plant Ind CSIRO ... Field Station Record. Division of Plant Industry. Commonwealth Scientific and Industrial Research Organisation [*A publication*] (APTA)
Field Stud ... Field Studies [*A publication*]
FIELecIE ... Fellow of the Institution of Electrical and Electronics Incorporated Engineers [*British*] (DBQ)
FIEM .... Federation Internationale de l'Enseignement Menager
FIEM .... Fellow of the Institute of Executives and Managers [*British*] (DBQ)
FIENA .... Fire Engineering [*A publication*]
FIEO .... Federation of Indian Export Organisations [*Canada*]
FIEP .... Federation Internationale pour l'Education des Parents [*International Federation for Parent Education - IFPE*] [*Sevres, France*] (EAIO)
FIEP .... Federation Internationale d'Education Physique [*International Federation for Physical Education*] (EAIO)
FIEP .... Federation Internationale des Etudiants en Pharmacie
FIEP .... Foundation for International Economic Policy (EA)
FIEP Bull ... FIEP [*Federation Internationale d'Education Physique*] Bulletin [*A publication*]
FIER .... Federation Internationale des Enseignants de Rythmique [*International Federation of Teachers of Rhythmics - IFTR*] (EA)
FIER .... Fieramente [*Boldly*] [*Music*] (ROG)
FIER .... Foundation for Instrumentation Education and Research [*Defunct*]
FIERE .... Fellow of the Institution of Electronic and Radio Engineers [*British*]
FIERF .... Forging Industry Educational and Research Foundation (EA)
FIES .... Fellow of the Illuminating Engineering Society [*Later, FIllumES*] [*British*]
Fie Sci Abs ... Fire Science Abstracts [*A publication*]
FIESP .... Federation Internationale des Etudiants en Sciences Politiques
FIET .... Federation Internationale des Employes, Techniciens, et Cadres [*International Federation of Commercial, Clerical, Professional, and Technical Employees*] [*Geneva, Switzerland*] (EAIO)

FIET .... Field Integration Engineering Test (MCD)
FIEWS ...... Food Information and Early Warning System [*FAO*] [*United Nations*]
FIEx .... Fellow of the Institute of Export [*British*] (DCTA)
FIExE .... Fellow of the Institute of Executive Engineers and Officers [*British*] (DBQ)
FIF .... Failure Indicating Fuse
FIF .... Feedback Inhibition Factor [*Immunochemistry*]
FIF .... Ferric Ion Free
FIF .... Fibroblast Interferon [*Genetics*]
FIF .... Fibroblast-Migration Inhibitory Factor [*Immunochemistry*]
FIF .... Fifteen [*Lawn tennis*] (DSUE)
FIF .... Financial News Composite Fund [*NYSE symbol*] (SPSG)
FIF .... First Irish Families
FIF .... Forced Inspiratory Flow [*Physiology*]
FIF .... Formaldehyde-Induced Fluorescence
FIF .... Fuji International Finance [*Japan*]
f-if--- .... Ifni [*MARC geographic area code*] [*Library of Congress*] (LCCP)
FIFA .... Federation Internationale du Film sur d'Art [*International Federation of Films on Art*]
FIFA .... Federation Internationale de Football Association [*International Federation of Association Football*] [*Zurich, Switzerland*] (EA)
FI FA .... Fieri Facias [*Cause to Be Made*] [*A writ commanding the sheriff to execute judgment*] [*Legal term*] [*Latin*]
FIFAO .... Fouilles de l'Institut Francais d'Archeologie Orientale [*A publication*]
FIFC .... First Fincorp, Inc. [*Kinston, NC*] [*NASDAQ symbol*] (NQ)
FIFC .... Fur Information and Fashion Council (EA)
FIFCLC .... Federation Internationale des Femmes de Carrieres Liberales et Commerciales [*International Federation of Business and Professional Women*]
FIFCQ .... Festival International du Film de la Critique Quebecoise [*International Festival of Quebec Film Critics*] [*Canada*]
FIFDU .... Federation Internationale des Femmes Diplomees des Universites [*International Federation of University Women - IFUW*] (EAIO)
FIFE .... American Institute of Fellows in Free Enterprise [*Houston, DE*] (EA)
FIFE .... Federation Internationale des Associations de Fabricants de Produits d'Entretien [*International Federation of Associations of Manufacturers of Household Products*] (EAIO)
FIFE .... Financial Federal Savings Bank [*Hartford, CT*] [*NASDAQ symbol*] (NQ)
FIFES .... Fifeshire [*County in Scotland*]
FIFI .... Field Image Feature Interface [*Photovoltaic energy systems*]
FIFirE .... Fellow of the Institution of Fire Engineers [*British*] (DCTA)
FIFO .... Fade In, Fade Out [*Films, television, etc.*]
FIFO .... First In, First Out [*Accounting*]
FIFO .... Flight Inspection Field Office [*FAA*]
FIFO .... Floating Input - Floating Output [*Data processing*]
FIFO-H .... Flight Inspection Field Office, High Altitude [*FAA*] (FAAC)
FIFOR .... Flight Forecast (FAAC)
FI (For Ital) ... FI (Forum Italicum) [*A publication*]
FIFP .... Filed IFR [*Instrument Flight Rules*] Flight Plan [*Aviation*] (FAAC)
FIFRA .... Federal Insecticide, Fungicide, and Rodenticide Act [*1947*] [*Department of Agriculture*]
FIFSP .... Federation Internationale des Fonctionnaires Superieurs de Police [*International Federation of Senior Police Officers*] [*France*]
FIFST .... Fellow of the Institute of Food Science and Technology [*British*]
Fifth Est ...... Fifth Estate [*A publication*]
FIG .... Federation Internationale de Genetique [*International Genetics Federation*] (EAIO)
FIG .... Federation Internationale des Geometres [*International Federation of Surveyors - IFS*] [*Edmonton, AB*] (EAIO)
FIG .... Federation Internationale de Gymnastique [*International Gymnastic Federation - IGF*] [*Lyss, Switzerland*] (EAIO)
FIG .... Figaro [*A publication*]
FIG .... Fighter Intercepter Group (MCD)
FIG .... Figurative
FIG .... Figure (AFM)
FIG .... Flight Inspection Group [*FAA*]
FIG .... Floated Integrating Gyro [*Aerospace*] (AAG)
FIG .... FORTH Interest Group (EA)
FIG .... Fraud Investigation Group [*Serious Fraud Office*] [*British*]
FIGA .... Fretted Instrument Guild of America (EA)
FIGA .... Iberian Federation of Anarchist Groups [*Spain*] (PD)
FIGAS .... Falkland Islands Government Air Service (EY)
FIGasE .... Fellow of the Institution of Gas Engineers [*British*]
FIGAZ .... Federation de l'Industrie du Gaz [*Gas Industry Federation*] [*Belgium*] (EY)
FIGCAD ...... Flore Iconographique des Champignons du Congo [*A publication*]
Fig Can ...... Figures Canadiennes [*A publication*]
FIGCM ...... Fellow of the Incorporated Guild of Church Musicians [*British*]
FIGD .... Fellow of the Institute of Grocery Distribution [*British*] (DBQ)

FIGE.......... Federation de l'Industrie Granitiere Europeenne [*Federation of the European Granite Industry*] (EAIO)

FIGE.......... Field Inversion Gel Electrophoresis [*Analytical biochemistry*]

FIGED....... Federation Internationale des Grandes et Moyennes Entreprises de Distribution [*International Federation of Retail Distributors*] (EAIO)

FIGeol........ Fellow of the Institution of Geologists [*British*] (DBQ)

FigEtym...... Figura Etymologica [*A publication*] (BJA)

FIGHT........ Family Interest Group - Head Trauma (EA)

FIGHTRON ... Fighting Squadron

FIGI.......... Figgie International, Inc. [*NASDAQ symbol*] (NQ)

FIGIEFA ... Federation Internationale des Grossistes, Importateurs, et Exportateurs Fournitures Automobiles [*International Federation of Wholesalers, Importers, and Exporters in Automobile Fittings*] (EAIO)

FIGIJ......... Federation Internationale de Gynecologie Infantile et Juvenile [*International Federation of Infantile and Juvenile Gynecology - IFIJG*] [*Sierre, Switzerland*] (EAIO)

Fig Litt....... Figaro Litteraire [*A publication*]

FIGLU....... Formimino-L-glutamic Acid [*Organic chemistry*]

FIGM........ Friends of Israel Gospel Ministry (EA)

FIGO .... Federation Internationale de Gynecologie et d'Obstetrique [*International Federation of Gynecology and Obstetrics*] [*London, England*] (EAIO)

FIGS......... Figures Shift [*Teleprinters*]

FIGS......... Future Income Growth Security [*Finance*]

FIGWA...... Forschung im Ingenieurwesen [*A publication*]

FIH.......... Fat-Induced Hyperglycemia [*Medicine*]

FIH.......... Federation Internationale de Handball [*International Handball Federation*]

FIH.......... Federation Internationale de Hockey [*International Hockey Federation*] [*Brussels, Belgium*] (EA)

FIH.......... Federation Internationale des Hopitaux [*International Hospital Federation*]

FIH .... Fellow of the Institute of Housing [*British*] (DBQ)

FIH .... Fellow of the Institute of Hygiene [*British*]

FIH .... Free in Harbor [*Navigation*]

FIH .... Kinshasa [*Zaire*] [*Airport symbol*] (OAG)

FIHC........ Federation Internationale Halterophile et Culturiste

FIHC........ Federation Internationale des Hommes Catholiques [*International Council of Catholic Men - ICCM*] [*Vatican City, Vatican City State*] (EAIO)

FIHC .... First Intermountain Holding [*NASDAQ symbol*] (NQ)

FIHE........ Fellow of the Institute of Health Education [*British*]

FIHE........ Foundation for Independent Higher Education (EA)

FiHK......... Kauppakorkeakoulu [*Helsinki School of Economics*], Helsinki, Finland [*Library symbol*] [*Library of Congress*] (LCLS)

FIHM .... Fellow of the Institute of Housing Managers [*Formerly, FIHsg*] [*British*]

FIHR .... Foundation for International Human Relations (EA)

FiHR......... Oy Rekolid, Mikrofilmipalvelu, Helsinki, Finland [*Library symbol*] [*Library of Congress*] (LCLS)

FIHS........ Fellow of the Institute of Hospital Secretaries [*British*]

FIHsg........ Fellow of the Institute of Housing [*Later, FIHM*] [*British*]

FIHT......... Fellow of the Institution of Highway Engineers [*British*] (DBQ)

FiHT .... Valtion Teknillinen Tutkimuskeskus, Helsinki, Finland [*Library symbol*] [*Library of Congress*] (LCLS)

FIHU .... Federation Internationale de l'Habitation et de l'Urbanisme

FiHU......... Helsingin Yliopisto [*University of Helsinki*], Helsinki, Finland [*Library symbol*] [*Library of Congress*] (LCLS)

FIHUAT.... Federation Internationale pour l'Habitation, l'Urbanisme et l'Amenagement des Territoires [*International Federation for Housing and Planning - IFHP*] [*The Hague, Netherlands*] (EA)

FIHUL....... Filmihullu [*A publication*]

FIHVE....... Fellow of the Institution of Heating and Ventilating Engineers [*British*]

FII .... FARMS International, Incorporated (EA)

FII .... Federal Item Identification

FII .... Fellow of the Imperial Institute [*British*] (DAS)

FII .... Fletcher Challenge Investments II [*Toronto Stock Exchange symbol*] [*Vancouver Stock Exchange symbol*]

FII .... Food Industry Institute [*Michigan State University*] [*Research center*] (RCD)

FII .... Franked Investment Income [*Accounting*]

FII .... Fussboden Zeitung [*A publication*]

FIIA .... Fellow of the Institute of Industrial Administration [*Later, FBIM*] [*British*]

FIIA .... Fellow of the International Institute of Accountants [*Australia*]

FIIA .... First Interstate of Iowa, Inc. [*Des Moines, IA*] [*NASDAQ symbol*] (NQ)

FIIC .... Federacion Interamericana de la Industria de la Construccion [*Inter-American Federation of the Construction Industry - IAFCI*] (EAIO)

FIIC .... Fellow of the Insurance Institute of Canada

FIIC .... Flight Inspector in Charge

FIICPI...... Federation Internationale des Ingenieurs-Conseils en Propriete Industrielle

FIID .... Federation Internationale d'Information et de Documentation [*International Federation for Information and Documentation - IFID*] (EAIO)

FIIF........... Florafax International, Inc. [*NASDAQ symbol*] (NQ)

FIIG .... Federal Item Identification Guides

FIIG .... Federal Item Inventory Group

FIIG .... Federation des Institutions Internationales Semi-Officielles et Privees Etablies a Geneve [*Federation of Semi-Official and Private International Institutions Established in Geneva*] [*Switzerland*] (EA)

FIIGMO .... Forget It, I've Got My Orders [*Bowdlerized version*] [*Military slang*]

FIIGS........ Federal Item Identification Guide System

FIIGSC...... Federal Item Identification Guides for Supply Cataloging (AABC)

FIIHE .... Federation Internationale des Instituts de Hautes Etudes [*International Federation of Institutes for Advanced Study*] (EAIO)

FIILS........ Full Integrity Instrument Landing System

FIIM .... Federation Internationale de l'Industrie du Medicament [*International Federation of Pharmaceutical Manufacturers Associations - IFPMA*] (EAIO)

FIIM .... Federation Internationale des Ingenieurs Municipaux [*International Federation of Municipal Engineers - IFME*] (EAIO)

FIIM .... Fellow of the Institution of Industrial Managers [*British*] (DCTA)

FIIN .... Federal Item Identification Number

FIInfSc...... Fellow of the Institute of Information Scientists [*British*]

FIInst .... Fellow of the Imperial Institute [*British*]

FIIP .... Federation Internationale de l'Industrie Phonographique

FIISE .... Fellow of the International Institute of Social Economics [*British*] (DBQ)

FIISec .... Fellow of the Institute of Industrial Security [*British*] (DBQ)

FIITA6 ...... Fauna d'Italia [*A publication*]

FIJ .... Federation Internationale des Journalistes [*International Federation of Journalists - IFJ*] [*Brussels, Belgium*] (EAIO)

FIJ .... Federation Internationale de Judo [*International Judo Federation*]

FIJ .... Fellow of the Institute of Journalists [*British*]

FIJ .... Fund for Investigative Journalism (EA)

FIJB.......... Fondation Internationale Jacques Brel [*International Jacques Brel Foundation - IJBF*] (EA)

FIJBT .... Federation Internationale des Jeunesse Bons Templiers [*International Good Templar Youth Federation*] (EAIO)

FIJC .... Federation Internationale de la Jeunesse Catholique

FIJET .... Federation Internationale des Journalistes et Ecrivains du Tourisme [*World Federation of Travel Journalists and Writers*] [*Paris, France*] (EA)

Fiji Agric J ... Fiji Agricultural Journal [*A publication*]

Fiji Archt ... Fiji Architect [*A publication*]

Fiji Dep Agric Bull ... Fiji. Department of Agriculture. Bulletin [*A publication*]

Fiji Geol Surv Dep Bull ... Fiji. Geological Survey Department. Bulletin [*A publication*]

Fiji Geol Surv Dep Econ Invest ... Fiji. Geological Survey Department. Economic Investigation [*A publication*]

Fiji Geol Surv Dep Econ Rep ... Fiji. Geological Survey Department. Economic Report [*A publication*]

Fiji LR........ Fiji Law Reports [*A publication*] (DLA)

Fiji Miner Resour Div Bull ... Fiji. Mineral Resources Division. Bulletin [*A publication*]

Fiji Timb .... Fiji Timbers and Their Uses [*A publication*]

FIJL.......... Federation Internationale des Journalistes Libres [*International Federation of Free Journalists*]

FIJM .... Federation Internationale des Jeunesses Musicales [*International Federation of Jeunesses Musicales*] (EAIO)

FIJPA .... Federation Internationale des Journalistes Professionnels de l'Aeronautique

FIJU .... Federation Internationale des Producteurs de Jus de Fruits [*International Federation of Fruit Juice Producers - IFFJP*] (EAIO)

Fik........... Families Including Kids [*Lifestyle classification*]

FIK........... Field Ionization Kinetics

FIK........... Financiele Koerier [*A publication*]

FIL .... Federal Industries Ltd. [*Toronto Stock Exchange symbol*]

FIL .... Federation Internationale de Laiterie [*International Dairy Federation - IDF*] (EAIO)

FIL .... Federation Internationale de Luge de Course [*International Luge Federation - ILF*] [*Rottenmann, Austria*] (EA)

FIL .... Fellow of the Institute of Linguists [*British*] (EY)

FIL .... Filament (KSC)

Fil........... Filiale [*Branch Office*] [*German*]

FIL........... Filigree [*Jewelry*] (ROG)

FIL........... Fillet (MSA)

FIL........ Fillister

F Il........... Films Illustrated [*A publication*]

Fil........... Filologia [*A publication*]

Fil........... Filologija [*A publication*]

Fil........... Filomata [*A publication*]

Fil........... Filosofia [*A publication*]

FIL........... Filter (AABC)

FIL........... Florida Instructional League [*Baseball*]

FIL............ Franklin Institute Laboratories (MUGU)
FIL............. Fuel Injection Line (MSA)
FIL............. National Film Archives, Film Canadiana [*UTLAS symbol*]
FIL............. Sanifill, Inc. [*NYSE symbol*] (SPSG)
FILA.......... Farm Improvement Loans Act [*Canada*]
FILA .... Federation Internationale de Lutte Amateur [*International Amateur Wrestling Federation*] [*Lausanne, Switzerland*] (EAIO)
FILA .... Fellow of the Institute of Landscape Architects [*British*]
FILAM ...... Fellow of the Institute of Leisure and Amenity Management [*British*] (DBQ)
Filam Fungi ... Filamentous Fungi [*A publication*]
Fil (BA)..... Filologia (Buenos Aires) [*A publication*]
FILBAS ..... Philippine Base [*Army*] [*World War II*]
FILBDLP .. Fondation Internationale Lelio Basso pour le Droit et la Liberation des Peuples [*International Lelio Basso Foundation for the Rights and Liberation of Peoples - ILBFRLP*] (EA)
FILCEN..... Filter Center
FILCO........ Film Coalition (EA)
FILD......... Federal Item Logistics Data
FILDIR...... Federation Internationale Libre des Deportes et Internes de la Resistance [*International Free Federation of Deportees and Resistance Internees*]
Fil Dr .... Doctor of Philology
FILDR .... Federal Item Logistics Data Record
FILE .... Family Inventory of Life Events and Changes
FILE .... Fast Index Location Educators
FILE .... Feature Identification and Landmark Experiment [*NASA*]
FILE .... Fellow of the Institute of Legal Executives [*British*] (DLA)
FILE .... FileNet Corp. [*NASDAQ symbol*] (NQ)
FILE .... Florida Institute for Law Enforcement [*St. Petersburg Junior College*] [*Research center*] (RCD)
FILE .... Future Identification and Location Experiment [*NASA*] (NASA)
FILEF........ Federazione Italiana Lavorati Emigrati Famiglie
FILER........ File Information Language Executive Routine [*Data processing*]
FILEX....... File Exchange
FILFP .... Forum International de Liaison des Forces de la Paix [*International Liaison Forum of Peace Forces - ILF*] [*Moscow, USSR*] (EAIO)
FILG .... Filing (ROG)
FILG .... Filling (FAAC)
FILH.......... Fillister Head [*Screws*]
FIL et HOER ... Filius [*or Filia*] et Hoeres [*Latin*] (ROG)
FIL-IDF (Fed Int Lait Int Dairy Fed) Bull ... FIL-IDF (Federation Internationale de Laiterie - International Dairy Federation) Bulletin [*A publication*]
FIL-IDF (Fed Int Lait Int Dairy Fed) Stand ... FIL-IDF (Federation Internationale de Laiterie - International Dairy Federation) Standards [*A publication*]
FILIS .... Federazione Italiana Lavoratori Informazione Spettacolo [*Italian Federation of Theatre Workers*] [*Italy*] (EY)
Fil Ist .... File de Istorie. Culegere de Studii, Articole si Comunicari [*A publication*]
Fil Kand ..... Candidate in Philosophy
Fil Koezl.... Filologiai Koezloeny [*A publication*]
FILL .... Filling
FILL .... Fleet Issue Load List [*Navy*]
Fil Lic......... Licentiate in Philosophy
FILLM....... Federation Internationale des Langues et Litteratures Modernes [*International Federation for Modern Languages and Literatures*] (EAIO)
FILLS .... Fast Inter-Library Loans and Statistics [*MacNeal Hospital*] [*Information service or system*] (IID)
FIllumES ... Fellow of the Illuminating Engineering Society [*Formerly, FIES*] [*British*]
FILM .... Capfilm, Inc. [*Lee, MA*] [*NASDAQ symbol*] (NQ)
FILM .... CSIRO [*Commonwealth Scientific and Industrial Research Organisation*] Films [*Database*]
FILM .... For Illustrating Legal Methods [*Student legal action organization*] (EA)
Film Appreciation News ... Film Appreciation Newsletter [*A publication*] (APTA)
Film C .... Film Criticism [*A publication*]
Film Comm ... Film Comment [*A publication*]
Film Crit .... Film Criticism [*A publication*]
Film Cult.... Film Culture [*A publication*]
Filmf .... Filmfacts [*A publication*]
Film J......... Film Journal [*A publication*]
Film Lib Q ... Film Library Quarterly [*A publication*]
Film Libr Q ... Film Library Quarterly [*A publication*]
Film Lit Ind ... Film Literature Index [*A publication*]
Film Lit Index ... Film Literature Index [*A publication*]
Filmmakers M ... Filmmakers' Monthly [*A publication*]
Film Mus .... Film Music [*A publication*]
Film Mus Notes ... Film Music Notes [*A publication*]
Filmnet....... Film Users Network [*Cine Information*] [*Information service or system*] (IID)
Fil Mod ...... Filologia Moderna [*A publication*]
Film Psych ... Film Psychology Review [*A publication*]

Film Q........ Film Quarterly [*A publication*]
Films & F ... Films and Filming [*A publication*]
FILMSORT ... Microfilm Sorter [*Electronics*]
Films in R .. Films in Review [*A publication*]
Film u Ton Mag ... Film und Ton Magazin [*A publication*]
Filo............ Filologica [*A publication*]
FILO........... First In, Last Out [*Accounting*]
Filol Vesti .. Filologiceskie Vesti [*A publication*]
Filos .... Filosofia [*A publication*]
Filos Nauc Kommunizm ... Filosofija i Naucnyj Kommunizm [*A publication*]
Filos Nauki ... Filosofskie Nauki [*A publication*]
Filosof Cas CSAV ... Filosoficky Casopis CSAV [*Ceskoslovesnska Akademie Ved*] [*A publication*]
Filos Probl Obsc Soznanija ... Filosofskie Problemy Obscestvennogo Soznanija [*A publication*]
Filos Probl Suchasnoho Pryrodozn ... Filosofski Problemy Suchasnoho Pryrodoznavstva [*A publication*]
Filos Probl Suchasnoho Przyr Mizhvid Nauk Zb ... Filosofichnii Problemy Suchasnoho Przyrodoznavstva Mizhvidomchyi Naukovyi Zbirnyk [*A publication*]
Filos Vopr Fiz Khim ... Filosofskie Voprosy Fiziki i Khimii [*A publication*]
Filos Vopr Medicin Biol ... Filosofskie Voprosy Mediciny i Biologii [*A publication*]
Filoz Cas .... Filozoficky Casopis [*A publication*]
Fil Pregl .... Filoloski Pregled [*A publication*]
Fil Ro .... Filologia Romanza [*A publication*]
FILS........... Federal Information Locator System
FILS........... Filologicke Studie [*A publication*]
FILS........... Flarescan Instrument Landing System
FilSbAlm ... Filologiceskij Sbornik [*Stat'i Aspirantov i Soiskatelej*]. Alma-Ata [*A publication*]
FILSG........ Fels Institute of Local and State Governments [*University of Pennsylvania*]
Filson Club Hist Q ... Filson Club History Quarterly [*A publication*]
Filson C Q ... Filson Club Quarterly [*A publication*]
FILSUA..... Forest Industry Lecture Series. University of Alberta Forestry Program [*A publication*]
FILT .... Federation Internationale de Lawn Tennis [*International Lawn Tennis Federation*]
FILT .... Federazione Italiana Sindacati dei Trasporti [*Transportation industry*] [*Italy*] (EY)
FILT .... Filtra [*Filter*] [*Pharmacy*]
FILTH .... For Improved Labeling to Terminate Hazards [*Student legal action organization*]
Filtration.... Filtration and Separation [*A publication*]
Filtr Eng..... Filtration Engineering [*A publication*]
Filtr Sep..... Filtration and Separation [*A publication*]
Filtr Tech Sep ... Filtration et Techniques Separatives [*France*] [*A publication*]
Filtr Tech Separatives ... Filtration et Techniques Separatives [*A publication*]
FILU.......... Four-BIT [*Binary Digit*] Interface Logic Unit
FILUP .... Franklin Institute Laboratories Universal Pulser (KSC)
FilZ .... Filologija (Zagreb) [*A publication*]
FIM............ Fabric Insulation Material
FIM............ Facing Identification Mark [*Postal Service*]
FIM............ Failure Indication Modules
FIM............ Fairness in Media (EA)
FIM............ Far-Infrared MASER [*Microwave Amplification by Stimulated Emission of Radiation*]
FIM............ Fault Isolation Meter (MCD)
FIM............ Fault Isolation Module (CAAL)
FIM............ Federation Internationale des Mineurs [*Miners' International Federation - MIF*] [*Brussels, Belgium*] (EAIO)
FIM............ Federation Internationale Motocycliste [*International Motorcycle Federation*] [*Geneva, Switzerland*] (EAIO)
FIM............ Federation Internationale des Musiciens [*International Federation of Musicians*] [*Zurich, Switzerland*] (EAIO)
FIM............ Fellow of the Institute of Metallurgists [*British*] (EY)
FIM............ Fellow of the Institute of Metals [*British*]
FIM............ Fellowship of Independent Missions (EA)
FIM............ Field Inspection Manual (NRCH)
FIM............ Field Instruction Memorandum
FIM............ Field Intensity Meter
FIM............ Field Ion Microscope [*or Microscopy*]
FIM............ Fillmore, CA [*Location identifier*] [*FAA*] (FAAL)
FiM............ Filologia Moderna [*A publication*]
FIM............ Financial Market Trends [*Paris*] [*A publication*]
FIM............ Finnmark [*Finnish Mark*] [*Monetary unit*]
FIM............ Flight Information Manual
FIM............ Foundation for Innovation in Medicine (EA)
FIM............ Foundation for International Meetings (EA)
FIM............ Front Interface Module [*Data processing*]
FIM............ Full Indicator Movement (MSA)
FIM............ Functional Independence Measure [*Occupational therapy*]
FIMA........ Fault Isolation Maintainability Analysis (MCD)
FIMA........ Fellow of the Institute of Mathematics and its Application [*British*]
FIMA........ Fellow of the Institute of Municipal Administration [*Australia*] (ADA)
FIMA........ Fellow of the Institute of Municipal Treasurers and Accountants [*British*]

FIMA........ Financial Institutions Marketing Association [*Chicago, IL*] (EA)
FIMA........ Fission Initial Metal Atom [*Nuclear energy*] (NRCH)
FIMA........ Future International Military/Civil Airfighter [*British*]
FIManf...... Fellow of the Institute of Manufacturing [*British*] (DBQ)
FIMARC... Federation Internationale des Mouvements d'Adultes Ruraux Catholiques [*International Federation of Adult Rural Catholic Movements*]
FIMarE... Fellow of the Institute of Marine Engineers [*British*]
FIMATE... Factory-Installed Maintenance Automatic Test Equipment
FIMBI...... Fellow of the Institute of Medical and Biological Illustration [*British*] (DBQ)
FIMBM..... Fellow of the Institute of Municipal Building Management [*British*] (DBQ)
FIMBRA... Financial Intermediaries, Managers, and Brokers Association [*British*] (ECON)
FIMC........ Federal Interagency Media Committee (EGAO)
FIMC........ Fellow of the Institute of Management Consultants [*British*]
FIMCAP... Federation Internationale de Communautes de Jeunesse Catholique Paroissiales [*International Federation of Catholic Parochial Youth Communities*] [*Antwerp, Belgium*] (EAIO)
FIMCEE.... Federation de l'Industrie Marbriere de la Communaute Economique Europeenne [*Federation of the Marble Industry of the European Economic Community*] (EAIO)
FIME........ Federation Internationale des Maisons de l'Europe [*International Federation of Europe Houses - IFEH*] (EAIO)
FIME........ Fellow of the Institute of Marine Engineers [*British*] (DCTA)
FIME........ Fluorouracil, ICRF-159 [*Razoxane*], MeCCNU [*Semustine*] [*Antineoplastic drug regimen*]
FI Mech E... Fellow of the Institution of Mechanical Engineers [*British*]
FIMEM..... Federation Internationale des Mouvements d'Ecole Moderne (EAIO)
FIMF........ Federacion Internacional de Medecina Fisica [*International Federation of Physical Medicine*]
FIMF........ Fellow of the Institute of Metal Finishing [*British*] (DBQ)
FIMG........ Facilities Installation Monitoring Group (MUGU)
FIMGTechE... Fellow of the Institution of Mechanical and General Technician Engineers [*British*] (DBQ)
FIMH........ Fellow of the Institute of Materials Handling [*British*] (DBQ)
FIMI.......... Fellow of the Institute of the Motor Industry [*Formerly, FIMT*] [*British*]
FIMIG-CEE... Federation of the Marble Industry of the European Economic Community (EAIO)
FIMinE...... Fellow of the Institution of Mining Engineers [*British*]
FIMIS........ Financial Management Information System [*Army*]
FIMIT....... Fellow of the Institute of Music Instrument Technology [*British*]
FIMITIC... Federation Internationale des Mutiles, des Invalides du Travail, et des Invalides Civils [*International Federation of Disabled Workmen and Civilian Handicapped*] [*Federal Republic of Germany*] (EAIO)
FIML........ Full-Information Maximum Likelihood [*Econometrics*]
FIMLS....... Fellow of the Institute of Medical Laboratory Sciences [*British*] (DBQ)
FIMM........ Federation Internationale de Medicine Manuelle [*International Federation of Manual Medicine*] [*Zurich, Switzerland*] (EAIO)
FIMM........ Fellow of the Institution of Mining and Metallurgy [*British*] (DBQ)
FIMM........ Mauritius Flight Information Center [*ICAO location identifier*] (ICLI)
FIMOC...... Federation Internationale des Mouvements Ouvriers Chretiens [*International Federation of Christian Workers Movements*]
FIMP........ Federation Internationale de Medecine Physique [*International Federation of Physical Medicine*]
F Imp.......... Field Imprisonment [*British military*] (DMA)
FIMP........ Mauritius/Sir Seewoosagur Ramgoolam International [*ICAO location identifier*] (ICLI)
FIMPACS... Fashion Integrated Merchandising Planning and Control System (BUR)
FIMPS...... Federation Internationale de Medecine Preventive et Sociale [*International Federation for Preventive and Social Medicine*] (EAIO)
FIMR........ Finnish Marine Research [*A publication*]
FIMR........ Rodriguez Island/Plaine Corail [*Mauritius*] [*ICAO location identifier*] (ICLI)
FIMS........ Facility Information Management System (MCD)
FIMS........ Fault Isolation and Monitoring System [*NGT*] (MCD)
FIMS........ Federation Internationale Medecine Sportive [*International Federation of Sportive Medicine*]
FIMS........ Fellow of the Institute of Management Specialists [*British*] (DBQ)
FIMS........ Fellowship of Interdenominational Missionary Societies
FIMS........ Field Intensity Measuring System
FIMS........ Field Ionization Mass Spectrometry [*Air-pollutant detector*]
FIMS........ Folklore Institute. Monograph Series [*A publication*]
FIMS........ Friendly Iron Moulders Society [*A union*] [*British*]
FIMT........ Fellow of the Institute of Motor Trade [*Later, FIMI*] [*British*]

FIMTA...... Fellow of the Institute of Municipal Treasurers and Accountants [*British*]
FIMunE.... Fellow of the Institution of Municipal Engineers [*British*]
FIN............ Ad Finem [*At or To the End*] [*Latin*] (ADA)
Fin............ De Finibus [*of Cicero*] [*Classical studies*] (OCD)
FIN............ Federal Item Name
FIN............ Fellow of the Institute of Navigation [*British*]
FIN............ Fiduciary Identification Number [*IRS*]
FIN............ Finance [*or Financial*] (AFM)
FIN............ Financial Corp. of America [*NYSE symbol*] (SPSG)
FIN............ Financieel Dagblad voor Handel, Industrie, Scheepvaart, en Cultures [*A publication*]
Fin............ Finanse [*A publication*]
Fin............ Finansije [*A publication*]
Fin............ Finch's English Chancery Reports [*1673-81*] [*A publication*] (DLA)
FIN............ Findlay College, Findlay, OH [*OCLC symbol*] (OCLC)
Fin............ Finger
FIN............ Finis [*The End*] [*Latin*]
FIN............ Finish (KSC)
FIN............ Finland [*ANSI three-letter standard code*] (CNC)
Fin............ Finlay's Irish Digest [*A publication*] (DLA)
fin............ Finnish [*MARC language code*] [*Library of Congress*] (LCCP)
FIN............ Finschhafen [*Papua New Guinea*] [*Airport symbol*] (OAG)
FIN............ Flight Interneuron [*Zoology*]
FIN............ Future Information Network [*Australia*]
FIN............ Futures Information Network [*Defunct*] (EA)
FINA........ Federation Internationale de Natation Amateur [*International Amateur Swimming Federation*] [*Vancouver, BC*]
FINA........ Following Items Not Available
FINAC...... Fast Interline Nonactivate Automatic Control [*AT & T*]
FinAF........ Finnish Air Force
Fin Agr...... Financing Agriculture [*A publication*]
FINAL........ Financial Analysis Language [*Data processing*]
FINALCL... Final Coordination Line [*Military*]
Final Control Elem... Final Control Elements [*A publication*]
FINAN...... Financial
Fin Anal J... Financial Analysts Journal [*A publication*]
Fin Analyst... Financial Analysts Journal [*A publication*]
Fin Analysts J... Financial Analysts Journal [*A publication*]
Financ Agric... Financing Agriculture [*A publication*]
Financ Anal J... Financial Analysts Journal [*A publication*]
Financ Analysts J... Financial Analysts Journal [*A publication*]
Financ Dag... Financieel Dagblad [*A publication*]
Finance & Dev... Finance and Development [*A publication*]
Finance Dev... Finance and Development [*A publication*]
Finance Trade R... Finance and Trade Review [*A publication*]
Financ Exec... Financial Executive [*A publication*]
Financ Executive... Financial Executive [*A publication*]
Financial E... Financial Executive [*A publication*]
Financial M... Financial Management [*A publication*]
Financial W... Financial Weekly [*A publication*]
Financ Mail... Financial Mail [*A publication*]
Financ Manage... Financial Management [*A publication*]
Financ Times... Financial Times [*London*] [*A publication*]
Financ Times Europ Energy Rep... Financial Times. European Energy Report [*A publication*]
Financ Trade Rev... Finance and Trade Review [*A publication*]
Financ Week... Finance Week [*A publication*]
Financ World... Financial World [*A publication*]
Finan Manag... Financial Management [*A publication*]
FINANSAT... Financial Satellite Corp. [*Washington, DC*] [*Telecommunications service*] (TSSD)
Finanstid.... Finanstidende [*A publication*]
Finan World... Financial World [*A publication*]
Finanzj....... Finanzjournal [*A publication*]
FINART.... Feria Internacional de Artesania (TSPED)
FINAST.... First National Stores, Inc.
FINAT....... Federation Internationale des Fabricants et Transformateurs d'Adhesifs et Thermocollants sur Papiers et Autres Supports [*International Federation of Manufacturers and Converters of Pressure-Sensitive and Heatseals on Paper and Other Base Materials*] (EAIO)
Fin Budget... National Budget for Finland [*A publication*]
Fin C........ Financial Code (DLA)
FINCEN.... Financial Crimes Enforcement Network [*Federal task force*]
Finch.......... English Chancery Reports Tempore Finch [*A publication*] (DLA)
Finch.......... Finch's Precedents in Chancery [*England*] [*A publication*] (DLA)
Finch Cas Cont... Finch's Cases on Contract [*1886*] [*A publication*] (DLA)
Finch Cas Contr... Finch's Cases on Contract [*1886*] [*A publication*] (DLA)
Finch (Eng)... English Chancery Reports Tempore Finch [*A publication*] (DLA)
Finch (Eng)... Finch's Precedents in Chancery [*England*] [*A publication*] (DLA)
Finch Ins Dig... Finch's Insurance Digest [*A publication*] (DLA)
Finch Law.. [*Sir Henry*] Finch. A Discourse of Law [*1759*] [*A publication*] (DLA)
Finch LC.... Finch's Land Cases [*A publication*] (DLA)
Finch Nomot... Finch's Nomotechnia [*A publication*] (DLA)

Finch Prec ... Precedents in Chancery, Edited by Finch [*A publication*]   (DLA)
Finch Sum CL ... Finch's Summary of the Common Law [*A publication*]   (DLA)
FINCISCOM ... Finance and Comptroller Information Systems Command [*Army*]
Fincl Mail .. Financial Mail [*A publication*]
FINCO....... Field Intelligence Non-Commissioned Officer [*British military*]   (DMA)
FINCOM... Finance Committee [*Institute of Electrical and Electronics Engineers*]   (IEEE)
F INC ST ... Fellow of the Incorporated Shorthand Teachers [*British*]   (ROG)
FIND .... Federal Item Name Directory
FIND .... File of Industrial Data [*Data processing*]
FIND .... File Interrogation of Nineteen-Hundred Data [*Data processing*]   (DIT)
FIND .... Flight Information Display
F Ind.......... Food Industries [*A publication*]
FIND .... Friendless, Isolated, Needy, Disabled [*Project of National Council on the Aging - acronym used as name of New York City coffeehouse*]
FIND .... Fugitive Intercept Net Deployment [*Philadelphia police program*]
FINDB...... Financial Institution Data Base [*Cates Consulting Analysts, Inc.*] [*Information service or system*]   (CRD)
Fin Dev...... Finance and Development [*A publication*]
Fin & Devel ... Finance and Development [*A publication*]
Fin and Development ... Finance and Development [*A publication*]
Fin Dig........ Finlay's Irish Digest [*A publication*]   (DLA)
F Ind Man .. Food Industries Manual [*A publication*]
FINDS....... Fault Inferring Nonlinear Detection System [*NASA*]
F Ind SA ... Food Industries of South Africa [*A publication*]
Fin & Dul ... Finnemore and Dulcken's Natal Law Reports [*A publication*]   (DLA)
FINE.......... Fighter Inertial Navigation System
FINE.......... Financial Institutions in the Nation's Economy [*Study initiated by House of Representatives*]
Fine Arts J ... Fine Arts Journal [*A publication*]
FINEBEL.. France, Italy, Netherlands, Belgium, and Luxembourg [*Economic agreement*]
FINEFTA ... Finland-European Free Trade Association Treaty
Fine Pt....... Fine Print [*A publication*]
Fine Wood ... Fine Woodworking [*A publication*]
FINEX....... Finish Exercise [*Military*]   (NVT)
FINEX....... Fundo de Financiamento e Exportacao [*Financing and Export Fund*] [*Brazil*]
Fin Exec..... Financial Executive [*A publication*]
FINF.......... Firmen- und Marktinformationen [*Company and Market Information Data Base*] [*Society for Business Information*] [*Information service or system*]   (IID)
Fin Fisk...... Finlands Fiskerier [*A publication*]
FINFO....... Flight Inspection National Field Office [*FAA*]
FINGA....... Fernmelde-Ingenieur [*A publication*]
Fin H........... [*H.*] Finch's Chancery Reports [*1673-81*] [*England*] [*A publication*]   (DLA)
FINH .... First NH [*Formerly, New Hampshire*] Banks, Inc. [*NASDAQ symbol*]   (NQ)
FINI........... Financial Industry Information Service [*Database*] [*Bank Marketing Association*] [*Information service or system*]
FINIF........ Field-Induced Negative Ion Formation
FINIS .... Financial Industry Information Service [*Database*] [*Bank Marketing Association*] [*Information service or system*]   (CRD)
Finish Ind .. Finishing Industries [*A publication*]
Finishing Ind ... Finishing Industries [*A publication*]
F/INJ.......... Fuel Injection [*Automotive engineering*]
Finkel Medical Cyc ... Finkel, et Alia. Lawyers' Medical Cyclopedia [*A publication*]   (DLA)
Fin Kemistsamf Medd ... Finska Kemistsamfundet. Meddelanden [*A publication*]
Fink Ev ...... Fink's Indian Evidence Act [*A publication*]   (DLA)
FINL.......... Financial
Fin Lakaresallsk Handl ... Finska Lakaresallskapets Handlingar [*A publication*]
Finlande Comm Geol Bull ... Finlande. Commission Geologique. Bulletin [*A publication*]
Finlay Rev Med-Hist Cubana ... Finlay Revista Medico-Historica Cubana [*A publication*]
Finl Ch Tr ... Finlason on Charitable Trusts [*A publication*]   (DLA)
Finl Com ..... Finlason on Commons [*A publication*]   (DLA)
Finl Dig ...... Finlay's Irish Digest [*A publication*]   (DLA)
Finl Fisk..... Finlands Fiskerier [*A publication*]
Finl Geodeettinen Laitos Julk ... Finland Geodeettinen Laitos. Julkaisuja [*A publication*]
Finl Geol Tutkimuslaitos Opas ... Finland Geologinen Tutkimuslaitos. Opas [*A publication*]
Finl Geol Tutkimuslaitos Bull ... Finland Geologinen Tutkimuslaitos. Bulletin [*A publication*]
Finl Jud Sys ... Finlason's Judicial System [*A publication*]   (DLA)
Finl LC....... Finlason's Leading Cases on Pleading [*A publication*]   (DLA)

Finl Ld Ten ... Finlason's History of Law of Tenures of Land [*1870*] [*A publication*]   (DLA)
Finl Mar L ... Finlason's Commentaries on Martial Law [*A publication*]   (DLA)
Finl Rep ..... Finlason's Report of the Gurney Case [*A publication*]   (DLA)
Finl Riot..... Finlay on Repression of Riot or Rebellion [*A publication*]   (DLA)
Finl Ten ..... Finlason's History of Law of Tenures of Land [*1870*] [*A publication*]   (DLA)
Finl Vesitutkimuslaitos Julk ... Finland Vesitutkimuslaitos. Julkaisuja [*A publication*]
Fin Mail (South Africa) ... Financial Mail (South Africa) [*A publication*]
Fin Mgt...... Financial Management [*A publication*]
Fin Mosskulturforen Arsb ... Finska Mosskulturforeningens Arsbok [*A publication*]
FINN .... Finnish [*Language, etc.*]
FINNAIR.. Aero O/Y [*Finnish airline*]
Finn Chem L ... Finnish Chemical Letters [*A publication*]
Finn Chem Lett ... Finnish Chemical Letters [*A publication*]
Finn Fish Res ... Finnish Fisheries Research [*A publication*]
Finn Found Alcohol Stud ... Finnish Foundation for Alcohol Studies [*A publication*]
Finn Game Res ... Finnish Game Research [*A publication*]
Finnish Pap Timber ... Finnish Paper and Timber Journal [*A publication*]
Finn J Dairy Sci ... Finnish Journal of Dairy Science [*A publication*]
Finn Mar Res ... Finnish Marine Research [*A publication*]
Finn Pap Timb ... Finnish Paper and Timber Journal [*A publication*]
Finn Pap Timber ... Finnish Paper and Timber Journal [*A publication*]
Finn Psychiatry ... Finnish Psychiatry [*A publication*]
FINO .... Finance Officer [*Army*]
FINO .... Weather Report Will Not Be Filed for Transmission [*Aviation*]   (FAAC)
Finommech-Mikrotech ... Finommechanika-Mikrotechnika [*A publication*]
FINP.......... Finnish Periodicals Index in Economics and Business [*Helsinki School of Economics Library*] [*Information service or system*]
Fin Paper ... Finnish Paper and Timber Journal [*A publication*]
Fin Planner ... Financial Planner [*A publication*]
Fin Planning Today ... Financial Planning Today [*A publication*]
Fin Plan Today ... Financial Planning Today [*A publication*]
Fin Post ..... Financial Post [*A publication*]
Fin Post M ... Financial Post Magazine [*A publication*]
Fin Post Mag ... Financial Post Magazine [*A publication*]
Fin Pr .... Finch's Precedents in Chancery [*England*] [*A publication*]   (DLA)
Fin Prec...... Finch's Precedents in Chancery [*England*] [*A publication*]   (DLA)
FINPRO .... Finnish Committee in Trade Procedures   (DS)
Fin R .... Financial Review [*A publication*]
FINRA....... Fishery Industrial Research [*United States*] [*A publication*]
Fin Ren ..... Finlay on Renewals [*A publication*]   (DLA)
FINREP..... Final Report
FINREP..... Reference Cited Message. Final Report Will Be Made as Soon as Possible   (AABC)
Fin Rep IANEC ... Final Report. Meeting. Inter-American Nuclear Energy Commission [*A publication*]
FINS .... Fishing Industry News Science [*A publication*]   (APTA)
Finshng Ind ... Finishing Industries [*A publication*]
Fins Kem Med ... Finska Kemistsamfundets Meddelanden [*A publication*]
Finskt Mus ... Finskt Museum [*A publication*]
Finsk Veterinaerts ... Finsk Veterinaertidskrift [*A publication*]
Finsk Veterinartidskr ... Finsk Veterinartidskrift [*A publication*]
Finsk Vet Tidskr ... Finsk Veterinaertidskrift [*A publication*]
Fin SSSR ... Finansy SSSR [*A publication*]
FINST .... Final Station [*Data processing*]
FInstAEA .. Fellow of the Institute of Automotive Engineer Assessors [*British*]   (DBQ)
FInstAM.... Fellow of the Institute of Administrative Management [*British*]   (DBQ)
FInstBB..... Fellow of the Institute of British Bakers   (DBQ)
FInstBCA .. Fellow of the Institute of Burial and Cremation Administration [*British*]   (DBQ)
FInstBiol.... Fellow of the Institute of Biology [*Later, FI Biol*] [*British*]
FInstBRM ... Fellow of the Institute of Baths and Recreation Management [*British*]   (DBQ)
FInstBTM ... Fellow of the Institute of Business and Technical Management [*British*]   (DBQ)
FInstC........ Fellow of the Institute of Commerce [*British*]
FInstCh...... Fellow of the Institute of Chiropodists [*British*]
F Inst CM .. Fellow of the Institute of Commercial Management [*British*]   (DCTA)
FInstD........ Fellow of the Institute of Directors [*British*]
F Inst Dir ... Fellow of the Institute of Directors [*British*]
FInstE........ Fellow of the Institute of Energy [*British*]   (DBQ)
F Inst F ...... Fellow of the Institute of Fuel [*British*]
FInstFF...... Fellow of the Institute of Freight Forwarders [*British*]   (DBQ)
F Inst L Ex ... Fellow of the Institute of Legal Executives [*British*]   (DCTA)
FInstM....... Fellow of the Institute of Marketing [*British*]
FInstM....... Fellow of the Institute of Meat [*British*]
FInstMC.... Fellow of the Institute of Measurement and Control [*British*]   (DBQ)

FInstMet.... Fellow of the Institute of Metals [*British*]
F Inst MSM ... Fellow of the Institute of Marketing and Sales Management [*Formerly, FSMA*] [*British*]
FInstNDT ... Fellow of the British Institute of Non-Destructive Testing (DBQ)
F Inst P ...... Fellow of the Institute of Physics and the Physical Society [*British*] (EY)
F Inst Pet ... Fellow of the Institute of Petroleum [*British*]
F Inst PI..... Fellow of the Institute of Patentees and Inventors [*British*] (EY)
FInstPS...... Fellow of the Institute of Purchasing and Supply [*British*]
FInstR........ Fellow of the Institute of Refrigeration [*British*] (DBQ)
FInstRE(Aust) ... Fellow of the Institution of Radio Engineers (Australia)
FInstSMM ... Fellow of the Institute of Sales Management [*British*] (DBQ)
F INST ST ... Fellow of the Institute of Shorthand Teachers [*British*] (ROG)
F Inst TA ... Fellow of the Institute of Transport Administration [*British*] (DCTA)
FInstW....... Fellow of the Institute of Welding [*British*]
FInstWM... Fellow of the Institute of Wastes Management [*British*] (DBQ)
FInstWM(Hon) ... Honorary Fellowship of the Institute of Wastes Management [*British*] (DBQ)
FINSUPSCOL ... Finance and Supply School [*Coast Guard*]
FInt .... Fiction International [*A publication*]
Fin T .... T. Finch's Precedents in English Chancery [*1689-1722*] [*A publication*] (DLA)
Fin Tax & Comp L ... Finance Taxation and Company Law [*Pakistan*] [*A publication*] (DLA)
FinTech...... Financial Technology [*Publisher*] [*British*]
FINTEL..... Financial Times Company Information Database [*Financial Times Business Information Ltd. and Predicasts*] [*Bibliographic database*] [*British*]
Fin Tid .... Finsk Tidskrift [*A publication*]
Fin Times... Financial Times [*A publication*]
Fin Trade ... Finnish Trade Review [*A publication*]
Fin and Trade R (South Africa) ... Finance and Trade Review (South Africa) [*A publication*]
FI Nucl E ... Fellow of the Institution of Nuclear Engineers [*British*]
FINUFO.... First-In/Not-Used/First-Out [*Replacement algorithm*] [*Data processing*] (BYTE)
Fin Wkly.... Financial Weekly [*A publication*]
Fin World... Financial World [*A publication*]
FINX......... Fingermatrix, Inc. [*NASDAQ symbol*] (NQ)
FIO .... Far-Infrared Observation
FIO .... Federacion Internacional de Oleicultura [*International Olive Oil Federation*] [*Rome, Italy*] (EA)
FIO .... Federation Internationale d'Oleiculture [*International Olive Growers Federation*]
FIO .... Fellow of the Institute of Ophthalmic Opticians [*British*]
FIO .... Field Intelligence Officer [*British military*] (DMA)
FIO .... Financieel Overheidsbeheer [*A publication*]
FIO .... Fleet Instruction Officer [*Navy*] [*British*]
FIO .... Fleet Intelligence Officer
FIO .... Florida Institute of Oceanography
FIO .... For Information Only (AAG)
FIO .... Foreign Intelligence Office
FIO .... Fraction Inspired Oxygen [*Physiology*]
FIO .... Free In and Out [*Shipping*]
FIO .... Furnished and Installed by Others (MCD)
FIO .... Paducah, KY [*Location identifier*] [*FAA*] (FAAL)
FIO$_2$ .... Forced Inspiratory Oxygen [*Physiology*]
FIOB......... Fellow of the Institute of Builders [*British*]
FIOC......... Fellow of the Institute of Carpenters [*British*] (DBQ)
FIOC......... Final Initial Operational Capability [*Aerospace*] (AAG)
FIOCC...... Federation Internationale des Ouvriers de la Chaussure et du Cuir [*International Shoe and Leather Worker's Federation*]
FIOCES..... Federation Internationale des Organisations de Correspondances et d'Echanges Scolaires [*International Federation of Organizations for School Correspondence and Exchange*] [*Paris, France*] (EA)
FIODS ...... Federation Internationale des Organisations de Donneurs de Sang Benevoles [*International Federation of Blood Donor Organizations - IFBDO*] [*Dole, France*] (EAIO)
FIOE......... Fraternite Internationale des Ouvriers en Electricite [*International Brotherhood of Electrical Workers - IBEW*] [*Canada*]
FIOM .... Federation Internationale des Organisations de Travailleurs de la Metallurgie [*International Metalworkers Federation - IMF*] [*Geneva, Switzerland*] (EAIO)
FIOM .... Federation Internationale des Ouvriers sur Metaux [*International Metalworkers' Federation*]
FIOP......... Fellow of the Institute of Plumbing [*British*] (DBQ)
FIOP......... Fellow of the Institute of Printing [*British*] (DBQ)
FIOP......... FORTRAN [*Formula Translating System*] Input-Output Package [*Data processing*] (IEEE)
FIOPM...... Federation Internationale des Organismes de Psychologie Medicale [*International Federation of the Psychological-Medical Organizations - IFPMO*] (EAIO)
FIORH ...... Federation Internationale pour l'Organisation de Rencontres de Handicapes [*International Federation for the Organization of Meetings for the Handicapped*]

FIOS .... Free In and Out and Stowed [*Shipping*]
FIOSH....... Fellow of the Institution of Occupational Safety and Health [*British*] (DCTA)
FIOSS........ Federation Internationale des Organisations de Sciences Sociales [*International Federation of Social Science Organizations - IFSSO*] (EAIO)
FIOST .... Federation Internationale des Organisations Syndicales du Personnel des Transporte [*International Federation of Trade Unions of Transport Workers - IFTUTW*] (EAIO)
FIOT.......... Fellow of the Institute of Operating Theatre Technicians [*British*]
FIOT.......... Free In and Out and Trimmed [*Shipping*]
FIOT.......... Free In and Out of Trucks [*Business term*]
FIOU .... Film Input/Output Unit
FiOU.......... Oulun Yliopisto [*Oulu University*], Oulu, Finland [*Library symbol*] [*Library of Congress*] (LCLS)
FIP .... Fact Issue Paper
FIP .... Fairly Important Person
FIP .... Family Involvement Process [*Used to encourage parental support in the education of handicapped children*]
FIP .... Far-Infrared Pointer
FIP .... Fastener Installation Procedure [*Manual*] (MCD)
FIP .... Fault Isolation Procedure
FIP .... Federacion Internacional de Periodistas [*International Federation of Journalists*]
FIP .... Federal Identity Program [*Canada*]
FIP .... Federation Internationale Pharmaceutique [*International Pharmaceutical Federation*] [*The Hague, Netherlands*] (EAIO)
FIP .... Federation Internationale de Philatelie [*International Federation of Philately*] (EAIO)
FIP .... Federation Internationale des Phonotheques [*International Federation of Record Libraries*]
FIP .... Federation Internationale des Pietons [*International Federation of Pedestrians*] [*Netherlands*]
FIP .... Federation Internationale de Podologie [*International Federation of Podology*]
FIP .... Federation Internationale de la Precontrainte [*International Federation of Prestressed Concrete*] (EAIO)
FIP .... Federazione Italiana della Pubblicita [*Italian Federation of Advertisers*] [*Italy*] (EY)
FIP .... Feline Infectious Peritonitis
FIP .... Fellow of the Institute of Physics [*British*]
FIP .... Fellowship in Prayer (EA)
FIP .... Field Inspection Procedure (NRCH)
FIP .... Finance Image Processor [*Data processing*] (IBMDP)
FIP .... Fleet Improvement Program [*Navy*]
FIP .... Fleet Indoctrination Program [*Navy*] (MCD)
FIP .... Fleet Information Program [*Navy*]
FIP .... Fleet Introduction Program [*Navy*]
FI/P .... Flight Inspection (Permanent) (FAAC)
FIP .... Flight Instruction Program [*Air Force*] (AFM)
FIP .... Foamed-in-Place [*Plastics technology*]
FIP .... Force Improvement Plan (MCD)
FIP .... Forestry Incentive Program [*US Forest Service*]
FIP .... Free Instrument Package
FIP .... Frente de Izquierda Popular [*Popular Left Front*] [*Argentina*] [*Political party*] (PPW)
FIP .... Fuel Injection Pressure (KSC)
FIP .... Fuel Injection Pump (MSA)
FIP .... Future Impact Point (MCD)
FIPA .... Federation of International Poetry Associations (EA)
FIPA .... Federation Internationale des Producteurs Agricoles [*International Federation of Agricultural Producers*]
FIPA .... Fellow of the Institute of Patent Attorneys [*Australia*]
FIPA .... Fellow of the Institute of Practitioners in Advertising [*British*]
FIPA .... Fellow of the Institute of Public Administration [*British*]
FIPACE..... Federation Internationale des Producteurs Auto-Consommateurs Industriels d'Electricite [*International Federation of Industrial Producers of Electricity for Own Consumption*]
FIPAD .... Fondation Internationale pour un Autre Developpement [*International Foundation for Development Alternatives - IFDA*] [*Nyon, Switzerland*] (EAIO)
FIPAGO .... Federation Internationale des Fabricants de Papiers Gommes [*International Federation of Manufacturers of Gummed Paper*] (EAIO)
FIPAH....... Federation des Importateurs et Producteurs d'Adjuvants et Additifs pour Coulis Mortier et Beton de Ciment [*Association of Importers and Producers of Admixtures*] (EAIO)
FIPA Nouv ... FIPA [*Federation Internationale des Producteurs Agricoles*] Nouvelles [*A publication*]
FIPC .... Federation Internationale des Pharmaciens Catholiques [*International Federation of Catholic Pharmacists*] [*Eupen, Belgium*] (EAIO)
FIPC .... Fellow of the Institute of Production Control [*British*] (DBQ)
FIPD .... Fellow of the Institute of Professional Designers
FIPE .... Fund for the Improvement of Postsecondary Education [*Department of Education*] (EGAO)

FIPEDX.....	FAO [*Food and Agriculture Organization of the United Nations*] Informes de Pesca [*A publication*]
FIPESO.....	Federation Internationale des Professeurs de l'Enseignement Secondaire Officiel [*International Federation of Secondary Teachers*] (EAIO)
FIPET........	Federacion Interamericana de Periodistas y Escritores de Turismo [*Interamerican Federation of Journalists and Writers in the Tourist Trade*]
FIPF..........	Federation Internationale des Professeurs de Francais [*International Federation of Teachers of French - IFTF*] (EAIO)
FIPFP........	Federation Internationale des Petits Freres des Pauvres [*International Federation of the Little Brothers of the Poor - IFLBP*] (EAIO)
FIPHE.......	Fellow of the Institution of Public Health Engineers [*British*]
FIPI	Fellow of the Institute of Professional Investigators [*British*] (DBQ)
FIPJF	Federation Internationale des Producteurs de Jus de Fruits [*International Federation of Fruit Juice Producers - IFFJP*]
FIPJP	Federation Internationale de Petanque et Jeu Provencal [*Marseille, France*] (EAIO)
FIPlantE....	Fellow of the Institution of Plant Engineers [*British*] (DBQ)
FIPLF........	Federation Internationale de la Presse de Langue Francaise [*EA*)
FIPLV........	Federation Internationale des Professeurs de Langues Vivantes [*International Federation of Modern Language Teachers*] [*Zurich, Switzerland*]
FIPM	Federation Internationale de la Philatelie Maritime [*International Federation of Maritime Philately - IFMP*] (EA)
FIPM	Federation Internationale de Psychotherapie Medicale [*International Federation for Medical Psychotherapy*]
FIPM	Fellow of the Institute of Personnel Management [*Later, CIPM*] [*British*]
FIPMEC....	Federation Internationale des Petites et Moyennes Entreprises Commerciales [*International Federation of Small and Medium-Sized Commercial Enterprises*]
FIPOL	Fonds International d'Indemnisation pour les Dommages dus a la Pollution par les Hydrocarbures [*International Oil Pollution Compensation Fund*] (EAIO)
FIPP	Far-Infrared Pointer Package
FIPP	Federation Internationale de la Presse Periodique [*International Federation of the Periodical Press*] (EAIO)
FIPP	Federation Internationale pour la Protection des Populations
FIPP	Fondation Internationale Penale et Penitentiaire [*International Penal and Penitentiary Foundation - IPPF*] [*Bonn, Federal Republic of Germany*] (EAIO)
FIPR	Fellow of the Institute of Public Relations [*British*]
FIPR	Foreign Intelligence Production Requirement [*Army*] (RDA)
FIPR	Foundation for International Potash Research [*Later, PI*] (EA)
FIPRA	Federation Internationale de la Presse Agricole
FIPRD	Fiber Producer [*A publication*]
FIPRECAN ...	Fire Prevention Canada Association
FIPREGA ...	Federation Internationale de la Presse Gastronomique et Vinicole [*International Federation of Gastronomical and Vinicultural Press*]
FIPRESCI ...	Federation Internationale de la Presse Cinematographique [*International Federation of the Cinematographic Press - IFCP*] (EAIO)
FIProdE....	Fellow of the Institution of Production Engineers [*British*]
FIPS..........	Federal Information Processing Standards [*National Institute of Standards and Technology*] [*Gaithersburg, MD*]
FIPS..........	Fellow of the Incorporated Phonographic Society [*British*] (ROG)
FIPS..........	First Independent Political Success [*Political campaigning*]
FIPS..........	Flight Inspection Positioning System
FIPS..........	Foreign Interest Payment Security [*Investment term*]
FIPSA........	Fellow of the Institute of Private Secretaries (Australia) (ADA)
FIPSCAC ..	Federal Information Processing Standards Coordinating and Advisory Committee [*National Institute of Standards and Technology*]
FIPSE........	Fund for the Improvement of Postsecondary Education [*Department of Education*]
FIPSG........	Falkland Islands Philatelic Study Group [*of the American Philatelic Society*] [*Fordingbridge, Hampshire, England*] (EAIO)
FIPS-PUB ...	Federal Information Processing Standards Publication [*National Institute of Standards and Technology*]
FIPSR........	Federal Information Processing Standards Register [*National Institute of Standards and Technology*]
FIPTP........	Federation Internationale de la Presse Technique et Periodique [*International Federation of the Technical and Periodical Press*] (DIT)
FIPUB	Flight Information Publication [*Air Force*] (NVT)
FIPV	Federacion Internacional de Pelota Vasca [*International Federation of Pelota Vasca - IFPV*] (EA)
FIPV	Feline Infectious Peritonitis Virus
FIQ	Federation Internationale des Quillieurs [*International Federation of Bowlers*]
FIQ	Fellow of the Institute of Quarrying [*British*] (DBQ)
FIQ	Morganton, NC [*Location identifier*] [*FAA*] (FAAL)
FIQA.........	Fellow of the Institute of Quality Assurance [*British*] (DBQ)
FIR...........	Facility Installation Review
FIR...........	Facility Interference Review
FIR...........	Far Infrared
FIR...........	Far-Infrared Radiometer
FIR...........	Fault Isolation Routine
FIR...........	Federation Internationale des Resistants [*International Federation of Resistance Movements*]
FIR...........	Fellow of the Institute of Population Registration [*British*] (DBQ)
FIR...........	Field Information Release (MCD)
FIR...........	Field Intensity Receiver
FIR...........	File Indirect Register
FIR...........	Films in Review [*A publication*]
FiR...........	Filologia Romanza [*A publication*]
FIR...........	Final Inspection Report (MCD)
FIR...........	Financial Inter-Relations Ratio
FIR...........	Financial Inventory Report
FIR...........	Finite Impulse Response [*Filter*] (MCD)
FIR...........	Finnish Reactor
FIR...........	Fired (MSA)
FIR...........	Firenze Ximeniano [*Florence*] [*Italy*] [*Seismograph station code, US Geological Survey*] (SEIS)
FIR...........	Firestone Tire & Rubber Co. [*NYSE symbol*] (SPSG)
FIR...........	Firkin
FIR...........	First City Trustco, Inc. [*Vancouver Stock Exchange symbol*]
FIR...........	Flight Information Region [*FAA*]
FIR...........	Flight Information Report
FIR...........	Flight Information Requirement (NVT)
FIR...........	Flight Inspection Report (NG)
FIR...........	Floating-In Rates
FIR...........	Food Irradiation Reactor
FIR...........	Forschungsinstitut fuer Rationalisierung [*Research Institute for Operations Management*] [*Research center*] [*Federal Republic of Germany*] (IRC)
FIR...........	Frente de Izquierda Revolucionaria [*Peru*]
FIR...........	Freshwater Institute Report [*United Nations*]
FIR...........	Fuel Indicator Reading
FIR...........	Full Indicator Reading
FIR...........	Functional Input Report (MCD)
FIR...........	Functional Item Replacement [*Program*] [*Navy*] (NG)
FIR...........	Future Issue Requirement
FIRA.........	Falciparum Interspersed Repeat Antigen [*Genetics*]
FIRA.........	Federation Internationale de Football-Rugby Amateur [*International Amateur Rugby Foundation*] (EA)
FIRA.........	Fontes Iuris Romani ante Iustiniani [*A publication*] (OCD)
FIRA.........	Foreign Investment Review Act [*1973*] [*Canada*] (IMH)
FIRA.........	Foreign Investment Review Agency [*Canada*]
FIRA.........	Freedom of Information Reform Act of 1986
FIRA....:....	Furniture Industry Research Association [*United Kingdom*] [*Research center*] (IRC)
FIRAA	Fire Insurance Research and Actuarial Association [*Later, ISO*] (EA)
FIRA Bull ..	FIRA [*Furniture Industry Research Association*] Bulletin [*A publication*]
FIRA Bull (Furn Ind Res Ass) ...	FIRA (Furniture Industry Research Association) Bulletin [*A publication*]
FIRAD.......	Fiziologiya Rastenii [*Moscow*] [*A publication*]
FIRA(Ind) ...	Fellow of the Institute of Railway Auditors and Accountants (India)
FIRAS........	Far-Infrared Absolute Spectrophotometer
FIRA Tech Rep (Furn Ind Res Ass) ...	FIRA (Furniture Industry Research Association) Technical Report [*A publication*]
FIRA Trans (Furn Ind Res Ass) ...	FIRA (Furniture Industry Research Association) Transaction [*A publication*]
FIRAV	Arrival Report Will Be Filed With _____ [*Aviation*] (FAAC)
FIRAV	First Available [*Military*]
FIRB	Flight Information Region Boundary (FAAC)
FIRB	Foreign Investment Review Board [*Australia*]
FIRC	Forest Industries Radio Communications [*Later, FIT*] (EA)
FIR/CPL ...	Flight Incident Recorder/Crash Position Locator [*Navy*] (RDA)
FIRD	Far-Infrared Detector
FIRD	Fault Isolation Requirement Document (MCD)
FIRE	Fellow of the Institution of Radio Engineers [*British*]
FIRE	Finance, Insurance, and Real Estate [*Insurance*]
FIRE	Fingerprint Reader
FIRE	First International Radiation Experiment [*Climatology*]
FIRE	First ISCCP [*International Satellite Cloud Climatology Project*] Regional Experiment [*National Oceanic and Atmospheric Administration*]
FIRE	Flight Investigation of the Reentry Environment
FIRE	Flight in a Radiation Environment
FIRE	Foundation for Insurance Reform and Education
FIRE	Fully Integrated Robotized Engine [*FIAT*]
FIRE (Aust) ...	Fellow of the Institution of Radio Engineers (Australia) [*Later, FIREE (Aust)*]
FIREC	Federation Internationale des Redacteurs en Chef
Fire & Cas Cas ...	Fire and Casualty Cases [*A publication*] (DLA)
Fire & Casualty Cas CCH ...	Fire and Casualty Cases. Commerce Clearing House [*A publication*]

FIREE (Aust) ... Fellow of the Institution of Radio and Electronics Engineers (Australia) [*Formerly, FIRE (Aust)*]
Fire Eng ..... Fire Engineering [*A publication*]
Fire Eng J .. Fire Engineers Journal [*A publication*]
Fire Engnrs J ... Fire Engineers Journal [*A publication*]
Fire J .... Fire Journal [*A publication*]
Fire J (Boston) ... Fire Journal (Boston) [*A publication*]
Fire Manage Notes USDA For Serv ... Fire Management Notes. United States Department of Agriculture. Forest Service [*A publication*]
Fire Mater ... Fire and Materials [*A publication*]
FIRE PLAN ... Fleet Improved Readiness by Expediting Procurement, Logistics, and Negotiations [*Navy*] (NG)
Fire Prev .... Fire Prevention [*England*] [*A publication*]
Fire Prev Sci Tech ... Fire Prevention Science and Technology [*A publication*]
Fire Prev Sci Technol ... Fire Prevention Science and Technology [*A publication*]
Fire Prot ..... Fire Protection [*A publication*]
Fire Protect ... Fire Protection [*A publication*]
Fire Prot Yearb ... Fire Protection Yearbook [*A publication*]
Fire Res Abstr & Rev ... Fire Research Abstracts and Reviews [*A publication*]
Fire Res (Lausanne) ... Fire Research (Lausanne) [*A publication*]
Fire Saf J ... Fire Safety Journal [*Switzerland*] [*A publication*]
Fire Sci Abs ... Fire Science Abstracts [*A publication*]
Fire Surv .... Fire Surveyor [*A publication*]
Fire Tech .... Fire Technology [*A publication*]
Fire Technol ... Fire Technology [*A publication*]
FIRETRAC ... Firing Error Trajectory Recorder and Computer
Fire Water Eng ... Fire and Water Engineering [*A publication*]
FIREX ...... Fire Extinguisher [*or Extinguishing*] System (AAG)
FIREX ...... Firing Exercise (NVT)
FIRF .... First Financial Savings Association [*NASDAQ symbol*] (NQ)
FIRFLT ..... First Fleet [*Pacific*] [*Navy*]
FIRG .... Firing (FAAC)
FIRI .... Fellow of the Institution of the Rubber Industry [*British*]
FIRIRCA ... Financial Institutions Regulatory and Interest Rate Control Act of 1978
FIRIV .... Arrival Report Will Be Filed With _____ [*Aviation*] (FAAC)
FIRL .... Fleet Issue Requirements List [*Navy*]
FIRL .... Franklin Institute Research Laboratories
FIRL/SG .... Fleet Issue Requirements List/Shopping Guide [*Navy*] (MCD)
FIRM .... Federation Internationale des Reconstructeurs de Moteurs [*International Federation of Engine Reconditioners - IFER*] (EAIO)
FIRM .... Financial Information for Resources Management (AFM)
FIRM .... Financial Institutions Resource Management [*Online database*]
FIRM .... Fleet Induction Replacement Model [*Navy*]
FIRM .... Flood Insurance Rate Map
FIRMA ...... Firepower and Maneuver [*Army*] (AABC)
FIRMCO ... Federal Information Requirements Management Council
FIRMR ...... Federal Information Resources Management Regulation Interagency Advisory Council [*Information Resources Management Service*] [*General Services Administration*] (EGAO)
FIRMS ...... Forecasting Information Retrieval of Management System (IEEE)
FIRMS ...... Foreign Intelligence Relations Management System (MCD)
FIRMS ...... Fourier Ion Resonance Mass Spectrometer
FIRO .... Far-Infrared Observation
FIRO .... First Ohio Bancshares, Inc. [*NASDAQ symbol*] (NQ)
FIRO .... Fundamental Interpersonal Relations Orientation [*Psychology*]
FIRO-B ...... Fundamental Interpersonal Relations Orientation - Behavior
FIRO-BC ... Fundamental Interpersonal Relations Orientation - Behavior Characteristics [*Personality development test*] [*Psychology*]
FIRO-F ...... Fundamental Interpersonal Relations Orientation - Feelings [*Personality development test*] [*Psychology*]
FIRP .... Far-Infrared Pointer
FIRP .... Functional Item Replacement Program [*Navy*]
FIRPP .... Far-Infrared Pointer Package
FIRPTA ..... Foreign Investment in Real Property Tax Act of 1980
FIRRE .... Financial Institutions Reform, Recovery, and Enforcement Act [*1989*] [*Also, FIRREA*] [*Pronounced "Fire"*]
FIRREA ..... Financial Institutions Reform, Recovery, and Enforcement Act [*1989*] [*Pronounced "fi-ree-a"*]
FIRS .... Far-Infrared Spectrometer
FIRS .... Federation Internationale de Roller-Skating [*International Roller Skating Federation*] (EAIO)
FIRS .... Field Incident Radio System [*Nuclear energy*] (NRCH)
FIRS .... File Interrogation and Reporting System [*Data processing*]
FIRS .... Forest Inventory and Regeneration System
FIRSE .... Fellow of the Institute of Railway Signal Engineers [*British*] (DBQ)
FIRSE .... Field Reference Scene Equipment (MCD)
FIRST .... Fabrication of Inflatable Reentry Structures for Test [*Air Force*]
FIRST .... Far-Infrared Search and Track
FIRST .... Fast Information Retrieval for Surface Transportation [*IBM Corp.*]
FIRST .... Fast Interactive Retrieval System Technology
FIRST .... Feeding Interaction Report, Scale, and Treatment [*Occupational therapy*]
FIRST .... Financial Information Reporting System [*Data processing*]

FIRST .... FIRST - Foundation for Ichthyosis and Related Skin Types (EA)
FIRST .... First Independent Research Support and Transition Award [*National Institutes of Health*]
FIRST .... Fleet Input and Reserve Support Training
FIRST .... Fourier Infrared Software Tools
FIRST .... Funding for Innovation Research and State Technology [*Australia*]
FIRST .... Futures Information Retrieval System [*Congressional Research Service*]
FIRSTA ..... Fund for the Improvement and Reform of Schools and Teaching Act [*1988*]
FIRSTASKFLT ... First Task Fleet
First Bk Judg ... First Book of Judgments [*1655*] [*England*] [*A publication*] (DLA)
First Book Judg ... First Book of Judgments [*1655*] [*England*] [*A publication*] (DLA)
First Chi ..... First Chicago Report [*A publication*]
First Internat Econ Hist ... First International Conference of Economic History [*A publication*]
First Nat City Bank ... First National City Bank [*Later, Citibank*] of New York. Monthly Economic Letter [*A publication*]
First Pt Edw III ... Part II of the Year Books [*A publication*] (DLA)
First Pt H VI ... Part VII of the Year Books [*A publication*] (DLA)
FIRSTS ..... Floating-Interest-Rate Short-Term Securities [*Shearson Lehman Brothers, Inc.*]
FIRT .... Federation Internationale pour la Recherche Theatrale [*International Federation for Theatre Research - IFTR*] (EAIO)
FIRT .... Fertilizer Industry Round Table (EA)
FIRTA .... Far-Infrared Technical Area [*Night Vision Laboratories*] [*Army*] (RDA)
FIRTA ...... Fishing Industry Research Trust Account [*Australia*]
FIRTE .... Fellow of the Institute of Road Transport Engineers [*British*]
FIRTS .... Following Individual Reported This Station [*Army*] (AABC)
FIS .... Facilities Inventory Study
FIS .... Facility Interface Sheet
FIS .... Fairy Investigation Society [*Inactive*] (EA)
FIS .... Family Income Supplement [*Great Britain*] [*Australia*]
FIS .... Far-Infrared Search
FIS .... Far-Infrared Spectrometer
FIS .... Farm Income Situation
FIS .... Fault Isolation Software (CAAL)
FIS .... Federation Internationale des Centres Sociaux et Communautaires [*International Federation of Settlements and Neighborhood Centers*]
FIS .... Federation Internationale du Commerce des Semences [*International Federation of the Seed Trade*]
FIS .... Federation Internationale de Sauvetage Aquatique [*Essen, Federal Republic of Germany*]
FIS .... Federation Internationale de Ski [*International Ski Federation*] [*Gumlingen, Switzerland*] (EA)
FIS .... Federazione Informazione Spettacolo [*Tourism industry*] [*Italy*] (EY)
FIS .... Fellow of the Institute of Statisticians [*British*]
FIS .... Fellow of the Institution of Surveyors [*British*]
FIS .... Fellowship of Independent Schools [*British*]
FIS .... Field Information System [*Data processing*]
FIS .... Field Infrared Spectrometer
FIS .... Field Installation Simulator
FIS .... Field Instruction System
FIS .... Fighter Identification System
FIS .... Fighter-Interceptor Squadron [*Air Force*]
FIS .... Financial Information System
FIS .... Financial Inventory Subsidiary
FIS .... Finite Intermediate Storage [*Industrial engineering*]
FIS .... Fire Island [*Alaska*] [*Seismograph station code, US Geological Survey*] [*Closed*] (SEIS)
FIS .... Fiscal
FIS .... Fiscal Information System
FIS .... Fischbach Corp. [*NYSE symbol*] (SPSG)
FIS .... Fleet Indoctrination Site [*Navy*]
FIS .... Fleet Information Service [*Navy*]
FIS .... Flexible Inspection System
FIS .... Flight Information Service (AFM)
FIS .... Floating-Point Instruction Set [*Data processing*] (MSA)
FIS .... Fluoroimmunosensor [*Analytical chemistry*]
FIS .... Flying Instrument School [*British military*] (DMA)
FIS .... Foam in System
FIS .... Fondation Internationale pour la Science [*International Foundation for Science - IFS*] (EAIO)
FIS .... Force Information Service [*Military*] (NVT)
FIS .... Foreign Instrumentation Signals (MCD)
FIS .... Foundations of Information Science [*American Society for Information Science*]
FIS .... Four-Impinging-Stream Reactor [*Chemical engineering*]
FIS .... Fourier Interferometric Stimulation [*Instrumentation*]
FIS .... Free in Store [*Business term*]
FIS .... Freedom Information Service (EA)
FIS .... Freight, Insurance, and Shipping Charges [*Business term*]
FIS .... Front Islamique de Salut [*Algeria*] [*Political party*]

FIS .... Functional Interface Specification [*Telecommunications*] (TEL)

FIS .... Key West, FL [*Location identifier*] [*FAA*] (FAAL)

Fis .... Physicist

FISA .... Federation Internationale des Semaines d'Art

FISA .... Federation Internationale des Societes Aerophilateliques [*International Federation of Aero-Philatelic Societies*] [*Zurich Airport, Switzerland*] (EAIO)

FISA .... Federation Internationale des Societes d'Aviron [*International Rowing Federation*] [*Neuchatel, Switzerland*] (EAIO)

FISA .... Federation Internationale du Sport Automobile [*Paris, France*] (EAIO)

FISA .... Fellow of the Incorporated Secretaries' Association [*British*]

FISA .... Financial Information Services Agency

FISA .... Financial Institutions Supervisory Act of 1966

FISA .... Fondation Internationale pour le Saumon de l'Atlantique [*International Atlantic Salmon Foundation*] [*Canada*]

FISA .... Food Industries Suppliers Association (EA)

FISA .... Foreign Intelligence Surveillance Act of 1978

FISAA .... Fellow of the Incorporated Society of Accountants and Auditors [*British*] (DAS)

FISAC .... Fellow of the Incorporated Society of Advertisement Consultants [*British*] (DAS)

FISAE .... Federation Internationale des Societes d'Amateurs d'Exlibris [*London, England*] (EAIO)

FISAIC .... Federation Internationale des Societes Artistiques et Intellectuelles de Cheminots [*International Federation of Railwaymen's Art and Intellectual Societies*]

FISAR .... Federal Institute for Snow and Avalanche Research

FISB .... Federal Internal Security Board [*Formerly, Subversive Activities Control Board*]

FISB .... Federation Internationale de Skibob [*Duisburg, Federal Republic of Germany*] (EAIO)

FISB .... First Indiana Corp. [*NASDAQ symbol*] (NQ)

FISC .... Fiscal (MUGU)

FISC .... Fisheries of Canada [*A publication*]

FISC .... Flight Instrument Signal Converter (MCD)

FISC .... Foundation for International Scientific Co-Ordination [*Paris, France*] (EAIO)

FISC .... Fuel Inspection and Sampling Cell [*Nuclear energy*] (NRCH)

FISCA .... Flexible Integrated Solar Cell Assembly

Fiscalite Eur ... Fiscalite Europeenne [*A publication*]

FISCETCV ... Federation Internationale des Syndicats Chretiens d'Employes, Techniciens, Cadres, et Voyageurs de Commerce [*International Federation of Christian Trade Unions of Salaried Employees, Technicians, Managers, and Commercial Travellers*]

Fisc Europ ... Fiscalite Europeenne [*A publication*]

Fischereiforsch Inf Prax ... Fischereiforschung. Informationen fuer der Praxis [*A publication*]

Fischer Taschenb ... Fischer Taschenbuecher [*A publication*]

Fisch-Forsch ... Fischerei-Forschung [*A publication*]

Fischwaren Feinkost Ind ... Fischwaren und Feinkost Industrie [*A publication*]

Fischwirtsch Fischind Fischereiwelt ... Fischwirtschaft mit die Fischindustrie und Fischereiwelt [*A publication*]

FISCM ...... Federation Internationale des Syndicats Chretiens de la Metalurgie [*International Federation of Christian Metalworkers Unions*]

FISCOA .... Federation Internationale des Syndicats Chretiens d'Ouvriers Agricoles [*International Federation of Christian Agricultural Workers Unions*]

FISCOBB .. Federation Internationale des Syndicats Chretiens d'Ouvriers du Batiment et du Bois [*International Federation of Christian Trade Unions of Building and Wood Workers*]

FIS-COV ... Fire Survivability for Ground Combat Vehicles (MCD)

FISCTTH ... Federation Internationale des Syndicats Chretiens des Travailleurs du Textile et de l'Habillement [*International Federation of Christian Trade Unions of Textile and Clothing Workers*]

FISD .... Federation Internationale de Stenographie et de Dactylographie [*International Federation of Shorthand and Typewriting*]

FISDO .... Flight Standards District Office [*FAA*]

FISE .... Federation Internationale Syndicale de l'Enseignement [*World Federation of Teachers' Unions*] [*Berlin, Federal Republic of Germany*] (EAIO)

FISE .... Fellow of the Institution of Sanitary Engineers [*British*]

FISE .... Fonds International de Secours a l'Enfance [*Also known as Fonds des Nations Unies pour l'Enfance*] [*Canada*]

FISEC .... Federation Internationale Sportive de l'Enseignement Catholique

FIS-ELF .... German Information System on Food, Agriculture, and Forestry [*Bonn*] [*Information service or system*] (IID)

FISEM .... Federation Internationale des Societes d'Ecrivains-Medecins

FISEMA .... Federation Internationale et Syndicale des Employes de Madagascar [*International Federation and Union of Malagasy Employees*] [*WFTU affiliate*]

FISF .... Family Interaction Summary Format

FISGV .... Federazione Internazionale della Stampa Gastronomica e Vinicola [*International Federation of Gastronomical and Vinicultural Press*]

FISH .... First-In, Still-Here [*Facetious extension of FIFO definition*] [*Accounting*]

FISH .... Fisheries

Fish .... Fisher's United States Patent Cases [*A publication*] (DLA)

Fish .... Fisher's United States Prize Cases [*A publication*] (DLA)

FISH .... Friends in Service Here

FISH .... Fully Instrumented Submersible Housing [*An oceanographic instrument*]

FISH .... North Atlantic Fisheries, Inc. [*Rochester, NY*] [*NASDAQ symbol*] (NQ)

Fish B .... Fishery Bulletin [*A publication*]

Fish Board Swed Inst Freshwater Res (Drottningholm) Rep ... Fishery Board of Sweden. Institute of Freshwater Research (Drottningholm). Report [*A publication*]

Fish Board Swed Inst Mar Res Rep ... Fishery Board of Sweden. Institute of Marine Research. Report [*A publication*]

Fish Board Swed Ser Hydrogr Rep ... Fishery Board of Sweden. Series Hydrography. Report [*A publication*]

Fish Boat Wld ... Fishing Boats of the World [*A publication*]

Fish Bull .... Fishery Bulletin [*A publication*]

Fish Bull (Dublin) ... Fisheries Bulletin (Dublin) [*A publication*]

Fish Bull FAO ... Fisheries Bulletin. Food and Agriculture Organization [*A publication*]

Fish Bull S Afr ... Fisheries Bulletin. South Africa [*A publication*]

FISHC .... Federation Internationale des Societes d'Histochimie et de Cytochimie [*International Federation of Societies for Histochemistry and Cytochemistry*] (EAIO)

Fish Cas ..... Fisher's Cases, United States District Courts [*A publication*] (DLA)

Fish CL Dig ... Fisher's Digest of English Common Law Reports [*A publication*] (DLA)

Fish Const ... Fisher on the United States Constitution [*A publication*] (DLA)

Fish Contr Vict ... Victoria. Fisheries and Wildlife Department. Fisheries Contribution [*A publication*] (APTA)

Fish Cop..... Fisher on Copyrights [*A publication*] (DLA)

Fish Crim Dig ... Fisher's Digest of English Criminal Law [*A publication*] (DLA)

FISHD .... Fisheries [*A publication*]

Fish Dig ..... Fisher's Digest of English Common Law Reports [*A publication*] (DLA)

Fisher......... Fisher on Mortgages [*A publication*] (DLA)

Fisher......... Fisher's United States Prize Cases [*A publication*] (DLA)

Fisheries .... Fisheries of the US [*A publication*]

Fisheries Nletter ... Fisheries Newsletter [*A publication*] (APTA)

Fisher & Lightwood ... Fisher and Lightwood on Mortgages [*9th ed.*] [*1977*] [*A publication*] (DLA)

Fisher Pat Cas (F) ... Fisher's United States Patent Cases [*A publication*] (DLA)

Fisher Pr Cas (F) ... Fisher's United States Prize Cases [*A publication*] (DLA)

Fisher Pr Cas (PA) ... Fisher. Pennsylvania Prize Cases [*A publication*] (DLA)

Fisher's Pat Cas ... Fisher's United States Patent Cases [*A publication*] (DLA)

Fishery Ind Res ... Fishery Industrial Research [*A publication*]

Fish Farming Int ... Fish Farming International [*A publication*]

Fish & GC ... Fish and Game Code [*A publication*] (DLA)

Fishg News Int ... Fishing News International [*A publication*]

Fish Ind Res ... Fishery Industrial Research [*A publication*]

Fish Invest Minist Agric Fish Food (GB) Ser ... Fishery Investigations. Ministry of Agriculture, Fisheries, and Food (Great Britain). Series II. Salmon and Freshwater Fisheries [*A publication*]

Fish Invest Minist Agric Fish Food (GB) Ser IV ... Fishery Investigations. Ministry of Agriculture, Fisheries, and Food (Great Britain). Series IV [*A publication*]

Fish Invest Ser II Mar Fish GB Minist Agric Fish Food ... Fishery Investigations. Series II. Marine Fisheries. Great Britain Ministry of Agriculture, Fisheries, and Food [*A publication*]

Fish & L Mort ... Fisher and Lightwood on Mortgages [*9th ed.*] [*1977*] [*A publication*] (DLA)

Fish Manage ... Fisheries Management [*A publication*]

Fish Mort... Fisher on Mortgages [*A publication*] (DLA)

Fish Mortg ... Fisher on Mortgages [*A publication*] (DLA)

Fish News .. Fisheries Newsletter [*A publication*] (APTA)

Fish News Int ... Fishing News International [*A publication*]

Fish Newsl ... Fisheries Newsletter [*A publication*]

Fish N Intnl ... Fishing News International [*A publication*]

Fish Notes ... Queensland. Department of Harbours and Marine. Fisheries Notes [*A publication*] (APTA)

Fish Notes Dep Prim Ind Qd ... Fisheries Notes. Department of Primary Industries. Queensland [*A publication*] (APTA)

Fish Notes Dep Prim Ind Queensl ... Fisheries Notes. Department of Primary Industries. Queensland [*A publication*] (APTA)

Fish Pap Dep Prim Ind ... Australia. Department of Primary Industry. Fisheries Paper [*A publication*] (APTA)

Fish Pat...... Fisher's United States Patent Cases [*A publication*] (DLA)

Fish Pat Cas ... Fisher's United States Patent Cases [*A publication*] (DLA)

Fish Pat Dig ... Fisher's Digest of Patent Law [*A publication*] (DLA)

Fish Pathol ... Fish Pathology [*A publication*]

Fish Pat R ... Fisher's United States Patent Reports [*A publication*] (DLA)

Fish Pat Rep ... Fisher's United States Patent Reports [*A publication*] (DLA)
FISHPATS ... Fisheries Patrols [*Canadian Navy*]
Fish Pr Cas ... Fisher's United States Prize Cases [*A publication*] (DLA)
Fish Prize... Fisher's United States Prize Cases [*A publication*] (DLA)
Fish Prize Cas ... Fisher's United States Prize Cases [*A publication*] (DLA)
Fish Rep Dep Agric ... Fisheries Report. Department of Agriculture [*A publication*] (APTA)
Fish Rep Dep Prim Ind ... Australia. Department of Primary Industry. Fisheries Report [*A publication*] (APTA)
Fish Res (Amst) ... Fisheries Research (Amsterdam) [*A publication*]
Fish Res Board Can Annu Rep ... Fisheries Research Board of Canada. Annual Report [*A publication*]
Fish Res Board Can ARO Circ ... Fisheries Research Board of Canada. ARO [*Atlantic Regional Office*] Circular [*A publication*]
Fish Res Board Can Bull ... Fisheries Research Board of Canada. Bulletin [*A publication*]
Fish Res Board Can Gen Ser Circ ... Fisheries Research Board of Canada. General Series Circular [*A publication*]
Fish Res Board Can Misc Spec Publ ... Fisheries Research Board of Canada. Miscellaneous Special Publication [*A publication*]
Fish Res Board Can Prog Rep Atl Coast Stn ... Fisheries Research Board of Canada. Progress Reports of the Atlantic Coast Stations [*A publication*]
Fish Res Board Can Prog Rep Pac Coast Stn ... Fisheries Research Board of Canada. Progress Reports of the Pacific Coast Station [*A publication*]
Fish Res Board Can Rev ... Fisheries Research Board of Canada. Review [*A publication*]
Fish Res Board Can Tech Pap ... Fisheries Research Board of Canada. Technical Paper [*A publication*]
Fish Res Board Can Tech Rep ... Fisheries Research Board of Canada. Technical Report [*A publication*]
Fish Res Bull ... Fisheries Research Bulletin [*A publication*] (APTA)
Fish Res Bull (West Aust Mar Res Lab) ... Fisheries Research Bulletin (Western Australia Marine Research Laboratories) [*A publication*]
Fish Res Div Occas Publ (NZ) ... Fisheries Research Division. Occasional Publication (New Zealand) [*A publication*]
Fish Res Ves Kapala Cruise Rep ... Cruise Report. Fisheries Research Vessel Kapala [*A publication*] (APTA)
FISHSTATS ... Fishery Statistics Data Base [*National Marine Fisheries Service*] [*Information service or system*] (CRD)
Fish Synopsis Div Fish Oceanogr CSIRO ... Fisheries Synopsis. Division of Fisheries and Oceanography. Commonwealth Scientific and Industrial Research Organisation [*A publication*] (APTA)
Fish Technol ... Fishery Technology [*A publication*]
Fish WA .... Fisher on the Will Act [*A publication*] (DLA)
Fish Wildl Pap (Victoria) ... Fisheries and Wildlife Paper (Victoria) [*A publication*]
Fish Wildl Serv (US) Res Rep ... Fish and Wildlife Service (United States). Research Report [*A publication*]
FISI........... Financial Institution Services [*NASDAQ symbol*] (NQ)
FISI........... Friends of India Society International (EA)
FISIER ...... Federation Internationale des Societes et Instituts pour l'Etude de la Renaissance [*International Federation of Societies and Institutes for the Study of the Renaissance*] (EA)
FISINT ...... FIS Intelligence (MCD)
Fisiol e Med ... Fisiologia e Medicina [*A publication*]
Fisiol Med (Rome) ... Fisiologia e Medicina (Rome) [*A publication*]
FISITA ...... Federation Internationale des Societes d'Ingenieurs des Techniques de l'Automobile [*International Federation of Automobile Engineers' and Technicians' Associations*]
FISK .... Fiskeridirektoratets Skrifter. Serie Havundersokelser [*A publication*]
Fisk Anal ... Fisk's Analysis of Coke on Littleton [*1824*] [*A publication*] (DLA)
Fisk Dir Skr ... Fiskeridirektoratets Skrifter [*A publication*]
Fiskeridir Skr Ser Ernaer ... Fiskeridirektoratets Skrifter. Serie Ernaering [*A publication*]
Fiskeridir Skr Ser Fisk ... Fiskeridirektoratets Skrifter. Serie Fiskeri [*A publication*]
Fiskeridir Skr Ser Havunders ... Fiskeridirektoratets Skrifter. Serie Havundersokelser [*A publication*]
Fiskeridir Skr Ser Teknol Unders ... Fiskeridirektoratets Skrifter. Serie Teknologiske Undersokelser [*A publication*]
FISL.......... Federally Insured Student Loan
FISLIB ...... FORTRAN [*Formula Translating System*] Interactive Subroutine Library [*Data processing*]
FISLP .... Federal Insured Student Loan Program
FISM .... Federation Internationale des Societes Magiques [*International Federation of Magical Societies - IFSM*] [*Paris, France*] (EAIO)
FISM .... Fellow of the Institute of Supervisory Management [*British*] (DBQ)
FISM .... International Federation of Sports Medicine (EA)
FISMA ...... Federazione Italiana Strumenti Musicali ed Accessori [*Italian Federation of Manufacturers of Musical Instruments and Parts*] (EY)

FISMARC ... Federation Internationale du Sport Medical pour l'Aide a la Recherche Cancerologique [*International Medical Sports Federation for Aid to Cancer Research*] [*Beziers, France*] (EAIO)
Fis Med...... Fisiologia e Medicina [*A publication*]
FISN .... Fisons PLC [*NASDAQ symbol*] (NQ)
FISO .... Force Integration Staff Officer [*Army*] (RDA)
FISP........... Family Income Security Plan
FISP........... Federation Internationale des Societes de Philosophie [*International Federation of Philosophical Societies - IFPS*] (EAIO)
FISq .... Fighter-Interceptor Squadron [*Air Force*] (AFM)
FISR .... Financial Interest and Syndication Rules [*FCC*]
FI & SS ...... Foreign Intelligence and Security Service (MCD)
FISSG .... Fleet Issue Ship Shopping Guide [*Navy*] (NVT)
FISSO........ Foreign Intelligence Special Security Office (MCD)
FIST........... Fault Isolation by Semiautomatic Techniques [*National Institute of Standards and Technology*]
FIST........... Federal Investigative Strike Team
FIST........... Federation of Interstate Truckers [*Acronym is title of film*]
FIST........... Fellow of the Institute of Science Technology [*British*]
FIST........... Field Artillery Fire Support Team [*Army*] (RDA)
FIST........... Field Intelligence Simulation Test (NATG)
FIST........... Fire Integration Support Team
FIST........... First-In, Still-There [*Facetious extension of FIFO definition*] [*Accounting*]
FIST........... First Stop Professional Services, Inc. [*Milwaukee, WI*] [*NASDAQ symbol*] (NQ)
FIST........... Fistula
FIST........... Flagship International Sports Television [*Phony TV station used as bait to capture fugitives*] [*Canada*]
FIST........... Fugitive Investigative Strike Team [*Operation conducted jointly by the US Marshals Service and local police*]
FIST........... Full Integral Simulation Test [*Nuclear energy*] (NRCH)
FIST........... Functional Integrated Systems Trainer (MCD)
FISTA........ Federation Internationale des Syndicats des Travailleurs Audiovisuel [*International Federation of Audio-Visual Workers Unions - IFAVWU*] (EAIO)
FIST ARM ... Fistula Armata [*Clyster-Pipe and Bladder Fitted for Use*] [*Pharmacy*] (ROG)
FISTB........ Field and Stream [*A publication*]
FISTC........ Fellow of the Institute of Scientific and Technical Communicators [*British*] (DBQ)
FISTC........ Fellow of the International Institute of Sports Therapy [*British*] (DBQ)
FISTD........ Fellow of the Imperial Society of Teachers of Dancing [*British*] (DBQ)
Fis e Tecnol ... Fisica e Tecnologia [*A publication*]
FISTM........ Fellow of the Institute of Sales Technology and Management [*British*] (DBQ)
FIStructE.... Fellow of the Institution of Structural Engineers [*British*]
FISTV........ Fire Support Team Vehicle [*Army*] (RDA)
FISU .... Federation Internationale du Sport Universitaire [*International University Sports Federation*] [*Brussels, Belgium*] (EAIO)
FISV .... FIserv, Inc. [*West Allis, WI*] [*NASDAQ symbol*] (NQ)
FISW .... Fellow of the Institute of Social Welfare [*British*] (DBQ)
FISYS........ Fairplay Information Systems Ltd. (IID)
FISZA........ Fizikai Szemle [*A publication*]
FIT............. Fab Industries, Inc. [*AMEX symbol*] (SPSG)
FIT............. Fabrication, Integration, and Test
FIT............. Fabrication in Transit (ADA)
FIT............. Failure in Time [*Telecommunications*] (TEL)
FIT............. Far-Infrared Track
FIT............. Fashion Institute of Technology
FIT............. Fault Isolation Test
FIT............. Federal Income Tax
FIT............. Federal Insurance Tax (DLA)
FIT............. Federation International Triathlon (EA)
FIT............. Federation Internationale des Traducteurs [*International Federation of Translators - IFT*] (EAIO)
FIT............. Federation Internationale de Trampoline [*International Trampoline Federation*] (EA)
FIT............. Federazione Italiana Trasporti [*Italian Federation of Transport*] [*Italy*] (EY)
FIT............. Fentanyl Isothiocyanate [*Biochemistry*]
FIT............. Field Installation and Test
FIT............. Fight Inflation Together [*Group opposing high food prices in 1973*]
FIT............. Fighter
FIT............. File Information Table [*Data processing*]
FIT............. File Inquiry Technique
FIT............. Finding in Transit
FIT............. First Computer Interface Tester (MCD)
FIT............. First Indication of Trouble
FIT............. Fitchburg, MA [*Location identifier*] [*FAA*] (FAAL)
FIT............. Fixed Interval Timer
FIT............. Flanagan Industrial Tests [*Aptitude and skills test*]
FIT............. Fleet Introduction Team [*Navy*] (NVT)
FI/T............ Flight Inspection (Temporary) (FAAC)
FIT............. Flight Instrument Trainer (AFM)
FIT............. Florida Institute of Technology [*Melbourne*]

FIT............	Flow Indicator Transmitter [*Nuclear energy*] (NRCH)
FIT............	Foreign Independent [*or Individual*] Travel [*Air travel term*]
FIT............	Forest Industries Telecommunications [*Eugene, OR*] (EA)
FIT............	Forward Inspection Team [*Military*]
FIT............	Foundation to Improve Television (EA)
FIT............	Fourier Integral Transform [*Physics*]
FIT............	Franchise Industry Training [*High school dropout program*] [*Department of Labor*]
FIT............	Free of Income Tax
FIT............	Free in Truck [*Business term*]
FIT............	Frequency, Intensity, and Time [*Exercise formula*] [*Army*]
FIT............	Frequent Independent Traveler
FIT............	Functional Integration Test
FIT............	Fusion at the Inferred Threshold [*Test*] [*Medicine*]
FiTA.........	Abo Akademi [*Swedish University of Abo*], Turku, Finland [*Library symbol*] [*Library of Congress*] (LCLS)
FITA.........	Fault Isolation Test Adapter (MCD)
FITA.........	Federal Interpreter and Translators Association [*Australia*]
FITA.........	Federation of International Trade Associations (EA)
FITA.........	Federation Internationale de Tir a l'Arc [*International Archery Federation*] [*Milan, Italy*] (EA)
FITA.........	Foreign Investors Tax Act of 1966
FITAC.......	Federacion Interamericana de Touring y Automovil Clubes [*Inter-American Federation of Touring and Automobile Clubs - IFTAC*] (EAIO)
FITAP.......	Federation Internationale des Transports Aeriens Prives [*International Federation of Private Air Transport*]
FITASC.....	Federation Internationale de Tir aux Arms Sportives de Chasse [*International Federation for Sport Shooting*] [*Paris, France*] (EAIO)
FITB.........	Federation Internationale des Techniciens de la Bonneterie [*International Federation of Knitting Technologists - IFKT*] (EAIO)
FITB.........	Fifth Third Bancorp [*NASDAQ symbol*] (NQ)
FITB.........	Fluorospar International Technical Bureau (EAIO)
FITBB.......	Federation Internationale des Travailleurs du Batiment et du Bois [*International Federation of Building and Woodworkers*]
FITC.........	Financial Trust Corporation [*Carlisle, PA*] [*NASDAQ symbol*] (NQ)
FITC.........	Fluorescein Isothiocyanate [*Organic chemistry*]
FITCA.......	Fire Technology [*A publication*]
FITCAL.....	Feel, Inspect, Tighten, Clean, Adjust, Lubricate [*A keyword representing operations in preventive maintenance of communications equipment*] [*Military*]
FITCE.......	Federation des Ingenieurs des Telecommunications de la Communaute Europeenne [*Federation of Telecommunications Engineers in the European Community*]
FITC-gARGG ...	Fluorescein Isothiocyanate Conjugated Goat Antiserum to Rabbit Gamma Globulin [*Immunology*]
Fitch RE Ag ...	Fitch on Real Estate Agency [*A publication*] (DLA)
FITD.........	Far-Infrared Target Detector
FITD.........	Fellow of the Institute of Training and Development [*British*] (DBQ)
FITDC.......	Footwear Industry Traffic and Distribution Council (EA)
FITE.........	Fair International Trade Employment Committee
FITE.........	Federacion Interamericana de Trabajadores del Espectaculo [*Interamerican Federation of Entertainment Workers*]
FITE.........	Forward Interworking Telephony Event [*Telecommunications*] (TEL)
FITEA.......	Fishery Technology [*India*] [*A publication*]
FITEC.......	Federation Internationale du Thermalisme et du Climatisme [*International Federation of Thermalism and Climatism*]
FITFIMS...	Federal Interagency Task Force on Inadvertent Modification of the Stratosphere
FITGO.......	Floating Input to Ground Output
FITH.........	Federation Internationale des Travailleurs de l'Habillement
FITH.........	Fire-in-the-Hole [*Burn*] [*NASA*]
FITH.........	First-in-the-Hole (MCD)
FITI.........	Far-Infrared Target Indicator
FITIM.......	Federacion Internacional de Trabajadores de las Industrias Metalurgicas [*International Metalworkers' Federation*]
FITITHC...	Federation Internationale des Travailleurs des Industries du Textile, de l'Habillement, et du Cuir [*International Textile, Garment, and Leather Workers' Federation*] [*Brussels, Belgium*]
FITITV......	Federacion Interamericana de Trabajadores de la Industria Textil, Vestuario, y Cuero [*Interamerican Textile, Garment, and Leather Workers Federation*]
FITITVCC ...	Federacion Interamericana de Trabajadores de la Industria Textil, Vestuario, Cuero, y Calzado [*Interamerican Textile, Leather, Garment, and Shoe Workers Federation - ITLGSWF*] (EA)
FiTK.........	Turun Yliopiston Kirjasto [*Turku School of Economics*], Turku, Finland [*Library symbol*] [*Library of Congress*] (LCLS)
Fitness Inst Bull ...	Fitness Institute. Bulletin [*A publication*]
FITNGSq ..	Fighter Interceptor Training Squadron [*Air Force*]
Fitopat Bras ...	Fitopatologia Brasileira [*A publication*]
Fitopatol.....	Fitopatologia [*A publication*]
Fitopatol Bras ...	Fitopatologia Brasileira [*A publication*]
Fitopatol Mex ...	Fitopatologia Mexicana [*A publication*]
Fitotec Latinoam ...	Fitotecnia Latinoamericana [*A publication*]
Fitotecnia Latinoam ...	Fitotecnia Latinoamericana [*A publication*]
FITP.........	Federation Internationale des Travailleurs du Petrole
FITP.........	Federation Internationale des Travailleurs des Plantations
FITPASC ..	Federation Internationale des Travailleurs des Plantations, de l'Agriculture, et des Secteurs Connexes [*International Federation of Plantation, Agricultural, and Allied Workers*]
FITPC.......	Federation Internationale des Travailleurs du Petrole et de la Chimie [*International Federation of Petroleum and Chemical Workers*]
FITPQ.......	Federacion Internacional de Trabajadores Petroleros y Quimicos [*International Federation of Petroleum and Chemical Workers*]
FITR.........	Foundation for International Trade Research (EA)
FITREP.....	Officer Fitness Report [*Navy*] (NVT)
FITRON....	Fighter Squadron [*Navy*] (MUGU)
FITS.........	Federation Internationale du Tourisme Social [*International Social Travel Federation - ISTF*] (EAIO)
FiTs.........	Finsk Tidskrift [*A publication*]
FITS.........	Functional Individual Training System [*Navy*] (NVT)
FITSA........	Fellow of the Institute of Trading Standards Administration [*British*] (DBQ)
F-I-T-T	Fearful, Irritable, Tense, and Tremulous [*Combat behavior disorder*] [*Military*] (INF)
FITT	Federation Internationale de Tennis de Table [*International Table Tennis Federation*]
FITT	Federation Internationale des Travailleurs de la Terre
FITT	Frequency, Intensity, Time, and Type [*Exercise formula*] [*Army*] (INF)
FITTC.......	Federation of International Trampoline Technical Committee (EA)
FITTHC	Federation Internationale des Travailleurs des Industries du Textile, de l'Habillement, et du Cuir [*International Textile, Garment, and Leather Workers' Federation - ITGLWF*] (EAIO)
FITTS........	Fittings (ADA)
FITU.........	Federation of Independent Trade Unions [*Lebanon*]
FITW.........	Federal Income Tax Withholding
FITWING ...	Fighter Wing [*Navy*] (NVT)
FITZ	Fitzgerald, DeArman & Roberts, Inc. [*NASDAQ symbol*] (NQ)
Fitz............	Fitzgibbon's King's Bench Reports [*England*] [*A publication*] (DLA)
Fitz	Fitzherbert's Abridgment [*1516*] [*A publication*] (DSA)
Fitz Abridg ...	Fitzherbert's Abridgment [*1516*] [*A publication*] (DLA)
Fitzad Jud Act ...	Fitzadams on the Judicature Act [*A publication*] (DLA)
Fitzg	Fitzgibbon's Irish Land Reports [*A publication*] (DLA)
Fitzg	Fitzgibbon's Irish Registration Appeals [*A publication*] (DLA)
Fitzg	Fitzgibbon's King's Bench Reports [*England*] [*A publication*] (DLA)
Fitzg Land R ...	Fitzgibbon's Irish Land Reports [*A publication*] (DLA)
Fitzg LG Dec ...	Fitzgibbon's Irish Local Government Decisions [*A publication*] (DLA)
Fitzg Pub H ...	Fitzgerald on the Public Health [*A publication*] (DLA)
Fitzg Reg Ca ...	Fitzgibbon's Irish Registration Appeals [*A publication*] (DLA)
Fitzh..........	Fitzherbert's Abridgment [*1516*] [*A publication*] (DLA)
Fitzh Abr....	Fitzherbert's Abridgment [*1516*] [*A publication*] (DLA)
Fitzh Nat Brev ...	Fitzherbert's Natura Brevium [*A publication*] (DLA)
Fitzh NB	Fitzherbert's Natura Brevium [*A publication*] (DLA)
Fitzh N Br ...	Fitzherbert's Natura Brevium [*A publication*] (DLA)
Fitz LG Dec ...	Fitzgibbon's Irish Local Government Decisions [*A publication*] (DLA)
FitzN.........	Fitzgerald Newsletter [*A publication*]
Fitz Nat Brev ...	Fitzherbert's Natura Brevium [*A publication*] (DLA)
FIU	Facility Interface Unit [*Telecommunications*]
FIU	Federation of Information Users [*Defunct*] (EA)
FIU	Field Intelligence Unit (MUGU)
FIU	Fighter Interception Unit [*RAF*] [*British*]
fiu	Finno-Ugrian [*MARC language code*] [*Library of Congress*] (LCCP)
FIU	Florida International University [*Miami*]
FIU	Forward Interpretation Unit [*Military*]
FIUC..........	Federation Internationale des Universites Catholiques [*International Federation of Catholic Universities - IFCU*] (EAIO)
FIU/CR	Caribbean Review. Florida International University. Office of Academic Affairs [*A publication*]
FIUN	First United, Incorporated [*NASDAQ symbol*] (NQ)
FIUO	For Internal Use Only (KSC)
FIUP..........	Foundation for Indiana University of Pennsylvania [*Research center*] (RCD)
FIUS..........	Flax Institute of the United States [*Defunct*] (EA)
FIUS..........	French Institute in the United States [*Later, FIAF*] (EA)
FIUV..........	Federation Internationale Una Voce (EA)
FIV	Federation Internationale de la Vieillesse [*International Federation on Ageing - IFA*] (EAIO)
FIV............	Feline Immunodeficiency Virus

FIV............. Fellow of the Institute of Valuers [*British*]
FIV............. Fuel Insolation Valves   (MCD)
f-iv---.......... Ivory Coast [*MARC geographic area code*] [*Library of Congress*]   (LCCP)
FIVA......... Federation Internationale des Vehicules Anciens   (EA)
FIVA......... Fluid Inject Valve Actuator
FIVB......... Federation Internationale de Volleyball [*International Volleyball Federation*] [*Switzerland*]
FIVC......... Festival International du Video-Clip [*The first festival entirely devoted to pop-music video, at San Tropez, October, 1984*]
FIVC......... First Valley Corporation [*NASDAQ symbol*]   (NQ)
FIVC......... Forced Inspiratory Vital Capacity [*Medicine*]
FIVD......... Fifth Dimension, Inc. [*NASDAQ symbol*]   (NQ)
FIVE......... Fifth Avenue Cards, Inc. [*NASDAQ symbol*]   (NQ)
FIVEATAF ... Fifth Allied Tactical Air Force, Southern Europe   (NATG)
Fi Vet Tidskr ... Finsk Veterinaertidskrift [*A publication*]
FIVGV......... Fan Inlet Variable Guide Vanes   (MCD)
FIVS.......... Federation Internationale des Vins et Spiritueux [*International Federation of Wines and Spirits - IFWS*]   (EAIO)
FIVT......... First Vermont Financial [*NASDAQ symbol*]   (NQ)
FIVU......... Federacion Internacional de Vivienda y Urbanismo [*International Federation for Housing and Planning*]
FIVV......... Federation Internationale de Vo Viet Nam [*An association*]   (EAIO)
FIVZ......... Federation Internationale Veterinaire de Zootechnie
FIW............. Fellow of the Welding Institute [*British*]
FIW............. Fiberglass-Insulated Wire
FIW............. Fighter-Interceptor Wing   (MCD)
FIW............. Forschungsinstitut fuer Wirtschaftsverfassung und Wettbewerb [*A publication*]
FIW............. Free in Wagon [*Business term*]
FIWC......... Fiji Industrial Workers' Congress
FIW Dok... FIW [*Forschungsinstitut fuer Wirtschaftsverfassung und Wettbewerb*] Dokumentation [*A publication*]
FIWE......... Fellow of the Institute of Water Engineers [*British*]
FIWHTE ... Fellow of the Institution of Works and Highways Technician Engineers [*British*]   (DBQ)
FIWI......... First Interstate Corp. of Wisconsin [*NASDAQ symbol*]   (NQ)
FIWM......... Fellow of the Institution of Works Managers [*British*]
FIWOA....... Financial World [*A publication*]
FIWSc....... Fellow of the Institute of Wood Science [*British*]
FIW Schr ... FIW [*Forschungsinstitut fuer Wirtschaftsverfassung und Wettbewerb*] Schriftenreihe [*A publication*]
FIWT......... Fellow of the Institute of Wireless Technology [*British*]   (DAS)
FIX............. Factor IX [*Hematology*]
FIX............. FID [*Federation Internationale de Documentation*] News Bulletin [*A publication*]
FIX............. Firing in Extension [*Missiles*]
FIX............. Fixture
FIXExpE ... Fellow of the Institute of Explosives Engineers [*British*]   (DBQ)
FIXIT........ Fostering, or Fighting, Innovations and Experiment in Teaching [*Game*]
FIXN......... Fixation
FIXRES..... Fixtures   (ROG)
FIXT......... Fixture
FIXWEX ... Fixed-Wing Evaluation Exercise [*Aviation*]
FIYTO........ Federation of International Youth Travel Organizations [*Copenhagen, Denmark*]   (EAIO)
FIZ............. Dritte Welt Frauensinformationszentrum [*Information Center for Third World Women*] [*Zurich, Switzerland*]   (EAIO)
FIZ............. Farhang-E Iran-Zamin [*Revue Trimestrielle des Etudes Iranologiques*] [*A publication*]
Fiz Aerodispersnykh Sist ... Fizika Aerodispersnykh Sistem [*A publication*]
Fiz Chastits Vys Energ ... Fizika Chastits Vysokikh Energii [*A publication*]
Fiz Chastits Vys Energ Akad Nauk Gruz SSR Inst Fiz ... Fizika Chastits Vysokikh Energii. Akademiya Nauk Gruzinskoi SSR. Institut Fiziki [*Georgian SSR*] [*A publication*]
FIZ Chemie ... Fachinformationszentrum Chemie GmbH [*Chemical Information Center*] [*Information service or system*]   (IID)
Fiz Chim Mech Mat ... Fiziko-Chimiceskaja Mechanika Materialov [*A publication*]
Fiz Dielektr Radiospektrosk ... Fizyka Dielektrykow i Radiospektroskopia [*A publication*]
Fiz Ehlem Chastits At Yad ... Fizika Elementarnykh Chastits i Atomnogo Yadra [*A publication*]
Fiz Elektron (Lvov) ... Fizichna Elektronika (Lvov) [*A publication*]
Fiz Elektron (Moscow) ... Fizicheskaya Elektronika (Moscow) [*A publication*]
Fiz Elem Chastits At Yadra ... Fizika Elementarnykh Chastits i Atomnogo Yadra [*A publication*]
Fiz Elementar Castic i Atom Jadra ... Fizika Elementarnyh Castic i Atomnogo Jadra [*A publication*]
Fiz Elementar Chastits i Atom Yadra ... Fizika Elementarnykh Chastits i Atomnogo Yadra. Obedinennyi Institut Yadernykh Issledovanii Dubna [*A publication*]
Fiz Energ Inst Rap FEI ... Fiziko-Energeticheskii Institut. Raport FEI [*Fiziko-Energeticheskii Institut*] [*A publication*]
Fiz Fiz-Khim Zhidk ... Fizika i Fiziko-Khimiya Zhidkostei [*A publication*]
Fiz Gazorazryadnoi Plazmy ... Fizika Gazorazryadnoi Plazmy [*A publication*]
Fiz Geogr ... Fizicheskaya Geografiya [*A publication*]

Fiz Geogr Geomorfol ... Fizichna Geografiya ta Geomorfologiya [*A publication*]
Fiz Gidrodin Kinet Zhidk ... Fizicheskaya Gidrodinamika i Kinetika Zhidkosti [*A publication*]
Fiz Goreniya Metody Ed Issled ... Fizika Goreniya i Metody. Ed. Issledovaniya [*USSR*] [*A publication*]
Fiz Goreniya & Vzryva ... Fizika Goreniya i Vzryva [*A publication*]
Fiz Gorn Porod Protsessov ... Fizika Gornykh Porod i Protsessov [*A publication*]
Fiz Gor Vzryva ... Fizika Goreniya i Vzryva [*A publication*]
FIZHD....... Fiziologicheskii Zhurnal [*Kiev*] [*A publication*]
Fiz Heohr Heomorfol Mizhvid Nauk Zb ... Fizycheskaya Heohrafiya ta Heomorfolohiya Mizhvidomchyi Naukovyi Zbirnykh [*A publication*]
Fizic Kult ... Fiziceskaja Kul'tura v Skole [*A publication*]
Fizic Z........ Fiziceskij Zurnal [*A publication*]
Fizika (Zagreb) Suppl ... Fizika (Zagreb). Supplement [*Yugoslavia*] [*A publication*]
Fiz Inst Rak ... Fizikas Instituta Raksti [*A publication*]
Fiziol Aktiv Veshchestva ... Fiziologicheski Aktivnye Veshchestva [*Ukrainian SSR*] [*A publication*]
Fiziol Akt Veshchestva ... Fiziologicheski Aktivnye Veshchestva [*A publication*]
Fiziol Biokhim Kul't Rast ... Fiziologiya i Biokhimiya Kul'turnykh Rastenii [*A publication*]
Fiziol Biokhim Osn Pitan Rast ... Fiziologo-Biokhimicheskie Osnovy Pitaniya Rastenii [*A publication*]
Fiziol Biokhim Osn Vzaimodeistviya Rast Fitotsenozakh ... Fiziologo-Biokhimicheskie Osnovy Vzaimodeistviya Rastenii e Fitotsenozakh [*A publication*]
Fiziol Biokhim Patol Endokr Sist ... Fiziologiya, Biokhimiya, i Patologiya Endokrinnoi Sistemy [*A publication*]
Fiziol Biokhim Sil's'kogospod Tvarin ... Fiziologiya i Biokhimiya Sil's'kogospodars'kikh Tvarin [*A publication*]
Fiziol Chel ... Fiziologiya Cheloveka [*A publication*]
Fiziol Drev Rast ... Fiziologiya Drevesnykh Rastenii [*A publication*]
Fiziol Fiz-Khim Mekh Regul Obmennykh Protsessov Org ... Fiziologicheskie i Fiziko-Khimicheskie Mekhanizmy Regulyatsii Obmennykh Protsessov Organizma [*USSR*] [*A publication*]
Fiziol Norm Patol ... Fiziologiya Normala si Patologica [*A publication*]
Fiziologiya Rast ... Fiziologiya Rastenii [*A publication*]
Fiziol Patol Vyssh Nervn Deyat ... Fiziologiya i Patologiya Vysshei Nervnoi Deyatel'nosti [*A publication*]
Fiziol Rast ... Fiziologiya Rastenii [*A publication*]
Fiziol Rast (Engl Transl Plant Physiol) ... Fiziologiya Rastenii (English Translation of Plant Physiology) (Moscow) [*A publication*]
Fiziol Rast (Mosc) ... Fiziologiya Rastenii (Moscow) [*A publication*]
Fiziol Rast (Sofia) ... Fiziologiya na Rasteniyata (Sofia) [*A publication*]
Fiziol Vodoobmena Ustoich Rast ... Fiziologiya Vodoobmena i Ustoichivosti Rastenii [*A publication*]
Fiziol Z....... Fiziologicheskii Zhurnal [*A publication*]
Fiziol Z....... Fiziolohicnyj Zurnal [*A publication*]
Fiziol Zh ... Fiziologichnyi Zhurnal [*A publication*]
Fiziol Zh Akad Nauk Ukr RSR ... Fiziologichnij Zhurnal. Akademiya Nauk Ukrainskoj RSR [*A publication*]
Fiziol Zh (Kiev) ... Fiziolohichnyi Zhurnal (Kiev) [*A publication*]
Fiziol Zh SSSR ... Fiziologicheskii Zhurnal SSSR Imeni I. M. Sechenova [*A publication*]
Fiziol Zh SSSR Im I M Sechenova ... Fiziologicheskii Zhurnal SSSR Imeni I. M. Sechenova [*A publication*]
FIZ Karlsruhe ... Fachinformationszentrum Energie, Physik, Mathematik GmbH [*Information Center for Energy, Physics, Mathematics*] [*Information service or system*]   (IID)
Fiz Khim .... Fizicheskaya Khimiya [*USSR*] [*A publication*]
Fiz Khim Issled Prir Sorbentov Ryada Anal Sist ... Fiziko-Khimicheskoe Issledovanie Prirodnykh Sorbentov i Ryada Analiticheskikh Sistem [*A publication*]
Fiz-Khim Mekh Liofil' Dispers Sist ... Fiziko-Khimicheskaya Mekhanika i Liofil'nost Dispersnykh Sistem [*A publication*]
Fiz-Khim Mekh Mater ... Fiziko-Khimicheskaya Mekhanika Materialov [*Ukrainian SSR*] [*A publication*]
Fiz Khim (Moscow) ... Fizicheskaya Khimiya (Moscow) [*A publication*]
Fiz i Khim Obrab Mater ... Fizika i Khimiya Obrabotki Materialov [*A publication*]
Fiz Khim Obrab Mater ... Fizika i Khimiya Obrabotki Materialov [*A publication*]
Fiz Khim Prir Sint Polim ... Fizika i Khimiya Prirodnykh i Sinteticheskikh Polimerov [*A publication*]
Fiz Khim Probl Krist ... Fiziko-Khimicheskie Problemy Kristallizatsii [*Kazakh SSR*] [*A publication*]
Fiz i Khim Stekla ... Fizika i Khimiya Stekla [*A publication*]
Fiz Khim Stekla ... Fizika i Khimiya Stekla [*A publication*]
Fiz Khim Svoistva Individ Uglevodorodov ... Fiziko Khimicheskie Svoistva Individual'nykh Uglevodorodov [*A publication*]
Fiz Khim Tekhnol Silik Neorg Mater ... Fizicheskaya Khimiya i Tekhnologiya Silikatnykh i Neorganicheskikh Materialov [*A publication*]
Fiz Kondens Sostoyaniya ... Fizika Kondensirovannogo Sostoyaniya [*A publication*]
Fiz Kurortnye Faktory Ikh Lech Primen ... Fizicheskie i Kurortnye Faktory i Ikh Lechebnow Primenenie [*A publication*]

Fiz Magn Plenok ... Fizika Magnitnykh Plenok [*A publication*]
Fiz Mat Inst Rak ... Fizikas un Matematikas Instituta Raksti [*A publication*]
Fiz-Mat Spis ... Fiziko-Matematichesko Spisanie [*Bulgaria*] [*A publication*]
Fiz Mekh ... Fizicheskaya Mekhanika [*USSR*] [*A publication*]
Fiz Met ...... Fizika Metallov i Metallovedenie [*A publication*]
Fiz Metallov Metalloved ... Fizika Metallov i Metallovedenie [*A publication*]
Fiz Metal M ... Fizika Metallov i Metallovedenie [*A publication*]
Fiz Met i Metalloved ... Fizika Metallov i Metallovedenie [*A publication*]
Fiz Met Metalloved Akad Nauk SSSR Ural Fil ... Fizika Metallov i
    Metallovedenie Akademiia Nauk SSSR Ural'skii Filial
    [*USSR*] [*A publication*]
Fiz Metody Issled Tverd Tela ... Fizicheskie Metody Issledovaniya Tverdogo
    Tela [*A publication*]
Fiz Miner ... Fizika Mineralov [*A publication*]
Fiz Mnogochastichnykh Sist ... Fizika Mnogochastichnykh Sistem [*A
    publication*]
Fiz Mol ...... Fizika Molekul [*A publication*]
Fiz Nizk Temp ... Fizika Nizkikh Temperatur [*A publication*]
Fiz Nizk Temp (Kiev) ... Fizika Nizkikh Temperatur (Kiev) [*Ukrainian SSR*]
    [*A publication*]
Fiz Plazmy (Moskva) ... Fizika Plazmy (Moskva) [*A publication*]
Fiz Plazmy Probl Upr Termoyad Sin ... Fizika Plazmy i Problemy
    Upravlyaemogo Termoyadernogo Sinteza [*Ukrainian SSR*]
    [*A publication*]
Fiz Plazmy (Tbilisi) ... Fizika Plazmy (Tbilisi) [*A publication*]
Fiz Poluprovodn Poluprovodn Elektron ... Fizika Poluprovodnikov i
    Poluprovodnikovaya Elektronika [*A publication*]
Fiz Prochn Plast Met Elektrodin Yavleniya Veshchestve ... Fizika Prochnosti
    Plastichnosti Metallov i Elektrodinamicheskie Yavleniya v
    Veshchestve [*A publication*]
Fiz Protsessy Gorn Proizvod ... Fizicheskie Protsessy Gornogo Proizvodstva
    [*A publication*]
Fiz Rezaniya Met ... Fizika Rezaniya Metallov [*A publication*]
Fiz Sb .... Fizicheskii Sbornik [*A publication*]
Fiz Sb L'vov Gos Univ ... Fizicheskii Sbornik. L'vovskii Gosudarstvennyi
    Universitet [*Ukrainian SSR*] [*A publication*]
Fiz Sk .... Fizika v Skole [*A publication*]
Fiz Sz .... Fizikai Szemle [*A publication*]
Fiz Szk .... Fizyka w Szkole [*Poland*] [*A publication*]
FIZ Technik ... Fachinformationszentrum Technik [*Technical Information
    Center*] [*Information service or system*]   (IID)
Fiz Tekhnol Vopr Kibern Semin ... Fiziko-Tekhnologicheskie Voprosy
    Kibernetiki. Seminar [*Ukrainian SSR*] [*A publication*]
Fiz Tekhn Poluprov ... Fizika i Tekhnika Poluprovodnikov [*A publication*]
Fiz Tekh Poluprovo ... Fizika i Tekhnika Poluprovodnikov [*A publication*]
Fiz i Tekh Poluprovodn ... Fizika i Tekhnika Poluprovodnikov [*A
    publication*]
Fiz-Tekh Probl Razrab Polez Iskop ... Fiziko-Tekhnicheskie Problemy
    Razrabotki Poleznykh Iskopaemykh [*A publication*]
Fiz Tverd T ... Fizika Tverdogo Tela [*A publication*]
Fiz Tverd Tel ... Fizika Tverdogo Tela [*A publication*]
Fiz Tverd Tela ... Fizika Tverdogo Tela [*A publication*]
FIZ-W .... Fachinformationszentrum Werkstoffe [*Information Center for
    Materials*] [*Information service or system*]   (IID)
Fiz Yad Reakt ... Fizika Yadernykh Reaktorov [*A publication*]
Fiz Z .... Fiziceskij Zurnal [*A publication*]
Fiz Zap .... Fizichni Zapiski [*A publication*]
Fiz Zemli ..... Fizika Zemli [*A publication*]
Fiz Zhidk Sostoyaniya ... Fizika Zhidkogo Sostoyaniya [*A publication*]
FJ .... Air Pacific Ltd. [*Fiji*] [*ICAO designator*]   (FAAC)
FJ .... Congregation of Daughters of Jesus [*Roman Catholic religious
    order*]
FJ .... Field Judge [*Football*]
FJ .... Fighter Jet
FJ .... Fiji [*ANSI two-letter standard code*]   (CNC)
fj .... Fiji [*MARC country of publication code*] [*Library of
    Congress*]   (LCCP)
FJ .... Filles de Jesus de Kermaria [*Daughters of Jesus of Kermaria -
    DJK*] [*Paris, France*]   (EAIO)
FJ .... Film Journal [*A publication*]
FJ .... First Judge [*Legal term*]   (DLA)
FJ .... Fisher-Johns [*Melting point method*]
FJ .... Flush Joint [*Diamond drilling*]
FJ .... Flute Journal [*A publication*]
FJ .... Forst und Jagd [*A publication*]
FJ .... Fort Smith Journal [*A publication*]
FJ .... Freeman's Journal [*A publication*]
FJ .... Friesisches Jahrbuch [*A publication*]
FJ .... Fused Junction
FJ .... Jacksonville Public Library System, Jacksonville, FL [*Library
    symbol*] [*Library of Congress*]   (LCLS)
FJA .... Fluid Jet Amplifier
FJA .... Functional Job Analysis
FJA .... Furniture Manufacturer [*A publication*]
FJA .... Future Journalists of America   (EA)
FJAA .... Fashion Jewelry Association of America   (EA)
FJAK .... Flakey Jake's, Inc. [*NASDAQ symbol*]   (NQ)
FJAP .... Federal and Judicial Appointments Project   (EA)
Fj-Ar .... Central Archives of Fiji, Suva, Fiji [*Library symbol*] [*Library of
    Congress*]   (LCLS)
FJB .... Frankfurter Judaistische Beitraege [*A publication*]

FJB .... West Jefferson, NC [*Location identifier*] [*FAA*]   (FAAL)
F & J Bank ... De Gex, Fisher, and Jones' English Bankruptcy Reports [*A
    publication*]   (DLA)
FJC .... Fairbury Junior College [*Nebraska*]
FJC .... Federal Judicial Center
FJC .... Fisher Junior College [*Boston, MA*]
FJC .... Flint Junior College [*Michigan*]
FJC .... Fraser's Reports, Justiciary Court [*Scotland*] [*A
    publication*]   (DLA)
FJC .... Freeman Junior College [*South Dakota*]
FJC .... Friendship Junior College [*South Carolina*]
FJC .... Fullerton Junior College [*Later, Fullerton College*] [*California*]
FJCC .... Fall Joint Computer Conference [*Replaced by National
    Computer Conference - NCC*]
FJCE.......... Forum Jeunesse des Communautes Europeennes [*Youth Forum
    of the European Communities - YFEC*]   (EAIO)
FJCEE....... Federation des Jeunes Chefs d'Entreprises d'Europe [*European
    Federation of Young Managers*]
FJCF......... Federation des Jeunes Canadiens-Francais [*Federation of
    French-Canadian Youth*]
FJCNY ...... Furriers Joint Council of New York   (EA)
FJCT .... Freedom and Justice for Cyprus Trust   (EA)
FJD .... Florida Junior College at Jacksonville, DTC, Jacksonville, FL
    [*OCLC symbol*]   (OCLC)
FJDG .... Diego Garcia [*British Indian Ocean Territory*] [*ICAO location
    identifier*]   (ICLI)
FJDKDW .. Bulletin. Faculty of Home Life Science. Fukuoka Women's
    University [*A publication*]
FJE .... Free Jet Expansion
FJF .... Farmworker Justice Fund   (EA)
FJF .... Florida Junior College at Jacksonville, Jacksonville, FL [*Library
    symbol*] [*Library of Congress*]   (LCLS)
FJF .... Forschungen zur Judenfrage [*A publication*]
FJG .... Fonda, Johnstown & Gloversville Railroad Co. [*AAR code*]
FJGS......... Church of Jesus Christ of Latter-Day Saints, Genealogical
    Society Library, Jacksonville Branch, Jacksonville, FL
    [*Library symbol*] [*Library of Congress*]   (LCLS)
FJI .... Fellow of the Journalists' Institute [*British*]   (ROG)
FJI .... Fiji [*ANSI three-letter standard code*]   (CNC)
FJI .... Frequency Jumper Identification
FJI .... Friends of Julio International   (EA)
FJK .... Florida Junior College at Jacksonville, Kent, Jacksonville, FL
    [*OCLC symbol*]   (OCLC)
FJM .... Friedman, John M., Hurricane WV [*STAC*]
FJM .... Friends of Johnny Mathis   (EA)
FJMC .... Federation of Jewish Men's Clubs   (EA)
FJMSA...... Fukushima Journal of Medical Science [*A publication*]
FJN .... Familial Juvenile Nephrophthisis [*Medicine*]
FJN .... Florida Junior College at Jacksonville, North, Jacksonville, FL
    [*OCLC symbol*]   (OCLC)
FJN .... Front Jednosci Narodowej [*Polish Front of National Unity*]
FJNA .... Front des Jeunes Nationalistes Africains [*National African
    Youth Front*]
FJNC .... First Jersey National Corporation [*NASDAQ symbol*]   (NQ)
FJNF .... Foundation for the Jewish National Fund   (EA)
FJO........... Offshore Power Systems, Jacksonville, FL [*Library symbol*]
    [*Library of Congress*]   (LCLS)
F Journal ... Film Journal [*A publication*]
FJP .... Federation of Jewish Philanthropies of New York   (EA)
FJPC......... Federation des Jeunes Progressistes-Conservateurs du Canada
    [*Progressive Conservative Youth Federation of Canada*]
FJPTFCG ... Federation of Jewish Philanthropies Task Force on Compulsive
    Gambling   (EA)
FJQ .... Fedders Corp. [*NYSE symbol*]   (SPSG)
FJR .... Factories Journal Reports [*India*] [*A publication*]   (DLA)
F of JR ...... Fourth of July Road
FJR .... Friends of James Rogers   (EA)
FJRM .... Full Joint Range of Movement [*Orthopedics*]
FJS............ First Jersey Securities
FJS............ Florida Junior College at Jacksonville, South, Jacksonville, FL
    [*OCLC symbol*]   (OCLC)
FJS............ Fort Jones, CA [*Location identifier*] [*FAA*]   (FAAL)
FJS............ Fu Jen Studies [*A publication*]
FJSRL .... Frank J. Seiler Research Laboratory [*US Air Force Academy,
    CO*]
FJSTEX....... Fu Jen Studies [*A publication*]
FJSTO....... Federation of Jewish Student Organizations [*Defunct*]   (EA)
FJT .... Familiarization Job Training   (AFIT)
FJT .... Flush Joint [*Technical drawings*]
FJT .... Free Jet Test
FJU .... Chicago, IL [*Location identifier*] [*FAA*]   (FAAL)
FJU .... Jacksonville University, Jacksonville, FL [*Library symbol*]
    [*Library of Congress*] [*OCLC symbol*]   (LCLS)
FJUNF ...... University of North Florida, Jacksonville, FL [*Library symbol*]
    [*Library of Congress*]   (LCLS)
FJUS .... International FJ Class Organization   (EA)
FJW .... Friends of Jackie Wilson   (EA)
FJWO .... Federation of Jewish Women's Organizations   (EA)
FK .... Europe Falcon Service [*France*] [*ICAO designator*]   (FAAC)
FK .... Faker Track   (MUGU)
FK .... Falkland Islands [*ANSI two-letter standard code*]   (CNC)

fk .... Falkland Islands [*MARC country of publication code*] [*Library of Congress*] (LCCP)
F & K .... Film and Kino [*A publication*]
FK .... Filologiai Koezloeny [*A publication*]
FK .... Flat Keel [*Shipbuilding*]
FK .... Fokker-VFW BV [*Netherlands*] [*ICAO aircraft manufacturer identifier*] (ICAO)
F o K .... Folk og Kultur [*A publication*]
FK .... Fork (MSA)
FK .... Friends of Karen (EA)
FK .... Fujisawa Pharmaceutical Co. [*Japan*] [*Research code symbol*]
FK .... Function Key (MCD)
FKAB .... Banyo [*Cameroon*] [*ICAO location identifier*] (ICLI)
FKAF .... Bafia [*Cameroon*] [*ICAO location identifier*] (ICLI)
FKAG .... Abong-M'Bang [*Cameroon*] [*ICAO location identifier*] (ICLI)
FKAL .... Lomie [*Cameroon*] [*ICAO location identifier*] (ICLI)
FKAM .... Meiganga [*Cameroon*] [*ICAO location identifier*] (ICLI)
FKAMA .... Finska Kemistsamfundet. Meddelanden [*A publication*]
FKAMAR ... Suomen Kemistiseuran Tiedonantoja [*A publication*]
FKAN .... N'Kongsamba [*Cameroon*] [*ICAO location identifier*] (ICLI)
FKAO .... Betare-Oya [*Cameroon*] [*ICAO location identifier*] (ICLI)
FKAY .... Yoko [*Cameroon*] [*ICAO location identifier*] (ICLI)
FKB .... Flight Display Keyboard [*NASA*] (NASA)
FKB .... Fredericksburg, TX [*Location identifier*] [*FAA*] (FAAL)
FKBI .... Fourdrinier Kraft Board Institute [*Later, CKPG*] (EA)
FKC .... Fellow of King's College [*London*]
FKC .... Friends of the Kennedy Center (EA)
FKCL .... Fellow of King's College, London
FKCM .... Franklin Consolidated Mining Co., Inc. [*NASDAQ symbol*] (NQ)
FKD .... Forked
FKD .... Forschungen zur Kirchen- und Dogmengeschichte [*A publication*]
FKDG .... Forschungen zur Kirchen- und Dogmengeschichte (Goettingen) [*A publication*]
FKDNEF ... Bulletin. Fukuoka University of Education. Part 3. Mathematics, Natural Sciences, and Technology [*A publication*]
FKDRA ...... Fukuoka Kyoiku Daigaku Kiyo, Dai-3-Bu, Rika-Hen [*A publication*]
FKDRAN... Bulletin. Fukuoka University of Education. Part 3. Natural Sciences [*A publication*]
FKE .... Foros Kyklou Ergasion [*Business Turnover Tax*] [*Greek*]
f-ke--- .... Kenya [*MARC geographic area code*] [*Library of Congress*] (LCCP)
FKF .... Finlands Kristliga Foerbund [*Finnish Christian League*] (PPE)
FKF .... Franklin Bluffs, AK [*Location identifier*] [*FAA*] (FAAL)
FKFD .... [*The*] Frankford Corp. [*NASDAQ symbol*] (NQ)
FKFRD2 .... Frankfurter Kakteen-Freund [*A publication*]
FKGG .... Forschungen zur Kirchen- und Geistesgeschichte [*A publication*]
FKG(NF) ... Forschungen zur Kirchen- und Geistesgeschichte (Neue Folge) [*A publication*]
FKHD .... Frederick and Herrud [*NASDAQ symbol*] (NQ)
FKI .... Fachverband Klebstoffindustrie [*Association of European Adhesives Manufacturers*] (EAIO)
FKI .... Kisangani [*Zaire*] [*Airport symbol*] (OAG)
F & Kino..... Film and Kino [*A publication*]
FKIZA .... Fukuoka Igaku Zasshi [*Japan*] [*A publication*]
FKJ .... Fukue [*Japan*] [*Seismograph station code, US Geological Survey*] (SEIS)
FKK .... Freie-Koerper-Kultur [*Nudism, a pre-NAZI fad in Germany*]
FKK .... Fukuoka [*Japan*] [*Seismograph station code, US Geological Survey*] (SEIS)
FKKA .... Maroua/Ville [*Cameroon*] [*ICAO location identifier*] (ICLI)
FKKAD...... Funtai Kogaku Kaishi [*A publication*]
FKKB .... Kribi [*Cameroon*] [*ICAO location identifier*] (ICLI)
FKKC .... Tiko [*Cameroon*] [*ICAO location identifier*] (ICLI)
FKKD .... Douala [*Cameroon*] [*ICAO location identifier*] (ICLI)
FKKE .... Eseka [*Cameroon*] [*ICAO location identifier*] (ICLI)
FKKF .... Mamfe [*Cameroon*] [*ICAO location identifier*] (ICLI)
FKKG .... Bali [*Cameroon*] [*ICAO location identifier*] (ICLI)
FKKH .... Kaele [*Cameroon*] [*ICAO location identifier*] (ICLI)
FKKI .... Batouri [*Cameroon*] [*ICAO location identifier*] (ICLI)
FKKJ .... Yagoua [*Cameroon*] [*ICAO location identifier*] (ICLI)
FKKK .... Douala [*Cameroon*] [*ICAO location identifier*] (ICLI)
FKKL .... Maroua/Salak [*Cameroon*] [*ICAO location identifier*] (ICLI)
FKKM .... Foumban/Nkounja [*Cameroon*] [*ICAO location identifier*] (ICLI)
FKKN .... N'Gaoundere [*Cameroon*] [*ICAO location identifier*] (ICLI)
FKKO .... Bertoua [*Cameroon*] [*ICAO location identifier*] (ICLI)
FKKR .... Garoua [*Cameroon*] [*ICAO location identifier*] (ICLI)
FKKS .... Dschang [*Cameroon*] [*ICAO location identifier*] (ICLI)
FKKT .... Tibati [*Cameroon*] [*ICAO location identifier*] (ICLI)
FKKU .... Bafoussam [*Cameroon*] [*ICAO location identifier*] (ICLI)
FKKV .... Bamenda [*Cameroon*] [*ICAO location identifier*] (ICLI)
FKKW........ Ebolowa [*Cameroon*] [*ICAO location identifier*] (ICLI)
FKKY .... Yaounde [*Cameroon*] [*ICAO location identifier*] (ICLI)
FKL .... Franklin [*Pennsylvania*] [*Airport symbol*] (OAG)
FKL .... Franklin Holding Corp. [*AMEX symbol*] (SPSG)
FKL .... Franklin, PA [*Location identifier*] [*FAA*] (FAAL)

FKLB .... Franklin National Bank of Washington DC [*NASDAQ symbol*] (NQ)
FKM .... Finanzkurzmeldung [*Short Financial Report*] [*German*]
FKM .... Fluke [*John*] Manufacturing Co., Inc. [*AMEX symbol*] (SPSG)
FKM .... Fort Knox Minerals Ltd. [*Vancouver Stock Exchange symbol*]
FKN .... Field-Koros-Noves [*Physical chemistry*]
FKN .... Franklin, VA [*Location identifier*] [*FAA*] (FAAL)
FKOMA .... Fizika i Khimiya Obrabotki Materialov [*A publication*]
FKP............ Finlands Kommunistiska Parti [*Finnish Communist Party*] (PPE)
FKP............ Foros Katharas Prosodou [*Tax on Net Income*] [*Greek*]
FKP............ Fueggetlen Kisgazda Part [*Independent Smallholders' Party*] [*Hungary*] (PPE)
FKP............ Hopkinsville, KY [*Location identifier*] [*FAA*] (FAAL)
FKQ .... Fak-Fak [*Indonesia*] [*Airport symbol*] (OAG)
FKQCP ...... Fellow of the King's and Queen's College of Physicians, Ireland
FKQCPI .... Fellow of the King's and Queen's College of Physicians, Ireland [*Later, FRCPI*] (ROG)
Fkr .... Filmkritik [*A publication*]
FKR............ Frankfort, IN [*Location identifier*] [*FAA*] (FAAL)
F KR.......... Krona [*Crown*] [*Monetary unit*] [*Faroe Islands*]
F & K RGA ... Fife and Kincardine Royal Garrison Artillery [*British military*]
FKS .... Friends of Kate Smith [*Later, Kate Smith/God Bless America Foundation*] (EA)
FKS .... Fukushima [*Japan*] [*Seismograph station code, US Geological Survey*] (SEIS)
FKT .... Fernseh- und Kino- Technik [*A publication*]
FKT........... Field Kitchen Trailer (MCD)
FKT........... Friends of Kristoffer Tabori (EA)
FKTU .... Federation of Korean Trade Unions [*South Korea*]
FKU .... Feminist Karate Union (EA)
F Kultura... Film Kultura [*A publication*]
F Kunst ...... Filmkunst [*A publication*]
FKV........... Gainesville, GA [*Location identifier*] [*FAA*] (FAAL)
FKw........... Monroe County Public Library, Key West, FL [*Library symbol*] (LCLS)
FKWBRC .. Florida Keys Wild Bird Rehabilitation Center (EA)
FKwH .... Ernest Hemingway Home, Key West, FL [*Library symbol*] [*Library of Congress*] (LCLS)
FKwHi .... Key West Art and Historical Society, Key West, FL [*Library symbol*] [*Library of Congress*] (LCLS)
FKYN .... First Kentucky National Corp. [*NASDAQ symbol*] (NQ)
FKZ........... Sacramento, CA [*Location identifier*] [*FAA*] (FAAL)
F & L.......... Aviation Fuels, Lubricants, and Associated Products [*NATO*] (NATG)
Fl h............ Dutch Florin [*or Guilder*] [*Monetary unit*] [*German*]
FL.............. Fail (NASA)
FL.............. Falconbridge Limited [*Toronto Stock Exchange symbol*] [*Vancouver Stock Exchange symbol*]
FL.............. Fall
FL.............. Fall [*A publication*]
FL.............. Falsa Lectio [*False Reading, in a text*] [*Latin*]
F u L........... Farbe und Lack [*A publication*]
FL.............. Fatigue Limit
FL.............. Fault Localization (CAAL)
FL.............. Federal League [*Major league in baseball, 1914-15*]
FL.............. Feed Lines (NASA)
Fl............... Feldspar [*A mineral*]
FL.............. Feline Lung (Cell) [*Cytology*]
fl............... Femtoliter [*One quadrillionth of a liter*]
F/L............ Fetch/Load [*Data processing*] (MDG)
F a L........... Field and Laboratory. Contributions from the Science Departments [*A publication*]
FL.............. Field Length
FL.............. Field Loss Contactor or Relay [*Industrial control*] (IEEE)
FL.............. Figaro Litteraire [*A publication*]
F/L............ Film Load (KSC)
FL.............. Filologia e Letteratura [*A publication*]
FL.............. Filter (CET)
FL.............. First Lady [*Imelda Marcos of The Philippines*]
FL.............. Fiscal Letter (OICC)
FL.............. Fish Lake [*Pisciculture*]
FL.............. Flag [*British naval signaling*]
FL.............. Flag Lieutenant [*Navy*]
FL.............. Flame (AAG)
FL.............. Flammable
FL.............. Flanker [*Football*]
Fl............... Flash (DAS)
FL.............. Flash Lamp
FL.............. Flashing Light [*Navigation signal*]
FL.............. Flat (MSA)
FL.............. Flauto [*Flute*] [*Music*] (ROG)
FL.............. Flawless [*Diamond clarity grade*]
FL.............. Flemish [*Language, etc.*] (ROG)
Fl............... Fleta. Seu Commentarius Juris Anglici [*1647*] [*England*] [*A publication*] (DLA)
FL.............. Flexion [*Medicine*]
FL.............. Flight Level
FL.............. Flight Lieutenant
F/L............ Flintlock [*British military*] (DMA)

FL............ Floating Landing (ROG)
FL............ Flood (MSA)
FL............ Floor
FL............ Floor Line (MSA)
fl............ Floren [or Floreny] [Florin or Florins] [Monetary unit] [Poland]
FL............ Flores [Flowers] [Latin]
FL............ Florida [Postal code]
fl............ Florim [Florin] [Monetary unit] [Portugal]
FL............ Florin [Monetary unit] [Netherlands]
FL............ Floruit [He Flourished] [Latin]
fl............ Floryn [Florin] [Monetary unit] [Afrikaans]
FL............ Flotilla Leader [British]
FL............ Flow (MSA)
FL............ Flow Line [Technical drawings]
fl............ Flower [Botany]
FL............ Fluid (KSC)
FL............ Fluidus [Fluid] [Pharmacy]
FL............ Fluorescence
FL............ Fluorine [Chemical element] [Symbol is F] (ROG)
fl............ Fluoro [As substituent on nucleoside] [Biochemistry]
Fl............ Fluorometric [or Fluorometry]
FL............ Flush (MSA)
FL............ Flute
FL............ Flute Lead (MSA)
FL............ Fluvio-Lacustrine Sandstone [Geology]
FL............ Focal Length [Photography]
FL............ Folia Linguistica [A publication]
FL............ Folk Life [A publication]
FL............ Folklore [A publication]
FL............ Follicular Lymphoma [Oncology]
FL............ Food Laboratory [Army]
FL............ Foot-Lambert [Illumination]
FL............ For Life [An association] (EA)
FL............ Foreign Language
FL............ Foreign Listing [Telecommunications] (TEL)
FL............ Form Letter
FL............ Forum der Letteren [A publication]
FL............ Foundations of Language [A publication]
FL............ France Libre [A publication]
FL............ France-Louisiane [Later, FLFADDFA] [France] (EAIO)
FL............ Franciscaans Leven [A publication]
FL............ Franciscansch Leven [A publication]
F/L............ Free Lance
FL............ Freedom League (EA)
F/L............ Freight Liner [British Railways Board] (DS)
FL............ Frontal Lobe [Brain anatomy]
FL............ Frontier Airlines, Inc. [ICAO designator]
FL............ Fuel (KSC)
FL............ Full Lift (KSC)
FL............ Full Liquid [Medicine]
F/L............ Full Load (KSC)
FL............ Funnel Length
FL............ Guilder [Florin] [Monetary unit] [Netherlands]
fl............ Gulden [Florin] [Monetary unit] [Netherlands]
FL............ Land Station [ITU designation] (CET)
FL............ Liechtenstein [IYRU nationality code] (IYR)
fl----............ Nile River and Basin [MARC geographic area code] [Library of Congress] (LCCP)
FL1............ Function Language One
FLA............ Air Florida [Miami, FL] [FAA designator] (FAAC)
FLA............ Fabric Laminators Association [Defunct]
FLA............ Federal Librarians Association [Defunct]
FLA............ Federal Loan Administration
FLA............ Federal Loan Agency [Abolished 1947, records transferred to Reconstruction Finance Corporation]
FLA............ Fellow of the Library Association [British]
FLA............ Feminists for Life of America [Later, FFL] (EA)
FLA............ Fiat Lege Artis [Let It Be Done According to the Rules of the Art] [Pharmacy]
FLA............ Firearms Lobby of America [Later, CCRKBA] (EA)
FLA............ First Lord of the Admiralty [British]
FLA............ Flats [Utah] [Seismograph station code, US Geological Survey] [Closed] (SEIS)
FLA............ Flight Article [Army] (AABC)
FLA............ Florencia [Colombia] [Airport symbol] (OAG)
FLA............ Florida (AFM)
FLA............ Florida East Coast Industries, Inc. [NYSE symbol] (SPSG)
Fla............ Florida Reports [A publication] (DLA)
FLA............ Fluid Levitation Accelerometer
FLA............ Fluorescent Lighting Association (EA)
FLA............ Foam Laminators Association (EA)
FLA............ Foreign Language Annals [A publication]
FLA............ Foreign Language Associates
FLA............ Frontline Ambulance [Army] (INF)
FLA............ Full Load Amperes (MSA)
FLA............ Librairies Flammarion [ACCORD] [UTLAS symbol]
FLAA............ Fellow of the Library Association of Australia
FLAA............ Fellow, London Association of Accountants
FLAA............ Fellow of the London Associaton of Certified and Corporate Accountants (DAS)

FLAAC............ Florida Lime and Avocado Administrative Committee (EA)
Fla Acad Sci Q J ... Florida Academy of Sciences. Quarterly Journal [A publication]
Fla Admin Code ... Florida Administrative Code [A publication] (DLA)
Fla Admin Code Ann ... Florida Administrative Code, Annotated [A publication]
Fla Admin Weekly ... Florida Administrative Weekly [A publication]
Fla Ag Dept Quar B ... Florida. Department of Agriculture. Quarterly Bulletin [A publication]
Fla Ag Exp ... Florida. Agricultural Experiment Stations. Publications [A publication]
Fla Agric Exp Stn Annu Rep ... Florida. Agricultural Experiment Stations. Annual Report [A publication]
Fla Agric Exp Stn Bull ... Florida. Agricultural Experiment Stations. Bulletin [A publication]
Fla Agric Exp Stn Circ ... Florida. Agricultural Experiment Stations. Circular [A publication]
Fla Agric Exp Stn Dep Soils Mimeo Rep ... Florida. Agricultural Experiment Station. Department of Soils. Mimeo Report [A publication]
Fla Agric Exp Stn Monogr Ser ... Florida. Agricultural Experiment Stations. Monograph Series [A publication]
Fla Agric Exp Stn Res Rep ... Florida. Agricultural Experiment Stations. Research Report [A publication]
Fla Agric Ext Serv Bull ... Florida. Agricultural Extension Service. Bulletin [A publication]
Fla Anthropol ... Florida Anthropologist [A publication]
FLAAR............ Foundation for Latin American Anthropological Research (EA)
Fla Archit... Florida Architect [A publication]
Fla B J .... Florida Bar Journal [A publication]
Fla Board Conserv Mar Lab Prof Pap Ser ... Florida Board of Conservation. Marine Research Laboratory. Professional Papers Series [A publication]
Fla Board Conserv Mar Res Lab Leafl Ser ... Florida Board of Conservation. Marine Research Laboratory. Leaflet Series [A publication]
Fla Board Conserv Mar Res Lab Spec Sci Rep ... Florida Board of Conservation. Marine Research Laboratory. Special Scientific Report [A publication]
Fla Board Conserv Mar Res Lab Tech Ser ... Florida Board of Conservation. Marine Research Laboratory. Technical Series [A publication]
Fla Bur Geol Geol Bull ... Florida Bureau of Geology. Geological Bulletin [A publication]
Fla Bur Geol Inf Circ ... Florida Bureau of Geology. Information Circular [A publication]
Fla Bur Geol Rep Invest ... Florida Bureau of Geology. Report of Investigation [A publication]
FLAC......... Flaccid
FLAC......... Florida Automatic Computer [Air Force]
Flac .... In Flaccum [of Philo Judaeus] (BJA)
Flac .... Pro Flacco [of Cicero] [Classical studies] (OCD)
Fla Cattlm Livest J ... Florida Cattleman and Livestock Journal [A publication]
Fla Conserv News ... Florida Conservation News [A publication]
FLACSO ... Facultad Latinoamericana de Ciencias Sociales [Latin American Faculty of Social Sciences] [San Jose, Costa Rica]
Fla Dent J ... Florida Dental Journal [A publication]
Fla Dep Agric Consum Serv Div Plant Ind Bienn Rep ... Florida. Department of Agriculture and Consumer Services. Division of Plant Industry. Biennial Report [A publication]
Fla Dep Agric Consum Serv Div Plant Ind Bull ... Florida. Department of Agriculture and Consumer Services. Division of Plant Industry. Bulletin [A publication]
Fla Dep Agric Consum Serv Div Plant Ind Entomol Circ ... Florida. Department of Agriculture and Consumer Services. Division of Plant Industry. Entomology Circular [A publication]
Fla Dep Agric Consum Serv Div Plant Ind Nematol Circ ... Florida. Department of Agriculture and Consumer Services. Division of Plant Industry. Nematology Circular [A publication]
Fla Dep Agric Consum Serv Div Plant Ind Plant Pathol Circ ... Florida. Department of Agriculture and Consumer Services. Division of Plant Industry. Plant Pathology Circular [A publication]
Fla Dep Nat Resour Bienn Rep ... Florida. Department of Natural Resources. Biennial Report [A publication]
Fla Dep Nat Resour Bur Geol Bull ... Florida. Department of Natural Resources. Bureau of Geology. Bulletin [A publication]
Fla Dep Nat Resour Bur Geol Rep Invest ... Florida. Department of Natural Resources. Bureau of Geology. Report of Investigations [A publication]
Fla Dep Nat Resour Bur Geol Spec Publ ... Florida. Department of Natural Resources. Bureau of Geology. Special Publication [A publication]
Fla Dep Nat Resour Educ Ser ... Florida. Department of Natural Resources. Educational Series [A publication]
Fla Dep Nat Resour Mar Res Lab Leafl Ser ... Florida. Department of Natural Resources. Marine Research Laboratory. Leaflet Series [A publication]

Fla Dep Nat Resour Mar Res Lab Prof Pap Ser ... Florida. Department of Natural Resources. Marine Research Laboratory. Professional Papers Series [*A publication*]

Fla Dep Nat Resour Mar Res Lab Tech Ser ... Florida. Department of Natural Resources. Marine Research Laboratory. Technical Series [*A publication*]

Fla Dept Nat Resour Mar Res Lab Spec Sci Rep ... Florida. Department of Natural Resources. Marine Research Laboratory. Special Scientific Report [*A publication*]

Fla Dig .... Thompson's Digest of Laws [*Florida*] [*A publication*] (DLA)

FLAE .... [*The*] Florida Employers Insurance Co. [*NASDAQ symbol*] (NQ)

Fla Ent ...... Florida Entomologist [*A publication*]

Fla Entomol ... Florida Entomologist [*A publication*]

Fla Environmental and Urban Issues ... Florida Environmental and Urban Issues [*A publication*]

Fla Field Nat ... Florida Field Naturalist [*A publication*]

Fla Food Resour Econ Coop Ext Serv Univ Fla ... Florida Food and Resource Economics. Cooperative Extension Service. University of Florida [*A publication*]

FLAG .... Family Liaison Action Group [*Inactive*] (EA)

FLAG .... Federal Lesbians and Gays (EA)

FLAG .... Female Liberal Arts Graduate

FLAG .... Feminist Legal Action Group [*Australia*]

FLAG .... First Federal Savings Bank of LaGrange [*NASDAQ symbol*] (NQ)

FLAG .... Flageolet [*Music*]

FLAG .... Flagstaff National Park Service Group

FLAG .... Flexible Hours Action Group [*British*]

FLAG .... FORTRAN [*Formula Translating System*] Load and Go [*Xerox Corp.*] [*Data processing*]

FLAG .... Foundation for Law and Government [*Organization on television series "Knight Rider"*]

FLAG .... Four London Airport Group [*British*]

FLAGCENT ... Flag Officer, Central Europe

FLAGE ...... Flexible Lightweight Agile-Guided Experiment Missile [*Military*] (SDI)

Fla Geol Surv Geol Bull ... Florida. Geological Survey. Geological Bulletin [*A publication*]

Fla Geol Surv Inf Circ ... Florida. Geological Survey. Information Circular [*A publication*]

Fla Geol Surv Inform Circ ... Florida. Geological Survey. Information Circular [*A publication*]

Fla Geol Surv Rep Invest ... Florida. Geological Survey. Report of Investigations [*A publication*]

Fla Geol Surv Spec Publ ... Florida. Geological Survey. Special Publication [*A publication*]

Fla Grower Rancher ... Florida Grower and Rancher [*A publication*]

FLAGRP ... Florida Group [*Navy*]

Fla G S An Rp ... Florida. Geological Survey. Annual Report [*A publication*]

FLAH .... Flah's Inc. [*NASDAQ symbol*] (NQ)

Fla His S .... Florida Historical Society. Quarterly [*A publication*]

Fla Hist Q ... Florida Historical Quarterly [*A publication*]

Fla Hist Quar ... Florida Historical Quarterly [*A publication*]

FLAI .... Fleet Aerospace, Inc. [*NASDAQ symbol*] (NQ)

FLAIR .... Fleet Location and Information Reporting [*Police term*]

FLAIRS ..... Food Launch Awareness in the Retail Sector [*Leatherhead Food Research Association*] [*Information service or system*] (CRD)

Fla Jur .... Florida Jurisprudence [*A publication*] (DLA)

Fla & K .... Flanagan and Kelly's Irish Rolls Court Reports [*1840-42*] [*A publication*] (DLA)

FLAK .... Fliegerabwehrkanone [*German word for antiaircraft gun; acronym used in English for antiaircraft fire and as a slang term for dissension*]

FLAK .... Fondest Love and Kisses [*Correspondence*]

Fla Laws ..... Laws of Florida [*A publication*]

Fla Lib .... Florida Libraries [*A publication*]

Fla Libr .... Florida Libraries [*A publication*]

Fla LJ .... Florida Law Journal [*A publication*] (DLA)

Fla L Rev ... Florida Law Review [*A publication*] (DLA)

FLAM .... Fault Location and Monitoring (AABC)

Flam .... Flamininus [*of Plutarch*] [*Classical studies*] (OCD)

FLAM .... Forward Launched Aerodynamic Missiles

Fla Mar Res Publ ... Florida Marine Research Publications [*A publication*]

Flamb .... Flambeau [*A publication*]

FLAME ..... Foundation of Light and Metaphysical Education (EA)

FLAME ..... Friendship Loans to Latin American Endeavors, Inc.

Flame Retardancy Polym Mater ... Flame Retardancy of Polymeric Materials [*A publication*]

Flamme Therm ... Flamme et Thermique [*France*] [*A publication*]

FLAMQ ..... Flame Industries, Inc. [*NASDAQ symbol*] (NQ)

FLAMR ..... Forward-Looking Advanced Multimode RADAR

FLAMTI .... Forward-Looking Airborne Moving Target Indication (NG)

Fla Nat .... Florida Naturalist [*A publication*]

Fla NBA .... Flather's New Bankrupt Act [*A publication*] (DLA)

Fland Ch J ... Flanders' Lives of the Chief Justices of the United States [*A publication*] (DLA)

Fland Const ... Flanders on the United States Constitution [*A publication*] (DLA)

Fland Fire Ins ... Flanders on Fire Insurance [*A publication*] (DLA)

Fland Mar L ... Flanders' Maritime Law [*A publication*] (DLA)

Fland Sh .... Flanders on Shipping [*A publication*] (DLA)

F Lang .... Foundations of Language [*A publication*]

Flan & K ..... Flanagan and Kelly's Irish Rolls Court Reports [*1840-42*] [*A publication*] (DLA)

Flan & Ke ... Flanagan and Kelly's Irish Rolls Court Reports [*1840-42*] [*A publication*] (DLA)

Flan & Kel ... Flanagan and Kelly's Irish Rolls Court Reports [*1840-42*] [*A publication*] (DLA)

Fla Nurse ... Florida Nurse [*A publication*]

FLAP .... Fear, Love, Anger, and Pain [*Cognitive system*]

FLAP .... Federacion Latinoamericana de Parasitologos

FLAP .... First Level Adaptive Program

FLAP .... Five-Lipoxygenase Activating Protein [*Biochemistry*]

FLAP .... Flight Application Software [*NASA*] (NASA)

FLAP .... Flores Assembly Program [*Data processing*]

FLAP .... Flow Analysis Program [*Data processing*]

FLAP .... Formula Algebraic Processor [*Data processing*] (CSR)

FLAP .... Light from the Ancient Past, the Archeological Background of Judaism and Christianity [*Jack Finegan*] [*A publication*] (BJA)

FLAPA9 .... Flora do Parana. Instituto Paranaense de Botanica Curitiba [*A publication*]

FLAPS ...... Flight Application Software [*NASA*] (NASA)

FLAPW ..... Full-Potential Linear Augmented Plane Wave [*Physical chemistry*]

FLAR .... Fault Location and Repair (AABC)

FLAR .... Flare, Inc. [*NASDAQ symbol*] (NQ)

Fla R .... Florida Reports [*A publication*] (DLA)

FLAR .... Forward-Looking Airborne RADAR

FLARE ...... Flight Anomalies Reporting (KSC)

FLARE ...... Florida Aquanaut Research Expedition [*National Oceanic and Atmospheric Administration*]

Fla Rep .... Florida Reports [*A publication*] (DLA)

FLAREX .... Flare Exercises [*Navy*]

FLAS .... Fellow of the Chartered Land Agents' Society [*British*]

Fla SBA Jo ... Florida State Bar Association. Journal [*A publication*] (DLA)

Fla SBALJ ... Florida State Bar Association. Law Journal [*A publication*] (DLA)

Fla Sci .... Florida Scientist [*A publication*]

Fla Sea Grant Coll Rep ... Florida Sea Grant College. Report [*A publication*]

Fla Sea Grant Mar Res Educ Advis Serv Tech Pap ... Florida Sea Grant Marine Research Education Advisory Services. Technical Paper [*A publication*]

Fla Sess Law Serv ... Florida Session Law Service (West) [*A publication*] (DLA)

Fla Sess Law Serv (West) ... Florida Session Law Service (West) [*A publication*]

FLASH ...... Facts Location and Summarized History [*General Motors Corp.*] [*Data processing*]

FLASH ...... Fast Luciferase Automated Assay of Specimens for Hospitals [*Bacteria analysis*] [*NASA*]

FLASH ...... Feeder Lighter Aboard Ship

FLASH ...... Flame Launched Assault Shoulder or Hip-Fired Weapon [*Army*]

FLASH ...... Flash Lights and Send Help [*Florida highway driving aid*]

FLASH ...... Foreign Fishing Vessel Licensing and Surveillance Hierarchical Information System [*Canada*] (MSC)

FLASH ...... List of Australian Subject Headings. First Edition [*A publication*] (APTA)

FLASH FIRE ... Flash Financial Report [*for prospective overruns*] [*Navy*]

FLASP ...... Flight Plan Support Specialist [*NASA*]

Fla Stat ...... Florida Statutes [*A publication*] (DLA)

Fla Stat Ann ... Florida Statutes, Annotated [*A publication*] (DLA)

Fla Stat Anno ... Annotations to Official Florida Statutes [*A publication*] (DLA)

Fla Stat Ann (West) ... Florida Statutes, Annotated (West) [*A publication*]

Fla State Board Conserv Bien Rep ... Florida. State Board of Conservation. Biennial Report [*A publication*]

Fla State Board Conserv Div Water Survey and Research Paper ... Florida. State Board of Conservation. Division of Water Survey and Research. Paper [*A publication*]

Fla State Board Health Monogr Ser ... Florida. State Board of Health. Monograph Series [*A publication*]

Fla State LJ ... Florida State Law Journal [*A publication*] (DLA)

Fla State L Rev ... Florida State University. Law Review [*A publication*]

Fla State Mus Biol Sci Bull ... Florida State Museum. Biological Sciences Bulletin [*A publication*]

Fla State Plant Bd ... Florida State Plant Board. Publications [*A publication*]

Fla State Univ Dep Geol Sedimentol Res Lab Contrib ... Florida State University. Department of Geology. Sedimentological Research Laboratory. Contribution [*A publication*]

Fla State Univ Studies ... Florida State University. Studies [*A publication*]

Fla St Hort Soc Q ... Florida. State Horticultural Society. Quarterly [*A publication*]

Fla St U LR ... Florida State University. Law Review [*A publication*]

Fla St U L Rev ... Florida State University. Law Review [*A publication*]

Fla St Univ Slavic Papers ... Florida State University. Slavic Papers [*A publication*]

Fla Supp ..... Florida Supplement [*A publication*] (DLA)

Fla Supp 2d ... Florida Supplement. Second Series [*A publication*]

FLAT .... Foreign Language Aptitude Test
FLAT .... Katete [*Zambia*] [*ICAO location identifier*]   (ICLI)
Fla Trend ... Florida Trend [*A publication*]
Fla Univ Agric Ext Serv Circ ... Florida. University. Agricultural Extension Service. Circular [*A publication*]
Fla Univ Eng Exp Sta Bull ... Florida. University. Engineering and Industrial Experiment Station. Bulletin [*A publication*]
Fla Univ Eng Ind Exp Stn Bull Ser ... Florida. University. Engineering and Industrial Experiment Station. Bulletin Series [*A publication*]
Fla Univ Eng Ind Exp Stn Leafl Ser ... Florida. University. Engineering and Industrial Experiment Station. Leaflet Series [*A publication*]
Fla Univ Eng Ind Exp Stn Tech Pap Ser ... Florida. University. Engineering and Industrial Experiment Station. Technical Paper Series [*A publication*]
Fla Univ Eng Ind Exp Stn Tech Prog Rep ... Florida. University. Engineering and Industrial Experiment Station. Technical Progress Report [*A publication*]
FLAV .... Flavus [*Yellow*] [*Pharmacy*]
Flavour Ind ... Flavour Industry [*A publication*]
Flavours Fruit Juices Spices Rev ... Flavours, Fruit Juices, and Spices Review [*A publication*]
FLAW .... Fleet Logistic Air Wing
FLAWP ..... French-Language Association of Work Psychology [*Viroflay, France*]   (EAIO)
FLAX .... Fleming International Airways, Inc. [*Air carrier designation symbol*]
Flax Reg ..... Flaxman's Registration of Births and Deaths [*1875*] [*A publication*]   (DLA)
FLB .... Brittany Revolutionary Front [*France*]
FLB .... Family Life Bureau   (EA)
FLB .... Federal Land Bank
FLB .... Federal Loan Bank
FLB .... Flight Line Bunker   (NATG)
FLB .... Flow Brazing
FLB .... Fluorescently Labelled Bacteria [*Microbiology*]
FLB .... Foreign Language Bulletin
FLB .... Funny Looking Beat [*Cardiology*]
f-lb--- .... Liberia [*MARC geographic area code*] [*Library of Congress*]   (LCCP)
FLBA .... Federal Land Bank Association
FL Bank ..... Florida Banker [*A publication*]
FLB-ARB .. Front de Liberation de la Bretagne - Armee Republicaine Bretonne [*Liberation Front of Brittany - Breton Republican Army*] [*France*]   (PD)
FL-BE .... Filter-Band Eliminator   (MUGU)
FLBIN .... Floating-Point Binary [*Data processing*]
FLBK .... Florida Commercial Banks, Inc. [*NASDAQ symbol*]   (NQ)
FLB-LNS... Front de Liberation de la Bretagne pour la Liberation Nationale et le Socialisme [*Liberation Front of Brittany for National Liberation and Socialism*] [*France*]   (PD)
FL-BP .... Filter-Bandpass   (MUGU)
FL Build ..... Florida Builder [*A publication*]
FLBWA ...... Fries Landbouwblad [*A publication*]
FLC .... Australian Family Law Cases [*A publication*]   (APTA)
FLC .... Family Law Council   (EA)
FLC .... Farm Labor Coalition   (EA)
FLC .... Fault Locator Cable
FLC .... Federal Laboratory Consortium for Technology Transfer
FLC .... Federal Library Committee [*Later, FLICC*] [*Library of Congress*] [*Washington, DC*]
FLC .... Federation of Lutheran Clubs   (EA)
FLC .... Federazione Lavoratori delle Costruzioni [*Italy*]   (EY)
FLC .... FEDLINK [*Federal Library and Information Network*], Washington, DC [*OCLC symbol*]   (OCLC)
FLC .... Fenway Library Consortium/Abbot Memorial Library [*Library network*]
FLC .... Fibrolamellar Carcinoma [*Oncology*]
FLC .... File Location Code [*Data processing*]
FLC .... FINFO Flight Inspection Aircraft [*Oklahoma City, OK*] [*FAA designator*]   (FAAC)
FLC .... First Line Check
FLC .... Flag-Lieutenant-Commander [*Navy*] [*British*]
FLC .... Flat Load Cell
FLC .... Fleet Loading Center
FLC .... Flight Crew   (KSC)
FLC .... Folklore (Calcutta) [*A publication*]
FLC .... Force Logistics Command [*Marine Corps*]   (NVT)
FLC .... Foreign Liquidation Commission
FLC .... Forward Load Control   (MCD)
FLC .... Frequency and Load Controller
FLC .... Friend Leukemia Cells [*Cytology*]
FLCA .... Funny Looking Child [*Medical slang*]
FLCA .... Forward Load Control Assembly   (MCD)
FLCB .... Frequency and Load Control Box   (MCD)
FLCCU ...... FIREX [*Fire Extinguisher*] and Launch Coolant Control Unit [*Aerospace*]
FLCFDQ ... Canadian Forestry Service. Pacific Forest Research Centre. Forest Pest Leaflet [*A publication*]
FLCH .... Choma [*Zambia*] [*ICAO location identifier*]   (ICLI)

FLCL .... Family Life Communications Line
FLCM .... Fellow of the London College of Music [*British*]
FLCO .... Chocha [*Zambia*] [*ICAO location identifier*]   (ICLI)
FLCO .... Finalco Group, Inc. [*NASDAQ symbol*]   (NQ)
FLCO .... Floor Cleanout [*Technical drawings*]
FL Constr Ind ... Florida Construction Industry [*A publication*]
FL Cont and Build ... Florida Contractor and Builder [*A publication*]
FLCP .... Chipata [*Zambia*] [*ICAO location identifier*]   (ICLI)
FLCP .... Falcon Products, Inc. [*NASDAQ symbol*]   (NQ)
FLCPN ...... French Language Congress of Psychiatry and Neurology [*Paris, France*]   (EAIO)
FLCR .... Fixed Length Cavity Resonance
FLCRA ...... Farm Labor Contractor Registration Act [*1963*] [*US Employment Service*] [*Department of Labor*]
FL CRS ..... Flat Cars [*Freight*]
FLCS .... Chinsali [*Zambia*] [*ICAO location identifier*]   (ICLI)
FLCS .... Front de Liberation de la Cote des Somalis [*Front for the Liberation of the Somali Coast*] [*Djibouti*]
FLCSP .... Fellow of the London and Counties Society of Physiologists [*British*]
FLCT .... Friends of Libraries Charitable Trust [*British*]
FLCTN ...... Fluctuation   (FAAC)
FLcV .... United States Veterans Administration Hospital, Lake City, FL [*Library symbol*] [*Library of Congress*]   (LCLS)
FLD .... Fairchild Gold [*Vancouver Stock Exchange symbol*]
FLD .... Fairlead   (MSA)
FLD .... Fault Logic Diagram
FLD .... Ferret LASER Detector
FLD .... Field [*Data processing*]   (AFM)
FLD .... Field Division [*Census*]   (OICC)
FLD .... Fieldcrest Cannon, Inc. [*NYSE symbol*]   (SPSG)
F & LD ...... Flight and Laboratory Development   (MCD)
FLD .... Flood   (MCD)
fld .... Flowered [*Botany*]
FLD .... Fluid   (AAG)
FLD .... Fond Du Lac, WI [*Location identifier*] [*FAA*]   (FAAL)
FLD .... Forming Limit Diagram [*Manufacturing term*]
FLD .... Fraunhofer Line Discriminator [*Physics*]
FLD .... Fuel Loading Data [*Nuclear energy*]   (NRCH)
FLD .... Functional Line Diagram   (KSC)
FLD .... Fund for Labor Defense   (EA)
FLD .... Newfoundland Tracking Station
FLDA .... Federal Land Development Authority [*Malaysia*]
FLDACTYSq ... Field Activity Squadron [*Air Force*]
Fld Amb ..... Field Ambulance [*British military*]   (DMA)
FLDARTYGRU ... Field Artillery Group
FLDBR ...... Field Branch
FldCH .... Field Champion [*Dog show term*]
FLDCK ...... Field Cook [*Marine Corps*]
FLDCK(B) ... Field Cook (Baker) [*Marine Corps*]
FLDCK(C) ... Field Cook (Commissary) [*Marine Corps*]
FLDCOMDASA ... Field Command, Defense Atomic Support Agency   (AABC)
FLDCOMDNA ... Field Command, Defense Nuclear Agency [*DoD*]   (AABC)
Fld Crop Abstr ... Field Crop Abstracts [*A publication*]
FLDE .... Delkin (Lusiwasi) [*Zambia*] [*ICAO location identifier*]   (ICLI)
FLDEC ...... Floating-Point Decimal [*Data processing*]
FLDEXT .... Fluidextractum [*Fluidextract*] [*Pharmacy*]
FLDG .... Folding   (MSA)
FLDGM ..... Folding Map [*Publishing*]
FLDI .... Flare Die
FLDK .... Flight Deck
FLDMAINTSq ... Field Maintenance Squadron [*Air Force*]
FLDMS ...... Field Maintenance Shop [*Army*]   (AABC)
FLDMSLMAINTSq ... Field Missile Maintenance Squadron [*Air Force*]
FLDNG ..... Flooding
FLDO .... Field Officer
FLDO .... Final Limit, Down
FLDP .... Federation of Liberal and Democratic Parties   (PPE)
FLDR .... Fluid Dram
FLDRTA ... Federated Long Distance Road Transport Association of Australia
FLDSD2 .... Ireland. Department of Fisheries and Forestry. Trade and Information Section. Fishery Leaflet [*A publication*]
FLDST .... Flood Stage   (FAAC)
Fld Stn Rec Div Plant Ind CSIRO ... Field Station Record. Division of Plant Industry. Commonwealth Scientific and Industrial Research Organisation [*A publication*]   (APTA)
Fld Stn Rec Div Pl Ind CSIRO ... Field Station Record. Division of Plant Industry. Commonwealth Scientific and Industrial Research Organisation [*A publication*]   (APTA)
Fld Stud ..... Field Studies [*A publication*]
FLDT .... Floodlight
FLDTNS ... Field Trains
FldUrd .... Fluorodeoxyuridine [*Floxuridine*] [*Also, FUDR*] [*Antineoplastic drug*]
FLDXT ...... Fluidextractum [*Fluidextract*] [*Pharmacy*]
FLE .... Fatigue Life Expectancy [*or Expended*]   (MCD)
FLe .... Fiera Letteraria [*A publication*]
FLE .... Fire, Lightning, and Explosion [*Insurance*]   (AIA)
FLE .... Fixed Leading Edge   (MCD)

FLE........... Fleetwood Enterprises, Inc. [*NYSE symbol*] (SPSG)
FLE........... Fletcher [*Vermont*] [*Seismograph station code, US Geological Survey*] (SEIS)
FLE........... Telemetering Land Station [*ITU designation*] (CET)
FLEA........ East One [*Zambia*] [*ICAO location identifier*] (ICLI)
FLEA........ Flux Logic Element Array
FLEACT.... Fleet Activities
FLEASWSCOL ... Fleet Antisubmarine Warfare School (MUGU)
FLEASWTACSCOL ... Fleet Antisubmarine Warfare Tactical School
FLEB .... East Two [*Zambia*] [*ICAO location identifier*] (ICLI)
FLEB .... Flebile [*Pensive*] [*Music*] (ROG)
FLEBALMISUBTRACEN ... Fleet Ballistic Missile Submarine Training Center
FLEC .... East Three [*Zambia*] [*ICAO location identifier*] (ICLI)
FLEC .... Frente de Libertacao do Enclave de Cabinda [*Front for the Liberation of the Cabinda Enclave*] [*Angola*] (PD)
FLECC........ Federal Libraries' Experiment in Cooperative Cataloging [*Later, FEDLINK*]
FLECDR ... Flora of Ecuador [*A publication*]
FLECHT ... Full Length Emergency Cooling Heat Transfer [*Nuclear energy*] (NRCH)
FLECOMPRON ... Fleet Composite Squadron [*Navy*]
FLECOMPUTPROGCEN ... Fleet Computer Programming Center (MCD)
FLECOMPUTPROGCENLANT ... Fleet Computer Programming Center, Atlantic [*Navy*]
FLECOMPUTPROGCENPAC ... Fleet Computer Programming Center, Pacific [*Navy*]
FL Econ Ind ... Florida Economic Indicators [*A publication*]
FLED........ East Four [*Zambia*] [*ICAO location identifier*] (ICLI)
FLED........ Family Life Educator [*A publication*]
FLEE........ East Five [*Zambia*] [*ICAO location identifier*] (ICLI)
FLEEP....... Flying Lunar Excursion Experimental Platform [*NASA*]
Fleet .... Fleet, Cars, Vans, and Utilities [*A publication*]
FLEETEX ... Fleet Exercise [*Navy*] (NVT)
FLEETSAT ... Fleet Communications Satellite [*Navy*] (MCD)
FLEETSATCOM ... Fleet Satellite Communications System [*DoD*]
FLEF........ East Six [*Zambia*] [*ICAO location identifier*] (ICLI)
FLEG........ East Seven [*Zambia*] [*ICAO location identifier*] (ICLI)
FLEH........ East Eight [*Zambia*] [*ICAO location identifier*] (ICLI)
Fleischw..... Fleischwirtschaft [*A publication*]
FLeL .... Lake-Sumter Community College, Leesburg, FL [*Library symbol*] [*Library of Congress*] (LCLS)
FLEM........ Flemish
FLEMATSUPPO ... Fleet Material Support Office [*Navy*]
FLEMATSUPPOFAGLANT ... Fleet Material Support Office, Fleet Assistance Group, Atlantic [*Navy*]
FLEMATSUPPOFAGPAC ... Fleet Material Support Office, Fleet Assistance Group, Pacific [*Navy*]
Flemish Vet J ... Flemish Veterinary Journal [*A publication*]
FLEND........ Flendist [*England*]
FLENUMWEAFAC ... Fleet Numerical Weather Facility (MUGU)
FL Env Urb Iss ... Florida Environmental and Urban Issues [*A publication*]
FLEOA...... Federal Law Enforcement Officers Association (EA)
FLEOPINTRACEN ... Fleet Operational Intelligence Training Center [*Navy*]
FLER......... Fractional Loss Exchange Ratio (MCD)
FLEREADREP ... Fleet Readiness Representative [*Navy*] (AFIT)
FLES......... Foreign Languages in Elementary Schools
FLESONARSCOL ... Fleet SONAR School [*Navy*]
FLESUBTRAFAC ... Fleet Submarine Training Facility [*Navy*]
Fleta.......... Fleta. Seu Commentarius Juris Anglici [*A publication*] (DLA)
FLETACSUPPRON ... Fleet Tactical Support Squadron [*Navy*]
FLETC....... Federal Law Enforcement Training Center [*Department of the Treasury*]
Fletcher Corporations ... Fletcher's Cyclopedia of Corporations [*A publication*] (DLA)
Fletcher Cyc Corp ... Fletcher's Cyclopedia of Corporations [*A publication*] (DLA)
Fletcher F... Fletcher Forum [*A publication*]
Fletch Tr .... Fletch on Trustees of Estates [*A publication*] (DLA)
Flet Mjeks Shquip ... Fletorja Mjeksore Shquiptare [*A publication*]
FLETRABASE ... Fleet Training Base
FLETRACEN ... Fleet Training Center [*Navy*]
FLETRAGRUWATE ... Fleet Training Group and Underway Training Element
FLett .... Fiera Letteraria [*A publication*]
Fleury Hist ... Fleury's History of the Origin of French Laws [*1724*] [*A publication*] (DLA)
FLEWEACEN ... Fleet Weather Center [*or Central*] [*NATO*] (NATG)
FLEWEAFAC ... Fleet Weather Facility [*NATO*] (NATG)
FLEWORKSTUDYGRULANT ... Fleet Work Study Group, Atlantic [*Navy*]
FLEX........ Federal Licensing Examination [*for physicians*]
FLEX........ Fladden Ground Experiment [*Oceanography*] (MSC)
FLEX........ Fleet Exercise [*Navy*] [*British*]
FLEX........ Flexible (AABC)
FLEX........ Flexion [*Medicine*]
FLEX........ Flexowriter Equipment (AABC)
FLEX........ Flextronics, Inc. [*NASDAQ symbol*] (NQ)
FLEX........ Flexure [*Mechanics*]
FLEX........ Free Lance Exchange
FLEX........ Free Learning Exchange [*An association*] [*Defunct*] (EA)
FLEXAR.... Flexible Adaptive RADAR (MCD)

FLEXEM... Flexible Energy Management (MCD)
FLF .... Fault Location Facility [*Aircraft*]
FLF .... Final Limit, Forward
FLF .... Fisheries Loan Fund [*National Oceanic and Atmospheric Administration*]
FLF .... Fixed-Length Field [*Data processing*] (BUR)
FLF .... Flin Flon Mines [*Vancouver Stock Exchange symbol*]
FLF .... Flip-Flop [*Data processing*] (DEN)
FLF .... Follow-the-Leader Feedback [*Circuit theory*] (IEEE)
FLF .... Four Lucky Fellows [*In company name, FLF Associates*] [*Investment group comprised of four sons of Lawrence Tisch*]
FLF .... Fran Lee Foundation (EA)
FLF .... Freedom Leadership Foundation (EA)
FLF .... Friendly Laotian Forces (CINC)
FLFAAN ... Flora og Fauna [*A publication*]
FLFADDFA ... France-Louisiane/Franco-Americaine - Defense et Developpement de la Francophonie Americaine (EAIO)
FLFC......... First Liberty Financial Corp. [*NASDAQ symbol*] (NQ)
FLFE.......... Flora Fennica [*A publication*]
FLFE.......... Florida Federal Savings Bank [*NASDAQ symbol*] (NQ)
FLFEAZ.... Flour and Feed [*A publication*]
FLFI......... Lusaka [*Zambia*] [*ICAO location identifier*] (ICLI)
FLFN........ Free Lance Finders Network (EA)
FLFNAS.... Flora Fennica [*A publication*]
Fl Forum ... Fletcher Forum [*A publication*]
FLFRB7.... Flore de France [*A publication*]
FLFSA9.... Folia Forestalia [*Helsinki*] [*A publication*]
FLFT........ Forklift (AABC)
FLFT........ Full Load Frame Time [*Term used in SAGE operations*]
FLFW........ Fiwila [*Zambia*] [*ICAO location identifier*] (ICLI)
FLG........... American Flag Flying, Inc. [*Ft. Lauderdale, FL*] [*FAA designator*] (FAAC)
FLG........... Falling (FAAC)
FLG........... Flag [*Data processing*] (MDG)
FLG........... Flag Range (MCD)
FLG........... Flagship [*Navy*] (NVT)
FLG........... Flagstaff [*Arizona*] [*Seismograph station code, US Geological Survey*] [*Closed*] (SEIS)
FLG........... Flagstaff [*Arizona*] [*Airport symbol*] (OAG)
FLG........... Flagstaff, AZ [*Location identifier*] [*FAA*] (FAAL)
FLG........... Flange (MSA)
FLG........... Flashing
FLG........... Fletcher Leisure Group, Inc. [*Toronto Stock Exchange symbol*]
FLG........... Flooring (KSC)
FLG........... Flying (AABC)
FLG........... Following
FLG........... Friends of Little Gidding (EA)
FLG........... Front de Libertacao de Guinee [*Guinean Liberation Front*] [*Portuguese Guinea*]
FLGA........ Fellow of the Local Government Association [*British*]
FLGA........ Florida Lychee Growers Association (EA)
FLGC........ Friends for Lesbian and Gay Concerns (EA)
FLGE........ Mukinge [*Zambia*] [*ICAO location identifier*] (ICLI)
FLGF .... Flagship Financial Corp. [*NASDAQ symbol*] (NQ)
FLGL........ [*The*] Flagler Bank Corp. [*West Palm Beach, FL*] [*NASDAQ symbol*] (NQ)
Flg Off .... Flying Officer [*Australia*]
FLGPAA ... Federation of Local Government Planners Associations of Australia
FLGRAB ... Flower Grower [*A publication*]
FLGSTF .... Flagstaff
FLGSTN ... Flagstone
FLGW........ Mpongwe [*Zambia*] [*ICAO location identifier*] (ICLI)
FLH .... Federacion Latinoamericana de Hospitales [*Latin American Hospital Federation*] (EAIO)
FLH .... Fife Light Horse [*British military*] (DMA)
FLH .... Final Limit, Hoist
FLH .... Flash
FLH .... Flat Head (MSA)
FLH .... Land Hydrological and Meteorological Station [*ITU designation*] (DEN)
FLHAA...... Finska Lakaresallskapets Handlingar [*A publication*]
FLHLS ...... Flashless [*NASA*] (KSC)
FL-HP ...... Filter-High Pass (MUGU)
FLHQ .... Lusaka [*Zambia*] [*ICAO location identifier*] (ICLI)
FLHS........ Fellow of the London Historical Society [*British*]
FLHS........ Flashless
FLHV .... Fife Light Horse Volunteers [*British military*] (DMA)
FLI .... Farm Labor Information [*US Employment Service*] [*Department of Labor*]
FLI .... Farm and Land Institute [*Later, RLI*] (EA)
FLI .... Fault Location Indicator
FLI .... Federation Lainiere Internationale [*International Wool Textile Organization - IWTO*] (EAIO)
FLI .... Fellow of the Landscape Institute [*British*] (DBQ)
FLI .... Film Literature Index [*A publication*]
FLI .... Flateyri [*Iceland*] [*Airport symbol*] (OAG)
FLI .... Flight Leader Identity [*RADAR*]
FLI .... Flint Rock Mines [*Vancouver Stock Exchange symbol*]
FLI .... Fluorescence-Line Imager [*Instrumentation*]

FLI .... Food Law Institute [*Later, FDLI*]   (EA)
FLI .... Foodservice and Lodging Institute   (EA)
FLI .... Foreign Language Index [*A publication*]
FLI .... Former Live-In
FLI .... Forward-Looking Infrared
FLI .... Funnel Length Index
FLIA .... Federation Life Insurance of America [*Milwaukee, WI*]   (EA)
F Lib Q ..... Film Library Quarterly [*New York*] [*A publication*]
F Lib Quarterly ... Film Library Quarterly [*A publication*]
FLIC .... Fault Location Indicating Console   (AABC)
FLIC .... Film Library Information Council [*Absorbed by EFLA*]   (EA)
FLIC .... Film Library Inter-College Cooperative of Pennsylvania
　　　　　　[*Library network*]
FLIC .... [*The*] First of Long Island Corp. [*NASDAQ symbol*]   (NQ)
FLIC .... Foreign Languages for Industry and Commerce
　　　　　　[*British*]   (DBQ)
FLICC .... Federal Library and Information Center Committee [*Library of
　　　　　　Congress*] [*Also, an information service or system*]   (IID)
FLICON .... Flight Control [*or Controller*]
FLICR .... Fluid Logic Industrial Control Relay
FLICS .... Farm Labor Interstate Clearance System [*US Employment
　　　　　　Service*] [*Department of Labor*]
FLID .... Front de la Lutte pour l'Independence du Dahomey [*Battle
　　　　　　Front for the Independence of Dahomey*]
FLIDAP.... Flight Data Position
FLIDEN .... Flight Data Entry [*Device*] [*SAGE*]
FLIDIT...... Flight Line Detection and Isolation Techniques
FLIFO .... Flight Information
FLIGA ...... Forced Landing Incidents - Ground Accidents
Flight Aircr Eng ... Flight and Aircraft Engineer [*A publication*]
Flight Int.... Flight International [*A publication*]
Flight Int (London) ... Flight International (London) [*A publication*]
FLIH......... First Level Interrupt Handler [*Data processing*]
FLIK .... Isoka [*Zambia*] [*ICAO location identifier*]   (ICLI)
FLIM .... Fast Library Maintenance
FLIM .... Florida Automative Marketing [*NASDAQ symbol*]   (NQ)
FLIMBAL ... Floated Inertial Measurement Ball
FLIN .... Florida Library Information Network [*Florida State Library*]
　　　　　　[*Tallahassee, FL*] [*Library network*]
FLin .... Folia Linguistica [*A publication*]
FLINBAL ... Fluid Inertial Balance   (MCD)
Flinders Inst Atmos Mar Sci Cruise Rep ... Cruise Report. Flinders Institute
　　　　　　for Atmospheric and Marine Science. Flinders University
　　　　　　of South Australia [*A publication*]   (APTA)
Flinders J Hist Polit ... Flinders Journal of History and Politics [*A
　　　　　　publication*]
FLING....... Frente da Luta pela Independencia Nacional da Guine
　　　　　　"Portuguesa" [*Front for the Fight for Guinea-Bissau's
　　　　　　National Independence*]   (PD)
FLINK .... Flash/Wink Signal [*Telecommunications*]   (TEL)
FLINKS..... Front de Liberation Nationale Kanake Socialiste [*National
　　　　　　Liberation Front of Socialist Kanakes*] [*New Caledonia*]
　　　　　　[*Political party*]
FLINT .... Floating Interpretive Language [*Princeton University*]
Flint Conv .. Flintoff's Introduction to Conveyancing [*A publication*]   (DLA)
Flint R Pr .. Flintoff's Real Property [*1839-40*] [*A publication*]   (DLA)
FLINTS..... Flintshire [*Former county in Wales*]
Flintshire Hist Soc Publ ... Flintshire Historical Society. Publications [*A
　　　　　　publication*]
FLIOP ...... Flight Operations Planner
FLIP .... Family Life Income Patterns [*Economics simulation game*]
FLIP .... Film Library Instantaneous Presentation [*Data processing*]
FLIP .... Financially Limited Plan   (NATG)
FLIP .... Flexible Loan Insurance Program
FLIP .... Flight Information Plan
FLIP .... Flight Information Publication [*Air Force*]
FLIP .... Flight Launched Infrared Probe
Flip............ Flippin's Circuit Court Reports [*United States*] [*A
　　　　　　publication*]   (DLA)
FLIP .... Floated Lightweight Inertial Platform
FLIP .... Floating Indexed Point Arithmetic [*Data processing*]
FLIP .... Floating Instrument Platform [*Navy*]   (NG)
FLIP .... Floating Laboratory Instrument Platform [*Movable
　　　　　　oceanographic research station*]
FLIP .... Floating-Point Interpretive Program [*Data processing*]
Flipp (F).... Flippin's Circuit Court Reports [*United States*] [*A
　　　　　　publication*]   (DLA)
FLIPPG ..... French-Language Infant Pneumology and Phthisiology Group
　　　　　　[*Yerres, France*]   (EAIO)
FLIPS .... Future Language Information Processing System   (BUR)
FLIPS .... Fuzzy Logical Inferences per Second [*Computer chip
　　　　　　technology*]
FLIR .... Flight Low-Level Image Receiver
FLIR .... Forward-Loading Infrared   (RDA)
FLIR .... Forward-Looking Infrared   (AFM)
FLIRAS..... Forward-Looking Infrared Attack Set
FLIRS........ Forward-Looking Infrared System
FLIRT........ Federal Librarians Round Table [*American Library
　　　　　　Association*]
FLIRT........ First Ladies' International Racing Team [*Group of women
　　　　　　racing at Le Mans, France*]

FLIRT........ FORTRAN [*Formula Translating System*] Logical Information
　　　　　　Retrieval Technique [*Data processing*]
FLIRTS ..... Forward-Looking Infrared Thermovision System   (MCD)
FLiS .... Suwannee River Regional Library, Live Oak, FL [*Library
　　　　　　symbol*] [*Library of Congress*]   (LCLS)
FLISAO..... Folia Limnologica Scandinavica [*A publication*]
FLIST .... File List Processor [*Data processing*]
FLIT .... Fault Location through Interpretive Testing [*Data processing*]
FLIT .... Flexowriter Interrogation Tape
FLIT .... Free Limiting Internal Truss [*Nuclear energy*]   (NRCH)
FLIT .... Frequency Line Tracker [*Military*]   (CAAL)
FLIT .... Functional Literacy [*Program to provide marginally literate
　　　　　　soldiers with minimal literacy skills*] [*Army*]   (RDA)
FLITE....... Federal Legal Information through Electronics [*Air
　　　　　　Force*]   (IID)
FLITE....... Future Lawyers Investigating Transportation Employment
　　　　　　[*Student legal action organization*]   (EA)
FLiv......... Folk-Liv [*A publication*]
FLIWR ...... Functional Listing and Interconnection Wiring Record
FLIXS .... Fleet Information Exchange System [*Navy*]   (MCD)
FLIZ .... F-Layer Irregularity Zone [*Geophysics*]
FLJ .... Canada Fortnightly Law Journal [*A publication*]   (DLA)
FLJ .... Federal Law Journal [*1939*] [*A publication*]   (DLA)
FLJ .... Federal Law Journal of India [*A publication*]   (DLA)
Fl J .... Flandre Judiciaire [*A publication*]
Fl J .... Folklore Journal [*A publication*]
FLJ (Can) .. Fortnightly Law Journal (Canada) [*A publication*]   (ILCA)
FLJ Ind...... Federal Law Journal of India [*A publication*]   (ILCA)
FLJTC ...... Freeland League for Jewish Territorial Colonization [*Later,
　　　　　　LYT*]   (EA)
FLK .... Falkland Islands [*ANSI three-letter standard code*]   (CNC)
FLK .... Fetal Lamb Kidney [*A cell line*]
Fl & K....... Flanagan and Kelly's Irish Rolls Court Reports [*1840-42*] [*A
　　　　　　publication*]   (DLA)
FLK .... Fleck Resources Ltd. [*Vancouver Stock Exchange symbol*]
FLK .... Funny Looking Kid [*Syndrome*] [*Medical slang*]
FLKB .... Kawambwa [*Zambia*] [*ICAO location identifier*]   (ICLI)
FLKD........ Fluked [*Naval architecture*]
FLKD........ Kalundu [*Zambia*] [*ICAO location identifier*]   (ICLI)
FLKE........ Kasompe [*Zambia*] [*ICAO location identifier*]   (ICLI)
FLKG........ Kalengwa [*Zambia*] [*ICAO location identifier*]   (ICLI)
FLKJ......... Kanja [*Zambia*] [*ICAO location identifier*]   (ICLI)
FLKK .... Kakumbi [*Zambia*] [*ICAO location identifier*]   (ICLI)
FLKL......... Kalabo [*Zambia*] [*ICAO location identifier*]   (ICLI)
FLKM........ Kapiri Mposhi [*Zambia*] [*ICAO location identifier*]   (ICLI)
FLKO........ Kaoma [*Zambia*] [*ICAO location identifier*]   (ICLI)
FLKS........ Kasama [*Zambia*] [*ICAO location identifier*]   (ICLI)
FLKU........ Kanyau [*Zambia*] [*ICAO location identifier*]   (ICLI)
FLKW........ Kabwe/Milliken [*Zambia*] [*ICAO location identifier*]   (ICLI)
FLKY........ Kasaba Bay [*Zambia*] [*ICAO location identifier*]   (ICLI)
FLKZ........ Lukuzi [*Zambia*] [*ICAO location identifier*]   (ICLI)
FLL........... Final Limit, Lower
FLL........... Flow Line
FLL........... Flux-Line Lattice [*Superconductivity*] [*Physics*]
FLL........... Fort Lauderdale [*Florida*] [*Airport symbol*]   (OAG)
FLL........... Harvard University, Frances Loeb Library, Cambridge, MA
　　　　　　[*OCLC symbol*]   (OCLC)
FLLA .... Luanshya [*Zambia*] [*ICAO location identifier*]   (ICLI)
FLLC .... Lusaka [*Zambia*] [*ICAO location identifier*]   (ICLI)
FLLD .... Full Load
FLLD .... Lundazi [*Zambia*] [*ICAO location identifier*]   (ICLI)
FLLI .... Livingstone [*Zambia*] [*ICAO location identifier*]   (ICLI)
FLLK .... Frustum Lifting Lug Kit   (MCD)
FLLK .... Lukulu [*Zambia*] [*ICAO location identifier*]   (ICLI)
FLLO........ Kalomo [*Zambia*] [*ICAO location identifier*]   (ICLI)
FL-LP....... Filter-Low Pass   (MUGU)
FL LR .... University of Florida. Law Review [*A publication*]
FLLS......... Family Location and Legal Service [*Formerly, FLS*]   (EA)
FLLS......... Finger Lakes Library System [*Library network*]
FLIS.......... Florida Southern College, Lakeland, FL [*Library symbol*]
　　　　　　[*Library of Congress*]   (LCLS)
FLLS.......... Lusaka/International [*Zambia*] [*ICAO location
　　　　　　identifier*]   (ICLI)
FLLS.......... Waterfalls [*Board on Geographic Names*]
FLLU......... Federation of Libyan Labor Unions
FLLU......... Luampa [*Zambia*] [*ICAO location identifier*]   (ICLI)
FLLY......... Lilayi [*Zambia*] [*ICAO location identifier*]   (ICLI)
FLM.......... Falmouth, KY [*Location identifier*] [*FAA*]   (FAAL)
FLM.......... Family Life Mission [*An association*]   (EAIO)
FLM.......... Federation Lutherienne Mondiale [*Lutheran World Foundation
　　　　　　- LWF*] [*Geneva, Switzerland*]   (EAIO)
FLM.......... Fetal Lung Maturity [*Physiology*]
FLM.......... Film
FLM.......... Flame   (MSA)
FLM.......... Fleming Companies, Inc. [*NYSE symbol*]   (SPSG)
FLM.......... Fleming International Airways, Inc. [*Lithonia, GA*] [*FAA
　　　　　　designator*]   (FAAC)
FLM.......... Flight Line Maintenance
FLM.......... Fluidic Logic Module
FLM.......... Fraction of Labeled Mitoses [*Measurement of cell labeling*]
FLM.......... Friends of the Louvre Museum   (EA)

FLM........... Frightened Little Man
FLM........... Functional Level Management
FLMA........ Mansa [*Zambia*] [*ICAO location identifier*] (ICLI)
FLMB........ Flammable (MSA)
FLMB........ Maamba [*Zambia*] [*ICAO location identifier*] (ICLI)
FLMC........ Federal Labor-Management Consultant [*A publication*]
FLMC........ Full Load Motor Current [*Kraus & Naimer Microelectronics*]
FLMD........ Musonda Falls [*Zambia*] [*ICAO location identifier*] (ICLI)
FLMECH ... Fluid Mechanical (MCD)
FLMF........ Mfuwe [*Zambia*] [*ICAO location identifier*] (ICLI)
FLM-FJC.. Fur, Leather and Machine Workers Unions - Furriers Joint
     Council (EA)
FLMG........ Mongu [*Zambia*] [*ICAO location identifier*] (ICLI)
FLMI........ Fellow, Life Management Institute [*Designation awarded by*
     Life Office Management Association]
FLMI........ Mukonchi [*Zambia*] [*ICAO location identifier*] (ICLI)
FLMK........ Mkushi [*Zambia*] [*ICAO location identifier*] (ICLI)
FLML........ Mufulira [*Zambia*] [*ICAO location identifier*] (ICLI)
FLMM........ Mwami [*Zambia*] [*ICAO location identifier*] (ICLI)
FLMO........ Monze [*Zambia*] [*ICAO location identifier*] (ICLI)
FL Monthly ... Florida Monthly [*A publication*]
FLMP........ Mpika [*Zambia*] [*ICAO location identifier*] (ICLI)
FLMPB2 .. Flora Malesiana. Series II. Pteridophyta [*A publication*]
FLMPRF... Flameproof (MSA)
FLMPRS... Film Processing
FLM RES .. Flame Resistant (MSA)
FLM RTD .. Flame Retardant (MSA)
FLMSD...... Film Sound
FLMT........ Flush Mount
FLMT........ Mutanda [*Zambia*] [*ICAO location identifier*] (ICLI)
FLMTHR .. Flamethrower (AABC)
FL/MTR.... Flow Meter (AAG)
FLMTT ...... Flame Tight
FLMU........ Mulobezi [*Zambia*] [*ICAO location identifier*] (ICLI)
FLMW........ Mwinilunga [*Zambia*] [*ICAO location identifier*] (ICLI)
FLMZ........ Mazabuka [*Zambia*] [*ICAO location identifier*] (ICLI)
FLN .... Flatten (MSA)
FLN .... Florianopolis [*Brazil*] [*Airport symbol*] (OAG)
FLN .... Flown
Fln............. Fluorene [*Biochemistry*]
FLN .... Fluorescence-Line Narrowed [*Spectrometry*]
FLN .... Following Landing Numbers [*Shipping*]
FLN .... Freelance Network (EA)
FLN .... Frente de Liberacion Nacional [*National Liberation Front*]
     [*Venezuela*] [*Political party*] (PD)
FLN .... Front de Liberation Nationale [*National Liberation Front*]
     [*Algeria*] [*Political party*] (PPW)
FLN .... Fuel Line
FLN .... La Foliniere [*France*] [*Seismograph station code, US Geological*
     Survey] (SEIS)
FLNA........ Ngoma [*Zambia*] [*ICAO location identifier*] (ICLI)
FLNC........ First Lincoln Financial Corporation [*NASDAQ symbol*] (NQ)
FLNC........ Front de Liberation Nationale Congolais [*Congolese National*
     Liberation Front] [*Zaire*] [*Political party*] (PD)
FLNC........ Front de Liberation Nationale de la Corse [*Corsican National*
     Liberation Front] [*Political party*] (PD)
FLND .... Ndola [*Zambia*] [*ICAO location identifier*] (ICLI)
FL (Neb).... Foreign Languages (Nebraska) [*A publication*]
FLNF........ Front de Liberation Nationale Francaise [*French National*
     Liberation Front] (PD)
FLNG .... Fueling
FLNK........ Force de Liberation Nationale Kamerunaise [*National*
     Cameroonian Liberation Force] [*Political party*] (PD)
FLNL........ Namwala [*Zambia*] [*ICAO location identifier*] (ICLI)
FLNMAV ... Flora Neotropica Monograph [*A publication*]
FLNY........ Nyimba [*Zambia*] [*ICAO location identifier*] (ICLI)
FLO .... Fault-Location Oscillator [*Bell System*]
FLO .... Film Liaison Officer [*Army*]
FLO .... Fleet Electrical Officer [*British military*] (DMA)
FLO .... Florence [*South Carolina*] [*Airport symbol*] (OAG)
FLO .... Florence, SC [*Location identifier*] [*FAA*] (FAAL)
Flo............. Florentinus [*Flourished, 2nd century*] [*Authority cited in pre-*
     1607 legal work] (DSA)
Flo............. Florianus de Sancto Petro [*Deceased, 1441*] [*Authority cited in*
     pre-1607 legal work] (DSA)
Flo............. Florilege [*Record label*]
FLO .... Florin [*Monetary unit*] [*Netherlands*] (ROG)
FLO .... Florissant [*Missouri*] [*Seismograph station code, US Geological*
     Survey] [*Closed*] (SEIS)
FLO .... Flowers Industries, Inc. [*NYSE symbol*] (SPSG)
Fl/O.......... Flying Officer [*British*] (DMA)
FLO .... Foreign Liaison Office [*Military*] (AABC)
FLO .... Frederick Law Olmsted [*American landscape architect, 1822-*
     1903]
FLO .... Fuel Lube Oil
FLO .... Functional Line Organization
f-lo---....... Lesotho [*MARC geographic area code*] [*Library of*
     Congress] (LCCP)
FLOA........ Federal Licensed Officers Association (EA)
FLOA........ Frederick Law Olmsted Association (EA)
FLOC........ Farm Labor Organizing Committee (EA)

FLOC........ Fault Localization
FLOC........ For Love of Children
FLOCC...... Flocculation
FLOCOM .. Floating Commutator
FLODAC... Fluid-Operated Digital Automatic Computer [*Sperry UNIVAC*]
Fl Offr........ Flying Officer [*British*] (DMA)
FLO/FLO .. Float On/Float Off
FLOG........ Falcon Oil & Gas Co., Inc. [*NASDAQ symbol*] (NQ)
FLOG .... Fleet Logistics
FLOGAIR ... Fleet Logistics Air Wing [*Navy*]
FLOGWING ... Fleet Logistics Air Wing [*Obsolete*] [*Navy*]
FLOGWINGLANT ... Fleet Logistics Air Wing, Atlantic [*Navy*]
FLOGWINGPAC ... Fleet Logistics Air Wing, Pacific [*Navy*]
Flojo........... Florence Griffith Joyner [*American track athlete and Olympic*
     gold medalist]
FLOK........ Flock Industries, Inc. [*NASDAQ symbol*] (NQ)
FLOLS...... Fresnel Lens Optical Landing System [*Navy*]
FLOOD...... Fleet Observation of Oceanographic Data [*Navy*]
Flood El Eq ... Flood. Equitable Doctrine of Election [*1880*] [*A*
     publication] (DLA)
Flood Lib.... Flood. Slander and Libel [*1880*] [*A publication*] (DLA)
Flood Wills ... Flood on Wills of Personal Property [*A publication*] (DLA)
Floor Fact... Facts from Flooring. Resilient Flooring Production Estimates [*A*
     publication]
FLOP........ Floating Octal Point [*IBM Corp.*]
FLOP........ Fresnel Lens Optical Practice [*Navy*]
FLOPF...... Fresnel Lens Optical Practice, Fleet [*Navy*]
FLOPS...... Floating-Point Operations per Second [*Data processing*]
FloQ......... Florida Quarterly [*A publication*]
FLOR........ Florence [*Italy*] (ROG)
FLOR........ Flores [*Flowers*] [*Latin*] (ROG)
Flor........... Florianus de Sancto Petro [*Deceased, 1441*] [*Authority cited in*
     pre-1607 legal work] (DSA)
FLOR........ Floriculture
Flor........... Florida [*of Apuleius*] [*Classical studies*] (OCD)
Flor........... Florida Reports [*A publication*] (DLA)
Flo R .... Florida Reports [*A publication*] (DLA)
FLOR........ Florist (ROG)
FLOR........ Floruit [*He Flourished*] [*Latin*]
FLORA...... Fire Location RADAR (NG)
Flora Allg Bot Ztg Abt A Physiol Biochem (Jena) ... Flora oder Allgemeine
     Botanische Zeitung. Abteilung A. Physiologie und
     Biochemie (Jena) [*A publication*]
Flora Allg Bot Ztg Abt B Morphol Geobot (Jena) ... Flora oder Allgemeine
     Botanische Zeitung. Abteilung B. Morphologie und
     Geobotanik (Jena) [*A publication*]
Flora Allg Bot Ztg (Jena) ... Flora oder Allgemeine Botanische Zeitung (Jena)
     [*A publication*]
Flora & Fauna Handb ... Flora and Fauna Handbook [*A publication*]
Flora Fenn ... Flora Fennica [*A publication*]
Flora (Jena) ... Flora oder Allgemeine Botanische Zeitung (Jena) [*A*
     publication]
Flora (Jena) Abt A ... Flora (Jena). Abteilung A. Physiologie und Biochemie
     [*East Germany*] [*A publication*]
Flora (Jena) Abt B ... Flora (Jena). Abteilung B. Morphologie und Geobotanik
     [*East Germany*] [*A publication*]
Flora Males Bull ... Flora Malesiana. Bulletin [*A publication*]
Flora Malesiana Ser II Pteridophyta ... Flora Malesiana. Series II.
     Pteridophyta [*A publication*]
Flora Malesiana Ser I Spermatophyta ... Flora Malesiana. Series I.
     Spermatophyta [*A publication*]
Flora Ned... Flora van Nederland [*A publication*]
Flora Neerl ... Flora Neerlandica [*A publication*]
Flora Neotrop Monogr ... Flora Neotropica Monograph [*A publication*]
Flora NSW ... Flora of New South Wales [*A publication*] (APTA)
Flora of NSW ... Flora of New South Wales [*A publication*] (APTA)
Flor Anthr ... Florida Anthropologist [*A publication*]
Flora Pak ... Flora of Pakistan [*A publication*]
Flora Parana Inst Parana Bot Curitiba ... Flora do Parana. Instituto
     Paranaense de Botanica Curitiba [*A publication*]
Flora Pol Rosl Naczyniowe Pol Ziem Osciennych ... Flora Polska Rosliny
     Naczyniowe Polski i Ziem Osciennych [*A publication*]
Flora Tex ... Flora of Texas [*A publication*]
Flora Timarit Isl Grasafraedi ... Flora Timarit um Islenzka Grasafraedi [*A*
     publication]
Flore........... Florentinus [*Flourished, 2nd century*] [*Authority cited in pre-*
     1607 legal work] (DSA)
Flore Fr...... Flore de France [*A publication*]
Flore Iconogr Champignons Congo ... Flore Iconographique des Champignons
     du Congo [*A publication*]
Flore Illus Champignons Afr Cent ... Flore Illustree des Champignons
     d'Afrique Centrale [*A publication*]
FLORENT ... Florentia [*Florence*] [*Latin*] (ROG)
FLOREX ... Technical Exhibition for Florists [*Brussels International Trade*
     Fair] (TSPED)
Flor Exc ... Florists' Exchange [*A publication*]
Flor Exch ... Florists' Exchange [*A publication*]
Flori .... Florianus de Sancto Petro [*Deceased, 1441*] [*Authority cited in*
     pre-1607 legal work] (DSA)
Floria .... Florianus de Sancto Petro [*Deceased, 1441*] [*Authority cited in*
     pre-1607 legal work] (DSA)

Florida .... Florida Reports [*A publication*] (DLA)
Florida Anthropol ... Florida Anthropologist [*A publication*]
Florida BJ ... Florida Bar Journal [*A publication*]
Florida Bur Geology Geol Bull ... Florida. Department of Natural Resources. Bureau of Geology. Geological Bulletin [*A publication*]
Florida Bur Geology Inf Circ ... Florida. Department of Natural Resources. Bureau of Geology. Information Circular [*A publication*]
FLORIDA COMCAT ... Florida Computer Catalog of Monographic Holdings [*Library network*]
Florida Geol Surv Bull ... Florida. Geological Survey. Bulletin [*A publication*]
Florida Geol Surv Inform Circ ... Florida. Geological Survey. Information Circular [*A publication*]
Florida Geol Surv Rep Invest ... Florida. Geological Survey. Report of Investigations [*A publication*]
Florida R.... Florida Reports [*A publication*] (DLA)
Florida Rep ... Florida Reports [*A publication*] (DLA)
Florida State Mus Bull Biol Sci ... Florida State Museum. Bulletin. Biological Sciences [*A publication*]
Florida State Univ Sedimentol Research Lab Contr ... Florida State University. Department of Geology. Sedimentological Research Laboratory. Contribution [*A publication*]
Florida Ti U ... Florida Times Union [*A publication*]
Florida Univ Eng Progr Bull ... Florida. University. Engineering Progress Bulletin [*A publication*]
Florida Univ Eng Progr Leafl ... Florida. University. Engineering Progress Leaflet [*A publication*]
Florida Univ Eng Progr Tech Pap ... Florida. University. Engineering Progress Technical Paper [*A publication*]
Florida Univ Eng Progr Tech Progr Rep ... Florida. University. Engineering Progress Technical Progress Report [*A publication*]
Florist Nursery Exch ... Florist and Nursery Exchange [*A publication*]
Florists Exch Hortic Trade World ... Florists' Exchange and Horticultural Trade World [*A publication*]
FLORL ...... Fluorescent Runway Lighting
Flor Nat ..... Florida Naturalist [*A publication*]
FlorQ .... Florida Quarterly [*A publication*]
Flor Rev ..... Florists' Review [*A publication*]
FLORSENT ... Fluorescent [*Freight*]
Flor Ti Jack ... Florida Times Union and Jacksonville Journal [*A publication*]
FLOS .... Fixed Line of Sight (KSC)
FLOSOST ... Fluorine One-Stage Orbital Space Truck (KSC)
FLOSY ...... Front for the Liberation of Occupied South Yemen (PD)
FLOT .... Flotation (KSC)
FLOT .... Flotilla (AABC)
FLOT .... Forward Line of Own Troops (MCD)
FLOTRAN ... Flowcharting FORTRAN [*Data processing*] (IEEE)
FLOTUS ... First Lady of the United States
FLOVTH ... Flush Oiltight Ventilation Hole
FLOW .... Flow International Corp. [*NASDAQ symbol*] (NQ)
Flower and Gard ... Flower and Garden. Northern Edition [*A publication*]
Flower Gard South Ed ... Flower and Garden. Southern Edition [*A publication*]
Flower Grow ... Flower Grower [*A publication*]
Flowering Plants Afr ... Flowering Plants of Africa [*A publication*]
Flower Nursery Rep Commer Grow Calif Univ Coop Ext ... Flower and Nursery Report for Commercial Growers. California University Cooperative Extension [*A publication*]
FLOX .... Fluorine-Liquid Oxygen
Floy Proct Pr ... Floyer's Proctors' Practice [*A publication*] (DLA)
FLOZ .... Fluid Ounce
FLP .... Fault Location Panel [*Aerospace*] (AAG)
FLP .... Featherly Pass [*Alaska*] [*Seismograph station code, US Geological Survey*] (SEIS)
FLP .... Festlegepunkt [*Reference point, a gunnery term*] [*German military - World War II*]
FLP .... Field Landing Practice
FLP .... Fighting Landplane
FLP .... Fiji Labour Party [*Political party*] (FEA)
FLP .... Finlands Landsbygdsparti [*Finnish Rural Party*] [*Political party*] (PPE)
FLP .... Flame Leak Proof
FLP .... Flap (NASA)
FLP .... Flight Line Printer
FLP .... Flippin, AR [*Location identifier*] [*FAA*] (FAAL)
FLP .... Floating Point [*Data processing*]
FLP .... Floating Point Systems, Inc. [*NYSE symbol*] (SPSG)
FLP .... Florida Law and Practice [*A publication*] (DLA)
Flp .... Fluorescent Pseudomonad
FLP .... Foreign Language Program
F/LP .... Freight/Luggage Panniers [*Hovercraft*]
FLP .... Frente de Liberacion de los Pobres [*Liberation Front of the Poor*] [*Ecuador*] [*Political party*] (PD)
FLP .... Front de Liberation Populaire [*Quebec separatist group*]
FLPA .... Flight Level Pressure Altitude
FLPA .... Foreign Language Press of America
FLPA .... Kasempa [*Zambia*] [*ICAO location identifier*] (ICLI)
FLPAU ...... Floating-Point Arithmetic Unit
FLPC .... Federal Local Port Controller
FLPE .... Petauke [*Zambia*] [*ICAO location identifier*] (ICLI)
FLPK .... Mporokoso [*Zambia*] [*ICAO location identifier*] (ICLI)

FLPL .... FORTRAN [*Formula Translating System*] List Processing Language [*Data processing*] (IEEE)
FLPMA ..... Federal Land Policy and Management Act [*1976*]
FLPO .... Kabompo [*Zambia*] [*ICAO location identifier*] (ICLI)
FLPOAD ... Flora Polska; Rosliny Naczyniowe Polski i Ziem Osciennych [*A publication*]
FLPP .... Foreign Language Proficiency Pay [*Army*] (INF)
FLPP/CWS ... Family Life and Population Program/Church World Service (EA)
FLPR .... Flapper
FLPS .... First Lot Procurement Status (AAG)
FLPS .... Flight Load Preparation System [*NASA*] (NASA)
FLQ .... Dallas-Fort Worth, TX [*Location identifier*] [*FAA*] (FAAL)
FLQ ..... Families Leaving Quebec [*Humorous interpretation for Front de Liberation du Quebec*]
FLQ .... Film Library Quarterly [*A publication*]
FLQ .... Front de Liberation de Quebec [*Quebec Liberation Front*] [*Separatist group*]
FLQRAR ... Fluoride Quarterly Reports [*A publication*]
FLQX .... Juvancourt [*France*] [*ICAO location identifier*] (ICLI)
FLR .... Failure (MSA)
FLR .... Fall River [*Massachusetts*] [*Seismograph station code, US Geological Survey*] (SEIS)
FLR .... Fall River, MA [*Location identifier*] [*FAA*] (FAAL)
FLR .... Fast Liner Reactor (MCD)
FLR .... Federal Law Reports [*A publication*] (APTA)
FLR .... Federal Law Review [*A publication*]
FLR .... Field Level Repair (NVT)
FLR .... Field Loss Relay
FLR .... Fiji Law Reports [*A publication*] (DLA)
FLR .... Filler (AABC)
FLR .... Final Limit, Reverse
FLR .... Fixed Loan Rate [*Business term*]
FLR .... Flares
FLR .... Flight Line Reference (NVT)
FLR .... Flight Load Recorder
FLR .... Floor
FLR .... Florence [*Italy*] [*Airport symbol*] (OAG)
FLR .... Flow Rate (AAG)
FLR .... Flower
FLR .... Fluor Corp. [*NYSE symbol*] (SPSG)
Fl R .... Folklore Record [*A publication*]
FLR .... Forward-Looking RADAR
FLR .... University of Florida. Law Review [*A publication*]
FLRA .... Federal Labor Relations Authority [*Independent government agency*]
FLRC .... Farm Labor Research Committee [*Defunct*] (EA)
FLRC .... Federal Labor Relations Council [*Later, FLRA*]
FLRD .... Flared
FLRD .... Front de Liberation et de Rehabilitation du Dahomey [*Dahomey Liberation and Rehabilitation Front*] [*Benin*] [*Political party*] (PD)
F L Rev ...... Federal Law Review [*A publication*]
FLRG .... Flaring
FLRG .... Rusangu [*Zambia*] [*ICAO location identifier*] (ICLI)
FLRNG ...... Flash Ranging
FLRNG ...... Flooring
FLRO .... Rosa [*Zambia*] [*ICAO location identifier*] (ICLI)
FLRP .... Farm Labor Research Project (EA)
FLRS .... Forward-Looking RADAR Set (NVT)
FLRT .... Fat Lip Readers Theater (EA)
FLRT .... Federal Librarians Round Table [*American Library Association*] (EA)
FL/RT .... Flow Rate (AAG)
FLRU .... Rufansa [*Zambia*] [*ICAO location identifier*] (ICLI)
FLRY .... Flurry [*Meteorology*] (FAAC)
FLS .... Faculty of Library and Information Science, University of Toronto [*UTLAS symbol*]
FLS .... Falls (MCD)
FLS .... False [*FBI standardized term*]
FLS .... Family Location Service [*Later, FLLS*] (EA)
FLS .... Farm Labor Service [*of USES*]
FLS .... Fault Locator System (AABC)
FLS .... Fellow of the Linnaean Society [*British*]
FLS .... Fibrous Long-Spacing Collagen
FLS .... Fighter Leader School [*British military*] (DMA)
FLS .... Financial Listing Service [*Prime Rating, Inc.*] [*Defunct*] [*Information service or system*] (CRD)
FLS .... Flashing Light System (AAG)
FLS .... Flashless
FLS .... Fleet Logistics Support Department [*Naval Weapons Support Center*]
FLS .... Flight Surgeon (MCD)
FLS .... Flinders Island [*Australia*] [*Airport symbol*] (OAG)
FLS .... Florida Specialized Carriers Rate Conference, Inc., Jacksonville FL [*STAC*]
FLS .... Florida State University, School of Library Science, Tallahassee, FL [*OCLC symbol*] (OCLC)
FLS .... Florida Steel Corp. [*NYSE symbol*] (SPSG)
FLS .... Florida Supplement [*A publication*] (DLA)
FLS .... Flow Switch

FLS	Forward Light Scatter
FLS	Foundation of Law and Society [*Defunct*] (EA)
FLS	Foundations of Linguistics Series [*Elsevier Book Series*] [*A publication*]
FLS	Free Line Signal [*Telecommunications*] (TEL)
FLS	French Literature Series [*Columbia, South Carolina*] [*A publication*]
FLS	Future Launching System [*Space flight*]
FLSA	Fair Labor Standards Act [*1938*]
FLSA	Follicular Lymphosarcoma [*Oncology*]
FLSA	Frankie Laine Society of America (EA)
FLSA	St. Anthony [*Zambia*] [*ICAO location identifier*] (ICLI)
FLSC	Federal Lake Survey Center
FLSC	Fixed Laboratory Standard Capacitor
FLSC	Flexible Linear Shaped Charge
FLSC	Folia Limnologica Scandinavica [*A publication*]
FLSE..........	Serenje [*Zambia*] [*ICAO location identifier*] (ICLI)
FLSG	Force Logistics Support Group [*Marine Corps*] (NVT)
FLSH.........	FLS Holdings, Inc. [*NASDAQ symbol*] (NQ)
FLSH.........	Shiwan'Gandu [*Zambia*] [*ICAO location identifier*] (ICLI)
FLSIP........	Fleet Logistic Support Improvement Program [*Navy*] (NG)
FLSJ	Sakeji [*Zambia*] [*ICAO location identifier*] (ICLI)
FLSM	St. Mary's [*Zambia*] [*ICAO location identifier*] (ICLI)
FLSMP......	French-Language Society of Medical Psychology (EA)
FLSN	Senanga [*Zambia*] [*ICAO location identifier*] (ICLI)
FLSND	French-Language Society of Nutrition and Dietetics (EAIO)
FLSO	Southdowns [*Zambia*] [*ICAO location identifier*] (ICLI)
FLSOA	Frankie Laine Society of America (EA)
FLSP..........	Flame Spraying [*Welding*]
FLSP..........	Flight Space
FLSP..........	Fluorescein-Labeled Serum Protein [*Clinical chemistry*]
FLSPT	Fellowship of the London School of Polymer Technology [*British*] (DBQ)
FLSS..........	Falcon Launching Saber System
FLSS..........	Flight Level Sensing System [*or Subsystem*] (MCD)
FLSS..........	Sesheke [*Zambia*] [*ICAO location identifier*] (ICLI)
FLSU	Force Logistics Support Unit [*Marine Corps*] (NVT)
FLSW	Fleet Logistic Support Wing [*Navy*]
FLSW	Flow Switch
FLSW	Solwezi [*Zambia*] [*ICAO location identifier*] (ICLI)
FLT	Faculty of Library and Information Science (Teaching), University of Toronto [*UTLAS symbol*]
FLT	Family Life Today [*A publication*]
FLT	Fault
FLT	Fault Location Technology [*or Test*] (IEEE)
FLT	Federacion Latinoamericana de Termalismo [*Latin American Federation of Thermalism and Climatism - LAFTC*] [*Buenos Aires, Argentina*] (EAIO)
FLT	Field Level Training
FLT	Filing Time [*Time a message is presented for transmission*]
FLT	Filter
FLT	Flashlight (MSA)
FLT	Flat [*Alaska*] [*Airport symbol*] (OAG)
FLT	Flat, AK [*Location identifier*] [*FAA*] (FAAL)
FLT	Flats
FLT	Fleet (CINC)
FLT	Fleet Aerospace Corp. [*Toronto Stock Exchange symbol*]
FLT	Fleetwood [*Alabama*] [*Seismograph station code, US Geological Survey*] (SEIS)
FLT	Flex-Lead Torque
FLT	Flight (AFM)
F/LT	Flight Lieutenant (ADA)
FLT	Flight Line Taxi
FLT	Flight Line Tester
FLT	Float (MSA)
FLT	Florida Institute of Technology, Melbourne, FL [*OCLC symbol*] (OCLC)
FLT	Fluorodeoxythymidine [*Antiviral*]
FLT	Foreign Labor Trends [*Department of Labor*] [*A publication*]
FLT	Forklift Truck
FLT	Foss Launch & Tug [*AAR code*]
FLTAC	Fleet Analysis Center [*Navy*] (CAAL)
FLTACT....	Fleet Activities
FLTASWTRACEN ...	Fleet ASW [*Antisubmarine Warfare*] Training Center [*Navy*]
FLTBCST ...	Fleet Broadcast [*Navy*] (NVT)
FLTBDCST ...	Fleet Broadcast [*Navy*] (NVT)
FLTBRG....	Float Bridge
FLTCERT ...	Flight Certificate
FLTCINC ...	Fleet Commander-in-Chief [*Navy*] (MCD)
FLTCK	Flight Check [*Aviation*]
Flt Cmdr	Flight Commander [*Australia*]
Flt Comdr...	Flight Commander (DAS)
FLTCON...	Fleet Control
FLTCON...	Flight Control
FLTCORGRU ...	Fleet Composite Operational Readiness Group [*Navy*] (CAAL)
FLTD........	Fluted (MSA)
FLTDEMO ...	Fleet Demonstration [*Navy*] (NVT)
FLTEX	Fleet Exercise [*Navy*] (NVT)
FLTG.........	Floating (AABC)

FLTGA9	Flora Timarit um Islenzka Grasafraedi [*A publication*]
FLTGUNSCH ...	Fleet Gunnery School
FLTGUNSCOL ...	Fleet Gunnery School
FLTI	[*The*] Flight International Group, Inc. [*Newport News, VA*] [*NASDAQ symbol*] (NQ)
Flt Intnl......	Flight International [*A publication*]
FLTL	Flight Line
Flt Lieut	Flight Lieutenant [*British military*] (DMA)
FLTLOSCAP ...	Fleet Liaison Officer, Supreme Commander Allied Powers [*World War II*]
Flt Lt	Flight Lieutenant [*Australia*]
FLTO........	Flight Officer [*Air Force*] (AFM)
FLTO........	Flight Orders [*Aviation*] (FAAC)
Flt Off	Flight Officer [*Australia*]
FL/TOT	Flow Totalizer
FLTP	Flush Type
FLTP	Foreign Language Training Program [*Air Force*]
FLT/PG...	Flight Programmer (AAG)
FLT PLN ..	Flight Plan (MSA)
FLTR	Filmstar, Inc. [*NASDAQ symbol*] (NQ)
FLTR	Filter (MSA)
FLTRACKCEN ...	Fleet Tracking Center [*Navy*]
FLTREADREP ...	Fleet Readiness Representative [*Navy*] (MCD)
FL Trend ...	Florida Trend [*A publication*]
FLTS	Flight Line Test Set [*Military*] (CAAL)
FLTSAT	Fleet Satellite [*Navy*] (MCD)
FLTSATCOM ...	Fleet Satellite Communications System [*DoD*]
FLTSERVSCOL ...	Fleet Service School [*Navy*]
FLTSEVOCOM ...	Fleet Secure Voice Communications [*Navy*] (NVT)
Flt Sgt	Flight Sergeant [*Australia*]
FLTSOUNDSCOL ...	Fleet Sound School
FLTST	Flight Steward
FLTSTRIKEX ...	Full General-Emergency Striking Force Exercise [*Navy*] (NVT)
FLTSURG ...	Flight Surgeon
FltSurgBad ...	Flight Surgeon Badge [*Military decoration*] [*Army*] (AABC)
FLTTRACEN ...	Fleet Training Center [*Navy*]
FLTTRAGRU ...	Fleet Training Group [*Navy*]
FLTWEPCEN ...	Fleet Weapons Center [*Navy*]
FLTWO.....	Flight Watch Outlet (FAAC)
FLTx..........	Fork Lift Truck (DS)
FLTXAQ ...	Flora of Texas [*A publication*]
FLU	Fault Location Unit [*Aerospace*] (AAG)
FLU	Federation of Labor Unions [*Lebanon*]
FLU	Final Limit, Up
FLU	First Line Unit (MCD)
FLU	Flight Loads Unit (MCD)
flu	Florida [*MARC country of publication code*] [*Library of Congress*] (LCCP)
FLU	Flunitrazepam [*A hypnotic*]
FLU	Front for Liberation and Unity [*Western Sahara*]
FLU	New York/Flushing, NY [*Location identifier*] [*FAA*] (FAAL)
FLUA........	Fellow of the Life Underwriters of Australia
FLUC........	Fluctuate
FLUD	Fluid Corp. [*NASDAQ symbol*] (NQ)
Flue Cured Tob Farmer ...	Flue-Cured Tobacco Farmer [*A publication*]
Flue SG......	Fluechtlingssiedlungsgesetz [*A publication*]
FLUG.........	Flugfelag Islands H.F. [*Iceland Airways Ltd.*]
Flug Rev.....	Flug Revue [*A publication*]
Flug-Rev Int ...	Flug-Revue International [*West Germany*] [*A publication*]
FLUID.......	Formed Lines Using Interactive Data (MCD)
Fluid Apparecchiature Idraul & Pneum ...	Fluid Apparecchiature Idrauliche e Pneumatiche [*A publication*]
Fluid Apparecch Idraul & Pneum ...	Fluid Apparecchiature Idrauliche e Pneumatiche [*A publication*]
Fluid Contr Inst FCI Stand ...	Fluid Controls Institute. FCI Standards [*A publication*]
Fluid Dyn...	Fluid Dynamics [*A publication*]
Fluid Dyn Trans ...	Fluid Dynamics. Transactions [*A publication*]
Fluid Eng ...	Fluid Engineering [*Japan*] [*A publication*]
FLUIDEXTER ...	Fluidextractum [*Fluidextract*] [*Pharmacy*] (ROG)
FLUIDEXTR ...	Fluidextractum [*Fluidextract*] [*Pharmacy*] (ROG)
Fluidics Q ..	Fluidics Quarterly [*A publication*]
Fluid Mech Sov Res ...	Fluid Mechanics. Soviet Research [*A publication*]
Fluidos Hidraul Neumatica Lubr ...	Fluidos Hidraulica Neumatica Lubricacion [*A publication*]
Fluid Phase Equilib ...	Fluid Phase Equilibria [*A publication*]
Fluid Phase Equilibria ...	Fluid Phase Equilibria [*Netherlands*] [*A publication*]
Fluid Power Int ...	Fluid Power International [*A publication*]
Fluid Pwr Int ...	Fluid Power International [*A publication*]
Fluid Q......	Fluidics Quarterly [*A publication*]
Fluids Handl ...	Fluids Handling [*A publication*]
Flui Handl ...	Fluid Handling [*A publication*]
FLUL........	Federation of Labor Unions in Lebanon
FLUOA4	Fluoride [*A publication*]
FLUOR.......	Fluorescent [*or Fluoresces or Fluorescence*] (KSC)
FLUOR......	Fluoroscopy
Fluoresc Miner Soc J ...	Fluorescent Mineral Society. Journal [*A publication*]
Fluoride Q Rep ...	Fluoride Quarterly Reports [*A publication*]
Fluorine Chem Rev ...	Fluorine Chemistry Reviews [*A publication*]

Fluorocarbon Relat Chem ... Fluorocarbon and Related Chemistry [*A publication*]
FLUR........ Fluorescent [*Technical drawings*]
FLURAM ... Fluorescamine [*Biochemical analysis*] [*Acronym is trademark of Roche Diagnostics*]
Flur BG ...... Flurbereinigungsgesetz [*A publication*]
FLUSOC ... Fluted Socket
FLUSOCH ... Fluted Socket Head
FLUT........ Flutter   (MSA)
FLV.......... Feline Leukemia Virus [*Also, FELV*]
FLV.......... Foreign Leave [*Military*]   (AABC)
FLV.......... Friend Leukemia Virus [*Also, FDV, FV*]
FLV.......... Leavenworth, KS [*Location identifier*] [*FAA*]   (FAAL)
FLVER ...... Vermont Foreign Language Association. Bulletin [*A publication*]
FL Vk........ Forschungen zur Deutschen Landes- und Volkskunde [*A publication*]
FLW.......... Fault Location Word   (MCD)
FLW.......... Feedlot Waste
FLW.......... Fellows, CA [*Location identifier*] [*FAA*]   (FAAL)
FLW.......... Fellows, CA [*TACAN station*]   (NASA)
FL/W........ Flash Welding [*Metallurgy*]
FLW.......... Flat Washer
FLW.......... Fleet Logistics Wing [*Navy*]
FLW.......... Flow Resources Ltd. [*Vancouver Stock Exchange symbol*]
FLW.......... Follow
FLW.......... Foulwind [*New Zealand*] [*Seismograph station code, US Geological Survey*] [*Closed*]   (SEIS)
FLW.......... International Fur and Leather Workers Union of United States and Canada
FLw.......... Lake Worth Public Library, Lake Worth, FL [*Library symbol*] [*Library of Congress*]   (LCLS)
FLW.......... Santa Cruz, Flores [*Azores*] [*Airport symbol*]   (OAG)
FLWA........ Frank Lloyd Wright Association [*Later, FLWN*]   (EA)
FLWA........ West One [*Zambia*] [*ICAO location identifier*]   (ICLI)
FLWB........ West Two [*Zambia*] [*ICAO location identifier*]   (ICLI)
FLWC........ West Three [*Zambia*] [*ICAO location identifier*]   (ICLI)
FLWD........ West Four [*Zambia*] [*ICAO location identifier*]   (ICLI)
FLWE........ West Five [*Zambia*] [*ICAO location identifier*]   (ICLI)
FLWF........ Feedlot Waste Filtrate
FLWF........ Frank Lloyd Wright Foundation   (EA)
FLWF........ West Six [*Zambia*] [*ICAO location identifier*]   (ICLI)
FLWFEA.. Fort Leonard Wood Facilities Engineer Activity
FLWG........ Following
FLWG........ West Seven [*Zambia*] [*ICAO location identifier*]   (ICLI)
FLWGA..... Finger Lakes Wine Growers Association   (EA)
FLWHSF... Frank Lloyd Wright Home and Studio Foundation   (EA)
FLWIS........ Flood Warnings Issued
FLWK........ Flat Work
FLWL........ Flower Length [*Botany*]
FLWN........ Frank Lloyd Wright Newsletter   (EA)
FLWO ...... Fred Lawrence Whipple Observatory [*Amado, AZ*] [*Smithsonian Institution*]   (GRD)
FLWP........ Follow-Up
FLwP .... Palm Beach Junior College, Lake Worth, FL [*Library symbol*] [*Library of Congress*]   (LCLS)
FLWR........ Flores de New Mexico, Inc. [*NASDAQ symbol*]   (NQ)
FLWR........ Flower
FLWW....... Waka Waka [*Zambia*] [*ICAO location identifier*]   (ICLI)
FLX............ Fallon, NV [*Location identifier*] [*FAA*]   (FAAL)
FLX............ Flavex Industries Ltd. [*Vancouver Stock Exchange symbol*]
FLX............ Flexible [*Technical drawings*]
FLX............ Flexible Bond Trust [*AMEX symbol*]   (SPSG)
FLX............ Flxible Historic Association [*Defunct*]   (EA)
FLXS .... Flexsteel Industries, Inc. [*NASDAQ symbol*]   (NQ)
FLXX......... Flexible Computer Corp. [*NASDAQ symbol*]   (NQ)
FLY............ Airlease Ltd. [*NYSE symbol*]   (SPSG)
FLY............ CHC Helicopter Corp. [*Toronto Stock Exchange symbol*]
fly .... Flinty [*Quality of the bottom*] [*Nautical charts*]
Fly .... Flying [*A publication*]
FLY............ Flying
FLY............ Flywheel [*Automotive engineering*]
f-ly--- .... Libya [*MARC geographic area code*] [*Library of Congress*]   (LCCP)
FLYA .... Samfya [*Zambia*] [*ICAO location identifier*]   (ICLI)
FLYCO...... Commander, Flying [*British military*]   (DMA)
FLYCO...... Flying Control [*Position*] [*British*]
FLYCON... Flight Control
F-Lyd-Bild ... Film-Lyd-Bilde [*A publication*]
Flyers .... Fun-Loving Youth En Route to Success [*Lifestyle classification*] [*Title of book by Lawrence Graham and Lawrence Hamdan*]
Flygtek Forsoksanst Medd ... Flygtekniska Forsoksanstalten. Meddelande [*A publication*]
FLYOBRPT ... Flying Object Report [*Air Force*]
fly stat .... Flying Status [*Military*]
FLYT.......... Flight Dynamics, Inc. [*NASDAQ symbol*]   (NQ)
FLYTAF.... Flying Training Air Force
FLYWHL.. Flywheel
FLYWT ..... Flyweight [*Boxing*]
FLZB .... Zambezi [*Zambia*] [*ICAO location identifier*]   (ICLI)

FLZO......... Farband Labor Zionist Order [*Later, Labor Zionist Alliance*]   (EA)
FM .... Commandement des Transports Aeriens Militaires Francais [*France*] [*ICAO designator*]   (FAAC)
FM .... Face Measurement
FM .... Facilities Maintenance
FM .... Facilities Management
FM .... Factory Manual
FM .... Factory Mutual System [*Formerly, AFMFIC*] [*Group of four insurance companies and an engineering organization*]
FM .... Fan Marker [*Aviation*]
F/M .... Farads per Meter
FM .... Farm
FM .... Farm-to-Market [*Texas highway*]
FM .... Fashion Merchandising, Fashion Design, and/or Interior Design Programs [*Association of Independent Colleges and Schools specialization code*]
FM .... Fathom
FM .... Fault Monitor   (TEL)
FM .... Faulty Magazine [*Military*]   (MCD)
F-M .... Federal-Mogul
FM .... Federated States of Micronesia [*ANSI two-letter standard code*]   (CNC)
FM .... Feedback Mechanism
F/M .... Feet per Minute   (ADA)
FM .... Femtometer [*Formerly, Fermi*]   (MCD)
FM .... Ferdinand Marcos [*Former president of The Philippines*]
Fm .... Fermium [*Chemical element*]
FM .... Ferrite Metal
FM .... Fetal Movement [*Gynecology*]
FM .... Fiat Mistura [*Let a Mixture Be Made*] [*Pharmacy*]
FM .... Fibrous Material
FM .... Field Magnet   (ROG)
FM .... Field Main   (AAG)
FM .... Field Maintenance   (MCD)
FM .... Field Manual [*Military*]
FM .... Field Manufacture   (AFIT)
FM .... Field Marshal
FM .... Field Memorandum
FM .... Field Modification   (AAG)
FM .... Field Moist Soil [*Agronomy*]
FM .... Field Music [*Marine Corps*]
FM .... Figure of Merit
FM .... Filament Midtop
FM .... File Maintenance [*Data processing*]   (BUR)
FM .... File Management
F M .... Film Making [*A publication*]
FM .... Filologia Moderna [*A publication*]
FM .... Filosofska Misul [*A publication*]
FM .... Financial Mail [*Johannesburg*] [*A publication*]
FM .... Financial Management
FM .... Fine Measurement
FM .... Fine Motor
FM .... Fire Main   (AAG)
FM .... Firm [*Horse racing*]
FM .... First Main [*Firefighting*]   (ROG)
F/M .... First Motion   (KSC)
FM .... Fissile Material
FM .... Flight Manual   (MCD)
FM .... Flight Mechanic
FM .... Flight Model
FM .... Flight Monitor
FM .... Floor Manager   (DEN)
FM .... Flow Meter   (KSC)
FM .... Fluorescence Microphotolysis
FM .... Foam Monitor   (DS)
FM .... Focolare Movement   (EA)
FM .... Focusing Mount [*Photography*]
F & M .... Force and Mission
FM .... Ford Motor Co. [*Toronto Stock Exchange symbol*]
FM .... Foreign Material   (MCD)
FM .... Foreign Military
FM .... Foreign Minister [*or Ministry*]
FM .... Foreign Mission
FM .... Form
FM .... Formation [*Lithology*]
FM .... Formerly Married
FM .... Forms Management
FM .... Fort Major [*British*]   (ROG)
FM .... Forward Motion
FM .... Foster Mother
FM .... Foundation Member
FM .... Franc Macon [*Freemasonry*] [*French*]   (ROG)
FM .... Franc Mali [*Monetary unit*] [*Mali*]
FM .... Francais Moderne [*A publication*]
F and M .... Franklin and Marshall College [*Pennsylvania*]
FM .... Fraternite Mondiale [*World Brotherhood*]
FM .... Free Men   (EA)
Fm .... Freeman [*A publication*]
FM .... Freemason   (ROG)
FM .... Freight Management [*A publication*]

FM .... Freimaurer [*Freemason*] [*German*]   (ROG)
FM .... Frequency Meter
FM .... Frequency Modulation [*Radio*]
FM .... Frequency Multiplex
FM .... Frisker-Monitor [*Radiation detection*]
FM .... From   (MUGU)
FM .... Front Matter [*Publishing*]
FM .... Full Moon [*Astronomy*]
FM .... Functional Manager   (MCD)
FM .... Functional Mathematical Programming System [*Data processing*]   (MCD)
FM .... Functional Megaspore [*Botany*]
FM .... Fusarium Multiformis [*A fungus*]
FM .... Fused to Metal [*Dentistry*]
FM .... Fusobacteria Micro-Organisms [*Medicine*]
FM .... Libya [*License plate code assigned to foreign diplomats in the US*]
FM .... Miami-Dade Public Library, Miami, FL [*Library symbol*] [*Library of Congress*]   (LCLS)
FM .... Shippers Forecasts [*Symbol*] [*National Weather Service*]
FM .... Titanium Tetrachloride [*Inorganic chemistry*]
FMA .... Average Female Mass [*Ecology*]
FMA .... Daughters of Mary, Help of Christians [*Salesian Sisters of St. John Bosco*] [*Roman Catholic religious order*]
FMA .... Fabricators and Manufacturers Association, International   (EA)
FMA .... Facilities Management Analysis
FMA .... Factory Materials Association
FMA .... Failure Mode Analysis
FMA .... Family Mediation Association   (EA)
FMA .... Farm Management Association [*British*]
FMA .... Federal Managers Association   (EA)
FMA .... Federation Mondiale des Annonceurs [*World Federation of Advertisers - WFA*] [*Brussels, Belgium*]   (EAIO)
FMA .... Fein-Marquart Associates [*Chemical Information Systems, Inc.*] [*Information service or system*]   (IID)
FMA .... Fellow of the Museums Association [*British*]   (EY)
FMA .... Ferrite Manufacturers Association
FMA .... Fertiliser Manufacturers Association [*Great Britain*]
FMA .... Field Maintenance Activity   (MCD)
FMA .... File Manufacturers Association [*Defunct*]   (EA)
FMA .... Financial Management [*A publication*]
FMA .... Financial Management Association [*Tampa, FL*]   (EA)
FMA .... Financial Marketing Association   (EA)
FMA .... First Medical Management [*Vancouver Stock Exchange symbol*]
FMA .... Flexicore Manufacturers Association   (EA)
FMA .... Flight Manual Allowance
FMA .... Fluorescein Mercury Acetate [*Analytical chemistry*]
FMA .... Food Management Area   (MCD)
FMA .... Food Manufacture [*A publication*]
FMA .... Food Merchandisers of America   (EA)
FMA .... Forging Manufacturers Association [*Later, ODFI*]
FMA .... Formosa [*Argentina*] [*Airport symbol*]   (OAG)
FMA .... Forum for Medical Affairs [*Formerly, CPOSMA*]   (EA)
FMA .... Forward Maintenance Area   (NATG)
FMA .... Foxon-Maddocks Associates   (IID)
FMA .... Fragrance Materials Association of the US   (EA)
FMA .... Fulfillment Management Association   (EA)
FMA .... Future Mailing Address
FMAA ...... Fleet Master-at-Arms [*British military*]   (DMA)
FMaC .... Chipola Junior College, Marianna, FL [*Library symbol*] [*Library of Congress*]   (LCLS)
FMAC....... Federation Mondiale des Anciens Combattants [*World Veterans Federation - WVF*] [*Paris, France*]   (EAIO)
FMAC....... Financial Management Advisory Committee
FMAC....... Frequency Management Advisory Council [*Department of Commerce*] [*Washington, DC*]   (EGAO)
FMACC..... Foreign Military Assistance Coordinating Committee [*Department of State*] [*Terminated, 1950*]
FMacn ...... Macnaghten's Hindu Law [*India*] [*A publication*]   (DLA)
FMAD ...... Flight Mission Assignments Document   (KSC)
FMadN...... North Florida Junior College, Madison, FL [*Library symbol*] [*Library of Congress*]   (LCLS)
FMAG ...... Fleet Maintenance Assistance Group [*Navy*]   (NVT)
FMAG ...... Fluxgate Magnetometer   (MCD)
F Ma G ..... Forschungen zur Mittelalterlichen Geschichte [*A publication*]
FMAGR..... Furniture Manufacturers Association of Grand Rapids [*Later, GRAFMA*]   (EA)
FMAHTS ... Flight Manifest and Hardware Tracking System   (MCD)
FMAI........ Fabricators and Manufacturers Association, International   (EA)
FMAID...... Financial Mail [*South Africa*] [*A publication*]
FMaJ .... Jackson County Public Library, Marianna, FL [*Library symbol*] [*Library of Congress*]   (LCLS)
FMAL....... Funds Management Audit List   (AFIT)
FMAM ...... Federation Mondiale des Amis de Musees [*World Federation of Friends of Museums - WFFM*]   (EAIO)
FMAMA ... Factory Management and Maintenance [*A publication*]
FMAN....... February, May, August, November [*Denotes quarterly payments of interest or dividends in these months*] [*Business term*]
FMAN .... Foreman   (AABC)

FMANA .... Fire Marshals Association of North America   (EA)
FMANU .... Federation Mondiale des Associations pour les Nations Unies [*World Federation of United Nations Associations - WFUNA*] [*Geneva, Switzerland*]   (EA)
FMAP........ Fan Marker Approach [*Aviation*]
FMAP........ Father Moriarty Asylum Project   (EA)
FMAP "DM" ... Fabrica Militar de Armas Portatiles "Domingo Matheu"
FMAS........ Field Museum of Natural History. Anthropological Series [*A publication*]
FMAS........ Florida Marine Aquarium Society
FMAS........ Fruehmittelalterliche Studien [*A publication*]
FMASC .... Foreign Military Assistance Steering Committee
FMAT........ First Matagorda Corp. [*NASDAQ symbol*]   (NQ)
FMAT........ Food Management Assistance Team [*Army*]   (INF)
FMATH .... Federation Mondiale de Travailleurs des Industries Alimentaires, du Tabac, et de l'Hotellerie [*World Federation of Workers in Food, Tobacco, and Hotel Industries - WFFTH*]   (EAIO)
FMAU .... Fluoro(methyl)arabinosyluracil [*Biochemistry*]
FMAW ...... First Marine Aircraft Wing
FMAW ...... Fleet Marine Air Wing
FMB .... Biscayne Chemical Laboratories, Inc., Miami, FL [*Library symbol*] [*Library of Congress*]   (LCLS)
FMB .... Factory Mutuals' Combined Fire-Boiler Policy [*Insurance*]
FMB .... Fast Missile Boat [*Navy*]
FMB .... Federal Maritime Board [*1950-1961; functions transferred to FMC*]
FMB .... Federal Maritime Board Reports [*United States Maritime Administration, Department of Commerce*] [*A publication*]   (DLA)
FMB .... Federation of Master Builders [*British*]   (DAS)
FMB .... Financial Management Board [*Air Force*]   (AFIT)
FMB .... Foreign Materiel Branch [*Military*]
FMB .... Frequency Management Branch [*White Sands Missile Range*]
FMB .... Frequency Modulation Broadcasters
FMB .... Full Maternal Behavior [*Physiology*]
FMB .... Fuze Management Board [*Army*]
FMBA....... 51st Medical Battalion Association   (EA)
FMBC....... Biscayne College, Miami, FL [*Library symbol*] [*Library of Congress*]   (LCLS)
FMBC....... First Michigan Bank Corporation [*NASDAQ symbol*]   (NQ)
FMBCAG ... Folia Medica Bialostocensia [*A publication*]
FMBH .... Baptist Hospital of Miami, Health Sciences Library, Miami, FL [*Library symbol*] [*Library of Congress*]   (LCLS)
FMBI........ First Midwest Bancorp, Incorporated [*NASDAQ symbol*]   (NQ)
FMBMA ... Fiziko-Matematichesko Spisanie (Bulgaria) [*A publication*]
FMbMS.... Mount Sinai Medical Center, Media Center, Miami Beach, FL [*Library symbol*] [*Library of Congress*]   (LCLS)
FMBRA ..... Flour Milling and Baking Research Association [*British*]   (IRUK)
FMBS........ Forward Mobile Base Stockage   (MCD)
FMBSA ..... Farmers and Manufacturers Beet Sugar Association   (EA)
FMBT....... Future Main Battle Tank   (NATG)
Fm Bull Indian Coun Agric Res ... Farm Bulletin. Indian Council of Agricultural Research [*A publication*]
FMC .... Decisions of the Federal Maritime Commission [*United States*] [*A publication*]   (DLA)
FMC .... Facilities Management Contract
FMC .... Fatstock Marketing Corporation [*British*]
FMC .... Federal Management Circular
FMC .... Federal Manufacturers Code   (MCD)
FMC .... Federal Maritime Commission [*Independent government agency*]
FMC .... Fellow of the Medical Council [*British*]
FMC .... Felt Manufacturers Council   (EA)
FMC .... Ferrite Memory Core
FMC .... Field Medical Card [*Army*]   (AABC)
FMC .... Film Magnetic Counter
FMC .... Film-Makers' Cooperative   (EA)
FMC .... Filter Manufacturers Council   (EA)
FMC .... Fire Mark Circle [*Liverpool, England*]   (EAIO)
FMC .... First Ministers' Conference [*Canada*]
FMC .... Fixed Message Format [*Telecommunications*]   (TEL)
FMC .... Fixed Mica Capacitor
FMC .... Fixed Mylar Capacitor
FMC .... Flexible Machining Center [*Manufacturing technology*]
FMC .... Flexible Monte Carlo [*Data processing*]
FMC .... Flexible Motor Coupling
FMC .... Flight Medicine Clinic
FMC .... Florida Memorial College, Miami, FL [*OCLC symbol*]   (OCLC)
FMC .... Flutter Mode Control [*Aviation*]
FMC .... FMC Corp. [*Formerly, Food Machinery Corporation*] [*NYSE symbol*]   (SPSG)
FMC .... Focus on Micronesia Coalition [*Later, MC*]   (EA)
FMC .... Food Management Compartment   (MCD)
FMC .... Force Missile Coordinator [*Navy*]   (CAAL)
FMC .... Force Mobile (Canadian Forces)
FMC .... Forces Motoring Club [*British military*]   (DMA)
FMC .... Ford Motor Co. of Canada Ltd. [*Toronto Stock Exchange symbol*]

FmC .... Forman Co., Monmouth, IL [*Library symbol*] [*Library of Congress*] (LCLS)
FMC .... Former Members of Congress [*US*] [*Later, AFMC*]
FMC .... Forward Motion Compensation
FMC .... Foundation for Medical Care [*Generic term*] (DHSM)
FMC .... Foundation for Mideast Communication [*Later, FMEC*] (EA)
FMC .... Four Mile Canyon [*Oregon*] [*Seismograph station code, US Geological Survey*] (SEIS)
FMC .... Franklin and Marshall College [*Pennsylvania*]
FMC .... Free Man of Color [*Term of reference for blacks after the Civil War*]
FMC .... Frequency-Modulated Cyclotron
FMC .... Fuel Management Computer (NG)
FMC .... Fully Mission Capable (MCD)
FMC .... Fund for Modern Courts (EA)
FMC .... Fundamental Material Controls
FMC .... Intertax [*A publication*]
FMCA .... Family Motor Coach Association (EA)
FMCA .... Fire Mark Circle of the Americas (EA)
FMCA .... Ford Mercury Club of America (EA)
FMCA .... [*The*] Forensic Medicine Consultant-Advisor [*Program*]
FMCARP .. Father Moriarty Central American Refugee Program [*Later, FMAP*] (EA)
FMC-in-C .. Field Marshal Commanding-in-Chief [*British military*] (DMA)
FMCC .... Ford Motor Credit Company
FMCE .... Federacion Mundial Cristiana de Estudiantes [*World Student Christian Federation*]
FMCF .... First Manned Captive Flight [*NASA*] (NASA)
FMCG .... Fast-Moving Consumer Goods (DS)
FMCH .... Moroni/Hahaia [*Comoros*] [*ICAO location identifier*] (ICLI)
Fm Chem .. Farm Chemicals [*A publication*]
FMCI .... Forms Manufacturers Credit Interchange (EA)
FMCI .... Moheli/Bandaressalam [*Comoros*] [*ICAO location identifier*] (ICLI)
FMCIM ..... Federation Mondiale des Concours Internationaux de Musique [*World Federation of International Music Competitions - WFIMC*] (EAIO)
FMCL .... Fleet Mechanical Calibration Laboratory
FMCMA .... Fraternal and Military Club Managers Association [*Defunct*] (EA)
FMCMS ..... F. Marion Crawford Memorial Society (EA)
FMCN ...... Moroni/Iconi [*Comoros*] [*ICAO location identifier*] (ICLI)
FMCO .... FMS Financial Corp. [*NASDAQ symbol*] (CTT)
FMCORP .. Field Music Corporal [*Marine Corps*]
FMCPL ...... Field Music Corporal [*Marine Corps*]
FMCR .... Fleet Marine Corps Reserve
FMCRAW ... Folia Medica Cracoviensia [*A publication*]
FMCS .... Federal Mediation and Conciliation Service [*Independent government agency*]
FMCS .... Fleet Management Control Systems, Inc. [*Software*]
FMCS .... Flight Management Computer System
FMCS .... Franklin Mint Collector's Society (EA)
FMCT .... Federation of Moulders and Collateral Trades [*A union*] [*British*]
FMCU .... Form Cutter
FMCV .... Anjouan/Ouani [*Comoros*] [*ICAO location identifier*] (ICLI)
FMCVC ..... Federation Mondiale des Communautes de Vie Chretienne [*World Federation of Christian Life Communities - WFCLC*] [*Rome, Italy*] (EAIO)
FMCW ...... Frequency-Modulated Continuous-Wave [*RADAR*] (KSC)
FMCZ .... Dzaoudzi/Pamanzi [*Mayotte*] [*ICAO location identifier*] (ICLI)
FMD .... Ferrous Metal Detector
FMD .... Ferry Movement Directive [*Navy*] (NVT)
FMD .... Fibromuscular Dysplasia [*Medicine*]
FMD .... Fixtures Manufacturers and Dealers (EA)
FMD .... Foot-and-Mouth Disease [*Veterinary medicine*]
FMD .... Force Modernization Division [*Military*] (MCD)
FMD .... Form Molding Die (MCD)
FMD .... Frequency Management Division [*White Sands Missile Range*]
FMD .... Frequency of Minimum Delay
FMD .... Frequency Modulation Discriminator
FMD .... Friends of Medieval Dublin [*Irish*]
FMD .... Front Militant Departementaliste [*Militant Departmentalist Front*] [*Reunion*] (PD)
FMD .... Fulcrum Development Ltd. [*Vancouver Stock Exchange symbol*]
FMD .... Function Management Data (IBMDP)
FMDA .... 1st Marine Division Association
FMDA .... 4th Marine Division Association WWII (EA)
FMDA .... FM Development Association [*Later, NRBA*]
FMDA Abt II Monographien ... FMDA [*Forschungen und Materialien zur Deutschen Aufklarung*] Abteilung II. Monographien [*A publication*]
FMDB .... First Maryland Bancorp [*NASDAQ symbol*] (NQ)
FMDC .... First Medical Devices Corp. [*NASDAQ symbol*] (NQ)
FMD & C ... Flight Mechanics, Dynamics, and Control (KSC)
FMDC .... Franciscan Missionary Sisters of the Divine Child [*Roman Catholic religious order*]
FMDI .... Form Die
FMDLAJ... Folia Mendeliana [*A publication*]

FMDM ...... Flex Multiplexer/Demultiplexer (MCD)
FMDM ...... Franciscan Missionaries of the Divine Motherhood [*Roman Catholic religious order*]
FMDM ...... Frequency Modulation Deviation Meter
FMDO .... Firmado [*Signed*] [*Spanish*]
FMDR .... Final Missile Deviation Report [*Aerospace*] (AAG)
FMDV .... Foot-and-Mouth Disease Virus [*Veterinary medicine*]
FMDZA.... Fortschritte der Medizin [*A publication*]
FME .... Failure Mode and Effects
FME .... Farnesyl Methyl Ether [*Juvenile hormone analog*]
FME .... Field Maintenance Equipment [*Military*]
FME .... Finished with Main Engines [*Navy*]
FME .... Fixed Mobile Experiment (MCD)
FME .... Foreign Materiel Exploitation (RDA)
FME .. Fort Meade, MD [*Location identifier*] [*FAA*] (FAAL)
FME .... Foundation for Management Education [*British*]
FME .... Frequency-Measuring Equipment
FME .... Full Mouth Extraction [*Dentistry*]
FMe .... Melbourne Public Library, Melbourne, FL [*Library symbol*] [*Library of Congress*] (LCLS)
FMEA .... Failure Mode and Effects Analysis
FMEA .... Flour Millers Export Association (EA)
FMEC .... Forward Master Events Controller [*NASA*] (NASA)
FMEC .... Foundation for Mideast Communication (EA)
FMEC .... Fur Merchants Employers Council (EA)
FMECA ..... Failure Mode, Effects, and Criticality Analyses
Fm Economist ... Farm Economist [*A publication*]
F Med .... Fortschritte der Medizin [*A publication*]
FMED .... Forward Medical Equipment Depot [*Military*] [*British*]
FMED .... Foster Medical Corp. [*NASDAQ symbol*] (NQ)
FMeE........ Eau Gallie Public Library, Melbourne, FL [*Library symbol*] [*Library of Congress*] (LCLS)
FMEE .... Saint-Denis/Gillot [*Reunion*] [*ICAO location identifier*] (ICLI)
FMeF .... Florida Institute of Technology, Melbourne, FL [*Library symbol*] [*Library of Congress*] (LCLS)
FMEF .... Fuels and Materials Examination Facility [*Department of Energy*]
F-MEL...... Friend Murine Erythroleukaemia [*Cell line*]
FMEM....... Federation Mondiale pour l'Enseignement Medical [*World Federation for Medical Education - WFME*] (EA)
FMeM ..... Meadowlane Community Library, Melbourne, FL [*Library symbol*] [*Library of Congress*] (LCLS)
FMEO .... Fleet Marine Engineering Officer [*Navy*] [*British*]
FMEP .... Foundation for Middle East Peace (EA)
FMEP .... Friction Mean Effective Pressure
FMEP .... Saint-Pierre-Pierrefonds [*Reunion*] [*ICAO location identifier*] (ICLI)
FMER....... Factory Mutual Engineering and Research
FMer .... French Mercury [*Record label*]
FMERDB .. Forstschutz-Merkblaetter [*A publication*]
FMERO ..... Factory Mutual Engineering and Research Organization (EA)
FMES .... Ferry Mission Equipment Store (MCD)
FMES .... Full Mission Engineering Simulator (KSC)
fMet .... Formylmethionyl [*Biochemistry*]
FMETA ..... Foreign Material Exploitation Tactical Air [*Military*] (CAAL)
FMETO..... Fleet Meteorological Officer [*Navy*] [*British*]
fMet-tRNA ... Ribonucleic Acid, Transfer - Formylmethionyl [*Biochemistry, genetics*]
FMEVA..... Floating-Point Means and Variance [*Biochemistry, genetics*]
FMEW....... Financial Management Executive Workshop
FMF......... Familial Mediterranean Fever
FMF .... Famous Science Fiction [*A publication*]
FMF .... Farm Management and Finance [*British*]
FMF .... Fetal Movement Felt [*Medicine*]
FMF .... First Mercantile Currency Fund, Inc. [*Toronto Stock Exchange symbol*]
FMF .... Flagler Memorial Library, Miami, FL [*Library symbol*] [*Library of Congress*] (LCLS)
FMF .... Fleet Marine Force [*Military*]
FMF .... Florida Mango Forum (EA)
FMF .... Flow Microfluorometer [*Instrumentation*]
FMF .... Fluid Modeling Facility [*Environmental Protection Agency*] (GRD)
FMF .... Food Manufacturers' Federation [*British*]
FMF .... Francis Marion National Forest [*South Carolina*] [*Seismograph station code, US Geological Survey*] [*Closed*] (SEIS)
FMF .... Free Market Foundation [*Saxonwold, South Africa*] (EAIO)
FMF .... Free Molecular Flow
FMF .... Fudan Museum Foundation (EA)
FMF .... Fuel Melt Fraction [*Nuclear energy*] (NRCH)
FMFB .... Frequency Modulation with Feedback
FMFC .... First Midwest Financial [*NASDAQ symbol*] (NQ)
FMFD....... Frequency Modulation Feedback Discriminator
F & M Feinwerktech Messtech ... F und M, Feinwerktechnik und Messtechnik [*A publication*]
F M-Feinw M ... F und M, Feinwerktechnik und Messtechnik [*A publication*]
FMFIA ...... Federal Managers Financial Integrity Act [*1982*]
FMFIC ...... Federation of Mutual Fire Insurance Companies (EA)
FMFIU ...... Florida International University, Miami, FL [*Library symbol*] [*Library of Congress*] (LCLS)

FMFLANT ... Fleet Marine Force, Atlantic [*Navy*]   (MCD)
FMFM....... Fleet Marine Force Manual [*Marine Corps*]   (MCD)
FMFM....... Florida Memorial College, Miami, FL [*Library symbol*] [*Library of Congress*]   (LCLS)
FM-FM ..... Frequency Modulation - Frequency Modulation
Fm Forest (Nigeria) ... Farm and Forest (Nigeria) [*A publication*]
FMFPAC... Fleet Marine Force, Pacific Fleet [*Navy*]
FMF Rev.... FMF [*Food Manufacturer's Federation*] Review [*A publication*]
FMFS........ F & M Financial Services Corp. [*Menomonee Falls, WI*] [*NASDAQ symbol*]   (NQ)
FMFWESTPAC ... Fleet Marine Force, Western Pacific [*Navy*]
FMG .... Fabricated Metal Goods
FMG .... Financial Management [*A publication*]
FMG .... Flakmessgerat [*Antiaircraft, gun-laying RADAR*] [*German*]
FMG .... Foreign Medical Graduate [*doing residency in US hospital*]
FMG .... Franc [*Monetary unit*] [*Malagasy Republic*]
FMG .... Frequency Modulation Generator
f-mg--- ...... Malagasi Republic [*Madagascar*] [*MARC geographic area code*] [*Library of Congress*]   (LCCP)
FMG(A)..... Fleet Maintenance Group (Atlantic) [*Canada*]
FMGEMS ... Foreign Medical Graduate Examination in Medical Sciences
FMGF........ Factorial Moment Generating Function [*Statistics*]
Fmg Forum ... Farming Forum [*A publication*]   (APTA)
FMGM ...... French MGM [*Record label*]
FMG(P)..... Fleet Maintenance Group (Pacific) [*Canada*]
Fmg Rev .... Farming Review [*A publication*]
FMGS........ Church of Jesus Christ of Latter-Day Saints, Genealogical Society Library, Miami Branch, Miami, FL [*Library symbol*] [*Library of Congress*]   (LCLS)
Fmg S Afr .. Farming in South Africa [*A publication*]
FMGTF ...... FMG Telecomputer Ltd. [*NASDAQ symbol*]   (NQ)
Fmg Zambia ... Farming in Zambia [*A publication*]
FMH.......... Falling Mass Hazard
FMH.......... Falmouth, MA [*Location identifier*] [*FAA*]   (FAAL)
FMH.......... Fat-Mobilizing Hormone [*Medicine*]
FMH.......... Federal Meteorological Handbook
FMH.......... Federation Mondiale de l'Hemophilie [*World Federation of Hemophilia*]   (EAIO)
FMH(P)...... Fetal Maternal Hemorrhage [*Medicine*]
FMH.......... Fluoromethylhistidine [*Biochemistry*]
FMH.......... Focus on Mental Health [*Quezon City*] [*A publication*]
FMH.......... Freemasons' Hall [*Freemasonry*]   (ROG)
FMH.......... Friends Meeting House [*Quakers*]
FMH.......... Radiobeacon Combined with Fan Marker [*Aviation*]   (FAAC)
FmHA........ Farmers Home Administration [*Formerly, FHA*] [*Department of Agriculture*]
FMHC ...... Federation of Mental Health Centers [*Defunct*]   (EA)
FMHiS ...... Historical Association of Southern Florida, Miami, FL [*Library symbol*] [*Library of Congress*]   (LCLS)
Fm Home Sci ... Farm and Home Science [*A publication*]
FMHS ...... Freely Moving Human Subject
FMHW ...... Federation of Mental Health Workers [*British*]
FMI........... Daughters of Mary Immaculate [*Marianist Sisters*] [*Roman Catholic religious order*]
FMI........... Failure Mode Indicator   (MUGU)
FMI........... Fils de Marie Immaculee [*Sons of Mary Immaculate*] [*Saint Fulgent, France*]   (EAIO)
FMI........... Financial Management Initiative [*British*]
FMI........... First Market Intelligence Ltd. [*Information service or system*]   (IID)
FMI........... Flexible Modular Interface
FMI........... Flow Measurement and Indication   (DEN)
FMI........... Fluid Metering, Incorporated
FMI........... Fonds Monetaire International [*International Monetary Fund*]
FMI........... Food Marketing Institute   (EA)
FMI........... Ford Marketing Institute
FMI........... Franciscan Sisters of Mary Immaculate of the Third Order of St. Francis of Assisi [*Roman Catholic religious order*]
FMI........... Franklin McLean Memorial Research Institute [*University of Chicago*] [*Research center*]   (RCD)
FMI........... Franklin Multi-Income Trust [*NYSE symbol*]   (SPSG)
FMI........... Free Motion Impedance
FMI........... Freight Management International [*Australia*]   (ADA)
FMI........... Frequency Modulation Intercity Relay Broadcasting
FMI........... Friedrich Miescher Institute [*Switzerland*]
FMI........... Functional Management Inspection [*Military*]
FMI........... Future Manned Interceptor [*Military*]
FMI........... Kalemi [*Zaire*] [*Airport symbol*]   (OAG)
FMi........... Merritt Island Public Library, Merritt Island, FL [*Library symbol*] [*Library of Congress*]   (LCLS)
FMIA......... Federal Meat Inspection Act
FMIAA ..... Fitness Motivation Institute of America Association   (EA)
FMiB .... Brevard County Library System, Merritt Island, FL [*Library symbol*] [*Library of Congress*]   (LCLS)
FMIC........ Flight Manual Interim Changes
FMIC........ Frequency Monitoring and Interference Control [*Radio*]
FMIC........ Front Malaysian Islamic Council [*Political party*]   (FEA)
FMICDK .. Fund Management Identification Code [*Military*]   (AFM)
FMICDK .. Food Microstructure [*A publication*]
FMICS ...... Financial Management Information and Control System [*Navy*]
FMILS........ Force Modernization Integrated Logistics Support

F Min........ Fortschritte der Mineralogie [*A publication*]
FMIP........ Financial Management Improvement Program
FMIR........ Frustrated Multiple Internal Reflectance
FMIRA...... Fighter Multifunctional Inertial Reference Assembly   (MCD)
FMI Rev .... FMI [*Federation of Malta Industries*] Review [*A publication*]
FMIS .... Farm Market Infodata Service [*Department of Agriculture*] [*Database*]
FMIS .... Financial Management Information System
FMIS .... Fiscal Management Information System
FMIS .... Fleet Management Information System [*Software*]
FMIS .... Force Modernization Information System   (MCD)
F MIST ..... Fiat Mistura [*Let a Mixture Be Made*] [*Pharmacy*]   (ROG)
FMIT........ Fusion Materials Irradiation Test Facility [*Proposed*]
FMJ........... Federation Museums Journal [*A publication*]
FMJ........... Financial Mail (Johannesburg) [*A publication*]
FMJ........... Folk Music Journal [*A publication*]
FMJC........ Federation Mondiale de Jeunesse Catholique [*World Federation of Catholic Youth*]
FMJD........ Federation Mondiale du Jeu de Dames [*World Draughts (Checkers) Federation - WDF*] [*Dordrecht, Netherlands*]   (EAIO)
FMJD........ Federation Mondiale de la Jeunesse Democratique [*World Federation of Democratic Youth - WFDY*] [*Budapest, Hungary*]   (EAIO)
FMJFC....... Federation Mondiale des Jeunesses Feminines Catholiques
FMJLR...... Federation Mondiale des Jeunesses Liberales et Radicales [*World Federation of Liberal and Radical Youth*]
F MK .... Markka [*Monetary unit*] [*Finland*]
FML........... Fault Message Line   (MCD)
FML........... Feedback, Multiple Loop
FML........... File Manipulation Language
FML........... Final Materials List [*NASA*]   (NASA)
FML........... Flexible Membrane Liner [*For waste containment*]
FML........... Flight Mechanics Laboratory [*Texas A & M University*] [*Research center*]   (RCD)
FML........... Fluid Mechanics Laboratory [*MIT*] [*Research center*]
FML........... Fluorometholone [*Anti-inflammatory drug*]
FML........... FM Resources Limited [*Vancouver Stock Exchange symbol*]
FML........... Fort Mill, SC [*Location identifier*] [*FAA*]   (FAAL)
FML........... French Men of Letters [*A publication*]
FML........... Front Mounting Light
f-ml---........ Mali [*MARC geographic area code*] [*Library of Congress*]   (LCCP)
FML........... University of Miami, Law Library, Coral Gables, FL [*OCLC symbol*]   (OCLC)
FMLC........ Fetal Mouse Liver Cell [*Bioassay*]
F/MLDG ... Finish Moulding [*Automotive engineering*]
FMLED7 ... FEMS [*Federation of European Microbiological Societies*] Microbiology Letters [*A publication*]
FMLF .... File Management Loading Facility
FMLM........ French Military Liaison Mission [*World War II*]
FMLN .... Frente Farabundo Marti de Liberacion Nacional [*Farabundo Marti National Liberation Front*] [*El Salvador*]   (ECON)
FMLN .... Frente Morazanista de Liberacion Nacional [*Morazanista National Liberation Front*] [*Honduras*] [*Political party*]   (PD)
FMLP .... Field Mirror Landing Practice
FMLP .... Formyl(methionyl)(leucyl)phenylalanine [*Biochemistry*]
FMLS .... Forum for Modern Language Studies [*A publication*]
FMLY........ Family
FMLY........ Family Bancorp [*NASDAQ symbol*]   (NQ)
FMLY........ Formerly
FMM .... [*From the Latin for*] Brothers of Mercy [*Roman Catholic religious order*]
FMM .... Fact. The Money Management Magazine [*A publication*]
FMM .... Federation of Malaysian Manufacturers   (DS)
FMM .... Ferromagnetic Material
FM & M...... Fibber McGee and Molly [*Radio program*]
FMM .... Filmmakers' Monthly [*A publication*]
FMM .... Financial Management Manual [*NASA*]
FMM .... Finite Message Machine [*Telecommunications*]
FMM .... First Maritime Mining Corp. Ltd. [*Toronto Stock Exchange symbol*]
FMM .... Fizika Metallov i Metallovedenie [*A publication*]
FMM .... Fort Morgan, CO [*Location identifier*] [*FAA*]   (FAAL)
FMM .... Framework Molecular Models
FMM .... Franciscan Missionaries of Mary [*Roman Catholic women's religious order*]
FMM .... French Military Mission   (NATG)
FMM .... University of Miami, Music Library, Coral Gables, FL [*OCLC symbol*]   (OCLC)
FMMA ...... Antananarivo/Arivonimamo [*Madagascar*] [*ICAO location identifier*]   (ICLI)
FMMA ...... Floor Machine Manufacturers Association
FMMC ...... Fixed Mylar Metallized Capacitor
FMMC ...... Malaimbandy [*Madagascar*] [*ICAO location identifier*]   (ICLI)
FMMD ...... Antananarivo [*Madagascar*] [*ICAO location identifier*]   (ICLI)
FMMD ...... Form Mandrel [*Tool*]   (AAG)
FMMD ...... Miami-Dade Community College, Miami, FL [*Library symbol*] [*Library of Congress*]   (LCLS)
FMME....... Antsirabe [*Madagascar*] [*ICAO location identifier*]   (ICLI)

FMME....... Fund for Multinational Management Education   (EA)

FMME....... Racal-Milgo, Inc., Miami, FL [*Library symbol*] [*Library of Congress*]   (LCLS)

FMMEA...... Fizika Metallov i Metallovedenie [*A publication*]

FMMF...... Flexure Monitor Mounting Fixture

FMMG...... Antsalova [*Madagascar*] [*ICAO location identifier*]   (ICLI)

Fm Mgmt... Farm Management [*A publication*]   (APTA)

FMMH....... Mahanoro [*Madagascar*] [*ICAO location identifier*]   (ICLI)

FMMI....... Antananarivo/Ivato [*Madagascar*] [*ICAO location identifier*]   (ICLI)

FMMJ....... Ambohijanahary [*Madagascar*] [*ICAO location identifier*]   (ICLI)

FMMK ...... Ankavandra [*Madagascar*] [*ICAO location identifier*]   (ICLI)

FMML....... Belo-Sur-Tsiribihina [*Madagascar*] [*ICAO location identifier*]   (ICLI)

FMMM ..... Antananarivo [*Madagascar*] [*ICAO location identifier*]   (ICLI)

FMMN ...... Miandrivazo [*Madagascar*] [*ICAO location identifier*]   (ICLI)

FMMO ...... Maintirano [*Madagascar*] [*ICAO location identifier*]   (ICLI)

FMMP....... Amparafaravola [*Madagascar*] [*ICAO location identifier*]   (ICLI)

FMMP....... Force Modernization Master Plan   (MCD)

FMMP....... Formylmethionyl (sulfonyl) Methyl Phosphate [*Biochemistry*]

FMMQ...... Ilaka-Est [*Madagascar*] [*ICAO location identifier*]   (ICLI)

FMMR ...... Morafenobe [*Madagascar*] [*ICAO location identifier*]   (ICLI)

FMMRI...... Franklin McLean Memorial Research Institute [*University of Chicago*] [*Research center*]

FMMRS .... Force Modernization Milestone Reporting System [*Army*]   (RDA)

FMMS...... Sainte-Marie [*Madagascar*] [*ICAO location identifier*]   (ICLI)

FMMT....... Toamasina [*Madagascar*] [*ICAO location identifier*]   (ICLI)

FMMTA..... Fizika Metallov i Metallovedenie [*A publication*]

FMMU...... Tambohorano [*Madagascar*] [*ICAO location identifier*]   (ICLI)

FMMV ...... Morondava [*Madagascar*] [*ICAO location identifier*]   (ICLI)

FMMX ...... Tsiroanomandidy [*Madagascar*] [*ICAO location identifier*]   (ICLI)

FMMY ...... Vatomandry [*Madagascar*] [*ICAO location identifier*]   (ICLI)

FMMZ ...... Ambatondrazaka [*Madagascar*] [*ICAO location identifier*]   (ICLI)

F/M/N....... Faith-Man-Nature [*from F/M/N Papers, National Council of Churches*]

FMN.......... Farmington [*New Mexico*] [*Airport symbol*]   (OAG)

FMN.......... Farmington, NM [*Location identifier*] [*FAA*]   (FAAL)

FMN.......... Federal Reserve Bank of Minneapolis. Quarterly Review [*A publication*]

FMN.......... Federation Mondiale de Neurologie [*World Federation of Neurology*]

FMN.......... Filmmakers' Newsletter [*A publication*]

FMN.......... Flavin Mononucleotide [*Biochemistry*]

FMN.......... Flight Motor Neuron [*Entomology*]

FMN.......... FMC Corp., Princeton, NJ [*OCLC symbol*]   (OCLC)

FMN.......... Formation

F MN .... Full Moon [*Astronomy*]   (ROG)

FMN.......... United States Department of Commerce, National Oceanic and Atmospheric Administration, Miami, FL [*Library symbol*] [*Library of Congress*]   (LCLS)

FMNA ...... Antsiranana/Arrachart [*Madagascar*] [*ICAO location identifier*]   (ICLI)

FMNBNA ... Frequency Modulation and Narrowband Noise Analyzer   (MCD)

FMNC .... Mananara-Nord [*Madagascar*] [*ICAO location identifier*]   (ICLI)

FMND....... Andapa [*Madagascar*] [*ICAO location identifier*]   (ICLI)

FMNE....... Ambilobe [*Madagascar*] [*ICAO location identifier*]   (ICLI)

FMNF....... Befandriana Nord [*Madagascar*] [*ICAO location identifier*]   (ICLI)

FMNG....... Port Berge [*Madagascar*] [*ICAO location identifier*]   (ICLI)

FMNH....... Antalaha [*Madagascar*] [*ICAO location identifier*]   (ICLI)

FMNH...... Field Museum of Natural History [*Chicago, IL*]

FMNH...... Flavin Mononucleotide [*Reduced*] [*Biochemistry*]

FMNHAS ... Field Museum of Natural History. Anthropological Series [*A publication*]

FMNJ....... Ambanja [*Madagascar*] [*ICAO location identifier*]   (ICLI)

FMNL...... Analalava [*Madagascar*] [*ICAO location identifier*]   (ICLI)

FMNM...... Mahajanga/Amborovy [*Madagascar*] [*ICAO location identifier*]   (ICLI)

FMNN....... Nosy-Be/Fascene [*Madagascar*] [*ICAO location identifier*]   (ICLI)

FMNO....... Soalala [*Madagascar*] [*ICAO location identifier*]   (ICLI)

FMNP....... Mampikony [*Madagascar*] [*ICAO location identifier*]   (ICLI)

FMNQ....... Besalampy [*Madagascar*] [*ICAO location identifier*]   (ICLI)

FMNR....... Maroantsetra [*Madagascar*] [*ICAO location identifier*]   (ICLI)

FMNS....... Sambava [*Madagascar*] [*ICAO location identifier*]   (ICLI)

FMNT ...... F & M National Corp. [*NASDAQ symbol*]   (NQ)

FMNT ...... Tsaratanana [*Madagascar*] [*ICAO location identifier*]   (ICLI)

FMNUAS ... Farmacia Nueva [*A publication*]

FMNV....... Vohemar [*Madagascar*] [*ICAO location identifier*]   (ICLI)

FMNW...... Antsohihy/Ambalabe [*Madagascar*] [*ICAO location identifier*]   (ICLI)

FMNX ...... Mandritsara [*Madagascar*] [*ICAO location identifier*]   (ICLI)

FMO.......... Facilities Maintenance Operations and Computerized Systems Show   (TSPED)

FMO .... Fast Moving Object

FMO .... Federal-Mogul [*NYSE symbol*]   (SPSG)

FMO .... Federation of Mobile Home Owners   (EA)

FMO .... Financial Management Office   (KSC)

FMO .... Fleet Mail Office [*British*]

FMO .... Fleet Maintenance Office [*or Officer*]

FMO .... Fleet Medical Officer

FMO .... Flight Management Office [*Air Force*]   (AFM)

FMO .... Flight Medical Officer [*Air Force*]

FMO .... Force Modernization Office [*Army*]   (RDA)

fmo .... Former Owner [*MARC relator code*] [*Library of Congress*]   (LCCP)

FMO .... Forms Management Officer [*Army*]   (AABC)

FMO .... Frequency Management Officer   (FAAC)

FMO .... Frontier Molecular Orbital Theory [*Physical chemistry*]

FMO .... Fuels Management Officer [*Air Force*]   (AFIT)

FMO .... Full Marching Order [*British military*]   (DMA)

FMO .... Fundamentals of Machine Operation [*John Deere Service Publications*] [*Moline, IL*] [*A publication*]

FMOC .... Fluorenylmethyloxycarbonyl [*Organic chemistry*]

FMod .... Filologia Moderna [*A publication*]

FMOF....... First Manned Orbital Flight [*NASA*]

FMOFEV .. First Manned Orbital Flight with EVA [*Extravehicular Activity*]   (MCD)

FMOFPL... First Manned Orbital Flight with Payload   (MCD)

FMOI .... Federation Mondiale des Organisations d'Ingenieurs [*World Federation of Engineering Organizations*]

FMonde ..... Francais dans le Monde [*A publication*]

F Moore ..... English King's Bench Reports [*72 English Reprint*] [*A publication*]   (DLA)

FMOP .... Frequency Modulation on the Pulse   (NG)

FMORAO ... Folia Morphologica [*Prague*] [*A publication*]

FMP.......... Ferrous Metal Powder

FMP.......... Field Maintenance Party [*Aviation*]

FMP.......... Field Marching Pack

FMP.......... Financial Management Plan

FMP.......... First Menstrual Period [*Medicine*]

FMP.......... Fishery Management Plan

FMP.......... Fleet Modernization Plan [*Navy*]

FMP.......... Fleet Modernization Program   (MCD)

FMP.......... Flight Mechanic's Panel

FMP.......... Fluid Motion Panel [*of the British Aeronautical Research Council*]   (MCD)

FMP.......... Force Modernization Program

FMP.......... Formable Metallized Plastics [*Industrial technology*]

FMP.......... FORSCOM [*Forces Command*] Mobilization Plan [*DoD*]

FMP.......... Freeport-McMoRan Oil & Gas Co. [*NYSE symbol*]   (SPSG)

FMP.......... Fructose Monophosphate [*Biochemistry*]

FMP.......... Fuel Maintenance Panel   (AAG)

FMP.......... Full Marching Pack [*Military*]

FMP.......... Functional Maintenance Procedure

FMPA........ Federated Master Plumbers of Australia

FMPA........ Federation Mondiale pour la Protection des Animaux [*World Federation for the Protection of Animals*] [*Also known as WFPA and WTB*]

FMPA........ Fellow of the Master Photographers Association [*British*]   (DBQ)

FMPC........ Federation of Motion Picture Councils   (EA)

FMPC........ Feed Materials Production Center [*AEC*]

FMPD........ Fort Monmouth Procurement Division

FMPEC ...... Financial Management Plan for Emergency Conditions [*Army*]

FMPI........ Future Medical Products, Incorporated [*NASDAQ symbol*]   (NQ)

FMPM....... Family Manned Planetary Mission

FM-PM ..... Frequency Modulation - Phase Modulation [*RADAR*]

FMPO........ Fort Monmouth Procurement Office

Fm Policy... Farm Policy [*A publication*]   (APTA)

FMPP........ Federal Merit Promotion Program

FMPP........ Flexible Multipipeline Processor

FMPP........ Foundation of Motion Picture Pioneers   (EA)

FMPS........ Federation of Modern Painters and Sculptors   (EA)

FMPS .... Form Pads [*Tool*]   (AAG)

FMPS .... FORTRAN [*Formula Translating System*] Mathematical Programming System [*Data processing*]   (IEEE)

FMPS .... Functional Mathematical Programming System [*Data processing*]

FMPT........ First Material Processing Test [*Japan*]

FMQ......... Fayalite Magnetite Quartz (Buffer) [*Geophysics*]

FMQ......... Federal Reserve Bank of Minneapolis. Quarterly Review [*A publication*]

FMQ......... Fichier MARC [*Machine-Readable Cataloging*] Quebecois [*Source file*] [*UTLAS symbol*]

FMQ......... Frequency-Modulated Quartz

FMQB .... Friday Morning Quarterback [*In title FMQB Album Report*]

FMR .... Failure and Malfunction Report [*NASA*]   (KSC)

FMR .... Fairbourne Miniature Railway [*Wales*]

FMR .... Fellow of the Association of Health Care Information and Medical Records Officers [*British*]   (DBQ)

FMR .... Ferromagnetic Resonance

FMR .... Field Modification Report

FMR .... Field Modification Request [*Military*]
FMR .... Fife Mounted Rifles [*British military*]   (DMA)
FMR .... Final Meteorological Radiation
FMR .... Financial Management Report   (AABC)
FMR .... Fire Movement Range   (MCD)
FMR .... Flanagan McAdam Resources, Inc. [*Toronto Stock Exchange symbol*]
FMR .... Former
FMR .... Franco Maria Ricci [*A publication*]
FMR .... Freeport-McMoRan Oil & Gas Royalty Trust [*NYSE symbol*]   (SPSG)
FMR .... Frequency-Modulated RADAR
FMR .... Frequency-Modulated Ranging   (MCD)
FMR .... Frequency-Modulated Receiver [*Telecommunications*]
FMR .... Frontier Mounted Rifles [*British military*]   (DMA)
FMR .... Function Maximum Rate   (NASA)
FMR .... Funds Management Record [*Military*]   (AFM)
FMR .... Les Fusiliers Mont Royal [*British military*]   (DMA)
f-mr--- .... Morocco [*MARC geographic area code*] [*Library of Congress*]   (LCCP)
FMRA .... Foreign Media Representatives Association
FMRC .... Fixed Motor Run Capacitor
FMRD .... Flight Mission Rules Document [*NASA*]   (KSC)
FMRD .... Fundmuenzen der Roemischen Zeit in Deutschland [*A publication*]
FMREC ..... Force Mobilization Review and Evaluation Committee [*Military*]   (MCD)
Fm Res News ... Farm Research News [*A publication*]
Fmr Forester ... Farmer and Forester [*A publication*]
FMRL .... Form Roll
FMRL .... Functional Machine Representation Language [*Data processing*]   (CSR)
FMRLA ..... Fortschritte der Mineralogie [*A publication*]
FMRLY ..... Formerly   (EY)
Fmrs Bull Dep Agric (Can) ... Farmer's Bulletin. Department of Agriculture (Canada) [*A publication*]
Fmr's Bull (Rhodesia) ... Farmer's Bulletin (Rhodesia) [*A publication*]
Fmrs Bull US Dep Agric ... Farmers' Bulletin. United States Department of Agriculture [*A publication*]
Fmrs Newsl ... Farmers' Newsletter [*A publication*]   (APTA)
Fmr Stk Breed ... Farmer and Stock Breeder [*A publication*]
FMRT .... Final Meteorological Radiation Tape
FMS .... Facilities Management System
FMS .... Factory Management System [*General Electric Co.*]
FMS .... Factory Mutual System [*Formerly, AFMFIC*] [*Group of four insurance companies and an engineering organization*]
FMS .... Fallout Monitoring Station [*Civil Defense*]
FMS .... Fat-Mobilizing Substance [*Medicine*]
FMS .... Fecal Management System [*NASA*]   (KSC)
FMS .... Federal Malay States [*A publication*]
FMS .... Federal Music Society   (EA)
FMS .... Federated Malay States
FMS .... Federation of Materials Societies   (EA)
FMS .... Federation Mondiale des Sourds [*World Federation of the Deaf - WFD*] [*Rome, Italy*]   (EA)
FMS .... Feline McDonough Sarcoma [*Virus*]
FMS .... Fellow of the Institute of Management Services [*British*]   (DBQ)
FMS .... Fellow of the Medical Society [*British*]
FMS .... Fellow of the Meteorological Society [*British*]
FMS .... Field Maintenance Shop [*Army*]   (NATG)
FMS .... Field Maintenance Squadron [*Air Force*]   (MCD)
FMS .... Field Music School [*Marine Corps*]
FMS .... Fighter Missile System
FMS .... File Maintenance System   (MCD)
FMS .... File Management Supervisor [*Honeywell, Inc.*]
FMS .... File Management System   (AFIT)
FMS .... Final Multiple Score   (NVT)
FMS .... Financial Management System
FMS .... Financial Managers Society   (EA)
FMS .... Financial Managers' Statement [*Financial Managers' Society*] [*A publication*]
FMS .... First Marathon, Inc. [*Toronto Stock Exchange symbol*]
FMS .... Fleet Material Support [*Navy*]
FMS .... Fleet Music School
FMS .... Flexible Manufacturing System
FMS .... Flight Management System
FMS .... Flight Mission Simulation Test   (MCD)
FMS .... Flight Motion Simulator
FMS .... Floating Machine Shop
FMS .... Floating Maintenance Shop   (MCD)
FMS .... Flow Measuring System
FMS .... Flux Monitoring System [*Nuclear energy*]   (NRCH)
FMS .... Food Management System [*or Subsystem*]   (MCD)
FMS .... Force Measuring System   (KSC)
FMS .... Foreign Military Sales   (AFM)
FMS .... Foreign Military Service   (MCD)
FMS .... Forms Management System [*Data processing*]
FMS .... Fort Myers Southern Railroad Co. [*AAR code*]
FMS .... FORTRAN [*Formula Translating System*] Monitor System [*Data processing*]

FMS .... Fratres Maristae Scholarum [*Marist Brothers of the Schools*] [*Also known as Little Brothers of Mary*]   (EAIO)
FMS .... Free-Machining Steel
FMS .... Frequency Mixer Stage
FMS .... Frequency-Multiplexed Subcarrier
FMS .... Frequency Multiplier Storer
FMS .... Full Mouth Series [*Dentistry*]
FMS .... Fuze Maintenance Spares   (NG)
FMSA .... Ambalavao [*Madagascar*] [*ICAO location identifier*]   (ICLI)
FMSA .... Fellow of the Mineralogical Society of America
FMSA .... First Mutual Savings Association of Florida [*NASDAQ symbol*]   (NQ)
FMSA .... Foreign Military Sales Act   (AFIT)
FMSA .... Future Military Systems Authority
FMSAEG ... Fleet Missile Systems Analysis and Evaluation Group [*Navy*]
FMSAEGA ... Fleet Missile Systems Analysis and Evaluation Group Annex [*Navy*]   (MCD)
FMSAEL... Fleet Missile Systems Analysis and Evaluation Laboratory   (MCD)
FMsB .... Barry College, Miami Shores, FL [*Library symbol*] [*Library of Congress*]   (LCLS)
FMSB .... Beroroha/Antsoa [*Madagascar*] [*ICAO location identifier*]   (ICLI)
FMSB .... First Mutual Savings Bank [*Bellevue, WA*] [*NASDAQ symbol*]   (NQ)
FMSC .... Federal Manual for Supply Cataloging   (AABC)
FMSC .... Federation Mondiale des Societes de Cuisiniers [*World Association of Cooks Societies - WACS*]   (EA)
FMSC .... Film Magazine Stowage Container   (MCD)
FMSC .... Fixed Motor Starting Capacitor
FMSC .... Franciscan Missionary Sisters of the Sacred Heart [*Roman Catholic religious order*]
FMSC .... Mandabe [*Madagascar*] [*ICAO location identifier*]   (ICLI)
FMSCD2 .. Canada. Fisheries and Marine Service. Industry Report [*A publication*]
FMSCR ..... Foreign Military Sales Credit [*Financing*]
FMSD .... Tolagnaro [*Madagascar*] [*ICAO location identifier*]   (ICLI)
FMSE .... Betroka [*Madagascar*] [*ICAO location identifier*]   (ICLI)
FMSF .... Fianarantsoa [*Madagascar*] [*ICAO location identifier*]   (ICLI)
FMSF .... Foreign Military Sales Financing
FMSG .... Farafangana [*Madagascar*] [*ICAO location identifier*]   (ICLI)
FMSGT ..... Field Music Sergeant [*Marine Corps*]
FMSHRD ... Federal Mine Safety and Health Review Decisions [*A publication*]   (DLA)
FMSI .... Fidelity Medical, Incorporated [*NASDAQ symbol*]   (NQ)
FMSI .... Filii Mariae Salutis Infirmorum [*Sons of Mary, Health of the Sick*] [*Roman Catholic religious order*]
FMSI .... Folk Music Society of Ireland   (EAIO)
FMSI .... Food Machinery Service Institute   (EA)
FMSI .... Friction Materials Standards Institute   (EA)
FMSI .... Ihosy [*Madagascar*] [*ICAO location identifier*]   (ICLI)
FMSJ .... Franciscan Missionaries of St. Joseph [*Mill Hill Sisters*] [*Roman Catholic religious order*]
FMSJ .... Manja [*Madagascar*] [*ICAO location identifier*]   (ICLI)
FMSK .... Manakara [*Madagascar*] [*ICAO location identifier*]   (ICLI)
FMSL .... Bekily [*Madagascar*] [*ICAO location identifier*]   (ICLI)
FMSL .... Fort Monmouth Signal Laboratory [*Army*]
FMSM .... Federation Mondiale pour la Sante Mentale [*World Federation for Mental Health*]
FMSM .... Mananjary [*Madagascar*] [*ICAO location identifier*]   (ICLI)
FMSMP .... Foreign Military Sales Management Plan   (AFIT)
FMSN .... Tanandava-Samangoky [*Madagascar*] [*ICAO location identifier*]   (ICLI)
FMSO .... Fleet Material Support Office [*Navy*]
FMSO .... Foreign Military Sales Order [*Army*]   (AABC)
FMSO .... Ranohira [*Madagascar*] [*ICAO location identifier*]   (ICLI)
FMSp .... Fiziko-Matematichesko Spisanie [*A publication*]
FMSP .... [*A*] Fool and His Money Are Soon Parted   (ROG)
FMSP .... Foreign Military Sales Program [*Army*]   (AABC)
FMSP .... Frequency Modulation Signal Processor   (NASA)
FMSPA4 ... Flora Malesiana. Series I. Spermatophyta [*A publication*]
FMSq .... Field Maintenance Squadron [*Air Force*]   (AFM)
FMSR .... Federated Malay States Reports [*A publication*]   (DLA)
FMSR .... Federation des Mouvements Socialistes Regionalistes de la Reunion [*Federation of Socialist Regionalist Movements of Reunion*] [*Political party*]   (PPW)
FMSR .... Formaster Corp. [*NASDAQ symbol*]   (NQ)
FMSR .... Morombe [*Madagascar*] [*ICAO location identifier*]   (ICLI)
FMSRDD .. Canada. Fisheries and Marine Service. Manuscript Report [*A publication*]
FMSS .... Financial Management Systems [*A publication*]
FMST .... Field Missile Specification Test
FMST .... Field Missile System Test
FMSt .... Folkmalsstudier [*A publication*]
FMST .... Foreign Military Sales Training
FMST .... Frequency Mass Spectrometer Tube
FM St .... Fruehmittelalterliche Studien [*A publication*]
FMST .... Toliara [*Madagascar*] [*ICAO location identifier*]   (ICLI)
FMSV .... Betioky [*Madagascar*] [*ICAO location identifier*]   (ICLI)
FMSVA ..... Fluid Mechanics. Soviet Research [*A publication*]

FMSVR	Federated Malay Straits Volunteer Reserve [*British military*] (DMA)
FMSWR	Flexible Mild Steel Wire Rope
FMSY	Ampanihy [*Madagascar*] [*ICAO location identifier*] (ICLI)
FMSZ	Ankazoabo [*Madagascar*] [*ICAO location identifier*] (ICLI)
FMT	Facilities Maintenance Team [*Military*]
FMT	Factory Marriage Test
FMT	Field Maintenance Technician
FMT	Field Modification Task (MCD)
FMT	Flight Management Team [*Skylab*] [*NASA*]
FMT	Flush Metal Threshold [*Technical drawings*]
FMT	Force Modernization Training [*Military*]
FMT	Foreign Material for Training (MCD)
FMT	Foreign Military Training (CINC)
FMT	Foremost Energy Corp. [*Vancouver Stock Exchange symbol*]
FMT	Format
FMT	Foundation for Medical Technology (EA)
FMT	Freemasons Tavern [*Freemasonry*] (ROG)
FMT	Frequency-Modulated Transmitter [*Telecommunications*]
FMT	Friction Measurement Test
FMTA	Federation Mondiale de Travailleurs Agricoles [*World Federation of Agricultural Workers - WFAW*] (EAIO)
FMTA	Flash Mass Thermal Analysis (KSC)
FMTC	Fairmont Chemical Co., Inc. [*Newark, NJ*] [*NASDAQ symbol*] (NQ)
FMTE	Field Maintenance Test Equipment
Fm Technol ...	Farm Technology [*A publication*]
FMTM	Friction Materials Test Machine
FMTNM ...	Federation Mondiale des Travailleurs Non-Manuels [*World Federation of Trade Unions of Non-Manual Workers - WFNMW*] [*Antwerp, Belgium*] (EAIO)
FMTO	Form Tool
FMTP	File Management Transaction Processor
FMTR	Florida Missile Test Range (MUGU)
FMTR	Formatter (MCD)
FMTS	Federation Mondiale des Travailleurs Scientifiques [*World Federation of Scientific Workers - WFSW*] (EAIO)
FMTS	Field Maintenance Test Set
FMTS	Field Maintenance Test Station [*Military*] (AFIT)
FMTS	Flat Moving Target Screen [*Weaponry*] (INF)
FMTV	Family of Medium Tactical Vehicles [*Military*] (RDA)
FMTV	Frequences Modulation and Television [*A publication*]
FMU	Files Management Unit [*Data processing*]
FMU	Financial Management Unit [*LIMRA*]
FMU	Force Measurement Unit
FMU	Function Memory Unit
FMU	Functional Mock-Up (KSC)
f-mu---	Mauritania [*MARC geographic area code*] [*Library of Congress*] (LCCP)
FMU	University of Miami, Coral Gables, FL [*Library symbol*] [*Library of Congress*] (LCLS)
FMU-L	University of Miami, Law Library, Coral Gables, FL [*Library symbol*] [*Library of Congress*] (LCLS)
F-MuLV....	Friend Murine Leukemia Virus
FMU-M.....	University of Miami, Medical Library, Miami, FL [*Library symbol*] [*Library of Congress*] (LCLS)
FMU-Mu...	University of Miami, Music Library, Coral Gables, FL [*Library symbol*] [*Library of Congress*] (LCLS)
FMU-R	University of Miami, Rosenstiel School of Marine and Atmospheric Sciences, Miami, FL [*Library symbol*] [*Library of Congress*] (LCLS)
FMUSIC ...	Federation of Military and United Services Institutes of Canada
F Music Ntbk ...	Film Music Notebook [*A publication*]
FMV	Fair Market Value [*Bargaining term*]
FMV	United States Veterans Administration Hospital, Miami, FL [*Library symbol*] [*Library of Congress*] (LCLS)
FMVEME ...	Federation of Malaya Volunteer Electrical and Mechanical Engineers [*British military*] (DMA)
FMVF Rpt ...	Federal Motor Vehicle Fleet Report [*United States*] [*A publication*]
FMVJ	Federation Mondiale des Villes Jumelees-Cites Unies [*United Towns Organisation - UTO*] (EA)
FMVRC.....	Federation of Malaya Volunteer Reconnaissance Corps [*British military*] (DMA)
FMVSS.....	Federal Motor Vehicle Safety Standard
FMVTAV ..	Farmacevtski Vestnik [*A publication*]
FMVTPS...	Federal Motor Vehicle Theft Prevention Standard [*Automotive engineering*]
FMW	Federation of Masons of the World (EA)
FMW	First Main Watch
f-mw---	Malawi [*MARC geographic area code*] [*Library of Congress*] (LCCP)
FMW	Mount Fremont [*Washington*] [*Seismograph station code, US Geological Survey*] (SEIS)
FMW	World University-Miami, Miami, FL [*Library symbol*] [*Library of Congress*] (LCLS)
FMWC	First Midwest Corporation [*NASDAQ symbol*] (NQ)
FMWF.......	Free Methodist World Fellowship (EA)
FMWWR ...	Fire, Mildew, Water, and Weather Resistant (MCD)
FMX	Frequency-Modulated Transmitter [*Telecommunications*] (KSC)
FMX	Full Mouth Radiograph [*Dentistry*]
FMXBAL ..	Frontiers of Matrix Biology [*A publication*]
FMY	Foreign Missons of Yarumal [*Colombia*] (EAIO)
FMY	Fort Myers [*Florida*] [*Airport symbol*] (OAG)
FMY	Fort Myers, FL [*Location identifier*] [*FAA*] (FAAL)
f-mz---	Mozambique [*MARC geographic area code*] [*Library of Congress*] (LCCP)
FN	Fabrique Nationale [*Belgium*]
FN	Falcon Jet Centre Ltd. [*Great Britain*] [*ICAO designator*] (FAAC)
FN	False Negative [*Medicine*]
FN	Fantastic Novels [*A publication*]
FN	Fence [*Technical drawings*]
FN	Fibronectin [*Biochemistry*]
FN	Film News [*A publication*]
FN	Filologiceskie Nauki [*A publication*]
FN	Filosofskie Nauki [*A publication*]
FN	Financial [*Rate*] [*Value of the English pound*]
FN	Find Number (MSA)
F-N	Finger to Nose Test [*Neurology*]
F to N	Finger to Nose Test [*Neurology*]
FN	Fireman [*Nonrated enlisted man*] [*Navy*]
FN	First Name
FN	First National Corporation of California [*AMEX symbol*] (SPSG)
FN	Flat or Nested [*Freight*]
FN	Flat Nose [*Projectile*]
FN	Flight Nurse
FN	Fog Nautophone [*Navigation charts*]
FN	Folklore. Rivista di Tradizioni Popolari (Naples) [*A publication*]
FN	Food and Nutrition [*A publication*]
FN	Footnote
FN	Fort Smith News [*A publication*]
FN	Fortid og Nutid [*A publication*]
Fn	Fortnightly [*A publication*]
FN	Franco-Nevada Mining Corp. [*Toronto Stock Exchange symbol*]
FN	Freelance Network (EA)
FN	French Navy (NATG)
FN	Friends of Nature (EA)
FN	Front National [*National Front*] [*France*] [*Political party*] (PPW)
FN	Fruitarian Network (EA)
FN	Full Employment [*Economics*]
FN	Functional Network
FN	Futures Network [*Ormskirk, Lancashire, England*] (EA)
Fn	[*The*] Holy Bible in Modern English (1903) [*Ferrar Fenton*] [*A publication*] (BJA)
FN	Night First Class [*Airline fare code*]
fn-----	Sudan (Region) [*MARC geographic area code*] [*Library of Congress*] (LCCP)
FNA	Federation of National Associations (EA)
FNA	Fellow of the Indian National Science Academy [*Formerly, FNI*]
FNA	Final Approach [*Aviation*]
FNA	Finanzarchiv [*A publication*]
FNA	Fine-Needle Aspiration [*Medicine*]
FNA	Flora North America Program [*Defunct*] (EA)
FNA	Florenville, LA [*Location identifier*] [*FAA*] (FAAL)
FNA	Following Named Airmen
FNA	For Necessary Action (ADA)
FNA	Freetown [*Sierra Leone*] [*Airport symbol*] (OAG)
FNA	French North Africa
FNA	Frequency Network Analyzer
FNA	Fujitsu Network Architecture [*Fujitsu Ltd.*] [*Japan*]
FNA	Fuming Nitric Acid (KSC)
FNA	Functional Name Addresses
FNAA	Fast Neutron Activation Analysis [*Analytical chemistry*]
FNAB	Fine-Needle Aspiration Biopsy [*Medicine*]
FNaC	Collier County Free Public Library, Naples, FL [*Library symbol*] [*Library of Congress*] (LCLS)
FNAC	Federation Nationale d'Achats des Cadres [*Initials alone now used as name of discount-store chain in France*] [*Pronounced "f-nak"*]
FNAC	First National Cincinnati Corp. [*NASDAQ symbol*] (NQ)
FNAEA......	Fellow of the National Association of Estate Agents [*British*] (DBQ)
FNAF........	Front National pour l'Algerie Francaise [*National Front for French Algeria*] [*Political party*]
FNAI..........	Federazione Nazionale Autoferrotranvieri Internavigatori [*National Federation of Bus, Railway, and Tram Workers*] [*Italy*] (EY)
FNAI..........	Florida Natural Areas Inventory [*Information service or system*] (EISS)
FNAL........	Fermi National Accelerator Laboratory [*Also, FERMILAB*] [*Batavia, IL*] [*Department of Energy*]
FNAM.......	Ambriz [*Angola*] [*ICAO location identifier*] (ICLI)
FNAMA	Arizona. Bureau of Mines. Field Notes [*A publication*]
FNAN	Luanda [*Angola*] [*ICAO location identifier*] (ICLI)

FNAO........ Fellow of the National Association of Opticians [*British*] (DAS)
FNAOE..... Federation of National AFS Organizations in Europe [*Brussels, Belgium*] (EAIO)
F/Nav......... Flight Navigator (AIA)
FNAWS.... Foundation for North American Wild Sheep (EA)
FNB .... Falls City, NE [*Location identifier*] [*FAA*] (FAAL)
FNB .... First Chicago Corp. [*NYSE symbol*] (SPSG)
FNB .... Fitzherbert's Natura Brevium [*A publication*] (DLA)
FNB .... Food and Nutrition Board (EA)
FNB .... Fort Necessity National Battlefield, Farmington, PA [*OCLC symbol*] (OCLC)
FNBA .... Fellow of the North British Academy (DAS)
FNBA .... First National Bancorp of Allentown [*NASDAQ symbol*] (NQ)
FNBC......... M'Banza-Congo [*Angola*] [*ICAO location identifier*] (ICLI)
FNBF.......... Florida National Banks of Florida, Inc. [*NASDAQ symbol*] (NQ)
FNBG......... Benguela [*Angola*] [*ICAO location identifier*] (ICLI)
FNBR......... Fast Neutron Breeder Reactor [*Nuclear energy*] (DEN)
FNBR......... FNB Rochester Corp. [*Rochester, NY*] [*NASDAQ symbol*] (NQ)
FNC .... Fast Neutron Cavity
FNC .... Financial Computing [*A publication*]
FNC .... Fine-Needle Cholangiography [*Gastroenterology*]
FNC .... Finlay Fork [*British Columbia*] [*Seismograph station code, US Geological Survey*] [*Closed*] (SEIS)
FNC .... Fixed Niobium Capacitor
FNC .... Flexible Nylon Coupling
FNC .... Focus National Mortgage Corp. [*Toronto Stock Exchange symbol*]
FNC .... Frente Nacional Constitucionalista [*National Constitutionalist Front*] [*Ecuador*] [*Political party*] (PPW)
FNC .... Frente Nacional Opositora [*National Opposition Front*] [*Panama*] [*Political party*] (PPW)
FNC .... Friends of Nicaraguan Culture (EA)
FNC .... Funchal [*Portugal*] [*Airport symbol*] (OAG)
FNCA .... Cabinda [*Angola*] [*ICAO location identifier*] (ICLI)
FNCA .... Federation of Nordic Commercial Agents [*Stockholm, Sweden*] (EA)
FNCA .... First National Corporation [*Mandeville, LA*] [*NASDAQ symbol*] (NQ)
FNCB......... Camembe [*Angola*] [*ICAO location identifier*] (ICLI)
FNCB......... First National City Bank [*Later, Citibank*] [*New York City*]
FNCC......... Cacolo [*Angola*] [*ICAO location identifier*] (ICLI)
FNCC......... Federation Nationale des Cooperatives de Cereales
FNCETA ...... Federation Nationale des Centres d'Etudes Techniques Agricoles
FNCH......... Chitato [*Angola*] [*ICAO location identifier*] (ICLI)
FNCI.......... Financial News Composite Index [*Pronounced "fancy"*] [*Financial News Network*]
FNCM .... Camabatela [*Angola*] [*ICAO location identifier*] (ICLI)
FNCM .... Fellow, National College of Music [*London, England*] (ADA)
FNCRT...... Fellow of the National College of Rubber Technology [*British*]
FNCTN...... Function (FAAC)
FNCUMA ... Federation Nationale des Cooperatives d'Utilisation de Materiel Agricole
FNCV .... Cuito Cuanavale [*Angola*] [*ICAO location identifier*] (ICLI)
FNCX......... Camaxilo [*Angola*] [*ICAO location identifier*] (ICLI)
FNCZ......... Cazombo [*Angola*] [*ICAO location identifier*] (ICLI)
FND.......... Baltimore, MD [*Location identifier*] [*FAA*] (FAAL)
FND.......... Facility Need Date (NASA)
FND.......... Fast Neutron Dose
FND.......... Fender[s] [*Freight*]
FND.......... Finnemore's Notes and Digest of Natal Cases [*A publication*] (DLA)
FND.......... Found
FND.......... Foundation [*Technical drawings*]
FND.......... Frank Nelson Doubleday [*American publisher*]
FND.......... Friends of Neil Diamond (EA)
FND.......... Frontul National Democratic [*National Democratic Front*] [*Romania*] [*Political party*] (PPE)
fnd .... Funder/Sponsor [*MARC relator code*] [*Library of Congress*] (LCCP)
FNDB .... Damba [*Angola*] [*ICAO location identifier*] (ICLI)
FNDD........ Founded
FNDD........ Funded (ROG)
FNDF......... Federal National Democratic Front [*Burma*] [*Political party*] (PD)
FNDG........ Founding
FNDG........ Funding (KSC)
FNDH......... Foreign National Direct Hire [*Military*]
FNDN........ Foundation
FNDP......... Frente Nacional Democratico Popular [*Popular National Democratic Front*] [*Mexico*] (PD)
FNDPA...... Foundations of Physics [*A publication*]
FNDR......... Fender [*Automotive engineering*]
FNDR .... Founder
FNDTS..... Fellow of the Non-Destructive Testing Society of Great Britain
FNDV-A.... Finance and Development [*A publication*]
F & NE....... Fairchild & Northeastern Railway

FNE .... Faisceaux Nationalistes Europeens [*European Nationalist Alliances*] [*France*] (PD)
FNE .... Fane [*Papua New Guinea*] [*Airport symbol*] (OAG)
fne .... Fine [*Quality of the bottom*] [*Nautical charts*]
FNE .... Following Named Enlisted Personnel
FNE .... Free Nerve Ending [*Anatomy*]
FNEA .... Federation of National Electrolysis Associations [*Defunct*] (EA)
FNECInst.. Fellow of the North East Coast Institution of Engineers and Shipbuilders [*British*]
FNEEAA ... Flora van Nederland/Flora Neerlandica [*A publication*]
FNEG .... False Negative [*Medicine*]
FNEORID ... Following Named Enlisted Member Organization Indicated
FNERAS ... Following Named Enlisted Members Are Relieved Assignment
FNES .... Field Network Evaluation Study [*Survey*]
FNET......... Fundsnet, Inc. [*NASDAQ symbol*] (NQ)
FNEUC..... Federation Nationale des Etudiants des Universites Canadiennes [*National Federation of Canadian University Students*]
F Neur Psyc ... Fortschritte der Neurologie, Psychiatrie, und Ihrer Grenzgebiete [*A publication*]
F News ...... Film News [*A publication*]
FNF............ Fidelity National Financial, Inc. [*AMEX symbol*] (SPSG)
FNF............ Foundation for the New Freeman (EA)
FNFA .... Fellow of the National Federation of Accountants [*British*] (DAS)
FNFC......... First National Financial Co. [*British*]
FNFC......... First Nationwide Financial Corporation [*NASDAQ symbol*] (NQ)
FNFL......... Forces Navales Francaises Libres [*Free French Naval Forces*] [*World War II*]
FNFP......... First Nations Financial Project (EA)
FNG .... Fada N'Gourma [*Upper Volta*] [*Airport symbol*] (OAG)
FNG .... Firan Corp. [*Toronto Stock Exchange symbol*]
FNG .... Fleet/Norstar Financial Group, Inc. [*NYSE symbol*] (SPSG)
f-ng--- .... Niger [*MARC geographic area code*] [*Library of Congress*] (LCCP)
FNGAA ..... Federation Nationale des Groupements Agricoles d'Approvisionnement
FNGB .... First Northern Savings Bank SA [*NASDAQ symbol*] (NQ)
FNGI .... N'Giva [*Angola*] [*ICAO location identifier*] (ICLI)
FNGP .... Federation Nationale des Gaullistes de Progres [*National Federation of Progressive Gaullists*] [*France*] [*Political party*] (PPW)
FNGU........ N'Gunza [*Angola*] [*ICAO location identifier*] (ICLI)
FNH.......... Flashless Nonhygroscopic [*Gunpowder*]
FNH.......... Focal Nodular Hyperplasia [*Medicine*]
FNHO........ Forum of National Hispanic Organizations (EA)
FNHP........ Federation of Nurses and Health Professionals (EA)
FNHU........ Huambo [*Angola*] [*ICAO location identifier*] (ICLI)
FNI .... Facial Nerve Involvement [*Medicine*]
FNI .... Fan In
FNI .... Federation Naturiste Internationale [*International Naturist Federation*]
FNI .... Fellow of the National Institute of Sciences in India [*Later, FNA*]
FNI .... Fellow of the Nautical Institute [*British*]
FNI .... FNI Fashion, Inc. [*Vancouver Stock Exchange symbol*]
FNI .... Following Named Individuals
FNI .... Foreign National Indirect (NVT)
FNI .... Nimes [*France*] [*Airport symbol*] (OAG)
FNIAL...... Fellow of the National Institute of Arts and Letters [*British*]
FNIB.......... Federation Nationale des Infirmieres Belges [*A publication*]
FNIC.......... Food and Nutrition Information Center [*Department of Agriculture*] (IID)
FNIF .... Florence Nightingale International Foundation (EA)
FNIH .... Federation Nationale de l'Industrie Hoteliere [*National Federation of the Hotel Industry*] [*France*] (EY)
FNIH .... Fellow of the National Institute of Hardware [*British*] (DBQ)
FNIMH ..... Fellow of the National Institute of Medical Herbalists [*British*]
FNIN .... Financial Industries Corp. [*NASDAQ symbol*] (NQ)
FNIN .... Fridtjof Nansen Institute. Newsletter [*A publication*]
FNiO.......... Okaloosa-Walton Junior College, Niceville, FL [*Library symbol*] [*Library of Congress*] (LCLS)
FNJ............ Fort Gordon, GA [*Location identifier*] [*FAA*] (FAAL)
FNJ............ Front National de la Jeunesse [*National Youth Front*] [*France*] (PD)
FNJ............ Pyongyang [*North Korea*] [*Airport symbol*] (OAG)
FNJ FDC... United States Food and Drug Administration. Notices of Judgment: Foods [*A publication*] (DLA)
FNK.......... Fin Creek, AK [*Location identifier*] [*FAA*] (FAAL)
FNKU........ Kuito/Bie [*Angola*] [*ICAO location identifier*] (ICLI)
FNL .... Fansteel, Inc. [*NYSE symbol*] (SPSG)
FNL .... Fantasy Newsletter [*A publication*]
FNL .... Final (NASA)
FNL .... Financial Mail [*A publication*]
FNL .... Fitzgerald Newsletter [*A publication*]
FNL .... Five New Laender [*Lands*] [*Name given to former East German territory after unification*] (ECON)
FNL .... Flight Navigator's Licence [*British*] (AIA)

FNL .... Fort Collins/Loveland, CO [*Location identifier*] [*FAA*]   (FAAL)
FNL .... Friends of the National Libraries [*British*]
FNL .... Fund for New Leadership   (EA)
FNLA .... Front National de Liberation de l'Angola [*Angolan National Liberation Front*]   (PD)
FNLB .... Front National de Liberation de Bretagne [*National Liberation Front of Brittany*] [*France*]   (PD)
FNLB .... Lobito [*Angola*] [*ICAO location identifier*]   (ICLI)
FNLG .... Forschungen zur Neueren Literaturgeschichte [*A publication*]
FNLG .... Front National de Liberation Guyanais [*Guiana National Liberation Front*] [*French Guiana*]   (PD)
FNLLP ...... Formyl(norleucyl)(leucyl)phenylalanine [*Biochemistry*]
FNLO .... French Naval Liaison Officer   (NATG)
FNLT .... Final Test, Inc. [*NASDAQ symbol*]   (NQ)
FNLU .... Luanda/4 De Fevereiro [*Angola*] [*ICAO location identifier*]   (ICLI)
FNLW........ Foundation for Non-Lethal Warfare   (EA)
FNM .... Fancamp Resources Ltd. [*Vancouver Stock Exchange symbol*]
FNM .... Fantastic Novels Magazine [*A publication*]
FNM .... Federal National Mortgage Association [*Wall Street slang name: "Fannie Mae"*] [*NYSE symbol*]   (SPSG)
FNM .... Ferrocarriles Nacionales de Mexico [*National Railways of Mexico*]
FNM .... Financial Network Manager   (BUR)
FNM .... Florence Nightingale Medal [*Australia*]
FNM .... Free National Movement [*Bahamas*] [*Political party*]   (PPW)
FNMA .... Federal National Mortgage Association
FNMA .... Front National Martiniquais pour l'Autonomie [*Martinique National Front for Autonomy*] [*Political party*]   (PPW)
FNMA .... Malanje [*Angola*] [*ICAO location identifier*]   (ICLI)
FNmB .... Barry College, North Miami, FL [*Library symbol*] [*Library of Congress*]   (LCLS)
FNME .... Menongue [*Angola*] [*ICAO location identifier*]   (ICLI)
FNMKA ..... Finommechanika-Mikrotechnika [*A publication*]
FNMO .... Mooamedes/Yuri Gagarin [*Angola*] [*ICAO location identifier*]   (ICLI)
FNMQ .... Maquela [*Angola*] [*ICAO location identifier*]   (ICLI)
FNN .... Financial News Network [*Cable-television system*]
FNN .... Franconia Notch [*New Hampshire*] [*Seismograph station code, US Geological Survey*] [*Closed*]   (SEIS)
FNNG .... Finnigan Corp. [*NASDAQ symbol*]   (NQ)
FNNG .... Negage [*Angola*] [*ICAO location identifier*]   (ICLI)
FNNI .... Financial News Network, Incorporated [*NASDAQ symbol*]   (NQ)
FNO .... Clinton, IA [*Location identifier*] [*FAA*]   (FAAL)
FNO .... Fan Out
FNO .... Following Named Officers
FNOA .... Following Named Officers and Airmen
FNOC .... Fleet Numerical Oceanographic Center [*Marine science*]   (MSC)
FNOGF ..... Federazione Nazionale Orafi Gioiellierei Fabbricanti [*Jewellers and Goldsmiths Federation*] [*Italy*]   (EY)
FNOIO ...... Fleet Naval Ordnance Inspecting Officer
FNP .... Family Nurse Practitioner
FNP .... Federazione Nazionale Pensionati [*National Federation of Pensioners' Union*] [*Italy*]   (EY)
FNP .... Fijian Nationalist Party [*Political party*]   (PPW)
FNP .... Floating Nuclear Plant [*or Powerplant*] [*ERDA*]
FNP .... Foundation for National Progress   (EA)
FNP .... Frente Nacional de Panama [*Panamanian National Front*] [*Political party*]   (PD)
FNP .... Front-End Network Processor
FNP .... Fusion Point
FNP .... University of North Florida, Jacksonville, FL [*OCLC symbol*]   (OCLC)
FNPA........ Foreign Numbering Plan Area [*AT & T*] [*Telecommunications*]   (TEL)
FNPA........ Porto Amboim [*Angola*] [*ICAO location identifier*]   (ICLI)
FNPB .... Sanza Pombo [*Angola*] [*ICAO location identifier*]   (ICLI)
FNPC........ [*The*] First National Pennsylvania Corp. [*NASDAQ symbol*]   (NQ)
FNPG .... Forschungen zur Neueren Philosophie und Ihrer Geschichte [*A publication*]
FNPGA...... Fortschritte der Neurologie, Psychiatrie, und Ihrer Grenzgebiete [*A publication*]
FNPH .... Foreningen Nordiska Pappershistoriker [*Association of Nordic Paper Historians - NPH*] [*Stockholm, Sweden*]   (EAIO)
FNPLAI..... Fauna Polski [*A publication*]
FNPLT ...... Front Nationaliste Progressiste pour la Liberation de la Tunisie [*Progressive Nationalist Front for the Liberation of Tunisia*] [*Political party*]   (PD)
FNP Newsl Food Nutr Health ... FNP [*Food & Nutrition Press, Inc.*] Newsletter. Food, Nutrition, and Health [*A publication*]
FNPO .... For NASA Personnel Only   (KSC)
FNPOR...... Federation of National Professional Organizations for Recreation   (EA)
FNPP........ Floating Nuclear Power Plant Study [*Marine science*]   (MSC)
FNPQAX... Folia Neuropsiquiatrica del Sur y Este de Espana [*A publication*]
FNPR........ Friends of National Public Radio   (EA)

FNPT......... Fusion Point
FNPTA...... Finnish Paper and Timber Journal [*A publication*]
FNQBAR... Faune du Quebec [*A publication*]
FNR .... File Next Register
FNR .... Ford Nuclear Reactor
FNR .... Foundations Resources [*Vancouver Stock Exchange symbol*]
FNR .... Funter Bay [*Alaska*] [*Airport symbol*]   (OAG)
FNR .... Funter Bay, AK [*Location identifier*] [*FAA*]   (FAAL)
f-nr--- .... Nigeria [*MARC geographic area code*] [*Library of Congress*]   (LCCP)
FNRA......... Federal National Railroad Association [*Proposed railroad corporation*] [*Nickname: Fannie Rae*]
FNRC......... Federated Natural Resources Corporation [*NASDAQ symbol*]   (NQ)
FNRI.......... Federation Nationale des Republicains Independants [*National Federation of Independent Republicans*] [*France*] [*Political party*]   (PPW)
FNRRDF ... Focus on Renewable Natural Resources [*A publication*]
FNS .... Agriculture, Food, and Nutrition Service. Publications [*A publication*]
FNS .... Failure Notification Sheet   (KSC)
FNS .... Family and Neighborhood Services
FNS .... Feedback Node Set
FNS .... Feminist News Service
FNS .... First National State Bancorporation [*NYSE symbol*]   (SPSG)
FNS .... Flash-Nitrogen Supply
FNS .... Food and Nutrition Service [*Department of Agriculture*]
FNS .... Frontier Nursing Service   (EA)
FNS .... Functional Neuromuscular Stimulation [*Physiotherapy*]
FNS .... Functional Nomenclature Signal
FNSA .... Frente Nacional Socialista Argentino [*Argentinian National Socialist Front*] [*Political party*]   (PD)
FNSA .... Saurimo [*Angola*] [*ICAO location identifier*]   (ICLI)
FNSBB ...... Federation Nationale des Syndicats du Batiment et du Bois, Inc. [*National Federation of Shipyard and Woodworkers Unions*]
FNSC......... Federation pour une Nouvelle Societe Caledonienne [*Federation for a New Caledonian Society*] [*Political party*]   (PPW)
FNSCA6 .... Forensic Science [*Later, Forensic Science International*] [*A publication*]
FNSF .... Fast Night Striking Force [*British military*]   (DMA)
FNSH .... Finish   (MSA)
FNSI .... Finding of No Significant Impact
FNSID .... Fellow of the National Society of Interior Designers
FNSII .... Federation Nationale des Syndicats d'Infirmieres et d'Infirmiers [*National Federation of Nurses' Unions - NFNU*]
FNSL .... Fixed Nozzle Slow [*or Short*] Landing   (MCD)
FNSO .... Soyo [*Angola*] [*ICAO location identifier*]   (ICLI)
FNT .... Failure Notification Telex   (MCD)
FNT .... Flight International, Inc. [*Atlanta, GA*] [*FAA designator*]   (FAAC)
FNT .... Flint [*Michigan*] [*Airport symbol*]   (OAG)
FNT .... Flint, MI [*Location identifier*] [*FAA*]   (FAAL)
FNT .... Foilseachain Naisiunta Tta [*A publication*]
Fnt............. Fonit [*Record label*] [*Italy*]
FNT .... Fort Nelson [*Hobart*] [*Tasmania*] [*Seismograph station code, US Geological Survey*] [*Closed*]   (SEIS)
FNT .... Front   (FAAC)
FNTBB ...... Federation Nordique des Travailleurs du Batiment et du Bois [*Nordic Federation of Building and Wood Workers - NFBWW*]   (EAIO)
FNTC .... Frente Nacional de Trabajadores y Campesinos [*National Workers' and Peasants' Front*] [*Peru*] [*Political party*]   (PPW)
FNTGNS... Frontogenesis [*Meteorology*]   (FAAC)
FNTLYS... Frontolysis [*Meteorology*]   (FAAC)
FNTM .... Funtime, Inc. [*NASDAQ symbol*]   (NQ)
FNTO .... Toto [*Angola*] [*ICAO location identifier*]   (ICLI)
FNU .... Family Nursing Unit
FNU........... First Name Unknown
FNU........... Forces des Nations Unies [*United Nations Forces*]
FNU........... Front National Uni [*United National Front*] [*The Comoros*]
FNUA .... Luau [*Angola*] [*ICAO location identifier*]   (ICLI)
FNUB .... Lubango [*Angola*] [*ICAO location identifier*]   (ICLI)
FNUE .... Fonds des Nations Unies pour l'Enfance [*United Nations Children's Fund*]   (EAIO)
FNUE .... Luena [*Angola*] [*ICAO location identifier*]   (ICLI)
FNUG........ Federation of NCR [*NCR Corp.*] User Groups   (EA)
FNUG........ Uige/Vige [*Angola*] [*ICAO location identifier*]   (ICLI)
FNUK .... Front National Uni des Komores [*National United Front of the Comoros*] [*Political party*]   (PD)
FNUR .... Fonds des Nations Unies pour les Refugies [*United Nations Funds for Refugees*]
F Nutr .... Food and Nutrition [*A publication*]
F Nutr Bull ... Food and Nutrition Bulletin [*A publication*]
FNV .... Partido Federacion Nacional Velasquista [*National Velasquista Federation*] [*Ecuador*] [*Political party*]   (PPW)
FNWA .... Federal Noxious Weed Act
FNWA .... Foreign National Weather Agency
FNWB .... FNW Bancorp, Inc. [*Elgin, IL*] [*NASDAQ symbol*]   (NQ)

FNWC .... Fleet Numerical Weather Center [*Monterey, CA*] [*Navy*]
FNWF .... Fleet Numerical Weather Facility
FNWK ...... Wako-Kungo [*Angola*] [*ICAO location identifier*] (ICLI)
FNX .... FINAIR [*Miami, FL*] [*FAA designator*] (FAAC)
FNX .... Fort Knox Gold Resources, Inc. [*Toronto Stock Exchange symbol*]
FNXA .... Xangongo [*Angola*] [*ICAO location identifier*] (ICLI)
FNY .... Federal Reserve Bank of New York. Quarterly Review [*A publication*]
FNY .... Food Policy [*A publication*]
FNY .... French Navy
FNZ .... Friends of the National Zoo (EA)
FNZ .... Huntingburg, IN [*Location identifier*] [*FAA*] (FAAL)
FNZ .... Zuivelzicht [*A publication*]
FNZE .... N'Zeto/N'Zeto [*Angola*] [*ICAO location identifier*] (ICLI)
FNZIA .... Fellow of the New Zealand Institute of Architects
FNZIAS.... Fellow of the New Zealand Institute of Agricultural Science
FNZIC ...... Fellow of the New Zealand Institute of Chemistry
FNZIE ...... Fellow of the New Zealand Institution of Engineers
FNZLA ...... Fellow of the New Zealand Library Association
FNZP........ Flunitrazepam [*A hypnotic*]
FO .... Alon, Inc. [*ICAO aircraft manufacturer identifier*] (ICAO)
FO .... Fabrication Order (MCD)
FO .... Fabrication Outline (MCD)
FO .... Factory Order
FO .... Facultad de Odontologia [*A publication*]
FO .... Faculty of Ophthalmologists [*British*]
FO .... Fade Out [*Films, television, etc.*]
FO .... Fail Open [*Nuclear energy*] (NRCH)
FO .... Fail Operation [*NASA*] (KSC)
FO .... Fairest One [*Genotype of Phlox paniculata*]
FO .... Fan Out
FO .... Faroe Islands [*ANSI two-letter standard code*] (CNC)
FO .... Fast Operating [*Relay*]
FO .... Fatty Oil
F/O .... Feature Film Only (ADA)
FO .... Federal Official
FO .... Fiber Optic [*Data transmission*] (TEL)
FO .... Field Office [*or Officer*]
FO .... Field Operational [*Test*] (NATG)
FO .... Field Order
FO .... Filter Output (AAG)
FO .... Finance Officer [*Army*]
F & O .... Financial and Operating Data for Investor-Owned Water Companies [*A publication*] (EAAP)
FO .... Fine Old
FO .... Firing Order
FO .... Firm Offer [*Business term*]
FO .... Firm Order [*Business term*]
FO .... First Officer (ADA)
FO .... First Open [*First class train compartment*] (DCTA)
FO .... Fishery Officer [*Ministry of Agriculture, Fisheries, and Food*] [*British*]
FO .... Fitting Out [*Navy*] (NG)
FO .... Fixed Oil
FO .... Flag Officer [*Navy*]
FO .... Flash Operate Relay
FO .... Flash Override [*Telecommunications*] (TEL)
FO .... Flat Oval [*Technical drawings*]
FO .... Fleet Operations [*Navy*] (MCD)
FO .... Flight Officer [*Air Force*]
FO .... Flight Order
FO .... Flight Orderly
FO .... Fluoroorotate [*Organic chemistry*]
FO .... Flying Officer [*British*]
FO .... Foldout (MSA)
FO .... Folia Orientalia [*A publication*]
FO .... Folio
Fo .... Folklore [*A publication*]
FO .... Foot Orthosis [*Medicine*]
FO .... For Orders
FO .... Foramen Ovale [*Anatomy*]
F/O .... Force Objective (CINC)
FO .... Force Out [*Baseball*]
FO .... Force Ouvriere [*A publication*]
FO .... Foreign Object
FO .... Foreign to Occupation [*Insurance*]
FO .... Foreign Office
FO .... Foreign Order (ADA)
Fo .... Forestry [*A publication*]
Fo .... Fornvaennen [*A publication*]
fo .... Forsterite [*CIPW classification*] [*Geology*]
FO .... Fortissimo [*Very Loud*] [*Music*] (ROG)
FO .... Fortune [*A publication*]
Fo .... Forum [*A publication*]
FO .... Forward Oblique (CAAL)
FO .... Forward Observer [*Military*]
Fo .... Fourier Number [*IUPAC*]
FO .... Fraction Optimizing
FO .... Fred. Olsen Flyselskap A/S [*Norway*] [*ICAO designator*] (FAAC)

FO .... Free Out [*Shipping*]
FO .... Free Overside
FO .... Frente Obrero [*Workers' Front*] [*Nicaragua*] [*Political party*] (PD)
FO .... Fridays Only [*British railroad term*]
FO .... Friends Outside (EA)
FO .... Fronto-Occipital [*Anatomy*]
FO .... Fuel Oil
F/O .... Fuel to Oxidizer [*Ratio*]
FO .... Full Organ [*Music*]
FO .... Full Out [*Typesetting*]
F/O .... Full Out Terms [*Business term*] [*British*] (ROG)
FO .... Functional Objective (KSC)
FO .... Oil-Immersed Forced-Oil-Cooled [*Transformer*] (IEEE)
FO .... Orlando Public Library, Orlando, FL [*Library symbol*] [*Library of Congress*] (LCLS)
FOA .... Faculty of Advocates [*British*] (DAS)
FOA .... Failure to Obtain Action (AAG)
FOA .... Federation of Orthodontic Associations (EA)
FOA .... Fellow of Advertising [*British*]
FOA .... Field Office Assistant [*Red Cross*]
FOA .... Field Operating Agency (MCD)
FOA .... Financial Operations Association (EA)
FOA .... First of America Bank [*NYSE symbol*] (SPSG)
FOA .... Fitting Out Availability [*Navy*]
FOA .... Flora, IL [*Location identifier*] [*FAA*] (FAAL)
FOA .... Fluoroorotic Acid [*Organic chemistry*]
FOA .... FOB Airport ["*INCOTERM,*" *International Chamber of Commerce official code*]
FOA .... Football Officials Association
FOA .... Forced Oil and Air (MSA)
FOA .... Foreign Affairs [*A publication*]
FOA .... Foreign Operations Administration [*Later, ICA*]
FOA .... Foresters of America
FOA .... Forsvarets Forskningsanstalt [*Research Institute of National Defense*] [*Information service or system*] (IID)
FOA .... Free on Aircraft [*Cargo delivery term for export traffic*] (DCTA)
FOA .... Friends of Animals (EA)
FOA .... Fugitive Other Authorities [*FBI standardized term*]
FOA .... Oil-Immersed Forced-Oil-Cooled with Forced-Air Cooler [*Transformer*] (IEEE)
FOAA .... Flying Optometrists Association of America (EA)
FOAC .... Flag Officer, Aircraft Carriers (NATG)
FOAC .... Flag Officer, Atlantic Coast [*Canada*]
FOADAS... FAO [*Food and Agriculture Organization of the United Nations*] Agricultural Development Paper [*A publication*]
FOAF........ Friend of a Friend [*Urban folklore term coined by Rodney Dale*]
FOAFB ..... Forbes Air Force Base [*Kansas*] (AAG)
FOAGB4 ... Foreign Agriculture [*A publication*]
FOAIB ...... Flag Officer, Admiralty Interview Board [*Navy*] [*British*]
FOALAI .... Folia Allergologica [*Later, Folia Allergologica et Immunologica Clinica*] [*A publication*]
FOAM .... Fluorouracil, Oncovin [*Vincristine*], Adriamycin, Mitomycin C [*Antineoplastic drug regimen*]
FOAM .... Fragmenting Offensive Aerial Mine (MCD)
FOAMP..... Foreign Aerospace Material Production (MCD)
FOAMP.... Fraternal Order of Air Mail Pilots [*Defunct*] (EA)
Fo-An-Si ... Forsterite-Anorthite-Silica [*Lunar geology*]
FOAP........ Foreign Aircraft Production (MCD)
FOAPH ..... Federation Ouest Africaine des Associations pour la Promotion des Personnes Handicapees [*West African Federation of Associations for the Advancement of Handicapped Persons - WAFAH*] [*Bamako, Mali*] (EAIO)
Foard Mer Sh ... Foard on Merchant Shipping [*A publication*] (DLA)
FOA Rep.... FOA [*Foersvarets Forskningsanstalt*] Reports [*A publication*]
FOASA5.... FAO [*Food and Agriculture Organization of the United Nations*] Agricultural Studies [*A publication*]
FOB .... Federal Office Building
FOB .... Feet out of Bed
FOB .... Fetal Occult Blood [*Medicine*]
FOB .... Fiber Optics Board (MCD)
FOB .... Fiberoptic Bronchoscopy [*Also, FB*] [*Medicine*]
FOB .... Fine Old Blend [*Wines and spirits*]
FOB .... First Overtone Band
FOB .... Flannery O'Connor Bulletin [*A publication*]
FOB .... Flight Operations Building [*NASA*] (KSC)
FOB .... Forward Observer Bombardment [*Military*]
FOB .... Forward Operating Base [*Air Force*] (AFM)
FOB .... Fractional Orbital Bombardment (MCD)
FOB .... Free on Board ["*INCOTERM,*" *International Chamber of Commerce official code*] [*Shipping*]
FOB .... Freight on Board (AAG)
FOB .... Fresh Off the Boat
FOB .... Front of Board (MSA)
FOB .... Frontiers of Biology [*Elsevier Book Series*] [*A publication*]
FOB .... Fuel on Board [*Aviation*]
FOB .... Full of Brooklyns [*Coined by baseball broadcaster Red Barber, initialism refers to bases loaded with Brooklyn Dodgers*] [*Obsolete*]

FOb............ Ormond Beach Public Library, Ormond Beach, FL [Library symbol] [Library of Congress]   (LCLS)
FOBA .... Free on Board Airport [Business term]
FOBAA...... Flag Officer, British Assault Area
FOBB......... First Oak Brook Bancshares, Inc. [Oak Brook, IL] [NASDAQ symbol]   (NQ)
FOBES ...... Fiber Optics Borehole Earth Strainmeter [Geology]
FOBGA8 ... Folia Biologica [Cracow] [A publication]
FOBLAN... Folia Biologica [Prague] [A publication]
FOBO .... Fort Bowie National Historic Site
FOBS .... Fiber Optics Borescope
FOBS .... Fractional Orbital Bombardment System
FOBSR ...... Forward Observer [Military]
FOBTSU ... Forward Observer Target Survey Unit [Military]
FOBu .... Flannery O'Connor Bulletin [A publication]
FOC .... 57 Oldsmobile Chapter   (EA)
FOC .... 505th Ordnance Company   (EA)
FOc .... Central Florida Regional Library, Ocala, FL [Library symbol] [Library of Congress]   (LCLS)
FOC .... Face of Concrete [Technical drawings]
FOC .... Faint-Object Camera [Astronomy]
FOC .... Farthest-On Circle   (NVT)
FOC .... Father of Chapel [Shop steward] [British]
FOC .... Ferrari Owners Club   (EA)
FOC .... Fiber Optics and Communications [Information Gatekeepers, Inc.] [Information service or system] [No longer available online]   (CRD)
FOC .... Fiber Optics Communications [Data transmission]   (TEL)
FOC .... Final Operational Capability [Military]   (AFM)
FOC .... Fire Offices Committee [British]   (AIA)
FOC .... Fixed Oil Capacitor
FOC .... Flag of Convenience   (ADA)
FOC .... Flight Operating Costs
FOC .... Flight Operations Center
FOC .... Focal   (MSA)
FOC .... Focsani [Romania] [Seismograph station code, US Geological Survey]   (SEIS)
Foc .... Focus [A publication]
FOC .... Focus   (KSC)
Foc............ Focus/Midwest [A publication]
FOC .... Follow-On Contract
FOC .... Foreign Object Check   (MCD)
FOC .... Foreign Operating Committee [World War II]
FOC .... Forward Observer COLIDAR [Coherent Light Detecting and Ranging]
FOC .... Free on Car [Shipping]
FOC .... Free of Charge [Business term]
FOC .... Friends of Community   (EA)
FOC .... From Own Correspondent
FOC .... Fuel Oil Cooler
FOC .... Full Operational Capability   (NASA)
FOC .... Full Operational Capability Program [Navy]   (NVT)
FOC .... Fuzhou [China] [Airport symbol]   (OAG)
FOCA .... Field Operating Cost Agency [Army]
FOCA .... Fiero Owners Club of America   (EA)
FOCA .... Formula One Constructors' Association [Australia]
FOCA .... Fort Caroline National Memorial
FOCA .... Free and Open Church Association [British]
FOCA .... Friends of the Origami Center of America   (EA)
FOCAAT... Folia Cardiologica [A publication]
FOCAF...... Flag Officer, Commander, Her Majesty's Australian Fleet   (CINC)
FOCAL...... Formula Calculator [Digital Equipment Corp.]   (CSR)
Focale Mag ... Focale Magazine [A publication]
FOCAP...... Federacion Odontologica Centro America y Panama [Odontological Federation of Central America and Panama]
FOCAS ...... Faint-Object Classification and Analysis System [Astronomy]
FOCAS ...... Fiber Optic Communications for Aerospace Systems   (MCD)
FOCAS ...... Flag Officer, Carriers and Amphibious Ships [Navy] [British]
FOCAS ...... Ford [Automobile] Operating Cost Analysis System
FOcC......... Central Florida Community College, Ocala, FL [Library symbol] [Library of Congress]   (LCLS)
FOCC......... Fiber Optic Coordinating Committee [American National Standards Institute] [Telecommunications]
FOCC......... Fleet Operations Control Center [Navy]
FOCCEUR ... Fleet Operations Control Center, Europe [Navy]
FOCCPAC ... Fleet Operations Control Center, Pacific Fleet [Navy]
Foc Exc Chi ... Focus on Exceptional Children [A publication]
Foc F .... Focus on Film [A publication]
FOCH......... Forward Channel [Telecommunications]
FOCHDJ... Food Chemistry [A publication]
FOCI......... Farrand Optical Company, Incorporated
FOCI......... Foreign Ownership, Control, or Influence
FOCIA ...... Folia Clinica Internacional [A publication]
FOCL......... Fort Clatsop National Memorial
FOC/LAN ... International Fiber Optics and Communications Exposition and Show on Local Area Networks [TSPED]
FOCM .... Feminists on Children's Media [Defunct]   (EA)
FOCMA .... Feline Orcornavirus-Associated Cell Membrane Antigen [Immunology]

FOCNAS... Flag Officer Commanding, North Atlantic Station [British military]   (DMA)
FOCNAY... Food in Canada [A publication]
FOCOA ... Fiero Owners Club of America   (EA)
FOCOBANK ... Foreign Commerce Bank [Switzerland]
FOCOHANA ... Fourier Coefficient Harmonic Analyzer
FO/COT... Firing Out/Consolidate Operability Tests   (MCD)
Foc Proj F .. Focus Project. Folklore Computerized Studies Technical Report [A publication]
FOCRIN.... Flag Officer Commanding, Royal Indian Navy [British military]   (DMA)
FOCS......... Fiber-Optic Chemical Sensor [Analytical chemistry]
FOCS......... Fiberchem, Inc. [NASDAQ symbol]   (NQ)
FOCSL ...... Fleet Oriented Consolidated Stock List [Navy]
FOCSL ...... Forecastle
FO'C'SLE ... Forecastle   (ROG)
FOCT......... Flag Officer, Carrier Training [British military]   (DMA)
FOCUS...... Financial and Operations Combined Uniform Single Report
FOCUS...... Fire Operational Characteristics Using Simulation [System for comparing organizations for wildland fire protection services in cost-effective terms] [Department of Agriculture, Forest Services]
Focus .... Focus on Indiana Libraries [A publication]
Focus .... Focus/Midwest [A publication]
FOCUS...... For Our Children's Unpaid Support   (EA)
FOCUS...... For Our Christian Understanding [Program]
FOCUS...... Forecasting Control and Updating Schedule   (MCD)
FOCUS...... Form of Control Users System   (MCD)
FOCUS...... Formal Officer Career Utilization Structure [Military]
FOCUS...... Forum of Control Data Users [Later, VIM, Inc.]
Focus AACN ... Focus on American Association of Critical Care Nurses [Later, Focus on Critical Care] [A publication]
Focus Crit Care ... Focus on Critical Care [A publication]
Focus Excep Child ... Focus on Exceptional Children [A publication]
Focus on F ... Focus on Film [A publication]
Focus Indiana Libr ... Focus on Indiana Libraries [A publication]
Focus Indo ... Focus on Indonesia [A publication]
Focus Jpn... Focus Japan [A publication]
Focus Renewable Nat Resour ... Focus on Renewable Natural Resources [A publication]
FOCWA .... Flag Officer Commanding West Africa [British]
FOD........... Fear of Death
FOD........... Field Officer of the Day [Army]   (AABC)
FOD........... Field Operations Department
FOD........... Flag Officer, Denmark   (NATG)
FOD........... Flashblindness Orientation Device
FOD........... Flight Operations Directorate [or Division] [Apollo] [NASA]
FOD........... Fluidic Output Device
FOD........... Foreign Object Damage
FOD........... Fort Dodge [Iowa] [Airport symbol]   (OAG)
FOD........... Fort Dodge, IA [Location identifier] [FAA]   (FAAL)
FOD........... Free of Damage [Business term]
FOD........... Free of Disease [Medicine]
FOD........... Functional Operational Design
FODA .... Fort Davis National Historic Site
FODAAS... Field Online Data Acquisition and Analysis System
FODC .... Friends of David Cassidy   (EA)
FODEDF... Folia Dendrologica [A publication]
F-O Dis...... Feeling-Oriented Discussion
FODL......... Fiber Optics Data Link   (MCD)
FODN......... Foothills Dempster Newsletter [A publication]
FODO......... Fort Donelson National Military Park
FoDokAB... Forschungsdokumentation zur Arbeitsmarkt- und Berufsforschung [Deutsche Bundesanstalt fuer Arbeit] [Federal Republic of Germany] [Information service or system]   (CRD)
FODS......... Fraud and Overservicing Detection System   (ADA)
FODW........ Friends of Dennis Wilson   (EA)
FOE .... Females Opposed to Equality
FOE .... Ferro Corp. [NYSE symbol]   (SPSG)
FOE .... Field Operational Evaluation
FOE .... Flight Operations Engineer   (MCD)
FOE .... Follow-On Evaluation
FOE .... Foreign-Object Elimination [Manufacturing]
FOE .... Friends of the Earth   (EA)
FOE .... Grand Aerie, Fraternal Order of Eagles   (EA)
FOE .... Topeka [Kansas] Forbes [Airport symbol]   (OAG)
FOE .... Topeka, KS [Location identifier] [FAA]   (FAAL)
FOEB......... Fuel Oil Equivalent Barrel
FOEG .... Forschungen zur Ost Europaeischen Geschichte [A publication]
FOEGAN .. Food Engineering [New York] [A publication]
FOEI......... Friends of the Earth International   (EAIO)
Foeldmuevel Min Allami Gazd Foeigazgatosaga (Budapest) ... Foeldmuevelesuegyi Miniszterium. Allami Gazdasagok Foeigazgatosaga (Budapest) [A publication]
Foel Dr Int ... Foelix. Droit International Prive [A publication]   (DLA)
Foelix Droit Int Princ ... Foelix. Droit International Prive [A publication]
FOEMA7... Faunistisch-Oekologische Mitteilungen [A publication]
FOENAA .. Folia Endocrinologica [A publication]
FOENIC.... Foeniculum [Fennel] [Pharmacy]   (ROG)

FOEP........	Frog Otolith Experiment Package [*NASA*]
FOES........	Fine Old Extra Special
FOET........	Follow-On Evaluation Test
FOEU	Foreign Organizations' Employees Union
FOF...........	Face of Finish [*Technical drawings*]
FOF...........	Factory-of-the-Future
FOF...........	Facts on File, Inc.
FOF...........	Field of Fire [*Military*] (MCD)
FOF...........	Field Observing Facility [*National Center for Atmospheric Research*]
FOF...........	First Operational Flight (MCD)
FOF...........	First Orbital Flight [*NASA*] (NASA)
FOF...........	Fish Oil Film
FOF...........	Flag Officer, Flotilla [*British military*] (DMA)
FOF...........	Flight Operations Facility
FoF...........	Foto File Systems, Inc., Kansas City, KS [*Library symbol*] [*Library of Congress*] (LCLS)
FOF...........	Friends of Families [*Defunct*] (EA)
FOF...........	Friends of the FBI (EA)
FOF...........	Friends of Freddy (EA)
FOF...........	Fukuoka Occupation Force
FOF...........	Full Octave Filter
FOF...........	Fund of Funds
FOFA........	Follow-On Forces Attack
FOFA........	Friends of Free Asia [*Defunct*]
FOFATUSA ...	Federation of Free African Trade Unions of South Africa
FOFAX......	Forecast Office Facsimile [*National Weather Service*]
FOFC........	Friends of Free China (EA)
FOFCC......	Federal Oceanographic Fleet Coordination Council
FOFEBA ...	Forward of the FEBA [*Forward Edge of the Battle Area*] [*Military*]
FOFF	50-Off Stores, Inc. [*NASDAQ symbol*] (NQ)
FOFL.........	Fauna och Flora [*A publication*]
FOFM........	Fog Foam
FO/FO/FS ...	Fail-Operational, Fail-Operational, Fail-Safe
FOFR........	Fort Frederica National Monument
FOFRAR ...	FAO [*Food and Agriculture Organization of the United Nations*] Fisheries Reports [*A publication*]
FO/FS	Fail-Operational, Fail-Safe (NASA)
FOFT.........	Florida Technological University, Orlando, FL [*Library symbol*] [*Library of Congress*] (LCLS)
FOFUA......	Funtai Oyobi Funmatsuyakin [*A publication*]
FOG...........	Fast Oxidative Glycolytic [*Fibers*] [*Neuroanatomy*]
FOG...........	Fats, Oils, and Grease [*Food plant effluent*]
FOG...........	Fiber Optics Guidance (MCD)
FOG...........	Field Operations Group
FOG...........	Flag Officer, Germany (NATG)
FOG...........	Flight Operations Group
FOG...........	Flow of Gold
FOG...........	FOG [*First Osborne Group*] International Computer Users Group (EA)
FOG...........	Forschungen zur Ost Europaeischen Geschichte [*A publication*]
FOG...........	Frequency Offset Generator
FOG...........	Shreveport, LA [*Location identifier*] [*FAA*] (FAAL)
FOGA........	Akieni [*Gabon*] [*ICAO location identifier*] (ICLI)
FOGA	Fashion Originators Guild of America [*Defunct*] (EA)
FOGAMM ...	Friends of the Geological and Mining Museum [*Australia*]
FOGB	Booue [*Gabon*] [*ICAO location identifier*] (ICLI)
FOGCO	Federal Oil & Gas Corporation
FOGD........	Fiber Optics Guidance Demonstration (RDA)
Fog Det Lt ...	Fog Detector Light [*Nautical charts*]
FOGE........	N'Dende [*Gabon*] [*ICAO location identifier*] (ICLI)
FOGF.........	Fougamou [*Gabon*] [*ICAO location identifier*] (ICLI)
FOGG........	Feed-Only-Good Generator [*Nuclear energy*] (NRCH)
Fogg..........	Fogg's Reports [*32-35 New Hampshire*] [*A publication*] (DLA)
FOGG	Mbigou [*Gabon*] [*ICAO location identifier*] (ICLI)
FOGGA	Fuel-, Orr-, Gegegyogyaszat [*A publication*]
Fogg Art Mus Acqu ...	Fogg Art Museum. Acquisitions [*A publication*]
Fogg Mus Bul ...	Fogg Art Museum. Bulletin [*Harvard University*] [*A publication*]
FOGI..........	Moabi [*Gabon*] [*ICAO location identifier*] (ICLI)
FOGJ.........	Ndjole [*Gabon*] [*ICAO location identifier*] (ICLI)
FOGK	Koula-Moutou/Mabimbi [*Gabon*] [*ICAO location identifier*] (ICLI)
FOGL	Leconi [*Gabon*] [*ICAO location identifier*] (ICLI)
FOG-M......	Fiber Optic Guided Missile [*Army*] (RDA)
FOGM	Mouila [*Gabon*] [*ICAO location identifier*] (ICLI)
FOGMA	Flag Officer, Gibraltar Mediterranean Area [*British*]
FOGO........	Oyem [*Gabon*] [*ICAO location identifier*] (ICLI)
Fogorv Sz ...	Fogorvosi Szemle [*A publication*]
FOGQ........	Okondja [*Gabon*] [*ICAO location identifier*] (ICLI)
FOGR........	Lambarene [*Gabon*] [*ICAO location identifier*] (ICLI)
FOGRA (Dtsche Forshungsges Druck Reproduktionstech) Mitt ...	FOGRA (Deutsche Forschungsgesellschaft fuer Druck und Reproduktionstechnik) Mitteilungen [*A publication*]
FOGS.........	Church of Jesus Christ of Latter-Day Saints, Genealogical Society Library, Orlando Branch, Orlando, FL [*Library symbol*] [*Library of Congress*] (LCLS)
FOGS........	Faint-Object Grism Spectrograph [*Astronomy*]
FOGS........	Function-on-Generator-Stop (RDA)
FOGSIG	Fog Signal Station [*Nautical charts*]
FOGT	First Order Gradient Technique
FOGU........	Moupoupa [*Gabon*] [*ICAO location identifier*] (ICLI)
FOGV........	Minvoul [*Gabon*] [*ICAO location identifier*] (ICLI)
FOGW	Wonga-Wongue [*Gabon*] [*ICAO location identifier*] (ICLI)
FOH...........	Columbia, MS [*Location identifier*] [*FAA*] (FAAL)
FOH...........	Focus on Holland [*A publication*]
FOH...........	Forced Outage Hours [*Electronics*] (IEEE)
FOH...........	Friends of Haiti (EA)
FOH...........	Front of House (ADA)
FOHBC	Federation of Historical Bottle Clubs (EA)
FOHC	Friends of Helix Club (EA)
FOHEAW ...	Folia Haematologica [*Leipzig*] [*A publication*]
FOHMD....	Fiber Optic Helmet Mounted Display [*Computer generated imagery*]
FOHO	For Oily Hair Only [*Trademark of The Gillette Co.*]
FOHPAV ..	Folia Hereditaria et Pathologica [*A publication*]
FOHWA....	Forst- und Holzwirt [*A publication*]
FOI	Field Operations Intelligence
FOI	Fighter Officer for Interceptors [*Member of the SAGE Command Post staff*]
FOI	Final Opinion Inventory [*Psychometrics*]
FOI	Fleet Operational Investigation [*NOO*]
FOI	Follow-On Interceptor [*Military*]
FOI	Forced Oil Injection
FOI	Foreign Object Inspection [*or Investigation*] (MCD)
FOI	Foreign Object Investigation
FoI	Forum Italicum [*A publication*]
FOI	Free of Interest [*Business term*]
FOI	Freedom of Information [*Army*]
FOI	Freedom of Information Act
FOI	Freedom of Information Center (EA)
FOI	Fuels Operating Instruction (AFIT)
FOIA	Freedom of Information Act [*1966*]
FOIA	Fund for Open Information and Accountability (EA)
FOIC	Flag Officer-in-Charge [*British-controlled port*]
FOIC.........	Freedom of Information Clearinghouse (EA)
FOICR.......	Freedom of Information Center. Reports [*A publication*] (DLA)
FOI Dig	FOI [*Freedom of Information*] Digest [*A publication*] (DLA)
FOIF.........	Free Oceanographic Instrument Float
FOIH.........	Flight Operations Integration Handbook (MCD)
FOIJA	Food Industries Journal [*A publication*]
FOIL.........	Field Oil Identification Laboratory [*Marine science*] (MSC)
FOIL.........	File-Oriented Interpretive Language [*1969*] [*Data processing*]
FOIL.........	First, Outer, Inner, Last [*Mathematical term used in factoring second degree trinomials*]
FOIL.........	Forest Oil Corp. [*NASDAQ symbol*] (NQ)
FOIP.........	Follow-On In-Plant [*Test*] (MCD)
FOIPA	Freedom of Information and Privacy Act
FOIR.........	Field-of-Interest Register [*DoD*]
FOIRA	Food Irradiation [*A publication*]
FOIRA8	Irradiation des Aliments [*English Edition*] [*A publication*]
FOITC	Fleet Operational Intelligence Training Center [*Navy*]
FOIU	Flowmeter Ordering and Indicating Unit
FOJ............	Fremont, MI [*Location identifier*] [*FAA*] (FAAL)
FOJ............	Fuse on Jam (MCD)
FOJE	Fort Jefferson National Monument
FOJT	Formal On-the-Job Training
FOK	Fill or Kill [*Stock options*] [*Investment term*]
FoK	Folk og Kultur. Arbog for Dansk Etnologi og Folkemindevidenskab [*A publication*]
FOK	Free of Knots
FOK	Prague Film and Concert Orchestra
FOK	Westhampton Beach, NY [*Location identifier*] [*FAA*] (FAAL)
FOKEU	Foreign Organizations Korean Employees' Union [*South Korea*]
FOKL.........	First Oklahoma Bancorporation, Inc. [*NASDAQ symbol*] (NQ)
FOKN	Fixation Optokinetic Nystagmus [*Eye movement*]
FOKOA9 ...	Foldtani Kozlony [*A publication*]
FOL	Facility Operating License [*Nuclear energy*] (NRCH)
FOL	[*The*] Facts of Life [*NBC television program*]
FOL	Festival of Lights [*Hanukkah*] [*Commemoration of the rededication of the Temple by Judas Maccabeus in 165BC*] (ADA)
FOL	Fiber Optics LASER
FOL	Fiber Optics Light
FOL	First Order Logic
Fol	Foley's English Poor Law Cases [*1556-1730*] [*A publication*] (DLA)
FOL	Folia [*Leaves*]
FOL	Foligno [*Italy*] [*Seismograph station code, US Geological Survey*] [*Closed*] (SEIS)
FOL	Folio
FOL	Folium [*or Foliorum*] [*Leaf (or Leaves)*] [*Pharmacy*] (ROG)
FoL	Folk Life [*Cardiff*] [*A publication*]
FOL	Follow (AFM)
FOL	Following [*Business term*]
FOL	Forward Operating Location [*Military*]
FoL............	Foundations of Language [*A publication*]

FOL .... Frente Obrero de Liberacion [*Workers' Liberation Front*] [*Netherlands Antilles*] [*Political party*] (PPW)
FOL .... Friends of the Land [*Later, IWLA*]
FOLA........ Fort Laramie National Historic Site
Fol Arch ..... Folia Archaeologica [*A publication*]
Fol Biol ...... Folia Biologica [*A publication*]
FolcL.......... Folclor Leterar [*A publication*]
Folder Mont State Coll Coop Ext ... Folder. Montana State College. Cooperative Extension Service [*A publication*]
Folder Univ Ariz Agric Exp Stn ... Folder. University of Arizona. Agricultural Experiment Station [*A publication*]
Folder Univ MO Coll Agr Ext Serv ... Folder. University of Missouri. College of Agriculture. Extension Service [*A publication*]
Fol Dic .... Kames and Woodhouselee's Folio Dictionary, Scotch Court of Session [*A publication*] (DLA)
Fol Dict ...... Kames and Woodhouselee's Folio Dictionary, Scotch Court of Session [*A publication*] (DLA)
Foldrajzi Ert ... Foldrajzi Ertesito [*A publication*]
Foldrajzi Ertes ... Foldrajzi Ertesito [*A publication*]
Foldrajzi Koezl ... Foldrajzi Koezlemenyek [*A publication*]
Foldt Koezl ... Foldtani Koezlony [*A publication*]
Foldt Kozl .. Foldtani Kozlony [*A publication*]
Foldt Kut.... Foldtani Kutatas [*A publication*]
FOLEM..... Flag Officer, Levant and Eastern Mediterranean [*British Marines*] [*World War II*]
Fol Endocr ... Folia Endocrinologica [*A publication*]
Fol Endocr Jap ... Folia Endocrinologica Japonica [*A publication*]
Fol Ent Hung ... Folia Entomologica Hungarica [*A publication*]
Fol Ent Mex ... Folia Entomologica Mexicana [*A publication*]
Fol For .... Folia Forestalia [*A publication*]
FOLG .... Fiber Optics LASER Gyro (MCD)
FOLG .... Following (ROG)
Fol Geobot Phytotax ... Folia Geobotanica et Phytotaxonomica [*A publication*]
Fol Geogr ... Folia Geographica [*A publication*]
Fol Haemat ... Folia Haematologica [*A publication*]
Folha Med ... Folha Medica [*A publication*]
Folha Med (Rio De Janeiro) ... Folha Medica (Rio De Janeiro) [*A publication*]
Folh Divulg Serv Flor Aquic (Portugal) ... Folhetas de Divulgacao. Servicos Florestais e Aquicolas (Portugal) [*A publication*]
Fol Hered Path ... Folia Hereditaria et Pathologica [*A publication*]
Fol Hist Art ... Folia Historiae Artium [*A publication*]
Fol Hist Cy ... Folia Histochemica et Cytochemica [*Later, Folio Histochemica et Cytobiologica*] [*A publication*]
Fol Hist Cytochem ... Folia Histochemica et Cytochemica [*Later, Folio Histochemica et Cytobiologica*] [*A publication*]
Fol Hum..... Folia Humanistica. Ciencias, Artes, Letras [*A publication*]
Fol Humanis ... Folia Humanistica [*A publication*]
Fo Li.......... Folia Linguistica [*A publication*]
FOLI.......... Foliage Plus, Inc. [*NASDAQ symbol*] (NQ)
Folia Allergol ... Folia Allergologica [*Later, Folia Allergologica et Immunologica Clinica*] [*A publication*]
Folia Allergol Immunol Clin ... Folia Allergologica et Immunologica Clinica [*A publication*]
Folia Anat Jpn ... Folia Anatomica Japonica [*A publication*]
Folia Anat Univ Conimbrigensis (Coimbra) ... Folia Anatomica Universitatis Conimbrigensis (Coimbra) [*A publication*]
Folia Arch ... Folia Archeologica [*Lodz*] [*A publication*]
Folia Archaeol ... Folia Archaeologica [*Budapest*] [*A publication*]
Folia Biochim Biol Graeca ... Folia Biochimica et Biologica Graeca [*A publication*]
Folia Biol ... Folia Biologica [*A publication*]
Folia Biol (Cracow) ... Folia Biologica (Cracow) [*A publication*]
Folia Biol (Prague) ... Folia Biologica (Prague) [*A publication*]
Folia Biol (Praha) ... Folia Biologica (Praha) [*A publication*]
Folia Cardiol ... Folia Cardiologica [*A publication*]
Folia Clin Biol ... Folia Clinica et Biologica [*A publication*]
Folia Clin Biol Nova Ser ... Folia Clinica et Biologica. Nova Serie [*A publication*]
Folia Clin Chim Microsc ... Folia Clinica. Chimica et Microscopica [*A publication*]
Folia Clin Int ... Folia Clinica Internacional [*A publication*]
Folia Clin Int (Barc) ... Folia Clinica Internacional (Barcelona) [*A publication*]
Folia Dendrol ... Folia Dendrologica [*A publication*]
Folia Endocrinol ... Folia Endocrinologica [*A publication*]
Folia Endocrinol Jpn ... Folia Endocrinologica Japonica [*A publication*]
Folia Endocrinol (Pisa) ... Folia Endocrinologica (Pisa) [*A publication*]
Folia Endocrinol (Rome) ... Folia Endocrinologica (Rome) [*A publication*]
Folia Ent Hung ... Folia Entomologica Hungarica [*A publication*]
Folia Ent Mex ... Folia Entomologica Mexicana [*A publication*]
Folia Entomol Hung ... Folia Entomologica Hungarica [*A publication*]
Folia Entomol Hung Rovartani Kozl ... Folia Entomologica Hungarica. Rovartani Kozlemenyek [*A publication*]
Folia Entomol Mex ... Folia Entomologica Mexicana [*A publication*]
Folia Fac Med ... Folia Facultatis Medicae [*A publication*]
Folia Fac Med Univ Comenianae Bratisl ... Folia Facultatis Medicae Universitatis Comenianae Bratislaviensis [*A publication*]
Folia Fac Sci Nat Univ Purkynianae Brun Biol ... Folia Facultatis Scientiarum Naturalium Universitatis Purkynianae Brunensis: Biologia [*A publication*]

Folia Fac Sci Nat Univ Purkynianae Brun Chem ... Folia. Facultatis Scientiarum Naturalium. Universitatis Purkynianae Brunensis. Chemia [*A publication*]
Folia Fac Sci Nat Univ Purkynianae Brunensis Phys ... Folia Facultatis Scientiarum Naturalium Universitatis Purkynianae Brunensis: Physica [*A publication*]
Folia For .... Folia Forestalia [*A publication*]
Folia For (Helsinki) ... Folia Forestalia (Helsinki) [*A publication*]
Folia For Inst For Fenn ... Folia Forestalia Instituti Forestalis Fenniae [*A publication*]
Folia For Polon (Drzewn) ... Folia Forestalia Polonica. Seria B (Drzewnictwo) [*A publication*]
Folia For Polon (Lesn) ... Folia Forestalia Polonica. Seria A (Lesnictwo) [*A publication*]
Folia For Pol Ser A (Lesn) ... Folia Forestalia Polonica. Seria A (Lesnictwo) [*A publication*]
Folia For Pol Ser B (Drzewnictwo) ... Folia Forestalia Polonica. Seria B (Drzewnictwo) [*A publication*]
Foliage Dig ... Foliage Digest [*A publication*]
Folia Geobot Phytotaxon ... Folia Geobotanica et Phytotaxonomica [*A publication*]
Folia Geogr Ser Geogr Phys ... Folia Geographica. Series Geographica-Physica [*A publication*]
Folia Gynaec (Pavia) ... Folia Gynaecologica (Pavia) [*A publication*]
Folia Haematol (Frankfurt Am Main) ... Folia Haematologica (Frankfurt Am Main) [*A publication*]
Folia Haematol (Leipz) ... Folia Haematologica (Leipzig) [*A publication*]
Folia Haematol (Leipzig) Arch ... Folia Haematologica (Leipzig). Archiv [*A publication*]
Folia Haematol (Leipzig) Zentralorgan ... Folia Haematologica (Leipzig). Zentralorgan [*A publication*]
Folia Hered Pathol ... Folia Hereditaria et Pathologica [*A publication*]
Folia Histochem Cytobiol ... Folia Histochemica et Cytobiologica [*A publication*]
Folia Histochem Cytochem ... Folia Histochemica et Cytochemica [*Later, Folia Histochemica et Cytobiologica*] [*A publication*]
Folia Histochem Cytochem (Krakow) ... Folia Histochemica et Cytochemica (Krakow) [*Later, Folia Histochemica et Cytobiologica*] [*A publication*]
Folia Hum ... Folia Humanistica. Ciencias, Artes, Letras [*A publication*]
Folia Limnol Scand ... Folia Limnologica Scandinavica [*A publication*]
Folia Med Bialostocensia ... Folia Medica Bialostocensia [*A publication*]
Folia Med Cracov ... Folia Medica Cracoviensia [*A publication*]
Folia Med Fac Med Univ Saraev ... Folia Medica Facultatis. Medicinae Universitatis Saraeviensis [*A publication*]
Folia Med Lodz ... Folia Medica Lodziensia [*A publication*]
Folia Med (Naples) ... Folia Medica (Naples) [*A publication*]
Folia Med Neerl ... Folia Medica Neerlandica [*A publication*]
Folia Med (Plovdiv) ... Folia Medica (Plovdiv) [*A publication*]
Folia Microbiol ... Folia Microbiologica [*A publication*]
Folia Microbiol (Prague) ... Folia Microbiologica (Prague) [*A publication*]
Folia Morph ... Folia Morphologica [*A publication*]
Folia Morphol (Prague) ... Folia Morphologica (Prague) [*A publication*]
Folia Morphol (Praha) ... Folia Morphologica (Praha) [*A publication*]
Folia Morphol (Warsaw) ... Folia Morphologica (Warsaw) [*A publication*]
Folia Mus Rerum Nat Bohemia Occident Geol ... Folia Musei Rerum Naturalium Bohemiae Occidentalis. Geologica [*A publication*]
Folia Neuropsiquiatr Sur Este Esp ... Folia Neuropsiquiatrica del Sur y Este de Espana [*A publication*]
Folia O .... Folia Orientalia [*A publication*]
Folia Ophthalmol ... Folia Ophthalmologica [*A publication*]
Folia Ophthalmol Jpn ... Folia Ophthalmologica Japonica [*A publication*]
Folia Ophthalmol (Leipz) ... Folia Ophthalmologica (Leipzig) [*A publication*]
Folia Orient ... Folia Orientalia [*A publication*]
Folia Parasit ... Folia Parasitologica [*A publication*]
Folia Parasitol (Prague) ... Folia Parasitologica (Prague) [*A publication*]
Folia Pharm ... Folia Pharmaceutica [*A publication*]
Folia Pharmacol Jpn ... Folia Pharmacologica Japonica [*A publication*]
Folia Pharm (Istanbul) ... Folia Pharmaceutica (Istanbul) [*A publication*]
Folia Phoniatr ... Folia Phoniatrica [*A publication*]
Folia Phoniatr (Basel) ... Folia Phoniatrica (Basel) [*A publication*]
Folia Primat ... Folia Primatologica [*A publication*]
Folia Primatol ... Folia Primatologica [*A publication*]
Folia Psychiatr Neurol Jpn ... Folia Psychiatrica et Neurologica Japonica [*A publication*]
Folia Quat ... Folia Quaternaria [*A publication*]
Folia Sci Afr Cent ... Folia Scientifica Africae Centralis [*Congo*] [*A publication*]
Folia Serol ... Folia Serologica [*A publication*]
Folia Soc Sci Lublinensis ... Folia Societatis Scientiarum Lublinensis [*A publication*]
Folia Univ .. Folia Universitaria [*A publication*]
Folia Univ Cochabamba ... Folia Universitaria Cochabamba [*A publication*]
Folia Vet ... Folia Veterinaria [*A publication*]
Folia Vet Lat ... Folia Veterinaria Latina [*A publication*]
Folia Vet (Prague) ... Folia Veterinaria (Prague) [*A publication*]
Folia Zool ... Folia Zoologica [*A publication*]
Folio Supp ... Folio. Guide to Magazine Suppliers [*A publication*]
FOLIS .... Following Information Is Submitted [*Army*] (AABC)
FOLK........ Folk. Dansk Ethnografisk Tidsskrift [*A publication*]

Folk............ Folklore [*A publication*]
FOLK........ Folks Restaurants, Inc. [*NASDAQ symbol*] (NQ)
Folk Harp J ... Folk Harp Journal [*A publication*]
Folk Inst .... Folklore Institute. Journal [*A publication*]
Folkkult ..... Folkkultur [*A publication*]
Folkl.......... Folklore [*London*] [*A publication*]
Folkl Am .... Folklore Americano [*A publication*]
Folkl Arch ... Folklore Archives [*A publication*]
Folkl Brabancon ... Folklore Brabancon [*A publication*]
Folkl (Calcutta) ... Folklore (Calcutta) [*A publication*]
Folkl Champagne ... Folklore de Champagne [*A publication*]
Folklore Am ... Folklore Americano [*A publication*]
Folklore C ... Folklore (Calcutta) [*A publication*]
Folk-Lore J ... Folk-Lore Journal [*A publication*]
Folkl St (P) ... Folklore Studies (Peking) [*A publication*]
Folkl Stud .. Folklore Studies [*A publication*]
Folkl Suisse ... Folklore Suisse [*A publication*]
Folkm......... Folkminner och Folktankar [*A publication*]
Folk Mus Arch ... Folklore and Folk Music Archivist [*A publication*]
Folk Music .... Folk Music Journal [*A publication*]
Folk Mus J .... Folk Music Journal [*A publication*]
Folk Pl .... Folkard's Loans and Pledges [*2nd ed.*] [*1876*] [*A publication*] (DLA)
FolkS .... Folklore Studies [*A publication*]
Folk St Sl... Folkard's Edition of Starkie on Slander and Libel [*A publication*] (DLA)
FOLL........ Following
Foll Divulg Inst For (Chile) ... Folleto de Divulgacion. Instituto Forestal (Santiago De Chile) [*A publication*]
FOLLG .... Following (ROG)
Fol Limnol Scand ... Folia Limnologica Scandinavica [*A publication*]
Fol Ling...... Folia Linguistica [*A publication*]
Foll Tec For ... Folletos Tecnicos Forestales [*A publication*]
Foll Tec For Adm Nac Bosques (Argent) ... Folletos Tecnicos Forestales. Administracion Nacional de Bosques (Argentina) [*A publication*]
FOLMA8... Folia Medica [*Plovdiv*] [*A publication*]
Fol Med ..... Folha Medica [*A publication*]
Fol Med ..... Folia Medica [*A publication*]
Fol Med Cracov ... Folia Medica Cracoviensia [*A publication*]
Fol Med Lodz ... Folia Medica Lodziensia [*A publication*]
Fol Med (Napoli) ... Folia Medica (Napoli) [*A publication*]
Fol Med Neerl ... Folia Medica Neerlandica [*A publication*]
Fol Mend .... Folia Mendeliana [*A publication*]
Fol Microb ... Folia Microbiologica [*A publication*]
Fol Microbiol ... Folia Microbiologica [*A publication*]
Fol Morph ... Folia Morphologica [*A publication*]
FOLNOAVAL ... Following Items Not Available
Fol Oecon Cracov ... Folia Oeconomica Cracoviensia [*A publication*]
Fol Or...... Folia Orientalia [*A publication*]
FOLPEN... Foliage Penetration [*RADAR*] (MCD)
FOLPES.... Foliage Penetration System [*Military*]
Fol Pharm J ... Folia Pharmacologica Japonica [*A publication*]
Fol Phoniat ... Folia Phoniatrica [*A publication*]
Fol PLC ..... Foley's English Poor Law Cases [*1556-1730*] [*A publication*] (DLA)
Fol PL Cas ... Foley's English Poor Law Cases [*1556-1730*] [*A publication*] (DLA)
Fol Primat ... Folia Primatologica [*A publication*]
FOLQ .... Foam Liquid
Fo LR .... Fordham Law Review [*A publication*]
FOLR......... Forward Observer LASER Range-Finder
FOLS........ Follows (NVT)
FOLS........ Fort Larned National Historic Site
Fol Tec Secr Agr Ganad Inst Nac Invest Agr (Mexico) ... Folleto Tecnico. Secretaria de Agricultura y Ganaderia. Instituto Nacional de Investigaciones Agricolas (Mexico) [*A publication*]
FOLUP....... Follow-Up
FOL USA .. Friends of Libraries USA (EA)
FOM.......... Face of Masonry [*Technical drawings*]
FOM.......... Factor of Merit [*Telecommunications*] (TEL)
FOM.......... Fault of Management
FOM.......... Fellowship of Missions (EA)
FOM.......... Fiber Optic MODEM [*Modulator-Demodulator*]
FOM.......... Field Operations Manual
FOM.......... Field Operations Memorandum
FOM.......... Fighter Officer for Missiles [*Member of the SAGE Command Post staff*]
FOM.......... Figure of Merit
FOM.......... Foreign Materiel Number [*Weapons*] (INF)
FOM.......... Forum Resources Ltd. [*Vancouver Stock Exchange symbol*]
FOMA .... Foreign Military Assistance (MCD)
FOMA ...... Fort Matanzas National Monument
FOMAAB .. Food Manufacture [*A publication*]
FOMAD ..... Food Market Awareness Databank [*Leatherhead Food Research Association*] [*Information service or system*] (CRD)
FOMC .... Federal Open Market Committee [*Also, OMC*] [*Federal Reserve System*]
FOMC .... Fort McHenry National Monument
FOMCAT ... Foreign Material Catalog
FOMDA .... Folia Medica [*A publication*]

FOMDAK ... Folia Medica [*Naples*] [*A publication*]
FOMEAN ... Folha Medica [*A publication*]
FOMi......... Fluorouracil, Oncovin [*Vincristine*], Mitomycin C [*Antineoplastic drug regimen*]
FOMIAZ... Folia Microbiologica [*A publication*]
FOMIE5... Food Microbiology [*London*] [*A publication*]
FOMIN ...... Foreign Minister (CINC)
FOMINPI ... Fomento Industrial do Piani, SA
FOMIS ...... Fitting Out Management Information System [*Navy*] (CAAL)
FOMNAG ... Folia Medica Neerlandica [*A publication*]
FOMOAJ ... Folia Morphologica [*Warsaw*] [*A publication*]
FOMOCO ... Ford Motor Company (MCD)
FOMP .... Fiber Optic Mortar Projectile [*Boeing Co.*] [*Military*]
FOMP .... Foreign Missile Production (MCD)
FOMR .... Flight Operations Management Room [*NASA*] (KSC)
FoMRHI.... Fellowship of Makers and Researchers of Historical Instruments [*Formerly, Fellowship of Makers and Restorers of Historical Instruments*] (EA)
FOMTR....... Formatter (MCD)
fon .... Fon [*MARC language code*] [*Library of Congress*] (LCCP)
FoN .... Fortid og Nutid [*A publication*]
FON.......... United States Navy, Naval Training Equipment Center, Orlando, FL [*Library symbol*] [*Library of Congress*] (LCLS)
FONA .... Friends of the US National Arboretum (EA)
FONAC ..... Flag Officer, Naval Air Command [*British*]
Fonaments ... Fonaments Prehistoria i Mon Antic als Paisos Catalans [*A publication*]
FONAP ..... Flag Officer, Naval Air, Pacific [*British*]
FONAR .... Field Focusing Nuclear Magnetic Resonance
Fon Art Mus ... Fontes Artis Musicae [*A publication*]
FONAS...... Flag Officer, Naval Air Stations [*British military*] (DMA)
FONASBA ... Federation of National Associations of Shipbrokers and Agents [*London, England*] (EAIO)
Fon BC ...... Fonblanque's Bankruptcy Cases [*1849-52*] [*A publication*] (DLA)
Fonb Eq..... Fonblanque's Equity [*England*] [*A publication*] (DLA)
Fonbl.......... Fonblanque on Medical Jurisprudence [*A publication*] (DLA)
Fonbl.......... Fonblanque's Equity [*England*] [*A publication*] (DLA)
Fonbl.......... Fonblanque's New Reports, English Bankruptcy [*1849-52*] [*A publication*] (DLA)
Fonbl (Eng) ... Fonblanque's Equity [*England*] [*A publication*] (DLA)
Fonbl Eq (Eng) ... Fonblanque's Equity [*England*] [*A publication*] (DLA)
Fonbl Med Jur ... Fonblanque on Medical Jurisprudence [*A publication*] (DLA)
Fonbl NR ... Fonblanque on Medical Jurisprudence [*A publication*] (DLA)
Fonbl NR ... Fonblanque's English Cases in Chancery [*A publication*] (DLA)
Fonbl NR ... Fonblanque's Equity [*England*] [*A publication*] (DLA)
Fonbl NR ... Fonblanque's New Reports, English Bankruptcy [*1849-52*] [*A publication*] (DLA)
Fonbl R ...... Fonblanque's Bankruptcy Cases (or New Reports) [*1849-52*] [*A publication*] (DLA)
Fonbl R & Wr ... Fonblanque's Rights and Wrongs [*1860*] [*A publication*] (DLA)
FONCON ... Telephone Conversation (MCD)
Fonderia Ital ... Fonderia Italiana [*A publication*]
Fondeur....... Fondeur d'Aujourd'hui [*A publication*]
Fond Giorgio Ronchi Att ... Fondazione Giorgio Ronchi. Atti [*A publication*]
Fondren Sci Ser ... Fondren Science Series [*A publication*]
Fonds Rech For Univ Laval Bull ... Fonds de Recherches Forestieres. Universite Laval. Bulletin [*A publication*]
Fonds Rech For Univ Laval Contrib ... Fonds de Recherches Forestieres. Universite Laval. Contribution [*A publication*]
Fond Univ Luxemb Ser Notes Rech ... Fondation Universitaire Luxembourgeoise. Serie Notes de Recherche [*A publication*]
FONE .... Farmstead Telephone Group, Inc. [*NASDAQ symbol*] (NQ)
FONE .... Fort Necessity National Battlefield
FONE .... Telephone (FAAC)
FONECON ... Telephone Conference [*or Conversation*]
FONF .... Flag Officer, Newfoundland [*British*]
FONN........ Federation of Ontario Naturalists. Newsletter [*A publication*]
FONOBP... Forest Notes. New Hampshire's Conservation Magazine [*A publication*]
FONOFF... Foreign Office
FONPLATA ... Fondo Financiero para el Desarrollo de la Cuenca del Plata [*Financial Fund for the Development of the Plata Basin*] (EAIO)
FONR .... Fonar Corp. [*NASDAQ symbol*] (NQ)
FONR .... Fund for Objective News Reporting (EA)
FONSI .... Finding of No Significant Impact [*Office of Surface Mining*]
Font........... Fontaine [*A publication*]
Font............ Fontes Iuris Romani Antiqui [*A publication*] (OCD)
Font............ Pro Fonteio [*of Cicero*] [*Classical studies*] (OCD)
Fontane Bl ... Fontane Blaetter [*A publication*]
Font A Pos ... Fontes Archaeologici Posnanienses [*A publication*]
Fontes .... Fontes Artis Musicae [*A publication*]
FontesArtisM ... Fontes Artis Musicae [*A publication*]
FONYA ..... Forskningsnytt [*A publication*]
FONZ........ Friends of the National Zoo

FOO.......... Fear of Obesity
FOO.......... Fleet Operations Officer [*Navy*] [*British*]
FOO.......... Food Processing [*A publication*]
FOO.......... Forward Observation Officer [*Military*]
FOO.......... Fraternal Order of Orioles   (EA)
FOO.......... Fundamental Order of Operation [*Mathematics game*]
FOO.......... Numfor [*Indonesia*] [*Airport symbol*]   (OAG)
FOOA....... Mouila [*Gabon*] [*ICAO location identifier*]   (ICLI)
FOOB....... Bitam [*Gabon*] [*ICAO location identifier*]   (ICLI)
FOOC....... Cocobeach [*Gabon*] [*ICAO location identifier*]   (ICLI)
FOOD....... Foodservice Organization of Distributors   (EA)
FOOD....... Moanda [*Gabon*] [*ICAO location identifier*]   (ICLI)
FOOD....... P & C Foods, Inc. [*Syracuse, NY*] [*NASDAQ symbol*]   (NQ)
Food Addit Contam ... Food Additives and Contaminants [*A publication*]
Food Agric Leg ... Food and Agricultural Legislation [*A publication*]
Food & Bev ... Food and Beverage Marketing [*A publication*]
Food Bus ... Food Business [*A publication*]
Food Can.... Food in Canada [*A publication*]
Food Canad ... Food in Canada [*A publication*]
Food Chem ... Food Chemistry [*A publication*]
Food Chem Microbiol Technol ... Food Chemistry, Microbiology, Technology [*A publication*]
Food Chem Toxicol ... Food and Chemical Toxicology [*A publication*]
Food Cosmet ... Food and Cosmetics Toxicology [*A publication*]
Food Cosmetics Toxicol ... Food and Cosmetics Toxicology [*A publication*]
Food Cosmet Toxicol ... Food and Cosmetics Toxicology [*A publication*]
Food Dev ... Food Development [*A publication*]
Food Devel ... Food Development [*A publication*]
Food Drug C ... Food, Drug, Cosmetic Law Journal [*A publication*]
Food Drug Cos L Rep ... Food, Drug, Cosmetic Law Reporter [*Commerce Clearing House*] [*A publication*]   (DLA)
Food Drug Cosmet Law Q ... Food, Drug, Cosmetic Law Quarterly [*A publication*]
Food Drug Cosm LJ ... Food, Drug, Cosmetic Law Journal [*A publication*]
Food Drug Cosm LQ ... Food, Drug, Cosmetic Law Quarterly [*A publication*]
Food Drug Cosm L Rep (CCH) ... Food, Drug, Cosmetic Law Reporter (Commerce Clearing House) [*A publication*]   (DLA)
Food Drug Cosm L Rep CCH ... Food, Drug, Cosmetic Law Reports. Commerce Clearing House [*A publication*]
Food Drugs Ind Bull ... Food and Drugs Industry Bulletin [*A publication*]
Food Eng.... Food Engineering [*A publication*]
Food Engin ... Chilton's Food Engineering [*A publication*]
Food Eng Int ... Food Engineering International [*A publication*]
Food Eng (NY) ... Food Engineering (New York) [*A publication*]
Food Eng (Philadelphia) ... Food Engineering (Philadelphia) [*A publication*]
Food Eng Syst ... Food Engineering Systems [*A publication*]
Food Farming Agric ... Food Farming and Agriculture. Journal for the Development of Food and Agriculture [*India*] [*A publication*]
Food Fish Mark Rev & Outl ... Food Fish Market Review and Outlook [*A publication*]
Food Flavour Ingredients Processing and Packaging ... Food: Flavouring Ingredients Processing and Packaging [*A publication*]
Food Hyg Stud ... Food Hygiene Study [*Japan*] [*A publication*]
Food Ind..... Food Industry [*A publication*]
Food Ind J ... Food Industries Journal [*A publication*]
Food Ind S Afr ... Food Industries of South Africa [*A publication*]
Food Ind (Tokyo) ... Food Industry (Tokyo) [*A publication*]
Food Irradiat ... Food Irradiation [*France*] [*A publication*]
Food Irradiat Inf ... Food Irradiation Information [*A publication*]
Food Irradiat (Jpn) ... Food Irradiation (Japan) [*A publication*]
Food Manage ... Food Management [*A publication*]
Food Manuf ... Food Manufacture [*A publication*]
Food Mater Equip ... Food Materials and Equipment [*A publication*]
Food Mfr .... Food Manufacture [*A publication*]
Food Microbiol (Lond) ... Food Microbiology (London) [*A publication*]
Food Microstruct ... Food Microstructure [*A publication*]
Food Mon .. Food Monitor [*A publication*]
FoodMonit ... Food Monitor [*A publication*]
Food & Nutr ... Food and Nutrition [*A publication*]
Food Nutr... Food and Nutrition [*A publication*]
Food Nutr Bull ... Food and Nutrition Bulletin [*A publication*]
Food Nutr News ... Food and Nutrition News [*A publication*]
Food Nutr Notes Rev ... Food and Nutrition. Notes and Reviews [*A publication*]   (APTA)
Food and Nutr Notes and Rev ... Food and Nutrition. Notes and Reviews [*A publication*]   (APTA)
Food & Nutr Notes Revs ... Food and Nutrition. Notes and Reviews [*A publication*]   (APTA)
Food Nutr (Rome) ... Food and Nutrition (Rome) [*A publication*]
Food PM.... Food Production/Management [*A publication*]
Food Pol..... Food from Poland [*A publication*]
Food Pol..... Food Policy [*A publication*]
Food Preservation Q ... Food Preservation Quarterly [*A publication*]   (APTA)
Food Preserv Q ... Food Preservation Quarterly [*A publication*]
Food Proc.... Food Processing Industry [*A publication*]
Food Proc... Food Processing News [*A publication*]
Food Process ... Food Processing [*A publication*]
Food Process (Chic) ... Food Processing (Chicago) [*A publication*]
Food Process Ind ... Food Processing Industry [*A publication*]

Food Processing Mktg ... Food Processing and Marketing [*Chicago*] [*A publication*]
Food Process Mark (Chic) ... Food Processing and Marketing (Chicago) [*A publication*]
Food Process Packag ... Food Processing and Packaging [*A publication*]
Food Prod .. Food Product Development [*A publication*]
Food Prod Dev ... Food Product Development [*A publication*]
Food Prod Devel ... Food Product Development [*A publication*]
Food Prod/Manage ... Food Production/Management [*A publication*]
Food Res .... Food Research [*A publication*]
Food Res Dep Div Food Res CSIRO ... Food Research Report. Division of Food Research. Commonwealth Scientific and Industrial Research Organisation [*A publication*]   (APTA)
Food Research Inst Studies ... Food Research Institute. Studies [*A publication*]
Food Res Inst Stud ... Food Research Institute. Studies [*A publication*]
Food Res Inst Stud Agric Econ Trade Dev (Stanford) ... Food Research Institute. Studies in Agricultural Economics, Trade, and Development (Stanford) [*A publication*]
Food Res Inst Stud (Stanford) ... Food Research Institute. Studies (Stanford) [*A publication*]
Food Rev .... Food Review [*A publication*]
Food Rev Int ... Food Reviews International [*A publication*]
Food Sci .... Food Science [*A publication*]
Food Sci (NY) ... Food Science (New York) [*A publication*]
Food Sci & Tech Abstr ... Food Science and Technology Abstracts [*International Food Information Service*] [*Bibliographic database*] [*A publication*]
Food Sci Technol ... Food Science and Technology [*A publication*]
Food Sci Technol Abstr ... Food Science and Technology Abstracts [*A publication*]
Food Sci Technol Ser Monogr ... Food Science and Technology. A Series of Monographs [*A publication*]
Food Sci & Technol (Zur) ... Food Science and Technology (Zurich) [*A publication*]
Food Serv Mark ... Food Service Marketing [*A publication*]
Food Serv Mkt ... Food Service Marketing [*A publication*]
Food S Mkt ... Food Service Marketing [*A publication*]
Foods Nutr Dent Health ... Foods, Nutrition, and Dental Health [*A publication*]
Food Tech .. Food Technology [*A publication*]
Food Tech Aust ... Food Technology in Australia [*A publication*]   (APTA)
Food Tech in Aust ... Food Technology in Australia [*A publication*]   (APTA)
Food Technol ... Food Technology [*A publication*]
Food Technol Aust ... Food Technology in Australia [*A publication*]
Food Technol NZ ... Food Technology in New Zealand [*A publication*]
Food Technology in Aust ... Food Technology in Australia [*A publication*]   (APTA)
Food Technol Rev ... Food Technology Review [*A publication*]
Food Tech NZ ... Food Technology in New Zealand [*A publication*]
Food Trade R ... Food Trade Review [*A publication*]
Food Trade Rev ... Food Trade Review [*A publication*]
Food Wld N ... Food World News [*A publication*]
FOOE........ Mekambo [*Gabon*] [*ICAO location identifier*]   (ICLI)
FOOG........ Port Gentil [*Gabon*] [*ICAO location identifier*]   (ICLI)
FOOH .... Omboue [*Gabon*] [*ICAO location identifier*]   (ICLI)
FOOHA....... Fueloil and Oil Heat [*A publication*]
FOOI .... Iguela [*Gabon*] [*ICAO location identifier*]   (ICLI)
FOOK .... Makokou/Epassengue [*Gabon*] [*ICAO location identifier*]   (ICLI)
FOOL .... Libreville/Leon M'Ba [*Gabon*] [*ICAO location identifier*]   (ICLI)
FOOM....... Mitzic [*Gabon*] [*ICAO location identifier*]   (ICLI)
FOON........ Franceville/Mvengue [*Gabon*] [*ICAO location identifier*]   (ICLI)
FOOO........ Libreville [*Gabon*] [*ICAO location identifier*]   (ICLI)
FOOPDZ... Folia Ophthalmologica [*Leipzig*] [*A publication*]
FOOR........ Lastourville [*Gabon*] [*ICAO location identifier*]   (ICLI)
Foord........ Foord's Supreme Court Reports [*Cape Colony, South Africa*] [*A publication*]   (DLA)
FOOS .... Force Out of Service [*Telecommunications*]   (TEL)
FOOS .... Function-Oriented Organizational Structure   (AAG)
FOOS .... Sette-Cama [*Gabon*] [*ICAO location identifier*]   (ICLI)
FOOT .... Follow-On Operational Test
FOOT .... Foothill Independent Bancorp [*NASDAQ symbol*]   (NQ)
FOOT .... Tchibanga [*Gabon*] [*ICAO location identifier*]   (ICLI)
Foote B & B ... Foote's Bench and Bar of the South and Southwest [*A publication*]   (DLA)
Foote & E Incorp Co ... Foote and Everett's Law of Incorporated Companies Operating under Municipal Franchises [*A publication*]   (DLA)
Foote Highw ... Foote's Law of Highways [*A publication*]   (DLA)
Foote Int Jur ... Foote on Private International Jurisprudence [*A publication*]   (DLA)
Foote Prints Chem Met Alloys Ores ... Foote Prints on Chemicals, Metals, Alloys, and Ores [*A publication*]
Foot Mouth Dis Bull ... Foot and Mouth Disease Bulletin [*A publication*]
FOOV .... Libreville [*Gabon*] [*ICAO location identifier*]   (ICLI)
FOOW .... Finding Our Own Ways [*An association*]   (EA)
FOOY .... Mayumba [*Gabon*] [*ICAO location identifier*]   (ICLI)
FOP .... Farthest on Point

FOP .... Festschrift fuer Otto Procksch (1934) [*A publication*]   (BJA)
FOP .... Fiber Optics Probe
FOP .... Fibrodysplasia Ossificans Progressiva [*Medicine*]
FOP .... Financial Operating Plan
F/OP .... Firing/Observation Port
FOP .... Flight Operations Panel
FOP .... Flight Operations Plan   (MCD)
FOP .... Follow-On Production   (NASA)
FOP .... Forensic Pathology [*Medicine*]   (DHSM)
FOP .... Forward Observation Post [*Military*]
FOP .... Fraternal Order of Police, Grand Lodge   (EA)
FOP .... Friends of Photography   (EA)
FOP .... Friendship Oil Pipeline [*Eastern Europe*]
FOP .... Fuel Oil Pump   (MSA)
FOP .... Grand Lodge, Ladies Auxiliary, Fraternal Order of Police   (EA)
FOPA .... Firearms Owners' Protection Act
FOPAAQ .... Food Packer [*A publication*]
FOPC .... Flag Officer, Pacific Coast [*Canada*]
FOPE .... Forgotten People [*A publication*]
FOPEN ...... Foliage Penetration [*RADAR*]   (MCD)
FOPG .... Flight Operations Planning Group [*NASA*]   (NASA)
FOPHA ..... Folia Phoniatrica [*A publication*]
FOPHAD .. Aktuelle Probleme der Phoniatrie und Logopaedie [*A publication*]
FOPHAD .. Folia Phoniatrica [*A publication*]
FOPI .... First-Order Polynomial Interpolator
FOPMAS .. Folia Pharmaceutica [*Istanbul*] [*A publication*]
FOPMBT ... Food Processing and Marketing [*Chicago*] [*A publication*]
FOPO .... Focal Points [*A publication*]
FOPOD3 ... Food Policy [*A publication*]
FOPP .... Fiber Optics Photo Pickup
FOPP .... First-Order Polynomial Predictor
FOPP .... Follow-On Parts Production   (NASA)
FOPPA ...... First-Order Polarization Propagator Approach [*Physics*]
FOP-PT ..... Front Oubangais Patriotique - Parti du Travail [*Oubangian Patriotic Front - Party of Labor*] [*Central Africa*]   (PD)
FOPR .... Full Outpatient Rate   (AFM)
FOPR .... Society of Friends of Puerto Rico   (EA)
FOPRA9 .... Food Processing [*Chicago*] [*A publication*]
FOPRB ..... Foret Privee [*A publication*]
FOPREP..... Force Packaging Report [*Military*]
FOPS .... Fair Organ Preservation Society [*British*]
FOPS .... Falling Object Protective Structure [*For mining machines*]
FOPS .... First Orbit Penetration System   (MCD)
FOPS .... Flight Operations and Planning Scheduling   (MCD)
FOPT .... Fiber Optics Photo Transfer
FOPU .... Fort Pulaski National Monument
FOPW .... Federation of Organizations for Professional Women   (EA)
FOQ .... Free on Quay [*Business term*]
FOQCV ..... Fuel Oil Quick Closing Valve   (NVT)
FOQUAN ... Folia Quaternaria [*A publication*]
FOR .... Farmer-Owned Reserve [*Business term*]
FOR .... Federacion Obrera Revolucionaria [*Mexican political party*]
FOR .... Federation of Outdoor Recreationists [*Defunct*]   (EA)
FOR .... Fellow of Operational Research [*British*]   (DBQ)
FOR .... Fellowship of Reconciliation   (EA)
FO & R ...... Fleet Operations and Readiness
FOR .... Flight Operations Review   (MCD)
FOR .... Force   (NVT)
FOR .... Force Resources Ltd. [*Vancouver Stock Exchange symbol*]
FOR .... Forced Outage Rate [*Electronics*]   (IEEE)
FOR .... Ford Foundation Library, New York, NY [*OCLC symbol*]   (OCLC)
FOR .... Fordham [*New York*] [*Seismograph station code, US Geological Survey*] [*Closed*]   (SEIS)
FOR .... Fore River Railroad Corp. [*AAR code*]
FOR .... Foreign
FOR .... Foreign Affairs [*A publication*]
FOR .... Forel Parchment [*Bookbinding*]   (ROG)
FOR .... Forensic Pathology [*Medicine*]
FOR .... Forest
FOR .... Forestry
FOR .... Forma Orbis Romanae. Carte Archeologique de la Gaule Romaine [*A publication*]   (OCD)
FOR .... Formica Corp. [*NYSE symbol*]   (SPSG)
For............. Fornax [*Constellation*]
For............. Forrester's English Chancery Cases Tempore Talbot [*A publication*]   (DLA)
For............. Forrest's English Exchequer Reports [*A publication*]   (DLA)
FOR .... Forskolin [*Also, FSK*] [*Organic chemistry*]
FOR .... Forsyth, MT [*Location identifier*] [*FAA*]   (FAAL)
FOR .... Fortaleza [*Brazil*] [*Airport symbol*]   (OAG)
FOR .... Forte [*Loud*] [*Music*]
For............. Fortescue. De Laudibus Legum Angliae [*A publication*]   (DLA)
FOR .... Fortune [*A publication*]
For............. Forum [*Record label*]
FOR .... Forward [*Business term*]
FOR .... Free on Rail/Free on Truck [*"INCOTERM," International Chamber of Commerce official code*]
FOR .... Friends of the River   (EA)
FOR .... Fuel Oil Return   (AAG)

FORA .... Families of Resisters for Amnesty   (EA)
FORA .... Fort Raleigh National Historic Site
For Abstr ... Forestry Abstracts [*A publication*]
FORAC...... For Action
FORACS .... Fleet Operational Readiness Accuracy Check Sites [*Navy*]
FORACS .... Force Accuracy Standards
For Aff ...... Foreign Affairs [*A publication*]
For Affairs ... Foreign Affairs [*A publication*]
For Aff Rep ... Foreign Affairs Reports [*A publication*]
Forage Res ... Forage Research [*A publication*]
For Agric... Foreign Agriculture [*A publication*]
FORAM .... Foraminiferal [*Geology*]
For Anim Dis Rep ... Foreign Animal Disease Report [*A publication*]
FORAST ... Forest Responses to Anthropogenic Stress [*Project sponsored by university and governmental research groups*]
FORAST ... Formula Assembler Translator [*Data processing*]
FORATOM ... Forum Atomique Europeen [*Association of European Atomic Forums*]   (EAIO)
Forb........... Forbes' Cases in St. Andrews Bishop's Court [*A publication*]   (DLA)
Forb........... Forbes' Court of Session Decisions [*Scotland*] [*A publication*]   (DLA)
Forb........... Forbes' Journal of the Session [*1705-13*] [*Scotland*] [*A publication*]   (DLA)
Forb Bills ... Forbes on Bills of Exchange [*A publication*]   (DLA)
Forbes .... Forbes' Journal of the Session [*1705-13*] [*Scotland*] [*A publication*]   (DLA)
Forb Inst .... Forbes' Institutes of the Law of Scotland [*A publication*]   (DLA)
For and Bird ... Forest and Bird [*New Zealand*] [*A publication*]
FORBLOC ... FORTRAN [*Formula Translating System*] Compiled Block-Oriented Simulation Language [*Data processing*]   (IEEE)
Forb Tr....... Forbes on Trustees and Post Office Savings Banks [*A publication*]   (DLA)
For Bull Dep For Clemson Univ ... Forestry Bulletin. Department of Forestry. Clemson University [*A publication*]
For Bur Aust For Res Notes ... Australia. Commonwealth Forestry and Timber Bureau. Forestry Research Notes [*A publication*]   (APTA)
For Bur Aust Leaf ... Australia. Commonwealth Forestry and Timber Bureau. Leaflet [*A publication*]   (APTA)
For Bur Aust Timber Supp Rev ... Australia. Commonwealth Forestry and Timber Bureau. Timber Supply Review [*A publication*]   (APTA)
FORC .... Fluorinator Off-Gas Recycle Compressor [*Nuclear energy*]   (NRCH)
FORC .... Forces. Hydro Quebec [*A publication*]
FORC .... Formula Coder [*Data processing*]
Forca .... [*Stephanus*] Forcatulus [*Deceased, 1574*] [*Authority cited in pre-1607 legal work*]   (DSA)
For Can Gt Lakes For Cent Inf Rep O-X ... Forestry Canada. Great Lakes Forestry Centre. Information Report O-X [*A publication*]
FORCAP ... Force Application Processor   (MCD)
FORCAP ... Force Combat Air Patrol [*Military*]   (NVT)
For Cas & Op ... Forsyth's Cases and Opinions on Constitutional Law [*A publication*]   (DLA)
FORCAST ... Flexible Operational Resolution for Combat Air Support [*Model*]   (MCD)
Forcat......... [*Stephanus*] Forcatulus [*Deceased, 1574*] [*Authority cited in pre-1607 legal work*]   (DSA)
FORCE...... FORTRAN [*Formula Translating System*] Conversational Environment [*Data processing*]
FORCE...... Western Federation of Regional Construction Employers
FORCEM ... Force Evaluation Model [*Army*]   (RDA)
FORC ENT ... Forcible Entry and Detainer [*Legal term*]   (DLA)
For Chron ... Forestry Chronicle [*A publication*]
For Comm .. Foreign Commerce Weekly [*A publication*]
For Comm Victoria Bull ... Forests Commission Victoria. Bulletin [*A publication*]
For Comm Victoria For Tech Pap ... Forests Commission Victoria. Forestry Technical Papers [*A publication*]
For Comp ... Forsyth on Composition with Creditors [*A publication*]   (DLA)
For Cons Law ... Forsyth's Cases and Opinions on Constitutional Law [*A publication*]   (DLA)
FOR CORP ... Foreign Corporation [*Legal term*]   (DLA)
Forc Sous M ... Forces Sous-Marines [*A publication*]
FOrD .... Dickinson Memorial Library, Orange City, FL [*Library symbol*] [*Library of Congress*]   (LCLS)
FORD .... Fix or Repair Daily [*Reference to the alleged defects of Ford automobiles*]
FORD .... Floating Ocean Research and Development [*Station*]
FORD .... Fordham [*England*]
FORD .... Foreign Office Research Department [*British*]
FORD .... Forward
FORD .... Forward Industries, Inc. [*NASDAQ symbol*]   (NQ)
FORD .... Found on Road Dead [*Reference to the alleged defects of Ford automobiles*]
FORDACS ... Fuel Oil Route Delivery and Control System [*Computer-based system*]
FORDAD .. Foreign Disclosure Automated Data [*System*]
FORDAP... FORTRAN [*Formula Translating System*] Debugging Aid Program [*Data processing*]

For Def....... For the Defense [*A publication*]
For De Laud ... Fortescue. De Laudibus Legum Angliae [*A publication*] (DLA)
For Dep Bull For Dep (Zambia) ... Forest Department Bulletin. Forest Department (Zambia) [*A publication*]
For Dep West Aust Res Pap ... Forests Department of Western Australia. Research Paper [*A publication*]
FORDEX... Formula Index [*Molecular formula indexing*]
Ford For Cent Mich Technol Univ Bull ... Ford Forestry Center. Michigan Technological University. Bulletin [*A publication*]
Ford For Cent Mich Technol Univ Res Notes ... Ford Forestry Center. Michigan Technological University. Research Notes [*A publication*]
Fordham Corp Inst ... Proceedings. Fordham Corporate Law Institute [*A publication*] (DLA)
Fordham Intl LF ... Fordham International Law Forum [*A publication*]
Fordham Int'l LJ ... Fordham International Law Journal [*A publication*]
Fordham L Rev ... Fordham Law Review [*A publication*]
Fordham Urban L J ... Fordham Urban Law Journal [*A publication*]
Fordham Urb LJ ... Fordham Urban Law Journal [*A publication*]
For Dig (Philippines) ... Forestry Digest (Philippines) [*A publication*]
FORDIMS ... Force Development Integrated Management System [*Military*]
For Div Tech Note For Div (Tanz) ... Forest Division Technical Note. Forest Division. (Dar Es Salaam, Tanzania) [*A publication*]
Ford L Rev ... Fordham Law Review [*A publication*]
Ford Oa...... Ford on Oaths [*8th ed.*] [*1903*] [*A publication*] (DLA)
FORDS........ Floating Ocean Research and Development Station
FORDTIS ... Foreign Disclosure and Technical Information System
FORDU ..... For Duty [*Military*]
Ford Urban LJ ... Fordham Urban Law Journal [*A publication*]
FORE........ Foundation for Oceanographic Research and Education
FORE........ Fraternity of Recording Executives (EA)
FOREAE ... Food Research [*A publication*]
Forecast Home Econ ... Forecast for Home Economics [*A publication*]
For Ecol Manage ... Forest Ecology and Management [*A publication*]
For Ecol & Mgt ... Forest Ecology and Management [*A publication*]
FORECON ... Forward Reconnaissance (NVT)
FORECONCO ... Force Reconnaissance Company [*Marine Corps*]
For Econ NY St Coll For ... Forestry Economics. New York State University. College of Forestry at Syracuse University [*A publication*]
For Econ Trd ... Foreign Economic Trends and Their Implications for the United States [*A publication*]
For of Educ ... Forum of Education [*A publication*] (APTA)
FOREG...... Foregoing (ROG)
FOREGE... Food Regulation Enquiries [*Leatherhead Food Research Association*] [*Information service or system*] (CRD)
Foreign Aff ... Foreign Affairs [*A publication*]
Foreign Aff Rep ... Foreign Affairs Reports [*A publication*]
Foreign Agr ... Foreign Agriculture. US Foreign Agricultural Service [*A publication*]
Foreign Agric ... Foreign Agriculture [*A publication*]
Foreign Agric Canned Fruits FCAN US Foreign Agric Serv ... Foreign Agriculture Circular. Canned Fruits. FCAN. United States Foreign Agricultural Service [*A publication*]
Foreign Agric Circ Dried Fruit FDF USDA Foreign Agric Serv ... Foreign Agriculture Circular. Dried Fruits. FDF. United States Department of Agriculture. Foreign Agricultural Service [*A publication*]
Foreign Agric Circ Grains FG US Dep Agric Foreign Agric Serv ... Foreign Agriculture Circular. Grains. FG. United States Department of Agriculture. Foreign Agricultural Service [*A publication*]
Foreign Agric Circ US Dep Agric ... Foreign Agriculture Circular. United States Department of Agriculture [*A publication*]
Foreign Agric Circ US Dep Agric Serv Spices FTEA ... Foreign Agricultural Circular. United States Department of Agriculture. Foreign Agricultural Services. Spices. FTEA [*A publication*]
Foreign Agric Econ Rep US Dep Agric Econ Res Serv ... Foreign Agricultural Economic Report. US Department of Agriculture. Economic Research Service [*A publication*]
Foreign Agric US Dep Agric Foreign Agric Serv ... Foreign Agriculture. US Department of Agriculture. Foreign Agricultural Service [*A publication*]
Foreign Agr Incl Foreign Crops Markets ... Foreign Agriculture. Including Foreign Crops and Markets. US Foreign Agricultural Service [*A publication*]
Foreign Agr Trade US ... Foreign Agriculture Trade of the United States [*A publication*]
Foreign Compd Metab Mamm ... Foreign Compound Metabolism in Mammals [*A publication*]
Foreign Econ Trends Their Implic US ... Foreign Economic Trends and Their Implications for the United States [*A publication*]
Foreign Lan ... Foreign Language Annals [*A publication*]
Foreign Lang Index ... Foreign Language Index [*A publication*]
Foreign Leg Per ... Foreign Legal Periodicals Index [*A publication*]
Foreign Pet Technol ... Foreign Petroleum Technology [*A publication*]
Foreign Pol ... Foreign Policy [*A publication*]
Foreign Sci Publ Natn Cent Sci Tech Econ Inf (Warsaw) ... Foreign Scientific Publication. National Center for Scientific, Technical, and Economic Information (Warsaw) [*Poland*] [*A publication*]
Foreign Tr ... Foreign Trade [*A publication*]

FOREM..... File Organization Evaluation Model
FOREM..... Force Requirements and Methodology [*Military*]
FOREMAN ... Form Retrieval and Manipulation Language
Foren Sci I ... Forensic Science International [*A publication*]
Forensic Sci ... Forensic Science [*Later, Forensic Science International*] [*A publication*]
Forensic Sci Int ... Forensic Science International [*A publication*]
Forensic Sci Soc J ... Forensic Science Society Journal [*A publication*]
For Environ Prot US For Serv North Reg ... Forest Environmental Protection. United States Forest Service. Northern Region [*A publication*]
For Equipm Note FAO ... Forestry Equipment Notes. FAO [*Food and Agriculture Organization of the United Nations*] [*A publication*]
FORESDAT ... Formerly Restricted Data [*Military*]
FOREST.... [*The*] Ancient Order of Foresters [*Freemasonry*] (ROG)
FOREST.... Fast Order Radiation Effects Sampling Technique
Forest Abstr ... Forestry Abstracts [*A publication*]
Forest Chro ... Forestry Chronicle [*A publication*]
Forester...... Chancery Cases Tempore Talbot [*England*] [*A publication*] (DLA)
Forester N Ire ... Forester. Ministry of Agriculture of Northern Ireland [*A publication*]
Forest Fire Losses Can ... Forest Fire Losses in Canada [*A publication*]
Forest Hist ... Forest History [*A publication*]
Forest Ind .. Forest Industries [*A publication*]
Forest PMT ... Forest Products Market Trends [*A publication*]
Forest Prod J ... Forest Products Journal [*A publication*]
Forest Products R ... Forest Products Review [*A publication*]
Forest Res News Midsouth ... Forest Research News for the Midsouth [*A publication*]
Forestry Abstr ... Forestry Abstracts [*A publication*]
Forestry Chron ... Forestry Chronicle [*A publication*]
Forestry Res Newsl ... Forestry Research Newsletter [*A publication*]
Forestry Res Rept Agr Expt Sta Univ Ill ... Forestry Research Report. Agricultural Experiment Station. University of Illinois [*A publication*]
Forestry Tech Paper ... Forestry Technical Papers [*A publication*] (APTA)
Forest Sci... Forest Science [*A publication*]
Forest Sci Monogr ... Forest Science Monographs [*A publication*]
Forest Timb ... Forest and Timber [*A publication*] (APTA)
Forest Tre Ser For Timb Bur ... Forest Tree Series. Forestry and Timber Bureau [*A publication*] (APTA)
Foret-Conserv ... Foret-Conservation [*A publication*]
FOREWAS ... Force and Weapon Analysis System (AABC)
FOREWON ... Forces and Weapons
FOREX..... Foreign Exchange [*Investment term*]
For Exch Bull ... Foreign Exchange Bulletin [*A publication*] (DLA)
FORF........ Forfeiture (AFM)
FORF........ Fortune Financial Group, Inc. [*NASDAQ symbol*] (NQ)
For Farmer ... Forest Farmer [*A publication*]
For Fire Control Abstr ... Forest Fire Control Abstracts [*A publication*]
For Fire News For Fire Atmos Sci Res For Serv USDA ... Forest Fire News. Forest Fire and Atmospheric Sciences Research. Forest Service. US Department of Agriculture [*A publication*]
For Focus ... Forest Focus [*A publication*] (APTA)
FOR/FOT ... Free on Rail/Free on Truck [*Business term*]
FORF & P ... Forfeiture and Penalties [*Legal term*] (DLA)
FORG........ Forgery [*Business term*]
FORG .... Forging (MSA)
F ORG .... Full Organ [*Music*]
FORGA .... Forages [*A publication*]
FORGE...... File Organization Generator
Forg Ind NR ... Forging Industry Association's News Release [*A publication*]
FORGN ...... Foreign
Forgn Agr... Foreign Agriculture [*A publication*]
FORGO..... FORTRAN [*Formula Translating System*] Load and Go System [*University of Wisconsin*] [*Data processing*] (IEEE)
FORGOV .. Foreign Government (AFIT)
Forg Top .... Forging Topics [*A publication*]
For Hort ... Forsyth's Hortensius [*A publication*] (DLA)
FORIAQ.... Forest Research in India [*A publication*]
FORIMS ... FORTRAN [*Formula Translating System*]-Oriented Information Management System [*Data processing*]
For Ind .... Forest Industries [*A publication*]
For Ind R.... Forest Industries Review [*Later, Forest Industries*] [*A publication*]
For Ind Rev ... Forest Industries Equipment Review [*A publication*]
For Indus Rev ... Forest Industries Review [*A publication*]
For Inf........ Forsyth's Custody of Infants [*A publication*] (DLA)
For Insect Dis Cond US ... Forest Insect and Disease Conditions in the United States [*A publication*]
For Insect Dis Leafl USDA For Serv ... Forest Insect and Disease Leaflet. United States Department of Agriculture. Forest Service [*A publication*]
For Inst For GB ... Forestry. Institute of Foresters of Great Britain [*A publication*]
For Int LJ .. Fordham International Law Journal [*A publication*]
For Investment R ... Foreign Investment Review [*A publication*]

FORIS .... Forest Information System [*Global Environmental Monitoring System*]
FORIS .... Forschungsinformationssystem Sozialwissenschaften [*Informationszentrum Sozialwissenschaften*] [*Database*]
FORJ .... Fellowship of Religious Journalists (EA)
For Jury Tr ... Forsyth's Trial by Jury [*A publication*] (DLA)
FOR KY Univ Coop Ext Serv ... FOR. Kentucky University Cooperative Extension Service [*A publication*]
FORL............ Foreland Corp. [*Ogden, UT*] [*NASDAQ symbol*] (NQ)
For L .... Forum Linguisticum [*A publication*]
For Ling ..... Forum Linguisticum [*A publication*]
For Log ..... Forestry Log [*A publication*] (APTA)
FORLOGMD ... Force Logistics Command [*Marine Corps*] (NVT)
For LR........ Fordham Law Review [*A publication*]
FORM .... Ferromagnetic Object Recognition Matrix
Form............ Forman's Reports [*1 Scammon, 2 Illinois*] [*A publication*] (DLA)
FORM .... Formation (MSA)
FORM .... Formerly (ROG)
FORM .... Formula
FORM .... [*The*] Forum Re Group, Inc. [*NASDAQ symbol*] (NQ)
FORMA .... FORTRAN [*Formula Translating System*] Matrix Analysis [*Data processing*]
FORMAC ... Formula Manipulation Compiler [*Programming language*] [*1962*] [*Data processing*]
Forma Functio ... Forma et Function [*A publication*]
Formage Trait Metaux ... Formage et Traitements des Metaux [*A publication*]
FORMAL ... Formula Manipulation Language [*1970*] [*Data processing*] (MDG)
Forman....... Forman's Reports [*1 Scammon, 2 Illinois*] [*A publication*] (DLA)
Forman (Ill) ... Forman's Reports [*1 Scammon, 2 Illinois*] [*A publication*] (DLA)
FORMAT ... Foreign Material (MCD)
FORMAT ... FORTRAN [*Formula Translating System*] Matrix Abstraction Technique [*Data processing*] (MCD)
Format Continue ... Formation Continue [*A publication*]
FORMAT-FORTRAN ... FORTRAN [*Formula Translating System*] Matrix Abstraction Technique-FORTRAN [*Data processing*] (CSR)
Formation Agric Develop Rur ... Formation pour l'Agriculture et le Developpement Rural [*A publication*]
Formazione Dom ... Formazione Domani [*A publication*]
FORMDEPS ... FORSCOM [*Forces Command*] Mobilization and Deployment Planning System (MCD)
FORMECU ... Forestry Management, Evaluation, and Co-Ordinating Unit [*Nigeria*] [*World Bank Assisted Project*] [*Federal Department of Rural Development*]
For Mgmt Note BC For Serv ... Forest Management Note. British Columbia Forest Service [*A publication*]
Formirov Celov Kom Obsc ... Formirovanie Celovska Kommunisticeskogo Obscestva [*A publication*]
FORMN .... Formation
Formosan Agr Rev ... Formosan Agricultural Review [*A publication*]
Formosan Sci ... Formosan Science [*A publication*]
FORMOST ... Force Mobilization Steering Committee [*Army*] (MCD)
FORMPATPAC ... Formosa Patrol Force, US Pacific Fleet
Form Pla ... Brown's Formulae Bene Placitandi [*A publication*] (ILCA)
Form Prop Gas Bubbles Conf ... Formation and Properties of Gas Bubbles Conference [*A publication*]
FORMS..... Field Office Reporting-Management System [*HUD*]
FORMSA.... Force Command Standards Activity
Forms Ind ... Present and Future of the Forms Industry [*A publication*]
Form Tech ... Form und Technik [*A publication*]
FORMUL ... Formulary
Formul Solen ... Formulae Solemnes [*A publication*] (DLA)
Forn............ Fornax [*Constellation*]
FORN .... Fornication [*FBI standardized term*]
FORNN ..... Forenoon (FAAC)
For Note Ill Agric Exp Sta ... Forestry Note. University of Illinois. Agricultural Experiment Station [*A publication*]
For Notes ... Forest Notes. New Hampshire's Conservation Magazine [*A publication*]
Fornv.......... Fornvaennen [*A publication*]
Foro Amm ... Foro Amministrativo [*A publication*]
For Occ Pap FAO ... Forestry Occasional Paper. FAO [*Food and Agriculture Organization of the United Nations*] [*A publication*]
FORODD.. Fortschritte der Ophthalmologie [*A publication*]
Foro Int...... Foro Internacional [*A publication*]
Foro Internac ... Foro Internacional [*A publication*]
Foro It .... Foro Italiano [*A publication*]
Foro Nap..... Foro Napoletano [*A publication*] (ILCA)
Foro Pad ..... Foro Padano [*A publication*]
Foro Pen..... Foro Penale [*A publication*]
For & Outdoors ... Forest and Outdoors [*A publication*]
FORP......... Forestry Report. Northern Forest Research Centre. Canadian Forestry Service [*Edmonton*] [*A publication*]
FORPA...... Force Planning System
FORPAC.... Forecasting Passenger and Cargo (MCD)
FORPC...... Frozen Onion Ring Packers Council [*Absorbed by AFFI*] (EA)
For Pest Leafl ... Forest Pest Leaflet [*A publication*]

For Pest Leafl US For Serv ... Forest Pest Leaflet. United States Forest Service [*A publication*]
For Pla .... Brown's Formulae Bene Placitandi [*A publication*] (DLA)
For Pol .... Foreign Policy [*A publication*]
For Policy... Foreign Policy [*A publication*]
For Policy Bul ... Foreign Policy Bulletin [*A publication*]
For Policy Rep ... Foreign Policy Reports [*A publication*]
FORPORT ... Forward Port Capabilities [*Navy*]
For Pr......... Foran. Code of Civil Procedure of Quebec [*A publication*] (DLA)
FORPRIDECOM ... Forest Products Research and Industries Development Commission
FORPRIDE Dig ... FORPRIDE [*Forest Products Research and Industries Development*] Digest [*A publication*]
For Prod J ... Forest Products Journal [*A publication*]
For Prod Ne Lett ... Forest Products News Letter [*A publication*]
For Prod Newsl ... Forest Products Newsletter. Commonwealth Scientific and Industrial Research Organisation. Division of Forest Products [*A publication*] (APTA)
For Prod Res ... Forest Products Research [*A publication*]
For Prod Res Bull (GB) ... Forest Products Research Bulletin (Great Britain) [*A publication*]
For Prod Res Dev Inst J ... Forest Products Research and Development Institute. Journal [*A publication*]
For Prod Res Ind Dev Dig ... Forest Products Research and Industries Development Digest [*A publication*]
For Prod Res No ... Forest Products Research Notes. Forest Research Institute [*New Zealand*] [*A publication*]
For Prod Res Rec Div For Prod (Zambia) ... Forest Products Research Record. Division of Forest Products (Zambia) [*A publication*]
For Prod Res Rep Dep For Res (Nigeria) ... Forest Products Research Reports. Department of Forest Research (Nigeria) [*A publication*]
For Prod Util Tech Rep US For Serv Coop For Div ... Forest Products Utilization Technical Report. United States Forest Service. Cooperative Forestry Division [*A publication*]
For Q.......... Foreign Quarterly Review [*A publication*]
FOR Q .... Forestry Quarterly [*New York*] [*A publication*]
For Quar ..... Forest Quarterly [*A publication*]
For R .... Foreign Review [*A publication*]
Forr .... Forrester's English Chancery Cases Tempore Talbot [*A publication*] (DLA)
Forr .... Forrest's English Exchequer Reports [*A publication*] (DLA)
FORRAJ ... Forest Record [*London*] [*A publication*]
For Rec For Comm (Lond) ... Forest Record. Forestry Commission (London) [*A publication*]
For Rec (Lond) ... Forest Record (London) [*A publication*]
For Recreat Res ... Forest Recreation Research [*A publication*]
For Res Bull For Dep (Zambia) ... Forest Research Bulletin. Forest Department (Zambia) [*A publication*]
For Res India ... Forest Research in India [*A publication*]
For Res Inf Pap Minist Natl Res (Ont) ... Forest Research Information Paper. Ministry of Natural Resources (Ontario) [*A publication*]
For Res Inst (Bogor) Commun ... Forest Research Institute (Bogor). Communication [*A publication*]
For Res Note Ont For Res Cent ... Forest Research Note. Ontario Forest Research Centre [*A publication*]
For Res Notes ... Forestry Research Notes [*A publication*]
For Res Notes Weyerhaeuser Timber Co ... Forestry Research Notes. Weyerhaeuser Timber Company [*A publication*]
For Res Note Wis Coll Agric ... Forestry Research Notes. University of Wisconsin. College of Agriculture [*A publication*]
For Resour Newslett ... Forest Resources Newsletter [*A publication*]
For Resour Rep US For Serv ... Forest Resource Report. United States Forest Service [*A publication*]
For Res Pamphl Div For Res (Zambia) ... Forest Research Pamphlet. Division of Forest Research (Zambia) [*A publication*]
For Res Rep ... Forest Resource Report. United States Forest Service [*A publication*]
For Res Rep Agric Exp Stn Univ Ill ... Forestry Research Report. Agricultural Experiment Station. University of Illinois [*A publication*]
For Res Rep Ont Minist Nat Resour ... Forest Research Report. Ontario Ministry of Natural Resources [*A publication*]
For Res Rev ... Forest Research Review. British Columbia Forest Service [*A publication*]
For Res Southeast US Southern For Exp Stn ... Forest Research in the Southeast. United States Southeastern Forest Experiment Station [*A publication*]
Forrest .... Forrest's English Exchequer Reports [*A publication*] (DLA)
Forrester .... Forrester's English Chancery Cases Tempore Talbot [*A publication*] (DLA)
For Res West US For Serv ... Forestry Research West. United States Forest Service [*A publication*]
For Res What's New West ... Forestry Research. What's New in the West [*A publication*]
For the Riverina Teach ... For the Riverina Teacher [*A publication*] (APTA)
FORS......... Fabrication Operations Requirements System (MCD)
FORS......... Faint Object Red Spectrograph [*Astronomy*]
FORS......... Fiber Optic Rate Sensors [*Instrumentation*]
FORS......... Forensic Science Database [*British Home Office Forensic Science Service*] [*Reading, Berkshire, England*] [*Information service or system*] (IID)

FORS......... Forestry

FORS......... Forschungsprojekte, Raumordnung, Stadtebau, Wohnungswesen [*Regional Planning, Town Planning, Housing, Research Projects Database*] [*Fraunhofer Society*] (IID)

FORS......... Fully Optimized Reaction Space

For S Afr..... Forestry in South Africa [*A publication*]

Fors Cas & Op ... Forsyth's Cases and Opinions on Constitutional Law [*A publication*] (DLA)

Forsch u Berat ... Forschung und Beratung. Forstwirtschaft [*A publication*]

Forsch Berat Forstw ... Forschung und Beratung. Forstwirtschaft [*A publication*]

Forsch Ber Evangel Studiengemeinsch ... Forschungen und Berichte. Evangelische Studiengemeinschaft [*A publication*]

Forsch Ber Staatl Mus Berlin ... Forschungen und Berichte. Staatliche Museen zu Berlin [*A publication*]

Forsch D Ld u Volksk ... Forschungen zur Deutschen Landes- und Volkskunde [*A publication*]

Forsch Dt Landeskde ... Forschungen zur Deutschen Landes- und Volkskunde [*A publication*]

Forsch F..... Forschungen und Fortschritte [*A publication*]

Forsch Fortschr ... Forschungen und Fortschritte [*A publication*]

Forsch u Fortschr ... Forschungen und Fortschritte [*A publication*]

Forsch Fortschr Dtsch Wiss ... Forschungen und Fortschritte. Nachrichtenblatt der Deutschen Wissenschaft und Technik [*A publication*]

Forsch Geb Ingenieurwes ... Forschung auf dem Gebiete des Ingenieurwesens [*A publication*]

Forsch Geogr Ges ... Forschungen. Geographische Gesellschaft in Luebeck [*A publication*]

Forsch Gesch Opt ... Forschungen zur Geschichte der Optik [*A publication*]

Forsch H Schiffst ... Forschungshefte fuer Schiffstechnik, Schiffbau, und Schiffsmaschinenbau [*A publication*]

Forsch H Stahlbau ... Forschungshefte aus dem Gebiete des Stahlbaues [*A publication*]

Forsch Ing ... Forschung auf dem Gebiete des Ingenieurwesens [*A publication*]

Forsch Ingenieurw ... Forschung im Ingenieurwesen [*A publication*]

Forsch Ingenieurwes ... Forschung im Ingenieurwesen [*A publication*]

Forsch Klin Lab ... Forschung in der Klinik und im Labor [*A publication*]

Forschn Fortschr ... Forschungen und Fortschritte [*A publication*]

Forsch Ost Eur G ... Forschungen zur Ost Europaeischen Geschichte [*A publication*]

Forsch Planen Bauen ... Forschen, Planen, Bauen [*A publication*]

Forschungsber Dtsch Forsch Versuchsant Luft-Raumfahrt ... Forschungsbericht. Deutsche Forschungs- und Versuchsanstalt fuer Luft- und Raumfahrt [*West Germany*] [*A publication*]

Forschungsber Fachbereich Bauwesen ... Forschungsbericht aus dem Fachbereich Bauwesen [*A publication*]

Forschungsber Landes Nordrhein-Westfalen ... Forschungsberichte des Landes Nordrhein-Westfalen [*A publication*]

Forschungsber Wirtsch Verkehrministr Nordrhein Westfalen ... Forschungsberichte des Wirtschafts- und Verkehrsministeriums Nordrhein-Westfalen [*A publication*]

Forschungsber Wirtsch Verkehrsminist Nordrhein-Westfalen ... Forschungsberichte des Wirtschafts- und Verkehrsministeriums Nordrhein-Westfalen [*A publication*]

Forschungsber Wirtsch Verkehrsminist Nordrh Westfalen ... Forschungsberichte des Wirtschafts- und Verkehrsministeriums Nordrhein-Westfalen [*West Germany*] [*A publication*]

Forschungsh Geb Stahlbaues ... Forschungshefte aus dem Gebiete des Stahlbaues [*A publication*]

Forschungsh Studienges Hoechstspannungsanlagen ... Forschungshefte. Studiengesellschaft fuer Hoechstspannungsanlagen [*A publication*]

Forsch Volks Land ... Forschungen zur Volks- und Landeskunde [*A publication*]

Forsch Vor und Fruehgesch ... Forschungen zur Vor- und Fruehgeschichte [*A publication*]

For Sci........ Forest Science [*A publication*]

For Sci Intl ... Forensic Science International [*A publication*]

For Sci Monogr ... Forest Science Monographs [*A publication*]

For Sci (Sofia) ... Forest Science (Sofia) [*A publication*]

FORSCOM ... Forces Command [*Formerly, CONARC*] [*Army*]

Fors Comp ... Forsyth on Composition with Creditors [*A publication*] (DLA)

For Serv Res Note NE Northeast For Exp Stn US Dep Agric ... Forest Service Research Note NE. Northeastern Forest Experiment Station. Forest Service. Department of Agriculture [*A publication*]

For Serv Res Pap NE (US) ... Forest Service Research Paper NE (United States) [*A publication*]

Fors u Fort ... Forschungen und Fortschritte [*A publication*]

Fors Hor .... Forsyth's Hortensius [*A publication*] (DLA)

FORSIC..... Forces Intelligence Center (AABC)

Fors Inf ...... Forsyth's Custody of Infants [*A publication*] (DLA)

FORSIZE ... Force Sizing Exercise [*Military*]

Forsk Fors Landbr ... Forskning og Forsok i Landbruket [*A publication*]

Forsk Fors Landbruket ... Forskning og Forsok i Landbruket [*A publication*]

Forsk Framsteg ... Forskning och Framsteg [*A publication*]

Forsk Groenl ... Forskning i Groenland [*Denmark*] [*A publication*]

Forsk Udvikling Uddannelse ... Forskning Udvikling Uddannelse [*A publication*]

For Social Agric Sci ... For Socialist Agricultural Science [*A publication*]

For Soils Jpn ... Forest Soils of Japan [*A publication*]

Forsokmeld Landbrukstek Inst ... Forsoksmelding. Landbruksteknisk Institutt [*A publication*]

FORSTAR ... Force Status and Identity Report

FORSTAT ... Force Status Report [*Military*]

Forst Cust .. Forster's Digest of the Laws of Customs [*A publication*] (DLA)

Forst Forsogvaes Dan ... Forstlige Forsogsvaesen i Danmark [*A publication*]

Forst- u Holzw ... Forst- und Holzwirt [*A publication*]

Forstl Bundesversuchsanst ... Forstliche Bundesversuchsanstalt [*A publication*]

Forstl Bundesversuchsanst Wien Jahresber ... Forstliche Bundesversuchsanstalt Wien. Jahresbericht [*A publication*]

Forstl Forsogsvaes Dan ... Forstlige Forsogsvaesen i Danmark [*A publication*]

Forstl Forsogsv Danm ... Forstlige Forsogsvaesen i Danmark [*A publication*]

Fors Tr .... Forsyth on Trusts and Trustees in Scotland [*A publication*] (DLA)

Fors Tr Jur ... Forsyth's History of Trial by Jury [*A publication*] (DLA)

FORSTRY ... Forestry

Forsttech Inf ... Forsttechnische Informationen [*A publication*]

Forsttech Inform ... Forsttechnische Informationen [*A publication*]

Forstw Centbl ... Forstwirtschaftliches Centralblatt [*A publication*]

Forstwirtsch Holzwirtsch ... Forstwirtschaft Holzwirtschaft [*A publication*]

Forstwiss Cbl ... Forstwissenschaftliches Centralblatt [*A publication*]

Forstwiss Centralbl (Hamb) ... Forstwissenschaftliches Centralblatt (Hamburg) [*A publication*]

Forstwiss Forsch ... Forstwissenschaftliche Forschungen [*A publication*]

Forstwiss Forsch Beih Forstwiss Centralbl ... Forstwissenschaftliche Forschungen. Beihefte zum Forstwissenschaftlichen Centralblatt [*A publication*]

Forstwiss Zentbl ... Forstwissenschaftliches Zentralblatt [*A publication*]

For Surv Note BC For Serv ... Forest Survey Notes. British Columbia Forest Service [*A publication*]

Fort .... Fortescue's English King's Bench Reports [*92 English Reprint*] [*1695-1738*] [*A publication*] (DLA)

FORT........ Fortification

FORT........ Fortis [*Strong*] [*Pharmacy*]

FORT........ Fortune 44 Co. [*NASDAQ symbol*] (NQ)

FORT........ Full Out Rye Terms [*Grain trade*]

FORTA........ Fortune [*A publication*]

For Tax Bull ... Foreign Tax Law Bi-Weekly Bulletin [*A publication*] (DLA)

For Tax L S-W Bull ... Foreign Tax Law Semi-Weekly Bulletin [*A publication*] (DLA)

For Tax LS Weekly Bull ... Foreign Tax Law Semi-Weekly Bulletin [*A publication*] (DLA)

For Tax LW Bull ... Foreign Tax Law Weekly Bulletin [*A publication*] (DLA)

Fortbildungskurse Rheumatol ... Fortbildungskurse fuer Rheumatologie [*A publication*]

Fortbildungskurse Schweiz Ges Psychiatr ... Fortbildungskurse. Schweizerische Gesellschaft fuer Psychiatrie [*A publication*]

Fort De Laud ... Fortescue. De Laudibus Legum Angliae [*A publication*] (DLA)

Fort Dodge Bio-Chem Rev ... Fort Dodge Bio-Chemic Review [*A publication*]

FORTE...... File Organization Technique (BUR)

For Tech Note NH Agric Exp Sta ... Forestry Technical Notes. University of New Hampshire. Agricultural Experiment Station [*A publication*]

For Tech Pap ... Forestry Technical Papers [*A publication*] (APTA)

For Tech Pap For Comm Vict ... Forestry Technical Papers. Forests Commission of Victoria [*A publication*]

FORTEL ... Formatted Teletypewriter (CET)

Fortes .... Fortescue's English Courts Reports [*A publication*] (DLA)

Fortesc ...... Fortescue's English King's Bench Reports [*92 English Reprint*] [*1695-1738*] [*A publication*] (DLA)

Fortesc De LL Angl ... Fortescue. De Laudibus Legum Angliae [*A publication*] (DLA)

Fortescue.... Fortescue's English King's Bench Reports [*92 English Reprint*] [*1695-1738*] [*A publication*] (DLA)

Fortescue (Eng) ... Fortescue's English King's Bench Reports [*92 English Reprint*] [*1695-1738*] [*A publication*] (DLA)

Fortes De Laud ... Fortescue. De Laudibus Legum Angliae [*A publication*] (DLA)

Fortes Rep ... Fortescue's English King's Bench Reports [*92 English Reprint*] [*1695-1738*] [*A publication*] (DLA)

FORTFLAC ... Fellowship of Reconciliation Task Force on Latin America and Caribbean (EA)

FORTH ..... [*A*] programming language [*1968*] (CSR)

Fort Hare Pap ... Fort Hare Papers [*A publication*]

Fort Hays Stud New Ser Sci Ser ... Fort Hays Studies. New Series. Science Series [*A publication*]

Forthcoming Int Sci & Tech Conf ... Forthcoming International Scientific and Technical Conference [*A publication*]

Forth Nat Hist ... Forth Naturalist and Historian [*A publication*]

For and Timb ... Forest and Timber [*A publication*] (APTA)

For Timb .... Forest and Timber [*A publication*] (APTA)

For Timber ... Forest and Timber [*A publication*]

FORTIS..... Fortissimo [*Very Loud*] [*Music*]
FORTISS .. Fortissimo [*Very Loud*] [*Music*]   (ROG)
FORTISS .. Fortissimus [*Strongest*] [*Pharmacy*]   (ROG)
FORTL...... Force Requirement Troop List Reporting System   (AABC)
Fort LJ...... Fortnightly Law Journal [*A publication*]   (DLA)
FORTN ..... Fortnightly
Fortn .... Fortnightly Review [*A publication*]
Fortnightly LJ ... Fortnightly Law Journal [*A publication*]   (DLA)
Fortn LJ..... Fortnightly Law Journal [*A publication*]   (DLA)
FortnR........ Fortnightly Review [*A publication*]
Fortn Rev Chic Dent Soc ... Fortnightly Review of the Chicago Dental Society [*A publication*]
Fortpflanz Besamung Aufzucht Haustiere ... Fortpflanzung Besamung und Aufzucht der Haustiere [*A publication*]
Fortpflanz Zuchthyg Haustierbesamung ... Fortpflanzung, Zuchthygiene, und Haustierbesamung [*A publication*]
Fort Pierce ARC Res Rep R1 Univ Fla Agric Res Cent ... Fort Pierce ARC Research Report R1. University of Florida. Agricultural Research Center [*A publication*]
FORTRAN ... Formula Translating System [*Programming language*] [*1953-54*]   (CSR)
FORTRANSIT ... FORTRAN [*Formula Translating System*] and Internal Translator System [*Data processing*]   (IEEE)
For Tree Improv ... Forest Tree Improvement [*A publication*]
For Tree Ser Div For Res CSIRO ... Forest Tree Series. Division of Forest Research. Commonwealth Scientific and Industrial Research Organisation [*A publication*]   (APTA)
Fort Rev ..... Fortnightly Review [*A publication*]
FORTRPS ... Force Troops
FORTRUNCIBLE ... FORTRAN [*Formula Translating System*] Style Runcible [*Data processing*]
Fortsch-Ber VDI Z Reihe ... Fortschritt-Berichte. VDI [*Verein Deutscher Ingenieure*] Zeitschriften. Reihe [*West Germany*]
Fortsch Klin Pharmakol ... Fortschritte der Klinischen Pharmakologie [*A publication*]
Fortsch Ophthalmol ... Fortschritte der Ophthalmologie [*A publication*]
Fortschr Acker Pflanzenb ... Fortschritte im Acker und Pflanzenbau [*A publication*]
Fortschr Acker- Pflanzenbau ... Fortschritte im Acker- und Pflanzenbau [*A publication*]
Fortschr Allergiel ... Fortschritte der Allergielehre [*A publication*]
Fortschr Androl ... Fortschritte der Andrologie [*A publication*]
Fortschr Anorg Chem Ind ... Fortschritte in der Anorganisch Chemischen Industrie [*A publication*]
Fortschr Antimikrob Antineoplast Chemother ... Fortschritte der Antimikrobiellen und Antineoplastischen Chemotherapie [*A publication*]
Fortschr Arzneimittelforsch ... Fortschritte der Arzneimittelforschung [*A publication*]
Fortschr Augenheilkd ... Fortschritte der Augenheilkunde [*A publication*]
Fortschrber Landw ... Fortschrittsberichte fuer die Landwirtschaft [*A publication*]
Fortschr Ber VDI Z ... Fortschritt-Berichte. VDI [*Verein Deutscher Ingenieure*] Zeitschrift [*A publication*]
Fortschr Ber VDI Zeitschr Reihe 2 ... Fortschritt-Berichte. VDI [*Verein Deutscher Ingenieure*] Zeitschriften. Reihe 2 [*A publication*]
Fortschr-Ber VDI Z Reihe 4 ... Fortschritt-Berichte. VDI [*Verein Deutscher Ingenieure*] Zeitschriften. Reihe 4. Bauingenieurwesen [*West Germany*] [*A publication*]
Fortschr Bot ... Fortschritte der Botanik [*A publication*]
Fortschr Chem Forsch ... Fortschritte der Chemischen Forschung [*A publication*]
Fortschr Chem Org Natr ... Fortschritte der Chemie Organischer Naturstoffe [*A publication*]
Fortschr Chem Org Natstoffe ... Fortschritte der Chemie Organischer Naturstoffe [*A publication*]
Fortschr Chem Org Naturst ... Fortschritte der Chemie Organischer Naturstoffe [*A publication*]
Fortschr Chem Phys Phys Chem ... Fortschritte der Chemie, Physik, und Physikalischen Chemie [*A publication*]
Fortschr Evolutionsforsch ... Fortschritte der Evolutionsforschung [*A publication*]
Fortschr Exp Theor Biophys ... Fortschritte der Experimentellen und Theoretischen Biophysik [*A publication*]
Fortschr Exp Tumorforsch ... Fortschritte der Experimentellen Tumorforschung [*A publication*]
Fortschr Geb Roentgenstr ... Fortschritte auf dem Gebiete der Roentgenstrahlen [*A publication*]
Fortschr Geb Roentgenstr Nuklearmed ... Fortschritte auf dem Gebiete der Roentgenstrahlen und der Nuklearmedizin [*A publication*]
Fortschr Geb Roentgenstr Ver Roentgenprax ... Fortschritte auf dem Gebiete der Roentgenstrahlen Vereinigt mit Roentgenpraxis [*A publication*]
Fortschr Geburtshilfe Gynaekol ... Fortschritte der Geburtshilfe und Gynaekologie [*A publication*]
Fortschr Geol Rheinland Westfalen ... Fortschritte in der Geologie von Rheinland und Westfalen [*A publication*]
Fortschr Geol Rheinl Westfalen ... Fortschritte in der Geologie von Rheinland und Westfalen [*A publication*]

Fortschr Hals- Nasen Ohrenheilkd ... Fortschritte der Hals- Nasen- Ohrenheilkunde [*A publication*]
Fortschr Hochpolym-Forsch ... Fortschritte der Hochpolymeren-Forschung [*A publication*]
Fortschr Immunitaetsforsch ... Fortschritte der Immunitaetsforschung [*A publication*]
Fortschritt Ber VDI Zeitschr Reihe 11 ... Fortschritt-Berichte. VDI [*Verein Deutscher Ingenieure*] Zeitschriften. Reihe 11 [*A publication*]
Fortschritt Ber VDI Zeitschr Reihe 8 ... Fortschritt-Berichte. VDI [*Verein Deutscher Ingenieure*] Zeitschriften. Reihe 8 [*A publication*]
Fortschrittsber Chem Ztg ... Fortschrittsberichte der Chemiker-Zeitung [*A publication*]
Fortschrittsber Kolloide Polym ... Fortschrittsberichte ueber Kolloide und Polymere [*A publication*]
Fortschrittsber Landwirtsch ... Fortschrittsberichte fuer die Landwirtschaft [*A publication*]
Fortschr Kardiol ... Fortschritte der Kardiologie [*A publication*]
Fortschr Kiefer Gesichtschir ... Fortschritte der Kiefer und Geschichts Chirurgie [*A publication*]
Fortschr Kieferorthop ... Fortschritte der Kieferorthopaedie [*A publication*]
Fortschr Krebsforsch ... Fortschritte der Krebsforschung [*A publication*]
Fortschr Landwirtsch ... Fortschritte der Landwirtschaft [*A publication*]
Fortschr Med ... Fortschritte der Medizin [*A publication*]
Fortschr Med Mikrobiol ... Fortschritte der Medizinischen Mikrobiologie [*A publication*]
Fortschr Med Virusforsch ... Fortschritte der Medizinischen Virusforschung [*A publication*]
Fortschr Mineral ... Fortschritte der Mineralogie [*A publication*]
Fortschr Mineral Beihe ... Fortschritte der Mineralogie. Beiheft [*A publication*]
Fortschr Mineral Kristallogr Petrogr ... Fortschritte der Mineralogie, Kristallographie, und Petrographie [*A publication*]
Fortschr Miner Beih ... Fortschritte der Mineralogie. Beiheft [*A publication*]
Fortschr Neurol Psychiatr ... Fortschritte der Neurologie, Psychiatrie, und Ihrer Grenzgebiete [*A publication*]
Fortschr Neurol Psychiatr Grenzgeb ... Fortschritte der Neurologie, Psychiatrie, und Ihrer Grenzgebiete [*A publication*]
Fortschr Neurol Psychiatr Ihrer Grenzgeb ... Fortschritte der Neurologie, Psychiatrie, und Ihrer Grenzgebiete [*A publication*]
Fortschr Pflanzenzuecht ... Fortschritte der Pflanzenzuechtung [*A publication*]
Fortschr Ph ... Fortschritte der Physik [*A publication*]
Fortschr Phys ... Fortschritte der Physik [*A publication*]
Fortschr Phys Chem ... Fortschritte der Physikalischen Chemie [*A publication*]
Fortschr Phys Dtsche Phys Ges ... Fortschritte der Physik. Deutsche Physikalische Gesellschaft [*A publication*]
Fortschr Physik ... Fortschritte der Physik [*A publication*]
Fortschr Psychosom Med ... Fortschritte der Psychosomatischen Medizin [*A publication*]
Fortschr Ther ... Fortschritte der Therapie [*A publication*]
Fortschr Tierphysiol Tierernaehr ... Fortschritte in der Tierphysiologie und Tierernaehrung [*A publication*]
Fortschr Tuberkuloseforsch ... Fortschritte der Tuberkuloseforschung [*A publication*]
Fortschr Verfahrenstech ... Fortschritte der Verfahrenstechnik [*A publication*]
Fortschr Verhaltensforsch ... Fortschritte der Verhaltensforschung [*A publication*]
Fortschr Veterinaermed ... Fortschritte der Veterinaermedizin [*A publication*]
Fortschr Wasserchem Ihrer Grenzgeb ... Fortschritte der Wasserchemie und Ihrer Grenzgebiete [*East Germany*] [*A publication*]
Fortschr Wasserchem Ihrer Grenzgebie ... Fortschritte der Wasserchemie und Ihrer Grenzgebiete [*A publication*]
Fortschr Zool ... Fortschritte der Zoologie [*A publication*]
Fortschr Zool Syst Evolutionsforsch ... Fortschritte in der Zoologischen Systematik und Evolutionsforschung [*A publication*]
FORTSK ... For Task Force [*Military*]   (AABC)
Fortu .... Fortunius Garcia de Erzila [*Flourished, 16th century*] [*Authority cited in pre-1607 legal work*]   (DSA)
Fortuna Ital ... Fortuna Italiana [*A publication*]
FORTUNE ... FORTRAN [*Formula Translating System*] Tuner [*Data processing*]
Fortune Sp ... Fortune Special Issue. Investor's Guide [*A publication*]
FORUM .... Formula for Optimizing through Real-Time Utilization of Multiprogramming
Forum......... Forum: Bench and Bar Review [*A publication*]   (DLA)
Forum......... Forum. Dickinson School of Law [*A publication*]   (DLA)
Forum......... Forum for the Discussion of New Trends in Education [*A publication*]
Forum......... Forum Law Review [*A publication*]   (DLA)
Forum......... International Trade Forum [*A publication*]
Forum Disc New Trends Educ ... Forum for the Discussion of New Trends in Education [*A publication*]
Forum Ed ... Forum of Education [*A publication*]
Forum Educ ... Forum of Education [*A publication*]   (APTA)
Forum Ekon Tek ... Forum foer Ekonomi och Teknik [*A publication*]
ForumH ... Forum (Houston) [*A publication*]
Forum LR ... Forum Law Review [*A publication*]   (DLA)
Forum M.... Forum Musicum [*A publication*]
Forum Med ... Forum on Medicine [*A publication*]

Forum Microbiol ... Forum Microbiologicum [*A publication*]
Forum Mikrobiol ... Forum Mikrobiologie [*West Germany*] [*A publication*]
Forum Mod L ... Forum for Modern Language Studies [*A publication*]
Forum Pub Aff ... Forum on Public Affairs [*A publication*]
Forum Rep Sci Ind Forum Aust Acad Sci ... Australian Academy of Science. Science and Industry Forum. Forum Report [*A publication*]   (APTA)
Forum Rep Sci Ind Forum Aust Acad Sci ... Forum Report. Science and Industry Forum. Australian Academy of Science [*A publication*]
Forum Rev ... Forum Law Review [*A publication*]   (ILCA)
ForumS ...... Forum: A Ukrainian Review (Scranton, Pennsylvania) [*A publication*]
Forum Sekolah Pasca Sarjana Inst Pertanian Bogor ... Forum Sekolah Pasca Sarjana Institut Pertanian Bogor [*A publication*]
Forum Staedte Hyg ... Forum Staedte Hygiene [*A publication*]
Forum Umwelt Hyg ... Forum Umwelt Hygiene [*A publication*]
Forum Umw Hyg ... Forum Umwelt Hygiene [*A publication*]
ForumZ ...... Forum (Zagreb) [*A publication*]
For Urb LJ ... Fordham Urban Law Journal [*A publication*]
FORWARD ... Forces Organized Ready for War and Able to Rapidly Deploy   (MCD)
FORWEPCON ... Forward Weapons Controller [*Military*]   (NVT)
FORWEPCORD ... Force Weapons Coordinator [*Navy*]   (NVT)
FORY .... Flag Officer, Royal Yachts [*Navy*] [*British*]
FORZ .... Forzato [*Strongly Accented*] [*Music*]
FOS .... Face of Studs [*Technical drawings*]
FOS .... Faint Object Spectrograph [*Astronomy*]
FOS .... Fall of Shot   (NVT)
FOS .... Family of Small Arms [*Military*]   (MCD)
FOS .... Fats and Oils Situation
FOS .... Field Officers School [*Formerly, AOS*] [*LIMRA*]
FOS .... File Organization System   (DIT)
FOS .... Final Operating System   (MCD)
FOS .... Flight Operations Support   (KSC)
FOS .... Follow-On Spares   (AFM)
FOS .... FORTRAN [*Formula Translating System*] Operating System [*Data processing*]
FOS .... Free on Ship [*or Steamer*] [*Shipping*]
FOS .... Free on Station
FOS .... Full Operational Status
FOS .... Functional Operational Specification [*Military*]   (CAAL)
FOSA .... Family of Small Arms [*Military*]
FOSA .... Formula One Spectators Association   (EA)
FOSAT ...... Fitting Out Supply Assistance Team [*Navy*]
FOSATLANT ... Fitting Out Supply Assistance Team, Atlantic [*Navy*]
FOSATPAC ... Fitting Out Supply Assistance Team, Pacific [*Navy*]
FOSC .... From Other Service Centers [*IRS*]
FOSC .... Full Overlap Slotted Container [*Packaging*]
FOSCAD ... Forest Science [*A publication*]
FOSCAN ... Food News Scanning Database [*Leatherhead Food Research Association*] [*Information service or system*]   (CRD)
FOSCAS .... Foreign Ship Construction and Shipyards   (MCD)
FOSCDG ... Food Science [*New York*] [*A publication*]
FOSD .... Field Operations and Support Division [*Environmental Protection Agency*]
FOSD .... Functional Operational Sequence Diagram
FOSDIC .... Film Optical Sensing Device for Input to Computers [*National Institute of Standards and Technology*]
FOSE .... Federal Office Systems Expo [*National Trade Productions*]   (TSPED)
FOSF .... Field Observing Support Facility [*National Center for Atmospheric Research*]
FOSF .... Friends of Old St. Ferdinand   (EA)
FOSFA ...... Federation of Oils, Seeds, and Fats Associations [*British*]
FOSGEN ... Fog Oil Smoke Generator
Fo-Si .... Forsterite-Silica [*Lunar geology*]
FOSIC .... Fleet Ocean Surveillance Information Center [*Navy*]   (CAAL)
FOSIF .... Fleet Ocean Surveillance Information Facilities [*Navy*]
FOSL .... Fossil Oil & Gas Co. [*NASDAQ symbol*]   (NQ)
FOSM .... Flag Officer, Submarines [*Navy*] [*British*]
FOSM .... Fort Smith National Historic Site
FOSMA9 ... Forest Science Monographs [*A publication*]
FOSMEF .... Flag Officer, Soviet Middle East Forces
FOSN .... Fabrication Order Special Number
FOSO .... Flight Operations Scheduling Office [*NASA*]   (MCD)
FOSO .... Flight Operations Scheduling Officer [*NASA*]   (NASA)
FOSOL ...... Florian's Own Statistically Oriented Language [*Data processing*]   (CSR)
FOSP .... Fabrication Outline Special Purpose
FOSP .... Flight Operations Support Personnel   (MCD)
Fo-Sp-Crd-Pl ... Forsterite-Spinel-Cordierite-Plagioclase [*Lunar geology*]
FOSPSL .... Follow-On Spare Parts Selection List   (MCD)
FOSS .... Family of Systems Studies [*Military*]   (RDA)
FOSS .... Fiber Optics SONAR System   (MCD)
Foss .... [*E.*] Foss. Biographia Juridica [*1 vol.*] [*1870*] [*A publication*]   (DLA)
Foss .... [*E.*] Foss. The Judges of England [*9 vols.*] [*1848-64*] [*A publication*]   (DLA)
Foss Bio Jur ... [*E.*] Foss. Biographia Juridica [*1 vol.*] [*1870*] [*A publication*]   (DLA)

FOSSCS .... Field Office Sales and Service Costs Study [*LIMRA*]
Foss Judg ... [*E.*] Foss. The Judges of England [*9 vols.*] [*1848-64*] [*A publication*]   (DLA)
FOSSL ...... Follow-On Spares Support List   (AFIT)
FOST .... Flag Officer, Sea Training [*Navy*] [*British*]
FOST .... Flight Operations Support Team   (MCD)
Fost .... Foster's English Crown Law Cases [*168 English Reprint*] [*1743-61*] [*A publication*]   (DLA)
Fost .... Foster's Legal Chronicle Reports [*Pennsylvania*] [*A publication*]   (DLA)
Fost .... Foster's New Hampshire Reports [*A publication*]   (DLA)
Fost .... Foster's Reports [*5, 6, and 8 Hawaii*] [*A publication*]   (DLA)
Fost CL ..... Foster's English Crown Law Cases [*168 English Reprint*] [*1743-61*] [*A publication*]   (DLA)
Fost CL (Eng) ... Foster's English Crown Law Cases [*168 English Reprint*] [*1743-61*] [*A publication*]   (DLA)
Fost Cr Law ... Foster's English Crown Law Cases [*168 English Reprint*] [*1743-61*] [*A publication*]   (DLA)
Fost Doct Com ... Foster on Doctors' Commons [*A publication*]   (DLA)
Fost El Jur ... Foster's Elements of Jurisprudence [*1853*] [*A publication*]   (DLA)
Foster .... Foster's English Crown Law Cases [*168 English Reprint*] [*1743-61*] [*A publication*]   (DLA)
Foster .... Foster's New Hampshire Reports [*A publication*]   (DLA)
Foster .... Legal Chronicle Reports, Edited by Foster [*Pennsylvania*] [*A publication*]   (DLA)
Foster Fed Pr ... Foster on Federal Practice [*A publication*]   (DLA)
Foster Mo Ref ... Foster's Monthly Reference Lists [*A publication*]
Foster (PA) ... Foster's Legal Chronicle Reports [*Pennsylvania*] [*A publication*]   (DLA)
Fost & F ..... Foster and Finlason's English Nisi Prius Reports [*175, 176 English Reprint*] [*A publication*]   (DLA)
Fost Fed Prac ... Foster's Treatise on Pleading and Practice in Equity in Courts of the United States [*A publication*]   (DLA)
Fost & F (Eng) ... Foster and Finlason's English Nisi Prius Reports [*175, 176 English Reprint*] [*A publication*]   (DLA)
Fost & Fin .. Foster and Finlason's English Nisi Prius Reports [*175, 176 English Reprint*] [*A publication*]   (DLA)
FOSTG ...... Freedom of Ocean Science Task Group [*NAS-NRC*]   (NOAA)
Fost (Haw) ... Foster's Reports [*5, 6, and 8 Hawaii*] [*A publication*]   (DLA)
Fost Jt Own ... Foster on Joint Ownership and Partition [*A publication*]   (DLA)
Fost (NH) .. Foster's New Hampshire Reports [*A publication*]   (DLA)
Fost Sci Fa ... Foster on the Writ of Scire Facias [*1851*] [*A publication*]   (DLA)
Fost on Sci Fa ... Foster on the Writ of Scire Facias [*1851*] [*A publication*]   (DLA)
FOSU .... Fort Sumter National Monument
FOSWAC .. Family of Special Weapons Atomic Contractors
FOSZAE ... Fogorvosi Szemle [*A publication*]
FOT .... Face of Template   (MCD)
FOT .... Fifth-Order Theory
FOT .... Flight Operations Team   (MCD)
FOT .... Follow-On Operational Test   (AFM)
FOT .... Fortuna, CA [*Location identifier*] [*FAA*]   (FAAL)
FOT .... Fortune [*A publication*]
FOT .... Forward Transfer [*Telecommunications*]   (TEL)
FOT .... Free of Tax
FOT .... Free on Truck [*See also FOR*] [*Business term*]
FOT .... Frequency of Optimum Operation   (MCD)
FOT .... Frequency Optimum Traffic
FOT .... Frequency on Target
FOT .... Fuel Oil Tank   (MSA)
FOT .... Fuel Oil Transfer
FOT .... Units of English System [*Aviation code*]   (FAAC)
FOTA .... Fuels Open Test Assembly [*Nuclear energy*]   (NRCH)
FOTALI .... Flag Officer, Taranto and Adriatic and for Liaison
FOTC .... Forward Observer Training Center [*Army*]   (INF)
FOTC .... Friends of Terra Cotta   (EA)
FOT & E .... Follow-On Test and Evaluation   (MCD)
FOTEAO .... Food Technology [*A publication*]
FOTEGLLD ... Forward Observer Team Equipped with Ground LASER Locator Designator   (MCD)
FOTELSYS ... Foreign Telecommunications Systems   (MCD)
FOTF .... Folded Other Than Flat [*Freight*]
FOTIB3 ..... Forest and Timber [*A publication*]
FOTJ .... Formal On-the-Job
FOTM .... Friends of Old-Time Music [*Later, Society for Traditional Music*]   (EA)
FOTO .... Forced Oscillation in a Tightening Oscillator [*Chemical kinetics*]
FOTO .... Seattle FilmWorks, Inc. [*NASDAQ symbol*]   (NQ)
Fotogr Italiana ... Fotografia Italiana [*A publication*]
Fotokhim Prom ... Fotokhimicheskaya Promyshlennost [*A publication*]
Foto Mag ... Foto Magazin [*A publication*]
FOTR .... Friends of Old-Time Radio   (EA)
FOTR .... Friends of the River   (EA)
FOTS .... Fiber Optic Transmission System [*Consists of modulated light signals sent through glass fibers and demodulated by photo-diodes*] [*Data transmission*]
FOTS .... Freeman Overseas Testing Services [*Australia*]

FOTU .... Fotus [*A Fermentation*] [*A publication*]   (ROG)
FOU .... Fougamou [*Gabon*] [*Airport symbol*]   (OAG)
FOU .... Foundation [*A publication*]
Foulk Act ... Foulke's Action at Law [*A publication*]   (DLA)
FOUN .... Foreland Corp. [*NASDAQ symbol*]   (NQ)
FOUN .... Fort Union National Monument
Foun .... Foundations [*Baptist*] [*A publication*]
FOUNA .... Foundry [*A publication*]
FOUND .... Foundation
Found Control Eng ... Foundations of Control Engineering [*Poland*] [*A publication*]
FOUNDEX ... International Foundry Exhibition   (TSPED)
Found Facts ... Foundation Facts [*A publication*]
Found Fundam Res Matter Yearb ... Foundation for Fundamental Research on Matter. Yearbook [*A publication*]
Found Inst Nucl Res Yearb ... Foundation Institute for Nuclear Research. Yearbook [*A publication*]
Found Lang ... Foundations of Language [*A publication*]
Found Language ... International Journal of Language and Philosophy. Foundations of Language [*A publication*]
Found L Rev ... Foundation Law Review [*A publication*]   (DLA)
FOUNDN ... Foundation
Found News ... Foundation News [*A publication*]
Found Phys ... Foundations of Physics [*A publication*]
Foundry Manage Technol ... Foundry Management and Technology [*A publication*]
Foundry Pract ... Foundry Practice [*A publication*]
Foundry Trade J ... Foundry Trade Journal [*A publication*]
Found Sci Research Surinam and Netherlands Antilles Pub ... Foundation for Scientific Research in Surinam and the Netherlands Antilles. Publication [*A publication*]
Found Trade J ... Foundry Trade Journal [*A publication*]
Fount .... Fountainhall's Decisions, Scotch Court of Session [*1678-1712*] [*A publication*]   (DLA)
Fount Dec ... Fountainhall's Decisions, Scotch Court of Session [*1678-1712*] [*A publication*]   (DLA)
FOUO .... For Official Use Only [*Army*]
FOUR .... Forum Group, Inc. [*NASDAQ symbol*]   (NQ)
FOURATAF ... Fourth Allied Tactical Air Force, Central Europe
Four Corners Geol Soc Bull ... Four Corners Geological Society. Bulletin [*A publication*]
Four Corners Geol Soc Field Conf Guideb ... Four Corners Geological Society. Field Conference. Guidebook [*A publication*]
Four Qt ...... Four Quarters [*A publication*]
Four Quart ... Four Quarters [*A publication*]
Fourrages Actual ... Fourrages Actualites [*A publication*]
FOUS .... Fort Union Trading Post National Historic Site
FOUSA .... Finance Officer, United States Army
FOUVAC ... Folia Universitaria Cochabamba [*A publication*]
FOV .... Field of View [*or Vision*]
FOV .... First Orbital Vehicle [*NASA*]   (NASA)
FOV .... Flyable Orbital Vehicle
FOV .... Forward Observer Vehicle [*Military*]   (MCD)
FOV .... Valencia Community College, Orlando, FL [*Library symbol*] [*Library of Congress*]   (LCLS)
FOV .... Visserijnieuws [*A publication*]
FOVA .... Fort Vancouver National Historic Site
FOVEANT ... Foveantur [*Let Them Be Fermented*] [*Pharmacy*]   (ROG)
FOVES ... Fine Old Very Extra Special [*Designation on brandy labels*]
FOVH .... Flush Oiltight Ventilation Hole   (MSA)
FOW .... Family of Weapons   (MCD)
FOW .... Fenestration Oval Window [*Otology*]
FOW .... First Open Water [*Shipping*]
FOW .... Forge Welding
FOW .... Formation Ordnance Workshop [*British military*]   (DMA)
FOW .... Free on Wagon [*Business term*]
FOW .... Free on Water [*Business term*]
FOW .... Free on Wharf [*Business term*]   (ROG)
FOW .... Friends of the Wilderness [*Defunct*]   (EA)
FOW .... Morristown, MN [*Location identifier*] [*FAA*]   (FAAL)
FOW .... Oil-Immersed Forced-Oil-Cooled with Forced-Water Cooler [*Transformer*]   (IEEE)
FOWABPF ... Flag Officer, Western Area, British Pacific Fleet
FOWHM ... Fuel Oil and Water Heater Manufacturers Association   (EA)
FOWJ .... Foothills Wilderness Journal [*A publication*]
Fowl Col ..... Fowler. Collieries and Colliers [*4th ed.*] [*1884*] [*A publication*]   (DLA)
Fowl L Cas ... Fowler's Leading Cases on Collieries [*A publication*]   (DLA)
Fowl Pews .. Fowler on Church Pews [*A publication*]   (DLA)
Fowl Pr ...... Fowler's Exchequer Practice [*A publication*]   (DLA)
FOWSAB .. Federation of Women Shareholders in American Business [*New York, NY*]   (EA)
FOX .... Focus [*A publication*]
FOX .... Fox, AK [*Location identifier*] [*FAA*]   (FAAL)
FOX .... [*The*] Foxboro Co. [*NYSE symbol*]   (SPSG)
Fox .... Fox's Circuit and District Court Decisions [*United States*] [*A publication*]   (DLA)
Fox .... Fox's Patent, Trade Mark, Design, and Copyright Cases [*Canada*] [*A publication*]   (DLA)
Fox .... Fox's Registration Cases [*England*] [*A publication*]   (DLA)
FOX .... Futures and Options Exchange [*British*]

Fox Breeders Gaz ... Fox Breeders Gazette [*A publication*]
Fox Chase Cancer Cent Sci Rep ... Fox Chase Cancer Center. Scientific Report [*A publication*]
Fox Dig Part ... Fox's Digest of the Law of Partnership [*A publication*]   (DLA)
FOXI .... Foxmoor International Films Ltd. [*NASDAQ symbol*]   (NQ)
FOXM ...... Foxmeyer Corp. [*NASDAQ symbol*]   (NQ)
Fox Pat C ... Fox's Patent, Trade Mark, Design, and Copyright Cases [*Canada*] [*A publication*]   (DLA)
Fox Pat Cas ... Fox's Patent, Trade Mark, Design, and Copyright Cases [*Canada*] [*A publication*]   (DLA)
Fox PC ...... Fox's Patent, Trade Mark, Design, and Copyright Cases [*Canada*] [*A publication*]   (DLA)
Fox Reg Ca ... Fox's Registration Cases [*England*] [*A publication*]   (DLA)
Fox & S ... Fox and Smith's Irish King's Bench Reports [*1822-24*] [*A publication*]   (DLA)
Fox & S (Ir) ... Fox and Smith's Irish King's Bench Reports [*1822-24*] [*A publication*]   (DLA)
Fox & Sm ... Fox and Smith's Irish King's Bench Reports [*1822-24*] [*A publication*]   (DLA)
Fox & Sm ... Fox and Smith's Registration Cases [*1886-95*] [*A publication*]   (DLA)
Fox & Sm RC ... Fox and Smith's Registration Cases [*1886-95*] [*A publication*]   (DLA)
Fox & S Reg ... Fox and Smith's Registration Cases [*1886-95*] [*A publication*]   (DLA)
FOXT .... Fox Technology, Inc. [*Dayton, OH*] [*NASDAQ symbol*]   (NQ)
FOXY .... Fraction-Optimizing X-Y Collector [*Spectroscopy*]
FOY .... FGGE [*First Global Atmospheric Research Program Global Experiment*] Operational Year [*Marine science*]   (MSC)
FOY .... Foya [*Liberia*] [*Airport symbol*]   (OAG)
FOY .... Foyer   (MSA)
FOYB .... Foothills Yukon Bulletin [*A publication*]
FOzM .... Ozona Microfilm, Inc., Ozona, FL [*Library symbol*] [*Library of Congress*]   (LCLS)
FOZODJ ... Folia Zoologica [*A publication*]
FP .... Aeroleasing SA [*Switzerland*] [*ICAO designator*]   (FAAC)
FP .... Faceplate   (IEEE)
FP .... Factory Pass   (AAG)
FP .... Fair Play [*Signature used on warning letters sent by George Metesky, the "Mad Bomber" of New York City in 1940's and 1950's*]
FP .... Faithful Performance
FP .... False Positive [*Medicine*]
FP .... False Pretenses
FP .... Family Planning
FP .... Family Practice [*or Practioner*]
FP .... Fast Processor [*Instrumentation*]
FP .... Fatherhood Project   (EA)
FP .... Fecal Pellet
FP .... Federal Parliament   (DLA)
FP .... Federal Party [*Namibia*]   (PPW)
FP .... Federazione della Funzione Pubblica [*Italy*]   (EY)
FP .... Fee Paid [*Classified advertising*]
FP .... Feedback Positive [*Data processing*]
FP .... Feedback Potentiometer
FP .... Fellowship Party [*British*]
FP .... Fellowship in Prayer [*An association*]   (EA)
FP .... Female Penitentiary [*British*]   (ROG)
FP .... Female Protein [*Biochemistry*]
FP .... Feminist Press [*An association*]   (EA)
FP .... Ferriprotoporphyrin [*Biochemistry*]
FP .... Festpunkt [*Reference point, a surveying term*] [*German military - World War II*]
FP .... Fiat Pilula [*Let a Pill Be Made*] [*Pharmacy*]
FP .... Fiat Potio [*Let a Potion Be Made*] [*Pharmacy*]
FP .... Fibrinopeptide
FP .... Fibrous Plaster   (ADA)
FP .... Field Potential [*Neuroelectricity*]
FP .... Field Protective   (AAG)
FP .... Field Punishment [*Military*]
FP .... Fighter Prop
FP .... File Processor [*Data processing*]   (BUR)
FP .... File Protect
FP .... Film Pack [*Photography*]
FP .... Filoil Pipeline [*Manila*] [*A publication*]
FP .... Filoloski Pregled [*Belgrade*] [*A publication*]
FP .... Filter Paper
fp .... Fin Prochain [*At the End of Next Month*] [*Business term*] [*French*]
FP .... Financial Plan
FP .... Financial Post Magazine [*A publication*]
FP .... Fine Paper
FP .... Fine Pointing   (MCD)
FP .... Fire Plug
F/P .... Fire Policy [*Insurance*]
FP .... Fire Protection Equipment [*Nuclear energy*]   (NRCH)
FP .... Fireplace [*Real estate*]
Fp .... Fireproof   (DAS)
FP .... First Monthly Payment
FP .... First Performance [*Music*]
FP .... First Proof   (ADA)

FP...............	Fischer & Porter Co. [*AMEX symbol*] (SPSG)	
FP...............	Fission Product	
FP...............	Fixed Point (MCD)	
FP...............	Fixed Price	
FP...............	Flag Plot	
FP...............	Flag Post (MCD)	
FP...............	Flagpole	
FP...............	Flameproof (AAG)	
FP...............	Flash Photolysis [*Chemical kinetics*]	
FP...............	Flash Point	
FP...............	Flat Pad	
FP...............	Flat Panel [*Data processing*]	
F/P.............	Flat Pattern	
FP...............	Flat Plate [*Medicine*]	
FP...............	Flat Point [*Technical drawings*]	
FP...............	Flavin Phosphate [*Biochemistry*]	
FP...............	Flavoprotein [*Biochemistry*]	
FP...............	Flavor Profile [*Sensory test method developed by A. D. Little, Inc.*]	
FP...............	Fleet Paymaster [*Navy*] [*British*] (ROG)	
FP...............	Flight Pay	
FP...............	Flight Plan [*Aviation*]	
F/P.............	Flight Programmer (AAG)	
FP...............	Flight Progress (KSC)	
FP...............	Floating Open Marine Policy [*Insurance*] (DS)	
FP...............	Floating Point [*Data processing*] (BUR)	
FP...............	Floating Policy [*Insurance*]	
FP...............	Florid Papillomatosis [*Medicine*]	
FP...............	Fluorescence Polarization	
FP...............	Fluorescent Particle	
FP...............	Fluorescent Pseudomonad spp.	
FP...............	Fluoropolymers [*Organic chemistry*]	
FP...............	Flying Psychologists [*Inactive*] (EA)	
FP...............	Focal Plane [*Photography*]	
FP...............	Fokker-Planck Equation [*Mathematics*]	
FP...............	Food Poisoning [*Medicine*]	
FP...............	Food Policy [*British*]	
FP...............	Food Production [*British*]	
FP...............	Foot Patrol (AFM)	
FP...............	Foot-Pound [*Unit of work*]	
FP...............	Footpath (ADA)	
FP...............	For Private Use (ROG)	
FP...............	Forbidden Planet [*Bookstore chain*] [*British*]	
FP...............	Fordyce & Princeton Railroad Co. [*AAR code*]	
FP...............	Fore Perpendicular	
fp................	Forearm Pronated [*Medicine*]	
FP...............	Foreign Policy	
FP...............	Forepeak [*Naval architecture*]	
F/P.............	Forest Patrol [*Activity of Civil Air Patrol*]	
FP...............	Forfeiture of Pay	
FP...............	Former Priest	
FP...............	Former Pupil [*Alumnus*] [*British*]	
FP...............	Forte Piano [*Loud, then Soft*] [*Music*]	
FP...............	Forward Perpendicular	
FP...............	Frame Pointer [*Data processing*]	
FP...............	Frame Protected [*Insurance classification*]	
FP...............	Franklin Pierce [*US president, 1804-1869*]	
FP...............	Free Pardon (ADA)	
FP...............	Free Piston [*Machinery*] (DS)	
FP...............	Free Play [*Military*] (CAAL)	
FP...............	Free Port [*Shipping*]	
FP...............	Free Propellers (AAG)	
FP...............	Freezing Point	
FP...............	Freight and Passenger Vessels [*Army*]	
FP...............	Fremskrittspartiet [*Progress Party*] [*Norway*] [*Political party*] (PPE)	
FP...............	French Patent	
fp................	French Polynesia [*MARC country of publication code*] [*Library of Congress*] (LCCP)	
FP...............	Fresh Paragraph (ADA)	
FP...............	Friendly Peersuasion [*Girls Club of America*] (EA)	
FP...............	[*The*] Friends Program (EA)	
FP...............	Friends' Provident Life Office [*Insurance*] [*British*]	
FP...............	Frog Pond - Frog Collectors Club (EA)	
FP...............	Frozen Plasma [*Medicine*]	
FP...............	Fruition Project (EA)	
FP...............	Fuel Pressure (NASA)	
FP...............	Fuel Pump Gasket [*Automotive engineering*]	
FP...............	Full Pay [*Military*] [*British*] (ROG)	
FP...............	Full Pension [*Hotel rate*]	
FP...............	Full Period	
FP...............	Full Power	
FP...............	Full Price (ADA)	
FP...............	Fully Paid [*Business term*]	
FP...............	Functional Path (NASA)	
FP...............	Fungus Proof	
FP...............	Fusing Point	
FP...............	Pipefitter [*Navy*]	
FP...............	Public Forecasts [*Symbol*] [*National Weather Service*]	
FP1.............	Floating Platform No. 1 [*English bilingual film made in Germany with actor Conrad Veidt, 1933*]	
FP-25	People's Forces of 25 April [*Portugal*] (PD)	
FP-31	Frente Popular 31 de Enero [*31st January Popular Front*] [*Guatemala*] (PD)	
FPA	Facilities Procurement Application (AAG)	
FPA	Failure Probability Analysis (MCD)	
FPA	Families for Private Adoption (EA)	
FPA	Family Planning Association	
FPA	Far Point of Accommodation [*Ophthalmology*]	
FPA	Federal Physicians Association (EA)	
FPA	Federal Preparedness Agency [*FEMA*]	
FPA	Federal Professional Association [*Later, FEPA*]	
FPA	Federal Property Assistance [*Department of Health and Human Services*]	
FPA	Federation of Professional Athletes [*Later, NFLPA*] (EA)	
FPA	Fibrinopeptide A [*Biochemistry*]	
FPA	Field Profit Analysis	
FPA	Fill Producers' Association	
FPA	Filter Paper Activity	
FPA	Final Power Amplifier	
FPA	Financial Printers Association (EA)	
FPA	Fire Protection Association [*British*]	
FPA	First Pennsylvania Corp. [*NYSE symbol*] (SPSG)	
FPA	First Point of Aries [*Navigation*]	
FPA	First Production Article (MCD)	
FPA	Flat-Plate Antenna [*or Array*]	
FPA	Flexible Packaging Association (EA)	
FPA	Flight Path Accelerometer	
FPA	Flight Path Analysis	
FPA	Flight Path Angle (MCD)	
FPA	Flight Plan Approval [*Aviation*] (AFM)	
FPA	Floating-Point Accelerator [*Data processing*] (BYTE)	
FPA	Floating-Point Arithmetic	
FPA	Fluorophenylalanine [*Biochemistry*]	
FPA	Flying Pharmacists of America [*Defunct*] (EA)	
FPA	Flying Physicians Association (EA)	
FPA	Focal-Plane Array (MCD)	
FPA	Food Production Administration [*World War II*]	
FPA	Force Planning Analysis [*Army*] (AABC)	
FPA	Foreign Policy Association (EA)	
FPA	Foreign Press Association (EA)	
FPA	Forest Products Abstracts [*Oxford, England*] [*A publication*]	
FPA	Formalin-Propionic Acid-Alcohol [*Fixative*] [*Botany*]	
FPA	Foundation for Public Affairs (EA)	
FPA	Franklin Pierce Adams [*1881-1960*] [*American newspaper columnist*]	
FPA	Free Pacific Association (EA)	
FPA	Free of Particular Average [*Insurance*]	
FPA	Free Press Association (EA)	
FPA	Friends of the Peaceful Alternatives [*Defunct*] (EA)	
FPA	Funding Program Advice [*Military*] (AABC)	
FPA	Fusion Power Associates (EA)	
FPa	Larimer Memorial Library, Palatka, FL [*Library symbol*] [*Library of Congress*] (LCLS)	
FPAA	Federacion Panamericana de Asociaciones de Arquitectos [*Panamerican Federation of Architects' Associations*] (EA)	
FPAA	Final Procurement Action Approval (MCD)	
FPAA	First Printings of American Authors [*A publication*]	
FPAA	Flat-Plate Array Antenna	
FPAA	Flight Path Analysis Area [*Space Flight Operations Facility, NASA*]	
FPAA	Fort Polk Army Airfield [*Fort Polk, LA*]	
FPAAC	Free of Particular Average, American Conditions [*Insurance*]	
FPAC	Flight Path Analysis and Command [*Team*] [*NASA*]	
FPAD.........	Freight Payable at Destination [*Business term*]	
FPAD.........	Fret Payable a Destination [*Freight Payable at Destination*] [*French*] [*Business term*]	
FPAD.........	Fund for Peaceful Atomic Development [*Defunct*]	
FPAEC.......	Free of Particular Average, English Conditions [*Insurance*]	
FPAF	Fixed Price Award Fee [*Contract*]	
FPAH	Foundation for Preservation of the Archeological Heritage (EA)	
FPANY......	Film Producers Association of New York [*Defunct*] (EA)	
FPANZ......	Fellow, Public Accountant, New Zealand	
FPAP	Floating-Point Array Processor [*Data processing*]	
FPAPVD...	Flight Plan Approved [*Aviation*] (FAAC)	
FPARA9 ...	Folia Parasitologica [*Prague*] [*A publication*]	
FPAS	Fail-Passive Autoland System [*Aviation*]	
FPAS	Fellow of the Pakistan Academy of Sciences	
FPAS	Front for Popular Armed Struggle [*Iraq*]	
FPASA	Federal Property and Administrative Services Act [*1949*]	
FPB	Fast Patrol Boat [*Navy*] (NVT)	
FPB	Federal Petroleum Board [*Department of the Interior*]	
FPB	Federation of Podiatry Boards [*Later, FPMB*] (EA)	
FPB	Femoral Popliteal Bypass [*Medicine*]	
FPB	Fixed Price Basis	
FPB	Flexor Pollicis Brevis [*Anatomy*]	
FPB	Flight Progress Board [*Aviation*]	
FPB	Foreign Policy Briefs	
FPB	Forum of Private Business [*British*]	
FPB	Fuel Preburner (KSC)	

FPBAA ...... Folding Paper Box Association of America [*Later, PPC*]　(EA)
FPBCCA .... Famous Personalities' Business Card Collectors of America　(EA)
FPBD .... Fibrous Plasterboard
FPBG .... Final Program and Budget Guidance
FPBOV ...... Fuel Preburner and Oxidizer Valve　(NASA)
FPBRS .... Fels Parent Behavior Rating Scales [*Psychology*]
FPBT .... Fountain Powerboat Industries, Inc. [*Washington, NC*] [*NASDAQ symbol*]　(NQ)
FPc .... Bay County Public Library, Panama City, FL [*Library symbol*] [*Library of Congress*]　(LCLS)
FPC .... Facility Power Control　(AAG)
FPC .... Fall Planting Council　(EA)
FPC .... Familial Polyposis Coli [*Later, FAP*] [*Medicine*]
FPC .... Family Planning Clinic [*British*]
FPC .... Family Practitioner Committee [*British*]
FPC .... Federal Pacifist Council [*Australia*]
FPC .... Federal Personnel Council [*Abolished, 1954*] [*Civil Service Commission*]
FPC .... Federal Power Commission [*Superseded by Department of Energy, 1977*]
FPC .... Federal Power Commission Reports [*A publication*]　(DLA)
FPC .... Federal Property Council [*Terminated, 1977*]
FPC .... Federal Publisher's Committee　(EA)
FPC .... Fellow of Pembroke College [*British*]　(ROG)
FPC .... Feminist Party of Canada
FPC .... Ferrite Pot Core
FPC .... Field Petroleum Corp. [*Vancouver Stock Exchange symbol*]
FPC .... Field Press Censorship
FPC .... Final Processing Center
FPC .... Financial Print & Communications Ltd. [*British*]
FPC .... Fire Pump Control　(IEEE)
FPC .... Firestone Plastics Company
FPC .... Firestone Polyvinyl Chloride
FPC .... Fiscal Policy Council　(EA)
FPC .... Fish Protein Concentrate [*For use in antistarvation programs*]
FPC .... Fixed Paper Capacitor
FPC .... Fixed Partial Charge [*Physical chemistry*]
FPC .... Fixed Photoflash Capacitor
FPC .... Fixed Point Calculation
FPC .... Fixed Polycarbonate Capacitor
FPC .... Fixed Precision Capacitor
FPC .... Fixed Price Call
FPC .... Fixed Price Contracts
FPC .... Fixed Program Computer
FPC .... Flexible Printed Circuit
FPC .... Flight Path Control
FPC .... Flight Programmer Computer
FPC .... Floating-Point Calculation
FPC .... Florida Presbyterian College [*Later, Eckerd College*]
FPC .... Florida Progress Corporation [*Formerly, Florida Power Corporation*] [*NYSE symbol*]　(SPSG)
FPC .... Fluid Power Centre [*University of Bath*] [*British*]　(CB)
FPC .... Fluids Pressure Control　(NASA)
FPC .... Focal Plane Camera　(ROG)
FPC .... Food Packaging Council　(EA)
FPC .... Food Protein Council [*Later, SPC*]　(EA)
FPC .... For Private Circulation
FPC .... Forced Pair Copulation [*Sociobiology*]
FPC .... Forward Power Controller　(MCD)
FPC .... Foundation for Philosophy of Creativity　(EA)
FPC .... Frank Phillips College [*Texas*]
FPC .... Free Polymer-Derived Carbon [*Chemistry*]
FPC .... French Pressure Cell
FPC .... Frente Popular Costarricense [*Costa Rican Popular Front*] [*Political party*]　(PPW)
FPc .... Friends Peace Committee　(EA)
FPC .... Front Panel Control
FPC .... Frozen Pea Council [*Defunct*]
FPC .... Fuel Pool Cooling [*Nuclear energy*]　(NRCH)
FPC .... Functional Progression Chart [*Telecommunications*]　(TEL)
FPC .... Future Physicians Clubs　(EA)
FPC .... United States Federal Power Commission Opinions and Decisions [*A publication*]　(DLA)
FPC's .... Functions/Parameters/Characteristics　(MCD)
FPCA .... Federal Post Card Application [*For an absentee ballot*]　(AABC)
FPCA .... Federation of Parents and Citizens Associations [*Australia*]
FPCA .... Fiber Producers Credit Association　(EA)
FPCA .... Forward Power Control Assembly　(MCD)
FPCA .... Foundation of Pharmacists and Corporate America for AIDS [*Acquired Immune Deficiency Syndrome*] Education　(EA)
FP-CART .. Federal/Provincial Committee on Atlantic Region Transportation [*Canada*]
FPCC .... Fair Play for Cuba Committee [*Defunct*]
FPCC .... Financial Performance Corporation [*New York, NY*] [*NASDAQ symbol*]　(NQ)
FPCC .... First Portuguese Canadian Club
FPCC .... Fixed Polycarbonate Capacitor
FPCC .... Fixed Printed Circuit Capacitor
FPCC .... Flight/Propulsion Acronym Coupling [*Air Force*]

FPCC .... Fuel Pool Cooling and Cleanup [*Nuclear energy*]　(NRCH)
FPCCM ...... Flight Planning and Cruise Control Manual　(MCD)
FPCCS .... Fuel Pool Cooling and Cleanup System [*Nuclear energy*]　(NRCH)
FPCE .... Fission Products Conversion and Encapsulation [*Plant*] [*Nuclear energy*]
FPcG .... United States Department of Commerce, National Oceanic and Atmospheric Administration, Gulf Coastal Fisheries Center, Panama City, FL [*Library symbol*] [*Library of Congress*]　(LCLS)
FPCH .... Foreign Policy Clearing House [*Defunct*]
FPCI .... Fluid Power Consultants International　(EA)
FPCL .... Front Paisanu di Liberazione [*Corsica*]
FPCLANT ... Fleet Programming Center, Atlantic
FPCM .... Fibroblast Populated Collagen Matrix [*Biology*]
FPcN .... Northwest Regional Library, Panama City, FL [*Library symbol*] [*Library of Congress*]　(LCLS)
FPcNM ...... United States Navy, Mine Defense Laboratory, Technical Library, Panama City, FL [*Library symbol*] [*Library of Congress*]　(LCLS)
FPCO .... Facilities Procuring Contracting Officer [*Military*]　(AFIT)
FPCO .... Florida Partners Corporation [*Coral Gables, FL*] [*NASDAQ symbol*]　(NQ)
FPCORP ... Financial Post Canadian Corporate Database [*Financial Post Corporation Service Group*] [*Information service or system*]　(CRD)
FPCP .... Ferrocene Polymer Cure Process
FPCR .... Federal Power Commission Reports
FPCS .... Focal-Plane Crystal Spectrometer
FPCS .... Free Polar Corticosteroids [*Endocrinology*]
FPCS .... Freezing Point Calibration Standard
FPCS .... Fuel Pool Cooling System [*Nuclear energy*]　(IEEE)
FPCS .... Full-Page Composition System [*Data processing*]
FPCSTL .... Fission Product Control Screening Test Loop [*Nuclear energy*]　(NRCH)
FPCU .... Fuel Pump Control Unit　(MCD)
FP & D .... Facility Planning and Design　(KSC)
FPD .... Federacion Popular Democratica [*Popular Democratic Federation*] [*Spain*] [*Political party*]　(PPE)
FPD .... Federal Pattern Description　(AAG)
FPD .... Ferrite Phase Driver
FPD .... Flame Photometric Detector
FPD .... Flat Pack Diode
FPD .... Friction Pressure Drop
FPD .... Full Page Display　(BYTE)
FPD .... Full Paid [*Stock exchange term*]　(SPSG)
FPD .... Full Power Days [*Nuclear energy*]　(NRCH)
FPDA .... Finnish Plywood Development Association
FPDA .... Fluid Power Distributors Association　(EA)
FP & DB .... Facilities Planning and Development Branch [*BUPERS*]
FPDC .... Federal Procurement Data Center [*Database*]
FPDD .... Final Project Design Description　(NRCH)
FPDG .... Foreign Policy Discussion Group　(EA)
FPDI .... Flight Path Deviation Indicator [*Navigation*]
FPDI .... Food Processing Development Irradiator
FPDL .... Federacion de Partidos Democraticas y Liberales [*Federation of Democratic and Liberal Parties*] [*Spain*] [*Political party*]　(PPE)
FPDL .... Fission Products Development Laboratory [*ORNL*]
FPDP .... Flight Path Design Program
FPDS .... Federal Procurement Data System [*Database*]　(EISS)
FPDS .... Fleet Probe Data System [*Navy*]　(NG)
FPE .... Fairport, Painesville & Eastern Railway Co. [*AAR code*]
FPE .... Federal Pioneer Ltd. [*Toronto Stock Exchange symbol*]
FPE .... Federal Procurement Eligibility
FPE .... Federation des Pecheurs de l'Est [*Eastern Fishermen's Federation - EFF*] [*Canada*]
FPE .... Final Prediction Error [*Statistics*]
FPE .... Fixed Potential Electrode [*Electrochemistry*]
FPE .... Fixed Price with Escalation
FP & E .... Food Products and Equipment [*A publication*]
FPE .... Foot-Pounds of Energy
FPE .... Force Planning Estimate　(MCD)
FPE .... Friends Peace Exchange　(EA)
FPE .... Functional Program Elements [*NASA*]
FPe .... Pensacola Public Library, Pensacola, FL [*Library symbol*] [*Library of Congress*]　(LCLS)
FPEA .... Ford Philpot Evangelistic Association　(EA)
FPEB .... Family Planning Evaluation Branch [*Public Health Service*]　(IID)
FPEB .... Fuel Pool Exhaust Blower [*Nuclear energy*]　(NRCH)
FPEC .... Federal Pacific Electric Company　(KSC)
FPEC .... Fixed Porcelain Enamel Capacitor
FPeC .... Pensacola Junior College, Pensacola, FL [*Library symbol*] [*Library of Congress*]　(LCLS)
FPED .... Family Planning Evaluation Division [*HEW*]　(IID)
FPEG .... Fast Pulse Electron Gun　(MCD)
FPeGS .... Church of Jesus Christ of Latter-Day Saints, Genealogical Society Library, Pensacola Branch, Pensacola, FL [*Library symbol*] [*Library of Congress*]　(LCLS)

FPeJC....... Pensacola Junior College, Pensacola, FL [*Library symbol*] [*Library of Congress*] (LCLS)
FPeN......... United States Naval Air Station, Pensacola, FL [*Library symbol*] [*Library of Congress*] (LCLS)
FPeN-M .... United States Navy, Naval Aerospace Medical Institute, Pensacola, FL [*Library symbol*] [*Library of Congress*] (LCLS)
FPERR ...... Field Personnel Record
FPeU......... University of West Florida, Pensacola, FL [*Library symbol*] [*Library of Congress*] (LCLS)
FPeW .... West Florida Regional Library, Pensacola, FL [*Library symbol*] [*Library of Congress*] (LCLS)
FPEX .... Fortune Petroleum Corp. [*NASDAQ symbol*] (NQ)
FPF .... Familial Pulmonary Fibrosis
FPF .... Feathered Pipe Foundation (EA)
FPF .... Fibroblast Pneumonocyte Factor [*Biochemistry*]
FPF .... Final Protective Fire [*Artillery term*]
FPF .... Fine Pointing Facility [*NASA*] (KSC)
FPF .... First Philippine Fund [*NYSE symbol*] (SPSG)
FPF .... Fixed Price Firm (AFM)
FPF .... Flexible Polyurethane Foam
FPF .... Fuel Packaging Facility [*Nuclear energy*]
FPF .... Full Power Frequency
FPFC .... Fixed Photoflash Capacitor
FPFC .... Flight Patrol Fan Club (EA)
FPFGBI ..... French Polishers' Federation of Great Britain and Ireland [*A union*]
FPG .... Fasting Plasma Glucose [*Medicine*]
FPG .... Federal Pecan Growers
FPG .... Fire Philatelic Group (EA)
FPG .... Fluorescence plus Giemsa [*Cell-staining technique*]
FPG .... Force Planning Guide [*Army*] (AABC)
FPG .... Fragmenta Philosophorum Graecorum [*A publication*] (OCD)
FPG .... Frank Porter Graham Child Development Center [*University of North Carolina at Chapel Hill*] [*Research center*] (RCD)
f-pg--- .... Portuguese Guinea [*Guinea-Bissau*] [*MARC geographic area code*] [*Library of Congress*] (LCCP)
FPGA........ Field Programmable Gate Array [*Data processing*]
FPGAUS ... Federated Pecan Growers' Associations of the United States (EA)
FPGEC ..... Foreign Pharmacy Graduate Examination Commission (EA)
FPGL........ Flight Plan Gas Load [*Air Force*]
FPGN .... Focal Proliferative Glomerulonephritis [*Medicine*]
FPGPAX ... Family Planning Perspectives [*A publication*]
FPH .... Failures per Hour [*Military*]
FPH .... First Pacific Holdings [*Bank*] [*Hong Kong*]
FPH .... Fish Protein Hydrolysate
FPH .... Floating-Point Hardware [*Data processing*]
FPH .... Fredericks Place Holdings [*British*]
FPH .... Frente Patriotico Hondureno [*Honduran Patriotic Front*] [*Political party*] (PD)
FPH .... Friends of Patrick Henry (EA)
FPH .... Full Power Hours [*Nuclear energy*] (DEN)
FPHA .... Federal Public Housing Authority [*Functions transferred to Public Housing Administration, 1947*]
FPharmS ... Fellow of the Pharmaceutical Society [*British*]
FPHB........ Flight Procedures Handbook (MCD)
FPHC........ Foreign Personal Holding Company
FPHE........ Formalin-Treated Pyruvaldehyde-Stabilized Human Erythrocytes [*Immunology*]
FPHO .... First Phone Corp. [*NASDAQ symbol*] (NQ)
F Phon....... Folia Phoniatrica [*A publication*]
FPHS........ Fallout Protection in Houses
F Ph S .... Fellow of the Philosophical Society [*British*]
F Phys S.... Fellow of the Physical Society [*British*]
F PHYS SOC ... Fellow, Physical Society [*British*] (ROG)
FPI .... Fabry-Perot Interferometer
FPI .... Faded Prior to Interception [*RADAR*]
FPI .... Family Pitch In [*Indicates family may eat freely of a certain dish at a meal where guests are present*]
FPI .... Fast Processor Interface [*Computer chip*]
FPI .... Federal Personnel Intern [*Program*] [*Civil Service Commission*]
FPI .... Federal Prison Industries, Inc. [*Department of Justice*]
FPI .... Federal Procurement Institute [*Later, FAI*] (MCD)
FPI .... Federation Prohibitionniste Internationale [*International Prohibition Federation*]
FPI .... Fellow of the Plastics Institute [*British*]
FPI .... First Periodic Inspection (AAG)
FPI .... Fisheries Products International [*Canada*]
FPI .... Fixed Price Incentive
FPI .... Flexible Pavements (EA)
FPI .... Flexion Producing Interneuron [*Neurology*]
FPI .... Flight Path Indicator [*Aviation*] (AIA)
FPI .... Fluorescent Penetrant Inspection (MSA)
FPI .... Food Processors Institute (EA)
FPI .... Foodservice and Packaging Institute (EA)
FPI .... Forest Products Industry
FPI .... Fountain Powerboat Industries, Inc. [*AMEX symbol*] (SPSG)
FPI .... Frames per Inch [*Data processing*]
FPI .... Friends of Pioneering Israel

FPI .... Fuel Pressure Indicator
FPi .... Pinellas Park Public Library, Pinellas Park, FL [*Library symbol*] [*Library of Congress*] (LCLS)
FPIA .... 504th Parachute Infantry Association (EA)
FPIA .... 542nd Parachute Infantry Association (EA)
FPIA .... Family Planning International Assistance (EA)
FPIA .... Fluorescence Polarization Immunoassay
FPIC .... Financial Post Information Centre [*MacLean-Hunter Ltd.*] [*Information service or system*] (IID)
FPIC .... Fixed Price Incentive Contract
FPIC .... Fuel and Power Industries Committee [*British*] (DCTA)
FPIECE ..... Frontispiece [*Publishing*] (ROG)
FPIF .... Fixed Price Incentive Fee
FPIF......... Fixed Price Incentive Firm [*Award*] [*Government contracting*]
FPIF .... Fixed Price Incentive Force (AFM)
F PIL .... Fiat Pilula [*Let a Pill Be Made*] [*Pharmacy*]
FPIS.......... Family Planning and Information Service
FPIS.......... Fixed Price Incentive Successive Targets
FPIS.......... Forward Propagation by Ionospheric Scatter [*Radio communications technique*]
FPJ .... Pensacola Junior College, Pensacola, FL [*OCLC symbol*] (OCLC)
FPJMC..... Four Power Joint Military Commission (AABC)
FPJOAB.... Forest Products Journal [*A publication*]
FPJPA ...... Fully Proceduralized Job Performance Aid (MCD)
FPJU .... Fonds Special pour la Jeunesse de l'UNESCO [*UNESCO Special Fund for Youth*] (EAIO)
FPK .... Fixed Position Keyboard
FPK .... Flash Pack Ltd. [*Vancouver Stock Exchange symbol*]
FPK .... Folding Pocket Kodak [*Photography*] (ROG)
FPK .... Processed Prepared Food [*A publication*]
FPL .... Family Protection League of USA [*Defunct*] (EA)
FPL .... Feline Panleukopenia
FPL .... Ferry-Porter Law [*Physics*]
FPL .... Field Flight Plan
FPL .... Filed Flight Plan Message [*Aviation code*]
FPL .... Final Parts List (MCD)
FPL .... Final Protective Line [*Military*]
FPL .... Financial Planning [*A publication*]
FPL .... Findlay-Hancock County District Public Library, Findlay, OH [*OCLC symbol*] (OCLC)
FPL .... Fire Plug (AAG)
FPL .... Fireplace [*Real estate*]
FPL .... Fisons Pharmaceuticals Limited
FPL .... Flexor Pollicis Longus [*Anatomy*]
FPL .... Flight Propulsion Laboratory
FPL .... Floor Plate [*Technical drawings*]
FPL .... Fluid Power Laboratory [*Ohio State University*] [*Research center*] (RCD)
FPL .... Forced-Choice Preferential Looking
FPL .... Forest Pest Leaflets
FPL .... Forest Products Laboratory [*Department of Agriculture*]
FPL .... Fox Programming Language
FPL .... FPI Ltd. [*Toronto Stock Exchange symbol*]
FPL .... FPL Group, Inc. [*NYSE symbol*] (SPSG)
FPL .... Fragmenta Poetarum Latinorum Epicorum et Lyricorum [*A publication*] (OCD)
FPL .... Frequency Phase Lock
FPL .... Fuerzas Populares de Liberacion Farabundo Marti [*Farabundo Marti Popular Liberation Forces*] [*El Salvador*] (PD)
FPL .... Full Power Level [*NASA*] (NASA)
FPL .... Full Power Load (NASA)
FPLA .... Fair Packaging and Labeling Act [*1966*]
FPLA .... Field-Programmable Logic Array [*Data processing*]
fpla .... Fireplace [*Real estate*]
FPLAAD ... Flowering Plants of Africa [*A publication*]
FPLC .... Fast Protein, Peptide, and Polynucleotide Liquid Chromatography
FPLE .... Field-Programmable Logic Element [*Military*]
FPLF......... Field Programmable Logic Family (TEL)
FPLIF....... Field Pack, Large, with Internal Frame [*Army*] (INF)
FPLN .... Frente Patriotica de Libertacao Nacional [*Portugal*]
FPLP......... Frente Patriotico de Libertacao de Portugal [*Patriotic Front for the Liberation of Portugal*] [*Political party*] (PPE)
FPLS......... Federal Parent Locator Service [*HEW*]
FPLY .... Foothills Pipe Lines (Yukon) Limited. News Releases [*A publication*]
FPM .... Facility Power Monitor (AAG)
FPM .... Federal Personnel Manual
FPM.......... Federation Patronale Monegasque [*Employers' Federation of Monaco*] (EY)
FPM .... Feet per Minute
FPM......... File Protect Memory [*Data processing*] (BUR)
FPM......... Filter Paper Microscopic [*Test*] [*Medicine*]
FPM......... Fine Particulate Matter [*Pisciculture*]
FPM.......... First Pacific Mortgage Ltd. [*Australia*]
FPM.......... Flexible Payment Mortgage
FPM.......... Flight Path Marker
F & PM ..... Flint & Pere Marquette Railroad
FPM.......... Fluid Phase Marker
FPM.......... Folding Platform Mechanism (MCD)

FPM............ Force Packaging Methodology [*Military*]
FPM............ Forest Pest Management [*Program*] [*Forest Service*]
FPM............ Fratres Presentationis Mariae [*Presentation Brothers - PB*]   (EAIO)
FPM............ Free Papau Movement [*Indonesia*] [*Political party*]
FPM............ Frequency Position Modulation [*Telecommunications*]   (IEEE)
FPM............ Functional Planning Matrices   (IEEE)
FPMADL .. US Forest Service. Forest Pest Management. Nothern Region Report [*A publication*]
FPMB........ Federation of Podiatric Medical Boards   (EA)
FPMC........ Fixed Paper Metallized Capacitor
FPMH........ Failures per Million Hours [*Telecommunications*]   (TEL)
FPMI........ Fellow of the Pensions Management Institute [*British*]   (DBQ)
FPMI........ Fireplace Manufacturers, Inc. [*NASDAQ symbol*]   (NQ)
FPMI........ Forest Pest Management Institute [*Environment Canada*] [*Research center*]   (RCD)
FPMIS....... Federal Personnel Management Information System [*Civil Service Commission*]
FPML........ Forest Products Marketing Laboratory [*Forest Service*]
FPMMA.... Fortschritte der Psychosomatischen Medizin [*A publication*]
FPMMAK .. Advances in Psychosomatic Medicine [*A publication*]
FPMO........ Free of Poundage Money Order
FPMR........ Federal Property Management Regulations
FPMR........ Frente Patriotico Manuel Rodriguez [*Manuel Rodriguez Patriotic Front*] [*Political party*] [*Chile*]
FPMS .... Federal Personnel Manual Systems   (OICC)
FPMS .... Flood Plain Management Services [*Army*]
FPMS .... Fueled Prototype Mock-Up System
FPM & SA ... Food Processing Machinery and Supplies Association   (EA)
F/Pn.......... Factor of Production [*Economics*]
FPN .... Fairview Park [*Nevada*] [*Seismograph station code, US Geological Survey*] [*Closed*]   (SEIS)
FPN .... Falange Patria Nova [*New Fatherland Phalange*] [*Brazil*]   (PD)
FPN .... Financial Planning [*A publication*]
FPN .... Fixed Pulse RADAR Navigation Aid   (FAAC)
FPN .... Frederick Point, AK [*Location identifier*] [*FAA*]   (FAAL)
FPN .... Frente Patriotico Nacional [*National Patriotic Front*] [*Nicaragua*] [*Political party*]   (PPW)
FPN .... Friends of Peace Now   (EA)
FPn .... Fryske Plaknammen [*A publication*]
FPNE........ First Phone of New England [*Telecommunications service*]   (TSSD)
FPNJ .... First Peoples Finance Corp. [*NASDAQ symbol*]   (NQ)
FPNJAG ... Folia Psychiatrica et Neurologica Japonica [*A publication*]
FPNO .... Flight Plan Not Received [*Aviation*]   (FAAC)
FPO .... Federal Protective Officer [*General Services Administration*]
FPO .... Federation of Prosthodontic Organizations   (EA)
FPO .... Field Placement Officer
FPO .... Field Post Office [*Military*] [*British*]
FPO .... Field Project Officer
FPO .... Financial Post [*Toronto*] [*A publication*]
FPO .... Fire Prevention Officer [*British*]
FPO .... Fixed Path of Operation
FPO .... Fixed Point Operation
FPO .... Fixed Price Open
FPO .... Fleet Post Office [*Navy*]
FPO .... Forces Post Office [*Military*] [*British*]
FPO .... FPA Corp. [*AMEX symbol*]   (SPSG)
FPO .... Freeport [*Bahamas*] [*Airport symbol*]   (OAG)
FPO .... Freezing Point Osmometer
FPO .... Freiheitliche Partei Oesterreichs [*Liberal Party of Austria (or Austrian Freedom Party)*] [*Political party*]   (PPW)
FPO .... Frequency Planning Organisation [*Telecommunications*] [*British*]
FPO .... Fuel Pressure Out
FPO .... Fuerza Popular Organizada [*Organized Popular Force*] [*Guatemala*] [*Political party*]   (PPW)
FPO .... Future Projects Office [*NASA*]
FPOA........ Federal Probation Officers Association   (EA)
FPOA........ Fentanyl/Pancuronium/Oxygen Anesthesia
FPoCG ..... Charlotte-Glades Library System, Port Charlotte, FL [*Library symbol*] [*Library of Congress*]   (LCLS)
FPOE........ First Port of Entry   (AFM)
F/POL ...... Fire Policy [*Insurance*]   (DCTA)
FPOM .... Fine Particulate Organic Matter
FPORD...... Fusion Power Report [*A publication*]
FPOT........ Facility Power Out Test   (KSC)
FPOT........ Feedback Potentiometer   (MSA)
FPOV........ Fuel Preburner and Oxidizer Valve   (MCD)
FPP .... Facility Power Panel   (AAG)
FPP .... Fast Prepotential [*Neurophysiology*]
FPP .... Field Promotion Program [*FAA*]   (FAAC)
FPP .... Firepower Potential   (AABC)
FPP .... Fixed-Path Protocol [*Telecommunications*]
FPP .... Floating-Point Processor [*Data processing*]
FPP .... Food Processing and Packaging   (IMH)
FPP .... Force Planning Package [*Military*]   (RDA)
FPP .... Foster Parents' Plan   (EA)
FPP .... Freon Pump Package   (MCD)
FPP .... Friends of Palestinian Prisoners   (EA)
FPP .... Friends of Peace Pilgrim   (EA)

FPP .... From Present Position [*Aviation*]   (FAAC)
FPPA .... Porto Alegre [*Sao Tome*] [*ICAO location identifier*]   (ICLI)
FPPC......... Fair Political Practices Commission   (OICC)
FPPCA ..... Fuel and Purchased Power Cost Adjustment
FPPH........ Fire Protection Pumphouse [*Nuclear energy*]   (NRCH)
FPPI .... Frozen Potato Products Institute   (EA)
FPPO......... Federation of Postal Police Officers   (EA)
FPPOD...... Financial Planners and Planning Organizations Directory [*A publication*]
FPPPH ...... Foundation for the Preservation and Protection of the Przewalski Horse   (EA)
FPPR .... Fishpaper [*Insulation*]
FPPR .... Fixed Price, Price Redetermination [*or Revision*]
FPPR .... Principe [*Principe*] [*ICAO location identifier*]   (ICLI)
FPPS......... Flight Plan Processing System [*British*]
FPPTE....... Federation of Public Passenger Transport Employees [*British*]   (DCTA)
FPPVS....... Fuel Pool Pump Ventilation System [*Nuclear energy*]   (NRCH)
FPQA........ Fixed Portion Queue Area [*Data processing*]
FPQI......... Federal Plant Quarantine Inspectors National Association [*Later, NAAE*]
FPQINA .... Federal Plant Quarantine Inspectors National Association [*Later, NAAE*]   (EA)
FPR........... Failure/Problem Report
FPR........... Fan Pressure Ratio [*Aviation*]
FPR........... Farm Publications Reports   (EA)
FPR........... Federal Procurement Regulations
FPR........... Feet per Revolution
FPR........... Field Personnel Record
FPR........... Final Progress Report
FPR........... Financial Public Relations Consultants Retained
FPR........... Fixed Point Representation
FPR........... Fixed Price Redeterminable   (NG)
FPR........... Fixed Problem Report   (MCD)
FPR........... Flat-Plate Radiometer
FPR........... Flexible Plastic Reactor   (NRCH)
FPR........... Flight Planned Route [*Aviation*]   (FAAC)
FPR........... Floating-Point Register
FPR........... Floating-Point Routine
FPR........... Fluid Properties Research, Inc.
FPR........... Fluorescence Photobleaching Recovery
FPR........... Foliage Penetration RADAR
FPR........... Folin Phenol Reagent [*For protein assay*]
FPR........... Force Program Review [*DoD*]
FPR........... Foreign Projects Newsletter [*A publication*]
FPR........... Fort Pierce, FL [*Location identifier*] [*FAA*]   (FAAL)
FPR........... Fragmenta Poetarum Romanorum [*A publication*]   (OCD)
FPR........... Frente Patriotico para la Revolucion [*Patriotic Front for the Revolution*] [*Nicaragua*] [*Political party*]   (PPW)
FPR........... Frente Popular Contra la Represion [*Popular Front Against Repression*] [*Honduras*] [*Political party*]   (PD)
FPR........... Fuerzas Populares Revolucionarias Lorenzo Zelaya [*Lorenzo Zelaya Popular Revolutionary Forces*] [*Honduras*] [*Political party*]   (PD)
FPR........... Full Power Response
FPR........... Full Propellant Requirement
FPRA........ Fifty-Plus Runners Association   (EA)
FPRA........ Financial Public Relations Association [*Later, BMA*]   (EA)
FPRA........ First-Pass Radionuclide Angiogram [*Medicine*]
FPRA........ Fixed Price Redeterminable Article
FPRA........ Forward Pricing Rate Agreement
FPRAC ...... Federal Prevailing Rate Advisory Committee [*Washington, DC*]   (EGAO)
FPRB .... Food Prices Review Board
FPRC......... Fixed Price Redetermination Contract
FPRC......... Fluid Power Research Center [*Oklahoma State University*] [*Research center*]   (RCD)
FPRC......... Flying Personnel Research Committee [*British*]   (MCD)
FPRC......... For Possible Reclearance [*Aviation*]   (FAAC)
FPRDAI .... Food Product Development [*A publication*]
FPRDC...... Food Protein Research and Development Center [*Texas A & M University*]
FPRDI J .... FPRDI [*Forest Products Research and Development Institute*] Journal [*A publication*]
FPRF .... Fats and Proteins Research Foundation   (EA)
FPRF .... Fireproof   (AABC)
FP-RF .... Flash Photolysis-Resonance Fluorescence Technique [*Physics*]
FPRF .... Fusion Plasma Research Facility [*Department of Energy*]
FPRI .... Fellow of the Plastics and Rubber Institute [*British*]   (DBQ)
FPRI/O ..... Orbis. Foreign Policy Research Institute [*A publication*]
FPRL .... Fish Pesticide Research Laboratory [*Department of the Interior*]
FPRL .... Forest Products Research Laboratory [*British*]
FPRM....... Flexible Parts Repair Material [*Automotive engineering*]
FPRMAB .. Folia Primatologica [*A publication*]
FPRO........ Federal-Provincial Relations Office [*Canada*]
F-PROM ... Field-Programmable Read-Only Memory [*Data processing*]   (MCD)
FPRP .... Fixed-Price-Redeterminable-Prospective   (MCD)
FPRR .... Fixed-Price-Redeterminable-Retroactive   (MCD)
FPRRE ...... Foundation for Public Relations Research and Education   (EA)

FPRS .... Federal Property Resources Service [*General Services Administration*]
FPRS .... Federation of Professional Railway Staff [*A union*] [*British*]
FPRS .... Forest Products Radio Service
FPRS .... Forest Products Research Society   (EA)
FPRY .... First Federal Savings Bank of Perry [*NASDAQ symbol*]   (NQ)
FPS .... Faculty of Physicians and Surgeons [*British*]   (ROG)
FPS .... Fast Packet Switching [*Telecommunications*]
FPS .... Fast-Payback System   (MCD)
FPS .... Fauna Preservation Society [*Later, FFPS*]   (EA)
FPS .... Federal Prison System   (MCD)
FPS .... Federal Protective Service [*General Services Administration*]
FPS .... Feet per Second
FPS .... Fellow of the Pathological Society of Great Britain
FPS .... Fellow of the Pharmaceutical Society [*British*]
FPS .... Fellow of the Philological Society [*British*]
FPS .... Fellow of the Philosophical Society [*British*]
FPS .... Fellow of the Physical Society [*British*]
FPS .... Ferrite Phase Shifter
FPS .... Field Power Supply
FPS .... Financial Planning System [*IBM Corp.*]
FPS .... Fine Particle Society   (EA)
FPS .... Fire Protection System [*Nuclear energy*]   (NRCH)
FPS .... First Preferred Stock [*Investment term*]
FPS .... Fiscal Pay Services of Armies [*World War II*]
FPS .... Fixed Plasma Sheath
FPS .... Fixed Point Station [*RADAR*]
FPS .... Fixed Point System
FPS .... Fixed Price Supply
FPS .... Fixed Pulse RADAR Search Equipment   (FAAC)
FPS .... Flash Photolysis System
FPS .... Flight Path Stabilization   (MCD)
FPS .... Flight Power Subsystem
FPS .... Flight Preparation Sheet   (MCD)
FPS .... Flight Progress Strip [*Aviation*]
FPS .... Flight per Second   (NASA)
FPS .... Floating-Point Systems, Inc.
FPS .... Fluid Power Society   (EA)
FPS .... Fluid Power Supply
FPS .... Fluid Power System
FPS .... Fluid Purification System
FPS .... Fluor Power Services, Inc.   (NRCH)
FPS .... Focus Projection and Scanning
FPS .... Foot-Pound-Second [*System*]
FPS .... Forces Postal Service [*British*]
FPS .... Forests Protection Society [*Australia*]
FPS .... Forward Power Supply   (MCD)
FPS .... Foundation for the Private Sector [*San Diego, CA*]   (EA)
FPS .... Frames per Second [*Data processing*]
FPS .... Franciscan Preparatory Seminary
FPS .... Francophone Primatological Society [*See also SFDP*] [*Plelan Le Grand, France*]   (EAIO)
FPS .... Front Populaire Soudanais [*Sudanese Popular Front*]
FPS .... Full Pressure Suit [*Aerospace*]
FPS .... Fusion Power Systems   (MCD)
FPS1117 .... Federal Procurement Disc [*Alde Publishing*] [*Information service or system*]   (IID)
FPSB .... Financial Products Standards Board   (EA)
FPSC .... Family Policy Studies Centre [*British*]   (CB)
FPSC .... Foreign Petroleum Supply Committee [*Terminated, 1976*]
FPSC .... Forest Products Safety Conference   (EA)
FPSG .... Focus Policy Study Group [*British*]
FPSG .... Food Processors and Suppliers Group   (EAIO)
FPSK .... Frequency and Phase Shift Keying
FPSL .... Fission Product Screening Loop [*Nuclear energy*]   (NRCH)
FPSM .... Fleet Program Support Material
FPSO .... Floating Production, Storage, and Offloading System [*Petroleum technology*]
FPSO .... Forms and Publications Supply Office [*Military*]   (CINC)
FPSP .... Federation of Postal Security Police [*Later, FPPO*]   (EA)
FPSP .... (Fluoropropyl)spiperone [*Organic chemistry*]
FPSP .... Future Problem Solving Program   (EA)
FPSPS .... Feet per Second per Second
FPS/S .... Feet per Second per Second
FP-ST .... Flash Photolysis-Shock Tube Experiment [*For study of chemical kinetics*]
FPST .... Sao Tome [*Sao Tome*] [*ICAO location identifier*]   (ICLI)
FPSTB .... Fire Prevention Science and Technology [*A publication*]
FPSTR ...... Fund to Promote Scientific and Technical Research [*Ouagadougou, Burkina Faso*]   (EAIO)
FPSTU ...... Full Pressure Suit Training Unit [*Military*]
FPSUEA... Facial Plastic Surgery [*A publication*]
FPSV .... Flow Path Selector Valve   (MCD)
FPt .... Far Point [*A publication*]
FPT .... Federazione Poste e Telecomunicazioni [*Italy*]   (EY)
FPT .... Feedwater Pump Turbine [*Nuclear energy*]   (NRCH)
FPT .... Female Pipe Thread   (MSA)
FPT .... Finite Perturbation Theory [*Physics*]
FPT .... First Preferred Trust [*Vancouver Stock Exchange symbol*]
FPT .... Fluidic Proportional Thruster
FPT .... Forward Peak Tank [*On ships*]

FPT .... Foundation for Physical Therapy   (EA)
FPT .... Four Picture Test [*Psychology*]
FPT .... Franklin Principal Maturity [*NYSE symbol*]   (SPSG)
FPT .... Freight Pass-Through [*Publishing*]
FPT .... Fruit Pressure Tester
FPT .... Full Period Termination   (CAAL)
FPT .... Full Power Trial
FPT .... Functional Performance Time
FPT .... Fundamental Parameters Technique
FPTA .... Forest Products Traffic Association   (EA)
FPTA .... Fully Proceduralized Troubleshooting Aids [*Military*]
FPTC .... Forest Products Trucking Council   (EA)
FPTE .... Facility Portable Test Equipment   (AAG)
FPTED ...... Fuel Processing Technology [*A publication*]
FPTG .... Free Patellar Tendon Graft [*Sports medicine*]
FPTP .... Flight Proof Test Plan   (AAG)
FPTPI....... Fiberglass Petroleum Tank and Pipe Institute   (EA)
FPTS......... Fixed Point Test Site [*Military*]   (CAAL)
FPTS......... Forward Propagation by Tropospheric Scatter [*Radio communications technique*]
FPTU .... Federation of Progressive Trade Unions [*Zanzibar*]
FPU .... Film Production Unit [*British military*]   (DMA)
FPU .... First Production Unit
FPU .... Floating-Point Unit [*Data processing*]   (MCD)
FPU .... Florida Public Utilities Co. [*AMEX symbol*]   (SPSG)
FPU .... Folkepartiets Ungdomsforbund [*Liberal Youth*] [*Political party*]   (EAIO)
FPU .... Francis Peak [*Utah*] [*Seismograph station code, US Geological Survey*]   (SEIS)
FPU .... Fuel Purification Unit [*Aerospace*]   (AAG)
FPU .... Future Publication Uncertain
FPUB .... Franklin Electronic Publishers, Inc. [*NASDAQ symbol*]   (SPSG)
FPUP .... Federal Photovoltaics Utilization Program [*Department of Energy*]
FPUR........ For the Purpose Of
FPV .... Feed Water Regulation Valve   (IEEE)
FPV .... Feline Panleukopenia Virus
FPV .... Fishery Protection Vessel
FPV .... Flow Proportioning Value   (MCD)
FPV .... Fowl Plague Virus
FPV .... French Polydor Variable Micrograde [*Record label*]
FPV .... Front Progressiste Voltaique [*Upper Volta Progressive Front*] [*Political party*]   (PPW)
FPV .... Functional Proofing Vehicle
FPVB .... Femoral Popliteal Vein Bypass [*Medicine*]
FPVN........ Vila Das Neves [*Sao Tome*] [*ICAO location identifier*]   (ICLI)
FPVPC...... Federation of Paint and Varnish Production Clubs [*Later, FSCT*]
FPV/S...... Floating Production Vessel/System   (DS)
FPW.......... Fields Point [*Washington*] [*Seismograph station code, US Geological Survey*]   (SEIS)
FPW.......... Firing Port Weapon
FPW.......... Flat Pack Welder
FPW.......... Free Progressive Wave
FPWA .... Federation of Professional Writers of America   (EA)
FPWA .... Federation of Protestant Welfare Agencies   (EA)
FPWA .... Further Particulars When Available
FPWS .... Flat Pack Welder System
FPWT .... Fire Protection Water Tank   (IEEE)
FPWT .... Fuel Pool Water Treatment [*Nuclear energy*]   (NRCH)
FPY .... Failures per Year [*Telecommunications*]   (TEL)
FPY .... Perry, FL [*Location identifier*] [*FAA*]   (FAAL)
FPYKA ...... Fortschritte der Physik [*A publication*]
FPZ........... Fluphenazine [*Tranquilizer*]
FPZ........... Free Port Zone [*Shipping*]   (DS)
fq----.......... Africa, Equatorial [*MARC geographic area code*] [*Library of Congress*]   (LCCP)
FQ .... Faerie Queene [*A publication*]
FQ .... Fare Quotation [*Airline*]
FQ .... Film Quarterly [*A publication*]
FQ .... First Quarter [*Moon phase*]
FQ .... Fiscal Quarter   (AFM)
FQ .... Flight Qualification
FQ .... Florida Quarterly [*A publication*]
FQ .... Formal Qualification
FQ .... Four Quarters [*A publication*]
FQ .... French Quarterly [*A publication*]
FQ .... Frequency [*Online database field identifier*]
FQ .... Fused Quartz
FQ .... Societe Minerve [*France*] [*ICAO designator*]   (FAAC)
FQA .... Fuqua Industries, Inc. [*NYSE symbol*]   (SPSG)
FQAG .... Angoche [*Mozambique*] [*ICAO location identifier*]   (ICLI)
FQBE........ Beira [*Mozambique*] [*ICAO location identifier*]   (ICLI)
FQBI........ Bilene [*Mozambique*] [*ICAO location identifier*]   (ICLI)
FQBR........ Beira [*Mozambique*] [*ICAO location identifier*]   (ICLI)
FQCB........ Cuamba [*Mozambique*] [*ICAO location identifier*]   (ICLI)
FQCH .... Chimoio [*Mozambique*] [*ICAO location identifier*]   (ICLI)
FQES......... Estima [*Mozambique*] [*ICAO location identifier*]   (ICLI)
FQF .... Front du Quebec Francais
FQFU......... Furancungo [*Mozambique*] [*ICAO location identifier*]   (ICLI)

FQG .... University of Miami, Coral Gables, FL [*OCLC symbol*]   (OCLC)
FQH .... Filled Quartz Helix
FQHE .... Fractional Quantum Hall Effect [*Solid-state physics*]
FQI .... Flight Qualification Instrumentation   (MCD)
FQI .... Fuel Quantity Indicator
FQIA .... Inhaca [*Mozambique*] [*ICAO location identifier*]   (ICLI)
FQIL .... Fused Quartz Incandescent Lamp
FQIN .... Inhambane [*Mozambique*] [*ICAO location identifier*]   (ICLI)
FQL .... Functional Query Language [*1978*] [*Data processing*]   (CSR)
FQLC .... Lichinga [*Mozambique*] [*ICAO location identifier*]   (ICLI)
FQLU .... Lumbo [*Mozambique*] [*ICAO location identifier*]   (ICLI)
FQM .... Four-Quadrant Multiplier
FQM .... University of Miami, School of Medicine, Miami, FL [*OCLC symbol*]   (OCLC)
FQMA ...... Maputo [*Mozambique*] [*ICAO location identifier*]   (ICLI)
FQMD ...... Mueda [*Mozambique*] [*ICAO location identifier*]   (ICLI)
FQML .... Fort Worth Qualified Material List [*NASA*]   (KSC)
FQMP .... Mocimboa Da Praia [*Mozambique*] [*ICAO location identifier*]   (ICLI)
FQMR ...... Marrupa [*Mozambique*] [*ICAO location identifier*]   (ICLI)
FQMS .... Farrier Quartermaster-Sergeant [*British military*]   (DMA)
FQMU ...... Mutarara [*Mozambique*] [*ICAO location identifier*]   (ICLI)
FQNC .... Nacala [*Mozambique*] [*ICAO location identifier*]   (ICLI)
FQNP .... Nampula [*Mozambique*] [*ICAO location identifier*]   (ICLI)
FQNZA ..... Frequenz [*A publication*]
FQ & P ...... Flight Qualities and Performance
FQPA .... Flight Quality Photomultiplier Assembly
FQPB .... Pemba [*Mozambique*] [*ICAO location identifier*]   (ICLI)
FQPO .... Ponta Do Ouro [*Mozambique*] [*ICAO location identifier*]   (ICLI)
FQPR .... Frequency Programmer   (IEEE)
FQQL .... Quelimane [*Mozambique*] [*ICAO location identifier*]   (ICLI)
FQQPRI .... Final Qualitative and Quantitative Personnel Requirements Information
FQR .... Fabrication Quality Record
FQR .... Flight Qualification Recorder   (KSC)
FQR .... Flight Qualification Reviews   (MCD)
FQR .... Formal Qualification Reviews   (MCD)
FQR .... Functional Qualification Review
FQRSD5 .... Faune du Quebec. Rapport Special [*A publication*]
FQS .... Flight Qualified System   (MCD)
FQSG .... Songo [*Mozambique*] [*ICAO location identifier*]   (ICLI)
FQT .... Formal Qualification Test   (KSC)
FQT .... Frequent
FQT .... Fused Quartz Tubing
FQTE .... Tete [*Mozambique*] [*ICAO location identifier*]   (ICLI)
FQTR .... Flight Qualification Tape Recorder [*NASA*]   (KSC)
FQTT .... Tete/Chingozi [*Mozambique*] [*ICAO location identifier*]   (ICLI)
F Quarterly ... Film Quarterly [*A publication*]
Fque .... Fabrique [*Factory*] [*Business term*] [*French*]
FQUG .... Ulongwe [*Mozambique*] [*ICAO location identifier*]   (ICLI)
FQV .... Plattsburgh, NY [*Location identifier*] [*FAA*]   (FAAL)
FQVL .... Vilanculos [*Mozambique*] [*ICAO location identifier*]   (ICLI)
FQXA .... Xai-Xai [*Mozambique*] [*ICAO location identifier*]   (ICLI)
FR .... Australian Financial Review [*A publication*]   (APTA)
FR .... Facilities Report [*or Request*]
FR .... Faculty Rating
FR .... Failure Rate
FR .... Failure Report
FR .... Fair   (ROG)
fr .... Faire Reporter [*Carry Over*] [*Stock exchange term*] [*French*]
F and R ...... Faith and Reason [*A publication*]
FR .... Family Room [*Real estate*]
FR .... Family Rosary   (EA)
FR .... Fargo Resources Ltd. [*Vancouver Stock Exchange symbol*]
FR .... Fast Recovery
FR .... Fast Release [*Relay*]
FR .... Father
FR .... Fatigue Resistant
FR .... Feather River [*AAR code*]
FR .... Federal Register [*A publication*]
FR .... Federal Reporter [*A publication*]   (DLA)
FR .... Federal Representative [*Job Training and Partnership Act*]   (OICC)
FR .... Federal Republic   (EY)
FR .... Federal Reserve
FR .... Felix Ravenna [*A publication*]
FR .... Ferry Range   (MCD)
FR .... Field Report
FR .... Field Resistance   (DEN)
FR .... Field Retrofit   (MCD)
FR .... Field Reversing   (AAG)
FR .... Fighter Reconnaissance [*Air Force*]
FR .... File Register
FR .... Filing Requirement [*IRS*]
F u R .... Film und Recht [*A publication*]
FR .... Film Recording
FR .... Film Report   (AFM)
FR .... Final Release   (AAG)

FR .... Final Report
F/R .... Financial Responsibility
FR .... Fineness Ratio
FR .... Fire Resistant [*or Retardant*]
FR .... Fire Resistive
FR .... Fireman Recruit [*Navy rating*]
FR .... Firing Room [*NASA*]   (KSC)
FR .... First Reader
FR .... First Renewal
FR .... Fixed Ratio
FR .... Flame Retardant
F/R .... Flared Rudder   (NASA)
FR .... Flash Ranging
FR .... Flat Rack Container [*Shipping*]   (DS)
FR .... Fleet Readiness [*Navy*]   (AFIT)
FR .... Fleet Reserve [*Navy*]
FR .... Flight Readiness
FR .... Flight Recorder   (MCD)
FR .... Flight Refueling   (MCD)
FR .... Flight Reliability   (MCD)
FR .... Flight Rule   (MCD)
FR .... Flocculation Reaction [*Obsolete test for liver function*]
FR .... Flood Relief Punt [*Coast Guard*]
FR .... Flow Rate
FR .... Flow Recorder
FR .... Flow Regulator [*Nuclear energy*]   (NRCH)
FR .... Fluid Resistant
FR .... Fluorescence
fr .... Fluorite [*CIPW classification*] [*Geology*]
FR .... Folio Recto [*Right-Hand Page*] [*Latin*]
FR .... Food Ratio
Fr .... Foraminifera [*Quality of the bottom*] [*Nautical charts*]
FR .... Force Release [*Telecommunications*]   (TEL)
F & R .... Force and Rhythm [*of Pulse*] [*Medicine*]
FR .... Forced Removal
FR .... Fordham Law Review [*A publication*]
FR .... Foreign Relations   (DLA)
FR .... Foreign Relations Committee [*US Senate*]
FR .... Foreign Requirements
FR .... Forest Rangers [*British military*]   (DMA)
FR .... Formation Pennant [*Navy*] [*British*]
FR .... Forming Rolls   (MCD)
FR .... Fort   (ROG)
FR .... Fortnightly Review [*A publication*]
FR .... Forum Romanum [*The Roman Forum*]
FR .... Fossil Record
Fr .... Fragmenta [*of Aristotle*] [*Classical studies*]   (OCD)
FR .... Fragmentum [*Fragment*] [*Latin*]   (ROG)
FR .... Frame   (MSA)
FR .... Frame Reset [*Telecommunications*]   (TEL)
FR .... Framework Region [*Genetics*]
FR .... Franc [*Monetary unit*] [*France*]   (EY)
FR .... France [*ANSI two-letter standard code*]   (CNC)
fr .... France [*MARC country of publication code*] [*Library of Congress*]   (LCCP)
Fr .... Franciscus de Telese [*Flourished, 1270-82*] [*Authority cited in pre-1607 legal work*]   (DSA)
Fr .... Francium [*Chemical element*]
Fr .... Franklin [*Also, sC, statC*] [*Unit of electric charge*]
FR .... Frater [*Brother*] [*Latin*]
FR .... Free   (ADA)
FR .... Free Response
FR .... Free Ribosomes [*Cytology*]
Fr .... Freeman's English King's Bench and Chancery Reports [*A publication*]   (DLA)
FR .... Freight Release
FR .... French
FR .... French Research [*Satellite*]
FR .... French Review [*A publication*]
FR .... French Rite [*Freemasonry*]   (ROG)
FR .... Frequency Measuring Devices [*JETDS nomenclature*] [*Military*]   (CET)
FR .... Frequency Range
FR .... Frequency Response
FR .... Frequent
FR .... Fresh
FR .... Friar
FR .... Friday
FR .... Frigate
fr .... Frigorie [*Unit of rate of extraction of heat*] [*Thermodynamics*]
FR .... From   (AFM)
FR .... Front
FR .... Frontispiece [*Publishing*]
FR .... Fructus [*Fruit*] [*Latin*]   (ROG)
fr .... Fruit
FR .... Fuel Remaining [*Aviation*]
FR .... Full Range   (MCD)
FR .... Full-Rate [*Telegrams and cables*]
FR .... Fully Registered
FR .... Functional Requirements
F & R .... Functions and Responsibilities

FR .... Fund Raising [*Red Cross*]
FR .... Fund for the Republic [*Later, Robert Maynard Hutchins Center for the Study of Democratic Institutions*]   (EA)
FR .... Fundamental Resonance   (MCD)
FR .... Funding Request
FR .... Furlough Rations [*Army*]
FR .... Furness Railway [*Scotland*]
FR .... Furtwaengler und Reichhold, Griechische Vasenmalerei [*A publication*]
FR .... Receiving station only, connected with the general network of telecommunications channels [*ITU designation*]   (CET)
fr----- .... Rift Valley [*MARC geographic area code*] [*Library of Congress*]   (LCCP)
FR .... Suffix to regular Air Force officers' service number and prefix to airmen's service number
FR .... Swiss Air Ambulance Ltd. Zurich [*ICAO designator*]   (FAAC)
FRA .... Farah, Inc. [*NYSE symbol*]   (SPSG)
FRA .... Father's Rights of America   (EA)
FRA .... Federal Railroad Administration
FRA .... Federal Regular Army [*Federation of South Arabia*]
FRA .... Federal Reports Act   (DLA)
FRA .... Federal Reserve Act [*1913*]
FRA .... Fibrinogen-Related Antigen [*Immunology*]
FRA .... Financial Research Associates
FRA .... Fleet Reserve Association   (EA)
FRA .... Flow Recorder and Alarm [*Nuclear energy*]   (NRCH)
FRA .... Fluorescent Rabies Antibody [*Immunology*]
FRA .... Fontes Rerum Austriacarum [*A publication*]
FRA .... Footwear Retailers of America [*Later, FDRA*]   (EA)
FRA .... Force Recon Association   (EA)
FRA .... Foreign Resources Associates
FRA .... Forward Rate Agreement [*Banking*]
FRA .... Forward Refueling Area
FRAS .... Fos-Related Antigens [*Biochemistry*]
FRA .... Fra Randers Amt [*A publication*]
Fr A .... Fraenkische Alb [*A publication*]
FRA .... Framycetin [*Neomycin B*] [*Antibacterial compound*]
FRA .... France [*ANSI three-letter standard code*]   (CNC)
FrA .... France-Asie [*A publication*]
Fra .... Francis' Maxims of Equity [*1722-46*] [*A publication*]   (DLA)
Fra .... Franciscus de Telese [*Flourished, 1270-82*] [*Authority cited in pre-1607 legal work*]   (DSA)
FRA .... Frankfurt [*West Germany*] [*Airport symbol*]   (OAG)
FRA .... Frente Radical Alfarista [*Radical Alfarista Front*] [*Ecuador*] [*Political party*]   (PPW)
FRA .... Friant, CA [*Location identifier*] [*FAA*]   (FAAL)
FRA .... Friction Reducing Agent [*Chemicals*]
FRA .... Functional Residual Air   (ADA)
FRA .... Funded Reimburseable Authority   (MCD)
FRAA .... Fleet Reserve Association Auxiliary
FRAA .... Furniture Rental Association of America   (EA)
FRAACA ... Foundation for Research in the Afro-American Creative Arts   (EA)
Fra Ac F ..... Franciscus de Accursio (Filius) [*Deceased, 1293*] [*Authority cited in pre-1607 legal work*]   (DSA)
FRAB .... Banque Franco-Arabe d'Investissements Internationaux
FRAB .... Fuel Receiving Air Blowers [*Nuclear energy*]   (NRCH)
FRAC .... Food Research and Action Center   (EA)
Frac .... Fracastoro [*A publication*]
FRAC .... Fractional   (MSA)
FRAC .... Fractionator Reflux Analog Computer
FRAC .... Fracture [*Medicine*]
FRACA ...... Fracastoro [*A publication*]
FRACAS.... Filter Response Analysis for Continuously Accelerating Spacecraft [*NASA*]
FRACDS ... Fellow of the Royal Australian College of Dental Surgeons
FRACHE ... Federation of Regional Accrediting Commissions of Higher Education [*Later, COPA*]   (EA)
FRACI .... Fellow of the Royal Australian Chemical Institute [*Formerly, FACI*]
FRACMA ... Fellow of the Royal Australian College of Medical Administrators
FRACO ...... Framycetin [*Neomycin B*], Colistin [*Antineoplastic drug regimen*]
FRACON... Framycetin [*Neomycin B*], Colistin, Nystatin [*Antineoplastic drug regimen*]
FRACP ...... Fellow of the Royal Australasian College of Physicians
FRACR ...... Fellow of the Royal Australasian College of Radiologists
FRACS ...... Fellow of the Royal Australasian College of Surgeons
FRACT ...... Fraction
FRACT ...... Fracture [*Medicine*]
FRACT DOS ... Fracti Dosi [*In Divided Doses*] [*Pharmacy*]
Fr Actuelle ... France Actuelle [*A publication*]
FRAD .... Fellow of the Royal Academy of Dancing [*British*]
FRADU ..... Fleet Requirements and Aircraft Direction Unit [*Navy*]   (MCD)
FrAE .... French Antarctic Expedition [*1903-05,1908-10,1948-*]
FRAeS .... Fellow of the Royal Aeronautical Society [*British*]   (EY)
FRAF .... Fuel Receiving Air Filters [*Nuclear energy*]   (NRCH)
Fra Fys Verden ... Fra Fysikkens Verden [*A publication*]
FRAG......... Fragile
FRAG......... Fragment [*Military*]   (AFM)

FRAG......... Fragment [*Used in correcting manuscripts, etc.*]
FRAGBOMB ... Fragmentation Bomb
FRAGM..... Fragments
Fragm Balcan ... Fragmenta Balcanica. Musei Macedonici Scientiarum Naturalium [*A publication*]
Fragm Balcan Prir Muz (Skopje) ... Fragmenta Balcanica. Prirodonaucen Muzej (Skopje) [*A publication*]
Fragm Balc Mus Macedonici Sci Nat ... Fragmenta Balcanica. Musei Macedonici Scientiarum Naturalium [*A publication*]
Fragm Bot ... Fragmenta Botanica [*A publication*]
Fragm Coleopterol ... Fragmenta Coleopterologica [*A publication*]
Fragm Coleopterol Jpn ... Fragmenta Coleopterologica Japonica [*A publication*]
Fragm Ent ... Fragmenta Entomologica [*A publication*]
Fragm Entomol ... Fragmenta Entomologica [*A publication*]
Fragm Faun ... Fragmenta Faunistica [*A publication*]
Fragm Faun Hung ... Fragmenta Faunistica Hungarica [*A publication*]
Fragm Faun Pol Akad Nauk Inst Zool ... Fragmenta Faunistica. Polska Akademia Nauk Instytut Zoologii [*A publication*]
Fragm Faun (Warsaw) ... Fragmenta Faunistica (Warsaw) [*A publication*]
Fragm Flor Geobot ... Fragmenta Floristica et Geobotanica [*A publication*]
Fragm Florist Geobot (Cracow) ... Fragmenta Floristica et Geobotanica (Cracow) [*A publication*]
Fragm Herbol Jugosl ... Fragmenta Herbologica Jugoslavica [*A publication*]
Fragm Mineral Palaeontol ... Fragmenta Mineralogica et Palaeontologica [*A publication*]
FRAGNET ... Fragmented Network   (MCD)
FRAGO ...... Fragmentary Order [*Military*]
Fra Gon ...... Franciscus Gonzaga [*Authority cited in pre-1607 legal work*]   (DSA)
Fr Agric...... France Agricole [*A publication*]
FRAGROC ... Fragmenting Warhead Rocket
FRAgSs...... Fellow of the Royal Agricultural Societies [*British*]
FRAHS..... Fellow of the Royal Australian Historical Society
FRAI.......... Fellow of the Royal Anthropological Institute [*British*]
FRAIA .... Fellow of the Royal Australian Institute of Architects
FRAIC .... Fellow of the Royal Architectural Institute of Canada
FRAIN...... Front Revolutionnaire Africain pour l'Independence Nationale des Colonies Portugaises [*African Revolutionary Front for the National Independence of Portuguese Colonies*]
FRAIPA..... Fellow of the Royal Australian Institute of Public Administration
FrAipNA.... Centre d'Etudes Nord-Americaines, Aix-En-Provence, France [*Library symbol*] [*Library of Congress*]   (LCLS)
FRAK........ Flak RADAR Automatic Kanon
FRAM....... Fellow of the Royal Academy of Music [*British*]
FRAM....... Ferroelectronic RAM [*Random-Access Memory*] [*Ramtron*]
FRAM....... Fleet Rehabilitation and Maintenance
FRAM....... Fleet Rehabilitation and Modernization [*Navy*]   (MCD)
Fra M........ Francis' Maxims of Equity [*1722-46*] [*A publication*]   (DLA)
FRAM2...... Field Records Administration Microform Mode
FRAMATOME ... Societe Franco-Americaine de Constructions Atomiques   (NRCH)
Fr Am Commer ... French American Commerce [*A publication*]
FRAME...... Fund for the Replacement of Animals in Medical Experiments
FRAME..... Fund for the Replacement of Animals in Medical Experiments. Technical News [*A publication*]
FRAMP..... Fleet Readiness Aircraft Maintenance Personnel [*Navy*]   (MCD)
FRAMP..... Fleet Readiness Aviation Maintenance Personnel [*Navy*]
FRAMP..... Fleet Rehabilitation and Modernization Program [*Navy*]
FRAMP..... Frampton [*England*]
F de Ramp ... Franciscus de Ramponibus [*Deceased, 1401*] [*Authority cited in pre-1607 legal work*]   (DSA)
FRAMPO ... Frente Amplio Popular [*Broad Popular Front*] [*Panama*] [*Political party*]   (PPW)
Fr Am Rev ... French American Review [*A publication*]
FRAN .... Fleet Readiness Analysis [*NORRS*]
Fran........... Franciscus de Telese [*Flourished, 1270-82*] [*Authority cited in pre-1607 legal work*]   (DSA)
Fran........... Franciscus Vercellensis [*Flourished, 13th century*] [*Authority cited in pre-1607 legal work*]   (DSA)
Fran........... Franciscus Zabarella [*Deceased, 1417*] [*Authority cited in pre-1607 legal work*]   (DSA)
Fran Anz .... Franciscus Anzolellus [*Authority cited in pre-1607 legal work*]   (DSA)
Fran Anzol ... Franciscus Anzolellus [*Authority cited in pre-1607 legal work*]   (DSA)
Fran de Are ... Franciscus de Accoltis de Aretio [*Deceased, 1486*] [*Authority cited in pre-1607 legal work*]   (DSA)
Fran Aret ... Franciscus de Accoltis de Aretio [*Deceased, 1486*] [*Authority cited in pre-1607 legal work*]   (DSA)
Fran de Aret ... Franciscus de Accoltis de Aretio [*Deceased, 1486*] [*Authority cited in pre-1607 legal work*]   (DSA)
Franc.......... Franciscana [*A publication*]
Franc.......... Franciscus de Telese [*Flourished, 1270-82*] [*Authority cited in pre-1607 legal work*]   (DSA)
Franc Ac..... Franciscus de Accursio [*Deceased, 1293*] [*Authority cited in pre-1607 legal work*]   (DSA)
FRANC AD MOEN ... Francofurtum Ad Moenum [*Frankfort-On-The-Main*] [*Imprint*] [*Latin*]   (ROG)

Franc Anz .. Franciscus Anzolellus [*Authority cited in pre-1607 legal work*] (DSA)

Franc de Are ... Franciscus de Accoltis de Aretio [*Deceased, 1486*] [*Authority cited in pre-1607 legal work*] (DSA)

Franc Balb ... [*Johannes*] Franciscus Balbus [*Flourished, 16th century*] [*Authority cited in pre-1607 legal work*] (DSA)

Franc Conn ... Franciscus Connanus [*Deceased, 1551*] [*Authority cited in pre-1607 legal work*] (DSA)

France .... France's Reports [*3-11 Colorado*] [*A publication*] (DLA)

France Apic ... La France Apicole [*A publication*]

France As ... France-Asie; Revue de Culture et de Synthese Franco-Asiatique [*A publication*]

France (Colo) ... France's Reports [*3-11 Colorado*] [*A publication*] (DLA)

France Illus ... France Illustration [*A publication*]

France Illus Sup ... France Illustration. Supplement [*A publication*]

France Jud ... France Judiciaire [*1876-1910*] [*French*] [*A publication*] (DLA)

Fran Char .. Francis' Law of Charities [*2nd ed.*] [*1855*] [*A publication*] (DLA)

Franchise LJ ... Franchise Law Journal [*A publication*] (DLA)

Franchis'g .. Franchising in the Economy, 1983-1985 [*A publication*]

FRANCIS ... Fichier de Recherches Automatisees sur les Nouvautes, la Communication et l'Information en Sciences Sociales et Humaines [*French Retrieval Automated Network for Current Information in Social and Human Sciences*] [*Database*]

Francis Bald ... Franciscus Balduinus [*Deceased, 1572*] [*Authority cited in pre-1607 legal work*] (DSA)

FRANCIS: DOGE ... FRANCIS: Documentation Automatisee en Gestion des Entreprises [*Database*]

Francis Duar ... Franciscus Duarenus [*Deceased, 1559*] [*Authority cited in pre-1607 legal work*] (DSA)

Francis Max ... Francis' Maxims of Equity [*1722-46*] [*A publication*] (DLA)

FRANCIS: RESHUS ... FRANCIS: Reseau Documentaire en Sciences Humaines de la Sante [*French*] [*Database*]

Francis Sonsb ... Franciscus Sonsbeccius [*Flourished, 16th century*] [*Authority cited in pre-1607 legal work*] (DSA)

Franc Judg ... Francillon's County Court Judgments [*England*] [*A publication*] (DLA)

FrancLA ..... Studii Biblici Franciscani. Liber Annuus [*Jerusalem*] [*A publication*]

Franc Lev ... Franciscaans Leven [*A publication*]

Franc Mod ... Francais Moderne [*A publication*]

FRANCOF ... Francofortium [*Frankfort*] [*Imprint*] [*Latin*] (ROG)

Fran Coll LJ ... Franciso College Law Journal [*A publication*] (DLA)

Franc de Rampo ... Franciscus de Ramponibus [*Deceased, 1401*] [*Authority cited in pre-1607 legal work*] (DSA)

Franc S .... Franciscan Studies [*A publication*]

FrancSt ...... Franciscan Studies. Annual [*St. Bonaventure, New York*] [*A publication*]

Franc de T ... Franciscus de Telese [*Flourished, 1270-82*] [*Authority cited in pre-1607 legal work*] (DSA)

Franc de Tel ... Franciscus de Telese [*Flourished, 1270-82*] [*Authority cited in pre-1607 legal work*] (DSA)

Franc Viv ... Franciscus Vivius [*Flourished, 16th century*] [*Authority cited in pre-1607 legal work*] (DSA)

Franc Zoannet ... Franciscus Zoannettus [*Deceased, 1586*] [*Authority cited in pre-1607 legal work*] (DSA)

Fran Duar .. Franciscus Duarenus [*Deceased, 1559*] [*Authority cited in pre-1607 legal work*] (DSA)

Fran Eng Law ... Francillon's Lectures on English Law [*1860-61*] [*A publication*] (DLA)

FRANK ...... Frequency Regulation and Network Keying (IEEE)

FrankfAllg ... Frankfurter Allgemeine [*A publication*]

Frankf Hefte ... Frankfurter Hefte. Zeitschrift fuer Kultur und Politik [*A publication*]

Frankf Hist Forsch ... Frankfurter Historische Forschungen [*A publication*]

Frankf Kakteen-Freund ... Frankfurter Kakteen-Freund [*A publication*]

Frankfurter Ver Geog Jber ... Frankfurter Verein fuer Geographie und Statistik. Jahresbericht [*A publication*]

Frankfurt H ... Frankfurter Hefte [*A publication*]

Frankf Z Path ... Frankfurter Zeitschrift fuer Pathologie [*A publication*]

Frankf Z Pathol ... Frankfurter Zeitschrift fuer Pathologie [*A publication*]

Frankf Zt ... Frankfurter Allgemeine Zeitung fuer Deutschland [*A publication*]

Fran Max ... Francis' Maxims of Equity [*1722-46*] [*A publication*] (DLA)

Fran Mod ... Francais Moderne [*A publication*]

Fran Prec ... Francis' Common Law Precedents [*A publication*] (DLA)

Fran de Rampo ... Franciscus de Ramponibus [*Deceased, 1401*] [*Authority cited in pre-1607 legal work*] (DSA)

Fran Rip ..... [*Johannes*] Franciscus de Ripa [*Deceased, 1534*] [*Authority cited in pre-1607 legal work*] (DSA)

FRANS ...... Franciscan

FranS .... Franciscan Studies [*A publication*]

Fran Stds ... Franciscan Studies [*A publication*]

Fran Stud ... Franciscan Studies [*A publication*]

Fran Vercell ... Franciscus Vercellensis [*Flourished, 13th century*] [*Authority cited in pre-1607 legal work*] (DSA)

FRANY ...... Fashion Reporters Award - New York

FRANZ ...... Fellow, Registered Accountant, New Zealand

Franz Forsch ... Franziskanische Forschungen [*A publication*]

FranzS .... Franziskanische Studien [*Padeborn*] [*A publication*]

Franz St ..... Franziskanische Studien [*A publication*]

FRAP .... Fast Response Action Potential [*Psychology*]

FRAP .... Fellow of the Royal Academy of Physicians [*British*]

FRAP .... Fire Rescue Air Pack [*NASA*]

FRAP .... Flat Response Audio Pickup

FRAP .... Fleet Readiness Assistance Program (MCD)

FRAP .... Fleet Reliability Assessment Program [*Navy*] (MCD)

FRAP .... Fluorescence Recovery [*or Redistribution*] after Photobleaching [*Analytical biochemistry*]

FRAP .... Fluoride-Resistant Acid Phosphatase [*An enzyme*]

FRAP .... Frente de Accion Popular [*Popular Action Front*] [*Chile*]

FRAP .... Frente Revolucionario Antifascista Patriotica [*Anti-Fascist and Patriotic Revolutionary Front*] [*Spain*]

FRAP .... Front d'Action Politique

FRAP .... Fuel Rod Analysis Program [*Nuclear energy*] (NRCH)

FRAP .... Fuerzas Revolucionarias Armadas Populares [*People's Revolutionary Armed Forces*] [*Mexico*] (PD)

FRAPA ..... Forest Products Accident Prevention Association

FRAPRU ... Front d'Action Populaire en Reamenagement Urbain [*Canada*]

FRAP-S ..... Fuel Rod Analysis Program - Steady-State [*Nuclear energy*] (NRCH)

FRAP-T ..... Fuel Rod Analysis Program - Transient [*Nuclear energy*] (NRCH)

FRAR .... Fire Research Abstracts and Reviews [*A publication*]

FRARA ...... Fire Research Abstracts and Reviews [*A publication*]

Fr Ar Rev ... Fremantle Arts Review [*A publication*]

FRAS .... Fellow of the Royal Asiatic Society [*British*]

FRAS .... Fellow of the Royal Astronomical Society [*British*]

Fras .... Fraser's English Election Cases [*1776-77*] [*A publication*] (DLA)

Fra de Sax ... Franciscus de Saxolinis [*Flourished, 13th century*] [*Authority cited in pre-1607 legal work*] (DSA)

Fra de Saxolis ... Franciscus de Saxolinis [*Flourished, 13th century*] [*Authority cited in pre-1607 legal work*] (DSA)

FRASB ...... Fellow of the Royal Asiatic Society of Bengal

FRASCO ... Foundation for Religious Action in the Social and Civil Order (EA)

Fras Div ..... Fraser's Conflict of Laws in Cases of Divorce [*A publication*] (DLA)

Fras Dom Rel ... Fraser on Personal and Domestic Relations [*Scotland*] [*A publication*] (DLA)

FRASE ...... Fellow of the Royal Agricultural Society of England

Fras Elec Cas ... Fraser's English Election Cases [*1776-77*] [*A publication*] (DLA)

Fraser .... Fraser's English Cases of Controverted Elections [*1776-77*] [*A publication*] (DLA)

Fraser .... Fraser's Husband and Wife [*1876-78*] [*Scotland*] [*A publication*] (DLA)

Fraser .... Fraser's Magazine [*A publication*]

Fraser .... Fraser's Scotch Court of Sessions Cases, Fifth Series [*A publication*] (DLA)

Fraser of Allander Inst Q Econ Commentary ... Fraser of Allander Institute. Quarterly Economic Commentary [*A publication*]

Fraser (Scot) ... Fraser's English Cases of Controverted Elections [*1776-77*] [*A publication*] (DLA)

Fraser (Scot) ... Scotch Court of Session Cases, Fifth Series, by Fraser [*A publication*] (DLA)

Fras M & S ... Fraser on Master and Servant in Scotland [*A publication*] (DLA)

Fras Par & Ch ... Fraser's Parent and Child [*Scotland*] [*A publication*] (DLA)

FR and ASS ... Fellow of the Royal and Antiquarian Societies [*British*]

FRASS ...... Fraser Marketing Investments [*NASDAQ symbol*] (NQ)

Fra Sundhedsstyr ... Fra Sundhedsstyrelsen [*A publication*]

Fra Sundhedsstyr (Copenhagen) ... Fra Sundhedsstyrelsen (Copenhagen) [*A publication*]

FRAT .... Fraternity

FRAT .... Fraternize (DSUE)

FRAT .... Free Radical Assay Technique [*Clinical chemistry*]

Fra de Te .... Franciscus de Telese [*Flourished, 1270-82*] [*Authority cited in pre-1607 legal work*] (DSA)

Fra de Tels ... Franciscus de Telese [*Flourished, 1270-82*] [*Authority cited in pre-1607 legal work*] (DSA)

FRATU ...... Fleet Requirements and Aircraft Training Unit [*British military*] (DMA)

FRAUD ..... Fraudulent (MSA)

Frauen & F ... Frauen und Film [*A publication*]

FrAv .... Bibliotheque Calvet, Avignon, France [*Library symbol*] [*Library of Congress*] (LCLS)

Fraz .... Frazer's Admiralty Cases, Etc. [*Scotland*] [*A publication*] (DLA)

Fra Za .... Franciscus Zabarella [*Deceased, 1417*] [*Authority cited in pre-1607 legal work*] (DSA)

Fraz Adm ... Frazer's Admiralty Cases, Etc. [*Scotland*] [*A publication*] (DLA)

FRB .... Business Review. Federal Reserve Bank of Philadelphia [*A publication*]

FRB .... FABS Reference Bible [*FABS International, Inc.*] [*Information service or system*] (CRD)

FRB .... Failure to Return to Battery [*Study*] (MCD)

FRB .... Failure Review Board [*NASA*] (NASA)

FRB .... Fast Rise Balloon

FRB........... Federal Reserve Banks [of FRS]
FRB........... Federal Reserve Board [Later, BGFRS]
FRB........... Federal Reserve Bulletin [A publication]
FRB........... Federation of Radical Booksellers [British]
FRB........... Fiberglass Rotor Blade   (MCD)
FRB........... Fire-Resistant Brick [Technical drawings]
FRB........... Fireball Resources [Vancouver Stock Exchange symbol]
FRB........... First RepublicBank Corp. [NYSE symbol]   (SPSG)
FRB........... Fisheries Research Board of Canada [Marine science]   (MSC)
FRB........... Fitness Reports Branch [BUPERS]
FRB........... Flight Rated Bioinstrumentation
FRB........... Forbes [Australia] [Airport symbol]   (OAG)
FRB........... Forschungs-Reaktor Berlin
FRB........... Frobisher [Northwest Territories] [Seismograph station code,
                   US Geological Survey]   (SEIS)
Fr Baldui.... Franciscus Balduinus [Deceased, 1572] [Authority cited in pre-
                   1607 legal work]   (DSA)
Fr Bank...... Frank on the United States Bankrupt Act of 1867 [A
                   publication]   (DLA)
FRBC........ Franklin Bancorp of New Jersey [NASDAQ symbol]   (NQ)
FRBCB...... Fisheries Research Board of Canada. Bulletin [A publication]
FRBCTR.... Fisheries Research Board of Canada. Technical Report [A
                   publication]
FRBFC....... Foggy River Boys Fan Club   (EA)
FRBK........ Fairfield First Bank & Trust Co. [NASDAQ symbol]   (NQ)
FRBMRS... Fisheries Research Board of Canada. Manuscript Report Series
                   [A publication]
Fr Br.......... Front og Bro [A publication]
FRBRD....... Federal Reserve Bank of St. Louis. Review [A publication]
FRBS .... Fellow of the Royal Botanic Society [British]
FRBS .... Fellow of the Royal Society of British Sculptors
Fr Bul Stat ... Bulletin Mensuel de Statistique (France) [A publication]
Fr Bur Rech Geol Minieres Bull Ser 2 Sect 1 ... France. Bureau de Recherches
                   Geologiques et Minieres. Bulletin. Serie 2. Section 1.
                   Geologie de la France [A publication]
Fr Bur Rech Geol Minieres Bull Ser 2 Sect 4 ... France. Bureau de Recherches
                   Geologiques et Minieres. Bulletin. Serie 2. Section 4 [A
                   publication]
Fr Bur Rech Geol Minieres Mem ... France. Bureau de Recherches
                   Geologiques et Minieres. Memoires [A publication]
Fr Bur Rech Geol Min Mem ... France. Bureau de Recherches Geologiques et
                   Minieres. Memoires [A publication]
FRBW........ Federal Reserve Board Weekly [Database] [I. P. Sharp
                   Associates] [Information service or system]   (CRD)
FRC........... Control of Rents and Furnished Lets [British]
FRC........... Facility Review Committee
FRC........... Family Research Council   (EA)
FRC........... Family Resource Coalition   (EA)
FRC........... Family Rosary Crusade [Later, FR]   (EA)
FRC........... Fasteners Research Council [Defunct]   (EA)
FRC........... Fatah Revolutionary Council [Libyan-based terrorist
                   organization]
FRC........... Federal Radiation Council [Defunct]   (EA)
FRC........... Federal Radio Commission [Functions transferred to FCC,
                   1934]
FRC........... Federal Ranch [British Columbia] [Seismograph station code,
                   US Geological Survey] [Closed]   (SEIS)
FRC........... Federal Records Center [General Services
                   Administration]   (AABC)
FRC........... Federal Records Council
FRC........... Federal Regional Center [Office of Civil Defense]
FRC........... Federal Regional Council [for federal-state-local interchange]
                   [Abolished, 1983]
FRC........... Federal Reserve Bank of Philadelphia, Philadelphia, PA [OCLC
                   symbol]   (OCLC)
FRC........... Fiber-Reinforced Composite
FRC........... Filipino Rehabilitation Commission [Post-World War II]
FRC........... Final Routing Center [Telecommunications]   (TEL)
FRC........... First Republic Bancorp, Inc. [AMEX symbol]   (SPSG)
FRC........... Fishery Research Craft
FRC........... Fixed Radio Communication
FRC........... Flag Research Center   (EA)
FRC........... Flat Rock Consultants, Inc. [Information service or
                   system]   (IID)
FRC........... Fletcher Challenge Finance Canada, Inc. [Toronto Stock
                   Exchange symbol]
FRC........... Flight Research Center [Later, DFRC] [NASA]
FRC........... Flow Recorder Controller
FRC........... Flowers' Roguish Cultivator
FRC........... Franca [Brazil] [Airport symbol]   (OAG)
FRC........... Franklin Research Center [Research center]   (RCD)
FRC........... Frederick Research Center   (KSC)
FRC........... Free Carrier [Followed by a named point] ["INCOTERM,"
                   International Chamber of Commerce official code]
FRC........... Free Residual Chlorine
FRC........... Frequency Response Curve
FRC........... Fresnel Reflection Coefficient [Optics]
FRC........... Frozen Red Cells [Medicine]
FRC........... Fuels Research Council [Defunct]
FRC........... Full Route Clearance Necessary [Aviation]   (FAAC)

FRC........... Functional Reserve [or Residual] Capacity [of the lungs]
                   [Physiology]
FRC........... Spokane, WA [Location identifier] [FAA]   (FAAL)
FRCA........ Family Research Council of America [Later, FRC]   (EA)
FRCA........ Fellow of the Royal College of Art [British]
FRCA........ Fire Retardant Chemicals Association   (EA)
FRCATS.... Fellow of the Royal College of Advanced Technology, Salford
                   [British]
FRCC........ Federal Research Contract Center
FRCC........ First Financial Caribbean Corp. [NASDAQ symbol]   (CTT)
FRCC........ Free of Riots and Civil Commotions [Insurance]
FR & CC .... Free of Riots and Civil Commotions [Insurance]
FRCD........ Fellow of the Royal College of Dentists [British]
FRCD........ Floating Rate Certificate of Deposit
FRCD(C) ... Fellow of the Royal College of Dentists (Canada)
Fr Cent Natl Exploit Oceans Publ Result Compagnes Mer ... France. Centre
                   National pour l'Exploitation des Oceans. Publications.
                   Resultats des Compagnes a la Mer Brest [A publication]
Fr Cent Natl Exploit Oceans Rapp Annu ... France. Centre National pour
                   l'Exploitation des Oceans. Rapport Annuel [A publication]
Fr Cent Rech Zones Arides Publ Ser Geol ... France. Centre de Recherches sur
                   les Zones Arides. Publications. Serie Geologie [A
                   publication]
FRCF .... Federation of Reconstructionist Congregations and Fellowships
                   [Later, FRCH]   (EA)
FRCGP ...... Fellow of the Royal College of General Practitioners [British]
FRCH .... Federation of Reconstructionist Congregations and
                   Havurot   (EA)
FR CH ...... Free Church   (ROG)
Fr Ch.......... Freeman's English Chancery Reports [A publication]   (DLA)
Fr Ch.......... Freeman's Mississippi Chancery Reports [A
                   publication]   (DLA)
FRCH .... Frenchtex, Inc. [NASDAQ symbol]   (NQ)
FrChr........ Freier Christentum [A publication]
Fr Chy .... Freeman's English Chancery Reports [A publication]   (DLA)
Fr Chy .... Freeman's Mississippi Chancery Reports [A
                   publication]   (DLA)
FRCI .... Fellow of the Royal Colonial Institute [British]
FRCI .... Fibrous Refractory Composite Insulation
FRCJ .... Fiber-Reinforced Composite Junction
FRCM .... Fellow of the Royal College of Music [British]
FRCM........ Firecom, Inc. [NASDAQ symbol]   (NQ)
FRCO .... Fellow of the Royal College of Organists [British]
FRCOA ...... Fruit Color (No Green to Mostly Green) [Botany]
FRCOB...... Fruit Color (Greenish Red to Dark Red) [Botany]
FRCO(CHM) ... Fellow of the Royal College of Organists (Choir-Training
                   Diploma) [British]
FRCOG ...... Fellow of the Royal College of Obstetricians and Gynaecologists
                   [British]
Fr Cosci...... Franciscus Coscius [Deceased, 1556] [Authority cited in pre-
                   1607 legal work]   (DSA)
FRCOUSA ... Federation of Russian Charitable Organizations of the United
                   States of America [Defunct]   (EA)
FRCP .... Facility Remote Control Panel   (AAG)
FRCP .... Federal Rules of Civil Procedure [A publication]   (DLA)
FRCP .... Fellow of the Royal College of Physicians [British]
FRCP .... Fellow of the Royal College of Preceptors [British]
FRCPA ...... Fellow, Royal College of Pathologists, Australasia
FRC Path ... Fellow of the Royal College of Pathologists [British]
FRCP(C).... Fellow of the Royal College of Physicians (Canada)
FRCPCan .. Fellow of the Royal College of Physicians of Canada
FRCPE ...... Fellow of the Royal College of Physicians of Edinburgh
FRCPEd .... Fellow of the Royal College of Physicians of Edinburgh
FRCP Edin ... Fellow of the Royal College of Physicians of Edinburgh
FRCPGlas ... Fellow of the Royal College of Physicians and Surgeons of
                   Glasgow
FRCPI .... Fellow of the Royal College of Physicians, Ireland   (ROG)
FRCP Irel .. Fellow of the Royal College of Physicians of Ireland
FRCP Lond ... Fellow of the Royal College of Physicians of London [British]
FRCPS(Hon) ... Honorary Fellow of the Royal College of Physicians and
                   Surgeons [Glasgow]
FRC Psych ... Fellow of the Royal College of Psychiatrists [British]
FRCR........ Fellow of the Royal College of Radiologists [British]
FRCRAX ... Forestry Chronicle [A publication]
FRCS .... Federal Reserve Communications System
FRCS .... Fellow of the Royal College of Surgeons [British]
FRCS .... Flow Recording Controller Switch [Nuclear energy]   (NRCH)
FRCS .... Forward Reaction Control Subsystem [NASA]   (NASA)
FRCS .... Francs [Monetary units]   (ROG)
FRCS(C).... Fellow of the Royal College of Surgeons (Canada)
FRCSCan... Fellow of the Royal College of Surgeons of Canada
FRCSE ...... Fellow of the Royal College of Surgeons of Edinburgh
FRCS Ed.... Fellow of the Royal College of Surgeons of Edinburgh
FRCSEd(C/Th) ... Fellow of the Royal College of Surgeons of Edinburgh,
                   Specialising in Cardiothoracic Surgery [British]   (DBQ)
FRCS Edin ... Fellow of the Royal College of Surgeons of Edinburgh
FRCSEd(Orth) ... Fellow of the Royal College of Surgeons of Edinburgh,
                   Specialising in Orthopaedic Surgery [British]   (DBQ)
FRCSEd(SN) ... Fellow of the Royal College of Surgeons of Edinburgh,
                   Specialising in Surgical Neurology [British]   (DBQ)
FRCS Eng ... Fellow of the Royal College of Surgeons of England

FRCSGlas ...	Fellow of the Royal College of Surgeons of Glasgow
FRCSI	Fellow of the Royal College of Surgeons in Ireland
FRCS Irel ..	Fellow of the Royal College of Surgeons in Ireland
FRCSL	Fellow of the Royal College of Surgeons of London
FRCSoc	Fellow of the Royal Commonwealth Society [*British*]
FRCTF	Fast Reactor Core Test Facility [*Nuclear energy*]
FRCU	Fractocumulus [*Meteorology*]
FRCUS	Fellow of the Royal College of University Surgeons [*Denmark*]
FRCVS	Fellow of the Royal College of Veterinary Surgeons [*British*]
FRCwlthS ..	Fellow of the Royal Commonwealth Society
FRD	Facilities Requirements Documents (MCD)
FRD	Failure Rate Data (KSC)
FRD	Federal Reserve Bank of Dallas, Dallas, TX [*OCLC symbol*] (OCLC)
FRD	Federal Reserve District
FRD	Federal Rules Decisions [*A publication*]
FRD	Field Remount Depot [*British military*] (DMA)
FRD	Fix-Radial-Distance (FAAC)
FRD	Flight Readiness Demonstration
FRD	Flight Requirements Document (MCD)
FRD	Fluid Rate Damper
FRD	Ford Motor Co. [*Detroit, MI*] [*FAA designator*] (FAAC)
FRD	Formerly Restricted Data [*Military*]
FRD	Fraction Reliability Deviation
FRD	Fraud [*FBI standardized term*]
FRD	Fredericksburg [*Virginia*] [*Geomagnetic observatory code*]
FRD	Free Rural Delivery [*British*]
FRD	Friday Harbor [*Washington*] [*Airport symbol*] (OAG)
FRD	Friedman Industries, Inc. [*AMEX symbol*] (SPSG)
FRD	Friend (AABC)
FRD	Functional Reference Device (IEEE)
FRDB	Failure Rate Data Bank [*GIDEP*]
FRDCA	Fridericiana [*A publication*]
FRDF	Fonds de Recherches et de Developpement Forestier [*Forest Research and Development Foundation*] [*Canada*]
FRDF	Forest Research and Development Foundation [*Canada*]
FRDI	Flight Research and Development Instrumentation (KSC)
FRDLT	Fraudulent (ROG)
FRDM	Fast Retrieval and Data Manipulator (MCD)
FRDM	Freedom Savings & Loan Association [*NASDAQ symbol*] (NQ)
FRDN	Ferdinand Railroad Co. [*AAR code*]
FRE	Facteur Respiratoire Equilibre [*Ingredient in a cosmetic by Chanel*]
FRE	Facture [*Invoice*] [*Business term*] [*French*]
FRE	Federal Home Loan Mortgage Senior Participating Preferred [*NYSE symbol*] (SPSG)
FRE	Federal Rules of Evidence
FRE	Fera Island [*Solomon Islands*] [*Airport symbol*] (OAG)
FRE	Field Representative Europe
FRE	Flight Related Element (MCD)
FRE	Format Request Element (MCD)
FRE	Frederick Community College, Frederick, MD [*OCLC symbol*] (OCLC)
FRE	French
fre	French [*MARC language code*] [*Library of Congress*] (LCCP)
FRE	Frequency
FRE	Fresno [*California*] [*Seismograph station code, US Geological Survey*] [*Closed*] (SEIS)
FRE	Friends of R. [*Ralph*] Emery (EA)
F Reader ..	Film Reader [*A publication*]
FREB	Federal Real Estate Board [*Abolished, 1951*]
FREB	Field Repairable - Expendable Rotor Blade (RDA)
FREC	Federal Radio Education Committee
Fr EC	Fraser's English Election Cases [*1776-77*] [*A publication*] (DLA)
FR Econ S ..	Fellow of the Royal Economic Society [*British*]
FR Econ Soc ...	Fellow of the Royal Economic Society [*British*] (ROG)
FR Ec S	Fellow of the Royal Economic Society [*British*]
FRED	Fare Reduction Enhancement Device [*Travel industry software*] [*CompuCheck Corp.*]
FRED	Fast Reactivity Exclusion Device [*Nuclear energy*]
FRED	Fast Realistic Editor [*Word processing program*] (ADA)
FRED	Fiendishly Rapid Electronic Device
FRED	Figure Reading Electronic Device [*Information retrieval*]
FRED	Foolish Rear End Device [*Bowdlerized version*] [*Electronic caboose replacement*]
FRED	Fractionally Rapid Electronic Device
FRED	Fredericton [*City in Canada*] (ROG)
Fred	Fredonia [*Record label*]
FRED	Friendly Recoton Entertainment Decoder [*Television stereo adapter*]
FRED	Friendly Robot Educational Device [*Androbot, Inc.*]
FRED	Front End for Databases [*GTE usage*]
FRED	Fund for Rural Economic Development [*Canada*]
FREDA	Freddo [*A publication*]
Fred Code ...	Frederician Code [*Prussia*] [*A publication*] (DLA)
FREDDIE MAC ...	Federal Home Loan Mortgage Corp. (ECON)
FREDI	Flight Range and Endurance Data Indicator
FREDS	Flight Readiness Evaluation Data System (MCD)
FREE	Fabric Retailers, Etc., Etc. [*Trade group*]
FREE	Feasibility of Rocket Energy Employment (MCD)
FREE	Fellowship for Racial and Economic Equality [*Later, Southeast Institute*] (EA)
FREE	Feminist Resources on Energy and Ecology [*Defunct*] (EA)
FREE	Foundation for Rational Economics and Education (EA)
FREE	Foundation for Research on Economics and the Environment [*Research center*] (RCD)
Free	Freeman's English Chancery Reports [*A publication*] (DLA)
Free	Freeman's English King's Bench Reports [*89 English Reprint*] [*1670-1704*] [*A publication*] (DLA)
Free	Freeman's Reports [*31-96 Illinois*] [*A publication*] (DLA)
FREE	Fund for Renewable Energy and the Environment (EA)
FREE	Fund to Restore an Educated Electorate (EA)
Free Assoc ..	Free Association [*A publication*]
FREEBD ...	Freeboard (KSC)
FreeCATS ...	Free Catecholamines Column Test
Free CC	Freeman's English Chancery Reports [*A publication*] (ILCA)
Free Ch	Freeman's English Chancery Reports [*A publication*] (DLA)
Free Ch	Freeman's Mississippi Chancery Reports [*A publication*] (DLA)
Free China R ...	Free China Review [*A publication*]
Freedom Soc ...	Freedom Socialist [*A publication*]
Free Inq	Free Inquiry [*A publication*]
Free KB	Freeman's English King's Bench Reports [*89 English Reprint*] [*1670-1704*] [*A publication*] (DLA)
Free L	Free Lance [*A publication*]
Free Lbr Wld ...	Free Labour World [*A publication*]
Freem	Freeman's English Chancery Reports [*A publication*] (DLA)
Freem	Freeman's Mississippi Chancery Reports [*A publication*] (DLA)
Freeman Ch R ...	Freeman's Mississippi Chancery Reports [*A publication*] (DLA)
Freeman's (Miss) Rep ...	Freeman's Mississippi Chancery Reports [*A publication*] (DLA)
Freem CC ...	Freeman's English Chancery Cases [*A publication*] (DLA)
Freem Ch ...	Freeman's English Chancery Reports [*A publication*] (DLA)
Freem Chan ...	Freeman's Mississippi Chancery Reports [*A publication*] (DLA)
Freem Ch (Eng) ...	Freeman's English Chancery Reports [*A publication*] (DLA)
Freem Ch (Miss) ...	Freeman's Mississippi Chancery Reports [*A publication*] (DLA)
Freem Ch R ...	Freeman's Mississippi Chancery Reports [*A publication*] (DLA)
Freem Compar Politics ...	Freeman. Comparative Politics [*A publication*] (DLA)
Freem Cot ..	Freeman on Cotenancy and Partition [*A publication*] (DLA)
Freem Eng Const ...	Freeman's Growth of the English Constitution [*3rd ed.*] [*1876*] [*A publication*] (DLA)
Freem Ex ...	Freeman on Executors [*A publication*] (DLA)
Freem (Ill) ...	Freeman's Reports [*31-96 Illinois*] [*A publication*] (DLA)
Freem Judgm ...	Freeman on Judgments [*A publication*] (DLA)
Freem KB ...	Freeman's English King's Bench and Common Pleas Reports [*89 English Reprint*] [*A publication*] (DLA)
Freem (Miss) ...	Freeman's Mississippi Chancery Reports [*A publication*] (DLA)
Freem Pr	Freeman's Practice [*Illinois*] [*A publication*] (DLA)
Free News ..	Freedom News [*A publication*]
FREEP	Los Angeles Free Press [*A publication*]
Free Soc	Freedom Socialist [*A publication*]
Free Spir	Freeing the Spirit [*A publication*]
FREE-TH ...	Free-Thinker [*or Free-Thinking*] (ROG)
FREEY	Free State Geduld Mines Ltd. [*NASDAQ symbol*] (NQ)
FREI	Fellow of the Real Estate Institute [*Australia*]
FREIA	Fellow of the Real Estate Institute of Australia
Freiberger Forsch H ...	Freiberger Forschungshefte [*A publication*]
Freiberger Forsch Ser C ...	Freiberger Forschungshefte. Series C. Geologie. Geophysik. Mineralogie-Lagerstaettenlehre und Paleontologie [*A publication*]
Freiberger Forschungsh B Metall ...	Freiberger Forschungshefte. Reihe B. Metallurgie [*A publication*]
Freiberg Forschungsh B ...	Freiberger Forschungshefte. Reihe B [*East Germany*] [*A publication*]
Freiberg Forschungsh C ...	Freiberger Forschungshefte. Reihe C [*A publication*]
Freiberg Forschungsh D ...	Freiberger Forschungshefte. Reihe D [*East Germany*] [*A publication*]
Freiberg Forschungsh Reihe A ...	Freiberger Forschungshefte. Reihe A [*A publication*]
Freiberg Forschungsh Reihe C ...	Freiberger Forschungshefte. Reihe C [*A publication*]
Freib FH	Freiberger Forschungshefte [*A publication*]
Freibl	Freibleibend [*Optional*] [*Business term*] [*German*]
FreibRu	Freiburger Rundbrief [*Freiburg Im Breisgau*] [*A publication*]
Freib Symp Med Univ Klin ...	Freiburger Symposion an der Medizinischen Universitaets-Klinik [*A publication*]
FreibThSt ..	Freiburger Theologische Studien [*A publication*]
Freiburger Geog Mitt ...	Freiburger Geographische Mitteilungen [*A publication*]
FreibZ	Freiburger Zeitschrift fuer Philosophie und Theologie [*A publication*]

Freight & Container Transp ... Freight and Container Transportation [*A publication*]   (APTA)
Freight Mgmt ... Freight Management [*A publication*]
FREIR .... Federal Research on Biological and Health Effects of Ionizing Radiations
FREIT .... Finite-Life Real Estate Investment Trust
Frei Z Phil Theol ... Freiburger Zeitschrift fuer Philosophie und Theologie [*A publication*]
FREJID .... Frequency Jumper Identification
FREL .... Feltman Research and Engineering Laboratory [*Picatinny Arsenal*] [*Army*]
FRELATOR ... Frequency Translator
FRELIMO ... Frente da Libertacao de Mocambique [*Mozambique Liberation Front*] [*Political party*]   (PPW)
FRELP .... Flexible Real Estate Loan Plan
FREM .... Fleet Readiness Enlisted Maintenance [*Trainees*] [*Navy*]
FREM .... Fremington [*England*]
FREM .... Fremitus Vocalis [*Vocal Fremitus*] [*Medicine*]
FREMEC .. Frequent Traveller's Medical Card [*British*]
FRENATRACA ... Frente Nacional de Trabajadores y Campesinos [*National Workers' and Peasants' Front*] [*Peru*] [*Political party*]   (PD)
French Am Rev ... French American Review [*A publication*]
French Hist St ... French Historical Studies [*A publication*]
French (NH) ... French's Reports [*6 New Hampshire*] [*A publication*]   (DLA)
French Pln ... Ninth Plan for Economic and Social Development, 1984-1988 (France) [*A publication*]
French R .... French Review [*A publication*]
French Tech Building Civ Engng & Town Planning ... French Techniques. Building, Civil Engineering, and Town Planning [*A publication*]
French Tech Electr Engn & Electron Ind ... French Techniques. Electrical Engineering and Electronics Industries [*A publication*]
French Tech Mech Hydraul & Consult Engng Ind ... French Techniques. Mechanical, Hydraulic, and Consultant Engineering Industries [*A publication*]
French Tech Metal Ind ... French Techniques. Metal Industries [*A publication*]
French Tech Misc Ind & Consum Goods ... French Techniques. Miscellaneous Industries and Consumer Goods [*A publication*]
French Tech Tranp Stud & Res ... French Techniques. Transportation Studies and Research [*A publication*]
Frend & W Prec ... Frend and Ware's Precedents of Instruments Relating to the Transfer of Land to Railway Companies [*2nd ed.*] [*1866*] [*A publication*]   (DLA)
Freno .... Frente Nacional Opositora [*National Opposition Front*] [*Panama*] [*Political party*]   (PPW)
FRENSIT .. Friendly Situation   (MCD)
FR Ent S .... Fellow of the Royal Entomological Society [*British*]
FRENU ...... Frente Nacional de Unidad [*National Unity Front*] [*Guatemala*] [*Political party*]   (PPW)
FREP .... Fleet Return Evaluation Program
FREPAS .... Forest Range Environmental Production Analytical System   (MCD)
FREPSOG ... Free Play Scenario Generator   (MCD)
FREQ .... Frequency [*or Frequent*]   (AFM)
Freq .... Frequenz [*A publication*]
FREQCONV ... Frequency Converter   (MCD)
FREQDIV ... Frequency Divider   (MCD)
FREQLY .. Frequently   (ROG)
FREQM ...... Frequency Meter
FREQMULT ... Frequency Multiplier   (KSC)
FREQ OCC ... Frequenter Occurrit [*It Occurs Frequently*] [*Latin*]   (ROG)
FREQSCANRA ... Frequency Scan RADAR   (MCD)
FREQT .... Frequent   (ROG)
FRERDC ... Forest Recreation Research [*A publication*]
FRES .... Federal Regulation of Employment Service [*A publication*]   (DLA)
FRES .... Fellow of the Royal Economic Society [*British*]
FRES .... Fellow of the Royal Empire Society [*British*]   (EY)
FRES .... Fellow of the Royal Entomological Society [*British*]   (ROG)
FRES .... Fire Resistant
F Res .... Food Research [*A publication*]
FRES .... Forward Recoil Spectrometry [*Measurement method*]
FRES .... Freres [*Brothers*] [*French*]
FRESCA .... Fermi-Level Referenced Electron Spectroscopy for Chemical Analysis
FRESCA .... Field-Emitter Referenced Electron Spectroscopy for Chemical Analysis
FRESCAN ... Frequency Scanning
FRESCANNAR ... Frequency Scanning RADAR
Fresenius Z Anal Chem ... Fresenius' Zeitschrift fuer Analytische Chemie [*A publication*]
FRESH ...... Foil Research Supercavitating Hydrofoil
FRESH ...... Force Requirements Expert System [*Navy*]
FRESHW .. Freshwell [*England*]
Freshwater Biol ... Freshwater Biology [*A publication*]
Freshwater Biol Assoc Annu Rep ... Freshwater Biology Association. Annual Report [*A publication*]
Freshwater Biol Assoc Sci Publ ... Freshwater Biology Association. Scientific Publication [*A publication*]

Freshwater Fish Newsl ... Freshwater Fisheries Newsletter [*A publication*]   (APTA)
Freshwater Invertebr Biol ... Freshwater Invertebrate Biology [*A publication*]
Freshwat Fish Newsl ... Freshwater Fisheries Newsletter [*A publication*]   (APTA)
Freshw Biol ... Freshwater Biology [*A publication*]
Freshw Biol Assoc Annu Rep ... Freshwater Biological Association. Annual Report [*A publication*]
Freshw Biol Assoc Sci Publ ... Freshwater Biological Association. Scientific Publication [*A publication*]
FRETURN ... Function Return [*Data processing*]
Freunde Naturw Ber (Haidinger) ... Freunde der Naturwissenschaften in Wien. Berichte ueber die Mittheilungen (W. Haidinger) [*A publication*]
Fr Eurafr .... France-Eurafrique [*A publication*]
FRF .... Fernando Rielo Foundation   (EAIO)
FRF .... Fertility Research Foundation   (EA)
FRF .... Filter Replacement Fluid
FRFM .... Fire-Resistant Fuels   (RDA)
FRF .... Flight Readiness Firing [*NASA*]   (NASA)
FRF .... Flight Readiness Firing Test [*NASA*]   (AFM)
FRF .... Follicle-Stimulating Hormone Releasing Factor [*Also, FSH-RF, FSH-RH*] [*Endocrinology*]
FRF .... Fragrance Research Fund   (EA)
FRF .... France Growth Fund [*NYSE symbol*]   (SPSG)
FRF .... Free French [*World War II*]
FRF .... Free Running Frequency
FRF .... Freedom to Read Foundation
Fr F .... French Forum [*A publication*]
FRF .... Frequency Response Function [*Statistics*]
FRF .... Fuel Reprocessing Facility [*Nuclear energy*]   (NRCH)
FRF .... Functional Renal Failure [*Medicine*]
FRFA .... Federal Regulatory Flexibility Act   (IEEE)
FRFD .... First Community Bancorp, Inc. [*Rockford, IL*] [*NASDAQ symbol*]   (NQ)
FRFDS .... Fund Raising and Financial Development Section [*Library Administration and Management Association*]
FRFE .... Field Representative Far East
FRFE .... Freedom Federal Savings Bank [*Oak Brook, IL*] [*NASDAQ symbol*]   (NQ)
FrFM .... French Forum Monographs [*A publication*]
Fr For NW Dt Zahn Ae ... Freies Forum. Nordwestdeutscher Zahnaerzte [*A publication*]
Fr Forum ..... French Forum [*A publication*]
FRFPS .... Fellow of the Royal Faculty of Physicians and Surgeons [*British*]
FRFPS(G) ... Fellow of the Royal Faculty of Physicians and Surgeons of Glasgow
FRFPSGlas ... Fellow of the Royal Faculty of Physicians and Surgeons of Glasgow
FRFS .... Fast Reaction Fighting System   (NATG)
FRFT .... Flight Readiness Firing Test   (MCD)
FRG .... Emerging Germany Fund [*NYSE symbol*]   (SPSG)
FRG .... Farmingdale, NY [*Location identifier*] [*FAA*]   (FAAL)
FRG .... Federal Republic of Germany   (AABC)
FRG .... Federal Reserve System, Board of Governors, Washington, DC [*OCLC symbol*]   (OCLC)
FRG .... Fergana [*USSR*] [*Seismograph station code, US Geological Survey*]   (SEIS)
FRG .... Floated Rate Gyro [*Aerospace*]   (AAG)
FR(g) .... Flow Rate of Sparge Gas
FRG .... Focus on Robert Graves [*A publication*]
FRG .... Force Requirements Generator
FRG .... Forge
frg .... Forger [*MARC relator code*] [*Library of Congress*]   (LCCP)
FRG .... Long Island Republic [*New York*] [*Airport symbol*]   (OAG)
FRG .... Revista de Filologie Romanica si Germanica [*Bucarest*] [*A publication*]
FRGB .... First Regional Bancorp [*NASDAQ symbol*]   (NQ)
FRGN .... Foreign
Fr Gon .... Franciscus Gonzaga [*Authority cited in pre-1607 legal work*]   (DSA)
FRGp .... Field Record Group [*Air Force*]   (AFM)
FRGR .... Frozen Granular Snow [*Skiing condition*]
Fr Graph .... France Graphique
FrGrU .... Universite de Grenoble, Bibliotheque Droit-Lettres, St.-Martin d'Heres, France [*Library symbol*] [*Library of Congress*]   (LCLS)
FRGS .... Fellow of the Royal Geographical Society [*British*]   (ROG)
FRGS .... Forked River Generating Station [*Nuclear energy*]   (NRCH)
FRGS(C) ..... Fellow of the Royal Geographical Society (Canada)
FRGSS .... Fellow of the Royal Geographical Society, Scotland   (ROG)
FRH .... Fellowship of Religious Humanists   (EA)
FRH .... Flying Runway Heading [*Aviation*]   (FAAC)
Fr H .... Frankfurter Hefte [*A publication*]
FrH .... Franzoesisch Heute [*A publication*]
FRH .... French Lick, IN [*Location identifier*] [*FAA*]   (FAAL)
FRH .... Frequency Response Histogram [*Biometrics*]
FRH .... Fruehauf Canada, Inc. [*Toronto Stock Exchange symbol*]
FRH .... Fuller, R. H., Los Angeles CA [*STAC*]

f-rh--- .... Rhodesia [*Southern Rhodesia*] [*MARC geographic area code*] [*Library of Congress*] (LCCP)
FRHB .... Foundation for Research on Human Behavior (EA)
FRHEAJ ... Facsimile Reprints in Herpetology [*A publication*]
FRHED ...... Frankfurter Hefte [*A publication*]
FRHGT ..... Free Height
Fr Hist .... Fragmenta Historica [*of Aristoxenus*] [*Classical studies*] (OCD)
FRHistS.... Fellow of the Royal Historical Society [*British*] (ROG)
FRHistSoc ... Fellow of the Royal Historical Society [*British*]
Fr Hist Stu ... French Historical Studies [*A publication*]
Fr Hist Stud ... French Historical Studies [*A publication*]
FRHortS .... Fellow of the Royal Horticultural Society [*British*]
FRHS........ Fellow of the Royal Historical Society [*British*] (ROG)
FRHS........ Fellow of the Royal Horticultural Society [*British*] (ROG)
FRI .... Family Relations Indicator [*Psychology*]
FRI .... Family Relationship Inventory [*Psychology*]
FRI .... Feeling Rough Inside [*Slang*]
FRI .... Fellow of the Canadian Institute of Realtors
FRI .... Fellow of the Royal Institution [*British*]
FRI .... Financial Real Estate Insurance
FRI .... Fisheries Research Institute [*University of Washington*] [*Research center*]
FRI .... Flight Refueling, Incorporated
FRI .... Focal Region Investigation
FRI .... Food Research Institute [*University of Wisconsin - Madison*] [*Research center*] (RCD)
FRI .... [*The*] Food Research Institute [*Agricultural Research Council*] [*British*]
FRI .... Food Research Institute [*Canada*] (ARC)
FRI .... Formal Reading Inventory [*Educational test*]
FRI .... Fort Riley, KS [*Location identifier*] [*FAA*] (FAAL)
FRI .... Freeport Resources, Incorporated [*Vancouver Stock Exchange symbol*]
FRI .... Frente Revolucionaria de Izquierda [*Left Revolutionary Front*] [*Bolivia*] [*Political party*] (PPW)
FRI .... Friant [*California*] [*Seismograph station code, US Geological Survey*] (SEIS)
FRI .... Friday (EY)
FRI .... Friendly Initiated [*Incident*] [*Vietnam*]
fri. .... Frisian [*MARC language code*] [*Library of Congress*] (LCCP)
FRI .... Fulmer Research Institute (AAG)
FRIA .... Finnish Radio Industries Association
FRIA .... Firearms Research and Identification Association (EA)
FRIAI .... Fellow of the Royal Institute of Architects of Ireland
FRIAS .... Fellow of the Royal Institute of Architects of Scotland
FRIBA ...... Fellow of the Royal Institute of British Architects (ROG)
FRIC .... Fellow of the Royal Institute of Chemistry [*Formerly, FIC*] [*British*]
FRICAND ... Fricandus [*To Be Rubbed*] [*Pharmacy*] (ROG)
FRICC .... Federal Research Internet Coordinating Committee [*National Science Foundation*]
FRICENT ... Fricentur [*Let Them Be Rubbed*] [*Pharmacy*] (ROG)
FRICS........ Fellow of the Royal Institution of Chartered Surveyors [*Formerly, FSI*] [*British*]
FRICT .... Friction
Frict Wear Mach ... Friction and Wear in Machinery [*A publication*]
FRID........ Friday (ADA)
Fridericiana Z Univ Karlsruhe ... Fridericiana. Zeitschrift der Universitaet Karlsruhe [*A publication*]
FRIED........ Friedman Test [*for pregnancy*] [*Obstetrics*]
Fried G Bl .. Friedberger Geschichtsblaetter [*A publication*]
Friends Hist Assoc Bull ... Friends Historical Association. Bulletin [*A publication*]
Friends PI Nixon Med Hist Libr ... Friends of the P. I. Nixon Medical Historical Library [*A publication*]
FRIES........ Friesian [*Language, etc.*] (ROG)
Fries Landbouwbl ... Fries Landbouwblad [*Netherlands*] [*A publication*]
Fries Tr .... Trial of John Fries (Treason) [*A publication*] (DLA)
FRIF .... Furnished Recurring Intelligence File (MCD)
FRIG........ Frigidus [*Cold*] [*Pharmacy*]
FRIH .... Fellow of the Royal Institute of Horticulture [*New Zealand*]
FRIJ........ Frost i Jord/Frost Action in Soils [*A publication*]
FRILAB.... Indian Forest Leaflet [*A publication*]
Fri Memo .... Friday Memo [*A publication*]
FRIMP ...... Flexible Reconfigurable Interconnected Multiprocessor
FRIN........ Fellow of the Royal Institution of Navigation [*British*] (DBQ)
FRIN........ Firing Research Investigation, Navy
FRIN........ FRI [*Fuel Research Institute*] News [*A publication*]
FRINA .... Fellow of the Royal Institute of Naval Architects [*British*]
Fr Ind .... Annuaire de Statistique Industrielle (France) [*A publication*]
Fr Ind .... France-Inde [*A publication*]
Fr Ind .... France-Indochine [*A publication*]
Fr Ind M .... Bulletin Mensuel de Statistique Industrielle (France) [*A publication*]
FRINEL.... Food Reviews International [*A publication*]
FRINGE.... File and Report Information Processing Generator [*Data processing*]
Fr Inst Natl Propr Ind Bull Off Propr Ind Abr ... France. Institut National de la Propriete Industrielle. Bulletin Officiel de la Propriete Industrielle. Abreges [*A publication*]

FRIP .... Fleet Readiness Improvement Plan
FRIPA .... Fellow of the Royal Institute of Public Administration [*British*] (ADA)
FRIPH ...... Fellow of the Royal Institute of Public Health [*British*] (ADA)
FRIPHH.... Fellow of the Royal Institute of Public Health and Hygiene [*British*]
Fri Report .. Friday Report [*A publication*]
FRIS .... Fire Research Information Services [*National Institute of Standards and Technology*] (IID)
FRIS .... Friesland [*County in the Netherlands*] (ROG)
Fris............. Frigisinga [*A publication*]
FRIS .... Frisian [*Language, etc.*]
FRIS .... Stanford University Food Research Institute Studies [*A publication*]
FRISCO..... Fast Reaction Integrated Submarine Control [*Navy*]
FRISCO..... San Francisco [*California*] (ROG)
FRIT .... Fritzi of California [*NASDAQ symbol*] (NQ)
FRITALUX ... Union Economique France, Italie, Benelux
Frith .... United States Opinions Attorneys-General (Frith) [*Pt. 2., Vol. 21*] [*A publication*] (DLA)
Friuli Med ... Friuli Medico [*A publication*]
Friul Med.... Friuli Medico [*A publication*]
FRIVOL .... Frivolous (DSUE)
FRIVOLS ... Frivolities [*Slang*] (DSUE)
FRJ .... Oklahoma City, OK [*Location identifier*] [*FAA*] (FAAL)
FRJD .... Forward Reaction Jet Driver (MCD)
FRJM .... Full Range Joint Movement [*Occupational therapy*]
Fr Jud .... France Judiciaire [*1876-1910*] [*French*] [*A publication*] (DLA)
Fr J Water Sci ... French Journal of Water Science [*A publication*]
FRK .... Federal Reserve Bank of Kansas City, Kansas City, MO [*OCLC symbol*] (OCLC)
FRK .... Florida Rock Industries, Inc. [*AMEX symbol*] (SPSG)
FRK .... Folkstone Resources Limited [*Vancouver Stock Exchange symbol*]
FRK .... Fork
FRK .... Fregate Island [*Seychelles Islands*] [*Airport symbol*] (OAG)
FRKT .... Florida Rock & Tank Lines, Inc. [*Jacksonville, FL*] [*NASDAQ symbol*] (NQ)
FRL .... Feltman Research Laboratory [*Picatinny Arsenal*] [*Army*] (RDA)
FRL .... Field Requirements List
FRL .... Fire Resistance Level
FRL .... Flight Research Laboratory [*University of Kansas*] [*Research center*] (RCD)
FRL .... Forest Research Laboratory [*Oregon State University*] [*Research center*] (RCD)
FRL .... Forest Resources Laboratory [*Pennsylvania State University*] [*Research center*] (RCD)
FRL .... Forschungen zur Religion und Literatur des Alten und Neuen Testaments [*A publication*]
FRL .... Forum Retirement Partnership LP [*AMEX symbol*] (SPSG)
FRL .... Fraeulein [*Miss*] [*German*]
FRL .... Frame Reference Line (MCD)
FRL .... Frame Representation Language [*Data processing*]
FrL .... France Latine [*A publication*]
Fr L .... Frank Leslie's Popular Monthly [*A publication*]
FRL .... Fuels Research Laboratory [*MIT*] (MCD)
FRL .... Fuselage Reference Line [*Aviation*]
FRL .... Jackson, MS [*Location identifier*] [*FAA*] (FAAL)
FRL .... Mobil Research & Development Corp., Dallas, TX [*OCLC symbol*] (OCLC)
FRLA .... Federal Regulation of Lobbying Act
FRLANT ... Forschungen zur Religion und Literatur des Alten und Neuen Testaments [*A publication*]
FRLD........ Foreland
Frld .... Frankenland [*A publication*]
FrLemU .... Universite du Maine, Le Mans, France [*Library symbol*] [*Library of Congress*] (LCLS)
FrLimU ..... Universite de Limoges, Limoges, France [*Library symbol*] [*Library of Congress*] (LCLS)
FrLimU-L ... Universite de Limoges, Bibliotheque des Lettres, Limoges, France [*Library symbol*] [*Library of Congress*] (LCLS)
Fr Lit Ser ... French Literature Series [*A publication*]
FrLiU .... Universite de Lille, Bibliotheque de Section Droit-Lettres, Domaine Universitaire, Litteraire, et Juridique, Lille, France [*Library symbol*] [*Library of Congress*] (LCLS)
Fr LM .... French Literature on Microfiche [*A publication*]
FrLy .... Bibliotheque Municipale de Lyon, Lyon, France [*Library symbol*] [*Library of Congress*] (LCLS)
FrLyU .... Universite de Lyon, Bibliotheque Centrale, Lyon, France [*Library symbol*] [*Library of Congress*] (LCLS)
FRM .... Fairmont [*Minnesota*] [*Airport symbol*] (OAG)
FRM .... Fairmont, MN [*Location identifier*] [*FAA*] (FAAL)
FRM .... Farm (ADA)
FRM .... Fault Reporting Module (TEL)
FRM .... Federal Reference Method
FRM .... Federation of Retail Merchants (EA)
FRM .... Fiber-Reinforced Material
FRM .... Fiber-Reinforced Metal [*Materials science*]
FRM .... Field Reversed Mirror (MCD)
FRM .... Film Reading Machine

FRM	Fire Room
FRM	First America Mining Corp. [*Vancouver Stock Exchange symbol*]
FRM	First Mississippi Corp. [*NYSE symbol*] (SPSG)
FRM	Fixed Rate Mortgage
FRM	Flat River [*Missouri*] [*Seismograph station code, US Geological Survey*] [*Closed*] (SEIS)
FRM	Force Reaction Motor
FRM	Form (FAAC)
FRM	Foucault Rotating Mirror [*Physics*]
FRM	Frame
FRM	Framingham Public Library, Framingham, MA [*OCLC symbol*] (OCLC)
Fr M	Francais Moderne [*A publication*]
FRM	France Alimentaire [*A publication*]
Fr M	Francis' Maxims of Equity [*1722-46*] [*A publication*] (DLA)
frm..............	French, Middle [*MARC language code*] [*Library of Congress*] (LCCP)
FRM	Frequency Meter
FRM	From
FRM	Fund Raising Management [*A publication*]
FRMB........	Forum Re Group (Bermuda) Ltd. [*NASDAQ symbol*] (NQ)
FRMBA	Farmacia (Bucharest) [*A publication*]
FRM Bericht ...	Forschungsreaktor Muenchen. Bericht [*A publication*]
FrMC.........	Institut National de la Propriete Industrielle, Centre Regional, Marseilles, France [*Library symbol*] [*Library of Congress*] (LCLS)
FRMCM....	Fellow of the Royal Manchester College of Music [*British*]
FRMCSL...	Fellow of the Royal Medical and Chirurgical Society, London (ROG)
FRMD	Formed
FRMD	Framed
FRME........	First Merchants Corp. [*NASDAQ symbol*] (NQ)
Fr Med	France Medicale [*A publication*]
FRMedSoc ...	Fellow of the Royal Medical Society [*British*]
FR Met S ...	Fellow of the Royal Meteorological Society [*British*]
FR Met Soc ...	Fellow of the Royal Meteorological Society [*British*] (ROG)
FRMG	FirstMiss Gold, Inc. [*NASDAQ symbol*] (NQ)
FRMG	Forming (FAAC)
FRMG	Framing [*of a ship*] (DS)
FRMI.........	Frontier Mining & Oil Corp. [*NASDAQ symbol*] (NQ)
FRMIA	Fellow of the Retail Management Institute of Australia
Fr Minist Agric Bull Tech Inf ...	France. Ministere de l'Agriculture. Bulletin Technique d'Information [*A publication*]
FRML........	Freymiller Trucking, Inc. [*NASDAQ symbol*] (NQ)
FRMN	Formation (FAAC)
FRMNTN ...	Fermentation
FRMO	Fleet Royal Marines Officer [*Navy*] [*British*]
Fr Mo	Francais dans le Monde [*A publication*]
FRMR........	Former (MSA)
FRMR........	Frame Reject
FRMS	Federation of Rocky Mountain States
FRMS	Fellow of the Royal Meteorological Society [*British*]
FRMS	Fellow of the Royal Microscopical Society [*British*] (ROG)
FRMT........	Format
FRMT........	Fremont General Corp. [*NASDAQ symbol*] (NQ)
FrN	Bibliotheque Municipale, Nantes, France [*Library symbol*] [*Library of Congress*] (LCLS)
FRN	Federal Register Notice (NRCH)
FRN	Federal Reserve Note
FRN	Feed Rate Number (MCD)
FRN	Feminist Radio Network [*Defunct*] (EA)
FRN	Fernie [*British Columbia*] [*Seismograph station code, US Geological Survey*] [*Closed*] (SEIS)
FRN	Floating Rate Note
FRN	Floating Round
FRN	Force Requirement Number [*Army*] (AABC)
FRN	Foreign-Rate Note
FRN	Fort Richardson, AK [*Location identifier*] [*FAA*] (FAAL)
FRN	France Fund, Inc. [*NYSE symbol*] (SPSG)
FRN	Fredonia Oil & Gas [*Vancouver Stock Exchange symbol*]
FRN	Frontul Renasterii Nationale [*Front of National Rebirth*] [*Romania*] [*Political party*] (PPE)
FRN	Full-Round Nose [*Diamond drilling*]
FRNA	Foreign Rations Not Available (AABC)
FrNanU	Universite de Nancy, Bibliotheque Centrale, Nancy, France [*Library symbol*] [*Library of Congress*] (LCLS)
FrNanU-L ...	Universite de Nancy, Bibliotheque des Lettres-Droit-Sciences, Nancy, France [*Library symbol*] [*Library of Congress*] (LCLS)
FRNB........	First National Bancorp of Louisiana [*NASDAQ symbol*] (NQ)
FRNC........	Fortune National Corporation [*NASDAQ symbol*] (NQ)
FRNCM......	Fellow of the Royal Northern College of Music [*British*] (DBQ)
FRND	Friend
FRNG	Firing
FRNG	Fringe (MSA)
FrNiU-D....	Universite de Nice, Bibliotheque de Droit, Nice, France [*Library symbol*] [*Library of Congress*] (LCLS)
FrNiU-S.....	Universite de Nice, Bibliotheque des Sciences, Nice, France [*Library symbol*] [*Library of Congress*] (LCLS)
FRNM	Foundation for Research on the Nature of Man (EA)

FRNM Bull ...	FRNM [*Foundation for Research on the Nature of Man*] Bulletin [*A publication*]
FRNS.........	Fellow of the Royal Numismatic Society [*British*] (EY)
FRNT.........	Frontier Savings Association [*NASDAQ symbol*] (NQ)
FRNTA......	Frontiers [*A publication*]
FrNU	Universite de Nantes, Section Droit-Lettres, Nantes, France [*Library symbol*] [*Library of Congress*] (LCLS)
FrNU-M	Universite de Nantes, Section Medecine, Nantes, France [*Library symbol*] [*Library of Congress*] (LCLS)
FrNU-S......	Universite de Nantes, Section Sciences, Nantes, France [*Library symbol*] [*Library of Congress*] (LCLS)
FRNWC.....	French Naval War College
FRNZ.........	Frantz Manufacturing Co. [*Sterling, IL*] [*NASDAQ symbol*] (NQ)
FRO	Faroe Islands [*ANSI three-letter standard code*] (CNC)
FRO	Fleet Records Office [*Navy*]
FRO	Fleet Recreation Officer [*British*]
FRO	Fleet Resources Office
FRO	Flexible Response Options (MCD)
FRO	Flight Radio Officer [*Aviation*]
FRO	Floro [*Norway*] [*Airport symbol*] (OAG)
FRO	Food Rationing Order [*British*]
fro..............	Franco [*Shipping Cost Paid*] [*Business term*] [*French*]
fro..............	French, Old [*MARC language code*] [*Library of Congress*] (LCCP)
FRO	Front
FRO	Frozya Industries [*Vancouver Stock Exchange symbol*]
FROC	Federated Russian Orthodox Clubs (EA)
FROD	Functionally Related Observable Difference [*between weapons*]
Froebel J	Froebel Journal [*A publication*]
F Roent Nuk ...	Fortschritte auf dem Gebiete der Roentgenstrahlen und der Nuklearmedizin [*A publication*]
FROF.........	Fire Risk on Freight [*Insurance*]
FROF.........	Freight Office
Fr Off Rech Sci Tech Outre-Mer Cah Ser Pedol ...	France. Office de la Recherche Scientifique et Technique d'Outre-Mer. Cahiers. Serie Pedologie [*A publication*]
Fr Off Rech Sci Tech Outre-Mer Monogr Hydrol ...	France. Office de la Recherche Scientifique et Technique d'Outre-Mer. Monographies Hydrologiques [*A publication*]
FROG	Free Ranging on Grid [*Computer-controlled transport system*]
FROG	Free Rocket over Ground [*USSR missile*]
Frog............	Frogerius [*Rogerius Beneventanus*] [*Flourished, 12th century*] [*Authority cited in pre-1607 legal work*] (DSA)
FROG	Frontier Energy Corp. [*NASDAQ symbol*] (NQ)
FROGS......	Fund Raising Organization Graphics Service
Froid Clim ...	Froid et la Climatisation [*A publication*]
FROIN.......	Frost on Indicator [*Aviation*] (FAAC)
FROKA......	First Republic of Korea Army
FROLINAT ...	Front de Liberation Nationale [*Chad*]
FROLIZI...	Front for the Liberation of Zimbabwe
FRom	Filologia Romanza [*A publication*]
FROM	Full Range of Motion [*or Movement*] [*Occupational therapy*]
FROM	Fusable Read-Only Memory [*Data processing*] (MDG)
Fr O-Mer ...	France d'Outre-Mer [*A publication*]
Frommanns Klassiker ...	Frommann's Klassiker der Philosophie [*A publication*]
FRON	Frontier
FRON	Frontier Adjusters of America, Inc. [*Phoenix, AZ*] [*NASDAQ symbol*] (NQ)
FRONASA ...	Front for National Salvation [*Uganda*]
Fron Matrix Biol ...	Frontiers of Matrix Biology [*A publication*]
Front	Frontier [*A publication*]
FRONT	Frontispiece [*Publishing*]
Front Aging Ser ...	Frontiers in Aging Series [*A publication*]
Front Biol...	Frontiers of Biology [*A publication*]
Front Clin Neurosci ...	Frontiers of Clinical Neuroscience [*A publication*]
Front Diabetes ...	Frontiers in Diabetes [*A publication*]
Front Gastrointest Res ...	Frontiers of Gastrointestinal Research [*A publication*]
Front Health Serv Manage ...	Frontiers of Health Services Management [*A publication*]
Front Horm Res ...	Frontiers of Hormone Research [*A publication*]
Frontiers in Phys ...	Frontiers in Physics [*A publication*]
Frontiers Plant Sci ...	Frontiers of Plant Science [*A publication*]
Frontiers in Systems Res ...	Frontiers in Systems Research [*A publication*]
Frontin	Frontinus [*First century AD*] [*Classical studies*] (OCD)
FRONTIS ...	Frontispiece [*Publishing*]
Front Matrix Biol ...	Frontiers of Matrix Biology [*A publication*]
Front Nauki Tekh ...	Front Nauki i Tekhniki [*USSR*] [*A publication*]
Front Neuroendocrinol ...	Frontiers in Neuroendocrinology [*A publication*]
Front Nurs Serv Q Bull ...	Frontier Nursing Service. Quarterly Bulletin [*A publication*]
Front Oral Physiol ...	Frontiers of Oral Physiology [*A publication*]
Front Phys ...	Frontiers in Physics [*A publication*]
Front Plant Sci ...	Frontiers of Plant Science [*A publication*]
Front Plant Sci Conn Agric Exp Stn (New Haven) ...	Frontiers of Plant Science. Connecticut Agricultural Experiment Station (New Haven) [*A publication*]
Front Radiat Ther Oncol ...	Frontiers of Radiation Therapy and Oncology [*A publication*]

Front Sl...... Front Slobode [*A publication*]
FROPA...... Frontal Passage [*Meteorology*] (FAAC)
FR ORD.... French Ordinances [*A publication*] (DLA)
Fr ORSTOM Cah Ser Geophys ... France. Office de la Recherche Scientifique et Technique d'Outre-Mer. Cahiers. Serie Geophysique [*A publication*]
Fr ORSTOM Cah Ser Hydrol ... France. Office de la Recherche Scientifique et Technique d'Outre-Mer. Cahiers. Serie Hydrologie [*A publication*]
Fr ORSTOM Cah Ser Pedol ... France. Office de la Recherche Scientifique et Technique d'Outre-Mer. Cahiers. Serie Pedologie [*A publication*]
Fr ORSTOM Monogr Hydrol ... France. Office de la Recherche Scientifique et Technique d'Outre-Mer. Monographies Hydrologiques [*A publication*]
FROS......... Fleet Resources Office Subsystem (MCD)
FROSFC.... Frontal Surface [*Meteorology*] (FAAC)
FROST...... Floating Repair and Oil Storage Terminal
FROST...... Food Reserves on Space Trips
Frost......... Frost and Sullivan News. American Market [*A publication*]
FROSTI..... Food RA Online Scientific and Technical Information [*Leatherhead Food Research Association*] [*Information service or system*] (CRD)
Frozen and Chilled Fds ... Frozen and Chilled Foods [*A publication*]
Frozen Fd Di ... Frozen Food Digest [*A publication*]
Frozen Fds ... Frozen Foods [*A publication*]
Frozen Food ... Frozen Foods [*A publication*]
FRP............ Faculty Research Participation [*National Science Foundation program*]
FRP............ Fairfield Public Library, Supervisor of Technical Services, Fairfield, CT [*OCLC symbol*] (OCLC)
FRP............ Famous Records of the Past [*Record label*]
FRP............ Fast Rise Pulse
FRP............ Fault Report Point (TEL)
FRP............ Feather River Project
FRP............ Feature Recognition Processor
FRP............ Federal Radionavigation Plan
FRP............ Federation des Republicains de Progres [*Federation of Progressive Republicans*] [*France*] [*Political party*] (PPW)
FRP............ Ferritin Repressor Protein [*Biochemistry*]
FRP............ Fiberglass-Reinforced Plastic
FRP............ Fiberglass-Reinforced Plywood
FRP............ Filament-Reinforced Plastic
FRP............ Flag Register Processing
FRP............ Fleet Replacement Pilot [*Navy*] (NVT)
FRP............ Follicle Regulatory Protein [*Endocrinology*]
FRP............ Force Rendezvous Point [*Military*] (AFM)
FRP............ Foreign Report [*A publication*]
FRP............ Forward Refueling Point
FRP............ Fragmentation Bomb, Parachute
Fr P.......... France-Pologne [*A publication*]
FRP............ Free Radical Photography
FRP............ Freeport-McMoRan Resource Partnership LP [*NYSE symbol*] (SPSG)
FRP............ Fremont Peak [*California*] [*Seismograph station code, US Geological Survey*] (SEIS)
FRP............ Frequency Reference Protection
FRP............ Frequency Response Plotter
FROPA...... Fresh Water Bay [*Alaska*] [*Airport symbol*] (OAG)
FRP............ Fuel Reprocessing Plant [*Nuclear energy*] (NRCH)
FRP............ Fully Refined Paraffinic Wax [*Petroleum technology*]
FRP............ Functional Refractory Period [*Neurophysiology*]
FRP............ Fuselage Reference Plane [*Aviation*] (MCD)
FRP............ Parachute Fragmentation Bomb [*Air Force*]
FRPA......... Family Rights and Privacy Act [*1974*] (OICC)
FRPA......... Fiberglass Reinforced Panel Association (EA)
FRPA......... Fixed Radiation Pattern Antenna
FrPBA....... Bibliotheque de l'Arsenal, Paris, France [*Library symbol*] [*Library of Congress*] (LCLS)
FrPBN ...... Bibliotheque Nationale, Paris, France [*Library symbol*] [*Library of Congress*] (LCLS)
FRPD........ Finitely Repeated Prisoner's Dilemma [*Psychology*]
FRPE .... Fellow of the Royal Society of Painter-Etchers and Engravers [*British*] (ROG)
FrPE-C ...... Ecole Normale Superieure, Laboratoire de Chimie, Paris, France [*Library symbol*] [*Library of Congress*] (LCLS)
FrPED .... Institut National d'Etudes Demographiques, Paris, France [*Library symbol*] [*Library of Congress*] (LCLS)
FR-PET ..... Fiber-Reinforced Polyethylene Terephthalate [*Glass*]
FR Ph........ Forschungen zur Romanischen Philologie [*A publication*]
Fr Pharm ... France-Pharmacie [*A publication*]
FRPO........ Front-Panel Operation [*Data processing*] (PCM)
FrPoU .... Universite de Poitiers, Bibliotheque de Droit-Lettres, Poitiers, France [*Library symbol*] [*Library of Congress*] (LCLS)
FRPP .... Flame Retardant Phosphonitratic Polymer
FRPP .... FRP Properties, Inc. [*NASDAQ symbol*] (NQ)
FRPPAO .... Farmaco. Edizione Pratica [*A publication*]
FRPR .... Australian Financial Review Property Review [*A publication*] (ADA)
FRPS .... Fellow of the Royal Photographic Society [*British*] (ROG)

FrPS........... Sirco-France, Paris, France [*Library symbol*] [*Library of Congress*] (LCLS)
FRPSAX.... Farmaco. Edizione Scientifica [*A publication*]
FRPSL....... Fellow of the Royal Philatelic Society, London
FRPTNG ... Fleet Replacement Pilot Training [*Navy*] (NVT)
FrPU .... Universite de Paris a la Sorbonne, Bibliotheque de la Faculte des Lettres et de la Faculte des Sciences, Paris, France [*Library symbol*] [*Library of Congress*] (LCLS)
FrPU-AL ... Institut des Hautes Etudes de l'Amerique Latine, Universite de Paris, Paris, France [*Library symbol*] [*Library of Congress*] (LCLS)
FrPU-M..... Universite de Paris a la Sorbonne, Faculte de Medecine, Paris, France [*Library symbol*] [*Library of Congress*] (LCLS)
FrPU-OS... Universite de Paris, Faculte des Sciences, (Orsay), Orsay, France [*Library symbol*] [*Library of Congress*] (LCLS)
FrPU-P ...... Universite de Paris a la Sorbonne, Faculte des Sciences Pharmaceutiques et Biologiques de Paris-Luxembourg, Paris, France [*Library symbol*] [*Library of Congress*] (LCLS)
FRPV .... Full-Range Picture Vocabulary Test [*Intelligence test*]
FRPVT ...... Full-Range Picture Vocabulary Test [*Education*]
FRQ........... Frequent
FRQMULT ... Frequency Multiplier (KSC)
FRR........... Failure and Rejection Report
FRR........... Failure Reporting Review (KSC)
FRR........... False Removal Rate (CAAL)
FRR........... Federal Register Reprint
FRR........... Federal Research Report [*Business Publishers, Inc.*] [*Information service or system*] (CRD)
FRR........... Federal Reserve Bank of Richmond, Richmond, VA [*OCLC symbol*] (OCLC)
FRR........... Firariana [*Madagascar*] [*Seismograph station code, US Geological Survey*] (SEIS)
FRR........... Fitchburg Railroad
FRR........... Flight Readiness Review (KSC)
FRR........... Force Readiness Report [*DoD*]
FRR........... Foreign Receiving Report (MCD)
FRR........... Forester Resources, Inc. [*Vancouver Stock Exchange symbol*]
FRR........... Front Royal, VA [*Location identifier*] [*FAA*] (FAAL)
FRR........... Full Reimbursement Rate (AFM)
FRR........... Functional Recovery Routine [*Data processing*] (BUR)
FRR........... Royal Irish Fusiliers Reserve Regiment [*Military unit*] [*British*] (DMA)
FRRA........ Federal Regional Reconstitutional Area
Fr Railw Tech ... French Railway Techniques [*A publication*]
FRRB........ Fast Rise Reflective Balloon
FR & RC .... Family Resource and Referral Center [*National Council on Family Relations*] [*Information service or system*] (IID)
FRRE .... Field and Reservoir Reserve Estimate [*US Geological Survey*]
Fr Rev .... French Review [*A publication*]
FRRG........ First Railroad & Bank of Georgia [*NASDAQ symbol*] (NQ)
FRRID ...... Flight Readiness Review Item Description [*NASA*] (NASA)
FRRID ...... Flight Readiness Review Item Disposition [*NASA*] (NASA)
FRRIO ...... Fleet Replacement RADAR Intercept Officer [*Navy*] (NVT)
FRRRB ...... Fast Rise RADAR Reflective Balloon
FRRS .... Frequency Resource Records System
FRRS .... Full Remaining Radiation Service [*Unit*] [*Military*]
Fr Ru .... Freiburger Rundbrief [*A publication*]
FRRU......... Freight Receiving and Redistribution Unit
FRRV .... Fast-Response Relief Valve (MCD)
FRS .... Facilities Requirements Study
FRS .... Failure Reporting System (MCD)
FRS .... Fall Reaction Spheres (AAG)
FRS .... Fast Reactor Safety [*Nuclear energy*] (NRCH)
FRS .... Fast Retrieval Storage [*Data processing*]
FRS .... Fault Repair Service [*Telecommunications*] [*British*]
FRS .... Federal Reserve Bank of St. Louis, St. Louis, MO [*OCLC symbol*] (OCLC)
FRS .... Federal Reserve System [*Independent government agency*]
FRS .... Fellow of the Royal Society [*British*] (ROG)
FRS .... Ferrite Resonance Switch
FRS .... Financial Relations Society [*Defunct*] (EA)
FRS .... Fire Research Station [*United Kingdom*] [*Research center*] (IRC)
FRS .... First Readiness State (AAG)
FRS .... Fisheries Research Station [*British*]
FRS .... Fixed Radial Shield [*Nuclear energy*] (NRCH)
FRS .... Flash Ranging System
FRS .... Fleet Readiness Squadron [*Navy*] (NVT)
FRS .... Fleet Repair Service [*Navy*] (NVT)
FRS .... Flight Radio Subsystem
FRS .... Flores [*Guatemala*] [*Airport symbol*] (OAG)
FR(s).......... Flow Rate of Sample
FRS .... Fluidic Rate Sensor (MCD)
FRS .... Flying Relay Station
FRS .... Forced Response Simulation [*Data processing*]
FRS .... Fortress Resources [*Vancouver Stock Exchange symbol*]
FRS .... Forward Ready Signal [*Telecommunications*] (TEL)
FRS .... Foundation Research Service
FRS .... Fragility Response Spectrum (IEEE)
FRS .... Franz Rosenzweig Society (EA)

FRS............ Fraternitatis Regiae Socius [*Fellow of the Royal Society*] [*Latin*]
FRS............ Frente Republicana e Socialista [*Republican and Socialist Front*] [*Portugal*] [*Political party*] (PPW)
FRS............ Frequency Response Survey (CET)
FRS............ Frisch's Restaurants, Inc. [*AMEX symbol*] (SPSG)
FRS............ Frisian [*or Frisic*] [*Language, etc.*]
FRS............ Frozen Foods [*A publication*]
FRS............ Fuel Receiving Station [*Nuclear energy*] (NRCH)
FRS............ Functional Requirement Specification (AAG)
FRSA......... Fellow of the Royal Society of Arts [*British*] (EY)
FRSABT.... Food Research Institute. Studies in Agricultural Economics, Trade, and Development [*Stanford*] [*A publication*]
FRSAI....... Fellow of the Royal Society of Antiquaries of Ireland
FRSAIrel... Fellow of the Royal Society of Antiquaries, Ireland (ROG)
FRSanI...... Fellow of the Royal Sanitary Institute [*Later, FRSH*] [*British*]
FRSAS...... Fast-Response Solar Array Simulator
FRS et AS ... Fraternitatis Regiae Socius et Associatus [*Fellow and Associate of the Royal Society*] [*Latin*] (ROG)
FRSB .... Federal Reserve System Bank
FRSC......... Fellow of the Royal Society, Canada (ROG)
FRSC......... Fellow of the Royal Society of Chemistry [*British*] (DBQ)
FRSCan .... Fellow of the Royal Society of Canada
FRSCh ...... Fellow of the Royal Society of Chemists [*Australia*]
Fr Sci N...... French Science News [*A publication*]
FRSCM...... Fellow of the Royal School of Church Music [*British*]
FRSE .... Fellow of the Royal Society, Edinburgh (ROG)
FRS Edin ... Fellow of the Royal Society of Edinburgh
Fr Ses Parfums ... France et Ses Parfums [*A publication*]
FRSF......... Fuel Receiving and Storage Facility [*Nuclear energy*] (NRCH)
FRSGS...... Fellow of the Royal Scottish Geographical Society (ROG)
FRSH......... Fellow of the Royal Society of Health [*Formerly, FRSanI*] [*British*]
FRSH......... [*The*] Fresh Juice Co., Inc. [*Great Neck, NY*] [*NASDAQ symbol*] (NQ)
Frsh Wat Biol ... Freshwater Biology [*A publication*]
FRSI .... Fellow of the Royal Sanitary Institute [*British*] (ROG)
FRSI .... Felt Reusable Surface Insulation (MCD)
FRSI .... Flexible Reusable Surface Insulation (MCD)
FRSL .... Fellow of the Royal Society of Literature [*British*] (ROG)
FRSL .... Fellow of the Royal Society, London [*British*]
FRSL .... Forestry Remote Sensing Laboratory
FRSL .... Frost & Sullivan, Inc. [*NASDAQ symbol*] (NQ)
FRSM .... Fellow of the Royal Society of Medicine [*British*]
FrSM .... Franziskanische Studien (Munster) [*A publication*]
FRSNA ...... Fellow of the Royal School of Naval Architects [*British*] (ROG)
FRSNZ ...... Fellow of the Royal Society of New Zealand
FRSocMed ... Fellow of the Royal Society of Medicine [*British*]
FRSP .... Fredericksburg and Spotsylvania County Battlefield Memorial National Military Park
FRSS......... Fast Response Survey System [*Washington, DC*] [*Department of Education*] (GRD)
FRSS......... Federal Register Search System [*Chemical Information Systems, Inc.*] [*Information service or system*] (CRD)
FRSS......... Fellow of the Royal Statistical Society [*British*] (ROG)
FRSS......... Fire-Retardant and Smoke-Suppressant [*Chemicals*]
FRSS......... Flight Reference Stabilization Systems (KSC)
FRSSA ...... Fellow of the Royal Scottish Society of Arts (ROG)
FRSSAf ..... Fellow of the Royal Society of South Africa
FRSSS ...... Fellow of the Royal Statistical Society of Scotland (ROG)
FRST .... Fellow of the Royal Society of Teachers [*British*]
FRST .... FirsTier Finance, Inc. [*NASDAQ symbol*] (NQ)
FRST .... Forest
Fr St .... Franciscan Studies [*A publication*]
FrSt .... Franziskanische Studien [*A publication*]
Fr St .... French Studies [*A publication*]
FRST .... Frost (FAAC)
FRSTAH ... Forestry [*Oxford*] [*A publication*]
Fr Stat A .... Annuaire Statistique de la France [*A publication*]
FRSTM & H ... Fellow of the Royal Society of Tropical Medicine and Hygiene [*British*]
Fr Stud ...... French Studies. A Quarterly Review [*A publication*]
FRSUB ...... Fra Sundhedsstyrelsen [*A publication*]
FRT........... Fairbanks Rhyme Test [*Hearing*]
FRT........... Family Relations Test [*Psychology*]
FRT........... Faratahi [*Tuamotu Archipelago*] [*Seismograph station code, US Geological Survey*] (SEIS)
FRT........... Federal Realty Investment Trust SBI [*NYSE symbol*] (SPSG)
FRT........... Fine Range Tuning [*Military*] (CAAL)
FRT........... Fire Retardant [*Technical drawings*]
FRT........... Fire-Retardant Treated
FRT........... Flight Rating Test
FRT........ Flight Readiness Test
FRT........ Flight Readiness Training (MCD)
FRT........... Flow Recording Transmitter
FRT........... Fortnight
FRT........... Forward Repair Team [*Military*] [*British*]
Fr de T .... Franciscus de Telese [*Flourished, 1270-82*] [*Authority cited in pre-1607 legal work*] (DSA)
Frt .... Fraternite-Matin [*Abidjan*] [*A publication*]
FRT........... Freight (AFM)
FRT........... Frequency Response Test (MCD)

FRT........... Front [*Automotive engineering*]
FRT........... Front [*Telecommunications*] (TEL)
FRT........... Fruitteelt [*A publication*]
FRT........... Full Recovery Time [*Medicine*]
FRT........... Spartanburg, SC [*Location identifier*] [*FAA*] (FAAL)
FRTAA ...... Forstarchiv [*A publication*]
FRTC......... Finance Replacement Training Center [*World War II*]
Fr Tech ...... French Techniques [*A publication*]
FRTEF....... Fast Reactor Thermal Engineering Facility [*Nuclear energy*] (NRCH)
Fr Telephn ... Industries Francaises du Telephone, du Telegraphe, et de Leurs Applications Telematiques [*A publication*]
Fr Textil..... Statistique Generale de l'Industrie Textile Francaise [*A publication*]
FRTF .... Fixed Radio Transmission Facility
FRTFL....... FSS [*Flight Service Station*] Returns Control of Tower Frequencies and Lights [*Aviation*] (FAAC)
Frt Fwd ..... Freight Forward [*Shipping*] (DS)
FRTH .... Fourth Financial Corp. [*NASDAQ symbol*] (NQ)
FRTISO..... Floating-Point Root Isolation [*Data processing*] (MDG)
FRTL........ Fertil-A-Chron, Inc. [*NASDAQ symbol*] (NQ)
FRTN........ Front End
FRTO........ French Togoland
FRTP .... Fiberglass-Reinforced Thermoplastic
FRTP .... Fraction of Rated Power (IEEE)
FRTPI....... Fellow of the Royal Town Planning Institute [*British*]
FRTRDJ..... Great Britain. Ministry of Agriculture, Fisheries, and Food. Directorate of Fisheries Research. Fisheries Research Technical Report [*A publication*]
FRTX........ Frontier Texas Corp. [*NASDAQ symbol*] (NQ)
FRU .... Field Replaceable Unit [*IBM Corp.*]
FRU .... Fire and Rescue Unit [*Australia*]
FRU .... Fleet Radio Unit
FRU .... Fleet Requirements Units [*Aircraft*]
FRU .... Free Representation Unit [*Legal term*] (DLA)
FRu .... Freiburger Rundbrief [*A publication*]
Fru........... Fructose [*A sugar*]
FRU .... Fruit
Fru............ Fruits [*A publication*]
FRU .... Frunze [*USSR*] [*Seismograph station code, US Geological Survey*] (SEIS)
FRU .... Frunze [*USSR*] [*Airport symbol*] (OAG)
FRU .... Grand Junction, CO [*Location identifier*] [*FAA*] (FAAL)
Fruchtsaft Ind ... Fruchtsaft Industrie [*A publication*]
FRUCOM ... Federation Europeenne des Importateurs de Fruits Secs, Conserves, Epices et Miels [*European Federation of Importers of Dried Fruits, Preserves, Spices, and Honey*] [*Federal Republic of Germany*]
FRUCT...... Fructus [*Fruit*] [*Latin*]
Fruehma St ... Fruehmittelalterliche Studien [*A publication*]
Frueh Mit Alt St ... Fruehmittelalterliche Studien. Jahrbuch des Instituts fuer Fruehmittelalterforschung der Universitaet Muenster [*A publication*]
FRUGAL... FORTRAN [*Formula Translating System*] Rules Used as a General Applications Language [*Data processing*]
FRUI......... Fellow of the Royal University of Ireland (ROG)
FRUIA....... Fruits [*A publication*]
Fruit Grow ... Fruit Grower [*A publication*]
Fruit Notes Coop Ext Serv Univ Mass ... Fruit Notes. Cooperative Extension Service. University of Massachusetts [*A publication*]
Fruit Prod J Am Food Manuf ... Fruit Products Journal and American Food Manufacturer [*A publication*]
Fruit Prod J Am Vinegar Ind ... Fruit Products Journal and American Vinegar Industry [*A publication*]
Fruit Sci Rep (Skierniewice) ... Fruit Science Reports (Skierniewice) [*A publication*]
Fruit Situat US Dep Agric Econ Res Serv ... Fruit Situation TFS. United States Department of Agriculture. Economic Research Service [*A publication*]
Fruits Prim Afr Nord ... Fruits et Primeurs de l'Afrique du Nord [*A publication*]
Fruit Var Hortic Dig ... Fruit Varieties and Horticultural Digest [*A publication*]
Fruit Var J ... Fruit Varieties Journal [*A publication*]
Fruit Veg Honey Crop Mkt Rep ... Fruit, Vegetable, and Honey Crop and Market Report [*A publication*]
Fruit & Veg R ... Fruit and Vegetable Review [*A publication*] (APTA)
Fruit World Ann ... Fruit World Annual [*A publication*] (APTA)
Fruit World Annu Orchardists' Guide ... Fruit World Annual and Orchardists' Guide [*A publication*]
Fruit World Mark Grow ... Fruit World and Market Grower [*A publication*]
Fruit Yb...... Fruit Yearbook [*A publication*]
FRUM ...... Fratrum [*Of the Brothers*] [*Latin*] (ADA)
FRUMEL.. Fleet Radio Unit, Melbourne [*World War II*]
FRUMP..... Fast Reading and Understanding Memory Program [*Data processing*]
Fru O-Mer ... Fruits d'Outre-Mer [*A publication*]
FRUPAC... Fleet Radio Unit, Pacific
FRUS......... Foreign Relations of the United States [*A publication*]
FRUSA ...... Flexible Rolled-Up Solar Array [*Air Force*]
FRUST ...... Frustillatim [*In Little Pieces*] [*Pharmacy*] (ROG)

Frust Entomol Ist Entomol ... Frustula Entomologica. Istituto di Entomologia [*A publication*]
Frustula Entomol ... Frustula Entomologica [*A publication*]
F Rutan ...... Filmrutan [*A publication*]
FRU VEG .. Fruits or Vegetables [*Freight*]
FRV .... Financial Review [*A publication*]
FRV .... Fishing Research Vessel
FRV .... Flight Readiness Vehicle
FRV .... Future Reconnaissance Vehicle [*Army*]
FRVA .... Fellow of the Rating and Valuation Association [*British*] (DBQ)
FRVIA .... Fellow of the Royal Victorian Institute of Architects [*British*] (ROG)
FRW .... Faraway Gold Mines Ltd. [*Vancouver Stock Exchange symbol*]
FRW .... Francistown [*Botswana*] [*Airport symbol*] (OAG)
FRW .... Friction Welding
f-rw--- .... Rwanda [*MARC geographic area code*] [*Library of Congress*] (LCCP)
FrWAfr ...... French West Africa
Fr Warte ... Die Friedenswarte [*A publication*]
FRWD .... Foreword
FRWF .... Forecast Wind Factor [*Meteorology*] (FAAC)
FRWI .... Framingham Relative Weight Index [*Cardiology*]
FRWID ...... Fruit Width [*Botany*]
FRWIS ..... Frost Warnings Issued (NOAA)
FRWK .... Framework [*Also, FR*] [*Genetics*] (MSA)
FRWL .... Forest, Range, and Watershed Laboratory [*Laramie, WY*] [*Department of Agriculture*] (GRD)
FRWMA .... Fernwaerme International [*A publication*]
Fr & W Prec ... Frend and Ware's Precedents of Instruments Relating to the Transfer of Land to Railway Companies [*2nd ed.*] [*1866*] [*A publication*] (DLA)
FRWY .... Freeway
FRX .... Forest Laboratories, Inc. [*AMEX symbol*] (SPSG)
FRXAAJ .... Archivos. Fundacion Roux-Ocefa [*A publication*]
FRXD .... Fully Automatic Reperforator Transmitter Distributor [*Telecommunications*] (TEL)
FRXZZ ...... Archivos. Fundacion Roux-Ocefa [*A publication*]
FRY .... Fairlady Energy [*Vancouver Stock Exchange symbol*]
FRY .... Ferry
Fry .... Fry on Specific Performance of Contracts [*A publication*] (DLA)
FRY .... Fryeburg, ME [*Location identifier*] [*FAA*] (FAAL)
FRYA .... Frey Associates, Inc. [*NASDAQ symbol*] (NQ)
FRYI .... Fairfield Refugee Youth Inter-Agency [*Australia*]
Fry Lun ...... Fry on Lunacy [*A publication*] (DLA)
FryskJb ...... Frysk Jierboek [*A publication*]
Fry Sp Per ... Fry on Specific Performance of Contracts [*A publication*] (DLA)
Fry Vac ...... Fry on the Vaccination Acts [*A publication*] (DLA)
FRZ .... Freeze [*or Freezing*] (FAAC)
FRZ .... Zeitschrift fuer Familienrecht [*A publication*]
Fr Zabar ..... Franciscus Zabarella [*Deceased, 1417*] [*Authority cited in pre-1607 legal work*] (DSA)
FRZBAW .. Feddes Repertorium [*A publication*]
Frz F .... Franziskanische Forschungen [*A publication*]
FRZG .... Freezing
FRZKAP .... Farmatsevtychnyi Zhurnal [*Kiev*] [*A publication*]
FRZLVL .... Freezing Level (FAAC)
FRZN .... Frozen
FRZR .... Freezer (MSA)
FRZSScot .. Fellow of the Royal Zoological Society of Scotland
fs----- .... Africa, Southern [*MARC geographic area code*] [*Library of Congress*] (LCCP)
FS .... Fabian Society [*British*] (ILCA)
FS .... Facsimile (ADA)
FS .... Factor of Safety
FS .... Fail-Safe (NASA)
FS .... Fail to Synchronize (MCD)
FS .... Fairbairn-Sykes [*British military*] (DMA)
FS .... Faire Suivre [*Please Forward*] [*French*]
FS .... Fallschirm [*Parachute*] [*German military*]
FS .... Family Status (OICC)
FS .... Famous Sayings [*Psychological testing*]
FS .... Famous Scots [*A publication*]
FS .... Far Side
FS .... Farm Sanctuary (EA)
FS .... Fast Screening
FS .... Fast Slew
FS .... Fast Store [*Data processing*] (TEL)
FS .... Fast Supply [*Ships*]
FS .... Father of Sion [*Roman Catholic*]
FS .... Fault Summary (MCD)
FS .... Feasibility Study
FS .... Federal Specification
FS .... Federal Standard
FS .... Federal Supplement [*A publication*] (DLA)
FS .... Feedback, Stabilized
FS .... Feet per Second
F & S .... Feffer & Simons [*Publisher*]
FS .... Felix Schlag [*Designer's mark, when appearing on US coins*]

FS .... Female Servant
FS .... Female Soldered (MSA)
FS .... Female, Spayed
FS .... Femininity Study [*Psychology*]
FS .... Feminist Studies [*A publication*]
FS .... Fernschreiben [*or Fernschreiber*] [*Teletype Message or Teletype*] [*German military - World War II*]
fs .... Ferrosilite [*CIPW classification*] [*Geology*]
FS .... Ferrovie dello Stato [*Italian State Railways*]
Fs .... Festschrift [*A publication*] (BJA)
F/S .... Fetch and Send [*Telecommunications*] (TEL)
FS .... Fiber Society (EA)
FS .... Fiberstock [*Firearms*]
FS .... Field Aircraft Services Ltd. [*Great Britain*] [*ICAO designator*] (FAAC)
FS .... Field Security [*British Army detective police - a branch of Intelligence*]
FS .... Field Separator
FS .... Field Service
FS .... Field Sparrow [*Ornithology*]
FS .... Field Station
FS .... Fight for Sight [*Also known as NCCB*] (EA)
FS .... File Save [*Data processing*]
FS .... File Separator [*Data processing*]
FS .... File Source [*Data processing*]
FS .... Filing Status [*IRS*]
FS .... Filler for Smoke Shells [*Weaponry*] (NATG)
F/S .... Film and Sheet [*Plastics technology*]
FS .... Filmstrip
FS .... Filtration Society (EA)
FS .... Fin Stabilized [*Rocketry*]
FS .... Final Selector [*Telecommunications*]
FS .... Final Settlement
F/S .... Final Statement [*Army*]
FS .... Financial Scribe [*Freemasonry*] (ROG)
FS .... Financial Secretary
F/S .... Financial Statement
FS .... Finish Specification
FS .... Finishers' Society [*A union*] [*British*]
FS .... Fire Service
FS .... Fire Station [*Maps and charts*]
FS .... Fire Support
FS .... Fire Suppression (MCD)
FS .... Fire Switch (KSC)
FS .... Firing Set (NG)
FS .... Firing Station (MUGU)
FS .... First Stage [*Aerospace*]
FS .... First Step (MUGU)
FS .... First Sunday (EA)
FS .... Fiscal Service (IEEE)
FS .... Flagstaff
FS .... Flame Shielding
FS .... Flameless, Smokeless [*Gunpowder*]
F/S .... Fleet Status [*Navy*] (MCD)
FS .... Fleet Support [*Navy*]
FS .... Fleet Surgeon
FS .... Fleischner Society (EA)
FS .... Flexible Sigmoidoscopy [*Proctoscopy*]
FS .... Flight Safety (AFM)
FS .... Flight Sergeant [*RAF*] [*British*]
FS .... Flight Service
FS .... Flight Simulator (AFM)
FS .... Flight Standards Service [*FAA*] (FAAC)
FS .... Flight Surgeon
FS .... Flight System (MCD)
FS .... Float Switch [*Aerospace*] (AAG)
FS .... Floating Sign
FS .... Flood Stage
FS .... Flow Switch
FS .... Fluid Switch
FS .... Fluorescence Spectroscopy
FS .... Flying Scholarship [*British military*] (DMA)
FS .... Flying Status
FS .... Foaming Stability [*Food technology*]
FS .... Fog Signal [*Station*] [*Maps and charts*]
FS .... Fog Siren [*Navigation charts*]
FS .... Folio Society [*London, England*] (EAIO)
FS .... Folklore Studies [*A publication*]
FS .... Follow Sender [*Telecommunications*] (TEL)
FS .... Food Stamp
FS .... Foot-Second (ADA)
FS .... Foot Shock [*Biometrics*]
FS .... Foramen Spinosum [*Neuroanatomy*]
FS .... Force Structuring (MCD)
FS .... Forearm Supinated [*Medicine*]
FS .... Forecast/Surface (NATG)
FS .... Foreign Service [*Department of State*]
F of S .... Foreman of Signals [*Military*] [*British*]
FS .... Foresight (AAG)
F/S .... Forest/Savanna Soils [*Agronomy*]
FS .... Forest Science [*A publication*]

FS.............. Forest Service [*Later, Department of Natural Resources*] [*Department of Agriculture*]
FS.............. Forged Steel
FS.............. Form Separator [*Data processing*]   (PCM)
FS.............. Fort Simpson Journal [*A publication*]
FS.............. Fortune Society   (EA)
FS.............. Forward Scatter
FS.............. Forward Support
FS.............. Fourth Section [*of Interstate Commerce Act*]
F & S .... Fox and Smith's Irish King's Bench Reports [*1822-24*] [*A publication*]   (DLA)
F & S .... Fox and Smith's Registration Cases [*1886-95*] [*A publication*]   (DLA)
FS.............. Fractional Shortening [*Cardiology*]
FS.............. Fractostratus [*Meteorology*]
FS.............. Fracture, Simple [*Medicine*]
FS.............. Frame Scan   (DEN)
FS.............. Franc Suisse [*Swiss Franc*] [*Monetary unit*] [*French*]
FS.............. Franciscan Studies [*A publication*]
FS.............. Franklin Simon & Co. [*Retail clothing stores*]
FS.............. Franziskanische Studien [*A publication*]
FS.............. Fred Society   (EA)
FS.............. Free Safety [*Football*]
FS.............. Free by Servitude   (ADA)
FS.............. Free Standing   (ADA)
FS.............. Freestone   (ADA)
FS.............. Freight Ship
FS.............. Freight Supply Vessel [*Obsolete*] [*Navy*]
fs.............. French Southern and Antarctic Lands [*MARC country of publication code*] [*Library of Congress*]   (LCCP)
FS.............. French Studies [*A publication*]
FS.............. Freon Servicer   (MCD)
FS.............. Frequency Shift   (BUR)
FS.............. Frequency Stability
FS.............. Frequency Standard
FS.............. Friendly Society [*British*]   (ILCA)
FS.............. Friendly Status   (MCD)
FS.............. Friends of the Shakers   (EA)
FS.............. Friends of Solidarity   (EA)
F & S .... Frost & Sullivan, Inc. [*Information service or system*]   (IID)
FS.............. Frozen Section [*Medicine*]
FS.............. Fuel Saver [*Automotive engineering*]
FS.............. Fuel Storage Subsystem   (MCD)
FS.............. Full Scale [*Analog computers*]
FS.............. Full Size   (MSA)
FS.............. Full and Soft [*Dietetics*]
FS.............. Full Stop   (ADA)
FS.............. Fullrack System
FS.............. Funbericht aus Schwaben [*A publication*]
FS.............. Function Set
FS.............. Functional Schedules   (MCD)
FS.............. Functional Schematic
FS.............. Functional Selector
FS.............. Functional Specification [*Telecommunications*]   (TEL)
FS.............. Fundacion Servivienda   (EAIO)
F & S .... Funk & Scott Publishing Co. [*Detroit, MI*]
FS.............. Furman Studies [*A publication*]
FS.............. Furnace Soldering
FS.............. Fuse
FS.............. Fuselage Station [*Aviation*]
FS.............. Future System [*IBM Corp.*] [*Data processing*]
FS.............. Futures Spread [*Investment term*]
FS.............. Graduate of the Royal Air Force Staff College [*British*]
FS.............. Land station established solely for the safety of life [*ITU designation*]   (CET)
FS.............. Registry of Friendly Societies [*British*]
FS.............. Sarasota Public Library, Sarasota, FL [*Library symbol*] [*Library of Congress*]   (LCLS)
FS.............. Sulfur Trioxide Chlorsulfonic Acid [*Inorganic chemistry*]
F1S............ Finish One Side [*Technical drawings*]
F2S............ Finish Two Sides [*Technical drawings*]
FS³............ Future Strategic Strategy Study [*Military*]   (SDI)
F & SA ...... Engineering and Stores Association [*A union*] [*British*]
FSA............ Fabric Salesmen's Association   (EA)
FSA............ Fallout Shelter Analysis [*or Analyst*] [*Civil Defense*]
FSA............ Family Separation Allowance [*Military*]   (AABC)
FSA............ Family Service America   (EA)
FSA............ Family Support Administration [*Department of Health and Human Services*]
FSA............ Farm Security Administration [*Succeeded by Farmers Home Administration, 1946*]
FSA............ Federal Security Agency [*Functions and units transferred to HEW, 1953*]
FSA............ Federal Statutes, Annotated [*A publication*]   (DLA)
FSA............ Fellow of the Society of Actuaries [*Designation awarded by Society of Actuaries*]
FSA............ Fellow of the Society of Antiquaries [*British*]
FSA............ Fellow of the Society of Arts [*British*]
FSA............ Fertility Society of Australia
FSA............ Fetal Sulfoglycoprotein Antigen [*Oncology*]

FSA............ Fiat Secundum Artem [*Let It Be Done According to Art*] [*Pharmacy*]
FSa............ Fibrosarcoma [*Oncology*]
FSA............ Field Safety Activity   (MCD)
FSA............ Field Safety Agency   (MCD)
FSA............ Field Service Addition   (MCD)
FSA............ Field Support Activity [*Military*]   (NVT)
FSA............ Final Site Acceptance   (NATG)
FSA............ Finance Service, Army
FSA............ Financial Services Act [*British*]
FSA............ Financial Stationers Association   (EA)
FSA............ Financial Suppliers Association [*Later, FSF*]   (EA)
FSA............ Fire Science Abstracts [*Department of the Environment*] [*Information service or system*]   (IID)
FSA............ Fire Support Area [*Military*]
FSA............ Firearms Sports Association [*Australia*]
FSA............ Flared Slot Antenna
FSA............ Flat-Plate Solar Array
FSA............ Flexible Solar Array
FSA............ Flexible Spending Account [*Employer distribution of nontaxable income to employees*]
FSA............ Florida Statutes, Annotated [*A publication*]   (DLA)
FSA............ Fluid Sealing Association   (EA)
FSA............ Flux Switch Alternator
FSA............ Food Security Act [*of 1985*]
FSA............ Force Structure Allowance [*DoD*]
FSA............ Foreign Service Act
FSA............ Foreign Service Allowances [*British*]
FSA............ Foreign Service Availability [*Military*]
FSA............ Foreign Statesmen [*A publication*]
FSA............ Formosa Resources Corp. [*Vancouver Stock Exchange symbol*]
FSA............ Forward Sale Agreement [*EXFINCO*]
FSA............ Forward Skirt Adapter
FSA............ Forward Support Area [*Military*]
FSA............ Foster Aviation [*Nome, AK*] [*FAA designator*]   (FAAC)
FSA............ Fraternity Scholarship Association [*Later, College Fraternity Scholarship Officers Association*]   (EA)
FSA............ Free Support Area   (MUGU)
FSA............ French Society of Acoustics [*Formerly, Group of French-Speaking Acousticians*]   (EA)
FSA............ Frequency Stability Analyzer
FSA............ Friendly Societies Act [*British*]   (ILCA)
FSA............ Front Suspension Arm
FSA............ Fuel Storage Area   (AAG)
FSA............ Future Scientists of America [*Defunct*]   (EA)
f-sa--- .... South Africa [*MARC geographic area code*] [*Library of Congress*]   (LCCP)
FSAA .... Family Service Association of America [*Later, FSA*]   (EA)
FSAA .... Fellow of the Society of Incorporated Accountants and Auditors [*British*]   (EY)
FSAA .... Flight Simulator for Advanced Aircraft [*NASA*]
FSAA .... Folk-School Association of America [*Later, FEAA*]   (EA)
FSAC .... Federal Safety Advisory Council [*Later, FACOSH*]
FSAC .... Film Studies Association of Canada
FSAC .... Fire Support Armament Center [*Dover, NJ*] [*Army*]   (GRD)
FSAC .... Fourth Stowage Adapter Container
FSAC .... Freight Station Accounting Code [*Railroad term*]
FSAC .... From the Stone Age to Christianity [*A publication*]   (BJA)
FSAE .... Fellow of the National Society of Art Education [*British*]
FSAE .... Fellow of the Society of Antiquaries, Edinburgh
FSaF .... Flagler College, St. Augustine, FL [*Library symbol*] [*Library of Congress*]   (LCLS)
FSAF .... Future Scientists of America Foundation [*Defunct*]
FSAFA ...... Farming in South Africa [*A publication*]
FSaHi .... St. Augustine Historical Society, St. Augustine, FL [*Library symbol*] [*Library of Congress*]   (LCLS)
FSAI .... Fellow of the Society of Antiquaries, Ireland   (ROG)
F(SA)ICE .. Fellow of the South African Institution of Civil Engineers
FSAICU.... Federation of State Associations of Independent Colleges and Universities [*Later, NAICU*]   (EA)
F(SA)IEE .. Fellow of the South African Institute of Electrical Engineers
F(SA)IME ... Fellow of the South African Institution of Mechanical Engineers
FSAIT........ Fellow of the South Australian Institute of Technology
FSAK......... Franklin Savings Association [*NASDAQ symbol*]   (NQ)
FSAL .... Fellow of the Society of Antiquaries, London   (ROG)
FSALA ...... Fellow of the South African Library Association
FSAM .... Fellow of the Society of Art Masters [*British*]
FSAM .... First American Savings FA [*Jenkintown, PA*] [*NASDAQ symbol*]   (NQ)
FSAM .... Free South Africa Movement   (EA)
FSan.......... Sanford Public Library, Sanford, FL [*Library symbol*] [*Library of Congress*]   (LCLS)
FSanS .... Seminole Community College, Sanford, FL [*Library symbol*] [*Library of Congress*]   (LCLS)
FSAO........ Family Services and Assistance Officer   (AABC)
FSAO........ Fellow of the Scottish Association of Opticians   (DAS)
FSAP .... Factory Space Allocation Plan   (MCD)
FSAR .... Fiat Secundum Artem Reglas [*Let It Be Done According to the Rules of the Art*] [*Pharmacy*]
FSAR .... Final Safety Analysis Report [*NASA*]   (KSC)

FSARAU ...	Facsimile Reprint. Society for the Study of Amphibians and Reptiles [*A publication*]
FSArc.........	Fellow of the Society of Architects [*British*]
FSAS	Fellow of the Society of Antiquaries of Scotland
FSAS	Fluidic Stability Augmentation System [*for helicopters*]
FSAS	Fuel Savings Advisory System
FSASA.......	Fette - Seifen - Anstrichmittel [*A publication*]
FSASAX.....	Fette - Seifen - Anstrichmittel [*A publication*]
FSA Scot....	Fellow of the Society of Antiquaries of Scotland
FSASM......	Fellow of the South Australian School of Mines
FSASM (Met) ...	Fellow of the South Australian School of Mines (Metallurgy)
FSAT	Full-Scale Aerial [*or Afterburning*] Target
FSAT	FutureSat Industries, Inc. [*NASDAQ symbol*] (NQ)
FSAVC	Free-Standing Additional Voluntary Contribution [*Pension fund payment option*] [*British*]
FSAW........	First Savings Association of Wisconsin [*NASDAQ symbol*]
FSB...........	Falange Socialista Boliviana [*Bolivian Socialist Phalange*] [*Political party*] (PPW)
FSB...........	Fallout Studies Branch [*AEC*]
FSB...........	Federal Savings Bank
FSB...........	Federal Specification Board
FSB...........	Federal Supplemental Benefits
FSB...........	Female Sexual Biomass [*Botany*]
FSB...........	Field Selection Board [*Military*]
FSB...........	Field Service Bulletin (AAG)
FSB...........	Final Staging Base (AFM)
FSB...........	Financial Corporation of Santa Barbara [*NYSE symbol*] (SPSG)
FSB...........	Fire Support Base [*Army*] (AABC)
FSB...........	Fleet Satellite Broadcasting [*Navy*] (MCD)
FSB...........	Food Supply Board [*Ministry of Food*] [*British*] [*World War II*]
FSB...........	Foreign Science Bulletin
FSB...........	Forward Space Block (CMD)
FSB...........	Forward Support Base
FSB...........	Front Striker Bulletin [*An association*] (EA)
FSB...........	Fuel Storage Basin [*Nuclear energy*]
FSb...........	Functional Specification Block [*Telecommunications*] (TEL)
FSb...........	Satellite Beach Public Library, Satellite Beach, FL [*Library symbol*] [*Library of Congress*] (LCLS)
FSBA	Federal and State Business Assistance Database [*National Technical Information Service*] [*Information service or system*] (CRD)
FSBA	Finnsheep Breeders Association (EA)
FSBA	Fluorosulfonylbenzoyl Adenosine [*Biochemistry*]
FSBA	Food Service Brokers of America (EA)
FSBC	First Savings Bank FSB [*Clovis, NM*] [*NASDAQ symbol*] (NQ)
FSBD	First Federal Savings Bank of DeFuniak Springs [*NASDAQ symbol*] (NQ)
FSBF.........	First Savings Bank of Florida FSB [*NASDAQ symbol*] (NQ)
FSBG	First Federal Savings Bank of Georgia [*Winder, GA*] [*NASDAQ symbol*] (NQ)
FSBI.........	Falange Socialista Boliviana de Izquierda [*Bolivian Socialist Phalange of the Left*] [*Political party*] (PPW)
FSBI.........	Fisheries Society of the British Isles
FSBK	First Service Bank for Savings [*Leominster, MA*] [*NASDAQ symbol*] (NQ)
FSBL.........	Feasible (MSA)
FSBL.........	Fusible (MSA)
FSBO........	For Sale by Owner [*Real estate ads*] [*Pronounced "fizz-bo"*]
FSBS.........	Front Supply Base Sections (MCD)
FSBTh	Fellow of the Society of Health and Beauty Therapists [*British*] (DBQ)
FSBUDD ...	FAO [*Food and Agriculture Organization of the United Nations*] Soils Bulletin [*A publication*]
FSBX	Framingham Savings Bank [*Framingham, MA*] [*NASDAQ symbol*] (NQ)
FSC...........	Fabricated Steel Construction [*Bethlehem Steel Corp.*]
FSC...........	Fairmont State College [*West Virginia*]
FSC...........	Family Services Center [*Military*]
FSC...........	Fat-Storing Cell [*Liver anatomy*]
FSC...........	Fault Simulation Comparator
FSC...........	Federal Safety Council
FSC...........	Federal Simulation Center
FSC...........	Federal Stock [*or Supply*] Catalog (NG)
FSC...........	Federal Stock [*or Supply*] Classification [*Army*]
FSC...........	Federal Stock Control
FSC...........	Federal Supplemental Compensation [*Unemployment insurance*] (OICC)
FSC...........	Federal Supply Code (MCD)
FSC...........	Federation Socialiste Caledonienne [*Caledonian Socialist Federation*] [*Political party*] (PPW)
FSC...........	Federation of Southern Cooperatives [*Later, FSC/LAF*] (EA)
FSC...........	Fellowship of Southern Churchmen [*Later, Committee of Southern Churchmen*] (EA)
FSC...........	Fest Resources [*Vancouver Stock Exchange symbol*]
FSC...........	Fibrous Sausage Casing
FSC...........	Field Studies Council [*British*] (ARC)
FSC...........	Field Study Coordinator [*Military*] (MCD)
FSC...........	Field Survey Company [*British military*] (DMA)
FSC...........	Figari [*Corsica*] [*Airport symbol*] (OAG)

FSC...........	File System Control [*Data processing*]
FSC...........	Filing Status Code [*IRS*]
FSC...........	Film Stowage Container
FSC...........	Final Systems Check [*NASA*] (KSC)
FSC...........	Finnish Shippers Council (DS)
FSC...........	Fire Service College [*British*]
FSC...........	Fire Support Coordination [*Military*]
FSC...........	First-Stage Conduit [*Aerospace*]
FSC...........	Fixed Silicon Capacitor
FSC...........	Flame Spread Classification [*For polymers*]
FSC...........	Fleet Satellite Communications [*DoD*]
FSC...........	Fleet Systems Capable (NVT)
FSC...........	Flexible Shielded Cable
FSC...........	Flight Security Controller [*Military*]
FSC...........	Flight Service Center
FSC...........	Florida Southern College [*Lakeland*]
FSC...........	Florida Southern College, Lakeland, FL [*OCLC symbol*] (OCLC)
F-SC...........	Florida Supreme Court, Tallahassee, FL [*Library symbol*] [*Library of Congress*] (LCLS)
FSC...........	Fluid Storage Container
FSC...........	Flying Status Code (AFM)
FSC...........	Food Safety Council [*Defunct*] (EA)
FSC...........	Food Standards Committee [*British*]
FSC...........	Food Storage Cell
FSC...........	Food Supplement Company [*British*]
FSC...........	Force Structure Committee (AFM)
FSC...........	Foreign Sales Corporation [*See also Domestic International Sales Corporation - DISC*]
FSC...........	Foreign Service Credits [*Military*]
FSC...........	Foreign Staff College [*British*]
FSC...........	Forward Scatter (NATG)
FSC...........	Foundation for Student Communication [*Princeton, NJ*] (EA)
FSC...........	Foundation for the Study of Cycles (EA)
FSC...........	Fratres Scholarum Christianarum [*Institute of the Brothers of the Christian Schools*] [*Also known as Christian Brothers*] (EAIO)
FSC...........	Free Secreting Component [*Immunology*]
FSC...........	French Shippers Council (DS)
FSC...........	Frequency Shift Converter
FSC...........	Fresno Service Center [*IRS*]
FSC...........	Fresno State College [*Later, California State University, Fresno*]
FSC...........	Friends Service Council [*Quakers*]
FSC...........	Friends of the Superior Court (EA)
FSC...........	Fuel Scheduling Computer (MCD)
FSC...........	Fuel Systems Capability (MCD)
FSC...........	Full Scale
FSC...........	Full Systems Capable [*Military*] (CAAL)
FSC...........	Fully Self-Contained (ADA)
FSC...........	Funding Sources Clearinghouse, Inc. (IID)
FSC...........	Fuscaldo [*Italy*] [*Seismograph station code, US Geological Survey*] (SEIS)
FSC...........	Future Studies Centre [*British*] (CB)
FSC...........	Selected Judgments of the Federal Supreme Court [*1956-61*] [*Nigeria*] [*A publication*] (DLA)
FSCA	Fellow of the Society of Company and Commercial Accountants [*British*] (DCTA)
FSCB	File System Control Block [*Data processing*] (IBMDP)
FSCB	First Commercial Bancshares, Inc. [*NASDAQ symbol*] (NQ)
FSCC	Federal Supply Classification Code
FSCC	Federal Surplus Commodities Corporation
FSCC	Ferrous Scrap Consumers Coalition (EA)
FSCC	Figure Skating Coaches of Canada [*See also EPAC*]
FSCC	Fire Support Coordination Center [*Military*]
FSCC	First Federal Savings Bank of Charlotte County [*NASDAQ symbol*] (NQ)
FSCC	First-Stage Conduit Container [*Aerospace*]
FSCC	Food Surplus Commodities Corporation
FSCE	Fire Support Coordination Element [*Military*]
FSCE	Free-Solution Capillary Electrophoresis [*Physical chemistry*]
FSCEA.......	French-Speaking Comparative Education Association [*See also AFEC*] [*Sevres, France*] (EAIO)
FSCEN	Flight Service Center
FSCFC.......	Friends of Shaun Cassidy Fan Club (EA)
FSCG	Federal Supply Classification Group (AFM)
FSCH........	Fulbright Scholarship
Fsch PG	Forschungen zur Neueren Philosophie und Ihrer Geschichte [*A publication*]
FSCI	Frequency Space Characteristic Impedance
F Sci Abstr ...	Food Science Abstracts [*A publication*]
FSCIL........	Federal Supply Catalog Identification List (MSA)
FSCJ.........	Congregatio Filiorum Sacratissimi Cordis Jesu [*Sons of the Sacred Heart*] [*Verona Fathers*] [*Roman Catholic religious order*]
FSCJ.........	Friendly Society of Carpenters and Joiners [*A union*] [*British*]
FSCL.........	Federal Supply Classification Listing
FSCL	Fire Support Coordination Line [*Military*] (AABC)
FSC/LAF...	Federation of Southern Cooperatives and Land Assistance Fund (EA)
FSCM	Federal Supply Code for Manufacturers
FSCM	Fellow of the State Conservatorium of Music [*Australia*]

FSC/MMAC ...	Federal Supply Classification/Material Management Aggregation (MCD)
FSCN	Free State Consolidated Gold Mining Co. Ltd. [*New York, NY*] [*NASDAQ symbol*] (NQ)
FSC Ne	FSC [*Friends Service Council*] News [*A publication*]
FSCNHA...	Federal Service Campaign for National Health Agencies [*Later, National Health Agencies for the Combined Federal Campaign*] (EA)
FSC (Nig) ..	Judgments of the Federal Supreme Court [*1956-61*] [*Nigeria*] [*A publication*] (DLA)
FSCNM.....	Federal Supply Code for Non-Manufacturers
FSCO.........	First Security Corporation [*NASDAQ symbol*] (NQ)
FSCOORD ...	Fire Support Coordinator [*Military*] (AABC)
FSCP	Feasibility Study Change Proposal (MCD)
FSCP	Federal/State Cooperative Program for Population Estimates and Projections (OICC)
FSCP	Fellow of the Society of Certified Professionals [*British*] (DBQ)
FSCP	Fire Sensor Control Panel (MCD)
FSCP	Firing Site Command Post [*Army*] (AABC)
FSCP	Foolscap [*Paper*] (ROG)
FSCR	Federal Screw Works [*NASDAQ symbol*] (NQ)
FSCR	Field Select Command Register
FSCR	First Ship Configuration Review [*Navy*]
FSCR	Fuel Storage Control Room [*Nuclear energy*] (NRCH)
FSCS.........	Federal Supply Classification System
FSCS.........	Fire Support Coordination Section [*Military*]
FSCS.........	Flight Service Communications System
FSCS.........	Foresight Sierra Communications System (MCD)
FSCS.........	Frequency Shift Communications System
FSCS.........	Fuel Storage Cable Spread [*Nuclear energy*] (NRCH)
FSCS.........	Fundamental Studies in Computer Science [*Elsevier Book Series*] [*A publication*]
FSCT	Federation of Societies for Coatings Technology (EA)
FSCT	Fellow of the Society of Cardiological Technicians [*British*] (DBQ)
FSCT	Fellow of the Society of Commercial Teachers [*British*] (DBQ)
FSCT	Floyd Satellite Communications Terminal
FSCU.........	Frequency Select Control Unit (MCD)
FSCUSA.....	Flying Senior Citizens of United States of America (EA)
FSCV	Fire Support Combat Vehicle (MCD)
FSCWC	Florida Space Coast Writers Conference (EA)
FSCX	FastComm Communications Corp. [*NASDAQ symbol*] (NQ)
FSD............	Federation des Socialistes Democrates [*Federation of Democratic Socialists*] [*France*] [*Political party*] (PPE)
FSD............	First-Degree Stochastic Dominance [*Statistics*]
FSD............	Flight Simulation Division [*Johnson Space Center*] [*NASA*] (NASA)
FSD............	Fluidic Setting Device
FSD............	Flying Spot Digitizer
FSD............	Focal Skin Distance [*Radiology*]
FsD............	Fonetica si Dialectologie [*A publication*]
FSD............	Force Spectral Density
FSD............	Forecast Support Date
FSD............	Foreign Sea Duty
FSD............	Foster-Seeley Discriminator
FSD............	Fuel Supply Depot [*Military*]
FSD............	Full-Scale Deflection [*Instrumentation*]
FSD............	Full-Scale Development (MCD)
FSD............	Functional Sequence Diagram [*Data processing*]
FSD............	Sioux Falls [*South Dakota*] [*Airport symbol*] (OAG)
FSD............	Sioux Falls, SD [*Location identifier*] [*FAA*] (FAAL)
FSDB	Fishery Statistics Data Base [*National Marine Fisheries Service*] [*Information service or system*] (MSC)
FSDC	Federal Statistical Data Center (IEEE)
FSDC	Fellow of the Society of Dyers and Colourists [*British*]
FSDH	Fondation de la Sante et des Droits de l'Homme [*Foundation for Health and Human Rights*] (EA)
FSDLWG ..	Fundamental Standard Data Link Working Group [*NATO*] (NATG)
FSDO.........	Flight Standards District Office [*FAA*]
FSDR	Final Software Design Review
FSDS	Flagship Data System (MCD)
FSDU.........	Fur Skin Dressers' Union [*British*]
FSDVP	Freiheitlich Soziale Deutsche Volkspartei [*Liberal Social German People's Party*] [*Federal Republic of Germany*] [*Political party*] (PPW)
FSE............	[*From the Latin for*] Brothers of the Holy Eucharist [*Roman Catholic religious order*]
FSE............	Facilities System Engineer
FSE............	Facility Support Equipment
FSE............	Factory Support Equipment (KSC)
FSE............	Faculty of Surgeons of England
FSE............	Family Stop Eating [*A table signal at a meal where guests are present*]
FSE............	Fat-Specific Element [*Genetics*]
FSE............	Federal Reserve Bank of San Francisco. Economic Review [*A publication*]
FSE............	Fellow of the Society of Engineers [*British*]
FSE............	Fellow of the Society of Executives [*Australia*]
FSE............	Field Service Engineer [*Military*]
FSE............	Field Support Engineering

FSE............	Field Support Equipment [*Military*]
FSE............	Fill Start Entry [*Data processing*]
FSE............	Filles du Saint Esprit [*Institute of the Franciscan Sisters of the Eucharist*] [*Roman Catholic religious order*]
FSE............	Fire Support Element [*Military*] (AABC)
FSE............	First Star Energy [*Vancouver Stock Exchange symbol*]
FSE............	Fleet Supportability Evaluation (MCD)
FSE............	Flight Simulation Engineer (MCD)
FSE............	Flight Support Equipment (KSC)
FSE............	Florida Solar Energy Center, Cape Canaveral, FL [*OCLC symbol*] (OCLC)
FSE............	Fluid Shaft Encoder
FSE............	Forward Support Element
FSE............	Fosston, MN [*Location identifier*] [*FAA*] (FAAL)
FSE............	Fundamental Studies in Engineering [*Elsevier Book Series*] [*A publication*]
FSEA	Food Service Executives' Association [*Later, IFSEA*] (EA)
FSEB	First Home Federal Savings & Loan Association [*Sebring, FL*] [*NASDAQ symbol*] (NQ)
FSEB	Fuel Storage Exhaust Blower [*Nuclear energy*] (NRCH)
FSEC	Federal Software Exchange Center
FSEC	Federal Specifications Executive Committee
fsec............	Femtosecond [*One quadrillionth of a second*]
FSEC	Florida Solar Energy Center [*University of Central Florida*] [*Research center*] (RCD)
FSECO	First-Stage Engine Cutoff [*Aerospace*]
FSED	Full-Scale Engineering Development (MCD)
FSEE	Federal Service Entrance Examination [*Later, PACE*] [*Civil Service*]
FSEE	Field-Stimulated Exoelectron Emission [*Physics*]
FSEI...........	Food Service Equipment Industry [*Later, FEDA*] (EA)
FSEPA........	Filtration and Separation [*A publication*]
FSER	Field Service Engineering (AAG)
FSERI.........	Federal Solar Energy Research Institute [*Energy Research and Development Administration*]
FSERT.......	Fellow of the Society of Electronic and Radio Technicians [*British*] (DBQ)
FSES	Federation of Swiss Employees' Societies
FSES	Fire Safety Evaluation System [*National Institute of Standards and Technology*]
FSES	Friendly Society of Engravers and Sketchmakers [*Later, MPEA*]
FSF............	Fading Safety Factor [*Telecommunications*] (TEL)
F & SF........	Fantasy and Science Fiction [*A publication*]
FSF............	Federal Security Forces
FSF............	Fibrin-Stabilizing Factor [*Factor XIII*] [*Also, LLF*] [*Hematology*]
FSF............	Field Site Facility
FSF............	Financial Suppliers Forum (EA)
FSF............	Financial Suspense File [*Army*]
FSF............	First Static Firing (MCD)
FSF............	Fixed Sequence Format
FSF............	Flight Safety Foundation (EA)
FSF............	Forensic Sciences Foundation (EA)
FSF............	Forward Space File (CMD)
FSF............	Fuel Storage Facility [*Nuclear energy*] (NRCH)
FSF............	Magazine of Fantasy and Science Fiction [*A publication*]
f-sf---	Sao Tome and Principe [*MARC geographic area code*] [*Library of Congress*] (LCCP)
FS Fact Sheet Oreg State Univ Ext Serv ...	FS. Fact Sheet. Oregon State University. Extension Service [*A publication*]
FS/FB	Free Store/Food Bank (EA)
FSFC..........	First Security Financial Corporation [*Salisbury, NC*] [*NASDAQ symbol*] (NQ)
FSFC..........	Forester Sisters Fan Club (EA)
FSFI...........	First State Financial Services, Inc. [*NASDAQ symbol*] (NQ)
FSFLP	Farm Storage Facility Loan Program
FSFMA	Forskning och Framsteg [*A publication*]
FSFRAL	Far Seas Fisheries Research Laboratory. S Series [*A publication*]
FSFS	Falcon/Sciences, Inc. [*NASDAQ symbol*] (NQ)
FS & G	Farrar, Straus & Giroux [*Publisher*]
FSG..........	Fasting Serum Glucose [*Clinical chemistry*]
FSG..........	Federal Stock Group
FSG..........	Federal Supply Group [*Air Force*]
FSG..........	Fellow of the Society of Genealogists [*British*]
FSG..........	Field Supply Group
FSG..........	Finite State Grammar
FSG..........	Fiume Study Group (EA)
FSG..........	Flexible Space Garment
FSG............	Florida Sea Grant College [*University of Florida*] [*Research center*] (RCD)
FSG..........	Foreign Services Group [*British*]
FSG..........	Fortress Study Group (EAIO)
FSG..........	Freres de Saint Gabriel [*Brothers of Christian Instruction of St. Gabriel*] [*Rome, Italy*] (EAIO)
f-sg---	Senegal [*MARC geographic area code*] [*Library of Congress*] (LCCP)
FSGA	Four-Wire, Shipboard, General Use, Armored [*Cable*]
FSGB	Foreign Service Grievance Board [*Department of State*]
FSGBI........	Federation of Sailmakers of Great Britain and Ireland [*A union*]
FSGD........	Federation of Sports Goods Distributors [*British*] (DCTA)
FSGO.........	Floating Spherical Gaussian Orbitals [*Atomic physics*]

FSGp.......... Federal Supply Group [*Air Force*]   (AFM)
FSGS .... Flare/Shallow Glide Slope   (MCD)
FSGS .... Focal Segmental Glomerulosclerosis [*Nephrology*]
FSGT .... Federation Sportive et Gymnique du Travail
FSGT .... Fellow of the Society of Glass Technology [*British*]
F/Sgt.......... Flight Sergeant [*RAF*] [*British*]   (DMA)
FSH .... Fascioscapulohumeral [*Medicine*]
FSH .... Federacion de Sociedades Hispanas [*Defunct*]   (EA)
FSH .... Federation of Sterea Hellas   (EA)
FSH .... First-Stage Hydraulics [*Aerospace*]
Fsh stks...... Fishing Stakes [*Nautical charts*]
FSH .... Flight Services Handbook
FSH .... Follicle-Stimulating Hormone [*Endocrinology*]
FSH .... Forest Service Handbook [*Department of Agriculture, Forest Service*] [*A publication*]
FSH .... Foundation for Science and the Handicapped   (EA)
FSH .... Four Seasons Hotels, Inc. [*Toronto Stock Exchange symbol*]
f-sh--- .... Spanish Territories in Northern Morocco [*Spanish North Africa*]   (LCCP)
FSHAA...... Fellow of the Society of Hearing Aid Audiologists [*British*]   (DBQ)
FSHB........ Follicle-Stimulating Hormone Beta Subunit [*Endocrinology*]
FSHEW..... Federal Security Agency, Health, Education, and Welfare
FSHG .... Fisher Scientific Group, Inc. [*NASDAQ symbol*]   (NQ)
FSHIP .... Fellowship
FSHP........ Fellow of the Society of Hospital Pharmacists [*Australia*]
FSHRBI .... Follicle-Stimulating Hormone Receptor Binding Inhibitor [*Endocrinology*]
FSH-RF .... Follicle-Stimulating Hormone Releasing Factor [*Also, FRF, FSH-RH*] [*Endocrinology*]
FSH-RH .... Follicle-Stimulating Hormone Releasing Hormone [*Also, FRF, FSH-RF*] [*Endocrinology*]
FSHV........ Full-Scale Hydrodynamic Vehicle   (MCD)
FSI .... Faggan Studio Industries [*Database producer*]   (IID)
FSI .... Family Suffering Index [*Economic measurement based on unemployment rate, plus costs of food, fuel, and housing*]
FSI .... Federal Stock Item
FSI .... Federation Spirite Internationale [*International Spiritualist Federation*]
FSI .... Fellow of the Sanitary Institute [*British*]   (ROG)
FSI .... Fellow of the Surveyors' Institute [*Later, FRICS*] [*British*]
FSI .... Final Systems Installation [*NASA*]   (NASA)
FSI .... Fire Service Inspectorate [*British*]
FSI .... Fire Service Instructors
FSI .... Flightsafety International, Inc. [*Aerospace*] [*NYSE symbol*]   (SPSG)
FSI .... Fluid Structure Interaction [*Nuclear energy*]   (NRCH)
FSI .... Flutter Speed Index [*Aerodynamics*]
FSI .... Foam Stability Index [*Chemistry*]
FSI .... Food Sanitation Institute   (EA)
FSI .... Force Structure Increase [*Military*]
FSI .... Foreign Service Institute [*Department of State*]
FSI .... Formed Steel Institute
FSI .... Fort Sill, OK [*Location identifier*] [*FAA*]   (FAAL)
FSI .... Foundation for Savings Institutions [*Inactive*]   (EA)
FSI .... Frame Synchronization Indication
FSI .... Free Sons of Israel   (EA)
FSI .... Freelance Syndicate, Incorporated   (EA)
FSI .... Freestanding Insert [*Advertising*]
FSI .... Functionally Significant Items   (MCD)
FSI .... International Society of Fire Service Instructors   (EA)
FSIA .... Fellow of the Society of Industrial Artists [*British*]   (EY)
FSIA .... Fellow of the Society of Investment Analysts [*British*]   (DBQ)
FSIAD .... Fellow of the Society of Industrial Artists and Designers [*British*]
FSIB.......... Flight Safety Information Bulletin [*NASA*]
FSIC .... Foreign Service Inspection Corps [*Department of State*]
FSIC .... Franciscan Sisters of the Third Order of the Immaculate Conception [*Roman Catholic religious order*]
FSIF.......... Flight Suit with Integrated Flotation
FSIF.......... Friendly Society of Ironfounders of England, Ireland, and Wales [*A union*]
FSIG .... Franklin Signal Corp. [*NASDAQ symbol*]   (NQ)
FSIGT........ Frequently Sampled Intravenous Glucose Tolerance (Test) [*Clinical chemistry*]
FSII........... FSI International, Inc. [*NASDAQ symbol*]   (CTT)
FSII........... Fuel System Icing Inhibitor [*Aviation*]   (AFIT)
FSIM .... Functional Simulator   (NASA)
FSIMT....... Foundation for the Support of International Medical Training   (EA)
FSIND....... Forensic Science International [*A publication*]
FSINDR..... Forensic Science International [*A publication*]
FS-INFO ... Forest Service Information Network - Forestry Online [*US Forest Service*] [*Information service or system*]   (IID)
FSIO .... Foreign Service Information Officer [*Department of State*]
FSIP.......... Federal Service Impasses Panel
FSIP.......... Federal Shelter Incentive Program
FSIP.......... Fire Service in Philately [*An association*]
FSIR .... Force Status Identity Report   (MCD)
FSIS.......... First-Stage Ignition System [*Aerospace*]   (MCD)

FSIS.......... Food Safety and Inspection Service [*Formerly, FSQS*] [*Department of Agriculture*]
FSISI .... Foundation for the Study of Independent Social Ideas   (EA)
FSISWG.... Flight System Interface Working Group
FSIT......... First Spanish Investment Trust [*London Stock Exchange*]
FSIWA ...... Federation of Sewage and Industrial Wastes Associations [*Later, Water Pollution Control Federation*]
FSIWG ..... Flight System Interface Working Group   (MCD)
FSIZA....... Fukushima Igaku Zasshi [*A publication*]
FSJ............ Faculte Saint-Jean Library, University of Alberta [*UTLAS symbol*]
FSJ............ Feedback Summing Junction [*Data processing*]
FSJ............ Fellowship of St. James   (EA)
FSJ............ Fort St. James [*British Columbia*] [*Seismograph station code, US Geological Survey*]   (SEIS)
FSJ............ Fratres Sancti Joseph [*Brothers of St. Joseph*] [*Roman Catholic religious order*]
FSJ............ Free Supersonic Jet
f-sj--- .... Sudan [*MARC geographic area code*] [*Library of Congress*]   (LCCP)
FSJC......... Fort Scott Junior College [*Kansas*]
FSJC......... Fort Smith Junior College [*Arkansas*]
FSJM........ Society of Franciscan Servants of Jesus and Mary [*Anglican religious community*]
FSJOD ..... Fire Safety Journal [*A publication*]
FSK.......... Fatigue Scales Kit [*Psychology*]
FSK.......... Fisk University, Nashville, TN [*OCLC symbol*]   (OCLC)
FSK.......... Forskolin [*Also, FOR*] [*Organic chemistry*]
FSK.......... Fort Scott, KS [*Location identifier*] [*FAA*]   (FAAL)
FSK.......... Frequency Shift Keying [*Telecommunications*]
FSKLF....... Frequency Shift Keying Low-Frequency [*Converter*]   (NATG)
FSKY .... First Security Corporation of Kentucky [*NASDAQ symbol*]   (NQ)
FSL .... Family Strike Light [*Indicates family should take small portions at a meal where guests are present*]
FSL .... Federal Reserve Bank of St. Louis. Review [*A publication*]
FSL .... Federal Stock Listings
FSL .... Federation des Syndicats Libres des Travailleurs Luxembourgeois [*Free Luxembourg Workers' Federation*]
FSL .... Field Storage List   (MCD)
FSL .... Finite State Language
FSL .... Fire Control and Small Caliber Weapon Systems Laboratory [*Picatinny Arsenal, Dover, NJ*] [*Army*]   (INF)
FSL .... First Standard Mining Ltd. [*Vancouver Stock Exchange symbol*]
FSL .... Fixed Safety Level
FSL .... Fleet Street Letter [*A publication*]
FSL .... Flight Simulation Laboratory [*NASA*]   (NASA)
FSL .... Flight Systems Laboratory   (MCD)
FSL .... Florida State League [*Baseball*]
FSL .... Florida State University, Law Library, Tallahassee, FL [*OCLC symbol*]   (OCLC)
FSl............ Folia Slavica [*A publication*]
FS/L.......... Food Service/Lodging
FSL .... Foreign Service Leave [*British military*]   (DMA)
FSL .... Foreign Service Local   (CINC)
FSL .... Forestry Sciences Laboratory [*US Forest Service*] [*Research center*]   (RCD)
FSL .... Formal Semantic Language [*Data processing*]
FSL .... Free Shear Layer
FSL .... French Sign Language
FSL .... Full Stop Landing [*Aviation*]
FSL .... Full Supply Level   (ADA)
f-sl--- .... Sierra Leone [*MARC geographic area code*] [*Library of Congress*]   (LCCP)
FSLAET .... Fellow of the Society of Licensed Aircraft Engineers and Technologists [*British*]
FSlC......... Saint Leo College, Saint Leo, FL [*Library symbol*] [*Library of Congress*]   (LCLS)
FSLIC........ Federal Savings & Loan Insurance Corporation [*of FHLBB*] [*Pronounced "FIZ-lick"*] [*Functions transferred to SAIF, 1989*]
FSLMMC ... Friends of the Sea Lion Marine Mammal Center   (EA)
FSLN .... Frente Sandinista de Liberacion Nacional [*Sandinista National Liberation Front*] [*Nicaragua*] [*Political party*]   (PPW)
FSLP......... First Spacelab Payload [*NASA*]
FSLPAB .... Flora Slodkowodna Polski [*A publication*]
FSLPPS..... Federalist Society for Law and Public Policy Studies   (EA)
FSLR .... First Standard Mining Ltd. [*NASDAQ symbol*]   (NQ)
FSLT......... First Sea Level Test [*NASA*]   (NASA)
FSM .... Fairly Serious Monthly Magazine [*A publication*]
FSM .... Fantastic Story Magazine [*A publication*]
FSM .... Fast Settle Mode
FSM .... Fast Steering Mirror [*Optical instrumentation*]
FSM .... Federated States of Micronesia
FSM .... Federated States of Micronesia [*ANSI three-letter standard code*]   (CNC)
FSM .... Federation Sephardite Mondiale [*World Sephardi Federation - WSF*] [*Geneva, Switzerland*]   (EAIO)
FSM .... Federation Socialiste de la Martinique [*Socialist Federation of Martinique*] [*Political party*]   (PPW)

FSM.......... Federation Syndicale Mondiale [*World Federation of Trade Unions - WFTU*] [*French*]   (EAIO)
FSM.......... Fellow of the Society of Metaphysicians [*British*]
FSM.......... Fellowship Recorded Libraries of Sacred Music [*Record label*] [*Atlanta, GA*]
FSM.......... Field Service Manual [*British military*]   (DMA)
FSM.......... Field Strength Meter
FSM.......... Finite State Machine
FSM.......... First-Stage Motor [*Aerospace*]
FSM.......... First Surface Mirror
FSM.......... Flight System Mockup
FSM.......... Flying Spot Microscope   (ADA)
FSM.......... Folded Sideband Modulation
FSM.......... Foodarama Supermarkets, Inc. [*AMEX symbol*]   (SPSG)
FSM.......... Fort Smith [*Arkansas*] [*Airport symbol*]   (OAG)
FSM.......... Fort Smith, AR [*Location identifier*] [*FAA*]   (FAAL)
FSM.......... Frame-Scanning Mode [*Microscopy*]
FSM.......... Free Speech Movement [*University of California, Berkeley*]
FSM.......... Frequency Shift Modulation [*Radio*]
FSM.......... Friendly Society of Mechanics [*A union*] [*British*]
FSM.......... Fuel Supply Module   (MCD)
FSMA....... Farm Store Merchandising Association [*Commercial firm*]
FSMA....... Fellow of the Incorporated Sales Managers' Association [*Later, F Inst MSM*] [*British*]
FSMB....... Federation of State Medical Boards of the United States   (EA)
FSMBUS... Federation of State Medical Boards of the United States   (EA)
FSMC....... Federal Supply Manufacturers' Code [*DoD*]
FSMC....... Fellow of the Spectacle Makers Company
FSMC....... First-Stage Motor Container [*Aerospace*]
FSMC....... Fixed Silver Mica Capacitor
FSMG....... Foundry Supply Manufacturers Group   (EA)
FSMI......... Food Service Marketing Institute   (EA)
FSML....... Fleet Support Material List [*Navy*]
FSMNA..... Fishermen's News [*A publication*]
FSMO....... Field Service Marching Order [*British military*]   (DMA)
FSMR....... Field Station Materiel Requirements
FSMS........ Firing Set Maintenance Spares   (NG)
FSMT....... Feed System Maintenance Transfer   (MCD)
FSMT....... Fleet Service Mine Test [*Navy*]   (NG)
FSMWI..... Free Space Microwave Interferometer
FSMWO.... Field Service Modification Work Order
FSN.......... Factory Serial Number   (MCD)
FSN.......... Family Support Networks Project [*Australia*]
FSN.......... Federal Stock Number [*Later, NSN*]
FSN.......... Filler Sensor Nozzle
FSN.......... Financial Satellite Network
FSN.......... Fiscal Station Number [*Military*]
FSN.......... Foreign State National
FSN.......... Forward Sequence Number [*Telecommunications*]   (TEL)
FSN.......... French-Speaking Nations [*NATO*]
FSN.......... Fuel Service Nozzle   (MSA)
FSN.......... New College, Sarasota, FL [*Library symbol*] [*Library of Congress*]   (LCLS)
FSNFO...... Flight Standards National Field Office [*FAA*]   (FAAC)
FSNI......... Family Shopping Network, Inc. [*NASDAQ symbol*]   (NQ)
FSNMDR ... Federal Stock Number [*later, NSN*] Master Data Record
FSNOx...... Fuel-Specific Nitrogen Oxide Emissions [*Air pollution*]
FSNP........ Famous Spock Neck Pinch [*From television show "Star Trek"*]
FSNR........ [*The*] Forschner Group, Inc. [*NASDAQ symbol*]   (NQ)
FSNS........ French-Speaking Neuropsychological Society [*Paris, France*]   (EAIO)
FSO........... Fast Settle Operation
FSO........... Field Security Officer [*Military*]
FSO........... Field Service Operations   (NATG)
FSO........... Fire Support Officer [*Military*]
FSO........... Fleet Signals Officer [*Navy*]
FSO........... Fleet Supply Officer [*Navy*]
FSO........... Fleet Support Operations   (NVT)
FSO........... Flight Safety Officer   (MCD)
FSO........... Flight Services Officer   (ADA)
FSO........... Flying Safety Officer [*Air Force*]   (AFM)
FSO........... Flying Saucers from Other Worlds [*A publication*]
FSO........... Force Supply Officer
FSO........... Foreign Service Officer [*Department of State*]
FSO........... Frequency Sweep Oscillator
FSO........... Friends of the Sea Otter   (EA)
FSO........... Fuel Supply Office [*Military*]
FSO........... Full-Scale Output
FSO........... Functional Supplementary Objective   (MCD)
FSO........... Fund for Special Operations [*Inter-American Development Bank*]
f-so--- .... Somali [*MARC geographic area code*] [*Library of Congress*]   (LCCP)
FSOB........ Friendly Society of Operative Bricklayers [*A union*] [*British*]
FSOC........ Fixed Stand-Off Capacitor
FSOCM..... Friendly Society of Operative Cabinet Makers [*A union*] [*British*]
F Soc Rev ... Film Society Review [*A publication*]
FS Oe Th ... Forschungen zur Systematischen und Oekumenischen Theologie [*A publication*]

FSOH........ Flight Support Operations Handbook   (MCD)
FSor.......... French Cetra-Soria [*Record label*]
FSOS......... Free-Standing Operating System [*General Automation, Inc.*]
FSOSEIW ... Friendly Society of Operative Stonemasons of England, Ireland, and Wales [*A union*]
FSOT........ Friendly Society of Operative Tobacconists [*A union*] [*British*]
FSOTS....... Foreign Service Officers' Training School
FSP........... [*From the Latin for*] Brothers of St. Patrick [*Patrician Brothers*] [*Roman Catholic religious order*]
FSP........... Facility Security Program [*World War II*]
FSP........... Family Services Program [*Military*]
FSP........... Family Support Program [*Australia*]
FSP........... Fault Servicing Process   (TEL)
FSP........... Fault Summary Page   (MCD)
FSP........... Federal/State Programs [*Social Security Administration*]   (OICC)
FSP........... Fellow of Sheffield Polytechnic [*British*]
FSP........... Fellowship of St. Paul   (EA)
FSP........... Fibrinogen-Split Products [*Hematology*]
FSP........... Field Security Personnel
FSP........... Field Security Police
FSP........... Figlie de San Paolo [*Pious Society of the Daughters of Saint Paul - PSDSP*] [*Rome, Italy*]   (EAIO)
FSP........... Finger Sweat Print [*Psychometrics*]
FSP........... Fixed Sample-Size Procedure
FSP........... Flat Salary Payroll   (AAG)
FSP........... Flight Scheduling Precedence
FSP........... Flight Strip Printer   (FAAC)
FSP........... Food Stamp Program
FSP........... Force Sensing Probe
FSP........... Ford Satellite Plan [*Telecommunications*]
FSP........... Foreign Service Pay
f sp........... Forma Specialis [*Special Form*] [*Biology*]
FSP........... Forward Supply Point [*Military*]   (AFM)
FSP........... Foundation for the Peoples of the South Pacific   (EA)
FSP........... Freedom Socialist Party   (EA)
FSP........... French Socialist Party
FSP........... Frente Social Progresista [*Progressive Social Front*] [*Ecuador*] [*Political party*]   (PPW)
FSP........... Frente Socialista Popular [*Portugal*]
FSP........... Frequency Shift Pulsing
FSP........... Frequency Standard, Primary
FSP........... Fuel Storage Pool [*Nuclear energy*]   (NRCH)
FSP........... Full-Scale Production
FSP........... Full-Scale Prototype [*Military*]   (CAAL)
FSP........... Full-Screen Processing [*Data processing*]
FSP........... Functional Specification Package [*Data processing*]
FSp........... St. Petersburg Public Library, St. Petersburg, FL [*Library symbol*] [*Library of Congress*]   (LCLS)
FSPA .... Fellow, Society of Pension Actuaries [*Designation awarded by American Society of Pension Actuaries*]
FSPA .... Former Spouse Protection Act
FSPA .... Fuel Storage Personnel Area [*Nuclear energy*]   (NRCH)
FSPA .... Sisters of the Third Order of St. Francis of the Perpetual Adoration [*Roman Catholic religious order*]
FSPB......... Field Service Pocket Book [*British military*]   (DMA)
FSPB......... Forward Support Patrol Base
FSPB......... Fuel Storage Processing Building [*Nuclear energy*]   (NRCH)
FSPBC....... For a Separate Peace Before Carter [*Refers to Israeli-Egyptian agreements of 1978*]
FSPC......... Federal Science Policy Council [*Later, FCCSET*]
FSPC......... Foundation for the Study of Primitive Culture
FSpC......... St. Petersburg Junior College, St. Petersburg, FL [*Library symbol*] [*Library of Congress*]   (LCLS)
FSPCT....... Foundation for the Study of Presidential and Congressional Terms   (EA)
FSpE......... Eckerd College, St. Petersburg, FL [*Library symbol*] [*Library of Congress*]   (LCLS)
FSPG .... First Home Savings Bank, SLA [*NASDAQ symbol*]   (NQ)
FSPMA ..... Federal Services Podiatric Medical Association   (EA)
FSPMAM ... Fermentnaya i Spirtovaya Promyshlennost' [*A publication*]
FSPO........ Force Structure Planning Objective   (MUGU)
FSPP........ Fiske-Subbarow Positive Phosphorus [*Analytical chemistry*]
FSPPR....... Fast Supercritical Pressure Power Reactor
FSPQ........ Family Support Program (Queensland) [*Australia*]
FSPS......... Ferranti Sonobuoy Processing System   (MCD)
FSPS......... Foundation for the Study of Plural Societies   (EA)
FSPSO....... Federal Statistical Policy and Standards Office   (OICC)
FSPT......... Federation of Societies for Paint Technology [*Later, FSCT*]   (EA)
FSQ........... Atlanta, GA [*Location identifier*] [*FAA*]   (FAAL)
FSQ........... Fantastic Story Quarterly [*A publication*]
FS/Q......... Flight Standards and Qualification [*Army*]
FSq........... Flying Squadron
f-sq--- .... Swaziland [*MARC geographic area code*] [*Library of Congress*]   (LCCP)
FSQS .... Food Safety and Quality Service [*Later, FSIS*] [*Department of Agriculture*]
FSQS US Dep Agric Food Saf Qual Serve ... FSQS. United States Department of Agriculture. Food Safety and Quality Service [*A publication*]

FSR............ [*From the Latin for*] Brothers of the Holy Rosary [*Roman Catholic religious order*]
FSR............ False Signal Recognition [*RADAR technology*]
FSR............ Farming Systems Research
FSR............ Fast Slew Rate
FSR............ Feedback Shift Register
FSR............ Fellow of the Royal Society of Radiographers
FSR............ Fermi Selection Rules
FSR............ Field Service Regulations [*Army*]
FSR............ Field Service Report
FSR............ Field Service Representative   (AFM)
FSR............ Field Strength Radio
FSR............ File Storage Region [*Digital Equipment Corp.*]
FS & R .... Filling, Storage, and Remelt System [*Nuclear energy*]   (NRCH)
FSR............ Film Society Review [*A publication*]
FSR............ Fin Stabilized Rockets
FSR............ Final System Release   (MCD)
FSR............ Final System Run   (KSC)
FSR............ Financial Services Recorder [*Telecommunications*] [*British*]
FSR............ Financial Status Report   (OICC)
FSR............ First Soviet Reactor
FSR............ First Surrey Rifles [*Military unit*] [*British*]
FSR............ Firstar Corp. [*NYSE symbol*]   (SPSG)
FSR............ Fixed Sample Rate
FSR............ Fleet Spotter Reconnaissance [*British military*]   (DMA)
FSR............ Fleet Street Reports of Patent Cases [*England*] [*A publication*]   (DLA)
FSR............ Flight Safety Research
FSR............ Flight Safety Rules   (MCD)
FSR............ Flight Simulation Report
FSR............ Flight Solar Reflectometer
FSR............ Flight Specific Requirements   (MCD)
FSR............ Flight Support Request   (KSC)
FSR............ Floor Space Ratio
FSR............ Flux Sensitive Resistor
FSR............ Flying Saucer Review [*British*] [*A publication*]
FSR............ Force Service Regiment [*Marine Corps*]   (NVT)
FSR............ Foreign Separate Rations   (AABC)
FSR............ Foreign Service Reservists   (MUGU)
FSR............ Forward Space Record
FSR............ Foundation for Scientific Relaxation
FSR............ Four Seasons Resources Ltd. [*Vancouver Stock Exchange symbol*]
FSR............ Franciscan Sisters of Ringwood [*Roman Catholic religious order*]
FSR............ Frequency Scan RADAR
FSR............ Frequency Selective Relay
FSR............ Frequency Shift Receiver
FSR............ Frequency Shift Reflector
FSR............ Full-Scale Record [*Instrumentation*]
FSR............ Full-Scale Review
FSR............ Function Status Review   (MCD)
FSR............ Functional Stretch Reflex [*of muscles*]
FSR............ Fund for Stockowners Rights [*Later, FFSR*]   (EA)
FSR............ Fund Summary Record [*Military*]   (AFIT)
FSR............ John and Mable Ringling Museum of Art, Sarasota, FL [*Library symbol*] [*Library of Congress*]   (LCLS)
FSRA .... Federal Sewage Research Association [*Later, Federal Water Quality Association*]
FSRB .... Flight Safety Review Board
FSRC .... Ringling Museum of the Circus, Sarasota, FL [*Library symbol*] [*Library of Congress*]   (LCLS)
FSRDC ...... Full Straps Roosevelt Dime Club   (EA)
FSRG .... Fellow of the Society of Remedial Gymnasts [*British*]
FSRI .... Foreign Services Research Institute   (EA)
FSRM .... First-Stage Rocket Motor [*Aerospace*]
FSRN .... Forest Service Research Notes
FSRP .... Forest Service Research Paper
FS/RPNL .. Function Safe-Release Panel [*Aerospace*]   (AAG)
FSRR .... Flight Software Readiness Review   (MCD)
FSRR .... Flight System Readiness Review   (NASA)
FSRS......... Flight System Recording System   (MCD)
FSRS......... Force Structure Requirements Study [*Military*]
FSRS......... Frequency Selective Receiver System   (MCD)
FSRT .... Flight Systems Redundancy Test   (MCD)
FSRTS .... Fyra Svenska Reformationskrifter Tryckta i Stockholm Ar 1562 [*A publication*]
FSRU......... Foreign Service Reserve (Unlimited) [*Department of State*]
FSS .... Fabrication Statusing System   (MCD)
FSS .... Facility Security Supervision   (MCD)
FSS .... Family Security Service
FSS .... Fear Survey Schedule [*Psychology*]
FSS .... Federal Signal Corp. [*Formerly, Federal Sign & Signal Corp.*] [*NYSE symbol*]   (SPSG)
FSS .... Federal Supply Schedule
FSS .... [*Office of*] Federal Supply and Services [*GSA*]
FSS .... Fellow of the Royal Statistical Society [*British*]
FSS .... Field Service Section [*Military*]
FSS .... Field Spectrometer System   (MCD)
FSS .... Field Support System
FSS .... Financial Status Summary   (OICC)

FSS .... Fine Sun Sensor [*NASA*]
FSS .... Fire Support Ship
FSS .... Fire Support Station [*Navy*]   (NVT)
FSS .... Fire Suppression System   (MCD)
FSS .... First-Stage Separation [*Aerospace*]
FSS .... Fixed Satellite Service
FSS .... Fixed Service Structure   (MCD)
FSS .... Fleet Service School [*Navy*]
FSS .... Flight Security Supervisor [*Military*]
FSS .... Flight Service Station [*FAA*]
FSS .... Flight Standards Service [*FAA*]   (MCD)
FSS .... Flight Support Station [*For manned maneuvering unit*]   (NASA)
FSS .... Flight Support Structure   (MCD)
FSS .... Flight Support System   (MCD)
FSS .... Flight Systems Simulator [*NASA*]   (NASA)
FSS .... Floor Service Stations   (NRCH)
FSS .... Fluid Supply System   (MCD)
FSS .... Flutter Suppression System [*Aviation*]
FSS .... Flying Spot Scanner [*Optical character recognition*]
FSS .... Fog Signal Station [*Coast Guard*]
FSS .... Force Stratification System
FSS .... Force Structure Subsystem [*Military*]
FSS .... Foreign Shore Service
FSS .... Forensic Science Society   (EAIO)
FSS .... Forward Scatter System   (NATG)
FSS .... Forward Scattering Spectroscopy
FSS .... Forward Supply Support
FSS .... Four Sigma Society   (EA)
FSS .... Frame Storage System [*Television*]
FSS .... Franco-Scottish Society
FSS .... Fully Separated Subsidiary
FSS .... Seminole Community College, Sanford, FL [*OCLC symbol*]   (OCLC)
f-ss---.......... Spanish Sahara [*Western Sahara*] [*MARC geographic area code*] [*Library of Congress*]   (LCCP)
FSSA .... Federation des Syndicats du Secteur de l'Aluminium, Inc. [*Federation of Aluminum Sector Unions, Inc.*] [*Canada*]
FSSA .... Fellow of the Society of Science and Art [*British*]
FSSA .... Fire Suppression Systems Association   (EA)
FSSA .... Flying Scot Sailing Association   (EA)
FSSA .... French Studies in Southern Africa [*A publication*]
FSSC......... Federal Standard Stock Catalog
FSSC......... Foreign Student Service Council   (EA)
FSSCA ...... Fellow of the Society of Science and Arts, London [*British*]   (ROG)
FSSCOM... Flight Service Station Operations/Procedures Committee [*FAA*]   (FAAC)
FSSCT .... Forer Structured Sentence Completion Test [*Psychology*]
FSSD .... Federal Supply Storage Depot
FSSD .... First-Stage Separation Device [*Aerospace*]
FSSD .... Foreign Service Selection Date
FSSE .... Federation des Societes Suisses d'Employes [*Federation of Swiss Employees' Societies*]
FSSE .... Fellow of the Society of Senior Executives [*Australia*]
FSSE .... Foreign Service Sales Expense
FSSE .... Forward Service Support Element   (AABC)
FSSE .... Franciscan Sisters of St. Elizabeth [*Roman Catholic religious order*]
FSSF .... First Special Service Force   (MCD)
FSSFA ...... First Special Service Force Association   (EA)
FSSG .... Field Service Support Group [*USMC*]   (MCD)
FSSG .... Force Service Support Group [*Military*]   (NVT)
FSSI.......... Fellow of the Statistical Society of Ireland   (ROG)
FSSJ .... Franciscan Sisters of St. Joseph [*Roman Catholic religious order*]
FSSL.......... Financial Security Savings & Loan Association [*NASDAQ symbol*]   (NQ)
FSSN .... Fission   (MSA)
FSSP......... Fellowship of St. Paul   (EA)
FSSP......... Film Strip Sound Projector
FSSP......... Forward-Scattering Spectrometer Probe [*Aerosol measurement device*]
FSSP......... Fraternite Sacerdotale Saint Pie X [*International Sacerdotal Society Saint Pius X - ISSSP*]   (EAIO)
FSSP......... Fuel System Supply Point
FSSR .... Fellow of the Royal Statistical Society [*British*]
FSSR .... Flight Systems Software Requirement   (MCD)
FSSR .... Functional Subsystem Software Requirements   (NASA)
FSSRS .... Farm Structure Survey Retrieval System [*Information service or system*]   (EISS)
FSSS .... Family Support Services Scheme [*Australia*]
FSS/S .... Fine Sun Sensor/Signal Conditioner [*NASA*]   (MCD)
FSSS .... Fuse Set Subsystem
FSSS .... Mahe/Seychelles International   (ICLI)
FSSTMUK ... Friendly Society of Spade Tree Makers of the United Kingdom [*A union*]
FSSU .... Federated Superannuation Scheme for Universities [*British*]
FSSWT...... Full-Scale Subsonic Wind Tunnel
FST .... Far Eastern Resources Corp. [*Vancouver Stock Exchange symbol*]

FST .... Fast [*Horse racing*]
FST .... Federal Sales Tax [*Canada*]
FSt .... Feminist Studies [*A publication*]
FST .... Field Service Technician   (MCD)
FST .... Field Suitability Test
FST .... Field Supply Technician   (MCD)
FST .... Field Surgical Team [*Military*] [*British*]
FST .... Field Survey Team
FST .... File Status Table [*Data processing*]   (IBMDP)
FST .... File Systems Tree [*Data processing*]
FST .... Film Supertwist
FST .... Finite Sampling Time
FST .... Fire Support Team   (MCD)
FST .... First
FST .... First Class or Saloon Passengers [*Shipping*] [*British*]
FST .... Fixed Service Tower
FST .... Flatter, Squarer Tube [*Television picture tube*]
FST .... Fleurs Synthesis Telescope
FST .... Flight Support Tapes
FST .... Foam Stability Test
FST .... Follow-On Soviet Tank [*In FST-1, model name of a Russian "supertank" having improved armor and a 135-mm gun*] [*Introduced in the late 1980's*]
FST .... Foreign Service Tour [*Military*]
FST .... Forged Steel [*Technical drawings*]
FST .... Forstmann & Co. [*AMEX symbol*]   (SPSG)
FST .... Fort Stockton, TX [*Location identifier*] [*FAA*]   (FAAL)
FST .... Forward Support Team   (MCD)
FST .... Framingham State College, Framingham, MA [*OCLC symbol*]   (OCLC)
FSt .... Franciscan Studies [*A publication*]
F St .... Franziskanische Studien [*A publication*]
FST .... Free Southern Theater
FST .... Free Space Transfer   (MCD)
FST .... Freestate Aviation, Inc. [*Gaithersburg, MD*] [*FAA designator*]   (FAAC)
F St .... French Studies [*A publication*]
FST .... Frequency Shift Transmission
FST .... Full-Scale Tunnel [*Aerospace*]
FST .... Functional Simulator and Translator [*Data processing*]   (CSR)
FST .... Funkstelle [*Radio Station*] [*German military - World War II*]
FST .... Future Strategic Targets   (MCD)
FST .... Fuzed Silica Tube
FSTA .... Fellow of the Swimming Teachers' Association [*British*]   (DBQ)
FSTA .... Food Science and Technology Abstracts [*International Food Information Service*] [*Bibliographic database*] [*A publication*]
FSTA .... Force Structure Trade-Off Analysis   (MCD)
FSTA .... Four Star International, Inc. [*NASDAQ symbol*]   (NQ)
FStaB .... Bradford County Public Library, Starke, FL [*Library symbol*] [*Library of Congress*]   (LCLS)
FSTACOE ... Fleet Special Test and Checkout Equipment
FSTAD ...... Fire Support and Target Acquisition Division [*Human Engineering Laboratory*] [*Army*]
FSTC .... Farmington State Teachers College [*Merged with University of Maine*]
FSTC .... Fayetteville State Teachers College [*Later, Fayetteville State University*] [*North Carolina*]
FSTC .... Foreign Science and Technology Center [*Army*]
F & STD .... Fire and Safety Test Detachment [*Coast Guard*] [*Mobile, AL*]   (GRD)
FSTD .... Flight Simulation Test Data
FSTDY ...... Final Semester Temporary Duty [*Air Force*]   (AFM)
FSTE .... Factory Special Test Equipment   (NASA)
FSTE .... Field Support Test Equipment
FSTEB .... Fibre Science and Technology [*A publication*]
FSTH .... Firstsouth Federal Savings & Loan [*NASDAQ symbol*]   (NQ)
FS Th R ..... Forschungen zur Systematischen Theologie und Religionsphilosophie [*A publication*]
FSTI .... Formed Steel Tube Institute [*Later, WSTI*]
FSTI .... Free Search Terminal Interface [*Telecommunications*]
FSTK/SUP ... Friendly Strike or Support [*Military*]   (NVT)
FSTL .... Foreign Salable Technology and Licence [*Republic of Korea*] [*Information service or system*]   (IID)
FSTL .... Future Strategic Target List
FSTMA ...... Firearm and Security Trainers Management Association   (EA)
FSTNR ...... Fastener
FSTPW ...... Friendly Society of Tin Plate Workers [*A union*] [*British*]
FSTR .... Fallschirmtruppen [*Parachute Troops*] [*German military*]
FSTR .... Field Service Technical Report   (AAG)
FSTR .... Foster [*L. B.*] Co. [*NASDAQ symbol*]   (NQ)
FSTRE....... Field Service Trouble Report
FSTS.......... Federal Secure Telephone Service [*or System*] [*DoD*]
FSTS.......... Financial Services Terminals Support [*IBM Corp.*]
FSTS.......... Fitting Shop Trade Society [*A union*] [*British*]
FSTS.......... Flight Simulated Training System [*Military*]
FSTS.......... Future Space Transportation System
FSTS.......... Fuze Set Test Set
FSTTC....... Flight Safety Training and Test Center
F Stud........ Franziskanische Studien [*A publication*]

FStuM .... Martin County Public Library, Stuart, FL [*Library symbol*] [*Library of Congress*]   (LCLS)
FSTV .... Full-Scale Test Vehicle [*NASA*]
FSTXA ...... Faserforschung und Textiltechnik [*A publication*]
FSU........... Facsimile Switching Unit
FSU........... Fail Sheer Ultimate   (MCD)
FSU........... Family Service Unit [*Medicine*] [*British*]
FSU........... Fellowship for Spiritual Understanding   (EA)
FSU........... Ferry Service Unit
FSU........... Field Select Unit
FSU........... Field Storage Unit [*Military*]
FSU........... Final Signal Unit [*Telecommunications*]   (TEL)
FSU........... Flight Service Unit   (ADA)
FSU........... Flightline Support Unit   (MCD)
FSU........... Florida State University [*Tallahassee*]
FSU........... Fort Sumner, NM [*Location identifier*] [*FAA*]   (FAAL)
FSU........... Freisoziale Union - Demokratische Mitte [*Free Social Union - Democratic Center*] [*Federal Republic of Germany*] [*Political party*]   (PPW)
FSU........... Freon Servicing Unit   (NASA)
FSUC......... Full-Scale Unit   (KSC)
FSUC......... Federal Statistics Users' Conference [*Defunct*]   (EA)
FSUD........ Fort Street Union Depot Co. [*AAR code*]
FSUJPM ... Friendly Society of United Journeymen Platers and Moulders [*A union*] [*British*]
F Supp........ Federal Supplement [*A publication*]
FSUS......... Florida State University. Studies [*A publication*]
FSUSA ...... Finance School, United States Army
FSUSP....... Florida State University. Slavic Papers [*A publication*]
FSV........... Falciparum Sporozoite Vaccine [*Antimalarial*]
FSV........... Feline Fibrosarcoma Virus
FSV........... Final Stage Vehicle
FSV........... Fire Service Valve   (IEEE)
FSV........... Fire Support Vehicle [*Military*]   (MCD)
FSV........... Fort St. Vrain [*Nuclear plant*]   (NRCH)
FSV........... Frequency Selective Voltmeter
FSV........... Fujinami Sarcoma Virus
FSVA .... Fellow of the Incorporated Society of Valuers and Auctioneers [*British*]   (DBQ)
FSVA .... Fidelity Savings Association [*NASDAQ symbol*]   (NQ)
FSVB .... Fort Smith & Van Buren Railway Co. [*AAR code*]
FSVB .... Franklin Savings Bank, FSB [*NASDAQ symbol*]   (SPSG)
FSVNGS ... Fort St. Vrain Nuclear Generating Station   (NRCH)
FSVP......... FIND/SVP, Inc. [*New York, NY*] [*NASDAQ symbol*]   (NQ)
FSW.......... Faith in the Second World [*See also G2W*] [*Zollikon-Zurich, Switzerland*]   (EAIO)
FSW.......... Feet of Seawater [*Deep-sea diving*]
FSW.......... Field Switch
FSW.......... Fire Team Support Weapon   (MCD)
FSW.......... Fletcher Sutcliffe Wild [*Commercial firm*] [*British*]
FSW.......... Flexible Steel Wire
FSW.......... Flight Software   (MCD)
FSW.......... Forward Swept Wing
FSW.......... Frame Synchronization Word   (MSA)
FSW.......... Friendly Society of Watermen [*A union*] [*British*]
FSWC........ Foundry Sector Working Circle [*Australia*]
FSWD........ Foundation for the Study of Wilson's Disease [*Later, NCSWD*]   (EA)
FSWD........ Full-Scale Weapons Delivery [*Military*]
FSWEC...... Federal Software Exchange Center
FSWFS...... Field Standard Weight and Force System   (AAG)
FSWMA .... Fine and Specialty Wire Manufacturers Association [*Later, Specialty Wire Association*]   (EA)
FSWO........ Financial Secretary to the War Office [*British*]
FSWR........ Flexible Steel Wire Rope
FSWT........ Free Surface Water Tunnel
FSWW .... First Society of Whale Watchers [*Defunct*]   (EA)
FSX........... Fighter Support Experimental [*Military*]
f-sx--- .... South West Africa [*Namibia*] [*MARC geographic area code*] [*Library of Congress*]   (LCCP)
FSYCA3 .... Faraday Symposia of the Chemical Society [*A publication*]
FSYO......... Fleet Security Officer [*Navy*] [*British*]
FSz............ Folks-Sztyme [*A publication*]
f szla .... Folyo Szamla [*Current Account*] [*Hungarian*]
FT .... Factory Test
FT .... Fail Type [*Military*]   (AFIT)
FT .... Faint
FT .... Family Team [*Australia*]
FT .... Family Therapy
FT .... Fan Tek   (EA)
FT .... Faserforschung und Textiltechnik [*A publication*]
FT .... Fashion Television [*TV program*]
FT .... Fast [*Track condition*] [*Thoroughbred racing*]
FT .... Fast Track [*Insurance*]
FT .... Fatigue Time [*Sports medicine*]
FT .... Fault Tree   (MCD)
FT .... Federal Triangle [*Washington, DC*]
FT .... Feet [*or Foot*]   (AAG)
FT .... Feet Together [*Dance terminology*]
FT .... Feint [*of account book rulings*]
FT .... Fiant [*Let Them Be Made*] [*Pharmacy*]   (ROG)

FT .... Fiat [*Make*] [*Pharmacy*]
FT .... Fiat SpA [*Italy*] [*ICAO aircraft manufacturer identifier*] (ICAO)
FT .... Fibrous Tissue [*Medicine*]
FT .... Field Test (AAG)
FT .... Field Training [*AFROTC*] (AFM)
FT .... Field Trip
FT .... Filing Time [*Time a message is presented for transmission*]
FT .... Filipino Teacher [*A publication*]
FT .... Financial Times [*A publication*]
FT .... Fine Thermal [*Furnace*]
FT .... Finsk Tidskrift [*A publication*]
FT .... Fire Control Technician [*Navy rating*]
FT .... Fire Team [*Marine Corps*]
F & T .... Fire and Theft
FT .... Fire Thermostat (AAG)
FT .... Fire-Tube Boiler
FT .... Firing Tables [*Military*]
FT .... Fischer-Tropsch Synthesis [*Organic chemistry*]
FT .... Fitter and Turner [*Navy rating*] [*British*]
FT .... Fixed Tone
FT .... Flagon and Trencher (EA)
FT .... Flame Tight
FT .... Flanging Tube
FT .... Flat [*Paper*]
FT .... Flat Template
FT .... Flat-Topped [*Frames*] [*Optometry*]
FT .... Flexible Trunk [*Hovercraft*]
FT .... Flight Team (MCD)
FT .... Flight Termination
F/T .... Flight Test (KSC)
FT .... Flow Through
FT .... Flow Transducer [*Instrumentation*]
FT .... Flow Transmitter [*Nuclear energy*] (NRCH)
FT .... Fluorescent Target
FT .... Flush Threshold [*Technical drawings*]
FT .... Flushometer Tank
FT .... Flying Tiger Line, Inc. [*ICAO designator*]
FT .... Foam Tape
FT .... Fog Trumpet [*Navigation charts*]
F-T .... Follow Through
FT .... Foreign Theater
FT .... Foreign Transaction (AFM)
FT .... Forest Trust [*An association*] (EA)
FT .... Foretop [*Obsolete*]
FT .... Forint [*Monetary unit*] [*Hungary*]
FT .... Forklift Truck (DCTA)
FT .... Formal Toxoid [*Medicine*]
FT .... Formal Training [*Military*] (AFM)
FT .... Fort
FT .... Fort McMurray Today [*A publication*]
FT .... Fortification (ROG)
FT .... Forward Transfer [*Telecommunications*] (TEL)
FT .... Foundation of Thanatology (EA)
FT .... Fourier Transform
FT .... Franciscus Tigrini de Pisis [*Flourished, 13th-14th century*] [*Authority cited in pre-1607 legal work*] (DSA)
FT .... Franklin Universal Trust [*NYSE symbol*] (CTT)
FT .... Free Throw [*Basketball*]
FT .... Free Thyroxine [*Also, FT₄ Endocrinology*]
FT .... Free Trader (ROG)
FT .... Free Turbine (AAG)
FT .... Free Turn
FT .... Freight Ton
FT .... Freight Transport
FT .... French Telefunken [*Record label*]
ft .... French Territory of the Afars and Issas [*Djibouti*] [*MARC country of publication code*] [*Library of Congress*] (LCCP)
FT .... French Title [*Online database field identifier*]
FT .... Frequency and Time (IEEE)
FT .... Frequency Tolerance
FT .... Frequency Tracker (MSA)
FT .... Frequent Traveler [*on airlines*]
FT .... Friends of the Tango (EA)
FT .... Front [*Deltiology*]
FT .... Ftorafur [*Analog of 5-fluorourical deoxyribose*] [*Soviet anticancer drug*]
FT .... Fuel Tanking [*Aerospace*] (AAG)
FT .... Fuel Terms (DS)
F & T .... Fuel and Transportation [*Navy*]
FT .... Full Term [*Pregnancy*] [*Medicine*]
FT .... Full Tilt Container (DCTA)
FT .... Full Time [*Employment, education*]
FT .... Fully Tracked (NATG)
FT .... Fume-Tight [*Technical drawings*]
FT .... Functional Test [*Data processing*]
FT .... Fund Type [*Military*] (AFIT)
FT .... Fundic Type [*of epithelium*] [*Medicine*]
FT .... Funk-Technik [*A publication*]

FT .... Tampa-Hillsborough County Public Library, Tampa, FL [*Library symbol*] [*Library of Congress*] (LCLS)
FT .... Terminal Forecasts [*Symbol*] [*National Weather Service*]
FT1 .... Fire Control Technician, First Class [*Navy rating*]
FT2 .... Fire Control Technician, Second Class [*Navy rating*]
FT² .... Square Foot
FT3 .... Fire Control Technician, Third Class [*Navy rating*]
FT135 .... US Foreign Trade. FT 135. General Imports. Schedule A. Commodity by Country [*A publication*]
FT410 .... US Foreign Trade. FT 410. Exports. Schedule E. Commodity by Country [*A publication*]
FT610 .... US Foreign Trade. FT 610. Exports SIC Based Products by World Areas [*A publication*]
FTA............. Failed to Attend (ADA)
FTA............. Failure to Appear [*Court case*]
FTA............. Fast Time Analysis
FTA............. Fatigue Test Article (NASA)
FTA............. Fault Tree Analysis (NASA)
FTA............. Federation of Tax Administrators (EA)
FT/A............. Feet per Year
FTA............. Field to Advise [*Telecommunications*] (TEL)
FTA............. Field Technical Authority (NVT)
FTA............. Field Test Administration (AAG)
FTA............. Film Training Aid
FTA............. Fixed Time of Arrival [*Aviation*]
FTA............. Flexographic Technical Association (EA)
FTA............. Flight Test Article (KSC)
FTA............. Florida Trail Association (EA)
FTA............. Fluid Transpiration Arc
FTA............. Fluorescent Treponemal Antibody [*Clinical chemistry*]
FTA............. Food Technology in Australia [*A publication*]
FTA............. Food Trade Review [*A publication*]
FTA............. Food Tray Association [*Defunct*]
FTA............. Foreign Trade Association [*Cologne, Federal Republic of Germany*] (EAIO)
FTA............. Forward Transfer Admittance
FTA............. Foundation of the Twelve Apostles (EA)
FTA............. Free the Army [*Bowdlerized version*] [*Barracks graffiti; also, title of antimilitary play*]
FTA............. Free Thought Association (EA)
FTA............. Free Throws Attempted [*Basketball*]
FTA............. Free Trade Agreement [*or Arrangement*]
FTA............. Free Trade Area
FTA............. Free Trade Association [*European*]
FTA............. Freight Transport Association [*British*]
FTA............. Frontier Flying Service, Inc. [*Fairbanks, AK*] [*FAA designator*] (FAAC)
FTA............. Fuel Treatment Apparatus
FTA............. Fun, Travel, Adventure [*Sarcastic alternate to FTA - Free the Army*]
FTA............. Fur Takers of America (EA)
FTA............. Future Teachers of America [*Later, SAE*] (EA)
FTA............. Hot Springs, SD [*Location identifier*] [*FAA*] (FAAL)
FTaA............. Apalachee Community Mental Health Services, Inc., Tallahassee, FL [*Library symbol*] [*Library of Congress*] (LCLS)
FTA-ABS .. Fluorescent Treponemal Antibody - Absorption [*Test for syphilis*]
FTACCC ... Florida Technical Advisory Committee on Citrus Canker (EA)
FTACT ...... Financial Times Actuaries Share Indices [*Database*] [*Financial Times Business Enterprises Ltd.*] [*Information service or system*] (CRD)
FTAF .... Flying Training Air Force
FTaFA .... Florida A & M University, Tallahassee, FL [*Library symbol*] [*Library of Congress*] (LCLS)
FTaL .... Leon-Jefferson-Wakulla County Public Library, Tallahassee, FL [*Library symbol*] [*Library of Congress*] (LCLS)
FTAM .... File Transfer, Access, and Management [*Telecommunications*] (TSSD)
FTAM .... File Transfer Access Method [*Data processing*]
FTAO .... Foreign Technology Activity Office [*or Officer*] (AFM)
FTAR .... Following Transmitted as Received (FAAC)
FTAS .... Fast Time Analyzer System
FTAS .... Federation of Turkish-American Societies (EA)
FTaS .... Sunland Center, Tallahassee, FL [*Library symbol*] [*Library of Congress*] (LCLS)
FTaSU .... Florida State University, Tallahassee, FL [*Library symbol*] [*Library of Congress*] (LCLS)
FTaSU-L ... Florida State University, Law Library, Tallahassee, FL [*Library symbol*] [*Library of Congress*] (LCLS)
FTAT......... Facilities Technology Application Test [*Army*] (RDA)
FTAT......... Field Turn-Around Time (MCD)
FTAT......... Fluorescent Treponemal Antibody Test [*for syphilis*]
FTAT......... Furniture, Timber, and Allied Trades Union [*British*]
FTaT......... Tallahassee Community College, Tallahassee, FL [*Library symbol*] [*Library of Congress*] (LCLS)
FTATU....... Furniture, Timber, and Allied Trades Union [*British*]
FTAUAC... Food Technology in Australia [*A publication*]
FT-AWI.... Financial Times-Actuaries World Indices [*British*]
FTB............. Fails to Break
FTB............. Fast Torpedo Boat [*NATO*]

FTB............	Field Team Bulletin [*Military*] (CINC)
FTB............	Fighter Bomber [*Obsolete*]
FTB............	Film Transfer Boom [*NASA*]
FTB............	Fingertip Blood [*Medicine*]
FTB............	Fire Control Technician, Ballistic Missile [*Navy rating*]
FTB............	Fire-Tube Boiler (DS)
FTB............	First-Time-Buy (MCD)
FTB............	Fitchburg State College, Fitchburg, MA [*OCLC symbol*] (OCLC)
FTB............	Fleet Torpedo Bomber
FTB............	Flight [*or Flying*] Test Bed
FTB............	Freight Tariff Bureau
FTB............	Freight Traffic Bureau
FTB............	Frequency Time Base (DEN)
FTB............	Full to Bursting [*Reply to question, "Have you had enough to eat"*]
FTB............	Functional Training Branch [*BUPERS*]
F-TBA........	Fasting-Total Bile Acids [*Physiology*]
FTBA.........	Food Tray and Board Association [*Later, SSI*]
FT BAL......	Football [*Freight*]
FTBD........	Fit to Be Detained [*Medicine*]
FTBD........	Full Term Born Dead [*Medicine*]
FTBF.........	Frequency Tuned Bandpass Filter
FTBI.........	Financial Times Business Information [*London, England*]
FTBN........	First Tulsa Bancorp [*NASDAQ symbol*] (NQ)
FTBR........	Fort McMurray Today. Oil Sands Business Report [*A publication*]
FTBS	Fire-Tube Boiler Survey (DS)
FTBS	Free Throwers Boomerang Society (EA)
FTBSA.......	Fire Control Technician, Ballistic Missile Fire Control, Seaman Apprentice [*Navy rating*]
FTBSN	Fire Control Technician, Ballistic Missile Fire Control, Seaman [*Navy rating*]
FTC............	Facility Terminal Cabinet (AAG)
FTC............	False Target Can [*Navy*] (NVT)
FTC............	Fast Time Constant [*RADAR*]
FTC............	Fault-Tolerant Computing
FTC............	Federal Telecommunications System [*of GSA*] (NOAA)
FTC............	Federal Trade Commission [*Independent government agency*] [*OCLC symbol*]
FTC............	Federal Trade Commission Decisions [*A publication*] (DLA)
FT & C.......	Feint and Cash [*of account book rulings*]
FTC............	Field Training Command [*Military*]
FTC............	Financial Trustco Capital Ltd. [*Toronto Stock Exchange symbol*]
FTC............	Fire Control Technician, Chief [*Navy rating*]
FTC............	Fixed Tantalum Capacitor
FTC............	Fleet Training Center [*Navy*]
FTC............	Flight Test Center
FTC............	Flight Test Conductor (NASA)
FTC............	Flight Time Constant
FTC............	Florida Test Center [*NASA*] (KSC)
FTC............	Fluid-Bed Thermal Cracking [*A chemical process developed by the Institute of Gas Technology*]
FTC............	Flying Training Command [*Air Force*]
FT-C	Foot-Candle [*Illumination*]
FTC............	Force Track Coordinator [*Navy*] (NVT)
FTC............	Fordson Tractor Club (EA)
FTC............	Foreign Tax Credit
FTC............	Forest Tent Caterpillars
FT & C.......	Formal Training and Certification (MCD)
FTC............	Fort Collins [*Colorado*] [*Airport symbol*] (OAG)
FTC............	Fort Tejon [*California*] [*Seismograph station code, US Geological Survey*] [*Closed*] (SEIS)
FTC............	Frames to Come [*Optometry*]
FTC............	Freighter Travel Club of America (EA)
FTC............	Freon Tank Container
FTC............	Frequency Threshold Curve
FTC............	Frequency Time Control
FTC............	Fuel Transfer Canal [*Nuclear energy*] (NRCH)
FTC............	Full Technological Certificate [*British*]
FT & C.......	Functional Test and Calibration (IEEE)
FTCA........	Federal Tort Claims Act
FT CAT......	Fiat Cataplasma [*Let a Poultice Be Made*] [*Pharmacy*]
FTCC........	Fellow of Trinity College, Cambridge [*British*] (ROG)
FTCC........	First Trust Company [*NASDAQ symbol*] (NQ)
FTCC........	Fixed Temperature Compensating Capacitor
FTCC........	Flight Test Coordinating Committee [*Air Force*]
FTCC........	FTC Communications, Inc. [*New York, NY*] (TSSD)
FTCD........	Fellow of Trinity College, Dublin
FT CD........	Foot-Candela [*Foot-Candle*] [*Illumination*] (ADA)
FT CERAT ...	Fiat Ceratum [*Let a Cerate Be Made*] [*Pharmacy*]
FT CHART ...	Fiat Chartula [*Let a Powder Be Made*] [*Pharmacy*]
FTCL........	Fellow of Trinity College of Music, London (EY)
FTCLR	Financial Times Commercial Law Reports [*A publication*] [*British*]
FTCM........	Fire Control Technician, Master Chief [*Navy rating*]
FTCO........	Franklin Telecommunications Corp. [*NASDAQ symbol*] (NQ)
FT COLLYR ...	Fiat Collyrium [*Let an Eyewash Be Made*] [*Pharmacy*]
FTCP	Flight Test Change Proposal (MCD)
FTCR	Functional Test Change Request

FTCS	Fire Control Technician, Senior Chief [*Navy rating*]
FTCSS......	Flight Trace Contaminant Sensor System [*NASA*] (KSC)
FTC-TLTR ...	Freight Traffic Committee - Trunk Line Territory Railroads
FTD	Fails to Drain
FTD	Federal Tax Deposit [*IRS*]
FT/D	Feet per Day
FTD	Femoral Total Density
FTD	Field Training Detachment [*Program*] [*Air Force*]
FTD	Fire Technology Division [*National Institute of Standards and Technology*]
FTD	First Tridon Industry [*Vancouver Stock Exchange symbol*]
FTD	Fitted (MSA)
FTD	Flight Test Direction [*or Directive*] (AAG)
FTD	Flight Test Drawing (MCD)
FTD	Florists' Transworld [*formerly, Telegraph*] Delivery [*Trademark*]
FTD	Foreign Technical Department [*Navy*] (NVT)
FTD	Foreign Technology Division [*Air Force*] [*Wright-Patterson Air Force Base, Ohio*]
FTD	Foreign Trade Division [*Census*] (OICC)
FTD	Formal Technical Documents
FTD	Fort Dearborn Income Securities, Inc. [*NYSE symbol*] (SPSG)
FTD	Fortified
FTD	Freight Traffic Department
FTD	Freight Traffic Division [*Army*]
FTD	Frequency Translation Distortion
FTD	Full-Time Duty (ADA)
FTD	Functional Test Data
FTDA........	Fellow of the Theatrical Designers and Craftsmen's Association [*British*]
FTDA........	Florists' Transworld Delivery Association (EA)
FTDC........	Field Testing and Development Center
FTDIP	Flight Test Division, Internal Project [*Navy*] (MCD)
FTDMA.....	Frequency and Time-Division Multiple Access (MCD)
FTDR........	Flight Test Data Recorder (MCD)
FTDS	Flag Tactical Data System (MUGU)
FTDS	Formal Training Data System (NVT)
FTE...........	Facility Training Equipment
FTE...........	Factory Test Equipment (MCD)
FTE...........	FFTF [*Fast Flux Test Facility*] Test Engineering [*Nuclear energy*] (NRCH)
FTE...........	Flight Test Encoder
FTE...........	Flight Test Engineer (MCD)
FTE...........	Flight Test Equipment
FTE...........	Flight Test Evaluation
FTE...........	Florida Tomato Exchange (EA)
FTE...........	Flux Transfer Event [*Planetary physics*]
FTE...........	Follett, TX [*Location identifier*] [*FAA*] (FAAL)
FTE...........	Foote Mineral Co. [*AMEX symbol*] (SPSG)
FTE...........	Forced Test End (NASA)
FTE...........	Foundation for Teaching Economics (EA)
FTE...........	Frame Table Entry [*Data processing*] (IBMDP)
FTE...........	Free the Eagle [*Washington, DC*] (EA)
FTE...........	Free Thyroxine Equivalent [*Endocrinology*]
FTE...........	Full-Time Education
FTE...........	Full-Time Employee
FTE...........	Full-Time Equivalent
FTE...........	Functional Test Equipment
FTE...........	Fund for Theological Education (EA)
FTEC........	Federal Trial Examiners Conference [*Later, FALJC*] (EA)
FTEC........	Feminist Teacher Editorial Collective (EA)
FTEC........	Firetector, Inc. [*NASDAQ symbol*] (NQ)
FTEC........	Free Territory of Ely-Chatelaine [*An association*] (EA)
F Techn......	Food Technology [*A publication*]
FTECS.......	Field Training Equipment Concentration Site [*Army*] (AABC)
FTEE........	Full-Time Equivalency Enrollment [*Education*]
FTEF	Fair Tax Education Fund (EA)
F & Televisie ...	Film et Televisie [*A publication*]
FTEM........	Factory Test Equipment Manufacturing
FT EMULS ...	Fiat Emulsio [*Let an Emulsion Be Made*] [*Pharmacy*]
FTEN.........	First Tennessee National Corp. [*NASDAQ symbol*] (NQ)
FTEO........	Flight Test Engineering Order
FTET	Full-Time Equivalent Terminals [*Data processing*]
FTF...........	Fair Tax Foundation (EA)
FTF...........	Financial Times (Frankfurt) [*A publication*]
FTF...........	Flared Tube Fitting
FTF...........	Functional Test Flight (AFM)
FTF...........	Fundamental Train Frequency [*Machinery*]
FT-FAM....	Fourier Transform-Faradic Admittance Measurements [*Spectrometry*]
FTFC........	Field Training Feedback Components (MCD)
FTFC........	First Federal Capital Corp. [*NASDAQ symbol*] (NQ)
FTFC	Florida College, Tampa, FL [*Library symbol*] [*Library of Congress*] (LCLS)
FTFC	Functional Test Flight Checklist
FTFET.......	Four-Terminal Field-Effect Transistor (IEEE)
FTFF.........	Formaldehyde Task Force Fund [*Defunct*] (EA)
FTFFA.......	Florida Tropical Fish Farms Association (EA)
FT (Fft)......	Financial Times (Frankfurt Edition) [*A publication*]
FTFGS.......	Flared Tube Fitting Gasket Seal (MSA)

FTFLSU .... Fairy Tale-Folklore Study Unit [*American Topical Association*] (EA)
FTFSU .... Fairy Tale-Folklore Study Unit [*American Topical Association*] (EA)
FT³/(FT D) ... Cubic Feet per Foot Day
FT³/(FT² D) ... Cubic Feet per Square Foot Day
FTG .... Fairchild Tropical Garden
FTG .... Fire Control Technician, Gun [*Navy rating*]
FTG .... Fitting (MSA)
FTG .... Fleet Training Group [*Navy*]
FTG .... Fluid Thioglycolate [*Medium*] [*Microbiology*]
FTG .... Footing (KSC)
FTG .... Full Thickness Graft [*Medicine*]
f-tg--- .... Togo [*MARC geographic area code*] [*Library of Congress*] (LCCP)
FT GARG .. Fiat Gargarisma [*Let a Gargle Be Made*] [*Pharmacy*]
FTGBA ...... Fertigungstechnik und Betrieb [*A publication*]
FTGBG ...... Flareout and Terminal Glide Beam Guidance [*Aerospace*] (AAG)
FTGDV ...... Footage Dives [*Military*] (AABC)
FTGS .... Church of Jesus Christ of Latter-Day Saints, Genealogical Society Library, Tampa Branch, Tampa, FL [*Library symbol*] [*Library of Congress*] (LCLS)
FTGSVC .... Fleet Training Group Services (NVT)
FTH .... Fathom
FT/H .... Feet per Hour
FTH .... Fuel Tank Helicopter
FT²/H .... Square Feet per Hour
Ft Haust ..... Fiat Haustus [*Let a Drink Be Made*] [*Pharmacy*]
FTHF .... Formyltetrahydrofolate [*Biochemistry*]
FThL .... Forum Theologiae Linguisticae [*A publication*]
FTHM .... Fathom (ROG)
FThought ... Faith and Thought. Journal of the Victoria Institute [*Croydon, Surrey*] [*A publication*]
FTHR .... Farther (FAAC)
FTHR .... Further (FAAC)
FTHRD ..... Feathered (FAAC)
F Th St .... Freiburger Theologische Studien [*A publication*]
FTI .... Dansk Fiskeriteknologisk Institut [*Danish Institute of Fisheries Technology*] [*Information service or system*] (IID)
FTI .... Facing Tile Institute (EA)
FTI .... Federal Tax Included
FTI .... Fellow of the Textile Institute [*British*]
FTI .... Film Thickness Indicator
FTI .... Fixed Target Information [*Army*] (AABC)
FTI .... Foreign Trade Institute [*Mexico*]
FTI .... Foreign Traders Index [*Department of Commerce*] [*Washington, DC*] [*Information service or system*] (IID)
FTI .... France Telecom International, Inc. [*Telecommunications service*] (TSSD)
FTI .... Free Testosterone Index [*Endocrinology*]
FTI .... Free Thyroxine Index [*Endocrinology*]
FTI .... Frequency Time Indicator [*RADAR*]
FTI .... Frequency Time Intensity [*RADAR*]
FTI .... Frustration Tolerance Index [*Psychology*]
FTI .... FTI Foodtech International, Inc. [*Vancouver Stock Exchange symbol*]
FTi .... North Brevard Public Library, Titusville, FL [*Library symbol*] [*Library of Congress*] (LCLS)
f-ti--- .... Tunisia [*MARC geographic area code*] [*Library of Congress*] (LCCP)
FT-ICR ..... Fourier Transform-Ion Cyclotron Resonance [*Spectrometry*]
FTID .... Flame Thermionic Ionization Detector [*Instrumentation*]
FTID .... Flight Test Information Drawing (MCD)
FTIG .... Fort Indiantown Gap [*Army*] (AABC)
FTII .... Fellow of the Taxation Institute, Inc. [*British*] (DBQ)
FTIL .... First Illinois Corp. [*NASDAQ symbol*] (NQ)
FTIMA ...... Federal Tobacco Inspectors Mutual Association
FT INFUS ... Fiat Infusum [*Let an Infusion Be Made*] [*Pharmacy*]
FTIPA3...... Forest Tree Improvement [*A publication*]
FT & IR...... Flight Taxiing and Ingestion Risks [*Insurance*] (AIA)
FT-IR .... Fourier Transform Infrared [*Spectroscopy*]
FTIR .... Functional Terminal Innervation Ratio [*Psychiatry*]
FTIR-PAS ... Fourier Transform Infrared Photoacoustic Spectroscopy
FTIR-RAS ... Fourier Transform Infrared Reflection Absorption Spectroscopy
FTIS........... Flight Test Instrumentation System (NASA)
FTIT .... Fan Turbine Inlet Temperature (MCD)
FTIT .... Fellow of the Institute of Taxation [*British*] (DCTA)
FT₃IX........ Free Triiodothyronine Index
FT4IX .... Free Thyroxine Index [*Endocrinology*]
Ftiziol....... Ftiziologia [*A publication*]
FTK........... Field Test Kit
FTK........... Filtertek, Inc. [*NYSE symbol*] (SPSG)
FTK........... Fort Knox, KY [*Location identifier*] [*FAA*] (FAAL)
FTK........... Fuel Tank
FTK........... Futurtek Communications, Inc. [*Toronto Stock Exchange symbol*]
FTL........... Fast Transient Loader
FTL........... Fast Transit Link [*Rapid-transit term*]
FTL........... Faster Than Light [*Science fiction*] (AAG)

FTL........... Federal Telecommunications Laboratory [*Air Force*]
FTL........... Flying Thread Loom
FTL........... Flying Tiger Line, Inc.
FT-L.......... Foot-Lambert [*Illumination*]
FTL........... Foreign Theological Library [*A publication*]
FTL........... Formal Technical Literature
FTL........... Freeze Thaw Lysate [*Cytology*]
FTL........... Fruit of the Loom, Inc. [*AMEX symbol*] (SPSG)
FTL........... Full Term License [*For nuclear power plant*] (NRCH)
FTL........... Full Truck Loads
Ft Laud Nw ... Fort Lauderdale News [*A publication*]
FT-LB........ Foot-Pound [*Unit of work*] (AAG)
FT LBF ...... Foot-Pound Force
FT LB/H ... Foot-Pounds per Hour
FT LB/MIN ... Foot-Pounds per Minute
FT LB/S .... Foot-Pounds per Second
FTLD......... Faster-Than-Light Drive (AAG)
FT LINIM ... Fiat Linimentum [*Let a Linament Be Made*] [*Pharmacy*]
FT (London) ... Financial Times (London Edition) [*A publication*]
FTLR .... Financial Times Law Report [*A publication*] (DLA)
FTLV .... Feline T-Lymphotropic Lentivirus [*Later, FIV*]
FTLX .... Flying Tiger Line, Inc. [*Air carrier designation symbol*]
FTM .... Facilitated Transport Membrane [*Separation of chemicals*]
FTM .... Fan-Type Marker
FTM .... Film Thickness Monitor
FTM .... Fire Control Technician, Surface Missile [*Navy rating*]
FTM .... Flat-Tension Mask Screen (PCM)
FTM .... Fleet Training Missile (MUGU)
FTM .... Flexible Theatre Missile (AFM)
FTM .... Flight Test Manual
FTM .... Flight Test Matrix (MCD)
FTM .... Flight Test Missile [*Air Force*]
FTM .... Flight Training Mission (MCD)
FTM .... Fluid Thioglycolate Medium [*Microbiology*]
FTM .... Force/Torque Module [*NASA*]
FTM .... Fractional Test Meal [*Medicine*]
FTM .... Free to Member
FTM .... Free Throws Made [*Basketball*]
FTM .... Freight Traffic Manager
FTM .... French Training Mission [*Military*] (CINC)
FTM .... Frequency Time Modulation (DEN)
FTM .... FTM Resources, Inc. [*Vancouver Stock Exchange symbol*]
FTM .... Full-Time Manning (MCD)
FTM .... Functional Test Manager [*Hewlett-Packard Co.*]
FT MAS ..... Fiat Massa [*Let a Mass Be Made*] [*Pharmacy*]
FT MAS DIV in PIL ... Fiat Massa et Divide in Pilulae [*Let a Mass Be Made and Divided into Pills*] [*Pharmacy*]
FTMC........ Frequency and Time Measurement Counter
Ft McMurray News ... Fort McMurray News [*A publication*]
FTMEA ..... Formage et Traitements des Metaux [*A publication*]
FT/MIN ..... Feet per Minute
FT MIST ... Fiat Mistura [*Let a Mixture Be Made*] [*Pharmacy*]
FTMP........ Fault Tolerant Multiprocessor System [*Data processing*]
FTMS........ Fabrication Tracking and Management System (MCD)
FTMS........ Federal Test Method Standards (MCD)
FT/MS ...... Fourier Transform/Mass Spectrometry
FT-MW ..... Fourier Transform-Microwave [*Spectroscopy*]
FTN .... Family Therapy Network (EA)
FTN .... Flocculus Target Neuron [*Neuroanatomy*]
FTN .... Fortification (AABC)
FTN .... Fountain
FTNC........ First National Corp. [*NASDAQ symbol*] (NQ)
FTND........ Full Term Normal Delivery [*Medicine*]
FT-NMR ... Fourier Transform-Nuclear Magnetic Resonance [*Spectrometry*]
FTO .... Failed to Open (IEEE)
FTO .... Field Test Office (MCD)
FTO .... Field Test Operations [*Aerospace*] (KSC)
FTO .... First Toronto Capital Corp. [*Toronto Stock Exchange symbol*]
FTO .... Fleet Torpedo Officer [*British*]
FTO .... Flexible and Selective Targeting Options [*DoD*]
FTO .... Flight Test Objective (KSC)
FTO .... Flight Test Operations
FTO .... Foreign Technology Office [*Army Tank-Automotive Command*]
FTO .... Foreign Trade Organization (IMH)
FTO .... Foreign Training Officer [*Military*]
FTO .... Fort Yukon, AK [*Location identifier*] [*FAA*] (FAAL)
FTO .... Fourier Transform Operator
FTO .... Full-Time Officer [*of an organization*]
FTO .... Functional Test Objective (KSC)
FTOH .... Flight Team Operations Handbook (NASA)
FTOH .... Flight Test Operations Handbook (NASA)
FTOL........ Full Term Operating License (NRCH)
F & Ton..... Film und Ton [*A publication*]
FTOS......... Field Test Operations Support [*Aerospace*] (AAG)
FTP........... Factor/Test Procedure (MCD)
FTP........... Failure to Pay [*IRS*]
FTP........... Falling to Pieces [*Slang*]
FTP........... Federal Test Procedure
FTP........... Federal Theater Project

FTP............ FFTF [*Fast Flux Test Facility*] Test Procedure [*Nuclear energy*]   (NRCH)
FTP............ Field Test Operational Procedures [*Aerospace*]   (AAG)
FTP............ File Transfer Protocol [*Data processing*]
FTP............ Final Technical Proposal   (NATG)
FTP............ Fixed Term Plan   (BUR)
FTP............ Fixed Throttle Point [*NASA*]
FTP............ Fleet Training Publication [*Navy*]
FTP............ Flight Test Plan [*or Procedure or Program*]
FTP............ Florida Test Procedure [*Aerospace*]   (AAG)
FTP............ Fluorocarbons Technical Panel [*of Manufacturing Chemists Association*]
FTP............ Fly-to-Point   (NVT)
FTP............ Folded, Trimmed, Packed [*Books*]
FTP............ Fracture Toughness Parameter
FTP............ Fruit and Tropical Products [*A publication*]
FTP............ Fuel Tanking Panel [*Aerospace*]   (AAG)
FTP............ Fuel Transfer Pool [*Nuclear energy*]   (NRCH)
FTP............ Fuel Transfer Port [*Nuclear energy*]   (NRCH)
FTP............ Fuel Transfer Pump   (MSA)
FTP............ Full Throttle Position   (KSC)
FTP............ Full-Time Permanent [*Employment*]
FTP............ Full-Time Personnel [*Employment*]
FTP............ Full Transport Pack [*Military*]
FTP............ Function Test Procedure [*or Progress*]   (NASA)
FTP............ Functional Test Procedure [*or Program*]
FTPA........ Federal Timber Purchasers Association   (EA)
FTPA........ Fellow of the Town Planning Association [*British*]
FTPC......... Francs-Tireurs et Partisans Corses [*Corsican Guerrillas and Partisans*]   (PD)
FTPCS..... Failure to Pay Child Support
FT PDL...... Foot-Poundal [*Unit of work*]
FTP & E.... Flight Test Planning and Evaluation
FTPF.......... Federation des Travailleurs du Papier et de la Foret [*Federation of Paper and Forest Workers*] [*Canada*]
FTPI .... Flux Transitions per Inch
FTPI .... Future Time Perspective Inventory [*Psychology*]
FT PIL...... Fiat Pilulae [*Let Pills Be Made*] [*Pharmacy*]   (ROG)
FTPP .... Folklore. Tribuna del Pensamiento Peruano [*A publication*]
FTPPA....... Fizika i Teknika Poluprovodnikov [*Leningrad*] [*A publication*]
FTPR .... Federacion del Trabajo de Puerto Rico [*Puerto Rican Federation of Labor*]
FTPS.......... Fellow of the Technical Publishing Society
FTPTAG ... Advances in Animal Physiology and Animal Nutrition [*A publication*]
FT PULV... Fiat Pulvis [*Let a Powder Be Made*] [*Pharmacy*]
FT PULV SUBTIL ... Fiat Pulvis Subtilis [*Let a Fine Powder Be Made*] [*Pharmacy*]
FTQ .... Monterey/Fort Ord, CA [*Location identifier*] [*FAA*]   (FAAL)
FTR............ Australian Federal Tax Reporter [*A publication*]
FTR............ Factor   (KSC)
FTR............ Failed to Return [*British military*]   (DMA)
FTR............ Fails to Reproduce
FTR............ False Target Rate [*Military*]   (CAAL)
FTR............ Fan Thrust Reverser
FTR............ Fast Test Reactor
FTR............ Feather   (MSA)
FTR............ Federacion de Trabajadores Revolucionarios [*Revolutionary Workers' Federation*] [*El Salvador*]   (PD)
FTR............ Federal Telephone and Radio
FTR............ Federal Travel Regulations   (NRCH)
FTR............ Federal Trial Reports [*Maritime Law Book Company Ltd.*] [*Canada*] [*Information service or system*]   (CRD)
FTR............ Fighter   (AABC)
FTR............ Film Tracing Reproduction
FTR............ Final Technical Report
FTR............ Final Test Rack   (KSC)
FTR............ Finnish Trade Review [*Helsinki*] [*A publication*]
FTR............ Fixed Transom   (AAG)
FTR............ Flag Tower [*Maps and charts*]
FTR............ Flash Triangulation Reduction
FTR............ Flat-Tile Roof   (AAG)
FTR............ Flight Test Report
FTR............ Flight Test Requirements [*NASA*]   (NASA)
FTR............ Foreign Trade Reports
FTR............ Free-Text Retrieval [*Computer system alternative to Content-Addressable File Store*]
FTR............ Frontier Insurance Group, Inc. [*NYSE symbol*]   (SPSG)
FTR............ Frustrated Total Reflection
FTR............ Full-Time Regular [*Civil Service employee category*]
FTR............ Functional Test Report
FTR............ Functional Test Requirement   (IEEE)
F Tr .... Fusion Treaty [*European Communities*] [*1965*]   (ILCA)
FTRAC...... Full-Tracked Vehicle
FTRB .... Flight Test Review Board   (MCD)
FTRC........ Federal Telecommunications Records Center   (NRCH)
FTRD........ Flight Test Requirements Document [*NASA*]   (NASA)
FTRD........ Functional Test Requirements Document   (NASA)
FT Rep .... Foreign Trade Report [*A publication*]
FTRF .... Freedom to Read Foundation   (EA)

FT/RF........ Frequency Translator/Recursive Filter   (CAAL)
FTRF .... Full-Time Recruiting Force [*DoD*]
FTRFME..... Flight Test Rocket Facilities Mechanical Engineering   (AAG)
FTRG........ Flight Test Report Guide   (MCD)
FTRIA .... Fiziko-Tekhnicheskie Problemy Razrabotki Poleznykh Iskopaemykh [*A publication*]
FTRIA .... Flow and Temperature Removable Instrument Assembly [*Nuclear energy*]   (NRCH)
FTRM........ Flight Test Request Memorandum   (MCD)
FTRO........ Fighter Operations
FTRP .... Fighter Plans
FTRR & I... For Their Respective Rights and Interests [*Insurance*]   (AIA)
FTRT .... Flight Test Release Ticket   (MCD)
FTRW........ Flight Test Reports Writer   (MUGU)
FTRWPNSSq ... Fighter Weapons Squadron [*Air Force*]
FTS............ Facsimile Test Society
FTS............ Facteur Thymique Serique [*Synthetic Serum Thymic Factor*] [*Immunochemistry*] [*French*]
FTS............ Factory Test Set
FTS............ Factory Training School
FTS............ Faith Theological Seminary
FTS............ Fault Tolerance System
FTS............ Federal Telecommunications System [*of GSA*]
FTS............ Federal Telephone System   (KSC)
FTS............ Federal Teleprocessing Service [*GSA*]
FT/S .... Feet per Second
FTS............ Fellow of Technological Sciences
FTS............ Femtosecond Transition-State Spectroscope
FTS............ Femtosecond Transition-State Spectroscopy
FTS............ Field Computer Test Set
FTS............ Field Target Screen
FTS............ Field Test Support [*Aerospace*]   (AAG)
FTS............ Field Training Services [*Army*]   (AABC)
FTS............ Filled Thermal System [*Temperature sensor*]
FTS............ Financial Times [*A publication*]
FTS............ Financial Times. Supplements [*A publication*]
FTS............ Fine Track Sensor
FTS............ Fischer-Tropsch Synthesis [*Organic chemistry*]
FTS............ Fleet Training Squadron [*Navy*]
FTS............ Flexible Test Station
FTS............ Flight Telemetry Subsystem [*Spacecraft*]
FTS............ Flight Telerobotic Servicer [*NASA*]
FTS............ Flight Termination System   (AFM)
FTS............ Flight Test Sketch   (MCD)
FTS............ Flight Test Standard
FTS............ Flight Test Station   (MCD)
FTS............ Flight Test Support
FTS............ Flight Test System   (NASA)
FTS............ Flying Training School
FTS............ Foot Switch [*Industrial control*]   (IEEE)
FTS............ Ford's Theatre Society   (EA)
FTS............ Foreign Trade Statistics [*Bureau of Census*]
FTS............ Fortis, Inc. [*Toronto Stock Exchange symbol*]
FTS............ Fourier Transform Spectrometer [*or Spectroscopy*]
FTS............ Fourier Transform System
FTS............ Frame-Supported Tension Structure [*Tent*] [*Navy*]
FTS............ Free-Time System [*GE/PAC*]   (IEEE)
FTS............ Frequency Time Schedule   (NVT)
FTS............ Frequency Time Standard
FTS............ Frequency and Timing Subsystem [*Deep Space Instrumentation Facility, NASA*]
FTS............ Fuel Transfer System [*Nuclear energy*]   (NRCH)
FTS............ Full-Time Support
FTS............ Fulmer Technical Services [*Research center*] [*British*]   (IRC)
FTS............ Functional Test Specification   (KSC)
FTS............ Funds Transfer System
FTS............ Funeral Telegraph Service
FTS............ University of South Florida, Tampa, FL [*Library symbol*] [*Library of Congress*]   (LCLS)
FT²/S .... Square Feet per Second
FT³/S .... Cubic Feet per Second
FT & SA..... Fuel Transfer and Storage Assembly [*Nuclear energy*]   (NRCH)
FTSA .... Seaman Apprentice, Fire Control Technician, Striker [*Navy rating*]
FTSB .... First Federal Savings Bank of Tennessee [*NASDAQ symbol*]   (NQ)
FTSC .... Fault Tolerant Spaceborne Computer
FTSC .... Federal Telecommunications Standards Committee
FTSC .... Fellow in the Technology of Surface Coatings [*British*]   (DBQ)
FTSC .... First Savings Bank FSB [*NASDAQ symbol*]   (NQ)
FTSC .... [*US*] Foreign Trade Statistics, Classifications, and Cross-Classifications [*A publication*]
FT-SE .... Financial Times - Stock Exchange [*Stock index*] [*Pronounced "footsie"*] [*London, England*]
FT/SEC .... Feet per Second   (MCD)
FTSED ...... Filtration et Techniques Separatives [*A publication*]
FTSI.......... Fisher Transportation Services, Inc. [*NASDAQ symbol*]   (NQ)
FTS-M....... University of South Florida, College of Medicine, Tampa, FL [*Library symbol*] [*Library of Congress*]   (LCLS)
FTS-MC .... University of South Florida, Media Center, Tampa, FL [*Library symbol*] [*Library of Congress*]   (LCLS)

FTSMS...... Flying Training Student Management System [*Air Force*]
FTSN......... Seaman, Fire Control Technician, Striker [*Navy rating*]
FTSP......... First Team Sports, Inc. [*NASDAQ symbol*]   (NQ)
FTSq......... Flying Training Squadron [*Air Force*]
FTSR........ Foreign Trade Statistics Regulations
FTST......... Futurist [*A publication*]
FTSTP....... Flexible Test Station Test Procedure
FTT........... Failure to Thrive [*Syndrome*] [*Medicine*]
FTT........... Fanciful Tales of Time and Space [*A publication*]
FTT........... Fever Therapy Technician [*Navy*]
FTT........... Field Training Team [*Military*]   (CINC)
FTT........... Finning Ltd. [*Toronto Stock Exchange symbol*] [*Vancouver Stock Exchange symbol*]
FTT........... Finsk Teologisk Tidsskrift [*A publication*]
FTT........... Fischer-Tropsch Type [*Class of chemical reaction*]
FTT........... Five Task Test [*Psychology*]
FTT........... Fizika Tverdogo Tela [*A publication*]
FTT........... Flanged Tongue Terminal
FTT........... Flat Trim Template   (MSA)
FTT........... Free Territory of Trieste
FTT........... Fuel Transfer Tool
FTT........... Full-Time Temporary [*Civil Service employee category*]
FTT........... Fulton, MO [*Location identifier*] [*FAA*]   (FAAL)
FTTA........ Sarh [*Chad*] [*ICAO location identifier*]   (ICLI)
FTTB........ Bongor [*Chad*] [*ICAO location identifier*]   (ICLI)
FTTC........ Abeche [*Chad*] [*ICAO location identifier*]   (ICLI)
FTTD........ Full-Time Training Duty [*Army*]   (AABC)
FTTD........ Moundou [*Chad*] [*ICAO location identifier*]   (ICLI)
FTTE........ Biltine [*Chad*] [*ICAO location identifier*]   (ICLI)
FTTF........ Fada [*Chad*] [*ICAO location identifier*]   (ICLI)
FTtF.......... Florida College, Temple Terrace, FL [*Library symbol*] [*Library of Congress*]   (LCLS)
FTTF........ Freedom through Truth Foundation   (EA)
FTTG........ Goz-Beida [*Chad*] [*ICAO location identifier*]   (ICLI)
FTTH........ Lai [*Chad*] [*ICAO location identifier*]   (ICLI)
FTTI......... Ati [*Chad*] [*ICAO location identifier*]   (ICLI)
FTTJ......... N'Djamena [*Chad*] [*ICAO location identifier*]   (ICLI)
FTTK........ Bokoro [*Chad*] [*ICAO location identifier*]   (ICLI)
FTTL........ Bol [*Chad*] [*ICAO location identifier*]   (ICLI)
FTTM........ Few-Tube Test Model [*Nuclear energy*]   (NRCH)
FTTM........ Mongo [*Chad*] [*ICAO location identifier*]   (ICLI)
FTTN........ Am-Timan [*Chad*] [*ICAO location identifier*]   (ICLI)
FTTP......... Full-Time Temporary Personnel [*Employment*]
FTTP......... Pala [*Chad*] [*ICAO location identifier*]   (ICLI)
FTTPP....... Federation of Trainers and Training Programs in PsychoDrama   (EA)
FTTR......... Fretter, Inc. [*Livonia, MI*] [*NASDAQ symbol*]   (NQ)
FTTR......... Zouar [*Chad*] [*ICAO location identifier*]   (ICLI)
FT TROCH ... Fiat Trochisci [*Make Lozenges*] [*Pharmacy*]
FTTS......... Bousso [*Chad*] [*ICAO location identifier*]   (ICLI)
FTTS......... Flow-Through Tube Sampler [*Nuclear energy*]   (NRCH)
FTTT......... N'Djamena [*Chad*] [*ICAO location identifier*]   (ICLI)
FTTU........ Field Technical Training Unit   (MCD)
FTTU........ Mao [*Chad*] [*ICAO location identifier*]   (ICLI)
FTTV........ N'Djamena [*Chad*] [*ICAO location identifier*]   (ICLI)
FT & TW ... Desk, Combination Flat Top and Typewriter
FTTY......... Faya-Largeau [*Chad*] [*ICAO location identifier*]   (ICLI)
FTTZ........ Bardai-Zougra [*Chad*] [*ICAO location identifier*]   (ICLI)
FTU.......... Factory Training Unit   (KSC)
FTU.......... Fail Tension Ultimate   (MCD)
FTU.......... Federation of Theatre Unions [*British*]   (DCTA)
FTU.......... Federation of Trade Unions [*British*]   (DAS)
FTU.......... Ferry Training Unit [*British*]
FTU.......... Field Torpedo Unit
FTU.......... Field Transfusion Unit [*Military*] [*British*]
FTU.......... First Time Use
FTU.......... First Training Unit
FTU.......... First Union Corp. [*NYSE symbol*]   (SPSG)
FTU.......... Fleet Training Unit
FTU.......... Flight Test Unit   (KSC)
FTU.......... Fluorescein Thiourea [*Organic chemistry*]
FTU.......... Formazin Turbidity Unit [*Analytical chemistry*]
FTU.......... Fort Dauphin [*Madagascar*] [*Airport symbol*]   (OAG)
FTU.......... Freeman Time Unit [*Psychology*]
FTU.......... Frequency Transfer Unit
FTU.......... Fuel Transfer Unit [*NASA*]   (KSC)
FTU.......... University of Central Florida, Orlando, FL [*OCLC symbol*]   (OCLC)
FTU.......... University of Tampa, Tampa, FL [*Library symbol*] [*Library of Congress*]   (LCLS)
FTUB........ Free Trade Unions of Burma
FTUC........ Federal Trade Union Congress [*European*]
FT UNG .... Fiat Unguentum [*Make an Ointment*] [*Pharmacy*]
FTUP........ Free Trade Unions of the Philippines
FTURE...... Furniture   (ROG)
FTUS........ Full-Time Unit Support [*Army Reserve*]   (INF)
FT-UV/Vis ... Fourier-Transform Ultraviolet/Visible [*Spectrophotometer*]
FTV........... Fashion Television [*Video sales technique in the apparel industry*]
F & TV ...... Film et Televisie [*A publication*]
FTV........... Flight Television [*NASA*]   (KSC)

FTV........... Flight Test Vehicle [*Air Force*]
FTV........... Foxtail Mosaic Virus
FTV........... Functional Technical Validation   (SDI)
FTV........... Functional Technology Vehicle [*Army*]
FTV........... Masvingo [*Zimbabwe*] [*Airport symbol*]   (OAG)
FTV........... United States Veterans Administration Hospital, Tampa, FL [*Library symbol*] [*Library of Congress*]   (LCLS)
F & TV Kam ... Film und TV Kameramann [*A publication*]
FTVSP....... Flight Test Vehicle Safety Plan [*Air Force*]   (MCD)
F & TV Tech ... Film and Television Technician [*A publication*]
FTW.......... Fairmont [*Washington*] [*Seismograph station code, US Geological Survey*]   (SEIS)
FTW.......... Federation of Telephone Workers
FTW.......... Fighter Tactical Wing   (MCD)
FTW.......... Fizean Toothed Wheel
FTW.......... Footwall Exploration [*Vancouver Stock Exchange symbol*]
FTW.......... Foreign Trade Review [*A publication*]
FTW.......... Fort Worth, TX [*Location identifier*] [*FAA*]   (FAAL)
FTW.......... Forward Traveling Wave
FTW.......... Free Trade Wharf
FTW.......... Friends of the Third World   (EA)
FTWG....... Flight Test Working Group
FTWIAD ... Fort Wingate Army Depot [*New Mexico*]
FTWO....... Flight Test Work Order   (MCD)
FTWOAD ... Fort Worth Army Depot [*Texas*]
Ftwr File .... Men's, Women's, and Childrens' Footwear Fact File [*A publication*]
Ftwr News ... Footwear News [*A publication*]
FTWS .... Federal Train Wreck Statute
FTX.......... Field Test Exercise [*Military*]
FTX.......... Field Training Exercise [*Army*]   (INF)
FTX.......... Fleet Training Exercise
FTX.......... Fort Riley, KS [*Location identifier*] [*FAA*]   (FAAL)
FTX.......... Freeport-McMoRan, Inc. [*NYSE symbol*]   (SPSG)
FTX.......... Funnel-Web Spider Toxin
FTX.......... Owando [*Congo*] [*Airport symbol*]   (OAG)
FTY.......... Atlanta, GA [*Location identifier*] [*FAA*]   (FAAL)
FTY.......... Fookien Times Yearbook [*Manila*] [*A publication*]
FTY.......... Futurity Oils Ltd. [*Vancouver Stock Exchange symbol*]
FTyAF-T ... United States Air Force, Technical Library, Tyndall AFB, FL [*Library symbol*] [*Library of Congress*]   (LCLS)
FTZ.......... Federal Trade Zone
FTZ.......... Fernmeldetechnische Zeitschrift [*A publication*]
FTZ.......... Foreign Trade Zone [*New York City docks area*]
FTZ.......... Foristell, MO [*Location identifier*] [*FAA*]   (FAAL)
FTZ.......... Free Trade Zone   (IMH)
FTZ.......... Fushi Tarazu [*Not Enough Segments*] [*Genetics*] [*Japan*]
f-tz--- .... Tanzania [*MARC geographic area code*] [*Library of Congress*]   (LCCP)
FTZB .... Foreign Trade Zone Board
FU .... Air Littoral [*France*] [*ICAO designator*]   (FAAC)
FU .... Fecal Urobilinogen [*Clinical chemistry*]
FU .... Federal Union   (DAS)
Fu .... Finsen Unit [*for ultraviolet light*]
FU .... Firing Unit [*Military*]
FU .... Flight Unit   (MCD)
FU .... Fluorouracil [*Also, F*] [*Antineoplastic drug*]
FU .... Foederalistische Union [*Federal Union*] [*Federal Republic of Germany*] [*Political party*]   (PPE)
FU .... Folkuniversitetet
FU .... Follow-Up
FU .... Forecast Unit
FU .... Forecast Upper Air   (NATG)
FU .... Forstliche Umschau [*A publication*]
FU .... Fouled Up [*To describe a confused, mixed-up situation, person, or action*] [*Bowdlerized version*]
FU .... Fractional Urinalysis [*Medicine*]
FU .... Frame Unprotected [*Insurance classification*]
FU .... Frederick Ungar [*Publisher*]
FU .... Freeman Time Unit [*Psychology*]
FU .... Freie Union in Niedersachsen [*Free Union in Lower Saxony*] [*Federal Republic of Germany*] [*Political party*]   (PPW)
FU .... Freie Universitaet (Berlin) [*Free University (Berlin)*] [*Information retrieval*] [*Federal Republic of Germany*]
Fu .... Fucus [*Quality of the bottom*] [*Nautical charts*]
FU .... Fuel   (NASA)
FU .... Functional Unit [*Data processing*]
Fu .... Furche. Freie Kulturpolitische Wochenschrift [*A publication*]
FU .... Fuse   (MSA)
FU .... Smoke [*Aviation code*]   (FAAC)
fu----- .... Suez Canal [*MARC geographic area code*] [*Library of Congress*]   (LCCP)
FU .... University of Florida, Gainesville, FL [*Library symbol*] [*Library of Congress*]   (LCLS)
FUA .... Farm Underwriters Association [*Defunct*]
FUA .... Federal Unemployment Account [*Unemployment insurance*]
FUA .... Fire Unit Analyzer [*Military*]
FUA .... Follow-Up Amplifier
FUA .... Frente Unita Angolana [*Angolan United Front*]
FUA .... Fuel Use Act

f-ua--- .... United Arab Republic [*Egypt*] [*MARC geographic area code*] [*Library of Congress*] (LCCP)

FU-A .... University of Florida, Agricultural Experiment Station, Gainesville, FL [*Library symbol*] [*Library of Congress*] (LCLS)

FUA .... University of Florida, Agricultural Library, Gainesville, FL [*OCLC symbol*] (OCLC)

FUAA .... Filmmakers United Against Apartheid (EA)

FUAAV ...... Federation Universelle des Associations d'Agences de Voyages [*Universal Federation of Travel Agents' Associations - UFTAA*] (EAIO)

FUABBV ... Annali. Universita di Ferrara. Sezione III. Biologia Animale [*A publication*]

Fu Abstr ..... Fuel Abstracts [*A publication*]

Fu Abstr Curr Titl ... Fuel Abstracts and Current Titles. Institute of Fuel [*A publication*]

FUACE ...... Federation Universelle des Associations Chretiennes d'Etudiants [*Universal Federation of Christian Students Associations*]

FUAFA8 .... Annali. Universita di Ferrara. Sezione VI. Fisiologia e Chimica Biologica [*A publication*]

FUAI .... Front Uni pour l'Autonomie Interne [*United Front for Internal Autonomy*] [*French Polynesia*] [*Political party*] (PPW)

FUAM .... Freie und Angenommene Maurer [*Free and Accepted Mason*] [*German*] [*Freemasonry*]

FU (Amst) ... Free University Quarterly. A Quarterly of Christian Knowledge and Life (Amsterdam) [*A publication*]

FUB .... Facility Utilization Board (AFM)

FUB .... Federalist Union of Brittany [*See also UKB*] [*Bannalec, France*] (EAIO)

FUB .... Finance and Development [*A publication*]

Fu B .... Forschungen und Berichte. Staatliche Museen zu Berlin [*A publication*]

FUB .... Forward Utility Bridge (NASA)

FUB .... Front de l'Unite Bangala [*Bangala United Front*]

FUB .... Fube [*Japan*] [*Seismograph station code, US Geological Survey*] (SEIS)

FUB .... Fulleborn [*Papua New Guinea*] [*Airport symbol*] (OAG)

FUB .... Functional Uterine Bleeding [*Medicine*]

FUB .... Furman University. Bulletin [*A publication*]

FUB .... University of Florida, Law Library, Gainesville, FL [*OCLC symbol*] (OCLC)

FUBA .... Federal Unemployment Benefit and Allowance Account [*Unemployment insurance*]

FUBA .... Filologia. Instituto de Filologia Romancia Facultad de Filosofia y Letras. Universidad de Buenos Aires [*A publication*]

FUBAR ...... Fouled Up Beyond All Recognition [*Military slang*] [*Bowdlerized version*]

FUBB .... Fouled Up Beyond Belief [*Military slang*] [*Bowdlerized version*]

Fu Ber Bad Wuert ... Fundberichte aus Baden-Wuerttemberg [*A publication*]

Fu Ber Hessen ... Fundberichte aus Hessen [*A publication*]

Fu Ber Oe .... Fundberichte aus Oesterreich [*A publication*]

FUBX .... Fuse Box

FUCCO ..... First (United States Army Reserve) Company Chaplain Office

FUCL .... Fellow of University College, London [*British*] (ROG)

FUCO .... Fellow of University College, Oxford [*British*] (ROG)

FU-CP .... University of Florida, Chemistry-Pharmacy Library, Gainesville, FL [*Library symbol*] [*Library of Congress*] (LCLS)

FUD .... Fear, Uncertainty, and Doubt [*Factors hindering sales of lesser-known products*]

FUD .... Fellow of the University of Dublin (ROG)

FUD .... Fire Up Decoder

FUD .... First Use Date [*NASA*] (NASA)

FUD .... Frente Voluntario de Defensa [*Voluntary Defense Front*] [*Guatemala*] (PD)

Fudan J ...... Fudan Journal [*A publication*]

FUDD .... Fuddruckers, Inc. [*NASDAQ symbol*] (NQ)

FUDR .... Failure and Usage Data Report (IEEE)

FUDR .... Fluorodeoxyuridine [*Floxuridine*] [*Also, FldUrd*] [*Antineoplastic drug*]

FUDT .... Forensic Urine Drug Testing [*Analytical chemistry*]

FUE .... Federated Union of Employers [*Ireland*] (IMH)

FUE .... Fire Unit Effectiveness (MCD)

FUE .... First Unit Equipped (MCD)

FUE .... Fuerteventura [*Canary Islands*] [*Airport symbol*] (OAG)

Fu Econ Rev ... Fuel Economy Review [*A publication*]

FUED .... First Unit Equipped Date (MCD)

FUEL .... Fuel Users Emergency Line [*Pennsylvania*]

FUEL .... Griffith Consumers Co. [*Cheverly, MD*] [*NASDAQ symbol*] (NQ)

Fuel Abstr Curr Titles ... Fuel Abstracts and Current Titles [*A publication*]

Fuel Combust ... Fuel and Combustion [*Japan*] [*A publication*]

Fuel Econ ... Fuel Economy [*A publication*]

Fuel Econ 1925-1936 ... Fuel Economist (1925-1936) [*A publication*]

Fuel Econ Rev ... Fuel Economy Review [*A publication*]

Fuel Eff Bull ... Fuel Efficiency Bulletin [*A publication*]

Fuel Effic ... Fuel Efficiency [*A publication*]

Fuel & Energy Abstr ... Fuel and Energy Abstracts [*A publication*]

Fuel Oil J ... Fuel Oil Journal [*A publication*]

Fueloil & Oil Heat ... Fueloil and Oil Heat and Solar Systems [*A publication*]

Fueloil Oil Heat Sol Syst ... Fueloil and Oil Heat and Solar Systems [*A publication*]

Fuel Oil Temp J ... Fuel Oil and Temperature Journal [*A publication*]

Fuel- Orr- Gegegyogy ... Fuel-, Orr-, Gegegyogyaszat [*Hungary*] [*A publication*]

Fuel Processing Tech ... Fuel Processing Technology [*A publication*]

Fuel Process Technol ... Fuel Processing Technology [*Netherlands*] [*A publication*]

Fuel Res Inst (Pretoria) Bull ... Fuel Research Institute (Pretoria). Bulletin [*A publication*]

Fuel Res Inst S Afr Bull ... Fuel Research Institute of South Africa. Bulletin [*A publication*]

Fuel Sci Prac ... Fuel in Science and Practice [*A publication*]

Fuel Sci Pract ... Fuel in Science and Practice [*A publication*]

Fuels Furn ... Fuels and Furnaces [*A publication*]

Fuel Soc J .. Fuel Society Journal [*England*] [*A publication*]

FUEN .... Federal Union of European Nationalities [*Political party*] (PPW)

FUEV .... Foederalistische Union Europaeischer Volksgruppen [*Federal Union of European Nationalities*]

FUF .... Federation des Unions de Familles [*Federation of Family Unions*] [*Canada*]

FUF .... Federation for Universal French (EAIO)

FUF .... Finnisch-Ugrische Forschungen [*A publication*]

FuF .... Forschungen und Fortschritte [*A publication*]

FUFAB ..... Funk-Fachhaendler [*A publication*]

FUFO .... Fly-Under, Fly-Out (MCD)

FUFO .... Full Fuzing Option [*Air Force*]

FUFOD .... Fusion Forefront [*A publication*]

FUFOR .... Fund for UFO [*Unidentified Flying Object*] Research (EA)

FUFS .... First United Financial Services, Inc. [*Arlington Heights, IL*] [*NASDAQ symbol*] (NQ)

Fug .... De Fuga et Inventione [*Philo*] (BJA)

FUG .... Fuyang [*China*] [*Airport symbol*] (OAG)

f-ug--- .... Uganda [*MARC geographic area code*] [*Library of Congress*] (LCCP)

FUG .... University of Florida, Gainesville, FL [*OCLC symbol*] (OCLC)

Fugg Magyar ... Fuggetlen Magyarorszag [*A publication*] (APTA)

FUGIT .... First Union General Insurance Trust [*South Africa*] (ECON)

FUH .... University of Florida, Health Center Library, Gainesville, FL [*OCLC symbol*] (OCLC)

FU-HC .... University of Florida, J. Hillis Miller Health Center Library, Gainesville, FL [*Library symbol*] [*Library of Congress*] (LCLS)

FUHLR ..... Fuse Holder

FUHYD ..... Forum Umwelt Hygiene [*A publication*]

FUIF .... Fire Unit Integration Facility [*Military*]

FUINCA .... Fundacion para el Fomento de la Informacion Automatizada [*Foundation for the Promotion of Automated Information*] [*Information service or system*] (IID)

FUJ .... Front Upset Jaw (MSA)

FUJ .... Fuji Bank Bulletin [*Tokyo*] [*A publication*]

FUJ .... Fukue [*Japan*] [*Airport symbol*] (OAG)

Fu Jen Stud ... Fu Jen Studies [*A publication*]

FUJI .... Fuji Photo Film Co. Ltd. [*NASDAQ symbol*] (NQ)

Fuji Bank ... Fuji Bank Bulletin [*A publication*]

Fuji Bank Bul ... Fuji Bank Bulletin [*A publication*]

Fuji Electr J ... Fuji Electric Journal [*A publication*]

Fuji Electr Rev ... Fuji Electric Review [*A publication*]

Fujikura Tech Rev ... Fujikura Technical Review [*A publication*]

Fujitsu Sci Tech J ... Fujitsu Scientific and Technical Journal [*Japan*] [*A publication*]

FUJTA .... Fujitsu [*A publication*]

FUK .... Fukui [*Japan*] [*Seismograph station code, US Geological Survey*] (SEIS)

FUK .... Fukuoka [*Japan*] [*Airport symbol*] (OAG)

Fukien Acad Res Bull ... Fukien Academy. Research Bulletin [*A publication*]

Fukien Agric J ... Fukien Agricultural Journal [*A publication*]

Fukien Christ Univ Sci J ... Fukien Christian University. Science Journal [*A publication*]

FUKOB .... Funtai Kogaku [*A publication*]

Fukuoka Acta Med ... Fukuoka Acta Medica [*A publication*]

Fukushima J Med Sci ... Fukushima Journal of Medical Science [*A publication*]

Fukushima Med J ... Fukushima Medical Journal [*A publication*]

Fukush J Med Sci ... Fukushima Journal of Medical Science [*A publication*]

FUL .... Florida Union List of Serials, Gainesville, FL [*OCLC symbol*] [*Inactive*] (OCLC)

FUL .... Front Uni Liberateur de la Guinee Portuguesa et des Isles du Cap Vert [*United Liberation Front of Portuguese Guinea and Cape Verde*] [*Political party*]

FUL .... Fulcrum (MSA)

FUL .... Fullerton [*California*] [*Airport symbol*] (OAG)

FUL .... Fullerton, CA [*Location identifier*] [*FAA*] (FAAL)

FUL .... Funchal [*Madeira Island*] [*Seismograph station code, US Geological Survey*] (SEIS)

FU-L .... University of Florida, Law Library, Gainesville, FL [*Library symbol*] [*Library of Congress*] (LCLS)

Fulb Par ..... Fulbeck's Parallel [*A publication*] (DLA)

Fulbright Educ Dev Program Grantee Rep ... Fulbright Educational Development Program Grantee Reports [*A publication*] (APTA)

Fulbright Univ Adm Program Grantee Rep ... Fulbright University Administrator Program Grantee Reports [*A publication*] (APTA)

Fulb St Law ... Fulbeck's Study of the Law [*A publication*] (DLA)

FULC........ First Unit Loading Cost

Fulg............ [*Raphael*] Fulgosius [*Deceased, 1427*] [*Authority cited in pre-1607 legal work*] (DSA)

Fulgo......... [*Raphael*] Fulgosius [*Deceased, 1427*] [*Authority cited in pre-1607 legal work*] (DSA)

Fulgos........ [*Raphael*] Fulgosius [*Deceased, 1427*] [*Authority cited in pre-1607 legal work*] (DSA)

FULICO.... Fidelity Union Life Insurance Company

FULK........ Front Uni de Liberation Kanake [*Political party*] [*New Caledonia*] (FEA)

FULL........ Fuller [*H. B.*] Co. [*NASDAQ symbol*] (NQ)

Full BR...... Bengal Full Bench Rulings [*North-Western Provinces, India*] [*A publication*] (DLA)

Full Ch Hist ... Fuller's Church History [*A publication*] (DLA)

Fuller......... Fuller's Reports [*59-105 Michigan*] [*A publication*] (DLA)

Fuller (Mich) ... Fuller's Reports [*59-105 Michigan*] [*A publication*] (DLA)

Fulmer Res Inst Newsl ... Fulmer Research Institute. Newsletter [*A publication*]

Fulmer Res Inst Spec Rep ... Fulmer Research Institute. Special Report [*A publication*]

FulN.......... Fulbright Newsletter [*A publication*]

FULRO...... Front Unifie de la Lutte de la Race Opprime [*United Front for the Struggle of Oppressed Races*] (CINC)

FULS......... Florida Union List of Serials

FULT......... Fulton Financial Corp. [*Lancaster, PA*] [*NASDAQ symbol*] (NQ)

Fult............ Fulton's Supreme Court Reports, Bengal [*1842-44*] [*India*] [*A publication*] (DLA)

Fulton........ Fulton's Supreme Court Reports, Bengal [*1842-44*] [*India*] [*A publication*] (DLA)

FUM.......... Fluorouracil, Methotrexate [*Antineoplastic drug regimen*]

FUM.......... Friendly Union of Mechanics [*British*]

FUM.......... Friends United Meeting

FUM.......... Fumarate

FUM.......... Fumigate (AABC)

FUM.......... Functional User's Manual (AABC)

FUMIST ... Fellow of the University of Manchester Institute of Science and Technology [*British*]

FUMM...... [*The*] Fellowship of United Methodist Musicians (EA)

FUMRA2 .. FAO [*Food and Agriculture Organization of the United Nations*] General Fisheries Council for the Mediterranean. Studies and Reviews [*A publication*]

FUMTU .... Fouled Up More Than Usual [*See FU*] [*Bowdlerized version*]

FUN........... Atlanta, GA [*Location identifier*] [*FAA*] (FAAL)

FUN........... Cedar Fair Limited Partnership [*NYSE symbol*] (SPSG)

FUN........... Fantasy Unrestricted Network [*Cable-television system*]

FUN........... Forty Upward Network

FUN........... Fractional and Unknown Nuclear [*Material in meteorites*]

FUN........... Free University Network [*Later, LERN*] (EA)

FUN........... Frente de Unidad Nacional [*National Unity Front*] [*Guatemala*] [*Political party*] (PPW)

FUN........... Frente Unido Nacionalista [*Nationalist United Front*] [*Venezuela*] [*Political party*] (PPW)

FUN........... From Unknown Worlds [*A publication*]

FUN........... Funafuti Atol [*Tuvalu*] [*Airport symbol*] (OAG)

FUN........... Funatsu [*Kawaguchuko*] [*Japan*] [*Seismograph station code, US Geological Survey*] (SEIS)

FUN........... Function (MDG)

FUN........... Fundament [*Slang*] [*British*] (DSUE)

FUNA........ Front d'Union Nationale de l'Angola [*National Union Front of Angola*]

FUNAAO .. Fauna [*Oslo*] [*A publication*]

FUNC........ Force de l'Union National Cambodge [*Cambodia*] [*Political party*]

FUNC........ Function (AABC)

Func.......... Functions [*A publication*]

FUNCINPEC ... National United Front for an Independent National, Peaceful, and Cooperative Kampuchea [*Political party*] (PD)

FUNCT...... Function (KSC)

FUNCT...... Functional (NASA)

Funct Approx Comment Math ... Functiones et Approximatio Commentarii Mathematici [*A publication*]

Funct Approximatio Comment Math ... Functiones et Approximatio Commentarii Mathematici [*A publication*]

Functional Anal Appl ... Functional Analysis and Its Applications [*A publication*]

FUNCTLINE ... Functional Line Diagram (MCD)

Funct Orthod ... Functional Orthodontist [*A publication*]

Funct Photgr ... Functional Photography [*A publication*]

Funct Photogr ... Functional Photography [*A publication*]

Funct Polym ... Functional Polymer [*A publication*]

FUND........ America's All Season Fund, Inc. [*NASDAQ symbol*] (NQ)

FUND........ Fundamental (MSA)

Fundam Aerosp Instrum ... Fundamentals of Aerospace Instrumentation [*A publication*]

Fundam Appl Toxicol ... Fundamental and Applied Toxicology [*A publication*]

Fundam Aspects Pollut Control Environ Sci ... Fundamental Aspects of Pollution Control and Environmental Science [*A publication*]

Fundam Balneo Bioclimatol ... Fundamenta Balneo Bioclimatologica [*A publication*]

Fundam Cosmic Phys ... Fundamentals of Cosmic Physics [*A publication*]

Fundam Cosm Phys ... Fundamentals of Cosmic Physics [*A publication*]

Fundamentals Proc Design Dev ... Fundamentals, Process Design, and Development [*A publication*]

Fundamental Stud in Comput Sci ... Fundamental Studies in Computer Science [*A publication*]

Fundam Phenom Mater Sci ... Fundamental Phenomena in the Material Sciences [*A publication*]

Fundam Radiol ... Fundamental Radiologica [*A publication*]

Fundam Sci ... Fundamenta Scientiae [*A publication*]

Fund Bariloche Ser ... Fundacion Bariloche Series [*A publication*]

Fundber Hessen ... Fundberichte aus Hessen [*A publication*]

Fundber Oesterreich ... Fundberichte aus Oesterreich [*A publication*]

Fundber Schwaben ... Fundberichte aus Schwaben [*A publication*]

Fund Bras Conserv Nat Bol Inf ... Fundacao Brasileira para a Conservacao da Natureza Boletim Informativo [*A publication*]

Fundb Schwaben ... Fundberichte aus Schwaben [*A publication*]

Fund Inform ... Fundamenta Informaticae [*A publication*]

Fund Informat ... Fundamenta Informaticae [*A publication*]

Fund Math ... Fundamenta Mathematicae [*A publication*]

Fund Miguel Lillo Misc ... Fundacion Miguel Lillo Miscelanea [*A publication*]

Fund Raising Manage ... Fund Raising Management [*A publication*]

Fund Raising Mgt ... Fund Raising Management [*A publication*]

Fund Sci...... Fundamenta Scientiae [*A publication*]

FUNDWI .. Fund for the United Nations for the Development of West Irian

Fund Zoobot Rio Grande Do Sul Publ Avulsas ... Fundacao Zoobotanica do Rio Grande Do Sul. Publicacoes Avulsas [*A publication*]

Fung Herb Insect ... Fungicides, Herbicides, Insecticides [*A publication*]

FUNGIC.... Fungicide

Fungi Can ... Fungi Canadenses [*A publication*]

FUNILS .... Flinders University of South Australia, National Institute of Labour Studies

Funkc Anal ... Funkcional'nyj Analiz i Ego Prilozenija [*A publication*]

Funkcial Ekvac ... Funkcialaj Ekvaciog [*A publication*]

Funk Scott Annu Ind ... Funk and Scott Annual Index of Corporations and Industries [*A publication*]

Funk Scott Index Corp Ind ... Funk and Scott Index of Corporations and Industries [*A publication*]

Funk T .... Funk-Technik [*A publication*]

Funk-Tech ... Funk-Technik [*A publication*]

Funkt Morphol Organ Zelle ... Funktionelle und Morphologische Organisation der Zelle [*A publication*]

Funktsional Anal i Prilozhen ... Akademiya Nauk SSSR. Funktsional'nyi Analiz i ego Prilozheniya [*A publication*]

Funkts Org Usloviyakh Izmen Gazov Sredy ... Funktsii Organizma v Usloviyakh Izmenennoi Gazovoi Sredy [*A publication*]

FUNL........ Federation of Unions of Workers and Employees of North Lebanon

FUNL........ Funnel (MSA)

FUNLOG .. Functional Programming and Prolog

FUNN........ Pizza Entertainment Centers [*NASDAQ symbol*] (NQ)

FUNOP..... Full Normal Plot [*Data processing*]

FUNSA...... Fabrica Uruguaya de Neumaticos, Sociedad Anonima [*A tire manufacturer*]

FUNT........ French Underground Nuclear Test (MCD)

FUNU........ Force d'Urgence des Nations Unies

FUNY........ Free University of New York

FUO........... Fever of Undetermined Origin [*Medicine*]

FUO........... Follow-Up Output (NASA)

FUOFAA... Fauna och Flora [*Stockholm*] [*A publication*]

FUOP........ Fix Up on Printer [*Have technician add or change an effect by means of optical printing*] [*Motion-picture production*]

FUP........... Facility Utilization Plan (AFM)

FUP........... Falciparum Uganda - Palo Alto [*Plasmodium strain causing malaria*]

FUP........... Forming Up Place (MCD)

FUP........... Forward Unity Periscope

FUP........... Frente por la Unidad del Pueblo [*United Popular Front*] [*Colombia*] [*Political party*] (PPW)

FUP........... Fusion Point

FUPAC...... Federacion de Universidades Privadas de America Central

FUPCD...... Fonds un Pour Cent pour le Developpement [*One Percent for Development Fund*] (EAIO)

FUPOSAT ... Follow-Up on Supply Action Taken

FUPP......... Full-Up Powerpack [*Military*]

Fuppy......... Female Urban Professional [*Lifestyle classification*]

FUPRO...... Future Production (MCD)

FUQ........... Free University Quarterly. A Quarterly of Christian Knowledge and Life [*Amsterdam*] [*A publication*]

FUQ........... Fuquene [*Colombia*] [*Geomagnetic observatory code*]

FUQ........... Fuquene [*Colombia*] [*Seismograph station code, US Geological Survey*] (SEIS)
FUR .... Failure or Unsatisfactory Report
FUR .... File Utility Routines [*Data processing*]
FUR .... First Union Real Estate Equity & Mortgage Investments SBI [*NYSE symbol*] (SPSG)
FUR .... Follow-Up Report
FUR .... Forma Urbis Romae [*Rome*] [*A publication*] (OCD)
FUR .... Frente Unido de la Revolucion [*United Revolutionary Front*] [*Guatemala*] [*Political party*] (PPW)
FUR .... Fuerstenfeldbruck [*Federal Republic of Germany*] [*Geomagnetic observatory code*]
FUR .... Fuerstenfeldbruck [*Federal Republic of Germany*] [*Seismograph station code, US Geological Survey*] (SEIS)
Fur............. Furioso [*A publication*]
FUR .... Furlong [*Unit of distance*]
FUR .... Furnace (MSA)
FUR .... Furnished
FUR .... Furred [*Technical drawings*]
FUR .... Further (AABC)
FUR .... Futures [*A publication*]
FUR-30...... Frente Universitario Revolucionario 30 de Julio [*30th July Revolutionary University Front*] [*El Salvador*]
FURA .... Federal Utility Regulation, Annotated [*A publication*] (DLA)
FUra........... French Urania [*Record label*]
FURAM ..... Ftorafur [*Tegafur*], Adriamycin, Mitomycin C [*Antineoplastic drug regimen*]
FURAS...... For Further Assignment
FUREPT ... [*And*] Further Report To [*Army*] (AABC)
FURF......... Federation des Unions Royalistes de France [*Federation of Royalist Unions of France*] (PPW)
FURL......... Furlough [*Military*] (ROG)
Furl L & T ... Furlong on the Irish Law of Landlord and Tenant [*A publication*] (DLA)
FurmS .... Furman Studies [*A publication*]
FURN .... Furnace
FURN .... Furnish (AFM)
FURN .... Furniture
FURNC ...... Furnishing 2000, Inc. [*NASDAQ symbol*] (SPSG)
FURNIDEC ... International Fair of Furniture, Decoration, Lighting Fixtures, Machinery, and Equipment [*Hellexpo*] (TSPED)
Furnit Manuf ... Furniture Manufacturer [*A publication*]
Furniture Wkrs P ... Furniture Workers Press [*A publication*]
Furn Mfr.... Furniture Manufacturer [*A publication*]
FURN PTS ... Furniture Parts [*Freight*]
FURO......... Furioso [*Furiously*] [*Music*] (ROG)
FURPO...... Full Utilization of Rural Program Opportunities (EA)
FURPUR... File Utility Routines, Program Utility Routines [*Data processing*]
FURR........ Furrier
FURR........ Further
FURS......... Antonovich, Inc. [*NASDAQ symbol*] (NQ)
FURS......... Failure or Unsatisfactory Report System
FURS......... Follow-Up Reporting System (MCD)
FURTH ..... Further
FURTH C ... Further Care [*Medicine*]
Fur Trade J Can ... Fur Trade Journal of Canada [*A publication*]
FURTS ...... Furnished This Station [*Army*] (AABC)
Furukawa Electr Rev ... Furukawa Electric Review [*A publication*]
Furukawa Rev ... Furukawa Review [*A publication*]
FURWA ..... Furrow [*A publication*]
FUS............ Far Ultraviolet Spectrometer [*NASA*]
FUS............ Feline Urologic Syndrome
FUS............ Film Unit Secretary
FUS............ Firing Unit Simulator
FUS............ Focused Ultrasonic Surgery
FUS............ FORTRAN [*Formula Translating System*] Utility System [*Data processing*]
FUS............ Frontul Unitatii Socialiste [*Front of Socialist Unity*] [*Romania*] [*Political party*] (PPE)
FUS............ Fusa [*Let It Be Fused*] [*Pharmacy*] (ROG)
FUS............ Fuselage [*Aviation*] (AABC)
FUS............ Fusilier
FUSA......... First United States Army
FUSAC...... Finno-Ugrian Studies Association of Canada [*See also ACEFO*]
FUSAG...... First United States Army Group
FUSB......... First United Savings Bank FSB [*NASDAQ symbol*] (NQ)
FUSE......... Far Ultraviolet Satellite Experiment (MCD)
FUSE........ Federation for Unified Science Education (EA)
FUSES...... Fordham Urban Solar Eco-System
FUSF .... Fortsetzung und Schluss Folgen [*To Be Continued and Concluded*] [*German*]
FUSHA ..... Funkschau [*A publication*]
Fusion Energy Found Newsl ... Fusion Energy Foundation. Newsletter [*A publication*]
Fusion Power Assoc Exec Newsl ... Fusion Power Associates. Executive Newsletter [*A publication*]
Fusion Power Rep ... Fusion Power Report [*A publication*]
Fusion Technol ... Fusion Technology [*A publication*]
FUSLA ...... Friends of the United States of Latin America (EA)
FUS/LF ..... Fuselage, Lower Forward (MCD)

FUSLG ...... Fuselage [*Aviation*] (MSA)
FUSOB...... Friendly United Society of Operative Brickmakers [*A union*] [*British*]
FUSOD ..... Future of Scientific Ocean Drilling [*Marine science*] (MSC)
FUSRAP.... Formerly Utilized Sites Remedial Action Program [*Department of Energy*]
Fussboden Ztg ... Fussboden Zeitung [*West Germany*] [*A publication*]
FUST .... Full-Up System Test (RDA)
FUSTA ...... Fujitsu Scientific and Technical Journal [*Japan*] [*A publication*]
FUS/UF .... Fuselage, Upper Forward (MCD)
FUT .... Federal Unemployment Tax (MCD)
FUT .... Fire Until Touchdown [*Apollo*] [*NASA*]
FUT .... Fleet Utility [*Navy*]
FUT .... Futura Airlines Ltd. [*Vancouver, BC, Canada*] [*FAA designator*] (FAAC)
FUT .... Future
Fut............ Future Fiction [*A publication*]
Fut............ Futures [*A publication*]
Fut............ Futurist [*A publication*]
FUT .... University of Tampa, Tampa, FL [*OCLC symbol*] (OCLC)
FUTA........ Federal Unemployment Tax Act [*1954*]
FUTA........ Friends United through Astronomy (EA)
Fut Abstr... Future Abstracts [*A publication*]
FUTB........ Futbol Internacional [*Ministerio de Cultura*] [*Spain*] [*Information service or system*] (CRD)
FUTC........ Federacion Unica de Trabajadores Campesinos [*Single Federation of Peasant Workers*] [*Bolivia*] (PD)
FUTEA...... Funk-Technik [*A publication*]
FUTF........ Future Science Fiction [*A publication*]
FUTJA...... Foundry Trade Journal [*A publication*]
Fut L .... Future Life [*A publication*]
FUTR........ Jack Carl/312 Futures, Inc. [*Chicago, IL*] [*NASDAQ symbol*] (NQ)
FUTS........ Firing Unit Test Set
FUTS......... Futuristic Stories [*A publication*]
FUTU........ Futures [*A publication*]
FUTU........ Futures Information Service [*Institute for Futures Studies*] [*Information service or system*] [*Defunct*]
FUTUA ..... Futurist [*A publication*]
FUTUB ..... Futures [*A publication*]
FUTUD ..... Futuribles [*A publication*]
FUTURE... Friends United Toward Understanding, Rights, and Equality
Future Sur ... Future Survey [*A publication*]
FUU.......... Federacion de Universitarios de Uruguay [*Federation of University Students of Uruguay*] (PD)
FUU.......... Foundation of Universal Unity (EA)
FUV .... Far-Ultraviolet [*Spectra*]
FUV .... For Ultraviolet
f-uv--- .... Upper Volta [*MARC geographic area code*] [*Library of Congress*] (LCCP)
FUVD .... Far Ultraviolet Detector
FUW .... Federation of University Women
FUWOB .... Forward Unconventional Warfare Operations Base (MCD)
FUWPM.... Free University, Washington-Paris-Moscow [*An association*] (EA)
FUWW ...... Federal Union of Wire Weavers of the United Kingdom
FUY .... Fury Exploration Ltd. [*Vancouver Stock Exchange symbol*]
FUZ .... Frente Urbana Zapatista [*Mexico*]
FUZED...... Fussboden Zeitung [*A publication*]
Fuzzy Math ... Fuzzy Mathematics [*A publication*]
Fuzzy Sets and Syst ... Fuzzy Sets and Systems [*A publication*]
FV .... Aero Tour [*France*] [*ICAO designator*] (FAAC)
FV .... Face Value (ADA)
FV .... Fashion Victim [*Women's Wear Daily*]
Fv .... Femoral Vein [*Anatomy*]
FV .... Femtovolt (MDG)
FV .... Fighting Vehicle [*Bradley*] [*Army*]
FV .... Final Value
FV .... Finnaviation Oy [*Finland*] [*ICAO designator*] (FAAC)
FV .... Fired Vessel [*Insurance*]
FV .... Firing Velocity
FV .... Flight Vehicle
FV .... Flight Version (MCD)
FV .... Floor Valve (NRCH)
FV .... Fluid Volume
FV .... Flush Valve [*Technical drawings*]
FV .... Flux Valve
FV .... Folio Verso [*On the Back of the Page*] [*Latin*]
FV .... Forward Visibility
FV .... Freeze Voter (EA)
FV .... French RCA (Victor) [*Record label*]
F/V .... Frequency to Voltage (IEEE)
FV .... Friend Virus [*Also, FDV, FLV*]
FV .... Front View (MSA)
FV .... Fruit and Vegetable Division [*of Agricultural Research Service*] [*Department of Agriculture*]
FV .... Fuel Valve (AAG)
FV .... Full Above the Eaves (ROG)
FV .... Full Voltage (MSA)
FV .... Future Value [*Finance*]

fv---- .... Volta River and Basin [*MARC geographic area code*] [*Library of Congress*]   (LCCP)
FVA .... Air Virginia, Inc. [*Lynchburg, VA*] [*FAA designator*]   (FAAC)
FVA .... Fellow of the Valuers' Association [*British*]   (DAS)
FVA .... Fighting Vehicle Armament   (RDA)
FVA .... Film/Video Arts   (EA)
FVA .... Floor Valve Adapter   (NRCH)
FVA .... Flying Veterinarians Association   (EA)
FVA .... Fredonia Veterans Association   (EA)
FVB .... First Virginia Bankshares Corp. [*NYSE symbol*]   (SPSG)
FVB........... Fitzwilliam Virginal Book
FVB........... Future Villain Band [*Evil rock music group in 1978 film "Sgt. Pepper's Lonely Hearts Club Band"*]
FVBB .... Beit Bridge [*Zimbabwe*] [*ICAO location identifier*]   (ICLI)
FVBD........ Bindura [*Zimbabwe*] [*ICAO location identifier*]   (ICLI)
FVbF......... Florida Medical Entomology Laboratory, Vero Beach, FL [*Library symbol*] [*Library of Congress*]   (LCLS)
FVBU......... Bulawayo/Bulawayo [*Zimbabwe*] [*ICAO location identifier*]   (ICLI)
FVC........... Fixed Vacuum Capacitor
FVC........... Forced Vital Capacity [*Physiology*]
FVC........... Franciscan Vocation Conference [*Formerly, AFSV*] [*Defunct*]   (EA)
FVC........... Fraser Valley College Learning Resources Centre [*UTLAS symbol*]
FVC........... Frozen Vegetable Council   (EA)
FVC........... Valencia Community College, Orlando, FL [*OCLC symbol*]   (OCLC)
FVCH .... Chipinge [*Zimbabwe*] [*ICAO location identifier*]   (ICLI)
FVCM........ Fellow of the Victoria College of Music [*London*] [*British*]   (ROG)
FVCP .... Harare/Charles Prince [*Zimbabwe*] [*ICAO location identifier*]   (ICLI)
FVCV .... Chiredzi/Buffalo Range [*Zimbabwe*] [*ICAO location identifier*]   (ICLI)
FVD .... Front Vertex Back Focal Distance
FVD .... Fuel Vapor Detector
FVDE......... Fighting Vehicles Design Establishment [*British military*]   (DMA)
FVE........... Federation of Veterinarians of the EEC   (EAIO)
FVE........... Forced Volume, Expiratory [*Physiology*]
FVE........... Frenchville, ME [*Location identifier*] [*FAA*]   (FAAL)
F VENOES ... Fiat Venaesectio [*Let the Patient Be Bled*] [*Pharmacy*]   (ROG)
F-VF.......... Fine to Very Fine [*Philately*]
FVF........... Finevest Foods [*NYSE symbol*]   (SPSG)
FVF........... First Vertical Flight [*NASA*]   (NASA)
FVFA .... Victoria Falls/Victoria Falls [*Zimbabwe*] [*ICAO location identifier*]   (ICLI)
FVFP .... Filed VFR [*Visual Flight Rules*] Flight Plan [*Aviation*]   (FAAC)
FVFSA........ Fortschritte der Verfahrenstechnik [*A publication*]
FVGDCF ... Fishing Vessel and Gear Damage Compensation Fund [*National Oceanic and Atmospheric Administration*]
FVGO .... Gokwe [*Zimbabwe*] [*ICAO location identifier*]   (ICLI)
FVGR........ Mutare/Grand Reef [*Zimbabwe*] [*ICAO location identifier*]   (ICLI)
FVGW .... Gweru/Gweru [*Zimbabwe*] [*ICAO location identifier*]   (ICLI)
FVH.......... Fulminant [*or Fulminating*] Viral Hepatitis [*Medicine*]
FVHA .... Harare/Harare [*Zimbabwe*] [*ICAO location identifier*]   (ICLI)
FVHQ........ Harare [*Zimbabwe*] [*ICAO location identifier*]   (ICLI)
FVI............ Final Voluntary Indefinite [*Status*] [*Army*]   (INF)
FVI............ First Volar Interosseous Muscle [*Myology*]
FVI............ Forage Value Index [*Agriculture*]
FVIF .... Future Value Interest Factor [*Finance*]
FVIN.......... Bulawayo/Induna [*Zimbabwe*] [*ICAO location identifier*]   (ICLI)
FVIP .... Fishing Vessel Insurance Plan [*Canada*]
FVIRL .... Fruit and Vegetable Insects Research Laboratory [*Closed 1985*] [*Vincennes, IN*] [*Department of Agriculture*]   (GRD)
FVKA .... Karoi [*Zimbabwe*] [*ICAO location identifier*]   (ICLI)
FVKB .... Kariba/Kariba [*Zimbabwe*] [*ICAO location identifier*]   (ICLI)
FVKK .... Kwekwe [*Zimbabwe*] [*ICAO location identifier*]   (ICLI)
FVL........... Femoral Vein Ligation [*Medicine*]
FVL........... Flow Volume Loop [*Hemodialysis*]
FVL........... Forschungen zur Volks- und Landeskunde [*A publication*]
FVM .... Five-Mile Camp, AK [*Location identifier*] [*FAA*]   (FAAL)
FVM .... Fluid Vacancy Model
FVM .... French Village [*Missouri*] [*Seismograph station code, US Geological Survey*]   (SEIS)
FVMA .... Marondera [*Zimbabwe*] [*ICAO location identifier*]   (ICLI)
FVMF........ Friends of Vieilles Maisons Francaises   (EA)
FVMMA.... Floor and Vacuum Machinery Manufacturers' Association [*Defunct*]   (EA)
FVMS........ Fluid Volume Measurement System   (MCD)
FVMT........ Mutoko [*Zimbabwe*] [*ICAO location identifier*]   (ICLI)
FVMU........ Mutare/Mutare [*Zimbabwe*] [*ICAO location identifier*]   (ICLI)
FVMUDL ... Flora et Vegetatio Mundi [*A publication*]
FVMV........ Masvingo/Masvingo [*Zimbabwe*] [*ICAO location identifier*]   (ICLI)
FVNC .... Fondation Vietnam-Canada [*Vietnam-Canada Foundation*]
FVO .... Fluidic Valve Operator
FVO .... For Valuation Only [*Business term*]

FVOC .... Facel Vega Owners Club   (EA)
FVP........... Feasibility Validation Program
FVP........... Flash-Vacuum Pyrolysis
FVP........... Fluid Velocity Potential
FVP........... Freie Volkspartei [*Free People's Party*] [*Federal Republic of Germany*] [*Political party*]   (PPE)
FVPB .... Flight Vehicle Power Branch
FVPD........ Film/Video Producers and Distributors [*National Film Board of Canada*] [*Information service or system*]   (CRD)
FVPPA ...... Families of Vietnamese Political Prisoners Association   (EA)
FVR........... Feline Viral Rhinotracheitis [*Vaccine*]
FVR........... Fiber Volume Ratio
FVR........... Forearm Vascular Resistance [*Medicine*]
FVR........... Functional Vestibular Reserve [*Orientation*]
FVR........... Fuse Voltage Rating
FVRC .... Foreign Vehicle Resource Center [*Tank-Automotive Command*] [*Army*]
FVRDE...... Fighting Vehicles Research and Development Establishment [*British*]
FVRU .... Rusape [*Zimbabwe*] [*ICAO location identifier*]   (ICLI)
F VS........... Fiat Venaesectio [*Let the Patient Be Bled*] [*Pharmacy*]
FVS........... Fighting Vehicle Systems   (RDA)
FVS........... Flight Vehicles Systems   (MCD)
FVS........... Forer Vocational Survey [*Psychology*]
FVS........... Forest, MS [*Location identifier*] [*FAA*]   (FAAL)
FVSC .... Fraser Videotex Services [*Information service or system*]   (IID)
FVSC .... Fort Valley State College [*Georgia*]
FVSH......... Zvishavane [*Zimbabwe*] [*ICAO location identifier*]   (ICLI)
FVSNA ...... Friends Vegetarian Society of North America   (EA)
FVSV......... Victoria Falls/Spray View [*Zimbabwe*] [*ICAO location identifier*]   (ICLI)
FVT........... Family Viewing Time [*Television*]
FVT........... Field Validation Test
FVT........... Flash-Vacuum Thermolysis
FVT........... Functional Validation Test [*Army*]
FVTL......... Gweru/Thornhill [*Zimbabwe*] [*ICAO location identifier*]   (ICLI)
FVTLAQ ... Folia Veterinaria Latina [*A publication*]
FVTS .... Field Verification Test Set   (MCD)
FVU .... File Verification Utility [*Data processing*]
FVU .... Functional Verification Unit [*Photography*]
FVV .... Flight Verification Vehicle   (KSC)
FVVM........ Friends of the Vietnam Veterans Memorial   (EA)
FVW .... Forward Volume Wave [*Telecommunications*]   (TEL)
FVWN .... Hwange/Hwange National Park [*Zimbabwe*] [*ICAO location identifier*]   (ICLI)
FVWS .... Female Voice Warning System   (MCD)
FVWT .... Hiwange Town [*Zimbabwe*] [*ICAO location identifier*]   (ICLI)
FVWU .... Free Visayan Workers' Union [*Philippines*]
FVX........... Farmville, VA [*Location identifier*] [*FAA*]   (FAAL)
FVZC .... Zisco [*Zimbabwe*] [*ICAO location identifier*]   (ICLI)
fw----- .... Africa, West [*MARC geographic area code*] [*Library of Congress*]   (LCCP)
FW .... Face Width   (MSA)
FW .... Fascinating Womanhood [*Title of book by Helen Andelin and of antifeminist seminars*]
FW .... Feed Water   (KSC)
F & W........ Feeding and Watering [*Charge*] [*Business term*]
FW .... Felix-Weil [*Reaction*] [*Clinical chemistry*]
FW .... Field Weakening
FW .... Field Weld   (NRCH)
FW .... Field Worship [*Army*] [*British*]
FW .... Fighter Weapons   (MCD)
FW .... Filament Wound
FW .... Filter Wheels
FW .... Financial Weekly [*A publication*]
FW .... Financial World [*A publication*]
FW .... Fire Wall [*Technical drawings*]
FW .... Firmware [*Data processing*]
FW .... First Wachovia Corp. [*NYSE symbol*]   (SPSG)
FW .... First Word
FW .... Fixed Wavelength [*Electronics*]
FW .... Fixed Wing [*Aircraft*]
FW .... Flag Word   (MCD)
FW .... Flash Welding [*Metallurgy*]
FW .... Flight Weight
FW .... Floor Waste
FW .... Focke-Wulf [*A German fighter plane*]
FW .... Focke-Wulf GmbH [*Federal Republic of Germany*] [*ICAO aircraft manufacturer identifier*]   (ICAO)
FW .... Fog Whistle [*Navigation charts*]
FW .... Folktales of the World [*A publication*]
FW .... Foot Wide
FW .... Forced Whisper [*Medicine*]
FW .... Formula Weight [*Chemistry*]
FW .... Forward of Wing [*Aerospace*]   (AAG)
FW .... Frame Synchronization Word   (MUGU)
FW .... Framework
FW .... Franklin Watts Group [*Publishers*] [*British*]
FW .... Free Wheel   (ADA)
FW .... Fresh Water [*Technical drawings*]

FW .... Fresh Weight [*of fruit*] [*Botany*]
FW .... Freshwater [*Load line mark*]
FW .... Fuel Wasting (MCD)
FW .... Full Wave
FW .... International Freight Airways SA [*Belgium*] [*ICAO designator*] (FAAC)
FW .... Le Point Air [*France*] [*ICAO designator*] (ICDA)
FWA .... Factories and Workshops Acts [*Law*] [*British*] (ROG)
FWA .... Family Welfare Association [*British*] (ILCA)
FWA .... Far West Airlines [*Hillsboro, OR*] [*FAA designator*] (FAAC)
FWA .... Farmers and World Affairs [*An association*] [*Defunct*] (EA)
FWA .... Federal Works Agency [*Abolished, 1949*]
FWA .... Federation of Women Clerks [*A union*] [*British*]
FWA .... Fellow of the World Academy of Arts and Sciences
FWA .... Filler Wire Addition
FWA .... Film Weekly Award [*British*]
FWA .... Financial Women's Association of New York [*New York, NY*] (EA)
FWA .... Financial Working Arrangement
FWA .... First Word Address [*Data processing*]
FWA .... Flight Watch Area (FAAC)
FWA .... Fluorescent Whitening Agent [*Detergent*]
FWA .... Fort Wayne [*Indiana*] [*Airport symbol*] (OAG)
FWA .... Fort Wayne, IN [*Location identifier*] [*FAA*] (FAAL)
FWA .... Forward Wave Amplifier
FWA .... Fraud, Waste, and Abuse
FWA .... French West Africa
FWA .... Fresh Water Allowance (DS)
FWA .... Full-Wave Amplifier
FWA .... Future Weapons Agency [*Army*]
FWA .... University of West Florida, Pensacola, FL [*OCLC symbol*] (OCLC)
FWAA ...... Football Writers Association of America (EA)
FWAA ...... Fur Wholesalers Association of America (EA)
FWAC ...... Full-Wave Alternating Current
FWAD ...... Fort Wingate Army Depot [*New Mexico*] (AABC)
FWAF ...... Free World Armed Forces
FWAIS ...... Free World Air Intelligence Study (MCD)
FWAIT ...... Floating-Point Wait [*Data processing*]
FWAM ...... Fleet Weapon Armament Maintenance [*Navy*] (MCD)
FWAOB ... Free World Air Order of Battle (MCD)
FWAS ...... Failure Warning and Analysis System
FWAT .... Flexwatt Corp. [*NASDAQ symbol*] (NQ)
FWB.......... Fahrenheit Wet Bulb (KSC)
FWB.......... First Women's Bank [*New York City*]
FWB.......... Fort Worth Belt Railway Co. [*AAR code*]
FWB.......... Forum for Women in Bridge (EA)
FWB.......... Four-Wheel Brake
FWB.......... Free-Wheel Bicycle
FWB.......... Free-Will Baptists
FWB.......... Full Weight Bearing [*Medicine*]
FWB.......... University of Minnesota, Freshwater Biological Institute, Navarre, MN [*OCLC symbol*] (OCLC)
FWBA ...... Full-Wave Balanced Amplifier
FWBC ...... Fort Wayne Bible College [*Indiana*]
FW-BF .... Foster Wheeler-Bergbau Forschung [*Flue gas treatment*]
FWBG....... Bangula [*Malawi*] [*ICAO location identifier*] (ICLI)
FWBI .... First Western Bancorp, Inc. (NQ)
FWBLA ...... Freshwater Biology [*A publication*]
FWBO ...... Friends of the Western Buddhist Order (EA)
FWBPA ...... Free Will Baptist Press Association (EA)
FWBR ...... Full-Wave Bridge Rectifier
FWC .... Fair Weather Current
FWC .... Fairfield, IL [*Location identifier*] [*FAA*] (FAAL)
FWC .... Federal Warning Center (NATG)
FWC .... Feedwater Control [*Nuclear energy*] (NRCH)
FWC .... Fleet Weapons Center [*Navy*] (MCD)
FWC .... Fleet Weather Center [*Navy*] (NVT)
FWC .... Flight Warning Computer (MCD)
FWC .... Flying Wheel Casting [*Metallurgy*]
FWC .... Foil Wound Coil
FWC .... Force Weapons Coordinator [*Navy*] (NVT)
FWC .... Foster Wheeler Corporation [*NYSE symbol*] (SPSG)
FWC .... Fourdrinier Wire Council (EA)
FWC .... Free Wallenberg Committee (EA)
FWC .... Freshwater Cooling
FWC .... Friends World College [*Huntington, NY*] (EA)
FWC .... Fully Loaded Weight and Capacity [*Shipping*]
FWCC....... Chintheche [*Malawi*] [*ICAO location identifier*] (ICLI)
FWCC....... Friends World Committee for Consultation [*London, England*] (EAIO)
FWCC....... Friends of the World Council of Churches (EA)
FWCD ...... Chelinda [*Malawi*] [*ICAO location identifier*] (ICLI)
FWCH ...... First World Cheese, Inc. [*NASDAQ symbol*] (NQ)
FWCI ...... Feedwater Coolant Injection [*Nuclear energy*] (NRCH)
FWCI ...... Foundation of the Wall and Ceiling Industry (EA)
FWCI ...... Futura West, Incorporated [*Scottsdale, AZ*] [*NASDAQ symbol*] (NQ)
FWCL ...... Blantyre/Chileka [*Malawi*] [*ICAO location identifier*] (ICLI)
FWCL ...... Field Wire Command Link [*Army*] (AABC)
FWCM ...... Makokola Club [*Malawi*] [*ICAO location identifier*] (ICLI)

FWCNG .... Florida West Coast Nuclear Group
FWCS ...... Feedwater Control System [*Nuclear energy*] (NRCH)
FWCS ...... Flight Watch Control Station (FAAC)
FWCS ...... Ntchisi [*Malawi*] [*ICAO location identifier*] (ICLI)
FWCT ...... Chitipa [*Malawi*] [*ICAO location identifier*] (ICLI)
fwd............. Foreword (BJA)
FWD .... Fort Worth & Denver Railway Co. [*AAR code*]
FWD .... Forward (AFM)
FWD .... Four-Wheel Drive [*Vehicle*]
FWD .... Free Water Damage (ADA)
FWD .... Fresh Water Damage
FWD .... Front Wheel Drive
FWD .... Furniture World and Furniture Buyer and Decorator [*A publication*]
FWDA ...... Federal Wholesale Druggists Association [*Later, DWA*] (EA)
FWDA ...... Federated Wire Drawers' Association [*A union*] [*British*]
FWDBAA ... Forward Brigade Administrative Area [*British*]
FWDBL ...... Forward Bomb Line
FW & DC... Fort Worth & Denver City Railway Co.
FWDC ...... Forward Collect (FAAC)
FWDC ...... Full-Wave Direct Current
FWDCT..... Fresh Water Drain Collecting Tank
FWDD ...... Forwarded
FWDG ...... Forwarding
FWDHTSHLD ... Forward Heat Shield (MCD)
FWDP........ Foreign Weapon Development Program (NG)
FWDR ...... Forwarder
FWDT ...... Flight Worthiness Demonstration Test (KSC)
FWDW ...... Dwanga [*Malawi*] [*ICAO location identifier*] (ICLI)
FWDZ ...... Dedza [*Malawi*] [*ICAO location identifier*] (ICLI)
FWE........... Federation of Woman's Exchanges (EA)
FWE........... Finished with Engines
FWE........... Foreign Weapons Evaluation
FWE........... Friends of Waycross Express (EA)
FWEA ...... Finnish Workers' Educational Association [*Defunct*] (EA)
FWeldI....... Fellow of the Welding Institute [*British*] (DBQ)
FWEO ...... Fleet Weapons Engineering Officer [*Navy*] [*British*]
FWERAT .. Fourth World Educational and Research Association Trust (EA)
FWES ...... First Western Financial Corp. [*NASDAQ symbol*] (NQ)
FWF........... Far West Financial Corp. [*NYSE symbol*] (SPSG)
FWF........... Far Western Forum [*A publication*]
FWF........... Felicidades Wildlife Foundation (EA)
FWF........... Fleet Weather Facility [*Navy*]
FWF........... Fly without Fear [*Commercial firm*] (EA)
FWFHC..... Farm Workers Family Health Center
FWFWA..... Fresh Water Fish Wholesalers Association (EA)
FWG .... Facility Working Group
FWG .... Factory Work Group
FWG .... Feminist Writers' Guild (EA)
FWG .... Financial Working Group [*Military*] (AFIT)
FWG .... Flexible Waveguide
FWGE....... Fort Worth Grain Exchange (EA)
FWGE....... FREE [*Federated Republics of Earth and Its Environs*] World Government (EA)
FWH.......... Flexible Working Hours
FWH.......... Folklore of World Holidays [*A publication*]
FWH.......... Fort Worth, TX [*Location identifier*] [*FAA*] (FAAL)
FWH.......... Frank W. Horner Ltd. [*Canada*] [*Research code symbol*]
FWHC....... Feminist Women's Health Center [*Later, FWHC/WCC*] (EA)
FWHC/WCC ... Feminist Women's Health Center/Women's Choice Clinic [*Defunct*] (EA)
FWHF .... Federation of World Health Foundations (EA)
FWHM....... Full Width at Half Maximum [*Spectroscopy*]
FWHMA .... Feed Water Heater Manufacturers Association (EA)
FWHP....... Full Width at Half Peak [*Spectroscopy*] (DEN)
FWhP........ Polk Community College, Winter Haven, FL [*Library symbol*] [*Library of Congress*] (LCLS)
FWHQ....... Lilongwe [*Malawi*] [*ICAO location identifier*] (ICLI)
FWI........... Families and Work Institute (EA)
FWI........... Federation of West Indies
FWI........... Fellow of the Institute of Welfare Officers [*British*]
FWI........... Fixed-Weight Indexes
FWI........... French West Indies
FWI........... Fresh Water Institute [*Rensselaer Polytechnic Institute*] [*Research center*] (RCD)
FWI........... Roslyn, NY [*Location identifier*] [*FAA*] (FAAL)
FWIB........ Federal Women's Interagency Board (EA)
FWIC........ Federated Women's Institutes of Canada
FWIC........ Fighter Weapons Instructor Course [*Military*]
F Wiss Beit ... Filmwissenschaftliche Beitraege [*A publication*]
FWISU ...... Federation of Westinghouse Independent Salaried Unions (EA)
FWIT .... Federated Women in Timber (EA)
FWIT .... Fixed-Wing Tactical Transport [*Aviation*] (MUGU)
FWIW........ For What It's Worth
FWK.......... Field Weakening
FWK.......... Framework
FWKA....... Karonga [*Malawi*] [*ICAO location identifier*] (ICLI)
FWKB....... Katumbi [*Malawi*] [*ICAO location identifier*] (ICLI)
FWKG ...... Kasungu/Kasungu [*Malawi*] [*ICAO location identifier*] (ICLI)

FWKI......... Kamuzu International [*Malawi*] [*ICAO location identifier*] (ICLI)
FWKK........ Nkhotakota [*Malawi*] [*ICAO location identifier*] (ICLI)
FWL........... Far West Laboratory for Educational Research and Development [*Department of Education*] [*San Francisco, CA*] (GRD)
FWL........... Farewell [*Alaska*] [*Airport symbol*] (OAG)
FWL........... Farewell, AK [*Location identifier*] [*FAA*] (FAAL)
FWL........... Federation of Women Lawyers', Judicial Screening Panel (EA)
FWL........... Fixed Word Length [*Data processing*]
FWL........... Foilborne Water Line
FWL........... Foundation for World Literacy [*Defunct*]
FWL........... Fraternity of the Wooden Leg [*Inactive*] (EA)
F Wld Energy ... Free World Energy Survey [*A publication*]
FWLEEA... US Fish and Wildlife Service. Fish and Wildlife Leaflet [*A publication*]
FWLERD .. Far West Laboratory for Educational Research and Development [*Department of Education*]
FWLK........ Likoma [*Malawi*] [*ICAO location identifier*] (ICLI)
FWLL........ Lilongwe [*Malawi*] [*ICAO location identifier*] (ICLI)
FWLP........ Kasungu/Lifupa [*Malawi*] [*ICAO location identifier*] (ICLI)
FWM .... Fort William [*Scotland*] [*Airport symbol*] (OAG)
FWM .... Fourth World Movement [*Later, NI/FWM*] (EA)
FWMA ..... Free World Military Assistance (CINC)
FWMAC.... Free World Military Assistance Council
FWMAF.... Free World Military Assistance Forces [*Vietnam*]
FWMAO ... Free World Military Assistance Organization (MCD)
FWMC ...... Mchinji [*Malawi*] [*ICAO location identifier*] (ICLI)
FWMG ...... Mangochi [*Malawi*] [*ICAO location identifier*] (ICLI)
FWMQC ... Fixed-Wing Multiengine Qualification Course [*Aviation*]
FWMU ...... Fire-Weather Mobile Unit [*National Weather Service*] (NOAA)
FWMY ...... Monkey Bay [*Malawi*] [*ICAO location identifier*] (ICLI)
FWMZ....... Mzimba [*Malawi*] [*ICAO location identifier*] (ICLI)
FWN .... Footwear News [*A publication*]
FWN .... Futures World News [*Information service or system*] (CRD)
FWN .... Futures World News Network [*Information service or system*] (EISS)
FWNC .... Fort Wayne National Corporation [*Fort Wayne, IN*] [*NASDAQ symbol*] (NQ)
FWNEOFAP ... Funds Will Not Be Entrusted to Others for Any Purpose [*Army*] (AABC)
FWNY .... [*The*] First Women's Bank [*NASDAQ symbol*] (NQ)
FWO .... Fire-Weather Office [*National Weather Service*] (NOAA)
FWO .... First Wyoming Bancorporation [*AMEX symbol*] (SPSG)
FWO .... Fleet Wireless Officer [*British*]
FWOC .... Federation of Western Outdoor Clubs (EA)
FWOP .... Federal Women's Program Committee/Coordinator (AABC)
FWOP .... Furloughed without Pay
FWOS .... Free Will Offering Scheme (ROG)
FWOSR..... Flight Work Orders - Ships Records (MCD)
FWOTSC . First Woman on the Supreme Court [*Sandra Day O'Connor*]
FWP........... Fair-Witness Project (EA)
FWP........... Federal Women's Program
FWP........... Federal Writers' Project [*Obsolete*]
FWP........... Feed Water Pump (MSA)
FWP........... Flight Watch Point (FAAC)
FWP........... Fresh Water Pump (MSA)
FWP........... Fulcrum, Weight, Power
FWp........... Winter Park Public Library, Winter Park, FL [*Library symbol*] [*Library of Congress*] (LCLS)
FWPB........ Feedwater Pipe Break [*Nuclear energy*] (NRCH)
FWpb........ West Palm Beach Public Library, West Palm Beach, FL [*Library symbol*] [*Library of Congress*] (LCLS)
FWpbG ...... Good Samaritan Hospital, Medical Library, West Palm Beach, FL [*Library symbol*] [*Library of Congress*] (LCLS)
FWpbP....... Palm Beach County Public Library System, West Palm Beach, FL [*Library symbol*] [*Library of Congress*] (LCLS)
FWPC........ Federal Women's Program Committee/Coordinator
FWPCA..... Federal Water Pollution Control Act [*1965*] (NRCH)
FWPCA..... Federal Water Pollution Control Administration [*Later, OWP*] [*Department of the Interior*]
FWP J........ FWP [*Founding, Welding, Production Engineering*] Journal [*South Africa*] [*A publication*]
FWPJA...... FWP [*Founding, Welding, Production Engineering*] Journal [*A publication*]
FWPLN ..... Fairwater Planes
FWPO .... Federal Wildlife Permit Office [*Department of the Interior*]
FWPPAP... US Department of the Interior. Federal Water Pollution Control Administration. Water Pollution Control Research Series [*A publication*]
FWPR......... Field Work Performance Report
F & W Pr.... Frend and Ware's Precedents of Instruments Relating to the Transfer of Land to Railway Companies [*2nd ed.*] [*1866*] [*A publication*] (DLA)
FWpR .... Rollins College, Winter Park, FL [*Library symbol*] [*Library of Congress*] (LCLS)
FWpR-S..... Rollins College, Bush Science Library, Winter Park, FL [*Library symbol*] [*Library of Congress*] (LCLS)
FWQA .... Federal Water Quality Administration [*Later, OWP*] [*Environmental Protection Agency*]
FWQA .... Federal Water Quality Association (EA)

FWR .... Forest, Wildlife, and Range Experiment Station [*University of Idaho*] [*Research center*] (RCD)
FWR .... Free-Wheel Rectifier
FWR .... Full-Wave Rectifier [*or Rectification*]
FWRAP .... Federal Water Resources Assistance Program [*Australia*]
FWRC........ Federal Water Resources Council
FWRNG .... Fire Warning (FAAC)
FWRRC ..... University of Florida Water Resources Research Center [*Research center*] (RCD)
FWRS .... Fish and Wildlife Reference Service [*Fish and Wildlife Service*] [*Information service or system*] (MSC)
FWRS .... Flexible Wing Recovery System [*Aerospace*] (AAG)
FWRU ...... Full-Wave Rectified Unfiltered
FWS .... FAS [*Fixed Airlock Shroud*] Work Station
FWS .... Federal Wage Systems [*DoD*]
FWS .... Fighter Weapons School [*Military*]
FWS .... Filament-Wound Structure
FWS .... Filter Wedge Spectrometer
FWS .... Final Work Statement (MCD)
FWS .... Fire Water Service
FWS .... Fish and Wildlife Service [*Department of the Interior*]
F & WS .... Fish and Wildlife Service [*Department of the Interior*]
FWS .... Fleet Work Study [*Navy*] (NG)
FWS .... Flight Warning System (MCD)
FWS .... Flight Watch Specialist (FAAC)
FWS .... Flight and Weapons Simulator (MCD)
FWS .... Fluid Wetting and Spreading [*Lubrication*]
FWS .... Fly Wire Screen (ADA)
FWS .... Furtwangen [*Schwarzwald*] [*Federal Republic of Germany*] [*Seismograph station code, US Geological Survey*] (SEIS)
FWSAB ..... Federation of Women Shareholders in American Business (EA)
FWSCA .... Forstwissenschaftliches Centralblatt [*A publication*]
FWSDR..... Final Working System Design Review [*Nuclear energy*] (NRCH)
FWSFAA... Feldwirtschaft [*A publication*]
FWSG........ Fleet Work Study Group [*Navy*]
FWSH ...... Fresh Water Supply Header [*Nuclear energy*] (NRCH)
FW/SIFR .. Fixed-Wing Special Instrument Flight Rules [*Aviation*]
FWSJ........ Nsanje [*Malawi*] [*ICAO location identifier*] (ICLI)
FWSM....... Salima [*Malawi*] [*ICAO location identifier*] (ICLI)
FWS/OBS .. Fish and Wildlife Service/Office of Biological Services [*Department of the Interior*]
FWS/OBS US Fish Wildl Serv Off Biol Serv ... FWS/OBS. United States Fish and Wildlife Service. Office of Biological Services [*A publication*]
FWSSUSA ... Federation of Workers' Singing Societies of the USA (EA)
FWSU........ Nchalo/Sucoma [*Malawi*] [*ICAO location identifier*] (ICLI)
FWSV........ Funnel-Web Spider Venom
FW/SVFR ... Fixed-Wing Special Visual Flight Rules [*Aviation*]
FWT.......... Fair Wear and Tear
FWT.......... Far West Industries, Inc. [*Toronto Stock Exchange symbol*] [*Vancouver Stock Exchange symbol*]
FWT.......... Fast Walsh Transform [*Spectrometry*]
FWT.......... Forward Wave Tube
FWTC........ Far and Wide Tape Club (EA)
FWTC........ Fighter Weapons Training Command (MCD)
FWTM....... Full Width at Tenth Maximum (IEEE)
FWTT........ Fixed-Wing Tactical Transport [*Aviation*] (MCD)
FWTUC..... Free Workers' Trade Union Congress [*Aden*]
FWU .... Flight Watch Unit (FAAC)
FWU .... Fort Wayne Union [*AAR code*]
FWUU .... Mzuzu [*Malawi*] [*ICAO location identifier*] (ICLI)
FWV .... Farmerville, LA [*Location identifier*] [*FAA*] (FAAL)
FWVA....... Finnish War Veterans in America (EA)
FWW .... Federation of Wholefood Wholesalers [*British*]
FWW .... First Western Communications Corp. [*Vancouver Stock Exchange symbol*]
FWW .... First World War (DMA)
FWW .... Food, Water, and Waste [*NASA*] (MCD)
FWW .... Friends of Workshop Way (EA)
FWWM ...... Food, Water, and Waste Management [*NASA*] (NASA)
FWWMR .... Fire, Water, Weather, Mildew Resistant (MCD)
FWWMS... Food, Water, and Waste Management Subsystem [*NASA*] (NASA)
FWY .... Fairways Corp. [*Washington, DC*] [*FAA designator*] (FAAC)
FWY .... Fenway Resources Ltd. [*Vancouver Stock Exchange symbol*]
FWY .... Freeway (MCD)
FWZI........ Full Width at Zero Intensity [*Spectroscopy*]
F/X............ Effects [*Filmmaking and television*] [*Also title of a movie about special effects*]
FX .... Facsimile (KSC)
FX .... Field Exercise [*Military*] (MCD)
FX .... Fighter Experimental (MCD)
FX .... Fighter Export [*Military*]
FX .... Fix [*Navigation*]
FX .... Fixed Area [*of magnetic disk*]
FX .... Fixed Station [*ITU designation*] (CET)
FX .... Forecastle [*Navy*] [*British*]
FX .... Foreign Exchange [*Investment term*]
FX .... Foreign Exchange [*ADP Network Services, Inc.*] [*Information service or system*]

FX .... Foreign Exchange Rate Service [*Refco, Inc.*] [*Information service or system*]   (IID)

FX .... Four Island Air Ltd. [*Antigua, Barbuda*] [*ICAO designator*]   (FAAC)

FX .... Fracture [*Medicine*]

FX .... Freight Traffic Concurrence

FXBASE .... International Interest and Exchange Rate Database [*Citicorp Database Services*] [*Information service or system*]   (IID)

FXBB .... Bobete [*Lesotho*] [*ICAO location identifier*]   (ICLI)

Fx BB .... Fracture of Both Bones [*Medicine*]

FXBC .... ExecuFirst Bancorporation, Inc. [*NASDAQ symbol*]   (NQ)

FXBIN .... Fixed Binary   (DEN)

FXC........... Ferrox Cube [*Telecommunications*]   (TEL)

FXC........... Francis X. Curzio [*In company name FXC Investors Corp.*]

FXD .... Fixed   (AAG)

FXD .... Flash X-Ray Device

FXE........... Fort Lauderdale, FL [*Location identifier*] [*FAA*]   (FAAL)

FXE........... Telemetering Fixed Station [*ITU designation*]   (CET)

FXER........ Foreign Exchange Encashments Receipts [*Finance*]

FXF............ Flash X-Ray Facility

FXG .... Fixing   (ADA)

FXG .... Florida International University, Miami, FL [*OCLC symbol*]   (OCLC)

FXH .... Hydrological and Meteorological Fixed Station [*ITU designation*]   (CET)

FXKB .... Kolberg [*Lesotho*] [*ICAO location identifier*]   (ICLI)

FXLE .... Forecastle

FXLK .... Lebakeng [*Lesotho*] [*ICAO location identifier*]   (ICLI)

FXLR .... Leribe [*Lesotho*] [*ICAO location identifier*]   (ICLI)

FXLS .... Lesobeng [*Lesotho*] [*ICAO location identifier*]   (ICLI)

FXLT .... Letseng [*Lesotho*] [*ICAO location identifier*]   (ICLI)

FXM .... Flaxman Island, AK [*Location identifier*] [*FAA*]   (FAAL)

FXMA....... Matsaile [*Lesotho*] [*ICAO location identifier*]   (ICLI)

FXMF....... Mafeteng [*Lesotho*] [*ICAO location identifier*]   (ICLI)

FXMH .... Mohales'Hoek [*Lesotho*] [*ICAO location identifier*]   (ICLI)

FXMK .... Mokhotlong [*Lesotho*] [*ICAO location identifier*]   (ICLI)

FXML .... Malefiloane [*Lesotho*] [*ICAO location identifier*]   (ICLI)

FXMM .... Maseru Moshoeshoe International [*Lesotho*] [*ICAO location identifier*]   (ICLI)

FXMN ...... Mantsonyane [*Lesotho*] [*ICAO location identifier*]   (ICLI)

FXMP .... Mohlanapeng [*Lesotho*] [*ICAO location identifier*]   (ICLI)

FXMS .... Mashai Store [*Lesotho*] [*ICAO location identifier*]   (ICLI)

FXMT....... Matabeng Store [*Lesotho*] [*ICAO location identifier*]   (ICLI)

FXMU ...... Maseru/Leabua Jonathan [*Lesotho*] [*ICAO location identifier*]   (ICLI)

FXMV ...... Matabeng Village [*Lesotho*] [*ICAO location identifier*]   (ICLI)

FXN .... Florida International University, North Campus, North Miami, FL [*OCLC symbol*]   (OCLC)

FXNH .... Nohanas [*Lesotho*] [*ICAO location identifier*]   (ICLI)

FXNK .... Nkaus [*Lesotho*] [*ICAO location identifier*]   (ICLI)

FXP........... Fixed Point

FXP........... Fleet Exercise Publication [*Navy*]

FXPG........ Pelaneng [*Lesotho*] [*ICAO location identifier*]   (ICLI)

FXQG........ Quthing [*Lesotho*] [*ICAO location identifier*]   (ICLI)

FXQN .... Qachas' Nek [*Lesotho*] [*ICAO location identifier*]   (ICLI)

FXR........... Fox Resources Ltd. [*Vancouver Stock Exchange symbol*]

FXR........... Foxer [*Navy*] [*British*]

FXS........... Fox Sparrow [*Ornithology*]

FXS........... Fragile X Syndrome [*Genetics*]

FXSE .... Sehlabathebe [*Lesotho*] [*ICAO location identifier*]   (ICLI)

FXSH .... Sehonghong [*Lesotho*] [*ICAO location identifier*]   (ICLI)

FXSK .... Sekake [*Lesotho*] [*ICAO location identifier*]   (ICLI)

FXSM .... Semongkong [*Lesotho*] [*ICAO location identifier*]   (ICLI)

FXSR .... Foreign Exchange Sale Receipts [*Finance*]

FXSS .... Seshote [*Lesotho*] [*ICAO location identifier*]   (ICLI)

FXST .... St. Theresa [*Lesotho*] [*ICAO location identifier*]   (ICLI)

FXTA .... Thaba Tseka [*Lesotho*] [*ICAO location identifier*]   (ICLI)

FXTB .... Tebellong [*Lesotho*] [*ICAO location identifier*]   (ICLI)

FXTK .... Tlokoeng [*Lesotho*] [*ICAO location identifier*]   (ICLI)

FXTR .... Fixture   (MSA)

FXU .... F. W. Faxon Co. [*ACCORD*] [*UTLAS symbol*]

FXU .... Fixed-Point Unit

FXV........... Appleton, WI [*Location identifier*] [*FAA*]   (FAAL)

FXV........... Future Experimental Vehicle [*Toyota Motor Co.*]

FXX........... Foxx Industry, Inc. [*Vancouver Stock Exchange symbol*]

FXY........... Forest City, IA [*Location identifier*] [*FAA*]   (FAAL)

Fy .... Duffy [*Blood group*]

FY .... Fall Yearling [*Pisciculture*]

Fy .... Ferry [*Nautical charts*]

FY .... Fiscal Year [*Business term*]

FY .... Fishery Flag [*Navy*] [*British*]

FY .... Full Year

FY .... South Africa [*Later, BL*] [*License plate code assigned to foreign diplomats in the US*]

FY .... Transafrica SA [*Senegal*] [*ICAO designator*]   (FAAC)

FY1 .... Fort Yukon [*Alaska*] [*Seismograph station code, US Geological Survey*]

FY2 .... Fort Yukon [*Alaska*] [*Seismograph station code, US Geological Survey*]   (SEIS)

FY3 .... Fort Yukon [*Alaska*] [*Seismograph station code, US Geological Survey*]   (SEIS)

FY4 .... Fort Yukon [*Alaska*] [*Seismograph station code, US Geological Survey*]   (SEIS)

FY5 .... Fort Yukon [*Alaska*] [*Seismograph station code, US Geological Survey*]   (SEIS)

FYA .... First-Year Algebra [*National Science Foundation project*]

FYA .... For Your Attention [*Business term*]

FYA .... Yukon Air Service, Inc. [*Fairbanks, AK*] [*FAA designator*]   (FAAC)

FYB........... Albert Lea, MN [*Location identifier*] [*FAA*]   (FAAL)

FYBR .... Critical Industries, Inc. [*NASDAQ symbol*]   (NQ)

FYC........... Fission Yield Curve

FYCAB ...... Fyzikalny Casopis. Vydavatel'stvo Slovenskej Akademie Vied [*A publication*]

FYD .... Fellowship of Youth Development [*British*]   (DBQ)

FyD .... Finanzas y Desarrollo [*A publication*]

FYDA ...... Associate Fellowship of Youth Development [*British*]   (DBQ)

FYDO ...... Fiscal Year Design Objective

FYDO ...... Five-Year Design Objective

FYDP .... Fiscal Year Development Plan   (MCD)

FYDP .... Five-Year Defense Plan [*or Program*] [*Military*]

FYDS........ Fiscal Year Data Summary

FYE .... Fiscal Year Ending

FYF........... For Your Files

FYFC .... Faron Young Fan Club   (EA)

FYFSFP ..... Five-Year Force Structure and Financial Program [*Navy*]   (KSC)

FYFS & FP ... Five-Year Force Structure and Financial Program [*Navy*]

FYG .... Friends of Yesh Gvul   (EA)

FYI .... For Your Information

FYI .... News/Retrieval for Your Information [*Dow Jones & Co., Inc.*] [*Information service or system*]   (CRD)

FYIG .... For Your Information and Guidance

Fyiz Tverd Tyila ... Fyizika Tverdogo Tyila [*A publication*]

FYJKA .... Fysiokjemikeren [*A publication*]

FyL............ Filosofia y Letras [*A publication*]

FYM .... Fayetteville, TN [*Location identifier*] [*FAA*]   (FAAL)

FYM .... Fiscal Year Month

FYM .... Miami-Dade Community College, Miami, FL [*OCLC symbol*]   (OCLC)

FYMP .... Five-Year Materiel Program [*Military*]

FYN .... Fuyun [*China*] [*Airport symbol*]   (OAG)

Fyn Mind ... Fynske Minder [*A publication*]

FYO .... Fiscal Year Option

FYP........... Five-Year Plan [*Military*]

FYP........... Four-Year Plan

FYPB .... Five-Year Planning Base [*Military*]   (AABC)

FYPP .... Five-Year Procurement Program [*Military*]   (AABC)

FYPP .... Five-Year Program Plan

FYQ .... Rome, NY [*Location identifier*] [*FAA*]   (FAAL)

FYSA .... Foundation for Youth and Student Affairs [*Defunct*]   (EA)

Fysiatr Reumatol Vestn ... Fysiatricky a Reumatologicky Vestnik [*A publication*]

Fysiatr Vestn ... Fysiatricky Vestnik [*A publication*]

Fys Tidsskr ... Fysisk Tidsskrift [*A publication*]

FYTDP .... Five-Year Training Development Plan [*Army*]

FYTDY ...... Final Year Temporary Duty [*Military*]   (AFM)

FYTIA ...... Fysisk Tidsskrift [*Denmark*] [*A publication*]

FYTP .... Five-Year Test Program [*Military*]   (AABC)

FYTQ........ Fiscal Year Transition Quarter

FYU .... Fort Yukon [*Alaska*] [*Seismograph station code, US Geological Survey*]   (SEIS)

FYU .... Fort Yukon [*Alaska*] [*Airport symbol*]   (OAG)

FYU .... Fort Yukon, AK [*Location identifier*] [*FAA*]   (FAAL)

FYV.......... Fayetteville [*Arkansas*] [*Airport symbol*]   (OAG)

FYV.......... Fayetteville, AR [*Location identifier*] [*FAA*]   (FAAL)

FYVDA ...... Fra Fysikkens Verden [*A publication*]

Fyz Cas ...... Fyzikalny Casopis [*A publication*]

FZ .... Air Fret [*ICAO designator*]   (FAAC)

FZ .... Fetal Zone [*Medicine*]

FZ .... Float Zone [*Crystallization process*]

FZ .... Fluoresceinated Zymosan [*Clinical chemistry*]

FZ .... Flurazepam [*Organic chemistry*]

Fz .... Forzando [*or Forzato*] [*Strongly Accented*] [*Music*]

FZ .... Fracture Zone [*Geophysics*]

FZ .... Frankfurter Allgemeine Zeitung [*A publication*]

FZ .... Freezing

FZ .... Frigid Zone   (ROG)

FZ .... Furazolidone [*Antimicrobial drug*]

FZ .... Fuze   (MSA)

FZ .... Sfair [*France*] [*ICAO designator*]   (FAAC)

fz----- .... Zambezi River and Basin [*MARC geographic area code*] [*Library of Congress*]   (LCCP)

FZA........... Fellow of the Zoological Academy

FZA........... Free Zone Authority   (EA)

f-za--- .... Zambia [*MARC geographic area code*] [*Library of Congress*]   (LCCP)

FZAA........ Kinshasa/N'Djili [*Zaire*] [*ICAO location identifier*]   (ICLI)

FZAB........ Kinshasa/N'Dolo [*Zaire*] [*ICAO location identifier*]   (ICLI)

FZAD........ Celo-Zongo [*Zaire*] [*ICAO location identifier*]   (ICLI)

FZAE........ Kimpoko [*Zaire*] [*ICAO location identifier*]   (ICLI)

FZAF .... Nsangi [*Zaire*] [*ICAO location identifier*]   (ICLI)

FZAG......... Muanda [*Zaire*] [*ICAO location identifier*]　(ICLI)
FZAH .... Tshela [*Zaire*] [*ICAO location identifier*]　(ICLI)
FZAI .... Kitona-Base [*Zaire*] [*ICAO location identifier*]　(ICLI)
FZAJ .... Boma [*Zaire*] [*ICAO location identifier*]　(ICLI)
FZAL .... Luozi [*Zaire*] [*ICAO location identifier*]　(ICLI)
FZAM .... Matadi [*Zaire*] [*ICAO location identifier*]　(ICLI)
FZAN .... Inga [*Zaire*] [*ICAO location identifier*]　(ICLI)
FZAP .... Lukala [*Zaire*] [*ICAO location identifier*]　(ICLI)
FZAR .... Nkolo-Fuma [*Zaire*] [*ICAO location identifier*]　(ICLI)
FZAS .... Inkisi [*Zaire*] [*ICAO location identifier*]　(ICLI)
FZAU .... Konde [*Zaire*] [*ICAO location identifier*]　(ICLI)
FZAW .... Kwilu-Gongo [*Zaire*] [*ICAO location identifier*]　(ICLI)
FZAX .... Luheki [*Zaire*] [*ICAO location identifier*]　(ICLI)
FZAY .... Mvula-Sanda [*Zaire*] [*ICAO location identifier*]　(ICLI)
FZAZ......... Kinshasa [*Zaire*] [*ICAO location identifier*]　(ICLI)
FzB......... Forschung zur Bibel [*Wuerzburg*] [*A publication*]
FZBA......... Inongo [*Zaire*] [*ICAO location identifier*]　(ICLI)
FZBB......... Bongimba [*Zaire*] [*ICAO location identifier*]　(ICLI)
FZBC......... Bikoro [*Zaire*] [*ICAO location identifier*]　(ICLI)
FZBD......... Oshwe [*Zaire*] [*ICAO location identifier*]　(ICLI)
FZBE......... Beno [*Zaire*] [*ICAO location identifier*]　(ICLI)
FZBF......... Bontika [*Zaire*] [*ICAO location identifier*]　(ICLI)
FZBG......... Kempa [*Zaire*] [*ICAO location identifier*]　(ICLI)
FZBI......... Nioki [*Zaire*] [*ICAO location identifier*]　(ICLI)
FZBJ......... Mushie [*Zaire*] [*ICAO location identifier*]　(ICLI)
FZBK......... Bosobe-Boshwe [*Zaire*] [*ICAO location identifier*]　(ICLI)
FZBL......... Djokele [*Zaire*] [*ICAO location identifier*]　(ICLI)
FZBN......... Malebo [*Zaire*] [*ICAO location identifier*]　(ICLI)
FZBO......... Bandundu [*Zaire*] [*ICAO location identifier*]　(ICLI)
FZBP......... Ngebolobo [*Zaire*] [*ICAO location identifier*]　(ICLI)
FZBQ......... Bindja [*Zaire*] [*ICAO location identifier*]　(ICLI)
FZBS......... Semendua [*Zaire*] [*ICAO location identifier*]　(ICLI)
FZBT......... Kiri [*Zaire*] [*ICAO location identifier*]　(ICLI)
FZBU......... Ibeke [*Zaire*] [*ICAO location identifier*]　(ICLI)
FZBV......... Kempili [*Zaire*] [*ICAO location identifier*]　(ICLI)
FZBW......... Bokote/Basengele [*Zaire*] [*ICAO location identifier*]　(ICLI)
FZCA......... Kikwit [*Zaire*] [*ICAO location identifier*]　(ICLI)
FZCB......... Idiofa [*Zaire*] [*ICAO location identifier*]　(ICLI)
FZCD......... Vanga [*Zaire*] [*ICAO location identifier*]　(ICLI)
FZCE......... Lusanga [*Zaire*] [*ICAO location identifier*]　(ICLI)
FZCF......... Kahemba [*Zaire*] [*ICAO location identifier*]　(ICLI)
FZCI......... Banga [*Zaire*] [*ICAO location identifier*]　(ICLI)
FZCK......... Kajiji [*Zaire*] [*ICAO location identifier*]　(ICLI)
FZCL......... Banza-Lute [*Zaire*] [*ICAO location identifier*]　(ICLI)
FZCO......... Boko [*Zaire*] [*ICAO location identifier*]　(ICLI)
FZCP......... Popokabaka [*Zaire*] [*ICAO location identifier*]　(ICLI)
FZCR......... Busala [*Zaire*] [*ICAO location identifier*]　(ICLI)
FZCS......... Kenge [*Zaire*] [*ICAO location identifier*]　(ICLI)
FZCT......... Fatundu [*Zaire*] [*ICAO location identifier*]　(ICLI)
FZCU......... Ito [*Zaire*] [*ICAO location identifier*]　(ICLI)
FZCV......... Masi-Manimba [*Zaire*] [*ICAO location identifier*]　(ICLI)
FZCW......... Kikoka Sur Wamba [*Zaire*] [*ICAO location identifier*]　(ICLI)
FZCX......... Kimafu [*Zaire*] [*ICAO location identifier*]　(ICLI)
FZCY......... Yuki [*Zaire*] [*ICAO location identifier*]　(ICLI)
FZDA......... Malanga [*Zaire*] [*ICAO location identifier*]　(ICLI)
FZDB......... Kimbau [*Zaire*] [*ICAO location identifier*]　(ICLI)
FZDC......... Lukuni [*Zaire*] [*ICAO location identifier*]　(ICLI)
FZDD......... Wamba-Luadi [*Zaire*] [*ICAO location identifier*]　(ICLI)
FZDE......... Tono [*Zaire*] [*ICAO location identifier*]　(ICLI)
FZDF......... Nzamba [*Zaire*] [*ICAO location identifier*]　(ICLI)
FZDG......... Nyanga [*Zaire*] [*ICAO location identifier*]　(ICLI)
FZDH......... Ngi [*Zaire*] [*ICAO location identifier*]　(ICLI)
FZDJ......... Mutena [*Zaire*] [*ICAO location identifier*]　(ICLI)
FZDK......... Kipata' Katika [*Zaire*] [*ICAO location identifier*]　(ICLI)
FZDL......... Kolokoso [*Zaire*] [*ICAO location identifier*]　(ICLI)
FZDM......... Masamuna [*Zaire*] [*ICAO location identifier*]　(ICLI)
FZDN......... Mongo Wa Kenda [*Zaire*] [*ICAO location identifier*]　(ICLI)
FZDO......... Moanda [*Zaire*] [*ICAO location identifier*]　(ICLI)
FZDP......... Mukedi [*Zaire*] [*ICAO location identifier*]　(ICLI)
FZDS......... Yasa-Bonga [*Zaire*] [*ICAO location identifier*]　(ICLI)
FZDT......... Matari [*Zaire*] [*ICAO location identifier*]　(ICLI)
FZDU......... Kimpangu [*Zaire*] [*ICAO location identifier*]　(ICLI)
FZDY......... Misay [*Zaire*] [*ICAO location identifier*]　(ICLI)
FZDZ......... Freezing Drizzle [*Meteorology*]
FZEA......... Mbandaka [*Zaire*] [*ICAO location identifier*]　(ICLI)
FZEB......... Monieka [*Zaire*] [*ICAO location identifier*]　(ICLI)
FZEG......... Lokolela [*Zaire*] [*ICAO location identifier*]　(ICLI)
FZEI......... Ingende [*Zaire*] [*ICAO location identifier*]　(ICLI)
FZEM......... Yembe-Moke [*Zaire*] [*ICAO location identifier*]　(ICLI)
FZEN......... Basankusu [*Zaire*] [*ICAO location identifier*]　(ICLI)
FZEO......... Beongo [*Zaire*] [*ICAO location identifier*]　(ICLI)
FZEP......... Mentole [*Zaire*] [*ICAO location identifier*]　(ICLI)
FZER......... Kodoro [*Zaire*] [*ICAO location identifier*]　(ICLI)
FZES......... Float Zone Experiment System
FZFA......... Libenge [*Zaire*] [*ICAO location identifier*]　(ICLI)
FZFB......... Imasse [*Zaire*] [*ICAO location identifier*]　(ICLI)
FZFD......... Gbadolite [*Zaire*] [*ICAO location identifier*]　(ICLI)
FZFE......... Abumumbazi [*Zaire*] [*ICAO location identifier*]　(ICLI)
FZFF......... Bau [*Zaire*] [*ICAO location identifier*]　(ICLI)
FZFG......... Bokada [*Zaire*] [*ICAO location identifier*]　(ICLI)
FZFG......... Freezing Fog [*Meteorology*]

FZFH......... Mokaria-Yamoleta [*Zaire*] [*ICAO location identifier*]　(ICLI)
FZFJ......... Goyongo [*Zaire*] [*ICAO location identifier*]　(ICLI)
FZFK......... Gemena [*Zaire*] [*ICAO location identifier*]　(ICLI)
FZFL......... Kala [*Zaire*] [*ICAO location identifier*]　(ICLI)
FZFN......... Lombo [*Zaire*] [*ICAO location identifier*]　(ICLI)
FZFP......... Kotakoli [*Zaire*] [*ICAO location identifier*]　(ICLI)
FZFQ......... Mpaka [*Zaire*] [*ICAO location identifier*]　(ICLI)
FZFS......... Karawa [*Zaire*] [*ICAO location identifier*]　(ICLI)
FZFT......... Tandala [*Zaire*] [*ICAO location identifier*]　(ICLI)
FZFU......... Bumba [*Zaire*] [*ICAO location identifier*]　(ICLI)
FZFV......... Gbado [*Zaire*] [*ICAO location identifier*]　(ICLI)
FZFW......... Gwaka [*Zaire*] [*ICAO location identifier*]　(ICLI)
FZG .... Fitzgerald, GA [*Location identifier*] [*FAA*]　(FAAL)
FzG .... Forschungsberichte zur Germanistik [*Osaka-Kobe*] [*A publication*]
FZGA......... Lisala [*Zaire*] [*ICAO location identifier*]　(ICLI)
FZGB......... Bosondjo [*Zaire*] [*ICAO location identifier*]　(ICLI)
FZGD......... Bokenge [*Zaire*] [*ICAO location identifier*]　(ICLI)
FZGF......... Bokungu [*Zaire*] [*ICAO location identifier*]　(ICLI)
FZGG......... Mondombe [*Zaire*] [*ICAO location identifier*]　(ICLI)
FZGH......... Wema [*Zaire*] [*ICAO location identifier*]　(ICLI)
FZGI......... Yalingimba [*Zaire*] [*ICAO location identifier*]　(ICLI)
FZGN......... Boende [*Zaire*] [*ICAO location identifier*]　(ICLI)
FZGT......... Boteka [*Zaire*] [*ICAO location identifier*]　(ICLI)
FZGV......... Ikela [*Zaire*] [*ICAO location identifier*]　(ICLI)
FZGY......... Yemo [*Zaire*] [*ICAO location identifier*]　(ICLI)
FZI......... Fostoria, OH [*Location identifier*] [*FAA*]　(FAAL)
FZIA......... First Zen Institute of America　(EA)
FZIA......... Kisangani [*Zaire*] [*ICAO location identifier*]　(ICLI)
FZIC......... Kisangani/Bangoka [*Zaire*] [*ICAO location identifier*]　(ICLI)
FZIF......... Ubundu [*Zaire*] [*ICAO location identifier*]　(ICLI)
FZIK......... Katende [*Zaire*] [*ICAO location identifier*]　(ICLI)
FZIR......... Yangambi [*Zaire*] [*ICAO location identifier*]　(ICLI)
FZIZ......... Lokutu [*Zaire*] [*ICAO location identifier*]　(ICLI)
FZJA......... Isiro [*Zaire*] [*ICAO location identifier*]　(ICLI)
FZJB......... Doko [*Zaire*] [*ICAO location identifier*]　(ICLI)
FZJF......... Aba [*Zaire*] [*ICAO location identifier*]　(ICLI)
FZJH......... Isiro/Matari [*Zaire*] [*ICAO location identifier*]　(ICLI)
FZJI......... Watsha [*Zaire*] [*ICAO location identifier*]　(ICLI)
FZJK......... Faradje [*Zaire*] [*ICAO location identifier*]　(ICLI)
FZJR......... Kerekere [*Zaire*] [*ICAO location identifier*]　(ICLI)
FZKA......... Bunia [*Zaire*] [*ICAO location identifier*]　(ICLI)
FZKAA......... Fizika [*Zagreb*] [*A publication*]
FZKB......... Bambili-Dingila [*Zaire*] [*ICAO location identifier*]　(ICLI)
FZKC......... Mahagi [*Zaire*] [*ICAO location identifier*]　(ICLI)
FZKF......... Kilomines [*Zaire*] [*ICAO location identifier*]　(ICLI)
FZKI......... Yedi [*Zaire*] [*ICAO location identifier*]　(ICLI)
FZKJ......... Buta Zega [*Zaire*] [*ICAO location identifier*]　(ICLI)
FZKN......... Aketi [*Zaire*] [*ICAO location identifier*]　(ICLI)
FZKO......... Ango [*Zaire*] [*ICAO location identifier*]　(ICLI)
FZKP......... Bondo [*Zaire*] [*ICAO location identifier*]　(ICLI)
FZKSA......... Fizika [*Zagreb*]. Supplement [*A publication*]
FZLZA......... Fiziologicheskii Zhurnal SSSR Imeni I. M. Sechenova [*A publication*]
FZM......... Floating Zone Melting
FZMA......... Bukavu/Kavumu [*Zaire*] [*ICAO location identifier*]　(ICLI)
FZMB......... Butembo [*Zaire*] [*ICAO location identifier*]　(ICLI)
FZMC......... Mulungu [*Zaire*] [*ICAO location identifier*]　(ICLI)
FZMK......... Bulonge-Kigogo [*Zaire*] [*ICAO location identifier*]　(ICLI)
FZMP......... Kimano II [*Zaire*] [*ICAO location identifier*]　(ICLI)
FZMW......... Shabunda [*Zaire*] [*ICAO location identifier*]　(ICLI)
FZNA......... Goma [*Zaire*] [*ICAO location identifier*]　(ICLI)
FZNC......... Rutshuru [*Zaire*] [*ICAO location identifier*]　(ICLI)
FZNF......... Lubero [*Zaire*] [*ICAO location identifier*]　(ICLI)
FZNI......... Ishasha [*Zaire*] [*ICAO location identifier*]　(ICLI)
FZNK......... Katanda Sur Rutshuru [*Zaire*] [*ICAO location identifier*]　(ICLI)
FZNM......... Mweso [*Zaire*] [*ICAO location identifier*]　(ICLI)
FZNP......... Beni [*Zaire*] [*ICAO location identifier*]　(ICLI)
FZNPA......... Fiziologia Normala si Patologica [*A publication*]
FZNR......... Ruindi [*Zaire*] [*ICAO location identifier*]　(ICLI)
FZNT......... Mutwanga [*Zaire*] [*ICAO location identifier*]　(ICLI)
FZOA......... Kindu [*Zaire*] [*ICAO location identifier*]　(ICLI)
FZOB......... Tingi-Tingi [*Zaire*] [*ICAO location identifier*]　(ICLI)
FZOC......... Kalima-Kamisuku [*Zaire*] [*ICAO location identifier*]　(ICLI)
FZOD......... Kalima [*Zaire*] [*ICAO location identifier*]　(ICLI)
FZOE......... Kampene [*Zaire*] [*ICAO location identifier*]　(ICLI)
FZOF......... Kiapupe [*Zaire*] [*ICAO location identifier*]　(ICLI)
FZOG......... Lulingu-Tshioka [*Zaire*] [*ICAO location identifier*]　(ICLI)
FZOH......... Moga [*Zaire*] [*ICAO location identifier*]　(ICLI)
FZOJ......... Obokote [*Zaire*] [*ICAO location identifier*]　(ICLI)
FZOK......... Kasongo [*Zaire*] [*ICAO location identifier*]　(ICLI)
FZOO......... Kailo [*Zaire*] [*ICAO location identifier*]　(ICLI)
FZOP......... Punia [*Zaire*] [*ICAO location identifier*]　(ICLI)
FZOS......... Kasese [*Zaire*] [*ICAO location identifier*]　(ICLI)
FZPB......... Kamituga [*Zaire*] [*ICAO location identifier*]　(ICLI)
FZPT......... Freiburger Zeitschrift fuer Philosophie und Theologie [*A publication*]
FZQA......... Lubumbashi/Luano [*Zaire*] [*ICAO location identifier*]　(ICLI)
FZQC......... Pweto [*Zaire*] [*ICAO location identifier*]　(ICLI)
FZQD......... Mulungwishi [*Zaire*] [*ICAO location identifier*]　(ICLI)

FZQF......... Fungurume [*Zaire*] [*ICAO location identifier*]   (ICLI)
FZQG........ Kasenga [*Zaire*] [*ICAO location identifier*]   (ICLI)
FZQH......... Katwe [*Zaire*] [*ICAO location identifier*]   (ICLI)
FZQI.......... Kamatanda [*Zaire*] [*ICAO location identifier*]   (ICLI)
FZQJ .... Mwadingusha [*Zaire*] [*ICAO location identifier*]   (ICLI)
FZQM .... Kolwezi [*Zaire*] [*ICAO location identifier*]   (ICLI)
FZQN........ Mutshatsha [*Zaire*] [*ICAO location identifier*]   (ICLI)
FZQO........ Lubumbashi/Karavia [*Zaire*] [*ICAO location identifier*]   (ICLI)
FZQP......... Kisenge [*Zaire*] [*ICAO location identifier*]   (ICLI)
FZQU......... Lubudi [*Zaire*] [*ICAO location identifier*]   (ICLI)
FZQV......... Mitwaba [*Zaire*] [*ICAO location identifier*]   (ICLI)
FZQW........ Luishi [*Zaire*] [*ICAO location identifier*]   (ICLI)
FZRA........ Freezing Rain [*Meteorology*]
FZRA........ Manono [*Zaire*] [*ICAO location identifier*]   (ICLI)
FZRB......... Moba [*Zaire*] [*ICAO location identifier*]   (ICLI)
FZRC......... Mukoy [*Zaire*] [*ICAO location identifier*]   (ICLI)
FZRD........ Kabombo [*Zaire*] [*ICAO location identifier*]   (ICLI)
FZRF......... Kalemie [*Zaire*] [*ICAO location identifier*]   (ICLI)
FZRG........ Kania-Sominka [*Zaire*] [*ICAO location identifier*]   (ICLI)
FZRJ .... Pepa [*Zaire*] [*ICAO location identifier*]   (ICLI)
FZRK........ Kansimba [*Zaire*] [*ICAO location identifier*]   (ICLI)
FZRL......... Lusinga [*Zaire*] [*ICAO location identifier*]   (ICLI)
FZRM........ Kabalo [*Zaire*] [*ICAO location identifier*]   (ICLI)
FZRN........ Nyunzu [*Zaire*] [*ICAO location identifier*]   (ICLI)
FZRO........ Luvua [*Zaire*] [*ICAO location identifier*]   (ICLI)
FZRQ........ Kongolo [*Zaire*] [*ICAO location identifier*]   (ICLI)
FZRSA ...... Fiziologiya na Rasteniyata [*Sofia*] [*A publication*]
FZS.......... Fellow of the Zoological Society [*British*]
FZSA......... Kamina-Base [*Zaire*] [*ICAO location identifier*]   (ICLI)
FZSB......... Kamina-Ville [*Zaire*] [*ICAO location identifier*]   (ICLI)
FZSC......... Songa [*Zaire*] [*ICAO location identifier*]   (ICLI)
FZSD......... Sandoa [*Zaire*] [*ICAO location identifier*]   (ICLI)
FZSE......... Kanene [*Zaire*] [*ICAO location identifier*]   (ICLI)
FZSEDV.... Fortschritte in der Zoologischen Systematik und
            Evolutionsforschung [*A publication*]
FZSI .... Dilolo [*Zaire*] [*ICAO location identifier*]   (ICLI)
FZSJ.......... Kasaji [*Zaire*] [*ICAO location identifier*]   (ICLI)
FZSK......... Kapanga [*Zaire*] [*ICAO location identifier*]   (ICLI)
FZSL......... Fellow of the Zoological Society, London [*British*]   (ROG)
FZSTO ...... Frozen Storage
FZT........... United States Fish and Wildlife Service, Laurel, MD [*OCLC
            symbol*]   (OCLC)
FZTK........ Kaniama [*Zaire*] [*ICAO location identifier*]   (ICLI)
FZTL......... Luena [*Zaire*] [*ICAO location identifier*]   (ICLI)
FZTS......... Kasese/Kaniama [*Zaire*] [*ICAO location identifier*]   (ICLI)
FZU .... St. Louis, MO [*Location identifier*] [*FAA*]   (FAAL)
FZU .... United States Fish and Wildlife Service, Slidell, LA [*OCLC
            symbol*]   (OCLC)
FZUA .... Kananga [*Zaire*] [*ICAO location identifier*]   (ICLI)
FZUE......... Lubondaie [*Zaire*] [*ICAO location identifier*]   (ICLI)
FZUF......... Kasongo [*Zaire*] [*ICAO location identifier*]   (ICLI)
FZUG .... Luisa [*Zaire*] [*ICAO location identifier*]   (ICLI)
FZUH........ Moma [*Zaire*] [*ICAO location identifier*]   (ICLI)
FZUI.......... Mboi [*Zaire*] [*ICAO location identifier*]   (ICLI)
FZUJ......... Muambi [*Zaire*] [*ICAO location identifier*]   (ICLI)
FZUK........ Tshikapa [*Zaire*] [*ICAO location identifier*]   (ICLI)
FZUKA...... Fiziologichnii Zhurnal (Kiev) [*A publication*]
FZUL......... Bulape [*Zaire*] [*ICAO location identifier*]   (ICLI)
FZUM .... Mutoto [*Zaire*] [*ICAO location identifier*]   (ICLI)
FZUN........ Luebo [*Zaire*] [*ICAO location identifier*]   (ICLI)
FZUO .... Musese [*Zaire*] [*ICAO location identifier*]   (ICLI)
FZUR........ Tshibala [*Zaire*] [*ICAO location identifier*]   (ICLI)
FZUS......... Tshikaji [*Zaire*] [*ICAO location identifier*]   (ICLI)
FZUT......... Katubwe [*Zaire*] [*ICAO location identifier*]   (ICLI)
FZUU........ Lutshatsha [*Zaire*] [*ICAO location identifier*]   (ICLI)
FZUV........ Kalonda [*Zaire*] [*ICAO location identifier*]   (ICLI)
FZV........... Fraserfund Venture Capital Corp. [*Vancouver Stock Exchange
            symbol*]
FZV........... United States Fish and Wildlife Service, National Fishery
            Research Laboratory, La Crosse, WI [*OCLC
            symbol*]   (OCLC)
FZVA......... Lodja [*Zaire*] [*ICAO location identifier*]   (ICLI)
FZVC......... Kole Sur Lukenie [*Zaire*] [*ICAO location identifier*]   (ICLI)
FZVD........ Dingele [*Zaire*] [*ICAO location identifier*]   (ICLI)
FZVE......... Lomela [*Zaire*] [*ICAO location identifier*]   (ICLI)
FZVF......... Kutusongo [*Zaire*] [*ICAO location identifier*]   (ICLI)
FZVG........ Katako, Kombe [*Zaire*] [*ICAO location identifier*]   (ICLI)
FZVH .... Shongamba [*Zaire*] [*ICAO location identifier*]   (ICLI)
FZVI.......... Lusambo [*Zaire*] [*ICAO location identifier*]   (ICLI)
FZVJ .... Tshumbe [*Zaire*] [*ICAO location identifier*]   (ICLI)
FZVK........ Lukombe-Batwa [*Zaire*] [*ICAO location identifier*]   (ICLI)
FZVL......... Wasolo [*Zaire*] [*ICAO location identifier*]   (ICLI)
FZVM........ Mweka [*Zaire*] [*ICAO location identifier*]   (ICLI)
FZVN........ Wembo-Nyama [*Zaire*] [*ICAO location identifier*]   (ICLI)
FZVO .... Bena-Dibele [*Zaire*] [*ICAO location identifier*]   (ICLI)
FZVP......... Dikungu [*Zaire*] [*ICAO location identifier*]   (ICLI)
FZVR......... Basongo [*Zaire*] [*ICAO location identifier*]   (ICLI)
FZVS......... Ilebo [*Zaire*] [*ICAO location identifier*]   (ICLI)
FZVT......... Dekese [*Zaire*] [*ICAO location identifier*]   (ICLI)
FZVU......... Idumbe [*Zaire*] [*ICAO location identifier*]   (ICLI)

FZW .... United States Fish and Wildlife Service, Denver, CO [*OCLC
            symbol*]   (OCLC)
FZWA........ Mbuji-Mayi [*Zaire*] [*ICAO location identifier*]   (ICLI)
FZWB........ Bibanga [*Zaire*] [*ICAO location identifier*]   (ICLI)
FZWC........ Gandajika [*Zaire*] [*ICAO location identifier*]   (ICLI)
FZWE........ Mwene-Ditu [*Zaire*] [*ICAO location identifier*]   (ICLI)
FZWF........ Kipushia [*Zaire*] [*ICAO location identifier*]   (ICLI)
FZWI......... Kashia [*Zaire*] [*ICAO location identifier*]   (ICLI)
FZWR........ Kisengwa [*Zaire*] [*ICAO location identifier*]   (ICLI)
FZWS .... Lubao [*Zaire*] [*ICAO location identifier*]   (ICLI)
FZWT........ Kabinda/Tunta [*Zaire*] [*ICAO location identifier*]   (ICLI)
FZX........... Columbia National Fisheries Research Laboratory, Columbia,
            MO [*OCLC symbol*]   (OCLC)
FZY........... United States Fish and Wildlife Service, Portland, OR [*OCLC
            symbol*]   (OCLC)
FZZ........... United States Fish and Wildlife Service, Atlanta, GA [*OCLC
            symbol*]   (OCLC)
FZZA......... Zaire Fir [*Zaire*] [*ICAO location identifier*]   (ICLI)

DEVELOPING MANAGEMENT SKILLS

SEVENTH EDITION

David A. Whetten
BRIGHAM YOUNG UNIVERSITY

Kim S. Cameron
UNIVERSITY OF MICHIGAN

PEARSON
Prentice Hall

Pearson Education International

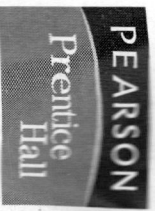

PEARSON
Prentice
Hall

Senior Acquisitions Editor: David Parker
VP/Editorial Director: ... elstad
Product Development Manager:
...shley Santora
Marketing Manager: ...ine Howard
Marketing Assistant: Susan Osterlitz
Associate Director, Production Editorial:
...dy Leale
Managing Editor: Renata Butera
Production Editor: Marcela Boos
Permissions Coordinator: Charles Morris
Associate Director, Manufacturing:
Vinc Scelta
Manufacturing Buyer: Michelle Klein

Manager, Creative Services:
Christy Mahon
Composition Liaison: Suzanne Duda
Interior Design: Suzanne Duda and
Michael J. Fruhbeis
Cover Design: Suzanne Duda
Cover Illustration/Photo: Jim Frazier
Composition: TexTech
Full-Service Project Management:
...tratford Publishing Services
Printer/Binder: Von Hoffmann Press
Cover Printer: Phoenix Color Corp.
Typeface: 10/12 Weidemann-Book

If you purchased this book within the United States or Canada you should be aware that it has been wrongfully imported without the approval of the Publisher or the Author.

Pearson Prentice Hall™ is a trademark of Pearson Education, Inc.
Pearson® is a registered trademark of Pearson plc
Prentice Hall® is a registered trademark of Pearson Education, Inc.

Pearson Education Ltd., London
Pearson Education Singapore, Pte. Ltd.
Pearson Education, Canada, Ltd.
Pearson Education—Japan

Pearson Education Australia PTY, Limited
Pearson Education North Asia Ltd.
Pearson Educación de Mexico, S.A. de C.V.
Pearson Education Malaysia, Pte. Ltd.
Pearson Education, Upper Saddle River, New Jersey

10 9 8 7 6 5 4 3 2 1
ISBN: 0-13-503280-6

BRIEF TABLE OF CONTENTS

Preface   xvii
Introduction   1

PART I   PERSONAL SKILLS   44

1   Developing Self-Awareness   45
2   Managing Personal Stress   109
3   Solving Problems Analytically and Creatively   171

PART II   INTERPERSONAL SKILLS   236

4   Building Relationships by Communicating Supportively   237
5   Gaining Power and Influence   283
6   Motivating Others   327
7   Managing Conflict   377

PART III   GROUP SKILLS   442

8   Empowering and Delegating   443
9   Building Effective Teams and Teamwork   493
10   Leading Positive Change   537

PART IV   SPECIFIC COMMUNICATION SKILLS   594

Supplement A   Making Oral and Written Presentations   595
Supplement B   Conducting Interviews   623
Supplement C   Conducting Meetings   655
Appendix I   Glossary   677
Appendix II   References   687
Name Index   709
Subject Index   713
Combined Index   717

CONTENTS

Preface   xvii

INTRODUCTION   1

THE CRITICAL ROLE OF MANAGEMENT SKILLS   3

The Importance of Competent Managers   6
The Skills of Effective Managers   7
Essential Management Skills   8
What Are Management Skills?   9
Improving Management Skills   12
An Approach to Skill Development   13
Leadership and Management   16
Contents of the Book   18
Organization of the Book   19
Practice and Application   21
Diversity and Individual Differences   21
Summary   23

SUPPLEMENTARY MATERIAL   24

Diagnostic Survey and Exercises   24
Personal Assessment of Management Skills (PAMS)   24
What Does It Take to Be an Effective Manager?   28
SSS Software In-Basket Exercise   30

SCORING KEY AND COMPARISON DATA   42

Personal Assessment of Management Skills   42
Scoring Key   42
Comparison Data   42
What Does It Take to Be an Effective Manager?   43
SSS Software In-Basket Exercise   43

PART I   PERSONAL SKILLS   44

1   DEVELOPING SELF-AWARENESS   45

SKILL ASSESSMENT   46

Diagnostic Surveys for Self-Awareness   46
Self-Awareness Assessment   46
Emotional Intelligence Assessment   47
The Defining Issues Test   48

v

The Learning Style Inventory 52
Locus of Control Scale 54
Tolerance of Ambiguity Scale 56
Core Self-Evaluation Scale (CSES) 57

SKILL LEARNING 58
Key Dimensions of Self-Awareness 58
The Enigma of Self-Awareness 59
The Sensitive Line 59
Understanding and Appreciating Individual Differences 61
Important Areas of Self-Awareness 62
Emotional Intelligence 63
Values 66
Ethical Decision Making and Values 74
Learning Style 75
Attitudes Toward Change 79
Core Self-Evaluation 83

SKILL ANALYSIS 88
Cases Involving Self-Awareness 88
Communist Prison Camp 88
Computerized Exam 89
Decision Dilemmas 90

SKILL PRACTICE 93
Exercises for Improving Self-Awareness Through Self-Disclosure 93
Through the Looking Glass 93
Diagnosing Managerial Characteristics 94
An Exercise for Identifying Aspects of Personal Culture:
A Learning Plan and Autobiography 96

SKILL APPLICATION 99
Activities for Developing Self-Awareness 99
Suggested Assignments 99
Application Plan and Evaluation 99

SCORING KEYS AND COMPARISON DATA 101
Self-Awareness Assessment 101
Scoring Key 101
Comparison Data 101
Emotional Intelligence Assessment 101
Scoring Key 101
Comparison Data 103
The Defining Issues Test 103
The Escaped Prisoner 103
The Doctor's Dilemma 104
The Newspaper 104
Learning Style Inventory 105
Scoring Key 105
Locus of Control 105
Scoring Key 105
Comparison Data 105
Tolerance of Ambiguity 106
Scoring Key 106
Comparison Data 106

Core Self-Evaluation Scale   106
  Scoring Key   106
  Comparison Data   107

2 MANAGING PERSONAL STRESS   109

SKILL ASSESSMENT   110

Diagnostic Surveys for Managing Stress   110
  Stress Management Assessment   110
  Time Management Assessment   111
  Type A Personality Inventory   112
  Social Readjustment Rating Scale   113
  Sources of Personal Stress   115

SKILL LEARNING   116

Improving the Management of Stress and Time   116
  The Role of Management   117
Major Elements of Stress   117
  Reactions to Stress   118
  Coping with Stress   119
Managing Stress   121
  Stressors   121
Eliminating Stressors   124
  Eliminating Time Stressors Through Time Management   125
  Eliminating Encounter Stressors Through Collaboration and Emotional Intelligence   132
  Eliminating Situational Stressors Through Work Redesign   134
  Eliminating Anticipatory Stressors Through Prioritizing, Goal Setting, and Small Wins   136
Developing Resiliency   138
  Physiological Resiliency   140
  Psychological Resiliency   143
  Social Resiliency   147
Temporary Stress-Reduction Techniques   148

SKILL ANALYSIS   151

Cases Involving Stress Management   151
  The Turn of the Tide   151
  The Case of the Missing Time   154

SKILL PRACTICE   159

Exercises for Long-Term and Short-Run Stress Management   159
  The Small-Wins Strategy   159
  Life-Balance Analysis   160
  Deep Relaxation   162
  Monitoring and Managing Time   163

SKILL APPLICATION   165

Activities for Managing Stress   165
  Suggested Assignments   165
  Application Plan and Evaluation   166

SCORING KEYS AND COMPARISON DATA   168

Stress Management Assessment   168
  Scoring Key   168
  Comparison Data   168
Time Management Assessment   168
  Scoring Key   168

Comparison Data 169
Type A Personality Inventory 169
   Scoring Key 169
   Comparison Data 169
Social Readjustment Scale 170
   Comparison Data 170
Source of Personal Stress 170

3 SOLVING PROBLEMS ANALYTICALLY AND CREATIVELY 171

SKILL ASSESSMENT 172
Diagnostic Surveys for Creative Problem Solving 172
   Problem Solving, Creativity, and Innovation 172
   How Creative Are You?© 173
   Innovative Attitude Scale 175
   Creative Style Assessment 176

SKILL LEARNING 178
Problem Solving, Creativity, and Innovation 178
Steps in Analytical Problem Solving 178
   Defining the Problem 178
   Generating Alternatives 180
   Evaluating Alternatives 180
   Implementing the Solution 181
Limitations of the Analytical Problem-Solving Model 182
Impediments to Creative Problem Solving 182
Multiple Approaches to Creativity 183
Conceptual Blocks 187
   Percy Spencer's Magnetron 189
   Spence Silver's Glue 189
   The Four Types of Conceptual Blocks 189
Review of Conceptual Blocks 198
Conceptual Blockbusting 198
   Stages in Creative Thought 198
   Methods for Improving Problem Definition 199
   Ways to Generate More Alternatives 203
International Caveats 206
Hints for Applying Problem-Solving Techniques 207
Fostering Creativity in Others 207
   Management Principles 208

SKILL ANALYSIS 214
Cases Involving Problem Solving 214
   Admiral Kimmel's Failure at Pearl Harbor 214
   Creativity at Apple 216

SKILL PRACTICE 219
Exercises for Applying Conceptual Blockbusting 219
   Individual Assignment—Analytical Problem Solving (10 minutes) 219
   Team Assignment—Creative Problem Solving (20 minutes) 220
   Moving Up in the Rankings 221
   Keith Dunn and McGuffey's Restaurant 222
   Creative Problem-Solving Practice 225

SKILL APPLICATION 227
Activities for Solving Problems Creatively 227
   Suggested Assignments 227
   Application Plan and Evaluation 227

SCORING KEYS AND COMPARISON DATA 229
Problem Solving, Creativity, and Innovation 229
  Scoring Key 229
  Comparison Data 229
How Creative Are You©️ 229
  Scoring Key 229
  Comparison Data 230
Innovative Attitude Scale 230
  Scoring Key 230
Creative Style Assessment 231
  Scoring Key 231
SKILL PRACTICE Applying Conceptual Blockbusting 231
  Observer's Feedback Form 231
Answer to Matchstick Problem in Figure 3.4 233
Answer to Shakespeare Riddle in Figure 3.5 233
Some Common Themes Applying to Water and Finance 233
Answer to Name That Ship Problem in Figure 3.6 234
Answer to Nine-Dot Problem in Figure 3.7 234
Answer to Embedded Pattern Problem in Figure 3.8 235

PART II   INTERPERSONAL SKILLS 236

4 BUILDING RELATIONSHIPS BY COMMUNICATING SUPPORTIVELY 237

SKILL ASSESSMENT 238
Diagnostic Surveys for Supportive Communication 238
  Communicating Supportively 238
  Communication Styles 239

SKILL LEARNING 242
Building Positive Interpersonal Relationships 242
The Importance of Effective Communication 243
  The Focus on Accuracy 244
What Is Supportive Communication? 246
Coaching and Counseling 248
  Coaching and Counseling Problems 249
  Defensiveness and Disconfirmation 250
Principles of Supportive Communication 251
  Supportive Communication Is Based on Congruence, not Incongruence 251
  Supportive Communication Is Descriptive, not Evaluative 252
  Supportive Communication Is Problem-oriented, not Person-oriented 254
  Supportive Communication Validates Rather than Invalidates Individuals 255
  Supportive Communication Is Specific (Useful), not Global (Nonuseful) 257
  Supportive Communication Is Conjunctive, not Disjunctive 258
  Supportive Communication Is Owned, not Disowned 259
  Supportive Communication Requires Listening, not One-Way Message Delivery 260
The Personal Management Interview 264
International Caveats 267

SKILL ANALYSIS 270
Cases Involving Building Positive Relationships 270
  Find Somebody Else 270
  Rejected Plans 271

SKILL PRACTICE 273
Exercises for Diagnosing Communication Problems and Fostering Understanding 273
    United Chemical Company 273
    Byron vs. Thomas 275
    Active Listening Exercise 276

SKILL APPLICATION 278
Activities for Communicating Supportively 278
    Suggested Assignments 278
    Application Plan and Evaluation 278

SCORING KEYS AND COMPARISON DATA 280
Communicating Supportively 280
    Scoring Key 280
    Comparison Data 280
Communication Styles 280
    Comparison Data 280
SKILL PRACTICE Diagnosing Problems and Fostering Understanding:
United Chemical Company and Byron vs. Thomas 281
    Observer's Feedback Form 281

5 GAINING POWER AND INFLUENCE 283

SKILL ASSESSMENT 284
Diagnostic Surveys for Gaining Power and Influence 284
    Gaining Power and Influence 284
    Using Influence Strategies 285

SKILL LEARNING 287
Building a Strong Power Base and Using Influence Wisely 287
A Balanced View of Power 287
    Lack of Power 287
    Abuse of Power 289
Strategies for Gaining Organizational Power 290
    The Necessity of Power and Empowerment 290
    Sources of Personal Power 292
    Sources of Position-Power 297
Transforming Power into Influence 302
    Influence Strategies: The Three Rs 302
    The Pros and Cons of Each Strategy 304
    Acting Assertively: Neutralizing Influence Attempts 308

SKILL ANALYSIS 314
Case Involving Power and Influence 314
    River Woods Plant Manager 314

SKILL PRACTICE 315
Exercise for Gaining Power 315
    Repairing Power Failures in Management Circuits 315
Exercise for Using Influence Effectively 316
    Ann Lyman's Proposal 317
Exercises for Neutralizing Unwanted Influence Attempts 318
    Cindy's Fast Foods 318
    9:00 to 7:30 319

SKILL APPLICATION   321
Activities for Gaining Power and Influence   321
   Suggested Assignments   321
   Application Plan and Evaluation   322

SCORING KEYS AND COMPARISON DATA   323
Gaining Power and Influence   323
   Scoring Key   323
   Comparison Data   324
Using Influence Strategies   324
   Scoring Key   324
SKILL PRACTICE Neutralizing Unwanted Influence Attempts   324
   Observer's Feedback Form   324

6   MOTIVATING OTHERS   327

SKILL ASSESSMENT   328
Diagnostic Surveys for Motivating Others   328
   Diagnosing Poor Performance and Enhancing Motivation   328
   Work Performance Assessment   329

SKILL LEARNING   330
Increasing Motivation and Performance   330
Diagnosing Work Performance Problems   330
Enhancing Individuals' Abilities   332
Fostering a Motivating Work Environment   334
Elements of an Effective Motivation Program   335
   Establish Clear Performance Expectations   336
   Remove Obstacles to Performance   338
   Reinforce Performance-Enhancing Behavior   341
   Provide Salient Rewards   349
   Be Fair and Equitable   352
   Provide Timely Rewards and Accurate Feedback   352

SKILL ANALYSIS   358
Case Involving Motivation Problems   358
   Electro Logic   358

SKILL PRACTICE   365
Exercises for Diagnosing Work Performance Problems   365
   Joe Chaney   367
   Work Performance Assessment   368
Exercise for Reshaping Unacceptable Behaviors   368
   Shaheen Matombo   368

SKILL APPLICATION   371
Activities for Motivating Others   371
   Suggested Assignments   371
   Application Plan and Evaluation   372

SCORING KEYS AND COMPARISON DATA   374
Diagnosing Poor Performance and Enhancing Motivation   374
   Scoring Key   374
   Comparison Data   374
Work Performance Assessment   375
   Scoring Key   375

Comparison Data 375
SKILL PRACTICE Exercise for Reshaping Unacceptable Behaviors 375
Observer's Feedback Form 375

7 MANAGING CONFLICT 377

SKILL ASSESSMENT 378
Diagnostic Surveys for Managing Conflict 378
Managing Interpersonal Conflict 378
Strategies for Handling Conflict 379

SKILL LEARNING 380
Interpersonal Conflict Management 380
Mixed Feelings About Conflict 380
Diagnosing the Type of Interpersonal Conflict 382
Conflict Focus 382
Conflict Source 384
Selecting the Appropriate Conflict Management Approach 387
Comparing Conflict Management and Negotiation Strategies 390
Selection Factors 390
Resolving Interpersonal Confrontations Using the Collaborative Approach 394
A General Framework for Collaborative Problem Solving 395
The Four Phases of Collaborative Problem Solving 396

SKILL ANALYSIS 409
Case Involving Interpersonal Conflict 409
Educational Pension Investments 409

SKILL PRACTICE 414
Exercise for Diagnosing Sources of Conflict 414
SSS Software Management Problems 414
Exercises for Selecting an Appropriate Conflict Management Strategy 422
Bradley's Barn 423
Avocado Computers 423
Phelps, Inc. 424
Exercises for Resolving Interpersonal Disputes 424
Freida Mae Jones 425
Can Larry Fit In? 427
Meeting at Hartford Manufacturing Company 428

SKILL APPLICATION 435
Activities for Improving Managing Conflict Skills 435
Suggested Assignments 435
Application Plan and Evaluation 436

SCORING KEYS AND COMPARISON DATA 438
Managing Interpersonal Conflict 438
Scoring Key 438
Comparison Data 439
Strategies for Handling Conflict 439
Scoring Key 439
SKILL PRACTICE Exercises for Resolving Interpersonal Disputes 439
Observer's Feedback Form 439

PART III GROUP SKILLS 442

8 EMPOWERING AND DELEGATING 443

SKILL ASSESSMENT 444
Diagnostic Surveys for Empowering and Delegating 444
   Effective Empowerment and Delegation 444
   Personal Empowerment Assessment 445

SKILL LEARNING 447
Empowering and Delegating 447
A Management Dilemma Involving Empowerment 447
   The Dirty Dozen 448
The Meaning of Empowerment 449
Historical Roots of Empowerment 450
Dimensions of Empowerment 451
   Self-Efficacy 451
   Self-Determination 452
   Personal Consequence 453
   Meaning 453
   Trust 454
   Review of Empowerment Dimensions 455
How to Develop Empowerment 455
   Articulating a Clear Vision and Goals 456
   Fostering Personal Mastery Experiences 457
   Modeling 458
   Providing Support 458
   Emotional Arousal 459
   Providing Information 460
   Providing Resources 461
   Connecting to Outcomes 461
   Creating Confidence 462
   Review of Empowerment Principles 463
Inhibitors to Empowerment 465
   Attitudes About Subordinates 466
   Personal Insecurities 466
   Need for Control 466
Delegating Work 467
   Advantages of Empowered Delegation 467
   Deciding When to Delegate 468
   Deciding to Whom to Delegate 469
   Deciding How to Delegate Effectively 469
   Review of Delegation Principles 474
International Caveats 475

SKILL ANALYSIS 478
Cases Involving Empowerment and Delegation 478
   Minding the Store 478
   Changing the Portfolio 479

SKILL PRACTICE 480
Exercises for Empowerment 480
   Executive Development Associates 480
   Empowering Ourselves 484
   Deciding to Delegate 485

SKILL APPLICATION 487
Activities for Empowerment and Delegation 487
   Suggested Assignments 487
   Application Plan and Evaluation 487

SCORING KEYS AND COMPARISON DATA 489
Effective Empowerment and Delegation 489
   Scoring Key 489
   Comparison Data 489
Personal Empowerment 489
   Scoring Key 489
   Comparison Data 490
SKILL PRACTICE Deciding to Delegate: Analysis of "An Emergency Request" 490
SKILL PRACTICE Analysis of Biological Warfare 490

9 BUILDING EFFECTIVE TEAMS AND TEAMWORK 493

SKILL ASSESSMENT 494
Diagnostic Surveys for Building Effective Teams 494
   Team Development Behaviors 494
   Diagnosing the Need for Team Building 495

SKILL LEARNING 497
Developing Teams and Teamwork 497
The Advantages of Teams 498
   An Example of an Effective Team 501
Team Development 502
   The Forming Stage 502
   The Norming Stage 503
   The Storming Stage 505
   The Performing Stage 507
Leading Teams 510
   Developing Credibility 511
   Establish SMART Goals and Everest Goals 513
   International Caveats 515
Team Membership 516
   Advantageous Roles 516
   Providing Feedback 520
   International Caveats 521

SKILL ANALYSIS 523
Cases Involving Building Effective Teams 523
   The Tallahassee Democrat's ELITE Team 523
   The Cash Register Incident 525

SKILL PRACTICE 527
Exercises in Building Effective Teams 527
   Team Diagnosis and Team Development Exercise 527
   Winning the War on Talent 528
   Team Performance Exercise 531

SKILL APPLICATION 533
Activities for Building Effective Teams 533
   Suggested Assignments 533
   Application Plan and Evaluation 534

SCORING KEYS AND COMPARISON DATA   535
Team Development Behaviors   535
   Scoring Key   535
   Comparison Data   535
Diagnosing the Need for Team Building   535
   Comparison Data   535

10   LEADING POSITIVE CHANGE   537

SKILL ASSESSMENT   538
Diagnostic Surveys for Leading Positive Change   538
   Leading Positive Change   538
   Reflected Best-Self Feedback™ Exercise   539
   A Sample E-mail Request for Feedback   539
   Machiavellianism Scale—MACH IV   540

SKILL LEARNING   542
Leading Positive Change   542
Ubiquitous and Escalating Change   543
The Need for Frameworks   543
Tendencies Toward Stability   544
A Framework for Leading Positive Change   546
   Establishing a Climate of Positivity   548
   Creating Readiness for Change   554
   Articulating a Vision of Abundance   557
   Generating Commitment to the Vision   561
   Institutionalizing the Positive Change   566

SKILL ANALYSIS   572
Cases Involving Leading Positive Change   572
   Corporate Vision Statements   572
   Lee Iacocca's Transformation of Chrysler—1979–1984   578

SKILL PRACTICE   585
Exercises in Leading Positive Change   585
   Reflected Best-Self Portrait   585
   Positive Organizational Diagnosis Exercise   586
   A Positive Change Agenda   587

SKILL APPLICATION   588
Activities for Leading Positive Change   588
   Suggested Assignments   588
   Application Plan and Evaluation   589

SCORING KEYS AND COMPARISON DATA   591
Leading Positive Change   591
   Scoring Key   591
   Comparison Data   591
Reflected Best-Self Feedback™ Exercise   591
Machiavellianism Scale—MACH IV   591
   Scoring Key   591
   Comparison Data   592
SKILL ANALYSIS Iacocca's Transformation of Chrysler—1979–1984   592

PART IV SPECIFIC COMMUNICATION SKILLS 594

Supplement A MAKING ORAL AND WRITTEN PRESENTATIONS 595

SKILL LEARNING 596

Making Oral and Written Presentations 596
Essential Elements of Effective Presentations 597

SKILL PRACTICE 613

Exercises for Making Effective Oral and Written Presentations 613
Speaking as a Leader 613
Quality Circles at Battle Creek Foods 614

Supplement B CONDUCTING INTERVIEWS 623

SKILL LEARNING 624

Planning and Conducting Interviews 624
Specific Types of Organizational Interviews 633

SKILL PRACTICE 638

Exercises for Conducting Special-Purpose Interviews 638
Evaluating the New Employee-Orientation Program 638
Performance-Appraisal Interview with Chris Jakobsen 641
Employment-Selection Interview at Smith Farley Insurance 647

Supplement C CONDUCTING MEETINGS 655

SKILL LEARNING 656

Conducting Effective Meetings:
A Short Guide for Meeting Managers and Meeting Participants 656
The Five Ps of Effective Meetings 656
Suggestions for Group Members 661

SKILL PRACTICE 664

Exercises for Conducting Meetings 664
Preparing and Conducting a Team Meeting at SSS Software 664
Role Diagnosis 664
Meeting Evaluation Worksheet 665

Appendix I GLOSSARY 677

Appendix II REFERENCES 687

NAME INDEX 709

SUBJECT INDEX 713

COMBINED INDEX 717

DEVELOPING MANAGEMENT SKILLS

SEVENTH EDITION

David A. Whetten
BRIGHAM YOUNG UNIVERSITY

Kim S. Cameron
UNIVERSITY OF MICHIGAN

Pearson Education International

Senior Acquisitions Editor: David Parker
VP/Editorial Director: Jeff Shelstad
Product Development Manager:
Ashley Santora
Marketing Manager: Anne Howard
Marketing Assistant: Susan Osterlitz
Associate Director, Production Editorial:
Judy Leale
Managing Editor: Renata Butera
Production Editor: Marcela Boos
Permissions Coordinator: Charles Morris
Associate Director, Manufacturing:
Vinnie Scelta
Manufacturing Buyer: Michelle Klein

Manager, Creative Services:
Christy Mahon
Composition Liaison: Suzanne Duda
Interior Design: Suzanne Duda and
Michael J. Fruhbeis
Cover Design: Suzanne Duda
Cover Illustration/Photo: Jim Frazier
Composition: TexTech
Full-Service Project Management:
Stratford Publishing Services
Printer/Binder: Von Hoffmann Press
Cover Printer: Phoenix Color Corp.
Typeface: 10/12 Weidemann-Book

Credits and acknowledgments borrowed from other sources and reproduced, with permission, in this textbook appear on the appropriate page within the text.

If you purchased this book within the United States or Canada you should be aware that it has been wrongfully imported without the approval of the Publisher or the Author.

Pearson Education Ltd. , London.
Pearson Education Singapore, Pte. Ltd.
Pearson Education, Canada, Ltd.
Pearson Education–Japan

Pearson Education Australia PTY, Limited
Pearson Education North Asia Ltd.
Pearson Educación de Mexico, S.A. de C.V.
Pearson Education Malaysia, Pte. Ltd.
Pearson Education, Upper Saddle River, New Jersey

10 9 8 7 6 5 4 3 2 1
ISBN: 0-13-503280-6

BRIEF TABLE OF CONTENTS

Preface   xvii

Introduction   1

PART I   PERSONAL SKILLS   44

1   Developing Self-Awareness   45

2   Managing Personal Stress   109

3   Solving Problems Analytically and Creatively   171

PART II   INTERPERSONAL SKILLS   236

4   Building Relationships by Communicating Supportively   237

5   Gaining Power and Influence   283

6   Motivating Others   327

7   Managing Conflict   377

PART III   GROUP SKILLS   442

8   Empowering and Delegating   443

9   Building Effective Teams and Teamwork   493

10 Leading Positive Change   537

PART IV   SPECIFIC COMMUNICATION SKILLS   594

Supplement A   Making Oral and Written Presentations   595

Supplement B   Conducting Interviews   623

Supplement C   Conducting Meetings   655

Appendix I   Glossary   677

Appendix II   References   687

Name Index   709

Subject Index   713

Combined Index   717

CONTENTS

Preface xvii

INTRODUCTION 1

THE CRITICAL ROLE OF MANAGEMENT SKILLS 3
The Importance of Competent Managers 6
The Skills of Effective Managers 7
Essential Management Skills 8
What Are Management Skills? 9
Improving Management Skills 12
An Approach to Skill Development 13
Leadership and Management 16
Contents of the Book 18
Organization of the Book 19
Practice and Application 21
Diversity and Individual Differences 21
Summary 23

SUPPLEMENTARY MATERIAL 24
Diagnostic Survey and Exercises 24
Personal Assessment of Management Skills (PAMS) 24
What Does It Take to Be an Effective Manager? 28
SSS Software In-Basket Exercise 30

SCORING KEY AND COMPARISON DATA 42
Personal Assessment of Management Skills 42
Scoring Key 42
Comparison Data 42
What Does It Take to Be an Effective Manager? 43
SSS Software In-Basket Exercise 43

PART I   PERSONAL SKILLS 44

1   DEVELOPING SELF-AWARENESS 45

SKILL ASSESSMENT 46
Diagnostic Surveys for Self-Awareness 46
Self-Awareness Assessment 46
Emotional Intelligence Assessment 47
The Defining Issues Test 48

The Learning Style Inventory   52
Locus of Control Scale   54
Tolerance of Ambiguity Scale   56
Core Self-Evaluation Scale (CSES)   57

SKILL LEARNING   58
Key Dimensions of Self-Awareness   58
The Enigma of Self-Awareness   59
    The Sensitive Line   59
Understanding and Appreciating Individual Differences   61
Important Areas of Self-Awareness   62
    Emotional Intelligence   63
    Values   66
    Ethical Decision Making and Values   74
    Learning Style   75
    Attitudes Toward Change   79
    Core Self-Evaluation   83

SKILL ANALYSIS   88
Cases Involving Self-Awareness   88
    Communist Prison Camp   88
    Computerized Exam   89
    Decision Dilemmas   90

SKILL PRACTICE   93
Exercises for Improving Self-Awareness Through Self-Disclosure   93
    Through the Looking Glass   93
    Diagnosing Managerial Characteristics   94
    An Exercise for Identifying Aspects of Personal Culture:
    A Learning Plan and Autobiography   96

SKILL APPLICATION   99
Activities for Developing Self-Awareness   99
    Suggested Assignments   99
    Application Plan and Evaluation   99

SCORING KEYS AND COMPARISON DATA   101
Self-Awareness Assessment   101
    Scoring Key   101
    Comparison Data   101
Emotional Intelligence Assessment   101
    Scoring Key   101
    Comparison Data   103
The Defining Issues Test   103
    The Escaped Prisoner   103
    The Doctor's Dilemma   104
    The Newspaper   104
Learning Style Inventory   105
    Scoring Key   105
Locus of Control   105
    Scoring Key   105
    Comparison Data   105
Tolerance of Ambiguity   106
    Scoring Key   106
    Comparison Data   106

Core Self-Evaluation Scale 106
Scoring Key 106
Comparison Data 107

2 MANAGING PERSONAL STRESS 109

SKILL ASSESSMENT 110

Diagnostic Surveys for Managing Stress 110
Stress Management Assessment 110
Time Management Assessment 111
Type A Personality Inventory 112
Social Readjustment Rating Scale 113
Sources of Personal Stress 115

SKILL LEARNING 116
Improving the Management of Stress and Time 116
The Role of Management 117
Major Elements of Stress 117
Reactions to Stress 118
Coping with Stress 119
Managing Stress 121
Stressors 121
Eliminating Stressors 124
Eliminating Time Stressors Through Time Management 125
Eliminating Encounter Stressors Through Collaboration and Emotional Intelligence 132
Eliminating Situational Stressors Through Work Redesign 134
Eliminating Anticipatory Stressors Through Prioritizing, Goal Setting, and Small Wins 136
Developing Resiliency 138
Physiological Resiliency 140
Psychological Resiliency 143
Social Resiliency 147
Temporary Stress-Reduction Techniques 148

SKILL ANALYSIS 151
Cases Involving Stress Management 151
The Turn of the Tide 151
The Case of the Missing Time 154

SKILL PRACTICE 159
Exercises for Long-Term and Short-Run Stress Management 159
The Small-Wins Strategy 159
Life-Balance Analysis 160
Deep Relaxation 162
Monitoring and Managing Time 163

SKILL APPLICATION 165
Activities for Managing Stress 165
Suggested Assignments 165
Application Plan and Evaluation 166

SCORING KEYS AND COMPARISON DATA 168
Stress Management Assessment 168
Scoring Key 168
Comparison Data 168
Time Management Assessment 168
Scoring Key 168

Comparison Data   169
Type A Personality Inventory   169
    Scoring Key   169
    Comparison Data   169
Social Readjustment Scale   170
    Comparison Data   170
Source of Personal Stress   170

3   SOLVING PROBLEMS ANALYTICALLY AND CREATIVELY   171

SKILL ASSESSMENT   172
Diagnostic Surveys for Creative Problem Solving   172
    Problem Solving, Creativity, and Innovation   172
    How Creative Are You?© 173
    Innovative Attitude Scale   175
    Creative Style Assessment   176

SKILL LEARNING   178
Problem Solving, Creativity, and Innovation   178
Steps in Analytical Problem Solving   178
    Defining the Problem   178
    Generating Alternatives   180
    Evaluating Alternatives   180
    Implementing the Solution   181
Limitations of the Analytical Problem-Solving Model   182
Impediments to Creative Problem Solving   182
Multiple Approaches to Creativity   183
Conceptual Blocks   187
    Percy Spencer's Magnetron   189
    Spence Silver's Glue   189
    The Four Types of Conceptual Blocks   189
    Review of Conceptual Blocks   198
Conceptual Blockbusting   198
    Stages in Creative Thought   198
    Methods for Improving Problem Definition   199
    Ways to Generate More Alternatives   203
International Caveats   206
Hints for Applying Problem-Solving Techniques   207
Fostering Creativity in Others   207
    Management Principles   208

SKILL ANALYSIS   214
Cases Involving Problem Solving   214
    Admiral Kimmel's Failure at Pearl Harbor   214
    Creativity at Apple   216

SKILL PRACTICE   219
Exercises for Applying Conceptual Blockbusting   219
    Individual Assignment—Analytical Problem Solving (10 minutes)   219
    Team Assignment—Creative Problem Solving (20 minutes)   220
    Moving Up in the Rankings   221
    Keith Dunn and McGuffey's Restaurant   222
    Creative Problem-Solving Practice   225

SKILL APPLICATION   227
Activities for Solving Problems Creatively   227
    Suggested Assignments   227
    Application Plan and Evaluation   227

SCORING KEYS AND COMPARISON DATA   229
Problem Solving, Creativity, and Innovation   229
  Scoring Key   229
  Comparison Data   229
How Creative Are You©   229
  Scoring Key   229
  Comparison Data   230
Innovative Attitude Scale   230
  Scoring Key   230
Creative Style Assessment   231
  Scoring Key   231
SKILL PRACTICE Applying Conceptual Blockbusting   231
  Observer's Feedback Form   231
Answer to Matchstick Problem in Figure 3.4   233
Answer to Shakespeare Riddle in Figure 3.5   233
Some Common Themes Applying to Water and Finance   233
Answer to Name That Ship Problem in Figure 3.6   234
Answer to Nine-Dot Problem in Figure 3.7   234
Answer to Embedded Pattern Problem in Figure 3.8   235

PART II   INTERPERSONAL SKILLS   236

4   BUILDING RELATIONSHIPS BY COMMUNICATING SUPPORTIVELY   237

SKILL ASSESSMENT   238
Diagnostic Surveys for Supportive Communication   238
  Communicating Supportively   238
  Communication Styles   239

SKILL LEARNING   242
Building Positive Interpersonal Relationships   242
The Importance of Effective Communication   243
  The Focus on Accuracy   244
What Is Supportive Communication?   246
Coaching and Counseling   248
  Coaching and Counseling Problems   249
  Defensiveness and Disconfirmation   250
Principles of Supportive Communication   251
  Supportive Communication Is Based on Congruence, not Incongruence   251
  Supportive Communication Is Descriptive, not Evaluative   252
  Supportive Communication Is Problem-oriented, not Person-oriented   254
  Supportive Communication Validates Rather than Invalidates Individuals   255
  Supportive Communication Is Specific (Useful), not Global (Nonuseful)   257
  Supportive Communication Is Conjunctive, not Disjunctive   258
  Supportive Communication Is Owned, not Disowned   259
  Supportive Communication Requires Listening, not One-Way Message Delivery   260
The Personal Management Interview   264
International Caveats   267

SKILL ANALYSIS   270
Cases Involving Building Positive Relationships   270
  Find Somebody Else   270
  Rejected Plans   271

SKILL PRACTICE   273
Exercises for Diagnosing Communication Problems and Fostering Understanding   273
   United Chemical Company   273
   Byron vs. Thomas   275
   Active Listening Exercise   276

SKILL APPLICATION   278
Activities for Communicating Supportively   278
   Suggested Assignments   278
   Application Plan and Evaluation   278

SCORING KEYS AND COMPARISON DATA   280
Communicating Supportively   280
   Scoring Key   280
   Comparison Data   280
Communication Styles   280
   Comparison Data   280
SKILL PRACTICE Diagnosing Problems and Fostering Understanding:
United Chemical Company and Byron vs. Thomas   281
   Observer's Feedback Form   281

5   GAINING POWER AND INFLUENCE   283

SKILL ASSESSMENT   284
Diagnostic Surveys for Gaining Power and Influence   284
   Gaining Power and Influence   284
   Using Influence Strategies   285

SKILL LEARNING   287
Building a Strong Power Base and Using Influence Wisely   287
A Balanced View of Power   287
   Lack of Power   287
   Abuse of Power   289
Strategies for Gaining Organizational Power   290
   The Necessity of Power and Empowerment   290
   Sources of Personal Power   292
   Sources of Position-Power   297
Transforming Power into Influence   302
   Influence Strategies: The Three Rs   302
   The Pros and Cons of Each Strategy   304
   Acting Assertively: Neutralizing Influence Attempts   308

SKILL ANALYSIS   314
Case Involving Power and Influence   314
   River Woods Plant Manager   314

SKILL PRACTICE   315
Exercise for Gaining Power   315
   Repairing Power Failures in Management Circuits   315
Exercise for Using Influence Effectively   316
   Ann Lyman's Proposal   317
Exercises for Neutralizing Unwanted Influence Attempts   318
   Cindy's Fast Foods   318
   9:00 to 7:30   319

SKILL APPLICATION 321
Activities for Gaining Power and Influence 321
    Suggested Assignments 321
    Application Plan and Evaluation 322

SCORING KEYS AND COMPARISON DATA 323
Gaining Power and Influence 323
    Scoring Key 323
    Comparison Data 324
Using Influence Strategies 324
    Scoring Key 324
SKILL PRACTICE Neutralizing Unwanted Influence Attempts 324
    Observer's Feedback Form 324

6 MOTIVATING OTHERS 327

SKILL ASSESSMENT 328
Diagnostic Surveys for Motivating Others 328
    Diagnosing Poor Performance and Enhancing Motivation 328
    Work Performance Assessment 329

SKILL LEARNING 330
Increasing Motivation and Performance 330
Diagnosing Work Performance Problems 330
Enhancing Individuals' Abilities 332
Fostering a Motivating Work Environment 334
Elements of an Effective Motivation Program 335
    Establish Clear Performance Expectations 336
    Remove Obstacles to Performance 338
    Reinforce Performance-Enhancing Behavior 341
    Provide Salient Rewards 349
    Be Fair and Equitable 352
    Provide Timely Rewards and Accurate Feedback 352

SKILL ANALYSIS 358
Case Involving Motivation Problems 358
    Electro Logic 358

SKILL PRACTICE 365
Exercises for Diagnosing Work Performance Problems 365
    Joe Chaney 367
    Work Performance Assessment 368
Exercise for Reshaping Unacceptable Behaviors 368
    Shaheen Matombo 368

SKILL APPLICATION 371
Activities for Motivating Others 371
    Suggested Assignments 371
    Application Plan and Evaluation 372

SCORING KEYS AND COMPARISON DATA 374
Diagnosing Poor Performance and Enhancing Motivation 374
    Scoring Key 374
    Comparison Data 374
Work Performance Assessment 375
    Scoring Key 375

Comparison Data   375
SKILL PRACTICE Exercise for Reshaping Unacceptable Behaviors   375
Observer's Feedback Form   375

7   MANAGING CONFLICT   377

SKILL ASSESSMENT   378
Diagnostic Surveys for Managing Conflict   378
Managing Interpersonal Conflict   378
Strategies for Handling Conflict   379

SKILL LEARNING   380
Interpersonal Conflict Management   380
Mixed Feelings About Conflict   380
Diagnosing the Type of Interpersonal Conflict   382
Conflict Focus   382
Conflict Source   384
Selecting the Appropriate Conflict Management Approach   387
Comparing Conflict Management and Negotiation Strategies   390
Selection Factors   390
Resolving Interpersonal Confrontations Using the Collaborative Approach   394
A General Framework for Collaborative Problem Solving   395
The Four Phases of Collaborative Problem Solving   396

SKILL ANALYSIS   409
Case Involving Interpersonal Conflict   409
Educational Pension Investments   409

SKILL PRACTICE   414
Exercise for Diagnosing Sources of Conflict   414
SSS Software Management Problems   414
Exercises for Selecting an Appropriate Conflict Management Strategy   422
Bradley's Barn   423
Avocado Computers   423
Phelps, Inc.   424
Exercises for Resolving Interpersonal Disputes   424
Freida Mae Jones   425
Can Larry Fit In?   427
Meeting at Hartford Manufacturing Company   428

SKILL APPLICATION   435
Activities for Improving Managing Conflict Skills   435
Suggested Assignments   435
Application Plan and Evaluation   436

SCORING KEYS AND COMPARISON DATA   438
Managing Interpersonal Conflict   438
Scoring Key   438
Comparison Data   439
Strategies for Handling Conflict   439
Scoring Key   439
SKILL PRACTICE Exercises for Resolving Interpersonal Disputes   439
Observer's Feedback Form   439

PART III   GROUP SKILLS   442

8   EMPOWERING AND DELEGATING   443

SKILL ASSESSMENT   444
Diagnostic Surveys for Empowering and Delegating   444
    Effective Empowerment and Delegation   444
    Personal Empowerment Assessment   445

SKILL LEARNING   447
Empowering and Delegating   447
A Management Dilemma Involving Empowerment   447
    The Dirty Dozen   448
The Meaning of Empowerment   449
Historical Roots of Empowerment   450
Dimensions of Empowerment   451
    Self-Efficacy   451
    Self-Determination   452
    Personal Consequence   453
    Meaning   453
    Trust   454
    Review of Empowerment Dimensions   455
How to Develop Empowerment   455
    Articulating a Clear Vision and Goals   456
    Fostering Personal Mastery Experiences   457
    Modeling   458
    Providing Support   458
    Emotional Arousal   459
    Providing Information   460
    Providing Resources   461
    Connecting to Outcomes   461
    Creating Confidence   462
    Review of Empowerment Principles   463
Inhibitors to Empowerment   465
    Attitudes About Subordinates   466
    Personal Insecurities   466
    Need for Control   466
Delegating Work   467
    Advantages of Empowered Delegation   467
    Deciding When to Delegate   468
    Deciding to Whom to Delegate   469
    Deciding How to Delegate Effectively   469
    Review of Delegation Principles   474
International Caveats   475

SKILL ANALYSIS   478
Cases Involving Empowerment and Delegation   478
    Minding the Store   478
    Changing the Portfolio   479

SKILL PRACTICE   480
Exercises for Empowerment   480
    Executive Development Associates   480
    Empowering Ourselves   484
    Deciding to Delegate   485

SKILL APPLICATION   487
Activities for Empowerment and Delegation   487
    Suggested Assignments   487
    Application Plan and Evaluation   487

SCORING KEYS AND COMPARISON DATA   489
Effective Empowerment and Delegation   489
    Scoring Key   489
    Comparison Data   489
Personal Empowerment   489
    Scoring Key   489
    Comparison Data   490
SKILL PRACTICE Deciding to Delegate: Analysis of "An Emergency Request"   490
SKILL PRACTICE Analysis of Biological Warfare   490

9 BUILDING EFFECTIVE TEAMS AND TEAMWORK   493

SKILL ASSESSMENT   494
Diagnostic Surveys for Building Effective Teams   494
    Team Development Behaviors   494
    Diagnosing the Need for Team Building   495

SKILL LEARNING   497
Developing Teams and Teamwork   497
The Advantages of Teams   498
    An Example of an Effective Team   501
Team Development   502
    The Forming Stage   502
    The Norming Stage   503
    The Storming Stage   505
    The Performing Stage   507
Leading Teams   510
    Developing Credibility   511
    Establish SMART Goals and Everest Goals   513
    International Caveats   515
Team Membership   516
    Advantageous Roles   516
    Providing Feedback   520
    International Caveats   521

SKILL ANALYSIS   523
Cases Involving Building Effective Teams   523
    The Tallahassee Democrat's *ELITE Team   523*
    The Cash Register Incident   525

SKILL PRACTICE   527
Exercises in Building Effective Teams   527
    Team Diagnosis and Team Development Exercise   527
    Winning the War on Talent   528
    Team Performance Exercise   531

SKILL APPLICATION   533
Activities for Building Effective Teams   533
    Suggested Assignments   533
    Application Plan and Evaluation   534

SCORING KEYS AND COMPARISON DATA   535
Team Development Behaviors   535
    Scoring Key   *535*
    Comparison Data   *535*
Diagnosing the Need for Team Building   535
    Comparison Data   *535*

10   LEADING POSITIVE CHANGE   537

SKILL ASSESSMENT   538
Diagnostic Surveys for Leading Positive Change   538
    Leading Positive Change   *538*
    Reflected Best-Self Feedback™ Exercise   *539*
    A Sample E-mail Request for Feedback   *539*
    Machiavellianism Scale—MACH IV   *540*

SKILL LEARNING   542
Leading Positive Change   542
Ubiquitous and Escalating Change   543
The Need for Frameworks   543
Tendencies Toward Stability   544
A Framework for Leading Positive Change   546
    Establishing a Climate of Positivity   *548*
    Creating Readiness for Change   *554*
    Articulating a Vision of Abundance   *557*
    Generating Commitment to the Vision   *561*
    Institutionalizing the Positive Change   *566*

SKILL ANALYSIS   572
Cases Involving Leading Positive Change   572
    Corporate Vision Statements   *572*
    Lee Iacocca's Transformation of Chrysler—1979–1984   *578*

SKILL PRACTICE   585
Exercises in Leading Positive Change   585
    Reflected Best-Self Portrait   *585*
    Positive Organizational Diagnosis Exercise   *586*
    A Positive Change Agenda   *587*

SKILL APPLICATION   588
Activities for Leading Positive Change   588
    Suggested Assignments   *588*
    Application Plan and Evaluation   *589*

SCORING KEYS AND COMPARISON DATA   591
Leading Positive Change   591
    Scoring Key   *591*
    Comparison Data   *591*
Reflected Best-Self Feedback™ Exercise   591
Machiavellianism Scale—MACH IV   591
    Scoring Key   *591*
    Comparison Data   *592*
SKILL ANALYSIS Iacocca's Transformation of Chrysler—1979–1984   592

PART IV SPECIFIC COMMUNICATION SKILLS 594

Supplement A MAKING ORAL AND WRITTEN PRESENTATIONS 595

SKILL LEARNING 596
Making Oral and Written Presentations 596
Essential Elements of Effective Presentations 597

SKILL PRACTICE 613
Exercises for Making Effective Oral and Written Presentations 613
Speaking as a Leader 613
Quality Circles at Battle Creek Foods 614

Supplement B CONDUCTING INTERVIEWS 623

SKILL LEARNING 624
Planning and Conducting Interviews 624
Specific Types of Organizational Interviews 633

SKILL PRACTICE 638
Exercises for Conducting Special-Purpose Interviews 638
Evaluating the New Employee-Orientation Program 638
Performance-Appraisal Interview with Chris Jakobsen 641
Employment-Selection Interview at Smith Farley Insurance 647

Supplement C CONDUCTING MEETINGS 655

SKILL LEARNING 656
Conducting Effective Meetings:
A Short Guide for Meeting Managers and Meeting Participants 656
The Five Ps of Effective Meetings 656
Suggestions for Group Members 661

SKILL PRACTICE 664
Exercises for Conducting Meetings 664
Preparing and Conducting a Team Meeting at SSS Software 664
Role Diagnosis 664
Meeting Evaluation Worksheet 665

Appendix I GLOSSARY 677

Appendix II REFERENCES 687

NAME INDEX 709

SUBJECT INDEX 713

COMBINED INDEX 717

Whetten and Cameron's *Developing Management Skills*, Seventh Edition, Delivers an Abundance of Self-assessments, Activities, and Applications to Help Your Students Learn by Doing

Management skills help current and future managers answer such difficult questions as: "How can I help others accept new goals, new ideas, new approaches?" "How can I invigorate those who feel outdated and left behind?" "How do I help the 'survivors' of a downsizing pick up the pieces and move on?" "How do I help people with very different agendas and philosophies work together, especially during periods of high stress and uncertainty?"

Which Management Skills Should I Learn and How Can I Best Learn Them?

Although different management jobs require somewhat different expertise, and each person's developmental needs are different, we have gleaned ten essential management skills, organized into three categories, from our years of research, teaching, and personal observation. Each chapter in this book addresses one of these skills.

Personal Skills

Developing Self-Awareness
Managing Personal Stress
Solving Problems Analytically and Creatively

Interpersonal Skills

Building Relationships by Communicating Supportively
Gaining Power and Influence
Motivating Others
Managing Conflict

Group Skills

Empowering and Delegating
Building Effective Teams and Teamwork
Leading Positive Change

In addition to these chapters, we have included three supplemental chapters focusing on specific, applied communications skills: Making Oral and Written Presentations, Conducting Interviews, and Conducting Meetings.

Skills Assessments Set the Stage for Each Chapter

The Skill Assessment surveys provided in this book, beginning with the PAMS instrument in the Introduction, will give you an indication of which topics warrant more careful study and more deliberate practice. For students with minimal work experience we caution you to avoid the "novice's bias"—"this doesn't look that difficult." As you will see in the Introduction, most studies of practicing managers indicate serious deficiencies in one or more of the areas covered in this book.

What's New in This Edition

Reviewers' comments, instructors' suggestions, and student feedback provide us with very useful information—on an ongoing basis—for how this book can be improved. We encourage you to send us your comments and suggestions for how we can assist you in making your learning and developing experiences more effective. In addition, you are welcome to participate in a Web-based discussion with other teachers using this book by sending a request to DMS@byu.edu. Based on input from these sources, we have made a number of changes to the seventh edition of *Developing Management Skills*.

SELF-ASSESSMENTS ONLINE AND INTERACTIVE

We have created a new access-code-protected Web site that gives students access to the book's self-assessments in an interactive format. This access code can be ordered with the text. When students log on, they will be asked a series of personal and demographic questions. Providing this information will allow students to receive personalized feedback, comparing their scores with similar students who have previously completed our diagnostic surveys. We are confident that students will appreciate the feedback they receive from this on-line, dynamic, normed database.

UPDATES CHAPTER BY CHAPTER

Chapter 1—"Developing Self-Awareness"—has been substantially revised. Two new assessment instruments have been added, one on emotional intelligence and one on core self-evaluation. As a result of copyright issues, the FIRO-B instrument has now been omitted. One additional case study—The Computerized Exam, which relates to ethical decision-making—has also been added in the Skill Analysis section of the chapter.

Chapter 3—"Solving Problems Analytically and Creatively"—has also been revised. A new assessment instrument for diagnosing personal creative style has been added, as has another skill practice exercise for fostering creative problem solving.

In Chapter 4—"Building Relationships By Communicating Supportively"—the revision has focused the chapter more on the development of flourishing interpersonal relationships than have past editions. A new Skill Practice exercise on active listening has also been added.

In Chapter 5, a new case study on effectively utilizing power and influence has been added.

Chapter 9 has been substantially rewritten and reorganized based on the phases of team development. A new Skill Practice exercise has been added that focuses on team-work and team coordination.

The revision in Chapter 10—"Leading Positive Change"—has been updated based on the recent work of the Center for Positive Organizational Scholarship at the University of Michigan. Additional resource material is available on the Reflected Best-Self Feedback exercise online from: http://www.reflectivelearning.com.

Supplements

INSTRUCTOR'S RESOURCE CENTER

At http://www.prenhall.com/irc, instructors can access a variety of print, media, and presentation resources available with this text in downloadable, digital format. Registration is simple and gives you immediate access to new titles and new editions. As a registered faculty member, you download resource files and receive immediate access and instructions for installing Course Management content on your campus server.

If you ever need assistance, our dedicated technical support team is ready to help with the media supplements that accompany this text. Visit http://www.247. prenhall.com for answers to frequently asked questions and toll-free user support phone numbers.

The following supplements are available to adopting instructors (for detailed descriptions, please visit http://www.prenhall.com/irc):

Instructor's Resource Center (IRC) on CD-ROM—ISBN: 0-13-229719-1

Printed Instructor's Manual—ISBN: 0-13-156069-7

Printed Test Item File—ISBN: 0-13-230726-X

TestGen Test Generating Software—Available at the IRC (online or on CD-ROM).

PowerPoint Slides—Both basic and enhanced versions are available at the IRC (online or on CD-ROM).

Custom Videos on DVD—ISBN: 0-13-239707-2

PASSWORD-PROTECTED ASSESSMENT WEB SITE

A new access-code-protected Web site has been developed to accompany the seventh edition. Once inside, students can take every assessment that is in the book online (with the exception of "Source of Personal Stress" from Chapter 2 and the "Best-Self Feedback Exercise" in Chapter 10 as these two do not lend themselves to interactive presentation) and compare their scores to those of students across the nation. Instructors are able to track student completion of self-assessments and review composite results. To order this access card, please contact your Prentice Hall Sales Representative.

SAFARIX ETEXTBOOKS ONLINE

Developed for students looking to save on required or recommended textbooks, SafariX eTextbooks Online saves students money off the suggested list price of the print text. Students simply select their eText by title or author and purchase immediate access to the content for the duration of the course using any major credit card. With a SafariX eText, students can search for specific keywords or page numbers, make notes online, print out reading assignments that incorporate lecture notes, and bookmark important passages for later review. For more information, or to purchase a SafariX eTextbook, visit http://www.safarix.com.

Feedback

The authors and the product team would appreciate hearing from you! Let us know what you think about this textbook by writing to college_marketing@prenhall.com. Please include "Feedback about Whetten/Cameron 7e" in the subject line.

If you have questions related to this product, please contact our customer service department online at http://www.247.prenhall.com.

Acknowledgments

In addition to the informal feedback that we have received from colleagues around the world, we would especially like to thank the following people who have formally reviewed material and provided valuable feedback:

Richard Allan, University of Tennessee—Chattanooga
Forrest F. Aven, University of Houston
Lloyd Baird, Boston University
Bud Baker, Wright State University
John D. Bigelow, Boise State University
Ralph R. Braithwaite, University of Hartford
Julia Britt, California State University
Tim Bothell, Brigham Young University
David Cherrington, Brigham Young University
John Collins, Syracuse University
Kerri Crowne, Temple University
Todd Dewett, Wright State University
Andrew J. Dubrin, Rochester Institute of Technology
Steven Edelson, Temple University
Norma Givens, Fort Valley State University
Barbara A. Gorski, St. Thomas University
David Hampton, San Diego State University
Stanley Harris, Auburn University
Richard E. Hunt, Rockhurst College
Daniel F. Jennings, Baylor University
Avis L. Johnson, University of Akron

Jay T. Knippen, University of South Florida
Roland Kushner, Lafayette College
Roy J. Lewicki, Ohio State University
Michael Lombardo, Center for Creative Leadership
Charles C. Manz, University of Massachusetts—Amherst
Ralph F. Mullin, Central Missouri State University
Thomas J. Naughton, Wayne State University
J. Randolph New, University of Richmond
Jon L. Pierce, University of Minnesota—Duluth
Lyman Porter, University of California—Irvine
Lyle F. Schoenfeldt, Appalachian State University
Jacop P. Siegel, University of Toronto
Charles Smith, Hofstra University
Noel M. Tichy, University of Michigan
Wanda V. Trenner, Ferris State University
Ulya Tsolmon, Brigham Young University
Kenneth M. York, Oakland University

We especially thank our collaborators who adapted the book for the European and Australian markets, as well as those who translated *Developing Management Skills* into Spanish, Russian, Chinese, and Dutch.

We are grateful for the assistance of many dedicated associates who have helped us continually upgrade and enhance *Developing Management Skills*. These include Nancy Keesham and Don Clement, both of the Fuqua School of Business at Duke University, for their work on the supplement on making oral and written presentations; Gretchen Spreitzer of the University of Southern California for her work on the chapter on gaining power and influence; Richard M. Steers of the University of Oregon for his work on the motivation chapter; Pat Seybolt and Troy Nielsen of the University of Utah for their work on the chapter on managing conflict; Cathy German of Miami University for her assistance in revising Supplement A, and John Tropman, University of Michigan, for taking the lead in revising Supplement C. Special thanks are also due to Susan Schor, Joseph Seltzer, and James Smither for writing the SSS Software In-Basket Exercise. Our long-time collaboration with Sue Campbell-Clark has been particularly rewarding.

We would like to thank David Parker, Ashley Santora, Nancy Welcher, Renata Butera, and Marcy Boos of Prentice Hall; and Simone Payment of Stratford Publishing for her expert assistance with this edition.

We also express appreciation to our families for their patience and support, which is reflected in their willingness to share their time with this competing "labor of love" and to forgive our own gaps between common sense and common practice.

David A. Whetten
Kim S. Cameron

MANAGEMENT CONCEPTS

- The Critical Role of Management Skills
- The Importance of Competent Managers
- The Skills of Effective Managers
- Essential Management Skills
- What Are Management Skills?
- Improving Management Skills
- An Approach to Skill Development
- Leadership and Management
- Contents of the Book
- Organization of the Book
- Practice and Application
- Diversity and Individual Differences
- Summary

SUPPLEMENTARY
MATERIAL

- Personal Assessment of Management Skills (PAMS)
- What Does It Take to Be an Effective Manager?
- SSS Software In-Basket Exercise

SCORING KEY AND
COMPARISON DATA

INTRODUCTION

The Critical Role of Management Skills

SKILL DEVELOPMENT OBJECTIVES

- INTRODUCE THE IMPORTANCE OF MANAGEMENT SKILLS
- IDENTIFY ESSENTIAL MANAGEMENT SKILLS
- EXPLAIN A LEARNING MODEL FOR DEVELOPING MANAGEMENT SKILLS
- REVIEW THE CONTENTS OF THE BOOK

Introduction

The Critical Role of Management Skills

[handwritten note: Use Drucker quote ... people need to understand themselves too]

No one doubts that the twenty-first century will continue to be characterized by chaotic, transformational, rapid-fire change. In fact, almost no sane person is willing to predict what the world will be like 50, 25, or even 15 years from now. Change is just too rapid and ubiquitous. The development of "nanobombs" have caused some people to predict that personal computers and desktop monitors will land on the scrap heap of obsolescence within 20 years. The new computers will be a product of etchings on molecules leading to personalized data processors injected into the bloodstream, implanted in eyeglasses, or included in wristwatches.

Predictions of the changes that will occur in the future are often notoriously wrong, of course, as illustrated by Charles Watson's (founder of IBM) prediction that only a few dozen computers would ever be needed in the entire world, Thomas Edison's prediction that the lightbulb would never catch on, or Irving Fisher's (preeminent Yale economist) prediction in 1929 that the stock market had reached "a permanently high plateau." When Neil Armstrong walked on the moon in 1969, most people predicted that we would soon be walking on Mars, establishing colonies in outer space, and launching probes from lunar pads. In 1973, with long lines at the gas pumps due to an OPEC-led fuel crisis, economists predicted that oil would sell for $100 a barrel in the United States by 1980. Most notorious of all, of course, was the prediction by the United States patent office in 1896 that it would soon close its doors since "everything that can be invented has been invented."

Warren Bennis, a colleague of ours, half-jokingly predicted that the factory of the future would have only two employees, a person and a dog. The person would be there to feed the dog. The dog would be there to keep the person from touching the equipment! Tom Peters counseled managers that, due to the chaotic pace of change, "If you're not confused, you're not paying attention." And Peter Drucker characterized the current environment this way: "We are in one of those great historical periods that occur every 200 or 300 years when people don't understand the world anymore, and the past is not sufficient to explain the future." Almost no one would argue that "permanent white water" best characterizes our current environment. Almost everything is in flux, from our technology and methods of transacting business to the nature of education and the definition of the family.

Despite all this change in our environment, there is something that has remained, and continues to remain, relatively constant. With minor variations and stylistic differences, what has not changed in several thousand years are the basic skills that lie at the heart of effective, satisfying, growth-producing human relationships. Freedom, dignity, trust, love, and honesty in relationships have always been among the goals of human beings, and the same principles that brought about those outcomes in the eleventh century still bring them about in the twenty-first century. Despite our circumstances, in other words, and despite the technological resources we have available to us, the same basic human skills still lie at the heart of effective human interaction.

In fact, human relationships are becoming more important, not less, as the information age unfolds and technologies encroach even more upon our daily lives. Most of us are exposed to more information each day than we can possibly pay attention to. Moreover, no mechanism exists to organize, prioritize, or interpret that information, so it is often unclear what is crucial and what can be ignored. Consequently, the relationship we have with the sources of that information is the key sense-making mechanism. Building trusting relationships is a critical part of coping with information overload.

It is a fact that when everything is changing, change becomes unmanageable. No one can manage constant, unorganized change. Think of being a pilot on an airplane. Everything is changing—the entire plane is in constant motion—as the plane moves through the air. Unless you can fix on something that is not changing—for example, the ground or the stars—it is impossible to fly the plane. Tragically, investigators found that John F. Kennedy Jr. unknowingly flew his plane into the Atlantic Ocean killing himself, his wife, and his sister-in-law because he lost sight of land and, consequently, lost perspective. He became unable to manage change because he did not have an established, unwavering point that helped him maintain his bearings.

We make sense of change by being able to identify a fixed, stable, permanent point that provides us with perspective. In our current "white water" environment, the skills discussed in this book serve as fixed points. They have changed very little in their effectiveness and relevance over several thousand years. And their relationship to effective human and organizational performance has been well-documented. Later in this Introduction we share some of the scientific research that confirms the power of these management skills in accounting for effective personal, interpersonal, and organizational performance.

The problem, of course, is that what is known is not always the same as what is demonstrated. Although we have known about the principles of effective relationships for a very long time, the history of humankind illustrates that these principles have not always been practiced. Especially in our current day, what we know and what we demonstrate do not always match. Dr. Bob Moorehead of Seattle's Overlake Christian Church, who resigned his own position under a cloud of accusations, described it this way:

The paradox of our time in history is that we have taller buildings but shorter tempers, wider freeways but narrower viewpoints. We spend more but have less; we buy more but enjoy it less. We have bigger houses and smaller families, more conveniences but less time. We have more degrees but less sense; more knowledge but less judgment; more experts but more problems; more medicine but less wellness. We drink too much, smoke too much, spend too recklessly, laugh too little, drive too fast, get too angry too quickly, stay up too late, get too tired, read too seldom, watch TV too much, and pray too seldom. We have multiplied our possessions, but reduced our values. We talk too much, love too seldom, and hate too often. We have learned how to make a living but not a life; we've added years to life but not life to years. We've been all the way to the moon and back but have trouble crossing the street to meet the new neighbor. We've conquered outer space but not inner space. We've done larger things but not better things. We've cleaned up the air but d the soul. We've split the atom but not our prejudice. We write more n less. We plan more but accomplish less. We've learned to rush but not to e build more computers to hold more information to produce more copies er but have less communication. These are the times of fast foods and slow n; tall men and short character; steep profits and shallow relationships. re the times of world peace but domestic warfare; more leisure but less fun; nds of food but less nutrition. These are the days of two incomes but more , of fancier houses but broken homes. These are the days of quick trips, dis- e diapers, throw-away morality, one-night stands, overweight bodies, and *pills that do everything from cheer to quiet to kill. It is a time when there is much in the show window and nothing in the stockroom. (Moorehead, n.d.)*

k is built on the presumption that developing management skills—that is, the to manage one's own life as well as relationships with others—is a ceaseless se skills were largely the same a century ago as they are today. The basic behav- s that lie at the foundation of these skills are timeless. That is one reason why bookstores and on-line newsletters are filled with prescriptions of how one e or one more company struck it rich or beat out the competition. Thousands et some special set of prescriptions for how to be successful in business, or in ese books have made it to the best-seller lists and have enjoyed lengthy stays. Our intention in this book is not to try to duplicate the popular appeal of the best-selling books nor to utilize the common formula of recounting anecdotal incidents of successful organizations and well-known managers. We have produced a book that remains true to, and is based on, social science and business research. We want to share with you what is known and what is not known about how to develop management skills and how to foster productive, healthy, satisfying, and growth-producing relationships with others in your work setting. *Developing Management Skills* is designed to help you actually improve your personal management competencies—to change your behavior. This book, therefore, serves more as a practicum or a guide to effective managerial behavior than a description of what someone else has done to successfully manage an organization. It will surely help you think, and it will provide examples of success, but it will have failed if it also does not help you *behave* more competently in your own life.

Whereas the skills focused on in this book are called "management skills," their relevance is not limited just to an organization or work setting. We focus mainly on work settings here because our primary goal is to help you prepare for and improve your own competency in a managerial role. You will discover, however, that these skills are applicable in most areas of your life—with families, friends, volunteer organizations, and your community.

In the next section we review some of the scientific evidence that demonstrates how management skills are associated with personal and organizational success, and we review several studies of the key management skills that seem to be the most important in our modern-day environment. It is those key skills that this book has targeted. We then describe a model and a methodology for helping you to develop management skills. A large number of management fads abound proclaiming a new way to be a leader, get rich, or both, but our intent is to rely on a proven methodology that has grounding in the scientific literature. We present what has been shown to be a superior process for improving management skills, and we base our claims on scholarly evidence. This Introduction concludes with a brief description of the organization of the rest of the book and the importance of keeping in mind individual differences among people.

The Importance of Competent Managers

In the last decade or so, an abundance of evidence has been produced that skillful management—especially those competent in the management of people in organizations—is *the* key determinant of organizational success. These studies have been conducted across numerous industry sectors, international settings, and organization types. The research findings now make it almost unquestionable that if organizations want to succeed, they must have competent, skillful managers.

For example, in one study of 968 firms, representing all major industries in the United States, organizations whose managers effectively managed their people—that is, they implemented effective people management strategies and demonstrated personal competency in management skills—had, on the average, a decrease in turnover of more than 7 percent, increased profits of $3,814 per employee, $27,044 more in sales per employee, and $18,641 more in stock market value per employee, compared to firms that had less effective people management (Huselid, 1995; Pfeffer & Veiga, 1999). In a follow-up study of 702 firms, shareholder wealth was an amazing $41,000 per employee higher in companies demonstrating strong people management skills than in firms that had a lower emphasis on people management (Huselid & Becker, 1997). A study of German firms in 10 industrial sectors produced similar results: "Companies that place workers at the core of their strategies produce higher long-term returns . . . than their industry peers" (Blimes, Wetzker, & Xhonneux, 1997). A study of five-year survivability in 136 nonfinancial companies that issued IPOs in the late 1980s found that the effective management of people was the most significant factor in predicting longevity, even when accounting for industry type, size, and profits. Firms that did a good job of managing people tended to survive; others did not (Welbourne & Andrews, 1996).

A study by Hanson (1986) investigated the factors that best accounted for financial success over a five-year span in 40 major manufacturing firms. The question being addressed was: "What explains the financial success of the firms that are highly effective?" The five most powerful predictors were identified and assessed. They included market share (assuming that the higher the market share of a firm, the higher its profitability); firm capital intensity (assuming that the more a firm is automated and up-to-date in technology and equipment, the more profitable it is); size of the firm in assets (assuming that economies of scale and efficiency can be used in large firms to increase profitability); industry average return on sales (assuming that firms would reflect the performance of a highly profitable industry); and the ability of managers to effectively manage their people (assuming that an emphasis on good people management helps produce profitability in firms). The results revealed that one factor—the ability to manage people effectively—was three times more powerful than all other factors combined in accounting for firm financial success over a five-year period! We repeat, good management was more important than all other factors taken together in predicting profitability.

Even research by the U.S. government confirms this management-effectiveness link. The U.S. Office of the Comptroller of the Currency studied the reasons for the failures of national banks in the United States during the 1980s. Two major factors were found to account for the record number of bank failures during that period: distressed economic conditions and poor management. The relative impact of those two factors, however, was somewhat surprising. Almost 90 percent of the failed banks were judged to have had poor management. Only 35 percent of the failures had experienced depressed economic conditions in the region in which they operated, and in only 7 percent of the cases was a depressed economic condition the sole cause of bank failure (U.S. Office of the Comptroller of the Currency, 1990).

Dramatic anecdotal evidence also abounds regarding the impact of effective management on workers and organizations. One of the most notable, for example, was the General Motors automobile assembly plant in Fremont, California. The plant was built in the 1950s and, at the beginning of the 1980s, was assembling the Chevrolet Nova model. The plant had a history of labor and productivity problems, however, and by the end of 1982 the performance statistics were dismal. Absenteeism was running at 20 percent. The number of formal grievances filed by employees totaled almost 5,000 (an average of more than 20 grievances per day for every workday of the year), and more than 2,000 grievances were still unresolved at year's end. An average of three to four wildcat strikes per year had occurred during the previous few years, and morale, productivity, and quality of production by the 5,000 employees were the worst in the corporation. Costs of assembling the automobile were about 30 percent above the Asian competitors. In light of these data, corporate headquarters issued an order to close the plant and lay off the workers.

Three years later, General Motors signed a joint operating agreement with one of its major competitors: Toyota Motors. Much had been written about the Japanese method of managing, so General Motors asked Toyota to reopen and manage the Fremont plant. Most of the former U.S. autoworkers were rehired, and a new management team was put in place. Workers were exposed to training in high-involvement work practices, and a former Ford Motor Company employee actually became the plant manager. The primary difference between the plant before it closed and after it reopened was that a new management team was in place and employee training had occurred. The workforce, in other words, remained essentially unchanged. One year after reopening, the organization's performance data looked like this:

Absenteeism:	2 percent
Grievances:	2 outstanding
Strikes:	None
Employees:	2,500 (producing 20 percent more cars)
Productivity:	Highest in the corporation
Quality:	Highest in the corporation
Costs:	Equal to those of the competition
Product:	Toyota Corolla—rated AAA's best car in its price range

The remarkable thing about this turnaround is that it did not take five or ten years to produce major improvements in productivity, cohesion, and commitment. It occurred in just over a year simply by changing the way workers were managed.

These studies indicate overwhelmingly that good management fosters financial success, whereas less effective management fosters financial distress. Successful organizations have managers with well-developed people management skills. In surveys of CEOs, executives, and business owners, results consistently show that the factor most responsible for business failure is "bad management" and the best way to ensure business success is to "provide better management." Moreover, the data are clear, management skills are more important than industry, environment, competition, and economic factors combined.

Surprisingly, however, finding people who effectively manage people is not as easy as might be expected. Pfeffer & Veiga (1999) concluded that: "Even as these research results pile up, trends in actual management practice are, in many instances, moving in a direction exactly opposite to what this growing body of evidence prescribes." Common sense and common knowledge are not necessarily common practice. Knowing and doing are not the same things. Being able to analyze a case, identify a problem, or recite a correct answer to a question is not equivalent to being able to actually implement effective management skills.

The Skills of Effective Managers

What, then, differentiates effective managers from less effective managers? If developing management skills is so crucial for organizational success, what skills ought to be the focus of attention?

The management literature is filled with lists of attributes, behaviors, orientations, and strategies for enhancing successful performance. For example, Pfeffer (1998) identified seven key practices associated with managerial and organizational effectiveness: ensure employment security, selectively hire people, foster decentralization and self-managing teams, institute high levels of pay based on performance, train extensively, reduce status differences, and share information. Quinn (2000) identified eight "seeds" of effective management and leadership: "envision the productive community," "first look within," "embrace the hypocritical self," "transcend fear," "embody a vision of the common good," "disturb the system," "surrender to the emergent process," and "entice through moral power." An international study of 6,052 managers from 22 countries focused on differences in managerial attributes and identified attributes such as inspirational, self-sacrificial, integrity, diplomatic, malevolent, visionary, administrative, self-centered, status conscious, autocratic, modest, and autonomous (Brodbeck et al., 2000). Rigby (1998) focused on the 25 most popular management tools and techniques in an investigation of the association between management tools and techniques and organizational performance. According to 4,137 managers in North America, Europe, and Asia, the tools associated with organization success were: strategic planning, pay for performance, strategic alliances, customer satisfaction measurement, shareholder value analysis, mission and vision statements, benchmarking, cycle time reduction, agile strategies, self-directed teams, and groupware.

These kinds of lists are useful, but they do not identify management *skills* per se. Instead, they enumerate organizational strategies, personality orientations, or philosophical approaches to management, and their implementation is usually outside the explicit control of the individual manager. Either they are complex sets of activities in which many people must be involved—for example, "ensuring employment security," "selectively hiring," or "shareholder value analysis"—or they are cognitive activities that are not behavioral in character—for example, "envisioning the productive community," "first looking within," or "avoiding malevolence." Some of the lists enumerate personality characteristics or styles—for example, inspirational, or autocratic—or they enumerate organizational practices—for example, pay for performance, or strategic planning. The effectiveness of the attributes on these kinds of lists depends on the manager's skill in implementing them, and that means being competent in fundamental management skills. Management skills form the vehicle by which management strategy, management practice, tools and techniques, personality attributes, and style work to produce effective outcomes in organizations. Management skills, in other words, are the building blocks upon which effective management rests. That is why the focus of this book is on developing management skills rather than on strategy, tools and techniques, or styles. Management skills are the means by which managers translate their own style, strategy, and favorite tools or techniques into practice.

Essential Management Skills

A variety of investigators have sought to identify what specific skills are characteristic of the most effective managers. In our own investigation, for example, we wanted to identify the skills and competencies that separate extraordinarily effective performers from the rest of us. We identified 402 individuals who were rated as highly effective managers in their own organizations in the fields of business, health care, education, and state government by asking senior officers to name the most effective managers in their own organizations. We then interviewed those people to determine what attributes were associated with managerial effectiveness. We asked questions such as:

❑ How have you become so successful in this organization?
❑ Who fails and who succeeds in this organization and why?

- If you had to train someone to take your place, what knowledge and what skills would you make certain that person possessed in order to perform successfully as your successor?
- If you could design an ideal curriculum or training program to teach you to be a better manager, what would it contain?
- Think of other effective managers you know. What skills do they demonstrate that explain their success?

Our analysis of the interviews produced about 60 characteristics of effective managers. The 10 identified most often are listed in Table 1. Not surprisingly, these 10 characteristics are all behavioral skills. They are not personality attributes or styles, nor are they generalizations such as "luck" or "timing." They also are common across industries, levels, and job responsibilities. The characteristics of effective managers are not a secret.

The management skills derived from our study are similar to those resulting from several other surveys published in the management literature. Table 2, for example, lists a representative sample of surveys that relied on a heterogeneous mix of respondents. Not surprisingly, the two lists are very similar. Regardless of whether respondents are CEOs or first-line supervisors, whether they work in the public sector or the private sector, their skills are quite easily identifiable and agreed upon by observers. It is not hard to recognize and describe the skills of effective managers.

What Are Management Skills?

There are several defining characteristics of management skills that differentiate them from other kinds of managerial characteristics and practices. First, management skills are *behavioral*. They are not personality attributes or stylistic tendencies. Management skills consist of identifiable sets of actions that individuals perform and that lead to certain outcomes. Skills can be observed by others, unlike attributes that are purely mental or are embedded in personality. Whereas people with different styles and personalities may apply the skills differently, there are, nevertheless, a core set of observable attributes in effective skill performance that are common across a range of individual differences.

Second, management skills are *controllable*. The performance of these behaviors is under the control of the individual. Unlike organizational practices such as "selectively

Table 1	Skills of Effective Managers—One Study
1. Verbal communication (including listening)	
2. Managing time and stress	
3. Managing individual decisions	
4. Recognizing, defining, and solving problems	
5. Motivating and influencing others	
6. Delegating	
7. Setting goals and articulating a vision	
8. Self-awareness	
9. Team building	
10. Managing conflict	

Table 2 | Critical Management Skills—A Sample of Studies

STUDY ❑ RESPONDENTS • FOCUS

RESULTS

❑ Luthans, Rosenkrantz, and Hennessey (1985)

- 52 managers in 3 organizations
- Participant observation of skills demonstrated by most effective versus least effective managers

Building power and influence	Communicating with insiders
Communicating with outsiders	Developing subordinates
Managing conflict	Processing paperwork
Decision making	Planning and goal setting

❑ Curtis, Winsor, and Stephens (1989)

- 428 members of the American Society of Personnel Administrators in the United States
- (1) Skills needed to obtain employment
- (2) Skills important for successful job performance
- (3) Skills needed to move up in the organization

Employment	*Job Success*
Verbal communication	Interpersonal skills
Listening	Verbal communication
Enthusiasm	Written communication
Written communication	Persistence/determination
Technical competence	Enthusiasm
Appearance	Technical competence

To Move Up	
Ability to work well with others one-on-one	Ability to present a good image for the firm
Ability to gather information and make a decision	Ability to use computers
Ability to work well in groups	Knowledge of management theory
Ability to listen and give counsel	Knowledge of finance
Ability to give effective feedback	Knowledge of marketing
Ability to write effective reports	Knowledge of accounting
Knowledge of the job	Ability to use business machines

❑ Van Velsor & Britain (1995)

- Summarizes 5 previous studies of "derailment"
- 20 US managers and 42 European managers
- Focus on skills causing "derailment" (the opposite of success)

Problems with interpersonal relationships
Failure to meet business objectives
Inability to build and lead a team
Inability to manage self-development or to adapt

❑ American Management Association (2000)

- 921 managers in the United States

Skill	Importance to Organizations	Managerial Competence	Gap
Customer Focus	1 (4.74)	1 (3.90)	22
Ability to use information to solve problems	2 (4.64)	2 (3.71)	15
Recognizing problems and implementing solutions	3 (4.56)	8 (3.52)	7
Credibility among peers, subordinates, colleagues	4 (4.45)	3 (3.69)	18
Ability to transform words into actions	5 (4.44)	5 (3.55)	11
Listening and asking questions	6 (4.40)	13 (3.36)	3
Contributing to firm mission/objectives	7 (4.39)	4 (3.57)	16
Working in teams (cooperation/commitment)	8 (4.34)	11 (3.40)	8
Identifying opportunities for innovation	9 (4.33)	14 (3.35)	4
Setting standards for self and subordinates	10 (4.32)	7 (3.53)	9
Coaching and mentoring skills	15 (4.21)	26 (2.99)	1
Time management	12 (4.27)	25 (3.19)	2
Implementing improvements	11 (4.29)	17 (3.33)	5
Setting priorities	14 (4.24)	20 (3.32)	6

Table 2	Critical Management Skills—A Sample of Studies	
STUDY ❑ RESPONDENTS • FOCUS	RESULTS	
❑ Andersen Consulting (2000)		
• Study of Andersen partners, consultants, and client leaders	*Employee skills* Creativity Team building Resilience/flexibility Technical competence Deal with ambiguity Speed Emotional intelligence Communication skills	*Leadership attributes* Less controlling Shares authority Culturally attuned Encourages challenge Clear vision Comfortable with risk Creates a motivated business Manages intellectual diversity Entrepreneurial

hiring," or cognitive activities such as "transcending fear," skills can be consciously demonstrated, practiced, improved, or restrained by individuals themselves. Skills may certainly engage other people and require cognitive work, but they are behaviors that people can control themselves.

Third, management skills are *developable*. Performance can improve. Unlike IQ or certain personality or temperament attributes that remain relatively constant throughout life, individuals can improvement their competency in skill performance through practice and feedback. Individuals can progress from less competence to more competence in management skills, and that outcome is the primary objective of this book.

Fourth, management skills are *interrelated* and *overlapping*. It is difficult to demonstrate just one skill in isolation from others. Skills are not simplistic, repetitive behaviors, but they are integrated sets of complex responses. Effective managers, in particular, must rely on combinations of skills to achieve desired results. For example, in order to effectively motivate others, skills such as supportive communication, influence, empowerment, and self-awareness may be required. Effective managers, in other words, develop a constellation of skills that overlap and support one another and that allow flexibility in managing diverse situations.

Fifth, management skills are sometimes *contradictory* or *paradoxical*. For example, the core management skills are neither all soft and humanistic in orientation nor all hard-driving and directive. They are oriented neither toward teamwork and interpersonal relations exclusively nor toward individualism and technical entrepreneurship exclusively. A variety of skills are typical of the most effective managers, and some of them appear incompatible.

To illustrate, Cameron and Tschirhart (1988) assessed the skill performance of more than 500 midlevel and upper-middle managers in about 150 organizations. The most frequently mentioned 25 management skills taken from about a dozen studies in the academic literature (such as those in Table 2) were measured. Statistical analyses revealed that the skills fell into four main groups or clusters. One group of skills focused on participative and human relations skills (for example, supportive communication and team building), while another group focused on just the opposite, that is, competitiveness and control (for example, assertiveness, power, and influence skills). A third group focused on innovativeness and individual entrepreneurship (for example, creative problem solving), while a fourth group emphasized the opposite type of skills, namely, maintaining order and rationality (for example, managing time and rational decision making). One conclusion from that study was that effective managers are required to demonstrate paradoxical skills. That is, the most effective managers are both participative and hard-driving, both nurturing and competitive. They were able to be flexible and creative while also being controlled, stable, and rational (see Cameron, Quinn, DeGraff, & Thakor, 2006). Our objective in this book is to help you develop that kind of behavioral competency and complexity.

Improving Management Skills

It is a bit unnerving that while average IQ scores have increased in the population over the last half-century, social and emotional intelligence scores have actually declined. In the population in general, people are less skilled at managing themselves and managing others than they were 50 years ago (Goleman, 1998). While average IQ scores have jumped approximately 25 points, emotional intelligence scores (EQ) among young people and adults has fallen. Moreover, whereas the "technological float" has shrunk dramatically— that is, the time between the introduction of a new technology and its being copied and revised is constantly decreasing and is now measured in weeks rather than years—the "human float" has changed very little. It still takes about the same amount of time to develop behavioral skills and human competencies as it always has. No shortcuts or quick fixes have emerged, and the effort and practice that are required to become more emotionally intelligent and interpersonally skilled is substantial. Progress regarding how to cope with and manage issues relating to other people has not kept pace with technological progress, and it remains the biggest challenge for managers.

The good news is that improvement in developing management skills has been found in both students and managers who have been exposed to a curriculum such as the one advocated in *Developing Management Skills*. For example, MBA students showed improvement of from 50 to 300 percent on social skills over the course of two years by enrolling in two courses based on the approach to developing management skills presented here. A greater amount of improvement occurred among students who applied these skills to multiple aspects of their lives outside the classroom, and people who were more competent to begin with made the most progress. In addition, a cohort of 45- to 55-year-old executives produced the same results as the MBA students. That is, they also improved dramatically in their management skills even though most were already experienced in senior managerial positions (Boyatzis, 1996, 2000, 2005; Boyatzis, Cowen, & Kolb, 1995; Boyatzis, Leonard, Rhee, & Wheeler, 1996; Leonard, 1996; Rhee, 1997; Wheeler, 1999).

On the other hand, exposure to a traditional cognitive-based curriculum without exposure to management skills development does not correlate with improvements in social competence, management skills, or career success. For example, Cohen (1984) summarized the results of 108 studies of the relationship between performance in college courses (as measured by grade-point average) and subsequent life success. Life success was measured by a variety of factors, including job performance, income, promotions, personal satisfaction, eminence, and graduate degrees. The mean correlation between performance in school and performance in life in these studies was .18, and in no case did the correlation exceed .20. These low correlations suggest that school performance and successful performance in subsequent life activities are related only marginally.

The data, in other words, appear quite compelling. Attending school merely to achieve high grades in cognitive courses—while important—is not sufficient for management, career, or life success. Going into debt for a formal education or achieving an additional set of letters behind your name without also developing and improving your management skills will be an unfortunate lost opportunity. That is why we feel so strongly that in the management curriculum of universities, students should be exposed to a learning model such as the one we describe here. Our strong feelings, of course, are not based on blind optimism. Scientific evidence exists that such exposure can make a difference both to individuals and to the bottom-line performance of companies.

An Approach to Skill Development

Successful management development, of course, is more than just following a cookbook list of sequential behaviors. Developing highly competent management skills is much more complicated than developing skills such as those associated with a trade (for example, welding) or a sport (for example, shooting baskets). Management skills are: (1) linked to a more complex knowledge base than other types of skills and (2) inherently connected to interaction with other (frequently unpredictable) individuals. A standardized approach to welding or shooting free throws may be feasible, but no standardized approach to managing human beings is possible.

On the other hand, what all skills do have in common is the potential for improvement through practice. Any approach to developing management skills, therefore, must involve a heavy dose of practical application. At the same time, practice without the necessary conceptual knowledge is sterile and ignores the need for flexibility and adaptation to different situations. Therefore, developing competencies in management skills is inherently tied to both conceptual learning and behavioral practice.

The method that has been found to be most successful in helping individuals develop management skills is based on social learning theory (Bandura, 1977; Boyatzis et al., 1995; Davis & Luthans, 1980). This approach marries rigorous conceptual knowledge with opportunities to practice and apply observable behaviors. It relies on cognitive work as well as behavioral work. Variations on this general approach have been used widely in on-the-job supervisory training programs, and they are common in executive education programs and corporate universities—less so in business schools.

This learning model, as originally formulated, consisted of four steps: (1) the presentation of behavioral principles or action guidelines, generally using traditional instruction methods; (2) demonstration of the principles by means of cases, films, scripts, or incidents; (3) opportunities to practice the principles through role plays or exercises; and (4) feedback on performance from peers, instructors, or experts.

Our own experience in teaching complex management skills, as well as recent research on management skills development among MBA students (e.g., Boyatzis, et al., 1995; Vance, 1993) has convinced us that three important modifications are necessary in order for this model to be most effective. First, the behavioral principles must be grounded in social science theory and in reliable research results. Common sense generalizations and panacea-like prescriptions appear regularly in the popular management literature. To ensure the validity of the behavioral guidelines being prescribed, the learning approach must include scientifically based knowledge about the effects of the management principles being presented.

Second, individuals must be aware of their current level of skill competency and be motivated to improve upon that level in order to benefit from the model. Most people receive very little feedback about their current level of skill competency. Most organizations provide some kind of annual or semiannual evaluation (for example, course grades in school or performance appraisal interviews in firms), but these evaluations are almost always infrequent and narrow in scope, and they fail to assess performance in most critical skill areas. To help a person understand what skills to improve and why, therefore, an assessment activity must be part of the model. In addition, most people find change uncomfortable and therefore avoid taking the risk to develop new behavior patterns. An assessment activity in the learning model helps encourage these people to change by illuminating their strengths and weaknesses. People then know where weaknesses lie and what things need to be improved. Assessment activities generally take the form of self-evaluation instruments, case studies, or problems that help highlight personal strengths and weaknesses in a particular skill area.

Third, an application component is needed in the learning model. Most management skill training takes place in a classroom setting where feedback is immediate, and it is relatively safe to try out new behaviors and make mistakes. Therefore, transferring learning to an actual job setting is often problematic. Application exercises help to apply classroom learning to examples from the real world of management. Application exercises often take the form of an outside-of-class intervention, a consulting assignment, self-analysis through journal writing, or a problem-centered intervention, which the student then analyzes to determine its degree of success or failure.

In summary, evidence suggests that a five-step learning model is most effective for helping individuals develop management skills (see Cameron & Whetten, 1984; Kolb, 1984; Vance, 1993; Whetten & Cameron, 1983). Table 3 outlines such a model. Step 1 involves the *assessment* of current levels of skill competency and knowledge of the behavioral principles. Step 2 consists of the presentation of validated, scientifically based *principles and guidelines* for effective skill performance. Step 3 is an *analysis* step in which models or cases are made available in order to analyze behavioral principles in real organizational settings. This step also helps demonstrate how the behavioral guidelines can be adapted to different personal styles and circumstances. Step 4 consists of *practice* exercises in which experimentation can occur and immediate feedback can be received in a relatively safe environment. Step 5, finally, is the *application* of the skill to a real-life setting outside the classroom with follow-up analysis of the relative success of that application.

Research on the effectiveness of training programs using this general learning model has shown that it produces results superior to those based on more traditional lecture-discussion-case method approaches (Boyatzis et al., 1995; Burnaska, 1976; Kolb, 1984; Latham & Saari, 1979; Moses & Ritchie, 1976; Porras & Anderson, 1981; Smith, 1976; Vance, 1993). In addition, evidence suggests that management skill training can have significant impact on the bottom-line performance of a firm. The U.S. Postal Service completed a study a few years ago in which 49 of the largest 100 post offices in America were evaluated. An important question in the study was, "How can we make post offices more effective?" Productivity and service quality were both monitored over a period of five years. The two major factors that had impact on these effectiveness measures were (1) degree of automation, and (2) investment in training. Two kinds of training were provided: technical training (operating and maintaining the equipment) and management training (developing management skills). The study found that management training was more important than technical training in accounting for improved productivity and service in the post offices, and both kinds of training were more important than having up-to-date equipment in the post office. Low-tech

Table 3	A Model for Developing Management Skills	
Components	**Contents**	**Objectives**
1. Skill assessment	Survey instruments Role plays	Assess current level of skill competence and knowledge; create readiness to change.
2. Skill learning	Written text Behavioral guidelines	Teach correct principles and present a rationale for behavioral guidelines.
3. Skill analysis	Cases	Provide examples of appropriate and inappropriate skill performance. Analyze behavioral principles and reasons they work.
4. Skill practice	Exercises Simulations Role plays	Practice behavioral guidelines. Adapt principles to personal style. Receive feedback and assistance.
5. Skill application	Assignments (behavioral and written)	Transfer classroom learning to real-life situations. Foster ongoing personal development.

offices outperformed high-tech offices when managers were provided with management skill training. In short, its five-year study convinced the U.S. Postal Service that helping employees to develop management skills was the best way to improve organizational effectiveness (Cameron & Ulrich, 1986).

This is consistent with the conclusion drawn by Eric Greenberg, Director of Surveys for the American Management Association, upon summarizing the lessons learned from years of surveys of American managers:

> *Where companies increased their training activity, the chances were much, much better that they were going to increase their operating profits and that they were going to increase their shareholder value. Product quality, market share, and productivity all tend to rise as training budgets go up. Companies that don't make the investment are apt to see disappointing results. (Greenberg, 1999)*

More than thirty years ago, Mintzberg (1975) made a similar point about the curriculum needed in business schools. Things have not changed.

> *Management schools will begin the serious training of managers when skill training takes its place next to cognitive learning. Cognitive learning is detached and informational, like reading a book or listening to a lecture. No doubt much important cognitive material must be assimilated by the manager-to-be. But cognitive learning no more makes a manager than it does a swimmer. The latter will drown the first time he jumps into the water if his coach never takes him out of the lecture hall, gets him wet, and gives him feedback on his performance. Our management schools need to identify the skills managers use, select students who show potential in these skills, put the students into situations where these skills can be practiced, and then give them systematic feedback on their performance. (p. 60)*

A senior executive in a major consulting firm similarly observed:

> *The higher up the organization you go, the less relevant technical knowledge becomes. It is important for your first couple of promotions, but after that, people skills are what count.*

A recent graduate from a Big Ten management school also reported:

> *I can't believe it. I went for my second interview with a company last week, and I spent the first half-day participating in simulation exercises with ten other job candidates. They videotaped me playing the role of a salesman handling an irate customer, a new director of personnel putting down a revolt by the "old guard," and a plant manager trying to convince people of the need to install a radically new production process. Boy, was I unprepared for that!*

The message behind these personal observations is clear: from almost every perspective, competence in personal, interpersonal, and group skills is a critical prerequisite for success in management. Strong analytical and quantitative skills are important, but they are not sufficient. Successful managers must be able to work effectively with people. Unfortunately, interpersonal and management skills have not always been a high priority for business school students and aspiring executives. In a recent survey of 110 *Fortune* 500 CEOs, 87 percent were satisfied with the level of competence and analytic skills of business school graduates, 68 percent were satisfied with conceptual skills of graduates, but only 43 percent of the CEOs were satisfied with graduates' management skills, and only 28 percent were satisfied with their interpersonal skills and EQ!

To assist you in improving your own management skills, this book emphasizes practicing management skills, rather than just reading about them. We have organized the book with this specific approach in mind.

Leadership and Management

Before outlining the organization of this book, we want to discuss briefly the place of leadership in this volume. Some writers have differentiated between the concepts of "leadership" and "management" (Bass, 1990; Katzenbach, 1995; Nair, 1994; Quinn, 2000; Tichy, 1999). Some have wondered why we concentrate on "management" skills instead of "leadership" skills in this book. We have also been asked by professors, business executives, and students why we have not either changed the title of the book to *Developing Leadership Skills*, or at least included one chapter on leadership in this volume. These queries and suggestions are important and have motivated us to clarify at the outset of the book what we mean by management, and why we believe our focus on management skills lies at the heart of leadership as typically defined.

One of the most popular models of leadership is based on the "Competing Values Framework," an organizing framework for leadership and managerial skills. It was developed by examining the criteria used to evaluate organizational and managerial performance (Cameron et al., 2006; Quinn & Rohrbaugh, 1983). Extensive research has been conducted on this framework over the past two decades, and a brief explanation will help clarify the relationship between management and leadership skills. You should be aware that this framework has been used on several continents to help managers and organizations improve their effectiveness, and a database of more than 80,000 managers has now been compiled (Cameron & Quinn, 2006). That research has shown that leadership and management skills fall into four clusters or categories as illustrated in Figure 1. In order to be an effective manager, in other words, individuals must be competent in: (1) clan skills, or a

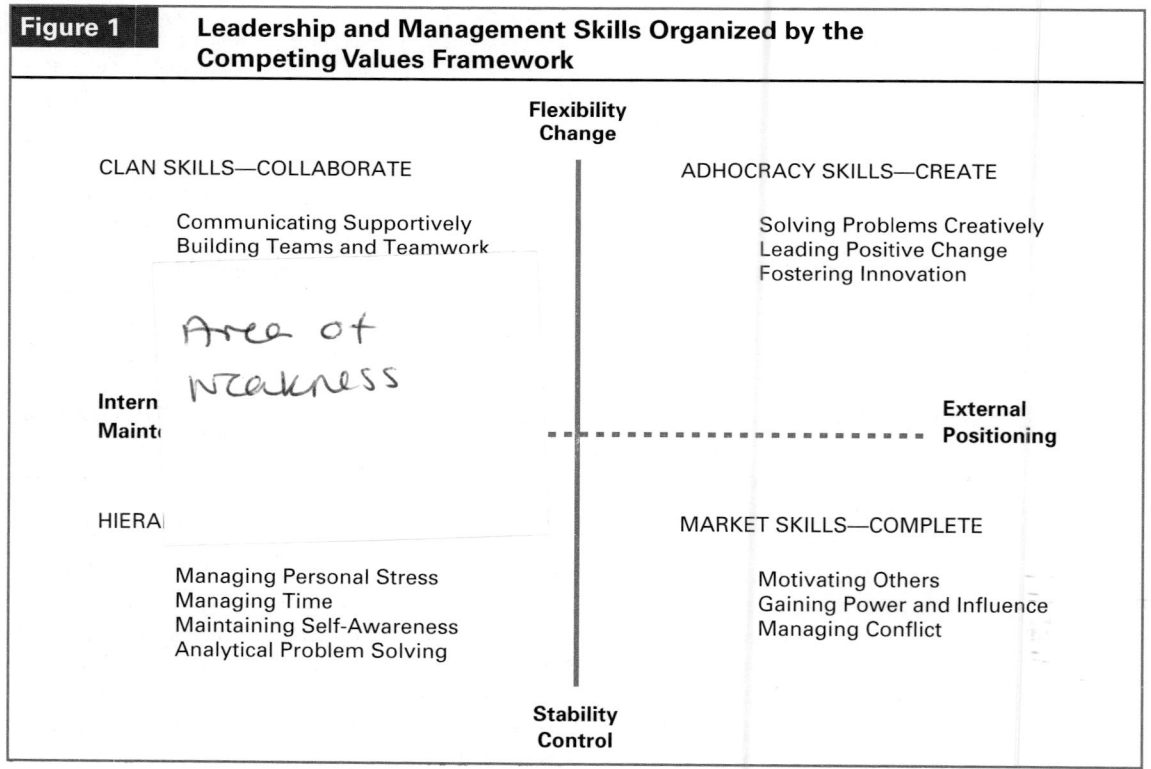

Figure 1 **Leadership and Management Skills Organized by the Competing Values Framework**

Flexibility
Change

CLAN SKILLS—COLLABORATE

Communicating Supportively
Building Teams and Teamwork

ADHOCRACY SKILLS—CREATE

Solving Problems Creatively
Leading Positive Change
Fostering Innovation

Area of weakness

Intern
Maint

External
Positioning

HIERA

MARKET SKILLS—COMPLETE

Managing Personal Stress
Managing Time
Maintaining Self-Awareness
Analytical Problem Solving

Motivating Others
Gaining Power and Influence
Managing Conflict

Stability
Control

focus on collaboration; (2) adhocracy skills, or a focus on creation; (3) market skills, or a focus on competition; and (4) hierarchy skills, or a focus on control.

Clan skills include those required to build effective interpersonal relationships and develop others (e.g., building teamwork, communicating supportively). Adhocracy skills include those required to manage the future, innovate, and promote change (e.g., solving problems creatively, articulating an energizing vision). Market skills include those required to compete effectively and manage external relationships (e.g., motivating others, using power and influence). Hierarchy skills include those required to maintain control and stability (e.g., managing personal stress and time, solving problems rationally) (see Cameron & Quinn, 2006).

In Figure 1, the two top quadrants in the Competing Values Framework—clan and adhocracy—are usually associated with leadership. The two bottom quadrants—market and hierarchy—are usually associated with management. In other words, traditionally, leadership has been used to describe what individuals do under conditions of change. When organizations are dynamic and undergoing transformation, people at the top are expected to exhibit leadership (i.e., pay attention to clan and adhocracy issues). Management, on the other hand, has traditionally been used to describe what executives do under conditions of stability. Thus, management has been linked with the status quo (i.e., pay attention to market and hierarchy issues). In addition, leadership has sometimes been defined as "doing the right things," whereas management has been defined as "doing things right." Leaders have been said to focus on setting the direction, articulating a vision, transforming individuals and organizations, and creating something new. Managers have been said to focus on monitoring, directing, and refining current performance. Leadership has been equated with dynamism, vibrancy, and charisma; management with hierarchy, equilibrium, and control.

However, the recent research is clear that such distinctions between leadership and management, which may have been appropriate in previous decades, are no longer useful (Quinn, 2000; Tichy, 1993, 1999). Managers cannot be successful without being good leaders, and leaders cannot be successful without being good managers. No longer do organizations and individuals have the luxury of holding on to the status quo; worrying about doing things right but failing to do the right things; keeping the system stable instead of leading change and improvement; monitoring current performance instead of formulating a vision of the future; concentrating on equilibrium and control instead of vibrancy and charisma. Effective management and leadership are inseparable. The skills required to do one are also required of the other. No organization in a postindustrial, hyperturbulent, twenty-first-century environment will survive without executives capable of providing both management and leadership. Leading change and managing stability, establishing vision and accomplishing objectives, breaking the rules and monitoring conformance, although paradoxical, all are required to be successful.

Figure 2 illustrates one major reason for this assertion. By staying the same, we tend to get worse. Because our circumstances are constantly changing and expectations for performance are continually escalating, the traditional definition of management is outmoded and irrelevant today. Effective managers and leaders do much the same things in dealing effectively with constant change and constant stability.

All of us, in other words, need to develop competencies that will enhance our ability to be both leaders and managers. The specific skills in this book represent all four quadrants in the Competing Values Framework of leadership. They serve as the foundation for effective management and for effective leadership. The book could appropriately include the word "leadership" in the title, therefore, based on the skills being covered. *The skills contained in this book cover both the management and the leadership ground.* We have chosen, appropriately or not, to use the label "management skills" to subsume the skills associated with leadership as well as with management.

Figure 2 | **The Necessity of Developing Leadership and Management Skills**

PERSONAL OR ORGANIZATIONAL PERFORMANCE

[handwritten note: Nice way of depicting performances]

Contents of the Book

Again, this book focuses on the skills that research has identified as critically important for successful management and leadership. Part I contains three chapters on personal skills: Developing Self-Awareness, Managing Personal Stress, and Solving Problems Analytically and Creatively. These skills focus on issues that may not involve other people but instead relate to the management of the self—hence they are called personal skills. Each chapter, however, really includes a cluster of related behaviors, not just one single, simple skill. These clusters of interrelated behaviors comprise the overall management skill indicated in the chapter's title. Figure 3 also points out that each skill cluster is related to and overlaps with other personal management skills, so each relies at least partially on the others to be performed successfully.

Part II focuses on interpersonal skills: Building Relationships by Communicating Supportively, Gaining Power and Influence, Motivating Others, and Managing Conflict. These skills focus primarily on issues that arise in your interactions with other people. Overlap exists among these skills, of course, so that you must rely on parts of many skill areas in order to perform any one skill effectively.

Part III includes three chapters on group skills: Empowering and Delegating, Building Effective Teams and Teamwork, and Leading Positive Change. These skills focus on key issues that arise when you are involved with groups of people either as a leader or as a member of the group. As with all the skills in the book, overlap occurs among the group skills as well as with the personal and interpersonal skills. In other words, as you progress from personal to interpersonal to group skills, the core competencies developed in the previous skill area help support successful performance of the new skill area.

In addition to the ten core management skills in Parts I, II, and III, the supplemental Part IV chapters contain three additional communications skills: Making Oral and Written Presentations, Conducting Interviews, and Conducting Meetings. These supplements cover specialized communication skills that are especially relevant for students who have had little managerial experience or skill training. These supplements foster skill development needed to implement assignments typically included in a management skill-building course. Writing reports, giving class presentations, interviewing managers, and conducting group meetings are all prerequisites for building skills in the core management skill areas, so we have provided material on these three topics that students will find helpful.

Figure 3 | **A Model of Essential Management Skills**

Appendix I contains a glossary of key terms in the text; and Appendix for excerpted material in the book.

Acknowledge further areas for development

Organization of the Book

Each chapter is organized on the basis of the learning model summarized in Table 4. Each chapter begins with *Skill Assessment* instruments. Their purpose is to highlight areas of personal competence as well as areas needing improvement in both knowledge and performance. As you complete the instruments in the Skill Assessment section, you will discover areas in which you will want to establish personal learning goals, and areas in which your competency is already well developed. As pointed out earlier, however, research has demonstrated that the most competent managers tend to progress the most when engaging in skill development exercises, so don't dismiss a skill just because you feel that it is an area of strength. We encourage you to take time to complete these assessment instruments. You will be surprised with what you learn if you complete them honestly and as accurately as you can.

Table 4	The Organization of Each Chapter	
SECTION	**CONTENTS**	
Skill Assessment	Instruments designed to identify your current level of skill competency, your styles, and/or key dimensions of the skill. These instruments can be used to identify individual differences, issues surrounding diversity, and areas for personal improvement plans.	
Skill Learning	Behavioral guidelines and key principles associated with the skill are explained. Scientific research is used as the basis for prescribed skill performance. Clarifying how to successfully develop and perform the skill is the purpose of this section.	
Skill Analysis	Cases and examples are presented in order to provide examples of successful and unsuccessful skill performance. Analytic problem solving is facilitated as recommendations are made for what the key issues are, how performance might be modified, and why success was achieved.	
Skill Practice	Exercises and role plays make it possible for individuals to actually practice the skill. Feedback from peers and the instructor will facilitate improvement of the skill in a setting where failure is not costly.	
Skill Application	Suggested assignments are provided so that the skill can be applied in a real-life setting. A feedback mechanism is also suggested so that individuals analyze their own success in applying the skill outside the classroom. Improvement plans should always be associated with the application exercises.	

Second, an explanation of the key behavioral guidelines, as well as a rationale for why these guidelines work, is found in the *Skill Learning* section of each chapter. This section explains the core behavioral principles associated with each skill. We present a research-based model of each skill, along with evidence from research that the principles identified are effective in practice. Our objective is to provide a sound rationale for the action guidelines summarized at the end of the section. We have not relied on popular anecdotes or stories from the popular press in presenting these guidelines and principles. Instead, we rely on scientific research that identifies what behaviors must be performed in order to foster effective outcomes.

In the *Skill Analysis* section, you will find brief case histories that illustrate both effective and ineffective applications of the behavioral principles. The purpose of this section is to bridge the gap between intellectual understanding and behavioral application. Critiquing a manager's performance in a real-life case enhances your understanding of the skill learning material. Each case provides a model of effective or ineffective performance and helps identify ways that the skill can be adapted to your personal style. In analyzing these cases, focus less on trying to find a "right" answer and more on determining how you might behave in similar circumstances.

The *Skill Practice* section provides exercises, problems, and role-play assignments. The goal of this section is to provide opportunities to practice the behavioral guidelines in simulated managerial situations and to receive feedback from peers and instructors. Practicing these managerial skills in a classroom setting is not only safer and less costly than in a real-life management job, but others' observation and feedback can be more precise and more timely as well. Many of these types of exercises can seem "gamey" or superficial, of course, unless you take them seriously as ways to improve your skill performance. We encourage you to use the feedback of others to critique your performance and help you find ways to enhance your skill competencies.

The last section of each chapter is *Skill Application*. It contains a form to help you generate your own improvement agenda, as well as assignments and ideas for applying the skill in an out-of-class situation. The purpose of these assignments is to help you transfer behavioral guidelines into everyday practice. You may be directed to teach the skill to someone else, consult with another manager to help resolve a relevant problem, or apply the skill in an organization or family.

Practice and Application

The philosophy of this book is that improvement in management ski[ll is the] learner's responsibility. If the application of the principles covered in this [book is not consci]entiously applied outside the classroom, little or no progress can be achie[ved. Our goal,] therefore, is to have the course carry over into the life activities of learne[rs. Effectiveness in] management is no different from effectiveness in most other human ente[rprises. It takes] the same kinds of skills to live a productive and successful life as it does to manage people effectively. That is why, even though some users of this book may not presently be managers of other employees—and indeed may never become managers—they shou[ld neither dis]miss these skills as irrelevant nor wait until they become managers before [they begin to] practice them.

Psychological research has confirmed that when we are forced to perfo[rm under stress,] we rely on what is called a "dominant response pattern" (Staw, Sandela[nds, and Dutton,] 1981; Weick, 1995). That is, we rely on the behavior patterns that a[re most deeply] ingrained in our response repertoire. For example, if a person who has bee[n accustomed to] responding to conflict combatively—but who has recently begun practi[cing a more sup]portive response pattern—is faced with an intense, emotional confronta[tion, that person] may begin by reacting supportively. But as pressure mounts, he or she is likely to revert to the more practiced, combative style. That is why, it is said, that people always curse in their native language. Stress causes us to revert to our fundamental, most reinforced behaviors.

Thus it is important that learners not make the mistake of thinking they can delay applying skill training until they become managers. When problems and conflicts occur then, it is too late to change behaviors to handle issues effectively. We enco[urage you, there]fore, to practice and apply the skills discussed in this book to part-time job[s, to clubs, to stu]dent organizations, families, church groups, and so forth. If you are in a m[anagement job, you] will want to use the guidelines provided here with your coworkers, mana[gers, subordinates,] and customers. With conscientious practice, following the behavior[al guidelines will] become second nature.

A second reason that nonmanagers should not delay the applicatio[n of management] skills is that we all learn faster and remember better that which we ex[perience emotion]ally as well as intellectually. That is, people learn best the things that a[ffect them person]ally, and they feel affected by something if they see an immediate effect on their lives. For example, we can more quickly acquire a working knowledge of a foreign language and retain it longer if we spend a summer living in a country where the language is spoken than if we merely take a language course in our own country. Simply stated, application is a crucial component of the skill improvement process, but it generally takes extra effort and ingenuity to make application exercises effective and worthwhile. We encourage you to put that extra effort into improving your management skills.

Diversity and Individual Differences

One reason developing management skills is difficult is because all of us possess our own unique styles, personalities, and inclinations. We all know that everyone doesn't react in the same way to similar circumstances. We can freely choose to behave differently than expected or than we did in the past. It is impossible, therefore, to manage each relationship

[Handwritten margin notes: "Justification for choice of skill development"; "Responding under stress"; "Affects me personally — so more likely to benefit"]

in exactly the same way, or even to behave the same way from one encounter to the next. Sensitivity to individual differences is an important part of an effective manager's repertoire.

A great deal of research has been conducted on cultural differences, gender differences, ethnic differences, and age differences in organizations (e.g., Cox, 1994; Cox & Beal, 1997). While we will not summarize that extensive research, we do want to highlight the importance of being sensitive to individuality. Two kinds of sensitivities are necessary: one to the uniqueness displayed by each person, and the other to distinctive but general patterns of behavior that characterize groups of people. For example, it is essential that effective managers not only become aware of, but also value and capitalize on the differences that characterize people with whom they work. In this book we will encourage you to develop sensitivity to the diversity that people display as they interact with you. In addition, you will also become skilled at diagnosing certain generalized patterns of behavior among people with different experiences, nationalities, genders, ethnic backgrounds, and ages. These generalized patterns can be used inappropriately to stereotype or categorize people, of course, and that may lead to deterioration in interpersonal sensitivity and emotional intelligence. On the other hand, being aware of national, cultural, ethnic, gender, or age differences can also be extremely useful to you as you engage in managerial roles.

We have included in each chapter a framework for diagnosing individual differences across cultures and summaries of some extensive crossnational research by Trompenaars and Hampden-Turner (1998). We include this framework to assist you in diagnosing some key differences that affect behavior. Knowing that the general tendency of people is to fear or oppose those who are different from them, our main objective in providing this information is to help us all better understand and appreciate differences. We don't emphasize so much *managing diversity* as we do *diagnosing individual differences* so they can be valued, understood, and appreciated.

In Chapter 1, Developing Self-Awareness, we explain the Trompenaars model, which relies on seven dimensions found to differ across national and cultural boundaries. These dimensions have been found to be very helpful in assisting people to understand key differences in others. They are: universalism versus particularism, individualism versus communitarianism, specificity versus diffuseness, neutral versus affective, achievement versus ascription oriented, internal versus external, and past versus present versus future time emphasis. These dimensions will help you to remain sensitive to the personal variations that may require alternation of some of the ways in which you practice core management skills. Whereas the behavioral principles upon which the management skills are based are applicable across cultures, genders, ethnic groups, and age cohorts, important nuances may be required of you as you practice among people characterized by these differences. Women may not behave the same as men. Japanese colleagues may not respond the same as German colleagues. Individuals in their sixties may not see the world the same as someone in their twenties. Stereotyping based on these categories, of course, is also dangerous and damaging, so being sensitive to and valuing individual differences is the key.

This means that you may want to pay special attention to the results of colleagues' Skill Assessment responses. You can identify the different patterns that arise among your own colleagues as you work your way through the book. Do you detect any general differences among men and women, among old and young, among different nationalities, among ethnic groups, among those with managerial experience and those without? People with high degrees of emotional intelligence have developed the ability to sense and empathize with the differences that are typical of different groups of people. We hope you will improve in this ability as well. Each of the sections of the chapters—Assessment, Learning, Analysis, Practice, and Application—can be useful to you in gaining insight into individual differences.

Summary

In sum, *Developing Management Skills* is not intended just for individuals who plan to enter managerial positions or who currently manage organizations. It is meant to help you better manage many aspects of your life and relationships. It is intended to help you actually change your behavior, to improve your competence, and to be more savvy in your relationships with different kinds of people. It is intended to improve your social and emotional intelligence. John Holt (1964) succinctly summarized our intention by equating management skill to intelligence:

> When we talk about intelligence, we do not mean the ability to get a good score on a certain kind of test or even the ability to do well in school; these are at best only indicators of something larger, deeper, and far more important. By intelligence we mean a style of life, a way of behaving in various situations. The true test of intelligence is not how much we know how to do, but how we behave when we don't know what to do. (p. 165)

Fostering the development of such intelligence is the goal of *Developing Management Skills.*

Diagnostic Survey and Exercises

Personal Assessment of Management Skills (PAMS)

Step 1: To get an overall profile of your level of skill competence, respond to the following statements using the rating scale below. Please rate your behavior as it is, not as you would like it to be. If you have not engaged in a specific activity, answer according to how you think you would behave based on your experience in similar activities. Be realistic; this instrument is designed to help you tailor your learning to your specific needs. After you have completed the survey, the scoring key at the end of the chapter will help you generate an overall profile of your management skill strengths and weaknesses.

Step 2: Get copies of the Associates' version of this instrument from your instructor. An alternate version has been provided in the Instructor's Manual that uses "he" or "she" instead of "I" in the questions. Give copies to at least three other people who know you well or who have observed you in a situation in which you have had to lead or manage others. Those people should complete the instrument by rating your behavior. Bring the completed surveys back to class and compare: (1) your own ratings to your associates' ratings, (2) your associates' ratings to the ratings received by others in the class, and (3) the ratings you received to those of a national norm group.

Subsections of this instrument appear in each chapter throughout the book.

Rating Scale

1 Strongly disagree
2 Disagree
3 Slightly disagree
4 Slightly agree
5 Agree
6 Strongly agree

In regard to my level of self-knowledge:

_____ 1. I seek information about my strengths and weaknesses from others as a basis for self-improvement.

_____ 2. In order to improve, I am willing to be self-disclosing to others (that is, to share my beliefs and feelings).

_____ 3. I am very much aware of my preferred style in gathering information and making decisions.

_____ 4. I have a good sense of how I cope with situations that are ambiguous and uncertain.

_____ 5. I have a well-developed set of personal standards and principles that guide my behavior.

When faced with stressful or time-pressured situations:

_____ 6. I use effective time-management methods such as keeping track of my time, making to-do lists, and prioritizing tasks.

_____ 7. I frequently affirm my priorities so that less important things don't drive out more important things.

_____ 8. I maintain a program of regular exercise for fitness.

_____ 9. I maintain an open, trusting relationship with someone with whom I can share my frustrations.

_____ 10. I know and practice several temporary relaxation techniques such as deep breathing and muscle relaxation.

_____ 11. I maintain balance in my life by pursuing a variety of interests outside of work.

When I approach a typical, routine problem:

_____ 12. I state clearly and explicitly what the problem is. I avoid trying to solve it until I have defined it.

_____ 13. I always generate more than one alternative solution to the problem, instead of identifying only one obvious solution.

_____ 14. I keep steps in the problem-solving process distinct; that is, I define the problem before proposing alternative solutions, and I generate alternatives before selecting a single solution.

When faced with a complex or difficult problem that does not have an easy solution:

_____ 15. I try out several definitions of the problem. I don't limit myself to just one way to define it.

_____ 16. I try to unfreeze my thinking by asking lots of questions about the nature of the problem before considering ways to solve it.

_____ 17. I try to think about the problem from both the left (logical) side of my brain and the right (intuitive) side of my brain.

_____ 18. I do not evaluate the merits of an alternative solution to the problem before I have generated a list of alternatives. That is, I avoid deciding on a solution until I have developed many possible solutions.

_____ 19. I have some specific techniques that I use to help develop creative and innovative solutions to problems.

When trying to foster more creativity and innovation among those with whom I work:

_____ 20. I make sure there are divergent points of view represented or expressed in every complex problem-solving situation.

_____ 21. I try to acquire information from individuals outside the problem-solving group who will be affected by the decision, mainly to determine their preferences and expectations.

_____ 22. I try to provide recognition not only to those who come up with creative ideas (the idea champions) but also to those who support others' ideas (supporters) and who provide resources to implement them (orchestrators).

_____ 23. I encourage informed rule-breaking in pursuit of creative solutions.

In situations where I have to provide negative feedback or offer corrective advice:

_____ 24. I am able to help others recognize and define their own problems when I counsel them.

_____ 25. I am clear about when I should coach someone and when I should provide counseling instead.

_____ 26. When I give feedback to others, I avoid referring to personal characteristics and focus on problems or solutions instead.

_____ 27. When I try to correct someone's behavior, our relationship is almost always strengthened.

_____ 28. I am descriptive in giving negative feedback to others. That is, I objectively describe events, their consequences, and my feelings about them.

_____ 29. I take responsibility for my statements and point of view by using, for example, "I have decided" instead of "They have decided."

_____ 30. I strive to identify some area of agreement in a discussion with someone who has a different point of view.

_____ 31. I don't talk down to those who have less power or less information than I.

_____ 32. When discussing someone's problem, I usually respond with a reply that indicates understanding rather than advice.

In a situation where it is important to obtain more power:

_____ 33. I always put forth more effort and take more initiative than expected in my work.

_____ 34. I am continually upgrading my skills and knowledge.

_____ 35. I strongly support organizational ceremonial events and activities.

_____ 36. I form a broad network of relationships with people throughout the organization at all levels.

_____ 37. In my work I consistently strive to generate new ideas, initiate new activities, and minimize routine tasks.

_____ 38. I consistently send personal notes to others when they accomplish something significant or when I pass along important information to them.

_____ 39. I refuse to bargain with individuals who use high-pressure negotiation tactics.

_____ 40. I always avoid using threats or demands to impose my will on others.

When another person needs to be motivated:

_____ 41. I always determine if the person has the necessary resources and support to succeed in a task.

_____ 42. I use a variety of rewards to reinforce exceptional performances.

_____ 43. I design task assignments to make them interesting and challenging.

_____ 44. I make sure the person gets timely feedback from those affected by task performance.

_____ 45. I always help the person establish performance goals that are challenging, specific, and time bound.

_____ 46. Only as a last resort do I attempt to reassign or release a poorly performing individual.

_____ 47. I consistently discipline when effort is below expectations and capabilities.

_____ 48. I make sure that people feel fairly and equitably treated.

_____ 49. I provide immediate compliments and other forms of recognition for meaningful accomplishments.

When I see someone doing something that needs correcting:

_____ 50. I avoid making personal accusations and attributing self-serving motives to the other person.

_____ 51. I encourage two-way interaction by inviting the respondent to express his or her perspective and to ask questions.

_____ 52. I make a specific request, detailing a more acceptable option.

When someone complains about something I've done:

_____ 53. I show genuine concern and interest, even when I disagree.

_____ 54. I seek additional information by asking questions that provide specific and descriptive information.

_____ 55. I ask the other person to suggest more acceptable behaviors.

When two people are in conflict and I am the mediator:

_____ 56. I do not take sides but remain neutral.

_____ 57. I help the parties generate multiple alternatives.

_____ 58. I help the parties find areas on which they agree.

In situations where I have an opportunity to engage people in accomplishing work:

_____ 59. I help people feel competent in their work by recognizing and celebrating their small successes.

_____ 60. I provide regular feedback and needed support.

_____ 61. I try to provide all the information that people need to accomplish their tasks.

_____ 62. I highlight the important impact that a person's work will have.

When delegating work to others:

_____ 63. I specify clearly the results I desire.

_____ 64. I specify clearly the level of initiative I want others to take (for example, wait for directions, do part of the task and then report, do the whole task and then report, and so forth).

_____ 65. I allow participation by those accepting assignments regarding when and how work will be done.

_____ 66. I avoid upward delegation by asking people to recommend solutions, rather than merely asking for advice or answers, when a problem is encountered.

_____ 67. I follow up and maintain accountability for delegated tasks on a regular basis.

When I am in the role of leader in a team:

_____ 68. I know how to establish credibility and influence among team members.

_____ 69. I am clear and consistent about what I want to achieve.

_____ 70. I build a common base of agreement in the team before moving forward with task accomplishment.

_____ 71. I articulate a clear, motivating vision of what the team can achieve along with specific short-term goals.

When I am in the role of team member:

_____ 72. I know a variety of ways to facilitate task accomplishment in the team.

_____ 73. I know a variety of ways to help build strong relationships and cohesion among team members.

When I desire to make my team perform well, regardless of whether I am a leader or member:

_____ 74. I am knowledgeable about the different stages of team development experienced by most teams.

_____ 75. I help the team avoid groupthink by making sure that sufficient diversity of opinions is expressed in the team.

_____ 76. I can diagnose and capitalize on my team's core competencies, or unique strengths.

_____ 77. I encourage the team to achieve dramatic breakthrough innovations as well as small continuous improvements.

When I am in a position to lead change:

_____ 78. I create positive energy in others when I interact with them.

_____ 79. I emphasize a higher purpose or meaning associated with the change I am leading.

_____ 80. I express gratitude frequently and conspicuously, even for small acts.

_____ 81. I emphasize building on strengths, not just overcoming weaknesses.

_____ 82. I use a lot more positive comments than negative comments.

_____ 83. When I communicate a vision, I capture people's hearts as well as their heads.

_____ 84. I know how to get people to commit to my vision of positive change.

What Does It Take to Be an Effective Manager?

The purpose of this exercise is to help you get a first-hand picture of the role of a manager and the skills required to perform that job successfully.

Your assignment is to interview at least three managers who are employed full-time. You should use the questions below in your interviews, plus use others that you think might help you identify effective management skills. The purpose of these interviews is to give you a chance to learn about critical managerial skills from those who have to use them.

Please treat the interviews as confidential. The names of the individuals do not matter— only their opinions, perceptions, and behaviors. Assure the managers that no one will be able to identify them from their responses. Keep written notes of your interviews. These notes should be as detailed as possible so you can reconstruct the interviews later. Be sure to keep a record of each person's job title and a brief description of his or her organization.

1. Please describe a typical day at work. What do you do all day?

2. What are the most critical problems you face as a manager?

3. What are the most critical skills needed to be a successful manager in your line of work?

4. What are the major reasons managers fail in positions like yours?

5. What are the outstanding skills or abilities of other effective managers you have known?

6. If you had to train someone to replace you in your current job, what key abilities would you focus on?

7. On a scale of 1 (very rarely) to 5 (constantly), can you rate the extent to which you use the following skills or behaviors during your workday?

_____ Managing personal time and stress

_____ Facilitating group decision making

_____ Creative problem solving

_____ Articulating an energizing vision

_____ Managing conflict

_____ Gaining and using power

_____ Delegating

_____ Active listening

_____ Holding interviews

_____ Building teams and teamwork

_____ Conducting meetings

_____ Fostering continuous improvement and quality

_____ Making analytical decisions

_____ Using interpersonal communication skills

_____ Motivating others

_____ Capitalizing on your self-awareness

_____ Facilitating organizational change

_____ Setting specific goals and targets

_____ Empowering others

_____ Giving speeches or presentations

_____ Defining and/or solving complex problems

_____ Negotiating

SSS Software In-Basket Exercise

NOTE: *The SSS Software exercise is used with permission. Copyright © 1995 by Susan Schor, Joseph Seltzer, and James Smither. All rights reserved.*

One way to assess your own strengths and weaknesses in management skills is to engage in an actual managerial work experience. The following exercise gives you a realistic glimpse of the tasks faced regularly by practicing managers. Complete the exercise, and then compare your own decisions and actions with those of classmates.

SSS Software designs and develops customized software for businesses. It also integrates this software with the customer's existing systems and provides system maintenance. SSS Software has customers in the following industries: airlines, automotive, finance/banking, health/hospital, consumer products, electronics, and government. The company has also begun to generate important international clients. These include the European Airbus consortium and a consortium of banks and financial firms based in Kenya.

SSS Software has grown rapidly since its inception eight years ago. Its revenue, net income, and earnings per share have all been above the industry average for the past several years. However, competition in this technologically sophisticated field has grown very rapidly. Recently, it has become more difficult to compete for major contracts. Moreover, although SSS Software's revenue and net income continue to grow, the rate of growth declined during the last fiscal year.

SSS Software's 250 employees are divided into several operating divisions with employees at four levels: Nonmanagement, Technical/Professional, Managerial, and Executive. Nonmanagement employees take care of the clerical and facilities support functions. The Technical/Professional staff performs the core technical work for the firm. Most Managerial employees are group managers who supervise a team of Technical/Professional employees working on a project for a particular customer. Staff who work in specialized areas such as finance, accounting, human resources, nursing, and law are also considered Managerial employees. The Executive level includes the 12 highest-ranking employees at SSS Software. An organization chart in Figure 4 illustrates SSS Software's structure. There is also an Employee Classification Report that lists the number of employees at each level of the organization.

In this exercise, you will play the role of Chris Perillo, Vice President of Operations for Health and Financial Services. You learned last Wednesday, October 13, that your predecessor, Michael Grant, had resigned and gone to Universal Business Solutions, Inc. You were offered his former job, and you accepted it. Previously, you were the Group Manager for a team of 15 software developers assigned to work on the Airbus consortium project in the Airline Services Division. You spent all of Thursday, Friday, and most of the weekend finishing up parts of the project, briefing your successor, and preparing for an interim report you will deliver in Paris on October 21.

It is now 7:00 A.M. Monday and you are in your new office. You have arrived at work early so you can spend the next two hours reviewing material in your in-basket (including some memos and messages to Michael Grant), as well as your voice mail and e-mail. Your daily planning book indicates that you have no appointments today or tomorrow but will have to catch a plane for Paris early Wednesday morning. You have a full schedule for the remainder of the week and all of next week.

Assignment

During the next two hours, review all the material in your in-basket, as well as your voice mail and e-mail. Take only two hours. Using the response form below as a model, indicate how you want to respond to each item (that is, via letter/memo, e-mail, phone/voice mail, or personal meeting). If you decide not to respond to an item, check "no response"

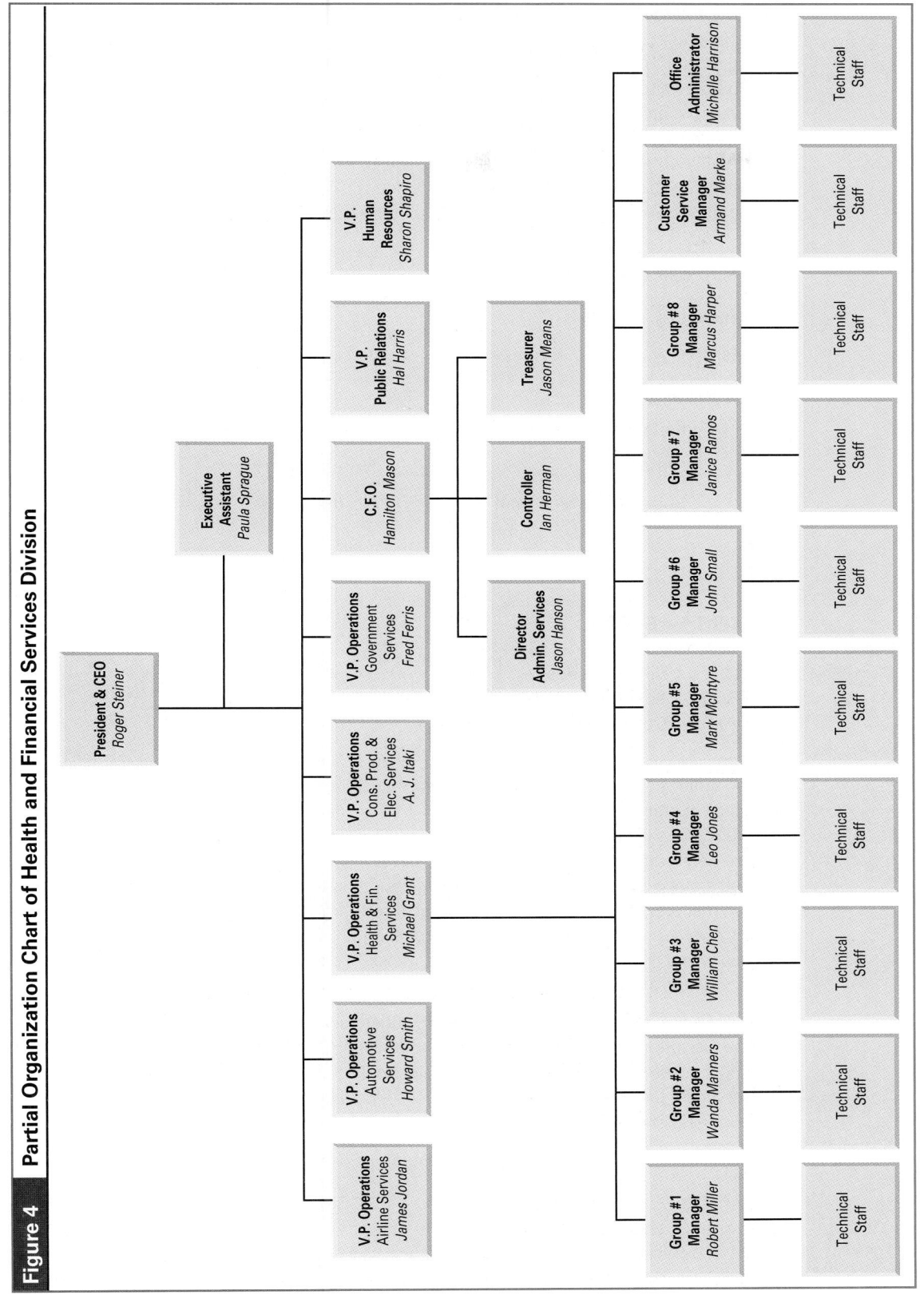

Figure 4   Partial Organization Chart of Health and Financial Services Division

President & CEO
Roger Steiner

Executive Assistant
Paula Sprague

V.P. Operations
Airline Services
James Jordan

V.P. Operations
Automotive Services
Howard Smith

V.P. Operations
Health & Fin. Services
Michael Grant

V.P. Operations
Cons. Prod. & Elec. Services
A. J. Itaki

V.P. Operations
Government Services
Fred Ferris

V.P.
Public Relations
Hal Harris

V.P.
Human Resources
Sharon Shapiro

C.F.O.
Hamilton Mason

Director
Admin. Services
Jason Hanson

Controller
Ian Herman

Treasurer
Jason Means

Group #1 Manager
Robert Miller

Group #2 Manager
Wanda Manners

Group #3 Manager
William Chen

Group #4 Manager
Leo Jones

Group #5 Manager
Mark McIntyre

Group #6 Manager
John Small

Group #7 Manager
Janice Ramos

Group #8 Manager
Marcus Harper

Customer Service Manager
Armand Marke

Office Administrator
Michelle Harrison

Technical Staff

on the response form. All your responses must be written on the response forms. Write your precise, detailed response (do not merely jot down a few notes). For example, you might draft a memo or write out a message that you will deliver via phone/voice mail. You may also decide to meet with an individual (or individuals) during the limited time available on your calendar today or tomorrow. If so, prepare an agenda for a personal meeting and list your goals for the meeting. As you read through the items, you may occasionally observe some information that you think is relevant and want to remember (or attend to in the future) but that you decide not to include in any of your responses to employees. Write down such information on a sheet of paper titled "note to self."

Sample Response Form

Relates to:

Memo # _____   E-mail # _____   Voice mail # _____

Response form:

_____ Letter/Memo   _____ Meet with person (when, where)

_____ E-mail   _____ Note to self

_____ Phone call/Voice mail   _____ No response

ITEM 1 – E-MAIL

TO: All Employees
FROM: Roger Steiner, Chief Executive Officer
DATE: October 15

I am pleased to announce that Chris Perillo has been appointed as Vice President of Operations for Health and Financial Services. Chris will immediately assume responsibility for all operations previously managed by Michael Grant. Chris will have end-to-end responsibility for the design, development, integration, and maintenance of custom software for the health and finance/banking industries. This responsibility includes all technical, financial, and staffing issues. Chris will also manage our program of software support and integration for the recently announced merger of three large health maintenance organizations (HMOs). Chris will be responsible for our recently announced project with a consortium of banks and financial firms operating in Tanzania. This project represents an exciting opportunity for us, and Chris's background seems ideally suited to the task.

Chris comes to this position with an undergraduate degree in Computer Science from the California Institute of Technology and an M.B.A. from the University of Virginia. Chris began as a member of our technical/professional staff six years ago and has most recently served for three years as a Group Manager supporting domestic and international projects for our airlines industry group, including our recent work for the European Airbus consortium.

I am sure you all join me in offering congratulations to Chris for this promotion.

ITEM 2 – E-MAIL

TO: All Managers
FROM: Hal Harris, Vice President, Community and Public Relations
DATE: October 15

For your information, the following article appeared on the front page of the business section of Thursday's Los Angeles Times.

In a move that may create problems for SSS Software, Michael Grant and Janice Ramos have left SSS Software and moved to Universal Business Solutions Inc. Industry analysts see the move as another victory for Universal Business Solutions Inc. in their battle with SSS Software for share of the growing software development and integration business. Both Grant and Ramos had been with SSS Software for over 7 years. Grant was most recently Vice President of Operations for all SSS Software's work in two industries: health and hospitals, and finance and banking. Ramos brings to Universal Business Solutions Inc. her special expertise in the growing area of international software development and integration.

Hillary Collins, an industry analyst with Merrill Lynch, said "the loss of key staff to a competitor can often create serious problems for a firm such as SSS Software. Grant and Ramos have an insider's understanding of SSS Software's strategic and technical limitations. It will be interesting to see if they can exploit this knowledge to the advantage of Universal Business Solutions Inc."

ITEM 3 – E-MAIL

TO: Chris Perillo
FROM: Paula Sprague, Executive Assistant to Roger Steiner
DATE: October 15

Chris, I know that in your former position as a Group Manager in the Airline Services Division, you probably have met most of the group managers in the Health and Financial Services Division, but I thought you might like some more personal information about them. These people will be your direct reports on the management team.

Group #1: Bob Miller, 55-year-old white male, married (Anna) with two children and three grandchildren. Active in local Republican politics. Well regarded as a "hands-off" manager heading a high-performing team. Plays golf regularly with Mark McIntyre, John Small, and a couple of V.P.s from other divisions.

Group #2: Wanda Manners, 38-year-old white female, single with one school-age child. A fitness "nut" has run in several marathons. Some experience in Germany and Japan. Considered a hard-driving manager with a constant focus on the task at hand. Will be the first person to show up every morning.

Group #3: William Chen, 31-year-old male of Chinese descent, married (Harriet), two young children from his first marriage. Enjoys tennis and is quite good at it. A rising star in the company, he is highly respected by his peers as a "man of action" and a good friend.

Group #4: Leo Jones, 36-year-old white male, married (Janet) with an infant daughter. Recently returned from paternity leave. Has traveled extensively on projects, since he speaks three languages. Has liked hockey ever since the time he spent in Montreal. Considered a strong manager who gets the most out of his people.

Group #5: Mark McIntyre, 45-year-old white male, married (Mary Theresa) to an executive in the banking industry. No children. A lot of experience in Germany and Eastern Europe. Has been writing a mystery novel. Has always been a good "team player," but several members of his technical staff are not well respected and he hasn't addressed the problem.

Group #6: John Small, 38-year-old white male, recently divorced. Three children living with his wife. A gregarious individual who likes sports. He spent a lot of time in Mexico and Central America before he came to SSS Software. Recently has been doing mostly contract work with the federal government. An average manager, has had some trouble keeping his people on schedule.

Group #7: This position vacant since Janice Ramos left. Roger thinks we ought to fill this position quickly. Get in touch with me if you want information on any in-house candidates for any position.

Group #8: Marcus Harper, 42-year-old black male, married (Tamara) with two teenage children. Recently won an award in a local photography contest. Considered a strong manager who gets along with peers and works long hours.

Customer Services: Armad Marke, 38-year-old male, divorced. A basketball fan. Originally from Armenia. Previously a Group Manager. Worked hard to establish the Technical Services Phone Line, but now has pretty much left it alone.

Office Administrator: Michelle Harrison, 41-year-old white female, single. Grew up on a ranch and still rides horses whenever she can. A strict administrator.

There are a number of good folks here, but they don't function well as a management team. I think Michael played favorites, especially with Janice and Leo. There are a few cliques in this group and I'm not sure how effectively Michael dealt with them. I expect you will find it a challenge to build a cohesive team.

ITEM 4 – E-MAIL

TO: Chris Perillo
FROM: Wanda Manners, Group 2 Manager
DATE: October 15

CONFIDENTIAL AND RESTRICTED

Although I know you are new to your job, I feel it is important that I let you know about some information I just obtained concerning the development work we recently completed for First National Investment. Our project involved the development of asset management software for managing their international funds. This was a very complex project due to the volatile exchange rates and the forecasting tools we needed to develop.

As part of this project, we had to integrate the software and reports with all their existing systems and reporting mechanisms. To do this, we were given access to all of their existing software (much of which was developed by Universal Business Solutions Inc.). Of course, we signed an agreement acknowledging that the software to which we were given access was proprietary and that our access was solely for the purpose of our system integration work associated with the project.

Unfortunately, I have learned that some parts of the software we developed actually "borrow" heavily from complex application programs developed for First National Investment by Universal Business Solutions Inc. It seems obvious to me that one or more of the software developers from Group 5 (that is, Mark McIntyre's group) inappropriately "borrowed" algorithms developed by Universal Business Solutions Inc. I am sure that doing so saved us significant development time on some aspects of the project. It seems very unlikely that First National Investment or Universal Business Solutions Inc. will ever become aware of this issue.

Finally, First National Investment is successfully using the software we developed and is thrilled with the work we did. We brought the project in on time and under budget. You probably know that they have invited us to bid on several other substantial projects.

I'm sorry to bring this delicate matter to your attention, but I thought you should know about it.

ITEM 5A – E-MAIL

TO: Chris Perillo
FROM: Paula Sprague, Executive Assistant to Roger Steiner
DATE: October 15

RE: Letter from C.A.R.E. Services (copies attached)

Roger asked me to work on this C.A.R.E. project and obviously wants some fast action. A lot of the staff are already booked solid for the next couple of weeks. I knew that Elise Soto and Chu Hung Woo have the expertise to do this system and when I checked with them, they were relatively free. I had them pencil in the next two weeks and wanted to let you know. Hopefully, it will take a "hot potato" out of your hands.

ITEM 5B – COPY OF FAX

C.A.R.E.
Child and Adolescent Rehabilitative and Educational Services
A United Way Member Agency
200 Main Street
Los Angeles, California 90230

DATE: October 11
Roger Steiner, CEO
SSS Software
13 Miller Way
Los Angeles, California 90224

Dear Roger,

This letter is a follow-up to our conversation after last night's board meeting. I appreciated your comments during the board meeting about the need for sophisticated computer systems in nonprofit organizations and I especially appreciate your generous offer of assistance to have SSS Software provide assistance to deal with the immediate problem with our accounting system. Since the board voted to fire the computer consultant, I am very worried about getting our reports done in time to meet the state funding cycle.

Thanks again for your offer of help during this crisis.

Sincerely yours,

Janice Polocizwic

Janice Polocizwic
Executive Director

ITEM 5C – COPY OF A LETTER

SSS SOFTWARE
13 Miller Way
Los Angeles, CA 90224

DATE: October 12

Janice Polocizwic
Executive Director, C.A.R.E. Services
200 Main Street
Los Angeles, California 90230

Dear Janice,

I received your fax of October 11. I have asked Paula Sprague, my executive assistant, to line up people to work on your accounting system as soon as possible. You can expect to hear from her shortly.

Sincerely,

Roger Steiner

Roger Steiner
cc: Paula Sprague, Executive Assistant

ITEM 6 – E-MAIL

TO: Michael Grant
FROM: Harry Withers, Group 6 Technical Staff
DATE: October 12

PERSONAL AND CONFIDENTIAL

Our team is having difficulty meeting the submission deadline of November 5 for the Halstrom project. Kim, Fred, Peter, Kyoto, Susan, Mala, and I have been working on the project for several weeks, but we are experiencing some problems and may need additional time. I hesitate to write this letter, but the main problem is that our group manager, John Small, is involved in a relationship with Mala. Mala gets John's support for her ideas and brings them to the team as required components of the project. Needless to say, this has posed some problems for the group. Mala's background is especially valuable for this project, but Kim and Fred, who have both worked very hard on the project, do not want to work with her. In addition, one member of the team has been unavailable recently because of child-care needs. Commitment to the project and team morale have plummeted. However, we'll do our best to get the project finished as soon as possible. Mala will be on vacation the next two weeks, so I'm expecting that some of us can complete it in her absence.

ITEM 7 – VOICE MAIL MESSAGE

Hello, Michael. This is Jim Bishop of United Hospitals. I wanted to talk with you about the quality assurance project that you are working on for us. When Jose Martinez first started talking with us, I was impressed with his friendliness and expertise. But recently, he doesn't seem to be getting much accomplished and has seemed distant and on-edge in conversations. Today, I asked him about the schedule and he seemed very defensive and not entirely in control of his emotions. I am quite concerned about our project. Please give me a call.

ITEM 8 – VOICE MAIL MESSAGE

Hi, Michael. This is Armand. I wanted to talk with you about some issues with the Technical Services Phone Line. I've recently received some complaint letters from Phone Line customers whose complaints have included long delays while waiting for a technician to answer the phone, technicians who are not knowledgeable enough to solve problems, and, on occasion, rude service. Needless to say, I'm quite concerned about these complaints.

I believe that the overall quality of the Phone Line staff is very good, but we continue to be understaffed, even with the recent hires. The new technicians look strong, but are working on the help-line before being fully trained. Antolina, our best tech, often brings her child to work, which is adding to the craziness around here.

I think you should know that we're feeling a lot of stress here. I'll talk with you soon.

ITEM 9 – VOICE MAIL MESSAGE

Hi, Chris, it's Pat. Congratulations on your promotion. They definitely picked the right person. It's great news—for me, too. You've been a terrific mentor so far, so I'm expecting to learn a lot from you in your new position. How about lunch next week?

ITEM 10 – VOICE MAIL MESSAGE

Chris, this is Bob Miller. Just thought you'd like to know that John's joke during our planning meeting has disturbed a few of the women in my group. Frankly, I think the thing's being blown out of proportion, especially since we all know this is a good place for both men and women to work. Give me a call if you want to chat about this.

ITEM 11 – VOICE MAIL MESSAGE

Hello. This is Lorraine Adams from Westside Hospital. I read in today's Los Angeles Times that you will be taking over from Michael Grant. We haven't met yet, but your division has recently finished two large million-dollar projects for Westside. Michael Grant and I had some discussion about a small conversion of a piece of existing software to be compatible with the new systems. The original vendor had said that they would do the work, but they have been stalling, and I need to move quickly. Can you see if Harris Wilson, Chu Hung Woo, and Elise Soto are available to do this work as soon as possible? They were on the original project and work well with our people.

Um. . . (long pause) I guess I should tell you that I got a call from Michael offering to do this work. But I think I should stick with SSS Software. Give me a call.

ITEM 12 – VOICE MAIL MESSAGE

Hi, Chris, this is Roosevelt Moore calling. I'm a member of your technical/professional staff. I used to report to Janice Ramos, but since she left the firm, I thought I'd bring my concerns directly to you. I'd like to arrange some time to talk with you about my experiences since returning from six weeks of paternity leave. Some of my major responsibilities have been turned over to others. I seem to be out of the loop and wonder if my career is at risk. Also, I am afraid that I won't be supported or seriously considered for the opening created by Janice's departure. Frankly, I feel like I'm being screwed for taking my leave. I'd like to talk with you this week.

ITEM 13 – E-MAIL

TO: Michael Grant
FROM: Jose Martinez, Group 1 Technical Staff
DATE: October 12

I would like to set up a meeting with you as soon as possible. I suspect that you will get a call from Jim Bishop of United Hospitals and want to be sure that you hear my side of the story first. I have been working on a customized system design for quality assurance for them using a variation of the J-3 product we developed several years ago. They had a number of special requirements and some quirks in their accounting systems, so I have had to put in especially long hours. I've worked hard to meet their demands, but they keep changing the ground rules. I keep thinking, this is just another J-3 I'm working on, but they have been interfering with an elegant design I have developed. It seems I'm not getting anywhere on this project. Earlier today, I had a difficult discussion with their Controller. He asked for another major change. I've been fighting their deadline and think I am just stretched too thin on this project. Then Jim Bishop asked me if the system was running yet. I was worn out from dealing with the Controller, and I made a sarcastic comment to Jim Bishop. He gave me a funny look and just walked out of the room.

I would like to talk with you about this situation at your earliest convenience.

ITEM 14 – E-MAIL

TO: Chris Perillo
FROM: John Small, Group 6 Manager
DATE: October 15

Welcome aboard, Chris. I look forward to meeting with you. I just wanted to put a bug in your ear about finding a replacement for Janice Ramos. One of my technical staff, Mala Abendano, has the ability and drive to make an excellent group manager. I have encouraged her to apply for the position. I'd be happy to talk with you further about this, at your convenience.

ITEM 15 – E-MAIL

TO: Chris Perillo
FROM: Paula Sprague, Executive Assistant to Roger Steiner
DATE: October 15

Roger asked me to let you know about the large contract we have gotten in Tanzania. It means that a team of four managers will be making a short trip to determine current needs. They will assign their technical staff the tasks of developing a system and software here over the next six months, and then the managers and possibly some team members will be spending about 10 months on site in Tanzania to handle the implementation. Roger thought you might want to hold an initial meeting with some of your managers to check on their interest and willingness to take this sort of assignment. Roger would appreciate an e-mail of your thoughts about the issues to be discussed at this meeting, additional considerations about sending people to Tanzania, and about how you will put together an effective team to work on this project. The October 15 memo I sent to you will provide you with some information you'll need to start making these decisions.

ITEM 16 – E-MAIL

TO: Chris Perillo
FROM: Sharon Shapiro, V.P. of Human Resources
DATE: October 15

RE: Upcoming meeting

I want to update you on the rippling effect of John Small's sexual joke at last week's planning meeting. Quite a few women have been very upset and have met informally to talk about it. They have decided to call a meeting of all people concerned about this kind of behavior throughout the firm. I plan to attend, so I'll keep you posted.

ITEM 17 – E-MAIL

TO: All SSS Software Managers
FROM: Sharon Shapiro, V.P. of Human Resources
DATE: October 15

RE: Promotions and External Hires

Year-to-Date (January through September) Promotions and External Hires

Level	Race				Native	Sex		Total
	White	Black	Asian	Hispanic	American	M	F	
Hires into Executive Level	0 (0%)	0 (0%)	0 (0%)	0 (0%)	0 (0%)	0 (0%)	0 (0%)	0
Promotions to Executive Level	0 (0%)	0 (0%)	0 (0%)	0 (0%)	0 (0%)	0 (0%)	0 (0%)	0

Level	Race				Native	Sex		Total
	White	Black	Asian	Hispanic	American	M	F	
Hires into Management Level	2 (67%)	1 (33%)	0 (0%)	0 (0%)	0 (0%)	2 (67%)	1 (33%)	3
Promotions to Management Level	7 (88%)	0 (0%)	1 (12%)	0 (0%)	0 (0%)	7 (88%)	1 (12%)	8
Hires into Technical/ Professional Level	10 (36%)	6 (21%)	10 (36%)	2 (7%)	0 (0%)	14 (50%)	14 (50%)	28
Promotions to Technical/ Professional Level	0 (0%)	0 (0%)	0 (0%)	0 (0%)	0 (0%)	0 (0%)	0 (0%)	0
Hires into Non- Management Level	4 (20%)	10 (50%)	2 (10%)	4 (20%)	0 (0%)	6 (30%)	14 (70%)	20
Promotions to Non- Management Level	NA	NA	NA	NA	NA	NA	NA	NA

SSS Software Employee (EEO) Classification Report as of June 30

Level	Race					Sex		Total
	White	Black	Asian	Hispanic	Native American	M	F	
Executive Level	11 (92%)	0 (0%)	1 (8%)	0 (0%)	0 (0%)	11 (92%)	1 (8%)	12
Management Level	43 (90%)	2 (4%)	2 (4%)	1 (2%)	0 (0%)	38 (79%)	10 (21%)	48
Technical/ Professional Level	58 (45%)	20 (15%)	37 (28%)	14 (11%)	1 (1%)	80 (62%)	50 (38%)	130
Non- Management Level	29 (48%)	22 (37%)	4 (7%)	4 (7%)	1 (2%)	12 (20%)	48 (80%)	60
Total	141 (56%)	44 (18%)	44 (18%)	19 (8%)	2 (1%)	141 (56%)	109 (44%)	250

Personal Assessment of Management Skills

Scoring Key

SKILL AREA	ITEMS	ASSESSMENT	
		PERSONAL	ASSOCIATES
Developing Self-Awareness	**1–5**		
Self-disclosure and openness	1–2		
Awareness of self	3–5		
Managing Stress	**6–11**		
Eliminating stressors	6–7		
Developing resiliency	8–9		
Short-term coping	10–11		
Solving Problems Creatively	**12–23**		
Rational problem solving	12–14		
Creative problem solving	15–19		
Fostering innovation and creativity	20–23		
Communicating Supportively	**24–32**		
Coaching and counseling	24–25		
Effective negative feedback	26–28		
Communicating supportively	29–32		
Gaining Power and Influence	**33–40**		
Gaining power	33–37		
Exercising influence	38–40		
Motivating Others	**41–49**		
Managing Conflict	**50–58**		
Initiating	50–52		
Responding	53–55		
Mediating	56–58		
Empowering and Delegating	**59–67**		
Empowering	59–62		
Delegating	63–67		
Building Effective Teams and Teamwork	**68–77**		
Leading teams	68–71		
Team membership	72–73		
Teamwork	74–77		
Leading Positive Change	**78–84**		
Foster positive deviance	78–80		
Lead positive change	81–82		
Mobilize others	83–84		

Comparison Data

Compare your scores with at least four referents: (1) If you asked others to rate you using the Associates' version, compare how you rated yourself with how your associates rated you. (2) Compare the ratings you received to those received by other students in the class. (3) Compare the ratings you received to a norm group of approximately 1,500 business school students (see the information below). (4) Compare your score against the maximum possible (510).

For the survey as a whole, if you scored

394.35	=	mean
422 or above	=	you are in the top quartile.
395–421	=	you are in the second quartile.
369–394	=	you are in the third quartile.
368 or below	=	you are in the bottom quartile.

What Does It Take to Be an Effective Manager

This exercise does not have a solution or scoring data. Answers will vary among students.

SSS Software In-Basket Exercise

This exercise does not have a solution or scoring data. Answers will vary among students.

Part I

Personal Skills

CHAPTERS

1 DEVELOPING SELF-AWARENESS

Assessing emotional intelligence
Determining values and priorities
Identifying learning style
Assessing attitude toward change
Understanding core self-evaluation

2 MANAGING PERSONAL STRESS

Coping with stressors
Managing time
Developing resiliency

3 SOLVING PROBLEMS ANALYTICALLY AND CREATIVELY

Using the rational approach
Using the creative approach
Fostering innovation in others

SKILL **ASSESSMENT** ▶

- Self-Awareness Assessment
- Emotional Intelligence Assessment
- The Defining Issues Test
- The Learning Style Inventory
- Locus of Control Scale
- Tolerance of Ambiguity Scale
- Core Self-Evaluation Scale

SKILL **LEARNING** ■

- Key Dimensions of Self-Awareness
- The Enigma of Self-Awareness
- Understanding and Appreciating Individual Differences
- Important Areas of Self-Awareness
- Summary
- Behavioral Guidelines

SKILL **ANALYSIS**

- Communist Prison Camp
- Computerized Exam
- Decision Dilemmas

SKILL **PRACTICE**

- Through the Looking Glass
- Diagnosing Managerial Characteristics
- An Exercise for Identifying Aspects of Personal Culture: A Learning Plan and Autobiography

SKILL **APPLICATION**

- Suggested Assignments
- Application Plan and Evaluation

SCORING KEYS AND *COMPARISON DATA* ■

1

Developing Self-Awareness

SKILL DEVELOPMENT OBJECTIVES

Increase personal awareness of your:

- SENSITIVE LINE
- EMOTIONAL INTELLIGENCE
- PERSONAL VALUES AND MORAL MATURITY
- LEARNING STYLE
- ORIENTATION TOWARD CHANGE
- CORE SELF-EVALUATION

DIAGNOSTIC SURVEYS FOR SELF-AWARENESS

SELF-AWARENESS ASSESSMENT

Step 1: Before you read the material in this chapter, please respond to the following statements by writing a number from the rating scale below in the left-hand column (Pre-assessment). Your answers should reflect your attitudes and behavior as they are now, not as you would like them to be. Be honest. This instrument is designed to help you discover how self-aware you are so you can tailor your learning to your specific needs. When you have completed the survey, use the scoring key at the end of the chapter to identify the skill areas discussed in this chapter that are most important for you to master.

Step 2: After you have completed the reading and the exercises in this chapter and, ideally, as many of the Skill Application assignments at the end of this chapter as you can, cover up your first set of answers. Then respond to the same statements again, this time in the right-hand column (Post-assessment). When you have completed the survey, use the scoring key at the end of the chapter to measure your progress. If your score remains low in specific skill areas, use the behavioral guidelines at the end of the Skill Learning section to guide further practice.

Rating Scale

1 Strongly disagree
2 Disagree
3 Slightly disagree
4 Slightly agree
5 Agree
6 Strongly agree

Assessment

Pre-   Post-

_____ _____ 1. I seek information about my strengths and weaknesses from others as a basis for self-improvement.

_____ _____ 2. When I receive negative feedback about myself from others, I do not get angry or defensive.

_____ _____ 3. In order to improve, I am willing to be self-disclosing to others (that is, to share my beliefs and feelings).

_____ _____ 4. I am aware of my personal learning style and how I learn best.

_____ _____ 5. I have a good grasp of what it means to be emotionally mature, and I demonstrate that capability.

_____ _____ 6. I have a good sense of how I cope with situations that are ambiguous and uncertain.

_____ _____ 7. I have a well-developed set of personal standards and principles that guide my behavior.

_____ _____ 8. I feel in charge of what happens to me, good and bad.

_____ _____ 9. I seldom, if ever, feel angry, depressed, or anxious without knowing why.

_____ _____ 10. I am conscious of the areas in which conflict and friction most frequently arise in my interactions with others.

_____ _____ 11. I have a close personal relationship with at least one other person with whom I can share personal information and personal feelings.

EMOTIONAL INTELLIGENCE ASSESSMENT

Please reply to each item below by selecting the one alternative that is most likely to be your response. Think about the way you usually respond to these kinds of situations, not the way you would like to respond or the way you think you should respond. No correct answers exist for any of the items, and your scores will be most useful if you provide an accurate assessment of your typical behavior. Mark only one answer per item.

1. When I get really upset, I . . .
   a. _____ Analyze why I am so disturbed.
   b. _____ Blow up and let off steam.
   c. _____ Hide it and remain calm.

2. In a situation in which a colleague takes credit in public for my work and my ideas, I would probably . . .
   a. _____ Let it slide and do nothing in order to avoid a confrontation.
   b. _____ Later—in private—indicate that I would appreciate being given credit for my work and ideas.
   c. _____ Thank the person in public for referencing my work and ideas and then elaborate on my contributions.

3. When I approach another person and try to strike up a conversation but the other person doesn't respond, I . . .
   a. _____ Try to cheer up the person by sharing a funny story.
   b. _____ Ask the person if he or she wants to talk about what's on his or her mind.
   c. _____ Leave the person alone and find someone else to talk to.

4. When I enter a social group I usually . . .
   a. _____ Remain quiet and wait for people to talk to me.
   b. _____ Try to find something complimentary I can tell someone.
   c. _____ Find ways to be the life of the party or the source of energy and fun.

5. On important issues I usually . . .
   a. _____ Make up my own mind and ignore others' opinions.
   b. _____ Weigh both sides, and discuss it with others before making a decision.
   c. _____ Listen to my friends or colleagues and make the same decision they do.

6. When someone that I do not particularly like becomes romantically attracted to me, I usually . . .
   a. _____ Tell that person directly that I am not interested.
   b. _____ Respond by being friendly but cool or aloof.
   c. _____ Ignore the person and try to avoid him or her.

7. When I am in the company of two people who have diametrically opposing points of view about an issue (for example, politics, abortion, war) and are arguing about it, I . . .

   a. _____ Find something upon which they can both agree and emphasize it.

   b. _____ Encourage the verbal battle.

   c. _____ Suggest that they stop arguing and calm down.

8. When I am playing a sport and the game comes down to my last-second performance, I . . .

   a. _____ Get very nervous and hope that I don't choke.

   b. _____ See this as an opportunity to shine.

   c. _____ Stay focused and give it my best effort.

9. In a situation in which I have an important obligation and need to leave work early, but my colleagues ask me to stay to meet a deadline, I would probably . . .

   a. _____ Cancel my obligation and stay to complete the deadline.

   b. _____ Exaggerate a bit by telling my colleagues that I have an emergency that I can't miss.

   c. _____ Require some kind of compensation for missing the obligation.

10. In a situation in which another person becomes very angry and begins yelling at me, I . . .

    a. _____ Get angry in return. I don't take that from anyone.

    b. _____ Walk away. It doesn't do any good to argue.

    c. _____ Listen first, and then try to discuss the issue.

11. When I encounter someone who has just experienced a major loss or tragedy, I . . .

    a. _____ Really don't know what to do or say.

    b. _____ Tell the person I feel very sorry and try to provide support.

    c. _____ Share a time when I experienced a similar loss or tragedy.

12. When someone makes a racist joke or tells a crude story about a member of the opposite sex in mixed company, I usually . . .

    a. _____ Point out that this is inappropriate and not acceptable, and then change the subject.

    b. _____ Ignore it so I don't cause a scene.

    c. _____ Get really upset and tell the person just what I think of what he or she said.

THE DEFINING ISSUES TEST

This instrument assesses your opinions about controversial social issues. Different people make decisions about these issues in different ways. You should answer the questions for yourself without discussing them with others. You are presented with three stories. Following each story are 12 statements or questions. Your task after reading the story is to rate each statement in terms of its importance in making a decision. After rating each statement, select the four most important statements and rank them from one to four in the spaces provided. Each statement should be ranked in terms of its relative importance in making a decision.

Some statements will raise important issues, but you should ask yourself whether the decision should rest on that issue. Some statements sound high and lofty but are largely gibberish. If you cannot make sense of a statement, or if you don't understand its meaning, mark it 5—"Of no importance."

For information about interpreting and scoring the Defining Issues Test, refer to the scoring key at the end of the chapter. Use the following rating scale for your response.

Rating Scale

1	Of great importance	This statement or question makes a crucial difference in making a decision about the problem.
2	Of much importance	This statement or question is something that would be a major factor (though not always a crucial one) in making a decision.
3	Of some importance	This statement or question involves something you care about, but it is not of great importance in reaching a decision.
4	Of little importance	This statement or question is not very important to consider in this case.
5	Of no importance	This statement or question is completely unimportant in making a decision. You would waste your time thinking about it.

The Escaped Prisoner

A man had been sentenced to prison for 10 years. After one year, however, he escaped from prison, moved to a new area of the country, and took on the name of Thompson. For eight years he worked hard, and gradually he saved enough money to buy his own business. He was fair to his customers, gave his employees top wages, and gave most of his own profits to charity. Then one day, Ms. Jones, an old neighbor, recognized him as the man who had escaped from prison eight years before and for whom the police had been looking.

Should Ms. Jones report Mr. Thompson to the police and have him sent back to prison? Write a number from the rating scale on the previous page in the blank beside each statement.

_____ Should report him
_____ Can't decide
_____ Should not report him

Importance

_____   1. Hasn't Mr. Thompson been good enough for such a long time to prove he isn't a bad person?

_____   2. Every time someone escapes punishment for a crime, doesn't that just encourage more crime?

_____   3. Wouldn't we be better off without prisons and the oppression of our legal system?

_____   4. Has Mr. Thompson really paid his debt to society?

_____   5. Would society be failing what Mr. Thompson should fairly expect?

_____   6. What benefit would prison be apart from society, especially for a charitable man?

_____   7. How could anyone be so cruel and heartless as to send Mr. Thompson to prison?

_____   8. Would it be fair to prisoners who have to serve out their full sentences if Mr. Thompson is let off?

_____   9. Was Ms. Jones a good friend of Mr. Thompson?

_____ 10. Wouldn't it be a citizen's duty to report an escaped criminal, regardless of the circumstances?

_____ 11. How would the will of the people and the public good best be served?

_____ 12. Would going to prison do any good for Mr. Thompson or protect anybody?

From the list of questions above, select the four most important:
_____ Most important
_____ Second most important
_____ Third most important
_____ Fourth most important

The Doctor's Dilemma

A woman was dying of incurable cancer and had only about six months to live. She was in terrible pain, but was so weak that a large dose of a pain killer such as morphine would probably kill her. She was delirious with pain, and in her calm periods, she would ask her doctor to give her enough morphine to kill her. She said she couldn't stand the pain and that she was going to die in a few months anyway.

What should the doctor do? (Check one.)
_____ He should give the woman an overdose that will make her die
_____ Can't decide
_____ Should not give the overdose

Importance

_____ 1. Is the woman's family in favor of giving her the overdose?

_____ 2. Is the doctor obligated by the same laws as everybody else?

_____ 3. Would people be better off without society regimenting their lives and even their deaths?

_____ 4. Should the doctor make the woman's death from a drug overdose appear to be an accident?

_____ 5. Does the state have the right to force continued existence on those who don't want to live?

_____ 6. What is the value of death prior to society's perspective on personal values?

_____ 7. Should the doctor have sympathy for the woman's suffering, or should he care more about what society might think?

_____ 8. Is helping to end another's life ever a responsible act of cooperation?

_____ 9. Can only God decide when a person's life should end?

_____ 10. What values has the doctor set for himself in his own personal code of behavior?

_____ 11. Can society afford to let anybody end his or her life whenever he or she desires?

_____ 12. Can society allow suicide or mercy killing and still protect the lives of individuals who want to live?

From the list of questions above, select the four most important:
_____ Most important
_____ Second most important
_____ Third most important
_____ Fourth most important

The Newspaper

Rami, a senior in high school, wanted to publish a mimeographed newspaper for students so that he could express his opinions. He wanted to speak out against military build-up and some of the school's rules, such as the rule forbidding boys to wear long hair.

When Rami started his newspaper, he asked his principal for permission. The principal said it would be all right if before every publication Rami would turn in all his articles for the principal's approval. Rami agreed and turned in several articles for approval. The principal approved all of them and he published two issues of the paper in the next two weeks.

But, the principal had not expected that Rami's newspaper would receive so much attention. Students were so excited by the paper that they began to organize protests against the government, hair regulation, and other school rules. Angry parents objected to Rami's opinions. They phoned the principal telling him that the newspaper was unpatriotic and should not be published. As a result of the rising excitement, the principal wondered if he should order Rami to stop publishing on the grounds that the controversial newspaper articles were disrupting the operation of the school.

What should the principal do? (Check one.)

_____ Should stop it
_____ Can't decide
_____ Should not stop it

Importance

_____   1. Is the principal more responsible to the students or to the parents?

_____   2. Did the principal give his word that the newspaper could be published for a long time, or did he just promise to approve the newspaper one issue at a time?

_____   3. Would the students start protesting even more if the principal stopped the newspaper?

_____   4. When the welfare of the school is threatened, does the principal have the right to give orders to students?

_____   5. Does the principal have the freedom of speech to say no in this case?

_____   6. If the principal stopped the newspaper, would he be preventing full discussion of important problems?

_____   7. Would the principal's stop order make Rami lose faith in him?

_____   8. Is Rami really loyal to his school and patriotic to his country?

_____   9. What effect would stopping the paper have on the students' education in critical thinking and judgment?

_____   10. Is Rami in any way violating the rights of others in publishing his own opinions?

_____   11. Should the principal be influenced by some angry parents when it is the principal who knows best what is going on in the school?

_____   12. Is Rami using the newspaper to stir up hatred and discontent?

From the list of questions above, select the four most important:

_____ Most important
_____ Second most important
_____ Third most important
_____ Fourth most important

Source: *Adapted from Rest, 1979.*

THE LEARNING STYLE INVENTORY

This inventory will be more helpful to you if you think about situations in which you are presently learning. These may be situations at school, at work, at home, or in some other context. Take a few minutes to think about these situations and make note of your answers to the following questions: Where are you learning? What are some important things that you have learned in the past year? How do you approach new learning opportunities?

In the following assessment instrument you are asked to complete 12 sentences that describe learning. Each has four endings. To respond to these sentences, consider some of the recent learning situations you have just written about. Then rank the endings for each sentence according to how well you think the ending describes the way you learned. Write *4* next to the sentence ending that describes how you learn *best*, and so on down to *1* for the sentence ending that seems *least* like the way you learned. Be sure to rank all the endings for each sentence unit. Do not make ties. (Remember: 4 = best; 1 = worst.)

EXAMPLE: When I learn:

    a. __2__ I am happy

    b. __4__ I am careful

    c. __1__ I am fast

    d. __3__ I am logical

1. When I learn:

    a. _____ I like to deal with my feelings

    b. _____ I like to think about ideas

    c. _____ I like to be doing things

    d. _____ I like to watch and listen

2. I learn best when:

    a. _____ I listen and watch carefully

    b. _____ I rely on logical thinking

    c. _____ I trust my hunches and feelings

    d. _____ I work hard to get things done

3. When I am learning:

    a. _____ I tend to reason things out

    b. _____ I am responsible about things

    c. _____ I am quiet and reserved

    d. _____ I have strong feelings and reactions

4. I learn by:

    a. _____ feeling

    b. _____ doing

    c. _____ watching

    d. _____ thinking

5. When I learn:

    a. _____ I am open to new experiences

b. _____ I look at all sides of issues

c. _____ I like to analyze things, break them down into their parts

d. _____ I like to try things out

6. When I am learning:

a. _____ I am an observing person

b. _____ I am an active person

c. _____ I am an intuitive person

d. _____ I am a logical person

7. I learn best from:

a. _____ observation

b. _____ personal relationships

c. _____ rational theories

d. _____ a chance to try out and practice

8. When I learn:

a. _____ I like to see results from my work

b. _____ I like ideas and theories

c. _____ I take my time before acting

d. _____ I feel personally involved in things

9. I learn best when:

a. _____ I rely on my observations

b. _____ I rely on my feelings

c. _____ I can try things out for myself

d. _____ I rely on my ideas

10. When I am learning:

a. _____ I am a reserved person

b. _____ I am an accepting person

c. _____ I am a responsible person

d. _____ I am a rational person

11. When I learn:

a. _____ I get involved

b. _____ I like to observe

c. _____ I evaluate things

d. _____ I like to be active

12. I learn best when:

a. _____ I analyze ideas

b. _____ I am receptive and open-minded

c. _____ I am careful

d. _____ I am practical

Source: *Copyright, 1999 by David A. Kdb, Experience Based Learning Systems, Inc. All rights reserved.*

LOCUS OF CONTROL SCALE

This questionnaire assesses your opinions about certain issues. Each item consists of a pair of alternatives marked with *a* or *b*. Select the alternative with which you most agree. If you believe both alternatives to some extent, select the one with which you most strongly agree. If you do not believe either alternative, mark the one with which you least strongly disagree. Since this is an assessment of opinions, there are obviously no right or wrong answers. When you have finished each item, turn to the scoring key at the end of the chapter for instructions on how to tabulate the results and for comparison data.

This questionnaire is similar, but not identical, to the original locus of control scale developed by Julian Rotter. The comparison data provided in the scoring key comes from research using Rotter's scale instead of this one. However, the two instruments assess the same concept, are the same length, and their mean scores are similar.

1. a. Leaders are born, not made.
   b. Leaders are made, not born.

2. a. People often succeed because they are in the right place at the right time.
   b. Success is mostly dependent on hard work and ability.

3. a. When things go wrong in my life, it's generally because I have made mistakes.
   b. Misfortunes occur in my life regardless of what I do.

4. a. Whether there is war or not depends on the actions of certain world leaders.
   b. It is inevitable that the world will continue to experience wars.

5. a. Good children are mainly products of good parents.
   b. Some children turn out bad no matter how their parents behave.

6. a. My future success depends mainly on circumstances I can't control.
   b. I am the master of my fate.

7. a. History judges certain people to have been effective leaders mainly because circumstances made them visible and successful.
   b. Effective leaders are those who have made decisions or taken actions that resulted in significant contributions.

8. a. Avoiding punishing children guarantees that they will grow up irresponsible.
   b. Spanking children is never appropriate.

9. a. I often feel that I have little influence over the direction my life is taking.
   b. It is unreasonable to believe that fate or luck plays a crucial part in how my life turns out.

10. a. Some customers will never be satisfied no matter what you do.
    b. You can satisfy customers by giving them what they want when they want it.

11. a. Anyone can get good grades in school by working hard enough.
    b. Some people are never going to excel in school no matter how hard they try.

12. a. Good marriages result when both partners continually work on the relationship.
    b. Some marriages are going to fail because the partners are just incompatible.

13. a. I am confident that I can improve my basic management skills through learning and practice.
    b. It is a waste of time to try to improve management skills in a classroom.

14. a. More management skills courses should be taught in business schools.

    b. Less emphasis should be put on skills in business schools.

15. a. When I think back on the good things that happened to me, I believe they happened mainly because of something I did.

    b. The bad things that have happened in my life have mainly resulted from circumstances outside my control.

16. a. Many exams I took in school were unconnected to the material I had studied, so studying hard didn't help at all.

    b. When I prepared well for exams in school, I generally did quite well.

17. a. I am sometimes influenced by what my astrological chart says.

    b. No matter how the stars are lined up, I can determine my own destiny.

18. a. Government is so big and bureaucratic that it is very difficult for any one person to have any impact on what happens.

    b. Single individuals can have a real influence on politics if they will speak up and let their wishes be known.

19. a. People seek responsibility in work.

    b. People try to get away with doing as little as they can.

20. a. The most popular people seem to have a special, inherent charisma that attracts people to them.

    b. People become popular because of how they behave.

21. a. Things over which I have little control just seem to occur in my life.

    b. Most of the time I feel responsible for the outcomes I produce.

22. a. Managers who improve their personal competence will succeed more than those who do not improve.

    b. Management success has very little to do with the competence possessed by the individual manager.

23. a. Teams that win championships in most sports are usually the teams that, in the end, have the most luck.

    b. More often than not, teams that win championships are those with the most talented players and the best preparation.

24. a. Teamwork in business is a prerequisite to success.

    b. Individual effort is the best hope for success.

25. a. Some workers are just lazy and can't be motivated to work hard no matter what you do.

    b. If you are a skillful manager, you can motivate almost any worker to put forth more effort.

26. a. In the long run, people can improve this country's economic strength through responsible action.

    b. The economic health of this country is largely beyond the control of individuals.

27. a. I am persuasive when I know I'm right.

    b. I can persuade most people even when I'm not sure I'm right.

28. a. I tend to plan ahead and generate steps to accomplish the goals that I have set.

    b. I seldom plan ahead because things generally turn out OK anyway.

29. a. Some things are just meant to be.

    b. We can change anything in our lives by hard work, persistence, and ability.

TOLERANCE OF AMBIGUITY SCALE

Please respond to the following statements by indicating the extent to which you agree or disagree with them. Fill in the blanks with the number from the rating scale that best represents your evaluation of the item. The scoring key is at the end of the chapter.

Rating Scale

1 Strongly disagree
2 Moderately disagree
3 Slightly disagree
4 Neither agree nor disagree
5 Slightly agree
6 Moderately agree
7 Strongly agree

_____ 1. An expert who doesn't come up with a definite answer probably doesn't know too much.

_____ 2. I would like to live in a foreign country for a while.

_____ 3. There is really no such thing as a problem that can't be solved.

_____ 4. People who fit their lives to a schedule probably miss most of the joy of living.

_____ 5. A good job is one where what is to be done and how it is to be done are always clear.

_____ 6. It is more fun to tackle a complicated problem than to solve a simple one.

_____ 7. In the long run it is possible to get more done by tackling small, simple problems rather than large and complicated ones.

_____ 8. Often the most interesting and stimulating people are those who don't mind being different and original.

_____ 9. What we are used to is always preferable to what is unfamiliar.

_____ 10. People who insist upon a yes or no answer just don't know how complicated things really are.

_____ 11. A person who leads an even, regular life in which few surprises or unexpected happenings arise really has a lot to be grateful for.

_____ 12. Many of our most important decisions are based upon insufficient information.

_____ 13. I like parties where I know most of the people more than ones where all or most of the people are complete strangers.

_____ 14. Teachers or supervisors who hand out vague assignments give one a chance to show initiative and originality.

_____ 15. The sooner we all acquire similar values and ideals the better.

_____ 16. A good teacher is one who makes you wonder about your way of looking at things.

Source: _Tolerance of Ambiguity Scale_, S. Budner (1962), _"Intolerance of Ambiguity as a Personality Variable,"_ from Journal of Personality, _30: 29–50. Reprinted with the permission of Blackwell Publishing, Ltd._

CORE SELF-EVALUATION SCALE (CSES)

Below are several statements with which you may agree or disagree. Using the response scale below, indicate your level of agreement or disagreement with each statement.

Rating Scale

1 Strongly disagree
2 Disagree
3 Neutral
4 Agree
5 Strongly agree

_____ 1. I am confident I get the success I deserve in life.

_____ 2. Sometimes I feel depressed.

_____ 3. When I try, I generally succeed.

_____ 4. Sometimes when I fail I feel worthless.

_____ 5. I complete tasks successfully.

_____ 6. Sometimes, I do not feel in control of my work.

_____ 7. Overall, I am satisfied with myself.

_____ 8. I am filled with doubts about my competence.

_____ 9. I determine what will happen in my life.

_____ 10. I do not feel in control of my success in my career.

_____ 11. I am capable of coping with most of my problems.

_____ 12. There are times when things look pretty bleak and hopeless to me.

Source: *Judge, Erez, Bono, and Thoreson, 2003. Courtesy of Personnel Psychology.*

Who do I think

I am vs

Who I am
(I am 20).

...s of Self-Awareness

...rs, knowledge of the self has been ... ... at the very core of human behavior. The ancient dictum "Know thyself" has been variously attributed to Plato, Pythagoras, Thales, and Socrates. Plutarch noted that this inscription was carved on the Delphic Oracle, that mystical sanctuary where kings and generals sought advice on matters of greatest importance to them. As early as 42 B.C., Publilius Syrus proposed: "It matters not what you are thought to be, but what you are." Alfred Lord Tennyson said: "Self-reverence, self-knowledge, self-control, these three alone lead to sovereign power." Probably the most oft-quoted passage on the self is Polonius' advice in Hamlet: "To thine own self be true, and it must follow as the night the day, thou canst not then be false to any man."

Messinger reminded us: "He that would govern others must first master himself." **Self-awareness** lies at the heart of the ability to master oneself, but it is not sufficient. While self-management depends first and foremost on self-awareness, as illustrated in Figure 1.1, other self-management skills are closely linked to and build upon self-awareness. Developing self-control, for example, and clarifying priorities and goals, help individuals create direction in their own lives. Effectively managing time and stress make it possible for individuals to adapt to and organize their surroundings.

This chapter centers on the core aspects of self-management and serves as the foundation for the following chapter on stress and time management.

Moreover, as Figure 1.1 illustrates, when problems arise in personal management, the easily recognized symptoms are often time pressures or experienced stress. However, those symptoms are often linked to more fundamental problems with self-awareness and out-of-balance priorities so we begin with a focus on enhancing knowledge of oneself.

Despite the research cited above, students of human behavior have long known that knowledge of oneself—self-awareness, self-insight, self-understanding—is essential to one's productive personal and interpersonal functioning, and in understanding and empathizing with other people. A host of techniques and methods for achieving self-knowledge have long been available—including group methods, meditation techniques, altered consciousness procedures, aromatherapy, assorted massages, physical exercise regimens, and biofeedback. A 1993 *New England Journal of Medicine* article estimated that Americans alone spent approximately $12 billion on such therapies in 1990, and *Forbes* magazine estimated the figure at more than $15 billion in 1995. In this chapter we do not summarize those various approaches to enhanced self-awareness, nor do we espouse any one procedure in particular. Instead, our objective is to help you understand the importance of self-awareness if you are to be a successful manager—or a successful individual—and to provide you with some powerful self-assessment instruments that are related to managerial success. Our emphasis is on scientifically validated information linking self-awareness to the behavior of managers, and we try to avoid generalizations that have not been tested in research.

Figure 1.1   A Hierarchy of Personal Life-Management Skills

The Enigma of Self-Awareness

Erich Fromm (1939) was one of the first behavioral scientists to observe the ~~[obscured]~~ tween one's self-co~~[obscured]~~ rs: "Hatred agains~~[obscured]~~ ~~[obscured]~~ed against others~~[obscured]~~ d that self-awaren~~[obscured]~~ tes for psychologi~~[obscured]~~ ability to know a~~[obscured]~~ ested that the basi~~[obscured]~~ which he found to~~[obscured]~~ ases than physiolog~~[obscured]~~ Brouwer (1964, p. 156) asserted:

The function of self-examination is to lay the groundwork for insight, without which no growth can occur. Insight is the "Oh, I see now" feeling which must consciously or unconsciously precede change in behavior. Insights— real, genuine glimpses of ourselves as we really are—are reached only with difficulty and sometimes with real psychic pain. But they are the building blocks of growth. Thus, self-examination is a preparation for insight, a groundbreaking for the seeds of self-understanding which gradually bloom into changed behavior.

There is little question that the knowledge we possess about ourselves, which makes up our self-concept, is central to improving our management skills. We cannot improve ourselves or develop new capabilities unless and until we know what level of capability we currently possess. Considerable empirical evidence exists that individuals who are more self-aware are more healthy, perform better in managerial and leadership roles, and are more productive at work (Boyatzis, 1982; Cervone, 1997; Spencer & Spencer, 1993).

On the other hand, self-knowledge may inhibit personal improvement rather than facilitate it. The reason is that individuals frequently evade personal growth and new self-knowledge. They resist acquiring additional information in order to protect their self-esteem or self-respect. If they acquire new knowledge about themselves, there is always the possibility that it will be negative or that it will lead to feelings of inferiority, weakness, evilness, or shame. So they avoid new self-knowledge. As Maslow (1962, p. 57) notes:

We tend to be afraid of any knowledge that would cause us to despise ourselves or to make us feel inferior, weak, worthless, evil,

shameful. We protect ours~~[obscured]~~ image of ourselves by repr~~[obscured]~~ defenses, which are essen~~[obscured]~~ which we avoid becom~~[obscured]~~ unpleasantness or dangero~~[obscured]~~

We avoid personal growth, ~~[obscured]~~ finding out that we are not all th~~[obscured]~~ If there is a better way to be, ~~[obscured]~~ therefore be inadequate or inferior. The realization that one is not totally adequate or knowledgeable is difficult for many people to accept. This resistance is the "denying of our best side, of our talents, of our finest impulses, of our highest potentialities, of our creativeness. In brief, this is the struggle against our own greatness" (Maslow, 1962, p. 58). Freud (1956) asserted that to be completely honest with oneself is the best effort an individual can make, because complete honesty requires a continual search for more information about the self and a desire for self-improvement. The results of that search are usually uncomforta~~[obscured]~~

Seeking knowledg~~[obscured]~~ be an enigma. It is a ~~[obscured]~~ growth and improveme~~[obscured]~~ and improvement. It n~~[obscured]~~ fear of knowing more ~~[obscured]~~ be accomplished? How~~[obscured]~~ oped if the self-knowl~~[obscured]~~ ment of those skills is n~~[obscured]~~

THE SENSITIVE LINE

One answer relies on the concept of the **sensitive line**. This concept refers to the point at which individuals become defensive or protective when encountering information about themselves that is inconsistent with their self-concept or when encountering pressure to alter their behavior. Most people regularly experience information about themselves that doesn't quite fit or that is marginally inconsistent. For example, a friend might say, "You look tired today. Are you feeling okay?" If you are feeling fine, the information is inconsistent with your self-awareness. But because the discrepancy is relatively minor, it would not be likely to offend you or evoke a strong defensive reaction. That is, it would probably not require that you reexamine and change your self-concept.

On the other hand, the more discrepant the information or the more serious its implications for your self-concept, the closer it would approach your sensitive line, and you would feel a need to defend yourself against it. For exampl[e] [...] incompetent as a ma[nager...] line if you think you [...] ager. This would be es[pecially...] an influential person. [...] to defend yourself ag[ainst...] the image you hold of [...]

This response is [called a threat-rigidity] **response** (Staw, San[ton, & Dutton,] 1993). When individuals are threatened, when they encounter uncomfortable information, or when uncertainty is created, they tend to become rigid. They hunker down, protect themselves, and become risk averse. Consider what happens when you are startled or suddenly shocked by something unexpected. Physically, your body tends to become rigid in order to protect itself. It tightens up to safeguard stability. Similarly, individuals also become rigid—psychologically and emotionally—when they encounter information that is a threat to their self-concept. They tend to redouble their efforts to protect what is comfortable and familiar (Cameron, 1994; Cameron, Kim, & Whetten, 1987; Weick & Sutcliffe, 2000). They rely on first-learned or most reinforced behavior patterns and emotions. When discrepancies in the self-image are encountered, in other words, the validity of the information or its source is denied, or other kinds of defense mechanisms are used to ensure that the self-concept remains stable. Crossing the sensitive line creates rigidity and self-preservation.

In light of this defensiveness, then, how can increased self-knowledge and personal change ever occur? There are at least two answers. One is that information that is verifiable, predictable, and controllable is less likely to cross the sensitive line than information without those characteristics. That is, if an individual can test the validity of the discrepant information (for example, if some objective standard exists for evaluating the accuracy of the information), if the information is not unexpected or "out-of-the-blue" (for example, if it is received at regular intervals), and if there is some control over what, when, and how much information is received (for example, if it is requested), the feedback is more likely to be heard and accepted. The information you receive about yourself in this chapter possesses those three characteristics. You have already completed several self-assessment instruments that have been used extensively in research. Their reliability and validity have been established. Moreover, they have been found to be associated with managerial success. Therefore, as you analyze your scores and seek honestly to understand more about your underlying attributes, you can gain important insight that will prove to be very useful.

A second answer to the problem of overcoming resistance to self-examination lies in the role other people can play in helping insight to occur. It is almost impossible to increase skill in self-awareness unless we interact with and disclose ourselves to others. Unless one is willing to open up to others, to discuss aspects of the self that seem ambiguous or unknown, little growth can ever occur. **Self-disclosure**, therefore, is a key to improvement in self-awareness. Harris (1981) points out:

> *In order to know oneself, no amount of introspection or self-examination will suffice. You can analyze yourself for weeks, or meditate for months, and you will not get an inch further—any more than you can smell your own breath or laugh when you tickle yourself.*
>
> *You must first be open to the other person before you catch a glimmering of yourself. Our self-reflection in a mirror does not tell us what we are like; only our reflection in other people. We are essentially social creatures, and our personality resides in association, not in isolation.*

As you engage in the practice exercises in this chapter, therefore, you are encouraged to discuss your insights with someone else. A lack of self-disclosure not only inhibits self-awareness but also may affect adversely other aspects of managerial skill development. For example, several studies have shown that low self-disclosers are less healthy and more self-alienated than high self-disclosers. College students give the highest ratings for interpersonal competence to high self-disclosers. Individuals who are high self-disclosers are liked best, and excessive or insufficient self-disclosure results in less liking and acceptance by others (see, for example, Covey, 1989; Goleman, 1998b; Kelley, 1999).

Some of the exercises in this chapter will require you to discuss your experiences with others. This is because involving others in the process of self-understanding will be a critical aspect of your personal growth. These interactions, of course, should be sincere, honest, and motivated by self-understanding and self-improvement. Never should the information you share or receive be used to judge or wound another person. Maintaining a trusting relationship with someone with whom you can share is a critical prerequisite to self-understanding.

[handwritten margin note: need to involve others to Self-awareness]

The enigma of self-awareness can be managed, then, by exercising some control over when and what kind of information you receive about yourself, and by involving others in your pursuit of self-understanding. The support and feedback individuals receive from others during the process of self-disclosure, besides helping to increase feedback and self-awareness, helps information contribute to greater self-awareness without crossing the sensitive line.

Understanding and Appreciating Individual Differences

Another important reason for focusing on self-awareness is to help you develop the ability to diagnose impor[tant differences among] others with whom you interac[t] [tha]t an individual's [...] [c]losely related to [...] [appr]eciate, and ultima[tely] [...] [diffe]rences among oth[ers] [...] in the manageme[nt] [...] [ma]naging diversity." [...] [prog]ressed through a [...] [plet]hora of statistics demonstrating the extent to [which,] and the specific ways in which, the workforce is becoming more diverse. This was followed by evidence-based arguments touting the merits of a diverse group of workers contributing to the performance of a work group (Cox, 1994). The primary sources of diversity discussed in this literature are gender, age, culture, and ethnicity.

In this chapter, and throughout the book, we use broader, more inclusive, and less ambiguous terminology that is more conducive to skill development. Whereas it is difficult, for example, to understand all the ramifications of "managing diversity," it is not difficult to be sensitive to certain important differences that affect the way you manage others. In other words, this chapter has two objectives: (1) to help you better understand your own uniqueness as an individual—to become better equipped to manage yourself—and (2) to help you diagnose, value, and utilize the differences you find in other people.

Self-knowledge will help you understand your own taken-for-granted assumptions, trigger points, sensitive line, comfort zone, strengths and weaknesses, and so forth. This knowledge is useful for all of us, not because we can or should change fundamental dimensions of ourselves, but because it helps make our interactions with others more effective and insightful. It also helps us gain a more complete understanding of our

potential for contributing value in our future career roles and our special strengths relative to others. It is not unusual for many of us to feel intimidated at times, for example, by heroic or luminary figures whose success is attributed to charisma, intelligence, or style. We feel we are somehow diminished and less able because of what we see in others. Self-knowledge allows us to recognize our own special gifts and strengths and to capitalize on our talents.

Diagnosing fundamental differences in others is, similarly, an important part of being an effective manager. Being aware of, and empathetic toward, the different perspectives, needs, and inclinations of other people is a key part of emotional intelligence and interpersonal maturity. Most people, however, have a tendency to interact with individuals who are like themselves, to choose similar people to work with them, and to exclude others who seem to be different (Berscheid & Walster, 1978). The history of human warfare and conflict testifies to the fact that differences are usually interpreted as frightening or threatening. However, although fostering similarity seemingly makes it easier to interact with other people, especially in a work setting, it also reduces creativity, complex problem solving, and the likelihood that working colleagues will challenge the perspective of the authority figure. Research on organizational failure has repeatedly demonstrated that a lack of diversity in the composition of key decision-making bodies makes it difficult for them to recognize changes in their environment and to respond in appropriately new and novel ways (Cameron, Kim, & Whetten, 1987).

One key to helping individuals feel comfortable discussing ways in which they are different is by sharing a commitment to focusing on *differences* not *distinctions*. We observe differences; we create distinctions. Differences help us understand potential sources of misunderstanding between people and give us clues for how we can work together more effectively. Distinctions create social barriers between people for the express purpose of creating (or reinforcing) advantages and disadvantages. When someone discounts the opinion of a coworker, for example, on the grounds that the person is "a member of the old boys' club," "from marketing," "a woman," or "doesn't have a college degree," he or she is creating a distinction that is not only potentially hurtful on a personal basis but ineffective for the organization.

The creation of such distinctions destroys trust among people, even if the distinctions refer to individuals who are not present. If you were to apply distinctions that belittled someone in another group, for example, that action plants a seed of mistrust in the minds of

[handwritten annotation: To become better equipped to manage myself]

people who are present regarding what distinctions you may be privately using to discount them. The point is, recognizing differences is not the same as evaluating distinctions. One is helpful; the other is hurtful. Moreover, when others feel that self-disclosing information could be used against them—that is, they could be placed on the disadvantaged side of a distinction—they will be reluctant to participate in any self-discovery process, especially one that requires them to share information about their personal characteristics.

To repeat, self-awareness and understanding differences cannot occur without self-disclosure, sharing, and trusting conversations. Self-knowledge requires an understanding and valuing of differences, not the creation of distinctions. We encourage you, therefore, to use the information you discover about yourself and others to build, grow, and value both of you in your interactions.

Important Areas of Self-Awareness

Of course, an innumerable quantity of personal dimensions is available to explore if one is to develop in-depth self-awareness. For example, numerous aspects of cognitive style have been measured; authors have identified more than a dozen "intelligences" (ranging from social and practical to cognitive and creative); literally thousands of pers~~~~~ factors have been investigated in the psychologica~~~~~~~~~~ ~~~~~human chromosome has~~~~~~~~~~ phys-iological di~~~~~~~~~~nding behavior; g~~~~~~~~~~rience differences~~~~~~~~~~impos-sible, of co~~~~~~~~~~or most central asp~~~~~~~~~~ternatives are just to~~~~~~~~~~ve focus here on five of the ~~~~ ~~~~~~~~~awareness that have been found to be key in developing successful management. They are: emotional intelligence, personal values, learning style, orientation toward change, and core self-evaluation. These areas represent a limited set of factors, of course, but they have been found to be among the most important predictors of various aspects of effective managerial performance—including achieving life success, performing effectively in teams, competent decision making, life-long learning and development, creativity, communication competency, job satisfaction, and job performance (Allan & Waclawski, 1999; Atwater & Yammarino, 1992; Goleman, 1998b; Judge et al., 2003; Parker & Kram, 1993; Sosik & Megerian, 1999).

Research on the concept of **emotional intelligence**—the ability to manage oneself and to manage relationships with others—has been identified as among the most important factors in accounting for success in leaders and managers (Boyatzis, Goleman, & Rhee, 2000; Goleman, 1998a). In particular, self-awareness has been identified as a crucial aspect of emotional intelligence, and it is more powerful than IQ in predicting success in life (Goleman, 1995). One study, for example, tried to identify differences between star performers and average managers in 40 companies. Emotional intelligence competencies, including self-awareness, were *twice* as important in contributing to excellence as cognitive intelligence (IQ) and expertise (Goleman, 1998a). In a study of a multinational consulting firm, superior performing partners were compared to average performing partners. Superior performers—who had significantly higher emotional intelligence and self-awareness scores—contributed more than twice the revenues to the firm and were four times more likely to be promoted than those with low self-awareness and emotional intelligence (Boyatzis, 1998).

Personal values are included here because they are "the core of the dynamics of behavior, and play so large a part in unifying personality" (Allport, Gordon, & Vernon, 1931, p. 2). That is, all other attitudes, orientations, and behaviors arise out of an individuals' values. Two major types of values are considered: *instrumental* and *terminal* (Rokeach, 1973). We present research findings that relate personal development in these two types of values to successful managerial performance. The assessment instrument that assesses your values development is discussed, along with information concerning the scores of other groups of people. You will want to compare your scores with individuals who are close to you, as well as with successful managers. Some comparison data is provided for that purpose. Because this discussion of values development is connected to ethical decision making, the implications of managerial ethics are also discussed in this section.

A third area of self-awareness is **learning style**, which refers to the manner in which individuals gather and process information. A discussion of the critical dimensions of learning style is presented, based on the assessment instrument that you completed to assess your own style. Empirical research linking learning style to managerial behavior is discussed, and your scores are compared to other successful managers in a variety of organizations.

Fourth, a discussion of **orientation toward change** focuses on the methods people use to cope with change in their environment. In the twenty-first century, of cou_____ idi- tions (Peters, _____ me aware of your _____ on- ditions. Two i_____ _trol_ and _intoleranc_____ by two assessme_____ ing these two dim_____ dis- cussed in the s_____

[handwritten: Core Self- evaluation · + EI]

Finally, **core self-evaluation** is a recently developed construct that captures the essential aspects of personality. More than 50,000 studies have been conducted on what has been referred to as "the Big Five" personality dimensions—neuroticism, extroversion, conscientiousness, agreeableness, and openness—but an underlying factor has been found to account for the effects of these personality dimensions. It is referred to as core self-evaluation (Judge et al., 2003), and we provide an instrument that assesses your core self-evaluation. Some important research on this construct is explained in this chapter relating to how scores correlate with success at work and in life. By analyzing your scores, you not only learn about your underlying personality dimensions, but you also will learn about how they are associated with other important behaviors such as motivation, problem solving, creativity, life satisfaction, and work performance.

These five areas of self-awareness—emotional intelligence, personal values, learning style, orientation toward change, and core self-evaluation—constitute the very core of the self-concept. Emotional intelligence identifies the extent to which people are able to recognize and control their own emotions, as well as to recognize and respond appropriately to the emotions of others. Values identify an individual's basic standards about what is good and bad, worthwhile and worthless, desirable and undesirable, true and false, moral and immoral. Learning style identifies individual thought processes, perceptions, and methods for acquiring and storing information. It determines not only what kind of information is received by an individual, but how that individual interprets, judges, and responds to the information. Orientation toward change identifies the adaptability of individuals. It includes the extent to which individuals are tolerant of ambiguous, uncertain conditions, and the extent to which they are inclined to accept personal responsibility for their actions under changing conditions. Core

self-evaluation identifies the general personality orientation that guides behavior. It uncovers levels of self-esteem, self-efficacy, emotional stability, and self-control that have important effects on individuals' happiness as well as managerial effectiveness. Figure 1.2 summarizes these five aspects of self-awareness, along with their functions in de_____

Again, many o_____ be considered in th_____ the self are related _____ cepts discussed he_____ about ourselves, ho_____ we want to achieve_____ are strongly influenc_____ values, learning style_____ core self-evaluation. These are among the most important building blocks upon which other aspects of the self emerge.

[handwritten: Maybe do an 'indepth self-awareness' test. Done- Myers Briggs]

On the other hand, if you want to do a more in-depth analysis of multiple aspects of self-awareness, instruments such as the Strong-Campbell Vocational Inventory, the Minnesota Multiphasic Personality Inventory, the Myers-Briggs Type Indicator, the Stanford-Binet Intelligence Test, and a host of other instruments are available in most college counseling centers or testing centers. Be careful, however, of the multiple assessment instruments you can find on numerous Web sites. Most are not reliable or valid. On the other hand, no one, it should be emphasized, can get too much self-knowledge.

EMOTIONAL INTELLIGENCE

Emotional intelligence has become a very popular topic that, unfortunately, suffers from the problem that almost all trendy concepts encounter. Its meaning and measurement have become very confusing and ambiguous. Emotional intelligence has come to encompass almost everything that is noncognitive—including social, emotional, behavioral, attitudinal, and personality factors—so the extent to which it can be adequately measured and predictive of outcomes remains cloudy. Since the publication of Daniel Goleman's book *Emotional Intelligence* in 1995, interest in the concept of emotional intelligence has mushroomed (even though the concept was introduced in 1990 by Salovey and Mayer). More than 500 books have been published on the topic, and scores of consulting companies and executive coaches now advertise themselves as experts in helping others develop emotional intelligence. The number of instruments available to assess emotional

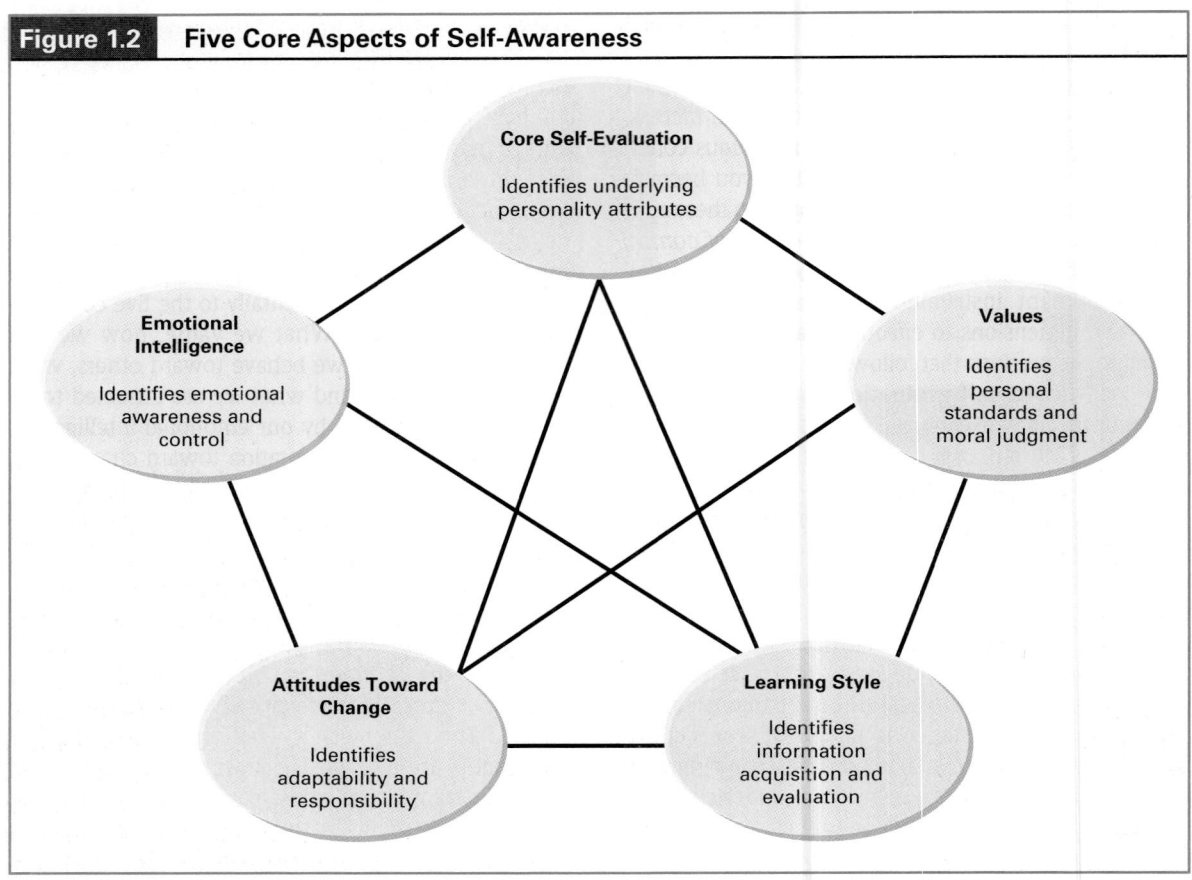

Figure 1.2   Five Core Aspects of Self-Awareness

Core Self-Evaluation

Identifies underlying personality attributes

Emotional Intelligence

Identifies emotional awareness and control

Values

Identifies personal standards and moral judgment

Attitudes Toward Change

Identifies adaptability and responsibility

Learning Style

Identifies information acquisition and evaluation

intelligence is voluminous (more than 100), although only three or four have been scientifically validated and used in any systematic investigations.

In particular, only Bar-On's *EQ-I* measure (Bar-On, 1997)—a self-report instrument that defines emotional intelligence as an array of noncognitive skills; Salovey's *Multifactor Emotional Intelligence Scale* (Salovey & Mayer, 1990)—a behavioral assessment that defines emotional intelligence as "a form of social intelligence that involves the ability to monitor one's own and others' feelings and emotions, to discriminate among them, and to use this information to guide one's thinking and action"(p. 185); and Goleman and Boyatzis' *Emotional Competence Inventory* (Boyatzis et al., 2000)—a 360-degree assessment that defines emotional intelligence as "the composite set of capabilities that enable a person to manage himself or herself and others," (p. 344) have been scientifically validated. The trouble is, each of these instruments is far too lengthy to be included in this text, and each is protected under copyright. Virtually all other instruments, including the one included in this book, are designed merely to provide a general estimate of

particular dimensions of emotional intelligence, and extensive research has not yet been published.

As you can tell by the widely differing definitions associated with the three major assessment instruments described above, the concept of emotional intelligence has been defined as embracing almost everything. A scan of the scientific and popular writing on emotional intelligence confirms this conclusion—almost everything and anything is defined as an aspect of emotional intelligence. Our colleagues Richard Boyatzis and Daniel Goleman, for example—two of the chief researchers in the field of emotional intelligence—explicitly include all capabilities that help people manage themselves and others. These include, for example, leadership, influence, conflict management, communication, self-confidence, and teamwork. Other scholars limit emotional intelligence to a much narrower set of factors. Mayer, Caruso, and Salovey (1998) for example, reduce emotional intelligence to the ability to adequately diagnose and react to emotions.

One way to clarify this problem of multiple definitions is to differentiate between *emotional intelligence* and *emotional competence.* Emotional intelligence refers to the ability to diagnose, understand, and manage emotional cues. Emotional competence refers to the noncognitive capabilities and skills—including social skills—that affect human functioning. The first definition is the one we have adopted in this chapter because the remainder of this book is focused on helping you develop competency and capability in skills that some would include under the emotional competence umbrella. That is, the management skills covered in this text—which have been well-researched and found to predict the success of managers and leaders—are sometimes included in discussions of the impact of emotional intelligence. In this regard, we agree that they are critical. These noncognitive skills and abilities are, in fact, among the most important factors in explaining why some people succeed as leaders and managers and others do not.

On the other hand, a much narrower treatment of emotional intelligence limits it to *emotions*, not to social or interpersonal skills. This is the position we adopt in this chapter. We will help you assess, in an in-depth and rigorous way, other social and behavioral skills throughout the remainder of the book. It is important to point out that a certain degree of emotional *intelligence* is necessary in order for people to develop emotional *competencies* (i.e., social and behavioral competencies), so this aspect of self-awareness is an important prerequisite to your developing other management skills.

Emotional intelligence, then, refers to: (1) the ability to diagnose and recognize your own emotions, (2) the ability to control your own emotions, (3) the ability to recognize and diagnose the emotions displayed by others, and (4) the ability to respond appropriately to those emotional cues. These abilities are not in-born but can be developed and improved. Unlike IQ, for example, which remains relatively constant over a lifetime, emotional intelligence can be enhanced with practice. With concerted effort, people can change their levels of emotional intelligence. The instrument you completed in the Pre-assessment section assesses these four dimensions, and we briefly explain them below.

One of our acquaintances, who now readily admits having made progress in developing emotional intelligence, had a great deal of difficulty recognizing and diagnosing her own emotions. When something seemed to go wrong and she was asked, "Are you upset?", she would invariably deny her feelings—"No, I'm fine." She had never learned to accurately diagnose her own emotional state. This ability is simply the capacity to identify and label your own emotions. Try, for example, to identify the emotion you are feeling

right now. Can you label it? Emotionally intelligent people are able to get in touch with and accurately *diagnose* their own internal feelings.

Emotionally intelligent people are also able to *regulate* and control their emotions. They are less likely to blow up and lose control, less likely to experience debilitating depression and anxiety, and more likely to manage their own emotional states than those with less emotional intelligence. Think of how you behave in a sporting event, for example, when the officials make a bad call; when someone gets angry at you and berates you; when you are criticized for something you did; or, alternatively, when you receive special accolades and recognition. Emotionally intelligent people remain in control of their emotions, whereas less emotionally intelligent people lose control. This ability does not mean being bland or even-tempered all the time—emotionally intelligent people may display a wide range of emotions and intensity. Instead, it means that a person can control his or her emotions so that they are not unrestrained.

Emotionally intelligent people are also able to accurately diagnose and empathize with the feelings of others. They are sensitive to what others are experiencing, and they can share in those feelings. Empathy refers to the ability to understand and connect with others' feelings. It does not mean sympathizing or adopting the same feelings, and it is not based on a memory of having experienced the same emotions. If someone has experienced a tragedy or loss, for example, emotionally intelligently people can empathize, share in, and understand those feelings even if they have never experienced something similar. They need not be depressed themselves, for example, in order to understand the depression of others.

Emotionally intelligent people also *respond* appropriately to the emotions of others. Their responses match the intensity of the emotions other people feel, and they support and encourage emotional expressions. That is, if others are excited and happy, they do not remain aloof and withdrawn. They endorse the expression of emotions in others, rather than suppressing or censoring those emotions. On the other hand, they are not merely manipulated in their feelings and responses by the emotions of others. They don't respond merely on the basis of others' feelings. Rather, they remain in personal control of their responses. They advance a sense of caring for, and acceptance of, the other person by means of their emotional responses.

One reason emotional intelligence is so important is that general competency levels seem to have deteriorated over time. Whereas average IQ points have increased almost 25 points over the last 100 years—people tend to be smarter now than 100 years ago—emotional intelligence scores have actually declined (Goleman, 1998a). Think, for example, of the amount of litigation, conflict, disrespect, and divorce that characterizes our society. Less emphasis is placed on emotional intelligence development now than in the past. This is a problem because emotional intelligence has strong predictive power regarding success in management and in work setting—much stronger, in fact, than IQ scores. For example, it is estimated that IQ accounts for only about 10 percent of the variance in job performance and in life success (Sternberg, 1996), but by adding emotional intelligence (EQ) to the equation, we can account for four times more variance.

For example, a study was conducted of 450 boys who grew up in a small town in Massachusetts. Two thirds of the boys lived in welfare families and one third had IQ scores below 90. They were followed over 40 years, and it was found that IQ had almost nothing to do with life success. Emotional intelligence, on the other hand, was the most predictive factor (Snarey & Vaillant, 1985). Another study of 80 PhDs in science who attended the University of California at Berkeley in the 1950s found that what accounted for life success 40 years after graduation was mainly emotional intelligence scores. Emotional intelligence was four times more important than IQ in determining who had achieved in their careers, were evaluated by experts as being highly successful, and were listed in sources such as *Who's Who* and *American Men and Women of Science* (Feist & Barron, 1996). A study of workers followed over 20 years found that employees who were better at empathizing with others—that is, demonstrating a key aspect of emotional intelligence—were more successful in their work, as well as in their social lives (Rosenthal, 1977).

Emotional intelligence has also been found to be an important predictor of managerial success. In a study of managers on three continents, for example, 74 percent of successful managers had emotional intelligence as their most salient characteristic, whereas this was the case in only 24 percent of the failures. A study at PepsiCo found that company units headed by managers with well-developed emotional intelligence skills outperformed yearly revenue targets by 15 to 20 percent. Those with underdeveloped skills underperformed their targets by about the same amount (Goleman, Boyatzis, & McKee, 2002). A McBer study comparing outstanding managers with average managers found that 90 percent of the difference was accounted for by emotional intelligence. In a worldwide study of what companies were

looking for in hiring new employees, 67 percent of the most desired attributes were emotional intelligence competencies (Goleman et al., 2002). In a study of highly emotionally intelligent partners in a consulting firm, in which they were compared to partners with average emotional intelligence, 41 percent of the high emotional intelligence group had been promoted after two years whereas only 10 percent of the low emotional intelligence partners had been promoted. More importantly, high emotional intelligence partners contributed more than twice as much revenue to the company as did the low emotional intelligence partners (Boyatzis, 1982). The point should be clear: effective managers have developed high levels of competency in emotional intelligence.

The Emotional Intelligence Assessment instrument that you completed in the Pre-assessment section provides an evaluation of your competency in the four general areas of emotional intelligence—emotional awareness, emotional control or balance, emotional diagnosis or empathy, and emotional response. Of course, a fully accurate and valid measure of these factors would require an instrument many times longer than the one included here, so this assessment merely provides a glimpse or an incomplete evaluation of your emotional intelligence capability. Your scores should help you identify areas of strength but also motivate you to pursue the development of your emotional intelligence. This may effectively be done by consciously practicing emotional diagnosis, control, and response in yourself and others, but, especially, it may also be significantly enhanced by learning, and improving the skills discussed in this book. They are, according to a variety of writers (e.g., Goleman, 1998b; Boyatzis et al., 2000), critical components of the broad definition of emotional intelligence.

VALUES

Values are among the most stable and enduring characteristics of individuals. They are the foundation upon which attitudes and personal preferences are formed. They are the basis for crucial decisions, life directions, and personal tastes. They help define our morality and our conceptions of what is "good." Much of what we are is a product of the basic values we have developed throughout our lives.

The trouble with values, unfortunately, is that they are taken for granted, and people are often unaware of them. Unless a person's values are challenged, the values being held remain largely undetected. People especially are not aware that they hold some values as being more important than others. This unawareness leads to actions or behaviors that are sometimes contrary to values, or even to confusion about values. Until people encounter a contradiction or a threat to their basic values, they seldom articulate their values or seek to clarify them.

The values held by each of us are affected by a variety of factors, and a number of ways have been used to measure and describe values. We point out several ways in this chapter—each of which has been widely used in research and in management circles. The first is a framework for describing the broad, general value orientations that characterize large groups, such as nationalities, ethnic groups, industries, or organizations. Much research has been done, for example, on identifying the differences in values that arise across cultural groups. The point of this research is to identify ways in which nationalities differ from one another, since almost all managers now face the need to manage across national boundaries. In your own life, it is likely that you will interact more and more with individuals who do not share your birth country, and knowing something about their value orientations will help your interactions be more effective. It has been discovered that values differ systematically across national cultures, and these differences are a strong influence in predicting the values each of us hold ourselves. At least some of our values are affected significantly by the country and culture in which we are raised.

Cultural Values

Trompenaars (1996; Trompenaars & Hampden-Turner, 1998) identified seven value dimensions upon which significant differences exist among national cultures. Data are based upon 30,000 managers in 55 countries, and results show that certain cultures emphasize some values more than others do. Table 1.1 identifies Trompenaars' seven dimensions, and we provide examples of countries that represent each of the value dimensions. No national culture emphasizes one of

Table 1.1	**Cultural Values Dimensions**	
VALUE DIMENSIONS	**EXPLANATION**	**EXAMPLE OF COUNTRIES WITH DOMINANCE**
Universalism	Societal rules and norms are valued.	United States, Switzerland, Norway, Sweden
Particularism	Individual relationships are valued.	Korea, Venezuela, China, Indonesia
Individualism	Individual contributions are valued.	United States, Nigeria, Denmark, Austria
Collectivism	Team contributions are valued.	Mexico, Indonesia, Japan, Philippines
Affective	Showing emotions is valued.	Iran, Spain, France, Switzerland
Neutral	Unemotional responses are valued.	Korea, Ethiopia, China, Japan
Specific	Segregating life's roles is valued	Holland, Sweden, Denmark, United Kingdom
Diffuse	Integrating life's role is valued.	China, Nigeria, Singapore, Korea
Achievement	Personal accomplishment is valued.	United States, Norway, Canada, Austria
Ascription	Inherent attributes are valued.	Egypt, Indonesia, Korea, Czech Republic
Past and Present	Past is tightly connected to future.	France, Japan, United Kingdom
Future	Future is disconnected but valued.	United States, Holland
Internal	Individual control is valued.	United States, Canada, Austria, United Kingdom
External	Control comes from outside forces.	Czech Republic, Japan, Egypt, China

Source: *C. Hampden-Turner and F. Trompenaars, (1998) "Riding the waves of culture." Reprinted with the permission of McGraw-Hill Companies.*

these dimensions to the exclusion of another, but there are clear differences in the amount of emphasis placed on each dimension.

The first five dimensions of the model refer to how individuals relate to other people. For example, some countries (e.g., the United States, Norway, Sweden, Switzerland) emphasize a value of **universalism**, in which other people's behavior is governed by universal standards and rules—e.g., do not lie, do not cheat, do not run a red light, even if no one is coming the other way. General societal rules govern behavior. Other countries (e.g., Korea, China, Indonesia, Singapore) hold a value of **particularism**, in which the relationship with an individual governs behavior—e.g., is the other person a friend, a family member, a relative? To illustrate the differences, consider your answer to this question: *You are driving in a car with a close friend who hits a pedestrian while going 40 miles an hour in a 25-mile-an-hour zone. There are no witnesses, and your friend's lawyer says that if you'll testify that he was only traveling 25 miles an hour, he'll get off. Will you lie for him?* People in universalistic cultures are more likely to refuse than people in particularistic cultures. For example 97 percent of the Swiss and 93 percent of North Americans (Canada and the United States) would refuse to testify, whereas 32 percent of Venezuelans and 37 percent of South Koreans would refuse.

A second value dimension differentiates cultures that value **individualism**—an emphasis on the self, on independence, and on uniqueness—versus **collectivism**—an emphasis on the group, the combined unit, and on joining with others. Individualistic values hold the contributions of individuals to be most valued, whereas collectivism values team contributions. In general, individual responsibility dominates much more in Western cultures than in Eastern cultures. For example, consider your answer to this question: *What kind of job is found most frequently in your organization, one where everyone works together and you do not get individual credit, or one where everyone is allowed to work individually and you receive individual recognition?* Eastern Europeans (e.g, Russia, Czech Republic, Hungary, Poland) average above 80 percent in agreeing that individual credit is received, whereas Asians (e.g., Japan, India, Nepal) average below 45 percent. (The United States score is 72 percent.)

A third value dimension refers to the display of feelings in public. It identifies an **affective** versus **neutral** orientation. Cultures with high affective values tend to show emotions openly and to deal in emotional ways with problems. Loud laughter, anger, and intense passion may all be displayed in the course of a business negotiation, for example. Cultures with neutral values are more rational and stoic in their approach to problem solving. Instrumental, goal directed behaviors rather than emotions dominate interactions. For example, *if you became very upset at work or in class—say you feel slighted, offended, or angry—how likely would you be to display your feelings openly in public?* Managers in Japan, Ethiopia, and Hong Kong, for example, average 64 percent, 74 percent, and 81 percent respectively in refusing to show emotions publicly. On the other hand, 15 percent of Kuwait managers, 18 percent of Egyptian managers, and 19 percent of Spanish managers would refuse. (The United States score is 43 percent.)

A fourth dimension—**specific** versus **diffuse**—describes the difference between cultures that segregate the different roles in life so as to maintain privacy and personal autonomy compared to cultures that integrate and merge their roles. Cultures with specific values separate work relationships from family relationships, for example, whereas diffuse cultures entangle work and home relationships. People with specific values may seem hard to get to know because they keep a boundary between their personal lives and their work lives. People with diffuse values may seem too forward and too superficial because they seem to share personal information freely. Interestingly, diffuse cultures have lower turnover rates among employees and higher degrees of loyalty to an employer because work and personal relationships are more intertwined. To illustrate the difference, how would you respond to this question: *Your boss asks you to come to her home to help her paint her house. You don't want to do it since you hate painting. Would you refuse?* More than 90 percent of the Dutch and Swedes would refuse, whereas only 32 percent of the Chinese and 46 percent of Nigerians would refuse. (In the United States, 82 percent would refuse.)

A fifth value dimension differentiates cultures that emphasize an **achievement** orientation versus an **ascription** culture. People tend to acquire high status based on their personal accomplishments in some cultures, whereas in other cultures status and prestige are based more on ascribed characteristics such as age, gender, family heritage, or ethnic background. Who you know (ascription) versus what you can do (achievement) helps identify the difference on this value dimension. For example, the following statement helps highlight achievement versus ascription value differences: *It is important to act the way you are, to be consistent with your true self, even if you do not accomplish the task at hand.* Only 10 percent of managers from Uruguay, 12 percent from Argentina, and 13 percent from Spain disagree with the statement, whereas 77 percent of

Norwegians and 75 percent of managers from the United States disagree.

A sixth value dimension relates to how people interpret and manage time. It distinguishes the emphasis placed on the past, present, or future in various cultures. Some cultures, for example, value past and tradition more than future; other cultures place more value on the future than the past. What you have achieved in the past matters more in some cultures than where you are headed in the future. Time differences also exist regarding short- versus long-time horizons. For example, some people are oriented toward very short time horizons where they think in terms of minutes and hours (a short-time horizon). Other people think in terms of months or years (a long-time horizon). Complete the following brief exercise, for example, to get a sense of your own time horizon. *Use the following scale and give a number to each of the following statements: My past started _____ ago, and ended _____ ago. My present started _____ ago and ended _____ from now. My future will start _____ from now and will end _____ from now. Use this rating scale: 7 = years, 6 = months, 5 = weeks, 4 = days, 3 = hours, 2 = minutes, 1 = seconds.*

By way of comparison, people in the Philippines averaged 3.40 on the scale, Irish managers averaged 3.82, and Brazilians averaged 3.85. On the other hand, managers in Hong Kong averaged 5.71, Portugal averaged 5.62, and Pakistan averaged 5.47. (People in the United States averaged 4.30.)

The seventh and final value dimension focuses on internal and external control. We will discuss this value dimension in more detail later in the chapter. It differentiates cultures that presume that individuals are in control of their own destinies from those that presume that nature or external forces control much of what happens. For example, some countries emphasize the value of individuals inventing or creating things themselves (internal control), whereas other countries emphasize the value of taking what already exists or has been created elsewhere and then refining or improving it (external control). Two statements that illustrate this difference are the following: *(1) What happens to me is my own doing. (2) Sometimes I feel that I do not have enough control over the directions my life is taking.* More than 80 percent of managers from Uruguay, Norway, Israel, and the United States agree with the first statement, whereas less than 40 percent of Venezuelans, Chinese, and Nepalese agree.

Throughout this book we will refer back to some of the differences that have been discovered among various cultures. We encourage you to begin using these dimensions to raise your awareness of individual differences around you. Because virtually every manager will be faced with the opportunity to interact with and manage individuals born in other cultures, being aware of value differences, and being able to diagnose and manage those differences, is an important prerequisite for success in the twenty-first century. Of course, stereotyping people based on their national culture, or overgeneralizing based on trends such as those reported here, can be dangerous and misleading. None of us would like to be pigeonholed based on a general country profile. These dimensions, as you will see, are most useful for increasing sensitivity and helping with diagnosis rather than to place people in categories.

Like countries, organizations, too, have value systems, referred to as an **organizational culture**. Research has found that employees who hold values that are congruent with their organization's values are more productive and satisfied (Cable & Judge, 1996; Cameron & Quinn, 2006; Nwachukwu & Vitell, 1997; Posner & Kouzes, 1993). Holding values that are inconsistent with company values, on the other hand, is a major source of frustration, conflict, and nonproductivity. Being aware of your own priorities and values, the values of your organization, and the general value priorities of your country, are important if you expect to achieve compatibility at work and in a long-term career (Fisher, Macrosson, & Yusuff, 1996; Lobel, 1992). We will not spend time here discussing the various models available for assessing organizational culture. If you are interested in this topic, see Cameron and Quinn (2006).

Personal Values

Rokeach (1973) argued that the total number of values people possess is relatively small and that all individuals possess the same values, but in different degrees. For example, everyone values peace, but some make it a higher priority than others. Two general types of values were identified by Rokeach, and independent priority ratings have been found to exist for each type (that is, the two sets of values are largely unrelated). One general type of values is labeled instrumental, or means-oriented; the other type is terminal, or ends-oriented.

Instrumental values prescribe desirable standards of conduct or methods for attaining an end. Two types of instrumental values relate to morality and competence. Violating moral values (for example, behaving wrongly) causes feelings of guilt, while violating competence values (for example, behaving incapably) brings about feelings of shame.

Terminal values prescribe desirable ends or goals for the individual. There are fewer of them, according to Rokeach, than there are instrumental values, so the sum total for all individuals in all societies can be identified. Terminal values are either personal (for example, peace of mind) or social (for example, world peace). Rokeach has found that an increase in the priority of one personal value tends to increase the priority of other personal values and decrease the priority of social values. Conversely, an increase in the priority of one social value tends to increase the priority of other social values and decrease the value of personal values. Individuals who increase their priority for "a world at peace," for example, would also increase their priority for "equality" while decreasing their priority for "pleasure" or "self-respect." People tend to differ, in other words, in the extent to which they are self- versus others-orientated in their values. Table 1.2 lists the 18 terminal values "judged to represent the most important values in American society" (Rokeach, 1973, p. 29).

In one study of 567 managers in 12 nations, the instrumental values "broadminded," "capable," and "courageous" were held in the highest esteem by managers from all 12 nations, but significant national differences were found on 75 percent of the values (Bigoness & Blakely, 1996). Another study of 658 Egyptians, 132 Americans, 43 Africans, and 101 Arabs found significant national differences on both instrumental and terminal values, with Egyptians being least like Americans (Elsayed-Elkhouly & Buda, 1997).

In a national study of 1,460 American managers, Schmidt and Posner (1982) assessed which of these values were most important in the workplace. Using Rokeach's instrumental values list, they asked managers to identify those that were most desired in the workplace. "Responsible" and "honest" were by far the most desired values in employees (over 85 percent of the managers selected them), followed by "capable" (65 percent), "imaginative" (55 percent), and "logical" (49 percent). "Obedient," "clean," "polite," and

Table 1.2	Terminal and Instrumental Values	
TERMINAL VALUES	**INSTRUMENTAL VALUES**	
A comfortable life (a prosperous life)	Ambitious (hard-working, aspiring)	
An exciting life (a stimulating, active life)	Broadminded (open-minded)	
A sense of accomplishment (lasting contribution)	Capable (competent, effective)	
A world at peace (free of war and conflict)	Cheerful (lighthearted, joyful)	
A world of beauty (beauty of nature and the arts)	Clean (neat, tidy)	
Equality (brotherhood, equal opportunity for all)	Courageous (standing up for your beliefs)	
Family security (taking care of loved ones)	Forgiving (willing to pardon others)	
Freedom (independence, free choice)	Helpful (working for the welfare of others)	
Happiness (contentedness)	Honest (sincere, truthful)	
Inner harmony (freedom from inner conflict)	Imaginative (daring, creative)	
Mature love (sexual and spiritual intimacy)	Independent (self-reliant, self-sufficient)	
National security (protection from attack)	Intellectual (intelligent, reflective)	
Pleasure (an enjoyable, leisurely life)	Logical (consistent, rational)	
Salvation (saved, eternal life)	Loving (affectionate, tender)	
Self-respect (self-esteem)	Obedient (dutiful, respectful)	
Social recognition (respect, admiration)	Polite (courteous, well-mannered)	
True friendship (close companionship)	Responsible (dependable, reliable)	
Wisdom (a mature understanding of life)	Self-controlled (restrained, self-disciplined)	

Source: *Rokeach (1973). Reprinted with permission. Copyright © 1973 by The Free Press. All rights reserved.*

"forgiving" were the least important, being selected by fewer than 10 percent of the managers.

Different groups of people tend to differ in the values they hold. For example, in other studies, business school students and professors tend to rate "ambition," "capability," "responsibility," and "freedom" higher than people in general. They tend to place lower importance than people in general on concern and helpfulness to others, aesthetics and cultural values, and overcoming social injustice. In a study that compared highly successful, moderately successful, and unsuccessful managers, highly successful managers gave significantly higher scores to values relating to economic (for example, a comfortable life) and political values (for example, social recognition) than less successful managers.

Compared to the population in general, managers place substantially more value on "sense of accomplishment," "self-respect," "a comfortable life," and "independence." The instrumental value managers held highest for themselves, in fact, was "ambition"; their highest held terminal value was "sense of accomplishment." In other words, personal values (rather than social values) and those oriented toward achievement predominate among managers (Bilsky & Schwartz, 1994; Cable & Judge, 1996; Cavanaugh, 1980; Clare & Sanford, 1979). In the population in general, one study found that "openness to experience"—that is, a combination of a positive emphasis on broadmindedness, imagination, freedom, and self- direction coupled with a negative emphasis on recognition, obedience, and conformity—was the dominating value held by most people (Dollinger, Leong, & Ulicni, 1996). Interestingly, no gender differences have been found on the Rokeach instrument (Johnston, 1995).

These value preferences may explain why business students and even managers themselves have been criticized for being too self-centered and impatient for personal achievement and promotion (see Introduction). A balance of personal values and social values, such as justice and helpfulness, may characterize a more adaptable manager in the future.

Simply esteeming certain personal and achievement-oriented values does not mean, of course, that one will be a successful manager. On the other hand, it is clear that values do affect individual behavior. For example, sharing values among team members, as well as compatibility of instrumental and terminal values among team members, was found to be associated with significantly more effective teams (Fisher et al., 1996). More importantly, several authors have argued that the behavior displayed by individuals (that is, the means used to achieve their valued ends) is a product of their level of **values maturity** (e.g., Kohlberg, 1969; Kohlberg & Ryncarz, 1990). Individuals differ in their level of values development, according to these authors, so different sets of instrumental values are held by individuals at different stages of development. People progress from one level of maturity to another, and as they do, their value priorities change. Individuals who have progressed to more mature levels of values development possess a qualitatively different set of instrumental values than individuals who are at less mature levels. This theory of values maturity or moral development has received a great deal of attention from researchers, and research findings have some important implications for self-awareness and managerial effectiveness. Therefore, we shall discuss in some detail this notion of values maturity.

Values Maturity

Kohlberg's model is the best known and most widely researched approach to values maturity. It focuses on the kind of reasoning used to reach a decision about an issue that has value or moral connotations. The model consists of three major levels, each of which contains two stages. Table 1.3 summarizes the characteristics of each stage. In brief, the stages are sequential (for example, a person can't progress to stage 3 before passing through stage 2), and each stage represents a higher level of maturity. Kohlberg uses the terms *preconventional*, *conventional*, and *postconventional* to describe these three levels. In the following discussion, we have chosen to use different terms that capture the dominant characteristics of each stage.

The first level of maturity, the *self-centered level*, includes the first two stages of values development. Moral reasoning and instrumental values are based on personal needs or wants and on the consequences of an act. For example, something could be judged as right or good if it helped an individual obtain a reward or avoid punishment and if the consequences were not negative for someone else. Stealing $50,000 is worse than stealing $500 in the self-centered level because the consequences (that is, the losses) are more negative for someone else.

The second level, or *conformity level*, includes stages 3 and 4. Moral reasoning is based on conforming to and upholding the conventions and expectations of society. This level is sometimes referred to as the "law and order" level because the emphasis is on conformity to laws and norms. Right and wrong are judged on the basis of whether or not behaviors conform to the rules

Table 1.3	Classification of Moral Judgment into Stages of Development
LEVEL BASIS OF MORAL JUDGMENT	**STAGE OF DEVELOPMENT**
A *PRECONVENTIONAL LEVEL (SELF-CENTERED)* Moral value resides in external factors, and consequences, not persons or relationships.	1. *Punishment and Obedience* Right is determined by avoiding punishment and not breaking an authority's rules. 2. *Individual Instrumental Purpose and Exchange* Right is meeting one's own immediate interests, and what is fair or equal for others.
B *CONVENTIONAL LEVEL (CONFORMITY)* Moral value resides in duty, maintaining social contracts, keeping commitments.	3. *Mutual Interpersonal Expectations, Relationships, and Conformity* Right is being concerned about others' feelings and maintaining trust by keeping expectations and commitments. The Golden Rule is relevant. 4. *Social System and Conscience Maintenance* Right is doing one's duty to society and upholding the social order.
C *POSTCONVENTIONAL (PRINCIPLED)* Moral value resides in commitment to freely selected standards, rights, and duties.	5. *Prior Rights and Social Contract or Utility* Right is upholding the rights, values, and contracts of others in society; moral behavior is freely chosen. 6. *Universal Ethical Principles* Right is guided by internal, universal ethical principles. When laws violate principles, the laws are ignored.

Source: *Adapted from Kohlberg (1981).*

of those in authority. Respect from others based on obedience is a prized outcome. Stealing $50,000 and stealing $500 are equally wrong in this level because both violate the law. Most American adults function at this level of values maturity.

Third is the *principled level*. It includes the final two stages of maturity and represents the most mature level of moral reasoning and the most mature set of instrumental values. Right and wrong are judged on the basis of the internalized principles of the individual. That is, judgments are made on the basis of a set of principles or core values that have been developed from individual experience. In the highest stage of maturity, this set of principles is comprehensive (it covers all contingencies), consistent (it is never violated), and universal (it does not change with the situation or circumstance). Thus, stealing $50,000 and stealing $500 are still judged to be wrong, but the basis for the judgment is not the violation of laws or rules; rather, it is the violation of a set of comprehensive, consistent, universal principles developed by the individual. Few individuals, according to Kohlberg, reach this highest level of maturity on a consistent basis.

In short, self-centered individuals view rules and laws as outside themselves, but they obey because, by doing so, they may obtain rewards or avoid punishment. Conformist individuals view rules and laws as outside themselves, but they obey because they have learned and accepted those rules and laws, and they seek the respect of others. Principled individuals examine the rules and laws and develop a set of internal principles that they believe are morally right. If there is a choice to be made between obeying a law or obeying a principle, they choose the principle. Internalized principles supersede rules and laws in principled individuals.

To understand the different levels of values maturity, consider the following story used by Kohlberg (1969):

In Europe a woman was near death from a special kind of cancer. There was one drug that the doctors thought might save her. It was a form of radium that a druggist in the same town had recently discovered. The drug was expensive to make, but the druggist was charging ten times what the drug cost to make. He *paid $200 for radium and charged $2,000 for a small dose of the drug. The sick woman's husband, Heinz, went to everyone he knew to borrow the money, but he could get together only about $1,000, which was half of what it cost. He told the druggist that his wife was dying and begged him to sell the drug at a lower price or let him pay later. But the druggist said, "No, I discovered the drug and I'm going to make money from it." So Heinz grew desperate and began to think about breaking into the store to steal the drug for his wife.*

Now answer the following questions in reaction to the story:

YES	NO	
_____	_____	1. Would it be wrong for Heinz to break into the store?
_____	_____	2. Did the druggist have the right to charge that much for the product?
_____	_____	3. Did Heinz have an obligation to steal the drug for his wife?
_____	_____	4. What if Heinz and his wife did not get along? Should Heinz steal the drug for her?
_____	_____	5. Suppose Heinz's best friend were dying of cancer, rather than Heinz's wife. Should Heinz steal the drug for his friend?
_____	_____	6. Suppose the person dying was not personally close to Heinz. Should Heinz steal the drug?
_____	_____	7. Suppose Heinz read in the paper about a woman dying of cancer. Should he steal the drug for her?
_____	_____	8. Would you steal the drug to save your own life?
_____	_____	9. Suppose Heinz was caught breaking in and brought before a judge. Should he be sentenced to jail?

For individuals in the self-centered level of maturity, stealing the drug might be justified because Heinz's wife had instrumental value: she could provide companionship, help rear the children, and so on. A stranger, however, would not have the same instrumental value

for Heinz, so it would be wrong to steal the drug for a stranger. Individuals in the conformity level would base their judgments on the closeness of the relationship and on law and authority. Heinz has an obligation to steal for family members, according to this reasoning, but not for nonfamily members. A governing principle is whether or not an action is against the law (or society's expectations). Principled individuals base their judgments on a set of universal, comprehensive, and consistent principles. They may answer any question yes or no, but their reasoning will be based on their own internal principles, not on externally imposed standards or expectations. (For example, they might feel an obligation to steal the drug for anyone because they value human life more than property.)

Research on Kohlberg's model of values development reveals some interesting findings that have relevance to managerial behavior. For example, moral judgment stories were administered to college students who had earlier participated in Milgram's (1963) obedience study. Under the guise of a reinforcement-learning experiment, Milgram's subjects had been directed to give increasingly intense electric shocks to a person who was observed to be in great pain. Of the respondents at the principled level (stages 5 and 6), 75 percent refused to administer the shocks (i.e., to hurt someone), while only 12.5 percent of the respondents at the conformity level refused. Higher levels of values development were associated with more humane behavior toward other people.

It should also be noted that Kohlberg's model has been criticized by Carol Gilligan (1979, 1980, 1982, 1988) as containing a male bias. In her investigations of moral dilemmas among women, Gilligan indicated that women tend to value care, relationships, and commitment more highly than do males. The Kohlberg model, which tends to emphasize justice as the highest moral value, is more typical of males than females, she claimed. Whereas Gilligan's criticisms are somewhat controversial among researchers, they are less relevant to our discussion here because of our emphasis on the development of internalized principles for guiding behavior, whatever their basis. For our purposes in this chapter, the debate about whether justice is a male value and caring is a female value is largely beside the point.

Becoming more mature in values development requires that individuals develop a set of internalized principles by which they can govern their behavior. The development of those principles is enhanced and values maturity is increased as value-based issues are confronted, discussed, and thought about. Lickona (1976, p. 25) notes, "Simply increasing the amount of reciprocal communication that occurs among people is likely to enhance moral development."

To help you determine your own level of values maturity, an instrument developed by James Rest at the University of Minnesota's Moral Research Center was included in the Assessment section. It has been used extensively in research because it is easier to administer than Kohlberg's method for assessing maturity. According to Kohlberg (1976, p. 47), "Rest's approach does give a rough estimate of an individual's moral maturity level." Rather than placing a person on one single level of values maturity, it identifies the stage that the person relies on most. That is, it assumes that individuals use more than one level of maturity (or set of instrumental values), but that one level generally predominates. By completing this instrument, therefore, you will identify your predominant level of values maturity. To determine your maturity level, refer to the self-scoring instructions in the Appendix at the end of this chapter. An exercise in the Skill Practice section will help you develop or refine principles at the stage 5 and stage 6 level of maturity.

ETHICAL DECISION MAKING AND VALUES

In addition to its benefits for self-understanding, awareness of your own level of values maturity also has important practical implications for **ethical decision making.** By and large, the American public rates the honesty, integrity, and concern for moral values of American business executives as abysmal. A large majority of the public indicates that they think executives are dishonest, overly profit-oriented, and willing to step on other people to get what they want (Andrews, 1989; Harris & Sutton, 1995; Lozano, 1996). Although nine out of 10 companies have a written code of ethics, evidence exists to support public perceptions that these documents are not influential in assuring high moral conduct.

In December 2001, Enron, the seventh largest U.S. corporation at the time, declared bankruptcy. Tragically, a once great company has become a synonym for managerial greed and corporate fraud. The Enron debacle spawned more than 30 major pieces of legislation designed to clamp down on financial loopholes exploited by Enron executives, as well as numerous books and articles criticizing Enron-like unethical business practices (Elliott & Schroth, 2002; Mitchell, 2002).

While Enron was arguably one of the largest corporate scandals in U.S. history, it is hardly the only lapse of ethical judgment staining the image of business. Martha Stewart's insider trading transaction, for example, netted her less than $50,000 in personal wealth but cost her firm billions of dollars in lost stock value. Ford Motor Company refused to alter the dangerous gas tank on the Pinto in order to save $11 per car. It cost Ford millions of dollars in lawsuits and cost many people their lives. Equity Funding tried to hide 64,000 phony insurance claims, but went bankrupt when the truth came out. Firestone denied that its 500-series tire was defective, but eventually took losses in the millions when the accident reports were publicized. A. H. Robins knew of problems with its Dalkon Shield for years before informing the public. The billion dollars set aside for lawsuits against the company was dwarfed by the actual claims, and the company filed Chapter 11. E. F. Hutton, General Dynamics, General Electric, Rockwell, Martin Marietta, Tyco, Lockheed, Bank of Boston, Dow Corning, and a host of other firms have also been in the news for violating ethical principles. One cartoon that seems to summarize these goings-on shows a group of executives sitting at a conference table. The leader remarks, "Of course, honesty is one of the better policies."

Corporate behavior that exemplifies unethical decision making is not our principal concern here. More to the point is a study by the American Management Association that included 3,000 managers in the United States. It reported that most individual managers felt they were under pressure to compromise personal standards to meet company goals (Harris & Sutton, 1995). Moreover, most individuals have encountered someone else violating ethical standards, but in a majority of cases, nothing is reported. For example, in a survey of federal employees asked whether they had observed any of the following activities in the last year, more than 50 percent answered yes to seeing: stealing funds, stealing property, accepting bribes, sexual harassment, ineligible people receiving funds, deficient goods or services, use of position for personal benefit, taking unfair advantage of a contractor, serious violation of the law. More than two thirds did not report what they saw. As an illustration, consider the following true incident (names have been changed). How would you respond? Why?

Dale Monson, a top manufacturing manager at Satellite Telecommunications, walked into the office of Al Lake, the head of quality control. Dale was carrying an assembled part that was to be shipped to a customer on the West Coast. Dale handed Al the part and said, "Look Al, this part is in perfect shape electronically, but the case has a gouge in it. I've seen engineering and they say that the mark *doesn't affect form, fit, or function. Marketing says the customer won't mind because they are just going to bury the unit anyway. We can't rework it, and it would cost $75,000 to make new cases. We will only do 23 units, and they're already made. The parts are due to be shipped at the end of the week." Al responded, "Well, what do you want from me?" "Just sign off so we can move forward," said Dale. "Since you're the one who needs to certify acceptable quality, I thought I'd better get this straightened out now rather than waiting until the last minute before shipping."*

Would you ship the part or not? Discuss this with your class members. Generate a recommendation for Al.

This case exemplifies the major values conflict faced over and over again by managers. It is a conflict between maximizing the economic performance of the organization (as indicated by revenues, costs, profits, and so forth) or the social performance of the organization (as indicated by obligations to customers, employees, suppliers, and so forth). Most ethical tradeoffs are conflicts between these two desirable ends: economic versus social performance (Hosmer, 2003). Making these kinds of decisions effectively is not merely a matter of selecting between right and wrong alternatives or between good and bad choices. Most of these choices are between right and right or between one good and another. Individuals who effectively manage these kinds of ethical trade-offs are those who have a clear sense of their own values and who have developed a principled level of moral maturity. They have articulated and clarified their own internal set of universal, comprehensive, and consistent principles upon which to base their decisions. It is seldom the case, of course, that a manager could choose economic performance goals every time or that he or she could choose social performance goals every time. Trade-offs are inevitable.

It is not a simple matter, on the other hand, to generate a personal set of universal, comprehensive, and consistent principles that can guide decision making. According to Kohlberg's research, most adults have neither constructed, nor do they follow, a well-developed set of principles in making decisions. One reason is that they have no model or example of what such principles might be. We offer some standards against which to test your own principles for making moral or ethical choices. These standards are neither comprehensive nor absolute, nor are they independent of one another. They simply serve as reference against which to test the principles that you include in your personal values statement.

❑ *Front page test:* Would I be embarrassed if my decision became a headline in the local newspaper? Would I feel comfortable describing my actions or decision to a customer or stockholder?

❑ *Golden rule test:* Would I be willing to be treated in the same manner?

❑ *Dignity and liberty test:* Are the dignity and liberty of others preserved by this decision? Is the basic humanity of the affected parties enhanced? Are their opportunities expanded or curtailed?

❑ *Equal treatment test:* Are the rights, welfare, and betterment of minorities and lower status people given full consideration? Does this decision benefit those with privilege but without merit?

❑ *Personal gain test:* Is an opportunity for personal gain clouding my judgment? Would I make the same decision if the outcome did not benefit me in any way?

❑ *Congruence test:* Is this decision or action consistent with my espoused personal principles? Does it violate the spirit of any organizational policies or laws?

❑ *Procedural justice test:* Can the procedures used to make this decision stand up to scrutiny by those affected?

❑ *Cost-benefit test:* Does a benefit for some cause unacceptable harm to others? How critical is the benefit? Can the harmful effects be mitigated?

❑ *Good night's sleep test:* Whether or not anyone else knows about my action, will it produce a good night's sleep?

In the Skill Application section of this chapter, you may want to consider these alternatives when constructing your own set of comprehensive, consistent, and universalistic principles. You should be aware, however, that your set of personal principles will also be influenced by your orientation for acquiring and responding to the information you receive. This orientation is called learning style.

LEARNING STYLE

Each of us is constantly being exposed to an overwhelming amount of information, and only part of it can be given attention and acted upon at a time. For example, right now you have information entering your brain relating to the functioning of your physical body, the attributes of the room in which you are sitting, the words on this page, the ideas and memories that spring to mind as you read about self-awareness, long-held beliefs, recollections of recent events, and so on. Of course, not all of this information is conscious, otherwise your brain would become overloaded and you would go insane. Over time, we all develop strategies for suppressing some kinds of information and paying attention to other kinds. These strategies become habitual and ingrained, and they result in a particular kind of learning style for each of us.

Learning style refers to the inclination each of us has to perceive, interpret, and respond to information in a certain way. Learning style is based on two key dimensions: (1) the manner in which you gather information, and (2) the way in which you evaluate and act on information. An abundance of instruments exist to measure different dimensions of cognitive and learning styles (see Eckstrom, French, & Harmon, 1979; Sternberg & Zhang, 2000), but we are focusing here on the most fundamental dimensions of learning. We use the most widely employed assessment instrument to measure learning style. This instrument has been used in more than 1,000 studies of managerial and leadership behavior, and it has been shown to be an excellent predictor of learning and information processing styles.

One of the main reasons we focus on learning style is that, to be successful, everyone must be constantly learning. In the twenty-first century, it is clear that knowledge will be the most important sustaining competitive advantage. Because the half-life of knowledge is approaching three years (half of everything you know will be outdated in approximately three years), and the amount of knowledge available to the average person doubles about every three years, learning is a prerequisite for a productive life. If people stop learning, they quickly become outdated and out of touch. Constant, lifelong learning is a key requirement, therefore, to successful living, not to mention successful management.

You completed the Learning Styles Instrument (LSI) in the Pre-assessment section of this chapter. In order to help you interpret your scores and be clear about their relevance, you will want to know something about the theory of learning style and learning cycles. This theory was developed and refined by David Kolb and his colleagues at Case Western Reserve University. It assumes that when individuals encounter information, they are more inclined to concentrate on and learn from certain kinds of inputs more than others. In addition, individuals are inclined to react to that information in different ways as they

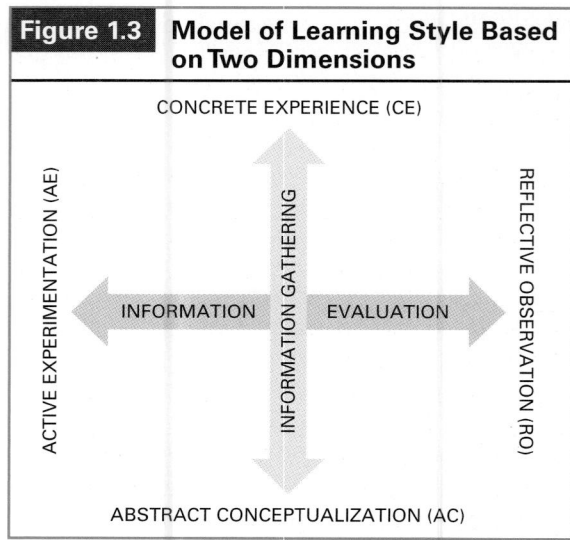

Figure 1.3 Model of Learning Style Based on Two Dimensions

CONCRETE EXPERIENCE (CE)

ACTIVE EXPERIMENTATION (AE)

INFORMATION GATHERING

INFORMATION   EVALUATION

REFLECTIVE OBSERVATION (RO)

ABSTRACT CONCEPTUALIZATION (AC)

try to understand and interpret it. Figure 1.3 illustrates two dimensions of learning: the information-gathering dimension, which distinguishes *concrete experience (CE)* from *abstract conceptualization (AC)*, and the information-response dimension, which distinguishes *reflective observation (RO)* from *active experimentation (AE)*.

Let us first consider the information-gathering dimension. Some people are more inclined to take in information through direct experience. They learn by tangible, concrete, sensual encounters. The perceptible, felt qualities of information are easiest to capture, so they tend to immerse themselves in situations in order to learn from them. We would describe these individuals as having an inclination toward **concrete experience**. They learn best through experience and involvement.

On the other hand, some people tend to take in information best that is abstract, symbolic, or theoretical. They learn most effectively when they encounter ideas and theories and then have a chance to think about them logically and analytically. They are more likely to learn from information that they can rationally examine or intellectually explore. We would describe these individuals as having an inclination toward **abstract conceptualization**. People who are inclined to learn from concrete experience are likely to interact with people to get their information, whereas abstract conceptualizers are more likely to get their information from books.

The second dimension of the learning model refers to strategies for interpreting, evaluating, and responding to information. Differences on this dimension arise from reliance on a particular problem-solving pattern. For example, after encountering information, some people are inclined to examine it from different perspectives, to ruminate about it, and to explore the various meanings that might be present. They are inclined to observe and scrutinize information or to engage in **reflective observation**. Quick judgments are avoided, and pondering and reflecting about the information is typical.

On the other hand, some people are inclined to act immediately on the information they receive. They respond by being proactive, by testing out the new information, or by applying it to an immediate problem or situation. They experiment to investigate the implications and utility of the information. By actively applying it, they can form alternative hypotheses about it. We would describe these people as having an inclination toward **active experimentation**.

Each orientation or inclination represents a choice. It is almost impossible, for example, to simultaneously drive a car (concrete experience) while analyzing the properties of the motor and its torque (abstract conceptualization). Similarly, thoughtfully examining implications of information (reflective observation) is opposite from taking immediate action to test out the usefulness of information (active experimentation).

Research on these cognitive dimensions has found that no matter what type of problem they face, most individuals use their preferred learning style to approach it. They prefer, and even seek, decision situations and problem types that are consistent with their own learning style (for example, individuals scoring high on AC and AE prefer problems with a step-by-step method of solution). In one study, for example, managers who were more RO and AC (lower-right part of Figure 1.3) than AE and CE (upper-left part of Figure 1.3) implemented more computer-based systems and rational procedures for decision making. Managers in another study defined identical problems differently depending on their different learning styles (e.g., some thought the problem required action, while others thought it required thoughtful analysis). Another study found that differences in learning style led to significantly different decision-making processes in managers (see Chenhall & Morris, 1991; Henderson & Nutt, 1980; Ruble & Cosier, 1990).

Figure 1.4 provides you with a scoring profile upon which you can plot your scores from the LSI. On the figure, find the point on the vertical CE axis that corresponds with your score. Do the same for your RO score, your AC score, and your AE score. By plotting your scores on each axis of the figure and joining those points together, you will have produced some kind of

"kite-shaped" profile. This profile identifies your learning style. It is compared to about 1,500 practicing managers and graduate students in management school. Your scores are compared to a large data set that has emerged from hundreds of studies using this learning style instrument.

In Figure 1.4, the lines connecting the hash marks represent approximately 20 percentile points. For example, if you scored 32 on the CE dimension, you would be between the 60th and 80th percentiles. In other words, between 60 and 80 percent of people would have lower scores than you on this dimension. If you scored 19 on the RO dimension, you would be at about the 20th percentile. Approximately 80 percent of the people would score higher than you on this dimension.

Using your plot, you can now identify your particular preference or inclination toward learning. The quadrant in Figure 1.4 that takes up the largest area in your "kite" profile is your strongest learning style. Research over the last 30 years has identified four common types of learners that encompass the vast majority of people—diverging, assimilating, converging, and accommodating learning styles (Kolb, 1984; 1999).

Diverging The **diverging** learning style has dominant scores on the concrete experience (CE) and reflective observation (RO) dimensions. People with this learning style are best at viewing concrete situations from many different points of view. It is labeled diverging because these individuals perform better in situations that require idea generation and the creation of alternative perspectives. They excel at creative, inventive activities with problems that can be viewed from a variety of perspectives. People with this style like to gather lots of information and engage in brainstorming, they are inductive thinkers, and they usually have very broad-based interests. Research shows that these people tend to be imaginative and emotional, tend toward specializing in the arts, and prefer working in groups so as to hear a broad array of different opinions. In college, divergers tend to major in the arts, history, political science, English, and psychology. They tend to select careers in social services (e.g., psychology, nursing, public policy) and in arts and communication (e.g., theater, literature, journalism), and they prefer jobs in which personal interactions predominate (Kolb, Boyatzis, & Mainemelis, 2000).

Assimilating The **assimilating** style has dominant scores on the reflective observation (RO) and the abstract conceptualization (AC) dimensions. People with this learning style are best at processing a wide

| Figure 1.4 | Scoring the LSI |

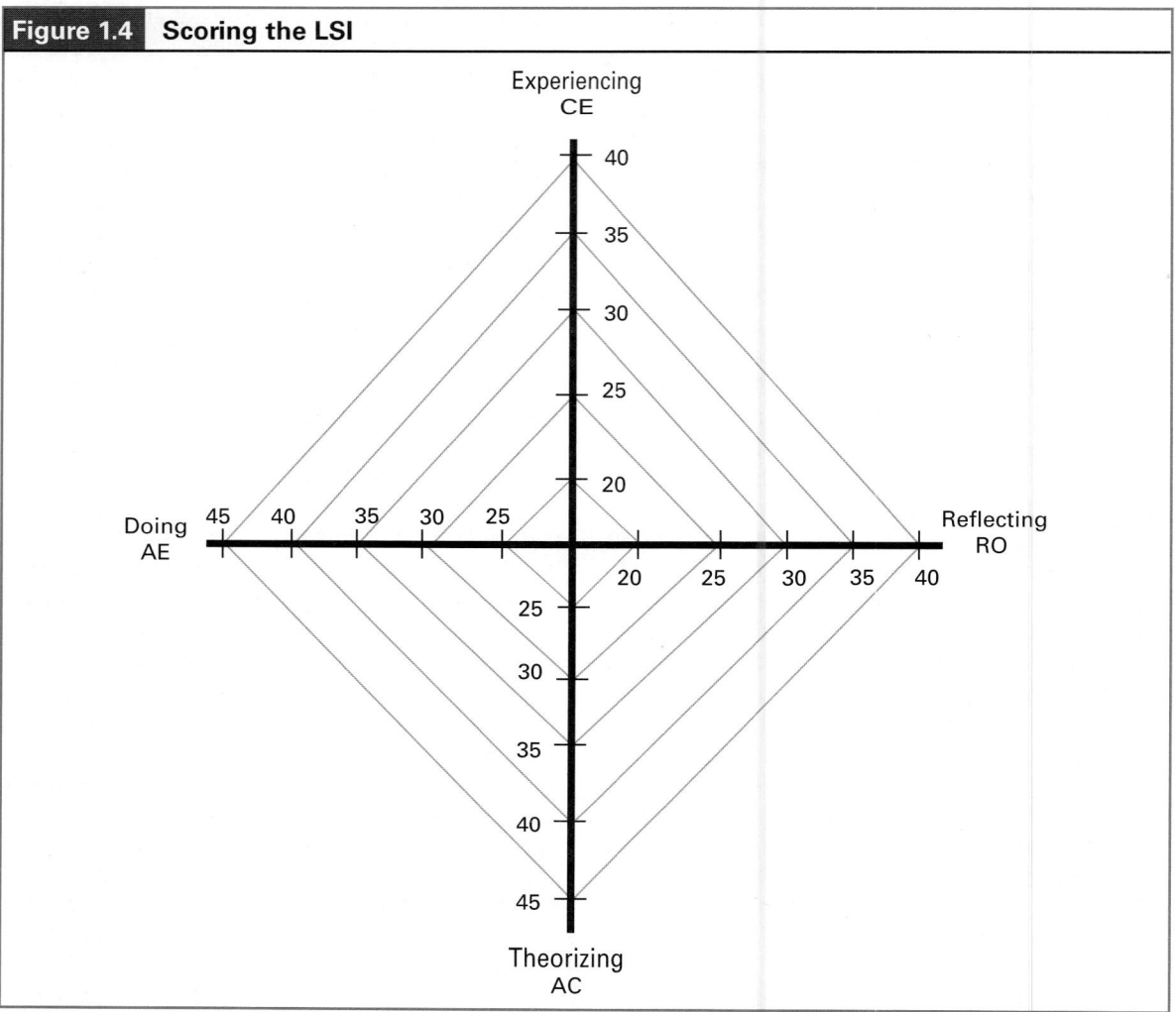

range of information and putting it into a concise, cohesive, logical form. They are less inclined toward acquiring information by interacting with people and more interested in thinking through abstract ideas and concepts. They excel at inductive reasoning and organizing material into a consistent whole. They find it more important to have a theory with logical soundness than practical or utilitarian value. Research has shown that assimilators are inclined toward information and science careers, and they prefer lectures, readings, analytical models, and thinking time as their learning activities. In college, assimilators tend to major in economics, mathematics, sociology, and chemistry. They tend to select careers in the information sciences and in research fields (e.g., educational research, law, theology), and they prefer jobs in which information gathering predominates (e.g., research and analysis) (Kolb et al., 2000).

Converging The **converging** style has dominant scores on the abstract conceptualization (AC) and active experimentation (AE) dimensions. People with this learning style are best at finding practical uses for ideas and theories. They are problem solvers and decision makers who prefer to deal with technical tasks and pre-scribed problems rather than social or interpersonal issues. They excel at the practical application of ideas and at problems that have one correct answer. Research has suggested that these individuals are inclined toward careers in technology and engineering. In formal learning situations, they prefer simulations, laboratory assignments, and practical application problems. In college, convergers tend to major in physical sciences, engineering, and computers. They tend to select careers in technology fields (e.g., engineering, computer science, medical technology), economics, and environmental science, and they prefer jobs that have a technical problem-solving emphasis (Kolb et al., 2000).

Accommodating   The **accommodating** style has dominant scores on the active experimentation (AE) and concrete experience (CE) dimensions. People with this learning style are best at hands-on experience. They enjoy carrying out plans and involving themselves in new and challenging experiences. They tend to act on gut feeling more than on logical analysis, and they have an inclination toward solving problems by interacting with other people rather than performing their own systematic critique. They excel at activities in which risk taking and adaptation are required, such as in entrepreneurial endeavors. Research has found that accommodators are inclined toward careers in marketing and sales and managerial roles. In formal learning situations accommodators prefer to work with others to accomplish assignments, to establish goals, to engage in field projects, and to test out various approaches to a problem. In college, accommodators tend to major in business and management. They tend to select careers in business (e.g., management, finance, marketing) and in organizational administration (e.g., government, public service, educational administration), and they prefer jobs that have a leadership or executive component (e.g., task accomplishment and decision making) (Kolb et al., 2000).

These descriptions of style are general, of course, and your learning style is not the only factor that is relevant in selecting a path for your future. A great deal of variety exists among people in various college majors, job types, and career choices, so do not interpret your scores on the LSI as determining your destiny. On the other hand, your learning profile can help you identify the ways in which you learn best, the types of learning activities you are likely to prefer, and the ways in which you will have the easiest time assimilating and responding to information. It may also help you determine the kinds of people you want to work with you as you build an effective learning team (see Chapter 9 in this book).

Another important aspect of Kolb's learning model is explaining how we can use each of the four dimensions in sequence to improve learning. The four types of learning depicted in Figure 1.5 describe a learning cycle that has proven to be successful in improving learning. Research has confirmed that if this learning process is followed, people learn more effectively,

retain learning for longer periods, and develop more effective behavioral skills (Kolb & Kolb, 1999). The stages in the learning cycle are as follows.

When a person has an experience (step 1, CE), little learning occurs unless some kind of reflective observation accompanies it (step 2, RO). Organizing the information and interpreting its meaning is an important step in learning from experience. This step is followed by forming theories about the information, relating it to other experiences that may be similar, and drawing conclusions about the relevance and usefulness of the experience (step 3, AC). Generalizing from the specific experience allows it to be applied or to have meaning in more than a single idiosyncratic situation. Finally, testing out the conclusions, generalizations, or theories that were formulated helps identify their applicability (step 4, AE).

Experimenting with the learning in new situations, in other words, leads to another concrete experience (step 1), and the cycle begins again. A person may enter the learning cycle at any point, of course, not just at the CE step. The point is to engage in all four steps in the learning process in order for learning to be most effective.

Most schools overemphasize the reflective observation (RO) and abstract conceptualization (AC) steps in the learning process in that most concentrate a great deal of their learning activities in the classroom. Most colleges and universities, in fact, exhibit a bias toward admitting people who score high on those learning styles (as recorded on ACT, SAT, or GMAT exams). Moreover, focusing a curriculum entirely on the case study method, for example, or on experiential exercises to teach students about effective management and leadership, has been shown to be much less effective than having learning activities that represent each of these four steps (see Kolb & Kolb, 1999). The best management skills curriculum, for example, has opportunities for action learning and student experimentation (CE and AE), as well as class discussion, readings, and examinations (RO and AC).

ATTITUDES TOWARD CHANGE

In order to capitalize fully on the strengths of your own learning style, you also should be aware of your orientation toward change. This is important because, as the environment in which managers operate continues to become more chaotic, more temporary, more complex, and more overloaded with information, your ability to process information is at least partly constrained by your fundamental attitude about change.

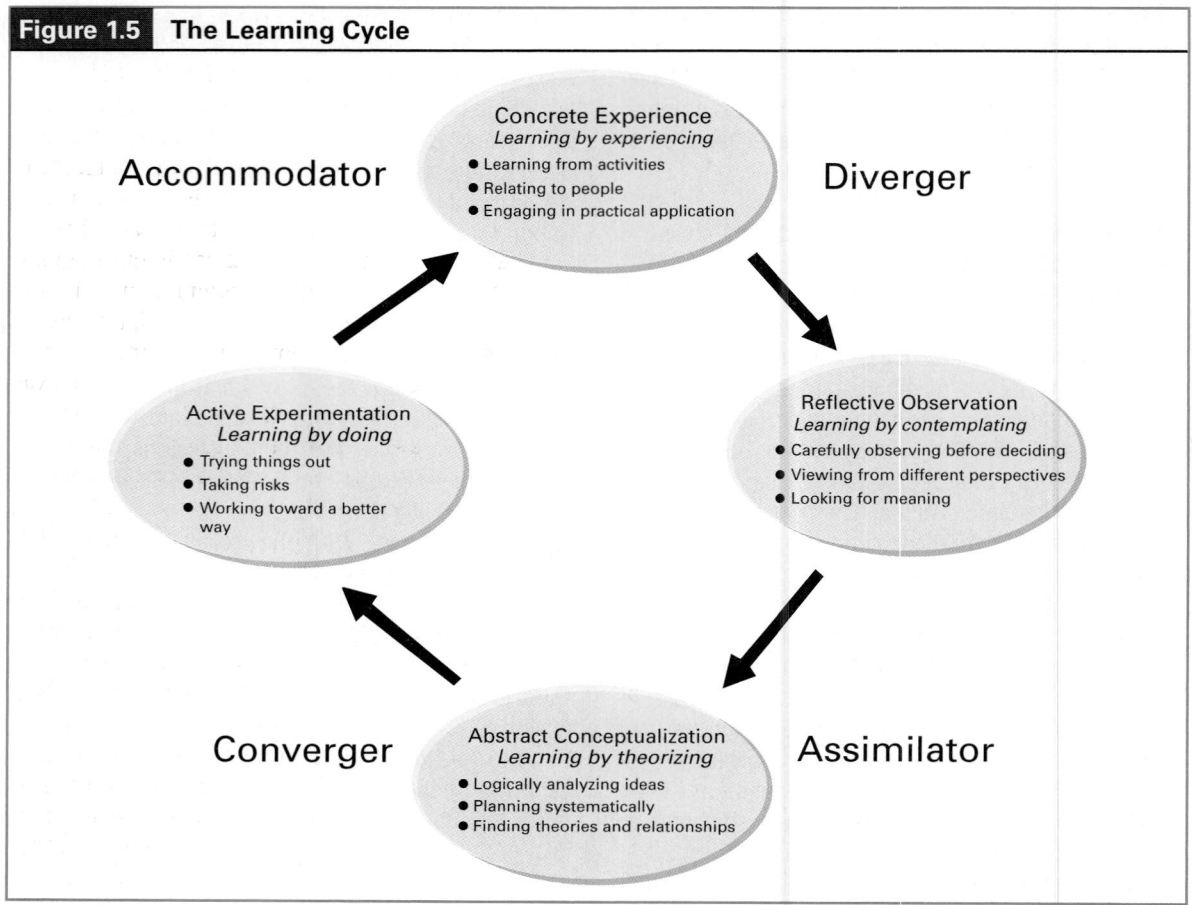

Almost no one disagrees with the prediction that change will increase in the future, both in pace and scope. The challenge of students and managers at the beginning of the twenty-first century is to prepare for a world that cannot be predicted by the experiences of the past. This condition, according to Peter Drucker (father of modern management), occurs no more frequently than every 200 to 300 years. The last times such conditions were encountered were at the dawn of the Renaissance and the outset of the industrial revolution. The world changed dramatically, unpredictably. The patterns of the past could not be used to predict the trends of the future. Dramatic, transformational change occurred. Similarly, graduates of management schools will face an environment in the decades ahead unlike one that any person has ever experienced before.

As pointed out earlier, both the half-life of knowledge and the amount of knowledge available to people are changing at incredible speeds. Even the half-life of most information technologies is now less than one year. (Consider how up-to-date your current computer is, regardless of how recently you purchased it.) It is estimated that in a decade, for example, personal computers will become anachronistic as etching on molecules replaces etching on silicon. It is predicted that computers as small as a pencil head will be implanted in the body to govern, for example, heart rate, or in eyeglasses to display the name of every person you pass by on the street.

Educated people who read the *Wall Street Journal*, *New York Times*, or *Herald Tribune* are now exposed to more information in one day than a person was exposed to in a lifetime in the eighteenth century. Most of the world's population has never known a world without a computer, remote control, unlimited TV channels, and satellite transmission, yet the population group that is growing the fastest and that controls most of society's wealth is over 60 years old and have just encountered the information revolution in the last half of their lives. Alarmingly, a large majority of the world's population can only dream of having access to current information technology, and even a majority of the U.S.

population cannot afford a computer. Hence, we face a real danger of perpetuating technological apartheid both in the United States and throughout the world.

In business organizations, no manager at the beginning of the twenty-first century would boast of being stable, constant, or maintaining the status quo. Even now, stability is interpreted more as stagnation than steadiness, and organizations not in the business of major transformation and revolution are generally viewed as recalcitrant. The frightening uncertainty that has always accompanied major change is now superseded by a fear of staying the same.

All this is to say that the environment of the twenty-first century will be characterized by turbulence, gigantic change, rapid-fire decisions, and chaos. No one will have time to read and analyze a case study. E-business has changed the rules of the game. For example, it is now possible for competitors in almost any business to emerge on the Internet within 24 hours. No one can predict the competitive environment anymore. Customers are no longer geographically constrained, and the standards for servicing them have changed completely. Speed to market and competing against time have begun to dominate the traditional competitive advantages learned in business schools. Rapid decision making, mostly without the benefit of adequate information and careful analysis, is becoming the norm.

In the midst of this chaotic pace of change—what some refer to as "permanent white water"—being aware of your own orientation toward change is an important prerequisite for successfully coping with it. Two dimensions of change orientation particularly relevant for managers are discussed on the following pages.

Tolerance of Ambiguity

The first important dimension is **tolerance of ambiguity**, which refers to the extent to which individuals are threatened by or have difficulty coping with situations that are ambiguous, where change occurs rapidly or unpredictably, where information is inadequate or unclear, or where complexity exists. Stimulus-rich and information-overloaded environments (for example, air traffic control towers) are examples. Regardless of their cognitive style, people vary in their aptitude for operating in such circumstances.

People differ in the extent to which they are "cognitively complex" or in the extent to which they can cope with ambiguous, incomplete, unstructured, dynamic situations. Individuals who have a high tolerance of ambiguity also tend to be more cognitively

complex. They tend to pay attention to more information, interpret more cues, and possess more sense-making categories than less complex individuals do. Research has found that cognitively complex and tolerant individuals are better transmitters of information, more sensitive to internal (nonsuperficial) characteristics of others when evaluating their performance at work, and more behaviorally adaptive and flexible under ambiguous and overloaded conditions than less tolerant and less cognitively complex individuals. Managers with higher tolerance-of-ambiguity scores are more likely to be entrepreneurial in their actions, to screen out less information in a complex environment, and to choose specialties in their occupations that possess less-structured tasks. They also cope more effectively with major organizational change, downsizing, and role stress and conflict (Armstrong-Stassen, 1998; Haase, Lee, & Banks, 1979; Teoh & Foo, 1997; Timothy, Thoresen, Pucik, and Welbourne, 1999).

It also should be pointed out, however, that individuals who are more tolerant of ambiguity have more difficulty focusing on a single important element of information—they are inclined to pay attention to a variety of items—and they may have somewhat less ability to concentrate without being distracted by interruptions. However, for the most part, in an information-rich environment, tolerance of ambiguity and cognitive complexity are more adaptive than the opposite characteristics.

In the Skill Assessment section of this chapter, a Tolerance of Ambiguity Scale (Budner, 1962) assesses the extent to which you have a tolerance for these kinds of complex situations. In scoring the Tolerance of Ambiguity Scale (see the scoring key at the end of the chapter) three different subscale scores are assessed. One is the *novelty* score, which indicates the extent to which you are tolerant of new, unfamiliar information or situations. The second subscale is the *complexity* score, which indicates the extent to which you are tolerant of multiple, distinctive, or unrelated information. The third subscale is the *insolubility* score, which indicates the extent to which you are tolerant of problems that are very difficult to solve because, for example, alternative solutions are not evident, information is unavailable, or the problem's components seem unrelated to each other. In general, the more tolerant people are of novelty, complexity, and insolubility, the more likely they are to succeed as managers in information-rich, ambiguous environments. They are less overwhelmed by ambiguous circumstances.

It is important to note that cognitive complexity and tolerance for ambiguity are not related to cognitive intelligence, and your score on the Tolerance of Ambiguity Scale is not an evaluation of how smart you are. Most important, individuals can learn to tolerate more complexity and more flexibility in their information-processing abilities. The first step toward increasing tolerance is becoming aware of where you are now by completing the Skill Assessment section. Then the Skill Analysis and Skill Practice sections of this chapter, along with discussions such as the one in the chapters on problem solving and creativity, provide ways to improve your tolerance for ambiguity and your cognitive complexity. It is also interesting to note that a positive correlation exists between tolerance of ambiguity and the second dimension of orientation toward change discussed here, internal locus of control.

Locus of Control

The second dimension of orientation toward change is **locus of control**. It is one of the most studied and written-about aspects of orientation toward change. Locus of control refers to the attitude people develop regarding the extent to which they are in control of their own destinies. When individuals receive information about the success or failure of their own actions, or when something changes in the environment, they differ in how they interpret that information. People receive reinforcements, both positive or negative, as they attempt to make changes around them. If individuals interpret the reinforcement they receive to be contingent upon their own actions, it is called an **internal locus of control** (that is, "I was the cause of the success or failure of the change"). If they interpret the reinforcement as being a product of outside forces, it is called an **external locus of control** (that is, "Something or someone else caused the success or failure"). Over time, people develop a "generalized expectancy" about the dominant sources of the reinforcements they receive. Thus, they become largely internally focused or largely externally focused with regard to the source of control they perceive in a changing environment.

Over 10,000 studies have been done using the locus of control scale. In general, the research suggests that managers in North America have a far greater tendency to have an internal locus of control than, say, Middle Eastern and Far East managers (Trompenaars, 1996). In Japan, for example, an external locus of control has been associated with high levels of stress and violence among teenagers, presumably due to less emphasis on self-control (Tubbs, 1994). In American culture, internal locus of control is associated with the most successful managers (for reviews of the literature,

see Hendricks, 1985; Spector, 1982). For example, people with an internal locus of control are more likely to (1) be attentive to aspects of the environment that provide useful information for the future, (2) engage in actions to improve their environment, (3) place greater emphasis on striving for achievement, (4) be more inclined to develop their own skills, (5) ask more questions, and (6) remember more information than people with an external locus of control.

In the management literature, individuals who have an internal locus of control are less alienated from the work environment, more satisfied with their work, and experience less job strain and more position mobility (promotions and job changes) than do individuals with an external locus of control (Bernardi, 1997; Coleman, Irving, & Cooper, 1999; Newton & Keenan, 1990; Seeman, 1982). A study of leadership and group performance found that internals were more likely to be leaders and that groups led by internals were more effective than those led by externals (Anderson & Schneider, 1978; Blau, 1993). Internals also were found to outperform externals in stressful situations, to engage in more entrepreneurial activity, to be more active in managing their own careers, and to have higher levels of job involvement than externals (Bonnett & Furnham, 1991; Boone & Brabander, 1997; Cromie, Callahan, & Jansen, 1992; Hammer & Vardi, 1981; Kren, 1992). Differences have also been found regarding how power and authority are utilized by externals and internals (see Chapter 5: Gaining Power and Influence). External leaders tend to use coercive power and threat, whereas internal leaders rely more on persuasion and expertise as a source of power (Sweeney, McFarlin, & Cotton, 1991). Moreover, internals both demonstrate and are more satisfied with a participative management style than externals are (Judge, Erez, Bono, & Thoreson, 2002).

A study of locus of control among top executives found that the firms led by internals engaged in more innovation, more risky projects, more leadership in the marketplace, longer planning horizons, more scanning of the environment, and a more highly developed technology than external-led firms did (Miller, Kets de Vries, & Toulouse, 1982). In summarizing the results of this massive array of research on locus of control, the conclusion is consistent: in American culture, people are handicapped by an external locus of control.

On the other hand, research also has found that an internal locus of control is not a panacea for all management problems. Internal locus of control is not always a positive attribute. For example, individuals with an external locus of control have been found to be more inclined to initiate structure as leaders (to help clarify roles). Internals are less likely to comply with leader directions and are less accurate in processing feedback about successes and failures than are externals. Internals also have more difficulty arriving at decisions with serious consequences for someone else (Coleman, et al., 1999; Rothenberg, 1980; Wheeler & Davis, 1979).

It is important to note that locus of control can shift over time, particularly as a function of the position held at work, and that external locus of control does not inhibit individuals from attaining positions of power and influence at the top of organizations. Therefore, no matter what your internal–external score, you can be a successful manager in the right setting, or you can alter your locus of control. Research has shown that people who interpret information about change as if they are in control of it, and who perceive themselves to be in charge of their own performance (and hence able to control outcomes related to that performance), are more likely to be effective managers in most circumstances in our culture.

The Locus of Control Scale in the Skill Assessment section helps you generate a score showing the extent to which you have an internal or external locus of control. The scoring key and some comparison information are located at the end of the chapter.

In summary, two key attitudes toward change—tolerance of ambiguity and locus of control—have been found to be associated with success in management roles. Knowing your scores on these two factors can help you capitalize on your strengths and enhance your potential for management success. While substantial research exists associating some positive managerial behaviors with internal locus of control and tolerance of ambiguity, possessing these orientations is neither an assurance of success as a manager nor a solution to the problems that managers face. By knowing your scores, however, you will be able to choose situations in which you are more likely to feel comfortable, perform effectively, and understand the point of view of those whose perspectives differ from yours. Self-understanding is a prerequisite to self-improvement and change.

CORE SELF-EVALUATION

Every person has a distinct personality. This concept of *personality* refers to the relatively enduring combination of traits that makes an individual unique and at the same time produces consistencies in his or her thoughts and behaviors. We are all aware of the differences in personalities among the people around us. These differences are manifest in certain kinds of behaviors, attitudes,

emotional reactions, and thought patterns. Collectively, we refer to these unique patterns as a person's personality. Usually, personality refers to a "trait" of individuals inasmuch as it is relatively enduring and stable, even though it may be changed and developed through conscious effort. There is much disagreement about how much of our personality is learned as opposed to being biologically or genetically determined. Some explanation for what makes us unique can certainly be attributed to the genetic predispositions we bring with us when we are born. Yet, a sizable portion of our behavioral make-up is learned and can be changed. We focus in this chapter on factors over which we have some control and can change if we determine to do so.

In the field of personality psychology, there has been a gradual convergence around a few major dimensions of personality. A review of the literature in 2001, for example, found that more than 50,000 studies had been conducted on just three attributes of personality—self-esteem, locus of control, and neuroticism or emotional stability (Bono & Judge, 2003). More than 100 studies a month are published on the topic of self-esteem alone! It has become popular in psychology to refer to the "Big Five" personality attributes as being the most important aspects of personality, although there is no scientific evidence that such a conclusion is merited. These Big Five attributes are the most researched, however, and they include *extroversion* (the extent to which people are inclined toward gregariousness and being outgoing instead of quiet and reserved), *agreeableness* (the extent to which people are friendly and affable as opposed to being disagreeable and aggressive), *conscientiousness* (the extent to which people are careful, task oriented, and orderly as opposed to being disorganized, flexible, and unreliable), *neuroticism* (the extent to which people are emotionally fragile, negative, and fearful as opposed to being optimistic, positive, and emotionally stable), and *openness* (the extent to which people are curious and open to new ideas as opposed to being rigid or dogmatic). Individuals tend to differ on these five attributes, and scores on these five factors have been used to predict a variety of outcomes including behavioral performance, life success, job satisfaction, interpersonal attraction, and intellectual achievement.

Timothy Judge and his colleagues have found, however, that differences in scores on these Big Five personality attributes can be explained by a more foundational personality factor. It is referred to as core self-evaluation, or the fundamental evaluation each person has developed about himself or herself. According to Judge and colleagues (2003), core evaluations influence people's appraisals of themselves, the world, and others, but these evaluations operate subconsciously. For the most part, people are not aware of their own core self-evaluations. Yet, when people respond to certain cues—including personality surveys, behavioral signals, or mental stimuli—their responses are determined to a nontrivial extent by this deeper and more fundamental self-appraisal. In fact, core self-evaluations have been found to predict individuals' scores on the Big Five personality attributes as well as a variety of other unique personal differences. Most people are not aware of the influence that their core self-evaluations have on their perceptions and behaviors, so the assessment instrument at the beginning of this chapter will be very useful in helping you identify your own core self-evaluation.

Core self-evaluation is sometimes referred to as overall positive self-regard—or the extent to which people value themselves and feel proficient as individuals. It is comprised of four components: (1) *self-esteem*, or the extent to which people see themselves as capable, successful, and worthy (Harter, 1990); (2) *generalized self-efficacy*, or the sense of one's ability to perform capably across a variety of circumstances (Locke, McClear, & Knight, 1996); (3) *neuroticism*, which is reversed-scored, or the tendency to have a negative outlook and pessimistic approach to life (Watson, 2000); and (4) *locus of control*, which has been discussed earlier, referring to a person's belief's about the extent to which he or she can control his or her own experiences (Rotter, 1966). Whereas these four personality traits have been studied separately in psychology, it has been discovered that there is a great deal of overlap, and, in combination, they create a single, powerful factor that lies at the core of personality (Judge et al., 2002, 2003). This factor is called a "latent" attribute that lies at the foundation of personality manifestations.

The commonalties among the four factors that make up core self-evaluation are not difficult to understand. That is, when people view themselves in a positive way, or when they possess high self-esteem, they also tend to feel capable of performing effectively across a variety of situations (generalized self-efficacy), they feel in control of their circumstances (locus of control), and they feel emotionally stable (the opposite of neuroticism). Each of these factors by itself has a slightly different meaning, of course, but the overlap and shared meaning among them is the thing being measured by the Core Self-Evaluation Survey. In other words, core self-evaluation assesses the extent to which you possess positive self-regard, or that you feel valuable, capable, stable, and in control. The instrument

you completed in the Pre-assessment section captures the commonality among these four factors rather than their unique meaning. That is, your scores reflect your own core self-evaluation rather than any one of the components by themselves.

Of course, we have all met people who are self-centered, braggarts, or narcissistic. They seem to possess an abundance of positive self-regard, and we might be tempted to think of them as having very high scores in core self-evaluation. However, these people also are likely to be insensitive to their abrasive impact on others. When threatened, they emphasize winning or getting their way. They tend to look in the mirror more often than others, spend more time thinking about themselves and the impressions they convey, and work to make themselves look good or be in the spotlight. They tend to be manipulative in their relationships with others. They are, in a word, selfish people. This is not the same as having a positive core self-evaluation. Rather, a positive core self-evaluation implies sensitivity to others and to the environment so that relationships with others are strengthened rather than weakened, developed rather than destroyed. As summarized in Figure 1.6, strong, confident people are better able to lead, to manage, and to form supportive relationships with others.

Evidence for this fact comes from the studies of the relationships between core self-evaluation and the effectiveness of individuals at work. A great deal of research has been conducted using this Core Self-Evaluation Survey, and its validity has been established in a variety of settings (Judge et al., 2003). Research findings indicate that individuals with high core self-evaluations tend to be more satisfied with their jobs. One explanation for this result is that people are more satisfied with their jobs when they are performing more rewarding work and when they have more complex and challenging work. As it turns out, people with higher core self-evaluation scores tend to select more challenging jobs and they tend to find the work in which they are engaged to be more intrinsically fulfilling. Their work is simply more rewarding and more stimulating to them.

In addition to job satisfaction, core self-evaluation is also strongly related to job performance. That is, people who score higher in core self-evaluation tend to perform more successfully at work as employees and as managers (Judge & Bono, 2001). One reason for this result is that high core self-evaluation scores are strongly associated with motivation, and motivated people (as you will see in Chapter 6) tend to perform better. Similarly, people with higher core self-evaluation

| Figure 1.6 | The Effects of Core Self-Evaluation |

Figure 1.6 **The Effects of Core Self-Evaluation**

Core Self-Evaluation
Positive Self-Regard

- Self-esteem
- Self-efficacy
- Emotional stability
- Locus of control

- Personality uniqueness
- Job satisfaction
- Job performance
- Life happiness

scores tend to have higher levels of task motivation (a desire to accomplish a task), persistence (the inclination to spend the time needed to accomplish a task), productivity in the task itself (producing more output), goal setting (establishing goals for themselves), goal commitment (commitment to accomplishing a goal), and activity level (energized work behavior) (Erez & Judge, 2001). They tend also to be more effective at overcoming obstacles and challenges, in solving problems, and in adapting to organizational change. People with high core self-evaluation scores have also been found to have higher levels of life satisfaction and personal happiness and lower levels of personal stress on the job and experienced strain (headaches, backaches, and somatic symptoms). Higher salary levels, less career plateauing, and more organizational commitment have also been found to be associated with higher core self-evaluation scores.

In summary, core self-evaluation scores tend to be a very important predictor of personality differences, job satisfaction, job performance, and life happiness. When people have developed a positive self-regard—when they feel valuable, capable, stable, and in control—they tend to function better at work, in relationships, and in life. Developing management skills and acquiring the competency to perform effectively in work settings is one way to enhance feelings of positive self regard.

Summary

Corporate America increasingly has begun to discover the power of developing self-awareness among its managers. Each year, millions of executives complete instruments designed to increase self-awareness in companies such as Apple, AT&T, Citicorp, Exxon, General Electric, Honeywell, 3M, and the U.S. Army. An awareness of how individuals differ in their emotional maturity, values priorities and values maturity, learning style, orientation toward change, and personality has helped many companies cope better with interpersonal conflicts, botched communications, breakdowns in trust, and misunderstandings. For example, after requiring his top 100 managers to undergo self-awareness training, the president of the computer reservations company of Hilton Hotels and Budget Rent-a-Car stated:

We had some real morale problems. I realized I had a mixed bag of people reporting to me and that this training could help us better understand each other and also understand how we make decisions. We wouldn't have made it through [a recent company crisis] without self-awareness training (Moore, 1987).

Not only does self-awareness training assist individuals in their ability to understand, and thereby manage, themselves, but it also is important in helping individuals develop understanding of the differences in others. Most people will regularly encounter individuals who possess different styles, different sets of values, and different perspectives than they do. Most work forces are becoming more, not less, diverse. Self-awareness training as discussed in this chapter, therefore, can be a valuable tool in helping individuals develop empathy and understanding for the expanding diversity they will face in work and school settings. Self-awareness is a key component of and a prerequisite for successful management. The relationship between the five critical areas of self-awareness and these management outcomes is summarized in Figure 1.7.

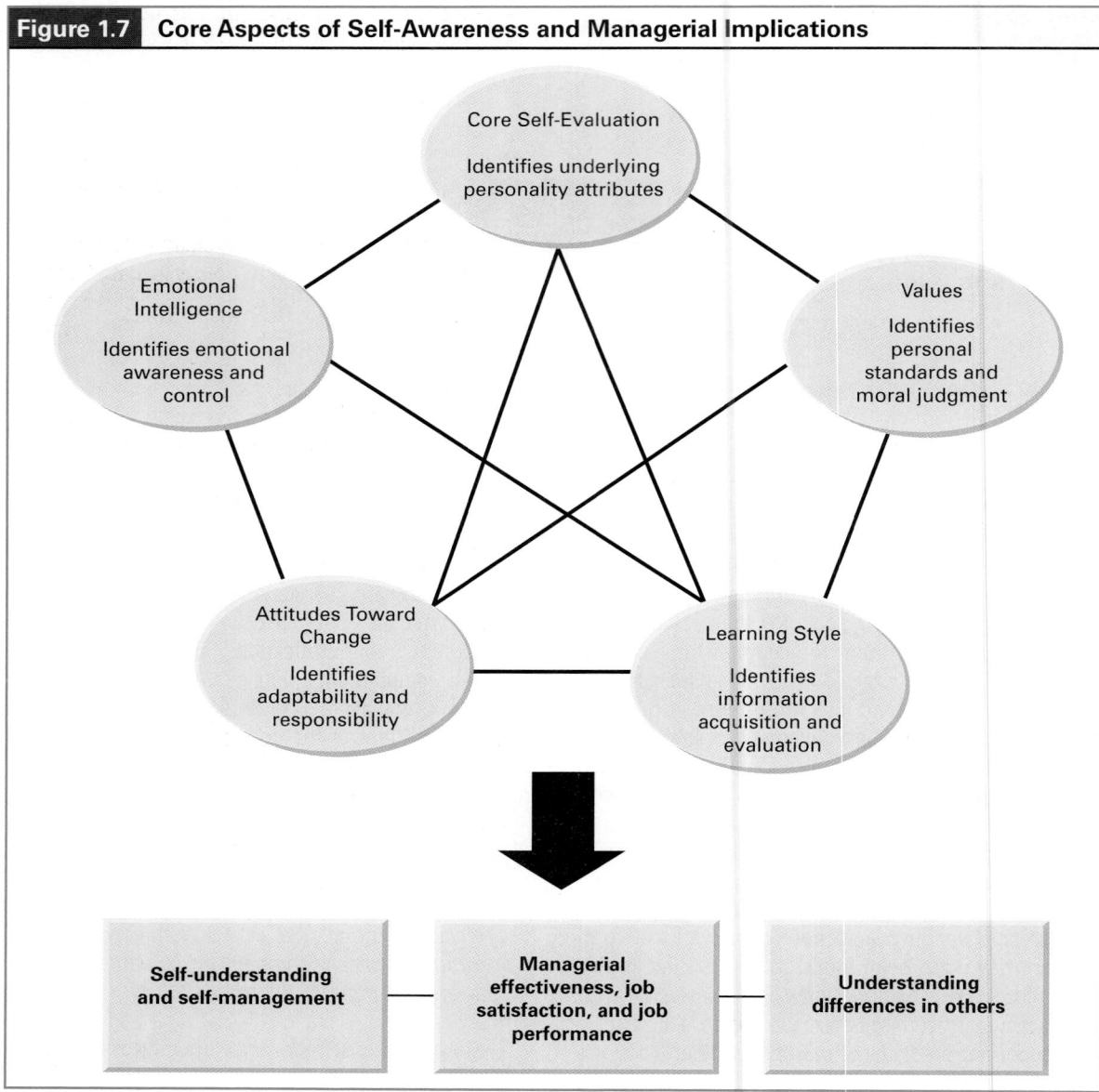

Figure 1.7 Core Aspects of Self-Awareness and Managerial Implications

Core Self-Evaluation

Identifies underlying personality attributes

Emotional Intelligence

Identifies emotional awareness and control

Values

Identifies personal standards and moral judgment

Attitudes Toward Change

Identifies adaptability and responsibility

Learning Style

Identifies information acquisition and evaluation

Self-understanding and self-management

Managerial effectiveness, job satisfaction, and job performance

Understanding differences in others

Most of the following chapters relate to skills in interpersonal or group interaction, but successful skill development in those areas will occur only if individuals have a firm foundation in self-awareness. In fact, there is an interesting paradox in human behavior: we can know others only by knowing ourselves, but we can know ourselves only by knowing others. Our knowledge of others, and therefore our ability to manage or interact successfully with them, comes from relating what we see in them to our own experience. If we are not self-aware, we have no basis for knowing certain things about others. Self-recognition leads to recognition and understanding of others. As Harris (1981) puts it:

Nothing is really personal that is not first interpersonal, beginning with the infant's shock of separation from the umbilical cord. What we know about ourselves comes only from the outside, and is interpreted by the kind of experiences we have had; and what we know about others comes only from analogy with our own network of feelings.

Behavioral Guidelines

Following are the behavioral guidelines relating to the improvement of self-awareness. These guidelines will be helpful to you as you engage in practice and application activities designed to improve your self-awareness.

1. Identify your sensitive line. Determine what information about yourself you are most likely to defend against.

2. Use the seven dimensions of national culture to diagnose differences between your own values orientation and that of individuals from other cultures, age categories, or ethnic groups.

3. Identify a comprehensive, consistent, and universal set of principles on which you will base your behavior. Identify the most important terminal and instrumental values that guide your decisions.

4. Expand your learning style, your tolerance of ambiguity, and your internal locus of control by increasing your exposure to new information and engaging in different kinds of activities than you are used to. Seek ways to expand and broaden yourself.

5. Enhance your emotional intelligence by consciously monitoring your own emotional responses and by practicing the diagnosis of others' emotional cues.

6. Develop a healthy core self-evaluation and positive self-regard by consciously capitalizing on your personal strengths, and by highlighting and building on your successful accomplishments.

7. Engage in honest self-disclosure with someone who is close to you and accepting of you. Check out aspects of yourself that you are not sure of.

8. Keep a journal, and make time regularly to engage in self-analysis. Balance life's activities with some time for self-renewal.

LEARNING

CASES INVOLVING SELF-AWARENESS

Communist Prison Camp

To understand the development of increased self-awareness, it is helpful to consider the opposite process, that is, the destruction of self-awareness. Understanding the growth process is often enhanced by understanding the deterioration process. Hence, in the case below, a process of psychological self-destruction is described as it occurred among prisoners of war during the Korean War. Consider how these processes that destroy self-awareness can be reversed to create greater self-awareness. The setting is a prisoner-of-war camp managed by the Communist Chinese.

In such prisons the total regimen, consisting of physical privation, prolonged interrogation, total isolation from former relationships and sources of information, detailed regimentation of all daily activities, and deliberate humiliation and degradation, was geared to producing a confession of alleged crimes, the assumption of a penitent role, and the adoption of a Communist frame of reference. The prisoner was not informed what his crimes were, nor was he permitted to evade the issue by making up a false confession. Instead, what the prisoner learned he must do was reevaluate his past from the point of view of the Communists and recognize that most of his former attitudes and behavior were actually criminal from this point of view. For example, a priest who had dispensed food to needy peasants in his mission church had to "recognize" that he was actually a tool of imperialism and was using his missionary activities as cover for exploitation of the peasants. Even worse, he had used food as blackmail to accomplish his aims.

The key technique used by the Communists to produce social alienation to a degree sufficient to allow such redefinition and reevaluation to occur was to put the prisoner into a cell with four or more other prisoners who were somewhat more advanced in their "thought reform" than he. Such a cell usually had one leader who was responsible to the prison authorities, and the progress of the whole cell was made contingent upon the progress of the least "reformed" member. This condition meant in practice that four or more cell members devoted all their energies to getting their least "reformed" member to recognize "the truth" about himself and to confess. To accomplish this they typically swore at, harangued, beat, denounced, humiliated, reviled, and brutalized their victim 24 hours a day, sometimes for weeks or months on end. If the authorities felt that the prisoner was basically uncooperative, they manacled his hands behind his back and chained his ankles, which made him completely dependent on his cellmates for the fulfillment of his basic needs. It was this reduction to an animal-like existence in front of other humans which constituted the ultimate humiliation and led most reliably to the destruction of the prisoner's image of himself. Even in his own eyes he became something that was not worthy of the regard of his fellow man.

If, to avoid complete physical and personal destruction, the prisoner began to confess in the manner desired of him, he was usually forced to prove his sincerity by making irrevocable behavioral commitments, such as denouncing and implicating his friends and relatives in his own newly recognized crimes. Once he had done this he became further alienated from his former self, even in his own eyes, and could seek security only in a new identity and new social relationships. Aiding this process of confessing was the fact that the crimes gave the prisoner something concrete to which to attach the free-floating guilt that the accusing environment and his own humiliation usually stimulated.

A good example was the plight of the sick and wounded prisoners of war who, because of their physical confinement, were unable to escape from continual conflict with their interrogator or instructor, and who therefore often ended up forming a close relationship with him. Chinese Communist instructors often encouraged prisoners to take long walks or have informal talks with them and offered as incentives cigarettes, tea, and other rewards. If the prisoner was willing to cooperate and become a "progressive," he could join with other "progressives" in an active group life.

Within the political prison, the group cell not only provided the forces toward alienation but also offered the road to a "new self." Not only were there available among the fellow prisoners individuals with whom the prisoner could identify because of their shared plight, but once he showed any tendency to seek a new identity by truly trying to reevaluate his past, he received again a whole range of rewards, of which perhaps the most important was the interpersonal information that he was again a person worthy of respect and regard.

Source: *Schein, 1960.*

Discussion Questions

1. What specific techniques were used to bring about the destruction of self-awareness among the prisoners?
2. What opposite processes could be used to create the reverse process, that is, a strengthening of the self-concept?
3. Assume that you are charged with the orientation of a cohort of new managers in your organization. How would you help them understand their own strengths and inclinations and how they could best contribute to the firm?
4. What mechanisms do people use, and what mechanisms could the prisoners of war have used, to resist a change in their self-concepts?
5. What could be done to reform or rebuild the self-awareness of these prisoners? What can be done to help individuals without self-awareness to improve that skill?

Computerized Exam

Graduate business school students were all required to take a one-credit-hour current events course. Like other courses in the business school, the final exam was administered on a computer. From a memory bank containing 350 questions, the computer was programmed to select 40 questions for each student, flashing them on the screen one at a time. Students could take the exam any time after the course began in January, whenever they felt ready.

Unfortunately, problems arose. When the test was computerized, a "skip feature" was added to the computer program. This feature was designed so that students could pass over a question they didn't want to answer immediately. The question, theoretically, would return to the screen at a later time, simulating the way in which students skip over and then return to questions on a written exam. However, the skip feature didn't work correctly. Instead of recycling skipped questions back to the student, the computer simply threw them out. Thus, the skip feature became a way for students to avoid any questions they couldn't answer.

Another snafu in the program was that when a certain number of questions were skipped during the exam—apparently between six and ten—the computer automatically ended the test. Scores were immediately flashed to the student and recorded in the computer memory. Scores were calculated on a percentage basis, only counting the questions that the student answered. Skipped questions were not counted as correct or incorrect. Therefore, a student who answered ten questions, nine of them correctly, and skipped enough other questions to trigger the automatic computer shutoff, received a score of 90 percent.

Knowledge of the skip command apparently was widely distributed well before the end of the term. One person estimated that at least half the students knew about it. Upon review, 77 out of 139 members of the graduating class answered fewer than the required 40 questions when they took the exam. When questioned, some students said that they didn't realize that a programming error had occurred and didn't keep track of how many questions were asked in total. Others argued that "it is like filling out an income tax form. People hire accountants all the time to find loopholes that they can use. That is not illegal, even if the government doesn't advertise the loopholes. The commuter program allowed for this loophole, and we did what we did."

1. *If you were one of the students in the class:*
   a. Would you tell the instructor about the programming error before the end of the term?
   b. Report the names of the other students you knew who cheated?
   c. Admit that you cheated?

2. *If you were the instructor for the course, which of the following would you do?*
   a. Flunk the 77 students who did not complete 40 questions.
   b. Require the 77 students to retake the exam, but let them graduate.
   c. Require all 139 students to retake the course since no student reported the problem, a violation of the student ethical code.
   d. Change the computer program, but do nothing to the students.
   e. Select another alternative.

3. *What is your rationale for the decisions you made in questions 1 and 2 above? Discuss your rationale with your colleagues.*

4. *What level of values maturity is displayed? What ethical principles are applied?*

Decision Dilemmas

For each of the five scenarios below, select the choice you would make if you were in the situation.

1. A young manager in a high-technology firm was offered a position by the firm's chief competitor for almost double her salary. Her firm sought to prevent her from changing jobs, arguing that her knowledge of certain specialized manufacturing processes would give the competitor unfair advantage. Since she had acquired that knowledge through special training and unique opportunities in her current position, the firm argued that it was unethical for her to accept the competitor's offer. What should the young manager do?

   _____ Accept the offer

   _____ Reject the offer

2. A consumer advocate organization conducted a survey to determine whether Wendy's hamburgers were really any more "hot and juicy" than any other hamburgers. After testing a Big Mac, a Whopper, a Teen Burger, and a Wendy's Hot and Juicy, each hamburger brand received approximately the same number of votes for being the juiciest. The consumer group advocated that Wendy's not advertise its hamburgers to be the juiciest. The company indicated that its own tests showed different results and that the image of the burger was the important thing, not the test results. Should the advertisements cease or not?

_____ Cease to advertise

_____ Continue to advertise

3. After several profitable years, the Bob Cummings Organic Vitamin Company was made available for sale. Bob's movie and TV appearances precluded him from keeping track of a large company, and it became apparent that, if present trends continued, the company would either have to expand substantially or lose a large share of the market. Several firms were interested in purchasing the company for the asking price, but one firm was particularly aggressive. It sponsored several parties and receptions in Bob's honor; a 35-foot yacht was made available for his use during the summer; and several gifts for family members arrived during the holidays. Bob's wife questioned the propriety of these activities. Was it appropriate for Bob to accept the gifts? Should he sell to that firm?

_____ Proper to accept

_____ Not proper

_____ Should not sell

_____ Should sell

4. John Waller was hired to coach football. After two seasons, he was so successful that he was named coach of the year by UPI, *Sporting News*, and ESPN. He was also very vocal about the need to clean up cheating in college athletics, especially among competitor schools in his own conference. He heard rumors about inappropriate alumni gifts to some of his own athletes, but after confronting those involved, he received assurances that the rumors weren't true. At the beginning of the next season, however, he received conclusive evidence that seven of the starters on his team, including an All-American, had received financial benefits from a wealthy booster. What should Waller do?

_____ Kick them off the team

_____ Suspend them for several games

_____ Warn them but do nothing

5. Roger's company had been battered by competition from Asian firms. Not only were Asian products selling for less money, but their quality was substantially higher. By investing in some high-technology equipment and fostering better union–management relations, Roger was relatively certain that the quality gap could be overcome. But his overhead rate was more than 40 percent above that of the competitor firms. He reasoned that the most efficient way to lower costs would be to close one of his older plants, lay off the employees, and increase production in the newer plants. He knew just which plant would be the one to close. The trouble was, the community was dependent on that plant as its major employer and had recently invested a great deal of money for highway repair and

streetlight construction around the plant. Most of the work force were older people who had lived in the area most of their lives. It was improbable that they could obtain alternative employment in the same area. Should Roger close the plant or not?

_____ Close the plant

_____ Do not close

Discussion Questions

Form a small group and discuss the following questions regarding these five scenarios:

1. Why did you make the choices you did in each case? Justify each answer.
2. What principles or basic values for decision making did you use in each case?
3. What additional information would you need in order to be certain about your choices?
4. What circumstances might arise to make you change your mind about your decision? Could there be a different answer to each case in a different circumstance?
5. What do your answers tell you about your own emotional intelligence, values, cognitive style, attitude toward change, and core self-evaluation?

EXERCISES FOR IMPROVING SELF-AWARENESS THROUGH SELF-DISCLOSURE

Through the Looking Glass

In the nineteenth century, the concept of "looking-glass self" was developed to describe the process used by people to develop self-awareness. It means that other people serve as a looking glass for each of us. They mirror back our actions and behaviors. In turn, we form our opinions of ourselves as a result of observing and interpreting this mirroring. The best way to form accurate self-perceptions, therefore, is to share your thoughts, attitudes, feelings, actions, and plans with others. This exercise helps you do that by asking you to analyze your own styles and inclinations and then share and discuss them with others. This sharing exercise will provide insights that you haven't recognized before.

Assignment

In a group of three or four, share your scores on the Skill Assessment instruments. Determine what similarities and differences exist among you. Do systematic ethnic or gender differences exist? Now read aloud the 11 statements listed below. Each person should complete each statement, but take turns going first. The purpose of your completing the statements aloud is to help you articulate aspects of your self-awareness and to receive reactions to them from others.

1. In taking the assessment instruments, I was surprised by . . .

2. Some of my dominant characteristics captured by the instruments are . . .

3. Among my greatest strengths are . . .

4. Among my greatest weaknesses are . . .

5. The time I felt most successful was . . .

6. The time I felt least competent was . . .

7. My three highest priorities in life are . . .

8. The way in which I differ most from other people is . . .

9. I get along best with people who . . .

10. From what the others in this group have shared, here is an impression I have formed about each:

Diagnosing Managerial Characteristics

This exercise is designed to give you practice in diagnosing differences in others' styles and inclinations. Being aware of the styles, values, and attitudes of others will help you manage them more effectively. Below are brief descriptions of four successful managers. They differ in values, learning styles, orientations toward change, and interpersonal orientation. After reading the scenarios, form small groups to discuss the questions that follow.

Michael Dell

Michael Dell is the kind of guy people either love or hate. He is worth more than $13 billion, loves to go to work each day, and is as likely to tear a computer apart and put it back together again as to read a financial report. More than 15 years after he started assembling computers in his dorm room, Michael is still fascinated with the hardware. Despite his billionaire status, "if anyone believes that he is not the chief technologist in this company, they are naive," says Robert McFarland, vice president of Dell's federal sales group. Although Dell Computer is the quintessential lean-and-mean company, Michael does not play the part of the whipcracker. After recently receiving an award from the Austin, Texas, Chamber of Commerce, for example, Michael and his wife stayed long after the program was over to chat with everyone who wanted to meet him. He has been described as shy and quiet and not inclined toward public hyperbole. "Michael has a genuine shyness . . . he is a genuinely mild-mannered, low-key person who was very focused on reaching his objectives," says Brian Fawkes, a former Dell employee. Admittedly, Dell has experienced several missteps and losses, but Michael has been unafraid to learn from missteps. "Michael makes mistakes. He just never makes the same mistake twice," says Mark Tebbe, president of a firm Dell recently acquired.

SOURCE: *Adapted from Darrow, 1998.*

Patrick M. Byrne

As president and chairman of Overstock.com in Salt Lake City, Utah, Byrne was a Marshall Scholar who received his PhD in philosophy from Stanford University. His management style, personality, and core values are illustrated in his interview with *Fast Company*: "Learning philosophy has been useful in teaching me how to get to the heart of things—to be able to deconstruct what the real issues are. People think we're endless debaters, but what we're really doing is refining concepts in order to reach agreement. With negotiations, instead of trying to fight someone on every one of the issues, most of the time it turns out he cares about a whole bunch of things that you don't care about. Make those trade-offs, and he'll think you're being too generous when in fact you're just giving him the sleeves off your vest. Ultimately, philosophy is about values, and that definitely has its place in business. I consider myself a far outsider to Wall Street. There's a whole lot of obfuscation involved. In August, I spoke out on how the Wall Street system was corrupt and how the financial press was co-opted. Because of it I got called a buffoon and wacky; then a lot of lies came out about my being gay, taking cocaine, and hiring a stripper. That's sort of the fifth-grade level we're operating on. It doesn't bother me. When you decide to stand for things, you have to be prepared to face criticism, mockery, and derision."

SOURCE: Adapted from Fast Company, 2005.

Maurice Blanks

When Maurice started architecture school, one of the professors said that only 25 percent of the students would make it. Sure enough, Maurice dropped out in his forties after operating his own office in Chicago. He moved to Minneapolis to devote himself full time to Blu Dot, a company he helped create. His discussion about architecture reveals a great deal about his personal attributes. "Architecture is about keeping track of thousands of pieces of information and making sure they're all covered in the design. The implications of failure are pretty high if you don't—people could get hurt. Therefore, you learn that you must be very efficient with information and organization, which naturally translates to running the day-to-day operations of a company. It's funny how the word 'sell' is never used in architecture school, but to me the critiques were kind of informal lessons in sales. For exams, you'd present your work to a jury—professors, peers, local architects, and so on. Their job was to shell you; your job was to defend yourself. It's pretty brutal. Tears are not uncommon. But it taught me how to communicate ideas quickly and tailor information to an audience."

SOURCE: Adapted from Fast Company, 2005.

Gordon Bethune

Gordon Bethune has been described as the *other* earthy, exuberant, hard-drinking Texas CEO who turned around an airline that is now famous for good service, happy employees, and admirable profitability. Herb Kelleher at Southwest Airlines is the best known, but Gordon Bethune at Continental Airlines is the most successful. A high school dropout mechanic who spent years in the Navy, Gordon took over a twice-bankrupt airline in 1994 and led it from a $960 million loss to more than $600 million profit in five years. Even from his early years as a Navy mechanic, Gordon was known as superb motivator of people and a network builder. "He had a web of relationships that enabled him to get whatever he needed," said a former commanding officer. At Continental, Gordon turned around a culture where morale was in the pits, on-time performance was abysmal, and everything from the planes to the meals were a mess. Part of the turnaround was due to Gordon's personal attention to employees—for example, he attends the graduation ceremonies of every new class of flight attendants, hands out candy canes to employees during the Christmas season, shows up regularly at employee birthday parties, and holds a monthly open house in his office to encourage employee communication. "Anybody who's worked here longer than two months can recognize Gordon," says a baggage handler in Newark. When he walks through an airport, employees wave and call out his name. Whereas Gordon is known as an irreverent and wild guy, he demands precision and standardized levels of service in every place in the company. When he discovered slightly larger white coffee cups in a Houston airport lounge, for example, he was told that they were needed to fit the new coffee maker. He demanded that the coffee maker be changed so that the standard blue cups could be used. No exceptions."

SOURCE: *Adapted from O'Reilly, 1999.*

Discussion Questions

1. Rank these individuals from highest to lowest in terms of:
   - Emotional intelligence
   - Values maturity
   - Tolerance of ambiguity
   - Core self-evaluation

   Justify your evaluations in a discussion with your colleagues and compare your scores.

2. What is your prediction about the dominant learning styles of each of these individuals? What data do you use as evidence?

3. If you were assigned to hire a senior manager for your organization and this was your candidate pool, what questions would you ask to identify these individuals':
   - Learning styles
   - Values orientations
   - Orientation toward change
   - Core self-evaluation

   Which one of these people would you hire if you wanted a CEO for your company? Why?

4. Assume that each of these individuals were members of your team. What would be the greatest strengths and weaknesses of your team? What kinds of attributes would you want to add to your team to ensure that it was optimally heterogeneous?

An Exercise for Identifying Aspects of Personal Culture: A Learning Plan and Autobiography

The purpose of this exercise is to assist you in articulating your key goals and aspirations as well as identifying a personal learning plan to facilitate your success. Because continuous learning is so important for you to succeed throughout your life, we want to help you identify some specific ambitions and to develop a set of procedures to help you reach your potential.

This exercise is accomplished in three steps:

Step 1: (Aspirations): Write an autobiographical story that might appear in *Fortune Magazine, Fast Company*, or the *Wall Street Journal* on this date 15 years from now. This story should identify your notable accomplishments and your newsworthy successes. What will you have achieved that will fulfill your dreams? What outcomes would make you ecstatically happy? What legacy do you want to be known for?

Step 2: (Characteristics): Review your scores on the Pre-assessment instruments. Using Figure 1.8, identify the extent to which you are satisfied with your scores on these various

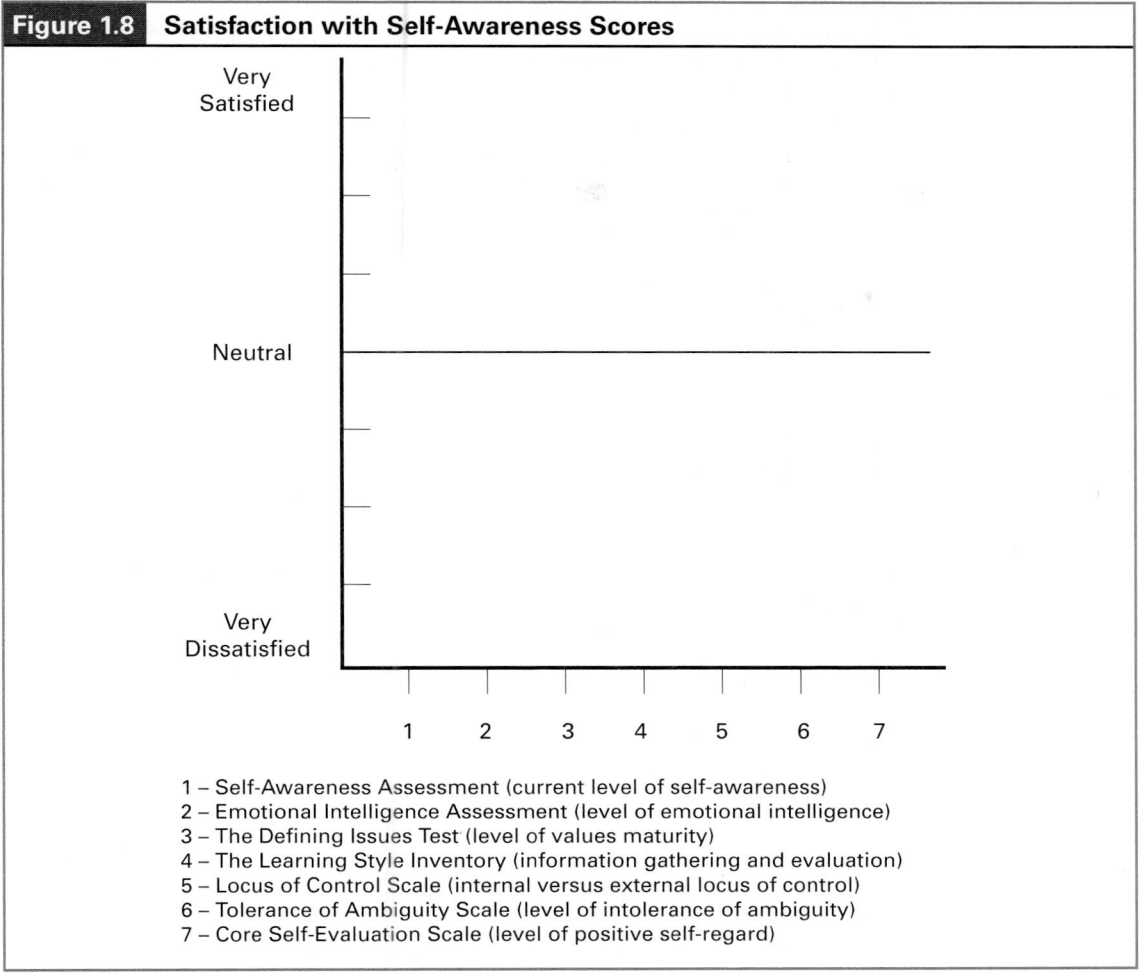

Figure 1.8 **Satisfaction with Self-Awareness Scores**

Very
Satisfied

Neutral

Very
Dissatisfied

1   2   3   4   5   6   7

1 – Self-Awareness Assessment (current level of self-awareness)
2 – Emotional Intelligence Assessment (level of emotional intelligence)
3 – The Defining Issues Test (level of values maturity)
4 – The Learning Style Inventory (information gathering and evaluation)
5 – Locus of Control Scale (internal versus external locus of control)
6 – Tolerance of Ambiguity Scale (level of intolerance of ambiguity)
7 – Core Self-Evaluation Scale (level of positive self-regard)

instruments. The vertical axis in the figure ranges from Very Satisfied to Very Dissatisfied. The horizontal axis identifies the five areas of self-awareness being assessed in this chapter. For each of the seven instruments, plot your satisfaction level with how you scored. By joining those points together, you will have created a Self-Awareness Satisfaction Profile. This will help you highlight areas in which you will want to improve.

Based on that plot, identify your distinctive competencies, your strengths, and your unique attributes. What are the values, styles, and attitudes that will assist you in achieving the aspirations you have identified in Step 1?

Step 3: (Feedback): Interview a member of your family or someone who knows you very well. Ask that person to describe what they see as your unique strengths and capabilities. What does he or she see for you in your future? Include the following questions in your interview:

- Who do you know that you admire a great deal because of their success in life? What capabilities and attributes do they possess?

- Who do you know that has failed to achieve their potential? What do you see as the most significant causes of their failure?

- What do you see as the distinctive and notable capabilities that I possess?

- In what areas do you think I should focus my improvement and development efforts?
- What do you see me doing in 15 years?

Step 4: (Planning): Now identify the developmental activities in which you will engage if you are to achieve your aspirations. With the insight you have gained from steps 2 and 3, identify the things you must do to help you achieve what you hope to accomplish. Consider the following activities.

- What courses will you take?
- What people will you get to know?
- In what extracurricular or life-balance activities will you engage?
- What will you read?
- What spiritual activities will be most meaningful?

This written product should be handed in to your instructor, or it should be given to a family member for safekeeping. Open and reread this document in five years to determine the extent to which you are on track.

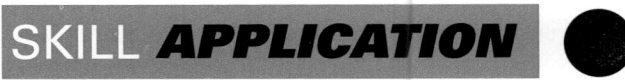
ACTIVITIES FOR DEVELOPING SELF-AWARENESS

Suggested Assignments

1. Keep a journal for at least the remainder of this course. Record significant discoveries, insights, learnings, and personal recollections, not daily activities. Write in your journal at least twice a week. Give yourself some feedback.

2. Ask someone you know well to complete the assessment instruments wherein that person rates you on each item. Compare your scores and those of this other person. Discuss differences, strengths, and areas of confusion. The goal is to help you increase your self-awareness by getting a picture of yourself from the standpoint of someone else.

3. Write down the comprehensive, consistent, and universal principles that guide your behavior under all circumstances. What core principles will you rarely violate?

4. After completing the personal assessment instruments and discussing their implications with someone else, write an essay responding to the following four questions: (1) Who am I? (2) What are my main strengths and weaknesses? (3) What do I want to achieve in my life? (4) What legacy do I want to leave?

5. Spend an evening with a close friend or relative discussing your emotional intelligence, values, learning style, attitude toward change, and core self-evaluation. You may want to have that person complete the instruments, giving his or her impressions of you, so you can compare and contrast your scores. Discuss implications for your future and for your relationship.

6. Teach someone else the value of self-awareness in managerial success and explain the relevance of emotional intelligence, values maturity, learning style, attitudes toward change, and core self-evaluation. Describe the experience in your journal.

Application Plan and Evaluation

The intent of this exercise is to help you apply this cluster of skills in a real-life, out-of-class setting. Now that you have become familiar with the behavioral guidelines that form the

APPLICATION

basis of effective skill performance, you will improve most by trying out those guidelines in an everyday context. Unlike a classroom activity, in which feedback is immediate and others can assist you with their evaluations, this skill application activity is one you must accomplish and evaluate on your own. There are two parts to this activity. Part 1 helps prepare you to apply the skill. Part 2 helps you evaluate and improve on your experience. Be sure to write down answers to each item. Don't short-circuit the process by skipping steps.

Part 1. Planning

1. Write down the two or three aspects of this skill that are most important to you. These may be areas of weakness, areas you most want to improve, or areas that are most salient to a problem you face right now. Identify the specific aspects of this skill that you want to apply.

2. Now identify the setting or the situation in which you will apply this skill. Establish a plan for performance by actually writing down a description of the situation. Who else will be involved? When will you do it? Where will it be done?

    Circumstances:
    Who else?
    When?
    Where?

3. Identify the specific behaviors in which you will engage to apply this skill. Operationalize your skill performance.

4. What are the indicators of successful performance? How will you know you have been effective? What will indicate you have performed competently?

Part 2. Evaluation

5. After you have completed your implementation, record the results. What happened? How successful were you? What was the effect on others?

6. How can you improve? What modifications can you make next time? What will you do differently in a similar situation in the future?

7. Looking back on your whole skill practice and application experience, what have you learned? What has been surprising? In what ways might this experience help you in the long term?

SCORING KEYS AND COMPARISON DATA

Self-Awareness Assessment

Scoring Key

SKILL AREA	ITEMS	ASSESSMENT	
		PRE-	POST-
Self-disclosure and openness to feedback	1, 2, 3, 9, 11	_____	_____
Awareness of own values, emotional intelligence, change orientation, and core self-evaluation	4, 5, 6, 7, 8, 10	_____	_____
	Total Score	_____	_____

Comparison Data (N = 1,500 students)

Compare your scores to three standards:
1. The maximum possible score = 66
2. The scores of other students in the class.
3. Norm data from more than 1,500 business school students.

Pre-Test				Post-Test
51.47	=	mean	=	54.52
56 or above	=	top quartile	=	60 or above
52–55	=	second quartile	=	56–59
48–51	=	third quartile	=	51–55
47 or below	=	bottom quartile	=	50 or below

Emotional Intelligence Assessment

Scoring Key

The statements below have been reorganized according to the key dimension of emotional intelligence being assessed. The numbers next to each alternative indicate the number of points attached to that alternative. Circle which alternatives you selected, and then add up the points for these 12 items.

ITEM	ALTERNATIVE	POINTS

Emotional Awareness

1	a	10
	b	0
	c	0

EXPLANATION: Only alternative (a) indicates that you are aware of what's going on inside emotionally.

5	a	5
	b	10
	c	0

EXPLANATION: Alternative (a) may be OK if you are clear about your priorities, but alternative (b) indicates that you are aware of possible alternative points of view.

9	a	0
	b	0
	c	10

EXPLANATION: Only alternative (c) indicates that you are aware of your own emotional reactions and will require compensation for the inevitable upset it will create.

Emotional Control (Balance)

2	a	0
	b	5
	c	10

EXPLANATION: Alternative (c) implies that you are confident enough to handle the situation on the spot. Alternative (b) confronts the issue but not in the presence of those affected.

6	a	10
	b	5
	c	0

EXPLANATION: Alternative (a) is honest if it is done skillfully and avoids being harsh. Alternative (b) relies on the other person getting an indirect hint.

10	a	0
	b	0
	c	10

EXPLANATION: Only alternative (c) demonstrates emotional control.

Emotional Diagnosis (Empathy)

3	a	5
	b.	10
	c	0

EXPLANATION: Alternative (a) may be appropriate in some circumstances, but alternative (b) indicates sensitivity to a possible emotional issue on the part of the other person.

7	a	10
	b	5
	c	0

EXPLANATION: Alternative (a) indicates an ability to recognize different emotions but to not let them get carried away. Alternative (b) acknowledges different emotional perspectives but may engender bad feelings or emotional casualties. Alternative (c) does not acknowledge the different emotional commitments.

11	a	0
	b	10
	c	0

EXPLANATION: Only alternative (b) empathetically acknowledges the other person's feelings.

Emotional Response

4	a	0
	b	10
	c	0

EXPLANATION: Alternatives (a) and (c) may indicate that you are not sensitive to the emotional climate of the group, and your behavior may be inappropriately.

8	a	0
	b	5
	c	10

EXPLANATION: Alternative (b) may be appropriate if it isn't a sign of narcissism, but alternative (c) is clearly an indication of emotional control.

12	a	10
	b	0
	c	5

EXPLANATION: Alternative (b) implies losing emotional control, whereas (a) indicates remaining under control.

Total _____

Comparison Data

Mean score:	70
Top quartile:	86 or higher
Second quartile:	71–85
Third quartile:	55–70
Bottom quartile:	54 or lower

The Defining Issues Test

The possibility of misusing and misinterpreting this instrument is high enough that its author, James Rest, maintains control over the scoring procedure associated with its use. Some people may interpret the results of this instrument to be an indication of inherent morality, honesty, or personal worth, none of which the instrument is intended to assess. A scoring manual may be obtained from James Rest, Minnesota Moral Research Center, Burton Hall, University of Minnesota, Minneapolis, MN 55455.

Our purpose is to help you become aware of the stage of moral development you rely on most when facing moral dilemmas. To help determine that, the following lists present the stage of moral development each statement associated with each story reflects. By looking at the four statements you selected as most important in deciding what action to take in each situation, you can determine which stage of development you use most often.

After you have done this, you should discuss which action you would take in each situation and why, and why you selected the statements you did as the most important ones to consider.

The Escaped Prisoner

1. Hasn't Mr. Thompson been good enough for such a long time to prove he isn't a bad person? (Stage 3)

2. Every time someone escapes punishment for a crime, doesn't that just encourage more crime? (Stage 4)
3. Wouldn't we be better off without prisons and the oppression our legal system? (Indicates antiauthoritarian attitudes.)
4. Has Mr. Thompson really paid his debt to society? (Stage 4)
5. Would society be failing what Mr. Thompson should fairly expect? (Stage 6)
6. What benefits would prison be apart from society, especially for a charitable man? (Nonsense alternative, designed to identify people picking high-sounding alternatives.)
7. How could anyone be so cruel and heartless as to send Mr. Thompson to prison? (Stage 3)
8. Would it be fair to all the prisoners who had to serve out their full sentences if Mr. Thompson was let off? (Stage 4)
9. Was Ms. Jones a good friend of Mr. Thompson? (Stage 3)
10. Wouldn't it be a citizen's duty to report an escaped criminal, regardless of circumstances? (Stage 4)
11. How would the will of the people and the public good best be served? (Stage 5)
12. Would going to prison do any good for Mr. Thompson or protect anybody? (Stage 5)

The Doctor's Dilemma

1. Whether the woman's family is in favor of giving her an overdose or not. (Stage 3)
2. Is the doctor obligated by the same laws as everybody else if giving her an overdose would be the same as killing her? (Stage 4)
3. Whether people would be much better off without society regimenting their lives and even their deaths. (Indicates antiauthoritarian attitudes.)
4. Whether the doctor could make it appear like an accident. (Stage 2)
5. Does the state have the right to force continued existence on those who don't want to live? (Stage 5)
6. What is the value of death prior to society's perspective on personal values? (Nonsense alternative, designed to identify people picking high-sounding alternatives.)
7. Whether the doctor has sympathy for the woman's suffering or cares more about what society might think. (Stage 3)
8. Is helping to end another's life ever a responsible act of cooperation? (Stage 6)
9. Whether only God should decide when a person's life should end. (Stage 4)
10. What values the doctor has set for himself in his own personal code of behavior. (Stage 5)
11. Can society afford to let everybody end their lives when they want to? (Stage 4)
12. Can society allow suicides or mercy killing and still protect the lives of individuals who want to live? (Stage 5)

The Newspaper

1. Is the principal more responsible to students or to the parents? (Stage 4)
2. Did the principal give his word that the newspaper could be published for a long time, or did he promise to approve the newspaper one issue at a time? (Stage 4)
3. Would the students start protesting even more if the principal stopped the newspaper? (Stage 2)
4. When the welfare of the school is threatened, does the principal have the right to give orders to students? (Stage 4)
5. Does the principal have the freedom of speech to say "no" in this case? (Nonsense alternative, designed to identify people picking high-sounding alternatives.)

6. If the principal stopped the newspaper, would he be preventing full discussion of important problems? (Stage 5)
7. Whether the principal's order would make Rami lose faith in the principal. (Stage 3)
8. Whether Rami was loyal to his school and patriotic to his country. (Stage 3)
9. What effect would stopping the paper have on the students' education in critical thinking and judgment? (Stage 5)
10. Whether Rami was in any way violating the rights of others in publishing his own opinions. (Stage 5)
11. Whether the principal should be influenced by some angry parents when it is the principal who knows best what is going on in the school. (Stage 4)
12. Whether Rami was using the newspaper to stir up hatred and discontent. (Stage 3)

Learning Style Inventory

Scoring Key

Add your scores for each of the four categories, then plot those scores on Figure 1.4 on page 34.

LEARNING STYLE DIMENSION	1	2	3	4	5	6	7	8	9	10	11	12	TOTAL
Concrete Experience	a	c	d	a	a	c	b	d	b	b	a	b	Total CE
Reflective Observation	d	a	c	c	b	a	a	c	a	a	b	c	Total RO
Abstract Conceptualization	b	b	a	d	c	d	c	b	d	d	c	a	Total AC
Active Experimentation	c	d	b	b	d	b	d	a	c	c	d	d	Total AE

Locus of Control Scale

Scoring Key

Count up the number of items you selected from the list below:

2a	5b	9a	12b	16a	20a	23a	28b
3b	6a	10a	13b	17a	21a	25a	29a
4b	7a	11b	15b	18a	22b	26b	

Total Score _____

Comparison Data (N = 1,500 students)

Mean score:	5.19 (SD = 3.04)
Top quartile:	7 or above
Third quartile:	5–6
Second quartile:	3–4
Bottom quartile:	2 or below

SAMPLE	MEAN	SD	SOURCE
Ohio State psychology students (N=1,180)	8.29	3.97	1966
Connecticut psychology students (N=303)	9.22	3.88	1966
Peace Corps trainees (N=155)	5.95	3.96	1966
National high school students (N=1,000)	8.50	3.74	1966
Municipal administrators, Alberta, Canada (N=50)	6.24	3.31	1971
Business executives (N=71)	8.29	3.57	1980
Career military officers (N=261)	8.28	3.86	1980
Students using *Developing Management Skills*	5.19	3.04	2006

Tolerance of Ambiguity Scale

Scoring Key

High scores indicate an intolerance of ambiguity. Having high intolerance means that you tend to perceive situations as threatening rather than promising. Lack of information or uncertainty would tend to make you uncomfortable. Ambiguity arises from three primary sources: novelty, complexity, and insolubility. These three subscales are measured by the instrument.

In scoring the instrument, the *even-numbered* items must be reversed. That is, 7 becomes 1, 6 becomes 2, 5 becomes 3, 3 becomes 5, 2 becomes 6, and 1 becomes 7. After reversing the appropriate items, sum all 16 items to get your score.

ITEM	SUBSCALE	ITEM	SUBSCALE	ITEM	SUBSCALE	ITEM	SUBSCALE
1	I	5	C	9	N	13	N
2	N	6	C	10	C	14	C
3	I	7	C	11	N	15	C
4	C	8	C	12	I	16	C

N = Novelty Score (2, 9, 11, 13) _____
C = Complexity Score (4, 5, 6, 7, 8, 10, 14, 16) _____
I = Insolubility Score (1, 3, 12) _____
Total Score _____

Comparison Data (N = 1,500 students)

Mean score:	56.47
Top quartile:	63 or above
Third quartile:	57–62
Second quartile:	50–56
Bottom quartile:	49 or below

Core Self-Evaluation Scale

Scoring Key

Sum your scores for all 12 items, making certain that you reverse your scores for items 2, 4, 6, 8, 10, 12. That is, for these items, 1 becomes 5, 2 becomes 4, 4 becomes 2, and 5 becomes 1. Divide the sum by 12 to produce an average CSES score.

1. _____ I am confident I get the success I deserve in life.
2. _____ Sometimes I feel depressed. **(reverse)**
3. _____ When I try, I generally succeed.
4. _____ Sometimes when I fail I feel worthless. **(reverse)**
5. _____ I complete tasks successfully.
6. _____ Sometimes, I do not feel in control of my work. **(reverse)**
7. _____ Overall, I am satisfied with myself.
8. _____ I am filled with doubts about my competence. **(reverse)**
9. _____ I determine what will happen in my life.
10. _____ I do not feel in control of my success in my career. **(reverse)**
11. _____ I am capable of coping with most of my problems.
12. _____ There are times when things look pretty bleak and hopeless to me. **(reverse)**

Total _____
÷12 _____ (Average Score)

Comparison Data

(Compared to psychology students, business students, practicing managers)

Mean score: 3.88
Top quartile: 4.41 or above
Third quartile: 3.88 and 4.40
Second quartile: 3.35 and 3.87
Bottom quartile: 3.34 or below

Managing Personal Stress

SKILL ASSESSMENT

- Stress Management Assessment
- Time Management Assessment
- Type A Personality Inventory
- Social Readjustment Rating Scale
- Sources of Personal Stress

SKILL LEARNING

- Improving the Management of Stress and Time
- Major Elements of Stress
- Managing Stress
- Eliminating Stressors
- Developing Resiliency
- Temporary Stress-Reduction Techniques
- Summary
- Behavioral Guidelines

SKILL ANALYSIS

- The Turn of the Tide
- The Case of the Missing Time

SKILL PRACTICE

- The Small-Wins Strategy
- Life-Balance Analysis
- Deep Relaxation
- Monitoring and Managing Time

SKILL APPLICATION

- Suggested Assignments
- Application Plan and Evaluation

SCORING KEYS AND COMPARISON DATA

SKILL DEVELOPMENT OBJECTIVES

- ELIMINATE STRESSORS
- DEVELOP RESILIENCY
- COPE WITH STRESS IN THE SHORT TERM

DIAGNOSTIC SURVEYS FOR MANAGING STRESS

STRESS MANAGEMENT ASSESSMENT

Step 1: Before you read the material in this chapter, please respond to the following statements by writing a number from the rating scale below in the left-hand column (Pre-assessment). Your answers should reflect your attitudes and behavior as they are now, not as you would like them to be. Be honest. This instrument is designed to help you discover your level of competency in stress management so you can tailor your learning to your specific needs. When you have completed the survey, use the scoring key at the end of the chapter to identify the skill areas discussed in this chapter that are most important for you to master.

Step 2: After you have completed the reading and the exercises in this chapter and, ideally, as many as you can of the Skill Application assignments at the end of this chapter, cover up your first set of answers. Then respond to the same statements again, this time in the right-hand column (Post-assessment). When you have completed the survey, use the scoring key at the end of the chapter to measure your progress. If your score remains low in specific skill areas, use the behavioral guidelines at the end of the Skill Learning section to guide further practice.

Rating Scale

1 Strongly disagree
2 Disagree
3 Slightly disagree
4 Slightly agree
5 Agree
6 Strongly agree

Assessment

Pre-   Post-

When faced with stressful or time-pressured situations:

_____ _____ 1. I use effective time-management methods such as keeping track of my time, making to-do lists, and prioritizing tasks.

_____ _____ 2. I maintain a program of regular exercise for fitness.

_____ _____ 3. I maintain an open, trusting relationship with someone with whom I can share my frustrations.

_____ _____ 4. I know and practice several temporary relaxation techniques such as deep breathing and muscle relaxation.

_____ _____ 5. I frequently affirm my priorities so that less important things don't drive out more important things.

_____ _____ 6. I maintain balance in my life by pursuing a variety of interests outside of work.

_____ _____ 7. I have a close relationship with someone who serves as my mentor or advisor.

_____ _____ 8. I effectively utilize others in accomplishing work assignments.

_____ _____ 9. I encourage others to generate recommended solutions, not just questions, when they come to me with problems or issues.

_____ _____ 10. I strive to redefine problems as opportunities for improvement.

TIME MANAGEMENT ASSESSMENT

In responding to the statements below, fill in each blank with the number from the rating scale that indicates the frequency with which you do each activity. Assess your behavior as it is, not as you would like it to be. How useful this instrument will be to you depends on your ability to accurately assess your own behavior.

Please note that the *first* section of the instrument can be completed by anyone. The *second* section applies primarily to individuals currently serving in a managerial position.

Turn to the end of the chapter to find the scoring key and an interpretation of your scores.

Rating Scale

0 Never
1 Seldom
2 Sometimes
3 Usually
4 Always

Section I

_____ 1. I read selectively, skimming the material until I find what is important, then highlighting it.

_____ 2. I make a list of tasks to accomplish each day.

_____ 3. I keep everything in its proper place at work.

_____ 4. I prioritize the tasks I have to do according to their importance and urgency.

_____ 5. I concentrate on only one important task at a time, but I do multiple trivial tasks at once (such as signing letters while talking on the phone).

_____ 6. I make a list of short five- or ten-minute tasks to do.

_____ 7. I divide large projects into smaller, separate stages.

_____ 8. I identify which 20 percent of my tasks will produce 80 percent of the results.

_____ 9. I do the most important tasks at my best time during the day.

_____ 10. I have some time during each day when I can work uninterrupted.

_____ 11. I don't procrastinate. I do today what needs to be done.

_____ 12. I keep track of the use of my time with devices such as a time log.

_____ 13. I set deadlines for myself.

_____ 14. I do something productive whenever I am waiting.

_____ 15. I do redundant "busy work" at one set time during the day.

_____ 16. I finish at least one thing every day.

_____ 17. I schedule some time during the day for personal time alone (for planning, meditation, prayer, exercise).

_____ 18. I allow myself to worry about things only at one particular time during the day, not all the time.

_____ 19. I have clearly defined long-term objectives toward which I am working.

_____ 20. I continually try to find little ways to use my time more efficiently.

_____ 1. I hold routine meetings at the end of the day.

_____ 2. I hold all short meetings standing up.

_____ 3. I set a time limit at the outset of each meeting.

_____ 4. I cancel scheduled meetings that are not necessary.

_____ 5. I have a written agenda for every meeting.

_____ 6. I stick to the agenda and reach closure on each item.

_____ 7. I ensure that someone is assigned to take minutes and to watch the time in every meeting.

_____ 8. I start all meetings on time.

_____ 9. I have minutes of meetings prepared promptly after the meeting and see that follow-up occurs promptly.

_____ 10. When subordinates come to me with a problem, I ask them to suggest solutions.

_____ 11. I meet visitors to my office outside the office or in the doorway.

_____ 12. I go to subordinates' offices when feasible so that I can control when I leave.

_____ 13. I leave at least one-fourth of my day free from meetings and appointments I can't control.

_____ 14. I have someone else who can answer my calls and greet visitors at least some of the time.

_____ 15. I have one place where I can work uninterrupted.

_____ 16. I do something definite with every piece of paper I handle.

_____ 17. I keep my workplace clear of all materials except those I am working on.

_____ 18. I delegate tasks.

_____ 19. I specify the amount of personal initiative I want others to take when I assign them a task.

_____ 20. I am willing to let others get the credit for tasks they accomplish.

TYPE A PERSONALITY INVENTORY

Rate the extent to which each of the following statements is typical of you most of the time. Focus on your general way of behaving and feeling. There are no right or wrong answers. When you have finished, turn to the end of the chapter to find the scoring key and an interpretation of your scores.

Rating Scale

3 The statement is very typical of me.
2 The statement is somewhat typical of me.
1 The statement is not at all typical of me.

_____ 1. My greatest satisfaction comes from doing things better than others.

_____ 2. I tend to bring the theme of a conversation around to things I'm interested in.

_____ 3. In conversations, I frequently clench my fist, bang on the table, or pound one fist into the palm of another for emphasis.

_____ 4. I move, walk, and eat rapidly.

_____ 5. I feel as though I can accomplish more than others.

_____ 6. I feel guilty when I relax or do nothing for several hours or days.

_____ 7. It doesn't take much to get me to argue.

_____ 8. I feel impatient with the rate at which most events take place.

_____ 9. Having more than others is important to me.

_____ 10. One aspect of my life (e.g., work, family care, school) dominates all others.

_____ 11. I frequently regret not being able to control my temper.

_____ 12. I hurry the speech of others by saying "Uh huh," "Yes, yes," or by finishing their sentences for them.

_____ 13. People who avoid competition have low self-confidence.

_____ 14. To do something well, you have to concentrate on it alone and screen out all distractions.

_____ 15. I feel others' mistakes and errors cause me needless aggravation.

_____ 16. I find it intolerable to watch others perform tasks I know I can do faster.

_____ 17. Getting ahead in my job is a major personal goal.

_____ 18. I simply don't have enough time to lead a well-balanced life.

_____ 19. I take out my frustration with my own imperfections on others.

_____ 20. I frequently try to do two or more things simultaneously.

_____ 21. When I encounter a competitive person, I feel a need to challenge him or her.

_____ 22. I tend to fill up my spare time with thoughts and activities related to my work (or school or family care).

_____ 23. I am frequently upset by the unfairness of life.

_____ 24. I find it anguishing to wait in line.

Source: *Tolerance of Ambiguity Scale, S. Budner (1962), "Intolerance of Ambiguity as a Personality Variable,"* from Journal of Personality, 30: 29–50. Reprinted with the permission of Blackwell Publishing, Inc.

SOCIAL READJUSTMENT RATING SCALE*

Circle any of the following you have experienced in the past year. Using the weightings at the left, total up your score.

Mean Value	Life Event
87	1. Death of spouse/mate
79	2. Death of a close family member
78	3. Major injury/illness to self
76	4. Detention in jail or other institution
72	5. Major injury/illness to a close family member
71	6. Foreclosure on loan/mortgage
71	7. Divorce
70	8. Being a victim of crime
69	9. Being a victim of police brutality

*This assessment is not available online.

69	10. Infidelity
69	11. Experiencing domestic violence/sexual abuse
66	12. Separation or reconciliation with spouse/mate
64	13. Being fired/laid-off/unemployed
62	14. Experiencing financial problems/difficulties
61	15. Death of a close friend
59	16. Surviving a disaster
59	17. Becoming a single parent
56	18. Assuming responsibility for sick or elderly loved one
56	19. Loss of or major reduction in health insurance/benefits
56	20. Self/close family member being arrested for violating the law
53	21. Major disagreement over child support/custody/visitation
53	22. Experiencing/involved in an auto accident
53	23. Being disciplined at work/demoted
51	24. Dealing with unwanted pregnancy
50	25. Adult child moving in with parent/parent moving in with adult child
49	26. Child develops behavior or learning problem
48	27. Experienced employment discrimination/sexual harassment
47	28. Attempting to modify addictive behavior of self
46	29. Discovering/attempting to modify addictive behavior of close family member
45	30. Employer reorganization/downsizing
44	31. Dealing with infertility/miscarriage
43	32. Getting married/remarried
43	33. Changing employers/careers
42	34. Failure to obtain/qualify for a mortgage
41	35. Pregnancy of self/spouse/mate
39	36. Experiencing discrimination/harassment outside the workplace
39	37. Release from jail
38	38. Spouse/mate begins/ceases work outside the home
37	39. Major disagreement with boss/coworker
35	40. Change in residence
34	41. Finding appropriate child care/day care
33	42. Experiencing a large unexpected monetary gain
33	43. Changing positions (transfer, promotion)
33	44. Gaining a new family member
32	45. Changing work responsibilities
30	46. Child leaving home
30	47. Obtaining a home mortgage
30	48. Obtaining a major loan other than home mortgage

28	49. Retirement
26	50. Beginning/ceasing formal education
22	51. Receiving a ticket for violating the law

Total of Circled Items: _____

Source: *Social Readjustment Rating Scale, Hobson, Charles Jo, Joseph Kaen, Jane Szotek, Carol M. Nethercutt, James W. Tiedmann and Susan Wojnarowicz (1998) "Stressful Life Events: A Revision and Update of the Social Readjustment Rating Scale"* International Journal of Stress Management, *5: 1–23.*

SOURCES OF PERSONAL STRESS

1 Identify the factors that produce the most stress for you right now. What is it that creates feelings of stress in your life?

Source of Stress   Rating

2 Now give each of those stressors above a rating from 1 to 100 on the basis of how powerful each is in producing stress. Refer to the Social Readjustment Rating Scale for relative weightings of stressors. A rating of 100, for example, might be associated with the death of a spouse or child, while a rating of 10 might be associated with the overly slow driver in front of you.

3 Use these specific sources of stress as targets as you discuss and practice the stress management principles presented in the rest of the chapter.

Improving the Management of Stress and Time

Managing stress and time is one of the most crucial, yet neglected, management skills in a competent manager's repertoire. Here is why: The National Institute for Occupational Safety and the American Psychological Association estimate that the growing problem of stress on the job siphons off more than $500 billion from the nation's economy. Almost half of all adults suffer adverse health effects due to stress; the percentage of workers feeling "highly stressed" more than doubled from 1985 to 1990 and doubled again in the 1990s. In one survey, 37 percent of workers reported that their stress level at work increased last year, while less than 10 percent say their stress level decreased. Between 75 and 90 percent of all visits to primary care physicians are for stress-related complaints or disorders. An estimated one million workers are absent on an average working day because of stress-related complaints, and approximately 550,000,000 workdays are lost each year due to stress. In one major corporation, more than 60 percent of absences were found to be stress related, and in the United States as a whole, about 40 percent of worker turnover is due to job stress. Between 60 and 80 percent of industrial accidents are attributable to stress, and worker compensation claims have skyrocketed in the last two decades, with more than 90 percent of the lawsuits successful. It is estimated that businesses in the United States alone will spend more than $12 billion on stress management training and products this year (American Institute of Stress, 2000). Name any other single factor that has such a devastating and costly effect on workers, managers, and organizations.

A review of the chapters in a recent medical book on stress illustrates the wide-ranging and devastating effects of stress: stress and the cardiovascular system, stress and the respiratory system, stress and the endocrine system, stress and the gastrointestinal tract, stress and the female reproductive system, stress and reproductive hormones, stress and male reproductive functioning, stress and immunodepression, stress and neurological disorders, stress and addiction, stress and malignancy, stress and immune functions with HIV-1, stress and dental pathology, stress and pain, and stress and anxiety disorders (Hubbard & Workman,

1998). Almost no part of life or health is immune from the effects of stress.

As an illustration of the debilitating effects of job-related stress, consider the following story reported by the Associated Press.

Baltimore (AP) The job was getting to the ambulance attendant. He felt disturbed by the recurring tragedy, isolated by the long shifts. His marriage was in trouble. He was drinking too much.

One night it all blew up.

He rode in back that night. His partner drove. Their first call was for a man whose leg had been cut off by a train. His screaming and agony were horrifying, but the second call was worse. It was a child-beating. As the attendant treated the youngster's bruised body and snapped bones, he thought of his own child. His fury grew.

Immediately after leaving the child at the hospital, the attendants were sent out to help a heart attack victim seen lying in a street. When they arrived, however, they found not a cardiac patient but a drunk—a wino passed out. As they lifted the man into the ambulance, their frustration and anger came to a head. They decided to give the wino a ride he would remember.

The ambulance vaulted over railroad tracks at high speed. The driver took the corners as fast as he could, flinging the wino from side to side in the back. To the attendants, it was a joke.

Suddenly, the wino began having a real heart attack. The attendant in back leaned over the wino and started shouting. "Die, you sucker!" he yelled. "Die!"

He watched as the wino shuddered. He watched as the wino died. By the time they reached the hospital, they had their stories straight. Dead on arrival, they said. Nothing they could do.

The attendant, who must remain anonymous, talked about that night at a recent counseling session on "professional burnout"— a growing problem in high-stress jobs.

As this story graphically illustrates, stress can produce devastating effects. Personal consequences can range from inability to concentrate, anxiety, and depression to stomach disorders, low resistance to illness, and heart disease. For organizations, consequences range from absenteeism and job dissatisfaction to high accident and turnover rates.

THE ROLE OF MANAGEMENT

Amazingly, a 25-year study of employee surveys revealed that incompetent management is the largest cause of workplace stress! Three out of four surveys listed employee relationships with immediate supervisors as the worst aspect of the job. Moreover, research in psychology has found that stress not only affects workers negatively, but it also produces less visible (though equally detrimental) consequences for managers themselves (Auerbach, 1998; Staw, Sandelands, & Dutton, 1981; Weick, 1993b). For example, when managers experience stress, they tend to:

❏ Selectively perceive information and see only that which confirms their previous biases

❏ Become very intolerant of ambiguity and demanding of right answers

❏ Fixate on a single approach to a problem

❏ Overestimate how fast time is passing (hence, they often feel rushed)

❏ Adopt a short-term perspective or crisis mentality and cease to consider long-term implications

❏ Have less ability to make fine distinctions in problems, so that complexity and nuances are missed

❏ Consult and listen to others less

❏ Rely on old habits to cope with current situations

❏ Have less ability to generate creative thoughts and unique solutions to problems

Thus, not only do the results of stress negatively affect employees in the workplace, but they also drastically impede effective management behaviors such as listening, making good decisions, solving problems effectively, planning, and generating new ideas. Developing the skill of managing stress, therefore, can have significant payoffs. The ability to deal appropriately with stress not only enhances individual self-development but can also have an enormous bottom-line impact on entire organizations.

Unfortunately, most of the scientific literature on stress focuses on its consequences. Too little examines how to cope effectively with stress, and even less addresses how to prevent stress (Hepburn, McLoughlin, & Barling, 1997). We begin our discussion by presenting a framework for understanding stress and learning how to cope with it. This model explains the major types of stressors faced by managers, the primary reactions to stress, and the reasons some people experience more negative reactions than others do. The last section presents principles for managing and adapting to stress, along with specific examples and behavioral guidelines.

Major Elements of Stress

One way to understand the dynamics of stress is to think of it as the product of a "force field" (Lewin, 1951). Kurt Lewin suggested that all individuals and organizations exist in an environment filled with reinforcing or opposing forces (i.e., stresses). These forces act to stimulate or inhibit the performance desired by the individual. As illustrated in Figure 2.1, a person's level of performance in an organization results from factors that may either complement or contradict one another. Certain forces drive or motivate changes in behavior, while other forces restrain or block those changes.

According to Lewin's theory, the forces affecting individuals are normally balanced in the force field. The strength of the driving forces is exactly matched by the strength of the restraining forces. (In the figure, longer arrows indicate stronger forces.) Performance changes when the forces become imbalanced. That is, if the driving forces become stronger than the restraining forces, or more numerous or enduring, change occurs. Conversely, if restraining forces become stronger or more numerous than driving forces, change occurs in the opposite direction.

Feelings of stress are a product of certain stressors inside or outside the individual. These stressors can be thought of as driving forces in the model. That is, they exert pressure on the individual to change present levels of performance physiologically, psychologically, and interpersonally. Unrestrained, those forces can lead to pathological results (e.g., anxiety, heart disease, and mental breakdown). However, most people have developed a certain amount of resiliency or restraining forces to counter stressors and inhibit pathological results. These restraining forces include behavior patterns, psychological characteristics, and supportive social relationships. Strong restraining forces lead to low heart rates, good interpersonal relationships, emotional stability, and

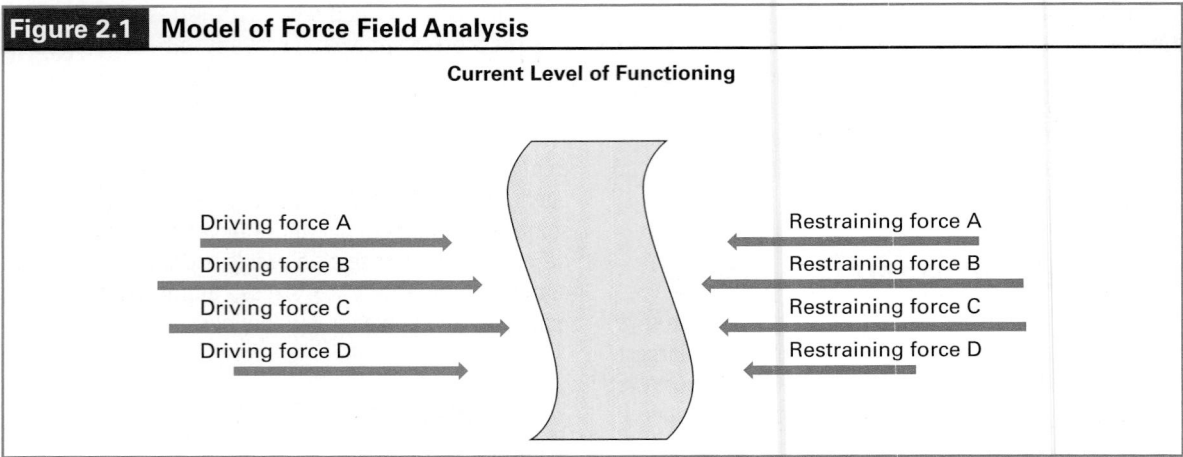

| Figure 2.1 | Model of Force Field Analysis |

Current Level of Functioning

Driving force A   Restraining force A

Driving force B   Restraining force B

Driving force C   Restraining force C

Driving force D   Restraining force D

effective stress management. An absence of restraining forces leads to the reverse.

Of course, stress produces positive as well as negative effects. In the absence of any stress, people feel completely bored and lack any inclination to act. Even when high levels of stress are experienced, equilibrium can be restored quickly if there is sufficient resiliency. In the case of the ambulance driver, for example, multiple stressors overpowered the available restraining forces and burnout occurred. Before reaching such an extreme state, however, individuals typically progress through three stages of reactions: an alarm stage, a resistance stage, and an exhaustion stage (Auerbach, 1998; Cooper, 1998; Selye, 1976).

REACTIONS TO STRESS

The **alarm stage** is characterized by acute increases in anxiety or fear if the stressor is a threat, or by increases in sorrow or depression if the stressor is a loss. A feeling of shock or confusion may result if the stressor is particularly acute. Physiologically, the individual's energy resources are mobilized and heart rate, blood pressure, and alertness increase. These reactions are largely self-correcting if the stressor is of brief duration. However, if it continues, the individual enters the **resistance stage**, in which defense mechanisms predominate and the body begins to store up excess energy.

Five types of defense mechanisms are typical of most people who experience extended levels of stress. The first is *aggression*, which involves attacking the stressor directly. It may also involve attacking oneself, other people, or even objects (e.g., whacking the computer). A second is *regression*, which is the adoption of a behavior pattern or response that was successful at some earlier

time (e.g., responding in childish ways). A third defense mechanism, *repression*, involves denial of the stressor, forgetting, or redefining the stressor (e.g., deciding that it isn't so scary after all). *Withdrawal* is a fourth defense mechanism, and it may take both psychological and physical forms. Individuals may engage in fantasy, inattention, or purposive forgetting, or they may actually escape from the situation itself. A fifth defense mechanism is *fixation*, which is persisting in a response regardless of its effectiveness (e.g., repeatedly and rapidly redialing a telephone number when it is busy).

If these defense mechanisms reduce a person's feeling of stress, negative effects such as high blood pressure, anxiety, or mental disorders are never experienced. The primary evidence that prolonged stress has occurred may simply be an increase in psychological defensiveness. However, when stress is so pronounced as to overwhelm defenses or so enduring as to outlast available energy for defensiveness, *exhaustion* may result, producing pathological consequences.

While each reaction stage may be experienced as temporarily uncomfortable, the exhaustion stage is the most dangerous one. When stressors overpower or outlast the resiliency capacities of individuals, or their ability to defend against them, chronic stress is experienced and negative personal and organizational consequences generally follow. Such pathological consequences may be manifest physiologically (e.g., heart disease), psychologically (e.g., severe depression), or interpersonally (e.g., dissolution of relationships). These changes result from the damage done to an individual for which there was no defense (e.g., psychotic reactions among prisoners of war), from an inability to defend continuously against a stressor (e.g., becoming exhausted), from an overreaction (e.g., an ulcer produced by excessive secretion of

Figure 2.2 **A General Model of Stress**

EXPERIENCING STRESS

Stressors
• Anticipatory
• Encounter
• Time
• Situational

Reactions
• Physiological
• Psychological

Resiliency
• Physical
• Psychological
• Social

MANAGING STRESS

	Enactive Strategies	Proactive Strategies	Reactive Strategies
Purpose	Eliminate stressors	Develop resiliency strategies	Learn temporary coping mechanisms
Effects	Permanent	Long term	Short term
Approach	Enactive	Proactive	Reactive
Time Required	Long time	Moderate time	Immediate

body chemicals), or from lack of self-awareness so that stress is completely unacknowledged.

Figure 2.2 identifies the major categories of stressors (driving forces) that managers experience, as well as the major attributes of resiliency (restraining forces) that inhibit the negative effects of stress. Each of these forces is discussed in some detail in this chapter, so that it will become clear how to identify stressors, how to eliminate them, how to develop more resiliency, and how to cope with stress on a temporary basis.

COPING WITH STRESS

Individuals vary in the extent to which stressors lead to pathologies and dysfunctions. Some people are labeled "hot reactors," meaning they have a predisposition to experience extremely negative reactions to stress (Adler & Hillhouse, 1996; Eliot & Breo, 1984). For others, stress is experienced more favorably. Their physical condition, personality characteristics, and social support mechanisms mediate the effects of stress and produce resiliency, or the capacity to cope effectively with stress.

In effect, resiliency serves as a form of inoculation against the effects of stress. It eliminates exhaustion. This helps explain why some athletes do better in "the big game," while others do worse. Some managers appear to be brilliant strategists when the stakes are high; others fold under the pressure.

An elaboration of the differences in dispositions toward stress reactions comes from a set of studies in which hot reactors were more likely to be women (men reacted more quickly to stress, but more factors produced stress in women); individuals with low self esteem and who viewed themselves as less attractive; and children who had been neglected, fearful, or in chaotic or broken homes (Adler, 1999). Physician Frank Trieber reported: "If you come from a family that's somehow chaotic, unstable, not cohesive, harboring grudges, very early on, it's associated later with greater blood pressure reactivity to various types of stress."

In managing stress, using a particular hierarchy of approaches has been found to be most effective (Kahn & Byosiere, 1992; Lehrer, 1996). First, the best way to manage stress is to eliminate or minimize stressors with

enactive strategies. These create, or enact, a new environment for the individual that does not contain the stressors. The second most effective approach is for individuals to enhance their overall capacity to handle stress by increasing their personal resiliency. These are called **proactive strategies** and are designed to initiate action that resists the negative effects of stress. Finally, developing short-term techniques for coping with stressors is necessary when an immediate response is required. These are **reactive strategies**; they are applied as on-the-spot remedies to reduce temporarily the effects of stress.

To understand why this hierarchy of stress management techniques is recommended, consider the physiological processes that occur when stress is encountered. Experiencing a stressor is like stepping on the accelerator pedal of an automobile: the engine "revs up." Within seconds, the body prepares for exertion by having blood pressure and heart rate rise substantially. The liver pours out glucose and calls up fat reserves to be processed into triglycerides for energy. The circulatory system diverts blood from nonessential functions, such as digestion, to the brain and muscles. The body's intent is to extinguish the stress by either "fight or flight." However, if the stressor is not eliminated as a result of these physiological responses, the elevated blood pressure begins to take its toll on arteries. Moreover, because the excess fat and glucose don't get metabolized right away, they stay in the blood vessels. Heart disease, stroke, and diabetes are common consequences. If the stress continues, minutes later a second, less severe physiological response occurs. The hypothalamus signals the pituitary to produce a substance called ACTH. This substance stimulates the adrenal cortex to produce a set of hormones known as glucocorticoids. The action of ACTH serves to stimulate a part of the brain vital to memory and learning, but an excess actually can be toxic. That's why impaired memory and lower levels of cognition occur under conditions of high stress. People actually get dumber! These same glucocorticoids also suppress parts of the immune system, so chronic stress leaves people more vulnerable to infections. Figure 2.3 summarizes these physiological consequences.

Individuals are better off if they can eliminate harmful stressors and the potentially negative effects of frequent, potent stress reactions. However, because most individuals do not have complete control over their environments or their circumstances, they can seldom eliminate all harmful stressors. Their next-best alternative, therefore, is to develop a greater capacity to withstand the negative effects of stress and to mobilize the energy generated by stressors. Developing personal resiliency that helps the body return to normal levels of activity more quickly—or that directs the "revved up engine" in a productive direction—is the next best strategy to eliminating the stressors altogether.

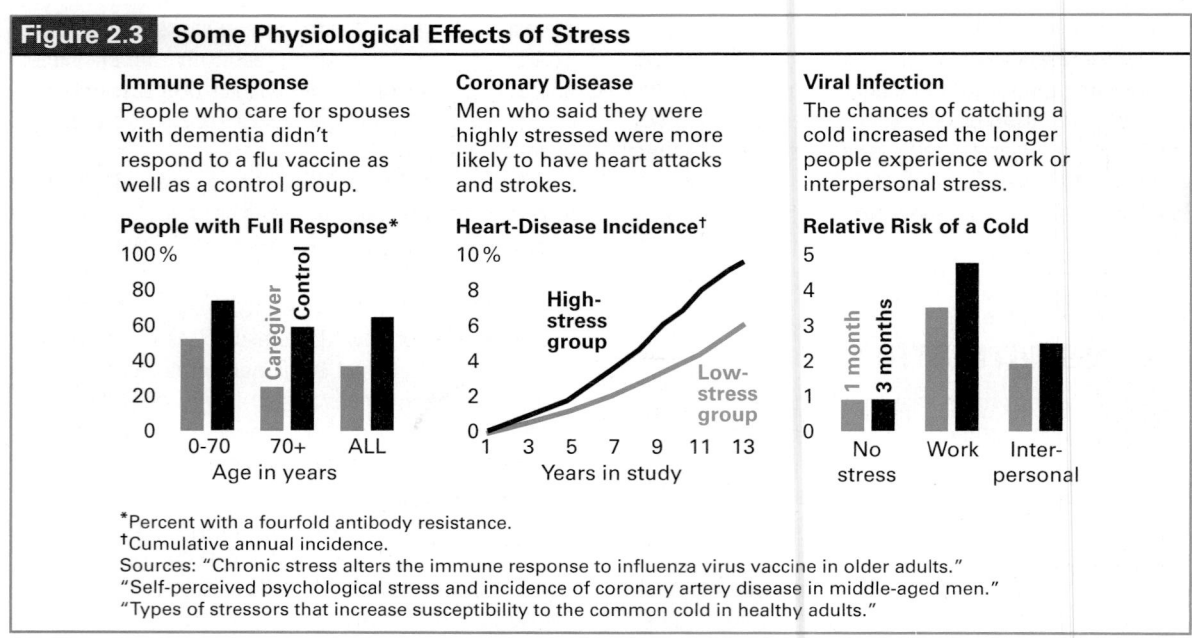

Figure 2.3   Some Physiological Effects of Stress

Immune Response
People who care for spouses with dementia didn't respond to a flu vaccine as well as a control group.

People with Full Response*

Coronary Disease
Men who said they were highly stressed were more likely to have heart attacks and strokes.

Heart-Disease Incidence†

Viral Infection
The chances of catching a cold increased the longer people experience work or interpersonal stress.

Relative Risk of a Cold

*Percent with a fourfold antibody resistance.
†Cumulative annual incidence.
Sources: "Chronic stress alters the immune response to influenza virus vaccine in older adults."
"Self-perceived psychological stress and incidence of coronary artery disease in middle-aged men."
"Types of stressors that increase susceptibility to the common cold in healthy adults."

Source: *American Institute of Stress (2000)*, http://www.stress.org/problem.htm.

Finally, on a temporary basis, individuals can respond to the revved-up state by using constructive strategies such as temporary relaxation techniques and mind control. Such techniques are designed to help the "engine" return to idle more quickly, at least for a short time.

Unfortunately, most people reverse the order of coping strategies presented above—that is, they rely first on temporary reactive methods to cope with stress because these actions can be implemented immediately. But reactive strategies also have to be repeated whenever stressors are encountered because their effects are short-lived. Moreover, some common reactive strategies, such as drinking, taking sleeping pills, or letting off steam through anger, can become habit-forming and harmful in themselves. Without more long-term strategies, relying on repetitive reactive strategies can create a vicious circle.

It takes more effort to develop proactive resiliency strategies, but the effects are more long lasting. However, resiliency strategies can take time to implement; hence, the payoff, while substantial, is not immediate. The best and most permanent strategies are those that eliminate stressors altogether. They require the longest time to implement, and they may involve complex arrangements. But because stress is purged, the payoff is enduring.

Managing Stress

In the following sections, each of the three major strategies for managing stress is discussed in detail. Each section first describes the elements of the model in Figure 2.2 and then discusses specific techniques for effectively managing that aspect of stress. Because elimination of stress is the most important stress management tool, we cover it in the most detail.

STRESSORS

Table 2.1 lists the four main types of stressors illustrated in the story of the ambulance driver. The first, **time stressors**, generally result from having too much to do in too little time. These are the most common and most pervasive sources of stress faced by managers in corporations (Kahn & Byosiere, 1992; Mintzberg, 1973; Stalk & Hout, 1990; Vinton, 1992). One reason for time stressors is that Western culture is extremely time conscious and continues to be even more so year by year. Fifteen years ago, when asked for the time, a person might have responded, "It's about 2:30." Now the

response is more likely to be, "It's 2:28," or even, "It's 15 seconds before 2:28." The emphasis on time is also evidenced by the many ways we have of talking about time. We have time, keep time, buy time, save time, mark time, spend time, sell time, waste time, kill time, pass time, give time, take time, and make time.

This fascination with time makes it an important source of stress. A variety of researchers, for example, have studied the relationships between role overload and chronic time pressures, on the one hand, and psychological and physiological dysfunction on the other (Fisher & Gitelson, 1983; French & Caplan, 1972; Kahn et al., 1964; Singh, 1993, 1998). They found significant relationships between the presence of time stressors and job dissatisfaction, tension, perceived threat, heart rate, cholesterol levels, skin resistance, and other factors.

In the story of the ambulance drivers presented earlier, time stressors were evidenced by the drivers' work overload—that is, they felt compelled to accomplish a large number of tasks in a short time and were not in control of the time available. When experienced on a daily basis, time stressors can be highly detrimental. The presence of temporary time stressors may serve as motivators for getting work done, and some individuals accomplish much more when faced with an immediate deadline than when left to work at their own pace. However, a constant state of time pressure—having too much to do and not enough time to do it—is usually harmful.

Table 2.1	Four Key Sources of Stress
Time Stressors	
• Work overload	
• Lack of control	
Encounter Stressors	
• Role conflicts	
• Issue conflicts	
• Action conflicts	
Situational Stressors	
• Unfavorable working conditions	
• Rapid change	
Anticipatory Stressors	
• Unpleasant expectations	
• Fear	

As mentioned in the first chapter on self-awareness, time stressors are experienced differently in different national cultures (Trompenaars,1996; Trompenaars & Hampden-Turner, 1998). Some cultures, for example, have an orientation toward a short time horizon where time stressors are more prevalent (e.g., Philippines, the United States, Ireland, Brazil, India, Australia). In cultures with a longer time horizon (e.g., Hong Kong, Czech Republic, Austria, Sweden, Portugal), on the other hand, the immediacy of time demands is less prevalent. Long-term planning and extended time horizons make time stressors very different. Americans are more inclined to pack a day full of short-term activities, for example, each of which has a completion point. Japanese or Polynesian people, on the other hand, may have busy days, but their orientation is less toward immediate task completion than a long-term wholeness.

Encounter stressors are those that result from interpersonal interactions. Most people have experienced the debilitating effects of a quarrel with a friend, roommate, or spouse; of trying to work with an employee or supervisor with whom there has been an interpersonal conflict; or of trying to accomplish a task in a group that is divided by lack of trust and cohesion. Each of these stressors results from some kind of conflictual interpersonal encounter. Encounter stressors are especially common for managers. They generally arise from three types of conflicts: role conflicts, in which roles performed by group members are incompatible; issue conflicts, in which disagreement exists over how to define or solve a problem; and interaction conflicts, in which individuals fail to get along well because of mutual antagonism (Balzer, Doherty, & O'Connor, 1989; Cordes & Dougherty, 1993; Fisher & Gitelson, 1983; Singh, 1998).

Our own research has revealed that encounter stressors in organizations have significant negative effects on productivity and satisfaction (Cameron, 1994; Cameron, Whetten, & Kim, 1987), and encounter stressors have been found by other researchers to be at the very heart of most organizational dysfunction (Likert, 1967; Peters, 1988; Pfeffer, 1998; Thoits, 1995). Not surprisingly, encounter stressors more frequently affect managers with responsibility for people rather than equipment. The highest levels of encounter stress exist among managers who interact frequently with other people and have responsibility for individuals in the workplace (French & Caplan, 1972; Singh, 1998). Poor relationships with others cause particularly high levels of stress. Mishra (1992) reviewed literature on interpersonal trust, for example, and reported that lack of trust among individuals not only blocks high quality communication, information sharing, decision competence, and problem-solving capabilities, but also results in high levels of personal stress.

Differences have also been discovered among national cultures with regard to encounter stressors (Trompenaars & Hampden-Turner, 1998). The cultures that are *egalitarian*, for example, and emphasize interpersonal relationships as a way to accomplish work (e.g., the United States, Norway, Ireland, and Finland) face more encounter stress as a general rule than countries with a *hierarchical* or position-based orientation (e.g., South Korea, India, Spain, and Israel). Similarly, country cultures emphasizing *affectivity* as opposed to *neutrality* (e.g., Iran and Mexico rather than China and Japan), also have a tendency toward more encounter stress due to the outward expression of emotions. Reacting personally or emotionally to issues tends to increase encounter stress in the workplace. The point to keep in mind in managing stress is that some people will experience certain kinds of stress more than others. National culture is one predictive factor. Thus, whereas encounter stress is a key for everyone, it will be more typical of some people than others.

In a national survey of workers in the United States by Northwestern National Life (1992), encounter stressors were cited as a major cause of burnout. Table 2.2 summarizes the results of that study. When workers reported not feeling free to interact socially, experienced workplace conflict, didn't talk openly to managers, felt unsupported by fellow employees, were stifled by red tape, and did not feel recognized, burnout was significantly higher than when those encounter stressors were not present. Of the 10 most significant stressors associated with burnout, 7 dealt with encounter stressors. The other 3 were situational stressors, to which we turn next.

The third category of stressors, **situational stressors**, arises from the environment in which a person lives or from an individual's circumstances. One of the most common forms of situational stress is unfavorable working conditions. For the ambulance drivers, these would include continual crises, long hours, and isolation from colleagues. In addition, wide-reaching and increasingly rapid change also creates an increase in stress. Cameron and his colleagues (1987, 1991, 1994), for example, reported that a large majority of organizations in industrialized nations have downsized or restructured since the beginning of the 1990s. Their research identified an almost universal

Table 2.2	Causes of Burnout	
WORK SITE CHARACTERISTICS		**PERCENTAGE OF EMPLOYEES REPORTING BURNOUT**
Employees are not free to talk with one another.		48%
Employees are free to talk with one another.		28%
Personal conflicts on the job are common.		46%
Personal conflicts on the job are rare.		22%
Employees are given too little control.		46%
Employees are given enough control.		25%
Staffing or expense budgets are inadequate.		45%
Staffing or expense budgets are adequate.		21%
Management and employees do not talk openly.		44%
Management and employees talk openly.		20%
Management is unsupportive of employees.		44%
Management is supportive of employees.		20%
Sick and vacation benefits are below average.		44%
Sick and vacation benefits are average or better.		26%
Employee benefits have been reduced.		42%
Employee benefits have been maintained.		24%
Dealing with red tape is common.		40%
Dealing with red tape is rare.		22%
Employees are not recognized and rewarded.		39%
Employees are recognized and rewarded.		20%

Sample size: 1,299 private-sector employees in 37 organizations.

increase in situational stress as a result. The following quotation from one employee is illustrative:

My husband and I both work for a huge conglomerate. We are carrying workloads that used to be handled by three or four employees. We come home exhausted after putting in 12-hour days, drag ourselves behind lawn mowers and vacuum cleaners at 9:00 at night, miss our children's soccer games and school plays, and barely see each other. Because of today's business climate, we feel totally helpless to make a move. Nobody dares quit a job these days. It's too risky. But the stress is killing us.

One of the most well-researched links between situational stressors and negative consequences involves rapid change, particularly the effects of changes in life events (Hobson et al., 1998; Holmes & Rahe, 1970; Wolff, Wolf, & Hare, 1950). The Social Readjustment Rating Scale (SRRS) was introduced in 1967 to track the number of changes individuals had experienced over the past 12 months. Since changes in some events were thought to be more stressful than others, a scaling method was used to assign weights to each life event. More than 3,100 studies have been published just since 1995 among a variety of cultures, age groups, and occupations using this SRRS instrument. More recently, Hobson and colleagues (1998) revised the SRRS so that the weightings of individual items have been updated. The instrument was expanded from the original 43 items in the Holmes and Rahe work to 51 items. Confirmation of the item weights was produced by 3,122 adults of various cultural, ethnic, socioeconomic, and gender backgrounds. The weightings are similar and consistent across each of these various groups. (Females have slightly higher stress scores than males, for example, but the differences are so small as to be nonmeaningful.) In other words, we can have some confidence that the revised instrument matches the situational stress experienced by most people in the twenty-first century (also see Adler & Hillhouse, 1996; Rahe, Ryman, & Ward, 1980). (You completed this revised instrument in the Assessment section.)

Statistical relationships between the amount of life-event change and physical illness and injury have been found consistently among managers, sports figures, naval personnel, and the general population. For example, on the original instrument, scores of 150 points or below resulted in a probability of less than 37 percent that a serious illness would occur in the next year, but the probability increased to about 50 percent with scores of 150–300. Those who scored over 300 on the SRRS had an 80 percent chance of serious illness (Holmes & Rahe, 1967; Kobasa, 1979). Evidence for the revised SRRS are the same. High scores are strongly associated with illness and/or injury, whereas low scores are much less likely to experience illness or injury.

Several studies have been conducted using college and high school football players to determine if life-event change is related to injury as well as to illness (Bramwell, Masuda, Wagner, & Holmes, 1975; Coddington & Troxell, 1980). Bramwell and colleagues found that college players with the lowest scores on the SRRS had a rate of injury (they missed three or more practices) of 35 percent. Those with medium scores had an injury rate of 44 percent, and those with high scores were injured at the amazing rate of 72 percent. Coddington and Troxell's results showed an injury rate five times as great for high scorers on the SRRS as for low scorers among high school athletes. Cordes and Dougherty (1993) reported findings about the extent to which daily health changes occurred as a result of life-event changes. Rather than focusing on major illness or injuries, they recorded minor symptoms such as headache, nausea, fever, backache, eyestrain, and so forth over 1,300 workdays. The results revealed high correlations between scores in life-event changes and the chronic presence of these symptoms.

We must caution, of course, that scoring high on the SRRS does not necessarily mean a person is going to become ill or be injured. A variety of coping skills and personal characteristics, to be discussed later, may counteract those tendencies. The point to be made here is that situational stressors are important factors to consider in learning to manage stress skillfully.

Anticipatory stressors, the fourth category, includes potentially disagreeable events that threaten to occur—unpleasant things that have not yet happened, but might happen. Stress results from the anticipation or fear of the event. In the case of the ambulance drivers, the constant threat of anticipating having to witness one more incident of human suffering or death served as an anticipatory stressor. In organizations that experience rapid change, restructuring, or downsizing, anticipatory stressors are also pervasive. People fear that they will lose their jobs, they fear that their friends will be ousted from the company, they become anxious about new reporting and interpersonal relationships that result from restructuring, and they worry that the future will be unpredictable and frightful. Brockner and Weisenfeld (1993) documented the negative effects of layoffs and plant closings on survivors (those who kept their jobs), and a paramount problem they identified is the presence of anticipatory stressors.

In other contexts, Schein (1960) reported that dramatic behavioral and psychological changes occurred in American prisoners in the Korean War. He identified anticipatory stressors (e.g., threat of severe punishment) as major contributors to psychological and physiological pathology among the prisoners (see the Skill Analysis section of Chapter 1, Communist Prison Camp). Stress levels in organizations that announce layoffs, mergers, or the introduction of new technologies skyrocket as employees anticipate potential job changes, layoffs, or new skills requirements (Cameron, 1998; Latack, Kinicki, & Prussia, 1995).

Anticipatory stressors need not be highly unpleasant or severe, however, to produce stress. Investigators have induced high levels of stress by telling individuals that they would experience a loud noise or a mild shock or that someone else might become uncomfortable because of their actions (Milgram, 1963). Fear of failure or fear of embarrassment in front of peers is a common anticipatory stressor. Anxieties about retirement and losing vitality during middle age have been identified by Levinson (1978), Hall (1976), and others as common stress producers as well.

Eliminating Stressors

Because eliminating **stressors** is a permanent stress reduction strategy, it is by far the most desirable. Although it is impossible, and even undesirable, for individuals to eliminate all the stressors they encounter, they can effectively eliminate those that are harmful. One way is to "enact" the environment rather than merely "react" to it. That is, individuals can actively work to create more favorable environmental circumstances in which to work and live. By so doing, they can rationally and systematically eliminate stressors.

Table 2.3	Management Strategies for Eliminating Stressors	
TYPE OF STRESSOR	**ELIMINATION STRATEGY**
Time	Effective time management
	Efficient time management
	Delegating
Encounter	Collaboration and team building
	Emotional intelligence
Situational	Work redesign
Anticipatory	Goal setting
	Small wins

Table 2.3 outlines several ways to eliminate each of the four types of stressors.

ELIMINATING TIME STRESSORS THROUGH TIME MANAGEMENT

As pointed out earlier, time is usually the greatest source of stress for managers. With a literal explosion of time management books, organizers, consultants, efficiency enhancers, and technological time savers, you'd expect most of us to be pretty good at managing our time. We certainly have all the gadgets and advice we can use. The trouble is, most of us are getting worse. Just look around you. Whom do you know who is a terrific time manager, who isn't overloaded, or who doesn't complain about being stressed because of time? Which of your acquaintances is not increasingly stressed by a perceived absence of time? We're hard-pressed to name many. How about you?

It's no surprise that time stress is escalating because of the rapidity of change and the overwhelming amounts of information that people encounter in the twenty-first century. Most of us are moving pretty fast just to keep up, and most of us feel inadequate because we find it impossible to completely keep up. The Hilton Time Value Survey found that 77 percent of people identified their top goal in the coming decade as "spending more time with family and friends." Two thirds of the respondents indicated a desire to put more emphasis on "having free time" (Davidson, 1995). The trouble is, another study showed that the average manager was required to engage in between 237 and 1,073 separate incidents a day. More than a third of managers

indicated that they don't accomplish what they set out to do each day. Time stress results. In this section we review some time management principles that can enable you to gain control over your time and organize your fragmented, chaotic environment.

Two sets of skills are important for effectively managing time and for eliminating time stressors. One set focuses on *efficiently* using time each day. The other set focuses on *effectively* using time over the long term. Because the effectiveness approach to time management serves as the foundation for the efficiency approach, we explain it first. Then we review the tools and techniques for achieving efficiency in time use.

Effective Time Management

Almost everyone suffers now and then from a pervasive feeling of time stress. Along with the information age has come an increasing sense that each of us is falling behind. For example, this week more books will be published in the United States alone than you could read in the remainder of your life. Consequently, we all have the feeling that we just can't quite keep up. Somehow, no matter how much time is available, it seems to get filled up and squeezed out. Currently, the most commonly prescribed solutions for attacking problems of time stress are to use calendars and planners, to generate to-do lists, and to learn to say "no." Although almost all of us have tried such tactics, however, almost all of us still claim to be under enormous time stress. This is not to say that calendars, lists, and saying "no" are never useful. They are, however, examples of an efficiency approach to time management rather than an effectiveness approach. In eliminating time stressors, efficiency without effectiveness is fruitless.

Managing time with an effectiveness approach means that (1) individuals spend their time on important matters, not just urgent matters; (2) people are able to distinguish clearly between what they view as important versus what they view as urgent; (3) results rather than methods are the focus of time management strategies; and (4) people have a reason not to feel guilty when they must say "no."

A number of time management experts have pointed out the usefulness of a "time management matrix" in which activities are categorized in terms of their relative importance and urgency (Covey, 1989; Lakein, 1989). *Important* activities are those that produce a desired result. They accomplish a valued end, or they achieve a meaningful purpose. *Urgent* activities are those that demand immediate attention.

They are associated with a need expressed by someone else, or they relate to an uncomfortable problem or situation that requires a solution as soon as possible. Figure 2.4 outlines this matrix and provides examples of types of activities that fit in each quadrant.

Activities such as handling employee crises or customer complaints are both urgent and important (Cell 1). A ringing telephone, the arrival of the mail, or unscheduled interruptions might be examples of urgent but potentially unimportant activities (Cell 2). Important but nonurgent activities include developmental opportunities, innovating, planning, and so on (Cell 3). Unimportant and nonurgent activities are escapes and routines that people may pursue but which produce little valuable payoff: for example, small talk, daydreaming, shuffling paper, or arguing (Cell 4).

Activities in the Important/Urgent quadrant (Cell 1) usually dominate the lives of managers. They are seen as "have to" activities that demand immediate attention. Attending a meeting, responding to a call or request, interacting with a customer, or completing a report might all legitimately be defined as Important/Urgent activities. The trouble with spending all one's time on activities in this quadrant, however, is that they all require the manager to react. They are usually controlled by someone else, and they may or may not lead to a result the manager wants to achieve.

The problem is even worse in the Unimportant/Urgent quadrant (Cell 2). Demands by others that may meet their needs but that serve only as deflections or interruptions to the manager's agenda only escalate a sense of time stress. Because they may not achieve results that are meaningful, purposeful, and valued—in other words, important—feelings of time stress will never be overcome. Experiencing overload and loss of control can be guaranteed. Managers are merely reactive. Moreover, when these time stressors are experienced over an extended period of time, people generally try to escape into Nonimportant/Nonurgent activities (Cell 4) to relieve the stress. They escape, shut out the world, or put everything on hold. However, although feelings of stress may be temporarily relieved, no long-term solutions are implemented, so time stress is never permanently reduced. That means lives are spent battling crises 95 percent of the time and escaping 5 percent of the time. A better alternative is to focus on activities in the Important/Nonurgent quadrant (Cell 3). Activities that are Important/Nonurgent might be labeled opportunities instead of problems. They are oriented toward accomplishing high-priority results. They prevent problems from occurring or build processes that eliminate problems rather than just reacting to them. Preparation, preventive maintenance, planning, building resiliency, and organizing are all "non-have-to" activities that are crucial for long-term success. Because they are not urgent, however, they often get driven out of managers' time schedules. Important/Nonurgent activities should be the top priority on the time management agenda. By ensuring that these kinds of activities get priority, the urgent problems being encountered can be reduced. Time stressors can be eliminated.

Figure 2.4   Types of Activities That Determine Time Use

		URGENCY	
		High	**Low**
IMPORTANCE	**High**	1 Crises Customer complaints	3 Developmental opportunities Innovating Planning
	Low	2 Mail Ringing telephone Unscheduled interruptions	4 Escapes Routines Arguments

One of the most difficult yet crucially important decisions you must make in managing time effectively is determining what is important and what is urgent. There are no rules for dividing all activities, demands, or opportunities into those neat categories. Problems don't come with an "Important/Nonurgent" tag attached. In fact, every problem or time demand is important to someone. But if you let others determine what is and is not important, you will never effectively manage your time.

Barry Sullivan, CEO at First Chicago, for example, reorganized the way he manages his time. Instead of leaving his appointments calendar in the control of his secretary, he now decides what activities he wants to accomplish, then he allocates specific blocks of time to work on those activities. Only after he has made these determinations does he make his calendar available to his secretary to schedule other appointments. Jan Timmer, recent CEO of Philips Electronics, assigned an auditor keep track of the way he used his time. He reported to the entire company quarterly the percent of his time he spent on key company objectives.

The question still remains, however: How can people make certain that they focus on activities that are important, not just urgent? The answer is to identify clear and specific personal priorities. In Chapter 1, Developing Self-Awareness, we pointed out how important it is for people to be aware of their own core values and to establish a set of basic principles to guide their behavior. In order to determine what is important in time management, those core values, basic principles, and personal priorities must be clearly identified. Otherwise, individuals are at the mercy of the unremitting demands that others place upon them.

In order to help you articulate clearly the basis for judging the importance of activities, consider the following questions:

1. What do I stand for? What am I willing to die (or live) for?
2. What do I care passionately about?
3. What legacy would I like to leave? What do I want to be remembered for?
4. What do I want to have accomplished 20 years from now?
5. If I could persuade everyone in the world to follow a few basic principles, what would they be?

Answering these questions can help you create a personal principles statement. A personal principles statement is an articulation of the criteria you use for evaluating what is important. Other people generally help determine what is urgent. But judging importance must be done in relation to a set of personal principles and values. Table 2.4 presents two different types of personal principles statements. They are provided as examples of the kinds of principles statements you can write for yourself. At the end of the Developing Self-Awareness chapter,

Table 2.4	Examples of Personal Principles Statements

From Mahatma Gandhi

Let then our first act every morning be to make the following resolve for the day:

- I shall not fear anyone on earth.
- I shall fear only God.
- I shall not bear ill will toward anyone.
- I shall not submit to injustice from anyone.
- I shall conquer untruth by truth.
- And in resisting untruth I shall put up with all suffering.

From William Rolfe Kerr

Prime Personal and Professional Principles:

- Succeed at home first.
- Seek and merit Divine help.
- Never compromise with honesty.
- Remember the people involved.
- Plan tomorrow today.
- Develop one new proficiency a year.
- Attain visibility by productivity.
- Hustle while I wait.
- Facilitate the success of my colleagues.
- Pursue excellence in all my endeavors.
- Be sincere and gentle yet decisive.
- Be a creative and innovative person.
- Don't fear mistakes.
- Concentrate all abilities on the task at hand.
- Obtain the counsel of others.
- Defend those who are absent.
- Listen twice as much as I speak.
- Be orderly in work and person.
- Maintain a positive attitude and sense of humor.

we urged you to take time to develop a statement of your own basic principles. These are the criteria upon which you judge activities to be important. Without such a statement, it is unlikely that you will be able to overcome the tyranny of urgent time demands.

Basing time management on core principles that serve to judge the importance of activities is also the key to being able to say "no" without feeling guilty. When you have decided what it is that you care about passionately, what it is you most want to accomplish, and what legacy you want to leave, you can more easily say "no" to activities that aren't congruent with those principles. We are always saying "no" to something anyway. But usually we are saying "no" to Important/Nonurgent activities (Cell 3) that are most congruent with our personal objectives or missions. People who experience the most time stress are those who allow others to generate their personal principles statement for them through their demands for time. Clarifying your core principles and making them public not only helps make them more powerful, but it also provides a basis for saying "no" without feeling guilty. You can opt for prevention, planning, personal development, and continuous improvement, knowing that these Important/Nonurgent activities will help eliminate and prevent the problems that create time stress. Effectiveness in time management, then, means that you accomplish what you *want* to accomplish with your time. How you achieve those accomplishments relates to efficiency of time use, to which we now turn.

Efficient Time Management

In addition to approaching time management from the point of view of effectiveness (i.e., aligning time use with core personal principles), it is also important to adopt an efficiency point of view (i.e., accomplishing more by reducing wasted time). Many techniques are available to help managers utilize more efficiently the time they have each day.

One way to enhance efficient time use is to be alert to your own tendencies to use time inefficiently. The list of propositions in Table 2.5 shows general

Table 2.5	Typical Patterns of Time Use

- We do what we like to do before we do what we don't like to do.
- We do the things we know how to do faster than the things we do not know how to do.
- We do the things that are easiest before things that are difficult.
- We do things that require a little time before things that require a lot of time.
- We do things for which the resources are available.
- We do things that are scheduled (e.g., meetings) before nonscheduled things.
- We sometimes do things that are planned before things that are unplanned.
- We respond to demands from others before demands from ourselves.
- We do things that are urgent before things that are important.
- We readily respond to crises and to emergencies.
- We do interesting things before uninteresting things.
- We do things that advance our personal objectives or that are politically expedient.
- We wait until a deadline before we really get moving.
- We do things that provide the most immediate closure.
- We respond on the basis of who wants it.
- We respond on the basis of the consequences to us of doing or not doing something.
- We tackle small jobs before large jobs.
- We work on things in the order of arrival.
- We work on the basis of the squeaky-wheel principle (the squeaky wheel gets the grease).
- We work on the basis of consequences to the group.

patterns of behavior for most individuals in their use of time. In many situations, these tendencies may represent appropriate responses. In others, however, they can get in the way of efficient time management and increase time stressors unless individuals are aware of them and their possible consequences.

For example, if we do things that are planned before things that are unplanned, some important tasks may never get done unless consciously scheduled. Because many people have a tendency to do things that are urgent before things that are important, they may find themselves saying "no" to important things in order to attend to urgent things, thereby perpetuating feelings of overload. If we do the things that are easiest before the things that are difficult, our time may be taken up dealing with mundane and easy-to-resolve issues while difficult but important problems go unresolved.

To help you identify your own time management practices, and to help you determine the efficiency with which you use your time, we included in the Assessment section an instrument to help you diagnose your time management competency: The Time Management Survey. The first part of that survey applies to everyone in daily life. The second part is most applicable to individuals who have managed or worked in an organization. The scoring information at the end of the chapter will show you how well you manage your time compared to others. The rules set forth below correspond to the item numbers in the assessment survey.

The Time Management Survey lists guidelines or techniques that have been derived from research on the management of time. Whereas one kind of time stressor is having too much time available (i.e., boredom), that is not usually the one facing managers and students. The rules in this survey, therefore, relate to the opposite problem, that is, having too little time available due to an overloaded schedule.

Of course, no individual can or should implement all of these time management techniques at once. The amount of time spent trying to implement all the techniques would be so overwhelming that time stressors would only increase. Therefore, it is best to incorporate just a few of these techniques at a time into your everyday life. Implement those hints first that will lead to the most improvement in your use of time. Saving just 10 percent more time or using an extra 30 minutes a day more wisely can produce astounding results over months and years. Saving 30 minutes per day is the equivalent of one full year over a 48-year work life. That's one full year's time, nonstop, without sleep or eating! Effective time management, then, not only

helps a person accomplish more in a typical work day but also helps eliminate feelings of stress and overload that are so detrimental to personal accomplishment and satisfaction.

What follows is a brief discussion of these 40 techniques. The first 20 are applicable to anyone in all aspects of life; the remaining relate more directly to managers and the management role.

Rule 1 Read selectively. This applies mainly to individuals who find themselves with too much material they must read such as mail, magazines, newspapers, books, brochures, instructions, and so on. Except when you read for relaxation or pleasure, most reading should be done the way you read a newspaper, that is, skim most of it, but stop to read what seems most important. Even the most important articles don't need a thorough reading because important points are generally at the beginnings of paragraphs or sections. Furthermore, if you underline or highlight what you find important, you can review it quickly when you need to.

Rule 2 Make a list of things to accomplish today. Focus on what you want to achieve, not just on what you want to do. This is a commonsense rule that implies that you need to do some advance planning each day and not rely solely on your memory. (It also suggests that you should have only one list, not multiple lists on multiple scraps of paper.)

Rule 3 Have a place for everything and keep everything in its place. Letting things get out of place robs you of time in two ways: you need more time to find something when you need it, and you are tempted to interrupt the task you are doing to do something else. For example, if material for several projects is scattered on top of your desk, you will be continually tempted to switch from one project to another as you shift your eyes or move the papers.

Rule 4 Prioritize your tasks. Each day you should focus first on important tasks and then deal with urgent tasks. During World War II, with an overwhelming number of tasks to perform, General Dwight D. Eisenhower successfully managed his time by following rule 4 strictly. He focused his attention rigorously on important matters that only he could resolve, while leaving urgent, but less important matters to be dealt with by subordinates.

Rule 5 Do one important thing at a time but several trivial things simultaneously. You can accomplish a lot by doing more than one thing at a time when tasks are routine, trivial, or require little thought. This rule allows managers to get rid of multiple trivial tasks in less time (e.g., signing letters while talking on the phone). However, take a cue from great flight attendants, retail clerks, or food servers: give one important item, or person, all your attention.

Rule 6   Make a list of some 5- or 10-minute discretionary tasks. This helps use the small bits of time almost everyone has during his or her day (waiting for something to begin, between meetings or events, talking on the telephone, etc.). Beware, however, of spending all your time doing these small discretionary tasks while letting high-priority items go unattended.

Rule 7   Divide up large projects. This helps you avoid feeling overwhelmed by large, important, urgent tasks. Feeling that a task is too big to accomplish contributes to a feeling of overload and leads to procrastination.

Rule 8   Determine the critical 20 percent of your tasks. Pareto's law states that only 20 percent of the work produces 80 percent of the results. Therefore, it is important to analyze which tasks make up the most important 20 percent and spend the bulk of your time on those.

Rule 9   Save your best time for important matters. Time spent on trivial tasks should not be your "best time." Do routine work when your energy level is low, your mind is not sharp, or you aren't on top of things. Reserve your high-energy time for accomplishing the most important and urgent tasks. Many of us are often like puppets whose strings are being pulled by a crowd of unknown and unorganized people. Don't let others interrupt your best time with unwanted demands. You, not others, should control your best time.

Rule 10   Reserve some time during the day when others don't have access to you. Use this time to accomplish Important/Nonurgent tasks, or spend it just thinking. This might be the time before others in the household get up, after everyone else is in bed, or at a location where no one else comes. The point is to avoid being in the line of fire all day, every day, without personal control over your time.

Rule 11   Don't procrastinate. If you do certain tasks promptly, they will require less time and effort than if you put them off. Of course, you must guard against spending all your time on trivial, immediate concerns that crowd out more important tasks. The line between procrastination and time wasting is a fine one, but don't get in the habit of deciding that "I'll get to this later."

Rule 12   Keep track of your time. This is one of the best time management strategies. It is impossible to improve your management of time or decrease time stressors unless you know how you spend your time.

You should keep time logs in short enough intervals to capture the essential activities, but not so short that they create a recording burden. Try keeping track of what you do every 30 minutes or hour. Parts of the Skill Practice and Skill Application sections suggest that you keep a time log for at least two weeks. Eliminate activities that don't help you accomplish your desired outcomes, or your statement of personal principles.

Rule 13   Set deadlines. This helps improve your efficient use of time. Work always expands to fill the time available, so if you don't specify a termination time, tasks tend to continue longer than they need to.

Rule 14   Do something productive while waiting. It has been estimated that up to 20 percent of an average person's time is spent in waiting. During such time, try reading, planning, preparing, rehearsing, reviewing, outlining, or doing other things that help you accomplish your work.

Rule 15   Do busy work at one set time during the day. Because it is natural to let simple tasks drive out difficult tasks (see Table 2.5), specify a certain period of time to do busy work. Refusing to answer mail or read the newspaper until a specified time, for example, can help ensure that those activities don't supersede priority time.

Rule 16   Reach closure on at least one thing every day. Reaching the end of a day with nothing completely finished (even a 10-minute task) serves to increase a sense of overload and time stress. Finishing a task, on the other hand, produces a sense of relief and releases stress.

Rule 17   Schedule some personal time. You need some time when no interruptions will occur, when you can get off the "fast track" for awhile and be alone. This time should be used to plan, prioritize, take stock, pray, meditate, or just relax. Among other advantages, personal time also helps you maintain self-awareness.

Rule 18   Don't worry about anything on a continuing basis. Allow yourself to worry only at a specified time and avoid dwelling on a worrisome issue at other times. This keeps your mind free and your energy focused on the task at hand. It may seem difficult, but controlling your worry time will do wonders to make your time use more efficient and relieve your stress.

Rule 19   Write down long-term objectives. This helps you maintain consistency in activities and tasks. You can be efficient and organized but still accomplish nothing unless you have a clear direction in mind. Writing down your long-term objectives helps make them real and lets them constantly serve as reminders.

Rule 20   Be on the alert for ways to improve your management of time. Read a list of time management hints periodically. All of us need reminding, and it will help make continuous improvement in your time use a part of your lifestyle.

Efficient Time Management for Managers

The second list of rules encompasses the major activities in which managers engage at work. The first nine rules deal with conducting meetings, since managers report that approximately 70 percent of their time is spent in meetings (Cooper & Davidson, 1982; Mintzberg, 1973).

Rule 1   Hold routine meetings at the end of the day. Energy and creativity levels are highest early in the day and shouldn't be wasted on trivial matters. Furthermore, an automatic deadline—quitting time—will set a time limit on the meeting.

Rule 2   Hold short meetings standing up. This guarantees that meetings will be kept short. Getting comfortable helps prolong meetings.

Rule 3   Set a time limit. This establishes an expectation of when the meeting should end and creates pressure to conform to a time boundary. Set such limits at the beginning of every meeting and appointment.

Rule 4   Cancel meetings once in a while. Meetings should be held only if they are needed. If the agenda isn't full or isn't going to help you achieve your objectives, cancel it. This way, meetings that are held will be more productive and more time efficient. (Plus, people get the idea that the meeting really will accomplish something—a rare outcome.)

Rules 5, 6, and 7   Have agendas, stick to them, and keep track of time. These rules help people prepare for a meeting, stick to the subject, and remain work oriented. Many things will be handled outside of meetings if they have to appear on the agenda to be discussed. You can set a verbal agenda at the beginning of even impromptu meetings (i.e., "Here is what I want to cover in this meeting"). Keeping a record of the meeting ensures that assignments are not forgotten, that follow-up and accountability occur, and that everyone is clear about expectations. Keeping track of the time motivates people to be efficient and conscious of ending at the stated time.

Rule 8   Start meetings on time. This helps guarantee that people will arrive on time. (Some managers set meetings for odd times, such as 10:13 A.M., to make attendees

time conscious.) Starting on time rewards people who arrive on time rather than waiting for laggards.

Rule 9   Prepare minutes of the meeting and follow up. This practice keeps items from appearing again in a meeting without having been resolved. It also creates the expectation that accountability for accomplishments is expected and that some work should be done outside the meeting. Commitments and expectations made public through minutes are more likely to be fulfilled.

Rule 10   Insist that subordinates suggest solutions to problems. This rule is discussed in the Empowering and Delegating chapter (Chapter 8). The purpose of this rule is to eliminate the tendency toward upward delegation, that is, for your subordinates to delegate difficult problems back to you. They do this by sharing the problem and asking for your ideas and solutions rather than recommending solutions. It is more efficient to choose among alternatives devised by subordinates than to generate your own.

Rule 11   Meet visitors in the doorway. This practice helps you maintain control of your time by controlling the use of your office space. It is easier to keep a meeting short if you are standing in the doorway rather than sitting in your office.

Rule 12   Go to subordinates' offices for brief meetings. This is useful if it is practical. The advantage is that it helps you control the length of a meeting by being free to leave when you choose. Of course, if you spend a great deal of time traveling between subordinates' offices, the rule is not practical.

Rule 13   Don't overschedule the day. You should stay in control of at least some of your time each workday. Others' meetings and demands can undermine the control you have over your schedules unless you make an effort to maintain it. This doesn't mean that you can create large chunks of time when you're free. But good time managers take the initiative for, rather than responding to, schedule requirements.

Rule 14   Have someone else answer telephone calls and scan e-mail. Not being a slave to the telephone provides you with a buffer from interruptions for at least some part of the day. Having someone else scan e-mail helps eliminate the nonimportant items that can be eliminated or require perfunctory replies.

Rule 15   Have a place to work uninterrupted. This helps guarantee that when a deadline is near, you can concentrate on your task and concentrate uninterrupted. Trying to get your mind focused once more on a task or project after interruptions wastes a lot of time. "Mental gearing up" is wasteful if required repeatedly.

Rule 16 Do something definite with every piece of paperwork handled. This keeps you from shuffling the same items over and over. Not infrequently, "doing something definite" with a piece of paper means throwing it away.

Rule 17 Keep the workplace clean. This minimizes distractions and reduces the time it takes to find things.

Rules 18, 19, and 20 Delegate work, identify the amount of initiative recipients should take with the tasks they are assigned, and give others credit for their success. These rules all relate to effective delegation, a key time management technique. These last three rules are also discussed in the Empowering and Delegating chapter.

Remember that these techniques for managing time are a means to an end, not the end itself. If trying to implement techniques creates more rather than less stress, they should not be applied. However, research has indicated that managers who use these kinds of techniques have better control of their time, accomplish more, have better relations with subordinates, and eliminate many of the time stressors most managers ordinarily encounter (Davidson, 1995; Lehrer, 1996; Turkington, 1998). Remember that saving just 30 minutes a day amounts to one full year of free time during your working lifetime. That's 8,760 hours of free time! You will find that as you select a few of these hints to apply in your own life, the efficiency of your time use will improve and your time stress will decrease.

Most time management techniques involve single individuals changing their own work habits or behaviors by themselves. Greater effectiveness and efficiency in time use occurs because individuals decide to institute personal changes; the behavior of other people is not involved. However, effective time management must often take into account the behavior of others, because that behavior may tend to inhibit or enhance effective time use. For this reason, effective time management sometimes requires the application of other skills discussed in this book. The Empowering and Delegating chapter provides principles for efficient time management by involving other people in task accomplishment. The Motivating Employees chapter explains how to help others be more effective and efficient in their own work. The Communicating Supportively chapter identifies ways in which interpersonal relationships can be strengthened, thus relieving stressors resulting from interpersonal conflicts. It is to these encounter stressors that we now turn.

ELIMINATING ENCOUNTER STRESSORS THROUGH COLLABORATION AND EMOTIONAL INTELLIGENCE

We pointed out earlier that dissatisfying relationships with others, particularly with a direct manager or supervisor, are prime causes of job stress among workers. These encounter stressors result directly from abrasive, conflictual, nonfulfilling relationships. Even though work is going smoothly, when encounter stress is present, everything else seems wrong. It is difficult to maintain positive energy when you are fighting or at odds with someone, or when feelings of acceptance and amiability aren't typical of your important relationships at work.

Collaboration

One important factor that helps eliminate encounter stress is membership in a stable, closely-knit group or community. When people feel a part of a group, or accepted by someone else, stress is relieved. For example, it was discovered 35 years ago by Dr. Stewart Wolf that in the town of Roseto, Pennsylvania, residents were completely free from heart disease and other stress-related illnesses. He suspected that their protection sprang from the town's uncommon social cohesion and stability. The town's population consisted entirely of descendants of Italians who had moved there 100 years ago from Roseto, Italy. Few married outside the community, the firstborn was always named after a grandparent, conspicuous consumption and displays of superiority were avoided, and social support among community members was a way of life.

Wolf predicted that residents would begin to display the same level of stress-related illnesses as the rest of the country if the modern world intruded. It did, and they did. By the mid-1970s, residents in Roseto had Cadillacs, ranch-style homes, mixed marriages, new names, competition with one another, and a rate of coronary disease the same as any other town's (Farnham, 1991). They had ceased to be a cohesive, collaborative clan and instead had become a community of selfishness and exclusivity. Self-centeredness, it was discovered, was dangerous to health.

The most dramatic psychological discovery resulting from the Vietnam and the Persian Gulf wars related to the strength associated with small, primary work teams. In Vietnam, unlike the Persian Gulf, teams of soldiers did not stay together and did not form the strong bonds that occurred in the Persian Gulf War. The constant injection of new personnel into squadrons, and the constant transfer of soldiers from one location to another, made soldiers feel isolated, without loyalty, and vulnerable to stress-related illnesses. In the Persian Gulf War, by contrast, soldiers were kept in the same unit throughout the campaign, brought home together, and given lots of time to debrief together after the battle. Using a closely knit group to provide interpretation of, and social support for, behavior was found to be the most powerful deterrent to postbattle trauma. David Marlowe, chief of psychiatry at Walter Reed Army Institute of Research, indicated that "Squad members are encouraged to use travel time en route home from a war zone to talk about their battlefield experience. It helps them detoxify. That's why we brought them back in groups from Desert Storm. Epistemologically, we know it works" (Farnham, 1991).

Developing collaborative, clan-like relationships with others is a powerful deterrent to encounter stress. One way of developing this kind of relationship is by applying a concept described by Stephen Covey (1989)—an emotional bank account. Covey used this metaphor to describe the trust or feeling of security that one person develops for another. The more "deposits" made in an emotional bank account, the stronger and more resilient the relationship becomes. Conversely, too many "withdrawals" from the account weaken relationships by destroying trust, security, and confidence. "Deposits" are made through treating people with kindness, courtesy, honesty, and consistency. The emotional bank account grows when people feel they are receiving love, respect, and caring. "Withdrawals" are made by not keeping promises, not listening, not clarifying expectations, or not allowing choice. Because disrespect and autocratic rule devalue people and destroy a sense of self-worth, relationships are ruined because the account becomes overdrawn.

The more people interact, the more deposits must be made in the emotional bank account. When you see an old friend after years of absence, you can often pick up right where you left off, because the emotional bank account has not been touched. But when you interact with someone frequently, the relationship is constantly being fed or depleted. Cues from everyday interactions are interpreted as either deposits or withdrawals. When the emotional account is well stocked, mistakes, disappointments, and minor abrasions are easily forgiven and ignored. But when no reserve exists, those incidents may become creators of distrust and contention.

The commonsense prescription, therefore, is to base relationships with others on mutual trust, respect, honesty, and kindness. Make deposits into the emotional bank accounts of others. Collaborative, cohesive communities are, in the end, a product of the one-on-one relationships that people develop with each other. As Dag Hammarskjöld, former Secretary-General of the United Nations, stated: "It is more noble to give yourself completely to one individual than to labor diligently for the salvation of the masses." That is because building a strong, cohesive relationship with an individual is more powerful and can have more lasting impact than leading masses of people. Feeling trusted, respected, and loved is, in the end, what most people desire as individuals. We want to experience those feelings personally, not just as a member of a group. Therefore, because encounter stressors are almost always the products of abrasive individual relationships, they are best eliminated by building strong emotional bank accounts with others.

Social and Emotional Intelligence

As we discussed in the previous chapter, emotional intelligence is an important attribute of healthy and effective individuals. It is part of a repertoire of "intelligences" that have been identified by psychologists as predicting success in life, work, and managerial roles. As we mentioned before, emotional intelligence has become the catchall phrase that incorporates multiple intelligences—for example, practical intelligence, abstract intelligence, moral intelligence, interpersonal intelligence, spiritual intelligence, and mechanical intelligence (Gardner, 1993; Sternberg, 1997). Therefore, it is convenient to use the term *emotional intelligence* to refer to a group of noncognitive abilities and skills that people need to develop to be successful. It is clear from studies of various aspects of emotional intelligence that it is an important strategy for eliminating encounter stress. Most importantly, developing the social aspects of emotional intelligence—or *social intelligence*—helps people manage the stresses that arise from interpersonal encounters (Cantor & Kihlstrom, 1987; Goleman, 1998; Saarni, 1997).

Simply put, social intelligence refers to the ability to manage your relationships with other people. It consists of four main dimensions:

1. An accurate perception of others' emotional and behavioral responses.
2. The ability to cognitively and emotionally understand and relate to others' responses.
3. Social knowledge, or an awareness of what is appropriate social behavior.
4. Social problem solving, or the ability to manage interpersonal difficulties.

A large number of studies have confirmed that we all have multiple intelligences, the most common of which is IQ, or cognitive intelligence. By and large, cognitive intelligence is beyond our control, especially after the first few years of life. It is a product of the gifts with which we were born or our genetic code. Interestingly, above a certain threshold level, the correlation between IQ and success in life (e.g., achieving high occupational positions, accumulated wealth, luminary awards, satisfaction with life, performance ratings by peers and superiors) is essentially zero. Very smart people have no greater likelihood of achieving success in life or of achieving personal happiness than people with low IQ scores (Goleman, 1998; Spencer & Spencer, 1993; Sternberg, 1997). On the other hand, social and emotional intelligence have strong positive relationships to success in life and to a reduced degree of encounter stress.

For example, in a study at Stanford University, four-year-old children were involved in activities that tested aspects of their emotional intelligence. (In one study, a marshmallow was placed in front of them, and they were given two choices: eat it now, or wait until the adult supervisor returned from running an errand, then the child would get two marshmallows.) A follow-up study with these same children 14 years later, upon graduation from high school, found that students who demonstrated more emotional intelligence (i.e., postponed gratification in the marshmallow task) were less likely to fall apart under stress, became less irritated and less stressed by interpersonally abrasive people, were more likely to accomplish their goals, and scored an average of 210 points higher on the SAT college entrance exam (Shoda, Mischel, & Peake, 1990). The IQ scores of the students did not differ significantly, but the emotional intelligence scores were considerably different. Consistent with other studies, emotional intelligence predicted success in life as well as the ability to handle encounter stress for these students.

In another study, the social and emotional intelligence scores of retail store managers was assessed and found to be the largest factor in accounting for their abilities to handle personal stress and manage socially stressful events. These abilities, in turn, predicted profits, sales, and employee satisfaction in their stores (Lusch & Serpkenci, 1990). Social and emotional intelligence predicted managerial success. When managers were able to accurately identify others' emotions and respond to them, they were found to be more successful in their personal lives as well as in their work lives (Rosenthal, 1977), and were evaluated as the most desired and competent managers (Pilling & Eroglu, 1994).

If social and emotional intelligence are so important, how does one develop them? The answer is neither simple nor simplistic. Each of the chapters in this book contains answers to that question. The skills we hope to help you develop are among the most important competencies that comprise social and emotional intelligence. In other words, by improving your abilities in the management skills covered in this book—e.g., self-awareness, problem solving, supportive communication, motivating self and others, managing conflict, empowering others, and so on—your social and emotional competence scores will increase. This is important because a national survey of workers found that employees who rated their manager as supportive and interpersonally competent had lower rates of burnout, lower stress levels, lower incidence of stress-related illnesses, higher productivity, more loyalty to their organizations, and more efficiency in work than employees with nonsupportive and interpersonally incompetent managers (NNL, 1992). Socially and emotionally intelligent managers affect the success of their employees as much as they affect their own success.

The point we are making is a simple one: eliminating encounter stressors can be effectively achieved by developing social and emotional intelligence. Fewer conflicts arise, individuals with whom we interact are more collaborative, and more effective and satisfying interpersonal relationships are developed among those with whom we work. The remaining chapters in this book provide the guidelines and techniques to help you improve your interpersonal competence and your social and emotional intelligence. After completing the book, including engaging in the practice and application exercises, you will have improved your ability to eliminate many forms of encounter stress.

ELIMINATING SITUATIONAL STRESSORS THROUGH WORK REDESIGN

Most of us would never declare that we feel less stress now than a year ago, that we have less pressure, or that we are less overloaded. We all report feeling more stress than ever at least partly because it is the "in" thing to be stressed. "I'm busier than you are" is a common theme in social conversations. On the other hand, these feelings are not without substance for most people. A third of U.S. workers are thinking of quitting their jobs, repeated downsizings have introduced new threats to the workplace, highways are increasingly congested, financial pressures are escalating, crime is pervasive, and worker compensation claims for stress-related illness are ballooning. Unfortunately, in medical treatment and time lost, stress-related illnesses are almost twice as expensive as workplace injuries because of longer recovery times, the need for psychological therapy, and so on (Farnham, 1991). Situational stressors, in other words, are costly. And they are escalating.

For decades, researchers in the area of occupational health have examined the relationship between job strain and stress-related behavioral, psychological, and physiological outcomes. Studies have focused on various components of job strain, including level of task demand (e.g., the pressure to work quickly or excessively), the level of individual control (e.g., the freedom to vary the work pace), and the level of intellectual challenge (e.g., the extent to which work is interesting).

Research in this area has challenged the common myth that job strain occurs most frequently in the executive suite (Karasek et al., 1988). A federal government study of nearly 5,000 workers found that after controlling for age, sex, race, education, and health status (measured by blood pressure and serum cholesterol level), low-level workers tended to have a higher incidence of heart disease than their bosses who were in high-status, presumably success-oriented, managerial or professional occupations. This is true because certain characteristics of lower-level positions—high demand, low control, low discretion, and low interest—tend to produce higher levels of job strain.

A review of this research suggests that the single most important contributor to stress is lack of freedom (Adler, 1989; French & Caplan, 1972; Greenberger & Stasser, 1991). In a study of administrators, engineers, and scientists at the Goddard Space Flight Center, researchers found that individuals provided with more discretion in making decisions about assigned tasks experienced fewer time stressors (e.g., role overload), situational stressors (e.g., role ambiguity), encounter stressors (e.g., interpersonal conflict), and anticipatory stressors (e.g., job-related threats). Individuals without discretion and participation experienced significantly more stress.

In response to these dynamics, Hackman, Oldham, Janson, and Purdy (1975) proposed a model of job redesign that has proved effective in reducing stress and in increasing satisfaction and productivity. A detailed discussion of this job redesign model is provided in the chapter on Motivating Employees. It consists of five aspects of work—**skill variety** (the opportunity to use multiple skills in performing work), **task identity** (the opportunity to complete a whole task), **task significance** (the opportunity to see the impact of the work being performed), **autonomy** (the opportunity to choose how and when the work will be done), and **feedback** (the opportunity to receive information on

the success of task accomplishment). Here we briefly provide an overview of the applicability of this model to reducing stress-producing job strain. To eliminate situational stressors at work:

Combine Tasks When individuals are able to work on a whole project and perform a variety of related tasks (e.g., programming all components of a computer software package), rather than being restricted to working on a single repetitive task or subcomponent of a larger task, they are more satisfied and committed. In such cases, they are able to use more skills and feel a pride of ownership in their job.

Form Identifiable Work Units Building on the first step, when teams of individuals performing related tasks are formed, individuals feel more integrated, productivity improves, and the strain associated with repetitive work is diminished. When these groups combine and coordinate their tasks, and decide internally how to complete the work, stress decreases dramatically. This formation of natural work units has received a great deal of attention in Japanese auto plants in America as workers have combined in teams to assemble an entire car from start to finish, rather than do separate tasks on an assembly line. Workers learn one another's jobs, rotate assignments, and experience a sense of completion in their work.

Establish Customer Relationships One of the most enjoyable parts of a job is seeing the consequences of one's labor. In most organizations, producers are buffered from consumers by intermediaries, such as customer relations departments and sales personnel. Eliminating those buffers allows workers to obtain firsthand information concerning customer satisfaction as well as the needs and expectations of potential customers. Stress resulting from filtered communication also is eliminated.

Increase Decision-Making Authority Managers who increase the autonomy of their subordinates to make important work decisions eliminate a major source of job stress for them. Being able to influence the what, when, and how of work increases an individual's feelings of control. Cameron, Freeman, and Mishra (1991) found a significant decrease in experienced stress in firms that were downsizing when workers were given authority to make decisions about how and when they did the extra work required of them.

Open Feedback Channels A major source of stress is not knowing what is expected and how task performance is being evaluated. As managers communicate their expectations more clearly and give timely and accurate feedback, subordinates' satisfaction and performance improve. A related form of feedback in production tasks is quality control. Firms that allow the individuals who assemble a product to test its quality, instead of shipping it off to a separate quality assurance group, find that quality increases substantially and that conflicts between production and quality control personnel are eliminated. The point is, providing more information to people on how they are doing always reduces stress.

These practices are used widely today in all types of organizations, from the Social Security Administration to General Motors. When Travelers Insurance Companies implemented a job redesign project, for example, productivity increased dramatically, absenteeism and errors fell sharply, and the amount of distractions and stresses experienced by managers decreased significantly (Hackman and Oldham, 1980; Singh 1998). In brief, work redesign can effectively eliminate situational stressors associated with the work itself.

ELIMINATING ANTICIPATORY STRESSORS THROUGH PRIORITIZING, GOAL SETTING, AND SMALL WINS

While redesigning work can help structure an environment where stressors are minimized, it is much more difficult to eliminate entirely the anticipatory stressors experienced by individuals. Stress associated with anticipating an event is more a product of psychological anxiety than current work circumstances. To eliminate that source of stress requires a change in thought processes, priorities, and plans. In the Developing Self-Awareness chapter, for example, we discussed the central place of learning style (thought processes), values (priorities), and moral maturity (personal principles) for effective management.

Earlier in this chapter, we discussed the central importance of establishing clear personal priorities, such as identifying what is to be accomplished in the long term, what cannot be compromised or sacrificed, and what lasting legacy one desires. Establishing this core value set or statement of basic personal principles helps eliminate not only time stressors but also eliminates anticipatory stress by providing clarity of direction. When traveling on an unknown road for the first time, having a road map reduces anticipatory stress. You don't have to figure out where to go or where you are by trying to identify the unknown landmarks along the roadside. In the same way, a personal principles statement acts as a map or guide. It makes clear where you will eventually end up. Fear of the unknown, or anticipatory stress, is thus eliminated.

Goal Setting

Similarly, establishing short-term plans also helps eliminate anticipatory stressors by focusing attention on immediate goal accomplishment instead of a fearful future. Short-term planning, however, implies more than just specifying a desired outcome. Several action steps are needed if short-term plans are to be achieved (Locke & Latham, 1990). The model in Figure 2.5 outlines the four-step process associated with successful short-term planning.

The first step is to identify the desired goal or objective. Most goal setting, performance appraisal, or management by objectives (MBO) programs begin with that step, but most also stop at that point. Unfortunately, this first step alone is not likely to lead to goal achievement or stress elimination. Merely establishing a goal, while helpful, is not sufficient. When people fail to achieve their goals, it is almost always because they have not followed through on steps 2, 3, and 4.

Step 2 is to identify, as specifically as possible, the activities and behaviors that will lead toward accomplishing the goal. The more difficult the goal is to accomplish, the more rigorous, numerous, and specific should be the behaviors and activities.

A friend once approached one of us with a problem. She was a wonderfully sensitive, caring, competent single woman of about 25 who was experiencing a high degree of anticipatory stress because of her size. She weighed well over 350 pounds, but she had experienced great difficulty losing weight over the last several years. She was afraid of both the health consequences and the social consequences of not being able to reduce her weight. With the monitoring of a physician, she set a goal, or short-term plan, to lose 100 pounds in the next 12 months. Because it was to be such a difficult goal to reach, however, she asked us for help in achieving her ambitious objective. We first identified a dozen or so specific actions and guidelines that would facilitate the attainment of the goal: for example, never shop alone nor without a menu, never carry more than 50 cents in change (in order to avoid the temptation to buy a doughnut), exercise with friends each day at 5:30 P.M., arise each morning at 7:00 A.M. and eat a specified breakfast with a friend, forgo watching TV to reduce the temptation to snack, and go to bed by 10:30 P.M. The behaviors were rigid, but the goal was so difficult that they were

Figure 2.5   A Model for Short-Term Planning and Goal Setting

1
Establish a goal

2
Specify actions
and
behavioral requirements

3
Generate accountability
and
reporting mechanisms

4
Identify criteria of success
and a reward

necessary to ensure progress. In each case, these specific behaviors could be seen as having a direct effect on the ultimate goal of losing 100 pounds.

Step 3 involves establishing accountability and reporting mechanisms. If no one else will ever know if the goal was achieved, chances are it will not be. The principle at the foundation of this step is: "Make it more difficult to stay the same than to change." This is done by involving others in ensuring adherence to the plan, establishing a social support network to obtain encouragement from others, and instituting penalties for nonconformance. In addition to announcing to coworkers, friends, and a church group that she would lose the 100 pounds, for example, our friend had her doctor register her for a hospital stay at the end of the 12-month period. If she did not achieve the goal on her own, she was to go on an intravenous feeding schedule in the hospital to lose the weight, at a cost of over $250 per day. Because of her public commitments, her self-imposed penalties, and the potential high medical expenses, it became more uncomfortable and costly not to succeed than to accomplish the goal.

Step 4 involves establishing an evaluation and reward system. This means identifying the evidence that the goal has been accomplished. In the case of losing weight, it's a matter of simply getting on the scales. But for improving management skills, becoming a better friend, developing more patience, establishing more effective leadership, and so on, the criteria of success are not so easily identified. That is why this step is crucial. "I'll know it when I see it" isn't good enough. Specific indicators of success, or specific changes that will have been produced when the goal is achieved, must be identified. (For example, I'll know I have become more patient when I reinterpret the situation and refuse to get upset when my spouse, or friend, is late for an appointment.) Carefully outlining these criteria serves as a motivation toward goal accomplishment by making the goal more observable and measurable.

The purpose of this short-term planning model is to eliminate anticipatory stress by establishing a focus and direction for activity. The anxiety associated with uncertainty and potentially negative events is dissipated when mental and physical energy are concentrated on purposeful activity. (By the way, the last time we saw our friend, her weight was below 200 pounds.)

Small Wins

Another principle related to eliminating anticipatory stressors is the small-wins strategy (Weick, 1984). By "small win," we mean a tiny but definite change made in a desired direction. We begin by changing something that is relatively easy to change. Then we change a second thing that is easy to change, and so on. Although each individual success may be relatively modest when considered alone, the multiple small gains eventually mount up, generating a sense of momentum that creates the impression of substantial movement toward a desired goal. This momentum helps convince our-selves, as well as others, of our ability to accomplish our objective. The fear associated with anticipatory change is eliminated as we build self-confidence through small wins. We also gain the support of others as they see progress being made.

In the case of our overweight friend, one key was to begin changing what she could change, a little at a time. Tackling the loss of 100 pounds all at once would have been too overwhelming a task. But she could change the time she shopped, the time she went to bed, and the menu she ate for breakfast. Each success-ful change generated more and more momentum that, when combined, led to the larger change that she desired. Her ultimate success was a product of multiple small wins.

Similarly, Weick (1993b) has described Poland's peaceful transition from a communistic command-type economy to a capitalistic free-enterprise economy as a product of small wins. Not only is Poland now one of the most thriving economies in eastern Europe, but it made the change to free enterprise without a single shot being fired, a single strike being called, or a single political upheaval. One reason for this is that long before the Berlin Wall fell, small groups of volunteers in Poland began to change the way they lived. They adopted a theme that went something like this: "If you value free-dom, then behave freely; if you value honesty, then speak honestly; if you desire change, then change what you can."

Polish citizens organized volunteer groups to help at local hospitals, assist the less fortunate, and clean up parks. They behaved in a way that was outside the control of the central government but reflected their free choice. Their changes were not on a large enough scale to attract attention and official opposition from the central government. But their actions nevertheless reflected their determination to behave in a free, self-determining way. They controlled what they could control, namely, their own voluntary service. These voluntary service groups spread throughout Poland, so when the transition from communism to capitalism occurred, a large number of people in Poland had already gotten used to behaving in a way consistent with self-determination. Many of these people simply stepped into positions where independent-minded managers were needed. The transition was smooth because of the multiple small wins that had previously spread throughout the country relatively unnoticed.

In summary, the rules for instituting small wins are simple: (1) identify something that is under your control; (2) change it in a way that leads toward your desired goal; (3) find another small thing to change, and change it; (4) keep track of the changes you are making; and (5) maintain the small gains you have made. Anticipatory stressors are eliminated because the fearful unknown is replaced by a focus on immediate successes.

Developing Resiliency

Now that we have examined various causes of stress and outlined a series of preventive measures, we turn our attention to a second major strategy for managing stress as shown in Figure 2.2, the development of **resiliency** to handle stress that cannot be eliminated. When stressors are long lasting or are impossible to remove, coping requires the development of personal resiliency. This is the capacity to withstand or manage the negative effects of stress, to bounce back from adversity, and to endure difficult situations (Masten & Reed, 2002). The first studies of resiliency emerged from investigations of children in abusive, alcoholic, poverty, or mentally ill parent circumstances. Some of these children surprised researchers by rising above their circumstances and developing into healthy, well-functioning adolescents and adults. They were referred to as highly resilient individuals (Masten & Reed, 2002).

We all differ widely in our ability to cope with stress. Some individuals seem to crumble under pres-sure, while others appear to thrive. A major predictor of which individuals cope well with stress and which do not is the amount of resiliency that they have developed. Two categories of factors explain differ-ences in resiliency. One is personal factors—such as positive self-regard and core self-evaluation, good cog-nitive abilities, and talents valued by society—and the second is personal coping strategies—such as improv-ing relationships and social capital, and a reduction in risk factors such as abuse, neglect, homelessness, and crime (Masten & Reed, 2002). Several of the first set of factors were measured in Chapter 1, including aspects of personality, self-efficacy, values maturity, and so on. The second set of factors is more behavioral and can be summarized by Figure 2.6. The figure illustrates that resiliency is fostered by achieving balance in the vari-ous aspects of life.

The wheel in Figure 2.6 represents the key activi-ties that characterize most people's lives. Each seg-ment in the figure identifies an important aspect of life that must be developed in order to achieve resiliency. The most resilient individuals are those who have achieved a certain degree of **life balance**. They

Figure 2.6 | Balancing Life Activities

Ideal Level of Development

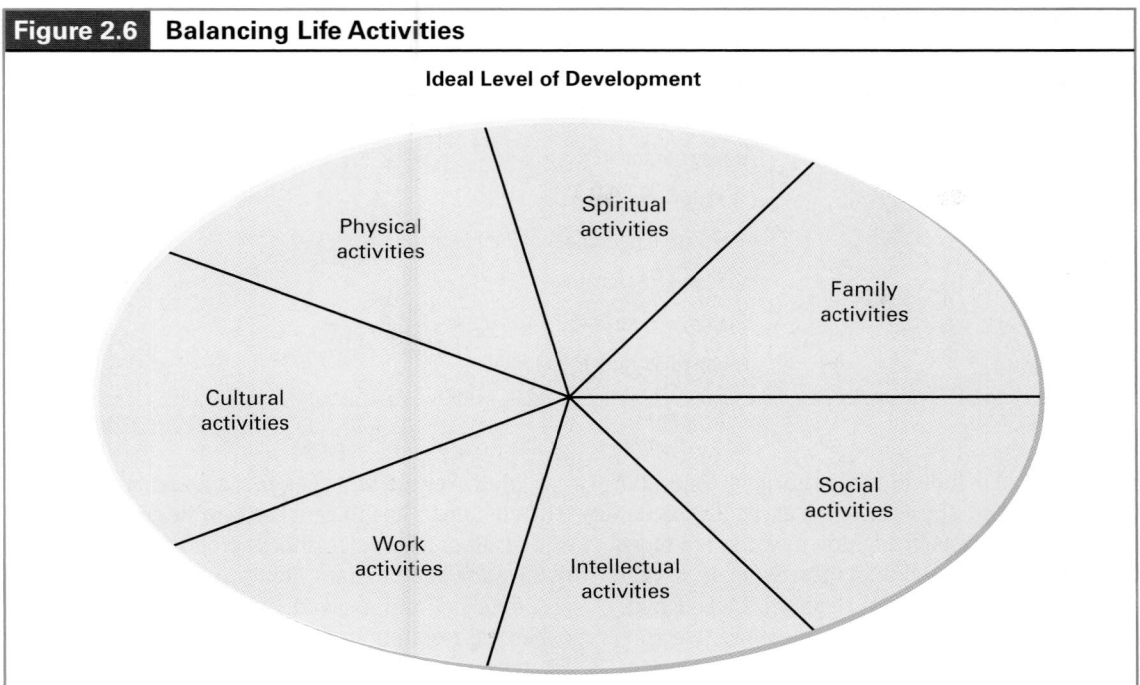

actively engage in activities in each segment of the circle so that they achieve a degree of balance in their lives. For example, assume that the center of the figure represents the zero point of involvement and the outside edge of the figure represents maximum involvement. Shading in a portion of the area in each of the seven segments would represent the amount of attention paid to each area. (This exercise is included in the Skill Practice section.) Individuals who are best able to cope with stress would shade in a substantial portion of each segment, indicating they have spent time developing a variety of dimensions of their lives. The pattern of shading in this exercise, however, should also be relatively balanced. A lopsided pattern is as much an indicator of nonresiliency as not having some segments shaded at all. Overemphasizing one or two areas to the exclusion of others often creates more stress than it eliminates. Life balance is key (Lehrer, 1996; Murphy, 1996; Rostad & Long, 1996).

This prescription, of course, is counterintuitive. Generally, when we are feeling stress in one area of life, such as an overloaded work schedule, we respond by devoting more time and attention to it. While this is a natural reaction, it is counterproductive for several reasons. First, the more we concentrate exclusively on work, the more restricted and less creative we become. We lose perspective, cease to take fresh points of view,

and become overwhelmed more easily. As we shall see in the discussion of creativity in Chapter 3, many breakthroughs in problem solving come from the thought processes stimulated by unrelated activities. That is why several major corporations send senior managers on high-adventure wilderness retreats, invite thespian troupes to perform plays before the executive committee, require volunteer community service, or encourage their managers to engage in completely unrelated activities outside of work.

Second, refreshed and relaxed minds think better. A bank executive commented recently during an executive development workshop that he gradually has become convinced of the merits of taking the weekend off from work. He finds that he gets twice as much accomplished on Monday as his colleagues who have been in their offices all weekend. He encourages members of his unit to take breaks, get out of the office periodically, and make sure to use their vacation days.

Third, the cost of stress-related illness decreases markedly when employees participate in well-rounded wellness programs. A study by the Association for Fitness in Business concluded that companies receive an average return of $3 to $4 on each dollar invested in health and wellness promotion. AT&T, for example, expects to save $72 million in the next 10 years as a result of investment in wellness programs for employees.

Table 2.6	Resiliency: Moderating the Effects of Stress		
PHYSIOLOGICAL RESILIENCY	**PSYCHOLOGICAL RESILIENCY**		**SOCIAL RESILIENCY**
Cardiovascular conditioning	Balanced lifestyle		Supportive social relations
Proper diet	Hardy personality		Mentors
	• High internal control		Teamwork
	• Strong personal commitment		
	• Love of challenge		
	Small-wins strategy		
	Deep-relaxation techniques		

Well-developed individuals, who give time and attention to cultural, physical, spiritual, family, social, and intellectual activities in addition to work, are more productive and less stressed than those who are workaholics (Adler & Hillhouse, 1996; Hepburn, McLoughlin, and Barling, 1997). In this section, therefore, we concentrate on three common areas of resiliency development for managers: physical resiliency, psychological resiliency, and social resiliency. Development in each of these areas requires initiative on the part of the individual and takes a moderate amount of time to achieve. These are not activities that can be accomplished by lunchtime or by the weekend. Rather, achieving life balance and resiliency requires ongoing initiative and continuous effort. Components of resiliency are summarized in Table 2.6.

PHYSIOLOGICAL RESILIENCY

One of the most crucial aspects of resiliency development involves one's physical condition because physical condition significantly affects the ability to cope with stress. Two aspects of physical condition combine to determine physical resiliency: cardiovascular conditioning and dietary control.

Cardiovascular Conditioning

Henry Ford is reputed to have stated, "Exercise is bunk. If you are healthy, you don't need it. If you are sick, you shouldn't take it." Fortunately, American business has not taken Ford's advice; thousands of major corporations now have in-house fitness facilities. An emphasis on physical conditioning in business has resulted partly from overwhelming evidence that individuals in good physical condition are better able to cope with stressors than those in poor physical condition. Table 2.7 shows the benefits of regular physical exercise.

Mesa Petroleum experienced an annual saving of $1.6 million in health care costs for its 650 employees as a result of its physical fitness program. As a result of its Live for Life program, Johnson & Johnson lowered absenteeism and slowed the rate of health care expenses, resulting in savings of $378 per employee. Exercisers at General Electric Aircraft in Cincinnati were absent from work 45 percent fewer days than nonexercisers. Prudential Life Insurance found a 46 percent reduction in major medical expenses over five years resulting from a workplace fitness program. The Scoular Grain Company opened a fitness center for its 600 employees and reaped an annual saving in health care costs of a million dollars—$1,500 per employee. The advantages of physical conditioning, both for individuals and for companies, are irrefutable (Rostad & Long, 1996).

Three primary purposes exist for a regular exercise program: maintaining optimal weight, increasing psychological well being, and improving the cardiovascular system.

We mentioned earlier that ongoing stress tends to make us fat. Recall that excess fat is released by the body when we encounter a stressor, and when it is not expended, that fat tends to settle around our middles. The rest of our bodies may be trim, but stress creates potbellies and pear-shapes. Couple that with the sedentary life style that many people live, and we face significant health concerns. For example, an office worker burns up only about 1,200 calories during an eight-hour day. That is fewer calories than are contained in the typical lunch of a hamburger, french fries, and a milkshake. More than 90 million adults watch at least two hours of television per day (and, parenthetically, by the age of 6 children have spent more time watching television than they will spend speaking to their fathers over their entire lifetimes), so it is easy to predict the

Table 2.7	Confirmed Benefits of Regular Vigorous Exercise

- Blood pressure is lowered.
- Resting heart rate is lowered; the heart is better able to distribute blood where needed under stress.
- Cardiac output is increased; the heart is better able to distribute blood where needed under stress.
- Number of red blood cells is increased; more oxygen can be carried per quart of blood.
- Elasticity of arteries is increased.
- Triglyceride level is lowered.
- Blood cholesterol level is decreased. High-density cholesterol, which is more protective of blood vessels than low-density cholesterol, is proportionately increased.
- Adrenal secretions in response to emotional stress are lowered.
- Lactic acid is more efficiently eliminated from the muscles. (This has been associated with decreased fatigue and tension.)
- Fibrin, a protein that aids in the formation of blood clots, is decreased.
- Additional routes of blood supply are built up in the heart.

Source: *Rostad & Long, 1996. Courtesy of Edizione Posse.*

long-term physical and psychological effects. It is little wonder that almost half of adult Americans are at least 10 percent overweight and more than half report excessive levels of stress. The resulting strain on both the heart and the self-image makes overweight individuals more vulnerable to stressors.

An advantage of regular physical exercise as a resiliency development strategy is that it improves mental as well as physical outlook. It increases self-esteem. It gives individuals the energy to be more alert and attentive throughout the day. Episodes of depression are far less frequent. Exercise fosters the necessary energy to cope with the stresses of both unexpected events and dull routine. Physically active individuals are less prone to anxiety, have less illness, and miss fewer days of work (Griest et al., 1979; Murphy, 1996). Researchers have found a chemical basis for the psychological benefit of exercise: the brain releases endorphins (similar to morphine) during periods of intense physical activity. This substance numbs pain and produces a feeling of well being, sometimes referred to as "jogger's high," which is a euphoric, relaxed feeling reported by long-distance runners (Rostad & Long, 1996).

Another vital benefit of exercise is a strengthened cardiovascular system (Greenberg, 1987). The best results come from aerobic exercises that do not require more oxygen than a person can take in comfortably (as compared with all-out sprinting or long-distance swimming). This type of exercise includes brisk walking, jogging, riding a bicycle, or climbing stairs. However, the cardiovascular system is improved by exercise only when the following two conditions are met:

1. The target heart rate is sustained throughout the exercise. This rate is 60–80 percent of the heart's maximum. To figure your target rate, subtract your age in years from 220, then take 60–80 percent of that number. You should begin your exercise program at the 60-percent level and gradually increase to the 80-percent rate. To check your heart rate during your exercise, periodically monitor your heartbeat for 6 seconds and multiply by 10.
2. The exercise occurs for 20 to 30 minutes, three or four days each week. Since cardiovascular endurance decreases after 48 hours, it is important to exercise at least every other day.

Dietary Control

The adage that "You are what you eat" is sobering, especially given the fact that Americans annually consume an average of 100 pounds of refined sugar, 125 pounds of fat, 36 gallons of carbonated beverages, and 25 times more salt than the human body requires (Adler & Hillhouse, 1996). Since diet has received a great deal of attention among Americans in the past decade or so, most people are well informed about healthy foods and eating habits, but the key principles can't be repeated too often. Here are some of the key prescriptions agreed upon by most medical professionals (see Adler, 2005; Adler & Hillhouse, 1996; Hubbard & Workman, 1998).

Eat a Variety of Foods   There are approximately 40–60 nutrients you need to stay healthy. Nutritionists recommend the following balanced diet for adults each day: five or six servings of fruits and vegetables; four servings of bread or cereal; two servings of milk, cheese, or yogurt; and two servings of meat, poultry, fish, eggs, beans, or peas.

Maintain Optimal Weight   Optimal weight is best maintained through a combination of proper diet and exercise. To lose a pound in a week, you need to burn 500 more calories a day than you consume. Although there are a number of fad diets, sound and simple practices that can help individuals avoid overeating include:

❏ Start each meal with a filling, low-calorie appetizer, such as a clear broth or salad.

❏ Curb between-meal hunger pangs with large glasses of water or fruit juices.

❏ A half-hour before mealtime, eat a carbohydrate food such as two soda crackers or half a wheat bagel.

❏ Use vegetables to provide low-calorie bulk in a meal.

❏ Eat slowly. (It takes approximately 20 minutes after you begin eating for your brain to get the message that you are doing so.)

❏ Eat regularly (every three to five hours) to avoid binge eating.

❏ Eat smaller portions. Concentrate on your eating (rather than, for example, on watching TV) so you are aware of how much you've eaten.

❏ Don't eat to cope with being bored, angry, tired, or anxious. Try exercise instead.

Reduce Fat Intake   Fat is an essential nutrient, but Americans tend to eat too much of it. They get approximately 45 percent of their calories from fat, whereas a healthy diet should contain no more than about 30 percent fat. Current medical research indicates that saturated fats (those that are solid at room temperature, such as meat fat, butter, and heavy cream) tend to elevate the level of "bad" cholesterol in the blood, contributing to heart disease.

Eat More Whole Foods   These include raw or lightly steamed vegetables, fruits, whole grains and cereals, brown rice, beans, dried peas, nuts, and seeds. These are complex-carbohydrate foods that contain a mix of starch, fiber, sugar, vitamins, and minerals. Simple-carbohydrate foods to avoid are white flour, white rice, refined sugar, processed fruit products, and overcooked vegetables.

Reduce Sugar Intake   Americans get 25 percent of their calories from sugar in various forms, consuming an average of 160 pounds of sugar a year per adult. Sugar gives people a boost of energy and a feeling of restlessness. However, it also stimulates the pancreas to produce insulin, which counteracts the sugar in the blood. Sixty percent of the population have pancreases that overreact, creating feelings of irritability, depression, nausea, anxiety, and, potentially, diabetes.

Reduce Sodium Intake   Sodium is an important mineral, but Americans, on the average, consume approximately 10 times more than they need. Sodium is found in table salt (40 percent sodium), as well as many condiments, processed foods, soft drinks, and salty snacks. Consuming more than five grams a day is unwise, especially for individuals with high blood pressure.

Avoid Alcohol   Alcohol is high in calories and low in other nutrients. It also depletes the body of Vitamin B, which is important for coping with stress.

Restrict Caffeine Intake   Caffeine is a stimulant that chemically induces the fight or flight reaction. In addition, it also depletes the body's supply of Vitamin B. Although many people seek a cup of coffee or a cola drink when they are under stress, caffeine actually makes stress worse. Moreover, recent medical research links caffeine to health risks such as heart disease, hypertension, and various kinds of cancer.

Take Vitamin and Mineral Supplements   Although there is disagreement among nutritionists regarding the need for supplemental vitamins and minerals, most people don't eat a well-balanced diet on a regular basis. It is a good idea, therefore, to make sure you are getting an adequate supply of supplemental nutrients during periods of high stress. Deficiencies in the B vitamins, Vitamin C, and calcium/magnesium have been linked to stress-related symptoms such as insomnia, irritability, depression, and fatigue.

Make Eating a Relaxing Time   Take time to enjoy nutritious meals eaten in peaceful surroundings. Frequent, small meals, associated with periods of relaxation, are more beneficial than two or three large, frantic meals.

PSYCHOLOGICAL RESILIENCY

Another important moderator of the effects of stress is an individual's psychological resiliency. Individuals with certain psychological characteristics, sometimes referred to as "resilient personality types," tend to handle stress better than others. We will focus on two examples that show best the relationship between personality and vulnerability to stress: the hardy personality and the Type A personality. First we will introduce the concept of "hardiness" and use it to discuss general psychological attributes that foster resiliency. Then we will focus on three stress-prone elements of the Type A personality and outline techniques for eliminating them.

Hardiness

Psychological resiliency has recently begun to be studied much more than in the past (for example, see Gittell, Cameron, & Lim, 2006; Sutcliffe & Vogus, 2003), but one of the best sources for learning how to develop psychological resiliency remains a book that is more than two decades old. In *The Hardy Executive*, Maddi and Kobasa (1984) described three elements that characterize a hardy, or highly stress-resistant, personality. **Hardiness** results from (1) feeling in control of one's life, rather than powerless to shape external events; (2) feeling committed to and involved in what one is doing, rather than alienated from one's work and other individuals; and (3) feeling challenged by new experiences rather than viewing change as a threat to security and comfort. According to these authors, hardy individuals tend to interpret stressful situations positively and optimistically, and they respond to stress constructively. As a result, their incidence of illness and emotional dysfunction under stressful conditions is considerably below the norm.

These three concepts—control, commitment, and challenge—are central to the development of a variety of management skills, and are crucial for mitigating the harmful effects of stress (Cowley, 2000; Kobasa, 1979, 1982). As we discussed in the Developing Self-Awareness chapter, individuals who score high on internal locus of control feel that they are in charge of their own destinies. They take responsibility for their actions and feel they can neutralize negative external forces. They generally believe that stressors are the result of their personal choices rather than uncontrollable, capricious, or even malicious external forces. The belief that one can influence the course of events is central to developing high self-esteem. Self-esteem, in turn, engenders self-confidence and the optimistic

view that bad situations can be improved and that problems can be overcome. Confidence in one's own efficacy produces low fear of failure, high expectations, willingness to take risks, and persistence under adversity (Anderson, 1977; Bandura 1997; Ivancevich & Matteson, 1980; Mednick, 1982; Sorenson, 1998), all of which contribute to resiliency under stress. Holding a positive self-regard or having a high core self-evaluation score is strongly related to psychological resiliency (Judge & Bono, 2001).

Commitment implies both selection and dedication. Hardy individuals not only feel that they choose what they do, but they also strongly believe in the importance of what they do. This commitment is both internal (that is, applied to one's own activities) and external (that is, applied to a larger community). The feeling of being responsible to others is an important buffer against stress. Whereas self-esteem and a sense of purpose help provide a psychological support system for coping with stressful events, an individual's belief that others are counting on him or her to succeed and that he or she belongs to a larger community fosters psychological resiliency during stressful periods. Feeling part of a group, feeling cared about, and feeling trusted by others engender norms of cooperation and commitment and encourage constructive responses to stress (Bandura, 1997).

Hardy people also welcome challenge. They believe that change, rather than stability, is the normal and preferred mode of life. Therefore, much of the disruption associated with a stressful life event is interpreted as an opportunity for personal growth rather than as a threat to security. This mode of thinking is consistent with the Chinese word for crisis, which has two meanings: "threat" and "opportunity." Individuals who seek challenges search for new and interesting experiences and accept stress as a necessary step toward learning. Because these individuals prefer change to stability, they tend to have high tolerance for ambiguity and high resiliency under stress (Ivancevich & Ganster, 1987; Maddi & Kobasa, 1984). The three characteristics of hardy personalities—control, commitment, and challenge—have been found to be among the most powerful mitigators of the adverse consequences of stress. By contrast, a different complex of personality attributes, the so-called Type A Syndrome, is associated with reduced hardiness and higher levels of psychological stress.

The Type A Personality

A second important aspect of psychological resiliency relates to a personality pattern many individuals develop as they enter the competitive worlds of advanced education and of management. By far, the most well-known connection between personality and resiliency relates to a combination of attributes known as the **Type A personality**. For more than four decades, scientists have been aware of a link between certain personality attributes and stress-related behavioral, psychological, and physiological problems such as anxiety, deteriorating relationships, and heart disease (Friedman & Rosenman, 1974). Table 2.8 summarizes the primary attributes of Type A personalities that have emerged from the research.

The manner in which Friedman and Rosenman (both cardiologists) discovered the link between personality and heart disease is intriguing. Observing that their waiting room was becoming a bit shabby, they decided to have their chairs reupholstered. The decorator pointed out that only the front edges of the chairs were worn. The doctors suddenly realized that their patients seemed to be "on edge," literally sitting on the edges of their seats, prepared for action.

Following up their observations with intensive interviews, they noted that during interviews, many of their patients showed signs of impatience and hostility such as fidgeting, eye blinking, grimaces, rapid or explosive speech, interrupting, and filling in incomplete sentences during a pause. The opposite personality types, which they labeled Type B, appeared more relaxed, patient, and able to listen without interrupting. Over 15 percent of Friedman and Rosenman's Type A's had had heart attacks, compared to 7 percent of Type B's.

Subsequent research has found that in America about 70 percent of men and 50 percent of women exhibit Type A personality traits, such as extreme competitiveness, strong desires for achievement, haste, impatience, restlessness, hyperalertness, explosiveness of speech, tenseness of facial muscles, free-floating hostility, and so on. Rosenman suggested that anger, impatience, and competitiveness were the most debilitating factors in the Type A personality although other factors such as hostility, blaming, and feelings of urgency also have been identified as causes of continuous adrenaline secretions in the body. Regardless of the key ingredient, the Type A personality is certainly a high risk factor in maintaining personal well-being (Friedman, 1996; Siegman & Smith, 1994; William & Williams, 1998).

In one of the most extensive studies of personality effects on heart disease ever conducted, an eight-year survey of 3,400 men found that Type A individuals in the

Table 2.8	Characteristics of the Type A Personality

- Signs of personal tension, such as a clenched jaw, tight muscles, tics.
- Personal commitment to having, rather than being.
- Unawareness of the broader environment.
- Ignorance of elements outside the immediate task.
- Strong need to be an expert on a subject; otherwise, lack of involvement.
- Compulsion to compete with other Type A's rather than understand and cooperate with them.
- Speech characterized by explosive accentuation, acceleration of the last few words of a sentence, impatience when interrupted.
- Chronic sense of being in a hurry.
- Polyphasic thoughts and actions, that is, a tendency to do several things simultaneously.
- Impatience with the normal pace of events. Tendency to finish others' sentences.
- Doing everything rapidly.
- Feelings of guilt when relaxing.
- Tendency to evaluate all activities in terms of measurable results.
- Belief that Type A attributes are what lead to success.
- Frequent knee-jiggling or finger-tapping.
- Determination to win every game, even when playing with those who are less skilled or experienced.

39- to 49-year age group had approximately 6.5 times the likelihood of heart disease as Type B's. Even when factors such as cigarette smoking, parental medical history, blood pressure, and cholesterol levels were factored out, the Type A personality still accounted for a two to three times greater likelihood of heart disease. This research concluded that personality is a better predictor than physiology of cardiovascular illness (Friedman, 1996; Friedman & Rosenman, 1974). Ironically, subsequent research has also found that whereas Type A personalities are more prone to experience heart attacks, they are also more likely to recover from them.

Most Type A individuals believe it is their Type A personality that has led to their success. Many are unwilling to give up that orientation because hard-driving, intense, persistent action is generally admired and valued among managers. This has often been associated with the traditional male management role, but it has also been connected to the disproportionately high incidence of heart disease among men. In fact, several researchers initially linked Type A personality characteristics to certain sex-linked behavior patterns (Friedman, 1996; Goldberg, 1976; Jourard, 1964; Siegman & Smith, 1994).

Specifically, males or females who followed stereotypic views of appropriate male behavior were found to be more likely to experience stress-related illness. They tended to equate low self-disclosure, low emotional involvement, low display of feelings, high defensiveness, and high insensitivity to the acquisition of power and control—the presumed prerequisites for success. These were so typical of male behavior in the workplace that they became known as "the lethal aspects of the male role." As more women began to enter the workforce, this same pattern became less and less gender-linked. Many women also behaved as if acceptance in the workplace required "acting as masculine" as their male counterparts. As a result, the gap between stress-related illness among professional men and women has narrowed. In recent years, female stress-related illnesses (e.g., heart attacks, suicides, migraine headaches) actually have surpassed those of males in some professions. This trend is not only tragic but ironic, because corporations are spending millions of dollars each year on training workshops designed to encourage their managers to become more sensitive, understanding, and supportive. The folly of the Type A approach to management, and to life, is illustrated in the following story from the lore of Zen Buddhism.

Matajura wanted to become a great swordsman, but his father said he wasn't quick enough and could never learn. So Matajura went to the famous dueler, Banzo, and asked to become his pupil. "How long will it take me to become a master?" he asked. "Suppose I become your servant, and spend every minute with you; how long?"

"Ten years," said Banzo.

"My father is getting old. Before 10 years have passed, I will have to return home to take care of him. Suppose I work twice as hard; how long will it take me?"

"Thirty years," said Banzo.

"How is that?" asked Matajura. "First you say 10 years. Then when I offer to work twice as hard, you say it will take three times as long. Let me make myself clear: I will work unceasingly; no hardship will be too much. How long will it take?"

"Seventy years," said Banzo. "A pupil in such a hurry learns slowly."

This Type A sense of urgency, of being able to overcome any obstacle by working harder and longer, works against the ability to develop psychological hardiness. When stressors are encountered, arousal levels increase, and the tendency is to combat them by increasing arousal levels, or effort, even further. But at high arousal levels, coping responses become more primitive (Staw, Sandelands, & Dutton, 1981; Weick, 1995). Patterns of response that were learned most recently are the first ones to disappear, which means that the responses that are most finely tuned to the current stressful situation are the first ones to go. The ability to distinguish among fine-grained stimuli actually deteriorates, so the extra energy expended by individuals trying to cope becomes less and less effective. Weick (1984, 1995) pointed out that highly stressed people consequently find it difficult to learn new responses, to brainstorm, to concentrate, to resist relying on old non-adaptive behavior patterns, to perform complex responses, to delegate, and to avoid the vicious spiral of escalating arousal. Resiliency deteriorates.

The Small-Wins Strategy

An effective antidote to this Type A escalation problem is working for "small wins," discussed earlier in this chapter. When individuals work for incremental accomplishments rather than trying to achieve a major milestone or "hit a home run," they consciously remain sensitive to the progress they are making, they can celebrate victories, and they can develop a sense of making progress, all the while coping with a major stressor.

A hypothetical example introduced by Kuhn and Beam (1982, pp. 249–250) illustrates the power of small wins.

Your task is to count out a thousand sheets of paper while you are subject to periodic interruptions. Each interruption causes you to lose track of the count and forces you to start over. If you count the thousand as a single sequence, then an interruption could cause you to lose count of as many as 999. If the sheets are put into stacks of 100, however, and each stack remains undisturbed by interruptions, then the worst possible count loss from interruption is 108. That number represents the recounting of nine stacks of 100 each plus 99 single sheets. Further, if sheets are first put into stacks of 10, which are then joined into stacks of 100, the worst possible loss from interruption would be 27. That number represents nine stacks of 100 plus nine stacks of 10 plus nine single sheets. Not only is far less recounting time lost by putting the paper into "subsystems" of tens and hundreds, but the chances of completing the count are vastly higher.

When individuals work for a small, concrete outcome, giving them a chance to enjoy visible success, they develop heightened confidence, excitement, and optimism, which motivate an attempt to accomplish another small win. By itself, a small win may seem unimportant. A series of wins at seemingly insignificant tasks, however, reveals a pattern that tends to attract allies, deter opponents, and lower resistance to further action. Once a small win has been accomplished, forces are set in motion that favor another small win. When one solution has been identified, the next solvable problem often becomes more visible. Additional resources also tend to flow toward winners, so the probability of additional successes increases.

Research clearly demonstrates that a small-wins strategy is superior to a strategy of trying to cope with stressors in large chunks (Weick, 1984, 1995). For example, successive small requests are more likely to be approved and achieve compliance than one large request. Positions advocated within the latitude of acceptance (i.e., that are only slightly different from current positions) modify opinions more than does advocacy of a position that exceeds those limits (i.e., large differences exist between current and proposed positions). People whose positions are close to one's own tend to be the targets of the most intensive persuasion attempts, while those whose positions are farther away are dismissed, isolated, or derogated. Cognitive therapy is most successful when the patient is persuaded to do just one thing differently that changes his or her pattern of coping up to that point. Learning tends to occur in small increments rather than in large, all-or-nothing chunks. Retention of learning is better when individuals are in an emotional state similar to the one in which they learned the original material. Over 75 percent of the changes and improvements in both individuals and organizations over time can be accounted for by minor improvements, not major alterations. The point is that the incremental approach used in a small-wins strategy is the most basic and the one most compatible with human preferences for learning, perception, motivation, and change.

What does this have to do with hardiness and resiliency? A small-wins strategy both engenders hardiness and helps overcome the Type A personality syndrome, which is basically a large-win, winner-takes-all approach to stress. Recall that hardiness is composed of control, commitment, and challenge. The deliberate cultivation of a strategy of small wins helps produce precisely those psychological states. Small wins reinforce the perception that individuals can influence what happens to them (being in control); it helps motivate further action by building on the confidence of past successes (which creates commitment); and it produces changes of manageable size that serve as incentives to broaden, learn, and seek new opportunities or challenges. "Continuing pursuit of small wins can build increasing resistance to stress in people not originally predisposed toward hardiness" (Weick, 1984, p. 46).

Deep-Relaxation Strategies

In addition to a small-wins strategy, a second approach to building psychological resiliency is to learn and practice a deep-relaxation technique. Research demonstrates a marked decrease in Type A personality characteristics for regular users of meditation and deep-relaxation techniques. Using the automotive analogy, individuals who use deep-relaxation exercises find that when stress occurs, their "engines" don't rev up as high, and they return to idle faster (Curtis & Detert, 1981; Davis, Eshelman, & McKay, 1980; Greenberg, 1987). Deep-relaxation techniques differ from temporary, short-term relaxation techniques, which we will discuss later.

Deep-relaxation techniques include meditation, yoga, autogenic training or self-hypnosis, biofeedback, and so on. Considerable evidence exists that individuals who practice such techniques regularly are able to condition their bodies to inhibit the negative effects of stress (Beary & Benson, 1977; Cooper & Aygen, 1979; Deepak, 1995; Dellbeck & Shatkin, 1991; Orme-Johnson, 1973; Stone & Deleo, 1976; Yogi, 1994). Most of these deep-relaxation techniques must be practiced over a period of time to develop fully, but they are not difficult to learn. Most deep-relaxation techniques require the following conditions:

1. A quiet environment in which external distractions are minimized.

2. A comfortable position so that muscular effort is minimized.

3. A mental focus. Transcendental meditation (TM) advocates recommend concentrating on one word, phrase, or object. Benson (1975) suggests the word "one." Others suggest picturing a plain vase. The ancient Chinese used a carved jade object that resembled a mountain and sat on a desktop. The purpose of focusing on a word or object is to rid the mind of all other thoughts.

4. Controlled breathing (i.e., deliberate breathing) with pauses between breaths. Thoughts are focused on rhythmic breathing, which helps clear the mind and aids concentration.

5. A passive attitude, so that if other thoughts enter the mind, they are ignored.

6. Focused bodily changes. While meditation uses the mind to relax the body, autogenic training uses bodily sensations of heaviness and warmth to change the psychological state. Feelings of warmth and heaviness are induced in different parts of the body, which, in turn, create deep relaxation.

7. Repetition. Because physiological and psychological results depend on consistent practice, the best results occur when such techniques are practiced from 20 to 30 minutes each day.

The Skill Practice section contains an example of a deep-relaxation exercise.

SOCIAL RESILIENCY

The third factor moderating the harmful effects of stress and contributing to resiliency involves developing close social relationships. Individuals who are embedded in supportive social networks are less likely to experience stress and are better equipped to cope with its consequences (Cordes & Dougherty, 1993; Lehrer, 1996; Singh, 1993). Supportive social relations provide opportunities to share one's frustrations and disappointments, to receive suggestions and encouragement, and to experience emotional bonding. Such supportive interactions provide the empathy and bolstering required to cope with stressful events. They are formed most easily among individuals who share close emotional ties (e.g., family members) or common experiences (e.g., coworkers).

Poignant testimony to the value of social support systems during periods of high stress comes from the experiences of soldiers captured during World War II and the Korean and Vietnam wars. When it was possible for prisoners to form permanent, interacting groups, they maintained better health and morale and were able to resist their captors more effectively than when they were isolated or when groups were unstable. Indeed, the well-documented technique used by the Chinese during the Korean War for breaking down soldiers' resistance to their indoctrination efforts involved weakening group solidarity through planting seeds of mistrust and doubt about members' loyalty.

Aside from personal friendships or family relations, two types of social support systems can be formed as part of a manager's job. One is a mentor relationship; the other is a task team. Most individuals, with the possible exception of the most senior managers, can profit from a mentoring relationship. The research is clear, in fact, that career success, work satisfaction, and resiliency to stress are enhanced by a mentoring relationship (Bell, 1998; Hendricks, 1996; Kram, 1985). Individuals need someone else in the organization that can provide a role model, from whom they can learn, and from whom they can receive personal attention and a reinforcement of self-worth, especially under uncertain, crucial, and stressful situations.

Many organizations formally prescribe a mentoring system by assigning a senior manager to shepherd a younger manager when he or she enters the organization. With rare exceptions, when the contact is one-way, from the top down, these relationships don't work out (Kram, 1985). The junior manager must actively seek and foster the mentoring relationship as well. The junior manager can do this, not by demonstrating overdependence or overingratiation, but by expressing a desire to use the senior person as a mentor and then by making certain that the relationship does not become a one-way street. The subordinate can pass along important information and resources to the potential mentor, while both will share in working out solutions to problems. That way, the mentoring relationship becomes mutually satisfying and mutually beneficial for both parties, and resiliency to stress is enhanced because of the commitment, trust, and cooperation that begin to characterize the relationship. A mentor's guidance can both help avoid stressful situations and provide support for coping with them.

Smoothly functioning work teams also enhance social resiliency. The social value of working on a team has been well documented in research, and Chapter 9 in this book reviews some of that evidence (also see Dyer, 1987; Katzenbach & Smith, 1993). The more cohesive the team, the more support it provides its members. Members of highly cohesive teams communicate with one another more frequently and more positively and report higher satisfaction, lower stress, and higher commitment levels than do individuals who do not feel as though they are part of a work team (Lawler, Mohrman, and Ledford, 1992).

The value of work teams has been amply demonstrated in practice as well. In the Introductory chapter, for example, we recounted a dramatic change that occurred in the Fremont, California, plant of General Motors when U.S. workers came under Japanese management. In just one year, marked improvements in productivity, morale, and quality occurred, due in large part to the use of effective work teams. Relationships were formed based not only on friendship but on a common commitment to solving work-related problems and to generating ideas for improvement. Teams met regularly during work hours to discuss ideas for improvement and to coordinate and resolve issues.

Similar dynamics have been fostered in most of the successful companies in the United States and abroad. The productivity and success of the East Asian economies, for example, has been attributed largely to the effective use of work teams. Almost every company that has won the Malcolm Baldrige National Quality Award (e.g., Motorola, Ritz Carlton, Westinghouse, Xerox, Millikin) has fostered teamwork among employees as a crucial part of its improvement efforts. The marked improvements that occur in individual satisfaction and lowered stress levels suggest that each person should likewise help facilitate similar teamwork in his or her work setting as part of a social resiliency repertoire.

To foster teamwork in your own work settings, you might consider involving others in defining the challenges (stressors) tasks or issues you encounter, encourage broad participation and two-way feedback with every person involved, share information and resources broadly so that knowledge sharing occurs, and cultivate a feeling of cohesion and commitment among team members by identifying team rewards or positive outcomes rather than focusing on individual accomplishment. A detailed discussion of these and other team dynamics is found in Chapter 9 on Building Effective Teams.

Temporary Stress-Reduction Techniques

Thus far, we have emphasized eliminating sources of stress and developing resiliency to stress. These are the most desirable stress-management strategies because they have a permanent or long-term effect on your well being. However, the occurrence of stressors is sometimes beyond our control so it may be impossible to eliminate them. Moreover, developing resiliency takes time, so sometimes we must use temporary reactive mechanisms in order to maintain equilibrium. Although increased resilience can buffer the harmful effects of stress, we must sometimes take immediate action in the short term to cope with the stress we encounter.

Implementing short-term strategies reduces stress temporarily so that longer-term stress-elimination or resiliency strategies can operate. Short-term strategies are largely reactive and must be repeated whenever stressors are encountered because, unlike other strategies, their effects are only temporary. On the other hand, they are especially useful for immediately calming feelings of anxiety or apprehension. You can use them when you are asked a question you can't answer, when you become embarrassed by an unexpected event, when you are faced with a presentation or an important meeting, or almost any time you are suddenly stressed and must respond in a short period of time. Although more than 5,000 books have been published on temporary stress-reduction techniques since 1990, we review only five of the best-known and easiest to learn techniques here. The first two are physiological; the last three are psychological.

Muscle relaxation involves easing the tension in successive muscle groups. Each muscle group is tightened for five or ten seconds and then completely relaxed. Starting with the feet and progressing to the calves, thighs, stomach, and on to the neck and face, one can relieve tension throughout the entire body. All parts of the body can be included in the exercise. One variation is to roll the head around on the neck several times, shrug the shoulders, or stretch the arms up toward the ceiling for five to ten seconds, then release the position and relax the muscles. The result is a state of temporary relaxation that helps eliminate tension and refocus energy.

A variation of muscle relaxation involves **deep breathing**. This is done by taking several successive, slow, deep breaths, holding them for five seconds, and exhaling completely. You should focus on the act of breathing itself, so that your mind becomes cleared for a brief time while your body relaxes. After each deep breath, muscles in the body should consciously be relaxed.

A third technique uses **imagery and fantasy** to eliminate stress temporarily by changing the focus of your thoughts. Imagery involves visualizing an event, using "mind pictures." An increasingly common practice for athletes is to visualize successful performance or to imagine themselves achieving their goal. Research has confirmed both the stress-reduction advantages of this technique as well as the performance enhancement benefits (e.g., Deepak, 1995).

In addition to visualization, imagery also can include recollections of sounds, smells, and textures. Your mind focuses on pleasant experiences from the past (e.g., a fishing trip, family vacation, visit with relatives, day at the beach) that can be recalled vividly. Fantasies, on the other hand, are not past memories but make-believe events or images. It is especially well known, for example, that children often construct imaginary friends, make-believe occurrences, or special wishes that are comforting to them when they encounter stress. Adults also use daydreams or other fantasy experiences to get them through stressful situations. The purpose of this technique is to relieve anxiety or pressure temporarily by focusing on something pleasant so that other, more productive stress-reducing strategies can be developed for the longer term.

The fourth technique is called **rehearsal**. Using this technique, people work themselves through potentially stressful situations, trying out different scenarios and alternative reactions. Appropriate reactions are rehearsed, either in a safe environment before stress occurs, or "off-line," in private, in the midst of a stressful situation. Removing oneself temporarily from a stressful circumstance and working through dialogue or reactions, as though rehearsing for a play, can help one regain control and reduce the immediacy of the stressor.

A final strategy, **reframing**, involves temporarily reducing stress by optimistically redefining a situation as manageable. Reframing serves as a key to developing "hardiness" and "emotional intelligence" discussed earlier. Although reframing is difficult in the midst of a stressful situation, it can be facilitated by using the following cues:

- ❏ "I understand this situation."
- ❏ "I've solved similar problems before."
- ❏ "Other people are available to help me get through this situation."
- ❏ "Others have faced similar situations and made it through."
- ❏ "In the long run, this really isn't so critical."
- ❏ "I can learn something from this situation."
- ❏ "There are several good alternatives available to me."

Each of these statements can assist you in reframing a situation in order to develop long-term proactive or enactive strategies.

Summary

We began this chapter by explaining stress in terms of a relatively simple model. Four kinds of stressors—time, encounter, situational, and anticipatory—cause negative physiological, psychological, and social reactions in individuals. These reactions are moderated by the resiliency that individuals have developed for coping with stress. The best way to manage stress is to eliminate it through time management, delegation, collaboration, interpersonal competence, work redesign, prioritizing, goal setting, and small wins. This strategy has permanent consequences, but it often takes an extended period of time to implement.

The next most effective stress management strategy is improving one's resiliency. Physiological resiliency is strengthened through increased cardiovascular conditioning and improved diet. Psychological resiliency and hardiness are improved by practicing small-wins strategies and deep relaxation. Social resiliency is increased by fostering mentoring relationships and teamwork among coworkers. These strategies produce long-term benefits, but they also take quite a long time to implement.

When circumstances make it impossible to apply longer-term strategies for reducing stress, short-term relaxation techniques can temporarily alleviate the symptoms of stress. These strategies have short-term consequences, but they can be applied immediately and repeated over and over again.

Behavioral Guidelines

Following are specific behavioral guidelines for improving one's stress management skills.

LEARNING

1. Use effective time management practices. Make sure that you use time effectively as well as efficiently by generating your own personal mission statement. Make sure that low-priority tasks do not drive out time to work on high-priority activities. Make better use of your time by using the guidelines in the Time Management Survey in the Assessment Section.

2. Build collaborative relationships with individuals based on mutual trust, respect, honesty, and kindness. Make "deposits" into the "emotional bank accounts" of other people. Form close, stable relationships among those with whom you work.

3. Consciously work to improve your emotional intelligence by learning and practicing the principles discussed in other chapters of this book.

4. Try redesigning your work to increase its skill variety, importance, task identity (comprehensiveness), autonomy, and feedback. Make the work itself stress reducing, rather than stress inducing.

5. Reaffirm priorities and short-term plans that provide direction and focus to activities. Give important activities priority over urgent ones.

6. Increase your general resiliency by leading a balanced life and consciously developing yourself in physical, intellectual, cultural, social, family, and spiritual areas, as well as in your work.

7. Increase your physical resiliency by engaging in a regular program of exercise and proper eating.

8. Increase your psychological resiliency and hardiness by implementing a small-wins strategy. Identify and celebrate the small successes that you and others achieve.

9. Learn at least one deep-relaxation technique and practice it regularly.

10. Increase social resiliency by forming an open, trusting, sharing relationship with at least one other person. Facilitate a mentoring relationship with someone who can affirm your worth as a person and provide support during periods of stress.

11. Establish a teamwork relationship with those with whom you work or study by identifying shared tasks and structuring coordinated action among team members.

12. Learn at least two short-term relaxation techniques and practice them consistently.

CASES INVOLVING STRESS MANAGEMENT

The Turn of the Tide

Not long ago I came to one of those bleak periods that many of us encounter from time to time, a sudden drastic dip in the graph of living when everything goes stale and flat, energy wanes, enthusiasm dies. The effect on my work was frightening. Every morning I would clench my teeth and mutter: "Today life will take on some of its old meaning. You've got to break through this thing. You've got to!"

But the barren days went by, and the paralysis grew worse. The time came when I knew I had to have help. The man I turned to was a doctor. Not a psychiatrist, just a doctor. He was older than I, and under his surface gruffness lay great wisdom and compassion. "I don't know what's wrong," I told him miserably, "but I just seem to have come to a dead end. Can you help me?"

"I don't know," he said slowly. He made a tent of his fingers and gazed at me thoughtfully for a long while. Then, abruptly, he asked, "Where were you happiest as a child?"

"As a child?" I echoed. "Why, at the beach, I suppose. We had a summer cottage there. We all loved it."

He looked out the window and watched the October leaves sifting down. "Are you capable of following instructions for a single day?"

"I think so," I said, ready to try anything.

"All right. Here's what I want you to do."

He told me to drive to the beach alone the following morning, arriving not later than nine o'clock. I could take some lunch; but I was not to read, write, listen to the radio, or talk to anyone. "In addition," he said, "I'll give you a prescription to be taken every three hours."

He then tore off four prescription blanks, wrote a few words on each, folded them, numbered them, and handed them to me. "Take these at nine, twelve, three, and six."

"Are you serious?" I asked.

He gave a short bark of laughter. "You won't think I'm joking when you get my bill!"

The next morning, with little faith, I drove to the beach. It was lonely, all right. A northeaster was blowing; the sea looked gray and angry. I sat in the car, the whole day stretching emptily before me. Then I took out the first of the folded slips of paper. On it was written: LISTEN CAREFULLY.

I stared at the two words. "Why," I thought, "the man must be mad." He had ruled out music and newscasts and human conversation. What else was there? I raised my head and I did listen. There were no sounds but the steady roar of the sea, the creaking cry of a gull, the drone of some aircraft high overhead. All these sounds were familiar. I got out of the car. A gust of wind slammed the door with a sudden clap of sound. "Am I supposed to listen carefully to things like that?" I asked myself.

I climbed a dune and looked out over the deserted beach. Here the sea bellowed so loudly that all other sounds were lost. And yet, I thought suddenly, there must be sounds beneath sounds—the soft rasp of drifting sand, the tiny wind-whisperings in the dune grasses—if the listener got close enough to hear them.

On an impulse I ducked down and, feeling fairly ridiculous, thrust my head into a clump of sea-oats. Here I made a discovery: If you listen intently, there is a fractional moment in which everything seems to pause, wait. In that instant of stillness, the racing thoughts halt. For a moment, when you truly listen for something outside yourself, you have to silence the clamorous voices within. The mind rests.

I went back to the car and slid behind the wheel. LISTEN CAREFULLY. As I listened again to the deep growl of the sea, I found myself thinking about the white-fanged fury of its storms.

I thought of the lessons it had taught us as children. A certain amount of patience: you can't hurry the tides. A great deal of respect: the sea does not suffer fools gladly. An awareness of the vast and mysterious interdependence of things: wind and tide and current, calm and squall and hurricane, all combining to determine the paths of the birds above and the fish below. And the cleanness of it all, with every beach swept twice a day by the great broom of the sea.

Sitting there, I realized I was thinking of things bigger than myself—and there was relief in that.

Even so, the morning passed slowly. The habit of hurling myself at a problem was so strong that I felt lost without it. Once, when I was wistfully eyeing the car radio, a phrase from Carlyle jumped into my head: "Silence is the element in which great things fashion themselves."

By noon the wind had polished the clouds out of the sky, and the sea had merry sparkle. I unfolded the second "prescription." And again I sat there, half amused and half exasperated. Three words this time: TRY REACHING BACK.

Back to what? To the past, obviously. But why, when all my worries concerned the present or the future?

I left the car and started tramping reflectively along the dunes. The doctor had sent me to the beach because it was a place of happy memories. Maybe that was what I was supposed to reach for: the wealth of happiness that lay half-forgotten behind me.

I decided to experiment: to work on these vague impressions as a painter would, retouching the colors, strengthening the outlines. I would choose specific incidents and recapture as many details as possible. I would visualize people complete with dress and gestures. I would listen (carefully) for the exact sound of their voices, the echo of their laughter.

The tide was going out now, but there was still thunder in the surf. So I chose to go back 20 years to the last fishing trip I made with my younger brother. (He died in the Pacific during World War II and was buried in the Philippines.) I found that if I closed my eyes and really tried, I could see him with amazing vividness, even the humor and eagerness in his eyes that far-off morning.

In fact, I could see it all: the ivory scimitar of beach where we were fishing; the eastern sky smeared with sunrise; the great rollers creaming in, stately and slow. I could feel the backwash swirl warm around my knees, see the sudden arc of my brother's rod as he struck a fish, hear his exultant yell. Piece by piece I rebuilt it, clear and unchanged under the transparent varnish of time. Then it was gone.

I sat up slowly. TRY REACHING BACK. Happy people were usually assured, confident people. If, then, you deliberately reached back and touched happiness, might there not be released little flashes of power, tiny sources of strength?

This second period of the day went more quickly. As the sun began its long slant down the sky, my mind ranged eagerly through the past, reliving some episodes, uncovering others that had been completely forgotten. For example, when I was around 13 and my brother 10, Father had promised to take us to the circus. But at lunch there was a phone call: Some urgent business required his attention downtown.

We braced ourselves for disappointment. Then we heard him say, "No, I won't be down. It'll have to wait."

When he came back to the table, Mother smiled. "The circus keeps coming back, you know."

"I know," said Father. "But childhood doesn't."

Across all the years I remembered this and knew from the sudden glow of warmth that no kindness is ever wasted or ever completely lost.

By three o'clock the tide was out and the sound of the waves was only a rhythmic whisper, like a giant breathing. I stayed in my sandy nest, feeling relaxed and content—and a little complacent. The doctor's prescriptions, I thought, were easy to take.

But I was not prepared for the next one. This time the three words were not a gentle suggestion. They sounded more like a command. REEXAMINE YOUR MOTIVES.

My first reaction was purely defensive. "There's nothing wrong with my motives," I said to myself. "I want to be successful—who doesn't? I want to have a certain amount of recognition—but so does everybody. I want more security than I've got—and why not?"

"Maybe," said a small voice somewhere inside my head, "those motives aren't good enough. Maybe that's the reason the wheels have stopped going around."

I picked up a handful of sand and let it stream between my fingers. In the past, whenever my work went well, there had always been something spontaneous about it, something uncontrived, something free. Lately it had been calculated, competent—and dead. Why? Because I had been looking past the job itself to the rewards I hoped it would bring. The work had ceased to be an end in itself, it had been merely a means to make money, pay bills. The sense of giving something, of helping people, of making a contribution, had been lost in a frantic clutch at security.

In a flash of certainty, I saw that if one's motives are wrong, nothing can be right. It makes no difference whether you are a mailman, a hairdresser, an insurance sales-man, a housewife—whatever. As long as you feel you are serving others, you do the job well. When you are concerned only with helping yourself, you do it less well. This is a law as inexorable as gravity.

For a long time I sat there. Far out on the bar I heard the murmur of the surf change to a hollow roar as the tide turned. Behind me the spears of light were almost horizontal. My time at the beach had almost run out, and I felt a grudging admiration for the doctor and the "prescriptions" he had so casually and cunningly devised. I saw, now, that in them was a therapeutic progression that might well be of value to anyone facing any difficulty.

LISTEN CAREFULLY: To calm a frantic mind, slow it down, shift the focus from inner problems to outer things.

TRY REACHING BACK: Since the human mind can hold but one idea at a time, you blot out present worry when you touch the happiness of the past.

REEXAMINE YOUR MOTIVES: This was the hard core of the "treatment," this challenge to reappraise, to bring one's motives into alignment with one's capabilities and conscience. But the mind must be clear and receptive to do this—hence the six hours of quiet that went before.

The western sky was a blaze of crimson as I took out the last slip of paper. Six words this time. I walked slowly out on the beach. A few yards below the high water mark I stopped and read the words again: WRITE YOUR TROUBLES ON THE SAND.

I let the paper blow away, reached down and picked up a fragment of shell. Kneeling there under the vault of the sky, I wrote several words on the sand, one above the other. Then I walked away, and I did not look back. I had written my troubles on the sand. And the tide was coming in.

SOURCE: *Gordon, 1959.*

ANALYSIS

Discussion Questions

1. What is effective about these strategies for coping with stress, and why did they work?
2. What troubles, challenges, or stressors do you face right now to which these prescriptions might apply?
3. Are these prescriptions effective coping strategies or merely escapes?
4. What other prescriptions could the author take besides the four mentioned here? Generate your own list based on your own experiences with stress.

The Case of the Missing Time

At approximately 7:30 A.M. on Tuesday, June 23, 1959, Chet Craig, manager of the Norris Company's Central Plant, swung his car out of the driveway of his suburban home and headed toward the plant located some six miles away, just inside the Midvale city limits. It was a beautiful day. The sun was shining brightly and a cool, fresh breeze was blowing. The trip to the plant took about 20 minutes and sometimes gave Chet an opportunity to think about plant problems without interruption.

The Norris Company owned and operated three printing plants. Norris enjoyed a nationwide commercial business, specializing in quality color work. It was a closely held company with some 350 employees, nearly half of whom were employed at the Central Plant, the largest of the three Norris production operations. The company's main offices were also located in the Central Plant building.

Chet had started with the Norris Company as an expediter in its Eastern Plant in 1948, just after he graduated from Ohio State. After three years Chet was promoted to production supervisor, and two years later he was made assistant to the manager of the Eastern Plant. Early in 1957 he was transferred to the Central Plant as assistant to the plant manager and one month later was promoted to plant manager when the former manager retired (see Figure 2.7).

Chet was in fine spirits as he relaxed behind the wheel. As his car picked up speed, the hum of the tires on the newly paved highway faded into the background. Various thoughts occurred to him, and he said to himself, "This is going to be the day to really get things done."

He began to run through the day's work, first one project, then another, trying to establish priorities. After a few minutes he decided that the open-end unit scheduling was probably the most important, certainly the most urgent. He frowned for a moment as he recalled that on Friday the vice president and general manager had casually asked him if he had given the project any further thought. Chet realized that he had not been giving it much thought lately. He had been meaning to get to work on this idea for over three months, but something else always seemed to crop up. "I haven't had much time to sit down and really work it out," he said to himself. "I'd better get going and hit this one today for sure." With that he began to break down the objectives, procedures, and installation steps of the project. He grinned as he reviewed the principles involved and calculated roughly the anticipated savings. "It's about time," he told himself. "This idea should have been followed up long ago." Chet remembered that he had first conceived of the open-end unit scheduling idea nearly a year and a half ago, just prior to his leaving Norris's Eastern Plant. He had spoken to his boss, Jim Quince, manager of the Eastern Plant, about it then, and both agreed that it was worth looking into. The idea was temporarily shelved when he was transferred to the Central Plant a month later.

Figure 2.7 | **Organization Chart**

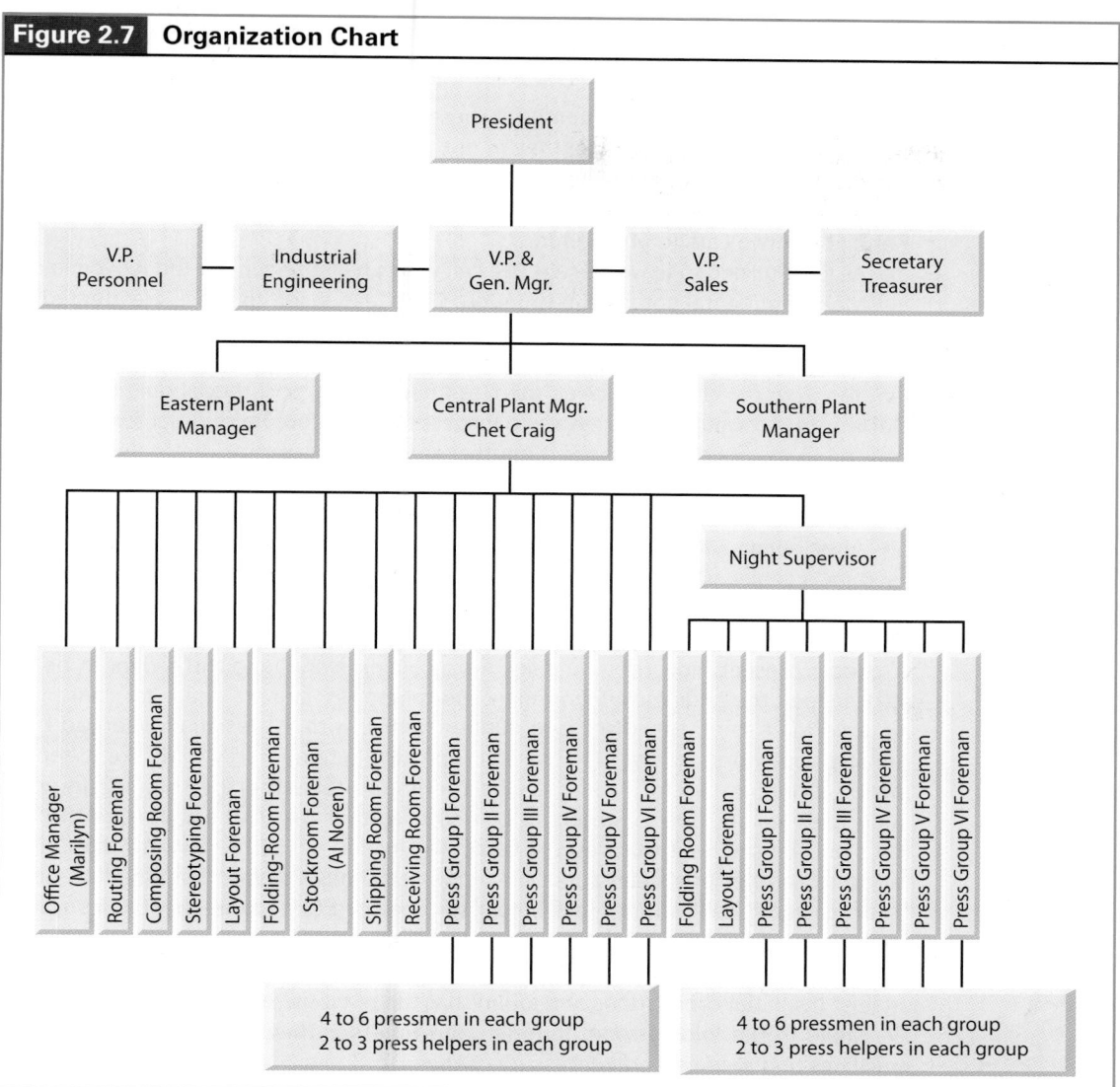

A blast from a passing horn startled him, but his thoughts quickly returned to other plant projects he was determined to get underway. He started to think through a procedure for simpler transport of dies to and from the Eastern Plant. Visualizing the notes on his desk, he thought about the inventory analysis he needed to identify and eliminate some of the slow-moving stock items, the packing controls that needed revision, and the need to design a new special-order form. He also decided that this was the day to settle on a job printer to do the simple outside printing of office forms. There were a few other projects he couldn't recall offhand, but he could tend to them after lunch, if not before. "Yes, sir," he said to himself, "this is the day to really get rolling."

Chet's thoughts were interrupted as he pulled into the company parking lot. When he entered the plant Chet knew something was wrong as he met Al Noren, the stockroom foreman, who appeared troubled. "A great morning, Al," Chet greeted him cheerfully.

"Not so good, Chet; my new man isn't in this morning," Noren growled.

"Have you heard from him?" asked Chet.

"No, I haven't," replied Al.

Chet frowned as he commented, "These stock handlers assume you take it for granted that if they're not here, they're not here, and they don't have to call in and verify it. Better ask Personnel to call him."

Al hesitated for a moment before replying, "Okay, Chet, but can you find me a man? I have two cars to unload today."

As Chet turned to leave he said, "I'll call you in half an hour, Al, and let you know."

Making a mental note of the situation, Chet headed for his office. He greeted the group of workers huddled around Marilyn, the office manager, who was discussing the day's work schedule with them. As the meeting broke up, Marilyn picked up a few samples from the clasper, showed them to Chet, and asked if they should be shipped that way or if it would be necessary to inspect them. Before he could answer, Marilyn went on to ask if he could suggest another clerical operator for the sealing machine to replace the regular operator, who was home ill. She also told him that Gene, the industrial engineer, had called and was waiting to hear from Chet.

After telling Marilyn to go ahead and ship the samples, he made a note of the need for a sealer operator for the office and then called Gene. He agreed to stop by Gene's office before lunch and started on his routine morning tour of the plant. He asked each foreman the types and volumes of orders they were running, the number of people present, how the schedules were coming along, and the orders to be run next; helped the folding-room foreman find temporary storage space for consolidating a carload shipment; discussed quality control with a pressman who had been running poor work; arranged to transfer four people temporarily to different departments, including two for Al in the stockroom; and talked to the shipping foreman about pickups and special orders to be delivered that day. As he continued through the plant, he saw to it that reserve stock was moved out of the forward stock area, talked to another pressman about his requested change of vacation schedule, had a "heart-to-heart" talk with a press helper who seemed to need frequent reassurance, and approved two type and one color-order okays for different pressmen.

Returning to his office, Chet reviewed the production reports on the larger orders against his initial productions and found that the plant was running behind schedule. He called in the folding-room foreman and together they went over the lineup of machines and made several necessary changes.

During this discussion, the composing-room foreman stopped in to cover several type changes, and the routing foreman telephoned for approval of a revised printing schedule. The stockroom foreman called twice, first to inform him that two standard, fast-moving stock items were dangerously low, later to advise him that the paper stock for the urgent Dillion job had finally arrived. Chet made the necessary subsequent calls to inform those concerned.

He then began to put delivery dates on important and difficult inquiries received from customers and salesmen. (The routine inquiries were handled by Marilyn.) While he was doing this he was interrupted twice, once by a sales correspondent calling from the West Coast to ask for a better delivery date than originally scheduled, once by the personnel vice president asking him to set a time when he could hold an initial training and induction interview with a new employee.

After dating the customer and salesmen inquiries, Chet headed for his morning conference in the executive offices. At this meeting he answered the sales vice president's questions in connection with "hot" orders, complaints, and the status of large-volume orders and potential new orders. He then met with the general manager to discuss a few ticklish policy matters and to answer "the old man's" questions on several specific production and personnel problems. Before leaving the executive offices, he stopped at the office of the secretary-treasurer to inquire about delivery of cartons, paper, and boxes and to place a new order for paper.

On the way back to his own office, Chet conferred with Gene about two current engineering projects concerning which he had called earlier. When he reached his desk, he looked at his watch. It was 10 minutes before lunch, just time enough to make a few notes of the details he needed to check in order to answer the knotty questions raised by the sales manager that morning.

After lunch Chet started again. He began by checking the previous day's production reports, did some rescheduling to get out urgent orders, placed appropriate delivery dates on new orders and inquiries received that morning, and consulted with a foreman on a personal problem. He spent some 20 minutes at the TWX going over mutual problems with the Eastern Plant.

By midafternoon Chet had made another tour of the plant, after which he met with the personnel director to review with him a touchy personal problem raised by one of the clerical employees, the vacation schedules submitted by his foremen, and the pending job-evaluation program. Following this conference, Chet hurried back to his office to complete the special statistical report for Universal Waxing Corporation, one of Norris' best customers. As he finished the report, he discovered that it was 10 minutes after six and he was the only one left in the office. Chet was tired. He put on his coat and headed through the plant toward the parking lot; on the way he was stopped by both the night supervisor and night layout foremen for approval of type and layout changes.

With both eyes on the traffic, Chet reviewed the day he had just completed. "Busy?" he asked himself. "Too much so—but did I accomplish anything?" His mind raced over the day's activities. "Yes and no" seemed to be the answer. "There was the usual routine, the same as any other day. The plant kept going and I think it must have been a good production day. Any creative or special-project work done?" Chet grimaced as he reluctantly answered, "No."

With a feeling of guilt, he probed further. "Am I an executive? I'm paid like one, respected like one, and have a responsible assignment with the necessary authority to carry it out. Yet one of the greatest values a company derives from an executive is his creative thinking and accomplishments. What have I done about it? An executive needs some time for thinking. Today was a typical day, just like most other days, and I did little, if any, creative work. The projects that I so enthusiastically planned to work on this morning are exactly as they were yesterday. What's more, I have no guarantee that tomorrow night or the next night will bring me any closer to their completion. This is the real problem and there must be an answer."

Chet continued, "Night work? Yes, occasionally. This is understood. But I've been doing too much of this lately. I owe my wife and family some of my time. When you come down to it, they are the people for whom I'm really working. If I am forced to spend much more time away from them, I'm not meeting my own personal objectives. What about church work? Should I eliminate that? I spend a lot of time on this, but I feel I owe God some time, too. Besides, I believe I'm making a worthwhile contribution in this work. Perhaps I can squeeze a little time from my fraternal activities. But where does recreation fit in?"

Chet groped for the solution. "Maybe I'm just rationalizing because I schedule my own work poorly. But I don't think so. I've studied my work habits carefully and I think I plan intelligently and delegate authority. Do I need an assistant? Possibly, but that's a long-term project and I don't believe I could justify the additional overhead expenditure. Anyway, I doubt whether it would solve the problem."

By this time Chet had turned off the highway onto the side street leading to his home—the problem still uppermost in his mind. "I guess I really don't know the answer," he told himself as he pulled into his driveway. "This morning everything seemed so simple, but now . . . " His thoughts were interrupted as he saw his son running toward the car calling out, "Mommy, Daddy's home."

SOURCE: McNichols, 1973.

Discussion Questions

1. What principles of time and stress management are violated in this case?
2. What are the organizational problems in the case?
3. Which of Chet's personal characteristics inhibit his effective management of time?
4. If you were hired as a consultant to Chet, what would you advise him?

EXERCISES FOR LONG-TERM AND SHORT-RUN STRESS MANAGEMENT

In this section, we provide four relatively short exercises to help you practice good stress management. We strongly urge you to complete the exercises with a partner who can give you feedback and who will monitor your progress in improving your skill. Because managing stress is a personal skill, most of your practice will be done in private. But having a partner who is aware of your commitment will help foster substantial improvement.

The Small-Wins Strategy

An ancient Chinese proverb states that long journeys are always made up of small steps. In Japan, the feeling of obligation to make small, incremental improvements in one's work is known as kaizen. In this chapter the notion of small wins was explained as a way to break apart large problems and identify small successes in coping with them. Each of these approaches represents the same basic philosophy—to recognize incremental successes—and each helps an individual build up psychological resiliency to stress.

Assignment

Answer the following questions. An example is given to help clarify each question, but your response need not relate to the example.

1. What major stressor do you currently face? What creates anxiety or discomfort for you? (For example, "I have too much to do.")

2. What are the major attributes or components of the situation? Divide the major problem into smaller parts or subproblems. (For example, "I have said 'yes' to too many things. I have deadlines approaching. I don't have all the resources I need to complete all my commitments right now.")

3. What are the subcomponents of each of those subproblems? Divide them into yet smaller parts. (For example, "I have the following deadlines approaching: a report due, a large amount of reading to do, a family obligation, an important presentation, a need to spend some personal time with someone I care about, a committee meeting that requires preparation.")

PRACTICE ◆

Attribute 1:

Attribute 2:

Attribute 3:

And so on:

4. What actions can I take that will affect any of these subcomponents? (For example, "I can engage the person I care about in helping me prepare for the presentation. I can write a shorter report than I originally intended. I can carry the reading material with me wherever I go.")

5. What actions have I taken in the past that have helped me cope successfully with similar stressful circumstances? (For example, "I have found someone else to share some of my tasks. I have gotten some reading done while waiting, riding, and eating. I have prepared only key elements for the committee meeting.")

6. What small thing should I feel good about as I think about how I have coped or will cope with this major stressor? (For example, "I have accomplished a lot when the pressure has been on in the past. I have been able to use what I had time to prepare to its best advantage.")

Repeat this process when you face major stressors. The six specific questions may not be as important to you as (1) breaking the problem down into incremental parts and then breaking those parts down again, and (2) identifying actions that can be done that will be successful in coping with components of the stressor.

Life-Balance Analysis

The prescription to maintain a balanced life seems both intuitive and counterintuitive. On the one hand, it makes sense that life should have variety and that each of us should develop multiple aspects of ourselves. Narrowness and rigidity are not highly valued by anyone. On the other hand, the demands of work, school, or family, for example, can be so overwhelming that we don't have time to do much except respond to those demands. Work could take all of our time. So could school. So could family. The temptation for most of us, then, is to focus on only a few areas of our lives that demand our attention and leave the other areas undeveloped. This exercise helps you discover which areas those might be and which areas need more attention.

Assignment

Use Figure 2.8 below to complete this exercise. In responding to the four items in the exercise, think of the amount of time you spend in each area, the amount of experience and development you have had in the past in each area, and the extent to which development in each area is important to you.

1. In Figure 2.8, shade in the portion of each section that represents the extent to which that aspect of your life has been well developed. In other words, rate how satisfied you are that each aspect is adequately cultivated.

2. Now write down at least one thing you can start doing to improve your development in the areas that need it. For example, you might do more outside reading to develop culturally, invite a foreign visitor to your home to develop socially, engage in regular prayer or meditation to develop spiritually, begin a regular exercise program to develop physically, and so on.

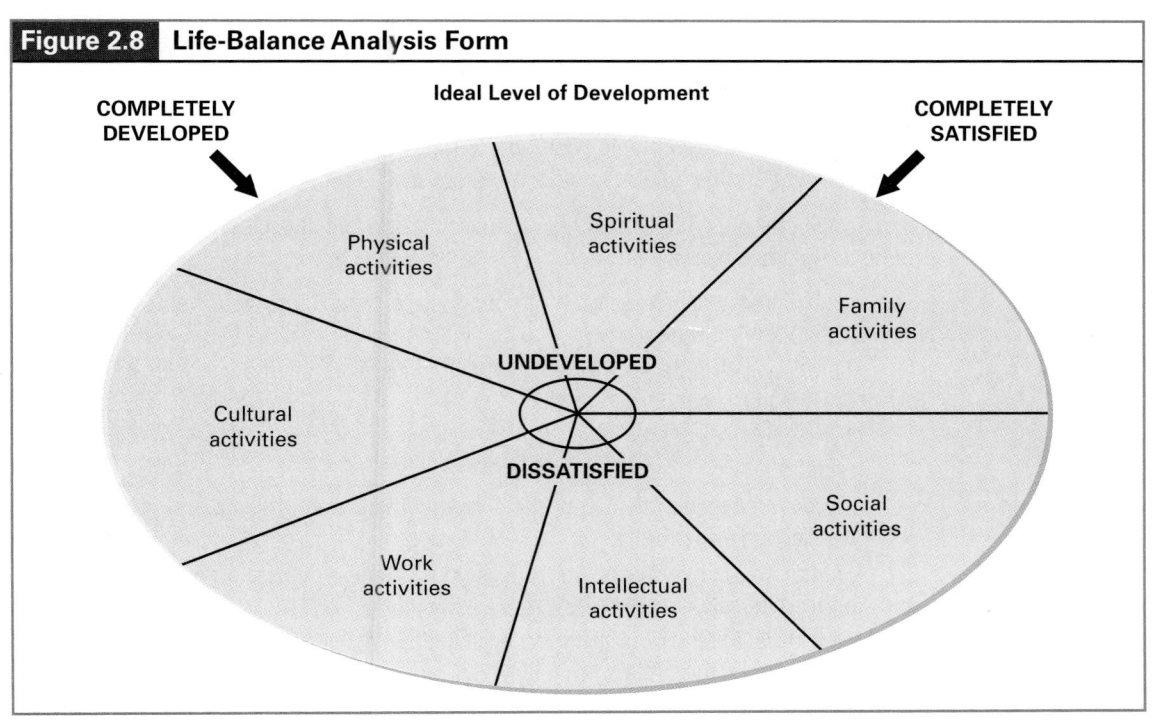

Figure 2.8 **Life-Balance Analysis Form**

3. Because the intent of this exercise is not to add more pressure and stress to your life but to increase your resiliency through life balance, identify the things you will *stop* doing in various areas that will make it possible to achieve better life balance.

4. To make this a practice exercise and not just a planning exercise, do something today that you have on your list for items 2 and 3 above. Write down specifically what you'll do and when. Don't let the rest of the week go by without implementing something you've written.

Deep Relaxation

To engage in deep relaxation, you need to reserve time that can be spent concentrating on relaxation. Cognitive control and physiological control are involved. By focusing your mind, you can positively affect both your mental and physical states (Davis, Eshelman, & McKay, 1980). This exercise describes one technique that is easily learned and practiced.

The deep-relaxation technique presented below combines key elements of several well-known formulas. It is recommended that this technique be practiced for 20 minutes a day, three times a week. Reserve at least 30 minutes to engage in this exercise for the first time.

Find a quiet spot with a partner. You may want to do this in the classroom itself the first time. Have that person read the instructions below. Do not rush through the instructions. Allow time between each step to complete it unrushed. When you have finished, switch roles. (Since you will be practicing this exercise later in a different setting, you may want to make a tape recording of these instructions. Alternatively, agree to do the exercise regularly with a friend or a spouse.)

Assignment

Step 1: Assume a comfortable position. You may lie down. Loosen any tight clothing. Close your eyes and be quiet. Slow down and let go.

Step 2: Focus on your body and on relaxing specific muscles. Tune out all other thoughts. Assume a passive attitude.

Step 3: Now tense and relax each of your muscle groups for five to ten seconds each. Do it in the following order:

> *Forehead.* Wrinkle your forehead. Try to make your eyebrows touch your hairline for five seconds, then relax.
>
> *Eyes and nose.* Close your eyes as tightly as you can for five seconds, then relax.
>
> *Lips, cheeks, and jaw.* Draw the corners of your mouth back and grimace for five seconds, then relax.
>
> *Hands.* Extend your arms in front of you. Clench your fists tightly for five seconds, then relax.
>
> *Forearms.* Extend your arms out against an invisible wall and push forward for five seconds, then relax.

Upper arms. Bend your elbows and tense your biceps for five seconds, then relax.

Shoulders. Shrug your shoulders up to your ears for five seconds, then relax.

Back. Arch your back off the floor for five seconds, then relax.

Stomach. Tighten your stomach muscles by lifting your legs off the ground about two inches for five seconds, then relax.

Hips and buttocks. Tighten your hip and buttock muscles for five seconds, then relax.

Thighs. Tighten your thigh muscles by pressing your legs together as tightly as you can for five seconds, then relax.

Feet. Bend your ankles toward your body as far as you can for five seconds, then point your toes for five seconds, then relax.

Toes. Curl your toes as tightly as you can for five seconds, then relax.

Step 4: Focus on any muscles that are still tense. Repeat the exercise for that muscle group three or four times until it relaxes.

Step 5: Now focus on your breathing. Do not alter it artificially, but focus on taking long, slow, deep breaths. Breathe through your nose and exhale through your mouth. Concentrate exclusively on the rhythm of your breathing until you have taken at least 45 breaths.

Step 6: Now focus on the heaviness and warmth of your body. Let all the energy in your body seep away. Let go of your normal tendency to control your body and mobilize it toward activity.

Step 7: With your body completely relaxed, relax your mind. Picture a plain object such as a glass ball, an empty white vase, the moon, or some favorite thing. Don't analyze it; don't examine it; just picture it. Concentrate fully on the object for at least three minutes without letting any other thoughts enter your mind. Begin now.

Step 8: Now open your eyes, slowly get up, and return to your hectic, stressful, anxiety-ridden, Type-A environment better prepared to cope with it effectively.

Monitoring and Managing Time

Time management is the most often identified problem faced by managers and business school students. Most people feel overwhelmed at least part of the time with having too much to accomplish in too little time. It is interesting, however, that even though people may be extremely busy, if they feel that their time is *discretionary*—that is, it can be used in any way that they choose, such as in recreation, playing with friends or family, or by themselves—they feel less stress. Increasing discretionary time, therefore, is a key to effective time management.

This exercise helps you identify and better manage your discretionary time. It takes one full week to complete. It requires that you record how you spend your time for the next seven days. Virtually every executive who is a good time manager has completed this exercise and, in fact, regularly repeats this exercise.

Assignment

Complete the following five steps, then use a partner to get feedback and ideas for improving and refining your plans.

Step 1: Beginning today, keep a time log for one full week. Record how you spend each 30-minute block in the next seven 24-hour periods. Using the following format, record the log in your own notebook, diary, or journal. Simply write down what you did during the 30-minute period. If you did multiple things, record them one above the other.

TIME	ACTIVITY	REQUIRED/ DISCRETIONARY	PRODUCTIVE/ UNPRODUCTIVE
12:00–1:00			
1:00–1:30			
1:30–2:00			
2:00–3:00			
.			
.			
.			
23:00–23:30			
23:30–24:00			

Step 2: Beneath the heading "Required/Discretionary," write whether the time spent in each 30-minute block was required by someone or something else (R) or was discretionary (D). That is, to what extent did you have choice about whether or not you would engage in this activity? You don't have a choice about a certain amount of sleep, for example, or attending class. But you do have a choice about watching TV or spending time socializing.

Step 3: Beneath the heading "Productive/Unproductive," rate the extent to which each activity was productive. That is, identify the extent to which the activity achieved what it was intended to achieve. To what extent did the activity accomplish your own goals or lead to improvements of some kind ? Use the following scale for your rating:

    4 Time was used productively
    3 Time was used somewhat productively
    2 Time was used somewhat unproductively
    1 Time was used unproductively

Step 4: Draw up a plan for increasing the amount of discretionary time you have during the week. Refer to the Time Management Survey in the Assessment Section for suggestions. Write down the things you will *stop* doing and *start* doing.

Step 5: Identify ways in which you can use your discretionary time more productively, especially any blocks of time you rated 1 or 2 in step 3. What will you do to make sure the time you control is used for more long-term benefit? What will you stop doing that impedes your effective use of time?

ACTIVITIES FOR MANAGING STRESS

Suggested Assignments

1. Do a systematic analysis of the stressors you face in your job, family, school, and social life. List the types of stressors you face, and identify strategies to eliminate or sharply reduce them. Record this analysis in your journal.

2. Find someone you know well who is experiencing a great deal of stress. Teach him or her how to manage that stress better by applying the concepts, principles, techniques, and exercises in this chapter. Describe what you taught and record the results in your journal.

3. Implement at least three of the time management techniques suggested in the Time Management Survey or elsewhere that you are not currently using but think you might find helpful. In your time log, keep track of the amount of time these techniques save you over a one-month period. Be sure to use that extra time productively.

4. With a coworker or colleague, identify ways in which your work at school, job, or home can be redesigned to reduce stress and increase productivity. Use the hints provided in the chapter to guide your redesign.

5. Write a personal principles statement. Specify precisely your core principles; those things you consider to be central to your life and your sense of self-worth; and the legacy you want to leave. Identify at least one thing that you want to accomplish in your life that you would like to be known for. Begin working on it today.

6. Establish a short-term goal or plan that you wish to accomplish this year. Make it compatible with the top priorities in your life. Specify the behavioral action steps, the reporting and accounting mechanisms, and the criteria of success and rewards as outlined in Figure 2.5. Share this plan with others you know so that you have an incentive to pursue it even after you finish this class.

7. Get a physical examination, then outline and implement a regular physical fitness and diet program. Even if it is just regular walking, do some kind of physical exercise at least three times a week. Preferably, institute a regular, vigorous cardio-vascular fitness program. Record your progress in your journal.

8. Pick at least one long-term deep-relaxation technique. Learn it and practice it on a regular basis. Record your progress in your journal.

9. Establish a mentoring relationship with someone with whom you work or go to school. Your mentor may be a professor, a senior manager, or someone who has been around longer than you have. Make certain that the relationship is reciprocal and that it will help you cope with the stresses you face at work or school.

Application Plan and Evaluation

The intent of this exercise is to help you apply this cluster of skills in a real-life, out-of-class setting. Now that you have become familiar with the behavioral guidelines that form the basis of effective skill performance, you will improve most by trying out those guidelines in an everyday context. Unlike a classroom activity, in which feedback is immediate and others can assist you with their evaluations, this skill application activity is one you must accomplish and evaluate on your own. There are two parts to this activity. Part 1 helps prepare you to apply the skill. Part 2 helps you evaluate and improve on your experience. Be sure to write down answers to each item. Don't short-circuit the process by skipping steps.

Part 1. Planning

1. Write down the two or three aspects of this skill that are most important to you. These may be areas of weakness, areas you most want to improve, or areas that are most salient to a problem you face right now. Identify the specific aspects of this skill that you want to apply.

2. Now identify the setting or the situation in which you will apply this skill. Establish a plan for performance by actually writing down a description of the situation. Who else will be involved? When will you do it? Where will it be done?
   Circumstances:
   Who else?
   When?
   Where?

3. Identify the specific behaviors in which you will engage to apply this skill. Operationalize your skill performance.

4. What are the indicators of successful performance? How will you know you have been effective? What will indicate you have performed competently?

Part 2. Evaluation

5. After you have completed your implementation, record the results. What happened? How successful were you? What was the effect on others?

6. How can you improve? What modifications can you make next time? What will you do differently in a similar situation in the future?

7. Looking back on your whole skill practice and application experience, what have you learned? What has been surprising? In what ways might this experience help you in the long term?

Stress Management Assessment

Scoring Key

Skill Area	Items	Assessment	
		Pre-	Post-
Eliminating stressors	1, 5, 8, 9	_____	_____
Developing resiliency	2, 3, 6, 7	_____	_____
Short-term coping	4, 10	_____	_____
	Total Score	_____	_____

Comparison Data (N = 1,500 students)

Compare your scores to three standards:
1. The maximum possible score = 60
2. The scores of other students in the class.
3. Norm data from more than 1,500 business school students.

Pre-Test				Post-Test
41.11	=	mean	=	47.84
48 or above	=	top quartile	=	53 or above
44–47	=	third quartile	=	48–52
39–43	=	second quartile	=	44–47
38 or below	=	bottom quartile	=	43 or below

Time Management Assessment

Scoring Key

To see how effective you are as a manager of your time, give yourself the following number of points for the boxes you checked:

Points	Frequency
0	Never
1	Seldom
2	Sometimes
3	Usually
4	Always

If you completed only Section 1 of the assessment, double the scores for each category. Add up your total points for the 40 items.

First half score   _____

Second half score   _____

Total score   _____

Comparison Data (N = 1,500 students)

Mean score:	92
Top quartile:	108 or above
Second quartile:	93–107
Third quartile:	78–92
Bottom quartile:	77 or below

Note: Sometimes people have markedly different scores in the two sections of this instrument. That is, they are better time managers at the office than in their personal lives, or vice versa. Compare your scores for each half of the instrument separately, and discuss with your colleagues how you interpret those scores.

Type A Personality Inventory

Scoring Key

The Type A Personality Inventory costs of four behavioral tendencies: extreme competitiveness, significant life imbalance (typically coupled with high work involvement), strong feelings of hostility and anger, and an extreme sense of urgency and impatience. Scores above 12 in each area suggest that you have a pronounced tendency. Research suggests that the hostility tendency is the most damaging to personal health.

COMPETITIVENESS		WORK INVOLVEMENT		HOSTILITY/ANGER		IMPATIENCE/URGENCY	
ITEM	SCORE	ITEM	SCORE	ITEM	SCORE	ITEM	SCORE
1	_____	2	_____	3	_____	4	_____
5	_____	6	_____	7	_____	8	_____
9	_____	10	_____	11	_____	12	_____
13	_____	14	_____	15	_____	16	_____
17	_____	18	_____	19	_____	20	_____
21	_____	22	_____	23	_____	24	_____
Total	_____	Total	_____	Total	_____	Total	_____

Total Score _____

Comparison Data (N = 1,500 students)

Scores above 12 in each of the four areas indicate a pronounced tendency toward that factor and, consequently, a detrimental effect on physiological, psychological, and social health.

Mean score:	45.83
Top quartile:	51 or above
Third quartile:	45–50

| Second quartile: | 40–44 |
| Bottom quartile: | 39 or below |

Social Readjustment Rating Scale

Scores of 150 points or below resulted in a probability of less than 37 percent that a serious illness would occur in the next year, but the probability increased to about 50 percent with scores of 150–300. Those who scored over 300 on the SRRS had an 80 percent chance of serious illness. Research results also show an injury rate among athletes five times as great for high scorers on the SRRS as for low scorers.

Comparison Data (N = 1,500 students)

Mean score:	257.76
Top quartile:	347 or above
Third quartile:	222–346
Second quartile:	123–221
Bottom quartile:	122 or below

Source of Personal Stress

This exercise does not have a solution or scoring data. Answers will vary among students. Solutions for this exercise are not available online.

3

Solving Problems Analytically and Creatively

SKILL *ASSESSMENT* ▶

- Problem Solving, Creativity, and Innovation
- How Creative Are You?
- Innovative Attitude Scale
- Creative Style Assessment

SKILL *LEARNING* ■

- Problem Solving, Creativity, and Innovation
- Steps in Analytical Problem Solving
- Limitations of the Analytical Problem-Solving Model
- Impediments to Creative Problem Solving
- Multiple Approaches to Creativity
- Conceptual Blocks
- Conceptual Blockbusting
- International Caveats
- Hints for Applying Problem-Solving Techniques
- Fostering Creativity in Others
- Summary
- Behavioral Guidelines

SKILL *ANALYSIS* ▶

- Admiral Kimmel's Failure at Pearl Harbor
- Creativity at Apple

SKILL *PRACTICE* ◆

- Individual Assignment—Analytical Problem Solving
- Team Assignment—Creative Problem Solving
- Moving Up in the Rankings
- Keith Dunn and McGuffey's Restaurant
- Creative Problem-Solving Practice

SKILL *APPLICATION* ●

- Suggested Assignments
- Application Plan and Evaluation

SCORING KEYS AND *COMPARISON DATA* ■

SKILL DEVELOPMENT OBJECTIVES

- INCREASE PROFICIENCY IN ANALYTICAL PROBLEM SOLVING
- RECOGNIZE PERSONAL CONCEPTUAL BLOCKS
- ENHANCE CREATIVITY BY OVERCOMING CONCEPTUAL BLOCKS
- FOSTER INNOVATION AMONG OTHERS

DIAGNOSTIC SURVEYS FOR CREATIVE PROBLEM SOLVING

PROBLEM SOLVING, CREATIVITY, AND INNOVATION

Step 1: Before you read the material in this chapter, please respond to the following statements by writing a number from the rating scale below in the left-hand column (Pre-assessment). Your answers should reflect your attitudes and behavior as they are now, not as you would like them to be. Be honest. This instrument is designed to help you discover your level of competency in problem solving and creativity so you can tailor your learning to your specific needs. When you have completed the survey, use the scoring key at the end of the chapter to identify the skill areas discussed in this chapter that are most important for you to master.

Step 2: After you have completed the reading and the exercises in this chapter and, ideally, as many as you can of the Skill Application assignments at the end of this chapter, cover up your first set of answers. Then respond to the same statements again, this time in the right-hand column (Post-assessment). When you have completed the survey, use the scoring key at the end of the chapter to measure your progress. If your score remains low in specific skill areas, use the behavioral guidelines at the end of the Skill Learning section to guide further practice.

Rating Scale

1 Strongly disagree
2 Disagree
3 Slightly disagree
4 Slightly agree
5 Agree
6 Strongly agree

Assessment

Pre-   Post-

When I encounter a routine problem:

_____   _____   1. I state clearly and explicitly what the problem is. I avoid trying to solve it until I have defined it.

_____   _____   2. I always generate more than one alternative solution to the problem, instead of identifying only one obvious solution.

_____   _____   3. I keep in mind both long-term and short-term consequences as I evaluate various alternative solutions.

_____   _____   4. I gather as much information as I can about what the problem is before trying to solve it.

_____   _____   5. I keep steps in the problem-solving process distinct; that is, I define the problem before proposing alternative solutions, and I generate alternatives before selecting a single solution.

When faced with an ambiguous or difficult problem that does not have an easy solution:

_____ _____ 6. I try out several definitions of the problem. I don't limit myself to just one way to define it.

_____ _____ 7. I try to be flexible in the way I approach the problem by trying out several different alternative methods rather than relying on the same approach every time.

_____ _____ 8. I try to find underlying patterns among elements in the problem so that I can uncover underlying dimensions or principles that help me understand the problem.

_____ _____ 9. I try to unfreeze my thinking by asking lots of questions about the nature of the problem before considering ways to solve it.

_____ _____ 10. I try to think about the problem from both the left (logical) side of my brain and the right (intuitive) side of my brain.

_____ _____ 11. To help me understand the problem and generate alternative solutions, I use analogies and metaphors that help me identify what else this problem is like.

_____ _____ 12. I sometimes reverse my initial definition of the problem to consider whether or not the exact opposite is also true.

_____ _____ 13. I do not evaluate the merits of an alternative solution to the problem before I have generated a list of alternatives. That is, I avoid selecting one solution until I have developed several possible solutions.

_____ _____ 14. I often break down the problem into smaller components and analyze each one separately.

_____ _____ 15. I have some specific techniques that I use to help develop creative and innovative solutions to problems.

When trying to foster more creativity and innovation among those with whom I work:

_____ _____ 16. I help arrange opportunities for individuals to work on their ideas outside the constraints of their normal job assignments.

_____ _____ 17. I make sure there are divergent points of view represented or expressed in every complex problem-solving situation.

_____ _____ 18. I sometimes make outrageous suggestions to stimulate people to find new ways of approaching problems.

_____ _____ 19. I try to acquire information from individuals outside the problem-solving group who will be affected by the decision, mainly to determine their preferences and expectations.

_____ _____ 20. I sometimes involve outsiders (e.g., customers or recognized experts) in problem-solving discussions.

_____ _____ 21. I try to provide recognition not only to those who come up with creative ideas (the idea champions) but also to those who support others' ideas (supporters) and who provide resources to implement them (orchestrators).

_____ _____ 22. I encourage informed rule-breaking in pursuit of creative solutions.

HOW CREATIVE ARE YOU?©

How creative are you? The following test helps you determine if you have the personality traits, attitudes, values, motivations, and interests that characterize creativity. It is based on several years' study of attributes possessed by men and women in a variety of fields and occupations who think and act creatively.

For each statement, write in the appropriate letter:

A Agree
B Undecided or Don't Know
C Disagree

Be as frank as possible. Try not to second-guess how a creative person might respond. Turn to the end of the chapter to find the answer key and an interpretation of your scores.

1. I always work with a great deal of certainty that I am following the correct procedure for solving a particular problem.
2. It would be a waste of time for me to ask questions if I had no hope of obtaining answers.
3. I concentrate harder on whatever interests me than do most people.
4. I feel that a logical step-by-step method is best for solving problems.
5. In groups I occasionally voice opinions that seem to turn some people off.
6. I spend a great deal of time thinking about what others think of me.
7. It is more important for me to do what I believe to be right than to try to win the approval of others.
8. People who seem uncertain about things lose my respect.
9. More than other people, I need to have things interesting and exciting.
10. I know how to keep my inner impulses in check.
11. I am able to stick with difficult problems over extended periods of time.
12. On occasion I get overly enthusiastic.
13. I often get my best ideas when doing nothing in particular.
14. I rely on intuitive hunches and the feeling of "rightness" or "wrongness" when moving toward the solution of a problem.
15. When problem solving, I work faster when analyzing the problem and slower when synthesizing the information I have gathered.
16. I sometimes get a kick out of breaking the rules and doing things I am not supposed to do.
17. I like hobbies that involve collecting things.
18. Daydreaming has provided the impetus for many of my more important projects.
19. I like people who are objective and rational.
20. If I had to choose from two occupations other than the one I now have, I would rather be a physician than an explorer.
21. I can get along more easily with people if they belong to about the same social and business class as myself.
22. I have a high degree of aesthetic sensitivity.
23. I am driven to achieve high status and power in life.
24. I like people who are sure of their conclusions.
25. Inspiration has nothing to do with the successful solution of problems.
26. When I am in an argument, my greatest pleasure would be for the person who disagrees with me to become a friend, even at the price of sacrificing my point of view.
27. I am much more interested in coming up with new ideas than in trying to sell them to others.
28. I would enjoy spending an entire day alone, just "chewing the mental cud."
29. I tend to avoid situations in which I might feel inferior.
30. In evaluating information, the source is more important to me than the content.
31. I resent things being uncertain and unpredictable.
32. I like people who follow the rule "business before pleasure."
33. Self-respect is much more important than the respect of others.
34. I feel that people who strive for perfection are unwise.
35. I prefer to work with others in a team effort rather than solo.

_____ 36. I like work in which I must influence others.

_____ 37. Many problems that I encounter in life cannot be resolved in terms of right or wrong solutions.

_____ 38. It is important for me to have a place for everything and everything in its place.

_____ 39. Writers who use strange and unusual words merely want to show off.

_____ 40. Below is a list of terms that describe people. Choose 10 words that best characterize you.

energetic	persuasive	observant
fashionable	self-confident	persevering
original	cautious	habit-bound
resourceful	egotistical	independent
stern	predictable	formal
informal	dedicated	forward-looking
factual	open-minded	tactful
inhibited	enthusiastic	innovative
poised	acquisitive	practical
alert	curious	organized
unemotional	clear-thinking	understanding
dynamic	self-demanding	polished
courageous	efficient	helpful
perceptive	quick	good-natured
thorough	impulsive	determined
realistic	modest	involved
absent-minded	flexible	sociable
well-liked	restless	retiring

Source: _Exerpted from_ How Creative Are You? _By Eugene Raudsepp. Copyright ©1981 by Eugene Raudsepp._

INNOVATIVE ATTITUDE SCALE

Indicate the extent to which each of the following statements is true of either your actual behavior or your intentions at work. That is, describe the way you are or the way you intend to be on the job. Use the scale for your responses.

Rating Scale

5 Almost always true
4 Often true
3 Not applicable
2 Seldom true
1 Almost never true

_____ 1. I openly discuss with my fellow students and colleagues how to get ahead.

_____ 2. I try new ideas and approaches to problems.

_____ 3. I take things or situations apart to find out how they work.

_____ 4. I welcome uncertainty and unusual circumstances related to my tasks.

_____ 5. I maintain an open dialogue with others who disagree with me.

_____ 6. I can be counted on to find a new use for existing methods or equipment.

_____ 7. I will usually be the first to try out a new idea or method among my colleagues or fellow students.

_____ 8. I take the opportunity to incorporate ideas from other fields or disciplines in my work.

_____ 9. I demonstrate originality in my work.

_____ 10. I will willingly work on a problem that has caused others great difficulty.

_____ 11. I provide important input regarding new solutions when working in a group.

_____ 12. I avoid jumping to conclusions about others' proposed ideas.

_____ 13. I develop contacts with experts outside my area of interest or specialty.

_____ 14. I use personal contacts to expand my options for new jobs or assignments.

_____ 15. I make time to pursue my own pet ideas or projects.

_____ 16. I set aside resources for pursuing a risky project that interests me.

_____ 17. I tolerate people who depart from organizational routine.

_____ 18. I speak out in class and in meetings.

_____ 19. I am good at working in teams to solve complex problems.

_____ 20. If my fellow students or colleagues are asked, they will say I am a wit.

Source: *Adapted from Ettlie & O'Keefe, 1982.*

CREATIVE STYLE ASSESSMENT

Four alternatives exist in each of the items below. You should divide 100 points among each of the four alternatives depending on which alternative is most similar to you. Rate yourself as you are right now, not as you would like to be or as you think you should be. No correct answers exist, so be as accurate as you can. For example, in question 1, if you think alternative "A" is very similar to you, "B" is somewhat similar, and "C" and "D" are hardly similar at all, you might give 50 points to A, 30 points to B, and 10 points each to C and D. Any combination of numbers is acceptable, including 100, 0, 0, 0, or 25, 25, 25, 25. **Just be sure that for each question, the total points add up to 100.**

1. I usually approach difficult problems by:

_____ a. Brainstorming solutions

_____ b. Carefully evaluating alternatives

_____ c. Engaging other people

_____ d. Responding quickly

100

2. My friends and colleagues usually think of me as:

_____ a. Creative

_____ b. Systematic

_____ c. Collaborative

_____ d. Competitive

100

3. I am good at:

_____ a. Experimenting

_____ b. Administering

_____ c. Empowering people

_____ d. Meeting challenges

100

4. When I complete a project or an assignment, I am likely to:

_____ a. Come up with a new project

_____ b. Review the results to see how I might be able to improve them

_____ c. Share what I have learned with others

_____ d. Determine the grade or the evaluation of the results

100

5. I would describe myself as:

_____ a. Flexible

_____ b. Organized

_____ c. Supportive

_____ d. Driven

100

6. I like to work on projects that:

_____ a. Let me invent something new

_____ b. Create practical improvements

_____ c. Get other people involved

_____ d. Can be completed quickly

100

7. When solving a problem, I:

_____ a. Enjoy exploring a lot of options

_____ b. Collect a lot of data

_____ c. Communicate a lot with others

_____ d. Emphasize getting the job done

100

Source: *Adapted from DeGraff & Lawrence, 2002.*

Problem Solving, Creativity, and Innovation

Problem solving is a skill that is required of every person in almost every aspect of life. Seldom does an hour go by without an individual's being faced with the need to solve some kind of problem. The manager's job, in particular, is inherently a problem-solving job. If there were no problems in organizations, there would be no need for managers. Therefore, it is hard to conceive of an incompetent problem solver succeeding as a manager.

In this chapter we offer specific guidelines and techniques for improving problem-solving skills. Two kinds of problem solving—analytical and creative—are addressed. Effective managers are able to solve problems both analytically and creatively, even though different skills are required for each type of problem. First we discuss analytical problem solving—the kind of problem solving that managers use many times each day. Then we turn to creative problem solving, a kind of problem solving that occurs less frequently. Yet this creative problem-solving ability often separates career successes from career failures, heroes from goats, and achievers from derailed executives. It can also produce a dramatic impact on organizational effectiveness. A great deal of research has highlighted the positive relationship between creative problem solving and successful organizations (Sternberg, 1999). This chapter provides guidelines for how you can become a more effective problem solver, both analytical and creative, and concludes with a brief discussion of how managers can foster creative problem solving and innovation among the people with whom they work.

Steps in Analytical Problem Solving

Most people, including managers, don't particularly like problems. Problems are time consuming, they create stress, and they never seem to go away. In fact, most people try to get rid of problems as soon as they can. Their natural tendency is to select the first reasonable solution that comes to mind (Koopman, Broekhuijsen, & Weirdsma, 1998; March, 1994; March & Simon, 1958). Unfortunately, that first solution is often not the best one. In typical problem solving, most people implement a marginally acceptable or merely

satisfactory solution instead of the optimal or ideal solution. In fact, many observers have attributed the extensive failures of Internet and dot.com firms—as well as more established companies—to the abandonment of correct problem-solving principles by managers. Shortcuts in analytical problem solving by managers and entrepreneurs, they argue, have had a major negative effect on company survival (Goll & Rasheed, 1997). Malcolm Gladwell, in his intriguing book entitled *Blink* (2005), argued that people are able to make decisions and reach conclusions on very, very little data—thin slices of behavior—because of their intuitive sense. In a one or two seconds people can reach a conclusion that is as valid as the one made after studying a problem for a long time. First impressions count, he argued, and are valid a lot of the time. These first impressions and instantaneous judgments are valid, however, mainly when problems are not complex, when people have experience with the issue they are judging, and when they have developed an attunement to their own internal cues (that is, they have developed adequate self-awareness and emotional intelligence). Most of the time, the problems we face are complicated, multifaceted, and ambiguous. In such instances, effective problem-solving techniques are required, and they rely on a systematic and logical approach. This approach involves at least four steps, which are explained next.

DEFINING THE PROBLEM

The most widely accepted model of analytical problem solving is summarized in Table 3.1. This method is well known and widely utilized in firms, and it lies at the heart of the quality improvement movement. It is widely asserted that to improve effectiveness of individuals and organizations, an essential step is to learn and apply this analytical method of problem solving (see, for example, Juran, 1988; Riley, 1998). Many large organizations (e.g., Ford Motor Company, General Electric, Hewlett Packard), for example, spend millions of dollars to teach their managers this type of problem solving as part of their productivity and improvement process. Variations on this four-step approach have been implemented in various firms (e.g., Ford uses an eight-step approach), but all the steps are merely derivations of the standard model we discuss here.

Table 3.1   A Model of Problem Solving

STEP	CHARACTERISTICS
1. Define the problem.	• Differentiate fact from opinion.
	• Specify underlying causes.
	• Tap everyone involved for information.
	• State the problem explicitly.
	• Identify what standard is violated.
	• Determine whose problem it is.
	• Avoid stating the problem as a disguised solution.
2. Generate alternative solutions.	• Postpone evaluating alternatives.
	• Be sure all involved individuals generate alternatives.
	• Specify alternatives that are consistent with goals.
	• Specify both short-term and long-term alternatives.
	• Build on others' ideas.
	• Specify alternatives that solve the problem.
3. Evaluate and select an alternative.	• Evaluate relative to an optimal standard.
	• Evaluate systematically.
	• Evaluate relative to goals.
	• Evaluate main effects and side effects.
	• State the selected alternative explicitly.
4. Implement and follow up on the solution.	• Implement at the proper time and in the right sequence.
	• Provide opportunities for feedback.
	• Engender acceptance of those who are affected.
	• Establish an ongoing monitoring system.
	• Evaluate based on problem solution.

The first step is to *define* a problem. This involves diagnosing a situation so that the focus is on the real problem, not just its symptoms. For example, suppose you must deal with an employee who consistently fails to get work done on time. Slow work might be the problem, or it might be only a symptom of another underlying problem such as bad health, low morale, lack of training, or inadequate rewards. Defining the problem, therefore, requires a wide search for information. The more relevant information that is acquired, the more likely it is that the problem will be defined accurately. As Charles Kettering put it, "It ain't the things you don't know that'll get you in trouble, but the things you know for sure that ain't so."

Following are some attributes of good problem definition:

1. Factual information is differentiated from opinion or speculation. Objective data are separated from perceptions and suppositions.
2. All individuals involved are tapped as information sources. Broad participation is encouraged.
3. The problem is stated explicitly. This often helps point out ambiguities in the definition.
4. The problem definition clearly identifies what standard or expectation has been violated. Problems, by their very nature, involve the violation of some standard or expectation.

5. The problem definition must address the question "Whose problem is this?" No problems are completely independent of people. Identify for whom this is a problem.
6. The definition is not simply a disguised solution. Saying "The problem is that we need to motivate slow employees" is inappropriate because the problem is stated as a solution. The problem should be described, not resolved.

Managers often propose a solution before an adequate definition of a problem has been given. This may lead to solving the wrong problem or to reaching conclusions that are misleading or inadequate. Effectively identifying the problem in Iraq, for example, or in the merger of Daimler and Chrysler into one company, required careful analysis. Premature problem definition can become problematic. The definition step in problem solving, therefore, is extremely important.

GENERATING ALTERNATIVES

The second step is to generate alternative solutions. This requires postponing the selection of any one solution until several alternatives have been proposed. Much research on problem solving (e.g., March, 1999) supports the prescription that the quality of solutions can be significantly enhanced by considering multiple alternatives. Judgment and evaluation, therefore, must be postponed so the first acceptable solution suggested isn't the one immediately selected. The problem with evaluating and selecting an alternative too early is that we may rule out some good ideas by just not getting around to thinking about them. We hit on an idea that sounds good and we go with it, thereby never even thinking of alternatives that may be better in the long run.

Many alternative solutions should be produced before any of them are evaluated. A common problem in managerial decision making is that alternatives are evaluated as they are proposed, so the first acceptable (although frequently not optimal) one is chosen.

Some attributes of good alternative generation follow:

1. The evaluation of each proposed alternative is postponed. All relevant alternatives should be proposed before evaluation is allowed.
2. Alternatives are proposed by all individuals involved in the problem. Broad participation in proposing alternatives improves solution quality and group acceptance.

3. Alternative solutions are consistent with organizational goals or policies. Subversion and criticism are detrimental to both the organization and the alternative generation process.
4. Alternatives take into consideration both short-term and long-term consequences.
5. Alternatives build on one another. Bad ideas may become good ones if they are combined with or modified by other ideas.
6. Alternatives solve the problem that has been defined. Another problem may also be important, but it should be ignored if it does not directly affect the problem being considered.

EVALUATING ALTERNATIVES

The third problem-solving step is to evaluate and select an alternative. This step involves careful weighing of the advantages and disadvantages of the proposed alternatives before making a final selection. In selecting the best alternative, skilled problem solvers make sure that alternatives are judged in terms of the extent to which they will solve the problem without causing other unanticipated problems; the extent to which all individuals involved will accept the alternative; the extent to which implementation of the alternative is likely; and the extent to which the alternative fits within organizational constraints (e.g., is consistent with policies, norms, and budget limitations). Care is taken not to short-circuit these considerations by choosing the most conspicuous alternative without considering others. The classic description of the difficulty with problem solving—made almost 50 years ago—still remains as a core principle in problem solving (March & Simon, 1958):

> Most human decision making, whether individual or organizational, is concerned with the discovery and selection of satisfactory alternatives; only in exceptional cases is it concerned with the discovery and selection of optimal alternatives. To optimize requires processes several orders of magnitude more complex than those required to satisfy. An example is the difference between searching a haystack to find the sharpest needle in it and searching the haystack to find a needle sharp enough to sew with.

Given the natural tendency to select the first satisfactory solution proposed, this step deserves particular attention in problem solving. Some attributes of good evaluation are:

1. Alternatives are evaluated relative to an optimal, rather than a satisfactory standard. Determine what is best rather than just what will work.

2. Evaluation of alternatives occurs systematically so each alternative is given due consideration. Short-circuiting evaluation inhibits selection of optimal alternatives, so adequate time for evaluation and consideration should be allowed.

3. Alternatives are evaluated in terms of the goals of the organization and the needs and expectations of the individuals' involved. Organizational goals should be met, but individual preferences should also be considered.

4. Alternatives are evaluated in terms of their probable effects. Both side effects and direct effects on the problem are considered, as well as long-term and short-term effects.

5. The alternative ultimately selected is stated explicitly. This can help ensure that everyone involved understands and agrees with the same solution, and it uncovers ambiguities.

IMPLEMENTING THE SOLUTION

The final step is to implement and follow up on the solution. A surprising amount of the time, people faced with a problem will try to jump to step 4 before having gone through steps 1 through 3. That is, they react to a problem by trying to implement a solution before they have defined it, analyzed it, or generated and evaluated alternative solutions. It is important to remember, therefore, that "getting rid of the problem" by solving it will not occur successfully without the first three steps in the process.

Implementing any problem solution requires sensitivity to possible resistance from those who will be affected by it. Almost any change engenders some resistance. Therefore, the best problem solvers are careful to select a strategy that maximizes the probability that the solution will be accepted and fully implemented. This may involve ordering that the solution be implemented by others, "selling" the solution to others, or involving others in the implementation. Several authors (e.g., Dutton & Ashford, 1993; Miller, Hickson, & Wilson, 1996; Vroom & Yetton, 1973) have provided guidelines for managers to determine which of these implementation behaviors is most appropriate under which circumstances. Generally speaking, participation by others in

the implementation of a solution will increase its acceptance and decrease resistance (Black & Gregersen, 1997).

Effective implementation is usually most effective when it is accomplished in small steps or increments. Weick (1984) introduced the idea of "small wins" in which solutions to problems are implemented little by little. The idea is, implement a part of the solution that is easy to accomplish, then make the successful implementation public. Follow that up by implementing another part of the solution that is easy to accomplish, and publicize it again. Continue implementing incrementally to achieve small wins. This strategy decreases resistance (small changes are usually not worth fighting over), creates support as others observe progress (a bandwagon effect occurs), and reduces costs (failure is not career-ending, and large allocations of resources are not required before success is assured). It also helps ensure persistence and perseverance in implementation. Calvin Coolidge's well-known quotation is apropos:

> *Nothing in the world can take the place of perseverance. Talent will not; nothing is more common than unsuccessful people with talent. Genius will not; unrewarded genius is almost a proverb. Education will not; the world is full of educated derelicts. Persistence and determination alone are omnipotent.*

Of course, any implementation requires follow-up to prevent negative side effects and ensure solution of the problem. Follow-up not only helps ensure effective implementation, but it also serves a feedback function by providing information that can be used to improve future problem solving.

Some attributes of effective implementation and follow-up are:

1. Implementation occurs at the right time and in the proper sequence. It does not ignore constraining factors, and it does not come before steps 1, 2, and 3 in the problem-solving process.

2. Implementation occurs using a "small wins" strategy in order to discourage resistance and engender support.

3. The implementation process includes opportunities for feedback. How well the solution works is communicated and recurring information exchange occurs.

4. Participation by individuals affected by the problem solution is facilitated in order to create support and commitment.

5. An ongoing measurement and monitoring system is set up for the implemented solution. Long-term as well as short-term effects are assessed.

6. Evaluation of success is based on problem solution, not on side benefits. Although the solution may provide some positive outcomes, it is unsuccessful unless it solves the problem being considered.

Limitations of the Analytical Problem-Solving Model

Most experienced problem solvers are familiar with the preceding steps in analytical problem solving, which are based on empirical research results and sound rationale (March, 1994; Miller, Hickson, & Wilson, 1996; Mitroff, 1998; Zeitz, 1999). Unfortunately, managers do not always practice these steps. The demands of their jobs often pressure managers into circumventing some steps, and problem solving suffers as a result. When these four steps are followed, however, effective problem solving is markedly enhanced.

On the other hand, simply learning about and practicing these four steps does not guarantee that an individual will effectively solve all types of problems. These problem-solving steps are most effective mainly when the problems faced are straightforward, when alternatives are readily definable, when relevant information is available, and when a clear standard exists against which to judge the correctness of a solution. The main tasks are to agree upon a single definition, gather the accessible information, generate alternatives, and make an informed choice. But many managerial problems are not of this type. Definitions, information, alternatives, and standards are seldom unambiguous or readily available. In a complex, fast-paced, digital world, these conditions appear less and less frequently. Hence, knowing the steps in problem solving and being able to implement them are not necessarily the same thing.

For example, problems such as discovering why morale is so low, determining how to implement downsizing without antagonizing employees, developing a new process that will double productivity and improve customer satisfaction, or identifying ways to overcome resistance to change are common—and often very complicated—problems faced by most managers. Such problems may not always have an easily identifiable definition or set of alternative solutions available. It may not be clear how much information is needed, what the complete set of alternatives is, or

how one knows if the information being obtained is accurate. Analytical problem solving may help, but something more is needed to address these problems successfully. Tom Peters said, in characterizing the modern world faced by managers: "If you're not confused, you're not paying attention."

Table 3.2 summarizes some reasons why analytical problem solving is not always effective in day-to-day managerial situations. Constraints exist on each of these four steps and stem from other individuals, from organizational processes, or from the external environment that make it difficult to follow the prescribed model. Moreover, some problems are simply not amenable to systematic or rational analysis. Sufficient and accurate information may not be available, outcomes may not be predictable, or means-ends connections may not be evident. In order to solve such problems, a new way of thinking may be required, multiple or conflicting definitions may be needed, and unprecedented alternatives may have to be generated. In short, creative problem solving must be used.

Impediments to Creative Problem Solving

As mentioned in the beginning of the chapter, analytical problem solving is focused on getting rid of problems. Creative problem solving is focused on generating something new (DeGraff & Lawrence, 2002). The trouble is, most people have trouble solving problems creatively. There are two reasons why. First, most of us misinterpret creativity as being one-dimensional—that is, creativity is limited to generating new ideas. We are not aware of the multiple strategies available for being creative, so our repertoire is restricted. Second, all of us have developed certain conceptual blocks in our problem-solving activities, of which we are mostly not aware. These blocks inhibit us from solving certain problems effectively. These blocks are largely personal, as opposed to interpersonal or organizational, so skill development is required to overcome them.

In this chapter, we focus primarily on the individual skills involved in becoming a better creative problem solver. A large literature exists on how managers and leaders can foster creativity in organizations, but this is not our focus (Zhou & Shalley, 2003). Rather, we are interested in helping you strengthen and develop your personal skills and expand your repertoire of creative problem-solving alternatives. We spend most of our time in this chapter on the problem of conceptual blocks inasmuch as it is the obstacle people have the most difficulty addressing. However, the first problem—the need to

Table 3.2	Some Constraints on the Analytical Problem-Solving Model
STEP	**CONSTRAINTS**
1. Define the problem.	• There is seldom consensus as to the definition of the problem.
	• There is often uncertainty as to whose definition will be accepted.
	• Problems are usually defined in terms of the solutions already possessed.
	• Symptoms get confused with the real problem.
	• Confusing information inhibits problem identification.
2. Generate alternative solutions.	• Solution alternatives are usually evaluated one at a time as they are proposed.
	• Few of the possible alternatives are usually known.
	• The first acceptable solution is usually accepted.
	• Alternatives are based on what was successful in the past.
3. Evaluate and select an alternative.	• Limited information about each alternative is usually available.
	• Search for information occurs close to home—in easily accessible places.
	• The type of information available is constrained by factors such as primacy versus recency, extremity versus centrality, expected versus surprising, and correlation versus causation.
	• Gathering information on each alternative is costly.
	• Preferences of which is the best alternative are not always known.
	• Satisfactory solutions, not optimal ones, are usually accepted.
	• Solutions are often selected by oversight or default.
	• Solutions often are implemented before the problem is defined.
4. Implement and follow up on the solution.	• Acceptance by others of the solution is not always forthcoming.
	• Resistance to change is a universal phenomenon.
	• It is not always clear what part of the solution should be monitored or measured in follow-up.
	• Political and organizational processes must be managed in any implementation effort.
	• It may take a long time to implement a solution.

develop multiple approaches to creativity—is also important and is addressed in the section that follows.

Multiple Approaches to Creativity

One of the most sophisticated approaches to creativity identifies four distinct methods for achieving it. This approach is based on the Competing Values Framework (Cameron, Quinn, DeGraff, & Thakor, 2006), which identifies competing or conflicting dimensions that describe people's attitudes, values, and behaviors. Figure 3.1 describes the four different types of creativity and the relationships. These four types were developed by our colleague Jeff DeGraff (DeGraff & Lawrence, 2002).

For example, achieving creativity through **imagination** refers to the *creation* of new ideas, breakthroughs, and radical approaches to problem solving. People who pursue creativity in this way tend to be experimenters, speculators, and entrepreneurs,

Figure 3.1 | Four Types of Creativity

Flexibility

Incubation
Be sustainable

capitalize on teamwork,
involvement,
coordination and
cohesion, empowering
people, building trust

Imagination
Be new

experimentation,
exploration, risk taking,
transformational ideas,
revolutionary thinking,
unique visions

Internal ──────────────────────────── **External**

Improvement
Be better

incremental
improvements, process
control, systematic
approaches, careful
methods, clarifying
problems

Investment
Be first

rapid goal achievement,
faster responses than
others, competitive
approaches, attack
problems directly

Control

Source: *Adapted from DeGraff & Lawrence, 2002.*

and they define creativity as exploration, new product innovation, or developing unique visions of possibilities. When facing difficult problems in need of problem solving, their approach is focused on coming up with revolutionary possibilities and unique solutions. Well-known examples include Steve Jobs at Apple, the developer of the iPod and the Macintosh computer, and Walt Disney, the creator of animated movies and theme parks. Both of these people approached problem solving by generating radically new ideas and products that created entirely new industries. The most famous design firm in the world—*Ideo* in Palo Alto, California—produces more than 90 new products a year and has become renowned for creating product designs that no one had ever thought of before—neat-squeeze toothpaste containers, computer mouses, flat-screen monitors, Nerf footballs. They hire radical thinkers, rule breakers, and risk takers to think "outside the box."

People may also achieve creativity, however, through opposite means—that is, by developing incrementally better alternatives, *improving* on what already exists, or clarifying the ambiguity that is associated with the problem. Rather than being revolutionaries and risk takers, they are systematic, careful, and thorough. Creativity comes by finding ways to improve processes or functions. An example is Ray Kroc, the magician behind McDonald's remarkable success. As a salesman in the 1950s, Kroc bought out a restaurant in San Bernardino, California, from the McDonald brothers and, by creatively changing the way hamburgers were made and served, he created the largest food service company in the world. He didn't invent fast food— White Castle and Dairy Queen had long been established—but he changed the processes. Creating a limited, standardized menu, uniform cooking procedures, consistent service quality, cleanliness of facilities, and inexpensive food—no matter where in the country (and now, in the world) you eat—demonstrated a very different approach to creativity. Instead of breakthrough ideas, Kroc's secret was incremental improvements on existing ideas. This type of creativity is referred to as **improvement**.

A third type of creativity is called **investment**, or the pursuit of rapid goal achievement and *competitiveness*. People who approach creativity in this way meet challenges head on, adopt a competitive posture, and focus on achieving results faster than others. People achieve creativity by working harder than the competition, exploiting others' weaknesses, and being first to offer a product, service, or idea. The advantages of being a "first mover" company are well-known. This kind of creativity can be illustrated by Honda President Kawashima in the "Honda-Yamaha Motorcycle War." Honda became the industry leader in motorcycles in Japan in the 1960s but decided to enter the automobile market in the 1970s. Yamaha saw this as an opportunity to overtake Honda in motorcycle market share in Japan. In public speeches at the beginning of the 1980s, Yamaha's President Koike promised that Yamaha would soon overtake Honda in motorcycle production because of Honda's new focus on automobiles. "In a year we will be the domestic leader, and in two years we will be number one in the world," touted Koike in his 1982 shareholders' meeting. At the beginning of 1983, Honda's president replied: "As long as I am president of this company, we will surrender our number one spot to no one . . . *Yamaha wo tubusu*!"—meaning, we will smash, break, annihilate, destroy Yamaha. In the next year, Honda introduced 81 new models of motorcycles and discontinued 32 models for a total of 113 changes to its product line. In the following year, Honda introduced 39 additional models and added 18 changes to the 50cc line. Yamaha's sales plummeted 50 percent and the firm endured a loss of 24 billion yen for the year. Yamaha's president conceded: "I would like to end the Honda-Yamaha war . . . From now on we will move cautiously and ensure Yamaha's relative position as second to Honda." Approaching creativity through investment—rapid response, competitive maneuvering, and being the first mover—characterized Honda president Kawashima's approach to creativity.

The fourth type of creativity is **incubation**. This refers to an approach to creative activity through teamwork, involvement, and coordination among individuals. Creativity occurs by unlocking the potential that exists in interactions among networks of people. Individuals who approach creativity through incubation encourage people to work together, foster trust and cohesion, and empower others. Creativity arises from a collective mindset and shared values. For example, Mahatma Gandhi was probably the only person in modern history who has single-handedly stopped a war. Lone individuals have started wars, but Gandhi was creative enough to stop one. He did so by mobilizing networks of people to pursue a clear vision and set of values. Gandhi would probably have been completely noncreative and ineffective had he not been adept at capitalizing on incubation dynamics. By mobilizing people to march to the sea to make salt, or to burn passes that demarcated ethnic group status, Gandhi was able to engender creative outcomes that had not been considered possible. He was a master at incubation by connecting, involving, and coordinating people. The same could be said for Bill Wilson, the founder of Alcoholics Anonymous, whose 12-step program is the foundation for almost all addiction treatment organizations around the world—gambling addiction, drug addiction, eating disorders, and so on. To cure his own alcoholism, Wilson began meeting with others with the same problem and, over time, developed a very creative way to help himself as well as other people overcome their dependencies. The genius behind Alcoholics Anonymous is the creativity that emerges when human interactions are facilitated and encouraged.

Figure 3.2 helps place these four types of creativity into perspective. You will note that imagination and improvement emphasize opposite approaches to creativity. They differ in the *magnitude* of the creative ideas being pursued. Imagination focuses on new, revolutionary solutions to problems. Improvement focuses on incremental, controlled solutions. Investment and incubation are also contradictory and opposing in their approach to creativity. They differ in *speed* of response. Investment focuses on fast, competitive responses to problems, whereas incubation emphasizes more developmental and deliberate responses.

It is important to point out that no one approach to creativity is best. Different circumstances call for different approaches. For example, Ray Kroc and McDonald's would not have been successful with an imagination strategy (revolutionary change), and Walt Disney would not have been effective with an incubation strategy (group consensus). Kawashima at Honda could not afford to wait for an incubation strategy (slow, developmental change), whereas it would have made no sense for Gandhi to approach creativity using investment (a competitive approach). Different circumstances require different approaches. Circumstances in which each of these four approaches to creativity are most effective are listed in Figure 3.3.

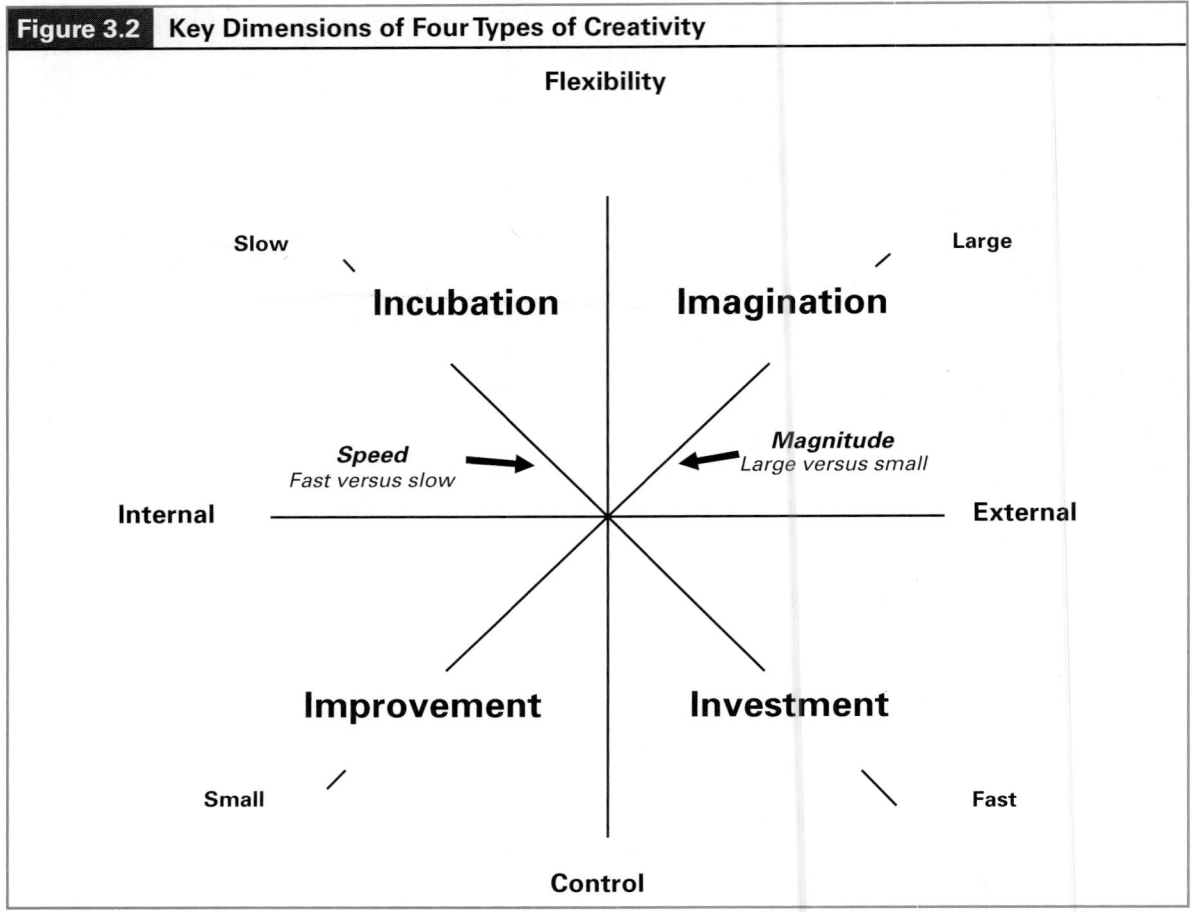

Figure 3.2 | **Key Dimensions of Four Types of Creativity**

Flexibility

Slow

Incubation **Imagination**

Large

Speed
Fast versus slow

Magnitude
Large versus small

Internal ——————————————————————— External

Improvement **Investment**

Small

Fast

Control

Source: *Adapted from DeGraff & Lawrence, 2002.*

This figure shows that imagination is the most appropriate approach to creativity when breakthroughs are needed and when original ideas are necessary—being new. The improvement approach is most appropriate when incremental changes or tightening up processes are necessary—being better. The investment approach is most appropriate when quick responses and goal achievement takes priority—being first. And, the incubation approach is most appropriate when collective effort and involvement of others is important—being sustainable.

The Creativity Assessment survey that you completed in the Pre-assessment section helps identify your own preferences regarding these different approaches to creativity. You were able to create a profile showing the extent to which you are inclined toward imagination, improvement, investment, or incubation as you approach problems calling for creativity. Your profile

will help you determine which kinds of problems you are inclined to solve when creativity is required. Of course, having a preference is not the same as having ability or possessing competence in a certain approach, but the remainder of this chapter as well as several additional chapters in this book will help with your creative competence development.

Your profile is in the shape of a kite, and it identifies your most preferred style of creativity. The quadrant in which you score highest is your preferred approach but you will notice that you do not have a single approach. No one gives all of their points to a single alternative. Just as you have points in each of the four quadrants on the creativity profile, you also have an inclination to approach creativity in multiple ways. However, most people have certain dominant inclinations toward creativity, and those inclinations are helpful guides to you as you approach problems.

Figure 3.3   **Examples of Situations in Which Each Approach Is Effective**

Incubation
Be sustainable

Existence of a diverse community with strong values; need for collective effort and consensus; empowered workforce

Imagination
Be new

Need for brand-new, breakthrough products or services; emerging markets; resources needed for experimentation

Internal ———————————————————— **External**

Improvement
Be better

Requirement for quality, safety, and reliability; high technical specialization; effective standardized processes

Investment
Be first

Fast results are a necessity; highly competitive environments; emphasis on bottom-line outcomes

Source: *Adapted from DeGraff & Lawrence, 2002.*

Most of us are not aware that we can be creative in multiple ways, yet anyone can be creative and add value to problem solving. Just because you are not a clever producer of unique ideas, for example, does not mean that you are not creative and cannot add value to the creative process.

Conceptual Blocks

The trouble is, each of these different approaches to creativity can be inhibited. That is, in addition to being unaware of the multiple ways in which we can be creative, most of us have difficulty in solving problems creatively because of the presence of **conceptual blocks.** Conceptual blocks are mental obstacles that constrain the way problems are defined, and they can inhibit us from being effective in any of the four types of creativity. Conceptual blocks limit the number of alternative solutions that people think about (Adams, 2001). Every individual has conceptual blocks, but some people have more numerous and more intense ones than others. These blocks are largely unrecognized or unconscious, so the only way individuals can

be made aware of them is to be confronted with problems that are unsolvable because of them. Conceptual blocks result largely from the thinking processes that problem solvers use when facing problems. Everyone develops some conceptual blocks over time. In fact, we need some of them to cope with everyday life. Here's why.

At every moment, each of us is bombarded with far more information than we can possibly absorb. For example, you are probably not conscious right now of the temperature of the room, the color of your skin, the level of illumination overhead, or how your toes feel in your shoes. All of this information is available to you and is being processed by your brain, but you have tuned out some things and focused on others. Over time, you must develop the habit of mentally filtering out some of the information to which you are exposed; otherwise, information overload would drive you crazy. These filtering habits eventually become conceptual habits or blocks. Though you are not conscious of them, they inhibit you from registering some kinds of information and, therefore, from solving certain kinds of problems.

Paradoxically, the more formal education individuals have, and the more experience they have in a job, the less able they are to solve problems in creative ways. It has been estimated that most adults over 40 display less than two percent of the creative problem-solving ability of a child under five years old. That's because formal education often prescribes "right" answers, analytic rules, or thinking boundaries. Experience in a job often leads to "proper" ways of doing things, specialized knowledge, and rigid expectation of appropriate actions. Individuals lose the ability to experiment, improvise, or take mental detours. Consider the following example:

> If you place in a bottle half a dozen bees and the same number of flies, and lay the bottle down horizontally, with its base to the window, you will find that the bees will persist, till they die of exhaustion or hunger, in their endeavor to discover an issue through the glass; while the flies, in less than two minutes, will all have sallied forth through the neck on the opposite side. . . . It is [the bees'] love of light, it is their very intelligence, that is their undoing in this experiment. They evidently imagine that the issue from every prison must be there when the light shines clearest; and they act in accordance, and persist in too logical an action. To them glass is a supernatural mystery they never have met in nature; they have had no experience of this suddenly impenetrable atmosphere; and the greater their intelligence, the more inadmissible, more incomprehensible, will the strange obstacle appear. Whereas the feather-brained flies, careless of logic as of the enigma of crystal, disregarding the call of the light, flutter wildly, hither and thither, meeting here the good fortune that often waits on the simple, who find salvation where the wiser will perish, necessarily end by discovering the friendly opening that restores their liberty to them (Weick, 1995, p. 59).

This illustration identifies a paradox inherent in learning to solve problems creatively. On the one hand, more education and experience may inhibit creative problem solving and reinforce conceptual blocks. Like the bees in the story, individuals may not find solutions because the problem requires less "educated," more "playful" approaches. On the other hand, as several researchers have found, training focused on improving thinking significantly enhances creative problem-solving abilities and managerial effectiveness (Albert & Runco,

1999; Mumford, Baughman, Maher, Costanza, & Supinski, 1997; Nickerson, 1999; Smith, 1998).

For example, research has found that training in thinking increased the number of good ideas produced in problem solving by more than 125 percent (Scope, 1999). Creativity in art, music composition, problem finding, problem construction, and idea generation have been found to improve substantially when training in creative problem solving and thinking skills is received (de Bono, 1973, 1992; Finke, Ward, & Smith, 1992; Getzels & Csikszentmihalyi, 1976; Nickerson, 1999; Starko, 2001). Moreover, substantial data also exists that such training can enhance the profitability and efficiency of organizations (Williams & Yang, 1999). Many organizations—such as Microsoft, General Electric, and AT&T—now send their executives to creativity workshops in order to improve their creative-thinking abilities. Creative problem-solving experts are currently hot properties on the consulting circuit, and about a million copies of books on creativity are sold each year in North America. Several well-known products have been produced as a direct result of this kind of training: for example, NASA's Velcro snaps, G.E.'s self-diagnostic dishwashers, Mead's carbonless copy paper, and Kodak's Trimprint film.

Resolving this paradox is not just a matter of more exposure to information or education. Rather, people must master the process of thinking about certain problems in a creative way. As Csikszentmihalyi (1996, p. 11) observed:

> Each of us is born with two contradictory sets of instructions: a conservative tendency, made up of instincts for self-preservation, self-aggrandizement, and saving energy, and an expansive tendency made up of instincts for exploring, for enjoying novelty and risk—the curiosity that leads to creativity belongs to this set. We need both of these programs. But whereas the first tendency requires little encouragement or support from the outside to motivate behavior, the second can wilt if it is not cultivated. If too few opportunities for curiosity are available, if too many obstacles are placed in the way of risk and exploration, the motivation to engage in creative behavior is easily extinguished.

In the next section, we focus on problems that require creative rather than analytical solutions. These are problems for which no acceptable alternative seems to be available, all reasonable solutions seem to be blocked, or no obvious best answer is accessible. Analytical problem solving just doesn't seem to apply. This situation often exists because conceptual blocks inhibit the range of solutions thought possible. We introduce some tools and techniques that help overcome conceptual blocks and unlock problem-solving creativity. First consider these two examples that illustrate creative problem solving and breaking through conceptual blocks.

PERCY SPENCER'S MAGNETRON

During World War II, the British developed one of the best-kept military secrets of the war, a special radar detector based on a device called the magnetron. This radar was credited with turning the tide of battle in the war between Britain and Germany and helping the British withstand Hitler's Blitzkrieg. In 1940, Raytheon was one of several U.S. firms invited to produce magnetrons for the war effort.

The workings of magnetrons were not well understood, even by sophisticated physicists. Even among the firms that made magnetrons, few understood what made them work. A magnetron was tested, in those early days, by holding a neon tube next to it. If the neon tube got bright enough, the magnetron tube passed the test. In the process of conducting the test, the hands of the scientist holding the neon tube got warm. It was this phenomenon that led to a major creative breakthrough that eventually transformed lifestyles throughout the world.

At the end of the war, the market for radar essentially dried up, and most firms stopped producing magnetrons. At Raytheon, however, a scientist named Percy Spencer had been fooling around with magnetrons, trying to think of alternative uses for the devices. He was convinced that magnetrons could be used to cook food by using the heat produced in the neon tube. But Raytheon was in the defense business. Next to its two prize products—the Hawk and Sparrow missiles—cooking devices seemed odd and out of place. Percy Spencer was convinced that Raytheon should continue to produce magnetrons, even though production costs were prohibitively high. But Raytheon had lost money on the devices, and now there was no available market for magnetrons. The consumer product Spencer had in mind did not fit within the bounds of Raytheon's business.

As it turned out, Percy Spencer's solution to Raytheon's problem produced the microwave oven and a revolution in cooking methods throughout the world. Later, we will analyze several problem-solving techniques illustrated by Spencer's creative triumph.

SPENCE SILVER'S GLUE

A second example of creative problem solving began with Spence Silver's assignment to work on a temporary project team within the 3M company. The team was searching for new adhesives, so Silver obtained some material from AMD, Inc., which had potential for a new polymer-based adhesive. He described one of his experiments in this way: "In the course of this exploration, I tried an experiment with one of the monomers in which I wanted to see what would happen if I put a lot of it into the reaction mixture. Before, we had used amounts that would correspond to conventional wisdom" (Nayak & Ketteringham, 1986). The result was a substance that failed all the conventional 3M tests for adhesives. It didn't stick. It preferred its own molecules to the molecules of any other substance. It was more cohesive than adhesive. It sort of "hung around without making a commitment." It was a "now-it-works, now-it-doesn't" kind of glue.

For five years, Silver went from department to department within the company trying to find someone interested in using his newly found substance in a product. Silver had found a solution; he just couldn't find a problem to solve with it. Predictably, 3M showed little interest. The company's mission was to make adhesives that adhered ever more tightly. The ultimate adhesive was one that formed an unbreakable bond, not one that formed a temporary bond.

After four years the task force was disbanded, and team members were assigned to other projects. But Silver was still convinced that his substance was good for something. He just didn't know what. As it turned out, Silver's solution has become the prototype for innovation in American firms, and it has spawned a multibillion-dollar business for 3M—in a unique product called Post-It Notes.

These two examples are positive illustrations of how solving a problem in a unique way can lead to phenomenal business success. Creative problem solving can have remarkable effects on individuals' careers and on business success. To understand how to solve problems creatively, however, we must first consider the blocks that inhibit creativity.

THE FOUR TYPES OF CONCEPTUAL BLOCKS

Table 3.3 summarizes four types of conceptual blocks that inhibit creative problem solving. Each is discussed and illustrated below with problems or exercises. We encourage you to complete the exercises and solve the

Table 3.3   Conceptual Blocks That Inhibit Creative Problem Solving

1. *Constancy*

   - Vertical thinking — Defining a problem in only one way without considering alternative views.
   - One thinking language — Not using more than one language to define and assess the problem.

2. *Commitment*

   - Stereotyping based on past experience — Present problems are seen only as the variations of past problems.
   - Ignoring commonalities — Failing to perceive commonalities among elements that initially appear to be different.

3. *Compression*

   - Distinguishing figure from ground — Not filtering out irrelevant information or finding needed information.
   - Artificial constraints — Defining the boundaries of a problem too narrowly.

4. *Complacency*

   - Noninquisitiveness — Not asking questions.
   - Nonthinking — A bias toward activity in place of mental work.

problems as you read the chapter, because doing so will help you become aware of your own conceptual blocks. Later, we shall discuss in more detail how you can overcome those blocks.

Constancy

One type of conceptual block occurs because individuals become wedded to one way of looking at a problem or using one approach to define, describe, or solve it. It is easy to see why **constancy** is common in problem solving. Being constant, or consistent, is a highly valued attribute for most of us. We like to appear at least moderately consistent in our approach to life, and constancy is often associated with maturity, honesty, and even intelligence. We judge lack of constancy as untrustworthy, peculiar, or airheaded. Some prominent psychologists theorize, in fact, that a need for constancy is the primary motivator of human behavior (Festinger, 1957; Heider, 1946; Newcomb, 1954). Many psychological studies have shown that once individuals take a stand or employ a particular approach to a problem, they are highly likely to pursue that same course without deviation in the future (see Cialdini, 2001, for multiple examples).

On the other hand, constancy can inhibit the solution of some kinds of problems. Consistency sometimes drives out creativity. Two illustrations of the constancy block are vertical thinking and using only one thinking language.

Vertical Thinking   The term **vertical thinking** was coined by Edward de Bono (1968, 2000). It refers to defining a problem in a single way and then pursuing that definition without deviation until a solution is reached. No alternative definitions are considered. All information gathered and all alternatives generated are consistent with the original definition. De Bono contrasted lateral thinking to vertical thinking in the following ways: vertical thinking focuses on continuity, lateral thinking focuses on discontinuity; vertical thinking chooses, lateral thinking changes; vertical thinking is concerned with stability, lateral thinking is concerned with instability; vertical thinking searches for what is right, lateral thinking searches for what is different; vertical thinking is analytical, lateral thinking is provocative; vertical thinking is concerned with where an idea came from, lateral thinking is concerned with where the idea is going; vertical thinking moves in the most likely directions, lateral thinking moves in the least likely directions; vertical thinking develops an idea, lateral thinking discovers the idea.

In a search for oil, for example, vertical thinkers determine a spot for the hole and drill the hole deeper and deeper until they strike oil. Lateral thinkers, on the other hand, drill a number of holes in different places in search of oil. The vertical-thinking conceptual block arises from not being able to view the problem from multiple perspectives—to drill several holes—or to think laterally as well as vertically in problem solving.

Plenty of examples exist of creative solutions that occurred because an individual refused to get stuck with a single problem definition. Alexander Graham Bell was trying to devise a hearing aid when he shifted definitions and invented the telephone. Harland Sanders was trying to sell his recipe to restaurants when he shifted definitions and developed his Kentucky Fried Chicken business. Karl Jansky was studying telephone static when he shifted definitions, discovered radio waves from the Milky Way galaxy, and developed the science of radio astronomy.

In developing the microwave industry described earlier, Percy Spencer shifted the definition of the problem from "How can we save our military radar business at the end of the war?" to "What other applications can be made for the magnetron?" Other problem definitions followed, such as: "How can we make magnetrons cheaper?" "How can we mass-produce magnetrons?" "How can we convince someone besides the military to buy magnetrons?" "How can we enter a consumer products market?" "How can we make microwave ovens practical and safe?" And so on. Each new problem definition led to new ways of thinking about the problem, new alternative approaches, and, eventually, to a new microwave oven industry.

Spence Silver at 3M is another example of someone who changed problem definitions. He began with "How can I get an adhesive that has a stronger bond?" but switched to "How can I find an application for an adhesive that doesn't stick firmly?" Eventually, other problem definitions followed: "How can we get this new glue to stick to one surface but not another (e.g., to notepaper but not normal paper)?" "How can we replace staples, thumbtacks, and paper clips in the workplace?" "How can we manufacture and package a product that uses nonadhesive glue?" "How can we get anyone to pay $1.00 a pad for scratch paper?" And so on.

Shifting definitions is not easy, of course, because it is not natural. It requires individuals to deflect their tendency toward constancy. Later, we will discuss some hints and tools that can help overcome the constancy block while avoiding the negative consequences of inconsistency.

A Single Thinking Language
A second manifestation of the constancy block is the use of only one **thinking language**. Most people think in words—that is, they think about a problem and its solution in terms of verbal language. **Analytical problem solving** reinforces this approach. Some writers, in fact, have argued that thinking cannot even occur without words (Feldman, 1999; Vygotsky, 1962). Other thought languages are available, however, such as nonverbal or symbolic languages (e.g., mathematics), sensory imagery (e.g., smelling or tactile sensation), feelings and emotions (e.g., happiness, fear, or anger), and visual imagery (e.g., mental pictures). The more languages available to problem solvers, the better and more creative will be their solutions. As Koestler (1964, p. 177) puts it, "[Verbal] language can become a screen which stands between the thinker and reality. This is the reason that true creativity often starts where [verbal] language ends."

Percy Spencer at Raytheon is a prime example of a visual thinker:

> One day, while Spencer was lunching with Dr. Ivan Getting and several other Raytheon scientists, a mathematical question arose. Several men, in a familiar reflex, pulled out their slide rules, but before any could complete the equation, Spencer gave the answer. Dr. Getting was astonished. "How did you do that?" he asked. "The root," said Spencer shortly. "I learned cube roots and squares by using blocks as a boy. Since then, all I have to do is visualize them placed together." (Scott, 1974, p. 287)

The microwave oven depended on Spencer's command of multiple thinking languages. Furthermore, the new oven would never have gotten off the ground without a critical incident that illustrates the power of visual thinking. By 1965, Raytheon was just about to give up on any consumer application of the magnetron when a meeting was held with George Foerstner, president of the recently acquired Amana Refrigeration Company. In the meeting, costs, applications, manufacturing obstacles, and production issues were discussed. Foerstner galvanized the entire microwave oven effort with the following statement, as reported by a Raytheon vice president.

> George says, "It's no problem. It's about the same size as an air conditioner. It weighs about the same. It should sell for the same. So we'll price it at $499." Now you think that's silly, but you stop and think about it. Here's a man who really didn't understand the technologies. But there is about the same amount of copper involved, the same amount of steel as an air conditioner. And these are basic raw

materials. It didn't make a lot of difference how you fit them together to make them work. They're both boxes; they're both made out of sheet metal; and they both require some sort of trim. (Nayak & Ketteringham, 1986, p. 181)

In several short sentences, Foerstner had taken one of the most complicated military secrets of World War II and translated it into something no more complex than a room air conditioner. He had painted a picture of an application that no one else had been able to capture by describing a magnetron visually, as a familiar object, not as a set of calculations, formulas, or blueprints.

A similar occurrence in the Post-It Note chronology also led to a breakthrough. Spence Silver had been trying for years to get someone in 3M to adopt his unsticky glue. Art Fry, another scientist with 3M, had heard Silver's presentations before. One day while singing in North Presbyterian Church in St. Paul, Minnesota, Fry was fumbling around with the slips of paper that marked the various hymns in his book. Suddenly, a visual image popped into his mind.

I thought, "Gee, if I had a little adhesive on these bookmarks, that would be just the ticket." So I decided to check into that idea the next week at work. What I had in mind was Silver's adhesive. . . . I knew I had a much bigger discovery than that. I also now realized that the primary application for Silver's adhesive was not to put it on a fixed surface like bulletin boards. That was a secondary application. The primary application concerned paper to paper. I realized that immediately." (Nayak & Ketteringham, 1986, pp. 63–64)

Years of verbal descriptions had not led to any applications for Silver's glue. Tactile thinking (handling the glue) also had not produced many ideas. However, thinking about the product in visual terms, as applied

to what Fry initially called "a better bookmark," led to the breakthrough that was needed.

This emphasis on using alternative thinking languages, especially visual thinking, has become a new frontier in scientific research (McKim, 1997). With the advent of the digital revolution, scientists are more and more working with pictures and simulated images rather than with numerical data. "Scientists who are using the new computer graphics say that by viewing images instead of numbers, a fundamental change in the way researchers think and work is occurring. People have a lot easier time getting an intuition from pictures than they do from numbers and tables or formulas. In most physics experiments, the answer used to be a number or a string of numbers. In the last few years the answer has increasingly become a picture" (Markoff, 1988, p. D3).

To illustrate the differences among thinking languages, consider the following simple problem:

Figure 3.4 shows seven matchsticks. By moving only one matchstick, make the figure into a true equality (i.e., the value on one side equals the value on the other side). Before looking up the answers in the section at the end of the chapter with scoring keys and comparison data, try defining the problem by using different thinking languages. What thinking language is most effective?

Commitment

Commitment can also serve as a conceptual block to creative problem solving. Once individuals become committed to a particular point of view, definition, or solution, it is likely that they will follow through on that commitment. Cialdini (2001) reported a study, for example, in which investigators asked Californians to put a large, poorly lettered sign on their front lawns saying DRIVE CAREFULLY. Only 17 percent agreed to do so. However,

Figure 3.4	The Matchstick Configuration

after signing a petition favoring "keep California beautiful," the people were again asked to put the DRIVE CAREFULLY sign on their lawns, and 76 percent agreed to do so. Once they had committed to being active and involved citizens (i.e., to keeping California beautiful), it was consistent for these people to agree to the large unsightly sign as visible evidence of their commitment. Most people have the same inclination toward being consistent and maintaining commitments.

Two forms of commitment that produce conceptual blocks are stereotyping based on past experiences and ignoring commonalities.

Stereotyping Based on Past Experiences March (1999) pointed out that a major obstacle to innovative problem solving is that individuals tend to define present problems in terms of problems they have faced in the past. Current problems are usually seen as variations on some past situation, so the alternatives proposed to solve the current problem are ones that have proven successful in the past. Both problem definitions and proposed solutions are therefore restricted by past experience. This restriction is referred to as **perceptual stereotyping** (Adams, 2001). That is, certain preconceptions formed on the basis of past experience determine how an individual defines a situation.

When individuals receive an initial cue regarding the definition of a problem, all subsequent problems are frequently framed in terms of the initial cue. Of course, this is not all bad, because perceptual stereotyping helps organize problems on the basis of a limited amount of data, and the need to consciously analyze every problem encountered is eliminated. On the other hand, perceptual stereotyping prevents individuals from viewing a problem in novel ways.

The creation of microwave ovens and of Post-It Notes provide examples of overcoming stereotyping based on past experiences. Scott (1974) described the first meeting of John D. Cockcroft, technical leader of the British radar system that invented magnetrons, and Percy Spencer of Raytheon.

Cockcroft liked Spencer at once. He showed him the magnetron, and the American regarded it thoughtfully. He asked questions—very intelligent ones—about how it was produced, and the Britisher answered at length. Later Spencer wrote, "The technique of making these tubes, as described to us, was awkward and impractical." Awkward and impractical! Nobody else dared draw such a judgment about a product of undoubted scientific brilliance, produced and displayed by the leaders of British science.

Despite his admiration for Cockcroft and the magnificent magnetron, Spencer refused to abandon his curious and inquisitive stance. Rather than adopting the position of other scientists and assuming that since the British invented it and were using it, they surely knew how to produce a magnetron, Spencer broke out of the stereotypes and pushed for improvements.

Similarly, Spence Silver at 3M described his invention in terms of breaking stereotypes based on past experience.

The key to the Post-It adhesive was doing the experiment. If I had sat down and factored it out beforehand, and thought about it, I wouldn't have done the experiment. If I had really seriously cracked the books and gone through the literature, I would have stopped. The literature was full of examples that said you can't do this. (Nayak & Ketteringham, 1986, p. 57)

This is not to say that one should avoid learning from past experience or that failing to learn the mistakes of history does not doom us to repeat them. Rather, it is to say that commitment to a course of action based on past experience can sometimes inhibit viewing problems in new ways, and can even prevent us from solving some problems at all. Consider the following problem as an example.

Assume that there are four volumes of Shakespeare on the shelf (see Figure 3.5). Assume that the pages of each volume are exactly two inches thick, and that the covers of each volume are each one-sixth of an inch thick. Assume that a bookworm began eating at page 1 of Volume 1, and it ate straight through to the last page of Volume IV. What distance did the worm cover? Solving this problem is relatively simple, but it requires that you overcome a stereotyping block to get the correct answer. (See the end of the chapter for the correct answer.)

Ignoring Commonalities A second manifestation of the commitment block is failure to identify similarities among seemingly disparate pieces of data. This is among the most commonly identified blocks to creativity. It means that a person becomes committed to a particular point of view, to the fact that elements are different, and, consequently, becomes unable to make connections, identify themes, or perceive commonalities.

The ability to find one definition or solution for two seemingly dissimilar problems is a characteristic of creative individuals (see Sternberg, 1999). The inability to do this can overload a problem solver by requiring

Figure 3.5 | Shakespeare Riddle

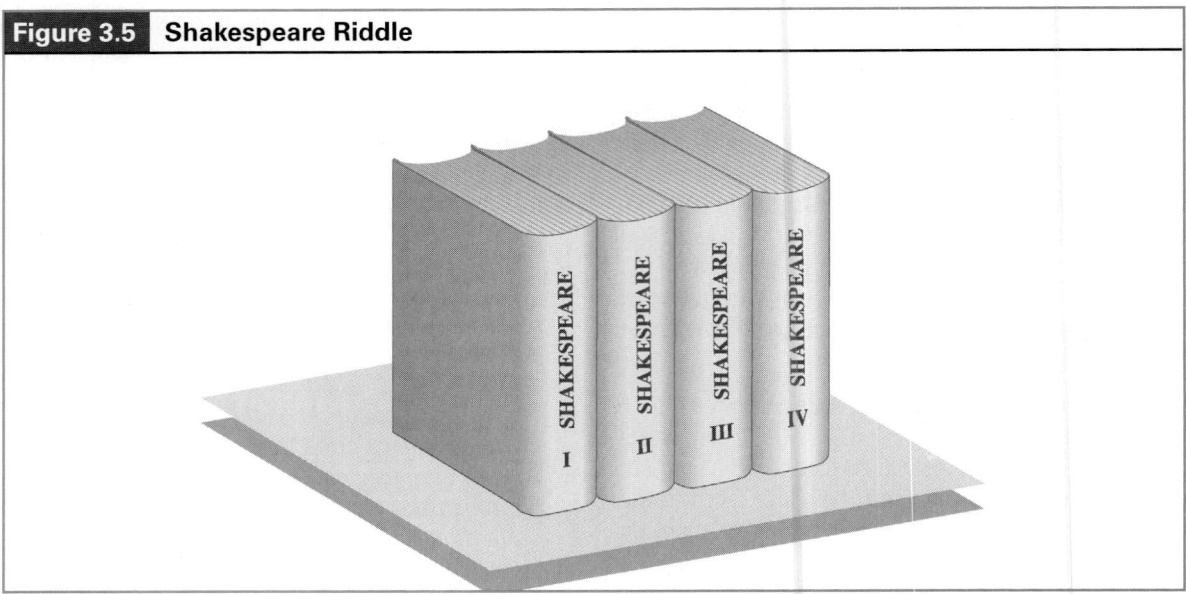

Source: "Shakespeare Riddle" from CREATIVE GROWTH GAMES by Eugene Raudsepp and George P. Haugh, Copyright © 1977 by Eugene Raudsepp & George P. Haugh, Jr. Used with permission of Berkley Publishing Group, a division of Penguin Group (USA) Inc.

that every problem encountered be solved individually. The discovery of penicillin by Sir Alexander Fleming resulted from his seeing a common theme among seemingly unrelated events. Fleming was working with some cultures of staphylococci that had accidentally become contaminated. The contamination, a growth of fungi, and isolated clusters of dead staphylococci led Fleming to see a relationship no one else had ever seen previously and thus to discover a wonder drug. The famous chemist Friedrich Kekule saw a relationship between his dream of a snake swallowing its own tail and the chemical structure of organic compounds. This creative insight led him to the discovery that organic compounds such as benzene have closed rings rather than open structures (Koestler, 1964).

For Percy Spencer at Raytheon, seeing a connection between the heat of a neon tube and the heat required to cook food was the creative connection that led to his breakthrough in the microwave industry. One of Spencer's colleagues recalled: "In the process of testing a bulb [with a magnetron], your hands got hot. I don't know when Percy really came up with the thought of microwave ovens, but he knew at that time—and that was 1942. He [remarked] frequently that this would be a good device for cooking food." Another colleague described Spencer this way: "The way Percy Spencer's mind worked is an interesting thing. He had a mind that allowed him to hold an extraordinary array of associations on phenomena and relate them to one another"

(Nayak & Ketteringham, 1986, pp. 184, 205). Similarly, the connection Art Fry made between a glue that wouldn't stick tightly and marking hymns in a choir book was the final breakthrough that led to the development of the revolutionary Post-It Note business.

To test your own ability to see commonalities, answer the following two questions: (1) What are some common terms that apply to both the substance water and the field of finance? (For example, "financial float.") (2) In Figure 3.6, using the code letters for the smaller ships as a guide, what is the name of the larger ship? (Some of the answers are at the end of the chapter.)

Compression

Conceptual blocks also occur as a result of **compression** of ideas. Looking too narrowly at a problem, screening out too much relevant data, and making assumptions that inhibit problem solution are common examples. Two especially cogent examples of compression are artificially constraining problems and not distinguishing figure from ground.

Artificial Constraints Sometimes people place boundaries around problems, or constrain their approach to them, in such a way that the problems become impossible to solve. Such constraints arise from hidden assumptions people make about problems they encounter. People assume that some problem definitions or alternative solutions are off limits, so

Figure 3.6 Name That Ship!

G E B A H

D W R V J

L U F I K

N S P O M

T X C Q Y

Source: *Ship Shapes; Bodycombe, D.J. (1997). Appears by permission of the publisher Constable & Robinson Ltd., London.*

they ignore them. For an illustration of this conceptual block, look at Figure 3.7. This is a problem you have probably seen before. Without lifting your pencil from the paper, draw four straight lines that pass through all nine dots. Complete the task before reading further.

By thinking of the figure as more constrained than it actually is, the problem becomes impossible to solve. It is easy if you break out of your own limiting assumptions on the problem. Now that you have been cued, can you do the same task with only three lines? What limiting constraints are you placing on yourself?

If you are successful, now try to do the task with only one line. Can you determine how to put a single straight line through all nine dots without lifting your pencil from the paper? Both the three-line solution and some one-line solutions are provided at the end of the chapter.

Artificially constraining problems means that the problem definition and the possible alternatives are limited more than the problem requires. Creative problem solving requires that individuals become adept at

recognizing their hidden assumptions and expanding the alternatives they consider—whether they imagine, improve, invest, or incubate.

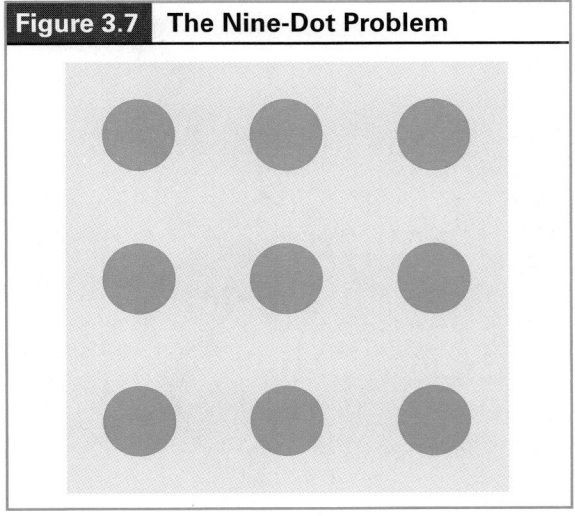

Figure 3.7 The Nine-Dot Problem

Separating Figure from Ground Another illustration of the compression block is the reverse of artificial constraints. It is the inability to constrain problems sufficiently so that they can be solved. Problems almost never come clearly specified, so problem solvers must determine what the real problem is. They must filter out inaccurate, misleading, or irrelevant information in order to define the problem correctly and generate appropriate alternative solutions. The inability to separate the important from the unimportant, and to compress problems appropriately, serves as a conceptual block because it exaggerates the complexity of a problem and inhibits a simple definition.

How well do you filter out irrelevant information and focus on the truly important part of a problem? Can you ask questions that get to the heart of the matter? Consider Figure 3.8. For each pair, find the pattern on the left that is embedded in the more complex pattern on the right. On the complex pattern, outline the embedded pattern. Now try to find at least two figures in each pattern. (See the end of the chapter for some solutions.)

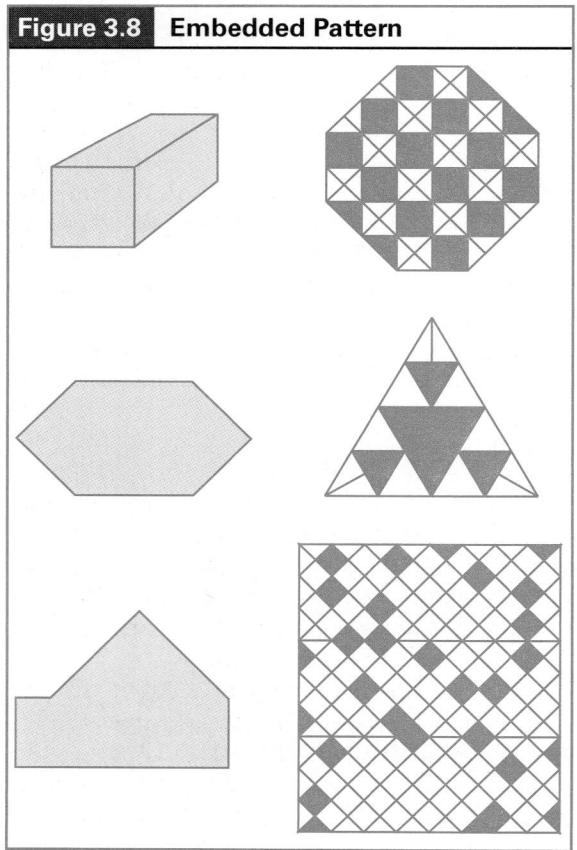

Figure 3.8 | Embedded Pattern

Overcoming this compression block—separating figure from ground and artificially constraining problems—was an important explanation for the microwave oven and Post-It Note breakthroughs. George Foerstner's contribution to the development and manufacture of the microwave oven was to compress the problem, that is, to separate out all the irrelevant complexity that constrained others. Whereas the magnetron was a device so complicated that few people understood it, Foerstner focused on its basic raw materials, its size, and its functionality. By comparing it to an air conditioner, he eliminated much of the complexity and mystery, and, as described by two analysts, "He had seen what all the researchers had failed to see, and they knew he was right" (Nayak & Ketteringham, 1986, p. 181).

On the other hand, Spence Silver had to add complexity, to overcome compression, in order to find an application for his product. Because the glue had failed every traditional 3M test for adhesives, it was categorized as a useless configuration of chemicals. The potential for the product was artificially constrained by traditional assumptions about adhesives—more stickiness, stronger bonding is best—until Art Fry visualized some unconventional applications—a better bookmark, a bulletin board, scratch paper, and, paradoxically, a replacement for 3M's main product, tape.

Complacency

Some conceptual blocks occur not because of poor thinking habits or inappropriate assumptions but because of fear, ignorance, insecurity, or just plain mental laziness. Two especially prevalent examples of the **complacency** block are a lack of questioning and a bias against thinking.

Noninquisitiveness Sometimes the inability to solve problems results from an unwillingness to ask questions, obtain information, or search for data. Individuals may think they will appear naïve or ignorant if they question something or attempt to redefine a problem. Asking questions puts them at risk of exposing their ignorance. It also may be threatening to others because it implies that what they accept may not be correct. This may create resistance, conflict, or even ridicule by others.

Creative problem solving is inherently risky because it potentially involves interpersonal conflict. It is risky also because it is fraught with mistakes. As Linus Pauling, the Nobel laureate, said, "If you want to have a good idea, have a lot of them, because most of them will be bad ones." Years of nonsupportive socialization, however, block the adventuresome and inquisitive stance in most people. Most of us are not rewarded for bad ideas. To illustrate, answer the following questions for yourself:

1. When would it be easier to learn a new language, when you were five years old or now? Why?
2. How many times in the last month have you tried something for which the probability of success was less than 50 percent?
3. When was the last time you asked three "why" questions in a row?

To illustrate the extent of our lack of inquisitiveness, how many of the following commonly experienced questions can you answer?

❑ Why are people immune to their own body odor?
❑ What happens to the tread that wears off tires?
❑ Why doesn't sugar spoil or get moldy?
❑ Why doesn't a two-by-four measure two inches by four inches?
❑ Why is a telephone keypad arranged differently from that of a calculator?
❑ Why do hot dogs come 10 in a package while buns come 8 in a package?
❑ How do military cadets find their caps after throwing them in the air at football games and graduation?
❑ Why is Jack the nickname for John?

Most of us adopt a habit of being a bit complacent in asking such questions, let alone finding out the answers. We often stop being inquisitive as we get older because we learn that it is good to be intelligent, and being intelligent is interpreted as already knowing the answers, instead of asking good questions. Consequently, we learn less well at 25 than at 5, take fewer risks, avoid asking why, and function in the world without really trying to understand it. Creative problem solvers, on the other hand, are frequently engaged in inquisitive and experimental behavior. Spence Silver at 3M described his attitude about the complacency block this way:

People like myself get excited about looking for new properties in materials. I find that very satisfying, to perturb the structure slightly and just see what happens. I have a hard time talking people into doing that—people who are more highly trained. It's been my

experience that people are reluctant just to try, to experiment—just to see what will happen. (Nayak & Ketteringham, 1986, p. 58)

Bias Against Thinking A second manifestation of the complacency block is in an inclination to avoid doing mental work. This block, like most of the others, is partly a cultural bias as well as a personal one. For example, assume that you passed by your roommate's or colleague's office one day and noticed him leaning back in his chair, staring out the window. A half-hour later, as you passed by again, he had his feet up on the desk, still staring out the window. And 20 minutes later, you noticed that his demeanor hadn't changed much. What would be your conclusion? Most of us would assume that the fellow was not doing any work. We would assume that unless we saw action, he wasn't being productive.

When was the last time you heard someone say, "I'm sorry. I can't go to the ball game (or concert, dance, party, or movie) because I have to think?" Or, "I'll do the dishes tonight. I know you need to catch up on your thinking"? That these statements sound silly illustrates the bias most people develop toward action rather than thought, or against putting their feet up, rocking back in their chair, looking off into space, and engaging in solitary cognitive activity. This does not mean daydreaming or fantasizing, just thinking.

A particular conceptual block exists in Western cultures against the kind of thinking that uses the right hemisphere of the brain. **Left-hemisphere thinking**, for most people, is concerned with logical, analytical, linear, or sequential tasks. Thinking using the left hemisphere is apt to be organized, planned, and precise. Language and mathematics are left-hemisphere activities. **Right-hemisphere thinking**, on the other hand, is concerned with intuition, synthesis, playfulness, and qualitative judgment. It tends to be more spontaneous, imaginative, and emotional than left-hemisphere thinking. The emphasis in most formal education is toward left-hemisphere thought development even more in Eastern cultures than in Western cultures. Problem solving on the basis of reason, logic, and utility is generally rewarded, while problem solving based on sentiment, intuition, or pleasure is frequently considered tenuous and inferior.

A number of researchers have found that the most creative problem solvers are **ambidextrous** in their thinking. That is, they use both left- and right-hemisphere thinking and easily switch from one to the other (Hermann, 1981; Hudspith, 1985; Martindale, 1999). Creative ideas arise most frequently in the right

Table 3.4	Exercise to Test Ambidextrous Thinking
LIST 1	**LIST 2**
sunset	decline
perfume	very
brick	ambiguous
monkey	resources
castle	term
guitar	conceptual
pencil	about
computer	appendix
umbrella	determine
radar	forget
blister	quantity
chessboard	survey

hemisphere but must be processed and interpreted by the left, so creative problem solvers use both hemispheres equally well.

Try the exercise in Table 3.4. It illustrates this ambidextrous principle. There are two lists of words. Take about two minutes to memorize the first list. Then, on a piece of paper, write down as many words as you can remember. Now take about two minutes and memorize the words in the second list. Repeat the process of writing down as many words as you can remember.

Most people remember more words from the first list than from the second. This is because the first list contains words that relate to visual perceptions. They connect with right-brain activity as well as left-brain activity. People can draw mental pictures or fantasize about them. The same is true for creative ideas. The more both sides of the brain are used, the more creative the ideas.

REVIEW OF CONCEPTUAL BLOCKS

So far, we have suggested that certain conceptual blocks prevent individuals from solving problems creatively and from engaging in the four different types of creativity. These blocks narrow the scope of problem definition, limit the consideration of alternative solutions, and constrain the selection of an optimal solution. Unfortunately, many of these conceptual blocks are unconscious, and it is only by being confronted with problems that are

unsolvable because of conceptual blocks that individuals become aware that they exist. We have attempted to make you aware of your own conceptual blocks by asking you to solve some simple problems that require you to overcome these mental barriers. These conceptual blocks are not all bad, of course; not all problems should be addressed by creative problem solving. But research has shown that individuals who have developed creative problem-solving skills are far more effective with complex problems that require a search for alternative solutions than others who are conceptually blocked (Basadur, 1979; Collins & Amabile, 1999; Sternberg, 1999; Williams & Yang, 1999).

In the next section, we provide some techniques and tools that help overcome these blocks and improve creative problem-solving skills.

Conceptual Blockbusting

Conceptual blocks cannot be overcome all at once because most blocks are a product of years of habit-forming thought processes. Overcoming them requires practice in thinking in different ways over a long period of time. You will not become a skilled creative problem solver just by reading this chapter. On the other hand, by becoming aware of your conceptual blocks and practicing the following techniques, research has demonstrated that you can enhance your **creative problem-solving** skills.

STAGES IN CREATIVE THOUGHT

A first step in overcoming conceptual blocks is recognizing that creative problem solving is a skill that can be developed. Being a creative problem solver is not an inherent ability that some people naturally have and others do not have. Jacob Rainbow, an employee of the U.S. Patent Office who has more than 200 patents by himself, described the creative process as follows:

> So you need three things to be an original thinker. First, you have to have a tremendous amount of information—a big data base if you like to be fancy. Then you have to be willing to pull the ideas, because you're interested. Now, some people could do it, but they don't bother. They're interested in doing something else. It's fun to come up with an idea, and if nobody wants it, I don't give a damn. It's just fun to come up with something strange and different. And then you must have the ability to get rid of the trash which you think of. You cannot only

think of good ideas. And by the way, if you're not well-trained, but you've got good ideas, and you don't know if they're good or bad, then you send them to the Bureau of Standards, National Institute of Standards, where I work, and we evaluate them. And we throw them out. (Csikszentmihalyi, 1996, p. 48)

In other words, gather a lot of information, use it to generate a lot of ideas, and sift through your ideas and get rid of the bad ones. Researchers generally agree that creative problem solving involves four stages: *preparation, incubation, illumination,* and *verification* (see Albert & Runco, 1999; Nickerson, 1999; Poincare, 1921; Ribot, 1906; Wallas, 1926). The **preparation stage** includes gathering data, defining the problem, generating alternatives, and consciously examining all available information. The primary difference between skillful creative problem solving and analytical problem solving is in how this first step is approached. Creative problem solvers are more flexible and fluent in data gathering, problem definition, alternative generation, and examination of options. In fact, it is in this stage that training in creative problem solving can significantly improve effectiveness because the other three steps are not amenable to conscious mental work (Adams, 2001; Ward, Smith, & Finke, 1999). The following discussion, therefore, is limited primarily to improving functioning in this first stage. The **incubation stage** involves mostly unconscious mental activity in which the mind combines unrelated thoughts in pursuit of a solution. Conscious effort is not involved. **Illumination**, the third stage, occurs when an insight is recognized and a creative solution is articulated. **Verification** is the final stage, which involves evaluating the creative solution relative to some standard of acceptability.

In the preparation stage, two types of techniques are available for improving creative problem-solving abilities. One technique helps individuals think about and *define problems more creatively;* the other helps individuals gather information and *generate more alternative solutions* to problems.

One major difference between effective, creative problem solvers and other people is that creative problem solvers are less constrained. They allow themselves to be more flexible in the definitions they impose on problems and the number of solutions they identify. They develop a large repertoire of approaches to problem solving. In short, they engage in what Csikszentmihalyi (1996) described as "playfulness and childishness." They try more things and worry less about their false

starts or failures. As Interaction Associates (1971, p. 15) explained:

> *Flexibility in thinking is critical to good problem solving. A problem solver should be able to conceptually dance around the problem like a good boxer, jabbing and poking, without getting caught in one place or "fixated." At any given moment, a good problem solver should be able to apply a large number of strategies [for generating alternative definitions and solutions]. Moreover, a good problem solver is a person who has developed, through his understanding of strategies and experiences in problem solving, a sense of appropriateness of what is likely to be the most useful strategy at any particular time.*

As a perusal through any bookstore will show, the number of books suggesting ways to enhance creative problem solving is enormous. We now present a few tools and hints that we have found to be especially effective and relatively simple for business executives and students to apply. Although some of them may seem game-like or playful, a sober pedagogical rationale underlies all of them. Our purpose is to address your own personal skills as a creative problem solver, not to discuss how creativity can be fostered in an organizational setting. These tools, therefore, will help to unfreeze you from your normal skeptical, analytical approach to problems and increase your playfulness. They relate to (1) defining problems and (2) generating alternative solutions.

METHODS FOR IMPROVING PROBLEM DEFINITION

Problem definition is probably the most critical step in creative problem solving. Once a problem is defined, solving it is often relatively simple. However, as explained in Table 3.2, individuals tend to define problems in terms with which they are familiar. Even well-trained scientists suffer from this problem: "Good scientists study the most important problems they think they can solve" (Medawar, 1967). When a problem is faced that is new or complex or does not appear to have an easily identified solution, the problem either remains undefined or is redefined in terms of something familiar. Unfortunately, new problems may not be the same as old problems, so relying on past definitions may impede the process of solving current problems, or lead to solving the wrong problem. Applying techniques for creative problem definition can help individuals see problems in alternative ways so their definitions are less narrowly constrained. Three such techniques for improving and expanding the definition process are discussed below.

Make the Strange Familiar and the Familiar Strange

One well-known, well-tested technique for improving creative problem solving is called **synectics** (Gordon, 1961; Roukes, 1988). The goal of synectics is to help you put something you don't know in terms of something you do know, then reverse the process back again. The point is, by analyzing what you know and applying it to what you don't know, you can develop new insights and perspectives. The process of synectics relies on the use of analogies and metaphors, and it works this way.

First you form a definition of a problem (make the strange familiar). Then you try to transform that definition so it is made similar to something completely different that you know more about (make the familiar strange). That is, you use analogies and metaphors (synectics) to create this distortion. Postpone the original definition of the problem while you examine the analogy or the metaphor. Then impose this same analysis on the original problem to see what new insights you can uncover.

For example, suppose you have defined a problem as low morale among members of your team. You may form an analogy or metaphor by answering questions such as the following about the problem:

❏ What does this remind me of?
❏ What does this make me feel like?
❏ What is this similar to?
❏ What is this opposite of?

Your answers, for example, might be: This problem reminds me of trying to get warm on a cold day (I need more activity). It makes me feel like I do when visiting a hospital ward (I need to smile and go out of my way to empathize with people). It is similar to the loser's locker room after an athletic contest (I need to find an alternative purpose or goal). This isn't like a well-tuned automobile (I need to do a careful diagnosis). And so on. Metaphors and analogies should connect what you are less sure about (the original problem) to what you are more sure about (the metaphor). By analyzing the metaphor or analogy, you may identify attributes of the problem that were not evident before. New insights can occur and new ideas can come to mind.

Many creative solutions have been generated by such a technique. For example, William Harvey was the first to apply the "pump" analogy to the heart, which led to the discovery of the body's circulatory system. Niels Bohr compared the atom to the solar system and supplanted Rutherford's prevailing "raisin pudding" model of matter's building blocks. Consultant Roger von Oech (1986) helped turn around a struggling computer company by applying a restaurant analogy to the company's operations. The real problems emerged when the restaurant, rather than the company, was analyzed. Major contributions in the field of organizational behavior have occurred by applying analogies to other types of organization, such as machines, cybernetic or open systems, force fields, clans, and so on. Probably the most effective analogies (called parables) were used by Jesus to teach principles that otherwise were difficult for individuals to grasp (for example, the prodigal son, the good Samaritan, a shepherd and his flock).

Some hints to keep in mind when constructing analogies include:

❏ Include action or motion in the analogy (e.g., driving a car, cooking a meal, attending a funeral).
❏ Include things that can be visualized or pictured in the analogy (e.g., circuses, football games, crowded shopping malls).
❏ Pick familiar events or situations (e.g., families, kissing, bedtime).
❏ Try to relate things that are not obviously similar (e.g., saying an organization is like a big group is not nearly as rich a simile as saying that an organization is like, say, a psychic prison or a poker game).

Four types of analogies are recommended as part of synectics: **personal analogies**, in which individuals try to identify themselves as the problem ("If I were the problem, how would I feel, what would I like, what could satisfy me?"); **direct analogies**, in which individuals apply facts, technology, and common experience to the problem (e.g., Brunel solved the problem of underwater construction by watching a shipworm tunneling into a tube); **symbolic analogies**, in which symbols or images are imposed on the problem (e.g., modeling the problem mathematically or diagramming the process flow); and **fantasy analogies**, in which individuals ask the question "In my wildest dreams, how would I wish the problem to be resolved?" (e.g., "I wish all employees would work with no supervision.").

Elaborate on the Definition

There are a variety of ways to enlarge, alter, or replace a problem definition once it has been specified. One way is to force yourself to generate at least two alternative hypotheses for every problem definition. That is, specify at least two plausible definitions of the problem in addition to the one originally accepted. Think in plural rather than singular terms. Instead of asking, "What is the problem?" "What is the meaning of this?" "What will be the result?" ask instead questions such as: "What are the problems?" "What are the meanings of this?" "What will be the results?"

As an example, look at Figure 3.9. Select the figure that is different from all the others.

A majority of people select B first. If you did, you're right. It is the only figure that has all straight lines. On the other hand, quite a few people pick A. If you are one of them, you're also right. It is the only figure with a continuous line and no points of discontinuity. Alternatively, C can also be right, with the rationale that it is the only figure with two straight and two curved lines. Similarly, D is the only one with one curved and one straight line, and E is the only figure that is non-symmetrical or partial. The point is, there can often be more than one problem definition, more than one right answer, and more than one perspective from which to view a problem.

Another way to elaborate definitions is to use a question checklist. This is a series of questions designed to help you think of alternatives to your accepted definitions. Several creative managers have shared with us some of their most fruitful questions, such as:

- ❏ Is there anything else?
- ❏ Is the reverse true?
- ❏ Is this a symptom of a more general problem?
- ❏ Who sees it differently?

Nickerson (1999) reported an oft-used acronym— SCAMPER—designed to bring to mind questions having to do with **S**ubstitution, **C**ombination, **A**daptation, **M**odification (Magnification–Minimization), **P**utting to other uses, **E**limination, and **R**earrangement.

As an exercise, take a minute now to think of a problem you are currently experiencing. Write it down so it is formally defined. Now manipulate that definition by answering the four questions in the checklist. If you can't think of a problem, try the exercise with this one. "I am not as attractive/intelligent/creative as I would like to be." How would you answer the four questions?

Reverse the Definition

A third tool for improving and expanding problem definition is to reverse the definition of the problem. That is, turn the problem upside down, inside out, or back to front. Reverse the way in which you think of the problem. For example, consider the following problem:

> A tradition in Sandusky, Ohio, for as long as anyone could remember was the Fourth of July Parade. It was one of the largest and most popular events on the city's annual calendar. Now, in 1988, the city mayor was hit with some startling and potentially disastrous news. The State of Ohio was mandating that liability insurance be carried on every attraction—floats, bands, majorettes—that participated in the parade. To protect against the possibility of injury or accident of any parade participant, each had to be covered by liability insurance.
>
> The trouble, of course, was that taking out a liability insurance policy for all parade participants would require far more expense than the city could afford. The amount of insurance required for that large a number of participants and equipment made it impossible for the city to carry the cost. On the one hand, the mayor hated to cancel an important tradition that everyone in town looked forward to. On the

---

Figure 3.9	The Five-Figure Problem

Of the five figures below, select the one that is different from all of the others.

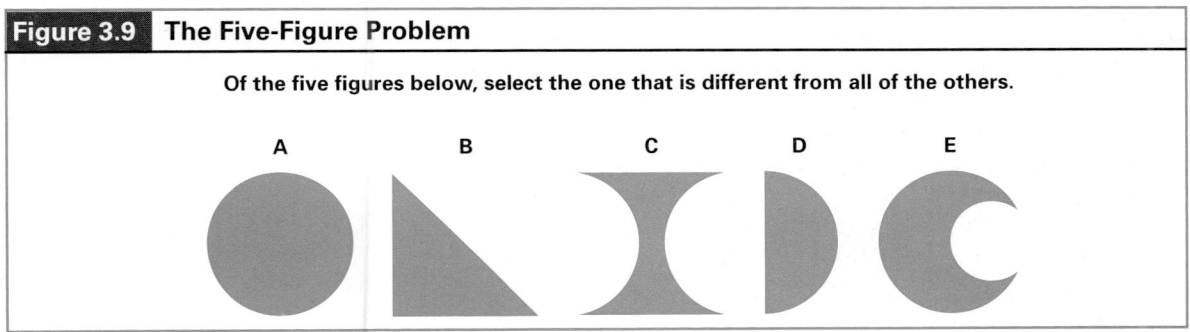

A   B   C   D   E

other hand, to hold the event would break the city budget. If you were a consultant to the mayor, what would you suggest?

Commonly suggested alternatives in this problem include the following:

1. Try to negotiate with an insurance company for a lower rate. (However, the risk is merely being transferred to the insurance company.)
2. Hold fund-raising events to generate enough money to purchase the insurance policy, or find a wealthy donor to sponsor the parade. (However, this may deflect potential donations away from, or may compete with, other community service agencies such as United Way, Red Cross, or local churches that also sponsor fund raisers and require donations.)
3. Charge a "participation fee" to parade participants to cover the insurance expense. (However, this would likely eliminate most high school, middle school, and elementary school bands and floats. It would also reduce the amount of money float builders and sponsoring organizations could spend on the actual float. Such a requirement would likely be a parade killer.)
4. Charge a fee to spectators of the parade. (However, this would require restricted access to the parade, an administrative structure to coordinate fee collection and ticketing, and the destruction of the sense of community participation that characterized this traditional event.)

Each of these suggestions is good, but each maintains a single definition of the problem. Each assumes that the solution to the problem is associated with solving the financial problem associated with the liability insurance requirement. Each suggestion, therefore, brings with it some danger of damaging the traditional nature of the parade or eliminating it altogether. If the problem is reversed, other answers normally not considered become evident. That is, the need for liability insurance at all could be addressed.

Here is an excerpt from a newspaper report of how the problem was addressed:

Sandusky, Ohio (AP) *The Fourth of July parade here wasn't canceled, but it was immobilized by liability insurance worries. The band marched in place to the beat of a drum, and a country fair queen waved to her subjects from a float moored to the curb.*

The Reverse Community Parade began at 10:00 A.M. Friday along Washington Row at the north end of the city and stayed there until dusk. "Very honestly, it was the issue of liability," said Gene Kleindienst, superintendent of city schools and one of the celebration's organizers. "By not having a mobile parade, we significantly reduced the issue of liability," he said.

The immobile parade included about 20 floats and displays made by community groups. Games, displays, and food booths were in an adjacent park. Parade chairman Judee Hill said some folks didn't understand, however. "Someone asked me if she was too late for the parade, and she had a hard time understanding the parade is here all day," she said.

Those who weren't puzzled seemed to appreciate the parade for its stationary qualities. "I like this. I can see more," said 67-year-old William A. Sibley. "I'm 80 percent blind. Now I know there's something there," he said pointing to a float.

Spectator Emmy Platte preferred the immobile parade because it didn't go on for "what seemed like miles," exhausting participants. "You don't have those little drum majorettes passing out on the street," she commented.

Baton twirler Tammy Ross said her performance was better standing still. "You can throw better. You don't have to worry about dropping it as much," she explained.

Mr. Kleindienst said community responses were favorable. "I think we've started a new tradition," he said.

By reversing the definition, Sandusky not only eliminated the problem without damaging the tradition and without shifting the risk to insurance companies or other community groups, it added a new dimension that allowed at least some people to enjoy the event more than ever.

This reversal is similar to what Rothenberg (1979, 1991) referred to as **Janusian thinking**. Janus was the Roman god with two faces that looked in opposite directions. Janusian thinking means thinking contradictory thoughts at the same time: that is, conceiving two opposing ideas to be true concurrently. Rothenberg claimed, after studying 54 highly creative artists and scientists (e.g., Nobel Prize winners), that most major scientific breakthroughs and artistic masterpieces are products of Janusian thinking. Creative people who actively formulate antithetical ideas and then resolve them produce the most valuable contributions to the scientific and artistic worlds. Quantum leaps in knowledge often occur.

An example is Einstein's account (1919, p. 1) of having "the happiest thought of my life." He developed the concept that, "for an observer in free fall from the roof of a house, there exists, during his fall, no gravitational field. . . in his immediate vicinity. If the observer releases any objects, they will remain, relative to him, in a state of rest. The [falling] observer is therefore justified in considering his state as one of rest." Einstein concluded, in other words, that two seemingly contradictory states could be present simultaneously: motion and rest. This realization led to the development of his revolutionary general theory of relativity.

In another study of creative potential, Rothenberg and Hausman (2000) found that when individuals were presented with a stimulus word and asked to respond with the word that first came to mind, highly creative students, Nobel scientists, and prize-winning artists responded with antonyms significantly more often than did individuals with average creativity. Rothenberg argued, based on these results, that creative people think in terms of opposites more often than do other people (also see research by Blasko & Mokwa, 1986).

For our purposes, the whole point is to reverse or contradict the currently accepted definition in order to expand the number of perspectives considered. For instance, a problem might be that morale is too high instead of (or in addition to) too low in our team (we may need more discipline), or maybe employees need less motivation (more direction) instead of more motivation to increase productivity. Opposites and backward looks often enhance creativity.

These three techniques for improving creative problem definition are summarized in Table 3.5. Their purpose is not to help you generate alternative definitions just for the sake of alternatives but to broaden your perspectives, to help you overcome conceptual blocks, and to produce more elegant (i.e., high-quality and parsimonious) solutions. They are tools or techniques that you can easily use when you are faced with the need to solve problems creatively.

WAYS TO GENERATE MORE ALTERNATIVES

Because a common tendency is to define problems in terms of available solutions (i.e., the problem is defined as already possessing a certain set of possible solutions, e.g., March & Simon, 1958; March 1999), most of us consider a minimal number and a narrow range of alternatives in problem solving. Most experts agree, however, that the primary characteristics of effective creative problem solvers are their **fluency** and their **flexibility of thought** (Sternberg, 1999). Fluency refers to the number of ideas or concepts produced in a given length of time. Flexibility refers to the diversity of ideas or concepts generated. While most problem solvers consider a few homogeneous alternatives, creative problem solvers consider many heterogeneous alternatives.

The following techniques are designed to help you improve your ability to generate a large number and a wide variety of alternatives when faced with problems, whether they be imagination, improvement, investment, or incubation. They are summarized in Table 3.6.

Defer Judgment

Probably the most common method of generating alternatives is the technique of *brainstorming* developed by Osborn (1953). This tool is powerful because most people make quick judgments about each piece of information or each alternative solution they encounter. Brainstorming is designed to help people generate alternatives for problem solving without prematurely evaluating, and hence discarding, them. It is practiced by having a group of people get together and simply begin sharing ideas about a problem—one at a time, with

Table 3.5	Techniques for Improving Problem Definition

1. **Make the strange familiar and the familiar strange** (for example, analogies and metaphors).

2. **Elaborate on the definition** (for example, question checklists and SCAMPER).

3. **Reverse the definition** (for example, Janusian thinking and opposition).

Table 3.6	Techniques for Generating More Alternatives

1. **Defer judgment** (for example, brainstorming).

2. **Expand current alternatives** (for example, subdivision).

3. **Combine unrelated attributes** (for example, morphological synthesis and relational algorithm).

someone recording the ideas that are suggested. Four main rules govern brainstorming:

1. No evaluation of any kind is permitted as alternatives are being generated. Individual energy is spent on generating ideas, not on defending them.
2. The wildest and most divergent ideas are encouraged. It is easier to tighten alternatives than to loosen them up.
3. The quantity of ideas takes precedence over the quality. Emphasizing quality engenders judgment and evaluation.
4. Participants should build on or modify the ideas of others. Poor ideas that are added to or altered often become good ideas.

The idea of brainstorming is to use it in a group setting so individuals can stimulate ideas in one another. Often, after a rush of alternatives is produced at the outset of a brainstorming session, the quantity of ideas often rapidly subsides. But to stop at that point is an ineffective use of brainstorming. When easily identifiable solutions have been exhausted, that's when the truly creative alternatives are often produced in brainstorming groups. So keep working. Apply some of the tools described in this chapter for expanding definitions and alternatives. Brainstorming often begins with a flurry of ideas that then diminish. If brainstorming continues and members are encouraged to think past that point, breakthrough ideas often emerge as less common or less familiar alternatives are suggested. After that phase has unfolded in brainstorming, it is usually best to terminate the process and begin refining and consolidating ideas.

Recent research has found that brainstorming in a group may be less efficient and more time consuming than alternative forms of brainstorming due to free riders, unwitting evaluations, production blocking, and so on. One widely used alternative brainstorming technique is to have individual group members generate ideas on their own then submit them to the group for exploration and evaluation (Finke, Ward, & Smith, 1992). Alternatively, electronic brainstorming in which individuals use chat rooms or their own computer to generate ideas has shown positive results as well (Siau, 1995). What is clear from the research is that generating alternatives in the presence of others produces more and better ideas than can be produced alone.

The best way to get a feel for the power of brainstorming groups is to participate in one. Try the following exercise based on an actual problem faced by a group of students and university professors. Spend at least 10 minutes in a small group, brainstorming your ideas.

The business school faculty has become increasingly concerned about the ethics associated with modern business practice. The general reputation of business executives is in the tank. They are seen as greedy, dishonest, and untrustworthy. What could the faculty or the school do to affect this problem?

How do you define the problem? What ideas can you come up with? Generate as many ideas as you can following the rules of brainstorming. After at least 10 minutes, assess the fluency (the number) and flexibility (the variety) of the ideas you generated as a team.

Expand Current Alternatives

Sometimes, brainstorming in a group is not possible or is too costly in terms of the number of people involved and hours required. Managers facing a fast-paced twenty-first-century environment may find brainstorming to be too inefficient. Moreover, people sometimes need an external stimulus or way to break through conceptual blocks to help them generate new ideas. One useful and readily available technique for expanding alternatives is **subdivision**, or dividing a problem into smaller parts. This is a well-used and proven technique for enlarging the alternative set.

For example, March and Simon (1958, p. 193) suggested that subdivision improves problem solving by increasing the speed with which alternatives can be generated and selected.

The mode of subdivision has an influence on the extent to which planning can proceed simultaneously on the several aspects of the problem. The more detailed the factorization of the problem, the more simultaneous activity is possible, hence, the greater the speed of problem solving.

To see how subdivision helps develop more alternatives and speeds the process of problem solving, consider the problem, common in the creativity literature, of listing alternative uses for a familiar object. For example, in one minute, how many uses can you list for a Ping-Pong ball? Ready . . . go.

The more uses you identify, the greater is your fluency in thinking. The more variety in your list, the greater is your flexibility in thinking. You may have included the following in your list: bob for a fishing line, Christmas ornament, toy for a cat, gearshift knob, model for a molecular structure, wind gauge when hung from a string, head for a finger puppet, miniature basketball. Your list will be much longer.

Now that you have produced your list, apply the technique of subdivision by identifying the specific characteristics of a Ping-Pong ball. That is, divide it into its component attributes. For example, weight, color, texture, shape, porosity, strength, hardness, chemical properties, and conduction potential are all attributes of Ping-Pong balls that help expand the uses you might think of. By dividing an object mentally into more specific attributes, you can arrive at many more alternative uses (e.g., reflector, holder when cut in half, bug bed, ball for lottery drawing, inhibitor of an electrical current, and so on).

One exercise we have used with students and executives to illustrate this technique is to have them write down as many of their leadership or managerial strengths as they can think of. Most people list 10 or 12 attributes relatively easily. Then we analyze the various aspects of the manager's role, the activities in which managers engage, the challenges that most managers face from inside and outside the organization, and so on. We then ask these same people to write down another list of their strengths as managers. The list is almost always more than twice as long as the first list. By identifying the subcomponents of any problem, far more alternatives can be generated than by considering the problem as a whole. Try this by yourself. Divide

your life into the multiple roles you play—student, friend, neighbor, leader, brother or sister, and so on. If you list your strengths associated with each role, your list will be much longer than if you just create a general list of personal strengths.

Combine Unrelated Attributes

A third technique focuses on helping problem solvers expand alternatives by forcing the integration of seemingly unrelated elements. Research in creative problem solving has shown that an ability to see common relationships among disparate factors is a major factor differentiating creative from noncreative individuals (Feldman, 1999). Two ways to do this are through morphological synthesis (Koberg & Bagnall, 2003) and the relational algorithm (Crovitz, 1970). (For literature reviews, see Finke, Ward, & Smith, 1992; and Starko, 2001.)

With **morphological synthesis**, a four-step procedure is involved. First, the problem is written down. Second, attributes of the problem are listed. Third, alternatives to each attribute are listed. Fourth, different alternatives from the attributes list are combined together.

This seems a bit complicated so let us illustrate the procedure. Suppose you are faced with the problem of an employee who takes an extended lunch break almost every day despite your reminders to be on time. Think of alternative ways to solve this problem. The first solution

---

Table 3.7 Morphological Synthesis

Step 1. Problem statement: The employee takes extended lunch breaks every day with friends in the cafeteria.

Step 2. Major attributes of the problem:

AMOUNT OF TIME	START TIME	PLACE	WITH WHOM	FREQUENCY
More than 1 hour	12 noon	Cafeteria	Friends	Daily

Step 3. Alternative attributes:

AMOUNT OF TIME	START TIME	PLACE	WITH WHOM	FREQUENCY
30 minutes	11:00	Office	Coworkers	Weekly
90 minutes	11:30	Conference Room	Boss	Twice a Week
45 minutes	12:30	Restaurant	Management Team	Alternate Days

Step 4. Combining Attributes:

1. A 30-minute lunch beginning at 12:30 in the conference room with the boss once a week.

2. A 90-minute lunch beginning at 11:30 in the conference room with coworkers twice a week.

3. A 45-minute lunch beginning at 11:00 in the cafeteria with the management team every other day.

4. A 30-minute lunch beginning at 12:00 alone in the office on alternate days.

that comes to mind for most people is to sit down and have a talk with (or threaten) the employee. If that doesn't work, most of us would reduce the person's pay, demote or transfer him or her, or just fire the person. However, look at what other alternatives can be generated by using morphological synthesis (see Table 3.7).

You can see how many more alternatives come to mind when you force together attributes that aren't obviously connected. The matrix of attributes can create a very long list of possible solutions. In more complicated problems—for example, how to improve quality, how to better serve customers, how to improve the reward system, how to land a great job—the potential number of alternatives is even greater, and, hence, more creativity is required to analyze them.

The second technique for combining unrelated attributes in problem solving, the **relational algorithm**, involves applying connecting words that force a relationship between two elements in a problem. For example, the following is a list of some words that connect other words together. They are called "relational" words.

about	across	after
against	opposite	or
out	among	and
as	at	over
round	still	because
before	between	but
so	then	though
by	down	for
from	through	till
to	if	in
near	not	under
up	when	now
of	off	on
where	while	with

To illustrate the use of this technique, suppose you are faced with the following problem: *Our customers are dissatisfied with our service.* The two major subjects in this problem are *customers* and *service.* They are connected by the phrase *are dissatisfied with.* With the relational algorithm technique, the relational words in the problem statement are removed and replaced with other relational words to see if new ideas for alternative solutions can be identified. For example, consider the following connections where new relational words are used:

❏ Customers *among* service (e.g., customers interact with service personnel).

❏ Customers *as* service (e.g., customers deliver service to other customers).

❏ Customers *and* service (e.g., customers and service personnel work collaboratively together).

❏ Customers *for* service (e.g., customer focus groups can help improve service).

❏ Service *near* customers (e.g., change the location of the service to be nearer customers).

❏ Service *before* customers (e.g., prepare personalized service before the customer arrives).

❏ Service *through* customers (e.g., use customers to provide additional service).

❏ Service *when* customers (e.g., provide timely service when customers want it).

By connecting the two elements of the problem in different ways, new possibilities for problem solution can be formulated.

International Caveats

The perspective taken in this chapter has a clear bias toward Western culture. It focuses on analytical and creative problem solving as methods for addressing specific issues. Enhancing creativity has a specific purpose, and that is to solve certain kinds of problems better. Creativity in Eastern cultures, on the other hand, is often defined differently. Creativity is focused less on creating solutions than on uncovering enlightenment, one's true self, or the achievement of wholeness or self-actualization (Chu, 1970; Kuo, 1996). It is aimed at getting in touch with the unconscious (Maduro, 1976). In both the East and the West, however, creativity is viewed positively. Gods of creativity are worshipped in West African cultures (Olokun) and among Hindus (Vishvakarma), for example (Ben-Amos, 1986; Wonder & Blake, 1992), and creativity is often viewed in mystical or religious terms rather than managerial or practical terms.

In fostering creative problem solving in international settings or with individuals from different countries, Trompenaars and Hampden-Turner's (1987, 2004) model is useful for understanding the caveats that must be kept in mind. Countries differ, for example, in their orientation toward *internal control* (Canada, United States, United Kingdom) versus *external control* (Japan, China, Czech Republic). In internal cultures, the environment is assumed to be changeable, so creativity focuses on attacking problems directly. In external cultures, because individuals assume less control of the environment, creativity focuses less on problem resolution and more on achieving insight or oneness with nature. Changing the environment is not the usual objective.

Similarly, cultures emphasizing a *specific orientation* (Sweden, Denmark, United Kingdom, France) are more likely to challenge the status quo and seek new ways to address problems than cultures emphasizing a *diffuse culture* (China, Nigeria, India, Singapore) in which loyalty, wholeness, and long-term relationships are more likely to inhibit individual creative effort. This is similar to the differences that are likely in countries emphasizing *universalism* (Korea, Venezuela, China, India) as opposed to *particularism* (Switzerland, United States, Sweden, United Kingdom, Germany). Cultures emphasizing universalism tend to focus on generalizable outcomes and consistent rules or procedures. Particularistic cultures are more inclined to search for unique aberrations from the norm, thus having more of a tendency toward creative solution finding. Managers encouraging conceptual blockbusting and creative problem solving, in other words, will find some individuals more inclined toward the rule-oriented procedures of analytical problem solving and less inclined toward the playfulness and experimentation associated with creative problem solving than others.

Hints for Applying Problem-Solving Techniques

Not every problem is amenable to these techniques and tools for conceptual blockbusting, of course, nor is every individual equally inclined or skilled. Our intent in presenting these six suggestions is to help you expand the number of options available to you for defining problems and generating additional alternatives. They are most useful with problems that are not straightforward, are complex or ambiguous, or are imprecise in their definitions. All of us have enormous creative potential, but the stresses and pressures of daily life, coupled with the inertia of conceptual habits, tend to submerge that potential. These hints are ways to help unlock it again.

Reading about techniques or having a desire to be creative is not, alone, enough to make you a skillful creative problem solver, of course. Although research has confirmed the effectiveness of these techniques for improving creative problem solving, they depend on application and practice as well as an environment that is conducive to creativity. Here are six practical hints that will help facilitate your own ability to apply these techniques effectively and improve your creative problem solving ability.

1. *Give yourself some relaxation time.* The more intense your work, the more your need for

complete breaks. Break out of your routine sometimes. This frees up your mind and gives room for new thoughts.

2. *Find a place (physical space) where you can think.* It should be a place where interruptions are eliminated, at least for a time. Reserve your best time for thinking.

3. *Talk to other people about ideas.* Isolation produces far fewer ideas than does conversation. Make a list of people who stimulate you to think. Spend some time with them.

4. *Ask other people for their suggestions about your problems.* Find out what others think about them. Don't be embarrassed to share your problems, but don't become dependent on others to solve them for you.

5. *Read a lot.* Read at least one thing regularly that is outside your field of expertise. Keep track of new thoughts from your reading.

6. *Protect yourself from idea-killers.* Don't spend time with "black holes"—that is, people who absorb all of your energy and light but give nothing in return. Don't let yourself or others negatively evaluate your ideas too soon.

You'll find these hints useful not only for enhancing creative problem solving but for analytical problem solving as well. Figure 3.10 summarizes the two problem-solving processes—analytical and creative—and the factors you should consider when determining how to approach each type of problem. In brief, when you encounter a problem that is straightforward—that is, outcomes are predictable, sufficient information is available, and means-ends connections are clear—analytical problem-solving techniques are most appropriate. You should apply the four distinct, sequential steps. On the other hand, when the problem is not straightforward—that is, information is ambiguous or unavailable and alternative solutions are not apparent—you should apply creative problem-solving techniques in order to improve problem definition and alternative generation.

Fostering Creativity in Others

Unlocking your own creative potential is important but insufficient, of course, to make you a successful manager. A major challenge is to help unlock it in other people as well. Fostering creativity among those with whom you work is at least as great a challenge as increasing your own creativity. In this last section of the

Figure 3.10 A Model of Analytical and Creative Problem Solving

Yes

Problem Assessment
- Outcomes predictable?
- Sufficient information present?

No

Constraints
- Definitional problems
- Solution-generation problems
- Evaluation and selection problems
- Implementation and follow-up problems

Conceptual Blocks
- Constancy
- Commitment
- Compression
- Complacency

Analytical Problem Solving
- Define the problem
- Generate alternative solutions
- Evaluate and select alternatives
- Implement and follow up on the solution

Four Approaches to Creativity
- Imagination
- Improvement
- Investment
- Incubation

Creative Problem-Solving Tools
- To improve problem definition:
  - Make the familiar strange and the strange familiar
  - Elaborate definitions
  - Reverse the definition
- To improve the generation of alternatives:
  - Defer judgment
  - Expand current alternatives
  - Combine unrelated attributes

chapter, we briefly discuss some principles that will help you better accomplish the task of fostering creativity.

MANAGEMENT PRINCIPLES

Neither Percy Spencer nor Spence Silver could have succeeded in his creative ideas had there not been a support system present that fostered creative problem solving. In each case, certain characteristics were present in their organizations, fostered by managers around them, which made their innovations possible. In this section we will not discuss the macro-organizational issues associated with innovation (e.g., organization design, strategic orientation, and human resource systems). Excellent discussions of those factors are reviewed in sources such as Amabile (1988), DeGraff and Lawrence (2002), McMillan (1985), Tichy (1983), Tushman and Anderson (1997), and Van de Ven (1997). Instead, we'll focus on activities in which individual managers can engage that foster creativity. Table 3.8 summarizes three management principles that help engender creative problem solving among others.

Table 3.8	Three Principles for Fostering Creativity
PRINCIPLE	**EXAMPLES**
1. Pull people apart; put people together.	• Let individuals work alone as well as with teams and task forces.
	• Encourage minority reports and legitimize "devil's advocate" roles.
	• Encourage heterogeneous membership in teams.
	• Separate competing groups or subgroups.
2. Monitor and prod.	• Talk to customers.
	• Identify customer expectations both in advance and after the sale.
	• Hold people accountable.
	• Use "sharp-pointed" prods.
3. Reward multiple roles.	• Idea champion
	• Sponsor and mentor
	• Orchestrator and facilitator
	• Rule breaker

Pull People Apart; Put People Together

Percy Spencer's magnetron project involved a consumer product closeted away from Raytheon's main-line business of missiles and other defense contract work. Spence Silver's new glue resulted when a polymer adhesive task force was separated from 3M's normal activities. The Macintosh computer was developed by a task force taken outside the company and given space and time to work on an innovative computer. Many new ideas come from individuals being given time and resources and allowed to work apart from the normal activities of the organization. Establishing bullpens, practice fields, or sandlots is as good a way to develop new skills in business as it has proven to be in athletics. Because most businesses are designed to produce the 10,000th part correctly or to service the 10,000th customer efficiently, they do not function well at producing the first part. That is why pulling people apart is often necessary to foster innovation and creativity. This principle is the same as providing autonomy and discretion for other people to pursue their own ideas.

On the other hand, forming teams (putting people together) is almost always more productive than having people work by themselves. Such teams should be characterized by certain attributes, though. For example, Nemeth (1986) found that creativity increased markedly when minority influences were present in the team, for example, when "devil's advocate" roles were legitimized, when a formal minority report was always included in final recommendations, and when individuals assigned to work on a team had divergent backgrounds or views. "Those exposed to minority views are stimulated to attend to more aspects of the situation, they think in more divergent ways, and they are more likely to detect novel solutions or come to new decisions" (Nemeth, 1986, p. 25). Nemeth found that those positive benefits occur in groups even when the divergent or minority views are wrong. Similarly, Janis (1971) found that narrow-mindedness in groups (dubbed **groupthink**) was best overcome by establishing competing groups working on the same problem, participation in groups by outsiders, assigning a role of critical evaluator in the group, and having groups made up of cross-functional participants. The most productive groups are those characterized by fluid roles, lots of interaction among members, and flat power structures. On the other hand, too much diversity, too much disagreement, and too much fluidity can sidetrack groups, so devil's advocates must be aware of when to line up and support the decision of the group. Their role is to help groups rethink quick decisions or solutions that have not been considered carefully enough, not to avoid making group decisions or solving problems.

You can help foster creativity among people you manage, therefore, by pulling people apart (e.g., giving them a bullpen, providing them with autonomy, encouraging individual initiative) as well as putting people together (e.g., putting them in teams, enabling minority influence, and fostering heterogeneity).

Monitor and Prod

Neither Percy Spencer nor Spence Silver was allowed to work on their projects without accountability. Both men eventually had to report on the results they accomplished with their experimentation and imagination. At 3M, for example, people are expected to allocate 15 percent of their time away from company business to work on new, creative ideas. They can even appropriate company materials and resources to work on them. However, individuals are always held accountable for their decisions. They need to show results for their "play time."

Holding people accountable for outcomes, in fact, is an important motivator for improved performance. Two innovators in the entertainment industry captured this principle with these remarks: "The ultimate inspiration is the deadline. That's when you have to do what needs to be done. The fact that twice a year the creative talent of this country is working until midnight to get something ready for a trade show is very good for the economy. Without this kind of pressure, things would turn to mashed potatoes" (von Oech, 1986, p. 119). One way Woody Morcott, former CEO at Dana Corporation, held people accountable for creativity was to require that each person in the company submit at least two suggestions for improvement each month. At least 70 percent of the new ideas had to be implemented. Woody admitted that he stole the idea during a visit to a Japanese company where he noticed workers huddled around a table scribbling notes on how some ideas for improvement might work. At Dana, this requirement is part of every person's job assignment. Rewards are associated with such ideas as well. A plant in Chihuahua, Mexico, for example, rewards employees with $1.89 for every idea submitted and another $1.89 if the idea is used. "We drill into people that they are responsible for keeping the plant competitive through innovation," Morcott said (personal communication).

In addition to accountability, creativity is stimulated by what Gene Goodson at Johnson Controls called "sharp-pointed prods." After taking over the automotive group at that company, Goodson found that he could stimulate creative problem solving by issuing certain mandates that demanded new approaches to old tasks. One such mandate was, "There will be no more forklift trucks allowed in any of our plants." At first hearing, that mandate sounded absolutely outrageous. Think about it. You have a plant with tens of thousands of square feet of floor space. The loading docks are on one side of the building, and many tons of heavy raw materials are unloaded weekly and moved from the loading docks to work stations throughout the entire facility. The only way it can be done is with forklifts. Eliminating forklift trucks would ruin the plant, right?

Wrong. This sharp-pointed prod demanded that individuals working in the plant find ways to move the work stations closer to the raw materials, to move the unloading of the raw materials closer to the work stations, or to change the size and amounts of material being unloaded. The innovations that resulted from eliminating forklifts saved the company millions of dollars in materials handling and wasted time; dramatically improved quality, productivity, and efficiency; and made it possible for Johnson Controls to capture some business from their Japanese competitors.

One of the best methods for generating useful prods is to regularly monitor customer preferences, expectations, and evaluations. Many of the most creative ideas have come from customers, the recipients of goods and services. Identifying their preferences in advance and monitoring their evaluations of products or services later are good ways to get creative ideas and to foster imagination, improvement, investment, and incubation. All employees should be in regular contact with their own customers, asking questions and monitoring performance.

By customers, we don't mean just the end users of a business product or service. In fact, all of us have customers, whether we are students in school, members of a family, players on a basketball team, or neighbors in an apartment complex. Customers are simply those we serve or for whom we are trying to produce something. Students, for example, can count their instructors, class members, and potential employers as customers whom they serve. A priori and post hoc monitoring of their expectations and evaluations is an important way to help foster new ideas for problem solving. This monitoring is best done through one-on-one meetings, but it can also be done through follow-up calls, surveys, customer complaint cards, suggestion systems, and so on.

In summary, you can foster creativity by holding people accountable for new ideas and by stimulating them with periodic prods. The most useful prods generally come from customers.

Reward Multiple Roles

The success of Post-It Notes at 3M is more than a story of the creativity of Spence Silver. It also illustrates the necessity of people playing multiple roles in enabling creativity and the importance of recognizing and rewarding those who play such roles. Without a number of people playing multiple roles, Spence Silver's glue would probably still be on a shelf somewhere.

Four crucial roles for enabling creativity in others include the **idea champion** (the person who comes up with creative problem solutions), the **sponsor** or mentor (the person who helps provide the resources, environment, and encouragement for the idea champion to work on his idea), the **orchestrator** or facilitator (the person who brings together cross-functional groups and necessary political support to facilitate implementation of creative ideas), and the **rule breaker** (the person who goes beyond organizational boundaries and barriers to ensure success of the creative solution). Each of these roles is present in most important innovations in organizations, and all are illustrated by the Post-It Note example.

This story has four major parts.

1. Spence Silver, while fooling around with chemical configurations that the academic literature indicated wouldn't work, invented a glue that wouldn't stick. Silver spent years giving presentations to any audience at 3M that would listen, trying to pawn off his glue on some division that could find a practical application for it. But nobody was interested.

2. Henry Courtney and Roger Merrill developed a coating substance that allowed the glue to stick to one surface but not to others. This made it possible to produce a permanently temporary glue, that is, one that would peel off easily when pulled but would otherwise hang on forever.

3. Art Fry found a problem that fit Spence Silver's solution. He found an application for the glue as a "better bookmark" and as a note pad. No equipment existed at 3M to coat only a part of a piece of paper with the glue. Fry therefore carried 3M equipment and tools home to his own basement, where he designed and made his own machine to manufacture the forerunner of Post-It Notes. Because the working machine became too large to get out of his basement, he blasted a hole in the wall to get the equipment back to 3M. He then brought together engineers, designers, production managers, and machinists to demonstrate the prototype machine and generate enthusiasm for manufacturing the product.

4. Geoffrey Nicholson and Joseph Ramsey began marketing the product inside 3M. They also submitted the product to the standard 3M market tests. The product failed miserably. No one wanted to pay $1.00 for a pad of scratch paper. But when Nicholson and Ramsey broke 3M rules by personally visiting test market sites and giving away free samples, the consuming public became addicted to the product.

In this scenario, Spence Silver was both a rule breaker and an idea champion. Art Fry was also an idea champion, but more importantly, he orchestrated the coming together of the various groups needed to get the innovation off the ground. Henry Courtney and Roger Merrill helped sponsor Silver's innovation by providing him with the coating substance that would allow his idea to work. Geoff Nicholson and Joe Ramsey were both rule breakers and sponsors in their bid to get the product accepted by the public. In each case, not only did all these people play unique roles, but they did so with tremendous enthusiasm and zeal. They were confident of their ideas and willing to put their time and resources on the line as advocates. They fostered support among a variety of constituencies, both within their own areas of expertise as well as among outside groups. Most organizations are inclined to give in to those who are sure of themselves, persistent in their efforts, and savvy enough to make converts of others.

Not everyone can be an idea champion. But when managers reward and recognize those who sponsor and orchestrate the ideas of others, creativity increases in organizations. Teams form, supporters replace competitors, and innovation thrives. Facilitating multiple role development is the job of the managers who want to foster creativity. Figure 3.11 summarizes this process.

Summary

In the twenty-first century, almost no manager or organization can afford to stand still, to reply on past practices, and to avoid innovation. In a fast-paced environment in which the half-life of knowledge is about three years and the half-life of almost any technology is counted in weeks and months instead of years, creative problem solving is increasingly a prerequisite for success. The digital revolution makes the rapid production of new ideas almost mandatory. This is not to negate the importance of analytical problem solving, of course. The quality revolution of the 1980s and 1990s taught us important lessons about carefully proscribed, sequential, and analytic problem-solving processes. Error rates, response times, and missed deadlines dropped dramatically when analytical problem solving was institutionalized in manufacturing and service companies.

In this chapter we have discussed a well-developed model for solving problems. It consists of four separate

Figure 3.11 | **Enabling Creativity in Others**

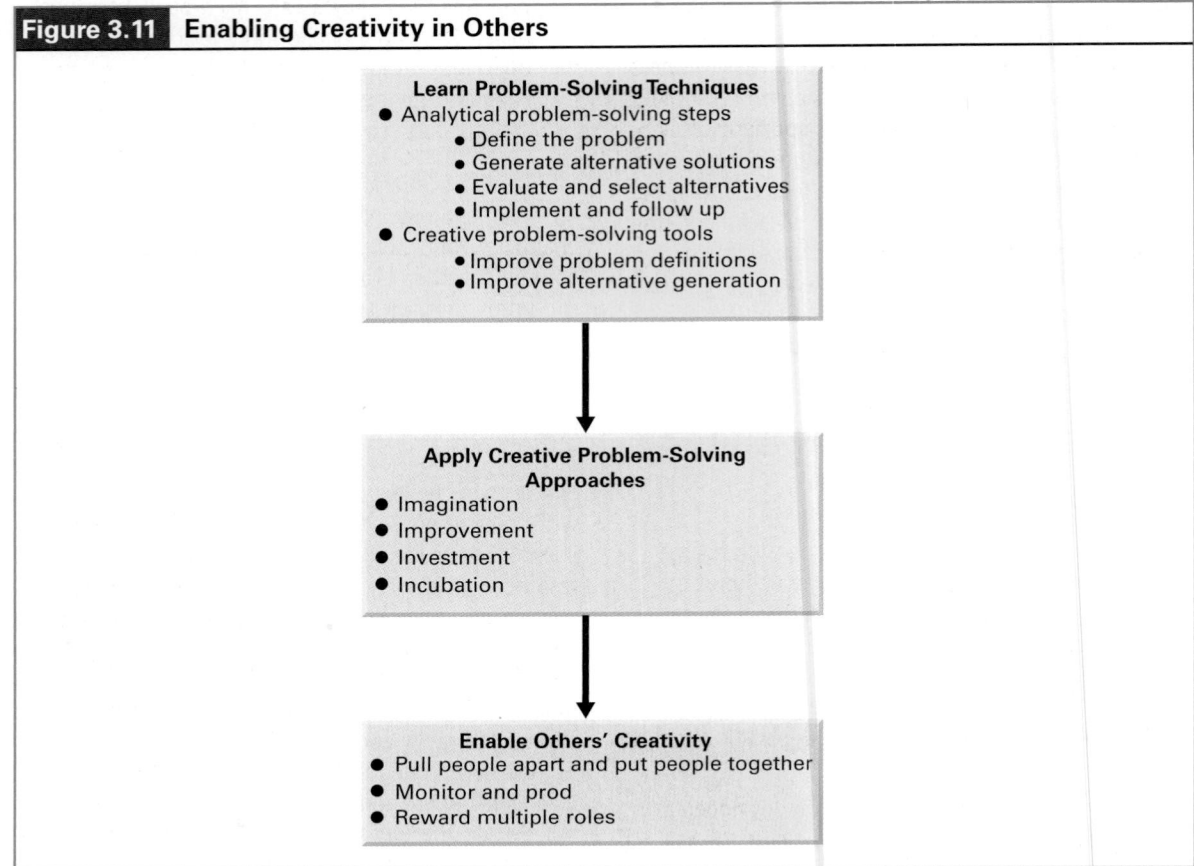

Learn Problem-Solving Techniques
- Analytical problem-solving steps
  - Define the problem
  - Generate alternative solutions
  - Evaluate and select alternatives
  - Implement and follow up
- Creative problem-solving tools
  - Improve problem definitions
  - Improve alternative generation

Apply Creative Problem-Solving Approaches
- Imagination
- Improvement
- Investment
- Incubation

Enable Others' Creativity
- Pull people apart and put people together
- Monitor and prod
- Reward multiple roles

and sequential stages: defining a problem; generating alternative solutions; evaluating and selecting the best solution; and implementing the chosen solution. This model, however, is mainly useful for solving straightforward problems. Many problems faced by managers are not of this type, and frequently managers are called on to exercise creative problem-solving skills. That is, they must broaden their perspective of the problem and develop alternative solutions that are not immediately obvious.

We have discussed four different types of creativity and encouraged you to consider all four when faced with the need to be creative. However, we have also illustrated eight major conceptual blocks that inhibit most people's creative problem-solving abilities. Conceptual blocks are mental obstacles that artificially constrain problem definition and solution and that keep most people from being effective creative problem solvers.

Overcoming these conceptual blocks is a matter of skill development and practice in thinking, not a matter of innate ability. Everyone can become a skilled creative

problem solver with practice. Becoming aware of these thinking inhibitors helps individuals overcome them. We also discussed three major techniques for improving creative problem definition and three major techniques for improving the creative generation of alternative solutions. Specific suggestions were offered that can help implement these six techniques.

We concluded by offering some hints about how to foster creativity among other people. Becoming an effective problem solver yourself is important, but effective managers can also enhance this activity among those with whom they work.

Behavioral Guidelines

Below are specific behavioral action guidelines to help guide your skill practice in analytical and creative problem solving.

1. Follow the four-step procedure outlined in Table 3.1 when solving straightforward problems. Keep the steps separate, and do not take short-

cuts—define the problem, generate alternative solutions, evaluate the alternatives, select and implement the optimal solution.

2. When approaching a difficult or complex problem, remember that creative solutions need not be a product of revolutionary and brand-new ideas. Four different types of creativity are available to you—imagination, improvement, investment, and incubation.

3. Try to overcome your conceptual blocks by consciously doing the following:
   ❏ Use lateral thinking in addition to vertical thinking
   ❏ Use several thought languages instead of just one
   ❏ Challenge stereotypes based on past experiences
   ❏ Identify underlying themes and commonalities in seemingly unrelated factors
   ❏ Delete superfluous information and fill in important missing information when studying the problem
   ❏ Avoid artificially constraining problem boundaries
   ❏ Overcome any unwillingness to be inquisitive
   ❏ Use both right- and left-brain thinking

4. To enhance creativity, use techniques that elaborate problem definition such as:
   ❏ Making the strange familiar and the familiar strange by using metaphors and analogies
   ❏ Developing alternative (opposite) definitions and applying a question checklist
   ❏ Reversing the definition

5. To enhance creativity, use techniques that elaborate possible alternative solutions such as:
   ❏ Deferring judgment
   ❏ Subdividing the problem into its attributes
   ❏ Combining unrelated problem attributes

6. Foster creativity among those with whom you work by doing the following:
   ❏ Providing autonomy, allowing individuals to experiment and try out ideas
   ❏ Putting people together who hold different perspectives into teams to work on problems
   ❏ Holding people accountable for innovation
   ❏ Using sharp-pointed prods to stimulate new thinking
   ❏ Recognizing, rewarding, and encouraging multiple roles including idea champions, sponsors, orchestrators, and rule breakers

LEARNING

CASES INVOLVING PROBLEM SOLVING

Admiral Kimmel's Failure at Pearl Harbor

In the summer of 1941, as relations between the United States and Japan were rapidly deteriorating, Admiral Kimmel, Commander in Chief of the Pacific Fleet, received many warnings concerning the imminence of war. During this period he worked out a plan in collaboration with his staff at Pearl Harbor that gave priority to training key personnel and supplying basic equipment to U.S. outposts in the Far East. The plan took account of the possibility of a long, hard war with Japan and the difficulties of mobilizing scarce resources in manpower and material. At that time, Admiral Kimmel and his staff were keenly aware of the risks of being unprepared for war with Japan, as well as the high costs and risks involved in preparing for war. They appear to have been relatively optimistic about being able to develop a satisfactory military plan and about having sufficient time in which to implement it. In short, all the conditions were present for vigilance, and it seems likely that this coping pattern characterized their planning activity.

But, during the late fall of 1941, as warnings became increasingly more ominous, a different pattern of coping behavior emerged. Admiral Kimmel and his staff continued to cling to the policy to which they had committed themselves, discounting each fresh warning and failing to note that more and more signs were pointing to Pearl Harbor as a possible target for a surprise air attack. They repeatedly renewed their decision to continue using the available resources primarily for training green sailors and soldiers and for supplying bases close to Japan, rather than instituting an adequate alert that would give priority to defending Pearl Harbor against enemy attack.

Knowing that neither their own sector nor the rest of the U.S. military organization was ready for a shooting war, they clung to an unwarranted set of rationalizations. The Japanese, they thought, would not launch an attack against any American possession; and if by some remote chance they decided to do so, it certainly wouldn't be at Pearl Harbor. Admiral Kimmel and his staff acknowledged that Japan could launch a surprise attack in any direction, but remained convinced that it would not be launched in their direction. They saw no reason to change their course. Therefore, they continued to give peacetime weekend leave to the majority of the naval forces in Hawaii and allowed the many warships in the Pacific Fleet to remain anchored at Pearl Harbor, as sitting ducks. Kimmel regularly discussed each warning with members of his staff. At times he became emotionally aroused and obtained reassurance from the members of his in-group. He shared with them a number of rationalizations that bolstered his decision to ignore the warnings. On November 27, 1941, for example, he received an explicit "war warning" from the chief of naval operations in Washington, which stirred up his concern but did not impel him to take any new protective action. This message was intended as a strong follow-up to an earlier warning, which Kimmel had received only three days earlier, stating that war with Japan was imminent and that "a surprise aggressive movement in any direction, including attack on Philippines or Guam, is a possibility." The new warning asserted that "an aggressive move by Japan is expected within the next few days" and instructed Kimmel to "execute appropriate defensive deployment" preparatory to carrying out the naval war plan.

The threat conveyed by this warning was evidently strong enough to induce Kimmel to engage in prolonged discussion with his staff about what should be done.

But their vigilance seems to have been confined to paying careful attention to the way the warning was worded. During the meeting, members of the staff pointed out to Kimmel that Hawaii was not specifically mentioned as a possible target in either of the two war warnings, whereas other places—the Philippines, Malaya, and other remote areas—were explicitly named. Kimmel went along with the interpretation that the ambiguities they had detected in the wording must have meant that Pearl Harbor was not supposed to be regarded as a likely target, even though the message seemed to be saying that it was. The defensive quality that entered into this judgment is revealed by the fact that Kimmel made no effort to use his available channels of communication in Washington to find out what really had been meant. He ended up agreeing with the members of his advisory group that there was no chance of a surprise air attack on Hawaii at that particular time.

Since he judged Pearl Harbor not to be vulnerable, Kimmel decided that the limited-alert condition that had been instituted months earlier would be sufficient. He assumed, however, that all U.S. Army units in Hawaii had gone on full alert in response to this war warning, so that antiaircraft and radar units under army control would be fully activated. But, again, reflecting his defensive lack of interest in carrying out tasks that required acknowledging the threat, Kimmel failed to inquire of Army headquarters exactly what was being done. As a result, he did not discover until after the disaster on December 7 that the Army, too, was on only limited alert, designed exclusively to protect military installations against local sabotage.

On December 3, 1941, Kimmel engaged in intensive discussion with two members of his staff upon receiving a fresh warning from naval headquarters in Washington stating that U.S. cryptographers had decoded a secret message from Tokyo to all diplomatic missions in the United States and other countries, ordering them to destroy their secret codes. Kimmel realized that this type of order could mean that Japan was making last-minute preparations before launching an attack against the United States. Again, he and his advisors devoted considerable attention to the exact wording of this new, worrisome warning. They made much of the fact that the dispatch said "most" of the codes but not "all." They concluded that the destruction of the codes should be interpreted as a routine precautionary measure and not as a sign that Japan was planning to attack an American possession. Again, no effort was made to find out from Washington how the intelligence units there interpreted the message. But the lengthy discussions and the close attention paid to the wording of these messages imply that they did succeed in at least temporarily inducing decisional conflict.

By December 6, 1941, the day before the attack, Kimmel was aware of a large accumulation of extremely ominous signs. In addition to receiving the official war warnings during the preceding week, he had received a private letter three days earlier from Admiral Stark in Washington stating that both President Roosevelt and Secretary of State Hull now thought that the Japanese were getting ready to launch a surprise attack. Then on December 6, Kimmel received another message from Admiral Stark containing emergency war orders pertaining to the destruction of secret and confidential documents in American bases on outlying Pacific islands. On that same day, the FBI in Hawaii informed Kimmel that the local Japanese consulate had been burning its papers for the last two days. Furthermore, Kimmel's chief naval intelligence officer had reported to him that day, as he had on the preceding days, that despite fresh efforts to pick up Japanese naval signal calls, the whereabouts of all six of Japan's aircraft carriers still remained a mystery. (U.S. Naval Combat Intelligence had lost track of the Japanese aircraft carriers in mid-November, when they started to move toward Hawaii for the planned attack on Pearl Harbor.)

Although the various warning signs, taken together, clearly indicated that Japan was getting ready to launch an attack against the United States, they remained ambiguous as to exactly where the attack was likely to be. There was also considerable "noise" mixed in with the warning signals, including intelligence reports that huge Japanese naval forces were moving toward Malaya. But, inexplicably, there was a poverty of imagination on the part of Kimmel and his staff with regard to considering the possibility that Pearl Harbor itself might be one of the targets of a Japanese attack.

The accumulated warnings, however, were sufficiently impressive to Kimmel to generate considerable concern. On the afternoon of December 6, as he was pondering alternative courses of action, he openly expressed his anxiety to two of his staff officers. He told them he was worried about the safety of the fleet at Pearl Harbor in view of all the disturbing indications that Japan was getting ready for a massive attack somewhere. One member of the staff immediately reassured him that "the Japanese could not possibly be able to proceed in force against Pearl Harbor when they had so much strength concentrated in their Asiatic operations." Another told him that the limited-alert condition he had ordered many weeks earlier would certainly be sufficient and nothing more was needed. "We finally decided," Kimmel subsequently recalled, "that what we had [already] done was still good and we would stick to it." At the end of the discussion, Kimmel "put his worries aside" and went off to a dinner party.

SOURCE: Reprinted with the permission of the Free Press, a division of Simon & Schuster Adult Publishing Group, from DECISION MAKING: A Psychological Analysis of Conflict, Choice and Commitment by Irving L. Janis and Leon Mann. Copyright © 1977 by the Free Press. All rights reserved.

Discussion Questions

1. Identify the conceptual blocks that are illustrated in this case.
2. Outline the problem-solving steps followed by Kimmel and his advisors. What steps in analytical problem solving were skipped or short-circuited?
3. If you were Admiral Kimmel's advisor, knowing what you know about problem solving, what would you have suggested to help his problem-solving processes? What kinds of conceptual blockbusters could have been useful to Kimmel?
4. What do you learn from this case that would help you advise Microsoft in its anti-competitive case with the federal government, or advise Barnes & Noble.com to help it displace Amazon.com, or advise American Greetings to become the dominant player in the greeting card business? What practical hints, in other words, do you derive from this classic case of analytical problem solving gone awry?

Creativity at Apple

In his annual speech in Paris in 2003, Steven Jobs, the lionized CEO of Apple Computer, Inc., proudly described Apple in these terms: "Innovate. That's what we do." And innovate they have. Jobs and his colleagues, Steve Wozniak and Mike Markkula, invented the personal computer market in 1977 with the introduction of the Apple II. In 1980, Apple was the number one vendor of personal computers in the world. Apple's success, in fact, helped spawn what became known as Silicon Valley in California, the mother lode of high technology invention and production for the next three decades.

Apple has always been a trailblazing company whose innovative products are almost universally acknowledged as easier to use, more powerful, and more elegant than those of its rivals. In the last ten years, Apple has been granted 1,300 patents, half as many as Microsoft, a company 145 times the size of Apple. Dell Computer, by contrast, has been granted half as many patents as Apple. Apple has invented, moreover, more businesses than just the personal computer. In 1984, Apple created the first computer network with its Macintosh machines, whereas Windows-based PC's didn't network until the mid-1990s. A decade ago, Apple introduced the first handheld, pen-based computing device known as the Newton and followed that up with a wireless mouse, ambient-lit keyboards for working in the dark, and the fastest computer on the market in 2003. In 2003, Apple also introduced the first legal, digital music store for downloading songs—iTunes—along with its compatible technology, iPods. In other words, Apple has been at the forefront of product and technological innovation for almost 30 years. Apple has been, hands down, the most innovative company in its industry and one of the most innovative companies on the planet.

Here's the problem. Today, Apple commands just two percent of the $180 billion worldwide market for PCs. Apple's rivals have followed its creative leads and snatched profits and market share from Apple with astonishing effectiveness. From its number one position two decades ago, Apple currently ranks as the ninth largest PC firm—behind name-brand firms such as Dell, Hewlett-Packard, and IBM, but embarrassingly, also behind no-name firms such as Acer and Legend. These clone-makers, from Taiwan and China respectively, have invented no new products.

Moreover, whereas Apple was once among the most profitable companies in the PC industry, its operating profits have shrunk from 20 percent in 1981 to 0.4 percent in 2004, one-tenth the industry average. Its chief competitor in software—Microsoft—sold $2.6 billion in software in the most recent quarter compared to $177 million for Apple.

What could possibly be wrong? If one takes seriously the messages being declared loudly and prominently in the business press and in the broader global society today, innovation and creativity are the keys to success. "Change or die." "Innovate or get passed over." "Be creative to be successful." A key tenet upon which progressive, market-based, capitalistic societies are based is the idea of creative destruction. That is, without creativity and innovation, individuals and organizations become casualties of the second law of thermodynamics—they disintegrate, wither, disorganize, and die. New products are needed to keep consumers happy. Obsolescence is ubiquitous. Innovation and creativity, consequently, are touted as being at the very heart of success. For more evidence, just skim over the more than 49,000 book titles when you log onto Amazon and search using the key word "innovation."

On the other hand, consider some of the most innovative companies in recent American history. Xerox Corporation's famed Palo Alto Research Center gave the world laser printing, the Ethernet, Windows-type software, graphical user interfacing, and the mouse, yet it is notorious for not having made any money at all. Polaroid introduced the idea of instant images, yet it filed for bankruptcy in 2001. The Internet boom in the late 1990s was an explosion of what is now considered to be worthless innovation. And, Enron may have been the most innovative financial company ever.

On the other hand, Amazon, Southwest Airlines, eBay, Wal-Mart, and Dell are examples of incredibly successful companies, but did not invent any new products or technologies. They are acknowledged as innovative and creative companies, but they don't hold a candle to Apple. Instead of new products, they have invented new processes, new ways to deliver products, new distribution channels, new marketing approaches. It is well known that Henry Ford didn't invent the automobile. He simply invented a new way to assemble a car at a cost affordable to his own workers. The guy who invented the automobile hardly made a dime.

The trouble is, creativity as applied to business processes—manufacturing methods, sales and marketing, employee incentive systems, or leadership development—are usually seen as humdrum, nitty gritty, uncool, plodding, unimaginative, and boring. Creative people and creative companies that capture headlines are usually those that come up with great new product ideas or splashy features. But, look at the list of

Fortune 500 companies and judge how many are product champions versus process champions. Decide for yourself which is the driver of economic growth: good innovation or good management.

SOURCE: Adapted from Hawn, 2004.

Discussion Questions:

1. Consider the four approaches to creativity. What approach(es) has Apple relied upon? What alternatives have other firms in the industry pursued? What other alternatives could Apple implement?

2. Assume you were a consultant to the CEO at Apple. What advice would you give on how Apple could capitalize on its creativity? How can Apple make money based on its own inclination to pursue creativity in certain ways?

3. What are the major obstacles and conceptual blocks that face Apple right now? What do employees need to watch out for?

4. What tools for fostering creative problem solving are applicable to Apple, and which would not be workable? Which ones do you think are used the most there?

EXERCISES FOR APPLYING CONCEPTUAL BLOCKBUSTING

The purpose of this exercise is to have you practice problem solving—both analytical and creative. Two actual scenarios are provided below. Both present real problems faced by real managers. They are very likely the same kinds of problems faced by your own business school and by many of your local businesses. Your assignment in each case is to identify a solution to the problem. You will approach the problem in two ways: first using analytical problem solving techniques; second, using creative problem-solving techniques. The first approach—analytical problem solving—you should accomplish by yourself. The second approach—creative problem solving—you should accomplish in a team. Your task is to apply the principles of problem solving to come up with realistic, cost-efficient, and effective solutions to these problems. Consider each scenario separately. You should take no more than ten minutes to complete the analytical problem-solving assignment. Then take twenty minutes to complete the creative problem-solving assignment.

Individual Assignment—Analytical Problem Solving (10 minutes)

1. After reading the first case, write down a specific problem definition. What precisely worded problem are you going to solve? Complete the sentence: The problem I am going to solve is . . .

2. Now identify at least four or five alternative solutions. What ideas do you have for resolving this problem? Complete this sentence: Possible ways to resolve this problem are . . .

3. Next, evaluate the alternatives you have proposed. Make sure you don't evaluate each alternative before proposing your complete set. Evaluate your set of alternatives on the basis of these criteria: Will this alternative solve the problem you have defined? Is this alternative realistic in terms of being cost-effective? Can this solution be implemented in a short time frame?

PRACTICE

4. Now write down your proposed solution to the problem. Be specific about what should be done and when. Be prepared to share that solution with other team members.

Team Assignment—Creative Problem Solving (20 minutes)

1. Now form a team of four or five people. Each team member should share his or her own definition of the problem. It is unlikely that they will all be the same, so make sure you keep track of them. Now add at least three more plausible definitions of the problem. In doing so, use at least two techniques for expanding problem definition discussed in the text. Each problem definition should differ from the others in what the problem is, not just a statement of different causes of the problem.

2. Now examine each of the definitions you have proposed. Select one that the entire team can agree upon. Since it is unlikely that you can solve multiple problems at once, select just one problem definition that you will work on.

3. Share the four or five proposed solutions that you generated on your own, even if they don't relate to the specific problem your team has defined. Keep track of all the different alternatives proposed by team members. After all team members have shared their alternatives, generate at least five additional alternative solutions to the problem you have agreed upon. Use at least two of the techniques for expanding alternatives discussed in the text.

4. Of all the alternatives your team proposed, select the five that you consider to be the most creative and having the highest probability of success.

5. Select one team member from each team to serve as a judging panel. This panel is charged with selecting the team with the most creative and potentially successful alternatives to the problem. Team members cannot vote for their own team.

6. Each team now shares their five alternatives with the class. The judging panel selects the winner.

Moving Up in the Rankings

Business schools seem to have lost the ability to evaluate their own quality and effectiveness. With the emergence of rankings of business schools in the popular press, the role of judging quality seems to have been captured by publications such as *Business Week, U.S. News and World Report*, and the *Financial Times*. The accreditation association for business schools, AACSB, mainly assesses the extent to which a school is accreditable or not, a 0–1 distinction, so a wide range in quality exists among accredited business schools. More refined distinctions have been made in the popular press by identifying the highest rated 50, the first, second, or third tiers, or the top 20. Each publication relies on slightly different criteria in their rankings, but a substantial portion of each ranking rests on name recognition, visibility, or public acclaim. In some of the polls, more than 50 percent of the weighting is placed on the reputation or notoriety of the school. This is problematic, of course, because reputation can be deceiving. One recent poll rated the Harvard and Stanford undergraduate business programs among the top three in the country, even though neither school has an undergraduate business program. Princeton's law school has been rated in the top five in several polls, even though, you guessed it, no such law school exists.

Other criteria sometimes considered in various ranking services include student selectivity, percent of students placed in jobs, starting salaries of graduates, tuition costs compared to graduates' earnings, publications of the faculty, student satisfaction, recruiter satisfaction, and so on. By and large, however, name recognition is the single most crucial factor. It helps predict the number of student applicants, the ability to hire prominent faculty members, fund-raising opportunities, corporate partnerships, and so on.

Many business schools have responded to this pressure to become better known by creating advertising campaigns, circulating internal publications to other business schools and media outlets, and hiring additional staff to market the school. Most business school deans receive an average of 20 publications a week from other business schools, for example, and an editor at *Business Week* reported receiving more than 100 per week. Some deans begrudge the fact that these resources are being spent on activities other than improving the educational experience for students and faculty. Given constrained resources and tuition increases that outstrip the consumer price index every year, spending money on one activity precludes it from being spent on others. On the other hand, most deans acknowledge that this is the way the game must be played.

As part of a strategy to increase visibility, one business school hired world-renowned architect Frank O. Gehry to design a new business school building. Photographs of models of the building are reproduced below. It is a $70 million building that houses all the educational activities of the school. Currently this particular school does not appear in the top 20 on the major rankings lists. However, like about 75 other business schools in the world, it would very much like to reach that level. That is, the school would like to displace another school currently listed in the top 20. One problem with this new landmark building is that it is so unusual, so avant-garde, that it is not even recognized as a building. Upon seeing a photograph for the first time, some people don't even know what they're looking at. On the other hand, it presents an opportunity to leapfrog other schools listed higher in the rankings if the institution is creative in its approach. The challenge, of course, is that no one is sure exactly how to make this happen.

Keith Dunn and McGuffey's Restaurant

Keith Dunn knew exactly what to expect. He knew how his employees felt about him. That's why he had sent them the questionnaire in the first place. He needed a shot of confidence, a feeling that his employees were behind him as he struggled to build McGuffey's Restaurants, Inc., beyond two restaurants and $4 million in annual sales.

Gathering up the anonymous questionnaires, Dunn returned to his tiny corporate office in Asheville, North Carolina. With one of his partners by his side, he ripped open the first envelope as eagerly as a Broadway producer checking the reviews on opening night. His eyes zoomed directly to the question where employees were asked to rate the three owners' performance on a scale of 1 to 10.

A zero. The employee had scrawled in a big, fat zero. "Find out whose handwriting this is," he told his partner, Richard Laibson.

He ripped open another: zero again. And another. A two. "We'll fire these people," Dunn said to Laibson coldly. Another zero.

A one.

"Oh, go work for somebody else, you jerk!" Dunn shouted.

Soon he had moved to fire 10 of his 230 employees. "Plenty of people seemed to hate my guts," he says.

Over the next day, though, Dunn's anger subsided. "You think, I've done all this for these people and they think I'm a total jerk who doesn't care about them," he says. "Finally, you have to look in the mirror and think, 'Maybe they're right.'"

For Dunn, that realization was absolutely shattering. He had started the company three years earlier out of frustration over all the abuse he had suffered while working at big restaurant chains. If Dunn had one overriding mission at McGuffey's, it was to prove that restaurants didn't have to mistreat their employees.

He thought he had succeeded. Until he opened those surveys, he had believed that McGuffey's was a place where employees felt valued, involved, and appreciated. "I had no idea we were treating people so badly," he says. Somewhere along the way, in the day-to-day running of the business, he had lost his connection with them and left behind the employee-oriented company he thought he was running.

Dunn's 13-year odyssey through some big restaurant chains left him feeling as limp as a cheeseburger after a day under the heat lamps. Ponderosa in Georgia. Bennigan's in Florida and Tennessee. TGI Friday's in Texas, Tennessee, and Indiana. Within one six-month period at Friday's, he got two promotions, two bonuses, and two raises; then his boss left, and he got fired. That did it. Dunn was fed up with big chains.

At the age of 29, he returned to Atlanta, where he had attended Emory University as an undergraduate and where he began waiting tables at a local restaurant.

There he met David Lynn, the general manager of the restaurant, a similarly jaded 29-year-old who, by his own admission, had "begun to lose faith." Lynn and Dunn started hatching plans to open their own place, where employees would enjoy working as much as customers enjoyed eating. They planned to target the smaller markets that the chains ignored. With financing from a friend, they opened McGuffey's.

True to their people-oriented goals, the partners tried to make employees feel more appreciated than they themselves had felt at the chains. They gave them a free drink and a meal at the end of every shift, let them give away appetizers and desserts, and provided them a week of paid vacation each year.

A special camaraderie developed among the employees. After all, they worked in an industry in which a turnover rate of 250 percent was something to aspire to. The night before McGuffey's opened, some 75 employees encircled the ficus tree next to the bar, joined hands, and prayed silently for two minutes. "The tree had a special energy," says Dunn.

Maybe so. By the third night of operation, the 230-seat McGuffey's had a waiting list. The dining room was so crowded that after three months the owners decided to add a 58-seat patio. Then they had to rearrange the kitchen to handle the volume. In its first three and a half months, McGuffey's racked up sales of about $415,000, ending the year just over $110,000 in the red, mostly because the partners paid back the bulk of their $162,000 debt right away.

Word of the restaurant's success reached Hendersonville, North Carolina, a town of 30,000 about 20 miles away. The managing agent of a mall there—*the* mall there—even stopped by to recruit the partners. They made some audacious requests, asking him to spend $300,000 on renovations, including the addition of a patio and upgraded equipment. The agent agreed. With almost no market research, they opened the second McGuffey's 18 months later. The first, in Asheville, was still roaring, having broken the $2 million mark in sales its first year, with a marginal loss of just over $16,000.

By midsummer, the 200-seat Hendersonville restaurant was hauling in $35,000 a week. "Gee, you guys must be getting rich," the partners heard all around town. "When are you going to buy your own jets?" "Everyone was telling us we could do no wrong," says Dunn. The Asheville restaurant, though, was developing some problems. Right after the Hendersonville McGuffey's opened, sales at Asheville fell 15 percent. But the partners shrugged it off; some Asheville customers lived closer to Hendersonville, so one restaurant was probably pulling some of the other's customers. Either way, the customers were still there. "We're just spreading our market a little thinner," Dunn told his partners. When Asheville had lost another 10 percent and Hendersonville 5 percent, Dunn blamed the fact that the drinking age had been raised to 21 in Asheville, cutting into liquor sales.

By the end of that year, the company recorded nearly $3.5 million in sales, with nominal losses of about $95,000. But the adulation and the expectation of big money and fancy cars were beginning to cloud the real reason they had started the business. "McGuffey's was born purely out of frustration," says Dunn. Now, the frustration was gone. "You get pulled in so many directions that you just lose touch," says Laibson. "There are things that you simply forget."

What the partners forgot, in the warm flush of success, were their roots.

"Success breeds ego," says Dunn, "and ego breeds contempt." He would come back from trade shows or real-estate meetings all pumped up. "Isn't this exciting?" he'd ask an employee. "We're going to open a new restaurant next year." When the employee stared back blankly, Dunn felt resentful. "I didn't understand why they weren't thrilled," he says. He didn't see that while his world was constantly growing and expanding, his employees' world was sliding downhill. They were still busing tables or cooking burgers and thinking, "Forget the new restaurant; you haven't said hello to me in months; and by the way, why don't you fix the tea machine?"

"I just got too good, and too busy, to do orientation," he says. So he decided to tape orientation sessions for new employees, to make a film just like the one he had been subjected to when he worked at Bennigan's. On tape, Dunn told new employees one of his favorite stories, the one about the customer who walks into a chain restaurant and finds himself asking questions of a hostess sign because he can't find a human. The moral: "McGuffey's will never be so impersonal as to make people talk to a sign." A film maybe, but never a sign.

PRACTICE

Since Dunn wasn't around the restaurants all that much, he didn't notice that employees were leaving in droves. Even the departure of Tom Valdez, the kitchen manager in Asheville, wasn't enough to take the shine off his "glowing ego," as he calls it.

Valdez had worked as Dunn's kitchen manager at TGI Friday's. When the Hendersonville McGuffey's was opening up, Dunn recruited him as kitchen manager. A few months later, Valdez marched into Dunn's office and announced that he was heading back to Indianapolis. "There's too much b.s. around here," he blurted out. "You don't care about your people." Dunn was shocked. "As soon as we get this next restaurant opened, we'll make things the way they used to be," he replied. But Valdez wouldn't budge. "Keith," he said bitterly, "you are turning out to be like all the other companies." Dunn shrugged. "We're a big company, and we've got to do big-company things," he replied.

Valdez walked out, slamming the door. Dunn still didn't understand that he had begun imitating the very companies that he had so loathed. He stopped wanting to rebel against them; under the intense pressure of growing a company, he just wanted to master their tried-and-true methods. "I was allowing the company to become like the companies we hated because I thought it was inevitable," he says.

Three months later, McGuffey's two top managers announced that they were moving to the West Coast to start their own company. Dunn beamed, "Our employees learn so much," he would boast, "that they are ready to start their own restaurants."

Before they left, Dunn sat down with them in the classroom at Hendersonville. "So," he asked casually, "how do you think we could run the place better?" Three hours later, he was still listening. "The McGuffey's we fell in love with just doesn't exist anymore," one of them concluded sadly.

Dunn was outraged. How could his employees be so ungrateful? Couldn't they see how everybody was sharing the success? Who had given them health insurance as soon as the partners could afford it? Who had given them dental insurance this year? And who—not that anyone would appreciate it—planned to set up profit sharing next year?

Sales at both restaurants were still dwindling. This time, there were no changes in the liquor laws or new restaurants to blame. With employees feeling ignored, resentful, and abandoned, the rest rooms didn't get scrubbed as thoroughly, the food didn't arrive quite as piping hot, the servers didn't smile so often. But the owners, wrapped up in themselves, couldn't see it. They were mystified. "It began to seem like what made our company great had somehow gotten lost," says Laibson.

Shaken by all the recent defections, Dunn needed a boost of confidence. So he sent out the one-page survey, which asked employees to rate the owners' performance. He was crushed by the results. Out of curiosity, Dunn later turned to an assistant and asked a favor. Can you calculate our turnover rate? Came the reply: "220 percent, sir."

Keith Dunn figured he would consult the management gurus through their books, tapes, and speeches. "You want people-oriented management?" he thought. "Fine. I'll give it to you."

Dunn and Laibson had spent a few months visiting 23 of the best restaurants in the Southeast. Driving for hours, they'd listen to tapes on management, stop them at key points, and ask, "Why don't we do something like this?" At night, they read management books, underlining significant passages, looking for answers.

"They were all saying that people is where it's at," says Dunn. "We've got to start thinking of our people as an asset," they decided. "And we've got to increase the value of that asset." Dunn was excited by the prospect of forming McGuffey's into the shape of a reverse pyramid, with employees on top. Keeping employees, he now knew, meant keeping employees involved.

He heard one consultant suggest that smart companies keep managers involved by tying their compensation to their performance. McGuffey's had been handing managers goals every quarter; if they hit half the goals, they pocketed half their bonus. Sound reasonable?

No, preached the consultant, you can't reward managers for a halfhearted job. It has to be all or nothing. "From now on," Dunn told his managers firmly, "there's no halfway."

Dunn also launched a contest for employees. Competition, he had read, was a good way of keeping employees motivated.

So the CUDA (Customer Undeniably Deserves Attention) contest was born. At Hendersonville and Asheville, he divided the employees into six teams. The winning team would win $1,000, based on talking to customers, keeping the restaurant clean, and collecting special tokens for extra work beyond the call of duty.

Employees came in every morning, donned their colors, and dug in for battle. Within a few weeks, two teams pulled out in front. Managers also seemed revitalized. To Dunn, it seemed like they would do anything, anything, to keep their food costs down, their sales up, their profit margins in line. This was just what all the high-priced consultants had promised.

But after about six months, only one store's managers seemed capable of winning those all-or-nothing bonuses. At managers' meetings and reviews, Dunn started hearing grumblings. "How come your labor costs are so out of whack?" he'd ask. "Heck, I can't win the bonus anyway," a manager would answer, "so why try?" "Look, Keith," another would say, "I haven't seen a bonus in so long, I've forgotten what they look like." Some managers wanted the bonus so badly that they worked understaffed, didn't fix equipment, and ran short on supplies.

The CUDA contest deteriorated into jealousy and malaise. Three teams lagged far behind after the first month or so. Within those teams people were bickering and complaining all the time: "We can't win, so what's the use?" The contest, Dunn couldn't help but notice, seemed to be having a reverse effect than the one he had intended. "Some people were really killing themselves," he says. About 12, to be exact. The other 100-plus were utterly demoralized.

Dunn was angry. These were the same employees who, after all, had claimed he wasn't doing enough for them. But OK, he wanted to hear what they had to say. "Get feedback," the management gurus preached; "find out what your employees think." Dunn announced that the owners would hold informal rap sessions once a month.

"This is your time to talk," Dunn told the employees who showed up—all three of them. That's how it was most times, with three to five employees in attendance, and the owners dragging others away from their jobs in the kitchen. Nothing was sinking in, and Dunn knew it. He now was clear about what didn't work. He just needed to become clear about what would work.

SOURCE: INC: THE MAGAZINE FOR GROWING COMPANIES by J. HYATT. Copyright 1989 by MANSUETO VENTURES LLC. Reproduced with permission of MANSUETO VENTURES LLC in the format CD-ROM via Copyright Clearance Center.

Creative Problem-Solving Practice

In a team of colleagues, apply as many of the creative problem-solving tools as you can in developing alternative solutions to any of the following problems. Different teams may take different problems and then report their solutions to the entire class. You may substitute a current pressing issue you are facing instead of one of these problems if you choose. Try consciously to break through your conceptual blocks and apply the hints that can help you expand your problem definition and the alternatives you consider to be relevant. Keep in mind the four different approaches to creativity.

Problem 1: Consumers now have access to hundreds of television channels and thousands of shows on demand. The average person is lost. Without major advertising dollars, many networks, not to mention many programs, simply get ignored. How could you address this problem?

Problem 2: At least 20 different rankings of schools appear periodically in the modern press. Students are attracted to schools that receive high rankings, and resources tend to flow to the top schools more than to the bottom schools. What could be done to affect the rankings of your own school?

Problem 3: In the last five years, Virgin Atlantic Airlines has been growing at double digit rates while most U.S.-based airlines have struggled to make any money at all. What could the U.S. airline industry do to turn itself around?

Problem 4: The newspaper industry has been slowly declining over the past several decades. People rely less and less on newspapers to obtain the news. What be done to reverse this trend?

Have a team of observers watch the analytical and creative problem-solving process as it unfolds. Use the Observers' forms at the end of the chapter to provide feedback to the individuals and the teams on the basis of how well they applied the analytical and creative problem solving techniques.

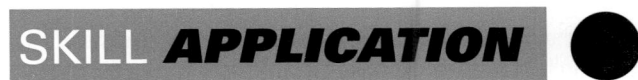

ACTIVITIES FOR SOLVING PROBLEMS CREATIVELY

Suggested Assignments

1. Teach someone else how to solve problems creatively. Explain the guidelines and give examples from your own experience. Record your experience in your journal.

2. Think of a problem that is important to you right now for which there is not an obvious solution. It may relate to your family, your classroom experiences, your work situation, or some interpersonal relationship. Use the principles and techniques discussed in the chapter to work out a creative solution to that problem. Spend the time it takes to do a good job, even if several days are required. Describe the experience in your journal.

3. Help direct a group (your family, roommates, social club, church, etc.) in a carefully crafted analytical problem-solving process—or a creative problem-solving exercise—using techniques discussed in the chapter. Record your experience in your journal.

4. Write a letter to your dean or a CEO of a firm identifying solutions to some perplexing problem facing his or her organization right now. Write about an issue that you care about. Be sure to offer suggested solutions. This will require that you apply in advance the principles of problem solving discussed in the chapter.

Application Plan and Evaluation

The intent of this exercise is to help you apply this cluster of skills in a real-life, out-of-class setting. Now that you have become familiar with the behavioral guidelines that form the basis of effective skill performance, you will improve most by trying out those guidelines in an everyday context. Unlike a classroom activity, in which feedback is immediate and others can assist you with their evaluations, this skill application activity is one you must accomplish and evaluate on your own. There are two parts to this activity. Part 1 helps prepare you to apply

APPLICATION

the skill. Part 2 helps you evaluate and improve on your experience. Be sure to write down answers to each item. Don't short-circuit the process by skipping steps.

Part 1. Planning

1. Write down the two or three aspects of this skill that are most important to you. These may be areas of weakness, areas you most want to improve, or areas that are most salient to a problem you face right now. Identify the specific aspects of this skill that you want to apply.

2. Now identify the setting or the situation in which you will apply this skill. Establish a plan for performance by actually writing down a description of the situation. Who else will be involved? When will you do it? Where will it be done?

> Circumstances:
> Who else?
> When?
> Where?

3. Identify the specific behaviors in which you will engage to apply this skill. Operationalize your skill performance.

4. What are the indicators of successful performance? How will you know you have been effective? What will indicate you have performed competently?

Part 2. Evaluation

5. After you have completed your implementation, record the results. What happened? How successful were you? What was the effect on others?

6. How can you improve? What modifications can you make next time? What will you do differently in a similar situation in the future?

7. Looking back on your whole skill practice and application experience, what have you learned? What has been surprising? In what ways might this experience help you in the long term?

Problem Solving, Creativity, and Innovation

Scoring Key

SKILL AREA	ITEMS	ASSESSMENT	
		PRE-	POST-
Analytical Problem Solving	1, 2, 3, 4, 5	_____	_____
Creative Problem Solving	6, 7, 8, 9, 10, 11, 12, 13, 14, 15	_____	_____
Fostering Creativity	16, 17, 18, 19, 20, 21, 22	_____	_____
	Total Score	_____	_____

Comparison Data (N = 1,500 students)

Compare your scores to three standards:
1. The maximum possible score = 132
2. The scores of other students in the class.
3. Norm data from more than 1,500 business school students.

Pre-Test				Post-Test
98.59	=	mean	=	107.47
114 or above	=	top quartile	=	118 or above
106–113	=	second quartile	=	109–117
102–105	=	third quartile	=	98–108
101 or below	=	bottom quartile	=	97 or below

How Creative Are You?©

Scoring Key

Circle and add up the values assigned to each item below.

ITEM	A AGREE	B UNDECIDED/ DON'T KNOW	C DISAGREE	ITEM	A AGREE	B UNDECIDED/ DON'T KNOW	C DISAGREE
1	0	1	2	21	0	1	2
2	0	1	2	22	3	0	−1
3	4	1	0	23	0	1	2
4	−2	0	3	24	−1	0	2
5	2	1	0	25	0	1	3
6	−1	0	3	26	−1	0	2

Continued

ITEM	A AGREE	B UNDECIDED/ DON'T KNOW	C DISAGREE	ITEM	A AGREE	B UNDECIDED/ DON'T KNOW	C DISAGREE
7	3	0	−1	27	2	1	0
8	0	1	2	28	2	0	−1
9	3	0	−1	29	0	1	2
10	1	0	3	30	−2	0	3
11	4	1	0	31	0	1	2
12	3	0	−1	32	0	1	2
13	2	1	0	33	3	0	−1
14	4	0	−2	34	−1	0	2
15	−1	0	2	35	0	1	2
16	2	1	0	36	1	2	3
17	0	1	2	37	2	1	0
18	3	0	−1	38	0	1	2
19	0	1	2	39	−1	0	2
20	0	1	2				

40. These words have values of 2:

energetic	perceptive		
resourceful	innovative		
original	self-demanding		
enthusiastic	persevering		
dynamic	dedicated		
flexible	courageous		
observant	curious		
independent	involved		

These words have values of 1:

self-confident	informal
thorough	alert
	forward-looking
restless	open-minded

The remaining words have a value of 0.

Total Score:

Comparison Data (N = 1,500 students)

Mean score:	55.99
Top quartile:	65 or above
Second quartile:	55–64
Third quartile:	47–54
Bottom quartile:	46 or below

Innovative Attitude Scale

Scoring Key

Add up the numbers associated with your responses to the 20 items. When you have done so, compare your scores to the norm group of approximately 1,500 graduate and undergraduate business school students.

Mean score:	72.41
Top quartile:	79 or above

Second quartile:	73–78
Third quartile:	66–72
Bottom quartile:	65 or below

Creative Style Assessment

Scoring Key

Add up the points you gave to all of the "A" alternatives, the "B" alternatives, the "C" alternatives, and the "D" alternatives. Then divide by 7 to get an average score for each of the alternatives. Plot your score on the profile below, connecting the lines so that you produce some kind of kite-like shape.

Total of As: _____ ÷ 7   Average score for A: _____

Total of Bs: _____ ÷ 7   Average score for B: _____

Total of Cs: _____ ÷ 7   Average score for C: _____

Total of Ds: _____ ÷ 7   Average score for D: _____

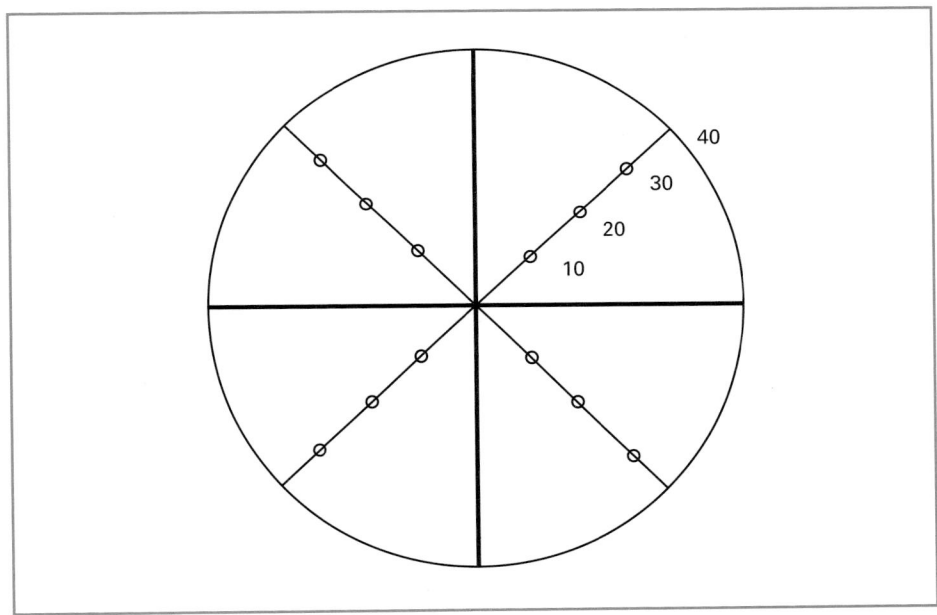

SKILL PRACTICE Applying Conceptual Blockbusting

The following Observer's Feedback Form can be used for each of the cases within the Skill Practice section (Moving Up in the Rankings, Keith Dunn and McGuffey's Restaurant).

Observer's Feedback Form

After the group has completed its problem-solving task, take the time to give the group feedback on its performance. Also provide feedback to each individual group member, either by means of written notes or verbal comments.

Group Observation

1. Was the problem defined explicitly?
   a. To what extent was information sought from all group members?
   b. Did the group avoid defining the problem as a disguised solution?
   c. What techniques were used to expand or alter the definitions of the problem?

2. Were alternatives proposed before any solution was evaluated?
   a. Did all group members help generate alternative solutions without judging them one at a time?
   b. Did people build on the alternatives proposed by others?
   c. What techniques were used to generate more creative alternatives for solving the problem?

3. Was the optimal solution selected?
   a. Were alternatives evaluated systematically?
   b. Was consideration given to the realistic long-term effects of each alternative?

4. Was consideration given to how and when the solution could be implemented?
   a. Were obstacles to implementation discussed?
   b. Was the solution accepted because it solved the problem under consideration, or for some other reason?

5. How creative was the group in defining and solving the problem?

6. What techniques of conceptual blockbusting did the group use?

Individual Observation

1. What violations of the rational problem-solving process did you observe in this person?

2. What conceptual blocks were evident in this person?

3. What conceptual blockbusting efforts did this person make?

4. What was especially effective about the problem-solving attempts of this person?

5. What could this individual do to improve problem-solving skills?

Answer to Matchstick Problem in Figure 3.4

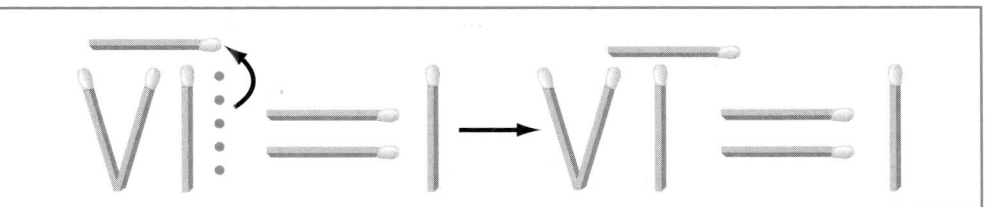

Placing the match at the top turns the figure into a square root sign. The square root of 1 equals 1. ($\sqrt{1}=1$).

Answer to Shakespeare Riddle in Figure 3.5

The answer is 5 inches. Be careful to note where page 1 of Volume I is and where the last page of Volume IV is.

Some Common Themes Applying to Water and Finance (page 194)

banks	capital drain
currency	sinking funds
cash flow	liquid assets
washed up	slush fund
deposits	financial float
frozen assets	underwater pricing
float a loan	

SCORING KEYS AND COMPARISON DATA

Answer to Name That Ship Problem in Figure 3.6

Comparing each part of the ship with the parts from the smaller ships, we find that the ship's name is DISCOVERY:

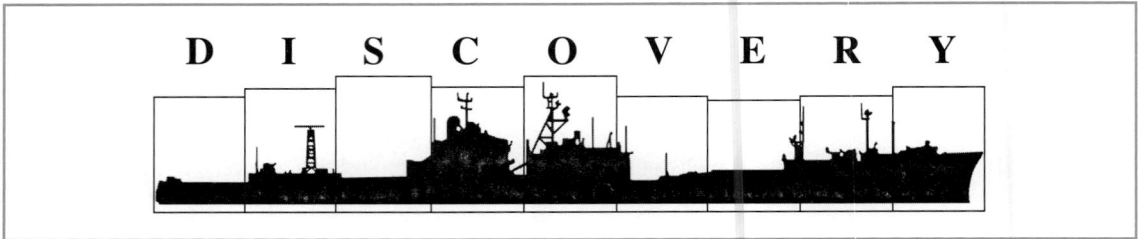

Answer to Nine-Dot Problem in Figure 3.7

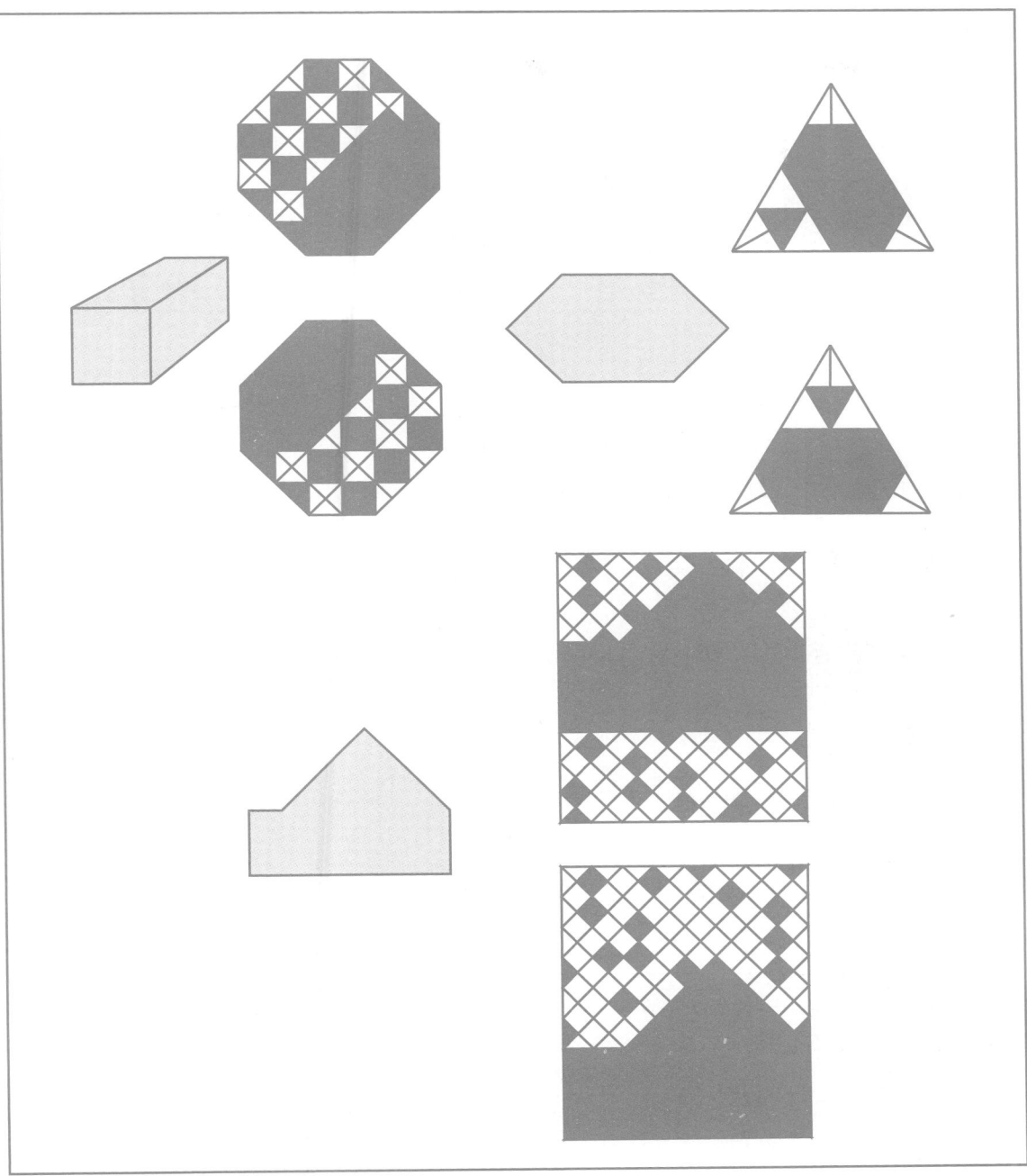

Part II

Interpersonal Skills

CHAPTERS

4 BUILDING RELATIONSHIPS BY COMMUNICATING SUPPORTIVELY

Coaching
Counseling
Listening

5 GAINING POWER AND INFLUENCE

Gaining power
Exercising influence
Increasing authority

6 MOTIVATING OTHERS

Diagnosing poor performance
Creating a motivating environment
Rewarding accomplishments

7 MANAGING CONFLICT

Identifying sources
Selecting strategies
Resolving confrontations

SKILL *ASSESSMENT* ▶

- Communicating Supportively
- Communication Styles

SKILL *LEARNING* ■

- Building Positive Interpersonal Relationships
- The Importance of Effective Communication
- What Is Supportive Communication?
- Coaching and Counseling
- Principles of Supportive Communication
- The Personal Management Interview
- International Caveats
- Summary
- Behavioral Guidelines

SKILL *ANALYSIS* ▶

- Find Somebody Else
- Rejected Plans

SKILL *PRACTICE* ◆

- United Chemical Company
- Byron vs. Thomas
- Active Listening Exercise

SKILL *APPLICATION* ●

- Suggested Assignments
- Application Plan and Evaluation

SCORING KEYS AND *COMPARISON DATA* ■

4

Building Relationships by Communicating Supportively

SKILL DEVELOPMENT OBJECTIVES

- BUILD SUPPORTIVE RELATIONSHIPS EVEN WHEN DELIVERING NEGATIVE FEEDBACK
- AVOID DEFENSIVENESS AND DISCONFIRMATION IN INTERPERSONAL COMMUNICATION
- IMPROVE ABILITY TO APPLY PRINCIPLES OF SUPPORTIVE COMMUNICATION
- IMPROVE RELATIONSHIPS BY USING PERSONAL MANAGEMENT INTERVIEWS

DIAGNOSTIC SURVEYS FOR SUPPORTIVE COMMUNICATION

COMMUNICATING SUPPORTIVELY

Step 1: Before you read the material in this chapter, please respond to the following statements by writing a number from the rating scale below in the left-hand column (Pre-assessment). Your answers should reflect your attitudes and behavior as they are now, not as you would like them to be. Be honest. This instrument is designed to help you discover your level of competency in communicating supportively so you can tailor your learning to your specific needs. When you have completed the survey, use the scoring key at the end of the chapter to identify the skill areas discussed in this chapter that are most important for you to master.

Step 2: After you have completed the reading and the exercises in this chapter and, ideally, as many as you can of the Skill Application assignments at the end of this chapter, cover up your first set of answers. Then respond to the same statements again, this time in the right-hand column (Post-assessment). When you have completed the survey, use the scoring key at the end of the chapter to measure your progress. If your score remains low in specific skill areas, use the behavioral guidelines at the end of the Skill Learning section to guide further practice.

Rating Scale

1 Strongly disagree
2 Disagree
3 Slightly disagree
4 Slightly agree
5 Agree
6 Strongly agree

Assessment

Pre-   Post-

In situations where I have to provide negative feedback or offer corrective advice:

_____   _____   1. I am clear about when I should coach someone and when I should provide counseling instead.

_____   _____   2. I am able to help others recognize and define their own problems when I counsel them.

_____   _____   3. I am able to be completely honest in the feedback that I give to others, even when it is negative.

_____   _____   4. When I give feedback to others, I avoid referring to personal characteristics and focus on problems or solutions instead.

_____   _____   5. I always link negative feedback to a standard or expectation that has been violated.

_____   _____   6. When I try to correct someone's behavior, our relationship is almost always strengthened.

_____   _____   7. I am descriptive in giving negative feedback to others. That is, I objectively describe events, their consequences, and my feelings about them.

_____ _____ 8. I always suggest specific alternatives to individuals whose behavior I'm trying to correct.

_____ _____ 9. I reinforce other people's sense of self-worth and self-esteem in my communication with them.

_____ _____ 10. I convey genuine interest in the other person's point of view, even when I disagree with it.

_____ _____ 11. I don't talk down to those who have less power or less information than I.

_____ _____ 12. Even when I feel strongly about my point of view, I convey to others that I am flexible and open to new information.

_____ _____ 13. I strive to identify some area of agreement in a discussion with someone who has a different point of view.

_____ _____ 14. My feedback is always specific and to the point, rather than general or vague.

_____ _____ 15. I don't dominate conversations with others.

_____ _____ 16. I take ownership of my statements and point of view by using personal words such as, "I think" instead of impersonal words such as "they think."

_____ _____ 17. When discussing someone's problem, I usually respond with a reply that indicates understanding rather than advice.

_____ _____ 18. When asking questions of others in order to understand their viewpoints better, I generally ask "what" questions instead of "why" questions.

_____ _____ 19. I hold regular, private meetings with people with whom I work and with whom I live.

_____ _____ 20. I understand clearly when it is appropriate to offer advice and direction to others and when it is not.

COMMUNICATION STYLES

This assessment instrument is divided into two parts.

In Part 1, four people complain about problems they face in their jobs. Following each complaint are five possible responses. Rank three of the responses you would be most likely to make, with 3 being your first choice, 2 being your second choice, and 1 being your third choice.

Part 2 of the assessment describes a particular situation. Several pairs of statements follow. Place a check mark next to the statement in each pair that you would most likely use in responding to that situation. Don't identify your preference. Rather, mark the alternatives that are most like your current behavior.

To score the Communication Styles instrument, turn to the end of the chapter to find the answer key and an interpretation of your scores.

Part 1

1. I've been in this job now for six months, and I hardly know anyone at all in the organization. I just can't seem to make friends or to be accepted by other people. Most people are extremely busy and don't take time to socialize. I feel isolated and excluded from what's going on.

    _____ a. Don't be concerned about not making friends so soon. Things will get better the longer you're with the organization, you'll see.

    _____ b. When you first meet people, what do you say? Are you the one to be friendly first?

    _____ c. Because organization members are so busy, probably no one has time to get close socially. You shouldn't expect too much.

_____ d. So you're feeling that people haven't accepted you in the organization?

_____ e. When I first joined the organization it took me more than six months to get adjusted. I still don't know some of the people in several departments.

2. I can't stand my boss. He is the most autocratic, demanding person you can imagine. I've never worked around anyone who cared less for his employees than he does. His complete insensitivity and lack of humanity have made this a miserable place to work.

_____ a. You sound as if you're having difficulty dealing with rigid control and authority.

_____ b. I know how you feel because last year we had a woman in our department who would drive anybody crazy. She was the ultimate domineering boss.

_____ c. You're going to have problems unless you work this out. I think you should go to him and tell him how you feel.

_____ d. You really are having a hard time adjusting to your boss, aren't you?

_____ e. Why is it you feel so strongly about him?

3. What I want to know is, what happened on that last promotion decision? I thought I was in line for it. I'm sure no else in the department has my experience, and the scuttlebutt I heard indicated the job was mine for the asking. I'm really disappointed that you brought in someone from the outside over me. I don't think it's fair. What does it take to get promoted around here anyway?

_____ a. What was it that made you think this promotion was yours? Are you aware of the requirements of the job and what kind of person we were looking for?

_____ b. Don't be discouraged. Your work is good, and if you're patient I'm sure other chances will come along. I'll try to help you be ready the next time around.

_____ c. I think you have the wrong impression about this. The criteria were very clear for the new position, and the other person was just a better fit.

_____ d. In other words, you feel kind of puzzled about where you stand with the company.

_____ e. Are you interpreting this promotion decision as a challenge to your technical competence?

4. Hey, what's the idea of not approving my request for a new personal computer? I really need it in the office. We've got far more work to do than one machine can handle, and we're doing things manually that ought to be done on a spreadsheet. And don't give me that old story about tight company resources again. I've been in line for new equipment for a long time now.

_____ a. I understand that you are really upset about not getting your request approved.

_____ b. Why do you need a new computer? Can you borrow one during the times you really feel the crunch?

_____ c. You know, others are facing the same problem. We're having a terrible time trying to get the necessary work accomplished with the existing machines.

_____ d. If you'll be patient, I'm sure I can work out a solution to your problem.

_____ e. We turned you down because resources are really tight. You'll just have to make do.

Part 2

You are the manager of Carole Schulte, a 58-year-old supervisor who has been with the company for 21 years. She will retire at age 62, the first year she's eligible for a full pension. The trouble is, her performance is sliding, she is not inclined to go the extra mile by putting in extra time when required, and occasionally her work is even a little slipshod. Several line workers and customers have complained that she's treated them rather abruptly and without much sensitivity, even though superior customer service is a hallmark of your organization. She doesn't do anything bad enough to be fired, but she's just not performing up to levels you expect. Assume that you are having your monthly one-on-one meeting with her in your office. Which of the statements in each pair would you be most likely to use?

_____ 1. a. I've received complaints from some of your customers that you have not followed company standards in being responsive to their requests.

   b. You don't seem to be motivated to do a good job any more, Carole.

_____ 2. a. I know that you've been doing a great job as supervisor, but there's just one small thing I want to raise with you about a customer complaint, probably not too serious.

   b. I have some concerns about several aspects of your performance on the job, and I'd like to discuss them with you.

_____ 3. a. When one of your subordinates called the other day to complain that you had criticized his work in public, I became concerned. I suggest that you sit down with that subordinate to work through any hard feelings that might still exist.

   b. You know, of course, that you're wrong to have criticized your subordinate's work in public. That's a sure way to create antagonism and lower morale.

_____ 4. a. I would like to see the following changes in your performance: (1), (2), and (3).

   b. I have some ideas for helping you to improve; but first, what do you suggest?

_____ 5. a. I must tell you that I'm disappointed in your performance.

   b. Several of our employees seem to be unhappy with how you've been performing lately.

SKILL *LEARNING*

Building Positive Interpersonal Relationships

A great deal of research supports the idea that **positive interpersonal relationships** are a key to creating positive energy in people's lives (Baker, 2000; Dutton, 2003). When people experience positive interactions—even if they are just temporary encounters—they are elevated, revitalized, and enlivened. Positive relationships create positive energy. All of us have experienced people who give us energy—they are pleasant to be around, they lift us, and they help us flourish. We also have encountered people who have the reverse effect—we feel depleted, less alive, and emotionally exhausted when we interact with them. Such encounters are personally de-energizing.

The effects of positive relationships are much stronger and more long-lasting than just making people feel happy or uplifted, however. When individuals are able to build relationships that are positive and that create energy, important physiological, emotional, intellectual, and social consequences result. For example, people's physical well-being is significantly affected by their interpersonal relationships. Individuals in positive relationships recover from surgery twice as fast as those in conflicting or negative relationships. They have fewer incidences of cancer and fewer heart attacks, and they recover faster if they experience them. They contract fewer minor illnesses such as colds, flu, or headaches; they cope better with stress; and they actually have fewer accidents (i.e., being in the wrong place at the wrong time). As might be expected, they also have a longer life expectancy. These benefits occur because positive relationships actually strengthen the immune system, the cardiovascular system, and the hormonal system (Dutton, 2003; Heaphy & Dutton, 2006; Reis & Gable, 2003).

Positive relationships also help people perform better in tasks and at work, and learn more effectively. That is, positive relationships help people feel safe and secure, so individuals are more able to concentrate on the tasks at hand. They are less distracted by feelings of anxiety, frustration, or uncertainty that accompany almost all relationships that are nonpositive. People are more inclined to seek information and resources from people who are positively energizing, and they are less

likely to obtain what they need to succeed if it means interacting with energy-depleting people. The amount of information exchange, participation, and commitment with other people is significantly higher when relationships are positive, so productivity and success at work are also markedly higher (see Dutton, 2003, for a review of studies).

Positive emotions—such as joy, excitement, and interest—are a product of positive relationships, and these emotions actually expand people's mental capacities. Feelings of joy and excitement, for example, create a desire to act, to learn, and to contribute to others. Moreover, the amount of information people pay attention to, the breadth of data they can process, and the quality of the decisions and judgments they make are all enhanced in conditions in which positive relationships are present. People's intellectual capacities are actually broadened (mental acuity expands), they learn more and more efficiently, and they make fewer mental errors when experiencing positive relationships (Fredrickson, 2001).

Not surprisingly, the performance of organizations is also enhanced by the presence of positive relationships among employees. Positive relationships foster cooperation among people, so the things that get in the way of highly successful performance—such as conflict, disagreements, confusion and ambiguity, unproductive competition, anger, or personal offense—are minimized. Employees are more loyal and committed to their work and to the organization when positive relationships exist, and information exchange, dialogue, and knowledge transfer are significantly enhanced. Creativity and innovation, as well as the ability of the system to adapt to change, are substantially higher when positive relationships characterize the workforce (Gittell, 2003; Gittell, Cameron, & Lim, 2006).

It is hard to find a reason why people would *not* want to build and enhance positive relationships with other human beings. Many advantages and very few liabilities are associated with positive interpersonal relationships. Creating such relationships sounds like a simple prescription, of course, but it is much easier said than done. It is not difficult to build positive relationships with people who are like us, to whom we are attracted, or who behave according to our expectations. But when we encounter people who are abrasive, who are not easy to like, or who make a lot of errors or blunders, building relationships is more difficult. In other words, building positive relationships in negative circumstances or with negative people requires special skill.

Arguably the most important skill in building and strengthening positive relationships is the ability to communicate with people in a way that enhances feelings of trust, openness, and support. In this chapter we focus on helping you develop and improve this skill. Of course, all of us communicate constantly, and we all feel that we do a reasonably good job of it. We haven't gotten this far in life without being able to communicate effectively. On the other hand, in study after study, communication problems are identified as the single biggest impediment to positive relationships and positive performance in organizations (Carrell & Willmington, 1996; Thorton, 1966). We focus in this chapter on this most important skill that effective managers must possess: the ability to communicate supportively.

The Importance of Effective Communication

In an age of electronic communication, the most frequently used means of passing messages to other people is via electronic technology (Gackenbach, 1998). E-mail now dominates communication channels in organizations, and it is purported to enhance information flow, the sharing of knowledge, consistency of communication, quality of feedback, and speed or cycle time (Council of Communication Management, 1996; Synopsis Communication Consulting of London, 1998). However, international surveys indicate that face-to-face communication is still the second most frequent form of communication, but it remains the most problematic (Rosen, 1998). One report concluded: "Technology is ahead of people's ability to cope and use it; it's becoming part of the problem, not part of the solution" (Synopsis Communication Consulting of London, 1998).

The problems with electronic communication are that: (1) people are bombarded with an overabundance of information, often poorly presented, so they are less willing to consume all the messages aimed at them; (2) no one puts all these rapid-fire messages in context, so much of the information lacks significance or meaning; and (3) effective interpretation and use of the information still depends on the relationship the recipient has with the sender. Accurate interpretation and effective message delivery depends on relationships of trust and shared context. Technology doesn't make messages more useful unless good interpersonal relationships are in place first. Simply put, relationships determine meaning.

Of course, some relationships can be created electronically, but meaningful relationships based on trust are the exceptions rather than the rule. In a study of problems in marital relationships, for example, 87 percent said that communication problems were the root, double that of any other kind of problem (Beebe, Beebe, & Redmond, 1996). For the most part, the conclusion of an international study of communications in the workplace summarizes the key to effective communication: "To make the most of electronic communication requires learning to communicate better face to face" (Rosen, 1998).

Surveys have consistently shown that the ability to effectively communicate face to face is the characteristic judged by managers to be most critical in determining promotability (see surveys reported by Bowman, 1964; Brownell, 1986, 1990; Hargie, 1997; Randle, 1956; Steil, Barker, & Watson, 1983). Frequently, the quality of communication between managers and their employees is fairly low (Schnake, Dumler, Cochran, & Barnett, 1990). This ability may involve a broad array of activities, from writing to speech-making to body language. Whereas skill in each of these activities is important, for most managers it is face-to-face, one-on-one communication that dominates all the other types in predicting managerial success. In a study of 88 organizations, both profit and nonprofit, Crocker (1978) found that, of 31 skills assessed, interpersonal communication skills, including listening, were rated as the most important. Spitzberg (1994) conducted a comprehensive review of the interpersonal competence literature and found convincing and unequivocal evidence that incompetence in interpersonal communication is "very damaging personally, relationally, and socially." Thorton (1966, p. 237) summarized a variety of survey results by stating, "A manager's number-one problem can be summed up in one word: communication."

At least 80 percent of a manager's waking hours are spent in verbal communication, so it is not surprising that serious attention has been given to a plethora of procedures to improve interpersonal communication. Scholars and researchers have written extensively on communicology, semantics, rhetoric, linguistics, cybernetics, syntactics, pragmatics, proxemics, and canalization; and library shelves are filled with books on the physics of the communication process—encoding, decoding, transmission, media, perception, reception, and noise. Similarly, volumes are available on effective public-speaking techniques, making formal presentations, and the processes of organizational communication. Most colleges and universities have academic departments dedicated to the field of speech communication; most business schools provide a business communication curriculum; and many organizations have public communication departments and intraorganizational communication specialists such as newsletter editors and speech writers.

Even with all this available information about the communication process and the dedicated resources in many organizations for fostering better communication, most managers still indicate that poor communication is their biggest problem (Schnake et al., 1990). In a study of major manufacturing organizations undergoing large-scale changes, Cameron (1994) asked two key questions: (1) What is your major problem in trying to get organizational changes implemented? and (2) What is the key factor that explains your past success in effectively managing organizational change? To both questions, a large majority of managers gave the same answer: communication. All of them agreed that more communication is better than less communication. Most thought that over-communicating with employees was more a virtue than a vice. It would seem surprising, then, that in light of this agreement by managers about the importance of communication, communication remains a major problem for managers. Why might this be?

One reason is that most individuals feel that they are very effective communicators. They feel that communication problems are a product of others' weaknesses, not their own (Brownell, 1990; Carrell & Willmington, 1996; Golen, 1990). Haney (1992) reported on a survey of over 8,000 people in universities, businesses, military units, government agencies, and hospitals in which "virtually everyone felt that he or she was communicating at least as well as and, in many cases, better than almost everyone else in the organization. Most people readily admit that their organization is fraught with faulty communication, but it is almost always 'those other people' who are responsible" (p. 219). Thus, while most agree that proficiency in interpersonal communication is critical to managerial success, most individuals don't seem to feel a strong need to improve their own skill level (Spitzberg, 1994).

THE FOCUS ON ACCURACY

Much of the writing on interpersonal communication focuses on the *accuracy* of the information being communicated. The emphasis is generally on making certain that messages are transmitted and received with little alteration or variation from original intent. The communication skill of most concern is the ability to transmit clear, precise messages. The following incidents illustrate problems that result from inaccurate communication:

A motorist was driving on the Merritt Parkway outside New York City when his engine stalled. He quickly determined that his battery was dead and managed to stop another driver who consented to push his car to get it started.

"My car has an automatic transmission," he explained, "so you'll have to get up to 30 or 35 miles an hour to get me started."

The second motorist nodded and walked back to his own car. The first motorist climbed back into his car and waited for the good Samaritan to pull up behind him. He waited— and waited. Finally, he turned around to see what was wrong.

There was the good Samaritan—coming up behind his car at about 35 miles an hour!

The damage amounted to $3,800. (Haney, 1992, p. 285)

A woman of 35 came in one day to tell me that she wanted a baby but had been told that she had a certain type of heart disease that, while it might not interfere with a normal life, would be dangerous if she ever had a baby. From her description, I thought at once of mitral stenosis. This condition is characterized by a rather distinctive rumbling murmur near the apex of the heart and especially by a peculiar vibration felt by the examining finger on the patient's chest. The vibration is known as the "thrill" of mitral stenosis.

When this woman had undressed and was lying on my table in her white kimono, my stethoscope quickly found the heart sounds I had expected. Dictating to my nurse, I described them carefully. I put my stethoscope aside and felt intently for the typical vibration which may be found in a small and variable area of the left chest.

I closed my eyes for better concentration and felt long and carefully for the tremor. I did not find it, and with my hand still on the woman's bare breast, lifting it upward and out of the way, I finally turned to the nurse and said: "No thrill."

The patient's black eyes snapped, and with venom in her voice, she said, "Well, isn't that just too bad! Perhaps it's just as well you don't get one. That isn't what I came for."

My nurse almost choked, and my explanation still seems a nightmare of futile words. (Loomis, 1939, p. 47)

In a Detroit suburb, a man walked onto a private plane and greeted the co-pilot with, "Hi, Jack!" The salutation, picked up by a microphone in the cockpit and interpreted as "hijack" by control tower personnel, caused police, the county sheriff's SWAT team, and the FBI all to arrive on the scene with sirens blaring. (Time, 2000, p. 31)

In the English language, in particular, we face the danger of miscommunicating with one another merely because of the nature of our language. For example, Table 4.1 lists 22 examples of the same word whose meaning and pronunciation are completely different, depending on the circumstances. No wonder individuals from other cultures and languages have trouble communicating accurately in the United States.

This doesn't account, of course, for the large number of variations in English-language meaning throughout the world. For example, because in England a billion is a million million, whereas in the United States and Canada a billion is a thousand million, it is easy to see how misunderstanding can occur regarding financial performance. Similarly, in an American meeting, if you "table" a subject, you postpone its discussion. In a British meeting, to "table" a topic means to discuss it now.

A Confucian proverb states: "Those who speak do not know. Those who know do not speak." It is not difficult to understand why Americans are often viewed as brash and unsophisticated in Asian cultures. A common problem for American business executives has been to announce, upon their return home, that a business deal has been struck, only to discover that no agreement was made at all. Usually it is because Americans assume that when their Japanese colleagues say "hai," the Japanese word for "yes," it means agreement. To the Japanese, it often means "Yes, I am trying to understand you (but I may not necessarily agree with you)."

When accuracy is the primary consideration, attempts to improve communication generally center on improving the mechanics: transmitters and receivers, encoding and decoding, sources and destinations, and noise. Improvements in voice recognition software have made accuracy a key factor in electronic communication. One cardiologist friend, who always records his diagnoses via voice recognition software, completed a

procedure to clear a patient's artery by installing a shunt (a small tube in the artery). He then reported in the patient's record: "The patient was shunted and is recovering nicely." The next time he checked the record, the software had recorded: "The patient was shot dead and is recovering nicely."

Fortunately, much progress has been made recently in improving the transmission of accurate messages—that is, in improving their clarity and precision. Primarily through the development of a sophisticated information-based technology, major strides have been taken to enhance communication speed and accuracy in organizations. Computer networks with multimedia

Table 4.1	Inconsistent Pronunciations in the English Language

- We polish Polish furniture.
- He could lead if he would get the lead out.
- A farm can produce produce.
- The dump was so full it had to refuse refuse.
- The Iraqi soldiers decided to desert in the desert.
- The present is a good time to present the present.
- In the college band, a bass was painted on the head of a bass drum.
- The dove dove into the bushes.
- I did not object to that object.
- The insurance for the invalid was invalid.
- The bandage was wound around the wound.
- There was a row among the oarsmen about how to row.
- They were too close to the door to close it.
- The buck does funny things when the does are present.
- They sent a sewer down to stitch the tear in the sewer line.
- She shed a tear because of the tear in her skirt.
- To help with planting, the farmer taught his sow to sow.
- The wind was to strong to be able to wind the sail.
- After a number of Novocaine injections, my jaw got number.
- I had to subject the subject to a series of tests.
- How can I intimate this to my most intimate friend?
- I spent last evening evening out a pile of dirt.

capabilities now enable members of an organization to transmit messages, documents, video images, and sound almost anywhere in the world. The technology that enables modern companies to share, store, and retrieve information has dramatically changed the nature of business in just a decade. Customers and employees routinely expect information technology to function smoothly and the information it manages to be reliable. Sound decisions and competitive advantage depend on such accuracy.

However, comparable progress has not occurred in the interpersonal aspects of communication. People still become offended at one another, make insulting statements, and communicate clumsily. The interpersonal aspects of communication involve the nature of the relationship between the communicators. Who says what to whom, what is said, why it is said, and how it is said all have an effect on the relationships between people. This has important implications for the effectiveness of the communication, aside from the accuracy of the statement.

Similarly, irrespective of the availability of sophisticated information technologies and elaborately developed models of communication processes, individuals still frequently communicate in abrasive, insensitive, and unproductive ways. Rather than building and enhancing positive relationships, they damage relationships. More often than not, it is the interpersonal aspect of communication that stands in the way of effective message delivery rather than the inability to deliver accurate information (Golen, 1990).

Ineffective communication may lead individuals to dislike each other, be offended by each other, lose confidence in each other, refuse to listen to each other, and disagree with each other, as well as cause a host of other interpersonal problems. These interpersonal problems, in turn, generally lead to restricted communication flow, inaccurate messages, and misinterpretations of meanings. Figure 4.1 summarizes this process.

To illustrate, consider the following situation. Latisha is introducing a new goal-setting program to the organization as a way to overcome some productivity problems. After Latisha's carefully prepared presentation in the management council meeting, Jose raises his hand. "In my opinion, this is a naive approach to solving our productivity issues. The considerations are much more complex than Latisha seems to realize. I don't think we should waste our time by pursuing this plan any further." Jose's opinion may be justified, but the manner in which he delivers the message will probably eliminate any hope of its being dealt with objectively. Instead, Latisha will probably hear a message such as, "You're naive," "You're stupid," or "You're incompetent." Therefore, we wouldn't be surprised if Latisha's response was defensive or even hostile. Any good feelings between the two have probably been jeopardized, and their communication will probably be reduced to self-image protection. The merits of the proposal will be smothered by personal defensiveness. Future communication between the two will probably be minimal and superficial.

What Is Supportive Communication?

In this chapter, we focus on a kind of interpersonal communication that helps you communicate accurately and honestly, especially in difficult circumstances, without jeopardizing interpersonal relationships. It is not hard to communicate supportively—to express confidence, trust, and openness—when things are going well and when people are doing what you like. But when you have to correct someone else's behavior, when you have to deliver negative feedback, or when you have to point out shortcomings of another person, communicating in a way that builds and strengthens the relationship is more difficult. This type of communication is called **supportive communication**. Supportive communication seeks to preserve or enhance a positive relationship

Figure 4.1   Relationships Between Unskillful Communication and Interpersonal Relationships

between you and another person while still addressing a problem, giving negative feedback, or tackling a difficult issue. It allows you to communicate information to others that is not complimentary, or to resolve an uncomfortable issue with another person but, in the process, strengthen your relationship.

Supportive communication has eight attributes, which are summarized in Table 4.2. Later in the chapter we expand on each attribute. When supportive communication is used, not only is a message delivered accurately, but the relationship between the two communicating parties is supported, even enhanced, by the interchange. Positive interpersonal relationships result. People feel energized and uplifted, even when the information being communicated is negative.

The goal of supportive communication is not merely to be liked by other people or to be judged to be a nice person. Nor is it used merely to produce social

Table 4.2	The Eight Attributes of Supportive Communication		
• Congruent, Not Incongruent			
A focus on honest messages where verbal statements match thoughts and feelings.			
Example: "Your behavior really upset me."		*Not*	"Do I seem upset? No, everything's fine."
• Descriptive, Not Evaluative			
A focus on describing an objective occurrence, describing your reaction to it, and offering a suggested alternative.			
Example: "Here is what happened; here is my reaction; here is a suggestion that would be more acceptable."		*Not*	"You are wrong for doing what you did."
• Problem-Oriented, Not Person-Oriented			
A focus on problems and issues that can be changed rather than people and their characteristics.			
Example: "How can we solve this problem?"		*Not*	"Because of you a problem exists."
• Validating, Not Invalidating			
A focus on statements that communicate respect, flexibility, collaboration, and areas of agreement.			
Example: "I have some ideas, but do you have any suggestions?"		*Not*	"You wouldn't understand, so we'll do it my way."
• Specific, Not Global			
A focus on specific events or behaviors and avoid general, extreme, or either-or statements.			
Example: "You interrupted me three times during the meeting."		*Not*	"You're always trying to get attention."
• Conjunctive, Not Disjunctive			
A focus on statements that flow from what has been said previously and facilitate interaction.			
Example: "Relating to what you just said, I'd like to raise another point."		*Not*	"I want to say something (regardless of what you just said)."
• Owned, Not Disowned			
A focus on taking responsibility for your own statements by using personal ("I") words.			
Example: "I have decided to turn down your request because . . . "		*Not*	"You have a pretty good idea, but it wouldn't get approved."
• Supportive Listening, Not One-Way Listening			
A focus on using a variety of appropriate responses, with a bias toward reflective responses.			
Example: "What do you think are the obstacles standing in the way of improvement?		*Not*	"As I said before, you make too many mistakes. You're just not performing."

acceptance. As pointed out above, positive interpersonal relationships have practical, instrumental value in organizations. Researchers have found, for example, that organizations fostering supportive interpersonal relationships enjoy higher productivity, faster problem solving, higher-quality outputs, and fewer conflicts and subversive activities than do groups and organizations in which relationships are less positive. Moreover, delivering outstanding customer service is almost impossible without supportive communication. Customer complaints and misunderstandings frequently require supportive communication skills to resolve. Not only must managers be competent in using this kind of communication, therefore, but they must help their subordinates develop this competency as well.

One important lesson that American managers have been taught by foreign competitors is that good relationships among employees, and between managers and employees, produce bottom-line advantages (Ouchi, 1981; Peters, 1988; Pfeffer, 1998). Hanson (1986) found, for example, that the presence of good interpersonal relationships between managers and subordinates was three times more powerful in predicting profitability in 40 major corporations over a five-year period than the four next most powerful variables— market share, capital intensity, firm size, and sales growth rate—combined. Supportive communication, therefore, isn't just a "nice-person technique," but a proven competitive advantage for both managers and organizations.

Coaching and Counseling

One of the ways to illustrate the principles of supportive communication is to discuss two common roles performed by managers (and parents, friends, and coworkers): coaching and counseling others. In coaching, managers pass along advice and information, or they set standards to help others improve their work skills. In counseling, managers help others recognize and address problems involving their level of understanding, emotions, or personalities. Thus, coaching focuses on abilities, counseling on attitudes.

The skills of coaching and counseling also apply to a broad array of activities, of course, such as motivating others, handling customer complaints, passing critical or negative information upward, handling conflicts between other parties, negotiating for a certain position, and so on. Because most managers—and most people—are involved in coaching and counseling at some time, however, we will use them to illustrate and explain the behavioral principles involved.

Skillful coaching and counseling are especially important in (1) rewarding positive performance and (2) correcting problem behaviors or attitudes. Both of these activities are discussed in more detail in the chapter on Motivating Others. In that chapter, we discuss the *content* of rewarding and correcting behavior (i.e., *what* to do), whereas in our present discussion we focus on the *processes* of rewarding and correcting behavior (i.e., *how* to do it).

Coaching and counseling are more difficult to perform effectively when individuals are not performing up to expectations, when their attitudes are negative, when their behavior is disruptive, or when their personalities clash with others in the organization. Whenever managers have to help people change their attitudes or behaviors, coaching or counseling is required. In these situations, managers face the responsibility of providing negative feedback to others or getting them to recognize problems that they don't want to acknowledge. Managers must reprimand or correct employees, but in a way that facilitates positive work outcomes, positive feelings, and positive relationships.

What makes coaching and counseling so challenging is the risk of offending or alienating other people. That risk is so high that many managers ignore completely the feelings and reactions of others by taking a directive, hard-nosed, "shape up or ship out" approach. Alternatively, they soft-pedal, avoid confrontations, or drop hints for fear of hurting feelings and destroying relationships—the "don't worry be happy" approach. The principles we describe in this chapter not only facilitate accurate message delivery in sensitive situations, but their effective use can produce higher levels of motivation, increased productivity, and better interpersonal relationships.

Of course, coaching and counseling skills are also required when negative feedback is not involved, such as when other people ask for advice, need someone to listen to their problems, or want to register complaints. Sometimes just listening is the most effective form of coaching or counseling. Although the risk of damaged relationships, defensiveness, or hurt feelings is not as likely as when negative feedback is given, these situations still require competent supportive communication skills. Guidelines for how to implement supportive communication effectively in both negative and positive coaching and counseling situations are discussed in the rest of this chapter.

To illustrate, consider the following two scenarios:

Jagdip Ahwal is the manager of the division sales force in your firm, which makes and sells components for the aerospace industry. He reports directly to you. Jagdip's division consistently misses its sales projections, its revenues per salesperson are below the firm average, and Jagdip's monthly reports are almost always late. You make another appointment to visit with Jagdip after getting the latest sales figures, but he isn't in his office when you arrive. His secretary tells you that one of Jagdip's sales managers dropped by a few minutes ago to complain that some employees are coming in late for work in the morning and taking extra-long coffee breaks. Jagdip had immediately gone with the manager to his sales department to give the salespeople a "pep talk" and to remind them of performance expectations. You wait for 15 minutes until he returns.

Betsy Christensen has an MBA from a prestigious Big Ten school and has recently joined your firm in the financial planning group. She came with great recommendations and credentials. However, she seems to be trying to enhance her own reputation at the expense of others in her group. You have heard increasing complaints lately that Betsy acts arrogantly, is self-promotional, and is openly critical of other group members' work. In your first conversation with her about her performance in the group, she denied that there is a problem. She said that, if anything, she was having a positive impact on the group by raising its standards. You schedule another meeting with Betsy after this latest set of complaints from her coworkers.

What are the basic problems in these two cases? Which one is primarily a coaching problem and which is primarily a counseling problem? How would you approach them so that the problems got solved and, at the same time, your relationships with Jagdip and Betsy are strengthened? What would you say, and how would you say it, so that the best possible outcomes result? This chapter can help you improve your skill in handling such situations effectively.

COACHING AND COUNSELING PROBLEMS

The two cases above help identify the two basic kinds of interpersonal communication problems faced by managers. Although no situation is completely one

thing versus the other, in the case with Jagdip Ahwal, the basic need is primarily for **coaching**. Coaching situations are those in which managers must pass along advice and information or set standards for others. People must be advised on how to do their jobs better and to be coached to better performance. Coaching problems are usually caused by lack of ability, insufficient information or understanding, or incompetence on the part of individuals. In these cases, the accuracy of the information passed along by managers is important. The other person must understand clearly what the problem is and how to overcome it.

In the Jagdip Ahwal case, Jagdip was accepting upward delegation from his subordinates, and he was not allowing them to solve their own problems. In the chapter on Managing Personal Stress, we learned that upward delegation is one of the major causes of ineffective time management. By not insisting that his subordinates bring recommendations for solutions to him instead of problems, and by intervening directly in the problems of his subordinate's subordinates, Jagdip became overloaded himself. He didn't allow his subordinates to do their jobs. Productivity almost always suffers in cases in which one person is trying to resolve all the problems and run the whole show. Jagdip needs to be coached regarding how to avoid upward delegation and how to delegate responsibility as well as authority effectively. The chapter on Motivating Employees gives some guidelines for diagnosing the reasons for poor performance, and these guidelines could help guide the coaching suggestions.

The Betsy Christensen case illustrates primarily a **counseling** problem. Managers need to counsel others instead of coach them when the problem stems from attitudes, personality clashes, defensiveness, or other factors tied to emotions. Betsy's competency or skill is not a problem, but her unwillingness to recognize that a problem exists or that a change is needed on her part requires counseling by the manager. Betsy is highly qualified for her position, so coaching or giving advice would not be a useful approach. Instead, an important goal of counseling is to help Betsy recognize that a problem exists, that her attitude is of critical importance, and to identify ways in which that problem might be addressed.

Coaching applies to ability problems, and the manager's approach is, "I can help you do this better." Counseling applies to attitude problems, and the manager's approach is, "I can help you recognize that a problem exists."

Although many problems involve both coaching and counseling, it is important to recognize the difference between these two types of problems because a mismatch of problem with communication approach can aggravate, rather than resolve, a problem. Giving direction or advice (coaching) in a counseling situation often increases defensiveness or resistance to change. For example, advising Betsy Christensen about how to do her job or about the things she should not be doing (such as criticizing others' work) will probably only magnify her defensiveness because she doesn't perceive that she has a problem. Similarly, counseling in a situation that calls for coaching simply side-steps the problem and doesn't resolve it. Jagdip Ahwal knows that a problem exists, for example, but he doesn't know how to resolve it. Coaching, not problem recognition, is needed.

The question that remains, however, is, "How do I effectively coach or counsel another person? What behavioral guidelines help me perform effectively in these situations?" Both coaching and counseling rely on the same set of key supportive communication principles summarized in Table 4.1, which we'll now examine more closely.

DEFENSIVENESS AND DISCONFIRMATION

If principles of supportive communication are not followed when coaching or counseling subordinates, two major obstacles result that lead to a variety of negative outcomes (Brownell, 1986; Cupach & Spitzberg, 1994; Gibb, 1961; Sieburg, 1978; Steil et al., 1983). These two obstacles are defensiveness and disconfirmation (see Table 4.3).

Defensiveness is an emotional and physical state in which one is agitated, estranged, confused, and inclined to strike out (Gordon, 1988). Defensiveness arises when one of the parties feels threatened or punished by the communication. For that person, self-protection becomes more important than listening, so defensiveness blocks both the message and the interpersonal relationship. Clearly a manager's coaching or counseling will not be effective if it creates defensiveness in the other party. But defensive thinking may be pervasive and entrenched within an organization. Overcoming it calls for awareness by managers of their own defensiveness and vigorous efforts to apply the principles of supportive communication described in this chapter (Argyris, 1991).

The second obstacle, **disconfirmation**, occurs when one of the communicating parties feels put down, ineffectual, or insignificant because of the communication. Recipients of the communication feel that their self-worth is being questioned, so they focus more on building themselves up rather than listening. Reactions are often self-aggrandizing or show-off behaviors, loss of motivation, withdrawal, and loss of respect for the offending communicator.

The eight attributes of supportive communication, which we'll explain and illustrate in the following pages, serve as behavioral guidelines for overcoming defensiveness and disconfirmation. Competent coaching and counseling depend on knowing and practicing these guidelines. They also depend on maintaining a balance among the guidelines, as we will illustrate.

Table 4.3	Two Major Obstacles to Effective Interpersonal Communication

Supportive communication engenders feelings of support, understanding, and helpfulness. It helps overcome the two main obstacles resulting from poor interpersonal communication:

Defensiveness

• One individual feels threatened or attacked as a result of the communication.

• Self-protection becomes paramount.

• Energy is spent on constructing a defense rather than on listening.

• Aggression, anger, competitiveness, and avoidance are common reactions.

Disconfirmation

• One individual feels incompetent, unworthy, or insignificant as a result of the communication.

• Attempts to reestablish self-worth take precedence.

• Energy is spent trying to portray self-importance rather than on listening.

• Showing off, self-centered behavior, withdrawal, and loss of motivation are common reactions.

1. SUPPORTIVE COMMUNICATION IS BASED ON CONGRUENCE, NOT INCONGRUENCE

Most researchers and observers agree that the best interpersonal communications, and the best relationships, are based on **congruence**. That is, what is communicated, verbally and nonverbally, matches exactly what the individual is thinking and feeling (Dyer, 1972; Hyman, 1989; Knapp & Vangelisti, 1996; Rogers, 1961; Schnake et al.,1990). Congruence simply means being honest. It means communicating what you intend.

Two kinds of **incongruence** are possible: One is a mismatch between what one is experiencing and what one is aware of. For example, an individual may not even be aware that he or she is experiencing anger or hostility toward another person, even though the anger or hostility is really present. In severe cases, therapists must help individuals reach greater congruence between experience and awareness. A second kind of incongruence, and the one more closely related to supportive communication, is a mismatch between what one thinks or feels and what one communicates. For example, an individual may be aware of a feeling of anger but deny saying that the feeling exists.

When building interpersonal relationships, and when coaching and counseling others, genuine, honest statements are always better than artificial or dishonest statements. Managers who hold back their true feelings or opinions, or who don't express what's really on their minds, create the impression that a hidden agenda exists. Other people sense that there is something else not being said, or that an opinion or thought is not being expressed. Therefore, they trust the communicator less and focus on trying to figure out what the hidden message is, not on listening or trying to improve. The relationship between the two communicators stays superficial and distrusting.

The chapter on Managing Personal Stress discussed Covey's (1989) "emotional bank account" in which individuals make deposits in an account that builds the relationship with another person. These deposits help establish mutual trust and respect in the relationship. Similarly, communication cannot be genuinely supportive unless it is based on trust and respect and is also *perceived* as trusting and respectful. Otherwise, false impressions and miscommunication result. Congruence

is a prerequisite of trust. Genuineness and authenticity lie at the heart of positive relationships.

Rogers (1961) suggested that congruence in communication lies at the heart of "a general law of interpersonal relationships." After 40 years of clinical treatment of psychological problems in patients, Rogers concluded that this one law was the fundamental key to positive interpersonal relationships.

The greater the congruence of experience, awareness, and communication on the part of one individual, the more the ensuing relationship will involve a tendency toward reciprocal communication with increasing congruence; a tendency toward more mutually accurate understanding of the communications; improved psychological adjustment and functioning in both parties; mutual satisfaction in the relationship.

Conversely, the greater the communicated incongruence of experience and awareness, the more the ensuing relationship will involve further communication with the same quality; disintegration of accurate understanding; less adequate psychological adjustment and functioning in both parties; mutual dissatisfaction in the relationship. (pp. 344–345)

Congruence also relates to matching the content of the words spoken to the communicator's manner and tone of voice. "What a nice day" can mean the opposite if muttered sarcastically. "I'm just here to help" can mean the opposite if said without sincerity, especially if the history of the relationship suggests otherwise.

Striving for congruence, being honest and open, or demonstrating authenticity does not mean, of course, that we should blow off steam immediately upon getting upset, nor does it mean that we cannot repress certain inappropriate feelings (e.g., keeping anger, disappointment, or aggression under wraps). Other principles of supportive communication must also be practiced, and achieving congruence at the expense of all other consideration is not productive. On the other hand, in problematic interactions, when reactive feedback must be given, or when correcting someone else's behavior, individuals are more likely to express too little congruence than too much. This is because many people are afraid to respond in a completely honest way or are not sure how to communicate congruently without being offensive. It is often a matter of not knowing *how* to be congruent. Saying exactly what we feel, of course, can sometimes offend the other person.

Consider the problem of a person who is not performing up to expectations and displays a nonchalant attitude even after having been given hints that the organization's rating is being negatively affected. What could you say that would strengthen the relationship with this person and still resolve the problem? How could you express honest feelings and opinions and still remain nonjudgmental? How can you ever be completely honest without offending another person? This is even more difficult when you consider how to respond supportively to someone who constantly has bad breath or displays poor manners while eating. The more personal the feedback, the more difficult it is to be completely congruent. This is where skillful communication is important. Other principles of supportive communication provide some guidelines.

2. SUPPORTIVE COMMUNICATION IS DESCRIPTIVE, NOT EVALUATIVE

It is difficult to be congruent in isolation—that is, without using other rules of thumb for supportive communication. If your friend asks you, "How did I do?" and he or she didn't do so well, it is difficult to know how to respond honestly without being offensive. **Evaluative communication** makes a judgment or places a label on other individuals or on their behavior: "You are doing it wrong," or "You are incompetent." Such evaluation generally makes other people feel under attack and, consequently, respond defensively. They see the communicator as judgmental. Examples of probable responses are, "I am *not* doing it wrong," or "I am more capable than *you* are." Arguments, bad feelings, and a deterioration in the interpersonal relationship result—"No, I'm not." "Yes, you are." "No, I'm not." "Yes, you are." And so on.

The tendency to evaluate others is strongest when the issue is emotionally charged or when a person feels personally attacked. For example, it is more threatening to provide negative messages when others may be emotionally wounded. Sometimes people try to resolve their own bad feelings or anxieties by placing a label on others: "You are dumb" implies "Therefore, I am smart," and it makes me feel better. They may have such strong feelings that they want to punish the other person for violating their expectations or standards: "What you have done deserves to be punished. You have it coming." Most often, evaluations occur merely because people don't have any other alternatives in mind. They don't know how to be congruent without being judgmental or evaluating the other person.

The problem with evaluative communication is that it is likely to be self-perpetuating. Placing a label on someone else generally leads that person to place a label on you, which makes you defensive in return. When you are defensive and the other person is defensive, it's not hard to see why effective communication does not occur. Both the accuracy of the communication and quality of the relationship weaken. Arguments ensue.

An alternative to evaluation is **descriptive communication**. It is difficult to avoid evaluating other people without having an alternative strategy, so descriptive communication is designed to reduce the tendency to evaluate and to perpetuate a defensive interaction. It allows a person to be congruent and authentic as well as being helpful. Descriptive communication involves three steps, summarized in Table 4.4.

First, *describe objectively your observation of the event that occurred or the behavior that you think needs to be modified*. As objectively and dispassionately as possible, talk about *what* happened instead of about the person involved. This description should identify elements of the behavior that can be confirmed by someone else. Behavior should be compared to accepted standards rather than to personal opinions or preferences. Subjective impressions or attributions to the motives of another person should be avoided. The description "You have finished fewer projects this month than anyone else in the division" can be confirmed by an objective record. It relates strictly to the behavior and to an objective standard, not to the motives or personal characteristics of the subordinate. There is less likelihood of the other person feeling unfairly treated, since no evaluative label is placed on the behavior or the person. Describing a behavior, as opposed to evaluating a behavior, is relatively neutral, as long as the manager's manner is congruent with the message.

Second, *describe your (or others') reactions to the behavior or describe the consequences of the behavior*. Rather than projecting onto another person the cause of the problem, focus on the reactions or consequences the behavior has produced. This requires that communicators are aware of their own reactions and are able to describe them. Using one-word descriptions for feelings is often the best method: "I'm concerned about our productivity." "Your level of accomplishment frustrates me." Similarly, the consequences of the behavior can be pointed out: "Profits are off this month," "Department quality ratings are down," or "Two customers have called in to express dissatisfaction." Describing feelings or consequences also lessens the likelihood of defensiveness since the problem is

Table 4.4	Descriptive Communication

Step 1: Describe objectively the event, behavior, or circumstance.

- Avoid accusations.
- Present data or evidence.

Example: Three clients have complained to me this month that you have not responded to their requests.

Step 2: Focus on the behavior and your reaction, not on the other person's attributes.

- Describe your reactions and feelings.
- Describe the objective consequences that have resulted or will result.

Example: I'm worried because each client has threatened to go elsewhere if we aren't more responsive.

Step 3: Focus on solutions.

- Avoid discussing who's right or wrong.
- Suggest an acceptable alternative.
- Be open to other alternatives.

Example: We need both to win back their confidence and to show them you are responsive. I suggest you offer to do a free analysis of their systems.

framed in the context of the communicator's feelings or objective consequences, not the attributes of the subordinate. If those feelings or consequences are described in a nonaccusing way, the major energies of the communicators can be focused on problem solving rather than on defending against evaluations. That is, if *I* am concerned, *you* have less of a reason to feel defensive.

Third, *suggest a more acceptable alternative.* This focuses the discussion on the suggested alternative, not on the person. It also helps the other person save face and avoid feeling personally criticized because the individual is separated from the behavior. Self-esteem is preserved because it is the behavior—something controllable—not the person, that should be modified. Of course, care should be taken not to give the message, "I don't like the way things are, so what are *you* going to do about it?" The change need not be the responsibility of only one of the communicating parties. Instead, the emphasis should be on finding a solution that is acceptable to both people, not on deciding who is right and who is wrong or who should change and who shouldn't. For example, "I suggest that you identify what it would take to complete six more projects than you did last month," or "I would like to help you identify the things that are standing in the way of higher performance."

One concern that is sometimes expressed regarding descriptive communication is that these steps may not work unless the other person knows the rules, too. We have heard people say that if both people know about supportive communication, it works; otherwise the person who doesn't want to be supportive can subvert any positive result. For example, the other person might say, "I don't care how you feel," or "I have an excuse for what happened, so it's not my fault," or "It's too bad if this annoys you. I'm not going to change." How might you respond to these responses? Do you abandon principles of descriptive communication and become evaluative and defensive in return? Do you engage in the "Yes, you are"; "No, I'm not"; "Yes, you are"; "No, I'm not" kind of argument?

There is an alternative. This display of lack of concern, or a defensive reaction, now becomes the priority problem. The problem of low performance will be very difficult to address as long as the more important interpersonal problem between these two people is blocking progress. In effect, the focus must shift from coaching to counseling, from focusing on ability to focusing on attitude. If two people cannot work on the problem together, no amount of communication about the consequences of poor performance will be productive. Instead, the focus of the communication should be shifted to the lack of concern in the relationship, or the obstacles that inhibit working together to improve performance. Staying focused on the problem, remaining congruent, and using descriptive language become critical.

Effective supportive communicators do not abandon the three steps. They simply switch the focus. They might respond, "I'm surprised to hear you say that you don't care how I feel about this problem (step 1). Your response concerns me, and I think it might have important implications for the productivity of our team (step 2). I suggest we spend some time trying to identify the obstacles you feel might be inhibiting our ability to work together on this problem (step 3)."

It has been our experience that few individuals are completely recalcitrant about wanting to improve, and few are completely unwilling to work on problem solving when they believe that the communicator has their interests at heart. A common criticism of American managers, however, is that compared to their Asian counterparts, many do not believe in these assumptions. They do not accept the fact that employees are "doing the best that they can," that "people want to get along with one another," and that "people are motivated by opportunities for improvement." In Trompenaars' (1996, 1998) terms, national cultures differ in the extent to which they focus on individual achievement ("I'll do what's best for me") versus the collective good ("I'm concerned about what is best for the group"). These are also similar to McGregor's (1960) Theory Y assumptions (e.g., individuals can be trusted to do what is right) as opposed to Theory X assumptions (e.g., individuals should be mistrusted since it takes threats of punishment to motivate change). In our experience, regardless of the national culture, most people want to perform successfully, to be a part of a productive and satisfying team, and to be contributors. When managers use supportive communication principles, not as manipulative devices but as genuine techniques to foster development and improvement, we have seldom found that people will not accept these genuine, authentic, congruent expressions. This applies to cultures all over the globe.

It is important to keep in mind, however, that the steps of descriptive communication do not imply that one person should do all the changing. Frequently a middle ground must be reached on which both individuals are satisfied (e.g., one person becomes more tolerant of deliberate work, and the other person becomes more conscious of trying to work faster). It is important to follow up these kinds of interaction sessions with discussions to monitor and clarify what was heard, what the reactions were, and whether progress is being made. A person's performance problems, for example, may stem from poor work habits developed over time. Such habits are not likely to change abruptly even if a coaching sessions goes especially well. Moreover, it is important to ensure that misinterpretation of the message or its intent did not occur after the fact.

Reinforcing a sense of caring and genuine concern is an important follow-up step.

When it is necessary to make evaluative statements, the evaluations should be made in terms of some established criteria (e.g., "Your behavior does not meet the prescribed standard"), some probable outcomes (e.g., "Continuation of your behavior will lead to worse consequences"), or some past successes by the same individual (e.g., "This behavior is not as good as your past behavior"). The important point is to avoid disconfirming the other person or arousing defensiveness.

3. SUPPORTIVE COMMUNICATION IS PROBLEM-ORIENTED, NOT PERSON-ORIENTED

Problem-oriented communication focuses on problems and solutions rather than on personal traits. Person-oriented communication focuses on the characteristics of the individual, not the event. "This is the problem" rather than "You are the problem" illustrates the difference between problem and person orientation. Problem-oriented communication is useful even when personal appraisals are called for because it focuses on behaviors and events. Person-oriented communication, on the other hand, often focuses on things that cannot be changed or controlled, and it can send the message that the individual is inadequate.

Statements such as "You are dictatorial" and "You are insensitive" describe the person, while "I am being left out of decision making" and "We don't seem to see things the same way" describe problems. Imputing motives is person-oriented ("It's because you want to control other people"), whereas describing overt behaviors is problem-oriented ("You made several sarcastic comments in the meeting today").

One problem with person-oriented communication is that, while most people can change their behavior, few can change their basic personalities. Because nothing can generally be done to accommodate person-oriented communication, it leads to a deterioration in the relationship rather than to problem solving. Person-oriented messages often try to persuade the other individual that "this is how you should feel" or "this is what kind of person you are" (e.g., "You are an incompetent manager, a lazy worker, or an insensitive office mate"). But since most individuals accept themselves pretty much as they are, their common reaction to person-oriented communication is to defend themselves against it or reject it outright. Even when communication is positive (e.g., "You are a wonderful person"), it may not be viewed as trustworthy if it is not tied to a behavior or an accomplishment (e.g., "I think you are a terrific person because of the extra-mile service you rendered to our organization"). The absence of a meaningful referent is the key weakness in person-oriented communication.

In building positive, supportive relationships, problem-oriented communication should also be linked to accepted standards or expectations rather than to personal opinions. Personal opinions are more likely to be interpreted as person-oriented and arouse defensiveness than statements in which the behavior is compared to an accepted standard or performance. For example, the statement, "I don't like the way you dress" is an expression of a personal opinion and will probably create resistance, especially if the listener does not feel that the communicator's opinions are any more legitimate than his or her own. On the other hand, "Your dress is not in keeping with the company dress code," or "In this firm, everyone is expected to wear a tie to work," are comparisons to external standards that have some legitimacy. Feelings of defensiveness are less likely to arise since the problem, not the person, is being addressed. In addition, other people are more likely to support a statement based on a commonly accepted standard.

Supportive communicators need not avoid expressing personal opinions or feelings about the behavior or attitudes of others. When doing so, however, they should keep in mind the following additional principles.

4. SUPPORTIVE COMMUNICATION VALIDATES RATHER THAN INVALIDATES INDIVIDUALS

Validating communication helps people feel recognized, understood, accepted, and valued. Communication that is **invalidating** arouses negative feelings about self-worth, identity, and relatedness to others. It denies the presence, uniqueness, or importance of other individuals. Especially important are communications that invalidate people by conveying superiority, rigidity, indifference, and imperviousness (Brownell, 1986; Cupach & Spitzberg, 1994; Sieburg, 1978; Steil et al., 1983). Barnlund's (1968) observation more than a quarter century ago is even more true today:

> People often do not take time, do not listen, do not try to understand, but interrupt, anticipate, criticize, or disregard what is said; in their own remarks they are frequently vague,

> inconsistent, verbose, insincere, or dogmatic. As a result, people often conclude conversations feeling more inadequate, more misunderstood, and more alienated than when they started. (p. 618)

Communication that is superiority oriented gives the impression that the communicator is informed while others are ignorant, adequate while others are inadequate, competent while others are incompetent, or powerful while others are impotent. It creates a barrier between the communicator and those to whom the message is sent.

Superiority-oriented communication can take the form of put-downs, in which others are made to look bad so that the communicator looks good. Or it can take the form of "one-upmanship," in which the communicator tries to elevate himself or herself in the esteem of others. One form of one-upmanship is withholding information, either boastfully ("If you knew what I knew, you would feel differently") or coyly to trip people up ("If you had asked me, I could have told you the executive committee would disapprove of your proposal"). Boasting almost always makes others uncomfortable, mainly because it is designed to convey superiority.

Another common form of superiority-oriented communication is the use of jargon, acronyms, or words in such a way as to exclude others or to create barriers in a relationship. Doctors, lawyers, government employees, and many professionals are well known for their use of jargon or acronyms, designed to exclude others or to elevate themselves rather than to clarify a message. Speaking a foreign language in the presence of individuals who don't understand it may also be done to create the impression of exclusiveness or superiority. In most circumstances, using words or language that a listener can't understand is bad manners because it invalidates the other person.

Rigidity in communication is the second major type of invalidation: The communication is portrayed as absolute, unequivocal, or unquestionable. No other opinion or point of view could possibly be considered. Individuals who communicate in dogmatic, "know-it-all" ways often do so in order to minimize others' contributions or to invalidate others' perspectives. It is possible to communicate rigidity, however, in ways other than just being dogmatic. Rigidity is also communicated by:

❏ Reinterpreting all other viewpoints to conform to one's own.

❏ Never saying, "I don't know," but having an answer for everything.

LEARNING

- Appearing unwilling to tolerate criticisms or alternative points of view.
- Reducing complex issues to simplistic definitions or generalizations.
- Placing exclamation points after statements so the impression is created that the statement is final, complete, or unqualified.
- Resistance to receiving personal feedback.

Indifference is communicated when the other person's existence or importance is not acknowledged. A person may do this by using silence, by making no verbal response to the other's statements, by avoiding eye contact or any facial expression, by interrupting the other person frequently, by using impersonal words ("one should not" instead of "you should not"), or by engaging in unrelated activity during a conversation. The communicator appears not to care about the other person and gives the impression of being impervious to the other person's feelings or perspectives. To be indifferent is to exclude others, to treat them as if they are not even present.

Imperviousness means that the communicator does not acknowledge the feelings or opinions of the other person. They are either labeled illegitimate— "You shouldn't feel that way" or "Your opinion is incorrect"—or they are labeled as ignorant—"You don't understand," "You've been misinformed," or (worse yet) "Your opinion is naive." Being impervious means to ignore or make unimportant the personal feelings or thoughts of another. It serves to exclude the other person's contribution to the conversation or the relationship, and it makes the other person feel illegitimate or unimportant.

Communication is invalidating when it denies the other person an opportunity to establish a mutually satisfying relationship or when contributions cannot be made by both parties. When one person doesn't allow the other to finish a sentence, adopts a competitive, win-or-lose stance, sends confusing messages, or disqualifies the other person from making a contribution, communication is invalidating and, therefore, dysfunctional for effective problem solving.

Invalidation is even more destructive in interpersonal relationships than criticism or disagreement because criticism and disagreement do, in fact, validate the other person by recognizing that what was said or done is worthy of correction, response, or notice. As William James (1965) stated, "No more fiendish punishment could be devised, even were such a thing physically possible, than that one could be turned loose in a society and remain absolutely unnoticed by all the members thereof."

Validating communication, on the other hand, helps people feel recognized, understood, accepted, and valued (see also the chapter on Empowering and Delegating). It has four attributes: It is *egalitarian, flexible, two-way*, and *based on agreement.*

Respectful, egalitarian communication (the opposite of superiority-oriented communication) is especially important when a person with a higher status interacts with a person of a lower status. When a hierarchical distinction exists between individuals, for example, it is easy for subordinates to feel invalidated since they have access to less power and information than their managers. Supportive communicators, however, help subordinates feel that they have a stake in identifying problems and resolving them by communicating an egalitarian stance. They treat subordinates as worthwhile, competent, and insightful and emphasize joint problem solving rather than projecting a superior position. They can do this merely by asking for opinions, suggestions, and ideas. Another way they do this is by using flexible (rather than rigid) statements.

Even without hierarchical differences, however, communicating respectfully and in an egalitarian way is important. When people of different nationalities, ethnic groups, or genders are communicating, for example, some people are almost always vulnerable to feeling excluded or inferior. In those circumstances, egalitarian and inclusive statements are especially important in order to foster supportive relationships.

Flexibility in communication is the willingness of a person to communicate an understanding that the other party may possess additional data and other alternatives that may make significant contributions both to the problem solution and to the relationship. It simply implies being receptive to other people. It means communicating genuine humility—not self-abasement or weakness— and a willingness to learn and to be open to new experience. It means remaining open to new insights. As Benjamin Disraeli noted, "To be conscious that you are ignorant is a first great step toward knowledge."

Perceptions and opinions are not presented as facts in flexible communication, but are stated provisionally. No claim is made for the absolute truthfulness of opinions or assumptions. Rather, they are identified as being changeable if more data should become available. Flexible communication conveys a willingness to enter into joint problem solving rather than to control the other person or to assume a master–teacher role. However, being flexible is not synonymous with being wishy-washy. "Gee, I can't make up my mind" is wishy-washy, whereas "I have my own opinions, but what do you think?" suggests flexibility.

Two-way communication is an implied result of respectfulness and flexibility. Individuals feel validated when they are asked questions, given "air time" to express their opinions, and encouraged to participate actively in the interpersonal interaction. Two-way interchange communicates the message that the other person is valued, which is a prerequisite for building collaboration and teamwork (see the chapter on Building Effective Teams and Teamwork).

Finally, one person's communication validates another when it *identifies areas of agreement* and joint commitment. One way to express validation based on agreement is to identify positive behaviors, positive attitudes, and positive consequences. Almost all models of negotiation, teambuilding, and conflict resolution prescribe finding areas of agreement upon which everyone can concur. Agreement makes progress possible. Similarly, highlighting positive factors also provides positive energy and a willingness to invest in conversation. Some examples include pointing out important points made by the other person before pointing out trivial ones, areas of agreement before areas of disagreement, advantages of the other person's statements before disadvantages, compliments before criticisms, and positive next steps before past mistakes. The point is, validating other people helps create feelings of self-worth and self-confidence that can translate into self-motivation and improved performance. Positive relationships result. Invalidation, on the other hand, seldom produces such positive outcomes, yet it is a common form of response when people encounter something that they feel a need to criticize or correct.

5. SUPPORTIVE COMMUNICATION IS SPECIFIC (USEFUL), NOT GLOBAL (NONUSEFUL)

Specific statements are supportive because they identify something that can be easily understood and acted upon. In general, the more specific a statement is, the more effective it is in motivating improvement. For example, the statement "You have trouble managing your time" is too general to be useful, whereas "You spent an hour scheduling meetings today when that could have been done by your assistant" provides specific information that can serve as a basis for behavioral change. "Your communication needs to improve" is not nearly as useful

as a more specific "In this role play exercise, you used evaluative statements 60 percent of the time and descriptive statements 10 percent of the time."

Specific statements avoid extremes and absolutes. The following are extreme or global (and nonuseful) statements that lead to defensiveness or disconfirmation:

> A: "You never ask for my advice."
> B: "Yes, I do. I always consult you before making a decision."
>
> A: "You have no consideration for others' feelings."
> B: "I do so. I am always considerate."
>
> A: "This job stinks."
> B: "You're wrong. It's a great job."

Another common type of global communication is the either–or statement, such as "You either do what I say or I'll fire you," "Life is either a daring adventure or nothing" (Helen Keller), and "If America doesn't reduce its national debt, our children will never achieve the standard of living we enjoy today."

The problem with extreme and either–or statements is that they deny any alternatives. The possible responses of the recipient of the communication are severely constrained. To contradict or deny the statement generally leads to defensiveness and arguments. A statement by Adolf Hitler in 1933 illustrates the point: "Everyone in Germany is a National Socialist; the few outside the party are either lunatics or idiots." On the other hand, a friend of ours was asked to serve as a consultant to a labor and management committee. As he entered the room and was introduced as a professor, the union president declared: "Either he goes or I go."

What would you do? How would you use supportive communication when the union president has made a global statement that either excludes you or cancels the negotiations? Our friend's reply was, "I hope there are more alternatives than that. Why don't we explore them?" This response provided a way for communicatation to continue and for the possibility of a supportive relationship to be formed.

Specific statements are more useful in interpersonal relationships because they focus on behavioral events and indicate gradations in positions. More useful forms of the examples above are the following:

> A: "You made that decision yesterday without asking for my advice."
> B: "Yes, I did. While I generally like to get your opinion, I didn't think it was necessary in this case."

A: "By using sarcasm in your response to my request, you gave me the impression you don't care about my feelings."

B: "I'm sorry. I know I am often sarcastic without thinking how it affects others."

A: "The pressure to meet deadlines affects the quality of my work."

B: "Since deadlines are part of our work, let's discuss ways to manage the pressure."

Specific statements may not be useful if they focus on things over which another person has no control. "I hate it when it rains," for example, may relieve some personal frustration, but nothing can be done to change the weather. Similarly, communicating the message (even implicitly) "The sound of your voice (or your personality, your weight, your tastes, the way you are, etc.) bothers me" only proves frustrating for the interacting individuals. Such a statement is usually interpreted as a personal attack. The reaction is likely to be, "What can I do about that?" or "I don't even understand what you mean." Specific communication is useful to the extent that it focuses on an identifiable problem or behavior about which something can be done (e.g., "It bothers me when you talk so loudly in the library that it disturbs others' concentration").

Even when offering compliments to another person, being specific is better than being global or general. For example, providing positive feedback to someone by saying "You are a nice person" is not nearly as helpful as describing an incident or a behavior that created that impression; for example, "You seem to always smile when I see you, and you express interest in my work." Whereas both statements are pleasant to hear, the specific comment is much more helpful than the general comment.

6. SUPPORTIVE COMMUNICATION IS CONJUNCTIVE, NOT DISJUNCTIVE

Conjunctive communication is joined to previous messages in some way. It flows smoothly. **Disjunctive communication** is disconnected from what was stated before.

Communication can become disjunctive in at least three ways. First, there can be a lack of equal opportunity to speak. When one person interrupts another, when someone dominates by controlling "air time," or when two or more people try to speak at the same time, the communication is disjunctive. The transitions between exchanges do not flow smoothly. A smooth transition does not occur between one statement and the next. Second, extended pauses are disjunctive. When speakers pause for long periods in the middle of their speeches or when there are long pauses before responses, the communication is disjunctive. Pauses need not be total silence; the space may be filled with "umm," "aaah," or a repetition of something stated earlier, but the communication does not progress. Third, topic control can be disjointed. When one person decides unilaterally what the next topic of conversation will be (as opposed to having it decided bilaterally), the communication is disjunctive. Individuals may switch topics, for example, with no reference to what was just said, or they may control the other person's communication topic by directing what should be responded to. Sieburg (1969) found that more than 25 percent of the statements made in small-group discussions failed to refer to or even acknowledge prior speakers or their statements.

These three factors—taking turns speaking, management of timing, and topic control—contribute to what Wiemann (1977) called "interaction management." They have been found to be crucial in supportive communication. In an empirical study of perceived communication competence, Wiemann (1977, p. 104) found that "the smoother the management of the interaction, the more competent the communicator was perceived to be." People who took turns, who did not dominate with pauses or excessive air time, and who connected what they said to what others had said in the past were judged as competent communicators. In fact, interaction management was concluded to be the most powerful determinant of perceived communication competence in his experimental study. Individuals who used conjunctive communication were rated as being significantly more competent in interpersonal communication than were those whose communication was disjunctive.

This suggests that people who are good at building positive relationships use several kinds of behaviors in managing communication situations so they are conjunctive rather than disjunctive. For example, they foster conjunctive communication in an interaction by asking questions that are based directly on the subordinate's previous statement, by waiting for a sentence to be completed before beginning a response (e.g., not finishing a sentence for someone else), and by saying only three or four sentences at a time before pausing to give the other person a chance to add input. All of us have been in interactions in which one person goes on and on and on without allowing others to comment

Figure 4.2 The Continuum of Conjunctive Statements

The communicator's statement or question . . .

Most Conjunctive

. . . refers to an immediately preceding statement.

. . . refers to a statement that was made earlier in the conversation.

. . . refers to something not stated previously but that both parties understand or share in common.

. . . refers to nothing that has been said or that the parties share in common.

Disjunctive

or contribute. Almost always it produces discomfort because it is disjunctive. Interaction, exchange, and give-and-take are necessary for supportive communication to occur. In other words, supportive communicators avoid long pauses, their statements refer to what has been said before, and they take turns speaking. Figure 4.2 illustrates the continuum of conjunctive and disjunctive statements.

By using conjunctive communication, managers confirm the worth of the other person's statements, thereby helping to foster joint problem solving and teamwork.

7. SUPPORTIVE COMMUNICATION IS OWNED, NOT DISOWNED

Taking responsibility for one's statements and acknowledging that the source of the ideas is oneself and not another person or group is **owning communication**. Using first-person words, such as "I," "me," "mine," indicates owning communication. **Disowning communication** is suggested by use of third-person or first-person-plural words: "We think," "They said," or "One might say." Disowned communication is attributed to an unknown person, group, or to some external source (e.g., "Lots of people think"). The communicator avoids taking responsibility for the message and therefore avoids investing in the interaction. This may convey the

message that the communicator is aloof or uncaring about the receiver or is not confident enough in the ideas expressed to take responsibility for them.

Glasser (1965, 2000) based his approach to mental health—reality therapy—on the concept of taking responsibility for, or owning, communication and behavior. According to Glasser, people's mental health depends on their accepting responsibility for their statements and behaviors. The basic assumption of reality therapy is that taking responsibility for your own communication builds self-confidence and a sense of self-worth. The opposite, attributing what one feels or says to someone or something else (e.g., "My being cranky isn't my fault because my roommate stayed up all night playing loud music") leads to poor mental health and loss of self-control. Ownership and responsibility are keys to personal growth and to trusting and effective interpersonal relationships. You will trust me more if you know that I take responsibility for my statements.

One result of disowned communication is that the listener is never sure whose point of view the message represents: "How can I respond if I don't know to whom I am responding?" "If I don't understand the message, whom can I ask since the message represents someone else's point of view?" Moreover, an implicit message associated with disowned communication is, "I want to keep distance between you and me." The speaker communicates as a representative rather than as a person, as a message-conveyer rather than an interested individual. Owned communication, on the other hand, indicates a willingness to invest oneself in a relationship and to act as a colleague or helper.

This last point suggests that coaches or counselors should encourage others to own their own statements. This can be done by example but also by asking the other person to restate disowning statements, as in this exchange:

> SUBORDINATE: *Everyone else says my work is fine.*
> MANAGER: *So no one besides me has ever expressed dissatisfaction with your work or suggested how to improve it?*
> SUBORDINATE: *Well . . . Mark complained that I took shortcuts and left him to clean up after me.*
> MANAGER: *Was his complaint fair?*
> SUBORDINATE: *Yeah, I guess so.*
> MANAGER: *What led you to take shortcuts?*
> SUBORDINATE: *My work was piling up, and I felt I had too much to do.*
> MANAGER: *Does this happen often, that your work builds up and you look for shortcuts?*
> SUBORDINATE: *More than I'd like.*

Here the manager has used conjunctive questions to guide the subordinate away from disowning responsibility toward acknowledging a behavior that may be affecting others' performance.

8. SUPPORTIVE COMMUNICATION REQUIRES SUPPORTIVE LISTENING, NOT ONE-WAY MESSAGE DELIVERY

The previous seven attributes of supportive communication all focus on message delivery, where a message is initiated by the coach or counselor. But another aspect of supportive communication—that is, *listening and responding* effectively to someone else's statements—is at least as important as delivering supportive messages. As Maier, Solem, and Maier (1973, p. 311) stated: "In any conversation, the person who talks the most is the one who learns the least about the other person. The good supervisor therefore must become a good listener."

Haas and Arnold (1995) found that in the workplace, about one-third of the characteristics people use to judge communication competence have to do with listening. Kramer (1997) found that good listening skills accounted for 40 percent of the variance in effective leadership. In short, good listeners are more likely to be perceived to be skillful communicators. In fact, people who are judged to be the most "wise," or to possess the attribute of wisdom—and, therefore, are the most sought-after people with whom to interact—are also the best listeners (Kramer, 2000; Sternberg, 1990).

In a survey of personnel directors in 300 businesses and industries conducted to determine what skills are most important in becoming a manager, Crocker (1978) reported that effective listening was ranked highest. Despite its importance in managerial success, however, and despite the fact that most people spend at least 45 percent of their communication time listening, most people have underdeveloped listening skills. Tests have shown, for example, that individuals are usually about 25 percent effective in listening; that is, they listen to and understand only about a fourth of what is being communicated (Bostrom, 1997; Huseman, Lahiff, & Hatfield, 1976). Geddie (1999) reported that in a survey across 15 countries, listening was found to be the poorest communication skill. When asked to rate the extent to which they are skilled listeners, 85 percent of all individuals rate themselves as average or worse. Only 5 percent rate themselves as highly skilled (Steil, 1980). It is particularly unfortunate that listening skills are often poorest when people interact with those closest to them, such as family members and coworkers. They interrupt and jump to conclusions more frequently (i.e., they stop listening) with people close to them than with others.

When individuals are preoccupied with meeting their own needs (e.g., saving face, persuading someone else, winning a point, avoiding getting involved), when they have already made a prior judgment, or when they hold negative attitudes toward the communicator or the message, they don't listen effectively. Because a person listens at the rate of 500 words a minute but speaks at a normal rate of only 125 to 250 words a minute, the listener's mind can dwell on other things half the time. Therefore, being a good listener is neither easy nor automatic. It requires developing the ability to hear and understand the message sent by another person, while at the same time helping to strengthen the relationship between the interacting parties.

Rogers and Farson (1976) suggest that this kind of listening conveys the idea that:

> *I'm interested in you as a person, and I think what you feel is important. I respect your thoughts, and even if I don't agree with them, I know they are valid for you. I feel sure you*

have a contribution to make. I think you're worth listening to, and I want you to know that I'm the kind of person you can talk to. (p. 99)

People do not know they are being listened to unless the listener makes some type of response. This can be simple eye contact and nonverbal responsiveness such as smiles, nods, and focused attention. However, competent managers who must coach and counsel also select carefully from a repertoire of verbal response alternatives that clarify the communication as well as strengthen the interpersonal relationship. The mark of a supportive listener is the competence to select appropriate responses to others' statements (Bostrom, 1997).

The appropriateness of a response depends to some degree on whether the focus of the interaction is primarily coaching or counseling. Of course, seldom can these two activities be separated from one another completely—effective coaching often involves counseling and effective counseling sometimes involves coaching—and attentive listening involves the use of a variety of responses. Some responses, however, are more appropriate under certain circumstances than others.

Figure 4.3 lists four major response types and arranges them on a continuum from most directive and closed to most nondirective and open. Closed responses eliminate discussion of topics and provide direction to individuals. They represent methods by which the listener can control the topic of conversation. Open responses, on the other hand, allow the communicator, not the listener, to control the topic of conversation. Each of these response types has certain

advantages and disadvantages, and none is appropriate all the time under all circumstances.

Most people get in the habit of relying heavily on one or two response types, and they use them regardless of the circumstances. Moreover, most people have been found to rely first and foremost on evaluative or judgmental responses (Bostrom, 1997; Rogers, 1961). That is, when they encounter another person's statements, most people tend to agree or disagree, to pass judgment, or to immediately form a personal opinion about the legitimacy or veracity of the statement. On the average, about 80 percent of most people's responses have been found to be evaluative. Supportive listening, however, avoids evaluation and judgment as a first response. Instead, it relies on flexibility in response types and the appropriate match of responses to circumstances. The four major types of responses are discussed below.

Advising

An **advising response** provides direction, evaluation, personal opinion, or instructions. Such a response imposes on the communicator the point of view of the listener, and it creates listener control over the topic of conversation. The advantages of an advising response are that it helps the communicator understand something that may have been unclear before, it helps identify a problem solution, and it can provide clarity about how the communicator should act or interpret the problem. It is most appropriate when the listener has expertise that the communicator doesn't possess or when the communicator is in need of direction. Supportive listening sometimes means that the listener does the talking, but this is usually appropriate only

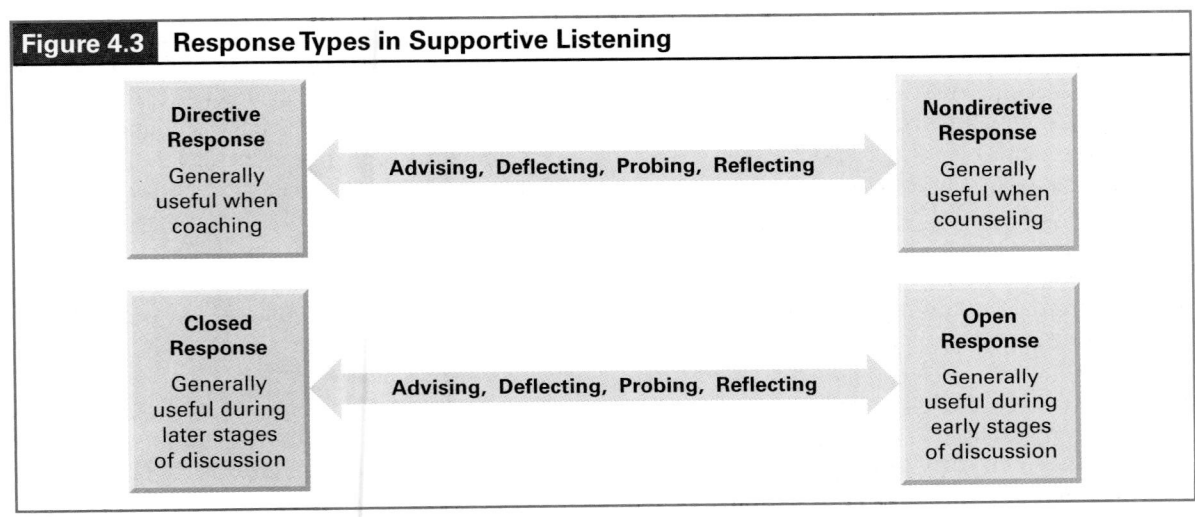

Figure 4.3   Response Types in Supportive Listening

Directive Response	Advising, Deflecting, Probing, Reflecting	Nondirective Response
Generally useful when coaching		Generally useful when counseling

Closed Response	Advising, Deflecting, Probing, Reflecting	Open Response
Generally useful during later stages of discussion		Generally useful during early stages of discussion

LEARNING

when advice or direction is specifically requested. Most listeners have a tendency to offer much more advice and direction than is appropriate.

One problem with advising is that it can produce dependence. Individuals get used to having someone else generate answers, directions, or clarifications. They are not permitted to figure out issues and solutions for themselves. A second problem is that advising also creates the impression that the communicator is not being understood by the listener. Rogers (1961) found that most people, even when they seem to be asking for advice, mainly desire understanding and acceptance, not advice. They want the listener to share in the communication but not take charge of it. The problem with advising is that it removes from the communicator the opportunity to stay focused on the issue that is on the communicator's mind. Advice shifts the control of the conversation away from the communicator. A third problem with advising is that it shifts focus from the communicator's issue to the listener's advice. When listeners feel advising is appropriate, they concentrate more on the legitimacy of the advice or on the generation of alternatives and solutions than on simply listening attentively. When listeners are expected to generate advice and direction, they may focus more on their own experience than on the communicator's experience, or on formulating their advice more than on the nuances of the communicator's message. It is difficult to simultaneously be a good listener and a good adviser. A fourth potential problem with advising is that it can imply that communicators don't have the necessary understanding, expertise, insight, or maturity, so they need help because of their incompetence.

One way to overcome the disadvantages of advising is to avoid giving advice as a first response. Almost always advising should follow other responses that allow communicators to have control over the topics of conversation, that show understanding and acceptance, and that encourage analysis and self-reliance on the part of communicators. First communicating concern and personal interest, for example, makes much more likely that any advice being offered will be heard and accepted.

In addition, advice should either be connected to an accepted standard or should be tentative. An accepted standard means that communicators and listeners both acknowledge that the advice will lead to a desired outcome and that it is inherently good, right, or appropriate. When this is impossible, the advice should be communicated as the listener's opinion or feeling, and as only one option (i.e., with flexibility), not as the only option. This permits communicators to

accept or reject the advice without feeling that the advisor is being invalidated or rejected if the advice is not accepted.

Deflecting

A **deflecting response** switches the focus from the communicator's problem to one selected by the listener. Listeners deflect attention away from the original problem or the original statement. The listener essentially changes the subject. Listeners may substitute their own experience for that of the communicator (e.g., "Let me tell you something similar that happened to me") or introduce an entirely new topic (e.g., "That reminds me of [something else]"). The listener may think the current problem is unclear to the communicator and that the use of examples or analogies will help. Or, the listener may feel that the communicator needs to be reassured that others have experienced the same problem and that support and understanding are available.

Deflecting responses are most appropriate when a comparison or some reassurance is needed. They can provide empathy and support by communicating the message "I understand because of what happened to me (or someone else)." They can also convey the assurance "Things will be fine. Others have also had this experience." Deflection is also often used to avoid embarrassing either the communicator or the listener. Changing the subject when either party becomes uncomfortable or answering a question other than the one asked are common examples.

The disadvantages of deflecting responses, however, are that they can imply that the communicator's message is not important or that the experience of the listener is more significant than that of the communicator. They may produce competitiveness or feelings of being one-upped by the listener. Deflection can be interpreted as, "My experience is more worthy of discussion than yours." Or it may simply change the subject from something that is important and central to the communicator to a topic that is not as important. ("I want to talk about something important to me, but you changed the subject to your own experience.")

Deflecting responses are most effective when they are conjunctive—that is, when they are clearly connected to what the communicator just said, when the listener's response leads directly back to the communicator's concerns, and when the reason for the deflection is made clear. That is, deflecting can produce desirable outcomes if the communicator feels supported and understood, not invalidated, by the change in topic focus.

Probing

A **probing response** asks a question about what the communicator just said or about a topic selected by the listener. The intent of a probe is to acquire additional information, to help the communicator say more about the topic, or to help the listener foster more appropriate responses. For example, an effective way to avoid being evaluative and judgmental and to avoid triggering defensive reactions is to continue to ask questions. Questioning helps the listener adopt the communicator's frame of reference so that in coaching situations suggestions can be specific (not global) and in counseling situations statements can be descriptive (not evaluative). Questions tend to be more neutral in tone than direct statements. A study of top management team communication, for example, found that high-performing teams had a balance between inquiry (asking questions or probing) and advocacy (declaring or advocating a perspective), so that questions and probes received equal time. Low-performing teams were heavily oriented toward advocacy and away from inquiry and probing (Losada & Heaphy, 2004).

Questioning, however, can sometimes have the unwelcome effect of switching the focus of attention from the communicator's statement to the reasons behind it. The question "Why do you think that way?" for example, might pressure the communicator to justify a feeling or a perception rather than just report it. Similarly, probing responses can serve as a mechanism for escaping discussion of a topic or for maneuvering the topic around to one the listener wants to discuss (e.g., "Instead of discussing your feelings about your job, tell me why you didn't respond to my memo"). Probing responses can also allow the communicator to lose control of the conversation, especially when difficult subjects need to be addressed (e.g., "Why aren't you

performing up to your potential?" allows all kinds of other issues to be raised that may or may not be apropos.)

Two important hints should be kept in mind to make probing responses more effective. One is that "why" questions are seldom as effective as "what" questions. "Why" questions lead to topic changes, escapes, and speculations more often than to valid information. For example, the question "Why do you feel that way?" can lead to off-the-wall statements such as "Because I am a redhead," or "Because my father was an alcoholic and my mother beat me," or "Because Dr. Laura said so." These are silly examples, but they illustrate how ineffective "why" questions can be. "What do you mean by that?" is likely to be more fruitful.

A second hint is to tailor the probes to fit the situation. Four types of probes are useful in interviewing. When the communicator's statement does not contain enough information, or part of the message is not understood, an **elaboration probe** should be used (e.g., "Can you tell me more about that?"). When the message is not clear or is ambiguous, a **clarification probe** is best (e.g., "What do you mean by that?"). A **repetition probe** works best when the communicator is avoiding a topic, hasn't answered a previous question, or a previous statement is unclear (e.g., "Once again, what do you think about this?"). A **reflection probe** is most effective when the communicator is being encouraged to keep pursuing the same topic in greater depth (e.g., "You say you are discouraged?"). Table 4.5 summarizes these four kinds of questions or probes.

Probing responses are especially effective in turning hostile or conflictive conversations into supportive conversations. Asking questions can often turn attacks into consensus, evaluations into descriptions, general statements into specific statements, disowning statements into owning statements, or person-focused declarations

Table 4.5	Four Types of Probing Responses
TYPE OF PROBE	**EXPLANATION**
Elaboration Probe	Use when more information is needed. ("Can you tell me more about that?")
Clarification Probe	Use when the message is unclear or ambiguous. ("What do you mean by that?")
Repetition Probe	Use when topic drift occurs or statements are unclear. ("Once again, what do you think about this?")
Reflection Probe	Use to encourage more in-depth pursuit of the same topic. ("You say you are having difficulty?")

into problem-focused declarations. In other words, probes can often be used to help others use supportive communication when they have not been trained in advance to do so.

Reflecting

The primary purpose of the **reflecting response** is to mirror back to the communicator the message that was heard and to communicate understanding and acceptance of the person. Reflecting the message *in different words* allows the speaker to feel listened to, understood, and free to explore the topic in more depth. Reflective responding involves paraphrasing and clarifying the message. Instead of simply mimicking the communication, supportive listeners also contribute meaning, understanding, and acceptance to the conversation while still allowing communicators to pursue topics of their choosing. Athos and Gabarro (1978); Brownell (1986); Steil, Barker, and Watson (1983); Wolvin and Coakley (1988); and others argue that this response should be most typical in supportive communication and should dominate coaching and counseling situations. It leads to the clearest communication, the most two-way exchanges, and the most supportive relationships. For example:

> SUPERVISOR: Jerry, I'd like to hear about any problems you've been having with your job over the last several weeks.
> SUBORDINATE: Don't you think they ought to do something about the air conditioning in the office? It gets to be like an oven in here every afternoon! They said they were going to fix the system weeks ago!
> SUPERVISOR: It sounds like the delay is really beginning to make you angry.
> SUBORDINATE: It sure is! It's just terrible the way maintenance seems to being goofing off instead of being responsive.
> SUPERVISOR: So it's frustrating ... and discouraging.
> SUBORDINATE: Amen. And by the way, there's something else I want to mention. ...

A potential disadvantage of reflective responses is that communicators can get an impression opposite from the one intended. That is, they can get the feeling that they are not being understood or listened to carefully. If they keep hearing reflections of what they just said, their response might be, "I just said that. Aren't you listening to me?" Reflective responses, in other words, can be perceived as an artificial "technique" or as a superficial response to a message.

The most effective listeners keep the following rules in mind when using reflective responses.

1. Avoid repeating the same response over and over, such as "You feel that ... ," "Are you saying that ... ?" or "What I heard you say was. ..."

2. Avoid mimicking the communicator's words. Instead, restate what you just heard in a way that helps ensure that you understand the message and the communicator knows that you understand.

3. Avoid an exchange in which listeners do not contribute equally to the conversation, but serve only as mimics. (One can use understanding or reflective responses while still taking equal responsibility for the depth and meaning of the communication.)

4. Respond to the personal rather than the impersonal. For example, to a complaint by a subordinate about close supervision and feelings of incompetence and annoyance, a reflective response would focus on personal feelings before supervision style.

5. Respond to expressed feelings before responding to content. When a person expresses feelings, they are the most important part of the message. They may stand in the way of the ability to communicate clearly unless acknowledged.

6. Respond with empathy and acceptance. Avoid the extremes of complete objectivity, detachment, or distance on the one hand, or over-identification (accepting the feelings as one's own) on the other.

7. Avoid expressing agreement or disagreement with the statements. Use reflective listening and other listening responses to help the communicator explore and analyze the problem. Later you can draw on this information to help fashion a solution.

The Personal Management Interview

Not only are the eight attributes of supportive communication effective in normal discourse and problem-solving situations, but they can be most effectively applied when specific interactions with subordinates are planned and conducted frequently. One important difference between effective and ineffective managers is the extent to which they provide their subordinates with opportunities to receive regular feedback, to feel supported and bolstered, and to be coached and counseled. Providing these opportunities is difficult, however, because of the tremendous time demands most managers face. Many managers want to coach, counsel, train, and develop subordinates, but they simply never find the time. Therefore, one important mechanism for applying supportive communication and for providing subordinates with development and feedback opportunities is to implement a **personal management interview (PMI) program**. This program is probably the most frequently adopted tool that managers employ in the executive education programs we teach when they commit themselves to improving relationships with their subordinates and team members. We have received more feedback about the success of the PMI program than almost any other management improvement technique we have shared. It is a very simple and straightforward technique for implementing supportive communication and building positive relationships in a manager's role. Most importantly, however, it has also been proven to be equally effective in family settings, community groups, church

service, or peer teams. Many people have implemented the PMI system in their own families with their children, for instance.

A PMI program is a regularly scheduled, one-on-one meeting between a manager and his or her subordinates. In a study of the performance of working departments and intact teams in a variety of organizations, Boss (1983) found that effectiveness increased significantly when managers conducted regular, private meetings with subordinates on a biweekly or monthly basis. In a study of health care organizations holding these regular personal management interviews compared to those that did not, significant differences were found in organizational performance, employee performance and satisfaction, and personal stress management scores. The facilities that had instituted a PMI program were significantly higher performers on all the personal and organizational performance dimensions. Figure 4.4 compares the performance effectiveness of teams and departments that implemented the program versus those that did not.

Our own personal experience is also consistent with the empirical findings. We have conducted personal management interviews with individuals for whom we have responsibility in a variety of professional,

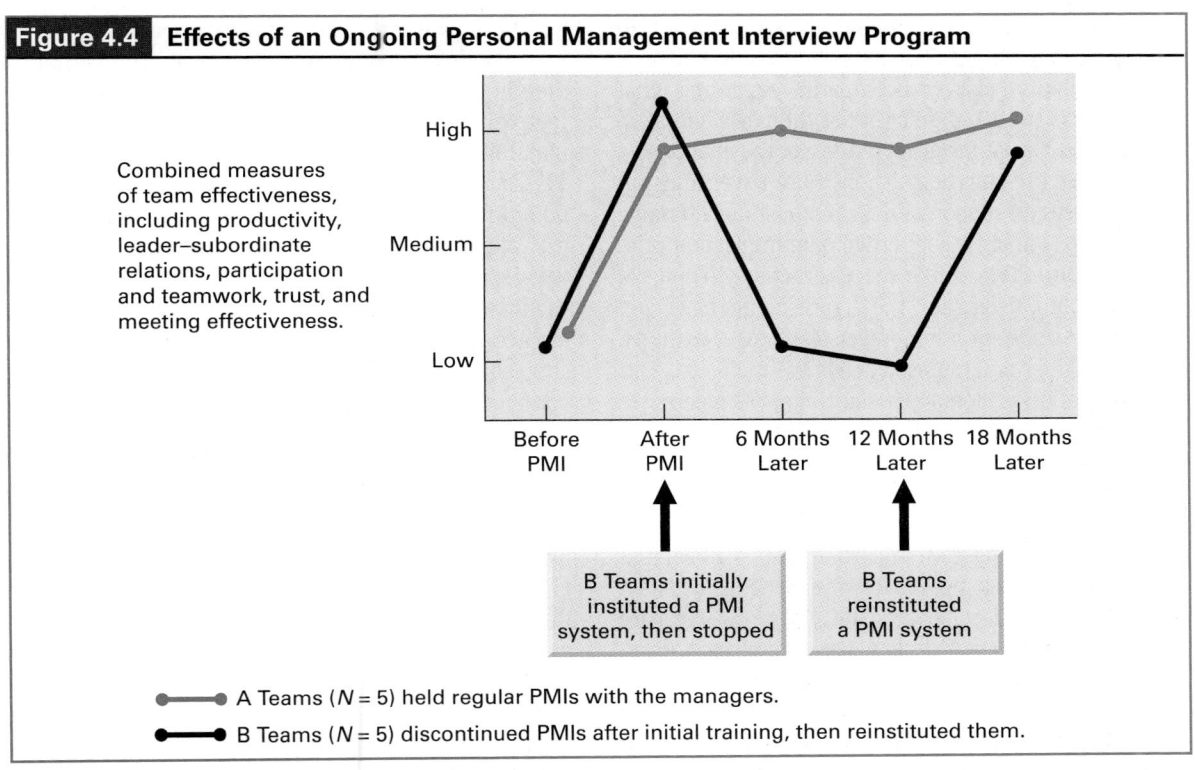

Figure 4.4   Effects of an Ongoing Personal Management Interview Program

Combined measures of team effectiveness, including productivity, leader–subordinate relations, participation and teamwork, trust, and meeting effectiveness.

B Teams initially instituted a PMI system, then stopped

B Teams reinstituted a PMI system

A Teams (N = 5) held regular PMIs with the managers.

B Teams (N = 5) discontinued PMIs after initial training, then reinstituted them.

Source: *Journal of Applied Behavioral Science, Online.*

community, and church organization settings. We also have conducted these sessions with our individual family members. Rather than being an imposition and an artificial means of communication, these sessions—held one-on-one with each child or each member of the unit—have been incredibly productive. Close bonds have resulted, open sharing of information and feelings has emerged, and the meetings themselves are eagerly anticipated by both us and those with whom we have conducted the PMI.

Instituting a PMI program consists of two steps. First, a role-negotiation session is held in which expectations, responsibilities, standards of evaluation, reporting relationships, and so on, are clarified. If possible, this meeting is held at the outset of the relationship. Unless such a meeting is held, most subordinates do not have a clear idea of exactly what is expected of them or on what basis they will be evaluated. In our own experiences with managers and executives, few have expressed confidence that they know precisely what is expected of them or how they are being evaluated in their jobs. In a role-negotiation session, that uncertainty is addressed. The manager and subordinate negotiate all job-related issues that are not prescribed by policy or by mandate. A written record is made of the agreements and responsibilities that result from the meeting that can serve as an informal contract between the manager and the subordinate. The goal of a role-negotiation session is to obtain clarity between both parties regarding what each expects from the other, what the goals and standards are, and what the ground rules for the relationship are. Because this role negotiation is not adversarial but rather focuses on supportiveness and building a positive relationship, the eight supportive communication principles should characterize the interaction. When we hold PMIs in our families, these agreements have centered on household chores, planned vacations, father–daughter or father–son activities, and so on. This role-negotiation session, to repeat, is simply a meeting to establish ground rules, spell out expectations, and clarify standards. It provides a foundation upon which the relationship can be built and helps foster better performance on the part of the manager as well as the subordinate.

The second, and most important, step in a PMI program is a set of ongoing, one-on-one meetings between the manager and each subordinate. These meetings are regular (not just when a mistake is made or a crisis arises) and private (not overheard by others). It is not a department staff meeting, a family gathering, or an end-of-the-day check-up. The meeting occurs one-on-one. We have never seen this program work when these meetings have been less frequent than once per month—both in organizations and in families. Many times managers choose to hold them more frequently than that, depending on the life cycle of their work and the time pressures they face. This meeting provides the two parties with a chance to communicate freely, openly, and collaboratively. It also provides managers with the opportunity to coach and counsel subordinates and to help them improve their own skills or job performance. Therefore, each meeting lasts from 45 to 60 minutes and focuses on items such as the following: (1) managerial and organizational problems, (2) information sharing, (3) interpersonal issues, (4) obstacles to improvement, (5) training in management skills, (6) individual needs, (7) feedback on job performance and personal capabilities, and (8) personal concerns or problems.

This meeting is not just a time to sit and chat. It has two overarching—and crucial—objectives: to foster improvement and to strengthen relationships. If improvement does not occur as a result of the meeting, it is not being held correctly. If relationships are not strengthened over time, something is not working as it should. The meeting always leads toward action items to be accomplished before the next meeting, some by the subordinate and others by the manager. Those action items are reviewed at the end of the meeting and reviewed again at the beginning of the next meeting. Accountability is maintained for improvement. This is not a meeting just to hold a meeting. Without agreements as to specific actions that will be taken, and the accountability that will be maintained, it can be a waste of both people's time. This means both parties prepare for the meeting, and both bring agenda items to be discussed. It is not a formal appraisal session called by the manager, but a development and improvement session in which both the manager and subordinate have a stake. It does not replace formal performance appraisal sessions, but it supplements them. The purposes of PMIs are not to conduct evaluation or performance appraisals. Rather, they provide a chance for subordinates to have personal time with the manager to work out issues, report information, receive coaching and counseling, and improve performance. Consequently, they help eliminate unscheduled interruptions and long, inefficient group meetings. At each subsequent meeting, action items are reviewed from previous meetings, so that continuous improvement is encouraged. The meetings, in other words, become an institutionalized continuous improvement activity. They are also a key to building the collaboration and teamwork needed in organizations. Table 4.6 summarizes the characteristics of the personal management interview program.

Table 4.6	Characteristics of a Personal Management Interview Program

- The interview is regular and private.
- The major intent of the meeting is continuous improvement in personal, interpersonal, and organizational performance, so the meeting is action oriented.
- Both the manager and the subordinate prepare agenda items for the meeting. It is a meeting for improving both of them, not just for the manager's appraisal.
- Sufficient time is allowed for the interaction, usually about an hour.
- Supportive communication is used so that joint problem solving and continuous improvement result (in both task accomplishment and interpersonal relationships).
- The first agenda item is a follow-up on the action items generated by the previous meeting.
- Major agenda items for the meeting might include:
  - Managerial and organizational problems
  - Organizational values and vision
  - Information sharing
  - Interpersonal issues
  - Obstacles to improvement
  - Training in management skills
  - Individual needs
  - Feedback on job performance
  - Personal concerns and problems
- Praise and encouragement are intermingled with problem solving but are more frequently communicated.
- A review of action items generated by the meeting occurs at the end of the interview.

LEARNING

The major objection to holding these PMI sessions, of course, is lack of time. Most people think that they simply cannot impose on their schedules a group of one-on-one meetings with each of their team members, subordinates, or children. Boss' research (1983) found, however, that a variety of benefits resulted in teams that instituted this program. It not only increased their effectiveness, but it improved individual accountability, department meeting efficiency, and communication flows. Managers actually found that more discretionary time became available because the program reduced interruptions, unscheduled meetings, mistakes, and problem-solving time. Furthermore, participants defined it as a success experience in itself. When correction or negative feedback had to be communicated, and when coaching or counseling was called for (which is typical of almost every manager–subordinate relationship at some point), supportive communication helped strengthen the interpersonal relationship at the same time that problems were solved and performance improved. In summary, setting aside time for formal, structured interaction between managers and their subordinates in which supportive communication played a part produced markedly improved bottom-line results in those organizations that implemented the program.

International Caveats

We point out in other chapters that it is important to keep in mind that cultural differences sometimes call for a modification of the skills discussed in this book. We noted, for example, that Asian managers are often less inclined to be open in initial stages of a conversation, and they consider managers from the United States or Latin America to be a bit brash and aggressive because they may be too personal too soon. Similarly, certain types of response patterns may differ among cultures—for example, deflecting responses are more typical of Eastern cultures than Western cultures. The language patterns and language structures across cultures can be dramatically different, and remember that considerable evidence exists that individuals are most effective interpersonally, and they display the greatest amount of emotional intelligence, when they recognize, appreciate, and capitalize on these differences among others.

On the other hand, whereas stylistic differences may exist among individuals and among various cultures, certain core principles of effective communication are, nevertheless, critical to effective communication. The research on interpersonal communication among various cultures and nationalities confirms that the eight attributes of supportive communication are effective in all cultures and nationalities (Gudykunst, Ting-Toomey, & Nishida, 1996; Triandis, 1994). These eight factors have almost universal applicability in solving interpersonal problems.

We have used Trompenaars' (1996, 1998) model of cultural diversity to identify key differences among people raised in different cultural contexts. (Chapter 1 in this book provides a more detailed explanation of these value dimensions.) Differences exist, for example, on an *affectivity orientation* versus a *neutral orientation*. Affective cultures (e.g., the Middle East, Southern Europe, South Pacific) are more inclined to be expressive and personal in their responses than neutral cultures (e.g., East Asia, Scandinavia). Sharing personal data and engaging quickly in sensitive topics may be comfortable for people in some cultures, for example, but very uncomfortable in others. The timing and pace of communication will vary, therefore, among different cultures. Similarly, *particularistic* cultures (e.g., Korea, China, Indonesia) are more likely to allow individuals to work out issues in their own way compared to *universalistic* cultures (e.g., Norway, Sweden, United States) where a common pattern or approach is preferred. This implies that reflective responses may be more common in particularistic cultures and advising responses more typical of universalistic cultures. When individuals are assumed to have a great deal of individual autonomy, for example, coaching responses (directing, advising, correcting) are less common than counseling responses (empathizing, probing, reflecting) in interpersonal problem solving.

Trompenaars (1996), Gudykunst & Ting-Toomey (1988), and others' research clearly points out, however, that the differences among cultures are not great enough to negate or dramatically modify the principles outlined in this chapter. Regardless of the differences in cultural background of those with whom you interact, being problem centered, congruent, descriptive, validating, specific, conjunctive, owned, and supportive in listening are all judged to indicate managerial competence and serve to build strong interpersonal relationships.

Sensitivity to individual differences and styles is an important prerequisite to effective communication.

Summary

The most important barriers to effective communication in organizations are interpersonal. Much technological progress has been made in the last two decades in improving the accuracy of message delivery in organizations, but communication problems still persist among people, regardless of their relationships or roles. A major reason for these problems is that a great deal of communication does not support a positive interpersonal relationship. Instead, it frequently engenders distrust, hostility, defensiveness, and feelings of incompetence and low self-esteem. Ask any manager about the major problems being faced in their organizations, and communication problems will most assuredly appear near the top of the list.

Dysfunctional communication is seldom associated with situations in which compliments are given, congratulations are made, a bonus is awarded, or other positive interactions occur. Most people have little trouble communicating effectively in positive or complimentary situations. The most difficult, and potentially harmful, communication patterns are most likely to emerge when you are giving feedback on poor performance, saying "no" to a proposal or request, resolving a difference of opinion between two subordinates, correcting problem behaviors, receiving criticism from others, providing feedback that could hurt another person's feelings, or encountering other negative interactions. Handling these situations in a way that fosters interpersonal growth and engenders stronger positive relationships is one mark of an effective manager. Rather than harming a relationship, using supportive communication builds and strengthens the relationship even when delivering negative news.

In this chapter, we pointed out that effective managers adhere to the principles of supportive communication. Thus, they ensure greater clarity and understanding of messages while making other persons feel accepted, valued, and supported. Of course, it is possible to become overly concerned with technique in trying to incorporate these principles and thereby to defeat the goal of being supportive. One can become artificial, inauthentic, or incongruent by focusing on technique alone, rather than on honest, caring communication. But if the principles are practiced and consciously implemented in everyday interactions, they can be important tools for improving your communication competence.

Behavioral Guidelines

The following behavioral guidelines will help you practice supportive communication:

1. Differentiate between coaching situations, which require giving advice and direction to help foster behavior change, and counseling situations, in which understanding and problem recognition are the desired outcomes.

2. Use problem-oriented statements rather than person-oriented statements; that is, focus on behavioral referents or characteristics of events, not attributes of the person.

3. Communicate congruently by acknowledging your true feelings without acting them out in destructive ways. Make certain that your statements match your feelings and thoughts and that you communicate authentically.

4. Use descriptive, not evaluative, statements. Describe objectively what occurred, describe your reactions to events and their objective consequences, and suggest acceptable alternatives.

5. Use validating statements that acknowledge the other person's importance and uniqueness. Communicate your investment in the relationship by demonstrating your respect of the other person and your flexibility and humility is being open to new ideas or new data. Foster two-way interchanges rather than dominating or interrupting the other person. Identify areas of agreement or positive characteristics of the other person before pointing out areas of disagreement or negative characteristics.

6. Use specific rather than global (either–or, black-or-white) statements, and, when trying to correct behavior, focus on things that are under the control of the other person rather than factors that cannot be changed.

7. Use conjunctive statements that flow smoothly from what was said previously. Ensure equal speaking opportunities for others participating in the interaction. Do not cause long pauses that dominate the time. Be careful not to completely control the topic being discussed. Acknowledge what was said before by others.

8. Own your statements, and encourage the other person to do likewise. Use personal words ("I") rather than impersonal words ("management").

9. Demonstrate supportive listening. Make eye contact and be responsive nonverbally. Use a variety of responses to others' statements, depending on whether you are coaching or counseling someone else. Have a bias toward the use of reflective responses.

10. Implement a personal management interview program with people for whom you have responsibility, and use supportive communication to coach, counsel, foster personal development, and build strong positive relationships.

LEARNING

CASES INVOLVING BUILDING POSITIVE RELATIONSHIPS

Find Somebody Else

Ron Davis, the relatively new general manager of the machine tooling group at Parker Manufacturing, was visiting one of the plants. He scheduled a meeting with Mike Leonard, a plant manager who reported to him.

RON: Mike, I've scheduled this meeting with you because I've been reviewing performance data, and I wanted to give you some feedback. I know we haven't talked face-to-face before, but I think it's time we review how you're doing. I'm afraid that some of things I have to say are not very favorable.

MIKE: Well, since you're the new boss, I guess I'll have to listen. I've had meetings like this before with new people who come in my plant and think they know what's going on.

RON: Look, Mike, I want this to be a two-way interchange. I'm not here to read a verdict to you, and I'm not here to tell you how to do your job. There are just some areas for improvement I want to review.

MIKE: OK, sure, I've heard that before. But you called the meeting. Go ahead and lower the boom.

RON: Well, Mike, I don't think this is lowering the boom. But there are several things you need to hear. One is what I noticed during the plant tour. I think you're too chummy with some of your female personnel. You know, one of them might take offense and level a sexual harassment suit against you.

MIKE: Oh, come on. You haven't been around this plant before, and you don't know the informal, friendly relationships we have. The office staff and the women on the floor are flattered by a little attention now and then.

RON: That may be so, but you need to be more careful. You may not be sensitive to what's really going on with them. But that raises another thing I noticed—the appearance of your shop. You know how important it is in Parker to have a neat and clean shop. As I walked through this morning, I noticed that it wasn't as orderly and neat as I would like to see it. Having things in disarray reflects poorly on you, Mike.

MIKE: I'll stack my plant up against any in Parker for neatness. You may have seen a few tools out of place because someone was just using them, but we take a lot of pride in our neatness. I don't see how you can say that things are in disarray. You've got no experience around here, so who are you to judge?

RON: Well, I'm glad you're sensitive to the neatness issue. I just think you need to pay attention to it, that's all. But regarding neatness, I notice that you don't dress like a plant manager. I think you're creating a substandard impression by not wearing a tie, for example. Casualness in dress can be used as an excuse for workers to come to work in really grubby attire. That may not be safe.

MIKE: Look, I don't agree with making a big separation between the managers and the employees. By dressing like people out on the shop floor, I think we eliminate a lot of barriers. Besides, I don't have the money to buy clothes that might get oil on them every day. That seems pretty picky to me.

RON: I don't want to seem picky, Mike. But I do feel strongly about the issues I've mentioned. There are some other things, though, that need to get corrected. One is the appearance of the reports you send into division headquarters. There are often mistakes, misspellings, and, I suspect, some wrong numbers. I wonder if you are paying attention to these reports. You seem to be reviewing them superficially.

MIKE: If there is one thing we have too much of, it's reports. I could spend three-quarters of my time filling out report forms and generating data for some bean counter in headquarters. We have reports coming out our ears. Why don't you give us a chance to get our work done and eliminate all this paperwork?

RON: You know as well as I do, Mike, that we need to carefully monitor our productivity, quality, and costs. You just need to get more serious about taking care of that part of your responsibility.

MIKE: OK. I'm not going to fight about that. It's a losing battle for me. No one at headquarters will ever decrease their demand for reports. But, listen, Ron, I also have one question for you.

RON: OK. What's that?

MIKE: Why don't you go find somebody else to pick on? I need to get back to work.

Discussion Questions

1. What principles of supportive communication and supportive listening are violated in this case?
2. If you were to change this interaction to make it more productive, what would you change?
3. Categorize each of the statements by naming the rule of supportive communication that is either illustrated or violated.
4. Conduct a role play. Handle the key issues that exist between Ron and Mike. Identify the principles that you used to make this a productive conversation. If you were Ron, what would you do in your follow-up meeting with Mike?

Rejected Plans

The following dialogue occurred between two employees in a large firm. The conversation illustrates several characteristics of supportive communication.

SUSETTE: How did your meeting go with Mr. Schmidt yesterday?

LEONARDO: Well, uh, it went . . . aaah . . . it was no big deal.

SUSETTE: It looks as if you're pretty upset about it.

LEONARDO: Yeah, I am. It was a totally frustrating experience. I, uh, well, let's just say I would like to forget the whole thing.

SUSETTE: Things must not have gone as well as you had hoped they would.

LEONARDO: I'll say! That guy was impossible. I thought the plans I submitted were very clear and well thought out. Then he rejected the entire package.

SUSETTE: You mean he didn't accept any of them?

LEONARDO: You got it.

SUSETTE: I've seen your work before, Leonardo. You've always done a first-rate job. It's hard for me to figure out why your plans were rejected by Schmidt. What did he say about them?

LEONARDO: He said they were unrealistic and too difficult to implement, and . . .

SUSETTE: Really?

ANALYSIS

LEONARDO: Yeah, and when he said that I felt he was attacking me personally. But, on the other hand, I was also angry because I thought my plans were very good, and, you know, I paid close attention to every detail in those plans.

SUSETTE: I'm certain that you did.

LEONARDO: It just really ticks me off.

SUSETTE: I'll bet it does. I would be upset, too.

LEONARDO: Schmidt has something against me.

SUSETTE: After all the effort you put into those plans, you still couldn't figure out whether Schmidt was rejecting you or your plans, right?

LEONARDO: Yeah. Right. How could you tell?

SUSETTE: I can really understand your confusion and uncertainty when you felt Schmidt's actions were unreasonable.

LEONARDO: I just don't understand why he did what he did.

SUSETTE: Sure. If he said your plans were unrealistic, what does that mean? I mean, how can you deal with a rationale like that? It's just too general—meaningless, even. Did he mention anything specific? Did you ask him to point out some problems or explain the reasons for his rejection more clearly?

LEONARDO: Good point, but, uh, you know . . . I was so disappointed at the rejection that I was kinda like in outer space. You know what I mean?

SUSETTE: Yeah. It's an incapacitating experience. You have so much invested personally that you try to divest as fast as you can to save what little self-respect is left.

LEONARDO: That's it all right. I just wanted to get out of there before I said something I would be sorry for.

SUSETTE: Yet, in the back of your mind, you probably figured that Schmidt wouldn't risk the company's future just because he didn't like you personally. But then, well . . . the plans were good! It's hard to deal with that contradiction on the spot, isn't it?

LEONARDO: Exactly. I knew I should have pushed him for more information, but, uh, I just stood there like a dummy. But what can you do about it now? It's spilled milk.

SUSETTE: I don't think it's a total loss, Leonardo. I mean, from what you have told me—what he said and what you said—I don't think that a conclusion can be reached. Maybe he doesn't understand the plans, or maybe it was just his off day. Who knows? It could be a lot of things. What would you think about pinning Schmidt down by asking for his objections, point by point? Do you think it would help to talk to him again?

LEONARDO: Well, I would sure know a lot more than I know now. As it is, I wouldn't know where to begin revising or modifying the plans. And you're right, I really don't know what Schmidt thinks about me or my work. Sometimes I just react and interpret with little or no evidence.

SUSETTE: Maybe, uh . . . maybe another meeting would be a good thing, then.

LEONARDO: Well, I guess I should get off my duff and schedule an appointment with him for next week. I am curious to find out what the problem is, with the plans, or me. (Pause) Thanks, Susette, for helping me work through this thing.

Discussion Questions

1. Categorize each statement in the case according to the supportive communication characteristic or type of response it represents. For example, the first statement by Leonardo obviously is not very congruent, but the second one is much more so.

2. Which statements in the conversation were most helpful? Which were least helpful, or could have produced defensiveness or closed off the conversation?

3. If you were the coach of Susette, how would you assist her in being more competent as a supportive communicator? How would you coach Leonardo to be more supportive even though it is he who faces the problem?

EXERCISES FOR DIAGNOSING COMMUNICATION PROBLEMS AND FOSTERING UNDERSTANDING

United Chemical Company

The role of manager encompasses not only one-on-one coaching and counseling with an employee but also frequently entails helping other people understand coaching and counseling principles for themselves. Sometimes it means refereeing interactions and, by example, helping other people learn about correct principles of supportive communication. This is part of the task in this exercise. In a group setting, coaching and counseling become more difficult because multiple messages, driven by multiple motives, interact. Skilled supportive communicators, however, help each group member feel supported and understood in the interaction, even though the solution to an issue may not always be the one he or she would have preferred.

Assignment

In this exercise you should apply the principles of supportive communication you have read about in the chapter. First, you will need to form groups of four people each. Next, read the case and assign the following roles in your group: Max, Marquita, Keeshaun, and an observer. Assume that a meeting is being held with Max, Marquita, and Keeshaun immediately after the end of the incidents in the following case. Play the roles you have been assigned and try to resolve the problems. The observer should provide feedback to the three players at the end of the exercise. An Observer's Feedback Form can be found at the end of the chapter.

The Case

The United Chemical Company is a large producer and distributor of commodity chemicals, with five production plants in the United States. The main plant in Baytown, Texas, is not only a production plant but also the company's research and engineering center.

The process design group consists of eight male engineers and their supervisor, Max Kane. The group has worked together steadily for a number of years, and good relationships have developed among all the members. When the workload began to increase, Max hired a new design engineer, Marquita Davis, a recent master's degree graduate from one of the foremost engineering schools in the country. Marquita was assigned to a project that would expand the capacity of one of the existing plant facilities. Three other design engineers were assigned to the project along with Marquita: Keeshaun Keller (age 38, 15 years with the company), Sam Sims (age 40, 10 years with the company), and Lance Madison (age 32, 8 years with the company).

As a new employee, Marquita was very enthusiastic about the opportunity to work at United. She liked her work very much because it was challenging and it offered her a chance to apply much of the knowledge she had gained in her university studies. On the job, Marquita kept mostly to herself and her design work. Her relations with her fellow project members were friendly, but she did not go out of her way to have informal conversations with them during or after working hours.

PRACTICE

Marquita was a diligent employee who took her work seriously. On occasions when a difficult problem arose, she would stay after hours in order to come up with a solution. Because of her persistence, coupled with her more current education, Marquita usually completed her portion of the various project stages several days ahead of her colleagues. This was somewhat irritating to her because on these occasions she had to go to Max to ask for additional work to keep her busy until her coworkers caught up to her. Initially, she had offered to help Keeshaun, Sam, and Lance with their assignments, but each time she was abruptly turned down.

About five months after Marquita had joined the design group, Keeshaun asked to see Max about a problem the group was having. The conversation between Max and Keeshaun went as follows:

MAX: Keeshaun, I understand you want to discuss a problem with me.

KEESHAUN: Yes, Max, I don't want to waste your time, but some of the other design engineers want me to discuss Marquita with you. She is irritating everyone with her know-it-all, pompous attitude. She's just not the kind of person we want to work with.

MAX: I can't understand that, Keeshaun. She's an excellent worker, and her design work is always well done and usually flawless. She's doing everything the company wants her to do.

KEESHAUN: The company never asked her to disrupt the morale of the group or to tell us how to do our work. The animosity in our group could eventually result in lower-quality work for the whole unit.

MAX: I'll tell you what I'll do. Marquita has a meeting with me next week to discuss her six-month performance. I'll keep your thoughts in mind, but I can't promise an improvement in what you and the others believe is a pompous attitude.

KEESHAUN: Immediate improvement in her behavior is not the problem; it's her coaching others when she has no right to. She publicly shows others what to do. You'd think she was lecturing an advance class in design with all her high-powered, useless equations and formulas. She'd better back off soon, or some of us will quit or transfer.

During the next week, Max thought carefully about his meeting with Keeshaun. He knew that Keeshaun was the informal leader of the design engineers and generally spoke for the other group members. On Thursday of the following week, Max called Marquita into his office for her mid-year review. One portion of the conversation went as follows:

MAX: There is one other aspect I'd like to discuss with you about your performance. As I just related to you, your technical performance has been excellent; however, there are some questions about your relationships with the other workers.

MARQUITA: I don't understand. What questions are you talking about?

MAX: Well, to be specific, certain members of the design group have complained about your apparent "know-it-all attitude" and the manner in which you try to tell them how to do their job. You're going to have to be patient with them and not publicly call them out about their performance. This is a good group of engineers, and their work over the years has been more than acceptable. I don't want any problems that will cause the group to produce less effectively.

MARQUITA: Let me make a few comments. First of all, I have never publicly criticized their performance to them or to you. Initially, when I finished ahead of them, I offered to help them with their work but was bluntly told to mind my own business. I took the hint and concentrated only on my part of the work. What you don't understand is that after five months of working in this group I have come to the conclusion that what is going on is a rip-off of the company. The other engineers are goldbricking; they're setting a work pace much slower than they're capable of. They're more interested in the music from Sam's radio, the local football team, and the bar they're going to go to for TGIF. I'm sorry, but this is just not the way I was raised or trained. And finally, they've never looked on me as a qualified engineer, but as a woman who has broken their professional barrier.

SOURCE: SZILAGYI, ORGANIZATIONAL BEHAVIOR AND PERFORMANCE, THIRD EDITION, 3rd, © 1983. Electronically reproduced by permission of Pearson Education, Inc. Upper Saddle River, New Jersey.

Byron vs. Thomas

Effective one-on-one coaching and counseling are skills that are required in many settings in life, not just in management. It is hard to imagine a parent, roommate, Little League coach, room mother, or good friend who would not benefit from training in supportive communication. Because there are so many aspects of supportive communication, however, it is sometimes difficult to remember all of them. That is why practice, with observation and feedback, is so important. These attributes of supportive communication can become a natural part of your interaction approach as you conscientiously practice and receive feedback from a colleague.

Assignment

In the following exercise, one individual should take the role of Hal Byron, and another should take the role of Judy Thomas. To make the role-play realistic, do not read each other's role descriptions. When you have finished reading, hold a meeting between Hal Byron and Judy Thomas. A third person should serve as the observer. An Observer's Feedback Form to assist in providing feedback is at the end of the chapter.

Hal Byron, Department Head

You are Hal Byron, head of the operations group—the "back room"—in a large bank corporation. This is your second year on the job, and you have moved up rather quickly in the bank. You enjoy working for this firm, which has a reputation for being one of the finest in the region. One reason is that outside opportunities for management development and training are funded by the bank. In addition, each employee is given an opportunity for a personal management interview each month, and these sessions are usually both productive and developmental.

One of the department members, Judy Thomas, has been in this department for 19 years, 15 of them in the same job. She is reasonably good at what she does, and she is always punctual and efficient. She tends to get to work earlier than most employees in order to peruse the *American Banker* and *USA Today*. You can almost set your watch by the time Judy visits the rest room during the day and by the time she makes her phone call to her daughter every afternoon.

Your feeling about Judy is that although she is a good worker, she lacks imagination and initiative. This has been indicated by her lack of merit increases over the last five years and by the fact that she has had the same job for 15 years. She's content to do just what is assigned, nothing more. Your predecessor must have given hints to Judy that she might be in line for a promotion, however, because Judy has raised this with you more than once. Because she has been in her job so long, she is at the top of her pay range, and without a promotion, she cannot receive a salary adjustment above the basic cost-of-living increase.

The one thing Judy does beyond the basic minimum job requirements is to help train young people who come into the department. She is very patient and methodical with them, and she seems to take pride in helping them learn the ropes. She has not been hesitant to point out this contribution to you. Unfortunately, this activity does not qualify Judy for a promotion, nor could she be transferred into the training and development department. Once you suggested that she take a few courses at the local college, paid for by the bank, but she

PRACTICE

matter-of-factly stated that she was too old to go to school. You surmise that she might be intimidated because she doesn't have a college degree.

As much as you would like to promote Judy, there just doesn't seem to be any way to do that in good conscience. You have tried putting additional work under her control, but she seems to be slowing down in her productivity rather than speeding up. The work needs to get done, and expanding her role just puts you behind schedule.

This interview coming up is probably the time to level with Judy about her performance and her potential. You certainly don't want to lose her as an employee, but there is not going to be a change in job assignment for a long time unless she changes her performance dramatically.

Judy Thomas, Department Member

You are a member of the operations group in a large bank corporation. You have been with the bank now for 19 years, 15 of them in the same job. You enjoy the company because of its friendly climate and because of its prestigious image in the region. It's nice to be known as an employee of this firm. However, lately you have become more dissatisfied as you've seen person after person come into the bank and get promoted ahead of you. Your own boss, Hal Byron, is almost 20 years your junior. Another woman who joined the bank the same time you did is now a senior vice president. You can't understand why you've been neglected. You are efficient and accurate in your work, you have a near-perfect attendance record, and you consider yourself to be a good employee. You have gone out of your way on many occasions to help train and orient young people who are just joining the bank. Several of them have written letters later telling you how important your help was in getting them promoted. A lot of good that does you!

The only thing you can figure out is that there is a bias against you because you haven't graduated from college. On the other hand, others have moved up without a diploma. You haven't taken advantage of any college courses paid for by the bank, but after a long day at work, you're not inclined to go to class for another three hours. Besides, you only see your family in the evenings, and you don't want to take time away from them. It doesn't take a college degree to do your job, anyway.

Your monthly personal management interview is coming up with your department head, Hal Byron, and you've decided the time has come to get a few answers. Several things need explaining. Not only haven't you been promoted, but you haven't even received a merit increase for five years. You're not getting any credit for the extra contributions you make with new employees, nor for your steady, reliable work. Could anyone blame you for being a little bitter?

Active Listening Exercise

Form a trio of colleagues who hold differing opinions about any of the following topics. Hold a 10- or 15-minute conversation about any of the topics. Take a position on the issue. Make a case for your point of view. Convince your partners that you are right. When you are finished, complete the short questionnaire below, and discuss the results together. Offer any helpful feedback to your colleagues that you think may be appropriate.

1. Should the United States have invaded Iraq in 2003?
2. Should late-term abortions be performed?
3. Is global warming a critical issue?
4. Should the United States prosecute and deport illegal aliens?
5. Should English become the national language in the United States?
6. Does the international media have a liberal bias, and does it matter either way?

7. Are business school rankings helpful or harmful?
8. Who is the world's most dangerous person?
9. Should professional athletes be allowed to compete in the Olympics?
10. Should the United Nations exist?

Rate your two colleagues on the following items using this response scale:

1 = *Strongly disagree*
2 = *Disagree*
3 = *Neither*
4 = *Agree*
5 = *Strongly agree*

ITEM	COLLEAGUE 1	COLLEAGUE 2
My colleague . . .		
1. Maintained eye contact and interest	1 2 3 4 5	1 2 3 4 5
2. Used inquiry more than advocacy	1 2 3 4 5	1 2 3 4 5
3. Interrupted	1 2 3 4 5	1 2 3 4 5
4. Displayed appropriate emotional engagement	1 2 3 4 5	1 2 3 4 5
5. Used a variety of response types	1 2 3 4 5	1 2 3 4 5
6. Used reflective responses	1 2 3 4 5	1 2 3 4 5

Reverse the scoring for item 3, and add up the scores for each colleague. Provide those scores to one another and discuss the results. Provide helpful feedback to one another.

PRACTICE

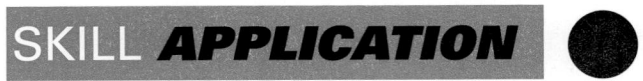

SKILL *APPLICATION*

ACTIVITIES FOR COMMUNICATING SUPPORTIVELY

Suggested Assignments

1. Tape record an interview with someone such as a coworker, friend, or spouse. Focus on an issue or challenge faced right now by that person. Diagnose the situation to determine if you should be a coach or a counselor. (Our bet is that it will be the latter.) Conduct a conversation in which you apply the principles of supportive communication discussed in the chapter. (The Rejected Plans case provides an example of such an interview.) Use the tape to determine how you could improve your own supportive communication skill.

2. Teach someone you know the concepts of supportive communication and supportive listening. Provide your own explanations and illustrations so the person understands what you are talking about. Describe your experience in your journal.

3. Identify a person with whom you have had a disagreement, some difficulty in the past, or some discomfort in your relationship. This could be a roommate, parent, friend, or instructor. Approach that person and ask to hold a conversation in which you discuss the interpersonal problem. To be successful, you'll discover how crucial supportive communication is in the conversation. When you have finished, write up the experience in as much detail as possible. What did you say and what did the other person say? What was especially effective and what didn't work so well? Identify areas in which you need to improve.

4. Write two mini–case studies. One should recount an effective coaching or counseling situation. The other should recount an ineffective coaching or counseling situation. The cases should be based on a real event, either from your own personal experience or from the experience of someone you know well. Use principles of supportive communication and listening in your cases.

Application Plan and Evaluation

The intent of this exercise is to help you apply this cluster of skills in a real-life, out-of-class setting. Now that you have become familiar with the behavioral guidelines that form the basis of effective skill performance, you will improve most by trying out those guidelines in an everyday context. Unlike a classroom activity, in which feedback is immediate and others can assist you with their evaluations, this skill application activity is one you must accomplish and evaluate on your own. There are two parts to this activity. Part 1 helps prepare you to apply the skill. Part 2 helps you evaluate and improve on your experience. Be sure to write down answers to each item. Don't short-circuit the process by skipping steps.

Part 1. Planning

1. Write down the two or three aspects of this skill that are most important to you. These may be areas of weakness, areas you most want to improve, or areas that are most salient to a problem you face right now. Identify the specific aspects of this skill that you want to apply.

2. Now identify the setting or the situation in which you will apply this skill. Establish a plan for performance by actually writing down a description of the situation. Who else will be involved? When will you do it? Where will it be done?

   Circumstances:
   Who else?
   When?
   Where?

3. Identify the specific behaviors in which you will engage to apply this skill. Operationalize your skill performance.

4. What are the indicators of successful performance? How will you know you have been effective? What will indicate you have performed competently?

Part 2. Evaluation

5. After you have completed your implementation, record the results. What happened? How successful were you? What was the effect on others?

6. How can you improve? What modifications can you make next time? What will you do differently in a similar situation in the future?

7. Looking back on your whole skill practice and application experience, what have you learned? What has been surprising? In what ways might this experience help you in the long term?

APPLICATION

Communicating Supportively

Scoring Key

SKILL AREA	ITEMS	ASSESSMENT PRE-	POST-
Knowledge of Coaching and Counseling	1, 2, 20	_____	_____
Providing Effective Negative Feedback	3, 4, 5, 6, 7, 8	_____	_____
Communicating Supportively	9, 10, 11, 12, 13, 14, 15, 16, 17, 18, 19	_____	_____
	Total Score	_____	_____

Comparison Data (N = 1,500 Students)

Compare your scores to three standards:
1. The maximum possible score = 120
2. The scores of other students in the class.
3. Norm data from more than 1,500 business school students.

Pre-Test				**Post-Test**
90.91	=	mean	=	99.75
99 or above	=	top quartile	=	108–120
92–98	=	second quartile	=	100–107
84–91	=	third quartile	=	93–99
83 or below	=	bottom quartile	=	92 or below

Communication Styles

Comparison Data

Identify the type of response pattern that you rely on the most by adding the numbers you gave to each response alternative in Part I. The chapter discusses the advantages and disadvantages of each of these response types. The most skilled supportive communicators score 9 or above on Reflecting responses and 6 or above on Probing responses. They score 2 or less on Advising responses and 4 or less on Deflecting responses.

In Part II, circle the alternative that you chose. The most skilled supportive communicators select alternatives 1a, 2b, 3a, 4b, and 5a.

Part I

1. a. Deflecting response
   b. Probing response
   c. Advising response
   d. Reflecting response
   e. Deflecting response

2.   a. Reflecting response

    b. Deflecting response

    c. Advising response

    d. Reflecting response

    e. Probing response

3.   a. Probing response

    b. Deflecting response

    c. Advising response

    d. Reflecting response

    e. Probing response

4.   a. Reflecting response

    b. Probing response

    c. Deflecting response

    d. Deflecting response

    e. Advising response

Part II

1.   a. Problem-oriented statement

    b. Person-oriented statement

2.   a. Incongruent–minimizing statement

    b. Congruent statement

3.   a. Descriptive statement

    b. Evaluative statement

4.   a. Invalidating statement

    b. Validating statement

5.   a. Owned statement

    b. Disowned statement

SKILL PRACTICE Diagnosing Problems and Fostering Understanding: United Chemical Company and Byron vs. Thomas

Observer's Feedback Form

As the observer, rate the extent to which each of the role players displayed the following behaviors effectively. Use the following numerical rating scale for each person. Identify specific things that each person can do to improve his or her performance.

1 = Strongly disagree

2 = Disagree

3 = Neither

4 = Agree

5 = Strongly agree

COMMUNICATION ATTRIBUTE	ROLE 1	ROLE 2	ROLE 3
1. Communicated congruently.	_____	_____	_____
2. Used descriptive communication.	_____	_____	_____

SCORING KEYS AND COMPARISON DATA

	Role 1	Role 2	Role 3
3. Used problem-oriented communication.	_____	_____	_____
4. Used validating communication.	_____	_____	_____
5. Used specific and qualified communication.	_____	_____	_____
6. Used conjunctive communication.	_____	_____	_____

COMMUNICATION ATTRIBUTE	ROLE 1	ROLE 2	ROLE 3
7. Owned statements and used personal words.	_____	_____	_____
8. Listened inventively.	_____	_____	_____
9. Used a variety of response alternatives appropriately.	_____	_____	_____

Comments:

SKILL *ASSESSMENT*

- Gaining Power and Influence
- Using Influence Strategies

SKILL *LEARNING*

- Building a Strong Power Base and Using Influence Wisely
- A Balanced View of Power
- Strategies for Gaining Organizational Power
- Transforming Power into Influence
- Summary
- Behavioral Guidelines

SKILL *ANALYSIS*

- River Woods Plant Manager

SKILL *PRACTICE*

- Repairing Power Failures in Management Circuits
- Ann Lyman's Proposal
- Cindy's Fast Foods
- 9:00 to 7:30

SKILL *APPLICATION*

- Suggested Assignments
- Application Plan and Evaluation

SCORING KEYS AND *COMPARISON DATA*

5

Gaining Power and Influence

SKILL DEVELOPMENT OBJECTIVES

- ENHANCE PERSONAL AND POSITION POWER
- USE INFLUENCE APPROPRIATELY TO ACCOMPLISH EXCEPTIONAL WORK
- NEUTRALIZE INAPPROPRIATE INFLUENCE ATTEMPTS

DIAGNOSTIC SURVEYS FOR GAINING POWER AND INFLUENCE

GAINING POWER AND INFLUENCE

Step 1: Before you read this chapter, respond to the following statements by writing a number from the rating scale that follows in the left-hand column (Pre-assessment). Your answers should reflect your attitudes and behavior as they are now, not as you would like them to be. Be honest. This instrument is designed to help you discover your level of competency in gaining power and influence so you can tailor your learning to your specific needs. When you have completed the survey, use the scoring key at the end of the chapter to identify the skill areas discussed in this chapter that are most important for you to master.

Step 2: After you have completed the reading and the exercises in this chapter and, ideally, as many of the Skill Application assignments at the end of this chapter as you can, cover up your first set of answers. Then respond to the same statements again, this time in the right-hand column (Post-assessment). When you have completed the survey, use the scoring key at the end of the chapter to measure your progress. If your score remains low in specific skill areas, use the behavioral guidelines at the end of the Skill Learning section to guide your further practice.

Rating Scale

1 Strongly disagree
2 Disagree
3 Slightly disagree
4 Slightly agree
5 Agree
6 Strongly agree

Assessment

Pre-   Post-

In a situation in which it is important to obtain more power:

_____ _____ 1. I strive to become highly proficient in my line of work.

_____ _____ 2. I express friendliness, honesty, and sincerity toward those with whom I work.

_____ _____ 3. I put forth more effort and take more initiative than expected in my work.

_____ _____ 4. I support organizational ceremonial events and activities.

_____ _____ 5. I form a broad network of relationships with people throughout the organization at all levels.

_____ _____ 6. I send personal notes to others when they accomplish something significant or when I pass along important information to them.

_____ _____ 7. In my work I strive to generate new ideas, initiate new activities, and minimize routine tasks.

_____ _____ 8. I try to find ways to be an external representative for my unit or organization.

_____ _____ 9. I am continually upgrading my skills and knowledge.

_____ _____ 10. I strive to enhance my personal appearance.

_____ _____ 11. I work harder than most coworkers.

_____ _____ 12. I encourage new members to support important organizational values by both their words and their actions.

_____ _____ 13. I gain access to important information by becoming central in communication networks.

_____ _____ 14. I strive to find opportunities to make reports about my work, especially to senior people.

_____ _____ 15. I maintain variety in the tasks that I do.

_____ _____ 16. I keep my work connected to the central mission of the organization.

When trying to influence someone for a specific purpose:

_____ _____ 17. I emphasize reason and factual information.

_____ _____ 18. I feel comfortable using a variety of different influence techniques, matching them to specific circumstances.

_____ _____ 19. I reward others for agreeing with me, thereby establishing a condition of reciprocity.

_____ _____ 20. I use a direct, straightforward approach rather than an indirect or manipulative one.

_____ _____ 21. I avoid using threats or demands to impose my will on others.

When resisting an inappropriate influence attempt directed at me:

_____ _____ 22. I use resources and information I control to equalize demands and threats.

_____ _____ 23. I refuse to bargain with individuals who use high-pressure negotiation tactics.

_____ _____ 24. I explain why I can't comply with reasonable-sounding requests by pointing out how the consequences would affect my responsibilities and obligations.

When trying to influence those above me in the organization:

_____ _____ 25. I help determine the issues to which they pay attention by effectively selling the importance of those issues.

_____ _____ 26. I convince them that the issues on which I want to focus are compatible with the goals and future success of the organization.

_____ _____ 27. I help them solve problems that they didn't expect me to help solve.

_____ _____ 28. I work as hard to make them look good and be successful as I do for my own success.

USING INFLUENCE STRATEGIES

Indicate, by writing the appropriate number in the blank, how often you use each of the following strategies for getting others to comply with your wishes. Choose from a scale of 1 to 5, with 1 being "rarely," 3 being "sometimes," and 5 being "always." After you have completed the survey, use the scoring key at the end of the chapter to tabulate your results.

_____ 1. "If you don't comply, I'll make you regret it."

_____ 2. "If you comply, I will reward you."

_____ 3. "These facts demonstrate the merit of my position."

_____ 4. "Others in the group have agreed; what is your decision?"

_____ 5. "People you value will think better (worse) of you if you do (do not) comply."

_____   6. "The group needs your help, so do it for the good of us all."

_____   7. "I will stop nagging you if you comply."

_____   8. "You owe me compliance because of past favors."

_____   9. "This is what I need; will you help out?"

_____   10. "If you don't act now, you'll lose this opportunity."

_____   11. "I have moderated my initial position; now I expect you to be equally reasonable."

_____   12. "This request is consistent with other decisions you've made."

_____   13. "If you don't agree to help out, the consequences will be harmful to others."

_____   14. "I'm only requesting a small commitment [now]."

_____   15. "Compliance will enable you to reach a personally important objective."

Building a Strong Power Base and Using Influence Wisely

"The difference between someone who can get an idea off the ground and accepted in an organization and someone who can't isn't a question of who has the better idea. It's a question of who has political competence. Political competence isn't something you're born with, but a skill you learn. It's an out-in-the-open process of methodically mapping the political terrain, building coalitions, and leading them to get your idea adopted." So says Samuel Bacharach, a Cornell University professor who has spent his career negotiating the halls of powerful New York businesses and labor unions (Bacharach, 2005, p. 93).

The skill of political competence is particularly relevant for today's workforce, which, according to a recent *Fortune* magazine report, includes large numbers of "fearless and ambitious unseasoned twenty-somethings flooding the managerial job market." These new managers are taking positions traditionally reserved for battle-tested pros who understand from experience the ins and outs of gaining power and influence. Nearly 12 percent of employed 20- to 34-year-olds held management positions in 1998. These young, inexperienced managers report difficulties managing "up"—getting their bosses to respect them—as well as managing "down"—getting their older subordinates to respect their position (Leger, 2000).

Professor John Kotter of Harvard University, who teaches a course on power, agrees with this assessment. "It makes me sick to hear economists tell students that their job is to maximize shareholder profits," he says. "Their job is going to be managing a whole host of constituencies: bosses, underlings, customers, suppliers, unions, you name it. Trying to get cooperation from different constituencies is an infinitely more difficult task than milking your business for money" (Gelman, 1985).

Bogdan J. Dawidowicz, a young senior systems analyst at General Motors, is grateful he took Professor Kotter's course during his Harvard MBA program. He credits it for his ability to handle extremely delicate assignments. For example, when he was told to evaluate product scheduling at a GM plant, he knew that plant management would not take kindly to an outsider's disrupting their routine, demanding information, and critiquing their performance. So he called the plant superintendent and enlisted his support. Following an extended discussion, the superintendent took the lead in scheduling appointments with his staff and compiling all the necessary information prior to the visit (Buell & Cowan, 1985).

A Balanced View of Power

It should come as no surprise that many authorities argue that the effective use of power is the most critical element of management. One such authority, Warren Bennis, seeking the quintessential ingredients of effective leaders, interviewed 90 individuals who had been nominated by peers as the most influential leaders in all walks of our society. Bennis found that these individuals shared one significant characteristic: They made others feel powerful. These leaders were powerful because they had learned how to build a strong power base in their organizations or institutions. They were influential because they used their power to help peers and subordinates accomplish exceptional tasks. It requires no particular power, skill, or genius to accomplish the ordinary. But it is difficult to do the truly unusual without political clout (Bennis & Nanus, 2003).

LACK OF POWER

John Gardner has observed, "In this country—and in most democracies—power has such a bad name that many people persuade themselves they want nothing to do with it" (1990). For these people, power is a "four-letter word," conjuring up images of vindictive, domineering bosses and manipulative, cunning subordinates. It is associated with dirty office politics engaged in by ruthless individuals who use as their handbooks for corporate guerrilla warfare books such as *Winning Through Intimidation*, and who subscribe to the philosophy of Heinrich von Treitschke: "Your neighbor, even though he may look upon you as a natural ally against another power which is feared by you both, is always ready, at the first opportunity, as soon as it can be done with safety, to better himself at your expense. . . . Whoever fails to increase his power, must decrease it, if others increase theirs" (Korda, 1991, p. 4).

Those with a distaste for power argue that teaching managers and prospective managers how to increase their power is tantamount to sanctioning the use of primitive forms of domination. They support this argument by noting the nasty political fight between Lewis Glucksman and Peter Peterson for control of Lehman Brothers that cost Lehman its independence; the conflict between cofounders Steven Jobs and John Sculley that turned Apple Computer into a battleground; and the firing of Frank Biondi, the president of Viacom, by its power-hungry chairperson Sumner Redstone.

This negative view of "personal power" is especially common in cultures that place a high value on ascription, rather than achievement, and on collectivism, rather than individualism (Triandis, 1994; Trompenaars, 1996). People who view interpersonal relations through the lens of ascription believe that power resides in stable, personal characteristics, such as age, gender, level of education, ethnic background, or social class. Hence, focusing the attention of organizational members on "getting ahead," "taking charge," and "making things happen" seems contrary to the natural social order. Those who place a high value on collectivism are also likely to feel uncomfortable with our approach, but for a different reason. Their concern would be that placing too much emphasis on increasing a single individual's power might not be in the best interests of the larger group.

We acknowledge that this chapter has a very "American" orientation. Consequently, it might not be an appropriate skill development framework for all readers. For those who feel uncomfortable modeling their own behavior after the principles and guidelines in this chapter, we suggest you think of this as a useful "translation guide" for helping you understand how American business managers view power and how American corporations treat power. In addition, we hope that readers who might be tempted to assume that our approach is the only reasonable approach will understand that they are likely to interact with individuals from different cultures who will probably believe that some of these strategies are ineffective and/or inappropriate.

There are many American business leaders and scholars who make a persuasive case for operating from a position of power in an organization. Robert Dilenschneider, president and chief executive officer (CEO) of a leading public relations firm, states: "The use of influence is itself not negative. It can often lead to a great good. Like any powerful force—from potent medicine to nuclear power—it is the morality with which influence is used that makes all the difference" (Dilenschneider, 1990, p. xviii). Power need not be associated with aggression, brute force, craftiness, or deceit. Power can also be viewed as a sign of personal efficacy. It is the ability to mobilize resources to accomplish productive work. People with power shape their environment, whereas the powerless are molded by theirs. Rollo May, in *Power and Innocence* (1998), suggests that those who are unwilling to exercise power and influence are condemned to experience unhappiness throughout their lives.

There is nothing more demoralizing than feeling you have a creative new idea or a unique insight into a significant organizational problem and then coming face-to-face with your organizational impotence. This face of power is seen by many young college graduates, who annually flood the corporate job market. They are energetic, optimistic, and supremely confident that their "awesome" ability, state-of-the-art training, and indefatigable energy will rocket them up the corporate ladder. However, many soon become discouraged and embittered. They blame "the old guard" for protecting their turf and not being open to new ideas. Their feelings of frustration prompt many to look for greener pastures of opportunity in other companies—only to be confronted anew with rejection and failure. One such "victim" stated dejectedly, "Hell is knowing you have a better solution than someone else but not being able to get the votes."

These individuals learn quickly that only the naive believe that the best recommendation always gets selected, the most capable individual always gets the promotion, and the deserving unit gets its fair share of the budget. These are political decisions heavily influenced by the interests of the powerful.

Astute managers understand that in the long run no one benefits from lopsided distributions of power. One seasoned veteran of organizational power games summarized his experience: "Powerless members of an organization either get angry and try to tear down the system, or they become apathetic and withdraw. Either way, everyone loses."

Rosabeth Kanter (1979) has pointed out that powerful managers not only can accomplish more personally, but can also pass on more information and make more resources available to subordinates. For this reason, people tend to prefer bosses with "clout." Subordinates tend to feel that they have higher status in an organization and their morale is higher when they perceive that their boss has considerable upward influence. In contrast, Kanter argues, powerlessness tends to foster bossiness, rather than true leadership. "In large organizations,

Table 5.1	Indicators of a Manager's Upward and Outward Power

Powerful managers can

- Intercede favorably on behalf of someone in trouble.
- Get a desirable placement for a talented subordinate.
- Get approval for expenditures beyond the budget.
- Get items on and off the agenda at policy meetings.
- Get fast access to top decision makers.
- Maintain regular, frequent contact with top decision makers.
- Acquire early information about decisions and policy shifts.

Source: *Reprinted by permission of Harvard Business Review. Indicators of a Manager's Upward and Outward Power. From "Power failures in management circuits" by R. Kanter, 57. Copyright © 1979 by the Harvard Business School Publishing Corporation; all rights reserved.*

at least," she notes, "it is powerlessness that often creates ineffective, desultory management and petty, dictatorial, rules-minded managerial styles" (p. 65).

Kanter (1979) has identified several indicators of a manager's upward and outward power in an organization. These are shown in Table 5.1. In some respects, these serve as a set of behavioral objectives for our discussion of power and influence.

ABUSE OF POWER

But what about Lord Acton's well-known dictum, "Power corrupts, and absolute power corrupts absolutely"? Hardly a week goes by that new evidence of this seemingly ageless observation isn't reflected in news headlines. Doesn't that suggest that effective managers should avoid power because "abuse of office," with a likely fall from power, will inevitably follow?

This certainly appears to be an ageless lesson of history. In the Greek plays of Sophocles, for instance, the viewer is confronted with the image of great and powerful rulers transformed by their prior success so that they are filled with a sense of their own worth and importance—with hubris—which causes them to be impatient of the advice of others and unwilling to listen to opinions different from their own. Yet in the end they are destroyed by events that they discover, to their anguish, they cannot control. Oedipus is destroyed soon after the crowds say (and he believes) that "he is almost like a God"; King Creon, at the zenith of his political and military power, is brought down as a result of his unjust and unfeeling belief in the infallibility of his judgments.

Headlines of business trade periodicals regularly trumpet claims of modern-day hubris among business elites (Bunker, Kram, & Ting, 2002). One of the most frequently mentioned examples is the "slash and burn" management style of Al Dunlap at Scott Paper and Sunbeam Electric. He takes pride in being responsible for thousands of employees losing their jobs while he takes home multimillion-dollar bonuses (DeGeorge, 1999).

Sophocles warns us never to be envious of the powerful until we see the nature of their endings. Support for the modern-day relevance of this timeless warning that arrogance tends to be self-checking is reflected in the results of studies of both successful and failed corporate executives (McCall & Lombardo, 1983; Shipper & Dillard, 2000). In the first study of its kind, scholars at the Center for Creative Leadership identified approximately 20 executives who had risen to the top of their firms and matched them with a similar group of 20 executives who had failed to reach their career aspirations. Earlier, both groups had entered their respective organizations with equal promise. There were no noticeable differences in their preparation, expertise, education, and so forth. However, over time, the second group's careers had become "derailed" by the personal inadequacies shown in Table 5.2.

It is sobering to note how many of these problems relate to the ineffective use of power in interpersonal relationships. In general, this group tends to support Lord Acton's dictum as well as the warnings of Sophocles. They were given a little authority, and they failed the test of worthy stewardship.

This observation is consistent with the research findings of David McClelland, who has spent many years studying what he considers to be one of the fundamental human needs, the "need for power" (McClelland & Burnham, 2003). According to McClelland, managers

Table 5.2	Characteristics That Derail Managers' Careers

- Insensitive to others; abrasive and intimidating
- Cold, aloof, and arrogant
- Betraying others' trust
- Overly ambitious; playing politics and always trying to move up
- Unable to delegate to others or to build a team
- Overdependent on others (e.g., a mentor)

Source: *REPRODUCED WITH PERMISSION From Psychology Today, Copyright © 2006 www.psychologytoday.com.*

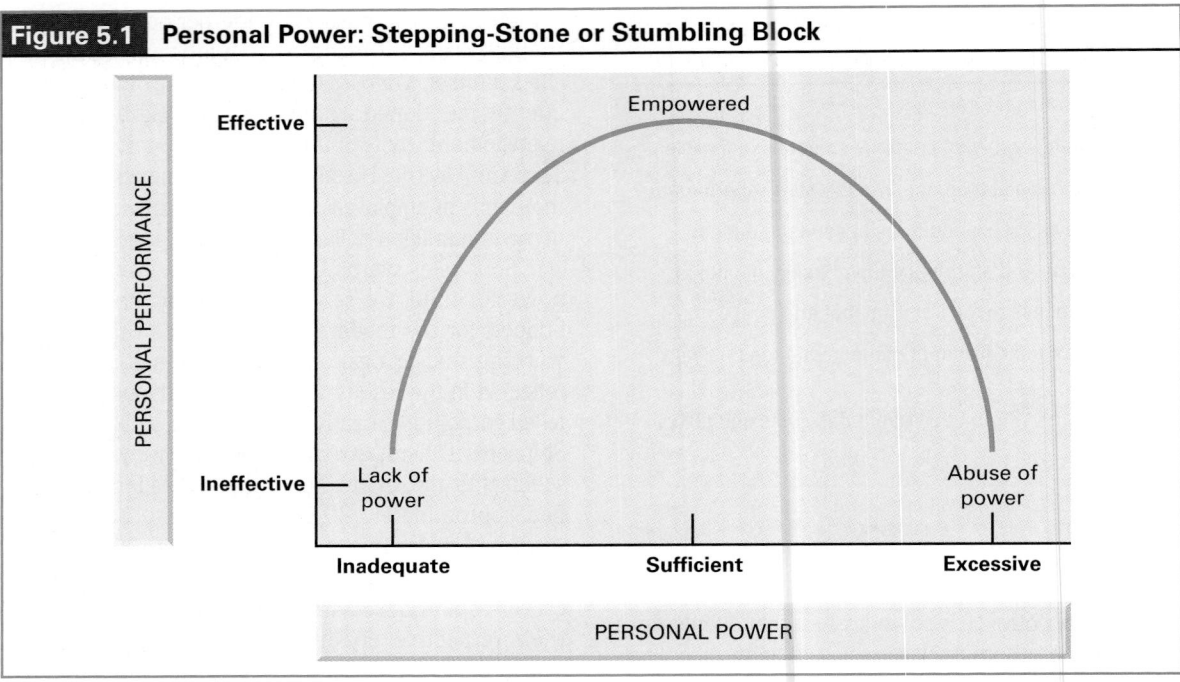

Figure 5.1 | **Personal Power: Stepping-Stone or Stumbling Block**

PERSONAL PERFORMANCE

Effective — Empowered

Ineffective — Lack of power — Abuse of power

Inadequate — Sufficient — Excessive

PERSONAL POWER

with an *institutional power* orientation use their power to advance the goals of the organization, whereas those with a *personal power* view of power tend to use their power for personal gain. For example, he found that although leaders with both orientations are likely to exhort their subordinates to engage in heroic endeavors, the "institutional power" leaders tend to link those efforts to organizational objectives, whereas the "personal power" leaders are more likely to use their subordinates' accomplishments to further enhance their own power base.

The relationship between power and personal effectiveness that we have described is depicted in Figure 5.1. Both a lack of power and the abuse of power are equally debilitating and counterproductive. In contrast, empowerment uses sufficient amounts of personal power to achieve high levels of effectiveness.

The purpose of this chapter is to help managers "stay on top of the power curve," as represented by the indicators of organizational power reported by Kanter in Table 5.1. This is accomplished with the aid of two specific management skills:

1. Gaining power (overcoming feelings of power-lessness)
2. Converting power effectively into interpersonal influence in ways that avoid the abuse of power

Strategies for Gaining Organizational Power

We will define power as the potential to influence behavior. This is an important departure from a more traditional definition that focuses on authority-based control of behavior, as in "powerful" bosses having authority over their subordinates or "powerful" parents having control over their children. We believe there are several trends in organizations that warrant this shift in the definition of power from "having authority over others" to "being able to get things done."

THE NECESSITY OF POWER AND EMPOWERMENT

Our discussion to this point should be viewed as a cautionary warning, reminiscent of similar concerns expressed about the potential harm resulting from the unintentional, improper use of medicine or the deliberate, harmful misapplication of powerful information technologies. Despite these legitimate concerns, people generally believe in and benefit from medicine and information technologies. The implication for our current discussion is not that we need to avoid the use of power, but that we need to learn how to use it wisely.

1. Organizations are becoming less hierarchical, or flatter, as they downsize layers of management (especially middle managers) and as they outsource work that can be done more cheaply by someone else. Rather than adding to their full-time employment ranks, many organizations are choosing to grow through the use of temporary and part-time workers who can more easily be let go during tough economic times. These leaner organizations are staffed by fewer managers who must learn to yield influence to lower-level employees in order to get the work of the organization done (Stewart, 1992).

2. Information technology, such as computers, is helping to decentralize the flow of information to lower levels of the organizational hierarchy. This not only gives lower-level employees more influence, but also increases their flexibility. Today, more and more workers are telecommuting, or working out of their homes but staying linked to the organization through the use of computers, faxes, and phones. When employees are off-site, managers must cede more decision-making control and discretion to them.

3. Traditional boundaries within and between organizations are becoming blurred. The "boundaryless" organization is becoming in vogue as we see evidence of the virtual organization composed of a network of different entities (Tully, 1993). Such an organization will exist only for the life of a project (say, a motion picture) and then disband upon its completion. These structural changes shift the nature of authority relationships as well.

4. The percentage of the workforce working in companies with fewer than 100 employees is increasing. In a small business where the organization's survival depends on good customer relations, imaginative ideas for new products, and favorable financial agreements with banks, personal characteristics are often the predominant source of power. The work of each employee is highly visible and the unique contribution of the aggressive salesperson or the problem-solving engineer will likely be recognized and rewarded. This may be why we see more and more MBAs choosing to forgo employment with blue-chip firms for smaller, entrepreneurial ventures (Labich, 1995).

Each of these changes is contributing to the evolution of the role of the typical manager from director to coach and mentor. Under these conditions, power is likely to come less from someone's formal position in the organization than from one's ability to perform. The conditions make the notion of empowerment particularly important for your effectiveness in today's organizations.

Two basic factors determine a person's power in an organization: personal attributes and position characteristics. Naturally, the importance of each factor varies depending on the organizational context. For example, position title is extremely important in a strong hierarchical system, such as the military or civil service. The saying "Rank has its privileges" illustrates the fact that in these organizations many rewards are allocated more on the basis of position title than personal performance. However, given the trends noted above, you will notice that our discussion of position power is very nonhierarchical. By this we mean that rather than focusing on the level of authority attached to a position, we focus on the opportunities embedded in a position or a job.

Although the trend in American firms is toward person-based views of power, there are cultural reasons why individuals might prefer a position-based orientation regarding power. Research has shown that people who have been raised in different cultures are likely to hold different views regarding the determinants of success (Chiu, 2001; Choi, Nisbett, & Norenzayan, 1999). Specifically, it has been shown that Eastern cultures encourage contextual, or situational, logic ("He was promoted because he got to know lots of people while working in headquarters"), whereas Western cultures foster personal, or dispositional, explanations ("He was promoted because he is the smartest engineer in the company"). This comparison was summarized by Chiu (1972) as follows: "Chinese are situation-centered. They are obliged to be sensitive to their environment. Americans are individual-centered. They expect their environment to be sensitive to them" (p. 236).

The strength of this "dispositional bias" in Western thought is reflected in research showing that Americans are willing to make very confident predictions about future behavior on the basis of a very small sample of past behavior and that they consistently overestimate the predictive power of personality traits (Choi et al., 1999, p. 55). Psychologists have also observed that Japanese and American college students describe themselves in very different ways. For example, phrases like "I am curious" and "I am sincere" appeared three times more often in the Americans' descriptions. In contrast, Japanese students were far more likely to describe themselves in terms of their social identities (e.g., "I am a Keiyo student") or in terms of a specific context (e.g., "One who plays mah-jongg on Friday nights") (Choi et al., 1999, p. 49).

It is worth noting that there are differences of opinion among organizational scholars regarding the relative importance of these two sources of power: who you are versus where you are (Bolman & Deal, 1997; Kanter, 1979; Kotter, 1977; Pfeffer, 1981, 1992). We have found the distinction between human capital and social capital useful in sorting out these competing claims (Adler & Kwon, 2002; Burt, 1997). **Human capital** refers to an individual's abilities and competencies, whereas **social capital** refers to a person's social connections within and outside an organization. In a sense, this is the difference between saying "I know the answer to that question" versus "I know someone who does." Burt's underlying argument is that managers with high social capital (what we are calling high position power) are in a better position to capitalize on their human capital (personal power) because their social connections allow them to leverage their personal knowledge and abilities. Hence, it makes sense for managers seeking to increase their influence in an organization to increase both sources of power.

SOURCES OF PERSONAL POWER

Four personal characteristics are important sources of power. As Table 5.3 shows, these are *expertise, personal attraction, effort,* and *legitimacy.* Expertise reflects knowledge and capabilities; personal attraction involves affective appeal; effort suggests personal commitment and motivation; and legitimacy conveys credibility.

Expertise

It is self-evident that in an era of technological sophistication expertise is an important source of power. In an e-commerce business environment, in which the most highly sought-after skills are more likely possessed by teenagers who have never had a real job than by their parents who have been working for 20 years, and in which the median age of millionaires will soon be closer

to 30 than to 60, it is hard to dispute the claim that expertise is the ascending "coin of the realm" in business. Increasingly, what you know is more important than who you know in getting a job and what you can do technically is the key to what you can become organizationally. **Expertise**, or work-related knowledge, is the great organizational equalizer because it can come from formal education, self-directed learning, or on-the-job experience. In addition, the universally understood and accessible standard of competence is the basis for evaluation and the antecedent of accomplishment.

Because the preponderance of management positions are not in small "dot-com" companies, but in larger, more diversified businesses, our focus will be on expertise as a source of personal power in that organizational setting. Expertise is especially salient in established business organizations because of their preference for a highly rationalized decision-making process (Bunderson, 2002; Pfeffer, 1977). In an environment in which choices are supposed to be made by objectively considering information supporting each alternative, a person possessing knowledge readily accrues power. This can become problematic when subordinates have more expertise than their bosses. The skillful subordinate makes knowledge available to the superior in a manner that does not threaten the boss' right to make the final decision but at the same time reinforces the subordinate's position as an expert. In essence, expert knowledge is deemed to be reliable information—something decision makers can bank on because it comes from someone whose expertise inspires trust.

That staff specialists gain power by virtue of their expertise points out the importance of examining both position and personal sources of power. If you examined only the position-power of staff specialists, you might conclude that they have very little power. Their role in the organization is not very visible, compared to line management; their jobs are often routine; and their tasks, by themselves, are generally not linked to the most central objectives and concerns of the firm. However, a staff specialist can compensate for weak

Table 5.3	Determinants of Personal Power	
CHARACTERISTIC	DESCRIPTION
Expertise	Task-relevant knowledge or experience
Personal attraction	Desirable characteristics associated with friendship
Effort	Higher-than-expected commitment of time
Legitimacy	Behavior consistent with key organizational values

position-power by developing expertise in a particular aspect of organizational life. This might involve a new accounting system, tax loopholes, safety and pollution regulations, or recent legal precedents in acquisitions.

There is, however, a catch-22 associated with expert power. Becoming an expert on a subject typically requires considerable time and effort, and in organizations using rapidly changing technologies, individuals must continually upgrade their expertise to avoid the "sell-by date" of their knowledge (Grove, 1983). Given the investment required to stay up to date in a particular area of specialization, it is easy to become typecast as a specialist. If you are interested in moving into general management positions, this perception can be a hindrance. The increasing boundarylessness of today's organizations may especially devalue overspecialization. Given the dynamic environment facing today's organizations, overspecialization may be a recipe for obsolescence. Aspiring young managers must be careful not to limit advancement opportunities by focusing their attention on very narrow aspects of a business' activities. This is tempting for individuals who are overly anxious to establish a power base. There are always small niches in an organization to which power-hungry novices can quickly lay claim. Only when they have fallen into the specialist trap do they recognize the value of building a broad base of knowledge about a wide variety of organizational activities to enhance their long-term attractiveness for promotion.

Attraction

We will consider three ways in which interpersonal **attraction** is a source of personal power: charisma, agreeable behavior, and physical characteristics. The charismatic leader has been the subject of extensive scholarly study (Yukl, 2002). The three definitions of *charisma* in the Oxford dictionary are instructive: (1) the ability to inspire followers with devotion and enthusiasm; (2) an attractive aura; great charm; (3) a divinely conferred power or talent. These definitions reflect the Greek origin of the word, which meant favor or grace from God.

The notion that charismatic leaders are favored by God stems from the common observation that their uncommon ability to engender devotion and enthusiasm stems from an innate gift—a seemingly mystical quality that cannot be acquired in a skill development workshop. This quality is reflected in comments like the following: "When she makes a presentation in a management meeting, her presence is so powerful any message sounds good"; "His magnetic personality enables him to attract the most qualified and dedicated people to his department—everyone wants to work for him."

Given that charisma is an attribution made by others, it is natural to wonder what characteristics of leaders tend to be associated with this label. Research on this topic (Conger & Kanungo, 1998) has found that leaders are more likely to be considered charismatic if they (1) express a vision that is inspiring, (2) incur personal sacrifice and even risk their personal well-being in pursuing their vision, (3) recommend the use of unconventional, nontraditional approaches to achieving shared goals, (4) have a seemingly uncanny feel for what is possible, including an acute sense of timing, (5) demonstrate sensitivity to members' needs and concerns.

The implication of this research is that it is a mistake to treat charisma as a personal, innate trait. Although it is uncommon to refer to a leader as charismatic (and one is not likely to receive flyers advertising weekend workshops for "aspiring charismatic leaders"), the behaviors and characteristics associated with this type of leader are far from mystical or even mysterious.

A related source of interpersonal attraction is much more mundane, but equally powerful. Social psychologists who have done research on interpersonal attraction have isolated several critical behaviors that determine what they call *agreeable behavior*. These behaviors are the kinds one would normally associate with friendship. Indeed, much of this research has been motivated by a desire to understand the essential ingredients of friendships. Studies of this type have identified several major factors that foster interpersonal attraction. Some of these are shown in Table 5.4 (Anderson, John, Keltner, & Kring, 2001; Canfield & LaGaipa, 1970; Furman, 2001).

Table 5.4	**Characteristics of Likable People**

We like people when we have reason to believe they will:

- Support an open, honest, and loyal relationship.
- Foster intimacy by being emotionally accessible.
- Provide unconditional, positive regard and acceptance.
- Endure some sacrifices if the relationship should demand them.
- Provide social reinforcement in the form of sympathy or empathy.
- Engage in the social exchanges necessary to sustain a relationship.

Source: *Adapted from Canfield and LaGaipa, 1970.*

LEARNING

How can we relate this information on friendship to the supposedly hard-nosed world of management? Does this imply that you must become good friends with your coworkers, subordinates, or boss? Not necessarily. Very often, people choose to work with others because of their demonstrated expertise, even when they know they will have difficulty getting along with them. Furthermore, it is often inappropriate to establish a close friendship with someone in your office. Thus, one need not become friends with everyone at work, but people who possess personality characteristics that are attractive to their coworkers (the kind that, if circumstances permitted, would likely lead to a strong friendship) will likely feel empowered (Hogg, 2001; Mechanic, 1962).

This proposition has been corroborated by an impressive amount of evidence. For example, individuals making persuasive arguments are more likely to be effective if they are liked by their audience. This stems from the fact that likable individuals are viewed as more trustworthy and impartial than disliked individuals. Subordinates who are liked by their supervisor also tend to be given the benefit of the doubt in performance appraisals. This benevolent orientation is also manifest in the fact that bosses use rewards rather than coercion to influence subordinates they like (Allinson, Armstrong, & Hayes, 2001; Tedeschi, 1974).

We don't want to overemphasize this point, nor do we mean to suggest that "good guys" always win, but there is an impressive amount of evidence that individuals with agreeable personalities become more influential than those with disagreeable personalities. Their arguments are given more credence, their influence attempts are less likely to evoke resistance, and coworkers seem less threatened if they are promoted.

In general, given a strong cultural distrust of individuals with power, leaders with likable personalities tend to put others at ease and, in so doing, gain greater trust and influence. This pattern is consistent with the explanations for promising management candidates ending up as "derailed executives" (Table 5.2) because they were perceived to be insensitive to others, abrasive and intimidating, as well as cold, aloof, and arrogant.

The third basis for interpersonal attraction, *physical appearance,* operates independently of personality or even behavior (Hosoda, Stone-Romero, & Coats, 2003; Langlois et al., 2000). Studies have shown that people judged to have an attractive appearance are also judged to have socially desirable personality characteristics and to lead highly successful lives. It is further assumed that they hold prestigious jobs and are highly successful marriage partners and parents. In addition, attractive individuals are judged to

be masters of their own fate—pursuing their own goals, imbued with a sense of mission—rather than being buffeted by environmental forces. In general, it appears that people assume attractive individuals are also virtuous and efficacious.

There is considerable evidence that these are not merely fanciful attributions. In some respects, attractive people are more successful. Research has found that, on the average, physically attractive people are paid more than their counterparts in organizations. Attractive students are assumed by teachers to be intelligent and disinclined to get into mischief. In a work setting, the written work of attractive people is more likely to be judged of high quality, and attractive people are more likely to receive high performance appraisals from their supervisors than are other people (Hosoda et al., 2003; Langlois et al., 2000).

Findings on personal attraction are obviously the most difficult to transform into concrete suggestions for personal development. There is not much one can do as an adult to radically transform one's basic appearance. However, this information is still highly relevant for managers for two reasons. First, in many of these studies, attractiveness was achieved through dress and grooming (Thompson, 2001, p. 141). Hence, it appears unnecessary for most people to resort to plastic surgery and other artificial forms of physical enhancement to boost their self-confidence. Second, one can become more sensitive to the way others form impressions and make evaluations. If you suspect you do not measure up very well in this category, despite your best efforts at "accentuating the positive," it is a good idea to compensate by emphasizing other sources of power. If, indeed, self-confidence is the primary mechanism for transforming personal attractiveness into organizational power, then other personal and positional characteristics can contribute in a similar manner to one's self-confidence.

Effort

A high level of personal **effort** is one of the most highly prized characteristics of employees because it means they are dependable, reliable human resources. If individuals can be counted on to stay late to get out a delivery following a technological breakdown, to catch an early-morning flight to visit a promising new customer, or to take a night class to learn a new software program, they earn the trust of their coworkers and their supervisors. Being known as a person who will do "whatever it takes" to get the job done is a valuable personal asset, especially in today's highly uncertain and rapidly changing business climate.

There are a variety of other ways by which effort fosters personal power. In a seminal article entitled "Sources of Power of Lower Participants," David Mechanic (1962) described a particular process whereby members of organizations often obtain more power than is warranted by their position in the hierarchy. His observation is based on the premise that because senior members of an organization are unable to attend to all their important business, they are forced to rely on junior members to perform many tasks critical to the goals of the organization. The senior officers thus become highly dependent on their subordinates. If subordinates do not perform well, it reflects poorly on their bosses' judgment and ability to supervise. As a result, subordinates are in a position to increase their power by working hard on these vital assignments, thereby gaining favor with their supervisors.

In addition to creating a sense of indebtedness, or obligation, a high level of effort can enhance other personal characteristics. For example, individuals who work hard at a task tend to increase their knowledge of the subject. Therefore, they are more likely to be sought out for their advice on that topic. They are also more apt to gather information that is relevant to other members of the organization. This information often can be the key to reducing another person's uncertainty.

The efficacy of personal effort is borne out in the career of Gordon McGovern, CEO of Campbell Soup and erstwhile president of Pepperidge Farms. During the 1960s, when he was a young executive rising through the ranks at Pepperidge Farms, McGovern liked to get up before dawn and hop aboard one of the company's bread delivery trucks. "I'd talk to the distributors and to the store managers to see what people were buying," he recalls. In addition, as a trainee, he learned how to mix bread in 10-quart bowls and knead it by hand. This extra effort gave McGovern personal knowledge of the production process, the distribution system, and customers' preferences (Miller, 1985). Similarly, Herb Kelleher, CEO of Southwest Airlines, is known for his "management by walking around." He frequently serves customers on flights and visits baggage handlers and gate agents to listen to their concerns.

An extraordinary level of personal effort can also result in increased responsibility and opportunity through a process known as cognitive dissonance reduction. A fundamental principle of psychology is that individuals strive to reduce inconsistencies between their own personal beliefs and personal behavior and between their expectations of others and the behavior of others. Applied to our discussion of effort, this principle has an important implication. When individuals

exert more effort to perform their jobs than is expected, according to organizational policy or office norms, an inconsistency exists. Because the person's rewards are based on completion of the amount of work normally expected, the inconsistency can be eliminated only by reduced effort or increased responsiblity. While it is quite common for "rate-busters" in blue-collar jobs to be informed by their coworkers that their extra effort is unacceptable because it makes the rest of the group look bad, this approach to dissonance reduction is less common in managerial ranks. At that level, extraordinary effort is viewed as a sign of commitment and dedication that should be encouraged and rewarded.

Before leaving this topic, we want to make a distinction between extraordinary effort and extraordinary image. The former focuses on enhanced performance, the latter on enhanced regard (without performance). The objective of the first is enhancing the boss; the objective of the second is impressing the boss. Based on their intensive examination of effective boss–subordinate relationships in major corporations, Jack Gabarro and John Kotter (1980) suggest several highly relevant guidelines for directing your efforts to the benefit of your boss. As shown in Table 5.5, these

Table 5.5	Managing the Relationship with Your Boss

Make sure you understand your boss, including:
- Your boss's goals and objectives.
- The pressures on him or her.
- Your boss's strengths, weaknesses, blind spots.
- His or her preferred work style.

Assess yourself, including:
- Your own strengths and weaknesses.
- Your personal style.
- Your predisposition toward dependence on authority figures.

Develop and maintain a relationship that:
- Fits the needs and styles of you both.
- Is characterized by mutual expectations.
- Keeps your boss informed.
- Is based on dependability and honesty.
- Selectively uses your boss's time and resources.

Source: Adapted and reprinted by permission of Harvard Business Review. From Gabarro, J. J. and Kotter, J. P. Managing the Relationship with Your Boss, May–June 1993. Copyright 1993 by the Harvard Business School Publishing Corporation; all rights reserved.

LEARNING

include understanding your boss's pressures and priorities as well as assessing your own needs and strengths. This knowledge helps you improve your performance by targeting your efforts to maximize their impact.

Legitimacy

Actions that are congruent with the prevailing value system are deemed credible, or legitimate, by other organizational members. They are taken for granted, rather than challenged or scrutinized. Therefore, **legitimacy** increases acceptance, and acceptance is a key to personal influence. Organizational leaders are vigilant in defending core organizational values and in socializing newcomers to proper modes of thinking and acting. Often, new members or outsiders fail to understand the critical role an organization's culture plays in articulating, and defending, its raison d'être. Conventional thinking may appear peculiar or arbitrary until it is examined from both a historical and a strategic perspective.

Managers understand that a precondition for their organization's becoming a market leader is to be perceived as a unique player in the market (e.g., not just another computer company). They strive to create a distinctiveness that merits attention from the financial community, potential employees, and customers. This may involve placing a premium on quality, economy, value, service, loyalty to employees, or civic involvement. This uniqueness is the basis for internal organizational pride and external projections of excellence.

This perspective is initially articulated as the vision of a dominant leader (often the founder) and institutionalized as the organization's culture (Deal & Kennedy, 1982; Peters, 1978; Schein, 1999). It typically focuses on the "hows" and "whys" of doing business the "right" way. Values are proclaimed via the insistent message of a strong leader. For example, Harold Geneen at ITT stressed, "Search for the unshakable facts"; Tom Jones at Northrop emphasized, "Everybody at Northrop is in marketing"; John DeButts at AT&T drummed into employees, "The system is the solution"; and Ed Rust at State Farm frequently asked colleagues, "How would a good neighbor handle this?"

New members of an organization are taught what is acceptable behavior through stories (the engineer who worked for 72 hours straight to save a project), rites (graduation or promotion ceremonies), and symbols (uniforms, no private offices for managers). The savvy newcomer looks beyond formal position statements, probing for answers to questions such as: "What are the organization's 'sacred cows'?" "What's the quickest way to get into trouble?" "What is the source of organizational pride?" "Who are the corporate heroes?" "What are the revered traditions?"

Many required organizational practices make sense only when viewed as symbolic support for fundamental values. For example, a large insurance firm stipulates that no one can be promoted above a certain level in any department unless he or she has completed the requirements for insurance industry professional certification (i.e., Certified Life Underwriter). Young employees in data processing, accounting, or personnel who chafe under the edict to take classes on the details of the insurance business miss the symbolic meaning of this requirement. The founders of the firm felt that the organization's key to success was a workforce deeply committed to delivering the best product and backing it with the best service. They further believed that the natural tendency for some individuals to identify more closely with their department's interests than with the insurance business undermined this corporate objective. They feared organizational factions would lose sight of the overarching goal. Therefore, commitment to taking insurance courses has become synonymous with commitment to the organization's mission, and organizational commitment is a litmus test for organizational advancement.

This does not mean that a nonconformist can't get ahead in the corporate world. It simply suggests that he or she will be held to a higher standard in terms of other sources of personal power, such as expertise and effort. A conversation during a promotion review meeting in a major corporation reflects this attitude: "Sometimes I don't know where he's coming from, but he is so blasted smart and he works so darn hard, we have no choice but to promote him."

Such an outcome appears less sinister and more rational when one considers that organizations abhor uncertainty, both in their environment and internally. Espoused values and beliefs help reduce uncertainty. They provide a framework for interpreting the behavior of others, communicate a consistent set of priorities, and increase the efficiency of the interpersonal transactions. Individuals who fail to conform to these organizational expectations create "noise" in the system. Their inconsistency makes communication and interaction problematic, because, in common parlance, colleagues "don't know where they're coming from." Consequently, these individuals tend to become bypassed and isolated. In fact, Jack Welch, recent CEO of General Electric, proclaimed that managers at GE who "make their numbers" but who do not espouse the value system of GE will not be promoted as they have been in the past.

Before leaving the subject of organizational culture and personal legitimacy, it is important to note that the discussion so far has been descriptive rather than normative. That is, we have described what it takes to become empowered in an organization, especially one with strong cultural values. That doesn't mean that strict conformity is morally right or that it is necessarily in the best long-term interests of the firm. In fact, evidence suggests that successful organizations have members who are capable of both gaining power by fitting in and using that power to challenge the prevailing belief system that, in some sense, has been responsible for their gaining power (Pascale, 1985). Unchallenged organizational beliefs often interfere with a company's necessary adaptation to changing competitive and regulatory conditions. However, challenges are most successful when mounted by members whose commitment to the organization has been the most loyal. "Paying your dues" creates legitimacy, and legitimacy is a prerequisite for effective criticism.

In summary, we have highlighted four sources of personal power, in the sense that they are organizational-valued assets attributed to individuals, not to the positions they occupy or the titles they carry. These personal characteristics have one thing in common—they are the antecedents of trust (Dirks & Ferrin, 2001; Hosmer, 1995). The relationship between trust and power is central to the overall view of power and influence espoused in this chapter. One meaning of the term *trustworthy* is "being above suspicion." Hence, individuals who are deemed trustworthy by their peers are likely candidates for positions of power and influence in organizations because organizational authority in their hands is less threatening. As shown in Table 5.6, there is a direct relationship between the four bases of personal power we've discussed and the requirements for personal trust. Basically, the trustworthiness of an individual's claims, promises, or commitments is a function of two factors: (1) How likely is it that the person *can* do what he or she says? and (2)

How likely is it that the person *will* do what he or she says? In other words, questions of trust devolve into assessments of probable performance informed by judgments regarding ability and motivation. This is why organizations place a great deal of emphasis on placing proven performers in positions of high trust (read: power).

SOURCES OF POSITION-POWER

Not all power stems from personal characteristics. In addition, the nature of one's position and task assignments play an important role. This is illustrated by the standard practice in most organizations of placing limits on how much position holders at different hierarchical levels can spend, or on the size of the exception they can authorize. Four important characteristics of a position account for its power potential in an organization: *centrality, flexibility, visibility,* and *relevance* (Fiol, O'Connor, & Aguinis, 2001; Kanter, 1979; Pfeffer, 1992). These are shown in Table 5.7.

Centrality

Based on data collected since 1993, Right Management Consultants reports that, "Failure to build strong relationships and teamwork with peers and subordinates is the chief culprit in 61% of new hires and promotions that don't work out" (Fisher, 2005). As suggested by this study, one of the most important ways of gaining power in an organization is by occupying a position of **centrality** in a broad network of task and interpersonal relationships. Networks are critical to effective performance for one compelling reason: except for routine jobs, no one has all the necessary information and resources to accomplish what's expected of him or her. Indeed, one investigation of the determinants of effective management performance concluded that a key factor distinguishing high and low performers was the ability to establish informal relationships via networks.

Table 5.6	The Relationship Between the Sources of Personal Power and Personal Trustworthiness	
SOURCES OF PERSONAL POWER	**RELATED PERSONAL CHARACTERISTIC**	**REQUIREMENTS FOR PERSONAL TRUSTWORTHINESS**
Expertise	Reliable	Ability: *Can* they make good on their commitments?
Effort	Dependable	
Attraction	Likable	Motivation: *Will* they make good on their commitments?
Legitimacy	Acceptable	

Table 5.7	Determinants of Position-Power	
CHARACTERISTIC	**DESCRIPTION**
Centrality	Access to information in a communication network
Flexibility	Amount of discretion vested in a position
Visibility	Degree to which task performance is seen by influential people in the organization
Relevance	Alignment of assigned tasks and organizational priorities

Isolates in informal networks were unable to gather the information, resource commitments, and personal support necessary to accomplish unusual, important tasks (Kaplan & Mazique, 1983; Sparrowe, Liden, & Kraimer, 2001). On the other hand, those who have extensive diverse social networks in their work earn higher salaries and are more successful than those with extensive but narrow contact with others (Pfeffer & Konrad, 1991; Sparrowe et al., 2001).

Power is accrued via horizontal and vertical network relationships by virtue of one's location and function in the network. Horizontal networks link positions with similar levels of authority, whereas vertical networks include positions with different levels of authority. The more central a position is to the flow of information throughout a network, and the more critical the function is to the performance of others in a network, the more power will be accrued. This view of organizational power is referred to as *strategic contingencies* (Pfeffer, 1992). It argues that the reason for the uneven distribution of power in organizations is that units and positions differ in their ability to control strategic contingencies (e.g., the securing of information, expertise, financing) critical to the effective performance of others. Few important activities occur in isolation; what happens in one unit affects another. It follows that the more pervasive the effect of a position's activities throughout the organization, the greater is its power base.

Increasing the power of a position by increasing its centrality in a communication or work-flow network represents a very different approach from conventional strategies. Typically, young aspiring members of an organization think only in terms of increasing their power by moving up the organizational career ladder. They mistakenly assume that power is the exclusive right of hierarchical position. If they are not promoted as quickly as they would like, they assume their ability to accomplish the unusual is thereby curtailed. Inexperienced, ineffective organizational members grumble about not having enough formal power to get

work done, and they covet the influence wielded on higher levels. In contrast, savvy organizational members realize that informal network power is available to individuals at all levels. Furthermore, they understand that informal personal power generally precedes, rather than follows from, formal organizational power. A promotion is simply a formal recognition by senior management that an individual has demonstrated the ability to get work done using informal networks.

The merits of building a horizontal power base became clear to Alan Brewer, a business manager in the medical supplies division of Hewlett-Packard (HP), when his initiatives were blocked by senior managers. He suggested to a manager in the medical instruments division that the reusable electrodes on HP electrocardiograph machines be replaced with disposable electrodes, which were becoming much more popular. The reply was, "It's too expensive to make the switch." Alan had done enough research to know this wasn't true. Further investigation revealed the real problem. The man who had helped develop the disposable electrodes was abrasive, and he had alienated members of the instruments division. Now, members were unwilling to take any action that would make this person look good.

Alan overcame this problem by asking people in his division to develop a new electrode—one that would not be burdened by association with an unpopular executive. During the development stage, he actively served as a mediator, keeping colleagues in other divisions abreast of his progress. Several suggestions for enhancements were incorporated during this phase. After building a broad base of support for the new product throughout the organization, he had no difficulty getting the second request approved (Gelman, 1985).

This example illustrates the merits of establishing broad networks of organizational contacts. One of the biggest mistakes individuals make at the outset of their management careers is to become isolated. Such people assume that getting ahead in their department is sufficient for getting ahead in the organization. As a result, they concentrate all their attention on building strong relations with their immediate coworkers. If you reconsider organizations in terms of horizontal structures, you will see how isolated a communication network in a single department is. It is important to become a central actor in the organization's communication network, not just the department's. This can be done by going to lunch with people in other departments, reading the annual reports of all the divisions, volunteering for interdepartmental task forces, and seeking out boundary-spanning positions that require you to work with other departments.

It is important that managers seeking to form wide-reaching social networks understand that social relations look very different in different cultural settings. Specifically, research has shown that members of different cultures differ in terms of how many friendships they are likely to form at work, the extent to which they are likely to mix socioemotional and instrumental social ties, the strength and longevity of their social relations, and the likelihood of their forming social networks that are upward, lateral, or downward directed (Morris, Podolny, & Ariel, 2000). For example, American business relationships are characterized by the norms of the marketplace (they must be profitable). In contrast, Chinese business relationships are characterized by a familial orientation (doing whatever is good for the organization), German relationships are characterized by a legal-bureaucratic orientation (play by the rules), and Spanish relationships are characterized by an affiliative orientation (sociability and friendship) (Morris et al., 2000).

Flexibility

A critical requirement for building a power base is **flexibility**, or discretion—that is, freedom to exercise one's judgment. A person who has little latitude to improvise, to innovate, or to demonstrate initiative will find it extremely difficult to become powerful (except in unusual situations in which meticulous obedience to rules disrupts the system, as in the case of air traffic controllers' slowdowns). Power can be lost because circumstances often change more readily than people or their jobs can change to keep up with the new times (Pfeffer, 1992). A flexible position has few rules or established routines governing how work should be done. In addition, when a manager needs to make a nonroutine decision, it is not necessary to seek a senior manager's approval. Flexibility tends to be associated with certain types of work assignments, particularly tasks that are high in variety and novelty

(Hinings, Hickson, Pennings, & Schneck, 1974). People in such positions are assigned several types of activities, each of which requires the use of considerable judgment. The more routine the work and the fewer the tasks assigned a person, the easier it is to preprogram the job to eliminate the need for discretion.

Flexibility is also correlated with the life cycle of a position. New tasks are much more difficult to routinize than old ones. Similarly, the number of rules governing a position tends to be positively correlated with the number of individuals who have previously occupied it. Because the intention of rules is to expose exceptions, the longer a position has been in existence, the more likely it is that exceptions have been discovered.

The same logic applies to the life cycle of a decision-making process. The longer a group has been meeting to discuss an issue, the more difficult it is to have any significant amount of influence over its deliberations, unless the decision-making process becomes hopelessly stalemated. The critical decisions about how discussions will be conducted, what evidence should be examined, and which alternatives are germane are all made early in a group's history. To make a difference, therefore, it is important to be a participant from the beginning.

One indication of the amount of flexibility inherent in a position is the reward system governing it. If people occupying a position are rewarded for being reliable and predictable, that suggests the organization will penalize people who use discretion. On the other hand, if people are rewarded for unusual performance and innovation, discretion is encouraged. A "reliable performance" reward system uses as its performance criterion conformity to a set of prescribed means for performing a task, such as a detailed procedure for assembling an electronic circuit. In contrast, an "unusual performance" reward system eschews consistency in favor of initiative. For example, a company may teach salespeople how to close a deal but at the same time encourage them to figure out better ways to do the task. Individuals with a high need for power should avoid a job that is governed by the reliable performance criterion, no matter how attractive it might appear in other aspects, because it will strip them of a necessary prerequisite of power.

Visibility

A sage corporate executive once counseled a young, aspiring MBA, "The key formula for promotion is excellent performance multiplied by visibility." Obviously, a highly visible, poor performance will not lead to promotion, but the real message of this advice is that an excellent, but obscure, performance won't either. This advice is supported by a Chicago consultant, Karolus Smejda, who is frequently brought into organizations to coach "competent but invisible" young managers. "The boss will say to me, 'Karolus, this guy is a wonderful worker, but he's just not visible enough.' My job is to make that person aware of the need to become well connected," he says (Gelman, 1985).

One measure of **visibility** is the number of influential people with whom you normally interact in your organization. This helps explain why people-oriented positions are often more powerful than task-oriented positions. Of course, contacts with some members of an organization are more important than with others. It is critical that a position foster frequent contact with senior officials, decision makers, and informal leaders. This can be accomplished through participation in company or outside programs, meetings, and conferences. Many a young career has been secured by a strong presentation at a trade association convention or board meeting.

Recognizing this point, an enterprising junior executive in a large Chicago conglomerate seized on a chance occurrence to impress the chairman of the board. By a strange set of circumstances, the young executive was asked to fill in for the secretary of the board of directors and take notes at a stockholders' meeting. Making sure that he arrived early, he greeted every person who entered the boardroom and then introduced that person to every other member in the room. The fact that this young man was able to put everyone at ease (not to mention remember the names of a large number of strangers) so impressed the chairman that he subsequently provided several opportunities for him to advance rapidly in the organization.

This example points out an important distinction between centrality and visibility. The purpose of becoming central in a broad communication network is to tap into a rich flow of information so you can satisfy the information needs of others. In contrast, from the point of view of visibility, being in a position that allows you to interact with a large number of influential people increases your power by making your accomplishments more evident to the people who allocate resources, such as desirable assignments and promotions.

The value of visibility is clearly demonstrated in the position of an executive secretary. For example, Jean C. Jones, while serving as executive secretary to the chairman of Intel Corporation, decided each day how many of the 125 telephone calls would gain Gordon Moore's ear and how much of the 30-inch stack of mail he would see. The power inherent in this gatekeeping role is also reflected in the fact that Kathleen Kallmer parlayed her job as executive secretary to Beatrice Company's chairman James L. Dutt into an assistant vice presidency in four years (Baum & Byre, 1986).

By far, the best way to gain visibility is by means of direct contact, and face-to-face communication is the most influential means to accomplish this. Inexperienced managers often assume that credit for writing an excellent report automatically goes to the author. Unfortunately for good writers, this is not always the case. If one member of a group composes a very good report and another member gives a very good presentation of the report to an executive committee, the presenter will likely receive a disproportionately large share of the credit for the work. Busy executives tend to be more impressed by what they see in a meeting than by what they read in their offices. They have fewer distractions in meetings (no stacks of other reading material or interruptions by phone calls), and a slightly positive personal evaluation of a presentation can be transformed into a very strong positive evaluation by the approving nods and smiles of other executives in the meeting.

Another important opportunity for gaining visibility is participation in problem-solving task forces. Being asked to serve in this capacity conveys to others that you have valuable expertise. More importantly, if the task force's report is received well by senior officials, your name will be associated with the group responsible for the "breakthrough." Using the language of the strategic contingencies model, problem solvers gain power by helping others cope with uncertainty. For example, those heads of government whose accomplishments stand out dramatically in a historical perspective are those who proposed remedies during major crises. Consider that Winston Churchill is credited with helping Britain survive World War II. On the smaller scale of a business firm, this truism is equally reliable. The visibility of a person's performance is directly proportional to the significance of the tasks performed and the popularity of the causes championed.

An additional source of visibility is name recognition. Elected officials recognize the value of keeping their names before the electorate, so they place signs at state and city boundaries and entrances to public transportation terminals welcoming travelers. In organizations there are analogous opportunities for enhancing your visibility. For example, if your office regularly sends information to the public or other departments, try enclosing a signed cover note. If you are new to an organization, introduce yourself to other members. If you have a good idea, formally communicate it to the appropriate parties in person, as well as in a follow-up memo. If someone has recently accomplished something significant, send a note expressing congratulations and appreciation.

Relevance

This leads us to the fourth critical characteristic of powerful positions, **relevance**, which means being associated with activities that are directly related to the central objectives and issues in an organization. As one manager put it, "My peers are responsive to me because the functions that I manage are the lifeblood of the organization. I manage the people who provide readings on their vital signs; consequently, my presence in their office implies that there's a vital concern of one sort or another that needs to be dealt with" (Kaplan & Mazique, 1983, p. 10).

A noted organizational sociologist, Charles Perrow (1970), argues that, in an advanced consumer products–oriented economy, sales and marketing represent the central concerns of most businesses. Because other activities in the organization are dependent on revenues from sales, the work performed by sales personnel is most relevant to the central concern of organizational survival.

Refining this general proposition, Paul Lawrence and Jay Lorsch (1986) identified the "dominant competitive issue" for companies using different types of technology. The dominant competitive issue is the organizational activity that most accounts for the firm's ability to compete effectively with other members of its industry. Companies using a flow-process form of technology, such as oil refineries and chemical plants, were found to be most dependent on effective marketing because of their sizable capital investment and small range of product alternatives. In contrast, companies using a standard mass-production (assembly-line) form of technology, with a stable line of products and established customers, were most dependent on the efficiency of their production process. Finally, high-tech firms, or companies producing custom-designed products, were most successful when they had strong research and development departments.

This general principle accounts for a significant recent shift in the power of the human resources department in large corporations. In the past, human resource executives occupied the outer circle in the corporate power structure. They ran a staff of personnel specialists, occupying the lower floors of the headquarters building. Today, a great many report directly to the CEO and play a key role in strategic decisions. The reason for this dramatic change is that with the increase in acquisitions, mergers, and divestments, corporations must base strategic decisions on human resource considerations. These include matching high-priced skills with critical jobs, keeping key personnel after a merger, solving human resource problems that arise from introducing new technology or closing a plant, and formulating agreements with the unions of an acquired firm (Conner & Ulrich, 1996).

According to business authorities, "The rise of the human resources function is the most dramatic change in managerial function since financial executives rose to power in the 1960s during the 'conglomerate era,' when asset management was the pressing problem in corporations" (Hoerr, 1985).

These results have significant implications for task relevance. An individual who seeks influential positions must be sensitive to the relevance of his or her department's activities for the company. For example, a design engineer who works for an oil company is less likely to become influential than one who works for an electronics firm, and operations researchers will have more influence in companies with established product lines and an assembly-line production process. Computer scientists are more likely to feel empowered in a software development firm than if they are working for an insurance company or a public utility. In the latter organization, computer programming is viewed as a support function, with only an indirect effect on profitability.

There are other indications of the relevance of assigned activities besides their relationship to the firm's dominant competitive issue. For example, the role of representative or advocate is powerful because it enables a person to become identified with important causes. Another key role is that of evaluator. Positions designated by the organization as checkpoints become powerful by virtue of the fact that they create dependence. The approval controlled by people in these positions is highly relevant to those individuals who must receive it to obtain organizational rewards.

The role of trainer or mentor to new members of a work unit is another powerful position. It places you in a critical position to reduce uncertainty for newcomers and substantially enhance their performance. Newcomers are generally apprehensive, and they will appreciate your showing them the ropes. Also, successful performance in this developmental role earns you the respect and admiration of those colleagues who stand to benefit from your effective training.

To summarize, we have discussed four aspects of organizational positions that are critical to the achievement of power. As Table 5.7 shows, centrality and relevance encourage the gaining of power through horizontal relationships. That is, a position's potential for power is based on its relationship to other lateral positions and activities in the organization. However, visibility and flexibility are linked to hierarchical power. Flexibility reflects the amount of discretion vested in a position by superiors. Positions that are closely supervised provide a poor vantage point for establishing a power base. A highly visible position has close ties with higher levels of authority, so a noteworthy performance in a visible position receives more recognition, which is an important prerequisite for an individual's upward mobility in an organization.

Transforming Power into Influence

Having discussed the skill of gaining power, we now turn our attention to converting power into influence. This concept requires an understanding of the difference between power and influence. As indicated at the beginning of this chapter, many popular books on this subject suggest that power is an end in itself. They bring to mind the old commercials about "98-pound weaklings" who take up body building to punish bullies for stealing their girlfriends.

Our goal here is not to help people gain power for its own sake. When the weak seek power simply because they are tired of being pushed around, tyranny generally follows their ascension. Our interest, instead, is in helping people accomplish the exceptional in organizations, recognizing that this generally requires political clout. The well-meaning but politically naive seldom make major contributions to organizations. Consequently, our focus is on how you can become influential as well as powerful.

However, we cannot talk about influence without first understanding power, because power is a necessary precondition for influence. Influential people have power, but not all powerful people have influence. Influence entails actually securing the consent of others to work with you in accomplishing an objective. Many powerful people cannot do that, as evidenced by the chronic inability of American presidents to convince Congress to pass what the president considers to be essential legislation. The skill of transforming power into influence hinges on securing the consent of others in ways that engender support and commitment, instead of resistance and resentment.

INFLUENCE STRATEGIES: THE THREE Rs

Power is converted into influence when the target individual consents to behave according to the desires of the power holder. The influence strategies used by managers to obtain compliance fall into three broad categories: *retribution, reciprocity,* and *reason* (Allen, Madison, Porter, Renwick, & Mayer, 1979; Kipnis, 1987; Kipnis, Schmidt, & Wilkinson, 1980). Table 5.8 lists these strategies and the corresponding direct and indirect approaches. Specific examples of these strategies are shown in Table 5.9 (Cialdini, 2001; Marwell & Schmitt, 1967).

You may have mixed reactions to these lists. Some strategies will probably strike you as particularly effective; others may seem inappropriate or even manipulative or dishonest. Our purpose in listing these is not to imply that all strategies within a category ought to be used. Rather, the full arsenal of influence strategies is presented so that you can informatively choose those with which you feel most comfortable, and so that you can be aware when others are attempting to influence you.

These three influence strategies rely on different mechanisms for obtaining compliance. Fear of **retribution** is based on personal threat, which typically stems from formal authority. The direct form of this approach, *coercion*, involves an explicit threat to impose sanctions if the manager's will is not obeyed.

Table 5.8	Influence Strategies		
STRATEGIES		**DIRECT APPROACH**	**INDIRECT APPROACH**
Retribution: Force others to do what you say		1. Coercion (threaten)	2. Intimidation (pressure)
Reciprocity: Help others want to do what you say		3. Bargaining (exchange)	4. Ingratiation (obligate)
Reason: Show others that it makes sense to do what you say		5. Present facts (or needs)	6. Appeal to personal values (or goals)

Table 5.9   Examples of Influence Strategies

RETRIBUTION (COERCION AND INTIMIDATION)

General form:	"If you don't do X, you will regret it!"
Threat:	"If you do not comply, I will punish you."
Social pressure:	"Others in your group have agreed; what's your decision?"
Had enough?:	"I will stop nagging you if you comply."
Perceived scarcity and time pressure:	"If you don't act now, you'll lose this opportunity/cause problems for others."
Avoid causing pain to others:	"If you don't agree, others will be hurt/disadvantaged."

RECIPROCITY (EXCHANGE AND INGRATIATION)

General form:	"If you do X, you'll receive Y."
Promise:	"If you comply, I will reward you."
Esteem:	"People you value will think better (worse) of you if you do (do not) comply."
Pregiving:	"I will do something you like for you; then will you do this for me?"
Obligation:	"You owe me compliance because of past favors." (Even though I implied there would be no future obligation.)
Reciprocal compromise:	"I have lowered my initial offer/price, and now I expect you to reciprocate" (no matter how unreasonable my initial position was).
Escalation of commitment:	"I'm only interested in a small commitment." (But I'll be back later for more.)

REASON (PERSUASION BASED ON FACTS, NEEDS, OR PERSONAL VALUES)

General form:	"I want you to do X, because it's consistent with/good for/necessary to . . ."
Evidence:	"These facts/experts' opinions demonstrate the merits of my position/request."
Need:	"This is what I need; will you help me out?"
Goal attainment:	"Compliance will enable you to reach a personally important objective."
Value congruence:	"This action is consistent with your commitment to X."
Ability:	"This endeavor would be enhanced if we could count on your ability/experience."
Loyalty:	"Because we are friends/minorities, will you do this?"
Altruism:	"The group needs your support, so do it for the good of us all."

Recognizing their vulnerability to sanctions controlled by the boss, subordinates generally comply, reluctantly. The threat usually involves either the denial of expected rewards or the imposition of punishment.

Intimidation is an indirect form of retribution because the threat is only implied. Behind the manager's forceful request is the possibility of organizationally based sanctions for noncompliance, but the dominant feature of the demand is an intimidating interpersonal style. Intimidation can take many forms: a manager publicly criticizes a subordinate's report, a member of a management committee is systematically ignored during meetings, or junior executives are given impossible tasks by insecure senior executives.

Acts of intimidation are generally accompanied by special emphasis on the authority of the power holder. Assignments are typically given in the boss's office, in a highly formal manner, with reference to the vulnerability of the target (e.g., mentioning his junior grade or short tenure with the organization). This sets the stage for an implicit threat (e.g., "If people aren't willing to work overtime on this project, corporate headquarters is going to pull the plug on our budget and a number of younger employees will get hurt").

Intimidation can also occur through peer pressure. Managers who know that a majority of their subordinates support a controversial action can use group dynamics to secure the compliance of the minority. This is done by telling the majority that a decision must be unanimous and it's their responsibility to demonstrate leadership by securing the commitment of all members. Or, the manager can apply pressure directly to the holdout members of the group by stressing the need for harmony, mutual support, and working for the common good.

The second strategy extracts compliance from others by invoking the norm of **reciprocity**. Reciprocity operates on the principle of satisfying the self-interest of both parties. The direct form of this approach involves straightforward *bargaining* in which each party gains something from the exchange. In bargaining, both parties are aware of the costs and benefits associated with striking a deal, and their negotiations focus on reaching an agreement that is satisfactory to both. *Ingratiation*, however, is more subtle. It involves using friendliness and favors to incur social obligations. When compliance is required or support is needed, previous benefactors are then reminded of their debts.

Reciprocity is used in many ways in organizations. These include striking deals with influential opinion leaders to support a new program, asking subordinates to work overtime in exchange for an extended weekend, doing small favors for the boss so one can occasionally take longer lunch hours, and formally negotiating with staff members to get them to accept undesirable assignments (Cohen & Bradford, 2003).

Although the retribution and reciprocity strategies are both grounded in the manager's control of outcomes valued by others, the dynamics of these strategies are different. Retribution strategies exploit a subordinate's natural desire to avoid pain or unpleasantness, while strategies of reciprocity are used to make the outcomes desired by the manager seem desirable and attractive to the subordinate. Retribution strategy ignores the rights of others and the norm of fairness, whereas reciprocity strategy honors both. An emphasis on retribution leads to ignoring the quality of the ongoing relationship between the parties, while reciprocity implies a recognition of the value of strengthening their interdependence.

The third approach is based on the manager's persuasive ability. Instead of seeking compliance by making the instrumental nature of their relationship salient to the target person, this approach appeals to **reason**. The manager argues that compliance is warranted because of the inherent merits of the request. Here, the focus is on helping others to see why your ideas make sense. This is most likely to occur if the manager is perceived as knowledgeable on the subject and if his or her personal characteristics are attractive to the target person. The direct approach to persuasion relies on the compelling nature of the *facts or needs* supporting the case. A convincing statement is made, coupled with a specific request. For example, "If your shift doesn't work overtime tonight, we will lose $5,000 worth of product. Will you pitch in and help us solve this problem?" In the indirect form, the manager appeals to the other person's *personal values or goals*. These might include being altruistic, a loyal team member, respected as an expert; and helping to keep the plant nonunion or keeping customers satisfied.

Because persuasion is sometimes confused with manipulation, it is important here to distinguish between the two. A persuasive appeal is explicit and direct, while a manipulative act is implicit and deceptive. The persuader respects the autonomy of decision makers and trusts their ability to judge evidence effectively. In contrast, a manipulator has low regard for the abilities of decision makers and doesn't trust them to make good decisions. Manipulators have the same objectives as authoritarian leaders—they simply use more subtle tactics. Manipulative managers, therefore, often appear to the casual observer to be using a democratic leadership style. In fact, they are actually "illusory democrats" because, while their actions may appear democratic, they have no inclination to share power. They use a democratic style only because it makes others less defensive and therefore more vulnerable to their power initiatives (Dyer, 1972).

THE PROS AND CONS OF EACH STRATEGY

As Table 5.10 notes, each approach has advantages and limitations (Cuming, 1984; Mulder, Koppelaar, de Jong, & Verhage, 1986). The retribution strategy produces immediate action, and work is performed exactly

Table 5.10	Comparisons Among Influence Strategies			
INFLUENCE STRATEGY	**WHEN TO USE IT**	**POSSIBLE ADVANTAGES**	**POSSIBLE DISADVANTAGES**	**POSSIBLE COMPLAINTS**
Retribution	• Unequal power, in influencer's favor • Commitment and quality not important • Tight time constraints • Serious violation • Issue not important to target • If issue is important, retribution not likely • Specific, unambiguous request • Resistance to request is likely	• Quick, direct action	• Stifles commitment, creativity • Insecurity of boss • Engenders resentment • Must increase seriousness of threats to maintain pressure	• Violation of rights • Ethical violations
Reciprocity	• Parties mutually dependent • Each party has resources valued by other • Adequate time for negotiating • Established exchange norms exist • Parties viewed as trustworthy • Commitment to broad goals and values not critical • Needs are specific and short-term	• Low incidence of resentment • Justification for request not required	• Engenders instrumental view of work (expectation of specific rewards for specific actions) • Encourages people to feel that the terms of assignments are open for negotiation	• Unfairness, dashed expectations, manipulation
Reason	• Adequate time for extensive discussion • Common goals/values • Parties share mutual respect/credibility • Parties share ongoing relationship	• Need for surveillance enhanced	• Considerable time required to build trust (time increases as number of people increases) • Requires common goals and values	• Difference of opinions, conflicting perceptions of priorities

according to the manager's specifications. But the retribution strategy comes with high costs. Of the three strategies, it is the most likely to engender resistance. Most people do not like to be forced to do something. Effective managers use this approach sparingly, generally reserving it for crises or as a last resort when the other strategies have failed. It is best suited to situations in which the goals of the parties are competing or independent. This approach is effective only when the target person perceives that the manager has both the power and the will to follow through on his or her threat. Otherwise, the person being influenced may be tempted to call the manager's bluff. Also, the threatened sanctions must be sufficiently severe that disobedience is unthinkable.

When used repeatedly, the retribution approach produces resentment and alienation, which frequently generates overt or covert opposition. Consequently, it should be used extensively only when the ongoing commitment of the target person is not critical, when opposition is acceptable (the target person can be replaced if necessary), and when extensive surveillance is possible. Because these conditions tend to stifle initiative and innovative behavior—even when individual compliance is obtained—organizational performance is likely to suffer because affected individuals have little incentive to bring emerging problems resulting from changing conditions to their supervisor's attention.

The reciprocity strategy allows the manager to obtain compliance without causing resentment, since both parties benefit from the agreement. Also, because of the instrumental nature of the exchange, it is not necessary to take time to justify the manager's actions. It is most appropriate when each party controls some outcomes valued by the other party and established rules govern the transaction, including provisions for adjudication of grievances. Even under these conditions, such exchanges—especially agreements that are not formally documented—require some degree of trust. If individuals have reneged on past agreements, their credibility as negotiating partners becomes suspect. Reciprocity is also best suited to situations in which the power holder needs the target person to perform specific unambiguous assignments. Consequently, neither a long-term commitment to general goals and values nor the extensive use of personal judgment is required. An agreement to perform certain tasks according to specified terms is sufficient.

The chief disadvantage of this approach, when used frequently, is that it engenders a highly instrumental view of work. The other person begins to expect that every request is open for negotiation and that every completed assignment will generate a reward of equal value. As a result, the reciprocal approach tends to undercut internalized commitment as members take on a highly calculative orientation and downplay the value of working hard to achieve organizational goals, regardless of personal gain.

The assets and liabilities of the third approach—reason—are more complicated. The objective of the rational strategy is a higher form of compliance, that is, internalized commitment. While the focus of compliance is acceptable behavior, commitment requires shared understanding. Commitment relies on teaching correct principles and explaining legitimate needs and then trusting the good intent and sound judgment of subordinates to act appropriately. In its ideal form, commitment decreases the need for surveillance based on accountability and enhances the subordinate's initiative, commitment, and creativity. This approach works best when the worst thing the other person can do is turn down the request, since he or she has little incentive to hurt the manager. Also, the target person should feel there is little potential for the manager to cause harm, as is typically the case when the target person is the manager's coworker or superior. However, when the target person is a subordinate, the manager must demonstrate his or her unwillingness to rely on coercion and intimidation in seeking compliance.

The principal disadvantage of the rational, or reason, approach is the amount of time required to build the trust and mutual understanding required to make it operate effectively. This time increases as the number of involved individuals expands. Also, because the success of this strategy requires congruence of goals and values (rather than the rewards or sanctions a person controls), this approach is difficult to implement when the parties have dissimilar backgrounds, subscribe to competing philosophies, or are assigned conflicting responsibilities, such as maintaining quality versus meeting deadlines.

In their classic studies on influence strategies, Schmidt and Kipnis (1987; Kipnis & Schmidt, 1988), provided compelling evidence supporting the superior benefits of the approach based on reason. Individuals who rely primarily on reason and logic to influence others are rated as highly effective by their bosses, and they report low levels of job-related stress and high levels of job satisfaction. In contrast, individuals who persistently use any other approach to get their way tend to receive lower performance ratings and experience higher levels of personal stress and job dissatisfaction.

Although the evidence is not clear-cut, it does appear that a more general rule can be proposed.

Higher-numbered strategies in Table 5.8 are more effective than lower-numbered strategies. This ordering reflects the overall value system portrayed here: direct is better than indirect; open is better than closed; exchange is better than intimidation; and sincere requests are better than guile.

One justification for this conclusion is that the higher-numbered strategies are more likely to be perceived as fair and just, because they are more likely to be accompanied by an explanation. Research on organizational change has consistently shown that people are more willing to change when they understand why. For example, in a study of 187 employees in seven business firms that had just been relocated, they rated the process as fair, even though they felt the move was unfavorable, when they understood the reasons behind the action (Daly, 1995).

It is important to point out how cultural preferences need to be factored into your choice of influence strategy. First, your influence strategy needs to be congruent with your personal cultural values. Second, it needs to be congruent with the cultural values of the influence "target." Third, it needs to be congruent with the general context in which your relationship is embedded. As an extreme case of these three situational factors, one can imagine a Japanese manager trying to influence an African employee in an auto plant in Germany. To illustrate the importance of cultural congruence, our claims regarding the merits and liabilities of these influence attempts are clearly bounded by traditional American cultural norms, including egalitarian relations, direct communication, and individualism. In contrast, members of cultures that place a high value on social obligation would be more prone to favor the reciprocity influence strategies. In addition, cultures that emphasize indirect communication methods, such as storytelling and inference making, would likely prefer the indirect over the direct strategies. Similarly, individuals who place particular importance on hierarchical relationships may feel more comfortable with the forcing strategies (Thompson, 2001).

Exercising Upward Influence—A Special Case of the Reason Strategy

There is a particular form of influence that warrants special attention. Our discussion of the "Three Rs" has largely assumed that the influence attempt involved a peer or a subordinate. The role that is obviously missing from this set of influence targets is "the boss." Given Kanter's (1979) notion discussed earlier in this chapter that organizational power can be measured in terms of

one's control over making "exceptions to the rule," it is important that we examine strategies for getting exceptional requests granted by exerting upward influence. As you recall, Table 5.1 listed a number of exceptions that subordinates believed were the result of having a "boss with clout," including actions like interceding favorably on behalf of someone in trouble, getting a desirable placement for a talented subordinate, and getting approval for expenditures beyond the budget. Given the stress we've placed on using our power to have a positive, constructive influence in an organization, it is important to underscore the merits of managers using their power to benefit their subordinates by exerting upward and outward influence. If subordinates perceive that their unit leader's clout will shield them from outside, disruptive pressures and help them break down artificial organizational barriers to getting the job done right, then they are naturally inclined to strengthen their boss' power base.

The synergy in this "win–win" process should be obvious. Unfortunately, the means whereby bosses can effectively influence their superiors is far from obvious. One approach that has received a great deal of attention is called **issue selling** (Dutton & Ashford, 1993). Effective issue selling draws attention to those issues or problems that concern you, notwithstanding the numerous other issues that compete for your superior's time and attention. The issues that busy leaders believe warrant their attention are those that they perceive are most consequential. Effectively influencing upward, therefore, means that you need to convince your boss that a particular issue you espouse is so important that it requires his or her attention. Table 5.11 contains a summary of the key strategies that can be used to exercise upward influence through effective issue selling (Dutton & Ashford, 1993; Dutton & Duncan, 1987).

There is another important reason to exercise upward influence. In today's decentralized and exceptionally complex corporate environment, uninformed bosses are prone to make bad decisions. As a consequence, the organization as a whole suffers and subordinates and their units may become demoralized and discouraged. According to Michael Useem, Director of the Center for Leadership and Change Management, too often subordinates could prevent or reverse bad decisions, but they remain silent. In an interview regarding his book, *Leading Up: How to Lead Your Boss So You Both Win*, Useem says, bluntly, "If people are afraid to help their leaders lead, their leaders will fail" (Breen, 2001). He offers several tips for what he calls "trickle-up leadership." First, you've got to speak up to lead up. Too often people with good ideas or with

Table 5.11 Ways to Sell Issues Upward

PRINCIPLE	EXPLANATION
Congruence	The issue must be congruent with your position and role. A person in the marketing department trying to sell an issue relating to computers would be less effective than would an information specialist.
Credibility	Maintain credibility by being honest, open, non-self-serving, and straightforward. Demonstrate that your interest in the issue is not mere personal gain. Issues that seem self-serving are more difficult to sell.
Communication	Gain or maintain access to a broad communication network. Use multiple communication channels, including face-to-face conversations, written memos, e-mail, conferences, news clippings, and so on.
Compatibility	Select issues that are compatible and in harmony with the organization. Avoid issues that contradict the company culture.
Solvability	The issue must be solvable. Make it clear that the issue can be solved. Show that solution alternatives are available. Unresolvable issues don't capture attention.
Payoff	Clearly point out the long-term payoff, for the organization or the manager, of addressing the issue. The higher the potential payoff appears to be, the more likely the issue will receive attention.
Expertise	Identify the expertise needed to solve the problem. Issues are more likely to capture attention if it is clear that the expertise necessary to resolve them resides in the organization, or better still, under the purview of the top manager or boss.
Responsibility	Point out the responsibility that top managers have to address the issue. Emphasize the negative consequences associated with ignoring the issue or leaving it unresolved.
Presentation	Ensure that the issue is presented succinctly, in emotionally positive terms, with supporting data and novel information. Complex and convoluted information does not capture attention, so the issue must be explained in precise, simple terms.
Bundling	Bundle similar issues together with other important issues that interest top managers. Point out the relationship between your issue and other issues already being addressed.
Coalitions	The issue must be sponsored by other people who will help see the issue. Building coalitions of supporters makes the issue hard to ignore.
Visibility	Present and sell the issue in a public forum rather than in a private meeting. The more individuals who hear about the issue, the more likely it is to reach the boss's agenda.

Source: *Adapted from Dutton and Ashford, 1993.*

knowledge regarding a misinformed decision or misinterpreted report elect to remain silent. He notes that even in the Marine Corps officers are expected to speak up if their superior issues a flawed order. Second, before you lead up, you've got to team up. When the implications of your message will require a major change of course, it is particularly important to work with allies, especially those who add credibility to your argument. Third, lead up, don't argue up. When offering a contrary perspective, disagree without being disagreeable. By modeling open-mindedness, support, and trustworthiness, your example of how you disagree may be your most important message, especially during times of high stress and conflict. Fourth, try to be all things to

everyone, and you'll be nothing to anybody. Superiors are more willing to hear bad news from subordinates whose judgment they can trust and whose loyalty is unquestioned. Trying to keep everyone happy or working on too many agendas can cloud one's judgment and lead others to question your loyalty.

ACTING ASSERTIVELY: NEUTRALIZING INFLUENCE ATTEMPTS

In general, managers are more effective when they assume others are reasonable, well meaning, and motivated. Unfortunately, in some cases, these assumptions are proven false. When this happens, it is important to be prepared to protect ourselves from unwanted, inappropriate efforts by others to influence our actions. Therefore, it is not only important to learn how to influence others effectively, but we must also understand how to protect ourselves against the undesirable attempts of others to influence us. As we discussed earlier, one-sided dependence is the antithesis of empowerment. Recalling Figure 5.1, feelings of lack of power are just as harmful to personal performance as flagrant, excessive use of power. Therefore, it is just as important to be skillful at resisting unwanted influence attempts as it is to influence the behavior of others effectively and appropriately. This skill is particularly relevant in work situations in which maintaining personal initiative is difficult in the face of strong countervailing pressures.

Tables 5.8 and 5.9 contain an impressive arsenal of influence strategies. Is it possible to neutralize the impact of such a highly developed, well-conceived set of tools? Many people succumb to these influence attempts, either because they are unaware of the social dynamics affecting their decisions or because they feel compelled to give in without offering any resistance. To avoid this plight, it is important to develop the skill of resisting inappropriate efforts to control your behavior. Assertiveness increases self-determination by thwarting exploitation at the hands of overpowering bosses, manipulative sales personnel, and high-pressured negotiators (Cialdini, 2001). This is consistent with the time-honored sociological theory that power is the opposite of dependence, and hence the pathway to empowerment involves throwing off the choice-limiting constraints imposed by dependence (Emerson, 1962).

The importance of avoiding relationships in which individuals in power positions attempt to foster dependency in others has been the subject of recent research on the "toxic effects of tyranny in organizations" (Bies & Tripp, 1998). A summary of the characteristics of abusive bosses, from this study, is shown in Table 5.12. Given the tendency for most leaders to occasionally take advantage of their position of power, we include this as a tool for identifying situations in which excess has become the norm. As you examine the following strategies for neutralizing inappropriate influence attempts, you might find it useful to use these characteristics of abusive relationships as a frame of reference.

Neutralizing Retribution Strategies Used by Others

Coercive and intimidating actions are intended to create a power imbalance by substituting dependence for interdependence. This is the most detrimental form of influence, and therefore it should be resisted most vigorously and directly. You can use several approaches. These tend to form a hierarchy of responses, as follows (begin with the first and progress to the others if the initial response fails):

1. **Use countervailing power to shift dependence to interdependence.** The primary reason individuals (particularly bosses) rely heavily on the threat of retribution as an influence strategy is because they perceive an inequality in power. Obviously, the boss in an organization has the final say, but the larger the perceived discrepancy in power, the greater the temptation to exploit the powerless. The first half of this chapter outlined several techniques for increasing your power base. However, when exploitation occurs, the time for planning how to increase your power base has passed. Ideally, you are in a position to focus your boss' attention on your mutual

Table 5.12	Characteristics of Abusive Bosses

- Micromanager—obsessed with details and perfection.
- Inexplicit direction with decisive delivery—treats everything as a priority, requiring immediate, careful attention.
- Mercurial mood swings—responses are very unpredictable.
- Obsession with loyalty and obedience—believes, "You are either for me or against me."
- Status derogation—criticizes subordinates in public, to the point of ridicule.
- Capricious actions—known for arbitrariness and hypocrisy.
- Exercises raw power for personal gain—feels entitled to the "spoils of victory."

Source: *Adapted from Bies and Tripp, 1988.*

LEARNING

dependence, that is, your interdependence. Point out the negative consequences of failing to respect your rights and acting cooperatively. As part of this discussion, it may be appropriate to discuss more acceptable means of satisfying the boss's demands.

2. **Confront the exploiting individual directly.** All individuals, no matter what their job or organizational status, must protect their personal rights. One of those rights is to be treated as an intelligent, mature, responsible adult. To initiate a complaint effectively, key elements include describing the problem in terms of behaviors, consequences, and feelings, persisting until understood, and making specific suggestions. These techniques can be used in this situation to stress the seriousness of your concerns. If necessary, you should specify actions you are willing to take to stop coercive behavior. For example, whistle-blowing involves registering a complaint with an external governing body.

3. **Actively resist.** As a last resort, you should consider "fighting fire with fire." This is obviously a sensitive matter, but there are some individuals who will keep pushing others until they meet resistance. A work slowdown, deliberate disobedience to orders, or reporting the problem to a senior manager might be necessary. Again, this step should be pursued only after all other efforts to counter unwanted threats and demands have failed.

Neutralizing Reciprocity Strategies by Others

Many of the persuasion strategies used in sales and advertising fall into this category. In the marketplace, your concern is to avoid being duped. In the workplace, your concern is to avoid being manipulated. The following hierarchically arranged actions should be helpful in either situation. Once again, begin with the first response and follow with others if necessary.

1. **Examine the intent of any gift or favor-giving activity.** When a favor or gift is offered, you should consider the motives of the person, the appropriateness of the behavior, and the probable consequences. You should ask yourself questions such as "Is the giver likely to profit from this?" "Is this transaction inappropriate, unethical, or illegal?" "Is there a stated or implied expectation of reciprocation, and

would I feel good about complying if the gift or favor were not offered?" In brief, when in doubt about a benefactor's motives, ask questions or decline the gift.

2. **Confront individuals who are using manipulative bargaining tactics.** Common ploys used in these situations are escalating commitments ("I'm only interested in a small commitment [now]") and reciprocal compromises ("I've lowered my [extreme] initial position; now I expect you [in the spirit of fair play] to also offer a compromise"). Simply drawing attention to these attempts at manipulation will enhance your power in the relationship. State that you do not approve of the manipulative strategy; then propose an alternative exchange, with emphasis on the merits of the case or the true value of the product rather than on the craftiness of the negotiators. You will thus be able to reshape the exchange process and avoid being manipulated.

3. **Refuse to bargain with individuals who use high-pressure tactics.** If steps 1 and 2 have failed, refuse to continue the discussion unless high-pressure tactics, such as imposing unrealistic time constraints or emphasizing the limited supply of the commodity or service, are dropped. If you suspect that the dynamics of the negotiation process may be clouding your judgment about the value of the object or the importance of the issue, ask yourself, "Would I be interested in this item if there were an unlimited supply and no decision-making deadline?" If the answer is negative, either disengage from the negotiation process or focus your attention on its inequality. By shifting attention from content to process, you neutralize the advantage of a more experienced or powerful bargainer. By refusing to continue unless artificial constraints of time and supply are removed, you can establish fairer terms of trade.

Neutralizing Reason Strategies by Others

Although strategies based on reason are the most egalitarian of influence attempts, they can still create or exacerbate conditions of inequity. The following ordered guidelines should help you avoid these situations:

1. **Explain the adverse effects of compliance on performance.** Often, others' pressing priorities are your incidentals. The fact that someone

can present a legitimate, convincing case does not mean you should comply with the request. For example, a request may be reasonable, but its timing bad; compliance would mean your having to miss important personal deadlines or neglect your customers. You should discuss these concerns with the influencer. By acknowledging the other person's need, explaining your concerns about personal compliance, and then, helping to find alternatives, you avoid becoming overcommitted without giving offense.

2. **Defend your personal rights.** If you have used step 1 and your petitioner persists, focus the discussion on your personal rights. If individuals frequently come to you for help because they mismanage their time or resources, appeal to their sense of fairness. Ask if it is right to ask you to get behind in your own work in order to bail them out of their predicaments. Coworkers have the right to request your help in a pinch, but you also have the right to say no when even reasonable requests place you at a serious disadvantage or when they stem from the negligence or overdependence of others.

3. **Firmly refuse to comply with the request.** If your efforts to explain why you are unable to comply have not worked, you should firmly restate your refusal and terminate the discussion. Some people believe that their case is so compelling, they have difficulty believing others won't comply. If your coworker still "won't take no for an answer," it's probably because your "no" was not firm enough. As a last resort, you may have to seek the support of a higher authority.

Summary

In Figure 5.2, the two skills discussed in this chapter—gaining power and translating power into influence—are highlighted. We began by discussing sources of power, such as personal attributes and position characteristics. Both of these must be developed if one is to maximize one's potential as a power holder. A strong person in a weak position and a weak person in a

Figure 5.2 Model of Power and Influence

GAINING POWER

Sources of Personal Power
- Expertise
- Personal attraction
- Effort
- Legitimacy

Sources of Position Power
- Centrality
- Flexibility
- Visibility
- Relevance

POWER OF AN INDIVIDUAL

TRANSFORMING POWER INTO INFLUENCE

Selection of proper strategy to influence others

Increasing authority via upward influence

Assertive responses to inappropriate influence attempts by others

INFLUENCE OVER OTHERS

strong position are both at a disadvantage. Ideally, one should become a strong person in a strong position.

A manager must establish a power base in order to get work accomplished and obtain commitments to important objectives. But power without influence is not sufficient. Consequently, we discussed how to translate power into influence by selecting an appropriate influence strategy and implementing it in such a way that resistance is minimized. In general, this is most likely to occur when managers use the higher-numbered strategies in Table 5.8. Persuasion tends to build trust and encourage internalized commitment, while coercion and intimidation erode trust, produce only superficial compliance, and encourage servility.

The unbridled use of power tends to increase resistance among subordinates, which in turn erodes the manager's power base. It also transforms the nature of the manager's stewardship over subordinates. The more a manager dominates subordinates, the more dependent they become on management's initiatives. As a result, managers tend to overvalue their contribution to their workers' job-performance activities ("Without me, they would be lost"). This inflated sense of self-importance encourages abuse of power that weakens the manager's influence and may even lead others to demand the manager's resignation. Thus, the abuse of power is both organizationally and personally destructive.

Power need not be abused, however. Managers, by definition, are located somewhere above the midpoint in the range of organizational levels (from the CEO at the top to hourly employees at the bottom). Managers who shun initiative and refuse to take responsibility for their actions see themselves as the "janitors" for the management pyramid above them. Their job, as they see it, is to clean up messes and carry out orders. Their attitude and demeanor reflect that of their bosses. In contrast, managers characterized by high initiative, personal responsibility, and influence see themselves as presidents of the organizational pyramid below them. They work within acknowledged constraints, but they figure out ways to do things right. They take full responsibility for their subordinates' performance, as well as for their commitment to their work and their membership in the organization.

Translating power into influence should not only be directed downward (i.e., toward organizational subordinates) but also upward (i.e., toward organizational superiors). Incompetent attempts to influence upward can quickly derail a manager's career, while competent upward influence can markedly enhance it. By helping to set the agenda of senior managers (issue selling) and by working for senior management's success (benefiting the boss), a manager's influence can increase significantly. When applying these two principles, however, managers should be motivated not by a thirst for mere self-aggrandizement, but by an honest desire to benefit their companies and strengthen their bosses' position.

The counsel of the late A. Bartlett Giamatti, former president of Yale University and commissioner of Major League Baseball, serves as a particularly fitting conclusion to this discussion: "Far better to conceive of power as consisting in part of the knowledge of when not to use all the power you have . . . Whoever knows how to restrain and effectively release power finds . . . that power flows back to him" (1981, p. 169).

Behavioral Guidelines

Effective management within an organization includes both gaining power and exercising influence wisely. Key guidelines for gaining power include:

1. Enhance your personal power in the organization by:
   - ❑ Developing your knowledge and skills to the point of becoming an acknowledged expert.
   - ❑ Enhancing your attractiveness to others, for example, by fostering the attributes of friendship (genuineness, intimacy, acceptance, validation of self-worth, tolerance, and social exchange).
   - ❑ Being extremely dependable and, when appropriate, putting forth more effort than expected.
   - ❑ Increase your legitimacy by aligning your behaviors and decisions with core organizational values.

2. Increase the centrality of your position by:
   - ❑ Expanding your network of communication contacts.
   - ❑ Staying abreast of relevant information.
   - ❑ Serving as the source of information for others.

3. Increase the latitude and flexibility of your job by:
   - ❑ Reducing the percentage of routine activities.
   - ❑ Expanding task variety and novelty.
   - ❑ Initiating new ideas.
   - ❑ Getting involved in new projects.
   - ❑ Participating in the early stages of decision-making processes.
   - ❑ Seeking unusual and design-oriented jobs, rather than those that are repetitive and maintenance oriented.

4. Increase the visibility of your job performance by:
   - ❏ Expanding the number of contacts you have with senior people.
   - ❏ Making oral presentations of written work.
   - ❏ Participating in problem-solving task forces.
   - ❏ Inviting senior managers to help you recognize important accomplishments within your work group.
   - ❏ Sending personal notes of congratulations or cover notes accompanying reports or useful information.

5. Increase the relevance of your tasks to the organization by:
   - ❏ Becoming an internal coordinator or external representative.
   - ❏ Providing services and information to other units.
   - ❏ Monitoring and evaluating activities within your own unit.
   - ❏ Expanding the domain of your work activities.
   - ❏ Becoming involved in activities central to the organization's top priorities.
   - ❏ Becoming a trainer or mentor for new members.

   The general guidelines for influencing others effectively involve matching your influence strategy to specific situations, acting assertively when others attempt to influence you inappropriately, and empowering others. In general, use reason strategies more often than reciprocity strategies, and reciprocity more than threats of retribution. Use open, direct approaches in preference to indirect, manipulative approaches.

6. Use reason strategies when:
   - ❏ There are few time constraints.
   - ❏ Initiative and innovation are vital.
   - ❏ Interpersonal trust is high.
   - ❏ The relationship is long term.
   - ❏ Interpersonal conflict is not high.
   - ❏ Personal goals are congruent and/or respected by both parties.
   - ❏ It is important for the other person to understand why the request is being made.

7. Use reciprocity strategies when:
   - ❏ The parties are mutually dependent.
   - ❏ There are clearly specified rules governing interpersonal transactions.
   - ❏ Long-term commitment to common goals and values is not important.

❏ There is sufficient time to reach satisfactory agreements.

8. Use retribution strategies when:
   - ❏ There is a substantial imbalance of power between the parties.
   - ❏ The ongoing commitment of the other person is not critical.
   - ❏ Quality and innovation are not important.
   - ❏ Opposition is acceptable (e.g., when personnel replacement is possible, if necessary).
   - ❏ Extensive surveillance is possible.
   - ❏ No other alternatives exist.

9. To neutralize reason influence strategies of others:
   - ❏ Explain the negative consequences of compliance.
   - ❏ Defend your rights.
   - ❏ Firmly refuse to comply with request.

10. To neutralize reciprocal influence strategies of others:
    - ❏ Examine the context of any gift- or favor-giving activity.
    - ❏ Confront individuals using escalating or compromising tactics.
    - ❏ Refuse to bargain with individuals using high-pressure tactics.

11. To neutralize retribution influence strategies of others:
    - ❏ Use countervailing power to shift dependence to interdependence.
    - ❏ Confront the exploitative individual directly.
    - ❏ Actively resist.

12. To sell issues to your superiors:
    - ❏ Select issues that are congruent with your position or role.
    - ❏ Present the issue honestly and without being self-serving.
    - ❏ Communicate the issue broadly.
    - ❏ Select an issue that is compatible with the culture.
    - ❏ Select a solvable issue.
    - ❏ Clarify the payoff to be achieved.
    - ❏ Identify the needed expertise.
    - ❏ Point out senior managers' responsibility for the issue.
    - ❏ Be succinct, use emotional imagery, and provide supporting data and novel information.
    - ❏ Bundle the issue with other similar important issues.
    - ❏ Find like-minded supporters.
    - ❏ Use public forums.

CASE INVOLVING POWER AND INFLUENCE

River Woods Plant Manager

Heritage Appliance Company recently announced plans to construct the River Woods manufacturing plant, replacing the company's original, flagship facility adjacent to the company headquarters in Edgemont. In announcing the new plant, the company stated that to the extent possible it would be staffed by Edgemont plant personnel and that the excess personnel would be transferred to other Heritage plants in neighboring states.

Heritage management views the River Woods facility as the plant of the future, featuring new methods of production and lower processing costs and manpower requirements. In a recent press release, the Heritage CEO noted that they were replacing one of the least automated plants in the industry with a plant using new forms of production not previously seen in appliance manufacturing.

Heritage Appliance is also using the River Woods plant to pilot a new decentralized management structure. In the past the firm's marketing activities were directed from the home office by a vice president. Manufacturing operations and certain other departments were under the control of the company's senior vice president. In this centralized, functional, arrangement none of the company's four plants had a general manager. Instead, each department in a plant reported on a line basis to its functional counterpart at the home office (e.g., director of production, director of engineering). In contrast, the new River Woods plant manager will be responsible for the management of all functions and personnel, except marketing and sales.

There is general consensus among the top management team that the long-term viability of the firm depends on the success of this initiative. However, some have expressed concerns about the difficulty of the task facing the River Woods general manager. They point to the shift from functional lines of communication and accountability to a plant-level focus, as well as the challenges of upgrading the skills of the Edgemont plant personnel, working out the bugs in new applications of advanced manufacturing processes to appliance design and production, and dealing with the inevitable complaints from employees in a small company town who are not satisfied with their new assignments and who might serve as the catalyst for unionizing the only nonunion U.S. appliance manufacturing firm.

Discussion Questions

1. If you were part of the selection committee for the River Woods plant manager position, based on what you've learned about the sources of personal power in this chapter, describe what you'd consider to be the ideal candidate's qualifications.
2. If you were offered the new River Woods plant manager position, based on what you've learned about the sources of position power, what actions would you take to insure that as the company's first general manager you had the necessary clout to accomplish your assigned duties?
3. Using the information on influence strategies in the second half of this chapter as your guide, strategize how you would address the challenges you are likely to encounter if you accepted the position of River Woods plant manager.

EXERCISE FOR GAINING POWER

Repairing Power Failures in Management Circuits

Rosabeth Kanter (1979) argues that much of what is labeled "poor management" in organizations is simply individuals protecting their diminished power bases. Instead of criticizing these managers as incompetent, she proposes that we bolster their feelings of personal power. If we solve the real problem of perceived lack of power, the undesirable symptoms of poor leadership often evaporate. This point of view is consistent with the principles discussed in this chapter.

Assignment

In this exercise, you are asked to give advice to individuals who feel powerless. For each of the situations below, form groups to explore opportunities for enhancing the power base of these three individuals. Prepare to report your recommendations.

Situation 1: First-Line Supervisor

Kate Shalene has been a first-line supervisor for six months. She was proud of her new promotion but surprised to discover she felt increasingly powerless. Instead of being a stepping stone, this position was feeling more and more like a dead end. Managers above her were about her age and the hoped-for company expansion never materialized. She was not a central part of the organization, and she felt that no one ever noticed her unless she messed up. She was expected to be supportive of her subordinates, but they never returned the favor. She was expected to absorb their flack without support from above. In general, she felt as though she was constantly "getting it from both ends." Her job was extremely rule-bound, so she had little discretion in what she did or how she did it. She had only modest control over the pay or benefits of her subordinates, because their union agreement left very little flexibility. So she felt powerless to reward them or punish them in ways that really mattered.

    As a result, she found she was more and more apt to impose rules to get subordinates to do what she wanted. She became increasingly jealous of any successes and recognition achieved by her subordinates, so she tended to isolate them from people higher up in the organization and from complete information. She lost her penchant for informality and became increasingly rigid in following standard operating procedures. Predictably, her subordinates were becoming more resentful and less productive.

Situation 2: Staff Professional

Shawn Quinn came to the organization a year ago as a staff professional. He believed it might be a way for him to achieve considerable visibility with the top brass, but instead he felt isolated and forgotten. As a staff officer, he had almost no decision-making authority except in his narrow area of expertise. Most of what went on in the organization occurred without his involvement. Innovation and entrepreneurial activity were completely out of his realm. While some of the line officers were given opportunities for professional development, no one seemed to care about his becoming more experienced and capable. They saw him only as a specialist. Because his job didn't require that he work with others, he had little opportunity to cultivate relationships that might lead to contacts with someone near the top.

What hurt was that a consultant had been hired a few times to work on projects that were part of his area. If consultants could be brought in to do his work, he thought, he must not be very important to the organization.

Shawn found himself being more and more turf conscious. He didn't want others encroaching on his area of expertise. He tried to demonstrate his competence to others, but the more he did so, the more he became defined as a specialist, outside the mainstream of the organization. Overall, he felt that he was losing ground in his career.

Situation 3: Top Executive

May Phelps has been a top executive for three years now. When she obtained the position, she felt that her ultimate career goal had been achieved. Now she was not so sure. Surprisingly, she discovered myriad constraints limiting her discretion and initiative. For example, the job had so many demands and details associated with it that she never had time to engage in any long-term planning. There always seemed to be one more crisis that demanded her attention. Unfortunately, most of the constraints were from sources she couldn't control, such as government regulations, demands for greater accountability made by the board of directors and by stockholders, union relationships, equal opportunity statutes, and so on. She had built her reputation as a successful manager on being entrepreneurial, creative, and innovative, but none of those qualities seemed appropriate for the demands of her current work. Furthermore, because she was so mired in operations, she had become more and more out of touch with the information flow in the organization. Some things had to remain confidential with her, but her secrecy made others unwilling to share information with her. She had assistants who were supposed to be monitoring the organization and providing her with information, but she often felt they only told her what she wanted to hear.

May had begun to hear rumors that certain special-interest groups were demanding her removal from the top job. She responded by becoming more dictatorial and defensive, with the result that the organization was becoming more control-oriented and conservative. She felt that she was on a downward spiral, but she couldn't find a way to reverse the trend. "I always thought the saying 'It's lonely at the top' was just a metaphor," she mused.

EXERCISE FOR USING INFLUENCE EFFECTIVELY

Managers are given formal power in an organization by virtue of their position of authority. However, they often find that this authority does not readily translate into actual influence. Particularly when they are working with peers, they find it necessary to develop informal relationships through making deals, persuasive arguments, and so forth. These relationships form the basis of real influence in an organization.

Assignment

After reading the following case, assume the roles of Ann's staff members. Divide into small groups and conduct an informal staff discussion in which you design a plan for influencing

Ann's colleagues and superiors to support her proposal. First, decide which general influence strategy (or combination of strategies) is most appropriate for this situation. Second, using Table 5.7, recommend specific actions for implementing your general strategy. Prepare to present your suggestions, including justifications.

Ann Lyman's Proposal

Ann Lyman was recently hired by the Challenge Products Corporation (CPC) as a senior marketing executive for the electronic housewares division. Her previous experience at Pearces, a major competitor, had earned her a reputation for being a creative and hardworking manager. Her department at Pearces had increased in sales at least 15 percent per year over the past five years, and she had been featured in a lead article in *Contemporary Management.* This combination of competence and visibility was what attracted the attention of John Dilworth, the CEO of Challenge. John was troubled about the two-quarter decline in electronic sales. This was the core of CPC's business, and he could not risk losing market share.

In the past, CPC's products had dominated such a large share of their markets that, ironically, marketing wasn't considered very important. Production touted its high quality and low costs, purchasing emphasized its contribution to keeping costs low, and engineering stressed the durability of its designs. CPC products, it was argued by many, "sold themselves."

But that was before the cheaper, "look-alike" products from Asia flooded the discount stores. No longer could CPC expect high customer loyalty simply because it was the oldest, best-known, most reliable name brand on the shelf. Ann was convinced that in order for CPC to stay competitive, the company needed to expand its product line, offering more options at different price levels. She felt it also needed to branch out into "trend designs" that appealed to the contemporary lifestyle of young adults. These options would require the company to find new channels of distribution, such as specialty mail-order catalogs, as well as manufacture generic products for department stores' private labels.

These changes had far-reaching ramifications for other departments at CPC. For one thing, they meant that engineering would have to shorten its design cycle, provide support for a broader range of products, and emphasize customer-oriented, rather than functional, features. These changes would obviously not sit well with the production department, which jealously protected its long production runs based on standard orders and relatively few model changes. It also stressed ease of fabrication and assembly. In addition, purchasing would be required to find new sourcing alternatives for nonstandard parts, which would make it more difficult to get volume discounts and ensure quality.

After three months on the job, Ann felt she was ready to make her proposal to John. She pushed her staff hard to add the finishing touches before John left on his two-week vacation to Lake Tahoe. She wasn't disappointed—he thought it was a winner. He was excited and ready to "sign on." But he was also realistic about the difficulty they faced convincing others that these changes were necessary. Ann's counterparts in production, purchasing, and engineering would certainly object. "It'll be a hard sell, but I think you have some good ideas," he concluded. "While I'm away, I'd like you to design a plan for getting the cooperation of the other departments. You can count on me for general support, but the culture in this organization isn't consistent with sending out an edict. You'll have to figure out how to get their support some other way."

EXERCISES FOR NEUTRALIZING UNWANTED INFLUENCE ATTEMPTS

An important aspect of becoming empowered and influential is reducing inappropriate dependence. Obviously, social and work interdependence are integral parts of organizational life. Most forms of interdependence are natural and healthy. However, sometimes individuals attempt to turn interdependence into dependence by exercising inappropriate influence. Their objective is to increase their power over us by creating a significant imbalance of power.

Assignment

Following are two role-play exercises. In each case, assume the role of the person who needs to resist unwanted influence (Betty or Pat). Prior to the beginning of the role play, review the relevant behavioral guidelines, determine which combination is most appropriate, and plan your strategy for dealing with this problem. Do not read the other role descriptions (Bill or Lynn). Following the role play, an assigned observer will give you feedback using the Observer's Feedback Form (found at the end of the chapter) as a guide.

Cindy's Fast Foods

Betty, Assistant Manager

You are the assistant manager of Cindy's, a fast-food franchise in a college town. You are one of the few student employees who has stayed on after graduation. You weren't ready to move on, and there weren't that many good jobs in elementary education, anyway. The spring before graduation, the owner offered you the job of assistant manager. The timing was perfect because the offer would relieve the pressure on you to pursue teaching jobs in which you really weren't interested. Your work at Cindy's had sparked your interest in business, and your student-teaching experience had not been very successful. Even though your parents weren't too pleased about paying four years' tuition at an expensive private liberal arts college to have you end up "cooking hamburgers" for a career, their feelings mellowed when you explained the opportunities you would have to advance and possibly purchase a franchise. "Besides," you told them, "I'll only be in this position for three years, and then I can decide whether I want to apply for a manager's position or try again for a teaching job."

It's hard to believe it's been two years since graduation. Your manager, Bill, has done a conscientious job helping you learn the ropes as a manager. He has worked you hard, but trained you well. You feel indebted to him for his help. You have become quite close friends, although his occasional dirty jokes and sexist comments with the guys on break in the back room make you feel uncomfortable.

One night you are finishing your book work for the day, after the rest of the crew has gone home. These late nights are the one really bad feature of your job. Just as you are about to turn out the lights, Bill comes in. It is not unusual for him to stop by at closing. He is single, likes to bowl after work, and sometimes drops by later on his way home. You are just putting on your coat when he asks you to come into his office. He shuts the door, and pulls up a chair next to you. "Betty, I've been watching your performance very closely. You're a hard worker. The employees enjoy your management style. And I've taken a liking to you as well. I think I have a good shot at transferring to a much larger store in Cincinnati. I'll be glad to get out of this one-horse town and gain more visibility closer to corporate headquarters."

You start getting a little nervous as he moves his chair closer to yours. "I think you would be a really good replacement for me, but you haven't completed your full term as assistant. So I'll need to ask for a special exception to the corporate policy. And I'll have to put in a good word for you with the owner. However, there's some risk involved for me, because the regional manager is a real stickler on rules, and I've asked him to recommend me for the Cincinnati job. But I'd be willing to take that risk under certain conditions." As he waits for a response, you know very well where this conversation is headed.

Bill, Manager

You have been attracted to Betty for some time. You find her very attractive, and you enjoy her company. You have several times manufactured excuses to have personal chats with her or to be alone with her. You think Betty finds you attractive, also. It seems that she has been extra friendly lately. You figure she's either bucking for your job or sending you signals that she'd like to expand your relationship beyond strictly business—or both.

Besides, you feel she owes you something. You have worked extra hard to train her, and you've been dropping hints to the owner that you think Betty might be ready to move up.

9:00 to 7:30

Pat Simpson, Loan Officer

You are a member of a small consumer-loan company. The staff consists of you, another loan officer, and a secretary. Last month, a larger financial institution acquired your firm and made some personnel changes. The other loan officer, with whom you had worked for four years, was replaced by Lynn Johnson. Having entered the company at about the same time, you and Lynn have known each other for years. In fact, you worked in the Ann Arbor office together for a year. During that time, you were both single, and together you enjoyed the night life of Detroit. You learn that Lynn is still single and "living the life of Riley." In contrast, you have been married for about three years. You looked forward to working with Lynn again but wondered if your lack of interest in the local night scene would affect your relationship. Lynn has the reputation of being capable but lazy. She's known for taking in lots of loan applications and then striking bargains with or cajoling coworkers into helping out with the dreaded credit-checking process. You wonder if this practice has anything to do with the fact that her uncle was a founding partner in the bank.

After Lynn arrives, you are shocked at the difference in your work attitudes and lifestyles. "Boy, what a difference three years makes!" you think to yourself. You and your previous office mate, Jim, were both married, and both of you favored a vigorous working tempo from 9:00 to 5:15, taking lunch when convenient. You and Jim had a great working relationship, and the loan volume in your office increased steadily. There was even some discussion of expanding the size of the staff. In contrast, Lynn prefers leisurely mornings that begin in earnest around 10:30, luncheons as long as Mexican siestas, and a flurry of activity between 4:00 and 7:30 P.M.

You and your spouse are experiencing some marital turbulence, and you feel it is very important to be home in the evenings. Your spouse has begun attending night classes and leaves for school at 8:00 P.M. The educational program is an extremely intense three-year ordeal. Unfortunately, the stress level already seems unbearable. When you stay at the office late, you not only miss dinner together but you don't even see each other until after class, when you are both so tired there is no opportunity for quality time. It seems as though most weekends are devoted to homework.

Because the office staff is so small, the difference in workday rhythms is creating a serious hardship on you. Lynn doesn't function very well in the morning and has begun expressing irritation when you rush out the door at closing time. Lately, your relationship

PRACTICE

has become strained. You handle most of the walk-in business early in the morning, eat lunch at your desk, and have your paperwork done by 5:30 at the latest. In contrast, Lynn is just getting into high gear about 4:00. Because company rules require checking each other's loan approvals, Lynn becomes testy when you say you can't stay after 5:30 to check her work. Some evenings you have relented and stayed until 7:00 or 8:00, but your spouse got very upset. When you don't stay late, you are greeted by a stack of paperwork on your desk in the morning, which makes it difficult for you to meet with new customers. Several times Lynn has tried to get you to do the credit checks on her loan applications, saying that the press of new business was too great.

Something has got to change! You decide to go to lunch with Lynn today and tell her how you feel.

Lynn Johnson, Loan Officer

You have worked for this firm for 10 years, and you are very good at your work. During that time, you have passed up offers from larger financial institutions because you like the flexibility of working in a small office. Besides, your family is well-to-do, so you aren't concerned about making a lot of money.

In every other office, your coworkers have been willing to accommodate your work style. They recognize that you are one of the top loan officers in the company—and having the right last name doesn't hurt any—so they make allowances for your idiosyncrasies.

But your new office mate (and, you thought, old friend) is an exception. Since you arrived, the relationship has been testy because of your different schedules. You don't understand why there can't be more tolerance for your work style. After all, you get the job done, and that's what counts. Besides, your requests for assistance are not that unreasonable; other coworkers have always been willing to comply.

Thinking about the impending discussion, you realize how important it is for you to get Pat to change her work habits to conform with yours. You certainly hope you can convince Pat to pitch in and help you when you get behind. "I mean, that's what coworkers (and old friends) are for, right?" you muse on the way to work. During the discussion, you plan to stress the reasonableness of your requests. Others have never objected strenuously; why should Pat? If that doesn't work, you plan to try and work out a bargain. Maybe you could put in a good word for Pat with your uncle, a founder of the company. Pat's career hasn't exactly skyrocketed, and she is probably itching to move to a larger office in a metropolitan city. Possibly, her title could be upgraded to Senior Loan Officer.

ACTIVITIES FOR GAINING POWER AND INFLUENCE

Suggested Assignments

1. Select a friend or associate who has complained to you about feeling powerless in an organizational position. This might be a person who holds a relatively insignificant leadership position in a campus organization or a low-level position in a work organization. Perhaps the individual feels his or her personal abilities do not command respect in that position. Sit down with this person and teach him or her the guidelines for gaining power in an organization. (You might use the Assessment Survey at the beginning of this chapter as a diagnostic instrument.) As part of this conversation, design a specific plan of action for increasing both the position and personal bases of power. Discuss the outcomes of this plan with your friend and report on his or her success.

2. Using the guidelines for gaining power, develop a plan for increasing your power in an organizational setting. Describe the setting, including the factors you feel account for your feelings of powerlessness. Use your score on the Assessment Survey as a diagnostic aid. Formulate a detailed strategy for increasing your positional and personal power. Report on your results and describe the benefits of becoming more empowered.

3. Over time, analyze your efforts to influence other people. Use the "Three Rs" model to catalog your strategies. Consider why you used each strategy. Did you repeatedly rely on one of two strategies, or did you vary your approach according to circumstances? Keep track of the outcome of each attempt. Did you seem to have more success with one of the strategies? Next, select a person you have attempted to influence, one with whom you have a close, ongoing relationship. Discuss the alternative influence strategies with that person and ask him or her what effect the frequent use of each approach might have on your relationship.

4. Watch at least two realistic dramas (movies, plays, TV). Observe the influence strategies used by various characters. Which form of influence did they use most frequently, and why? Did certain people demonstrate a preference for a particular strategy? If so, was this based on personality traits, gender roles, authority relationships, or other situational factors? How successful were these influence attempts, and what impact did they have on ongoing relationships?

5. Identify a specific relationship in which you are regularly asked to do things that you feel are inappropriate. Using the relevant guidelines for resisting unwanted influence, formulate a strategy for assertively responding to the next attempt. Role-play this approach with a friend or coworker and incorporate his or her suggestions. After you implement your plan, report on the outcome. What was the reaction? Were you successful in communicating your position? Was an understanding reached regarding future interactions that is more fair? Based on this experience, examine other relationships for which this approach might be appropriate.

Application Plan and Evaluation

The intent of this exercise is to help you apply this cluster of skills in a real-life, out-of-class setting. Now that you have become familiar with the behavioral guidelines that form the basis of effective skill performance, you will improve most by trying out those guidelines in an everyday context. Unlike a classroom activity, in which feedback is immediate and others can assist you with their evaluations, this skill application activity is one you must accomplish and evaluate on your own. There are two parts to this activity. Part 1 helps prepare you to apply the skill. Part 2 helps you evaluate and improve on your experience. Be sure to write down answers to each item. Don't short-circuit the process by skipping steps.

Part 1. Planning

1. Write down the two or three aspects of this skill that are most important to you. These may be areas of weakness, areas you most want to improve, or areas that are most salient to a problem you face right now. Identify the specific aspects of this skill that you want to apply.

2. Now identify the setting or the situation in which you will apply this skill. Establish a plan for performance by actually writing down a description of the situation. Who else will be involved? When will you do it? Where will it be done?
   Circumstances:
   Who else?
   When?
   Where?

3. Identify the specific behaviors you will engage in to apply this skill. Operationalize your skill performance.

4. What are the indicators of successful performance? How will you know you have been effective? What will indicate you have performed competently?

Part 2. Evaluation

5. After you have completed your implementation, record the results. What happened? How successful were you? What was the effect on others?

6. How can you improve? What modifications can you make next time? What will you do differently in a similar situation in the future?

7. Looking back on your whole skill practice and application experience, what have you learned? What has been surprising? In what ways might this experience help you in the long term?

Gaining Power and Influence

Scoring Key

SKILL AREA	ITEM	ASSESSMENT	
		PRE-	POST-
Gaining power			
(Personal characteristics)	1	_____	_____
Expertise	9	_____	_____
Interpersonal attraction	2	_____	_____
	10	_____	_____
Effort	3	_____	_____
	11	_____	_____
Legitimacy	4	_____	_____
	12	_____	_____
(Position characteristics) Centrality	5	_____	_____
	13	_____	_____
Visibility	6	_____	_____
	14	_____	_____
Flexibility	7	_____	_____
	15	_____	_____
Relevance	8	_____	_____
	16	_____	_____
Using influence	17	_____	_____
	18	_____	_____
	19	_____	_____
	20	_____	_____
	21	_____	_____
Resisting influence	22	_____	_____
	23	_____	_____
	24	_____	_____
Increasing authority	25	_____	_____
	26	_____	_____
	27	_____	_____
	28	_____	_____
Total Score		_____	_____

SCORING KEYS AND COMPARISON DATA

Comparison Data (N = 1,500 Students)

Compare your scores to three comparison standards:
1. The maximum possible score = 168.
2. The scores of other students in your class.
3. Norm data from more than 1,500 business school students.

Pre-Test				Post-Test
134.93	=	mean	=	142.95
145 or above	=	top quartile	=	154 or above
136–144	=	second quartile	=	144–153
126–135	=	third quartile	=	134–143
125 or below	=	bottom quartile	=	133 or below

Using Influence Strategies

Scoring Key

RETRIBUTION		RECIPROCITY		REASON	
ITEM	SCORE	ITEM	SCORE	ITEM	SCORE
1	_____	2	_____	3	_____
4	_____	5	_____	6	_____
7	_____	8	_____	9	_____
10	_____	11	_____	12	_____
13	_____	14	_____	15	_____
Total	_____	Total	_____	Total	_____

Primary influence strategy (highest score): _____

Secondary influence strategy (second highest score): _____

SKILL PRACTICE Neutralizing Unwanted Influence Attempts

Observer's Feedback Form

Rating

1 = Low
5 = High

Neutralizing Retribution Strategies

_____ 1. Used countervailing power to shift dependence to interdependence. (Focused on the value of mutual respect and cooperation. Pointed out the negative consequences to both parties of exploitation. If appropriate, suggested alternatives.)

_____ 2. Confronted exploitative individuals directly. (Challenged the right to intimidate and threaten. Stated what he/she was willing to do to stop actions.)

_____ 3. If necessary, actively resisted. (If 1 and 2 failed, did what was necessary to stop retribution attempts. Minimized consequences of resistance on others.)

Neutralizing Reciprocity Strategies

_____ 4. Examined the intent of any gift-or favor-giving activity. (Asked questions to determine the motivation behind favors.)

_____ 5. Confronted unfair bargaining practices, for example, escalating or reciprocally compromising tactics. (Questioned unfair bargaining tactics. Explored alternative ground rules.)

_____ 6. If necessary, refused to bargain with individuals who used high-pressure tactics. (If 4 and 5 failed, terminated the negotiation process.)

Neutralizing Reason Strategies

_____ 7. Explained the negative effect of compliance on performance. (Described effects on personal responsibilities of complying with request. If appropriate, suggested options.)

_____ 8. Defended personal rights. (Assertively restated position, emphasizing personal rights.)

_____ 9. If necessary, refused to comply with request. (If 7 and 8 failed, politely but firmly terminated discussion.)

Comments:

SKILL *ASSESSMENT* ▶

- Diagnosing Poor Performance and Enhancing Motivation
- Work Performance Assessment

SKILL *LEARNING* ■

- Increasing Motivation and Performance
- Diagnosing Work Performance Problems
- Enhancing Individuals' Abilities
- Fostering a Motivating Work Environment
- Elements of an Effective Motivation Program
- Summary
- Behavioral Guidelines

SKILL *ANALYSIS* ▶

- Electro Logic

SKILL *PRACTICE* ◆

- Joe Chaney
- Work Performance Assessment
- Shaheen Matombo

SKILL *APPLICATION* ●

- Suggested Assignments
- Application Plan and Evaluation

SCORING KEYS AND *COMPARISON DATA* ■

6

Motivating Others

SKILL DEVELOPMENT OBJECTIVES

- DIAGNOSE WORK PERFORMANCE PROBLEMS

- ENHANCE THE WORK-RELATED ABILITIES OF OTHERS

- FOSTER A MOTIVATING WORK ENVIRONMENT

DIAGNOSTIC SURVEYS FOR MOTIVATING OTHERS

DIAGNOSING POOR PERFORMANCE AND ENHANCING MOTIVATION

Step 1: Before you read the material in this chapter, respond to the following statements by writing a number from the rating scale that follows in the left-hand column (Pre-assessment). Your answers should reflect your attitudes and behavior as they are now, not as you would like them to be. Be honest. This instrument is designed to help you discover your level of competency in motivating others so you can tailor your learning to your specific needs. When you have completed the survey, use the scoring key at the end of the chapter to identify the skill areas discussed in this chapter that are most important for you to master.

Step 2: After you have completed the reading and the exercises in this chapter and, ideally, as many as you can of the Skill Application assignments at the end of the chapter, cover up your first set of answers. Then respond to the same statements again, this time in the right-hand column (Post-assessment). When you have completed the survey, use the scoring key at the end of the chapter to measure your progress. If your score remains low in specific skill areas, use the behavioral guidelines at the end of the Skill Learning section to guide your further practice.

Rating Scale

1 Strongly disagree
2 Disagree
3 Slightly disagree
4 Slightly agree
5 Agree
6 Strongly agree

Assessment

Pre-   Post-

When another person needs to be motivated:

_____   _____   1. I approach a performance problem by first establishing whether it is caused by a lack of motivation or ability.

_____   _____   2. I establish a clear standard of expected performance.

_____   _____   3. I offer to provide training and information, without offering to do tasks myself.

_____   _____   4. I am honest and straightforward in providing feedback on performance and assessing advancement opportunities.

_____   _____   5. I use a variety of rewards to reinforce exceptional performances.

_____   _____   6. When discipline is required, I give specific suggestions for improvement.

_____   _____   7. I design task assignments to make them interesting and challenging.

_____   _____   8. I provide the rewards that each person values.

_____	_____	9. I make sure that people feel fairly and equitably treated.
_____	_____	10. I make sure that people get timely feedback from those affected by task performance.
_____	_____	11. I carefully diagnose the causes of poor performance before taking any remedial or disciplinary action.
_____	_____	12. I help people establish performance goals that are challenging, specific, and time bound.
_____	_____	13. Only as a last resort do I attempt to reassign or release a poorly performing individual.
_____	_____	14. Whenever possible, I make sure valued rewards are linked to high performance.
_____	_____	15. I discipline when effort is below expectations and below capabilities.
_____	_____	16. I combine or rotate assignments so that people can use a variety of skills.
_____	_____	17. I arrange for an individual to work with others in a team, for the mutual support of all.
_____	_____	18. I make sure that people use realistic standards for measuring fairness.
_____	_____	19. I provide immediate compliments and other forms of recognition for meaningful accomplishments.
_____	_____	20. I determine if a person has the necessary resources and support to succeed in a task.

WORK PERFORMANCE ASSESSMENT

Respond to the following statements, based on your current (or recent) work situation. Then turn to the scoring key at the end of this chapter.

Rating Scale

1 Strongly disagree
2 Disagree
3 Neutral
4 Agree
5 Strongly agree

_____ 1. My supervisor and I agree on the quality of my performance.

_____ 2. I feel I have adequate training to perform my current job assignments.

_____ 3. I believe that my native skills and abilities are matched very well with my job responsibilities.

_____ 4. I believe that I have adequate resources and supplies to do my job well.

_____ 5. I understand my boss' expectations and generally feel they are realistic.

_____ 6. I believe that rewards are distributed fairly, on the basis of performance.

_____ 7. The rewards and opportunities available to me if I perform well are attractive to me personally.

_____ 8. My supervisor indicates that I am not performing as well as I should, but I disagree.

_____ 9. I could do a much better job if I had more training.

_____ 10. I believe that my job is too difficult for my ability level.

_____ 11. I believe that my job performance is hindered by a lack of supplies and resources.

_____ 12. I believe my boss' expectations are unclear and unrealistic.

_____ 13. I believe my boss plays favorites in allocating rewards.

_____ 14. I do not find the rewards and opportunities available to high performers very appealing.

Increasing Motivation and Performance

Focus groups at Intermountain Health Care (IHC), a Utah-based health care organization with more than 23,000 employees, revealed that a majority of front-line workers would not leave their jobs unless another employer offered them a 20 percent increase in pay and a 30 percent increase in benefits. Such commitment and motivation toward employed work is an extremely valued commodity in our current economy. Most organizations struggle to retain their best employees and to motivate them to high performance. The comments from three front-line workers at IHC reveal that their commitment has been won through the motivating and rewarding work environment they experience and the values IHC reinforces (Interview with Alison Mackey).

"I have never worked at a place where people have been so concerned about their employees. And because of that we can turn around and give the same to our customers."

"I think [IHC] is a system that's concerned about its employees and as a result it can attract employees with strong technical and people-based knowledge and experience."

"The values that IHC stands for make me never want to leave" (IHC Employee Opinion Survey Database).

The efforts IHC has taken to create such a motivating work environment have improved its clinical care and its bottom line. *Modern Healthcare* honored IHC in January 2000 as the number-one integrated health care system in America. President and chief executive officer (CEO) William H. Nelson attributes its clinical success and national recognition to its employees (IHC Annual Report, 1999).

Organizations like IHC that have highly motivated and committed employees are well equipped to compete in any market, be it health care or heavy industry. But like any distinctive competence, employee commitment is difficult to achieve—if it were otherwise it would have no competitive value. The focus of this chapter is on creating work environments where employees are highly productive and highly motivated.

After winning an unprecedented seventh NBA title as a coach, Phil Jackson was asked what his method was for motivating professional basketball players. "I don't motivate my players. You cannot motivate someone, all you can do is provide a motivating environment and the players will motivate themselves" (Jackson, 2000). We believe the imagery of "manager-as-coach" and "motivation-as-facilitation" suggested by this interview with one of the most successful coaches of our time provides the appropriate backdrop for our discussion. Whether managers are working with a group of steel workers, computer programmers, artists, or basketball players, they face a common challenge of fostering a motivating work environment.

The core of this chapter outlines a six-step process for accomplishing this goal. But first, to set the stage for this discussion, we begin with one of the most nettlesome problems facing managers—how to correctly identify the underlying causes of a specific employee's poor performance.

Diagnosing Work Performance Problems

Let's begin by examining the case for managers sharpening their skills for diagnosing work performance problems. There is a tendency for supervisors to attribute the cause of poor performance to low motivation (Bitter & Gardner, 1995). That is, when employees fail to meet performance expectations, supervisors tend to blame this outcome on insufficient effort—often expressed in terms of a lack of interest or commitment. The tendency to make assumptions about why things happen, without the benefit of scrutiny, is an example of what psychologists call an attribution bias (Choi, Nisbett, & Norenzayan, 1999). Because supervisors generally believe that if they work harder they will perform better, they assume their own experience applies to other organizational positions and work environments. The problem with this approach to problem diagnosis is that it lends itself to simplistic solutions, reminiscent of the Chinese proverb, "For every hundred men hacking away at the leaves of a diseased tree, only one man stoops to inspect the roots."

Let's consider one increasingly common set of work conditions that illustrates the need to "stoop and inspect the roots" of observed poor worker performance. It is estimated that one-third of American workers are assigned to irregular schedules (often involving night work), commonly known as shift work. In a recent article on the challenges facing shift workers, the story was told of a supervisor who sought permission from the human resources department to fire a worker because he didn't "stay on task," often walked around talking to others, and occasionally fell asleep on the job. Research on shift workers suggests the need to look beyond a simplistic "poor performance equals low motivation and commitment" explanation for this worker's unacceptable behavior. For example, shift workers sleep two to three hours less per night than day workers, they are four to five times more likely to experience digestive disorders due to eating the wrong foods at the wrong times, chronic fatigue is reported by 80 percent of shift workers, 75 percent of shift workers report feeling isolated on the job, and drug and alcohol abuse are three times greater among permanent shift workers (Perry, 2000).

To avoid falling prey to simplistic, ill-informed diagnoses of work performance problems, managers need a model, or framework, to guide their inquiry process. Various organizational scholars (e.g., Gerhart, 2003; Steers, Porter, & Bigley, 1996; Vroom, 1964) have summarized the determinants of task performance as follows:

Performance = Ability × Motivation (Effort)

where

Ability = Aptitude × Training × Resources

Motivation = Desire × Commitment

According to these formulas, **performance** is the product of ability multiplied by motivation, **ability** is the product of aptitude multiplied by training and resources, and **motivation** is the product of desire and commitment. The multiplicative function in these formulas suggests that all elements are essential. For example, workers who have 100 percent of the motivation and 75 percent of the ability required to perform a task can perform at an above-average rate. However, if these individuals have only 10 percent of the ability required, no amount of motivation will enable them to perform satisfactorily.

Aptitude refers to the native skills and abilities a person brings to a job. These involve physical and mental capabilities; but for many people-oriented jobs, they also include personality characteristics. Most of our inherent abilities can be enhanced by education and *training*. Indeed, much of what we call native ability in adults can be traced to previous skill-enhancement

experiences, such as modeling the social skills of parents or older siblings. Nevertheless, it is useful to consider training as a separate component of ability, since it represents an important mechanism for improving employee performance. Ability should be assessed during the job-matching process by screening applicants against the skill requirements of the job. If an applicant has minor deficiencies in skill aptitude but many other desirable characteristics, an intensive training program can be used to increase the applicant's qualifications to perform the job.

Our definition of ability is broader than most. We are focusing on the ability to perform, rather than the performer's ability. Therefore, our definition includes a third, situational component: adequate *resources*. Frequently, highly capable and well-trained individuals are placed in situations that inhibit job performance. Specifically, they aren't given the resources (technical, personnel, political) to perform assigned tasks effectively.

Motivation represents an employee's *desire* and *commitment* to perform and is manifested in job-related effort. Some people want to complete a task but are easily distracted or discouraged. They have high desire but low commitment. Others plod along with impressive persistence, but their work is uninspired. These people have high commitment but low desire.

The first diagnostic question that must be asked by the supervisor of a poor performer is whether the person's performance deficiencies stem from lack of ability or lack of motivation. Managers need four pieces of information in order to answer this question (Michener, Fleishman, & Vaske, 1976):

1. How difficult are the tasks being assigned to the individual?
2. How capable is the individual?
3. How hard is the individual trying to succeed at the job?
4. How much improvement is the individual making?

In terms of these four questions, low ability is generally associated with very difficult tasks, overall low individual ability, evidence of strong effort, and lack of improvement over time.

The answer to the question "Is this an ability or motivation problem?" has far-reaching ramifications for manager–subordinate relations. Research on this topic has shown that managers tend to apply more pressure to a person if they feel that the person is deliberately not performing up to expectations, rather than not performing effectively due to external, uncontrollable forces. Managers sometimes justify their choice of a forceful influence strategy on the grounds that the subordinate has a poor attitude, is hostile to authority, or lacks dedication.

Unfortunately, if the manager's assessment is incorrect and poor performance is related to ability rather than motivation, the response of increased pressure will worsen the problem. If poor performers feel that management is insensitive to their problems—that they lack resources, adequate training, or realistic time schedules—they may respond counterproductively to any tactics aimed at increasing their effort. Quite likely they will develop a motivational problem—that is, their desire and commitment will decrease—in response to management's insensitive, "iron-fisted" actions. Seeing this response, management will feel that their original diagnosis is confirmed, and they will use even stronger forms of influence to force compliance. The resulting vicious cycle is extremely difficult to break and underscores the high stakes involved in accurately diagnosing poor performance problems.

In this chapter, we will examine the two components of performance in more detail, beginning with ability. We'll discuss manifestations of low ability and poor motivation, their causes, and some proposed remedies. We'll devote more attention to motivation, since motivation is more central to day-to-day manager–subordinate interactions. While ability tends to remain stable over long periods of time, motivation fluctuates; therefore, it requires closer monitoring and frequent recharging.

Enhancing Individuals' Abilities

A person's lack of ability might inhibit good performance for several reasons. Ability may have been assessed improperly during the screening process prior to employment, the technical requirements of a job may have been radically upgraded, or a person who performed very well in one position may be promoted into a higher-level position that is too demanding. (The Peter Principle states that people are typically promoted one position above their level of competence.) In addition, human and material resource support may have been reduced because of organizational budget cutbacks.

As noted by Quick (1977, 1991), managers should be alert for individuals who show signs of ability deterioration. Following are three danger signals for management positions:

1. **Taking refuge in a specialty.** Managers show signs of insufficient ability when they respond to situations not by managing, but by retreating to their technical specialty. This often occurs when general managers who feel insecure address problems outside their area of expertise and experience. Anthony Jay, in *Management and Machiavelli* (1967), dubs this type of manager "George I," after the King of England who, after assuming the throne, continued to be preoccupied with the affairs of Hanover, Germany, whence he had come.

2. **Focusing on past performance.** Another danger sign is measuring one's value to the organization in terms of past performance or on the basis of former standards. Some cavalry commanders in World War I relied on their outmoded knowledge of how to conduct successful military campaigns and, as a result, failed miserably in mechanized combat. This form of obsolescence is common in organizations that fail to shift their mission in response to changing market conditions.

3. **Exaggerating aspects of the leadership role.** Managers who have lost confidence in their ability tend to be very defensive. This often leads them to exaggerate one aspect of their managerial role. Such managers might delegate most of their responsibilities because they no longer feel competent to perform them well. Or they might become nuts-and-bolts administrators who scrutinize every detail to an extent far beyond its practical value. Still others become "devil's advocates," but rather than stimulating creativity, their negativism thwarts efforts to change the familiar.

There are five principal tools available for overcoming poor performance problems due to lack of ability: *resupply, retrain, refit, reassign,* and *release.* We will discuss these in the order in which a manager should consider them.

Once a manager has ascertained that lack of ability is the primary cause of someone's poor performance, a performance review interview should be scheduled to explore these options, beginning with resupplying and retraining. Unless the manager has overwhelming evidence that the problem stems from low aptitude, it is wise to assume initially that it is due to a lack of resources or training. This gives the subordinate the benefit of the doubt and reduces the likely defensive reaction to an assessment of inadequate aptitude.

The **resupply** option focuses on the support needs of the job, including personnel, budget, and political clout. Asking "Do you have what you need to perform this job satisfactorily?" allows the subordinate to express his or her frustration related to inadequate support. Given the natural tendency for individuals to blame external causes for their mistakes, managers should explore their subordinates' complaints about lack of support in detail to determine their validity. Even if employees exaggerate their claims, starting your discussion of poor performance in this manner signals your willingness to help them solve the problem from their perspective rather than to find fault from your perspective.

The next least threatening option is to **retrain**. American companies with more than 100 employees budgeted in excess of $60 billion for formal training. To deliver this training, these firms spent $42 billion on corporate trainers and an additional $14.3 billion on commercial trainers (Reese, 1999; Tomlinson, 2002). This is a sizeable expenditure for American corporations, but the reasons for these expenditures are clear. First of all, technology is changing so quickly that employees' skills can soon become obsolete. It has been estimated that 50 percent of employees' skills become outdated within three to five years (Moe & Blodget, 2000). Second, employees will typically fill a number of different positions throughout their careers, each demanding different proficiencies. Finally, demographic changes in our society will lead to an increasingly older workforce. In order for companies to remain competitive, more and more of them must retrain their older employees.

Training programs can take a variety of forms. For example, many firms are using computer technology more in education. This can involve interactive technical instruction and business games that simulate problems likely to be experienced by managers in the organization. More traditional forms of training include subsidized university courses and in-house technical or management seminars. Some companies have experimented with company sabbaticals to release managers or senior technical specialists from the pressures of work so they can concentrate on retooling. The most rapidly increasing form of training is "distance learning," in which formal courses are offered over the Internet. Web-based corporate learning is expected to soon top $11 billion (Moe & Blodget, 2000). In their most recent report, the U.S. Department of Education states that 1,680 academic institutions offered 54,000 online courses in 1998— for which 1.6 million students enrolled. That marked a 70 percent increase since 1995 (Boehle, Dobbs, & Stamps, 2000).

In many cases, resupplying and retraining are insufficient remedies for poor performance. When this happens, the next step should be to explore **refitting** poor performers to their task assignments. While the subordinates remain on the job, the components of their work are analyzed, and different combinations of tasks and abilities that accomplish organizational objectives and provide meaningful and rewarding work are explored. For example, an assistant may be brought in to handle many of the technical details of a first-line supervisor's position, freeing up more time for the supervisor to focus on people development or to develop a long-term plan to present to upper management.

If a revised job description is unworkable or inadequate, the fourth alternative is to **reassign** the poor performer, either to a position of less responsibility or to one requiring less technical knowledge or interpersonal skills. For example, a medical specialist in a hospital who finds it increasingly difficult to keep abreast of new medical procedures but has demonstrated management skills might be shifted to a full-time administrative position.

The last option is to **release**. If retraining and creative redefinition of task assignments have not worked and if there are no opportunities for reassignment in the organization, the manager should consider releasing the employee from the organization. This option is generally constrained by union agreements, company policies, seniority considerations, and government regulations. Frequently, however, chronic poor performers who could be released are not because management chooses to sidestep a potentially unpleasant task. Instead, the decision is made to set these individuals "on the shelf," out of the mainstream of activities, where they can't cause any problems. Even when this action is motivated by humanitarian concerns ("I don't think he could cope with being terminated"), it often produces the opposite effect. Actions taken to protect an unproductive employee from the embarrassment of termination just substitute the humiliation of being ignored. Obviously, termination is a drastic action that should not be taken lightly. However, the consequences for the unproductive individuals and their coworkers of allowing them to remain after the previous four actions have proven unsuccessful should be weighed carefully in considering this option.

This approach to managing ability problems is reflected in the philosophy of Wendell Parsons, CEO of Stamp-Rite. He argues that one of the most challenging aspects of management is helping employees recognize that job enhancements and advancements are not always possible. Therefore, he says, "If a long-term employee slows down, I try to turn him around by saying how much I value his knowledge and experience, but pointing out that his production has slipped too much. If boredom has set in and I can't offer the employee a change, I encourage him to face the fact and consider doing something else with his life" (Nelton, 1988).

Fostering a Motivating Work Environment

The second component of employee performance is motivation. While it is important to see to the training and the support needs of subordinates and to be actively involved in the hiring and the job-matching processes to ensure adequate aptitude, the influence of a manager's actions on the day-to-day motivation of subordinates is equally vital. Effective managers devote considerable time to gauging and strengthening their subordinates' motivation, as reflected in their effort and concern.

In one of the seminal contributions to management thought, Douglas McGregor (1960) introduced the term *Theory X* to refer to a management style characterized by close supervision. The basic assumption of this theory is that people really do not want to work hard or assume responsibility. Therefore, in order to get the job done, managers must coerce, intimidate, manipulate, and closely supervise their employees. In contrast, McGregor espoused a *Theory Y* view of workers. He argued that workers basically want to do a good job and assume more responsibility; therefore, management's role is to assist workers to reach their potential by productively channeling their motivation to succeed. Unfortunately, McGregor believed, most managers subscribe to *Theory X* assumptions about workers' motives.

The alleged prevalence of the *Theory X* view brings up an interesting series of questions about motivation.

What is the purpose of teaching motivation skills to managers? Should managers learn these skills so they can help employees reach their potential? Or are we teaching these skills to managers so they can more effectively manipulate their employees' behavior? These questions naturally lead to a broader set of issues regarding employee–management relations. Assuming a manager feels responsible for maintaining a given level of productivity, is it also possible to be concerned about the needs and desires of employees? In other words, are concerns about employee morale and company productivity compatible, or are they mutually exclusive?

Contemporary research, as well as the experience of highly acclaimed organizational motivation programs (Harter, Schmidt, & Hayes, 2002), supports the position that concerns about morale and performance can coexist. As Figure 6.1 shows, effective motivational programs not only can, but must focus on increasing both satisfaction and productivity. A high emphasis on satisfaction with a low emphasis on performance represents an irresponsible view of the role of management. Managers are hired by owners to look after the owners' interests. This entails holding employees accountable for producing satisfactory results. Managers who emphasize satisfaction to the exclusion of performance will be seen as nice people, but their **indulging** management style undermines the performance of their subordinates.

Bob Knowling, former head of a group of internal change agents at Ameritech that reported directly to the CEO, joined US West in February 1996 as vice president of network operations and technology. His new job was to lead more than 20,000 employees in a large-scale change effort to improve service to US West's more than 25 million customers.

When asked what the biggest challenge facing companies is, even successful ones, he responded: "For me, it begins with changing a culture of entitlement into

| Figure 6.1 | Relationship Between Satisfaction and Performance |

a culture of accountability. My first week on the job [at US West] it was immediately apparent that nobody had been accountable for the reengineering effort. Beyond that, no one had been accountable for meeting customer expectations or for adhering to a cost structure. It was acceptable to miss budgets. Service was in the tank, we were overspending our budgets by more than $100 million—yet people weren't losing their jobs and they still got all or some of their bonuses. That's very much like Ameritech had been. When people failed, we moved them to human resources or sent them to international. When I got to US West, I felt like I was walking into the same bad movie" (Tichy, 1997).

A strong emphasis on performance to the exclusion of satisfaction is equally ineffective. This time, instead of indulging, the manager is **imposing**. In this situation, managers have little concern for how employees feel about their jobs. The boss issues orders, and the employees must follow them. Exploited employees are unhappy employees, and unhappy employees may seek employment with the competition. Thus, while exploitation may increase productivity in the short run, its long-term effects generally decrease productivity through increased absenteeism, employee turnover, and in some cases, even sabotage and violence.

Jim Stuart, who ran several companies before accepting the position of executive director of the Florida Aquarium in 1995, reflects on how life's experiences convinced him to alter his authoritarian leadership style.

My classmates at Harvard Business School used to call me the Prussian General: For many years, that was my approach to leadership. Then I was hit by a series of personal tragedies and professional setbacks. My wife died. A mail-order venture that I had started went bankrupt. The universe was working hard to bring a little humility into my life. Rather than launch another business, I accepted a friend's offer to head an aquarium project in Tampa. I spent the next six years in a job that gave me no power, no money, and no knowledge. That situation forced me to draw on a deeper part of myself. We ended up with a team of people who were so high-performing that they could almost walk through walls. Why, I wondered, was I suddenly able to lead a team that was so much more resilient and creative than any team that I had run before? The answer: Somewhere, amid all of my trials, I had begun to trust my colleagues as much as I trusted myself. (McCauley, 1999)

When managers emphasize neither satisfaction nor performance, they are **ignoring** their responsibilities and the facts at hand. The resulting neglect reflects a lack of management. There is no real leadership, in the sense that employees receive neither priorities nor direction. Paralyzed between what they consider to be mutually exclusive options of emphasizing performance or satisfaction, managers choose neither. The resulting neglect, if allowed to continue, may ultimately lead to the failure of the work unit.

The **integrating** motivation strategy emphasizes performance and satisfaction equally. Effective managers are able to combine what appear to be competing forces into integrative, synergistic programs. Instead of accepting the conventional wisdom that says competing forces cancel each other out, they capitalize on the tension between the combined elements to forge new approaches creatively. However, this does not mean that both objectives can be fully satisfied in every specific case. Some trade-offs occur naturally in ongoing work situations. However, in the long run, both objectives should be given equal consideration.

The integrative view of motivation proposes that while the importance of employees' feeling good about what they are doing and how they are being treated cannot be downplayed, this concern should not overshadow management's responsibility to hold people accountable for results. Managers should avoid the twin traps of working to engender high employee morale for its own sake or pushing for short-term results at the expense of long-term commitment. The best managers have productive people who are also satisfied with their work environment (Kotter, 1996).

Elements of an Effective Motivation Program

We now turn to the core of this discussion: a step-by-step program for creating an integrative, synergistic motivational program grounded in the belief that employees can simultaneously be high performers and personally satisfied. The key assumptions underlying our framework are summarized in Table 6.1.

It is useful to note that the prevailing wisdom among organizational scholars regarding the relationships between motivation, satisfaction, and performance has changed dramatically over the past several decades. When the authors took their first academic courses on this subject, they were taught the following model:

Satisfaction → Motivation → Performance

Table 6.1	Key Assumptions Underlying Our Framework

1. Employees typically start out motivated. Therefore, a lack of motivation is a learned response, often fostered by misunderstood or unrealistic expectations.

2. The role of management is to create a supportive, problem-solving work environment in which facilitation, not control, is the prevailing value.

3. Rewards should encourage high personal performance that is consistent with management objectives.

4. Motivation works best when it is based on self-governance.

5. Individuals should be treated fairly.

6. Individuals deserve timely, honest feedback on work performance.

However, over the course of our careers we have observed the following criticisms of this "contented cows give more milk" view of employee performance.

First, as researchers began collecting longitudinal data on the predictors of performance, they discovered that the satisfaction, motivation, performance causal logic was wrong. For reasons we will discuss later in this chapter, it is now believed that:

Motivation → Performance → Satisfaction

Second, the correlations among these three variables was very low, suggesting that there were a large number of additional factors that needed to be added to this basic model. For example, we now know that high performance leads to high satisfaction if workers believe that their organization reinforces high performance by contingently linking it to valued rewards. ("I want X and I am more likely to get X if I perform well.") In other words, performance leads to satisfaction when it is clear that rewards are based on performance, as compared with seniority or membership. The addition of this intermediate link between performance and rewards (more generally referred to as outcomes) has so dramatically improved our understanding of the organizational dynamics associated with work performance that it has been incorporated in a revised model:

Motivation → Performance → Outcomes → Satisfaction

The remainder of this chapter is basically an account of the improvements that have been made

over the past few decades in this basic "four factors" model of work motivation. We will not only discuss in more detail the causal logic linking these core variables, but we will also introduce several additional factors that we now know must also be included in a comprehensive motivation program. For example, earlier in this chapter we introduced the notion that people's performance is a function of *both* their motivation and their ability. This suggests that we need to add ability to the basic model as a second factor (besides motivation) contributing to performance. Each of the following sections of this chapter introduce additional variables that, like ability, need to be added to the basic, four-factor model. Table 6.2 shows the key building blocks of the complete model, in the form of six diagnostic questions, organized with reference to the "four-factor" model of motivation. A model encapsulating these questions will be used to summarize our presentation at the end of the chapter (Figure 6.5), and a diagnostic tool based on these questions will be described in the Skill Practice section (Figure 6.7).

ESTABLISH CLEAR PERFORMANCE EXPECTATIONS

As shown in Table 6.2, the first two elements of our comprehensive motivational program focus on the Motivation → Performance link. We begin by focusing on the manager's role in establishing clear expectations and then shift to the manager's role in enabling members of a work group to satisfy those expectations.

It is important to point out that we're not just talking about hourly employees. Based on data collected since 1993, Right Management Consultants report that one third of all managers who change jobs fail in their new positions within 18 months (Fisher, 2005). According to this study, the number-one tip for getting off to a good start is asking your boss exactly what's expected of you and how soon you're supposed to deliver it. In fact, there tends to be a negative correlation between the level of one's position in an organization and the likelihood of receiving a job description or detailed performance expectations. Too often the boss' attitude is, "I pay people to know without being told."

Discussions of goal setting often make reference to an insightful conversation between Alice in Wonderland and the Cheshire Cat. When confronted with a choice among crossing routes, Alice asked the Cat which one she should choose. In response, the Cat asked Alice where she was heading. Discovering that Alice had no real destination in mind, the Cat appropriately advised her that any choice would do. It is surprising how often

Table 6.2	Six Elements of an Integrative Motivation Program

MOTIVATION → PERFORMANCE

1. Establish moderately difficult goals that are understood and accepted.

   Ask: "Do subordinates understand and accept my performance expectations?"

2. Remove personal and organizational obstacles to performance.

   Ask: "Do subordinates feel it is possible to achieve this goal or expectation?"

PERFORMANCE → OUTCOMES

3. Use rewards and discipline appropriately to extinguish unacceptable behavior and encourage exceptional performance.

   Ask: "Do subordinates feel that being a high performer is more rewarding than being a low or average performer?"

OUTCOMES → SATISFACTION

4. Provide salient internal and external incentives.

   Ask: "Do subordinates feel the rewards used to encourage high performance are worth the effort?"

5. Distribute rewards equitably.

   Ask: "Do subordinates feel that work-related benefits are being distributed fairly?"

6. Provide timely rewards and specific, accurate and honest feedback on performance.

   Ask: "Are we getting the most out of our rewards by administering them on a timely basis as part of the feedback process?"

   Ask: "Do subordinates know where they stand in terms of current performance and long-term opportunities?"

supervisors violate the commonsense notion that they need to make sure individuals under their charge not only understand which road they should take but what constitutes an acceptable pace for the journey.

With this parable in mind, managers should begin assessing the motivational climate of their work environment by asking, "Is there agreement on, and acceptance of, performance expectations?" The foundation of an effective motivation program is proper **goal setting** (Locke & Latham, 2002). Across many studies of group performance it was shown that the average performance of groups that set goals is significantly higher than that of groups that didn't set goals. Goal-setting theory suggests that goals are associated with enhanced performance because they mobilize effort, direct attention, and encourage persistence and strategy development (Sue-Chan & Ong, 2002). The salience of goal setting is so well recognized that it has been incorporated in several formal management tools, such as management by objectives (MBO). Effective goal setting has three critical components: *goal-setting process, goal characteristics*, and *feedback*.

A common theme in this book is, "The way you do things is very often as important as what you do." Applied to the **goal-setting process**, this means that the manner by which goals are established must be

considered carefully. The basic maxim is that goals must be both understood and accepted if they are to be effective. To that end, research has shown that subordinates are more likely to "buy into" goals if they feel they were part of the goal-setting process. It has been well documented that the performance of work groups is higher when they choose their goals rather than have them assigned (Sue-Chan & Ong, 2002).

The motivating potential of chosen goals is especially important if the work environment is unfavorable for goal accomplishment (Latham, Erez, & Locke, 1988). For example, a goal might be inconsistent with accepted practice, require new skills, or exacerbate poor management–employee relations. To be sure, if working conditions are highly conducive to goal accomplishment, subordinates may be willing to commit themselves to the achievement of goals in whose formulation they did not participate. However, such acceptance usually occurs only when management demonstrates an overall attitude of understanding and support. When management does not exhibit a supportive attitude, the imposed goals or task assignments are likely to be viewed as unwelcome demands. As a result, subordinates will question the premises underlying the goals or assignments and will comply only reluctantly with the demands.

Sometimes it is difficult to allow for extensive participation in the establishment of work goals. For example, a manager frequently is given directions regarding new tasks or assignment deadlines that must be passed on. However, if subordinates believe management is committed to involving them in all discretionary aspects of the governance of their work unit, they are more willing to accept top-down directions regarding the nondiscretionary aspects of work assignments. For example, a computer programming unit may not have any say about which application programs are assigned to the group or what priority is assigned each incoming assignment. However, the manager can still involve unit members in deciding how much time to allocate to each assignment ("What is a realistic goal for completing this task?") or who should receive which job assignment ("Which type of programs would you find challenging?").

Shifting from process to content, research has shown that **goal characteristics** significantly affect the likelihood that the goal will be accomplished (Locke & Latham, 2002). Effective goals are *specific, consistent*, and *appropriately challenging*.

Goals that are **specific** are measurable, unambiguous, and behavioral. Specific goals reduce misunderstanding about what behaviors will be rewarded. Admonitions such as "be dependable," "work hard," "take initiative," or "do your best" are too general and too difficult to measure and are therefore of limited motivational value. In contrast, when a new vice president of operations was appointed at a major midwestern steel factory, he targeted three goals: Reduce finished product rejection by 15 percent (quality); reduce average shipment period by two days (customer satisfaction); and respond to all employee suggestions within 48 hours (employee involvement).

Goals should also be **consistent**. An already hardworking assistant vice president in a large metropolitan bank complains that she cannot increase both the number of reports she writes in a week and the amount of time she spends "on the floor," visiting with employees and customers. Goals that are inconsistent—in the sense that they are logically impossible to accomplish simultaneously—or incompatible—in the sense that they both require so much effort that they can't be accomplished at the same time—create frustration and alienation. When subordinates complain that goals are incompatible or inconsistent, managers should be flexible enough to reconsider their expectations.

One of the most important characteristics of goals is that they are **appropriately challenging** (Knight, Durham, & Locke, 2001). Simply stated, hard goals are more motivating than easy goals. One explanation for this is called "achievement motivation" (Atkinson, 1992; Weiner, 2000). According to this perspective, workers size up new tasks in terms of their chances for success and the significance of the anticipated accomplishment.

Based only on perceived likelihood of success, one would predict that those who seek success would choose an easy task to perform because the probability for success is the highest. However, these individuals also factor into their decisions the significance of completing the task. To complete a goal that anyone can reach is not rewarding enough for highly motivated individuals. In order for them to feel successful, they must believe that an accomplishment represents a meaningful achievement. Given their desire for success and achievement, it is clear that these workers will be most motivated by challenging, but reachable, goals.

Although there is no single standard of difficulty that fits all people, it is important to keep in mind that high expectations generally foster high performance and low expectations decrease performance (Davidson & Eden, 2000). As one experienced manager said, "We get about what we expect." Warren Bennis, author of *The Unconscious Conspiracy: Why Leaders Can't Lead*, agrees. "In a study of schoolteachers, it turned out that when they held high expectations of their students, that alone was enough to cause an increase of 25 points in the students' IQ scores" (Bennis, 1984, 2003).

In addition to selecting the right type of goal, an effective goal program must also include **feedback**. Feedback provides opportunities for clarifying expectations, adjusting goal difficulty, and gaining recognition. Therefore, it is important to provide benchmark opportunities for individuals to determine how they are doing. These along-the-way progress reports are particularly critical when the time required to complete an assignment or reach a goal is very long. For example, feedback is very useful for projects such as writing a large computer program or raising a million dollars for a local charity. In these cases, feedback should be linked to accomplishing intermediate stages or completing specific components.

REMOVE OBSTACLES TO PERFORMANCE

One of the key ingredients of an effective goal program is a supportive work environment. After setting goals, managers should shift their focus to facilitating successful accomplishment by focusing on the ability part of the performance formula. From a diagnostic perspective, this can be done by asking, "Do subordinates feel it is possible to achieve this goal?" Help from management must come in many forms, including making sure the worker has the aptitude required for the job, providing the necessary training, securing needed resources, and encouraging cooperation and support from other work units. It is the manager's job to make the paths leading toward the targeted goals easier for the subordinate to travel.

This management philosophy can be illustrated readily with examples from sports. Instead of assuming the role of the star quarterback who expects the rest of the team to make him look good, the facilitative manager is more like the blocking fullback or the pulling guard who specializes in downfield blocking and punching holes in the opposition's defenses. In a basketball example, this type of leader is like the player who takes more pride in his number of assists than in the number of points he has scored.

This view is reflected in the management philosophy of Stew Leonard, star of management films on effective motivation, Dale Carnegie ads, and one of 11 businessmen honored at the White House. His dairy sells $100 million worth of food a year—the largest sales volume per square foot in the grocery business. When asked for his management philosophy, Stew downplays gimmicks and high pressure in favor of "genuine caring" for customers and employees. This involves overcoming the natural tendency to worry about "What's in it for me?" The man who helped make Paul Newman's salad dressing famous offers this

management advice: "Don't go into business to get rich. Do it to enrich people. It will come back to you." Stew Leonard understands that the more we focus on our rewards, the less rewarding our focus becomes (Levering & Moskowitz, 2003; *News-Gazette*, 1987).

However, as with all general management guidelines, effective results follow from sensitive, informed implementation tailored to specific circumstances. In this case, the manner in which this enabling, facilitative role should be implemented varies considerably among individuals, organizational settings, and tasks. When subordinates believe that strong management support is needed, leaders who are not aware of the obstacles to performance, or not assertive enough to remove them, probably will be perceived as part of the employee's problem, rather than the source of solutions. By the same token, when management intervention is not needed or expected, managers who are constantly involved in the details of subordinates' job performance will be viewed as meddling and unwilling to trust. This view of management is incorporated in the "path goal" theory of leadership (House & Mitchell, 1974; see also, Schriesheim & Neider, 1996; Shamir, House, & Arthur, 1993), shown in Figure 6.2. The key question it addresses is, "How much help should a manager provide?" In response, the model proposes that the level of involvement should vary according to how much subordinates need to perform a specific task; how much they expect, in general; and how much support is available to them from other organizational sources.

Figure 6.2 | Leader Involvement and Subordinate Performance

The key task characteristics of the path-goal model are structure and difficulty. A task that is highly structured, as reflected in the degree of built-in order and direction, and relatively easy to perform does not require extensive management direction. If managers offer too much advice, they will come across as controlling, bossy, or nagging, because from the nature of the task itself, it is already clear to the subordinates what they should do. On the other hand, for an unstructured and difficult task, management's direction and strong involvement in problem-solving activities will be seen as constructive and satisfying.

The second factor that influences the appropriate degree of management involvement is the expectations of the subordinates. Three distinct characteristics influence expectations: desire for autonomy, experience, and ability. Individuals who prize their autonomy and independence prefer managers with a highly participative leadership style because it gives them more latitude for controlling what they do. In contrast, people who prefer the assistance of others in making decisions, establishing priorities, and solving problems prefer greater management involvement.

The connection between a worker's ability and experience levels and preferred management style is straightforward. Capable and experienced employees feel they need less assistance from their managers because they are adequately trained, know how to obtain the necessary resources, and can handle political entanglements with their counterparts in other units. They appreciate managers who "give them their head" but periodically check to see if further assistance is required. On the other hand, it is frustrating for relatively new employees, or those with marginal skills, to feel that their manager has neither the time nor interest to listen to basic questions.

An important concept in the path-goal approach to leadership is that management involvement should complement, rather than duplicate, organizational sources of support. Specifically, managers should provide more "downfield blocking" in situations wherein work-group norms governing performance are not clear, organizational rewards for performance are insufficient, and organizational controls governing performance are inadequate.

One of the important lessons from this discussion of the path-goal model is that managers must tailor their management style to specific conditions, such as those shown in Table 6.3. Although managers should focus on facilitating task accomplishment, their level of direct involvement should be calibrated to the nature of the work and the availability of organizational support, as well as the ability and experience of the individuals. If managers are insensitive to these contingencies, they probably will be perceived by some subordinates as interfering with their desires to explore their own way, while others will feel lost.

This conclusion underscores how important it is that managers understand the needs and expectations of their subordinates. Bill Dyer, a leading business consultant, observed that effective managers regularly ask their subordinates three simple questions: "How is your work going?" "What do you enjoy the most/least?" "How can I help you succeed?" Asking these questions communicates a supportive style; hearing the answers allows managers to fine-tune their facilitative actions.

Table 6.3	Factors Influencing Management Involvement	
CONTINGENCIES	CONDITIONS APPROPRIATE FOR HIGH MANAGEMENT INVOLVEMENT	CONDITIONS APPROPRIATE FOR LOW MANAGEMENT INVOLVEMENT
Task structure	Low	High
Task mastery	Low	High
Subordinate's desire for autonomy	Low	High
Subordinate's experience	Low	High
Subordinate's ability	Low	High
Strength of group norms	Low	High
Effectiveness of organization's controls and rewards	Low	High

REINFORCE PERFORMANCE-ENHANCING BEHAVIOR

Referring back to the basic "four-factor" model of motivation, we now shift our focus from the antecedents of work performance (the Motivation → Performance link) to its consequences (the Performance → Outcomes link). Once clear goals have been established and the paths to goal completion have been cleared by management, the next step in an effective motivational program is to encourage goal accomplishment by contingently linking performance to extrinsic outcomes (rewards and discipline) and fostering intrinsic outcomes. Given our overall emphasis in this book on improving management skills that are used day in and day out, the majority of this section will focus on linking performance to extrinsic outcomes.

The relevant diagnostic question here is, "Do subordinates feel that being a high performer is more rewarding than being a low or average performer?" Our discussion of this important element of an effective motivational program is based on two related principles: (1) in general, managers should link rewards to performance, rather than seniority or membership; and (2) managers should use discipline to extinguish counterproductive behaviors and use rewards to reinforce productive behaviors.

Use Rewards as Reinforcers

Here is the key to encouraging high performance: behaviors that positively affect performance should be contingently reinforced, using highly desirable rewards. When rewards are linked to desired behaviors, they reinforce (strengthen; increase the frequency of) that behavior (Luthans & Stajkovic, 1999; Stajkovic & Luthans, 2001). If an organization rewards all people identically, or on some basis other than performance, then high performers are likely to feel they are receiving fewer "rewards" than they deserve. Obviously, high performers are the key to the success of any organization. Therefore, motivational schemes should be geared to keeping this employee group satisfied. This observation has led some organizational consultants to use the performance ratings of individuals leaving an organization as an index of the organization's motivational climate.

Ed Lawler, one of the foremost authorities on reward systems, underscores this point when he says, "Often the early reward systems of an organization are particularly important in shaping its culture. They reinforce certain behavior patterns and signal how highly valued different individuals are by the organization. They also attract a certain type of employee and in a host of little ways indicate what the organization stands for and values" (Lawler, 2000a, p. 39).

The principle that rewards should be linked to performance points to a need for caution regarding the practice in some organizations of minimizing distinctions between workers. Some "progressive" organizations have received considerable publicity for motivational programs that include providing recreational facilities, library services, day care, and attractive stock option programs for all employees. These organizations work hard to reduce status distinctions by calling everyone "associates" or "partners," eliminating reserved parking places, and instituting a company uniform. Although there are obvious motivational benefits from employees feeling they are receiving basically the same benefits ("perks") regardless of seniority or level of authority, this motivational philosophy, when carried to an extreme or implemented indiscriminately, runs the risk of undermining the motivation of high performers. In an era of egalitarianism, managers often overlook the vital link between performance and rewards and as a consequence find it difficult to attract and retain strong performers (Pfeffer, 1995).

Fortunately, many firms recognize this pitfall. In a survey, 42 percent of 125 organizations contacted indicated they had made changes in their compensation plan during the previous three years to achieve a better link between pay and performance (Murlis & Wright, 1985). These respondents reported that an interesting set of pressures were prompting them to move in this direction. Hard-charging, typically younger managers were insisting on tighter control over employee performance; executives were determined to "get more bang for the buck" during periods of shrinking resources; personnel managers were trying to reduce the number of grievances focusing on "unfair" pay decisions; and employees were trying to eliminate what they considered to be discrimination in the workplace.

A sampling of the creative methods firms are using to establish closer connections between individual performance and pay includes sales commissions that include follow-up customer satisfaction ratings; pay increases linked to the acquisition of new knowledge, skills, and/or demonstrated competencies; compensating managers based on their ability to mentor new group members and resolve difficult intergroup relationships; and linking the pay of key employees to the accomplishment of new organizational goals or strategic initiatives (Zingheim & Schuster, 1995).

In an attempt to examine the impact of one of these innovative compensation programs, a study was conducted in which the productivity, quality, and labor costs of companies using skill-based pay were compared with comparable firms. The results indicated that firms using this type of pay plan benefited from 58 percent greater productivity, 16 percent lower labor costs per part produced, and an 82 percent better level of quality (Murray & Gerhart, 1998).

Technological constraints sometimes make it difficult to perfectly link individual performance with individual rewards. For example, people working on an automobile assembly line or chemists working on a group research project have little control over their personal productivity. In these situations, rewards linked to the performance of the work group will foster group cohesion and collaboration and partially satisfy the individual members' concerns about fairness (Lawler, 1988, 2000b). When it is not possible to assess the performance of a work group (work shift, organizational department), it is advisable to consider an organization-wide performance bonus. While the merits and technical details of various group and organizational reward systems are beyond the scope of this chapter, managers should link valued rewards and good performance at the most appropriate level of aggregation (Steers et al., 1996).

This discussion of the appropriate unit for measuring and rewarding performance reminds us of the need to take into consideration cultural values and expectations. For example, individuals from collectivist cultures tend to see the group as the appropriate target for improving performance (Graham & Trevor, 2000; Parker, 2001; Triandis, 1994). This implies that in addition to examining contextual factors that might make it difficult to reward individual workers, it is also important to take into consideration different culturally based assumptions about what is the appropriate unit of analysis (group or individual) for measuring and rewarding performance. If a manager of a sales department is concerned about heading off a slump in new orders that has traditionally occurred in the organization during the coming eight-week period, and if she has reason to believe that department members would respond positively to a bonus program targeting that time period, she still has to decide if the bonus should be linked to group performance or individual performance. If this particular work unit consists of a mixture of individuals holding collectivist and individualist value perspectives, the manager should look for ways to factor these conflicting perspectives into the design of the bonus program.

It is also important to point out that not nonfinancial rewards (often treated as awards) need to be included in an effective performance-reinforcing program. Lawler argues that firms will get the greatest motivational impact from awards programs if they follow these guidelines: (1) give the awards publicly, (2) use awards infrequently, (3) embed them in a credible reward process, (4) use the awards presentation to acknowledge past recipients, and (5) make sure the award is meaningful within the organization's culture (Lawler, 2000a, p. 72–73).

The Role of Managers' Actions as Reinforcers

An effective motivational program goes beyond the design of the formal organizational reward system, including such things as pay, promotions, and the like. Managers must also recognize that their daily interactions with subordinates constitute an important source of motivation. It is difficult for even highly sensitive and aware managers to understand fully the impact of their actions on the behavior and attitudes of subordinates. Unfortunately, some managers don't even try to monitor these effects. The danger of this lack of awareness is that it may lead to managerial actions that actually reinforce undesirable behaviors in their subordinates. This has been called "the folly of rewarding A while hoping for B" (Kerr, 1995). For example, a vice president of research and development with a low tolerance for conflict and uncertainty may unwittingly undermine the company's avowed objective of developing highly creative products by punishing work groups that do not exhibit unity or a clear, consistent set of priorities. Further, while avowing the virtue of risk, the manager may punish failure; while stressing creativity, he or she may kill the spirit of the idea champion. These actions will encourage a work group to avoid challenging projects, suppress debate, and routinize task performance.

The do's and don'ts for encouraging subordinates to assume more initiative, shown in Table 6.4, demonstrate the power of managers' actions in shaping behavior. Actions and reactions that might appear insignificant to the boss often have strong reinforcing or extinguishing effects on subordinates. Hence the truism, "Managers get what they reinforce, not what they want," and its companion, "People do what is inspected, not what is expected." Indeed, the reinforcing potential of managers' reactions to subordinates' behaviors is so strong that it has been argued, "The best way to change an individual's behavior in a work setting is to change his or her manager's behavior" (Thompson, 1978, p. 52).

Table 6.4 Guidelines for Fostering Subordinate Initiative

Do	Don't
Ask "How are we going to do this? What can I contribute to this effort? How will we use this result?," thus implying your joint stake in the work and results.	Imply that the task is the employee's total responsibility, that they hang alone if they fail. Individual failure means organizational failure.
Use an interested, exploring manner, asking questions designed to bring out factual information.	Play the part of an interrogator, firing questions as rapidly as they can be answered. Also, avoid asking questions that require only "yes" or "no" replies.
Keep the analysis and evaluation as much in the employees' hands as possible by asking for their best judgment on various issues.	React to their presentations on an emotional basis.
Present facts about organization needs, commitments, strategy, and so on, which permit them to improve and interest them in improving what they propose to do.	Demand a change or improvement in a preemptory tone of voice or on what appears to be an arbitrary basis.
Ask them to investigate or analyze further if you feel that they have overlooked some points or overemphasized others.	Take their planning papers and cross out, change dates, or mark "no good" next to certain activities.
Ask them to return with their plans after factoring these items in.	Redo their plans for them unless their repeated efforts show no improvement.

Source: *Reprinted with the permission of Simon & Schuster Adult Publishing Group, from PUTTING MANAGEMENT THEORIES TO WORK by Marion S. Kellogg, revised by Irving Burstiner. Copyright © 1979 by Prentice Hall. All rights reserved.*

Given the considerable leverage managers have over their subordinates' motivation to reach optimal performance, it is important that they learn how to use rewards and punishments effectively to produce positive, intended results consistently.

Use Rewards and Discipline Appropriately

Psychologists call the process of linking rewards and punishments with behaviors in such a manner that the behaviors are more or less likely to persist "operant conditioning" (Komaki, Coombs, & Schepman, 1996). This approach uses a wide variety of motivational strategies that involve the presentation or withdrawal of positive or negative reinforcers or the use of no reinforcement whatsoever. Although there are important theoretical and experimental differences in these strategies, such as between negative reinforcement and punishment, for the purposes of our discussion we will focus on three types of management responses to employee behavior: no response (ignoring), negative response (disciplining), and positive response (rewarding).

The trickiest strategy to transfer from the psychologist's laboratory to the manager's work environment is "no response." Technically, what psychologists refer to as "extinction" is defined as a behavior followed by no response whatsoever. However, in most managerial

situations, people develop expectations about what is likely to follow their actions based on their past experience, office stories, and so forth. Consequently, what is intended as a nonresponse, or a neutral response, generally is interpreted as either a positive or negative response. For example, if a subordinate comes into your office complaining bitterly about a coworker, and you attempt to discourage this type of behavior by changing the subject or responding in a low, unresponsive monotone voice, the subordinate may view this as a form of rejection. If your secretary sheepishly slips a delinquent report on your desk, and you ignore her behavior because you are busy with other business, she may be so relieved at not being reprimanded for her tardiness that she actually feels reinforced.

These simple examples underscore an important point: any behavior that is repeatedly exhibited in front of a boss is being rewarded, regardless of the boss's intention ("I don't want to encourage that type of behavior, so I'm purposely ignoring it"). By definition, if a behavior persists, it is being reinforced. Thus, if an employee is chronically late or continually submits sloppy work, the manager must ask where the reinforcement for this behavior is coming from. Consequently, while extinction plays an important role in the learning process when conducted in strictly controlled laboratory conditions, it is a less useful technique in organizational settings because the interpretation of a supposedly neutral

LEARNING

Figure 6.3   Behavior-Shaping Strategies

Reprimand   Redirect   Reinforce

Discipline   Reward

−   0   +

Unacceptable
Behavior

Acceptable
Behavior

Exceptional
Behavior

response is impossible to control. Thus, the focus of our discussion will be on the proper use of disciplining and rewarding strategies, as shown in Figure 6.3.

The **disciplining** approach involves responding negatively to an employee's behavior with the intention of discouraging future occurrences of that behavior. For example, if an employee is consistently late, a supervisor may reprimand him with the hope that this action will decrease the employee's tardiness. Nagging subordinates for their failure to obey safety regulations is another example.

The **rewarding** approach consists of linking desired behaviors with employee-valued outcomes. When a management trainee completes a report in a timely manner, the supervisor should praise his promptness. If a senior executive takes the initiative to solve a thorny, time-consuming problem on her own, she could be given some extra time to enjoy a scenic location at the conclusion of a business trip. Unfortunately, even simple rewards like these appear to be the exception, not the rule. Dr. Noelle Nelson, the author of a book on the power of appreciation in the workplace (2005), points out that according to U.S. Department of Labor data, the number-one reason people leave their job is that they do not feel appreciated. She also points to a Gallup poll report that 65 percent of workers say they didn't receive a single word of praise or recognition during the past year. Elaborating on these data, Nelson argues that even the most energetic and effective employees get worn down when they are rarely acknowledged for their good work and only singled out when they make mistakes.

Disciplining and rewarding are both viable and useful techniques and each has its place in the effective manager's motivational repertoire. However, as Figure 6.3 shows, each technique is associated with different behavior-shaping goals. Discipline should be used to extinguish unacceptable behaviors. However, once an individual's behavior has reached an acceptable level, negative responses will not push the behavior up to the exceptional level. It is difficult to encourage employees to perform exceptional behaviors through nagging, threatening, or related forms of discipline. The left-hand side of Figure 6.3 shows that subordinates work to remove an aversive response rather than to gain a desired reward. Only through positive reinforcement do employees have control over achieving what they want and, therefore, the incentive to reach a level of exceptional performance.

The emphasis in Figure 6.3 on matching discipline and rewards with unacceptable and acceptable behaviors, respectively, highlights two common misapplications of reinforcement principles. First, it helps us better understand why top performers frequently get upset because they feel "management is too soft on those guys who are always screwing things up." Thinking that it is good management practice always to be upbeat and optimistic and to discourage negative interactions, some managers try to downplay the seriousness of mistakes by ignoring them, by trying to temper the consequences by personally fixing errors, or by encouraging the high performers to be more tolerant and patient. Other managers feel so uncomfortable with confronting personal performance problems that they are willing to overlook all but the most egregious mistakes.

Although there is a lot to be said for managers having a positive attitude and giving poor performers the benefit of the doubt, their failure to reprimand and redirect inappropriate behaviors leads to two undesirable outcomes: the work unit's morale is seriously threatened, and the poor performers' behaviors are not improved.

Just as some managers find it unpleasant to issue reprimands for poor performance, other managers have difficulty praising exceptional performance. As a result, subordinates complain, "Nothing ever satisfies him." This second misapplication of the negative-response behavior-shaping strategy is just as dysfunctional as the indiscriminate use of praise. These managers mistakenly believe that the best way to motivate people is by always keeping expectations a little higher than their subordinates' best performance and then chiding them for their imperfection. In the process, they run the risk of burning out their staff or inadvertently encouraging lower performance ("We'll get chewed out anyway, so why try so hard?"). Furthermore, the irony is that this method creates a competitive, self-defeating situation in which subordinates look forward to the boss's making mistakes—the bigger the better!

Unfortunately, many managers genuinely believe that this is the best way to manage in all situations. They define their role as that of a "sheepdog," circling the perimeter of the group, nipping at the heels of those who begin to stray. They establish a fairly broad range of acceptable behaviors and then limit their interactions with employees to barking at those who exceed the boundaries. This negative, desultory style of management creates a demoralizing work environment and does not foster exceptional performance. Instead, workers are motivated to stay out of the boss' way and to avoid doing anything unusual or untried. Innovation and involvement are extinguished, and mundane performance becomes not only acceptable but desirable.

Having looked at the consequences of misapplying rewards and discipline, we will now turn our attention to the proper use of behavior-shaping techniques. The mark of exceptional managers is their ability to foster exceptional behavior in their subordinates. This is best accomplished by using a nine-step behavior-shaping process, which can be applied to the full range of subordinates' behaviors. They can be used either to make unacceptable behaviors acceptable or to transform acceptable behaviors into exceptional ones. They are designed to avoid the harmful effects typically associated with the improper use of discipline discussed in the previous section (Wood & Bandura, 1989). They also ensure the appropriate use of rewards.

Strategies for Shaping Behavior

Table 6.5 shows the nine steps for improving behaviors. These are organized into three broad initiatives: *reprimand, redirect,* and *reinforce.* As shown in Figure 6.3, steps 1 through 6 (reprimand and redirect) are used to extinguish unacceptable behaviors and

Table 6.5	Guidelines for Improving Behaviors

Reprimand

1. Identify the specific inappropriate behavior. Give examples. Indicate that the action must stop.

2. Point out the impact of the problem on the performance of others, on the unit's mission, and so forth.

3. Ask questions about causes and explore remedies.

Redirect

4. Describe the behaviors or standards you expect. Make sure the individual understands and agrees that these are reasonable.

5. Ask if the individual will comply.

6. Be appropriately supportive. For example, praise other aspects of their work, identify personal and group benefits of compliance; make sure there are no work-related problems standing in the way of meeting your expectations.

Reinforce

7. Identify rewards that are salient to the individual.

8. Link the attainment of desirable outcomes with incremental, continuous improvement.

9. Reward (including using praise) all improvements in performance in a timely and honest manner.

replace them with acceptable ones. Steps 4 through 9 (redirect and reinforce) are used to transform acceptable behaviors into exceptional behaviors.

An important principle to keep in mind when issuing a **reprimand** is that discipline should immediately follow the offensive behavior and focus exclusively on the specific problem. This is not an appropriate time to dredge up old concerns or make general, unsubstantiated accusations. The focus of the discussion should be on eliminating a problem behavior, not on making the subordinate feel bad. This approach increases the likelihood that the employee will associate the negative response with a specific act rather than viewing it as a generalized negative evaluation, which will reduce the hostility typically engendered by being reprimanded.

Second, it is important to **redirect** inappropriate behaviors into appropriate channels. It is important that people being reprimanded understand how they can receive rewards in the future. The process of redirection reduces the despair that occurs when people feel they are likely to be punished no matter what they do. If expected behaviors are not made clear, then workers may stop the inappropriate behavior but feel lost, not knowing how to improve. Keep in mind that the ultimate goal of any negative feedback should be to transform inappropriate behaviors into appropriate behaviors, in contrast to simply punishing a person for causing a problem or making the boss look bad. The lingering negative effects of a reprimand will quickly wear off if the manager begins using rewards to **reinforce** desirable behaviors shortly thereafter. This goal can be achieved only if workers know how they can receive positive outcomes and perceive that the available rewards are personally salient (a subject we'll discuss in detail shortly).

Experienced managers know it is just as difficult to transform acceptable behaviors into exceptional ones. Helping an "OK, but uninspired" subordinate catch the vision of moving up to a higher level of desire and commitment can be very challenging. This process begins at step 4 (redirect) by first clearly describing the goal or target behavior. The goal of skilled managers is to avoid having to administer any negative responses and especially to avoid trial-and-error learning among new subordinates. This is done by clearly laying out their expectations and collaboratively establishing work objectives. In addition, it is a good idea to provide an experienced mentor, known for exceptional performance, as a sounding board and role model.

Foster Intrinsic Outcomes

So far our discussion of the Performance → Outcomes link has focused on **extrinsic outcomes**. These are things like pay and promotions and praise that are controlled by someone other than the individual performer. In addition, the motivating potential of a task is affected by its associated **intrinsic outcomes**, which are experienced directly by an individual as a result of successful task performance. They include feelings of accomplishment, self-esteem, and the development of new skills. Although our emphasis has been on the former, a complete motivational program must take into account both types of outcomes.

Effective managers understand that the person–job interface has a strong impact on work performance. No matter how many externally controlled rewards managers use, if individuals find their jobs uninteresting and unfulfilling, performance will suffer. This is particularly true for certain individuals. For example, researchers have discovered that the level of job satisfaction reported by highly intelligent people is closely linked to the degree of difficulty they encounter in performing their work (Ganzach, 1998). In addition, attention to intrinsic outcomes is particularly important in situations in which organizational policies do not permit a close link between performance and rewards; for example, in a strong seniority personnel system. In these cases, it is often possible to compensate for lack of control over extrinsic outcomes by fine-tuning the person–job fit.

Motivating Workers by Redesigning Work

Work design is the process of matching job characteristics and workers' skills and interests. One popular work-design model proposes that particular job dimensions cause workers to experience specific psychological reactions called "states." In turn, these psychological reactions produce specific personal and work outcomes. Figure 6.4 shows the relationship between the core job dimensions, the critical psychological states they produce, and the resulting personal and work outcomes (Hackman & Oldham, 1980). A variety of empirical research has found that the five core job dimensions—skill variety, task identity, task significance, autonomy, and feedback—are positively related to job satisfaction.

The more variety in the skills a person can use in performing work, the more the person perceives the task as meaningful or worthwhile. Similarly, the more an individual can perform a complete job from beginning to

Figure 6.4   Designing Highly Motivating Jobs

Source: *Hackman/Oldham, WORK REDESIGN, © 1980. Reprinted by permission of Pearson Education, Inc. Upper Saddle River, NJ.*

end (task identity) and the more the work has a direct effect on the work or lives of other people (task significance), the more the employee will view the job as meaningful. On the other hand, when the work requires few skills, only part of a task is performed, or there seems to be little effect on others' jobs, experienced meaningfulness is low.

The more autonomy in the work (freedom to choose how and when to do particular jobs), the more responsibility workers feel for their successes and failures. Increased responsibility results in increased commitment to one's work. Autonomy can be increased by instituting flexible work schedules, decentralizing decision making, or selectively removing formalized controls, such as the ringing of a bell to indicate the beginning and end of a workday.

Finally, the more feedback individuals receive about how well their jobs are being performed, the more knowledge of results they have. Knowledge of results permits workers to understand the benefits of the jobs they perform. Employees' knowledge of results may be enhanced by increasing their direct contact with clients or by giving them feedback on how their jobs fit in and contribute to the overall operation of the organization.

By enhancing the core job dimensions and increasing critical psychological stages, employees' job fulfillment is increased. Job fulfillment (high internal work motivation) is associated with other outcomes valued by management. These include high-quality work performance, high employee satisfaction with their jobs, and low absenteeism and turnover. Employees who have well-designed jobs enjoy doing them because they are intrinsically satisfying.

This discussion of work design suggests five managerial action guidelines that can help increase desirable personal and work outcomes. These are summarized in Table 6.6. The first one is to *combine tasks.* A combination of tasks is by definition a more challenging and complex work assignment. It requires workers to use a wider variety of skills, which makes the work seem more challenging and meaningful. Telephone directories at the former Indiana Bell Telephone company used to be compiled in 21 steps along an assembly line. Through job redesign, each worker was given responsibility for compiling an entire directory.

A related managerial principle is to *form identifiable work units* so that task identity and task significance can be increased. Clerical work in a large insurance firm was

Table 6.6	Strategies for Increasing the Motivational Potential of Assigned Work		
Combine tasks	→	Increase skill variety and task significance	
Form identifiable work units	→	Increase task identity and significance	
Establish client relationships	→	Increase autonomy, task identity, and feedback	
Increase authority	→	Increase autonomy, task significance, and task identity	
Open feedback channels	→	Increase autonomy and feedback	

handled by 80 employees organized by functional task (e.g., opening the mail, entering information into the computer, sending out statements). Work was assigned, based on current workload, by a supervisor over each functional area. To create higher levels of task identity and task significance, the firm reorganized the clerical staff into eight self-contained groups. Each group handled all business associated with specific clients.

The third guideline for enhancing jobs is to *establish client relationships.* A client relationship involves an ongoing personal relationship between an employee (the producer) and the client (the consumer). The establishment of this relationship can increase autonomy, task identity, and feedback. Take, for example, research and development (R&D) employees. While they may be the ones who design a product, feedback on customer satisfaction generally is routed through their managers or a separate customer relations unit. At Caterpillar, Inc., members of each division's R&D group are assigned to make regular contacts with their major clients.

The fourth suggestion, *increase authority,* refers to granting more authority for making job-related decisions to workers. When we speak here of "vertical," we refer to the distribution of power between a subordinate and a boss. As supervisors delegate more authority and responsibility, their subordinates' perceived autonomy, task significance, and task identity increase. Historically, workers on auto assembly lines have had little decision-making authority. However, in conjunction with increased emphasis on quality, many plants now allow workers to adjust their equipment, reject faulty materials, and even shut down the line if a major problem is evident.

The final managerial suggestion is to *open feedback channels.* Workers need to know how well or how poorly they are performing their jobs if any kind of improvement is expected. Thus, it is imperative that they receive timely and consistent feedback, which allows them to make appropriate adjustments in their behavior so they can receive desired rewards. The

traditional approach to quality assurance in American industry is to "inspect it in." A separate quality assurance group is assigned to check the production team's quality. The emerging trend is to give producers responsibility for checking their own work. If it doesn't meet quality standards, they immediately fix the defect. Following this procedure, workers receive immediate feedback on their performance.

A different approach to job design focuses on matching individuals' "deeply embedded life interests" with the task characteristics of their work (Butler & Waldroop, 1999). The proponents of this approach argue that for too long people have been advised to select careers based on what they are good at, rather than what they enjoy. The assumption behind this advice is that individuals who excel at their work are satisfied with their jobs. However, critics of this perspective argue that many professionals are so well educated and achievement oriented that they could succeed in virtually any job. This suggests that people stay in jobs because they become involved in activities that are consistent with their long-held, emotionally driven passions, intricately entwined with their personality.

Setting aside the differences among the various approaches to matching workers and their work, the overall record of job redesign interventions is impressive. In general, firms typically report a substantial increase in productivity, work quality, and worker satisfaction (reflected in lower rates of absenteeism). For example, the Social Security Administration increased productivity 23.5 percent among a group of 50 employees; General Electric realized a 50 percent increase in product quality as a result of a job redesign program; and the absenteeism rate among data-processing operators at Travelers Insurance decreased 24 percent (Kopelman, 1985).

In summary, managers should recognize that both extrinsic and intrinsic outcomes are necessary ingredients of effective motivational programs. For example, because most people desire interesting and challenging work activities, good wages and job security will do little to overcome the negative effects of individuals' feeling that their abilities are being underutilized. In addition, recognizing that individual preferences for outcomes vary, managers should not assume that a narrow-gauged, outcomes-contingent, performance-reinforcing motivation program will satisfy the needs and interests of a broad group of individuals. This brings us to the subject of reward salience.

PROVIDE SALIENT REWARDS

Having established a link between performance and outcomes (rewards and discipline) as part of an integrative motivational program, we now move to the final link in the four-factor model of motivation: Outcomes → Satisfaction. In the following sections we will discuss the three remaining elements of our motivational program, as shown in Table 6.2. Each of these elements has been shown to affect how satisfied individuals are with their work-related outcomes, and as a set they help us understand the key distinction between a reward and a reinforcer. The likelihood that a "reward" (so labeled by the reward giver) will actually reinforce a specific performance-enhancing behavior depends on the extent to which the reward recipient: (1) actually values the specific outcome, (2) believes that the reward allocation process was handled fairly, and (3) receives the reward in a timely manner.

We begin this discussion, with diagnostic question 4, "Do subordinates feel the rewards used to encourage high performance are worth the effort?" One of the biggest mistakes that can be made in implementing a "reward program" is assuming that managers understand their subordinates' preferences. For example, while it is assumed that most people prefer cash incentives, according to a 2004 study conducted by the University of Chicago, performance increases much faster when it is linked to noncash rewards (14.6 percent increase for cash vs. 38.6 percent increase for noncash) (*Cook*, 2005, p. 6). On an individual level, the manager's lament "What does Joe expect, anyway? I gave him a bonus, and he's still complaining to other members of the accounting department that I don't appreciate his superior performance," indicates an apparent miscalculation of what Joe really values. This miscalculation also suggests that the manager needs a better understanding of the relationship between personal needs and personal motivation.

Personal Needs and Personal Motivation

One of the most enduring theories of motivation is based on our scientific understanding of human needs.

One way to categorize the various theories of human needs is by whether the theories assume that needs are arranged in a hierarchical fashion. The logic of a **hierarchical needs model** is that people are motivated to satisfy their most basic unfulfilled need. That is, until a lower-level need has been satisfied, a higher-level need won't become activated. Probably the best-known example of a hierarchical needs model was proposed by Abraham Maslow (1970). He posited five levels of needs, beginning with *physiological,* followed by *safety, belongingness, esteem,* and *self-actualization.* Clay Alderfer proposed a more parsimonious hierarchical model (1977) that contained only three levels, or categories: *existence, relatedness,* and *growth.* Like Maslow, Alderfer proposed that satisfied needs become dormant unless a dramatic shift in circumstances increases their salience. For example, a middle-level executive who is fired during a hostile takeover may suddenly find that her interest in personal growth is overwhelmed by a pressing need for security. The problem with hierarchical needs theories is that although they help us understand general developmental processes, from child to adult, they aren't very useful for understanding the day-to-day motivation levels of adult employees. A comparison of these hierarchical needs models is shown in Table 6.7.

An alternative perspective can be found in Murray's **manifest needs model** (McClelland, 1971, p. 13). Murray proposed that individuals can be classified according to the strengths of their various needs. In contrast to hierarchical models, in which needs are categorized based on their inherent strength (hunger is a stronger need than self-actualization), Murray posited that people have divergent and often conflicting needs. Murray proposed about two dozen needs, but later studies have suggested that only three or four of them are relevant to the workplace, including the needs for *achievement, affiliation,* and *power.* Another important distinction of Murray's conception is his belief that these

Table 6.7	Comparison of Hierarchical Needs Theories	
MASLOW	**ALDERFER**
Self-actualization	Growth
Esteem	
Belongingness	Social
Safety	
Physiological	Existence

needs are primarily learned, rather than inherited, and that they are activated by cues from the environment. That is, if a person has a high need for achievement it will become manifest, or an active motivational force, only if the environment cues achievement-oriented behavior.

The **need for achievement** is defined as "behavior toward competition with a standard of excellence" (McClelland, Arkinson, Clark, & Lowell, 1953, p. 111). This suggests that individuals with a high need for achievement would be characterized by: (1) a tendency to set moderately difficult goals, (2) a strong desire to assume personal responsibility for work activities, (3) a single-minded focus on accomplishing a task, and (4) a strong desire for detailed feedback on task performance. The level of a person's need for achievement (high to low) has been shown to be a good predictor of job performance. In addition, it is highly correlated with a person's preference for an enriched job with greater responsibility and autonomy.

The second of Murray's needs, **need for affiliation**, involves attractions to other individuals in order to feel reassured and acceptable (Birch & Veroff, 1966, p. 65). It has been suggested that people with a high need for affiliation are characterized by: (1) a sincere interest in the feelings of others; (2) a tendency to conform to the expectations of others, especially those whose affiliation they value; and (3) a strong desire for reassurance and approval from others. One would expect individuals with a high need for affiliation to gravitate toward jobs that provide a high degree of interpersonal contact. It is useful to point out that in contrast to the need for achievement, the need for affiliation does not seem to be correlated with job performance.

Rounding out Murray's model is the **need for power**, which represents a desire to influence others and to control one's environment. Individuals with a high need for power seek leadership positions and tend to influence others in a fairly open, direct manner. McClelland and Burnham (2003) suggest that there are two manifestations of the general need for power. Individuals with a high need for *personal power* tend to seek power and influence for its own sake. To them, control and dominance and conquest are important indicators of personal efficacy. These leaders inspire their subordinates to perform heroic feats, but for the sake of the leader, not the organization. In contrast, individuals with high *institutional power* needs are more oriented toward using their influence to advance the goals of the group or organization. These individuals are described by McClelland as follows: (1) they are organization minded, feeling personally responsible for advancing the purposes of the organization; (2) they enjoy work and accomplish-

ing tasks in an orderly fashion; (3) they are often willing to sacrifice their own self-interests for the good of the organization; (4) they have a strong sense of justice and equity; and (5) they seek expert advice and are not defensive when their ideas are criticized.

Using Need Theory to Identify Personally Salient Outcomes

An understanding of need theory helps managers understand whether organizational rewards are salient reinforcers for specific individuals. Simply put, if a reward satisfies an activated personal need, it can be used to reinforce desired individual behaviors. In practice this means that managers need to understand what motivates each of their subordinates. Table 6.8 demonstrates the difficulty of this task. These research results highlight differences in what various types of organizational members tend to see as highly motivating aspects of their work. For example, while on average the employees in this study placed the highest value on "interesting work" and the lowest value on "sympathetic help with personal problems," we see significant differences in the ratings for these two outcomes across gender, age, and income categories. It is easy to spot equally disparate outcome preferences expressed by different groups of workers for many of the other benefits and rewards, in the left-hand column, commonly used by business firms to attract, retain, and motivate employees.

In the abstract it is not surprising to learn that individuals with different demographic and economic profiles have different needs and, thus, bring different expectations to the workplace. The relevance of this data for effective motivational practices is underscored by a parallel research study suggesting that managers are not particularly good at predicting how their subordinates would rank the outcomes shown in Table 6.8 (LeDue, 1980). More particularly, this research suggests that managers tend to base their answers to the question, "What motivates your subordinates?" on two faulty assumptions. First, they assume that the outcome preferences among their subordinates are fairly homogenous, and second, they assume that their personal outcome preferences are similar to those held by their subordinates. Knowing this, the data shown in Table 6.8 illustrates how easy it is for managers with a certain gender, age, and income profile to systematically misread the salient needs of subordinates characterized by a different profile. Furthermore, it is not difficult to imagine individual circumstances that would result in a person's preferences being significantly different from those of others with a similar demographic and economic profile. In summary,

Table 6.8 What Workers Want, Ranked by Subgroups*

	All Employees	Men	Women	Under 30	31–40	41–50	Over 50	Under $25,000	$25,001–$40,000	$45,001–$50,000	Over $50,000	Blue-Collar Unskilled	Blue-Collar Skilled	White-Collar Unskilled	White-Collar Skilled	Lower Nonsupervisory	Middle Nonsupervisory	Higher Nonsupervisory
Interesting work	1	1	2	4	2	3	1	5	2	1	1	2	1	1	2	3	1	1
Full appreciation of work done	2	2	1	5	3	2	2	4	3	3	2	1	6	3	1	4	2	2
Feeling of being in on things	3	3	3	6	4	1	3	6	1	2	4	5	2	5	4	5	3	3
Job security	4	5	4	2	1	4	7	2	4	4	3	4	3	7	5	2	4	6
Good wages	5	4	5	1	5	5	8	1	5	6	8	3	4	6	6	1	6	8
Promotion and growth in organization	6	6	6	3	6	8	9	3	6	5	7	6	5	4	3	6	5	5
Good working conditions	7	7	10	7	7	7	4	8	7	7	6	9	7	2	7	7	7	4
Personal loyalty to employees	8	8	8	9	9	6	5	7	8	8	5	8	9	9	8	8	8	7
Tactful discipline	9	9	9	8	10	9	10	10	9	9	10	7	10	10	9	9	9	10
Sympathetic help with personal problems	10	10	3	10	8	10	6	9	10	10	9	10	8	8	10	10	10	9

*Ranked from 1 (highest) to 10 (lowest).

Source: Courtesy of Prof. K. A. Kovach. George Mason University. Results are from a study of 1000 employees conducted in 1995.

this data underscores the importance of managers getting to know their subordinates well enough that they can effectively match individual and group performance expectations with personally salient outcomes.

The importance of gaining this person-specific information is illustrated in the case of a stockbroker who was promoted to office manager because upper management in the home office felt he was "the most qualified and most deserving." Unfortunately, they failed to ask him if he wanted to be promoted. They assumed that because they had worked hard to qualify for their management positions that all hard workers were similarly motivated. Two weeks after receiving his "reward" for outstanding performance, the supersalesman-turned-manager was in the hospital with a stress-related illness.

Effective managers gain information about active needs and personal values through frequent, supportive, generally informal, discussions with their subordinates. One approach used by some managers is to discuss with subordinates recent significant changes in the roles or work assignments of common acquaintances, possibly involving a promotion, a change of work assignment, or a transfer to a new location or work unit. Subordinates' responses to the consequences of these changes, including level of pay, type of pay (e.g., sales commissions vs. salary), travel expectations, responsibilities for coordinat-ing the work of others, level of pressure to produce, capitalizing on old skills vs. learning new ones, an individual vs. team-oriented work environment, opportunities for promotion, and so forth, often provide insights into their own personal preferences. When engaging in discussions such as these, keep in mind that information regarding preferred trade-offs is particularly useful. In the abstract, everyone values everything. In reality, we have to make choices and those choices reflect our underlying needs and values. Thus, it is particularly instructive to see how someone responds to the prospect that a colleague's new job provides opportunities for more pay, but at the expense of being away from home three nights a week. Or, that the opportunity to be involved with the design of a new product line also means longer hours at work, higher levels of personal stress, and the possibility that the failure to meet high expectations may reflect negatively on the team members.

The data reported in Table 6.8 is also relevant for individuals in a position to shape the pay and benefits package for an entire organization. Scanning these results, it is easy to pick out differences between the ratings of blue-collar vs. white-collar, unskilled and skilled, lower and higher level employees. Recognizing the wide diversity in outcome preferences within the employee ranks of most large businesses, many firms, ranging from investment banks, like Morgan Stanley, to manufacturing firms, like American Can, have experimented with "cafeteria-style" incentive systems (Abbott, 1997; Lawler, 1987). This approach takes much of the guesswork out of linking an individual's organizational membership and work performance with personally salient outcomes, by allowing employees some say in the matching process. Using this approach, employees receive a certain number of work credits based on performance, seniority, or task difficulty, and they are allowed to trade those in for a variety of benefits, including upgraded insurance packages, financial planning services, disability income plans, extended vacation benefits, tuition reimbursement for educational programs, and so forth.

BE FAIR AND EQUITABLE

Once appropriate rewards have been determined for each employee, managers must then consider how to distribute those rewards (Cropanzano & Folger, 1996). This brings us to concerns about equity. Any positive benefits of salient rewards will be negated if workers feel they are not receiving their fair share. The relevant diagnostic question here is, "Do subordinates feel that work-related benefits are distributed fairly?" (As in the previous section, we will focus here only on rewards. However, the same principles also apply to the equitable use of discipline.)

Equity refers to workers' perceptions of the fairness of rewards. Evaluations of equity are based on a social comparison process in which workers individually compare what they are getting out of the work relationship (outcomes) to what they are putting into the work relationship (inputs). Outcomes include such items as pay, fringe benefits, increased responsibility, and prestige, while inputs may include hours worked and work quality, as well as education and experience. The ratio of outcomes to inputs is then compared to corresponding ratios of other individuals, judged to be an appropriate comparison group. The outcome of this comparison is the basis for beliefs about fairness.

If workers experience feelings of inequity, they will behaviorally or cognitively adjust their own or fellow workers' inputs and/or outputs. In some cases, this may lead to a decrease in motivation and performance. For example, if employees believe that they are underpaid, they have a number of options. Cognitively, they may rationalize that they really are not working as hard as they thought they were; thus, they reduce the perceived value of their own inputs. Alternatively, they might convince themselves that coworkers are actually working

harder than they thought they were. Behaviorally, workers can request a pay raise (increase their outcomes), or they can decrease their inputs by leaving a few minutes early each day, decreasing their effort, deciding not to complete an optional training program, or finding excuses not to accept difficult assignments.

The significance of this aspect of motivation underscores the need for managers to monitor closely subordinates' perceptions of equity (Janssen, 2001). In some cases, these conversations may uncover faulty comparison processes. For example, employees might misunderstand the value placed on various inputs, such as experience versus expertise or quantity versus quality; or they might have unrealistic views of their own or others' performance. It has been noted that most people believe their leadership skills are better than those of most of the population.

However, just as often these discussions uncover real inequities. For example, the hourly rate of a worker may not be keeping up with recent skill upgrades or increased job responsibilities. The act of identifying and correcting legitimate inequities generates enormous commitment and loyalty. For example, a manager in the computer industry felt he had been unfairly passed over for promotion by a rival. Utilizing the company's open-door policy, he took his case to a higher level in the firm. After a thorough investigation, the decision was reversed and the rival reprimanded. The individual's response was, "After they went to bat for me, I could never leave the company."

The important thing to keep in mind about equity and fairness is that we are dealing with perceptions. Consequently, whether they are accurate or distorted, legitimate or ill-founded, they are both accurate and legitimate in the mind of the perceiver until proven otherwise. A basic principle of social psychology states: "That which is perceived as being real is real in its consequences." Therefore, effective managers should constantly perform "reality checks" on their subordinates' perceptions of equity, using questions such as: "What criteria for promotions, pay raises, and so on do you feel management should be placing more/less emphasis on?" "Relative to others similar to you in this organization, do you feel your job assignments, promotions, and so on are appropriate?" "Why do you think Alice was recently promoted over Jack?"

PROVIDE TIMELY REWARDS AND ACCURATE FEEDBACK

Up to this point, we have emphasized that employees need to understand and accept performance standards;

they should feel that management is working hard to help them reach their performance goals; they should feel that available internal and external rewards are personally attractive; they should believe that rewards and reprimands are distributed fairly; and they should feel that these outcomes are administered primarily on the basis of performance.

All these elements are necessary for an effective motivational program, but they are not sufficient. As we noted earlier, a common mistake is to assume that all rewards are reinforcers. In fact, the reinforcing potential of a "reward" depends on its being linked in the mind of the reward recipient to the specific behaviors the reward giver desires to strengthen. ("When I did behavior X, I received outcome Y. And, because I value Y, I am going to repeat X.") The ability of reward recipients to make this reinforcing (X behavior–Y outcome) mental connection is related to two specific aspects of how the reward is administered: (1) the length of time between the occurrence of the desirable behavior and the receipt of the reward, and (2) the specificity of the explanation for the reward. These are the two final components of our motivational program. Hence, the sixth and final diagnostic question contains two parts. The first is, "Are we getting the most out of our rewards by administering them on a timely basis as part of the feedback process?"

As a general rule, the longer the delay in the administration of rewards the less reinforcement value they have. Even if the recipient greatly values the recognition and the reward giver clearly identifies the behaviors being rewarded, unless the reward is received soon after the behavior has been exhibited (or the goal accomplished), the intended reinforcement value of the reward is diminished.

Ironically, in a worst-case situation, the mistiming of a reward may actually reinforce undesirable behaviors. Giving a long overdue, fully warranted raise to a subordinate during an interview in which she or he is complaining about the unfairness of the reward system may reinforce complaining rather than good work performance. Moreover, failure to give a reward when a desired behavior occurs will make it even more difficult to sustain that behavior in the future. If the owners of a new business have delayed the implementation of a promise to grant stock options for the core start-up cadre as compensation for their low wages and 70- to 80-hour workweeks, the workers' willingness to sustain such a pace on promises and dreams alone may begin to wane.

The importance of timing becomes obvious when one considers that all the research findings supporting the value of operant conditioning as a motivational system assume that outcomes immediately follow behaviors. Imagine how little we would know about behavior-shaping processes if, in the experiments with birds and rats described in psychology textbooks, the food pellets were dropped into the cage several minutes after the desired behavior occurred.

Today's managers have a number of technological tools that can be used to speed up feedback. Hatim Tyabji, while serving as CEO of Verifone, used e-mail to reinforce important contributions. "We recently had a major win in a market where we hadn't been having much success. Against all odds, we went after a big customer and won. When I got word that we had won—and I'm so enmeshed in the organization that people just ignore the hierarchy and e-mail me that kind of news—my first reaction, apart from pure joy, was: Why did we win? My next question was: Who are the key people who made the difference? Then I immediately sent out a message of congratulations. The e-mails and phone calls I got back were enough to make my eyes moist. That to me is what makes us tick" (Adria, 2000; Nelson, 2000; Taylor, 1995).

Unfortunately, although timing is a critical contributor to the reinforcement potential of a reward, it is frequently ignored in everyday management practice. The formal administrative apparatus of many organizations often delays for months the feedback on the consequences of employee performance. It is customary practice to restrict in-depth discussions of job performance to formally designated appraisal interviews, which generally take place every six or twelve months. ("I'll have to review this matter officially later, so why do it twice?") The problem with this common practice is that the resulting delay between performance and outcomes dilutes the effectiveness of any rewards or discipline dispensed as a result of the evaluation process.

In contrast, effective managers understand the importance of immediate, spontaneous rewards. They use the formal performance evaluation process to discuss long-term trends in performance, solve problems inhibiting performance, and set performance goals. But they don't expect these infrequent general discussions to significantly alter an employee's motivation. For this, they rely on brief, frequent, highly visible performance feedback. At least once a week they seek some opportunity to praise desirable work habits among their subordinates.

Peters and Waterman, in their classic book *In Search of Excellence* (1988), stress the importance of immediacy by relating the following amusing anecdote:

At Foxboro, a technical advance was desperately needed for survival in the company's early days. Late one evening, a scientist rushed into the president's office with a working prototype. Dumbfounded at the elegance of the solution and bemused about how to reward it, the president bent forward in his chair, rummaged through most of the drawers in his desk, found something, leaned over the desk to the scientist, and said, "Here!" In his hand was a banana, the only reward he could immediately put his hands on. From that point on, the small "gold banana" pin has been the highest accolade for scientific achievement at Foxboro. (pp. 70–71)

The implication for effective management is clear: effective rewards are spontaneous rewards. Reward programs that become highly routinized, especially those linked to formal performance appraisal systems, lose their immediacy.

There is a second critical aspect of reinforcement timing: the consistency of reward administration. Administering a reward every time a behavior occurs is called continuous reinforcement. Administering rewards on an intermittent basis (the same reward is always used but is not given every time it is warranted) is referred to as partial, or intermittent, reinforcement. Neither approach is clearly superior; both approaches have trade-offs. Continuous reinforcement represents the fastest way to establish new behavior. For example, if a boss consistently praises a subordinate for writing reports using the manager's preferred format, the subordinate will readily adopt that style in order to receive more and more contingent rewards. However, if the boss suddenly takes an extended leave of absence, the learned behavior will be highly vulnerable to extinction because the reinforcement pattern is broken. In contrast, while partial reinforcement results in very slow learning, it is very resistant to extinction. The persistence associated with gambling behavior illustrates the addictive nature of a partial reinforcement schedule. Not knowing when the next payoff may come preserves the myth that the jackpot is only one more try away.

This information about reinforcement timing derived from experimental research has important implications for effective management. First, it is important to realize that continuous reinforcement systems are very rare in organizations unless they are mechanically built into the job, as in the case of the piece-rate pay plan. Seldom are individuals rewarded every time they make a good presentation or effectively handle a customer's complaint. When we recognize that most non-assembly-line work in an organization is typically governed by a partial reinforcement schedule, we gain new insights into some of the more frustrating aspects of a manager's role. For example, it helps explain why new employees seem to take forever to catch on to how the boss wants things done. It also suggests why it is so difficult to extinguish outdated behaviors, particularly in older employees.

Second, given how difficult it is for one manager to reinforce consistently the desired behaviors in a new employee (or an employee who is going through a reprimand, redirect, reward cycle), it is generally a good idea to use a team effort. By sharing your developmental objectives with other individuals who interact with the target employee, you increase the likelihood of the desired behaviors being reinforced during the critical early stages of improvement. For example, if a division head is trying to encourage a new member of her staff to become more assertive, she might encourage other staff members to respond positively to the newcomer's halting efforts in meetings or private conversations.

This brings us to the second half of the sixth diagnostic question, related to the accuracy of feedback, "Do subordinates know where they stand in terms of current performance and long-term opportunities?" In addition to the timing of feedback, the content of feedback significantly affects its reinforcement potential. As a rule of thumb, to increase the motivational potential of performance feedback, be very specific—including examples whenever possible. Keep in mind that feedback, whether positive or negative, is itself an outcome. The main purpose for giving people feedback on their performance is to reinforce productive behaviors and extinguish counterproductive behaviors. But this can only occur if the feedback focuses on specific behaviors. To illustrate this point, compare the reinforcement value of the following, equally positive, messages. "You are a great member of this team—we couldn't get along without you." "You are a great member of this team. In particular, you are willing to do whatever is required to meet a deadline."

It is especially important that managers provide accurate and honest feedback when a person's performance is marginal or substandard. There are many reasons why managers are reluctant to "tell it like it is" when dealing with poor performers. It is unpleasant to deliver bad news of any kind. It is especially painful to give negative feedback regarding a person's performance. Therefore, it is easy to justify sugarcoating negative information, especially when it is unexpected, on the basis that you are doing the recipient a favor. In practice, it is rarely the case that a poor performer is better off not receiving detailed, honest, accurate feedback. If the feedback is very general, or if it contains mixed signals, improvement is frustratingly difficult. And if a person truly is not well suited for a particular job, then no one benefits from delaying a shift in responsibilities or encouragement to seek other work opportunities.

When managers are reluctant to share unflattering or unhopeful feedback, it is often because they are unwilling to spend sufficient time with individuals receiving negative feedback to help them thoroughly understand their shortcomings, put them in perspective, consider options, and explore possible remedies. It is sometimes easier to pass on an employee with a poor performance record or unrealistic expectations to the next supervisor than it is to confront the problem directly, provide honest and constructive feedback, and help the individual respond appropriately. Therefore, many individuals feel that supportive communication of negative performance information is the management skill which is most difficult to master—and therefore the one most highly prized. If you are particularly interested in polishing this skill, we recom-

mend you review the specific techniques described under the heading "Use Rewards and Discipline Appropriately."

Summary

Our discussion of enhancing work performance has focused on specific analytical and behavioral management skills. We first introduced the fundamental distinction between ability and motivation. Then we discussed several diagnostic questions for determining whether inadequate performance was due to insufficient ability. A five-step process for handling ability problems (resupply, retrain, refit, reassign, and release) was outlined. We introduced the topic of motivation by stressing the need for placing equal emphasis on concerns for satisfaction and performance. The remainder of this chapter focused on the second skill by presenting six elements of an integrative approach to motivation.

The summary model shown in Figure 6.5 (and its "diagnostic" version discussed in the Skill Practice section as Figure 6.7) highlights our discussion of an expanded version of the basic "four factors" model of

Figure 6.5 Integrative Model of Motivation Enhancement

1–6: Key to six diagnostic questions in Table 6.2.

motivation. The resulting comprehensive model underscores the necessary role of, as well as the interdependence among, the various components. Skilled managers incorporate all components of this model into their motivational efforts rather than concentrating only on a favorite subset. There are no shortcuts to effective management. All elements of the motivation process must be included in a total, integrated program for improving performance and satisfaction.

The fact that the flowchart begins with motivation is important, because it makes explicit our assumption that individuals are initially motivated to work hard and do a good job. Recall that motivation is manifested as work effort and that effort consists of desire and commitment. This means that motivated employees have the desire to initiate a task and the commitment to do their best. Whether their motivation is sustained over time depends on the remaining elements of the model, which are actually amplifications of the Motivation → Performance link, the Performance → Outcomes link, and the Outcomes → Satisfaction link. These crucial links in the motivational process can best be summarized as questions pondered by individuals asked to work harder, change their work routine, or strive for a higher level of quality: First, "If I put forth more effort, am I likely to be able to perform up to performance expectations?" Second, "Will my level of performance matter in this organization?" Third, "Will the experience of being a high performer likely be personally rewarding?"

Beginning on the left side of the model, we see that the combination of goals and ability determines the extent to which effort is successfully transformed into performance. In the path-goal theory of leadership, the importance of fitting the right job to the right person and providing necessary resources and training is emphasized. These factors must be combined with effective goal setting (understanding and accepting moderately difficult goals) if increased effort is to result in increased performance.

The next section of the model focuses on reinforcing good performance, in terms of both increasing the frequency of performance-enhancing behaviors and linking outcomes to successful goal accomplishment. It is important to keep in mind that people are, in general, motivated by both extrinsic and intrinsic outcomes. In addition, the effective manager is adept at using the full range of behavior-shaping tools, spanning the spectrum from discipline to rewards. Although our discussion focused more on rewards than discipline, when faced with the challenge of providing constructive but negative performance feedback, and developing an accompanying plan for remediation, Table 6.5 provides a useful set of guidelines.

Proceeding to the Outcomes → Satisfaction segment of the model, the importance of perceived equity and reward salience stand out. Individuals must believe that the rewards offered are appropriate, not only for their personal performance level but also in comparison to the rewards achieved by "similar" others. The subjective value that individuals attach to incentives for performance reflects their personal relevance, or salience. Rewards with little personal value have low motivational potential. These subjective factors combine with the timeliness and accuracy of feedback to determine the overall motivational potential of rewards.

Based on their perceptions of outcomes, workers will experience varying degrees of satisfaction or dissatisfaction. Satisfaction creates a positive feedback loop, increasing the individual's motivation, as manifested by increased effort. Dissatisfaction, on the other hand, results in decreased effort and, therefore, lower performance and rewards. If uncorrected, this pattern may ultimately result in absenteeism or turnover.

Behavioral Guidelines

This discussion is organized around key diagnostic models and questions that serve as the basis for enhancing the following skills: (1) properly diagnosing performance problems; (2) initiating actions to enhance individuals' abilities; and (3) strengthening the motivational aspects of the work environment.

Table 6.2 summarizes the process for properly diagnosing the causes of poor work performance in the form of six diagnostic questions. (A "decision tree" version of these questions is included in the Skill Practice section as Figure 6.7.)

The key guidelines for creating a highly motivating work environment are:

1. Clearly define an acceptable level of overall performance or specific behavioral objective.
   - ❏ Make sure the individual understands what is necessary to satisfy expectations.
   - ❏ Formulate goals and expectations collaboratively, if possible.
   - ❏ Make goals as challenging and specific as possible.
2. Help remove all obstacles to reaching performance objectives.
   - ❏ Make sure the individual has adequate technical information, financial resources, personnel, and political support.

- ❏ If a lack of ability appears to be hindering performance, use the resupply, retrain, refit, reassign, or release series of remedies.
- ❏ Gear your level of involvement as a leader to how much help a person expects, needs, and how much help is otherwise available.
3. Make rewards and discipline contingent on high performance or drawing nearer to the performance objective.
   - ❏ Carefully examine the behavioral consequences of your nonresponses. (Ignoring a behavior is rarely interpreted as a neutral response.)
   - ❏ Use discipline to extinguish counterproductive behavior and rewards to reinforce productive behaviors.
4. When discipline is required, treat it as a learning experience for the individual.
   - ❏ Specifically identify the problem and explain how it should be corrected.
   - ❏ Use the reprimand and redirect guidelines in Table 6.5.
5. Transform acceptable into exceptional behaviors.
   - ❏ Reward each level of improvement.

- ❏ Use the redirect and reward guidelines in Table 6.5.
6. Use reinforcing rewards that appeal to the individual.
   - ❏ Allow flexibility in individual selection of rewards.
   - ❏ Provide salient external rewards as well as satisfying and rewarding work (intrinsic satisfaction).
   - ❏ To maintain salience, do not overuse rewards.
7. Periodically check subordinates' perceptions regarding the equity of reward allocations.
   - ❏ Correct misperceptions related to equity comparisons.
8. Provide timely rewards and accurate feedback.
   - ❏ Minimize the time lag between behaviors and feedback on performance, including the administration of rewards or reprimands. (Spontaneous feedback shapes behavior best.)
   - ❏ Provide specific, honest, and accurate assessments of current performance and long-range opportunities.

CASE INVOLVING MOTIVATION PROBLEMS

Electro Logic

Electro Logic (EL) is a small R&D firm located in a midwestern college town adjacent to a major university. Its primary mission is to perform basic research on, and development of, a new technology called "Very Fast, Very Accurate" (VFVA). Founded four years ago by Steve Morgan, an electrical engineering professor and inventor of the technology, EL is primarily funded by government contracts, although it plans to market VFVA technology and devices to nongovernmental organizations within the year.

The government is very interested in VFVA, as it will enhance radar technology, robotics, and a number of other important defense applications. EL recently received the largest small-business contract ever awarded by the government to research and develop this or any other technology. Phase I of the contract has just been completed, and the government has agreed to Phase II contracting as well.

The organizational chart of EL is shown in Figure 6.6. Current membership is 75, with roughly 88 percent in engineering. The hierarchy of engineering titles and requirements for each are listed in Table 6.9. Heads of staff are supposedly appointed based on their knowledge of VFVA technology and their ability to manage people. In practice, the president of EL hand-picks these people based on what some might call arbitrary guidelines: most of the staff leaders were or are the president's graduate students. There is no predetermined time frame for advancement up the hierarchy. Raises are, however, directly related to performance appraisal evaluations.

Working directly with the engineers are the technicians. These people generally have a high school degree, although some also have college degrees. They are trained on the job, although some have gone through a local community college's program on microtechnology fabrication. The technicians perform the mundane tasks of the engineering department: running tests, building circuit boards, manufacturing VFVA chips, and so on. Most are full-time, hourly employees.

The administrative staff is composed of the staff head (with an MBA from a major university), accountants, personnel director, graphic artists, purchasing agent, project

Table 6.9	Engineering Titles and Requirements
TITLE	**REQUIREMENT**
Member of Technical Staff	BSEE, MSEE
Senior Member of Technical Staff	PhD, MSEE with 2 years of industrial experience; BSEE with 5 years of industrial experience
Research Engineer	PhD with 2 years of industrial experience
	BSEE or MSEE with 7 years of industrial experience
Research Scientist	PhD with appropriate experience in research
Senior Research Scientist	PhD with appropriate industrial and research experience

Figure 6.6   Electro Logic Organization Chart

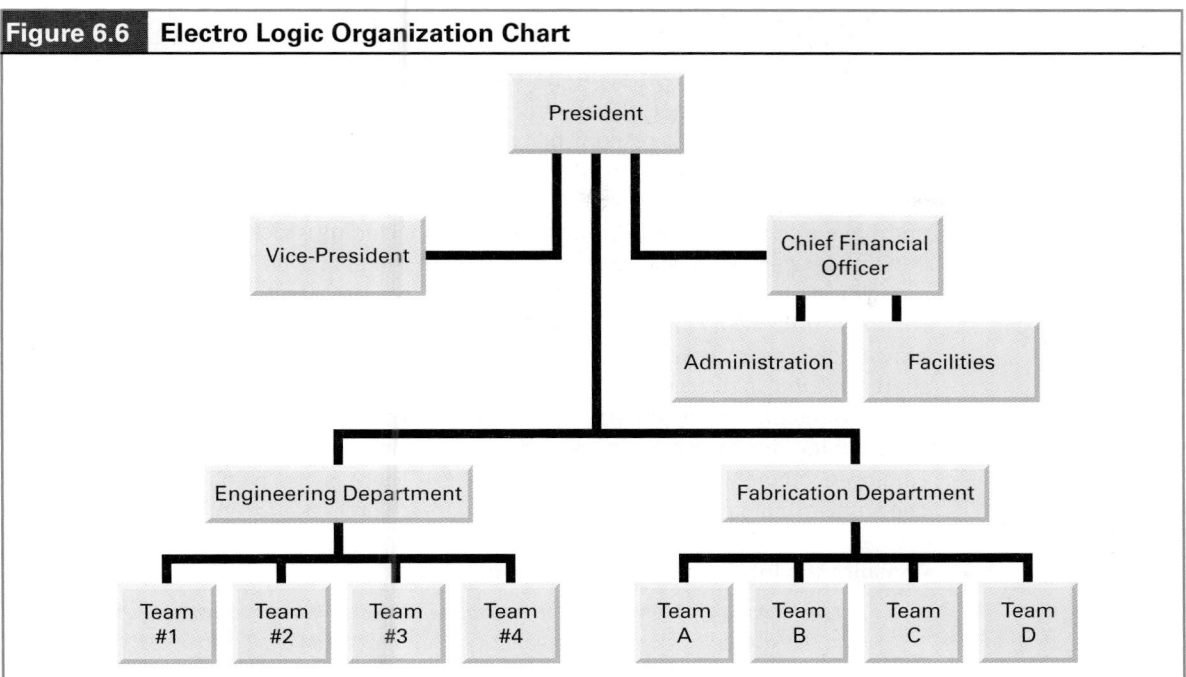

controller, technical writers/editors, and secretaries. Most of the people in the administrative staff are women. All are hourly employees except the staff head, personnel director, and project controller. The graphic artists and technical writer/editor are part-time employees.

The facilities staff is composed of the staff head and maintenance personnel. EL is housed in three different buildings, and the primary responsibility of the facilities staff is to ensure that the facilities of each building are in good working order. Additionally, the facilities staff is often called upon to remodel parts of the buildings as the staff continues to grow.

EL anticipates a major recruiting campaign to enhance the overall staff. In particular, it is looking for more technicians and engineers. Prior to this recruiting campaign, however, the president of EL hired an outside consultant to assess employee needs as well as the morale and overall effectiveness of the firm. The consultant has been observing EL for about three weeks and has written up some notes of her impressions and observations of the company.

Consultant's Notes from Observations of Electro Logic

Facilities: Electro Logic (EL) is housed in three different buildings. Two are converted houses, and one is an old school building. Senior managers and engineers are in the school, and others are scattered between the houses.

Meetings: Weekly staff meetings are held in the main building to discuss objectives and to formulate and review milestone charts.

Social interaction: A core group of employees interact frequently on a social basis; for example, sports teams, parties. The administrative staff celebrate birthdays at work. The president occasionally attends.

Work allocation: Engineers request various tasks from the support staff, which consists of technicians and administrative unit personnel. There is obviously some discretion used by the staff in assigning priorities to the work requests, based on rapport and desirability of the work.

Turnover: The highest turnover is among administrative personnel and technicians. Exit interviews with engineers indicate they leave because of the company's crisis-management style, better opportunities for career advancement and security in larger organizations, and overall frustration with EL's "pecking order." Engineers with the most responsibility and authority tend to leave.

Salary and benefits: In general, wages at EL are marginal by national and local standards. A small group of scientists and engineers do make substantial salaries and have a very attractive benefits package, including stock options. Salaries and benefits for new engineers tend to be linked to the perceived level of their expertise.

Offices and facilities: Only EL's president, vice president, and chief financial officer have their own offices. Engineers are grouped together in "pods" by project assignment. There is very little privacy in these work areas, and the noise from the shared printer is distracting. The head of administration shares a pod with the personnel director, facilities head, and the project controller. One to three secretaries per building are located in or near the reception areas. The large building has an employee lounge with three vending machines. There is also a coffee-and-tea station. The smaller buildings have only a soft-drink machine in the reception area.

Consultant's Interviews with Employees

After making these observations, the consultant requested interviews with a cross-section of the staff for the purpose of developing a survey to be taken of all employees. Presented below are excerpts from those interviews.

Pat Klausen, Senior Member of the Technical Staff

CONSULTANT: What is it about Electro Logic (EL) that gives you the most satisfaction?

PAT: I really enjoy the work. I mean, I've always liked to do research, and working on VFVA is an incredible opportunity. Just getting to work with Steve (EL's president and VFVA's inventor) again is exciting. I was his graduate student about six years ago, you know. He really likes to work closely with his people—perhaps sometimes too closely. There have been times when I could have done with a little less supervision.

CONSULTANT: What's the least satisfying aspect of your work?

PAT: Probably the fact that I'm never quite sure that we'll be funded next month, given the defense budget problems and the tentativeness of our research. I've got a family to consider, and this place isn't the most stable in terms of its financial situation. Maybe it'll change once we get more into commercial production. Who knows?

CONSULTANT: You've offered some general positives and negatives about EL. Can you be more specific about day-to-day dealings? What's good and bad about working here on a daily basis?

PAT: You're sure this isn't going to get back to anyone? Okay. Well, in general I'm not satisfied with the fact that too often we end up changing horses in the middle of the stream, if you know what I mean. In the past seven months, three of my engineers and four of my techs have been pulled off my project onto projects whose deadlines were nearer than mine. Now I'm faced with a deadline, and I'm supposed to be getting more staff. But I'll have to spend so much time briefing them that it might make more sense for me to just finish the project myself. On the other hand, Steve keeps telling me that we have to be concerned with EL's overall goals, not just our individual concerns—you know, we have to be "team players," "good members of the family." It's kind of hard to deal with that, though, when deadlines are bearing down and you know your butt's on the line, team player or not. But if you go along with this kind of stuff and don't complain, the higher-ups treat you well. Still, it seems to me there's got to be a better way to manage these projects.

CONSULTANT: What are the positive aspects of your daily work?

PAT: Well, the people here are all great to work with. They know their stuff or can learn quickly. I tend to be a social person and I really like socializing with these people. We play softball and basketball together and do happy hours and stuff. I like that. I've got some good friends here, which helps get my work orders filled quickly, if you know what I mean.

Bob Christensen, Member of the Technical Staff

CONSULTANT: You said earlier that Steve was your advisor for your M.S. So you've known him a long time.

BOB: Yes, that's right. I've known Professor Morgan—Steve—for about eight years. I had him for a few undergraduate classes; then, of course, he was my advisor for my two-year master's program, and now I've worked at Electro Logic (EL) for two years.

CONSULTANT: It seems as if you enjoy working with Steve.

BOB: Oh, yeah. But I really don't get to work directly with him anymore. I'll see him at meetings and such, but that's about it.

CONSULTANT: So he's not your immediate supervisor?

BOB: No, but for the amount of time I spend with my supervisor, Steve might as well be. My boss and I meet maybe once every three weeks for about an hour to see if all is well. And that's it. The rest of the time, I'm on my own. I used to talk to Steve when I had questions, but he's gotten so busy now that it's hard to see him—you need to make an appointment a few days in advance.

CONSULTANT: Do you think your supervisor treats all his staff this way?

BOB: To be honest, I have heard some complaints. In fact, about six months ago, the situation was so bad, some other people and I had a meeting with him. He promised that he would be more available to us and was, for about a month. Then we got involved in a new proposal, so he made himself scarce again. So nothing's really changed. We're coming up on finalizing the proposal now, and it's important that I see him, ask him questions. The last few drafts I've submitted to him, he's returned, rewritten in his own way, and with no explanation of the changes. Sometimes I think he treats me like somebody who doesn't know anything, as if I had no training whatsoever. I realize his neck is on the line with this project, but sometimes it seems that he uses being busy to avoid talking to me.

Chris Chen, Research Scientist

CONSULTANT: What kind of characteristics should a person have if he/she wants to work as a research scientist at Electro Logic (EL)?

CHRIS: Well, certainly technical knowledge is important. When I've interviewed recent college grads for entry-level positions, I am always concerned with their GPA. I like to see straight-A averages, if possible. But for experienced research scientists, technical knowledge shows up in their publication records, mostly. So I'll read their papers. I also think a research scientist has to be highly self-motivated, not look to others for praise and such. Particularly here. If you want someone to tell you you've done a good job, you'll be waiting a long time. It's not clear to me that research scientists really get the support we need from the rest of the staff here. Work orders are often lost or put off for one reason or another. Senior members seem to get more techs than scientists do, and they certainly get more attention from Steve. The rumor is that these guys also get higher raises than the scientists; allegedly, this is to keep pay at an equitable rate—you know, they're supposedly more valuable to the company. Of course, everybody knows that most of the senior members are Steve's old graduate students, and so he takes care of them really well. One of the things that

ANALYSIS

really galls me is that I need to keep up my publication record to maintain my career options. But publishing is frowned on because it takes time away from your work. I've even been told that my work can't be published because of proprietary rights or that the defense department considers the information classified. However, if somebody important is working with me and needs the publication, then it's full steam ahead.

CONSULTANT: You sound pretty disgruntled with your work.

CHRIS: It's not my work so much. I'm really very happy doing this work—it's cutting-edge, after all. The problem is that I'm never quite sure where the work is going. I do my part of a project, and unless I go out of my way to talk to other people, I never find out the final results of the total project. That's just something you learn to live with around here—being part of a system that's not particularly open.

Meg Conroy, Assistant to the Head of Administration

CONSULTANT: You've only been here a short time, is that correct?

MEG: That's right—just a little over a year.

CONSULTANT: Why did you take the job?

MEG: Well, I was in my last semester of college and was looking for a job, like most college seniors. My fiancé at the time—now he's my husband—was already working for Electro Logic (EL) and found out that there was an opening. So I applied.

CONSULTANT: So you were a business major in school?

MEG: Oh, no. I was a history major.

CONSULTANT: Do you like your job?

MEG: It has a lot to offer. I get paid pretty well for what I'm doing. And I'm learning a lot. I just wish the company would let me take some classes in administration, like accounting. The auditors ask some pretty tough questions. Steve says we should hire that expertise, but I'd still be responsible for supervising the people.

CONSULTANT: Is there any particular aspect about your job that you really find satisfying?

MEG: Well, let me think. I guess I like the fact that I get to do a lot of different tasks so that things don't get so boring. I would hate to have to do the same thing, day in and day out. A lot of times, I go to the library to do research on different things, and that's nice because it gets me out of the office.

CONSULTANT: What don't you like about your job?

MEG: Well, I often get the feeling that administration isn't taken seriously. You know, the engineers could get along without us quite nicely, or so they seem to think. The whole structure of the department shows that we're the catch-all department: if you don't fit anywhere else, they put you in here. Perhaps some of that is because our department is primarily women—in fact, I've been told that 95 percent of all the female employees are in administration. Sometimes it's hard to work with the engineers because they treat you like you don't know anything, and they always want things to be done their way. Clearly, the engineers get the money and consideration and yet, well, we do contribute quite a lot to the whole team, as Steve would say. But words of praise just aren't as impressive as actions. Sure, we get our birthday parties, but that still seems to be a little patronizing. We rarely get to see what's going on in the research area. I've asked a number of engineers specific questions, and they just kind of look at me with a blank stare and give me some really simplified answer. It seems to me if you want to build a family, like the president says, you can't treat administration like a bad relation.

P. J. Ginelli, Technician

CONSULTANT: I gather you've just been through your semiannual performance appraisal. How did it go?

P. J.: Like I expected. No surprises.

CONSULTANT: Do you find these appraisals useful?

P. J.: Sure. I get to find out what he thinks of my work.

CONSULTANT: Is that all?

P. J.: Well, I suppose it's a nice opportunity to understand what my supervisor wants. Sometimes he's not so clear during the rest of the year. I suppose he's been given specific goals from higher-ups before he talks with me, so he's clear and then I'm clear.

CONSULTANT: Do you like what you're doing?

P. J.: Oh yeah. The best part is that I'm not at the main building and so I don't have to put up with the "important" people, you know? I've heard from other techs that those guys can be a real pain—trying to be nice and all, but really just being a bother. I mean, how can you get your stuff done when the president's looking over your shoulder all the time? On the other hand, if the president knows your name, I suppose that's a good thing when it comes to raises and promotions. But my boss sticks up for his techs; we get a fair deal from him.

CONSULTANT: Do you think you'll be able to get ahead at Electro Logic (EL)?

P. J.: Get ahead? You mean become an engineer or something? No, and I really don't want to do that. Everyone around here keeps pushing me to move up. I'm afraid to tell people how I really feel for fear they'll decide I don't fit into this high-tech environment. I don't want to be the "black sheep of the family." I like where I am, and if the raises keep coming, I'll keep liking it. One of my kids is starting college next year, and I need the money to help her out. I get a lot of overtime, particularly when contract deadlines are near. I suppose the rush toward the end of contracts gives some people big headaches, but for me, I don't mind. The work is pretty slow otherwise, and so at least I'm working all the time and then some. But my family wishes my schedule was more predictable.

CONSULTANT: Do you think you'll continue working for EL?

P. J.: I'm not sure I want to answer that. Let's just say that my ratings on the performance appraisal were good, and I expect to see an improvement in my pay. I'll stay for that.

Chalida Montgomery, Technician

CONSULTANT: In general, what are your feelings about the work you do for Electro Logic (EL)?

CHALIDA: Well, I feel my work is quite good, but I also feel that I perform rather boring, tedious tasks. From what my supervisor says, the kinds of things I do are what electrical engineering students do in their last year of classes. I gather their final project is to make a circuit board, and that's what I do, day in and day out.

CONSULTANT: What is it that you would like to do?

CHALIDA: Well, it would be nice to be able to offer some input into some of the designs of these boards. I know I don't have a PhD or anything, but I do have lots of experience. But because I'm a tech, the engineers don't really feel I've got much to offer—even though I build the boards and can tell from the design which one will do what the designer wants it to do. I also would like to maybe supervise other technicians in my department. You know, some kind of advancement would be nice. As it is, lots of techs ask me how to do things, and of course I help, but then they get the credit. Around here, you have to have a piece of paper that says you're educated before they let you officially help other people.

Discussion Questions

1. Using the behavioral guidelines and Figure 6.5 as diagnostic aids, what are the strengths and weaknesses of Electro Logic (EL) from a motivational perspective?
2. What are the high-priority action items you would include in a consulting report to Steve Morgan, president of EL? Focus on specific actions that he could initiate that would better use the abilities of the staff and foster a more motivating work environment.

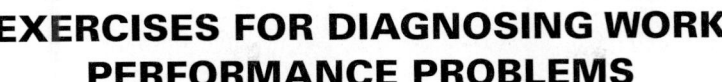
EXERCISES FOR DIAGNOSING WORK PERFORMANCE PROBLEMS

Proper diagnosis is a critical aspect of effective motivation management. Often, managers become frustrated because they don't understand the causes of observed performance problems. They might experiment with various "cures," but the inefficiency of this trial-and-error process often only increases their frustration level. In addition, the accompanying misunderstanding adds extra strain to the manager–subordinate relationship. This generally makes the performance problem even more pronounced, which in turn prompts the manager to resort to more drastic responses, and a vicious downward spiral ensues.

The performance diagnosis model in Figure 6.7 offers a systematic way for managers and subordinates to pinpoint collaboratively the causes of dissatisfaction and performance problems. It assumes that employees will work hard and be good performers if the work environment encourages these actions. Consequently, rather than jumping to conclusions about poor performance stemming from deficiencies in personality traits or a bad attitude, this diagnostic process helps managers focus their attention on improving the selection, job design, performance evaluation, and reward-allocation systems. In this manner, the specific steps necessary to accomplish work goals and management's expectations are examined to pinpoint why a worker's performance is falling short.

The manager and low-performing subordinate should follow the logical discovery process in the model, step by step. They should begin by examining the current perceptions of performance, as well as the understanding of performance expectations, and then proceed through the model until the performance problems have been identified. The model focuses on seven of these problems.

1. **Perception Problem:** "Do you agree your performance is below expectations?" A perception problem suggests that the manager and subordinate have different views of the subordinate's current performance level. Unless this disagreement is resolved, it is futile to continue the diagnostic process. The entire problem-solving process is based on the premise that both parties recognize the existence of a problem and are interested in solving it. If agreement does not exist, the manager should focus on resolving the discrepancy in perceptions, including clarifying current expectations (Problem 5).

2. **Resources Problem:** "Do you have the resources necessary to do the job well?" Ability has three components, and these should be explored in the order shown in the model. This order reduces a subordinate's defensive reactions. Poor performance may stem from a lack of resource support. Resources include material and personnel support as well as cooperation from interdependent work groups.

3. **Training Problem:** "Is a lack of training interfering with your job performance?" Individuals may be asked to perform tasks that exceed their current skill or knowledge level. Typically, this problem can be overcome through additional training or education.

4. **Aptitude Problem:** "Do you feel this is the right job/blend of work assignments for you?" This is the most difficult of the three ability problems to resolve because it is the most basic. If the resupply (providing additional resources) and retraining solutions have been explored without success, then more drastic measures may be

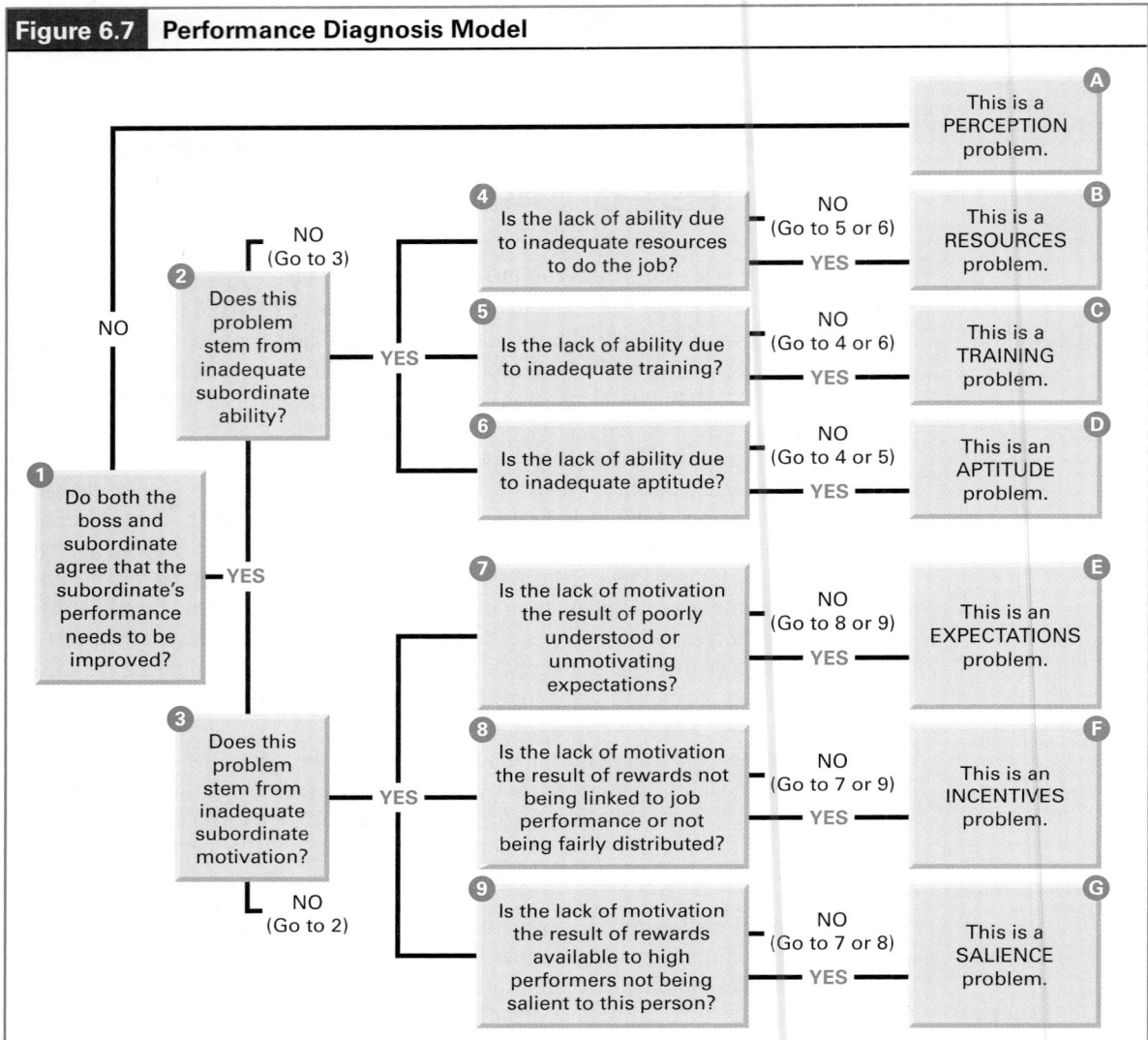

Figure 6.7 Performance Diagnosis Model

A This is a PERCEPTION problem.

4 Is the lack of ability due to inadequate resources to do the job?
— NO (Go to 5 or 6)
— YES —
B This is a RESOURCES problem.

2 Does this problem stem from inadequate subordinate ability?
NO (Go to 3)

5 Is the lack of ability due to inadequate training?
— NO (Go to 4 or 6)
— YES —
C This is a TRAINING problem.

6 Is the lack of ability due to inadequate aptitude?
— NO (Go to 4 or 5)
— YES —
D This is an APTITUDE problem.

NO

YES

1 Do both the boss and subordinate agree that the subordinate's performance needs to be improved?
YES

7 Is the lack of motivation the result of poorly understood or unmotivating expectations?
— NO (Go to 8 or 9)
— YES —
E This is an EXPECTATIONS problem.

3 Does this problem stem from inadequate subordinate motivation?
YES

8 Is the lack of motivation the result of rewards not being linked to job performance or not being fairly distributed?
— NO (Go to 7 or 9)
— YES —
F This is an INCENTIVES problem.

NO (Go to 2)

9 Is the lack of motivation the result of rewards available to high performers not being salient to this person?
— NO (Go to 7 or 8)
— YES —
G This is a SALIENCE problem.

required. These include refitting the person's current job requirements, reassigning him or her to another position, or, finally, releasing him or her from the organization.

5. **Expectations Problem:** "What are your performance expectations for this position? What do you think my expectations are?" This problem results from poor communication regarding job goals or job requirements. In some cases, the stated goals may be different from the desired goals. In other words, the employee is working toward one goal while the supervisor desires another. This often occurs when subordinates are not sufficiently involved in the goal- or standard-setting process. When this results in unrealistic, imposed expectations, motivation suffers.

6. **Incentives Problem:** "Do you believe rewards are linked to your performance in this position?" Either the individual does not believe that "performance makes a difference" or insufficient performance feedback and reinforcement have been given. The manager should also ask, "Do you feel rewards are being distributed equitably?" This provides an opportunity to discuss subordinates' criteria for judging fairness. Often, unrealistic standards are being used.

7. **Salience Problem:** "Are the performance incentives attractive to you?" Salience refers to the importance an individual attaches to available rewards. Often, the incentives offered to encourage high performance are not highly valued by a particular individual. Managers need to be creative in generating a broad range of rewards and flexible in allowing subordinates to choose among rewards.

Assignment
Option 1:

Read the case, "Joe Chaney," and privately use the diagnostic model (see Figure 6.7) to pinpoint plausible performance problems. Next, discuss in small groups your individual assessments and list specific questions you should ask Joe to accurately identify, from his point of view, the obstacles to his high performance. Finally, brainstorm ideas for plausible solutions. Prepare to represent your group in role-playing a problem-solving interview with Joe.

Option 2:

Administer the Work Performance Assessment survey to several employees. Using the scoring key at the end of this chapter, categorize the obstacles to high performance and satisfaction reported by the respondents. Then get together in small groups, with each group assuming the role of a management task force charged with the responsibility to analyze this employee survey data. Discuss the patterns in the data as well as possible remedies for these problems, using the behavioral guidelines and motivational models in the chapter as guides. Prepare a report on your analysis and recommendations for specific changes.

Joe Chaney

Joe Chaney joined your architectural firm two years ago as a draftsman. He is 35 years old and has been a draftsman since graduating from a two-year technical school right after high school. He is married and has four children. He has worked for four architectural firms in 12 years.

Joe came with mediocre recommendations from his previous employer, but you hired him anyway because you needed help desperately. Your firm's workload has been extremely high due to a local construction boom. The result is that a lot of the practices that contribute to a supportive, well-managed work environment have been overlooked. For instance, you can't remember the last time you conducted a formal performance review or did any career counseling. Furthermore, the tradition of closing the office early on Friday for a social hour was dropped long ago. Unfortunately, the tension in the office runs pretty high some days due to unbearable time pressures and the lack of adequate staff. Night and weekend work have become the norm rather than the exception.

Overall, you have been pleasantly surprised by Joe's performance. Until recently, he worked hard and consistently produced high-quality work. Furthermore, he frequently volunteered for special projects, made lots of suggestions for improving the work environment, and has demonstrated an in-depth practical knowledge of architecture and the construction business. However, during the past few months, he has definitely slacked off. He doesn't seem as excited about his work, and several times you have found him daydreaming at his desk. In addition, he has gotten into several heated arguments with architects about the specifications and proper design procedures for recent projects.

After one of these disagreements, you overheard Joe complaining to his officemate, "No one around here respects my opinion. I'm just a lowly draftsman. I know as much as these hotshot architects, but because I don't have the degree, they ignore my input, and I'm stuck doing the grunt work. Adding insult to injury, my wife has had to get a job to help support our family. I must be the lowest-paid person in this firm." In response to a question from a coworker regarding why he didn't pursue a college degree in architecture,

Joe responded, "Do you have any idea how hard it is to put bread on the table, pay a Seattle mortgage, work overtime, be a reasonably good father and husband, plus go to night school? Come on, be realistic!"

Work Performance Assessment

Respond to the following statements, based on your current work situation.

Rating Scale

1 Strongly disagree

2 Disagree

3 Neutral

4 Agree

5 Strongly agree

_____ 1. My supervisor and I agree on the quality of my performance.

_____ 2. I feel I have adequate training to perform my current job assignments.

_____ 3. I believe that my native skills and abilities are matched very well with my job responsibilities.

_____ 4. I believe that I have adequate resources and supplies to do my job well.

_____ 5. I understand my boss' expectations and generally feel they are realistic.

_____ 6. I believe that rewards are distributed fairly, on the basis of performance.

_____ 7. The rewards and opportunities available to me if I perform well are attractive to me personally.

_____ 8. My supervisor indicates that I am not performing as well as I should, but I disagree.

_____ 9. I could do a much better job if I had more training.

_____ 10. I believe that my job is too difficult for my ability level.

_____ 11. I believe that my job performance is hindered by a lack of supplies and resources.

_____ 12. I believe my boss' expectations are unclear and unrealistic.

_____ 13. I believe my boss plays favorites in allocating rewards.

_____ 14. I do not find the rewards and opportunities available to high performers very appealing.

EXERCISE FOR RESHAPING UNACCEPTABLE BEHAVIORS

Shaheen Matombo

One of the most challenging aspects of management is transforming inappropriate behaviors into appropriate behaviors. Managers commonly take insufficient action to transform negative actions into positive ones. Some of these insufficient responses include assuming that ignoring an employee's shortcomings will make them go away; praising positive aspects of an individual's performance in hopes that this will encourage him or her to rechannel unproductive energies; discussing problems in vague, general terms in a group meeting, in hopes that the unproductive person will "take a hint" and change; and getting upset with an individual and demanding that he or she "shape up."

Assignment

Assume the role of Andre Tate in the following case. After reading the case, review the applicable behavioral guidelines shown on the Observer's Feedback Form at the end of the chapter. In small groups, discuss how you would resolve this problem. Prepare to role-play your discussion with Shaheen Matombo. After the discussion, assigned observers will provide feedback on your performance, using the Observer's Feedback Form as a guide. Unless you are assigned to play her role, do not read the role instructions for Shaheen prior to the interview.

Andre Tate, Manager

Shaheen has been a member of your staff for only three months. You don't know much about her other than that she is a single parent who has recently entered the workforce after a difficult divorce. She is often 10 to 20 minutes late for work in the morning. You are the manager of a very hectic customer relations office for a utility company. The phones start ringing promptly at 8:00. When she is late for work, you have to answer her phone, and this interrupts your work schedule. This morning, you are particularly annoyed. She is 25 minutes late, and the phones are ringing like crazy. Because you have been forced to answer them, it will be difficult for you to complete an important assignment by the noon deadline. You are getting more upset by the minute.

While you are in the middle of a particularly unpleasant phone conversation with an irate customer, you look out your window and see Shaheen bounding up the steps to the building. You think to yourself, "This is ridiculous, I've got to put a stop to her tardiness. Maybe I should just threaten to fire her unless she shapes up." Upon further reflection, you realize that would be impractical, especially during this period of retrenchment after the rate hike was turned down. Given the rumors about a possible hiring freeze, you know it may be difficult to refill any vacancies.

Also, Shaheen is actually a pretty good worker when she is there. She is conscientious and has a real knack with cranky callers. Unfortunately, it has taken her much longer than expected to learn the computer program for retrieving information on customer accounts. She frequently has to put callers on hold while she asks for help. These interruptions have tended to increase an already tense relationship with the rest of the office staff. She has had some difficulty fitting in socially; the others are much younger and have worked together for several years. Shaheen is the first new hire in a long time, so the others aren't used to breaking someone in. Three of your staff have complained to you about Shaheen's constant interruptions. They feel their productivity is going down as a result. Besides, she seems to expect them to drop whatever they are doing every time she has a question. They had expected their workload to be lighter when a new person was hired, but now they are having second thoughts. (In the past, you have had enough time to train new hires, but your boss has had you tied up on a major project for almost a year.)

Shaheen enters the office obviously flustered and disheveled. She has "I'm sorry" written all over her face. You motion for her to pick up the blinking phone line and then scribble a note on a tablet while you complete your call: "See me in my office at 12:00 sharp!" It's time you got to the bottom of Shaheen's disruptive influence on an otherwise smooth-flowing operation.

Shaheen Matombo, Staff Member

Boy, what a morning! Your babysitter's father died during the night, and she called you from the airport at 6:30 A.M. saying she would be out of town for three or four days. You tried three usually available backups before you finally found someone who could take Keen, your 3-year-old. Then Shayla, your seventh-grader, went through five outfits before she was satisfied that she had just the right look for her first yearbook picture. It's a miracle that Buddy, your oldest, was able to pull himself out of bed after getting only five hours of sleep. On top of football and drama, he's now joined the chess team, and they had their first tournament last night. Why did it have to fall on the night before his final in physics? This morning you wished you had his knack for juggling so many activities. By the time you got the kids delivered, you were already 10 minutes behind schedule. Then there was this incredible accident on the expressway that slowed traffic to a crawl.

As you finally pull off the downtown exit ramp, you notice you're almost 20 minutes late for work. "My kingdom for a cell phone!" you groan. "Although by now I probably couldn't get an open line into the office, anyway." As you desperately scan the side streets for a parking space, you begin to panic. "How am I going to explain this to Andre? He'll be furious. I'm sure he's upset about my chronic lateness. On top of that, he's obviously disappointed with my lack of computer skills, and I'm sure the others complain to him about having to train a newcomer." You're sure that one of the reasons you got the job was that you had completed a computer class at the local community college. Unfortunately, there hadn't been much carryover to the incredibly complex computer program you use at work. (It seems to defy every convention of logic.)

"What am I going to tell him about my being late for work so often?" Unfortunately, there isn't an easy answer. "Maybe it will get better as the kids and I get used to this new routine. It's just very difficult to get the kids to the bus stop and the sitter, commute 20 minutes, and arrive precisely at 8:00. I wonder if he would allow me to come in at 8:30 and only take a half-hour lunch. Staying late wouldn't work because they close down the computers at 5:00, unless there was some paperwork I could do for half an hour."

Then what about the problems with the computer and the other staff members? "Sooner or later he's going to get on my case about those things. Is it my fault I don't think like a computer? Some people might be able to sit down and figure this program out in a couple of hours, but not me. So is that my fault or should someone be giving me more training? I wish the others weren't so cliquish and unwilling to help me out. I wonder why that's the case. It's like they're afraid I'll become as good as they are if they share their experience with me. I wish Andre had more time to help me learn the ropes, but he seems to always be in meetings."

"Well, I'm probably going to catch it this morning. I've never been this late. Maybe I'll be back home full time sooner than I expected."

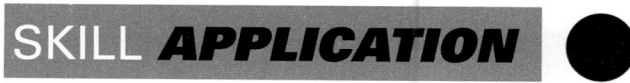
ACTIVITIES FOR MOTIVATING OTHERS

Suggested Assignments

1. Identify a situation in which you have some responsibility for another person whose performance is significantly below your expectation. Using the Work Performance Assessment Survey included in the Skill Practice section, collect information on the individual's perceptions of the situation. Using the diagnostic model (decision tree) in that section, specifically identify the perceived performance problems. Compare these results with your own views of the situation. Conduct an interview with the individual and discuss the results, highlighting areas of disagreement. Based on this discussion, formulate a plan of action that both parties accept. If inadequate ability is a problem, follow the resupply, retrain, refill, reassign, and release remedial steps. If insufficient effort is a problem, use the steps for reprimanding, redirecting, and rewarding discussed in this chapter as a resource for this discussion. Implement this plan for a period of time and then report on the results.

2. Focus on some aspect of your own work in which you feel performance is below your (or others') expectations. Using the Work Performance Assessment survey (Skill Assessment), identify the specific obstacles to improved performance. Then formulate a plan for overcoming these obstacles, including getting commitments from others. Discuss your plan with individuals affected by it and arrive at a set of actions all parties accept. Implement the plan for a period of time and report on your results. How successful were you in making the changes? Did your performance improve as expected? Based on this experience, identify other aspects of your work that you could improve on in a similar fashion.

3. Identify four or five situations in which you are typically provoked to exhibit punishing behavior. These might involve friends, family members, or work associates. Examine these situations and identify one in which punishment (discipline) is not working. Using the guidelines for reprimanding, redirecting, and rewarding, design a specific plan for shaping the other person's behaviors so you can begin rewarding positive actions. Report on your results. Based on this experience, consider how you might be able to use this strategy in other similar situations.

4. Using the six-step model for creating a motivational work environment (see Table 6.2), design a specific plan for managing a new relationship (e.g., a new subordinate) or a new phase in an old relationship (e.g., friend, family member, or subordinate about to begin work on a new project). Write down specific directions for yourself for implementing each of the six steps. Discuss your plan with this individual

and ask for suggestions for improvement. Make sure your perceptions of the key aspects of the plan are consistent with his or hers. Implement your plan for a period of time and then report on the consequences. Based on this experience, identify changes that would be appropriate in similar situations.

Application Plan and Evaluation

The intent of this exercise is to help you apply this cluster of skills in a real-life, out-of-class setting. Now that you have become familiar with the behavioral guidelines that form the basis of effective skill performance, you will improve most by trying out those guidelines in an everyday context. Unlike a classroom activity, in which feedback is immediate and others can assist you with their evaluations, this skill application activity is one you must accomplish and evaluate on your own. There are two parts to this activity. Part 1 helps prepare you to apply the skill. Part 2 helps you evaluate and improve on your experience. Be sure to write down answers to each item. Don't short-circuit the process by skipping steps.

Part 1. Planning

1. Write down the two or three aspects of this skill that are most important to you. These may be areas of weakness, areas you most want to improve, or areas that are most salient to a problem you face right now. Identify the specific aspects of this skill that you want to apply.

2. Now identify the setting or the situation in which you will apply this skill. Establish a plan for performance by actually writing down a description of the situation. Who else will be involved? When will you do it? Where will it be done?

   Circumstances:
   Who else?
   When?
   Where?

3. Identify the specific behaviors you will engage in to apply this skill. Operationalize your skill performance.

4. What are the indicators of successful performance? How will you know you have been effective? What will indicate you have performed competently?

Part 2. Evaluation

5. After you have completed your implementation, record the results. What happened? How successful were you? What was the effect on others?

6. How can you improve? What modifications can you make next time? What will you do differently in a similar situation in the future?

7. Looking back on your whole skill practice and application experience, what have you learned? What has been surprising? In what ways might this experience help you in the long term?

APPLICATION

Diagnosing Poor Performance and Enhancing Motivation

Scoring Key

SKILL AREA	ITEM	ASSESSMENT	
		PRE-	POST-
Diagnosing performance problems	1	_____	_____
	11	_____	_____
Establishing expectations and setting goals	2	_____	_____
	12	_____	_____
Facilitating performance (Enhancing ability)	3	_____	_____
	13	_____	_____
	20	_____	_____
Linking performance to rewards and discipline	5	_____	_____
	14	_____	_____
	6	_____	_____
	15	_____	_____
Using salient internal and external incentives	7	_____	_____
	16	_____	_____
	8	_____	_____
	17	_____	_____
Distributing rewards equitably	9	_____	_____
	18	_____	_____
Providing timely and straightforward performance feedback	4	_____	_____
	10	_____	_____
	19	_____	_____
Total Score		_____	_____

Comparison Data (N = 1,500 Students)

Compare your scores to three comparison standards:
1. The maximum possible score = 120.
2. The scores of other students in your class.
3. Norm data from more than 1,500 business school students.

Pre-Test				Post-Test
96.33	=	mean	=	103.23
104 or above	=	top quartile	=	112 or above
97–103	=	second quartile	=	104–111
90–96	=	third quartile	=	97–103
89 or below	=	bottom quartile	=	96 or below

Work Performance

STEP 1: Enter your score from each line below, as follows:

Regular scoring: Enter the number for your response on the survey.

Reverse scoring: Subtract the number of your response from 6 and enter the result.

ITEMS	SCORE		ITEMS	SCORE	
1.	Reverse	_____	8.	Regular	_____
2.	Reverse	_____	9.	Regular	_____
3.	Reverse	_____	10.	Regular	_____
4.	Reverse	_____	11.	Regular	_____
5.	Reverse	_____	12.	Regular	_____
6.	Reverse	_____	13.	Regular	_____
7.	Reverse	_____	14.	Regular	_____

STEP 2: Combine your scores according to the type of performance problem. Problems with scores higher than 7 are obstacles to high performance. Total scores over 50 suggest significant, broad-based motivational deficiencies.

TYPE OF PERFORMANCE PROBLEM	SCORES ON ITEMS		TOTAL OF TWO ITEMS
Perception	1. _____	8. _____	_____
Training	2. _____	9. _____	_____
Aptitude	3. _____	10. _____	_____
Resources	4. _____	11. _____	_____
Expectations	5. _____	12. _____	_____
Incentives	6. _____	13. _____	_____
Reward salience	7. _____	14. _____	_____
		Total Score	_____

Comparison Data (N = 1,500 Students)

Mean score:	29.94
Top quartile:	36 or above
Second quartile:	30–35
Third quartile:	24–29
Bottom quartile:	23 or below

SKILL PRACTICE Exercise for Reshaping Unacceptable Behaviors

Observer's Feedback Form

RATING

1 = Low
5 = High

Reprimand

_____ 1. Identified the specific inappropriate behavior. Gave examples. Indicated that the action must stop.

_____ 2. Pointed out the impact of the problem on the performance of others, the unit's mission, and so forth.

_____ 3. Asked questions about causes and explored remedies.

Redirect

_____ 4. Described the behaviors or standards expected. Made sure the individual understood and agreed that these are reasonable.

_____ 5. Asked if the individual would comply.

_____ 6. Was appropriately supportive. For example, praised other aspects of the person's work, identified personal and group benefits of compliance, and made sure there were no legitimate obstacles in the way of meeting stated expectations.

Reinforce

_____ 7. Identified rewards that were salient to the individual.

_____ 8. Linked the attainment of desirable outcomes with incremental, continuous improvement.

_____ 9. Rewarded (including using praise) all improvements in performance in a timely and honest manner.

Comments:

SKILL *ASSESSMENT* ▶

- Managing Interpersonal Conflict
- Strategies for Handling Conflict

SKILL *LEARNING* ■

- Interpersonal Conflict Management
- Diagnosing the Type of Interpersonal Conflict
- Selecting the Appropriate Conflict Management Approach
- Resolving Interpersonal Confrontations Using the Collaborative Approach
- Summary
- Behavioral Guidelines

SKILL *ANALYSIS* ▶

- Educational Pension Investments

SKILL *PRACTICE* ◆

- SSS Software Management Problems
- Bradley's Barn
- Avocado Computers
- Phelps, Inc.
- Freida Mae Jones
- Can Larry Fit In?
- Meeting at Hartford Manufacturing Company

SKILL *APPLICATION* ●

- Suggested Assignments
- Application Plan and Evaluation

SCORING KEYS AND *COMPARISON DATA* ■

Managing Conflict

SKILL DEVELOPMENT OBJECTIVES

- DIAGNOSE THE FOCUS AND SOURCE OF CONFLICTS
- UTILIZE APPROPRIATE CONFLICT MANAGEMENT STRATEGIES
- RESOLVE INTERPERSONAL CONFRONTATIONS THROUGH COLLABORATION

DIAGNOSTIC SURVEYS FOR MANAGING CONFLICT

MANAGING INTERPERSONAL CONFLICT

Step 1: Before you read this chapter, respond to the following statements by writing a number from the rating scale that follows in the left-hand column (Pre-assessment). Your answers should reflect your attitudes and behavior as they are now, not as you would like them to be. Be honest. This instrument is designed to help you discover your level of competency in managing conflict so you can tailor your learning to your specific needs. When you have completed the survey, use the scoring key at the end of the chapter to identify the skill areas discussed in this chapter that are most important for you to master.

Step 2: After you have completed the reading and the exercises in this chapter and, ideally, as many of the Skill Application assignments at the end of this chapter as you can, cover up your first set of answers. Then respond to the same statements again, this time in the right-hand column (Post-assessment). When you have completed the survey, use the scoring key at the end of the chapter to measure your progress. If your score remains low in specific skill areas, use the behavioral guidelines at the end of the Skill Learning section to guide your further practice.

Rating Scale

1 Strongly disagree
2 Disagree
3 Slightly disagree
4 Slightly agree
5 Agree
6 Strongly agree

Assessment

Pre-   Post-

When I see someone doing something that needs correcting:

_____ _____ 1. I avoid making personal accusations and attributing self-serving motives to the other person.

_____ _____ 2. When stating my concerns, I present them as my problems.

_____ _____ 3. I succinctly describe problems in terms of the behavior that occurred, its consequences, and my feelings about it.

_____ _____ 4. I specify the expectations and standards that have been violated.

_____ _____ 5. I make a specific request, detailing a more acceptable option.

_____ _____ 6. I persist in explaining my point of view until it is understood by the other person.

_____ _____ 7. I encourage two-way interaction by inviting the respondent to express his or her perspective and to ask questions.

_____ _____ 8. When there are several concerns, I approach the issues incrementally, starting with easy and simple issues and then progressing to those that are difficult and complex.

When someone complains about something I've done:

_____ _____ 9. I look for our common areas of agreement.

_____ _____ 10. I show genuine concern and interest, even when I disagree.

_____ _____ 11. I avoid justifying my actions and becoming defensive.

_____ _____ 12. I seek additional information by asking questions that provide specific and descriptive information.

_____ _____ 13. I focus on one issue at a time.

_____ _____ 14. I find some aspects of the complaint with which I can agree.

_____ _____ 15. I ask the other person to suggest more acceptable behaviors.

_____ _____ 16. I reach agreement on a remedial plan of action.

When two other people are in conflict and I am the mediator:

_____ _____ 17. I acknowledge that conflict exists and treat it as serious and important.

_____ _____ 18. I help create an agenda for a problem-solving meeting by identifying the issues to be discussed, one at a time.

_____ _____ 19. I do not take sides, but remain neutral.

_____ _____ 20. I help focus the discussion on the impact of the conflict on work performance.

_____ _____ 21. I keep the interaction focused on problems rather than on personalities.

_____ _____ 22. I make certain that neither party dominates the conversation.

_____ _____ 23. I help the parties generate multiple alternatives.

_____ _____ 24. I help the parties find areas on which they agree.

STRATEGIES FOR HANDLING CONFLICT

Indicate how often you use each of the following by writing the appropriate number in the blank. Choose a number from a scale of 1 to 5, with 1 being "rarely," 3 being "sometimes," and 5 being "always." After you have completed the survey, use the scoring key at the end of the chapter to tabulate your results.

_____ 1. I argue my position tenaciously.

_____ 2. I put the needs of others above my own.

_____ 3. I arrive at a compromise both parties can accept.

_____ 4. I don't get involved in conflicts.

_____ 5. I investigate issues thoroughly and jointly.

_____ 6. I find fault in other persons' positions.

_____ 7. I foster harmony.

_____ 8. I negotiate to get a portion of what I propose.

_____ 9. I avoid open discussions of controversial subjects.

_____ 10. I openly share information with others in resolving disagreements.

_____ 11. I enjoy winning an argument.

_____ 12. I go along with the suggestions of others.

_____ 13. I look for a middle ground to resolve disagreements.

_____ 14. I keep my true feelings to myself to avoid hard feelings.

_____ 15. I encourage the open sharing of concerns and issues.

_____ 16. I am reluctant to admit I am wrong.

_____ 17. I try to help others avoid "losing face" in a disagreement.

_____ 18. I stress the advantages of "give and take."

_____ 19. I encourage others to take the lead in resolving controversy.

_____ 20. I state my position as only one point of view.

Interpersonal Conflict Management

A conflict over issues is not only likely within top-management teams but also valuable. Such conflict provides executives with a more inclusive range of information, a deeper understanding of the issues, and a richer set of possible solutions. [In our ten-year study] we found that the alternative to conflict is usually not agreement but apathy and disengagement. In fast paced markets, successful strategic decisions are most likely to be made by teams that promote active and broad conflict over issues without sacrificing speed. The key to doing so is to mitigate interpersonal conflict. (Eisenhardt, Kahwajy, & Bourgeois, 1997, pp. 84–85)

One of the leading causes of business failure among major corporations is too much agreement among top management. They have similar training and experience, which means they tend to view conditions the same way and pursue similar goals. The resulting lack of tension between competing perspectives can foster a climate of complacency. This problem is often compounded by boards of directors' failing to play an aggressive oversight role. They avoid conflict with the internal management team who appear unified on key issues and very confident of their positions. What we learn from the study of business failures is that the absence of disagreement is often viewed by managers as a sign of good leadership, when in reality it is a leading indicator of being out of touch with significant changes in the marketplace (Argenti, 1976).

Interpersonal conflict is an essential, ubiquitous part of organizational life. In fact, given the current business trends toward workforce diversity, globalization, and joint ventures, how managers from different organizations and cultures deal with conflict is an increasingly important predictor of organizational success (Seybolt, Derr, & Nielson, 1996; Tjosvold, 1991). Organizations in which there is little disagreement regarding important matters generally fail in competitive environments. Members are either so homogeneous that they are ill-equipped to adapt to changing environmental conditions or so complacent that they see no need to improve the status quo. Conflict is the lifeblood of vibrant, progressive, stimulating organizations. It sparks creativity, stimulates innovation, and encourages personal improvement (Blackard & Gibson, 2002; Pascale, 1990; Wanous & Youtz, 1986).

This view is clearly in line with the management philosophy of Andrew Grove, former president of Intel. "Many managers seem to think it is impossible to tackle anything or anyone head-on, even in business. By contrast, we at Intel believe that it is the essence of corporate health to bring a problem out into the open as soon as possible, even if this entails a confrontation. Dealing with conflicts lies at the heart of managing any business. As a result, confrontation—facing issues about which there is disagreement—can be avoided only at the manager's peril. Workplace politicking grows quietly in the dark, like mushrooms; neither can stand the light of day" (Grove, 1984).

However, we all have ample evidence that conflict often produces harmful results. For example, some people have a very low tolerance for disagreement. Whether this is the result of family background, cultural values, or personality characteristics, interpersonal conflict saps their energy and demoralizes their spirit. Also, some types of conflicts, regardless of frequency, generally produce dysfunctional outcomes. These include personality conflicts and arguments over things that can't be changed.

As Figure 7.1 shows, scholars generally agree that some conflict is both inevitable and beneficial in effective organizations (Brown, 1983). As illustrated in this figure, holding constant the nature of the conflict and how well it is resolved, a moderate level of conflict appears to be healthy for most organizations.

MIXED FEELINGS ABOUT CONFLICT

With this general observation in mind, it is interesting to note that a well-known American psychologist, Abraham Maslow (1965), has observed a high degree of ambivalence regarding the value of conflict. On the one hand, he notes that managers intellectually appreciate the value of conflict and competition. They agree it is a necessary ingredient of the free-enterprise system. However, their actions demonstrate a personal preference for avoiding

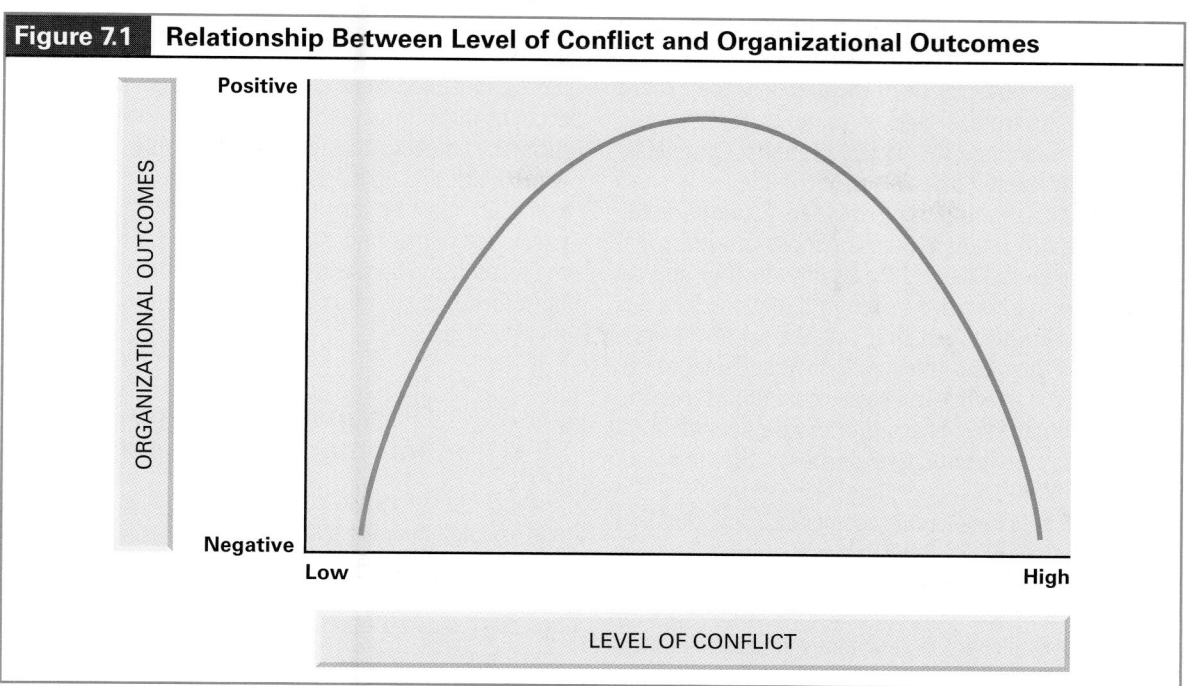

Figure 7.1 | Relationship Between Level of Conflict and Organizational Outcomes

ORGANIZATIONAL OUTCOMES

Positive

Negative

Low

High

LEVEL OF CONFLICT

conflicts whenever possible. This ambivalent view of conflict appears to be reflected in the following account.

In 1984 Ross Perot, an outspoken self-made billionaire, sold Electronic Data Systems (EDS) to General Motors (GM) for $2.5 billion and immediately became GM's largest stockholder and member of the board. GM needed EDS's expertise to coordinate its massive information system. Roger Smith, GM's chairman, also hoped that Perot's fiery spirit would reinvigorate GM's bureaucracy. Almost immediately, Perot became a severe critic of GM policy and practice. He noted that it takes longer for GM to produce a car than it took the country to win WWII. He was especially critical of GM's bureaucracy, claiming it fostered conformity at the expense of getting results. By December 1986, Roger Smith had apparently had enough of Perot's "reinvigoration." Whether his criticisms were true, or functional, the giant automaker paid nearly twice the market value of his stock ($750 million) to silence him and arrange his resignation from the board. (Perot, 1988)

The seemingly inherent tension between the intellectual acceptance of the merits of conflict and the emotional rejection of its enactment is illustrated in a classic study of decision making (Boulding, 1964). Several groups of managers were formed to solve a complex problem. They were told their performance would be judged by a panel of experts in terms of the quantity and quality of solutions generated. The groups were identical in size and composition, with the exception that half of them included a "confederate." Before the experiment began, the researcher instructed this person to play the role of "devil's advocate." This person was to challenge the group's conclusions, forcing the others to examine critically their assumptions and the logic of their arguments. At the end of the problem-solving period, the recommendations made by both sets of groups were compared. The groups with the devil's advocates had performed significantly better on the task. They had generated more alternatives, and their proposals were judged as superior. After a short break, the groups were reassembled and told that they would be performing a similar task during the next session. However, before they began discussing the next problem, they were given permission to eliminate one member. In every group containing a confederate, he or she was the one asked to leave. The fact that every high-performance group expelled their unique competitive advantage because that member made others feel uncomfortable demonstrates a widely shared reaction to conflict: "I know it has positive outcomes for the performance of the organization, as a whole, but I don't like how it makes me feel, personally."

We believe that much of the ambivalence toward conflict stems from a lack of understanding of the causes of conflict and the variety of modes for managing it effectively, and from a lack of confidence in one's personal skills for handling the tense, emotionally charged environment typical of most interpersonal confrontations. It is natural for an untrained or inexperienced person to avoid threatening situations, and it is generally acknowledged that conflict represents the most severe test of a manager's interpersonal skills. The task of the effective manager, therefore, is to maintain an optimal level of conflict, while keeping conflicts focused on productive purposes (Kelly, 1970; Thomas, 1976).

This view of conflict management is supported by a 10-year study conducted by Kathy Eisenhardt and her colleagues at Stanford University (Eisenhardt et al., 1997). In their *Harvard Business Review* article, they report, "The challenge is to encourage members of management teams to argue without destroying their ability to work together" (p. 78). What makes this possible? These authors identify several key "rules of engagement" for effective conflict management.

- ❏ Work with more, rather than less, information.
- ❏ Focus on the facts.
- ❏ Develop multiple alternatives to enrich the level of debate.
- ❏ Share commonly agreed-upon goals.
- ❏ Inject humor into the decision process.
- ❏ Maintain a balanced power structure.
- ❏ Resolve issues without forcing consensus.

Thus far, we have determined that: (1) interpersonal conflict in organizations is inevitable; (2) conflicts over issues or facts enhance the practice of management; (3) despite the intellectual acceptance of the value of conflict, there is a widespread tendency to avoid it; and (4) the key to increasing one's comfort level with conflict is to become proficient in managing all forms of interpersonal disputes (both productive and unproductive conflicts).

Following our skill-development orientation, the remainder of this chapter focuses on increasing your competence-based confidence. Drawing upon a large body of research on this subject, it appears that effective conflict managers must be proficient in the use of three essential skills. First, they must be able to accurately diagnose the types of conflict, including their causes. For example, managers need to understand how cultural differences and other forms of demographic diversity can spark conflicts in organizations. Second, having identified the sources of conflict and taken into account the context and personal preferences for dealing with conflict, managers must be able to select an appropriate conflict management strategy. Third, skillful managers must be able to settle interpersonal disputes effectively so that underlying problems are resolved and the relationship between disputants is not damaged. We now turn our attention to these three broad management proficiencies.

Diagnosing the Type of Interpersonal Conflict

Because interpersonal conflicts come in assorted lots, our first skill-building task involves the art of diagnosis. In any type of clinical setting, from medicine to management, it is common knowledge that effective intervention is predicated upon accurate diagnosis. Figure 7.2 presents a categorizing device for diagnosing the *type of conflict*, based on two critical identifying characteristics: focus and source. By understanding the *focus of the conflict*, we gain an appreciation for the substance of the dispute (what is fueling the conflict), and by learning more about the origins, or *source of the conflict*, we better understand how it got started (the igniting spark).

CONFLICT FOCUS

It is common to categorize conflicts in organizations in terms of whether they are primarily focused on *people* or *issues* (Eisenhardt et al., 1997; Jehn & Mannix, 2001). By this distinction we mean: is this a negotiation-like conflict over competing ideas, proposals, interests, or resources; or is this a dispute-like conflict stemming from what has transpired between the parties?

One of the nice features of the distinction between people-focused and issue-focused conflicts is that it helps us understand why some managers believe that conflict is the lifeblood of their organization, while others believe that each and every conflict episode sucks blood from their organization. Research has shown that people-focused conflicts threaten relationships, whereas issue-based conflicts enhance relationships, provided that people are comfortable with it, including feeling able to manage it effectively (de Dreu & Weingart, 2002; Jehn, 1997). Therefore, in general, when we read about the benefits of "productive conflict," the authors are referring to issue-focused conflict.

Although, by definition, all interpersonal conflicts involve people, **people-focused conflict** refers to the

Figure 7.2   **Categorizing Different Types of Conflict**

Figure 7.2   Categorizing Different Types of Conflict

LEARNING

"in your face" kind of confrontations in which the affect level is high and the intense emotional heat is likely fueled by moral indignation. Accusations of harm, demands for justice, and feelings of resentment are the common markers of personal disputes. Hence, personal disputes are extremely difficult to resolve, and the long-term effects of the dispute on interpersonal relations can be devastating. The longer this type of dispute goes on, the larger the gulf between the parties becomes and the more supporters begin showing up, arm in arm, on either side.

You might wonder how likely it is that you will actually become embroiled in a nasty, interpersonal confrontation. Isn't this something that just gets stirred up by cantankerous, insecure crackpots and only gets under the skin of defensive, closed-minded people? Although effective application of the skills covered in this book should lessen the likelihood of your interpersonal relationships becoming entangled in the web of personal disputes, the following information is sobering.

In response to the question, "In general, what percentage of management time is wasted on resolving personality conflicts?" Max Messmer, chairman of Accountemps, reports an average response of 18 percent from a large sample of organizations, compared with 9.2 percent a decade earlier. He laments the fact that approximately nine weeks of management time each year is consumed by this nonproductive activity ("The boss as referee," 1996).

Coming at the subject from a different angle, a recent article entitled, "Is Having Partners a Bad Idea?"

reported the results of an *Inc.* magazine poll in which nearly two-thirds of the small business owners surveyed said, notwithstanding the potential benefits, they preferred not adding a partner because of the increased potential for interpersonal conflict. In a second poll reported in this article, researchers at the University of Minnesota uncovered similar misgivings in family businesses. About half of the second-generation family members working in such companies were having second thoughts about the wisdom of joining the firm because, again, they were worried about their business careers being marred by interpersonal conflicts (Gage, 1999).

Whereas we have characterized people-focused conflicts as emotional disputes, **issue-focused conflicts** are more like rational negotiations, which can be thought of as "an interpersonal decision-making process by which two or more people agree how to allocate scarce resources" (Thompson, 2001, p. 2). In issue-based conflicts, manager–negotiators are typically acting as agents, representing the interests of their department, function, or project. Although negotiators have conflicting priorities for how the scarce resource should be utilized, in most day-to-day negotiations within an organization the negotiators recognize the need to find an amicable settlement that appears fair to all parties. Because the negotiation outcome, if not the process itself, is generally public knowledge, the negotiators recognize that there is no such thing as one-time-only negotiations. One veteran manager observed that he uses a simple creed to govern his dealings with others, "It's a small world and a long life"—meaning there is no long-term personal advantage to short-term gains won through unfair means.

Although our discussion of conflict management draws liberally on the negotiations literature, our objective is to prepare readers for highly charged emotional confrontations in which untrained initiators attempt to transfer their frustration to someone else by alleging that great harm has been caused by the offender's self-serving motives or incompetent practices. Being on the receiving end of a "surprise personal attack" is debilitating, and so the unskilled respondent is likely to fight back, escalating the conflict with counteraccusations or defensive retorts. That's why experienced mediators agree that when a disagreement "gets personal," it often becomes intractable.

CONFLICT SOURCE

We now shift our diagnostic lens from understanding the focus, or content, of a conflict ("What's this about?") to the source, or origin, of the conflict ("How did it get started?"). Managers, especially those who feel uncomfortable with conflict, often behave as though interpersonal conflict is the result of personality defects. They label people who are frequently involved in conflicts "troublemakers" or "bad apples" and attempt to transfer or dismiss them as a way of resolving disagreements. While some individuals seem to have a propensity for making trouble and appear to be cantankerous under even the best of circumstances, "sour dispositions" actually account for only a small percentage of organizational conflicts (Hines, 1980; Schmidt & Tannenbaum, 1965).

This proposition is supported by research on performance appraisals (Latham & Wexley, 1994). It has been shown that managers generally attribute poor performance to personal deficiencies in workers, such as laziness, lack of skill, or lack of motivation. However, when workers are asked the causes of their poor performance, they generally explain it in terms of problems in their environment, such as insufficient supplies or uncooperative coworkers. While some face-saving is obviously involved here, this line of research suggests that managers need to guard against the reflexive tendency to assume that bad behaviors imply bad people. In fact, aggressive or harsh behaviors sometimes observed in interpersonal confrontations often reflect the frustrations of people who have good intentions but are unskilled in handling intense, emotional experiences.

In contrast to the personality-defect theory of conflict, we propose four sources of interpersonal conflict in Table 7.1. These are *personal differences, informational deficiencies, role incompatibility*, and *environmental stress*. **Personal differences** are a common source of

Table 7.1	Sources of Conflict
Personal differences	Perceptions and expectations
Informational deficiencies	Misinformation and misrepresentation
Role incompatibility	Goals and responsibilities
Environmental stress	Resource scarcity and uncertainty

conflict because individuals bring different backgrounds to their roles in organizations. Their values and needs have been shaped by different socialization processes, depending on their cultural and family traditions, level of education, breadth of experience, and so forth. As a result, their interpretations of events and their expectations about relationships with others in the organization will vary considerably. Conflicts stemming from incompatible personal values and needs are some of the most difficult to resolve. They often become highly emotional and take on moral overtones. Under these conditions, a disagreement about what is *factually correct* easily turns into a bitter argument over *who is morally right*.

The distinction between people-focused conflict and personal differences as a source of conflict may seem a bit confusing. It might help to think of personal differences as a set of lenses that each member of an organization uses to make sense of daily experiences and to make value judgments, in terms of what is good and bad, appropriate and inappropriate. Because these conclusions are likely to become strongly held beliefs that conflict with equally strong beliefs held by coworkers, it is easy to see how these could spark interpersonal conflicts. However, parties to a dispute still have choices regarding what path their dispute will take, in terms of focusing on the issues (e.g., conflicting points of view reflecting different values and needs) or the people (e.g., questioning competence, intent, acceptance, understanding, etc.). It is precisely because conflicts stemming from personal differences tend to become person-focused that effective conflict managers need to understand this analytical distinction so they can help disputants frame their conflict in terms of offending (troublesome) issues, not offensive (troublemaking) people.

This observation is particularly relevant for managers working in an organizational environment characterized by broad demographic diversity. Why? It has been observed that: (1) a diverse workforce can be a strategic organizational asset, and (2) very different people tend to engage in very intense conflicts—which can become an organizational liability (Lombardo & Eichinger, 1996; Pelled, Eisenhardt, & Xin, 1999). On the positive side, the more heterogeneous the demographic profile of an employee population is, the more diversity of experience and perspective contained in the organization (Cox, 1994). From various studies of diversity in organizations (Cox & Blake, 1991; Morrison, 1996), some of the consistently cited benefits of an effectively managed, diverse workforce include:

❏ Cost savings from reducing turnover rates among minority employees

❏ Improved creativity and problem-solving capabilities due to the broader range of perspectives and cultural mindsets

❏ Perceptions of fairness and equity in the workplace

❏ Increased flexibility that positively affects motivation and minimizes conflict between work and nonwork demands (e.g., family, personal interest, leisure)

But few beneficial changes come without commensurate challenges. The old saying, "To create a spark, strike two unlike substances together," speaks to the notion that a diverse workforce will increase creativity and innovation. This saying also reminds us that "sparks can hurt." That's why its particularly important to look beneath the surface of interpersonal differences for a better understanding of why people from very different backgrounds often find themselves embroiled in debilitating interpersonal conflicts.

To begin with, people from different ethnic and cultural groups often have very different views about the value of, and justifications for, interpersonal disputes (Adler, 2002; Trompenaars, 1994, 1996). To state this observation more broadly, conflict is largely a culturally defined event (Sillars & Weisberg, 1987; Weldon & Jehn, 1995; Wilmot & Hocker, 2001), in the sense that our cultural background colors our views about what is worth "fighting for" and what constitutes "a fair fight."

In addition, when the everyday business of an organization requires people with very different demographic profiles to interact frequently, it is likely that their interactions will be marred by misunderstanding and mistrust due to a lack of understanding of and appreciation for each other's needs and values. The potential for harmful conflict is even greater when confrontations involve members of majority and minority groups within

an organization. This is where "diversity-sensitive" managers can help out by considering questions like: Are both participants from the majority culture of the organization? If one is from a minority culture, to what extent is diversity valued in the organization? To what extent do members of these minority and majority cultures understand and value the benefits of a diverse workforce for our organization? Has this particular minority group or individual had a history of conflict within the organization? If so, are there broader issues regarding the appreciation of personal differences that need to be addressed?

It is not difficult to envision how core differences in employees' personal identities could become manifest in organizational conflicts. For example, if a U.S. firm receives a very attractive offer from the Chinese government to build a major manufacturing facility in that country, it is very likely that a 35-year-old Chinese manager in that firm, who was exiled from China following the 1989 riots in Tiananmen Square, would strongly oppose this initiative. This example illustrates a conflict between a majority and minority member of an organization. It also exemplifies disputes in which differences in personal experiences and values lead one party to support a proposal because it is a good business decision and the other party to oppose the action because it is a bad moral decision.

The second source or cause of conflict among members of an organization is **informational deficiencies**. An important message may not be received, a boss's instructions may be misinterpreted, or decision makers may arrive at different conclusions because they use different databases. Conflicts based on misinformation or misunderstanding tend to be factual; hence, clarifying previous messages or obtaining additional information generally resolves the dispute. This might entail rewording the boss' instructions, reconciling contradictory sources of data, or redistributing copies of misplaced messages. This type of conflict is common in organizations, but it is also easy to resolve. Because value systems are not challenged, such confrontations tend to be less emotional. Once the breakdown in the information system is repaired, disputants are generally able to resolve their disagreement with a minimum of resentment.

For example, UOP, Inc., made an agreement with Union Carbide in 1987 that doubled its workforce. Conflicts over operating procedures surfaced immediately between the original employees and the new employees from Union Carbide. This, combined with traditional conflicts between functional groups in the organization, led UOP to begin a new training program in which groups of employees met to discuss quality improvements. "We discovered that the main problem had been a lack of communication," said one senior official. "No one had any idea what other groups were up to, so they all assumed that their way was best" (Caudron, 1992, p. 61).

The complexity inherent in most organizations tends to produce conflict between members whose tasks are interdependent but who occupy incompatible roles. This type of conflict is exemplified by the classic goal conflicts between line and staff, production and sales, and marketing and research and development (R&D). Each unit has different responsibilities in the organization, and as a result each places different priorities on organizational goals (e.g., customer satisfaction, product quality, production efficiency, compliance with government regulations). It is also typical of firms whose multiple product lines compete for scarce resources.

During the early days at Apple Computer, the Apple II division accounted for a large part of the company's revenue. It viewed the newly created Macintosh division as an unwise speculative venture. The natural rivalry was made worse when a champion of the Macintosh referred to the Apple II team as "the dull and boring product division." Because this type of conflict stems from the fundamental incompatibility of the job responsibilities of the disputants, it can often be resolved only through the mediation of a common superior.

Role incompatibility conflicts may overlap with those arising from personal differences or information deficiencies. The personal differences members bring to an organization generally remain dormant until they are triggered by an organizational catalyst, such as interdependent task responsibilities. One reason members often perceive that their assigned roles are incompatible is that they are operating from different bases of information. They communicate with different sets of people, are tied into different reporting systems, and receive instructions from different bosses.

Another major source of conflict is **environmentally induced stress**. Conflicts stemming from personal differences and role incompatibilities are greatly exacerbated by a stressful environment. When an organization is forced to operate on an austere budget, its members are more likely to become embroiled in disputes over domain claims and resource requests. Scarcity tends to lower trust, increase ethnocentrism, and reduce participation in decision making. These are ideal conditions for incubating interpersonal conflict (Cameron, Kim, & Whetten, 1987).

When a large eastern bank announced a major downsizing, the threat to employees' security was so severe that it disrupted long-time, close working relationships. Even friendships were not immune to the effects of the scarcity-induced stress. Long-standing golf foursomes and car pools were disbanded because tension among members was so high.

Another environmental condition that fosters conflict is uncertainty. When individuals are unsure about their status in an organization they become very anxious and prone to conflict. This type of "frustration conflict" often stems from rapid, repeated change. If task assignments, management philosophy, accounting procedures, and lines of authority are changed frequently, members find it difficult to cope with the resulting stress, and sharp, bitter conflicts can easily erupt over seemingly trivial problems. This type of conflict is generally intense, but it dissipates quickly once a change becomes routinized and individuals' stress levels are lowered.

When a major pet-food manufacturing facility announced that one-third of its managers would have to support a new third shift, the feared disruption of personal and family routines prompted many managers to think about sending out their résumés. In addition, the uncertainty of who was going to be required to work at night was so great that even routine management work was disrupted by posturing and infighting.

Before concluding this discussion of various sources of interpersonal conflicts, it is useful to point out that the seminal research of Geert Hofstede (1980) on cultural values suggests how people from any given cultural background might be drawn into different types of conflict. For example, one of the primary dimensions of cultural values emerging from Hofstede's research was tolerance for uncertainty. Some cultures, such as in Japan, have a high uncertainty avoidance, whereas other cultures, like the United States, are much more uncertainty tolerant. Extrapolating from these findings, if an American firm and a Japanese firm have created a joint venture in an industry known for highly volatile sales (e.g., short-term memory chips), one would expect that the Japanese managers would experience a higher level of uncertainty-induced conflict than their American counterparts. In contrast, because American culture places an extremely high value on individualism (another of Hofstede's key dimensions of cultural values), one would expect that the U.S. managers in this joint venture would experience a higher level of conflict stemming from their role interdependence with their Japanese counterparts.

To illustrate how various types of conflict actually get played out in an organization and how devastating their impact on a firm's performance can be, let's take a look at the troubles encountered by First Boston, one of the top seven investment banks dominating the New

York capital market. This venerable firm became embroiled in conflict between two important revenue divisions: trading and investment banking. After the stock market crash in 1987, the investment banking division, which accounted for the bulk of First Boston's profits in the 1980s through mergers and acquisitions, asked that resources be diverted from trading (an unprofitable line) to investment banking. They also asked for allocation of computer costs on the basis of usage instead of splitting the costs in half, since investment banking did not use computers very much. A review committee, including the CEO (a trader by background) reviewed the problem and finally decided to reject the investment banking proposals. This led to the resignations of the head of the investment division and several of the senior staff, including seven leveraged-buyout specialists.

This interdepartmental conflict was exacerbated by increasing frictions between competing subcultures within the firm. In the 1950s, when First Boston began, it was "WASPish" in composition, and its business came chiefly through the "old-boy network." In the 1970s, First Boston recruited a number of innovative "whiz kids"—mostly Jews, Italians, and Cubans. These individuals generated innovative ways to package mergers and acquisitions, which are now the mainstay of the current business in the investment area. These were less aristocratic people, many even wearing jeans to the office. The tension between the new "high flyers" and the "old guard" appeared to color many decisions at First Boston.

As a result of these conflicts, First Boston lost a number of key personnel. "The quitters claim that as the firm has grown, it has become a less pleasant place to work in, with political infighting taking up too much time" ("Catch a Falling Star," 1988).

Selecting the Appropriate Conflict Management Approach

Now that we have examined various types of conflict in terms of their focus and sources, it is natural to shift our attention to the common approaches for managing conflict of any type. As revealed in the Pre-assessment survey, people's responses to interpersonal confrontations tend to fall into five categories: *forcing, accommodating, avoiding, compromising,* and *collaborating* (Volkema & Bergmann, 2001). These responses can be organized along two dimensions, as shown in Figure 7.3 (Ruble &

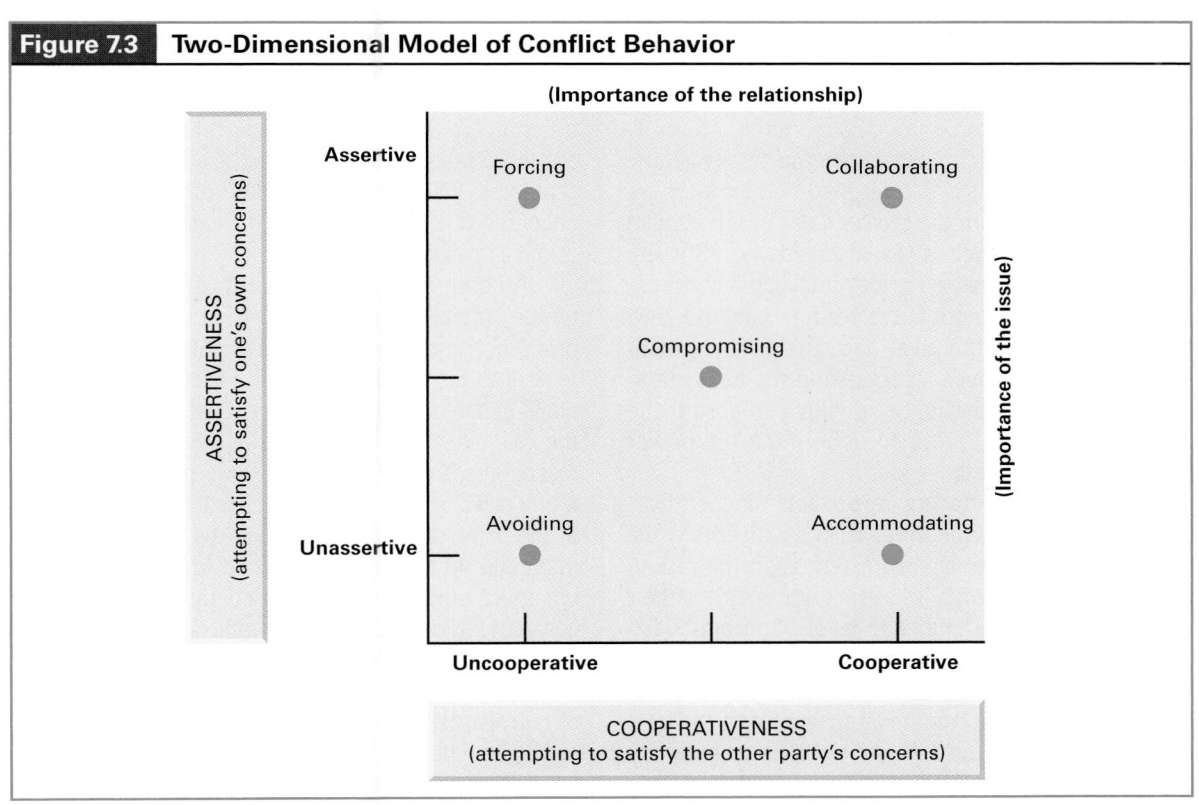

Figure 7.3 Two-Dimensional Model of Conflict Behavior

Source: *Adapted from Ruble & Thomas, 1976.*

Thomas, 1976). These five approaches to conflict reflect different degrees of cooperativeness and assertiveness. A cooperative response is intended to satisfy the needs of the interacting person, whereas an assertive response focuses on the needs of the focal person. The cooperativeness dimension reflects the importance of the relationship, whereas the assertiveness dimension reflects the importance of the issue.

The **forcing response** (assertive, uncooperative) is an attempt to satisfy one's own needs at the expense of the needs of the other individual. This can be done by using formal authority, physical threats, manipulation ploys, or by ignoring the claims of the other party. The blatant use of the authority of one's office ("I'm the boss, so we'll do it my way") or a related form of intimidation is generally evidence of a lack of tolerance or self-confidence. The use of manipulation or feigned ignorance is a much more subtle reflection of an egoistic leadership style. Manipulative leaders often appear to be democratic by proposing that conflicting proposals be referred to a committee for further investigation. However, they ensure that the composition of the committee reflects their interests and preferences so that what appears to be a selection based on merit is actually an authoritarian act. A related ploy some managers use is to ignore a proposal that threatens their personal interests. If the originator inquires about the disposition of his or her memo, the manager pleads ignorance, blames the mail clerk or new secretary, and then suggests that the proposal be redrafted. After several of these encounters, subordinates generally get the message that the boss isn't interested in their ideas.

The problem with the repeated use of this conflict management approach is that it breeds hostility and resentment. While observers may intellectually admire authoritarian or manipulative leaders because they appear to accomplish a great deal, their management styles generally produce a backlash in the long run as people become increasingly unwilling to absorb the emotional costs and work to undermine the power base of the authoritarian leader.

The **accommodating approach** (cooperative, unassertive) satisfies the other party's concerns while neglecting one's own. Unfortunately, as in the case of boards of directors of failing firms who neglect their interests and responsibilities in favor of accommodating the wishes of management, this strategy generally results in both parties' "losing." The difficulty with the habitual use of the accommodating approach is that it emphasizes preserving a friendly relationship at the expense of critically appraising issues and protecting personal rights. This may result in others' taking advantage of you, which lowers your self-esteem as you observe yourself being used by others to accomplish their objectives while you fail to make any progress toward your own.

The **avoiding response** (uncooperative, unassertive) neglects the interests of both parties by sidestepping the conflict or postponing a solution. This is often the response of managers who are emotionally ill-prepared to cope with the stress associated with confrontations, or it might reflect recognition that a relationship is not strong enough to absorb the fallout of an intense conflict. The repeated use of this approach causes considerable frustration for others because issues never seem to get resolved, really tough problems are avoided because of their high potential for conflict, and subordinates engaging in conflict are reprimanded for undermining the harmony of the work group. Sensing a leadership vacuum, people from all directions rush to fill it, creating considerable confusion and animosity in the process.

The **compromising response** is intermediate between assertiveness and cooperativeness. A compromise is an attempt to obtain partial satisfaction for both parties, in the sense that both receive the proverbial "half loaf." To accommodate this, both parties are asked to make sacrifices to obtain a common gain. While this approach has considerable practical appeal to managers, its indiscriminate use is counterproductive. If subordinates are continually told to "split the difference," they may conclude that their managers are more interested in resolving disputes than solving problems. This creates a climate of expediency that encourages game playing, such as asking for twice as much as you need.

A common mistake made in mergers is placing undue emphasis on "being fair to both sides" by compromising on competing corporate policies and practices as well as on which redundant staff members get laid off. When decisions are made on the basis of "spreading the pain evenly" or "using half of your procedures and half of ours," rather than on the basis of merit, then harmony takes priority over value. Ironically, actions taken in the name of "keeping peace in the merged families" often end up being so illogical and impractical that the emerging union is doomed to operate under a pall of constant internal turmoil and conflict.

The **collaborating approach** (cooperative, assertive) is an attempt to address fully the concerns of both parties. It is often referred to as the "problem-solving" mode. In this mode, the intent is to find solutions to the cause of the conflict that are satisfactory to both parties rather than to find fault or assign blame. In this way, both parties can feel that they have "won." This is the only win–win strategy among the five. The avoiding mode results in a lose–lose outcome and the compromising, accommodating, and forcing modes all represent win–lose outcomes. Although the collaborative approach is not appropriate for all situations, when used appropriately, it has the most beneficial effect on the involved parties. It encourages norms of collaboration and trust while acknowledging the value of assertiveness. It encourages individuals to focus their disputes on problems and issues rather than on personalities. Finally, it cultivates the skills necessary for self-governance, so that effective problem solvers feel empowered. The collaborative approach to problem solving and conflict resolution works best in an environment supporting openness, directness, and equality. In an interview with Steven Jobs, the editors of *Inc.* magazine quizzed the man they heralded as the "entrepreneur of the decade" regarding the perils of being a celebrity boss. ["It must help you in attracting the best minds to your new computer firm (NeXT), but once they're there, aren't they intimidated, working for a legend?"]

It all depends on the culture. The culture at NeXT definitely rewards independent thought, and we often have constructive disagreements—at all levels. It doesn't take a new person long to see that people feel fine about openly disagreeing with me. That doesn't mean I can't disagree with them, but it does mean that the best ideas win. Our attitude is that we want the best. Don't get hung up on who owns the idea. Pick the best one, and let's go. (Gendron & Burlingham, 1989)

Table 7.2 shows a comparison of the five conflict management approaches. In this table, the fundamentals of each approach are laid out, including its objective, how that objective is reflected in terms of an expressed point of view, and a supporting rationale. In addition, the likely outcomes of each approach are summarized.

Table 7.2	A Comparison of Five Conflict Management Approaches			
APPROACH	**OBJECTIVE**	**POINT OF VIEW**	**SUPPORTING RATIONALE**	**LIKELY OUTCOME**
1. Forcing	Get your way.	"I know what's right. Don't question my judgment or authority."	It is better to risk causing a few hard feelings than to abandon an issue you are committed to.	You feel vindicated but other party feels defeated and possibly humiliated.
2. Avoiding	Avoid having to deal with conflict.	"I'm neutral on that issue." "Let me think about it." "That's someone else's problem."	Disagreements are inherently bad because they create tension.	Interpersonal problems don't get resolved, causing long-term frustration manifested in a variety of ways.
3. Compromising	Reach an agreement quickly.	"Let's search for a solution we can both live with so we can get on with our work."	Prolonged conflicts distract people from their work and engender bitter feelings.	Participants become conditioned to seek expedient, rather than effective, solutions.
4. Accommodating	Don't upset the other person.	"How can I help you feel good about this encounter?" "My position isn't so important that it is worth risking bad feelings between us."	Maintaining harmonious relationships should be our top priority.	The other person is likely to take advantage of you.
5. Collaborating	Solve the problem together.	"This is my position. What is yours?" "I'm committed to finding the best possible solution." "What do the facts suggest?"	The positions of both parties are equally important (though not necessarily equally valid). Equal emphasis should be placed on the quality of the outcome and the fairness of the decision-making process.	The problem is most likely to be resolved. Also, both parties are committed to the solution and satisfied that they have been treated fairly.

LEARNING

COMPARING CONFLICT MANAGEMENT AND NEGOTIATION STRATEGIES

Although we have already noted that there is not a one-to-one correspondence between our focus on interpersonal confrontations and the negotiations literature, we believe our understanding of the five conflict management approaches is enriched by the following comparison (Savage, Blair, & Sorenson, 1989; Smith, 1987). **Negotiation strategies** are commonly categorized according to two broad perspectives: *integrative* and *distributive*. Stated succinctly, negotiation perspectives serve as an overarching value, or attitude, held by adversaries, that bound their set of acceptable approaches for resolving their differences and that give meaning to the outcomes of the conflict resolution process.

Negotiators who focus on dividing up a "fixed pie" reflect a **distributive bargaining perspective**, whereas parties using an **integrative perspective** search for collaborative ways of "expanding the pie" by avoiding fixed, incompatible positions (Bazerman & Neale, 1992; Murnighan, 1992, 1993; Thompson, 2001). One way to think about this distinction is that the distributive perspective focuses on the relative, individual scores for both sides (A versus B), whereas the integrative perspective focuses on the combined score (A + B). Hence, distributive negotiators assume an adversarial, competitive posture. They believe that one of the parties can improve only at the other party's expense. In contrast, integrative bargainers use problem-solving techniques to find "win–win" outcomes. They are interested in finding the best solution for both parties, rather than picking between the parties' preferred solutions (de Dreu, Koole, & Steinel, 2000; Fisher & Brown, 1988).

As Table 7.3 shows, four of the five conflict management strategies are distributive in nature. One or both parties must sacrifice something in order for the conflict to be resolved. Compromise occurs when both parties make sacrifices in order to find a common ground. Compromisers are generally more interested in finding an expedient solution than they are in finding an integrative solution. Forcing and accommodating demand that one party give up its position in order for the conflict to be resolved. When parties to a conflict avoid resolution, they do so because they assume that the costs of resolving the conflict are so high that they are better off not even attempting resolution. The "fixed pie" still exists, but the individuals involved view attempts to divide it as threatening, so they avoid decisions regarding the allocation process altogether.

Table 7.3	Comparison Between Negotiation and Conflict Management Strategies	
Negotiation Strategies	Distributive	Integrative
Conflict Management Strategies	Compromising Forcing Accommodating Avoiding	Collaborating

SELECTION FACTORS

A comparison of alternative approaches inevitably leads to questions like "Which one is the best?" or "Which one should I use in this situation?" Although, in general, the collaborative approach produces the fewest negative side effects, each approach has its place. The appropriateness of a management strategy depends on its congruence with both personal preferences and situational considerations. We will begin by discussing the most limiting consideration; how comfortable do individuals feel actually using each of the conflict management approaches or strategies?

Personal Preferences

As reflected in the "Strategies for Handling Conflict" survey in the Skill Assessment section of this chapter, it is important that we understand our personal preferences for managing conflict. If we don't feel comfortable with a particular approach, we are not likely to use it, no matter how convinced we are that it is the best available tool for a particular conflict situation. Although there are numerous factors that affect our personal preferences for how we manage conflict, three correlates of these choices have been studied extensively: ethnic culture, gender, and personality.

Research on conflict management styles reports that *ethnic culture* is reflected in individual preferences for the five responses we have just discussed (Seybolt et al., 1996; Weldon & Jehn, 1995). For example, it has been shown that individuals from Asian cultures tend to prefer the nonconfrontational styles of accommodating and avoiding (Rahim & Blum, 1994; Ting-Toomey et al., 1991; Xie, Song & Stringfellow, 1998), whereas, by comparison, Americans and South Africans prefer the forcing approach (Rahim & Blum, 1994; Seybolt et al., 1996; Xie et al., 1998). In general, compromise is the most commonly preferred approach across cultures (Seybolt et al., 1996), possibly because compromising may be viewed as the least costly alternative and the approach that most quickly reaches acceptable levels of fairness to both parties.

The research on the relationship between preferred conflict management style and *gender* is less clear cut. Some studies report that males are more likely to use the forcing response, whereas females tend to select the compromising approach (Kilmann & Thomas, 1977; Ruble & Schneer, 1994). In contrast, other studies found gender to have little influence on an individual's preferred responses to conflict (Korabik, Baril, & Watson, 1993). From a review of the growing literature on conflict styles and gender, Keashly (1994) draws five conclusions:

1. There is little evidence of gender differences in abilities and skills related to conflict management.
2. Evidence suggests that sex-role expectations appear to influence behavior and perceptions of behavior in particular conflict situations.
3. Influences and norms other than sex-role expectations may affect and influence conflict and behavior.
4. The experience and meaning of conflict may differ for women and men.
5. There is a persistence of beliefs in gender-linked behavior even when these behaviors are not found in research.

In summary, there is a widely shared belief that gender differences are correlated with conflict management style preferences, but this perception is only modestly supported by the results of recent research.

The third correlate of personal preferences is *personality type*. One line of research on this topic has linked conflict management style with three distinct personality profiles (Cummings, Harnett, & Stevens, 1971; Porter, 1973).

The *altruistic–nurturing* personality seeks gratification through promoting harmony with others and enhancing their welfare, with little concern for being rewarded in return. This personality type is characterized by trust, optimism, idealism, and loyalty. When altruistic–nurturing individuals encounter conflict, they tend to press for harmony by accommodating the demands of the other party.

The *assertive–directing* personality seeks gratification through self-assertion and directing the activities of others with a clear sense of having earned rewards. Individuals with this personality characteristic tend to be self-confident, enterprising, and persuasive. It is not

surprising that the assertive–directing personality tends to challenge the opposition by using the forcing approach to conflict management.

The *analytic–autonomizing* personality seeks gratification through the achievement of self-sufficiency, self-reliance, and logical orderliness. This personality type is cautious, practical, methodical, and principled. Individuals with this type of personality tend to be very cautious when encountering conflict. Initially, they attempt to resolve the problem rationally. However, if the conflict intensifies they will generally withdraw and break contact.

The Advantage of Flexibility

It is important to point out that none of these correlates of personal preferences are deterministic—they suggest general tendencies across various groups of people, but they do not totally determine individual choices. This is an important distinction because given the variety of causes, or forms, of conflict, one would suppose that effective conflict management would require the use of more than one approach or strategy.

The research on this matter is illuminating. In a classic study on this topic, 25 executives were asked to describe two conflict situations—one with bad results and one with good (Phillips & Cheston, 1979). These incidents were then categorized in terms of the conflict management approach used. As Figure 7.4 shows, there were 23 incidents of forcing, 12 incidents of problem solving, 5 incidents of compromise, and 12 incidents of avoidance. Admittedly, this was a very small sample of managers, but the fact that there were almost twice as many incidents of forcing as problem solving and nearly five times as many as compromising is noteworthy. It is also interesting that the executives indicated that forcing and compromising were equally as likely to produce good as bad results, whereas problem solving was always linked with positive outcomes, and avoidance generally led to negative results.

It is striking that, despite the fact that forcing was as likely to produce bad as good results, it was by far the most commonly used conflict management mode. Since this approach is clearly not superior in terms of results, one wonders why these senior executives reported a propensity for using it.

A likely answer is expediency. Evidence for this supposition is provided by a study of the preferred influence strategies of more than 300 managers in three countries (Kipnis & Schmidt, 1983). This study reports that when subordinates refuse or appear reluctant to comply with a request, managers become

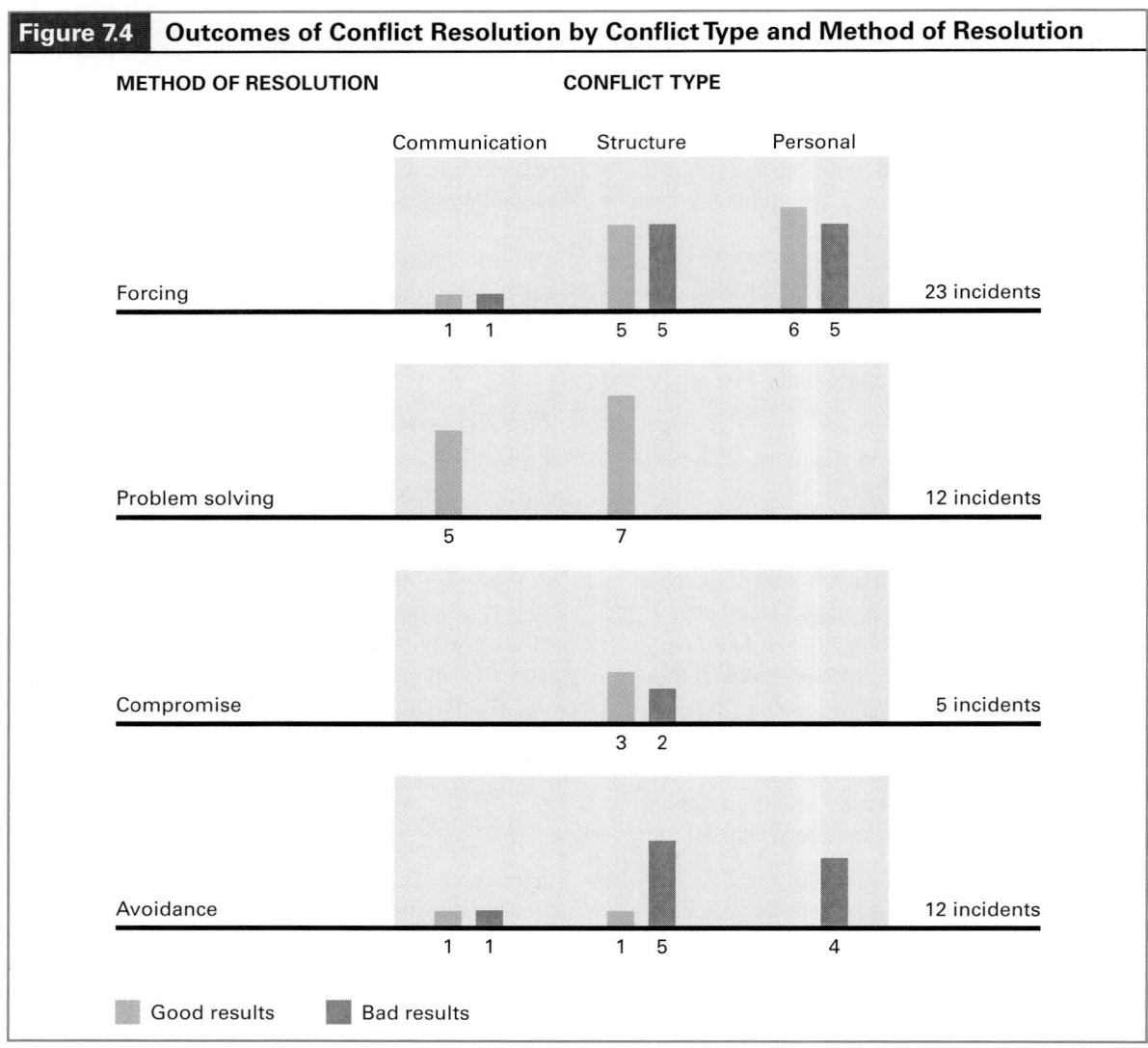

Figure 7.4 Outcomes of Conflict Resolution by Conflict Type and Method of Resolution

METHOD OF RESOLUTION   CONFLICT TYPE

Communication   Structure   Personal

Forcing   23 incidents
          1   1   5   5   6   5

Problem solving   12 incidents
          5   7

Compromise   5 incidents
                    3   2

Avoidance   12 incidents
          1   1   1   5   4

■ Good results   ■ Bad results

Source: © 1979 by The Regents of the University of California. Reprinted from the California Management Review. Vol 21, No. 4. By permission of The Regents.

directive. When resistance in subordinates is encountered, managers tend to fall back on their superior power and insist on compliance. So pervasive was this pattern that the authors of this study proposed an "Iron Law of Power: The greater the discrepancy in power between influence and target, the greater the probability that more directive influence strategies will be used" (p. 7).

A second prominent finding in Figure 7.4 is that some conflict management approaches were never used for certain types of issues. In particular, the managers did not report a single case of problem solving or compromising when personal problems were the source of the conflict. These approaches were used primarily for managing conflicts involving incompatible goals and conflicting reward systems between departments.

Two conclusions can be drawn from the research on the use of different conflict management approaches. First, no one approach is most effective for managing every type of conflict. Second, managers are more effective in dealing with conflicts if they feel comfortable using a variety of approaches (Savage et al., 1989).

These conclusions point out the need to understand the conditions under which each conflict management technique is most effective. This knowledge allows one to match the characteristics of a conflict incident with the management techniques best suited for those characteristics. The salient situational circumstances to consider are summarized in Table 7.4.

	CONFLICT MANAGEMENT APPROACH				
SITUATIONAL CONSIDERATIONS	FORCING	ACCOMMODATING	COMPROMISING	COLLABORATING	AVOIDING
Issue Importance	High	Low	Med	High	Low
Relationship Importance	Low	High	Med	High	Low
Relative Power	High	Low	Equal	Low-High	Equal
Time Constraints	Med-High	Med-High	Low	Low	Med-High

Table 7.4 | **Matching the Conflict Management Approach with the Situation**

Situational Considerations

Table 7.4 identifies four important incident-specific circumstances that can be used to select the appropriate conflict management approach. These can be stated in the form of diagnostic questions, with accompanying examples of high and low responses.

1. How important is the disputed issue? (High: Extremely important; Low: Not very important)
2. How important is the relationship? (High: Critical, ongoing, one-of-a-kind, partnership; Low: One-time transaction, for which there are readily available alternatives)
3. What is the relative level of power, or authority, between the disputants? (High: Boss to subordinate; Equal: Peers; Low: Subordinate to boss)
4. To what extent is time a significant constraint in resolving the dispute? (High: Must resolve the dispute quickly; Low: Time is not a salient factor)

The advantage of this table is that it allows you to quickly assess a situation and decide if a particular conflict management approach is suitable. As noted in the following descriptions, it is important to keep in mind that not all of the situational considerations are equally important for selecting a particular approach.

The forcing approach is most appropriate when a conflict involves values or policies and one feels compelled to defend the "correct" position; when a superior–subordinate relationship is involved; when maintaining a close, supportive relationship is not critical; and when there is a sense of urgency. An example of such a situation might be a manager insisting that a summer intern follow important company safety regulations.

The accommodating approach is most appropriate when the importance of maintaining a good working relationship outweighs all other considerations. While this could be the case regardless of your formal relationship with the other party, it is often perceived as being the only option for subordinates of powerful bosses. The nature of the issues and the amount of time available play a secondary role in determining the choice of this strategy. Accommodation becomes especially appropriate when the issues are not vital to your interests and the problem must be resolved quickly.

Trying to reach a compromise is most appropriate when the issues are complex and moderately important, there are no simple solutions, and both parties have a strong interest in different facets of the problem. The other essential situational requirement is adequate time for negotiation. The classic case is a bargaining session between representatives of management and labor to avert a scheduled strike. While the characteristics of the relationship between the parties are not essential factors, experience has shown that negotiations work best between parties with equal power who are committed to maintaining a good long-term relationship.

The collaborating approach is most appropriate when the issues are critical, maintaining an ongoing supportive relationship between peers is important, and time constraints are not pressing. Although collaboration can also be an effective approach for resolving conflicts between a superior and subordinate, it is important to point out that when a conflict involves peers, the collaborative mode is more appropriate than either the forcing or accommodating approach.

The avoidance approach is most appropriate when one's stake in an issue is not high and there is not a strong interpersonal reason for getting involved, regardless of whether the conflict involves a superior, subordinate, or peer. A severe time constraint becomes a contributing factor because it increases the likelihood of using avoidance, by default. While one might prefer other strategies that have a good chance of resolving problems without damaging relationships, such as compromise and collaboration, these are ruled out because of time pressure.

Now, admittedly, this is a very rational view of how to select the appropriate approach(es) for resolving a conflict. You might wonder if it is realistic to believe that in the heat of an emotional confrontation a person is likely to step back and make this type of deliberate, systematic assessment of the situation. Actually, it is because we share this concern that we are placing so much emphasis on a highly analytical approach to conflict management. Our purpose is to prepare you to effectively manage conflict, which often means overcoming natural tendencies, including allowing one's heightened emotional state to override the need for systematic analysis.

Although we are encouraging you to take a thoughtful, analytical approach to resolving disputes, that doesn't mean you can count on the other parties to the dispute agreeing with your analysis of the situation. For example, when conflicts involve individuals from very different cultural traditions, it is not uncommon for their lack of agreement on how to resolve their differences, or even on how important it is to resolve these differences, to make the prospect of achieving a truly collaborative solution seem remote. Given that several of our proposed diagnostic tools for selecting appropriate conflict management approaches also happen to represent major fault lines between cultural value systems, it is important that you factor into this decision-making process the cultural differences between disputants. If parties to a conflict hold very different views regarding time, power, ambiguity, the rule of norms, or the importance of relationships, one can expect they will have difficulty agreeing on the appropriate course of action for resolving their dispute (Trompenaars, 1994). Put simply: if you don't agree on *how* you are going to reach an agreement, it doesn't do you much good to discuss *what* that agreement might look like. Therefore, we hope that our ongoing discussion of various sources of differences in perspectives will help you to be sensitive to situations in which it is important to clarify assumptions, interpretations, and expectations early in the conflict management process.

To summarize this section, there are two key factors to take into consideration in selecting a conflict management approach or strategy. First, your choice of alternative approaches will be influenced by your comfort level with the various possibilities—referred to here as your personal preference. In general, personal preferences reflect personal characteristics, such as ethnic culture, gender, and personality. However, given that the use of multiple approaches appears to be a requirement of effective conflict management, it is important to stretch your "comfort zone" and become

proficient in the application of the full range of choices. The more you feel comfortable doing this, the more likely it is that you will seriously consider the second key selection factor—matching your choice of conflict management strategy with the salient situational considerations, including issue and relationship importance, relative power, and time constraints. Finally, it is important for parties of a dispute to discuss their assumptions regarding the appropriate process for resolving their differences, especially when they come from very different backgrounds.

Resolving Interpersonal Confrontations Using the Collaborative Approach

We now shift our attention from a consideration of when to use each of the approaches to how one can effectively implement the collaborative approach. We have chosen to focus on this approach for our skill development purposes for two reasons. First, as noted throughout our discussion, collaboration is the best overall approach. In a sense, effective managers treat this approach as their "default option"—unless there is a compelling reason to try something else, they will use this strategy. It is important to underscore the point that the collaborative approach is the appropriate "default option" for both issue-focused and people-focused conflicts. It seems quite natural to think of collaborating with someone with a different point of view regarding a troublesome issue. However, when someone is challenging your competence motivation, complaining about your "lack of sensitivity," or accusing you of being unfair, it seems like an unnatural act to collaborate with "the enemy." Instead, the natural tendency is to either "run away" (avoid or accommodate) or to "fight fire with fire" (force).

The second reason we are emphasizing the collaborative approach is that it is the hardest approach to implement effectively, under any circumstances. In the study by Kipnis and Schmidt (1983), discussed earlier, most managers expressed general support for the collaborative approach, but when it appeared that things were not going their way, they reverted back to a directive approach. By comparison, it is a fairly simple matter for managers to either give in or impose their will, but resolving differences in a truly collaborative manner is a complicated and taxing process. As a result, when situational conditions indicate that the collaborative approach is most appropriate, unskilled managers will often opt for less challenging approaches. To help you gain proficiency in using the collaborative approach, the remainder of this chapter describes behavioral guidelines for effectively resolving interpersonal confrontations in a collaborative manner.

A GENERAL FRAMEWORK FOR COLLABORATIVE PROBLEM SOLVING

The addition of "problem solving" to this title warrants a brief explanation. When two disputants agree to work toward a collaborative solution, they are basically agreeing to share an attitude or value. For example, collaborating disputants would not use asymmetrical sources of advantage (e.g., power, information, resources, etc.) to force the other party to accept a one-sided solution. But skill development requires more than an attitude adjustment—we need to understand the actual competencies required for effective conflict resolution. That is the benefit of incorporating the problem-solving process into our discussion of the collaborative approach. The problem-solving process provides a structured framework for an orderly, deliberate, reasoned approach to dispute resolution that enables disputants to make good on their commitment to work together. The merits of this structured approach are particularly useful when it is applied to people-focused conflicts. In these situations, it is helpful to have a framework to organize your thoughts and to discipline your emotions.

We will begin our discussion of the collaborative problem-solving process by introducing a general, six-step framework adapted from the integrative bargaining literature discussed earlier (Stroh, Northcraft, & Neale, 2002). We will then use this broad outline to develop a more a detailed set of problem-solving guidelines.

1. **Establish superordinate goals**. In order to foster a climate of collaboration, both parties to a dispute need to focus on what they share in common. Making more salient their shared goals of increased productivity, lower costs, reduced design time, or improved relations between departments sensitizes the parties to the merits of resolving their differences to avoid jeopardizing their mutual goals. The step is characterized by the general question, "What common goals provide a context for these discussions?"

2. **Separate the people from the problem**. Having clarified the mutual benefits to be gained by successfully resolving a conflict, it is useful to focus attention on the real issue at hand: solving a problem. Interpersonal confrontations are more likely to result in mutual satisfaction if the parties depersonalize their disagreement by suppressing their personal desires for revenge or one-upmanship. In other words, the other party is viewed as the advocate of a point of view, rather than as a rival. The problem solver would say, "That is an unreasonable position" rather than, "You are an unreasonable person."

3. **Focus on interests, not positions.** Positions are demands or assertions; interests constitute the reason behind the demands. Experience shows that it is easier to establish agreement on interests, given that they tend to be broader and multifaceted. This step involves redefining and broadening problems to make them more tractable. When a variety of issues are examined, parties are better able to understand each other's point of view and place their own views in perspective. A characteristic collaborative statement is, "Help me understand why you advocate that position."

4. **Invent options for mutual gains.** This step focuses on generating unusual, creative solutions. By focusing both parties' attention on brainstorming alternative, mutually agreeable solutions, the interpersonal dynamics naturally shift from competitive to collaborative. In addition, the more options and combinations there are to explore, the greater the probability of finding common ground. This step can be summarized as, "Now that we better understand each other's underlying concerns and objectives, let's brainstorm ways of satisfying both our needs."

5. **Use objective criteria for evaluating alternatives.** No matter how collaborative both parties may be, there are bound to be some incompatible interests. Rather than seizing on these as opportunities for testing wills, it is far more productive to determine what is fair. This requires both parties to examine how fairness should be judged. A shift in thinking from "getting what I want" to "deciding what makes most sense" fosters an open, reasonable attitude. It encourages parties to avoid overconfidence or overcommitment to their initial position. This approach is characterized by asking, "What is a fair way to evaluate the merits of our arguments?"

6. **Define success in terms of real gains, not imaginary losses.** If a manager seeks a 10 percent raise and receives only 6 percent, that outcome can be viewed as either a 6 percent improvement or a 40 percent shortfall. The first interpretation focuses on gains, the second on losses (in this case, unrealized expectations). The outcome is the same, but the manager's satisfaction with it varies substantially. It is important to recognize that our satisfaction with an outcome is affected by the standards we use to judge it. Recognizing this, the collaborative problem solver facilitates resolution by judging the value of proposed solutions against reasonable standards. This perspective is reflected in the question, "Does this outcome constitute a meaningful improvement over current conditions?"

THE FOUR PHASES OF COLLABORATIVE PROBLEM SOLVING

Notice how the problem-solving approach encourages collaboration by keeping the process focused on *shared problems* and *sharing solutions*. These are important themes to remember, especially when you utilize the collaborative approach to resolve a people-focused conflict. Because of the degree of difficulty inherent in this undertaking, we will continue using the people-focused conflict context in our remaining discussion. For information on how to manage issue-focused conflicts using various negotiation strategies, see Murnighan (1992, 1993) and Thompson (2001).

We have organized our detailed discussion of behavioral guidelines around the four phases of the **problem-solving process**: (1) *problem identification*, (2) *solution generation*, (3) *action plan formulation and agreement*, and (4) *implementation and follow-up*. In the midst of a heated exchange, the first two phases are the most critical steps, as well as the most difficult to implement effectively. If you are able to achieve agreement on what the problem is and how you intend to resolve it, the details of the agreement, including a follow-up plan, should follow naturally. In other words, we are placing our skill-building emphasis where skillful implementation is most critical.

We have also elected to identify specific problem-solving guidelines for each role in a dispute, because by definition, their orientations are discrepant during the initial stages of this process. A dyadic confrontation involves two actors, an **initiator** and a **responder**. For

example, a subordinate might complain about not being given a fair share of opportunities to work overtime; or the head of production might complain to the head of sales about frequent changes in order specifications. A dyadic conflict represents a greater challenge for responders because they have responsibility for transforming a complaint into a problem-solving discussion. This requires considerable patience and self-confidence, because unskilled initiators will generally begin the discussion by blaming the responder for the problem. In this situation, an unskilled responder will naturally become defensive and look for an opportunity to "even the score."

If these lose–lose dynamics persist, a **mediator** is generally required to cool down the dispute, reestablish constructive communication, and help the parties reconcile their differences. The presence of a mediator removes some pressure from the responder because an impartial referee provides assistance in moving the confrontation through the problem-solving phases.

The following guidelines provide a model for acting out the initiator, responder, and mediator roles in such a way that problem solving can occur. In our discussion of each role, we will assume that other participants in the conflict are not behaving according to their prescribed guidelines.

Initiator—Problem Identification

I1 Maintain Personal Ownership of the Problem
It is important to recognize that when you are upset and frustrated, this is your problem, not the other person's. You may feel that your boss or coworker is the source of your problem, but resolving your frustration is your immediate concern. The first step in addressing this concern is acknowledging accountability for your feelings. Suppose someone enters your office with a smelly cigar without asking if it is all right to smoke. The fact that your office is going to stink for the rest of the day may infuriate you, but the odor does not present a problem for your smoking guest. One way to determine ownership of a problem is to identify whose needs are not being met. In this case, your need for a clean working environment is not being met, so the smelly office is your problem.

The advantage of acknowledging ownership of a problem when registering a complaint is that it reduces defensiveness (Adler, Rosenfeld, & Proctor, 2001; Alder & Rodman, 2003). In order for you to get a problem solved, the respondent must not feel threatened by your initial statement of that problem. By beginning the conversation with a request that the responder help solve your problem, you immediately establish a problem-solving atmosphere. For example, you might say, "Bill, do you have a few minutes? I have a problem I need to discuss with you."

I2 Succinctly Describe Your Problem in Terms of Behaviors, Consequences, and Feelings

A useful model for remembering how to state your problem effectively has been prescribed by Gordon (2000): "I have a problem. When you do X, Y results, and I feel Z." Although we don't advocate the memorization of set formulas for improving communication skills, keeping this model in mind will help you implement three critical elements in your "problem statement."

First, describe the specific behaviors (X) that present a problem for you. This will help you avoid the reflexive tendency when you are upset to give feedback that is evaluative and not specific. One way to do this is to specify the expectations or standards that have been violated. For example, a subordinate may have missed a deadline for completing an assigned task, your boss may gradually be taking over tasks previously delegated to you, or a colleague in the accounting department may have repeatedly failed to provide you with data required for an important presentation.

Second, outline the specific, observable consequences (Y) of these behaviors. Simply telling others that their actions are causing you problems is often sufficient stimulus for change. In fast-paced work environments, people generally become insensitive to the impact of their actions. They don't intend to cause offense, but they become so busy meeting deadlines associated with "getting the product out the door" that they tune out subtle negative feedback from others. When this occurs, bringing to the attention of others the consequences of their behaviors will often prompt them to change.

Unfortunately, not all problems can be resolved this simply. At times, offenders are aware of the negative consequences of their behaviors, yet they persist in them. In such cases, this approach is still useful in stimulating a problem-solving discussion because it presents concerns in a nonthreatening manner. Possibly, the responders' behaviors are constrained by the expectations of their boss or by the fact that the department is currently understaffed. Responders may not be able to change these constraints, but this approach will encourage them to discuss them with you so you can work on the problem together.

Third, describe the feelings (Z) you experience as a result of the problem. It is important that the responder understand that the behavior is not just inconvenient. You need to explain how it is affecting you personally by engendering feelings of frustration, anger, or insecurity.

Explain how these feelings are interfering with your work. They may make it more difficult for you to concentrate, to be congenial with customers, to be supportive of your boss, or to be willing to make needed personal sacrifices to meet deadlines.

We recommend using this three-step model as a general guide. The order of the components may vary, and you should not use the same words every time. Obviously, it would get pretty monotonous if everyone in a work group initiated a discussion about an interpersonal issue with the words, "I have a problem." Observe how the key elements in the "XYZ" model are used in different ways in Table 7.5.

I3 Avoid Drawing Evaluative Conclusions and Attributing Motives to the Respondent

When exchanges between two disputing parties become vengeful, each side often has a different perspective about the justification of the other's actions. Typically, each party believes that it is the victim of the other's aggression. In international conflicts, opposing nations often believe they are acting defensively rather than offensively. Similarly, in smaller-scale conflicts, each side may have distorted views of its own hurt and the motives of the "offender" (Kim & Smith, 1993). Therefore, in presenting your problem, avoid the pitfalls of making accusations, drawing inferences about motivations or intentions, or attributing the responder's undesirable behavior to personal inadequacies. Statements such as, "You are always interrupting me," "You haven't been fair to me since the day I disagreed with you in the board meeting," and "You never have time to listen to our problems and suggestions because you manage your time so poorly" are good for starting arguments but ineffective for initiating a problem-solving process.

Another key to reducing defensiveness is to delay proposing a solution until both parties agree on the nature of the problem. When you become so upset with someone's behavior that you feel it is necessary to initiate a complaint, it is often because the person has seriously violated your ideal role model. For example, you might feel that your manager should have been less dogmatic and listened more during a goal-setting interview. Consequently, you might express your feelings in terms of prescriptions for how the other person should behave and suggest a more democratic or sensitive style.

Besides creating defensiveness, the principal disadvantage to initiating problem solving with a suggested remedy is that it hinders the problem-solving process. Before completing the problem-articulation phase, you have immediately jumped to the solution-generation

Table 7.5	Examples of the "XYZ" Approach to Stating a Problem

Model:

"I have a problem. When you do X (behavior), Y results (consequences), and I feel Z."

Examples:

I have to tell you that I get upset [feelings] when you make jokes about my bad memory in front of other people [behavior]. In fact, I get so angry so that I find myself bringing up your faults to get even [consequences].

I have a problem. When you say you'll be here for our date at six and don't show up until after seven [behavior], the dinner gets ruined, we're late for the show we planned to see [consequences], and I feel hurt because it seems as though I'm just not that important to you [feelings].

The employees want to let management know that we've been having a hard time lately with the short notice you've been giving when you need us to work overtime [behavior]. That probably explains some of the grumbling and lack of cooperation you've mentioned [consequences]. Anyhow, we wanted to make it clear that this policy has really got a lot of the workers feeling pretty resentful [feeling].

Source: *Adapted from Adler, 1977.*

phase, based on the assumption that you know all the reasons for, and constraints on, the other person's behavior. You will jointly produce better, more acceptable, solutions if you present your statement of the problem and discuss it thoroughly before proposing potential solutions.

I4 Persist Until Understood   There are times when the respondent will not clearly receive or acknowledge even the most effectively expressed message. Suppose, for instance, that you share the following problem with a coworker:

> *Something has been bothering me, and I need to share my concerns with you. Frankly, I'm uncomfortable [feeling] with your heavy use of profanity [behavior]. I don't mind an occasional "damn" or "hell," but the other words bother me a lot. Lately I've been avoiding you [consequences], and that's not good because it interferes with our working relationship, so I wanted to let you know how I feel.*

When you share your feelings in this nonevaluative way, it's likely that the other person will understand your position and possibly try to change behavior to suit your needs. On the other hand, there are a number of less satisfying responses that could be made to your comment:

> *Listen, these days everyone talks that way. And besides, you've got your faults, too, you know! [Your coworker becomes defensive, rationalizing and counterattacking.]*
>
> *Yeah, I suppose I do swear a lot. I'll have to work on that someday. [Gets the general*

drift of your message but fails to comprehend how serious the problem is to you.]

> *Listen, if you're still angry about my forgetting to tell you about that meeting the other day, you can be sure that I'm really sorry. I won't do it again. [Totally misunderstands.]*
>
> *Speaking of avoiding, have you seen Chris lately? I wonder if anything is wrong with him. [Is discomfited by your frustration and changes the subject.]*

In each case, the coworker does not understand or does not wish to acknowledge the problem. In these situations, you must repeat your concern until it has been acknowledged as a problem to be solved. Otherwise, the problem-solving process will terminate at this point and nothing will change. Repeated assertions can take the form of restating the same phrase several times or reiterating your concern with different words or examples that you feel may improve comprehension. To avoid introducing new concerns or shifting from a descriptive to an evaluative mode, keep in mind the "XYZ" formula for feedback. Persistence is most effective when it consists of "variations on a theme," rather than "variation in themes."

I5 Encourage Two-Way Discussion   It is important to establish a problem-solving climate by inviting the respondent to express opinions and ask questions. There may be a reasonable explanation for another's disturbing behavior; the person may have a radically different view of the problem. The sooner this information is introduced into the conversation, the more likely it is that the issue will be resolved. As a rule of thumb, the longer the initiator's opening statement, the longer it will take the two parties to work through their problem. This is because the lengthier the problem statement, the more likely it is to encourage a defensive reaction. The longer we talk, the more worked up we get, and the more likely we are to violate principles of supportive communication. As a result, the other party begins to feel threatened, starts mentally outlining a rebuttal or counterattack, and stops listening empathetically to our concerns. Once these dynamics enter the discussion, the collaborative approach is usually discarded in favor of the accommodation or forcing strategies, depending on the circumstances. When this occurs, it is unlikely that the actors will be able to reach a mutually satisfactory solution to their problem without third-party intervention.

I6 Manage the Agenda: Approach Multiple or Complex Problems Incrementally
One way to shorten your opening statement is to approach complex problems incrementally. Rather than raising a series of issues all at once, focus initially on a simple or rudimentary problem. Then, as you gain greater appreciation for the other party's perspective and share some problem-solving success, you can discuss more challenging issues. This is especially important when trying to resolve a problem with a person who is important to your work performance but does not have a long-standing relationship with you. The less familiar you are with the other's opinions and personality, as well as the situational constraints influencing his or her behaviors, the more you should approach a problem-solving discussion as a fact-finding and rapport-building mission. This is best done by focusing your introductory statement on a specific manifestation of a broader problem and presenting it in such a way that it encourages the other party to respond expansively. You can then use this early feedback to shape the remainder of your agenda. For example, "Bill, we had difficulty getting that work order processed on time yesterday. What seemed to be the problem?"

Initiator—Solution Generation

I7 Focus on Commonalities as the Basis for Requesting a Change
Once a problem is clearly understood, the discussion should shift to the solution-generation phase. Most disputants share at least some personal and organizational goals, believe in many of the same fundamental principles of management, and operate under similar constraints. These commonalities can serve as a useful starting point for generating solutions. The most straightforward approach to changing another's offensive behavior is making a request. The legitimacy of

a request will be enhanced if it is linked to common interests. These might include shared values, such as treating coworkers fairly and following through on commitments, or shared constraints, such as getting reports in on time and operating within budgetary restrictions. This approach is particularly effective when the parties have had difficulty getting along in the past. In these situations, pointing out how a change in the respondent's behavior would positively affect your shared fate will reduce defensiveness: "Jane, one of the things we have all worked hard to build in this audit team is mutual support. We are all pushed to the limit getting this job completed by the third-quarter deadline next week, and the rest of the team members find it difficult to accept your unwillingness to work overtime during this emergency. Because the allocation of next quarter's assignments will be affected by our current performance, would you please reconsider your position?"

Responder—Problem Identification

Now we shall examine the problem-identification phase from the viewpoint of the person who is supposedly the source of the problem. In a work setting, this could be a manager who is making unrealistic demands, a new employee who has violated critical safety regulations, or a coworker who is claiming credit for ideas you generated. The following guidelines for dealing with someone's complaint show how to shape the initiator's behavior so you can have a productive problem-solving experience.

R1 Establish a Climate for Joint Problem Solving by Showing Genuine Interest and Concern
When a person complains to you, do not treat that complaint lightly. While this may seem self-evident, it is often difficult to focus your attention on someone else's problems when you are in the middle of writing an important project report or concerned about preparing for a meeting scheduled to begin in a few minutes. Consequently, unless the other person's emotional condition necessitates dealing with the problem immediately, it is better to set up a time for another meeting if your current time pressures will make it difficult to concentrate.

In most cases, the initiator will be expecting you to set the tone for the meeting. You will quickly undermine collaboration if you overreact or become defensive. Even if you disagree with the complaint and feel it has no foundation, you need to respond empathetically to the initiator's statement of the problem. This is done by conveying an attitude of interest and receptivity through your posture, tone of voice, and facial expressions.

One of the most difficult aspects of establishing the proper climate for your discussion is responding appropriately to the initiator's emotions. Sometimes you may need to let a person blow off steam before trying to address the substance of a specific complaint. In some cases, the therapeutic effect of being able to express negative emotions to the boss will be enough to satisfy a subordinate. This occurs frequently in high-pressure jobs in which tempers flare easily as a result of the intense stress.

However, an emotional outburst can be very detrimental to problem solving. If an employee begins verbally attacking you or someone else, and it is apparent that the individual is more interested in getting even than in solving an interpersonal problem, you may need to interrupt and interject some ground rules for collaborative problem solving. By explaining calmly to the other person that you are willing to discuss a genuine problem but that you will not tolerate personal attacks or scapegoating, you can quickly determine the initiator's true intentions. In most instances, he or she will apologize, emulate your emotional tone, and begin formulating a useful statement of the problem.

R2 Seek Additional, Clarifying Information About the Problem by Asking Questions
As shown in Figure 7.5, untrained initiators typically present complaints that are so general and evaluative that they aren't useful problem statements. It is difficult to understand how you should respond to a general,

vague comment like "You never listen to me during our meetings," followed by an evaluative, critical comment like "You obviously aren't interested in what I have to say." In addition to not providing detailed descriptions of your offending actions, inflamed initiators often make attributions about your motives and your personal strengths and weaknesses from a few specific incidents. If the two of you are going to transform a personal complaint into a joint problem, you must redirect the conversation from general and evaluative accusations to descriptions of specific behaviors.

The problem is that when you are getting steamed up over what you believe are unfair and unjustified accusations, it is difficult to avoid fighting back. ("Oh yeah, well I haven't wanted to say this about you before, but since you've brought up the subject . . . ") The single best way to keep your mind focused on transforming a personal attack into a jointly identified problem is to limit your responses to questions. If you stick with asking clarifying questions you are going to get better-quality information and you are going to demonstrate your commitment to joint problem solving.

As shown in Figure 7.5, one of the best ways of doing this is to ask for examples ("Can you give me an example of what I did during a staff meeting that led you to believe I wasn't listening to what you had to say?"). Building on our discussion of the "XYZ" model in the initiator's guidelines, you might find it useful to ask for examples of your offending actions and their harmful consequences, including damaged feelings ("Can you give me a specific example of my behavior that concerns you?" "When I did that, what were the

---

| Figure 7.5 | Respondents' Effective Use of Clarifying Questions |

Transform Complaints . . .

From		*To*
General	→	Specific
Evaluative	→	Descriptive
Motives and Reasons	→	Actions and Consequences

Using Clarifying Questions:

"Can you give me an example?"
"What do you mean by that label/term?"
"Can you help me understand what your conclusion is based on?"
"When did this first become a problem for you?"
"How often has this occurred?"
"What specific actions have led you to believe that I'm taking sides in this issue?"
"What were some of the harmful consequences of my decision?"

specific consequences for your work?" "How did you feel when that happened?").

When a complaint is both serious and complex, it is especially critical for you to understand it completely. In these situations, after you have asked several clarifying questions, check your level of understanding by summarizing the initiator's main points and asking if your summary is correct.

Sometimes it is useful to ask for additional complaints: "Are there any other problems in our relationship you'd like to discuss?" If the initiator is just in a griping mood, this is not a good time to probe further; you don't want to encourage this type of behavior. But if the person is seriously concerned about improving your relationship, if your discussion to this point has been helpful, and if you suspect that the initiator is holding back and not talking about the really serious issues, you should probe deeper. Often, people begin by complaining about a minor problem to "test the waters." If you blow up, the conversation is terminated, and the critical issues aren't discussed. However, if you are responsive to a frank discussion about problems, the more serious issues are likely to surface.

R3 Agree with Some Aspect of the Complaint

This is an important point that is difficult for some people to accept because they wonder how it is possible to agree with something they don't believe is true. They may also be worried about reinforcing complaining behavior. In practice, this step is probably the best test of whether a responder is committed to using the collaborative approach to conflict management rather than the avoiding, forcing, or accommodating approach. People who use the forcing mode will grit their teeth while listening to the initiator, just waiting to find a flaw they can use to launch a counterattack. Or they will simply respond, "I'm sorry, but that's just the way I am. You'll simply have to get used to it." Accommodators will apologize profusely and ask for forgiveness. People who avoid conflicts will acknowledge and agree with the initiator's concerns, but only in a superficial manner because their only concern is how to terminate the awkward conversation quickly.

In contrast, collaborators will demonstrate their concerns for both cooperation and assertiveness by looking for points in the initiator's presentation with which they can genuinely agree. Following the principles of supportive communication, you will find it possible to accept the other person's viewpoint without conceding your own position. Even in the most blatantly malicious and hostile verbal assault (which may be more a reflection of the initiator's insecurity than evidence of your inadequacies), there is generally a

grain of truth. A few years ago, a junior faculty member in a business school who was being reviewed for promotion received a very unfair appraisal from one of his senior colleagues. Since the junior member knew that the critic was going through a personal crisis, he could have dismissed the criticism as irrelevant and tendentious. However, one particular phrase—"You are stuck on a narrow line of research"—kept coming back to his mind. There was something there that couldn't be ignored. As a result of turning a vindictive reproach into a valid suggestion, the junior faculty member made a major career decision that produced very positive outcomes. Furthermore, by publicly giving the senior colleague credit for the suggestion, he substantially strengthened the interpersonal relationship.

There are a number of ways you can agree with a message without accepting all of its ramifications (Adler et al., 2001). You can find an element of truth, as in the incident related above. Or you can agree in principle with the argument: "I agree that managers should set a good example" or "I agree that it is important for salesclerks to be at the store when it opens." If you can't find anything substantive with which to agree, you can always agree with the initiator's perception of the situation: "Well, I can see how you would think that. I have known people who deliberately shirked their responsibilities." Or you can agree with the person's feelings: "It is obvious that our earlier discussion greatly upset you."

In none of these cases are you necessarily agreeing with the initiator's conclusions or evaluations, nor are you conceding your position. You are trying to understand, to foster a problem-solving, rather than argumentative, discussion. Generally, initiators prepare for a complaint session by mentally cataloguing all the evidence supporting their point of view. Once the discussion begins, they introduce as much evidence as necessary to make their argument convincing; that is, they keep arguing until you agree. The more evidence that is introduced, the broader the argument becomes and the more difficult it is to begin investigating solutions. Consequently, establishing a basis of agreement is the key to culminating the problem-identification phase of the problem-solving process.

Responder—Solution Generation

R4 Ask for Suggestions of Acceptable Alternatives Once you are certain you fully understand the initiator's complaint, move on to the solution-generation phase by asking the initiator for recommended solutions. This triggers an important transition in the discussion by shifting attention from the negative to the positive and from the past to the future. It also communicates your regard for the initiator's opinions. This step is a key element in the joint problem-solving process. Some managers listen patiently to a subordinate's complaint, express appreciation for the feedback, say they will rectify the problem, and then terminate the discussion. This leaves the initiator guessing about the outcome of the meeting. Will you take the complaint seriously? Will you really change? If so, will the change resolve the problem? It is important to eliminate this ambiguity by agreeing on a plan of action. If the problem is particularly serious or complex, it is useful to write down specific agreements, including assignments and deadlines, as well as providing for a follow-up meeting to check progress.

Frequently, it is necessary for managers to mediate a dispute (Karambayya & Brett, 1989; Kressel & Pruitt, 1989; Stroh et al., 2002). While this may occur for a variety of reasons, we will assume in this discussion that the manager has been invited to help the initiator and responder resolve their differences. While we will assume that the mediator is the manager of both disputants, this is not a necessary condition for the guidelines we shall propose. For example, a hairstylist in a college-town beauty salon complained to the manager about the way the receptionist was favoring other beauticians who had been there longer. Since this allegation, if true, involved a violation of the manager's policy of allocating walk-in business strictly on the basis of beautician availability, the manager felt it necessary to investigate the complaint. In doing so, she discovered considerable animosity between the two employees, stemming from frequent disagreements regarding the amount of work the stylist had done on a given day. The stylist felt that the receptionist was keeping sloppy records, while the receptionist blamed the problem on the stylist's forgetting to hand in her credit slip when she finished with a customer. The problems between the stylist and the receptionist appeared serious enough to the participants and broad enough in scope that the manager decided to call both parties into her office to help them resolve their differences. The following guidelines are intended to help mediators avoid the common pitfalls associated with this role, which are shown in Table 7.6.

Mediator—Problem Identification

M1 Acknowledge That a Conflict Exists and Propose a Problem-Solving Approach for Resolving It
When a mediator is called in, it means the disputants have failed as problem solvers. Therefore, the first requirement of effective mediation is to establish a problem-solving framework. To that end, it is vital that the mediator take seriously the problems between conflicting parties. If they feel they have a serious problem, the mediator should not belittle its significance. Remarks such as, "I'm surprised that two intelligent people like you have not been able to work out your disagreement. We have more important things

Table 7.6	Ten Ways to Fail as a Mediator
1. After you have listened to the argument for a short time, begin to nonverbally communicate your discomfort with the discussion (e.g., sit back, begin to fidget).	
2. Communicate your agreement with one of the parties (e.g., through facial expressions, posture, chair position, reinforcing comments).	
3. Say that you shouldn't be talking about this kind of thing at work or where others can hear you.	
4. Discourage the expression of emotion. Suggest that the discussion would better be held later after both parties have cooled off.	
5. Suggest that both parties are wrong. Point out the problems with both points of view.	
6. Suggest partway through the discussion that possibly you aren't the person who should be helping solve this problem.	
7. See if you can get both parties to attack you.	
8. Minimize the seriousness of the problem.	
9. Change the subject (e.g., ask for advice to help you solve one of your problems).	
10. Express displeasure that the two parties are experiencing conflict (e.g., imply that it might undermine the solidarity of the work group).	

Source: *Adapted from Morris & Sashkin, 1976.*

to do here than get all worked up over such petty issues" will make both parties defensive and interfere with any serious problem-solving efforts. While you might wish that your subordinates could have worked out their disagreement without bothering you, this is not the time to lecture them on self-reliance. Inducing guilt feelings by implying personal failure during an already emotional experience tends to distract the participants from the substantive issues at hand. Seldom is this conducive to problem solving.

One early decision a mediator has to make is whether to convene a joint problem-solving session or meet separately with the parties first. The diagnostic criteria shown in Table 7.7 should help you weigh the trade-offs. First, what is the current position of the disputants? Are both aware that a problem exists? Are they equally motivated to work on solving the problem? The more similar the awareness and motivation of the parties, the more likely it is that a joint session will be productive. If there is a serious discrepancy in awareness and motivation, the mediator should work to reduce that discrepancy through one-on-one meetings before bringing the disputants together.

Second, what is the current relationship between the disputants? Does their work require them to interact frequently? Is a good working relationship critical for their individual job performance? What has their relationship been in the past? What is the difference in their formal status in the organization? As we discussed earlier, joint problem-solving sessions are most productive between individuals of equal status who are required to work together regularly. This does not mean that joint meetings should not be held between a supervisor and subordinate, only that greater care needs to be taken in preparing for such a meeting. Specifically, if a department head becomes involved in a dispute between a worker and a supervisor, the department head should make sure that the worker does not feel this meeting will serve as an excuse for two managers to gang up on an hourly employee.

Separate fact-finding meetings with the disputants prior to a joint meeting are particularly useful when the parties have a history of recurring disputes, especially if these disputes should have been resolved without a mediator. Such a history often suggests a lack of conflict management or problem-solving skills on the part of the disputants, or it might stem from a broader set of issues that are beyond their control. In these situations, individual coaching sessions prior to a joint meeting will increase your understanding of the root causes and improve the individuals' abilities to resolve their differences. Following up these private meetings with a joint problem-solving session in which the mediator coaches the disputants through the process for resolving their conflicts can be a positive learning experience.

Third, what is the nature of the problem? Is the complaint substantive in nature and easily verifiable? If the problem stems from conflicting role responsibilities

Table 7.7	Choosing a Format for Mediating Conflicts		
FACTORS		HOLD JOINT MEETINGS	HOLD SEPARATE MEETINGS FIRST
Awareness and Motivation			
• Both parties are aware of the problem.		Yes	No
• They are equally motivated to resolve the problem.		Yes	No
• They accept your legitimacy as a mediator.		Yes	No
Nature of the Relationship			
• The parties hold equal status.		Yes	No
• They work together regularly.		Yes	No
• They have an overall good relationship.		Yes	No
Nature of the Problem			
• This is an isolated (not a recurring) problem.		Yes	No
• The complaint is substantive in nature and easily verified.		Yes	No
• The parties agree on the root causes of the problem.		Yes	No
• The parties share common values and work priorities.		Yes	No

and the actions of both parties in question are common knowledge, then a joint problem-solving session can begin on a common information and experimental base. However, if the complaint stems from differences in managerial style, values, personality characteristics, and so forth, bringing the parties together immediately following a complaint may seriously undermine the problem-solving process. Complaints that are likely to be interpreted as threats to the self-image of one or both parties (Who am I? What do I stand for?) warrant considerable individual discussion before a joint meeting is called. To avoid individuals' feeling as though they are being ambushed in a meeting, you should discuss serious personal complaints with them ahead of time, in private.

M2 In Seeking Out the Perspective of Both Parties, Maintain a Neutral Posture Regarding the Disputants—If Not the Issues

Effective mediation requires impartiality. If a mediator shows strong personal bias in favor of one party in a joint problem-solving session, the other party may simply walk out. However, such personal bias is more likely to emerge in private conversations with the disputants. Statements such as, "I can't believe he really did that!" and "Everyone seems to be having trouble working with Charlie these days" imply that the mediator is taking sides, and any attempt to appear impartial in a joint meeting will seem like mere window dressing to appease the other party. No matter how well-intentioned or justified these comments might be, they destroy the credibility of the mediator in the long run. In contrast, effective mediators respect both parties' points of view and make sure that both perspectives are expressed adequately.

Occasionally, it is not possible to be impartial on issues. One person may have violated company policy, engaged in unethical competition with a colleague, or broken a personal agreement. In these cases, the challenge of the mediator is to separate the offense from the offender. If a person is clearly in the wrong, the inappropriate behavior needs to be corrected, but in such a way that the individual doesn't feel his or her image and working relationships have been permanently marred. This can be done most effectively when correction occurs in private.

M3 Serve as a Facilitator, Not as a Judge

When parties must work closely and have a history of chronic interpersonal problems, it is often more important to teach problem-solving skills than to resolve a specific dispute. This is done best when the mediator adopts the posture of facilitator. The role of judge is to render a verdict regarding a problem in the past, not to teach people how to solve problems in the future. While some disputes obviously involve right and wrong actions, most interpersonal problems stem from differences in perspective. In these situations, it is important that the mediator avoid being seduced into "rendering a verdict" by comments such as, "Well, you're the boss; tell us which one is right," or more subtly, "I wonder if I did what was right?" The problem with a mediator's assuming the role of judge is that it sets in motion processes antithetical to effective interpersonal problem solving. The parties focus on persuading the mediator of their innocence and the other party's guilt rather than striving to improve their working relationship with the assistance of the mediator. The disputants work to establish facts about what happened in the past rather than to reach an agreement about what ought to happen in the future. Consequently, a key aspect of effective mediation is helping disputants explore multiple alternatives in a nonjudgmental manner.

M4 Manage the Discussion to Ensure Fairness—Keep the Discussion Issue Oriented, Not Personality Oriented

It is important that the mediator maintain a problem-solving atmosphere throughout the discussion. This is not to say that strong emotional statements don't have their place. People often associate effective problem solving with a calm, highly rational discussion of the issues and associate a personality attack with a highly emotional outburst. However, it is important not to confuse affect with effect. Placid, cerebral discussions may not solve problems, and impassioned statements don't have to be insulting. The critical point about process is that it should be centered on the issues and the consequences of continued conflict on performance. Even when behavior offensive to one of the parties obviously stems from a personality quirk, the discussion of the problem should be limited to the behavior. Attributions of motives or generalizations from specific events to personal proclivities distract participants from the problem-solving process. It is important that the mediator establish and maintain these ground rules.

It is also important for a mediator to ensure that neither party dominates the discussion. A relatively even balance in the level of inputs improves the quality of the final outcome. It also increases the likelihood that both parties will accept the final decision, because there is a high correlation between feelings about the problem-solving process and attitudes about the final solution. If one party tends to dominate a discussion, the mediator can help balance the exchange by asking the less talkative individual direct questions: "Now that we have heard Bill's view of that incident, how do you see it?" "That's an important point, Brad, so let's make sure Brian agrees. How do you feel, Brian?"

Mediator—Solution Generation

M5 Explore Options by Focusing on Interests, Not Positions As noted earlier in this section, positions are demands, whereas interests are the underlying needs, values, goals, or concerns behind the demands. Often, conflict resolution is hampered by the perception that incompatible positions necessarily entail irreconcilable differences. Mediation of such conflicts can best be accomplished by examining the interests behind the positions. It is these interests that are the driving force behind the conflict, and these interests are ultimately what people want satisfied.

It is the job of the mediator to discover where interests meet and where they conflict. Interests often remain unstated because they are unclear to the participants. In order to flesh out each party's interests, ask "why" questions: "Why have they taken this position?" "Why does this matter to them?" Understand that there is probably no single, simple answer to these questions. Each side may represent a number of constituents, each with a special interest.

After each side has articulated its underlying interests, help the parties identify areas of agreement and reconcilability. It is common for participants in an intense conflict to feel that they are on opposite sides of all issues—that they have little in common. Helping them recognize that there are areas of agreement and reconcilability often represents a major turning point in resolving long-standing feuds.

M6 Make Sure All Parties Fully Understand and Support the Solution Agreed Upon, and Establish Follow-Up Procedures The last two phases of the problem-solving process are (1) agreement on an action plan and (2) follow-up. These will be discussed here within the context of the mediator's role, but they are equally relevant to the other roles.

A common mistake of ineffective mediators is terminating discussions prematurely, on the supposition that once a problem has been solved in principle, the disputants can be left to work out the details on their own. Or a mediator may assume that because one party has recommended a solution that appears reasonable and workable, the second disputant will be willing to implement it.

To avoid these mistakes, it is important to stay engaged in the mediation process until both parties have agreed on a detailed plan of action. You might consider using the familiar planning template—Who, What, How, When, and Where—as a checklist for making sure the plan is complete. If you suspect any hesitancy on the part of either disputant, this needs to be explored explicitly ("Tom, I sense that you are somewhat less enthusiastic than Sue about this plan. Is there something that bothers you?").

When you are confident that both parties support the plan, check to make sure they are aware of their respective responsibilities and then propose a mechanism for monitoring progress. For example, you might schedule another formal meeting, or you might stop by both individuals' offices to get a progress report. Without undermining the value of the agreement you've obtained, it is generally a good idea to encourage "good faith" modifications of the proposal to accommodate unforeseen implementation issues. Consider using a follow-up meeting to celebrate the successful resolution of the dispute and to discuss "lessons learned" for future applications.

Summary

Conflict is a difficult and controversial topic. In most cultures, it has negative connotations because it runs counter to the notion that we should get along with people by being kind and friendly. Although many people intellectually understand the value of conflict, they feel uncomfortable when confronted by it. Their discomfort may result from a lack of understanding of the conflict process as well as from a lack of training in how to handle interpersonal confrontations effectively. In this chapter, we have addressed these issues by introducing both analytical and behavioral skills.

A summary model of conflict management, shown in Figure 7.6, contains four elements: (1) diagnosing the sources of conflict and the associated situational considerations; (2) selecting an appropriate conflict management strategy, based on the results of the diagnosis combined with personal preferences; (3) effectively implementing the strategy, in particular the collaborative problem-solving process, which should lead to (4) a successful resolution of the dispute. Note that the final outcome of our model is successful dispute resolution. Given our introductory claim that conflict plays an important role in organizations, our concluding observation is that the objective of effective conflict management is the successful resolution of disputes, not the elimination of conflict altogether.

The diagnostic element of our summary model contains two important components. First, assessing the source or type of conflict provides insights into the

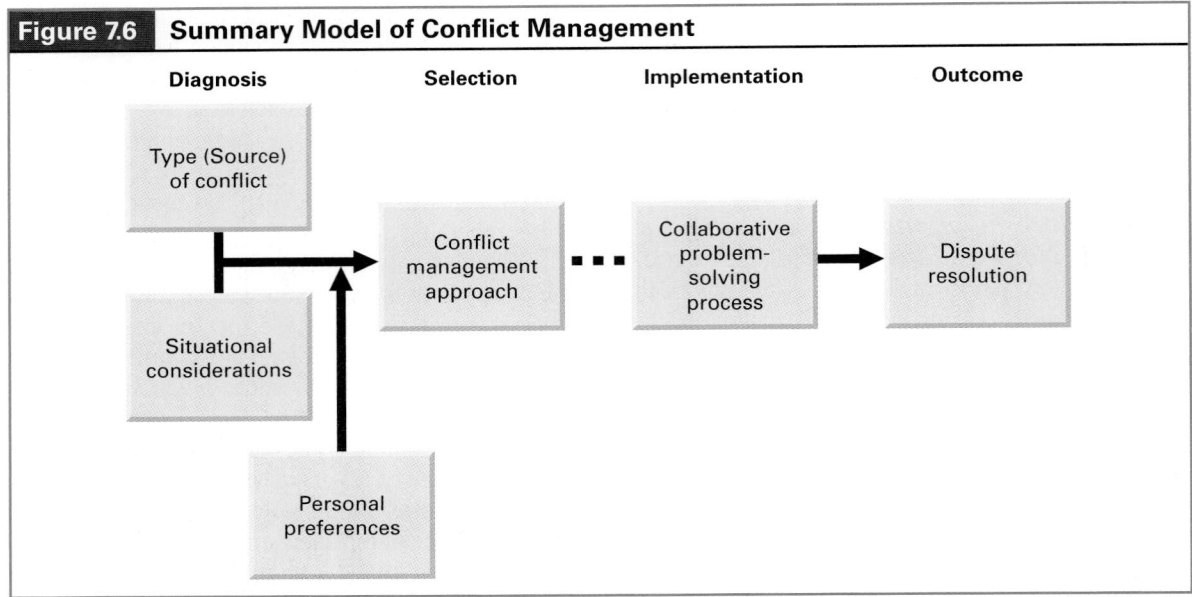

Figure 7.6   Summary Model of Conflict Management

Diagnosis   Selection   Implementation   Outcome

Type (Source) of conflict

Situational considerations

Personal preferences

Conflict management approach

Collaborative problem-solving process

Dispute resolution

"whys" behind a confrontation. Conflict can be "caused" by a variety of circumstances. We have considered four of these: irreconcilable personal differences, discrepancies in information, role incompatibilities, and environmentally induced stress. These "types" of conflict differ in both frequency and intensity. For example, information-based conflicts occur frequently, but they are easily resolved because disputants have low personal stakes in the outcome. In contrast, conflicts grounded in differences of perceptions and expectations are generally intense and difficult to defuse.

The second important component of the diagnostic process is assessing the relevant situational considerations, so as to determine the feasible set of responses. Important contextual factors that we considered included the importance of the issue, the importance of the relationship, the relative power of the disputants, and the degree to which time was a limiting factor.

The purpose of the diagnostic phase of the model is to wisely choose between the five conflict management approaches: avoiding, compromising, collaborating, forcing, and accommodating. These reflect different degrees of assertiveness and cooperativeness, or the priority given to satisfying one's own concerns versus the concerns of the other party, respectively.

As shown in Figure 7.6, personal preferences, reflecting a person's ethnic culture, gender, and personality play a key role in our conception of effective conflict management. One's personal comfort level with using the various conflict management approaches is both an enabling and a limiting factor. If we feel comfortable with

an approach, we are likely to use it effectively. Because effective problem solvers need to feel comfortable using a variety of tools, however, one shouldn't pass over an appropriate tool because its use might be discomforting. For this reason, it is important for conflict managers to stretch their natural "comfort zone" through skill development activities.

That is why, as shown in the figure, we elected to focus on the effective implementation of the specific conflict management approach that is both the most effective, all-purpose tool, and the most difficult to use comfortably and skillfully—collaborative problem solving. It takes little skill to impose your authority on another person, to withdraw from a confrontation, to split the difference between opponents, or to abandon your position at the slightest sign of opposition. Therefore, the behavioral guidelines for resolving an interpersonal confrontation involving complaints and criticisms by using a problem-solving approach have been described in detail.

Behavioral Guidelines

Effective conflict management involves both analytic and behavioral elements. The analytic process involves diagnosing the true causes of a conflict, as well as understanding the key situational considerations and personal preferences that need to be factored into selecting the appropriate conflict management approach. The behavior element of the process involves implementing the chosen strategy effectively to effect a successful resolution of the dispute. Skillful implementation is especially critical for the collaborative problem-solving process advocated in this chapter.

Behavioral guidelines for the diagnosis and selection aspects of conflict management include the following:

1. Collect information on the sources of conflict. Identify the source by examining the focus of the dispute. The four sources, or types of conflict, are personal differences (perception and expectations), information deficiency (misinformation and misinterpretation), role incompatibility (goals and responsibilities), and environmental stress (resource scarcity and uncertainty).

2. Examine relevant situational considerations, including the importance of the issue, the importance of the relationship, the relative power of the disputants, and the degree to which time is a factor.

3. Take into consideration your personal preferences for using the various conflict management approaches. These preferences tend to reflect important elements of your personal identity, including ethnic culture, gender, and personality.

4. Utilize the collaborative approach for managing conflict unless specific conditions dictate the use of an alternative approach.

Behavioral guidelines for effectively implementing the collaborative (problem-solving) approach to conflict management are summarized below. These are organized according to three roles. Guidelines for the problem-identification and solution-generation phases of the problem-solving process are specified for each role. Guidelines for the action plan and follow-up phases are the same for all three roles.

INITIATOR

Problem Identification

1. Maintain personal ownership of the problem.
   - ❏ Succinctly describe your problem in terms of behaviors, consequences, and feelings. ("When you do X, Y happens, and I feel Z.")
   - ❏ Stick to the facts (e.g., use a specific incident to illustrate the expectations or standards violated).
   - ❏ Avoid drawing evaluative conclusions and attributing motives to the respondent.

2. Persist until understood; encourage two-way discussion.
   - ❏ Restate your concerns or give additional examples.

- ❏ Avoid introducing additional issues or letting frustration sour your emotional tone.
- ❏ Invite the respondent to ask questions and express another perspective.

3. Manage the agenda carefully.
   - ❏ Approach multiple problems incrementally, proceeding from simple to complex, easy to difficult, concrete to abstract.
   - ❏ Don't become fixated on a single issue. If you reach an impasse, expand the discussion to increase the likelihood of an integrative outcome.

Solution Generation

4. Make a request.
   - ❏ Focus on those things you share in common (principles, goals, constraints) as the basis for recommending preferred alternatives.

RESPONDER

Problem Identification

1. Establish a climate for joint problem solving.
   - ❏ Show genuine concern and interest. Respond empathetically, even if you disagree with the complaint.
   - ❏ Respond appropriately to the initiator's emotions. If necessary, let the person "blow off steam" before addressing the complaint.

2. Seek additional information about the problem.
   - ❏ Ask questions that channel the initiator's statements from general to specific and from evaluative to descriptive.

3. Agree with some aspect of the complaint.
   - ❏ Signal your willingness to consider making changes by agreeing with facts, perceptions, feelings, or principles.

Solution Generation

4. Ask for suggestions and recommendations.
   - ❏ To avoid debating the merits of a single suggestion, brainstorm multiple alternatives.

MEDIATOR

Problem Identification

1. Acknowledge that a conflict exists.
   - ❏ Select the most appropriate setting (one-on-one conference versus group meeting) for coaching and fact-finding.

❑ Propose a problem-solving approach for resolving the dispute.

2. Maintain a neutral posture.
   ❑ Assume the role of facilitator, not judge. Do not belittle the problem or berate the disputants for their inability to resolve their differences.
   ❑ Be impartial toward disputants and issues (provided policy has not been violated).
   ❑ If correction is necessary, do it in private.

3. Manage the discussion to ensure fairness.
   ❑ Focus discussion on the conflict's impact on performance and the detrimental effect of continued conflict.
   ❑ Keep the discussion issue oriented, not personality oriented.
   ❑ Do not allow one party to dominate the discussion. Ask directed questions to maintain balance.

Solution Generation

4. Explore options by focusing on the interests behind stated positions.
   ❑ Explore the "why's" behind disputants' arguments or demands.

❑ Help disputants see commonalities among their goals, values, and principles.
❑ Use commonalities to generate multiple alternatives.
❑ Maintain a nonjudgmental manner.

ALL ROLES
Action Plan and Follow-Up

1. Ensure that all parties support the agreed-upon plan.
   ❑ Make sure the plan is adequately detailed (Who, What, How, When, and Where).
   ❑ Verify understanding of, and commitment to, each specific action.

2. Establish a mechanism for follow-up.
   ❑ Create benchmarks for measuring progress and ensuring accountability.
   ❑ Encourage flexibility in adjusting the plan to meet emerging circumstances.

CASE INVOLVING INTERPERSONAL CONFLICT

Educational Pension Investments

Educational Pension Investments (EPI), located in New York, invests pension funds for educational institutions. In 1988, it employed approximately 75 people, 25 of whom were responsible for actual investment activities. The company managed about $1.2 billion of assets and derived an income of about $2.5 million.

The firm was incorporated in 1960 by a group of academic professionals who wanted to control the destiny of their retirement years. They solicited pension funds under the assumption that their investments would be consistent and safe. Through their nearly three decades in the business, they have weathered rapid social and technological change as well as economic volatility. Through it all, they have resisted opportunities to "make it big" and instead stayed with less profitable but relatively secure investments.

Dan Richardson has an MBA from Wharton and is one of the original founders of EPI. He started out working in the research department and has worked in every department since then. The other partners, comfortable with Dan's conservative yet flexible nature, elected him to the position of CEO in the spring of 1975. After that, Dan became known as "the great equalizer." He worked hard to make sure that all the partners were included in decisions and that strong relations were maintained. Over the years, he became the confidant of the other seniors and the mentor of the next generation. He took pride in his "people skills," and EPI's employees looked to Dan for leadership and direction.

Dan's management philosophy is built on the concept of loyalty—loyalty to the organization, loyalty to its members, and loyalty to friends. As he is fond of saying, "My dad was a small town banker. He told me, 'Look out for the other guys and they'll look out for you.' Sounds corny, I know, but I firmly believe in this philosophy."

Dan, bolstered by the support of the other founding members of EPI, continued the practice of consistent and safe investing. This meant maintaining low-risk investment portfolios with moderate income. However, EPI's growth increasingly has not kept pace with other investment opportunities. As a result, Dan has reluctantly begun to consider the merits of a more aggressive investment approach. This consideration was further strengthened by the expressions of several of the younger analysts who were beginning to refer to EPI as "stodgy." Some of them were leaving EPI for positions in more aggressive firms.

One evening, Dan talked about his concern with his racquetball partner and longtime friend, Mike Roth. Mike also happened to be an investment broker. After receiving his MBA from the University of Illinois, Mike went to work for a brokerage firm in New York, beginning his career in the research department. His accomplishments in research brought him recognition throughout the firm. Everyone respected him for his knowledge, his work ethic, and his uncanny ability to predict trends. Mike knew what to do and when to do it. After only two years on the job, he was promoted to the position of portfolio manager. However, he left that firm for greener pastures and had spent the last few years moving from firm to firm.

When Mike heard Dan's concerns about EPI's image and need for an aggressive approach, he suggested to his friend that what EPI needed was some fresh blood, someone who could infuse enthusiasm into the organization—someone like him. He told Dan, "I can help you get things moving. In fact, I've been developing some concepts that would be perfect for EPI."

Dan brought up the idea of hiring Mike at the next staff meeting, but the idea was met with caution and skepticism. "Sure, he's had a brilliant career on paper," said one senior partner. "But he's never stayed in one place long enough to really validate his success. Look at his résumé. During the past seven years, he's been with four different firms, in four different positions."

"That's true," said Dan, "but his references all check out. In fact, he's been described as a rising star, aggressive, productive. He's just what we need to help us explore new opportunities."

"He may have been described as a comer, but I don't feel comfortable with his apparent inability to settle down," said another. "He doesn't seem very loyal or committed to anyone or anything."

Another partner added, "A friend of mine worked with Mike a while back and said that while he is definitely good, he's a real maverick—in terms of both investment philosophy and lifestyle. Is that what we really want at EPI?"

Throughout the discussion, Dan defended Mike's work record. He repeatedly pointed out Mike's impressive performance. He deflected concerns about Mike's reputation by saying that he was a loyal and trusted friend. Largely on Dan's recommendation, the other partners agreed, although somewhat reluctantly, to hire Mike. When Dan offered Mike the job, he promised Mike the freedom and flexibility to operate a segment of the fund as he desired.

Mike took the job and performed his responsibilities at EPI in a superior manner. Indeed, he was largely responsible for increasing the managed assets of the company by 150 percent. However, a price was paid for this increase. From the day he moved in, junior analysts enjoyed working with him very much. They liked his fresh, new approach, and were encouraged by the spectacular results. This caused jealousy among the other partners, who thought Mike was pushing too hard to change the tried-and-true traditions of the firm. It was not uncommon for sharp disagreements to erupt in staff meetings, with one or another partner coming close to storming out of the room. Throughout this time, Dan tried to soothe ruffled feathers and maintain an atmosphere of trust and loyalty.

Mike seemed oblivious to all the turmoil he was causing. He was optimistic about potential growth opportunities. He believed that computer chips, biotechnology, and laser engineering were the "waves of the future." Because of this belief, he wanted to direct the focus of his portfolio toward these emerging technologies. "Investments in small firm stocks in these industries, coupled with an aggressive market timing strategy, should yield a 50 percent increase in performance." He rallied support for this idea not only among the younger members of EPI, but also with the pension fund managers who invested with EPI. Mike championed his position and denigrated the merits of the traditional philosophy. "We should compromise on safety and achieve some real growth while we can," Mike argued. "If we don't, we'll lose the investors' confidence and ultimately lose them."

Most of the senior partners disagreed with Mike, stating that the majority of their investors emphasized security above all else. They also disagreed with the projected profits, stating that "We could go from 8 to 12 percent return on investment (ROI); then again, we could drop to 4 percent. A lot depends on whose data you use." They reminded Mike, "The fundamental approach of the corporation is to provide safe and moderate-income mutual funds for academic pension funds to invest in. That's the philosophy we used to solicit the investments originally, and that's the approach we are obligated to maintain."

Many months passed, and dissension among the managers grew. Mike's frustration over the lack of support among the senior partners began to undermine the day-to-day operations of EPI. He began to criticize detractors in discussions with younger EPI employees. In addition, he assigned research department employees tasks related to technological investments, distracting them from investigating more traditional alternatives. He gradually implemented his ideas within his portfolio, which accounted for approximately 35 percent of EPI's revenues. This disrupted the operations of other managers in EPI because the performance of their funds relied on the timely input of the researchers and other support staff. The other managers bristled when the research staff began tracking the ROI of the various investments on a chart prominently displayed on the conference room wall.

Amidst a rapidly spreading undercurrent of tension, one of the founding partners, Tom Watson, approached Dan one day. Conservative in his ways, Watson is the partner who walks the office and always has time to stop and chat. He began the conversation.

"Dan, I speak for most of the senior staff when I say that we are very troubled by Mike's approach. We've expressed ourselves well enough for Mike to understand, but his actions defy everything we've said. He's a catastrophe just waiting to happen."

"I can understand your concern, Tom," replied Dan. "I'm troubled, too. We have an opportunity to attract new business with some of Mike's new ideas. And the younger staff love working on his projects. But he has stirred up a lot of turmoil."

Tom agreed. "The real issue is that EPI is no longer presenting a unified image. Mike is willfully defying the stated objectives of our organization. And some of our oldest clients don't like that."

"That's true, Tom. On the other hand, some of our newer clients are really encouraged by Mike's approach—and his track record is extremely impressive."

"Come on, Dan. You and I both know that many experts feel the market is overheating. Mike's paper profits could quickly be incinerated if the budget and trade deficits don't turn around. We can't stake the reputation of the firm on a few high-flying technology stocks. Dan, the other senior partners agree. Mike must either conform to the philosophy and management practices of this organization or else resign."

Reflecting on the situation, Dan realized he faced the most difficult challenge of his career. He felt a strong personal investment in helping Mike succeed. Not only had he hired Mike over the objections of several colleagues; he had personally helped him "learn the ropes" at EPI. Beyond that, Dan was haunted by his promise to Mike that he would have the freedom and flexibility to perform the requirements of the position as he pleased. However, this flexibility had clearly caused problems within EPI.

Finally, bowing to the pressure of his peers, Dan called Mike in for a meeting, hoping to find some basis for compromise.

DAN: I gather you know the kinds of concerns the senior partners have expressed regarding your approach.

MIKE: I guess you've talked with Tom. Well, we did have a small disagreement earlier this week.

DAN: The way Tom tells it, you're willfully defying corporate objectives and being insubordinate.

MIKE: Well, it's just like Watson to see progressive change as an attempt to take away his power.

DAN: It's not quite that simple, Mike. When we founded EPI, we all agreed that a conservative stance was best. And right now, with the economic indicators looking soft, many experts agree that it may still be the best alternative.

MIKE: Dan, what are you going to rely on—predictions or performance? These concerns are just smokescreens to deflect attention away from the sub-par records of other portfolio managers. Old views need to be challenged and ultimately discarded. How else are we going to progress and keep up with our competitors?

DAN: I agree we need to change, Mike—but gradually. You have great ideas and terrific instincts, but you can't change a 30-year-old firm overnight. You can help me promote change, but you're pushing so fast, others are digging in their heels. The rate of change is just as important as the direction.

MIKE: You're telling me. And at this rate, it doesn't make much difference which direction we're headed in.

DAN: Come on, Mike. Don't be so cynical. If you'd just stop rubbing people's noses in your performance record and try to see things from their perspective, we could calm things down around here. Then maybe we could start building consensus.

Mike's emotions betray his impatience with the pace of the organization; he becomes agitated.

MIKE: I've always admired your judgment, and I value your friendship, but I honestly think you're kidding yourself. You seem to think you can get this firm to look like it's progressive—shrugging off its stodgy image—without taking any risks or ruffling any feathers. Are you interested in appearance or substance? If you want appearance, then hire a good PR person. If you want substance, then back me up and we'll rewrite the record book. Get off the fence, Dan, before your butt's full of slivers.

DAN: Mike, it simply isn't that easy. I'm not EPI, I'm simply its caretaker. You know we make decisions around here by consensus; that's the backbone of this organization. To move ahead, the confidence of the others has to be won, especially the confidence of the seniors. Frankly, your reputation as a maverick makes it hard to foster confidence in, and loyalty to, your plans.

MIKE: You knew my style when you hired me. Remember how you made it a point to promise me flexibility and autonomy? I'm not getting that any more, Dan. All I'm getting is grief, even though I'm running circles around your conservative cronies.

DAN: Well, that may be true. But your flamboyance . . .

MIKE: Oh, yeah. The sports car, the singles lifestyle, the messy office. But, again, that's appearance, Dan, not substance. Performance is what counts. That's what got me this far, and that's my ticket out. You know I could walk into any firm in town and write my own plan.

DAN: Well, there's no reason to be hasty.

MIKE: Do you honestly believe this can be salvaged? I think not. Maybe it's time for me to be moving on. Isn't that why you called me in here anyway?

Dan, feeling uncomfortable, breaks eye contact and shifts his gaze to the New York skyline. After a long pause, he continues, still gazing out of the window.

DAN: I don't know, Mike. I feel I've failed. My grand experiment in change has polarized the office; we've got two armies at war out there. On the other hand, you really have done a good job here. EPI will no doubt lose a good part of its customer base if you leave. You have a loyal following, with both customers and staff. If you go, so do they—along with our shot at changing our image.

MIKE: It's just like you, Dan, to take this problem personally. Blast it, you take everything personally. Even when I beat you at racquetball. Your heart's in the right place—you just can't ever seem to make the cutthroat hit. You know and I know that EPI needs a change in image. But it doesn't appear to be ready for it yet. And I'm certainly not willing to move slowly.

DAN: Yeah. Maybe. It's just hard to give up . . . [long pause]. Well, why don't we talk more about this after the reception tonight? Come on over and see Joanie and the kids. Besides, I'm dying to show off my new boat.

MIKE: What you see in sailing is beyond me. It's a waste of time, lazily drifting on gentle breezes.

DAN: Save it for later, "Speed King." I've got to get ready for tonight.

Discussion Questions

1. What are the sources of conflict in this case?
2. What approaches to conflict management are used by the actors in this situation? How effective was each?
3. Based on the behavioral guidelines for the collaborative approach, how could Dan have managed this conflict more effectively?

SKILL *PRACTICE*

EXERCISE FOR DIAGNOSING SOURCES OF CONFLICT

SSS Software Management Problems

In order to manage conflict between others effectively, it is important to be aware of early warning signs. It is also important to understand the underlying causes of disagreements. Conflict that is unmanaged, or managed ineffectively, interferes with work-group performance. A key to managing conflict effectively is recognizing it in its early stages and understanding its roots.

Assignment

Read the memos, faxes, voice mail, and e-mail messages that follow. As you examine each of these documents, look for evidence of organizational conflicts. Identify the two conflicts that you think are most significant for you to address in your role as Chris Perillo. Begin your analysis of these conflicts by identifying their likely sources or causes. Use Figure 7.2 as a diagnostic tool for identifying the type of conflict, based on its source and focus. Prepare to present your analysis, along with supporting evidence from the memos. Also, share your ideas regarding how this analysis of the causes of conflict would influence your approach to resolving the conflict.

SSS Software In-Basket Memos, E-mails, Faxes, and Voice Mails

ITEM 1 – E-MAIL

TO: All Employees
FROM: Roger Steiner, Chief Executive Officer
DATE: October 15

I am pleased to announce that Chris Perillo has been appointed as Vice President of Operations for Health and Financial Services. Chris will immediately assume responsibility for all operations previously managed by Michael Grant. Chris will have end-to-end responsibility for the design, development, integration, and maintenance of custom software for the health and finance/banking industries. This responsibility includes all technical, financial, and staffing issues. Chris will also manage our program of software support and integration for the recently announced merger of three large health maintenance organizations (HMOs). Chris will be responsible for our recently announced project with a consortium of banks and financial firms operating in Tanzania. This project represents an exciting opportunity for us, and Chris's background seems ideally suited to the task.

Chris comes to this position with an undergraduate degree in Computer Science from the California Institute of Technology and an MBA from the University of Virginia. Chris began as a member of our technical/professional staff six years ago and has most recently served for three years as a group manager supporting domestic and international projects for our airlines industry group, including our recent work for the European Airbus consortium.

I am sure you all join me in offering congratulations to Chris for this promotion.

ITEM 2 – E-MAIL

TO: All Managers
FROM: Hal Harris, Vice President, Community and Public Relations
DATE: October 15

For your information, the following article appeared on the front page of the business section of Thursday's *Los Angeles Times*.

In a move that may create problems for SSS Software, Michael Grant and Janice Ramos have left SSS Software and moved to Universal Business Solutions Inc. Industry analysts see the move as another victory for Universal Business Solutions Inc. in their battle with SSS Software for share of the growing software development and integration business. Both Grant and Ramos had been with SSS Software for over seven years. Grant was most recently Vice President of Operations for all SSS Software's work in two industries: health and hospitals, and finance and banking. Ramos brings to Universal Business Solutions Inc. her special expertise in the growing area of international software development and integration.

Hillary Collins, an industry analyst with Merrill Lynch, said "the loss of key staff to a competitor can often create serious problems for a firm such as SSS Software. Grant and Ramos have an insider's understanding of SSS Software's strategic and technical limitations. It will be interesting to see if they can exploit this knowledge to the advantage of Universal Business Solutions Inc."

ITEM 3 – E-MAIL

TO: Chris Perillo
FROM: Paula Sprague, Executive Assistant to Roger Steiner
DATE: October 15

Chris, I know that in your former position as a group manager in the Airline Services Division, you probably have met most of the group managers in the Health and Financial Services Division, but I thought you might like some more personal information about them. These people will be your direct reports on the management team.

Group #1: Bob Miller, 55-year-old white male, married (Anna) with two children and three grandchildren. Active in local Republican politics. Well regarded as a "hands-off" manager heading a high-performing team. Plays golf regularly with Mark McIntyre, John Small, and a couple of VPs from other divisions.

Group #2: Wanda Manners, 38-year-old white female, single with one school-age child. A fitness "nut" has run in several marathons. Some experience in Germany and Japan. Considered a hard-driving manager with a constant focus on the task at hand. Will be the first person to show up every morning.

Group #3: William Chen, 31-year-old male of Chinese descent, married (Harriet), two young children from his first marriage. Enjoys tennis and is quite good at it. A rising star in the company, he is highly respected by his peers as a "man of action" and a good friend.

Group #4: Leo Jones, 36-year-old white male, married (Janet) with an infant daughter. Recently returned from paternity leave. Has traveled extensively on projects, since he speaks three languages. Has liked hockey ever since the time he spent in Montreal. Considered a strong manager who gets the most out of his people.

Group #5: Mark McIntyre, 45-year-old white male, married (Mary Theresa) to an executive in the banking industry. No children. A lot of experience in Germany and Eastern

PRACTICE

Europe. Has been writing a mystery novel. Has always been a good "team player," but several members of his technical staff are not well respected and he hasn't addressed the problem.

Group #6: John Small, 38-year-old white male, recently divorced. Three children living with his wife. A gregarious individual who likes sports. He spent a lot of time in Mexico and Central America before he came to SSS Software. Recently has been doing mostly contract work with the federal government. An average manager, has had some trouble keeping his people on schedule.

Group #7: This position vacant since Janice Ramos left. Roger thinks we ought to fill this position quickly. Get in touch with me if you want information on any in-house candidates for any position.

Group #8: Marcus Harper, 42-year-old black male, married (Tamara) with two teenage children. Recently won an award in a local photography contest. Considered a strong manager who gets along with peers and works long hours.

Customer Services: Armand Marke, 38-year-old male, divorced. A basketball fan. Originally from Armenia. Previously a group manager. Worked hard to establish the Technical Services Phone Line, but now has pretty much left it alone.

Office Administrator: Michelle Harrison, 41-year-old white female, single. Grew up on a ranch and still rides horses whenever she can. A strict administrator.

There are a number of good folks here, but they don't function well as a management team. I think Michael played favorites, especially with Janice and Leo. There are a few cliques in this group, and I'm not sure how effectively Michael dealt with them. I expect you will find it a challenge to build a cohesive team.

ITEM 4 – E-MAIL

TO: Chris Perillo
FROM: Wanda Manners, Group 2 Manager
DATE: October 15

CONFIDENTIAL AND RESTRICTED

Although I know you are new to your job, I feel it is important that I let you know about some information I just obtained concerning the development work we recently completed for First National Investment. Our project involved the development of asset management software for managing their international funds. This was a very complex project due to the volatile exchange rates and the forecasting tools we needed to develop.

As part of this project, we had to integrate the software and reports with all their existing systems and reporting mechanisms. To do this, we were given access to all of their existing software (much of which was developed by Universal Business Solutions Inc.). Of course, we signed an agreement acknowledging that the software to which we were given access was proprietary and that our access was solely for the purpose of our system integration work associated with the project.

Unfortunately, I have learned that some parts of the software we developed actually "borrow" heavily from complex application programs developed for First National Investment by Universal Business Solutions Inc. It seems obvious to me that one or more of the software developers from Group 5 (that is, Mark McIntyre's group) inappropriately "borrowed" algorithms developed by Universal Business Solutions Inc. I am sure that doing so saved us significant development time on some aspects of the project. It seems very unlikely that First National Investment or Universal Business Solutions Inc. will ever become aware of this issue.

Finally, First National Investment is successfully using the software we developed and is thrilled with the work we did. We brought the project in on time and under budget. You probably know that they have invited us to bid on several other substantial projects.

I'm sorry to bring this delicate matter to your attention, but I thought you should know about it.

ITEM 5A – E-MAIL

TO: Chris Perillo
FROM: Paula Sprague, Executive Assistant to Roger Steiner
DATE: October 15
RE: Letter from C.A.R.E. Services (copies attached)

Roger asked me to work on this C.A.R.E. project and obviously wants some fast action. A lot of the staff are already booked solid for the next couple of weeks. I knew that Elise Soto and Chu Hung Woo have the expertise to do this system and when I checked with them, they were relatively free. I had them pencil in the next two weeks and wanted to let you know. Hopefully, it will take a "hot potato" out of your hands.

ITEM 5B – Copy of Fax

C.A.R.E.
Child and Adolescent Rehabilitative and Educational Services
A United Way Member Agency
200 Main Street
Los Angeles, California 90230

DATE: October 11
Roger Steiner, CEO
SSS Software
13 Miller Way
Los Angeles, California 90224

Dear Roger,

This letter is a follow-up to our conversation after last night's board meeting. I appreciated your comments during the board meeting about the need for sophisticated computer systems in nonprofit organizations and I especially appreciate your generous offer of assistance to have SSS Software provide assistance to deal with the immediate problem with our accounting system. Since the board voted to fire the computer consultant, I am very worried about getting our reports done in time to meet the state funding cycle.

Thanks again for your offer of help during this crisis.

Sincerely yours,

Janice Polocizwic

Janice Polocizwic
Executive Director

ITEM 5C – COPY OF A LETTER

SSS SOFTWARE
13 Miller Way
Los Angeles, CA 90224

DATE: October 12

Janice Polocizwic
Executive Director, C.A.R.E. Services
200 Main Street
Los Angeles, California 90230

Dear Janice,

I received your fax of October 11. I have asked Paula Sprague, my executive assistant, to line up people to work on your accounting system as soon as possible. You can expect to hear from her shortly.

Sincerely,

Roger Steiner

Roger Steiner
cc: Paula Sprague, Executive Assistant

ITEM 6 – E-MAIL

TO: Michael Grant
FROM: Harry Withers, Group 6 Technical Staff
DATE: October 12

PERSONAL AND CONFIDENTIAL

Our team is having difficulty meeting the submission deadline of November 5 for the Halstrom project. Kim, Fred, Peter, Kyoto, Susan, Mala, and I have been working on the project for several weeks, but we are experiencing some problems and may need additional time. I hesitate to write this letter, but the main problem is that our group manager, John Small, is involved in a relationship with Mala. Mala gets John's support for her ideas and brings them to the team as required components of the project. Needless to say, this has posed some problems for the group. Mala's background is especially valuable for this project, but Kim and Fred, who have both worked very hard on the project, do not want to work with her. In addition, one member of the team has been unavailable recently because of child-care needs. Commitment to the project and team morale have plummeted. However, we'll do our best to get the project finished as soon as possible. Mala will be on vacation the next two weeks, so I'm expecting that some of us can complete it in her absence.

ITEM 7 – VOICE MAIL MESSAGE

Hello, Michael. This is Jim Bishop of United Hospitals. I wanted to talk with you about the quality assurance project that you are working on for us. When Jose Martinez first started talking with us, I was impressed with his friendliness and expertise. But recently, he doesn't seem to be getting much accomplished and has seemed distant and on-edge in conversations. Today, I asked him about the schedule and he seemed very defensive and not entirely in control of his emotions. I am quite concerned about our project. Please give me a call.

ITEM 8 – VOICE MAIL MESSAGE

Hi, Michael. This is Armand. I wanted to talk with you about some issues with the Technical Services Phone Line. I've recently received some complaint letters from Phone Line customers whose complaints have included long delays while waiting for a technician to answer the phone, technicians who are not knowledgeable enough to solve problems, and, on occasion, rude service. Needless to say, I'm quite concerned about these complaints.

I believe that the overall quality of the Phone Line staff is very good, but we continue to be understaffed, even with the recent hires. The new technicians look strong, but are working on the help-line before being fully trained. Antolina, our best tech, often brings her child to work, which is adding to the craziness around here.

I think you should know that we're feeling a lot of stress here. I'll talk with you soon.

ITEM 9 – VOICE MAIL MESSAGE

Hi, Chris, it's Pat. Congratulations on your promotion. They definitely picked the right person. It's great news—for me, too. You've been a terrific mentor so far, so I'm expecting to learn a lot from you in your new position. How about lunch next week?

ITEM 10 – VOICE MAIL MESSAGE

Chris, this is Bob Miller. Just thought you'd like to know that John's joke during our planning meeting has disturbed a few of the women in my group. Frankly, I think the thing's being blown out of proportion, especially since we all know this is a good place for both men and women to work. Give me a call if you want to chat about this.

ITEM 11 – VOICE MAIL MESSAGE

Hello. This is Lorraine Adams from Westside Hospital. I read in today's *Los Angeles Times* that you will be taking over from Michael Grant. We haven't met yet, but your division has recently finished two large million-dollar projects for Westside. Michael Grant and I had some discussion about a small conversion of a piece of existing software to be compatible with the new systems. The original vendor had said that they would do the work, but they have been stalling, and I need to move quickly. Can you see if Harris Wilson, Chu Hung Woo, and Elise Soto are available to do this work as soon as possible? They were on the original project and work well with our people.

Um . . . (long pause) I guess I should tell you that I got a call from Michael offering to do this work. But I think I should stick with SSS Software. Give me a call.

PRACTICE

ITEM 12 – VOICE MAIL MESSAGE

Hi, Chris, this is Roosevelt Moore calling. I'm a member of your technical/professional staff. I used to report to Janice Ramos, but since she left the firm, I thought I'd bring my concerns directly to you. I'd like to arrange some time to talk with you about my experiences since returning from six weeks of paternity leave. Some of my major responsibilities have been turned over to others. I seem to be out of the loop and wonder if my career is at risk. Also, I am afraid that I won't be supported or seriously considered for the opening created by Janice's departure. Frankly, I feel like I'm being screwed for taking my leave. I'd like to talk with you this week.

ITEM 13 – E-MAIL

TO: Michael Grant
FROM: Jose Martinez, Group 1 Technical Staff
DATE: October 12

I would like to set up a meeting with you as soon as possible. I suspect that you will get a call from Jim Bishop of United Hospitals and want to be sure that you hear my side of the story first. I have been working on a customized system design for quality assurance for them using a variation of the J-3 product we developed several years ago. They had a number of special requirements and some quirks in their accounting systems, so I have had to put in especially long hours. I've worked hard to meet their demands, but they keep changing the ground rules. I keep thinking, this is just another J-3 I'm working on, but they have been interfering with an elegant design I have developed. It seems I'm not getting anywhere on this project. Earlier today, I had a difficult discussion with their Controller. He asked for another major change. I've been fighting their deadline and think I am just stretched too thin on this project. Then Jim Bishop asked me if the system was running yet. I was worn out from dealing with the Controller, and I made a sarcastic comment to Jim Bishop. He gave me a funny look and just walked out of the room.

I would like to talk with you about this situation at your earliest convenience.

ITEM 14 – E-MAIL

TO: Chris Perillo
FROM: John Small, Group 6 Manager
DATE: October 15

Welcome aboard, Chris. I look forward to meeting with you. I just wanted to put a bug in your ear about finding a replacement for Janice Ramos. One of my technical staff, Mala Abendano, has the ability and drive to make an excellent group manager. I have encouraged her to apply for the position. I'd be happy to talk with you further about this, at your convenience.

ITEM 15 – E-MAIL

TO: Chris Perillo
FROM: Paula Sprague, Executive Assistant to Roger Steiner
DATE: October 15

Roger asked me to let you know about the large contract we have gotten in Tanzania. It means that a team of four managers will be making a short trip to determine current needs. They will assign their technical staff the tasks of developing a system and software here over the next six months, and then the managers and possibly some team members will be spending about 10 months on site in Tanzania to handle the implementation. Roger thought you might want to hold an initial meeting with some of your managers to check on their interest and willingness to take this sort of assignment. Roger would appreciate an e-mail of your thoughts about the issues to be discussed at this meeting, additional considerations about sending people to Tanzania, and about how you will put together an effective team to work on this project. The October 15 memo I sent to you will provide you with some information you'll need to start making these decisions.

ITEM 16 – E-MAIL

TO: Chris Perillo
FROM: Sharon Shapiro, VP of Human Resources
DATE: October 15
RE: Upcoming meeting

I want to update you on the rippling effect of John Small's sexual joke at last week's planning meeting. Quite a few women have been very upset and have met informally to talk about it. They have decided to call a meeting of all people concerned about this kind of behavior throughout the firm. I plan to attend, so I'll keep you posted.

ITEM 17 – E-MAIL

TO: All SSS Software Managers
FROM: Sharon Shapiro, VP of Human Resources
DATE: October 15
RE: Promotions and External Hires

Year-to-Date (January through September) Promotions and External Hires

Level	Race					Sex		
	White	Black	Asian	Hispanic	Native American	M	F	Total
Hires into Executive Level	0 (0%)	0 (0%)	0 (0%)	0 (0%)	0 (0%)	0 (0%)	0 (0%)	0
Promotions to Executive Level	0 (0%)	0 (0%)	0 (0%)	0 (0%)	0 (0%)	0 (0%)	0 (0%)	0
Hires into Management Level	2 (67%)	1 (33%)	0 (0%)	0 (0%)	0 (0%)	2 (67%)	1 (33%)	3
Promotions to Management Level	7 (88%)	0 (0%)	1 (12%)	0 (0%)	0 (0%)	7 (88%)	1 (12%)	8
Hires into Technical/ Professional Level	10 (36%)	6 (21%)	10 (36%)	2 (7%)	0 (0%)	14 (50%)	14 (50%)	28

Level	Race White	Black	Asian	Hispanic	Native American	Sex M	F	Total
Promotions to Technical/ Professional Level	0 (0%)	0 (0%)	0 (0%)	0 (0%)	0 (0%)	0 (0%)	0 (0%)	0
Hires into Non-Management Level	4 (20%)	10 (50%)	2 (10%)	4 (20%)	0 (0%)	6 (30%)	14 (70%)	20
Promotions to Non-Management Level	NA	NA	NA	NA	NA	NA	NA	NA

SSS Software Employee (EEO) Classification Report as of June 30

Level	Race White	Black	Asian	Hispanic	Native American	Sex M	F	Total
Executive Level	11 (92%)	0 (0%)	1 (8%)	0 (0%)	0 (0%)	11 (92%)	1 (8%)	12
Management Level	43 (90%)	2 (4%)	2 (4%)	1 (2%)	0 (0%)	38 (79%)	10 (21%)	48
Technical/ Professional Level	58 (45%)	20 (15%)	37 (28%)	14 (11%)	1 (1%)	80 (62%)	50 (38%)	130
Non-Management Level	29 (48%)	22 (37%)	4 (7%)	4 (7%)	1 (2%)	12 (20%)	48 (80%)	60
Total	141 (56%)	44 (18%)	44 (18%)	19 (8%)	2 (1%)	141 (56%)	109 (44%)	250

NOTE: The SSS Software exercise is used with permission. Copyright © 1995 by Susan Schor, Joseph Seltzer, and James Smither. All rights reserved.

EXERCISES FOR SELECTING AN APPROPRIATE CONFLICT MANAGEMENT STRATEGY

Not all conflicts are alike; therefore, they cannot all be managed in exactly the same way. Effective managers are able to assess accurately the true causes of conflict and to match each type of conflict with an appropriate management strategy.

Assignment

For each of the following brief scenarios, select the most appropriate conflict management strategy. Refer to Table 4 for assistance in matching situational factors with strategies.

Bradley's Barn

You have decided to take your family out to the local steakhouse, Bradley's Barn, to celebrate your son's birthday. You are a single parent, so getting home from work in time to prepare a nice dinner is very difficult. On entering the restaurant, you ask the hostess to seat you in the nonsmoking section because your daughter, Shauna, is allergic to tobacco smoke. On your way to your seat, you notice that the restaurant seems crowded for a Monday night.

After you and your children are seated and have placed your orders, your conversation turns to family plans for the approaching holiday. Interspersed in the general conversation is a light banter with your son about whether or not he is too old to wear "the crown" during dinner—a family tradition on birthdays.

Suddenly you become aware that your daughter is sneezing and her eyes are beginning to water. You look around and notice a lively group of business people seated at the table behind you; all of them are smoking. Your impression is that they are celebrating some type of special occasion. Looking back at Shauna, you realize that something has to be done quickly. You ask your son to escort Shauna outside while you rush to the front of the restaurant and find the hostess.

Discussion Questions

1. What are the salient situational factors?
2. What is the most appropriate conflict management strategy?

Avocado Computers

When the head of Avocado Computers ran into production problems with his automated production facility, he hired you away from a competitor. It meant a significant increase in pay and the opportunity to manage a state-of-the-art production facility. What's more, there were very few other female production managers in Silicon Valley. Now you've been on the job a year, and it's been exciting to see your staff start working together as a team to solve problems, improve quality, and finally get the plant up to capacity. In general, Bill, the owner, has also been a plus. He is energetic, fair, and a proven industry leader. You feel fortunate to be in a coveted position, in a "star" firm, in a growth industry.

However, there is one distraction that bugs you. Bill is a real stickler about cleanliness, order, and appearance. He wants the robots all painted the same color, the components within the computer laid out perfectly on a grid, the workers wearing clean smocks, and the floor "clean enough to eat off." You are troubled by this compulsion. "Sure," you think, "it might impress potential corporate clients when they tour the production facility, but is it really that important? After all, who's ever going to look at the inside of their computer? Why should customers care about the color of the robot that built their computers? And who, for Pete's sake, would ever want to have a picnic in a factory?"

Today is your first yearly performance appraisal interview with Bill. In preparation for the meeting, he has sent you a memo outlining "Areas of Strength" and "Areas of Concern." You look with pride at the number of items listed in the first column. It's obvious that Bill likes your work. But you are a bit miffed at the single item of concern: "Needs to maintain a cleaner facility, including employee appearance." You mull over this "demerit" in your mind, wrestling with how to respond in your interview.

Discussion Questions

1. What are the salient situational factors?
2. What is the most appropriate conflict management strategy?

Phelps, Inc.

You are Philip Manual, the head of sales for an office products firm, Phelps, Inc. Your personnel sell primarily to small businesses in the Los Angeles metropolitan area. Phelps is doing about average for this rapidly growing market. The firm's new president, Jose Ortega, is putting a lot of pressure on you to increase sales. You feel that a major obstacle is the firm's policy on extending credit. Celeste, the head of the credit office, insists that all new customers fill out an extensive credit application. Credit risks must be low; credit terms and collection procedures are tough. You can appreciate her point of view, but you feel it is unrealistic. Your competitors are much more lenient in their credit examinations; they extend credit to higher risks; their credit terms are more favorable; and they are more lenient in collecting overdue payments. Your sales personnel frequently complain that they aren't "playing on a level field" with their competition. When you brought this concern to Jose, he said he wanted you and Celeste to work things out. His instructions didn't give many clues to his priorities on this matter. "Sure, we need to increase sales, but the small business failure in this area is the highest in the country, so we have to be careful we don't make bad credit decisions."

You decide it's time to have a serious discussion with Celeste. A lot is at stake.

Discussion Questions

1. What are the salient situational factors?
2. What is the most appropriate conflict management strategy?

EXERCISES FOR RESOLVING INTERPERSONAL DISPUTES

The heart of conflict management is resolving intense, emotionally charged confrontations. We have discussed guidelines for utilizing the collaborative (problem-solving) approach to conflict management in these situations. Assuming that the collaborative approach is appropriate for a particular situation, the general guidelines can be used by an initiator, a responder, or a mediator.

Assignment

Following are three situations involving interpersonal conflict and disagreement. After you have finished reading the assigned roles, review the appropriate behavioral guidelines. Do not read any of the role descriptions except those assigned to you.

In the first exercise (Freida Mae Jones), students assigned to play Freida Mae will practice applying the guidelines for the initiator's role. In the second exercise (Can Larry Fit In?), students assigned to play the role of Larry's boss, Melissa, will practice the guidelines for the respondent's role. In the third exercise (Meeting at Hartford Manufacturing Company), students assigned to play the role of Lynn Smith will practice the guidelines for resolving conflicts among subordinates. For each exercise an observer will be assigned to give students playing the roles of Freida Mae, Melissa, or Lynn feedback on their performance, using the Observer's Feedback Form at the end of the chapter as their guide.

Freida Mae Jones

Freida Mae Jones, Assistant Manager, Branch Operations

Freida Mae Jones was born in her grandmother's Georgia farmhouse on June 1, 1949. She was the sixth of George and Ella Jones's 10 children. Mr. and Mrs. Jones moved to New York City when Freida was four because they felt that the educational and career opportunities for their children would be better in the North. With the help of some cousins, they settled in a five-room apartment in the Bronx. George worked as a janitor at Lincoln Memorial Hospital, and Ella was a part-time housekeeper in a nearby neighborhood. George and Ella were conservative, strict parents. They kept a close watch on their children's activities and demanded they be home by a certain hour. The Joneses believed that because they were Black, the children would have to perform and behave better than their peers to be successful. They believed that their children's education would be the most important factor in their success as adults.

Freida entered Memorial High School, a racially integrated public school, in September 1963. Seventy percent of the student body was Caucasian, 20 percent black, and 10 percent Hispanic. About 60 percent of the graduates went on to college, of which 4 percent were Black, Hispanic, and male. In her senior year, Freida was the top student in her class. Following school regulations, Freida met with her guidance counselor to discuss plans upon graduation. The counselor advised her to consider training in a "practical" field such as housekeeping, cooking, or sewing, so that she could find a job.

George and Ella Jones were furious when Freida told them what the counselor had advised. Ella said, "Don't they see what they are doing? Freida is the top-rated student in her whole class and they are telling her to become a manual worker. She showed that she has a fine mind and can work better than any of her classmates and still she is told not to become anybody in this world. It's really not any different in the North than back home in Georgia, except that they don't try to hide it down South. They want her to throw away her fine mind because she is a Black girl and not a White boy. I'm going to go up to her school tomorrow and talk to the principal."

As a result of Mrs. Jones's visit to the principal, Freida was assisted in applying to 10 Eastern colleges, each of which offered her full scholarships. In September 1966, Freida entered Werbley College, an exclusive private women's college in Massachusetts. In 1970, Freida graduated summa cum laude in history. She decided to return to New York to teach grade school in the city's public school system. Freida was unable to obtain a full-time position, so she substituted. She also enrolled as a part-time student in Columbia University's Graduate School of Education. In 1975, she had attained her master of arts degree in teaching from Columbia but could not find a permanent teaching job. New York City was laying off teachers and had instituted a hiring freeze because of the city's financial problems.

Feeling frustrated about her future as a teacher, Freida decided to get an MBA. She thought that there was more opportunity in business than in education. Churchill Business School, a small, prestigious school located in upstate New York, accepted Freida into its MBA program.

Freida completed her MBA in 1977 and accepted an entry-level position at the Industrialist World Bank of Boston in a fast-track management development program. The three-year program introduced her to all facets of bank operations, from telling to loan training and operations management. She was rotated to branch offices throughout New England. After completing the program, she became an assistant manager for branch operations in the West Springfield branch office.

During her second year in the program, Freida had met James Walker, a Black doctoral student in business administration at the University of Massachusetts. Her assignment to West Springfield precipitated their decision to get married. They originally anticipated that they would marry when James finished his doctorate and could move to Boston. Instead, they decided he would pursue a job in the Springfield–Hartford area.

Freida was not only the first Black but also the first woman to hold an executive position in the West Springfield branch office. Throughout the training program Freida felt somewhat uneasy although she did very well. There were six other Blacks in the program, five men and one woman, and she found support and comfort in sharing her feelings with them. The group spent much of their free time together. Freida had hoped that she would be located near one or more of the group when she went out into the "real world." She felt that although she was able to share her feelings about work with James, he did not have as full an appreciation or understanding as her coworkers. However, the nearest group member was located 100 miles away.

Freida's boss in Springfield was Stan Luboda, a 55-year-old native New Englander. Freida felt that he treated her differently than he did the other trainees. He always tried to help her and took a lot of time (too much, according to Freida) explaining things to her. Freida felt that he was treating her like a child and not like an intelligent and able professional.

"I'm really getting frustrated and angry about what is happening at the bank," Freida said to her husband. "The people don't even realize it, but their prejudice comes through all the time. I feel as if I have to fight all the time just to start off even. Luboda gives Paul Cohen more responsibility than me and we both started at the same time with the same amount of training. He's meeting customers alone and Luboda has accompanied me to each meeting I've had with a customer."

"I run into the same thing at school," said James. "The people don't even know that they are doing it. The other day I met with a professor on my dissertation committee. I've known and worked with him for more than three years. He said he wanted to talk with me about a memo he had received. I asked him what it was about and he said that the records office wanted to know about my absence during the spring semester. He said that I had to sign some forms. He had me confused with Martin Jordan, another Black student. Then he realized that it wasn't me, but Jordan he wanted. All I could think was that we all must look alike to him. I was angry. Maybe it was an honest mistake on his part, but whenever something like that happens, and it happens often, it gets me really angry."

"Something like that happened to me," said Freida. "I was using the copy machine, and Luboda's secretary was talking to someone in the hall. She had just gotten a haircut and was saying her hair was now like Freida's—short and kinky—and that she would have to talk to me about how to take care of it. Luckily, my back was to her. I bit my lip and went on with my business. Maybe she was trying to be cute, because I know she saw me standing there, but comments like that are not cute, they are racist."

"I don't know what to do," said James. "I try to keep things in perspective. Unless people interfere with my progress, I try to let it slide. I only have so much energy and it doesn't make sense to waste it on people who don't matter. But that doesn't make it any easier to function in a racist environment. People don't realize that they are being racist. But a lot of times their expectations of Black people or women, or whatever, are different because of skin color or gender. They expect you to be different, although if you were to ask them they would say that they don't. In fact, they would be highly offended if you implied that they were racist or sexist. They don't see themselves that way."

"Luboda is interfering with my progress," said Freida. "The kinds of experiences I have now will have a direct effect on my career advancement. If decisions are being made because I am Black or a woman, then they are racially and sexually biased. It's the same kind of attitude that the guidance counselor had when I was in high school, although not as blatant." In September 1980, Freida decided to speak to Luboda about his treatment of her. She met with him in his office. "Mr. Luboda, there is something that I would like to discuss with you, and I feel a little uncomfortable because I'm not sure how you will respond to what I am going to say."

Stan Luboda, Manager, Branch Operations

Stan Luboda is a 55-year-old native New Englander who has managed the Springfield branch for more than a decade and has extensive ties to a tightly knit western Massachusetts community. Stan feels that he is liberal and open-minded, and is proud that he recruited Freida Mae Jones, one of only two African-American females in the Industrialist World Bank of Boston management development program. Stan feels that his working relationship with all of his assistant branch managers is cordial and working smoothly. He has structured the work so that each assistant branch manager is specialized in one part of the business.

He has assigned Paul Cohen to some established accounts as well as having him work on securing new customers, while he has Freida Mae Jones managing the important processing department and supervising a staff of clerical and accounting personnel. While having lunch with Garland Smith, his boss who was visiting from the Boston head office, the subject of why Stan had assigned Cohen the more visible customer contact assignments while assigning Jones to the backroom operations role came up.

"Look Garland, you know I'm not a naive person, and I'm very open-minded, which is why I'm so pleased to have Freida Mae on my staff," said Luboda. "You know the way the world works. There are some things that need to be taken more slowly than others. There are some assignments for which Cohen has been given more responsibility, and there are some assignments for which Jones is given more responsibility than Cohen."

"Don't you think Cohen's career will advance more quickly than Jones' because of the assignments that he gets?" Smith replied.

"That is not true," said Luboda. "Jones' career will not be hurt because she is getting different responsibilities than Cohen. Both of them need the different kinds of experiences they are getting. And you have to face the reality of the banking business. We are in a conservative business. When we speak to customers, we need to gain their confidence, and we put the best people for the job in the positions to achieve that end. If we don't get their confidence, they can go down the street to our competitors and do business with them. Their services are no different than ours. It's a competitive business in which you need every edge you have. It's going to take time for people to change some of their attitudes about whom they borrow money from or where they put their money. I can't change the way people feel. I am running a business, but believe me, I won't make any decisions that are detrimental to the bank."

SOURCE: *Copyright © Dr. Martin R. Moser, Associate Professor of Management, University of Massachusetts Lowell, Lowell, MA 01854. martin_moser@uml.edu.*

Can Larry Fit In?

Melissa, Office Manager

You are the manager of an auditing team sent to Bangkok, Thailand, to represent a major international accounting firm headquartered in New York. You and Larry, one of your auditors, were sent to Bangkok to set up an auditing operation. Larry is about seven years older than you and has five more years' seniority in the firm. Your relationship has become very strained since you were recently designated as the office manager. You feel you were given the promotion because you have established an excellent working relationship with the Thai staff as well as a broad range of international clients. In contrast, Larry has told other members of the staff that your promotion simply reflects the firm's heavy emphasis on affirmative action. He has tried to isolate you from the all-male accounting staff by focusing discussions on sports, local night spots, and so forth.

PRACTICE

You are sitting in your office reading some complicated new reporting procedures that have just arrived from the home office. Your concentration is suddenly interrupted by a loud knock on your door. Without waiting for an invitation to enter, Larry bursts into your office. He is obviously very upset, and it is not difficult for you to surmise why he is in such a nasty mood.

You recently posted the audit assignments for the coming month, and you scheduled Larry for a job you knew he wouldn't like. Larry is one of your senior auditors, and the company norm is that they get the choice assignments. This particular job will require him to spend two weeks away from Bangkok in a remote town, working with a company whose records are notoriously messy.

Unfortunately, you have had to assign several of these less desirable audits to Larry recently because you are short of personnel. But that's not the only reason. You have received several complaints from the junior staff (all Thais) recently that Larry treats them in a condescending manner. They feel he is always looking for an opportunity to boss them around, as if he were their supervisor instead of an experienced, supportive mentor. As a result, your whole operation works more smoothly when you can send Larry out of town on a solo project for several days. It keeps him from coming into your office and telling you how to do your job, and the morale of the rest of the auditing staff is significantly higher.

Larry slams the door and proceeds to express his anger over this assignment.

Larry, Senior Auditor

You are really ticked off! Melissa is deliberately trying to undermine your status in the office. She knows that the company norm is that senior auditors get the better jobs. You've paid your dues, and now you expect to be treated with respect. And this isn't the first time this has happened. Since she was made the office manager, she has tried to keep you out of the office as much as possible. It's as if she doesn't want her rival for leadership of the office around. When you were asked to go to Bangkok, you assumed that you would be made the office manager because of your seniority in the firm. You are certain that the decision to pick Melissa is yet another indication of reverse discrimination against white males.

In staff meetings, Melissa has talked about the need to be sensitive to the feelings of the office staff as well as the clients in this multicultural setting. "Where does she come off preaching about sensitivity! What about my feelings, for heaven's sake?" you wonder. This is nothing more than a straightforward power play. She is probably feeling insecure about being the only female accountant in the office and being promoted over someone with more experience. "Sending me out of town," you decide, "is a clear case of 'out of sight, out of mind.'"

Well, it's not going to happen that easily. You are not going to roll over and let her treat you unfairly. It's time for a showdown. If she doesn't agree to change this assignment and apologize for the way she's been treating you, you're going to register a formal complaint with her boss in the New York office. You are prepared to submit your resignation if the situation doesn't improve.

Meeting at Hartford Manufacturing Company

Hartford Manufacturing Company is the largest subsidiary of Connecticut Industries. Since the end of World War I, when it was formed, Hartford Manufacturing has become an industrial leader in the Northeast. Its sales currently average approximately $25 million a year, with an annual growth of approximately six percent. There are more than 850 employees in production, sales and marketing, accounting, engineering, and management.

Lynn Smith is general manager. He has held his position for a little over two years and is well respected by his subordinates. He has the reputation of being firm but fair. Lynn's training in college was in engineering, so he is technically minded, and he frequently likes to walk around the production area to see for himself how things are going. He has also been known to roll up his sleeves and help work on a problem on the shop floor. He is not opposed to rubbing shoulders with even the lowest-level employees. On the other hand, he tries to run a tight company, and employees pretty well stick to their assigned tasks. He holds high expectations for performance, especially from individuals in management positions.

Richard Hooton is the director of production at Hartford Manufacturing. He has been with the company since he was 19 years old, when he worked on the dock. He has worked himself up through the ranks and now, at age 54, is the oldest of the management personnel. Hooton has his own ideas of how things should be run in production, and he is reluctant to tolerate any intervention from anyone, even Lynn Smith. Because he has been with the company so long, he feels he knows it better than anyone else, and he believes he has had a hand in making it the success that it is. His main goal is to keep production running smoothly and efficiently.

Barbara Price is the director of sales and marketing. She joined the company about 18 months ago, after completing her MBA at Dartmouth. Before going back to school for a graduate degree, she held the position of assistant manager of marketing at Connecticut Industries. Price is a very conscientious employee and is anxious to make a name for herself. Her major objective, which she has never hesitated to make public, is to be a general manager some day. Sales at Hartford Manufacturing have increased in the past year to near-record levels under her guidance.

Chuck Kasper is the regional sales director for the New York region. He reports directly to Barbara Price. The New York region represents the largest market for Hartford Manufacturing, and Chuck is considered the most competent salesperson in the company. He has built personal relationships with several major clients in his region, and it appears that some sales occur as much because of Chuck Kasper as because of the products of Hartford Manufacturing. Chuck has been with the company for 12 years, all of them in sales.

This is Friday afternoon, and tomorrow Lynn Smith leaves for Copenhagen at noon to attend an important meeting with potential overseas investors. He will be gone for two weeks. Before he leaves, there are several items in his in-basket that must receive attention. He calls a meeting with Richard Hooton and Barbara Price in his office. Just before the meeting begins, Chuck Kasper calls and asks if he may join the meeting for a few minutes, since he is in town and has something important to discuss that involves both Lynn Smith and Richard Hooton. Smith gives permission for him to join the meeting, since there may not be another chance to meet with Kasper before the trip. The meeting convenes, therefore, with Smith, Hooton, Price, and Kasper all in the room.

Assignment

Groups of four individuals should be formed. Each person should take the role of one of the characters in the management staff of Hartford Manufacturing Company. A fifth person should be assigned to serve as an observer to provide feedback at the end of the meeting, using the Observer's Feedback Form at the end of the chapter as a guide. The letters described in the case that were received by Lynn Smith are shown in Figures 7.7, 7.8, and 7.9. Only the person playing the role of Lynn Smith should read the letters, and no one should read the instructions for another staff member's role. (The letters will be introduced by Lynn Smith during the meeting.)

Figure 7.7

T. J. Koppel, Inc.
General Accountants
8381 Spring Street
Hartford, Connecticut 06127

February 10, 2001

Mr. Lynn Smith
General Manager
Hartford Manufacturing Company
7450 Central Avenue
Hartford, CT 06118

Dear Mr. Smith:

As you requested last month, we have now completed our financial audit of Hartford Manufacturing Company. We find accounting procedures and fiscal control to be very satisfactory. A more detailed report of these matters is attached. However, we did discover during our perusal of company records that the production department has consistently incurred cost overruns during the past two quarters. Cost per unit of production is approximately 5 percent over budget. While this is not a serious problem given the financial solvency of your company, we thought it wise to bring it to your attention.

Respectfully,

T. J. Koppel

TJK: srw

Lynn Smith, General Manager

Three letters arrived today, and you judge them to be sufficiently important to require your attention before you leave on your trip. Each letter represents a problem that requires immediate action, and you need commitments from key staff members to resolve these problems. You are concerned about this meeting because these individuals don't work as well together as you'd like.

For example, Richard Hooton is very difficult to pin down. He always seems suspicious of the motives of others and has a reputation for not making tough decisions. You sometimes wonder how a person could become the head of production in a major manufacturing firm by avoiding controversial issues and blaming others for the results.

Figure 7.8

ZODIAK INDUSTRIES
6377 Atlantic Avenue
Boston, Massachusetts 02112

February 8, 2001

Mr. Lynn Smith
General Manager
Hartford Manufacturing Company
7450 Central Avenue
Hartford, CT 06118

Dear Mr. Smith:

We have been purchasing your products since 1975, and we have been very satisfied with our relations with your sales personnel. However, we have had a problem of late that requires your attention. Your sales representative for the Boston region, Sam St. Clair, has appeared at our company the last three times looking and smelling like he was under the influence of alcohol. Not only that, but our last order was mistakenly recorded, so we received the wrong quantities of products. I'm sure you don't make it a practice to put your company's reputation in the hands of someone like Sam St. Clair, so I suggest you get someone else to cover this region. We cannot tolerate, and I'm sure other companies in Boston cannot tolerate, this kind of relationship. While we judge your products to be excellent, we will be forced to find other sources if some action is not taken.

Sincerely yours,

Miles Andrew
Chief of Purchasing

:ms

PRACTICE

In contrast, Barbara Price is very straightforward. You always know exactly where she stands. The problem is that sometimes she doesn't take enough time to study a problem before making a decision. She tends to be impulsive and anxious to make a decision, whether it's the right one or not. Her general approach to resolving disagreements between departments is to seek expedient compromises. You are particularly disturbed by her approach to the sales incentive problem. You felt strongly that something needed to be done to increase sales during the winter months. You reluctantly agreed to the incentive program because you didn't want to dampen her initiative. But you aren't convinced this is the right answer, because, frankly, you're not yet sure what the real problem is.

Chuck Kasper is your typical, aggressive, "take no prisoners" sales manager. He is hard-charging and uncompromising. He is great in the field because he gets the job done, but he

Figure 7.9

HARTFORD MANUFACTURING COMPANY
7450 Central Avenue
Hartford, Connecticut 06118

"A subsidiary of CONNECTICUT INDUSTRIES"

Memorandum

TO: Lynn Smith, General Manager
FROM: Barbara Price, General Supervisor, Sales and Marketing
DATE: February 11, 2001

Mr. Smith:

In response to your concerns, we have instituted several incentive programs among our sales force to increase sales during these traditionally slow months. We have set up competition among regions, with the sales people in the top region being honored in the company newsletter and given engraved plaques. We have instituted a "vacation in Hawaii" award for the top salesperson in the company. And we have instituted cash bonuses for any salesperson who gets a new customer order. However, in the last month these incentives have been in operation, sales have not increased at all. In fact, in two regions they have decreased by an average of 5 percent.

What do you suggest now? We have advertised the incentives as lasting through this quarter, but they seem to be doing no good. Not only that, but we cannot afford to provide the incentives within our current budget, and unless sales increase, we will be in the red.

Regretfully, I recommend dropping the program.

sometimes ruffles the feathers of the corporate staff with his uncompromising, "black-and-white" style. He is also fiercely loyal to his sales staff, so you're sure he'll take the complaint about Sam St. Clair hard.

In contrast to the styles of these others, you have tried to use an integrating approach to problem solving: focusing on the facts, treating everyone's inputs equally, and keeping conversations about controversial topics problem-focused. One of your goals since taking over this position two years ago is to foster a "team" approach within your staff.

[*Note*: For more information about how you might approach the issues raised by these letters in your staff meeting, review the collaborating approach in Table 7.2 as well as the mediator's behavioral guidelines at the end of the Skill Learning section of this chapter.]

Richard Hooton, Director of Production

The only times you have had major problems in production are when the young know-it-alls fresh from college have come in and tried to change things. With their scientific management concepts coupled with fuzzy-headed human relations training, they have more often made a mess of things than helped to improve matters. The best production methods have been practiced for years in the company, and you have yet to see anyone who could improve on your system.

On the other hand, you have respect for Lynn Smith as the general manager. Because he has experience and the right kind of training, and is involved in the production part of the organization, he often has given you good advice and has shown special interest. He mostly lets you do what you feel is best, however, and he seldom dictates specific methods for doing things.

Your general approach to problems is to avoid controversy. You feel uncomfortable when production is made the scapegoat for problems in the company. Because this is a manufacturing business, it seems as if everyone tries to pin the blame for problems on the production department. You've felt for years that the firm was getting away from what it does best: mass producing a few standard products. Instead, the trend has been for marketing and sales to push for more and more products, shorter lead times, and greater customization capability. These actions have increased costs and caused significant production delays as well as higher rejection rates.

[*Note*: During the upcoming meeting, you should adopt the avoidance approach shown in Table 7.2. Defend your turf, place blame on others, defer taking a stand, and avoid taking responsibility for making a controversial decision.]

Barbara Price, Director of Sales and Marketing

You are anxious to impress Lynn Smith because you have your eye on a position that is opening up at the end of the year in the parent company, Connecticut Industries. It would mean a promotion for you. A positive recommendation from Lynn Smith would carry a lot of weight in the selection process. Given that both Hartford Manufacturing and Connecticut Industries are largely male dominated, you are pleased with your career advancement so far, and you are hoping to keep it up.

One current concern is Lynn Smith's suggestion some time ago that you look into the problem of slow sales during the winter months. You implemented an incentive plan that was highly recommended by an industry analyst at a recent trade conference. It consists of three separate incentive programs: (1) competition among regions in which the salesperson in the top region would have his or her picture in the company newsletter and receive an engraved plaque, (2) a vacation in Hawaii for the top salesperson in the company, and (3) cash bonuses for salespeople who obtained new customer orders. Unfortunately, these incentives haven't worked. Not only have sales not increased for the company as a whole, but sales for two regions are down an average of five percent. You have told the sales force that the incentives will last through this quarter, but if sales don't improve, your budget will be in the red. You haven't budgeted for the prizes, since you expected the increased sales to more than offset the cost of the incentives.

Obviously, this was a bad idea—it isn't working—and it should be dropped immediately. You are a bit embarrassed about this aborted project. But it is better to cut your losses and try something else rather than continue to support an obvious loser.

In general, you are very confident and self-assured. You feel that the best way to get work done is through negotiation and compromise. What's important is making a decision quickly and efficiently. Maybe everyone doesn't get exactly what he or she wants, but at least they can get on with their work. There are no black and whites in this business—only "grays" that can be traded off to keep the management process from bogging down with "paralysis by analysis." You are impatient over delays caused by intensive studies and investigations of detail. You agree with Tom Peters: action is the hallmark of successful managers.

[*Note*: During this meeting, use the compromise approach shown in Table 7.2. Do whatever is necessary to help the group make a quick decision so you can get on with the pressing demands of your work.]

Chuck Kasper, Regional Sales Director

You don't get back to company headquarters often because your customer contacts take up most of your time. You regularly work 50 to 60 hours a week, and you are proud of the job you do. You also feel a special obligation to your customers to provide them with the best product available in the timeliest fashion. This sense of obligation comes not only from your commitment to the company but also from your personal relationships with many of the customers.

Lately, you have been receiving more and more complaints about late deliveries of Hartford Manufacturing's products to your customers. The time between their ordering and delivery is increasing, and some customers have been greatly inconvenienced by the delays. You have made a formal inquiry of production to find out what the problem is. They replied that they are producing as efficiently as possible, and they see nothing wrong with past practices. Richard Hooton's assistant even suggested that this was just another example of the sales force's unrealistic expectations.

Not only will sales be negatively affected if these delays continue, but your reputation with your customers will be damaged. You have promised them that the problem will be quickly solved and that products will begin arriving on time. Since Richard Hooton is so rigid, however, you are almost certain that it will do no good to talk with him. His subordinate probably got his negative attitude from Hooton.

In general, Hooton is a 1960s production worker who is being pulled by the rest of the firm into the new age. Competition is different, technology is different, and management is different, but Richard is reluctant to change. You need shorter lead times, a wider range of products, and the capacity to do some customized work. Sure, this makes production's work harder, but other firms are providing these services with the use of just-in-time management processes, robots, and so forth.

Instead of getting down to the real problems, the home office, in their typical high-handed fashion, announced an incentives plan. This implies that the problem is in the field, not the factory. It made some of your people angry to think they were being pressed to increase their efforts when they weren't receiving the backup support in Hartford to get the job done. Sure, they liked the prizes, but the way the plan was presented made them feel as if they weren't working hard enough. This isn't the first time you have questioned the judgment of Barbara, your boss. She certainly is intelligent and hard-working, but she doesn't seem very interested in what's going on out in the field. Furthermore, she doesn't seem very receptive to "bad news" about sales and customer complaints.

[*Note*: During this meeting, use the forcing approach to conflict management and negotiations shown in Table 7.2. However, don't overplay your part, because you are the senior regional sales manager, and if Barbara continues to move up fast in the organization, you may be in line for her position.]

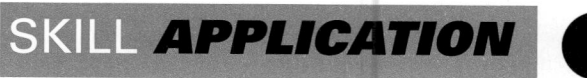
ACTIVITIES FOR IMPROVING MANAGING CONFLICT SKILLS

Suggested Assignments

1. Select a specific conflict with which you are very familiar. Using the framework for identifying the sources of conflict discussed in this chapter, analyze this situation carefully. It might be useful to compare your perceptions of the situation with those of informed observers. What type of conflict is this? Why did it occur? Why is it continuing? Next, using the guidelines for selecting an appropriate conflict management strategy, identify the general approach that would be most appropriate for this situation. Consider both the personal preferences of the parties involved and the relevant situational factors. Is this the approach that the parties have been using? If not, attempt to introduce a different perspective into the relationship and explain why you feel it would be more productive. If the parties have been using this approach, discuss with them why it has not been successful thus far. Share information on specific behavioral guidelines or negotiation tactics that might increase the effectiveness of their efforts.

2. Select three individuals whom you know who are from diverse cultural backgrounds and have experience working in American companies. Discuss with them the sources (especially the personal differences) of previous conflicts they have experienced at work. Ask them about their preferences in dealing with conflict situations. What strategies do they prefer to use? How do they generally attempt to resolve disputes? What relevant situational factors influence the way they manage conflict situations with individuals from other cultures and with individuals of their own cultures? With the help of these three persons, identify specific behavioral guidelines for managing conflict more effectively with other persons from their respective cultures.

3. Identify a situation in which another individual is doing something that needs to be corrected. Using the respondent's guidelines for collaborative problem solving, construct a plan for discussing your concerns with this person. Include specific language designed to state your case assertively without causing a defensive reaction. Role-play this interaction with a friend and incorporate any suggestions for improvement. Make your presentation to the individual and report on your results. What was the reaction? Were you successful in balancing assertiveness with support and responsibility? Based on this experience, identify other situations you feel need to be changed and follow a similar procedure.

4. Volunteer to serve as a mediator to resolve a conflict between two individuals or groups. Using the guidelines for implementing the collaborative approach to mediation, outline a plan of action prior to your intervention. Be sure to consider carefully whether or not private meetings with the parties prior to your mediation session are appropriate. Report on the situation and your plan. How did you feel? Which specific actions worked well? What was the outcome? What would you do differently? Based on this experience, revise your plan for use in related situations.

5. Identify a difficult situation involving negotiations. This might involve transactions at work, at home, or in the community. Review the guidelines for integrative bargaining and identify the specific tactics you plan to use. Write down specific questions and responses to likely initiatives from the other party. In particular, anticipate how you might handle the possibility of the other party's using a distributive negotiation strategy. Schedule a negotiation meeting with the party involved and implement your plan. Following the session, debrief the experience with a coworker or friend. What did you learn? How successful were you? What would you do differently? Based on this experience, modify your plan and prepare to implement it in related situations.

Application Plan and Evaluation

The intent of this exercise is to help you apply this cluster of skills in a real-life, out-of-class setting. Now that you have become familiar with the behavioral guidelines that form the basis of effective skill performance, you will improve most by trying out those guidelines in an everyday context. Unlike a classroom activity, in which feedback is immediate and others can assist you with their evaluations, this skill application activity is one you must accomplish and evaluate on your own. There are two parts to this activity. Part 1 helps prepare you to apply the skill. Part 2 helps you evaluate and improve on your experience. Be sure to write down answers to each item. Don't short-circuit the process by skipping steps.

Part 1. Planning

1. Write down the two or three aspects of this skill that are most important to you. These may be areas of weakness, areas you most want to improve, or areas that are most salient to a problem you face right now. Identify the specific aspects of this skill that you want to apply.

2. Now identify the setting or the situation in which you will apply this skill. Establish a plan for performance by actually writing down a description of the situation. Who else will be involved? When will you do it? Where will it be done?

   Circumstances:
   Who else?
   When?
   Where?

3. Identify the specific behaviors you will engage in to apply this skill. Operationalize your skill performance.

4. What are the indicators of successful performance? How will you know you have been effective? What will indicate you have performed competently?

Part 2. Evaluation

5. After you have completed your implementation, record the results. What happened? How successful were you? What was the effect on others?

6. How can you improve? What modifications can you make next time? What will you do differently in a similar situation in the future?

7. Looking back on your whole skill practice and application experience, what have you learned? What has been surprising? In what ways might this experience help you in the long term?

APPLICATION

Managing Interpersonal Conflict

Scoring Key

SKILL AREA	ITEM	ASSESSMENT	
		PRE-	POST-
Initiating a complaint	1	_____	_____
	2	_____	_____
	3	_____	_____
	4	_____	_____
	5	_____	_____
	6	_____	_____
	7	_____	_____
	8	_____	_____
Responding to a criticism	9	_____	_____
	10	_____	_____
	11	_____	_____
	12	_____	_____
	13	_____	_____
	14	_____	_____
	15	_____	_____
	16	_____	_____
Mediating a conflict	17	_____	_____
	18	_____	_____
	19	_____	_____
	20	_____	_____
	21	_____	_____
	22	_____	_____
	23	_____	_____
	24	_____	_____
	Total Score	_____	_____

Comparison Data (N = 1,500 Students)

Compare your scores to three comparison standards:
1. The maximum possible score = 144
2. The scores of other students in your class.
3. Norm group data from more than 1,500 practicing managers and business school students.

Pre-Test				Post-Test
113.20	=	mean	=	122.59
122 or above	=	top quartile	=	133 or above
114–121	=	second quartile	=	123–132
105–113	=	third quartile	=	115–122
104 and below	=	bottom quartile	=	114 or below

Strategies for Handling Conflict

Scoring Key

FORCING		ACCOMMODATING		COMPROMISING	
Item	*Score*	*Item*	*Score*	*Item*	*Score*
1	_____	2	_____	3	_____
6	_____	7	_____	8	_____
11	_____	12	_____	13	_____
16	_____	17	_____	18	_____
Total	_____	**Total**	_____	**Total**	_____

AVOIDING		INTEGRATING	
ITEM	*SCORE*	*ITEM*	*SCORE*
4	_____	5	_____
9	_____	10	_____
14	_____	15	_____
19	_____	20	_____
Total	_____	**Total**	_____

Primary conflict management strategy (highest score): _____
Secondary conflict management strategy (next-highest score): _____

SKILL PRACTICE Exercises for Resolving Interpersonal Disputes

Observer's Feedback Form

Rating

1 = Low
5 = High

Initiator

_____ Maintained personal ownership of the problem, including feelings

_____ Avoided making accusations or attributing motives; stuck to the facts

_____ Succinctly described the problem (behaviors, outcomes, feelings)

_____ Specified expectations or standards violated

_____ Persisted until understood

_____ Encouraged two-way interaction

_____ Approached multiple issues incrementally (proceeded from simple to complex, easy to hard)

_____ Appealed to what the disputants had in common (goals, principles, constraints)

_____ Made a specific request for change

Respondent

_____ Established a climate for joint problem solving

_____ Showed genuine concern and interest

_____ Responded appropriately to the initiator's emotions

_____ Avoided becoming defensive or overreacting

_____ Sought additional information about the problem (shifted general to specific, evaluative to descriptive)

_____ Focused on one issue at a time, gradually broadened the scope of the discussion, searched for integrative solution

_____ Agreed with some aspect of the complaint (facts, perceptions, feelings, or principles)

_____ Asked for suggestions for making changes

_____ Proposed a specific plan of action

Mediator

_____ Acknowledged that a conflict exists; treated the conflict and disputants seriously

_____ Broke down complex issues, separated the critical from the peripheral; began with a relatively easy problem

_____ Helped disputants avoid entrenched positions by exploring underlying interests

_____ Remained neutral (facilitator, not judge) and impartial towards issues and disputants

_____ Kept the interaction issue oriented (e.g., pointed out the effect of the conflict on performance)

_____ Made sure that neither party dominated conversation, asked questions to maintain balance

_____ Kept conflict in perspective by emphasizing areas of agreement

_____ Helped generate multiple alternatives, drawn from common goals, values, or principles

_____ Made sure that both parties were satisfied and committed to the proposed resolution

Comments:

Part III

Group Skills

CHAPTERS

8 EMPOWERING AND DELEGATING

Empowering others
Delegating
Sharing power

9 BUILDING EFFECTIVE TEAMS AND TEAMWORK

Diagnosing team development
Building teamwork
Fostering effective team leadership

10 LEADING POSITIVE CHANGE

Creating positive deviance
Leading positive change
Mobilizing the capabilities of others

SKILL *ASSESSMENT*

- Effective Empowerment and Delegation
- Personal Empowerment Assessment

SKILL *LEARNING*

- Empowering and Delegating
- A Management Dilemma Involving Empowerment
- The Meaning of Empowerment
- Historical Roots of Empowerment
- Dimensions of Empowerment
- How to Develop Empowerment
- Inhibitors to Empowerment
- Delegating Work
- International Caveats
- Summary
- Behavioral Guidelines

SKILL *ANALYSIS*

- Minding the Store
- Changing the Portfolio

SKILL *PRACTICE*

- Executive Development Associates
- Empowering Ourselves
- Deciding To Delegate

SKILL *APPLICATION*

- Suggested Assignments
- Application Plan and Evaluation

SCORING KEYS AND *COMPARISON DATA*

8

Empowering and Delegating

SKILL DEVELOPMENT OBJECTIVES

- EMPOWER OTHERS
- EMPOWER YOURSELF
- DELEGATE EFFECTIVELY

443

DIAGNOSTIC SURVEYS FOR EMPOWERING AND DELEGATING

EFFECTIVE EMPOWERMENT AND DELEGATION

Step 1: Before you read the material in this chapter, please respond to the following statements by writing a number from the rating scale below in the left-hand column (Pre-assessment). Your answers should reflect your attitudes and behavior as they are now, not as you would like them to be. Be honest. This instrument is designed to help you discover your level of competency in empowering and delegating so you can tailor your learning to your specific needs. When you have completed the survey, use the scoring key at the end of the chapter to identify the skill areas discussed in this chapter that are most important for you to master.

Step 2: After you have completed the reading and the exercises in this chapter and, ideally, as many as you can of the Skill Application assignments at the end of this chapter, cover up your first set of answers. Then respond to the same statements again, this time in the right-hand column (Post-assessment). When you have completed the survey, use the scoring key at the end of the chapter to measure your progress. If your score remains low in specific skill areas, use the behavioral guidelines at the end of the Skill Learning section to guide further practice.

Rating Scale

1 Strongly disagree
2 Disagree
3 Slightly disagree
4 Slightly agree
5 Agree
6 Strongly agree

Assessment

Pre-   Post-

In situations in which I have an opportunity to engage others in accomplishing work:

_____ _____ 1. I help people develop personal mastery in their work by involving them first in less complex tasks, and then in more difficult tasks.

_____ _____ 2. I help people feel competent in their work by recognizing and celebrating their small successes.

_____ _____ 3. I serve as an example of successful task accomplishment.

_____ _____ 4. I identify other successful people who can serve as role models.

_____ _____ 5. I frequently praise, encourage, and express approval of other people.

_____ _____ 6. I provide regular feedback and needed support to other people.

_____ _____ 7. I try to foster friendships and informal interaction.

_____ _____ 8. I highlight the important impact that a person's work will have on others and on goals.

_____ _____ 9. I try to provide all the information that people need to accomplish their tasks.

_____ _____ 10. As I become aware of it, I pass along relevant information to people on a continuous basis.

_____ _____ 11. I ensure that people have the necessary resources (equipment, space, and time) to succeed.

_____ _____ 12. I help people get access to needed resources that I may not have available personally.

_____ _____ 13. I help people become involved in teams in order to increase their participation.

_____ _____ 14. I encourage teams to make decisions and implement their own recommendations.

_____ _____ 15. I foster confidence by being fair and equitable in my decisions.

_____ _____ 16. I exhibit caring and personal concern for each person with whom I have dealings.

When delegating work to others:

_____ _____ 17. I specify clearly the results I desire.

_____ _____ 18. I specify clearly the level of initiative I want others to take (e.g., wait for directions, do part of the task and then report, do the whole task and then report, etc.).

_____ _____ 19. I allow participation by those accepting assignments regarding when and how work will be done.

_____ _____ 20. I make certain that the amount of authority I give matches the amount of responsibility I expect for producing results.

_____ _____ 21. I work within existing organizational structures when delegating assignments, and I never bypass someone without informing him or her.

_____ _____ 22. I identify constraints and limitations that people will face but also provide needed support.

_____ _____ 23. I maintain accountability for results, not for methods used.

_____ _____ 24. I delegate consistently—not just when I'm overloaded.

_____ _____ 25. I avoid upward delegation by asking people to recommend solutions, rather than merely asking for advice or answers, when a problem is encountered.

_____ _____ 26. I make clear the consequences of success and failure.

PERSONAL EMPOWERMENT ASSESSMENT

This instrument helps identify the extent to which you are empowered in your own work. You should respond to the items based on your own job, or, if you are in school, the work you do as a student. The items listed below describe different orientations people can have with respect to their work roles. Using the following scale, indicate the extent to which you believe each is true of you.

Rating Scale

1 Very strongly disagree
2 Strongly disagree
3 Disagree
4 Neutral
5 Agree
6 Strongly agree
7 Very strongly agree

Assessment

_____ 1. The work that I do is very important to me.

_____ 2. I am confident about my ability to do my work.

_____ 3. I have significant autonomy in determining how I do my job.

_____ 4. I have significant impact on what happens in my work unit.

_____ 5. I trust my coworkers to be completely honest with me.

_____ 6. My work activities are personally meaningful to me.

_____ 7. My work is within the scope of my competence and capabilities.

_____ 8. I can decide how to go about doing my own work.

_____ 9. I have a great deal of control over what happens in my work unit.

_____ 10. I trust my coworkers to share important information with me.

_____ 11. I care about what I do in my work.

_____ 12. I am confident in my capabilities to successfully perform my work.

_____ 13. I have considerable opportunity for independence and freedom in how I do my work.

_____ 14. I have significant influence over what happens in my work unit.

_____ 15. I trust my coworkers to keep the promises they make.

_____ 16. The work I do has special meaning and importance to me.

_____ 17. I have mastered the skills necessary to do my work.

_____ 18. I have a chance to use personal initiative in carrying out my work.

_____ 19. My opinion counts in my work unit's decision making.

_____ 20. I believe that my coworkers care about my well-being.

Empowering and Delegating

Many management books are oriented toward helping managers know how to control others' behavior. They focus on how managers can increase employees' performance, engender conformity, or motivate employees to achieve certain objectives. This book, too, includes skills that will help you motivate people to do what you want them to do (see the chapter on Motivating Others) or achieve power and influence over them (see the Gaining Power and Influence chapter). The present chapter, however, focuses on a skill called **empowerment** and on a special form of empowerment called **delegation**.

Empowerment is based on a set of assumptions that are in contrast to those normally made by managers. Empowerment means providing freedom for people to do successfully what they want to do, rather than getting them to do what you want them to do. Managers who empower people remove controls, constraints, and boundaries for them instead of motivating, directing, or stimulating their behavior. Rather than being a "push" strategy, in which managers induce employees to respond in desirable ways through incentives and influence techniques, empowerment is a "pull" strategy. It focuses on ways that managers can design a work situation so that it energizes and provides intrinsic encouragement to employees. In the context of such a strategy, workers accomplish tasks because they are intrinsically attracted by them, not because of an extrinsic reward system or influence technique.

Empowering others, however, can lead to dilemmas. On the one hand, evidence shows that empowered employees are more productive, more satisfied, and more innovative, and that they create higher-quality products and services than unempowered employees (Greenberger & Stasser, 1991; Kanter, 1983; Sashkin, 1982, 1984; Spreitzer, 1992). Organizations are more effective when an empowered workforce exists (Conger & Kanungo, 1988; Gecas, 1989; Thomas & Velthouse, 1990). On the other hand, empowerment means giving up control and letting others make decisions, set goals, accomplish results, and receive rewards. It means that other people probably will get credit for success. Managers with high needs for power and control (see McClelland, 1975) face a challenge when they are expected to sacrifice their needs for someone else's gain. They may ask themselves: "Why should others get the goodies when I am in charge? Why should I allow others to exercise power, and even facilitate their acquiring more power, when I naturally want to receive rewards and recognition myself?"

The answer is that although empowering others is neither easy nor natural (we aren't born knowing how to do it), it need not require a great amount of self-sacrifice. You don't need to sacrifice desired rewards, recognition, or effectiveness in order to be a skillful empowering manager. On the contrary, through real empowerment, managers actually multiply their own effectiveness. They and their organizations become more effective than they could have been otherwise. Nevertheless, for most managers, empowerment is a skill that must be developed and practiced, because despite the high visibility of the concept of empowerment in popular literature, its actual practice is all too rare in modern management.

Evidence for this assertion comes from a national survey by the Louis Harris organization, reported in *Business Week* for January 18, 1993. According to this survey, feelings of powerlessness and alienation among workers rose sharply through the 1990s and, according to more recent Harris polls, have not reversed themselves in the twenty-first century (Harris Poll, 2002). The percentage of workers answering "yes" to the questions in Table 8.1 illustrates this trend.

In this chapter, we begin by discussing the core dimensions of empowerment and, in particular, how to effectively accomplish empowerment. In the second part of this section, we discuss a special situation in which empowerment is essential: the delegation of responsibility. We conclude with a summary model of empowerment and delegation and a list of behavioral guidelines for successfully empowering and delegating to others.

A Management Dilemma Involving Empowerment

One of the most well-researched findings in organization and management science over the last four decades has shown that when environments are predictable and stable, organizations can function as routine, controlled, mechanistic units. Under such conditions, workers can be expected to follow rules and procedures and to engage in standardized, formalized behavior. Managers can maintain control and issue top-down mandates regarding the strategy and direction to be pursued by

Table 8.1	Powerlessness and Alienation Survey			
QUESTION		1972	1985	1992
What I think doesn't count very much anymore.		50%	62%	62%
Most people with power take advantage of people like myself.		43%	65%	71%
The people in charge don't really care what happens to me.		46%	65%	71%
I'm left out of things going on around me.		25%	48%	48%

the organization. However, the modern business environment is often described using terms such as *hyperturbulence, complexity, speed, competition*, and *revolutionary change*. Under such conditions, prescriptions for organizational and management effectiveness call for a flexible, autonomous, entrepreneurial workforce (DeGraff & Lawrence, 2002; Drucker, 1988; Quinn, 2005), rather than one that relies on management for direction and control. Less-centralized decision making, less top-down direction, and less-autocratic leadership are all prescribed as prerequisites for high-performing modern organizations.

When environments are unstable and unpredictable—when they change a lot or in unpredictable ways—organizations must be more flexible and organic. Workers are expected to be adaptable and self-managing. Managers must involve others in decision making and facilitate broad participation and accountability (Eisenhart, & Galunic, 1993; Lawrence & Lorsch, 1967). The workers' flexibility must match the flexibility of the environment (Ashby, 1956).

Our own research has shown, however, that instead of becoming adaptable, flexible, autonomous, and self-managing, individuals in rapidly changing, complex environments tend to behave in opposite ways than they should in order to succeed. Both managers and employees tend to become less flexible, less adaptable, less autonomous, less self-managing, more stable, more rigid, and more defensive when they face turbulence and change (Cameron, Whetten, & Kim, 1987; Cameron, Kim, & Whetten, 1987; Cameron, 1998).

In our research on how organizations are managed when they face decline, turbulence, downsizing, and change, we have identified 12 negative attributes or attitudes, which we label the **dirty dozen**. Table 8.2 summarizes these negative attitudes.

THE DIRTY DOZEN

Among the dirty dozen attributes is a "threat-rigidity" response (Staw, Sandelands, & Dutton, 1981; Weick,

1993), in which people become conservative. They hunker down and become self-protective and increasingly rely on old, first-learned habits and past behaviors. In reaction to a perceived threat, they do that which they know how to do best or that which has worked best in the past. Despite new circumstances in which old behaviors may not be effective, there is an escalating commitment to habitual behavior. People consider fewer options, look for information that confirms their previous biases, and become more narrow-minded in their perspectives.

In addition, less communication occurs among workers. When individuals in organizations are divulging information, they become vulnerable by putting their personal expertise or untested ideas at risk. This sense of vulnerability magnifies the feeling of uncertainty brought about by changing conditions. Under such circumstances, people are less likely to become contributing team members and to try out new, innovative ideas. Fear and conflict increase, while trust, morale, and productivity decrease. A "mean mood" is typical of most interactions, as loyalty and commitment to the organization erode. The tendency in such circumstances is for most important decisions to be made at the top of the organizational hierarchy because managers at the top feel an increasing need to be in control and to be closer to decisions. On the other hand, people at lower organizational levels become hesitant to make decisions without getting approval from a superior.

How can we ever expect a workforce in the modern, changing environment to develop the prescribed characteristics for effectiveness—that is, to be adaptable, flexible, autonomous, and self-managing? If people become more rigid and resistant in uncertain times rather than more independent and flexible, how can we ever foster effective performance?

The answer to these questions is to use empowerment. If managers are skilled at empowering workers, the inertia that drives organizations toward dysfunctional dirty dozen attitudes is counteracted. Workers

Table 8.2	The Dirty Dozen: Outcomes of Stress in Organizations
ATTRIBUTE	**EXPLANATION**
Centralization	Decision making is pulled toward the top of the organization. Less power is shared.
Threat-rigidity response	Conservative, self-protective behaviors predominate. Old habits are relied upon. Change is resisted.
Loss of innovativeness	Trial and error learning stops. Low tolerance for risk and creativity occurs.
Decreasing morale	In-fighting and a mean mood permeate the organization. It isn't fun.
Politicized environment	Special interest groups organize and become vocal. Everything is negotiated.
Loss of trust	Leaders lose the confidence of subordinates. Distrust predominates among employees.
Increased conflict	Infighting and competition occur. Self-centeredness predominates over the good of the organization.
Restricted communication	Only good news is passed upward. Information is not widely shared and is held close to the vest.
Lack of teamwork	Individualism and disconnectedness inhibit teamwork. Lack of coordination occurs.
Loss of loyalty	Commitment to the organization and to the leader erodes. Focus is on defending oneself.
Scapegoating leaders	Leadership anemia occurs as leaders are criticized, priorities become less clear, and a siege mentality occurs.
Short-term perspective	A crisis mentality is adopted. Long-term planning and flexibility are avoided.

Adapted from: *Cameron et al., 1987.*

become more effective, even in the face of trying times. Empowerment is a key to unlocking the potential of a successful workforce in an era of chaotic change and escalating competitive conditions.

But what is empowerment? What does it mean to be an empowered worker? What is the set of management skills associated with empowerment?

The Meaning of Empowerment

To empower means to enable; it means to help people develop a sense of self-confidence; it means to help people overcome feelings of powerlessness or helplessness; it means to energize people to take action; it means to mobilize intrinsic motivation to accomplish a task. Empowered people not only possess the wherewithal to accomplish something, but they also think of themselves differently than they did before they were empowered.

Empowerment is different from merely giving power to someone. Like empowerment, power connotes the ability to get things done (see the chapter on Gaining Power and Influence). But power and empowerment are not the same things. Table 8.3 contrasts the concepts of power and empowerment so as to highlight their differences. People may have power and also be empowered. However, although one can give someone else power, one must accept empowerment for oneself. You cannot empower me; you can only create the circumstances in which I can empower myself.

As explained in the chapter on Gaining Power and Influence, the acquisition of power is based on several personal factors and certain position attributes. In each case, other people need to acknowledge your power, follow your lead, and acquiesce to your influence in order for you to have power. The underlying source of your power is other people. For example, you may have power because you have more resources or political support than someone else. Thus you can reward others and have *reward power*. Alternatively, you may have the ability to penalize or sanction others as a result of your strength or support so you have *sanctioning power*. Your title or position may give you power over others, thus giving you *traditional power*. You may possess more knowledge or information than others, giving you *expertise power*. Or, you may be personally attractive or charismatic, thus having *referent power*. French and Raven (1960) identified these five factors as being the primary bases of power. Regardless of whether these are the five factors or

Table 8.3	The Difference Between Power and Empowerment	
POWER	**EMPOWERMENT**
External source	Internal source
Ultimately, few people have it	Ultimately, everyone can have it
The capacity to have others do what you want	The capacity to have others do what they want
To get more implies taking it away from someone else	To get more does not affect how much others have
Leads to competition	Leads to cooperation

whether there are others, each can be conveyed to another person. Each depends on others acknowledging it. Each can be delegated to someone else.

In the case of empowerment, however, people can be empowered even if no one acknowledges their personal attributes or positions. Victor Frankl, Nelson Mandela, and Mahatma Gandhi are examples of individuals who, despite the absence of the attributes of power, maintained complete empowerment in dismal circumstances (i.e., in prison and in bigoted environments). This is because the source of empowerment is internal. Its source is within the individual, not as a result of social acceptance, political support, or title. One accepts empowerment for oneself.

In addition, if I become more powerful, that generally means you become less powerful. If I have the power to get someone to do what I want, but that differs from what you want, my power and your power come into conflict. That's why, ultimately, relatively few people have power. Power gets concentrated among a few in most organizations. Furthermore, power struggles are almost universal in organizations and even small groups. Who gets enough power to have his or her way is a common problem, and it almost always leads toward conflict. Power games become a clash of wills or a battle to see who will win and reign supreme. On the other hand, every person can be empowered without affecting any other person's position or stature. It merely leads to each of us being enabled to accomplish what we choose. Empowerment, in fact, is more likely to lead to cooperation and collaboration than to conflict.

Historical Roots of Empowerment

The word *empowerment* came into vogue in the 1980s and 1990s but has since taken on the image of a faddish and even outdated concept. In our own consulting and executive education teaching, many managers will respond when introducing the concept of empowerment, "We already tried that." Or "That's a 1990s

term, isn't it?" Because the concept of empowerment was so widely used in so many different contexts, it tended to become almost any management practice relating to employee involvement. Empowerment became associated with everything from team-building to entrepreneurship to flexible benefits. The word became so overused that its precise meaning became obscured. It may be helpful, therefore, to provide a brief background of the roots of empowerment because it is by no means a new concept. This should help us avoid confusing empowerment with other related management behaviors.

Empowerment has roots in the disciplines of psychology, sociology, and theology dating back for centuries. In the field of psychology, Adler (1927) developed the concept of *mastery motivation*, emphasizing the striving that people have for competence in dealing with their world. Similar concepts introduced several decades ago include *effectance motivation*, an intrinsic motivation to make things happen (White, 1959); *psychological reactance*, which refers to seeking freedom from constraints (Brehm, 1966); *competence motivation*, a striving to encounter and master challenges (Harter, 1978); and *personal causation*, a drive to experience free agency (DeCharms, 1979). In each of these studies, the root concepts are similar to the notion of empowerment discussed in this chapter; that is, the inclination of people to experience self-control, self-importance, and self-liberation.

In sociology, notions of empowerment have been fundamental to most rights movements (e.g., Civil Rights, Women's Rights, Gay Rights) (see Bookman & Morgan, 1988; Solomon, 1976), in which people campaign for freedom and control of their own circumstances. Moreover, much of the writing attacking societal problems through social change has centered fundamentally on the empowerment of groups of people (Alinsky, 1971; Marx, 1844). That is, people seek social change in order to increase their access to an empowered condition.

In theology, issues of free will versus determinism, self-will versus submissiveness, predestination versus faith and works, and humanism versus positivism have been hotly debated for centuries. At their root, they are all variations on a theme of empowerment versus helplessness. The more recent literature on "liberation theology" (Friere & Faundez, 1989) emphasizes the empowerment of individuals to take charge of their own destinies, rather than relying solely and completely on the dictates of an all-controlling, supernatural force. This does not mean that people who believe in a Supreme Being cannot feel empowered; rather, empowered people couple a sense of self-mastery and self-determination with their faith in God.

Empowerment is not a new concept. It has appeared in various forms throughout modern management literature. In the 1950s, for example, management literature was filled with prescriptions that managers should be friendly to employees (human relations); in the 1960s, that managers should be sensitive to the needs and motivations of people (sensitivity training); in the 1970s, that managers should ask employees for help (employee involvement); in the 1980s, that managers should form teams and hold meetings (quality circles), and in the 1990s, that employees should become entrepreneurial and flexible. All of these emphases were associated with the notion of empowerment. Despite the continuing emphasis on various versions of employee involvement and empowerment, however, the ability to empower employees is still not common in most managers' repertoire of skills. Empowerment is more rarely seen than prescribed (Quinn & Spreitzer, 1997).

Dimensions of Empowerment

In one of the best empirical studies of empowerment to date, Spreitzer (1992) identified four dimensions of empowerment. We have added one dimension to her model, based on the research of Mishra (1992). In this section, we explain these five key dimensions of empowerment. In order for managers to empower others successfully, they must engender these five qualities in those they intend to empower. Skillful empowerment means producing (1) a sense of *self-efficacy*, (2) a sense of *self-determination*, (3) a sense of *personal consequence*, (4) a sense of *meaning*, and (5) a sense of *trust* (see Table 8.4). When these five dimensions of empowerment are present, empirical evidence is clear: individuals perform better and organizations perform better than normal.

When managers are able to foster these five attributes in others, they create a condition that is highly

Table 8.4	Five Core Dimensions of Empowerment
DIMENSION	**EXPLANATION**
Self-efficacy	A sense of personal competence
Self-determination	A sense of personal choice
Personal consequence	A sense of having impact
Meaning	A sense of value in activity
Trust	A sense of security

empowering, or that makes it easy for others to become empowered. No one can force another to be empowered, of course, but fostering an environment where these five factors are present makes it likely that people will accept empowerment for themselves. Empowered people not only can more effectively accomplish tasks, but they also think differently about themselves. They are more confident, they feel more freedom, they feel more important, and they feel more comfortable in their work and work setting.

After explaining these five dimensions, we provide guidelines for engendering each of them.

SELF-EFFICACY

When people are empowered, they have a sense of **self-efficacy**, or the feeling that they possess the capability and competence to perform a task successfully. Empowered people not only feel *competent*, they feel *confident* that they can perform adequately. They are more self-assured. They feel a sense of personal mastery and believe they can learn and grow to meet new challenges (see Bandura, 1989; Bennis & Nanus, 1985; Conger & Kanungo, 1988; Gecas, 1989; Zimmerman, 1990). Some writers believe that this is the most important element in empowerment because having a sense of self-efficacy determines whether people will try and persist in attempting to accomplish a difficult task.

The strength of people's conviction in their own effectiveness is likely to affect whether they would even try to cope with given situations. . . . They get involved in activities and behave assuredly when they judge themselves capable of handling situations that would otherwise be intimidating. . . . Efficacy expectations determine how much effort people will expend and how long they will persist in the face of obstacles and aversive experiences. (Bandura, 1977, pp. 193–194)

Our colleague Roger Goddard and his associates found that a sense of efficacy among students in a classroom—what he referred to as "collective efficacy"—is a more powerful predictor of success in school than any other single factor (Goddard, Hoy, & Hoy, 2002). That is, when students believe in themselves, when they have confidence that they can succeed and when they have faith that a successful outcome will occur, they are significantly higher performers in their academic work. Their grades are higher, their test scores are higher in math and reading, and their absenteeism and tardiness are lower. Collective efficacy is a more important factor in determining these outcomes than race; gender; socioeconomic status; attending a large or small, inner-city or suburban school; or ethnic makeup of the class.

A great deal of additional research has been done on the consequences of self-efficacy and its opposite, powerlessness, in relation to physical and psychological health. For example, self-efficacy has been found to be a significant factor in overcoming phobias and anxieties (Bandura, 1986), alcohol and drug abuse (Seeman & Anderson, 1983), eating disorders (Schneider & Agras, 1985), smoking addiction (DiClemente, 1985), depression (Seligman, 1975), as well as increasing tolerance for pain (Neufeld & Thomas, 1977). Recovery from illness and injury, as well as coping with job loss or disruptions, is more effective and more rapid among people who have developed a strong sense of self-efficacy, because they are more physically and psychologically resilient and are better able to change negative behaviors (Gecas, Seff, & Ray, 1988; Schwalbe & Gecas, 1988).

Bandura (1977) suggested that three conditions are necessary for people to feel a sense of self-efficacy: (1) a belief that they have the ability to perform a task, (2) a belief that they are capable of putting forth the necessary effort, and (3) a belief that no outside obstacles will prevent them from accomplishing the task. In other words, people feel empowered when they develop a sense of self-efficacy by having a basic level of competence and capability, a willingness to put forth effort to accomplish a task, and the absence of overwhelming inhibitors to success. We will suggest ways later for enhancing self-efficacy.

SELF-DETERMINATION

Empowered people also have a sense of **self-determination**. Whereas self-efficacy refers to a sense of competence, self-determination refers to feelings of *having a choice*. "To be self-determining means to experience a sense of choice in initiating and regulating one's own actions" (Deci, Connell, & Ryan, 1989, p. 580). People feel self-determined when they can voluntarily and intentionally involve themselves in tasks, rather than being forced or prohibited from involvement. Their actions are a consequence of personal freedom and autonomy. Empowered individuals have alternatives and a sense of freedom; therefore, they develop a sense of responsibility for and ownership of their activities (Rappoport, Swift, & Hess, 1984; Rose & Black, 1985; Staples, 1990; Zimmerman, 1990). They see themselves as proactive self-starters. They are able to take initiative on their own accord, make independent decisions, and try out new ideas (Conger & Kanungo, 1988; Thomas & Valthouse, 1990; Vogt & Murrell, 1990). Rather than feeling that their actions are predetermined, externally controlled, or inevitable, they experience themselves as the locus of control. In any task or situation, a sense self-determination can be engendered and enhanced, so people do not have to have high internal locus of control scores to feel a sense of empowerment.

Research shows that a strong sense of self-determination is associated with less alienation in the work environment (Maddux, 2002), more work satisfaction (Organ & Green, 1974), higher levels of work performance (Anderson, Hellreigel, & Slocum, 1977), more entrepreneurial and innovative activity (Hammer & Vardi, 1981), high levels of job involvement (Runyon, 1973), and less job strain (Gemmill & Heisler, 1972). In medical research, recovery from severe illness has been found to be associated with having the patient "reject the traditional passive role and insist on being an active participant in his own therapy" (Gecas, 1989, p. 298). People who are helped to feel that they can have personal impact on what happens to them, even with regard to the effects of disease, are more likely to experience positive outcomes than those who lack this feeling.

Self-determination is associated most directly with having choices about the *methods* used to accomplish a task, the amount of *effort* to be expended, the *pace* of the work, and the *time frame* in which it is to be accomplished. Empowered individuals have a feeling of ownership for tasks because they can determine how they are accomplished, when they are accomplished, and how quickly they are completed. Having a choice is the critical component of self-determination. Later we will offer specific suggestions for fostering self-determination.

PERSONAL CONSEQUENCE

Empowered people have a sense that when they act, they can produce a result. Think of an assembly line job where a worker screws a nut on a bolt, but if he makes an error, someone down the line will correct it. Such a person will have little sense that he can have any effect on the outcome of the product or that his efforts have an effect on the end product. He will feel little personal control over the outcome. On the other hand, people with a sense of personal consequence believe that expending effort produce a result. Personal consequence is "an individual's beliefs at a given point in time in his or her ability to effect a change in a desired direction" (Greenberger, Stasser, Cummings, & Dunham, 1989, p. 165). It is the conviction that through one's own actions, a person can influence what happens. A sense of personal consequence, then, refers to a perception of *impact*.

Empowered individuals do not believe that obstacles in the external environment control their actions; rather, they believe that those obstacles can be controlled. They have a feeling of *active control*—which allows them to bring their environment into alignment with their wishes—as opposed to *passive control*—in which their wishes are brought into alignment with environmental demands (see Greenberger & Stasser, 1991; Rappoport et al., 1984; Rothbaum, Weisz, & Snyder, 1982; Thomas & Velthouse, 1990; Zimmerman & Rappoport, 1988). Instead of being reactive to what they see around them, people with a sense of personal consequence try to maintain command over what they see. For individuals to feel empowered, they must not only feel that what they do produces an effect, but that they can produce the effect themselves. That is, they must feel that they are in control of producing the consequence in order for that consequence to be associated with a sense of empowerment.

Having a sense of personal consequence is related to internal locus of control discussed in the chapter on self-awareness. (You completed that instrument earlier in the book.) Unlike internal locus of control, however, a sense of personal consequence can be developed in association with a particular task. Managers can help other people develop this sense of having control over their work outcomes. Internal locus of control is a more fundamental and difficult-to-change personality attribute. This is, most people have developed an orientation toward internal or external locus of control, which characterizes their general approach to life. In helping people succeed in specific tasks, however, those who successfully empower others help them develop a sense that they can produce a desired result. Some ideas for how to foster a sense of consequence are discussed later.

Research on personal control suggests that people are intrinsically motivated to seek personal control (White, 1959). They fight to maintain a sense of control of themselves and their situations. Prisoners of war, for example, have been known to do strange things such as refusing to eat certain foods, not walking in a certain place, or developing secret communication codes, in order to maintain a sense of personal control. A certain amount of personal control is necessary for people to maintain psychological and physical well-being. When people lose personal control, we usually label them as insane and psychopathic.

Even small losses of personal control can be harmful physically and emotionally. For example, loss of control has been found to lead to depression, stress, anxiety, low morale, loss of productivity, burnout, learned helplessness, and even increased death rates (see Greenberger & Stasser, 1991; Langer, 1983). Having a sense of personal control, then, appears necessary for health as well as for empowerment. On the other hand, even the most empowered people are not able to control totally everything that happens to them. No one is in complete control of the outcomes in his or her life. Nevertheless, empowerment helps people increase the number of personal outcomes that they can control. Often, this is as much a matter of identifying areas in which personal consequence is possible as it is of manipulating or changing the external environment to increase control over it.

MEANING

Empowered people have a sense of meaning. They value the purpose or goals of the activity in which they are engaged. Their own ideals and standards are perceived as consistent with what they are doing. The activity "counts" in their own value system. Not only do they feel that they can produce a result, but empowered individuals believe in and care about what they produce. They invest psychic or spiritual energy in the activity, and they feel a sense of personal significance from their involvement. They experience personal connectedness and personal integrity as a result of engaging in the activity (Bennis & Nanus, 1985; Block, 1987; Conger & Kanungo, 1988; Manz & Sims, 1989). Meaningfulness, then, refers to a perception of *value*.

Activities infused with meaning create a sense of purpose, passion, or mission for people. They provide a source of energy and enthusiasm, rather than draining energy and enthusiasm from people. Merely getting paid, helping an organization earn money, or just doing a job does not create a sense of meaning for most people. Something more fundamental, more personal, and more value-laden must be linked to the activity. It must be associated with something more human. Almost all people want to feel that they are spending their time on something that will produce lasting benefit, that will make the world a better place, or that is associated with a personal value.

Acquiring personal benefit from an activity does not guarantee meaning. For example, service to others may bring no personal reward, yet it may be far more meaningful than work that produces a hefty paycheck. Involvement in activities without meaning, on the other hand, creates dissonance and annoyance, and produces a sense of disengagement from the work. People become bored or exhausted. Other incentives—such as rules, supervision, or extra pay—are required to get people to invest in the work. Unfortunately, these extra incentives are costly to organizations and represent non-value-added expenses that constrain organizational efficiency and effectiveness. It costs companies a lot of money to require work that has little or no meaning to workers. Self-estrangement results from lack of meaning; vigor and stimulation result from meaningful work (see Brief & Nord, 1990; Hackman & Oldham, 1980; Kahn, 1990; Thomas & Velthouse, 1990).

Research on meaningfulness in work has found that when individuals engage in work that they feel is meaningful, they are more committed to it and more involved in it. They have a higher concentration of energy and are more persistent in pursuing desired goals than when a sense of meaningfulness is low. People feel more excitement and passion for their work and have a greater sense of personal significance and self-worth because of their association with activity that is meaningful. Individuals empowered with a sense of meaningfulness also have been found to be more innovative, upwardly influential, and personally effective than those with low meaningfulness scores (Bramucci, 1977; Deci & Ryan, 1987; Pratt & Ashforth, 2003; Spreitzer, 1992; Vogt & Murrell, 1990; Wrzesniewski, 2003).

TRUST

Finally, empowered people have a sense of trust. They are confident that they will be treated fairly and equitably. They maintain an assurance that even if they are in subordinate positions, the ultimate outcome of their actions will be justice and goodness as opposed to harm or damage. Usually, this means they have confidence that those holding authority or power positions will not harm or injure them, and that they will be treated impartially. However, even in circumstances in which individuals holding power positions do not demonstrate integrity and fairness, empowered people still maintain a sense of assurance. Trust means, in other words, having a sense of *personal security*. Trust also implies that individuals place themselves in a position of vulnerability (Zand, 1972), and have faith that, ultimately, no harm will come to them as a result of that trust (Barber, 1983; Deutsch, 1973; Luhmann, 1979; Mishra, 1992).

How can a person maintain trust and a sense of security even when caught in a circumstance that seems unfair, inequitable, or even dangerous? In his attempts to gain independence for India, for example, Gandhi determined that he would burn the passes that the British government required be carried by all native Indians but not by British citizens. Gandhi called a meeting and publicly announced his intent to resist this law by burning the passes of each of his Indian supporters. In a now-famous incident, after Gandhi burned several of the passes, the British police intervened by clubbing him with nightsticks. Despite the beating, Gandhi continued to burn passes. Where is the trust or sense of security in this case? How can Gandhi be empowered in the process of being beaten by the police? In what did Gandhi have trust? Was Gandhi empowered or not? Gandhi's sense of security came not from the British authorities but from his faith in the principles that he espoused. His sense of security was associated with his belief that doing the right thing always leads, ultimately, to the right consequence.

Research on trust has found that trusting individuals are more apt to replace superficiality and facades with directness and intimacy; they are more apt to be open, honest, and congruent rather than deceptive or shallow. They are more search-oriented and self-determining, more self-assured and willing to learn. They have a larger capacity for interdependent relationships, and they display a greater degree of cooperation and risk-taking in groups than do those with low trust. Trusting people are more willing to try to get along with others and to be a contributing part of a team. They are also more self-disclosing, more honest in their own communication, and more able to listen carefully to others. They have less resistance to change and are better able to cope with unexpected traumas than are those with low levels of trust. Individuals who trust others are more likely to be trustworthy themselves and to maintain high personal ethical standards (see Gibb & Gibb, 1969; Golembiewski & McConkie, 1975; Mishra, 1992).

Because "trusting environments allow individuals to unfold and flourish" (Golembiewski & McConkie, 1975, p. 134), empowerment is closely tied to a sense of trust. Having a feeling that the behavior of others is consistent and reliable, that information can be held in confidence, and that promises will be kept all are a part of developing a sense of empowerment in people. Trusting others allows people to act in a confident and straightforward manner, without wasting energy on self-protection, trying to uncover hidden agendas, or playing politics. In brief, a sense of trust empowers people to feel secure.

REVIEW OF EMPOWERMENT DIMENSIONS

The main point of our discussion thus far is to make the point that fostering the five attributes of empowerment in individuals—*self-efficacy* (a sense of competence), *self-determination* (a sense of choice), *personal consequence* (a sense of impact), *meaning* (a sense of value), and *trust* (a sense of security)—produces very positive outcomes. Research findings associated with each of the five dimensions of empowerment indicate that both personal and organizational advantages result when people feel empowered. Negative consequences occur, on the other hand, when people experience the opposite of empowerment, such as powerlessness, helplessness, and alienation. Helping people feel a certain way about themselves and their work helps them to be more effective in the behaviors they display.

Some authors have gone so far as to claim that helping others develop this feeling of empowerment is at the very root of managerial effectiveness. Without it, they claim, neither managers nor organizations can be successful in the long term (Bennis & Nanus, 1985; Block, 1987; Conger, 1989; Kanter, 1983; Quinn & Spreitzer, 1997). As a psychological state, however, empowerment is never under the complete control of a manager. Individuals can refuse to feel empowered. In fact, some cynical students (but few practicing managers) have stated that empowering people is naïve since many people will not accept empowerment and will try to get along as a "free rider." Many people, they say, are not inclined to want empowerment.

This Theory X-like assumption is neither consistent with our own experience with thousands of practicing managers nor with the empirical research. People who don't want to get involved or who reject opportunities for empowerment—free-riders—exist in teams or classes, for example, when they do not value the outcome that has been assigned (absence of a sense of value), they believe that someone else will produce the result without their input (absence of a sense of personal consequence), or they don't believe that they have anything to contribute (absence of self-efficacy). When the five dimensions of empowerment are present, on the other hand, almost all people will become actively engaged. Research by Hackman and Oldham (1980) found that more than 80 percent of workers have high "growth need strength," or a desire to grow and contribute in their jobs. Providing opportunities for empowerment to people helps respond to this inherent need for growth and contribution.

A sense of empowerment can be influenced significantly by the conditions in which people find themselves. For that reason, the next section of this chapter discusses specific actions managers can take to facilitate empowerment in others.

How to Develop Empowerment

People are most in need of empowerment when they are faced with situations they perceive to be threatening, unclear, overly controlled, coercive, or isolating; when they experience inappropriate feelings of dependency or inadequacy; when they feel stifled in their ability to do what they would like to do; when they are uncertain about how to behave; when they feel that some negative consequence is imminent; and when they feel unrewarded and unappreciated.

Ironically, most large organizations engender these kinds of feelings in people, because, as Block (1987) noted, bureaucracy encourages dependency and submission. Rules, routines, and traditions define what can be done, stifling and supplanting initiative and discretion. In such circumstances, the formal organization—not the individual—is the recipient of empowerment. Therefore, in large organizations, empowerment is especially needed.

But empowerment is also key in environments outside of vast bureaucracies. For example, studies demonstrate positive effects of empowerment on child development, learning in school, coping with personal stress, and changing personal habits (see Ozer & Bandura, 1990).

Despite the applicability of empowerment in many different contexts including school and family life, our discussion considers ways in which managers can empower those with whom they work. We focus on empowerment mainly as a management skill, even though people in other roles, such as parents, teachers, coaches, tutors, and friends, can also benefit by developing the skills of empowerment.

Research by Kanter (1983), Hackman and Oldham (1980), Bandura (1986), Quinn and Spreitzer (1997), Wrzesniewski (2003), and others has produced at least nine specific prescriptions for fostering empowerment; that is, producing a sense of competence, choice, impact, value, and security. These include: (1) articulating a clear vision and goals, (2) fostering personal mastery experiences, (3) modeling, (4) providing support, (5) creating emotional arousal, (6) providing necessary information, (7) providing necessary resources, (8) connecting to outcomes, and (9) creating confidence. Each of these prescriptions is discussed below. Figure 8.1 illustrates their relationships to the five core dimensions of empowerment.

Some of these prescriptions are similar to the guidelines found in the chapters on Building Relationships by Communicating Supportively, Gaining Power and Influence, and Motivating Others. Because a completely separate and unique set of managerial skills does not exist for communicating with, influencing, and motivating others, some commonality and overlap is inevitable. On the other hand, the context of empowerment sheds a different light on some of the guidelines you have read about before.

ARTICULATING A CLEAR VISION AND GOALS

Creating an environment in which individuals can feel empowered requires that they be guided by a clearly articulated vision of where the organization is going and how they can contribute as individuals. All of us desire to know the purpose of the activities in which we engage, what the ultimate objective is, and how we fit into that objective. The worst circumstance we can experience is one with a total lack of direction, where people do whatever comes to mind, or where no common objective or goal is evident. This is the classical condition—labeled *anomie*—that leads to anarchy, chaos, and even death (Durkheim, 1963). To avoid such chaotic conditions, a clear vision and an established set of goals must be articulated so that behavior remains congruent with organizational purposes.

Cameron and Quinn (2006); Martin, Feldman, Hatch, and Sitkin (1983); and others have reported that several studies confirm that the most effective way to articulate a vision in a clear and energizing way is by using word pictures, stories, metaphors, and real-life examples. That is, individuals are more likely to

Figure 8.1 **Relationships Between Dimensions and Prescriptions for Empowerment**

Self-Efficacy (competence)
Self-Determination (choice)
Personal consequence (impact)
Meaningfulness (value)
Trust (security)

Vision and values
Personal mastery experiences
Model
Provide support
Emotional arousal
Provide information
Provide resources
Connect to outcomes
Create confidence

understand a vision if it has both right brain (intuitive, pictorial, story-based) as well as left brain (logical, reasonable, performance-based) elements associated with it. Not only do people understand communication more clearly when it contains stories and examples as well as descriptions, but they develop more of a sense of self-determination ("I can see the alternatives available"), a sense of personal consequence ("I can see how I can influence the outcomes"), and a sense of meaning ("I can see why this is so important").

Empowerment is also enhanced as specific behavioral goals are identified that help guide individuals' behavior as they work on their tasks. Goals specify desired outcomes as well as accountability. Locke and Latham (1990) identified the attributes of the most effective goals, and the acronym **SMART goals** best summarizes these attributes.

❏ *Specific goals*—those that are identifiable, behavioral, and observable.
❏ *Measurable goals*—those that have outcome criteria associated with them, that can be assessed objectively, and where the degree of successful accomplishment can be determined. One can evaluate the accomplishment of measurable goals.
❏ *Aligned goals*—those that are congruent with the overall purposes and vision of the organization. Their accomplishment contributes to the broader good.
❏ *Realistic goals*—realistic goals, those that are not so far above the capacity of the individual that they become discouraging at best and considered nonsense at worst. Realistic does not mean easily achieved, because research is clear that difficult goals—stretch goals—are better motivators of behavior and predict higher levels of accomplishment than do easy goals (Locke & Latham, 1990).
❏ *Time-bound goals*—that is, a time for accomplishing the goals is specified. Goals that have no ending point are not effective; a deadline for achievement is clear.

The point is: individuals are empowered as they are provided a clear vision of the future and some specific, behavioral goals that help clarify how they can get there.

FOSTERING PERSONAL MASTERY EXPERIENCES

Bandura (1986) found that the single most important thing a manager can do to empower other people is to help them experience personal mastery over some challenge or problem. By successfully accomplishing a task, defeating an opponent, or resolving a problem, people develop a sense of mastery. Personal mastery can be fostered by providing people with the opportunity to accomplish successively more difficult tasks that eventually lead to the accomplishment of desirable goals. The key is to start with easy tasks and then progress by small steps to more difficult tasks until the person experiences a sense of mastery over an entire complex of problems.

Managers can help others feel increasingly empowered by helping them develop an awareness that they can succeed. One way to do this is by breaking apart large tasks and giving workers only one part at a time. The manager watches for small successes achieved by workers and then highlights and celebrates them. Jobs can be expanded incrementally so that tasks become broader and more complex as workers master the basic elements. Other people are given further problem-solving responsibility as they succeed in resolving rudimentary difficulties. Managers can also provide opportunities for people to direct or lead others in a project, task force, or committee.

When managers adopt a **small-wins strategy**, individuals get opportunities to succeed in small ways, even though an overall challenge may be formidable (Weick, 1984). Small wins can occur when large problems are divided up into limited units that can be attacked individually. Small wins may seem insignificant by themselves, but they generate a sense of movement, progress, and success. The recognition and celebration of small wins generates momentum that leads people to feel empowered and capable.

Lee Iacocca used this strategy to turn around a failing Chrysler Corporation in the early 1980s. An analysis of his speeches to the top management team at Chrysler over a period of five years reveals that even though Chrysler was losing money, costs were too high, and quality was a major problem, Iacocca continued to celebrate small successes. (A transcript of these speeches is contained in the Skill Analysis section of the chapter on Leading Positive Change.) For example, he regularly announced that a certain amount of money was saved, a particular improvement was produced, a certain executive was hired away from the competition, or a compliment was received from a Wall Street analyst, even though the firm was losing a billion dollars a year. A great deal of emphasis was placed on succeeding at small things, all of which were aimed at eventually toppling the much larger challenge of company survival. In this case, continual small wins led to a big achievement.

MODELING

Another way to empower people is to model or demonstrate the correct behavior that they are to perform. Observing someone else succeed at challenging activities, Bandura (1977) found, provides a forceful impetus for others to believe that they, too, can succeed. It helps people presume that a task is do-able, that a job is within their capabilities, and that success is possible.

The manager may serve as the role model by demonstrating desired behaviors. On the other hand, it may not be possible for a manager to model desired behaviors personally for every single person with whom he or she interacts. The manager may not see an employee often enough to show him or her how to accomplish work or to frequently demonstrate success. Alternatively, however, managers may be able to draw peoples' attention to other individuals who have been successful in similar circumstances. They might make it possible for people to associate with senior or visible role models who could serve as examples, and they could provide opportunities for workers to be coached by these successful people. They can partner their people with mentors who can discuss their own past experiences that were similar to those of the person being mentored.

In other words, empowering people involves making available examples of past success. This is consistent with the learning model upon which this book is based. The Skill Analysis step of the learning model exemplifies appropriate and inappropriate behavior engaged in by others. It provides a model of people who have succeeded in accomplishing the desired skill. This modeling function helps foster a sense of empowerment in individuals who are trying to develop and improve management skills by showing ways in which such skills can be showcased successfully.

Think of what happens when a barrier is broken. In track and field athletics, for example, once John Thomas broke the seven-foot high jump mark and Roger Bannister broke the four-minute mile record, a host of other athletes quickly exceeded that standard. But before the first person broke those barriers, they were considered insurmountable. It took someone to demonstrate that the standard could be exceeded in order for others to experience the empowerment necessary to replicate the accomplishment themselves.

PROVIDING SUPPORT

A fourth technique for helping others experience empowerment is providing them with social and emotional support. If people are to feel empowered, managers should praise them, encourage them, express approval of them, back them, and reassure them. Kanter (1983) and Bandura (1986) each found that a crucial part of empowerment is having responsive and supportive managers. Managers seeking to empower others should find ways to praise their performance regularly. They can write letters or notes to workers, to members of their unit, or even to their family indicating that the person's good work has been noticed. They can provide feedback to people about their abilities and competencies. They can arrange for opportunities for individuals to receive social support from others by becoming part of a team or social unit. They can express confidence in people by monitoring them less closely or by allowing longer time intervals to elapse before requiring them to report results. Managers can hold regular ceremonies where individuals' achievements are recognized. It may simply be a matter of listening to people and trying to understand their feelings and points of view.

Managers can empower others, then, by engendering a feeling that they are accepted, that they are a valued asset, and that they are an integral part of the overall organizational mission or objective. This support can come from either the manager or colleagues.

Cameron, Freeman, and Mishra (1991), for example, described a variety of support activities undertaken by a highly effective manager who was forced to lay off workers due to a corporate downsizing mandate. Understandably, the layoffs resulted in undermined employee trust, increased skepticism, and an escalated sense of powerlessness. Because the announcement came down from the parent company, workers felt that they had lost the ability to control their own destinies. In short, they felt unempowered. Following the layoff, the manager held personal meetings with each remaining employee to reaffirm his or her value to the organization. People were told in a straightforward manner that they were considered valuable human resources, not human liabilities, to the company. A special "Build with Pride" week was held in which outsiders—the press, government officials, family members, school classes—were invited to tour the facility and provide feedback (which, by the way, consistently took the form of praise) to the employees for the products and services they were producing. An impromptu hot dog roast was held one lunch hour to recognize and celebrate the extra-mile efforts of one group of employees in the facility. People were assured that counseling, training, and assistance would be provided when job assignments changed or positions were merged as a result of the downsizing. In general, this notable manager attempted to re-empower his workforce by providing social and emotional support in a variety of ways. He helped provide the assistance people needed to cope with the uncertainty resulting from this uncontrollable event. Predictably, both organizational and individual performance results did not deteriorate after downsizing. Instead, contrary to what happens in most organizations that downsize, performance actually improved.

EMOTIONAL AROUSAL

Emotional arousal means replacing negative emotions such as fear, anxiety, or crabbiness with positive emotions such as excitement, passion, or anticipation. To empower people, managers help make the work environment fun and attractive. They ensure that the purpose behind the work is clear. They ensure that people's right brain (the side that controls emotions and passions) is involved in the work as well as their left brain (the side that controls logic and analysis). They provide positive energy to people. Bandura (1977) found that the absence of positive emotional arousal makes it difficult, if not impossible, for individuals to feel empowered. Baker, Cross, and Wooten (2003), on the other hand, found that positively energizing people enhances performance markedly and is even more important than providing people with powerful positions or special information in their work. Positive energy is easy to detect in people. When we interact with some people they seem to give us life and vigor. Other people seem to be life-depleting or negatively energizing. Emotional arousal is associated with being a positive energy source for people.

The visible celebrations of employee accomplishments and motivational events in marketing firms such as Mary Kay Cosmetics, Shaklee Products, and Amway are well known. However, emotional arousal doesn't simply mean tooting horns, increasing the decibel levels, listening to speeches, or superficially creating excitement. Instead, emotional arousal occurs more likely when what individuals are doing is connected to values they hold dear. To feel a sense of empowerment, workers must see how what they are doing every day is associated with their basic beliefs. Employees can get more excited, for example, about working for the betterment of humankind, for the improvement of the quality of people's lives, and for personal growth and development, than they can for a 10 percent return to institutional investors. This is not to say that revenue for stockholders is unimportant. But emotional arousal is associated more with personal values than with organizational profitability.

Managers can also increase workers' sense of empowerment by holding periodic social gatherings to foster friendships among coworkers. In their official communications, they can occasionally include a joke or lighthearted message to relieve tension. They can use superlatives in providing feedback or describing successes (e.g., say "terrific" instead of "good"; "awesome" instead of "acceptable"). They can make sure that employees are clear about how their work will affect the company's customers. They can help identify external threats or challenges that need to be met.

Successful emotional arousal is often associated with athletic teams. Chuck Coonradt (1985) observed that "people are willing to pay for the privilege of working harder than they will work when they are paid." That is, individuals will actually pay money in order to work at a more demanding level than the level at which they work when they are receiving a salary. Here is one example.

In the frozen food business, people are hired to work in refrigerated warehouses in terrible working conditions at near-zero temperatures. But the unions and OSHA have done much to make conditions bearable. Companies are required to provide insulated clothing and boots. They are required to provide hot drinks within so many feet of cold work areas. Workers must have a ten-minute break every hour. It's tough to get people to work in those kinds of conditions. Yet, whenever a winter snowstorm passes over . . . the mountains, followed by clearing skies and plunging temperatures, there is a sudden jump in employee absenteeism, particularly among young workers. Instead of staying home to avoid the freezing temperatures, they migrate up the local canyons to test the new and famous powder snow. . . . Equipped with hundreds of dollars of equipment, they gladly take a reduction in pay for the day off and a chance to buy a $40 pass to spend the day outside in subfreezing temperatures. There are no hot-drink vending machines on the slopes, nor does anyone demand a ten-minute break every hour. (Coonradt, 1985, p. 1)

Thus, people actually end up working harder, in worse conditions—and paying for the privilege—than when they are at work getting paid. Why is this so? Why does recreation produce such energy, such commitment, and such sense of empowerment?

LEARNING

Part of the explanation relates to the emotional arousal that results from several characteristics of sports. For example, all recreation has a clear *goal* (e.g., winning, exceeding a personal best). Without a clearly defined goal, no one gets excited. That goal is always pitted against a standard that people care about (e.g., winning the NCAA championship, bowling a 300 game). In recreation, the *scorekeeping* and *feedback* systems are objective, self-administered, and continuous. In a basketball game, for example, everyone knows that a free throw always counts one point, that the winner is the team that makes the most baskets, and that there is never a time when everyone can't find out the exact score of the game. One reason why people get so excited watching athletic events is because of the scorekeeping and feedback systems. In recreation, the *out-of-bounds* is clearly identified. Everyone knows the consequence of kicking a soccer ball over the end line, of hitting a ball to the left side of third base, or of stepping over the end of the takeoff board in the long jump. They are all out-of-bounds, and everyone knows that out-of-bounds behavior stops action.

Managers can help empower people through emotional arousal, not just by being a cheerleader, delivering charismatic speeches, and keeping the work climate fun, but also by capitalizing on some of the principles of recreation that create excitement: clear goals; objective, self-administered, and continuous scorekeeping and feedback; and clearly defined out-of-bounds behavior.

PROVIDING INFORMATION

Kanter (1983) identified information as one of the most crucial managerial "power tools." Acquiring information, particularly information that is viewed as central or strategic in an organization, can be used to build a power base and to make oneself indispensable and influential in that organization. On the other hand, when managers provide their people with more, rather than less information, those people gain a sense of empowerment and are more likely to work productively, successfully, and in harmony with the manager's wishes. The manager actually enhances his or her power base by involving others in the pursuit of desirable outcomes. With more information, people tend to experience more self-determination, personal control, and trust. The resulting sense of empowerment enhances the probability that they will not resist the manager, defend against his or her power, or work at protecting themselves. Rather, they are likely to collaborate with the empowering manager.

Therefore, a manager who wishes to increase an employee's sense of empowerment will make sure that the employee is given all task-relevant information needed to carry out an assignment. The empowering manager will make available, on an ongoing basis, pertinent technical information and data collected by others.

Such a manager keeps workers informed about what is happening in other areas of the organization that might affect what the worker is doing. Managers will keep employees informed of policy-making meetings and senior-level discussions related to their area of responsibility. Workers can be given access to sources closest to the information they need: for example, senior level people in the organization, customers, or the market research staff. Historical or "context" information can be shared in order to give the worker as broad a background as possible. Managers should make certain that employees have information about the effects of their own behavior on others and on the organization's goals.

To be sure, it is possible to overload people with information and to create anxiety and burnout with too much data. But our experience has been that most people suffer from too little information instead of too much. Furthermore, if the information is relevant in this context, overload is less likely to occur. Spreitzer (1992) found, for example, that people who received relevant information about costs, customers, and strategy felt significantly more empowered than those who did not. Block (1987) argued:

> Sharing as much information as possible is the opposite of the military notion that only those who "need to know" should be informed. Our goal is to let people know our plans, ideas, and changes as soon as possible. . . . If we are trying to create the mindset that everyone is responsible for the success of this business, then our people need complete information. (p. 90)

Our own research further confirms the importance of providing information to enhance empowerment (Cameron, Freeman, & Mishra, 1993). In one study, for example, we interviewed CEOs of large, well-known companies every six months to assess organizational changes and strategies they were using to cope with declining revenues. In one firm, not much progress was being made in improving the financial outlook. The CEO was very careful to share information on financial, productivity, cost, and climate indicators in the company only with his senior management team. No one else in the firm had access to that information. A change of CEO, however, led to a dramatic change in information-sharing policy. The new CEO began to provide information to every single employee in the firm who desired it. No data were treated as the sole possession of senior management. The sweepers had the same access as the vice presidents. The resulting empowerment that employees experienced led to dramatic results. Employee-initiated improvements increased markedly, morale and commitment surged, and the resulting financial turnaround made the CEO look like a genius. He attributed his success to his willingness to empower employees by sharing the information they needed to know to improve.

PROVIDING RESOURCES

In addition to providing information, empowerment is also fostered by providing people with other kinds of resources that help them accomplish their tasks. In this sense, managers who empower others act more like blocking backs on a football team than quarterbacks. They are less directors and commanders than they are resource providers (creating time to throw a pass or make a handoff) and obstacle eliminators (blocking onrushing defensive linemen). One of the primary missions of empowering managers, then, is to help others accomplish their objectives.

Managers attempting to enhance other peoples' empowerment by providing them with needed resources will ensure that they receive adequate and ongoing training and development experiences. Sufficient technical and administrative support will be provided to ensure success. Managers will give their people space, time, or equipment that may not be readily available otherwise. They will ensure that these people have access to communication or interpersonal networks that will make their jobs easier. Individuals can also be given discretion to spend monies or commit resources to activities that they consider important.

It is unrealistic, of course, to assume that everyone can have everything he or she desires. Very few successful organizations have excess resources to be distributed at will. On the other hand, the most important resources that empowering managers can provide are those that help people achieve control over their own work and lives; that is, foster a sense of self-efficacy and self-determination. When individuals feel that they have what they need to be successful and that they have the freedom to pursue what they want to accomplish, performance is significantly higher than when these types of resources are not available (Spreitzer, 1992).One of the best examples of using resources to empower comes from Carl Sewell, one of the most successful car salesmen in the United States,

who described his approach to empowerment through providing resources:

> *Not many people get to see our service repair shop—our insurance company wants to keep traffic there to a minimum—but those who do always comment on its cleanliness. And, in fact, it's immaculate. Why? Because, while customers rarely see it, our technicians do. They live and work there every day. Where would you like to spend your day—in a place that's dirty or one that's spotless? But it's more than just aesthetics. If we make the technicians' work environment more professional, more pleasant, more efficient, if we provide them with the very best equipment and tools, we're going to be able to hire the best technicians. . . . All this gives them another reason for working for us instead of our competition. (Sewell, 1990, p. 53)*

One reason Carl Sewell has been so dramatically successful is that he provides each individual with everything necessary to accomplish desired goals. This is true whether Sewell is dealing with mechanics or top salespersons, and whether his company is selling Cadillacs and Lexuses or Hyundais and Geos. It is not only *need*-to-have resources that Sewell provides, but also some *nice*-to-have resources. The point is: "Resources lead to empowerment."

CONNECTING TO OUTCOMES

One of the important lessons learned by U.S. manufacturing companies as a result of the Japanese entrance into the North American automobile and consumer electronics industries is that workers experience more empowerment when they can see the outcomes of their work. It was often a surprise to U.S. companies, for example, that their Japanese counterparts regularly visited customers in their homes or place of business, regularly observed how the products that the workers produced were used, and regularly received feedback directly from end users. This connection to the ultimate customer helped workers feel more empowered as well as provided a valuable source of improvement ideas. The importance of connecting workers with customers was confirmed, as mentioned in the chapter on Motivating Others, by Hackman and Oldham's (1980) research on job design and job enrichment. These investigators found that people are motivated at work when they can interact with ultimate customers in order to see the effects of their work.

A related idea is to provide employees with the authority to resolve problems on the spot. Studies at IBM, Ford Motor Company, Carl Sewell's auto dealerships, and other companies indicated that allowing employees to address customer concerns at the time the complaint was registered positively affected both employee and customer. When employees were given discretion to resolve a problem, respond immediately to a customer's complaint, fix the error instantly, or commit a certain level of company resources in pursuing customer satisfaction, not only was customer satisfaction dramatically increased (an average improvement of 300 percent), but workers felt far more empowered as well. Employees were given the necessary authority to go along with their responsibility for customer satisfaction, and they were provided with an opportunity to affect outcomes directly.

Hackman, Oldham, Janson, and Purdy (1975) suggested that another of the highly effective ways to enhance employee motivation and satisfaction is to create **task identity**, that is, the opportunity to accomplish a whole task. Individuals become frustrated and lack a sense of empowerment when they work on only part of a task, never see the end result of their work, and are blocked from observing the impact that their job creates. One of us has a colleague who quit a very lucrative job in a prestigious Wall Street firm because he became frustrated with his inability to see the results of his work. He was regularly given assignments to accomplish the first few steps in a complicated job and then had to hand the work off to a senior executive who completed the work and received most of the recognition. Not only was this colleague denied deserved rewards, but more important to him, he was unable to feel that he had completed a whole job. Task identity and the resulting sense of empowerment were completely lacking.

Having task identity implies that individuals can plan, implement, and evaluate the success of their efforts. The effects of what is accomplished can be assessed as well as the outcome. To feel empowered, in other words, I want to know whether I successfully completed my assigned job as well as whether that job made any difference to the overall success of my work unit. The more clear that connection is, the more I will feel empowered.

In sum, clarifying the connections between individuals' work and their outcomes and effects fosters empowerment by helping others develop a sense of self-efficacy (they feel more capable and competent) and a sense of personal consequence (a sense of having personal impact).

CREATING CONFIDENCE

One additional technique to be mentioned here—among many others—for engendering empowerment is to create a sense of confidence among workers in the trustworthiness of the manager. Rather than being on guard and suspicious, workers are secure in their feeling that the manager and the organization are honorable. This confidence helps drive out uncertainty, insecurity, and ambiguity in the relationships between employees and the manager.

There are at least two reasons why individuals feel more empowered as they develop greater confidence in their manager. First, the wasteful, unproductive behaviors associated with mistrust and suspicion are avoided. When people distrust one another, they don't listen, they don't communicate clearly, they don't try hard, and they don't collaborate. On the other hand, when trust exists, individuals are free to experiment, to learn, and to contribute without fear of retribution. Second, individuals who are admirable and honorable always create positive energy for others and make them feel more capable. Not without reason do universities trumpet the number of Nobel Prize winners on their faculties, the past Heisman trophy winners on their football teams, the number of outstanding faculty members in their business schools, and the notable achievements of their best students. Although other members of the university may have nothing to do with the achievements being publicized, they gain an enhanced self-image and a sense of empowerment because they are affiliated with the same organization. For the same reasons, creating confidence in a manager helps employees develop a sense of empowerment.

In creating such a sense of confidence and trustworthiness, five factors are especially important: (1) *reliability*, (2) *fairness*, (3) *caring*, (4) *openness*, and (5) *competence*. Managers create confidence, and thereby engender empowerment in others, as they display these five characteristics which are associated with being honorable.

❏ *Reliability.* Managers who wish their people to develop confidence in them need to exhibit reliability. The managers' behavior must be consistent, dependable, and stable. Their actions are congruent with their words and attitudes.

❏ *Fairness.* Good managers also need to be fair and must not take wrongful advantage of anyone. They are equitable in their actions. Workers are clear about the criteria used by the manager in making judgments as well as how the manager applies those criteria. Managers must make clear the standards by which workers will be judged and ensure that those standards are applied in an unbiased way.

❑ *Caring.* Managers must show a sense of personal concern for others and help each one feel important to the manager. Managers validate the points of view of other people and avoid denigrating them as individuals. When correction is needed, caring managers focus on the mistake or the behavior, not on the individual's personal characteristics.

❑ *Openness.* Confidence-building managers are open in their relationships. No harmful secrets exist, and relevant information is shared openly and honestly with employees. This does not suggest that a manager cannot keep confidences. But it does mean that other people should not have to worry about hidden agendas that could negatively affect them because their manager is straightforward and honest.

❑ *Competence.* People should be made aware of the manager's competence. They need to be assured that the manager has the necessary ability, experience, and knowledge to perform tasks and to solve problems. Without flaunting their expertise, skillful managers inspire a feeling on the part of employees that their confidence in the expertise and proficiency of their leader is not misplaced.

The power of creating confidence in others is illustrated by several CEOs who were interviewed regarding their keys to successful organizational change. Each CEO had managed a downsizing or redesign of his organization and was attempting to maintain a healthy, productive workforce in the midst of turmoil. The key role of trust and confidence in management is hard to miss (see Cameron et al., 1993; Mishra, 1992).

If they don't believe what I'm telling them, if they think it's all a bunch of bull, don't expect them to go out there and work a little harder. They won't work a little different. They're not going to be receptive to change unless they understand and trust the things that we're talking about are true. I think trust is the biggest single issue.

I had a boss one time who said, "What you do speaks so much louder than what you say." I've always stuck that in the back of my mind. I believe that. The people watch very

closely what you do. And, boy, you cannot underestimate that.

What's most important in my organization is this: being truthful. Don't b.s. anyone. Tell them what it is. Right or wrong or different. Tell them the truth.

My people are all 150 percent dedicated to helping one another. Because no one of them can do it alone, they need each other badly. But here comes the openness and trust. You have to talk about those things. I don't think you can go in and accomplish things without talking about what the barriers are going to be in trying to make a change or set a new direction.

Successful managers create confidence in themselves among their colleagues. They are authentic, honorable, and trustworthy.

REVIEW OF EMPOWERMENT PRINCIPLES

Table 8.5 summarizes the list of actions that we have discussed on the previous pages in relation to the nine prescriptions for empowerment. It provides a list of things managers can do to empower other people. Not all of these suggestions are relevant in every circumstance or with every person, of course, but developing the skill of empowerment at least partly depends on knowing what alternatives are available to empower people, as well as knowing how to implement them. This list is not comprehensive; other activities may be equally effective in empowering people. But the nine prescriptions and the suggestions associated with each of them represent actions that you will want to practice as you try to improve your competence in the skill of empowerment. The Skill Practice section of this chapter provides an opportunity for you to do this.

Research suggests that empowered individuals are most inclined to empower others. For that reason, we included an Assessment instrument at the beginning of this chapter that measures the extent to which you experience empowerment in your own work. Your scores on the instrument entitled Personal Empowerment Assessment indicate how much your own work is empowering for you in terms of self-efficacy, self-determination, personal control, meaning, and trust. Knowing what provides a sense of empowerment for you can be helpful as you consider ways in which you, in turn, can empower others. The other instrument that you completed in the Skill Assessment section

Table 8.5	Practical Suggestions for Empowering Others

Articulate a Clear Vision and Goals

- Create a picture of a desired future.
- Use word pictures and emotional language to describe the vision.
- Identify specific actions and strategies that will lead to the vision.
- Establish SMART goals.
- Associate the vision and goals with personal values.

Foster Personal Mastery Experiences

- Break apart large tasks and assign one part at a time.
- Assign simple tasks before difficult tasks.
- Highlight and celebrate small wins.
- Incrementally expand job responsibilities.
- Give increasingly more responsibility to solve problems.

Model Successful Behaviors

- Demonstrate successful task accomplishment.
- Point out other people who have succeeded.
- Facilitate interaction with other role models.
- Find a coach.
- Establish a mentor relationship.

Provide Support

- Praise, encourage, express approval for, and reassure.
- Send letters or notes of praise to family members or coworkers.
- Regular provide feedback.
- Foster informal social activities to build cohesion.
- Supervise less closely and provide time-slack.
- Hold recognition ceremonies.

Arouse Positive Emotions

- Foster activities to encourage friendship formation.
- Periodically send light-hearted messages.
- Use superlatives in giving feedback.
- Highlight compatibility between important personal values and organizational goals.
- Clarify impact on the ultimate customer.
- Foster attributes of recreation in work: clear goals, effective scorekeeping and feedback systems, and out-of-bounds behavior.

Provide Information

- Provide all task-relevant information.
- Continuously provide technical information and objective data.
- Pass along relevant cross-unit and cross-functional information.
- Provide access to information or people with senior responsibility.

Table 8.5   Practical Suggestions for Empowering Others

- Provide access to information from its source.
- Clarify effects of actions on customers.

Provide Resources

- Provide training and development experiences.
- Provide technical and administrative support.
- Provide needed time, space, or equipment.
- Ensure access to relevant information networks.
- Provide more discretion to commit resources.

Connect to Outcomes

- Provide a chance to interact directly with those receiving the service or output.
- Provide authority to resolve problems on the spot.
- Provide immediate, unfiltered, direct feedback on results.
- Create task identity, or the opportunity to accomplish a complete task.
- Clarify and measure effects as well as direct outcomes.

Create Confidence

- Exhibit reliability and consistency.
- Exhibit fairness and equity.
- Exhibit caring and personal concern.
- Exhibit openness and honesty.
- Exhibit competence and expertise.

(Effective Empowerment and Delegation) identifies the extent to which you behave in ways that empower people with whom you work and the extent to which you delegate work effectively. How much you actually engage in the behaviors discussed above is assessed, as well as the extent to which you are an effective delegator.

Inhibitors to Empowerment

If the data are clear that empowering people produces superior results, and if techniques for enhancing empowerment are clear, why then is empowerment is organizations so rare? Why do a majority of people feel that they are alienated from their work, unengaged, and not flourishing (Cameron, Dutton, & Quinn, 2003). In his book on managerial empowerment, Peter Block (1987) noted that empowerment is very difficult to accomplish:

> *Many, increasingly aware of the price we pay for too many controls, have had the belief that if*

some of these controls were removed, a tremendous amount of positive energy in service of the organization would be released. While in many cases this has happened, too often our attempts at giving people more responsibility have been unwelcome and met with persistent reluctance. Many managers have tried repeatedly to open the door of participation to their people, only to find them reluctant to walk through it. [In a study of managers who were offered total responsibility for their work areas], about 20 percent of the managers took the responsibility and ran with it, about 50 percent of the managers cautiously tested the sincerity of the offer and then over a period of six months began to make their own decisions. The frustrating part of the effort was that the other 30 percent absolutely refused to take the reins. They clutched tightly to their dependency and continued to complain that top management did not really mean it, they were not given enough people or resources

to really do their job, and the unique character-
istics of their particular location made efforts
at participative management unreasonable.
(p. 154)

As Block noted, many managers and employees are reluctant to accept empowerment, but they are even more reluctant to offer empowerment. One reason for this is the personal attitudes of managers. Several management surveys, for example, have examined the reasons managers have for not being willing to empower their employees (Byham, 1988; Newman & Warren, 1977; Preston & Zimmerer, 1978). These reasons can be organized into three broad categories.

ATTITUDES ABOUT SUBORDINATES

Managers who avoid empowering others often believe their subordinates are not competent enough to accomplish the work, aren't interested in taking on more responsibility, are already overloaded and unable to accept more responsibility, would require too much time to train, or shouldn't be involved in tasks or responsibilities typically performed by the boss. They feel that the problem of nonempowerment lies with the employees, not with themselves. This is typical of the classic distinction between Theory X managers and Theory Y managers first pointed out by Douglas McGregor (1960) which was discussed in the chapter on Motivating Others. Most managers, McGregor claimed, are characterized by these kinds of assumptions—that is, that workers try to avoid work and cannot be trusted to take initiative to perform work on their own. The rationale is: I'm willing to empower my people, but they just won't accept the responsibility. On the other hand, as pointed out above, these assumptions are far more typical of managers who use them as an excuse to avoid empowering than they are of people in general. A vast majority of people seek empowerment.

PERSONAL INSECURITIES

Some managers fear they will lose the recognition and rewards associated with successful task accomplishment if they empower others. They are unwilling to share their expertise or "trade secrets" for fear of losing power or position. They have an intolerance for ambiguity which leads them to feel that they personally must know all the details about projects assigned to them. They prefer working on tasks by themselves rather than getting others involved, or they are unwilling to absorb the costs associated with subordinates

making mistakes. The rationale is: I'm willing to empower people, but when I do, they either mess things up or try to grab all the glory. Unfortunately, when people try to be the heroes, obtain all the glory for themselves, or avoid involving other people, they almost never accomplish what they could have by capitalizing on the expertise and energy of others. The empirical data are abundant showing that empowered teams do better than even the most competent individual (see the chapter on Building Effective Teams and Teamwork).

NEED FOR CONTROL

Nonempowering managers also often have a high need to be in charge and to direct and govern what is going on. They presume that an absence of clear direction and goals from the boss and a slackening of controls will lead to confusion, frustration, and failure on the part of employees. They feel that direction from the top is mandatory. Moreover, they often see short-lived, disappointing results from pep talks, work teams, suggestion systems, job enrichment programs, and other fix-it activities ("We tried that, and it didn't work"). The rationale is: I'm willing to empower people, but they require clear directions and a clear set of guidelines; otherwise, the lack of instructions leads to confusion. Whereas it is true that clear goals and specific directions enhance performance, self-established goals are always more motivating than those prescribed by someone else. Thus, people will perform better if they are empowered to establish their own goals rather than to have the manager superimpose them as a prerequisite to success.

The rationale associated with each of these inhibitors may be partially true, of course, but they nevertheless inhibit managers from achieving the success associated with skillful empowerment. Even if managers demonstrate the willingness and courage to empower others, success still requires skillful implementation. Incompetent empowerment, in fact, can undermine rather than enhance the effectiveness of an organization and its employees. For example, such incompetent empowerment as giving employees freedom without clear directions or resources has been found to lead to psychological casualties among individuals, as manifested by increased depression (Alloy, Peterson, Abrahamson, & Seligman, 1984), heightened stress (Averill, 1973), decreased performance and job satisfaction (Greenberger et al., 1989), lowered alertness, and even increased mortality (Langer & Rodin, 1976). Of course, these negative consequences are not solely associated with incompetent empowerment. They have been noted, nevertheless, in situations in which attempted empowerment was ineffective and unskillful.

For example, when managers associated empowerment with behaviors such as "simply letting go," refusing to clarify expectations, abdicating responsibility, having an absence of ground rules, or giving inflexible or inconsistent directions—none of which are consistent with skillful empowerment—the results were not only unsuccessful, but even harmful. Because of the negative psychological and physiological consequences for workers resulting from nonempowerment or from incompetent empowerment, Sashkin (1984) labeled skillful empowerment "an ethical imperative" for managers.

Delegating Work

The situation in which empowerment is most needed is when other people must become involved in accomplishing work. Obviously, if a person is doing a task alone, knowing how to empower others is largely irrelevant. On the other hand, it is impossible for a manager to perform all the work needed to carry out an organization's mission, so work and the responsibility to carry it out must be delegated to others. All managers, therefore, are required to empower their employees if they are to accomplish the tasks of the organization. Without delegation and the empowerment that must accompany it, no organization and no manager can enjoy long-term success. Delegation involves the assignment of work to other people, and it is an activity inherently associated with all managerial positions.

In this section, we discuss the nature of delegation as well as ways in which delegation can be most effectively empowered. Delegation normally refers to the assignment of a task. It is work-focused. Empowerment, on the other hand, may involve nonwork activities, emotions, and relationships. It involves the way people think about themselves. We have previously discussed ways in which managers can affect people's sense of being empowered. We will now discuss ways in which managers can get work accomplished effectively through empowered delegation.

We begin by pointing out that although delegation is commonly practiced by managers, it is by no means always competently performed. In fact, one of the grand masters of management, Lester Urwick (1944, p. 51), claimed that the "lack of courage to delegate properly, and of knowledge of how to do it, is one of the most general causes of failures in organizations." Moreover, as pointed out by Leana (1987), researchers have paid little attention to delegation, and less is known about the relationships between delegation and management effectiveness than many other common management skills (Locke & Schweiger, 1979).

ADVANTAGES OF EMPOWERED DELEGATION

Learning to become a competent delegator who can simultaneously empower others has several important advantages for managers. It obviously helps managers accomplish more work than they could accomplish otherwise and can be used as a time-management tool to free up discretionary time. On the other hand, if delegation occurs only when managers are overloaded, those receiving the delegated tasks may feel resentful and sense that they are being treated only as objects to meet the managers' ends. In such cases, they will experience a sense of disempowerment. However, skillful use of empowered delegation can provide significant benefits to organizations, managers, and individuals receiving assigned tasks. Table 8.6 summarizes these advantages.

Table 8.6	Advantages of Delegation
ADVANTAGE	**EXPLANATION**
Time	Increases the discretionary time of the manager
Development	Develops knowledge and capabilities of delegates
Trust	Demonstrates trust and confidence in delegates
Commitment	Enhances commitment of delegates
Information	Improves decision making with better information
Efficiency	Enhances efficiency and timeliness of decisions
Coordination	Fosters work integration by manager coordination

Empowered delegation can help develop subordinates' capabilities and knowledge so that their effectiveness is increased. It can be a technique to encourage personal mastery experiences. Delegation also can be used to demonstrate trust and confidence in the person receiving the assignment. Mishra (1992) and Gambetta (1988) summarized research showing that individuals who felt trusted by their managers were significantly more effective than those who didn't feel that way. Empowered delegation can be used to enhance the commitment of individuals receiving work. Beginning with the classic study of participation by Coch and French (1948), research has consistently demonstrated a positive relationship between having an opportunity to participate in work and subsequent satisfaction, productivity, commitment, acceptance of change, and desire for more work.

Empowered delegation also can be used to improve the quality of decision making by bringing to bear more information, closer to the source of the problem, than the manager has alone. Delegating tasks to those who have direct access to relevant information can enhance efficiency (i.e., require less time and fewer resources) as well as effectiveness (i.e., result in a better decision).

Finally, empowered delegation can increase the coordination and integration of work by funneling information and final accountability through a single source. Empowering managers, in other words, can ensure that no cross-purposes occur in delegation and that different tasks are not producing contradictory effects. Competently administered, empowered delegation can produce all five dimensions of empowerment: a sense of competence, choice, impact, value, and security.

On the other hand, when delegation is ineffectively performed, several negative consequences can result that not only inhibit empowerment but also subvert the ability to get work accomplished at all. For example, instead of freeing up time, ineffective delegation may require even more time to supervise, evaluate, correct, and arbitrate disagreements among employees. Employees may find themselves spending a longer time to accomplish a task because of lack of know-how, experience, or information. Stress levels and interpersonal conflict may increase when tasks, accountability, or expectations are unclear. Managers may find themselves out of touch with what is really going on with employees, may lose control, and may find goals being pursued that are incompatible with the rest of the organization. Chaos, rather than coordination, can result. Subordinates may also begin to expect that they should be involved in all decisions and that any decision the manager makes alone is autocratic and unfair.

In this section, we identify ways in which the positive outcomes of delegation can be cultivated and the potential negative outcomes of poor delegation avoided. Empowerment and delegation must be linked in the accomplishment of work. We will present guidelines for deciding *when* to delegate, *to whom* to delegate, and, finally, *how* to delegate.

DECIDING WHEN TO DELEGATE

Empowered delegating involves deciding, first of all, when to delegate tasks to others and when to perform them oneself. When should subordinates be assigned to design and perform work or make decisions? To determine when delegation is most appropriate, managers should ask five basic questions (Vroom & Yetton, 1973; Vroom & Jago, 1974). Research indicates that when delegation occurs based on these questions, successful results are almost four times more likely than when these questions are not considered. These questions are equally applicable whether assigned work is to be delegated to a team or to a single subordinate.

1. *Do subordinates have the necessary (or superior) information or expertise?* In many cases, subordinates may actually be better qualified than their managers to make decisions and perform tasks because they are more familiar with customer preferences, hidden costs, work processes, and so forth, due to being closer to actual day-to-day operations.

2. *Is the commitment of subordinates critical to successful implementation?* Participation in the decision-making process increases commitment to the final decision. When employees have some latitude in performing a task (i.e., what work they do, and how and when they do it), they generally must be involved in the decision-making process to ensure their cooperation. Whereas participation usually will increase the time required to make a decision, it will substantially decrease the time required to implement it.

3. *Will subordinates' capabilities be expanded by this assignment?* Delegation can quickly get a bad name in a work team if it is viewed as a mechanism used by the boss to get rid of undesirable tasks. Therefore, delegation should be consistent, not just when overloads occur.

It should reflect an overall management philosophy emphasizing employee development. Enhancing the abilities and interests of subordinates should be a central motive in delegating tasks.

4. *Do subordinates share with management and each other common values and perspectives?* If subordinates do not share a similar point of view with one another and with their manager, unacceptable solutions, inappropriate means, and outright errors may be perpetuated. In turn, this produces a need for closer supervision and frequent monitoring. Articulating a clear mission and objective for subordinates is crucial. In particular, managers must be clear about why the work is to be done. Coonradt (1985) found that important people are always told why, but less important people are merely told what, how, or when. Telling subordinates why the work is meaningful creates a common perspective.

5. *Is there sufficient time to do an effective job of delegating?* It takes time to save time. To avoid misunderstanding, managers must spend sufficient time explaining the task and discussing acceptable procedures and options. Time must be available for adequate training, for questions and answers, and for opportunities to check on progress.

Empowered delegation depends on a positive answer to each of the preceding questions. If any of these conditions is not present when delegation is being considered, the probability is greater that it will not be effective. More time will be required, lower quality will result, more frustration will be experienced, and less empowerment will occur. However, a negative answer to any of the preceding questions does not necessarily mean that effective delegation is forever precluded because managers can change situations so that subordinates get more information, develop common perspectives, have adequate time to receive delegation, and so forth.

DECIDING TO WHOM TO DELEGATE

Having decided to delegate a task, managers must then consider whether to involve only a single individual or a team of subordinates. If the decision is made to form a team, it is also important to decide how much authority to give the members of the team. For example, managers should determine if the team will only investigate the problem and explore alternatives or if it will make the final decision. Managers must also outline whether or not they will participate in the team's deliberations. Figure 8.2 presents a model for helping managers decide who should receive delegated tasks—individuals or teams—and whether the manager should be an active participant in a team if it is formed.

Figure 8.2 is constructed as a "tree diagram" that allows a manager to ask questions and, as a result of the answer to each question, move along a path until a final alternative is selected (Huber, 1980; Vroom & Jago, 1974). Here is how it works.

If you were a manager determining whether to involve others in accomplishing a task or making a decision, you should look over the considerations below the question, "Should I involve others in the task or the decision?" If you decide that subordinates do not possess relevant information or skills, that their acceptance is not important, that no personal development can occur for members of the team, that time is tight, or that conflicts will arise among subordinates, you should answer "no" to this question. The tree then prescribes that you perform the task or make the decision yourself. However, if you answer "yes" to this question, you then move on to the next question: "Should I direct my subordinates to form a team?" Look over the five considerations below that question and then continue through the model. Any of the considerations below a question can result in a "no" answer. The most participative and empowering alternative is to delegate work to a team and then participate as an equal member of the team. The least empowering response, of course, is to do the work yourself.

DECIDING HOW TO DELEGATE EFFECTIVELY

When a decision has been made to delegate a task, and the appropriate recipients of the delegation have been identified, empowered delegation has just begun. Positive outcomes of empowered delegation are contingent upon managers following 10 proven principles throughout the process.

1. *Begin with the end in mind.* Managers must articulate clearly the desired results intended from the delegated task. Being clear about what is to be accomplished and why it is important is a necessary prerequisite for empowered delegation. If fact, unless people know why a task is important and what is to be achieved by performing it, they are unlikely to

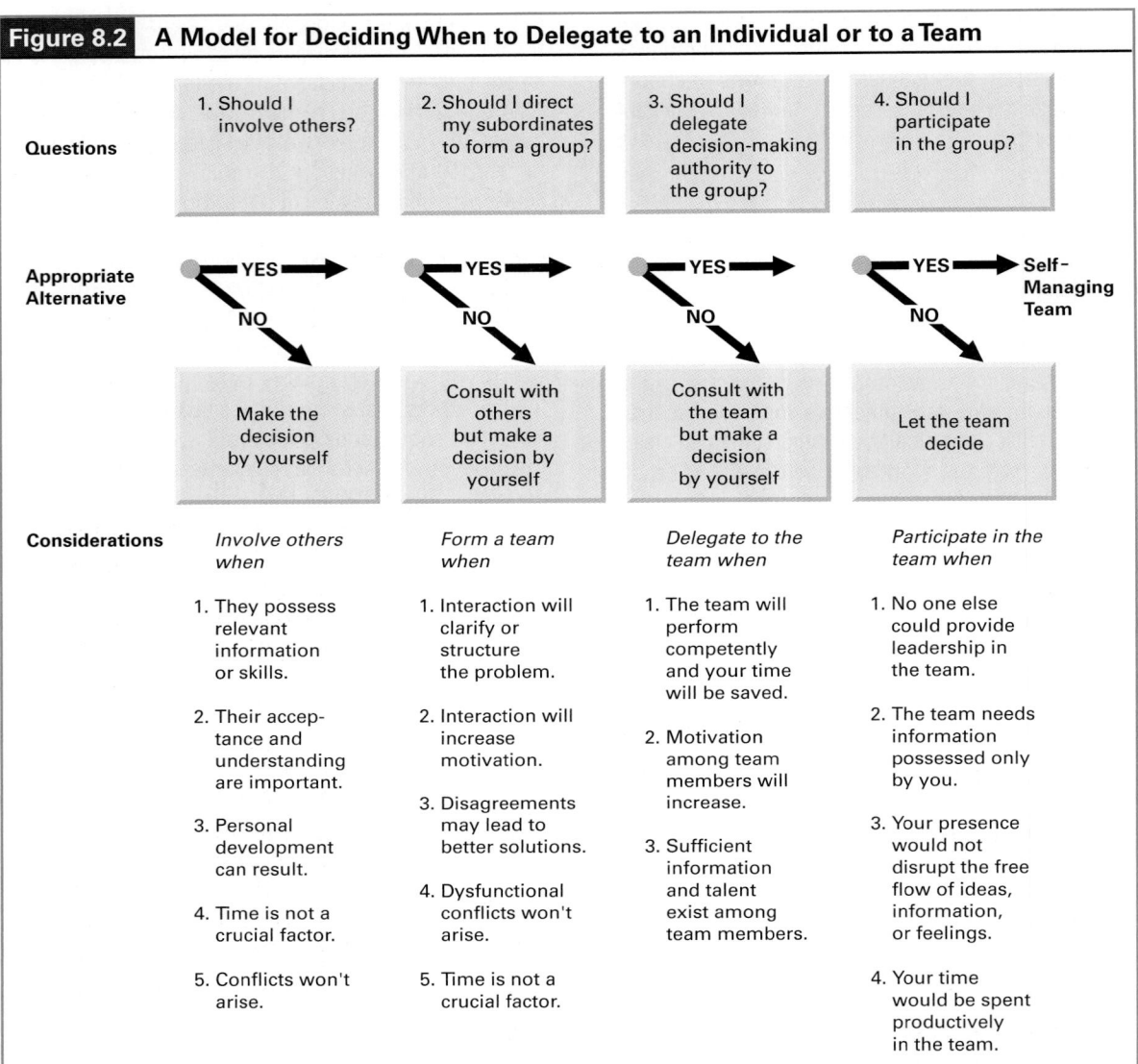

Figure 8.2   A Model for Deciding When to Delegate to an Individual or to a Team

Questions	1. Should I involve others?	2. Should I direct my subordinates to form a group?	3. Should I delegate decision-making authority to the group?	4. Should I participate in the group?

Appropriate Alternative

YES → ... YES → ... YES → ... YES → Self-Managing Team

NO ↓ ... NO ↓ ... NO ↓ ... NO ↓

Make the decision by yourself	Consult with others but make a decision by yourself	Consult with the team but make a decision by yourself	Let the team decide

Considerations

Involve others when	*Form a team when*	*Delegate to the team when*	*Participate in the team when*
1. They possess relevant information or skills.	1. Interaction will clarify or structure the problem.	1. The team will perform competently and your time will be saved.	1. No one else could provide leadership in the team.
2. Their acceptance and understanding are important.	2. Interaction will increase motivation.	2. Motivation among team members will increase.	2. The team needs information possessed only by you.
3. Personal development can result.	3. Disagreements may lead to better solutions.	3. Sufficient information and talent exist among team members.	3. Your presence would not disrupt the free flow of ideas, information, or feelings.
4. Time is not a crucial factor.	4. Dysfunctional conflicts won't arise.		4. Your time would be spent productively in the team.
5. Conflicts won't arise.	5. Time is not a crucial factor.		

act at all. No voluntary action ever persists unless these two elements are present. We don't stick with work, school, assignments, or other activities unless we have an idea of the purposes and intended outcomes involved. At a minimum, recipients of delegation will infer or fabricate a purpose or desired outcome, or the task will not be performed at all. To ensure that the ends desired by a manager are likewise perceived as desirable by others, the manager should point out the personal benefits to be achieved, the connection of task accomplishment to the organization's mission, or the important values represented by the task (e.g., service, learning, growth).

2. *Delegate completely.* In addition to the desired ends, managers must clearly specify the constraints under which the tasks will be performed. Every organization has rules and procedures, resource constraints, or boundaries that limit the kind of action that can be taken. These should be clarified when the task is delegated. In particular, managers must be clear about deadlines and the time frame for reporting back. When should the task be completed, who should receive the report, and to whom is accountability being assigned? No empowerment can occur without employees knowing what these boundaries are. Managers also must specify precisely the level of initiative

expected. No other oversight in the delegation process causes more confusion than the failure to delineate expectations regarding the level of initiative expected or permitted. At least five levels of initiative are possible, each of which may vary in terms of the amount of empowerment available to subordinates. These initiative levels differ in terms of the amount of control permitted over the timing and content of the delegated task. The five alternatives are:

❏ *Wait to be told what to do.* Take action only after specific directions are given. This is the least empowering form of delegation because it permits no initiative on the part of the subordinate. There is no control over timing, that is, when the task is to be accomplished, or content, that is, what is to be done.

❏ *Ask what to do.* Some discretion is provided to subordinates in that they have some control over the timing of the task, but not its content. Subordinates may formulate ideas for approaching the task, but because no action can be taken until the manager gives approval, empowerment is highly constrained.

❏ *Recommend, then take action.* This alternative is more empowering because subordinates are given some freedom over both the timing and the content of the delegated task. However, at least three different types of recommendations are possible, each with a different level of empowerment. One is for subordinates to simply gather information, present it to the manager, and let him or her decide what needs to be done. Another is for subordinates to determine alternative courses of action for each part of the task, leaving the manager to choose which course will be followed. Still another possibility is to outline a course of action for accomplishing the entire task and have the whole package approved at once. Progressively more empowerment is associated with each of these three recommendation types.

❏ *Act, then report results immediately.* Subordinates are given the freedom to act on their own initiative, but they are required to report to the manager immediately upon completion to ensure that their actions are correct and compatible with other organizational work. Subordinates may be permitted to perform only one part of a task at a time, reporting the results of each individual step. Or, they may be given the discretion to perform the entire task, reporting only when the final result has been accomplished. The latter alternative, of course, is the most empowering. But it may not be possible unless subordinates possess the necessary ability, information, experience, or maturity.

❏ *Initiate action, and report only routinely.* Subordinates receive complete control over timing and over content of the tasks assigned. Reporting occurs only in a routine fashion to maintain coordination. With sufficient ability, information, experience, and maturity among subordinates, this level of initiative is not only the most empowering but also the likeliest to produce high satisfaction and motivation among subordinates (Hackman & Oldham, 1980).

The important point for managers to remember is that they must be very clear about which of these levels of initiative they expect of their subordinates.

3. *Allow participation in the delegation of assignments.* Subordinates are more likely to accept delegated tasks willingly, perform them competently, and experience empowerment when they help decide what tasks are to be delegated to them and when. Often, managers cannot give subordinates complete choice about such matters, but providing opportunities to decide when tasks will be completed, how accountability will be determined, when work will begin, or what methods and resources will be used in task accomplishment increases employees' empowerment. Such participation should not be manipulative; that is, opportunities for participation should not be provided merely to convince subordinates of decisions already made. Rather, managers should promote participation when task requirements allow it and when acceptance and personal development can result.

Bernard (1938) formulated an "acceptance theory of authority" in which he proposed that people will accept and fulfill assignments only if four conditions are met. First, subordinates must *understand* what they are being asked to do. Second, subordinates must perceive that the assignment is *consistent* with the purpose of the organization. Third, subordinates must believe that the assignment is *compatible* with their own interests. Fourth, subordinates must be *able* to perform the assignment.

Bernard's theory underscores the importance of two-way communication during the delegation process. Not only should subordinates be encouraged to ask questions and seek information regarding delegated assignments, but they should also feel free to express ideas about the parameters of the work to be delegated. Expecting subordinates to seek answers to questions or providing guidance on every aspect of the delegated assignment can perpetuate overdependence if the manager answers every detailed question or provides continual advice. On the other hand, managers who remain available for consultation and idea interchange, foster two-way communication, and encourage a climate of openness and sharing make the delegation process empowering.

4. *Establish parity between authority and responsibility.* The oldest and most general rule of thumb in delegation is to match the amount of responsibility given with the amount of authority provided. Commonly, managers assign responsibility for work to subordinates without furnishing a corresponding amount of discretion to make decisions and authority to implement those decisions. If subordinates are to be successful, they must have as much authority as they need to accomplish the tasks assigned to them. An important part of developing a sense of self-determination and a sense of personal control—both critical dimensions of empowerment—is ensuring this match. Of course, managers also must take care not to delegate more authority than responsibility, thereby giving subordinates more authority, discretion, resources, or information than they can use. Such a mismatch leads to lack of accountability, potential abuses of power, and confusion on the part of subordinates. For example, without the necessary responsibility, providing a child with a loaded gun, or a $50 bill in a candy shop, could result in actions that would not lead to desirable outcomes.

Although managers cannot delegate *ultimate* accountability for delegated tasks, they can delegate *prime* accountability. This means that "the buck stops," eventually, at the manager's desk. Final blame for failure cannot be given away. This is ultimate accountability. On the other hand, managers can delegate prime

accountability, which means that subordinates can be given responsibility for producing desired short-term results. Their accountability is to the manager who delegated to them. Giving subordinates prime accountability is an important part of empowered delegation.

5. *Work within the organizational structure.* Another general rule of empowered delegation is to delegate to the lowest organizational level at which a job can be done. The people who are closest to the actual work being performed or the decision being made should be involved. They are usually the ones with the largest, most accurate fund of information. By definition, this increases efficiency (lower labor and information collection costs), and it frequently increases effectiveness (better understanding of problems). Whereas managers have a broader overall view of problems, the detailed knowledge needed to accomplish many tasks is most likely to reside with those who are lower in the organizational hierarchy.

In delegating a task down more than one level in an organization, it is important that the organizational chain of command be followed. In other words, delegation must occur *through* subordinates, not *around* them. If a senior manager circumvents the formal hierarchy, bypassing a manager to communicate directly with that manager's subordinate, the manager becomes unempowered. The subordinate now becomes accountable to the senior manager, not the manager with direct responsibility for the subordinate. The entire accountability system is thus destroyed. Following the chain of command by involving those at affected levels of the hierarchy in delegation is important for empowered delegation.

All individuals affected by a decision must be informed that it has been delegated. This applies to cross-functional coordination as well as hierarchical coordination. If a subordinate has been delegated responsibility, others who may have needed information, who may influence the results, or who may implement the recommendations must be notified of the delegation. If delegation occurs but no one knows about it, authority is essentially nullified.

6. *Provide adequate support for delegated tasks.* When authority is delegated to subordinates, managers must provide as much support to them as possible. As discussed earlier, this

involves making public announcements and presenting clearly stated expectations. It also means continuously providing relevant information and resources to help subordinates accomplish tasks. Reports, recent news clippings, customer data, articles, and even random thoughts that pertain to the delegated task should be passed on as they become available. This support not only aids task accomplishment but also communicates interest and concern for subordinates. Managers should help subordinates learn where to acquire needed resources, since the manager alone cannot be the sole source of all the support that subordinates will need.

Agreeing on the limits of resource use is also important. Since unlimited access to resources is never possible, managers must be clear about the limit beyond which no further resources can be used. Formulating a budget or establishing a set of specifications is a common way to specify limits.

Another form of support that managers can provide is to bestow credit—but not blame—publicly. Even though prime accountability has been delegated, pointing out mistakes or faults in front of others embarrasses workers, creates defensiveness, fosters the impression that the manager is trying to pass the buck and get rid of final accountability, and guarantees that workers will be less willing to initiate action on their own in the future. Correcting mistakes, critiquing work, and providing negative feedback on task performance of subordinates should be done in private, where the probability of problem solving and training can be enhanced.

7. *Focus accountability on results.* Once tasks are delegated and authority is provided, managers generally should avoid closely monitoring the way in which subordinates accomplish tasks. Excessive supervision of methods destroys the five dimensions of empowerment: self-efficacy, self-determination, personal control, meaningfulness, and trust. Successful accomplishment of a task, after all, rather than use of the manager's preferred procedures, is the primary goal of delegation. To be sure, harmful or unethical means for accomplishing tasks cannot be tolerated, nor can methods be used that obstruct other employees or subvert organizational rules. For the most part, though, managers

should focus primarily on results achieved by subordinates, rather than on the techniques used to achieve those results.

In order for accountability to be maintained, there must be agreement on acceptable levels of performance. Managers must clearly specify what level of performance is expected, what constitutes unacceptable performance, and what requirements are associated with the result. Without such specifications, it becomes difficult for managers not to worry about means as well as ends. By allowing subordinates to exercise initiative regarding how to tackle a task, their sense of empowerment is enhanced, and innovation and originality are more likely as well.

8. *Delegate consistently.* The time for managers to delegate is before they have to. Sometimes, when managers have time to do work themselves, they do just that, even though that work could and should be delegated. Two problems result. First, delegation becomes simply a method for relieving the manager's workload and stress. A primary reason for delegation— empowering subordinates—is forgotten. Employees begin to feel that they are merely "pressure valves" for managers rather than valued team members. Secondly, when delegation occurs only under pressure, there is no time for training, providing needed information, or engaging in two-way discussions. Clarity of task assignments may be impaired. Workers' mistakes and failures increase, and managers are tempted to perform tasks alone, in order to ensure quality. When managers delay delegating until they are overloaded, they create pressure on themselves to perform delegatable tasks personally, thereby increasing their own overload.

Another key to consistent delegation is for managers to delegate both pleasant and unpleasant tasks. Sometimes managers keep for themselves the tasks they like to perform and pass less-desirable work along to subordinates. It is easy to see the detrimental consequences this has on morale, motivation, and performance. When individuals feel that they are being used only to perform "dirty work," follow-through on delegated tasks is less likely. On the other hand, managers must not be afraid to share difficult or unpleasant tasks with subordinates. Playing the role of martyr by refusing to involve others in disagreeable tasks or drudgery creates unrealistic expectations for employees and isolates managers. Consistency of delegation, then, means that managers delegate tasks continuously, not just when overworked, and that they delegate both pleasant and unpleasant tasks.

9. *Avoid upward delegation*. Although it is crucial for subordinates to participate in the delegation process in order to become empowered, managers must conscientiously resist all so-called upward delegation, in which subordinates seek to shift responsibility for delegated tasks back onto the shoulders of the superior who did the initial delegating. Managers who fail to forestall upward delegation will find their time being tied up doing subordinates' work rather than their own.

Suppose a worker comes to a manager after delegation has occurred and says, "We have a problem. This assignment just isn't turning out very well. What do you suggest I do?" If the manager replies, "Gee, I'm not sure. Let me think about it, and I'll get back to you," the original delegated task has now been shifted from the employee back to the manager. Note that the manager has promised to report to the employee, that is, to maintain prime accountability, and the employee is now in a position to follow up on the manager's commitment, that is, supervising the manager. Thus, the subordinate has become the manager, and the manager the subordinate. Managers, in the hope of being helpful to, and supportive of, their subordinates, often get caught in the trap of upward delegation.

One way to avoid upward delegation is to insist that workers always take the initiative for developing their own solutions. Instead of promising the subordinate a report on the manager's deliberations, a more appropriate response would have been, "What do you recommend?" "What alternatives do you think we should consider?" "What have you done so far?" "What do you think would be a good first step?" Rather than sharing problems and asking for advice, subordinates should be required to share *proposed solutions* or to ask permission to implement them. Managers should refuse to solve delegated tasks. That is why specifying the expected level of initiative (see Rule 2) is so important. Not only does this avoid upward delegation, but it also helps

managers train employees to become competent problem solvers and to avoid working on tasks for which someone else has prime accountability. Yielding to upward delegation does not empower subordinates but, rather, makes them more dependent.

10. *Clarify consequences*. Subordinates should be made aware of the consequences of the tasks being delegated to them. They are more likely to accept delegation and be motivated to take initiative if it is clear what the rewards for success will be, what the opportunities might be, what the impact on the ultimate customer or the organization's mission can be, and so on. In particular, managers should help employees understand the connection between successful performance and financial rewards, opportunities for advancement, learning and developmental opportunities, informal recognition, and so forth. Most specific delegated assignments do not result in a direct payoff from the formal reward system, of course. But associating some desirable consequence—as minor as a pat on the back or a congratulatory mention in a staff meeting or as major as a financial bonus or incentive—enhances successful delegation.

Clarifying consequences also can help ensure an understanding that delegation not only implies task accomplishment, but enhancement of interpersonal relationships as well. Relationships with others in the organization, on the team, or with the manager individually should be strengthened as a result of task accomplishment. Accomplishing assignments in the course of damaging or destroying relationships creates more long-term costs than any organization can bear. Therefore, a desirable consequence of any delegation experience is the enhancement of interpersonal relationships and a strengthening of the organization.

REVIEW OF DELEGATION PRINCIPLES

The 10 principles summarizing *how* to delegate, preceded by the five criteria for determining *when* to delegate, and the four questions for identifying *to whom* to delegate, provide guidelines for ensuring not only that subordinates will experience a sense of empowerment but that other positive consequences will result as well. In particular, research results clearly show that empowered delegation leads to the following consequences:

- Delegated tasks are readily accepted by subordinates.
- Delegated tasks are successfully completed.
- Morale and motivation remain high.
- Workers' problem-solving abilities are increased.
- Managers have more discretionary time.
- Interpersonal relationships are strengthened.
- Organizational coordination and efficiency are enhanced.

Figure 8.3 summarizes the relationships among these principles.

International Caveats

Empowerment and empowered delegation are sometimes misinterpreted as a soft approach to management, an abrogation of responsibility by leaders, an invitation to the inmates to run the asylum, and a prescription for chaos. Strong leadership, visionary managers, and take-charge bosses are usually the ones we read about in the newspapers and business magazines. A great deal of attention is given to people who "take command of the situation" and "stay out front of the troops." With such a definition, empowerment is not a popular alternative in many cultures where, for example, an emphasis on *universalism, individualism, specificity,* and *ascription* are dominant. (Recall from earlier chapters that the Trompenaars [1996, 1998] model differentiates cultures on the basis of seven dimensions: *universalism* versus *particularism, individualism* versus *communitarianism, neutrality* versus *affectivity, specificity* versus *diffuseness, achievement* versus *ascription, internal* versus *external* control, and *past, present,* or *future* time orientation. Chapter 1 in this book provides a more detailed explanation of these value dimensions.)

Empowerment is sometimes viewed as contrary to some of these values in that maintaining consistency with rules and procedures (universalism) rather than

Figure 8.3 Relationships Among Principles of Effective Delegation

Deciding When
Subordinates have needed information.
Commitment is crucial.
Subordinates' capabilities will be expanded.
Common values are shared.
Sufficient time is available.

Deciding to Whom (Alternatives)
Involve no one.
Consult with other individuals, but decide alone.
Consult with a team, but decide alone.
Let the team decide.
Participate as a member of the team.

Deciding How
Begin with the end in mind.
Delegate completely.
Allow for participation.
Match authority with responsibility.
Work within the structure.
Provide support.
Focus accountability on results.
Delegate consistently.
Avoid upward delegation.
Clarify consequences.

Effective Outcomes of Delegation
Readily acceptable assignments.
High morale and motivation.
Organizational coordination and efficiency.
Increased problem-solving abilities.
More discretionary time for managers.
Stronger interpersonal relationships.
Successful task completion.

encouraging experimentation and team innovation may seem to make empowerment less desirable. Focusing on individual performance (individualism) rather than team or collective effort may be viewed as contrary to empowerment. Involving only a limited amount of the self in the work setting or task assignment (specificity) rather than engaging multiple roles and in-depth relationships with individuals with whom one is working also may be interpreted as inconsistent with empowerment and empowered delegation. A focus on ascribed status, title, and traditional position (ascription) rather than a blurring of hierarchical lines and focusing on merit or contribution also appears to contradict the aims of empowerment. Hence, empowerment may seem to be a concept that is more acceptable in cultures with a strong orientation toward particularism, collectivity, diffuseness, and achievement orientation.

On the other hand, the principles of empowerment and empowered delegation that we have discussed in this chapter are applicable across most, if not all, cultures. It is a misconception to believe that these principles do not work effectively in Eastern cultures as well as Western cultures, in Western Europe as well as South America, in Africa as well as the Polynesian Islands. Principles of empowerment are relevant to old and young, male and female, foreign and domestic. This is because the five principles of empowerment are connected to fundamental human needs that transcend national or ethnic cultures. Virtually everyone has needs for, and performs better when they are exposed to, an environment in which they: (1) feel capable, confident, and competent, (2) experience freedom, discretion, and choice, (3) believe they can make a difference, have an impact, and achieve a desired result, (4) sense meaning, value, and a higher purpose in their activities, and (5) trust that they will not be harmed or abused, but honored and respected. In other words, the keys to effective empowerment are also keys to effective human performance at a very fundamental level. Strong leaders are not lone rangers so much as they are savvy individuals who know how to mobilize those they lead and manage. Therefore, whereas individual differences must certainly be taken into account, and the pace at which empowerment and empowered delegation can be fully implemented may vary with the circumstances, these principles of empowerment are essential to effective managerial performance.

Summary

Empowerment means helping to develop in others a sense of self-efficacy, self-determinism, personal control, meaning, and trust. The current business environment is not particularly compatible with the principles of managerial empowerment. Because of the turbulent, complex, competitive circumstances that many organizations face, managers frequently experience a tendency to be less, rather than more, empowering. When managers feel threatened, they become rigid and seek more control over other people, not less. However, without empowered employees, organizations cannot succeed in the long run. Learning how to be a competent empowering manager is therefore a critical skill for individuals who probably will face a predilection not to practice empowerment.

Nine prescriptions that managers can use to empower others were discussed. We also offered a series of principles and criteria for ensuring empowered delegation, which results in better acceptance of delegated tasks by subordinates, enhanced motivation and morale, improved coordination and efficiency, better development of subordinates, increased discretionary time, strengthened relationships, and successful task performance. Producing a sense of empowerment in others and delegating in a way that empowers subordinates also brings desirable outcomes for organizations as well as employees. Empowered employees are more productive, psychologically and physically healthy, proactive and innovative, persistent in work, trustworthy, interpersonally effective, intrinsically motivated, and have higher morale and commitment than employees who are not empowered. Figure 8.4 illustrates the relationships among the various elements of empowerment and delegation.

Behavioral Guidelines

As you practice empowering others and carry out empowered delegating, you will want to use the following guidelines as cues. *To ensure empowerment in others, follow these guidelines.*

1. Foster self-efficacy or a sense of competence by fostering personal mastery experiences and pointing out successful role models.
2. Foster self-determination or a sense of personal choice by providing alternatives and information to people.
3. Foster personal consequence or a sense of personal impact by allowing people to see the effects of their work on end users or on those affected by the results.
4. Foster meaningfulness or a sense of value by clarifying vision and values and connecting to something of inherent value.

Figure 8.4 **Relationships Among the Elements of Empowerment and Empowered Delegation**

Guidelines for Empowering
- Mastery experiences
- Modeling
- Support
- Emotional arousal
- Information
- Resources
- Connect to outcomes
- Confidence

Delegation Principles
- Deciding when to delegate
- Deciding to whom to delegate
- Deciding how to delegate

Experienced Empowerment
- Self-efficacy
- Self-determinism
- Personal consequence
- Meaningfulness
- Trust

Empowered Delegation
- Task acceptance
- Motivation and morale
- Coordination and efficiency
- Subordinate development
- Discretionary time
- Strengthened relationships
- Successful performance

Desired Outcomes
- Productivity
- Psychological and physical health
- Proactivity and innovativeness
- Persistence in work
- Trustworthiness
- Interpersonal effectiveness
- Intrinsic motivation
- High morale and commitment

LEARNING

5. Foster trust or a sense of security by providing support and creating confidence, primarily by being consistent, honest, open, and fair.
6. Delegate work effectively by using the guidelines provided in the chapter to determine to whom the work should be delegated and when it should be delegated.

CASES INVOLVING EMPOWERMENT AND DELEGATION

Minding the Store

> On January 1, Ruth Cummings was formally named branch manager for the Saks Fifth Avenue store in a suburb of Denver. Her boss, Ken Hoffman, gave her this assignment on her first day: "Ruth, I'm putting you in charge of this store. Your job will be to run it so that it becomes one of the best stores in the system. I have a lot of confidence in you, so don't let me down."

One of the first things Ruth did was to hire an administrative assistant to handle inventories. Because this was such an important part of the job, she agreed to pay her assistant slightly more than the top retail clerks were making. She felt that having an administrative assistant would free her to handle marketing, sales, and personnel matters—areas she felt were crucial if the store was to be a success.

Within the week, however, she received a call from Hoffman: "Say, Ruth, I heard that you hired an administrative assistant to handle inventories. Don't you think that is a bit risky? Besides, I think paying an assistant more than your top sales clerk is damaging to morale in the store. I wish you had cleared this with me before you made the move. It sets a bad precedent for the other stores, and it makes me look like I don't know what is going on in the branches."

Three weeks later, Ruth appeared on a local noontime talk show to discuss new trends in fashion. She had worked hard to make contact with the hosts of the show, and she felt that public exposure like this would increase the visibility of her store. Although the TV spot lasted only 10 minutes, she was pleased with her performance and with the chance to get public exposure.

Later that night at home, she received another phone call from Hoffman: "Don't you know the policy of Saks? Any TV appearances made on behalf of the store are to be cleared through the main office. Normally, we like to have representatives from the main store appear on these kinds of shows because they can do a better job of plugging our merchandise. It's too bad that you didn't notify someone of your intentions. This could be very embarrassing for me."

Just before Easter, Ruth was approached in the store by one of the sales clerks. A customer had asked to charge approximately $3,000 worth of china as a gift for his wife. He had been a customer of the store for several years and Ruth had seen him on several occasions, but store rules indicated that no charge could be made for more than $1,000 for any reason. She told the customer that she was not authorized to okay a charge of that amount, but that if he would visit the main store in Denver, maybe arrangements could be made.

Later in the day, an irate Hoffman called again: "What in the world are you thinking about, Ruth? Today we had a customer come into the main store and say that you wouldn't make a sale to him because the charge was too much. Do you know how long he has been a customer of ours? Do you know how much he spends in the store every year? I certainly hope we have not lost him as a customer because of your blunder. This makes me very upset. You've just got to learn to use your head."

Ruth thought about the conversation for several days and finally decided that she needed to see Ken Hoffman. She called his secretary to schedule an appointment for the following day.

Discussion Questions

1. What guidelines related to empowerment were violated by Ken Hoffman? By Ruth Cummings?
2. What guidelines related to delegation were violated by Ken Hoffman? By Ruth Cummings?
3. What should Ruth Cummings and Ken Hoffman discuss in their meeting? Identify specific agenda items that should be raised.
4. What are the questions that Ruth should ask Ken to help her acquire the necessary elements of empowerment? What questions should Ken ask Ruth to be better able to ensure her success?
5. If you were an outside consultant attending the meeting, what advice would you give Ken? What advice would you give Ruth?

Changing the Portfolio

You are head of a staff unit reporting to the vice president of finance. He has asked you to provide a report on the firm's current portfolio, including recommendations for changes in the current selection criteria. Doubts have been raised about the efficiency of the existing system given the current market conditions, and there is considerable dissatisfaction with prevailing rates of return.

You plan to write the report, but at the moment you are perplexed about the approach to take. Your own specialty is the bond market, and it is clear to you that detailed knowledge of the equity market, which you lack, would greatly enhance the value of the report. Fortunately, four members of your staff are specialists in different segments of the equity market. Together, they possess a vast amount of knowledge about the intricacies of investment. However, they seldom agree on the best way to achieve anything when it comes to investment philosophy and strategy.

You have six weeks before the report is due. You have already begun to familiarize yourself with the firm's current portfolio and have been provided by management with a specific set of constraints that any portfolio must satisfy. Your immediate problem is to come up with some alternatives to the firm's present practices and to select the most promising for detailed analysis in your report.

Discussion Questions

1. Should this decision be made by you alone? Why or why not?
2. If you answered the question, "Should I involve others?" affirmatively, which alternative in Figure 8.2 should be used in making a decision? Justify your choice.
3. What are the most important considerations in deciding whom to involve in this task?
4. If others are to become involved, how much empowerment should they have? What would you do specifically to achieve the appropriate level of empowerment?

EXERCISES FOR EMPOWERMENT

Executive Development Associates

Assume that you are Mary Ann O'Connell, General Manager at Executive Development Associates. Your firm provides outplacement, training and development, career planning, and head-hunting services for a large number of Fortune 500 companies. You have been at the corporate board meeting for the last three days in the Rocky Mountains, and you relied on your secretary to screen out all but the most important or urgent messages. You slipped into the office on the way home from the airport Monday evening, just to check your electronic messages and your mail. Aside from a host of phone calls to return, here is the collection of messages that your secretary retrieved from your e-mail file and mail box.

Assignment

1. For each message, outline specifically the plan you will implement to empower others effectively to solve these problems. Determine who should be involved, what level of initiative should be taken, what actions you can take to ensure empowerment, how accountability should be maintained, and so on.

2. Write out the actions you'd take in response to each item. A worksheet has been provided below to remind you of what you should consider as you record your responses.

3. After you have completed your own responses to each item, form a team of fellow students and share your plans. Provide feedback to one another on what is especially good, what could be improved, and what could be added to each person's action plan. In particular, what principles of empowerment are included, which are omitted, and which are contradicted?

Solving Problems Through Empowerment Worksheet

For each message, write out your plan of action. This plan should include answers to the questions listed below. Not every question is relevant to each message, but most are, and they can guide your action plan. After you have formed your own responses, form a team of fellow students and share these plans in turn. Provide feedback to one another on what is especially good, what could be improved, and what could be added to each action plan.

1. Who should be involved in resolving this issue? Will you form a team?

2. What kinds of personal mastery experiences can be provided for whoever you involve? Can you model successful behavior?

3. What kinds of support, information, and resources can be provided?

4. How will you create emotional arousal and create confidence in others?

5. What are the main considerations in deciding if you should delegate each task?

6. If you opt for delegation, what will you do to:

   Begin with the end in mind?
   Delegate completely?
   Allow participation?
   Match authority with responsibility?
   Work within the structure?
   Provide support?
   Maintain accountability?
   Ensure consistency of delegation?
   Avoid upward delegation?
   Clarify consequences?

INTEROFFICE MEMORANDUM

Data Processing Center

DATE: 15 June
TO: Mary Ann O'Connell,
        General Manager
FROM: Roosevelt Monroe,
        for the Data Processing Staff

After looking over last quarter's audit, it is clear that the number of complaints our group is receiving from individuals throughout the company is escalating. The problem is an obvious one to us. It is, simply, that several incompatible software systems have evolved over the last several years in various departments, and it is becoming increasingly difficult to coordinate across units. As you know, some data have to be retyped two or three times into different systems because of these incompatibilities.

The trouble is, our own employees, not to mention our customers, are becoming increasingly impatient with our slow turnaround time. They focus squarely on our group as the bottleneck. We think the rising complaint numbers in the quarterly audit are misleading, however, and they divert us from the real cause of the problem.

We're writing this memo to you to collectively urge you to address this issue as soon as possible. At a minimum, it should be discussed at our upcoming staff meeting on Tuesday. So far, the data processing staff is taking the blame for not getting data processed fast enough, yet it is really the fault of the system, not our unit.

We'll look forward to hearing from you on Tuesday.

INTEROFFICE MEMORANDUM

Human Resources Department

DATE: 15 June
TO: Mary Ann
FROM: Lucy

I was excited by your speech at the senior management meeting last week in which you established a new challenge for all senior executives. With the new competitive environment that we face, the vision that you articulated for our future is both exciting and challenging and, I think, an important step forward. It really makes clear the key success factors that should drive our business.

In particular, I think your directive for all senior executives to disseminate the vision throughout the organization to their own subordinates is a good way to get the message delivered. However, you made a statement in your speech that has me troubled. You said, "We used to pay you on the basis of new accounts generated, quarterly earnings, customer satisfaction ratings, and new product designs. Our new barometer is going to be how you're doing in disseminating the vision throughout your own units."

Frankly, I'm perplexed as to how we'll ever measure this directive. As the one who has to administer the appraisal and compensation systems, I'm not sure what criteria we'll look for or what indicators we'll use to determine success. I'm afraid that we'll create dissatisfaction if we don't have something specific outlined. Our people, especially those who may not perform, will think it is purely arbitrary. Do you really mean to have us change the appraisal and compensation systems to include this new criterion? How do you propose we measure effective performance? What would you like me to do to support your statement? Did you mean to make the statement that you did?

This is rather urgent because I have a staff meeting Tuesday afternoon, and I promised to have a response by then. I've already stalled until I had a chance to talk to you.

COPY OF A LETTER

Midwest State University

24 May

Dear Ms. O'Connell:

I am happy to be joining Executive Development Associates after several years at Midwest State University. As you know, leaving Midwest State has been quite traumatic for me, and that is what motivated me to make a request of you. I'm convinced that the reason I didn't receive tenure at Midwest State is because the expectations were never clear about what my responsibilities were and what the criteria were for success.

I know your company is very professional and employees are pretty much on their own, but I'm feeling a need to get some specific performance requirements outlined for me. I'm sure that I can be a good addition to your company, but I want to be clear about what your expectations are.

I have set a meeting with you on Tuesday through your secretary. Would you please outline a specific set of responsibilities and expectations for my job as instructor in the training and development department? If possible, I'd like it in writing to avoid any misunderstanding. Regardless, I'll look forward to talking to you Tuesday.

Thank you for your consideration.

Sincerely,

Lester Frost

INTEROFFICE MEMORANDUM

Training and Development

DATE: Monday, A.M.
TO: Mary Ann
FROM: Pam
RE: Tom Kinnir's Jury Duty

I know you're just getting back, but we've got an emergency on our hands.

I was just notified this morning by Tom that he has been selected for jury duty and that (can you believe it) he is being sequestered! Holy cow, Mary Ann, this couldn't come at a worse time. As our expert on activity-based costing, Tom is the only guy we have who can teach the topic. So what's the trouble, you say? The trouble is that we have over 100 corporate trainers showing up here for a seminar on Friday, and the seminar isn't prepared yet. Tom said that he has some notes and a few transparencies on his desk, but he had planned to spend this entire week designing and preparing it. Not only don't any of us know the topic very well, but we're not even sure what information we need, what data still needs to be gathered, who's got what, and how we go about filling in. Help! We're counting on this seminar to make budget this quarter, and we're feeling a little ticked off at Tom for waiting until the last minute. What do we do next?

By the way, how were the Rocky Mountains???

INTEROFFICE MEMORANDUM

Outplacement Department

DATE: Monday, A.M.
TO: Mary Ann O'Connell
FROM: Aneil Mishra
RE: Pending Plant Closure

You may have missed the news over the weekend. It was announced in the paper that Detroit Manufacturing has filed for Chapter 11 protection and that they're closing their Toledo plant. That means about 4,000 people will be out of work.

If we want the business, we've got to get moving right away. They will be looking at proposals from outplacement firms next week. We've got to get our proposal together, identify staff, determine a budget, and prepare a presentation in the next day or two.

Sound's like a great opportunity. I'll stop by tomorrow when you get back.

Empowering Ourselves

In this exercise, your task is to identify ways in which the empowerment of members of the graduating students this year in your own institution can be enhanced. You should use the principles of empowerment in the chapter to identify specific ways in which the empowerment of this group of people can be increased. What can be done, practically speaking, to effect empowerment?

Make certain that you don't merely identify what others could do, what the administration could implement, or what hypothetically could occur. Rather, identify very practical and realistic factors that could empower this graduating class. What could they do as a group? What could you do? What personal responsibility could they take for their own empowerment?

Do not treat this exercise as hypothetical or fantasy. Actually identify behaviors that you can implement that will enhance empowerment. Use the suggestions in the text as well as others that you add to those lists.

	Things That Can Be Done to Enhance the Empowerment of the Graduating Class
Self-Efficacy (personal competence)	
Self-Determination (personal choice)	
Personal Consequence (personal impact)	
Meaningfulness (personal value)	
Trust (personal security)	

Now form a team with three or four colleagues. Share your ideas with the group. For each dimension of empowerment, identify the most powerful ideas you hear from the team members. Add at least one new idea to your list. Also, identify when and how you'll actually implement your list. Use your team to help specify actual behaviors that you can implement.

Deciding to Delegate

Delegation is one of the most deceiving management skills because it seems so easy to accomplish. Just tell someone what to do, and they'll do it, right? Unfortunately, highly competent delegators are rare, and this exercise is designed to help you determine when and how to delegate more effectively. To accomplish this exercise you'll need to use the framework in Figure 8.2.

For each of the two scenarios that follow, ask the following questions:

❑ *Should I involve others or make the decision by myself?*
❑ *If I involve others, should I direct them to form a team, or should I consult them individually and make the decision by myself?*
❑ *If I form a team, should I delegate decision-making authority to the team, or should I consult with the team but make the decision by myself?*
❑ *If I delegate to the team, should I participate in the team, or should I let the team decide?*

After you have made a decision about how to handle each of these two scenarios, form a team of colleagues. Share your decision and your rationale with the team. Reach a consensus regarding the most appropriate strategy to use in each of these two cases. For comparison purposes, an analysis by experts for the Emergency Request case is contained at the end of the chapter. It is provided only to enhance your team discussion. No comparative analysis is provided for the Biological Warfare case.

An Emergency Request

You are a general plant supervisor and seven product lines involving four of your eight foremen must be disrupted to satisfy an emergency request from an important client. You naturally wish to minimize the disruption. No additional personnel are available, and time limits to complete the new project are restrictive. The plant is new and is the only industrial plant in an economically depressed area dominated by farming. You can count on everyone pulling his or her own weight. The wages in the plant are substantially above farm wages, and the workers' jobs depend on the profitability of this plant—the first new industrial development in the area in 15 years. Your subordinates are relatively inexperienced, and you have been supervising them more closely than you might if the plant had been in a well-established industrial area and your subordinates were more experienced. The changes involve only standard procedures and are routine for someone of your experience. Effective supervision poses no problems. Your problem is how to reschedule the work to meet this emergency within the time limit with minimum disruption of the existing product lines. Your experience in such matters should enable you to figure out a way of meeting the request that will minimize the disruption of existing product lines.

Biological Warfare

You are the executive vice president of a small pharmaceutical manufacturer. You have the opportunity to bid on a contract for the Defense Department pertaining to biological warfare. The contract is outside the mainstream of your business; however, it could make economic sense, since you do have unused capacity in one of your plants, and the manufacturing processes are not dissimilar. You have written the document to accompany the bid and now have the problem of determining the dollar value of the quotation you think will win the job for your company. If the bid is too high, you will undoubtedly lose to one of your competitors. If it is too low, you could lose money on the program. There are many factors to consider in making this decision, including the cost of the new raw materials and the additional administrative burden of relationships with a new client, not to speak of factors that are likely to influence the bids of your competitors, such as how much they need this particular contract. You have been busy assembling the necessary data to make this decision, but there remain several unknowns, one of which involves the manager of the plant in which the new products will be manufactured. Of all your subordinates, only he can estimate the costs of adapting the present equipment to its new purpose, and his cooperation and support will be necessary if the specifications of the contract are to be met. However, in an initial discussion with him when you first learned of the possibility of the contract, he seemed adamantly opposed to the idea. His experience has not particularly equipped him to evaluate projects like this one, so you were not overly influenced by his opinions. From the nature of his arguments, you inferred that his opposition was ideological rather than economic. You recall that he was once involved in a local peace organization and was one of the most vocal opponents in the company to the Vietnam and the Persian Gulf Wars.

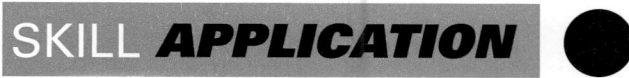
ACTIVITIES FOR EMPOWERMENT AND DELEGATION

Suggested Assignments

1. Teach someone else (your spouse, a colleague, your boss) how to empower others and delegate effectively. Include the principles in Table 8.5 in your discussion. Use your own examples and illustrations.

2. Interview a manager about his or her empowerment practices. Try to determine what is especially effective, what doesn't work, what comes off as condescending, and what motivates people to perform. Identify the extent to which the manager knows and uses the principles discussed in the Skill Learning section of this chapter.

3. Think of a situation you now face with which you would like some help. It may be a task you want to accomplish, a tough decision you need to make, or a team you want to form. Make sure you think of something that requires the involvement of other people. Write down specific things you can do to empower other people to help you. How can you help them do what they want to do, while simultaneously have them do what you want them to do?

4. Schedule a meeting with a manager who is not very good at empowerment. (Finding such a person shouldn't be difficult, because most leaders tend to be more authoritarian and bureaucratic than empowering.) As a student who has learned about and practiced empowerment and delegation, share what you have learned and offer suggestions that could help this manager improve.

Application Plan and Evaluation

The intent of this exercise is to help you apply this cluster of skills in a real-life, out-of-class setting. Now that you have become familiar with the behavioral guidelines that form the basis of effective skill performance, you will improve most by trying out those guidelines in an everyday context. Unlike a classroom activity, in which feedback is immediate and others can assist you with their evaluations, this skill application activity is one you must accomplish and evaluate on your own. There are two parts to this activity. Part 1 helps prepare you to apply the skill. Part 2 helps you evaluate and improve on your experience. Be sure to write down answers to each item. Don't short-circuit the process by skipping steps.

APPLICATION

Part 1. Planning

1. Write down the two or three aspects of this skill that are most important to you. These may be areas of weakness, areas you most want to improve, or areas that are most salient to a problem you face right now. Identify the specific aspects of this skill that you want to apply.

2. Now identify the setting or the situation in which you will apply this skill. Establish a plan for performance by actually writing down a description of the situation. Who else will be involved? When will you do it? Where will it be done?

   Circumstances:
   Who else?
   When?
   Where?

3. Identify the specific behaviors in which you will engage to apply this skill. Operationalize your skill performance.

4. What are the indicators of successful performance? How will you know you have been effective? What will indicate you have performed competently?

Part 2. Evaluation

5. After you have completed your implementation, record the results. What happened? How successful were you? What was the effect on others?

6. How can you improve? What modifications can you make next time? What will you do differently in a similar situation in the future?

7. Looking back on your whole skill practice and application experience, what have you learned? What has been surprising? In what ways might this experience help you in the long term?

SCORING KEYS AND COMPARISON DATA

Effective Empowerment and Delegation

Scoring Key

SKILL AREA	ITEMS	ASSESSMENT	
		PRE-	POST-
Personal mastery experiences	1, 2	_____	_____
Modeling	3, 4	_____	_____
Providing support	5, 6	_____	_____
Arousing positive emotions	7, 8	_____	_____
Providing information	9, 10	_____	_____
Providing resources	11, 12	_____	_____
Organizing teams	13, 14	_____	_____
Creating confidence	15, 16	_____	_____
Delegating work	17–26	_____	_____
Total Score		_____	_____

Comparison Data (N = 1,500 Students)

Compare your scores to three standards:
1. The maximum possible score = 156
2. The scores of other students in the class.
3. Norm data from more than 1,500 business school students.

Pre-Test				Post-Test
129.54	=	mean	=	138.03
139 or above	=	top quartile	=	149 or above
130–138	=	second quartile	=	140–148
121–129	=	third quartile	=	129–139
120 or below	=	bottom quartile	=	128 or below

Personal Empowerment

Scoring Key

SKILL AREA	ITEMS	MEAN (TOTAL ÷ 4)
Self-efficacy (competence)	2, 7, 12, 17	_____
Self-determination (choice)	3, 8, 13, 18	_____
Personal consequence (impact)	4, 9, 14, 19	_____
Meaningfulness (value)	1, 6, 11, 16	_____
Trust (security)	5, 10, 15, 20	_____

Comparison Data

Scores are compared to approximately 3,000 middle managers in manufacturing and service organizations.

SKILL AREA	MEAN	TOP THIRD	BOTTOM THIRD
Self-efficacy	5.76	>6.52	<5.00
Self-determination	5.50	>6.28	<4.72
Personal control	5.49	>6.34	<4.64
Meaningfulness	5.88	>6.65	<5.12
Trust	5.33	>6.03	<4.73

SKILL PRACTICE Deciding to Delegate: Analysis Of "An Emergency Request"

QUESTION:	ANALYSIS:
Is it a group or individual problem?	Group because the task affects subordinates.
Is there a quality requirement?	Yes, because one way is better than another.
Does the manager have needed information?	Yes; the manager has experience.
Is the problem structured or unstructured?	Structured, because routine changes are required.
Do subordinates have to accept the decision?	No, because they have no discretion in implementation.
Are subordinates likely to accept the decision?	Yes, because close supervision is accepted.
Does everyone share a common goal?	Yes; all want the firm to be profitable.
Is conflict among subordinates likely?	No, since there is no investment in a prior alternative.
Do subordinates have needed information?	No; subordinates are inexperienced.

Choice: Make an individual decision if time is the important factor. If training of subordinates is the important factor, form a team and participate in the team's discussions.

SKILL PRACTICE Analysis of Biological Warfare

QUESTION:	ANALYSIS:
Is it a group or individual problem?	Group because the task affects many employees.
Is there a quality requirement?	Yes, because one bid may clearly be better than another.
Does the manager have needed information?	No; the manager must obtain information from others.

Is the problem structured or unstructured?	Structured, because standard routines are involved.
Do subordinates have to accept the decision?	Yes, because they will have discretion in implementation.
Are subordinates likely to accept the decision?	Yes, probably, because of the benefit to the firm.
Does everyone share a common goal?	No; whereas all want the firm to be profitable, some are ideologically opposed to this kind of business.
Is conflict among subordinates likely?	Yes, since ideological factors may become relevant.
Do subordinates have needed information?	No; subordinates are inexperienced.

Choice: Make a decision by yourself, without sharing the problem with subordinates, after having obtained the necessary information. You may or may not share the problem with subordinates to discuss alternatives, but regardless, the decision should be yours alone.

SKILL **ASSESSMENT**

- Team Development Behaviors
- Diagnosing the Need for Team Building

SKILL **LEARNING**

- Developing Teams and Teamwork
- The Advantages of Teams
- Team Development
- Leading Teams
- Team Membership
- Summary
- Behavioral Guidelines

SKILL **ANALYSIS**

- The Tallahassee Democrat's ELITE Team
- The Cash Register Incident

SKILL **PRACTICE**

- Team Diagnosis and Team Development Exercise
- Winning the War on Talent
- Team Performance Exercise

SKILL **APPLICATION**

- Suggested Assignments
- Application Plan and Evaluation

SCORING KEYS AND **COMPARISON DATA**

9

Building Effective Teams and Teamwork

SKILL DEVELOPMENT OBJECTIVES

- DIAGNOSE AND FACILITATE TEAM DEVELOPMENT
- BUILD HIGH-PERFORMANCE TEAMS
- FACILITATE TEAM LEADERSHIP
- FOSTER EFFECTIVE TEAM MEMBERSHIP

DIAGNOSTIC SURVEYS FOR BUILDING EFFECTIVE TEAMS

TEAM DEVELOPMENT BEHAVIORS

Step 1: Before you read the material in this chapter, please respond to the following statements by writing a number from the rating scale below in the left-hand column (Pre-assessment). Your answers should reflect your attitudes and behavior as they are now, not as you would like them to be. Be honest. This instrument is designed to help you discover your level of competency in building effective teams so you can tailor your learning to your specific needs. When you have completed the survey, use the scoring key at the end of the chapter to identify the skill areas discussed in this chapter that are most important for you to master.

Step 2: After you have completed the reading and the exercises in this chapter and, ideally, as many as you can of the Skill Application assignments at the end of this chapter, cover up your first set of answers. Then respond to the same statements again, this time in the right-hand column (Post-assessment). When you have completed the survey, use the scoring key at the end of the chapter to measure your progress. If your score remains low in specific skill areas, use the behavioral guidelines at the end of the Skill Learning section to guide further practice.

Rating Scale

1 Strongly disagree
2 Disagree
3 Slightly disagree
4 Slightly agree
5 Agree
6 Strongly agree

Assessment

Pre-   Post-

When I am in the role of leader in a team:

_____   _____   1. I know how to establish credibility and influence among team members.

_____   _____   2. I behave congruently with my stated values and I demonstrate a high degree of integrity.

_____   _____   3. I am clear and consistent about what I want to achieve.

_____   _____   4. I create positive energy by being optimistic and complimentary of others.

_____   _____   5. I build a common base of agreement in the team before moving forward with task accomplishment.

_____   _____   6. I encourage and coach team members to help them improve.

_____   _____   7. I share information with team members and encourage participation.

_____   _____   8. I articulate a clear, motivating vision of what the team can achieve, along with specific short-term goals.

When I am in the role of team member:

_____ _____ 9. I know a variety of ways to facilitate task accomplishment in the team.

_____ _____ 10. I know a variety of ways to help build strong relationships and cohesion among team members.

_____ _____ 11. I confront and help to overcome negative, dysfunctional, or blocking behaviors by others.

_____ _____ 12. I shift roles from facilitating task accomplishment to helping build trusting relationships among members, depending on what the team needs to move forward.

When I desire to make my team perform well, regardless of whether I am a leader or member:

_____ _____ 13. I am knowledgeable about the different stages of team development experienced by most teams.

_____ _____ 14. I help establish clear expectations and purpose as well as help team members feel comfortable with one another at the outset of a team.

_____ _____ 15. I encourage team members to become as committed to the success of the team as to their own personal success.

_____ _____ 16. I help team members become committed to the team's vision and goals.

_____ _____ 17. I help the team avoid groupthink by making sure that sufficient diversity of opinions are expressed in the team.

_____ _____ 18. I can diagnose and capitalize on my team's core competencies, or unique strengths.

_____ _____ 19. I encourage the team to continuously improve as well as to seek for dramatic innovations.

_____ _____ 20. I encourage exceptionally high standards of performance and outcomes that far exceed expectations.

DIAGNOSING THE NEED FOR TEAM BUILDING

Teamwork has been found to dramatically affect organizational performance. Some managers have credited teams with helping them to achieve incredible results. On the other hand, teams don't work all the time in all organizations. Therefore, managers must decide when teams should be organized. To determine the extent to which teams should be built in your organization, complete the instrument below.

Think of an organization in which you participate (or will participate) that produces a product or service. Answer these questions with that organization in mind. Write a number from a scale of 1 to 5 in the blank at the left; 1 indicates that there is little evidence; 5 indicates there is a lot of evidence. Comparison data is provided at the end of the chapter.

_____ 1. Output has declined or is lower than desired.

_____ 2. Complaints, grievances, or low morale are present or are increasing.

_____ 3. Conflicts or hostility between members is present or is increasing.

_____ 4. Some people are confused about assignments, or their relationships with other people are unclear.

_____ 5. Lack of clear goals and lack of commitment to goals exist.

_____ 6. Apathy or lack of interest and involvement by members is in evidence.

_____ 7. Insufficient innovation, risk taking, imagination, or initiative exists.

_____ 8. Ineffective and inefficient meetings are common.

_____ 9. Working relationships across levels and units are unsatisfactory.

_____ 10. Lack of coordination among functions is apparent.

_____ 11. Poor communication exists; people are afraid to speak up; listening isn't occurring; and information isn't being shared.

_____ 12. Lack of trust exists among members and between members and senior leaders.

_____ 13. Decisions are made that some members don't understand, or with which they don't agree.

_____ 14. People feel that good work is not rewarded or that rewards are unfairly administered.

_____ 15. People are not encouraged to work together for the good of the organization.

_____ 16. Customers and suppliers are not part of organizational decision making.

_____ 17. People work too slowly and there is too much redundancy in the work being done.

_____ 18. Issues and challenges that require the input of more than one person are being faced.

_____ 19. People must coordinate their activities in order for the work to be accomplished.

_____ 20. Difficult challenges that no single person can resolve or diagnose are being faced.

Source: *Adapted from Dyer, 1987. Reprinted with permission of Addison-Wesley.*

Developing Teams and Teamwork

Near the home of one of the authors of this book, scores of Canada geese spend the winter. They fly over the house to the nature pond nearby almost every morning. What is distinctive about these flights is that the geese always fly in a V pattern. The reason for this pattern is that the flapping wings of the geese in front create an updraft for the geese that follow. This V pattern increases the range of the geese collectively by 71 percent compared to flying alone. On long flights, after the lead goose has flown at the front of the V for a while, it drops back to take a place in the V where the flying is easier. Another goose then takes over the lead position, where the flying is most strenuous. If a goose begins to fly out of formation, it is not long before it returns to the V because of the resistance it experiences when not supported by the wing flapping of the other geese.

Another noticeable feature of these geese is the loud honking that occurs when they fly. Canada geese never fly quietly. One can always tell when they are in the air because of the noise. The reason for the honking is not random, however. It occurs among geese in the rear of the formation in order to encourage the lead goose. The leader doesn't honk—just those who are supporting and urging on the leader. If a goose is shot, becomes ill, or falls out of formation, two geese break ranks and follow the wounded or ill goose to the ground. There they remain, nurturing their companion, until it is either well enough to return to the flock or it dies.

This remarkable phenomenon serves as an apt metaphor for our chapter on teamwork. The lessons garnered from the flying V formation help highlight important attributes of effective teams and skillful teamwork. For example:

❑ *Effective teams have interdependent members.* Like geese, the productivity and efficiency of an entire unit is determined by the coordinated, interactive efforts of all its members.

❑ *Effective teams help members be more efficient working together than alone.* Like geese, effective teams outperform even the best individual's performance.

❑ *Effective teams function so well that they create their own magnetism.* Like geese, team members desire to affiliate with a team because of the advantages they receive from membership.

❑ *Effective teams do not always have the same leader.* As with geese, leadership responsibility often rotates and is shared broadly as teams develop over time.

❑ *In effective teams, members care for and nurture one another.* No member is devalued or unappreciated. All are treated as an integral part of the team.

❑ *Effective teams have members who cheer for and bolster the leader, and vice versa.* Mutual encouragement is given and received by each member.

❑ *Effective teams have a high level of trust among members.* Members demonstrate integrity and are interested in others' success as well as their own.

Because any metaphor can be carried to extremes, we don't wish to overemphasize the similarities between Canada geese and work teams. On the other hand, these seven attributes of effective teams do serve as the nucleus of this chapter. They will help us identify ways for you to improve your abilities to lead a team, to be an effective team member, and to foster effective team processes. Our intent is to identify proven techniques and skills that will help you function more effectively in team settings.

One important reason for this emphasis on teams is that participation in teams is fun for most people. There is something inherently attractive about being engaged in teamwork. Consider, for example, the two advertisements that appeared next to one another in a metropolitan newspaper, both seeking to fill the same type of position. They are reproduced in Figure 9.1. While neither advertisement is negative or inappropriate, they are noticeably different. Which job would you rather take? Which firm would you rather work for? For most of us, the team-focused job seems much more desirable. This chapter focuses on helping you to flourish in these kinds of team settings.

Our Team Needs One Good Multiskilled Maintenance Associate

Our Team is down one good player. Join our group of multiskilled Maintenance Associates who work together to support our assembly teams at American Automotive Manufacturing.

We are looking for a versatile person with skills in one or more of the following: ability to set up and operate various welding machinery, knowledge in electric arc and M.I.G. welding, willingness to work on detailed projects for extended time periods, and general overall knowledge of the automobile manufacturing process. Willingness to learn all maintenance skills a must. You must be a real team player, have excellent interpersonal skills, and be motivated to work in a highly participative environment.

Send qualifications to:

AMM

American Automotive Manufacturing
P.O. Box 616
Ft. Wayne, Indiana 48606
Include phone number. We respond to all applicants.

Maintenance Technician/Welder

Leading automotive manufacturer looking for Maintenance Technician/Welder. Position requires the ability to set up and operate various welding machinery and a general knowledge of the automobile production process. Vocational school graduates or 3–5 years of on-the-job experience required. Competitive salary, full benefits, and tuition reimbursement offered.

Interviews Monday, May 6, at the Holiday Inn South, 3000 Semple Road, 9:00 A.M. to 7:00 P.M. Please bring pay stub as proof of last employment.

NMC

National Motors Corporation
5169 Blane Hill Center
Springfield, Illinois 62707

The Advantages of Teams

Whether one is a manager, a subordinate, a student, or a homemaker, it is almost impossible to avoid being a member of a team. Some form of teamwork permeates most people's daily lives. Most of us are members of discussion groups, friendship groups, neighborhood groups, sports teams, or even families in which tasks are accomplished and interpersonal interaction occurs. Teams, in other words, are simply groups of people who are interdependent in the tasks they perform, affect one another's behavior through interaction, and see themselves as a unique entity. What we discuss in this chapter is applicable to team activity in most kinds of settings, although we focus mainly on teams and teamwork in employing organizations rather than in homes, classrooms, or in the world of sports. The principles of effective team performance, team leadership, and team participation we address here, however, are virtually the same across all these kinds of teams.

For example, empowered teams, autonomous work groups, semiautonomous teams, self-managing teams, self-determining teams, crews, platoons, cross-functional teams, top management teams, quality circles, project teams, task forces, virtual teams, emergency response teams, and committees are all examples of the various manifestations of teams and teamwork that appear in the scholarly literature, and research has been conducted on each of these forms of teams. Our focus is on helping you develop skills that are relevant in most or all these kinds of situations, whether as a team leader or a team member.

Developing team skills is important because of the tremendous explosion in the use of teams in work organizations over the last decade. For example, 79 percent of *Fortune* 1000 companies reported that they used self-managing work teams, and 91 percent reported that employee work groups were being utilized (Lawler, 1998; Lawler, Mohrman, & Ledford, 1995). More than two thirds of college students participate in an organized team, and almost no one can graduate from a business school anymore without participating in a team project or a group activity. Teams are ubiquitous in both work life and at school.

Possessing the ability to lead and manage teams and teamwork, in other words, has become a commonplace requirement in most organizations. In one survey, the most desired skill of new employees was found to be the ability to work in a team (Wellins, Byham, & Wilson, 1991).

One noted management consultant, Tom Peters (1987), even asserted:

Are there any limits to the use of teams? Can we find places or circumstances where a team structure doesn't make sense? Answer: No, as far as I can determine. That's unequivocal, and meant to be. Some situations may seem to lend themselves more to team-based management than others. Nonetheless, I observe that the power of the team is so great that it is often wise to violate apparent common sense and force a team structure on almost anything. (p. 306)

One reason for the escalation in the desirability of teamwork is that increasing amounts of data show improvements in productivity, quality, and morale when teams are utilized. Many companies have attributed their improvements in performance directly to the institution of teams in the workplace (Cohen & Bailey, 1997; Guzzo & Dickson, 1996; Hamilton, Nickerson, & Owan, 2003; Katzenbach & Smith, 1993; Senge, 1991). For example, by using teams in their organizations:

❏ Shenandoah Life Insurance Company in Roanoke, Virginia, saved $200,000 annually because of reduced staffing needs, while increasing its volume 33 percent.
❏ Westinghouse Furniture Systems increased productivity 74 percent in three years.
❏ AAL increased productivity by 20 percent, cut personnel by 10 percent, and handled 10 percent more transactions.
❏ Federal Express cut service errors by 13 percent.
❏ Carrier reduced unit turnaround time from two weeks to two days.
❏ Volvo's Kalamar facility reduced defects by 90 percent.
❏ General Electric's Salisbury, North Carolina, plant increased productivity by 250 percent compared to other GE plants producing the same product.
❏ Corning cellular ceramics plant decreased defect rates from 1,800 parts per million to 9 parts per million.

❏ AT&T's Richmond operator service increased service quality by 12 percent.
❏ Dana Corporation's Minneapolis valve plant trimmed customer lead time from six months to six weeks.
❏ General Mills plants became 40 percent more productive than plants operating without teams.
❏ A garment-making plant increased its productivity 14 percent by adopting a team-based production system.

Table 9.1 reports the positive relationships between employee involvement in teams and several dimensions of organizational and worker effectiveness. Lawler, Mohrman, and Ledford (1995) found that among firms that were actively using teams, both organizational and individual effectiveness were above average and improving in virtually all categories of performance. In firms without teams or in which teams were infrequently used, effectiveness was average or low in all categories.

Of course, a variety of factors can affect the performance and usefulness of teams. Teams are not inherently effective just because they exist. A *Sports Illustrated* cover story, for example, labeled the Los Angeles Clippers NBA basketball team the worst team in the history of professional sports from inception to the year 2000 (Lidz, 2000)—evidence that just because a group of talented people get together does not mean that an effective team can be created. Hackman (1993) identified a set of common inhibitors to effective team performance, including rewarding and recognizing individuals instead of the team, not maintaining stability of membership over time, not providing team members with autonomy, not fostering interdependence among team members, and failing to orient all team members. In contradiction to Peters' comments about the universal utility of teams, Verespei (1990) observed:

All too often corporate chieftains read the success stories and ordain their companies to adopt work teams—NOW. Work teams don't always work and may even be the wrong solution to the situation in question.

The instrument, called "*Diagnosing the Need for Team Building*" in the Skill Assessment section of this chapter, helps identify the extent to which the work teams in which you are involved are performing effectively, and the extent to which they need team building. Often, teams can take too long to make decisions, they

Table 9.1	Impact of Involvement in Teams on Organizations and Workers
PERFORMANCE CRITERIA	**PERCENT INDICATING IMPROVEMENT**
Changed management style to more participatory	78
Improved organizational processes and procedures	75
Improved management decision making	69
Increased employee trust in management	66
Improved implementation of technology	60
Elimination of layers of management supervision	50
Improved safety and health	48
Improved union-management relations	47
PERFORMANCE CRITERIA	**PERCENT INDICATING POSITIVE IMPACT**
Quality of products and services	70
Customer service	67
Worker satisfaction	66
Employee quality of work life	63
Productivity	61
Competitiveness	50
Profitability	45
Absenteeism	23
Turnover	22

(N = 439 of the *Fortune* 1000 firms)

Source: *Impact of involvement in teams on organizations and workers, Lawler, E. E., Mohman, S. A., & Ledford, G. E. (1992). Creating high performance organizations: Practices and results of employee involvement and total quality in Fortune 1000 companies. San Francisco: Reprinted with permission of John Wiley & Sons, Inc.*

can drive out effective action by becoming too insular, and they can create confusion, conflict, and frustration for their members. All of us have been irritated by being members of an inefficient team, a team dominated by a single person, a team with slothful members, or a team in which standards are compromised in order to get agreement from everyone. The common adage that "a camel is a horse designed by a team" illustrates one of the many potential liabilities of a team.

On the other hand, a great deal of research has been conducted to identify the factors associated with high performance in teams. Factors such as team composition (e.g., heterogeneity of members, size of the team, familiarity among team members), team motivation (e.g., team potency, team goals, team feedback), team type (e.g., virtual teams, cockpit crews, quality circles) and team structure (e.g., team member autonomy, team norms, team decision-making processes) have been studied to determine how best to form and lead teams (see comprehensive reviews by Cohen & Bailey,

1997; Guzzo & Dickson, 1996; Hackman, 2003). Several thousand studies of groups and teams have appeared in just the last decade. Self-managing work teams, problem-solving teams, therapy groups, task forces, interpersonal growth groups, student project teams, and many other kinds of teams have been studied extensively. Studies have ranged from teams meeting for just one session to teams whose longevity extends over several years. Membership in teams has varied widely, ranging from children to aged people, top executives to line workers, students to instructors, volunteers to prison inmates, professional athletes to playground toddlers. The analyses have included a variety of predictors of performance such as team-member roles, unconscious cognitive processes, group dynamics, problem-solving strategies, communication patterns, leadership actions, interpersonal needs, decision-making quality, innovativeness, and productivity (e.g., Ancona & Caldwell, 1992; Gladstein, 1984; Senge, 1991; Wellins et al., 1991).

We will not spend time in this chapter reviewing the extensive literature associated with teams, nor the multitude of factors that have been associated with team performance. Instead, we focus on a few key skills that will help you lead and participate effectively in most kinds of teams. We particularly focus here on teams that are faced with a task to accomplish. This may be a work team at your job, a project team composed of fellow students, an ad hoc team discussing an issue, or a self-managing team in a service organization. Regardless of the form of the team, you will want to improve your skills in helping the team become a high-performing unit. We will concentrate first on helping you understand the development of teams and how to diagnose the key issues present in each of four stages of team development. Then we focus on helping you improve your capability to lead teams in these various stages, and to become a more effective member of a team.

AN EXAMPLE OF AN EFFECTIVE TEAM

To illustrate some of the principles we discuss in this chapter, we briefly describe one of the most effective team efforts we know about. It is the team formed to plan and conduct the logistical support for the United States' engagement in the 1990 Persian Gulf War (Desert Storm)—the original conflict motivated by Iraq's threatened invasion of Kuwait. General Gus Pagonis was the designated leader of this team, which was organized as a result of the first President George Bush's announcement that the United States would send troops to Saudi Arabia in order to confront the Iraqi aggression into Kuwait.

The tasks Pagonis faced were daunting. He was charged with building a team that could transport more than half a million people and their personal belongings to the other side of the world, on short notice. But transporting the people was only part of the challenge. Supporting them once they arrived, moving them into position for a surprise attack, supporting their battle plans, and then getting them and their equipment back home in record time were even greater challenges.

More than 122 million meals had to be planned, moved, and served—approximately the number eaten by all the residents of Wyoming and Vermont in three months. Fuel (1.3 billion gallons) had to be pumped—about the same amount used in Montana, North Dakota, and Idaho in a year—in order to support soldiers driving 52 million miles. Tanks, planes, ammunition, carpenters, cashiers, morticians, social workers, doctors, and a host of support personnel had to be

transported, coordinated, fed, and housed. More than 500 new traffic signs had to be constructed and installed in order to help individuals speaking several different languages navigate the relatively featureless terrain of Saudi Arabia. Five hundred tons of mail had to be sorted and processed each day. More than 70,000 contracts with suppliers had to be negotiated and executed. All green-colored equipment—more than 12,000 tracked vehicles and 117,000 wheeled vehicles—had to be repainted desert brown and then repainted green when shipped home. Soldiers had to be trained to fit in with an unfamiliar culture that was intolerant of typical soldier-relaxation activity. Supplies had to be distributed at a moment's notice to several different locations, some of them behind enemy lines, in the heat of battle. Traffic control was monumental, as evidenced by one key checkpoint near the front where 18 vehicles per minute passed, seven days a week, 24 hours a day, for six weeks. More than 60,000 enemy prisoners of war had to be transported, cared for, and detained.

Because the war ended far sooner than predicted, an even more daunting challenge presented itself—getting all those supplies and personnel back home. Most of the equipment, ammunition, and food had to be brought back home because it had been unpacked but was mostly unused. That required thorough scrubbing to remove microorganisms or pests and reshrinkwrapping a huge amount of supplies. Since large, bulk containers had been broken up into smaller units during the war, it took twice as long to gather and ship materials out of Saudi Arabia as it did to ship them in. Yet, personnel were eager to return home at the end of the campaign, so the pressure for speed was at least as great as at the outset of the war. In short, Pagonis' team faced a set of tasks that had never before been accomplished on that scale, and they were to do it in a time frame that would have been laughable if it weren't factual.

The team building and teamwork skills used to accomplish these tasks was detailed in Pagonis' 1993 book, *Moving Mountains*. Pagonis was awarded a third star during Desert Storm as a result of his outstanding leadership in the field of battle. He helped plan and execute the famous "end run" that took the Iraqi army completely by surprise. Most observers now agree that it was the success of the logistics team that really won the Persian Gulf War for the United States in 1991 and saved tens of thousands, if not hundreds of thousands, of lives. We use excerpts from his description of this team's functioning to illustrate principles of effective team building and team leadership in the sections that follow.

Team Development

Regardless of whether you play the role of team leader or team member, in order to function effectively in a team it is important that you understand that all teams progress through stages of development. These stages cause the dynamics within the team to change, the relationships among team members to shift, and effective leader behaviors to be modified. In this section we outline the four major stages that teams pass through from early stages of development—when a team is still struggling to become a coherent entity—to a more mature stage of development—when the team has become a highly effective, smoothly functioning unit. The skill we want you to develop is to be able to diagnose the stage of your team's development so that you will know what kinds of behaviors will most effectively enhance your team's performance.

Evidence of predictable patterns of team development has been available since the early part of this century (Dewey, 1933; Freud, 1921). In fact, despite the variety in composition, purpose, and longevity of the teams investigated in a large array of studies, the stages of group and team development have been strikingly similar (Cameron & Whetten, 1984; Hackman, 2003; Quinn & Cameron, 1983). The research shows that teams tend to develop through four separate, sequential stages. These stages were first labeled by Tuckman (1965) as **forming, norming, storming,** and **performing.** Because of their rhyme and parsimony, these labels are still widely used today. (Tuckman's second and third stages are reversed in this chapter based on the research of Greiner, 1972, and Cameron & Whetten, 1981.)

Table 9.2 summarizes the four main stages of team development. In order for teams to be effective and for team members to benefit most from team membership, teams must progress through the first three stages of development to achieve Stage 4. In each separate stage, unique challenges and issues predominate, and it is by successfully diagnosing and managing these issues and challenges that a team matures and becomes more effective. For each of the four stages, we first identify major team member issues and questions, then we identify the management responses that help the team effectively transcend that stage of development.

THE FORMING STAGE

When team members first come together, they are much like an audience at the outset of a concert. They are not a team but an aggregation of individuals sharing a common setting. Something must happen for them to feel that they are a cohesive unit. When you meet with a group of people for the first time, for example, chances are that you do not feel integrated with the group right away. Several questions are probably on your mind, such as:

- ❏ Who are these other people?
- ❏ What is expected of me?
- ❏ Who is going to lead?
- ❏ What is supposed to happen?

The questions uppermost in the minds of participants in a new team have to do with establishing a sense of security and direction, getting oriented, and

Table 9.2	Four Stages of Team Development
STAGE	**EXPLANATION**
Forming	The team is faced with the need to become acquainted with its members, its purpose, and its boundaries. Relationships must be formed and trust established. Clarity of direction is needed from team leaders.
Norming	The team is faced with creating cohesion and unity, differentiating roles, identifying expectations for members, and enhancing commitment. Providing supportive feedback and fostering commitment to a vision are needed from team leaders.
Storming	The team is faced with disagreements, counterdependence, and the need to manage conflict. Challenges include violations of team norms and expectations and overcoming groupthink. Focusing on process improvement, recognizing team achievement, and fostering win/win relationships are needed from team leaders.
Performing	The team is faced with the need for continuous improvement, innovation, speed, and capitalizing on core competencies. Sponsoring team members' new ideas, orchestrating their implementation, and fostering extraordinary performance are needed from the team leaders.

becoming comfortable with the new situation. Sometimes, new team members can articulate these questions, while at other times they are little more than general feelings of discomfort or disconnectedness. Uncertainty and ambiguity tend to predominate as individuals seek some type of understanding and structure. Because there is no shared history with the team, there is no unity among members. Thus, the typical interpersonal relationships that predominate in this stage are:

❏ Silence
❏ Self-consciousness
❏ Dependence
❏ Superficiality

Even though some individuals may enter a team situation with great enthusiasm and anticipation, they are usually hesitant to demonstrate their emotions to others until they begin to feel at ease. Moreover, without knowing the rules and boundaries, it feels risky to speak out or to even ask questions. Seldom are new members willing to actively query a leader when a team first meets together, even though uncertainty prevails. When a leader asks questions of team members, rarely does someone jump at the chance to give an answer. When answers are given, they are likely to be brief. Little interaction occurs among team members themselves, most communication is targeted at the team leader or person in charge, and each individual is generally thinking more of himself or herself than of the team. Interactions tend to be formal and guarded. Congruent behaviors are masked in the interest of self-protection.

Individuals cannot begin to feel like a team until they become familiar with the rules and boundaries of their setting. They don't know whom to trust, who will take initiative, what constitutes normal behavior, or what kinds of interactions are appropriate. They are not yet a real team but only a collection of individuals. Therefore, the task of the team in this stage is less focused on producing an output than on developing the team itself. Helping team members become comfortable with one another takes precedence over task accomplishment. A team faces the following kinds of task issues in its first stage of development:

❏ Orienting members and getting questions answered
❏ Establishing trust
❏ Establishing relationships with the leader(s)
❏ Establishing clarity of purpose, norms, procedures, and expectations

This stage may be brief, but it is not a time to rely on free and open discussion and consensus decision making to accomplish an outcome. Direction, clarity, and structure are needed instead. The first task is to ensure that all team members know one another and that their questions are answered. Because relatively little participation may occur during this stage, the temptation may be to rush ahead or to short-circuit introductions and instructions. However, teams tend to flounder later if the challenges of this stage are not adequately managed.

In the case of the Persian Gulf logistics team, the first critical task was to make certain that objectives, rules and regulations, time frames, and resources were clearly laid out. Each member of the team had to become comfortable with his or her team membership:

The team got down to work with a redoubled sense of urgency. They were soon fully familiar with the plan that had been roughed out. We quickly got to a joint understanding of what I took to be our role in the theater. Our session . . . was very successful, mainly because from the outset we had a well-defined structure for invention. We worked toward several clearly expressed goals, and there was an imposed time limit to keep us on track. And finally, our various experiences were complementary. We needed each other and we knew it. (Pagonis, 1993, pp. 82–83)

THE NORMING STAGE

Once team members have become oriented, achieved clarity about the team's goals, and accepted their place in the team, the main challenge of the team is to create a cohesive unit or a "sense of team." Norms, rules, and expectations are clarified in the first stage, but an underlying team culture and informal relationships among members must also be developed. The need to move the team from a group of individuals sharing a common goal to a highly cohesive unit is the motivation that leads the team to a new stage of development—the norming stage. The more team members interact with one another, the more they develop common behaviors and perspectives. They experience a certain amount of pressure to conform to the expectations of other team members, so the team begins to develop a character and culture of its own. We all have experienced strong peer pressure, the clearest example of the dynamics in this stage of team development. A new cohesive team culture affects the amount of work done by the team, its style of communicating, approaches to problem solving, and even team member dress.

The major focus of team members, in other words, shifts from overcoming uncertainty in the forming stage to developing the norms of a unified group. Typical questions in team members' minds during this stage include:

❏ What are the norms and values of the team?
❏ How can I best get along with everyone else?
❏ How can I show my support to others?
❏ How can I fit in?

During the norming stage, team members become contented with team membership and begin to value the team's goals more than their own personal goals. Individual needs are met through the team's accomplishments. The team, rather than the leader or a single person, takes responsibility for solving problems, confronting and correcting mistakes, and ensuring success. Agreement and a willingness to go along characterize the climate of the team. Individuals experience feelings of loyalty to the team, and the interpersonal relationships that most characterize team members include:

❏ Cooperativeness
❏ Conformity to standards and expectations
❏ Heightened interpersonal attraction
❏ Ignoring disagreements

This norming stage is a time when effective teams encourage relationship-building roles. Participation by all team members is encouraged, and the team takes responsibility for ensuring that it:

❏ Maintains unity and cohesion
❏ Facilitates participation and empowerment
❏ Shows support to team members
❏ Provides feedback on team and team member performance

A major problem may arise in this stage of development, however, especially if the team refuses to move on. That problem is an increasing inability to engender diversity and varied perspectives in the team. Whereas team members may feel extremely satisfied with their tightly bonded unit, the team risks a danger of developing groupthink (Janis, 1972). Groupthink occurs when the cohesiveness and inertia developed in a team drives out good decision making and problem solving. The preservation of the team takes precedence over accurate decisions or high-quality task accomplishment. Not enough differentiation and challenge to the team's mindset occurs.

Irv Janis (1972) conducted research in which he chronicled several high-performing teams that in one instance performed in a stellar fashion, but performed disastrously in another instance. His classic example was the cabinet of President John F. Kennedy. This team worked through what is often considered one of the best sets of decisions ever made in handling the Cuban Missile Crisis, in which the former Soviet Union was inhibited from placing warhead missiles in Cuba by means of a high-stakes confrontation by Kennedy and his cabinet. This was also the same team, however, that earlier had made the disastrous decisions related to the Bay of Pigs fiasco, in which a planned overthrow of Fidel Castro's government in Cuba became a logistical nightmare, a confluence of indecision, and an embarrassing defeat for the same subsequently high-functioning team.

What was the difference? Why did the same team do so well in one circumstance and so poorly in another? Janis' answer is groupthink. Groupthink typically occurs when the following attributes develop in teams that are stuck in the norming stage.

❏ *Illusion of invulnerability.* Members feel assured that the team's past success will continue. ("Because of our track record, we cannot fail.")
❏ *Shared stereotypes.* Members dismiss disconfirming information by discrediting its source. ("These people just don't understand these things.")
❏ *Rationalization.* Members rationalize away threats to an emerging consensus. ("This is the reason they don't agree with us.")
❏ *Illusion of morality.* Members believe that they, as moral individuals, are not likely to make wrong decisions. ("This team would never knowingly make a bad decision or do anything immoral.")
❏ *Self-censorship.* Members keep silent about misgivings and try to minimize doubts. ("I must be wrong if others think that way.")
❏ *Direct pressure.* Sanctions are imposed on members who explore deviant viewpoints. ("If you don't agree, why don't you leave the team?")
❏ *Mind guarding.* Members protect the team from being exposed to disturbing ideas. ("Don't listen to them. We need to keep the rabble rousers at bay.")

- *Illusion of unanimity.* Members conclude that the team must have reached a consensus since the most vocal members are in agreement. ("If Dave and Melissa agree, there must be a consensus.")

The problem with groupthink is that it leads teams to commit more errors than normal. For example, consider the following commonly observed scenario. Not wanting to make a serious judgment error, a leader convenes a meeting of his or her team. In the process of discussing an issue, the leader expresses a preference for one option. Other team members, wanting to appear supportive, present arguments justifying the decision. One or two members tentatively suggest alternatives, but they are strongly overruled by the majority. The decision is carried out with even greater conviction than normal because everyone is in agreement, but the consequences are disastrous. How did this happen? While the leader brought the team together to avoid making a bad decision, the presence of groupthink actually made a bad decision more likely. Without the social support provided by the team, the leader may have been more cautious in implementing a personally preferred but uncertain decision.

To manage this tendency to develop groupthink, the team must move through the norming stage into the storming stage. The team must develop attributes that will foster diversity, heterogeneity, and even conflict in the team's processes. In particular, Janis makes the following suggestions for addressing groupthink:

- *Critical evaluators.* At least one team member should be assigned to perform the role of critic or evaluator of the team's decisions.
- *Open discussion.* The team leader should not express an opinion at the outset of the team meeting but should encourage open discussion of differing perspectives by team members.
- *Subgroups.* Multiple subgroups in the team may be formed to develop independent proposals.
- *Outside experts.* Invite outside experts to listen to the rationale for the team's decision and critique it.
- *Devil's advocate.* Assign at least one team member to play devil's advocate during the discussion if it seems that too much homogeneity exists in the team's discussion.
- *Second-chance meetings.* Sleep on the team's decision and revisit it afresh the next day. The expression of team members' second thoughts should be encouraged.

In other words, teams in the norming stage become cohesive and highly integrated entities, and this may create a tendency to preserve high involvement and good feeling at the expense of all else. Having a cohesive family feeling is necessary to pull the separate members together and to create a singular identity. However, it can prove disastrous if important information is filtered out, contrary points of view are squelched, or nonconformity in any form is punished. Effective teams must also move on to the next stage, the storming stage of development.

THE STORMING STAGE

Whereas the comfortable climate that team members develop in the norming stage can lead to an excessive amount of agreement and homogeneity, it also can lead to the opposite phenomenon. That is, once team members begin to feel comfortable with the team, they often begin to explore different roles. Some may tend toward task facilitation, for example, while others may tend toward relationship building. This differentiation of team members' roles invariably leads the team into a stage of potential conflict and counterdependence— a storming stage.

Playing different roles causes team members to develop different perspectives and to develop ideas that challenge the leadership and direction of the team. Virtually every effective team goes through a stage in which team members question the legitimacy of the team's direction, the leader, the roles of other team members, the opinions or decisions of others, and the task objectives. Up to now, the team was largely characterized by harmony and consensus. Individual differences were suppressed in order to create a sense of team. However, such a condition will not last forever without team members becoming uncomfortable about losing their individual identity, subjugating their feelings, or stifling differing perspectives. The team's long-term success, therefore, will depend on how well it manages the storming stage of development. Typical questions that arise in team members' minds during this stage are:

- How will we handle dissension?
- How can we make decisions amidst disagreement?
- How will we communicate negative information?
- Do I want to maintain my membership in the team?

An old Middle Eastern proverb states: "All sunshine makes a desert." Similarly, team development

LEARNING

implies that some struggles must occur, some discomfort must be experienced, and some obstacles must be overcome for the team to prosper. The team must learn to deal with adversity—especially that produced by its own members. Tendencies toward groupthink must be attacked head-on. If team members are more interested in keeping peace than in solving problems and accomplishing tasks, the team will never become effective. No one wants to remain in a team that will not allow for individuality and uniqueness and that wants to maintain harmony more than it wants to accomplish its goals. Consequently, harmony is sometimes sacrificed as the team attacks problems and accomplishes objectives.

Of course, team members do not cease to care about one another, and they remain committed to the team and its success. But they do begin to take sides on issues, to find that they are more compatible with some team members than others, and to align themselves with certain points of view. This leads to:

❏ Coalitions or cliques being formed
❏ Competition among team members
❏ Disagreement with the leader
❏ Challenging others' points of view

During Desert Storm, for example, a relatively rigid military command hierarchy—along with the urgency of the mission to be performed—inhibited large deviations from established norms and rules, but small aberrations began to emerge as Pagonis' team developed. Logistics team members painted personal logos on some tanks and trucks, insider code names were given to people and locations as a bit of sarcasm, and challenges to top-brass mandates became more common in briefing rooms. This testing of norms and boundaries is sometimes merely an expression of a need for individuality, while in other instances it is a product of strong feelings that the team can be improved. The main task issues to be addressed by the team in this stage include:

❏ Managing conflict
❏ Legitimizing productive expressions of individuality
❏ Turning counterdependence into interdependence
❏ Fostering consensus-building processes

Conflict, coalition formation, and counterdependence create conditions that may lead to the norms and values of the team being questioned. Rather than being stifled or resisted, however, effective teams encourage members to turn those challenges into constructive suggestions for improvement. It is important for team members to feel that they can legitimately express their personal uniqueness and idiosyncrasies, so long as they are not destructive to the overall team. It is clear from research on teams that when they face difficult or complex problems, teams are more effective if membership is heterogeneous than if all team members act, believe, and see things the same way (Campion, Medsker, & Higgs, 1993; Hackman, 2003). Diversity is productive in fostering creativity, individuality, and solutions to difficult problems (Cox, 1994). It has been said that "teams make complex problems simple." The trouble is, "teams also make simple problems complex," so diversity and heterogeneity are not universally appropriate. The first two stages of team development, in fact, are purposeful in minimizing diversity and heterogeneity. In this stage, however, maintaining flexibility in the team implies that tolerance for individuality is acceptable and that changes and improvements are promoted. General Pagonis' philosophy about the way to manage differences was to encourage their expression:

The key is to be open to different experiences and perspectives. If you can't tolerate different kinds of people, you're not likely to learn from different kinds of perspectives. Effective leaders encourage contrary opinions, an important source of vitality. This is especially true in the military where good ideas come in an incredible variety of packages. (Pagonis, 1993, p. 24)

In the storming stage of development, tensions arise between forces pushing the team toward cohesion and forces pushing it toward differentiation. At the same time strong bonds of team unity have been fostered, individuals begin differentiating themselves from one another and adopting unique roles in the team. They become complementary. This complementarity of roles may actually foster team cohesion and productivity rather than conflict, however, if the team:

❏ Identifies an external enemy (rather than one another) as a target for competition
❏ Reinforces team commitment with recognition of team-level performance
❏ Maintains visibility of vision and superordinate goals
❏ Turns students into teachers by having team members teach the group's values and vision to others

Pagonis' logistics team illustrates the value of the first three suggestions above—identifying an external enemy, team-level recognition, and vision.

In the presence of the enemy, our strength was flexibility, both as individuals and as a group. Organizations must be flexible enough to adjust and conform when their environments change. But the flexibility can degenerate into chaos in the absence of well-established goals. . . . Once everyone in the organization understands the goals of the organization, then each person sets out several objectives by which to attain those goals within his or her own sphere of activity. . . . When it works, cooperation and collegiality are enhanced, and in-fighting and suboptimization are minimized. (Pagonis, 1993, p. 83)

The fourth suggestion above is illustrated well by a process used effectively by Xerox Corporation to address stiff competition from external competitors—mainly Canon. Figure 9.2 illustrates a process implemented by Xerox where students were turned into teachers in order to ensure that a common vision and common processes were implemented throughout the company. To ensure that all units and all managers were working in harmony, the company divided itself into hierarchical family teams. A four-step process was then implemented:

1. *Learn.* Core principles, vision, and values were taught and discussed.
2. *Apply.* Action plans were formed and an improvement agenda was implemented.
3. *Teach.* The principles and successful experiences were taught to the next-lower family team.
4. *Inspect.* The performance and action plans of this lower family team were measured and monitored.

Teams were exposed to the desired information four times: when they learned it, when they applied it, when they taught it, and when they inspected it. More importantly, because team members were engaged in teaching others, their commitment to the team, even in light of differentiated roles, was enhanced.

THE PERFORMING STAGE

The performing stage of development represents highly effective and efficient team functioning. Because the team has worked through the issues embedded in each of the previous stages of development, it is able to work

Figure 9.2   The Xerox Dissemination Process

Family Group 1: Learn — Apply — Teach — Measure

Family Group 2: Learn — Apply — Teach — Measure

Family Group 3: Learn — Apply — Teach — Measure

Each person is exposed to information four times:
- When they get trained
- When they apply it
- When they teach it
- When they measure someone else's application

at a high level of performance. The team has overcome issues of skepticism, uncertainty, nonparticipativeness, dependence, and self-centeredness typical of the first, or forming stage of development. It has developed a clear mission, personal commitment to the team, a high degree of loyalty and morale, and has overcome tendencies toward groupthink that can occur in the norming stage. It has fostered differentiation and variety while also overcoming tendencies toward counterdependence, conflict, polarization, and disharmony typical of the storming stage. It now has the potential to develop the attributes of a high-performing team.

A listing of attributes of high-performance teams is provided in Table 9.3, based on research summarized

---

Table 9.3 Some Attributes of High-Performing Teams

- *Performance outcomes*

  High-performing teams do things. They produce something; they don't just discuss it. Without accomplishment, teams dissolve and become ineffective over time.

- *Specific, shared purpose and vision*

  The more specific the purpose, the more commitment, trust, and coordination can occur. Individuals don't work for themselves; they work for one another in pursuit of the shared purpose. The shared purpose can also be the same as a motivating vision of what the team should achieve.

- *Mutual, internal accountability*

  The sense of internal accountability is far greater than any accountability imposed by a boss or outsider. Self-evaluation and accountability characterize a high-performing team.

- *Blurring of formal distinctions*

  Team members do whatever is needed to contribute to the task, regardless of previous positions or titles. Team membership and team roles are more predominant than outside status.

- *Coordinated, shared work roles*

  Individuals always work in coordination with others on the team. The desired output is a single group product, not a set of individual products.

- *Inefficiency leading to efficiency*

  Because teams allow for lots of participation and sharing, mutual influence about purpose, and blurring of roles, they may initially be inefficient. As the team develops, because they come to know one another so well and can anticipate each other's moves, they become much more efficient than single people working alone.

- *Extraordinarily high quality*

  Teams produce outcomes above and beyond current standards of performance. They surprise and delight their various constituencies with quality levels not expected and never before obtained. An intolerance of mediocrity exists, so standards of performance are very high.

- *Creative continuous improvement*

  Large-scale innovations as well as never-ending small improvements characterize the team's processes and activities. Dissatisfaction with the status quo leads to a constant flow of new ideas, experimentation, and a quest for progress.

- *High credibility and trust*

  Team members trust one another implicitly, defend members who are not present, and form interdependent relationships with one another. Personal integrity and honesty characterize team activities and team member interactions.

- *Clarity of core competence*

  The unique talents and strategic advantages of the team and its members are clear. The ways in which these competencies can be utilized to further the team's objectives are well understood. Extraneous activities and deflections from the team's core mission are given low priority.

Source: *Adapted from Hackman, 1990, 2003; Katzenbach & Smith, 1993; Lawler, 1998, 2003.*

in Cohen and Bailey (1997), Guzzo and Dickson (1996), Hackman (1990; 2003), Katzenbach and Smith (1993), Parker (1996), and Yeatts and Hyten (1998). These attributes are those that produce the benefits enumerated earlier in the chapter (e.g., productivity improvements, quality achievements, speed, and cost reductions). By and large, teams produce the dramatic successes in organizations reported in the best-practice literature only if they reach the performing stage of development.

The team in the performing stage is not, of course, free of challenges. The common issues that tend to dominate members of high-performing teams are:

❏ How can we help our members thrive?
❏ How can we foster continuous improvement and creativity?
❏ How can we build on our core competence?
❏ How can we maintain a high level of energy in the team?

Team members' questions in this stage change from being static to being dynamic. They shift in focus from merely accomplishing objectives to fostering change and improvement and achieving extraordinarily positive performance. Continuous improvement replaces accomplishment as an objective. Up to this point, the team has been trying to manage and resolve issues that lead to three key outcomes: (1) accomplishing tasks or objectives, (2) coordinating and integrating team members' roles, and (3) assuring the personal well-being of all team members. It can now turn its attention to achieving a level of performance above the ordinary. The interpersonal relationships of team members are characterized by:

❏ High mutual trust
❏ Unconditional commitment to the team
❏ Mutual training and development
❏ Entrepreneurship

Team members in this stage exhibit a sense of shared responsibility and concern for one another as they carry out their work. Their relationships are not limited merely to accomplishing a task together, but also extend to ensuring that each team member is learning, developing, and flourishing. Coaching and assisting one another is common. In General Pagonis' high-performing team, for example, team members were continuously teaching one another and helping the team and its individuals members become more competent.

I arranged to take a day or two away from headquarters with a group of key people from the command [the team]. We use this brief respite from our everyday activities to take a long look at what our organization is doing. These sessions . . . gave us a chance to work as a group, in a focused way. . . . From Day One, I held large, open classes where we discussed scenarios and potential solutions. I would pose a question to the group: "O.K., you have a ship that docked at Ad Dammam this morning. It's ready to be unloaded, and the onboard crane breaks. What's our response?" Collectively, the group would work toward one of several solutions. . . . These group sessions served several useful purposes at once. Obviously, they brought potential challenges into the open so we could better prepare for them. . . . Equally important, they promoted collaborative discussion across ranks and disciplines. (Pagonis, 1993, pp. 101, 177)

In addition to multifaceted relationships and unconditional commitment to one another, high-performing team members also take responsibility individually for continuously improving the team and its processes. Experimentation, trial-and-error learning, freewheeling discussions of new possibilities, and personal responsibility by everyone for upgrading performance is typical. The team adopts a set of behaviors that help to foster and perpetuate this stage of development, including:

❏ Capitalizing on core competence
❏ Fostering innovation and continuous improvement
❏ Enhancing flourishing relationships
❏ Encouraging positive deviance

The most effective teams in this stage develop the capacity to perform beyond the norm. They achieve outcomes that are extraordinary. They extend the boundaries of what is possible. They become positively deviant. After having moved through the first three stages of development in the Persian Gulf War, for example, General Pagonis' logistics team moved into a stage characterized by activities that extended beyond the norm. On one occasion, for example, Pagonis directed two team members to generate a solution to the problem of how to provide combat troops with decent meals on the front lines.

Imagine that you've been at some remote and desolate desert site for weeks, or even months, consuming dehydrated or vacuum-packed military rations. One day, unannounced, an odd-looking vehicle with the word "Wolfmobile" painted on it comes driving into your camp. The side panels open up, and a smiling crew inside offers to cook you a hamburger to order. "Side of fries? How about a Coke?" Morale shot up everywhere the Wolfmobiles pulled in—a little bit of home in the desert. (Pagonis, 1993, p. 129)

This incident illustrates the major opportunity associated in the fourth stage of development—to help team members expand their focus from merely accomplishing their work and maintaining good interpersonal relationships to upgrading and elevating the team's performance. This level of performance unlocks positive energy and makes it impossible to ever return to a lower level of performance again.

An example of the power of high-performing teams and their effects of members is a story told by our friend Bob Quinn (2005) in which an upper-level executive in a major manufacturing organization was expressing frustration with his company. "The trouble with my firm," lamented the executive, "is that they cannot stand excellence." He illustrated his frustration by recounting the following incident.

One day in his plant, a major problem occurred on the assembly line, and the line had to be shut down and repaired. The issue was serious and required personnel from multiple shifts to come to the plant to work on the problem. As a gesture of good will on his part, this executive purchased lunch—pizza, hot dogs, and soft drinks—for these employees who were going the extra mile for the company. They completed the task at the highest levels of quality and in record time. Sometime later, a representative from the finance department entered the office of this executive, slapped a piece of paper down on the desk, and exclaimed, "We can't pay this bill for the food. You know that it is against corporate policy to purchase food for employees from your budget. This bill will not be reimbursed." Of course, no one could fault the finance department representative—he was simply doing his job and reinforcing the rules. Flabbergasted, however, the executive responded: "Look, I cannot do the same things we have always done and expect different results. I have to break rules once in a while in the service of achieving excellence or extraordinary performance. Buying lunch made all the difference to these employees. It's what accounted for our success."

"This incident just proves," stated the executive, "that my firm cannot stand excellence. They cannot tolerate being extraordinary." Our friend Bob offered this executive some advice. He simply proposed that the executive give up and conform to the rules and expectations. Stop trying to achieve extraordinary levels of success. The executive's reply was telling, however, and illustrates the power of high-performing teams in this fourth stage of development. His reply was: "I can't quit trying. Once I have experience excellence, normal performance is just not good enough anymore. I can't stand still and not to strive for extraordinary results."

Teams in this fourth stage of development are not all outstanding, of course, and unfortunately, are quite rare, yet their power and influence on team members is transformational. Once a person experiences this kind of excellence, team performance stuck in the first three stages of development will never be satisfactory again. Some of the prescriptions for achieving these levels of extraordinary success are highlighted in the sections below as we discuss skills involved in leading teams and in being an effective member of teams.

Leading Teams

In highly effective teams, members' behavior is interdependent, and personal goals are subservient to the accomplishment of the team goal. A commitment to and desire for team membership is present. Even though individuals may be formally designated as a team, if they act so as to bring exclusive credit to themselves, to accomplish their own objectives instead of the team's objective, or to maintain independence from others, they are not truly a team, regardless of the name of the group. A key challenge, then, is to find ways to create the elements of a highly effective team—interdependence, efficiency, magnetism, shared responsibility, positive energy, mutual encouragement, and trust—when individuals may have had no prior commitment to one another or to a common task.

One important factor in creating effective teams, of course, is the role of the leader. As pointed out by Hackman (2003), however, it is not the style of the leader that makes a difference. Multiple leadership styles can be effective, and no one style has particular advantages over others. Rather, it is the skills and capabilities of the leader, or the tools and techniques put into practice that account for effective versus ineffective team performance. We highlight two especially critical aspects of team leadership here. Not only are these two aspects of team leadership observable in General Pagonis, but they have emerged in the scholarly literature as critical factors in leading almost any kind of team (Edmonson, 1999; Hackman, 1990). The first is developing credibility and influence among team members. The second is establishing a motivating vision and goals for the team.

DEVELOPING CREDIBILITY

Effective leaders have the respect and commitment of team members. That is, they develop credibility (Kouzes & Posner, 1987). Establishing credibility and the capacity to influence team members are the first key challenges faced by leaders of teams. Except in rare circumstances (e.g., in a crisis), leading a team by command or direct control is much less effective than leading through influence and indirect control (Druskat & Wheeler, 2000; Hackman, 1987). Consequently, we focus on ways that you can be effective by working *with* team members rather than working *on* team members. Giving directions, articulating goals, or trying to motivate team members are all wasted efforts if you have not established credibility and respect. General Pagonis described this leadership challenge in the following way:

> *I have found, time and time again in commands around the world, that my troops are more invested in their work and better motivated when they understand and buy into the ultimate goals of the operation. Reason counts for far more than rank, when it comes to motivation. And motivation is the root of all organizational progress. Over the years I have developed a very distinctive leadership style. Gus Pagonis' command style, like everyone else's, is unique. This meant that I had choices to make. Would I rather have the world's best port operation officer, if he was someone who didn't already know*

> *my style? Or would I rather have the world's second best port operation officer who knew my style intimately and was comfortable with it? The answer was obvious; we couldn't waste time fighting our own systems. Equally important, we couldn't afford the time that would be wasted as a new person tried to impress me, or get on my good side. We needed an instant body of leaders, strengthened by a united front. We needed to know that we could depend on one another unconditionally. We needed the confidence that the mission, and not personal advancement, would always be paramount in the mind of each participant. (Pagonis, 1993, p. 78, 84)*

In earlier chapters we identified ways to enhance a manager's influence (Chapter 5) and trust (Chapter 8), which are components of credibility. In this chapter we highlight additional behaviors you can use to help establish leadership credibility in a team. Team members, of course, will not follow a person whom they don't trust, who is hypocritical or dishonest, or whose motives appear to be personal aggrandizement instead of the welfare of the team. In fact, Posner and Kouzes (1987) identified credibility as the single most important requirement for leadership effectiveness. Once credibility has been established, then goals for the team can be articulated and the team can move toward high performance. The seven behaviors summarized in Table 9.4 are keys to building and maintaining credibility and influence among team members. Whereas they are simple and straightforward, much scholarly evidence exists that support their efficacy (see Cialdini, 1995; Druskat & Wheeler, 2000; Hackman, 2003; Katzenbach & Smith, 1993; Kramer, 1999; Manz & Sims, 1987; Turner, 2000).

Table 9.4	Ways to Build Team Leader Credibility

Team leaders build credibility with their team members by:

• Demonstrating integrity, representing authenticity, and displaying congruence.

• Being clear and consistent about what they want to achieve.

• Creating positive energy by being optimistic and complimentary.

• Building a base of agreement among team members before moving on, with a focus on task accomplishment.

• Managing agreement and disagreement among team members by using one-sided and two-sided arguments appropriately—one-sided in situations when all team members agree, two-sided when consensus is not preexisting.

• Encouraging and coaching team members to help them improve.

• Sharing information about the team itself, providing perspective from external sources, and encouraging participation.

1. *Demonstrate integrity.* Chief among the behaviors that create leadership credibility is the demonstration of integrity. Integrity means that you do what you say, you behave congruently with your values, and you are believable in what you espouse. Some people call this "walking the talk" or "talking the walk." Credibility is dependent on having team members believe that the leader is trustworthy, that hidden agendas or unspoken motives are absent, and that the leader demonstrates justice and fairness. Individuals who appear to say one thing and do another, who are not honest in their feedback, or who do not follow through with promises are perceived to lack integrity and are ineffective as leaders of teams.

2. *Be clear and consistent.* Expressing certainty about what you want and where you are going, without being dogmatic or stubborn, helps produce confidence on the part of others. Being wishy-washy or inconsistent in your viewpoints inhibits credibility. The electorate in most countries throughout the world rate their politicians as very low in credibility because most candidates appear to be inconsistent in their statements, changing perspectives depending on the audience (Cialdini, 1995). Credible people, on the other hand, can be trusted to be consistent and predictable. A passionate point of view, it is said, is worth 50 IQ points. That's because being clear about what you want reduces uncertainty, fosters clarity, and creates consistency that leads to trust of the part of team members. Articulating and reinforcing an unwavering and persistent point of view is much more effective than changing opinions or preferences depending on whether or not others agree with you.

3. *Create positive energy.* Stay optimistic and complimentary. Most teams do not perform effectively when there is a climate of criticism, cynicism, or negativity. Criticizing team members, past leaders, others outside the team, or even being critical of the circumstances in which the team finds itself are usually not effective ways to help a team perform well. Individuals and teams perform better when positive energy exists—optimism, compliments, celebrations of success, and recognition of progress. This does not mean being unrealistic or a "Pollyanna." Instead, it means that when you are seen as a source of positive energy and enthusiasm, you have more credibility and influence among team members. People are more attracted to positive than negative forces for the same reason they are more likely to say "yes" to a request if they have said "yes" to previous requests (Cialdini, 1995). Team members are more likely to be agreeable and committed to your agenda if you, as the leader, are agreeable and optimistic.

4. *Use commonality and reciprocity.* If you express views in the team that are held in common with team members, they are more likely to agree with your later statements. If you want to foster team change, or move the team toward an outcome that appears to be risky or uncomfortable, begin by expressing views with which other team members agree. It can be as simple as "I know you all have very busy schedules." Or, "We have a lot of diversity of opinion in our team on this issue." These kinds of statements work because of the principle of reciprocity. Team members have a tendency to agree with you more if they have received something from you in advance, even if that is merely your agreement with their point of view. After you have expressed agreement with them, you can then lead them toward goals or targets that may stretch them or that may be uncomfortable or uncertain. Your credibility will have been established if your initial statements are seen as consistent with the values and perspectives of other team members. This is also a fundamental strategy in effective negotiations.

5. *Manage agreement and disagreement.* When team members initially agree with you, you are more effective if you use a one-sided argument. That is, present only one point of view and support it with evidence. When team members tend to disagree with you at the outset, use two-sided arguments. That is, first present both sides of the case and then show how your own point of view is superior to the contrary perspective. Keep in mind that when team members agree with you, the first statements you make tend to hold more weight and are remembered the longest. When they disagree with you, the last statements made tend to carry the most weight.

6. *Encourage and coach.* Providing encouragement to team members has been found to be among the most powerful predictors of effective

team leadership. Encouragement means to help others develop courage—to tackle uncertainty, to achieve beyond their current performance, to disrupt the status quo. Encouraging team members not only involves compliments and supportive statements, it also involves coaching and assistance. Coaching, as pointed out in Chapter 4, means helping to show the way, providing information or advice, and assisting team members with task requirements. It doesn't mean that the team leader becomes controlling or takes over. It means that coaches help others perform well while not being actively involved themselves. Effective encouragement, then, is more than cheerleading. It involves giving both positively reinforcing comments and helpful advice or direction.

7. *Share information.* Credible team leaders are knowledgeable, mainly about the preferences and talents that reside in the team and about the task facing the team. Building credibility means coming to understand the perspectives of team members as well as a sense of their talents and resources. Coming to know your team members well is crucial for successful leadership. One way to do this is to use the principle of "frequent checking." This merely involves asking questions and checking with team members regularly to determine levels of agreement, obstacles, dissatisfactions, needs, and interpersonal or team issues. Credibility is also built by having knowledge about the tasks and the external environment facing the team. This kind of knowledge can be achieved by playing the roles of "ambassador" and "scout" for the team, representing the team to outsiders, and obtaining information from external sources. Importantly, however, credibility grows as knowledge is shared. Being the source from which others can acquire needed information builds credibility and influence, so sharing is crucial. Of course, no leader can be an expert on all topics relevant to the team, but effective leaders continually increase and expand their storehouse of knowledge about the team and its environment.

As stated by General Pagonis:

Keeping [team members] abreast of your actions, as well as the rationale behind those actions, puts everybody on an equal information footing. I believe that information *is power, but only if it is shared. . . . Very early on I had gotten in the habit of sneaking John Carr into these briefing sessions with CINC [General Schwarzkopf and others] by having Carr flip my slides in and out of the overhead projector. That way, he stayed as smart and as current about the CINC's plans as I did. (Pagonis, 1993, p. 88, 131)*

ESTABLISH SMART GOALS AND EVEREST GOALS

Once team members have confidence in the leader, it is then possible for that leader to identify goals that the team can achieve and levels of performance to which team members can aspire. Katzenbach and Smith (1993), in an outstanding study of high-performing teams, reinforced this point of view:

The best teams invest a tremendous amount of time and effort exploring, shaping, and agreeing on a goal that belongs to them collectively and individually. . . . With enough time and sincere attention, one or more broad, meaningful aspirations invariably arise that motivate teams to provide a fundamental reason for their extra effort. (p. 50)

There are two kinds of goals that characterize high-performing teams, and leaders must identify and espouse both kinds. The first are called **SMART** goals and the second are called **Everest goals.** The purpose for establishing clear goals is so that every person on the team can give a similar answer to the question: What are we trying to achieve? Leaders who clearly articulate the desired outcomes for and with the team are more likely to experience high performance from the team. Goal-directed performance, in fact, always exceeds performance disassociated with goals (Locke, 1990). Figure 9.3 illustrates this point.

It shows that when people are given *no goals* ("Here is your task. Go do it."), their performance tends to be low, even though most people will perform at a minimum level even when they are not certain of the standard that they should achieve. However, being provided with an *easy goal* ("The average is 10 per day, but you can shoot for 4.") leads to even lower performance. People tend to work toward the standard that has been established, and when it is easy, they slack off. Establishing *general goals* ("Do your best.") result in improved performance over easy goals, but identifying *difficult goals* ("The average is 10 per day, but you

LEARNING

Figure 9.3   The Effect of Goals on Performance

Low ◄————————————————————————————► High
Performance

Type of Goal

No Goals

Easy Goals

General Goals

Difficult Goals

Difficult SMART Goals

Source: University of Michigan, Positive Organizational Scholarship: Kim Cameron.

should shoot for 12.") produces far higher levels of performance. The kinds of goals that produce the highest levels of performance, however are difficult goals that possess five characteristics. The acronym SMART identifies these attributes. SMART goals are:

- **S**pecific—The goal is clear, and precise targets and standards are identified.
- **M**easurable—The goal can be assessed and quantified. The extent to which the goal has been achieved is obvious.
- **A**ligned—The goal is supportive of and consistent with the goals of the broader organization. People are not pursuing their own objectives independent of their team.
- **R**ealistic—While being difficult and causing performance to stretch, the goal is not foolhardy or a fantasy.
- **T**ime-bound—An end point is identified or a completion date established so that goal achievement is not open-ended.

Consider the difference between goal statements such as "We will be the best in our industry," compared to a goal statement that is SMART: "We will achieve a 5% improvement in the on-time delivery of our products by the end of the quarter." The latter provides a more motivating goal in that it is specific, measurable, aligned with key outcomes, realistic, and time-bound. It gives people something they can easily understand and shoot for. It is important to keep in mind, however, that articulating motivating goals and identifying the methods to achieve them are different. The former specifies the target. The latter specifies the means for achieving the target. The former is crucial to

successful team leadership. The latter is often lethal. Pagonis' team illustrates this well:

> *I never tell a subordinate how to carry out a specific goal. Dictating terms to a subordinate undermines innovation, decreases the subordinate's willingness to take responsibility for his or her actions, increases the potential for sub-optimization of resources, and increases the chances that the command will be dysfunctional if circumstances change dramatically. Our first month in the theater only underscored my sense that our [team] would have to be incredibly elastic. (Pagonis, 1993, p. 119)*

The second type of goal that effective team leaders articulate is called an Everest goal. An Everest goal goes beyond normal goal setting. It represents an ultimate achievement, an extraordinary accomplishment, or a beyond-the-norm outcome. Achieving it requires everything one can give. Like setting your sights on getting to the summit of Mount Everest, an Everest goal is clear and compelling: serves as a unifying focal point; builds team spirit; engages people; and creates positive energy and excitement. An Everest goal is stimulating because it connects to a profound passion. People get it right away, with little explanation. An Everest goal is visionary, not just tactical or strategic, and it leaves people better for having engaged in its pursuit. It requires extraordinary effort to achieve, and maybe a little luck.

Examples of Everest goals include Henry Ford's goal of democratizing the automobile industry so that his workers could afford to purchase cars in the 1920s; Masaru Ibuka's goal of helping Sony to become the company that overcame the image of poor Japanese quality in the 1960s and 1970s; Steven Jobs' goal of one person, one computer throughout the world in the 1980s; or Sam Walton's goal in the 1990s of having Wal-Mart become the first trillion-dollar company.

Team leaders can identify stretch targets, of course, such as: "We will be #1 or #2 in our industry," or "We will be the world's best software team," or "We will achieve 100 percent customer satisfaction." These are very difficult goals to achieve and certainly extend beyond the norm. However, Everest goals have a very important attribute that supplements these goal statements. This attribute is illustrated by the following quotation from a climber who finally made it to the top of Mount Everest after three failed attempts:

I realized something on that night in the dark on Everest. What I realized was that real winning had nothing to do with beating someone else, or crossing the finish line first, or standing on top. Winning wasn't anything external at all. It was an internal satisfaction, a deep inner sense of pride and joy. Success can only be measured within ourselves, by ourselves. It has nothing to do with other people's perception of our achievements. It has everything to do with our own perceptions of our efforts . . . Success isn't standing on the podium, or hearing the cheers of others, or standing on the summit at all. It's giving it your all. . . . I think that in anything in life, if you give it everything you possibly can, you really do succeed. . . . Our business in life is not to get ahead of others but to get ahead of ourselves, to break our own records, to outstrip our yesterday by our today, to do our work with more force than ever before. We took comfort in the words of Gandhi: 'Full effort is full victory'. . .

I have come to understand that for me this notion of success is upside down. In fact, a traditional end—the summit, an Olympic gold medal, or wealth—only serves as a navigational tool, a marker to give the process direction. The end for me is a greater depth and breadth of character. I measure this in terms of greater integrity, better business and communication skills, and a higher personal motivation to become stronger. More simply, my aim is to become as internally knowledgeable and as externally aware as possible. The process, the experience, the struggle, the hard-won lessons, these are ends in themselves. (Clarke & Hobson, 2005, pp. 168, 169)

Everest goals are not merely stretch targets, but they possess the ability to elevate human performance far beyond the norm. People achieve what they could not previously have thought possible. They thrive personally in ways that would not have been feasible otherwise. Typical Everest goals:

❏ Capture deep inner commitment of people because they are tied to something about which they care deeply

❏ Require supreme effort and a passionate commitment

❏ Depend on complete honesty and authenticity, since achieving them cannot be accomplished by trying to be something artificial or false

❏ Motivate learning and wisdom, allowing people to learn new things about themselves and their capabilities in the pursuit of the goal

❏ Enhance positive human relationships—it is impossible to achieve an Everest goal alone, so they require support and interdependence with others

❏ Lead people beyond probabilities into the realm of possibilities, so that previously unconsidered levels of accomplishment become realistic

Identifying such a goal, of course, is neither automatic nor easy. Such goals don't just roll off the tips of our tongues. Most people identify few of these in a lifetime. These goals are often connected to: (1) producing a human benefit for others, (2) a core personal value, (3) producing an impact that extends beyond the immediate, even over a lifetime, (4) virtues such as love, faith, integrity, compassion, hope, or (5) producing a ripple effect, so that the achievement is reproduced over and over again. Establishing Everest goals requires that you get in touch with your personal values, your core mission or purpose in life, and that which provides you profound meaning. Everest goals help you reach those ultimate aspirations.

In summary, being an effective leader of a team requires two key skills: (1) developing credibility among team members and (2) articulating SMART goals and Everest goals for the team. Whereas these are obviously not the only skills that effective team leaders possess, without these two core capabilities, it is unlikely that the teams you lead will be successful.

INTERNATIONAL CAVEATS

We have pointed out throughout the book that individuals in different cultures exhibit differences in values and orientations (Trompenaars, 1996, 1998). Diagnosing, understanding, and capitalizing on individual differences, we repeat, is a crucial skill of competent managers. The seven value orientations identified by Trompenaars provide a useful tool for identifying those individual differences. That is, you can understand differences among people by assessing them on the extent to which they emphasize one value orientation over its opposite: *universalism* versus *particularism*, *individualism* versus *communitarianism*, *neutrality* versus *affectivity*, *specificity* versus *diffuseness*, *achievement* versus *ascription*, *internal* versus *external* control, and *past*, *present*, or *future* time orientation. The first chapter in this book provides a more detailed explanation of these value dimensions.

Individual differences may require that some modification be made in these team leadership behaviors. For example, if you are leading a team with members from cultures that tend to have a *collectivist* (e.g., Mexico, Japan, France, Philippines) as opposed to an *individualist* orientation, team members will expect to be involved in the creation and articulation of the goals. They will be less comfortable with the goals coming from a single leader, regardless of his or her credibility and influence. Consequently, the Everest goal and its accompanying SMART goals should be designed with active participation of team members. Similarly, team members from countries where a *neutral* (e.g., Korea, China, Japan, New Zealand) as opposed to an *affective* culture predominates, may be less energized by language filled with superlatives and passion. Their orientation toward task accomplishment and factual data may mute their responses to emotional language. Consequently, being sensitive to the wording of your Everest goal statement will help make it more motivating.

On the other hand, the differences in cultural values among different nationalities are not so great as to negate the overall effectiveness of the two key skills mentioned above—building credibility and articulating two types of goals. The data from thousands of managers worldwide supports the effectiveness of these two key skills for team leaders, regardless of national differences (see Trompenaars & Hampden-Turner, 1998). You may need to be sensitive to the potential need to modify your behaviors based on the composition of your team, but team composition will not have as strong an influence on team effectiveness as the leadership skills you display. (For one review of team composition influences, see Guzzo & Dickson, 1996.)

Team Membership

Most of the time, most of us will not serve as the leader of the teams in which we participate. Whereas you will want to prepare for the leadership roles you will play in the future, the vast majority of the time you will be an active member of a team, working for the common good of the group, rather than the person in charge. You will be valuable to your team because of the contributions you make in nonleadership roles. Fortunately, you can be at least as effective as a member of a team as you can be as the team's leader in having an effect on its performance. One of the most amazing statements made by General Pagonis as he reviewed the outcomes of Desert Storm related to the performance of his team, even when he was not the active leader:

I meet with skepticism, even disbelief, when I tell people that I didn't issue a single order during the ground war. This is only slightly a stretch of the truth. Yes, people sought and got guidance. But the people in my command knew exactly what they were supposed to do in almost every conceivable circumstance. They had been trained and encouraged to think on their feet. I felt they could even deal with the inconceivable. (Pagonis, 1993, p. 148)

Team members were not only guided by an overarching goal and a clear understanding of what they were to accomplish, but they had become an extraordinarily high-performing team because of the roles played by team members. Pagonis described it this way: "Truth be told, we spent less of our time as logisticians, and more of our time as managers, fixers, firefighters, father confessors, and cheerleaders. There was simply nobody else around to play those roles" (p. 87). In this section, we point out two main skills associated with team membership—playing advantageous roles, and providing helpful feedback to others. Once again, these skills are not complicated, but they have been found to be highly effective in helping team members foster team success (see Parker, 1996).

ADVANTAGEOUS ROLES

Work teams face two main challenges: accomplishing the task that has been assigned and building unity and collaboration among the team members. As a member of a team you can enhance or inhibit those two challenges at least as much as you can as the team leader. All of us have experienced teams that just seemed to click, that were able to get results quickly and effectively, and were fun to be in. Those dynamics don't happen by chance but depend on certain key roles played by team members.

A great deal of research has been done on the power of group pressure and the influence of team members on one another. The classic Solomon Asch experiments (1951) were among the first to highlight the influence of team members on one another. The Asch experiments showed, for example, that when other team members verbalized agreement with a statement that was obviously false—say, "The federal government controls the stock market"—the person being observed also tended to verbalize agreement with the

obviously false statement. Team members' behavior dramatically influenced the behaviors of one another. Most teams don't operate on the basis of blatant pressure tactics, of course, but team performance can be markedly enhanced by having team members play certain roles that facilitate task accomplishment and group cohesion.

Two main types of roles exist that enhance team performance: ***task-facilitating roles*** and ***relationship-building roles*** (Schein, 1976). It is difficult for team members to emphasize both types of roles equally, and most people tend to contribute in one area more than the other. That is, some team members tend to be more task-focused whereas others tend to be more relationship-focused. Task-facilitating roles are those that help the team accomplish its outcomes or objectives. Table 9.5 identifies the most common task-facilitating roles. They include:

Table 9.5	Task-Facilitating Roles
ROLE	EXAMPLES
Direction giving	"This is the way we were instructed to approach our task."
	"Everyone write down your ideas, then share them."
Information seeking	"What did you mean by that?"
	"Does anyone else have more information about this?"
Information giving	"Here are some relevant data."
	"I want to share some information that may be helpful."
Elaborating	"Building on your idea, here is an additional alternative."
	"An example of what you just said is . . ."
Urging	"We have only 10 minutes left, so we need to move more quickly."
	"We can't quit now. We're close to finalizing our proposal."
Monitoring	"You maintain accountability for the first recommendation, and I'll handle the second."
	"Here are some criteria we can use to judge our success."
Process analyzing	"It seems as if the energy level in the team is beginning to decline."
	"I've noticed that the females are participating less than the males in our team."
Reality testing	"Let's see if this is really practical."
	"Do you think this is workable given our resources?"
Enforcing	"We're beginning to wander in our comments; let's stay on task."
	"Since we agreed not to interrupt one another, I suggest we stick to our pact."
Summarizing	"It seems to me that these are the conclusions we have reached."
	"In summary, you have made three points . . ."

- *Direction giving.* Identifying ways to proceed or alternatives to pursue and clarifying goals and objectives.
- *Information seeking.* Asking questions, analyzing knowledge gaps, requesting opinions, beliefs, and perspectives.
- *Information giving.* Providing data, offering facts and judgments, and highlighting conclusions.
- *Elaborating.* Building on the ideas expressed by others; providing examples and illustrations.
- *Urging.* Imploring team members to stay on task and to achieve team goals.
- *Monitoring.* Checking on progress, developing measures of success and helping to maintain accountability for results.
- *Process analyzing.* Analyzing processes and procedures used by the team in order to improve efficiency and timeliness.
- *Reality testing.* Exploring whether ideas presented are practical or workable; grounding comments in reality.
- *Enforcing.* Helping to reinforce team rules, reinforcing standards, and maintaining agreed-upon procedures.
- *Summarizing.* Combining ideas and summing up points made in the team; helping members understand the conclusions that have been reached.

Performing task-facilitating roles helps the team work more efficiently and effectively in achieving its objectives. Without having at least one team member displaying task-facilitating behaviors, teams tend to take longer to achieve their objectives and have difficulty staying focused. In your role as a team member, you will find it useful to sometimes play the role of task facilitator. Sometimes keeping the team "on task" is the most important thing you can do. These roles are especially important when: progress toward goal accomplishment is slow, when the team is being deflected from its task, when time pressures exist, when the assignment is complex or ambiguous and it is not clear how to proceed, or when no one else is helping the team move toward task accomplishment. One doesn't have to be a task master to be an effective facilitator of outcomes. In fact, just recognizing that the team is in need of task facilitation is a big part of being an effective team member. In most effective teams, you will find several members performing these task-facilitation roles.

In addition to task accomplishment, high-performing teams also have a certain amount of interpersonal cohesion and collaboration. An overwhelming amount of evidence exists to suggest that high-performing teams are cohesive, interdependent, and have positive affect among team members (Cohen & Bailey, 1997; Druskat & Wolff, 1999; Gully, Divine, & Whitney, 1995; Mullen & Copper, 1994; Parker, 1996). Relationship-building roles are those that emphasize the interpersonal aspects of the team. They focus on assisting team members to feel good about one another, enjoy the team's work, and maintain a tension-free climate. These roles are especially important when disagreement is prevalent, tension is high, or team members are not contributing to the team's performance. Table 9.6 identifies the most common relationship-building roles:

- *Supporting.* Praising the ideas of others, showing friendliness, and pointing out others' contributions.
- *Harmonizing.* Mediating differences between others, and finding a common ground in disputes and conflicting points of view.
- *Tension relieving.* Using jokes and humor to reduce tension and put others at ease.
- *Confronting.* Challenging unproductive or disruptive behaviors; helping to ensure proper behavior in the team.
- *Energizing.* Motivating others toward greater effort; exuding enthusiasm.
- *Developing.* Assisting others to learn, grow, and achieve; orienting and coaching members of the team.
- *Consensus building.* Helping build solidarity among team members, encouraging agreement, and helping interactions to be smooth.
- *Empathizing.* Reflecting group feelings and expressing empathy and support for team members.

All of us have been on a team, or in a class, when a fellow participant was funny, actively engaging with others, or especially supportive of others on the team or in the class. The chemistry of the group just seems to improve under such conditions. It becomes easier to work and more enjoyable to be a team member. A certain amount of magnetism and positive energy exists. People tend to take more responsibility, collaborate more readily, and try harder to find consensual outcomes. These are the results that are intended by performing relationship-building roles. They are not designed to deflect attention away from the task,

Table 9.6	Relationship-Building Roles
ROLE	**EXAMPLES**
Supporting	"Your ideas are terrific!"
	"I really appreciate your honesty and openness. It's refreshing."
Harmonizing	"I hear the two of you saying essentially the same thing."
	"The disagreements being expressed don't seem to be all that crucial."
Tension relieving	"Hey folks, let's lighten up!"
	"This reminds me of the new conference table we bought. It sleeps 12."
Confronting	"How does your comment address the topic we are discussing?"
	"You are not taking as much responsibility as the other team members."
Energizing	"Your insights are terrific!"
	"This team is the most enjoyable group I've been in for a long time."
Developing	"How can I help you?"
	"Let me give you some assistance with that."
Consensus building	"It seems like we're all saying pretty much the same thing."
	"Can we all at least agree on point number 1, even if we disagree on the rest?"
Empathizing	"I know how you feel."
	"This must be a very sensitive topic for you given your personal experience."

but they assist the team in working more effectively together.

Without both task-facilitating and relationship-building roles, teams struggle to perform effectively. Some members must ensure that the team accomplishes its tasks, while others must ensure that members remain bonded together interpersonally. These are usually not the same individuals, and at certain points in time, different roles may become more dominant than others. The key is to have a balance between task-oriented roles and relationship-building roles displayed in the team. The downfall of many teams is that they become unidimensional—for example, they emphasize task accomplishment exclusively—and do not give equal attention to both types of roles.

Of course, each role can also have a downside if performed ineffectively or in inappropriate circumstances. For example, *elaborating* may be disruptive if the team is trying to reach a quick decision; *tension relieving* may be annoying if the team is trying to be serious; *enforcing* may create resistance when the team is already experiencing high levels of pressure; *consensus building* may mask real differences of opinion and tension among team members. However, it is even more likely that team members will display other unproductive roles rather than inappropriately play task or relationship roles. Unproductive roles inhibit the team or its members from achieving what they could have achieved, and they destroy morale and cohesion. They are called **blocking roles.** We point out a few of them here because, as you analyze the teams to which you belong, you may recognize these roles being performed and be able to confront them. Among the common blocking roles are:

- ❏ *Dominating.* Excessive talking, interrupting, or cutting others off.
- ❏ *Overanalyzing.* Splitting hairs and examining every detail excessively.
- ❏ *Stalling.* Not allowing the group to reach a decision or finalize a task by sidetracking the discussion, being unwilling to agree, repeating old arguments, and so on.
- ❏ *Remaining passive.* Not being willing to engage in the team's task. Staying on the fringe or refusing to interact with other team members. Expecting others to do the team's work.
- ❏ *Overgeneralizing.* Blowing something out of proportion and drawing unfounded conclusions.
- ❏ *Faultfinding.* Being unwilling to see the merits of others' ideas or criticizing others excessively.

❏ *Premature decision making*. Making decisions before goals are stated, information is shared, alternatives are discussed, or problems are defined.

❏ *Presenting opinions as facts*. Failing to examine the legitimacy of proposals and labeling personal opinions as truth.

❏ *Rejecting*. Rejecting ideas based on the person who stated them rather than on their merits.

❏ *Pulling rank*. Using status, expertise, or title to get ideas accepted rather than discussing and examining their value.

❏ *Resisting*. Blocking all attempts to change, to improve, or to make progress. Being disagreeable and negative about virtually all suggestions from other team members.

❏ *Deflecting*. Not staying focused on the topic of the team's discussion. Changing the subject of discussion or making comments that deflect attention away from the main points.

Each of these blocking roles has the potential to inhibit a team from efficiently and effectively accomplishing its task by crushing morale, destroying consensus, creating conflict, hampering progress, and making ill-informed decisions. Effective team members recognize when blocking roles are displayed, confront and isolate dysfunctional members, and provide feedback to those who are inhibiting effective team performance. Knowing the most effective ways in which that feedback can be delivered is the second key skill of team members.

PROVIDING FEEDBACK

It is not easy to provide feedback to someone who is behaving inappropriately or disruptively. Whereas it is much easier to provide positive feedback or give compliments, helping others correct their negative behavior or pointing out the dysfunctions of blocking roles is difficult. Most of us are afraid of offending others, of making the problem worse, or of creating conflict that may destroy team unity. (The chapter on building positive relationships by supportively communicating addressed this issue in detail.) While no set of behaviors are guaranteed to be effective in every situation or with every individual, of course, certain principles for providing feedback—usually negative feedback—have been found to be especially effective (Dew, 1998; Hayes, 1997; Yeatts & Hyten, 1998). They are summarized in Table 9.7.

❏ *Focus feedback on behavior rather than persons*. Individuals can control and change their behavior. They cannot change their personalities or physical characteristics. For example, "Your comments are not on the topic" is more effective than "You are completely naive."

❏ *Focus feedback on observations rather than inferences and on descriptions rather than judgments*. Facts and objective evidence are more trustworthy and acceptable than opinions and conjectures. For example, "The data don't support your point" is more effective than "You just don't get it, do you?"

❏ *Focus feedback on behavior related to a specific situation, preferably to the "here-and-now," rather than on abstract or past behavior*. It will merely frustrate people if they cannot pinpoint a specific incident or behavior to which you are referring. Similarly, people cannot change something that has already happened and is "water under the bridge." For example, "You have yet

Table 9.7 Rules for Effective Team Feedback	
EFFECTIVE FEEDBACK	**INEFFECTIVE FEEDBACK**
Focus on behaviors	Focus on the person
Focus on observations	Focus on inferences
Focus on descriptions	Focus on evaluations
Focus on a specific situation or incident	Focus on abstract or general situations
Focus on the here-and-now	Focus on the past
Focus on sharing ideas and information	Focus on giving advice
Give feedback that is valuable to the receiver	Give feedback that provides an emotional release
Give feedback at an appropriate time and place	Give feedback when it is convenient for you

to agree with anyone's comments" is more effective than "You have always been a problem in this team."

❑ *Focus feedback on sharing ideas and information rather than giving advice.* Explore alternatives together. Unless requested, avoid giving direct instructions demands. Instead, help recipients identify changes and improvements themselves. For example, "How do you suggest we can break this logjam and move forward?" is more effective than "This is what we must do now."

❑ *Focus feedback on the amount of information that the recipient can use, rather than on the amount you might like to give.* Information overload causes people to stop listening. Not enough information leads to frustration and misunderstanding. For example, "You seem to have reached a conclusion before all the facts have been presented" is more effective than "Here are some data you should consider, and here are some more, and here are some more, and here are some more."

❑ *Focus feedback on the value it may have to the receiver, not on the emotional release it provides for you.* Feedback should be for the good of the recipient, not merely for you to let off steam. For example, "I must say that your excessive talking is very troublesome to me and not helpful to the group" is more effective than "You are being a jerk and are a big cause of our team's difficulty in making any progress."

❑ *Focus feedback on time and place so that personal data can be shared at appropriate times.* The more specific feedback is, or the more it can be anchored in a specific context, the more helpful it can be. For example, "During a break I would like to chat with you about something" is more effective than "You think your title gives you the right to force the rest of us to agree with you, but it's just making us angry."

INTERNATIONAL CAVEATS

These team member skills may require some modification in different international settings or with teams comprised of international members (Trompenaars & Hampen-Turner, 1998). Whereas the team member skills discussed above have been found to be effective in a global context, it is naive to expect that everyone will react the same way to team member roles.

For example, in cultures that emphasize *affectivity* (e.g., Iran, Spain, France, Italy, Mexico), personal confrontations and emotional displays are more acceptable than in cultures that are more *neutral* (e.g., Korea, China, Singapore, Japan), where personal references are more offensive. Humor and displaying enthusiastic behavior is also more acceptable in affective cultures than neutral cultures. Similarly, status differences are likely to play a more dominant role in *ascription*-oriented cultures (e.g., Czech Republic, Egypt, Spain, Korea), than in *achievement*-oriented cultures (e.g., United States, Norway, Canada, Australia, United Kingdom), in which knowledge and skills tend to be more important. Appealing to data and facts in the latter cultures will carry more weight than in the former cultures. Some misunderstanding may also arise, for example, in cultures emphasizing different *time frames*. Whereas some cultures emphasize just-in-time, short-term time frames (e.g., United States), others emphasize long-term future time frames (e.g., Japan). The story is told of the Japanese proposal to purchase Yosemite National Park in California. The first thing the Japanese submitted was a 250-year business plan. The reaction of the California authorities was, "Wow, that's 1,000 quarterly reports." The urgency to move a team forward toward task accomplishment, in other words, may be seen differently by different cultural groups. Some cultures (e.g., Japan) are more comfortable spending substantial amounts of time on relationship-building activities before moving toward task accomplishment.

Summary

All of us are members of multiple teams—at work, at home, and in the community. Teams are becoming increasingly prevalent in the workplace and in the classroom because they have been shown to be powerful tools to improve the performance of individuals and organizations. Consequently, it is important to become proficient in leading and participating in teams. It is obvious that merely putting people together and giving them an assigned task does not make them into a team. Students often complain about an excessive amount of teamwork in business schools, but most of it is less real teamwork than a repetitive experience of aggregating people together and assigning them a task. In this chapter we have reviewed three types of team skills: diagnosing and facilitating team development, leading a team, and being an effective team member. Figure 9.4 illustrates the relationship of these three key skills to high performing team performance. These three skills are ones that you have no doubt engaged in

LEARNING

Figure 9.4   Management Skills for High-Performing Teams

Leading Teams
- Develop credibility
- Articulate a vision

Team Membership
- Play task-facilitation roles
- Play relationship-building roles
- Provide feedback

Team Development
- Diagnose stage development
- Foster team development and high performance

High-Performing Teams
- Desired outcomes
- Shared purpose
- Accountability
- Blurred distinctions
- Coordinated roles
- Efficiency and participation
- High quality
- Creative continuous improvement
- Credibility and trust
- Core competence

before, but to be a skillful manager, you will need to hone your ability to perform each of these skill activities competently.

Behavioral Guidelines

1. Learn to diagnose the stage in which your team is operating in order to help facilitate team development and perform your role appropriately. Know the key characteristics of the forming, norming, storming, and performing stages of development.

2. Provide structure and clarity in the forming stage, support and encouragement in the norming stage, independence and exploration in the storming stage, and foster innovation and positive deviance in the performing stage.

3. When leading a team, first develop credibility as a prerequisite to having team members follow you.

4. Based on your established credibility, establish two types of goals for and with your team: SMART goals and Everest goals.

5. As a team member, facilitate task performance in your team by encouraging the performance of different roles listed in Table 9.5.

6. As a team member, facilitate the development of good relationships in your team by encouraging the performance of different roles listed in Table 9.6.

7. When encountering team members who block the team's performance with disruptive behaviors, confront the behavior directly and/or isolate the disruptive member.

8. Provide effective feedback to unhelpful team members that has characteristics listed in Table 9.7.

CASES INVOLVING BUILDING EFFECTIVE TEAMS

The *Tallahassee Democrat*'s ELITE Team

Katzenbach and Smith (1993, pp. 67–72), as part of their extensive research on teams, observed the formation of a team at the Tallahassee Democrat, *the only major newspaper left in Tallahassee, Florida. Here is their description of how the team, which called itself "ELITE Team," performed over time. All incidents and names are factual. As you read the description, look for evidence of team development stages.*

Fred Mott, general manager of the *Democrat*, recognized [the declining profitability and distribution of most major metropolitan newspapers] earlier than many of his counterparts. In part, Mott took his lead from Jim Batten, who made "customer obsession" the central theme of his corporate renewal effort shortly after he became Knight-Ridder's CEO. But the local marketplace also shaped Mott's thinking. The *Democrat* was Tallahassee's only newspaper and made money in spite of its customer service record. Mott believed, however, that further growth could never happen unless the paper learned to serve customers in ways "far superior to anything else in the marketplace." The ELITE Team story actually began with the formation of another team made up of Mott and his direct reports. The management group knew they could not hope to build a "customer obsession" across the mile-high barriers isolating production from circulation from advertising without first changing themselves. It had become all too common, they admitted, for them to engage in "power struggles and finger pointing."

Using regularly scheduled Monday morning meetings, Mott's group began to "get to know each other's strengths and weaknesses, bare their souls, and build a level of trust." Most important, they did so by focusing on real work they could do together. For example, early on they agreed to create a budget for the paper as a team instead of singly as function heads.

Over time, the change in behavior at the top began to be noticed. One of the women who later joined the ELITE Team, for example, observed that the sight of senior management holding their "Monday morning come-to-Jesus" meetings really made a difference to her and others. "I saw all this going on and I thought, 'What are they so happy about?'"

Eventually, as the team at the top got stronger and more confident, they forged a higher aspiration: to build customer focus and break down the barriers across the broad base of the paper. . . .

A year after setting up the new [team], however, Mott was both frustrated and impatient. Neither the Advertising Customer Service department, a series of customer surveys, additional resources thrown against the problem in the interim, nor any number of top management exhortations had made any difference. Ad errors persisted, and sales reps still complained of insufficient time with customers. In fact, the new unit had turned into another organizational barrier.

Customer surveys showed that too many advertisers still found the *Democrat* unresponsive to their needs and too concerned with internal procedures and deadlines. People at the paper also had evidence beyond surveys. In one instance, for example, a sloppily prepared ad arrived through a fax machine looking like a "rat had run across the page." Yet the ad passed through the hands of seven employees and probably would have found its way into print if it had not been literally unreadable! As someone commented, "It was not anyone's job to make sure it was right. If they felt it was simply their job to type or paste it up, they just passed it along." This particular fax, affectionately know as the "rat tracks fax," came to symbolize the essential challenge at the *Democrat*. . . .

At the time, Mott was reading about Motorola's quality programs and the goal of zero defects. He decided to heed Dunlap's advice by creating a special team of workers charged with eliminating all errors in advertisements. Mott now admits he was skeptical that frontline people could become as cohesive a team as he and his direct reports. So he made Dunlap, his trusted confidante, the leader of the team that took on the name ELITE for "ELIminate The Errors."

A year later, Mott was a born-again believer in teams. Under ELITE's leadership, advertising accuracy, never before tracked at the paper, had risen sharply and stayed above 99 percent. Lost revenues from errors, previously as high as $10,000 a month, had dropped to near zero. Ad sales reps had complete confidence in the Advertising Customer Service department's capacity and desire to treat each ad as though the *Democrat*'s existence were at stake. And surveys showed a huge positive swing in advertiser satisfaction. Mott considered all of this nothing less than a minor miracle.

The impact of ELITE, however, went beyond numbers. It completely redesigned the process by which the *Democrat* sells, creates, produces, and bills for advertisements. More important yet, it stimulated and nurtured the customer obsession and cross-functional cooperation required to make the new process work. In effect, this team of mostly frontline workers transformed an entire organization with respect to customer service.

ELITE had a lot going for it from the beginning. Mott gave the group a clear performance goal (eliminate errors) and a strong mix of skills (12 of the best people from all parts of the paper). He committed himself to follow through by promising, at the first meeting, that "whatever solution you come up with will be implemented." In addition, Jim Batten's customer obsession movement helped energize the task force.

But it took more than a good sendoff and an overarching corporate theme to make ELITE into a high-performance team. In this case, the personal commitments began to grow, unexpectedly, over the early months as the team grappled with its challenge. At first, the group spent more time pointing fingers at one another than coming to grips with advertising errors. Only when one of them produced the famous "rat tracks fax" and told the story behind it did the group start to admit that everyone—not everyone else—was at fault. Then, recalls one member, "We had some pretty hard discussions. And there were tears in those meetings."

The emotional response galvanized the group to the task at hand and to one another. And the closer it got, the more focused it became on the challenge. ELITE decided to look carefully at the entire process by which an ad was sold, created, printed, and billed. When it did, the team discovered patterns in the errors, most of which could be attributed to time pressures, bad communication, and poor attitude. . . .

Commitment to one another drove ELITE to expand its aspirations continually. Having started with the charge to eliminate errors, ELITE moved on to break down functional barriers, then to redesigning the entire advertising process, then to refining new standards and measures for customer service, and, finally, to spreading its own brand of "customer obsession" across the entire *Democrat*. . . . Inspired by ELITE, for example, one production crew started coming to work at 4 A.M. to ease time pressures later in the day. . . .

To this day, the spirit of ELITE lives on at the *Democrat*. "There is no beginning and no end," says Dunlap. "Every day we experience something we learn from."

ELITE's spirit made everyone a winner—the customers, the employees, management, and even Knight-Ridder's corporate leaders. CEO Jim Batten was so impressed that he agreed to pay for managers from other Knight-Ridder papers to visit the *Democrat* to learn from ELITE's experience. And, of course, the 12 people who committed themselves to one another and their paper had an impact and an experience none of them will ever forget.

Discussion Questions

1. What were the stages of development of the ELITE Team? Identify specific examples of each of the four stages of team development in the case.
2. How do you explain the team's reaching a high-performance condition? What were the major predictive factors?
3. Why didn't Mott's top management team reach a high level of performance? What was his team lacking? Why was an ELITE team needed?
4. Make recommendations about what Mott should do now to capitalize on the ELITE Team experience. If you were to become a consultant to the *Tallahassee Democrat*, what advice would you give Mott about how he can capitalize on team building?

The Cash Register Incident

Read the following scenario by yourself. Then complete a three-step exercise, the first two steps by yourself, and the third step with a team. A time limit is associated with each step.

> *A store owner had just turned off the lights in the store when a man appeared and demanded money. The owner opened a cash register. The contents of the cash register were scooped up, and the man sped away. A member of the police force was notified promptly.*

Step 1: After reading these instructions, close your book. Without looking at the scenario, rewrite it as accurately as you can. Describe the incident as best you can using your own words.

Step 2: Assume that you observed the incident described in the paragraph above. Later, a reporter asks you questions about what you read in order to write an article for the local newspaper. Answer the questions from the reporter by yourself. Do not talk with anyone else about your answers. Put a Y, N, or DK in the response column. Since reporters are always pressed for time, take no more than two minutes to complete step 2.

	Answer
Y	Yes, or true
N	No, or false
DK	Don't know, or there is no way to tell

Step 3: The reporter wants to interview your entire team together. As a team, discuss the answers to each question and reach a consensus decision—that is, one with which everyone on the team agrees. Do not vote or engage in horse-trading. The reporter wants to know what you all agree upon. Complete your team discussion in ten minutes.

Statements About the Incident

"As a reporter, I am interested in what happened in this incident. Can you tell me what occurred? I'd like you to address the following eleven questions."

Statement

Alone   *Team*

_____   _____   1. Did a man appear after the owner turned off his store lights?

_____   _____   2. Was the robber a man?

_____   _____   3. Is it true that the man did not demand money?

_____   _____   4. The man who opened the cash register was the owner, right?

_____   _____   5. Did the store owner scoop up the contents of the cash register?

_____   _____   6. OK, so someone opened the cash register, right?

_____   _____   7. Let me get this straight, after the man who demanded the money scooped up the contents of the cash register, he ran away?

_____   _____   8. The contents of the cash register contained money, but you don't know how much?

_____   _____   9. Did the robber demand money of the owner?

_____   _____   10. OK, by way of summary, the incident concerns a series of events in which only three persons are involved: the owner of the store, a man who demanded money, and a member of the police force?

_____   _____   11. Let me be sure I understand. Is it true that the following events occurred: Someone demanded money, the cash register was opened, its contents were scooped up, and a man dashed out of the store?

When you have finished your team decision making and mock interview with the reporter, the instructor will provide correct answers. Calculate how many answers you got right as an individual, and then calculate how many right answers your team achieved. Also go back and compare your own description of the incident with the actual wording of the scenario. How did you do? How accurate were you in your description?

Discussion Questions

1. How many individuals did better than the team as a whole? (In general, more than 80 percent of people do worse than the team.)
2. What changes would be needed in order for your team score to be even better?
3. How do you explain the superior performance of most teams over even the best individuals?
4. Under what conditions would individuals do better than teams in making decisions?

EXERCISES IN BUILDING EFFECTIVE TEAMS

Team Diagnosis and Team Development Exercise

In order to help you develop the ability to diagnose team stage development, consider a team in which you are now a member. If you belong to a team as part of this class, select that one. You may also select a team at your employment, in your church or community, or a team in another class in school. Complete the following three-step exercise:

Step 1: Use the following questions to help you determine the stage of development in which your team is operating. Create a score for your team for each stage of development. Identify the stage in which the team seems to operate the most.

Step 2: Identify what actions or interventions would lead your team to the next higher stage of development. Specify what dynamics need to change, what team members need to do, and/or how the team leader could foster more advanced team development.

Step 3: Share your scores and your suggestions with others in class in a small-group setting, and add at least one good idea from someone else's diagnosis to your own design. Use the following scale in your rating of your team right now.

Rating Scale

1 Not typical at all of my team
2 Not very typical of my team
3 Somewhat typical of my team
4 Very typical of my team

Stage 1

_____ 1. Not everyone is clear about the objectives and goals of the team.

_____ 2. Not everyone is personally acquainted with everyone else in the team.

_____ 3. Only a few team members actively participate.

_____ 4. Interactions among team members are very safe or somewhat superficial.

_____ 5. Trust among all team members has not yet been established.

_____ 6. Many team members seem to need direction from the leader in order to participate.

Stage 2

_____ 7. All team members know and agree with the objectives and goals of the team.

_____ 8. Team members all know one another.

_____ 9. Team members are very cooperative and actively participate in the activities of the team.

_____ 10. Interactions among team members are friendly, personal, and non-superficial.

_____ 11. A comfortable level of trust has been established among team members.

_____ 12. A strong unity exists in the team, and team members feel very much a part of a special group.

Stage 3

_____ 13. Disagreements and differing points of view are openly expressed by team members.

_____ 14. Competition exists among some team members.

_____ 15. Some team members do not follow the rules or the team norms.

_____ 16. Subgroups or coalitions exist within the team.

_____ 17. Some issues create major disagreements when discussed by the team, with some members on one side and others on the other side.

_____ 18. The authority or competence of the team leader is being questioned or challenged.

Stage 4

_____ 19. Team members are committed to the team and actively cooperate to improve the team's performance.

_____ 20. Team members feel free to try out new ideas, experiment, share something crazy, or do novel things.

_____ 21. A high level of energy is displayed by team members and expectations for performance are very high.

_____ 22. Team members do not always agree, but a high level of trust exists and each person is given respect, so disagreements are resolved productively.

_____ 23. Team members are committed to helping one another succeed and improve, so self-aggrandizement is at a minimum.

_____ 24. The team can make fast decisions without sacrificing quality.

Scoring

Add up the scores for the items in each stage of team development. Generally, one stage clearly stands out as having the highest scores. Team stages develop sequentially, so the highest stage in which scores occur is usually the dominant stage of development. Based on these scores, identify ways to move the team to the next level.

Total of Stage 1 items _____

Total of Stage 2 items _____

Total of Stage 3 items _____

Total of Stage 4 items _____

Winning the War on Talent

In this exercise, you will form teams of six members. Your team will have an overall objective to achieve, and each team member will have individual objectives. The exercise is accomplished in seven steps and it should take a total of 50 minutes to complete steps 1 through 6.

Step 1: In your team, read the scenario below about the problem of attracting and retaining talented employees in twenty-first century organizations. Your team objective is to generate two innovative but workable ideas for how to retain good teachers in the public school system. You will have 15 minutes to develop the ideas.

Step 2: When each team has completed the assignment, each is given two minutes to present the two ideas. These ideas will be evaluated, and a winning team will be selected based on the following criteria:

❑ The ideas are workable and affordable.

❑ The ideas are interesting, innovative, and unusual.

❑ The ideas have a good chance of making a difference if they are implemented.

Step 3: In addition to the team assignment, each team member is assigned to play three team member roles during the discussion. A role assignment schedule is listed below. Team members may select the roles they wish to play, or an instructor can assign the roles. One purpose of this individual assignment is to give team members practice in playing either task-facilitation roles or relationship-building roles in a team setting, so you should take these assignments seriously. Remember, however, that you have only 15 minutes. When your team has completed its task, each team member will rate the effectiveness of every other team member in how well they played their roles and how much they helped the team accomplish its task. You will have five minutes to complete the ratings.

TEAM MEMBER NAME	ROLES	PERFORMANCE RATING (1) LOW–(10) HIGH PERFORMANCE FEEDBACK
1	Direction giving	
	Urging	
	Enforcing	
2	Information seeking	
	Information giving	
	Elaborating	
3	Monitoring	
	Reality testing	
	Summarizing	
4	Process analyzing	
	Supporting	
	Confronting	
5	Harmonizing	
	Tension relieving	
	Energizing	
6	Developing	
	Consensus building	
	Empathizing	

PRACTICE

Step 4: Each team member uses the form above to rate the performance of, and provide feedback to, every other member of the team. In completing the form, make sure you focus on how well each person performed his or her assigned roles. Identify at least one thing you noticed about the performance of each team member so that you can provide personal feedback to each one. Remember that the overall purpose of this exercise is to give you practice in playing effective roles in teams and providing feedback to team members. You are given five minutes for this rating task.

Step 5: When each team has completed its task, one representative from each team is selected to form a judging team. This judging team evaluates the quality of the ideas produced by each team. A winning team is announced as a result of their deliberations. (Other class members will want to observe and rate the performance of this judging team and its members as they make their selection.) The judging team will be given 10 minutes to select the winning team.

Step 6: Teams meet again so that personal feedback can be given. Each team member takes a total of three minutes to give feedback to the other members of his or her team based on the evaluation form above. A total of 20 minutes will be required to provide this feedback.

Step 7: Hold a class discussion about what you observed regarding team members' roles. Especially, reflect on your own experience trying to play those roles and what seemed to be most effective in facilitating task accomplishment and in building team cohesion.

The Problem Scenario

Almost to a person, the chief concern expressed by senior executives in most "old economy" firms is how to attract and retain managerial talent. With the economy expected to grow at almost three times the growth of the job market, finding competent employees will be a continuing challenge for the next several years. The allure of dot.com firms, high-growth companies, and high-risk–high-return ventures has created an incredibly difficult environment for organizations whose chief competitive advantage is intellectual capital and human talent. Headhunters, venture capitalists, and even firms' customers are aggressively trying to lure away management talent any way they can. A recent survey of Wall Street investment bankers revealed that more than half had been approached by an Internet company. Armed with venture capital dollars and business plans promising swift public offerings, it is easy to see why many are succeeding in attracting managerial talent away from traditional companies. Compensation packages in the seven figures are not unusual.

In this highly competitive environment where intellectual capital is at a premium, consider the difficulty faced by not-for-profit organizations, local or state governments, arts organizations, or educational institutions whose budgets are constrained far below the high-priced world of the "new economy." How will they compete for talent when they cannot come close to the salaries of firms whose market capitalization exceeds the GDP of many African countries?

In particular, the U.S. public education system has suffered tremendously in this environment. Currently the United States spends more per child than any other country, and the costs of education are increasing far faster than the consumer price index. However, it is well known that more than a quarter of public school students drop out before high school graduation, and of those who remain, the percent passing proficiency exams is woefully low—in some school districts, less than 10 percent. The average tenure of public school teachers is less than seven years, and that number is dropping rapidly as these knowledge workers can find positions elsewhere at triple and quadruple their school salaries. Add to that the difficulties escalating in the classroom resulting from students in single-parent homes, marginal economic circumstances, threats of violence, and behavioral disruptions, and it is clear why teaching is a difficult profession, even if monetary compensation were higher.

Numerous alternatives have been proposed, but few have addressed the problem of teacher attraction and retention. Your task as a team is to identify two answers to the question: How can we attract and retain teachers in the public schools of the United States? You may want to consider what is being done in the school systems in other countries or in highly effective school systems in America.

Team Performance Exercise

The purpose of this exercise is to help you practice the dynamics of team formation, development, and effective performance. The most important part of the exercise is having you practice effective team leadership and team membership, and accurately diagnosing the stages of team development so you can behave appropriately.

Your instructor will form you into teams of five members each. Your task as a team is to create a five-pointed star in the form that you drew when you were a child (see Figure 9.5). You will do this with a piece of rope that has been tied at the ends to form a circle. Here is how this exercise will occur:

1. You will find a 50-foot piece of rope on the floor. Each member of your team will surround the rope and take hold of it with both hands. Once you have taken hold of the rope, you cannot let go until the exercise has been completed.

2. You will be given five minutes to plan how you are going to create the star, with all the appropriate crisscrosses. You may not move at all during this five-minute planning period. You must stay exactly where you are. Practicing is not permitted.

3. Once you have finished the five-minute planning session, you may not talk out loud again. The task must be completed in complete silence. You may not communicate verbally with any other member of your team. Only nonverbal communication is permitted. Remember, once you have taken hold of the rope, you cannot let go with either hand.

4. When the instructor gives the signal, you will start moving in order to create your five-sided star. When you have finished, you will place the rope down on the floor in exactly the position in which you are standing. You may not rearrange or move the rope on the floor. The rope should accurately represent your team members' positions.

5. The quality of your results will be evaluated by the instructor and the winning team announced.

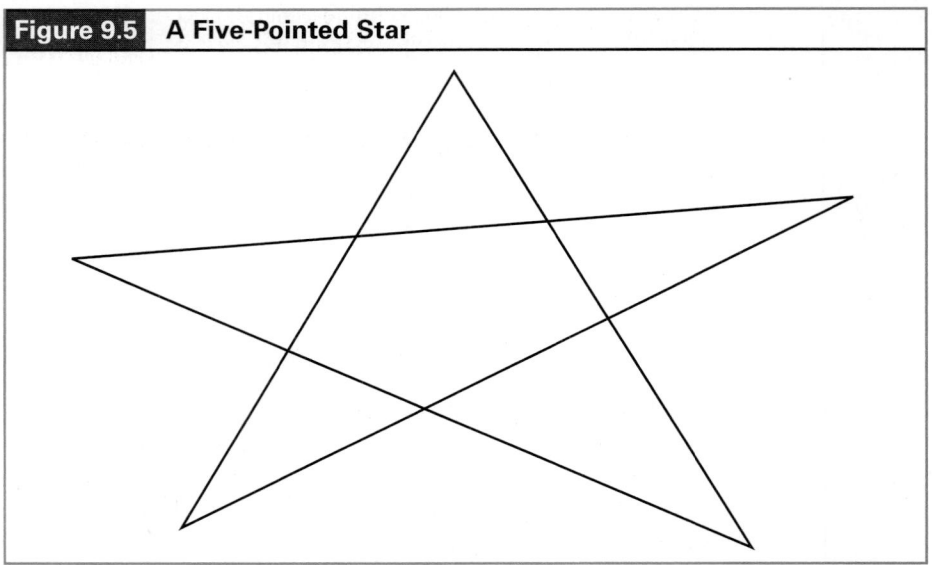

Figure 9.5   A Five-Pointed Star

When you have finished the task, discuss the following questions:

1. As a team, what was especially effective, and what was especially ineffective in planning for task accomplishment in advance?

2. What hints about initial stages of team development were utilized?

3. What happened to your team dynamics over the duration of the activity? Did they change from one stage to another? Did you end up as a high-performing team?

4. What team leadership and membership roles did each of your team members play? Which were the most effective?

5. What were the differences between teams that accomplished the task the most quickly and with the highest quality compared to the others?

6. How did you make up for the inability to communicate as a team during the task?

7. What do you wish you could do differently to be more efficient and more effective if you were to do another task together?

ACTIVITIES FOR BUILDING EFFECTIVE TEAMS

Suggested Assignments

1. Teach someone else how to determine which stage of development a team is in and what behaviors are most effective in each separate stage.

2. Analyze the characteristics of a team in which you are a member. Determine in what ways its functioning could be improved. Based on the attributes of high-performance teams, identify what could be done to improve its performance.

3. Conduct a role analysis of a real team meeting in which members are trying to make a decision, solve a problem, or examine an issue. Who performed what roles? Which team members were most helpful? Which team members were least helpful? Provide feedback to the team on what roles you saw being played, what roles were missing, and what improvements could have made the team more effective.

4. Write out a formal vision statement for a team you are leading. Make certain that the vision possesses the attributes of effective, energizing vision statements discussed in the chapter. Identify specifically what you can do to get team members to commit to that vision.

5. Do an in-depth analysis of an effective team leader you know. Focus specifically on the ways in which he or she has developed credibility and continues to influence team members. Identify what followers say about credibility, not just the leader.

6. Teach someone, or coach someone, on how to become an effective leader of a team, and how to become an effective team member. Demonstrate or exemplify the skills you teach that person.

7. For a team in which you participate, identify the basic services that it must deliver, the performance services that it should deliver, and the excitement services that it could deliver to its customers if it were not only to satisfy, but also to surprise and delight them.

APPLICATION

Application Plan and Evaluation

The intent of this exercise is to help you apply this cluster of skills in a real-life, out-of-class setting. Now that you have become familiar with the behavioral guidelines that form the basis of effective skill performance, you will improve most by trying out those guidelines in an everyday context. Unlike a classroom activity, in which feedback is immediate and others can assist you with their evaluations, this skill application activity is one you must accomplish and evaluate on your own. There are two parts to this activity. Part 1 helps prepare you to apply the skill. Part 2 helps you evaluate and improve on your experience. Be sure to write down answers to each item. Don't short-circuit the process by skipping steps.

Part 1. Planning

1. Write down the two or three aspects of this skill that are most important to you. These may be areas of weakness, areas you most want to improve, or areas that are most salient to a problem you face right now. Identify the specific aspects of this skill that you want to apply.

2. Now identify the setting or the situation in which you will apply this skill. Establish a plan for performance by actually writing down a description of the situation. Who else will be involved? When will you do it? Where will it be done?
   Circumstances:
   Who else?
   When?
   Where?

3. Identify the specific behaviors in which you will engage to apply this skill. Operationalize your skill performance.

4. What are the indicators of successful performance? How will you know you have been effective? What will indicate you have performed competently?

Part 2. Evaluation

5. After you have completed your implementation, record the results. What happened? How successful were you? What was the effect on others?

6. How can you improve? What modifications can you make next time? What will you do differently in a similar situation in the future?

7. Looking back on your whole skill practice and application experience, what have you learned? What has been surprising? In what ways might this experience help you in the long term?

Team Development Behaviors

Scoring Key

SKILL AREA	ITEMS	ASSESSMENT	
		PRE-	POST-
Leading the team	1–8	_____	_____
Being an effective team member	9–12	_____	_____
Diagnosing and facilitating team development	13–20	_____	_____
	Total Score	_____	_____

Comparison Data (N = 1,500 Students)

Compare your scores to three standards:
1. The maximum possible score = 120
2. The scores of other students in the class.
3. Norm data from more than 1,500 business school students.

Pre-Test				**Post-Test**
96.97	=	mean	=	104.07
105 or above	=	top quartile	=	113 or above
98–104	=	second quartile	=	106–112
90–97	=	third quartile	=	98–105
89 or below	=	bottom quartile	=	97 or below

Diagnosing the Need for Team Building

Comparison Data (N = 1,500 Students)

Mean score:	54.22
Top quartile:	70 or above
Second quartile:	53–69
Third quartile:	39–52
Bottom quartile:	38 or below

10

Leading Positive Change

SKILL ASSESSMENT ▶

- Leading Positive Change
- Reflected Best-Self Feedback Exercise
- Machiavellianism Scale—MACH IV

SKILL LEARNING ■

- Leading Positive Change
- Ubiquitous and Escalating Change
- The Need for Frameworks
- Tendencies Toward Stability
- A Framework for Leading Positive Change
- Summary
- Behavioral Guidelines

SKILL ANALYSIS ▶

- Corporate Vision Statements
- Lee Iacocca's Transformation of Chrysler—1979–1984

SKILL PRACTICE ◆

- Reflected Best-Self Portrait
- Positive Organizational Diagnosis Exercise
- A Positive Change Agenda

SKILL APPLICATION ●

- Suggested Assignments
- Application Plan and Evaluation

SCORING KEYS AND COMPARISON DATA ■

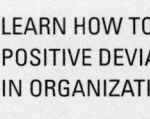

SKILL DEVELOPMENT OBJECTIVES

- LEARN HOW TO CREATE POSITIVE DEVIANCE IN ORGANIZATIONS

- DEVELOP THE CAPABILITY TO LEAD POSITIVE CHANGE

- ACQUIRE THE ABILITY TO MOBILIZE THE CAPABILITIES OF OTHERS IN ACHIEVING POSITIVE CHANGE

DIAGNOSTIC SURVEYS FOR LEADING POSITIVE CHANGE

LEADING POSITIVE CHANGE

Step 1: Before you read the material in this chapter, please respond to the following statements by writing a number from the rating scale below in the left-hand column (Pre-assessment). Your answers should reflect your attitudes and behavior as they are now, not as you would like them to be. Be honest. This instrument is designed to help you discover your level of competency in problem solving and creativity so you can tailor your learning to your specific needs. When you have completed the survey, use the scoring key at the end of the chapter to identify the skill areas discussed in this chapter that are most important for you to master.

Step 2: After you have completed the reading and the exercises in this chapter and, ideally, as many as you can of the Skill Application assignments at the end of this chapter, cover up your first set of answers. Then respond to the same statements again, this time in the right-hand column (Post-assessment). When you have completed the survey, use the scoring key at the end of the chapter to measure your progress. If your score remains low in specific skill areas, use the behavioral guidelines at the end of the Skill Learning section to guide further practice.

Rating Scale

1 Strongly disagree
2 Disagree
3 Slightly disagree
4 Slightly agree
5 Agree
6 Strongly agree

Assessment

Pre-   Post-

When I am in a leadership position required to lead change:

_____ _____ 1. I create positive energy in others when I interact with them.

_____ _____ 2. I know how to unlock the positive energy in other people.

_____ _____ 3. I express compassion toward people who are facing pain or difficulty.

_____ _____ 4. I help promote compassionate responses in others when it is appropriate.

_____ _____ 5. I emphasize a higher purpose or meaning associated with the change I am leading.

_____ _____ 6. I forgive others for the harm they may have produced or the mistakes they made.

_____ _____ 7. I maintain high standards of performance, even though I am quick to forgive.

_____ _____ 8. The language I use encourages virtuous actions by people.

_____ _____ 9. I express gratitude frequently and conspicuously, even for small acts.

_____ _____ 10. I keep track of things that go right, nor just things that go wrong.

_____ _____ 11. I frequently give other people positive feedback.

_____ _____ 12. I emphasize building on strengths, not just overcoming weaknesses.

_____ _____ 13. I use a lot more positive comments than negative comments.

_____ _____ 14. I compare my own (or my group's) performance against the highest standards.

_____ _____ 15. When I communicate a vision, I capture people's hearts as well as their heads.

_____ _____ 16. I work to close abundance gaps—the difference between good performance and great performance.

_____ _____ 17. I exemplify absolute integrity.

_____ _____ 18. I know how to get people to commit to my vision of positive change.

_____ _____ 19. I take advantage of a small-wins strategy in all my change initiatives.

_____ _____ 20. I have developed a teachable point of view for subjects I care about.

REFLECTED BEST-SELF FEEDBACK™ EXERCISE*

All of us can recall our own extraordinary moments, those moments when we felt that our best self was brought to light, affirmed by others, and put into practice. These memories are seared into our minds as moments in which we have felt alive, true to our deepest selves, and pursuing our full potential as human beings. Over time, we collect these experiences into a portrait of who we are when we are at our personal best. To help compose a best-self portrait, it is important to draw on the perceptions of significant others who have unique and valuable insights into our strengths and enduring talents. The Reflected Best-Self Feedback Exercise creates an opportunity for us to receive feedback regarding who we are when we are at our best. A detailed explanation of this exercise, including the research that supports its effectiveness in helping people become better leaders, can be found at: www.bus.umich.edu/positive. Look under POS teaching and learning tools.

In this exercise, you will gather information about yourself from other people who know you well. In the Skill Practice section of the chapter, you will be asked to develop a best self-portrait based on this feedback. The first step is to gather the information. Here is how you go about it.

Identify 20 people who know you well. These may be colleagues (former or current), friends (old or recent), family members, neighbors, class members, or anyone who has had extended contact with you. Think about who will give you an honest opinion. The more diverse the group, the better. Also, realize that due to time constraints, everyone may not be able to respond. You need at least 10 responses to complete this part of the assignment, so ask enough people to ensure at least 10 responses, but try for 20.

Compose the feedback request (see the example request below), and send it to the 20 people you select. While this request may seem awkward or difficult for you, people have found this assessment to be a profound learning activity, and other people are quite willing to participate in this exercise. You will find that this actually strengthens your relationships in many instances.

Source: _Roberts et al., 2005._

A SAMPLE E-MAIL REQUEST FOR FEEDBACK

I am taking a course that requires me to construct a profile of my unique strengths. I have been asked to contact twenty people who know me well. I would like to invite you to

* This assessment is not available online.

help me with this exercise. I am to request that each person provide me with three stories of when I was at my best.

This will require that you think about your interactions with me and identify times when you saw me at my very best. Please provide examples so I can understand the situation and the characteristics you are describing. I have attached some examples of what these stories could look like. Please use these only as a guide.

Feedback Examples:

   1. *One of your greatest strengths is:* *The ability to get people to work together and give all they have to a task.*
   For example, I think of the time that: *We were doing the Alpha project. We were getting behind and the stress was building. We started to close down and get very focused on just meeting our deadline. You noticed that we were not doing our best work and stopped the group to rethink our approach. You asked whether we wanted to just satisfy the requirements or whether we wanted to really do good and important work. You reminded us of what we were capable of doing and how each of us could contribute to a better outcome. No one else in that room would have thought to do that. As a result, we did meet the deadline and created a result we all feel proud of.*

   2. *One of your greatest strengths is:* *Being happy all the time.*
   For example, I think of the time that: *We had just lost the league championship game, and we were all really down in the dumps. All of us knew we could have played better, and we were really in a funk. You were the one who pumped us up and made us feel better—not in a superficial or silly way, but by expressing genuine pleasure at having a chance to play and being together as friends. I really admire you for being able to see the good in a situation and being such a positive person.*

   3. *One of your greatest strengths is:* *The capacity to persist in the face of adversity.*
   For example, I think of the time that: *We were past our deadline on a major report. Frank quit and we were left short-handed. Instead of getting discouraged, you became more focused than I have ever seen anyone get. I think you went 48 hours without sleep. I was amazed that you could produce such a quality product under those conditions.*

Your feedback to me: Please provide me with three examples of the strengths you observed by completing the following statements.

   1. One of your greatest strengths is:
      For example, I think of the time that:
   2. One of your greatest strengths is:
      For example, I think of the time that:
   3. One of your greatest strengths is:
      For example, I think of the time that:

Please e-mail your responses to me by [insert a date]. Thank you very much for your cooperation. I will be sure to share with you what I learn.

When you have obtained this feedback, you will be guided in developing a best-self portrait in the Skill Practice section of this chapter.

Source: *Adapted from Quinn, Dutton, & Spreitzer, 2003.*

MACHIAVELLIANISM SCALE—MACH IV

Listed below are a number of statements. Each represents a commonly held opinion, but there are no right or wrong answers. Indicate the extent to which you agree or disagree with each item using this scale. Comparison data is provided at the end of the chapter.

+3   Agree strongly
+2   Agree somewhat
+1   Agree slightly
−1   Disagree slightly
−2   Disagree somewhat
−3   Disagree strongly

If you find that the numbers to be used in answering do not adequately indicate your own opinion, use the one which is closest to the way you feel.

1. Never tell anyone the real reason you did something unless it is useful to do so. +3 +2 +1 −1 −2 −3

2. The best way to handle people is to tell them what they want to hear. +3 +2 +1 −1 −2 −3

3. One should take action only when sure it is morally right. +3 +2 +1 −1 −2 −3

4. Most people are basically good and kind. +3 +2 +1 −1 −2 −3

5. It is safest to assume that all people have a vicious streak and it will come out when they are given a chance. +3 +2 +1 −1 −2 −3

6. Honesty is the best policy in all cases. +3 +2 +1 −1 −2 −3

7. There is no excuse for lying to someone else. +3 +2 +1 −1 −2 −3

8. Generally speaking, people won't work hard unless they're forced to do so. +3 +2 +1 −1 −2 −3

9. All in all, it is better to be humble and honest than to be important and dishonest. +3 +2 +1 −1 −2 −3

10. When you ask someone to do something for you, it is best to give the real reasons for wanting it rather than giving reasons which carry more weight. +3 +2 +1 −1 −2 −3

11. Most people who get ahead in the world lead clean, moral lives. +3 +2 +1 −1 −2 −3

12. Anyone who completely trusts anyone else is asking for trouble. +3 +2 +1 −1 −2 −3

13. The biggest difference between most criminals and other people is that the criminals are stupid enough to get caught. +3 +2 +1 −1 −2 −3

14. Most people are brave. +3 +2 +1 −1 −2 −3

15. It is wise to flatter important people. +3 +2 +1 −1 −2 −3

16. It is possible to be good in all respects. +3 +2 +1 −1 −2 −3

17. Barnum was wrong when he said that there's a sucker born every minute. +3 +2 +1 −1 −2 −3

18. It is hard to get ahead without cutting corners here and there. +3 +2 +1 −1 −2 −3

19. People suffering from incurable diseases should have the choice of being put painlessly to death. +3 +2 +1 −1 −2 −3

20. Most people forget more easily the death of their father than the loss of their property. +3 +2 +1 −1 −2 −3

Source: *Christie & Lehman, 1970.*

Leading Positive Change

The word **leadership** is often used as a catch-all term to describe almost any desirable behavior by a manager. "Good leadership" is frequently the explanation given for the success of almost any positive organizational performance—from stock price increases to upward national economic trends to happy employees. Magazine covers trumpet the remarkable achievements of leaders, and the person at the top is almost always credited as being the cause of the success or failure. Coaches are fired when players don't perform, CEOs lose their jobs when customers choose a competitor, and presidents are voted out of office when the economy goes south. Contrarily, leaders are often given hero status when their organizations succeed (e.g., Gandhi, Welch, Buffett). The leader as scapegoat, and hero, is an image that is alive and well in modern society. Rationally speaking, however, most of us recognize that there is much more to organizational success than the leader's behavior, but we also recognize that leadership is one of the most important influences in helping organizations perform well (Cameron & Lavine, 2006; Pfeffer, 1998).

Some writers have differentiated between the concepts of leadership and management (Kotter, 1999; Tichy, 1993, 1997). *Leadership* has often been described as what individuals do under conditions of change. When organizations are dynamic and undergoing transformation, people exhibit leadership. *Management,* on the other hand, has traditionally been associated with the status quo. Maintaining stability is the job of the manager. Leaders have been said to focus on setting direction, initiating change, and creating something new. Managers have been said to focus on maintaining steadiness, controlling variation, and refining current performance. Leadership has been equated with dynamism, vibrancy, and charisma; management with predictability, equilibrium, and control. Hence, leadership is often defined as "doing the right things," whereas management is often defined as "doing things right."

Recent research is clear, however, that such distinctions between leadership and management, which may have been appropriate in previous decades, are no longer useful (Cameron & Lavine, 2006; Cameron & Quinn,1999; Quinn, 2000, 2004). Managers cannot be successful without being good leaders, and leaders cannot be successful without being good managers. No longer do organizations and individuals have the luxury of holding on to the status quo; worrying about doing things right without also doing the right things; keeping the system stable without also leading change and improvement; maintaining current performance without also creating something new; concentrating on equilibrium and control without also concentrating on vibrancy and charisma. Effective management and leadership are largely inseparable. The skills required to do one are also required for the other. No organization in a postindustrial, hyperturbulent, twenty-first century environment will survive without individuals capable of providing both management and leadership. Leading change and managing stability, establishing vision and accomplishing objectives, breaking the rules and monitoring conformance, although paradoxical, all are required to be successful. Individuals who are effective managers are also effective leaders much of the time. The skills required to be effective as a leader and as a manager are essentially identical.

On the other hand, Quinn (2004) has reminded us that no person is a leader all of the time. Leadership is a *temporary* condition in which certain skills and competencies are displayed. When they are demonstrated, leadership is present. When they are not demonstrated, leadership is absent. In other words, regardless of a person's title or formal position, people may act as leaders or not, depending on the behaviors they display. Most of the time people are not displaying leadership behaviors. People choose to enter a state of leadership when they choose to adopt a certain mindset and implement certain key skills.

> *Understanding that leadership is a temporary, dynamic state brings us to a radical redefinition of how we think about, enact, and develop leadership. We come to discover that most of the time, most people, including CEOs, presidents, and prime ministers, are not leaders. We discover that anyone can be a leader. Most of the time, none of us are leaders. (Quinn, 2004: xx)*

In this chapter, we focus on the most common activity that demonstrates leadership—leading change.

It is while engaging in this task that the temporary state of leadership is most likely to be revealed. That is, despite the heroic image of leaders, every person can develop the skills needed to lead change. No one was born as either a leader or absent the abilities that would enable him or her to be a leader. Everyone can, and most everyone does, become a leader at some point. On the other hand, effectively leading change involves a complex and difficult-to-master set of skills, so assistance is required in order to do it successfully. That is because of the difficulties associated with change.

Ubiquitous and Escalating Change

It is not news that we live in a dynamic, turbulent, and even chaotic world. Almost no one would try to predict with any degree of certainty what the world will be like in ten years. Things change too fast. We know that the technology currently exists, for example, to put the equivalent of a full-size computer in a wristwatch, or inject the equivalent of a laptop computer into the bloodstream. New computers are beginning to be etched on molecules instead of silicon wafers. The half-life of any technology you can name—from complex computers to nuclear devices to software—is less than six months. Anything can be reproduced in less than a half a year.

The mapping of the human genome is probably the greatest source for change, for not only can we now change a banana into an agent to inoculate people against malaria, but new organ development and physiological regulation promise to dramatically alter population life styles. As of this writing, more than 100 whole animals have been patented. Patents have exploded from an overwhelming 4,000 applications in 1991 to 22,000 in 1995, but one year later they mushroomed to 500,000 per year, with exponential growth expected to continue. Whereas it took ten years to produce a generic alternative to a normal pharmaceutical drug in 1965, the time was cut in half by 1980, cut in half again by 1990, and by the year 2000, generic alternatives could be produced for almost any pharmaceutical compound in about a week. In 1980 it took a year to assemble 12,000 DNA base pairs; by 1999 it took less than a minute, and by the end of 2000, 1,000 base pairs could be assembled in less than one second. Currently, computers are being configured that can sequence every major disease in a single day. Who can predict the changes that will result? Hence, not only is change ubiquitous and constant, but almost everyone predicts that it will escalate exponentially (see Enrique, 2000).

The Need for Frameworks

Frameworks or theories help provide stability and order in the midst of constant change. To illustrate the importance of frameworks, consider a simple experiment conducted by Nobel laureate Herbert A. Simon. Experimental subjects were shown a chess board as it appeared midgame. Some of these individuals were experienced chess players, some were novices. They were allowed to observe the chess board for ten seconds, and then the board was wiped clean. The subjects were asked to replace the pieces on the board exactly as they had appeared before the board was cleared. This experiment was actually conducted on a computer, so wiping the chess board clean was simple, and multiple trials could be generated for each person. Each trial showed a different configuration of a chess game midway through.

The question being investigated was: Which group was best at replacing the chess pieces, the novices or the experienced players? After looking at the board for ten seconds, which individuals would be most accurate in placing each piece in its previous location? An argument could be made for either group. On the one hand, the minds of novices would not be cluttered by preconceptions. They would look at the board with a fresh view. It is similar to the answer to the question: When is the best time to teach a person a new language, age 3 or age 30? The fact that 3-year-olds can learn a new language more quickly than 30-year-olds suggests that novices might also be better at this task because of their lack of preconceptions. On the other hand, the contrary argument is that experience ought to count for something, and the familiarity of experienced players with the chess board should allow them to be more successful.

The results of the experiment were dramatic. Novices accurately replaced the pieces less than five percent of the time. Experienced players were accurate more than 80 percent of the time. When experienced chess players looked at the board they saw familiar patterns, or what might be called frameworks. They said things like this: "This looks like the Leningrad defense, except this bishop is out of place and these two pawns are arranged differently." Experienced players identified the patterns quickly, and then they paid attention to the few exceptions on the board. Novices, on the other hand, needed to pay attention to every single piece as if it were an exception, since no pattern (or framework) was available to guide their decisions.

Frameworks serve the same function for managers. They clarify complex or ambiguous situations. Individuals who are familiar with frameworks can manage complex situations effectively because they can respond to fewer exceptions. Individuals without frameworks are left to react to every piece of information as a unique event or an exception. The best managers possess the most, and the most useful, frameworks. When they encounter a new situation, they do not become overwhelmed or stressed because they have frameworks that can help simplify and clarify the unfamiliar.

Tendencies Toward Stability

Organizations are designed like frameworks that allow exceptions to be managed effectively. They are intended to create stability, steadiness, and predictable conditions. They try to constrain as much change as possible. That is, organizations help specify what is expected of employees, who reports to whom, what the goals are, what procedures are to be employed, what rules apply, how the work gets done, and so on. These elements are all intended to reduce the ambiguity of changing conditions and to create predictability for employees so that the uncertainties of environmental change do not overwhelm them. Managers are obliged to try to ensure that steady, stable conditions are fostered.

Leading change, therefore, is contradictory to the common requirements of ensuring predictability and constancy. It disrupts the permanence of the system and creates more uncertainly. The skill of leading change, therefore, runs contrary to what organizations are fundamentally designed to do. Even more important, leading *positive* change is different from simply leading ordinary change in an organization. Change will always be widespread and constant, but leading positive change in organizations is unusual and difficult, and it requires special know-how and a special skill set.

To illustrate the difference between leading commonplace change and positive change, consider the continuum in Figure 10.1 (Cameron, 2003a). It shows a line depicting normal, healthy performance in the middle, with unhealthy, negative performance on the left and unusually positive performance on the right. Most organizations and most managers strive to maintain performance in the middle of the continuum. People and organizations strive to be healthy, effective, efficient, reliable, compatible, and ethical. It is in the middle of the continuum where things are most comfortable.

We usually refer to the left end of the continuum as **negative deviance**. To call someone a "deviant" usually means that he or she needs correction or treatment. Most managers strive to get deviant people to behave within a normal range. If they don't, if they continue to behave badly, they get transferred, punished, or fired. With few exceptions (e.g., athletes and heroic figures) the same pressure toward normal behavior exists on the right side of the continuum as

---

Figure 10.1 A Continuum of Negative and Positive Deviance

	Negative Deviance	Normal	Positive Deviance
Individual:			
Physiological *(Medical research)*	Illness	Health	Wellness
Psychological *(Psychological research)*	Illness	Health	Flow
Organizational and Managerial: *(Management and organizational research)*			
Revenues	Unprofitable	Profitable	Generous
Effectiveness	Ineffective	Effective	Excellent
Efficiency	Inefficient	Efficient	Extraordinary
Quality	Error-prone	Reliable	Flawless
Ethics	Unethical	Ethical	Virtuous
Relationships	Conflictual	Compatible	Caring
Adaptation	Threat-rigidity	Coping	Flourishing

Deficit gaps   *Abundance gaps*

Source: *Cameron, 2003b.*

well as the left. Pressure is always brought to bear to get people to behave in predictable, normal ways.

Think, for example, of people you have encountered who are positively deviant at work—flawless performers, flourishing in everything they do, and constantly extraordinary. They're too perfect. They make people feel uncomfortable. They make others feel guilty. They are rate-busters. We accuse them of showing up other people. There is a lot of pressure to get them back in line or within a normal range of performance. Most of the time we insist that others stay in the middle range. Being on either the right side or the left side of the continuum is usually interpreted as against the rules.

Not surprisingly, we know a lot more about the left side of the continuum than the right side. Consider the top line of Figure 10.1, for example, and think of your own physical health. If you're ill, you usually get treatment from a medical professional who provides medication or therapy until you return to normal health. When you're healthy you stop seeing the doctor and the doctor stops treating you. About 90 percent of all medical research has focused on how to get people from the left side of the continuum—illness—to the middle of the continuum—health. Yet, everyone knows that a condition exists on the right side of the continuum which is better than just being healthy. It is exemplified by people who can run a marathon, do 400 pushups, or compete at Olympic fitness levels. They are positively deviant on the health continuum. Much less serious attention in medical science has been paid to how people can reach this state of **positive deviance**. Leading positive change (from the middle point to the right side) is more uncertain than leading change from the left side to the middle point.

Similarly, the second line of the figure refers to psychological health. On the left is illness—depression, anxiety, burnout, paranoia, and so forth—and the middle depicts normal psychological functioning—being emotionally healthy or reasonably happy. Seligman (2002) reported that more than 99 percent of psychological research in the last 50 years has focused on the left and middle points on the continuum—that is, how to treat people who are ill in order to get them to a state of normality or health. Again, however, a positively deviant psychological condition is also possible. It is sometimes characterized by a state of **"flow"** (Csikszentmihalyi, 1990)—where people's minds are totally engaged in a challenging task so that they lose track of time, physical appetites, and outside influences—or they experience especially positive emotions (Fredrickson, 2003) such as joy, excitement, or love. Most people have experienced at some time being "in the zone," during which more of their brain capacity is used than at normal times. Such conditions represent positively deviant psychological states. A new movement in psychology studies positively deviant psychological states, and we will summarize some of those findings below. Most managers and most organizations, however, are in business to create normal behavior, not to foster deviant behavior. This is illustrated by the lower lines in Figure 10.1, which refer to organizations and managers.

The figure lists conditions ranging from unprofitable, ineffective, inefficient, and error-prone performance on the left side, to profitable, effective, efficient, and reliable performance in the middle. For the most part, leaders and managers are charged with the responsibility to ensure that their organizations are operating in the middle range. They are consumed with the problems and challenges that threaten their organizations from the left side of the continuum (e.g., unethical behavior, dissatisfied employees or customers, financial losses, and so on.) Most leaders and managers are content if they can get their organizations to that middle state—profitable, effective, reliable. In fact, almost all organizational and managerial research has focused on how to ensure that organizations can perform in the normal range. We don't have very good language to describe the right side of the organizational continuum. Instead of just being profitable, positively deviant organizations might strive to be generous, using their resources to do good. Instead of just being effective, efficient, reliable, they might strive to be benevolent, flourishing, and flawless.

The right side of the continuum is referred to as an **abundance approach** to performance. The left side of the continuum is referred to as a **deficit approach** to performance (Cameron & Lavine, 2006). Much more attention has been paid to solving problems, surmounting obstacles, battling competitors, eliminating errors, making a profit, and closing deficit gaps compared to identifying the flourishing and life-giving aspects of organizations, or closing abundance gaps. Our colleague Jim Walsh (1999) found, for example, that words such as "win," "beat," and "competition" have dominated the business press over the past two decades, whereas words such as "virtue," "caring," and "compassion" have seldom appeared at all. Less is known, therefore, about the right side of the continuum in Figure 10.1 and the concepts that characterize it. Most research on leadership, management, and organizations, therefore, has remained fixed on the left and center points of the continuum. Yet, it is on the right end that the skill of leading positive change becomes relevant. It is on that side of the continuum that our discussion will focus in this chapter.

Focusing on the right side of the continuum—or on abundance gaps—unlocks something called the heliotropic effect. This is a natural tendency in every living system to be inclined toward positive energy—toward light—and away from negative energy or from the dark. The reason is that light is life-giving and energy creating. Abundance creates positive energy. Deficits often do not. All living systems are inclined toward that which gives life, so abundance approaches to change enable the heliotropic effect to occur.

For example, with individuals, the heliotropic effect may be manifest physiologically as the *placebo effect*. A variety of studies have shown that if a person holds positive beliefs that a medication will be effective, it will, in fact, produce the desired effect about 60 percent of the time. Psychologically, the heliotropic effect is manifest as the *Pygmalion effect*. That is, not only does a person's biological system respond to his or her own positive expectations, but the expectations of others also can produce a heliotropic effect. A large amount of evidence suggests that when someone holds positive expectations for you—especially if that person is important to you—your behavior is altered positively.

The heliotropic effect is also manifest emotionally. Many studies have documented the fact that people with positive emotional states and optimistic outlooks experience fewer illness and accidents and, in fact, actually enjoy a longer and higher quality of life. Depressed, anxious, or angry people get sick more often than happy, joyful, upbeat people, even when exposed to the same number of cold viruses, and they tend more often to be in the wrong place at the wrong time and experience accidents.

The heliotropic effect can manifest itself in visualization. When people visualize themselves as succeeding—they see themselves hitting the ball, clearing the bar, making the shot, getting the right answer, or recovering from illness—they tend to succeed significantly more than otherwise. This heliotropic effect is explained in more detail in Cameron and Lavine (2006).

A Framework for Leading Positive Change

Leading positive change is a management skill that focuses on unlocking positive human potential. Positive change enables individuals to experience appreciation, collaboration, vitality, and meaningfulness in their work. It focuses on creating abundance and human well-being. It fosters positive deviance. It acknowledges that positive change engages the heart as well as the mind.

A Case Example   An example of this kind of change occurred in a New England hospital that faced a crisis of leadership when the popular vice president of operations was forced to resign (Cameron & Caza, 2002). Most employees viewed him as the most innovative and effective administrator in the hospital and as the chief exemplar of positive energy and change. Upon his resignation, the organization was thrown into turmoil. Conflict, backbiting, criticism, and adversarial feelings permeated the system. Eventually, a group of employees appealed to the board of directors to replace the current president and CEO with this ousted vice president. Little confidence was expressed in the current leadership, and the hospital's performance was deteriorating. Their lobbying efforts were eventually successful in that the president and CEO resigned under pressure, and the popular vice president was hired back as president and CEO.

Within six months of his return, however, the decimated financial circumstances at the hospital led to an announced downsizing aimed at reducing the workforce by 10 percent. The hospital faced millions of dollars in losses. This newly hired CEO had to eliminate the jobs of some of the very same people who supported his return. The most likely results of this action were an escalation in the negative effects of downsizing loss of loyalty and morale, perceptions of injustice and duplicity, blaming and accusations. Based on research on the effects of downsizing, a continuation of the tumultuous, antagonistic climate was almost guaranteed (Cameron, Whetten, & Kim, 1987).

Instead, the opposite results occurred. Upon his return, the new CEO made a concerted effort to lead positive change in the organization, not merely manage the required change. He institutionalized forgiveness, optimism, trust, and integrity. Throughout the organization, stories of compassionate acts of kindness and virtue were almost daily fare. One typical example involved a nurse who was diagnosed with terminal cancer. Respondents reported that when word spread of the man's illness, doctors and staff members from every area in the hospital donated vacation days and personal leave time so that he would continue to collect a salary even though he could not work. Ironically, the pool of days expired just before he died, so he was never terminated, and he received a salary right up to his last day.

Employees also reported that the personal and organizational damage done by the announced downsizing—friends losing jobs, budgets being cut—had been formally forgiven. Employees released grudges and moved on toward an optimistic future. One indication was the language used throughout the organization, which commonly included words such as love, hope, compassion, forgiveness, and humility, especially in reference to the leadership that announced the downsizing actions.

> *We are in a very competitive health care market, so we have differentiated ourselves through our compassionate and caring culture. . . . I know it sounds trite, but we really do love our patients. . . . People love working here, and their family members love us too. . . . Even when we downsized, [our leader] maintained the highest levels of integrity. He told the truth, and he shared everything. He got the support of everyone by his genuineness and personal concern. . . . It wasn't hard to forgive. (Representative responses from a focus group interview of employees, 2002)*

Even the redesigned physical architecture of the hospital reflected its positive approach to change, being designed to foster a more humane climate for patients and to communicate the virtuousness of the organization. For example, the maternity ward installed double beds (which didn't previously exist) so husbands could sleep with their wives rather than sitting in a chair all night; numerous communal rooms were created for family and friend gatherings; hallways and floors were all carpeted; volunteer pets were brought in to comfort and cheer up patients; original paintings on walls displayed optimistic and inspiring themes; nurses stations were all within eyesight of patients' beds; Jacuzzis were installed in the maternity ward; special meals were prepared to fit patients' dietary preferences; and so on. Employees indicate that the leadership of positive change—not merely the management of change—was the key to their recovery and thriving. Special language, activities, and processes were important parts of employees' explanations for the organization's renewal. Figure 10.2 illustrates the financial turnaround associated with the hospital's concentrated focus on virtuousness.

A Framework of Positive Change This chapter reviews the five key management skills and activities required to effectively lead positive change. They include: (1) establishing a climate of positivity, (2) creating readiness for change, (3) articulating a vision of abundance, (4) generating commitment to the vision, and (5) institutionalizing the positive

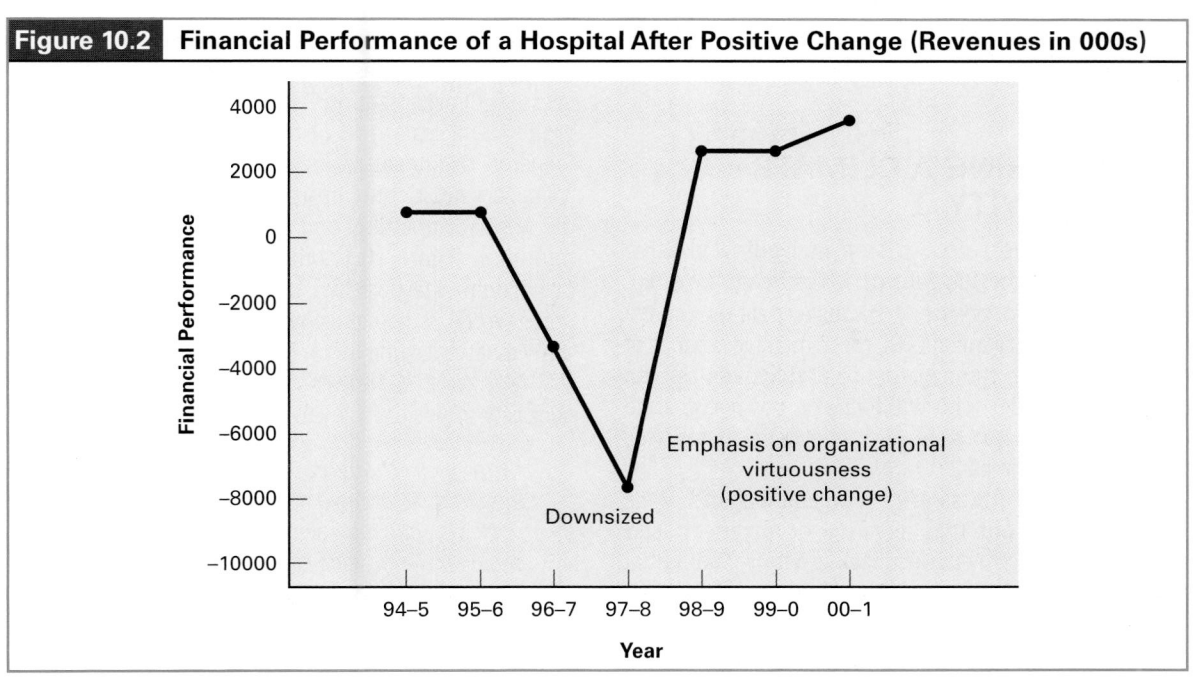

Figure 10.2 | **Financial Performance of a Hospital After Positive Change (Revenues in 000s)**

Source: *Cameron, Bright, & Caza, 2003.*

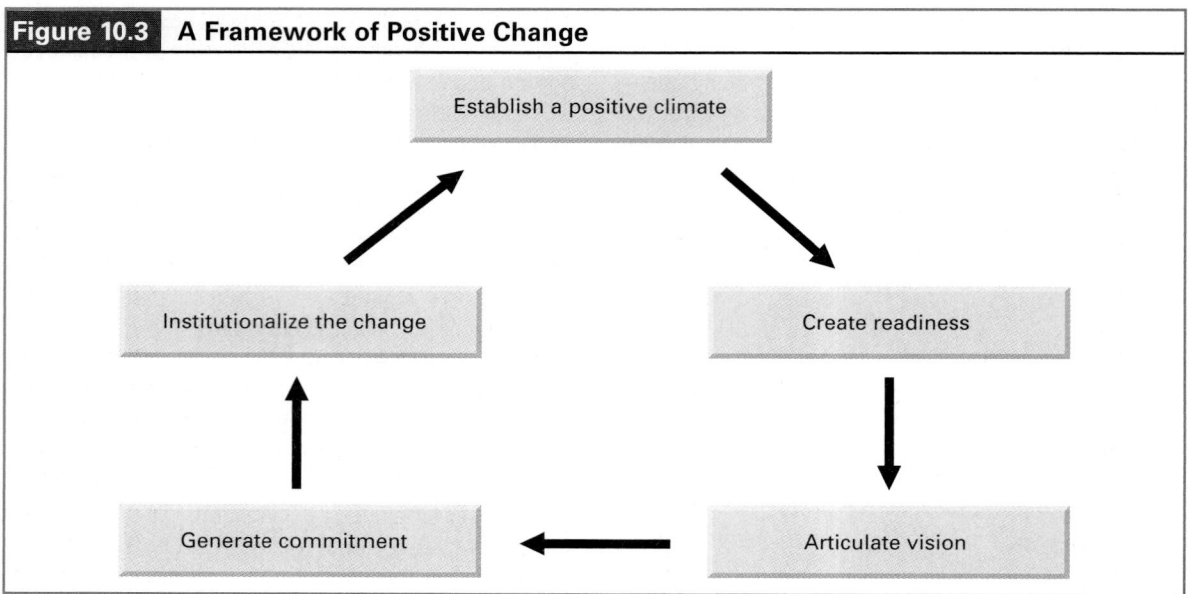

Figure 10.3   A Framework of Positive Change

Establish a positive climate

Institutionalize the change

Create readiness

Generate commitment

Articulate vision

change (Cameron & Ulrich, 1986). Figure 10.3 summarizes these steps, and we discuss them below. Leaders of positive change are not all CEOs, of course, nor are they in titled or powerful positions. On the contrary, the most important leadership demonstrated in organizations usually occurs in departments, divisions, and teams and by individuals who take it upon themselves to enter a temporary state of leadership (Meyerson, 2001; Quinn, 2004). These principles apply as much to the first-time manager, in other words, as to the experienced executive.

ESTABLISHING A CLIMATE OF POSITIVITY

The first and most crucial step in leading positive change is to set the stage for positive change by establishing a climate of positivity. Because constant change is typical of all organizations, most managers most of the time focus on the negative or problematic aspects of change. A leader who will focus on positive change is both rare and valuable. Not everyone masters it, although everyone can.

Baumeister, Bratslavsky, Finkenauer, and Vohs (2001) pointed out that negative occurrences, bad events, and disapproving feedback are more influential and longer lasting in people than positive, encouraging, and upbeat occurrences. For example, if someone breaks into your home and steals $1,000, it will affect you more, and will be more long-lasting in its effects,

than if someone sends you a $1,000 gift. If three people compliment you on your appearance and one person is critical, the one criticism will carry more weight than the three compliments. In other words, according to Baumeister's review of the literature, "bad is stronger than good." People tend to pay more attention to negative than positive phenomena, and for good reason. Ignoring a negative threat could cost you your life. Not attending to negative events could prove dangerous. Ignoring a positive, pleasant experience, on the other hand, would only result in regret. Consequently, managers and organizations—constantly confronted by problems, threats, and obstacles—have a tendency to focus on the negative much more than the positive. Managers must consciously choose to pay attention to the positive, uplifting, and flourishing side of the continuum in Figure 10.1, otherwise negative tendencies overwhelm the positive. Leading positive change, in other words, is going against the grain. It is not necessarily a natural thing to do. It requires skill and practice.

Mahatma Gandhi's statement illustrates the necessity of positivity, even though it is difficult:

Keep your thoughts positive, because your thoughts become your words. Keep your words positive, because your words become your behavior. Keep your behavior positive, because your behavior becomes your habits. Keep your habits positive because your habits become your values. Keep your values positive, because your values become your destiny. (Gold, 2002)

In order to establish a climate of positivity in an organization, managers must help establish at least three necessary conditions: (1) positive energy networks, (2) a climate of compassion, forgiveness, and gratitude, and (3) attention to strengths and the best self.

Create Positive Energy Networks

Have you ever been around a person who just makes you feel good? You leave every interaction happier, more energized, and uplifted? In contrast, do you know people who are constantly critical, negative, and discouraging? They seem to deplete your own reserve of positive energy? Recent research has discovered that people can be identified as "positive energizers" or "negative energizers" in their relationships with others (Baker, Cross, & Wooten, 2003). **Positive energizers** are those who strengthen and create vitality and liveliness in others. **Negative energizers** are people who deplete the good feelings and enthusiasm in other people and make them feel diminished, devalued, or drained. Research shows that positive energizers are higher performers, enable others to perform better, and help their own organizations succeed more than negative energizers (Baker et al., 2003). People who drain energy from others tend to be critical, express negative views, fail to engage others, and are more self-centered than positive energizers. Being a positive energizer is associated with being sensitive in interpersonal relationships, trustworthy, supportive to others in comments, actively (not passively) engaged in social interactions, flexible and tolerant in thinking, and unselfish. They are not necessarily charismatic, giddy, or just Pollyannaish. Rather, positive energy creators are optimistic and giving, and others feel better by being around them.

Here is why that is so important in leading positive change. Research by Wayne Baker (2001) has investigated the kinds of networks that exist in organizations. Most research investigates two kinds of networks—information networks and influence networks. If you are at the center of an information network, that means more information and communication flow through you than anyone else. You have access to a greater amount of information than others. Predictably, people at the center of an information network have higher performance and are more successful in their careers than people on the periphery. The same can be said for people at the center of influence networks. Influential people are not always people with the most prestigious titles, but they tend to be people who can

influence others to get things done (see Chapter 5 on power and influence). Recent research has discovered, however, that **positive energy networks** are far more powerful in predicting success than information or influence networks. In fact, being a positive energizer in an organization is four times more predictive of success than being at the center of an information network or even being the person with an important title or senior position. Displaying positive energy, in other words, tends to be a very powerful predictor of personal as well as organizational success.

Effective managers identify positive energizers and then make certain that networks of people are formed who associate with these energizers. Positive energizers are placed in positions where others can interact with them and be influenced by them. The research findings are clear that people who interact with positive energizers perform better, as well as do the positive energizers themselves, so make sure you and others rub shoulders with them often. In addition to forming positive energy networks, effective managers will also foster positive energy in other people by: (1) exemplifying or role modeling positive energy themselves, (2) recognizing and rewarding people who exemplify positive energy, and (3) providing opportunities for individuals to form friendships at work (which usually are positive energy creators).

Ensure a Climate of Compassion, Forgiveness, and Gratitude

A second aspect of a climate of positivity is the appropriate display of compassion, forgiveness, and gratitude in organizations. These terms may sound a bit saccharine and soft—even out of place in a serious discussion of developing management skills for the competitive world of business. Yet, recent research has found them to be very important predictors of organizational success. Companies that scored higher on these attributes performed significantly better than others (Cameron, 2003b). That is, when managers fostered compassionate behavior among employees, forgiveness for missteps and mistakes, and gratitude resulting from positive occurrences, their firms excelled in profitability, productivity, quality, innovation, and customer retention. Managers that reinforced these virtues were more successful in producing bottom-line results.

Paying attention to these concepts simply acknowledges that employees at work have human concerns—they feel pain, experience difficulty, and encounter injustice in their work and personal lives. Think of people you know, for example, who are currently managing a severe family illness, experiencing a failed relationship, coping with hostile and unpleasant coworkers or associates, or facing overload and burnout. Many organizations don't allow personal problems to get in the way of getting the job done. Human concerns take a back seat to work-related concerns. Regardless of what is happening personally, responsibilities and performance expectations remain the same. To lead positive change, however, managers must build a climate in which human concerns are acknowledged and where healing and restoration can occur. Because change always creates pain, discomfort, and disruption, leaders of positive change are sensitive to the human concerns that can sabotage many change efforts. Without a reserve of good will and positive feelings, almost all change fails. Therefore, unlocking people's inherent tendency to feel compassion, to forgive mistakes, and to express gratitude helps build the human capital and reserve needed to successfully lead positive change. How might that occur?

Compassion Kanov and colleagues (2003) found that **compassion** is built in organizations when managers foster three things: **collective noticing**, **collective feeling**, and **collective responding**. When people are suffering or experiencing difficulty, the first step is to notice or simply become aware of what is occurring. An iron-clad rule exists at Cisco Systems, for example, where CEO John Chambers must be notified within 48 hours of the death or serious illness of any Cisco employee or family member. People are on the lookout for colleagues who need help.

The second step is to enable the expression of collective emotion. Planned events where people can share feelings (for example, grief, support, or love) help build a climate of compassion. For example, a memorial service for a recently deceased executive at which the CEO shed tears was a powerful signal to organization members that responding compassionately to human suffering was important to the organization (Frost, 2003).

The third step is collective responding, meaning that the manager ensures that an appropriate response is made when healing or restoration is needed. In the aftermath of the 11 September 2001 tragedy, many examples of compassion—and noncompassion—were witnessed in organizations around the country. While some leaders modeled caring and compassion in the responses they fostered, others stifled the healing process (see Dutton, Frost, Worline, Lilius, & Kanov, 2002).

Forgiveness Most managers assume that **forgiveness** has no place in the work setting. Because of high

quality standards, the need to eliminate mistakes, and a requirement to "do it right the first time," managers assume that they cannot afford to let errors go unpunished. Forgiving mistakes will just encourage people to be careless and unthinking, they conclude. However, forgiveness and high standards are not incompatible. That is because forgiveness is not the same as pardoning, condoning, excusing, forgetting, denying, minimizing, or trusting (Enright & Coyle, 1998). To forgive does not mean relieving the offender of a penalty (i.e., pardoning), or saying that the offense is OK, not serious, or forgotten (i.e., condoned, excused, denied, minimized). The memory of the offense need not be erased for forgiveness to occur. Instead, forgiveness in an organization involves the capacity to abandon justified resentment, bitterness, and blame, and, instead, to adopt positive, forward-looking approaches in response to harm or damage (Cameron & Caza, 2002).

For example, because minor offenses and disagreements occur in almost all human interactions, especially in close relationships, most people are practiced forgivers. Without forgiveness, relationships could not endure and organizations would disintegrate into squabbles, conflicts, and hostilities. One explanation for the successful formation of the European Economic Union is forgiveness, for example (Glynn, 1994). Collectively speaking, the French, Dutch, and British forgave the Germans for the atrocities of World War II, as did other damaged nations. Likewise, the reciprocal forgiveness demonstrated by the United States and Japan after World War II helps explain the flourishing economic and social interchange that developed in subsequent decades. On the other hand, the lack of peace in certain war-torn areas of the world can be at least partly explained by the refusal of organizations and nations to forgive one another for past trespasses (Helmick & Petersen, 2001).

The importance of forgiveness in organizations, and societies, is illustrated by Nobel laureate Desmond Tutu in his description of postapartheid South Africa:

> Ultimately, you discover that without forgiveness, there is no future. We recognize that the past cannot be remade through punishment. . . . There is no point in exacting vengeance now, knowing that it will be the cause for future vengeance by the offspring of those we punish. Vengeance leads only to revenge. Vengeance destroys those it claims and those who become intoxicated with it . . . therefore, forgiveness is an absolute necessity for continued human existence. (Tutu, 1998, p. xiii; 1999, p. 155)

Forgiveness is enhanced in organizations when managers:

1. Acknowledge the trauma, harm, and injustice that their organization members have experienced, but they define the occurrence of hurtful events as an opportunity to move forward toward a new goal.

2. Associate the outcomes of the organization (e.g., its products and services) with a higher purpose that provides personal meaning for organization members. This higher purpose replaces a focus on self (e.g., retribution, self-pity) with a focus on a higher objective.

3. Maintain high standards and communicate the fact that forgiveness is not synonymous with tolerance for error or lowered expectations. Use forgiveness to facilitate excellence by refusing to focus on the negative and, instead, focus on achieving excellence.

4. Provide support by communicating that human development and human welfare are as important in the organization's priorities as the financial bottom line. This kind of support helps employees catch sight of a way to move past the injury.

5. Pay attention to language, so that terms such as forgiveness, compassion, humility, courage, and love are acceptable; this language provides a humanistic foundation upon which most forgiveness occurs.

An analysis of the several organizations' successful turnaround after the trauma of downsizing reveals these five steps being demonstrated in institutionalizing forgiveness.

Gratitude Observing acts of compassion and forgiveness—not to mention being the recipient of them—creates a sense of gratitude in people. **Gratitude** is crucial in organizations because it leads to reciprocal behavior, equity, and justice (e.g., returning a favor, doing good in return for receiving good, being fair). Simmel referred to gratitude as "the moral memory of mankind . . . if every grateful action . . . were suddenly eliminated, society (at least as we know it) would break apart" (1950, p. 388).

Feelings of gratitude have been found to have dramatic effects on individual and organizational performance. For example, Emmons (2003) induced feelings of gratitude in students by assigning them to keep journals as part of a semester-long assignment. Some of the students were required to keep "gratitude journals" on a daily or weekly basis. That is, they wrote down events or incidents that happened during the day (or week) for which they were grateful. Other students were assigned to write down events or incidents that were frustrating, and still other students were assigned to write down events or incidents that were merely neutral. Students keeping gratitude journals, compared to frustrated students and neutral students, experienced fewer physical symptoms such as headaches, colds, and so on; felt better about their lives as a whole; were more optimistic about the coming week; had higher states of alertness, attentiveness, determination, and energy; reported fewer hassles in their lives; engaged in more helping behavior toward other people; experienced better sleep quality; and had a sense of being more connected to others. In addition, they were absent and tardy less often and had higher grade point averages. Feelings of gratitude had significant impact on student classroom performance as well as people's personal lives.

McCraty and Childre (2004) helped explain one reason why the positive effect of gratitude occurs in people's lives. They studied heart rhythms of people when they experienced frustrating or stressful work conditions, and compared those heart rhythms to changes that occurred when people were induced into a gratitude condition. Figure 10.4 shows the differences. For the first 100 seconds, the erratic and disordered heartbeat pattern shows a condition of frustration and stress, whereas for the next 100 seconds the heartbeat pattern shows a condition of appreciation and gratitude. It is easy to see why performance and health are enhanced by gratitude.

Emmons also found that expressions of gratitude by one person tend to motivate others to express gratitude, so a self-perpetuating, virtuous cycle occurs when gratitude is expressed. Gratitude elicits positive behaviors on the part of other people (e.g., they are more likely to loan money, provide compassionate support, as well as behave reciprocally). For example, a hand-written "thank you" on a restaurant bill by the server elicits about 11 percent higher tips, and visits by case workers and social workers are 80 percent higher if they are thanked for coming (McCullough, Emmons, & Tsang, 2002). People respond positively to expressions of gratitude. Thus, not only does gratitude help people *feel* good but *do* good as well.

Managers engender gratitude in an organization simply by expressing gratitude frequently and conspicuously themselves, even for small acts and small successes, and by keeping track of things that go right (not just things that go wrong) and expressing gratitude for them. Elaborate programs are not needed, just frequent thank yous.

Figure 10.4 Heart Rhythms in Frustration and in Gratitude Conditions

These are actual heart rhythm patterns resulting from in an induced state of frustration followed by an induced gratitude condition.

Source: *McCraty & Childre, 2004.*

Pay Attention to Strengths and the Best Self

Identifying people's strengths (or what they do right) and then building on them creates more benefit than identifying weaknesses (or what people do wrong) and trying to correct them. For example, managers who spend more time with their strongest performers (rather than their weakest performers) achieved double the productivity. In organizations where workers have a chance to "do what they do best every day," productivity is one-and-a-half times greater than in normal organizations. People who are given feedback on their strengths are significantly more likely to feel highly engaged and to be more productive than people who are given feedback on their weaknesses. Students who are given feedback on their talents have fewer days of absenteeism, are tardy less often, and have higher GPAs than students who get no feedback on their talents. The strongest readers make more improvement in a speed-reading class designed to improve reading than the poor readers (Clifton & Harter, 2003).

Another illustration of this principle that building on positive strengths is more effective than concentrating on overcoming weaknesses is a classic study of (American) bowling (Kirschenbaum, 1984). To explain the study, let's assume that we decided to take a group of people to a bowling alley. The objective is to help these folks improve their bowling scores. We ask them all to bowl three games, and as they bowl, we videotape each person. Then, we ask that the entire group practice bowling for the next six months in order to improve their scores. However, to assist them, we will show them videotape of the three games we filmed. For half the group, we show them only video footage of when they rolled strikes, or knocked all the pins down. For the other half of the

group, we show them only video footage of when they did not roll strikes, or they did not knock all the pins down. Half the people are trying to capitalize on what they did right. Half the group is trying to correct mistakes. After six months of practice, we bring all the people back together and ask them to bowl three more games. We would discover that there is a statistically significant difference between the two groups. One group would bowl significantly better than the other. Which would you predict would do the best?

The research indicates that those who watched their past successes—they saw footage of their strikes—improved significantly more than those who watched footage of mistakes. That's because when we start out almost any activity, we mostly make mistakes. Yet, we tend to learn how to do it right over time. We tend to make more and more strikes, hit the ball down the center of the fairway, swish the free throw, or improve our public speaking ability, even though we make a lot of mistakes in the beginning. In other words, focusing on the positive will bring superior results to focusing on the negative. The trouble is, most people, most of the time, are inclined to pay attention to what's wrong, the problems, the negative feedback, or the failures they experience. The research, however, demonstrates the potency of the positive.

An even more dramatic finding resulted from a study of top management teams engaged in strategic planning for their organizations. Losada and Heaphy (2003) studied 60 teams of senior executives who met to set objectives, refine budgets, and identify plans for the upcoming year. The research focused on investigating why some teams, and their organizations, performed better than others. The teams used in the research were executives and top managers in well-recognized corporations.

The teams were categorized into three groups based on six measures of performance, such as firm profitability, productivity, managerial capability, and so on. The three groups were: those that performed well, those that performed about average, and those that performed poorly. To explain differences among the groups, the communication patterns of the teams was carefully monitored and analyzed. The single most important factor in predicting success—which was four times more powerful in predicting success than any other factor—was the ratio of positive comments to negative comments. Positive comments are those that express appreciation, support, helpfulness, or compliments. Negative comments express criticism, disapproval, or blame. The results of the research were dramatic. In high-performing teams, the ratio of positive to negative comments was 5:1. Five times more positive comments were made than negative comments. In medium-performing teams, the ratio was 1:1. In low-performing teams, the ratio was 0.36:1. In other words, in low-performing teams, there were three negative comments for every positive comment.

What these results show is that high-performing teams have an abundance of positive comments compared to negative comments. Effective teams are far more complimentary and supportive than ineffective teams. It's not that correction and criticism are entirely absent—it's not Pollyanna or rose-colored glasses all the time—but the positive outweighs the negative by a ratio of 5 to 1. Teams that performed moderately well had about an equal number of positive and negative comments, and teams that performed poorly had more negative than positive comments. The same ratio, by the way, has been found in successful marriages. Marriages that are strong also have a ratio of 5 to 1 positive interactions. Marriages that end in divorce have more negative than positive comments (Gottman, 1994).

Obviously, the management skill demonstrated by effective leaders of positive change is to bias their communication toward positive, supportive comments rather than negative and corrective comments. Remember, however, that the ratio is not 100:1 or 5:0. That is, critical, confrontive, and corrective comments need to be present and cannot be ignored. It's just that effective managers are, by and large, more focused on positive than negative communication.

Reflected Best-Self Feedback One technique that managers can use to enhance positivity and focus on strengths is called **"reflected best-self feedback"**

(Quinn, Dutton, & Spreitzer, 2003) It is a technique developed and used extensively at the University of Michigan Business School and recently adopted at the Harvard Business School, MIT, and several major corporations. It is designed to provide people with feedback on their strengths and unique capabilities. This kind of information is not frequently given to people, if ever, but receiving it allows individuals to build on their unique strengths in a positive way. Figure 10.5 illustrates the kind of feedback resulting from this exercise.

Begin at the bottom of the figure. Most of us have a lot of weaknesses—areas that are underdeveloped, areas in which we are uninformed, areas in which we have little skill. Most feedback systems provide information on what those areas are and how we compare to other people's capabilities in the same areas. Those are labeled **weaknesses** in Figure 10.5. We also all have areas in which we perform competently. We do fine—not stellar, but good enough. Those are area of **competence**. A third category is areas of well-developed skill. We're outstanding performers in some areas. We have special capabilities or talents, and we do better than most people. These are areas of **strength**. Finally, we all have areas that are unique to us. If we don't contribute what we have, or if we don't share our capacities and gifts, no one else has the ability to do so. Our talent or skill is special. We refer to this area as **uniquenesses**. Research indicates that capitalizing on our strengths and uniquenesses produces more success than trying to work on and overcome weaknesses—even though weaknesses may be more numerous and more obvious (Clifton & Harter, 2003).

You engaged in the reflected best-self feedback process as part of the Skill Pre-assessment section of this chapter. In this technique each person is asked to identify 20 other individuals who are acquaintances. These can be friends, coworkers, neighbors, or family members. Each of these acquaintances is asked to write three stories responding to this question: "When you have seen me at my best, or when you have seen me make a real contribution, what strengths did I display?" In other words, the 20 people write three stories about when the person was his or her best self. Those 60 stories identify the key strengths and unique talents of the individual—information that is both rare and extremely valuable. This information is analyzed by the person receiving the stories and summarized into a few key themes. Those themes represent the best-self strengths and uniquenesses of the person. The feedback comes in the form of incidents and stories, not numbers or trend lines, so it is

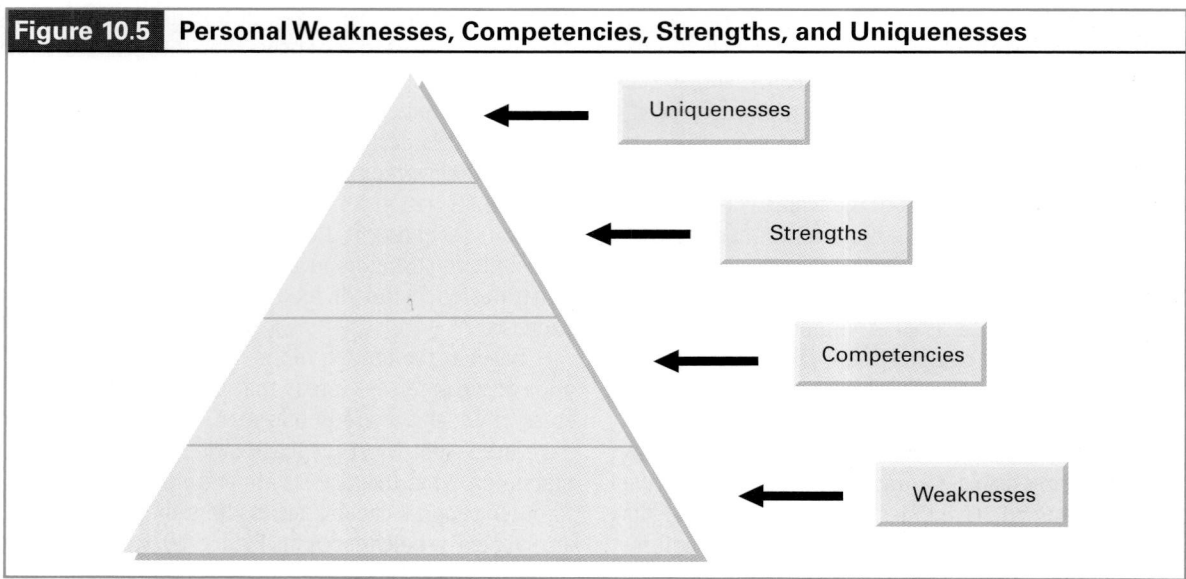

Figure 10.5 Personal Weaknesses, Competencies, Strengths, and Uniquenesses

connected directly to behaviors that the person has displayed in the past and which can be repeated and enhanced in the future. It captures emotions and feelings as well as intentional actions. These are the strengths and uniquenesses that can be built upon and enhanced. This kind of feedback does not even mention weaknesses or shortcomings. It does not motivate people to overcome areas of deficiency. Rather, it emphasizes the positive and helps people develop strategies to capitalize on it.

Of course, completely ignoring weaknesses and inadequacies is not healthy either. Focusing exclusively on the positive and disregarding critical weaknesses is not apt to be healthy in the long run. It's just that most individuals, and most organizations, concentrate almost exclusively on the negative and are likely to ignore, or at least short-change, the positive. The reflective best-self feedback technique is a way to counterbalance that tendency.

Summary Not everyone, and maybe even very few people, live or work in a positive organizational climate in which people flourish and experience positive energy. The role of the leader of positive change, therefore, is to facilitate and engender these characteristics. Table 10.1 summarizes some specific behaviors that can be implemented.

Being a source of positive energy and building positive energy networks leads to higher levels of personal success and organizational success. Similarly, the expression of compassion, forgiveness, and gratitude in organizations is also associated with superior performance,

personally and organizationally. And, focusing on strengths and talents—celebrating successes, complimenting what is going right, recognizing what folks do well—produces superior performance as well. Therefore, as the first step in leading positive change, establishing a positive climate is a crucial prerequisite. Without it, resistance and negativity are almost certain to present major obstacles. The tendency of most people is to focus on the problems, challenges, and negative issues associated with change. With a positive climate, however, positive change is much more likely to be successful. Figure 10.6 shows the relationship among these three aspects of positive climate.

Receiving feedback on strengths and successes produces feelings of gratitude and compassion which, in turn, leads to being positively energized. Each factor, in turn, affects performance directly, as well as in combination with the other factors.

CREATING READINESS FOR CHANGE

In addition to establishing a climate of positivity, individuals must feel a need for the change and to understand its importance and urgency. A positive climate is a crucial foundation, but leading positive change requires engaging individuals in the actual process of change. The second step in leading positive change, therefore, is to create readiness among those to be involved in the change. Many techniques are available, but three are mentioned here.

Table 10.1   Establishing a Climate of Positivity

1. Create positive energy networks.

  • Place positive energizers in places where others can interact with them and be influenced by them.

  • Model positive energy yourself.

  • Recognize and reward positive energizers.

  • Provide opportunities for people to form close friendships at work.

2. Ensure a climate of compassion, forgiveness, and gratitude.

  • Enable collective noticing of human concerns.

  • Enable the expression of collective emotion.

  • Enable the collective responding to difficulty, pain, or distress.

  • Publicly and personally acknowledge trauma and harm.

  • Identify higher purpose outcomes that people can point toward.

  • Maintain high standards and look toward the future after mistakes.

  • Provide personal support to people who have been harmed.

  • Pay attention to language so that virtuous words are acceptable.

  • Express gratitude frequently and conspicuously, even for small acts.

  • Keep track of things that go right (not just that go wrong).

3. Identify and give people feedback on their strengths and unique competencies.

  • Implement a reflected best-self feedback process.

  • Spend the most time with the strongest performers.

  • Work to capitalize on strengths rather than focusing on overcoming weaknesses.

  • Use five positive comments for every negative comment in your interactions with others.

LEARNING

Figure 10.6   Relationships Among Factors in a Climate of Positivity

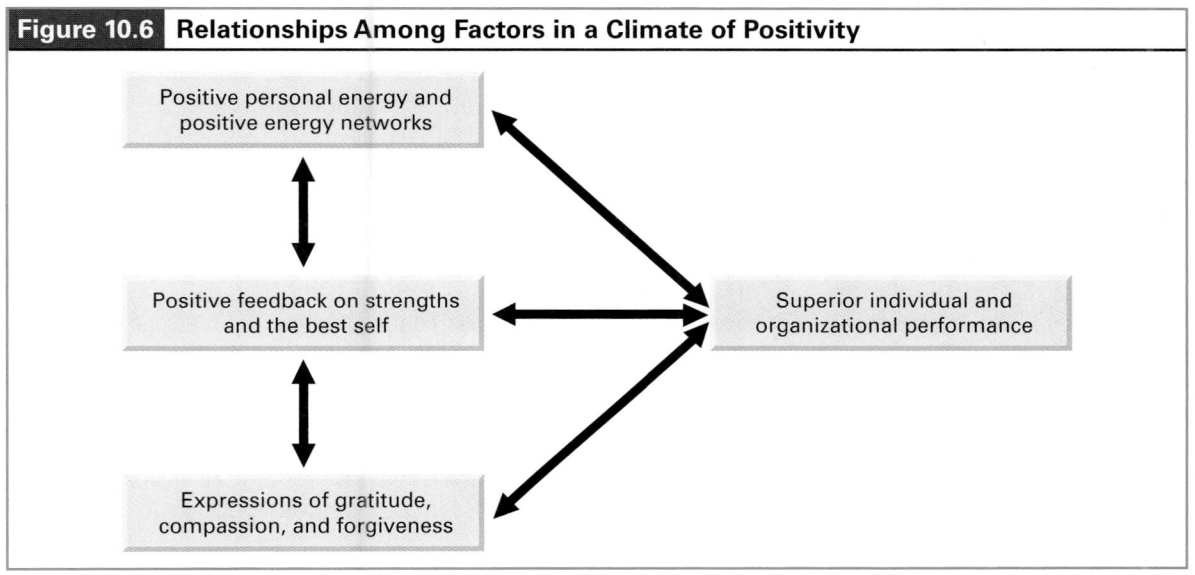

Benchmark Best Practice, and Compare Current Performance to the Highest Standards

One way to create readiness for change is to compare current levels of performance to the highest standards you can find. Identifying who else performs at spectacular levels helps set a standard toward which people can aspire. It identifies a target of opportunity. This is referred to as **benchmarking**, and it involves finding best practice, studying it in detail, and then planning to exceed that performance. "Shooting ahead of the duck" is the principle. Identifying best practice doesn't mean copying it. It means learning from it and exceeding it. Planned performance goes beyond the best practice, otherwise benchmarking is merely mimicking. Several different kinds of best practice standards are available for comparison.

- ❑ **Comparative standards**, or comparing current performance to similar individuals or organizations (e.g., "Here is how we are doing relative to our best competitors.")
- ❑ **Goal standards**, or comparing current performance to the publicly stated goals (e.g., "Here is how we are doing compared to the goals we have established.")
- ❑ **Improvement standards**, or comparing current performance with improvements made in the past (e.g., "Here is how we are doing compared to our improvement trends of the past year.")
- ❑ **Ideal standards**, or comparing current performance with an idea or perfect standard (e.g., "Here is how we are doing relative to a zero defect standard.")
- ❑ **Stakeholder expectations**, or comparing current performance with the expectations of customers, employees, or other stakeholders (e.g., "Here is how we are doing in meeting customer demands.")

Which standard of comparison is most appropriate depends, of course, on what opportunities exist, which standard has the most legitimacy with organization members, and which standard is perceived to be reachable. The purpose of these comparisons is to highlight the opportunities available by finding a higher level of performance and showing the possibility of achieving it.

Identifying benchmark standards also helps ensure that new information, new ideas, and new perspectives will be imported, and that standards not considered possible before may become realistic. Studying others who may be doing the same job better than you may be accomplished by sponsoring visitors, holding learning events (symposia and colloquia) or conferences, creating study teams, and scheduling visits to other sites. The objective is to unfreeze people from reliance on past practice by learning that there may be a better way.

Institute Symbolic Events

Leaders of positive change must signal the end of the old way of doing things and the beginning of a new way of doing things by means of symbols. This means that an event is used to signify a positive change or a new future. The symbolic event should be tangible and clearly identified with the positive change.

For example, during the 1980s Chrysler was experiencing very dark days. The company was bankrupt, and no one knew for sure if it would survive. Lee Iacocca was hired to be the new CEO. Tens of thousands of cars sat idle in the "sales bank" (Chrysler's term for cars parked in vacant lots) waiting to be sold. In his first closed-door speech to senior executives, Iacocca announced that the sales bank would be abolished. All cars in the sales bank would be sold at "distressed prices." "But," he said, "I want to keep one. You know what people do when they pay off the mortgage; they burn it on the front lawn. I want to burn that last car on the front lawn of headquarters, so the whole world knows it's over!" (Cameron, 1985). A symbolic event was held, in fact, in which the last car in the sales bank was burned, symbolizing a new future under Iacocca.

In that same speech, Iacocca asked all top managers to take out a piece of paper and write down all they had achieved in Chrysler during the past 12 months. After they had done so, they were instructed to tear up that paper and throw it away. They were to take out another piece of paper and write down all the things they were going to achieve in the next 12 months for the company. That was the document Iacocca instructed them to hang on their wall and explain to their coworkers. Symbolically, Iacocca was communicating the message: "You may have succeeded in the past, but the future is where we will now put our emphasis." The symbolic imagery communicated that message far more powerfully than merely stating it in a speech. The point is, symbolic images capture hearts as well as heads, and that resource is required for positive change to occur.

Create a New Language

Another way to create readiness for change is to help organization members begin to use different language to describe old realities. When new language is used, perspectives change. For example, a key goal for the theme park division at Disney Corporation is to provide the best service in the world. The trouble is, most of Disney's theme park employees in the summer months are college students working at temporary jobs and not particularly invested in being a park sweeper or concession stand cashier. Disney addresses this challenge by making sure that all new employees at Disney are taught that they have been hired by central casting, not the personnel department. They are cast members, not employees. They wear costumes, not uniforms. They serve guests and audience members, not tourists. They work in attractions, not rides or arcades. They have roles in the show and play characters (even as groundskeepers), not merely work a job. During working hours, they are onstage and must go offstage to relax, eat, or socialize.

The intent of this alternative language is to change the way these employees think about their work, to place them in a mindset that they wouldn't have considered otherwise. At Disney, summer employees are in show business—on stage, playing a role, performing for an audience. Changing language helps unfreeze old interpretations and helps create new ones. Another example is CNN. When the network was first formed, employees were fined $100 if they ever spoke the word "foreign." The reason: at a worldwide news organization, no one is foreign. Thinking globally requires that language change, and foreign became a forbidden word. Leading positive change requires that optimistic words replace pessimistic words, and language that blocks progress is shunned. Intel, for example, forbids phrases such as "It can't be done"; "It won't work"; "It's just like an idea we already tried"; "It will never get approved." These phrases are all "creativity killers," and they inhibit positive change, innovation, and improvement.

Bennis and Nanus (1984) observed that the most successful leaders in education, government, business, the arts, and the military are those who have developed a special language. Most notable is the absence in their vocabularies of the word *failure*. These individuals simply haven't allowed themselves, or others around them, to accept the possibility of failure. Alternative descriptors are used, such as temporary slowdown, false start, miscue, error, blooper, stumble, foul-up, obstacle, disappointment, or nonsuccess. These leaders use an alternative language in order to interpret reality for their organizations, to foster a willingness to try again, and to foster an inclination toward positive change. This language communicates the fact that failure is not an option. Success is just around the corner.

Summary

Creating readiness is a step designed to mobilize individuals in the organization to actively engage in the positive change process. It involves more than merely unfreezing people. Making people uncomfortable is a frequent prescription for getting people ready for change, and it often works. Making people uncomfortable, however, usually involves creating fear, crisis, or negative conditions. There is no doubt, of course, that change also creates its own discomfort. Interpersonal relationships, power and status, and routine ways of behaving are disrupted by change, so change is usually interpreted as anything but a positive condition. Leading positive change, on the other hand, focuses on ways to create readiness in ways that unlock positive motivations rather than resistance, and provides optimistic alternatives rather than fear. Benchmarking best practice, positive symbols, and new language are three practical ways to do it, as summarized in Table 10.2.

Establishing a climate of positivity and creating readiness for change does little good, of course, if there is not a clear idea of where the positive change is heading. That is why the third step in the framework refers to articulating a clear, motivating vision of abundance.

ARTICULATING A VISION OF ABUNDANCE

Positive change seldom occurs without a leader articulating a **vision of abundance** (see Figure 10.1). By abundance we mean a vision of a positive future, a flourishing condition, and a legacy about which people care passionately. This kind of vision helps unleash human wellsprings of potential since it addresses a basic human desire—to do something that makes a difference, something that outlasts one's own life, and something that has enduring impact. Visions of abundance are different from visions of goal achievement or effectiveness—such as earning a certain percent profit, becoming number one in the marketplace, or receiving personal recognition. Rather, these are visions that speak to the heart as well as the head.

For example, the vision of Richard Bogomolny, the CEO of Finast Supermarkets in Cleveland, Ohio, was to

Table 10.2	**Creating Readiness in Others to Pursue Positive Change**

1. Benchmark best practice, and compare current performance to the highest standards.

   - Use comparable others as standards.
   - Use stated goals as standards.
   - Use past improvement as a standard.
   - Use an ideal as a standard.
   - Use others' expectations as a standard.

2. Institute symbolic events to signal the positive change.

   - Interpret events or activities as indicators of the beginning of a new era.
   - Manage people's interpretations and mental images of incidents so that they reinforce the intended change.
   - Pay as much attention to the meaning of change as the substance of the change.

3. Create a new language that illustrates the positive change.

   - Use words associated with the change that capture people's imagination.
   - Use passionate and inspiring language.
   - Use words that communicate and reinforce a new direction.

improve the quality of life for residents of blighted areas of Cleveland who would otherwise never have access to a reasonably priced grocery store with competitive prices. He invested in new, state-of-the-art supermarkets in poor urban neighborhoods, stocking shelves with ethnic foods that were not popular in suburban stores, and providing an environment of safety and cleanliness along with offering prices competitive with suburban shopping centers. Finast stores have now become the social gathering places for entire neighborhoods, have provided training and employment for the chronically unemployed, and, at the same time, have become a highly profitable investment for the company (Bollier, 1996). Without the leader's clear statement of a vision of abundance, the overwhelming tendencies toward addressing obstacles, problem solving, and negative feedback drive out positive change.

Most organizations have some kind of mission statement or have established goals, but a **vision statement** is something different. Visions include the universalistic values and principles that will guide behavior. They provide a sense of direction. They help identify what the future holds. They provide glimpses of possibilities, not just probabilities. They evoke deeper meaning than mission statements or goals. They provide optimism and hope.

For example, goals that call for a 20 percent increase in ROI, an improvement in product quality,

timelier responses to customers, or lower costs all are valuable and important to organizations. Yet, they are not visions. They are examples of targets that the organization wants to achieve. Visions, on the other hand, are focused on helping individuals' *think* differently about themselves and about their future. They possess several important characteristics that are central to the positive change process.

Include Left-Brain and Right-Brain Features

Many years ago, neurosurgeons discovered that the brain consists of two hemispheres that can actually work independently when surgically separated. The left hemisphere controls the right side of the body, but it also controls rational cognitive activities such as sequential thinking, logic, deduction, numeric thought, and so on. Activities such as reading, solving math problems, and rational analysis are dominated by *left-brain thinking*.

The right hemisphere, on the other hand, controls the left side of the body as well as nonrational cognitive activities such as intuition, creativity, fantasy, emotions, pictorial images, and imagination. Composing music, storytelling, and artistic creation are most likely tied to *right-brained thinking.*

Of course, neither hemisphere operates autonomously from the other, and both kinds of mental activity are required in complex tasks. But that is precisely the point. Vision statements of leaders must contain rational targets, goals, and action plans (left-brain components), as well as metaphors, colorful language, and imagination (right-brain components). Unfortunately, most managers and most organizations emphasize the left-brain side in their mission statement or strategic planning documents (they focus, for example, on increased market share, becoming number one in the industry, or raising quality standards). Fewer paint pictures of the future, use exciting language, and speak to the imaginations of members. In the Skill Analysis section of this chapter, several corporate vision statements are provided for you to analyze. Note the differences among them in the relative emphasis on right-brain versus left-brain thinking.

Articulating the *left-brained* side of the vision is facilitated by answering the following questions:

❏ What are our most important strengths as an organization? Where do we have a strategic advantage?
❏ What major problems and obstacles do we face? What stands in the way of significant improvement?
❏ What are the primary resources that we need? What information is required?
❏ Who are our key customers? What must be done to respond to their expectations?
❏ What measurable outcomes will we accomplish? What are the criteria to be monitored?

Articulating the *right-brained* side of the vision is aided by answering the following questions:

❏ What is the best we can achieve? What represents peak performance?
❏ What stories or events can we tell that characterize what we stand for?
❏ What metaphors or analogies can we use that will identify what the future of our organization will look like?
❏ What symbols are appropriate for helping capture people's imaginations?
❏ What colorful and inspirational language can exemplify what we believe in?

The most motivating vision statements—for example, Churchill's "Never Give In" speech, Kennedy's "Ask Not What Your Country Can Do for You" speech, Mandela's "A Dream for Which I Am Prepared to Die" speech, Martin Luther King's "I Have a Dream" speech—all contain both left-brained and right-brained elements. Leaders of positive change pay attention to both in articulating their vision statements.

Make Vision Statements Interesting

Murray Davis (1971) published a now-classic article on what causes some kinds of information to be judged interesting or uninteresting. The truth or veracity of the information has little to do with that judgment, according to Davis. Rather, what's interesting depends on the extent to which the information contradicts weakly held assumptions and challenges the status quo. If new information is consistent with what is already known, people tend to dismiss it as common sense. If new information is obviously contradictory to strongly held assumptions, or if it blatantly challenges the core values of the organization's members, it is labeled ridiculous, silly, or blasphemous. Information that helps create new ways to view the future, that challenges the current state of things (but not core values), is viewed as interesting. New insights are created and people are drawn to the information because it makes them think, or it uncovers a new way to think.

Inspiring vision statements are interesting. They contain challenges and prods that confront and alter the ways people think about the past and the future. They are not outlandish or cavalier in their message, just provocative. For example, Ralph Peterson, CEO of CH2MHill (a large environmental and engineering firm) indicated that "corporate immortality" was the ultimate objective of the company, meaning that the firm was in business to create outcomes that would last well beyond the lifetime of any individual. Jeffrey Schwartz, CEO of Timberland, the shoe and clothing company, espoused a vision related to doing good in order to do well—organizational virtuousness is equally important to organizational profitability. Tom Gloucer, CEO of Reuters, espoused the vision that Reuters would become the fastest company in the world. Ross Perot, while serving on the board of directors at General Motors, articulated his vision of the new GM if he were at the helm. "From this point forward, GM'ers will fight in the marketplace, not with each other. Starting today, GM'ers will work together using brains, wits, creative abilities, and initiative as substitutes for money. Starting today, as GM goes through a transformation, all sacrifices will start at the top" (1988).

These examples are not intended to illustrate the best vision statements, of course, nor even vision statements that energize you personally. But, in each case, they carried a strong and motivating message for those in the organizations mentioned. They helped paint a mental picture. One of the chief reasons is that these vision statements are interesting. They identify a message that people care about but which challenges the normal perception of things. The statements confront the status quo and provide a new way to think about what people do in the organization every day. The fact that they are interesting is what captures attention and positive energy.

Include Passion and Principles

Effective visions are grounded in core values that organization members believe in, and about which they feel passionate. Such vision statements increase people's desire to affiliate with the organization if they care deeply about the company's core principles. The principles espoused in the vision, therefore, must be personal. A vision focused on "increasing productivity" is less energizing and inspiring than a vision based on "changing people's lives." "Achieving profitability" is less magnetic than "making people happy." Furthermore, such principles are best phrased using superlatives. Notice the difference in how you feel about the following comparisons: "phenomenal performance" versus "successful." Or, "passionately engaged" versus "committed." Or, "explosive growth" versus "good progress." Or, "awesome products" versus "useful items." Visions based on the former phrases engender more enthusiasm and passion than those based on the latter phrases.

Consider as an example of such language the vision statement of John Sculley, former CEO of Apple Computer Company:

> *We are all part of a journey to create an extraordinary corporation. The things we intend to do in the years ahead have never been done before. . . . One person, one computer is still our dream. . . . We have a passion for changing the world. We want to make personal computers a way of life in work, education, and the home. Apple people are paradigm shifters. . . . We want to be the catalyst for discovering new ways for people to do things. . . . Apple's way starts with a passion to create awesome products with a lot of distinctive value built in. . . . We have chosen directions for Apple that will lead us to wonderful ideas we haven't as yet dreamed. (Sculley, 1987)*

Two specific hints for articulating inspiring, passionate, principle-centered visions include:

1. Ensure that the vision statement reinforces *core values* about which you feel strongly. Instead of focusing on end results such as profit growth, expanded market share, customer satisfaction measures, or goal accomplishment, for example, the vision statement should relate to something fundamental about which people can feel passionate. This is likely to be associated with human flourishing, interpersonal relationships, or an ultimate good—that is, things that make life worth living. These are things that outlast a single person's lifetime, or that create a ripple effect so that the impact extends far beyond the immediate situation. Outcomes such as assistance to mankind, helping to make life or work more rewarding, increasing the freedom of individuals, or improving the quality of life all are more attractive and motivational than instrumental outcomes. People can become passionate about these kinds of aspirations.

2. The vision statement must be straightforward and simple. A common error of leaders is to be too complicated, too lengthy, or too multifaceted in their vision statement. Most great leaders acknowledge that they have only three or four major objectives in mind. Their visions help people focus. Ronald Reagan, Michael Eisner (Disney), Jack Welch (GE), Bill Gates (Microsoft), Jim Hackett (Steelcase) all are well-known examples of leaders who publicly espoused a simple and straightforward vision—usually with only three or four key parts. Contrast that with the former CEO and chairman of Whirlpool Corporation who wrote a 15-page document outlining his vision for the company. Employees complained that they couldn't understand exactly what he wanted or where the company was going. It was difficult to sign up for 15 pages! One senior manager dismissed the document by stating, "He simply has too much vision!" It was only when the vision statement was condensed to four key points that it became credible in the organization.

Attach the Vision to a Symbol

Effective vision statements are associated with a symbol. This is more than a symbolic event that helps create readiness for change. Rather, people must associate the vision with something tangible they see or hear. Not only does the vision identify expectations and direction for individuals in their day-to-day activities, but they should be reminded of it regularly by the presence of a symbol. That symbol may be a logo, a phrase from a speech, a flag, a physical structure, or any number of things that can serve as a reminder of where the vision is taking the organization.

The turnaround at Ford Motor Company after William Clay Ford took over was symbolized by the resurrection of the blue Ford oval on the headquarters building. Chrysler returned to the classic Chrysler logo instead of the five-pointed star. Malden Mills reconstructed a plant that had been devastated by fire on the same property to symbolize human commitment and corporate compassion. The replacement structures for the World Trade Center towers are targeted specifically to symbolize a positive and uplifting future after the devastating tragedy. Logos such as the golden arches, Nike Swoosh, or Mickey Mouse are carefully publicized, even protected, because of the symbolic messages that they communicate about the companies they represent.

One of us served as a dean in a Midwest business school for a time, and a key responsibility was to articulate a motivating and energizing vision in order to set new direction for the school. The vision being articulated focused on enhancing the school's reputation, engendering a spirit of entrepreneurship and innovation, and building a sense of pride in scholarly excellence. Speeches were made about these aspirations—we have all heard these kinds of talks—but speeches given by the dean seldom if ever have lasting impact. A symbol was needed to make the vision real and to serve as a constant reminder. That symbol was the construction of a new building, designed by the world's most famous architect. The new building symbolized a best-in-class, one-of-a-kind structure, and it signified that the school would be an innovative, entrepreneurial, out-of-the-box kind of place. Pride in being unique in the world was an important symbolic message. To get a sense of how a building could serve as a symbol of such things, look at the final building model in Figure 10.7.

You can see that this design can communicate strong messages to both internal and external constituencies. It was interpreted as representing the twenty-first century rather than the eighteenth or nineteenth century (which are more typical of most ivy-covered college campuses in America). It was used to represent innovation and the entrepreneurial spirit. It communicates humaneness, comfort, and interaction. It symbolizes movement, fluidity, and dynamism. It epitomizes best-in-class. The building was designed to foster lots of interaction, representing the fact that

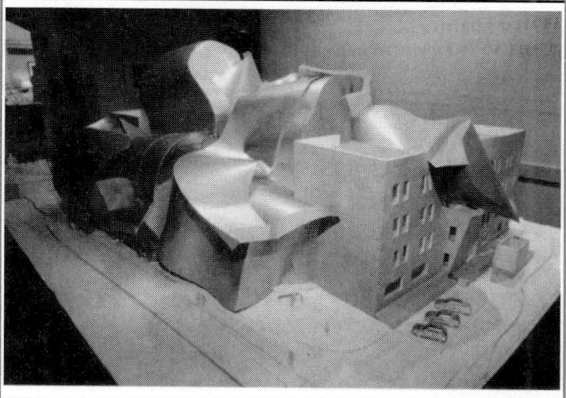

Figure 10.7   An Example: A Symbol of Positive Organizational Change

learning is mainly a social activity. It touches the whole person—emotions and spirit as well as intellect. It stimulates extraordinary thinking (Cameron, 2003b). Speeches about a vision, in other words, were not nearly as powerful as a visible symbol that could be experienced every day by the people who saw it.

Table 10.3 summarizes some specific behaviors you can use in articulating a high-impact vision of abundance.

GENERATING COMMITMENT TO THE VISION

Once this vision of abundance has been articulated, it is necessary for leaders to help organization members commit to that vision, to sign up, to adopt the vision as their own, and to work toward its accomplishment. The whole intent of a vision is to mobilize the energy and human potential of individuals who are to implement and be affected by it. Among the ways to generate commitment to a vision are four discussed below. Others are discussed in depth in the chapters on motivation, empowerment, and teamwork.

Apply Principles of Recreation

An interesting truism was identified by Chuck Coonradt (1985): "*People will pay for the privilege of working harder than they will work when they are paid.*" Think about that for a minute. "People will pay for the privilege of working harder than they will work when they are paid." In other words, under certain circumstances, individuals are more committed to doing work that actually costs them money than they are to doing work for which they receive remuneration.

Table 10.3	Articulating a Vision of Abundance

1. Focus on creating positive deviance rather than correcting negative deviance.

   • Focus on possibilities more than probabilities.

   • Focus on extraordinary, spectacular achievement rather than just winning or being seen as successful.

2. Include left-brain images by asking questions such as:

   • What are our most important strengths as an organization?

   • Where do we have a strategic advantage?

   • What major problems and obstacles do we face?

   • What stands in the way of significant improvement?

   • What are the primary resources that we need?

   • What information is required?

   • Who are our key customers?

   • What must be done to respond to customers' expectations?

   • What measurable outcomes will we accomplish?

   • What are the criteria to be monitored?

3. Include right-brain images by asking questions such as:

   • What is the best we can achieve?

   • What represents peak performance?

   • What stories or events can we tell that characterize what we stand for?

   • What metaphors or analogies can we use that will identify what the future of our organization will look like?

   • What symbols are appropriate for helping capture people's imaginations?

   • What colorful and inspirational language can exemplify what we believe in?

4. Make the vision interesting by challenging weakly held assumptions.

5. Ensure credibility of the vision through demonstrating:

   • Integrity in adhering to a consistent set of principles.

   • Knowledge regarding the implications of the vision.

   • Enthusiasm and personal passion for the vision.

   • Association with core personal values.

   • A straightforward and simple message.

   • Exciting and energizing language.

6. Attach the vision to a symbol to constantly remind people of the vision.

   • Create visual images such as logos, flags, or signs.

   • Make certain that the visual symbol is closely associated with the vision so it remains a constant reminder.

Sometimes people will pay to work when they will not work when they are paid. How can that be? In what circumstances might that be the case?

Consider the following hypothetical example. Suppose you live in Utah in the winter and, as you arrive at work, your find that the furnace is out of order. As the temperature falls to 65 degrees Fahrenheit you put on a coat. At 60 degrees you complain that it is too cold to work. At 55 degrees you leave, confident that no one could expect you to perform in such adverse conditions. Then you put on your $300 ski outfit, grab your $750 skis and boots, race off to the slopes in order to pay $75 for a lift ticket, $25 for gas, and $30 for a junk-food lunch. You will spend all day long in 10-degree weather working much harder skiing than you would have worked at the firm where you could have been paid. If this sounds unusual, consider the skyrocketing absenteeism rates in companies and schools when the first big snow falls in ski areas, when the surf is up in cities close to the beach, or the first day of hunting or fishing season. People regularly choose to pay to work harder than they would consider working when they are paid.

Well, you say, that's because it's fun. It's recreation. And you're right. But there is no reason why the work performed in a regular job cannot be characterized by the same principles that characterize recreation. In other words, what causes people to *want* to engage in recreational work can also be what causes them to be equally committed to their occupational work. At least five characteristics are typical of **recreational work** (Coonradt, 1985).

1. Goals are clearly defined
2. Scorekeeping is objective, self-administered, peer-audited, and compared to past performance
3. Feedback is frequent
4. Personal choice is present; rules are consistent and don't change until the season is over
5. A competitive environment is present

Consider the game of (American) football. Each year the University of Michigan averages about 106,000 fans per game, every one of whom knows exactly what the goal is—to score more points than the opponent. There is no need for a periodic performance appraisal system, because the score changes only when a team crosses the goal line or kicks a field goal. There is no guessing about how to get ahead. Feedback is not only frequent, it is continuous. If the clock goes down, they stop the game. No one would consider playing if the time and the score were not kept continuously. Within the rules of the game, every participant and fan has personal choice. Players can go full speed or not; fans can cheer or not; the team can run the ball or pass. No one forces people to perform a role that they don't want to perform. Coordination and control occur because everyone knows the rules, and the rules don't change. Off-side is off-side, a first down is a first down, and a touchdown is a touchdown. When a receiver is wide open and makes an easy catch in the end zone, no one could imagine an NCAA committee deliberating about

how many points the score is worth. No one would say, "Easy catch; wide open; worth only 4.5 points." No one would stand for that, and 106,000 people would go crazy. The rules simply don't change in recreation. Plus, the environment is one of competition—both against an opponent and against personal past performance. The stimulation of competing against something is fun. Playing against someone who is markedly less skilled—beating them 100 to 0, is not as much fun.

Despite the inherent motivation and commitment associated with these principles, many leaders behave inconsistently with them. Their vision is not stated clearly and precisely. There is no objective, self-administered evaluation system. The scorekeeping system is controlled hierarchically, by managers one step above, instead of being peer-audited and continuous, as in recreation. Criteria of evaluation are vague and inconsistently administered. Organization feedback often comes only when quarterly earnings statements are tabulated, and then it is often focused on what went wrong. Personal freedom is too often constrained, as evidenced by the elaborate bureaucratic structures that typify most large organizations. It is not unusual to have the criteria of success change in the middle of the game, especially if a new manager takes over. And, most employees never see how what they do makes any difference at all in obtaining the ultimate goal, or winning against a competitor.

The point is, one way for leaders to generate commitment to the vision is to identify clear, consistent goals associated with the vision; identify the criteria that will indicate progress toward reaching the vision which each organization member can monitor; provide mechanisms for frequent feedback to organization members; give individuals personal choice and the maximum discretion possible; maintain a consistency and stability of the rules of the game and expectations; and identify a competitive standard against which performance can be evaluated. Like commitment to recreation, commitment to visions, if based on similar principles, will also become strong and long-lasting.

Ensure Public Commitments

Another well-documented way to enhance commitment to a vision is to have people state their commitments aloud, in public. Individuals are motivated to behave consistently with their public declarations (Salancik, 1977). The internal need for congruence ensures that public statements will be followed by consistent actions. After making public pronouncements, individuals are more committed and more consistent in their behavior to that which they have espoused (Baker, 2001; Cialdini, 2000).

For example, during World War II, good cuts of meat were in short supply in the United States. Lewin (1951) found that a significant difference existed between the commitment level of shoppers who promised out loud to buy more plentiful but less desirable cuts of meat (e.g., liver, kidneys, brains) compared to those who made the same promise in private. In another study, students were divided in a college class into two groups. All students set goals for how much they would read and what kinds of scores they would get on exams. Only half the students were allowed to state these goals publicly to the rest of the class. By midsemester, the students who stated their goals publicly averaged 86 percent improvement. The nonpublic goal-setting students averaged 14 percent improvement.

When the Tennessee Valley Authority (TVA) was attempting to build a dam in the late 1940s, it found that local farmers vehemently resisted the efforts because of the land that would be flooded. To overcome this resistance and elicit farmers' commitment to the project, the TVA made local farmers members of the board that would supervise the construction efforts. These local farmers began to make public statements on behalf of the TVA project and, over time, became strongly committed to it (Selznick, 1949).

This point is, leaders of positive change look for opportunities to have others make public statements in favor of the vision, or to restate the vision themselves. Assigning individuals to represent the vision to outside groups or to other employees, or forming discussion groups so that others can help refine or clarify the vision, are examples of how opportunities for public statements can be fostered in order to enhance commitment.

Institute a Small-Wins Strategy

People become committed to change when they see progress being made or success being achieved. We are all more committed to winners than to losers. Fans attend more games when the team has a good record than when it has a poor record. The number of people claiming to have voted for a winning candidate always exceeds by a large margin the actual number of votes received. In other words, when we see success, or progress being made, we are more committed to respond positively, to continue that path, and to offer our support.

Leaders of positive change create this kind of support by identifying small wins—a strategy that was discussed in Chapter 2 on managing stress, as well as being mentioned in discussions of problem solving and empowerment. This small-wins strategy is applicable in a variety of skill-building activities, so we repeat part of the discussion here. The key message is that surfacing and publicizing small wins creates commitment and builds momentum for desired change (Weick, 1981). For example, we have observed leaders, when beginning a major change initiative, starting with small changes such as a new coat of paint, abolishing reserved parking spaces, adding a display case for awards, flying a flag, holding regular social events, instituting a suggestion system, and so on. Each of these small changes (and hundreds more) is designed to create commitment to the visualized change.

A small-wins strategy, in other words, is designed to create a sense of momentum by creating minor, quick changes. As a refresher, the basic rule of thumb for small wins is: *Find something that is easy to change. Change it. Publicize it, or recognize it publicly. Then, find a second thing that's easy to change, and repeat the process.*

Small wins create commitment because: (1) they reduce the importance of any one change ("It is no big deal to make this change."); (2) they reduce demands on any group or individual ("There isn't a lot to do."); (3) they improve the confidence of participants ("At least I can do that."); (4) they help avoid resistance or retaliation ("Even if they disagree, it's only a small loss."); (5) they attract allies and create a bandwagon effect ("I want to be associated with this success."); (6) they create the image of progress ("Things seem to be moving forward."); (7) if they don't work they only create a small flop ("No major harm is done and no long-lasting effects occur."); (8) they provide initiatives in multiple arenas ("Resistance cannot be coordinated or organized in a single area.") (Weick, 1993).

Communicate the Vision

Effective leaders of positive change communicate the vision, then they communicate it again, then again, and then again. If leaders stop communicating the vision, or if they change themes as they address organization members, the members tend to think that the vision isn't important anymore. Unless leaders continually and consistently articulate and rearticulate the vision, it loses its power and commitment erodes. Being accused of repetition is much less serious than being accused of neglect. Persistent and continuous delivery of the vision message is required, but surprisingly, it is a frequent shortcoming of leaders. They give a speech or hand out a sheet on which the vision is written; then they think their job is complete. In reality, it has only begun. No one ever heard Nelson Mandela speak in South Africa, for example, without having him rearticulate his vision of human dignity and equal treatment for all persons.

Communicating the vision must also occur using a variety of methods. This means referring to the vision in public statements, newsletters, celebrations and ceremonies, speeches, memos, and everyday interactions. Leaders model the vision in their personal behavior. There should be no questions, by observing and listening to leaders, what the vision is. From example, Jan Carlzon, the former president of Scandinavian Airlines (SAS), took control of the airline when it was losing $20 million a year. In the first year he increased revenues by $80 million and led his company to being voted "the best airline in the world" by *Fortune* magazine. Here is what he said about communicating his vision.

Good leaders spend more time communicating than anything else. From my first day at SAS I've made communicating, particularly with our employees, a top priority. In fact, during the first year I spent exactly half my working hours out in the field talking to SAS people. The word going around was that any time three employees gathered, Jan Carlzon would probably show up and begin talking with them.

When we began reorganizing SAS, our critics scoffed at our efforts as mere promotional gimmicks. They claimed we had become too marketing oriented, but in fact we hadn't increased our marketing budget one cent. Rather, we were spending our money more effectively on messages that were easily understood. (Carlzon, 1987, p. 88, 92)

Creating commitment is enhanced, in other words, by applying principles of recreational work, providing opportunities for public statements of commitment, instituting small wins, and communicating the vision frequently, consistently, and broadly. In essence, as summarized in Table 10.4, leaders will

Table 10.4	Generating Commitment to the Vision

1. Apply principles of recreation to the work associated with the vision:
   - Clearly define goals.
   - Ensure that scorekeeping is objective, self-administered, peer-audited, and compared to past performance.
   - Ensure frequent (or continuous) feedback.
   - Provide opportunity for personal choice.
   - Ensure that rules are consistent and don't change.
   - Provide a competitive environment.
2. Provide opportunities for people to publicly commit to the vision.
   - Hold events where people can verbalize their commitment.
   - Ask people to teach others about, or recruit others to sign up for, the vision.
3. Institute a strategy of small wins.
   - Find something easy to change.
   - Change it.
   - Publicize it.
   - Repeat the process multiple times.
4. Communicate the vision frequently.
   - Never give a public speech or presentation without mentioning the vision.
   - Make certain that all your written messages contain references to the vision.
   - Avoid changing messages.

achieve commitment to that which they *say*, that which they *do*, and that which they *reward*, but without consistency and frequency, not necessarily to that which they *want*.

INSTITUTIONALIZING THE POSITIVE CHANGE

The final challenge for leaders of positive change is to make the change a part of ongoing organizational life. General officers in the United States Army refer to this step as **"creating irreversible momentum"**; that is, ensuring that the positive change gains such momentum that it cannot be thwarted (U.S. Army, 2003). The challenge is to separate the vision from the visionary, to get others to own and become champions of the change, to create processes that reinforce the positive change without having to continually rely on the leader. The objective is to ensure that even if the leader leaves, the positive change will continue because of the sustainable impetus put in place. If Bill Gates was incarcerated for unfair business competition, Jan Carlzon got in an airplane crash, Lee Iacocca was run over by a car, or Jack Welch was electrocuted by a faulty refrigerator wire, Microsoft, SAS, Chrysler, and General Electric would not have missed a step. The positive changes championed by these leaders would still have been pursued because they had become embedded in their organizations' cultures. They were institutionalized and had gained irreversible momentum.

Institutionalizing change doesn't happen quickly, of course, and the four previous steps in positive change—establishing a climate of positivity, creating readiness, articulating a vision, and generating commitment—all must be successfully accomplished first. However, institutionalization is the necessary final step if the organization is to successfully achieve positive change. How do leaders institutionalize their positive changes? Three hints are provided.

Turn Students into Teachers

Most of the time we assume that it is the leader's responsibility to articulate the vision of abundance, and everyone else listens to it and accepts it. Teachers teach what students need to know and students learn it for the exam. The chief gives direction and the rest of us follow.

The most effective leaders, however, provide an opportunity for everyone in the organization to articulate the vision, or to teach others about the desired positive change. This process requires that every person develop "a teachable point of view" (Tichy, 1997). Developing one's own teachable point of view means that individuals come to believe in something, and they can clearly explain what it is and why. In other words, people get to the point where they can articulate the vision in their own words. They are given opportunities to teach others what they understand the positive change to be. They are required to develop their own perspective on the positive change in a way that it can be explained and illustrated to someone else. They are transformed from students or listeners into teachers or visionaries.

Researchers at the National Training Laboratories in Bethel, Maine, developed a "learning stair" (see Figure 10.8). Their studies found that people remember 5 percent of what they hear in a lecture, 10 percent of what they read, 20 percent of what they view in a video, 30 percent of what they observe being demonstrated, 50 percent of what they discuss in a group, 75 percent of what they apply, and 90 percent of what they teach to others. That is, by teaching someone else about the vision or the intended positive change, individuals remember it, become committed to it, and make it a part of their own personal agenda.

One manifestation of this principle was at Xerox under Rex Kern, a remarkable leader who turned that company around in the late 1980s and early 1990s. Kern's focus was on rapidly institutionalizing a positive change process by turning students into teachers. He spent time sharing his vision of positive change with his top leadership team. Then these leaders were required to apply what they heard; that is, to implement personal action agendas and make personal changes. Then, most importantly, they were required to teach the positive change vision to someone else. Who would they teach? They taught the next level of leaders in the firm. They were also required to assess or monitor the positive change. This was in order to identify measurable indicators, milestones, and hard data to ensure that the positive change was really taking place. It was a way to guard against lip service with no real substance. What did they assess? It was the action agendas and managerial experiments implemented by the leaders they taught. The process continued down through all the organizational levels. Each person, in other words, was exposed to the vision four times: when they learned it from their leader; when they applied it; when they taught it; and when they assessed it. Within a year, Xerox achieved stunning results. It is widely acknowledged that this

Figure 10.8 The Learning Stairs (from the NTL Institute)

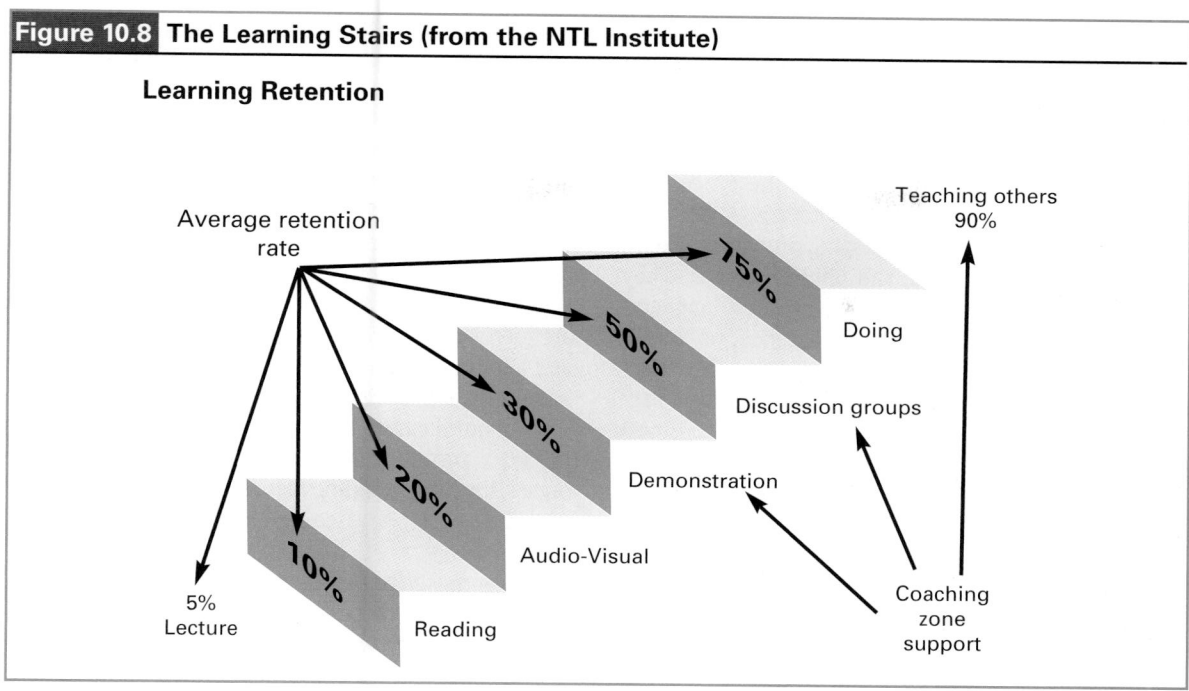

Learning Retention

Average retention rate

75% — Teaching others 90%

50% — Doing

30% — Discussion groups

20% — Demonstration

10% — Audio-Visual

5% Lecture — Reading

Coaching zone support

LEARNING

Source: *The Learning Stairs; NTL Institute; Bethel, ME.*

process was key in turning Xerox around as a company and in labeling Rex Kern as one of the great corporate leaders of the twentieth century.

This is similar to the process used by certain divisions within Hewlett-Packard. These divisions require engineers to spend time recruiting on college campuses. Having engineers actually recruit students—from disciplines in business, mathematics, physical sciences, arts and humanities, as well as engineering—is risky because engineers are not trained recruiters. However, the strategy pays off because HP engineers are required to articulate the vision, publicly praise Hewlett-Packard, and teach interested job candidates about the company. Former HP "students" are required to become the "teachers." These engineers may not convince many rookie recruits, but by articulating the HP Way, they internalize it themselves. As a result, Hewlett-Packard has the lowest turnover rate in the industry among engineers, one of its stated core competencies.

Build Human Capital

For positive change to have staying power, for it to last beyond the lifetime of the leader, people throughout the organization must have developed the capability to lead the vision themselves, to institute positive

change, and to carry on under their own initiative. In other words, well-developed human capital is always the chief predictor of growth in financial capital. The skill set of the people is the bedrock upon which organizational success is built. No company can make money over time without well-developed human capital—meaning capable and skilled employees. Institutionalizing positive change occurs as individuals throughout the organization develop the capacity to lead positive change themselves. This can happen in many ways, of course, but a good example of the core principle is illustrated by a large Asian company in which we conducted research.

This particular company requires that each time a senior manager is promoted, he or she is required to take a three-month leave of absence. The person must actually leave work for three full months. For one of the months the manager is required to intensively study religion or ethics, and then document it, usually with a written report. For another month the individual is required to study history or a major historical figure, and then document it. The third month must be spent studying business, broadly defined. So, at the end of three months, three documents have been prepared. If, after the three months, the business has run smoothly with no major hitches, then the promotion occurs. That is, the promotion occurs at the end of the three-month leave, not before. Why would a large company implement such a strange promotion system at substantial risk and expense? Why not just send the manager to a week-long executive education program at a university?

The reason is that this is part of the process for institutionalizing the vision of the company. A key value in the company relates to developing human capital, in addition to financial capital and physical capital. They know that human capital is the key driver of long-term success. The three-month leave of absence, of course, provides a chance for self-development, personal enrichment, and broadened perspective. Senior managers are required to study religion or ethics because all business decisions are based on some set of values or standards. The firm wants to make certain that these people have spent time intelligently thinking through their own value system. To avoid the trap of becoming short-term in orientation, studying history helps broaden viewpoints and helps assure that the mistakes of the past aren't repeated. Studying business principles helps expand the knowledge base and competence of the managers. Most importantly, however, the leave of absence is really a test. The key value in this company is that human capital must be developed if success is to be achieved, so the leave of absence serves as a test of whether the manager has really developed his or her employees. If the organization performs less well when subordinates are in charge, then the manager is not prepared to be promoted. All managers have the responsibility to help develop others to be as competent as they are in leading positive change, and managers are held accountable for that development.

The point is, a key to ensuring that positive change continues is to have capable people in place. Providing organization members with developmental opportunities—that is, chances to increase their own skill set—is an investment in the long-term future of the organization and in the continuing success of positive change.

Metrics, Measurement, Milestones

A third aspect of institutionalization is the establishment of **metrics** (or specific indicators of success), **measures** (or methods for assessing levels of success), and **milestones** (or benchmarks to determine when detectable progress will have occurred). These three factors help ensure accountability for change, make it clear whether or not progress is being made, and provide visible indicators that the change is successful. The adage "You get what you measure" is

an illustration of this principle. Change becomes institutionalized when it becomes a part of what people are held accountable to achieve. When it is clear what the measures are, people tend to respond to those measures. If I am measured on my test scores in a class but not on the extra reading I do, I will likely spend more effort and time studying for the exams than reading extra materials. It is only when I am measured on different criteria that I shift my focus. Consequently, institutionalizing positive change means that clear metrics are identified, a measurement system is put into place, and a milestone is identified for when the change must have been accomplished.

As an illustration of these points is Jan Carlzon's (1987) approach to institutionalizing his vision in the once-struggling Scandinavian Airlines.

Employees at all levels must understand exactly what the target is and how best to achieve it. Once the frontline personnel . . . have taken on the responsibility of making specific decisions, these employees must have an accurate feedback system for determining whether the decisions they are making are, in fact, the ones that will accomplish the company's overall goals. . . . The necessity of measuring results is particularly crucial for those employees who affect customer service but don't have face-to-face contact with these customers. Ticket agents get immediate feedback on their job performance hundreds of times a day from the customers they serve. However, other workers such as baggage handlers have no such advantages. In fact, loading and unloading cargo is probably the most thankless job we have at SAS. . . . The baggage handlers never come into contact with the passenger, and so they never get positive or negative feedback from them. Lacking this, they need clear targets and other means of measuring how well they are meeting their goals. (pp. 108–109)

The keys to establishing effective metrics, measures, and milestones for positive change are:

1. Identify two or three metrics or indicators that specify the result that is to be achieved. (A common mistake is to measure too many things. The key is to focus on a few core items.) These should not be metrics associated with effort or methods, but they should focus on results or

outcomes. Specifically, they should address the outcomes desired from the vision of abundance. At SAS Airlines, one metric includes the elapsed time between the plane pulling up to the gate and the first bag being delivered on the carousel.

2. Determine a measurement system. Data should be collected at certain time intervals in particular ways. This may be reports, surveys, or face-to-face meetings. At SAS, daily logs are kept of baggage handler performance. These measures do not focus on hours worked or how many bags are handled. They focus on the key outcomes desired, namely, speed and accuracy of delivery.

3. Milestones are specified, meaning that at a certain point in time, a measurable amount of progress will have been achieved. For example, by the end of the month baggage handler timeliness will have improved one percent. By the end of the year, it will have improved 15 percent. Milestones simply create a time frame for keeping track of real progress.

Institutionalizing a vision of abundance and positive change, in sum, depends on making it a part of daily life and the habitual behavior displayed by individuals throughout the organization. No positive change can survive if it depends solely on the leader. Therefore, helping people develop a teachable point of view about the positive change and providing opportunities for them to teach, building human capital through developing others' leadership skills, and instituting metrics, measurements, and milestones to ensure accountability all are actions that can help ensure successful institutionalization of positive change. Specific behaviors associated with these strategies are summarized in Table 10.5.

Summary

Most approaches to change focus on overcoming challenges, addressing obstacles, and solving problems. This chapter identifies an alternative approach to change in which the goal is to create abundance and extraordinarily positive change. It provides techniques and hints designed to help you achieve the best of the human condition or the highest potential of teams and organizations.

Leading positive change—that is, aiming for abundance-focused or positive targets rather than deficit-based or problem-centered targets—unlocks something called the *heliotropic effect*. To explain the heliotropic effect, let us pose this question: What happens over time when you put a plant in a window? The answer, of course, is that the plant begins to lean toward the light. That is, a natural inclination exists in every living system toward positive energy—toward light—and away from negative energy or from the dark. The reason is that light is life-giving and energy creating and all living systems are inclined toward that which gives life.

When you are able to foster positive change in organizations, you unleash the heliotropic effect and achieve outcomes that would be impossible otherwise.

Table 10.5	Institutionalizing the Vision and Creating Irreversible Momentum

1. Turn students into teachers.

- Provide opportunities for people to develop a teachable point of view.

- Make certain that others are required to articulate the vision themselves.

2. Build human capital.

- Ensure training and development opportunities for others so they can be leaders of positive change.

- Encourage the formation of networks and friendships that provide support.

3. Identify metrics, measures, and milestones.

- Identify when measurable progress will be achieved.

- Identify what the specific criteria will be for evaluating success.

- Determine how successful achievement of the vision will be ascertained.

- Maintain accountability for the success of the positive change.

Fostering virtuousness, positive energy, strengths, aspirational targets, and inspiring language, for example, are among the ways to unlock the heliotropic effect. This effect has been demonstrated in a variety of ways within organizations and individuals—physiologically, psychologically, emotionally, visually, and socially (see Cooperrider, 1990; Cameron, 2003b; Bright, Cameron, & Caza, 2006). It is also documented in a study by Cameron and Lavine (2006).

In this chapter we provided a simple and easily remembered framework for accomplishing positive change and unleashing the power of the heliotropic effect. Five sets of skills and activities were explained: (1) establishing a climate of positivity, (2) creating readiness for change, (3) articulating a vision of abundance, (4) generating commitment to the vision, and (5) institutionalizing the positive change. Specific behavioral guidelines for implementing this approach to change are provided next.

Behavioral Guidelines

Figure 10.9 summarizes the skill set involved in leading positive change. Because change is so pervasive in organizations, every leader must manage change much of the time. However, positive change cuts across the grain and goes against the tendencies of most leaders. Negative, problem-focused concerns consume most leaders and managers. Leading positive change requires a different skill set. The following are the behavioral guidelines for achieving positive change:

Figure 10.9 **A Framework for Leading Positive Change**

Establish a climate of positivity
• Create positive energy networks
• Ensure a climate of compassion, forgiveness, and gratitude
• Build on strengths and best-self

Create readiness
• Benchmark best practices
• Institute symbolic events
• Create a new language

Articulate a vision of abundance
• Focus on positive deviance
• Include left- and right-brain images
• Make the vision interesting
• Ensure source credibility
• Attach the vision to a symbol

Generate commitment
• Apply principles of recreational work
• Ensure public commitment
• Institute a small-wins strategy
• Communicate the vision frequently

Institutionalize the vision—Create irreversible momentum
• Turn students into teachers
• Build human capital
• Establish metrics, measures, and milestones

Positive change, positive deviance, exceptional performance

1. Establish a climate of positivity by creating positive energy networks; ensuring a climate of compassion, forgiveness, and gratitude; and identifying and giving feedback to people on their strengths and unique competencies.

2. Create readiness in others to pursue positive change by benchmarking best practice, and comparing current performance to the highest standards; instituting symbolic events to signal positive change; and creating a new language that illustrates the positive change.

3. Articulate a vision of abundance by focusing on creating positive deviance rather than correcting negative deviance; including right-brain as well as left-brain images; making the vision interesting by challenging weakly held assumptions; and ensuring credibility of the vision and the visionary.

4. Generate commitment to the vision by applying principles of recreational work associated with the vision; providing opportunities for people to publicly commit to the vision; instituting a strategy of small wins; and communicating the vision frequently.

5. Institutionalize the vision, or create irreversible momentum by turning students into teachers, helping people develop teachable points of view, and articulating the vision themselves; building human capital among others; and identifying metrics, measures, and milestones for success.

CASES INVOLVING LEADING POSITIVE CHANGE

Corporate Vision Statements

Here are examples of four vision statements by well-known leaders of companies in the United States—Apple, General Motors, Johnson & Johnson, and Microsoft. Each of these leaders was, at the time, considered to be among the most successful change leaders in the world. Analyze their statements in light of the principles discussed in the Skill Learning section of this chapter. How effective are each of these vision statements? What would be your prediction about the success of these firms based on the statements of their leaders?

Apple's Identity and Goals

John Sculley, Former Chairman, President, and CEO

Towards shared values . . .

We are all part of the journey to create an extraordinary corporation. The things we intend to do in the years ahead have never been done before by any other company on such a large scale. Many of us believe that Apple is poised to take off and the purpose of this document is to give everyone at Apple as clear a vision as we can as to where we are going. We expect the world ahead to be filled with changes but we need the stability of a clear corporate identity and a set or directional goals to give us a framework against which to judge how well we are doing. Our identity and directional goals also provide the foundation for establishing a shared set of values which we hope Apple people will also feel very good about.

Apple's Identity:

Apple's identity can be described using three important ideas. The first relates to what Apple does, the second to why it seeks to do that, and the third to how it goes about accomplishing it. First, with regards to "what":

I. We create great personal computer products.

One person, one computer is still our dream. Apple is an applied technology company. The purpose is to bring high-technology to individuals by making the power and control readily accessible to the individual. Apple creates products that people really want to use and enhances their knowledge and ability. These can be thought of as tools which empower people and whose elegance is brought about through simplicity.

With regards to "why" Apple wants to do this:

II. We have a passion for changing the world.

Apple wants to make personal computers a way of life in work, education, and the home. Apple wants to be a catalyst for change by improving the way people think, work, organize, communicate, and learn. There is a commitment to action and to changing the way things are done in the world.

The third aspect of Apple's identity is the "how":

III. We build an exciting environment.

At Apple, there is an opportunity to do and to be your best and to make a difference. In addition to being a fun, exciting, and rewarding environment, it's one where there's an openness and a shared vision. Learning and growth are the norm, not the exception. However, it's discipline that sets us free, and we recognize both individual and team contributions.

Apple people are paradigm shifters . . .

We offer the world alternative viewpoints on critical issues of productivity and learning. The traditional perspective on productivity focuses on institutions. It systemizes work flow using large scale data processing technology. Productivity is expected to increase by giving institutions the means to do complex work faster. Apple's alternative viewpoint on productivity focuses on people. We are a company that wants to be a catalyst in the process of discovering new ways for people to do things. We believe that increased productivity will result as people invent better ways to work with the enabling tools of better personal computer systems.

The traditional viewpoint on education focuses on institutions as the primary place of learning. Education is seen as a structured rule-bound process. The goal has been to prepare students for a life in the industrial economy. Apple's viewpoint on education is different. We see learning as a growing lifetime experience. Learning should be an interesting interactive process unbounded by rules and open to experimentation. We are interested in enabling people to turn information into knowledge and to prepare them for the information economy.

Apple Directional Goals:

We have established seven key directional goals which will be important in strengthening Apple's identity in the years ahead.

1. Independence

We believe we can best achieve our identity if we have the freedom of being an independent company. We are therefore not interested in acquisitions or mergers on only their financial merits. Innovation will be required across every area of our company and we must have the uncompromised commitment to take risks and try new things. This is hard to do if we were to become part of a different culture with a different identity and set of values.

2. High Market Capitalization

Market capitalization is the total value of a company as determined by the marketplace. It summarizes investor's assessment as to profitability, technology, growth, assets, management, and competitive position. In today's era of takeovers, a high market capitalization is one of the few ways we have of protecting our independence.

3. Superior Customer Value

We want to set an expectation for customer satisfaction that is vastly different and better than any of our competitors. Apple's way starts with a passion to create awesome products with a lot of distinctive value built in. Then we must learn to do new kinds of things in the future which will keep users satisfied after they have bought our products (e.g. ease of use, reliability, installation and service, etc.).

4. Exceptional Growth

We want Apple to consistently grow faster than the rest of the industry. To accomplish this we must make real strides in improving the functionality of our personal computer systems. We see ourselves in the role of creating phenomenal enabling tools which will stimulate people to learn new and better ways of doing things. We believe that meaningful differences, not better sameness, will be what drives our long-term growth.

5. 21st Century Model Company

In the second wave of management, large size was considered a strategic advantage. We believe that in the future, diversity and flexibility will be more important than corporate size in determining the winning companies.

We have a passion to make quality a building block in every area of our company.

We believe that outstanding individuals if given the charter, resources, and right environment can personally make a difference in the success of our enterprise.

In the process of pursuing Apple's identity and directional goals we believe we will pioneer many exciting new ways of doing things which may be adopted by the best companies in the twenty-first century. We are excited by the prospect of learning and experimenting with new ideas.

6. Dynamic Global Company

We have a passion to change the world, not just the USA. The parameters of the world's economy have shifted and we expect Apple to be leading the way as a powerful innovator for the future.

7. Grow Extraordinary People

Apple has always believed in attracting the most talented people to the company, and then providing them with an extraordinary environment in which to grow. Consequently, it's incumbent on us to provide comprehensive management training to the present employees who will run the company in the years ahead.

Let the journey be the guide . . .

We have chosen directions for Apple that will lead us to wonderful ideas we haven't as yet dreamed. Yet, how successful we are in making progress towards our directional goals will be the evidence of how well we are doing towards living up to the vision of our corporate identity. In other words, our directional goals are consistent with our identity yet do not set limits on our creativity.

Our overall corporate strategy is to use innovation to create growth by enabling people to create new ways of doing things. Innovation will be the basis of the meaningful differences which we believe should be sustainable over the long term.

Source: Courtesy of Apple.

Vision for General Motors
Ross Perot
(market share: 45%)

- Starting today, GM will become the finest car company in the world.
- Every GMer must understand that there are too many car plants in the world.
- From this point forward, GMers will fight in the marketplace, not with each other.
- Starting today, the power struggle between the financial staff and car builders will not be tolerated.
- Starting today, GM's relationship with the UAW will be a team relationship, not an adversarial one.

- Starting today, GM will listen to its customers, listen to its dealers who sell the cars to customers, listen to the men and women who build its cars in the factories, and listen to the engineers who design its cars.

- Starting today, any commitment made to GM people and customers will be kept.

- The first priority will be to fix every single substandard item on the existing cars being sold today.

- Starting today, GMers are going to work together, using brains, wits, creative abilities, and initiative as substitutes for money.

- GM will eliminate all waste, starting at the top and working through every level of the company.

- A new slate of outside directors will be prepared, who must have substantial stock in GM, for approval by stockholders.

- GM leaders will resign from any activity that takes them away from their responsibilities at the company.

- Starting today, words like management, labor, bonus-eligible, salaried, and hourly will no longer be used.

- As of today, people who manage in an authoritarian way will be fired.

- All bonuses and financial incentives will be determined by a single set of rules.

- From this point forward, the primary financial incentive offered will be GM stock.

- Starting today, as GM goes through a transition, all sacrifices will start at the top.

- Starting today, the word management will be replaced by the word leadership at GM.

- The leaders of GM, starting today, will accept full responsibility for the design and engineering of all GM cars.

- Starting today, most committees will be scrapped.

- No longer can a person rise to the top at GM by not doing anything wrong. The future belongs to people who are willing to step out front, take risks, and accept responsibility for their mistakes.

- Starting today, all copies of Sloan's book *My Years at General Motors* will be thrown away.

Johnson & Johnson
Our Credo
James Burke, CEO

We believe our first responsibility is to the doctors, nurses and patients,
to mothers and all others who use our products and services.

In meeting their needs everything we do must be of high quality.
We must constantly strive to reduce our costs in order to maintain reasonable prices.
Customers' orders must be serviced promptly and accurately.
Our suppliers and distributors must have an opportunity to make a fair profit.

We are responsible to our employees,
the men and women who work with us throughout the world.
Everyone must be considered as an individual.
We must respect their dignity and recognize their merit.
They must have a sense of security in their jobs.
Compensation must be fair and adequate, and working
conditions clean, orderly and safe.

We must be mindful of ways to help our employees
fulfill their family responsibilities.
Employees must feel free to make suggestions and complaints.
There must be equal opportunity for employment, development
and advancement for those qualified.
We must provide competent management,
and their actions must be just and ethical.

We are responsible to the communities in which we live and work
and to the world community as well.
We must be good citizens—support good works and charities
and bear our fair share of taxes.
We must encourage civic improvements and better health and education.
We must maintain in good order the property we are privileged to use,
protecting the environment and natural resources.

Our final responsibility is to our stockholders.
Business must make a sound profit.
We must experiment with new ideas.
Research must be carried on, innovative programs developed and mistakes paid for.
New equipment must be purchased, new facilities provided
and new products launched.
Reserves must be created to provide for adverse times.
When we operate according to these principles, the stockholders
should realize a fair return.

Johnson & Johnson

SOURCE: Courtesy of Johnson & Johnson.

Microsoft

Bill Gates
2004 Excerpts

Microsoft was built on innovation, and our future depends on it. We are in an extraordinary position to deliver even greater value to customers through a broad set of technologies, designed to complement each other and many third-party products and services. This is what we mean by *integrated innovation,* which is key to our business strategy.

To drive innovation, Microsoft has a long-term commitment to research and development. Our investment to date has brought about many of the successful products we offer today, and has built an increasingly valuable store of intellectual property. In fiscal 2004, we applied for more than 2,000 patents on some of our recent innovations. During the coming year, we plan to file for another 3,000 patents, which will make us one of the largest patent filers in the world. Our innovations are available for broad use in others' products through our patent licensing programs.

A key focus of our innovation is security. Beyond the advances in Windows XP SP2, we are developing advanced technologies that will help isolate computers from Internet attacks and make them more resilient when they are attacked. We are making it easier for customers to keep their systems updated with our latest, most secure software.

In addition, we are collaborating with other industry leaders to develop more effective community responses to security threats, and working closely with governments around the world to bring cybercriminals to justice. Through this broad, multipronged approach, our goal is to help bring significant improvements in security, and help preserve the benefits of technology for everyone.

Our innovation is also focused on exciting market opportunities across our businesses, which we believe hold great potential for growth over the next several years.

As we innovate in technology, we are equally focused on crisp execution. In particular, we are working to deliver an unparalleled customer and partner experience. Across the company, we have created new listening, feedback, and response systems to help us get closer to customers and respond quickly and appropriately. Using automated error-reporting technologies, we have fixed a large majority of the computer crashes and hangs reported by customers, and our strengthened field response system has favorably resolved most nontechnical issues reported by customers.

Microsoft competes vigorously, and we always will. At the same time, we are committed to maintaining positive relationships within our industry, including with competitors, and to forging strong relationships with governments. We are also committed to helping make technology safer and easier to use. We work to help protect the safety of children online, for example, through our partnership with the International Centre for Missing and Exploited Children. We are deeply engaged in industry efforts to protect peoples' privacy online, counter the problem of identify theft, and curb the spam epidemic.

SOURCE: Reprinted with permission from Microsoft Corporation.

Discussion Questions

First answer the following questions by yourself, and then form a team of colleagues and share your answers. Reach consensus regarding a rank ordering.

Step 1: Rank order these four firms based on these famous leaders' statements about their companies (1 = the best, and 4 = the worst).

	Apple	GM	J&J	Microsoft
1. Which of the vision statements do you think represents the most effective positive leadership?	____	____	____	____
2. Based on these statements, what is your prediction about future success in each firm in the next 10 years, from most to least successful? Ignore the health of the industry itself—e.g., computers, autos, software, pharmaceuticals—and predict how each firm will do in its own industry based on these statements.	____	____	____	____
3. Which statement has the clearest and most inspiring vision for the future?	____	____	____	____
4. Which statement do you believe has been institutionalized the most thoroughly, and the least thoroughly?	____	____	____	____

Step 2: Based on what you now know about leading positive change, what advice would you give each of these leaders if you were to make suggestions about how to could more effectively create readiness for change, articulate a vision of abundance, generate and so on?

Lee Iacocca's Transformation of Chrysler—1979–1984

This is a transcription of speeches by Chairman Lee Iacocca to Chrysler's top management team from the time he became CEO and chairman in 1979 until the dramatic transformation had been completed in 1984. The previously confidential videotapes were compiled and edited by Professor Kim S. Cameron at the University of Michigan and are used to exemplify the leadership of change. These speeches were intended by Mr. Iacocca only for an internal and confidential audience, not for the press, stockholders, or the general public. Duplication without permission of the University of Michigan Business School is strictly forbidden.

The transcript begins with the new president of Ford, Paul Bergmoser, explaining the state of the company and of the economy in 1979. He then introduced Mr. Iacocca to the top management team for the first time. The entire transcript from that point on is from Mr. Iacocca.

1979

Paul Bergmoser, President:

I don't have to tell you that we are meeting at a very critical time in the Corporation's history. You don't need a recitation of the problems that are facing us. At the same time that the volumes and penetrations are down, we are up against the most costly product program in Chrysler history. There is no margin for error as we plan for next year 1980. Our first slide today gives you a perspective of the current situation. It shows how we are doing thus far in 1979. I said thus far—the year isn't over yet. In our presentation to the government, we predicted we would lose a billion seventy-one million. That is about where we will come out if we move the sales bank, move the imports, get our manufacturing efficiencies, and meet all the commitments between now and December 31. In some areas we are coming in on target, others we are off. For example, our market share was less than we expected largely because the market went haywire. Consumers begin to lose confidence when our problems hit the headlines. We are looking at a sluggish economy, double-digit inflation, high interest rates that put a lot of pressure on both dealers and retail customers. Much has been written and much has been unspoken about the Chrysler crisis and its causes. A considerable amount of the rhetoric has dealt with past management as being one of the primary causes of that situation. Let me tell you how I stand on the matter at the moment. All of you fellows have survived personnel reductions and corporate reorganizations. You are, in the eyes of the outsider, now the new management. That goes for me, I am new, but every one of you is just as new in terms of the New Chrysler Corporation. We will be judged by what we do in 1980 and '81. We have stated to the government and to the world at large that those will be the years when Chrysler will recover from its current record loss position. We will not live to see 1981 if we don't do the job in 1980. So, in my view, it no longer serves any purpose to look back and reference your problems to the past management. Let Mr. Iacocca and let me handle the past. You will be a success or you will be a failure on the basis of what you do in 1980.

It is going to be a real tough year, a very tough year, perhaps, the toughest in the history of your corporate life! If you don't feel like being on my team in this fight, you had better come and see me very soon now, because I am counting on each and every one of you to do the job better than it has ever been done before. If the objectives are too tough, too hard, and too disciplined, come and see me now, because I need the help of every one of you. I am confident that we can carry it through. Now, fellows, in time, I think people are going to look back on this management team with respect and admiration for the job they have done. This is the New Chrysler Corporation. And I want to introduce the man who is providing the leadership and direction for all of us to carry out our day-to-day tasks, Chairman Lee Iacocca. Lee!

Lee Iacocca, CEO and Chairman:

As I said in my opening statement to Congress, this has not been a vintage year for me, for Chrysler, for the auto industry, or for the whole damn country. And, I guess that some of you must feel the same way. As Paul said, we lost a lot of money. Over a billion dollars is a lot of money. Our market penetration at the moment is down to what you might call deplorable levels. Some of our customers, or maybe I should say, some of our former customers, aren't really that confident that we are going to make it. Still, there are some good things to say about 1979. I believe it has been a year in which we did more than just survive. We reduced our fixed cost. We did proceed to put in place a product plan that will help us return to profitability. We took steps to improve our profit margins. In short, we invested a lot of time and money in our future.

First, I would like to give you an assessment of what is happening with our request for the loan guarantees* in Washington, and then second I want to expand on the concept of the "New Chrysler Corporation" mentioned by Paul in his presentation. There has been a lot of talk about our chances for getting legislation out of the Congress in time to help the Chrysler Corporation. Well, I want to tell you first hand that things, as of this afternoon at least, do look good. The energy picture is muddled and threatening as ever. I just saw in the paper this afternoon that Saudi Arabia is going to go for six dollars a barrel increase. That means the rest will go for seven or eight, and that's got to be bad news. The continuing crisis in Iran; production cut backs by other OPEC nations, Libya, Iraq and these way-out guys; and the lack of a sound, reasonable national energy policy right here; all of those put together are really what you would call bad news, not good news. But, what we have to do is survive, and more than survive, become profitable as soon as we can. And as Paul said, it won't be real easy. In fact, the first six months of 1980 will be pure hell, in my opinion, and I might as well tell it to you that way. There will be demanding challenges facing all of you, and me, in the months ahead. So this brings me to my second point today that I want to cover briefly.

When I say these are challenges facing us, I want you to know that the "us" is you and me. And, it is the new Chrysler Corporation. From the day that President Carter signs into law the Chrysler Loan Guarantee Program, a new era begins at Chrysler. And don't make any mistake about it, there will be a great deal to accomplish from that day forward. Much will be asked of you, and much will be expected of you. To begin with, we will have to re-launch Chrysler. We have to rebuild confidence, first amongst ourselves, then the rest of the Chrysler family, and most important with our customers. And this will not be easy. But, the early signals clearly show that it can be done. In spite of a dismal market this year, we have achieved some significant and positive results. We did take a hundred and thirty thousand orders for vehicles in November. We did move twenty thousand out of our sales bank.** And, I have to mention sales bank one more time, because it may be the last time you will hear me say it. That thing is in its death throes. I got to thinking on the way over here that we have plans to move those last ten thousand at distressed prices, and forget that we ever built them. And, I thought, I want him to keep one. And I want to do what they do when you finally pay off the mortgage, you burn it on the front lawn. I want to burn that last damn one on the front lawn of headquarters, so, the whole world knows it is over!

For the next ninety days each of you in this room has to play salesman. And, to do that, all you have to do is get in one of our cars, and expose it, and demonstrate it to somebody.

---

*Chrysler had appealed to the federal government to guarantee its bank loans, because the amount to be borrowed was more than the value of the company at the time.

**The sales bank refers to the excess inventory of unsold cars.

Those are our four new cars, and that market still is pretty good, even though it is down a little. And, those four cars—if you have driven them lately—are not just commercial, they are fine cars that everybody in this room should be proud of. They are good looking cars. They've got good features, and they don't rattle and leak as much as their predecessors the year before. At the new Chrysler Corporation we will build them better, and we will back them better. If we don't, nothing else is going to matter anyway, and we will have no one to blame but ourselves. What will be required to do these kind of things, to keep them as promises and not let them become just sales gimmicks, is hard work and dedication and, most of all, the realization that the new Chrysler Corporation is a team. A team that openly discusses its problems and freely exchanges ideas on how to improve our efforts and willingly accepts responsibility for performance. What will be required to rebuild confidence in this company is an active participation in its survival effort.

Over the next months the new Chrysler Corporation will be engaged in efforts to raise a lot of capital. But, with the products we have, with the improvements we have made, with the plans for the future, being as exciting as I believe they are—that money is going to be available to us. Count on it. In fact, what is happening with this corporation right now is unprecedented in the history of our industry and maybe the whole country. Just think of it. The UAW is willing now to reopen its contract settlement in order to participate in the effort of the new Chrysler Corporation and to make it profitable. Mayor Coleman Young has indicated that Detroit is willing to offer a hundred and fifty million dollars in Chrysler support. We expect a minimum of three hundred million dollars from Canada. I say three hundred million, but it could be as much as a $1.2 billion for Canadian operations so that we can go first class in a couple of programs we have planned. Other states with Chrysler plants and operations have expressed a willingness to help and their commitment comes up to about a hundred million dollars. We are confident that the Japanese banks will restore our letter of credit agreement under which we can continue to import vehicles from Mitsubishi. We are also offering right now, or will be very shortly I should say, a preferred stock offering to Chrysler suppliers and dealers. If we are as good as we think we are, we will sell four hundred million dollars of equity stock to our family, suppliers and dealers. If we are not good salesman, we sell two hundred. So the number is two hundred to four hundred million dollars. By mid-January we will discuss the role of the suppliers and the dealers in this offer. Our dealers' lobbying efforts in Washington in our behalf were nothing short of sensational, and I think that they will be a big part of turning this Congress around.

Before you go home for the holidays, I would like to ask you to do this. In just a few short minutes, I want you to ask yourselves, honestly, what have you done to help this company, your company, during the last twelve months. Put it down. Don't fight with it. Just put it down. Then throw it away. If you want to read it to your wife or your kids, fine but then throw it away. Then, after you have done that the more important part is get another piece of paper, a clean sheet of paper. Put down the things that you plan to do for your company, and for yourself, in the next twelve months, the year 1980. We will get the vote of confidence we need from the government. That is, I think, assured. It will then be up to all of us in the new Chrysler family to share that confidence, first amongst ourselves right in this room, then to spread it through all the family members, and eventually to the biggest family of them all, our customers out there. What I am saying to you is that we have all of the essentials in place. The basics are here. And more important, we have got the people, the team, to do it. Let me make it clear that this new Chrysler is not a mixed bag of hanger-ons mixed in with a little new talent from some other corporations. It is not that at all. It is a new, unified team that starts a new decade. Remember, on New Year's Eve January 1st, we start a new ten-year look.

One final thought to all of you. Somebody wrote a hit song called, "We Are Family," and Willie Stargell picked it up as a model to inspire his team to win the World Series

Championship. Well, the reason that I mentioned it to you is that we, the new Chrysler Corporation, are Family. Else, how is it possible to raise a billion and a half dollars from our own constituents? We do have a lot to do, and it is going to be tough. But because we are family, we can do it. So, that is all we have to say to you today except, have a nice Christmas all of you, and let's start the New Year with a Bang!

1980

While the economy was coming down around our ears, we put together a financing package to raise better than two billion dollars in non-guaranteed funds. We put together an operating plan that showed we can continue as a growing concern without any government help after 1983. Secretary Miller and Mr. Volcker said, it was by a long shot, the most complicated package in the entire history of American business. It involved the governments of five nations, local governments, more than four hundred lenders, and all the constituents of a very big industrial company—suppliers, dealers, employees, and the shareholders. We put the package together in record time. Within two weeks of the deadline that we set for ourselves, the Treasury Department, the Loan Guarantee Board, and some hardnosed consultants have scrutinized—and believe me they have scrutinized—all of our plans, every aspect of our business. And the hardheads, and the hard noses, came out and said they liked what they saw. No matter what you read in the press, that is what they ended up saying. They said that our operating plan code was realistic and feasible. They said that we demonstrated that we can continue as a growing concern, and that, simply stated, is why they gave us a guarantee. The guarantees give us a fighting chance we need to complete our rebuilding program.

In the meanwhile, we need to keep on doing right all of the other things that are so essential to our future. We talked about what that involved last December here, and I would like to take just a minute to look at the report card and see how we faired since we last met as a group. First, we talked about people. That is the strength of any business organization. We have kept almost, not all, but almost all of our top-flight people. We have been able to move some into key spots like Jack Withrow in engineering. We have attracted some very impressive new people at the organization to supplement our present staff. Don Dellerosa came on board as Vice President of Design. I worked with him for a long time. He is the best designer of small cars in the world. Dick Dow came on board as Executive VP of Diversified Operations. Dick has been in charge of production at VW-America, and before that he was at GM, where he was the youngest plant manager in their history. Dave Platt came on as Vice President of Procurement and Supply. He is experienced. He will make sure all of our suppliers meet their quality targets. I could go on and on, but the management, I am trying to say, is strong.

We have the plans and programs to meet our objectives, so I hope that everybody in this room knows and understands them. We have a great management team. I think it's the best in the business. We have the sales program. We are improving quality. Ford and GM will have to catch us from now on. We have the innovations to set us apart from the competition. We have the products that deliver the value that customers want today. So, in spite of all of the difficulties created for us, and all the obstacles put in our way, our plans are finally starting to come together. We see some real daylight.

The Loan Guarantee Board looked at a lot of factors when they considered our application—cost projections, industry volume, the debt load, the product plans. But when I talked to them privately, the most important consideration of all was whether this Chrysler Team had the guts, and the capacity, and the ability to see this program through to the end and to bring Chrysler back to profitability. The guy who asked me that most is a guy I admire a lot—Paul Volcker, of the Federal Reserve. He asked, "Are you really sure you have got the right people to stick it out?" They looked hard at us, at you really. They looked at what you have accomplished so far, and what's left to do. They must have seen *winners in some of you because they decided to put the country's money on you. Which is a big gamble. They put a billion and a half on the line.*

1982

Good evening. We announced our 1981 results this morning. For the total year we lost four hundred and seventy-six million. That is a little less than the analysts said that we would lose. They said that we would lose, for sure, five hundred million. One year ago— if you just stop to think about what was in the news four months ago—all of the smart money on Wall Street was betting that Volcker's scandalous interest rates, the advent of GM's new competition the 'J' car, and the total collapse of the car and truck market would certainly wipe out Chrysler in 1981. This was their year to die. The smart money was wrong again, because we not only survived this worse depression in the history of the automobile industry, but I think that you will agree we have come through as a stronger and more competitive company.

We continued our program to cut costs and become even more productive in the year '81. We performed major surgery to bring our cost under control. We looked at all of our operations, plant-by-plant and job-by-job, and over the last two years we have consolidated these operations. We have now closed a full twenty plants. We have cut our fixed cost by well over a half billion dollars in the last four months. And we have reduced our salaried employees by half, from about forty thousand to twenty-one thousand. Our break even is now half of what it was two years ago. We twenty thousand are doing the work of those forty thousand, but we are selling more cars and building more cars. What the hell were we doing wrong? Since the first of this year—we have taken several important actions to build an extra cash cushion to ride out the recession and protect our future programs. Last Friday we reached an agreement to sell Chrysler Defense, that is the tank business, to General Dynamics for three hundred and forty-eight point five million dollars. I have to say to you; gentlemen and ladies, that decision was a tough call. Chrysler Defense is a strong subsidiary with some great people, a lot of whom worked for this company for a lot of years. We have forty years of history tied up in the tank business. We were part of the Arsenal of Democracy in World War Two. I can tell you, our guys did design and build the best damn battle tank in the entire world. They had some very exciting and profitable new products on the drawing board, and we had some of the best talent in this organization running that place. Nobody wanted to give all of that up. But, in today's economic climate, we had to balance our attachment to that company against the need to build a substantial cash cushion with which to ride out this very serious economic depression that we are in. Our charter is to concentrate on cars and trucks. That is why we got the Loan Guarantees, and that is why we are here. Our job is to build the best cars and trucks, and take on the Japanese, even if just to be patriotic, but that's our job.

Here is our problem put as simply as I know how to put it. Today, it costs us exactly seventy-nine hundred dollars to build the average Chrysler car, and we sell them on an average for seventy-five hundred. We make our money today on Chrysler Financial, on Mexico, and on parts sales. We had better start to learn how to make money on cars and trucks, because that, again, is our business. We have to live within our budgets in '82, as tight as they are with no cost overruns, and that's nobody!

Now let me end with this note. We have all come through a hellish couple of years. I know we all feel that way, I do. But together, we have established Chrysler as a leader in the rebuilding of the American auto industry, and maybe of the entire American Industry. Together, we have set an example of what determined Americans can accomplish in the face of great adversity. We are on the edge of success. We are not quite there, but we are on the real sharp edge of success. If the management, the Union, all of our employees, and the dealers and the suppliers—all continue to work together towards our common goals, we can put the finishing touches on maybe the greatest chapter in the history of American business.

1983

We really are poised, no matter what the economy throws at us, no matter what the Japanese or Ford or General Motors throw at us, not only to stay in business but to prosper and do very, very, well. I also said to you late in July in a meeting with President Carter, that we now own our company again. I announced that we were paying off the loans, and that means that we are all alone now, and we can make our own decisions and we can make our own mistakes.

We have got to get this quality thing behind us. We have come a long, long, way. Warranty is down thirty eight percent the last couple of years, and our quality is up, but the track is fast, as you know. Ford is doing better on things gone wrong, and GM and we are a little worse than they are and Japan is still out-doing us all. So, we can have five and fifties, and we can have good power trains, and we can have five year warranties, and think about ten year warranties, but we have got to get rid of some of this crap we are doing. We've got some problems, but they are not big problems, I don't think.

I like to think that the officers, the first team, let's call it, the varsity, is good enough that each of us in the top senior management has ten charges out there. I can look around the room, and I feel that ten of you are my protégés. I watch to see what you are doing. I look at your future, and I get to know you well, and I take care of you, because you take of the company and me. At our level, this level, everybody is on the team. Everybody has gotten the message. Nobody believes there is an old way of doing it. Well, you have got your work cut out for you, and here is your assignment. It is a very general one, but it is the only thing that will make this company click. Out of the three hundred odd of you in here, each of you must accept as your charges ten subordinates. Ten times three hundred is three thousand, and that's the group we are looking at. The next three thousand has got to get the word. That is the only way we are going to continue to build on the progress that we have made, and we have made some fantastic progress. I hope that you are feeling that you are a big part of it, because you are. Every one of you, look to yourself, and look within yourself. When you manage, a good manager is a multiplier and a motivator. That is all he is. He can multiply himself, every day, wherever he is. People look up to him, and people work, because they know what their objective is, and they go out and hustle, and they do it because the boss is leading them and motivating them. Now, if you would just do that, we have got a big year ahead of us. While we are counting the two billion dollars back home, you will be really putting the seed corn in where it counts. Multiply yourselves times ten and nothing will stop us.

When the press asked me, what is the greatest thing you got out of the last five years, I say: "Hot a hell of a lot. It got tiring." But I did take one thing. It is the realization that six hundred thousand people, pulled in the same directions. Pulled the oars in the same way. Everybody felt they were getting the fair shake, the old equality of sacrifice. It is amazing how we can move a mountain. So, if you see anybody pulling apart, or they don't want to be on a team, you have got to straighten them out. I will end on this note. I will assure you that just as we are paying you for having reduced warranty costs, less engineering changes, and better market share, the new barometer will be how you are doing with your little nest of ten people. Some of you, I know, have twenty or thirty, but start with ten. I can settle for that right now if everybody in the room signed up for it.

1984

I would think that in the next five years, we start a new era. We have got to talk innovation in product, and we have got to talk innovation in service, and in manufacturing processes. I think that is going to be key to how well this corporation does. I think that we are on the threshold of doing great things together. I think that anytime any company, for whatever the reason, reports the one and a half plus billion dollars in six months, you should all be damned proud. As one of the reporters already said, "That is their peak."

Two analysts followed it up yesterday, and said "Chrysler will never make over eight hundred million dollars again in a three month period." They make it sound like I was a fluke. Well, we are going to show them that it is no fluke. True, it has been driven by volume, driven by rich mixes, but it has been driven by productivity improvements, and quality improvements, and having the right products for the market—rich convertibles and T–115s [minivans] that are a smash.

But the two areas that are not market driven but are management driven are the two you are not doing hot on. That is quality and market share. Market share, if you include T–115s, is doing pretty damn well. But we are not going to get to twelve percent. And quality is a disappointment. GM has caught up with us. The Japanese are way beyond us. And Ford is losing us in their dust right now. I take nothing from you or this managing team, but you have got to look at the whole cart now. Why is it, on the two toughies, competing head to head every day in the market, even with voluntary restraints on the part of the Japanese, against GM and Ford, we can't seem to meet our quality objectives, and in market share we are flunking out. Now, when I say it that way, we have come a long way from three years ago. Were shipping crap, frankly. And now you can be proud of what you are shipping. I am glad to hear it, I hope we don't do it every day, but I am glad to hear from time to time we shut a line down to get the message across that quality is not only the first priority but it could well be in the next twelve to twenty-four months our only priority.

We are going to have to join up with new technology, and we are going to have to cut out a position for ourselves at Chrysler in electronics, certainly new materials and composites of all kinds. That is on our strategy list. I asked one of our top people why can't I just order on a requisition tomorrow, a sports car, and I would like to do it in twenty-four months. You say, I can't do that. I say why? You say, we don't know how. But, what the hell, it is a car, and they're selling like hotcakes. We don't know how? Well, you have got to ask yourself, why not? You can't just claim that it's money. We've got plenty of money if we want to do something like that. While they are all reacting on our T–115, we have got to react back to them in some of these markets. Those aren't little niche markets. That may be the market of the future for young people.

Discussion Questions

1. In 1979, with the company in such bad shape and the economy so dismal, how did Iacocca create a climate of positivity? What symbols are used? What small wins were identified? What is interesting about his language?
2. In 1980, how did Iacocca ensure credibility? Who is the enemy? What is interesting about his language?
3. In 1982, how did Iacocca maintain positivity? What is the vision for the company? What symbolic events are used? How is commitment developed?
4. In 1983, how is the vision institutionalized? How does Iacocca personally exemplify the principles he espouses?
5. In 1984, given the dramatic turnaround of the company, why doesn't Iacocca celebrate? What is his motivation? Why does he mix confrontation and challenge in his positive message?

EXERCISES IN LEADING POSITIVE CHANGE

Reflected Best-Self Portrait

In the Skill Assessment section of this chapter you were asked to identify 20 people who could provide feedback to you regarding when you were at your very best. Now that you have obtained that feedback on your strengths, you will want to analyze that data to create a best-self portrait. Read all of your feedback and take notes on the key insights. Look for commonalities across the individuals who provided you with feedback. Create themes where you find commonalities, and link the examples to them. You may find it useful to use a table such as the following.

COMMONALITY/THEME	EXAMPLES GIVEN	MY INTERPRETATION
1. Creative	1. Innovative builder of new projects at work. 2. Found new solutions for old problems. 3. Guided the team in transforming itself.	My ideas tend to be interesting and creative. I tend to bring a new ideas to people with whom I work. I am innovative in my approach to problem solving.
2.	1. 2. 3.	
3.	1. 2. 3.	

Step 1: Now, create a portrait of your best self that captures the wisdom in your data. Identify when you are at your very best and what attributes and capabilities you display at your best. Write at least one paragraph describing yourself in third person using your best-self feedback as the data. The person you are reading about in this feedback is like this at his or her best. . . . Here are some reflective questions that you may want to consider as you craft your self portrait.

- ❏ What have you learned about your own key strengths and uniquenesses?
- ❏ What was surprising to you about your feedback?
- ❏ What circumstances bring out your best?
- ❏ How do you intend to follow up or capitalize on this feedback?
- ❏ What career or life implications does this feedback hold?
- ❏ What has changed, or could change, as a result of obtaining this feedback?

Write up your conclusions and your commitments as a result of reading through the feedback. Writing will have a clarifying and focusing effect, and you are not likely to get this

PRACTICE

kind of data very often in your life. Don't miss the opportunity to craft something meaningful for yourself.

Step 2: Read your best-self portrait with a team of colleagues. Get verbal feedback from them about what you have written. That is, your colleagues will help you clarify and become specific about your best-self attributes.

Source: www.bus.umich.edu/positive

Positive Organizational Diagnosis Exercise

Step 1: Select an organization that you can diagnose. If you are not currently working in one, volunteering in one, or leading one, select your own school or university. Your objective is to identify the strengths, peak experiences, and examples of positive deviance in the organization (rather than the problems and challenges). These kinds of data are seldom gathered in organizations, and people are not often asked to provide this kind of data. However, in every organization, something works well. When cued to do so, people can always identify things that are spectacular about their organization. Furthermore, the questions we ask and the language we use helps determine our vision of the future. People are more comfortable moving into the unknown future when they carry parts of the past forward. That is, when they have experienced success in the past, they are more willing to pursue a vision of the future, knowing that they have achieved extraordinary success some time in the past. They are confident that they can do it again.

Here are some examples of questions you should ask in diagnosing the positive aspects of an organization, a group, or even your own family.

- ❏ *Best-in-Class:* Put yourself in clients' or customers' shoes. What would they say makes this organization the best there is?
- ❏ *Careers:* What do you love about this organization that makes you want to come to work each day?
- ❏ *Leadership:* Who are the leaders in your organization you admire the most, and why? What do they do?
- ❏ *Communication:* When did you have an extremely satisfying and productive interchange with someone you care deeply about?
- ❏ *Teamwork:* When have you experienced delight at extraordinary cooperation and teamwork that emerged in this organization?
- ❏ *Culture:* What is especially fun, energizing, revitalizing about your culture? What turns you on?
- ❏ *Aspiration:* What are your highest aspirations for this organization? What do you really hope for?
- ❏ *Work:* What is the best you have ever seen accomplished in the work here? What was achieved that exceeded everyone's expectations?

When you ask these kinds of questions, you will detect more enthusiasm being displayed by the person responding, and you will note an unleashing of positive energy. This is in contrast to more typical questions used in organizational diagnosis:

- ❏ What are your major problems and challenges?
- ❏ Where are your deficits?
- ❏ What is troublesome to people in this organization?
- ❏ What needs fixing?
- ❏ In what areas are you missing your targets?

❑ Who is doing better than you are, and why?

Craft your own interview format for conducting a positive diagnosis of an organization, a group, or a family. Use the positive questions above as a guide. Interview a representative sample of people in that organization (or all the members of your family).

Step 2: Now, write up the equivalent of a best-self portrait for the organization. Address these questions regarding the organization.

❑ What are the strengths and unique qualities of this organization?
❑ In what ways can it capitalize on its competencies?
❑ What is the vision that drives the organization?
❑ What recommendations do you have for positive change?

A Positive Change Agenda

Write out a detailed plan for leading positive change in an organization in which you are participating. You need not be the formal leader of that organization, since most real change is initiated from places within the organization rather than the leader's office. Most great leaders simply capitalize on the ideas and agendas of their people.

In crafting your plan, address the following questions with very specific and actionable ideas. Do not simply say something like: "I'll treat people better." That is not specific enough and does not identify an action. Instead, say, "I will compliment someone every day." That's more doable and measurable.

1. In what ways will you work to create a positive climate? What will you actually do?
2. In what specific ways will you create readiness in others to pursue positive change?
3. What is your specific vision of abundance? How will you communicate it so that it is accepted and energizing to people?
4. How will you generate commitment to that vision among others? Identify specific actions.
5. What will you do to institutionalize and create irreversible momentum for your positive change?

Now, identify the specific things you will need to do personally to exemplify and model your positive change? How will you enhance your own credibility?

PRACTICE
◆

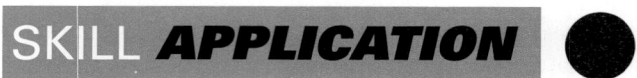

ACTIVITIES FOR LEADING POSITIVE CHANGE

Suggested Assignments

1. Find someone you know well who is working in an organization. Teach him or her the principles of leading positive change. Use the concepts, principles, techniques, and exercises provided in this chapter. Describe what you taught and record the results in your journal.

2. Give genuine positive feedback on a regular and consistent basis to one or more of your colleagues. Do it at least daily. Observe the extent to which your relationship changes over the next month.

3. Do a systematic analysis of the things that occur in your life for which you are grateful. What is going right, and what makes life worth living? Consider your job, family, school, and social life. Keep a "gratitude journal" for at least a semester (a three-month period). Make an entry in it at least once a week. Note what else changes in your life compared to before you began the journal.

4. Identify at least one person in your circle of acquaintances who is positively energizing to you. When you are around this person, you simply feel better. Make certain that you interact with that person on a frequent and consistent basis.

5. Identify an example of best practice. That is, find someone or some organization that is unique in being the best there is at something. Try to identify what it is that accounts for that extraordinary performance. What factors could be generalized to others or to other settings?

6. Establish an abundance agenda that you aspire to accomplish this year. Make it compatible with the top priorities in your life. Specify the behavioral action steps, the reporting and accounting mechanisms, and the criteria of success that you will implement. Share this plan with others you know so that you have an incentive to pursue it even after you finish this class.

7. Identify a symbol that can serve as a constant reminder of your own—or your organization's—vision of abundance. Select something that is positively energizing and that can remind you every time you see it that you are pursuing a meaningful, uplifting vision.

8. Establish a close mentoring relationship with someone with whom you work or go to school. Your mentor may be a professor, a senior manager, or someone who has been around longer than you have. That relationship should build your self-esteem and be energizing to you. Make certain, however, that the relationship is reciprocal, not one-way.

Application Plan and Evaluation

The intent of this exercise is to help you apply this cluster of skills in a real-life, out-of-class setting. Now that you have become familiar with the behavioral guidelines that form the basis of effective skill performance, you will improve most by trying out those guidelines in an everyday context. Unlike a classroom activity, in which feedback is immediate and others can assist you with their evaluations, this skill application activity is one you must accomplish and evaluate on your own. There are two parts to this activity. Part 1 helps prepare you to apply the skill. Part 2 helps you evaluate and improve on your experience. Be sure to write down answers to each item. Don't short-circuit the process by skipping steps.

Part 1. Planning

1. Write down the two or three aspects of this skill that are most important to you. These may be areas of weakness, areas of strength, or areas that are most salient to a situation you face right now. Identify the specific aspects of this skill that you want to apply.

2. Now identify the setting or the situation in which you will apply this skill. Establish a plan for performance by actually writing down a description of the situation. Who else will be involved? When will you do it? Where will it be done?

   Circumstances:
   Who else?
   When?
   Where?

3. Identify the specific behaviors in which you will engage to apply this skill. Operationalize your skill performance.

4. What are the indicators of successful performance? How will you know you have been effective? What will indicate you have performed competently?

Part 2. Evaluation

5. After you have completed your implementation, record the results. What happened? How successful were you? What was the effect on others?

6. How can you improve? What modifications can you make next time? What will you do differently in a similar situation in the future?

7. Looking back on your whole skill practice and application experience, what have you learned? What has been surprising? In what ways might this experience help you in the long term?

Leading Positive Change Assessment

Scoring Key

SUBSCALES	ITEMS
Personal capability to lead positive change	2, 3, 5, 6, 7, 9, 10, 12, 13, 16, 17, 20
Ability to mobilize others toward positive change	1, 4, 8, 11
Capacity to create positive deviance in organizations	14, 15, 18, 19

Comparison Data (N = 1,500 Students)

Compare your scores to three standards:
1. The maximum possible score = 100
2. The scores of other students in the class.
3. Norm data from more than 1,500 business school students.

Pre-Test			Post-Test
98.33	=	mean =	105.24
106 or above	=	top quartile =	114 or above
99–105	=	second quartile =	107–113
92–98	=	third quartile =	99–106
91 or below	=	bottom quartile =	98 or below

Reflected Best-Self Feedback™ Exercise

This exercise does not have a solution or comparison data. Answers will vary among students.

Machiavellianism Scale—MACH IV

Scoring Key

This scale measures individuals' general orientation toward dealing with other people, especially the extent to which they tend to manipulate others in interpersonal situations. High scores on this scale are the opposite of the qualities needed for effective leadership of positive change. That is, authenticity, genuineness, optimism, gratitude, humility, and emotional sensitivity are all characteristics of effective leaders of positive change, but this scale measures the extent to which people are cynical, distrustful, and manipulative.

The lowest possible score is −60, and the highest possible score is +60. A score of 00 is a neutral point.

The three subscales in this instrument are:

Duplicity:	Items 1, 2, 3, 6, 7, 9, 10, 15, 17	(reverse score: 3, 6, 7, 9, 10)
Negativism:	Items 5, 8, 12, 13, 18, 19, 20	
Distrust:	Items 4, 11, 12, 14, 16	(reverse score: 4, 11, 14, 16)

Comparison Data (N = 1,500 Students)

Mean score:	−17.18
Top quartile:	−8 or above
Third quartile:	−18– −9
Second quartile:	−27– −19
Bottom quartile:	−28 or below

SKILL ANALYSIS Iacocca's Transformation of Chrysler—1979–1984

In a 2000 survey published in *USA Today,* Lee Iacocca was rated as the greatest salesperson of our time. The other five, listed in order, were: Bill Gates, Bill Clinton, Ronald Reagan, Michael Dell, and Ted Turner. In other words, Iacocca was viewed the quintessential example of positive influence.

Some facts that may be helpful as you analyze the case are:

1979: The name of the company was changed to symbolically signal a new era. The "sales bank" was simply excess inventory, and Chrysler really did burn the last car on the front lawn of headquarters. This was the first time in U.S. history when loan guarantees had been requested, and at the time of the speech, no support had been received whatsoever from the federal government or from Congress. It was only through the persuasive influence of Iacocca that the loan guarantees were granted.

1980: Iacocca's salary was $1 per year. The "why" was to build credibility. Consider how much of the time Iacocca spends on the right-brain aspects of his speeches versus the left-brain side. Normally laying people off and hiring new employees would antagonize current workers. Why did Iacocca's announcement have the opposite effect?

1982: Iacocca makes a loss of $476 million sound like a big win. How? Why did he sell the tank business? What did he do with the money? Did he pay off the creditors? He delivers a strong message: "I'll put my money where my mouth is." Why does he refer to patriotism?

1983: Iacocca is incredibly close to the customer, as evidenced by his knowledge of the hood-release problem. Can CEOs really do that? This speech has a great deal to do with institutionalizing the vision. How does he do that?

1984: Up to that point in history, no company had ever earned more than $1.6 billion in six months. This was an incredible achievement. Why, then, doesn't Iacocca celebrate? He is creating readiness for change all over again, and he treats change as a cyclical affair, not a one-time, linear achievement. His wife died in 1984; he was asked to run for president, then Congress; he chaired the Statue of Liberty celebration; so Chrysler faltered for the rest of the decade. But near the end of the 1990s, Iacocca again took the reins and pulled off another dramatic transformation of a sinking company. A decade after he left, the company merged with Daimler, a German company that makes Mercedes-Benz automobiles.

Part IV

Specific Communication Skills

SUPPLEMENTS

A **MAKING ORAL AND WRITTEN PRESENTATIONS**

Formulating strategy and structure utilizing an enhanced style

B **CONDUCTING INTERVIEWS**

Conducting general interviews
Conducting specific purpose interviews

C **CONDUCTING MEETINGS**

Conducting productive meetings

SKILL *LEARNING* ■

■ Making Oral and Written Presentations
■ Essential Elements of Effective Presentations
■ Summary and Behavioral Guidelines

SKILL *PRACTICE* ◆

■ Speaking as a Leader
■ Quality Circles at Battle Creek Foods

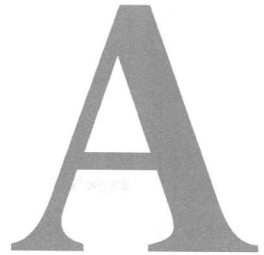

A

Making Oral and Written Presentations

SKILL DEVELOPMENT OBJECTIVES

■ MAKE INFORMATIVE ORAL PRESENTATIONS

■ WRITE CLEARLY AND PERSUASIVELY

■ RESPOND APPROPRIATELY TO QUESTIONS AND CHALLENGES

Making Oral and Written Presentations

Taylor Billingsley was hired as a sales representative in the Apex Communications Corporation in 1972. With training and hard work, she advanced through the levels of the corporation, finally landing the position of senior vice president in charge of personnel. Although she had anticipated that this position would require some adjustments, she was surprised at the kinds of changes she faced during her first few weeks on the job. Taylor had a lot of ideas about how to make the personnel division work more efficiently, but she realized almost immediately that she had to convince others to adopt them. In addition, she had to establish her own credibility—to make her employees and interested outsiders understand and appreciate her personal commitments and management style.

In the first few days on the job, Taylor had several opportunities to communicate her philosophy and expectations during a number of meetings with the departments in her division. Some of these meetings were formal, such as when she first accepted the position; others were more informal, including lunch meetings with the division heads. Immediately following the announcement of her appointment, she also wrote a memo to her division heads and their employees outlining some of her ideas for moving the department forward. In separate memos she addressed the personnel development and financial benefits departments, introducing a new project and encouraging them to move ahead full speed to develop a new policy on research teams.

Then Taylor began a round of visits with people who worked in her division. She talked individually with several workers and responded to the questions posed by informal groups. She was asked to write up her evaluation of morale among workers in her division and forward it to the corporate chief executive officer. The latest financial reports released by the company's controller's office revealed that quarterly figures were down unexpectedly; it seemed that certain costs had risen dramatically. Taylor was concerned and adjusted a report she had written for a scheduled meeting with the region's top executives to reflect these new developments.

Later, she spoke to an assembled employee group in the cafeteria in an effort to calm their fears about job cuts. At another facility located in a tough urban environment, the task proved more difficult. Workers were outspokenly critical of the company and challenged much of the information she presented. Following these meetings, Taylor was the featured dinner speaker at a regional Chamber of Commerce meeting.

Taylor Billingsley was experiencing the challenges of management in her new position. During her first two weeks, she addressed dozens of groups on a broad range of subjects; she wrote even more reports and memos. In most of this communication, Taylor was not simply presenting facts. Instead, she was conveying support, pointing a new direction, generating enthusiasm, communicating a sense of caring, building goodwill, and underscoring the value of teamwork. Some situations called for polite, ceremonial messages; others were confrontational. Some covered familiar material; others stretched her ability to find the right words to convey her ideas. At the end of her first two weeks, Taylor began to appreciate the importance of communication skills.

Managers have to master the basic elements of public communication and be flexible enough to adapt them to varying situations (Barrett, 1977; Mambert, 1976; Peoples, 1988; Sanford & Yeager, 1963; Wilcox, 1967). Like Taylor Billingsley, you may find yourself addressing many different audiences through speeches and in writing. Like Taylor Billingsley, you will probably discover very quickly that your effectiveness as a manager depends in large part upon your ability to communicate with your coworkers and customers. Unfortunately, new managers are often lacking in these skills. According to a survey of major business recruiters, the biggest deficiencies in college graduates were the lack of good oral communication and writing skills (*Endicott Report*, 1992). Considering that speaking and writing skills are central to good management and that many new employees are also relatively weak in these areas, we should turn our attention to how managers can develop these two critical skills. Let's focus first on the core ingredients of good communication and then examine the specific requirements of speaking and writing.

Essential Elements of Effective Presentations

How can one person meet all of the communication demands confronting a good manager? There are five basic steps to making effective presentations—we'll label them the Five *S*'s. These five *S*'s are sequential in the sense that each step builds upon the preceding steps. Good communication depends heavily on adequate forethought and preparation. As shown in Figure A.1, the first three steps involve preparation, the fourth and fifth focus on the spoken or written presentation itself. Adequate preparation is the cornerstone of effective communication (Collins and Devanna, 1990; Gelles-Cole, 1985; Wells, 1989).

1. Formulate a *strategy* for the specific audience and occasion. This is the phase in which you develop your purposes in relationship to the audience and situation.

2. Develop a clear *structure*. This step translates your broad strategy into specific content.

3. *Support* your ideas with examples, illustrations, and other material adapted to your audience. This will reinforce your ideas.

4. Prepare your material to create a presentation *style* that will enhance your ideas. How you present your ideas is often as important as what you present.

5. *Supplement* your presentation with confident, informed responses to questions and challenges. Your performance in a spontaneous, free-flowing discussion or exchange of memos should be as impressive and informative as your prepared presentation.

We have maintained throughout this book that effective personal performance is a function of skill, knowledge, and practice. This is especially the case with communication. The key to gaining confidence in making oral and written presentations is preparation and practice. If you follow the basic five steps, you should be on your way to delivering effective messages. Specific guidelines for implementing these five steps will be presented in the following sections.

FORMULATE A SPECIFIC STRATEGY

Identify Your Purpose

Michael Sheehan, a leading communications consultant whose clients include CEOs of major firms and presidential candidates, lists as his number-one rule for effective communication: "Know your objective, know your audience. It sounds easy, but it's really the hardest art of communications" (Reingold, 2004). In line with this recommendation, before collecting information or writing notes, you should clarify your general purpose for speaking or writing. Are you trying to motivate, inform, persuade, demonstrate, or teach? Your general purpose is to inform if you are providing information, demonstrating a technique, or delivering a report. When your purpose is to inform, you are concerned with the transmission and retention of ideas and facts. On the other hand, if you are motivating workers for higher production, convincing others to adopt your ideas, or stimulating pride in the company, your general purpose is to persuade. Persuasion requires the use of motivational language, convincing argument, and audience adaptation. Your general purpose may affect how you structure your message and how you supplement your ideas as well as your style of presentation. That is why it is important to identify your general purpose first.

Your specific purpose should be easier to determine once you have identified your general purpose (see Figure A.2). You can discover your specific purpose by asking, "What do I want my listeners to learn?" or "What behaviors or attitudes do I want my listeners to adopt?" You may answer, "I want my listeners or readers to learn the six steps in our new accounting procedure"

Figure A.1 The Five *S*'s Approach to an Effective Presentation

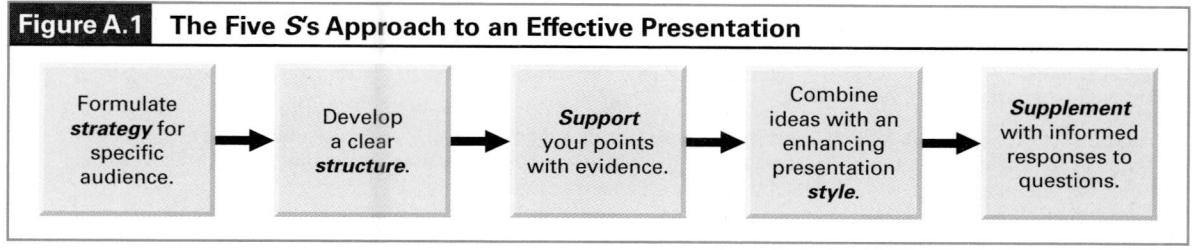

Formulate **strategy** for specific audience. → Develop a clear **structure**. → **Support** your points with evidence. → Combine ideas with an enhancing presentation **style**. → **Supplement** with informed responses to questions.

Figure A.2 | Determining Your Purpose

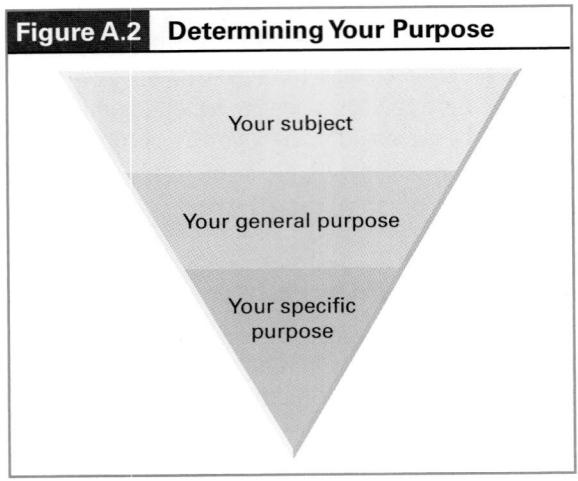

Your subject

Your general purpose

Your specific purpose

or "I want them to spend more time with customers." Each of these is a specific purpose. It determines how you will tailor the remainder of your preparation to your audience and the demands of the situation.

Tailor Your Message to Your Specific Audience

The success of your communication is partially dependent on your audience's understanding and receptivity.

The key to developing an audience-appropriate message is to understand their knowledge of the topic, their attitude toward your message, and their expectations of your presentation. If they already know what you are trying to teach them, they'll become bored and possibly hostile. Start with what they already know,

then expand on it. If you are teaching a new accounting procedure, begin with the one your listeners currently use, then add the new steps. Remember that audiences retain more information if the material is associated with something they already know, rephrased and repeated, reinforced with visual aids, and limited to three to five new ideas. Motivated listeners retain more so, early in your message, explain how they can use the information.

Your audience's attitudes toward your message are also critical to consider. Hostile receivers don't learn as readily as eager receivers. If your audience is hostile, start by setting realistic goals. If you try to do too much, you might trigger a boomerang effect in which your audience becomes even more hostile. Emphasize common ground by sharing similar values or parallel goals. For example, you might point out that increased profits are good for everyone in the company or that everyone has a stake in improving plant conditions.

For hostile or uncommitted listeners it is important to develop a two-sided message (see Table A.1). Present both sides of the issue. Use strong arguments built on logic and extensive evidence (Sprague & Stuart, 1996). Choose neutral language as you develop your ideas. In these situations, it is also important to build your credibility. Show yourself to be calm, fair, reasonable, and well informed. Use humor directed at yourself to ease tension (Sprague & Stuart, 1996).

Meet the Demands of the Situation

Your receivers' expectations of your presentation are also important. The situation frequently determines

Table A.1 | One-Sided Versus Two-Sided Messages

You should use a one-sided message when:

• Your audience already favors your position.

• Your audience is not well educated in general or on the topic.

• You require a public commitment from your audience.

You should use a two-sided message when:

• Your audience initially disagrees with your position.

• Your audience is well educated in general or on the topic.

• Your audience will experience counterpersuasion on the topic.

Research suggests that the best way to present a two-sided message is to first give the arguments that support your position. Organize those arguments beginning with the weakest and ending with the strongest. Then, present the argument of your opposition. Organize the opposition arguments beginning with the strongest and ending with the weakest. In this way, you take advantage of your listeners' tendency to remember the most recent thing they hear: your strong argument and your opponent's weak argument.

Source: *Adapted from Sproule, 1991.*

expectations, such as the level of formality. Some situations clearly demand more formal presentations. If you are expected to address a board meeting, you should prepare carefully. On the other hand, if you are asked for your off-the-cuff comments, a prepared speech is not appropriate or practical. In this case, it is permissible to present more spontaneous remarks. Written communication also involves certain expectations. Invitations to a company picnic can be posted on bulletin boards, but invitations to a board of directors meeting are sent individually. Some situations are tricky. For example, television often appears informal; however, you should carefully think out your comments. Banquets and ceremonies may encourage an informal, friendly atmosphere, but don't be fooled. These aren't the same settings as one-on-one or small-group events.

The settings of business presentations can create a number of constraints that you must anticipate. (Remember that forethought and preparation are keys to effective communication.) Consider these common occurrences. A meeting schedule runs over so that your 20-minute presentation must be condensed to 5 minutes. Be prepared with a short version that highlights information that will serve your strategy. After presenting your committee's proposal for changing customer service procedures, which the committee has studied for three months, an influential nonmember distributes an outline of a competing proposal. Be prepared to answer specific criticisms of your proposal while maintaining a tone of cordial professionalism.

Language is also affected by the situation. More formal language choices and more correct sentence structure are demanded by formal situations. Slang, colloquialisms, contractions, and less rigid grammar can add to the ease of informal settings. Determine your audience's expectations and adapt your language to them. Most experts agree that your language should be one step more intense than your audience's.

DEVELOP A CLEAR STRUCTURE
Begin with a Forecast

In general, an effective introduction does three things. First, it catches the listeners' attention and sets a tone for the message. Second, it provides your listeners with a reason for listening or reading. Finally, it gives them a road map or quick sketch of the message.

At a supervisor's meeting, you might start out your talk on a new plan for production changes this way: "Do you realize that we have not changed our basic production process in four years? In that time,

seven new competitors have entered the market, and we've lost 9 percent of market share. But with three changes, we can get more production, which will generate 3 percent more profits and pay raises in the next fiscal year. First, we reorganize Bay 2; second, we install a track between the parts room and the assembly line; and, third, we set up a phone connection between the parts room and the assembly line. Let me spend a few minutes filling out the details of each change and explaining why these changes will save us money."

This introduction gets your audience's attention because it portrays the immediacy of the problem and shows why your listeners have an important stake in what you have to say. By setting the larger context of increased competition, you intensify their reason for listening and counter possible resistance to change, which is common in organizations.

Choose an Appropriate Organizational Pattern

Organization is critical because it affects comprehension of the message. Learners retain more when messages are organized. Organization also affects your credibility as a speaker or writer. A person who is organized is viewed more positively than one who is not—and organization affects attitude change. Your receivers are more likely to be influenced by your viewpoint if it is organized. Finally, an organized message is more likely to be retained, and thus to influence the listener.

There are many patterns of organization to choose from (see Table A.2). In general, you should order your thoughts using continua such as time, direction, causal process, problem-solving sequence, complexity, space, or familiarity. A related technique is to organize your material as a series of answers to typical questions. Another common technique is called *sandwiching*. This involves three steps. First, you emphasize the advantages of the plan. Second, you realistically assess the risks or concerns associated with it. Third, you reinforce the benefits by showing how they outweigh the costs, demonstrate how risks can be minimized with proposed safeguards, or show how resistance to change can be overcome.

As you plan your message consider your listeners' orientation. The main question to ask is; "What does my audience already know or think?" Start from that point, then move closer to the desired knowledge or point of view.

Written and spoken communication vary in the amount of detailed information that can be conveyed in a single effort. Because a memo or report can be reread, the receiver doesn't have to remember all the

LEARNING

Table A.2 Common Patterns of Organization

STRATEGY	EXPLANATION
Chronological	Traces the order of events in a time sequence (such as past, present, and future or first step, second step, and third step).
Spatial	Arranges major points in terms of physical distance (such as north, central, and south) or direction from each other (such as internal and external).
Causal	Develops ideas from cause (such as diagnosing a disease from its causes) to effect or results to cause (such as from its symptoms to the disease).
Topical	Enumerates aspects of the topic (such as size, color, shape, or texture).
Monroe's Motivated Sequence	Follows a five-step process: 1. Gaining attention 2. Showing a need 3. Presenting a solution 4. Visualizing the results when the solution is implemented 5. Calling for action to implement the solution
Familiarity–acceptance order	Begins with what the listener knows or believes and moves on to new ideas.
Inquiry order	Develops the topic in steps the same way you acquire the information or solve a problem.
Question–answer	Raises and answers a series of listeners' questions.
Problem–solution	First establishes that a problem exists then develops a plan to solve the problem.
Elimination order	Surveys all the available solutions and systematically eliminates each possibility until one remains.

information. However, speeches can't be reheard. It's more important to limit the amount of information presented orally. How many points can you make in a speech? Three main points are preferred by most speakers, but many listeners can remember up to five main points. Seven chunks of information is about the limit of a person's immediate short-term memory at any one time. Since people must remember what you have said if they are to act on it, dividing your speech into no more than five major chunks should make your ideas easier to remember (Miller, 1967). If your presentation is long, consider using visual aids, such as overhead transparencies or handouts, to reinforce the message.

Use Transitions or Signposts to Signal Your Progress

It is important to give your audience a "road map" at the beginning of your message. Don't stop there. Continue to help them follow you through it. To do this, signal when you're moving from one idea to another by summarizing the first idea, then forecasting the new idea. This is especially important in oral communication, since listeners will only hear your message once; it is critical that you provide signposts during your speech. You should indicate major transitions between ideas, such as: "We've just seen how the two standard types of data storage operate, now let's look at the advantages and disadvantages of each storage system." In written form, you can signal transitions by indenting, numbering, or using bullets to highlight information. You can call your reader's attention to key words with italicized or bold print.

Conclude on a High Note

Two important psychological concepts are at work in communication—primacy and recency. Primacy is the first impression received and recency is the last. People tend to remember the first and last things they read or hear in messages. It's easy to understand why the most important parts of any presentation are the first and last impressions it creates. You establish an initial feeling in your introduction that colors the rest of the presentation, and the impression created during the conclusion influences the audience's overall evaluation of your message. Since these are the most important segments of your presentation, they warrant the most preparation. You should plan your message with the beginning and end in mind, that is, consider your specific purpose statement as you develop your introduction and conclusion. Some people write the conclusion first because this allows them to organize the rest of their material so it naturally flows into the conclusion.

Reach closure at the end of your speech or written message by summarizing your ideas for a final time. Research shows that this kind of reinforcement helps listeners retain information. Normally, people remember less than 20 percent of what they hear or read. If you preview the information in your introduction, reinforce it in internal summaries, and then summarize in the conclusion, you will increase the odds that your audience will remember your ideas.

The last statements you make after your summary should create a sense of closure and add to the memorability of your message. These statements can take a variety of forms. You can call for action, reinforce your audience's commitment to action, or establish feelings of goodwill (see Table A.3 for further suggestions). For example, you might emphasize legitimacy by highlighting several authoritative quotes, emphasize the "I'm here to help" theme, predict conditions in the future, underscore the utility of your proposal by emphasizing its impact on the bottom line, or use an emotional appeal to increase commitment and loyalty.

SUPPORT YOUR POINTS
Choose a Variety of Support

There are many reasons to use supporting materials, or evidence, as you develop your message. Most research concludes that supporting material makes a great difference in the impact of ideas. This is true even if you are not well known to your receivers or if they find your credibility moderate to low. What kind of support should you choose? Table A.4 illustrates some of the many kinds of supporting materials available. Messages are strongest when they are built upon a variety of supporting materials. For example, reinforce statistics on profit sharing with a specific instance, such as how those numbers will affect a person on the assembly line.

Consider Your Listeners When Choosing Your Support

The kinds of supporting materials you choose partially depends on your audience. If the evidence is new to them, it will have more impact. Videotapes, recordings,

Table A.3	Types of Introductions and Conclusions

When you select an introduction or conclusion, ask yourself if it orients your audience to your purposes and clearly signals the beginning or ending of your speech.

1. Refer to the subject or occasion.
2. Use a personal reference or greeting.
3. Ask a rhetorical question.
4. Make a startling statement.
5. Use a quotation.
6. Tell a humorous story.
7. Use an illustration.
8. Issue a challenge or appeal.
9. Use suspense.
10. Appeal to the listener's self-interest.
11. Employ a visual aid.
12. Refer to a recent incident.
13. Compliment the audience or a member of the audience.
14. Refer to the preceding speaker.
15. Request a specific action.

Table A.4	Types of Supporting Materials
Examples	Specific instances that illustrate the point or clarify the idea: For example, "Our plants in Detroit and Sacramento use Quality Circles."
Statistics	Numbers that express relationships of magnitude, segments, or trends: For example, "Currently, a full 32% of our workforce is involved in Quality Circle decision-making, and that is up 17% over the past two years."
Testimony	The opinions or conclusions of others, particularly experts: For example, "After studying our plants, professor Henry Wilson of the Harvard School of Business observed that American workers are not group motivated. He concluded that 'American workers cannot be expected to respond well to Quality Circles for that reason.'"

or photos also have greater impact. People who are highly dogmatic are more affected by evidence than those who are not so dogmatic. People are likely to believe evidence that agrees with their own position more than evidence that does not. So their initial position determines the extent to which they will find evidence believable. If your receivers find the source or types of evidence to be believable or credible, it will be more effective (see Table A.5).

Use Visual Aids as Support

There are as many reasons to use visual aids as there are types of visual aids (see Table A.6). Visual aids help people process and retain data (Seiler, 1971). In addition to enhancing comprehension and memory, visual aids can heighten the persuasive impact of your ideas if they engage receivers actively in the communicative exchange. Your credibility and your persuasiveness are enhanced by good visual aids. With these functions in mind, remember that visual aids should be simple, clear, and professional (see Table A.7). The purpose of a visual aid is to augment your presentation, not replace it or distract from it. Unfortunately, this last point is lost by many professionals who treat presentations as slide shows in which screen displays and even sound effects—not the presenter—become the center of attention.

Table A.5	Using Supporting Materials

There is a great deal of research on the use of supporting materials or evidence in oral presentations. The following patterns seem to emerge:

1. If you have low to moderate credibility, evidence will probably increase your persuasive effectiveness.

2. There seems to be minimal difference between emotional and logical evidence.

3. Using evidence is usually better than not using it.

4. There seems to be little difference between biased sources and objective sources in their final impact on audiences.

5. Good speech delivery may improve the potency of evidence when sources of the evidence are unknown or have low credibility.

6. Evidence can reinforce the long-term effectiveness of persuasion.

7. Evidence is most effective when listeners are not familiar with it.

8. People are more likely to believe evidence that agrees with their own position.

9. Highly dogmatic people are more affected by evidence than are less dogmatic people.

10. Evidence produces more attitude change when the course and source qualifications are provided.

11. Speakers with low credibility are seen as more credible when they cite evidence.

12. Using irrelevant evidence or poorly qualified sources may produce an effect opposite to what the speaker intends.

Source: *From Persuasion: Reception, and Responsibility* *6th edition* by Larson. © 1992. Reprinted with the permission of Wadsworth, a division of Thomson Learning: www.thomsonrights.com. Fax 800 730-2215.

Table A.6	Functions of Visual Aids

According to research, using effective visual aids in an oral presentation:

- Makes your presentation up to 50% more memorable.
- Significantly clarifies complex or detailed information.
- Portrays you as more professional and better prepared.
- Speeds up group decision making.
- Shortens meeting time by up to 28%.
- Makes your message 43% more persuasive.

Sources: *Osborn & Osborn, 1991, and Gronbeck et al., 1992.*

Computer-aided graphics make it easier than ever to supplement your main ideas with visual materials. They also make it easier to create cluttered, excessive visual and sound images that distract the audience from your strategic message. Select and design visual aids to reinforce your strategy and ideas, and to make them clearer. Keep in mind that each type of visual aid communicates information in a different way. In general, visual aids such as slides, photographs, and posters can help an audience *feel* the way you do. They enhance the emotional dimension of a presentation. On the other hand, descriptive or written materials help an audience *think* the way you do. Numbers and charts reinforce cognitive processes; photographs reinforce affective processes. Use tables and graphs to highlight relationships and patterns, not to convey comprehensive data. If necessary, use supplemental handouts of comprehensive tables and charts.

USE AN ENHANCING STYLE

Up to this point, the preparation of oral and written messages is very similar. Whether you intend to deliver

LEARNING

Table A.7	Checklist for Using Visual Aids

As you prepare your visual aids, ask yourself the following questions:

- ❏ Can I avoid making the visual aid the most important aspect of my speech? Will it be more than just an ornament?
- ❏ Can I translate complex numbers into bar or line graphs for easier comprehension?
- ❏ Am I comfortable with using the visual aid? Have I practiced with it so using it is natural, and it does not break the flow of ideas in my speech?
- ❏ Is it large enough to be seen by everyone without straining?
- ❏ Is all the printing short and neat?
- ❏ Is the visual aid colorful and involving? Studies show color highlights aid recall of information.
- ❏ Are my visual aids professional: neat, attractive, and accurate?
- ❏ Have I made the necessary arrangements for special visual aids in advance?
- ❏ Can I use the visual aid without blocking my audience's view of it? Will I be able to maintain good eye contact with my listeners while using the visual aid?
- ❏ Can I avoid reaching across my body or waving the visual aid in front of my face?
- ❏ Can I avoid distracting my listeners by keeping the visual aid covered or out of sight before and after I use it?
- ❏ What will I do if the visual aid fails to work? Am I prepared for unexpected contingencies such as a burned-out projector bulb or a room that cannot be darkened?
- ❏ Have I planned for assistance or volunteers in advance if they are needed?
- ❏ Will a pointer be needed?
- ❏ Will all charts be secured so I don't have to hunt for them on the floor in the middle of my speech?
- ❏ Am I using a variety of visual aids to increase my listeners' interest?
- ❏ If I'm using handouts, can I adjust to the distraction caused by passing them around? Can I compete with listeners who will read the handout rather than listen to me?
- ❏ Can I speak over the noise of a projector or other machine?

a speech or write a memo, you need to develop your strategy by identifying your purposes, structuring your message, and supporting your ideas with evidence. The fourth step requires separate treatment of oral and written messages because they are stylistically very different forms of communication. We'll first focus on oral presentations.

STYLE IN ORAL COMMUNICATION

Prepare Your Notes

The mark of effective presenters is the appearance of effortlessness. Some speakers have such command of their material it appears they are ad libbing. Most of us prefer such a conversational style (see Table A.8), but don't be fooled by appearances. Hours of preparation and practice preceded the actual performance. You've already been introduced to the three steps of preparation, but how do you develop the fourth stage of your preparation for oral communication?

After you have carefully considered your strategy, structure, and support, you should prepare your speaking notes. To do this, simply write your key points in a rough outline following the organizational pattern you have chosen. What you do next depends on your method of presentation. Most often, you will speak in a conversational manner that is not memorized or read; this is referred to as extemporaneous speaking. Extemporaneous presentation is desirable because it is natural and flexible; it applies to most situations. To prepare, copy key words on note cards to stimulate your memory; standard pages are often distracting. Write out quotations, statistics, or anything that requires exact wording. Highlight places where you intend to use visual aids, pause for questions, or present an exhibit. To rehearse, go through the speech, phrasing your ideas in language that seems natural. You may find yourself phrasing ideas with different words each time. That is okay. It will increase the conversational quality of your speech because your words will be typical of oral style and natural expression. It will help you develop flexibility, allowing you to adjust to different wording and flow of ideas.

If the occasion is formal and demands precise wording or exquisite prose, you should prepare a word-for-word manuscript to memorize or read. Then you should rehearse with the manuscript, trying to achieve as much natural flow in the dialogue as possible. This form of presentation is rare, but it may be required for discussing legal and financial issues, making announcements to the press, or conducting special ceremonies. Otherwise, avoid using written scripts and memorization for presentations because they disrupt the natural flow of conversational style and break eye contact with your listeners. Because manuscripts are prepared in written form first, they usually take on the style of written language. Unless you are a practiced speechwriter, your manuscript will sound like written rather than oral speech (see Table A.9).

Practice Your Presentation

It is a good idea to rehearse your presentation under simulated conditions—in a similar room, with listeners who can give you suggestions for improvement. Time your presentation so you know if it is necessary to cut or expand your ideas. Research shows that practicing a speech for short periods of time over the course of several days is more successful in reducing anxiety and improving memory than concentrated practice. So give the speech to yourself during breakfast, at your morning coffee break, as you walk to a midafternoon meeting, and before bed. Distributed practice is more efficient and yields better results than massed practice.

Table A.8	Differences Between Public Speaking and Conversation

Folk wisdom holds that giving a speech is just like talking to another person. While it is true that most people prefer a conversational style of public speaking, there are at least three noteworthy differences between giving speeches and holding conversations:

1. Public speaking is more highly structured. It requires more detailed planning and development. Specific time limits may be imposed, and the speaker does not have the advantage of being able to respond individually to listeners.

2. Public speaking requires more formal language. Slang, jargon, and poor grammar all lower speaker credibility, even in informal speech situations. Listeners usually react negatively to poor language choices. In fact, many studies show that some kinds of language, such as obscene language, dramatically lower a speaker's credibility.

3. Public speaking requires a different method of delivery. The speaker's voice must be adjusted in volume and projection, posture is more correct, and distracting mannerisms and verbal habits are avoided.

Source: *Adapted from Lucas, 1989.*

Table A.9 Differences Between Oral and Written Styles

Why do we instantly recognize a memorized speech? Why does a meeting transcript sound funny? The answer to both questions is that oral style differs from written style. Memorized speeches from manuscripts reveal their written style, and conversations that are read reveal their oral style. Oral style differs from written style in the following ways:

1. The average sentence length is shorter (about 16 words) in conversations.

2. Vocabulary is more limited in speaking than in writing. "I" and "you" make up almost 8% of the words used in speaking; fewer than 50 words make up almost half of the total vocabulary we use when we speak.

3. Spoken vocabulary consists of more short words.

4. Speakers use more words referring to themselves such as "I," "me," and "we"; listeners rate this as more interesting.

5. More qualifying terms (such as "much," "many," and "a lot") and allness terms (such as "none," "never," and "always") are used in speaking.

6. More phrases and terms indicating hesitation are apparent in speaking, such as "it seems to me," "apparently," "in my opinion," and "maybe."

7. Fewer precise numbers are used in speaking.

8. Speakers use more contractions and colloquial expressions such as "can't," "wouldn't," "wow," and "chill out."

One final note on language: There is some evidence that we use lexical diversity as a cue to a speaker's socioeconomic status, competence, and perceived similarity.

Source: Copyright 1978 From oral and written style by L. Einhorn. Reproduced by permission of Taylor & Francis Group, LLC. www.taylorandfrancis.com.

LEARNING

Practice Using Your Visual Aids

This will help you get used to managing them and give you some idea of how long your speech will take with the visual aids. Prepare for the totally unexpected. What if the roar of an overhead plane drowns out your voice? What if the microphone goes dead, a window blows open, or the room becomes extremely hot? Compensate for minor disruptions by slowing your rate, raising your volume a little, and continuing. You will encourage listeners to listen to your message rather than be temporarily distracted. For other disruptions, a good rule of thumb is to respond the same way you would if you were in the audience. Take off your jacket if it is too hot, close the window, raise your voice if listeners can't hear you, or pause to allow a complex idea to sink in.

As you practice, think about how you will channel your anxiety. Most speakers report feeling anxious before they speak; it's normal. To manage your anxiety, channel it into positive energy. Prepare well in advance for the speech—develop your ideas, support them, and practice your delivery. Even if you are anxious, you will have something important to say. It may help to visualize the speaking situation. Close your eyes, relax, and think about how it's going to feel and what your audience will look like as they watch you. Expect to feel a little momentary panic as you get up to speak; it will evaporate as you progress into the speech. Remember to think about your ideas rather than how nervous you feel. Focus on your message. Also remember that anxiety about speaking never really goes away. Most experienced speakers still get podium panic. The advantage of experience is that you learn how to cope by converting your anxiety into energy and enthusiasm. That gives you an extra sparkle as you speak. Above all, don't tell your listeners that you are nervous. This will divert their attention from your ideas to your anxiety. Usually, listeners can't tell that a speaker is nervous—only speakers know, and they should keep that secret.

Convey Controlled Enthusiasm for Your Subject

When a survey was given to 1,200 people asking them to identify the characteristics of effective presentations (Peoples, 1988), the results contained adjectives such as flexible, cooperative, audience-oriented, pleasant, and interesting. What was striking about these results is that only the last item on the list of 12 outstanding characteristics was specifically related to the content of the presentations. This suggests that the preceding discussion of effective format, while necessary, is not sufficient to guarantee your success. Put another way, a rambling, poorly organized presentation will surely produce an overall negative evaluation. On the other hand, a well-organized, highly logical, and easy-to-follow presentation that is poorly delivered will also be viewed negatively. This study suggests that style is extremely important in oral communication.

Years of research on student evaluations of classroom teaching performance have consistently shown that enthusiasm is the hallmark of a good teacher. Students will forgive other deficiencies if the teacher obviously loves the subject and is genuinely interested in conveying that appreciation to the students. The same holds true for presenters. Your posture, tone of voice, and facial expressions are all critical indicators of your attitude. Speak standing if you can, move occasionally, and use gestures to convey an attitude of earnestness. Remember, your audience will become infected with your enthusiasm.

Although enthusiasm is important, it must be controlled. Do not confuse enthusiasm with loudness. A good rule is to use vigorous but conversational tones of voice and inflections. Avoid bellowing or preaching at your listeners. Be sure you can be easily heard and that your tone is sufficiently emphatic to convey meaning effectively. In general, your speech should resemble an animated or lively conversation.

Use Delivery to Enhance Your Message

Another key to maintaining audience attention is effective delivery. Eye contact is the most important tool for establishing audience involvement. It makes listeners feel as if they are involved in a one-on-one, semiprivate discussion with you. In this culture, we value directness and honesty. One of the expressions of these values is direct eye contact. Effective eye contact means looking directly at members of the audience, one at a time, on a random, rotating basis. Generally, the smaller the group, the longer you can look at each person. Maintaining eye contact is also your primary source of audience feedback as you are presenting. If your audience appears puzzled, you may need to pause and review your key ideas.

It is important to use physical space and body movement to enhance your message. Remember that presentations are like movies, not snapshots. Alternate moving and standing still, speaking and listening, doing and thinking. Intersperse your lecture with chalkboard use, demonstration, audience participation, and audiovisual aids so that no single activity occupies a large portion of the presentation. Add some spice to your presentation by including personal anecdotes, references to members of the group, unusual facts, vital information, and vibrant images. Whenever appropriate, arrange the podium area to accommodate physical movement. Physical movement can be used to punctuate important points, signal transitions, build rapport with a person who asks a question, heighten the interest of particular segments of the audience, and help your listeners stay alert by refocusing their attention.

Other aspects of physical space affect the quality of your presentation. If possible, arrange the podium area and seating in the room to remove distractions. In more intimate settings, group participants so that there is less space between them. Eliminate unnecessary or distracting materials from the podium, such as unused equipment, signs, and displays. Keep your visual aids covered until they are used and keep the chalkboard clean. Focus your listeners' attention on you and your message.

You can use space to convey intimacy or distance. Position yourself roughly in the middle of your audience from left to right and in a spot where you can comfortably maintain eye contact. With this in mind, you can deliberately alter your presentation style to build rapport with members of the audience. Move closer if you intend to build intimacy or tension; move to a comfortable distance when your ideas are neutral.

Gestures can also add to a presentation. They should appear to be spontaneous and natural in order to enhance, rather than distract from, your message. They should be relaxed, not rigid. Use them to accentuate your normal mode of expression. To some extent, when you concentrate on your message, not your movements, the appropriate gestures will come naturally. Remember that your gestures should be smooth, relatively slow, and not too low (below your waist), too high (above your shoulders), or too wide (more than two feet from your body). If you are using a podium, step slightly behind or to the side of the podium so it does not block your listeners' view of your movement. The general rules for gestures change as your audience becomes larger. You must adapt to large groups by making larger, more dramatic gestures.

Avoid any gestures or movements that distract from your message. Irrelevant movement such as jingling change in a pocket, toying with notes, shifting from foot to foot, twisting hair, or adjusting eyeglasses are annoying. In fact, any movement repeated too often creates a distraction. Practice using a variety of body movements to illustrate or describe, enumerate, add emphasis, or direct attention. For variety, some gestures should involve the entire upper body, not just your dominant hand.

STYLE IN WRITTEN COMMUNICATION

Like oral communication, written communication is a skill; it can be learned. Written communication follows the same three preparation steps as oral communication. The writer determines strategies, structure, and support before actually putting pen to paper. As with effective presentations, good writing draws on careful analysis of the audience and situation. In a business setting, "every document is a response to a problem or opportunity requiring that some consensus be achieved or action taken" (Poor, 1992, p. 38).

There are significant differences between oral and written communication style. Although it lacks the interpersonal dimension of immediacy, written communication offers one tremendous advantage over oral communication—it lasts. Written documents can be retained, studied, duplicated, and filed for the future. This means that they are essentially capable of conveying much more detailed information. While written communication offers these advantages, it also makes different demands on the communicator; written communication demands precision.

Develop Mechanical Precision in Your Writing

Your professional image is judged by the appearance of your written communication. Cross outs, erasures, typographical errors, or other sloppiness detract from your written message, just as awkward mannerisms can distract from your oral message. Grammatical precision is also required—misspellings, punctuation errors, and poor grammar are marks of uneducated writers. This is certainly not an image you want to convey. You may expect a secretary or clerical worker to catch and correct all these things, and many times that happens. However, when you sign or otherwise endorse the final product, you alone are accountable for any errors it contains. It is essential to develop the habit of proofreading final drafts before you sign them.

Violations of the rules of grammar and punctuation may affect more than just your credibility. They can also disrupt your reader. If the reader is distracted by typos, confusing grammar, or ambiguous pronouns, your ideas may become lost; such errors can cripple the impact of your message. Some recruiters toss out résumés that contain mechanical errors. Their reasoning is that if job applicants can't take the time to proofread a short résumé, they may be sloppy on the job, too. Some readers are insulted by poor grammar; others automatically consider themselves superior to the writer. While these may not be logical reactions, they occur, and more important, they block your effectiveness. You may argue that correct grammar and punctuation are not vital. Maybe not, but you take a chance every time you present careless work to another reader. Consider the campaign of Charles Day for a seat on local government. His campaign flyers, delivered house to house, carried the banner, "Vote Charles Day for School Bord." Would you want a man who apparently can't spell make decisions on academic matters for your neighborhood schools? The impression is that if you don't have the time or incentive to check your own writing, you won't pay attention to details in the work of others.

Practice Factual Precision in Your Writing

Getting the facts right is important. If you send a memo calling for a meeting but record an incorrect meeting date, you'll suffer the consequences of inconveniencing others. Accuracy is critical, but that's just the beginning. It's up to the writer to create sentences that make the meaning unmistakably clear to the reader. Many times writers know the facts but omit important details in writing. Omission occurs when you have all the facts or circumstances but as you write, you assume the reader knows the facts. Write with your reader in mind. This assumes that you have analyzed who your readers are and understand what information they need and expect. What basic information is important for readers to know in order to understand your message? Instead of starting with the central part of the message, provide the background first, such as: "In response to your memo of February 2, requesting corrections to our policy on grievances, we have taken three actions. First . . . " If you're not sure what to include, ask someone who doesn't know the details of the situation to read what you have written.

Ambiguity is another barrier to clear writing. Many times we write as we speak, throwing in phrases as we would speak them. Unlike speakers, writers can't use nonverbal cues to convey specific meanings or associations. Since readers may not have the advantage of asking questions or getting immediate feedback, they are left to determine associations for themselves. Consider how ambiguity creates a lack of precise factual meaning in this memo:

The next meeting of the department is scheduled for next week. Matt Olsen has told Leo Robinson to report on the union elections. His report will follow announcements. We will elect new officers at our upcoming meeting.

LEARNING

This memo doesn't pass the standard test of clear writing. If the memo was sent on Friday and received on Monday, which week contains the meeting? Who is giving the report? The pronoun "his" causes confusion since it could refer to either Matt Olsen or Leo Robinson. Which "upcoming meeting" will result in the election of officers? Will it be the meeting called by the memo or another "upcoming meeting"? Because it can breed confusion, annoyance, and wasted time, such a sloppy memo can have an adverse effect on the relationship between the writer and recipients that can affect their subsequent communication. Seen in this light, the memos a manager routinely writes are an important factor in managing relationships strategically and productively.

Construct Written Messages with Verbal Precision

Achieving verbal precision is different from mechanical or factual precision. Verbal precision is based on the accuracy of the words chosen to express the ideas. In an ideal world, words would provide the exact meaning you intended, but words can't replicate reality. Rather, words are symbols of objects and ideas. Add to this inexact representation the reader's own subtle shadings of meaning, and you can see why it's difficult to achieve verbal precision. Put another way, a word has two levels of meaning: its denotation, or the meaning agreed upon by most people who use the word, and its connotation, or the personal dimension of meaning brought to the word by the receiver.

Communication depends on a blend of both denotative and connotative meanings. Consider the noun *Greenpeace*. Its denotative reference is to a specific international environmental organization. The connotative meaning varies widely. For many environmentalists, Greenpeace is leading a worthy crusade. However, for some governments and companies, the organization is, at best, a nuisance. These are the connotative references of a single word. Consider the difficulty in creating the right blend of denotative and connotative meaning in entire documents. You need to be aware of both types of meaning of the words you use. Frequently, you may recognize your own connotative meaning but be unaware of how others may react. While connotation is often a personal matter, you can attempt to judge this meaning by thinking from your receivers' viewpoint. What is their most likely reaction?

The key to verbal precision in writing is clarity. The fundamental questions you must ask yourself are: "Does the word or phrase convey my meaning without confusion?" or "Could anyone reading this memo for the first time understand the ideas directly and simply?" A secondary question is whether the written message conveys unintentional meanings stimulated by connotative meanings of words or phrases. The impact of connotations once more underlines the importance of knowing your audience and of being aware of what is appropriate for one audience or another.

Pay Attention to Tone

The tone of your writing is directly related to your diction, or word choices. For example, compare these two statements: "Our company will purchase the product" and "We'll buy it." The second sounds more informal because it uses pronouns and a contraction. In general, longer words and sentences tend to convey a more formal tone.

Using the appropriate level of formality in your writing calls for you to analyze the nature of the writing situation. An invitation to a reception for the company's board of directors calls for formal language. When you are writing to strangers or up the chain of command, it is safer to be formal. When you are communicating across or down the chain, you often may be informal. However, a letter of reprimand to a subordinate should be formal in tone.

Tone in business writing goes beyond its relative formality. It reflects on the nature of the writer as a person and therefore affects how the reader feels about the writer. Its impact can be significant and often unexpected. For example, a terse letter may be interpreted as sarcastic or angry even if the writer did not intend sarcasm or anger. Consider a customer who writes a long letter expressing problems with a product. What would the customer think if this response were mailed back: "Thank you for your letter of January 12. We always enjoy hearing from our customers." Although this response has the trappings of courtesy, it seems insincere and perhaps sarcastic. It hardly seems that the respondent read the customer's letter—there is nothing about its contents—or that the letter was "enjoyed." Although the response shows factual and mechanical precision, the tone is inappropriate and potentially damaging to the relationship with this customer.

In most cases, even disappointing news can be expressed in a positive way. Consider an employer who responds to a job applicant by writing, "In a company as well respected as ours, we rarely have time to consider applications such as yours." Not only is the news bad, the arrogant tone also needlessly humiliates the applicant. A response with a more positive tone might be: "We read your application with interest but currently do not have any openings in your specialties. Best wishes with your continued search." The news is still bad, but the polite tone shows respect for the applicant and promotes a professional image of the company.

Compare the following sentence and its more positive version: "Because of recent heavy demand, we will be unable to ship the items you ordered until July 15," and "Although recent demand has been heavy, we will be able to ship the items you ordered July 15." A slight variation in wording here changes a tone of helplessness to one of helpfulness.

Under most business writing conditions, you should be cordial. You should express tact and friendliness appropriate to your relationship with the reader. This attitude will have a positive effect on your word choices, which in turn will more likely convey an appropriate tone.

One area of modern business writing where failing to pay attention to tone has cost many bad feelings and lost time is electronic mail, or e-mail. By its nature, e-mail encourages rapid-fire exchanges, especially when busy workers face an in-box filled with messages, many of which are ill-considered and unclear. E-mail is not a phone conversation in which tone of voice and other cues can clarify your meaning and in which you can read the listener's vocal cues. However, many e-mailers seem to forget the difference. They don't state the context of their message; they don't give needed background information; they don't organize their message; they don't make careful word choices that convey a cordial tone. By not taking the time to consider their message in light of the situation and the receiver, e-mailers can convey inappropriately demanding tones or disapproving tones if their requests aren't met promptly. The antagonism created by the poor tone of e-mail messages can delay solving the business problem at hand and affect negatively the work relationships of the e-mailers.

Use the Proper Format

Like it or not, first impressions count, even in written communication. Sloppiness suggests that the writer doesn't take the message seriously; odd or unconventional formats hint that the writer is ignorant or unprofessional. You should become acquainted with the physical layout of letters, memos, proposals, and other common forms of written business communication. Others expect you to have this basic knowledge; many handbooks and computer software programs are available to guide you in the development of these formats. Some companies have style guides that precisely

prescribe the formats for all documents representing the company.

While there are several acceptable formats for written communication such as business letters, the reader should be able to pick up specific information at a glance. In the business letter, this information includes: the intended recipient of the letter, the sender, the sender's address for return correspondence, any enclosures, and recipients of copies of the letter. All of this information is separate from the body of the letter and should be clearly visible.

Because memos are intended to communicate within an organization, their format is different from that of letters. Instead of business letterhead, memo letterhead is used. Basic information can also be obtained at a glance. The top of the memo should include: To, From, Date, and Subject headings. Usually, salutations and closings are not considered necessary within an organization.

Proposals are much lengthier and require special attention to supporting information such as tables, graphs, and charts. The best ways to represent such data can be found in readily available resources on business writing.

Whatever the final format, there is one objective in all written business communication: Your message should be simple, direct, and clear. Anything that interrupts your reader's movement through your writing limits its effectiveness. Any imprecision—a mechanical blunder, a factual omission, or a strange word—calls attention to itself and, like an odd gesture in spoken communication, diverts attention away from your ideas. As a writer, you must aim at clear, direct transmission of your message.

SUPPLEMENT YOUR PRESENTATION BY RESPONDING TO QUESTIONS AND CHALLENGES

Prepare Thoroughly to Handle Questions

Answering questions and responding to objections is a vital part of the communication process because it allows us to interact directly with our listeners. We can learn about how our listeners are thinking and their responses to our ideas from their questions; it's a two-way street.

The key to formulating effective responses is the same as the key to developing good speeches—careful preparation. Read broadly and talk with experts in your field. Don't read just the material that supports your point of view but also read what the opposition is saying. The best defense can be a good offense, and this is no exception. Ask your colleagues to critique your material, discuss their questions and objections with them, and collect supporting documentation or evidence. You can also practice your responses. Begin by considering what your listeners might ask or find someone opposed to your position who will list questions for you. Then, practice your responses to these questions.

Despite your best efforts, you may get an overwhelmingly hostile response from your listeners. Don't be afraid to take a stand that disagrees with them. People may not agree with you but they will respect your sincerity. If someone throws you a curve, don't apologize or bluff your way through with an inadequate response. Be honest and direct, tell them if you don't have the answer. Invite them to discuss the problem further at a later time and follow up on your invitation. The next time someone asks the same question, you will be prepared.

Respond to Objections in an Orderly Manner

In general, answer questions as succinctly as possible. Rambling answers may make it appear as though you are hedging or unsure. They also suggest an inability to think concisely. You can answer objections in four steps:

1. *Restate the objection.* This gives you time to think, shows your interest, and makes sure that everyone understands the question. Restatement recognizes the objection and clarifies it for everyone in the audience.

2. *State your position.* Give a concise, direct statement of what you believe to make it clear where you stand.

3. *Offer support for your position.* This is the critical part of the response. Provide evidence that shows your position is the right one.

4. *Indicate the significance of your rebuttal.* Show the impact of adopting your position. Offer reasons for doing so.

Following the four steps we've outlined, a good response to an objection might take this form:

1. Joe has stated that a management-by-objectives system won't work in our factory because supervisors don't want input from the cutting floor (restatement of the objection).

2. I think that a management-by-objectives system will work and that it will increase worker satisfaction (statement of your position).

3. I'm basing my position on a group of studies done in our Newark plant last year. Output increased 0.5 percent during the first month, and more importantly, workers reported more job satisfaction. They had fewer sick days, too (support for the position).

4. If our plant is similar to the Newark plant—and I think it is—then I believe our supervisors will notice the same gains here. Until Joe can provide us with a reason to stick with the current system, I think we ought to give the new one a try—we stand to get more output and better job satisfaction (significance of rebuttal).

Practice this format until it becomes automatic. It builds up your own case while responding to the objection. Since this format rationally shores up your position, it increases your credibility as well. And, it increases the chances that others will agree with you.

Maintain Control of the Situation

You need to balance being sensitive to feedback and flexible enough to respond to legitimate concerns with avoiding prolonged, unproductive interchanges. Recognizing everyone's right to ask questions or offer alternative positions is important because it grants audience members respect. On the other hand, you also have every right to decide what is relevant for consideration. You shouldn't allow one or two members of your audience to dictate the pace or direction of your presentation. This places you in a position of weakness that undermines your credibility. If you should alter your position, make certain that the majority of your listeners view it as a responsible shift rather than an effort to placate a minority voice.

Keep exchanges on an intellectual level. Arguments and rebuttals can degenerate into name-calling in which little is settled. Effective communication is more likely to occur when the calm voice of reason dominates than when you squabble with your listeners.

You'll soon learn that people don't always ask questions just because they want information. Some people crave attention; others may sabotage your position if they perceive your ideas as a threat. Planning for these possibilities will give you more options; foresight enables you to respond appropriately. You might answer hostile questions with further questions, drawing out your interrogator and regaining the offensive.

Or you might broaden the discussion. Don't get trapped into an argument with one person. Involve others to determine if this is an isolated concern or a legitimate issue. Finally, you might express your willingness to discuss special or detailed issues but defer extensive discussion until the end of your presentation.

Summary and Behavioral Guidelines

A key aspect of management is communication, and formal presentations are an essential communication tool. Therefore, effective managers must be able to create effective informative and persuasive messages. You can enhance your speaking and writing with thorough preparation and repeated practice. This chapter has outlined a number of guidelines based on the Five *S*'s model:

1. Formulate a *strategy* for the specific audience and occasion.
2. Develop a clear *structure*.
3. *Support* your points with evidence adapted to your audience.
4. Practice presenting your material in a *style* that will enhance your ideas.
5. *Supplement* your presentation by effectively responding to questions and challenges.

Strategy

1. Identify your general and specific purposes.
2. Tailor your message to your audience.
   - ❏ Understand their needs, desires, knowledge level, and attitude toward your topic.
   - ❏ Make sure your approach is audience-centered.
   - ❏ Present both sides of the issue if your audience is hostile or uncommitted.
3. Meet the demands of the situation.
   - ❏ More formal situations demand formal language and sentence structure.
   - ❏ Informal situations allow slang and less rigid language use.

Structure

4. Begin with a forecast of your main ideas.
   - ❏ Catch your audience's attention as you begin.
   - ❏ Provide them with a reason for listening or reading.
   - ❏ Give them an outline of the message so they can follow along.

5. Choose your organizational pattern carefully.
   - ❏ Start with what your listeners already know or think.
   - ❏ Use organization to increase your credibility.
   - ❏ Move from familiar to unfamiliar, simple to complex, old to new, or use other continua for organizing your thoughts.
   - ❏ Make no more than three to five main points in oral communication.
6. Use transitions to signal your progress.
7. Conclude on a high note.
   - ❏ Take advantage of greater audience attention at the conclusion of your message.
   - ❏ Reach closure by reinforcing through a summary of your ideas.
   - ❏ Use your last statements to call for action, reinforce the commitment to action, or establish a feeling of goodwill.

Support

8. Choose a variety of support.
   - ❏ The most effective support is not well known to your listeners.
   - ❏ Support increases your credibility.
   - ❏ You may use a wide variety of supporting material.
9. Consider your audience when choosing your support.
   - ❏ New evidence and live videotapes have more impact.
   - ❏ The audience's initial position determines the extent to which they find evidence believable.
   - ❏ Using evidence is better than not using evidence.
10. Use visual aids as support.
    - ❏ Visual aids have a dramatic impact on comprehension and retention.
    - ❏ Visual aids also enhance persuasion.
    - ❏ Keep visual aids simple and effective.

Style in Oral Communication

11. Prepare your notes.
    - ❏ Remember, the crucial effect is conversational style.
    - ❏ Extemporaneous presentation requires limited notes combined with frequent delivery practice.
    - ❏ Formal occasions demand precise wording that requires a manuscript or memorized speech.

12. Practice your presentation.
    - ❏ Use distributed practice rather than massed practice.
    - ❏ Practice using your visual aids and plan for the unexpected.
    - ❏ Plan to channel your speaking anxiety.
13. Convey controlled enthusiasm for your subject.
    - ❏ Effective speakers communicate excitement about their topics.
    - ❏ Your posture, tone of voice, and facial expressions all indicate your attitude.
    - ❏ Your speech should resemble an animated conversation.
14. Engage your audience with effective delivery.
    - ❏ Eye contact is the most critical tool.
    - ❏ Use physical space and body movement to enliven your message.
    - ❏ Use space to convey intimacy or distance.
    - ❏ Use gestures to accentuate your normal mode of expression.
    - ❏ Avoid any movement that distracts from your message.

Style in Written Communication

15. Develop mechanical precision in your writing.
    - ❏ Project a professional image.
    - ❏ Errors may distract your readers and disrupt the impact of your message.
16. Practice factual precision in your writing.
    - ❏ Accuracy ensures that your meaning will be communicated clearly.
    - ❏ Ambiguity prevents factual precision.
17. Construct written messages with verbal precision.
    - ❏ Words cannot replicate reality.
    - ❏ Consider denotative and connotative meanings of words as you write them.
    - ❏ The key to verbal precision is clarity.
18. Pay attention to tone.
    - ❏ Tone is directly related to word choice.
    - ❏ Adjust the tone of your message to the formality of the situation.
    - ❏ Tone affects how readers feel about the writer.
    - ❏ Writing should express appropriate cordiality.
    - ❏ Positive phrasing is preferable to negativity.
19. Use the proper format.
    - ❏ You are responsible for creating an impression of professionalism.
    - ❏ Business letters, memos, and proposals all have special formats.

Supplement: Questions and Answers

20. Anticipate questions and thoroughly prepare responses.
    - ❏ Rehearse answers to difficult questions.
    - ❏ Handle hostile listeners with honesty and directness.
21. Respond to objections in an orderly fashion.
    - ❏ Restate the objection.
    - ❏ State your position.
    - ❏ Offer support for your position.
    - ❏ Indicate the significance of your rebuttal.
22. Maintain control of the situation.
    - ❏ Balance the demands of specific individuals with the interest of the group.
    - ❏ Keep exchanges on an intellectual level.
    - ❏ Plan for the questioner who has a personal agenda.

EXERCISES FOR MAKING EFFECTIVE ORAL AND WRITTEN PRESENTATIONS

Speaking as a Leader

As illustrated in the opening case about Taylor Billingsley at Apex Communications, one of the major challenges facing leaders is the requirement to deliver a wide range of presentations. Effective communicators must be skilled at both informing and inspiring. They must be able to hold their own with hostile audiences as well as impress content experts and instill confidence in novices. They must be skilled at building consensus, pointing out new directions, and explaining complex topics. This exercise, adapted from Richard Linowes, provides an opportunity to practice speaking on a variety of leadership topics.

Assignment

To practice playing this important leadership role, prepare a talk and a memo on one of the following topics. Your speech should last from three to five minutes, unless you are otherwise instructed. Your memo should not exceed two pages. Create a context for your communication by assuming a management role in a familiar organization. Before beginning, explain the details of the context to your audience (either orally or in a written summary). Briefly explain your organizational position, the makeup of the audience, and their expectations of your presentation. (For the memo, attach a one-page background statement.) The specific content of your communication is less important than how well it is prepared and how persuasively it is delivered. Prepare to respond to questions and challenges.

In preparing your presentation, review the behavioral guidelines at the end of the Skill Learning section. The checklist in this exercise may also be useful. You will receive feedback based on the criteria shown in the Observer's Feedback Form.

Topics for Leadership Talks

1. **Taking Charge of an Established Group.** The speaker is a manager newly assigned to a group that has worked together under other managers for some time.
2. **Announcing a New Project.** The speaker is announcing a new undertaking to members of his or her department and is calling on all to rally behind the effort.
3. **Calling for Better Customer Service.** The speaker is motivating all employees to be as attentive and responsive as possible to customers.
4. **Calling for Excellence and High-Quality Work.** The speaker is motivating all employees to perform their jobs with a commitment to meeting the highest possible standards.
5. **Announcing the Need for Cost Reductions.** The speaker is requesting that everyone look for ways to cut expenditures and immediately begin to slash spending.
6. **Commending a Job Well Done.** The speaker is extolling a group of people who have worked very hard for an extended period to produce outstanding results.
7. **Calming a Frightened Group of People.** The speaker is endeavoring to restore calm and confidence to those who feel panic in the face of distressing business developments.

PRACTICE

8. **Addressing a Challenging Opposition.** The speaker is presenting a heartfelt belief to a critical, even hostile, audience.

9. **Mediating Between Opposing Parties.** The speaker is serving as judge or arbiter between two groups who are bitterly opposed on a key issue.

10. **Taking Responsibility for Error.** The speaker is a spokesperson for an institution whose actions have produced an unfortunate result that affects the audience.

11. **Reprimanding Unacceptable Behavior.** The speaker is taking to task certain individuals who have failed to perform up to required levels.

12. **Petitioning for Special Allowances.** The speaker is presenting the case for an institution seeking certain rights that must be authorized by some external body.

Checklist for Developing Effective Presentations

1. What are my general and specific objectives?
2. What is the context of my communication? (My audience, the situation, etc.)
3. How will I open and close the communication?
4. How will I organize my information?
5. How will I get and keep the attention of my audience?
6. What supporting materials will I use?
7. What visual aids (graphs, charts, objects, etc.) will I use?
8. How will I tailor the presentation to this audience?
9. What format will I use in my presentation?
10. What questions or responses will likely occur?

Quality Circles at Battle Creek Foods

One of the newest innovations in group decision making, quality circles (QCs), has recently received considerable attention among U.S. manufacturers. Their interest in this technique stems from its having been described by the Japanese as critical to their recent manufacturing success. Ironically, Edward Deming, an American, first brought the notion of "statistical quality control," a management tool, to the Japanese in the early post–World War II years. The Japanese combined these ideas with the assumption that the person who performs a job is the one who best knows how to identify and correct its problems. As a result, the Japanese, with Deming's help, developed the "quality circle." A quality circle is a group of people (usually about 10) who meet periodically to discuss and develop solutions to problems related to quality, productivity, or product cost.

The purpose of this exercise is to give you an opportunity to make a presentation on this important topic.

Assignment

You are the director of personnel at Battle Creek Foods, a leading manufacturer of breakfast cereal. Productivity has been sagging industrywide, and your organization is starting to see its effect on profitability. In response, you have been asked by the corporate executive committee to make a 20-minute oral presentation (or prepare a five-page memo) on quality circles. The committee has heard that QCs have been initiated at several plants by your leading competitor, and it would like your recommendation as to whether Battle Creek Foods should follow suit. The committee's only previous exposure to QCs is what each member has read in the popular press. Using the following reference material, prepare a presentation on quality circles. Explain the QC structure and process, and the advantages and disadvantages of QCs. The final section of the presentation should include a recommendation regarding their adoption at your plants. Prepare to respond to questions and challenges.

In preparing your presentation, refer to the behavioral guidelines for effective presentations at the end of the Skill Learning section and the checklist in the preceding exercise. You will receive feedback based on the Observer's Feedback Form.

A Look at Some of the Evidence

Quality circles, on balance, appear to be making a positive contribution to product quality, profits, morale, and even improved employee attendance (DuBrin, 1985, pp. 174–185). The widespread attention QCs have received in recent years has led logically to their evaluation by both businesspeople and researchers. Here we will rely on several types of evaluation methods, sampling first the positive evidence, and then the negative.

Favorable Outcomes with QCs

Honeywell, a high-technology electronics firm, has become a pioneer in the application of QCs in North America. Honeywell currently operates several hundred QCs in the United States. Typically, about a half-dozen assembly workers are brought together every two weeks by a first-level supervisor or team leader. "We feel that this type of participatory management program not only increases productivity," says Joseph Riordan, director of Honeywell Corporate Productivity Services, "but it also upgrades the quality of work life for employees. Line workers feel that they are more a part of the action. As a result, we find that the quality of work improves and absenteeism is reduced. With this kind of involvement, we have, in many cases, been able to increase the capacity of a line without the addition of tooling or extra shifts."

Honeywell used the quality circle method to manage the problem of winning a renewable bid for a government contract. "Here was a situation," Riordan relates, "where we already had cut our rejects down, where all of the learning had effectively gone out of the process." The problem was assigned to the quality circle representing that particular work area. "They came up with a suggestion for further automating the process that enabled us to improve our competitive position by about 20 percent and win the contract."

In an attempt to determine the appropriateness of QCs to North American firms, a team of researchers set up a one-year field experiment at a metal fabricating facility of an electronics firm.

Eleven quality circles, averaging nine production employees each, were established. Performance was measured by a computerized monitoring system created from the company's existing employee performance reporting system. Both quantity and quality measurements were taken. Employee attitudes were also assessed, using the Motivating Potential Score (MPS) of the Hackman-Oldham Job Diagnostic Survey.

The major result of the circle program was its positive impact on reject rate, as shown in the top half of Figure A.3. Reject rates per capita for quality circle participants dropped by one-third to one-half of the former rates by the time the program had run three months. Surprisingly, the reject rates for the control group increased during the same period.

An explanation offered by the researchers for these results is that circle members tackled the issues of internal communication as a top priority item. For example, one of the initial projects implemented by the QCs was improving training manuals and procedures, including translating materials into a worker's native language if the worker desired. Careful attention to better training in fundamentals prevented many errors.

Circle members also made fewer errors. In addition, the defective parts the circle members did make tended to be less expensive to scrap or rework into usable parts. The explanation given for these results is that circle training instructs employees how to

PRACTICE

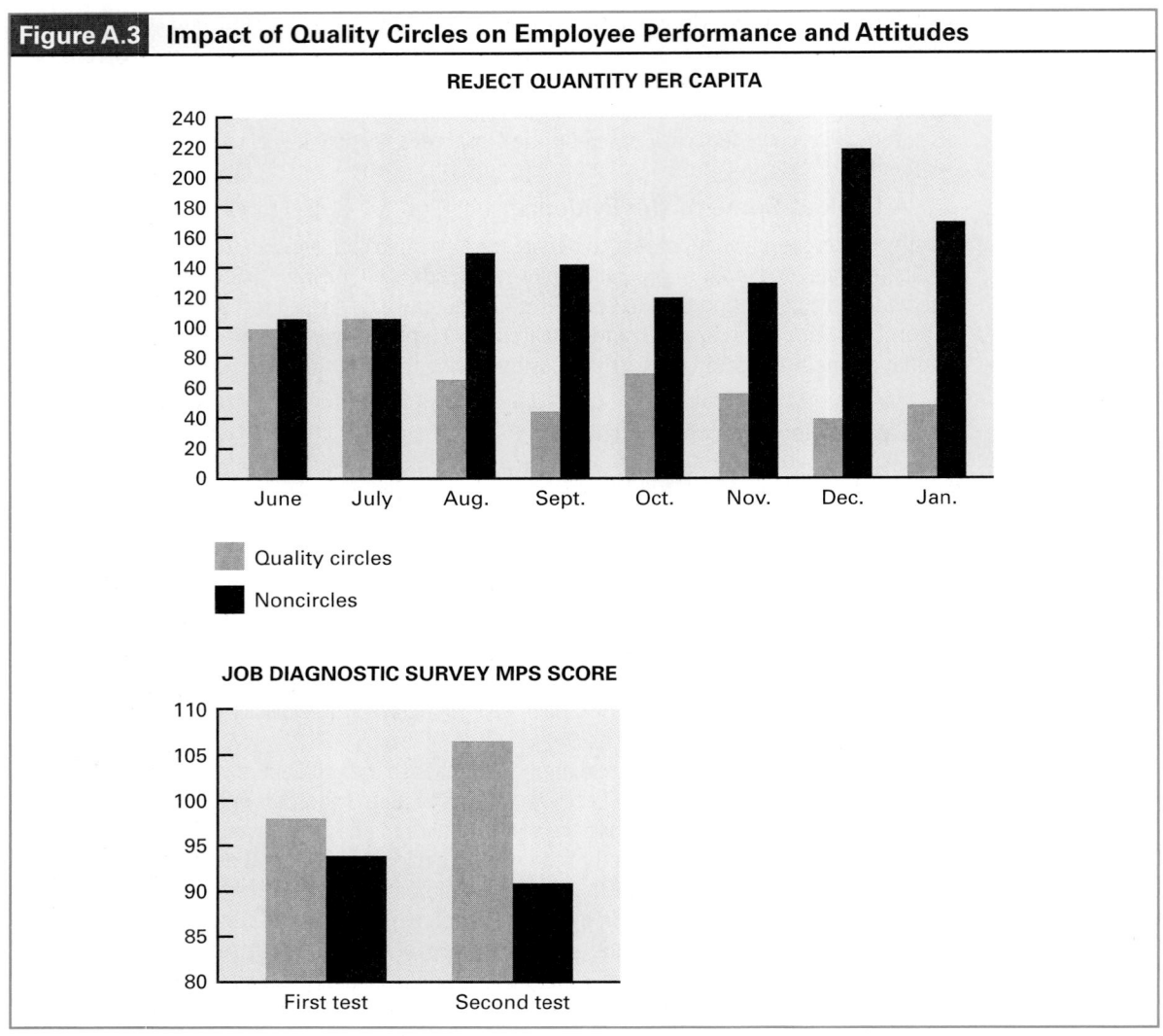

Figure A.3 Impact of Quality Circles on Employee Performance and Attitudes

REJECT QUANTITY PER CAPITA

Quality circles
Noncircles

JOB DIAGNOSTIC SURVEY MPS SCORE

prioritize problems on the basis of dollar impact on the company. The cost savings generated by the lower reject rate represented a 300 percent return on the cost of investment in the program.

The impact of QCs on participants' level of work satisfaction was equally impressive. Results shown in Figure A.3 indicate that the Motivating Potential Score (MPS) for the circle participants increased, while the control group showed a decrease. No other changes were present in the work environment that would impact the experimental group differently than the control group. The researchers therefore concluded that the improvement in employee job attitudes could be attributed to the circle training program and the problem-solving activity. The job characteristic most influenced by the quality activity was skill variety: the extent to which a job requires a variety of skills.

Negative Outcomes with Quality Circles

Despite the favorable outcomes reported, many negative results have also been reported. A review of the results of the first surge of QC activity in the United States revealed that as many as 75 percent of initially successful programs were no longer in operation after a few years. Even Lockheed, one of the American pioneers in this method, had decreased its involvement with quality circles. Robert Cole, a recognized authority on the Japanese workforce, made these pessimistic remarks:

> [The] fact is that the circles do not work very well in many Japanese companies. Even in those plants recognized as having the best operating programs, management knows that perhaps only one-third of the circles are working well, with another third borderline, and one-third simply making no contribution at all. For all of the rhetoric of voluntarism, in a number of companies the workers clearly perceive circle activity as coercive. Japanese companies face a continuing struggle to revitalize circle activity to ensure that it does not degenerate into ritualistic behavior.

A study of quality circles in 29 companies, conducted by Matthew Goodfellow, found only eight of them to be cost-effective in terms of gains in productivity. Management consultant Woodruff Imberman investigated the 21 unsuccessful QC efforts and found four major causes of failure. First, in many firms, the employees intensely disliked management. Their antagonism carried over into the quality circles, which some employees perceived to be a management ploy to reduce overtime and trim the workforce by increasing productivity.

Second, most organizations did a poor job of selling the QCs. Instead of conducting individual discussions with employees, they relied on flip charts, booklets, and formal management presentations. The workers were left wondering, "What's in it for me?"

Third, the supervisors chosen to lead the circles received some training in human relations and group dynamics, but they felt that little of this information satisfied the specific needs of their own departments.

Fourth, most of the 21 firms regarded the QC programs merely as a way of improving the efficiency of production techniques. They did not realize that QCs cannot succeed unless top management is willing to shift its philosophy toward emphasizing good relations among employees and between management and workforce. This last point hints at the importance of establishing the conditions that allow a quality circle program to succeed.

Key Elements of a Successful Program

Quality circle programs show some variation from company to company, whether these companies are engaged in manufacturing or service. They may differ in how frequently they meet, how much authority is granted to the team leader or supervisor, whether they use a group facilitator in addition to a supervisor, and how much coordination there is with the existing quality-control department. Based on the judgments of several observers, the successful programs have certain elements in common.

Quality circles work best in firms where good employee–management relations already exist. QCs are not likely to succeed in organizations suffering from acrimonious union–management conflict or high levels of distrust between employees and management.

Top management is committed to the program. Without commitment from top management, the initiation of a QC program is inadvisable. Instead, the director of a circle project should first prepare reports on other companies where QCs have been successful and present them to top management.

Circle leaders use a participative leadership style. Laurie Fitzgerald, a QC consultant, advocates the "leader as a worker for the members" concept. When the circle leader takes on a highly authoritarian role, the members are usually unresponsive.

The right people and the right area are selected. For quality circles to be effective, the program manager has to be enthusiastic, persistent, and hardworking. The facilitator or team leader must be energetic and cooperative. Also, another important step in getting the program off the ground is to select an area of the company where one can expect cooperation and enthusiasm from participants.

Program goals are stated explicitly. Objectives should be made clear in order to avoid confusion or unreasonable expectations from the circle program. Among the goals of QC programs are improving product quality, increasing productivity, improving communications between workers and supervisors, decreasing product costs, improving the quality of work life, and preparing people for future supervisory assignments.

The program is well publicized throughout the firm. Once the program is started, information about it should be disseminated widely throughout the company. Better communication results in less resistance and fewer negative rumors about the program. The content of the communication should be open and positive.

The program starts slowly and grows slowly. A gradual introduction of the program helps expose people to new concepts and helps reduce doubts about its intention and potential merit.

The QC program is customized to meet the needs of the firm. A subtle source of failure in some QC programs is the use of a canned set of procedures that don't fit local circumstances. A QC participant whose work is data processing may have difficulty with the translation of a case from the aerospace industry. A workable compromise is to use standard training as a framework and build on it with the unique problems of the firm in question.

Quality circles are used as a method of employee development. A key purpose of these circles is to foster personal development of the participating workers. If managers intend to install a QC as a tool for their own selfish gain, they would do better not to begin.

Management is willing to grant recognition for ideas originating in the circles. If management attempts to manipulate the circle volunteers or take away from them the credit for improvements, the program most likely will backfire. More will be lost than gained.

Membership is voluntary. As with job enrichment and all forms of participative management, employee preference is an influential factor. Employees who desire to contribute their ideas will generally perform better than employees who are arbitrarily assigned to a QC.

Achievements of quality circles are recognized as results of group, not individual, effort. Recognizing them as such decreases showboating and competitiveness and increases cooperation and interdependence within the group or department. Quality circles, not individual employees, receive credit for innovations and suggestions for improvement.

Ample training is provided. Program volunteers generally need some training in conference techniques or group dynamics. At a minimum, the circle leader will need skills in group participation methods. Otherwise, he or she will wind up lecturing about topics such as quality improvement and productivity improvement. Leaders and participants will also need training in the use of whatever statistical and problem-solving methods are to be used. Following are eight major problem-solving techniques and their purposes.

1. Brainstorming is used to identify all problems, even those beyond the control of circle members.
2. A check-sheet is used to log problems within the circle's sphere of influence within a certain time frame.
3. A Pareto chart graphically illustrates check-sheet data to identify the most serious problems; that is, the 20 percent of the problems that cause 80 percent of the major mistakes.

4. A cause-and-effect diagram graphically illustrates the cause of a particular problem.

5. Histograms or bar charts are graphed to show the frequency and magnitude of specific problems.

6. Scatter diagrams or "measles charts" identify major defect locations, which show up as dense dot clusters on the pictures of products.

7. Graph-and-control charts monitor a production process and are compared with production samples.

8. Stratification, generally accomplished by inspecting the same products from different production areas, randomizes the sampling process.

Creativity is encouraged. As illustrated above, brainstorming or variations thereof fit naturally into the quality circle method and philosophy. Maintaining an attitude of "anything goes" is particularly important, even if rough ideas must be refined later. If half-processed ideas are shot down by the leader or other members, idea generation will extinguish quickly.

Projects are related to members' actual job responsibilities. Quality circles are not arenas for amateur speculation about other people's work. People make suggestions about improving the quality of work for which they are already responsible. They should, however, be willing to incorporate information from suppliers and customers.

The Arguments For and Against Quality Circles

A major argument for quality circles is that they represent a low-cost, efficient vehicle for unleashing the creative potential of employees. In the process, highly desirable ends are achieved, such as improvements in the quality of both products and work life. Quality circles, in fact, are considered part of the quality of work life movement.

Another favorable feature of these circles is that they are perceived positively by all—management, workers, the union, and stockholders. A firm contemplating implementing such a program thus runs no risk of either internal or external opposition. (It is conceivable, however, that opposition will be forthcoming if management fails to act on quality circle suggestions.)

Quality circles contribute to organizational effectiveness in another important way. They have emerged as a useful method of developing present and future managers. Recently, a major computing manufacturing firm established a quality circle program. After the program had been operating for two years, the director of training observed that the supervisors who were quality circle leaders were significantly more self-confident, knowledgeable, and poised than other supervisors who were attending the regular training program. The director believed that the supervisors' involvement in the QC training programs and activities had been the major contributor to this difference.

One major criticism of quality circles is that many of them are not cost-effective. Furthermore, even more pessimistic is the criticism that the reported successes of QCs may be attributable to factors other than the actual quality circle program. One explanation is that the attention paid to employees by management may be the force behind the gains in productivity and morale (the well-known Hawthorne effect). Another possible explanation of the successes of quality circle programs is that the gains are due to improved group dynamics and problem-solving techniques. Therefore, an entire QC program need not be conducted just to achieve these gains.

A discouraging argument has been advanced that quality circles may not be suited to North American workers. Matsushita Electric, a leading user of the quality circle method in Japan, does not use circles in its U.S. plant (located in Chicago) because it does not consider the American worker suited to circle activities. Perhaps Matsushita management believes that Americans are too self-oriented to be group oriented.

Quality circles may prove to be breeding grounds for friction and role confusion between the quality-control department and the groups themselves. Unless management carefully defines the relationship of quality circles vis-à-vis the quality-control department, much duplication of effort (and therefore waste of resources) will inevitably result.

Exclusive reliance upon volunteers for the circles may result in the loss of potentially valuable ideas. Many nonassertive people may shy away from participation in the circles despite their having valid ideas for product improvement.

Some employees who volunteer to join quality circles may do so for the wrong reasons. The circle may develop the reputation of being "a good way to get away from the line for a while and enjoy a coffee break and a good bull session." (To counter such an abuse of the quality-circle program, QC group members might monitor the quality of input from their own group members.)

Guidelines for Action

An early strategic step in implementing a quality circle is to clarify relationships between the circle and the formal quality-control department. Otherwise, the quality-control department may perceive the circle as a redundancy or threat. One effective arrangement is for the quality circle to complement the quality-control department; the QC department thus does not become subject to the loss of authority.

Membership in the circle should be voluntary and on a rotating basis. In many instances, a team member will soon run out of fresh ideas for quality improvement. Rotating membership will result in a wider sampling of ideas being generated. Experience suggests that group size should be limited to nine.

Quality circles should be implemented on a pilot basis. As the circle produces results and wins the acceptance of managers and employees alike, it can be expanded as the demand for its output increases.

Do not emphasize quick financial returns or productivity increases from the output of the quality circles. The program should be seen as a long-range project that will raise the quality consciousness of the organization. (Nevertheless, as noted in the report from Honeywell, immediate positive results are often forthcoming.)

Management must make good use of many of the suggestions coming from the quality circle yet still define the limits of the power and authority of the circle. On the one hand, if none of the circle's suggestions is adopted, the circle will lose its effectiveness as an agent for change. Circle members will become discouraged because of their lack of clout. On the other hand, if the circle has too much power and authority, it will be seen as a governing body for technical change. Under the latter circumstances, people may use the circle for political purposes. An individual who wants to get a technical modification authorized may try to influence a member of the quality circle to suggest that modification during a circle meeting.

Training in group dynamics and methods of participative management will be particularly helpful. It may also prove helpful at the outset to appoint a group facilitator (an internal or external consultant) who can help the group run more smoothly.

RATING

1 = Low
5 = High

Strategy

_____ 1. Identified the general and specific purposes.

_____ 2. Tailored the message to the audience's needs, attitudes, knowledge level, and so forth.

_____ 3. Met the expectations of the audience by using appropriate language and style.

Structure

_____ 4. Began with a forecast of the main ideas and captivated the audience's interest by giving them an important reason to listen.

_____ 5. Chose an appropriate organizational structure; for example, moved from familiar to unfamiliar and simple to complex.

_____ 6. Used transitions, including internal summaries, to signal progress.

_____ 7. Concluded on a high note; reinforced major points; summarized key actions.

Support

_____ 8. Used a variety of supporting information, examples, and so forth, to increase the credibility and understanding of major points.

_____ 9. Used supporting material (both the content and format of evidence and illustrations) appropriate for the audience.

_____ 10. Used effective, simple visual aids to enhance comprehension and retention of the message.

Style in Oral Communication

_____ 11. Used notes to create a conversational style.

_____ 12. Presentation had obviously been well-rehearsed, including the use of visual aids, and so forth.

_____ 13. Conveyed controlled enthusiasm for the subject through the tone of voice, posture, and facial expressions.

_____ 14. Engaged the audience through effective eye contact, physical arrangement of the room, and appropriate gestures.

PRACTICE

Style in Written Communication

_____ 15. Document was mechanically precise; that is, it contained no errors that detracted from the message.

_____ 16. Document was factually precise; that is, the content was accurate.

_____ 17. The choice of words communicated the message clearly and unambiguously.

_____ 18. The tone matched the topic and the audience (e.g., formality, emotion, directness).

_____ 19. Used the appropriate format for the type of correspondence.

Supplement: Questions and Answers

_____ 20. Handled questions and challenges thoughtfully, candidly, and assertively.

_____ 21. Responded to objections in an orderly manner; for example, restated the objection, restated your position, offered further support for your position, and explained the significance of your rebuttal.

_____ 22. Maintained control of the meeting by balancing the demands of specific individuals with the interests of the group and keeping the discussion focused on the issues.

SKILL *LEARNING*

- Planning and Conducting Interviews
- Specific Types of Organizational Interviews
- Summary and Behavioral Guidelines

SKILL *PRACTICE* ◆

- Evaluating the New Employee-Orientation Program
- Performance Appraisal Interview with Chris Jakobsen
- Employment Selection Interview at Smith Farley Insurance

Conducting Interviews

SKILL DEVELOPMENT OBJECTIVES

- ADOPT GENERAL GUIDELINES FOR EFFECTIVE INTERVIEWS
- APPLY APPROPRIATE GUIDELINES FOR INFORMATION-GATHERING INTERVIEWS
- UTILIZE APPROPRIATE GUIDELINES FOR EMPLOYMENT-SELECTION INTERVIEWS
- IMPLEMENT APPROPRIATE GUIDELINES FOR PERFORMANCE-APPRAISAL INTERVIEWS

SKILL *LEARNING*

Planning and Conducting Interviews

Except for conversations, interviews are perhaps the most frequently occurring form of communication (Sincoff & Goyer, 1984); they certainly occur regularly in organizations. Individuals interview to obtain a position; they interview to gather information to perform their jobs; and managers interview subordinates to review their performance and provide counseling and coaching.

Interviews are so common that they are often taken for granted. People view interviews as simply conversations during which information is gathered. While interviews are similar to conversations, there are important differences. An **interview** is a specialized form of communication conducted for a specific task-related purpose (Downs, Smeyak, & Martin, 1980; Lopez, 1975). Indeed, one reason why some managers perform poorly as interviewers is that they treat this "purposeful communication" too casually, as though it were merely a conversation. As a result of poor planning and lack of attention to managing the interview process, they fail to accomplish their purpose and often alienate the interviewee in the process.

These outcomes are illustrated in the following counseling interview between Joe Van Orden, director of management services, and Kyle Isenbarger, a management consultant on his staff (DuBrin, 1981).

JOE: Kyle, I have scheduled this meeting with you because I want to talk about certain aspects of your work. My comments are not all that favorable.

KYLE: Since you have formal authority over me, I guess I don't have much choice. Go ahead.

JOE: I'm not a judge reading a verdict to you. I want your input.

KYLE: But you called the meeting; go ahead with your complaints. Particularly any with foundation. I remember once when we were having lunch you told me that you didn't like the fact that I wore a brown suit with a blue shirt. I would put that in the category of unfounded.

JOE: I'm glad you brought up appearance. I think you present a substandard impression to clients. A consultant is supposed to look sharp, particularly at the rates we charge clients. You often present the impression that you cannot afford good clothing. Your pants are baggy. Your ties are unstylish and often foodstained.

KYLE: The firm may charge those high rates, but the money I receive does not allow me to purchase fancy clothing. Besides, I have very little interest in trying to dazzle clients with my clothing. I have heard no complaints from them.

JOE: Nevertheless, I think that your appearance should be more businesslike. Now, let's talk about another concern. A routine audit of your expense account shows a practice that I think is improper. You charged one client for a Thursday night dinner for three consecutive weeks, yet your airline ticket receipt shows that you returned home at three in the afternoon each week. That kind of behavior is unprofessional. How do you explain your charges for these phantom dinners?

KYLE: The flight ticket may say 3 P.M., but with our unpredictable weather, the flight could very well be delayed. If I eat at the airport, then my wife won't have to run the risk of preparing a dinner for me that goes to waste. Food is very expensive.

JOE: But how can you eat dinner at 3 P.M. at the airport?

KYLE: I consider any meal after one in the afternoon to be dinner.

JOE: Okay for now. I want to comment on your reports to clients. They are much more careless than they should be. I know that you are capable of more meticulous work. I saw an article you prepared for publication that was first-rate and professional. Yet on one report you misspelled the name of the client company. That's unacceptable.

KYLE: A good secretary should have caught that mistake. Besides, I never claimed that I was able to write perfect reports. There are only so many hours in the working day to spend on writing up reports.

Effective interviews don't just happen. Like other purposeful communication activities, interviews must be properly planned and executed. To help you become an effective interviewer, this supplement includes a series of guidelines, organized according to the schema shown in Figure B.1. First, we present broad guidelines for planning and conducting interviews in general. These guidelines are divided into two steps: planning the interview and conducting the interview. Following this discussion, we will give more specific guidelines for conducting specialized interviews with limited purposes: gathering information, selecting new employees, and reviewing subordinate performance.

PLANNING THE INTERVIEW
Establish the Purpose and Agenda

As is the case with any kind of planned communication event, you need to define clearly your purpose for holding the interview. In an interview, as in an oral presentation, ask yourself what it is you want to accomplish. Do you want to gather information? Persuade? Counsel? Evaluate? Not only do you need to consider what you want to accomplish in terms of the *content* of the interview, you must also consider the *relationship* you want to develop with the other participant. Consider who your interview partner is and how what you say will affect the already existing relationship. This resembles the process of adapting your message to your audience in an oral presentation but is somewhat easier since there is only one member in your interview "audience." Also consider the situation in which the interview will occur. Are participants under pressures of deadlines? Can you arrange not to be interrupted?

Once you've determined your purpose, develop an agenda. Consider what kinds of information you need to obtain with respect to your purpose. Based on this, write out a list of topics that need to be covered in the interview. While these topics do not have to be listed in any particular order, you may want to prioritize them.

Create Good Questions That Encourage Information Sharing

Questions arise out of your purpose and agenda and are the fundamental means by which you obtain information in an interview. Any interviewer can ask questions; only well-prepared interviewers ask effective questions—ones that elicit the information they need. Make sure that the questions are worded clearly and that they ask for the information you want. Adapting to your interviewee is critical. Phrase your questions in language the interviewee can understand and in ways that will enhance your relationship with that person.

Different types of questions can be used for different effects and different types of information-gathering purposes. **Open questions** such as, "How is your work going?" or "How has the new regulation affected department morale?" elicit general information. Use open questions when you want to let the interviewee talk without restriction. They allow interviewees freedom to discuss how they feel, what their priorities are, and how much they know about a topic. Thus, open questions are useful for developing rapport. Remembering the answers to open questions is a problem, particularly if the interviewee talks on and on. Open questions are also time-consuming, and using them too often makes it difficult for the interviewer to control the interview. However, if you are looking for broad, general information, ask open questions.

If, on the other hand, you need specific information, ask closed questions. **Closed questions** such as, "Where were you last employed?" or "Would you rather work on Project A or Project Z?" restrict the possible answers an interviewee can give. They are appropriate when you have limited time or want to clarify a point made in an answer to an open question. Table B.1 suggests when to use open or closed questions.

Figure B.1 Guidelines for Effective Interviews

Follow General Guidelines for:
• Planning the interview
• Conducting the interview

Incorporate Specific Guidelines for:
• Information-gathering interview
• Performance-appraisal interview
• Employment-selection interview

Table B.1	When to Use Open and Closed Questions

Use open questions when you want to:

- Discover the interviewee's priorities.
- Discover the interviewee's frame of reference.
- Let the interviewee talk through his or her opinions without constraints.
- Ascertain the depth of the interviewee's knowledge.
- Ascertain how articulate the interviewee is.

Use closed questions when you want to:

- Save time, energy, and money.
- Maintain control over the interview situation.
- Obtain very specific information from the interviewee.
- Encourage the interviewee to reconstruct a specific event.
- Encourage a shy person to talk.
- Avoid extensive explanations on the part of the interviewee.
- Clarify a point made in answer to an open question.

Source: *Adapted from Downs, Smeyak, & Martin, 1980.*

As you plan your questions, pay close attention to how the questions are worded. Often, an unprepared interviewer will ask questions that are difficult to answer or prevent open, honest answers. One example is the **double-barreled question**:

- ❏ If there's anything that would make you stay, what would it be?
- ❏ If you had no choice but to use this system, how would you use it productively?
- ❏ Why should we adopt this insurance plan when none of our competitors has adopted it?

Each of these questions assumes a condition that the interviewee may not agree with but then calls for the interviewee to support or defend the condition. The first question assumes the interviewee is looking for a reason to stay; the second assumes the system can be used productively; the third suggests something is wrong with the plan. Such questions may lead to hypothetical answers that don't reflect the interviewee's honest position.

Another potentially problematic question is the **false bipolar question**. A bipolar question offers the interviewee two choices: "Did you vote yes or no on the union contract?" This can be a legitimate and appropriate question. However, suppose you asked this question: "Do you approve or disapprove of overtime

work?" Most people do not totally approve or disapprove of overtime work; yet this question forces interviewees to choose from limited, or false, options, neither of which likely represents their true stand on the issue. Thus, if you use bipolar questions, make sure that the options you offer are the only two possible options; otherwise, you will obtain inaccurate information.

A final type of problematic questions is the **leading question**, in which you let the interviewee know the answer you want to hear by how you phrase the question:

- ❏ Don't you think that using this plan will alleviate the problems we've been having?
- ❏ Are you in favor of this policy like all your coworkers?
- ❏ Of course, you want the best for your family, don't you?

It would not take an astute interviewee very long to figure out what you wanted to hear, and so you are likely to get biased responses. Leading questions can be useful when a biased answer is intended and desired. For instance, the question "Of course you want the best for your family, don't you?" would be useful in a sales interview if the interviewer tries to persuade a potential buyer to buy a set of encyclopedias. However, if you do not realize that you have asked a leading question, you will not know whether you are receiving a biased answer, which can create a serious problem. Table B.2 offers ways to reword these three types of badly constructed questions.

Structure the Interview Using Interviewing Aids

After determining the purpose and agenda, and after formulating your questions, the next step in preparing for an interview is to develop a structure. To do this, you need to think about three things: the interview guide, the questioning sequence, and transitions. The interview guide is an outline of the topics and subtopics you want to cover, usually with specific questions listed under each heading. In other words, it is the finalized version of the agenda. Alternative interview guide formats will be discussed later.

While you are constructing the interview guide, you will also need to be concerned with the sequence of questions; that is, how they will interconnect. The two most common types of question sequences are the **funnel sequence** and the **inverted funnel sequence**.

The funnel sequence begins with general questions and then moves toward increasingly specific questions. The inverted funnel sequence reverses this order,

Table B.2 Rewording Badly Constructed Questions

DOUBLE-BARRELED QUESTION	PROBLEM	BETTER QUESTION
1. If there's anything that would make you stay, what would it be?	The question ignores the reason behind the interviewee's decision and implies it can be changed.	Why do you want to leave our organization? (Let interviewee respond.) Is there anything I can do to change your mind?
2. If you had no choice but to use this system, how would you use it productively?	The question avoids an open analysis of the system and forces the interviewee to defend it.	What do you feel are the benefits of this system? (Let interviewee respond.) What do you feel are the disadvantages of this system?
3. Why should we adopt this insurance plan when none of our competitors has adopted it?	The question raises a suspicion that something is wrong with the plan and urges the interviewee to put the suspicion to rest rather than to evaluate the plan.	Do you think we should adopt this insurance? (Let interviewee respond.) Do you think that it offers us new benefits? (Let interviewee respond.) Have any of our competitors adopted it?
FALSE BIPOLAR QUESTION	**PROBLEM**	**BETTER QUESTION**
1. Do you prefer working with people or working alone?	The question assumes that there are only two possible choices.	Do you work well with other people? (Can be followed with appropriate probe.)
2. Do you approve or disapprove of the union contract?	The question assumes that there are only two ways to view the issue.	What are your feelings concerning the union contract?
LEADING QUESTION	**PROBLEM**	**BETTER QUESTION**
1. Don't you think that using this plan will alleviate the problems we've been having?	The question identifies the expected answer, making it difficult for the interviewee to disagree.	Do you think this plan will be useful in alleviating the problems we've been having?
2. Are you in favor of this policy like all your coworkers?	The question places interviewee in the position of siding with the "right" side.	What is your attitude toward this policy?
3. Of course, you want the best for your family, don't you?	The question associates response with a desirable goal (getting the best for the family), making it difficult for the interviewee to say no.	This product offers you some real advantages. Could I take some of your time to tell you about them?

Table B.3	Funnel and Inverted Funnel Question Sequences

Funnel: From General to Specific

How do you feel about the new regulations concerning smoking in the building?

Are these regulations fair?

How are these regulations curtailing smoking among employees?

Inverted Funnel: From Specific to General

How are these regulations curtailing smoking among employees?

Do you think the new smoking regulations are fair?

In general, how do you feel about these new regulations?

Use the funnel sequence when:

• You want to discover the interviewee's frame of reference.

• You want to avoid leading the interviewee.

• You want to maximize your ability to probe issues.

• The interviewee is willing to talk about the issues.

Use the interverted funnel sequence when:

• You want to get at specific facts before general reactions.

• You want to motivate a reluctant interviewee.

• You want to jog the interviewee's memory.

Source: *Adapted from Downs et al., 1980.*

beginning with specific questions and moving toward more open questions toward the end. Table B.3 shows examples of these two sequences. Your choice of which sequence to use depends on what you want to accomplish in the interview. Table B.3 also summarizes when you should use each of these sequences, depending on your goals.

After establishing the sequence of your questions, you should consider what kinds of transitions you can use to help the interviewee follow along. The transitions in an interview perform the same function as transitions in an oral presentation: They help listeners maintain focus and keep them aware of where the speaker is in terms of the overall organization. Transitions are difficult to prepare ahead in unstructured interviews, yet a good interviewer will keep in mind that transitions should be used when a topic change occurs. A simple statement such as, "I see what you're saying about that situation. Do you think you could help me with another issue?" allows you to move from one topic into the next. You may also use a brief summary of the interviewee's responses to wrap up one topic before moving to the next one.

Plan the Setting to Enhance Rapport

The interview location can have a major impact on the interview atmosphere and interview outcome. If you hold the interview in your office or an organizational meeting room, you will create a formal atmosphere. On the other hand, if you conduct the interview in a more neutral area, such as a restaurant, the climate will be more relaxed. The choice of setting depends on your goals for the interview. The most important point to remember about the setting is that, if at all possible, you should try to hold the interview in a setting that will be conducive to encouraging the kind of communication you seek.

Anticipate Problems and Prepare Responses

As you prepare for an interview, you should consider what kinds of problems you might encounter. Imagine how the interviewee might respond to what you have to ask, and prepare for his or her objections and questions. Consider the personality of the interviewee and how you might have to adapt to either draw the person out or to control his or her tendency to dominate. Anticipate how much time you will need to ask your questions and how much time your interviewee has to give you. Each interview will offer unique problems. If you can plan for some of these situations, you will be able to handle them better during the actual interview than if you had not considered them at all.

Table B.4 provides a checklist for helping prepare for an interview.

CONDUCTING THE INTERVIEW

Couple thorough preparation with sensitive implementation. Because an interview is an interpersonal communication situation, in this section we will first briefly review the concept of supportive communication as it applies to interviews. Then we will look at the three stages of the interview—the introduction, body, and conclusion—and discuss the functions of each. We will offer suggestions for developing the necessary skills to conduct an interview effectively. Finally, we will discuss ways of recording the interview information.

Establish and Maintain a Supportive Communication Climate

The climate of the interview refers to the tone of the interview and the general atmosphere in which the interview occurs. An interview, like any other interpersonal communication event, should be a supportive interaction, one in which participants feel free to communicate accurately. As the interviewer, you set the climate of the interview in the introduction when you begin to build rapport with the interviewee. In general, you should seek to build a comfortable, open climate, free of incongruence. Maintaining a supportive and productive climate requires that you constantly analyze and adapt to the interaction as it occurs. When you sense that the climate is no longer supportive, move away from the content level of the interview and address the relational level. Consider this excerpt from an information-gathering interview:

> INTERVIEWER: Thanks for taking the time to speak with me today.
>
> INTERVIEWEE: Oh, it's no problem at all. What can I do for you?
>
> INTERVIEWER: Well, I was wondering if you could tell me a little about the incident that occurred on the shop floor last week. First, do you have any idea how it started?
>
> INTERVIEWEE: No, not really. I was doing my job and then, all of a sudden, the two of them were at it.
>
> INTERVIEWER: I see. You didn't hear them talking before they began to fight?
>
> INTERVIEWEE: No. Like I said, it seemed to start out of the blue.
>
> INTERVIEWER: Weren't you paying attention?
>
> INTERVIEWEE: How was I to know they were going to fight?!

Table B.4	Interview Preparation Checklist
1. Have I determined my general purpose?	
2. Have I written out my specific purposes and agenda?	
a. Do I know exactly what I want to accomplish in terms of content?	
b. Do I know exactly what I want to accomplish in terms of the relationship with the interviewee?	
3. Do my questions all relate to my purposes and agenda?	
4. Are my questions clearly worded in language the interviewee can understand?	
5. Are my questions worded in an unbiased manner?	
6. Have I chosen an appropriate interview structure for the situation?	
7. Have I chosen an appropriate question sequence for the interview situation?	
8. Have I developed potential transitions to be used in the interview?	
9. Have I chosen a physical setting suited to the topics and the interviewee?	
10. Have I planned ways to deal with problems that could develop during the interview?	

By now, the questions are obviously beginning to irritate the interviewee. The interviewer has continued to probe an issue that the interviewee seems to think has already been covered sufficiently. The interviewer should move away from this one point and attempt to ease the interviewee's discomfort before continuing.

> INTERVIEWER: You're right. You really weren't in a position to anticipate this situation. Perhaps, though, you could describe to me what happened after the fight.

At this point, the interviewee may be hesitant to disclose fully. The interviewer may have to continue to strengthen relational support until the interviewee appears to be comfortable in answering the questions.

A supportive climate is not maintained solely by verbal behaviors. Listening analytically is also essential to maintaining the climate of an interview. If you do not show that you are listening and responding to what the interviewee is saying, he or she will not want to continue talking with you. In general, you should listen for *comprehension* of the content of the interview, for *empathy* with the interviewee, and for *evaluation* of information and feelings (Stewart & Cash, 1985).

Introduce the Interview

Supportive communication begins immediately in the introduction, where you establish the tone and set the climate of the interview. You should greet the interviewee in such a way as to build positive rapport. The impressions created in the initial minutes of an interview are crucial to its success (Stewart & Cash, 1985). Therefore, you should try to convey as favorable an impression as possible. After the greeting, you need to motivate the interviewee to participate willingly in the interview. Some common ways of doing this are to ask for the interviewee's help or tell the interviewee why he or she was chosen as a source of information. Finally, the introduction should contain an orientation to the total interview. You should tell an interviewee: (1) the purpose of the interview, (2) how he or she will help meet that purpose, and (3) how the information obtained during the interview will be used. The introduction should end with a transition into the body of the interview. Using a transition statement, such as, "Now then, let me begin by asking . . . " or "Now that you understand what's going to happen during the next few minutes, let's move on to the questions" tells the interviewee that the "real" interview is about to begin.

Conduct the Body of the Interview

Generally, the body of the interview will follow your interview guide, which is a predetermined sequence of questions. There are three types of guides: structured, semistructured, and unstructured. If the interview guide is structured, you will simply read the questions on the guide and record the interviewee's answers. A semistructured guide lists several recommended questions under each topic. The interviewer then selects the most appropriate questions for a specific candidate. A sample interview guide for a semistructured employment interview is shown in Table B.5.

If the interview guide is unstructured, then you will use the guide only as an agenda. For example, an unstructured interview guide for a termination interview might simply list a few general topics for discussion, for example, "What did he or she like and dislike about the work and the company?" "Why is he or she leaving?" "Any suggestions for improvement?" Particularly in an unstructured interview, an interviewee will need encouragement to answer your questions as fully as possible. In order to encourage complete answers, you will need to follow his or her initial responses with probing questions. Probing well depends directly on your ability to listen well and analyze the content and relational information the interviewee offers you. Probing questions are rarely planned ahead because you cannot predict how the interviewee will respond to your questions. You will want to probe when you feel that, for whatever reason, you are receiving an inadequate response to your question.

The kind of probing you do will depend on the responses given by your interviewee and the kind of information you are looking for. If you feel that the response is superficial or inadequate due to lack of information, you should use an **elaboration probe**, such as:

- ❑ "Tell me more about that issue."
- ❑ "Why do you suppose it happened that way?"
- ❑ "Was there anything else going on at the time?"

If you need to clarify the information given by the interviewee, use a **clarification probe**, such as:

- ❑ "What does job satisfaction mean to you?"
- ❑ "You said that you are unhappy with this policy. Can you tell me specifically what aspects make you feel this way?"
- ❑ "Earlier you mentioned that you enjoyed working with people. Can you provide a specific example?"

Table B.5 — Sample Interview Questions for an Employment Interview

EDUCATION	WORK EXPERIENCE	SELF-EVALUATION
• What was there about your major that appealed to you?	• How did you obtain your current job?	• What do you know about our industry or company?
• What was your most rewarding experience in college?	• What duties occupy most of your time?	• What interests you about our product or service?
• What subjects were the most difficult for you to master? Why?	• What part of your work do you like the most and the least?	• What is your long-term career objective?
• If you were starting college all over again, what courses would you take?	• What has been your greatest frustration and your greatest joy?	• What are your greatest strengths and weaknesses?
• What difficulties did you experience in getting along with other students and faculty?	• What things about your supervisor did you like and dislike?	• What have you done that has demonstrated initiative and willingness to work hard?
• What did you learn from your extracurricular activities?	• What criticisms of your work have you received?	• What do you think determines a person's progress in a good company?
		• What are your plans for self-improvement during this year?
		• What are the three most important things in your life?

A **reflective probe** is also used when you want elaboration or clarification. It is nondirective in nature and generally mirrors or repeats some aspect of the answer the interviewee just gave you:

❏ "You think, then, that this policy will work?"

❏ "Are you saying that your supervisor doesn't offer the kind of supervision you need?"

❏ "Is it correct to assume that you would be willing to relocate?"

If the interviewee does not answer your question, you may need to use a **repetition probe**. Simply paraphrase the question or repeat it verbatim. If you want the interviewee to keep on talking freely, use *silence* to encourage him or her to do so. Silence tends to communicate that you expect more from the interviewee. Be careful not to wait too long, though; give an interviewee enough time to think but not enough time to become uncomfortable. Responses such as "I see," "Hmmmm," and "Okay, go on" are nondirective and nonevaluative ways of encouraging the interviewee to speak. Table B.6 summarizes these probes and when to use them.

The effective use of probing questions is perhaps the most important skill an interviewer can develop. It is also the most difficult to develop. Too often, an interviewer leaves an interview and thinks about all the things that could have been discussed if only the topic had been followed up with appropriate probes. Or perhaps the interview was ineffective because the interviewer probed into irrelevant topics and thus spent too much time gathering relatively useless information. An effective interviewer needs to learn when to probe and when to stop. If you have planned appropriately, you will be aware of the issues you want to cover and at what depth. Follow your interviewee's cues as well as your agenda in determining when and how much to probe issues.

Conclude the Interview

The third stage of the interview is the conclusion. When you conclude an interview, you should accomplish four purposes. First, be sure you indicate explicitly that the interview is about to end. Say something such as, "Well, that's all the questions I have" or "You've been very helpful." This helps the interviewee understand that if he or she has any questions, they should be asked now. Second, try to summarize the information you obtained. This serves as a check on the accuracy of the information you have just obtained: the interviewee

LEARNING

Table B.6	Types of Probes and When to Use Them

• Use an *elaboration* probe when an answer seems superficial or inadequate in some way:

INTERVIEWER: How have you been able to adapt to your new job responsibilities?

INTERVIEWEE: Well, each day I find myself challenged by something new.

INTERVIEWER: Why don't you tell me more about a specific challenge.

• Use a *clarification* probe when you need to clarify information given by the interviewee:

INTERVIEWER: How do you feel about working overtime?

INTERVIEWEE: Well, it's okay some of the time.

INTERVIEWER: Can you tell me specifically when you would be willing to work overtime?

• Use a *reflective* probe when you want elaboration or clarification but want to obtain it in a nondirective manner:

INTERVIEWER: So how are you adapting to your new responsibilities?

INTERVIEWEE: Well, each day I find myself challenged by something new.

INTERVIEWER: Really? Something new each day?

• Use a *repetition* probe when the interviewee doesn't answer your question:

INTERVIEWER: What do you believe to be the most difficult aspect of your job?

INTERVIEWEE: Well, that's not an easy question. My supervisor says I have problems with meeting productivity quotas.

INTERVIEWER: But what do *you* believe to be the most difficult aspect of your job?

• Use *silence* when you want to encourage the interviewee to continue talking:

INTERVIEWER: Do you think that we should continue our policy concerning absenteeism?

INTERVIEWEE: Yes, I do.

INTERVIEWER: (pauses for 10 seconds)

INTERVIEWEE: Yes, I think it's good policy because . . .

can correct your impressions if they seem to be in error. Third, let the interviewee know what's going to happen next: Will you need to meet again? Will you make a report? Finally, make sure you continue to build the relationship by expressing appreciation for his or her time and thoughtful responses.

Record the Information

While you may have planned the interview perfectly and asked all the right questions and probes, if you cannot remember accurately the information obtained, the interview cannot be considered a success. After all, you prepared and conducted the interview to get information, not simply because you wanted to have a conversation with someone. The first point that you need to recognize concerning remembering interview information is simple: Memory alone will not work. Relying solely on memory leaves open the possibility of forgetting the information or readjusting it to meet your own needs. Even if you summarize the interview as soon as it is over, you run the risk of reinterpreting the information in ways that the interviewee did not mean. However, if summarizing the interview is your preferred choice, make sure you write your summary immediately after the interview. Additionally, you might want to use your interview guide as a basis for summarizing: Review your questions and write out the interviewee's answers.

A better way to remember information is to take notes during the interview. Make sure you advise the interviewee that you will take notes. Take notes as unobtrusively as possible so as not to make the interviewee uncomfortable. Learn how to write notes while still maintaining eye contact with the interviewee. This is a difficult skill to master, but it can be done; journalists use this skill frequently with great success. Develop your own shorthand so that you are, in fact, taking notes and not recording the interview verbatim. If you need a verbatim account of the interview, then you should use a tape recorder. First ask the interviewee if he or she minds being tape-recorded. Keep the recorder out of sight if possible so that neither you nor the interviewee feels threatened by it. One final way to help you remember the interview information is to have a second interviewer participate in the interview. After the interview, your discussion will function as a check on each other's memory of what occurred.

Specific Types of Organizational Interviews

The information presented in the preceding sections will help you plan and conduct almost any type of interview. However, there are some special types to plan and consider. In this section, we will briefly describe the most common types of organizational interviews and apply the general principles presented earlier to specific issues and circumstances.

INFORMATION-GATHERING INTERVIEWS

The information-gathering interview is the one most frequently held in organizations and is also the one that is most like a conversation. You might conduct this type of interview when you need to gather facts about an issue or to help in a problem-solving situation. If you treat these fact-finding missions as interviews, you will be in a better position to gather accurate, useful information because you will take the time to plan ahead. Clearly, you need to follow the planning steps discussed above: decide on a general purpose and create an agenda; develop questions; develop the structure of the interview; plan the setting; and anticipate problems.

Furthermore, the information-gathering interview is the only interview for which you can choose the expert. In other organizational interviews, such as the selection interview or the performance-appraisal interview, you have little choice of whom you will see. However, when you want to gather information about some topic or problem, you choose the interviewee. This choice is based on two factors: who *can* give you the information you need and who is *willing* to give you this information (Stano & Reinsch, 1982). Too often, interviewers will talk to interviewees who are willing but who do not have the necessary information. For instance, suppose your organization is considering the implementation of a flextime work schedule and you have been assigned to write a feasibility report. While you may get some interesting opinions from a colleague on the advantages of such a schedule, it would be better if you could find an expert on flextime for your interview. On the other hand, if you wanted to find out how well received such a change would be, then you would talk to colleagues rather than an expert.

The nature of an information-gathering interview is such that the interviewee may not realize he or she is being interviewed. Thus, it may be difficult to keep the interviewee on track and responsive to your questions. More so than in any other interview, you as the interviewer must remain flexible and adaptive to your interviewee. Choose a physical setting that will encourage talk and provide an appropriate climate. The funnel sequence works well in information-gathering interviews because of its ability to immediately elicit general information and the interviewee's feelings on the subject. However, the inverted funnel may be a better choice if you will be interviewing a number of people on the same topic and you need to maintain consistency in evaluating their responses.

EMPLOYMENT-SELECTION INTERVIEWS

The employment interview is used to help current organizational members choose new members. During the selection interview, the interviewer tries to assess whether job candidates will fit into the organization and if they have the appropriate skills for the job. In addition, the interviewer often tries to sell the organization itself to the interviewee. Questions asked during the selection interview address four general topics: prior work experience, education and training, personality characteristics, and related activities and interests. The nature of the job and the interviewee will dictate which topics will be emphasized.

As Table B.7 shows, there are three sources of information you should review when creating questions for a selection interview:

Table B.7	Formulating Selection Interview Questions

❑ Use the *job description* to formulate questions concerning task-related skills and personality characteristics.

❑ Use the selection interview *evaluation form* to formulate questions that can help you assess the applicant on the basis of your organization's general criteria for employees.

❑ Use the applicant's *résumé* and *cover letter* to formulate questions concerning the applicant's specific skills and prior work experience.

1. Review the *job description* to assess the technical skills and experience needed by the person. Also review the job environment to determine the desirable personal qualities required. Create your questions based on these reviews; avoid asking merely generic questions.

2. Look at the *evaluation form* your company uses to assess prospective employees. Make sure that some of your questions deal with the topics on this evaluation form. For instance, if one of the topics on this form is communication skills, create questions that specifically address this subject. In this case, you may want to ask the applicant about his or her writing skills and how he or she has used them in the past.

3. One final piece of information you should use for developing questions for a selection interview is the applicant's *résumé* and *cover letter*. Read these documents carefully. If there are gaps in time between jobs, ask the applicant about them. If the information on the résumé is too general, develop questions to get at the specifics. Remember that most people create résumés with a very specific goal in mind: to obtain an interview. Therefore, the information tends to be a summary of all the good aspects of that person's career to date. Additionally, all information tends to be written in glowing language. Be prepared to reach beyond this language to obtain clarifying information. For example, suppose you came across this line in a cover letter: "I've had years of experience in leadership positions." Clearly, you would want to ask this applicant for more specific information: "How many years?" "What kinds of positions were these?" "What were your specific leadership responsibilities?"

In constructing interview questions, be sure to include some that focus on specific experiences. For instance, you might want to ask something such as, "Can you tell me about a time when you successfully met a goal you set?" The interviewee may be reluctant to be specific, but you should probe until the interviewee offers you useful, specific, behavioral information.

Why is behavioral information so important? Many experts believe that the best way to assess future job performance is to assess past behavior: Past behavior predicts future performance. If you can find out how the interviewee behaved in real situations in the past that are similar to those he or she is likely to face

in your organization, you can determine if his or her style will fit into your organization and work well with other members.

Take care that you ask a balanced series of questions: Ask for negative information as well as positive. This will help you obtain a well-rounded picture of the interviewee and also expose hidden bias. For instance, you might want to follow the positive question with something like: "Well, now tell me about a time when you failed to meet a goal you set." Again, make sure the person gives you specific behavioral information.

In conclusion, remember that your primary purpose in a selection interview is to find a person who is qualified for a particular opening in your organization. Table B.8 details a six-step process (using the acronym PEOPLE) used by a major firm to help interviewers accomplish this purpose. It follows the general interviewing model outlined in the first half of this supplement.

PERFORMANCE-APPRAISAL INTERVIEWS

The performance-appraisal interview is usually part of a larger professional appraisal system. The goal of this system is to evaluate a member of an organization and often to provide feedback to a subordinate concerning ways to improve job performance. While every organization differs in the specifics of carrying out the performance-appraisal system, there are some common aspects.

Generally, prior to the performance-appraisal interview, written evaluations are prepared by the subordinate, the superior, or both people. There are any number of types of evaluation forms, including an essay form, on which the manager writes a description of the subordinate's work, with no real set format; *forced-choice ratings*, in which the manager chooses a statement from many which describes the subordinate in one area; or a *graphic rating scale*, in which the manager rates the subordinate on various areas on a 1–7 numerical scale. In most cases, though, you will be asked to back up your assessment of the subordinate with specific and concrete information. For instance, if you are using a graphic rating scale and indicate that the employee performed unsatisfactorily, you should write out in objective terms why you have made this assessment. The subordinate has a right to know, and you have the responsibility to back up your decisions with evidence.

It is the responsibility of the interviewer to prepare the structure of the performance-appraisal interview. The interviewer should set a definite time and place for the

Table B.8 Selection Interview Format (PEOPLE-Oriented Process)

P = Prepare

  1. Review application, résumé, transcripts, and other background information.

  2. Prepare both general and individual-specific questions.

  3. Prepare suitable physical arrangements.

E = Establish Rapport

  1. Try to make applicant comfortable.

  2. Convey genuine interest.

  3. Communicate supportive attitude with voice and manner.

O = Obtain Information

  1. Ask questions.

  2. Probe.

  3. Listen carefully.

  4. Observe the person (dress, mannerisms, body language).

P = Provide Information

  1. Describe current and future job opportunities.

  2. Sell positive features of firm.

  3. Respond to applicant's questions.

L = Lead to Close

  1. Clarify responses.

  2. Provide opportunity for final applicant input.

  3. Explain what happens next.

E = Evaluate

  1. Assess match between technical qualifications and job requirements.

  2. Judge personal qualities (leadership, maturity, team orientation).

  3. Make a recommendation.

interview, considering the effects these choices will have on the interview and the interviewee. The interviewer must decide on the general purpose of the interview and the agenda. Common topics that are often brought up in performance-appraisal interviews include job knowledge, job performance, job goals, career goals and opportunities, and interpersonal skills.

The difficult aspect of the performance-appraisal interview is that people tend to shy away from evaluating others or being evaluated in face-to-face situations. Both participants in a performance-appraisal interview may be apprehensive. As the interviewer, you need to reassure the interviewee that you are conducting the performance-appraisal interview as a means of assisting in the interviewee's development. Keep in mind that people do not like to be criticized, and balance your criticisms with reassurances and commendations.

In conducting a performance-appraisal interview, you must decide beforehand on your objectives. The objectives should then dictate the form of the interview. In general, three types of appraisal interviews seek to meet specific objectives (Maier, 1958), and a fourth type can be used to meet multiple objectives (Beer, 1987). These interview types are summarized in Table B.9.

The first type of appraisal interview is called the *tell-and-sell* interview. This approach is evaluative in nature. First, you *tell* the subordinate how you have

Table B.9	Types of Performance-Appraisal Interviews
Tell-and-Sell Interview	
Used for purely evaluative purposes. Manager tells the employee the evaluation and then persuades the employee to follow recommendations for improvement.	
Tell-and-Listen Interview	
Used for purely evaluative purposes. Manager tells the employee the evaluation and then listens to the employee's reactions to the evaluation in a nonjudgmental manner.	
Problem-Solving Interview	
Used for employee-development purposes. Manager does not offer evaluation but lets employee decide his or her weak areas and works with employee to develop plan for improvement.	
Mixed-Model Interview	
Used for both evaluative and development purposes. Manager begins interview with problem-solving session and concludes with a more directive tell-and-sell approach.	

evaluated him or her, and then you *sell* the subordinate on the ways you have chosen to improve his or her performance. This type of interview should be used when you must be very clear about your expectations. This format is also effective with young employees who find it difficult to evaluate themselves, with very loyal employees or those who strongly identify with the organization or the appraiser, and with employees who do not want to have a say in how to develop their job and role in the organization (Downs et al., 1980).

If, however, you want to let the subordinate respond to your evaluation, you would use the *tell-and-listen* appraisal format. In this interview, you first *tell* the employee your evaluation; then you *listen* to his or her reactions without displaying any agreement or disagreement. The objective of this interview is also evaluative, but you also want to hear the subordinate's viewpoints and work with the subordinate to help him or her accept your evaluation. Active listening directed at helping the subordinate work through his or her feelings about the evaluation and past performance will help you successfully complete a tell-and-listen appraisal. This type of interview works best with people who have a high need to participate in their jobs, with interviewees who are relatively close in status to the interviewer, and with subordinates who are highly educated (Downs et al., 1980).

The third general type of performance appraisal is the *problem-solving* interview. In this interview, evaluating the person is no longer the goal. Rather, the appraiser's role is to help the employee develop a plan for improving his or her performance. The performance deficiencies are determined by the subordinate, not the supervisor. Your goal as the interviewer is to avoid judgments and evaluations; rather, you offer suggestions for solutions to the problems defined by the interviewee. You form a partnership with the subordinate to solve the problems he or she brings up.

Finally, if your objectives are to both perform an evaluation and offer developmental coaching, you could choose to use a *mixed-model* interview (Beer, 1987). In this type of appraisal interview, you begin with a problem-solving framework and end the interview with a more directive tell-and-sell approach. In this way, you can both help a subordinate meet the development goals as well as offer your own evaluation and plan for development.

No matter which type of interview you choose, a performance-appraisal interview should contain all the elements of a general interview: build rapport and orient the interviewee to the subject; conduct the body of the interview in a supportive manner; conclude by specifying what is going to happen. Additionally, the performance-appraisal interview generally includes a discussion of a specific plan for improvement or change.

Summary and Behavioral Guidelines

While many people consider interviewing a process that just happens, we have argued that effective interviewing requires planning and thought. The steps shown in Figure B.1 provide a framework for enhancing your interviewing skills. The first step, thorough preparation, is essential for a successful interview. Planning involves deciding on your purposes, questions, structure, setting, and responses to anticipated problems. During the actual interview, work toward establishing and maintaining a supportive and productive climate. Keep in mind that every interview should have an introduction, body, and conclusion and that you need to develop ways to record the information you obtain during the interview.

There are a variety of organizational interviews, but the most common are the information-gathering interview, the employment-selection interview, and the performance-appraisal interview. Each of these interviews has very different objectives and specific means to reach them. Be flexible in how you conduct these interviews. As in any communication activity, you should adapt to the situation, your personality, and the person with whom you are conversing.

Interviewing is a vital management skill. When done well, an interview can provide you with information not otherwise available. This information can then better inform the decisions you make as you act out your role in the organization.

Following are general behavioral guidelines for planning and conducting interviews. Specific guidelines for specialized interviews are incorporated into the Observer's Feedback Forms in the Skill Practice exercises.

Planning the Interview

1. Specify your purposes and plan an agenda.
   - ❑ Determine your general purpose: to gather information, persuade, discipline, or evaluate.
   - ❑ Compose an agenda, prioritizing all topics.
2. Formulate questions.
   - ❑ Determine the type of questions (closed or open) that are consistent with the objectives.
   - ❑ Write specific questions for each topic on the agenda.
   - ❑ Use appropriate language in your questions.
   - ❑ Avoid biased or leading questions.
3. Develop the interview guide.
   - ❑ Select the appropriate format: structured, semistructured, or unstructured.
   - ❑ Use either the funnel or inverted funnel question sequence.
   - ❑ Formulate transition statements between topics.
4. Select a setting that is consistent with your objectives.
5. Identify potential complications that might occur during the interview and develop contingency plans.

Conducting the Interview

6. Establish and maintain a supportive climate.
   - ❑ Greet interviewee and initiate a brief social conversation.
   - ❑ Foster a positive communications climate by constant analysis of, and adaptation to, the interview process.
   - ❑ Use effective listening skills and nonverbal language (eye contact, posture, and gestures) to foster cooperation.
7. Introduce the interview.
   - ❑ State the purpose of the interview.
   - ❑ Clarify interviewee's and interviewer's roles.
   - ❑ Specify the time frame of the interview.
   - ❑ Indicate how the information will be used.
   - ❑ Use a transition to signal the beginning of the interview.
8. Conduct the interview.
   - ❑ Use the interview guide to manage the flow of the interview.
   - ❑ Use probing questions when elaboration or clarification are required.
   - ❑ Be flexible and adapt to the flow of the interview.
9. Conclude the interview.
   - ❑ Signal that the interview is about to end.
   - ❑ Summarize the information you have collected.
   - ❑ Clarify details or technical information.
   - ❑ Review what will happen as a result of the interview.
   - ❑ Strengthen the relationship by expressing appreciation.
10. Record the interview content, using the appropriate format.
    - ❑ Write a summary immediately after the interview.
    - ❑ Take notes during the interview (sustaining eye contact).
    - ❑ Use a tape recorder (with the interviewee's permission).
    - ❑ Use a second interviewer to improve your recall.

EXERCISES FOR CONDUCTING SPECIAL-PURPOSE INTERVIEWS

Evaluating the New Employee-Orientation Program

You work for a high-tech electronics firm that was recently purchased by a large, multibusiness conglomerate. Your company produces components for highly sophisticated communications equipment used by the government. This is an exciting, but somewhat confusing, period in the company's history. The new parent company, BETA Products, is known as a Japanese-like firm. It emphasizes high productivity, along with employee commitment and loyalty.

BETA is sending a human resources management team to inspect your organization in two weeks. In advance, they have sent a list of programs they want to review, including your new employee-orientation program. Your boss, the vice president of human resources, has given you the assignment of preparing a 30-minute briefing on this program to the BETA task force. Specifically, she has asked you to interview representatives of various groups in your organization to determine their perceptions of the program's merits and shortcomings.

Currently, when a new employee enters your organization, he or she goes through an extensive orientation session. During this session, the new employee meets with a member of the Human Resources Department to learn about company policies and procedures and receive the Employee's Handbook. This session can last from two to three hours, depending on the participants. At the end of the session, the new employee is assigned a mentor, a member of the new employee's department who has been with the organization for at least one year. The role of the mentor is to help the new employee become familiar with his or her new job and coworkers. The mentor is expected to meet with the new employee on a semiregular basis for at least six months. The relationship can continue if both parties agree. This orientation program has been used for about three years but has never been formally evaluated.

Assignment

To complete this assignment, you have scheduled interviews with several department heads, mentors, and current trainees. Prepare the interview you would conduct with the person from whom you are assigned to gather information about the orientation program. Before beginning this task, review the behavioral guidelines for planning an effective interview at the end of the Skill Learning section. You should also consult Tables B.1 through B.3, and Table B.6. In small groups, compare your questions with others. What did you leave out? What questions need to be reworded? What types of probes may be needed? After this discussion, split up into triads and take turns serving as the interviewer, interviewee, and observer. Do not look at the following role descriptions while planning this exercise. An observer will give feedback using the Observer's Feedback Form as a guide.

Role Descriptions for Interviewees
Trainee

You've just found out that you are going to be interviewed on the mentor program with which you've been involved for three months. You've been quite happy with the program and would like to see it continued; in fact, someday, you want to be a mentor to new employees.

Many of your friends have pointed out that you have a tendency to talk too fast, talk a lot, and tend to dominate a conversation. You realize that when you get nervous or involved in an issue, you do talk a lot. You are certainly nervous about this interview because you are very involved in the program and you've heard through the grapevine that the program might be cut. You feel that would be terrible. You really want to let the interviewer know how much you've learned from your mentor and the whole orientation program. What you have to say is important, and you want to make sure the interviewer hears all the good things you have to say about the program.

You are particularly positive about the program because it contrasts with your experience on your former job. In that organization, you were merely given a cursory overview of the company benefits through a videotape presentation. Furthermore, because there was no standardized mentoring program, new employees were left to fend for themselves. They were given no clear picture of what the company expected of them, no encouragement, and no sense of involvement in a group effort. As a result, a great deal of confusion and misunderstanding resulted. Here, in contrast, you have appreciated being able to get answers to your questions from one person. Overall, you feel as though this approach enabled you to become proficient in your job very quickly.

Department Head

You've just found out that you are going to be interviewed on the mentor program, and it couldn't have come at a worse time. You've just lost one of your best employees, and you have been scrambling to try to find a replacement. You're really not interested in spending time to think about this interview or participate in it. You'd rather use the time on employment interviews to find a new assistant.

In fact, you tend to be uncomfortable in interviews of any kind. Because you tend to be shy, this kind of one-on-one formal conversation always makes you feel uncomfortable. You don't mind it so much when you are the interviewer—at least then you have some control over the situation. But you don't feel you've ever been a really good interviewee. The direct questions always make you feel as if you are on trial; as a result, you withdraw and appear to be uncooperative, even defensive.

You think that the interviewer should be talking to people more directly involved in the program. You really don't have much to do with it anyway, except for matching up people. The program seems to work okay, but no doubt trainees would learn just as quickly if they sought out their own mentors. You know many of your staff members feel the program is worthwhile, so you'll back it up, albeit reluctantly. However, you would much rather write an evaluation of the program than have to talk about it to a relative stranger.

Mentor

You've just found out that you are going to be interviewed on the mentor program, a program with which you've been involved for six months. When you first became a mentor, you were excited about the possibilities. Now, however, experience has shown that the program is a waste of time. Too often, the trainees use their mentors as a crutch, both at work and in their social lives. The program inspires a dependency that you find counterproductive and time wasting.

You've found yourself in the position of practically taking over trainees' jobs because they got used to relying on your expertise. You've thought that this might simply be a result of your own personality—too willing to help, perhaps—but you've also noticed this behavior in other mentors and trainees.

Furthermore, you haven't noticed any significant difference in productivity between people who have gone through the program and people who haven't. In fact, because of

PRACTICE

the development of social relationships, your feeling is that productivity has probably declined: There is too much gossip and goofing off and not enough concentration on tasks.

You think the company ought to abandon the program. While a brief orientation might be useful to new hires, you no longer can justify the amount of time you put into the program, given the results. Even this evaluation of the program is taking up your valuable time.

Observer's Feedback Form

RATING

1 = Low
5 = High

Introduction

1. Did interviewer

_____ use a friendly greeting?

_____ begin to build rapport?

_____ state purpose?

_____ orient interviewee?

_____ refer to taking notes or recording interview?

Body

2. Did interviewer

_____ use appropriate question sequence?

_____ use a variety of question types?

_____ use internal summaries and transitions?

_____ respond to interviewee with good secondary questions (probes)?

_____ use silence when appropriate?

_____ maintain rapport with interviewee?

_____ handle problematic interviewee well?

Closing

3. Did interviewer

_____ sum up?

_____ maintain/encourage good interpersonal relationship?

_____ indicate what would happen with information?

_____ set up another meeting, if appropriate?

_____ thank interviewee?

Nonverbals

4. Did interviewer

_____ wear appropriate clothing?

_____ maintain eye contact with interviewee?

_____ use purposeful gestures?

_____ use appropriate tone of voice?

_____ maintain good posture?

_____ look enthusiastic and interested in what interviewee had to say?

| _____ | take notes inconspicuously? |
| _____ | avoid verbal pauses such as uh, uhm, and so forth? |

Comments:

Performance-Appraisal Interview with Chris Jakobsen

Background Information for Pat Ginelli

You are vice president of the Commercial Loan Division at Firstbank, a medium-sized, state-licensed bank. You have been with Firstbank for four years and have conducted a number of performance-appraisal interviews. During your tenure, you have increased your division's profits by 45 percent. Your goal is to increase this level by another 15 percent before the end of next year. In order to do so, you need to have aggressive, dynamic, and dedicated loan officers working for you.

Chris Jakobsen has been with Firstbank for three years. This will be your first review of Chris' performance because he was transferred to your department five months ago to fill a loan officer position vacated by Helen Smith, who had worked in the Personal Loan Division. You agreed to the transfer after reviewing Chris' credentials and past performance appraisal forms. Chris appeared to be qualified for the position, and the performance appraisal reports indicated that Chris' work was rated from above average to outstanding.

Unfortunately, you have been extremely disappointed with Chris' performance in your department. For a longtime bank employee, he seems surprisingly unfamiliar with standard procedures and protocol. Last week, he told a customer there shouldn't be any problem getting approval for her loan application. She wanted to open a boutique in a renovated building downtown. However, the review committee turned it down because the building hadn't met code yet.

There are several other deficiencies in Chris' performance. In contrast to Helen, Chris seems inattentive to detail. He has frequently left out important information on loan applications, causing needless delays in processing. Furthermore, he doesn't seem to be able to keep up with the workload. It takes him twice as long as it should to handle routine paperwork, and he seems totally ill at ease with your department's computerized information system. Due to a favorable investment environment and the recent opening of a local industrial park, your group's workload is up 50 percent from a year ago. You simply can't tolerate having to take extra time to make sure Chris is doing things right the first time.

In Chris' favor, he is extremely punctual and his attendance has been perfect. He also keeps a very neat work area and takes pride in his own appearance. Furthermore, as a native of the community and an active civic leader, he has very good contacts in the business community. It is also clear that everyone likes Chris. He is jovial and easygoing. He has a quick wit that livens up even the most routine and dull staff meeting. He loves treating coworkers during happy hour after work. Unfortunately, he sometimes loses perspective and gets carried away. Indeed, you've wondered at times how this free spirit ended up in a bank job. Certainly his attitude runs counter to your more formal and reserved personality, but it's hard to deny he has charm and class.

In general, Chris seems to have plenty of potential, but at best his current work performance is only average (an "expected" rating on your company's form). He just hasn't applied himself to his new position. You wonder if this is the right work for him or if perhaps he hasn't had adequate training. You spent some time orienting Chris to the group and assigned Jim, a veteran of the department, to act as his mentor. But, in retrospect, the local business boom has made it difficult for you and Jim to help Chris learn the ropes. Your days seem to be filled up with meetings with local investors and city planners. Still, it bugs you that he never asks questions. If he needs help with the technical aspects of the job, why doesn't he ever ask for assistance?

You have scheduled the interview with Chris for later in the day in your office. You know your review will make him very unhappy and probably put him on the defensive. He obviously has high aspirations for advancing in the bank and has received pretty positive feedback in the past. You've got to figure out some way to get him to improve. Your department is short-handed as it is, and everyone must contribute his or her share.

As you contemplate the unpleasant task ahead, you reflect, "Boy, I certainly miss Helen. I never had to have this type of conversation with her."

Assignment for Pat Ginelli

In preparation for this interview, complete a draft of the performance evaluation form in Exhibit 1 (the form is located after Chris' assignment). In keeping with standard practice, you have given a blank copy of the form to Chris and asked him to do a self-evaluation. He will bring his completed form to the interview.

After you have completed your draft, identify the type of performance-appraisal interview you feel is most appropriate for this situation (see Table B.9). Also, review the behavioral guidelines at the end of the Skill Learning section. Then formulate a series of questions consistent with your overall strategy. Finally, anticipate questions and objections Chris might initiate and prepare responses. Compare your plans in small groups and make revisions. Use the Interview Checklist in Table B.4 to guide your discussion.

Upon completion of your small-group discussion, prepare to conduct the interview with Chris. Do not look at the background information for Chris' role prior to the interview. An observer will use the Observer's Feedback Form to give you feedback.

Background Information for Chris Jakobsen

You have been with Firstbank, a medium-sized, state-licensed bank, for three years. For most of that time, you worked in the Personal Loan Division as a loan officer. You liked your job, your clients, and the people with whom you worked. You had hoped that your first move at Firstbank would be a promotion within the Personal Loan Division. However, five months ago, you were transferred to the Commercial Loan Division to replace a loan officer who had worked in that position for 10 years. You did not really want to transfer, but you realized that the move would, in fact, put you in a better position for the next upward move. Your former supervisor indicated that you would not have to stay in this position very long if you kept receiving good ratings on your performance appraisal forms, and you have always received outstanding or above-average ratings. He argued that you really needed to gain exposure to other departments in the bank as well as to other managers. Your new boss, Pat Ginelli, is a real rising star in the bank.

You expect your new supervisor, Pat, is going to be pretty tough on you. You feel frustrated and upset because you don't think there has been any change in your effort or commitment. Since you have been in the department, Pat's attitude toward you has seemed very distant and formal. You know that Pat thinks that the person you replaced was an excellent worker who contributed greatly to Pat's goal of achieving a 15 percent increase in profits this year. But certainly she doesn't expect you to immediately pick up where a 10-year veteran left off.

Then there's the problem of training. She promised to give you a thorough orientation when you arrived, but instead you were shunted off to Jim. He seemed sincere and interested in helping out, and he told you to come and ask questions whenever you needed help. However, when you asked about the department's loan-application procedure, he made you feel like an idiot for asking such a basic question, and you've never gone back. Furthermore, Pat always seems to be in meetings. You realize that she is bringing in important business for the bank, so you feel it would be inappropriate to distract her with your basic questions.

This lack of assistance has caused you to make some mistakes. These have primarily been due to the change in procedures between the Personal and Commercial Loan departments. You had much more autonomy and authority over there, probably because the loans were much smaller. In addition, there are many more government regulations to worry about over here. Besides, you really miss the close contact with people that was built into your old job. That's why you took your first job in the bank. You have always been a very people-oriented person and received great satisfaction from helping them. Now, you just seem to be buried in paperwork and committee meetings. Some days, you regret accepting the offer to transfer. You're not sure this stepping-stone to advancement is worth the lost enjoyment you received in your former position.

Assignment for Chris Jakobsen

Your interview with Pat is scheduled for her office. In preparation for the interview, Pat has asked you to complete a copy of the performance-appraisal form as a self-evaluation. Prior to the interview, complete the form in Exhibit 1. Do not review the background information for Pat's role.

Exhibit 1 Interview with Chris Jakobsen

Employee Performance Appraisal

DATA COMPLETED

NAME   Chris Jakobsen
DATE OF BIRTH   6/22/65
YEARS OF EMPLOYMENT   3
OFFICE LOCATION BRANCH 4   DEPARTMENTAL 9
DEPARTMENT   Commercial

PRESENT JOB TITLE   Loan Officer
CONVERSION CODE   32
YEARS IN PRESENT POSITION   6 months
SOC. SEC. NO.   555–33–9999
EDUCATION   B.A.—Business

Select the statement under each of the following categories that best describes the individual.

Quality of Work

General excellence of output with consideration to accuracy—thoroughness—dependability—without close supervision.

_____ Exceptionally high quality. Consistently accurate, precise, quick to detect errors in own and others' work.

_____ Work sometimes superior and usually accurate. Negligible amount needs to be redone. Work regularly meets standards.

_____ A careful worker. A small amount of work needs to be redone. Corrections made in reasonable time. Usually meets normal standards.

_____ Work frequently below acceptable quality. Inclined to be careless. Moderate amount of work needs to be redone. Excessive time to correct.

_____ Work often almost worthless. Seldom meets normal standards. Excessive amount needs to be redone.

Quantity of Work

Consider the amount of useful work over the period of time since the last appraisal. Compare the output of work to the standard you have set for the job.

_____ Output consistently exceeds standards. Unusually fast worker. Exceptional amount of output.

_____ Maintains a high rate of production. Frequently exceeds standards. More than normal effort.

_____ Output is regular. Meets standards consistently. Works at steady average speed.

_____ Frequently turns out less-than-normal amount of work. A low producer.

_____ A consistently low producer. Excessively slow worker. Unacceptable output.

Cooperation

Consider the employee's attitude toward the work, the employee's coworkers, and supervisors. Does the employee appreciate the need to understand and help solve problems with others?

_____ Always congenial and cooperative. Enthusiastic and cheerfully helpful in emergencies. Well-liked by associates.

_____ Cooperates well. Understands and complies with all rules. Usually demonstrates a good attitude. Liked by associates.

_____ Usually courteous and cooperative. Follows orders but at times needs reminding. Gets along well with associates.

_____ Does only what is specifically requested. Sometimes complains about following instructions. Reluctant to help others.

_____ Unfriendly and uncooperative. Refuses to help others.

Knowledge of the Job

The degree to which the employee has learned and understands the various procedures of the job and their objectives.

_____ Exceptional understanding of all phases. Demonstrates unusual desire to acquire information.

_____ Thorough knowledge in most phases. Has interest and potential toward personal growth.

_____ Adequate knowledge for normal performance. Will not voluntarily seek development.

_____ Insufficient knowledge of job. Resists criticism and instruction.

_____ No comprehension of the requirements of job.

Dependability

The reliability of the employee in performing assigned tasks accurately and within the allotted time.

_____ Exceptional. Can be left on own and will establish priorities to meet deadlines.

_____ Very reliable. Minimal supervision required to complete assignments.

_____ Dependable in most assignments. Normal supervision required. A profitable worker.

_____ Needs frequent follow-up. Excessive prodding necessary.

_____ Chronic procrastinator. Control required is out of all proportion.

Attendance and Punctuality

Consider the employee's record, reliability, and ability to conduct the job within the unit's work rules.

_____ Unusual compliance and understanding of work discipline. Routine usually exceeds normal.

_____ Excellent. Complete conformity with rules but cheerfully volunteers time during peak loads.

_____ Normally dependable. Rarely needs reminding of accepted rules.

_____ Needs close supervision in this area. Inclined to backslide without strict discipline.

_____ Unreliable. Resists normal rules. Frequently wants special privileges.

Knowledge of Company Policy and Objectives

Acceptance, understanding, and promotion of company policies and objectives in the area of the employee's job responsibilities.

_____ Thorough appreciation and implementation of all policies. Extraordinary ability to express objectives and encourage others to meet them.

_____ Reflects knowledge of almost all policies related to this position.

_____ Acceptable but fairly superficial understanding of job objectives.

_____ Limited insight into job or company goals. Mentally restricted.

_____ Not enough information or understanding to permit minimum efficiency.

Initiative and Judgment

The ability and interest to suggest and develop new ideas and methods; the degree to which these suggestions and normal decisions and actions are sound.

_____ Ingenious self-starter. Superior ability to think intelligently.

_____ Very resourceful. Clear thinker—usually makes thoughtful decisions.

_____ Fairly progressive, with normal sense. Often needs to be motivated.

_____ Rarely makes suggestions. Decisions need to be checked before implementation.

_____ Needs detailed instructions and close supervision. Tendency to assume and misinterpret.

Supervisory or Technical Potential

Consider the employee's ability to teach and increase skills of others, to motivate and lead, to organize and assign work, and to communicate ideas.

_____ An accomplished leader who can earn respect and inspire others to perform. An articulate and artful communicator, planner, and organizer.

_____ Has the ability to reach and will lead by example rather than technique. Speaks and writes well and can organize and plan with help.

_____ Fairly well informed on job-related subjects but has some difficulty communicating with others. Nothing distinctive about spoken or written word.

_____ Little ability to implement. Seems uninterested in teaching or helping others. Careless speech and writing habits.

_____ Unable to be objective or reason logically. Inarticulate and stilted in expression.

PRACTICE

Overall Rating

There are five alternatives in each category. The first alternative is worth 5 points, the last alternative is worth 1 point. Place a number from 1–5 by each of the selected alternatives and total the score for all nine categories. Then select the appropriate overall rating.

_____ Outstanding (45–39)

_____ Above Expected (38–32)

_____ Expected (31–23)

_____ Below Expected (22–16)

_____ Unsatisfactory (15–9)

Observer's Feedback Form

RATING

1 = Low

5 = High

Introduction

1. Did interviewer

_____ use appropriate greeting?

_____ build rapport?

_____ orient interviewee to the interview?

_____ refer to taking notes?

Body

2. Did interviewer

_____ praise individual's strengths?

_____ focus on specific concerns?

_____ compare perceptions of the problems?

_____ probe for underlying causes?

_____ reach agreement on performance expectations and goals?

_____ discuss specific plans of action for improving deficiencies?

_____ make specific references to the appraisal form?

Conclusion

3. Did interviewer

_____ provide opportunity for interviewee to make suggestions and ask questions?

_____ summarize interview?

_____ specify when next appraisal interview will be held?

Nonverbals

4. Did interviewer

_____ use nonverbal behaviors to maintain open climate and good rapport?

_____ avoid use of uhs and uhms?

_____ maintain good posture?

_____ maintain eye contact?

Comments:

Employment-Selection Interview at Smith Farley Insurance

Smith Farley is a rapidly growing insurance firm located in Peoria, Illinois. It offers general lines of insurance, including auto, fire, life, and health. It prides itself on its competitive rates, excellent agent relations, and fast claim service. Employees of the firm appreciate its no-layoff policy, generous pay and benefits, and family-oriented culture. Next to Caterpillar, it is the largest employer in the community, a source of employee pride.

Smith Farley has taken the lead in computerizing the insurance business. Agents and claim handlers conduct much of their business using laptop computers in their offices and in the field. Furthermore, the agents' and claim handlers' offices are all networked with one another as well as with the regional offices. This permits rapid transfer of information, including rate changes, new applications, and claims.

To support this massive computer system, the firm has installed state-of-the-art computer hardware in its 10 regional office centers. In addition, the company has a large software development and maintenance department which has doubled in size in the past five years and now employs 800 programmers. These programmers are generally recruited directly from college. Although they need no previous experience, any relevant experience can help new programmers move quickly into management or senior technical positions.

Programmer/analysts use typical programming languages to develop computer applications for the insurance business (e.g., new claim-handler and customer application forms), for the corporate headquarters staff (e.g., accounting and personnel records), and the computer system itself (internal procedures and controls). Data processing positions range from extremely technical design of complex computer networks to routine maintenance of existing programs.

All new programmers are put through a 16-week school in which they are oriented to the company and the data processing department, brought up to speed on the relevant programming languages and tools, and socialized into the corporate culture. To meet the heavy demand for computer applications, the data processing department has been authorized to hire two cohorts of 60 programmers a year.

To attract programmers to the firm, Smith Farley offers above-average starting salaries and rapid promotions during the first five years. After that, individuals can continue to pursue the technical career option, which leads to a senior analyst's position that pays about $10,000 above industry average, or they can move into management. The consistently high performance of the firm and its ongoing expansion of data processing afford ample opportunity for promotion into senior positions.

You are J. R. Henderson, a 20-year employee of Smith Farley. For the past 10 years you have been working in the personnel department, primarily interviewing job candidates for the data processing department. You enjoy your work—the constant contact with young, enthusiastic college graduates is invigorating—but sometimes you find the heavy travel schedule taxing.

For example, during the next week you will be traveling to three cities: first to nearby Bloomington, then to New Orleans and Atlanta. In addition to the regular campus interviews you have scheduled in these areas, you have received several résumés in response to local newspaper ads. In sifting through these inquiries, three résumés caught your interest. You have made arrangements to interview all three applicants during this trip.

Assignment

Review Exhibits 1 through 5 and prepare a list of questions you would ask these three job candidates. Using the Interview Guide planning form at the end of the chapter, review the general questions you should ask all three. In addition, identify several specific questions you would like to ask the candidate(s) you are assigned, based on their résumés and cover letters.

Review your proposed questions in small groups. What points did you overlook? What questions need to be reworded or discarded?

Using the questions you think are most appropriate, be prepared to conduct selection interviews with these job candidates in class. Prior to each interview, think about the questions each candidate is likely to ask you about the company, the community of Peoria, and the specific jobs available. In addition, identify your "selling points"—the specific features of the company, the community, and the jobs that you think each candidate would find most attractive. Also review the general behavioral guidelines and the six-step PEOPLE approach to selection interviews (Table B.8). Remember: The interviewing process influences the content of the information exchanged.

Following the interview, take a few minutes and grade the interviewee on each of the seven criteria on the Interview Guide (5 = high, 1 = low). Justify your grades with specific comments. Then make an oral report to the observer assigned to your interview; include a recommendation. (Assume the observer is the director of recruiting for your firm.) After your report, for those criteria related to the interview itself (as compared with the background of the assigned role), discuss your observations with the interviewee. Following this discussion, an observer will give you feedback on your performance as an interviewer using the Observer's Feedback Form as a guide.

Exhibit 1 Smith Farley Insurance Job Posting

A. POSITIONS OPEN

1. *Programmer/Analyst*—Auto & Life Company Data Processing Trainee openings leading to Programmer/Analyst positions at the conclusion of *16-week* training program. The DP Trainee is trained in the programming skills necessary to either develop new or to revise data-processing programs that help administer over 10 million auto, life, fire, and health insurance policies.

2. *Analyst*—Computer Operations Support Trainee opening leading to *Analyst* positions at conclusion of a *nine-month* training program. Computer Operations Support is responsible for technical operations support for the Regional Data Processing Offices, including: developing operator procedures, developing and administering training, problem resolution, and coordinating implementation of new systems and major changes for Regional Data Processing Offices.

B. MAJORS CONSIDERED

We are recruiting for three Data Processing Departments (Auto Data Processing, Life Data Processing, and Computer Operations Support), each having different requirements, which are as follows:

1. *Auto Data Processing:* Strongly prefer applied computer science, computer technology, and MIS majors, but will consider other majors with 12–15 hours of computer science academic background. Strongly prefer *3.0 overall GPA*.

   Logical analysis, problem-solving skills, and communication skills are important for expected job performance. Candidates should possess course work in *COBOL, C, C++,* and/or *Java*.

2. *Life Data Processing:* Most college majors are acceptable (i.e., mathematics, business or related majors, English, music, and science).

   Student must have a sincere interest in and aptitude for data processing. Only students with a *3.5 overall GPA* will be considered.

3. *Computer Operations Support:* Most business majors are acceptable (i.e., business, business administration, finance, economics, accounting, etc., with 6–10 hours of computer science academic background). Prefer a *3.0 overall GPA*.

Student must have a sincere interest in and aptitude for data processing.

C. CITIZENSHIP REQUIREMENTS

Must be citizens or permanent residents.

D. LOCATION

These positions will be located at the corporate headquarters in Peoria, Illinois.

Exhibit 2 Interview Guide for Data Processing (DP)

APPLICANT'S NAME _____   SCHOOL _____
INTERVIEW DATE _____   GPA _____
LOCATION _____ TIME _____   MAJOR _____

CRITERION	FOCUS	GENERAL QUESTIONS	APPLICANT-SPECIFIC QUESTIONS
Aptitude/ Knowledge	Determine if exposure to and retention of a high-level computer language and development methods are adequate.	Of the DP courses you have had, which was the most beneficial and why? Explain in detail the most difficult DP assignment you have had. How do you rate yourself as a programmer? Why?	
Interest/ Experience	Determine if interest and record of success in DP studies or work has been sustained (2+ years).	How did you first get interested in DP? What about it do you like the most? The least? Can you give me an example of a DP-related experience you have had that was satisfying? Not satisfying? What is your professional goal?	
Ability to work with others	Determine success of achieving results in team effort.	Do you feel you work more effectively on a one-to-one basis or in a group? Describe a situation in which you worked as a member of a team. What approach did you take to get people together and establish a common approach to the task?	

(Continued)

PRACTICE

CRITERION	FOCUS	GENERAL QUESTIONS	APPLICANT-SPECIFIC QUESTIONS
Commitment/ Initiative	Determine level of success in achieving task completion in light of task complexity, adversity, load, level of knowledge, and so forth.	What approaches do you use to get people to accept your ideas or goals? What is a big obstacle you had to overcome to get where you are today? Do you consider yourself a self-starter or are you better at implementing the plans of others?	
Communi-cation	Determine quality of written/spoken word.	Would you rather write a report or give a verbal report? Why? Do you think you are a good listener? What qualities do you need to be a good listener? How do you handle a situation when you are explaining something and the other person doesn't understand?	
Problem solving/ Decision making	Determine if applicant has a record of addressing relatively complex projects.	In your opinion, what are the most difficult problems with which a programmer/ analyst must deal? What particular strengths do you have that allow you to deal with these problems? What design methods do you use to create a program? Describe how to use them. Describe the most complex program you have ever written.	
Other:	Stability Maturity Leadership Personal appearance		

Exhibit 3 Résumé

William L. Henderson II

Campus
700 North Camden #107
Normal, IL 61761
(309) 454–6178

Home
1915 Western Hills
Arlington Heights, IL 60004
(312) 255–5738

OBJECTIVE	*Analyst/Data Processing*
EDUCATION	Illinois Wesleyan University, Bloomington, Illinois Expected Degree 1997

	Major: Computer Science	Major GPA: 3.75
	Business Administration	GPA: 3.03

EDUCATIONAL HIGHLIGHTS	Dean's List Spring Semester 1997 ACM Award Spring Semester 1997

STUDENT
ACTIVITIES
	ILLINOIS WESLEYAN UNIVERSITY
	Member of Gamma Ray Social Fraternity (3 years)
	    Pledge Class President; In-House Activities; Intramurals; Offset
	    Chairman; Social Committee.
	Member of Varsity Football Team (2 years)

WORK SUMMARY (Part time during college)	CENTRAL STATES INSURANCE, Bloomington, IL Auto/Divisional Programming—Corporate *Position:* DP—Intern ILLINOIS WESLEYAN UNIVERSITY, Bloomington, IL Office of Admissions *Position:* Admissions Counselor Aid Computer Lab *Position:* Lab Assistant
(Summers)	PREMIER CHECK PRINTERS, INC., Des Plaines, IL Printing presses (2 years) *Position:* Press Assistant/Operation SOFTWARE, ETC., Arlington Heights, IL Sales, Inventory, Shipping, Ordering, Partial Management *Position:* Salesman
AVAILABILITY	June 1998
REFERENCES	References available upon request

Exhibit 4 Résumé

Bryan E. Jensen
4364 Peachtree Place
Lilburn, Georgia 30247
Home (404) 381-8909

OBJECTIVE	*Project Leader/Systems Analyst* with supervision potential
BACKGROUND	Anticipated the decline in manufacturing jobs and retrained in computer science. Presently have two associate degrees and four years of in-depth experience. Accepted temporary position at Caterpillar to gain experience. The economic recession in the Midwest prompted my relocation to Atlanta. Accepted my present position to broaden my experience. I am now seeking a permanent career position with a midwest employer located in a "smaller" city. I will be an asset to a progressive company. I am well motivated, resourceful, versatile, work well with others, and accept responsibility readily.

HARDWARE	IBM 370—Models 3090E, 3083, 3084, 4341; IBM PC/XT; 486, Power PC
SOFTWARE	Case Tools: Knowledgeware GAMMA
	Databases: IMS-DL/I, DBII—SQL, Access, Oracle
	Communications: IMS—MFS, TSO—ISPF
	Languages: C, C++, Java
	Related: BTS, DDLTO, Fileaid-IMS, Datavatage, IMS-Online, SPUFI, QMF, OS/MVS-XA, JES2, Fileaid, Panvalet, Infopac, SDSF, JES-Master, Design/I, All-In-One,Diagram Master, Excel, Word PowerPoint
EXPERIENCE 03/97–	*Continental Service Corporation*, Macon, Georgia (Corporate) Senior Systems Analyst/Team Leader
	Guided planning, estimating, analysis, and development of major areas of IMB DB/DC Billing System. It has a 2.5 million customer base and is located in 42 states. Use Method/I life cycle/ methodology. Utilized Pacdesign (Yourdon) for system design and Pacbase for completion of deliverables and code generation.
01/94–03/97	*Federal Reserve Bank*, Savannah, Georgia (Corporate) Project Leader (10/96–03/97)
	Supervised eight analysts and programmers through the implementation of a billing system for Federal Reserve Districts throughout the United States. Presented written and verbal status reports, employee-performance reviews, and time-planning estimates/schedules to upper management.
	(09/95–10/96)
	Led development of IMS DB/DC billing system. Analyzed requirements to produce data-flow diagrams and logical data model. Participated in team presentation of system. Created program specifications. Investigated and resolved code-generation problems. Provided support to other team members.
	(01/95–08/95)
	Received Merit Award for outstanding performance. Designed, programmed, and tested accounting interface to all corporate IBM and branch Unisys applications. Provided training and support during parallel test and acceptance of accounting system. Redirected installation efforts for an accounting deposit module that had fallen behind. Provided production support of newly implemented accounting system.
	(04/94–12/94)
	Installed accounting software from tape. Modified all JCL to district standards. Installed and modified job-submission system. Documented and instructed the users on the system and the results of each job.
	(01/94–03/94)
	Designed, wrote, tested, and documented IMB DB/DC programs for system used to report the dollar amount of checks as they clear the Reserve.
03/93–12/93	*Caterpillar Tractor Company*, Chicago, Illinois (Corp.) Programmer

Programmed, tested, and documented IMS DB/DC programs from specifications for Man and Material Management System. (Due to be laid off 01/94)

04/87–06/91   Skilled Trades Machinist (last position held—layoff)

EDUCATION   Illinois Central College; East Peoria, Illinois—1991, Associate in Applied Science, Data Processing Technology Bradley University; Peoria, Illinois (1988–1989) Fifteen hours past Associate toward Manufacturing B.S. Illinois Central College; East Peoria, Illinois— 1985, Associates in Applied Science, Manufacturing Technology.

PERSONAL   Married, one child. Enjoy outdoor activities. Well motivated. References available upon request.

Exhibit 5 Résumé

Mary Lynn Smith
3922 North Blair Street
New Orleans, Louisiana 70117
(504) 945–6077

CAREER OBJECTIVES

Entry-level position in artificial intelligence research with an industrial firm and eventual managerial capacity in such a firm.

EDUCATION

Dillard University, Division of Natural Sciences, New Orleans, LA.
B.S. degree, Mathematics major with Computer Science minor, May 1989, G.P.A.: 3.58/4.0 (overall), 3.82/4.0 (major)

Courses in Mathematics:

Calculus I, II, III	Complex Variables	
Modern Algebra I & II	Real Algebra	Differential Equations
Advanced Calculus	Linear Algebra	Engineering Statistics

Courses in Computer Science:

Computer Fundamentals	BASIC	Advanced BASIC
Systems Analysis	Pascal	FORTRAN

HONORS AND ACTIVITIES

University academic scholarship, University and National Dean's Lists, Kappa Beta Alpha and Beta Kappa Tau Honor Societies, Kappa Delta Pi Mathematics Society, and Dillard University Concert Choir.

WORK EXPERIENCE

Computer Services, Inc., Systems Operator/Payroll Processor, Summer, 1997.
—Performed system backups, file verification, programming, and payroll processing.
—Verified payroll figures and prepared tax reports.

Black Computer Operators Association, Teacher, 8/96.
—Prepared the South New Orleans Computer Science Team for a national competition.

The South New Orleans Team placed first in the national competition.

Washington Elementary School, Summer Mini Camp, Teacher, 7/96–8/96.
—Taught children how to use computers and educational software.

Observer's Feedback Form

RATING

1 = Low
5 = High

Opening

1. Did interviewer

_____ use appropriate greeting?

_____ build rapport?

_____ orient interviewee to the interview?

_____ use appropriate transition to body of interview?

Body

2. Did interviewer

_____ clearly define structure of the interview?

_____ use transitions between topics?

_____ ask questions based on available information and needs?

_____ probe when necessary?

_____ solicit behavioral examples?

Closing

3. Did interviewer

_____ offer organizational or job information?

_____ invite questions?

_____ answer interviewee's questions appropriately and specifically?

_____ state when and how interviewee will be contacted?

Nonverbal

4. Did interviewer

_____ act poised?

_____ dress appropriately?

_____ speak articulately?

_____ act enthusiastically?

_____ use appropriate language style?

_____ maintain eye contact?

_____ use purposeful gestures?

Comments:

SKILL *LEARNING*

- Conducting Effective Meetings: A Short Guide for Meeting Managers and Meeting Participants
- The Five Ps of Effective Meetings
- Suggestions for Group Members
- Summary and Behavioral Guidelines

SKILL *PRACTICE*

- Preparing and Conducting a Team Meeting at SSS Software
- Role Diagnosis
- Meeting Evaluation Worksheet

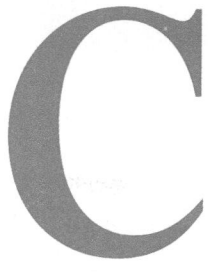

Conducting Meetings

SKILL DEVELOPMENT OBJECTIVES

- IMPLEMENT GUIDELINES FOR PLANNING AND CONDUCTING EFFECTIVE MEETINGS
- ENHANCE THE VALUE OF MEETINGS ATTENDED

Conducting Effective Meetings: A Short Guide for Meeting Managers and Meeting Participants

Becoming a skillful planner and conductor of meetings—a meeting manager—is a prerequisite for managerial and organizational effectiveness. There are several reasons this skill is a crucial one. One reason is because so much of a manager's time is spent in meetings. A 3M Company study, done in the late 1980s, found that meetings occupy a large percentage of a manager's workweek. These researchers found that the number of meetings had doubled over the last decade. As you move up the hierarchy, meeting demands increase substantially. The more senior the manager is, the more meetings he or she attends (3M, 1994).

A second reason is that meetings are a significant cost. This research found that the compensation for managers "just being there" had nearly tripled. About 15 percent of most companies' personnel budget was spent on meeting matters. And in the last decade these demands have increased substantially. With flatter organizations and an emphasis on teams and teamwork, the number of meetings has grown exponentially.

A third reason is that meetings are the place where most corporate decisions are actually made, or reviewed. Hence, the matter of decision quality—the amount of useful result from the meeting—becomes crucial for the health of the organization. The skilled meeting master can "produce" a meeting that results in high-quality decisions—not her or his decisions, but decisions that truly reflect the group.

A fourth reason relates to the concept of whole life, as opposed to work life. In these days of the boundaryless organization, skills that are useful at work are also useful and important away from work. Many people spend a substantial portion of their time in non-work-oriented meetings. For example, any community volunteer work; church activity; or participation in art councils, youth programs, and civic associations requires a lot of meetings. Failure here can have a great impact on our social fabric. Robert Putnam of Harvard University has developed a thesis about the decline in "social capital" in American society (Putnam, 2000). Collective activities seem to be on the decline across a wide range of organizations. One of the reasons for this decline is unorganized meetings that frustrate participants rather than help them contribute to the organization's goals. Folks may figure they just do not want to waste their time.

Because meetings are such a pervasive activity both in and out of work settings, being a skillful meeting manager has important rewards beyond those associated with team building. Meeting groups, if properly managed, can make higher-quality decisions than individuals. The phrase "if properly managed" is the key. If not properly managed, meetings become the supreme organizational and civic time waster. They can actually set the organization back by making rotten decisions when problematic processes such as folly (Tuchman, 1984), groupthink (Janis, 1983), the Abilene paradox (Harvey, 1974), the garbage can model of organizational choice (Cohen, March, & Olsen, 1972), or the "boiled frog syndrome" (Tichy & Devanna, 1986) come into play.

The Five *P*s of Effective Meetings

Effective meeting managers know the five steps in preparing for and conducting meetings: (1) purpose, (2) participants, (3) plan, (4) participation, and (5) perspective.

1. Purpose

Purpose refers to the reason for which a meeting is held. There are three functions a meeting performs—to make announcements, to make decisions, and to brainstorm. Of these three, only the second two count as reasons for actually holding a meeting. When information can be conveyed by a memo or phone call, when people are not prepared, when key people cannot attend, when the cost of a meeting is higher than the potential payoff, and when there is no advantage to holding a meeting, no meeting should be called (3M, 1994). In short, if there are no decisions to be made, nor any brainstorming to do, cancel the meeting.

Productive meetings *result* from good decision making and brainstorming. A meeting should be called when one or more of the following conditions applies.

We are grateful to John Tropman, who prepared this section based on the material that the authors had in the previous editions.

- *Information sharing.* When all needed information is not held by any single person, when ideas will be stimulated by getting people together, and when it is not clear what information is needed or available.
- *Commitment building.* When individuals need to become committed to a course of action and when they are involved in its planning and implementation.
- *Information disseminating and feedback.* When many people must receive the same message in the same way, e-mail is good. However, when the real issue is not the dissemination but gauging the reaction and allowing for "ventilation," then a meeting is very helpful.
- *Problem solving.* Groups outperform the best individuals in accomplishing complex tasks and making high-quality decisions where various policies or information are needed. Therefore, meetings should be called to manage complex problems and outline the options for decisions through brainstorming.

2. Participants

The second *P*, **participants**, refers to the individuals invited to attend a meeting. In conducting an effective meeting, it is important to determine the *size, composition*, and *skills* of the participants. Meetings can fail because too many or too few participants attend or because the wrong mix of people is present. If a meeting is too large, discussion may be superficial and diffuse; few people will be able to participate. If a meeting is too small, not enough information will be shared and problems will not be adequately solved. Odd numbers of participants work best because even numbers have a higher propensity of causing the group to polarize.

Meeting composition refers to three main dualistic dimensions:

- Homogeneity–Heterogeneity
- Competition–Cooperation
- Task–process

A homogeneous group is composed of members with similar backgrounds, personalities, knowledge, or values. Homogeneous groups produce less conflict and disagreement, but their outcomes may be mundane and unimaginative. On the other hand, heterogeneous groups produce more differences among individuals, which leads to criticisms and disputes but potentially to more novel, complex solutions to problems as well.

With regard to the competition–cooperation dimension, research on its effect in problem-solving meetings is compelling. Groups whose members are working toward a common goal and who adopt a cooperative stance toward one another perform more effectively and produce higher levels of member satisfaction than groups whose members are striving to fulfill individual needs or are pursuing competing goals. Cooperative groups also demonstrate more effective interpersonal communication, more complete divisions of labor, higher levels of involvement, and better task performance.

On the task–process dimension, meetings are more effective if they have participants who generate a balance of both task and process. Task-oriented participants are "all business." They have little tolerance for joking or for discussions of feelings and friendships. The task is accomplished efficiently, but satisfaction may be low. Process-oriented participants emphasize esprit de corps and participation. They are sensitive to participants' feelings and satisfaction. They may sacrifice accomplishment in favor of members' enjoyment. (This usually turns out to be a bad choice; the greatest enjoyment comes from accomplishment.) For meeting participants, one tip is not to refrain from using your default (or usual) style (task or process) but, rather, "Do what is not being done." If there is a lot of process going on, you can emphasize task. If there is an "all task" mind-set, then add a bit of process.

Skills address the competencies that participants bring to the meeting. We can think of *general* and *specific* skill sets. In general, the four generic skill sets that Cohen, March, and Olsen (1972) identify should be present in the meeting *at the same time*. First are the problem knowers—participants who have some sense of the problem under discussion. Second are the solution providers—participants who are creative and imaginative, but may not know the problems. Third are the resource controllers—participants who sign off on money, people, and resources needed for most decisions; therefore, they need to be in the loop. Finally, there are people called "decision-makers-looking-for-work"—the "organizational archbishops" who "bless" or affirm decisions. If all these skill sets are in the same room at the same time, and the process is a good one, the likelihood of a high-quality decision (timely, creative, participative) is great. In terms of specific skills, the particular knowledge that might be needed in a particular situation can be ascertained as one plans for the meeting, using the rule of halves, which will be mentioned later in this chapter. It is true that individuals may double up—and fit more than one of these categories. That is fine. Just be sure you have them all.

3. Planning

The third *P*, **planning**, refers to preparation of the meeting agenda. Often, the justification for a meeting is clear (e.g., we need to determine how to get fuel to troops at the front), and the appropriate individuals are in attendance, but the meeting still seems to flounder, wander aimlessly, or is unable to produce a final decision. Such meetings often begin with the leader saying, "We have a problem that I think we all need to sit down and discuss." The leader's erroneous assumption is that because a problem exists and all participants understand it, the meeting will be successful. Unfortunately, participants may come to the meeting unprepared, may be unaware of critical information, may be unclear about their specific roles, and may be confused about how to achieve the objective. Conversely, the meeting planner may try to cram too much into a single meeting, schedule too many presentations, handle too many documents, or cover too much business. Research suggests that there are a number of rules for planning meetings effectively (Tropman, 1996). The following is a list of the most important.

The Rule of Halves All agenda items for an upcoming meeting must be in the hands of the agenda scheduler no later than one-half of the time interval between the last meeting and the upcoming meeting. If meetings are held weekly, the person constructing the agenda should gather agenda items for the next meeting by the halfway mark in the week. This allows time to sort and cluster items, handle some items one-on-one outside the meeting, and produce and distribute an agenda in advance of the meeting. It also allows for the assembling of special skills, as driven by the developing agenda.

The Rule of Sixths Approximately two-thirds of the agenda should be focused on current agenda items. The remaining third should be subdivided into two-sixths. One of those sixths of meeting time should be spent on past agenda items and follow-up. The remaining sixth of the meeting should be spent on brainstorming for the future. Continuity is thus maintained and agenda items don't slip through the cracks.

The Reports Rule Meetings go better if the usual round of "reports" does *not* occur. Rather, the information that is contained in the "reports" is reorganized into specific items—announcement, decision, brainstorming.

The Rule of Three-Fourths Packets of information, including minutes from the past meeting and an agenda, should be sent to meeting participants at the three-quarter point between meetings. For example, if a weekly meeting is scheduled, the packet should be sent out approximately two days before the next meeting.

The Agenda Rule Agendas for meetings should be written with action verbs or sentence summaries, not with single words. Rather than saying "Minutes," for example, use "Approve Minutes." Rather than "Production Report," use "Determine Production Schedule." This provides clarity and impetus for what the meeting should accomplish. Figure C.1 illustrates this process.

The Rule of Thirds All meetings are divided into three parts: (1) a start-up period in which less difficult items are covered, latecomers arrive, and people get on board; (2) a heavy work period in which the most difficult items are considered; and (3) a decompression period in which the meeting begins to wind down. *Instructional items* should be handled in the first period, *items for decision* should be handled in the second period, and *items for discussion* should be handled in the third period.

Executive Summary Rule Reports circulated to meeting participants should always contain executive summaries or options memos. An executive summary highlights key points and conclusions of the report. An

Figure C.1	The Weekly Meeting	
1. Approve Minutes		2:00–2:05
2. Announcements		2:05–2:10
	New desks ordered	
	$1,000 each to your account	
3. Retreat Location (Action)		2:10–2:15
	Key West seems best	
4a. Vendor Selection (Action)		2:15–2:25
	A new vendor for gaskets	
	would like some business	
4b. Disposal of Broken Gaskets (Action)		2:25–2:35
	Trash? Sell abroad/fix?	
5. Permission to Ship (Action)		2:35–3:00
	Ship part with scratch?	
	Give discount?	
6. Improving Quality (Brains)		3:00–3:38
7. Adjourn		3:38–3:40

Source: *John Tropman.*

options memo summarizes alternatives to be discussed and decided on. This eliminates the need to sift through many pages to find relevant information and to spend meeting time shuffling through the report.

The Agenda Bell Rule   This rule is a more specific rule about when certain types of agenda items should be covered. Agenda items should be considered in order of ascending controversiality, then attention should be turned to discussion and decompression items. Figure C.2 shows a typical agenda bell for a meeting.

The Agenda Integrity Rule   All items on the agenda should be discussed, and items not on the agenda should not be discussed. This rule helps ensure that meeting participants do not sidetrack the meeting with items that are tangential, for which no one has prepared, or for which insufficient information is available.

The Temporal Integrity Rule   This rule is simple: Start on time and end on time. Follow a time schedule in the meeting itself. This ensures that all agenda items are given adequate time, that latecomers are not rewarded by having the meeting wait for them, and that people can count on finishing at a certain point.

The Minutes Rule   Minutes of meetings should have three characteristics: agenda relevance (information recorded is related to an agenda item), content relevance (minutes should be written in a form that follows the agenda so that it is easy to find pertinent material with a quick review), and decision focus (minutes should reflect decisions, conclusions, and actions agreed upon, rather than the processes by which the decisions are reached). After a brief summary of each item, skip a line and place the action or result in a box. Here is where names are named, times are timed, and so on. The key item is easy for everyone to see.

These 10 rules of meeting preparation help to ensure that when individuals arrive for a meeting and the meeting begins, a structure and plan will be in place to make the meeting productive and efficient.

4. Participation

The fourth *P*, **participation**, refers to the actual process of meetings and the methods used to ensure that meetings involve everyone present.

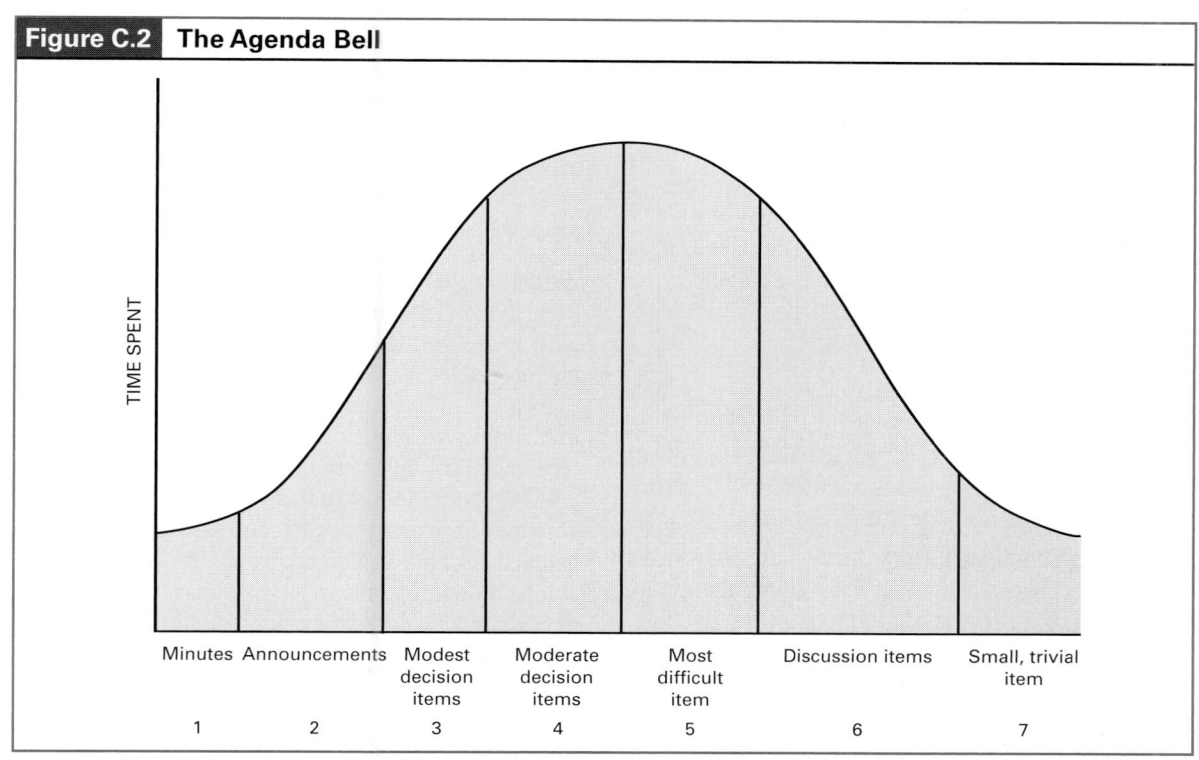

Figure C.2   The Agenda Bell

TIME SPENT

Minutes	Announcements	Modest decision items	Moderate decision items	Most difficult item	Discussion items	Small, trivial item
1	2	3	4	5	6	7

Source: *John Tropman.*

Provide Introductions Meeting participants should be introduced to each other and helped to feel comfortable together, especially if controversial issues are to be considered.

Establish Ground Rules It should be made clear what amount of participation is expected, what variations from the agenda will be tolerated, and what the time frame will be. Establishing a structure for the meeting at the outset helps keep the meeting on track.

Establish Decision Rules Decision rules are norms that make participants comfortable. Establish them at the beginning of the meeting. Because there are no neutral decision rules, meeting managers usually have to use several at once—a complex intellectual task. The most common are the extensive rule, the intensive rule, the involvement rule, the expert rule, and the power rule.

The *extensive rule* is majority rule. Each meeting participant votes on alternatives, and the alternatives with a majority of the votes wins. However, there are variations of this rule, which should be noted:

❏ *Highest total.* When more than two alternatives are being considered, none may get a majority of the votes. The alternative with the highest number of votes is adopted.

❏ *Straw vote.* A nonbinding vote is taken to get a sense of the participants' feelings toward various alternatives. This may happen several times before a decision is reached in order to eliminate nonsupported alternatives from consideration.

❏ *Weighted rating.* Meeting participants can divide 100 points among alternatives, so that the strength of their support can be tallied. If four alternatives exist, for example, a participant can give 90 points to one and 5 points to two others. The alternative with the most points wins.

❏ *Ranking.* Alternatives are rank ordered, and the alternative receiving the highest average ranking is adopted.

If the *intensive rule* is used, those who care most win. Through discussion, rather than voting, individuals who feel deeply can share that feeling with the group. Groups will try to be as accommodating as possible. However, problems occur if the majority cares a lot, but not "most," or if there are two groups that care deeply but differently. It requires a lot of imagination and attempts to come up with a solution that pleases the "shallow feelers" and the "deep feelers."

In the *involvement rule*, the person or subgroup that has to carry out any action gets to pick, or has it their way. Their downstream involvement gives them a particular view, which may not always be for the overall best. Using the *expert rule*, the participant with the law or science on his or her side wins. But neither law nor science is infallible by any means. Using the *power rule* means that the boss wins.

Any one of these rules can work, but quality decisions with the greatest buy-in (and hence, sticking power) usually come from consensus. Consensus, in this case, means that a decision is taken that meets, and can be shown to meet, each of the rules—it satisfied the greatest number of those who feel strongly, those who must carry it out, the experts, and the boss.

Sometimes it is necessary to proceed "in principle." Although agreement cannot be reached on all specific details, certain general principles can be agreed upon. The priniciples, rather than the entire proposal, are accepted. For example, you and your partner may decide in principle to have Italian food Friday night. Details (such as if you will go out, and if not, who will do the cooking) might remain unresolved for the moment while a range of details is explored.

Use a Variety of Media To maintain the interest of meeting participants, use various media to present information. Handouts, overhead transparencies, slides, flip charts, videos, and blackboard diagrams are all helpful in maintaining interest and increasing the efficiency with which information is presented and processed. Participants should be able to use at least two of their senses during a meeting (for example, seeing and hearing).

Encourage and Establish Participation Participation in a meeting should be equitable among participants, which does not mean that everyone must make exactly the same number of comments. Those with more information or those with vested interests in the topic will participate more. However, it is important to control the overparticipator or the person who dominates the discussion, as well as encourage those who may have something to contribute but may not be inclined to share it. Equity should also be maintained among different points of view, so that representatives of one side of an argument don't dominate the discussion. Ways to promote discussion among meeting participants include the following:

❏ Ask open-ended questions rather than questions that can be answered with a "yes" or a "no."

- Ask questions using the language of the participants rather than using jargon or recondite terminology.
- Encourage participants to share personal experiences that relate to the topic being considered.
- Use examples from your own experience to clarify points.
- Make eye contact with those to whom you are talking and summarize their points when they finish their statements.
- Ask group members for their reactions to points made by other meeting participants.
- When appropriate, involve others in answering a question asked of you.
- Remember that communication comes in a strand of two parts—the report part (information) and the rapport part (connection and feeling). Be sure to attend to both parts.
- As the leader, make certain that you facilitate the discussion rather than dominate it.

Summarize   Close the meeting by summarizing the decisions reached, tasks assigned, progress accomplished, key points discussed, and what was learned in the meeting. Review action items that will be reported on at the next meeting. Help meeting participants feel a sense of accomplishment for having spent their time in the meeting. This may be a good time to anticipate the next meeting by identifying when minutes and the next meeting's agenda will be distributed and what preparation will be required.

5. Perspective

The last *P* is **perspective**. Perspective directs us to view the meetings from a distance. It means evaluating each meeting and, every so often, the decisions of and process of the meeting series. At the end of each meeting, for example, you can use KSS methodology to do a quick and simple assessment. Pass out a piece of paper to each participant. Ask each participant to respond under each of the three letters—*K, S,* and *S. K* means "keep"—What went well about this meeting that we should keep or expand. *S* means "stop"—What about this meeting is nonproductive and should be stopped or phased out. *S* means "start"—What about this meeting is not happening and should be started. You may get the usual irreverent responses (for example, "better doughnuts"), but if you look for serious patterns of feedback, you can constantly improve the meeting series. The next week, give the participants

the results (in summary form) and let them know how you are using their feedback to improve the meeting.

Suggestions for Group Members

So far in this discussion of effective meeting management, we have focused on the role of the meeting manager—the person who calls, plans, and serves as the meeting's "conductor." This role is key to the success of any group activity. However, meeting participants also bear responsibility for the meeting's effectiveness. It is important for each participant to appreciate the impact of her or his contribution, both in shaping the short-term outcomes of meetings and affecting long-term career opportunities. The success of the meeting is the responsibility of everyone present, and even those not present, in the sense that these latter folks have the responsibility to let their views be known in advance. The best meetings are those in which meeting managers and other participants each take some responsibility for meeting leadership.

Following are several pointers for contributing to the effectiveness of meeting from a nonmanager's perspective.

1. *Determine if you need to attend the meeting.* Don't attend merely because you have been invited. If you have doubts about whether the meeting's agenda applies to you, discuss with the meeting manager why he or she believes your presence is important. Under the rule of three-fourths, you will know what is coming up in fairly specific detail. This information should help.

2. *Prepare.* Acquaint yourself with the agenda, and prepare any reports or information that will facilitate *others'* understanding of the issues. Come prepared with questions that will help you understand the issues.

3. *Be on time.* Stragglers not only waste the time of other participants by delaying the meeting or by requiring summaries of what has happened, but they also hinder effective team building and hurt morale.

4. *Ask for clarification on points that are unclear or ambiguous.* Often, you will find that others in this room have the same questions but were too timid to speak out.

5. *When giving information, be precise and to the point.* Don't bore everyone with anecdotes and details that add little to your point.

6. *Listen.* Keep eye contact with whoever is speaking, and try to ascertain the underlying ideas behind the comments. Be sensitive to the effect of your nonverbal behavior on speakers, such as slouching, doodling, or reading.

7. *Be supportive of other group members.* Following the guidelines on supportive communication, acknowledge and build on the comments of others. ("As Jane was saying . . . ")

8. *Assure equitable participation.* Take the lead in involving others so that everyone's talents are used. This is especially important if you know that critical information from particular points of view are not being included in the discussion. This can be rectified by encouraging those who rarely participate. ("Jim, your unit worked on something like this last year. What was your experience like?")

9. *Make disagreements principle-based.* If it is necessary to disagree with, or challenge, the comments of others, follow the guidelines for collaborative conflict management in the text. For example, base your comments on commonly held principles or values. ("That's an interesting idea, Bill, but how does it square with the president's emphasis on cost cutting?")

10. *Act and react in a way that will enhance the group performance.* Leave your personal agendas at the door and work toward the goals of the group.

Summary and Behavioral Guidelines

Meetings are a pervasive part of organizational life, especially for managers. Few important initiatives are forged without extensive and intensive group efforts. However, meetings are one of the most maligned aspects of organizational membership. To avoid poorly managed meetings, a Five-*P*'s approach was presented.

1. **Purpose** Use meetings to accomplish the following purposes:
   ❑ Decisions
      ❑ A complex problem needs to be resolved using the expertise of several people.
      ❑ Group members' commitment to a decision, or to each other, needs to be enhanced.
   ❑ Brainstorming
   ❑ Ideas about a problem need to be explored, such as:
      ❑ Precipitating and predisposing causes
      ❑ What is the root cause?

   ❑ Are there more effective and efficient ways we could approach this problem?
   ❑ What is the evidence?
   ❑ What does the evidence prove?
   ❑ Announcements
      ❑ Information needs to be shared simultaneously among several people.

2. **Participants** Make decisions regarding who and how many to invite based on the following:
   ❑ The size of the group should be comparable with the task. (For interactive groups, five to seven participants tend to work best.)
   ❑ A balance between individuals with strong task orientations and others with strong group-process orientations should be sought.
   ❑ Individuals should share some common goals or values.
   ❑ All relevant experience and knowledge need to be represented.
   ❑ The group's composition should reflect the goals of the meeting. (Homogeneity encourages solidarity and commitment; heterogeneity fosters creativity and innovation.)
   ❑ Be sure the general skills of problem knowing, problem solving, resource controlling, and key decision makers are on board.

3. **Plan** In preparing for the meeting, be sure to do the following:
   ❑ Provide for adequate physical space, audiovisual equipment, and so on.
   ❑ Establish priorities by sequencing agenda items and allotting time to each item.
   ❑ Prepare and distribute an agenda before, or at the beginning of, the meeting.
   ❑ Choose the most appropriate decision-making format structure for each item (for example, ordinary group discussion, brainstorming, or one of several consensus-building techniques).

4. **Process** In managing the group dynamics, specify the target time length, and highlight specific tasks by doing the following:
   ❑ Establish process ground rules, such as how decisions will be made.
   ❑ Allow members to become acquainted (if necessary) and make them feel comfortable.
   ❑ When critical thinking is important, refrain from expressing strong personal opinions. Also, assign the role of critical evaluator to group members.
   ❑ Sustain the flow of the meeting by using informational displays.

- Encourage the group not to stray from assigned tasks.
- Manage the discussion to achieve equitable participation.
- Discourage the premature evaluation of ideas.
- Prevent "social loafing" by assigning specific responsibilities and stressing the importance of group tasks.
- Discourage "conceptual misers"—those who opt for the "quick fix."
- Counteract the natural tendency for groups to make risky decisions by touching base with participants prior to the meeting so that discussion-induced trends can be detected. (The rule of halves helps with getting this information.)
- Deal with disruptive members by using supportive communication and collaborative conflict management skills.
- Conclude the meeting by summarizing what was accomplished, reviewing assignments, and making preparations for subsequent meetings, if necessary.

5. **Perspective** Evaluate each meeting using the KSS (Keep, Stop, Start) methodology by asking the following:
   - What went well in this meeting that we should keep?
   - What was nonproductive that we should stop or phase out?
   - What didn't happen in this meeting that we want to start in the future?

6. **Group Members** Foster constructive group dynamics as a participant by doing the following:
   - Take time to prepare for the meeting, and gain a clear understanding of the purposes of the meeting.
   - Respect other group members by arriving on time and leaving personal agendas at the door.
   - Listen to other group members, be supportive of them, and clarify and build upon points made by others.
   - Encourage participation by all members.

LEARNING

EXERCISES FOR CONDUCTING MEETINGS

Preparing and Conducting a Team Meeting at SSS Software

Part 1

Refer to the SSS Software In-Basket exercise at the end of this section. Assume the role of Chris Perillo. Since you are new to your position, you decide to hold a meeting with some or all of your direct reports tomorrow afternoon (Tuesday). You want to be brought up to date as well as to handle the items of business introduced in your e-mail, phone messages, and memos.

1. Review each of the 16 items in the SSS Software In-Basket exercise. This is the "business" to be covered in this meeting.
2. Determine the *purpose* of the meeting, the *participants* (who should attend), the *plan* (write an agenda; establish a time limit for the meeting) as well as the meeting *process* you will use, using the appropriate Behavioral Guidelines.

Part 2

3. Now select the nine other individuals that will be attending the meeting and assign them their roles in the Health and Financial Services Group. Each team member should realistically play the role assigned to him or her, even if not much specific information exists for the role in the memos. Each team member should play the role as though he or she were attending the first team meeting with a new leader. Each person should be prepared to make recommendations for each in-basket item pertaining to their role. The team should consist of:

   Chris Perillo, Vice President
   Bob Miller, Group 1 Manager
   Wanda Manners, Group 2 Manager
   William Chen, Group 3 Manager
   Leo Jones, Group 4 Manager
   Mark McIntyre, Group 5 Manager
   John Small, Group 6 Manager
   Marcus Harper, Group 8 Manager
   Armand Marke, Customer Service Manager
   Michelle Harrison, Office Administrator

4. At the conclusion of the meeting, assigned observers will provide feedback, using the Meeting Evaluation Worksheet as a guide.

Role Diagnosis

This exercise is intended to help you identify and practice effective role performance in meetings.

Listed below are a set of roles organized into three categories. As you are observing a team meeting, put check marks by the roles performed by the team members you are observing each time they make a comment or display behaviors that matches one of the roles listed below. If you are analyzing your own team after it has completed its meeting, put names of team members next to the roles they played. (See Chapter 9 for more information about these roles.)

Task-Facilitating Roles
Direction-giving
Information-seeking
Information-giving
Elaborating
Coordinating
Monitoring
Process-analyzing
Reality-testing
Enforcing
Summarizing

Process (Relationship-Building) Roles
Supporting
Harmonizing
Tension-relieving
Energizing
Developing
Facilitating
Processing

Blocking Roles
Overanalyzing
Overgeneralizing
Fault finding
Premature decision making
Presenting opinions as facts
Rejecting
Pulling rank
Dominating
Stalling

What suggestions do you have for improvement in the team members' performance? Identify some specific suggestions for more effective role performance in the meeting. Who could have done more and who could have done less? Why?

Meeting Evaluation Worksheet

It is important that individuals planning, conducting, and participating in meetings are asked periodically to evaluate the effectiveness of the time spent meeting together. The following worksheet can be used for this purpose.

To gain experience evaluating meetings, use the following questions to assess the effectiveness of a class or work-related project or staff meeting.

1. What is the specific purpose of the meeting?
2. Who was invited to attend? How are they contacted? Was the way in which the meeting announced appropriate (e.g., face-to-face, e-mail, secretary phone call)?

3. Was the agenda that was constructed consistent with the following rules?
   - ❏ The Agenda Rule (use action words)
   - ❏ The Rule of Sixths (two-thirds current items, one-third past and future items)
   - ❏ The Rule of Thirds (one-third warm up, one-third work, one-third wind down)
   - ❏ The Reports Rule (reports nonexistent; content reordered into specific items—announcements, decision, and brainstorm issues)
   - ❏ The Agenda Bell Rule (agenda ordered according to a bell-shaped "level of difficulty" process)
   - ❏ The Temporal Integrity Rule (start and stop on time)
   - ❏ The Minutes Rule (someone assigned to keep minutes)

4. What was done especially well in preparing for this meeting?

5. To what extent were the rules of effective meeting process followed in the meeting? Rate each step in terms of its effectiveness in the team meeting.

	Ineffective	Effective
1. Review purpose	_____	_____
2. Make introductions	_____	_____
3. Establish ground rules	_____	_____
4. Use informational displays	_____	_____
5. Ensure participation	_____	_____
6. Summarize conclusions	_____	_____

6. What could have been approved upon? What was omitted?

SSS Software In-Basket Memos, E-mails, Faxes, and Voice Mails

ITEM 1 – E-MAIL

TO: All Employees
FROM: Roger Steiner, Chief Executive Officer
DATE: October 15

I am pleased to announce that Chris Perillo has been appointed as Vice President of Operations for Health and Financial Services. Chris will immediately assume responsibility for all operations previously managed by Michael Grant. Chris will have end-to-end responsibility for the design, development, integration, and maintenance of custom software for the health and finance/banking industries. This responsibility includes all technical, financial, and staffing issues. Chris will also manage our program of software support and integration for the recently announced merger of three large health maintenance organizations (HMOs). Chris will be responsible for our recently announced project with a consortium of banks and financial firms operating in Tanzania. This project represents an exciting opportunity for us, and Chris's background seems ideally suited to the task.

Chris comes to this position with an undergraduate degree in Computer Science from the California Institute of Technology and an MBA from the University of Virginia. Chris began as a member of our technical/professional staff six years ago and has most recently served for three years as a group manager supporting domestic and international projects for our airlines industry group, including our recent work for the European Airbus consortium.

I am sure you all join me in offering congratulations to Chris for this promotion.

ITEM 2 – E-MAIL

TO: All Managers
FROM: Hal Harris, Vice President, Community and Public Relations
DATE: October 15

For your information, the following article appeared on the front page of the business section of Thursday's *Los Angeles Times*.

> *In a move that may create problems for SSS Software, Michael Grant and Janice Ramos have left SSS Software and moved to Universal Business Solutions Inc. Industry analysts see the move as another victory for Universal Business Solutions Inc. in their battle with SSS Software for share of the growing software development and integration business. Both Grant and Ramos had been with SSS Software for over seven years. Grant was most recently Vice President of Operations for all SSS Software's work in two industries: health and hospitals, and finance and banking. Ramos brings to Universal Business Solutions Inc. her special expertise in the growing area of international software development and integration.*

Hillary Collins, an industry analyst with Merrill Lynch, said "the loss of key staff to a competitor can often create serious problems for a firm such as SSS Software. Grant and Ramos have an insider's understanding of SSS Software's strategic and technical limitations. It will be interesting to see if they can exploit this knowledge to the advantage of Universal Business Solutions Inc."

ITEM 3 – E-MAIL

TO: Chris Perillo
FROM: Paula Sprague, Executive Assistant to Roger Steiner
DATE: October 15

Chris, I know that in your former position as a group manager in the Airline Services Division, you probably have met most of the group managers in the Health and Financial Services Division, but I thought you might like some more personal information about them. These people will be your direct reports on the management team.

Group #1: Bob Miller, 55-year-old white male, married (Anna) with two children and three grandchildren. Active in local Republican politics. Well regarded as a "hands-off" manager heading a high-performing team. Plays golf regularly with Mark McIntyre, John Small, and a couple of VPs from other divisions.

Group #2: Wanda Manners, 38-year-old white female, single with one school-age child. A fitness "nut" has run in several marathons. Some experience in Germany and Japan. Considered a hard-driving manager with a constant focus on the task at hand. Will be the first person to show up every morning.

Group #3: William Chen, 31-year-old male of Chinese descent, married (Harriet), two young children from his first marriage. Enjoys tennis and is quite good at it. A rising star in the company, he is highly respected by his peers as a "man of action" and a good friend.

Group #4: Leo Jones, 36-year-old white male, married (Janet) with an infant daughter. Recently returned from paternity leave. Has traveled extensively on projects, since he speaks three languages. Has liked hockey ever since the time he spent in Montreal. Considered a strong manager who gets the most out of his people.

Group #5: Mark McIntyre, 45-year-old white male, married (Mary Theresa) to an executive in the banking industry. No children. A lot of experience in Germany and Eastern Europe. Has been writing a mystery novel. Has always been a good "team player," but several members of his technical staff are not well respected and he hasn't addressed the problem.

Group #6: John Small, 38-year-old white male, recently divorced. Three children living with his wife. A gregarious individual who likes sports. He spent a lot of time in Mexico and Central America before he came to SSS Software. Recently has been doing mostly contract work with the federal government. An average manager, has had some trouble keeping his people on schedule.

Group #7: This position vacant since Janice Ramos left. Roger thinks we ought to fill this position quickly. Get in touch with me if you want information on any in-house candidates for any position.

Group #8: Marcus Harper, 42-year-old black male, married (Tamara) with two teenage children. Recently won an award in a local photography contest. Considered a strong manager who gets along with peers and works long hours.

Customer Services: Armand Marke, 38-year-old male, divorced. A basketball fan. Originally from Armenia. Previously a group manager. Worked hard to establish the Technical Services Phone Line, but now has pretty much left it alone.

Office Administrator: Michelle Harrison, 41-year-old white female, single. Grew up on a ranch and still rides horses whenever she can. A strict administrator.

There are a number of good folks here, but they don't function well as a management team. I think Michael played favorites, especially with Janice and Leo. There are a few cliques in this group, and I'm not sure how effectively Michael dealt with them. I expect you will find it a challenge to build a cohesive team.

ITEM 4 – E-MAIL

TO: Chris Perillo
FROM: Wanda Manners, Group 2 Manager
DATE: October 15

CONFIDENTIAL AND RESTRICTED

Although I know you are new to your job, I feel it is important that I let you know about some information I just obtained concerning the development work we recently completed for First National Investment. Our project involved the development of asset management software for managing their international funds. This was a very complex project due to the volatile exchange rates and the forecasting tools we needed to develop.

As part of this project, we had to integrate the software and reports with all their existing systems and reporting mechanisms. To do this, we were given access to all of their existing software (much of which was developed by Universal Business Solutions Inc.). Of course, we signed an agreement acknowledging that the software to which we were given access was proprietary and that our access was solely for the purpose of our system integration work associated with the project.

Unfortunately, I have learned that some parts of the software we developed actually "borrow" heavily from complex application programs developed for First National Investment by Universal Business Solutions Inc. It seems obvious to me that one or more of the software developers from Group 5 (that is, Mark McIntyre's group) inappropriately "borrowed" algorithms developed by Universal Business Solutions Inc. I am sure that doing so saved us significant development time on some aspects of the project. It seems very unlikely that First National Investment or Universal Business Solutions Inc. will ever become aware of this issue.

Finally, First National Investment is successfully using the software we developed and is thrilled with the work we did. We brought the project in on time and under budget. You probably know that they have invited us to bid on several other substantial projects.

I'm sorry to bring this delicate matter to your attention, but I thought you should know about it.

ITEM 5A – E-MAIL

TO: Chris Perillo
FROM: Paula Sprague, Executive Assistant to Roger Steiner
DATE: October 15
RE: Letter from C.A.R.E. Services (copies attached)

Roger asked me to work on this C.A.R.E. project and obviously wants some fast action. A lot of the staff are already booked solid for the next couple of weeks. I knew that Elise Soto and Chu Hung Woo have the expertise to do this system and when I checked with them, they were relatively free. I had them pencil in the next two weeks and wanted to let you know. Hopefully, it will take a "hot potato" out of your hands.

ITEM 5B – COPY OF FAX

C.A.R.E.
Child and Adolescent Rehabilitative and Educational Services
A United Way Member Agency
200 Main Street
Los Angeles, California 90230

DATE: October 11

Roger Steiner, CEO
SSS Software
13 Miller Way
Los Angeles, California 90224

Dear Roger,

This letter is a follow-up to our conversation after last night's board meeting. I appreciated your comments during the board meeting about the need for sophisticated computer systems in nonprofit organizations and I especially appreciate your generous offer of assistance to have SSS Software provide assistance to deal with the immediate problem with our accounting system. Since the board voted to fire the computer consultant, I am very worried about getting our reports done in time to meet the state funding cycle.

Thanks again for your offer of help during this crisis.

Sincerely yours,

Janice Polocizwic

Janice Polocizwic
Executive Director

ITEM 5C – COPY OF A LETTER

SSS SOFTWARE
13 Miller Way
Los Angeles, CA 90224

DATE: October 12

Janice Polocizwic
Executive Director, C.A.R.E. Services
200 Main Street
Los Angeles, California 90230

Dear Janice,

I received your fax of October 11. I have asked Paula Sprague, my executive assistant, to line up people to work on your accounting system as soon as possible. You can expect to hear from her shortly.

Sincerely,

Roger Steiner

Roger Steiner
cc: Paula Sprague, Executive Assistant

ITEM 6 – E-MAIL

TO: Michael Grant
FROM: Harry Withers, Group 6 Technical Staff
DATE: October 12

PERSONAL AND CONFIDENTIAL

Our team is having difficulty meeting the submission deadline of November 5 for the Halstrom project. Kim, Fred, Peter, Kyoto, Susan, Mala, and I have been working on the project for several weeks, but we are experiencing some problems and may need additional time. I hesitate to write this letter, but the main problem is that our group manager, John Small, is involved in a relationship with Mala. Mala gets John's support for her ideas and brings them to the team as required components of the project. Needless to say, this has posed some problems for the group. Mala's background is especially valuable for this project, but Kim and Fred, who have both worked very hard on the project, do not want to work with her. In addition, one member of the team has been unavailable recently because of child-care needs. Commitment to the project and team morale have plummeted. However, we'll do our best to get the project finished as soon as possible. Mala will be on vacation the next two weeks, so I'm expecting that some of us can complete it in her absence.

ITEM 7 – VOICE MAIL MESSAGE

Hello, Michael. This is Jim Bishop of United Hospitals. I wanted to talk with you about the quality assurance project that you are working on for us. When Jose Martinez first started talking with us, I was impressed with his friendliness and expertise. But recently, he doesn't seem to be getting much accomplished and has seemed distant and on edge in conversations. Today, I asked him about the schedule and he seemed very defensive and not entirely in control of his emotions. I am quite concerned about our project. Please give me a call.

ITEM 8 – VOICE MAIL MESSAGE

Hi, Michael. This is Armand. I wanted to talk with you about some issues with the Technical Services Phone Line. I've recently received some complaint letters from Phone Line customers whose complaints have included long delays while waiting for a technician to answer the phone, technicians who are not knowledgeable enough to solve problems, and, on occasion, rude service. Needless to say, I'm quite concerned about these complaints.

I believe that the overall quality of the Phone Line staff is very good, but we continue to be understaffed, even with the recent hires. The new technicians look strong, but are working on the help-line before being fully trained. Antolina, our best tech, often brings her child to work, which is adding to the craziness around here.

I think you should know that we're feeling a lot of stress here. I'll talk with you soon.

ITEM 9 – VOICE MAIL MESSAGE

Hi, Chris, it's Pat. Congratulations on your promotion. They definitely picked the right person. It's great news—for me, too. You've been a terrific mentor so far, so I'm expecting to learn a lot from you in your new position. How about lunch next week?

ITEM 10 – VOICE MAIL MESSAGE

Chris, this is Bob Miller. Just thought you'd like to know that John's joke during our planning meeting has disturbed a few of the women in my group. Frankly, I think the thing's being blown out of proportion, especially since we all know this is a good place for both men and women to work. Give me a call if you want to chat about this.

ITEM 11 – VOICE MAIL MESSAGE

Hello. This is Lorraine Adams from Westside Hospital. I read in today's *Los Angeles Times* that you will be taking over for Michael Grant. We haven't met yet, but your division has recently finished two large million-dollar projects for Westside. Michael Grant and I had some discussion about a small conversion of a piece of existing software to be compatible with the new systems. The original vendor had said that they would do the work, but they have been stalling, and I need to move quickly. Can you see if Harris Wilson, Chu Hung Woo, and Elise Soto are available to do this work as soon as possible? They were on the original project and work well with our people.

Um . . . (long pause) I guess I should tell you that I got a call from Michael offering to do this work. But I think I should stick with SSS Software. Give me a call.

ITEM 12 – VOICE MAIL MESSAGE

Hi, Chris, this is Roosevelt Moore calling. I'm a member of your technical/professional staff. I used to report to Janice Ramos, but since she left the firm, I thought I'd bring my concerns directly to you. I'd like to arrange some time to talk with you about my experiences since returning from six weeks of paternity leave. Some of my major responsibilities have been turned over to others. I seem to be out of the loop and wonder if my career is at risk. Also, I am afraid that I won't be supported or seriously considered for the opening created by Janice's departure. Frankly, I feel like I'm being screwed for taking my leave. I'd like to talk with you this week.

ITEM 13 – E-MAIL

TO: Michael Grant
FROM: Jose Martinez, Group 1 Technical Staff
DATE: October 12

I would like to set up a meeting with you as soon as possible. I suspect that you will get a call from Jim Bishop of United Hospitals and want to be sure that you hear my side of the story first. I have been working on a customized system design for quality assurance for them using a variation of the J–3 product we developed several years ago. They had a number of special requirements and some quirks in their accounting systems, so I have had to put in especially long hours. I've worked hard to meet their demands, but they keep changing the ground rules. I keep thinking, this is just another J–3 I'm working on, but they have been interfering with an elegant design I have developed. It seems I'm not getting anywhere on this project. Earlier today, I had a difficult discussion with their controller. He asked for another major change. I've been fighting their deadline and think I am just stretched too thin on this project. Then Jim Bishop asked me if the system was running yet. I was worn out from dealing with the controller, and I made a sarcastic comment to Jim Bishop. He gave me a funny look and just walked out of the room.

I would like to talk with you about this situation at your earliest convenience.

ITEM 14 – E-MAIL

TO: Chris Perillo
FROM: John Small, Group 6 Manager
DATE: October 15

Welcome aboard, Chris. I look forward to meeting with you. I just wanted to put a bug in your ear about finding a replacement for Janice Ramos. One of my technical staff,

Mala Abendano, has the ability and drive to make an excellent group manager. I have encouraged her to apply for the position. I'd be happy to talk with you further about this, at your convenience.

ITEM 15 – E-MAIL

TO: Chris Perillo
FROM: Paula Sprague, Executive Assistant to Roger Steiner
DATE: October 15

Roger asked me to let you know about the large contract we have gotten in Tanzania. It means that a team of four managers will be making a short trip to determine current needs. They will assign their technical staff the tasks of developing a system and software here over the next six months, and then the managers and possibly some team members will be spending about 10 months on site in Tanzania to handle the implementation. Roger thought you might want to hold an initial meeting with some of your managers to check on their interest and willingness to take this sort of assignment. Roger would appreciate an e-mail of your thoughts about the issues to be discussed at this meeting, additional considerations about sending people to Tanzania, and about how you will put together an effective team to work on this project. The October 15 memo I sent to you will provide you with some information you'll need to start making these decisions.

ITEM 16 – E-MAIL

TO: Chris Perillo
FROM: Sharon Shapiro, VP of Human Resources
DATE: October 15
RE: Upcoming meeting

I want to update you on the rippling effect of John Small's sexual joke at last week's planning meeting. Quite a few women have been very upset and have met informally to talk about it. They have decided to call a meeting of all people concerned about this kind of behavior throughout the firm. I plan to attend, so I'll keep you posted.

ITEM 17 – E-MAIL

TO: All SSS Software Managers
FROM: Sharon Shapiro, VP of Human Resources
DATE: October 15
RE: Promotions and External Hires

YEAR-TO-DATE (JANUARY THROUGH SEPTEMBER) PROMOTIONS AND EXTERNAL HIRES

| | Race | | | | | Sex | | |
Level	White	Black	Asian	Hispanic	Native American	M	F	Total
Hires into Executive Level	0	0	0	0	0	0	0	0
	(0%)	(0%)	(0%)	(0%)	(0%)	(0%)	(0%)	

Level	Race					Sex		
	White	Black	Asian	Hispanic	Native American	M	F	Total
Promotions to Executive Level	0 (0%)	0 (0%)	0 (0%)	0 (0%)	0 (0%)	0 (0%)	0 (0%)	0
Hires into Management Level	2 (67%)	1 (33%)	0 (0%)	0 (0%)	0 (0%)	2 (67%)	1 (33%)	3
Promotions to Management Level	7 (88%)	0 (0%)	1 (12%)	0 (0%)	0 (0%)	7 (88%)	1 (12%)	8
Hires into Technical/ Professional Level	10 (36%)	6 (21%)	10 (36%)	2 (7%)	0 (0%)	14 (50%)	14 (50%)	28
Promotions to Technical/ Professional Level	0 (0%)	0 (0%)	0 (0%)	0 (0%)	0 (0%)	0 (0%)	0 (0%)	0
Hires into Non-management Level	4 (20%)	10 (50%)	2 (10%)	4 (20%)	0 (0%)	6 (30%)	14 (70%)	20
Promotions to Nonmanagement Level	NA	NA	NA	NA	NA	NA	NA	NA

SSS SOFTWARE EMPLOYEE (EEO) CLASSIFICATION REPORT AS OF JUNE 30

Level	Race					Sex		
	White	Black	Asian	Hispanic	Native American	M	F	Total
Executive Level	11 (92%)	0 (0%)	1 (8%)	0 (0%)	0 (0%)	11 (92%)	1 (8%)	12
Management Level	43 (90%)	2 (4%)	2 (4%)	1 (2%)	0 (0%)	38 (79%)	10 (21%)	48
Technical/ Professional Level	58 (45%)	20 (15%)	37 (28%)	14 (11%)	1 (1%)	80 (62%)	50 (38%)	130

Level	Race					Sex		Total
	White	Black	Asian	Hispanic	Native American	M	F	
Non-management Level	29 (48%)	22 (37%)	4 (7%)	4 (7%)	1 (2%)	12 (20%)	48 (80%)	60
Total	141 (56%)	44 (18%)	44 (18%)	19 (8%)	2 (1%)	141 (56%)	109 (44%)	250

NOTE: The SSS Software exercise is used with permission. Copyright © 1995 by Susan Schor, Joseph Seltzer, and James Smither. All rights reserved.

PRACTICE

A

ability: the product of aptitude multiplied by training and opportunity.

abstract conceptualization: a way of gathering information of those who are inclined to take in information that is abstract, symbolic, or theoretical.

abundance approach: the right side of the performance continuum, characterized by concepts such as striving for excellence and being ethically virtuous, which are especially relevant to the skill of leading positive change.

accommodating: the learning style of those who are best at hands-on experience.

accommodating approach: a response to conflict that tries to preserve a friendly interpersonal relationship by satisfying the other party's concerns while ignoring one's own. It generally ends with both parties losing.

achievement orientation: an emphasis on personal accomplishment and merit as the basis for getting ahead, used in contrast to an ascription orientation. One of the key dimensions that identifies international culture differences.

active experimentation: a way of responding to information of those who are inclined to act immediately on information they receive.

advising response: a response that provides direction, evaluation, personal opinion, or instructions.

affectivity orientation: an emphasis on open displays of emotion and feeling as being acceptable, used in contrast to a neutral orientation. One of the key dimensions that identifies international culture differences.

alarm stage: initial response to stress characterized by increases in anxiety, fear, sorrow, or depression.

ambidextrous thinking: the use of both the left and right sides of the brain, indicative of the most creative problem solvers.

analytical problem solving: a method of solving problems that involves four steps: (1) defining the problem; (2) generating alternative solutions; (3) evaluating and selecting an alternative; and (4) implementing and following up on the solution.

anticipatory stressor: the anxious expectation of unfamiliar, uncertain, or disagreeable events.

appropriately challenging goals: one of the factors affecting the motivating potential of stated goals—hard goals tend to be more motivating than easy goals.

ascription orientation: an emphasis on attributes such as age, gender, or family background as the basis for getting ahead, used in contrast to achievement orientation. One of the key dimensions that identifies international culture differences.

assimilating: the learning style of those who are best at processing a wide range of information and putting it into a concise, cohesive, logical form.

attraction: also referred to as personal attraction, "likability" stemming from agreeable behavior and attractive physical appearance; a combination of behaviors normally associated with friendships that have been shown to contribute to managerial success.

autonomy: the freedom to choose how and when to do a particular task; one of the characteristics of an intrinsically satisfying job.

avoiding response: an unassertive, uncooperative reaction to conflict that neglects the interests of both parties by sidestepping the issue. The resulting frustration may engender power struggles as others rush to fill the leadership vacuum.

B

benchmarking: comparing current levels of performance to the highest standards available, by finding best practice, studying it in detail, and planning to exceed it.

bias against thinking: the inclination to avoid mental work, one indication of the conceptual block, complacency.

blocking roles: behaviors that stand in the way of or inhibit the effective performance of a team, or that subvert team member effectiveness.

brainstorming: a technique designed to help people solve problems by generating alternative solutions without prematurely evaluating and rejecting them.

C

centrality: the attribute of a position in which the occupant is a key member of informal networks of task-related and interpersonal relationships. The resulting access to information, resources, and the personal commitment of others is an important source of power.

clarification probe: question(s) designed to clarify information given by the interviewee.

closed questions: interview questions designed to elicit specific information from interviewees by restricting the possible answers the interviewee can give. Useful when time is limited and/or when answers to open questions need clarifying.

coaching: interpersonal communication used by managers to pass along advice and information or to set standards for subordinates.

cognitive style: the manner in which an individual gathers and evaluates information he/she receives.

collaborating approach: the cooperative, assertive, problem-solving mode of responding to conflict. It focuses on finding solutions to the basic problems and issues that are acceptable to both parties rather than on finding fault and assigning blame. Of the conflict management approaches, this is the only win–win strategy.

collective feeling: a feature of compassionate organizations, in which managers plan events where people can share feelings such as grief, support, or love.

collective noticing: a feature of compassionate organizations, in which managers notice or simply become aware when employees suffer or experience difficulty.

collective responding: a feature of compassionate organizations, in which managers ensure that an appropriate response is made when healing or restoration is needed.

collectivism orientation: an emphasis on the predominance of groups, families, or collectives over individuals, used in contrast to individualism orientation. One of the key dimensions that identifies international culture differences. Also referred to as communitarianism.

commitment: the conceptual block that results when an individual endorses a particular point of view, definition, or solution.

comparative standards: standards that compare current performance to similar individuals or organizations, one of several different kinds of best practice standards.

compassion: in an organization, the capacity to foster collective noticing, feeling, and responding.

competence: areas in which a person performs fine—not stellar, but good enough.

complacency: the conceptual block that occurs not because of poor thinking habits or inappropriate assumptions but because of fear, ignorance, self-satisfaction, or mental laziness.

compression: the conceptual block that results from an individual's looking at a problem too narrowly, screening out too much relevant data, or making assumptions that inhibit solving the problem.

compromising response: a reaction to conflict that attempts to find satisfaction for both parties by "splitting the difference." If overused, it sends the message that settling disputes is more important than solving problems.

conceptual blocks: mental obstacles that restrict the way a problem is defined and limit the number of alternative solutions that might otherwise be considered.

concrete experience: a way of gathering information of those who are inclined to take in information that is tangible, concrete, and sensual.

conformity level: the second level of values maturity, at which moral reasoning is based on agreement with and support of society's conventions and expectations.

congruence: exactly matching the communication, verbally and nonverbally, to what an individual is thinking and feeling.

conjunctive communication: connection of responses to previous messages in such a way that conversation flows smoothly.

consistent goals: one of the factors affecting the motivating potential of stated goals—it is difficult to pursue goals that are inconsistent or incompatible.

constancy: the conceptual block that results from using only one way to look at a problem—to approach, define, describe, or solve it.

continuous improvement: small, incremental changes team members initiate.

converging: the learning style of those who are best at finding practical uses for ideas and theories.

core competence: an aggregation of individual team member skills, including knowledge, styles, communication patterns, and ways of behaving.

core self-evaluation: a concept that captures the essential aspects of personality; it accounts for the five personality dimensions (neuroticism, extroversion, conscientiousness, agreeableness, and openness).

counseling: interpersonal communication used to help subordinates recognize their own problems rather than offering advice, direction, or a right answer.

creating irreversible momentum: ensuring that positive change gains such momentum that it becomes institutionalized and cannot be thwarted.

creative problem solving: a method of solving problems that involves four stages: preparation, incubation, illumination, and verification.

D

deep breathing: relaxation technique of taking several successive, slow deep breaths, then exhaling completely.

defensiveness: focusing on self-defense rather than listening; occurs when an individual feels threatened or punished by the communication.

deficit approach: the left side of the performance continuum, characterized by concepts such as solving problems and making a profit, which has garnered much more attention than the abundance approach but is less relevant to the skill of leading positive change.

deflecting response: a response that switches the focus from the communicator's subject to one selected by the listener; or simply the change of subject by the listener.

delegation: assignment of responsibility for tasks to subordinates.

descriptive communication: objective description of the event or behavior that needs modification; description of the reaction to the behavior or its consequences; and suggestion of a more acceptable alternative.

diffuseness orientation: an emphasis on integrating work, family, and personal roles in a society, used in contrast to specificity orientation. One of the key dimensions that identifies international culture differences.

dignity (and liberty): the ethical decision principle that a decision is right and proper if it preserves the basic humanity of individuals and provides the opportunity for them to have greater freedom.

direct analogies: a synectic problem-solving technique in which individuals apply facts, technology, and previous experience to solving a problem.

dirty dozen: twelve negative attributes found in companies facing decline, turbulence, downsizing, and change.

disciplining: a motivational strategy by which a manager reacts negatively to an employee's undesirable behavior in order to discourage further occurrences. Disciplining may be useful up to a point but does not encourage exceptional performance.

disconfirmation: a "put-down"; or the feeling resulting from communication that demeans or belittles the recipient and threatens his or her sense of self-worth.

disjunctive communication: responses that are disconnected from what was stated before. It can result from (1) a lack of equal opportunity to speak; (2) long pauses in a speech or before a response; or (3) when one person decides the topic of conversation.

disowned communication: attribution to an unknown person, group, or some external source; allows the communicator to avoid responsibility for the message and therefore avoid investing in the interaction.

distributive bargaining perspective: negotiation tactic that requires both parties to sacrifice something to resolve the conflict—to divide up a "fixed pie." (Contrast with the integrative approach.)

diverging: the learning style of those who are best at viewing concrete situations from many different points of view.

double-barreled question: a problematic question that actually consists of two questions that should be asked separately in order to avoid confusing the interviewee.

E

effort: an important source of power suggesting personal commitment.

elaboration probe: question(s) designed to pursue a topic further when an interviewee has responded with superficial or inadequate information.

emotional intelligence: the ability to manage oneself and to manage relationships with others.

empowerment: the use of acquired power to give others power in order to accomplish objectives; it strikes a balance between lack of power and abuse of power.

enactive strategy: a method of managing stress that creates a new environment by eliminating the stressors.

encounter stressor: the type of stressor that results from interpersonal conflict.

environmentally induced stress: conflict-fostering tension induced by such organizational factors as budget tightening or uncertainty caused by rapid, repeated change.

equity: workers' perceptions of the fairness of rewards based on the comparison of what they are getting out of the work relationship (outcomes) to what they are putting into it (input).

ethical decision making: a well-developed set of moral principles used when making decisions.

evaluative communication: a statement that makes a judgment about or places a label on other individuals or on their behavior.

Everest goals: goals that represent an ultimate achievement, an extraordinary accomplishment, or a beyond-the-norm outcome.

expertise: cognitive ability resulting from formal training and education or from on-the-job experience; an important source of power in a technological society.

extrinsic outcomes: rewards for performances that are controlled by someone other than the employee—usually the supervisor—such as appreciation, job security, or good working conditions. (Compare with internal motivators.)

F

false bipolar question: a poorly worded interview question, implying the choices are mutually exclusive, when in fact, the respondents are more likely to have mixed feelings (e.g., do you approve or disapprove of overtime work?).

fantasy analogies: a synetic problem-solving technique in which individuals ask, "In my wildest dreams, how would I wish the problem to be resolved?"

feedback: information regularly received by individuals from superiors about their performance on a job. Knowledge of results permits workers to understand how their efforts have contributed to organizational goals.

flexibility: the freedom to exercise one's judgment—an important prerequisite for gaining power in a position—particularly in tasks that are high in variety and novelty.

flexibility of thought: the diversity of ideas or concepts generated.

flexible communication: the result of the willingness of the coach or counselor to accept the existence of additional data or other alternatives and to acknowledge that other individuals may be able to make significant contributions both to the problem solution and to the relationship.

flow: a psychological state in which a person's mind is so totally engaged in a challenging task that he or she often loses track of time, physical appetites, and outside influences.

fluency of thought: the number of ideas or concepts produced in a given length of time.

forcing response: an assertive, uncooperative response to conflict that uses the exercise of authority to satisfy one's own needs at the expense of another's.

forgiveness: in an organization, the capacity to abandon justified resentment, bitterness, and blame, and instead, to adopt positive, forward-looking approaches in response to harm or damage.

forming stage: first stage of team development in which the team is oriented to each other and establishes clarity of purpose.

frameworks: familiar patterns that managers can use to clarify complex or ambiguous situations.

funnel sequence: a sequence of interview questions that begins with general questions and moves toward more and more specific questions.

G

goal characteristics: effective goals are specific, consistent, and appropriately challenging.

goal setting: the foundation of an effective motivational program, which consists of (1) including employees in the goal-setting process; (2) setting specific, consistent, and challenging goals; and (3) providing feedback.

goal-setting process: the critical consideration is that goals must be understood and accepted if they are to be effective.

goal standards: standards that compare current performance to publicly stated goals, one of several different kinds of best practice standards.

gratitude: in an organization, the frequent expression of thankfulness that leads to reciprocal behavior, equity, and justice.

groupthink: one of the pitfalls in group decision making that occurs when the pressure to reach consensus interferes with critical thinking. When the leader or the majority appear to prefer a particular solution, holders of dissenting views are reluctant to speak out.

H

hardiness: a combination of the three characteristics of a highly stress-resistant personality—control, commitment, and challenge.

hierarchical-needs model: a general theory of motivation, positing that behavior is oriented toward need fulfillment, and that human needs tend to be arranged hierarchically (i.e., lower-level needs must be fulfilled before higher-order needs become salient).

human capital: a person's abilities and competencies ("I know the answer to the question"). Compare with social capital.

I

idea champion: person who comes up with the innovative solutions to problems.

ideal standards: standards that compare current performance to an ideal or perfect standard, one of several different kinds of best practice standards.

ignoring: a manager's neglect of both the performance and the satisfaction of employees. Such a lack of effective leadership can paralyze a work unit.

ignoring commonalities: a manifestation of the commitment block—the failure to identify similarities among seemingly disparate situations or data.

illumination stage: in creative thought, the third stage, which occurs when an insight is recognized and a creative solution is articulated.

imagery and fantasy: a relaxation technique using visualization to change the focus of one's thoughts.

imagination creativity: the pursuit of new ideas, breakthroughs, and radical approaches to problem solving.

imperviousness in communication: the failure of the communicator to acknowledge the feelings or opinions of the listener.

imposing: a manager's exploitation of employees by assigning tasks with the sole emphasis on performance and without regard to their job satisfaction—usually disastrous in the long term.

improvement creativity: the pursuit of incremental improvements on existing ideas.

improvement standards: standards that compare current performance to improvements made in the past, one of several different kinds of best practice standards.

incongruence: a mismatch between what one is experiencing and what one is aware of, or a mismatch between what one feels and what one communicates.

incubation creativity: the pursuit of creativity through teamwork, involvement, and coordination among individuals.

incubation stage: an early stage in creative thought in which mostly unconscious mental activity combines unrelated thoughts in pursuit of a solution to a problem.

indifference: a type of communication in which the other person's existence or importance is not acknowledged.

individualism orientation: an emphasis on the self, uniqueness, and individuality, used in contrast to collectivism orientation. One of the key dimensions that identifies international cultural differences.

indulging: a manager's emphasis on employee satisfaction to the exclusion of employee performance; the resulting country club atmosphere hinders productivity.

informational deficiencies: breakdowns in interorganizational communication. Conflicts based on the resulting misunderstandings tend to be common but easy to resolve.

initiator role: the part played in a conflict management model by the individual who first registers a complaint with another person who is the "responder." (See Behavioral Guidelines in Chapter 7.)

innovation: large, visible, discontinuous changes; breakthroughs.

innovativeness: fostering new ideas among individuals by methods such as placing them in teams and separating them at least temporarily from the normal pressures of organizational life.

instrumental values: those values that prescribe desirable standards of conduct or methods to reach a goal.

integrating: a motivation strategy that emphasizes job performance and job satisfaction equally—a challenging strategy for a manager to implement, but one that can result in both high productivity and high morale of employees.

integrative perspective: negotiation tactic in which the focus is on collaborative ways of "expanding the pie" by avoiding fixed, incompatible positions. (Contrast with distributive approach.)

internal locus: the viewpoint of an individual who attributes the success or failure of particular behavior to his/her own actions.

interpersonal competence: the ability to manage conflict, to build and manage high-performance teams, to conduct efficient meetings, to coach and counsel employees, to provide negative feedback in constructive ways, to influence others' opinions, and to motivate and energize employees.

interpersonal orientation: the aspect of self-awareness that relates to behavior and relationships with other people.

interview: a specialized form of communication conducted for a specific, task-related purpose.

intrinsic outcomes: job characteristics inherent in the job itself, over which the manager has no control, and that determine whether or not a particular employee will find that job interesting and satisfying. (Compare with external motivators.)

intuitive strategy: a type of thinking that uses preconceived notions about the sort of information that will be relevant and looks for commonalities among the various elements of data.

invalidating communication: that which denies the other person the possibility of contributing to the communication.

inverted funnel sequence: a sequence of interview questions that begins with specific questions and moves toward more and more general questions.

investment creativity: the pursuit of rapid goal achievement and competitiveness.

issue-focused conflict: interpersonal conflicts that are substantive, or content, oriented. See people-focused conflict.

issue selling: influence strategy characterized by being the champion or representative of an issue.

J

Janusian thinking: thinking contradictory thoughts at the same time; conceiving two opposing ideas to be true concurrently.

L

leadership: a temporary, dynamic condition that can be developed and demonstrated by any person willing to choose to adopt a certain mind-set and implement certain key skills and competencies.

leading positive change: a management skill that focuses on unlocking positive human potential, creating abundance and human well-being, and acknowledging that positive change engages the heart as well as the mind.

leading question: a tricky interview question that includes the desired answer in the question itself. While useful in a sales interview, it can lead to biased answers in other types of interviews.

learning stair: a model, developed by researchers at the National Training Laboratories in Bethel, Maine, that grades learning retention; at the lowest level, people remember only 5 percent of what they hear in a lecture, while at the highest level, people remember 90 percent of what they teach to others.

learning style: the way in which individuals perceive, interpret, and respond to information. Four main learning styles exist.

left-hemisphere thinking: brain activity concerned with logical, analytic, linear, or sequential tasks.

legitimacy: conformity with an organization's value system and practices, which increases one's acceptance and thus one's influence in that organization.

level of initiative: the extent to which a subordinate is expected to take a task. At least five levels can be identified: (1) wait to be told; (2) ask what to do; (3) recommend, then act; (4) report after acting; and (5) act independently.

life balance: the development of resiliency in all areas of one's life in order to handle stress that cannot be eliminated.

locus of control: the second dimension of orientation toward change; the viewpoint from which an individual judges the extent to which he/she controls his/her own destiny.

M

manifest needs model: a general theory of motivation, positing that individuals can be classified according to the strengths of their various needs, which are often divergent and conflicting.

measures: methods for assessing levels of success.

mediator role: the conflict management role played by the third party who intervenes in a dispute between an "initiator" and a "responder."

metrics: specific indicators of success.

milestones: benchmarks to determine when detectable progress will have occurred.

morphological synthesis: a four-step process intended to expand the number of creative alternatives available for solving a problem. It involves combining the different attributes of a problem together in unique ways.

motivation: a combination of desire and commitment demonstrated by effort.

muscle relaxation: technique of relaxation by easing the tension in successive muscle groups.

N

need for achievement: an expressed desire for accomplishment and recognition.

need for affiliation: an expressed desire for social relations.

need for control: the desire to maintain for oneself a satisfactory balance of power and influence in relationships.

need for power: an expressed desire for control, or influence, over others.

negative deviance: change toward illness, error, conflict, and the like, usually depicted as a shift to the left along the continuum that shows normal, healthy performance in the middle.

negative energizers: people who deplete the good feelings and enthusiasm in others and make them feel diminished, devalued, or criticized.

negotiation strategies: two broad approaches or perspectives used for resolving differences or allocating scarce resources—integrative and distributive.

neutral orientation: an emphasis on rational and stoic approaches to problem solving, used in contrast to an affective orientation. One of the key dimensions that identifies international cultural differences.

noninquisitiveness: the failure to ask questions, obtain information or search for data; an example of the complacency block.

norming stage: the second stage of a team's development in which expectations become clear, a group identity is formed, and the norms become clear and accepted.

O

open questions: interview questions designed to elicit general information from interviewees—how they feel, what their priorities are, and how much they know about a topic. Useful for establishing rapport, they can be time-consuming.

orchestrator: person who brings together cross-functional groups and necessary political support to facilitate implementation of a creative idea.

organizational culture: the values and basic assumptions that typify an organization. It refers to the most basic elements of an organization, or "just the way things are around here."

orientation toward change: an individual's adaptability to ever-increasing levels of ambiguity and turbulence.

owned communication: statements for which a person takes responsibility, acknowledging that he or she is the source of the message; an indication of supportive communication.

P

participants: individuals invited to attend a meeting.

participation: the actual process of meetings and the methods used to ensure that meetings involve everyone present. The involvement of individuals—in addition to a single leader—in an activity.

particularism orientation: an emphasis on relationships and close personal connections to govern behavior, used in contrast to universalism orientation. One of the key dimensions that identifies international cultural differences.

people-focused conflict: interpersonal conflict that is personal (e.g., a clash between different personalities or interpersonal styles). See issue-focused conflict.

perceptual stereotyping: defining a problem by using preconceptions based on past experience, thus preventing the problem from being viewed in novel ways.

performance: the product of ability multiplied by motivation.

performing stage: stage of a team when it is able to function as a highly effective and efficient unit.

personal analogies: recommended as part of synectics, whereby individuals try to identify themselves as the problem, asking the question, "If I were the problem, what would I like? What would satisfy me?"

personal differences: variations among individuals' values and needs that have been shaped by different socialization processes. Interpersonal conflicts stemming from such incompatibilities are the most difficult for a manager to resolve.

personal management interview program: a regularly scheduled, one-on-one meeting between a manager and his or her subordinates.

personal values: an individual's standards that define what is good/bad, worthwhile/worthless, desirable/undesirable, true/false, moral/immoral.

perspective: the evaluation of a meeting from a distance.

planning: preparation for the meeting agenda.

positive deviance: change toward excellence, perfection, psychological "flow," and the like, usually depicted as a shift to the light along the continuum that shows normal, healthy performance in the middle.

positive energizers: people who strengthen and create vitality and liveliness in others.

positive energy networks: interconnected groups of vitality and liveliness creators, being a member of which has been shown to be more predictive of success than being at the center of an information network or influence network.

positive interpersonal relationships: relationships that create positive energy and physiological, emotional, intellectual, and social consequences.

preparation stage: a stage in creative thought that includes gathering data, defining the problem, generating alternatives, and consciously examining all available information.

principled level: the third and highest level of values maturity in which an individual judges right from wrong by following internalized principles developed from personal experience.

proactive strategy: a method of managing stress that initiates action in order to resist the negative effects of stress.

probing response: a response that asks a question about what the communicator just said or about a topic selected by the listener.

problem-solving process: an approach to conflict resolution that focuses on identifying underlying problems, or issues, and brainstorming solutions.

problem-solving teams: small groups of workers who meet for an hour or two each week to discuss ways to improve.

process: a sequential set of activities designed to lead to a specific outcome.

process improvement: stage in process management where process itself is changed so as to foster advancement.

purpose: the reason a meeting is held, including information sharing, commitment building, information disseminating, and problem solving and decision making.

Q

quality circles: Japanese problem-solving teams who meet to discuss issues and make recommendations to upper management.

R

reactive strategy: a method for managing stress that copes with the stressors immediately, temporarily reducing their effects.

reason: the influence strategy that relies on persuasion and appeals to rational consideration of the inherent merits of the request in order to gain compliance. It is explicit and direct, not manipulative.

reassigning: moving the poor performer to a position more consonant with his or her skill level and aptitude.

reciprocity: an influence strategy through which a manager uses bargaining as a tool for exacting a subordinate's compliance. This approach operates on the principle of self-interest and respect for the value of the interpersonal relationship.

recreational work: work that people willingly engage in due to characteristics such as clearly defined goals, objective evaluations, frequent feedback, the presence of personal choice, consistent rules, and a competitive environment.

redirection: a behavior-shaping process that follows a reprimand and gives the offender the opportunity to receive a future reward by modifying his or her behavior.

refitting: adapting the requirements of a job to an employee's abilities in order to improve poor performance.

reflected best-self feedback: a technique that managers can use to enhance positivity and focus on strengths, by providing people with feedback on their strengths and unique capabilities rather than their weaknesses.

reflecting response: a response that serves two purposes: (1) to confirm a message that was heard and (2) to communicate understanding and acceptance of the other person.

reflection probe: nondirective question(s) used for either elaboration or clarification of information; it generally mirrors or repeats some aspect of the interviewee's last answer.

reflective observation: a way of responding to information of those who are inclined to interpret and evaluate information they receive before responding.

reflective probe: a response to a communicator by reflecting back in one's own words what the communicator said. The purpose is to clarify the message and help the communicator feel open and safe in sharing more messages.

reframing: stress-reduction technique of redefining a situation as manageable.

rehearsal: relaxation technique of trying out stressful scenarios and alternative reactions.

reinforce: when rewards are linked to desired behaviors they are said to reinforce those behaviors (i.e., increase their frequency).

relational algorithm: a blockbusting technique for combining unrelated attributes in problem solving by connecting words to force a relationship between two elements in a problem.

relationship-building roles: those that emphasize the interpersonal aspects of the team.

relevance: the characteristic of a position whose tasks relate most closely to the dominant competitive goals of an organization and therefore enhance the power of the occupant.

repetition probe: a repeated or paraphrased question used if the interviewee has not directly answered a question the first time.

reprimand: a behavior-shaping approach used to transform unacceptable behaviors into acceptable ones; the discipline should be prompt and it should focus on the specific behavior.

resiliency: one's capacity to cope with stress.

resistance stage: response to stress in which defense mechanisms predominate.

respectful communication: treating subordinates as worthwhile, competent, and insightful by emphasizing joint problem solving rather than projecting a superior position.

responder role: the part played in a conflict management model by the person who is supposedly the source of the "initiator's" problem.

resupplying: managerial option for overcoming an employee's lack-of-ability problem that focuses on supplying the support needed to do the job.

retraining: a management tool for overcoming the problem of an employee's poor performance, especially needed in rapidly changing technical work environments.

retribution: an influence strategy that involves a threat—the denial of expected rewards or the imposition of punishment. It usually triggers an aversive response in the subordinate and the breakdown of the interpersonal relationship.

reverse the definition: a tool for improving and expanding problem definition by reversing the way you think of the problem.

rewarding: the motivational strategy that links desired behaviors with employee-valued outcomes. Such positive reinforcement gives an employee more incentive for exceptional accomplishment than does disciplining.

right-hemisphere thinking: mental activity concerned with intuition, synthesis, playfulness, and qualitative judgment.

rigidity in communication: a type of message that portrays the communication as absolute, unequivocal, or unquestionable.

role incompatibility: the conflict-producing difference between workers whose tasks are interdependent but whose priorities differ because their responsibilities within the organization differ. The mediation of a common superior is usually the best solution.

rule breaker: the person who goes beyond organizational boundaries and barriers to ensure success of the creative solution.

S

self-awareness: a knowledge of one's own personality and individuality.

self-centered level: the first level of values maturity. It contains two stages of values development, moral reasoning and instrumental values, which are based on personal needs or wants and the consequences of an act.

self-determination: feelings of having a choice.

self-disclosure: revealing to others ambiguous or inconsistent aspects of oneself, a process necessary for growth.

self-efficacy: empowered feeling of possessing the capability and competence to perform a task successfully.

self-managing teams: most advanced form of teamwork; maintain all responsibilities with the team that are normally spread across multiple levels and functions on an ongoing basis.

sensitive line: an invisible boundary around one's self-image, which, if threatened, will evoke a strong defensive reaction.

separating figure from ground: the ability to filter out inaccurate, misleading, or irrelevant information so the problem can be defined accurately and alternative solutions can be generated.

situational stressor: the type of stressor that arises from an individual's environment or circumstances, such as unfavorable working conditions.

skill variety: an attribute of a job that uses an individual's talents and abilities to the maximum and thus makes the job seem worthwhile and important.

small-wins strategy: a strategy for individuals to use for coping with stress; it involves celebrating each small successful step, especially changes that are easy to implement and that build momentum, in the attack on a large project.

SMART goals: goals that are specific, measurable, aligned, realistic, and time-bound.

social capital: a person's social connections ("I know someone who knows the answer to the question"). Compare with human capital.

source credibility: a judgment about the extent to which information can be believed, three attributes of which are trustworthiness, expertise, and dynamism.

specific goals: goals that are measurable, unambiguous, and behavioral.

specificity orientation: an emphasis on separating work, family, and personal roles in a society, used in contrast to diffusion orientation. One of the key dimensions that identifies international cultural differences.

sponsor: person who helps provide the resources, environment, and encouragement that the idea champion needs in order to work.

stakeholder expectations: a best-practice standard in which current performance is compared with the expectations of customers, employers, or other stakeholders.

storming stage: team development stage in which members question the team's direction, the leader, roles of other members, and task objectives.

strength: areas in which a person is an outstanding performer, has special capabilities or talents, and does better than most people.

stressors: stimuli that cause physiological and psychological reactions in individuals.

subdivision: the breaking apart of a problem into smaller parts.

superiority-oriented communication: a message that gives the impression that the communicator is informed while others are ignorant, adequate while others are inadequate, competent while others are incompetent, or powerful while others are impotent.

supportive communication: communication that helps managers share information accurately and honestly without jeopardizing interpersonal relationships.

symbolic analogies: symbols or images that are imposed on the problem; recommended as part of synectics.

synectics: a technique for improving creative problem solving by putting something you don't know in terms of something you do know.

T

task-facilitating roles: those that help the team accomplish its outcome objectives.

task identity: an attribute of a job that enables an individual to perform a complete job from beginning to end.

task significance: the degree to which the performance of a task affects the work or lives of other people. The greater its significance, the more meaningful the job is to the worker.

terminal values: those values that designate desirable ends or goals for an individual.

thinking languages: the various ways in which a problem can be considered, from verbal to nonverbal or symbolic languages as well as through sensory and visual imagery. Using only one thinking language is one indication of the constancy block.

threat-rigidity response: the tendency of almost all individuals, groups, and organizations to become rigid, meaning conservative and self-protective, when faced with a threat.

time stressor: the type of stressor generally caused by having too much to do in too little time.

tolerance of ambiguity: an individual's ability to cope with ambiguous, fast-changing, or unpredictable situations in which information is incomplete, unclear, or complex.

two-way communication: the result of respectfulness and flexibility.

Type A personality: a hard-driving, hostile, intense, highly competitive personality.

U

uniquenesses: areas in which a person has special capacities, gifts, talents, or skills.

universalism: the ethical decision principle that a decision is right and proper if everyone would be expected to behave in the same way under the same circumstances.

V

validating communication: a message that helps people feel recognized, understood, accepted, and valued. It is respectful, flexible, two-way, and based on agreement.

values maturity: the level of moral development displayed by individuals.

verification stage: the final stage in creative thought in which the creative solution is evaluated relative to some standard of acceptability.

vertical thinking: defining a problem in a single way and then pursuing that definition without deviation until a solution is reached.

visibility: the power-enhancing attribute of a position that can usually be measured by the number of influential people one interacts with in the organization.

vision of abundance: an image of a positive future, a flourishing condition, and a legacy about which people care passionately, which a leader articulates in order to promote positive change.

vision statement: a leadership document that outlines an organization's guiding values and principles, provides a sense of direction and possibilities, and inspires optimism and hope for a better future.

W

weaknesses: areas in which a person is underdeveloped, uninformed, or has little skill.

work design: the process of matching job characteristics and workers' skills and interests.

APPENDIX II
REFERENCES

INTRODUCTION REFERENCES

American Management Association. (2000). Managerial skills and competence. National survey by AMA, March–April 2000. (N = 921)

Andersen Consulting Company. (2000). *Skills needed for the e-business environment.* Chicago: Author.

Bandura, A. (1977). *A social learning theory.* Englewood Cliffs, NJ: Prentice Hall.

Bass, Bernard. (1990). *Handbook of leadership: Theory, research, and managerial applications* (3rd ed.). New York: Macmillan.

Blimes, L., K. Wetzker, and P. Xhonneux. (1997 February 10). Value in human resources. *Financial Times.*

Boyatzis, Richard E. (1996). Consequences and rejuvenation of competency-based human resource and organization development. In Richard Woodman and William A. Pasmore (Eds.), *Research in organizational change and development,* Vol. 9. Greenwich, CT: JAI Press.

Boyatzis, Richard E. (2000). Developing emotional intelligence. In C. Cherniss and D. Goleman (Eds.), *Development in emotional intelligence.* New York: Bantam.

Boyatzis, Richard E. (2005). Self-directed change and learning as a necessary meta-competency for success and effectiveness in the 21st century. In R. Sims and J.G. Veres (Eds.), *Keys to employee success in the coming decades.* Westport, CT: Greenwood Publishing.

Boyatzis, Richard E., Scott S. Cowen, and David A. Kolb. (1995). *Innovation in professional education: Steps on a journey from teaching to learning.* San Francisco: Jossey-Bass.

Boyatzis, Richard E., David Leonard, Ken Rhee, and Jane V. Wheeler. (1996). Competencies can be developed, but not in the way we thought. *Capability, 2*: 25–41.

Brodbeck, F., et al. (2000). Cultural variation of leadership prototypes across 22 countries. *Journal of Occupational and Organizational Psychology, 73*: 1–50.

Burnaska, R. F. (1976). The effects of behavioral modeling training upon managers' behavior and employees' perceptions. *Personnel Psychology, 29*: 329–335.

Cameron, Kim S., and Robert E. Quinn. (2006). *Diagnosing and changing organizational culture.* San Francisco: Jossey-Bass.

Cameron, K. S., R. E. Quinn, J. DeGraff, and A. V. Thakor. (2006). *Competing values leadership: Creating value in organizations.* New York: Edward Elgar.

Cameron, Kim, and Mary Tschirhart. (1988). Managerial competencies and organizational effectiveness. Working paper, School of Business Administration, University of Michigan.

Cameron, K. S., and D. O. Ulrich. (1986). Transformational leadership in colleges and universities. In J. Smart (Ed.), *Higher education: Handbook of theory and research* Vol. 2 (pp. 1–42). New York: Agathon.

Cameron, Kim S., and David A. Whetten. (1984). A model for teaching management skills. *Organizational Behavior Teaching Journal, 8*: 21–27.

Cohen, Peter A. (1984). College grades and adult achievement: A research synthesis. *Research in Higher Education, 20*: 281–291.

Cox, Taylor H. (1994). *Cultural diversity in organizations: Theory, research, and practice.* San Francisco: Barrett-Koehler.

Cox, Taylor H., and Ruby L. Beal. (1997). *Developing competency to manage diversity.* San Francisco: Barrett-Koehler.

Curtis, D. B., J. L. Winsor, and D. Stephens. (1989). National preferences in business and communication education. *Communication Education, 38*: 6–15.

Davis, T. W., and F. Luthans. (1980). A social learning approach to organizational behavior. *Academy of Management Review, 5*: 281–290.

Goleman, Daniel. (1998). *Working with emotional intelligence.* New York: Bantam.

Greenberg, Eric (1999) Broadcast Transcript, National Public Radio Morning Edition, October 26.

Hanson, Gary. (1986). *Determinants of firm performance: An integration of economic and organizational factors.* Unpublished doctoral dissertation, University of Michigan Business School.

Holt, John. (1964). *How children fail.* New York: Pitman.

Huselid, M. A. (1995). The impact of human resource management practices on turnover, productivity, and corporate financial performance. *Academy of Management Journal, 38*: 647.

Huselid, M. A., and B. E. Becker. (1997). The impact of high-performance work systems, implementing effectiveness, and alignment with strategy on shareholder wealth. *Academy of Management Best Papers Proceedings*: 144–148.

Katzenbach, J. R. (1995). *Real change leaders: How you can create growth and high performance in your company.* New York: New York Times Business, Random House.

Kolb, David A. (1984). *Experiential learning: Experience as the source of learning and development.* Englewood Cliffs, NJ: Prentice Hall.

Latham, Gary P., and L. P. Saari, (1979). Application of social learning theory to training supervisors through behavioral modeling. *Journal of Applied Psychology, 64*: 239–246.

Leonard, David. (1996). *The impact of learning goals on self-directed change in management development and education.* Unpublished doctoral dissertation, Weatherhead School of Management, Case Western Reserve University.

Luthans, Fred, Stuart A., Rosenkrantz, and Harry W. Hennessey. (1985). What do successful managers really do? An observation study of managerial activities. *Journal of Applied Behavioral Science, 21*: 255–270.

Mintzberg, Henry. (1975). The manager's job: Folklore and fact. *Harvard Business Review, 53*: 49–71.

Moorehead, B. (n.d.). http://www.snopes.com/politics/soapbox/paradox.asp

Moses, J. L., and R. J. Ritchie. (1976). Supervisory relationships training: A behavioral evaluation of a behavioral modeling program. *Personnel Psychology, 29*: 337–343.

Nair, K. (1994). *A higher standard of leadership.* San Francisco: Barrett-Koehler.

Pfeffer, Jeffrey. (1998). *The human equation: Building profits by putting people first.* Boston: Harvard Business School Press.

Pfeffer, Jeffrey, and John F. Veiga. (1999). Putting people first for organizational success. *Academy of Management Executive, 13*: 37–48.

Porras, Jerry I, and B. Anderson. (1991). Improving managerial effectiveness through modeling–based training. *Organizational Dynamics, 9*: 60–77.

Quinn, Robert E. (2000). *Change the world.* San Francisco: Jossey-Bass.

Quinn, R. E., and J. Rohrbaugh. (1983). A special model of effectiveness criteria: Towards a competing values approach to organizational analysis. *Management Science, 29*: 363–377.

Rhee, Ken. (1997). *Journey of Discovery: A longitudinal study of learning during a graduate professional program.* Unpublished doctoral dissertation, Weatherhead School of Management, Case Western Reserve University.

Rigby, Darrell. (1998). *Management tools and techniques.* Boston: Bain and Company.

Smith, P. E. (1976). Management modeling training to improve morale and customer satisfaction. *Personnel Psychology, 29*: 351–359.

Staw, Barry M., Lance Sandelands, and Jane Dutton. (1981). Threat-rigidity effects in organizational behavior: A multi-level analysis. *Administrative Science Quarterly, 26*: 501–524.

Tichy, Noel M. (1993). *Control your destiny or someone else will.* New York: Doubleday.

Tichy, Noel M. (1999). *The leadership engine.* New York: Harper Business.

Trompenaars, F., and C. Hampden-Turner. (1998). *Riding the waves of culture.* Understanding diversity in global business. New York: McGraw-Hill.

U.S. Office of the Comptroller of the Currency. (1990). http://www.occ.treas.gov

Vance, Charles M. (1993). *Mastering management education.* Newbury Park, CA: Sage.

Van Velsor, E., and L. Jean Britain. (1995). Why executives derail: Perspectives across time and culture. *Academy of Management Executive, 9*: 62–72.

Weick, Karl E. (1995). *Sensemaking in organizations.* Thousand Oaks, CA: Sage.

Welbourne, Teresa, and A. Andrews. (1996). Predicting performance of initial public offering firms: Should HRM be in the equation? *Academy of Management Journal, 39*: 891–919.

Wheeler, Jane V. (1999). *Organizational and environmental supports and opportunities for self-directed learning following graduate education.* Unpublished doctoral dissertation, Weatherhead School of Management, Case Western Reserve University.

Whetten, David A., and Kim S. Cameron. (1983). Management skill training: A needed addition to the management curriculum. *Organizational Behavior Teaching Journal, 8*: 10–15.

CHAPTER 1 REFERENCES

Allan, H., and Janine Waclawski. (1999). Influence behaviors and managerial effectiveness in lateral relations. *Human Resource Development Quarterly, 10*: 3–34.

Allport, G. R. Gordon, and P. Vernon. (1931, 1960). *The study of values manual.* Boston: Houghton Mifflin Co.

Anderson, Carl, and Craig E. Schneider. (1978). Locus of control, leader behavior, and leader performance among management students. *Academy of Management Journal, 21*: 690–698.

Andrews, Kenneth. (1989). Ethics in practice. *Harvard Business Review, September-October*: 99–104.

Armstrong-Stassen, Marjorie. (1998). Downsizing the federal government: A longitudinal study of managers' reactions. *Revue Canadienne des Sciences de l'Administration, 15*: 310–321.

Atwater, L., and F. Yammarino. (1992). Does self–other agreement on leadership perceptions moderate the validity of leadership and performance predictions? *Personnel Psychology, 45*: 141–164.

Bar-On, R. (1997). *Bar-On Emotional Quotient Inventory: User's manual.* Toronto: Multi-Health Systems.

Bernardi, Richard. (1997). The relationships among locus of control, perceptions of stress, and performance. *Journal of Applied Business Research, 13*: 108.

Berscheid, E., and E. H. Walster (1978). *Interpersonal attraction.* Reading, MA: Addison-Wesley.

Bigoness, William, and Gerald Blakely. (1996). A cross-national study of managerial values. *Journal of International Business Studies, 27*: 739–752.

Bilsky, W., and S. H. Schwartz. (1994). Values and personality. *European Journal of Personality, 8*: 163–181.

Blau, G. (1993). Testing the relationship of locus of control to different performance dimensions. *Journal of Occupational and Organizational Psychology, 66*: 125–138.

Bonnett, C., and A. Furnham. (1991). Who wants to be an entrepreneur? *Journal of Economic Psychology, 66*: 125–138.

Bono, J. E., and T. A. Judge. (2003). Core self-evaluations: A review of the trait and its role in job satisfaction and job performance. *European Journal of Personality, 17*: 5–18.

Boone, Christophe, and Bert de Brabander. (1997). Self reports and CEO locus of control research: A note. *Organizational Studies, 18*: 949–971.

Boyatzis, Richard E. (1982). *The competent manager: A model for effective performance.* New York: Wiley.

Boyatzis, Richard E. (1998). Self-directed change and learning as a necessary meta-competency for success and effectiveness in the 21st century. In R. Sims and J.G. Veres (Eds.), *Keys to employee success in the coming decade.* Westport, CT: Greenwood.

Boyatzis, Richard E., Daniel Goleman, and Ken Rhee. (2000). Clustering competence in emotional intelligence: Insights from the Emotional Intelligence Inventory. In R. Bar-On and J. D. A. Parker (Eds.), *Handbook of emotional intelligence* (pp. 343–352). San Francisco: Jossey-Bass.

Brouwer, P. J. (1964). The power to see ourselves. *Harvard Business Review, 42*: 156–165.

Budner, S. (1962). Intolerance of ambiguity as a personality variable. *Journal of Personality, 30*: 29–50.

Cable, D., and T.A. Judge. (1996). Person-organization fit, job choice decisions, and organizational entry. *Organizational Behavior and Human Decision Processes, 67*: 294–311.

Cameron, K. S. (1994). Strategies for successful organizational downsizing. *Human Resource Management Journal, 33*: 198–212.

Cameron, K. S., M. U. Kim, and D. A. Whetten. (1987). Organizational effects of decline and turbulence. *Administrative Science Quarterly, 32*: 222–240.

Cameron, K. S., and R. E. Quinn. (2006). *Diagnosing and changing organizational culture.* San Francisco: Jossey-Bass.

Cavanaugh, Gerald F. (1980). *American business values in transition.* Englewood Cliffs, NJ: Prentice Hall.

Cervone, Daniel. (1997). Social-cognitive mechanisms and personality coherence: Self-knowledge, situational beliefs, and cross-situational coherence in perceived self-efficacy. *Psychological Science, 8*: 156–165.

Chenhall, R., and D. Morris. (1991). The effect of cognitive style and sponsorship bias on the treatment of opportunity costs in resource allocation decisions. *Accounting, Organizations, and Society, 16*: 27–46.

Clare, D. A., and D. G. Sanford. (1979). Mapping personal value space: A study of managers in four organizations. *Human Relations, 32*: 659–666.

Coleman, Daniel, Gregory Irving, and Christine Cooper. (1999). Another look at the locus of control-organizational commitment relationship: It depends on the form of commitment. *Journal of Organizational Behavior, 20*: 995–1001.

Covey, Stephen R. (1989). *The seven habits of highly effective people.* New York: Simon & Schuster.

Cox, Taylor H. (1994). *Cultural diversity in organizations.* San Francisco: Barrett-Koehler.

Cromie, S., I. Callaghan, and M. Jansen. (1992). The entrepreneurial tendencies of managers. *British Journal of Management, 3*: 1–5.

Darrow, Barbara. (1998, November 16). Michael Dell. *Computer Reseller News*: 124–125.

Dollinger, S. J. , F. T. L. Leong, and S. K. Ulicni (1996). On traits and values: With special reference to openness to experience. *Journal of Research in Personality, 30*: 23–41.

Eckstrom, R. B., J. W. French, and H. H. Harmon. (1979). Cognitive factors: Their identification and replication. *Multivariate Behavioral Research Monographs, 72*: 3–84.

Elliott, A. L., and R. J. Schroth. (2002). *How companies lie: Why Enron is just the tip of the iceberg.* New York: Crown Business.

Elsayed-Elkhouly, Sayed M., and Richard Buda. (1997). A cross-cultural comparison of value systems of Egyptians, Americans, Africans, and Arab executives. *International Journal of Commerce and Management, 7*: 102–119.

Erez, A., and T. A. Judge. (2001). Relationship of core self-evaluations to goal setting, motivation, and performance. *Journal of Applied Psychology, 86*: 1270–1279.

Fast Company. (2005, December): 31.

Feist, G. J., and F. Barron. (1996). Emotional intelligence and academic intelligence in career and life success. Presented at the American Psychological Association Meetings, San Francisco.

Fisher, S. G., W. D. K. Macrosson, and M. R. Yusuff (1996). Team performance and human values. *Psychological Reports, 79*: 1019–1024.

Freud, Sigmund. (1956). *Collected papers* (Vols. 3 and 4). London: Hogarth.

Fromm, Erich. (1939). Selfishness and self-love. *Psychiatry, 2*: 507–523.

Gilligan, Carol. (1979). Women's place in man's life cycle. *Harvard Educational Review, 49*: 431–446.

Gilligan, Carol. (1980). Moral development in late adolescence: A critique and reconstruction of Kohlberg's theory. *Human Development, 23*: 77–104.

Gilligan, Carol. (1982). In a different voice: Women's conceptions of self and morality. *Harvard Educational Review, 47*: 481–517.

Gilligan, Carol. (1988). Two moral orientations: Gender differences and similarities. *Merrill-Palmer Quarterly, 34*: 223–237.

Goleman, Daniel. (1995). *Emotional intelligence.* New York: Bantam.

Goleman, Daniel. (1998a). What makes a leader? *Harvard Business Review, 76*: 92–102.

Goleman, Daniel. (1998b). *Working with emotional intelligence.* New York: Bantam.

Goleman, D., R. Boyatzis, and A. McKee. (2002). *Primal leadership.* Cambridge, MA: Harvard Business School Press.

Haase, Richard F., Dong Yul Lee, and Donald L. Banks. (1979). Cognitive correlates of polychronicity. *Perceptual and Motor Skills, 49*: 271–282.

Hammer, Tove H., and Yoav Vardi (1981). Locus of control and career self-management among nonsupervisory employees in industrial settings. *Journal of Vocational Behavior, 18*: 13–29.

Harris, J. R., and Sutton, C. (1995). Unraveling the ethical decision making process. *Journal of Business Ethics, 14*: 805–817.

Harris, S. (1981, October 6). Know yourself? It's a paradox. *Associated Press.*

Harter, S. (1990). Causes, correlates, and the functional role of global self-worth. In R.J. Sternberg and J. Kolligan (Eds.), *Competence reconsidered* (pp. 67–97). New Haven: Yale University Press.

Henderson, J. C., and Paul C. Nutt. (1980). The influence of decision style on decision making behavior. *Management Science*, 26: 371–386.

Hendricks, James A. (1985). Locus of control: Implications for managers and accountants. *Cost and Management*, May–June: 25–29.

Hosmer, L. T. (2003). *Ethics of Management.* Homewood, IL: Irwin.

Johnston, C. S. (1995). The Rokeach Value Survey: Underlying structure and multidimensional scaling. *Journal of Psychology*, 129: 583–597.

Judge, T. A., and Bono, J. E. (2001). Relationship of core self-evaluations traits—self-esteem, generalized self-efficacy, locus of control, and emotional stability—with job satisfaction and job performance: A meta-analysis. *Journal of Applied Psychology*, 86: 80–92.

Judge, T. A., A. Erez, J. E. Bono, and C. J. Thoreson. (2002). Are measures of self-esteem, neuroticism, locus of control, and generalized self-efficacy indicators of a common core construct? *Journal of Personality and Social Psychology*, 83: 693–710.

Judge, T. A., A. Erez, J. E. Bono, and C. J. Thoreson. (2003). The core self-evaluation scale: Development of a measure. *Personnel Psychology*, 56: 303–331.

Kelley, R. E. (1999). *How to be a star at work.* New York: Times Books.

Kohlberg, Lawrence. (1969). The cognitive-developmental approach to socialization. In D. A. Goslin (Ed.), *Handbook of socialization theory and research.* Chicago: Rand McNally.

Kohlberg, Lawrence, and Robert A. Ryncarz. (1990). Beyond justice reasoning: Moral development and consideration of a seventh stage. In Charles Alexander and Ellen J. Langer (Eds.), *Higher stages of human development.* New York: Oxford University Press.

Kolb, Alice, and David A. Kolb. (1999). *Bibliography of research on experiential learning theory and the learning style inventory.* Cleveland, OH: Weatherhead School of Management, Case Western Reserve University.

Kolb, David. (1999). *Kolb learning style inventory* 3rd ed. Philadelphia: Hay Group.

Kolb, David A., Richard E. Boyatzis, and Charalampos Mainemelis. (2000). Experiential learning theory: Previous research and new directions. In R. J. Sternberg and L. F. Zhang (Eds.), *Perspectives on cognitive, learning, and thinking styles.* Mahwah, NJ: Lawrence Erlbaum.

Kren, L. (1992). The moderating effects of locus of control on performance incentives and participation. *Human Relations*, 45: 991–1012.

Lickona, Thomas. (1976). Critical issues in the study of moral development and behavior. In T. Lickona (Ed.), *Moral development and behavior: Theory, research, and social issues.* New York: Holt, Rinehart & Winston.

Lobel, S. (1992). A value laden approach to integrating work and family life. *Human Resource Management Journal*, 31: 249–265.

Locke, E.A., K. McClear, and D. Knight. (1996). Self-esteem at work. *International Review of Industrial/Organizational Psychology*, 11: 1–32.

Lozano, J. M. (1996). Ethics and Management: A controversial issue. *Journal of Business Ethics*, 15: 227–236.

Maslow, Abraham H. (1962). *Toward a psychology of being.* Princeton, NJ: D. Von Nostrand Company.

Mayer, J. D., D. R. Caruso, and P. Salovey. (1998). Selecting a measure of emotional intelligence. In R. Bar-On and J. D. Parker (Eds.), *The handbook of emotional intelligence* (pp. 320–342). San Francisco: Jossey-Bass.

Milgram, Stanley. (1963). Behavioral study of obedience. *Journal of Abnormal and Social Psychology*, 67: 371–378.

Miller, Danny, Manfred F. R. Kets de Vries, and Jean-Marie Toulouse. (1982). Top executive locus of control and its relationship to strategy-making, structure, and environment. *Academy of Management Journal*, 25: 237–253.

Mitchell, L. E. (2002). *Corporate irresponsibility: America's newest export.* New Haven: Yale University Press.

Moore, Thomas. (1987, March 30). Personality tests are back. *Fortune*: 74–82.

Newton, T., and A. Keenan. (1990). The moderating effect of Type A behavior pattern and locus of control upon the relationship between change in job demands and change in psychological strain. *Human Relations*, 43: 1229–1255.

Nwachukwu, Saviour L. S., and Scott J. Vitell. (1997). The influence of corporate culture on managerial ethical judgments. *Journal of Business Ethics*, 16: 757–776.

O'Reilly, Brian. (1999). The mechanic who fixed Continental. *Fortune*, 140: 176–186.

Parker, V., and Kathy Kram. (1993). Women mentoring women. *Business Horizons*, 36: 101–102.

Peters, T. (1987). *Thriving on chaos.* New York: Knopf.

Posner, Barry, and James Kouzes. (1993). Values congruence and differences between the interplay of personal and organizational values. *Journal of Business Ethics*, 12: 341–347.

Rest, James R. (1979). *Revised manual for the Defining Issues Test: An objective test of moral judgment development.* Minneapolis: Minnesota Moral Research Projects.

Rogers, Carl R. (1961). *On becoming a person.* Boston: Houghton Mifflin Co.

Rokeach, Milton. (1973). *The nature of human values.* New York: Free Press.

Rosenthal, R. (1977). The PONS Test: Measuring sensitivity to nonverbal cues. In P. McReynolds (Ed.), *Advancement on psychological assessment.* San Francisco: Jossey-Bass.

Rothenberg, D. L. (1980). Professional achievement and locus of control: A tenuous relationship reconsidered. *Psychological Reports*, 46: 183–188.

Rotter, Julian B. (1966). Generalized expectancies for internal versus external control of reinforcement. *Psychological Monographs*, 80: 1–28.

Rotter, J. B. (1972). *Applications of a social learning theory of personality*. New York: Holt, Rinehart, and Winston.

Rotter, J. B. (1982). *Development and application of social learning theory selected papers*. Boston: Abbey Publishing.

Ruble, T., and R. Cosier. (1990). Effects of cognitive styles and decision settings on performance. *Organizational Behavior and Human Performance, 46*: 283–295.

Salovey, P., and J. Mayer. (1990). Emotional intelligence. *Imagination, Cognition, and Personality, 9*: 185–211.

Schein, Edgar H. (1960). Interpersonal communication, group solidarity, and social influence. *Sociometry, 23*: 148–161.

Schmidt, W. H., and B. Z. Posner. (1982). *Managerial values and expectations*. New York: American Management Association.

Seeman, M. (1982). On the personal consequences of alienation in work. *American Sociological Review, 32*: 273–285.

Snarey, J. R. and G. E. Vaillant. (1985). How lower- and working-class youth become middle-class adults: The association between ego defense mechanisms and upward social mobility. *Child Development, 56*: 899–910.

Spector, Paul E. (1982). Behavior in organizations as a function of employee's locus of control. *Psychological Bulletin, 47*: 487–489.

Spencer, Lyle M., and Signe M. Spencer. (1993). *Competence at work: Models for superior performance*. New York: Wiley.

Staw, B., L. Sandelands, and J. Dutton. (1981). Threat-rigidity effects in organizational behavior. *Administrative Science Quarterly, 26*: 501–524.

Sternberg, Robert J. (1996). *Successful intelligence*. New York: Simon & Schuster.

Sternberg, Robert J., and L. F. Zhang (Eds.). (2000). *Perspectives on cognitive, learning, and thinking styles*. Mahwah, NJ: Lawrence Erlbaum.

Sweeney, P., D. McFarlin, and J. Cotton. (1991). Locus of control as a moderator of the relationship between perceived influence and procedural justice. *Human Relations, 44*: 333–342.

Teoh, Hai Yap, and See Liang Foo. (1997). Moderating effects of tolerance for ambiguity and risk-taking propensity on the role conflict-perceived performance relationship: Evidence from Singaporean entrepreneurs. *Journal of Business Venturing, 12*: 67–81.

Timothy, A., Carl Thoresen, Vladimir Pucik, and Theresa Welbourne. (1999). Managerial coping with organizational change: A dispositional perspective. *Journal of Applied Psychology, 84*: 107–122.

Trompenaars, Frons. (1996). Resolving international conflict: Culture and business strategy. *Business Strategy Review, 7*: 51–68.

Trompenaars, Frons, and Charles Hampden-Turner (1998). *Riding the waves of culture*. New York: McGraw-Hill.

Tubbs, Walter. (1994). The roots of stress-death and juvenile delinquency in Japan: Disciplinary ambivalence and perceived locus of control. *Journal of Business Ethics, 13*: 507–522.

Watson, D. (2000). *Mood and temperament*. New York: Guilford.

Weick, Karl E. (1993). The collapse of sensemaking in organizations. *Administrative Science Quarterly, 38*: 628–652.

Weick, Karl E., and Kathleen Sutcliffe. (2000). High reliability: The power of mindfulness. *Leader to Leader, 17*: 33–38.

Wheeler, R. Wade, & John M. Davis (1979). Decision making as a function of locus of control and cognitive dissonance. *Psychological Reports, 44*: 499–502.

CHAPTER 2 REFERENCES

Adler, Christine, M., and Joel J. Hillhouse (1996). Stress, health, and immunity: A review of the literature. In Thomas W. Miller (Ed.), *Theory and assessment of stressful life events*. Madison, CT: International University Press.

Adler, J. (2005). *My prescription for anti-depressive living*. New York: Regan.

Adler, Jerry. (1999, June 14). Stress, *Newsweek*; 56–61.

Adler, V. (1989). Little control equals lots of stress. *Psychology Today, 23*: 18–19.

American Institute of Stress. (2000). www.stress.org/problem.htm

Anderson, C. R. (1977). Locus of control, coping behaviors and performance in a stress setting: A longitudinal study. *Journal of Applied Psychology, 62*: 446–451.

Auerbach, Stephen M. (1998). *Stress management: Psychological foundations*. Upper Saddle River, NJ: Prentice Hall.

Balzer, W. K., M. E. Doherty, and R. O'Connor. (1989). Effects of cognitive feedback on performance. *Psychological Bulletin, 106*: 410–433.

Bandura, A. (1997). *Self-efficacy: The exercise of control*. New York: W. H. Freeman.

Beary, J. F., and H. Benson. (1977). A simple psychophysiologic technique which elicits the hypometabolic changes in the relaxation response. *Psychosomatic Medicine, 36*: 115–120.

Bell, Chip R. (1998). *Managers as mentors*. San Francisco: Barrett-Koehler.

Benson, H. (1975). *The relaxation response*. New York: William Morrow.

Bramwell, S. T., M. Masuda, N. N. Wagner, and T. H. Holmes. (1975). Psychosocial factors in athletic injuries. *Journal of Human Stress, 1*: 6.

Brockner, Joel, and B. M. Weisenfeld. (1993). Living on the edge: The effects of layoffs on those who remain. In J. Keith Murnighan (Ed.), *Social psychology in organizations: Advances in theory and research*. Englewood Cliffs, NJ: Prentice Hall.

Cameron, Kim S. (1998). Strategic organizational downsizing: An extreme case. *Research in Organizational Behavior, 20*: 185–229.

Cameron, Kim S. (1994). Strategies for successful organizational downsizing. *Human Resource Management Journal, 33*: 189–212.

Cameron, Kim S., Sarah J. Freeman, and Aneil K. Mishra. (1991). Best practices in white-collar downsizing: Managing contradictions. *Academy of Management Executive, 5*: 57–73.

Cameron, Kim S., Myung U. Kim, and David A. Whetten. (1987). Organizational effects of decline and turbulence. *Administrative Science Quarterly, 32*: 222–240.

Cameron, Kim S., David A. Whetten, and Myung U. Kim. (1987). Organizational dysfunctions of decline. *Academy of Management Journal, 30*: 126–138.

Cantor, N., and J. F. Kihlstrom. (1987). *Personality and social intelligence*. Englewood Cliffs, NJ: Prentice Hall.

Coddington, R. D., and J. R. Troxell. (1980). The effect of emotional factors on football injury rates: A pilot study. *Journal of Human Stress, 6*: 3–5.

Cooper, C. L., and M. J. Davidson. (1982). The high cost of stress on women managers. *Organizational Dynamics, 11*: 44–53.

Cooper, Cary L. (1998). *Theories of organizational stress*. New York: Oxford University Press.

Cooper, M. J., and M. M. Aygen. (1979). A relaxation technique in the management of hypocholesterolemia. *Journal of Human Stress, 5*: 24–27.

Cordes, C. L., and T. W. Dougherty. (1993). Review and an integration of research on job burnout. *Academy of Management Review, 18*: 621–656.

Covey, Stephen. (1989). *Seven habits of highly effective people*. New York: Wiley.

Cowley, Jeffrey. (2000, June 14). Stress-busters: What works. *Newsweek*: 60.

Curtis, John D., and Richard A. Detert. (1981). *How to relax: A holistic approach to stress management*. Palo Alto: Mayfield Publishing Co.

Davidson, Jeff. (1995). *Managing your time*. Indianapolis: Alpha Books.

Davis, M., E. Eshelman, and M. McKay. (1980). *The relaxation and stress reduction workbook*. Richmond, CA: New Harbinger Publications.

Deepak, M. D. (1995). *Creating health: How to wake up the body's intelligence*. New York: Houghton Mifflin.

Dellbeck, Michael, and Susan Shatkin. (1991). *Scientific research on the transcendental meditation process*. Fairfield, IA: Maharishi International University of Management Press.

Dyer, William G. (1987). *Teambuilding*. Reading, MA: Addison-Wesley.

Eliot, Robert S., and Dennis L. Breo. (1984). *Is it worth dying for?* New York: Bantam Books.

Farnham, A. (1991, October 7). Who beats stress and how? *Fortune*: 71–86.

Fisher, Cynthia, and Richard Gitelson. (1983). A meta-analysis of the correlates of role conflict and role ambiguity. *Journal of Applied Psychology, 68*: 320–333.

French, J. R. R., and R. D. Caplan. (1972). Organizational stress and individual strain. In A. J. Marrow (Ed.), *The failure of success*. New York: AMACOM.

Friedman, M., and R. H. Rosenman. (1974). *Type A behavior and your heart*. New York: Knopf.

Friedman, M., & Ulmer, D. (1984). *Treating type A behavior and your heart*, New York: Alfred A. Knopf, 84–85.

Friedman, Meyer. (1996). *Type A behavior: Its diagnosis and treatment*. New York: Kluwer Academic Publishers.

Gardner, H. (1993). *Multiple intelligences: The theory in practice*. New York: Basic Books.

Gittell, J., K. Cameron, and S. Lim. (2006). Relationships, layoffs, and organizational resilience. *Journal of Applied Behavioral Science*.

Goldberg, H. (1976). *The hazards of being male*. New York: Nash.

Goleman, Daniel. (1998). *Working with emotional intelligence*. New York: Bantam Books.

Gordon, A. (1959). *A day at the beach*. Copyright © 1959 by Arthur Gordon. All rights reserved. Reprinted by permission of the author. First published in the *Reader's Digest*.

Greenberg, J. (1987). *Comprehensive stress management* (2nd ed.). Dubuque, IA: Wm. C. Brown Publishers.

Greenberger, D. B., and S. Stasser. (1991). The role of situational and dispositional factors in the enhancement of personal control in organizations. *Research in Organizational Behavior, 13*: 111–145.

Griest, J. H. et al. (1979). Running as treatment for depression. *Comparative Psychology, 20*: 41–56.

Hackman, J. R., G. R. Oldham, R. Janson, and K. Purdy. (1975). A new strategy for job enrichment. *California Management Review, 17*: 57–71.

Hackman, Richard J., and Gregory R. Oldham. (1980). *Work redesign*. Reading, MA: Addison-Wesley.

Hall, D. T. (1976). *Careers in organizations*. Santa Monica, CA: Goodyear.

Hendricks, William. (1996). *Coaching, mentoring, and managing*. Franklin Lakes, NJ: Career Press.

Hepburn, Gail C., Catherine A. McLoughlin, and Julian Barling. (1997). Coping with chronic work stress. In Benjamin H. Gottlieb (Ed.), *Coping with chronic stress*. (pp. 343–366). New York: Plenum.

Hobson, Charles J., Joseph Kamen, Jana Szostek, Carol M. Nethercutt, James W. Tiedmann, and Susan Wojnarowicz. (1998). Stressful life events: A revision and update of the Social Readjustment Rating Scale. *International Journal of Stress Management, 5*: 1–23.

Holmes, T. H., and R. H. Rahe. (1967). The social readjustment rating scale. *Journal of Psychosomatic Research, 11*: 213–218.

Holmes, T. H., and R. H. Rahe. (1970). The social readjustment rating scale. *Journal of Psychosomatic Research, 14*: 121–132.

Hubbard, John R., and E. A. Workman. (1998). *Handbook of stress medicine: An organ system approach*. Boca Raton, FL: CRC Press.

Ivancevich, John, and Daniel Ganster. (1987). *Job stress: From theory to suggestions*. New York: Haworth.

Ivancevich, John M., and Michael T. Matteson. (1980). *Stress & work: A managerial perspective*. Glenview, IL: Scott Foresman.

Jourard, S. M. (1964). *The transparent self*. Princeton, NJ: Von Nostrand.

Judge, T. A., and J. E. Bono. (2001). Relationship of core self-evaluations traits—self-esteem, generalized self-efficacy, locus of control, and emotional stability—with job satisfaction and job performance: A meta-analysis. *Journal of Applied Psychology, 86*: 80–92.

Kahn, R. L. et al. (1964). *Organizational stress: Studies in role conflict and ambiguity*. New York: Wiley.

Kahn, Robert L., and P. Byosiere. (1992). Stress in organizations. In Marvin Dunnette and L. M. Hough (Eds.), *Handbook of industrial and organizational psychology* (pp. 571–650). Palo Alto: Consulting Psychologists.

Karasek, R. A., T. Theorell, J. E. Schwartz, P. L. Schnall, C. F. Pieper, and J. L. Michela. (1988). Job characteristics in relation to the prevalence of myocardial infarction in the U.S. Health Examination Survey and the Health and Nutrition Examination Survey. *American Journal of Public Health, 78*: 910–918.

Katzenbach, Jon R., and Douglas K. Smith. (1993). *The wisdom of teams.* Boston: Harvard Business School Press.

Kobasa, S. C. (1979). Stressful life events, personality, and health: An inquiry into hardiness. *Journal of Personality and Social Psychology, 37*: 1–12.

Kobasa, Salvadore. (1982). Commitment and coping in stress resistance among lawyers. *Journal of Personality and Social Psychology, 42*: 707–717.

Kram, Kathy. (1985). *Mentoring at work.* Glenview, IL: Scott Foresman.

Kuhn, A., and R. D. Beam. (1982). *The logic of organizations.* San Francisco: Jossey-Bass.

Lakein, Dale. (1989). *How to get control of your time and your life.* New York: McKay.

Latack, Janina, Angelo J. Kinicki, and Gregory Prussia. (1995). An integrative process model of coping with job loss. *Academy of Management Review, 20*: 311–342.

Lawler, Edward E., Susan A. Mohrman, and Gerald E. Ledford. (1992). *Employee involvement and total quality management.* San Francisco: Jossey-Bass.

Lehrer, Paul M. (1996). *The Hatherleigh guide to issues in modern therapy.* New York: Hatherleigh Press.

Levinson, J. D. (1978). *Seasons of a man's life.* New York: Knopf.

Lewin, Kurt. (1951). *Field theory in social science.* New York: Harper & Row.

Likert, Rensis. (1967). *The human organization.* New York: McGraw-Hill.

Locke, Edward, and Gary Latham. (1990). *A theory of goal setting and task performance.* Englewood Cliffs, NJ: Prentice Hall.

Lusch, R. F., and R. R. Serpkenci. (1990). Personal differences, job tension, job outcomes, and store performance: A study of retail managers. *Journal of Marketing, 54*: 85–101.

Maddi, S., and S. C. Kobasa. (1984). *The hardy executive: Health under stress.* Homewood, IL: Dow Jones-Irwin.

Masten, A. S., and M. J. Reed. (2002). Resilience in development. In C. R. Snyder, and S. J. Lopez (Eds.), *Handbook of positive psychology* (pp. 74–88). New York: Oxford University Press.

McNichols, Thomas J. (1973). *The case of the missing time.* Evanston, IL: Northwestern University Kellogg School of Business.

Mednick, M. T. (1982). Woman and the psychology of achievement: Implications for personal and social change. In H. J. Bernardin (Ed.), *Women in the workforce.* New York: Praeger.

Milgram, Stanley. (1963). Behavioral study of obedience. *Journal of Abnormal and Social Psychology, 63*: 371–378.

Mintzberg, Henry. (1973). *The nature of managerial work.* New York: Harper & Row.

Mishra, Aneil K. (1992). *Organizational responses to crisis.* Unpublished doctoral dissertation, University of Michigan School of Business Administration.

Murphy, Lawrence R. (1996). Stress management in work settings: A critical review of health effects. *American Journal of Health Promotion, 11*: 112–135.

Northwestern National Life Insurance Company (NNL). (1992). *Employee burnout: Causes and cures.* Minneapolis, MN: Author.

Orme-Johnson, D. W. (1973). Autonomic stability and transcendental meditation. *Psychosomatic Medicine, 35*: 341–349.

Peters, Tom. (1988). *Thriving on chaos.* New York: Knopf.

Pfeffer, J. (1998). *The human equation: Building profits by putting people first.* Boston: Harvard Business School Press.

Pilling, B. K., and S. Eroglu. (1994). An empirical examination of the impact of salesperson empathy and professionalism and merchandise salability on retail buyer's evaluations. *Journal of Personal Selling and Sales Management, 14*: 55–58.

Rahe, R. H., D. H. Ryman, and H. W. Ward. (1980). Simplified scaling for life change events. *Journal of Human Stress, 6*: 22–27.

Rosenthal, R. (1977). The PONS Test: Measuring sensitivity to nonverbal cues. In P. McReynolds (Ed.), *Advances in psychological measurement.* San Francisco: Jossey-Bass.

Rostad, Faith G., and Bonita C. Long. (1996). Exercise as a coping strategy for stress: A review. *International Journal of Sport Psychology, 27*: 197–222.

Saarni, Carol. (1997). Emotional competence and self-regulation in childhood. In Peter Savoey and David J. Sluyter (Eds.), *Emotional development and emotional intelligence.* New York: Basic Books.

Schein, Edgar H. (1960). Interpersonal communication, group solidarity, and social influence. *Sociometry, 23*: 148–161.

Selye, Hans. (1976). *The stress of life* (2nd ed.). New York: McGraw-Hill.

Shoda, Y., W. Mischel, and P. K. Peake. (1990). Predicting adolescent cognitive and self-regulatory competencies from preschool delay of gratification: Identifying diagnostic conditions. *Developmental Psychology, 26*: 978–986.

Siegman, Aron Wolfe, and Timothy W. Smith (Eds.). (1994). *Anger, hostility, and the heart.* Mahwah, NJ: Lawrence Erlbaum and Associates.

Singh, Jagdip. (1993). Boundary role ambiguity: Facts, determinants, and impacts. *Journal of Marketing, 57*: 11–30.

Singh, Jagdip. (1998). Striking balance in boundary-spanning positions: An investigation of some unconventional influences of role stressors and job characteristics on job outcomes or salespeople. *Journal of Marketing, 62*: 69–86.

Sorenson, Marilyn J. (1998). *Breaking the chain of low self-esteem.* Stone Mountain, GA: Wolf Publications.

Spencer, Lyle M., and Signe M. Spencer. (1993). *Competence at work: Models for superior performance.* New York: Wiley.

Stalk, G., and T. M. Hout. (1990). *Competing against time.* New York: Free Press.

Staw, Barry M., Lance Sandelands, and Jane Dutton. (1981). Threat-rigidity effects in organizational behavior. *Administrative Science Quarterly, 26*: 501–524.

Sternberg, Robert. (1997). *Successful intelligence.* New York: Simon and Schuster.

Stone, R. A., and J. Deleo. (1976). Psychotherapeutic control of hypertension. *New England Journal of Medicine, 294*: 80–84.

Sutcliffe, K., and T. Vogus. (2003). Organizing for resilience. In K. S. Cameron, J. E. Dutton, and R. E. Quinn, (Eds.), *Positive organizational scholarship*. San Francisco: Barrett-Koehler.

Thoits, Peggy A. (1995). Stress, coping, and social support processes: Where are we? What next? *Journal of Health and Social Behavior, 36*: 53–79.

Trompenaars, Frons. (1996). Resolving international conflict: Culture and business strategy. *Business Strategy Review, 7*: 51–68.

Trompenaars, Frons, and Charles Hampden-Turner. (1998). *Riding the waves of culture*. New York: McGraw-Hill.

Turkington, Carol. (1998). *Stress management for busy people*. New York: McGraw-Hill.

Vinton, Donna E. (1992). A new look at time, speed, and the manager. *Academy of Management Executive, 6*: 1–16.

Weick, Karl. (1984). Small wins. *American Psychologist, 39*: 40–49.

Weick, Karl E. (1993a). The collapse of sensemaking in organizations. *Administrative Science Quarterly, 38*: 628–652.

Weick, Karl E. (1993b). The KOR experiment. Working paper, University of Michigan School of Business Administration.

Weick, Karl E. (1995). *Sensemaking in organizations*. Beverly Hills, CA: Sage.

William, Redford, and Virginia Williams. (1998). *Anger kills: 17 strategies to control the hostility that can harm your health*. New York: Harper Collins.

Wolff, H. G., S. G. Wolf, and C. C. Hare. (Eds.). (1950). *Life stress and bodily disease*. Baltimore: Williams and Wilkins.

Yogi, Mahesh. (1994). *Science of being and art of living: Transcendental meditation*. New Haven, CT: Meridian Books.

CHAPTER 3 REFERENCES

Adams, James L. (2001). *Conceptual blockbusting: A guide to better ideas*. Cambridge, MA: Perseus Publishing.

Albert, Robert S., and Mark A. Runco. (1999). A history of research on creativity. In Robert J. Sternberg (Ed.), *Handbook of creativity*. Cambridge: Cambridge University Press.

Amabile, Teresa M. (1988). A model of creativity and innovation in organizations. In Larry L. Cummings and Barry M. Staw (Eds.), *Research in Organizational Behavior, 10*: 123–167.

Basadur, M. S. (1979). *Training in creative problem solving: Effects of deferred judgment and problem finding and solving in an industrial research organization*. Unpublished doctoral dissertation, University of Cincinnati.

Ben-Amos, P. (1986). Artistic creativity in Benin Kingdom. *African Arts, 19*: 60–63.

Black, J. Stewart, and Hal B. Gregersen. (1997). Participative decision making: An integration of multiple dimensions. *Human Relations, 50*: 859–878.

Blasko, Vincent J., and Michael P. Mokwa. (1986). Creativity in advertising: A Janusian perspective. *Journal of Advertising, 15*: 43–50.

Bodycombe, David J. (1977). *The mammoth puzzle carnival*. New York: Carroll & Graf.

Cameron, K. S., R. E. Quinn, J. DeGraff, and A. V. Thakor. (2006). *Competing values leadership: Creating values in organizations*. New York: Edward Elgar.

Chu, Y-K. (1970). Oriented views of creativity. In A. Angloff and B. Shapiro (Eds.), *Psi factors in creativity* (pp. 35–50). New York: Parapsychology Foundation.

Cialdini, Robert B. (2001). *Influence: Science and practice*. Needham Heights, MA: Allyn and Bacon.

Collins, Mary Ann, and Teresa M. Amabile. (1999). Motivation and creativity. In Robert J. Sternberg (Ed.), *Handbook of creativity*. Cambridge, UK: Cambridge University Press.

Covey, Stephen R. (1998) "Creative orientation." *Executive Excellence, 1*: 13–14.

Crovitz, H. F. (1970). *Galton's walk*. New York: Harper & Row.

Csikszentmihalyi, Mihaly. (1996). *Creativity: Flow and the psychology of discovery and invention*. New York: Harper Collins.

de Bono, E. (1968). *New think*. New York: Basic Books.

de Bono, Edward. (1973). *CoRT thinking*. Blanford, England: Direct Educational Services.

de Bono, Edward. (1992). *Serious creativity*. New York: Harper Collins.

de Bono, Edward. (2000). *New Thinking for the New Millennium*. New York: New Millennium Press.

DeGraff, J., and K. A. Lawrence. (2002). *Creativity at work: Developing the right practices to make innovation happen*. San Francisco: Jossey-Bass.

Dutton, Jane E., and Susan J. Ashford. (1993). Selling issues to top management. *Academy of Management Review, 18*: 397–421.

Einstein, Albert. (1919). Fundamental ideas and methods of relativity theory, presented in their development. © 1919, G. Holton). Unpublished manuscript.

Ettlie, John E., and Robert D. O'Keefe. (1982). Innovative attitudes, values, and intentions in organizations. *Journal of Management Studies, 19*: 163–182.

Feldman, David Henry. (1999). The development of creativity. In Robert J. Sternberg (Ed.), *Handbook of creativity*. Cambridge, UK: Cambridge University Press.

Festinger, Leon. (1957). *A theory of cognitive dissonance*. Stanford: Stanford University Press.

Finke, R. A., T. B. Ward, and S. M. Smith. (1992). *Creative cognition: Theory, research, and applications*. Cambridge, MA: MIT Press.

Getzels, J. W., and Mihaly Csikszentmihalyi. (1976). *The creative vision: A longitudinal study of problem finding*. New York: Wiley.

Gladwell, M. (2005). *Blink*. Boston: Little Brown.

Goll, Irene, and Abdul M. A. Rasheed. (1997). Rational decision making and firm performance: The moderating role of environment. *Strategic Management Journal, 18*: 583–591.

Gordon, W. J. J. (1961). *Synectics: The development of creative capacity*. New York: Collier.

Hawn, Carleen. (2004, January). If he's so smart. . . *Fast Company*: 68–74.

Heider, Fritz. (1946). Attitudes and cognitive organization. *Journal of Psychology, 21*: 107–112.

Hermann, N. (1981). The creative brain. *Training and Development Journal, 35*: 11–16.

Hudspith, S. (1985). *The neurological correlates of creative thought.* Unpublished PhD Dissertation, University of Southern California.

Hyatt, J. (1989, February). The odyssey of an excellent man. *Inc.:* 63–68. Copyright © 1989 by Goldhirsch Group, Inc. Reprinted with permission of the publishers, 38 Commercial Wharf, Boston, MA 02110.

Interaction Associates. (1971). *Tools for change.* San Francisco: Author.

Janis, Irvin L. (1971). *Groupthink.* New York: Free Press.

Janis, Irvin L., and L. Mann. (1977). *Decision making: A psychological analysis of conflict, choice, and commitment.* New York: Free Press. Copyright © 1977 by the Free Press. Reprinted with the permission of the Free Press, an imprint of Simon and Schuster.

Juran, J. (1988). *Juran on planning management.* New York: Free Press.

Koberg, D., and J. Bagnall. (2003). *The universal traveler: A soft system guidebook to creativity, problem solving, and the process of design.* Los Aktos, CA: William Kaufmann.

Koestler, A. (1964). *The act of creation.* New York: Dell.

Koopman, Paul L., Jan Willem Broekhuijsen, and Andre F. M. Wierdsma. (1998). Complex decision making in organizations. In Pieter J. D. Drenth and Henk Thierry (Eds.), *Handbook of work and organizational psychology,* Vol. 4, (pp. 357–386). Hove, England: Psychology Press/Erlbaum.

Kuo, Y-Y. (1996). Toaistic psychology of creativity. *Journal of Creative Behavior, 30*: 197–212.

Maduro, R. (1976). *Artistic creativity in a Brahmin painter community* (Monograph 14). Berkeley: University of California Center for South and Southeast Asia Cultures.

March, James G. (1994). *A primer on decision making: How decisions happen.* New York: Free Press.

March, James G. (Ed.). (1999). *The pursuit of organizational intelligence.* New York: Blackwell.

March, James G., and Herbert A. Simon. (1958). *Organizations.* New York: Wiley.

Markoff, John. (1988, November 2). For scientists using supercomputers, visual imagery speeds discoveries. New York Times News Service, *Ann Arbor News,* D3.

Martindale, Colin. (1999). Biological bases of creativity. In Robert J. Sternberg (Ed.), *Handbook of creativity.* Cambridge, UK: Cambridge University Press.

McKim, Robert H. (1997). *Thinking visually: A strategy manual for problem solving.* Parsippany, NJ: Dale Seymour Publications.

McMillan, Ian. (1985). Progress in research on corporate venturing. Working paper, Center for Entrepreneurial Studies, New York University.

Medawar, P. B. (1967). *The art of the soluable.* London: Methuen.

Miller, Susan J., David J. Hickson, and David C. Wilson. (1996). Decision making in organizations. In Stewart R. Clegg and Cynthia Hardy (Eds.), *Handbook of organizational studies* (pp. 293–312). London: Sage.

Mitroff, Ian I. (1998). *Smart thinking for crazy times: The art of solving the right problems.* San Francisco: Barrett-Koehler.

Mumford, M. D., W. A. Baughman, M. A. Maher, D. P. Costanza, and E. P. Supinski. (1997). Process-based measures of creative problem solving skills. *Creativity Research Journal, 10:* 59–71.

Nayak, P. Ranganath, and John M. Ketteringham. (1986). *Breakthroughs!* New York: Rawson Associates.

Nemeth, C. J. (1986). Differential contributions of majority and minority influence. *Psychological Review, 93:* 23–32.

Newcomb, Theodore. (1954). An approach to the study of communicative acts. *Psychological Review, 60:* 393–404.

Nickerson, Raymond S. (1999). Enhancing creativity. In Robert J. Sternberg (Ed.), *Handbook of creativity.* Cambridge: Cambridge University Press.

Osborn, A. (1953). *Applied imagination.* New York: Scribner.

Poincare, H. (1921). *The foundation of science.* New York: Science Press.

Raudsepp, Eugene. (1981). *How creative are you?* New York: Perigee Books/G.P. Putnam's Sons. Copyright © 1981 by Eugene Raudsepp. Reprinted with the permission of the author, c/o Dominick Abel Literary Agency, Inc.

Raudsepp, Eugene, and G. P. Hough. (1977). *Creative growth games.* New York: Putnam.

Ribot, T. A. (1906). *Essay on the creative imagination.* Chicago: Open Court.

Riley, Susan. (1998). *Critical thinking and problem solving.* Upper Saddle River, NJ: Simon and Schuster.

Rothenberg, A. (1979). *The emerging goddess.* Chicago: University of Chicago Press.

Rothenberg, A. (1991). Creativity, health, and alcoholism. *Creativity Research Journal, 3:* 179–202.

Rothenberg, A., and C. Hausman. (2000). Metaphor and creativity. In M. A. Runco (Ed.), *Creativity research handbook,* Volume 2. Cresskill, NJ: Hampton.

Roukes, Nicholas. (1988). *Design synectics: Stimulating creativity in design.* Berkeley, CA: Davis Publications.

Scope, Ellis E. (1999). *A meta-analysis of research on creativity: The effects of instructional variables.* Ann Arbor, MI: Dissertation Abstracts International, Section A: Humanities and Social Sciences.

Scott, Otto J. (1974). *The creative ordeal: The story of Raytheon.* New York: Atheneum.

Siau, Keng L. (1995). Group creativity and technology. *Journal of Creative Behavior, 29:* 201–216.

Smith, G. F. (1998). Idea-generation techniques: A formulary of active ingredients. *Journal of Creative Behavior, 32:* 107–133.

Starko, A. J. (2001). *Creativity in the classroom: Schools of curious delight.* Mahwah, NJ: Lawrence Erlbaum.

Sternberg, Robert J. (Ed.), (1999). *Handbook of creativity.* Cambridge: Cambridge University Press.

Tichy, Noel. (1983). *Strategic human resource management.* New York: Wiley.

Trompenaars, F., and C. Hampden-Turner. (1987). *Riding the waves of culture: Understanding cultural diversity in business.* Yarmouth, ME: Nicholas Brealey Publishing.

Trompenaars, F., and C. Hampden-Turner. (2004). *Managing people across cultures.* Mankato, MN: Capstone Publishing.

Tushman, Michael L., and Philip Anderson. (1997). *Managing strategic innovation and change.* New York: Oxford University Press.

Van de Ven, Andrew. (1997). Technological innovation, learning, and leadership. In Raghu Garud, Praveen Rattan Nayyar, and Zur Baruch Shapira (Eds.), *Technological innovation: Oversights and foresights.* Cambridge: Cambridge University Press.

von Oech, Roger. (1986). *A kick in the seat of the pants.* New York: Harper & Row.

Vroom, V. H., and P. W. Yetton. (1973). *Leadership and decision making.* Pittsburgh: University of Pittsburgh Press.

Vygotsky, L. (1962). *Thought and language.* Cambridge, MA: MIT Press.

Wallas, G. (1926). *The art of thought.* London: C. A. Watts.

Ward, Thomas B., Steven M. Smith, and Ronald A. Finke. (1999). Creative cognition. In Robert J. Sternberg (Ed.), *Handbook of creativity.* Cambridge: Cambridge University Press.

Weick, K. E. (1979). *The social psychology of organizing.* Reading, Mass.: Addison-Wesley.

Weick, Karl. (1984). Small wins. *American Psychologist, 39*: 40–49.

Weick, Karl E. (1995). *Sensemaking in organizations.* Beverly Hills, CA: Sage.

Williams, Wendy M., and Lana T. Yang. (1999). Organizational creativity. In Robert J. Sternberg (Ed.), *Handbook of creativity.* Cambridge, UK: Cambridge University Press.

Wonder, J., and J. Blake. (1992). Creativity East and West: Intuition versus logic. *Journal of Creative Behavior, 26*: 172–185.

Zeitz, Paul. (1999). *The art and craft of problem solving.* New York: Wiley.

Zhou, J., and C. E. Shalley. (2003). Research on employee creativity: A critical review and directions or future research. *Research in Personnel and Human Resources Management, 22*: 165–217.

CHAPTER 4 REFERENCES

Argyris, Chris. (1991). Teaching smart people how to learn. *Harvard Business Review, 63*: 99–109.

Athos, Anthony, and John Gabarro. (1978). *Interpersonal behavior.* Englewood Cliffs, NJ: Prentice Hall.

Baker, W. (2000). *Achieving success through social capital.* San Francisco: Jossey-Bass.

Barnlund, D. C. (1968). *Interpersonal communication: Survey and studies.* Boston: Houghton Mifflin.

Beebe, Steven A., Susan J. Beebe, and Mark V. Redmond. (1996). *Interpersonal communication.* Boston: Allyn & Bacon.

Boss, Wayne L. (1983). Team building and the problem of regression: The personal management interview as an intervention. *Journal of Applied Behavioral Science, 19*: 67–83.

Bostrom, Robert N. (1997). The process of listening. In Owen D. W. Hargie (Ed.), *The handbook of communication skills.* London: Routledge.

Bowman, G. W. (1964). What helps or harms promotability? *Harvard Business Review, 42*: 14.

Brownell, J. (1986). *Building active listening skills.* Englewood Cliffs, NJ: Prentice Hall.

Brownell, J. (1990). Perceptions of effective listeners. *Journal of Business Communication, 27*: 401–415.

Cameron, K. S. (1994). Strategies for successful organizational downsizing. *Human Resource Management Journal, 33*: 89–122.

Carrell, Lori J., and S. Clay Willmington. (1996). A comparison of self-report and performance data in assessing speaking and listening competence. *Communication Reports, 9*: 185–191.

Council of Communication Management. (1996). Electronic communication is important, but face-to-face communication is still rated high. *Communication World, 13*: 12–13.

Covey, Stephen, R. (1989). *The seven habits of highly effective people.* New York: Simon & Schuster.

Crocker, J. (1978). Speech communication instruction based on employers' perceptions of the importance of selected communication skills for employees on the job. Paper presented at the Speech Communication Association meeting, Minneapolis, Minn.

Cupach, William R., and Brian H. Spitzberg. (1994). *The dark side of interpersonal communication.* Hillsdale, NJ: Lawrence Erlbaum.

Dutton, J. E. (2003). *Energize your workplace: How to create and sustain high quality relationships at work.* San Francisco: Jossey-Bass.

Dyer, W. G. (1972). Congruence. *In The sensitive manipulator.* Provo, UT: Brigham Young University Press.

Fredrickson, Barbara L. (2001). The role of positive emotions in positive psychology: The broaden-and-build theory of positive emotions. *American Psychologist, 56*: 218–226.

Gackenbach, Jayne. (1998). *Psychology and the Internet: Intrapersonal, interpersonal, and transpersonal implications.* New York: Academic Press.

Geddie, Tom. (1999). Moving communication across cultures. *Communication World, 16*: 37–40.

Gibb, J. R. (1961). Defensive communication. *Journal of Communication, 11*: 141–148.

Gittell, J. H. (2003). A theory of relational coordination. In K. S. Cameron, J. E. Dutton, and R. E. Quinn (Eds.), *Positive organizational scholarship.* San Francisco: Barrett-Koehler.

Gittell, J. H., K. S. Cameron, S. Lim. (2006). Relationships, layoffs, and organizational resilience: Airline industry responses to September 11th. *Journal of Applied Behavioral Science.*

Glasser, W. (1965). *Reality therapy: A new approach to psychiatry.* New York: Harper & Row.

Glasser, William. (2000). *Reality therapy in action.* New York: Harper Collins.

Golen, S. (1990). A factor analysis of barriers to effective listening. *Journal of Business Communication, 27*: 25–35.

Gordon, R. D. (1988). The difference between feeling defensive and feeling understood. *Journal of Business Communication, 25*: 53–64.

Gudykunst, William B., and Stella Ting-Toomey. (1988). *Culture and interpersonal communication.* Newbury Park, CA: Sage.

Gudykunst, William B., Stella Ting-Toomey, and Tsukasa Nishida. (1996). *Communication in personal relationships across cultures.* Thousand Oaks, CA: Sage.

Haas, J. W., and C. L. Arnold. (1995). An examination of the role of listening in judgments of communication competence in coworkers. *Journal of Business Communication, 32*: 123–139.

Haney, W. V. (1992). *Communication and interpersonal relations*. Homewood, IL: Irwin.

Hanson, Gary. (1986). *Determinants of firm performance: An integration of economic and organizational factors*. Unpublished doctoral dissertation, University of Michigan Business School.

Hargie, Owen D. W. (1997). Communication as skilled performance. In Owen D. W. Hargie (Ed.), *The handbook of communication skills*. London: Routledge.

Heaphy, E. D., and J. E. Dutton. (2006). Embodying social interactions: Integrating physiology into the study of positive connections and relationships at work. *Academy of Management Review* (in press).

Huseman, R. C., J. M. Lahiff, and J. D. Hatfield. (1976). *Interpersonal communication in organizations*. Boston: Holbrook Press.

Hyman, R. (1989). The psychology of deception. *Annual Review of Psychology, 40*: 133–154.

James, William, cited in Laing, D. R. (1965). Mystification, confusion, and conflict. In I. Boszormenya-Nagy and J. L. Franco (Eds.), *Intensive family therapy*. New York: Harper & Row.

Knapp, Mark L., and Anita L. Vangelisti. (1996). *Interpersonal communication and human relationships*. Boston: Allyn & Bacon.

Kramer, Deirdre A. (2000). Wisdom as a classical source of human strength: Conceptualization and empirical inquiry. *Journal of Social and Clinical Psychology, 19*: 83–101.

Kramer, Robert. (1997). *Leading by listening: An empirical test of Carl Rogers' theory of human relationship using interpersonal assessments of leaders by followers*. Ann Arbor, MI: Dissertation Abstracts International Section A: Humanities and Social Sciences, Volume 58.

Loomis, F. (1939). *The consultation room*. New York: Knopf.

Losada, M., and E. Heaphy. (2004). The role of positivity and connectivity in the performance of business teams. *American Behavioral Scientist, 47*: 740–765.

Maier, N. R. F., A. R. Solem, and A. A. Maier. (1973). Counseling, interviewing, and job contacts. In N. R. F. Maier (Ed.), *Psychology of industrial organizations*. Boston: Houghton Mifflin.

McGregor, Douglas. (1960). *The human side of enterprise*. New York: McGraw-Hill.

Ouchi, William. (1981). *Theory Z*. Reading, MA: Addison-Wesley.

Peters, Tom. (1988). *Thriving on chaos*. New York: Knopf.

Pfeffer, J. (1998). *The human equation: Building profits by putting people first*. Boston: Harvard Business School Press.

Randle, C. W. (1956). How to identify promotable executives. *Harvard Business Review, 34*: 122.

Reis, H., and S. L. Gable. (2003). Toward a positive psychology of relationships. In C. L. M. Keyes and J. Haidt. *Flourishing: Positive psychology and the life well-lived* (pp. 129–160). Washington, DC: American Psychological Association.

Rogers, Carl W. (1961). *On becoming a person*. Boston: Houghton Mifflin.

Rogers, Carl, and R. Farson. (1976). Active listening. Chicago: Industrial Relations Center.

Rosen, Sheri. (1998). A lump of clay. *Communication World, 15*: 58–59.

Schnake, M. E., M. P. Dumler, D. S. Cochran, and T. R. Barnett. (1990). Effects of differences in superior and subordinate perceptions of superiors' communication practices. *Journal of Business Communication, 27*: 37–50.

Sieburg, E. (1969). *Dysfunctional communication and interpersonal responsiveness in small groups*. Unpublished doctoral dissertation, University of Denver.

Sieburg, E. (1978). *Confirming and disconfirming organizational communication*. Working paper, University of Denver.

Spitzberg, Brian H. (1994). The dark side of (in)competence. In William R. Cupach and Brian H. Spitzberg (Eds.), *The dark side of interpersonal communication*. Hillsdale, NJ: Lawrence Erlbaum.

Steil, L. K. (1980). *Your listening profile*. Minneapolis: Sperry Corporation.

Steil, L., L. Barker, and K. Watson. (1983). *Effective listening: Key to your success*. New York: Addison-Wesley.

Sternberg, Robert J. (1990). *Wisdom: Its nature, origins, and development*. Cambridge: Cambridge University Press.

Synopsis Communication Consulting of London. (1998). *The human factor: New rules for the digital workplace*. London: Author.

Szligyi, A. D., and M. J. Wallace. (1983). *Organizational behavior and human performance*. Glenview, IL: Scott Foresman.

Time. (2000, June 19). Embarrassing miscue: 31.

Thorton, B. B. (1966). As you were saying: The number one problem. *Personnel Journal, 45*: 237–238.

Triandis, Harry C. (1994). *Culture and social behavior*. New York: McGraw-Hill.

Trompenaars, F. (1996). Resolving international conflict: Culture and business strategy. *Business Strategy Review, 7*: 51–68.

Trompenaars, F., and C. Hampden-Turner. (1998). *Riding the waves of culture*. New York: McGraw-Hill.

Wiemann, J. M. (1977). Explanation and test of a model of communication competence. *Human Communication Research, 3*: 145–213.

Wolvin, A., and C. Coakley. (1988). *Listening*. Dubuque: W. C. Brown.

CHAPTER 5 REFERENCES

Adler, P. S., and S. Kwon. (2002). Social capital: Prospects for a new concept. *Academy of Management Review, 27*: 17–40.

Allen, R. W., D. L. Madison, L. W. Porter, P. A. Renwick, and B. T. Mayer. (1979). Organizational politics: Tactics and characteristics of actors. *California Management Review, 22*: 77–83.

Allinson, C. W., S. J. Armstrong, and J. Hayes. (2001). The effects of cognitive style on leader-member exchange: A study of manager-subordinate dyads. *Journal of Occupational and Organizational Psychology, 74*: 201–220.

Anderson, C., O. P. John, D. Keltner, and A. M. Kring. (2001). Who attains social status? Effects of personality and physical attractiveness in social groups. *Journal of Personality and Social Psychology, 81*: 116–132.

Bacharach, S. B. (2005). Making things happen by mastering the game of day-to-day politics. *Fast Company*, May: 93.

Baum, L., and J. A. Byre. (1986, April). Executive secretary: A new rung on the corporate ladder; but hitching her star to the boss can work both ways. *BusinessWeek*: 74.

Bennis, W., and B. Nanus. (2003). *Leaders: Strategies for taking charge.* (2nd ed.). New York: HarperCollins.

Bies, R. J., and T. M. Tripp. (1998). Two faces of the powerless: Coping with tyranny in organizations. In R. M. Kramer, and M. A. Neale. (Eds.), *Power and influence in organizations.* Thousand Oaks, CA: Sage.

Bolman, L. G., and T. E. Deal. (1997). *Reframing organizations: Artistry, choice, and leadership.* San Francisco: Jossey-Bass.

Breen, B. (2001, November). Trickle-up leadership. *Fast Company*: 70.

Buell, B., and A. L. Cowan. (1985, August). Learning how to play the corporate power game. *BusinessWeek*: 54–55.

Bunderson, J. S. (2002). Team member functional background and involvement in management teams. *Academy of Management Proceedings, OB*: 11–16.

Bunker, K. A., K. E. Kram, and S. Ting. (2002). The young and the clueless. *Harvard Business Review, 80*: 80–87.

Burt, R. S. (1997). The contingent value of social capital. *Administrative Science Quarterly, 42*: 339–365.

Canfield, F. E., and J. J. LaGaipa. (1970). Friendship expectations at different stages in the development of friendship. Paper read at the annual meeting of the Southeastern Psychological Association, Louisville.

Chiu, L. H. (1972). A cross-cultural comparison of cognitive styles in Chinese and American children. *International Journal of Psychology, 8*: 235–242.

Chiu, L. (2001). Locus of control differences between American and Chinese adolescents. *Journal of Social Psychology, 128*: 411–413.

Choi, I., R. E. Nisbett, and A. Norenzayan. (1999). Causal attribution across cultures: Variation and universality. *Psychological Bulletin, 125*: 47–63.

Cialdini, R. B. (2001). *Influence: Science and practice* (4th ed.). Boston: Allyn & Bacon.

Cohen, A. R., and D. L. Bradford. (2003). Influence without authority: The use of alliances, reciprocity, and exchange to accomplish work. In B. M. Staw (Ed.), *Psychological dimensions of organizational behavior* (3rd ed.) (pp. 359–367). Englewood Cliffs, NJ: Prentice Hall.

Conger, J. A., and R. N. Kanungo. (1998). *Charismatic leadership in organizations.* Thousand Oaks, CA: Sage.

Conner, J., and D. Ulrich. (1996). Human resource roles: Creating value, not rhetoric. *Human Resource Planning, 19*: 38–49.

Cuming, P. (1984). *The power handbook.* Boston: CBI Publishing Co.

Daly, J. P. (1995). Explaining changes to employees: The influence of justifications and change outcomes on employees' fairness judgments. *Journal of Applied Behavioral Science, 31*: 415–428.

Deal, T. E., and A. A. Kennedy. (1982). *Corporate cultures: The rites and rituals of corporate life.* Reading, MA: Addison-Wesley.

DeGeorge, R. T. (1999). *Business ethics.* Upper Saddle River, NJ: Prentice Hall.

Dilenschneider, R. L. (1990). *Power and influence: Mastering the art of persuasion.* New York: Prentice Hall.

Dirks, K. T., and D. L. Ferrin. (2001). The role of trust in organizational settings. *Organization Science, 12*: 450–467.

Dutton, J. E., and S. J. Ashford. (1993). Selling issues to top management. *Academy of Management Review, 18*(3): 397–428.

Dutton, J. E., and R. B. Duncan. (1987). The creation of momentum for change through the process of strategic issue diagnosis. *Strategic Management Journal, 83*(3): 279–295.

Dyer, W. G. (1972). Congruence. In *The sensitive manipulator.* Provo, UT: Brigham Young University Press.

Emerson, R. M. (1962). Power-dependence relations. *American Sociological Review, 27*: 31–40.

Fisher, A. (2005, March 7). Starting a new job? Don't blow it. *Fortune*: 48.

Furman, W. (2001). Working models of friendship. *Journal of Social and Personal Relationships, 18*: 583–602.

Gabarro, J. J., and J. P. Kotter. (1980). Managing your boss. *Harvard Business Review, 58*: 92–100.

Gardner, J. (1990). *On leadership.* New York: Free Press.

Gelman, E. (1985, September). Playing office politics. *Newsweek*: 56.

Giamatti, A. B. (1981). *The university and public interest.* New York: Atheneum.

Grove, A. (1983). *High output management.* London: Souvenir Press.

Hinings, C. R., D. J. Hickson, J. M. Pennings, and R. E. Schneck. (1974). Structural conditions of intraorganizational power. *Administrative Science Quarterly, 21*: 22–44.

Hoerr, J. (1985, December). Human resource managers aren't corporate nobodies anymore. *BusinessWeek*: 58.

Hogg, M. A. (2001). A social identity theory of leadership. *Personality and Social Psychology Review, 5*: 184–200.

Hosmer, L. T. (1995). Trust: The connecting link between organizational theory and philosophical ethics. *Academy of Management Review, 20*: 379–403.

Hosoda, M., E. F. Stone-Romero, and G. Coats. (2003). The effects of physical attractiveness on job-related outcomes: A meta-analysis of experimental studies. *Personnel Psychology, 56*: 431–462.

Kanter, R. (1979). Power failures in management circuits. *Harvard Business Review, 57*: 65–75. Copyright © 1979 by The President and Fellows of Harvard College. Reprinted with the permission of *Harvard Business Review*. All rights reserved.

Kaplan, R. E., and M. Mazique. (1983). *Trade routes: The manager's network of relationships* (Technical Report # 22). Greensboro, NC: Center for Creative Leadership.

Kipnis, D. (1987). Psychology and behavioral technology. *American Psychologist, 42*: 30–36.

Kipnis, D., and S. M. Schmidt. (1988). Upward-influence styles: Relationship with performance evaluations, salary, and stress. *Administrative Science Quarterly, 33*: 528–542.

Kipnis, D., S. M. Schmidt, and I. Wilkinson. (1980). Intraorganizational influence tactics: Explorations in getting one's way. *Journal of Applied Psychology, 65*: 440–452.

Korda, M. (1991). *Power: How to get it, how to use it.* New York: Warner Books.

Kotter, J. P. (1977). Power, dependence and effective management. *Harvard Business Review, 55*: 125–136.

Labich, K. (1995, February 20). Kissing off corporate America. *Fortune, 131*: 44–52.

Langlois, J. H., L. Kalakanis, A. J. Rubenstein, A. Larson, M. Hallam, and M. Smoot. (2000). Maxims of myths of beauty? A meta-analytic and theoretical review. *Psychological Bulletin 126*: 390–423.

Lawrence, R. R., and J. W. Lorsch. (1986). *Organization and environment: Managing differentiation and integration*. Boston: Harvard University Press.

Leger, D. M. (2000, May). Help! I'm the new boss. *Fortune*: 281–284.

Marwell, G., and D. R. Schmitt, (1967). Dimensions of compliance-gaining strategies: A dimensional analysis. *Sociometry, 30*: 350–364.

May, R. (1998). *Power and innocence: A search for the sources of violence*. New York: Norton.

McCall, M. M., Jr., and M. M. Lombardo. (1983). What makes a top executive? *Psychology Today, 26*: 28–31. Copyright © 1983 by Sussex Publishers Inc. Reprinted with the permission of *Psychology Today*.

McClelland, D. C., and D. H. Burnham. (2003). Power is the great motivator. *Motivating People, 81*: 117–126.

Mechanic, D. (1962). Sources of power of lower participants in complex organizations. *Administrative Science Quarterly, 7*: 349–364.

Miller, R. (1985). Three who made a difference. *Management Review, 74*: 16–19.

Morris, M. W., J. M. Podolny, and S. Ariel. (2000). Missing relations: Incorporating relational constructs into models of culture. In P. C. Earley and H. Singh (Eds.), *Innovation in international and cross-cultural management*, (pp. 52–90). Thousand Oaks, CA: Sage.

Mulder, M., L. Koppelaar, R. V. de Jong, and J. Verhage. (1986). Organizational field study. *Journal of Applied Psychology, 7*: 566–570.

Pascale, R. (1985). The paradox of "corporate culture": Reconciling ourselves to socialization. *California Management Review, 27*: 26–41.

Perrow, C. (1970). Departmental power and perspectives in industrial firms. In M. N. Zold, (Ed.), *Power in organizations*. Nashville, TN: Vanderbilt University Press.

Peters, T. (1978). Symbols, patterns, and settings: An optimistic case for getting things done. *Organizational Dynamics, 7*: 3–22.

Pfeffer, J. (1977). Power and resource allocation in organizations. In B. Staw and G. Salancik, (Eds.), *New direction in organizational behavior*. Chicago: St. Clair Press.

Pfeffer, J. (1981). *Power in organizations*. Marshfield, MA: Pitman.

Pfeffer, J. (1992). *Managing with power: Politics and influence in organizations*. Boston: Harvard Business School Press.

Pfeffer, J., and A. Konrad. (1991). The effects of individual power on earnings. *Work and Occupations, 18*: 385–414.

Schein, E. H. (1999). *The corporate culture survival guide: Sense and nonsense about culture change*. San Francisco: Jossey-Bass.

Schmidt, S., and D. Kipnis. (1987). The perils of persistence. *Psychology Today, 21*: 32–33.

Shipper, F., and J. E. Dillard. (2000). A study of impending derailment and recovery of middle managers across career stages. *Human Resource Management, 39*: 331–345.

Sparrowe, R. T., R. C. Liden, and M. L. Kraimer. (2001). Social networks and the performance of individuals and groups. *Academy of Management Journal, 44*: 316–325.

Stewart, T. A. (1992, May 18). The search for the organization of tomorrow. *Fortune*: 92–98.

Tedeschi, J. T. (1974). Attributions, liking and power. In T. L. Huston (Ed.), *Foundations of interpersonal attraction*. New York: Academic Press.

Thompson, L. (2001). *The mind and heart of the negotiator*. Upper Saddle River, NJ: Prentice Hall.

Triandis, H. (1994). *Culture and social behavior*. New York: McGraw-Hill.

Trompenaars, F. (1996). Resolving international conflict: Culture and business strategy. *Business Strategy Review, 7*: 51–68.

Tully, S. (1993, February 8). The modular corporation. *Fortune*: 106–114.

Yukl, G. (2002). Leadership in organizations (5th ed.). Upper Saddle River, NJ: Prentice Hall.

CHAPTER 6 REFERENCES

Abbott, R. K. (1997). Flexible compensation: Past, present, and future. *Compensation & Benefits Management, 13*: 18–24.

Adria, M. (2000). Making the most of e-mail. *Academy of Management Executive, 14*: 153–154.

Alderfer, C. P. (1977). A critique of Salancik and Pfeffer's examination of need-satisfaction theories. *Administrative Science Quarterly, 22*: 658–672.

Atkinson, J. W. (1992). Motivational determinants of thematic apperception? In C. P. Smith (Ed.), *Motivation and personality: Handbook of thematic content analysis*. New York: Cambridge University Press.

Bennis, W. (1984). The four competencies of leadership. *Training and Development Journal, 38*: 15–19.

Bennis, W. (2003). *On becoming a leader*. Cambridge, MA: Perseus Books Group.

Birch, D., and J. Veroff. (1966). *Motivation: A study of action*. Monterey, CA: Brooks-Cole.

Bitter, M. E., and W. L. Gardner. (1995). A mid-range theory of the leader/member attribution process in professional service organizations: The role of the organizational environment and impression management. In M. J. Martinko, (Ed.), *Attribution theory: An organizational perspective*. Delray Beach, FL: St. Lucie Press.

Boehle, S., K. Dobbs, and D. Stamps. (2000). Two views of distance learning. *Training, 37*: 34.

Butler, T., and J. Waldroop. (1999). Job sculpting: The art of retaining your best people. *Harvard Business Review* (September–October): 144–152.

Choi, I., R. E. Nisbett, and A. Norenzayan. (1999). Causal attribution across cultures: Variation and universality. *Psychological Bulletin, 125*: 47–63.

Cook, A. (2005, May). Money's a sure-fire motivator—Isn't it? *Promotions and Incentives*: 56–59.

Cropanzano, R., and R. Folger. (1996). Procedural justice and worker motivation. In R. M. Steers, L. W. Porter, and G. A. Bigley (Eds.), *Motivation and leadership at work*. New York: McGraw-Hill.

Davidson, O. B., and D. Eden. (2000). Remedial self-fulfilling prophecy: Two field experiments to prevent golem effects among disadvantaged women. *Journal of Applied Psychology 85*: 386–398.

Fisher, A. (2005, March 7). Starting a new job? Don't blow it. *Fortune*: 5.

Ganzach, Y. (1998). Intelligence and job satisfaction. *Academy of Management Journal, 41*: 526–536.

Gerhart, Barry A. (2003). *Compensation: Theory, evidence, and strategic implications*. Thousand Oaks, CA: Sage.

Graham, M. E., and C. O. Trevor. (2000). Managing new pay program introductions to enhance the competitiveness of multinational corporations (MNCS). *Competitiveness Review, 10*: 136–154.

Hackman, J. R., and G. R. Oldham. (1980). *Work redesign*. Reading, MA: Addison-Wesley.

Harter, J. K., F. L. Schmidt, and T. L. Hayes. (2002). Business-unit-level relationship between employee satisfaction, employee engagement, and business outcomes: A meta-analysis. *Journal of Applied Psychology, 87*: 268–279.

House, R. J., and T. R. Mitchell. (1974). Path-goal theory of leadership. *Journal of Contemporary Business, 3*: 81–97.

Jackson, P. (2000). Interview with Phil Jackson by Bob Costas. MSNBC.

Janssen, O. (2001). Fairness perceptions as a moderator in the curvilinear relationships between job demands, and job performance and job satisfaction. *Academy of Management Journal, 44*: 1039–1050.

Jay, A. (1967). *Management and Machiavelli, an inquiry into the politics of corporate life*. New York: Holt, Rinehart & Winston.

Kerr, S. (1995). On the folly of rewarding A, while hoping for B. *Academy of Management Executive, 9*(1): 7–14.

Kerr, S. (1996, July 22). Risky business: The new pay game. *Fortune*, 94–97.

Kleiman, C. (2005, June 14). Awards for workers get better as they get personal. *Chicago Tribune*, 2.

Knight, D., C. C. Durham, and E. A. Locke. (2001). The relationship of term goals, incentives, and efficacy to strategic risk, tactical implementation, and performance. *Academy of Management Journal, 44*: 326–338.

Komaki, J., T. Coombs, and S. Schepman. (1996). Motivational implications of reinforcement theory. In R. M. Steers, L. W. Porter, and G. A. Bigley (Eds.), *Motivation and leadership at work*. New York: McGraw-Hill.

Kopelman, R. E. (1985). Job redesign and productivity: A review of evidence. *National Productivity Review* (Summer): 237–255.

Kotter, J. (1996, August 5). Kill complacency. *Fortune*: 168–170.

Latham, G., M. Erez, and E. Locke. (1988). Resolving scientific disputes by the joint design of crucial experiments by the antagonists: Application to the Erez-Latham disputes regarding participation in goal setting. *Journal of Applied Psychology, 73*: 753–772.

Lawler, E. E. (1987). The design of effective reward systems. In J. Lorsch (Ed.), *Handbook of organizational behavior*. Englewood Cliffs, NJ: Prentice Hall.

Lawler, E. E. (1988). Gainsharing theory and research: Findings and future directions. In W. A. Pasmore and E. R. Woodman (Eds.), *Research in organizational change and development* (Vol. 2). Greenwich, CT: JAI Press.

Lawler, E. E. (2000a). *Strategic pay*. San Francisco: Jossey-Bass.

Lawler, E. E., III. (2000b). *Pay strategies for the new economy*. San Francisco: Jossey-Bass.

LeDue, A. I., Jr. (1980). Motivation of programmers. *Data Base, 3*: 5.

Levering, R., and M. Moskowitz. (2003, January 20). 100 best companies to work for. *Fortune, 147*: 127.

Locke, E. A., and G. P. Latham. (2002, September). Building a practically useful theory of goal setting and task motivation. *American Psychologist, 57*: 705–717.

Luthans, F., and A. D. Stajkovic. (1999). Reinforce for performance: The need to go beyond pay and even rewards. *Academy of Management Executive, 13*(2): 49–57.

Maslow, A. H. (1970). *Motivation and personality* (2nd ed.). New York: Harper & Row.

McCauley, L. (1999). Next stop—the 21st century. *Fast Company, 27*: 108–112.

McClelland, D. (1971). *Assessing human motivation*. New York: General Learning Press.

McClelland, D. C., J. W. Arkinson, R. A. Clark, and E. L. Lowell. (1953). *The achievement motive*. New York: Appleton-Century-Crofts.

McClelland, D. C., and D. H. Burnham. (2003). Power is the great motivator. *Harvard Business Review, 81*: 117–126.

McGregor, D. (1960). *The human side of enterprise*. New York: McGraw-Hill.

Michener, H. A., J. A. Fleishman, and J. J. Vaske. (1976). A test of the bargaining theory of coalition formulation in four-person groups. *Journal of Personality and Social Psychology, 34*: 1114–1126.

Moe, M. T. and H. Blodget. (2000, May 23). *The knowledge web. Part 4: corporate e-learning—feeding hungry minds*. Merrill Lynch & Co.

Murlis, H., and A. Wright. (1985). Rewarding the performance of the eager beaver. *Personnel Management, 17*: 28–31.

Murray, B., and B. Gerhart. (1998). An empirical analysis of a skill-based pay program and plant performance outcomes. *Academy of Management Journal, 41*: 68–78.

Nelson, B. (2000). Are performance appraisals obsolete? *Compensation and Benefits Review, 32*: 39–42.

Nelson, N. (2005). *The power of appreciation in business: How an obsession with value increases performance, productivity, and profits*. Malibu, CA: MindLab Publishing.

Nelton, S. (1988, March). Motivating for success. *Nation's Business*: 25.

News-Gazette. (1987, January); 6.

Parker, G. (2001). Establishing remuneration practices across culturally diverse environments. *Compensation & Benefits Management, 17*: 23–27.

Perry, M. (2000, January). Working in the dark. *Training Media Review*: 13–14.

Peters, T. and R. H. Waterman. (1982). *In search of excellence*. New York: Warner Books.

Pfeffer, J. (1995). Producing sustainable competitive advantage through the effective management of people. *Academy of Management Executive, 9*: 55–71.

Quick, T. L. (1977). *Person to person managing*. New York: St. Martin's Press.

Quick, T. L. (1991). Motivation: Help your star performers shine even brighter. *Sales and Marketing Management, 143*: 96.

Reese, S. (1999, July). Getting your money's worth from training. *Business and Health*: 26–29.

Schriesheim, C. A., and L. L. Neider. (1996). Path-goal leadership theory: The long and winding road. *Leadership Quarterly, 7*: 317–321.

Shamir, B., R. J. House, and M. B. Arthur. (1993). The motivational effects of charismatic leadership: A self-concept based theory. *Organization Science, 4*(4): 577–594.

Stajkovic, A. D., and F. Luthans. (2001). Differential effects of incentive motivators on work performance. *Academy of Management Journal, 4*: 580–500.

Steers, R. M., L. W. Porter, and G. A. Bigley. (1996). *Motivation and leadership at work*. New York: McGraw-Hill.

Sue-Chan, C., and M. Ong. (2002). Goal assignment and performance: Assessing the mediating roles of goal commitment and self-efficacy and the moderating role of power distance. *Organizational Behavior and Human Decision Processes, 89*: 1140–1161.

Taylor, W. C. (1995). At Verifone it's a dog's life (and they love it?). *Fast Company, 1*: 115.

Thompson, D. W. (1978). *Managing people: Influencing behavior*. St. Louis, MO: C. V. Mosby Co.

Tichy, N. (1997, April). Bob Knowling's change manual. *Fast Company*: 76.

Tomlinson, A. (2002, March 25). T&D spending up in U.S. as Canada lags behind. *Canadian HR Reporter, 15*: 1–18.

Triandis, H. C. (1994). *Culture and social behavior*. New York: McGraw-Hill.

Vroom, V. (1964). *Work and motivation*. New York: Wiley.

Weiner, B. (2000). Intrapersonal and interpersonal theories of motivation from an attributional perspective. *Educational Psychology Review, 12*: 1–14.

Wood, R., and A. Bandura. (1989). Social cognitive theory of organizational management. *Academy of Management Review, 14*(3): 361–383.

Zingheim, P. K., and J. R. Schuster. (1995). Introduction: How are the new pay tools being deployed? *Compensation and Benefits Review* (July–August): 10–11.

CHAPTER 7 REFERENCES

Adler, N. J. (2002). *International dimensions of organizational behavior* 4th ed. Cincinnati, OH: South-Western.

Adler, R. B. (1977). Satisfying personal needs: Managing conflicts, making requests, and saying no. In *Confidence in communication: A guide to assertive and social skills*. New York: Holt, Rinehart & Winston.

Adler, R. B., L. B. Rosenfeld, R. F. Proctor. (2001). *Interplay: The process of interpersonal communication*. Fort Worth, TX: Harcourt, Inc.

Alder, R. B., and G. Rodman. (2003). *Understanding human communication* 8th ed. New York: Oxford University Press.

Argenti, J. (1976). *Corporate collapse: The causes and symptoms*. New York: Wiley.

Bazerman, M. H., and M. A. Neale. (1992). *Negotiating rationally*. New York: Free Press.

Blackard, K., and J. Gibson. (2002). *Capitalizing on conflict: Strategies and practices for turning conflict into synergy in organizations: A manager's handbook*. Palo Alto, CA: Davis-Black Publishing.

The boss as referee. [Accountemps survey]. (1996, September). *CMA Management Accounting Magazine, 70*(7): 32.

Boulding, E. (1964). Further reflections on conflict management. In R. L. Kahn and E. Boulding (Eds.), *Power and conflict in organizations*. New York: Basic Books.

Brown, L. D. (1983). *Managing conflict at organizational interfaces*. Reading, MA: Addison-Wesley.

Cameron, K. S., M. U. Kim, and D. A. Whetten. (1987). Organizational effects of decline and turbulence. *Administrative Science Quarterly, 32*: 222–240.

Catch a falling star. (1988, April 23). *The Economist*, 88–90.

Caudron, S. (1992). Subculture strife hinders productivity. *Personnel Journal, 71*(2): 60–64.

Cox, T. H. (1994). *Cultural diversity in organizations: Theory, research and practice*. San Francisco: Barrett-Koehler.

Cox, T. H., and Blake, S. (1991). Managing cultural diversity: Implications for organizational competitiveness. *Academy of Management Executive, 5*(3): 45–56.

Cummings, L. L., D. L. Harnett, and O. J. Stevens. (1971). Risk, fate, conciliation and trust: An international study of attitudinal differences among executives. *Academy of Management Journal, 14*: 285–304.

de Dreu, C. K. W., S. L. Koole, and W. Steinel. (2000). Unfixing the fixed pie: A motivated information-processing approach to integrative negotiation. *Journal of Personality and Social Psychology, 79*: 975–987.

de Dreu, C. K. W., and L. R. Weingart. (2002). Task versus relationship conflict: A meta-analysis. *Academy of Management Proceedings, CM*: B1–B6.

Eisenhardt, K. M., J. L. Kahwajy, and L. J. Bourgeois III. (1997). How management teams can have a good fight. *Harvard Business Review* (July–August): 77–85.

Fisher, R., and S. Brown. (1988). *Getting together: Building a relationship that gets to yes*. Boston: Houghton Mifflin.

Gage, D. (1999, December). Is having partners a bad idea? *Industry Week*, Growing Companies Edition: 46–47.

Gendron, G., and B. O. Burlingham. (1989, April). The entrepreneur of the decade: An interview with Steve Jobs. *Inc.;* 123.

The GM system is like a blanket of fog. (1988, February 15). *Fortune*, 48–49.

Gordon, T. (2000). *Parent effectiveness training*. New York: Three Rivers Press.

Grove, A. (1984, July). How to make confrontation work for you. *Fortune*: 74.

Hines, J. S. (1980). *Conflict and conflict management*. Athens: University of Georgia Press.

Hofstede, G. (1980). Motivation, leadership, and organization: Do American theories apply abroad? *Organizational Dynamics* (Summer): 42–63.

Jehn, K. A. (1997). A qualitative analysis of conflict types and dimensions of organizational groups. *Administrative Science Quarterly, 41*: 530–557.

Jehn, K., and E. A. Mannix. (2001). The dynamic nature of conflict: A longitudinal study of intragroup conflict and group performance. *Academy of Management Journal, 44*: 238–251.

Karambayya, R., and J. M. Brett. (1989). Managers handling disputes: Third party roles and perceptions of fairness. *Academy of Management Journal, 32*: 687–704.

Keashly, L. (1994). Gender and conflict: What does psychological research tell us? In A. Taylor and J. B. Miller (Eds.), *Conflict and gender*. Cresskill, NJ: Hampton Press.

Kelly, J. (1970). Make conflict work for you. *Harvard Business Review, 48* (July–August): 103–113.

Kilmann, R. H., and K. W. Thomas. (1977). Developing a forced-choice measure of conflict-handling behavior: The MODE instrument. *Educational and Psychological Measurement, 37*: 309–325.

Kim, S. H., and R. H. Smith. (1993). Revenge and conflict escalation. *Negotiation Journal. 9*: 37–44.

Kipnis, D., and S. Schmidt. (1983). An influence perspective in bargaining within organizations. In M. H. Bazerman, and R. J. Lewicki (Eds.), *Bargaining inside organizations*. Beverly Hills, CA: Sage.

Korabik, D., G. L. Baril, and C. Watson. (1993). Managers' conflict management style and leadership effectiveness: The moderating effects of gender. *Sex Roles, 29*(5/6): 405–420.

Kressel, K., and D. G. Pruitt. (1989). *Mediation research: The process and effectiveness of third party intervention*. San Francisco: Jossey-Bass.

Latham, G., and K. Wexley. (1994). *Increasing productivity through performance appraisal*. Reading, MA: Addison-Wesley.

Lombardo, M. M., and R. W. Eichinger. (1996). *The Career ARCHITECT Development Planner*. Minneapolis: Lominger Ltd.

Maslow, A. (1965). *Eupsychian management*. Homewood, IL: Irwin.

Morris, W., and M. Sashkin. (1976). *Organizational behavior in action*. St. Paul, MN: West Publishing.

Morrison, A. M. (1996). *The new leaders: Leadership diversity in America*. San Francisco: Jossey-Bass.

Murnighan, J. K. (1992). *Bargaining games: A new approach to strategic thinking in negotiations*. New York: William Morrow.

Murnighan, J. K. (1993). *The dynamics of bargaining games*. Upper Saddle River, NJ: Prentice Hall.

Pascale, R. (1990, February). Creating contention without causing conflict. *Business Month*: 69–71.

Pelled, L. H., K. M. Eisenhardt, and K. R. Xin. (1999). Exploring the black box: An analysis of work group diversity, conflict, and performance. *Administrative Science Quarterly, 44*: 1–28.

Perot, H. R. (1988, February). How I would turn around GM. *Fortune*: 48–49.

Phillips, E., and R. Cheston. (1979). Conflict resolution: What works. *California Management Review, 21*: 76–83.

Porter, E. H. (1973). *Manual of administration and interpretation for strength deployment inventory*. La Jolla, CA: Personal Strengths Assessment Service.

Rahim, M. A., and A. A. Blum. (1994). *Global perspectives on organizational conflict*. Westport, CT: Praeger.

Ruble, T., and J. A. Schneer. (1994). Gender differences in conflict-handling styles: Less than meets the eye? In A. Taylor, and J. B. Miller, (Eds.), *Conflict and gender*. Cresskill, NJ: Hampton Press.

Ruble, T., and K. Thomas. (1976). Support for a two-dimensional model of conflict behavior. *Organizational Behavior and Human Performance, 16*: 145.

Savage, G. T., J. D. Blair, and R. L. Sorenson. (1989). Consider both relationships and substance when negotiating strategically. *Academy of Management Executive. 3*: 37–48.

Schmidt, W. H., and R. Tannenbaum. (1965). Management of differences. *Harvard Business Review, 38* (November–December): 107–115.

Seybolt, P. M., C. B. Derr, and T. R. Nielson. (1996). Linkages between national culture, gender, and conflict management styles. Working paper, University of Utah.

Sillars, A., and J. Weisberg. (1987). Conflict as a social skill. In M. E. Roloff and G. R. Miller, (Eds.), *Interpersonal processes: New directions in communication research*. Beverly Hills, CA: Sage.

Smith, W. P. (1987). Conflict and negotiation: Trends and emerging issues. *Journal of Applied Social Psychology, 17*: 631–677.

Stroh, L. K., G. Northcraft, and M. Neale. (2002). *Organizational behavior: A management challenge* (3rd ed.). Mahwah, NJ: Lawrence Erlbaum Associates.

Thomas, K. (1976). Conflict and conflict management. In M. D. Dunnette (Ed.), *Handbook of industrial and organizational psychology*. London: Routledge and Kegan Paul.

Thompson, L. (2001). *The mind and heart of the negotiator* (2nd ed.). Upper Saddle River, NJ: Prentice Hall.

Ting-Toomey, S., G. Gao, P. Trubisky, Z. Yang, H. S. Kim, S. L. Lin, and T. Nishida. (1991). Culture, face maintenance, and styles of handling interpersonal conflict: A study in five cultures. *International Journal of Conflict Management, 2*: 275–296.

Tjosvold, D. (1991). *The conflict positive organization*. Reading, MA: Addison-Wesley.

Trompenaars, F. (1994). *Riding the waves of culture: Understanding diversity in global business*. New York: Irwin.

Trompenaars, F. (1996). Resolving international conflict: Culture and business strategy. *Business Strategy Review, 7*: 51–68.

Volkema, R. J., and T. J. Bergmann. (2001). Conflict styles as indicators of behavioral patterns in interpersonal conflicts. *Journal of Social Psychology, 135*: 5–15.

Wanous, J. P., and A. Youtz. (1986). Solution diversity and the quality of group decisions. *Academy of Management Journal, 1*: 149–159.

Weldon, E., and K. A. Jehn. (1995). Examining crosscultural differences in conflict management behavior: Strategy for future research. *International Journal of Conflict Management, 6*: 387–403.

Wilmot, W. W., and J. L. Hocker. (2001). *Interpersonal conflict*. New York: McGraw-Hill.

Xie, J., X. M. Song, and A. Stringfellow. (1998). Interfunctional conflict, conflict resolution styles, and new product success: A four-culture comparison. *Management Science, 44*: S192–S206.

CHAPTER 8 REFERENCES

Adler, Alfred. (1927). *Understanding human nature*. Garden City, NY: Garden City Publishing.

Alinsky, Saul D. (1971). *Rules for radicals: A pragmatic primer for realistic radicals*. New York: Vintage Books.

Alloy, L. B., C. Peterson, L. Y. Abrahamson, and M. E. P. Seligman. (1984). Attributional style and the generality of learned helplessness. *Journal of Personality and Social Psychology, 46*: 681–687.

Anderson, C., D. Hellriegel, and J. Slocum. (1977). Managerial response to environmentally induced stress. *Academy of Management Journal, 20*: 260–272.

Ashby, R. (1956). *Design for the brain*. London: Science Paperbacks.

Averill, J. R. (1973). Personal control over aversive stimuli and its relationships to stress. *Psychological Bulletin, 80*: 286–303.

Baker, W., R. Cross, and M. Wooten. (2003). Positive organizational network analysis and energizing relationships. In K. S. Cameron, J. E. Dutton, and R. E. Quinn (Eds.), *Positive Organizational Scholarship* (pp. 328–342). San Francisco: Barrett-Koehler.

Bandura, Alfred. (1977). Self-efficacy: Toward a unifying theory of behavioral change. *Psychological Review, 84*: 191–215.

Bandura, Alfred. (1986). *Social foundations of thought and action: A social cognitive theory*. Englewood Cliffs, NJ: Prentice Hall.

Bandura, Alfred. (1989). Human agency in social cognition theory. *American Psychologist, 44*: 1175–1184.

Barber, B. (1983). *The logic and limits of trust*. New Brunswick, NJ: Rutgers University Press.

Bennis, Warren, and Bert Nanus. (1985). *Leaders: The strategies for taking charge*. New York: Harper and Row.

Bernard, C. I. (1938). *The functions of the executive*. Cambridge, MA: Harvard University Press.

Block, Peter. (1987). *The empowered manager: Positive political skills at work*. San Francisco: Jossey-Bass.

Bookman, Ann, and Sandra Morgan. (1988). *Women and the politics of empowerment*. Philadelphia: Temple University Press.

Bramucci, R. (1977). A factorial examination of the self-empowerment construct. Unpublished doctoral dissertation, University of Oregon.

Brehm, J. W. (1966). *Response to loss of freedom: A theory of psychological reactance*. New York: Academic Press.

Brief, A., and W. Nord. (1990). *Meanings of occupational work*. Lexington, MA: Lexington Books.

Byham, William C. (1988). *Zapp! The lightening of empowerment*. New York: Harmony Books.

Cameron, Kim S. (1998). Strategic organizational downsizing: An extreme case. *Research in Organizational Behavior, 20*: 185–229.

Cameron, Kim S., Jane E. Dutton, and Robert E. Quinn. (2003). *Positive organizational scholarship*. San Francisco: Barrett-Koehler.

Cameron, Kim S., Sarah J. Freeman, and Aneil K. Mishra. (1991). Best practices in white-collar downsizing: Managing contradictions. *Academy of Management Executive, 5*: 57–73.

Cameron, Kim S., Sarah J. Freeman, and Aneil K. Mishra. (1993). Organization downsizing and redesign. In G. P. Huber, and W. Glick (Eds.), *Organizational change and design*. New York: Oxford University Press.

Cameron, Kim S., Myung U. Kim, and David A. Whetten. (1987). Organizational effects of decline and turbulence. *Administrative Science Quarterly, 32*: 222–240.

Cameron, Kim S., David A. Whetten, and Myung U. Kim. (1987). Organizational dysfunctions of decline. *Academy of Management Journal, 30*: 126–138.

Cameron, Kim S., and Robert E. Quinn. (2006). *Diagnosing and changing organizational culture*. San Francisco: Jossey-Bass.

Coch, L., and French, J. R. P. (1948). Overcoming resistance to change. *Human Relations, 11*: 512–532.

Conger, Jay A. (1989). Leadership: The art of empowering others. *Academy of Management Executive, 3*: 17–24.

Conger, Jay A., and Rabindra N. Kanungo. (1988). The empowerment process. *Academy of Management Review, 13*: 471–482.

Coonradt, Charles A. (1985). *The game of work*. Salt Lake City: Shadow Mountain Press.

DeCharms, R. (1979). Personal causation and perceived control. In L. C. Perlmuter and R. A. Monty (Eds.), *Choice and perceived control*. Hillsdale, NJ: Erlbaum.

Deci, E. L., and R. M. Ryan. (1987). The support of autonomy and control of behavior. *Journal of Personality and Social Psychology, 53*: 1024–1037.

Deci, Edward L., James P. Connell, and Richard M. Ryan. (1989). Self-determination in a work organization. *Journal of Applied Psychology, 74*: 580–590.

DeGraff, J., and Lawrence, K. A. (2002). *Creativity at work: Developing the right practices to make innovation happen*. San Francisco: Jossey-Bass.

Deutsch, Morton. (1973). *The resolution of conflict: Constructive and destructive processes*. New Haven, CT: Yale University Press.

DiClemente, C. C. (1985). Perceived efficacy in smoking cessation. Paper presented at the Annual meeting of the American Association for the Advancement of Science, Los Angeles.

Drucker, Peter. (1988). The coming of the new organization. *Harvard Business Review*, January–February: 45–53.

Durkheim, E. (1964). *The division of labor in Society*. New York: Free Press.

Eisenhart, Kathleen M., and D. Charlie Galunic. (1993). Renewing the strategy-structure-performance paradigm. *Research in organizational behavior*. Greenwich, CT: JAI Press.

French, J. P. R., Jr., and B. Raven. (1960). The bases of social power. In D. Cartwright and A. Zander (Eds.), *Group dynamics* (pp. 607–623). New York: Harper and Row.

Freire, P., and A. Faundez. (1989). *Learning to question: A pedagogy of liberation*. New York: Continuum Publishing.

Gambetta, Diego. (1988). *Trust: Making and breaking cooperative relations*. Cambridge, MA: Basil Blackwell.

Gecas, V., M. A. Seff, and M. P. Ray. (1988). Injury and depression: The mediating effects of self concept. Paper presented at the Pacific Sociological Association Meetings, Las Vegas.

Gecas, Viktor. (1989). The social psychology of self-efficacy. *Annual Review of Sociology, 15*: 291–316.

Gemmill, G. R., and W. J. Heisler. (1972). Fatalism as a factor in managerial job satisfaction. *Personnel Psychology, 25*: 241–250.

Gibb, J. R., and L. M. Gibb. (1969). Role freedom in a TORI group. In A. Burton (Ed.), *Encounter theory and practice of encounter groups*. San Francisco: Jossey-Bass.

Goddard, R. D., W. K. Hoy, and A. W. Hoy. (2003). Collective efficacy beliefs: Theoretical developments, empirical evidence, and future directions. *Educational Researcher, 33*: 3–13.

Golembiewski, R. T., and M. McConkie. (1975). The centrality of trust in group processes. In Cary Cooper (Ed.), *Theories of group processes*. New York: Wiley.

Greenberger, David B., and Stephen Stasser. (1991). The role of situational and dispositional factors in the enhancement of personal control in organizations. *Research in Organizational Behavior*, Volume 13, pp. 111–145. Greenwich, CT: JAI Press.

Greenberger, David B., Stephen Stasser, Larry L. Cummings, and Randall B. Dunham. (1989). The impact of personal control on performance and satisfaction. *Organizational Behavior and Human Decision Processes, 43*: 29–51.

Hackman, J. R., and G. R. Oldham. (1980). *Work design*. Reading, MA: Addison-Wesley.

Hackman, J. R., G. R. Oldham, R. Janson, and K. Purdy. (1975). A new strategy for job enrichment. *California Management Review, 17*: 57–71.

Hammer, T. H., and Y. Vardi. (1981). Locus of control and career self-management among nonsupervisory employees in industrial settings. *Journal of Vocational Behavior, 18*: 13–29.

Harris, L. (2002). *Harris Poll #31*. New York: Harris Interactive.

Harter, S. (1978). Effectance motivation reconsidered: Toward a developmental model. *Human Development, 21*: 34–64.

Huber, George P. (1980). *Managerial decision making*. Glenview, IL: Scott Foresman.

Kahn, W. A. (1990). Psychological conditions of personal engagement and disengagement at work. *Academy of Management Journal, 33*: 692–724.

Kanter, Rosabeth. (1983). *The change masters*. New York: Simon & Schuster.

Langer, E. J. (1983). *The psychology of control*. Beverly Hills, CA: Sage.

Langer, E. J., and J. Rodin. (1976). The effects of choice and enhanced personal responsibility. *Journal of Personality and Social Psychology, 34*: 191–198.

Lawler, Edward E. (1992) *The ultimate advantage: Creating the high involvement organization*. San Francisco: Jossey-Bass.

Lawrence, Paul, and Jay Lorsch. (1967). *Organizations and environments*. Homewood, IL: Irwin.

Leana, Carrie R. (1987). Power relinquishment versus power sharing: Theoretical clarification and empirical comparison on delegation and participation. *Journal of Applied Psychology, 72*: 228–233.

Locke, Edward A., and D. M. Schweiger. (1979). Participation in decision making: One more look. In B. M. Staw and L. L. Cummings. (Eds.), *Research in organizational behavior*, Vol. 1 (pp. 265–340). Greenwich, CT: JAI Press.

Luhmann, Niklas. (1979). *Trust and power*. New York: Wiley.

Maddux, J. E. (2002). Self-efficacy. In C. R. Snyder and S. J. Lopez, *Handbook of Positive Psychology* (pp. 277–287). New York: Oxford.

Manz, C. C. and H. Sims. (1989). *Super-leadership: Teaching others to lead themselves*. Englewood Cliffs, NJ: Prentice Hall.

Martin, J., M. Feldman, M. J. Hatch, and S. Sitkin. (1983). The uniqueness paradox of organizational stories. *Administrative Science Quarterly, 28*: 438–452.

Marx, Karl (1844). *Early writings*. Edited and translated by T. B. Bottomore. New York: McGraw-Hill.

McClellend, David. (1975). *Power: The inner experience*. New York: Irvington.

Mishra, Aneil K. (1992). Organizational response to crisis: The role of mutual trust and top management teams. Unpublished doctoral dissertation, University of Michigan.

Neufeld, R. W. J., and P. Thomas. (1977) Effects of perceived efficacy of a prophylactic controlling mechanism on self-control under painful stimulation. *Canadian Journal of Behavioral Science, 9*: 224–232.

Newman, W. H., and K. Warren. (1977). *The process of management*. Englewood Cliffs, NJ: Prentice Hall.

Organ, Dennis, and C. N. Greene. (1974). Role ambiguity, locus of control, and work satisfaction. *Journal of Applied Psychology, 59*: 101–112.

Ozer, E. M., and A. Bandura. (1990). Mechanisms governing empowerment effects: A self-efficacy analysis. *Journal of Personality and Social Psychology, 58*: 472–486.

Pratt, M. G., and B. E. Ashforth. (2003). Fostering meaningfulness in working and at work. In K. S. Cameron, J. E. Dutton, and R. E. Quinn (Eds.), *Positive organizational scholarship* (pp. 309–327). San Francisco: Barrett-Koehler.

Preston, P. and T. W. Zimmerer. (1978). *Management for supervisors*. Englewood Cliffs, NJ: Prentice Hall.

Quinn, R. E. (2005). *Building the bridge as you walk on it*. San Francisco: Jossey-Bass.

Quinn, Robert E., and Gretchen Spreitzer. (1997). The road to empowerment: Seven questions every leader should consider. *Organizational Dynamics, 25*: 37–49.

Rappoport, Julian, Carolyn Swift, and Robert Hess. (1984). *Studies in empowerment: Steps toward understanding and action*. New York: Haworth Press.

Rose, Stephen M. and Bruce L. Black. (1985). *Advocacy and empowerment: Mental health care in the community*. Boston: Routledge and Kegan Paul.

Rothbaum, F., J. R. Weisz, and S. S. Snyder. (1982). Changing the world and changing the self: A two-process model of perceived control. *Journal of Personality and Social Psychology, 42*: 5–37.

Runyon, K. E. (1973). Some interaction between personality variables and management style. *Journal of Applied Psychology, 57*: 288–294.

Sashkin, Marshall. (1982). *A manager's guide to participative management*. New York: American Management Association.

Sashkin, Marshall. (1984). Participative management is an ethical imperative. *Organizational Dynamics, 12*: 4–22.

Schneider, J. A., and W. W. Agras. (1985). A cognitive behavioral treatment of bulimia. *British Journal of Psychiatry, 146*: 66–69.

Schwalbe, M. L., and V. Gecas. (1988). Social psychological consequences of job-related disabilities. In J. T. Mortimer and K. M. Borman, (Eds.), *Work experience and psychological development through life span*. Boulder, CO: Westview.

Seeman, M., and C. S. Anderson. (1983). Alienation and alcohol. *American Sociological Review, 48*: 60–77.

Seligman, M. E. P. (1975). *Helplessness: On depression, development, and death*. San Francisco: Freeman.

Sewell, Carl. (1990). *Customers for life*. New York: Pocket Books.

Solomon, Barbara Bryant. (1976). *Black empowerment: Social work in oppressed communities*. New York: Columbia University Press.

Spreitzer, Gretchen M. (1992). *When organizations dare: The dynamics of individual empowerment in the workplace*. Unpublished doctoral dissertation, University of Michigan.

Staples, Lee H. (1990). Powerful ideas about empowerment. *Administration in Social Work, 14*: 29–42.

Staw, Barry, Lance Sandelands, and Jane Dutton. (1981). Threat-rigidity effects in organizational behavior: A multilevel analysis. *Administrative Science Quarterly, 26*: 501–524.

Thomas, Kenneth W., and Betty A. Velthouse. (1990). Cognitive elements of empowerment: An interpretive model of intrinsic task motivation. *Academy of Management Review, 15*: 666–681.

Trompenaars, Frons. (1996). Resolving international conflict: Culture and business strategy. *Business Strategy Review, 7*: 51–68.

Trompenaars, Frons, and Charles Hampden-Turner. (1998). *Riding the waves of culture*. New York: McGraw Hill.

Urwick, L. (1944). *Elements of administration*. New York: Harper and Brothers.

Vogt, Judith F., and Kenneth L. Murrell. (1990). *Empowerment in organizations*. San Diego: University Associates.

Vroom, V. H., and Jago, A. G. (1974). Decision making as social process: Normative and descriptive models of leader behavior. *Decision Sciences, 5*: 743–769.

Vroom, V. H., and Yetton, P. W. (1973). *Leadership and decision making*. Pittsburgh: University of Pittsburgh Press.

Weick, Karl E. (1979) *The social psychology of organizing*. Reading, MA: Addison-Wesley.

Weick, K. E. (1984). Small wins. *American Psychologist, 39*: 40–49.

Weick, K. E. (1993). Collapse of sense-making in organizations. *Administrative Science Quarterly, 38*: 628–652.

White, R. W. (1959). Motivation reconsidered: The concept of competence. *Psychological Review, 66*: 297–333.

Wrzesniewski, A. (2003). Finding positive meaning in work. In K. S. Cameron, J. E. Dutton, and R. E. Quinn (Eds.), *Positive organizational scholarship* (pp. 296–308). San Francisco: Barrett-Koehler.

Zand, Dale, E. (1972). Trust and managerial problem solving. *Administrative Science Quarterly, 17*: 229–239.

Zimmerman, M. A., and J. Rappaport. (1988). Citizen participation, perceived control, and psychological empowerment. *American Journal of Community Psychology, 16*: 725–750.

Zimmerman, Marc A. (1990). Taking aim on empowerment research: On the distinction between individual and psycho-logical conceptions. *American Journal of Community Psychology, 18*: 169–177.

CHAPTER 9 REFERENCES

Ancona, Deborah G., and David Caldwell. (1992). Bridging the boundary: External activity and performance in organizational teams. *Administrative Science Quarterly, 27*: 459–489.

Asch, Solomon E. (1951). Effects of group pressure upon the modification and distortion of judgments. In Harold Guetzkow (Ed.), *Groups, leadership, and men*. Pittsburgh: Carnegie Press.

Cameron, Kim S., and David A. Whetten. (1981). Perceptions of organizational effectiveness in organizational life cycles. *Administrative Science Quarterly, 27*: 524–544.

Cameron, Kim S., and David A. Whetten. (1984). Organizational life cycle approaches: Overview and applications to higher education. *Review of Higher Education, 6*: 60–102.

Campion, M. A., G. J. Medsker, and A. C. Higgs. (1993). Relations between work group characteristics and effectiveness: Implications for designing effective work groups. *Personnel Psychology, 46*: 823–850.

Cialdini, R. B. (1995). *Influence: Science and practice*, 3rd ed. Glenview, IL: Scott Foresman.

Clarke, J., and A. Hobson. (2005). *Above all else: The Everest dream*. Toronto: Stewart Publishing.

Cohen, Susan G., and Diane E. Bailey. (1997). What makes teams work: Group effectiveness research from the shop floor to the executive suite. *Journal of Management, 23*: 239–290.

Cox, Taylor H. (1994). *Cultural diversity in organizations: Theory, research, and practice*. San Francisco: Barrett-Koehler.

Dew, John R. (1998). *Managing in a team environment*. Westport, CT: Quorum.

Dewey, John. (1933). *How we think*. Boston: Heath.

Druskat, Vanessa, and Jane Wheeler. (2000). Effective leadership of self-managing teams: Behaviors that make a difference. Working paper, Weatherhead School of Management, Case Western Reserve University.

Druskat, Vanessa, and Steven Wolff. (1999). The link between emotions and team effectiveness: How teams engage members and build effective task processes. *Academy of Management Best Paper Proceedings*, Organizational Behavior Division.

Dyer, William, G. (1987). *Team building: Issues and alternatives*. Reading, MA: Addison-Wesley.

Edmonson, A. (1999). Psychological safety and learning behavior in work teams. *Administrative Science Quarterly, 44*: 350–383.

Freud, Sigmund. (1921). *Group psychology and the analysis of the ego*. London: Hogarth Press.

Gladstein, Deborah. (1984). Group in context: A model of task group effectiveness. *Administrative Science Quarterly, 29*: 497–517.

Greiner, Larry. (1972). Evolution and revolution as organizations grow. *Harvard Business Review, July–August*: 37–46.

Gully, S. M., D. S. Divine, and D. J. Whitney. (1995). A meta-analysis of cohesion and performance: Effects of level of analysis and task interdependence. *Small Group Research, 26*: 497–520.

Guzzo, Richard A., and Marcus W. Dickson. (1996). Teams in organizations: Recent research on performance and effectiveness. *Annual Review of Psychology, 47*: 307–338.

Hackman, J. Richard. (1987). The design of work teams. In Jay W. Lorsch (Ed.), *Handbook of organizational behavior.* Englewood Cliffs, NJ: Prentice Hall.

Hackman, J. Richard. (1990). *Groups that work (and those that don't).* San Francisco: Jossey-Bass.

Hackman, J. Richard. (1993). Teams and group failure. Presentation at the Interdisciplinary College on Organization Studies, University of Michigan, October.

Hackman, J. Richard. (2003). *Leading teams.* Cambridge, MA: Harvard Business School Press.

Hamilton, B. H., J. A. Nickerson, and H. Owan. (2003). Team incentives and worker heterogeneity: An empirical analysis of the impact of teams on productivity and participation. *Journal of Political Economy, 111*: 465–497.

Hayes, Nicky. (1997). *Successful team management.* Boston: International Thompson Business Press.

Janis, Irvin. (1972). *Victims of groupthink.* Boston: Houghton Mifflin.

Katzenbach, Jon R., and Douglas K. Smith. (1993). *The Wisdom of teams.* Boston: Harvard Business School Press.

Kouzes, James, and Barry Posner. (1987). *The leadership challenge.* San Francisco: Jossey-Bass.

Kramer, Rodrick M. (1999). Trust and distrust in organizations: Emerging perspectives, enduring questions. *Annual Review of Psychology, 50*: 569–598.

Lawler, Edward E. (1998). *Strategies for high performance organizations.* San Francisco: Jossey-Bass.

Lawler, E. E. (2003). *Treat people right.* San Francisco: Jossey-Bass.

Lawler, Edward E., Susan A. Mohrman, and Gerald E. Ledford. (1995). *Creating high performance organizations: Practices and results of employee involvement and total quality management in Fortune 1000 companies.* San Francisco: Jossey-Bass.

Lidz, Frank. (2000). Up and down in Beverly Hills. *Sports Illustrated, 92(16)*: 60–68.

Locke, E. (1990). *A theory of goal setting and task performance.* Upper Saddle River, NJ: Prentice Hall.

Manz, Charles, and Henry Sims. (1987). Leading workers to lead themselves: The external leadership of self-managing work teams. *Administrative Science Quarterly, 32*: 106–128.

Mullen, B., and C. Copper. (1994). The relation between group cohesiveness and performance: An integration. *Psychological Bulletin, 115*: 210–227.

Pagonis, W. G. (1993). *Moving mountains.* Cambridge, MA: Harvard Business School Press.

Parker, Glenn M. (1996). *Team players and teamwork: The new competitive business strategy.* San Francisco: Jossey-Bass.

Peters, Tom. (1987). *Thriving on chaos.* New York: Knopf.

Quinn, R. E. (2005). Building the bridge as you walk on it. San Francisco: Jossey-Bass.

Quinn, Robert E., and Kim S. Cameron. (1983). Organizational life cycles and shifting criteria of effectiveness: Some preliminary evidence. *Management Science, 29*: 33–51.

Schein, Edgar H. (1976). What to observe in a group. In Cyril R. Mill and Lawrence C. Porter (Eds.), *Reading book for human relations training.* Bethel, ME: NTL Institute.

Senge, Peter. (1991). *The fifth discipline.* New York: Doubleday.

Trompenaars, F. (1996). Resolving international conflict: Culture and business strategy. *Business Strategy Review, 7*: 51–68.

Trompenaars, F., and C. Hampden-Turner. (1998). *Riding the waves of culture.* New York: McGraw-Hill.

Tuckman, Bruce W. (1965). Developmental sequence in small groups. *Psychological Bulletin, 63*: 384–399.

Turner, M. E. (Ed.). (2000). *Groups at work: Advances in theory and research.* New York: Erlbaum.

Verespei, M. A. (1990, June 18). Yea, teams? Not always. *Industry Week:* 103–105.

Wellins, Richard S., William C. Byham, and Jeanne M. Wilson. (1991). *Empowered teams.* San Francisco: Jossey-Bass.

Yeatts, Dale E., and Cloyd Hyten (1998). *High performing self-managing work teams: A comparison of theory to practice.* Thousand Oaks, CA: Sage.

CHAPTER 10 REFERENCES

Baker, Wayne. (2001). *Achieving success through social capital.* San Francisco: Jossey-Bass.

Baker, Wayne, Rob Cross, and Melissa Wooten. (2003). Positive organizational network analysis and energizing relationships. In Kim S. Cameron, Jane E. Dutton, and Robert E. Quinn (Eds.), *Positive organizational scholarship: Foundations of a new discipline* (pp. 328–342). San Francisco: Barrett-Koehler.

Baumeister, Roy F., Ellen Bratslavsky, Catrin Finkenauer, and Kathleen D. Vohs. (2001). Bad is stronger than good. *Review of General Psychology, 5*: 323–370.

Bennis, Warren, and Bert Nanus. (1985). *Leaders: The strategies for taking charge.* New York: Harper & Row.

Bollier, David. (1996). *Aiming higher: Twenty-five stories of how companies prosper by combining sound management and social vision.* New York: Amacom.

Bright, David S., Kim S. Cameron, and Arran Caza. (2006). The ethos of virtuousness in downsized organizations. *Journal of Business Ethics, 64*: 249–269.

Cameron, Kim S. (1985). Iacocca's transformation of Chrysler; Excerpts from Lee Iacocca's speeches to his top management team, 1979–1984. (In possession of the author.)

Cameron, Kim S. (2003a). Ethics, virtuousness, and constant change. In Noel M. Tichy and Andrew R. McGill (Eds.), *The ethical challenge* (pp. 185–193). San Francisco: Jossey-Bass.

Cameron, Kim S. (2003b). Organizational virtuousness and performance. In Kim S. Cameron, Jane E. Dutton, and Robert E. Quinn (Eds.), *Positive organizational scholarship: Foundations of a new Discipline* (pp. 48–65). San Francisco: Barrett-Koehler.

Cameron, Kim S., and Arran Caza. (2002). Organizational and leadership virtues and the role of forgiveness. *Journal of Leadership and Organizational Studies, 9*: 33–48.

Cameron, Kim S., and Marc Lavine. (2006). *Making the impossible possible: Leading extraordinary performance—The Rocky Flats story.* San Francisco: Barrett-Koehler.

Cameron, Kim S., and Robert E. Quinn. (1999). *Diagnosing and changing organizational culture.* Reading, MA: Addison-Wesley.

Cameron, Kim S., and David O. Ulrich. (1986). Transformational leadership in colleges and universities. *Higher Education: Handbook of Theory and Research, 2*: 1–42.

Cameron, Kim S., David A. Whetten, and Myung U. Kim. (1987). Organizational effects of decline and turbulence. *Administration Science Quarterly, 32*: 222–240.

Carlzon, Jan. (1987). *Moments of truth.* Cambridge, MA: Ballinger.

Christie, R., and S. Lehman. (1970). The structure of Machiavellian orientations. In R. Christie and F. Geis (Eds.), *Studies in Machiavellianism* (pp. 359–387). New York: Academic Press.

Cialdini, R. B. (2000). *Influence: The science of persuasion.* New York: Allyn & Bacon.

Clifton, Donald O., and James K. Harter. (2003). Investing in strengths. In Kim S. Cameron, Jane E. Dutton, and Robert E. Quinn (Eds.), *Positive organizational scholarship: Foundations of a new discipline* (pp. 111–121). San Francisco: Barrett-Koehler.

Coonradt, Chuck. (1985). *The game of work.* Salt Lake City: Shadow Mountain Press.

Csikszentmihalyi, M. (1990). *Flow: The psychology of optimal experience.* New York: Harper Perennial.

Davis, Murray. (1971). That's interesting! *Philosophy of the Social Sciences, 1*: 309–344.

Dutton, Jane E., Peter J. Frost, Monica C. Worline, Jacoba M. Lilius, and Jason M. Kanov. (2002). Leading in times of trauma. *Harvard Business Review, January: 54–61.*

Emmons, Robert A. (2003). Acts of gratitude in organizations. In Kim S. Cameron, Jane E. Dutton, and Robert E. Quinn (Eds.), *Positive organizational scholarship: Foundations of a new discipline* (pp. 81–93). San Francisco: Barrett-Koehler.

Enright, Robert D., and C. Coyle. (1998). Researching the process model of forgiveness within psychological interventions. In Everett L. Worthington (Ed.), *Dimensions of forgiveness* (pp. 139–161). Philadelphia: Templeton Foundation Press.

Enrique, Juan. (2000). *As the future catches you.* New York: Crown Business.

Fredrickson, Barbara L. (2003). Positive emotions and upward spirals in organizations. In Kim S. Cameron, Jane E. Dutton, and Robert E. Quinn (Eds.), *Positive organizational scholarship: Foundations of a new discipline* (pp. 163–175). San Francisco: Barrett-Koehler.

Frost, Peter, J. (2003). *Toxic emotions at work: How compassionate managers handle pain and conflict.* Cambridge, MA: Harvard Business School Press.

Glynn, Patrick. (1994). Toward a politics of forgiveness. *American Enterprise, 5*: 48–53.

Gold, Taro. (2002). *Open your mind, open your life.* Springfield, IL: Andrews McNeel Publishing.

Gottman, J. (1994). *Why marriages succeed and fail.* New York: Simon and Schuster.

Helmick, R. G., and R. L. Petersen. (2001). *Forgiveness and reconciliation: Religion, public policy, and conflict.* Philadelphia: Templeton Foundation Press.

Kanov, Jason M., Sally Maitlis, Monica C. Worline, Jane E. Dutton, and Peter J. Frost. (2003). Compassion in organizational life. *American Behavioral Scientist*: 1–54.

Kirschenbaum, D. (1984). Self-regulation and sport psychology: Nurturing and emerging symbiosis. *Journal of Sport Psychology, 8*: 26–34.

Kotter, John. (1999). *John Kotter on what leaders really do.* Cambridge, MA: Harvard Business School Press.

Lewin, Kurt. (1951). *Field theory in social science.* New York: Harper & Row.

Losada, Marcial, and Emily Heaphy. (2003). The role of positivity and connectivity in the performance of business teams: A nonlinear dynamics model. *American Behavioral Scientist, 47*: 740–765.

McCraty, R., and Childre, D. (2004). The grateful heart. In R. A. Emmons and M. E. McCullough (Eds.), *The psychology of gratitude* (pp. 230–255). New York: Oxford University Press.

McCullough, Michael E., Robert A. Emmons, and J. Tsang. (2002). The grateful disposition: A conceptual and empirical topography. *Journal of Personality and Social Psychology, 82*: 112–127.

Meyerson, Deborah. (2001). *Tempered radicals.* Cambridge, MA: Harvard Business School Press.

Perot, H. R. (1988). A vision for General Motors. Internal company document. General Motors Corporation, Detroit, MI.

Pfeffer, Jeffrey. (1998). *The human equation: Building profits by putting people first.* Boston: Harvard Business School Press.

Quinn, Robert E. (2000). *Change the world.* San Francisco: Jossey-Bass.

Quinn, Robert E. (2004). *Building the bridge as you walk on it.* San Francisco: Jossey-Bass.

Quinn, R. E., J. E. Dutton, and G. M. Spreitzer. (2003). Reflected best-self exercise: Assignment and instructions for participants. Center for Positive Organizational Scholarship, Ross School of Business, University of Michigan. Product # 001B.

Roberts, Laura M., Gretchen Spreitzer, Jane Dutton, Robert Quinn, Emily Heaphy, and Brianna Barker. (2005). How to play to your strengths. *Harvard Business Review, 83*: 75–80.

Salancik, Gerald R. (1977). Commitment of control of organizational behavior and belief. In Barry M. Staw and Gerald R. Salancik (Eds.), *News directions in organizational behavior.* Chicago: St. Clair Press.

Sculley, J. (1987). Apple's identity and goals. Internal company document. Apple Computer, Inc., Cupertino, CA.

Seligman, M. E. P. (2002). *Authentic happiness.* New York: Free Press.

Selznick, Peter. (1949). *TVA and the grass roots.* Berkeley: University of California Press.

Simmel, Georg. (1950). *The sociology of Georg Simmel.* Glencoe, IL: Free Press.

Tichy, Noel M. (1993). *Control your destiny or someone else will.* New York: Doubleday.

Tichy, Noel M. (1997). *The leadership engine.* New York: Harper Collins.

Tutu, Desmond. (1998). Without forgiveness there is no future. In Robert D. Enright and Jane North (Eds.), *Exploring forgiveness.* Madison: University of Wisconsin Press.

Tutu, Desmond. (1999). *No future without forgiveness.* New York: Doubleday.

U. S. Army Strategic Leadership Program. (2003). Personal communication. Boston, MA.

Walsh, James P. (1999). Business must talk about its social role. In T. Dickson (Ed.), *Mastering strategy* (pp. 289–294). London: Financial Times/Prentice Hall.

Weick, Karl E. (1981). Small wins: Redefining the scale of social problems. *American Psychologist, 39*: 40–49.

Weick, Karl E. (1993). Small wins in organizational life. *Dividend, Winter*: 20–24.

SUPPLEMENT A REFERENCES

Barrett, H. (1977). *Practical uses of speech communication* 4th ed. New York: Holt, Rinehart & Winston.

Collins, E., and M. Devanna. (1990). *The portable MBA* New York: Wiley.

Dubrin, A. J. (1985). *Contemporary applied management*. Plano, TX: Business Publications, Inc.

Endicott Report. (1992). Baton Rouge: Louisiana State University Press.

Gelles-Cole, S. (1985). *The complete guide to executive manners.* New York: Rawson.

Gronbeck, B. E. et al. (1992). *Principles of speech communication* 11th ed. New York: Harper Collins.

Lucas, S. (1989). *The art of public speaking* (3rd ed.) New York: Random House.

Mambert, W. A. (1976). *Effective presentation.* New York: Wiley.

Miller, G. A. (1967). *The psychology of communication.* Baltimore: Penguin.

Osborn, M. and S. Osborn. (1991). *Public speaking.* Boston: Houghton Mifflin.

Peoples, D. A. (1988). *Presentations plus.* New York: Wiley.

Poor, E. (1992). *The executive writer: A guide to managing words, ideas, and people.* New York: Grove Weidenfeld.

Reingold, J. (2004). The man behind the curtain. *Fast Company, October*: 100–104.

Sproule, M. (1991). *Speechmaking: An introduction to rhetorical competence.* Dubuque, IA: William C. Brown.

Sanford, W. P., and W. H. Yeager. (1963). *Principles of effective speaking* (6th ed.) New York: Ronald Press.

Seiler, W. J. (1971). The effects of visual materials on attitudes, credibility, and retention. *Speech Monographs, 38*: 331–334.

Sprague, J., and D. Stuart. (1996). *The speaker's handbook* 4th ed. Fort Worth, TX: Harcourt Brace College Publishers.

Wells, W. (1989). *Communications in business* 5th ed. Belmont, CA: Wadsworth.

Wilcox, R. P. (1967). *Oral reporting in business and industry.* Upper Saddle River, NJ: Prentice Hall.

SUPPLEMENT B REFERENCES

Beer, M. (1987). *Meetings: How to make them work for you.* New York: Van Nostrand Reinholdt.

Downs, C. W., G. P. Smeyak, and E. Martin. (1980). *Professional interviewing.* New York: Harper & Row.

DuBrin, A. J. (1981). *Human relations: A job-oriented approach* 2nd ed. Reston, VA: Reston Publishing Company.

Lopez, R. M. (1975). *Personnel interviewing.* New York: McGraw-Hill.

Maier, N. R. F. (1958). Three types of appraisal interviews. *Personnel* (March/April): 27–40.

Sincoff, M. Z., and R. S. Goyer. (1984). *Interviewing.* New York: Macmillan.

Stano, M. E., and N. L. Reinsch, Jr. (1982). *Communication in interviews.* Upper Saddle River, NJ: Prentice Hall.

Stewart, C. J., and W. B. Cash, Jr. (1985). *Interviewing: Principles and practice* 4th ed. Dubuque, IA: Brown.

SUPPLEMENT C REFERENCES

Cohen, M., J. March and J. Olsen. (1972). A garbage can model of organizational choice. *Administrative Science Quarterly, 17*: 1–15.

DeBono, E. (1985). *The six thinking Hats.* Boston: Little, Brown.

De Tocqueville, A. (1841). *Democracy in America.* New York: Langley.

Harvey, J. (1974). The abilene paradox. *Organizational Dynamics*, (Summer); 63–80.

Janis, I. (1972). *Victims of groupthink.* Boston: Houghton Mifflin.

Janis, I. (1983). *Groupthink: Psychological studies of policy decisions and fiascoes*, Boston: Houghton Mifflin.

Putnam, R. (2000). *Bowling alone.* New York: Simon & Schuster.

Rothman, J., Erlich, J., & Tropman, J. (2000). Strategies of community intervention (6th ed.). Itasca, IL: F. E. Peacock.

3M Meeting Management Team. (1994). *Mastering meetings.* New York: McGraw-Hill.

Tichy, N., and M. Devanna. (1986). *The transformational leader.* New York: Wiley.

Tropman, J., Erlich, J., & Rothman, J. (2000). *Tactics of community intervention* (4th ed.). Itasca, IL: F. E. Peacock.

Tropman, J. E. (1996). *Effective meetings* 2nd ed. Thousand Oaks, CA: Sage.

Tuchman, B. (1984). *The march of folly: From Troy to Vietnam.* New York: Knopf.

A

AAL, 499
Abbott, R., 350
Acton, Lord, 289
Adams, J., 193, 199
Adler, C., 124, 135, 140, 141, 142, 385, 450
Adler, P., 292
Adler, R., 396, 401
Agras, W., 452
A. H. Robins, 74
Albert, R., 188, 199
Alderfer, Clay, 349
Alinsky, S., 450
Allan, H., 62
Allen, R., 302
Allinson, C., 294
Alloy, L., 466
Amabile, T., 198, 208
Amana Refrigeration Co., 191
Amazon, 217
American Management Association, 74
Ameritech, 334–335
Amway, 459
Ancona, D., 500
Anderson, C., 143, 293, 452
Anderson, P., 208
Apex Communications Corporation, 596
Apple Computer Inc., 216–218, 288, 386, 560, 572–574
Argenti, J., 380
Argyris, C., 250
Ariel, S., 299
Arkinson, J., 350
Armstrong, S., 294
Arnold, C., 260
Asch, S., 517
Ashford, S., 307
Ashforth, B., 454
AT&T, 499
Atkinson, J., 338
Atwater, L., 62
Auerbach, S. M., 117, 118
Averill, J., 466
Aygen, M., 147

B

Bacharach, S., 287
Bagnall, J., 205
Bailey, D., 499, 500, 509, 519
Baker, W., 242, 459, 549, 564
Balzer, W. K., 122
Bandura, A., 13, 143, 345, 451, 452, 455, 456, 457, 458, 459
Bannister, Roger, 458
Bar-On, R., 64
Barber, B., 454
Baril, G., 391
Barker, L., 243

Barling, J., 117, 140
Barnlund, D., 255
Basadur, M., 198
Baum, L., 300
Baumeister, R., 548
Bay of Pigs, 504
Bazerman, M., 390
Beal, R. L., 22
Beary, J., 147
Beatrice Company, 300
Beebe, S. A., 243
Beebe, S. J., 243
Beer, M., 635
Bell, Alexander Graham, 191
Bell, C., 147
Ben-Amos, P., 206
Bennis, Warren, 3, 287, 338, 451, 453, 455, 557
Benson, H., 147
Bergmoser, Paul, 578
Bernard, C., 471
Bethune, Gordon, 95–96
Bies, R., 309
Bigley, G., 331
Bigoness, W., 70
Billingsley, Taylor, 596
Bilsky, W., 71
Biondi, Frank, 288
Birch, D., 350
Black, B., 452
Black, J. S., 181
Blair, J., 390
Blake, J., 206, 385
Blakely, G., 70
Blanks, Maurice, 95
Blasko, V., 202
Blink, 178
Block, P., 453, 455, 460, 466
Blodget, H., 333
Blu Dot, 95
Blum, A., 390
Boehle, S., 333
Bogomolny, Richard, 558
Bohr, Niels, 200
Bollier, D., 558
Bolman, L., 292
Bono, J. E., 143
Bookman, A., 450
Boss, W., 264
Bostrom, R., 260, 261
Boulding, E., 381
Bourgeios, J., 380
Bowman, G., 243
Boyatzis, R. E., 13, 62, 64
Bradford, D., 304
Bramucci, R., 454
Branwell, S. T., 124
Breen, B., 307
Brehm, J., 450

Brett, J., 402
Brewer, Alan, 298
Brief, A., 454
Bright, D., 570
Brockner, J., 124
Broekhuijsen, J., 178
Brouwer, P. J., 59
Brown, L., 380
Brown, S., 390
Brownell, J., 243, 244, 250, 255
Buda, R., 70
Buell, B., 287
Bunderson, J., 292
Bunker, K., 289
Burlingham, B., 389
Burnham, D., 289, 350, 351
Burt, R., 292
Byham, W., 466
Byharn, W., 499
Byosiere, P., 121
Byre, J., 300
Byrne, Patrick, M., 95

C

Cable, D., 71
Caldwell, D., 500
Cameron, K. S., 11, 14, 16, 60, 61, 122, 122–123, 124, 135, 143, 183, 242, 386, 448, 456, 458, 460, 463, 465, 502, 542, 544, 545, 546, 548, 549, 550, 556, 561, 570
Campion, M., 506
Canfield, F., 293
Cantor, N., 133
Caplan, R.D., 121, 122, 135
Carlzon, J., 565, 566, 568
Carrell, L., 243, 244
Caruso, D. R., 64
Cash, W., 630
Caudron, S., 386
Cavanaugh, G. F., 71
Caza, A., 546, 550, 570
CH2MHill, 559
Chambers, John, 550
Cheston, R., 391
Childre, D., 551
Chiu, L., 291
Choi, I., 291, 292, 330
Chrysler, Corporation, 457, 556–557, 561, 578–584
Chu, Y-K., 206
Churchill, Winston, 300
Cialdini, R., 190, 192, 302, 309, 511, 512, 564
Cisco Systems, 550
Clare, D. A., 71
Clark, R., 350
Clarke, J., 515

Clifton, D., 553
CNN, 557
Coats, G., 294
Coch, L., 468
Cockcroft, John, D., 193
Coddington, R. D., 124
Cohen, A., 304
Cohen, M., 656, 657
Cohen, P. A., 12
Cohen, S., 499, 500, 509, 519
Collins, E., 597
Collins, M. A., 198
Conger, J., 293, 447, 451, 452, 453, 455
Connell, J., 452
Connor, J., 301
Continental Airlines, 95–96
Cook, A., 349
Coolidge, Calvin, 181
Coonradt, Chuck, 459, 469, 561–562
Cooper, C., 118, 131, 519
Cooper, M., 147
Cordes, C. L., 122, 147
Corning, 499
Council of Communication Management, 243
Courtney, Henry, 211–212
Covey, S., 126, 133, 251
Cowan, A., 287
Cowley, J., 143
Cox, T. H., 22, 385, 506
Coyle, C., 550
Creon, King, 289
Crocker, J., 243, 260
Cross, R., 459, 549
Crovitz, H., 205
Csikszentmihalyi, M., 188, 199, 545
Cuming, P., 304
Cummings, L., 391
Cupach, W., 250, 255
Curtis, J., 146

D

Daly, J., 307
Dana Corporation, 210, 499
Davidson, J., 125, 131, 132
Davidson, O., 338
Davis, Murray, 559
Davis, T. W., 13, 146
Dawidowicz, Bogdan, 287
De Bono, Edward, 190
De Dreu, C., 381, 390
Deal, T., 292, 296
DeButts, John, 296
DeCharms, R., 450
Deci, E., 452, 454
Deepak, M., 147, 149
DeGeorge, R., 289
DeGraff, J., 182, 183, 208, 448

Deleo, J., 147
Dell Computer, 94, 217
Dell, Michael, 94
Dellbeck, M., 147
Derr, C., 380
Detert, R., 146
Deutsch, M., 454
Devanna, M., 597, 656
Dew, J., 520
Dewey, J., 502
Dickson, M., 499, 500, 509, 516
DiClemente, C., 452
Dilenschneider, R., 288
Dillard, J., 289
Dirks, K., 297
Disney Corporation, 557
Disney, Walt, 184, 185
Disraeli, Benjamin, 256
Divine, D., 519
Dobbs, K., 333
Doherty, M. E., 122
Dollinger, S. J., 71
Downs, C., 624
Drucker, P., 448
Drucker, Peter, 3, 80
Druskat, V., 511, 519
DuBrin, A., 624
Duncan, R., 307
Dunlap, Al, 289
Dunn, Keith, 222–226
Durham, C., 338
Durkheim, E., 456
Dutt, James, L., 300
Dutton, J., 60, 117, 145, 242, 307,
    448, 465, 550, 553
Dyer, W., 148, 251, 304, 340

E
EBay, 217
Eden, D., 338
Edison, Thomas, 3
Edmonson, A., 511
Eichinger, R., 385
Einstein, Albert, 202
Eisenhardt, K., 380, 385, 448
Eisner, Michael, 560
Elsayed-Elkhouly, S. M., 70
Emerson, R., 309
Emmons, R., 551
Enright, R., 550
Enrique, J., 543
Enron, 74, 217
Equity Funding, 74
Eroglu, S., 134
Eshelman, E., 146

F
Farnham, A., 135
Farson, R., 260
Federal Express, 499
Feldman, D., 191, 205
Ferrin, D., 297
Festinger, L., 190
Finast Supermarkets, 558
Finke, R., 188, 199, 204, 205
Firestone, 74
First Boston, 386–387
First Chicago, 127
Fisher, C., 121, 122, 297, 336
Fisher, R., 390
Fleishman, J., 331
Fleming, Sir Alexander, 194
Foerstner, George, 191–192, 196
Ford, Henry, 140, 217, 514
Ford Motor Co., 74, 561
Ford, William Clay, 561
Frankl, Victor, 450
Fredrickson, B., 242, 545

Freeman, S. J., 135, 458, 460
French, J. R. R., 121, 122, 135,
    449, 468
Freud, S., 59, 502
Friedman, M., 144, 145
Fromm, Erich, 59
Fry, Art, 192, 194, 196, 211–212
Furman, W., 293

G
Gabarro, Jack, 295
Gable, S., 242
Gackenbach, J., 243
Gage, D., 383
Galunic, D. C., 448
Gambetta, D., 468
Gandhi, Mahatma, 127, 185, 450,
    454, 542, 548
Ganzach, Y., 346
Gardner, H., 133
Gardner, John, 287
Gates, Bill, 560, 566, 576–577
Gecas, V., 447, 451, 452
Geddie, T., 260
Gehry, Frank, 221
Gelles-Cole, S., 597
Gelman, E., 287, 298, 300
Gemmill, G., 452
Gendron, G., 389
Geneen, Harold, 296
General Electric, 296, 348, 499
General Electric Aircraft, 140
General Mills, 499
General Motors, 6–7, 148, 381,
    559–560, 574–576
Gerhart, B., 331, 342
Getzels, J., 188
Giamtti, A. Bartlett, 312
Gibb, J., 250, 454
Gibb, L., 454
Gilligan, C., 73
Gitelson, R., 121, 122
Gittell, J., 143, 242
Gladstein, D., 500
Gladwell, Malcolm, 178
Glasser, W., 259
Gloucer, Tom, 559
Glucksman, Lewis, 288
Glynn, P., 550
Goddard, Roger, 452
Goldberg, H., 145
Goleman, D., 60, 62, 63, 64, 66,
    133, 134
Golembiewski, R., 454, 455
Golen, S., 244
Goll, I., 178
Goodson, Gene, 210
Gordon, R., 250
Gottman, J., 553
Goyer, R., 624
Graham, M., 342
Greenberg, Eric, 15, 141, 146
Greenberger, D. B., 135, 453, 466
Greene, C., 452
Greengerger, D., 447
Gregersen, H., 181
Greiner, L., 502
Griest, J. H., 141
Grove, A., 293, 380
Gudykunst, W., 268
Gully, S., 519
Guzzo, R., 499, 500, 509, 516

H
Haas, J., 260
Hackett, Jim, 560
Hackman, J. R., 135, 136, 346, 454,
    455, 456, 461, 462, 471,

499, 500, 502, 506, 509,
    510, 511
Hall, D. T., 124
Hamilton, B., 499
Hammarskjold, Dag, 133
Hammer, T., 452
Hampton-Turner, C., 22, 67, 122, 206,
    516, 521
Haney, W., 244
Hanson, G., 6
Hare, C. C., 123
Hargie, O., 243
Harris, J. R., 74
Harris, S., 60, 86
Harter, J., 553
Harter, S., 84, 334, 450
Hartnett, D., 391
Harvey, J., 656
Harvey, William, 200
Hatfield, J., 260
Hausman, C., 202
Hayes, J., 294
Hayes, N., 520
Hayes, T., 334
Heaphy, E., 242, 263
Heider, F., 190
Heisler, W., 452
Hellreigel, C., 452
Helmick, R., 550
Hendricks, W., 147
Hepburn, G., 117, 140
Heritage Appliance Company, 314
Hermann, N., 197
Hess, R., 452
Hewlett-Packard, 298, 567
Hickson, D., 181, 182
Higgs, A., 506
Hillhouse, J. J., 124, 140, 141, 142
Hinings, C., 299
Hitler, Adolf, 257
Hobson, A., 515
Hobson, C. J., 123–124
Hocker, J., 385
Hoerr, J., 301
Hofstede, Geert, 386
Hogg, M., 294
Holmes, T. H., 123–124, 124
Holt, J., 23
Honda, 185
Hosoda, M., 294
House, R., 339
Hout, T. M., 121
Hoy, A., 452
Hoy, W., 452
Hubbard, J., 142
Huber, G., 469
Hudspith, S., 197
Huseman, R., 260
Hyman, R., 251
Hyten, C., 509, 520

I
Iacocca, Lee, 457, 556–557, 566,
    578–584
Ibuka, Masaru, 514–515
Ideo, 184
In Search of Excellence, 353–354
Intel Corporation, 300, 557
Interaction Associates, 199
Intermountain Health Care, 330
Ivancevich, J., 143

J
Jackson, Phil, 330
Jago, A., 468, 469
James, William, 256
Janis, I., 209, 504, 656
Jansky, Karl, 191

Janson, R., 135, 462
Jay, Anthony, 332
Jehn, K., 381, 385, 390
Jesus, 200
Jobs, Steve, 184, 216–218, 288, 389,
    515
Johnson & Johnson, 140
Johnson Controls, 210
Johnston, C. S., 71
Jones, Jean C., 300
Jones, Tom, 296
Jourard, S. M., 145
Judge, T. A., 62, 71, 83–84, 84, 143
Juran, J., 178

K
Kahn, R., 121, 454
Kahwajy, J., 380
Kalmer, Kathleen, 300
Kanov, J., 550
Kanter, Rosabeth, 288–289, 290,
    292, 297, 307, 315, 447,
    455, 456, 458, 460
Kanungo, R., 293, 447, 451, 452, 453
Kaplan, R., 298
Karambayya, R., 402
Karasek, R. A., 135
Katzenbach, J., 148, 499, 509, 511,
    513, 523
Keashly, L., 391
Kekule, Fredrich, 194
Kelleher, Herb, 95, 295
Kelley, R. E., 60
Kelly, J., 381
Kennedy, A., 296
Kennedy, John, F., 504
Kentucky Fried Chicken, 191
Kern, Rex, 566
Kerr, S., 342
Kerr, William Rolfe, 127
Kettering, Charles, 179
Ketteringham, J., 189, 192, 193, 196
Kihlstrom, J. F., 133
Kilmann, R., 391
Kim, M. U., 60, 61, 122, 386,
    448, 546
Kim, S., 397
Kimmel, Admiral, 214–216
Kinicki, A. J., 124
Kipnis, D., 302, 304, 391, 394
Kleiman, C., 351
Knapp, M., 251
Knight, D., 84, 338
Knowling, Bob, 334–335
Kobasa, S., 124, 143
Koberg, D., 205
Koestler, A., 191, 194
Kohlberg, L., 71–74, 75
Kolb, D. A., 14, 76, 79
Konrad, A., 298
Koole, S., 390
Koopman, P., 178
Kopelman, R., 348
Korabik, D., 391
Korda, M., 287
Kotter, John, 287, 292, 295, 335, 542
Kouzes, J., 511
Kraimer, M., 298
Kram, K., 62, 147, 289
Kramer, R., 260, 511
Kressel, K., 402
Kroc, Ray, 184–185
Kuo, Y. Y., 206
Kwon, S., 292

L
Labich, K., 291
LaGaipa, J., 293

Lahiff, J., 260
Lakein, D., 126
Langer, E., 453, 466
Langlois, J., 294
Latack, J., 124
Latham, G., 136, 337, 338, 457
Lavine, M., 570
Lawler, E., 148, 341, 342, 350, 498, 499
Lawrence, K., 182, 183, 208, 448
Lawrence, Paul, 301
Leana, C., 467
Ledford, G., 148, 498, 499
Leger, D., 287
Lehman Brothers, 288
Lehrer, P. M., 132, 147
Leonard, Stew, 339
Leong, F. T. L., 71
Levering, R., 339
Levine, M., 542, 545, 546
Levinson, J. D., 124
Lewin, Kurt, 117
Lickona, T., 73–74
Liden, R., 298
Lidz, F., 499
Likert, R., 122
Lim, S., 143, 242
Locke, E. A., 84, 136, 337, 338, 457,
    467, 513
Lombardo, M., 289, 385
Long, B., 140, 141
Loomis, F., 244–246
Lopez, R., 624
Lorsch, Jay, 301, 448
Los Angeles Clippers, 499
Losada, M., 263
Lowell, E., 350
Luhmann, N., 454
Lusch, R. F., 134
Luthans, F., 13, 341

M

Macintosh Computer, 209
Maddi, S., 143
Maddux, J., 452
Maduro, R., 206
Maier, A., 260
Maier, N., 260, 635
Malden Mills, 561
Management and Machiavelli, 332
Mandela, Nelson, 450, 565
Mannix, E., 381
Manz, C., 453, 511
March, J., 178, 180, 182, 202, 204,
    656, 657
Markoff, J., 192
Marlowe, David, 133
Martin, E., 624
Martin, J., 456
Martindale, C., 197
Marwell, G., 302
Marx, K., 450
Mary Kay Cosmetics, 459
Maslow, A. H., 59, 349, 380–381
Masten, A. S., 138
Masuda, M., 124
Matteson, M. T., 143
May, Rollo, 288
Mayer, J., 63, 64
Mazique, M., 298
McCall, M., 289
McCauley, L., 335
McClear, K., 84
McClelland, David, 289, 349, 350,
    351, 447
McConkie, M., 454, 455
McCraty, R., 551
McCullough, M., 551
McDonald's, 184–185

McGovern, Gordon, 295
McGregor, D., 254, 334, 466
McGuffey's Restaurant, 222–225
McKay, M., 146
McKim, R., 192
McLoughlin, C. A., 117, 140
McMillan, I., 208
Mechanic, D., 294, 295
Medawar, P., 199
Mednick, M. T., 143
Medsker, G., 506
Merrill, Roger, 211–212
Mesa Petroleum, 140
Meyerson, D., 548
Michener, H., 331
Microsoft, 576–577
Milgram, S., 73, 124
Miller, S., 181, 182
Mintzberg, H., 15, 121, 131
Mischel, W., 134
Mishra, A., 122, 135, 451, 454, 458,
    460, 463, 468
Mitchell, T., 339
Mitroff, I., 182
Moe, M., 333
Mohrman, S., 148, 498, 499
Mokwa, M., 202
Moore, Gordon, 300
Moore, T., 85
Moorehead, Dr. Bob, 4
Moral Research Center, University of
    Minnesota, 74
Morcott, Woody, 210
Morgan, S., 450
Morris, M., 299
Morrison, A., 385
Moskowitz, M., 339
Mulder, M., 304
Mullen, B., 519
Mumford, M., 188
Murlis, H., 341
Murnighan, J., 390, 396
Murphy, L. R., 141
Murray, B., 342
Murrell, K., 452, 454

N

Nanus, B., 287, 451, 453, 455, 557
National Training Laboratories, 566
Nayak, P., 189, 192, 193, 196
Neale, M., 390
Neider, L., 339
Nelson, Dr. Noelle, 344
Nelson, William, H., 330
Nemeth, C., 209
Neufeld, R., 452
Newcomb, T., 190
Newman, W., 466
Nicholson, Geoffrey, 212
Nickerson, J., 499
Nickerson, R., 188, 199, 201
Nielson, T., 380
Nisbett, R., 291, 330
Nishida, T., 268
Nord, W., 454
Norenzayan, A., 291, 330
Northwestern National Life, 122

O

O'Connor, R., 122
Oedipus, 289
Oldham, G. R., 135, 136, 346, 454,
    455, 456, 461, 462, 471
Olsen, J., 656, 657
Ong, M., 337
Organ, D., 452
Orme-Johnson, D., 147

Osborn, A., 202
Ouchi, W., 248
Overstock.com, 95
Owan, H., 499
Ozer, E., 455

P

Pagonis, Gen. Gus, 501, 503, 506–507,
    509–511, 511, 513, 514, 516
Parker, G., 509, 516, 519
Parker, V., 62, 342
Parsons, Wendell, 333–334
Pascale, A., 380
Pauling, Linus, 196
Peake, P. K., 134
Pearl Harbor, 214–216
Pelled, L., 385
Pepperidge Farms, 295
Perot, Ross, 381, 559–560, 574–576
Perrow, Charles, 301
Perry, M., 331
Peters, T., 122, 182, 248, 296, 499
Peters, Tom, 3
Peterson, Peter, 288
Peterson, Ralph, 559
Peterson, R. L., 550
Pfeffer, J., 8, 122, 248, 292, 297, 298,
    299, 341, 542
Phillips, E., 391
Phillips Electronics, 127
Pilling, B. K., 134
Plutarch, 58
Podolny, J., 299
Poincare, H., 199
Polaroid, 217
Polonius, 58
Poor, E., 607
Porter, L., 331
Posner, B. Z., 70, 511
Pratt, M., 454
Preston, P., 466
Proctor, R., 396
Prudential Life Insurance, 140
Pruitt, D., 402
Prussia, G., 124
Publilius Syrus, 58
Purdy, K., 135, 462
Putnam, R., 656

Q

Quick, T., 332
Quinn, R. E., 8, 16, 183, 451, 455, 456,
    465, 502, 510, 542, 548, 553

R

Rahe, R. H., 123–124
Rahim, M., 390
Rainbow, Jacob, 198–199
Ramsey, Joseph, 212
Randle, C., 243
Rappaport, J., 452, 453
Rasheed, A., 178
Raven, B., 449
Raytheon, 189, 191, 193, 194, 209
Reagan, Ronald, 560
Redmond, M., 243
Redstone, Sumner, 288
Reed, M. J., 138
Reese, S., 333
Reingold, J., 597
Reis, H., 242
Rest, J., 74
Reuters, 559
Ribot, T., 199
Rigby, D., 8
Riley, S., 178
Rodin, J., 466

Rogers, Carl, 59, 251, 260, 261, 262
Rohrbaugh, J., 16
Rokeach, M., 62, 69, 70
Rose, S., 452
Rosen, S., 243
Rosenfeld, L., 396
Rosenman, R. H., 144, 145
Rosenthal, R., 134
Rostad, F., 140, 141
Rothbaum, F., 453
Rothenberg, A., 201, 202
Rotter, Julian, 54, 84
Ruble, T., 391
Runco, M., 188, 199
Runyon, K., 452
Rust, Ed, 296
Ryan, R., 452, 454
Ryman, D. H., 124

S

Saarni, C., 133
Salancik, G., 564
Salovey, P., 63, 64
Sandelands, L., 60, 117, 145, 448
Sanders, Harland, 191
Sandusky, Ohio, 201–202
Sanford, D. G., 71
Sashkin, M., 447, 467
Savage, G., 390, 392
Scandiavian Airlines, 565, 568
Schein, E. H., 124, 296, 517
Schmidt, F., 334
Schmidt, S., 302, 304, 391, 394
Schmidt, W. H., 70
Schmitt, D., 302
Schnake, M., 243, 244, 251
Schneer, J., 391
Schneider, J., 452
Schriesheim, C., 339
Schuster, J., 341
Schwalbe, M., 452
Schwartz, Jeffrey, 559
Schwartz, S. H., 71
Schweiger, D., 467
Scott, O., 191, 193
Scoular Grain Company, 140
Sculley, John, 288, 560, 572–574
Seeman, M., 452
Seff, M., 452
Seligman, M., 452, 545
Seller, W., 602
Selye, H., 118
Selznik, P., 564
Senge, P., 499, 500
Serpkenci, R. R., 134
Sewell, Carl, 461, 462
Seybolt, P., 380, 390, 391
Shaklee Products, 459
Shalley, C., 182
Shamir, B., 339
Shatkin, S., 147
Shenandoah Life Insurance Co., 499
Shipper, F., 289
Shoda, Y., 134
Siau, K., 204
Sieburg, E., 250, 255, 258
Siegman, A. W., 144, 145
Sillars, A., 385
Silver, Spence, 189, 191, 192, 193, 196,
    209, 210–212
Simmel, G., 551
Simms, H., 453, 511
Simon, H., 178, 180, 202, 204, 543
Sincoff, M., 624
Singh, J., 122, 136, 147
Slocum, J., 452
Smejda, Karolus, 300
Smeyak, G., 624

Smith, D., 148, 499, 509, 511, 513, 523
Smith, G., 188
Smith, R., 397
Smith, Roger, 381
Smith, S., 188, 199, 204, 205
Smith, T., 144, 145
Smith, W., 390
Snyder, S., 453
Social Security Administration, 348
Solem, A., 260
Solomon, B., 450
Sophocles, 289
Sorenson, M. J., 143
Sorenson, R., 390
Sosik, J., 62
Southwest Airlines, 95, 217, 295
Sparrowe, R., 298
Spencer, L. M., 134
Spencer, Percy, 189, 191, 193, 194,
    209, 210
Spencer, S. M., 134
Spitzberg, B., 243, 244, 250, 255
Sprague, J., 597
Spreitzer, G., 447, 451, 454, 455, 456,
    460, 461, 553
SSS Software, 30–40, 664–675
Stajkovic, A., 341
Stalk, G., 121
Stamps, D., 333
Staples, L., 452
Starko, A., 188, 205
Stasser, S., 135, 447, 453
Staw, B., 60, 117, 145, 448
Steers, R., 331, 342
Steil, L., 243, 250, 260
Steinel, W., 390
Sternberg, R., 133, 134, 178, 193,
    198, 202, 260
Stewart, C., 630
Stewart, Martha, 74
Stewart, T., 291
Stone, R., 147
Stone-Romero, E., 294
Stroh, L., 402
Stuart, D., 598
Stuart, Jim, 335
Sue-Chan, C., 337
Sullivan, Barry, 127
Sutton, C., 74
Swift, C., 452
Synopsis Communication Consulting
    of London, 243

T
Tallahassee Democrat, 523–526
Tedeschi, J., 294
Tennessee Valley Authority, 564
Tennyson, Alfred Lord, 58
Thoits, P., 122
Thomas, John, 458
Thomas, K., 381, 391, 447, 452, 453,
    454
Thomas, P., 452
Thompson, D., 342
Thompson, L., 294, 307, 383,
    390, 396
Thorton, B., 243
3M, 189, 191, 192, 193, 196, 209,
    210, 656
Tichy, N., 208, 335, 542, 566, 656
Timberland, 559
Timmer, Jan, 127
Ting, S., 289
Ting-Toomey, S., 268, 390
Tjosvold, D., 380
Tomlinson, A., 333
Toyota Motors, 7
Travelers Insurance Co., 136, 348
Trevor, C., 342
Triandis, H., 268, 288, 342
Trieber, Frank, 119
Tripp, T., 309
Trompenaars, F., 22, 67, 122, 206,
    254, 268, 288, 385, 394,
    475, 516, 521
Tropman, J., 656, 658
Troxell, J. R., 124
Tsang, J., 551
Tschirhart, M., 11
Tuchman, B., 656
Tuckman, B., 502
Tully, S., 291
Turkington, C., 132
Turner, M., 511
Tushman, M., 208
Tutu, Desmond, 550
Tyabji, Hatim, 353

U
Ulicni, S. K., 71
Ulrich, D., 301, 548
Union Carbide, 385–386
United Chemical Company, 273–275,
    281–282
UOP Inc., 385–386

Urwick, Lester, 467
U.S. Postal Service, 14–15
U.S. public education system,
    530–531
US West, 334–335
Useem, Michael, 307

V
Van de Van, A., 208
Vance, C. M., 13, 14
Vangelisti, A., 251
Vardi, Y., 452
Vaske, J., 331
Velthouse, B., 447, 452, 453, 454
Verespei, M., 499
Verifone, 353
Veroff, J., 350
Viacom, 288
Vinton, D., 121
Vogt, J., 452, 454
Vogus, T., 143
Volvo, 499
Von Oech, Roger, 200, 210
Von Treitschke, Heinrich, 287
Vroom, V., 181, 331, 468, 469
Vygotsky, L., 191

W
Waclawski, J., 62
Wagner, N. N., 124
Wal-Mart, 217, 515
Wallas, G., 199
Walsh, J., 545
Walton, Sam, 515
Wanous, J., 380
Ward, H. W., 124
Ward, T., 188, 199, 204, 205
Warren, K., 466
Watson, C., 391
Watson, D., 84
Watson, K., 243
Weick, K. E., 60, 117, 137, 145, 146,
    188, 448, 457, 564
Weidsma, A., 178
Weiner, B., 338
Weingart, L., 381
Weisberg, J., 385
Weisenfeld, B. M., 124
Weisz, J., 453
Welch, Jack, 296, 542, 560, 566
Weldon, E., 385, 390
Wellins, R., 499, 500

Westinghouse Furniture Systems,
    499
Wheeler, J., 511
Whetten, D. A., 14, 60, 61, 122,
    386, 448, 502, 546
White, R., 450, 453
Whitney, D., 519
Wiemann, J., 258
Wilkinson, I., 302
William, R., 144
Williams, V., 144
Williams, W., 188, 198
Wilmington, S. C., 243, 244
Wilmot, W., 385
Wilson, Bill, 185
Wilson, D., 181, 182
Wilson, J., 499
Wolf, Dr. Stewart, 132
Wolf, S. G., 123
Wolff, H. G., 123
Wolff, S. G., 519
Wonder, J., 206
Wood, R., 345
Wooten, M., 459, 549
Workman, E. A., 142
World Trade Center, 561
Wright, A., 341
Wrzeniewski, A., 454, 456

X
Xerox Corporation, 217, 507, 566
Xie, J., 390
Xin, K., 385

Y
Yamaha, 185
Yammarino, F., 62
Yang, L., 188, 198
Yeatts, D., 509, 520
Yetton, P., 181, 468
Yogi, M., 147
Yountz, A., 380
Yuki, G., 293

Z
Zand, D., 454
Zeitz, P., 182
Zhou, J., 182
Zimmerer, T., 466
Zimmerman, M., 451, 452, 453
Zingheim, P., 341

SUBJECT INDEX

A

Ability, and performance, 331
Abstract conceptualization (AC), 76, 76–77, 78, 79
Abundance, vision of, 557–558
Accommodating, in conflict management, 388, 389t, 393
Accommodating learning style, 79
Accountability vs. entitlement, 334–335
ACTH, in stress reactions, 120
Active experimentation (AE), 76, 78, 79
Adhocracy skills, 16–17
Advising response, 261–262
Aggression, as stress mechanism, 118
Agreeableness, 83
Alarm stage, of stress, 118
Alice in Wonderland, 336–337
Alternatives, in analytical problem-solving, 178–182
Analogies, in problem-solving, 200
Analysis, and problem-solving, 108f, 178–182, 212
Anticipatory stressors, 124, 136–137
Aptitude, 331
Aspirations, in learning plan, 96
Assertiveness, and influence, 308–309
Assimilating learning style, 77–78
Attraction, as power source, 293–294
Attribution bias, 330
Authority, for decision-making, 135
Autonomy, at work, 135
Avoiding, in conflict management, 388, 389t, 393

B

Balance, in life, 138–139
Benchmarking, 556, 558t
Blocking roles, on teams, 519–520
Bosses, abusive, 309t
Brainstorming, and problem-solving, 203–204
Breathing, deep, to reduce stress, 149
Byron vs. Thomas, 275–276, 281–282

C

Cardiovascular conditioning, 140–141
Case of the Missing Time, the, 154–158
Center for Leadership and Change Movement, 307
Centrality, as power source, 297–299
Centralization, and empowerment, 449t
Change. See also Leadership, for positive change
    attitudes toward, 79–83
    effect on stress, 123
    and locus of control, 82–83
    managing, 4

predictions of, 3
and tolerance of ambiguity, 81–82
whitewater pace of, 4, 80
Characteristics, in learning plan, 96–97
Cheshire Cat, 336–337
Clan skills, 16–17
Clarification probe, for interviews, 630, 632t
Closed questions, for interviews, 625–626
Coaching, on communication, 248–250
Collaboration, in conflict management, 388–389, 393, 394–405
Collaboration, in stress management, 132–134
Collectivism, 68
Commitment, as conceptual block, 192–194
Commonalities, ignoring, as conceptual block, 193–194
Communication, and empowerment, 448, 449
Communication, supportive. See also Interviews, conducting
    accuracy and, 244–246
    attributes of, 246–248
    barriers to, 268
    behavioral guidelines for, 269
    coaching and counseling for, 248–250
    and congruence, 251–252
    conjunctive, 258–259
    consequences of ineffective, 246
    descriptive, 252–254
    effective, importance of, 242–243
    and electronic communication, 243
    international caveats for, 267–268
    and interpersonal relationships, 242–243
    listening and responding, 260–264, 276–277
    obstacles to, 250
    owned, 259–260
    personal management interview (PMI), 264–267
    problem-oriented, 254–255
    pronunciations, inconsistent, 245t
    scoring key for, 280–282, 280–282
    skill analysis for, 270–272
    skill application for, 278–279
    skill assessment for, 238–242
    skill practice for, 273–278
    specific, 257–258
    studies of, 243–244
    validating, 255–257
Communist prison camp, exercise on, 88–89

Compassion, and leadership, 549–550
Competing Values Framework, 16–17, 183
Compromising, in conflict management, 388, 389t, 393
Computerized exam, exercise on, 89–90
Conceptual blocks
    commitment as, 192–194
    complacency as, 195–198
    compression as, 194–196
    constancy as, 190–191
    defined, 187
    exercises to assess, 219–226
    and mental filtering, 187–188
    as mental obstacles, 212
    overcoming, 198–203, 212
    review of, 198
Conclusions, for a presentation, 601t
Concrete experience (CE), 76, 79
Conflict, and empowerment, 449t
Conflict management
    ambivalent view of, 380–382
    approaches to, 388–389, 393–395
    behavioral guidelines for, 406–408
    collaborative problem-solving and, 394–405
    and cultural diversity, 394
    and environmentally induced stress, 386–387
    flexibility in, 391–392
    and gender, 391
    and informational deficiencies, 385–386
    interpersonal, 380
    issue-focused, 383–384
    model for, 405–406
    and negotiation strategies, 389t
    people-focused, 382–383
    and personal differences, 384–385
    personal preferences for, 390–391, 406
    and role incompatibility, 386
    rules of engagement for, 382
    scoring key for, 439–441
    situational considerations for, 392–394
    skill analysis for, 409–413
    skill application for, 436–438
    skill assessment for, 378–379
    skill practice for, 414–435
    XYZ approach to, 397–398, 400–401
Congruence, and communication, 251–252
Conscientiousness, 83
Constancy, as conceptual block, 190–192

Constraints, artificial, as conceptual block, 194–195
Converging learning style, 78–79
Core self-evaluation, 63, 83–85
Core Self-Evaluation Scale, 57, 106–107
Core Self-Evaluation Survey, 84
Counseling, on communication, 248–250
Creativity, and problem-solving, 182–213
Credibility, and teamwork, 511–513
Cuban Missile Crisis, 504
Culture. See also Diversity
    affectivity in, 122
    and communication, 245
    and conflict management, 394
    egalitarian, 122
    hierarchical, 122
    personal, learning plan for, 96–98
    and power, 288
    as predictive factor in stress, 122
    sensitivity for, 22
    and teamwork, 516
    values of different, 66–68
Customer relationships, establishing, 135
Customer Undeniably Deserves Attention (CUDA), 225

D

Dalkon Shield, 74
Decision dilemmas, exercise on, 90–92
Defensiveness, and communication, 250
Defensiveness, and self-awareness, 60
Defining Issues Test, 48–51, 103–105
Definitions, reversing, 201–203
Deflecting response, 262
Delegation. See also Empowerment
    advantages of, 467–468
    behavioral guidelines for, 476–477
    principles for, 475f
    process for, 469–474
    relationship to empowerment, 477f
    scoring key for, 491–492
    skill analysis for, 478–479
    skill application for, 489–490
    skill assessment for, 444–446
    skill practice for, 486–488
    timing for, 468–469, 470f
Desert Storm. See Persian Gulf War
Deviance, negative and positive, 544–545
Dietary control, to combat stress, 141–142
Disconfirmation, and communication, 250
Distance learning, 333

Diverging learning style, 77
Diversity
  differences vs. distinctions, 61–62
  growth of, in workplace, 85
  and individual differences, 21–22
  and self-awareness, 61–62
  and Trompenaars model, 22
Doctor's dilemma, exercise on, 50, 104
Dominant response pattern, 21
Double-barreled questions, for
    interviews, 626, 627

E

E-mail, tone for, 609
Effort, as power source, 294–296
Egalitarian communication, 256
Elaboration probe, for interviews,
    630, 632t
Elaboration, used in problem-solving,
    201
ELITE team, 523–526
Embedded pattern puzzle, 196f, 235
Emotional bank account, 133
Emotional competence, 65
Emotional Competence Inventory, 64
Emotional Intelligence, 63, 64
Emotional Intelligence Assessment, 66
Emotional intelligence (EQ)
  assessment for, 101–103
  capabilities of those with, 65–66
  compared to IQ, 66
  and cultural diversity, 22
  defined, 65
  vs. emotional competence, 65
  EQ-I measure, 64
  as factor in success, 62, 63
  falling scores of, 12
  improving, 23
  refining concept of, 63–66
  skill assessment for, 46–48
  and stress management, 132–134
Empowerment. *See also* Delegation
  behavioral guidelines for, 476–477
  defined, 447
  developing, 455–465
    by connecting to outcomes,
      461–462, 465t
    by creating confidence, 462–463,
      465t
    with emotional arousal, 459–460,
      464t
    by fostering personal mastery, 457
    by modeling, 458, 464t
    by providing information,
      460–461, 464t–465t
    by providing resources, 461, 465t
    by providing support, 458–459,
      464t
    SMART goals for, 456–457, 464t
  inhibitors to, 465–467
  international caveats for, 475–476
  managers' dilemma with, 447–448
  and meaning, 453–454, 455
  negative attributes affecting,
    448–449
  and personal consequence, 453, 455
  vs. power, 449–450
  practical suggestions for, 463–465
  relationship to delegation, 477f
  roots of, 450–451
  scoring key for, 491–492
  and self-determination, 452, 455
  and self-efficacy, 451–452, 455
  skill analysis for, 478–479
  skill application for, 489–490
  skill assessment for, 444–446
  skill practice for, 480–486
  and trust, 454–455, 455

Encounter stressors, 122, 132–134
Energy, positive and negative, 549
Entitlement vs. accountability, 334–335
EQ-I measure, 64
Equity, and rewards, 352
Escaped prisoner, exercise on, 49–50,
    103–104
Ethics, and values, 75
Exercise, to combat stress, 141
Exhaustion, as stress mechanism, 118
Expertise, as power source, 292–293
Extraversion, 83

F

False bipolar questions, for interviews,
    626, 627
Feedback
  exercises for, 539–540
  in learning plan, 97–98
  and positivity, 555t
  of reflected best-self, 553–554
  in teams, 520–521
  at work, 135–136, 352–355
Fight or flight, as stress mechanism, 120
Figure from ground, separating, 196
Find Somebody Else exercise, 270–271
Five-figure problem, 201
Fixation, as stress mechanism, 118
Flexibility
  in communication, 256–257
  in conflict management, 391–392
  as power source, 299
  in problem-solving, 199, 203
Fluency, and problem-solving, 203
Forcing, in conflict management, 388,
    389t, 393
Forgiveness, and leadership, 550–551
Format, for presentations, 609
Forming stage, of team development,
    502–503
Frameworks, and leadership, 543–544

G

Gender, and conflict management, 391
Glossary, 677–685
Goals. *See also* Motivation; Performance
  characteristics of, 338
  Everest, 514–515
  motivating potential of, 337
  removing obstacles to, 338–340
  setting, to reduce stress, 136–137
  SMART, and teamwork, 513–514
  SMART, for empowerment, 457
Gratitude, and leadership, 551–552
Groupthink, 209, 504–505, 506, 508

H

Hardiness, and stress, 143
Heliotropic effect, on change, 546, 569
Hierarchal needs model, 349
Hierarchy skills, 16–17
Human resource departments,
    and power, 301

I

Idea champion, 211, 212
Illness, injury, 124, 134, 139, 145
Illumination, and creativity, 199
Imagery and fantasy, to reduce stress, 149
Imagination, and creativity, 183–184, 186
Imperviousness, in communication, 256
Implementation, in problem-solving,
    181–182
Improvement, and creativity, 184–185,
    186
Incubation, and creativity, 185, 186, 199
Indifference, in communication, 256
Individualism, 68

Influence
  behavioral guidelines for, 313
  model of, 311f
  neutralizing attempts at, 308–311
  and power, 302, 312
  scoring key for, 324–325
  skill analysis for, 314
  skill application for, 321–322
  skill assessment for, 284–286
  skill practice for, 316–320
  strategies for, 302–307
  and upward issue selling, 307–308,
    312
  using wisely, 287
Initiator, in conflict management,
    396–405, 407
Innovativeness, and empowerment, 449t
Intelligence quotient (IQ), 66, 133–134
Interviews
  behavioral guidelines for, 636–637
  and behavioral information, 634
  conducting. *See also* Communication,
    supportive
    probes for, 630–632
    recording, 632–633
    sections of, 630–632
    supportive climate for, 629–630
  defined, 624
  employee-orientation, 638–641
  employment-selection, 633–634,
    635t, 647–654
  information-gathering, 633
  performance-appraisal, 634–636,
    641–646
  planning
    checklist for, 629t
    failure to, 624–625
    funnel sequences for, 627–628,
      633
    problems with, 628–629
    purpose and agenda for, 625
    setting for, 628
    types of questions for, 625–627
  skill practice for, 638–654
Introductions, for a presentation, 601t
Investment, and creativity, 185, 186
Issue selling, as influence, 307–308, 312

J

Janusian thinking, and problem-solving,
    201–202

K

Kaizen, 159
Knowledge, half-life of, 76, 80
Korean War, 147

L

Language, for positive change, 557, 558t
Language, single thinking, as conceptual
    block, 191
Leadership, and management, 16, 17, 18f
Leadership, for positive change. *See also*
    Vision statements
  approaches to, abundance and
    deficit, 545–546
  behavioral guidelines for, 570–571
  and benchmarking, 556, 558t
  and change, escalating, 543
  defined, 542
  and deviance, negative and positive,
    544–545
  and frameworks, 543–544,
    546–548, 570f
  identifying strengths, 552–553
  institutionalizing
    creating momentum for, 566
    creating teachers for, 566–567

language for, 557, 558t
  and positivity, establishing, 548–554,
    555t
  and reflected best-self feedback,
    553–554
  scoring key for, 591–592
  skill analysis for, 572–584
  skill application for, 588–590
  skill assessment for, 538–541
  skill practice for, 585–587
  and small wins, 564, 565t
  and symbolism, 556–557, 558t
  as temporary position, 542–543
  and vision of abundance, 557–558,
    561–566
Leading questions, for interviews,
    626–627
Learning stair, 566, 567f
Learning style
  defined, 76
  dimensions of, 76–77
  institutionalizing
    human capital for, 567–568
    metrics, measurements,
      milestones for, 568–569
  and self-awareness, 62–63
  types of, 77–79, 80f
Learning Style Inventory, 52–53, 105
Learning Styles Instrument (LSI), 76,
    78f, 79
Legitimacy, as power source, 296–297
Life balance analysis, 160–162
Live for Life program, 140
Locus of control, 82–83, 84, 105–106
Locus of Control Scale, 54–55, 83
Logos, and vision, 561
Loyalty, and empowerment, 449t

M

Machiavellianism scale (MACH IV),
    540–541
Magnetron, 189, 194
Malcolm Baldrige National Quality
    Award, 148
Management
  as cause of stress, 117
  defined, 16, 17
  and leadership, 16, 17, 18f
Management by objectives, 337
Management skills
  applicable to daily life, 5
  based on research, 5
  characteristics of, 9, 11
  curriculum for improving, 12, 15
  defined, 8
  developing, 4–5
  diversity in, 21–22
  essential, 7–9
  exercises to assess, 24–43, 94–96
  importance for managers, 6
  improving, 12
  and leadership, 542
  learning model for developing, 13–14
  personal assessment for, 42–43
  for teams, teamwork, 521–522
  types and models of, 18–19
Managers. *See also* Leadership, for posi-
    tive change; Presentations,
    oral and written
  attitudes toward subordinates, 466
  effectiveness exercise for, 28–29
  essential skills of, 9, 10t–11t, 11
  importance of management skills for, 6
  insecurities of, 466
  need for control of, 466–467
  as reinforcers, 342–343
  teamwork skills for, 521–522
Manifest needs model, 349–350

Market skills, 16–17
Matchstick problem, 192, 233
Meaning, and empowerment, 453–454, 455
Mediator, in conflict management, 396–405
Meetings, conducting
　rules for group members in, 661–662, 663
　rules for managers in
　　participants, 657, 662
　　participation, 659–661
　　perspective, 661, 663
　　planning, 658–659, 662
　　process, 662–663
　　purpose, 656–657, 662
　skill practice for, 664–675
Mentoring, 147–148, 301–302, 458
Messages, one-sided, two-sided, 598
Microwave ovens, 189, 191, 194, 196
Minnesota Multiphasic Personality Inventory, 63
Mixed-mode interview, 636
Morale, and empowerment, 449t
Morphological synthesis, and problem-solving, 205–206
Motivation. See also Goals; Performance
　behavioral guidelines for, 356–357
　elements of program for, 335–338
　fostering environment of, 334–336
　and human needs, 349–352
　increasing, 330
　model for enhancing, 355f
　and performance, 331–332
　and rewards, 349, 350–355
　scoring key for, 374
　skill analysis for, 358–364
　skill application for, 371–373
　skill assessment for, 328–329
　skill practice for, 365–370
　and work design, 346–349
Moving Up in the Rankings, exercise on, 221
Multifactor Emotional Intelligence Scale, 64
Muscle relaxation, to reduce stress, 148–149
Myers-Briggs Type Indicator, 63

N
Name that ship problem, 194, 195f, 234
Nanobombs, 3
Neuroticism, 83, 84
Newspaper, the, exercise on, 51, 104–105
Nine-dot problem, 195, 234
Noninquisitiveness, as conceptual block, 196–197
Norming stage, of team development, 502, 503–505

O
Open questions, for interviews, 625–626
Openness, 83
Operant conditioning, 343
Orchestrator, 211, 212
Organization, for a presentation, 599–600
Orientation, toward change, 63

P
Particularism, 68
Penicillin, 194
Performance. See also Goals; Motivation
　ability deterioration and, 332
　ability-enhancing tools for, 332–334
　and behavior
　　discipline for, 343–345
　　managers as reinforcers of, 342–343

rewards for, 341–342, 343–345
　shaping and improving, 345–346
behavioral guidelines for, 356–357
diagnosing problems, 330–332
and extrinsic outcomes, 346
increasing, 330
scoring key for, 374–376
and shift work, 331
skill practice for, 365–370
Performing stage, in team development, 502
Persian Gulf War
　Pagonis's team in, 501, 503, 506–507, 509–510
　work teams in, 132–133
Personal Assessment of Management Skills (PAMS), 24–28
Personal consequence, 453, 455
Personal management interview (PMI), 264–267
Personality, and self-awareness, 83–84
Perspective, and empowerment, 449t
Peter Principle, The, 332
Ping-Pong puzzle, 204–205
Placebo effect, on change, 546
Planning, in learning plan, 98
Politicization, and empowerment, 449t
Post-It Notes
　breaking stereotypes to invent, 193, 196
　Fry's involvement with, 192, 194
　importance of teamwork to invent, 210–212
　invention of, 189
Power
　abuse of, 289–290, 312
　balanced view of, 287
　behavioral guidelines for, 312–313
　building base for, 287
　defined, 290
　in human resource department, 301
　and influence, 302, 312
　international caveats for, 291–292
　lack of, 287–289
　model of, 311f
　necessity of, 290–292
　personal
　　negative view of, 288
　　sources of, 292–297, 311–312
　　as stepping stone, 290
　position-power, sources of, 297–302
　and relationship with boss, 295t
　scoring key for, 323–324, 323–325
　skill analysis for, 314
　skill application for, 321–322
　skill assessment for, 284–286
　skill practice for, 315–316
Preparation, and creativity, 199
Presentations, oral and written
　behavioral guidelines for, 611–612
　necessity for, 596
　responding to questions on, 609–611
　skill practice for, 613–622
　strategies for, 597–599
　structure for, 599–601
　style for oral, 603–606
　style for written, 607–609
　supporting points for, 601–604
　visual aids for, 602–603, 605
Prioritizing, 136
Probing response, 263–264
Problem-oriented communication, 254–255
Problem solving. See also Conceptual blocks
　analytical
　　constraints on, 183t
　　exercise to assess, 219–220

limitations of, 182
　model of, 208f
　and single thinking language, 191
　steps in, 178–182
　success of, 212
　applying techniques for, 207
　behavioral guidelines for, 212–213
　in conflict management, 394–405
　creative
　　approaches to, 183–187
　　exercises to assess, 220–221, 225–226
　　fostering in others, 207–212
　　impediments to, 182–183
　　management principles for, 208–212
　　model of, 208f
　　as prerequisite for success, 212
　　stages of creative thought, 198–199
　　training for, 188–189
　and creativity, innovation, 178
　generating alternatives for, 203–206
　international caveats for, 206–207
　problem definition, improving, 199–204, 212
　scoring key for, 228–234, 229–235
　skill analysis for, 214–218
　skill application for, 227–228
　skill assessment for, 172–177
　skill practice for, 219–226
Problem-solving interview, 636
Pronunciation, inconsistent, 245t
Pygmalion effect, on change, 546

Q
Quality circles, exercises for, 614–622

R
Reality therapy, 259
Reason, as influence strategy, 303, 304–307, 310–311
Reassigning, for ability enhancement, 333
Reciprocity, as influence strategy, 303–307, 310
Recreation, and empowerment, 459–460
Recreation, and vision, 561–563, 565t
Redirect, to shape behavior, 345–346
Refitting, for ability enhancement, 333
Reflecting response, 264
Reflective observation (RO), 76, 79
Reflective probe, for interviews, 631, 632t
Reframing, to reduce stress, 149
Regression, as stress mechanism, 118
Rehearsal, to reduce stress, 149
Reinforce, to shape behavior, 345–346
Rejected Plans, 271–272
Relational algorithm, and problem-solving, 206
Relationship-building roles, on teams, 518–519
Relationship skills, developing, 4
Relaxation, deep, 146–147
Release, of employee, 333
Relevance, as power source, 301–302
Repetition probe, for interviews, 631, 632t
Repression, as stress mechanism, 118
Reprimand, to shape behavior, 345–346
Research, 5, 6
Resiliency, to deal with stress, 138–149, 147
Resistance stage, of stress, 118
Resources, and performance, 331
Responder, in conflict management, 396–405, 407
Resupply, for ability enhancement, 333

Retraining, for ability enhancement, 333
Retribution, as influence strategy, 302–307, 309–310
Rewards, for performance, 341–342, 350–355
Rigidity, in communication, 255–256
Rule breaker, 211, 212

S
Sandwiching, a presentation, 599
SCAMPER, used in problem-solving, 201
Scapegoating, and empowerment, 449t
Scoring keys
　for communication, supportive, 280–282
　for conflict management, 439–441
　for empowerment, delegation, 491–492
　for leadership, positive change, 591–592
　for motivation, 374
　for performance, 374–376
　for power and influence, 323–325
　for problem-solving, 228–234
　for stress, stress management, 167–168
　for teams, teamwork, 535
Self-awareness
　activities for developing, 99–100
　assessment for, 101
　behavioral guidelines for, 87
　change, attitudes toward, 79–83
　core aspects of, 64f
　and core self-evaluation, 83–86
　defined, 58
　dimensions of, 58
　and diversity, 61–62
　effectiveness of training for, 85
　enigma of, 59
　and learning style, 75–79
　and the sensitive line, 59–61
　skill analysis for, 88–92
　skill application for, 99–107
　skill assessment for, 46–47
　skill practice for, 93–98
　and values, 66–75
Self-determination, 452, 455
Self-disclosure, 60
Self-efficacy, 451–452, 455
Self-knowledge, 61
Self-portrait, best, 539
Sensitive line, the, 59–61
Shakespeare riddle, 193, 194f, 233
Shift work, 331
Silence, in interviews, 631, 632t
Situational stressors, 122–124, 134–136
Skill analysis
　for communication, supportive, 270–272
　for conflict management, 409–413
　for empowerment, delegation, 478–479
　for leadership, positive change, 572–584
　for motivation, 358–364
　for problem-solving, 214–218
　purpose of, 19
　for self-awareness, 88–92
　for stress management, 151–158
Skill application
　for communication, supportive, 278–279
　for conflict management, 436–438
　for empowerment, delegation, 489–490
　importance of, 21
　for leadership, positive change, 588–590

Skill application *(Continued)*
  for motivation, 371–373
  for power and influence, 321–322
  for problem-solving, 227–228
  purpose of, 19–20
  for self-awareness, 99–107
  for stress management, 165–167
  for teams, teamwork, 533–534
Skill assessment
  for communication, supportive, 238–242
  for conflict management, 378–379
  for empowerment, delegation, 444–446
  for leadership, positive change, 538–541
  for managing stress, 110–115
  for motivation, 328–329
  for power and influence, 284–286, 314
  for problem-solving, 172–177
  purpose of, 19
  for self-awareness, 46–57
  for teams, teamwork, 494–496, 523–526
  for time management, 111–112
Skill learning, purpose of, 19
Skill practice
  for communication, supportive, 273–278
  for conflict management, 414–435
  for empowerment, delegation, 480–488
  for influence, 316–320
  for interviews, 638–654
  for leadership, positive change, 585–587
  for meetings, conducting, 664–675
  for motivation, 365–370
  for performance, 365–370
  for power, 315–316
  for presentations, 613–622
  for problem-solving, 219–226
  purpose of, 19
  for self-awareness, 93–98
  for stress management, 159–164
  for teams, teamwork, 527–532
Skill variety, at work, 135
Small wins
  and commitment to change, 564, 565t
  and empowerment, 457
  exercise to assess, 159–160
  and problem-solving, 181
  strategy of, 137–138
  for Type A personalities, 145–146
Social Readjustment Rating Scale (SRRS), 113–114, 123–124
Soldiers, 132–133, 147
"Sources of Power of Lower Participants," 295

Sponsor, of creativity, 211, 212
Stanford-Binet Intelligence Test, 63
Stereotyping, as conceptual block, 193
Storming stage, of team development, 502, 505–507
Strategies, for presentations, 597–599
Stress, stress management. *See also* Time management
  anticipatory stressors
    defined, 124
    and goal setting, 136–137
    and prioritizing, 136
    and small wins, 137–138
  behavioral guidelines for, 149–150
  and burnout, 122, 123t
  coping strategies for, 119–121
  eliminating stressors, 124–125
  encounter stressors
    and collaboration, 132–134
    defined, 122
    and social and emotional intelligence, 133–134
  and illness, injury, 124, 134, 139, 145
  improving, 116–117
  and incompetent managers, 117
  model of, 119f
  physiological effects of, 120–121
  positive and negative elements of, 117–118
  reactions to stress, 118–119
  resiliency for, 138–149
  scoring key for, 167–168, 168
  situational stressors
    defined, 132–134
    and work redesign, 134–136
  skill analysis for, 151–158
  skill application for, 165–167
  skill assessment for, 110–115
  skill practice for, 159–164
  sources of, 115, 121–124
  temporary techniques for reduction of, 148–149
Strong-Campbell Vocational Inventory, 63
Structure, for presentations, 599–601
Subdivision, and problem-solving, 204–205
Success, organizational, 6
Superiority-oriented communication, 255
Symbolism, and leadership, 556–557, 558t
Synectics, and problem-solving, 200

T

Task facilitating roles, on teams, 517–518
Task identity, significance, 135, 347–348, 462
Teams, teamwork
  advantages of, 498–501
  advertisement for, 498f

  behavioral guidelines for, 522
  developing, 497–498
    forming stage, 502–503
    norming stage, 502, 503–505
    performing stage, 502, 507–510
    storming stage, 502, 505–507
  and empowerment, 449t
  examples of, 499
  feedback in, 520–521
  goals for, 513–515
  group pressure in, 517
  impact of, 500t
  international caveats for, 515–516, 521
  leading, 510–515
  management skills for, 521–522
  membership in, 516–521
  in Persian Gulf War, 501, 503, 506–507, 509–510
  roles in
    blocking, 519–520
    relationship-building, 518–519
    team-building, 517–518
  scoring key for, 535
  shortcomings of, 499–500
  skill analysis for, 523–526
  skill application for, 533–534
  skill assessment for, 494–496
  skill practice for, 527–532
  stretch targets for, 515
Tell-and-listen interview, 636
Tell-and-sell interview, 635–636
Theory X, Y assumptions, 254, 334, 455, 466
Thinking, bias against, as conceptual block, 196–197
Threat-rigidity response, 60, 448, 449
Through the Looking Glass, exercise on, 93–94
Time management. *See also* Stress, stress management
  effective
    and personal principles statement, 127–128
    and urgent/important matrix, 125–126
  efficient
    determining patterns, 128–129
    rules for all, 129–131
    rules for managers, 131–132
    Time Management Survey, 129
  eliminating stressors with, 125–132
  exercise to assess, 163–164
  improving, 116–117
  scoring key for, 168–169
  skill assessment for, 111–112
Time stressors, 121–122
Tolerance of ambiguity, 81–82, 106
Tolerance of Ambiguity Scale, 56, 81
Tone, in presentations, 608

Training, and performance, 331
Trompenaars model, 22
Trust, and empowerment, 449t, 454–455, 455
Turn of the Tide, exercise for, 151–154
Two-way communication, 257
Type A personality, and stress, 143–145
Type A Personality Inventory, 112–113, 169

U

Universalism, 68

V

Validating communication, 255–256
Values
  core organizational, 296
  cultural, 67–68
  dimensions of, 68–69
  and ethical decision-making, 74–75
  ethical standards test, 75
  as foundation, 66
  instrumental, 69, 70–71
  personal, 62, 63, 69–71
  terminal, 70, 71
Values maturity, levels and stages of, 71–72
Verification, and creativity, 199
Vertical, lateral thinking, as conceptual block, 190–191
Vietnam War, 147
Visibility, as power source, 299–301
Vision statements
  commitment to, 561–566
  defined, 558
  examples of, 559
  interest for, 559–560
  passion and principles for, 560
  symbols for, 561
Visual aids, 602–603, 605

W

Weight, and stress, 140–141, 142
Withdrawal, as stress mechanism, 118
Work design, 346–349
Work redesign, steps for, 135–136
Work teams, units
  attributes needed for, 209
  benefits of, 135
  and social resiliency, 148
  and task identity, 347–348
  in wartime, 132–133
World War II, 147, 300, 550, 564

X

XYZ approach, to conflict management, 397–398, 400–401

Z

Zen Buddhism, 145

COMBINED INDEX

A

AAL, 499
Abbott, R., 350
Ability, and performance, 331
Abstract conceptualization (AC), 76, 76–77, 78, 79
Abundance, vision of, 557–558
Accommodating, in conflict management, 388, 389t, 393
Accommodating learning style, 79
Accountability vs. entitlement, 334–335
ACTH, in stress reactions, 120
Active experimentation (AE), 76, 78, 79
Acton, Lord, 289
Adams, J., 193, 199
Adhocracy skills, 16–17
Adler, C., 124, 135, 140, 141, 142, 385, 450
Adler, P., 292
Adler, R., 396, 401
Advising response, 261–262
Aggression, as stress mechanism, 118
Agras, W., 452
Agreeableness, 83
A. H. Robins, 74
Alarm stage, of stress, 118
Albert, R., 188, 199
Alderfer, Clay, 349
Alice in Wonderland, 336–337
Alinsky, S., 450
Allan, H., 62
Allen, R., 302
Allinson, C., 294
Alloy, L., 466
Alternatives, in analytical problem-solving, 178–182
Amabile, T., 198, 208
Amana Refrigeration Co., 191
Amazon, 217
American Management Association, 74
Ameritech, 334–335
Amway, 459
Analogies, in problem-solving, 200
Analysis, and problem-solving, 108f, 178–182, 212
Ancona, D., 500
Anderson, C., 143, 293, 452
Anderson, P., 208
Anticipatory stressors, 124, 136–137
Apex Communications Corporation, 596
Apple Computer Inc., 216–218, 288, 386, 560, 572–574
Aptitude, 331
Argenti, J., 380
Argyris, C., 250
Ariel, S., 299
Arkinson, J., 350
Armstrong, S., 294

Arnold, C., 260
Asch, S., 517
Ashford, S., 307
Ashforth, B., 454
Aspirations, in learning plan, 96
Assertiveness, and influence, 308–309
Assimilating learning style, 77–78
AT&T, 499
Atkinson, J., 338
Attraction, as power source, 293–294
Attribution bias, 330
Atwater, L., 62
Auerbach, S. M., 117, 118
Authority, for decision-making, 135
Autonomy, at work, 135
Averill, J., 466
Avoiding, in conflict management, 388, 389t, 393
Aygen, M., 147

B

Bacharach, S., 287
Bagnall, J., 205
Bailey, D., 499, 500, 509, 519
Baker, W., 242, 459, 549, 564
Balance, in life, 138–139
Balzer, W. K., 122
Bandura, A., 13, 143, 345, 451, 452, 455, 456, 457, 458, 459
Bannister, Roger, 458
Bar-On, R., 64
Barber, B., 454
Baril, G., 391
Barker, L., 243
Barling, J., 117, 140
Barnlund, D., 255
Basadur, M., 198
Baum, L., 300
Baumeister, R., 548
Bay of Pigs, 504
Bazerman, M., 390
Beal, R. L., 22
Beary, J., 147
Beatrice Company, 300
Beebe, S. A., 243
Beebe, S. J., 243
Beer, M., 635
Bell, Alexander Graham, 191
Bell, C., 147
Ben-Amos, P., 206
Benchmarking, 556, 558t
Bennis, Warren, 3, 287, 338, 451, 453, 455, 557
Benson, H., 147
Bergmoser, Paul, 578
Bernard, C., 471
Bethune, Gordon, 95–96
Bies, R., 309

Bigley, G., 331
Bigoness, W., 70
Billingsley, Taylor, 596
Bilsky, W., 71
Biondi, Frank, 288
Birch, D., 350
Black, B., 452
Black, J. S., 181
Blair, J., 390
Blake, J., 206, 385
Blakely, G., 70
Blanks, Maurice, 95
Blasko, V., 202
Blink, 178
Block, P., 453, 455, 460, 466
Blocking roles, on teams, 519–520
Blodget, H., 333
Blu Dot, 95
Blum, A., 390
Boehle, S., 333
Bogomolny, Richard, 558
Bohr, Niels, 200
Bollier, D., 558
Bolman, L., 292
Bono, J. E., 143
Bookman, A., 450
Boss, W., 264
Boss.es, abusive, 309t
Bostrom, R., 260, 261
Boulding, E., 381
Bourgeios, J., 380
Bowman, R., 243
Boyatzis, R. E., 13, 62, 64
Bradford, D., 304
Brain, right and left hemispheres, 197–198, 457, 558–559
Brainstorming, and problem-solving, 203–204
Bramucci, R., 454
Branwell, S. T., 124
Breathing, deep, to reduce stress, 149
Breen, B., 307
Brehm, J., 450
Brett, J., 402
Brewer, Alan, 298
Brief, A., 454
Bright, D., 570
Brockner, J., 124
Broekhuijsen, J., 178
Brouwer, P. J., 59
Brown, L., 380
Brown, S., 390
Brownell, J., 243, 244, 250, 255
Buda, R., 70
Buell, B., 287
Bunderson, J., 292
Bunker, K., 289
Burlingham, B., 389

Burnham, D., 289, 350, 351
Burnout, as effect of stress, 122, 123t
Burt, R., 292
Byham, W., 466
Byharn, W., 499
Byosiere, P., 121
Byre, J., 300
Byrne, Patrick M., 95
Byron vs. Thomas, 275–276, 281–282

C

Cable, D., 71
Caldwell, D., 500
Cameron, K. S., 11, 14, 16, 60, 61, 122, 122–123, 124, 135, 143, 183, 242, 386, 448, 456, 458, 460, 463, 465, 502, 542, 544, 545, 546, 548, 549, 550, 556, 561, 570
Campion, M., 506
Canfield, F., 293
Cantor, N., 133
Caplan, R. D., 121, 122, 135
Cardiovascular conditioning, 140–141
Carlzon, J., 565, 566, 568
Carrell, L., 243, 244
Caruso, D. R., 64
Case of the Missing Time, the, 154–158
Cash, W., 630
Caudron, S., 386
Cavanaugh, G. F., 71
Caza, A., 546, 550, 570
Center for Leadership and Change Movement, 307
Centrality, as power source, 297–299
Centralization, and empowerment, 449t
CH2MHill, 559
Chambers, John, 550
Change. *See also* Leadership, for positive change
    attitudes toward, 79–83
    effect on stress, 123
    and locus of control, 82–83
    managing, 4
    predictions of, 3
    and tolerance of ambiguity, 81–82
    whitewater pace of, 4, 80
Characteristics, in learning plan, 96–97
Cheshire Cat, 336–337
Cheston, R., 391
Childre, D., 551
Chiu, L., 291
Choi, I., 291, 292, 330
Chrysler, Corporation, 457, 556–557, 561, 578–584
Chu, Y-K., 206
Churchill, Winston, 300

Cialdini, R., 190, 192, 302, 309, 511, 512, 564
Cisco Systems, 550
Clan skills, 16–17
Clare, D. A., 71
Clarification probe, for interviews, 630, 632t
Clark, R., 350
Clarke, J., 515
Clifton, D., 553
Closed questions, for interviews, 625–626
CNN, 557
Coaching, on communication, 248–250
Coats, G., 294
Coch, L., 468
Cockcroft, John D., 193
Coddington, R. D., 124
Cohen, A., 304
Cohen, M., 656, 657
Cohen, P. A., 12
Cohen, S., 499, 500, 509, 519
Collaboration, in conflict management, 388–389, 393, 394–405
Collaboration, in stress management, 132–134
Collectivism, 68
Collins, E., 597
Collins, M. A., 198
Commitment, as conceptual block, 192–194
Commonalities, ignoring, as conceptual block, 193–194
Communication, and empowerment, 448, 449
Communication, supportive. See also Interviews, conducting
  accuracy and, 244–246
  attributes of, 246–248
  barriers to, 268
  behavioral guidelines for, 269
  coaching and counseling for, 248–250
  and congruence, 251–252
  conjunctive, 258–259
  consequences of ineffective, 246
  descriptive, 252–254
  effective, importance of, 242–243
  and electronic communication, 243
  international caveats for, 267–268
  and interpersonal relationships, 242–243
  listening and responding, 260–264, 276–277
  obstacles to, 250
  owned, 259–260
  personal management interview (PMI), 264–267
  problem-oriented, 254–255
  pronunciations, inconsistent, 245t
  scoring key for, 280–282, 280–282
  skill analysis for, 270–272
  skill application for, 278–279
  skill assessment for, 238–242
  skill practice for, 273–278
  specific, 257–258
  studies of, 243–244
  validating, 255–257
Communist prison camp, exercise on, 88–89
Compassion, and leadership, 549–550
Competing Values Framework, 16–17, 183
Compromising, in conflict management, 388, 389t, 393
Computerized exam, exercise on, 89–90
Conceptual blocks

commitment as, 192–194
complacency as, 195–198
compression as, 194–196
constancy as, 190–191
defined, 187
exercises to assess, 219–226
and mental filtering, 187–188
as mental obstacles, 212
overcoming, 198–203, 212
review of, 198
Conclusions, for a presentation, 601t
Concrete experience (CE), 76, 79
Conflict, and empowerment, 449t
Conflict management
  ambivalent view of, 380–382
  approaches to, 388–389, 393–395
  behavioral guidelines for, 406–408
  collaborative problem-solving and, 394–405
  and cultural diversity, 394
  and environmentally induced stress, 386–387
  flexibility in, 391–392
  and gender, 391
  and informational deficiencies, 385–386
  interpersonal, 380
  issue-focused, 383–384
  model for, 405–406
  and negotiation strategies, 389t
  people-focused, 382–383
  and personal differences, 384–385
  personal preferences for, 390–391, 406
  and role incompatibility, 386
  rules of engagement for, 382
  scoring key for, 439–441
  situational considerations for, 392–394
  skill analysis for, 409–413
  skill application for, 436–438
  skill assessment for, 378–379
  skill practice for, 414–435
  XYZ approach to, 397–398, 400–401
Conger, J., 293, 447, 451, 452, 453, 455
Congruence, and communication, 251–252
Connell, J., 452
Connor, J., 301
Conscientiousness, 83
Constancy, as conceptual block, 190–192
Constraints, artificial, as conceptual block, 194–195
Continental Airlines, 95–96
Converging learning style, 78–79
Cook, A., 349
Coolidge, Calvin, 181
Coonradt, Chuck, 459, 469, 561–562
Cooper, C., 118, 131, 519
Cooper, M., 147
Cordes, C. L., 122, 147
Core self-evaluation, 63, 83–85
Core Self-Evaluation Scale, 57, 106–107
Core Self-Evaluation Survey, 84
Corning, 499
Council of Communication Management, 243
Counseling, on communication, 248–250
Courtney, Henry, 211–212
Covey, S., 126, 133, 251
Cowan, A., 287
Cowley, J., 143
Cox, T. H., 22, 385, 506
Coyle, C., 550

Creativity, and problem-solving, 182–213
Credibility, and teamwork, 511–513
Creon, King, 289
Crocker, J., 243, 260
Cross, R., 459, 549
Crovitz, H., 205
Csikszentmihalyi, M., 188, 199, 545
Cuban Missile Crisis, 504
Culture. See also Diversity
  affectivity in, 122
  and communication, 245
  and conflict management, 394
  egalitarian, 122
  hierarchical, 122
  personal, learning plan for, 96–98
  and power, 288
  as predictive factor in stress, 122
  sensitivity for, 22
  and teamwork, 516
  values of different, 66–68
Cuming, P., 304
Cummings, L., 391
Cupach, W., 250, 255
Curtis, J., 146
Customer relationships, establishing, 135
Customer Undeniably Deserves Attention (CUDA), 225

D

Dalkon Shield, 74
Daly, J., 307
Dana Corporation, 210, 499
Davidson, J., 125, 131, 132
Davidson, O., 338
Davis, Murray, 559
Davis, T. W., 13, 146
Dawidowicz, Bogdan, 287
De Bono, Edward, 190
De Dreu, C., 381, 390
Deal, T., 292, 296
DeButts, John, 296
DeCharms, R., 450
Deci, E., 452, 454
Decision dilemmas, exercise on, 90–92
Deepak, M., 147, 149
Defensiveness, and communication, 250
Defensiveness, and self-awareness, 60
Defining Issues Test, 48–51, 103–105
Definitions, reversing, 201–203
DeGeorge, R., 289
DeGraff, J., 182, 183, 208, 448
Delegation. See also Empowerment
  advantages of, 467–468
  behavioral guidelines for, 476–477
  principles for, 475f
  process for, 469–474
  relationship to empowerment, 477f
  scoring key for, 491–492
  skill analysis for, 478–479
  skill application for, 489–490
  skill assessment for, 444–446
  skill practice for, 486–488
  timing for, 468–469, 470f
Deleo, J., 147
Dell Computer, 94, 217
Dell, Michael, 94
Dellbeck, M., 147
Derr, C., 380
Descriptive communication, 252–254
Desert Storm. See Persian Gulf War
Detert, R., 146
Deutsch, M., 454
Devanna, M., 597, 656
Deviance, negative and positive, 544–545

Dew, J., 520
Dewey, J., 502
Dickson, M., 499, 500, 509, 516
DiClemente, C., 452
Dietary control, to combat stress, 141–142
Dilenschneider, R., 288
Dillard, J., 289
Dirks, K., 297
Disconfirmation, and communication, 250
Disney Corporation, 557
Disney, Walt, 184, 185
Disraeli, Benjamin, 256
Distance learning, 333
Diverging learning style, 77
Diversity
  differences vs. distinctions, 61–62
  growth of, in workplace, 85
  and individual differences, 21–22
  and self-awareness, 61–62
  and Trompenaars model, 22
Divine, D., 519
Dobbs, K., 333
Doctor's dilemma, exercise on, 50, 104
Doherty, M. E., 122
Dollinger, S. J., 71
Dominant response pattern, 21
Double-barreled questions, for interviews, 626, 627
Dougherty, T. W., 122, 147
Downs, C., 624
Drucker, P., 448
Drucker, Peter, 3, 80
Druskat, V., 511, 519
DuBrin, A., 624
Duncan, R., 307
Dunlap, Al, 289
Dunn, Keith, 222–226
Durham, C., 338
Durkheim, E., 456
Dutt, James, L., 300
Dutton, J., 60, 117, 145, 242, 307, 448, 465, 550, 553
Dyer, W., 148, 251, 304, 340

E

E-mail, tone for, 609
EBay, 217
Eden, D., 338
Edison, Thomas, 3
Edmonson, A., 511
Effort, as power source, 294–296
Egalitarian communication, 256
Eichinger, R., 385
Einstein, Albert, 202
Eisenhardt, K., 380, 385, 448
Eisner, Michael, 560
Elaboration probe, for interviews, 630, 632t
Elaboration, used in problem-solving, 201
ELITE team, 523–526
Elsayed-Elkhouly, S. M., 70
Embedded pattern puzzle, 196f, 235
Emerson, R., 309
Emmons, R., 551
Emotional bank account, 133
Emotional competence, 65
Emotional Competence Inventory, 64
Emotional Intelligence, 63, 64
Emotional Intelligence Assessment, 66
Emotional intelligence (EQ)
  assessment for, 101–103
  capabilities of those with, 65–66
  compared to IQ, 66
  and cultural diversity, 22

defined, 65
vs. emotional competence, 65
EQ-I measure, 64
as factor in success, 62, 63
falling scores of, 12
improving, 23
refining concept of, 63–66
skill assessment for, 46–48
and stress management, 132–134
Empowerment. *See also* Delegation
behavioral guidelines for, 476–477
defined, 447
developing, 455–465
    by connecting to outcomes,
        461–462, 465t
    by creating confidence, 462–463,
        465t
    with emotional arousal, 459–460,
        464t
    by fostering personal mastery, 457
    by modeling, 458, 464t
    by providing information,
        460–461, 464t–465t
    by providing resources, 461, 465t
    by providing support, 458–459,
        464t
    SMART goals for, 456–457, 464t
inhibitors to, 465–467
international caveats for, 475–476
managers' dilemma with, 447–448
and meaning, 453–454, 455
negative attributes affecting,
    448–449
and personal consequence, 453, 455
vs. power, 449–450
practical suggestions for, 463–465
relationship to delegation, 477f
roots of, 450–451
scoring key for, 491–492
and self-determination, 452, 455
and self-efficacy, 451–452, 455
skill analysis for, 478–479
skill application for, 489–490
skill assessment for, 444–446
skill practice for, 480–486
and trust, 454–455, 455
Encounter stressors, 122, 132–134
Energy, positive and negative, 549
Enright, R., 550
Enrique, J., 543
Enron, 74, 217
Entitlement vs. accountability, 334–335
EQ-I measure, 64
Equity, and rewards, 352
Equity Funding, 74
Eroglu, S., 134
Escaped prisoner, exercise on, 49–50,
    103–104
Eshelman, E., 146
Ethics, and values, 75
Exercise, to combat stress, 141
Exhaustion, as stress mechanism, 118
Expertise, as power source, 292–293
Extraversion, 83

F

False bipolar questions, for interviews,
    626, 627
Farnham, A., 135
Farson, R., 260
Federal Express, 499
Feedback
exercises for, 539–540
in learning plan, 97–98
and positivity, 555t
of reflected best-self, 553–554
in teams, 520–521

at work, 135–136, 352–355
Feldman, D., 191, 205
Ferrin, D., 297
Festinger, L., 190
Fight or flight, as stress mechanism, 120
Figure from ground, separating, 196
Finast Supermarkets, 558
Find Somebody Else exercise, 270–271
Finke, R., 188, 199, 204, 205
Firestone, 74
First Boston, 386–387
First Chicago, 127
Fisher, C., 121, 122, 297, 336
Fisher, R., 390
Five-figure problem, 201
Fixation, as stress mechanism, 118
Fleishman, J., 331
Fleming, Sir Alexander, 194
Flexibility
    in communication, 256–257
    in conflict management, 391–392
    as power source, 299
    in problem-solving, 199, 203
Float, human, 12
Fluency, and problem-solving, 203
Foerstner, George, 191–192, 196
Forcing, in conflict management, 388,
    389t, 393
Ford, Henry, 140, 217, 514
Ford Motor Co., 74, 561
Ford, William Clay, 561
Forgiveness, and leadership, 550–551
Format, for presentations, 609
Forming stage, of team development,
    502–503
Frameworks, and leadership, 543–544
Frankl, Victor, 450
Fredrickson, B., 242, 545
Freeman, S. J., 135, 458, 460
French, J. R. R., 121, 122, 135, 449, 468
Freud, S., 59, 502
Friedman, M., 144, 145
Fromm, Erich, 59
Fry, Art, 192, 194, 196, 211–212
Furman, W., 293

G

Gabarro, Jack, 295
Gable, S., 242
Gackenbach, J., 243
Gage, D., 383
Galunic, D. C., 448
Gambetta, D., 468
Gandhi, Mahatma, 127, 185, 450,
    454, 542, 548
Ganzach, Y., 346
Gardner, H., 133
Gardner, John, 287
Gates, Bill, 560, 566, 576–577
Gecas, V., 447, 451, 452
Geddie, T., 260
Gehry, Frank, 221
Gelles-Cole, S., 597
Gelman, E., 287, 298, 300
Gemmill, G., 452
Gender, and conflict management, 391
Gendron, G., 389
Geneen, Harold, 296
General Electric, 296, 348, 499
General Electric Aircraft, 140
General Mills, 499
General Motors, 6–7, 148, 381,
    559–560, 574–576
Gerhart, B., 331, 342
Getzels, J., 188
Giamtti, A. Bartlett, 312
Gibb, J., 250, 454

Gibb, L., 454
Gilligan, C., 73
Gitelson, R., 121, 122
Gittell, J., 143, 242
Gladstein, D., 500
Gladwell, Malcolm, 178
Glasser, W., 259
Glossary, 677–685
Gloucer, Tom, 559
Glucksman, Lewis, 288
Glynn, P., 550
Goals. *See also* Motivation; Performance
    characteristics of, 338
    Everest, 514–515
    motivating potential of, 337
    removing obstacles to, 338–340
    setting, to reduce stress, 136–137
    SMART, and teamwork, 513–514
    SMART, for empowerment, 457
Goddard, Roger, 452
Goldberg, H., 145
Goleman, D., 60, 62, 63, 64, 66,
    133, 134
Golembiewski, R., 454, 455
Golen, S., 244
Goll, I., 178
Goodson, Gene, 210
Gordon, R., 250
Gottman, J., 553
Goyer, R., 624
Graham, M., 342
Gratitude, and leadership, 551–552
Greenberg, Eric, 15, 141, 146
Greenberger, D. B., 135, 453, 466
Greene, C., 452
Greengerger, D., 447
Gregersen, H., 181
Greiner, L., 502
Griest, J. H., 141
Groupthink, 209, 504–505, 506, 508
Grove, A., 293, 380
Gudykunst, W., 268
Gully, S., 519
Guzzo, R., 499, 500, 509, 516

H

Haas, J., 260
Hackett, Jim, 560
Hackman, J. R., 135, 136, 346, 454,
    455, 456, 461, 462, 471, 499,
    500, 502, 506, 509, 510, 511
Hall, D. T., 124
Hamilton, B., 499
Hammarskjold, Dag, 133
Hammer, T., 452
Hampton-Turner, C., 22, 67, 122, 206,
    516, 521
Haney, W., 244
Hanson, G., 6
Hardiness, and stress, 143
Hare, C. C., 123
Hargie, O., 243
Harris, J. R., 74
Harris, S., 60, 86
Harter, J., 553
Harter, S., 84, 334, 450
Hartnett, D., 391
Harvey, J., 656
Harvey, William, 200
Hatfield, J., 260
Hausman, C., 202
Hayes, J., 294
Hayes, N., 520
Hayes, T., 334
Heaphy, E., 242, 263
Heider, F., 190
Heisler, W., 452

Heliotropic effect, on change, 546, 569
Hellriegel, C., 452
Helmick, R., 550
Hendricks, W., 147
Hepburn, G., 117, 140
Heritage Appliance Company, 314
Hermann, N., 197
Hess, R., 452
Hewlett-Packard, 298, 567
Hickson, D., 181, 182
Hierarchal needs model, 349
Hierarchy skills, 16–17
Higgs, A., 506
Hillhouse, J. J., 124, 140, 141, 142
Hinings, C., 299
Hitler, Adolf, 257
Hobson, A., 515
Hobson, C. J., 123–124
Hocker, J., 385
Hoerr, J., 301
Hofstede, Geert, 386
Hogg, M., 294
Holmes, T. H., 123–124, 124
Holt, J., 23
Honda, 185
Hosoda, M., 294
House, R., 339
Hout, T. M., 121
Hoy, A., 452
Hoy, W., 452
Hubbard, J., 142
Huber, G., 469
Hudspith, S., 197
Human float, 12
Human resource departments,
    and power, 301
Huseman, R., 260
Hyman, R., 251
Hyten, C., 509, 520

I

Iacocca, Lee, 457, 556–557, 566,
    578–584
Ibuka, Masaru, 514–515
Idea champion, 211, 212
Ideo, 184
Illness, injury, 124, 134, 139, 145
Illumination, and creativity, 199
Imagery and fantasy, to reduce
    stress, 149
Imagination, and creativity, 183–184,
    186
Imperviousness, in communication, 256
Implementation, in problem-solving,
    181–182
Improvement, and creativity, 184–185,
    186
In Search of Excellence, 353–354
Incubation, and creativity, 185, 186, 199
Indifference, in communication, 256
Individualism, 68
Influence
    behavioral guidelines for, 313
    model of, 311f
    neutralizing attempts at, 308–311
    and power, 302, 312
    scoring key for, 324–325
    skill analysis for, 314
    skill application for, 321–322
    skill assessment for, 284–286
    skill practice for, 316–320
    strategies for, 302–307
    and upward issue selling, 307–308,
        312
    using wisely, 287
Initiator, in conflict management,
    396–405, 407

Innovativeness, and empowerment, 449t
Intel Corporation, 300, 557
Intelligence quotient (IQ), 66, 133–134
Intelligence, types of, 133–134
Interaction Associates, 199
Intermountain Health Care, 330
Interviews
    behavioral guidelines for, 636–637
    and behavioral information, 634
    conducting. See also
        Communication, supportive
        probes for, 630–632
        recording, 632–633
        sections of, 630–632
        supportive climate for, 629–630
    defined, 624
    employee-orientation, 638–641
    employment-selection, 633–634,
        635t, 647–654
    information-gathering, 633
    performance-appraisal, 634–636,
        641–646
    planning
        checklist for, 629t
        failure to, 624–625
        funnel sequences for, 627–628,
            633
        problems with, 628–629
        purpose and agenda for, 625
        setting for, 628
        types of questions for, 625–627
    skill practice for, 638–654
Introductions, for a presentation, 601t
Investment, and creativity, 185, 186
Iron Law of Power, 392
Issue selling, as influence, 307–308, 312
Ivancevich, J., 143

J
Jackson, Phil, 330
Jago, A., 468, 469
James, William, 256
Janis, I., 209, 504, 656
Jansky, Karl, 191
Janson, R., 135, 462
Janusian thinking, and problem-solving,
    201–202
Jay, Anthony, 332
Jehn, K., 381, 385, 390
Jesus, 200
Jobs, Steve, 184, 216–218, 288,
    389, 515
Johnson & Johnson, 140
Johnson Controls, 210
Johnston, C. S., 71
Jones, Jean C., 300
Jones, Tom, 296
Jourard, S. M., 145
Judge, T. A., 62, 71, 83–84, 84, 143
Juran, J., 178

K
Kahn, R., 121, 454
Kahwajy, J., 380
Kaizen, 159
Kalmer, Kathleen, 300
Kanov, J., 550
Kanter, Rosabeth, 288–289, 290, 292,
    297, 307, 315, 447, 455, 456,
    458, 460
Kanungo, R., 293, 447, 451, 452, 453
Kaplan, R., 298
Karambayya, R., 402
Karasek, R. A., 135
Katzenbach, J., 148, 499, 509, 511,
    513, 523
Keashly, L., 391
Kekule, Fredrich, 194

Kelleher, Herb, 95, 295
Kelley, R. E., 60
Kelly, J., 381
Kennedy, A., 296
Kennedy, John, F., 504
Kentucky Fried Chicken, 191
Kern, Rex, 566
Kerr, S., 342
Kerr, William Rolfe, 127
Kettering, Charles, 179
Ketteringham, J., 189, 192, 193, 196
Kihlstrom, J. F., 133
Kilmann, R., 391
Kim, M. U., 60, 61, 122, 386, 448, 546
Kim, S., 397
Kimmel, Admiral, 214–216
Kinicki, A. J., 124
Kipnis, D., 302, 304, 391, 394
Kleiman, C., 351
Knapp, M., 251
Knight, D., 84, 338
Knowledge, half-life of, 76, 80
Knowling, Bob, 334–335
Kobasa, S., 124, 143
Koberg, D., 205
Koestler, A., 191, 194
Kohlberg, L., 71–74, 75
Kolb, D. A., 14, 76, 79
Konrad, A., 298
Koole, S., 390
Koopman, P., 178
Kopelman, R., 348
Korabik, D., 391
Korda, M., 287
Korean War, 147
Kotter, John, 287, 292, 295, 335, 542
Kouzes, J., 511
Kraimer, M., 298
Kram, K., 62, 147, 289
Kramer, R., 260, 511
Kressel, K., 402
Kroc, Ray, 184–185
Kuo, Y. Y., 206
Kwon, S., 292

L
Labich, K., 291
LaGaipa, J., 293
Lahiff, J., 260
Lakein, D., 126
Langer, E., 453, 466
Langlois, J., 294
Language, for positive change, 557, 558t
Language, single thinking, as conceptual
    block, 191
Latack, J., 124
Latham, G., 136, 337, 338, 457
Lavine, M., 570
Lawler, E., 148, 341, 342, 350,
    498, 499
Lawrence, K., 182, 183, 208, 448
Lawrence, Paul, 301
Leadership, and management, 16,
    17, 18f
Leadership, for positive change. See also
        Vision statements
    approaches to, abundance
        and deficit, 545–546
    behavioral guidelines for, 570–571
    and benchmarking, 556, 558t
    and change, escalating, 543
    defined, 542
    and deviance, negative and positive,
        544–545
    and frameworks, 543–544,
        546–548, 570f
    identifying strengths, 552–553
    institutionalizing

    creating momentum for, 566
        creating teachers for, 566–567
    language for, 557, 558t
    and positivity, establishing, 548–554,
        555t
    and reflected best-self feedback,
        553–554
    scoring key for, 591–592
    skill analysis for, 572–584
    skill application for, 588–590
    skill assessment for, 538–541
    skill practice for, 585–587
    and small wins, 564, 565t
    and symbolism, 556–557, 558t
    as temporary position, 542–543
    and vision of abundance, 557–558,
        561–566
Leading questions, for interviews,
    626–627
Leana, C., 467
Learning stair, 566, 567f
Learning style
    defined, 76
    dimensions of, 76–77
    institutionalizing
        human capital for, 567–568
        metrics, measurements,
            milestones for, 568–569
    and self-awareness, 62–63
    types of, 77–79, 80f
Learning Style Inventory, 52–53, 105
Learning Styles Instrument (LSI), 76,
    78f, 79
Ledford, G., 148, 498, 499
Leger, D., 287
Legitimacy, as power source,
    296–297
Lehman Brothers, 288
Lehrer, P. M., 132, 147
Leonard, Stew, 339
Leong, F. T. L., 71
Levering, R., 339
Levine, M., 542, 545, 546
Levinson, J. D., 124
Lewin, Kurt, 117
Lickona, T., 73–74
Lidz, F., 499
Liden, R., 298
Life balance analysis, 160–162
Likert, R., 122
Lim, S., 143, 242
Live for Life program, 140
Locke, E. A., 84, 136, 337, 338, 457,
    467, 513
Locus of control, 82–83, 84, 105–106
Locus of Control Scale, 54–55, 83
Logos, and vision, 561
Lombardo, M., 289, 385
Long, B., 140, 141
Loomis, F., 244–246
Lopez, R., 624
Lorsch, Jay, 301, 448
Los Angeles Clippers, 499
Losada, M., 263
Lowell, E., 350
Loyalty, and empowerment, 449t
Luhmann, N., 454
Lusch, R. F., 134
Luthans, F., 13, 341

M
Machiavellianism scale (MACH IV),
    540–541
Macintosh Computer, 209
Maddi, S., 143
Maddux, J., 452
Maduro, R., 206
Magnetron, 189, 194

Maier, A., 260
Maier, N., 260, 635
Malcolm Baldrige National Quality
    Award, 148
Malden Mills, 561
Management
    as cause of stress, 117
    defined, 16, 17
    and leadership, 16, 17, 18f
Management and Machiavelli, 332
Management by objectives, 337
Management skills
    applicable to daily life, 5
    based on research, 5
    characteristics of, 9, 11
    curriculum for improving, 12, 15
    defined, 8
    developing, 4–5
    diversity in, 21–22
    essential, 7–9
    exercises to assess, 24–43, 94–96
    importance for managers, 6
    improving, 12
    and leadership, 542
    learning model for developing, 13–14
    personal assessment for, 42–43
    for teams, teamwork, 521–522
    types and models of, 18–19
Managers. See also Leadership, for posi-
        tive change; Presentations,
        oral and written
    attitudes toward subordinates, 466
    effectiveness exercise for, 28–29
    essential skills of, 9, 10t–11t, 11
    importance of management skills for, 6
    insecurities of, 466
    need for control of, 466–467
    as reinforcers, 342–343
    teamwork skills for, 521–522
Mandela, Nelson, 450, 565
Manifest needs model, 349–350
Mannix, E., 381
Manz, C., 453, 511
March, J., 178, 180, 182, 202, 204,
    656, 657
Market skills, 16–17
Markoff, J., 192
Marlowe, David, 133
Martin, E., 624
Martin, J., 456
Martindale, C., 197
Marwell, G., 302
Marx, K., 450
Mary Kay Cosmetics, 459
Maslow, A. H., 59, 349, 380–381
Masten, A. S., 138
Masuda, M., 124
Matchstick problem, 192, 233
Matteson, M. T., 143
May, Rollo, 288
Mayer, J., 63, 64
Mazique, M., 298
McCall, M., 289
McCauley, L., 335
McClear, K., 84
McClelland, David, 289, 349, 350,
    351, 447
McConkie, M., 454, 455
McCraty, R., 551
McCullough, M., 551
McDonald's, 184–185
McGovern, Gordon, 295
McGregor, D., 254, 334, 466
McGuffey's Restaurant, 222–225
McKay, M., 146
McKim, R., 192
McLoughlin, C. A., 117, 140
McMillan, I., 208

Meaning, and empowerment, 453–454, 455
Mechanic, D., 294, 295
Medawar, P., 199
Mediator, in conflict management, 396–405
Mediator, in conflict management, 407–408
Mednick, M. T., 143
Medsker, G., 506
Meetings, conducting
  rules for group members in, 661–662, 663
  rules for managers in
    participants, 657, 662
    participation, 659–661
    perspective, 661, 663
    planning, 658–659, 662
    process, 662–663
    purpose, 656–657, 662
  skill practice for, 664–675
Mentoring, 147–148, 301–302, 458
Merrill, Roger, 211–212
Mesa Petroleum, 140
Messages, one-sided, two-sided, 598
Meyerson, D., 548
Michener, H., 331
Microsoft, 576–577
Microwave ovens, 189, 191, 194, 196
Milgram, S., 73, 124
Miller, S., 181, 182
Minnesota Multiphasic Personality Inventory, 63
Mintzberg, H., 15, 121, 131
Mischel, W., 134
Mishra, A., 122, 135, 451, 454, 458, 460, 463, 468
Mitchell, T., 339
Mitroff, I., 182
Mixed-mode interview, 636
Moe, M., 333
Mohrman, S., 148, 498, 499
Mokwa, M., 202
Moore, Gordon, 300
Moore, T., 85
Moorehead, Dr. Bob, 4
Moral Research Center, University of Minnesota, 74
Morale, and empowerment, 449t
Morcott, Woody, 210
Morgan, S., 450
Morphological synthesis, and problem-solving, 205–206
Morris, M., 299
Morrison, A., 385
Moskowitz, M., 339
Motivation. See also Goals; Performance
  behavioral guidelines for, 356–357
  elements of program for, 335–338
  fostering environment of, 334–336
  and human needs, 349–352
  increasing, 330
  model for enhancing, 355f
  and performance, 331–332
  and rewards, 349, 350–355
  scoring key for, 374
  skill analysis for, 358–364
  skill application for, 371–373
  skill assessment for, 328–329
  skill practice for, 365–370
  and work design, 346–349
Moving Mountains, 501
Moving Up in the Rankings, exercise on, 221
Mulder, M., 304
Mullen, B., 519
Multifactor Emotional Intelligence Scale, 64

Mumford, M., 188
Murlis, H., 341
Murnighan, J., 390, 396
Murphy, L. R., 141
Murray, B., 342
Murrell, K., 452, 454
Muscle relaxation, to reduce stress, 148–149
Myers-Briggs Type Indicator, 63

N
Name that ship problem, 194, 195f, 234
Nanobombs, 3
Nanus, B., 287, 451, 453, 455, 557
National Training Laboratories, 566
Nayak, P., 189, 192, 193, 196
Neale, M., 390
Neider, L., 339
Nelson, Dr. Noelle, 344
Nelson, William H., 330
Nemeth, C., 209
Neufeld, R., 452
Neuroticism, 83, 84
Newcomb, T., 190
Newman, W., 466
Newspaper, the, exercise on, 51, 104–105
Nicholson, Geoffrey, 212
Nickerson, J., 499
Nickerson, R., 188, 199, 201
Nielson, T., 380
Nine-dot problem, 195, 234
Nisbett, R., 291, 330
Nishida, T., 268
Noninquisitiveness, as conceptual block, 196–197
Nord, W., 454
Norenzayan, A., 291, 330
Norming stage, of team development, 502, 503–505
Northwestern National Life, 122

O
O'Connor, R., 122
Oedipus, 289
Oldham, G. R., 135, 136, 346, 454, 455, 456, 461, 462, 471
Olsen, J., 656, 657
Ong, M., 337
Open questions, for interviews, 625–626
Openness, 83
Operant conditioning, 343
Orchestrator, 211, 212
Organ, D., 452
Organization, for a presentation, 599–600
Orientation, toward change, 63
Orme-Johnson, D., 147
Osborn, A., 202
Ouchi, W., 248
Overstock.com, 95
Owan, H., 499
Ozer, E., 455

P
Pagonis, Gen. Gus, 501, 503, 506–507, 509–511, 511, 513, 514, 516
Parker, G., 509, 516, 519
Parker, V., 62, 342
Parsons, Wendell, 333–334
Particularism, 68
Pascale, R., 380
Pauling, Linus, 196
Peake, P. K., 134
Pearl Harbor, 214–216
Pelled, L., 385
Penicillin, 194

Pepperidge Farms, 295
Performance. See also Goals; Motivation
  ability deterioration and, 332
  ability-enhancing tools for, 332–334
  and behavior
    discipline for, 343–345
    managers as reinforcers of, 342–343
    rewards for, 341–342, 343–345
    shaping and improving, 345–346
  behavioral guidelines for, 356–357
  diagnosing problems, 330–332
  and extrinsic outcomes, 346
  increasing, 330
  scoring key for, 374–376
  and shift work, 331
  skill practice for, 365–370
Performing stage, in team development, 502
Performing stage, in team development, 507–510
Perot, Ross, 381, 559–560, 574–576
Perrow, Charles, 301
Perry, M., 331
Persian Gulf War
  Pagonis's team in, 501, 503, 506–507, 509–510
  work teams in, 132–133
Personal Assessment of Management Skills (PAMS), 24–28
Personal consequence, 453, 455
Personal management interview (PMI), 264–267
Personality, and self-awareness, 83–84
Perspective, and empowerment, 449t
Peter Principle, The, 332
Peters, T., 122, 182, 248, 296, 499
Peters, Tom, 3
Peterson, Peter, 288
Peterson, Ralph, 559
Peterson, R. L., 550
Pfeffer, J., 8, 122, 248, 292, 297, 298, 299, 341, 542
Phillips, E., 391
Phillips Electronics, 127
Pilling, B. K., 134
Ping-Pong puzzle, 204–205
Placebo effect, on change, 546
Planning, in learning plan, 98
Plutarch, 58
Podolny, J., 299
Poincare, H., 199
Polaroid, 217
Politicization, and empowerment, 449t
Polonius, 58
Poor, E., 607
Porter, L., 331
Posner, B. Z., 70, 511
Post-It Notes
  breaking stereotypes to invent, 193, 196
  Fry's involvement with, 192, 194
  importance of teamwork to invent, 210–212
  invention of, 189
Power
  abuse of, 289–290, 312
  balanced view of, 287
  behavioral guidelines for, 312–313
  building base for, 287
  defined, 290
  in human resource department, 301
  and influence, 302, 312
  international caveats for, 291–292
  lack of, 287–289
  model of, 311f
  necessity of, 290–292
  personal

negative view of, 288
  sources of, 292–297, 311–312
  as stepping stone, 290
  position-power, sources of, 297–302
  and relationship with boss, 295t
  scoring key for, 323–324, 323–325
  skill analysis for, 314
  skill application for, 321–322
  skill assessment for, 284–286
  skill practice for, 315–316
Pratt, M., 454
Preparation, and creativity, 199
Presentations, oral and written
  behavioral guidelines for, 611–612
  necessity for, 596
  responding to questions on, 609–611
  skill practice for, 613–622
  strategies for, 597–599
  structure for, 599–601
  style for oral, 603–606
  style for written, 607–609
  supporting points for, 601–604
  visual aids for, 602–603, 605
Preston, P., 466
Prioritizing, 136
Probing response, 263–264
Problem-oriented communication, 254–255
Problem solving. See also Conceptual blocks
  analytical
    constraints on, 183t
    exercise to assess, 219–220
    limitations of, 182
    model of, 208f
    and single thinking language, 191
    steps in, 178–182
    success of, 212
  applying techniques for, 207
  behavioral guidelines for, 212–213
  in conflict management, 394–405
  creative
    approaches to, 183–187
    exercises to assess, 220–221, 225–226
    fostering in others, 207–212
    impediments to, 182–183
    management principles for, 208–212
    model of, 208f
    as prerequisite for success, 212
    stages of creative thought, 198–199
    training for, 188–189
  and creativity, innovation, 178
  generating alternatives for, 203–206
  international caveats for, 206–207
  problem definition, improving, 199–204, 212
  scoring key for, 228–234, 229–235
  skill analysis for, 214–218
  skill application for, 227–228
  skill assessment for, 172–177
  skill practice for, 219–226
Problem-solving interview, 636
Proctor, R., 396
Pronunciation, inconsistent, 245t
Prudential Life Insurance, 140
Pruitt, D., 402
Prussia, G., 124
Publilius Syrus, 58
Purdy, K., 135, 462
Putnam, R., 656
Pygmalion effect, on change, 546

Q
Quality circles, exercises for, 614–622
Quick, T., 332

Quinn, R. E., 8, 16, 183, 451, 455, 456, 465, 502, 510, 542, 548, 553

R

Rahe, R. H., 123–124
Rahim, M., 390
Rainbow, Jacob, 198–199
Ramsey, Joseph, 212
Randle, C., 243
Rappaport, J., 452, 453
Rasheed, A., 178
Raven, B., 449
Ray, M., 452
Raytheon, 189, 191, 193, 194, 209
Reagan, Ronald, 560
Reality therapy, 259
Reason, as influence strategy, 303, 304–307, 310–311
Reassigning, for ability enhancement, 333
Reciprocity, as influence strategy, 303–307, 310
Recreation, and empowerment, 459–460
Recreation, and vision, 561–563, 565t
Redirect, to shape behavior, 345–346
Redmond, M., 243
Redstone, Sumner, 288
Reed, M. J., 138
Reese, S., 333
Refitting, for ability enhancement, 333
Reflecting response, 264
Reflective observation (RO), 76, 79
Reflective probe, for interviews, 631, 632t
Reframing, to reduce stress, 149
Regression, as stress mechanism, 118
Rehearsal, to reduce stress, 149
Reinforce, to shape behavior, 345–346
Reingold, J., 597
Reis, H., 242
Rejected Plans, 271–272
Relational algorithm, and problem-solving, 206
Relationship-building roles, on teams, 518–519
Relationship skills, developing, 4
Relaxation, deep, 146–147
Relaxation, deep, 162–163
Release, of employee, 333
Relevance, as power source, 301–302
Repetition probe, for interviews, 631, 632t
Repression, as stress mechanism, 118
Reprimand, to shape behavior, 345–346
Research, 5, 6
Resiliency, to deal with stress, 138–149, 147
Resistance stage, of stress, 118
Resources, and performance, 331
Responder, in conflict management, 396–405, 407
Rest, J., 74
Resupply, for ability enhancement, 333
Retraining, for ability enhancement, 333
Retribution, as influence strategy, 302–307, 309–310
Reuters, 559
Rewards, for performance, 341–342, 350–355
Ribot, T., 199
Rigby, D., 8
Rigidity, in communication, 255–256
Riley, S., 178
Rodin, J., 466
Rogers, Carl, 59, 251, 260, 261, 262
Rohrbaugh, J., 16

Rokeach, M., 62, 69, 70
Rose, S., 452
Rosen, S., 243
Rosenfeld, L., 396
Rosenman, R. H., 144, 145
Rosenthal, R., 134
Rostad, F., 140, 141
Rothbaum, F., 453
Rothenberg, A., 201, 202
Rotter, Julian, 54, 84
Ruble, T., 391
Rule breaker, 211, 212
Runco, M., 188, 199
Runyon, K., 452
Rust, Ed, 296
Ryan, R., 452, 454
Ryman, D. H., 124

S

Saarni, C., 133
Salancik, G., 564
Salovey, P., 63, 64
Sandelands, L., 60, 117, 145, 448
Sanders, Harland, 191
Sandusky, Ohio, 201–202
Sandwiching, a presentation, 599
Sanford, D. G., 71
Sashkin, M., 447, 467
Savage, G., 390, 392
SCAMPER, used in problem-solving, 201
Scandinavian Airlines, 565, 568
Scapegoating, and empowerment, 449t
Schein, E. H., 124, 296, 517
Schmidt, F., 334
Schmidt, S., 302, 304, 391, 394
Schmidt, W. H., 70
Schmitt, D., 302
Schnake, M., 243, 244, 251
Schneer, J., 391
Schneider, J., 452
Schriesheim, C., 339
Schuster, J., 341
Schwalbe, M., 452
Schwartz, Jeffrey, 559
Schwartz, S. H., 71
Schweiger, D., 467
Scoring keys
    for communication, supportive, 280–282
    for conflict management, 439–441
    for empowerment, delegation, 491–492
    for leadership, positive change, 591–592
    for motivation, 374
    for performance, 374–376
    for power and influence, 323–325
    for problem-solving, 228–234
    for stress, stress management, 167–168
    for teams, teamwork, 535
Scott, O., 191, 193
Scoular Grain Company, 140
Sculley, John, 288, 560, 572–574
Seeman, M., 452
Seff, M., 452
Self-awareness
    activities for developing, 99–100
    assessment for, 101
    behavioral guidelines for, 87
    change, attitudes toward, 79–83
    core aspects of, 64f
    and core self-evaluation, 83–86
    defined, 58
    dimensions of, 58
    and diversity, 61–62

effectiveness of training for, 85
    enigma of, 59
    and learning style, 75–79
    and the sensitive line, 59–61
    skill analysis for, 88–92
    skill application for, 99–107
    skill assessment for, 46–47
    skill practice for, 93–98
    and values, 66–75
Self-determination, 452, 455
Self-disclosure, 60
Self-efficacy, 451–452, 455
Self-knowledge, 61
Self-portrait, best, 539
Seligman, M., 452, 545
Seller, W., 602
Selye, H., 118
Selznik, P., 564
Senge, P., 499, 500
Sensitive line, the, 59–61
Serpkenci, R. R., 134
Sewell, Carl, 461, 462
Seybolt, P., 380, 390, 391
Shakespeare riddle, 193, 194f, 233
Shaklee Products, 459
Shalley, C., 182
Shamir, B., 339
Shatkin, S., 147
Shenandoah Life Insurance Co., 499
Shift work, 331
Shipper, F., 289
Shoda, Y., 134
Siau, K., 204
Sieburg, E., 250, 255, 258
Siegman, A. W., 144, 145
Silence, in interviews, 631, 632t
Sillars, A., 385
Silver, Spence, 189, 191, 192, 193, 196, 209, 210–212
Simmel, G., 551
Simms, H., 453, 511
Simon, H., 178, 180, 202, 204, 543
Sincoff, M., 624
Singh, J., 122, 136, 147
Situational stressors, 122–124, 134–136
Skill analysis
    for communication, supportive, 270–272
    for conflict management, 409–413
    for empowerment, delegation, 478–479
    for leadership, positive change, 572–584
    for motivation, 358–364
    for problem-solving, 214–218
    purpose of, 19
    for self-awareness, 88–92
    for stress management, 151–158
Skill application
    for communication, supportive, 278–279
    for conflict management, 436–438
    for empowerment, delegation, 489–490
    importance of, 21
    for leadership, positive change, 588–590
    for motivation, 371–373
    for power and influence, 321–322
    for problem-solving, 227–228
    purpose of, 19–20
    for self-awareness, 99–107
    for stress management, 165–167
    for teams, teamwork, 533–534
Skill assessment
    for communication, supportive, 238–242

for conflict management, 378–379
    for empowerment, delegation, 444–446
    for leadership, positive change, 538–541
    for managing stress, 110–115
    for motivation, 328–329
    for power and influence, 284–286, 314
    for problem-solving, 172–177
    purpose of, 19
    for self-awareness, 46–57
    for teams, teamwork, 494–496, 523–526
    for time management, 111–112
Skill learning, purpose of, 19
Skill practice
    for communication, supportive, 273–278
    for conflict management, 414–435
    for empowerment, delegation, 480–488
    for influence, 316–320
    for interviews, 638–654
    for leadership, positive change, 585–587
    for meetings, conducting, 664–675
    for motivation, 365–370
    for performance, 365–370
    for power, 315–316
    for presentations, 613–622
    for problem-solving, 219–226
    purpose of, 19
    for self-awareness, 93–98
    for stress management, 159–164
    for teams, teamwork, 527–532
Skill variety, at work, 135
Slocum, J., 452
Small wins
    and commitment to change, 564, 565t
    and empowerment, 457
    exercise to assess, 159–160
    and problem-solving, 181
    strategy of, 137–138
    for Type A personalities, 145–146
Smejda, Karolus, 300
Smeyak, G., 624
Smith, D., 148, 499, 509, 511, 513, 523
Smith, G.,, 188
Smith, R., 397
Smith, Roger, 381
Smith, S., 188, 199, 204, 205
Smith, T., 144, 145
Smith, W., 390
Snyder, S., 453
Social Readjustment Rating Scale (SRRS), 113–114, 123–124
Social Security Administration, 348
Soldiers, 132–133, 147
Solem, A., 260
Solomon, B., 450
Sophocles, 289
Sorenson, M. J., 143
Sorenson, R., 390
Sosik, J., 62
"Sources of Power of Lower Participants," 295
Southwest Airlines, 95, 217, 295
Sparrowe, R., 298
Spencer, L. M., 134
Spencer, Percy, 189, 191, 193, 194, 209, 210
Spencer, S. M., 134
Spitzberg, B., 243, 244, 250, 255
Sponsor, of creativity, 211, 212

Sprague, J., 597
Spreitzer, G., 447, 451, 454, 455, 456, 460, 461, 553
SSS Software, 30–40, 664–675
Stajkovic, A., 341
Stalk, G., 121
Stamps, D., 333
Stanford-Binet Intelligence Test, 63
Staples, L., 452
Starko, A., 188, 205
Stasser, S., 135, 447, 453
Staw, B., 60, 117, 145, 448
Steers, R., 331, 342
Steil, L., 243, 250, 260
Steinel, W., 390
Stereotyping, as conceptual block, 193
Sternberg, R., 133, 134, 178, 193, 198, 202, 260
Stewart, C., 630
Stewart, Martha, 74
Stewart, T., 291
Stone, R., 147
Stone-Romero, E., 294
Storming stage, of team development, 502, 505–507
Strategies, for presentations, 597–599
Stress, stress management. *See also* Time management
  anticipatory stressors
    defined, 124
    and goal setting, 136–137
    and prioritizing, 136
    and small wins, 137–138
  behavioral guidelines for, 149–150
  and burnout, 122, 123t
  coping strategies for, 119–121
  eliminating stressors, 124–125
  encounter stressors
    and collaboration, 132–134
    defined, 122
    and social and emotional intelligence, 133–134
  and illness, injury, 124, 134, 139, 145
  improving, 116–117
  and incompetent managers, 117
  model of, 119f
  physiological effects of, 120–121
  positive and negative elements of, 117–118
  reactions to stress, 118–119
  resiliency for, 138–149
  scoring key for, 167–168, 168
  situational stressors
    defined, 132–134
    and work redesign, 134–136
  skill analysis for, 151–158
  skill application for, 165–167
  skill assessment for, 110–115
  skill practice for, 159–164
  sources of, 115, 121–124
  temporary techniques for reduction of, 148–149
Stroh, L., 402
Strong-Campbell Vocational Inventory, 63
Structure, for presentations, 599–601
Stuart, D., 598
Stuart, Jim, 335
Subdivision, and problem-solving, 204–205
Success, organizational, 6
Sue-Chan, C., 337
Sullivan, Barry, 127
Superiority-oriented communication, 255
Sutcliffe, K., 143
Sutton, C., 74
Swift, C., 452

Symbolism, and leadership, 556–557, 558t
Synectics, and problem-solving, 200
Synopsis Communication Consulting of London, 243

T

Tallahassee Democrat, 523–526
Task facilitating roles, on teams, 517–518
Task identity, significance, 135, 347–348, 462
Teams, teamwork
  advantages of, 498–501
  advertisement for, 498f
  behavioral guidelines for, 522
  developing, 497–498
    forming stage, 502–503
    norming stage, 502, 503–505
    performing stage, 502, 507–510
    storming stage, 502, 505–507
  and empowerment, 449t
  examples of, 499
  feedback in, 520–521
  goals for, 513–515
  group pressure in, 517
  impact of, 500t
  international caveats for, 515–516, 521
  leading, 510–515
  management skills for, 521–522
  membership in, 516–521
  in Persian Gulf War, 501, 503, 506–507, 509–510
  roles in
    blocking, 519–520
    relationship-building, 518–519
    team-building, 517–518
  scoring key for, 535
  shortcomings of, 499–500
  skill analysis for, 523–526
  skill application for, 533–534
  skill assessment for, 494–496
  skill practice for, 527–532
  stretch targets for, 515
Tedeschi, J., 294
Tell-and-listen interview, 636
Tell-and-sell interview, 635–636
Tennessee Valley Authority, 564
Tennyson, Alfred Lord, 58
Theory X, Y assumptions, 254, 334, 455, 466
Thinking, bias against, as conceptual block, 196–197
Thoits, P., 122
Thomas, John, 458
Thomas, K., 381, 391, 447, 452, 453, 454
Thomas, P., 452
Thompson, D., 342
Thompson, L., 294, 307, 383, 390, 396
Thorton, B., 243
Threat-rigidity response, 60, 448, 449
3M, 189, 191, 192, 193, 196, 209, 210, 656
Through the Looking Glass, exercise on, 93–94
Tichy, N., 208, 335, 542, 566, 656
Timberland, 559
Time management. *See also* Stress, stress management
  effective
    and personal principles statement, 127–128
    and urgent/important matrix, 125–126
  efficient
    determining patterns, 128–129

  rules for all, 129–131
    rules for managers, 131–132
    Time Management Survey, 129
  eliminating stressors with, 125–132
  exercise to assess, 163–164
  improving, 116–117
  scoring key for, 168–169
  skill assessment for, 111–112
Time Management Survey, 129
Time stressors, 121–122
Timmer, Jan, 127
Ting, S., 289
Ting-Toomey, S., 268, 390
Tjosvold, D., 380
Tolerance of ambiguity, 81–82, 106
Tolerance of Ambiguity Scale, 56, 81
Tomlinson, A., 333
Tone, in presentations, 608
Toyota Motors, 7
Training, and performance, 331
Travelers Insurance Co., 136, 348
Trevor, C., 342
Triandis, H., 268, 288, 342
Trieber, Frank, 119
Tripp, T., 309
Trompenaars, F., 22, 67, 122, 206, 254, 268, 288, 385, 394, 475, 516, 521
Trompenaars model, 22
Tropman, J., 656, 658
Troxell, J. R., 124
Trust, and empowerment, 449t, 454–455, 455
Tsang, J., 551
Tschirhart, M., 11
Tuchman, B., 656
Tuckman, B., 502
Tully, S., 291
Turkington, C., 132
Turn of the Tide, exercise for, 151–154
Turner, M., 511
Tushman, M., 208
Tutu, Desmond, 550
Two-way communication, 257
Tyabji, Hatim, 353
Type A personality, and stress, 143–145
Type A Personality Inventory, 112–113, 169

U

Ulicni, S. K., 71
Ulrich, D., 301, 548
Union Carbide, 385–386
United Chemical Company, 273–275, 281–282
Universalism, 68
UOP Inc., 385–386
Urwick, Lester, 467
U.S. Postal Service, 14–15
U.S. public education system, 530–531
US West, 334–335
Useem, Michael, 307

V

Validating communication, 255–256
Values
  core organizational, 296
  cultural, 67–68
  dimensions of, 68–69
  and ethical decision-making, 74–75
  ethical standards test, 75
  as foundation, 66
  instrumental, 69, 70–71
  personal, 62, 63, 69–71
  terminal, 70, 71
Values maturity, levels and stages of, 71–72

Van de Van, A., 208
Vance, C. M., 13, 14
Vangelisti, A., 251
Vardi, Y., 452
Vaske, J., 331
Velthouse, B., 447, 452, 453, 454
Verespei, M., 499
Verification, and creativity, 199
Verifone, 353
Veroff, J., 350
Vertical, lateral thinking, as conceptual block, 190–191
Viacom, 288
Vietnam War, 147
Vinton, D., 121
Visibility, as power source, 299–301
Vision statements
  commitment to, 561–566
  defined, 558
  examples of, 559
  interest for, 559–560
  passion and principles for, 560
  symbols for, 561
Visual aids, 602–603, 605
Vogt, J., 452, 454
Vogus, T., 143
Volvo, 499
Von Oech, Roger, 200, 210
Von Treitschke, Heinrich, 287
Vroom, V., 181, 331, 468, 469
Vygotsky, L., 191

W

Waclawski, J., 62
Wagner, N. N., 124
Wal-Mart, 217, 515
Wallas, G., 199
Walsh, J., 545
Walton, Sam, 515
Wanous, J., 380
Ward, H. W., 124
Ward, T., 188, 199, 204, 205
Warren, K., 466
Watson, C., 391
Watson, D., 84
Watson, K., 243
Weick, K. E., 60, 117, 137, 145, 146, 188, 448, 457, 564
Weidsma, A., 178
Weight, and stress, 140–141, 142
Weiner, B., 338
Weingart, L., 381
Weisberg, J., 385
Weisenfeld, B. M., 124
Weisz, J., 453
Welch, Jack, 296, 542, 560, 566
Weldon, E., 385, 390
Wellins, R., 499, 500
Westinghouse Furniture Systems, 499
Wheeler, J., 511
Whetten, D. A., 14, 60, 61, 122, 386, 448, 502, 546
White, R., 450, 453
Whitney, D., 519
Wiemann, J., 258
Wilkinson, I., 302
William, R., 144
Williams, V., 144
Williams, W., 188, 198
Wilmington, S. C., 243, 244
Wilmot, W., 385
Wilson, Bill, 185
Wilson, D., 181, 182
Wilson, J., 499
Withdrawal, as stress mechanism, 118
Wolf, Dr. Stewart, 132
Wolf, S. G., 123

Wolff, H. G., 123
Wolff, S. G., 519
Wonder, J., 206
Wood, R., 345
Wooten, M., 459, 549
Work design, 346–349
Work redesign, steps for, 135–136
Work teams, units
  attributes needed for, 209
  benefits of, 135
  and social resiliency, 148
  and task identity, 347–348
  in wartime, 132–133
Workman, E. A., 142
World Trade Center, 561
World War II, 147, 300, 550, 564
Wright, A., 341
Wrzeniewski, A., 454, 456

X

Xerox Corporation, 217, 507, 566
Xie, J., 390
Xin, K., 385
XYZ approach, to conflict management, 397–398, 400–401

Y

Yamaha, 185
Yammarino, F., 62
Yang, L., 188, 198
Yeatts, D., 509, 520
Yetton, P., 181, 468
Yogi, M., 147
Yountz, A., 380
Yuki, G., 293

Z

Zand, D., 454
Zeitz, P., 182
Zen Buddhism, 145
Zhou, J., 182
Zimmerer, T., 466
Zimmerman, M., 451, 452, 453
Zingheim, P., 341